GENERAL INFORMATION

CHRYSLER MOTORS

FORD MOTOR CO.

GEN

JEEP

LATEST CHANGES & CORRECTIONS

Check these pages for updated information
in this and previous manuals.

1992 MITCHELL® DOMESTIC LIGHT TRUCKS & VANS SERVICE & REPAIR

Mitchell International

ACKNOWLEDGMENT | Mitchell International thanks the domestic manufacturers, distributors and dealers for their generous cooperation and assistance which make this manual possible.

Chrysler Motors
Ford Motor Company
General Motors Corporation

MARKETING

Director
David R. Koontz

EDITORIAL

Senior Vice President
& Editor-in-Chief
Larry Laumann

Manager, Annual Data Editorial
Thomas L. Landis

Manager, Special Product Editorial
Ronald E. Garrett

Senior Editors
Daniel D. Fleming
Chuck Vedra
Ramiro Gutierrez
John M. Fisher
Tom L. Hall
James A. Hawes
Serge G. Pirino

Technical Editors
Scott A. Olsen
Bob Reel
David W. Himes
Alex A. Solis

Technical Editors (Cont.)
Donald T. Pellettera
David C. Rust
Reginald L. Baldwin
Michael C. May
KC Rosendale
Scott A. Tiner
James R. Warren
James D. Boxberger
David M. Finley
Raymond C. Day
Bobby R. Gifford
Linda M. Murphy
Tim P. Lockwood
Dave L. Skora
Donald Lawler
Wayne D. Charbonneau
Sal Caloca

WIRING DIAGRAMS

Manager
Matthew Krimple
Senior Editor
Lloyd Adams
Electrical Editors
Leonard McVicker
Santiago Llano
Harry Piper
Richard B. Speake
Robert Klempan
Brian Durbin

QUALITY ASSURANCE

Manager
Daryl F. Visser
Sr. QA Specialist
Nick DiVerde
QA Specialists
Trang Nguyen
Brian W. Hutchins
Julia A. Kinneer
Julia R. Selverstone

PRODUCT COORDINATION

Roger Leftridge

TECHNICAL LIBRARIAN

Charlotte Norris

PRODUCT SUPPORT

Supervisor
Patrick G. San Nicolas
Product Specialists
Robert L. Rothgery
William E. Bond

GRAPHICS

Manager
Judie LaPierre
Supervisor
Ann Klimetz

Published By

MITCHELL INTERNATIONAL
9889 Willow Creek Road
P.O. Box 26260
San Diego, California 92196-0260

ISBN 0-8470-0738-3

Copyright © 1992 Mitchell International
All Rights Reserved

Customer Service Numbers:
Subscription/Billing Information:
1-800-648-8010 or 619-578-6550
Technical Information:
1-800-854-7030 or 619-578-6550
Or Write: P.O. Box 26260, San Diego, CA 92196-0260

1992 GENERAL INFORMATION
Computer Relearn Procedures

INTRODUCTION

ALL MODELS

Vehicles equipped with engine or transmission computers may require a relearn procedure after the vehicle battery is disconnected and reconnected. Many vehicle computers memorize and store vehicle operation patterns for optimum driveability and performance. When the vehicle battery is disconnected, this memory is lost. The computer will use default data until new data from each key start is stored. As the computer memorizes vehicle operation for each new key start, driveability is restored.

Driveability problems may occur during the relearn stage. Depending on the type and make of vehicle and how it is equipped, the following driveability problems may exist:

- Rough or unstable idle.
- Hesitation or stumble.
- Rich or lean running.
- Poor fuel mileage.
- Harsh or poor transmission shift quality.

Problems should decrease as vehicle is driven and drive cycles are completed. To accelerate relearn process, after battery removal and installation, vehicle should be road tested in the following manner:

- Warm-up vehicle to normal operating temperature or until cooling fan cycles.
- Accelerate at normal throttle position (20-50%).
- Cruise at light to medium throttle.
- Decelerate to a stop, downshifting and using brakes normally.

Some manufacturers identify specific relearn procedures that will help establish optimum driveability after the relearn cycle. See RELEARN PROCEDURES. Always complete the procedure before returning the vehicle to normal operation.

RELEARN PROCEDURES

CHRYSLER MOTORS

Transmission Shift Relearn Procedure – This procedure should be used on vehicles equipped with an A-604 transaxle. It will quickly optimize shift quality after disconnecting battery or loss of voltage supply to the transaxle controller.

1) Warm transaxle to normal operating temperature by allowing engine to idle for proper time depending on ambient temperature. See TRANSAXLE FLUID WARM-UP TIME table.

TRANSAXLE FLUID WARM-UP TIME

Ambient Temperature	Engine Idle Time (Minutes)
0°F (-18°C)	8
20°F (-7°C)	6
40°F (4°C)	4
60°F (16°C)	2
80°F (27°C)	0

CAUTION: DO NOT move accelerator pedal during transaxle upshifts.

2) Drive vehicle and maintain constant throttle opening during shifts. Accelerate vehicle with throttle opening angle in range of 10 to 50 degrees. Operate vehicle until transaxle performs 1-2, 2-3, and 3-4 upshifts at least 15-20 times.

CAUTION: Allow transaxle to operate in 2nd or 3rd gear at least 5 seconds before performing kickdown.

3) To set transaxle kickdown learn procedure, operate vehicle at less than 25 MPH, making 5-8 wide-open-throttle kickdowns to 1st gear from either 2nd or 3rd gear.

CAUTION: Operate transaxle in 4th gear for at least 5 seconds at steady throttle position before performing kickdown.

4) With vehicle speed greater than 25 MPH, make 5-8 part throttle to wide-open throttle kickdowns to either 3rd or 2nd gear from 4th gear (for example, 4-3 or 4-2 kickdowns).

FORD MOTOR CO.

Vehicle Preparation – Ensure all components are connected and transmission fluid level is correct. Warm engine to normal operating temperature. If vehicle has been repaired, perform KOEO test and continuous memory code self-test to ensure fault codes are not present. See appropriate article in ENGINE PERFORMANCE.

Engine Idle Relearn Procedure – Put transmission gear selector in Park (A/T) or Neutral (M/T). Start engine and allow to idle for at least one minute. Drive vehicle for 10 miles in stop and go traffic. Engine idle relearn procedure is complete.

Transmission Shift Relearn Procedure (E4OD Transmission) – **1)** With transmission gear selector in Drive, press Overdrive Cancel Switch (LED should light). Moderately accelerate vehicle to 40 MPH for a minimum of 15 seconds (30 seconds above 4000 ft. elevation). Transmission should be in 3rd gear.

2) While holding speed steady, press Overdrive Cancel Switch (LED should go off) and accelerate from 40 MPH to 50 MPH. Transmission should shift from 3rd gear to 4th gear. Hold speed steady for 15 seconds. While holding speed steady, lightly apply and release brakes to turn brake lights on. Maintain 50 MPH for about 5 seconds. Stop and park vehicle for a minimum of 20 seconds with transmission gear selector in Drive. Repeat procedure 5 times.

GENERAL MOTORS

NOTE: No specific relearn procedures are given to help establish optimum driveability after battery has been disconnected. See ALL MODELS in INTRODUCTION for road test procedure.

GENERAL INFORMATION

The term Parasitic Load refers to electrical devices that continue to use or draw current after the ignition switch is turned to OFF position. This small amount of continuous battery draw is expressed in milliamps (mA). On Ford Motor Co. and General Motors vehicles produced after 1980, a typical Parasitic Load should be no more than 50 milliamps (0.050 amps).

Vehicles produced since 1980 have memory devices that draw current with ignition off for as long as 20 minutes before shutting down the Parasitic Drain. When Parasitic Load exceeds normal specifications, the vehicle may exhibit dead battery and no-start condition.

Follow test procedure for checking Parasitic Loads to completion. A brief overview of a suggested test procedure is included along with some typical Parasitic Load specifications. Refer to GENERAL MOTORS PARASITIC LOAD TABLE chart.

TESTING FOR PARASITIC LOAD

CAUTION: Always turn ignition off when connecting or disconnecting battery cables, battery chargers or jumper cables. DO NOT turn test switch to OFF position (which causes current to run through ammeter or vehicle electrical system).

NOTE: Memory functions of various accessories must be reset after the battery is reconnected.

The battery circuit must be opened to connect test switch (shunt) and ammeter into the circuit. When a battery cable is removed, timer circuits within the vehicle computer are interrupted and immediately begin to discharge. If in doubt about the condition of the ammeter fuse, test it with an ohmmeter prior to beginning test. An open fuse will show the same reading (00.00) as no parasitic drain. Begin test sequence with the meter installed and on the 10-amp scale. Select lower scale to read parasitic draw.

TEST PROCEDURE USING TEST SWITCH

1) Turn ignition off. Remove negative battery terminal cable. Install Disconnect Tool (J-38758) test switch male end to negative battery cable. Turn test switch knob to OFF position (current through meter). Install negative battery cable to the female end of test switch.

2) Turn test switch knob to ON position (current through switch). Road test vehicle with vehicle accessories on (radio, air conditioner, etc). After road test, turn ignition switch to LOCKED position and remove key. Connect ammeter terminals to test switch terminals. *See Fig. 1.* Select 10-amp scale.

3) Turn off all electrical accessories. Turn off interior lights, underhood lamp, trunk light, illuminated entry, etc. To avoid damaging ammeter

or obtaining a false meter reading, all accessories must be off before turning test switch knob to OFF position.

4) Turn test switch knob to OFF position to allow current to flow through ammeter. If meter reads wrong polarity, turn test switch to ON position and reverse leads. Turn test switch to OFF position. Observe current reading. If reading is less than 2 amps, turn test switch to ON position to keep electrical circuits powered-up.

5) Select low amp scale. Switch lead to the correct meter position. Turn test switch to OFF position and compare results to normal current draw. See GENERAL MOTORS PARASITIC LOAD TABLE. If current draw is unusually high for the vehicle's overall electrical system, remove system fuses one at a time until current draw returns to normal.

6) Turn test switch to ON position each time door is opened or fuse is removed. Turn switch to OFF position to read current draw value through meter. When the cause of excessive current drain has been located and repaired, remove test switch and reconnect negative battery cable to the negative battery terminal.

INTERMITTENT PARASITIC LOAD PROBLEMS

Intermittent parasitic load can occur because of a memory device that does not power down with ignition off. With an intermittent parasitic load, battery draw can be greater than 1.0 amp.

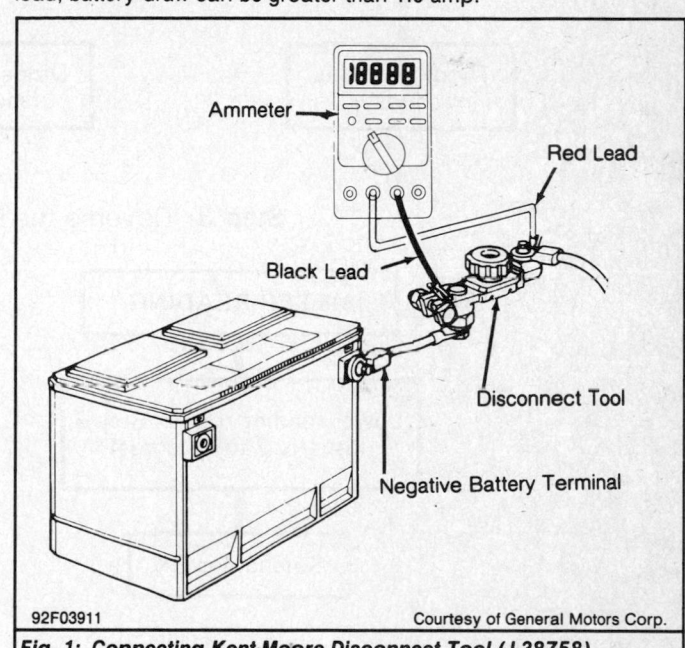

Ammeter

Red Lead

Black Lead

Disconnect Tool

Negative Battery Terminal

92F03911   Courtesy of General Motors Corp.

Fig. 1: Connecting Kent-Moore Disconnect Tool (J-38758)

GENERAL MOTORS PARASITIC LOAD TABLE (MILLIAMPS)

Component	Normal Draw	Maximum Draw	Time-Out (Minutes)
Anti-Theft System	0.4	1.0	
Auto Door Lock	1.0	1.0	
Body Control Module	3.6	12.4	20
Central Processing System	1.6	2.7	20
Electronic Control Module	5.6	10.0	
Electronic Level Control	2.0	3.3	20
Heated Windshield Module	0.3	0.4	
HVAC Power Module	1.0	1.0	
Illuminated Entry	1.0	1.0	1
Light Control Module	0.5	1.0	
Oil Level Module	0.1	0.1	
Multi-Function Chime	1.0	1.0	
Pass Key Decoder Module	0.75	1.0	
Power Control Module	5.0	7.0	
Retained Accessory Power	3.8	3.8	
Radio	7.0	8.0	15
Twilight Sentinel Module	1.0	1.0	
Voltage Regulator	1.4	2.0	

1992 GENERAL INFORMATION
Parasitic Load Explanation & Test Procedures (Cont.)

To find an intermittent problem requires that an ammeter and Disconnect Tool (J-38758) test switch be connected and left in the circuit. *See Fig. 1.* Road test vehicle. After road test, turn ignition off and remove key.

Monitor the milliamps scale for 15-20 minutes after ignition is turned off. This allows monitoring memory devices to determine if they time out and stop drawing memory current. The test switch is needed to protect ammeter when the vehicle is started.

DIODE CHECK & SOLENOID TEST

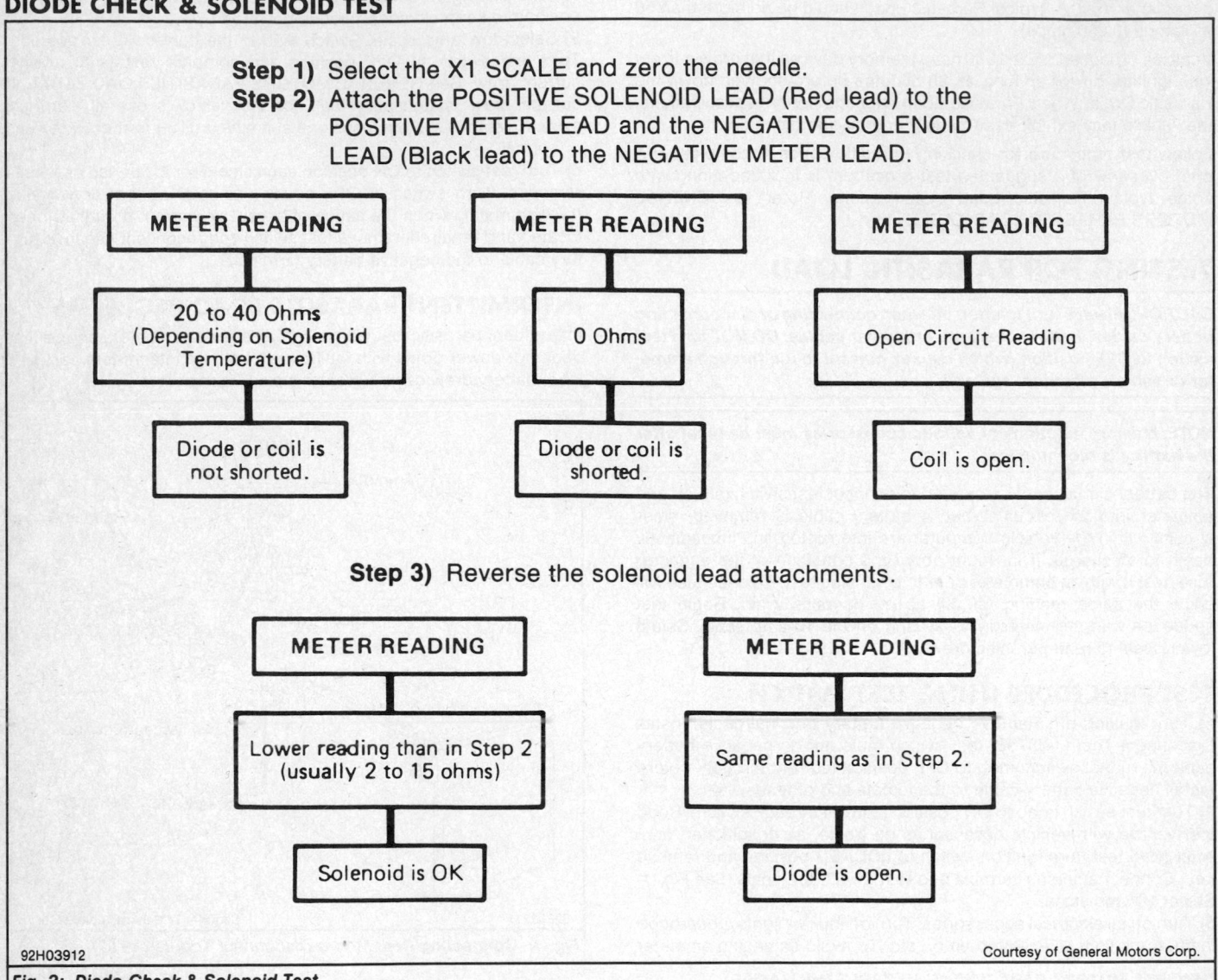

Step 1) Select the X1 SCALE and zero the needle.

Step 2) Attach the POSITIVE SOLENOID LEAD (Red lead) to the POSITIVE METER LEAD and the NEGATIVE SOLENOID LEAD (Black lead) to the NEGATIVE METER LEAD.

METER READING	METER READING	METER READING
20 to 40 Ohms (Depending on Solenoid Temperature)	0 Ohms	Open Circuit Reading
Diode or coil is not shorted.	Diode or coil is shorted.	Coil is open.

Step 3) Reverse the solenoid lead attachments.

METER READING	METER READING
Lower reading than in Step 2 (usually 2 to 15 ohms)	Same reading as in Step 2.
Solenoid is OK	Diode is open.

92H03912

Courtesy of General Motors Corp.

Fig. 2: Diode Check & Solenoid Test

QUAD DRIVER TEST

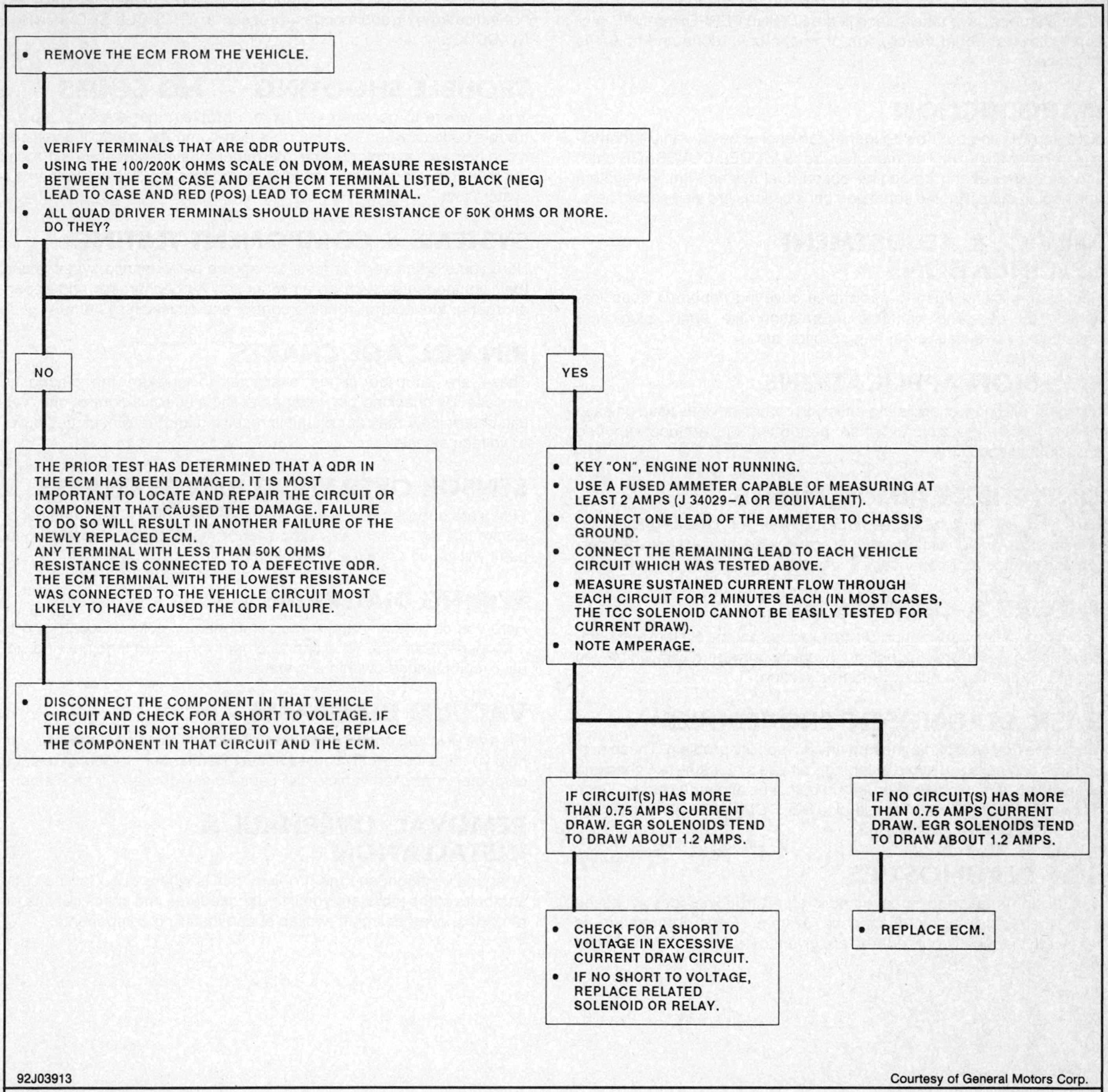

- REMOVE THE ECM FROM THE VEHICLE.

- VERIFY TERMINALS THAT ARE QDR OUTPUTS.
- USING THE 100/200K OHMS SCALE ON DVOM, MEASURE RESISTANCE BETWEEN THE ECM CASE AND EACH ECM TERMINAL LISTED, BLACK (NEG) LEAD TO CASE AND RED (POS) LEAD TO ECM TERMINAL.
- ALL QUAD DRIVER TERMINALS SHOULD HAVE RESISTANCE OF 50K OHMS OR MORE. DO THEY?

NO

YES

THE PRIOR TEST HAS DETERMINED THAT A QDR IN THE ECM HAS BEEN DAMAGED. IT IS MOST IMPORTANT TO LOCATE AND REPAIR THE CIRCUIT OR COMPONENT THAT CAUSED THE DAMAGE. FAILURE TO DO SO WILL RESULT IN ANOTHER FAILURE OF THE NEWLY REPLACED ECM.
ANY TERMINAL WITH LESS THAN 50K OHMS RESISTANCE IS CONNECTED TO A DEFECTIVE QDR. THE ECM TERMINAL WITH THE LOWEST RESISTANCE WAS CONNECTED TO THE VEHICLE CIRCUIT MOST LIKELY TO HAVE CAUSED THE QDR FAILURE.

- KEY "ON", ENGINE NOT RUNNING.
- USE A FUSED AMMETER CAPABLE OF MEASURING AT LEAST 2 AMPS (J 34029–A OR EQUIVALENT).
- CONNECT ONE LEAD OF THE AMMETER TO CHASSIS GROUND.
- CONNECT THE REMAINING LEAD TO EACH VEHICLE CIRCUIT WHICH WAS TESTED ABOVE.
- MEASURE SUSTAINED CURRENT FLOW THROUGH EACH CIRCUIT FOR 2 MINUTES EACH (IN MOST CASES, THE TCC SOLENOID CANNOT BE EASILY TESTED FOR CURRENT DRAW).
- NOTE AMPERAGE.

- DISCONNECT THE COMPONENT IN THAT VEHICLE CIRCUIT AND CHECK FOR A SHORT TO VOLTAGE. IF THE CIRCUIT IS NOT SHORTED TO VOLTAGE, REPLACE THE COMPONENT IN THAT CIRCUIT AND THE ECM.

IF CIRCUIT(S) HAS MORE THAN 0.75 AMPS CURRENT DRAW. EGR SOLENOIDS TEND TO DRAW ABOUT 1.2 AMPS.

IF NO CIRCUIT(S) HAS MORE THAN 0.75 AMPS CURRENT DRAW. EGR SOLENOIDS TEND TO DRAW ABOUT 1.2 AMPS.

- CHECK FOR A SHORT TO VOLTAGE IN EXCESSIVE CURRENT DRAW CIRCUIT.
- IF NO SHORT TO VOLTAGE, REPLACE RELATED SOLENOID OR RELAY.

- REPLACE ECM.

92J03913

Courtesy of General Motors Corp.

Fig. 3: Quad Driver Test

1992 GENERAL INFORMATION
How To Use The Engine Performance Section

We have redesigned Mitchell manuals to make them easier to use by organizing service and repair information by manufacturer. Also, major changes have taken place in the ENGINE PERFORMANCE section. Below is a brief description of what's been done and how it is organized.

INTRODUCTION

Here you will find out how to identify an engine by its Vehicle Identification Number (VIN). The manufacturer's MODEL COVERAGE chart lists each model and its engine option, fuel system, ignition system and engine code. Engine serial number locations are also shown here.

SERVICE & ADJUSTMENT SPECIFICATIONS

Here you will find easy-to-use tables covering *important* specifications. You can find valuable information like spark plug wire resistance, valve clearance, firing orders, etc.

EMISSION APPLICATIONS

Here you will find a chart listing emission control devices used on each model. These are helpful when performing government-required emissions inspections.

ON-VEHICLE ADJUSTMENTS

Here you will find adjustment procedures for checking/adjusting valves, base ignition timing and idle speed. Use this section when performing routine maintenance.

THEORY & OPERATION

Here you will find information on how various engine system and components work. Before diagnosing a vehicle or system with which you are not completely familiar, read this section.

BASIC DIAGNOSTIC PROCEDURES

This is the *first step* in diagnosing any driveability problem. These procedures can help you avoid skipping a simple step early, like checking base timing, which could be costly in both time and money later. Once all systems are "GO" here, proceed to SELF-DIAGNOSTICS or TROUBLE SHOOTING – NO CODES.

SELF-DIAGNOSTICS

Use this information to retrieve and interpret trouble codes accessed from the vehicle's self-diagnostic system. Once information is retrieved, diagnostic procedures are given to help pinpoint and repair computer system/component faults. Also included are steps for clearing trouble codes, once these faults are repaired. If there is a problem not indicated by trouble codes, proceed to TROUBLE SHOOTING – NO CODES.

TROUBLE SHOOTING – NO CODES

This is where to go when you have a problem that does not have a trouble code or when working on a non-computer controlled vehicle. It can help with symptoms and intermittent testing procedures. Procedures in this information should lead you to a specific component or system test.

SYSTEMS & COMPONENT TESTING

Here you will find various tests for engine performance systems and their components, such as air induction (turbochargers and superchargers), fuel control, ignition control and emission systems.

PIN VOLTAGE CHARTS

These are supplied (when available) to quicken the diagnostic process. By checking pin voltages at the electronic control unit, you can determine if the control unit is receiving and/or transmitting proper voltage signals.

SENSOR OPERATING RANGE CHARTS

These are supplied (when available) to determine if a sensor is out of calibration. An out-of-calibration sensor may not set a trouble code, but it will cause driveability problems.

WIRING DIAGRAMS

Here you can identify and trace component circuits or locate shorts and opens in circuits. They can also help you understand how individual circuits function within a system.

VACUUM DIAGRAMS

Here we give you underhood views of vacuum-hose routing which can help you find incorrectly routed hoses. Remember, a vacuum leak on computer-controlled vehicle can cause many driveability problems.

REMOVAL, OVERHAUL & INSTALLATION

After you've diagnosed the problem, this is where to go for the nuts-and-bolts of the job. Here you'll find procedures and specifications for removing, overhauling (if available) and installing components.

Engine Performance Safety Precautions

- Always refer to Engine Tune-Up Decal in engine compartment before performing tune-up. If manual and decal differ, always use decal specifications.
- Do not allow or create a condition of misfire in more than one cylinder for an extended period of time. Damage to converter may occur due to loading converter with unburned air/fuel mixture.
- Always turn ignition off and disconnect negative battery cable BEFORE disconnecting or connecting computer or other electrical components.
- DO NOT drop or shock electrical components such as computer, airflow meter, etc.
- DO NOT use fuel system cleaning compounds that are not recommended by the manufacturer. Damage to gaskets, diaphragm materials and catalytic converter may result.
- Before performing a compression test or cranking engine using a remote starter switch, disconnect coil wire from distributor and secure it to a good engine ground, or disable ignition.
- Before disconnecting any fuel system component, ensure fuel system pressure is released.
- Use a shop towel to absorb any spilled fuel to prevent fire.
- DO NOT create sparks or have an open flame near battery.
- If any EFI components such as hoses or clamps are replaced, ensure they are replaced with components designed for EFI use.
- Always reassemble throttle body components with new gaskets, "O" rings and seals.
- If equipped with an inertia switch, DO NOT reset switch until fuel system has been inspected for leaks.
- Wear safety goggles when drilling or grinding.
- Wear proper clothing which protects against chemicals and other hazards.

1992 GENERAL INFORMATION
Diagnostic Routine Outline

WHERE TO BEGIN DIAGNOSING A DRIVEABILITY PROBLEM?

STEP 1 – PERFORM BASIC INSPECTION

a) Verify Customer Complaint
b) Perform Visual Inspection
   (See BASIC DIAGNOSTIC PROCEDURES)
c) Test Engine Sub-Systems
   (See BASIC DIAGNOSTIC PROCEDURES)
   - Mechanical Condition (Compression)
   - Ignition Output
   - Fuel Delivery
d) Check Air Induction System For Leaks
e) Check & Adjust Basic Engine Settings
   (See ON-VEHICLE ADJUSTMENTS)
   - Ignition Timing
   - Idle Speed

STEP 2 – CHECK FOR TROUBLE CODES

a) If equipped with self-diagnostics, check for trouble codes. *(See SELF-DIAGNOSTICS)*
b) Repair cause of trouble codes.
c) Clear control unit memory.

STEP 3 – DIAGNOSE SYMPTOM

a) If self-diagnostics and trouble codes are not available, identify complaint by symptom.
b) See trouble shooting procedure to identify problem.
   (See TROUBLE SHOOTING – NO CODES)

STEP 4 – TEST & REPAIR SYSTEM

a) Perform required tests.
   (See SYSTEM & COMPONENT TESTING)
b) Verify complaint is repaired.

Compressed Natural Gas Safety Precautions

- DO NOT smoke or create sparks while servicing Compressed Natural Gas (CNG) fuel systems.

- Natural gas vapors at atmospheric pressure are lighter than air and will rise and disperse in open areas. In enclosed areas, natural gas vapor may collect and form a combustible mixture. If the vehicle is routinely placed in an enclosed area or if the facility is heated by open flame heaters, the area should be provided with adequate ventilation and/or a natural gas detection system. For long term storage, the manual shut-off valve and individual cylinder valves should be closed.

- Natural gas contains an odorant additive. If persistent natural gas odor is detected, a leak is indicated and should be located and repaired immediately.

- DO NOT return any vehicle to service that has been in an accident which may have damaged or dislocated any fuel system component until a thorough inspection and leak test has been made.

- DO NOT attempt to weld CNG fuel cylinders or any other part of fuel system.

- Any fuel system component, including the cylinders, that have been subjected to fire may not be returned to service due to reduced pressure capability.

- DO NOT use paint oven to cure paint repairs.

- DO NOT paint or undercoat any CNG fuel system component.

- Chrysler CNG fuel systems have a maximum capacity of 3000 psi compensated to a temperature of 70°F (21°C). Vehicles SHOULD ONLY be refueled using equipment incorporating temperature compensation to 70°F (21°C). Exceeding fuel system capacity will result in fuel system damage or personal injury.

- The fuel pressure regulator is under cooling system pressure. DO NOT attempt to remove hoses from regulator without relieving cooling system pressure.

- DO NOT park vehicle near a source of excessive heat or open flame.

- DO NOT attempt to force open fuel filler valve; a sudden release of natural gas will occur, possibly causing an explosion.

- When replacing threaded fuel system components on General Motors vehicles, always apply SWAK® anaerobic pipe sealant to new component threads, except compression fittings.

- When replacing threaded fuel system components on Chrysler vehicles, a go/no-go tool MUST be used to check for correct tightness of fittings.

- CNG fuel systems are under extremely high pressure. NEVER use steel, copper or brass tubing in place of stainless steel fuel tubes.

- NEVER use replacement fuel system components that are not manufactured to OEM standards.

1992 GENERAL INFORMATION
1980-92 Maintenance Reminder Lights

AMERICAN MOTORS

1980-81 MODELS

1) Every 30,000 miles, an emission maintenance reminder light will illuminate on the instrument panel, indicating oxygen sensor requires service. If sensor is faulty, it must be replaced. After servicing sensor, reset light activating switch.

2) Locate switch in engine compartment, between upper and lower speedometer cables, next to firewall. Slide rubber boot up. With small screwdriver, turn reset screw clockwise 1/4 turn until detent resets in switch. *See Fig. 1.*

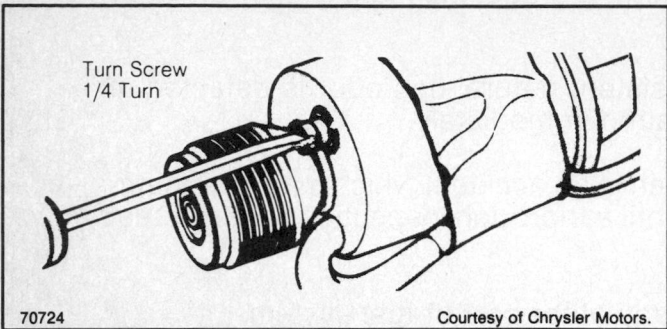

Fig. 1: Resetting Maintenance Reminder Switch (American Motors 1980-81 Models)

1982-84 MODELS (EXCEPT ALLIANCE & ENCORE)

1) The emission maintenance light illuminates after 1000 hours of engine operation, indicating oxygen sensor requires service. After servicing sensor, replace emission maintenance E-cell timer.

2) Locate timer in passenger compartment within the wire harness leading to the microprocessor. Remove E-cell timer from its enclosure and insert a replacement timer.

1987 EAGLE

1) An emission light timer will start flashing the O_2 sensor service light at 82,500 miles. At this time, O_2 sensor and timer should both be replaced. Locate timer under the dash panel (to right of steering column). Remove mounting screws and disconnect wiring.

CHRYSLER MOTORS & EAGLE

1980 PASSENGER CARS, 1980-87 LIGHT DUTY TRUCKS & RWD VANS

A mileage counter activates the emission reminder light between 12,000 and 30,000 mile intervals, depending on whether mechanical or electronic type is used. If equipped with mechanical type, see AMERICAN MOTORS 1980-81 MODELS reset procedure. *See Fig. 1.*
Electronic Type – 1) The electronic type uses a 9-volt battery which supplies power to the electronic counter, preventing memory loss when the vehicle battery is disconnected. On 1987 Dakota models, mileage counter in the odometer will illuminate reminder light at 52,500, 82,500 and 105,000 miles. On all other models, reminder light will illuminate between 12,000 and 30,000 mile intervals.

NOTE: Vehicle battery MUST be connected during resetting procedure to prevent power loss to memory.

2) To reset electronic type, locate Green, Red, White or Tan plastic case behind instrument panel in lower left cluster area. Slide case from bracket and open cover. Remove 9-volt battery, and insert a small rod or screwdriver into hole in switch, closing contacts. Replace battery with a new 9-volt alkaline type. Close case. Slide case back into bracket. *See Fig. 2.*

NOTE: Some models use a non-resettable mileage counter. Replace it with a resettable type.

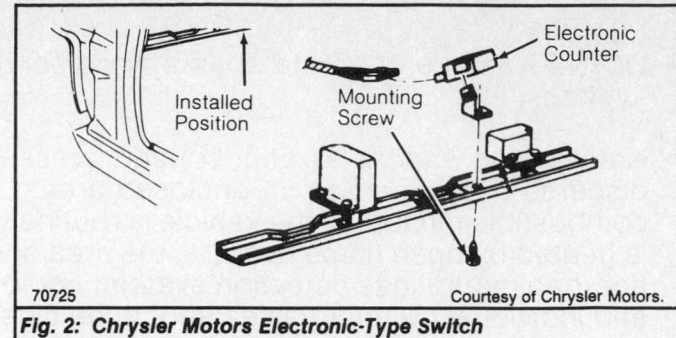

Fig. 2: Chrysler Motors Electronic-Type Switch

1987-88 FWD VANS & ALL 1988 LIGHT DUTY TRUCKS & VANS

CAUTION: There is no test procedure for this system. Any attempt to test this system will damage system components.

The Emission Maintenance Reminder (EMR) module is not an emissions warning system. It is only a reminder to perform emissions servicing. Components to be serviced include the EGR system, PCV valve, oxygen sensor, delay valves, and bi-level purge valve.

The EMR module will illuminate the MAINT REQD dash light after a predetermined time. The light will remain on until the EMR module is reset by inserting a small screwdriver into the hole in the module (RWD only) and/or depressing the reset switch (FWD and RWD).

The EMR module is located on the steering column, behind instrument panel on RWD vans and in the instrument cluster on FWD vans. *See Fig. 3 or 4.* On light trucks except Dakota, EMR module is located behind the far right side of dash panel next to the glove box. *See Fig. 5.* On Dakota models, module is located on bracket below headlight switch, on rear of instrument panel. *See Fig. 6.*

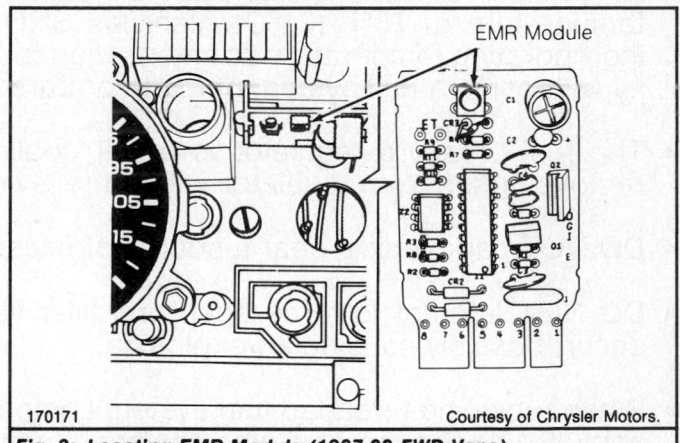

Fig. 3: Locating EMR Module (1987-88 FWD Vans)

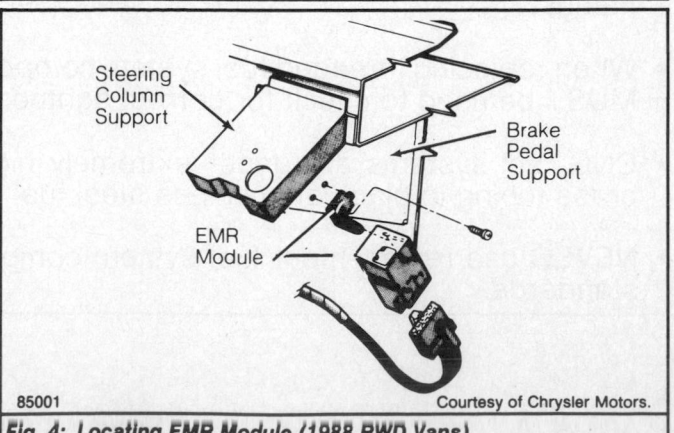

Fig. 4: Locating EMR Module (1988 RWD Vans)

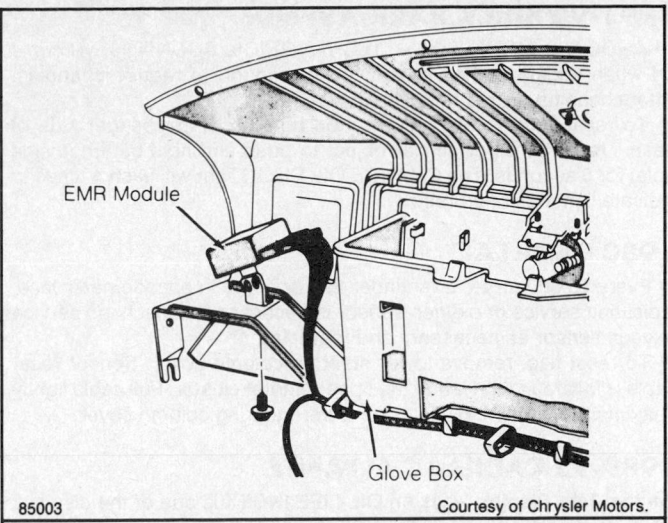

85003   Courtesy of Chrysler Motors.

Fig. 5: Locating EMR Module (1988 Light Trucks Except Dakota)

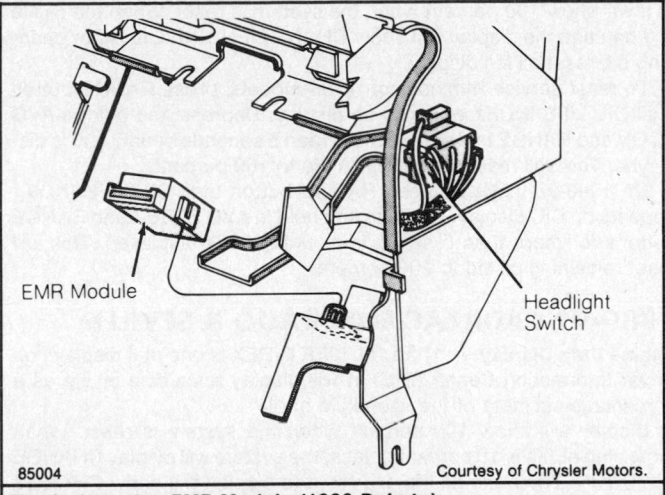

85004   Courtesy of Chrysler Motors.

Fig. 6: Locating EMR Module (1988 Dakota)

1989-92 LIGHT DUTY TRUCKS & VANS

Emission Maintenance Reminder (EMR) Light – The EMR light is designed to be a reminder to service the vehicle emissions control system. It is not an emissions warning system, only a reminder to perform emissions servicing.

The components to be serviced include the EGR system, PCV valve, oxygen sensor and some vacuum-operated components. EMR light will illuminate after a predetermined mileage. To reset EMR light, a Chrysler Diagnostic Readout Box (DRB-II) Tester (C-4805) or suitable scan tester is required.

NOTE: If DRB-II tester is used, go to RESET PROCEDURE. If any other scan tester is used, use procedure provide by scan tester manufacturer.

Reset Procedure – Attach DRB-II tester to diagnostic connector. Turn ignition on but do not start engine. Access SELECT SYSTEMS function of DRB-II tester. Select appropriate engine. Select with or without A/C. Select FUEL & IGNITION. Select ADJUSTMENTS. Select RESET EMR LIGHT. Reset EMR light. When DRB-II is finished resetting light, DRB-II display will read EMR LIGHT IS RESET.

NOTE: If Single Module Engine Controller (SMEC) or Single Board Engine Controller (SBEC) is replaced, vehicle mileage must be programmed back into the SMEC/SBEC. DRB-II tester MUST be used for this procedure. If the following procedure is not performed, EMR light will not turn on at the proper mileage intervals.

EMR Mileage Reset – **1)** Using DRB-II tester, select EMR MEMORY CHECK. DRB-II display will read, EMR MEMORY CHECK ARE YOU SURE?. Press YES key.
2) Display will read, WRITE TEST. Display will read, IS INSTRUMENT PANEL MILEAGE BETWEEN XXXXXX AND XXXXXX? If odometer mileage on vehicle is within specification, press YES key. DRB-II will display EMR MEMORY CHECK TEST COMPLETE.

NOTE: DRB-II may display EMR MEMORY WRITE FAILURE or EMR MEMORY CHECK WRITE REFUSED if there is a problem with SMEC/SBEC.

3) If odometer mileage on vehicle is not within specification shown on DRB-II, press NO key. DRB-II will read DO YOU WANT TO CORRECT EMR MILEAGE?. Press YES key on DRB-II. DRB-II will display ENTER MILEAGE SHOWN ON INSTRUMENT PANEL.
4) Enter mileage shown on instrument panel. DO NOT enter tenths. Press ENTER key on DRB-II. DRB-II will ask for verification of entry. If mileage entry was correct, DRB-II will display SETTING ENGINE DATA and EMR MEMORY CHECK TEST COMPLETE. Vehicle must be driven for at least 8 miles for mileage reset to be accepted.

1988-92 PREMIER & 1990-92 MONACO

Service Interval Reminder Light – Every 7500 miles, a Vehicle Maintenance Monitor (VMM) will illuminate a SERVICE interval reminder light. This indicates regular maintenance is due. After required service is performed, press RESET button on dash below VMM display. Hold button until a beep is heard. VMM display will now be clear.

FORD MOTOR CO.

1985-89 PASSENGER CARS

Service Interval Reminder Light – Every 5000 or 7500 miles, depending upon engine application, a SERVICE interval reminder light on the dash will illuminate (for approximately 30 seconds), or begin flashing, indicating an oil change is due.

To reset reminder light, turn ignition on. Simultaneously depress and hold TRIP (ODO SEL on Taurus and Sable, SYSTEM CHECK or CHECK OUT on Continental) and RESET or TRIP RESET buttons. On Probe models, depress and hold SERVICE RESET button, located on speed alarm keyboard. On all models, 3 beeps will verify that reminder light has been reset.

1990-92 CONTINENTAL

Service Interval Reminder Light – During system check sequence, the SERVICE symbol comes on and displays the number of miles to go before the next normal service. To reset the service interval reminder, press SYSTEM CHECK and RESET buttons simultaneously. The display should now show 7200 miles. Service interval reminder light has been reset.

1989-92 COUGAR & THUNDERBIRD

Vehicle Maintenance Monitor (VMM) – **1)** Turn ignition switch to ON position. Within 16 seconds of turning ignition on, insert small diameter shank into reset switch hole, and firmly push in switch. Reset switch hole is located on left side of VMM panel.
2) Keep switch depressed until left side of display stops flashing. If switch is not kept depressed until left side of display stops flashing, VMM will not be reset.

1990-92 PROBE
(WITH STANDARD INSTRUMENT CLUSTER)

Vehicle Maintenance Monitor (VMM) – **1)** The SERVICE light will come on approximately every 7500 miles, indicating routine service is required. The light will remain on for 3 minutes after vehicle is started.
2) To cancel the message and reset SERVICE light on 1990 models, depress and hold SERVICE RESET button until 3 beeps are sounded. This will verify that reminder light has been reset. SERVICE RESET button is located in VMM unit, in center of overhead console.

3) To cancel the message and reset SERVICE light on 1991-92 models, insert a small diameter shank into hole centered directly above VMM display lights, and press switch once.

1990-92 PROBE (WITH ELECTRONIC INSTRUMENT CLUSTER)

Vehicle Maintenance Monitor (VMM) – **1)** SERVICE INTERVAL will be displayed on system scanner every 7500 miles, indicating that routine service is due. At 7500 miles, the message will remain on for 3 minutes after vehicle is started.

2) To cancel message and reset service interval on 1990 models, press and hold ODO SEL and TRIP RESET buttons until 3 beeps are heard. Buttons are located on speed alarm keyboard.

3) To cancel message and reset service interval on 1991-92 models, press and hold SERV button until 3 tones are heard. SERV button is located on speed alarm keyboard.

1985-87 LIGHT DUTY TRUCKS, 1988 NON-EEC LIGHT DUTY TRUCKS & 1989-92 HEAVY DUTY TRUCKS

NOTE: 1980-84 trucks do not use an emission maintenance reminder light. Non-EEC vehicles for 1988 are the 2.0L Ranger, 2.3L Ranger, 6.1L and 7.0L gasoline trucks.

Maintenance Reminder Light – A maintenance reminder light is used to indicate emission system maintenance is required. Control unit (timer) for maintenance light is located under dash, near steering column or behind glove box. Some models use a non-resettable control unit. Replace it with a resettable type. After servicing emission system, reset light.

1) To reset light, turn ignition off. Remove tape over reset hole in timer. Lightly push a small Phillips screwdriver into hole in timer unit marked RESET. With light pressure on screwdriver, turn ignition switch to RUN position.

2) Light should stay on while screwdriver is pressed down. Hold screwdriver down for approximately 5 seconds. Remove screwdriver. Light should go out within 2-5 seconds. If light does not go out, repeat steps **1)** and **2)**.

3) Cycle ignition from OFF to RUN position. Light should glow for 2-5 seconds. This verifies proper reset of maintenance reminder light.

GENERAL MOTORS

NOTE: Most General Motors 1981-88 vehicles do not use an emission maintenance warning light.

1980 EXCEPT CADILLAC

1) Every 30,000 miles, a reminder flag appears in speedometer face, indicating service of oxygen sensor is necessary. *See Fig. 7.* Inspect and service oxygen sensor as necessary and reset flag.

2) To reset flag, remove instrument panel trim plate. Remove instrument cluster lens. Using pointed tool, apply light downward pressure on notches of flag until it is reset. An alignment mark will appear in left center of odometer window when flag is fully reset.

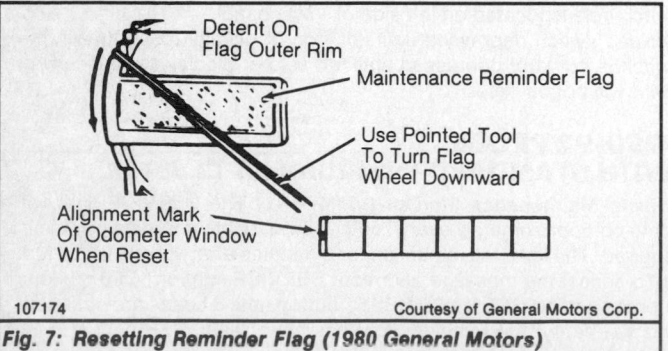

107174   Courtesy of General Motors Corp.

Fig. 7: Resetting Reminder Flag (1980 General Motors)

1991-92 BUICK PARK AVENUE

CHANGE OIL SOON Light – **1)** CHANGE OIL SOON light will come on when engine oil has broken down enough to require changing. After changing oil, reset oil life display.

2) To reset light, locate reset button hole under passenger side of dash. Use a pencil or similar object to push and hold button (inside hole) for 5 seconds. The CHANGE OIL SOON light will flash 4 times to indicate light has been reset.

1980 CADILLAC

1) Every 15,000 miles, a reminder flag appears in speedometer face, indicating service of oxygen sensor is necessary. Inspect and service oxygen sensor as necessary and reset flag.

2) To reset flag, remove lower steering column cover. Sensor reset cable is located to the left of the speedometer cluster. Pull cable lightly (maximum 2 lbs. force). Reinstall lower steering column cover.

1989-92 CADILLAC ALLANTÉ

Engine Data Display – **1)** An OIL LIFE INDEX is one of the displays on Driver Information Center (DIC). It will display remaining oil life as a percentage estimate of the useful life of oil.

2) It will show 100 percent when the system is reset. When the oil life is 0 percent, the display will show CHANGE ENGINE OIL. After changing oil, reset oil life display.

3) To reset service reminder on 1989 models, press RANGE button until OIL LIFE INDEX appears on display. Depress and hold in AVG ECON and RANGE buttons for more than 5 seconds or until 100 is displayed. This will reset remaining oil life to 100 percent.

4) On 1990-92 models, press RANGE button until OIL LIFE INDEX appears on DIC display. Depress and hold in AVG SPEED and RANGE buttons for more than 5 seconds or until 100 is displayed. This will reset remaining oil life to 100 percent.

1989-91 CADILLAC ELDORADO & SEVILLE

Engine Data Display – **1)** An OIL LIFE INDEX is one of 4 displays on Driver Information Center (DIC). It will display remaining oil life as a percentage estimate of the useful life of oil.

2) Display will show 100 percent when the system is reset. When remaining oil life is 10 percent or less, the system will display CHANGE OIL SOON. When the oil life expires, the display will show CHANGE ENGINE OIL. After changing oil, reset oil life display.

3) To reset oil life display, press ENG DATA button until OIL LIFE INDEX appears on DIC display. Depress and hold in ENG DATA and RANGE buttons until 100 is displayed. This will reset remaining oil life to 100 percent.

1992 CADILLAC ELDORADO & SEVILLE

Engine Data Display – **1)** Oil change reminder display is similar to 1990-91 models, but reset procedures are different. After changing oil, reset oil life display.

2) To reset, press INFORMATION button to display OIL LIFE INDEX. Press and hold STORE/RECALL button until 100 is displayed. This will reset oil life display to 100 percent.

1991-92 CADILLAC DEVILLE & FLEETWOOD

Engine Data Display – **1)** An OIL LIFE INDEX is one of the displays on Driver Information Center (DIC). It will display remaining oil life as a estimated percentage of the useful life of oil.

2) It will show 100 percent when the system is reset. When the oil life is 0 percent, the display will show CHANGE ENGINE OIL. After performing necessary services, reset service reminder.

3) To reset service reminder, depress and hold RANGE and FUEL USED buttons until OIL LIFE INDEX appears on DIC display. Depress and hold RANGE and RESET buttons for 5-60 seconds.

4) When CHANGE OIL SOON light flashes 4 times, remaining oil life index is reset to 100 percent. If CHANGE OIL SOON comes on and stays on for 5 seconds, display did not reset. Repeat step **3)**.

1990-91 CHEVROLET CORVETTE

Engine Oil Life Monitor – 1) Engine oil life monitor calculates engine oil temperature and RPM. It indicates when the oil is nearly worn out. A CHANGE OIL light on left side of instrument cluster is illuminated when it is time to change oil.

2) To reset oil life monitor, turn ignition on. Depress ENG MET button on trip monitor and release. Within 5 seconds, depress and release ENG MET button again. Within 5 seconds, depress and hold the RANGE button on trip monitor. The CHANGE OIL light should flash.

3) Hold the RANGE button depressed until the CHANGE OIL light stops flashing and goes out. When the light goes out, the engine oil life monitor is reset. This should take about 10 seconds. If the light does not reset, turn the ignition off and repeat the procedure.

1992 CHEVROLET CORVETTE

Engine Oil Life Monitor – 1) The CHANGE OIL light, located on left side of instrument cluster is illuminated when its time to change oil. When engine oil is changed, reset CHANGE OIL indicator even if indicator did not illuminate. This ensures indicator accuracy for next oil change.

2) To reset oil life monitor, turn ignition on. Press ENG MET button, located on the trip monitor, and release. Within 5 seconds, press and release ENG MET button again. Within another 5 seconds, press and hold the GAUGES button located on the trip monitor.

3) CHANGE OIL light will begin flashing. Hold GAUGES button pressed until CHANGE OIL light goes out. When light goes out, engine oil life monitor is reset. This should take about 10 seconds. If light does not reset, turn ignition off and repeat procedure.

1990-91 OLDSMOBILE CUTLASS CALAIS, CUTLASS SUPREME, CUTLASS CIERA, CUTLASS CRUISER, DELTA 88, NINETY-EIGHT & TOURING SEDAN

Engine Data Display – 1) An oil change reminder displays estimated percentage of the remaining useful life of the oil. When vehicle is started, a tone will sound and approximate distance to next oil change will be displayed.

2) When remaining oil life is 10 percent or less, the system will calculate distance to next oil change. When the oil life is 0 percent, the display will show CHANGE OIL NOW. After changing oil, reset oil life display.

3) To reset the display, press and hold in OIL button to select the oil life display. Then, press and hold in RESET and OIL buttons for at least 5 seconds. This will reset oil life display to 100 percent.

1992 OLDSMOBILE DELTA 88, NINETY-EIGHT

Engine Data Display – 1) Oil change reminder display is similar to 1990-91 models, but reset procedures are different. After changing oil, reset oil life display.

2) To reset the display, press and release the TEST button. Press and release the OIL button. Press and hold the RESET button for at least 5 seconds. This will reset oil life display to 100 percent.

1989-92 OLDSMOBILE TORONADO & TROFEO

Vehicles With Information Center Display – 1) OIL LIFE INDEX is one of 4 engine data displays used on models with Information Center display. It will display remaining oil life as estimated percentage of the useful life of oil. It will show 100 percent when the system is reset. After changing oil, reset oil life display.

2) To reset the display, press ENG DATA button (1989-90) or OPTIONS button (1991-92) until oil life index is displayed. Then, press and hold in ENG DATA and GAGE buttons (1989) or RESET/ENTER button (1990-92) for at least 5 seconds. This will reset remaining oil life to 100 percent.

Vehicles With Visual Information Center (VIC) – 1) OIL LIFE is one of the displays used on models with a VIC. It will display data regard-

ing previous oil change. A bar graph display shows full when oil is changed. Bar graph will go down as vehicle is driven and oil ages. When bar graph reaches CHANGE OIL mark, oil should be changed. After changing oil, reset oil life display.

2) To reset the display, press INFO hard key and then OIL LIFE soft key to display oil life index. Press RESET soft key. A reset confirmation page will appear and ask if oil has been changed. Press YES soft key to reset bar graph, and update last oil change date and mileage information.

1988-89 PONTIAC BONNEVILLE & 1987-89 6000 STE

Service Interval Reminder Light – 1) SERVICE REMINDER light is used on models with a Driver Information Center (DIC). After performing necessary services, reset service reminder light.

2) To reset service reminder, push DIC button until desired service item is displayed. Press and hold down the DIC button. With button pressed, the distance display will decrease in increments of 500 miles. Release button when desired distance is displayed on the DIC.

1990-91 PONTIAC BONNEVILLE

Service Interval Reminder Light – 1) SERVICE REMINDER light is used on models with a Driver Information Center (DIC). After performing necessary services, reset service reminder light.

2) To reset service reminder, push DIC button until service item preceding desired service item is displayed. Press and hold down the DIC button. This will advance display to desired service item and, with button pressed, the distance between service intervals will decrease in increments of 500 miles.

3) Release button when desired distance is displayed on the DIC. If the SERVICE REMINDER remains on after resetting, drive vehicle. Light should go out within 10 miles of driving.

JEEP

1988-90 CHEROKEE, COMANCHE, WAGONEER & WRANGLER

Emission Maintenance Indicator Light – 1) Vehicles are equipped with an emission maintenance indicator light on instrument cluster. This light will come on one time at 82,500 miles to alert driver that emission service is required. At this time, oxygen sensor and PCV valve must be replaced and all other emission components should be inspected and serviced or replaced as necessary.

2) Indicator timer is located under dash, near accelerator pedal or to right of steering column. Timer cannot be reset. To turn off light, timer must be replaced or disconnected. Since timer and sensor are interdependent, if timer should fail prematurely, oxygen sensor should be replaced at same time to preserve correct replacement interval.

3) To replace timer on Cherokee, Comanche and Wagoneer models, remove cruise control module (if equipped). Remove timer mounting screws. Disconnect electrical connector. On Wrangler models, remove timer mounting screws. Disconnect electrical connector. To install, reverse removal procedure.

1991-92 CHEROKEE, COMANCHE & WRANGLER

Emission Maintenance Indicator Light – Vehicles are equipped with an emission maintenance indicator light on instrument cluster. This light will come on one time at 82,500 miles to alert driver that emission service is required. At this time, oxygen sensor must be replaced and all other emission components should be inspected and serviced or replaced as necessary. Chrysler's Diagnostic Readout Box (DRB-II) tester is required to reset the emission maintenance indicator light.

Reset Procedure – Using DRB-II tester, access SELECT SYSTEMS. Select appropriate engine. Select with or without A/C. Select FUEL & IGNITION. Select ADJUSTMENTS. Select RESET EMR LIGHT. Reset EMR light. When DRB-II is finished resetting light, DRB-II display will read EMR LIGHT IS RESET.

1992 GENERAL INFORMATION
Using Mitchell's Wiring Diagrams

INTRODUCTION

Mitchell obtains wiring diagrams and technical service bulletins, containing wiring diagram changes, from the domestic and import manufacturers. These are checked for accuracy and are all redrawn into a consistent format for easy use.

All diagrams are arranged with the front of the vehicle at the left side of the first page and the rear of the vehicle at the right side of the last page. Accessories are shown near the end of the diagram.

Components are shown in their approximate location on the vehicle. Due to the constantly increasing number of components on vehicles today, it is impossible to show exact locations.

In the past, when cars were simpler, diagrams were simpler. All components were connected by wires, and diagrams seldom exceeded 4 pages in length. Today some wiring diagrams require more than 16 pages. It would be impractical to expect a service technician to trace a wire from page 1 across every page to page 16.

Removing some of the wiring maze reduces eyestrain and time wasted searching across several pages. Today, Mitchell wiring diagrams now follow a much improved format, which permits space for internal details of relays and switches.

Any wires that don't connect directly to their components are identified on the diagram to indicate where they go. There is a legend on the first page of each diagram, detailing component location. It refers you to sub-systems, using grid NUMBERS at the top and bottom of the page and grid LETTERS on each side. This grid system works in a manner similar to that of a road map.

HOW TO USE MITCHELL'S WIRING DIAGRAMS

1) On the first page of the diagram, you will find a listing of major electrical components or systems. Locate the specific component or system you wish to trace. A grid number and letter will follow the component's name.

2) Use the grid NUMBERS (arranged horizontally across the top and bottom of each page) to find the page of the wiring diagram that contains the component you're seeking. When you reach this page, use the grid LETTER/NUMBER combination to find the component's location.

3) Locate the circuit you need to service. The internals are shown for switches and relays to assist you in understanding how the circuit operates.

4) If the wires are not drawn all the way to another component (across several pages), a reference will tell you their final destination.

5) Again, use the legend on the first page of the wiring diagram to determine the grid number and letter of the referenced component. You can then turn directly to it without tracing wires across several pages.

6) The symbols shown in *Fig. 1* are called tie-offs. The first tie-off shown indicates that the circuit goes to the temperature sensor, and is also a ground circuit. The second symbol indicates that the circuit goes to the battery positive terminal. The third symbol leads to a particular component and the location is also given.

7) The lines shown in *Fig. 2* are called options. Which path or option to take depends on what engine or systems the vehicle has.

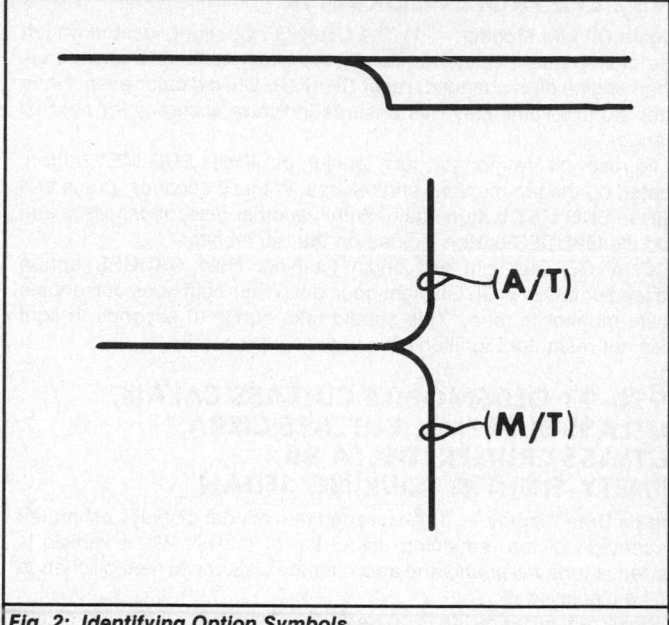

Fig. 2: Identifying Option Symbols

COLOR ABBREVIATIONS

Color	Normal	Optional
Black	BLK	BK
Blue	BLU	BU
Brown	BRN	BN
Clear	CLR	CR
Dark Blue	DK BLU	DK BU
Dark Green	DK GRN	DK GN
Green	GRN	GN
Gray	GRY	GY
Light Blue	LT BLU	LT BU
Light Green	LT GRN	LT GN
Orange	ORG	OG
Pink	PNK	PK
Purple	PPL	PL
Red	RED	RD
Tan	TAN	TN
Violet	VIO	VI
White	WHT	WT
Yellow	YEL	YL

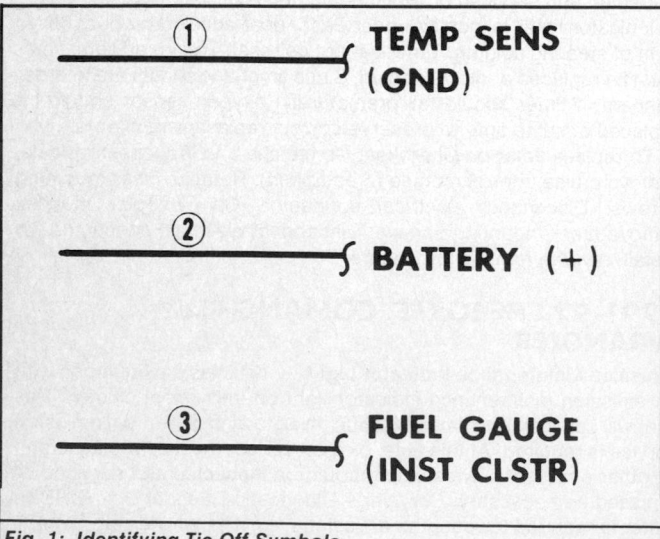

Fig. 1: Identifying Tie-Off Symbols

(Continued on Next Page)

IDENTIFYING WIRING DIAGRAM SYMBOLS

NOTE: Standard wiring symbols are used on Mitchell diagrams. The list below will help clarify any symbols that are not easily understood at a glance. Most components are labeled "Motor", "Switch" or "Relay" in addition to being drawn with the standard symbol.

 CIRCUIT BREAKER

 COIL (Internal)

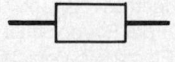 CONNECTOR

 DIODE (In-Line)

 DIODE (Internal)

 DIODE (Light Emitting)

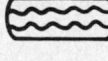 DEFOGGER GRID

 FUSE

 FUSIBLE LINK

 GROUND

 GLOW PLUG, RESISTOR (In-line), MIRROR HEATER

 INJECTOR, PHOTOCELL

 INTERNAL FUSE, THERMAL LIMITER

 LAMP (Dual Element)

 LAMP (Single Element)

 MOTOR

 RESISTOR (Internal)

 SENSOR, THERMISTOR

 SOLENOID

 SOLID STATE DEVICE, TRANSISTOR

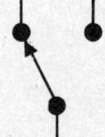 SWITCH (Internal)

 TWO PIN SWITCH

 VARIABLE RESISTOR OR POTENTIOMETER

IDENTIFYING WIRING DIAGRAM ABBREVIATIONS

NOTE: Abbreviations in Mitchell Wiring Diagrams are normally self-explanatory. To assist you, we have included a 2-page abbreviation list in this section.

1992 GENERAL INFORMATION
Commonly Used Abbreviations

"A"

A – Amperes
AAP – Auxiliary Accelerator Pump
AB – Air Bleed
ABDC – After Bottom Dead Center
ABS – Anti-Lock Brakes
ABRS – Air Bag Restraint System
Abs. – Absolute
AC – Alternating Current
A/C – Air Conditioning
ACCS – A/C Cycling Switch
ACCUM – Accumulator
ACCY – Accessory
ACT – Air Charge Temperature
 Sensor
ADJ – Adjust or Adjustable
ADV – Advance
AFS – Airflow Sensor
AI – Air Injection
AIR or A.I.R. – Air Injection
 Reactor
AIS – Air Injection System
ALCL – Assembly Line
 Communications Link
ALDL – Assembly Line
 Diagnostic Link
Alt. – Alternator or Altitude
Amp. – Ampere
ASCS – Air Suction Control Solenoid
ASD – Auto Shutdown
ASDM – Air Bag System
 Diagnostic Module
Assy. – Assembly
ASV – Air Suction Valve
A/T – Automatic Transmission/
 Transaxle
ATC – Automatic Temperature
 Control
ATDC – After Top Dead Center
ATF – Automatic Transmission Fluid
ATS – Air Temperature Sensor
Aux. – Auxiliary
Avg. – Average
AXOD – Automatic Transaxle
 Overdrive

"B"

BAC – By-Pass Air Control
BAP – Barometric Absolute
 Pressure Sensor
BARO – Barometric
Batt. – Battery
BBDC – Before Bottom Dead Center
Bbl. – Barrel (Example: 4-Bbl.)
BCM – Body Control Module
BDC – Bottom Dead Center
BHP – Brake Horsepower
Blst. – Ballast
BMAP – Barometric and Manifold
 Absolute Pressure Sensor
BOO – Brake On-Off Switch
B/P – Backpressure
BPS – Barometric Pressure Sensor
BPT – Backpressure Transducer
BTDC – Before Top Dead Center
BTU – British Thermal Unit
BVSV – Bimetallic Vacuum
 Switching Valve

"C"

°C – Celsius (Degrees)
Calif. – California
CANP – Canister Purge
CARB – California Air
 Resources Board
CAT – Catalytic Converter
CB – Circuit Breaker
CBD – Closed Bowl Distributor
CBVV – Carburetor Bowl Vent Valve
cc – cubic centimeter
CCC – Computer Command Control
CCD – Computer Controlled Dwell
CCOT – Cycling Clutch Orifice Tube
CCW – Counterclockwise
CDI – Capacitor Discharge Ignition
CEC – Computerized Engine Control
CID – Cubic Inch Displacement
CIS – Continuous Injection
 System
CIS-E – Continuous Injection
 System-Electronic
cm – Centimeter
CO – Carbon Monoxide
CO_2 – Carbon Dioxide
Cont. – Continued
CONV – Convertible
CP – Canister Purge
CPS – Crank Position Sensor
CTS – Coolant Temperature Sensor
Cu. In. – Cubic Inch
CVC – Constant Vacuum Control
CV – Check Valve or
 Constant Velocity
CW – Clockwise
CYL or Cyl. – Cylinder
C^3I – Computer Controlled
 Coil Ignition
C^4 – Computer Controlled
 Catalytic Converter

"D"

"D" – Drive
DBC – Dual Bed Catalyst
DC – Direct Current Or Discharge
DDD – Dual Diaphragm Distributor
Def. – Defrost
Defog. – Defogger
DERM – Diagnostic Energy
 Reserve Module
DFI – Digital Fuel Injection
Diag. – Diagnostic
DIC – Driver Information Center
DIS – Distributorless Ignition System
DIST – Distribution
DISTR – Distributor
DME – Digital Motor Electronics
 (Motronic System)
DOHC – Double Overhead Cam
DOT – Department of
 Transportation
DP – Dashpot
DRB-II – Diagnostic Readout Box
DVOM – Digital Volt-Ohmmeter

"E"

EAC – Electric Assist Choke
EACV – Electric Air Control Valve
EBCM – Electronic Brake
 Control Module
ECA – Electronic Control Assembly
ECM – Electronic Control Module
ECT – Engine Coolant
 Temperature Sensor
ECU – Electronic Control Unit
EDIS – Electronic Distributorless
 Ignition System
EEC – Electronic Engine Control
EECS – Evaporative Emission
 Control System
EEPROM – Electronically
 Erasable PROM
EFE – Early Fuel Evaporation
EGO – Exhaust Gas Oxygen Sensor
EGR – Exhaust Gas Recirculation
ESA – Electronic Spark Advance
ESC – Electronic Spark Control
EST – Electronic Spark Timing
EVAP – Fuel Evaporative System
EVIC – Electronic Vehicle
 Information Center
EVP – EGR Valve Position Sensor
Exc. – Except

"F"

°F – Fahrenheit (Degrees)
F/B – Fuse Block
FBC – Feedback Carburetor
Fed. – Federal
FI – Fuel Injection
FICD – Fast Idle Control Device
FIPL – Fuel Injector Pump Lever
FPR-VSV – Fuel Pressure Regulator
 Vacuum Switching Valve
Ft. Lbs. – Foot Pounds
FWD – Front Wheel Drive

"G"

g – grams
Gals. – gallons
GND or GRND – Ground
Gov. – Governor

"H"

HAC – High Altitude Compensation
HC – Hydrocarbons
H/D – Heavy Duty
HEGO – Heated Exhaust Gas
 Oxygen Sensor
HEI – High Energy Ignition
Hg – Mercury
Hgt. – Height
HLDT – Headlight
HO – High Output
HP – High Performance
HSC – High Swirl Combustion
HSO – High Specific Output
HTR – Heater
Hz – Hertz (Cycles Per Second)

"I"

IAC – Idle Air Control
IACV – Idle Air Control Valve
IC – Integrated Circuit
ID – Identification
I.D. – Inside Diameter
Ign. – Ignition
In. – Inches
INCH Lbs. – Inch Pounds
in. Hg – Inches of Mercury
Inj. – Injector
IP – Instrument Panel
IPC – Instrument Panel Cluster
ISC – Idle Speed Control
IVSV – Idle Vacuum Switching Valve

"J"

J/B – Junction Block

"K"

KAPWR – Keep Alive Power
k/ohms – 1000 ohms
　　　(kilo as in k/ohms)
kg – Kilograms (weight)
kg/cm² – Kilograms Per
　　　Square Centimeter
KM/H – Kilometers Per Hour
KOEO – Key On, Engine Off
KOER – Key On, Engine Running
KS – Knock Sensor

"L"

L – Liter
Lbs. – Pounds
LCD – Liquid Crystal Display
L/D – Light Duty
LED – Light Emitting Diode
LH – Left Hand

"M"

mA – Milliamps
MA or MAF – Mass Airflow
MAFS – Mass Airflow Sensor
MAP – Manifold Absolute Pressure
MAT – Manifold Air Temperature
MCU – Microprocessor Control Unit
MCV – Mixture Control Valve
Mem. – Memory
MEM-CAL – Memory Calibration
　　　Chip
mfd. – Microfarads
MFI – Multiport Fuel Injection
MIL – Malfunction Indicator Light
MPI – Multi-Point (Fuel) Injection
mm – Millimeters
MPH – Miles Per Hour
mV – Millivolts

"N"

NA – Not Available
N.m – Newton Meter
No. – Number
Nos. – Numbers
NOx – Oxides of Nitrogen

"O"

O – Oxygen
OC – Oxidation Catalyst
OD – Overdrive
O.D. – Outside Diameter
ODO – Odometer
OHC – Overhead Camshaft
O/S – Oversize
oz. – Ounce
ozs. – Ounces
O_2 – Oxygen

"P"

"P" – Park
PAV – Pulse Air Valve
P/C – Printed Circuit
PCM – Power Train Control Module
PCS – Purge Control Solenoid
PC-SOL – Purge Control Solenoid
PCV – Positive Crankcase
　　　Ventilation
PFI – Port Fuel Injection
PGM-CARB – Programmed
　　　Carburetor
PGM-FI – Programmed
　　　Fuel Injection
PIP – Profile Ignition Pick-up
P/N – Park/Neutral
PRNDL – Park Reverse Neutral
　　　Drive Low
PROM – Programmable
　　　Read-Only Memory
psi – Pounds Per Square Inch
P/S – Power Steering
PSPS – Power Steering
　　　Pressure Switch
PTC – Positive Temperature
　　　Coefficient
PTO – Power Take-Off
Pts. – Pints
Pwr. – Power

"Q"

Qts. – Quarts

R

RABS – Rear Anti-Lock Brake
　　　System
RECIRC – Recirculation
RH – Right Hand
RPM – Revolutions Per Minute
RWAL – Rear Wheel
　　　Anti-Lock Brake
RWD – Rear Wheel Drive

"S"

SBC – Single Bed Converter
SBEC – Single Board
　　　Engine Controller
SEN – Sensor
SES – Service Engine Soon
SFI – Sequential (Port) Fuel Injection
SIL – Shift Indicator Light
SIR – Supplemental Inflatable Restraint
SOHC – Single Overhead Cam
SOL or Sol. – Solenoid
SPFI – Sequential Port
　　　Fuel Injection
SPK – Spark Control
SPOUT – Spark Output
SRS – Supplemental
　　　Restraint System (Air Bag)
SSI – Solid State Ignition
STAR – Self-Test Automatic
　　　Readout
STO – Self-Test Output
SUB-O_2 – Sub Oxygen Sensor
Sw. – Switch
Sys. – System

"T"

TAB – Thermactor Air By-Pass
TAC – Thermostatic Air Cleaner
TAD – Thermactor Air Diverter
TBI – Throttle Body Injection
TCC – Torque Converter Clutch
TCCS – Toyota Computer
　　　Control System
TDC – Top Dead Center
Temp. – Temperature
TFI – Thick Film Ignition
THERMAC – Thermostatic Air
　　　Cleaner
TPS – Throttle Position
　　　Sensor/Switch
TS – Temperature Sensor
TV – Thermovalve
T.V. – Throttle Valve
TWC – Three-Way Catalyst

"V"

V – Valve
Vac. – Vacuum
VAF – Vane Airflow
VAPS – Variable Assist
　　　Power Steering
VCC – Viscous Converter Clutch
VIN – Vehicle Identification Number
VM – Vacuum Modulator
Volt. – Voltage
VOM – Volt-Ohmmeter (Analog)
VRV – Vacuum Regulator Valve
VSS – Vehicle Speed Sensor
VSV – Vacuum Switching Valve

"W"

W/ – With
W/O – Without
WAC – Wide Open Throttle
　　　A/C Switch
WOT – Wide Open Throttle

1992 GENERAL INFORMATION
Trouble Shooting

CHARGING SYSTEM

CHARGING SYSTEM TROUBLE SHOOTING

PROBLEM
Possible Cause   Action

NO START CONDITION
Dead Battery .... Check/Replace Battery
Bad Cable Connections .... Clean/Replace Cables
Ignition Switch/Circuit Fault .... Check Switch/Circuit

CHARGING SYSTEM WARNING LIGHT STAYS ON
Loose/Worn Alternator Belt .... Tighten/Replace Belt
Loose Alternator Connections .... Check/Repair Connections
Warning Light Wiring .... Check/Repair Wiring
Faulty Stator/Diodes .... Test/Repair Alternator
Faulty Voltage Regulator .... Test/Repair Regulator

WARNING LIGHT OFF WITH IGNITION SWITCH ON
Blown Fuse .... Check/Replace Fuse
Faulty Alternator .... Test Alternator
Bad Warning Light Bulb .... Test/Replace Bulb

WARNING LIGHT ON WITH IGNITION SWITCH OFF
Alternator Wiring Short .... Check/Repair Wiring
Faulty Rectifier Bridge .... Test/Repair Alternator

AMMETER INDICATES DISCHARGE
Loose/Worn Alternator Belt .... Tighten/Replace Belt
Loose Alternator Connections .... Check/Repair Connections
Faulty Ammeter .... Test/Replace Ammeter

NOISY ALTERNATOR
Loose Drive Pulley .... Check/Tighten Pulley Nut
Loose Mounting Bolts .... Tighten Mounting Bolts
Worn/Dirty Alternator
 Bearings .... Clean/Replace Alternator Bearings
Faulty Diodes/Stator .... Replace Diodes/Stator

BATTERY WON'T STAY CHARGED
Defective Battery .... Test/Replace Battery
Accessories Left ON .... Ensure Accessories OFF
Loose/Worn Alternator Belt .... Tighten/Replace Belt
Loose Alternator Connections .... Check/Repair Connections
Defective Alternator .... Test/Repair Alternator
Short in System .... Check/Repair Short

BATTERY OVERCHARGED
Defective Battery .... Replace Battery
Defective Alternator .... Test/Repair Alternator
Defective Regulator .... Test/Repair Regulator

STARTING SYSTEM

STARTING SYSTEM TROUBLE SHOOTING

PROBLEM
Possible Cause   Action

STARTER FAILS TO OPERATE
Dead Battery .... Check/Replace Battery
Bad Connections/Wiring .... Repair Connections/Wiring
Faulty Ignition Switch .... Check Switch Circuit
Faulty Solenoid/Relay .... Replace Solenoid/Relay
Faulty Ground .... Check/Repair Ground

STARTER FAILS TO OPERATE – LIGHTS DIM
Faulty Battery .... Replace Battery
Bad Cable Connections .... Check/Repair Connections
Grounded Starter Windings .... Test/Repair Starter
Faulty Bearing/Bushing .... Replace Bearing/Bushing
Faulty Ground .... Check/Repair Ground
Corroded Terminals .... Clean Terminals

STARTER TURNS – ENGINE DOES NOT
Faulty Starter Drive .... Replace Starter Drive
Broken Drive Housing .... Replace Drive Housing
Faulty Pinion Shaft .... Clean/Repair Shaft
Faulty Flywheel .... Check Flywheel/Starter

STARTING SYSTEM TROUBLE SHOOTING (Cont.)

PROBLEM
Possible Cause   Action

STARTER DOES NOT CRANK ENGINE
Faulty Starter Drive .... Replace Starter Drive
Broken Drive Housing .... Replace Drive Housing
Missing Flywheel Teeth .... Replace Flywheel
Faulty Ground .... Check/Repair Ground
Frozen Engine .... Check Engine
Liquid-Locked Engine .... Test Cooling System

STARTER ROTATES ENGINE SLOWLY
Faulty Battery .... Replace Battery
Bad Connections/Wiring .... Repair Connections/Wiring
Grounded Starter Windings .... Test/Repair Starter
Faulty Starter Bearings .... Replace Bearings
Faulty Ground .... Check/Repair Ground
Engine Overheated .... Check Cooling System
Timing Too Far Advanced .... Reset Timing
Burned Solenoid Contacts .... Replace Solenoid
High Current Draw .... Test Starter Draw

STARTER ENGAGES ENGINE MOMENTARILY
Timing Too Far Retarded .... Reset Timing
Missing Flywheel Teeth .... Replace Flywheel
Faulty Starter Drive .... Replace Starter Drive
Broken Drive Housing .... Replace Drive Housing
Weak Starter Solenoid .... Replace Starter Solenoid

STARTER DRIVE DOES NOT ENGAGE
Bad Solenoid Contacts .... Replace Solenoid
Bad Solenoid Ground .... Test Solenoid Ground

SOLENOID/RELAY DOES NOT CLOSE
Faulty Battery .... Replace Battery
Bad Connections/Wiring .... Repair Connections/Wiring
Faulty Safety Switch .... Replace Safety Switch
Faulty Solenoid/Relay .... Replace Solenoid/Relay

STARTER DRIVE WILL NOT DISENGAGE
Loose Starter Bolts .... Tighten Starter Bolts
Worn Drive End
 Bushing .... Replace Drive End Bushing
Missing Flywheel Teeth .... Check Flywheel/Drive
Faulty Ignition Switch .... Replace Ignition Switch

SOLENOID CLICKS
Weak Battery .... Charge/Replace Battery
Bad Solenoid Contacts .... Replace Solenoid
Bad Connections/Wiring .... Repair Connections/Wiring
Faulty Solenoid .... Replace Solenoid

HIGH CURRENT DRAW
Dragging Armature .... Replace Starter Bushings
Shorted Armature Windings .... Repair Starter

LOW CURRENT DRAW
Worn Starter Brushes .... Replace Brushes
Weak Brush Springs .... Replace Brush Springs
Faulty Engine Ground .... Check Ground Cable
High Resistance In Positive
 Battery Cable .... Replace Cable

STARTER WHINES DURING CRANKING
Starter Alignment .... Check Starter Alignment
Too Much Distance Between
 Starter Drive & Flywheel .... Ensure Flywheel is Okay
                                                        Ensure Starter is Correct

STARTER WHINES AFTER STARTING
Starter Alignment .... Check Starter Alignment
Too Little Distance Between
 Starter Drive & Flywheel .... Ensure Flywheel is Okay
                                                        Ensure Starter is Correct

TUNE-UP

TUNE-UP TROUBLE SHOOTING

PROBLEM
Possible Cause — **Action**

CARBON FOULED PLUGS
Rich Air/Fuel Mixture .... Adjust Air/Fuel Mixture
Faulty Choke .... Replace Choke Assembly
Clogged Air Filter .... Replace Air Filter
Incorrect Idle Speed .... Reset Idle Speed
Faulty Ignition Wiring .... Replace Ignition Wiring
Sticky Valves/Worn Valve Seal .... Check Valve Train
Fuel Injection Operation .... Check Fuel Injection

WET/OIL FOULED PLUGS
Worn Rings/Pistons .... Check Block Condition
Excessive Cylinder Wear .... Rebore/Replace Block

PLUG GAP BRIDGED
Combustion Chamber
  Carbon Deposits .... Clean Combustion Chamber

BLISTERED ELECTRODE
Engine Overheating .... Check Cooling System
Loose Spark Plugs .... Clean/Torque Plugs
Over-Advanced Timing .... Reset Timing
Wrong Plug Heat Range .... Install Correct Plug

MELTED ELECTRODES
Incorrect Timing .... Reset Timing
Burned Valves .... Replace Valves
Engine Overheating .... Check Cooling System
Wrong Plug Heat Range .... Install Correct Plug

ENGINE WON'T START
Loose Connections .... Check Connections
No Power .... Check Fuses/Battery

ENGINE RUNS ROUGH
Leaky/Clogged Fuel Lines .... Repair Fuel Lines
Incorrect Timing .... Reset Timing/Check Advance
Faulty Plugs/Wires .... Replace Plugs/Wires

COMPONENT FAILURE
Spark Arcing .... Replace Faulty Part
Defective Pick-Up Coil .... Replace Pick-Up Coil
Defective Ignition Coil .... Replace Ignition Coil
Defective Control Unit .... Replace Control Unit

IGNITION DIAGNOSIS BY SCOPE PATTERN

ALL FIRING LINES ABNORMALLY HIGH
Retarded Ignition Timing .... Reset Ignition Timing
Lean Air/Fuel Mixture .... Adjust Fuel Mixture
High Secondary Resistance .... Repair Secondary Ignition

ALL FIRING LINES ABNORMALLY LOW
Rich Air/Fuel Mixture .... Adjust Air/Fuel Mixture
Arcing Coil Wire .... Replace Coil Wire
Cracked Coil Arcing .... Replace Coil
Low Coil Output .... Replace Coil
Low Compression .... Check/Repair Engine

SEVERAL HIGH FIRING LINES
Fuel Mixture Unbalanced .... Adjust Fuel Mixture
EGR Valve Stuck Open .... Clean/Replace EGR Valve
High Plug Wire Resistance .... Replace Plug Wire
Cracked/Broken Plugs .... Replace Plugs
Intake Vacuum Leak .... Repair Leak

SEVERAL LOW FIRING LINES
Fuel Mixture Unbalanced .... Adjust Fuel Mixture
Plug Wires Arcing .... Replace Plug Wires
Cracked Coil Arcing .... Replace Coil
Low Compression .... Check/Repair Engine
Faulty Spark Plugs .... Replace Plugs

TUNE-UP TROUBLE SHOOTING (Cont.)

PROBLEM
Possible Cause — **Action**

CYLINDERS NOT FIRING
Cracked Distributor Cap .... Replace Cap
Shorted Plug Wires .... Replace Plug Wires
Mechanical Engine Fault .... Check/Repair Engine
Spark Plugs Fouled .... Replace Plugs
Carbon Track in Distributor Cap .... Replace Cap

HARD STARTING
Defective Ignition Coil(s) .... Replace Coil(s)
Fouled Spark Plugs .... Replace Plugs
Incorrect Timing .... Reset Ignition Timing

CARBURETOR

CARBURETOR TROUBLE SHOOTING

PROBLEM
Possible Cause — **Action**

ENGINE WON'T START
Choke Not Closing .... Check Choke/Linkage
Choke Linkage Bent .... Check Linkage
Float Dry .... Check/Reset Float Setting

ENGINE STARTS, THEN DIES
Choke Breaker Setting Too Wide .... Check Setting/Adjust
Fast Idle RPM Too Low .... Reset Fast Idle
Fast Idle Cam Index Incorrect .... Reset Fast Idle Cam Index
Vacuum Leak .... Check For Vacuum Leaks
Low Fuel Pump Output .... Repair/Replace Fuel Pump
Low Float Level .... Check/Reset Float Setting

ENGINE QUITS UNDER LOAD
Choke Breaker Setting Incorrect .... Reset Choke Breaker
Fast Idle Cam Index Incorrect .... Reset Fast Idle Cam Index
Hot Fast Idle Speed RPM Incorrect .... Reset Fast Idle RPM

ENGINE IDLES SLOWLY WITH BLACK SMOKE
Choke Breaker Setting Incorrect .... Reset Choke Breaker
Fast Idle Cam Index Incorrect .... Reset Fast Idle Cam Index
Hot Fast Idle RPM Too Low .... Reset Fast Idle RPM

COLD ENGINE STALLS IN GEAR
Choke Breaker Setting Incorrect .... Reset Choke Breaker
Fast Idle RPM Incorrect .... Reset Fast Idle RPM
Fast Idle Cam Index Incorrect .... Reset Fast Idle Cam Index

ACCELERATION SAG OR STALL
Defective Choke Heater .... Replace Choke Heater
Choke Breaker Setting .... Reset Choke Breaker
Float Level Too Low .... Adjust Float Level
Accelerator Pump Defective .... Repair Accelerator Pump

SAG OR STALL AFTER WARM-UP
Defective Choke Heater .... Replace Choke Heater
Faulty Accelerator Pump .... Replace Accelerator Pump
Float Level Too Low .... Adjust Float Level

WARM-UP BACKFIRING/BLACK SMOKE
Choke Stuck Shut .... Check/Replace Choke

TIP-IN HESITATION
Vacuum Leak .... Inspect Vacuum Lines
Accelerator Pump Weak .... Replace Accelerator Pump
Float Level Setting Too Low .... Reset Float Level
Metering Rods Sticking/Binding .... Inspect/Replace Rods
Idle Passages Plugged .... Clean/Rebuild Carburetor

WOT HESITATION
Faulty Accelerator Pump .... Replace Accelerator Pump
Large Vacuum Leak .... Check For Vacuum Leaks
Float Level Too Low .... Reset Float Level
Fuel Delivery Problem .... Inspect Pump, Lines, Filter

1992 GENERAL INFORMATION
Trouble Shooting (Cont.)

FUEL INJECTION

FUEL INJECTION TROUBLE SHOOTING

PROBLEM
Possible Cause — Action

ENGINE WON'T START
Cold Start Valve Inoperative .... Test Cold Start Valve
Poor Vacuum/Electrical Connection .... Repair Connections
Contaminated Fuel .... Test Fuel for Water/Alcohol
Bad Fuel Pump Relay/Circuit .... Test Relay/Wiring
Battery Voltage Low .... Charge/Test Battery
Low Fuel Pressure .... Test Press. Regulator/Pump
No Distributor Reference Pulse .... Repair Ignition System
Coolant Temp. Sensor Defective .... Test Temp. Sensor/Circuit
Shorted WOT Switch .... Check/Replace WOT Switch
Defective ECM .... Replace ECM

HARD STARTING
Defective Idle Air Control (IAC) .... Test IAC and Circuit
EGR Valve Open .... Test EGR Valve/Control Circuit
Stalls With A/C On .... Check A/C "On" Signal to ECM
Restricted Fuel Lines .... Inspect/Replace Fuel Lines
Poor MAP Sensor Signal .... Test MAP Sensor/Circuit
Engine Stalls During
  Parking Maneuver .... Check Power Steering Pressure
No Power To Injectors .... Check Injector Fuse/Relay

ROUGH IDLE
Poor MAP Sensor Signal .... Test MAP Sensor/Circuit
Intermittent Fuel Injector
  Operation .... Check Harness Connectors
Erratic Vehicle Speed Sensor
  Inputs .... Harness Too Close to Plug Wires
Poor Temperature Sensor Signal .... Test EGR Valve/Circuit
Poor O$_2$ Sensor Signal .... Test O$_2$ Sensor/Circuit
Faulty PCV System .... Check PCV Valve and Hoses

POOR HIGH SPEED OPERATION
Low Fuel Pump Volume .... Faulty Fuel Pump/Filter
Poor MAP Sensor Signal .... Test Speed Sensor/Circuit

ACCELERATION PING/KNOCK
Poor Knock Sensor Signal .... Test Knock Sensor/Circuit
Poor Baro Sensor Signal .... Test Baro Sensor/Circuit
Improper Ignition Timing .... Adjust Timing
Engine Overheating .... Check Cooling System

TURBOCHARGER

TURBOCHARGER TROUBLE SHOOTING

PROBLEM
Possible Cause — Action

Faulty Spark Advance System .... Check Distributor/Ignition
Defective EGR Operation .... Check EGR System
Air Inlet Restriction .... Clear Restriction
Excessive Boost .... Check/Adjust Boost Pressure
Fuel System Fault .... Check Fuel System
Internal Turbo Defect .... Repair/Replace Turbo

LOW ENGINE POWER
Faulty Spark Advance System .... Check Distributor/Ignition
Defective EGR Operation .... Check EGR System
Loose Turbo Bolts .... Check/Tighten Bolts

BLUE EXHAUST SMOKE
Oil Inlet Leak .... Check/Repair Fittings
Oil Drain Leak/Plugged .... Check/Repair Fittings
Turbo Seal Leak .... Check/Replace Seal

GAS ENGINE

GAS ENGINE TROUBLE SHOOTING

PROBLEM
Possible Cause — Action

ENGINE LOPES AT IDLE
Leaky Intake Gasket .... Replace Intake Gasket
Blown Head Gasket .... Replace Head Gasket
                                                         Test Cooling System
Worn Timing Chain/Gears .... Replace Timing Chain/Gears
Worn Timing Belt .... Inspect/Replace Belt
Worn Cam .... Inspect Valve Train
Overheated Engine .... Check Cooling System
Clogged PCV System .... Check/Clear PCV System
Leaking EGR Valve .... Check/Replace EGR Valve
Faulty Fuel Pump .... Replace Fuel Pump

ENGINE LACKS POWER
Low Fuel Pressure .... Replace Fuel Pump
Leaky Fuel Pump .... Replace Fuel Pump
Sticky Valves .... Inspect Valve Train
Worn Timing Chain/Gears .... Replace Timing Chain/Gears
Worn Piston Rings .... Check Compression
Weak Valve Springs .... Inspect Valve Train
Worn Cam .... Inspect Cam (Lifters)
Blown Head Gasket .... Replace Head Gasket
                                                         Check Cooling System
Clutch Slipping .... Adjust/Replace Clutch
Overheated Engine .... Check Cooling System
A/T Slipping .... Inspect/Repair A/T
Vacuum Leaks .... Repair Vacuum Leaks
Restricted Exhaust .... Clear Restriction

FAULTY HIGH SPEED OPERATION
Low Fuel Pressure .... Replace Fuel Pump
Leaky Fuel Pump .... Replace Fuel Pump
Sticky Valves .... Inspect Valve Train
Incorrect Valve Timing .... Inspect Valve Train
Intake Manifold Restricted .... Clear Restriction
Worn Distributor Shaft .... Replace Distributor

POOR ACCELERATION
Incorrect Ignition Timing .... Reset Timing
Leaky Valves .... Check Compression
Weak Fuel Pump .... Test/Replace Fuel Pump
Clogged Injectors .... Clean/Replace Injectors
Excessive Intake Valve Deposits .... Clean Valve Deposits

BACKFIRE IN INTAKE MANIFOLD
Improper Ignition Timing .... Adjust Timing
Improper Valve Timing .... Inspect Valve Train
Carbon Tracking/Crossfire .... Inspect Cap/Rotor/Plug Wires
Faulty Plug Wires .... Replace Plug Wires
Defective EGR Valve .... Replace EGR Valve
Lean Fuel Mixture .... Check/Adjust Mixture
Gas in Engine Oil .... Check Fuel System
Sticky Intake Valve .... Check Valve Train
Vacuum Leaks .... Check for Vacuum Leaks

BACKFIRE IN EXHAUST
Vacuum Leak .... Repair Vacuum Leak
Faulty Diverter Valve .... Replace Diverter Valve
Faulty Choke Operation .... Adjust Choke
Exhaust System Leak .... Repair Exhaust Leak
Carbon Tracking/Crossfire .... Inspect Cap/Rotor/Plug Wires

ENGINE DETONATION/PRE-IGNITION
Too Much Timing Advance .... Reset Timing
Faulty Ignition System .... Check Ignition System
Faulty Spark Plugs .... Replace Spark Plugs
Lean Fuel Mixture .... Check Fuel System
Carbon Deposit Build-Up .... Remove Carbon
Low Octane Fuel .... Try Different Fuel
Compression Too High .... Check Compression

GAS ENGINE (Cont.)

GAS ENGINE TROUBLE SHOOTING (Cont.)

PROBLEM
Possible Cause   **Action**

EXCESSIVE OIL CONSUMPTION
Worn Valve Guides/Stems .... Inspect Valve Train
Worn Piston Rings .... Inspect Engine Block
Worn Cylinder Walls .... Inspect Engine Block
Intake Manifold Leak .... Replace Gasket
Excessive Bearing Clearance .... Inspect Bearings/Crankshaft

NO OIL PRESSURE
Low Oil Level .... Add Oil/Check for Leaks
Faulty Oil Pump .... Replace Oil Pump
Oil Pick-Up Screen Blocked .... Clear Blockage
Loose Oil Pick-Up Tube .... Check "O" Ring
Blocked Oil Passages .... Inspect Engine Block
Faulty Pressure Relief Valve .... Replace Relief Valve
Faulty Oil Light/Gauge .... Check Light/Gauge
Worn Engine Bearings .... Check/Replace Bearings
Faulty Cooling System .... Check Cooling System
Excessive Backpressure .... Check Exhaust System

LOW OIL PRESSURE
Low Oil Level .... Fill to Proper Level
Faulty Oil Pump .... Replace Oil Pump
Oil Pick-Up Screen Blocked .... Clear Blockage
Loose Oil Pick-Up Tube .... Check "O" Ring
Blocked Oil Passages .... Inspect Engine Block
Faulty Pressure Relief Valve .... Replace Relief Valve
Faulty Oil Light/Gauge .... Check Light/Gauge
Worn Engine Bearings .... Check/Replace Bearings

HIGH OIL PRESSURE
Faulty Pressure Relief Valve .... Replace Relief Valve
Improper Grade of Oil .... Change Oil/Grade
Faulty Oil Light/Gauge .... Check Light/Gauge

NOISY MAIN BEARINGS
Low Oil Level .... Check Oil Level
Low Oil Pressure .... Check Oil Pressure
Worn Main Bearings .... Inspect Engine Block
Excessive Crankshaft End Play .... Check Main Bearings
Check Thrust Washer
Loose Flywheel/Torque Converter .... Check Flywheel/Converter
Worn Vibration Damper .... Replace Vibration Damper
Worn Crankshaft .... Replace Crankshaft/Bearings
Excessive Belt Tension .... Check/Loosen Belts

NOISY CONNECTING RODS
Low Oil Level .... Check/Fill Oil Level
Low Oil Pressure .... Check Oil Pressure
Worn Rod Bearings .... Inspect/Replace Bearings
Worn Crankshaft .... Check/Replace Crankshaft/Bearings
Misaligned Rod/Cap .... Check Rod/Cap
Excessive Belt Tension .... Check/Loosen Belts

NOISY VALVE TRAIN
Low Oil Pressure .... Check Oil Level/Pressure
Improper Valve Lash .... Check Valve Lash
Loose/Worn Timing
 Belt/Chain/Gears .... Check Belt/Chain/Gears
Worn/Bent Push Rods .... Check/Replace Push Rods
Worn Rocker Arms .... Check/Replace Rocker Arms
Bent Valve .... Check Valve Train/Head
Worn Camshaft .... Check Camshaft/Bearings
Broken Valve Spring .... Replace Valve Spring
Faulty Valve Lifters .... Check Lifters/Camshaft
Worn Valve Guides .... Check Valve Train
Missing Valve Keeper .... Replace Valve Keeper
Loose Rocker Arm Studs .... Replace Studs

DIESEL ENGINE

DIESEL ENGINE TROUBLE SHOOTING

PROBLEM
Possible Cause   **Action**

ENGINE WON'T CRANK
Bad Batteries .... Test/Replace Batteries
Bad Cable Connections .... Clean/Replace Cables
Bad Starter .... Test/Repair/Replace Starter
Bad Neutral Safety Switch .... Replace Neutral Safety Switch

ENGINE CRANKS SLOWLY
Bad Batteries .... Test/Replace Batteries
Bad Cable Connections .... Clean/Replace Cables
Bad Starter .... Test/Repair/Replace Starter

ENGINE CRANKS NORMALLY, WON'T START
Faulty Glow Plugs .... Test/Replace Glow Plugs
Faulty Glow Plug Controller .... Test/Replace Controller
No Fuel To Cylinders .... Test/Replace Injectors
No Fuel To Injector Pump .... Check Fuel Delivery System
Plugged Air Filter .... Replace Air Filter
Plugged Fuel Filter .... Replace Fuel Filter
Plugged Fuel Tank Filter .... Replace Tank Filter
Faulty Fuel Pump .... Test/Replace Fuel Pump
Fuel Return System Blocked .... Clear Restriction
No Voltage To Fuel Solenoid .... Check Fuel Solenoid Wiring
Manual Shut-Off Lever Engaged .... Disengage Shut-Off Lever
Incorrect/Contaminated Fuel .... Flush/Refill Tank
Incorrect Inj. Pump Timing .... Reset Inj. Pump Timing
Low Compression .... Check Engine Condition
Faulty Injection Pump .... Test/Replace Injection Pump
Fuel Solenoid Closed
 In RUN Position .... Test/Replace Fuel Solenoid

ENGINE STARTS, WON'T IDLE
Incorrect Slow Idle Setting .... Adjust Slow Idle Setting
Plugged Air Filter .... Replace Air Filter
Faulty Fast Idle Solenoid .... Test/Replace Fast Idle Solenoid
Air In Fuel System .... Bleed Air From System
Fuel Return System Blocked .... Clear Restriction
Glow Plugs Off Too Soon .... Test Glow Plugs
Incorrect Inj. Pump Timing .... Reset Inj. Pump Timing
No Fuel To Injector Pump .... Check Fuel Delivery System
Incorrect/Contaminated Fuel .... Flush/Refill Tank
Low Compression .... Check Engine Condition
Faulty Injection Pump .... Test/Replace Injection Pump

ENGINE STARTS, IDLES ROUGH
Incorrect Slow Idle Setting .... Adjust Slow Idle Setting
Plugged Air Filter .... Replace Air Filter
Fuel Leak at Injection Line .... Repair Fuel Leak
Fuel Return System Blocked .... Clear Restriction
Air In Fuel System .... Bleed Air From System
Incorrect/Contaminated Fuel .... Flush/Refill Tank
Faulty Injector Nozzle .... Test/Replace Injector Nozzle
Low Compression .... Check Engine Condition

ENGINE SMOKES, CLEARS AFTER WARM-UP
Incorrect Inj. Pump Timing .... Reset Inj. Pump Timing
Low Compression .... Check Engine Condition
Faulty Injector Nozzle .... Test/Replace Injector Nozzle
Air In Fuel System .... Bleed Air From System

ENGINE MISFIRES ABOVE IDLE
Plugged Fuel Filter .... Replace Fuel Filter
Incorrect Inj. Pump Timing .... Reset Inj. Pump Timing
Incorrect/Contaminated Fuel .... Flush/Refill Tank

ENGINE WON'T RETURN TO IDLE
Incorrect Fast Idle Setting .... Adjust Fast Idle Setting
Faulty Injection Pump .... Test/Replace Injection Pump
External Linkage Binding .... Check/Repair Linkage
Air In Fuel System .... Repair/Bleed Air From System

1992 GENERAL INFORMATION
Trouble Shooting (Cont.)

DIESEL ENGINE (Cont.)

DIESEL ENGINE TROUBLE SHOOTING (Cont.)

PROBLEM
Possible Cause — **Action**

ENGINE LACKS POWER

Possible Cause	Action
Restricted Air Intake	Clear Restriction
Faulty EGR Valve	Replace EGR Valve
Restricted Exhaust System	Repair Exhaust System
Blocked Fuel Cap Vent	Replace Fuel Cap
Restricted Fuel Supply From Tank to Injection Pump	Clear Restriction
Incorrect/Contaminated Fuel	Flush/Refill Tank
Faulty Injector Nozzle	Test/Replace Injector Nozzle
Low Compression	Check Engine Condition
Improper Throttle Linkage Adjustment	Adjust Throttle Linkage

CYLINDER KNOCKING NOISE

Possible Cause	Action
Injector Nozzles Stuck Open	Test/Replace Injectors
Low Injector Nozzle Pressure	Test/Replace Injectors
Loose Wrist Pin	Disassemble Engine
Piston Slap	Disassemble Engine

ENGINE OVERHEATING

Possible Cause	Action
Cooling System Leaks	Repair Cooling System
Loose/Damaged Belt	Tighten/Replace Belt
Plugged Radiator	Rod/Replace Radiator
Defective Fan	Replace Fan
Restricted Airflow Across Radiator	Clear Restriction
Thermostat Stuck Closed	Replace Thermostat
Leaking Head Gasket	Replace Head Gasket Test/Repair Cooling System

ENGINE WON'T SHUT OFF

Possible Cause	Action
Injector Pump Fuel Solenoid Does Not Shut Off Fuel Valve	Test/Repair Fuel Solenoid

VACUUM PUMP TROUBLE SHOOTING

PROBLEM
Possible Cause — **Action**

EXCESSIVE NOISE

Possible Cause	Action
Loose Pump Mounting	Tighten Pump Mounting
Loose Pump Tube	Tighten Pump Tube
Faulty Pump Valves	Replace Pump Valves

OIL LEAKAGE

Possible Cause	Action
Loose End Plug	Tighten End Plug
Bad Seal Crimp	Remove/Recrimp Seal

COOLING SYSTEM

COOLING SYSTEM TROUBLE SHOOTING

PROBLEM
Possible Cause — **Action**

OVERHEATING

Possible Cause	Action
Insufficient Coolant	Fill/Pressure Test System
Coolant Leak	Fill/Pressure Test System
Radiator Fins Clogged	Remove/Clean Radiator
Cooling Fan Malfunction	Test Cooling Fan/Circuit
Thermostat Stuck Closed	Replace Thermostat
Clogged Cooling System Passages	Clean/Flush Cooling System
Water Pump Malfunction	Replace Water Pump
Fan Clutch Malfunction	Replace Fan Clutch
Cooling Fan Motor Malfunction	Test Fan Motor
Cooling Fan Relay Malfunction	Test Fan Relay
Faulty Ignition Advance	Check/Replace Advance
Faulty Radiator Cap	Replace Radiator Cap
Broken/Slipping Fan Belt	Replace Fan Belt
Restricted Exhaust	Repair Exhaust System

CORROSION

Possible Cause	Action
Impurities in Coolant	Clean/Flush System

COOLING SYSTEM (Cont.)

COOLING SYSTEM TROUBLE SHOOTING (Cont.)

PROBLEM
Possible Cause — **Action**

COOLANT LEAKAGE

Possible Cause	Action
Damaged Hose	Replace Hose
Leaky Water Pump Seal	Replace Water Pump
Damaged Radiator Seam	Replace/Repair Radiator
Leaky Thermostat Cover	Replace Thermostat Cover
Cylinder Head Problem	Check Head/Head Gasket
Cylinder Block Problem	Check Cylinder Block
Air in Cooling System	Bleed Cooling System
Leaky Freeze Plugs	Replace Freeze Plugs

RECOVERY SYSTEM INOPERATIVE

Possible Cause	Action
Loose/Defective Radiator Cap	Replace Radiator Cap
Overflow Tube Clogged/Leaking	Repair Tube
Recovery Bottle Vent Restricted	Clean Vent

NO HEATER CORE FLOW

Possible Cause	Action
Collapsed Heater Hose	Replace Heater Hose
Plugged Heater Core	Clean/Replace Heater Core
Faulty Heater Valve	Replace Heater Valve

CLUTCH

CLUTCH TROUBLE SHOOTING

PROBLEM
Possible Cause — **Action**

CLUTCH CHATTERS/GRABS

Possible Cause	Action
Incorrect Pedal Adjustment	Adjust Free Play
Worn Input Shaft Spline	Replace Input Shaft
Binding Pressure Plate	Replace Pressure Plate
Binding Throw-Out Lever	Check Throw-Out Lever Check Throw-Out Bearing Check Bearing Retainer
Uneven Pressure Plate Contact With Flywheel	Align/Replace Worn Parts
Transmission Misaligned	Align Transmission
Worn Pressure Plate	Replace Clutch Assembly
Oil-Saturated Disc	Replace Clutch Assembly Repair Oil Leak
Loose Engine Mounts	Replace Engine Mounts

CLUTCH PEDAL STICKS DOWN

Possible Cause	Action
Clutch Cable Binding	Replace Clutch Cable
Weak Pressure Plate Springs	Replace Clutch Assembly
Binding Clutch Linkage	Lubricate Linkage
Broken Clutch Pedal Return Spring	Replace Return Spring

CLUTCH WILL NOT RELEASE

Possible Cause	Action
Oil-Saturated Disc	Replace Clutch Assembly Repair Oil Leak
Defective Disc Face	Replace Clutch Assembly
Disc Sticking on Input Shaft Splines	Replace Disc/Input Shaft
Binding Pilot Bearing	Replace Pilot Bearing
Faulty Clutch Master Cylinder	Replace Master Cylinder
Faulty Clutch Slave Cylinder	Replace Slave Cylinder
Blown Clutch Flex Hose	Replace Flexhose
Sticky Throw-Out Bearing Sleeve	Clean/Lube Sleeve
Clutch Cable Binding	Replace Clutch Cable
Broken/Loose Bellhousing	Check Bellhousing

RATTLING/SQUEAKING

Possible Cause	Action
Broken Throw-Out Lever Return Spring	Replace Return Spring
Faulty Throw-Out Bearing	Replace Throw-Out Bearing
Faulty Clutch Disc	Replace Clutch Disc
Faulty Pilot Bearing	Replace Pilot Bearing
Worn Throw-Out Bearing	Replace Throw-Out Bearing
Dry Bearing Retainer Slide For Throw-Out Bearing Sleeve	Lubricate Slide

CLUTCH (Cont.)

CLUTCH TROUBLE SHOOTING (Cont.)

PROBLEM
Possible Cause — Action

SLIPPING
Faulty Pressure Plate	Replace Clutch Assembly
Worn Clutch Disc	Replace Clutch Assembly
Incorrect Alignment	Realign Clutch Assembly
Faulty Clutch Slave Cylinder	Replace Slave Cylinder

NO PEDAL PRESSURE
Leaky Hydraulic System	Check Clutch Master Cylinder
	Check Clutch Slave Cylinder
	Check Clutch Flexhose
Broken Clutch Cable	Replace Clutch Cable
Faulty Throw-Out Lever	Replace Throw-Out Lever
Broken Clutch Linkage	Repair Clutch Linkage

NOISY CLUTCH PEDAL
Faulty Safety Switch	Check/Replace Switch
Noisy Self-Adj. Ratchet	Replace Ratchet
Dry Throw-Out Bearing	Replace Throw-Out Bearing
Dry Pilot Bearing	Replace Pilot Bearing
Worn Input Shaft	Replace Input Shaft

DRIVE AXLE (RWD)

DRIVE AXLE (RWD) TROUBLE SHOOTING

PROBLEM
Possible Cause — Action

KNOCKING OR CLUNKING
Differential Side Gear Clearance	Check Clearance
Worn Pinion Shaft	Replace Pinion Shaft
Axle Shaft End Play	Check End Play
Missing Gear Teeth	Check Diff./Replace Gear
Wrong Axle Backlash	Check Backlash
Misaligned Driveline	Realign Driveline

CLUNKING DURING ENGAGEMENT
Side Gear Clearance	Check Side Gear Clearance
Ring and Pinion Backlash	Check Backlash
Worn/Loose Pinion Shaft	Replace Shaft/Bearing
Bad "U" Joint	Replace "U" Joint
Sticking Slip Yoke	Lube Slip Yoke
Broken Rear Axle Mount	Replace Mount
Loose Drive Shaft Flange	Check Flange

CLICK/CHATTER ON TURNS
Differential Side Gear Clearance	Check Clearance
Worn Clutch Plates [1]	Replace Clutch Plates
Wrong Diff. Lubricant [1]	Change Lubricant

RHYTHMIC KNOCK OR CLICK
Flat Spot on Rear Wheel Bearing	Replace Wheel Bearing

HUM/LOW VIBRATION AT ALL SPEEDS
Faulty Wheel Bearings	Replace Bearings
Faulty "U" Joint	Replace "U" Joint
Faulty Drive Shaft	Balance Drive Shaft
Faulty Companion Flange	Replace Flange
Faulty Slip Yoke Flange	Replace Flange

[1] – Limited slip differential only.

DRIVE AXLE (FWD)

DRIVE AXLE (FWD) TROUBLE SHOOTING

PROBLEM
Possible Cause — Action

GREASE LEAKING
Ripped CV Boot	Replace Boot

CLICKING NOISE WHILE CORNERING
Dry/Worn CV Joints	Replace Outer CV Joints

CLUNK ON ACCELERATION
Dry/Worn CV Joints	Replace Inner CV Joints
Worn Trans. Gears/Bearings	Inspect Trans.

VIBRATION/SHUDDER ON ACCELERATION
Dry/Worn CV Joints	Replace CV Joints
Alignment Out	Check Alignment
Incorrect Spring Height	Check Spring Height

SQUEALING OR HUMMING
Dry/Worn CV Joints	Lube/Replace CV Joints
Faulty Wheel Bearing	Replace Wheel Bearing

BRAKE

BRAKE TROUBLE SHOOTING

PROBLEM
Possible Cause — Action

CAR PULLS WHILE BRAKING
Faulty Caliper	Rebuild/Replace Caliper
Restricted Brake Hose	Replace Hose
Faulty Rear Brakes	Inspect Rear Brakes
Worn Front Suspension	Check Suspension
Alignment Out	Check Alignment
Incorrect Tire Pressure	Check Pressure
Mismatched Tires	New Tires

HIGH-PITCHED SQUEAL (BRAKES OFF)
Wear Indicators Rubbing	Replace Disc Pads
Faulty Wheel Bearing	Replace Bearing

HIGH-PITCHED SQUEAL (BRAKES ON)
Worn Brake Pads	Replace Disc Pads
Glazed Rotors	Replace Pads/Resurface Rotor

CHATTERING/PULSATING
Faulty Rotors/Drums	Check Runout/Parallelism
Loose Wheel Bearings	Check Bearings
Poorly Installed Pads	Correct Installation

EXCESSIVE PEDAL EFFORT
Faulty Master Cylinder	Rebuild/Replace Cylinder
Faulty Power Booster	Repair/Replace Booster
Worn or Glazed Pads/Shoes	Replace Pads/Shoes
Frozen Caliper Piston	Replace Caliper
Poor Brake Adjustment	Adjust Brakes
Low Fluid Level	Fill Fluid/Inspect System
Air in Lines	Inspect/Bleed System
Heat Boiling Brake Fluid	Re-Route Brake Lines

1992 GENERAL INFORMATION
Trouble Shooting (Cont.)

BRAKE (Cont.)

BRAKE TROUBLE SHOOTING (Cont.)

PROBLEM
Possible Cause — **Action**

EXCESSIVE PEDAL TRAVEL
Brake Adjustment .... Adjust Brakes
Low Fluid Level .... Fill Fluid/Inspect System
Air in Lines .... Inspect/Bleed System
Faulty Master Cylinder .... Rebuild/Replace Cylinder
Faulty Brake Booster .... Repair/Replace Booster
Worn or Glazed Pads/Shoes .... Replace Pads/Shoes
Frozen Caliper Piston .... Replace Caliper
Booster Actuator Rod
  Adjustment .... Adjust Rod Clearance
Contaminated Fluid .... Flush/Bleed System

BRAKES DRAG
Faulty Master Cylinder .... Rebuild/Replace Cylinder
Restricted Brake Lines .... Clear Restrictions
Frozen Parking Brake Cables .... Replace Cables
Gear Oil-Soaked Pads/Shoes .... Repair Oil Leak
  Replace Pads/Shoes
Brake Fluid-Soaked Pads/Shoes .... Repair Fluid Leak
  Replace Pads/Shoes
Oil Accidentally Mixed
  With Brake Fluid .... Check/Replace All
  Cylinders/Calipers/Hoses
  Flush/Bleed System

BRAKES GRAB/UNEVEN ACTION
Faulty Combination Valve .... Replace Combination Valve
Faulty Power Booster .... Repair/Replace Booster
Binding Brake Pedal .... Check Pedal

WHEEL ALIGNMENT

WHEEL ALIGNMENT TROUBLE SHOOTING

PROBLEM
Possible Cause — **Action**

PREMATURE TIRE WEAR
Incorrect Tire Pressure .... Check Pressure
Alignment Out .... Check Alignment
Worn Front Suspension .... Check Suspension
Tires Out of Balance .... Balance Tires
Worn Steering Linkage .... Check/Replace Linkage
Improper Riding Height .... Check/Adjust Riding Height
Uneven/Worn Springs .... Replace Springs
Loose/Worn Wheel Bearings .... Replace Bearings
Bent Wheel/Rim .... Replace Wheel/Rim
Worn/Defective Shocks .... Replace Shocks

PULLS TO ONE SIDE
Incorrect Tire Pressure .... Check Pressure
Brake Drag .... Inspect Brakes
Mismatched Tires .... New Tires
Radial Belt Separation .... Replace Tires
Alignment Out .... Check Alignment
Frame Bent .... Check Frame Damage
Worn Front Suspension .... Check Suspension
Worn Steering Linkage .... Check/Replace Linkage
Uneven/Worn Springs .... Replace Springs
Loose/Worn Wheel Bearings .... Replace Bearings

STEERING TOO HARD
Tight Idler Arm Bushing .... Retorque Idler Arm
Tight Ball Joint .... Replace Ball Joint
Alignment Out .... Check Alignment
Power Steering Fluid Low .... Fill/Check Leaks
Power Steering Belt Loose .... Tighten Belt
Power Steering Pump Faulty .... Repair/Replace Pump
Faulty Steering Gear .... Repair/Replace Gear
Faulty Steering Knuckle .... Replace Steering Knuckle
Worn Front Suspension .... Check Suspension
Incorrect Tire Pressure .... Check Pressure

WHEEL ALIGNMENT (Cont.)

WHEEL ALIGNMENT TROUBLE SHOOTING (Cont.)

PROBLEM
Possible Cause — **Action**

VEHICLE WANDERS
Incorrect Tire Pressure .... Check Pressure
Loose/Worn Wheel Bearings .... Replace Bearings
Alignment Out .... Check Alignment
Loose Strut Rod (Bushings) .... Repair Strut Rod
Faulty Stabilizer Bar .... Repair Stabilizer Bar
Worn Spring/Shock .... Replace Spring/Shock
Worn Front Suspension .... Check Suspension

FRONT END SHIMMY
Tires Out of Balance .... Balance Tires
Radial Belt Separation .... Replace Tires
Excessive Wheel Runout .... Repair/Replace Wheel
Alignment Out .... Check Alignment
Worn Rack Bushings .... Replace Bushings
Worn Front Suspension .... Check Suspension
Loose/Worn Wheel Bearings .... Replace Bearings
Dry/Worn CV Joints .... Lube/Replace CV Joints

SUSPENSION

SUSPENSION TROUBLE SHOOTING

PROBLEM
Possible Cause — **Action**

FRONT END NOISE
Loose/Worn Wheel Bearings .... Replace Bearings
Worn Shocks/Struts .... Replace Shocks/Struts
Worn Strut Mountings .... Replace Mountings
Loose Steering Gear-to-Frame
  Mounting Bolts .... Check Mounting
Worn Control Arm Bushings .... Replace Bushings
Dry Ball Joints .... Lubricate Ball Joints

FRONT END SHIMMY
Tires Out of Balance .... Balance Tires
Excessive Wheel Runout .... Repair/Replace Wheel
Alignment Out .... Check Alignment
Worn Rack Bushings .... Replace Bushings
Worn Front Suspension .... Check Suspension
Loose/Worn Wheel Bearings .... Replace Bearings
Dry/Worn CV Joints .... Lube/Replace CV Joints

PULLS TO ONE SIDE
Incorrect Tire Pressure .... Check Pressure
Brake Drag .... Inspect Brakes
Mismatched Tires .... New Tires
Alignment Out .... Check Alignment
Frame Bent .... Check Frame Damage
Worn Front Suspension .... Check Suspension
Worn Steering Linkage .... Check/Replace Linkage
Uneven/Worn Springs .... Replace Springs
Loose/Worn Wheel Bearings .... Replace Bearings
Power Steering Unbalance .... Check Power Steering

SPRING NOISES
Loose "U" Bolts .... Check "U" Bolts
Loose/Worn Bushings .... Replace Bushings
Worn/Missing Leaf Spacers .... Replace Spacers

CAR LEANS/SWAYS ON CORNERS
Loose Stabilizer Bar .... Replace Bushings
Worn Shocks/Struts .... Replace Shocks/Struts
Worn Spring/Shock .... Replace Spring/Shock

STEERING COLUMN

STEERING COLUMN TROUBLE SHOOTING

PROBLEM
Possible Cause   **Action**

NOISE IN COLUMN
Coupling Pulled Apart .... Check Coupling
Column Incorrectly Aligned .... Align Column
Broken Lower Joint .... Replace Joint
Dry Horn Contact Ring .... Lube Contact Ring
Dry Column Bearings .... Lube/Replace Bearings
Shaft Snap Ring Loose .... Seat Snap Ring
Shroud Hits Wheel .... Realign Shroud
Lock Plate Ring Loose .... Seat Ring
Tight "U" Joint .... Replace "U" Joint

STEERING SHAFT BINDS
Column Misaligned .... Align Column
Shroud Misaligned .... Align Shroud
Faulty Column Bearings .... Replace Bearings
Tight "U" Joint .... Replace "U" Joint

SHIFT LEVER BINDS
Column Misaligned .... Align Column
Shroud Misaligned .... Align Shroud
Faulty Column Bearings .... Replace Bearings
Misadjusted Shifter .... Adjust Shifter
Damaged Shift Tube .... Replace Tube

EXCESS PLAY IN COLUMN
Mounting Bracket Loose .... Check Bolts
Broken Weld on Jacket .... Repair/Replace Column

IGNITION SWITCH STICKS
Poorly Installed Switch .... Check Switch Installation
Worn Key Switch .... Replace Key Switch

TILT STEERING COLUMN

TILT STEERING COLUMN TROUBLE SHOOTING

PROBLEM
Possible Cause   **Action**

STEERING WHEEL LOOSE
Housing/Pivot Pin Loose .... Check Clearance
Faulty Anti-Lash Springs .... Replace Springs
Upper Bearing Loose .... Seat Upper Bearing
Misadjusted Tilt Lock .... Adjust Tilt Lock
Loose Support Screws .... Tighten Screws
Missing/Broken Bearing Preload Spring .... Replace Spring
Housing Jacket Loose .... Tighten Screws

PLAY IN COLUMN MOUNT
Loose Support Screws .... Tighten Screws/Bracket
Loose Housing Shoes .... Check Housing Shoes
Loose Tilt Pivot Pins .... Check Pivot Pins
Loose Shoe Lock Pin .... Check Shoe Lock

HOUSING SCRAPES ON BOWL
Damaged Bowl .... Replace Bowl

WHEEL DOES NOT LOCK
Shoe Seized on Pivot Pin .... Check Shoe
Dirty/Damaged Shoe .... Clean/Replace Shoe
Faulty Shoe Lock Spring .... Replace Spring

WHEEL DOES NOT RETURN
Bound Pivot Pins .... Clean/Replace Pins
Damaged Tilt Spring .... Replace Tilt Spring
Turn Signal Switch Wires Too Tight .... Reset Wires

NOISE WHEN TILTING
Worn Upper Tilt Bumpers .... Replace Bumpers
Tilt Spring Rubs Housing .... Adjust Springs

MANUAL STEERING GEAR

MANUAL STEERING GEAR TROUBLE SHOOTING

PROBLEM
Possible Cause   **Action**

EXCESSIVE STEERING PLAY
Wheel Bearing Misadjusted .... Check Wheel Bearing
Worn/Loose Linkage .... Check Linkage
Worn/Loose Ball Joints .... Check Ball Joints
Loose Pitman Arm .... Check Arm/Gear Splines
Loose Pitman Shaft .... Check Gear
Loose Gear Mount .... Check Gear Mount
Loose Rack Mount .... Check Rack Mount

WHEEL CENTERS POORLY
Steering Gear Adjusted
  Too Tightly .... Check Gear Free Play
Dry Steering Linkage .... Lubricate/Replace Linkage
Dry Ball Joints Bind .... Lubricate/Replace Joints
Binding Rack Slide .... Inspect Rack
Shaft Contacts Seals .... Check Shaft/Replace Seal

POWER STEERING

POWER STEERING TROUBLE SHOOTING

PROBLEM
Possible Cause   **Action**

POWER STEERING PUMP GROWLS/GROANS
Air In System .... Bleed/Check System
Low Fluid Level .... Check Fluid/Leaks
High Pressure in Hoses .... Clear Restriction
Scored Pump Plates .... Check Pump Plates
Worn Cam Ring .... Replace Cam Ring

POWER STEERING PUMP RATTLES
Rotor Slot Vanes Sticking .... Clean/Replace Vanes

POWER STEERING PUMP SWISHES
Faulty Flow Control Valve .... Replace Valve

POWER STEERING PUMP SQUAWKS DURING TURN
Spool Valve "O" Ring Cut .... Replace "O" Ring

POWER STEERING PUMP MOANS/WHINES
Pump Shaft Bearing Scored .... Inspect Bearing
Air In Fluid .... Fill/Bleed System
Low Fluid Level .... Fill/Bleed System
Poor Bracket Alignment .... Correct Alignment

POWER STEERING PUMP HISSES DURING TURN
Internal Leakage in
  Steering Gear .... Check Steering Gear

POWER STEERING PUMP CHIRPS
Loose Power Steering Belt .... Tighten/Replace Belt

POWER STEERING PUMP BUZZES
Bearing Loose on Shaft .... Replace Bearing

POWER STEERING PUMP CLICKS
Broken Vane Springs .... Replace Springs
Worn/Nicked Rotors .... Replace Rotors

FLUID FOAMY/MILKY
Internal Pump Leakage .... Reseal Pump
Power Steering Belt Slipping .... Tighten/Replace Belt
Pump Output Low .... Check Pressure
Faulty Steering Gear .... Check Gear

WHEEL SURGES/JERKS
Low Fluid Level .... Check/Fill Fluid
Power Steering Belt Slipping .... Tighten/Replace Belt
Pump Output Low .... Check Pressure

1992 GENERAL INFORMATION
Engine Overhaul Procedures

DESCRIPTION

Examples used in this article are general in nature and do not necessarily relate to a specific engine or system. Illustrations and procedures have been chosen to guide mechanic through engine overhaul process. Descriptions of cleaning, inspection, and assembly processes are included.

ENGINE IDENTIFICATION

Engine may be identified from Vehicle Identification Number (VIN) stamped on a metal tab. Metal tab may be located in different locations depending on manufacturer. Engine identification number or serial number is located on cylinder block. Location varies with each manufacturer.

INSPECTION PROCEDURES

Engine components must be inspected to meet manufacturer's specifications and tolerances during overhaul. Proper dimensions and tolerances must be met to obtain proper performance and maximum engine life.

Micrometers, depth gauges and dial indicator are used for checking tolerances during engine overhaul. Magnaflux, Magnaglo, dye-check, ultrasonic and x-ray inspection procedures are used for parts inspection.

MAGNETIC PARTICLE INSPECTION

Magnaflux & Magnaglo – Magnaflux is an inspection technique used to locate material flaws and stress cracks. Component is subjected to a strong magnetic field. Entire component or a localized area can be magnetized. Component is coated with either a wet or dry material that contains fine magnetic particles.

Cracks which are outlined by the particles cause an interruption of magnetic field. Dry powder method of Magnaflux can be used in normal lighting and crack appears as a bright line.

Fluorescent liquid is used along with a Black light in the Magnaglo Magnaflux system. Darkened room is required for this procedure. The crack will appear as a glowing line. Complete demagnetizing of component upon completion is required on both procedures. Magnetic particle inspection applies to ferrous materials only.

PENETRANT INSPECTION

Zyglo – The Zyglo process coats material with a fluorescent dye penetrant. Component is often warmed to expand cracks that will be penetrated by the dye. Using darkened room and Black light, component is inspected for cracks. Crack will glow brightly.

Developing solution is often used to enhance results. Parts made of any material, such as aluminum cylinder heads or plastics, may be tested using this process.

Dye Check – Penetrating dye is sprayed on the previously cleaned component. Dye is left on component for 5-45 minutes, depending upon material density. Component is then wiped clean and sprayed with a developing solution. Surface cracks will show up as a bright line.

ULTRASONIC INSPECTION

If an expensive part is suspected of internal cracking, ultrasonic testing is used. Sound waves are used for component inspection.

X-RAY INSPECTION

This form of inspection is used on highly stressed components. X-ray inspection may be used to detect internal and external flaws in any material.

PRESSURE TESTING

Cylinder heads can be tested for cracks using a pressure tester. Pressure testing is performed by plugging all but one of the holes of cylinder head and injecting air or water into the open passage.

Leaks are indicated by the appearance of wet or damp areas when using water. When air is used, it is necessary to spray the head surface with a soap solution. Bubbles will indicate a leak. Cylinder head may also be submerged in water heated to specified temperature to check for cracks created during heat expansion.

CLEANING PROCEDURES

All components of an engine do not have the same cleaning requirements. Physical methods include bead blasting and manual removal. Chemical methods include solvent blast, solvent tank, hot tank, cold tank and steam cleaning of components.

BEAD BLASTING

Manual removal of deposits may be required prior to bead blasting, followed by some other cleaning method. Carbon, paint and rust may be removed using bead blasting method. Components must be free of oil and grease prior to bead blasting. Beads will stick to grease or oil soaked areas causing area not to be cleaned.

Use air pressure to remove all trapped residual beads from component after cleaning. After cleaning internal engine parts made of aluminum, wash thoroughly with hot soapy water. Component must be thoroughly cleaned as glass beads will enter engine oil resulting in bearing damage.

CHEMICAL CLEANING

Solvent tank is used for cleaning oily residue from components. Solvent blasting sprays solvent through a siphon gun using compressed air.

The hot tank, using heated caustic solvents, is used for cleaning ferrous materials only. DO NOT clean aluminum parts such as cylinder heads, bearings or other soft metals using the hot tank. After cleaning, flush parts with hot water.

A non-ferrous part will be ruined and caustic solution will be diluted if placed in the hot tank. Always use eye protection and gloves when using the hot tank.

Use of a cold tank is for cleaning aluminum cylinder heads, carburetors and other soft metals. A less caustic and unheated solution is used. Parts may be left in the tank for several hours without damage. After cleaning, flush parts with hot water.

Steam cleaning, with boiling hot water sprayed at high pressure, is recommended as the final cleaning process when using either hot or cold tank cleaning.

COMPONENT CLEANING

SHEET METAL PARTS

Examples of sheet metal parts are rocker covers, front and side covers, oil pan and bellhousing dust cover. Glass bead blasting or hot tank may be used for cleaning.

Ensure all mating surfaces are flat. Deformed surfaces should be straightened. Check all sheet metal parts for cracks and dents.

INTAKE & EXHAUST MANIFOLDS

Using solvent cleaning or bead blasting, clean manifolds for inspection. If intake manifold has an exhaust crossover, all carbon deposits must be removed. Inspect manifolds for cracks, burned or eroded areas, corrosion and damage to fasteners.

Exhaust heat and products of combustion cause threads of fasteners to corrode. Replace studs and bolts as necessary. On "V" type intake manifolds, sheet metal oil shield must be removed for proper cleaning and inspection. Ensure all manifold parting surfaces are flat and free of burrs.

CYLINDER HEAD REPLACEMENT

REMOVAL

Remove intake and exhaust manifolds and valve cover. Cylinder head and camshaft carrier bolts (if equipped) should be removed only when engine is cold. On many aluminum cylinder heads, removal while hot will cause cylinder head warpage. Mark rocker arm or overhead cam components for location.

Remove rocker arm components or overhead cam components. Components must be installed in original location. Individual design rocker arms may utilize shafts, ball-type pedestal mounts or no rocker arms. For all design types, wire components together and identify according to corresponding valve. Remove cylinder head bolts. Note length and location. Some applications require cylinder head bolts be removed in proper sequence to prevent cylinder head damage. *See Fig. 1.* Remove cylinder head.

INSTALLATION

Ensure all surfaces and head bolts are clean. Check that head bolt holes of cylinder block are clean and dry to prevent block damage when bolts are tightened. Clean threads with tap to ensure accurate bolt torque.

Install head gasket on cylinder block. Some manufacturers may recommend sealant be applied to head gasket prior to installation. Note that all holes are aligned. Some gasket applications may be marked so that certain area faces upward. Install cylinder head using care not to damage head gasket. Ensure cylinder head is fully seated on cylinder block.

Some applications require head bolts be coated with sealant prior to installation. This is done if head bolts are exposed to coolant passages. Some applications require head bolts be coated with light coat of engine oil.

Install head bolts. Head bolts should be tightened in proper steps and sequence to specification. *See Fig. 1.* Install remaining components. Tighten all bolts to specification. Adjust valves if required. See VALVE ADJUSTMENT in this article.

NOTE: Some manufacturers require that head bolts be retightened after specified amount of operation. This must be done to prevent head gasket failure.

73505　←　FRONT OF VEHICLE

Fig. 1: Typical Cylinder Head Tightening or Loosening Sequence

VALVE ADJUSTMENT

Engine specifications will indicate valve train clearance and temperature at which adjustment is to be made on most models. In most cases, adjustment will be made with a cold engine. In some cases, both a cold and a hot clearance will be given for maintenance convenience.

On some models, adjustment is not required. Rocker arms are tightened to specification and valve lash is automatically set. On some models with push rod actuated valve train, adjustment is made at push rod end of rocker arm while other models do not require adjustment.

Clearance will be checked between tip of rocker arm and tip of valve stem in proper sequence using a feeler gauge. Adjustment is made by rotating adjusting screw until proper clearance is obtained. Lock nut is then tightened. Engine will be rotated to obtain all valve adjustments to manufacturer's specifications.

Some models require hydraulic lifter to be bled down and clearance measured. Push rods of different length can be used to obtain proper clearance. Clearance will be checked between tip of rocker arm and tip of valve stem in proper sequence using a feeler gauge.

Overhead cam engines designed without rocker arms actuate valves directly on a cam follower. A hardened, removable disc is installed between the cam lobe and lifter. Clearance will be checked between cam heel and adjusting disc in proper sequence using a feeler gauge. Engine will be rotated to obtain all valve adjustments.

On overhead cam engines designed with rocker arms, adjustment is made at valve end of rocker arm. Ensure valve to be adjusted is riding on heel of cam on all engines. Clearance will be checked between tip of rocker arm and tip of valve stem in proper sequence using a feeler gauge. Adjustment is made by rotating adjusting screw until proper clearance is obtained. Lock nut is then tightened. Engine will be rotated to obtain all valve adjustments to manufacturer's specifications.

CYLINDER HEAD OVERHAUL

CYLINDER HEAD DISASSEMBLY

Mark valves for location. Using valve spring compressor, compress valve springs. Remove valve locks. Carefully release spring compressor. Remove retainer or rotator, valve spring, spring seat and valve. *See Fig. 2.*

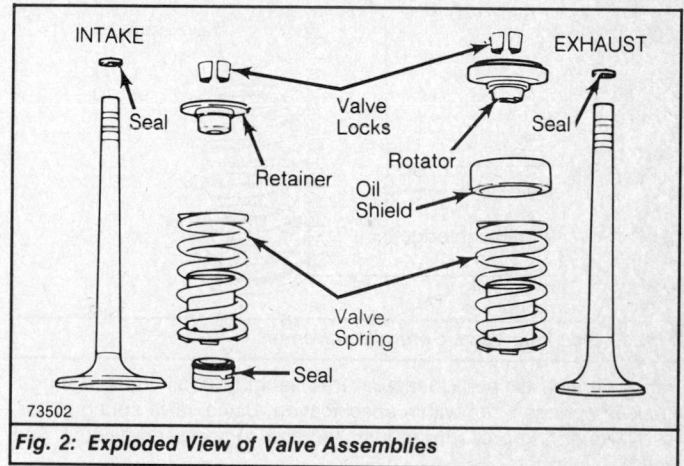

Fig. 2: Exploded View of Valve Assemblies

CYLINDER HEAD CLEANING & INSPECTION

Clean cylinder head and valve components using approved cleaning methods. Inspect cylinder head for cracks, damage or warped gasket surface. Place straightedge across gasket surface. Determine clearance at center of straightedge. Measure across both diagonals, longitudinal center line and across cylinder head at several points. *See Fig. 3.*

On cast iron cylinder heads, if warpage exceeds .003" (.08 mm) in a 6" span, or .006" (.15 mm) over total length, cylinder head must be resurfaced. On most aluminum cylinder heads, if warpage exceeds .002" (.05 mm) in any area, cylinder head must be resurfaced. Warpage specification may vary by manufacturer. If warpage exceeds specification on some cylinder heads, cylinder head must be replaced.

Cylinder head thickness should be measured to determine amount of material which can be removed before replacement is required. Cylinder head thickness must not be less than the manufacturer's specification.

If cylinder head required resurfacing, it may not align properly with intake manifold. On "V" type engines, misalignment is corrected by machining intake manifold surface that contacts cylinder head. Cylinder head may be machined on surface that contacts intake manifold. Using oil stone, remove burrs or scratches from all sealing surfaces.

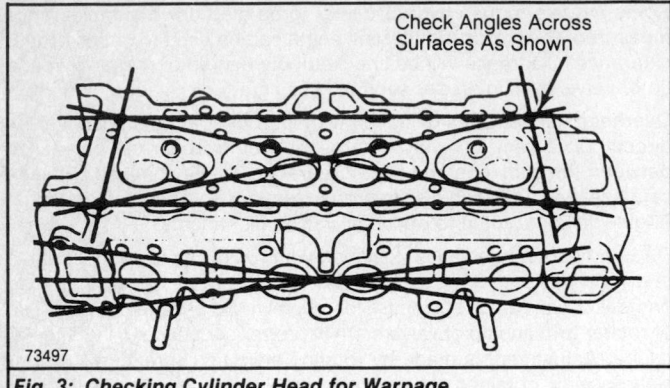

Check Angles Across Surfaces As Shown

73497

Fig. 3: Checking Cylinder Head for Warpage

VALVE SPRINGS

Inspect valve springs for corroded or pitted valve spring surfaces which may lead to breakage. Polished spring ends caused by a rotating spring indicate that spring surge has occurred. Replace springs showing evidence of these conditions.

Inspect valve springs for squareness using a 90 degree straightedge. See Fig. 4. Replace valve spring if out-of-square exceeds manufacturer's specification.

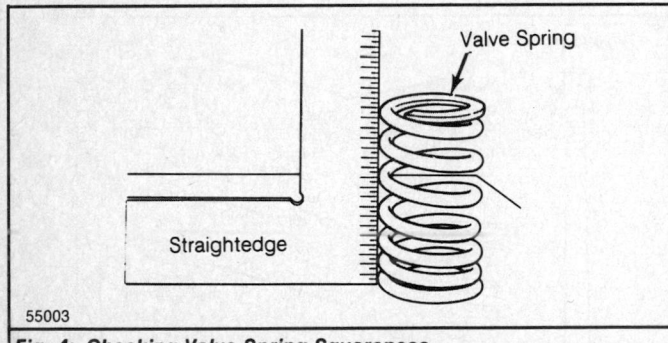

Valve Spring

Straightedge

55003

Fig. 4: Checking Valve Spring Squareness

Using vernier caliper, measure free length of all valve springs. Replace springs if not within specification. Using valve spring tester, test valve spring pressure at installed and compressed heights. See Fig. 5.

Usually compressed height is installed height minus valve lift. Replace valve spring if not within specification. It is recommended to replace all valve springs when overhauling cylinder head. Valve springs may need to be installed with color coded end or small coils at specified area according to manufacturer.

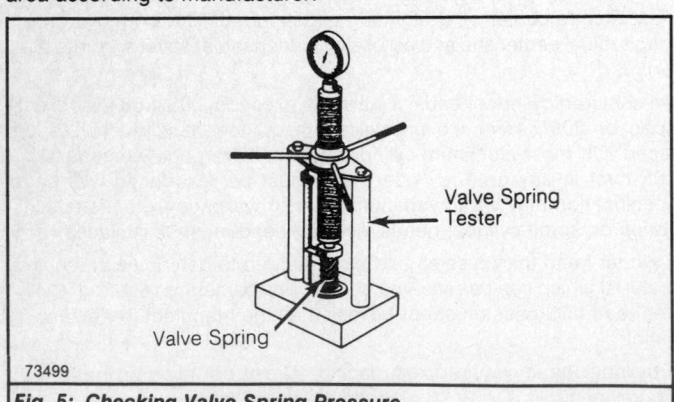

Valve Spring Tester

Valve Spring

73499

Fig. 5: Checking Valve Spring Pressure

VALVE GUIDE

Measuring Valve Guide Clearance – Check valve stem-to-guide clearance. Ensure valve stem diameter is within specification. Install valve in valve guide. Install dial indicator assembly on cylinder head with tip resting against valve stem just above valve guide. See Fig. 6.

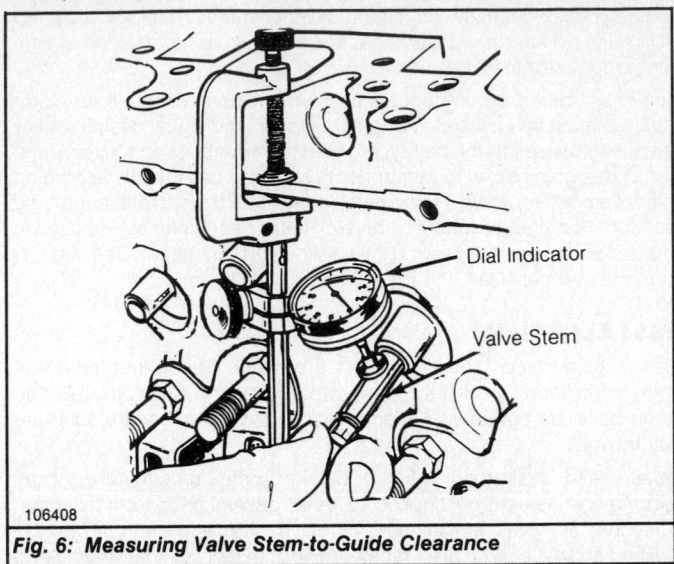

Dial Indicator

Valve Stem

106408

Fig. 6: Measuring Valve Stem-to-Guide Clearance

Lower valve approximately 1/16" below valve seat. Push valve stem against valve guide as far as possible. Adjust dial indicator to zero. Push valve stem in opposite direction and note reading. Clearance must be within specification.

If valve guide clearance exceeds specification, valves with oversize stems may be used and valve guides are reamed to larger size or valve guide must be replaced. On some applications, a false guide is installed, then reamed to proper specification. Valve guide reamer set is used to ream valve guide to obtain proper clearance for new valve.

Reaming Valve Guide – Select proper reamer for size of valve stem. Reamer must be of proper length to provide clean cut through entire length of valve guide. Install reamer in valve guide and rotate to cut valve guide. See Fig. 7.

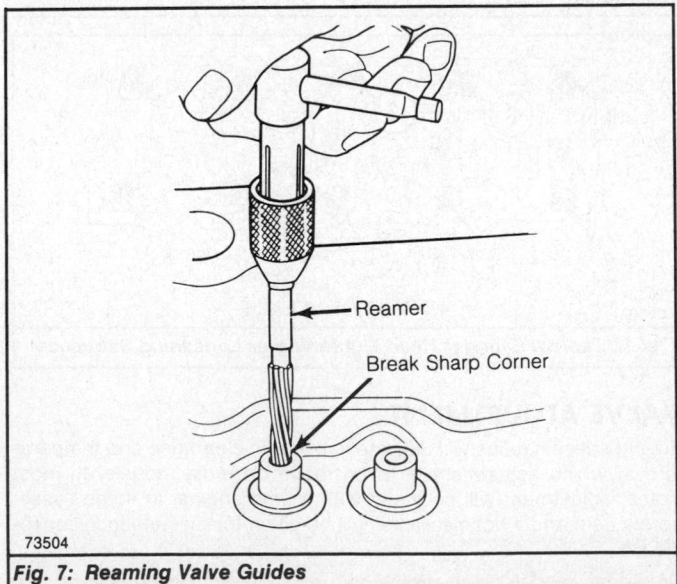

Reamer

Break Sharp Corner

73504

Fig. 7: Reaming Valve Guides

Replacing Valve Guide – Replace valve guide if clearance exceeds specification. Valve guides are either pressed, hammered or shrunk in place, depending upon cylinder head design and type of metal used.

Remove valve guide from cylinder head by pressing or tapping on a stepped drift. See Fig. 8. Once valve guide is installed, distance from cylinder head to top of valve guide must be checked. This distance must be within specification.

Aluminum heads are often heated before installing valve guide. Valve guide is sometimes cooled in dry ice prior to installation. Combination of a heated cylinder head and cooled valve guide ensures a tight guide fit upon assembly. The new guide must be reamed to specification.

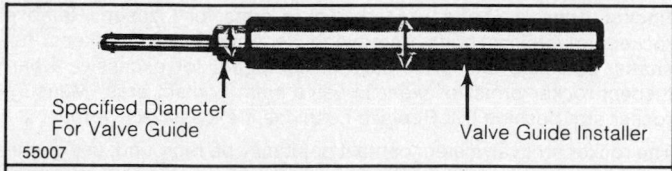

Specified Diameter For Valve Guide
Valve Guide Installer
55007

Fig. 8: Typical Valve Guide Remover & Installer

VALVES & VALVE SEATS

Valve Grinding – Valve stem O.D. should be measured in several areas to indicate amount of wear. Replace valve if not within specification. Valve margin area should be measured to ensure that valve can be ground. See Fig. 9.

If valve margin is less than specification, the valves will be burned. Valve must be replaced. Due to minimum margin dimensions during manufacture, some new type valves cannot be reground. Some manufacturers use stellite coated valves that must NOT be machined. Valves can only be lapped into valve seat.

CAUTION: Some valves are sodium filled. Extreme care must be used when disposing of damaged or worn sodium-filled valves.

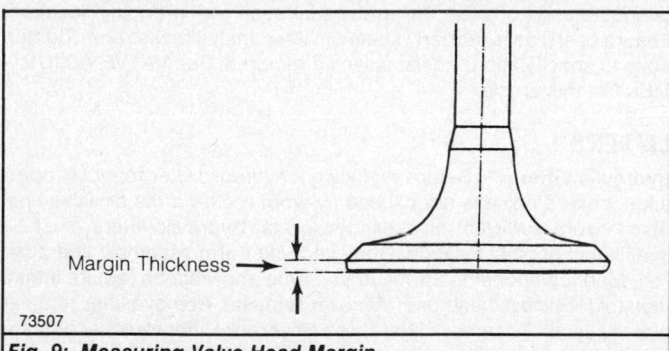

Margin Thickness
73507

Fig. 9: Measuring Valve Head Margin

Resurface valve to proper angle specification using valve grinding machine. Follow manufacturer's instructions for valve grinding machine. Specifications may indicate a different valve face angle than seat angle.

Measure valve margin after grinding. Replace valve if not within specification. Valve stem tip can be refinished using valve grinding machine.

Valve Lapping – During valve lapping of recently designed valves, be sure to follow manufacturer's recommendations. Surface hardening and materials used with some valves do not permit lapping. Lapping process will remove excessive amounts of the hardened surface.

Valve lapping is done to ensure adequate sealing between valve face and seat. Use either a hand drill or lapping stick with suction cup attached.

Moisten and attach suction cup to valve. Lubricate valve stem and guide. Apply a thin coat of fine valve grinding compound between valve and seat. Rotate lapping tool between the palms or with hand drill.

Lift valve upward off the seat and change position often. This is done to prevent grooving of valve seat. Lap valve until a smooth polished seat is obtained. Thoroughly clean grinding compound from components. Valve-to-valve seat concentricity should be checked. See VALVE SEAT CONCENTRICITY.

CAUTION: Valve guides must be in good condition and free of carbon deposits prior to valve seat grinding. Some engines contain an induction hardened valve seat. Excessive material removal will damage valve seats.

Valve Seat Grinding – Select coarse stone of correct size and angle for seat to be ground. Ensure stone is true and has a smooth surface. Select correct size pilot for valve guide dimension. Install pilot in valve guide. Lightly lubricate pilot shaft. Install stone on pilot. Move stone off and on the seat approximately 2 times per second during grinding operation.

Select a fine stone to finish grinding operation. Various angle grinding stones are used to center and narrow the valve seat as required. See Fig. 10.

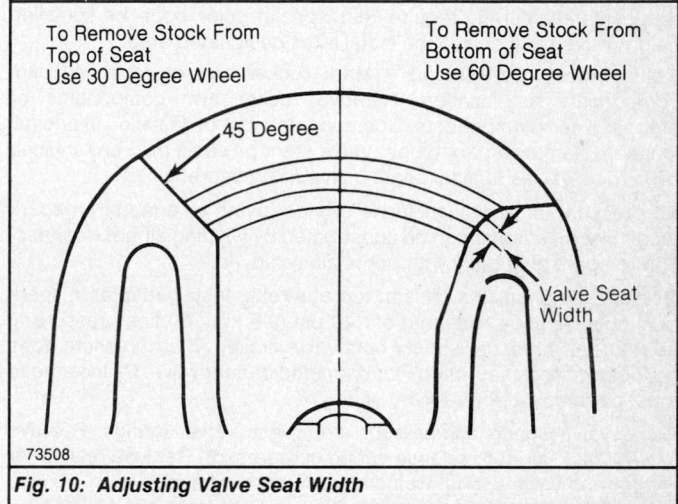

To Remove Stock From Top of Seat Use 30 Degree Wheel

To Remove Stock From Bottom of Seat Use 60 Degree Wheel

45 Degree

Valve Seat Width

73508

Fig. 10: Adjusting Valve Seat Width

Valve Seat Replacement – Replacement of valve seat inserts is done by cutting out the old insert and machining an oversize insert bore. Replacement oversize insert is usually cooled and the cylinder head is sometimes warmed. Valve seat is pressed into the head. This operation requires specialized machine shop equipment.

Valve Seat Concentricity – Using dial gauge, install gauge pilot in valve guide. Position gauge arm on the valve seat. Adjust dial indicator to zero. Rotate arm 360 degrees and note reading. Runout should not exceed specification.

To check valve-to-valve seat concentricity, coat valve face lightly with Prussian Blue dye. Install valve and rotate it on valve seat. If pattern is even and entire seat is coated at valve contact point, valve is concentric with the valve seat.

CYLINDER HEAD REASSEMBLY

Valve Stem Installed Height – Valve stem installed height must be checked when new valves are installed or when valves or valve seats have been ground. Install valve in valve guide. Measure distance from tip of valve stem to spring seat. See Fig. 11. Distance must be within specification to allow sufficient clearance for valve operation.

Remove valve and grind valve stem tip if height exceeds specification. Valve tips are surface hardened. DO NOT remove more than .010" (.25 mm) from tip. Chamfer sharp edge of reground valve tip. Recheck valve stem installed height.

VALVE STEM OIL SEALS

Valve stem oil seals must be installed on valve stem. See Fig. 2. Seals are needed due to pressure differential at the ends of valve guides. Atmospheric pressure above intake guide, combined with manifold vacuum below guide, causes oil to be drawn into the cylinder.

Exhaust guides also have pressure differential created by exhaust gas flowing past the guide, creating a low pressure area. This low pressure area draws oil into the exhaust system.

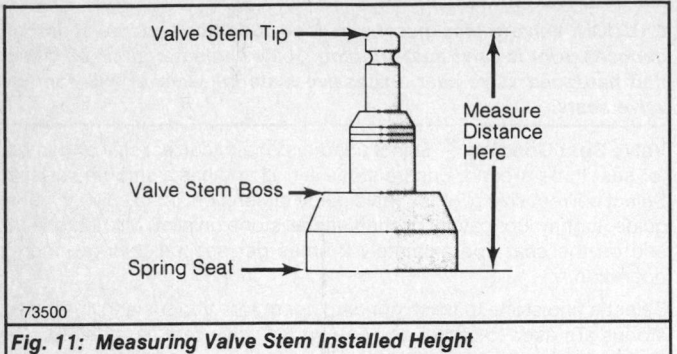

Fig. 11: Measuring Valve Stem Installed Height

Some manufacturers require that special color code or specified height valve stem oil seal be installed in designated area.

Replacement (On-Vehicle) – Mark rocker arm or overhead cam components for location. Remove rocker arm components or overhead cam components. Components must be installed in original location. Remove spark plugs. Valve stem oil seals may be replaced by holding valves against seats using air pressure.

Air pressure must be installed in cylinder using an adapter for spark plug hole. An adapter can be constructed by welding air hose connection to spark plug body with porcelain removed.

Rotate engine until piston is at top of stroke. Install adapter in spark plug hole. Apply a minimum of 140 psi (9.8 kg/cm²) line pressure to adapter. Air pressure should hold valve closed. If air pressure does not hold valve closed, check for damaged or bent valve. Cylinder head must be removed for service.

Using valve spring compressor, compress valve springs. Remove valve locks. Carefully release spring compressor. Remove retainer or rotator and valve spring. Remove valve stem oil seal.

If oversize valves have been installed, oversize oil seals must be used. Coat valve stem with engine oil. Install protective sleeve over end of valve stem. Install new oil seal over valve stem and seat on valve guide. Remove protective sleeve. Install spring seat, valve spring and retainer or rotator. Compress spring and install valve locks. Remove spring compressor. Ensure valve locks are fully seated.

Install rocker arms or overhead cam components. Tighten all bolts to specification. Adjust valves if required. Remove adapter. Install spark plugs, valve cover and gasket.

VALVE SPRING INSTALLED HEIGHT

Valve spring installed height should be checked during reassembly. Measure height from lower edge of valve spring to the upper edge. DO NOT include valve spring seat or retainer. Distance must be within specification. If valves and/or seats have been ground, a valve spring shim may be required to correct spring height. See Fig. 12.

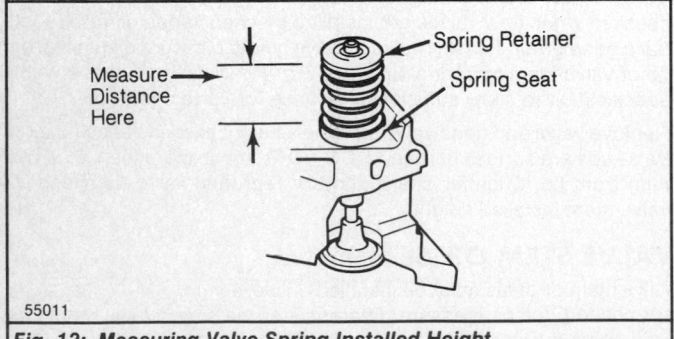

Fig. 12: Measuring Valve Spring Installed Height

ROCKER ARMS & ASSEMBLIES

Rocker Studs – Rocker studs are either threaded or pressed in place. Threaded studs are removed by locking 2 nuts on the stud.

Unscrew the stud by turning the jam nut. Coat new stud threads with Loctite and install. Tighten to specification.

Pressed-in stud can be removed using a stud puller. Ream stud bore to proper specification and press in a new oversize stud. Pressed-in studs are often replaced by cutting threads in the stud bore to accept a threaded stud.

Rocker Arms & Shafts – Mark rocker arms for location. Remove rocker arm retaining bolts. Remove rocker arms. Inspect rocker arms, shafts, bushings and pivot balls (if equipped) for excessive wear. Inspect rocker arms for wear in valve stem contact area. Measure rocker arm bushing I.D. Replace bushings if excessively worn.

The rocker arm valve stem contact point may be reground, using special fixture for valve grinding machine. Remove minimum amount of material as possible. Ensure all oil passages are clear. Install rocker arm components in original location. Ensure rocker arm is properly seated in push rod. Tighten bolts to specification. Adjust valves if required. See VALVE ADJUSTMENT in this article.

PUSH RODS

Remove rocker arms. Mark push rods for location. Remove push rods. Push rods can be steel or aluminum, solid or hollow. Hollow push rods must be internally cleaned to ensure oil passage to rocker arms is cleaned. Check push rods for damage, such as loose ends on steel tipped aluminum types.

Check push rod for straightness. Roll push rod on a flat surface. Using feeler gauge, check clearance at center. Replace push rod if bent. The push rod can also be supported at each end and rotated. A dial indicator is used to detect a bent area in the push rod.

Lubricate ends of push rod and install push rod in original location. Ensure push rod is properly seated in lifter. Install rocker arm. Tighten bolts to specification. Adjust valves if required. See VALVE ADJUSTMENT in this article.

LIFTERS

Hydraulic Lifters – Before replacing a hydraulic lifter for noisy operation, ensure noise is not caused by worn rocker arms or valve tips. Also ensure sufficient oil pressure exists. Hydraulic lifters must be installed in original location. Remove rocker arm assembly and push rod. Mark components for location. Some applications require intake manifold, cylinder head or lifter cover removal. Remove lifter retainer plate (if used). To remove lifters, use a hydraulic lifter remover or magnet. Different type lifters are used. See Fig. 13.

On sticking lifters, disassemble and clean lifter. DO NOT mix lifter components or positions. Parts are select-fitted and are not interchangeable. Inspect all components for wear. Note amount of wear in lifter body-to-camshaft contact area. Surface must have smooth and convex contact face. If wear is apparent, carefully inspect cam lobe.

Inspect push rod contact area and lifter body for scoring or signs of wear. If body is scored, inspect lifter bore for damage and lack of lubrication. On roller type lifters, inspect roller for flaking, pitting, loss of needle bearings and roughness during rotation.

Measure lifter body O.D. in several areas. Measure lifter bore I.D. Ensure components or oil clearance is within specification. Some models offer oversize lifters. Replace lifter if damaged.

If lifter check valve is not operating, obstructions may be preventing it from closing or valve spring may be broken. Clean or replace components as necessary.

Check plunger operation. Plunger should drop to bottom of the body by its own weight when assembled dry. If plunger is not free, soak lifter in solvent to dissolve deposits.

Lifter leak-down test can be performed on lifter. Lifter must be filled with special test oil. New lifters contain special test oil. Using lifter leak-down tester, perform leak-down test following manufacturer's instructions. If leak-down time is not within specifications, replace lifter assembly.

Lifters should be soaked in clean engine oil several hours prior to installation. Coat lifter base, roller (if equipped) and lifter body with ample amount of Molykote or camshaft lubricant. *See Fig. 13.* Install lifter in original location. Install remaining components. Valve lash adjustment is not required on most hydraulic lifters. Preload of hydraulic lifter is automatic. Some models may require adjustment.

NOTE: Some manufacturers require that a crankcase conditioner be added to engine oil and engine operated for specified amount of time to aid in lifter break-in procedure if new lifters or camshaft are installed.

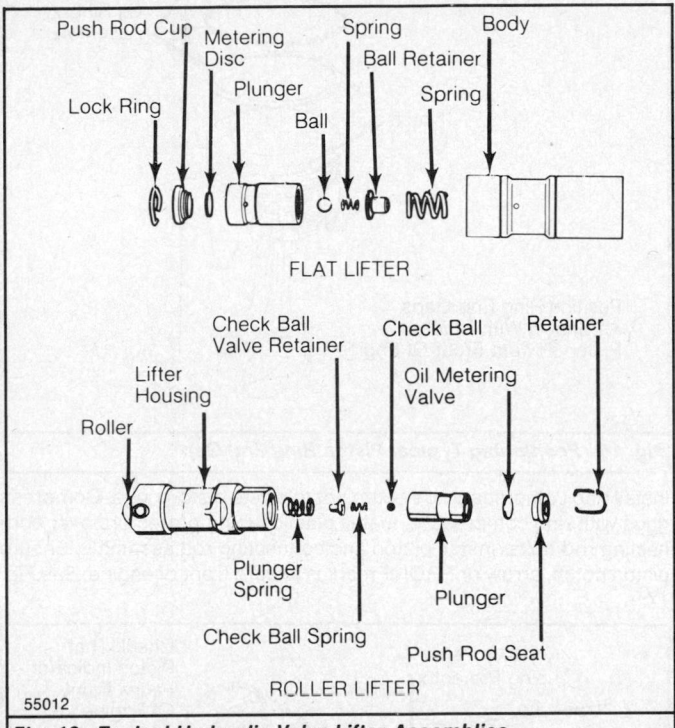

Fig. 13: Typical Hydraulic Valve Lifter Assemblies

Mechanical Lifters – Lifter assemblies must be installed in original locations. Remove rocker arm assembly and push rod. Mark components for location. Some applications require intake manifold or lifter cover removal. Remove lifter retainer plate (if used). To remove lifters, use lifter remover or magnet.

Inspect push rod contact area and lifter body for scoring or signs of wear. If body is scored, inspect lifter bore for damage and lack of lubrication. Note amount of wear in lifter body-to-camshaft contact area. Surface must have smooth and convex contact face. If wear is apparent, carefully inspect cam lobe.

Coat lifter base, roller (if equipped) and lifter body with ample amount of Molykote or camshaft lubricant. Install lifter in original location. Install remaining components. Tighten bolts to specification. Adjust valves. See VALVE ADJUSTMENT in this article.

PISTONS, CONNECTING RODS & BEARINGS

RIDGE REMOVAL

Ridge in cylinder wall must be removed prior to piston removal. Failure to remove ridge prior to removing pistons will cause piston damage in piston ring lands or grooves.

With piston at bottom dead center, place rag in bore to trap metal chips. Install ridge reamer in cylinder bore. Adjust ridge reamer using manufacturer's instructions. Remove ridge using ridge reamer. DO NOT remove an excessive amount of material. Ensure ridge is completely removed.

PISTON & CONNECTING ROD REMOVAL

Note top of piston. Some pistons may contain a notch, arrow or be marked FRONT. Piston must be installed in proper direction to prevent damage with valve operation.

Check that connecting rod and cap are numbered for cylinder location and which side of cylinder block the number faces. Proper cap and connecting rod must be installed together. Connecting rod cap must be installed on connecting rod in proper direction to ensure bearing lock procedure. Mark connecting rod and cap if necessary. Pistons must be installed in original location.

Remove cap retaining nuts or bolts. Remove bearing cap. Install tubing protectors on connecting rod bolts. This protects cylinder walls from scoring during removal. Ensure proper removal of ridge. Push piston and connecting rod from cylinder. Connecting rod boss can be tapped with a wooden dowel or hammer handle to aid in removal.

PISTON & CONNECTING ROD

Disassembly – Using ring expander, remove piston rings. Remove piston pin retaining rings (if equipped). Note direction of piston installation on connecting rod. On pressed type piston pins, special fixtures and procedures according to manufacturer must be used to remove piston pins. Follow manufacturer's recommendations to avoid piston distortion or breakage.

Cleaning – Remove all carbon and varnish from piston. Pistons and connecting rods may be cleaned in cold type chemical tank. Using ring groove cleaner, clean all deposits from ring grooves. Ensure all deposits are cleaned from ring grooves to prevent ring breakage or sticking. DO NOT attempt to clean pistons with wire brush.

Inspection – Inspect pistons for nicks, scoring, cracks or damage in ring areas. Connecting rod should be checked for cracks using Magnaflux procedure. Piston diameter must be measured in manufacturer's specified area.

Using telescopic gauge and micrometer, measure piston pin bore of piston in 2 areas, 90 degrees apart. This is done to check diameter and out-of-round.

Install proper bearing cap on connecting rod. Ensure bearing cap is installed in proper location. Tighten bolts or nuts to specification. Using inside micrometer, measure inside diameter in 2 areas, 90 degrees apart.

Connecting rod I.D. and out-of-round must be within specification. Measure piston pin bore I.D. and piston pin O.D. All components must be within specification. Subtract piston pin diameter from piston pin bore in piston and connecting rod to determine proper fit.

Connecting rod length must be measured from center of crankshaft journal inside diameter to center of piston pin bushing using proper caliper. Connecting rods must be the same length. Connecting rods should be checked on an alignment fixture for bent or twisted condition. Replace all components which are damaged or not within specification.

PISTON & CYLINDER BORE FIT

Ensure cylinder is checked for taper, out-of-round and properly honed prior to checking piston and cylinder bore fit. See CYLINDER BLOCK in this article. Using dial bore gauge, measure cylinder bore.

Measure piston skirt diameter at 90 degree angle to piston pin at specified area by manufacturer. Subtract piston diameter from cylinder bore diameter to determine piston-to-cylinder clearance. Clearance must be within specification. Mark piston for proper cylinder location.

ASSEMBLING PISTON & CONNECTING ROD

Install piston on connecting rod for corresponding cylinder. Ensure reference marking on top of piston corresponds with connecting rod and cap number. *See Fig. 14.*

Lubricate piston pin and install in connecting rod. Ensure piston pin retainers are fully seated (if equipped). On pressed type piston pins, follow manufacturer's recommended procedure to avoid distortion or breakage.

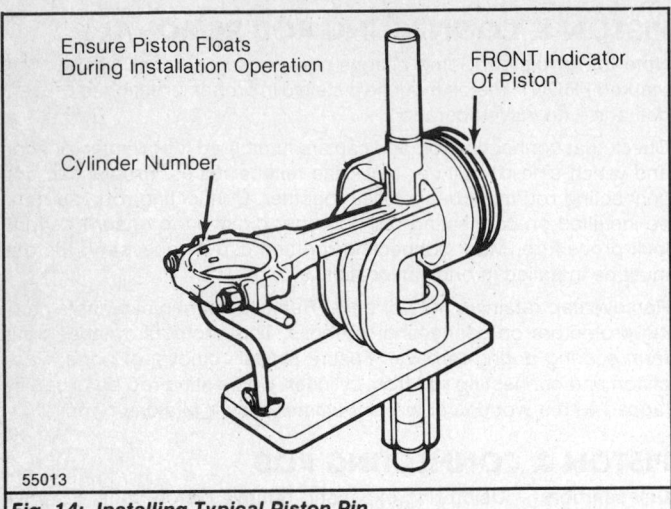

Ensure Piston Floats
During Installation Operation

FRONT Indicator
Of Piston

Cylinder Number

55013

Fig. 14: Installing Typical Piston Pin

CHECKING PISTON RING CLEARANCES

Piston rings must be checked for side clearance and end gap. To check end gap, install piston ring in cylinder in which it is to be installed. Using an inverted piston, push ring to bottom of cylinder in smallest cylinder diameter.

Using feeler gauge, check ring end gap. See Fig. 15. Piston ring end gap must be within specification. Ring breakage will occur if insufficient ring end gap exists.

Some manufacturers permit correcting insufficient ring end gap by using a fine file while other manufacturers recommend using another ring set. Mark rings for proper cylinder installation after checking end gap.

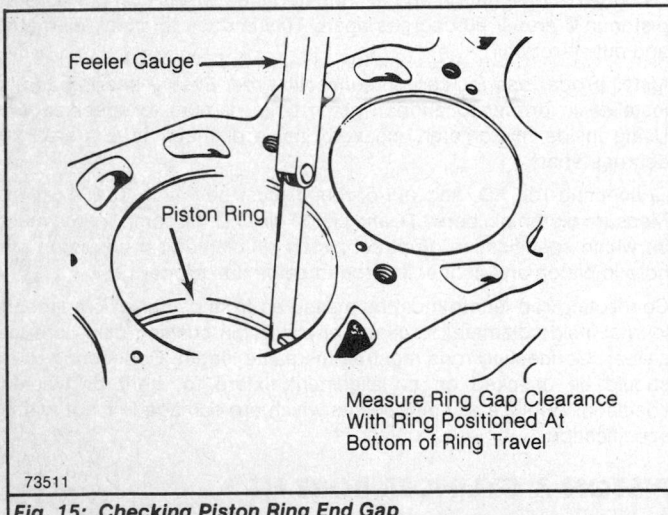

Feeler Gauge

Piston Ring

Measure Ring Gap Clearance
With Ring Positioned At
Bottom of Ring Travel

73511

Fig. 15: Checking Piston Ring End Gap

For checking side clearance, install rings on piston. Using feeler gauge, measure clearance between piston ring and piston ring land. Check side clearance in several areas around piston. Side clearance must be within specification.

If side clearance is excessive, piston ring grooves can be machined to accept oversize piston rings (if available). Normal practice is to replace piston.

PISTON & CONNECTING ROD INSTALLATION

Cylinders must be honed prior to piston installation. See CYLINDER HONING under CYLINDER BLOCK in this article.

Install upper connecting rod bearings. Lubricate upper bearings with engine oil. Install lower bearings in rod caps. Ensure bearing tabs are

properly seated. Position piston ring gaps according to manufacturer's recommendations. See Fig. 16. Lubricate pistons, rings and cylinder walls.

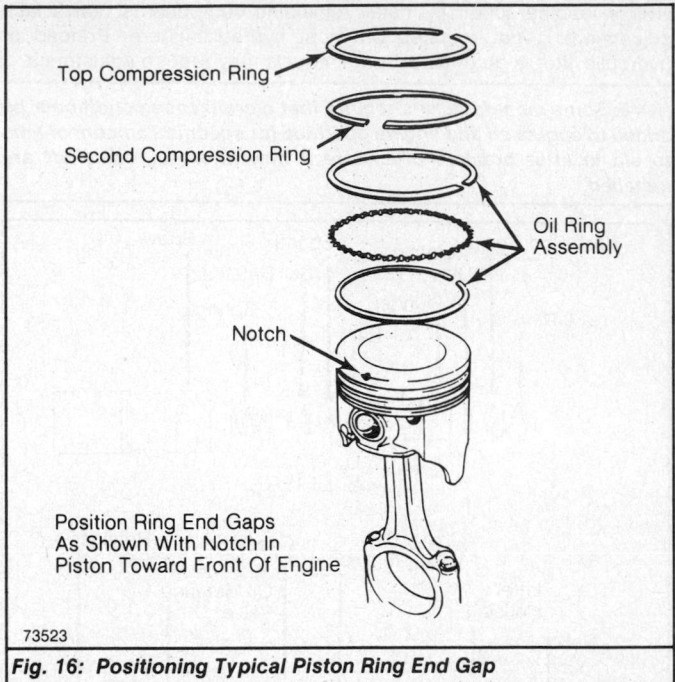

Top Compression Ring

Second Compression Ring

Oil Ring
Assembly

Notch

Position Ring End Gaps
As Shown With Notch In
Piston Toward Front Of Engine

73523

Fig. 16: Positioning Typical Piston Ring End Gap

Install ring compressor. Use care not to rotate piston rings. Compress rings with ring compressor. Install plastic tubing protectors over connecting rod bolts. Install piston and connecting rod assembly. Ensure piston notch, arrow or FRONT mark is toward front of engine. See Fig. 17.

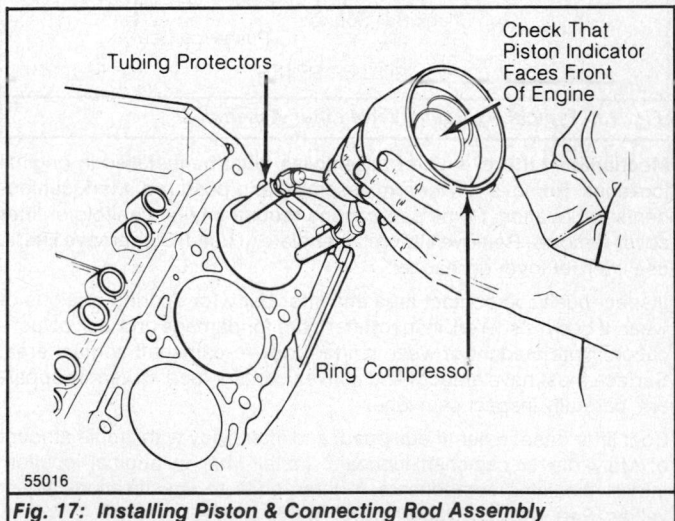

Tubing Protectors

Check That
Piston Indicator
Faces Front
Of Engine

Ring Compressor

55016

Fig. 17: Installing Piston & Connecting Rod Assembly

Carefully tap piston into cylinder until rod bearing is seated on crankshaft journal. Remove protectors. Install rod cap and bearing. Lightly tighten connecting rod bolts. Repeat procedure for remaining cylinders. Check bearing clearance. See MAIN & CONNECTING ROD BEARING CLEARANCE in this article.

Once clearance is checked, lubricate journals and bearings. Install bearing caps. Ensure marks are aligned on connecting rod and cap. Tighten rod nuts or bolts to specification. Ensure rod moves freely on crankshaft. Check connecting rod side clearance. See CONNECTING ROD SIDE CLEARANCE in this article.

CONNECTING ROD SIDE CLEARANCE

Position connecting rod toward one side of crankshaft as far as possible. Using feeler gauge, measure clearance between side of connecting rod and crankshaft. *See Fig. 18.* Clearance must be within specification.

Check for improper bearing installation, wrong bearing cap or insufficient bearing clearance if side clearance is insufficient. Connecting rod may require machining to obtain proper clearance. Excessive clearance usually indicates excessive wear at crankshaft. Crankshaft must be repaired or replaced.

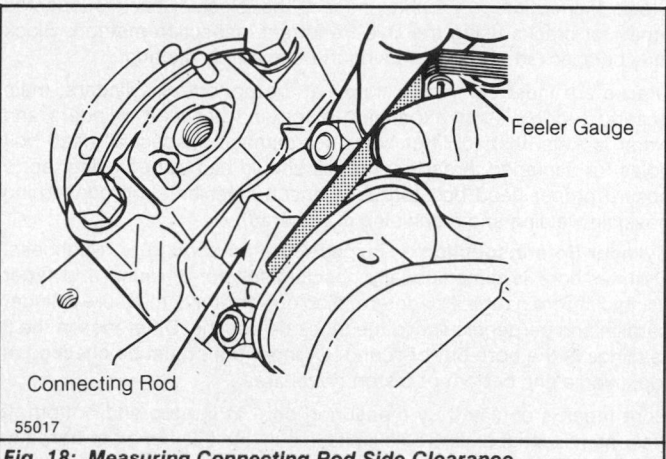

55017

Fig. 18: Measuring Connecting Rod Side Clearance

MAIN & CONNECTING ROD BEARING CLEARANCE

Plastigage Method – Plastigage method may be used to determine bearing clearance. Plastigage can be used with an engine in service or during reassembly. Plastigage material is oil soluble.

Ensure journals and bearings are free of oil or solvent. Oil or solvent will dissolve material and false reading will be obtained. Install small piece of Plastigage along full length of bearing journal. Install bearing cap in original location. Tighten bolts to specification.

CAUTION: DO NOT rotate crankshaft while Plastigage is installed. Bearing clearance will not be obtained if crankshaft is rotated.

Remove bearing cap. Compare Plastigage width with scale on Plastigage container to determine bearing clearance. *See Fig. 19.* Rotate crankshaft 90 degrees. Repeat procedure. This is done to check journal eccentricity. This procedure can be used to check oil clearance on both connecting rod and main bearings.

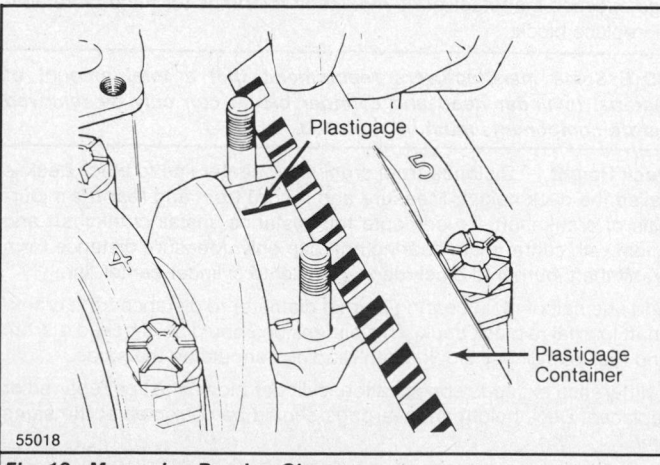

55018

Fig. 19: Measuring Bearing Clearance

Micrometer & Telescopic Gauge Method – A micrometer is used to determine journal diameter, taper and out-of-round dimensions of the crankshaft. See CLEANING & INSPECTION under CRANKSHAFT & MAIN BEARINGS in this article.

With crankshaft removed, install bearings and caps in original location on cylinder block. Tighten bolts to specification. On connecting rods, install bearings and caps on connecting rods. Install proper connecting rod cap on corresponding rod. Ensure bearing cap is installed in original location. Tighten bolts to specification.

Using a telescopic gauge and micrometer or inside micrometer, measure inside diameter of connecting rod and main bearings bores. Subtract each crankshaft journal diameter from the corresponding inside bearing bore diameter. This is the bearing clearance.

CRANKSHAFT & MAIN BEARINGS

REMOVAL

Ensure all main bearing caps are marked for location on cylinder block. Some main bearing caps have an arrow stamped on them. The arrow must face timing belt or timing chain end of engine. Remove main bearing cap bolts. Remove main bearing caps. Carefully remove crankshaft. Use care not to bind crankshaft in cylinder block during removal.

CLEANING & INSPECTION

Thoroughly clean crankshaft using solvent. Dry with compressed air. Ensure all oil passages are clear and free of sludge, rust, dirt, and metal chips.

Inspect crankshaft for scoring and nicks. Inspect crankshaft for cracks using Magnaflux procedure. Inspect rear seal area for grooving or damage. Inspect bolt hole threads for damage. If pilot bearing or bushing is used, check pilot bearing or bushing fit in crankshaft. Inspect crankshaft gear for damaged or cracked teeth. Replace gear if damaged. Check that oil passage plugs are tight (if equipped).

Using micrometer, measure all journals in 4 areas to determine journal taper, out-of-round and undersize. *See Fig. 20.* Some crankshafts can be reground to the next largest undersize, depending on the amount of wear or damage. Crankshafts with rolled fillet cannot be reground and must be replaced.

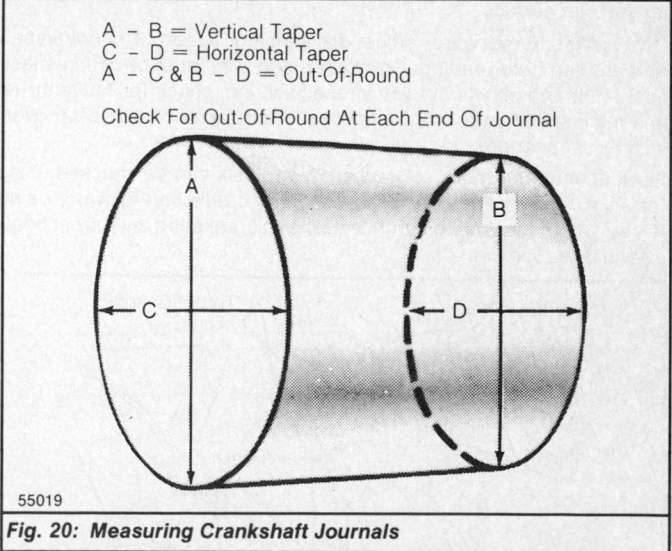

A – B = Vertical Taper
C – D = Horizontal Taper
A – C & B – D = Out-Of-Round

Check For Out-Of-Round At Each End Of Journal

55019

Fig. 20: Measuring Crankshaft Journals

Crankshaft journal runout should be checked. Install crankshaft in "V" blocks or bench center. Position dial indicator with tip resting on the main bearing journal area. *See Fig. 21.* Rotate crankshaft and note reading. Journal runout must not exceed specification. Repeat procedure on all main bearing journals. Crankshaft must be replaced if runout exceeds specification.

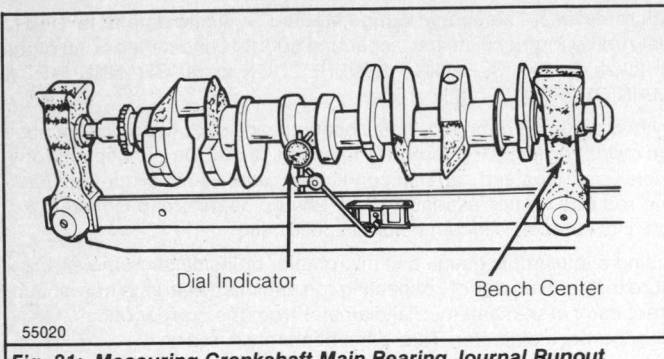

Dial Indicator   Bench Center

55020

Fig. 21: Measuring Crankshaft Main Bearing Journal Runout

INSTALLATION

Install upper main bearing in cylinder block. Ensure lock tab is properly located in cylinder block. Install bearings in main bearing caps. Ensure all oil passages are aligned. Install rear seal (if removed).

Ensure crankshaft journals are clean. Lubricate upper main bearings with clean engine oil. Carefully install crankshaft. Check each main bearing clearance using Plastigage method. See MAIN & CONNECTING ROD BEARING CLEARANCE in this article.

Once clearance is checked, lubricate lower main bearing and journals. Install main bearing caps in original location. Install rear seal in rear main bearing cap (if removed). Some rear main bearing caps require sealant to be applied in corners to prevent oil leakage.

Install and tighten all bolts except thrust bearing cap to specification. Tighten thrust bearing cap bolts finger tight only. Some models require that thrust bearing must be aligned. On most applications, crankshaft must be moved rearward then forward. Procedure may vary with manufacturer. Thrust bearing cap is then tightened to specification. Ensure crankshaft rotates freely. Crankshaft end play should be checked. See CRANKSHAFT END PLAY in this article.

CRANKSHAFT END PLAY

Dial Indicator Method – Crankshaft end play can be checked using dial indicator. Mount dial indicator on rear of cylinder block. Position dial indicator tip against rear of crankshaft. Ensure tip is resting against flat surface.

Pry crankshaft rearward. Adjust dial indicator to zero. Pry crankshaft forward and note reading. Crankshaft end play must be within specification. If end play is not within specification, check for faulty thrust bearing installation or worn crankshaft. Some applications offer oversize thrust bearings.

Feeler Gauge Method – Crankshaft end play can be checked using feeler gauge. Pry crankshaft rearward. Pry crankshaft forward. Using feeler gauge, measure clearance between crankshaft and thrust bearing surface. See Fig. 22.

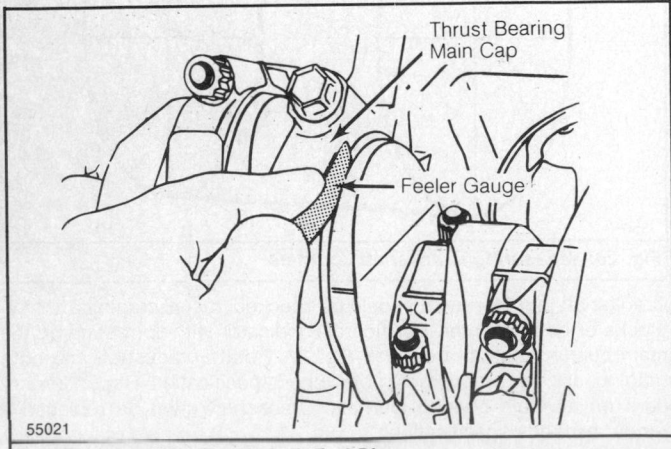

Thrust Bearing
Main Cap

Feeler Gauge

55021

Fig. 22: Checking Crankshaft End Play

Crankshaft end play must be within specification. If end play is not within specification, check for faulty thrust bearing installation or worn crankshaft. Some applications offer oversize thrust bearings.

CYLINDER BLOCK

Block Cleaning – Only cast cylinder blocks should be hot tank cleaned. Aluminum cylinder blocks should be cleaned using cold tank method. Cylinder block is cleaned in order to remove carbon deposits, gasket residue and water jacket scale. Remove oil gallery plugs, freeze plugs and cam bearings prior to block cleaning.

Block Inspection – Visually inspect the block. Check suspected areas for cracks using the Dye Penetrant inspection method. Block may be checked for cracks using the Magnaflux method.

Cracks are most commonly found at the bottom of cylinders, main bearing saddles, near expansion plugs and between cylinders and water jackets. Inspect lifter bores for damage. Inspect all head bolt holes for damaged threads. Threads should be cleaned using tap to ensure proper head bolt torque. Consult machine shop concerning possible welding and machining (if required).

Cylinder Bore Inspection – Inspect bore for scoring or roughness. Cylinder bore is dimensionally checked for out-of-round and taper using dial bore gauge. For determining out-of-round, measure cylinder parallel and perpendicular to the block center line. Difference in the 2 readings is the bore out-of-round. Cylinder bore must be checked at top, middle and bottom of piston travel area.

Bore taper is obtained by measuring bore at the top and bottom. If wear has exceeded allowable limits, block must be honed or bored to next available oversize piston dimension.

Cylinder Honing – Cylinder must be properly honed to allow new piston rings to properly seat. Cross-hatching at correct angle and depth is critical to lubrication of cylinder walls and pistons.

A flexible drive hone and power drill are commonly used. Drive hone must be lubricated during operation. Mix equal parts of kerosene and SAE 20W engine oil for lubrication.

Apply lubrication to cylinder wall. Operate cylinder hone from top to bottom of cylinder using even strokes to produce 45 degree cross-hatch pattern on the cylinder wall. DO NOT allow cylinder hone to extend below cylinder during operation.

Recheck bore dimension after final honing. Wash cylinder wall with hot soapy water to remove abrasive particles. Blow dry with compressed air. Coat cleaned cylinder walls with lubricating oil.

Deck Warpage – Check deck for damage or warped gasket surface. Place a straightedge across gasket surface of the deck. Using feeler gauge, measure clearance at center of straightedge. Measure across width and length of cylinder block at several points.

If warpage exceeds specifications, deck must be resurfaced. If warpage exceeds manufacturer's maximum tolerance for material removal, replace block.

NOTE: Some manufacturers recommend that a total amount of material (cylinder head and cylinder block) can only be removed before components must be replaced.

Deck Height – Distance from crankshaft center line to block deck is called the deck height. Measure and record front and rear main journals of crankshaft. To compute this distance, install crankshaft and retain with center main bearing and cap only. Measure distance from crankshaft journal to block deck, parallel to cylinder center line.

Add one half of main bearing journal diameter to distance from crankshaft journal to block deck. This dimension should be checked at front and rear of cylinder block. Both readings should be the same.

If difference exceeds specification, cylinder block must be repaired or replaced. Deck height and warpage should be corrected at the same time.

Main Bearing Bore & Alignment – For checking main bearing bore, remove all bearings from cylinder block and main bearing caps. Install main bearing caps in original location. Tighten bolts to specification.

Using inside micrometer, measure main bearing bore in 2 areas 90 degrees apart. Determine bore size and out-of-round. If diameter is not within specification, block must be align-bored.

For checking alignment, place a straightedge along center line of main bearing saddles. Check for clearance between straightedge and main bearing saddles. Block must be align-bored if clearance exists.

Expansion Plug Removal – Drill hole in center of expansion plug. Remove with screwdriver or punch. Use care not to damage sealing surface.

Expansion Plug Installation – Ensure sealing surface is free of burrs. Coat expansion plug with sealer. Using wooden dowel or pipe of slightly smaller diameter, install expansion plug. Ensure expansion plug is evenly located.

Oil Gallery Plug Removal – Remove threaded oil gallery plugs using appropriate wrench. Soft press-in plugs are removed by drilling into plug and installing a sheet metal screw. Remove plug with slide hammer or pliers.

Oil Gallery Plug Installation – Ensure threads or sealing surface is clean. Coat threaded oil gallery plugs with sealer and install. Replacement soft press-in plugs are installed with a hammer and drift.

CAMSHAFT

CLEANING & INSPECTION

Clean camshaft with solvent. Ensure all oil passages are clear. Inspect cam lobes and bearing journals for pitting, flaking or scoring. Using micrometer, measure bearing journal O.D.

Support camshaft at each end with "V" blocks. Position dial indicator with tip resting on center bearing journal. Rotate camshaft and note camshaft runout reading. If reading exceeds specification, replace camshaft.

Check cam lobe lift by measuring base circle of camshaft using micrometer. Measure again at 90 degree angle to tip of cam lobe. Cam lift can be determined by subtracting base circle diameter from tip of cam lobe measurement.

Different lift dimensions are given for intake and exhaust cam lobes. Reading must be within specification. Replace camshaft if cam lobes or bearing journals are not within specification.

Inspect camshaft gear for chipped, eroded or damaged teeth. Replace gear if damaged. On camshafts using thrust plate, measure distance between thrust plate and camshaft shoulder. Replace thrust plate if not within specification.

CAMSHAFT BEARINGS

Removal & Installation – Remove camshaft rear plug. Camshaft bearing remover is assembled with shoulder resting against bearing to be removed according to manufacturer's instructions. Tighten puller nut until bearing is removed. Remove remaining bearings, leaving front and rear bearings until last. These bearings act as a guide for camshaft bearing remover.

To install new bearings, puller is rearranged to pull bearings toward the center of block. Ensure all lubrication passages of bearing are aligned with cylinder block. Coat new camshaft rear plug with sealant. Install camshaft rear plug. Ensure plug is even in cylinder block.

CAMSHAFT INSTALLATION

Lubricate bearing surfaces and cam lobes with ample amount of Moly-kote or camshaft lubricant. Carefully install camshaft. Use care not to damage bearing journals during installation. Install thrust plate retaining bolts (if equipped). Tighten bolts to specification. On overhead camshafts, install bearing caps in original location. Tighten bolts to specification. On all applications, check camshaft end play.

CAMSHAFT END PLAY

Using dial indicator, check camshaft end play. Position dial indicator on front of engine block or cylinder head. Position indicator tip against camshaft. Push camshaft toward rear of cylinder head or engine and adjust indicator to zero.

Move camshaft forward and note reading. Camshaft end play must be within specification. End play may be adjusted by relocating gear, shimming thrust plate or replacing thrust plate depending on each manufacturer.

TIMING CHAINS & BELTS

TIMING CHAINS

Timing chains will stretch during operation. Limits are placed upon amount of stretch before replacement is required. Timing chain stretch will alter ignition timing and valve timing.

To check timing chain stretch, rotate crankshaft to eliminate slack from one side of timing chain. Mark reference point on cylinder block. Rotate crankshaft in opposite direction to eliminate slack from remaining side of timing chain. Force other side of chain outward and measure distance between reference point and timing chain. *See Fig. 23.* Replace timing chain and gears if not within specification.

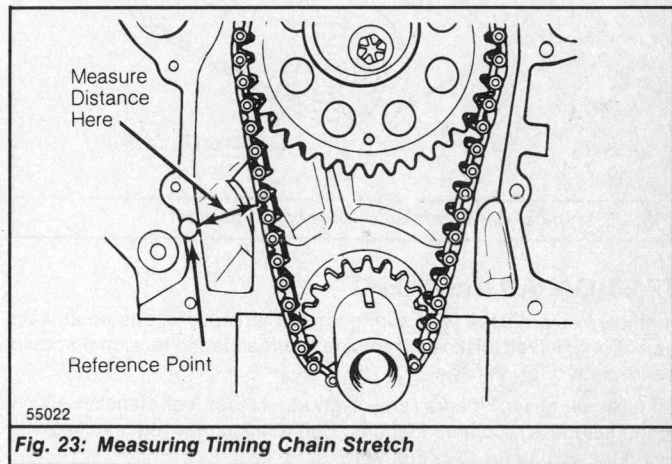

Fig. 23: Measuring Timing Chain Stretch

Timing chains must be installed so timing marks on camshaft gear and crankshaft gear are aligned according to manufacturer. *See Fig. 24.*

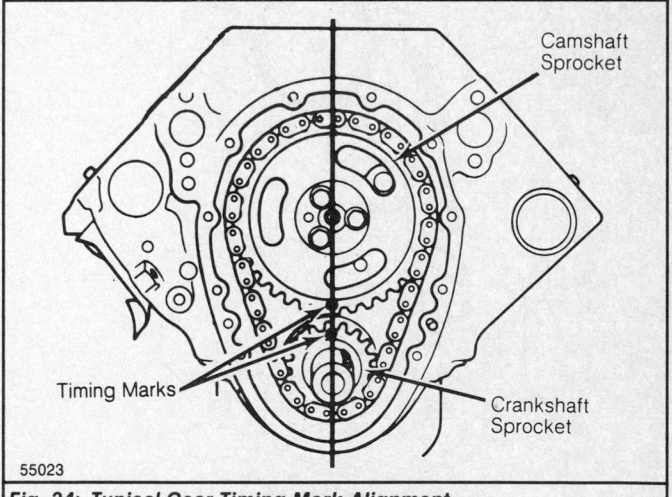

Fig. 24: Typical Gear Timing Mark Alignment

TIMING BELTS

Cogged tooth belts are commonly used on overhead cam engines. Inspect belt teeth for rounded corners or cracking. Replace belt if it is cracked, damaged, missing teeth, or oil soaked.

Used timing belt must be installed in original direction of rotation. Inspect all sprocket teeth for wear. Replace all worn sprockets.

Sprockets are marked for timing purposes. Engine is positioned so that crankshaft sprocket mark will be upward. Camshaft sprocket is aligned with reference mark on cylinder head or timing belt cover and then timing belt can be installed. *See Fig. 25.*

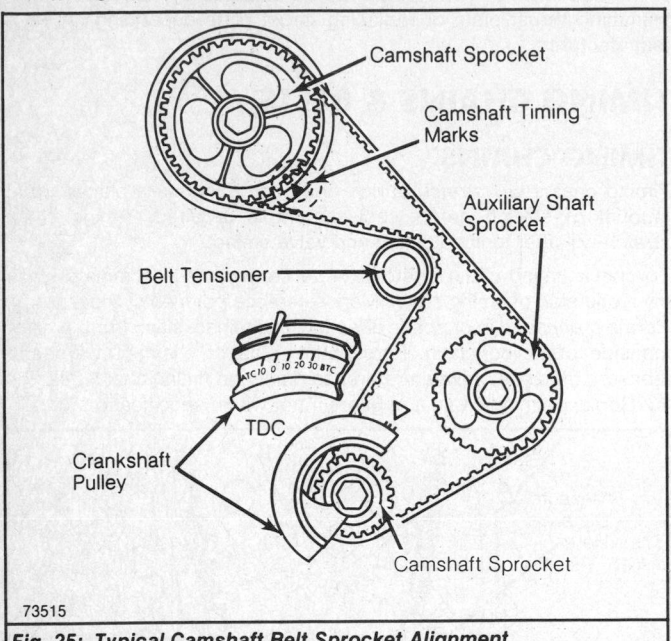

Fig. 25: Typical Camshaft Belt Sprocket Alignment

TENSION ADJUSTMENT

If guide rails are used with spring loaded tensioners, ensure at least half of original rail thickness remains. Spring loaded tensioner should be inspected for damage.

Ensure all timing marks are aligned. Adjust belt tension using manufacturer's recommendations. Belt tension may require checking using tension gauge. *See Fig. 26.*

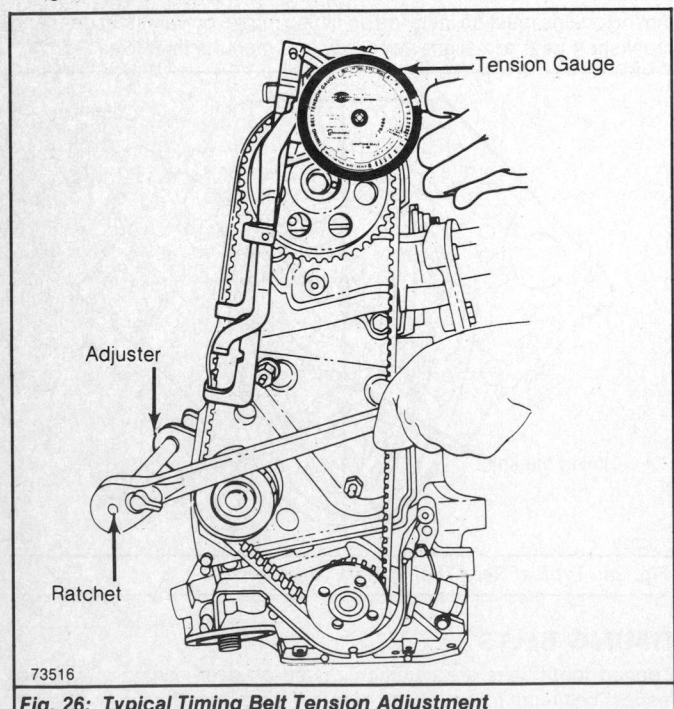

Fig. 26: Typical Timing Belt Tension Adjustment

TIMING GEARS

TIMING GEAR BACKLASH & RUNOUT

On engines where camshaft gear operates directly on crankshaft gear, gear backlash and runout must be checked. To check backlash, install dial indicator with tip resting on tooth of camshaft gear. Rotate camshaft gear as far as possible. Adjust indicator to zero. Rotate camshaft gear in opposite direction as far as possible and note reading.

To determine timing gear runout, mount dial indicator with tip resting on face edge of camshaft gear. Adjust indicator to zero. Rotate camshaft gear 360 degrees and note reading. If backlash or runout exceeds specification, replace camshaft and/or crankshaft gear.

REAR MAIN OIL SEAL INSTALLATION

One-Piece Type Seal – For one-piece type oil seal installation, coat block contact surface of seal with sealer if seal is not factory coated. Ensure seal surface is free of burrs. Lubricate seal lip with engine oil and press seal into place using proper oil seal installer. *See Fig. 27.*

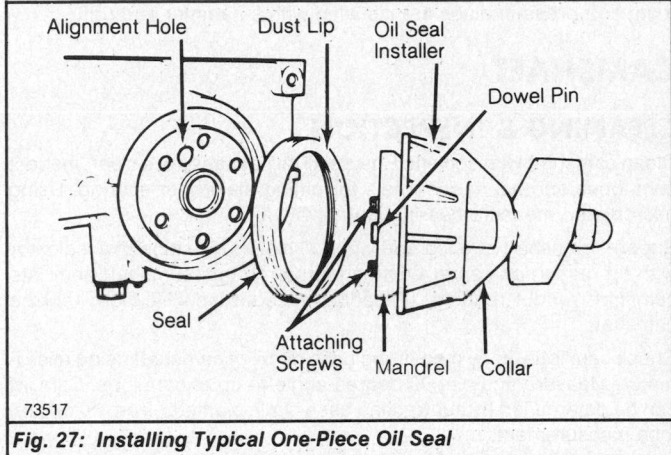

Fig. 27: Installing Typical One-Piece Oil Seal

Rope Type Seal – For rope type rear main oil seal installation, press seal lightly into seat area. Using seal installer, fully seat seal in bearing cap or cylinder block.

Trim seal ends even with cylinder block parting surface. Some applications require sealer to be applied on main bearing cap prior to installation. *See Fig. 28.*

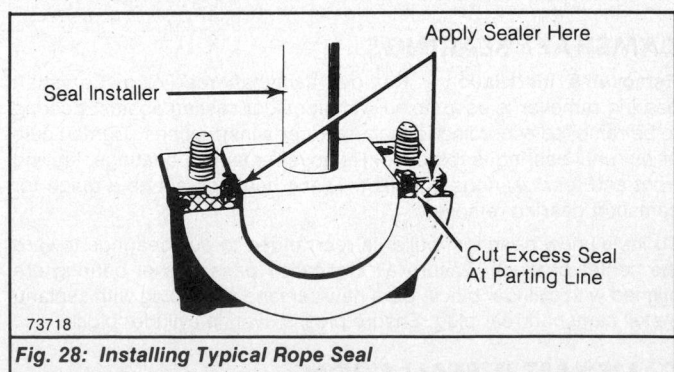

Fig. 28: Installing Typical Rope Seal

Split-Rubber Type Seal – Follow manufacturer's procedures when installing split-rubber type rear main oil seals. Installation procedures vary with manufacturer and engine type. *See Fig. 29.*

OIL PUMP

ROTOR TYPE

Mark oil pump rotor locations prior to removal. *See Fig. 30.* Remove outer rotor and measure thickness and diameter. Measure inner rotor

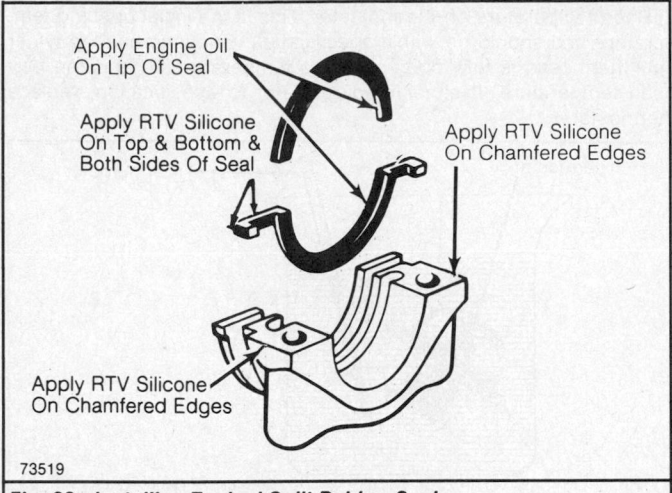

Fig. 29: Installing Typical Split-Rubber Seal

thickness. Inspect shaft for scoring or wear. Inspect rotors for pitting or damage. Inspect cover for grooving or wear. Replace worn or damaged components.

Measure outer rotor-to-body clearance. Replace pump assembly if clearance exceeds specification. Measure clearance between rotors. *See Fig. 31.* Replace shaft and both rotors if clearance exceeds specification.

Install rotors in pump body. Position straightedge across pump body. Using feeler gauge, measure clearance between rotors and straightedge. Pump cover wear is measured using a straightedge and feeler gauge. Replace pump if clearance exceeds specification.

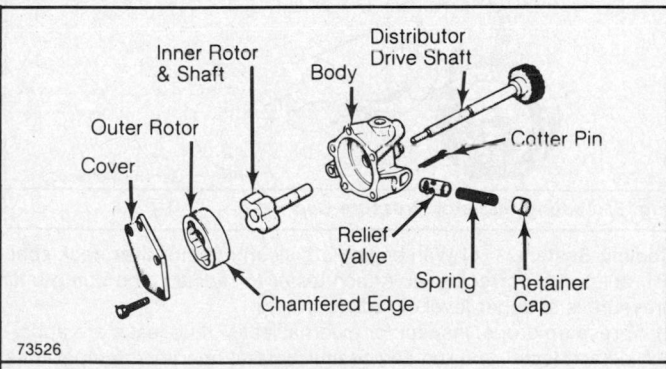

Fig. 30: Typical Rotor Type Oil Pump

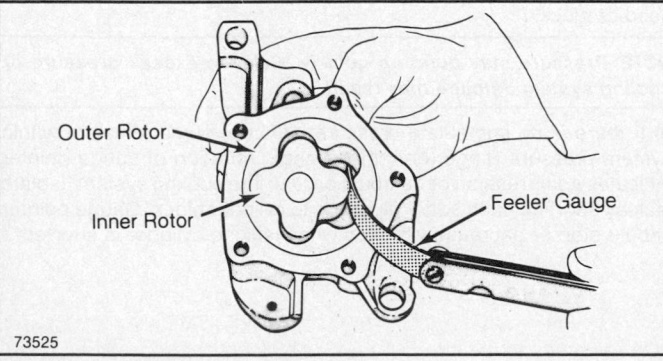

Fig. 31: Measuring Rotor Clearance

GEAR TYPE

Mark oil pump gear location prior to removal. *See Fig. 32.* Remove gears from pump body. Inspect gears for pitting or damage. Inspect cover for grooving or wear. Measure gear diameter and length. Measure gear housing cavity depth and diameter. *See Fig. 33.* Replace worn or damaged components.

Measure pump cover wear using a straightedge and feeler gauge. Replace pump or components if warpage/wear exceeds specification. Check pump mating surface for scratches or grooves.

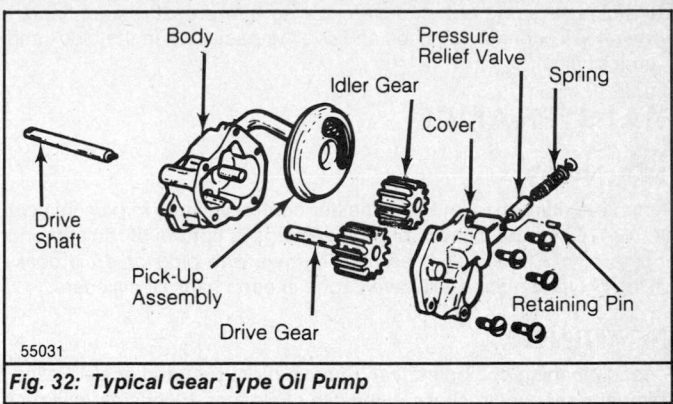

Fig. 32: Typical Gear Type Oil Pump

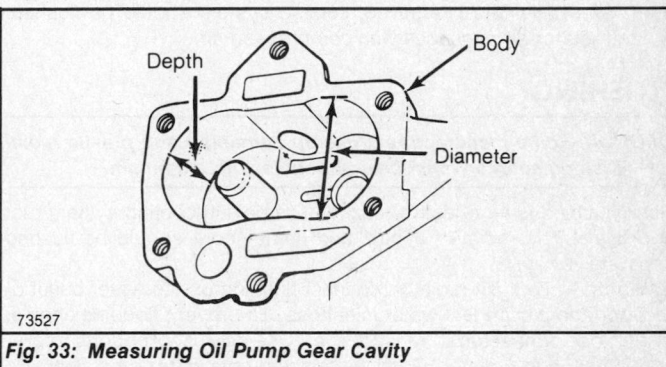

Fig. 33: Measuring Oil Pump Gear Cavity

BREAK-IN PROCEDURE

ENGINE PRE-OILING

Pre-oil engine prior to operation to prevent engine damage. A lightly oiled oil pump will cavitate unless oil pump cavities are filled with engine oil or petroleum jelly.

Engine pre-oiling can be done using pressure oiler (if available). Connect pressure oiler to oil pressure sending unit hole. Operate pressure oiler until oil fills crankcase. Check oil level while pre-oiling.

If pressure oiler is not available, disconnect ignition system. Remove oil pressure sending unit and install oil pressure test gauge. Using starter motor, rotate engine starter until gauge shows normal oil pressure for several seconds. DO NOT crank engine for more than 30 seconds to avoid starter motor damage. Ensure oil pressure has reached the furthest point from oil pump.

NOTE: If installing new lifters and camshaft, some manufacturers recommend adding a "crankcase conditioner" to engine oil.

INITIAL START-UP

Start engine and run at low RPM. Check for coolant, fuel and oil leaks. Stop engine. Recheck coolant and oil level. Fill if necessary.

CAMSHAFT

Break-in procedure is required when new or reground camshaft has been installed. Operate and maintain engine speed between 1500-2500 RPM for approximately 30 minutes.

PISTON RINGS

Piston rings require a break-in procedure to ensure seating of rings to cylinder walls. Follow piston ring manufacturer's recommended break-in procedure.

1992 GENERAL INFORMATION
General Cooling System Servicing

DESCRIPTION

The basic liquid cooling system consists of a radiator, water pump, thermostat, electric or belt-driven cooling fan, pressure cap, heater, and various connecting hoses and cooling passages in the block and cylinder head.

MAINTENANCE

DRAINING

Remove radiator cap and open heater control valve to maximum heat position. Open drain cocks or remove plugs in bottom of radiator and engine block. In-line engines usually have one plug or drain cock, while "V" type engines will have 2, one in each bank of cylinders.

CLEANING

A good cleaning compound can remove most rust and scale. Follow manufacturer's instructions in the use of cleaner. If considerable rust and scale have to be removed, cooling system should be flushed. Clean radiator air passages with compressed air.

FLUSHING

CAUTION: Some manufacturers use an aluminum and plastic radiator. Flushing solution must be compatible with aluminum.

Back flushing is an effective means of removing cooling system rust and scale. The radiator, engine and heater core should be flushed separately.
Radiator – To flush radiator, connect flushing gun to water outlet of radiator and disconnect water inlet hose. To prevent flooding engine, use a hose connected to radiator inlet. Use air in short bursts to prevent damage to radiator. Continue flushing until water runs clear.
Engine – To flush engine, remove thermostat and replace housing. Connect flushing gun to water outlet of engine. Flush using short air bursts until water runs clean.
Heater Core – Flush heater core as described for radiator. Ensure heater control valve is set to maximum heat position before flushing heater.

REFILLING

To prevent air from being trapped in engine block, engine should be running when refilling cooling system. After system is full, continue running engine until thermostat is open, then recheck fill level. Do not overfill system.

TESTING

THERMOSTAT

1) Remove and visually inspect thermostat for corrosion and proper sealing of valve and seat. If okay, suspend thermostat and thermometer in a 50/50 mixture of coolant and water. See Fig. 1. DO NOT allow thermostat or thermometer to touch bottom of container. Heat water until thermostat begins to open.

2) Read temperature on thermometer. This is the initial opening temperature and should be within specification. Continue heating water until thermostat is fully open and note temperature. This is the fully open temperature. If either reading is not to specification, replace thermostat.

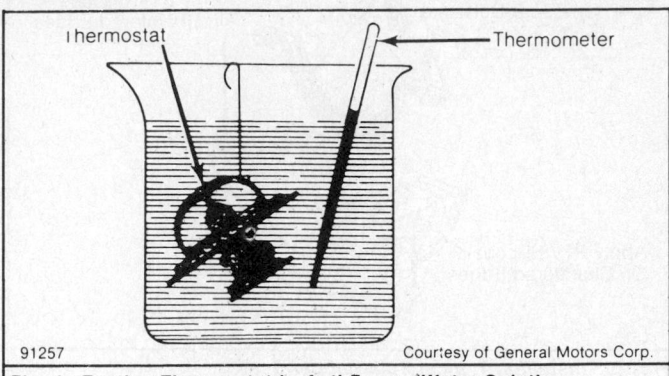

Fig. 1: Testing Thermostat in Anti-Freeze/Water Solution

PRESSURE TESTING

A pressure tester is used to check both radiator cap and complete cooling system. Follow pressure tester manufacturer's instructions and test components as follows:
Radiator Cap – Visually inspect radiator cap, then dip cap into water and connect to tester. Pump tester to bring pressure to upper limit of cap specification. See Fig. 2. If cap fails to hold pressure or releases at higher pressure than specification, replace cap.

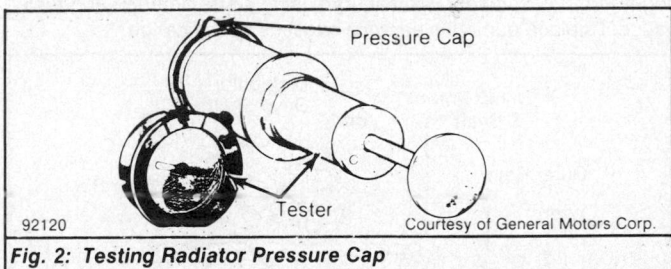

Fig. 2: Testing Radiator Pressure Cap

Cooling System – **1)** With engine off, clean radiator filler neck seat. Fill radiator to correct level. Attach tester to radiator and pump until pressure is at upper level of radiator rating.
2) If pressure drops, inspect for external leaks. If no leaks are apparent, detach tester and run engine until normal operating temperature is reached. Reattach tester and observe. If pressure builds up immediately, a possible leak exists from a faulty head gasket or crack in head or block.

NOTE: Pressure may build up quickly. Release excess pressure or cooling system damage may result.

3) If there is no immediate pressure build up, pump tester to within system pressure range (on radiator cap). Vibration of gauge pointer indicates compression or combustion leak into cooling system. Isolate leak by shorting each spark plug wire to cylinder block. Gauge pointer should stop or decrease vibration when leaking cylinder is shorted.

Gear Tooth Contact Patterns

INSPECTION

Wipe lubricant from internal parts. Rotate gears and inspect for wear or damage. Mount dial indicator to housing and check backlash at several points around ring gear. Backlash must be within specification at all points. If no defects are found, check gear tooth pattern contact.

NOTE: Drive pattern should be well centered on ring gear teeth. Coast pattern should be centered, but may be slightly toward toe of ring gear teeth.

Gear Tooth Contact Pattern – **1)** Paint ring gear teeth with marking compound. Wrap cloth or rope around drive pinion flange to act as brake. Rotate gear until clear contact pattern is obtained.
2) Contact pattern will indicate whether correct pinion bearing mounting shim has been installed and if drive gear backlash has been set properly. Backlash between drive gear pinion must be maintained within specified limits until correct tooth pattern is obtained.

ADJUSTMENTS

GEAR BACKLASH & PINION SHIM CHANGES

1) With no change in backlash, moving pinion further from ring gear moves drive pattern toward heel and top of tooth, and moves coast pattern toward toe and top of tooth.
2) With no change in backlash, moving pinion closer to ring gear moves drive pattern toward toe and bottom of tooth, and moves coast pattern toward heel and bottom of tooth.
3) With no change in pinion shim thickness, an increase in backlash moves ring gear further from pinion. Both drive and coast patterns move toward heel and top of tooth.
4) With no change in pinion shim thickness, a decrease in backlash moves ring gear closer to pinion gear. Both drive and coast patterns move toward toe and bottom of tooth.

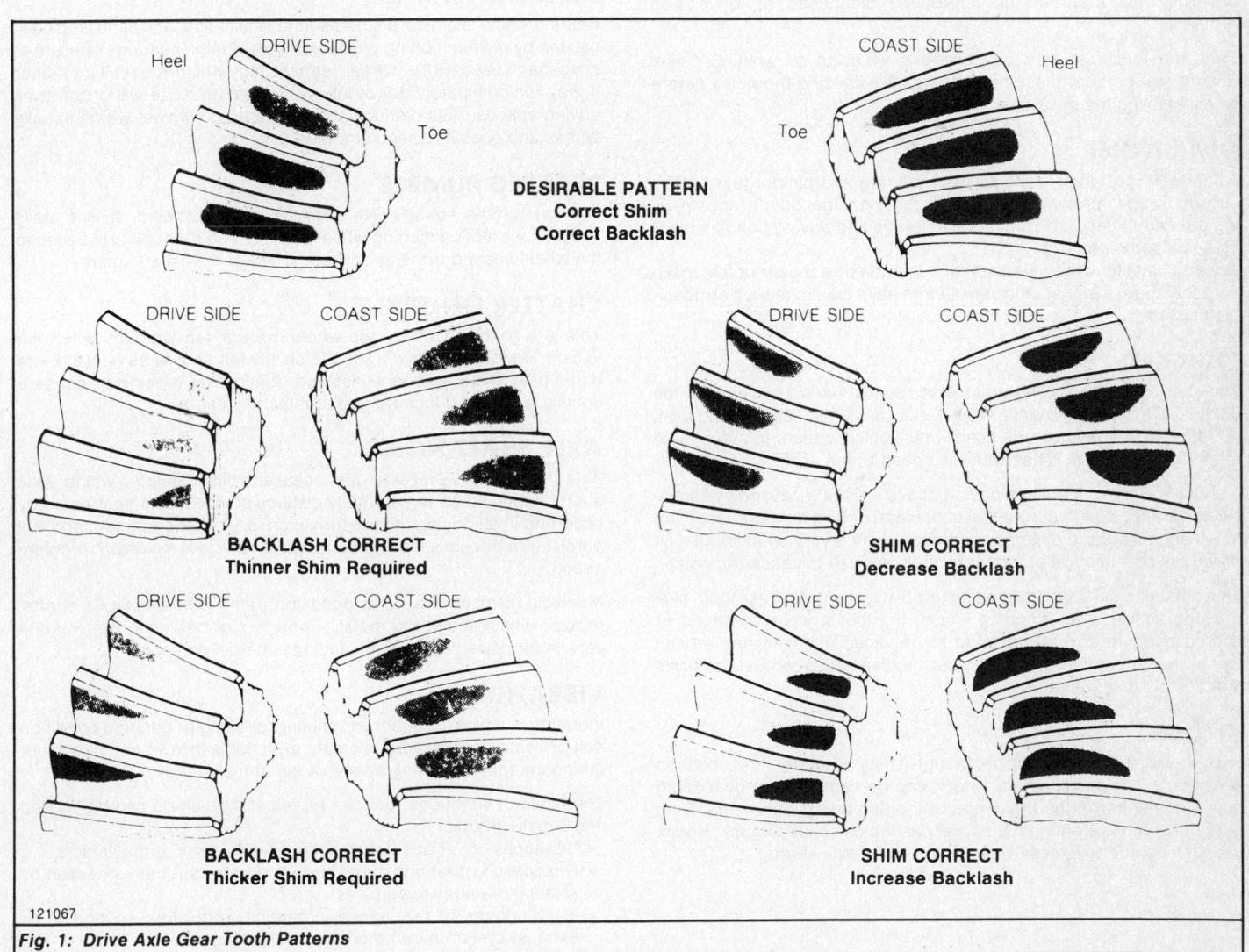

121067

Fig. 1: Drive Axle Gear Tooth Patterns

1992 GENERAL INFORMATION
Drive Axle Noise Diagnosis

UNRELATED NOISES

Some driveline trouble symptoms are also common to the engine, transmission, wheel bearings, tires, and other parts of the vehicle. Make sure that cause of trouble actually is in the drive axle before adjusting, repairing, or replacing any of its parts.

NON-DRIVE AXLE NOISES

A few conditions can sound just like drive axle noise and have to be considered in pre-diagnosis. The 4 most common noises are exhaust, tires, CV/universal joints and trim moldings.

In certain conditions, the pitch of the exhaust gases may sound like gear whine. At other times, it may be mistaken for a wheel bearing rumble.

Tires, especially radial and snow tires, can have a high-pitched tread whine or roar, similar to gear noise. Also, some non-standard tires with an unusual tread construction may emit a roar or whine.

Defective CV/universal joints may cause clicking noises or excessive driveline play that can be improperly diagnosed as drive axle problems.

Trim and moldings also can cause a whistling or whining noise. Ensure that none of these components are causing the noise before disassembling the drive axle.

GEAR NOISE

A "howling" or "whining" noise from the ring and pinion gear can be caused by an improper gear pattern, gear damage, or improper bearing preload. It can occur at various speeds and driving conditions, or it can be continuous.

Before disassembling axle to diagnose and correct gear noise, make sure that tires, exhaust, and vehicle trim have been checked as possible causes.

CHUCKLE

This is a particular rattling noise that sounds like a stick against the spokes of a spinning bicycle wheel. It occurs while decelerating from 40 MPH and usually can be heard until vehicle comes to a complete stop. The frequency varies with the speed of the vehicle.

A chuckle that occurs on the driving phase is usually caused by excessive clearance due to differential gear wear, or by a damaged tooth on the coast side of the pinion or ring gear. Even a very small tooth nick or a ridge on the edge of a gear tooth is enough to cause the noise.

This condition can be corrected simply by cleaning the gear tooth nick or ridge with a small grinding wheel. If either gear is damaged or scored badly, the gear set must be replaced. If metal has broken loose, the carrier and housing must be cleaned to remove particles that could cause damage.

KNOCK

This is very similar to a chuckle, though it may be louder, and occur on acceleration or deceleration. Knock can be caused by a gear tooth that is damaged on the drive side of the ring and pinion gears. Ring gear bolts that are hitting the carrier casting can cause knock. Knock can also be due to excessive end play in the axle shafts.

CLUNK

Clunk is a metallic noise heard when an automatic transmission is engaged in Reverse or Drive, or when throttle is applied or released. It is caused by backlash somewhere in the driveline, but not necessarily in the axle. To determine whether driveline clunk is caused by the axle, check the total axle backlash as follows:
1) Raise vehicle on a frame or twinpost hoist so that drive wheels are free. Clamp a bar between axle companion flange and a part of the frame or body so that flange cannot move.
2) On conventional drive axles, lock the left wheel to keep it from turning. On all models, turn the right wheel slowly until it is felt to be in drive condition. Hold a chalk marker on side of tire about 12" from center of wheel. Turn wheel in the opposite direction until it is again felt to be in drive condition.
3) Measure the length of the chalk mark, which is the total axle backlash. If backlash is one inch or less, clunk will not be eliminated by overhauling drive axle.

BEARING WHINE

Bearing whine is a high-pitched sound similar to a whistle. It is usually caused by malfunctioning pinion bearings. Pinion bearings operate at driveshaft speed. Roller wheel bearings may whine in a similar manner if they run completely dry of lubricant. Bearing noise will occur at all driving speeds. This distinguishes it from gear whine, which usually comes and goes as speed changes.

BEARING RUMBLE

Bearing rumble sounds like marbles being tumbled. It is usually caused by a malfunctioning wheel bearing. The lower pitch is because the wheel bearing turns at only about 1/3 of driveshaft speed.

CHATTER ON TURNS

This is a condition where the whole front or rear vibrates when the vehicle is moving. The vibration is plainly felt as well as heard. Extra differential thrust washers installed during axle repair can cause a condition of partial lock-up that creates this chatter.

AXLE SHAFT NOISE

Axle shaft noise is similar to gear noise and pinion bearing whine. Axle shaft bearing noise will normally distinguish itself from gear noise by occurring in all driving modes (drive, cruise, coast and float), and will persist with transmission in neutral while vehicle is moving at problem speed.

If vehicle displays this noise condition, remove suspect axle shafts, replace wheel seals and install a new set of bearings. Re-evaluate vehicle for noise before removing any internal components.

VIBRATION

Vibration is a high-frequency trembling, shaking or grinding condition (felt or heard) that may be constant or variable in level and can occur during the total operating speed range of the vehicle.

The types of vibrations that can be felt in the vehicle can be divided into 3 main groups:
- Vibrations of various unbalanced rotating parts of the vehicle.
- Resonance vibrations of the body and frame structures caused by rotating of unbalanced parts.
- Tip-in moans of resonance vibrations from stressed engine or exhaust system mounts or driveline flexing modes.

Anti-Lock Brake Safety Precautions

NOTE: Refer to appropriate Anti-Lock Brake System (ABS) article for description, operation, depressurizing, testing, system bleeding, trouble shooting and servicing of specific system. Failure to depressurize ABS could lead to physical injury.

- NEVER open a bleeder valve or loosen a hydraulic line while ABS is pressurized.

- NEVER disconnect or reconnect any electrical connectors while ignition is on. Damage to ABS control unit may result.

- DO NOT attempt to bleed hydraulic system without first referring to the appropriate article in your Mitchell service and repair manual.

- ONLY use specially designed brake hoses/lines on ABS equipped vehicles.

- DO NOT tap on speed sensor components (sensor, sensor rings). Speed rings must be pressed into hubs, NOT hammered into hubs. Striking these components can cause demagnetization or a loss of polarization, affecting the accuracy of the speed signal returning to the ABS control unit.

- DO NOT mix tire sizes. Increasing the width, as long as tires remain close to the original diameter, is acceptable. Rolling diameter must be identical for all 4 tires. Some manufacturers recommend tires of the same brand, style and type. Failure to follow this precaution may cause inaccurate wheel speed readings.

- DO NOT contaminate speed sensor components with grease. Only use recommended coating, when system calls for an anti-corrosion coating.

- When speed sensor components have been removed, ALWAYS check sensor-to-ring air gaps when applicable. These specifications can be found in each appropriate article.

- ONLY use recommended brake fluids. DO NOT use silicone brake fluids in an ABS equipped vehicle.

- When installing transmitting devices (CB's, telephones, etc.) on ABS equipped vehicles, DO NOT locate the antenna near the ABS control unit (or any control unit).

- Disconnect all on-board computers, when using electric welding equipment.

- DO NOT expose the ABS control unit to prolonged periods of high heat (185°F/85°C for 2 hours is generally considered a maximum limit).

1992 GENERAL INFORMATION
Wheel Alignment Theory & Operation

PRE-ALIGNMENT INSTRUCTIONS

Before adjusting wheel alignment, check the following:
- Ensure each axle uses tires of same construction and tread style, equal in tread wear and overall diameter. Using a dial indicator, verify that radial and axial runout of tires is not excessive. Inflation should be at manufacturer's specifications. *See Fig. 1.*
- Ensure steering linkage and suspension does not have excessive play. Check for wear in tie rod ends and ball joints. Springs must not be sagging. Check that control arm and strut rod bushings do not have excessive play.
- Vehicle must be on level floor with full fuel tank, no passenger load, spare tire in place and no load in trunk. Bounce front and rear end of vehicle several times. Confirm vehicle is at normal riding height.
- Ensure steering wheel is centered with wheels in straight ahead position. If required, shorten one tie rod adjusting sleeve and lengthen opposite sleeve (equal amount of turns). *See Fig. 2.*
- Ensure that wheel bearings have correct preload and that lug nuts are tightened to manufacturer's specifications. Adjust camber, caster and toe-in using this sequence. Follow instructions of the alignment equipment manufacturer.

CAUTION: DO NOT attempt to correct alignment by straightening parts. Damaged parts must be replaced.

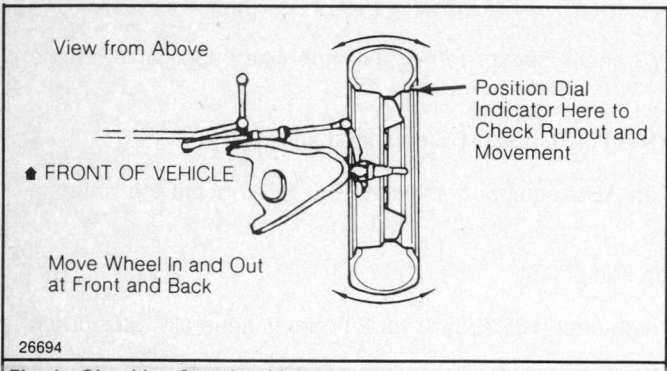

Fig. 1: Checking Steering Linkage

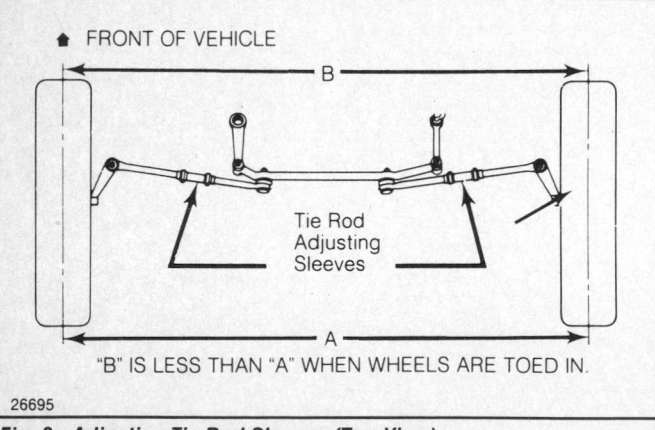

Fig. 2: Adjusting Tie Rod Sleeves (Top View)

CAMBER

1) Camber is the tilting of the wheel, outward at either top or bottom, as viewed from front of vehicle. *See Fig. 3.*
2) When wheels tilt outward at the top (from centerline of vehicle), camber is positive. When wheels tilt inward at top, camber is negative. Amount of tilt is measured in degrees from vertical.

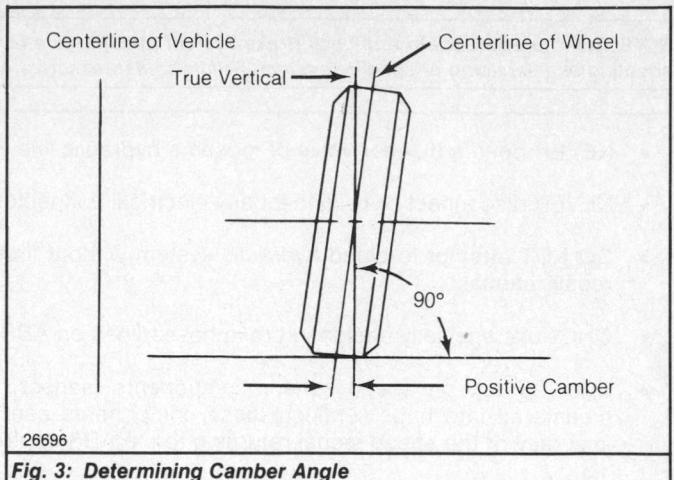

Fig. 3: Determining Camber Angle

CASTER

1) Caster is tilting of front steering axis either forward or backward from vertical, as viewed from side of vehicle. *See Fig. 4.*
2) When axis is tilted backward from vertical, caster is positive. This creates a trailing action on front wheels. When axis is tilted forward, caster is negative, causing a leading action on front wheels.

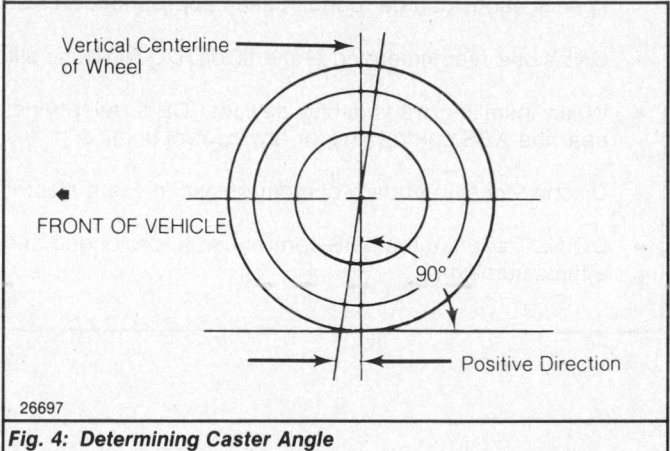

Fig. 4: Determining Caster Angle

TOE-IN ADJUSTMENT

Toe-in is the width measured at the rear of the tires subtracted by the width measured at the front of the tires at about spindle height. *See Fig. 5.* Toe-in specification is Dimension A less Dimension B. A positive figure would indicate toe-in and a negative figure would indicate toe-out. If the distance between the front and rear of the tires is the same, toe measurement would be zero. Use the following procedures to adjust toe-in:
1) Measure toe-in with front wheels in straight ahead position and steering wheel centered. To adjust toe-in, loosen clamps and turn adjusting sleeve or adjustable end on right and left tie rods. *See Figs. 2 and 5.*
2) Turn equally and in opposite directions to maintain steering wheel in centered position. Face of tie rod end must be parallel with machined surface of steering rod end to prevent binding.
3) When tightening clamps, make certain that clamp bolts are positioned so there will be no interference with other parts throughout the entire travel of the steering linkage.

Wheel Alignment Theory & Operation (Cont.)

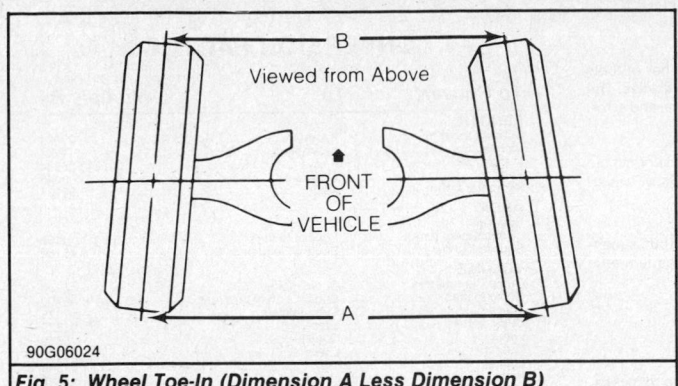

90G06024

Fig. 5: Wheel Toe-In (Dimension A Less Dimension B)

TOE-OUT ON TURNS

1) Toe-out on turns (turning radius) is a check for bent or damaged parts, and not a service adjustment. With caster, camber, and toe-in properly adjusted, check toe-out with weight of vehicle on wheels.
2) Use a full floating turntable under each wheel, repeating test with each wheel positioned for right and left turns. Incorrect toe-out generally indicates a bent steering arm. Replace steering arm, if necessary, and recheck wheel alignment.

STEERING AXIS INCLINATION

1) Steering axis inclination is a check for bent or damaged parts, and not a service adjustment. Vehicle must be level and camber should be properly adjusted. *See Fig. 6.*

2) If camber cannot be brought within limits and steering axis inclination is correct, steering knuckle is bent. If camber and steering axis inclination are both incorrect by approximately the same amount, the upper and lower control arms are bent.

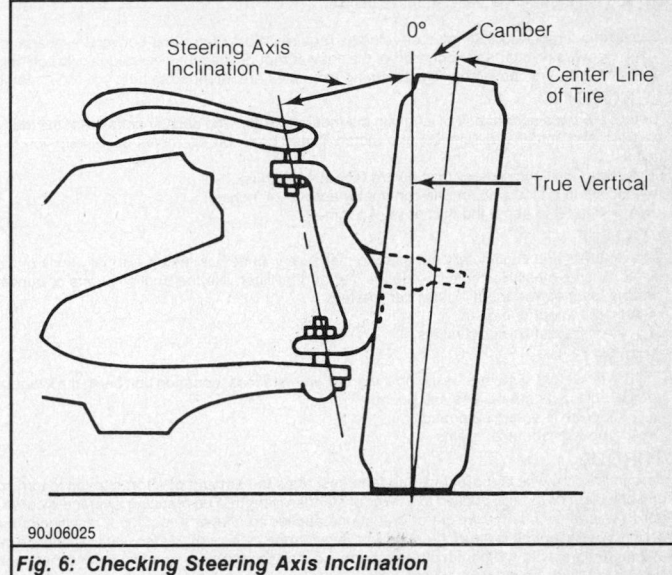

90J06025

Fig. 6: Checking Steering Axis Inclination

1992 GENERAL INFORMATION
English-Metric Conversion Chart

METRIC CONVERSIONS

Metric conversions are making life more difficult for the mechanic. In addition to doubling the number of tools required, metric-dimensioned nuts and bolts are used alongside English components in many new vehicles. The mechanic has to decide which tool to use, slowing down the job. The tool problem can be solved by trial and error, but some metric conversions aren't so simple.

Converting temperature, lengths or volumes requires a calculator and conversion charts, or else a very nimble mind. Conversion charts are only part of the answer though, because they don't help you "think" metric, or "visualize" what you are converting. The following examples are intended to help you "see" metric sizes:

LENGTH

Meters are the standard unit of length in the metric system. The smaller units are 10ths (decimeter), 100ths (centimeter), and 1000ths (millimeter) of a meter. These common examples might help you to visualize the metric units:

- A meter is slightly longer than a yard (about 40 inches).
- An aspirin tablet is about one centimeter across (.4 inches).
- A millimeter is about the thickness of a dime.

VOLUME

Cubic meters and centimeters are used to measure volume, just as we normally think of cubic feet and inches. Liquid volume measurements include the liter and milliliter, like the English quarts or ounces.

- One teaspoon is about 4 cubic centimeters.
- A liter is about one quart.
- A liter is about 61 cubic inches.

WEIGHT

The metric weight system is based on the gram, with the most common unit being the kilogram (1000 grams). Our comparable units are ounces and pounds:

- A kilogram is about 2.2 pounds.
- An ounce is about 28 grams.

TORQUE

Torque is somewhat complicated. The term describes the amount of effort exerted to turn something. A chosen unit of weight or force is applied to a lever of standard length. The resulting leverage is called torque. In our standard system, we use the weight of one pound applied to a lever a foot long, resulting in the unit called a foot-pound. A smaller unit is the inch-pound (the lever is one inch long). Metric units include the meter kilogram (lever one meter long with a kilogram of weight applied) and the Newton-meter (lever one meter long with force of one Newton applied). Some conversions are:

- A meter kilogram is about 7.2 foot pounds.
- A foot pound is about 1.4 Newton-meters.
- A centimeter kilogram (cmkg) is equal to .9 inch pounds.

PRESSURE

Pressure is another complicated measurement. Pressure is described as a force or weight applied to a given area. Our common unit is pounds per square inch. Metric units can be expressed in several ways. One is the kilogram per square centimeter (kg/cm²). Another unit of pressure is the Pascal (force of one Newton on an area of one square meter), which equals about 4 ounces on a square yard. Since this is a very small amount of pressure, we usually see the kiloPascal, or kPa (1000 Pascals). Another common automotive term for pressure is the bar (used by German manufacturers), which equals 10 Pascals. Thoroughly confused? Try the examples below:

- Atmospheric pressure at sea level is about 14.7 psi.
- Atmospheric pressure at sea level is about 1 bar.
- Atomospheric pressure at sea level is about 1 kg/cm².
- One pound per square inch is about 7 kPa.

CONVERSION FACTORS

To Convert	To	Multiply By
LENGTH		
Millimeters (mm)	Inches	.03937
Inches	Millimeters	25.4
Meters (M)	Feet	3.28084
Feet	Meters	.3048
Kilometers (Km)	Miles	.62137
AREA		
Square Centimeters (cm²)	Square Inches	.155
Square Inches	Square Centimeters	6.45159
VOLUME		
Cubic Centimeters	Cubic Inches	.06103
Cubic Inches	Cubic Centimeters	16.38703
Liters	Cubic Inches	61.025
Cubic Inches	Liters	.01639
Liters	Quarts	1.05672
Quarts	Liters	.94633
Liters	Pints	2.11344
Pints	Liters	.47317
Liters	Ounces	33.81497
Ounces	Liters	.02957
WEIGHT		
Grams	Ounces	.03527
Ounces	Grams	28.34953
Kilograms	Pounds	2.20462
Pounds	Kilograms	.45359
WORK		
Centimeter Kilograms	Inch Pounds	.8676
Pounds/Sq. Inch	Kilograms/Sq. Centimeter	.07031
Bar	Pounds/Sq. Inch	14.504
Pounds/Sq. Inch	Bar	.06895
Atmosphere	Pounds/Sq. Inch	14.696
Pounds/Sq. Inch	Atmosphere	.06805
TEMPERATURE		
Centigrade Degrees	Fahrenheit Degrees	$(C° \times {}^9/_5) + 32$
Fahrenheit Degrees	Centigrade Degrees	$(F°-32) \times {}^5/_9$

Inches	Decimals	mm
1/64	.016	.397
1/32	.031	.794
3/64	.047	1.191
1/16	.063	1.588
5/64	.078	1.984
3/32	.094	2.381
7/64	.109	2.778
1/8	.125	3.175
9/64	.141	3.572
5/32	.156	3.969
11/64	.172	4.366
3/16	.188	4.763
13/64	.203	5.159
7/32	.219	5.556
15/64	.234	5.953
1/4	.250	6.350
17/64	.266	6.747
9/32	.281	7.144
19/64	.297	7.541
5/16	.313	7.938
21/64	.328	8.334
11/32	.344	8.731
23/64	.359	9.128
3/8	.375	9.525
25/64	.391	9.992
13/32	.406	10.319
27/64	.422	10.716
7/16	.438	11.113
29/64	.453	11.509
15/32	.469	11.906
31/64	.484	12.303
1/2	.500	12.700
33/64	.516	13.097
17/32	.531	13.494
35/64	.547	13.891
9/16	.563	14.288
37/64	.578	14.684
19/32	.594	15.081
39/64	.609	15.478
5/8	.625	15.875
41/64	.641	16.272
21/32	.656	16.669
43/64	.672	17.066
11/16	.687	17.463
45/64	.703	17.859
23/32	.719	18.256
47/64	.734	18.653
3/4	.750	19.050
49/64	.766	19.447
25/32	.781	19.844
51/64	.797	20.241
13/16	.813	20.638
53/64	.828	21.034
27/32	.844	21.431
55/64	.859	21.828
7/8	.875	22.225
57/64	.891	22.622
29/32	.906	23.019
59/64	.922	23.416
15/16	.938	23.813
61/64	.953	24.209
31/32	.969	24.606
63/64	.984	25.003
1	1.000	25.400

WE ENCOURAGE PROFESSIONALISM

ASE CERTIFIED

THROUGH TECHNICIAN CERTIFICATION

MITCHELL INTERNATIONAL
9889 Willow Creek Road
P.O. Box 26260
San Diego, CA 92196-0260

CHRYSLER MOTORS

1992 CHRYSLER MOTORS CONTENTS

NOTE: Includes 1991-92 Cruise Control Systems.

GENERAL INFORMATION [1]

ENGINE PERFORMANCE

ENGINE PERFORMANCE (Cont.)

1992 CHRYSLER MOTORS CONTENTS (Cont.)

ENGINES (Cont.)

ENGINE COOLING

CLUTCHES

DRIVE AXLES

1992 CHRYSLER MOTORS CONTENTS (Cont.)

1992 MODEL COVERAGE

MODEL	BODY CODE	ENGINE	ENGINE ID	FUEL SYSTEM	IGNITION SYSTEM
Caravan [1]	S [2]	2.5L	K	TBI	Hall Effect [3]
		3.0L	3	PFI [4]	Optical
		3.3L	R	PFI [4]	DIS Magnetic [3]
Dakota	N	2.5L	K	TBI	Hall Effect [3]
		3.9L	X	PFI [4]	Magnetic [3]
		5.2L	Y	PFI [4]	Magnetic [3]
Pickup (D150/250/350 & W150/250/350)	D	3.9L	X	PFI [4]	Magnetic [3]
		5.2L	Y	PFI [4]	Magnetic [3]
		5.9L	Z	TBI	Hall Effect [3]
		5.9L [5]	5	TBI	Hall Effect [3]
		5.9L Diesel	8	Turbo DFI	N/A
Ramcharger (AD100/150 & AW100/150)	D	5.2L	Y	PFI [4]	Magnetic [3]
		5.9L	Z	TBI	Hall Effect [3]
RWD Van (B150/250/350) [6]	B	3.9L	X	PFI [4]	Magnetic [3]
		5.2L	Y	PFI [4]	Magnetic [3]
		5.2L CNG [7]	T	PFI	Magnetic [8]
		5.9L	Z	TBI	Hall Effect [3]
Town & Country	S	3.3L	R	PFI [4]	DIS Magnetic [3]
Voyager	S [2]	2.5L	K	TBI	Hall Effect [3]
		3.0L	3	PFI [4]	Optical
		3.3L	R	PFI [4]	DIS Magnetic [3]

[1] – Includes Caravan C/V, Extended Caravan, Cargo Van and Extended Cargo Van.
[2] – Available in 2WD or All-Wheel Drive (AWD).
[3] – Uses a Single Board Electronic Controller (SBEC) with a Hall Effect distributor.
[4] – Sequential Fuel Injection.
[5] – With heavy-duty emissions.
[6] – Includes Ram Wagon and Ram Van.
[7] – Compressed natural gas.
[8] – Uses a Powertrain Control Module (PCM) with a magnetic crankshaft position sensor.

VIN DEFINITION

1B7FB35X9NS000001
① ② ③ ④ ⑤ ⑥ ⑦ ⑧ ⑨ ⑩ ⑪ ⑫ ⑬ ⑭ ⑮ ⑯ ⑰

① Indicates Nation of Origin.
② Indicates Manufacturer.
③ Indicates Vehicle Type.
④ Indicates Gross Vehicle Weight Rating.
⑤ Indicates Vehicle Line.
⑥ Indicates Vehicle Series.
⑦ Indicates Body Type.
⑧ **Indicates Engine Code.**
⑨ Indicates Check Digit.
⑩ **Indicates Model Year.**
⑪ Indicates Assembly Plant.
⑫⑬⑭⑮⑯⑰ Indicate Plant Sequential Number.

MODEL YEAR VIN CODE APPLICATION

VIN Code	Model Year
L	1990
M	1991
N	1992

ENGINE CODE LOCATION

2.5L – Engine serial number is located on rear face of engine block, below cylinder head.
3.0L & 3.3L – Engine serial number is located on right front side of engine block, adjacent to exhaust manifold stud.
3.9L – Engine serial number is on a pad located on right side of block.
5.2L & 5.9L – Engine serial number is on left front corner of block, below cylinder head.

1992 ENGINE PERFORMANCE
Emission Applications

1992 CHRYSLER MOTORS

Engine & Fuel System	Emission Control Systems & Devices

2.5L TBI .... **PCV, TAC, EVAP, TWC,** [1] [2] **BP/EGR, SPK, O₂, CEC, EMR, CE,**
EVAP-CPCS, EVAP-VC, EVAP-PRRV, [1] BP/EGR-EET, SPK-CC

3.0L PFI .... **PCV, EVAP, TWC,** [2] [3] **BP/EGR, SPK, O₂, CEC, EMR, CE,**
EVAP-CPCS, EVAP-VC, EVAP-PRRV, BP/EGR-EET, SPK-CC

3.3L PFI .... **PCV, EVAP, TWC, SPK, O₂, CEC, EMR, CE,**
EVAP-CPCS, EVAP-VC, EVAP-PRRV, SPK-CC

3.9L PFI .... **PCV, EVAP, TWC,** [2] **BP/EGR, SPK, O₂, CEC, EMR, CE,**
EVAP-CPCS, EVAP-VC, EVAP-PRRV, BP/EGR-SOL, BP/EGR-EET, SPK-CC

5.2L PFI .... **PCV, EVAP, TWC,** [2] **BP/EGR, SPK, O₂, CEC, EMR, CE,**
EVAP-CPCS, EVAP-VC, EVAP-PRRV, BP/EGR-SOL, BP/EGR-EET, SPK-CC

5.2L PFI CNG [4] .... **PCV, TWC/OC, EGR, SPK, O₂, CEC, EMR, CE,**
[2] EGR-TRANS, SPK-CC

5.9L TBI .... **PCV, TAC, EVAP, TWC, BP/EGR, SPK, AP, O₂, CEC, EMR, CE,**
EVAP-CPCS, EVAP-VC, EVAP-PRRV, BP/EGR-SOL, BP/EGR-BPT,
SPK-CC, [5] AP-DV, [5] AP-ASS, [5] AP-ASRV

5.9L TBI (Heavy Duty) .... **PCV, TAC, EVAP, TWC, BP/EGR, SPK,** [6] **AP, O₂, CEC, EMR, CE,**
EVAP-CPCS, EVAP-VC, EVAP-PRRV, BP/EGR-SOL,
BP/EGR-BPT, SPK-CC, [5] AP-DV

5.9L Diesel Turbo .... **AIH**

[1] – Dakota only.
[2] – Elec. controlled.
[3] – Calif. A/T only.
[4] – Compressed natural gas.
[5] – Some models.
[6] – Equipped with dual air pump system.

NOTE: For quick reference, major emission control systems and devices are listed in bold type; components and other related devices are listed in light type.

AP – Air Pump
AIH – Air Intake Heaters
AP-ASS – AP Air Switching Solenoid
AP-DV – AP Diverter Valve
AP-ASRV – AP Air Switching Relief Valve
BP/EGR – Backpressure EGR
BP/EGR-BPT – BP/EGR Backpressure Transducer
BP/EGR-EET – BP/EGR Electronic EGR Transducer
BP/EGR-SOL – BP/EGR Solenoid

CE – CHECK ENGINE Light
CEC – Computerized Engine Controls
EGR – Exhaust Gas Recirculation
EGR-TRANS – EGR Transducer
EMR – Emission Maintenance Reminder Light
EVAP – Fuel Evaporative System
EVAP-CPCS – EVAP Canister Purge Control Solenoid
EVAP-PRRV – EVAP Pressure Relief Rollover Valve

EVAP-VC – EVAP Vapor Canister
O₂ – Oxygen Sensor
PCV – Positive Crankcase Ventilation
PFI – Port Fuel Injection
SPK – Spark Control System
SPK-CC – SPK Computer Controlled
TAC – Thermostatic Air Cleaner
TBI – Throttle Body Injection
TWC – Three-Way Catalyst
OC – TWC Oxidation Catalyst

1992 ENGINE PERFORMANCE
Service & Adjustment Specifications – Gasoline

**Caravan, Dakota, Pickup, Ramcharger,
RWD Van, Town & Country, Voyager**

INTRODUCTION

Use this article to quickly find specifications related to servicing and on-vehicle adjustments. This article may be used for quick reference when you are familiar with proper adjustment procedures and only need a specification.

CAPACITIES
BATTERY SPECIFICATIONS

Load Test (Amps)	[1] CCA Rating @ 0°F (Amps)	[2] Reserve Capacity (Min.)
200	500	110
250	600	120
300	600	120
315	685	125
375	750	125
405	810	133
535	1075	160

[1] – CCA rating is current a battery can deliver for 30 seconds and maintain a terminal voltage of 7.2 volts or greater at specified temperature.

[2] – Reserve capacity is length of time a battery can deliver 25 amps and maintain a minimum terminal voltage of 10.5 volts at 80°F (27°C).

FLUID CAPACITIES (AWD & FWD)

Application	Specification
Cooling System (Includes Recovery Tank)	
2.5L	[1] 9.5 Qts. (9.0L)
3.0L & 3.3L	[1] 10.0 Qts. (9.5L)
Crankcase (Includes Filter)	
All Models	4.5 Qts. (4.3L)
Automatic Transaxle (Dexron-II)	
3-Speed A-413/30TH & A670/31TH (Except Fleet)	8.5 Qts. (8.0L)
3-Speed A-413/30TH & A670/31TH (Fleet Only)	9.2 Qts. (8.7L)
4-Speed A-604/41TE	9.1 Qts. (8.6L)
Manual Transmission (SAE 5W-30 SG/API GL-4)	
5-Speed A-523	2.4 Qts. (2.3L)
Power Steering Fluid [2]	
All Models	1.7 Pts. (0.8L)

[1] – Add 1 qt. (.95L) if equipped with rear heater.

[2] – DO NOT use Automatic Transmission Fluid (ATF).

FLUID CAPACITIES (RWD & 4WD)

Application	Specification
Cooling System (Includes Recovery Tank)	
Dakota	
2.5L	9.8 Qts. (9.3L)
3.9L	14.0 Qts. (13.2L)
5.2L	14.3 Qts. (13.5L)
All Other Models	
3.9L	15.1 Qts. (14.3L)
5.2L 2WD	17.0 Qts. (16.1L)
5.2L 4WD	16.5 Qts. (15.6L)
5.9L 2WD [1]	15.5 Qts. (14.7L)
5.9L 4WD [1]	15.0 Qts. (14.2L)
Crankcase (Includes Filter)	
5.2L Dakota	5.0 Qts. (4.7L)
All Other Models	4.5 Qts. (4.3L)
Transfer Case (Dexron-II)	
NP-205	4.5 Pts. (2.1L)
NP-231	2.5 Pts. (1.2L)
NP-241	6.0 Pts. (2.8L)
Rear Axle (SAE 80W-90/API GL-4)	
Chrysler 7 1/4"	3.0 Pts. (1.4L)
Chrysler 8 1/4"	4.4 Pts. (2.0L)
Chrysler 9 1/4"	4.5 Pts. (2.1L)
Dana 60	6.0 Pts. (2.8L)
Dana 70	7.0 Pts. (3.3L)

[1] – Add 1 qt. (.95L) if equipped with rear heater.

FLUID CAPACITIES (RWD & 4WD) (Cont.)

Application	Specification
Front Axle (SAE 80W-90/API GL-4)	
Dakota	2.6 Pts. (1.2L)
All Others	
Spicer 44FBJ	5.6 Pts. (2.6L)
Spicer 60F	6.5 Pts. (3.1L)
Automatic Transmission (Dexron-II)	
A-500/42RH (3.9L)	10.2 Qts. (9.6L)
A-518/46RH (5.2L & 5.9L)	10.7 Qts. (10.2L)
A-727/36RH (5.2L & 5.9L)	8.4 Qts. (7.9L)
A-999/32RH (3.9L & 5.2L)	8.6 Qts. (8.1L)
Manual Transmission	
AX-15 [2]	[3]
Getrag 360 (5-Speed) [4]	3.5 Qts. (3.3L)
NP-2500 (5-Speed) [5]	2.0 Qts. (1.9L)
NV-4500 [6]	4.0 Qts. (3.8L)
Power Steering Fluid [7]	
Dakota RWD	1.7 Pts. (0.8L)
Dakota 4WD	2.5 Pts. (1.2L)
All Others	2.7 Pts. (1.3L)

[2] – Use SAE 75W-90 API GL-5 fluid.

[3] – Dakota, 3.3 qts. (3.1L). RWD Van, 3.4 qts. (3.2L).

[4] – Use SAE 5W-30 SG/API GL-4.

[5] – Use SAE 10W-30 API SG or SG/CD fluid.

[6] – Use synthetic 75W-90 API GL-4 fluid.

[7] – DO NOT use Automatic Transmission Fluid (ATF).

QUICK-SERVICE
SERVICE INTERVALS & SPECIFICATIONS
REPLACEMENT INTERVALS (AWD & FWD)

Component	Interval (Miles)
2.5L, 3.0L & 3.3L	
Air Filter	30,000
Coolant	[1] 52,500
Oil	7500
Oil Filter	[2] 15,000
Spark Plugs	30,000

[1] – Every 30,000 thereafter.

[2] – If mileage is less than 7500 miles (5000 miles on turbo) each 12 months, replace filter at each oil change.

REPLACEMENT INTERVALS (RWD & 4WD)

Component	Interval (Miles)
Light-Duty Service	
Air Filter	30,000
Coolant	30,000
Fuel Filter	As Necessary
Oil	7500
Oil Filter	[1] 15,000
Spark Plugs	30,000
Heavy-Duty Service	
Air Filter	24,000
Coolant	30,000
Fuel Filter	As Necessary
Oil	6000
Oil Filter	12,000
Spark Plugs	30,000

[1] – If mileage is less than 7500 miles each 12 months, replace filter at each oil change.

4-CYLINDER BELT TENSION ADJUSTMENT

Application	New Belt Lbs. (kg)	[1] Used Belt Lbs. (kg)
2.5L		
Dakota		
A/C Compressor	160 (72.6)	80 (36.3)
Alternator/Water Pump Poly "V"	160 (72.6)	80 (36.3)
Power Steering Pump	120 (54.4)	80 (36.3)
Caravan & Voyager		
A/C Compressor	125 (56.7)	80 (36.3)
Alternator/Water Pump Poly "V"	130 (60.0)	80 (36.3)
Power Steering Pump	105 (47.6)	80 (36.3)

[1] – Belt is considered used after 15 minutes of service.

V6 BELT TENSION ADJUSTMENT

Application	New Belt Lbs. (kg)	[1] Used Belt Lbs. (kg)
3.0L		
A/C Compressor	125 (56.7)	80 (36.3)
Serpentine	[2]	[2]
3.3L		
A/C Compressor	[2]	[2]
Serpentine	[2]	[2]
3.9L		
Serpentine	[2]	[2]

[1] – Belt is considered used after 15 minutes of service.
[2] – Dynamic tensioner equipped, no adjustment required.

V8 BELT TENSION ADJUSTMENT

Application	Tension Lbs. (kg)
5.2L	
Serpentine	[1]
5.9L	
All Belts	
New Belt	100-140 (45.4-63.5)
Used Belt [2]	60-90 (27.2-40.9)

[1] – Dynamic tensioner equipped, no adjustment required.
[2] – Belt is considered used after 15 minutes of service.

MECHANICAL CHECKS
ENGINE COMPRESSION

Check engine compression with engine at normal operating temperature at specified cranking speed, all spark plugs removed and throttle wide open.

COMPRESSION SPECIFICATIONS

Application	Specification
Compression Ratio	
2.5L	8.9:1
3.0L	8.85:1
3.3L	8.9:1
3.9L	9.1:1
5.2L	9.1:1
5.9L	8.1:1
Compression Pressure	
3.0L	[1] 178 psi (12.5 kg/cm²)
All Other Engines	[2] 100 psi (7.0 kg/cm²)

[1] – At 250 RPM.
[2] – Minimum compression pressure is given. Maximum difference between each cylinder should not exceed 25 percent.

VALVE CLEARANCE

All engines are equipped with hydraulic lifters and do not require valve adjustment. Valve clearance is zero lash with engine at operating temperature.

IGNITION SYSTEM
IGNITION COIL

IGNITION COIL RESISTANCE – Ohms @ 70-80°F (21-27°C)

Application	Primary	Secondary
2.5L & 3.0L		
Diamond	0.97-1.18	11,300-15,300
Toyodenso	0.95-1.20	11,300-13,300
3.3L		
Diamond	0.52-0.63	11,600-15,800
Toyodenso	0.51-0.61	11,500-13,500
3.9L & 5.2L		
Diamond	0.96-1.18	11,300-15,300
Toyodenso	0.95-1.20	11,300-13,300
5.9L		
Chrysler Essex	1.34-1.55	9000-12,200
Chrysler Prestolite	1.34-1.55	9400-11,720
Diamond	1.34-1.55	15,000-19,000

HIGH TENSION WIRE RESISTANCE
HIGH TENSION WIRE RESISTANCE

Application	Minimum Ohms	Maximum Ohms
All Wires	250 Per Inch	1000 Per Inch

SPARK PLUGS
SPARK PLUG TYPE

Application	Champion No.
2.5L	RN12YC
3.0L	
Standard	RN11YC4
Optional	BPR5ES-11
3.3L	RN16YC5
3.9L	RC12YC
5.2L & 5.9L	RC12YC

SPARK PLUG SPECIFICATIONS

Application	Gap In. (mm)	Torque Ft. Lbs. (N.m)
2.5L	.035 (.89)	20 (28)
3.0L	.035 (.89)	20 (28)
3.3L	.050 (1.27)	20 (28)
3.9L & 5.2L	.035 (.89)	20 (28)
5.9L	.035 (.89)	30 (41)

FIRING ORDER & TIMING MARKS

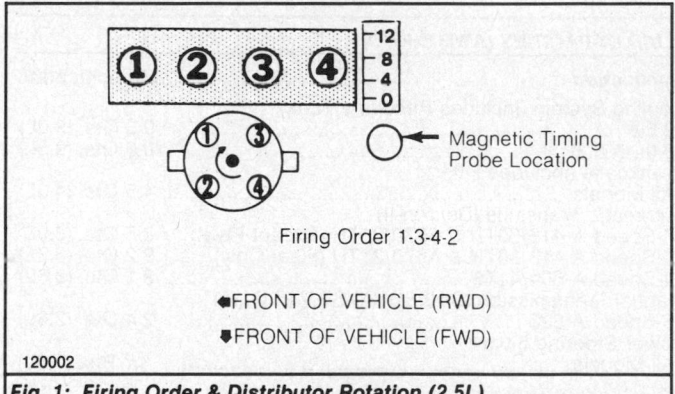

Firing Order 1-3-4-2

← FRONT OF VEHICLE (RWD)
↓ FRONT OF VEHICLE (FWD)

120002

Fig. 1: Firing Order & Distributor Rotation (2.5L)

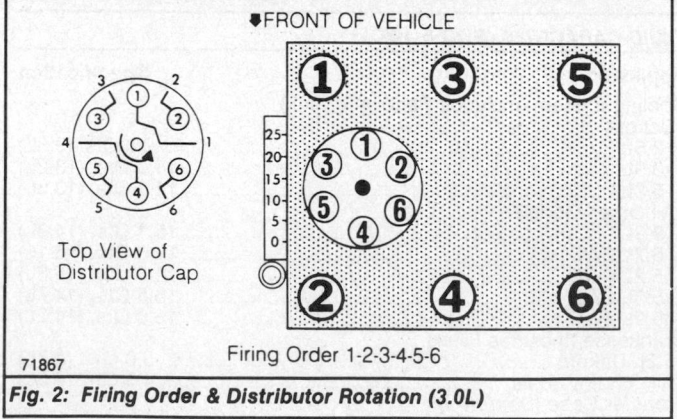

↓ FRONT OF VEHICLE

Top View of Distributor Cap

Firing Order 1-2-3-4-5-6

71867

Fig. 2: Firing Order & Distributor Rotation (3.0L)

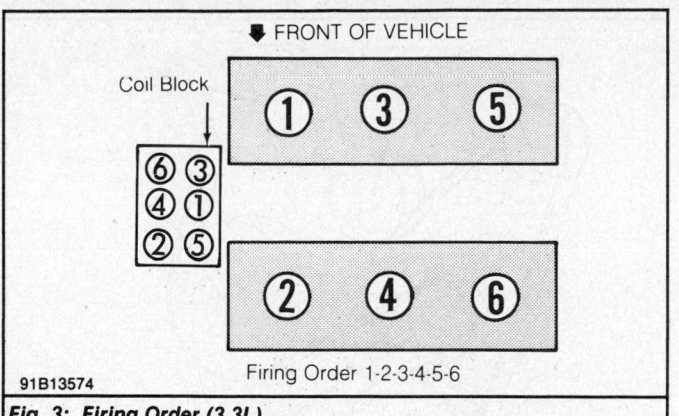

Fig. 3: Firing Order (3.3L)

FRONT OF VEHICLE

Coil Block

Firing Order 1-2-3-4-5-6

91B13574

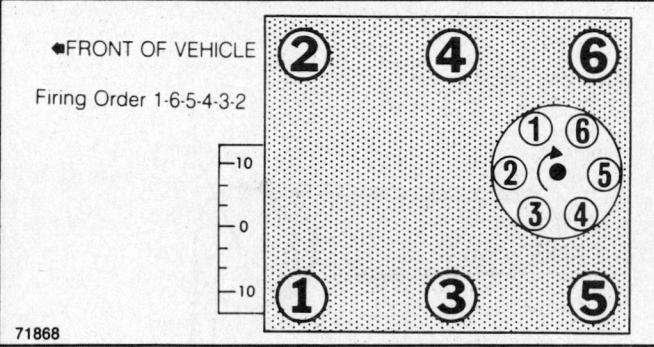

Fig. 4: Firing Order & Distributor Rotation (3.9L)

FRONT OF VEHICLE

Firing Order 1-6-5-4-3-2

71868

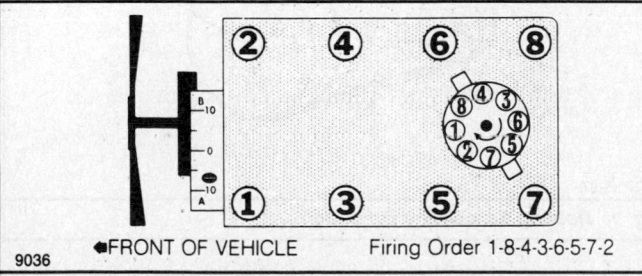

Fig. 5: Firing Order & Distributor Rotation (5.2L & 5.9L)

FRONT OF VEHICLE   Firing Order 1-8-4-3-6-5-7-2

9036

IGNITION TIMING

*NOTE: Always refer to Emission Control Label in engine compart-
ment before attempting service. If manual and label differ, always
use emission label specifications.*

IGNITION TIMING (Degrees BTDC @ RPM)

Application	Man. Trans.	Auto. Trans.
2.5L (Except Dakota)	10-14 @ 850	10-14 @ 850
2.5L (Dakota)	[1]	[1]
3.0L		10-14 @ 700
3.3L		[2]
3.9L & 5.2L	[2]	[2]
5.9L	8-12 [3]	8-12 [3]

[1] – See Emission Control Label in engine compartment.
[2] – Ignition timing is not adjustable.
[3] – At idle.

ELECTRONIC SPARK ADVANCE CHECK

*NOTE: Always refer to Emission Control Label in engine compart-
ment before attempting service. If manual and label differ, always
use emission label specifications.*

ELECTRONIC SPARK ADVANCE (Degrees BTDC @ RPM)

Application	Man. Trans.	Auto. Trans.
2.5L	17-25 @ 2000	17-25 @ 2000
3.0L		34-42 @ 2000
3.3L		N/A
3.9L, 5.2L & 5.9L	N/A	N/A

FUEL SYSTEM

FUEL PUMP

*NOTE: Fuel pump performance means fuel pressure and volume
availability (with vacuum removed), not regulated fuel pressure.*

FUEL PUMP PERFORMANCE

Application	Pressure psi (kg/cm²)
2.5L	49 (3.4)
3.0L & 3.3L	58 (4.1)
3.9L & 5.2L	49 (3.4)
5.9L	24.5 (1.7)

FUEL PUMP REGULATED PRESSURE

Application	Pressure psi (kg/cm²)
2.5L	39 (2.7)
3.0L & 3.3L	48 (3.4)
3.9L & 5.2L	39 (2.7)
5.9L	14.5 (1.0)

INJECTOR RESISTANCE
INJECTOR RESISTANCE

Application	Ohms	°F (°C)
3.9L & 5.2L	12.5-16.5	68 (20)
All Other Models	N/A	N/A

IDLE SPEED & MIXTURE

*NOTE: Mixture is controlled by Single Board Engine Controller
(SBEC). No adjustment is possible.*

CURB IDLE SPEED (RPM)

Application	Man. Trans.	Auto. Trans.
2.5L	1050-1250	1050-1250
3.0L		750-950
3.3L		750-950
3.9L, 5.2L & 5.9L	N/A	N/A

4-CYLINDER MINIMUM AIRFLOW RATE SPECIFICATIONS

Application	RPM
2.5L	1050-1250

V6 MINIMUM AIRFLOW RATE SPECIFICATIONS

Application	RPM
3.0L	750-950
3.3L	700-950

THROTTLE POSITION SENSOR
THROTTLE POSITION SENSOR VOLTAGE TEST

Application	Volts
All Models [1]	
At Idle	0.2-1.5
At Wide Open Throttle	3.4-5.0

[1] – Measure voltage at throttle position sensor center terminal.

1992 ENGINE PERFORMANCE
Service & Adjustment Specifications – Diesel

Pickup

INTRODUCTION

Use this article to quickly find specifications related to servicing and on-vehicle adjustments. This is a quick-reference article to use when you are familiar with an adjustment procedure and only need a specification.

CAPACITIES

BATTERY SPECIFICATIONS

Application	Cold Cranking Amperage
All Models	1075

FLUID CAPACITIES [1]

Application	Quantity
Cooling System (Includes Heater) [2]	
A/T	16.5 Qts. (15.7L)
M/T	15.5 Qts. (14.7L)
Crankcase (Includes Filter) [3]	12.0 Qts. (11.4L)
Automatic Transmission (Dexron-II) [4]	
37RH & 46RH	11.0 Qts. (10.4L)
Manual Transmission (SAE 5W-30 API SG Or SG/CD)	
G360	3.5 Qts. (3.3L)
Power Steering	2.7 Pts. (1.3L)
Transfer Case [5] (NP205)	4.5 Pts. (2.1L)
Front Axle [5]	6.5 Pts. (3.1L)
Rear Axle [5]	7.0 Pts. (3.3L)

[1] – All capacities are approximate.
[2] – Add 1 qt. (.95L) for coolant recovery tank.
[3] – Engine oil must meet API rating of CC/CD-SF, CD/SF, CE/SF or CE/SG. Use 15W-40 weight oil for temperatures exceeding 10°F (-12°C) and 10W-30 for temperature less than 10°F (-12°C). Maximum sulfated ash content of 1.85% is recommended. DO NOT use single grade oil.
[4] – Torque converters do not have drain plugs. DO NOT attempt to install drain plug. Add approximate amount of fluid and check fluid level several times while filling, and add fluid if necessary. Capacity is only approximate.
[5] – Use gear oil with API rating of GL-5. Use SAE 140 for temperatures greater than 90°F (32°C). Use SAE 90 for temperatures between -10°F (-23°C) and 90°F (32°C). Use SAE 80 for temperatures less than -10°F (-23°C).

QUICK-SERVICE

SERVICE INTERVALS & SPECIFICATIONS

ADJUSTMENT OR REPLACEMENT INTERVALS

Component	Interval
Adjust Bands (A/T)	12 Months Or 12,000 Miles
Adjust Valve Clearance	24 Months Or 24,000 Miles
Air Filter	24 Months Or 24,000 Miles
Automatic Transmission Fluid & Filter	
Normal Service	36,000 Miles
Severe Service	18,000 Miles
Coolant	24 Months Or 24,000 Miles
Fuel Filter	12 Months Or 12,000 Miles
Manual Transmission Fluid	
Normal Service	36,000 Miles
Severe Service	18,000 Miles
Oil & Filter	6 Months Or 6000 Miles
Transfer Case Fluid	36,000 Miles

BELT ADJUSTMENT

A single serpentine drive belt is used. Proper belt tension is maintained by automatic belt tensioner. Ensure serpentine drive belt is properly routed. *See Fig. 1.*

MECHANICAL CHECKS

ENGINE COMPRESSION

Information is not available from manufacturer.

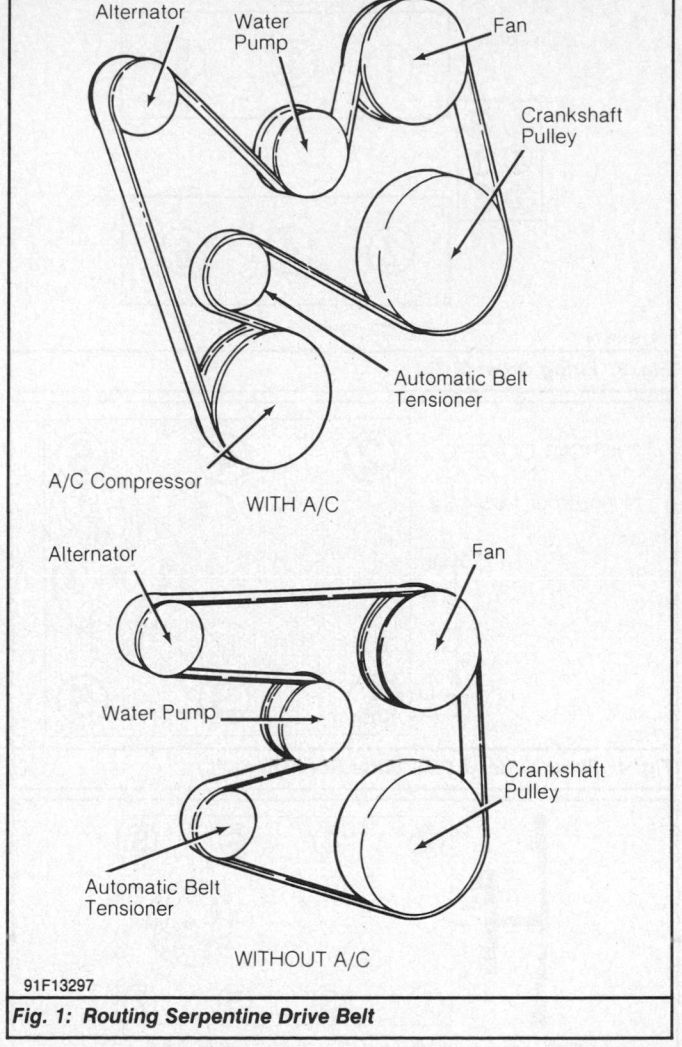

Fig. 1: Routing Serpentine Drive Belt

VALVE CLEARANCE

Valve clearance must be adjusted with engine temperature less than 140°F (60°C). For valve clearance adjusting procedure, see ON-VEHICLE ADJUSTMENTS – DIESEL article.

VALVE ADJUSTING SEQUENCE [1]

Procedure	Cylinder Numbers
Step 1 [2]	
Exhaust Valves	1, 3 & 5
Intake Valves	1, 2 & 4
Step 2 [3]	
Exhaust Valves	2, 4 & 6
Intake Valves	3, 5 & 6

[1] – Adjust valves with engine temperature less than 140°F (60°C).
[2] – Adjust with timing pin engaged and No. 1 cylinder at TDC.
[3] – Engine rotated 360 degrees from TDC of No. 1 cylinder and reference marks aligned.

VALVE CLEARANCE SPECIFICATIONS [1]

Application	In. (mm)
Exhaust Valves	.020 (.51)
Intake Valves	.010 (.25)

[1] – Adjust valves with engine temperature less than 140°F (60°C).

FIRING ORDER

NOTE: For firing order, see Fig. 2.

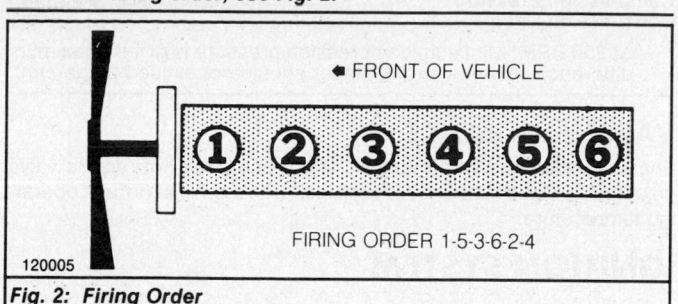

FRONT OF VEHICLE

FIRING ORDER 1-5-3-6-2-4

120005

Fig. 2: Firing Order

FUEL SYSTEM

FUEL INJECTOR

Fuel injector must have correct opening pressure. Fuel injector opening pressure should be 3550 psi (249 kg/cm²). If opening pressure is below specification, replace injector.

FUEL INJECTION PUMP TIMING

See ON-VEHICLE ADJUSTMENTS – DIESEL article.

FUEL LIFT PUMP

For fuel lift pump testing procedure, see SYSTEM & COMPONENT TESTING – DIESEL article.

FUEL LIFT PUMP SPECIFICATIONS

Application	Output
Pump Pressure	3 psi Minimum (.2 kg/cm²)
Volume Within 30 Seconds	.79 Qts. (.75L)

LOW IDLE SPEED

For low idle speed adjusting procedure, see ON-VEHICLE ADJUSTMENTS – DIESEL article. For specifications, see LOW IDLE SPEED SPECIFICATIONS table.

LOW IDLE SPEED SPECIFICATIONS [1]

Application	RPM
A/T	700
M/T	750

[1] – Check low idle speed with A/C on.

FULL THROTTLE SPEED

Check full throttle speed with A/C on. If engine will not meet full throttle speed and low-pressure fuel system and fuel injectors are operating correctly, fuel injection pump must be removed for service. See FULL THROTTLE SPEED SPECIFICATIONS table.

FULL THROTTLE SPEED SPECIFICATIONS [1]

Application	RPM
All Models	2825-2925

[1] – Check with A/C on.

THROTTLE POSITION SENSOR (TPS)

NOTE: Throttle position sensor is only used on intercooled models with automatic transmissions.

For throttle position sensor adjusting procedure, see ON-VEHICLE ADJUSTMENTS – DIESEL article.

TURBOCHARGER

For turbocharger testing procedures, see SYSTEM & COMPONENT TESTING – DIESEL article.

TURBOCHARGER SPECIFICATIONS

Application	In. (mm)
Shaft Clearances	
End Play	[1]
Radial Clearance	.012-.018 (.30-.46)
Turbine Shaft Minimum O.D.	.432 (10.97)

[1] – On turbochargers with serial No. 840637 and earlier, end play should be .004-.006" (.10-.15 mm). On turbochargers with serial No. 840638 and later, end play should be .001-.003" (.03-.08 mm).

1992 ENGINE PERFORMANCE
Service & Adjustment Specifications – CNG

RWD Van

INTRODUCTION

Use this article to quickly find specifications related to servicing and on-vehicle adjustments. This article may be used for quick reference when you are familiar with proper adjustment procedures and only need a specification.

CAPACITIES

BATTERY SPECIFICATIONS

Load Test (Amps)	[1] CCA Rating @ 0°F (Amps)	[2] Reserve Capacity (Minutes)
300	600	120
405	810	133

[1] – CCA rating is current a battery can deliver for 30 seconds and maintain a terminal voltage of 7.2 volts or greater at specified temperature.

[2] – Reserve capacity is length of time a battery can deliver 25 amps and maintain a minimum terminal voltage of 10.5 volts at 80°F (27°C).

FLUID CAPACITIES

Application	Specification
Automatic Transmission (Dexron-II)	
32RH	8.6 qts. (8.1L)
36RH	8.4 qts. (7.9L)
46RH	10.7 qts. (10.2L)
Cooling System (Includes Heater)	16.5 qts. (15.6L)
Crankcase (Includes Filter)	4.5 qts. (4.3L)
Manual Transmission (SAE 75W-90 SG/API GL-5)	
AX15 (5-Speed)	3.4 qts. (3.2L)
Power Steering	2.7 pts. (1.3L)
Rear Axle (SAE 80W-90/API GL-4)	
Chrysler 8 3/8"	4.4 pts. (2.1L)
Chrysler 9 1/4"	4.75 pts. (2.2L)
Dana 60	6.25 pts. (3.0L)

QUICK-SERVICE

SERVICE INTERVALS & SPECIFICATIONS

REPLACEMENT INTERVALS

Component	Interval (Miles)
Light-Duty Service	
Air Filter	30,000
Coolant	30,000
Fuel Filter	As Necessary
Oil	7500
Oil Filter	[1] 15,000
Spark Plugs	30,000
Heavy-Duty Service	
Air Filter	24,000
Coolant	30,000
Fuel Filter	As Necessary
Oil	6000
Oil Filter	12,000
Spark Plugs	30,000

[1] – If mileage is less than 7500 miles each 12 months, replace filter at each oil change.

BELT ADJUSTMENT

Application	Tension Lbs. (kg)
Alternator/Water & Power Steering Pumps	
New or Used Belt	[1]

[1] – Dynamic tensioner is used; adjustment is not necessary.

MECHANICAL CHECKS

ENGINE COMPRESSION

Check engine compression with engine at normal operating temperature at specified cranking speed, all spark plugs removed and throttle wide open.

COMPRESSION SPECIFICATIONS

Application	Specification
Compression Pressure [1]	100 psi (7.0 kg/cm²)
Compression Ratio	9.0:1

[1] – At 250 RPM. Minimum compression pressure is given. Maximum difference between each cylinder should not exceed 25 percent.

VALVE CLEARANCE

Engine is equipped with hydraulic lifters and does not require valve adjustment. Valve clearance is zero lash with engine at normal operating temperature.

IGNITION SYSTEM

IGNITION COIL

IGNITION COIL RESISTANCE – Ohms @ 70-80°F (21-27°C)

Application	Primary	Secondary
Diamond	0.96-1.18	11,300-15,300
Toyodenso	0.95-1.20	11,300-13,300

SPARK PLUGS

SPARK PLUG TYPE

Application	Champion No.
5.2L	RC12YC

SPARK PLUG SPECIFICATIONS

Application	Gap In. (mm)	Torque Ft. Lbs. (N.m)
5.2L	.035 (.90)	30 (41)

FIRING ORDER & TIMING MARKS

NOTE: For firing order and distributor rotation, see Fig. 1.

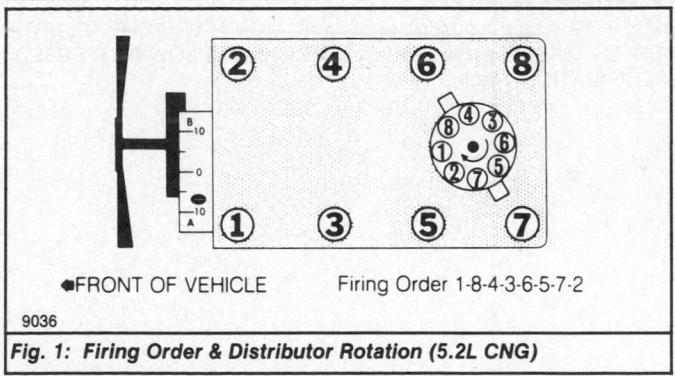

◄FRONT OF VEHICLE   Firing Order 1-8-4-3-6-5-7-2

9036

Fig. 1: Firing Order & Distributor Rotation (5.2L CNG)

IGNITION TIMING

IGNITION TIMING (Degrees BTDC @ RPM)

Application	Man. Trans.	Auto. Trans.
5.2L	[1] 10-14	[1] 10-14

[1] – At idle. Ignition timing is not adjustable.

FUEL SYSTEM

FUEL CAPACITY

FUEL CAPACITY

Application	Cu. In. (L)
Compressed Natural Gas	[1] 9144 (150)

[1] – Equivalent to approximately 11.0 gallons (41.6L) of gasoline.

FUEL PUMP

NOTE: Fuel system is under constant pressure; fuel pump is not required.

IDLE SPEED & MIXTURE

NOTE: Mixture is controlled by Single Board Engine Controller (SBEC). No adjustment is possible.

THROTTLE POSITION SENSOR
THROTTLE POSITION SENSOR VOLTAGE TEST

Terminals [1]	Volts
At Idle	1.0
At Wide Open Throttle	3.4

[1] – Measure voltage at throttle position sensor center terminal.

1992 ENGINE PERFORMANCE
On-Vehicle Adjustments – Gasoline

Caravan, Dakota, Pickup, Ramcharger, RWD Van, Town & Country, Voyager

ENGINE MECHANICAL

Before performing any on-vehicle adjustments to fuel or ignition systems, ensure engine mechanical condition is okay.

VALVE CLEARANCE

NOTE: All engines use hydraulic lifters. No adjustments are required.

IGNITION TIMING

NOTE: Always refer to emission control information label in engine compartment before service. If manual and emission label differ, use emission label specifications. Basic timing is not adjustable on 3.3L, 3.9L and 5.2L.

CAUTION: Timing light secondary connection should be made with inductive pick-up. DO NOT puncture cables, boots or nipples with test probes.

2.5L, 3.0L & 5.9L – 1) Connect a suitable timing light to No. 1 cylinder. Refer to equipment manufacturer's instructions for proper connection. Turn selector switch to appropriate cylinder position.

2) Start engine, and warm it to normal operating temperature. Connect tachometer, and ensure idle RPM is within specification. See CURB IDLE SPEED (RPM) table under IDLE SPEED & MIXTURE. Disconnect engine coolant sensor lead wire. Radiator fan should come on and CHECK ENGINE light should glow.

3) Check timing through timing window in bellhousing on 4-cylinder models or crankshaft pulley for other engines. See IGNITION TIMING table. DO NOT adjust timing if it is within 2 degrees of specification. If timing is incorrect, loosen distributor hold-down bolt and turn housing until specified timing is obtained.

4) Recheck timing after tightening distributor hold-down bolt. Reconnect coolant lead wire. Erase any fault codes. Recheck curb idle, and adjust if necessary. Remove diagnostic equipment.

IGNITION TIMING (Degrees BTDC @ RPM)

Application	Man. Trans.	Auto. Trans.
2.5L		
Caravan & Voyager	10-14 @ 850	10-14 @ 850
Dakota	[1]	[1]
3.0L		10-14 @ 700
3.3L		[2]
3.9L & 5.2L	[2]	[2]
5.9L	8-12 [3]	8-12 [3]

[1] – See emission control information label in engine compartment.
[2] – Ignition timing is not adjustable.
[3] – At idle.

IDLE SPEED & MIXTURE

NOTE: Mixture is controlled by Single Board Engine Controller (SBEC). No adjustment is possible.

Electronically fuel injected vehicles use an Automatic Idle Speed (AIS) motor or Idle Speed Control (ISC) actuator to regulate idle RPM. AIS or ISC is controlled by SBEC, which uses information received from various sensors to determine, among other things, idle speed. Curb idle speed is not adjustable. See appropriate SELF-DIAGNOSTICS article for diagnosis of incorrect idle speed.

IDLE RPM TEST

NOTE: Engine idle set RPM should be tested and recorded when vehicle is first brought into shop for testing. This will assist in diagnosing complaints of engine stalling, creeping and hard shifting on vehicles equipped with automatic transmission.

1) Connect tachometer Red lead to coil negative (–) terminal and tachometer Black lead to a chassis ground.

2) Turn selector switch to appropriate cylinder position of engine being tested. Start engine and warm to normal operating temperature. Turn tachometer RPM switch to 1000 RPM position.

3) With engine at normal operating temperature, momentarily open throttle and release to ensure linkage is not binding and throttle lever is fully against its stop.

4) Note engine RPM, and compare with specification. See CURB IDLE SPEED (RPM) table. If RPM is not within specification, see appropriate SELF-DIAGNOSTICS article.

CURB IDLE SPEED (RPM)

Application	Man. Trans.	Auto. Trans.
2.5L	850	850
3.0L	.....	700
3.3L	.....	750
3.9L, 5.2L & 5.9L	N/A	N/A

MINIMUM AIRFLOW

NOTE: Minimum airflow testing procedures are provided for 2.5L, 3.0L, 3.3L, 3.9L & 5.2L equipped with Automatic Idle Speed (AIS) motor on throttle body.

2.5L, 3.0L & 3.3L – 1) Set parking brake, and block front wheels. Warm engine to normal operating temperature. Disconnect and plug heated air door vacuum hose. Connect timing light and tachometer. Disconnect engine coolant temperature sensor. Set basic timing to 10-14 degrees BTDC. Turn engine off. Reconnect coolant temperature sensor.

2) With engine off, disconnect hose from PCV valve, and plug PCV valve nipple. Disconnect idle purge hose from vacuum harness "T". *See Fig. 1.* Attach Air Metering Fitting (6457) to manifold-mounted idle purge hose. Orifice size is .125" (3 mm). Connect Diagnostic Readout Box II (DRB-II) to vehicle.

3) Start engine. Let engine idle for at least one minute. Using DRB-II, access MINIMUM AIRFLOW IDLE SPEED. When this mode is accessed, AIS motor will fully close, spark advance will fix, fuel delivery will not change and engine RPM will be displayed on DRB-II.

4) Check minimum airflow. See MINIMUM AIRFLOW IDLE SPEED table. If minimum airflow idle speed is not within specification, replace throttle body.

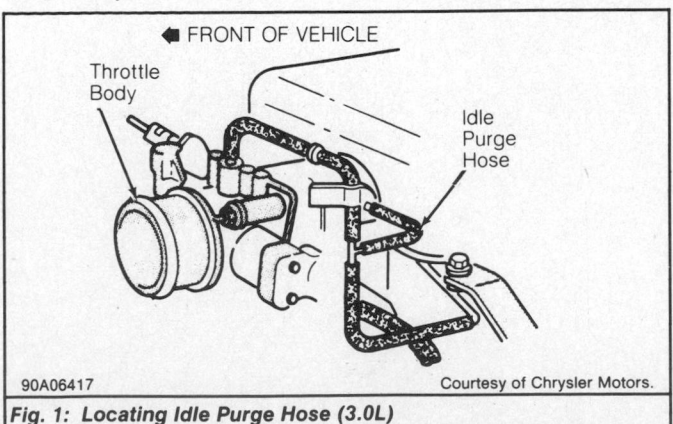

◄ FRONT OF VEHICLE

Throttle Body

Idle Purge Hose

90A06417   Courtesy of Chrysler Motors.

Fig. 1: Locating Idle Purge Hose (3.0L)

MINIMUM AIRFLOW IDLE SPEED

Application	RPM
2.5L	1050-1250
3.0L	750-950
3.3L	700-950

3.9L & 5.2L – 1) Set parking brake, and block front wheels. With engine off, disconnect AIS motor connector at throttle body. Connect Exerciser Tool (7558) harness connector to AIS motor. Connect Red clip of exerciser tool to positive battery terminal. Connect Black exerciser tool clip to negative battery terminal. Red light on exerciser tool will glow when tool is connected properly.

2) Start engine. With exerciser tool switch in HIGH or LOW position, Red tool light will flash. Move switch to HIGH position (engine speed should increase). Move switch to LOW position (engine speed should decrease). If engine speed changes, AIS motor is operating properly. Reconnect AIS motor connector at throttle body. If engine speed changes, test is complete. If engine speed does not change, go to next step.

3) DO NOT disconnect exerciser tool. Turn ignition to OFF position. Remove AIS motor from throttle body.

CAUTION: While testing AIS motor operation with AIS motor removed from throttle body, ensure pintle does not extend more than .250" (6.35 mm) from AIS motor body.

4) Cycle exerciser tool switch between HIGH and LOW positions and observe pintle. If pintle does not move, replace AIS motor. If pintle moves, check throttle body bore for blockage and clean as necessary. Install AIS motor, and retest system. If no blockage exists, see appropriate SELF-DIAGNOSTICS article.

THROTTLE POSITION SENSOR (TPS)

NOTE: Throttle Position Sensor (TPS) is not adjustable. Following procedures may be used to check TPS calibration.

1) Turn ignition switch to ON position. DO NOT start engine. Measure voltage at center terminal of TPS, with throttle valve fully closed against stop. Voltage should be within specification. See THROTTLE POSITION SENSOR VOLTAGE TEST table. If voltage is not within specification, replace TPS.

2) Slowly open throttle valve to wide open throttle. TPS voltage should gradually increase to at least 3.4 volts. If voltage does not gradually increase to at least 3.4 volts, replace TPS.

THROTTLE POSITION SENSOR VOLTAGE TEST

All Models [1]	Volts
At Idle	0.2-1.5
At Wide Open Throttle	3.4-5.0

[1] – Measure voltage at throttle position sensor center terminal.

1992 ENGINE PERFORMANCE
On-Vehicle Adjustments – Diesel

Pickup

ENGINE COMPRESSION

Information is not available from manufacturer.

VALVE CLEARANCE

NOTE: Valve clearance must be adjusted with engine temperature less than 140°F (60°C).

1) Engine can be rotated by removing dust cover from transmission adapter plate and installing Engine Barring Tool (3377462) in adapter plate. *See Fig. 1.* Rotate engine clockwise until No. 1 cylinder is at TDC. Engage timing pin.

CAUTION: Use care when engaging timing pin to avoid breaking tip of pin. Ensure timing pin is disengaged before rotating engine.

2) Remove rocker lever covers, and ensure No. 1 cylinder push rods are loose and valves are closed. If rods and valves are not okay, disengage timing pin, and rotate engine 360 degrees in clockwise direction. With No. 1 cylinder at TDC, check clearance on proper valves. See VALVE ADJUSTING SEQUENCE table. Adjust clearance using rocker lever adjusting screw if not within specification. See VALVE CLEARANCE SPECIFICATIONS table.

3) Once correct valves are checked and adjusted, place reference marks on vibration damper and front timing gear cover. Disengage timing pin and rotate engine 360 degrees (clockwise) and realign reference marks. Clearance must be checked on proper valves. See VALVE ADJUSTING SEQUENCE table. Adjust clearance if it is not within specification. See VALVE CLEARANCE SPECIFICATIONS table.

VALVE ADJUSTING SEQUENCE [1]

Procedure	Cylinder Number
Step 1 [2]	
Exhaust Valves	1, 3 & 5
Intake Valves	1, 2 & 4
Step 2 [3]	
Exhaust Valves	2, 4 & 6
Intake Valves	3, 5 & 6

[1] – Adjust valves with engine temperature less than 140°F (60°C).

[2] – Adjust with engine cold, timing pin engaged and No. 1 cylinder at TDC.

[3] – Engine rotated 360 degrees from TDC of No. 1 cylinder and reference marks aligned.

VALVE CLEARANCE SPECIFICATIONS

Application	In. (mm)
Exhaust Valves	[1] .020 (.51)
Intake Valves	[1] .010 (.25)

[1] – Adjust valves with engine temperature less than 140°F (60°C).

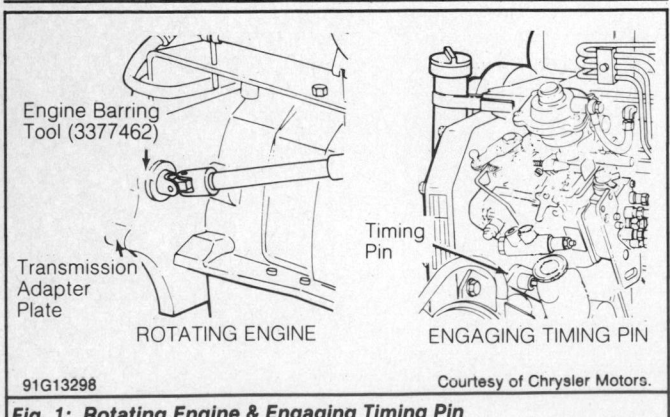

Fig. 1: Rotating Engine & Engaging Timing Pin

FUEL INJECTION PUMP TIMING

CAUTION: Special washer must be installed under lock bolt before rotating engine to allow fuel injection pump to rotate. If special washer is not installed, loosen lock bolt and install special washer. Tighten lock bolt to 10 ft. lbs. (14 N.m). See Fig. 3.

1) Ensure special washer is installed under lock bolt. *See Fig. 3.* Rotate engine clockwise until No. 1 cylinder is at TDC. Engage timing pin. *See Fig. 2.* Engine can be rotated by removing dust cover from transmission adapter plate and installing Engine Barring Tool (3377462) in adapter plate.

CAUTION: If removing some high-pressure fuel lines is necessary, ensure lines and fittings are thoroughly cleaned before removing. Cap all fuel lines and fittings when removed.

2) Remove plug from end of fuel injection pump. Install timing indicator in end of fuel injection pump. *See Fig. 2.* If necessary, remove some high-pressure fuel lines to install timing indicator.

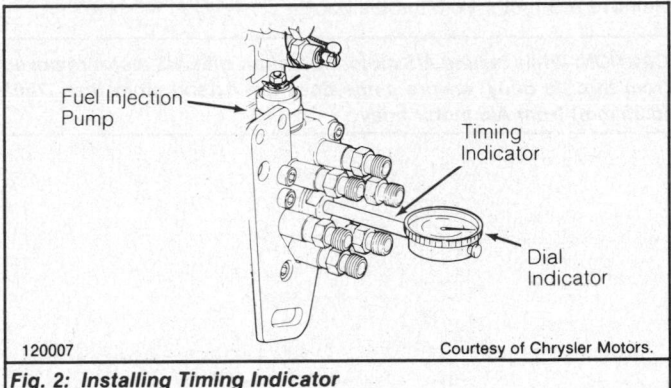

Fig. 2: Installing Timing Indicator

CAUTION: Note range of dial indicator and value of one revolution, as timing indicators may vary. Ensure timing indicator has at least .079" (2.00 mm) of travel.

3) Disengage timing pin. DO NOT rotate engine until timing pin is disengaged. Rotate engine in opposite direction of rotation until needle on dial indicator stops moving. Adjust dial indicator to zero.

4) Rotate engine in direction of normal rotation to TDC of No. 1 cylinder, while counting number of revolutions of dial indicator. Ensure timing pin can be engaged. Current dial reading, plus previous rotations, is the plunger lift.

5) Plunger lift should be **1.25 mm**. If lift is not within specification, loosen fuel injection pump mounting nuts, and rotate fuel injection pump on mounting studs to obtain correct plunger lift.

6) Tighten mounting nuts to **18 ft. lbs. (24 N.m)**. If installing new or replacement fuel injection pump, place timing mark on fuel injection pump flange to align with timing mark on gear housing. *See Fig. 3.*

7) Remove timing indicator, and install plug. Tighten plug to **84 INCH lbs. (10 N.m)**. Ensure timing pin is disengaged. Install and bleed high-

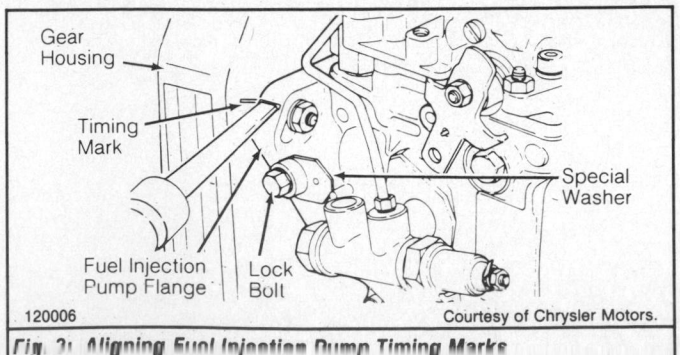

Fig. 3: Aligning Fuel Injection Pump Timing Marks

pressure fuel lines. See FUEL LINE BLEEDING in REMOVAL, OVERHAUL & INSTALLATION – DIESEL article.

IDLE SPEED

LOW IDLE SPEED

Using optical tachometer, ensure low idle speed is 700 RPM (A/T) or 750 RPM (M/T) with A/C on. Adjust if necessary using low idle speed screw. See Fig. 4.

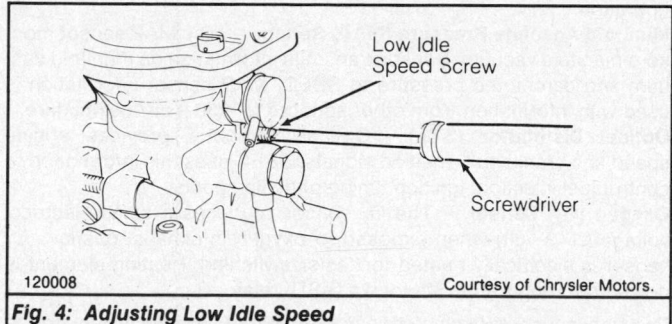

Fig. 4: Adjusting Low Idle Speed

THROTTLE LINKAGE

1) Proper throttle linkage adjustment is required to obtain full travel of throttle lever. Check low idle speed before adjusting throttle linkage.
2) Using optical tachometer, ensure low idle speed is 700 RPM (A/T) or 750 RPM (M/T) with A/C on. Adjust if necessary using low idle speed screw. See Fig. 4. Once low idle speed is correct, disconnect throttle cable from ball on fuel injection pump.

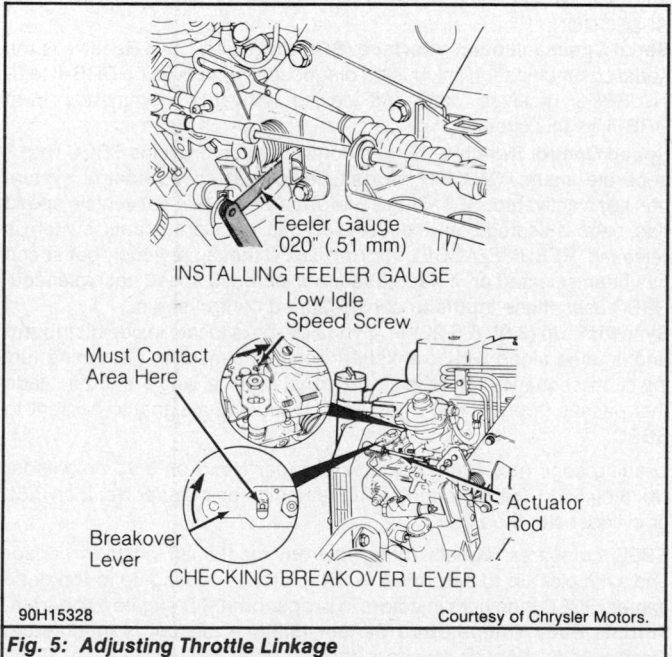

Fig. 5: Adjusting Throttle Linkage

3) Install a .020" (.51 mm) feeler gauge between throttle cam and cam stop. See Fig. 5. Ensure throttle lever contacts low idle speed screw and spring-loaded breakover lever has moved from stop area and is contacting breakover spring.
4) If low idle speed screw and breakover spring are not contacted, actuator rod must be adjusted. See Fig. 5. Hold rod while loosening lock nuts.

NOTE: One lock nut on actuator rod is left-hand thread. Flat area of actuator rod is marked "L" to indicate left-hand thread.

---

5) Adjust actuator rod to obtain correct adjustment. Tighten lock nuts. Remove feeler gauge. Reconnect throttle cable. Operate throttle and ensure breakover in both idle and full throttle positions. Ensure engine low idle speed is 700 RPM (A/T) or 750 RPM (M/T) with A/C on. Ensure full throttle speed is 2825-2925 RPM.

NOTE: If engine will does meet full throttle speed, and low pressure fuel system and fuel injectors are functioning correctly, fuel injection pump must be removed for service.

THROTTLE POSITION SENSOR (TPS)

NOTE: Throttle Position Sensor (TPS) is used on intercooled models with A/T only.

CAUTION: Before adjusting TPS, ensure throttle linkage is properly adjusted. See THROTTLE LINKAGE.

---

1) Connect negative probe of voltmeter to ground. Turn ignition on. Backprobe center wire terminal at TPS electrical connector. With control lever contacting low-speed screw (idle position), voltage should be at least one volt. If voltage is not at least one volt, adjust TPS to obtain correct voltage using 10-mm wrench. See Fig. 6.
2) Open throttle to full throttle position. Backprobe center wire terminal at TPS electrical connector. Voltage should be at least 2.25 volts more than voltage obtained with throttle in idle position. If voltage is not at least 2.25 volts more than idle position voltage, adjust TPS to obtain correct voltage. See Fig. 6.

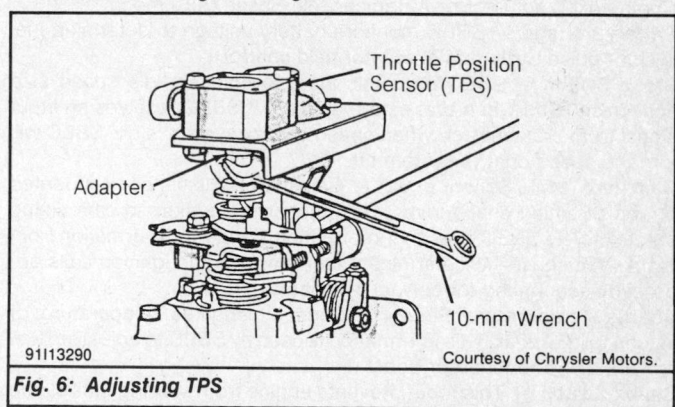

Fig. 6: Adjusting TPS

1992 ENGINE PERFORMANCE
Theory & Operation – Gasoline

Caravan, Dakota, Pickup, Ramcharger, RWD Van, Town & Country, Voyager

INTRODUCTION

This article covers the basic description and operation of engine performance related systems and components. Read this article before working on unfamiliar systems.

COMPUTERIZED ENGINE CONTROLS

SINGLE BOARD ENGINE CONTROLLER (SBEC)

SBEC is a digital computer that controls ignition timing, air/fuel ratio, emission control devices, cooling fan, charging system, idle speed, cruise control (if equipped), fuel pump and tachometer. The control unit is located in the engine compartment. SBEC uses data from various input sources to control output devices in order to achieve optimum engine performance for all operating conditions.

SBEC has voltage converters that convert battery voltage to regulated 5-volt and 8-volt outputs. The 8-volt output powers the distributor pick-up and crankshaft (angle/position) sensor. The 5-volt output powers coolant temperature sensor, charge temperature sensor, manifold absolute pressure sensor and throttle position sensor.

NOTE: *Basically, components are grouped into 2 categories. The first category, INPUT DEVICES, includes components that control or produce voltage signals monitored by the SBEC. The second category, OUTPUT SIGNALS, includes components controlled by the SBEC (this is accomplished by the SBEC grounding individual circuits).*

INPUT DEVICES

Vehicles are equipped with different combinations of input devices. Not all devices are used on all models. To determine the input usage on a specific model, see appropriate WIRING DIAGRAMS article in ENGINE PERFORMANCE. Available input signals include:

A/C Switch – Switch signals SBEC that A/C has been selected. SBEC then activates A/C compressor clutch relay and maintains idle speed at a scheduled RPM. This is done through control of Idle Speed Control (ISC) actuator or Automatic Idle Speed (AIS) motor.

Battery Voltage – SBEC monitors battery voltage to determine fuel injector pulse width and alternator field control.

Brake Switch – SBEC uses this input to maintain idle speed at a scheduled RPM when brakes are applied. If SBEC receives an input signal from brake switch when speed control system is on, SBEC will turn the speed control system off.

Camshaft Angle Sensor (3.3L) – Camshaft angle sensor is mounted on top of timing chain cover. This sensor reads slots in cam timing sprocket. The SBEC uses this information along with information from crankshaft sensor to determine if fuel injectors and ignition coils are properly sequenced for correct cylinders.

Charge Temperature Sensor – Sensor measures temperature of incoming intake air. This information is used by SBEC to adjust air/fuel mixture and turbocharger boost.

Clutch Switch – This input prevents engine from starting until clutch pedal is depressed.

Coolant Temperature Sensor (CTS) – The CTS monitors engine coolant temperature. Sensor is mounted in intake manifold, next to thermostat housing. SBEC uses coolant temperature information to adjust air/fuel mixture and idle speed and to control cooling fans as necessary.

Crankshaft (Angle/Position) Sensor (3.3L, 3.9L & 5.2L) – Crankshaft sensor is mounted on transaxle bellhousing. Sensor reads slots on flywheel/torque converter drive plate. SBEC uses this information to determine fuel injection sequence, ignition signal and spark timing.

Detonation Sensor (3.3L) – Sensor is mounted on engine block. Positioning of detonation sensor enables it to detect detonation in any cylinder. Sensor generates an input signal to SBEC when detonation occurs. The SBEC uses this input to adjust spark advance and to eliminate detonation.

Hall Effect Switch – Hall Effect switch, sometimes called a Hall Effect pick-up, is located inside distributor. This switch supplies SBEC with engine RPM data and ignition timing information. SBEC uses this information to advance or retard ignition timing as necessary.

Idle Contact Switch – Idle contact switch provides an input signal that enables SBEC to increase or decrease throttle stop angle in response to engine operating conditions.

Ignition Sense Circuit – Ignition sense circuit informs SBEC that ignition circuit has been activated. SBEC then prepares for engine operation.

Manifold Absolute Pressure (MAP) Sensor – The MAP sensor monitors manifold vacuum. Sensor transmits information on manifold vacuum and barometric pressure to SBEC. MAP sensor information is used with information from other sensors to adjust air/fuel mixture.

Optical Distributor (3.0L) – Optical distributor provides engine speed and crankshaft position signals. SBEC uses this information to control fuel injection, ignition timing and idle speed.

Oxygen (O_2) Sensor – The O_2 sensor produces a small electrical voltage (.1-.9 volt) when exposed to oxygen in exhaust gasflow. O_2 sensor is electrically heated for faster switching. Heating element is powered through Auto Shutdown (ASD) relay.

The O_2 sensor acts like a rich/lean (air/fuel ratio) switch by monitoring the oxygen content in exhaust gas. This information is used by SBEC to adjust air/fuel ratio.

The O_2 sensor produces a low voltage when oxygen content in exhaust gas is high. When oxygen content in exhaust gas is low, O_2 sensor produces a higher voltage.

Park/Neutral (P/N) Switch – Switch is available on automatic transmission vehicles only. The P/N switch is located on transmission housing. Switch prevents engine starter from engaging if vehicle is in any gear except Park or Neutral. Also see TRANSMISSION GEAR SELECTION.

Serial Communication Interface (SCI) Receive – SCI Receive is the serial communication link used if diagnosing vehicle using DRB-II tester. SBEC receives data and device activation commands from DRB-II on this circuit.

Speed Control Switch – Speed control switch provides SBEC with 3 separate inputs. ON/OFF informs SBEC that speed control system has been activated. SET/COAST informs SBEC that set vehicle speed has been selected, or if depressed will decelerate until switch is released. RESUME/ACCEL informs SBEC that a previously set speed has been selected or, if depressed, will increase speed until released. SBEC uses these inputs to control speed control servo.

Sync Pick-Up (3.9L & 5.2L) – Sync pick-up is locate inside distributor and is used along with crankshaft position sensor to determine fuel injection sequence. Sync pick-up consists of a single shutter blade that passes through Hall Effect switch causing a signal to be sent to SBEC.

Leading edge of shutter indicates cylinder No. 5 on 3.9L or cylinder No. 8 on 5.2L. Trailing edge of shutter indicates cylinder No. 2 on 3.9L or cylinder No. 5 on 5.2L.

SBEC compares signals received from crankshaft position sensor and sync pick-up to determine which piston is coming up to top dead center. SBEC then fires injectors in proper order for engine to operate.

Throttle Body Temperature Sensor (5.9L) – Sensor is mounted in throttle body. Sensor monitors throttle body temperature so SBEC can adjust air/fuel mixture for a hot restart condition.

Throttle Position Sensor (TPS) – TPS is mounted on throttle body and monitors opening angle of throttle valve. Sensor varies its output voltage according to angle of throttle blade opening. SBEC uses this information and other sensor inputs to adjust air/fuel ratio. If SBEC senses wide open throttle (WOT) position during cranking, it assumes engine is flooded and turns off fuel injectors until throttle is released.

Transmission Gear Selection – The P/N safety switch on the transmission housing provides an input to SBEC to indicate if transmission is in Park, Neutral or Drive. SBEC uses this input to determine necessary changes to idle speed, fuel injector pulse width and ignition timing advance. Also see PARK/NEUTRAL (P/N) SWITCH.

Transmission Overdrive Override Switch (A/T Models) – On models with Overdrive, SBEC regulates overdrive upshift and downshift through the overdrive solenoid. The transmission overdrive override switch is mounted in the instrument panel.

The switch is normally closed. If switch is depressed and switch opens, transmission will not enter Overdrive. Transmission will downshift if it is in Overdrive and switch is depressed.

Vehicle Speed Sensor (VSS) – The VSS generates 8 pulses per axle shaft revolution. SBEC interprets speed sensor input along with TPS closed throttle input.

This input enables SBEC to determine if a closed throttle deceleration or normal throttle idle (vehicle stopped) condition exists. During deceleration, SBEC controls Automatic Idle Speed (AIS) motor or Idle Speed Control (ISC) actuator to maintain a desired manifold pressure. During idle (vehicle stopped), SBEC controls AIS motor or ISC actuator to maintain a desired idle speed. SBEC also uses VSS signal to maintain set speed during cruise control operation.

OUTPUT SIGNALS

NOTE: Each vehicle may be equipped with different combinations of computer-controlled components. The following components may NOT be used on all models. For theory and operation on each output component, refer to the indicated system.

A/C Clutch Relay – See MISCELLANEOUS CONTROLS.
Air Switching Solenoid – See AIR INJECTION SYSTEM under EMISSION SYSTEMS.
Alternator – See MISCELLANEOUS CONTROLS.
Automatic Idle Speed (AIS) Motor – See IDLE SPEED under FUEL SYSTEM.
Auto Shutdown (ASD) Relay – See MISCELLANEOUS CONTROLS.
Canister Purge Solenoid – See EVAPORATIVE EMISSIONS SYSTEM under EMISSION SYSTEMS.
CHECK ENGINE Light – See SELF-DIAGNOSTIC SYSTEM.
Direct Ignition System – See IGNITION SYSTEM.
Electric EGR Transducer (EET) – See EXHAUST GAS RECIRCULATION (EGR) under EMISSION SYSTEMS.
Emission Maintenance Reminder (EMR) Light – See EMISSION MAINTENANCE REMINDER LIGHT under EMISSION SYSTEMS.
Exhaust Gas Recirculation (EGR) Solenoid – See EXHAUST GAS RECIRCULATION (EGR) under EMISSION SYSTEMS.
Fuel Injectors – See FUEL CONTROL under FUEL SYSTEM.
Idle Speed Control (ISC) Actuator – See IDLE SPEED under FUEL SYSTEM.
In-Tank Fuel Pump – See FUEL DELIVERY under FUEL SYSTEM.
Limp-In Mode – See MISCELLANEOUS CONTROLS.
Lock-Up Torque Converter Solenoid – See MISCELLANEOUS CONTROLS.
Magnetic Ignition System (Hall Effect) – See IGNITION SYSTEM.
Optical Ignition System – See IGNITION SYSTEM.
Overdrive Override Switch Indicator Light – See MISCELLANEOUS CONTROLS.
Overdrive Solenoid – See MISCELLANEOUS CONTROLS.
Radiator Fan Relay – See MISCELLANEOUS CONTROLS.
Serial Communication Interface (SCI) Transmit – See SELF-DIAGNOSTIC SYSTEM.
Shift Indicator Light – See MISCELLANEOUS CONTROLS.
Speed Control Servo – See MISCELLANEOUS CONTROLS.
Tachometer (Dakota) – See MISCELLANEOUS CONTROLS.

FUEL SYSTEM

FUEL DELIVERY

Auto Shutdown (ASD) Relay – See AUTO SHUTDOWN (ASD) RELAY under MISCELLANEOUS CONTROLS.
Fuel Pressure Damper (3.3L) – Damper is located downstream of fuel pressure regulator. *See Fig. 1.* Damper dampens fuel pressure pulsations caused by injectors opening and closing to keep fuel pressure constant across injectors. Pressure pulses are absorbed by an internal rubber diaphragm with air pocket on one side.

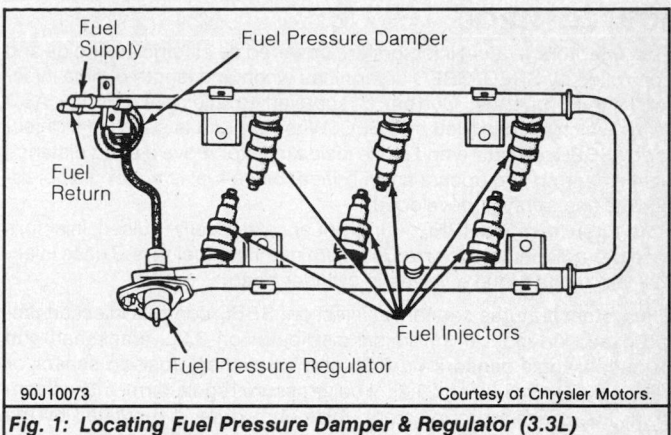

90J10073   Courtesy of Chrysler Motors.
Fig. 1: Locating Fuel Pressure Damper & Regulator (3.3L)

Fuel Pressure Regulator – Fuel pressure regulator is a mechanical device. Pressure regulator is located on top of throttle body on TBI engines. Pressure regulator is located on fuel injector rail on PFI engines. Regulator maintains constant fuel pressure across injectors. See FUEL PRESSURE table.

Inside pressure regulator is a spring-loaded diaphragm. When fuel pump is energized, fuel flows past fuel injectors into fuel pressure regulator. Pressure regulator restricts fuel from flowing any farther until proper pressure has been reached. *See Fig. 2.*

When proper fuel pressure is reached, fuel pressure pushes on spring behind diaphragm. As fuel pressure moves spring and diaphragm, a return line to fuel tank is uncovered. This allows excess fuel to return to fuel tank, keeping fuel pressure constant across injectors.

FUEL PRESSURE

Application	psi (kg/cm²)
2.5L, 3.9L & 5.2L	39.0 (2.7)
3.0L & 3.3L	48.0 (3.4)
5.9L	14.5 (1.0)

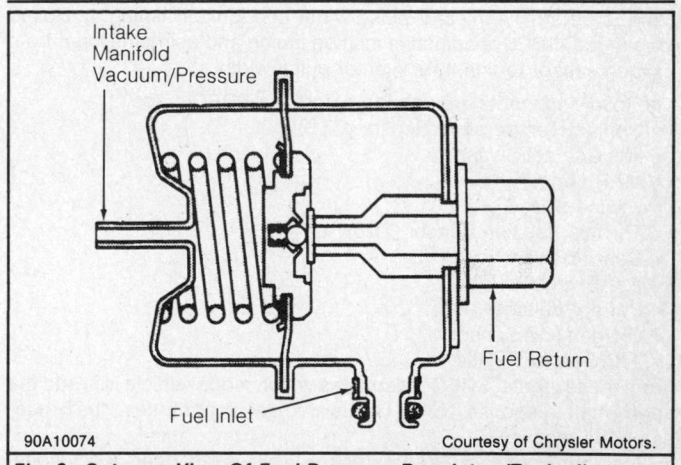

90A10074   Courtesy of Chrysler Motors.
Fig. 2: Cutaway View Of Fuel Pressure Regulator (Typical)

In-Tank Fuel Pump (PFI) – Fuel pump is a positive displacement, immersible gerotor pump with a permanent magnet motor. The pump incorporates a filter sock attached to pump pick-up. This fuel pump contains 2 check valves. One check valve is used to relieve internal pump pressure and regulate maximum fuel pump output. The other check valve, located near pump outlet, is used to restrict fuel movement in either direction when pump is not operational. Voltage to operate pump is supplied through ASD relay.
In-Tank Fuel Pump (TBI) – Fuel pump is an immersible electric pump with permanent magnet motor. The pump incorporates a sock attached to pump pick-up. Fuel pump also contains a check valve which restricts fuel movement in either direction to maintain fuel line pressure when pump is not operating. Voltage to operate pump is supplied through ASD relay.

1992 ENGINE PERFORMANCE
Theory & Operation – Gasoline (Cont.)

FUEL CONTROL

Fuel Injectors – Fuel injectors are powered by electric solenoids and controlled by SBEC. SBEC determines when and length of time injectors should operate. Current is supplied to injectors through ASD relay, which is controlled by SBEC. When ground is supplied to injector by SBEC, armature and pintle inside injector move a short distance against spring and open a small orifice. Since fuel is under high pressure, a fine spray is developed.

Port Fuel Injection (PFI) – Individual, electrically pulsed injectors (one per cylinder) are located in intake manifold fuel rails. These injectors are next to intake valves in cylinder head.

PFI system features sequential injection. SBEC controls injection timing based on input from optical distributor on 3.0L, crankshaft and camshaft angle sensors on 3.3L and crankshaft position sensor or sync pick-up on 3.9L and 5.2L. Fuel pressure regulator maintains constant fuel pressure to injectors. Air/fuel mixture is regulated by the length of time injector stays open (pulse width). ECM controls pulse width using information provided by various sensors.

Throttle Body Injection (TBI) – 2.5L uses single-injector throttle body. 5.9L uses dual-injector throttle body. Battery voltage is supplied to injector when ignition is on. SBEC energizes injector solenoid by providing a ground path through its internal circuitry. By regulating injector ground circuit, SBEC controls injector on-time (pulse width) to provide proper amount of fuel to engine.

Pressure regulator maintains pressure to injector at 39 psi (2.7 kg/cm²) on 2.5L and 14.5 psi (1.0 kg/cm²) on 5.9L. Excess fuel passes through pressure regulator and returns to fuel tank.

In the "run" mode, SBEC uses tach (RPM) signal to determine when to pulse injector. On models equipped with dual injectors in the throttle body, injectors are pulsed alternately.

Internal SBEC calibration controls fuel delivery during starting, clear flood mode, deceleration and heavy acceleration.

Modes Of Operation – As input signals to SBEC change, SBEC adjusts its response to the output devices. Modes of operation come in 2 types, open loop and closed loop. In open loop mode, SBEC is not using input from oxygen sensor and is responding to preset programming to determine injector pulse width and ignition timing. In closed loop mode, SBEC is adjusting ignition timing and using the input from oxygen sensor to fine tune injector pulse width.

The following inputs are used to determine SBEC mode.

- Coolant Temperature Sensor (CTS)
- Idle Contact Switch
- MAP Sensor
- Engine Speed
- Throttle Position Sensor (TPS)
- Gear Position
- A/C Switch
- Battery Voltage
- Oxygen (O₂) Sensor
- A/C Control Positions

From these inputs, SBEC determines which mode vehicle is in and the appropriate response. Not all inputs are used in all modes. The 8 modes of operation are:

- **Ignition Switch In ON Position** – This is an open loop mode. SBEC determines atmospheric pressure from MAP sensor and determines basic fuel strategy. SBEC modifies fuel strategy according to coolant temperature input.
- **Engine Start-Up** – This is an open loop mode. When starter is engaged, SBEC receives distributor signal and energizes Auto Shutdown (ASD) relay. See AUTO SHUTDOWN (ASD) RELAY under MISCELLANEOUS CONTROLS. Once ASD relay is energized, SBEC determines proper injector pulse width and ignition timing from input signals. During engine start-up, SBEC pulses each fuel injector 4 times per engine revolution instead of the normal 2 pulses per revolution.
- **Engine Warm-Up** – This is an open loop mode. SBEC determines injector pulse width using information from various inputs and fires each injector 2 times per engine revolution. SBEC controls engine idle speed, throttle stop angle and ignition timing.

- **Cruise** – When engine is at operating temperature, this is a closed loop mode. Using information from various inputs, SBEC determines injector pulse width and fires each injector 3 times per engine revolution. SBEC controls engine idle speed, throttle stop angle and ignition timing. SBEC determines proper air/fuel ratio using input from oxygen sensor.
- **Acceleration** – This is a closed loop mode on Dakota 2.5L and all FWD models. All other models are in open loop mode. When SBEC recognizes an abrupt increase in throttle position or manifold pressure as a demand for increased engine output, it increases injector pulse width in response to increased fuel demand.
- **Deceleration** – This is an open loop mode on Dakota 3.9L and 5.2L models. All other models are in closed loop mode. When SBEC receives inputs signaling a closed throttle and an abrupt decrease in manifold pressure, it may reduce injector firing to one pulse per engine revolution to lean air/fuel mixture. SBEC also prevents EGR and canister purge functions during deceleration by grounding EGR and evaporative purge solenoids. SBEC may cycle air switching solenoid for short periods of time in response to a high vacuum signal from MAP sensor.
- **Wide Open Throttle** – This is an open loop mode. When SBEC senses wide open throttle, it grounds EGR and evaporative purge solenoids to prevent EGR and canister purge functions. Oxygen sensor input is not utilized and SBEC adjusts injector pulse width to supply a predetermined amount of additional fuel.
- **Ignition Switch In OFF Position** – This is an open loop mode. All fuel injection is stopped. SBEC de-energizes auto shutdown (ASD) relay and extends Idle Speed Control (ISC) actuator (if equipped) in anticipation of next start-up.

IDLE SPEED

Automatic Idle Speed Motor (2.5L, 3.0L, 3.3L, 3.9L & 5.2L) – Automatic Idle Speed (AIS) motor adjusts idle speed to compensate for engine load and ambient temperature by adjusting amount of air flowing through by-pass in throttle body. SBEC uses coolant temperature, distance (speed) sensor, throttle position and various switch input operations to adjust AIS to obtain optimum idle conditions. Deceleration stall is prevented by increasing airflow when throttle is closed suddenly.

Idle Speed Control (ISC) Actuator (5.9L) – The ISC actuator is a motor mounted to throttle body and controlled by SBEC. Using inputs from various engine control system sensors, SBEC extends or retracts actuator to control engine idle speed and to set throttle stop angle during deceleration.

NOTE: DO NOT attempt to correct a high idle speed condition by turning ISC adjustment screw. This will not change idle speed of warm engine but may cause cold start problems due to restricted airflow.

IGNITION SYSTEM

DIRECT IGNITION SYSTEM (3.3L)

A Direct Ignition System (DIS) eliminates mechanical ignition components that can wear out. SBEC has complete ignition control and uses crankshaft and camshaft sensors to control ignition timing. Crankshaft position sensor senses slots (4 per cylinder, 20 degrees apart) around an extension of the drive plate. Basic timing is preset by crankshaft sensor position and is not adjustable. By using a crankshaft sensor, spark scatter has been eliminated.

A cam sensor is located on timing chain cover. Cam sensor senses slots on cam timing gear. Fuel injection synchronization and cylinder identification are provided through cam sensor. The unique combination of slots on cam gear are used to identify individual cylinders and initiate fuel and spark for start and run conditions.

This system uses 3 molded coils mounted on the intake manifold. Coil fires 2 spark plugs every power stroke. One cylinder is on compression stroke and the other cylinder is on exhaust stroke. A low primary resistance allows SBEC to fully charge ignition coil for each firing.

OPTICAL IGNITION SYSTEM (3.0L)

The timing member is a thin disc mounted on distributor shaft and driven at 1/2 crankshaft speed. Disc has 2 sets of slots on its surface. The outer, high data rate set of slots is positioned at intervals of 2 degrees of crankshaft rotation. Disc is used for ignition timing at engine speeds up to 1200 RPM to increase timing accuracy.

During cranking and idle, engine speed changes with firing pulse of each cylinder. High data rate signal is used to trigger ignition at correct crankshaft position regardless of these speed changes.

The inner, low data rate set contains 6 slots, which are correlated to piston TDC for each cylinder. This set is used to trigger fuel injection system operation at speeds greater than 1200 RPM, where speed changes because individual firing pulses are small. This set of slots is also used for ignition timing. Light Emitting Diodes (LEDs) and photo diodes are mounted in facing positions on opposite sides of disc, in-line with slots. *See Fig. 3.*

Masks over LEDs and photo diodes focus light beams onto photo diodes. As each slot passes between diodes, light beam is turned on and off. This creates an alternating voltage in each photo diode, which is converted into on-off pulses by an integrated circuit within distributor. SBEC uses these pulses to control timing.

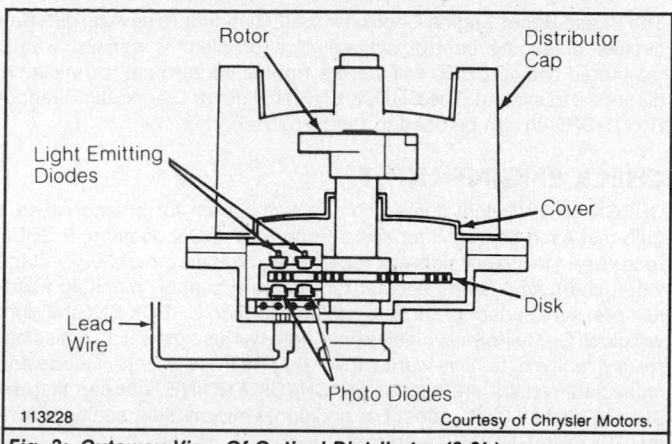

Fig. 3: Cutaway View Of Optical Distributor (3.0L)

MAGNETIC IGNITION SYSTEM (HALL EFFECT)

2.5L, 3.9L, 5.2L & 5.9L – Ignition timing is controlled by Single Board Engine Controller (SBEC). SBEC uses engine RPM data from the Hall Effect switch to control ignition timing. Hall Effect switch is located inside distributor on 2.5L and 5.9L and is incorporated into crankshaft position sensor on 3.9L and 5.2L.

Hall Effect distributor has a shutter attached to distributor shaft. On 2.5L and 5.9L, shutter contains one blade per engine cylinder. *See Fig. 4.* On 3.9L and 5.2L, a single-blade shutter is used. On all models, switch plate is mounted to distributor housing above shutter. Switch plate contains distributor pick-up (a Hall Effect device and magnet) through which shutter blade(s) rotate.

SBEC applies and monitors voltage to Hall Effect switch. As shutter blade(s) pass through pick-up, magnetic field is interrupted and monitored voltage is toggled between high and low. On 3.9L and 5.2L, same effect is generated when windows in flywheel pass magnet in crankshaft position sensor.

SBEC monitors voltage signal switching and uses these pulses to calculate engine speed (2.5L and 5.9L) or fuel injection sync signal (3.9L and 5.2L).

IGNITION TIMING CONTROL SYSTEM

The Single Board Engine Controller (SBEC) completely controls ignition system. During a crank/start mode, SBEC will set a fixed amount of spark advance for an efficient engine start.

Ignition Timing Advance Control – The amount of spark advance or retard is determined by inputs that SBEC receives from coolant

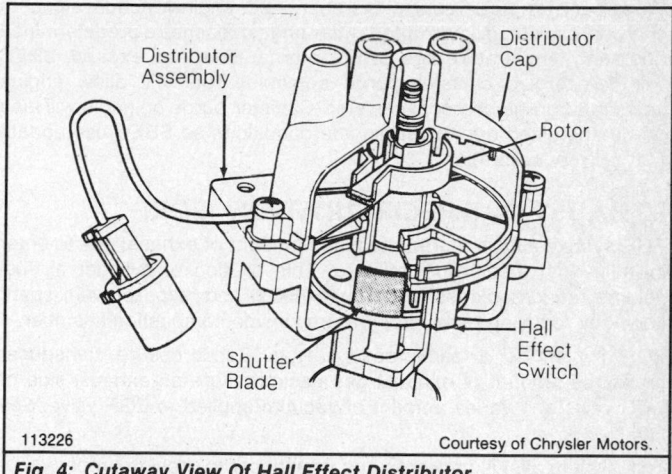

Fig. 4: Cutaway View Of Hall Effect Distributor (2.5L Shown; 5.9L Is Similar)

temperature, engine vacuum and engine RPM. During engine operation, SBEC can supply an infinite number of advance curves to ensure proper engine operation.

EMISSION SYSTEMS

AIR INJECTION SYSTEM

This system adds a controlled amount of air to exhaust gases to assist oxidation of hydrocarbons and carbon monoxide in exhaust stream. System does not interfere with ability of EGR system to control oxides of nitrogen emissions. Air is injected at either the exhaust manifold or the catalytic converter through air switching/relief valve. Air switching/relief valve is controlled by SBEC through air switching solenoid.
5.9L Heavy-Duty Emissions engines are equipped with a dual air pump system, which does not include air switching/relief valve.
Air Switching Solenoid – SBEC uses this solenoid to control discharge of air from air pump into exhaust system. This solenoid controls flow of vacuum to air switching/relief valve of air pump system. When solenoid is not energized, airflow is in downstream mode which means no vacuum is supplied to air switching/relief valve and air pump output is directed to catalytic converter. When solenoid is energized, airflow is in upstream mode, which means that vacuum is supplied to air switching/relief valve and air pump output is directed to exhaust manifolds.

EMISSION MAINTENANCE REMINDER LIGHT

SBEC activates the Emission Maintenance Reminder (EMR) light at scheduled mileage intervals to indicate need for servicing of certain emission system components. SBEC will also illuminate this light whenever a fault occurs in the emission systems.

To reset mileage interval, connect Diagnostic Readout Box II (DRB-II) to vehicle diagnostic connector. Turn ignition switch to RUN position. Access EMISSIONS EMR TESTS on DRB-II. Select EMR MEMORY CHECK. Select RESET EMR LIGHT. Reset EMR light.

EVAPORATIVE EMISSIONS SYSTEM

This system stores fuel vapors from fuel tank, preventing vapors from reaching the atmosphere. As fuel evaporates inside fuel tank, vapors are routed inside vent hoses to charcoal canister, located in wheelwell area, where they are stored until engine is started.
Canister Purge Solenoid – Charcoal canister purging is controlled by a canister purge solenoid. Canister purge solenoid is controlled by SBEC. During engine warm-up and for a short period after hot restarts, SBEC grounds canister purge solenoid winding causing solenoid to energize.

When canister purge solenoid is energized, engine vacuum signal to charcoal canister is interrupted. After engine reaches a predetermined operating temperature and SBEC internal timer has expired, SBEC will de-energize canister purge solenoid. This will allow engine vacuum to purge charcoal canister. Canister purge solenoid will also be de-energized during certain idle conditions so SBEC can update fuel delivery calibration.

EXHAUST GAS RECIRCULATION (EGR)

EGR system allows a predetermined amount of exhaust gas to enter cylinder with the air/fuel mixture. This dilution of cylinder air/fuel volume reduces oxides of nitrogen (NOx) and helps prevent spark knock by reducing peak temperatures inside combustion chamber.

EGR system is a backpressure type. Backpressure transducer measures amount of exhaust gas backpressure on exhaust side of EGR valve and varies amount of vacuum applied to EGR valve. See Fig. 5 or 6.

This system allows backpressure transducer to provide proper vacuum signal to EGR valve for all engine operating conditions. EGR system is controlled by an EGR vacuum solenoid using a manifold vacuum signal from throttle body.

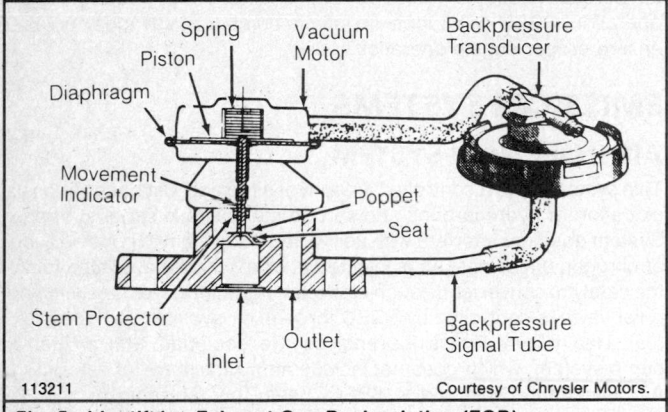

113211   Courtesy of Chrysler Motors.

Fig. 5: Identifying Exhaust Gas Recirculation (EGR) System Components (5.9L)

Exhaust Gas Recirculation (EGR) Solenoid (5.9L) – EGR solenoid does not allow EGR at idle. EGR system does not function when ambient temperature is less than 40°F (4°C). EGR system is activated when coolant temperature reaches 170°F (77°C).

Electric EGR Transducer (EET) – On 2.5L, 3.0L, 3.3L, 3.9L and 5.2L, EGR system uses an Electric EGR Transducer (EET). This system incorporates backpressure transducer and EGR solenoid into one unit. See Fig. 6.

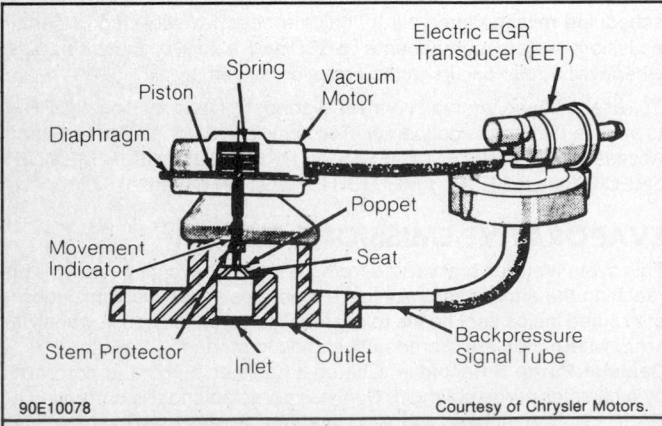

90E10078   Courtesy of Chrysler Motors.

Fig. 6: Identifying Electric EGR Transducer (EET) System Components (2.5L, 3.0L, 3.3L, 3.9L & 5.2L)

HEATED AIR INLET SYSTEM

This device is an air preheater that controls air temperature entering throttle body when ambient temperatures are low. By maintaining temperature, throttle body can be calibrated much leaner to reduce hydrocarbon and carbon monoxide emissions, improve engine warm-up characteristics and minimize icing.

The heated air inlet system is a 2-circuit airflow system. When ambient temperature is greater than control temperature, airflow is through outside air inlet alone. When air temperature is less than control temperature, airflow is through outside air inlet and through heated air inlet. The cooler the ambient temperature, the greater the flow through heated air inlet. Airflow is controlled by a vacuum-operated, heat-controlled door, located in snorkel.

POSITIVE CRANKCASE VENTILATION (PCV)

Crankcase blow-by gases are removed from crankcase with manifold vacuum. These gases are introduced into incoming air/fuel mixture and become part of the calibrated mixture. No fresh air enters crankcase with this PCV system.

SELF-DIAGNOSTIC SYSTEM

The Single Board Engine Controller (SBEC) monitors several different circuits of engine control system. If a problem is sensed with a monitored circuit, SBEC will store a trouble code to aid technician in diagnosis of system. The CHECK ENGINE light or Diagnostic Readout Box II (DRB-II) can be used to read trouble codes.

CHECK ENGINE LIGHT

CHECK ENGINE light comes on and remains on for 3 seconds as a bulb test each time ignition switch is turned to ON position. If SBEC receives an incorrect signal or receives no signal from battery voltage input, charging system, coolant temperature sensor, manifold absolute pressure sensor or throttle position sensor, CHECK ENGINE light will glow. On California vehicles only, light will also glow if an emission-related fault exists. This warns driver that SBEC is in limp-in mode and immediate repairs are necessary. CHECK ENGINE light can also be used to display fault codes. For additional information, see appropriate SELF-DIAGNOSTICS article.

SERIAL COMMUNICATIONS INTERFACE (SCI)

SCI circuit is used by SBEC to send data to and receive data and sensor activation signals from DRB-II tester. DRB-II uses signals sent on SCI to display fault codes, sensor voltages and device states (ON/OFF). DRB-II uses SCI to send solenoid and switch activation commands to SBEC so that devices and circuits can be tested. SCI is also used to reset Emission Maintenance Reminder (EMR) light and to write EMR mileage to SBEC.

MISCELLANEOUS CONTROLS

NOTE: Although not strictly considered part of engine performance system, some controlled devices can adversely affect driveability if they malfunction.

A/C CLUTCH RELAY

A/C clutch relay is controlled by SBEC and A/C switch. A/C relay is powered by condenser fan relay. This relay is energized during engine operation when A/C switch is closed and blower is on.

When SBEC senses low idle speed or wide open throttle through throttle position sensor, SBEC will de-energize A/C clutch relay, preventing A/C operation.

ALTERNATOR

Single Board Engine Controller (SBEC) controls voltage regulation.

AUTO SHUTDOWN (ASD) RELAY

The ASD relay is a cutoff relay for the following components.

- Electric Fuel Pump
- Fuel Injectors
- Ignition Coil
- O_2 Sensor Heating Element

When ignition switch is turned to RUN position, SBEC energizes ASD relay which powers these components. If SBEC does not receive a distributor signal (cam or crankshaft signal on 3.3L) shortly thereafter, SBEC will de-energize ASD relay and power to these components is cut off.

LIMP-IN MODE

Limp-in mode is the attempt by SBEC to compensate for failure of certain components by substituting information from other sources so that vehicle can still be operated. If SBEC senses incorrect data or no data at all from MAP sensor, throttle position sensor, coolant temperature sensor or battery voltage, system is placed into limp-in mode and CHECK ENGINE light on instrument panel is illuminated.

If faulty sensor comes back on line, SBEC will resume closed loop operation. On some vehicles, CHECK ENGINE will remain illuminated until ignition is shut off and vehicle is restarted. To prevent damage to catalytic converter, vehicle should NOT be driven for extended periods in limp-in mode.

LOCK-UP TORQUE CONVERTER SOLENOID

SBEC controls torque converter lock-up through lock-up solenoid. SBEC controls lock-up according to various operating conditions.

OVERDRIVE OVERRIDE SWITCH INDICATOR LIGHT

SBEC controls indicator light on overdrive override switch on models equipped with overdrive automatic transmission.

OVERDRIVE SOLENOID

On vehicles equipped with overdrive transmissions, SBEC controls the 3-4 overdrive upshift and downshift through the overdrive solenoid. SBEC determines optimum overdrive shift scheduling for all operating conditions.

RADIATOR FAN RELAY

Single Board Engine Controller (SBEC) controls radiator fan relay. Radiator fan relay is energized during the following conditions:

- Fan relay is energized when A/C clutch is engaged.
- On non-A/C vehicles and A/C vehicles with A/C not engaged, fan relay energizes when vehicle speed is greater than 40 MPH and coolant temperature reaches 230°F (110°C). Fan relay turns off when coolant temperature decreases to 220°F (104°C). When vehicle speed is less than 40 MPH, fan relay switches on at 210°F (99°C) and switches off at 200°F (93°C).
- Fan relay also prevents "steaming". "Steaming" occurs when moisture evaporates from outside of radiator and is not blown under the vehicle. Fan relay will energize when ambient temperature is less than 60°F (16°C), when coolant temperature is between 100-195°F (38-91°C), when engine is at idle and when vehicle is stopped. Fan relay will energize for 3 minutes only.

SHIFT INDICATOR LIGHT

SBEC provides ground for shift indicator light on models equipped with manual transmission. SBEC, based on engine speed, throttle position, and vehicle speed, turns shift indicator light on to advise driver to shift to a higher gear for optimum driveability.

SPEED CONTROL SERVO

System is electrically actuated and vacuum operated. The controls are located on the steering wheel. Controls consist of 3 buttons: OFF/ON, RESUME/ACCEL and SET/DECEL. Speed control servo is controlled by SBEC. System will operate at 35-85 MPH.

TACHOMETER (DAKOTA)

SBEC provides signal to drive tachometer on Dakota.

1992 ENGINE PERFORMANCE
Theory & Operation – Diesel

Pickup

INTRODUCTION

This article covers basic description and operation of engine performance-related systems and components. Read this article before diagnosing vehicles or systems with which you are not completely familiar.

AIR INDUCTION SYSTEM

TURBOCHARGERS

Turbocharger consists of turbine section, bearing housing and compressor section. *See Fig. 1.* Turbocharger is mounted on exhaust manifold where exhaust gases drive the turbine wheel. Turbine wheel rotates compressor wheel, taking in outside air and compressing it for increased airflow through intercooler and then into the cylinders. The intercooler lowers intake manifold air temperature before reaching the cylinders.

Pressurized engine oil lubricates turbocharger. Excess oil is returned into cylinder block. Data plate, located on compressor housing, contains assembly number, serial number and type. This information is necessary for ordering replacement parts.

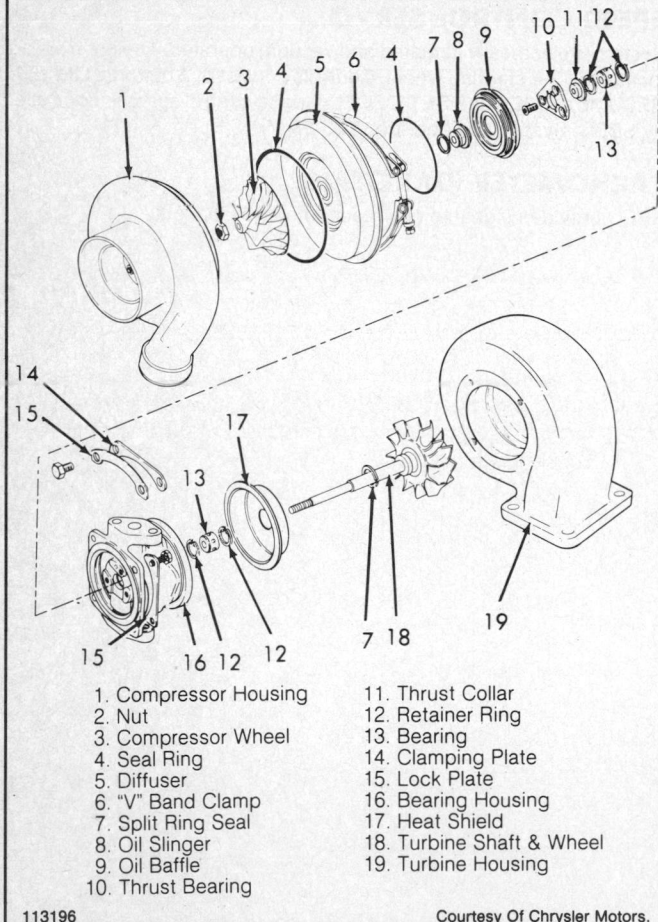

1. Compressor Housing
2. Nut
3. Compressor Wheel
4. Seal Ring
5. Diffuser
6. "V" Band Clamp
7. Split Ring Seal
8. Oil Slinger
9. Oil Baffle
10. Thrust Bearing
11. Thrust Collar
12. Retainer Ring
13. Bearing
14. Clamping Plate
15. Lock Plate
16. Bearing Housing
17. Heat Shield
18. Turbine Shaft & Wheel
19. Turbine Housing

113196   Courtesy Of Chrysler Motors.

Fig. 1: Exploded View Of Typical Turbocharger Assembly

INTERCOOLER

An intercooler is installed in front of the radiator. *See Fig. 2.* The intercooler is a heat exchanger, which is used to lower intake manifold air temperature before air reaches the cylinders.

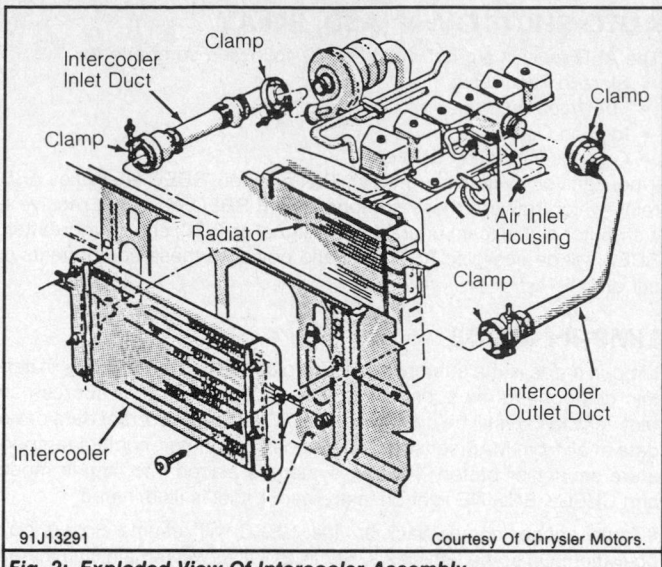

91J13291   Courtesy Of Chrysler Motors.

Fig. 2: Exploded View Of Intercooler Assembly

COMPUTERIZED ENGINE CONTROLS

SINGLE BOARD ENGINE CONTROLLER (SBEC)

SBEC is a microprocessor computer that controls speed control system, intake manifold heater relays and transmission overdrive solenoid. SBEC also operates WATER-IN-FUEL and WAIT-TO-START lights on message center in instrument panel. SBEC is located on left front corner of engine compartment, near horns on left fender.

SBEC uses various input signals for controlling various systems. SBEC contains a memory to store trouble codes if a system failure exists. Trouble codes can be retrieved for system diagnosis. For system diagnosis, see SELF-DIAGNOSTICS – DIESEL – INTERCOOLED article in ENGINE PERFORMANCE.

NOTE: Components are grouped in 2 categories. The first category covers INPUT DEVICES, which control or produce voltage signals monitored by SBEC. The second category covers OUTPUT SIGNALS, which are components controlled by SBEC.

INPUT DEVICES

Battery Voltage – Battery voltage provides power to operate SBEC. The battery voltage also indicates to SBEC that the engine is running. SBEC checks battery voltage after a crank signal is received from the starter relay.

If battery voltage is more than 12.66 volts, SBEC assumes engine is running. If battery voltage is less than 12.66 volts, SBEC will abort the postheat (ignition on, engine running) cycle of the intake manifold heater system.

Brake Switch – If SBEC receives an input signal from brake switch when speed control system is on, SBEC will turn the speed control system off.

Charge Air Temperature Sensor – Charge air temperature sensor is located in intake manifold cover. *See Fig. 3.* Charge air temperature sensor monitors intake manifold air temperature and sends a signal to SBEC. SBEC uses this input signal to determine when and how long to operate intake manifold heaters.

Crank Signal – The crank signal is delivered from starter relay to SBEC when engine is cranking. SBEC will energize intake manifold heater system for the postheat (ignition on, engine running) cycle. The postheat cycle will not begin unless SBEC receives crank signal from starter relay.

Crankshaft Position Sensor – Crankshaft position sensor, located on front of engine, generates engine RPM signal to SBEC. Sensor signal is used to control charging system, transmission overdrive, speed control and instrument panel tachometer.

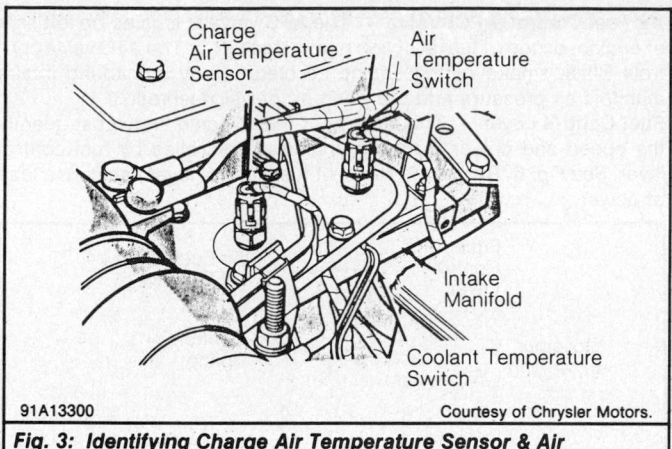

91A13300 Courtesy of Chrysler Motors.

Fig. 3: Identifying Charge Air Temperature Sensor & Air Temperature Switch

Ignition Signal – The ignition signal informs SBEC that ignition switch is in the RUN position.

Park/Neutral Switch (A/T) – The park/neutral switch is located on the side of transmission, near shift linkage. The park/neutral switch indicates to SBEC if transmission is in Drive, Neutral or Park. If transmission is in overdrive and driver shifts transmission in Neutral, and then back into gear, transmission will enter overdrive if SBEC determines all conditions are met.

SBEC uses input signal from park/neutral switch for speed control system operation. SBEC will disable speed control system if operator shifts transmission into Neutral. Speed control system will have to be reset if transmission is shifted into Neutral.

Serial Communication Interface (SCI) Receive – SCI receive is the serial communication link used when diagnosing vehicle with DRB-II tester. SBEC receives data and device activation commands from DRB-II on this circuit. SCI is also used to reset Emission Maintenance Reminder (EMR) light and to write EMR mileage to SBEC.

Throttle Position Sensor (A/T) – The Throttle Position Sensor (TPS) is mounted on top of the fuel injection pump. The TPS provides an input signal to SBEC ranging from one volt (idle position) to 5 volts (full throttle), depending on throttle position. SBEC uses input signal from TPS and vehicle speed sensor to determine transmission overdrive shift point.

Transmission Overdrive Override Switch (A/T) – On models with overdrive, SBEC regulates overdrive upshift and downshift through the overdrive solenoid. The transmission overdrive override switch is mounted in the instrument panel.

The switch is normally closed. If switch is depressed and switch opens, transmission will not go into overdrive. Transmission will downshift if transmission is in overdrive and switch is depressed.

NOTE: Transmission overdrive circuit also contains a transmission thermoswitch and coolant temperature switch. If either switch is open, transmission will not shift into overdrive or will downshift if already in overdrive. For more information, see TRANSMISSION THERMOSWITCH and COOLANT TEMPERATURE SWITCH under MISCELLANEOUS CONTROLS.

Vehicle Speed Sensor – Vehicle speed sensor is mounted on rear of transmission. SBEC uses input signal from vehicle speed sensor and TPS to determine transmission overdrive shift point (A/T models) and speed control system operation.

Water-In-Fuel Sensor – Water-in-fuel sensor is located in bottom of fuel/water separator filter. See Fig. 5. The water-in-fuel sensor sends an input signal to SBEC when water exists in fuel/water separator filter. SBEC monitors input signal when ignition is on and intake manifold heater postheat cycle is complete. If water is detected, SBEC will turn on WATER-IN-FUEL light on message center in the cab.

OUTPUT SIGNALS

A/C Clutch Relay – SBEC provides ground for A/C clutch relay to engage clutch. During wide open throttle operation, A/C clutch is disengaged to reduce power loss.

Auto Shutdown Relay – SBEC provides ground to energize auto shutdown relay. Relay is used to provide ground for alternator field circuit. SBEC cycles relay ON and OFF to maintain proper charging voltage.

Check Engine Light – CHECK ENGINE light comes on and remains on for 3 seconds as a bulb test each time ignition switch is turned to ON position. If SBEC receives an incorrect signal or receives no signal from battery voltage input, charging system, or certain sensors, CHECK ENGINE light will illuminate. CHECK ENGINE light can also be used to display fault codes. For additional information, see appropriate SELF-DIAGNOSTICS article.

Intake Manifold Heater Relays – Intake manifold heater relays are mounted on the inner wheelwell. See Fig. 4. Intake manifold heater relays are energized by SBEC, depending on intake manifold air temperature, which is monitored by the charge air temperature sensor. intake manifold heater relays are not energized during engine cranking. A clicking sound will be heard when intake manifold relays are energized.

CAUTION: Intake manifold heater relays should not be cycled (ignition turned off and then on) more than once within 15 minutes. Wait 15 minutes before turning ignition on.

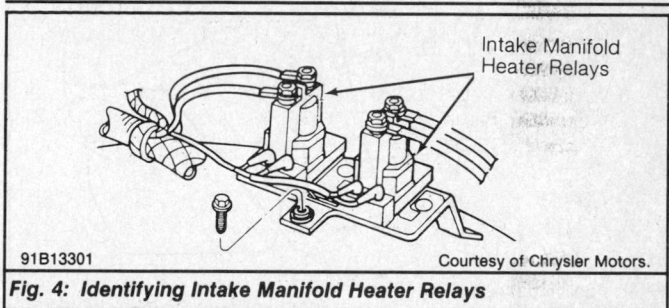

91B13301 Courtesy of Chrysler Motors.

Fig. 4: Identifying Intake Manifold Heater Relays

Overdrive Override Switch Indicator Light – SBEC controls indicator light on overdrive override switch on models equipped with overdrive automatic transmission.

Overdrive Solenoid (A/T) – SBEC controls the overdrive solenoid for overdrive operation.

Serial Communications Interface (SCI) Transmit – The SCI transmit allows SBEC to communicate with DRB-II for system diagnosis. DRB-II uses signals sent on SCI to display fault codes, sensor voltages and device states (ON/OFF).

Speed Control System – SBEC regulates vacuum and vent solenoid operation for speed control system operation. Vacuum solenoids maintain vacuum at a required pressure for speed control system operation. The vent solenoid allows vacuum to bleed off during deceleration, during brake application or when transmission is in gear or Neutral.

Tachometer – SBEC provides signal to drive tachometer in instrument panel.

WAIT-TO-START Light – SBEC operates the WAIT-TO-START light on the message center in the cab, based on signals received from charge air temperature sensor. The light is turned on when ignition is first turned on. Light will remain on for 2 seconds to check bulb and wiring circuit.

If signal from charge air temperature sensor indicates intake manifold air temperature is 59°F (15°C) or less, light and intake manifold heaters are turned on for the preheat cycle. Light will stay on until preheat cycle is completed.

Light will flash on and off if charge air temperature sensor signal to SBEC is less than or more than a given value. SBEC will store a trouble code in the memory when these conditions exist.

1992 ENGINE PERFORMANCE
Theory & Operation – Diesel (Cont.)

WATER-IN-FUEL Light – SBEC operates the WATER-IN-FUEL light on message center in the cab. The light will be turned on if SBEC receives an input signal from the water-in-fuel sensor, indicating water in bottom of fuel/water separator filter.

FUEL SYSTEM

FUEL DELIVERY

Fuel Injection Pump – The fuel injection pump contains a vane supply pump, governor, KSB valve, Air Fuel Control (AFC) valve, fuel control lever, shutoff solenoid valve and advance timing mechanism. *See Fig. 5.*

NOTE: On A/T models, a Throttle Position Sensor (TPS) is mounted above the fuel control lever.

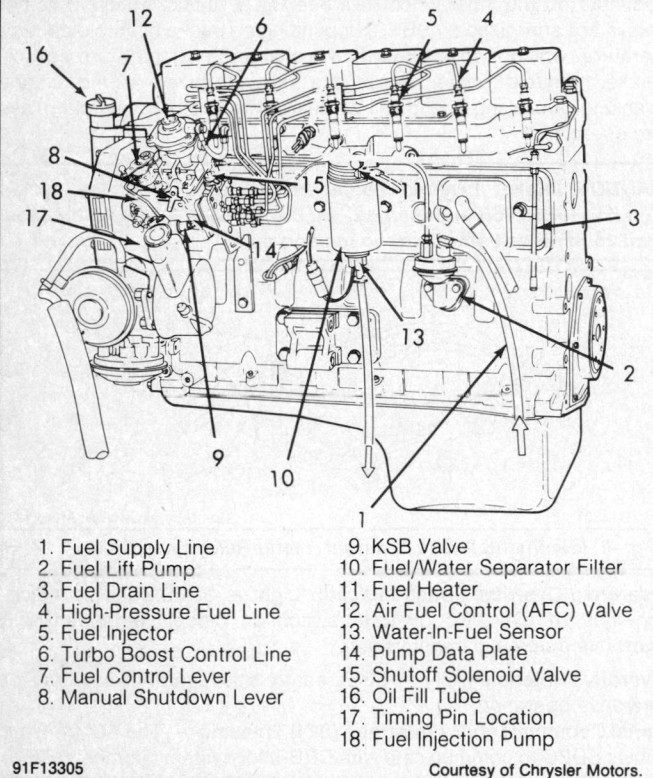

1. Fuel Supply Line
2. Fuel Lift Pump
3. Fuel Drain Line
4. High-Pressure Fuel Line
5. Fuel Injector
6. Turbo Boost Control Line
7. Fuel Control Lever
8. Manual Shutdown Lever
9. KSB Valve
10. Fuel/Water Separator Filter
11. Fuel Heater
12. Air Fuel Control (AFC) Valve
13. Water-In-Fuel Sensor
14. Pump Data Plate
15. Shutoff Solenoid Valve
16. Oil Fill Tube
17. Timing Pin Location
18. Fuel Injection Pump

91F13305   Courtesy of Chrysler Motors.

Fig. 5: Locating Fuel System Components

Fuel Lift Pump – Fuel lift pump is located on left side of engine block. *See Fig. 5.* The camshaft-driven fuel lift pump draws fuel from fuel tank to the fuel/water separator filter. Fuel lift pump contains a check valve to prevent fuel from bleeding back into fuel tank when engine is not operating. Fuel lift pump contains a hand lever for priming and bleeding air from fuel system. A defective fuel lift pump can create loss of engine power and long cranking periods.

Shutoff Solenoid Valve – Shutoff solenoid valve is located on rear side of fuel injection pump. *See Fig. 5.* Shutoff solenoid valve controls fuel flow to high-pressure head of fuel injection pump. With ignition on, battery voltage is supplied to shutoff solenoid valve, pulling plunger away from fuel passage and allowing fuel into high-pressure head for engine operation. When ignition is off, plunger is closed to stop fuel flow.

FUEL CONTROL

Advance Timing Mechanism – Regulated pressure produced by vane supply pump in fuel injection pump is used to advance timing. Timing advances as engine speed increases. A return spring is used to retard timing as engine speed is reduced.

Air Fuel Control (AFC) Valve – The AFC valve is located on left side of engine, on top of fuel injection pump. *See Fig. 5.* The AFC valve controls Black smoke during engine acceleration by monitoring intake manifold air pressure and providing proper air/fuel ratio.

Fuel Control Lever – The amount of fuel injected and subsequently the speed and power from the engine is controlled by fuel control lever. *See Fig. 6.* Restricted travel of fuel control lever can cause loss of power.

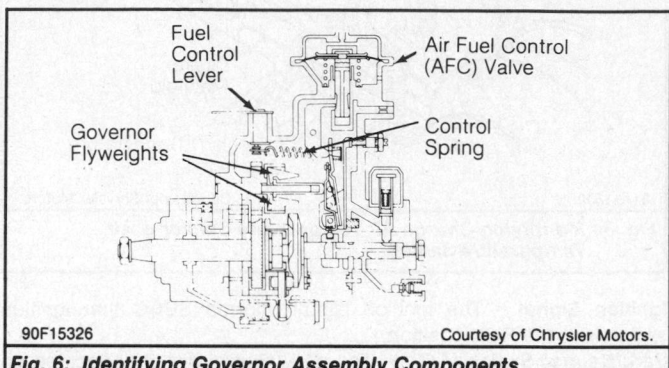

90F15326   Courtesy of Chrysler Motors.

Fig. 6: Identifying Governor Assembly Components

Fuel Injectors – During the fuel injection cycle, fuel injection pressure increases to fuel injector opening pressure or POP pressure of 3625 psi (254 kg/cm²). The opening pressure is pressure required to lift injector needle valve from its seat.

With injector needle valve off its seat, fuel is injected into cylinders. A spring is used to force needle valve closed as injection pressure drops below opening pressure. Fuel injector opening pressure is adjusted with shims above needle valve return spring.

Governor – Governor is located inside fuel injection pump. *See Fig. 6.* Balance between governor and fuel control lever position controls metering amount of fuel to be injected. Governor performance and setting can affect engine power.

Special tools and qualifications are required to adjust governor. If seals are broken on external adjustment screw, fuel rate may be out of adjustment. Warranty of pump governor and engine may be void if seals are tampered with or removed.

KSB Valve – Fuel pump timing is advanced at start-up by KSB valve to control White smoke. The KSB valve is located on side of the fuel injection pump. *See Fig. 5.* When intake manifold air temperature is less than 90°F (32°C), air temperature switch provides ground for KSB solenoid. Air temperature switch is located in the intake manifold cover. *See Fig. 3.*

When voltage is applied to KSB valve, valve closes and internal pressure in fuel injection pump increases. This causes fuel injection pump advance mechanism to advance fuel injection pump timing. Air temperature switch will open when intake manifold air temperature is greater than 90°F (32°C) and KSB solenoid will be de-energized. KSB valve will now open and fuel injection pump timing will return to normal operation.

CAUTION: DO NOT apply 12 volts to KSB valve. Wiring circuit contains a 3-ohm resistor to decrease voltage to KSB valve to 10 volts.

Manual Shutdown Lever – Fuel injection pump is equipped with a manual shutdown lever. This lever is spring loaded in the RUN position. There is no cable or rod connected to the lever. *See Fig. 5.* Engine can be shut down by rotating manual shutdown lever.

FUEL/WATER SEPARATOR FILTER

The fuel/water separator filter contains a water-in-fuel sensor and a water drain valve, located at bottom of fuel/water separator filter. *See Fig. 5.* The water-in-fuel sensor sends an input signal to SBEC when water exists in fuel/water separator filter.

SBEC will then turn on the WATER-IN-FUEL light on the message center in the cab. The WATER-IN-FUEL light informs operator to drain water from bottom of fuel/water separator filter or fuel system components may be damaged.

FUEL HEATER

Fuel flows from filter head and passes through the fuel heater, consisting of ceramic plates and a thermostat. Fuel heater is located between fuel/water separator filter and filter adapter on cylinder head. *See Fig. 5.* Voltage to operate fuel heater is provided from ignition switch.

A minimum of 7 volts is supplied from ignition switch to the ceramic plates. Thermostat senses fuel temperature and operates fuel heater to maintain a constant fuel viscosity to prevent fuel waxing. Fuel heater will turn on when temperature is approximately 43°F (6°C) and shut off at approximately 56°F (13°C).

EMISSIONS SYSTEMS

INTAKE MANIFOLD HEATER SYSTEM

Intake manifold heater is a grid heater installed between air inlet housing and intake manifold. The air inlet housing is attached to intercooler outlet duct which is connected to the intercooler. Intake manifold heater is used to warm intake manifold air before engine start-up.

A charge air temperature sensor monitors intake manifold air temperature and sends a signal to SBEC. The charge air temperature sensor is located in intake manifold cover. *See Fig. 3.* SBEC uses this input signal to determine when and how long to operate intake manifold heaters. SBEC is located on left front corner of engine compartment, near horns on left fender. Intake manifold heater relays are mounted on the inner wheelwell. *See Fig. 4.*

If signal from charge air temperature sensor indicates intake manifold air temperature is 59°F (15°C) or less, the WAIT-TO-START light on message center in the cab and intake manifold heater relays are energized. Intake manifold heater relays then energize the intake manifold heater. Intake manifold heater relays are not energized during engine cranking. A clicking sound will be heard when relays are energized.

CAUTION: Intake manifold heater relays should not be cycled (ignition turned off and then on) more than once within 15 minutes. Wait 15 minutes before turning ignition on.

SELF-DIAGNOSTIC SYSTEM

The Single Board Engine Controller (SBEC) monitors several different circuits and contains a self-diagnostic system. If a problem exists, SBEC will store a trouble code in the self-diagnostic system. Trouble code can be obtained using a DRB-II to determine circuit on which the problem exists. If problem is fixed, SBEC will cancel trouble code after 50 engine starts. For system diagnosis, see SELF-DIAGNOSTICS – DIESEL article in ENGINE PERFORMANCE.

MISCELLANEOUS CONTROLS

ALTERNATOR

Voltage regulation is controlled by Single Board Engine Controller (SBEC).

TRANSMISSION

Coolant Temperature Switch (A/T) – Coolant temperature switch is located in the cylinder head, below intake manifold, near air temperature switch. *See Fig. 3.* Coolant temperature switch opens when coolant temperature is less than 60°F (16°C).

When coolant temperature switch opens, transmission will not shift into overdrive. Transmission will downshift if it is in overdrive when coolant temperature switch opens.

Transmission Thermoswitch (A/T) – Transmission thermoswitch is located in transmission-to-radiator oil cooler line. Transmission thermoswitch opens when transmission fluid temperature is more than 273°F (134°C) and closes at 240°F (116°C).

If transmission is in overdrive and thermoswitch opens, transmission will downshift. Once switch closes, SBEC will send a signal to transmission to shift into overdrive.

1992 ENGINE PERFORMANCE
Theory & Operation – CNG

RWD Van

INTRODUCTION

This article covers the basic description and operation of engine performance related systems and components. Read this article before working on unfamiliar systems.

COMPUTERIZED ENGINE CONTROLS

POWERTRAIN CONTROL MODULE (PCM)

PCM is a digital computer that controls ignition timing, air/fuel ratio, emission control devices, cooling fan, charging system, idle speed, fuel pump and tachometer. The control unit is located in the engine compartment. PCM uses data from various input sources to control output devices in order to achieve optimum engine performance for all operating conditions.

PCM has voltage converters that convert battery voltage to regulated 5-volt and 8-volt outputs. The 8-volt output powers the distributor pick-up and crankshaft position sensor. The 5-volt output powers coolant temperature, charge temperature, fuel temperature, manifold absolute pressure and throttle position sensors.

FUEL INJECTOR DRIVER MODULE

Fuel injector driver module, located near PCM, supplies high current required for injector operation. PCM supplies low current fuel injector signal to fuel injector driver module.

SYSTEM COMPONENTS

The following engine components (as used on CNG vehicle) are identical to components used on RWD van equipped with a 5.2L Multiport Fuel Injection engine.
- Throttle Body
- Accelerator Linkage
- Manifold Absolute Pressure (MAP) Sensor
- Engine Coolant Temperature Sensor
- Intake Manifold
- Intake Manifold Charge Air Temperature Sensor
- Throttle Position Sensor
- Idle Air Control Motor (Automatic Idle Speed)
- Crankshaft Position Sensor
- Automatic Shut Down Relay
- Oxygen Sensor
- Vehicle Speed (Distance) Sensor
- Ignition Distributor
- All Air Conditioning Components
- All Speed Control Components
- All Overdrive Components
- Alternator (Generator)
- Park/Neutral Switch
- Brake Switch Controls

For service and component removal/installation procedures for shared components, see REMOVAL, OVERHAUL & INSTALLATION – GASOLINE article.

CNG fuel system uses these additional components.
- Unique Powertrain Control Module (PCM) Computer
- CNG Fuel Injector Driver Module
- CNG Fuel Shutoff Solenoid Relay
- High-Pressure Fuel Fill Receptacle With An Internal One-Way Check Valve
- Fuel Filter Mounted In Fuel Pressure Regulator
- Eight (8) Unique CNG Fuel Injectors
- High-Pressure, Stainless Steel Seamless Fuel Tubes
- Stainless Steel, Double-Ferrule, Compression-Type Fuel Tube Fittings (Not At All Fuel Tube Connections Or Components)
- Fuel Rail Mounted Fuel Low-Pressure Sensor
- Unique Fuel Rail To Mount Fuel Injectors
- Three (3) High-Pressure Fuel Cylinders
- Three (3) Manual Fuel Control Valves (On Each Fuel Cylinder)
- Manual (Mechanically Operated) 1/4 Turn Gas Shutoff Valve
- Fuel Rail Mounted Fuel Temperature Sensor
- Fuel Rail Mounted And Electrically Controlled Low-Pressure Fuel Shutoff Solenoid
- Fuel Pressure Regulator Mounted And Electrically Controlled High-Pressure Fuel Shutoff Solenoid
- Fuel Pressure Regulator Warmed By Engine Coolant
- Fuel Gauge High-Pressure Sensor Used To Operate Fuel Gauge.
- Separate Frame Rail Mounted Check Valve

INPUT DEVICES

Vehicles are equipped with different combinations of input devices. Not all devices are used on all models. To determine the input usage on a specific model, see appropriate wiring diagram in WIRING DIAGRAMS – CNG article. Available input signals include:

A/C Switch – Switch signals PCM that A/C has been selected. PCM then activates A/C compressor clutch relay and maintains idle speed at a scheduled RPM. This is done through control of Automatic Idle Speed (AIS) motor.

Battery Voltage – PCM monitors battery voltage to determine fuel injector pulse width and alternator field control.

Brake Switch – PCM uses this input to maintain idle speed at a scheduled RPM when brakes are applied. If PCM receives an input signal from brake switch when speed control system is on, PCM will turn the speed control system off.

Charge Temperature Sensor – Sensor measures temperature of incoming intake air. This information is used by PCM to adjust air/fuel mixture and turbocharger boost.

Clutch Switch – This input prevents engine from starting until clutch pedal is depressed.

Coolant Temperature Sensor (CTS) – The CTS monitors engine coolant temperature. Sensor is mounted in intake manifold, next to thermostat housing. PCM uses coolant temperature information to adjust air/fuel mixture and idle speed.

Crankshaft Position Sensor – Crankshaft sensor is mounted on transmission bellhousing. Sensor reads slots on torque converter drive plate. The PCM uses this information to determine fuel injection sequence, ignition pulse and spark timing.

Fuel Low-Pressure Sensor – Fuel low-pressure sensor monitors fuel pressure on the low-pressure side of the fuel system. Sensor is mounted in fuel rail inlet block. PCM uses fuel pressure sensor information to calculate injector timing.

Fuel Temperature Sensor – Fuel temperature sensor monitors fuel temperature. Sensor is mounted in fuel rail inlet block. PCM uses fuel temperature information to adjust air/fuel mixture and idle speed.

Oxygen (O_2) Sensor – The O_2 sensor produces a small electrical voltage (.1-.9 volt) when exposed to oxygen in exhaust gas flow. O_2 sensor is electrically heated for faster switching. Heating element is powered through Auto Shutdown (ASD) relay.

The O_2 sensor acts like a rich/lean (air/fuel ratio) switch by monitoring the oxygen content in exhaust gas. This information is used by PCM to adjust air/fuel ratio.

The O_2 sensor produces a low voltage when oxygen content in exhaust gas is high; when oxygen content in exhaust gas is low, sensor produces a higher voltage.

Park/Neutral (P/N) Switch – Switch is only available on A/T models. The P/N switch is located on transmission housing. Switch prevents engine starter from engaging if vehicle is in any gear except Park or Neutral. Also see TRANSMISSION GEAR SELECTION.

Serial Communication Interface (SCI) Receive – SCI Receive is serial communication link used if diagnosing vehicle using DRB-II tester. PCM receives data and device activation commands from DRB-II on this circuit.

Speed Control Switch – Speed control switch provides PCM with 3 separate inputs. ON/OFF informs PCM that speed control system has been activated. SET/COAST informs PCM that set vehicle speed has been selected, or if depressed will decelerate until switch is released. RESUME/ACCEL informs PCM that a previously set speed has been selected or, if depressed, will increase speed until released. PCM uses these inputs to control speed control servo.

Sync Pick-Up – Sync pick-up is locate inside distributor and is used along with crankshaft position sensor to determine fuel injection sequence. Sync pick-up consists of a single shutter blade that passes through Hall Effect switch causing a signal to be sent to PCM.

Leading edge of shutter indicates cylinder No. 8. Trailing edge of shutter indicates cylinder No. 5. PCM compares signals received from crankshaft position sensor and sync pick-up to determine which piston is coming up to top dead center. PCM then fires injectors in proper order for engine to operate.

Throttle Position Sensor (TPS) – TPS is mounted on throttle body and monitors opening angle of throttle valve. Sensor varies its output voltage according to angle of throttle blade opening. PCM uses this information and other sensor inputs to adjust air/fuel ratio. If PCM senses wide open throttle (WOT) position during cranking, it assumes engine is flooded and turns off fuel injectors until throttle is released.

Transmission Gear Selection – The P/N safety switch on the transmission housing provides an input to PCM to indicate if transmission gear selection is in Park, Neutral or Drive. PCM uses this input to determine necessary changes to idle speed, fuel injector pulse width and ignition timing advance. Also see PARK/NEUTRAL (P/N) SWITCH.

Transmission Overdrive Override Switch (A/T Models) – On models with overdrive, PCM regulates overdrive upshift and downshift through the overdrive solenoid. The transmission overdrive override switch is mounted in the instrument panel.

The switch is normally closed. If switch is depressed and switch opens, transmission will not go into overdrive. Transmission will downshift if transmission is in overdrive and switch is depressed.

Vehicle Speed Sensor (VSS) – The VSS generates 8 pulses per axle shaft revolution. PCM interprets speed sensor input along with TPS closed throttle input.

This input enables PCM to determine if a closed throttle deceleration or normal throttle idle (vehicle stopped) condition exists. During deceleration, PCM controls Automatic Idle Speed (AIS) motor to maintain a desired manifold pressure. During idle (vehicle stopped), PCM controls AIS motor to maintain a desired idle speed. PCM also uses VSS signal to maintain set speed during cruise control operation.

OUTPUT SIGNALS

NOTE: Each vehicle may be equipped with different combinations of computer-controlled components. The following components may NOT be used on all models. For theory and operation on each output component, refer to the indicated system.

A/C Clutch Relay – See MISCELLANEOUS CONTROLS.
Alternator – See MISCELLANEOUS CONTROLS.
Automatic Idle Speed (AIS) Motor – See IDLE SPEED under FUEL SYSTEM.
Auto Shutdown (ASD) Relay – See MISCELLANEOUS CONTROLS.
CHECK ENGINE Light – See SELF-DIAGNOSTIC SYSTEM.
Electric EGR Transducer (EET) – See EXHAUST GAS RECIRCULATION (EGR) SYSTEM under EMISSION SYSTEMS.
Emission Maintenance Reminder (EMR) Light – See EMISSION MAINTENANCE REMINDER LIGHT under EMISSION SYSTEMS.
Fuel Injectors – See FUEL CONTROL under FUEL SYSTEM.
Fuel Shutoff Solenoid Relay – See FUEL CONTROL under FUEL SYSTEM.
Magnetic Ignition System (Hall Effect) – See IGNITION SYSTEM.
Limp-In Mode – See MISCELLANEOUS CONTROLS.
Lock-Up Torque Converter Solenoid – See MISCELLANEOUS CONTROLS.
Overdrive Override Switch Indicator Light – See MISCELLANEOUS CONTROLS.
Overdrive Solenoid – See MISCELLANEOUS CONTROLS.
Serial Communication Interface (SCI) Transmit – See SELF-DIAGNOSTIC SYSTEM.

Shift Indicator Light – See MISCELLANEOUS CONTROLS.
Speed Control Servo – See MISCELLANEOUS CONTROLS.

FUEL SYSTEM

FUEL DELIVERY

NOTE: A decal indicating the location of the manual shutoff valve is affixed in front of the right rear wheelwell at the base of the side panel. A label indicating the type of fill nozzle required for fueling and the date the fuel cylinders are required to be tested is located on the fuel filler door.

Auto Shutdown (ASD) Relay – See AUTO SHUTDOWN (ASD) RELAY under MISCELLANEOUS CONTROLS.
Fuel Cylinders – Three high-pressure fuel cylinders are used to store natural gas at pressures up to approximately 3000 psi. Two of the cylinders are mounted transversely behind rear axle. The third cylinder is mounted longitudinally along left side of vehicle. Each cylinder is equipped with its own manually operated fuel control valve and pressure relief device.
Fuel Cylinder Control Valves – Each fuel cylinder is equipped with its own manually operated fuel control valve. The control valves are equipped with a pressure relief device. This device is designed to release excess cylinder pressure to atmosphere if temperature increases to more than about 217°F (103°C). Turn valve handle fully clockwise to stop gasflow. Turn handle fully counterclockwise to provide gasflow.
Fuel Fill Check Valves – Two different check valves are used with the CNG fuel system. One of the valves is located integrally with fuel fill receptacle. The other valve is located in fuel fill tube near top of left rear shock absorber. Both valves are used to keep fuel from escaping from fuel fill receptacle.
Fuel Injector Rail – A unique fuel injector rail is used with the CNG system. The rail can be disassembled for replacement of inlet blocks, connecting tubes and O-rings.
Fuel Filter – The fuel filter, located in fuel pressure regulator, requires service only when a fuel contamination problem is suspected.
Fuel Pressure Regulator – Fuel pressure regulator is located under right side of vehicle on frame rail. It is used to lower fuel cylinder pressure from approximately 3000 psi down to approximately 90-140 psi for system operation.

The regulator contains a pressure relief device located on low-pressure side of regulator. It is routed (by a tube) to right side of vehicle. This pressure relief device will release excess pressure to atmosphere when low-pressure side fuel pressure exceeds 175 psi.

Pressure regulator is warmed using engine coolant routed through regulator from cooling system. Two hoses teed into vehicle heater hoses are connected to fuel pressure regulator.
Fuel Tubes & Fittings – Due to the high-pressure requirements of CNG system, special stainless steel, SAE straight thread O-ring, double-ferrule, compression-type fuel tube fittings are used. These will connect all fuel tubes and components on high-pressure side of system (inlet side of fuel pressure regulator). High-pressure stainless steel, seamless fuel tubes are also used.

Standard NPT and 45-degree fittings are used on low-pressure side of system (outlet side of fuel pressure regulator).

Fittings with O-rings are used on the high-pressure side of system at:
- The main fuel tube-to-rear cylinder fuel control valve. This is a 90° fitting.
- The main fuel tube-to-side cylinder fuel control valve. This is a straight fitting.
- The connecting fuel tube between rear cylinder control valves. These are straight fittings.

High-Pressure Fuel Shutoff Solenoid – The high-pressure fuel shutoff solenoid is used as an on/off valve to electrically control high-pressure gas flowing through the fuel pressure regulator. It is located as an integral part of fuel pressure regulator and is operated by Powertrain Control Module (PCM) through CNG fuel shutoff solenoid relay.

Low-Pressure Fuel Shutoff Solenoid – Low-pressure fuel shutoff solenoid is controlled by the PCM through ASD Relay. The solenoid is mounted to inlet side of fuel injector rail. After cylinder pressure has been lowered by fuel pressure regulator, this solenoid is used as an on/off valve to electrically control fuel entering fuel rail assembly.

Manual Shutoff Valve – A manual one-quarter turn shutoff valve is located inboard of the right frame rail in front of the right rear wheelwell. Its location is identified by a label on the body. This valve isolates the fuel cylinders from the rest of the fuel system, the fuel fill tube and the tube to the engine.

FUEL CONTROL

Fuel Injectors – Fuel injectors are powered by electric solenoids and controlled by PCM. PCM determines when and time injectors should operate. Due to the higher amperage requirements of these injectors, a separate CNG fuel injector driver module (controlled by PCM) is used to supply current to injectors.

When ground is supplied to injector by PCM, armature and pintle inside injector move a short distance against spring and open a small orifice. Since fuel is under high pressure, a fine spray is developed.

Fuel Shutoff Solenoid Relay – Fuel shutoff solenoid relay, located in engine compartment, is comparable to fuel pump relay used on gasoline powered vehicles. Relay is controlled by PCM and is used to control the high-pressure fuel shutoff solenoid in the fuel pressure regulator.

Port Fuel Injection (PFI) – Individual, electrically pulsed injectors (one per cylinder) are located in intake manifold fuel rails. These injectors are next to intake valves in cylinder head.

PFI system features sequential injection. Injection timing is controlled by PCM based on input from crankshaft position sensor and sync pick-up. Constant fuel pressure to the injectors is maintained by the fuel pressure regulator. Air/fuel mixture is regulated by the length of time injector stays open (pulse width). The PCM controls pulse width using information provided by various sensors.

Modes Of Operation – As input signals to PCM change, PCM adjusts its response to the output devices. Modes of operation come in 2 types, open loop and closed loop. In open loop mode, PCM is not using input from oxygen sensor and is responding to preset programming to determine injector pulse width and ignition timing. In closed loop mode, PCM is adjusting ignition timing and using the input from oxygen sensor to fine tune injector pulse width.

The following inputs are used to determine PCM mode.
- Charge Temperature Sensor
- Coolant Temperature Sensor (CTS)
- Fuel Temperature Sensor
- Fuel Low-Pressure Sensor
- Idle Contact Switch
- MAP Sensor
- Engine Speed
- Throttle Position Sensor (TPS)
- Gear Position
- A/C Switch
- Battery Voltage
- Oxygen (O_2) Sensor
- A/C Control Positions

From these inputs, PCM determines which mode vehicle is in and the appropriate response. Not all inputs are used in all modes. The 8 modes of operation are as follows:
- **Ignition Switch In ON Position** – This is an open loop mode. PCM determines atmospheric pressure from MAP sensor and determines basic fuel strategy. PCM modifies fuel strategy according to ambient air temperature, coolant temperature, fuel temperature and fuel pressure inputs. PCM activates auto shutdown relay which in turn activates low-pressure fuel shutoff solenoid and ignition circuit for approximately 2 seconds unless engine is cranked. PCM also activates CNG fuel shutoff solenoid relay which in turn activates high pressure fuel shutoff solenoid and O_2 sensor heater element for approximately 2 seconds unless engine is cranked.

- **Engine Start-Up** – This is an open loop mode. When starter is engaged, PCM receives crankshaft position and distributor signal and energizes Auto Shutdown (ASD) relay. Once ASD relay is energized, PCM determines proper injector pulse width and ignition timing from input signals and sends a signal to fuel injector driver module to power up fuel injectors. PCM provides ground for injectors to fire in proper order. If PCM does not receive crankshaft position sensor signal within 3 seconds after engine begins cranking, fuel injection system is shut down and a fault code is set in PCM memory.

- **Engine Warm-Up** – This is an open loop mode. PCM determines injector pulse width using information from battery voltage, crankshaft position sensor, coolant, charge and fuel temperature sensors, MAP sensor and distributor pick-up. PCM also monitors A/C request, fuel low-pressure sensor and Park/Neutral switch (if equipped) signals for fuel calculation. PCM controls engine idle speed and ignition timing.

- **Idle** – This is an open loop mode. In idle mode PCM now adds O_2 sensor signal to the array of inputs. PCM maintains correct air/fuel ratio by adjusting injector pulse width and ignition timing. PCM also controls A/C clutch operation if A/C is requested.

- **Cruise** – When engine is at operating temperature, this is a closed loop mode. Using information from various inputs, PCM determines injector pulse width and ignition timing under different engine load conditions. PCM determines proper air/fuel ratio using input from O_2 sensor.

- **Acceleration** – This is an open loop mode. When PCM recognizes an abrupt increase in throttle position or manifold pressure as a demand for increased engine output, it increases injector pulse width through fuel injector driver module in response to increased fuel demand.

- **Deceleration** – This is an open loop mode. When PCM receives inputs signalling a closed throttle and an abrupt decrease in manifold pressure, it reduces injector pulse width to lean air/fuel mixture. Under certain RPM and closed throttle position conditions, O_2 sensor signals are ignored and PCM cuts off fuel injection until idle speed is reached. PCM also drives AIS motor for smooth transition to idle mode.

- **Wide Open Throttle** – This is an open loop mode. When PCM senses wide open throttle, it grounds EGR and evaporative purge solenoids to prevent EGR and canister purge functions. Oxygen sensor input is ignored and PCM adjusts injector pulse width to supply a predetermined amount of additional fuel.

- **Ignition Switch In OFF Position** – This is an open loop mode. All fuel injection is stopped and fuel flow is electrically shut down at both low-pressure and high-pressure fuel shutoff solenoids. PCM de-energizes auto shutdown relay and drives AIS motor into position in anticipation of next start-up.

IDLE SPEED

Automatic Idle Speed (AIS) Motor – AIS motor adjusts idle speed to compensate for engine load and ambient temperature by adjusting amount of air flowing through by-pass in throttle body. PCM uses coolant temperature, distance (vehicle speed) sensor, throttle position and various switch input operations to adjust AIS to obtain optimum idle conditions. Deceleration stall is prevented by increasing airflow when throttle is closed suddenly.

IGNITION SYSTEM

MAGNETIC IGNITION SYSTEM (HALL EFFECT)

Ignition timing is controlled by PCM. PCM uses engine RPM data from the Hall Effect switch to control ignition timing. Hall Effect switch is incorporated into crankshaft position sensor.

PCM applies and monitors voltage to Hall Effect switch. As windows in flywheel pass magnet in crankshaft position sensor magnetic field is interrupted and monitored voltage is toggled between high and low. PCM monitors voltage signal switching and uses these pulses to control ignition coil primary/secondary switching and spark timing and advance.

IGNITION TIMING CONTROL SYSTEM

The PCM completely controls ignition system. During a crank/start mode, PCM will set a fixed amount of spark advance for an efficient engine start.

Ignition Timing Advance Control – The amount of spark advance or retard is determined by inputs that PCM receives concerning coolant temperature, engine vacuum and engine RPM. During engine operation, PCM can supply an infinite number of advance curves to ensure proper engine operation.

EMISSION SYSTEMS

POSITIVE CRANKCASE VENTILATION (PCV) SYSTEM

Crankcase blow-by gases are removed from crankcase with manifold vacuum. These gases are introduced into incoming air/fuel mixture and become part of the calibrated mixture. No fresh air enters crankcase with this PCV system.

EMISSION MAINTENANCE REMINDER LIGHT

PCM activates the Emission Maintenance Reminder (EMR) light at scheduled mileage intervals to indicate need for servicing of certain emission system components. PCM will also illuminate this light whenever a fault occurs in the emission systems.

To reset mileage interval, connect Diagnostic Readout Box II (DRB-II) to vehicle diagnostic connector. Turn ignition switch to RUN position. Access EMISSIONS EMR TESTS on DRB-II. Select EMR MEMORY CHECK. Select RESET EMR LIGHT. Reset EMR light.

EXHAUST GAS RECIRCULATION (EGR) SYSTEM

EGR system allows a predetermined amount of exhaust gas to enter cylinder with the air/fuel mixture. This dilution of cylinder air/fuel volume reduces oxides of nitrogen (NOx) and helps prevent spark knock by reducing peak temperatures inside combustion chamber.

EGR system is a backpressure type. Backpressure transducer measures amount of exhaust gas backpressure on exhaust side of EGR valve and varies amount of vacuum applied to EGR valve.

This system allows backpressure transducer to provide proper vacuum signal to EGR valve for all engine operating conditions. EGR system is controlled by an EGR vacuum solenoid using a manifold vacuum signal from throttle body.

Electric EGR Transducer (EET) – EGR system uses an Electric EGR Transducer (EET). This system incorporates backpressure transducer and EGR solenoid into one unit.

SELF-DIAGNOSTIC SYSTEM

The PCM monitors several different circuits of engine control system. If a problem is sensed with a monitored circuit, PCM will store a trouble code to aid technician in diagnosis of system. The CHECK ENGINE light or DRB-II can be used to read trouble codes.

CHECK ENGINE LIGHT

CHECK ENGINE light comes on and remains on for 3 seconds as a bulb test each time ignition switch is turned to ON position. If PCM receives an incorrect signal or receives no signal from battery voltage input, charging system, coolant temperature sensor, manifold absolute pressure sensor or throttle position sensor, CHECK ENGINE light will glow. On California vehicles only, light will also glow if an emission-related fault exists. This warns driver that PCM is in limp-in mode and immediate repairs are necessary. CHECK ENGINE light can also be used to display fault codes. For additional information, see appropriate SELF-DIAGNOSTICS article.

SERIAL COMMUNICATIONS INTERFACE (SCI)

SCI circuit is used by PCM to send data to and receive data and sensor activation signals from DRB-II tester. DRB-II uses signals sent on SCI to display fault codes, sensor voltages and device states (ON/OFF). DRB-II uses SCI to send solenoid and switch activation commands to PCM so devices and circuits can be tested. SCI is also used to reset EMR light and write EMR mileage to PCM.

MISCELLANEOUS CONTROLS

NOTE: Although not strictly considered part of engine performance system, some controlled devices can adversely affect driveability if they malfunction.

A/C CLUTCH RELAY

A/C clutch relay is controlled by PCM and A/C switch. A/C relay is powered by condenser fan relay. This relay is energized during engine operation when A/C switch is closed and blower is on.

When PCM senses low idle speed or wide open throttle through throttle position sensor, PCM will de-energize A/C clutch relay, preventing A/C operation.

ALTERNATOR

Voltage regulation is controlled by Powertrain Control Module (PCM).

AUTO SHUTDOWN (ASD) RELAY

The ASD relay is a cutoff relay for the following components.
- Fuel Injector Driver Module
- Ignition Coil
- Low-Pressure Fuel Shutoff Solenoid

When ignition switch is turned to RUN position, PCM energizes ASD relay which powers these components. If PCM does not receive a crankshaft signal shortly thereafter, PCM will de-energize ASD relay and power to these components is cut off.

CNG FUEL SHUTOFF SOLENOID RELAY

The CNG fuel shutoff solenoid relay is a cutoff relay for the following components.
- High-Pressure Fuel Shutoff Solenoid
- O_2 Sensor Heating Element

When ignition switch is turned to RUN position, PCM energizes CNG fuel shutoff solenoid relay which powers these components. If PCM does not receive a crankshaft signal shortly thereafter, PCM will de-energize CNG fuel shutoff solenoid relay and power to these components is cut off.

LIMP-IN MODE

Limp-In mode is the attempt by PCM to compensate for failure of certain components by substituting information from other sources so that vehicle can still be operated. If PCM senses incorrect data or no data from MAP sensor, throttle position sensor, coolant temperature sensor or battery voltage, system is placed in Limp-In mode and CHECK ENGINE light on instrument panel is illuminated.

If faulty sensor comes back on line, PCM will resume closed loop operation. On some vehicles, CHECK ENGINE will remain illuminated until ignition is shut off and vehicle is restarted. To prevent damage to catalytic converter, vehicle should NOT be driven for extended periods in limp-in mode.

LOCK-UP TORQUE CONVERTER SOLENOID

PCM controls torque converter lock-up through lock-up solenoid. PCM controls lock-up according to various operating conditions.

OVERDRIVE OVERRIDE SWITCH INDICATOR LIGHT

PCM controls indicator light on overdrive override switch on models equipped with overdrive automatic transmission.

1992 ENGINE PERFORMANCE
Theory & Operation – CNG (Cont.)

OVERDRIVE SOLENOID

On vehicles equipped with overdrive transmissions, PCM controls the 3-4 overdrive upshift and downshift through the overdrive solenoid. PCM determines optimum overdrive shift scheduling for all operating conditions.

SHIFT INDICATOR LIGHT

PCM provides ground for shift indicator light on models equipped with manual transmission. PCM, based on engine speed, throttle position, and vehicle speed, turns shift indicator light on to advise driver to shift to a higher gear for optimum driveability.

SPEED CONTROL SERVO

System is electrically actuated and vacuum operated. The controls are located on the steering wheel. Controls consist of 3 buttons: OFF/ON, RESUME/ACCEL and SET/DECEL. PCM controls speed control servo. System will operate at 35-85 MPH.

Caravan, Dakota, Pickup, Ramcharger, RWD Van, Town & Country, Voyager

INTRODUCTION

Following diagnostic steps can help prevent overlooking a simple problem. Also use this article to begin diagnosis for a no-start condition. First step in diagnosing any driveability problem is verifying customer's complaint with a test drive under conditions during which problem reportedly occurs.

Before entering self-diagnostics, perform a careful and complete visual inspection. Most driveability or no-start problems are not related to computerized engine control systems, but are in fact simple mechanical, electrical, fuel or vacuum related faults. Most engine control problems are results of mechanical breakdowns, poor electrical connections or damaged or misrouted vacuum hoses. Before condemning computerized engine control system, perform each test listed in this article.

NOTE: All voltage tests should be performed with a Digital Volt-Ohmmeter (DVOM) with a minimum 10-megohm input impedance, unless stated otherwise in testing procedures.

PRELIMINARY INSPECTION & ADJUSTMENTS

VISUAL INSPECTION

Perform a visual inspection of all electrical wirings. Look for chafed, stretched, cut or pinched wiring. Inspect electrical connectors and connections for tight fit and corrosion. Repair as necessary. Inspect all vacuum hoses for proper routing, cuts or pinches. If necessary, see appropriate VACUUM DIAGRAMS article to verify routing and connections. Repair as necessary. Inspect air induction system for possible vacuum leaks.

MECHANICAL INSPECTION

Compression – Check engine mechanical condition using a compression gauge, vacuum gauge, or an engine analyzer capable of performing a relative compression test. See engine analyzer instruction manual for availability and description of relative compression feature.

CAUTION: Use a remote starter to crank engine during compression test; DO NOT use ignition switch. Fuel injectors on many models are triggered by ignition switch during engine cranking. This could create a fire hazard or cause engine flooding, crankcase contamination, hydrostatic lock or lubrication to be washed from cylinder walls.

ENGINE COMPRESSION

Application	psi (kg/cm²)
Minimum Compression Pressure	
2.5L, 3.3L, 3.9L, 5.2L & 5.9L	100 (7.0)
3.0L	178 (12.5)
Maximum Variation Between Cylinders	25 (1.8)

Exhaust System Backpressure – Check exhaust system using a vacuum gauge or pressure gauge. Remove O₂ sensor or air injection check valve (if equipped). Connect a 1-5 psi (.07-.35 kg/cm²) pressure gauge, and run engine at 2500 RPM. If exhaust system backpressure is greater than 1 3/4 - 2 psi (.12-.14 kg/cm²), exhaust system or catalytic converter is plugged.

If using a vacuum gauge, connect vacuum gauge hose to intake manifold vacuum port and start engine. Observe vacuum gauge. Open throttle part way and hold steady. If vacuum gauge reading slowly drops after stabilizing, check exhaust system for restriction.

FUEL SYSTEM

FUEL PRESSURE

WARNING: Always relieve fuel pressure before trying to open system for testing or component replacement. High fuel pressure may be present in fuel lines and components. DO NOT allow fuel to contact engine or electrical parts while testing fuel system components.

Fuel Pressure Release (2.5L, 3.0L, 3.3L & 5.9L) – **1)** Fuel pressure must be fully released before opening fuel system or removing any fuel-carrying components. To release pressure in tank, open fuel tank cap slowly.

2) To release remaining pressure in system, disconnect injector wiring harness. Using jumper wire, connect injector harness ground terminal No. 1 to ground. *See Fig. 1, 2 or 3.* Connect injector harness positive terminal No. 2 to positive battery terminal with second jumper wire.

3) DO NOT keep injector connector connected to positive battery terminal for longer than 5 seconds. Remove jumper wires. This releases system pressure. Continue fuel system service.

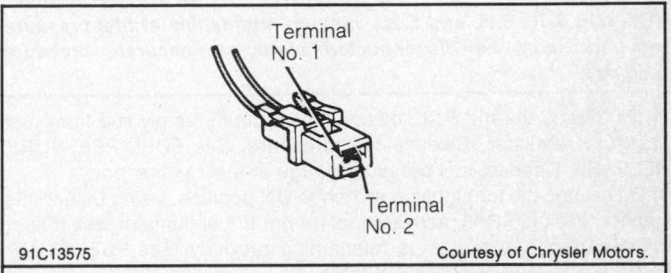

Fig. 1: Identifying Injector Harness Connector (2.5L)

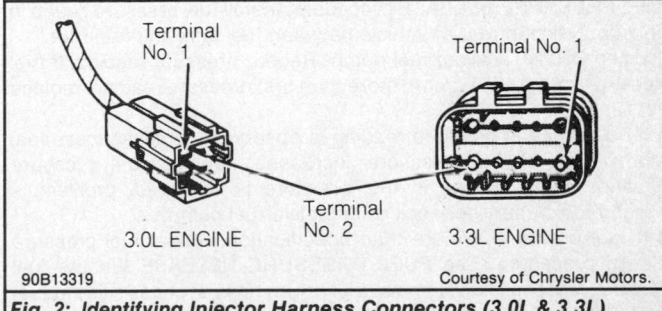

Fig. 2: Identifying Injector Harness Connectors (3.0L & 3.3L)

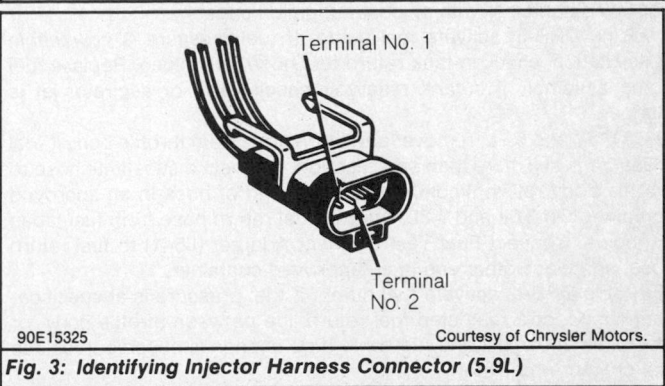

Fig. 3: Identifying Injector Harness Connector (5.9L)

WARNING: When battery is disconnected, vehicle computer and memory systems may lose memory data. Driveability problems may exist until computer systems have completed a relearn cycle. See COMPUTER RELEARN PROCEDURES article in GENERAL INFORMATION before disconnecting battery.

Fuel Pressure Release (3.9L & 5.2L) – **1)** Disconnect negative battery cable. Slowly open fuel cap to release fuel tank pressure. Remove protective cap from pressure test port on fuel rail.

CAUTION: To minimize fuel spill, wrap a shop towel around and under pressure test port.

2) Using Fuel Pressure Gauge/Hose Tool (5069) with gauge removed, place gauge end of hose into approved gasoline container. To release pressure, screw other end of hose onto pressure test port. After pressure is released, remove hose from test port and continue fuel system service. When servicing is completed, install protective cap on fuel rail test port.

WARNING: Before disconnecting any fuel line, or fuel system component, during testing, repeat FUEL PRESSURE RELEASE procedure. Perform FUEL PUMP TEST with fuel tank at least half full.

Fuel Pump Test – 1) Begin basic diagnosis of fuel system by determining fuel system pressure. On 2.5L, 3.0L and 5.9L engines, release fuel pressure. See FUEL PRESSURE RELEASE. Disconnect fuel supply hose. Connect fuel system pressure Gauge (C-4799-B) between fuel supply hose and engine fuel line.

NOTE: On 3.3L, 3.9L and 5.2L, vacuum supply line at fuel pressure regulator must be disconnected to obtain accurate pressure readings.

2) On 3.3L, 3.9L and 5.2L, disconnect vacuum supply line from fuel pressure regulator. Release fuel pressure. See FUEL PRESSURE RELEASE. Connect fuel pressure gauge at fuel rail test port.
3) On all models, turn ignition switch to ON position. Using Diagnostic Readout Box (DRB-II), activate fuel pump. If fuel pump pressure is at specification, fuel system is functioning properly. See FUEL PUMP PRESSURE SPECIFICATIONS table.
4) If fuel pressure is less than specification, record pressure. Repeat FUEL PRESSURE RELEASE procedure. Install fuel pressure gauge in fuel supply line at rear of vehicle between fuel tank and fuel filter.
5) Using DRB-II, activate fuel pump. Record pressure reading. If fuel pressure is 5 psi (.35 kg/cm²) more than first pressure reading, replace fuel filter.
6) If no change in pressure reading is observed, gently squeeze fuel return hose. If fuel pressure increases, replace fuel pressure regulator. If no change in fuel pressure is observed, problem is plugged fuel pump filter sock or defective fuel pump.
7) If fuel pressure is more than specification, repeat fuel pressure release procedure. See FUEL PRESSURE RELEASE. Ensure fuel tank is at least half full. Remove fuel return hose at chassis line at fuel tank. Connect an extension hose to return hose. Place hose in an approved container with at least a 2 gallon capacity.
8) Using DRB-II, activate fuel pump. If fuel pressure is now within specification, check in-tank return fuel hose for kinking. Replace fuel pump assembly if in-tank reservoir check valve or aspirator jet is plugged.
9) On 2.5L and 5.9L, remove fuel return hose from throttle body if fuel pressure is still more than specification. Connect a substitute hose to throttle body return nipple. Place other end of hose in an approved container. On 3.0L and 3.3L, remove fuel return hose from fuel tubes at engine. Connect Fuel Test Connect Adapter (6541) to fuel return hose, and place other end in an approved container.
10) Using DRB-II, activate fuel pump. If fuel pressure is at specification, check for a restricted fuel return line between throttle body, or fuel tubes at engine, and fuel tank. If no change is observed, replace fuel pressure regulator.

FUEL PUMP PRESSURE SPECIFICATIONS

Application	¹ psi (kg/cm²)
2.5L	39 (2.7)
3.0L & 3.3L	48 (3.4)
3.9L & 5.2L	39 (2.7)
5.9L	14.5 (1.0)

¹ – ± 2 psi (.14 kg/cm²).

AUTO SHUTDOWN (ASD) RELAY

NOTE: If ASD relay is suspected of causing a fuel or ignition system malfunction, use Diagnostic Readout Box (DRB-II) to diagnose ASD relay. See appropriate SELF-DIAGNOSTICS article.

2.5L, 3.0L, 3.9L, 5.2L & 5.9L – When distributor signal is not present with ignition switch in RUN position, ASD relay turns off power to electric fuel pump, fuel injectors, ignition coil and O_2 sensor heating element.
3.3L – When camshaft or crankshaft sensor signal does not exist with ignition switch in RUN position, ASD relay turns off power to electric fuel pump, fuel injectors, ignition coil and O_2 sensor heating element.

IGNITION CHECKS
TESTING SPARK AT COIL

NOTE: Ignition components may be damaged if test is performed with more than 1/4" clearance between wire and engine ground.

2.5L, 3.0L, 3.9L, 5.2L & 5.9L – 1) Remove coil wire from distributor cap. Hold end of cable 1/4" from engine ground. Crank engine and check for spark from coil wire. Spark should be present and constant.
2) If spark is present and constant, continue cranking engine. Slowly move coil wire away from ground. As coil wire is moved away from ground, check for arching at coil tower. If arching at coil tower is present, replace coil.
3) If spark is good and no arching is present, secondary ignition system is producing necessary voltage. Ensure spark reaches spark plugs by checking condition of rotor, cap, spark plug wires and spark plugs. Repair or replace as necessary. If ignition system components are in good condition, ignition system is okay. If vehicle still fails to start, proceed to NO-START TEST.

WARNING: 3.3L Direct Ignition System (DIS) generates approximately 40,000 volts. Direct contact with DIS could result in personal injury.

3.3L – 1) This system has 3 independent coils. These coils must be tested separately. Remove spark plug wire from No. 2 spark plug. Insert a clean screwdriver into spark plug boot.
2) Hold screwdriver approximately 1/4" from a ground. Crank engine, and watch for spark between screwdriver and ground. Repeat this test for No. 4 and No. 6 spark plug wires.
3) If no spark is present on any cylinder tested, go to NO-START TEST. If one or more cylinders has weak or no spark, go to next step.
4) Remove spark plug wires individually. Using an ohmmeter, measure resistance of each spark plug wire. Resistance should be 250-1,000 ohms per inch. Replace spark plug wire(s) if resistance is not within specification.
5) Disconnect electrical connector from coil pack. Measure resistance on primary side of each coil. Resistance should be .5-.7 ohm. Measure resistance between B+ terminal of ignition coil connector and corresponding cylinders. *See Fig. 4.* Replace coil if resistance is not within specification.

NOTE: Each coil tower is labeled with corresponding cylinder number.

6) Remove spark plug wires from coil one at a time. Measure secondary resistance of ignition coil between grouped cylinders and coil towers. Resistance should be 7000-15,800 ohms. Replace coil if resistance is not within specification. If ignition system components are in good condition, ignition system is okay. If vehicle still fails to start, proceed to NO-START TEST.

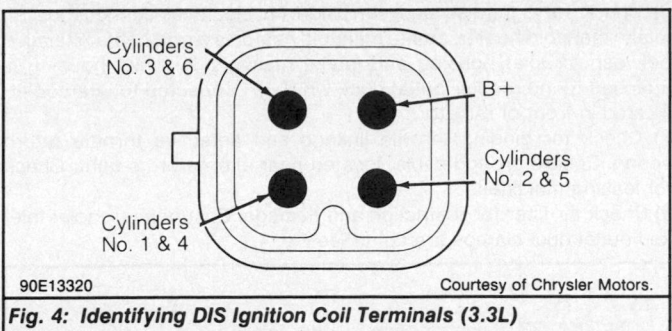

90E13320   Courtesy of Chrysler Motors.

Fig. 4: Identifying DIS Ignition Coil Terminals (3.3L)

NO-START TEST

NOTE: Perform TESTING SPARK AT COIL before proceeding with NO-START TEST.

2.5L, 3.0L, 3.9L, 5.2L & 5.9L – **1)** Unplug coil connector and coil. Connect a pair of jumper wires between coil and coil connector. Ensure sufficient battery voltage (12.4 volts) is available to crank engine and operate ignition systems. Crank engine for 5 seconds while monitoring voltage at coil positive terminal.

2) If voltage remains near zero during entire period of cranking, see appropriate SELF-DIAGNOSTICS article to check SBEC and ASD relay. If voltage is near battery voltage and drops to zero after 1-2 seconds of cranking, see appropriate SELF-DIAGNOSTICS article to check distributor pick-up circuit to SBEC.

3) If voltage remains near battery voltage during entire 5 seconds, turn ignition switch to OFF position. Disconnect SBEC 60-pin connector. Check 60-pin connector for loose terminals (push-outs).

4) Remove positive lead from coil. Connect a jumper wire between positive battery terminal and coil positive terminal. Using a specially constructed jumper wire, momentarily ground SBEC harness connector terminal No. 19. See Figs. 5 and 6. Spark should be generated when ground connection is disconnected.

5) If spark is generated, replace SBEC. If no spark is generated, use special jumper wire directly on coil negative terminal. If spark is produced, repair wiring harness for an open circuit. If no spark is produced, replace ignition coil.

Terminal No. 19

SBEC 60-PIN HARNESS CONNECTOR

90F13321   Courtesy of Chrysler Motors.

Fig. 5: Identifying SBEC 60-Pin Harness Connector Terminals

3.3L – **1)** Ensure sufficient battery voltage (12.4 volts) is available to operate cranking and ignition systems. Disconnect wiring connector from coil pack. Connect a test light between B+ coil pack wiring con-

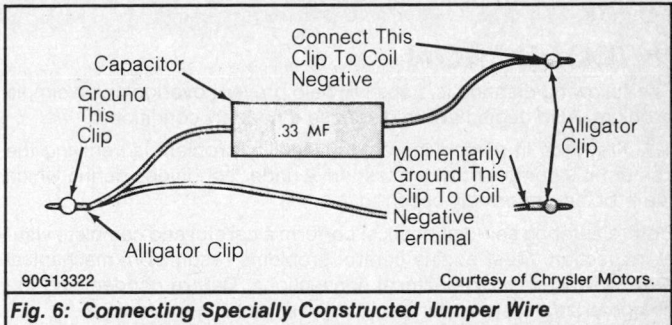

90G13322   Courtesy of Chrysler Motors.

Fig. 6: Connecting Specially Constructed Jumper Wire

nector terminal (Dark Green wire with Black tracer) and ground. See Fig. 7.

2) Turn ignition switch to ON position. DO NOT return ignition switch to OFF position. If test light flashes momentarily, SBEC energizes ASD relay, go to step **3)**. If test light does not flash, ASD relay did not energize, see appropriate SELF-DIAGNOSTICS article to check SBEC and ASD relay.

3) Crank engine for 5 seconds. If test light momentarily flashes during cranking, engine controller is not receiving signal. See appropriate SELF-DIAGNOSTICS article to check camshaft sensor and sensor circuits. If test light does not flash, unplug camshaft sensor connector.

4) Turn ignition switch to OFF position, then to ON position. Wait for test light to momentarily flash once then crank engine. If test light flashes once again, replace shorted camshaft sensor. If test light does not flash, see appropriate SELF-DIAGNOSTICS article to check crankshaft sensor/camshaft sensor 9-volt supply or crankshaft sensor 5-volt output to ground circuits.

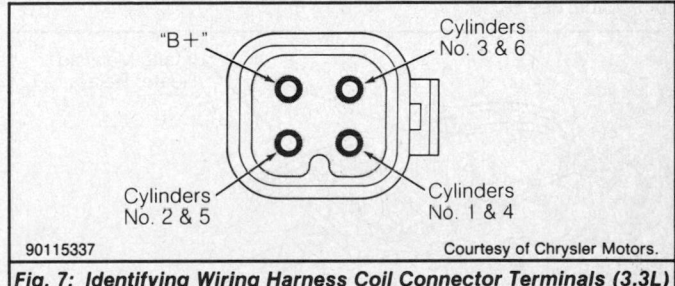

90115337   Courtesy of Chrysler Motors.

Fig. 7: Identifying Wiring Harness Coil Connector Terminals (3.3L)

IDLE SPEED & IGNITION TIMING

Ensure idle speed and ignition timing are set to specification. Always refer to emission control information label in engine compartment before servicing. If manual and emission label specifications differ, always use specifications on emission label. For adjustment procedures, see ON-VEHICLE ADJUSTMENTS – GASOLINE article.

SUMMARY

If no faults were found while performing BASIC DIAGNOSTIC PROCEDURES, proceed to appropriate SELF-DIAGNOSTICS article. If no hard codes are found in self-diagnostics, proceed to appropriate TROUBLE SHOOTING – NO CODES article for diagnosis by symptom (i.e., ROUGH IDLE, NO-START, etc.) or intermittent diagnostic procedures.

1992 ENGINE PERFORMANCE
Basic Diagnostic Procedures – Diesel

Pickup

INTRODUCTION

The following diagnostic steps will help prevent overlooking a simple problem. Also begin here to diagnose a no-start condition.

The first step in diagnosing any driveability problem is verifying the customer's complaint with a test drive under conditions during which the problem reportedly occurred.

Before entering self-diagnostics, perform a careful and complete visual inspection. Most engine control problems result from mechanical breakdowns or poor electrical connections. Before condemning the computerized system, perform each test listed in this article.

PRELIMINARY INSPECTION & ADJUSTMENTS

VISUAL INSPECTION

1) Ensure battery connections are tight and not corroded. Ensure 60-pin connector on Single Board Engine Controller (SBEC) is fully engaged and retaining screw is tight. Check for pushed-out connectors and bent terminals. SBEC is located in left front corner of engine compartment, near horns on left fender.

2) Ensure electrical connections on intake manifold heater relays are tight and not corroded. Intake manifold heater relays are mounted on inner wheelwell. See Fig. 1.

3) Check for loose or defective electrical connections on starter motor. Ensure electrical connections are installed on charge air temperature sensor and air temperature switch and wiring is okay. Charge air temperature sensor and air temperature switch are located in intake manifold cover. See Fig. 2.

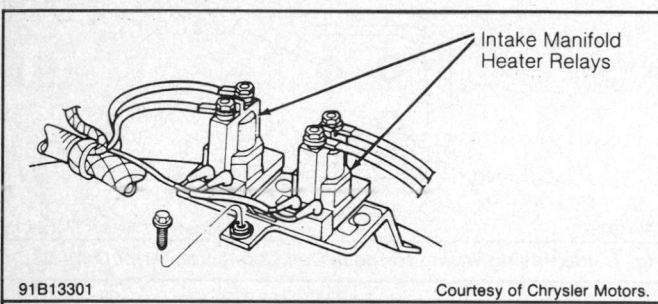

Fig. 1: Identifying Intake Manifold Heater Relays

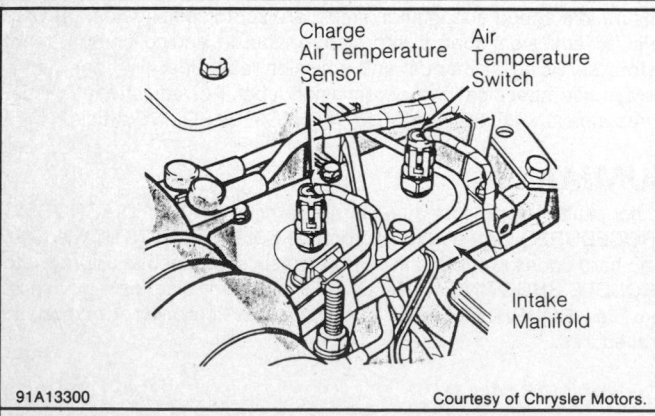

Fig. 2: Identifying Charge Air Temperature Sensor & Air Temperature Switch

4) Check for loose or defective electrical connection on engine speed sensor. Engine speed sensor is located on front of engine. Ensure electrical connector is installed on water-in-fuel sensor. Water-in-fuel sensor is located in bottom of fuel/water separator filter. See Fig. 3.

5) Ensure electrical connection is installed on shutoff solenoid valve and KSB valve on fuel injection pump. See Fig. 3.

6) Check for tightness and corrosion on electrical connections on intake manifold heater. Intake manifold heater is a grid heater installed between air inlet housing and intake manifold. Air inlet housing is attached to intercooler outlet duct, which is connected to intercooler, located in front of radiator.

7) Check for binding throttle linkage and defective throttle return spring. Ensure ground cable, located near alternator, is tight. Check for leaking fuel lines.

8) Check air filter for restriction and damage. Ensure intercooler inlet and outlet duct clamps are tight. See Fig. 4.

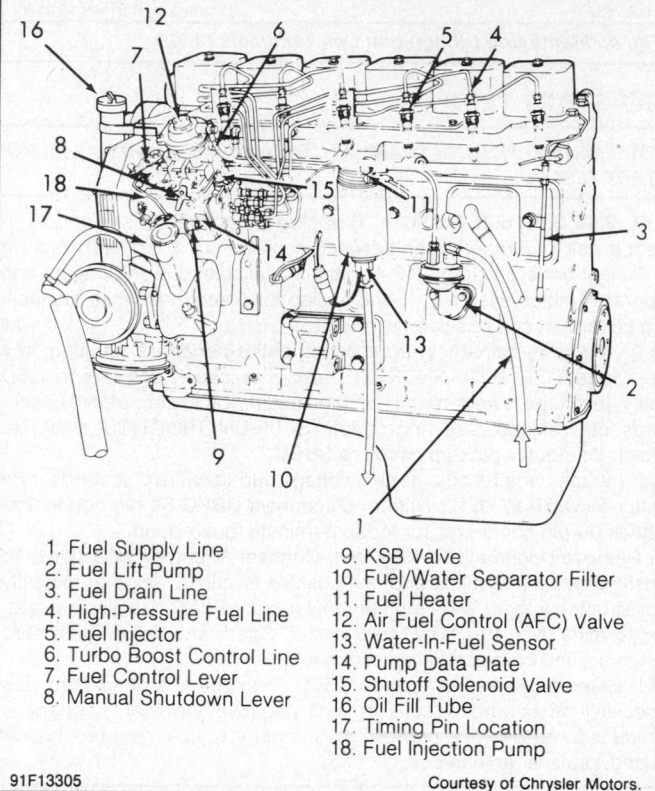

1. Fuel Supply Line
2. Fuel Lift Pump
3. Fuel Drain Line
4. High-Pressure Fuel Line
5. Fuel Injector
6. Turbo Boost Control Line
7. Fuel Control Lever
8. Manual Shutdown Lever
9. KSB Valve
10. Fuel/Water Separator Filter
11. Fuel Heater
12. Air Fuel Control (AFC) Valve
13. Water-In-Fuel Sensor
14. Pump Data Plate
15. Shutoff Solenoid Valve
16. Oil Fill Tube
17. Timing Pin Location
18. Fuel Injection Pump

Fig. 3: Locating Fuel System Components

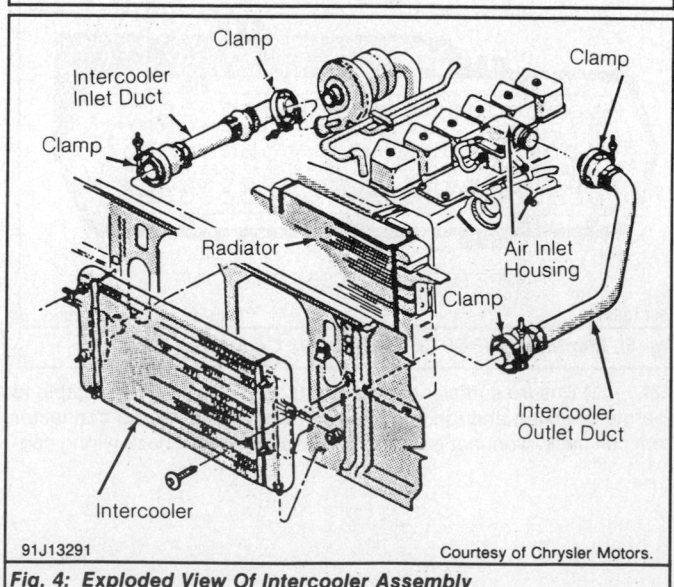

Fig. 4: Exploded View Of Intercooler Assembly

FUEL SYSTEM

FUEL/WATER SEPARATOR FILTER

Place drain pan under drain tube on fuel/water separator filter. *See Fig. 3.* With engine off, open drain valve on bottom of fuel/water separator filter until clean diesel fuel flows from drain tube. Close drain valve. It may be necessary to replace fuel/water separator filter if filter contains excessive water.

THROTTLE POSITION SENSOR (TPS)

TPS OPERATING VOLTAGE

NOTE: Throttle position sensor is located above fuel control lever on fuel injection pump and is used only on A/T models.

1) Before checking TPS, ensure cable rod is adjusted so control lever contacts low-speed screw when in idle position.
2) Ensure control lever moves over center position and rests against breakover spring when in full throttle position. If adjustment is required, see THROTTLE LINKAGE in ON-VEHICLE ADJUSTMENTS – DIESEL article.
3) Connect negative probe of voltmeter to ground. Turn ignition on. Backprobe center wire terminal at TPS electrical connector. With control lever contacting low-speed screw (idle position), voltage should be at least one volt. If voltage is not at least one volt, adjust TPS using 10-mm wrench to obtain correct voltage. *See Fig. 5.*
4) Open throttle to full throttle position. Backprobe center wire terminal at TPS electrical connector. Voltage should be at least 2.25 volts more than voltage obtained with throttle in idle position. If voltage is not at least 2.25 volts more than idle position voltage, adjust TPS to obtain correct voltage. Replace TPS if it cannot be adjusted.

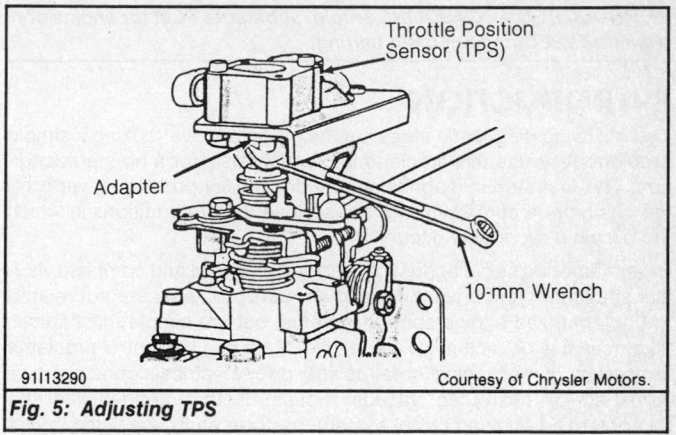

Fig. 5: Adjusting TPS

91113290   Courtesy of Chrysler Motors.

SUMMARY

If no faults were found while performing BASIC DIAGNOSTIC PROCEDURES, proceed to SELF-DIAGNOSTICS – DIESEL article. If no trouble codes are found in self-diagnostics, proceed to TROUBLE SHOOTING – NO CODES – DIESEL article for diagnosis by symptom (i.e., ROUGH IDLE, NO START, etc.).

1992 ENGINE PERFORMANCE
Basic Diagnostic Procedures – CNG

RWD Van

NOTE: Some tests in this article will refer to SELF-DIAGNOSTICS INTRODUCTION – GASOLINE article. Substitute PCM for engine controller or SBEC in diagnostic testing.

INTRODUCTION

The following diagnostic steps can help prevent overlooking a simple problem. Also use this article to begin diagnosis for a no-start condition. The first step in diagnosing any driveability problem is verifying the customer's complaint with a test drive under conditions in which the problem reportedly occurs.

Before entering self-diagnostics, perform a careful and complete visual inspection. Most driveability and no-start problems are not related to computerized engine control systems, but are simple mechanical, electrical, fuel or vacuum related faults. Most engine control problems are results of mechanical breakdowns, poor electrical connections or damaged or misrouted vacuum hoses. Before condemning the computerized engine control system, perform each test listed in this article.

NOTE: All voltage tests should be performed using a Digital Volt-Ohmmeter (DVOM) with a minimum 10-megohm input impedance unless stated otherwise in testing procedures.

PRELIMINARY INSPECTION & ADJUSTMENTS

VISUAL INSPECTION

Perform a visual inspection of all electrical wirings. Look for chafed, stretched, cut or pinched wiring. Inspect electrical connectors and connections for tight fit and corrosion. Repair as necessary. Inspect all vacuum hoses for improper routing, cuts and pinches. If necessary, see VACUUM DIAGRAMS – CNG article to verify routing and connections. Repair as necessary. Inspect air induction system for possible vacuum leaks.

MECHANICAL INSPECTION

Compression – Check engine mechanical condition using a compression gauge, vacuum gauge or an engine analyzer capable of performing a relative compression test. See engine analyzer instruction manual for availability and description of relative compression feature.

CAUTION: Use a remote starter to crank engine during compression test; DO NOT use ignition switch. Fuel injectors are triggered by ignition switch during engine cranking. This could create a fire hazard or cause engine flooding, crankcase contamination, hydrostatic lock or lubrication to be washed from cylinder walls.

ENGINE COMPRESSION

Application	psi (kg/cm²)
Minimum Compression Pressure	100 (7.0)
Maximum Variation Between Cylinders	25 (1.8)

Exhaust System Backpressure – Check exhaust system with a vacuum gauge or pressure gauge. Remove O_2 sensor or air injection check valve (if equipped). Connect a 1-5 psi pressure gauge, and run engine at 2500 RPM. If exhaust system backpressure is greater than 1 3/4-2 psi, exhaust system or catalytic converter is plugged.

If using a vacuum gauge, connect vacuum gauge hose to intake manifold vacuum port and start engine. Observe vacuum gauge. Open throttle part way and hold steady. If vacuum gauge reading slowly drops after stabilizing, check exhaust system for restriction.

FUEL SYSTEM

NO-START TEST (FUEL)

NOTE: Perform TESTING SPARK AT COIL under IGNITION CHECKS before proceeding with test.

1) Ensure sufficient battery voltage (12.4 volts) is available to crank engine and operate ignition system. Crank engine for 5 seconds while monitoring voltage at coil positive terminal.
2) If voltage remains near zero during entire period of cranking, see appropriate SELF-DIAGNOSTICS article to check PCM and ASD relay. If voltage is near battery voltage and drops to zero after 1-2 seconds of cranking, see appropriate SELF-DIAGNOSTICS article to check crankshaft position sensor circuit to PCM.
3) If voltage remains near battery voltage, ASD relay and crankshaft position sensor are functioning properly. Using a stethoscope, listen to a fuel injector while a helper cranks engine. If no "clicking" sound is heard from fuel injector, go to step **5)**. If fuel injector is clicking, go to next step.
4) While helper cranks engine, listen to injectors on same side as first injector. Stop cranking, and allow starter motor to cool. Crank engine and listen to injectors on opposite side of engine. If all injectors are clicking, go to FUEL PRESSURE. If some but not all injectors are clicking, go to next step.
5) If no "clicking" noise is evident from injector(s), ensure injector harness connector is fully connected. If connection appears okay, remove injector connector and inspect terminals for damage. If terminals are damaged, repair and retest injector. If wiring is okay, go to next step.
6) Disconnect fuel injector driver module 34-pin connector. Using an ohmmeter, check for continuity between chassis ground and fuel injector driver module pins No. 5, 8 and 15. See Fig. 1.
7) If resistance reading is not as specified, repair open circuit between fuel injector driver module and ground. If resistance reading on ALL pins is near zero, using a DVOM, check for voltage at pin No. 3 while a helper cranks engine for 5 seconds.
8) If battery voltage does not exist, repair open circuit between fuel injector driver module and pin No. 57 of PCM 60-pin connector. See Fig. 2. If battery voltage exists, go to next step.

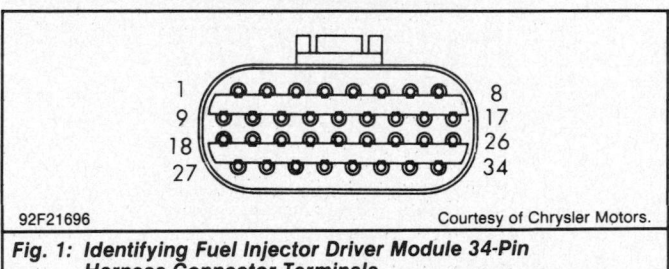

92F21696   Courtesy of Chrysler Motors.

Fig. 1: Identifying Fuel Injector Driver Module 34-Pin Harness Connector Terminals

PCM 60-PIN HARNESS CONNECTOR

92E21695   Courtesy of Chrysler Motors.

Fig. 2: Identifying PCM 60-Pin Harness Connector Terminals

9) While helper cranks engine, check for voltage on pins No. 1, 10, 18, 21, 26, 28, 31 and 33 of fuel injector driver module 34-pin connector. *See Fig. 1.* DO NOT crank engine longer than 15 seconds at a time.

10) If battery voltage does not exist on ALL pins, go to step **12)**. If battery voltage exists on some pins and no on others, repair open circuit between affected fuel driver module connector pin and PCM. See WIRING DIAGRAMS – CNG article in ENGINE PERFORMANCE.

11) If wiring is okay, check affected fuel injector for open circuit. Using an ohmmeter, connect leads across fuel injector terminals. If resistance reading is NOT 1.1-2.1 ohms, replace injector.

12) Disconnect PCM 60-pin connector. Using an ohmmeter, check for continuity between specified fuel injector driver module pins and PCM 60-pin connector pin No. 57. *See Fig. 2.*

13) If resistance reading on all pins is infinity, repair open circuit between PCM and fuel injector driver module. See WIRING DIAGRAMS – CNG article.

14) Check resistance between chassis ground and pins No. 1, 10, 18, 21, 26, 28, 31 and 33 of fuel injector driver module 34-pin connector. If resistance reading is less than infinity, repair short to ground between fuel injector driver module and PCM.

15) If fuel injector circuitry has tested okay so far, reconnect PCM 60-pin connector. While a helper cranks engine, check for voltage on pins No. 12, 20, 22, 24, 25, 30, 32 and 34 of fuel injector driver module 34-pin connector. DO NOT crank engine for more than 15 seconds.

16) Voltage reading should switch between some voltage and zero. If voltage reading is not as specified on ALL pins, repair open circuit or short to ground on affected wire between fuel injector driver module and PCM. If voltage reading is as specified, replace fuel injector driver module.

FUEL PRESSURE

Begin basic diagnosis of fuel system by determining fuel pressure.

WARNING: Always relieve fuel pressure before trying to open system for testing or component replacement. High pressure may exist in fuel lines and component parts. DO NOT allow fuel to flow onto engine or electrical parts while testing fuel system components.

Fuel System Purging – Before any part of compressed natural gas (CNG) fuel system is opened for repair, system must be purged of all natural gas. Fuel system must first be purged of natural gas if any of following components are to be removed or repaired.
- Any Fuel Tube Or Fuel Tube Fitting
- Fuel Injector Rail Assembly
- Fuel Temperature Sensor
- Fuel Low-Pressure Sensor
- Fuel Gauge Pressure Sensor
- Fuel Fill Receptacle
- Any Fuel Cylinder
- Manual Shutoff Valve
- Fuel Filter
- Any Or All Fuel Injectors
- Low-Pressure Fuel Shutoff Solenoid
- Fuel Pressure Regulator
- Either Fuel Fill Check Valve
- High-Pressure Fuel Shutoff Solenoid

Fuel Tube Purging – 1) Close control valve (clockwise) on side mounted fuel cylinder. Close control valves (clockwise) on both of rear mounted fuel cylinders. Open manual shutoff valve.

2) Start and operate engine until it runs out of fuel. Attempt 3 more engine starts. If check valve or fuel fill receptacle is to be serviced, slowly loosen inlet side of fuel fill tube fitting at check valve. It is normal for approximately 25 psi of natural gas pressure to flow from loosened fitting. All fuel tubes are now purged of natural gas between fuel cylinders and engine; fuel system may be opened for repair.

Fuel Cylinder Purging – 1) Open manual shutoff valve. Open only fuel control valves (counterclockwise) on fuel cylinders to be serviced. Close all control valves (clockwise) on fuel cylinders not being serviced.

2) Start and operate engine until it runs out of fuel. Attempt 3 more engine starts. All fuel tubes and opened cylinders are now purged of natural gas between fuel cylinders and engine; fuel system may be opened for repair.

Fuel System Pressure Test – 1) Purge fuel system. See FUEL TUBE PURGING. Remove engine cover. Remove fuel low-pressure sensor. *See Fig. 3.* Tee in a 0-300 psi pressure test gauge between sensor and fuel rail block. Install fuel low-pressure sensor to tee connection.

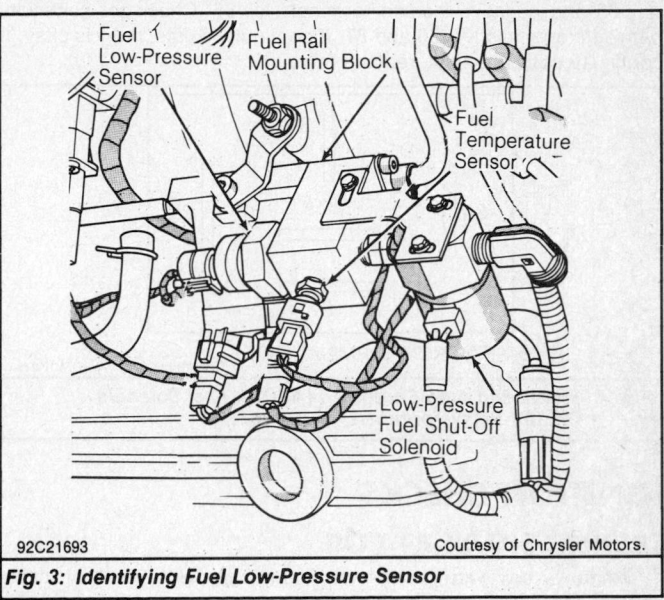

92C21693   Courtesy of Chrysler Motors.

Fig. 3: Identifying Fuel Low-Pressure Sensor

2) Repressurize fuel system, start engine and bring engine to full operating temperature. Note fuel pressure gauge reading. See FUEL PRESSURE SPECIFICATIONS table.

FUEL PRESSURE SPECIFICATIONS

Application	psi (kg/cm²)
Minimum	90 (6.3)
Maximum [1]	140 (9.8)

[1] – With fuel cylinders half full or more.

NOTE: Proper fuel system pressure depends on regulated fuel cylinder pressure at low-pressure side of fuel pressure regulator, ambient temperature, engine load and proper operation of high-pressure and low-pressure fuel shutoff solenoids.

3) If fuel pressure is greater than specified maximum, replace fuel pressure regulator. If fuel pressure is less than specified minimum, check for following items:
- Ensure cylinders have fuel.
- Ensure all 3 fuel cylinder control valves are open.
- Ensure manual valve is open.
- Check fuel tubes for kinks and restrictions.
- Check operation of high-pressure and low-pressure fuel shutoff solenoids.

4) After tests and repairs are complete, purge fuel system and remove gauge. Reinstall fuel low-pressure sensor, and check for leaks. Install engine cover.

AUTO SHUTDOWN (ASD) & FUEL SOLENOID SHUTOFF RELAY

NOTE: If ASD relay is suspected of causing a fuel or ignition system malfunction, use Diagnostic Readout Box (DRB-II) to diagnose ASD relay. See appropriate SELF-DIAGNOSTICS article. Perform NO-START TEST NS-1A or DRIVEABILITY TEST DR-1A test if fault code is present. If no fault code is present, perform NO-FAULT TEST NF-1A.

Relay Test – 1) Remove relay. Using an ohmmeter, check for continuity between terminals No. 85 and 86. *See Fig. 4.* If continuity exists, go to next step. If continuity does not exist, replace relay.

2) Check for continuity between terminals No. 30 and 87A. If continuity exists, go to next step. If continuity does not exist, replace relay.

3) Check for continuity between terminals No. 30 and 87. If continuity does not exist, go to next step. If continuity exists, replace relay.

4) Using a 12-volt power supply, connect positive lead to terminal No. 85 and negative lead to terminal No. 86. Check for continuity between terminals No. 30 and 87. If continuity exists, relay is okay. If continuity does not exist, replace relay.

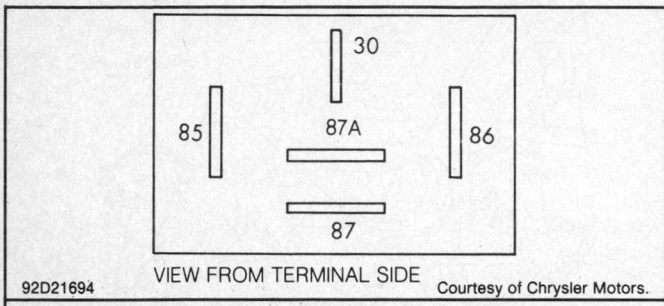

92D21694   VIEW FROM TERMINAL SIDE   Courtesy of Chrysler Motors.

Fig. 4: Identifying Auto Shutdown (ASD) & Fuel Solenoid Shutoff Relay Terminals

IGNITION CHECKS

TESTING SPARK AT COIL

1) Remove coil wire from distributor cap. Hold end of cable approximately 1/4" from ground. Crank engine and check for spark from coil wire. Spark should be present and constant. If spark does not exist, perform NO-START TEST (SPARK).

2) If spark is present and constant, continue cranking engine. Slowly move coil wire away from ground. As coil wire is moved away from ground, check for arching at coil tower. If arching at coil tower is present, replace coil.

3) If spark is good and no arching is present, secondary ignition system is producing necessary voltage. Ensure spark reaches spark plugs by checking condition of rotor, cap, spark plug wires and spark plugs. Repair or replace as necessary. If ignition system components are in good condition, ignition system is okay.

NO-START TEST (SPARK)

NOTE: Perform TESTING SPARK AT COIL before proceeding with test.

1) Ensure sufficient battery voltage (12.4 volts) is available to crank engine and operate ignition systems. Crank engine for 5 seconds while monitoring voltage at coil positive terminal.

2) If voltage remains near zero during entire period of cranking, see appropriate SELF-DIAGNOSTICS article to check PCM and ASD relay. If voltage is near battery voltage and drops to zero after 1-2 seconds of cranking, see appropriate SELF-DIAGNOSTICS article to check crankshaft position sensor circuit to PCM.

3) If voltage remains near battery voltage during entire 5 seconds, turn ignition off. Disconnect PCM 60-pin connector. Check 60-pin connector for loose terminals (push-outs).

4) Remove positive lead from coil. Connect a jumper wire between battery positive terminal and coil positive terminal. Using a specially constructed jumper wire, momentarily ground PCM harness connector terminal No. 19. *See Figs. 2 and 5.* Spark should be generated when ground connection is disconnected.

5) If spark is generated, replace PCM. If no spark is generated, use special jumper wire directly on coil negative terminal. If spark is produced, repair wiring harness for an open circuit. If no spark is produced, replace ignition coil.

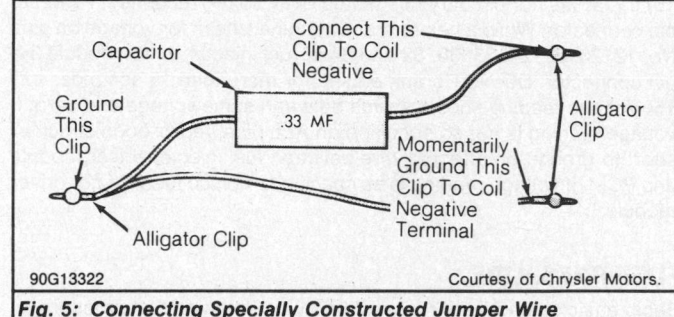

90G13322   Courtesy of Chrysler Motors.

Fig. 5: Connecting Specially Constructed Jumper Wire

IDLE SPEED & IGNITION TIMING

NOTE: Idle speed and ignition timing are controlled by PCM. No adjustments are required.

SUMMARY

If no faults were found while performing BASIC DIAGNOSTIC PROCEDURES, go to SELF-DIAGNOSTICS – CNG article. If no hard codes are found in self-diagnostics, go to TROUBLE SHOOTING – NO CODES – CNG article for diagnosis by symptom (i.e., ROUGH IDLE, NO-START, etc.) or intermittent diagnostic procedures.

Caravan, Dakota, Pickup, Ramcharger, Town & Country, RWD Van, Voyager

INTRODUCTION

If no faults were found while performing BASIC DIAGNOSTIC PROCEDURES, proceed with self-diagnostics. If no fault codes or only pass codes are present after entering self-diagnostics, proceed to appropriate TROUBLE SHOOTING – NO CODES article for diagnosis by symptom (i.e., ROUGH IDLE, NO START, etc.).

MODEL IDENTIFICATION

VEHICLE BODY IDENTIFICATION

Model Name	Body Type
Caravan, Town & Country, & Voyager	AS
Dakota	AN
Pickup	AD
Ramcharger	AD
RWD Van	AB

SELF-DIAGNOSTIC SYSTEM

WARNING: When battery is disconnected, vehicle computer and memory systems may lose memory data. Driveability problems may exist until computer systems have completed a relearn cycle. See COMPUTER RELEARN PROCEDURES article in GENERAL INFORMATION before disconnecting battery.

SELF-DIAGNOSTICS DIRECTORY

Application	Page
2.5L TBI	1-42
3.0L PFI	1-61
3.3L PFI	1-81
3.9L & 5.2L PFI	1-101
5.9L TBI	1-121

SYSTEM DIAGNOSTICS

The self-diagnostic capabilities of this system, if properly utilized, can simplify testing. The Single Board Engine Controller (SBEC) monitors several different engine control system circuits.

If a problem is sensed with a monitored circuit, SBEC memory stores a fault code, the CHECK ENGINE light glows and SBEC enters limp-in mode. In limp-in mode, SBEC compensates for component failure by substituting information from other sources. This allows vehicle operation until repairs can be made.

Once codes are known, see FAULT CODES table to determine the questionable circuit. Test circuits and repair or replace components as required. If problem is repaired or ceases to exist, the SBEC cancels fault code after 50 ignition on/off cycles. To clear codes, see CLEARING FAULT CODES.

A specific fault code results from a particular system failure. A fault code does not condemn a specific component. Component is not necessarily the reason for failure. Fault codes only call out a probable malfunction area.

Hard Failures – Hard failures cause CHECK ENGINE light to glow and remain on until the malfunction is repaired. If light comes on and remains on (light may flash) during vehicle operation, cause of malfunction must be determined using self-diagnostic tests. If a sensor fails, SBEC will use a substitute value in its calculations, allowing engine to operate in limp-in mode. In this condition, vehicle will run, but driveability may be poor. DRB-II will display key counter as zero.

Intermittent Failures – Intermittent failures may cause CHECK ENGINE light to flicker or stay on until the intermittent fault goes away. However, the corresponding fault code will be retained in SBEC memory. If related fault does not reoccur within a certain time frame, related fault code will be erased from SBEC memory. Intermittent failures can be caused by a faulty sensor, bad connector or wiring related

problems. DRB-II will display key counter as one or more. See TEST NF-1A in this article or INTERMITTENTS in appropriate TROUBLE SHOOTING – NO CODES article.

SERVICE PRECAUTIONS

Before proceeding with diagnosis, the following precautions must be followed:

- ALWAYS relieve fuel pressure before disconnecting any fuel injection-related component. DO NOT allow fuel to contact engine or electrical components. See FUEL PRESSURE RELEASE.
- When battery is disconnected, vehicle computer and memory systems may lose memory data. Driveability problems may exist until computer systems have completed a relearn cycle. See COMPUTER RELEARN PROCEDURES article in GENERAL INFORMATION before disconnecting battery.
- Vehicle must have a fully charged battery and functional charging system.
- Probe SBEC 60-pin connector from pin side. DO NOT backprobe SBEC connector.
- DO NOT cause short circuits when performing electrical tests. This will set additional fault codes, making diagnosis of original problem more difficult.
- DO NOT use a test light instead of a voltmeter.
- When checking for spark, ensure coil wire is NO more than 1/4" from ground. If coil wire is more than 1/4" from ground, damage to vehicle electronics and/or SBEC may result.
- DO NOT prolong testing of fuel injectors or engine may hydrostatically (liquid) lock.
- Always repair lowest fault code number (CHECK ENGINE light) or first fault displayed (DRB-II) first.
- Always perform VERIFICATION TEST after repairs are made.
- Always disconnect DRB-II after use.
- Always disconnect DRB-II before charging battery.

VISUAL INSPECTION

Most driveability problems in the engine control system result from faulty wiring, poor electrical connections or leaking air and vacuum hose connections. To avoid unnecessary component testing, perform a visual inspection before beginning self-diagnostic tests.

DIAGNOSTIC PROCEDURE

NOTE: DO NOT skip any steps in self-diagnostic tests or incorrect diagnosis may result.

Always perform a visual inspection before attempting to diagnose engine control system problems. See VISUAL INSPECTION. Enter on-board diagnostics, and retrieve fault code(s). See ENTERING ON-BOARD DIAGNOSTICS. If fault codes are not present and/or DRB-II (Diagnostic Readout Box-II) is used, proceed to one of the following tests:

- Go to TEST NS-1A (NO-START TEST 1A) if a no-start condition exists or engine stalls after start-up. Perform indicated VERIFICATION TEST after repairs have been made. Ensure self-diagnostic tests apply to engine being tested. See SELF-DIAGNOSTICS DIRECTORY table under SELF-DIAGNOSTIC SYSTEM.
- Go to TEST DR-1A (DRIVEABILITY TEST 1A) if engine runs but has performance problems. Perform indicated VERIFICATION TEST after repairs have been made. Ensure self-diagnostic tests apply to engine being tested. See SELF-DIAGNOSTICS DIRECTORY table under SELF-DIAGNOSTIC SYSTEM.
- Go to TEST NF-1A (NO FAULT CODE TEST 1A) if a driveability problem exits and no fault codes are present. Perform indicated VERIFICATION TEST after repairs have been made. Ensure self-diagnostic tests apply to engine being tested. See SELF-DIAGNOSTICS DIRECTORY table under SELF-DIAGNOSTIC SYSTEM.

1992 ENGINE PERFORMANCE
Self-Diagnostics Introduction – Gasoline (Cont.)

ENTERING ON-BOARD DIAGNOSTICS

NOTE: Although other scan testers are available, manufacturer recommends using DRB-II (Diagnostic Readout Box II) to diagnose the system. CHECK ENGINE light function can be used but has limited diagnostic usage.

CHECK ENGINE Light Diagnostic Mode – 1) Start engine (if possible). Move transmission shift lever through all positions, ending in PARK. Turn A/C switch on and then off (if equipped).

2) Turn engine off. Without starting engine again, turn ignition on, off, on, off and on. Record 2-digit fault codes as displayed by flashing CHECK ENGINE light.

3) For example, Code 23 is displayed as flash, flash, 4-second pause, flash, flash, flash. After a slightly longer pause, other codes stored are displayed in numerical order.

4) When CHECK ENGINE light begins to flash fault codes, it cannot be stopped. Start over if count is lost. Code 55 indicates end of fault code display. Refer to FAULT CODES table to translate trouble code number to a system fault description (DRB-II display).

5) Once trouble area is identified, refer to appropriate TEST NS-1A (NO-START TEST 1A) or TEST DR-1A (DRIVEABILITY TEST 1A) to diagnose problem. Use self-diagnostic test titles to find appropriate test.

6) As an example, a 3.0L engine starts and runs but has a driveability problem. CHECK ENGINE light indicates a Code 14. Refer to FAULT CODES table to translate trouble code number to a system fault description (DRB-II display).

7) When system fault description (DRB-II display) is obtained, refer to appropriate TEST DR-1A (DRIVEABILITY TEST DR-1A) since vehicle has a driveability problem. Select fault message and corresponding test from table, and proceed to appropriate test. To clear fault codes, see CLEARING FAULT CODES.

DRB-II Diagnostic Mode – 1) Turn ignition off. Connect DRB-II to engine diagnostic connector. Engine diagnostic connector is located in engine compartment, near SBEC on all models except Dakota. On Dakota models, diagnostic connector is located in right rear corner of engine compartment, taped to harness.

2) Start engine (if possible). With foot on brake, move transmission shift lever through all positions, ending in PARK. Turn A/C switch on and then off (if equipped).

3) Turn engine off. Without starting engine again, turn ignition on. Enter FUEL/IGN MENU. To enter FUEL/IGN MENU, see FUEL/IGN MENU under DRB-II TEST FUNCTIONS. At FUEL/IGN MENU, press "2" (READ FAULTS) key. Press ENTER key. After fault codes are accessed, see appropriate TEST NS-1A (NO-START TEST 1A) or TEST DR-1A (DRIVEABILITY TEST 1A) to diagnose problem.

4) To erase fault codes while in this mode, press ATM key. At DRB-II display, press "2" (ERASE) key. DRB-II will display ERASE FAULTS ARE YOU SURE? (ENTER TO ERASE). Press ENTER key.

FAULT CODES
FAULT CODES

Code	Display On DRB-II [1]	Fault Condition
11	NO REFERENCE SIGNAL DURING CRANKING	No Distributor Reference Signal Detected During Cranking.
13	SLOW CHANGE IN IDLE MAP SIGNAL	MAP Output Change Is Slower And/Or Smaller Than Expected.
	NO CHANGE IN MAP FROM START TO RUN	No Difference Recognized Between MAP Reading And Barometric (Atmospheric) Pressure Reading At Start-Up.
14	MAP VOLTAGE TOO LOW	MAP Sensor Input Less Than Minimum Acceptable Voltage.
	MAP VOLTAGE TOO HIGH	MAP Sensor Input More Than Maximum Acceptable Voltage.
15	NO VEHICLE SPEED SIGNAL	No Distance Sensor Signal Detected During Road Load Conditions.
17	ENGINE COLD TOO LONG	Coolant Temperature Stays Less Than Normal Operating Temperature During Vehicle Operation.
21	O$_2$ SIGNAL STAYS AT CENTER	No Rich Or Lean Signal Is Detected From O$_2$ Sensor Input.
	O$_2$ SIGNAL SHORTED TO VOLTAGE	O$_2$ Sensor Input Voltage Maintained At More Than Normal Operating Range.
22	COOLANT SENSOR VOLTAGE TOO LOW	Coolant Temperature Sensor Input Less Than Minimum Acceptable Voltage.
	COOLANT SENSOR VOLTAGE TOO HIGH	Coolant Temperature Sensor Input More Than Maximum Acceptable Voltage.
23	THROTTLE BODY TEMP VOLTAGE LOW	Throttle Body Temperature Sensor Input Less Than Minimum Acceptable Voltage.
	THROTTLE BODY TEMP VOLTAGE HIGH	Throttle Body Temperature Sensor Input More Than Maximum Acceptable Voltage.
24	TPS VOLTAGE LOW	TPS Sensor Input Less Than Minimum Acceptable Voltage.
	TPS VOLTAGE HIGH	TPS Sensor Input More Than Maximum Acceptable Voltage.
25	AIS MOTOR CIRCUITS	Open Or Shorted Condition Detected In One Or More Auto Idle Speed (AIS) Control Circuits.
27	INJECTOR CONTROL CIRCUIT	Injector Output Driver Does Not Respond Properly To SBEC Control Signal.
31	PURGE SOLENOID CKT	Open Or Shorted Condition Is Detected In Purge Solenoid Circuit.
32	EGR SOLENOID CIRCUIT	Open Or Shorted Condition Is Detected In Egr Solenoid Circuit.
	EGR SYSTEM FAILURE	SBEC Did Not Detect Required Air/Fuel Change During Diagnostic Test.
33	A/C CLUTCH RELAY CKT	Open Or Shorted Condition Detected In A/C Clutch Relay Circuit.
34	S/C SOLENOIDS CKT	Open Or Shorted Condition Detected In Speed Control (S/C) Vacuum Or Vent Solenoid Circuits.
35	RADIATOR FAN RELAY CKT	Open Or Shorted Condition Detected In Radiator Fan Relay Circuit.
37	TORQUE CONVERTER LOCK-UP SOLENOID CIRCUIT	An Open Or Shorted Condition Detected In Torque Converter Lock-Up Solenoid Circuit.
41 [2]	ALTERNATOR FIELD NOT SWITCHING PROPERLY	Alternator Field Not Switching Properly.
42	ASD RELAY CONTROL CIRCUIT	An Open Or Shorted Condition Detected In ASD Relay Circuit.
	NO ASD RELAY VOLTAGE SENSED AT CONTROLLER	No ASD Relay Voltage Sensed When ASD Relay Is Energized.
43	IGNITION COIL NO. 1 PRIMARY CKT	Peak Primary Circuit Current Not Achieved With Maximum Dwell Time.
	IGNITION COIL NO. 2 PRIMARY CKT	Peak Primary Circuit Current Not Achieved With Maximum Dwell Time.
	IGNITION COIL NO. 3 PRIMARY CKT	Peak Primary Circuit Current Not Achieved With Maximum Dwell Time.

[1] – Actual message displayed on DRB-II may vary between vehicles.
[2] – If code is displayed, charging system malfunction exists. See appropriate ALTERNATORS & REGULATORS article in ELECTRICAL.

FAULT CODES (Cont.)

Code	Display On DRB-II [1]	Fault Condition
44 [2]	BATTERY TEMP VOLTAGE	An Open Or Shorted Condition Exists In Coolant Temperature Sensor Circuit Or In SBEC Battery Temperature Voltage Circuit.
45	OVERDRIVE SOLENOID	Open Or Short Detected In Overdrive Solenoid Circuit.
46 [2]	CHARGING VOLTAGE TOO HIGH	Charging System Voltage Too High.
47 [2]	CHARGING VOLTAGE TOO LOW	Charging System Voltage Too Low.
51	O_2 SIGNAL STAYS BELOW CENTER (LEAN)	O_2 Sensor Input Indicates Lean Air/Fuel Ratio During Engine Operation.
	ADDITIVE ADAPTIVE MEMORY AT RICH LIMIT	Additive Adaptive Memory At Rich Limit
52	O_2 SIGNAL STAYS ABOVE CENTER (RICH)	O_2 Sensor Input Indicates Rich Air/Fuel Ratio During Engine Operation.
	ADDITIVE ADAPTIVE MEMORY AT LEAN LIMIT	Additive Adaptive Memory At Lean Limit.
53	INTERNAL CONTROLLER FAILURE	Internal Failure In Engine Controller.
54	NO SYNC PICK-UP SIGNAL	No Fuel Sync Signal Detected During Engine Rotation.
55	[3]	Completion Of Fault Code Display By CHECK ENGINE Light.
62	CONTROLLER FAILURE EMR MILES NOT STORED	Unsuccessful Attempt To Update EMR Mileage In SBEC.
63	CONTROLLER FAILURE EEPROM WRITE DENIED	Unsuccessful Attempt To Write To An EEPROM Location By SBEC.

[1] – Actual message displayed on DRB-II may vary between vehicles.
[2] – If code is displayed, charging system malfunction exists. See appropriate ALTERNATORS & REGULATORS article in ELECTRICAL.
[3] – No display on DRB-II.

5) When DRB-II is finished erasing fault codes, it will display FAULTS ERASED. This display will remain until ATM key is pressed. After ATM key is pressed, display will return to FUEL/IGN MENU screen.

CLEARING FAULT CODES

NOTE: Fault codes can also be cleared in READ FAULTS mode of DRB-II. To ensure all faults are read, use READ FAULTS mode to erase fault codes. See DRB-II DIAGNOSTIC MODE under ENTERING ON-BOARD DIAGNOSTICS.

1) If DRB-II is not available, go to step **3)**. If DRB-II is available, enter FUEL/IGN MENU. See FUEL/IGN MENU under DRB-II TEST FUNCTIONS. At FUEL/IGN MENU, press "5" (ADJUSTMENTS) key. Press ENTER key. At ADJUSTMENTS menu, press "1" (ERASE FAULTS) key. Press ENTER key.
2) DRB-II will display ERASE FAULTS ARE YOU SURE? (ENTER TO ERASE). Press ENTER key. When DRB-II is finished erasing fault codes, screen will display FAULTS ERASED.
3) If DRB-II is not available, fault codes may be cleared by disconnecting negative battery cable for at least 15 seconds, allowing SBEC to clear fault codes.

SUMMARY

If no hard fault codes (or only pass codes) are present, driveability symptoms exist or intermittent codes exist, proceed to appropriate TROUBLE SHOOTING – NO CODES article for diagnosis by symptom (i.e., ROUGH IDLE, NO START, etc.) or intermittent diagnostic procedures.

DRB-II TEST FUNCTIONS

WARNING: When battery is disconnected, vehicle computer and memory systems may lose memory data. Driveability problems may exist until computer systems have completed a relearn cycle. See COMPUTER RELEARN PROCEDURES article in GENERAL INFORMATION before disconnecting battery.

FUEL/IGN MENU

NOTE: DO NOT touch DRB-II keypad during DRB-II power-up sequence or an error message will result.

1) In order to perform self-diagnostic tests using DRB-II, DRB-II must be in the FUEL/IGN MENU. At the FUEL/IGN MENU, fault codes and DRB-II test functions can be accessed.

2) To reach FUEL/IGN MENU, turn ignition off. Connect DRB-II to engine diagnostic connector, located in engine compartment, near SBEC on all models except Dakota. On Dakota models, diagnostic connector is located in right rear corner of engine compartment, taped to harness. Turn ignition switch to RUN position.
3) All DRB-II character positions will glow and copyright information will appear on screen for a few seconds. If screen is blank or any error messages appear, see DRB-II PROBLEMS & ERROR MESSAGES.
4) After a few seconds, DRB-II menu will appear. At DRB-II menu, press "4" (SELECT SYSTEM) key. Press ENTER key. At SELECT SYSTEM menu, press "1" (ENGINE) key. Press ENTER key. DRB-II screen will indicate engine year, size, type of transmission and SBEC part number.
5) After a few seconds, AIR COND menu will appear. Press "1" (WITH A/C) or "2" (WITHOUT A/C). DRB-II display will change to ENGINE SYSTEMS menu. At ENGINE SYSTEMS menu, press "1" (FUEL/IGNITION) key. Press ENTER key.
6) Display will change to FUEL/IGN MENU. At FUEL/IGN MENU of engine diagnostic program, specific test functions programmed into DRB-II can be performed. The following DRB-II modes can be accessed: SYSTEM TESTS, READ FAULTS, STATE DISPLAY, ACTUATOR TESTS and ADJUSTMENTS.
SYSTEM TESTS Mode – This mode is not available in the engine diagnostics program.
READ FAULTS Mode – This mode allows user to read and erase fault codes. A fault counter will appear along with fault displayed. As an example, DRB-II will display 1 OF 2 FAULTS. SBEC will store up to 8 fault messages. Faults are numbered in reverse order of setting. The most recent fault to occur will be displayed first. Vehicles without air conditioning will always have A/C CLUTCH RELAY CKT (circuit) stored in memory. This fault will always be displayed first if vehicle is not equipped with A/C. If no fault messages are stored, DRB-II will display NO FAULTS DETECTED and start counter will show 0 STARTS SINCE ERS (erased).

A start counter will appear below DRB-II fault counter display. Start counter counts the number of times vehicle is started since faults were last set or erased or battery was disconnected. This helps determine if fault is intermittent. Memory space limits start counter to first 3 faults. Start counter of zero equals a hard fault. Start counter of more than zero indicates an intermittent fault. Start counter will count up to 255 starts. If no fault messages are stored, DRB-II will display NO FAULTS DETECTED and start counter will show 0 STARTS SINCE ERS (erased).

STATE DISPLAY Mode – This mode provides access to FUEL/IGN STATE menu. FUEL/IGN STATE menu permits viewing groups of data regarding the SBEC, sensor and switch inputs, controlled outputs, and predetermined or user selectable groups of data. The following modes can be accessed from the FUEL/IGN STATE menu: MODULE INFO, SENSORS, INPUTS/OUTPUTS, MONITORS and CUSTOM DISPLAYS. For information about the function of these modes, see FUEL/IGN STATE MENU.

ACTUATOR TESTS Mode – This mode allows the user to check for proper operation of output circuits or devices which the SBEC cannot internally recognize. DRB-II allows SBEC to activate these outputs or devices, allowing an observer to verify proper operation.

Most of the tests available in this mode provide an audible or visual indication of device operation (click of relay contacts, spray fuel, etc.). With the exception of an intermittent condition, if a device functions properly during its test, the device, wiring and its driver circuit are presumably functioning properly.

ADJUSTMENTS Mode – This mode allows the opportunity to make adjustments to SBEC memory. The following modes can be accessed from the ADJUSTMENTS menu: ERASE FAULTS, RESET MEMORY and EMR MEMORY CHECK. For information about the function of these modes, see ADJUSTMENTS MENU.

ADJUSTMENTS MENU

ERASE FAULTS Mode – This mode erases fault messages which are stored in SBEC memory. Once this mode is selected, DRB-II displays ARE YOU SURE?. If fault erasure is not desired, press ATM key. If fault erasure is desired, press ENTER key. All faults and secondary indicators will be erased.

RESET MEMORY Mode – This mode provides a sub-menu listing resettable memories. As vehicle is operated, SBEC learns to adjust fuel delivery, automatic idle speed motor position and minimum throttle position sensor signal voltage to compensate for different engine operating conditions. The following modes can be accessed from the RESET MEMORY menu: ADAPTIVE FUEL, AIS COUNTER, MINIMUM TPS and ALL VALUES. For additional information about the function of these modes, see RESET MEMORY MENU.

EMR MEMORY CHECK Mode – This mode allows the user to check and correct mileage stored in SBEC (if necessary). See EMISSION MAINTENANCE REMINDER (EMR) MILEAGE TRANSFER.

FUEL/IGN STATE MENU

MODULE INFO Mode – Mode displays model year, engine displacement, emission type, transmission type and SBEC part number.

SENSORS Mode – This mode provides a list of sensors and their input value to the SBEC.

INPUTS/OUTPUTS Mode – This mode provides a list of input switch and output device circuits and status.

MONITORS Mode – This mode provides access to MONITORS menu. MONITORS menu displays up to 12 inputs and outputs relating to a specific area of fuel and ignition system performance. The following modes can be accessed from the MONITORS menu: FUEL CONTROL, ADVANCE, RPM, ADAPTIVE MEM, NO START, INTERROGATOR and SEC INDICATORS. For additional information about the function of these modes, see MONITORS MENU.

CUSTOM DISPLAYS Mode – This mode allows the user to customize DRB-II display. The user can select up to 4 different displays which can be shown on a single screen. Any item from inputs/output list, sensor list or actuator list can be selected from custom display. Once selected, custom display will be retained in memory until changed. Up to 2 custom display screens can be customized by user.

MONITORS MENU

FUEL CONTROL Mode – This mode allows the user to display inputs and outputs which affect fuel delivery.

ADVANCE Mode – This mode allows the user to display inputs and outputs which affect ignition timing advance.

RPM Mode – This mode allows the user to display inputs and outputs which affect engine speed.

ADAPTIVE MEM Mode – This mode allows the user to display inputs and outputs which affect adaptive memory. As a vehicle is operated, SBEC learns to adjust fuel delivery, automatic idle speed motor posi-

tion and minimum throttle position sensor signal voltage to compensate for different engine operating conditions.

NO START Mode – This mode allows user to display inputs and outputs which affect engine starting.

INTERROGATOR Mode – This mode displays selectable inputs and outputs for use during the engineering process. This mode is not available in the engine diagnostics program.

SEC INDICATORS Mode – This mode allows user to display inputs and outputs which are not within optimum parameters but have not yet become faults. Secondary indicators are monitored by the DRB-II at all times after engine is selected in SELECT SYSTEM menu. When a secondary indicator is generated, DRB-II will emit 5 short beeps. If a secondary indicator becomes a hard fault, DRB-II red LED (light emitting diode) will glow.

RESET MEMORY MENU

ADAPTIVE FUEL Mode – This mode allows the user to erase SBEC memory of learned fuel delivery. As a vehicle is operated, SBEC learns to adjust fuel delivery, automatic idle speed motor position and minimum throttle position sensor signal voltage to compensate for different engine operating conditions.

AIS COUNTER Mode – This mode allows the user to erase SBEC memory of start-up Automatic Idle Speed (AIS) motor steps.

MINIMUM TPS Mode – This mode allows the user to erase SBEC memory of lowest Throttle Position Sensor (TPS) voltage.

ALL VALUES Mode – This mode allows the user to erase SBEC memory of adaptive fuel delivery, automatic idle speed motor position and minimum throttle position sensor signal voltage.

DRB-II VOLT/OHMMETER

1) To access volt/ohmmeter mode of DRB-II, connect Red volt/ohmmeter test lead to Red port, located on right top side of DRB-II.

NOTE: Because DRB-II is grounded through engine diagnostic connector, only one volt/ohmmeter test lead is required when using volt/ohmmeter option. DRB-II volt/ohmmeter should only be used when self-diagnostic tests require the use of this option.

2) To access voltmeter, press VOLT/OHM key once. DRB-II is now in voltmeter mode. Touch test probe to connector or wire to be measured. Read voltage on DRB-II display. When voltage testing is complete, press VOLT/OHM key 3 times to exit voltmeter mode.

3) To access ohmmeter, press VOLT/OHM key twice. DRB-II is now in ohmmeter mode. Touch test probe to connector or wire to be measured. Read resistance to circuit ground on DRB-II display. When resistance testing is complete, press VOLT/OHM key twice to exit ohmmeter mode.

DRB-II Continuity Meter Mode – Press VOLT/OHM key 3 times. Display will read NO CONTINUITY. Touch test probe to connector or wire to be measured. Read continuity on DRB-II display. When continuity testing is complete, press VOLT/OHM key once to exit continuity meter mode.

DRB-II PROBLEMS & ERROR MESSAGES

Blank Message Screen – **1)** Connect DRB-II to a different vehicle. If message screen is still blank, DRB-II or cable adapter is faulty. Substitute to find faulty component.

2) If message screen is not blank, DRB-II and cable adapter are functioning properly. Inspect diagnostic connector for proper wire placement, damaged terminals and pushed-out pins. Repair as necessary.

3) If engine diagnostic connector is okay, check for continuity between Black/tracer wire (tracer color may vary) and ground at engine diagnostic connector using an ohmmeter. If continuity does not exist, repair open in Black/tracer wire.

NO RESPONSE Message – **1)** Connect DRB-II to another vehicle. If DRB-II displays NO RESPONSE message again, DRB-II or cable adapter are faulty. Substitute to find faulty component. If message screen does not display NO RESPONSE, DRB-II and cable adapter are functioning properly. Go to next step.

2) Turn ignition off. Disconnect DRB-II. Using an ohmmeter, check Pink wire for continuity between SBEC connector terminal No. 25 and engine diagnostic connector. Check Pink wire for a short to ground. If continuity does not exist or wire is shorted to ground, repair open/shorted in Pink wire.

3) If continuity exists and wire is not shorted to ground, check Light Green wire for continuity between SBEC connector terminal No. 45 and engine diagnostic connector. Check Light Green wire for a short to ground. If continuity does not exist or wire is shorted to ground, repair open/shorted in Light Green wire. If all systems check okay, replace SBEC. Reset EMR mileage.

Other Failure Messages – If BAD FRAMING, CARTRIDGE ERROR, LOW BATTERY, BAD OP CODE, HIGH BATTERY, RAM TEST FAILURE, COMMAND REJECTED or KEYPAD TEST FAILURE Message is displayed, see VEHICLE COMMUNICATIONS article in ENGINE PERFORMANCE.

EMISSION MAINTENANCE REMINDER (EMR) MILEAGE TRANSFER

1) When SBEC is replaced, vehicle mileage must be copied from odometer to replacement SBEC memory. Transfer of vehicle mileage will enable new SBEC to operate EMR light properly.

2) Using DRB-II, enter FUEL/IGN MENU. See DRB-II TEST FUNCTIONS. At FUEL/IGN menu, press "5" (ADJUSTMENTS) key. Press ENTER key. At ADJUSTMENTS menu, press "3" (EMR MEMORY CHECK) key. Press ENTER key. DRB-II will display EMR MEMORY CHECK ARE YOU SURE? ENTER TO CONTINUE.

3) Press ENTER key. DRB-II will display IS INSTRUMENT PANEL MILEAGE BETWEEN XXXXX AND XXXXX? If vehicle mileage is within specification, EMR memory check is complete. Press YES key. If vehicle mileage is not within specification, go to next step.

4) Press NO key. DRB-II will display ENTER MILEAGE SHOWN ON INSTRUMENT PANEL, USE ENTER KEY TO END. Enter vehicle mileage. DO NOT enter tenths. When correct vehicle mileage is entered, press ENTER key.

5) DRB-II will ask for verification of mileage entry. If mileage entry was accurate, press ENTER key. DRB-II will display EMR MEMORY CHECK TEST COMPLETE. Vehicle must travel at least 8 miles for reset to occur.

FUEL PRESSURE RELEASE

WARNING: Always relieve fuel pressure before disconnecting any fuel injection-related component. DO NOT allow fuel to contact engine or electrical components.

Relieving Fuel Pressure (2.5L, 3.0L, 3.3L & 5.9L) – 1) Slowly open fuel tank cap to release pressure in tank. To release remaining pressure in system, disconnect injector wiring harness connector. Ground injector harness connector terminal No. 1 using jumper wire. *See Figs. 1-3.*

2) Using a second jumper wire, apply battery voltage to injector harness connector terminal No. 2. DO NOT apply battery voltage to terminal No. 2 for more than 5 seconds. Remove jumper wires. Connect injector wiring harness connector. Fuel pressure is now fully released.

Relieving Fuel Pressure (3.9L & 5.2L) – 1) Disconnect negative battery cable. Slowly open fuel tank cap to release pressure in tank. To release remaining pressure in system, remove protective cap from pressure test port on fuel rail. Remove gauge from hose in Fuel Pressure Gauge Set (5069).

2) Place one end of hose into an approved gasoline container. Place shop towel under test port. To release fuel pressure, screw other end of hose onto fuel pressure test port. After fuel pressure has been released, remove hose from test port. Install protective cap on pressure test port.

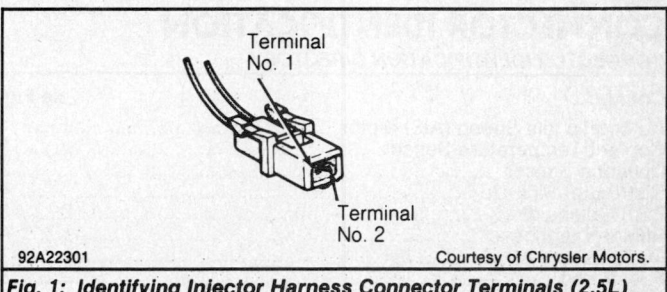

92A22301   Courtesy of Chrysler Motors.

Fig. 1: Identifying Injector Harness Connector Terminals (2.5L)

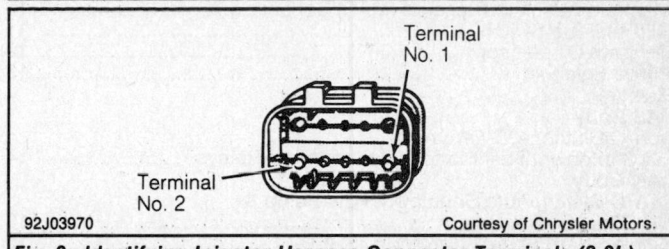

92J03970   Courtesy of Chrysler Motors.

Fig. 2: Identifying Injector Harness Connector Terminals (3.0L)

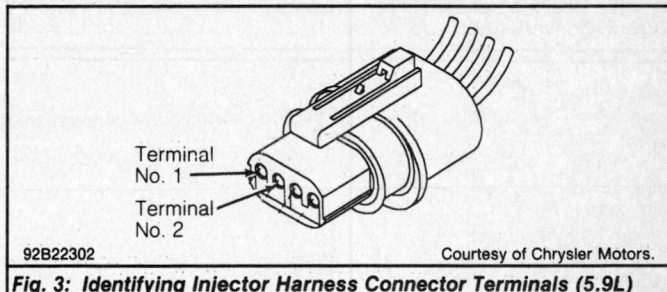

92B22302   Courtesy of Chrysler Motors.

Fig. 3: Identifying Injector Harness Connector Terminals (5.9L)

1992 ENGINE PERFORMANCE
Self-Diagnostic Tests – 2.5L TBI

WARNING: *When battery is disconnected, vehicle computer and energy systems may lose memory data. Driveability problems may exist until computer systems have completed a relearn cycle. See* **COMPUTER RELEARN PROCEDURES** *article in* **GENERAL INFORMATION** *before disconnecting battery.*

SELF-DIAGNOSTIC DIRECTORY
SELF-DIAGNOSTIC DIRECTORY

CONNECTOR IDENTIFICATION
CONNECTOR IDENTIFICATION DIRECTORY

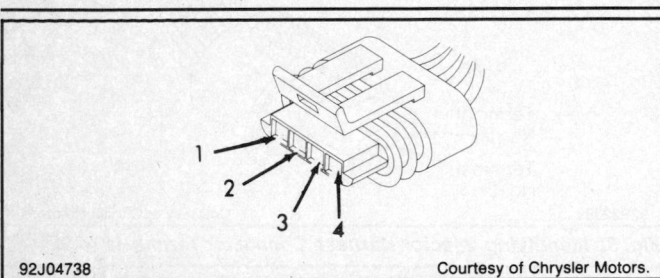

92J04738   Courtesy of Chrysler Motors.

Fig. 1: Identifying Automatic Idle Speed (AIS) Motor Connector Terminals

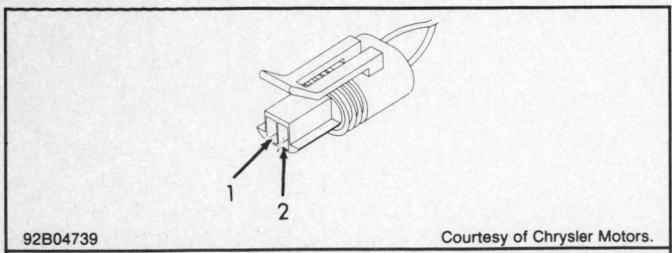

92B04739   Courtesy of Chrysler Motors.

Fig. 2: Identifying Coolant Temperature Sensor Connector Terminals

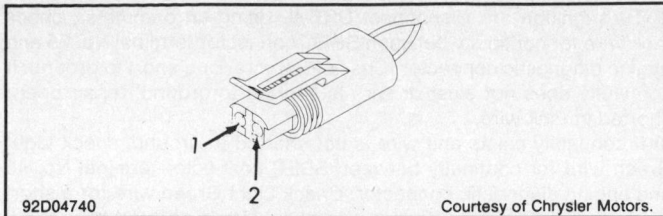

92D04740   Courtesy of Chrysler Motors.

Fig. 3: Identifying Distance Sensor Connector Terminals

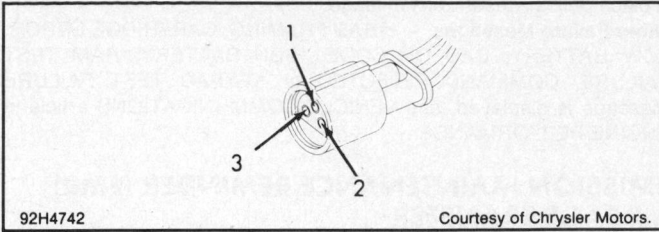

92H4742   Courtesy of Chrysler Motors.

Fig. 4: Identifying Distributor Pick-Up Connector Terminals

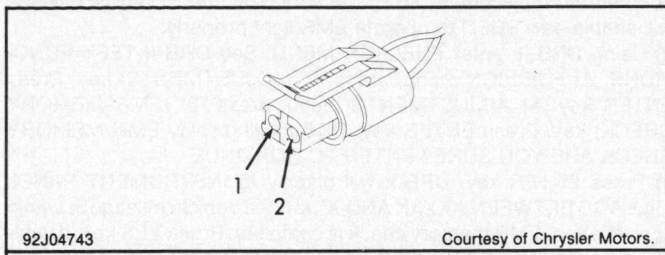

92J04743   Courtesy of Chrysler Motors.

Fig. 5: Identifying EGR Solenoid Connector Terminals

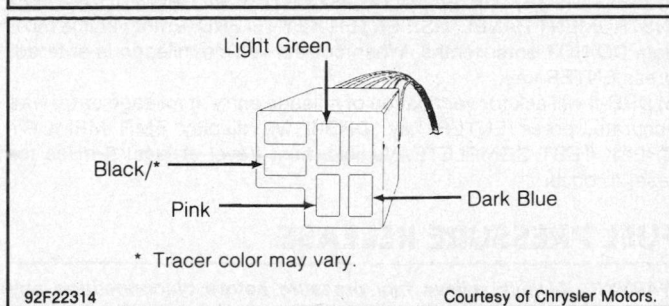

Light Green

Black/*

Pink

Dark Blue

* Tracer color may vary.

92F22314   Courtesy of Chrysler Motors.

Fig. 6: Identifying Engine Diagnostic Connector Terminals

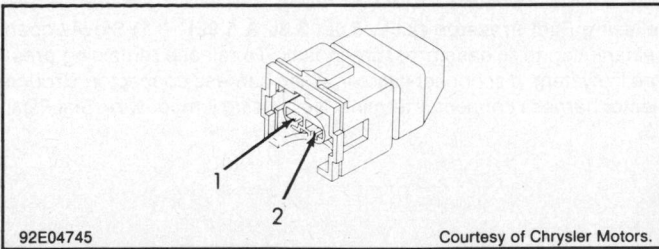

92E04745   Courtesy of Chrysler Motors.

Fig. 7: Identifying Fuel Injector Connector Terminals

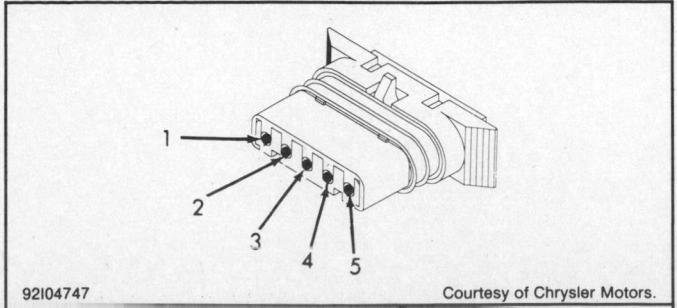

92I04747   Courtesy of Chrysler Motors.

Fig. 8: Identifying Fuel Pump Harness Connector Terminals

1992 ENGINE PERFORMANCE
Self-Diagnostic Tests – 2.5L TBI (Cont.)

CHRY
1-43

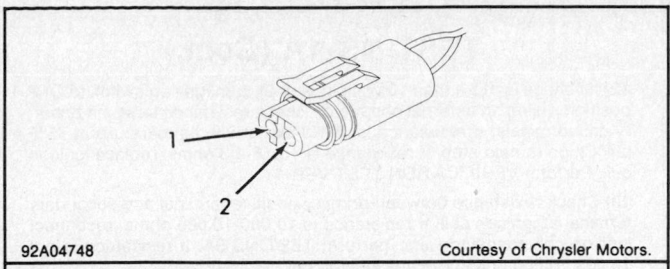

92A04748   Courtesy of Chrysler Motors.

Fig. 9: Identifying Ignition Coil Connector Terminals

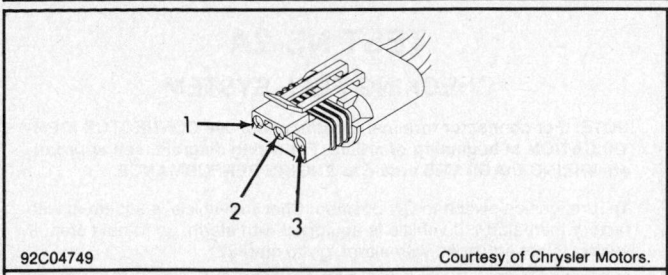

92C04749   Courtesy of Chrysler Motors.

Fig. 10: Identifying Manifold Absolute Pressure (MAP) Sensor Connector Terminals

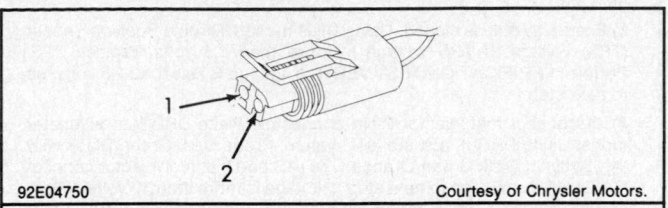

92E04750   Courtesy of Chrysler Motors.

Fig. 11: Identifying Oil Pressure Switch Connector Terminals

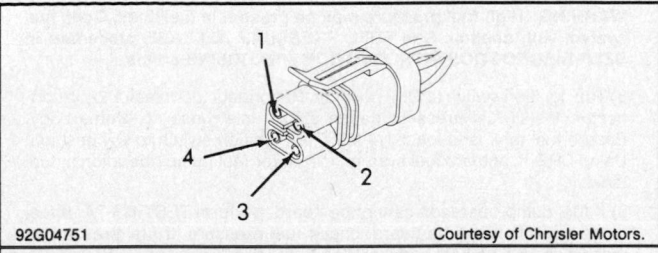

92G04751   Courtesy of Chrysler Motors.

Fig. 12: Identifying Oxygen (O₂) Sensor Connector Terminals

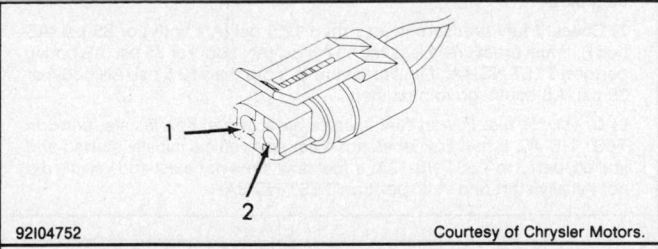

92I04752   Courtesy of Chrysler Motors.

Fig. 13: Identifying Purge Solenoid Connector Terminals

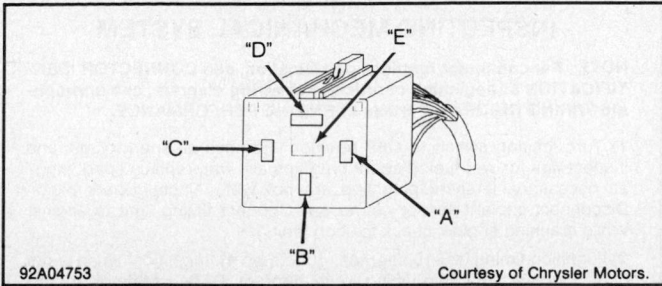

92A04753   Courtesy of Chrysler Motors.

Fig. 14: Identifying Relay Connector Terminals (AS Body)

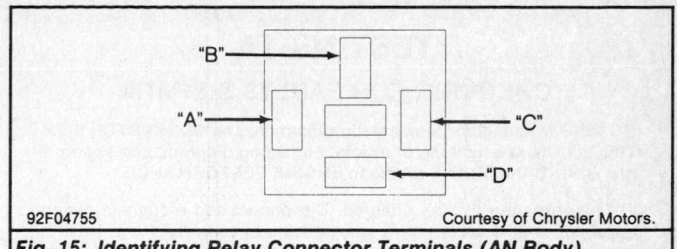

92F04755   Courtesy of Chrysler Motors.

Fig. 15: Identifying Relay Connector Terminals (AN Body)

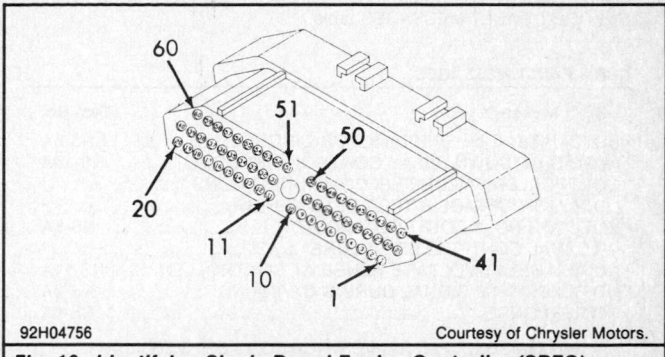

92H04756   Courtesy of Chrysler Motors.

Fig. 16: Identifying Single Board Engine Controller (SBEC) Connector Terminals

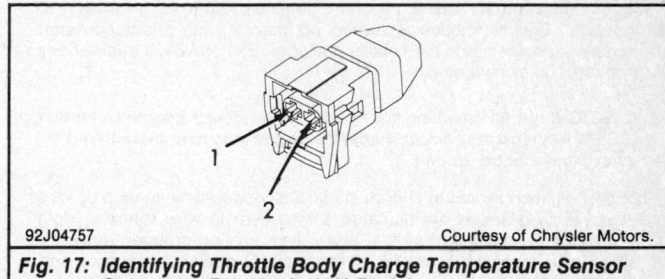

92J04757   Courtesy of Chrysler Motors.

Fig. 17: Identifying Throttle Body Charge Temperature Sensor Connector Terminals (AN Body)

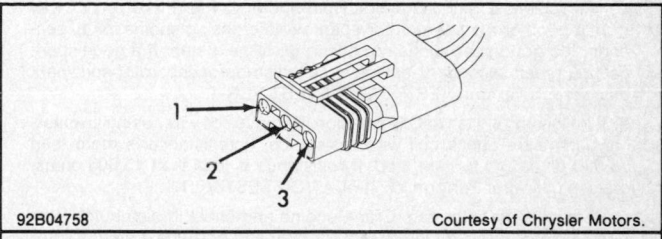

92B04758   Courtesy of Chrysler Motors.

Fig. 18: Identifying Throttle Position Sensor Connector Terminals

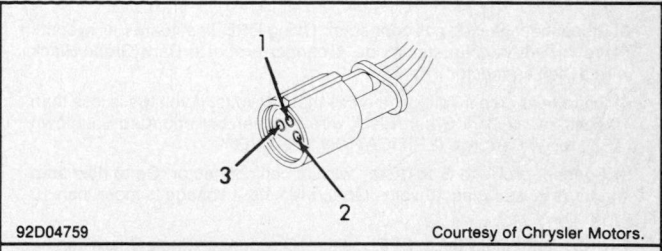

92D04759   Courtesy of Chrysler Motors.

Fig. 19: Identifying Torque Converter Lock-Up Solenoid Connector Terminals

SELF-DIAGNOSTIC TESTS

NOTE: In the following self-diagnostic tests, illustrations are courtesy of Chrysler Motors.

1992 ENGINE PERFORMANCE
Self-Diagnostic Tests – 2.5L TBI (Cont.)

TEST NS-1A

CHECKING FOR FAULTS & SPARK

NOTE: For connector terminal identification, see CONNECTOR IDEN-
TIFICATION at beginning of article. For wiring diagram, see appropriate WIRING DIAGRAMS article in ENGINE PERFORMANCE.

1) Ensure battery is fully charged. Disconnect and reconnect battery
quick disconnect cable. Try to start engine by cranking for at least 10
seconds. Ensure ignition is turned off before each attempt to start
engine. Turn ignition switch to ON position. Read faults using DRB-II.
See DRB-II FAULT MESSAGES table.

DRB-II FAULT MESSAGES

DRB-II Message	Test No.
AUTOMATIC IDLE SPEED MOTOR CIRCUITS	NS-6A
AUTO SHUTDOWN RELAY CONTROL CIRCUIT	NS-10A
CONTROLLER FAILURE SPI COMMUNICATIONS	1
COOLANT VOLTAGE & TPS VOLTAGE HIGH	2
INJECTOR NO. 1 CONTROL CIRCUIT	NS-5A
INTERNAL CONTROLLER FAILURE	1
NO ASD RELAY VOLTAGE SENSE AT CONTROLLER	NS-11A
NO REFERENCE SIGNAL DURING CRANKING	NS-9A
NO RESPONSE	NS-8A

1 - Replace SBEC. Perform VERIFICATION TEST VER-1.
2 - Repair open Black/Light Blue wire at SBEC connector terminal
   No. 4. Perform VERIFICATION TEST VER-1.

2) If no faults are displayed, try to start engine by cranking for at least 10
seconds. Ensure ignition is turned off before each attempt to start
engine. If engine starts then stalls, perform TEST NS-2A. If engine does
not start, go to next step.

**CAUTION: When checking for spark, Single Board Engine Controller
(SBEC) damage may occur if spark plug cable is held more than 1/4"
away from a good ground.**

3) Turn ignition switch to OFF position. Disconnect any spark plug wire
at spark plug. Insert an insulated screwdriver in wire terminal. Hold
screwdriver a maximum of 1/4" away from a good ground. Watch for
spark while cranking engine for 10 seconds. If a good spark occurs, perform TEST NS-2A. If a good spark does not occur, go to next step.

4) Turn ignition switch to OFF position. Reconnect spark plug wire. Disconnect coil wire from distributor. Hold coil wire a maximum of 1/4" away
from a good ground. Watch for spark while cranking engine for 10 seconds. If a good spark does not occur, go to next step. If a good spark
occurs, repair secondary ignition circuit (distributor cap, rotor and spark
plug wires). Perform VERIFICATION TEST VER-1.

5) Turn ignition switch to OFF position. Remove coil wire. Using an external ohmmeter, check coil wire resistance. If resistance is more than
15,000 ohms, go to next step. If resistance is less than 15,000 ohms,
replace coil wire. Perform VERIFICATION TEST VER-1.

6) Remove distributor cap. Crank engine and check if distributor rotor
turns. If rotor turns, install distributor cap, and go to next step. If rotor
does not turn, repair distributor drive components. Perform VERIFICA-
TION TEST VER-1.

7) Disconnect ignition coil connector. Using DRB-II, actuate fuel system.
Place DRB-II in voltmeter mode. Connect probe to Dark Green/Black
wire at coil connector.

8) Go to next step if voltage is more than 10 volts. If voltage is less than
10 volts, repair Dark Green/Black wire between coil and Auto Shutdown
(ASD) relay. Perform VERIFICATION TEST VER-1.

9) Connect probe to Black/Gray wire at coil connector. Go to next step
if voltage is less than 10 volts. Go to step **12)** if voltage is more than 10
volts.

10) Turn ignition switch to OFF position. Disconnect Single Board Engine
Controller (SBEC) connector. Place DRB-II in ohmmeter mode. Connect
ohmmeter probe to terminal No. 19 (Black/Gray wire) at SBEC connector. If resistance is less than 10 ohms, go to next step. If resistance is
more than 10 ohms, repair short to ground in ignition coil circuit. Perform
VERIFICATION TEST VER-1.

11) Check resistance at Black/Gray wire between coil connector and terminal
No. 19 at SBEC connector using an external ohmmeter. Replace
SBEC if resistance is more than 10 ohms. If resistance is less than 10
ohms, repair open in Black/Gray wire. Perform VERIFICATION TEST
VER-1.

TEST NS-1A (Cont.)

12) If voltage is more than 10 volts in step **9)**, turn ignition switch to OFF
position. Using an external ohmmeter, check resistance between primary coil terminals. If resistance is .8-1.3 ohms with temperature at 75°F
(24°C), go to next step. If resistance is not .8-1.3 ohms, replace ignition
coil. Perform VERIFICATION TEST VER-1.

13) Check resistance between primary positive terminal and secondary
terminal at ignition coil. If resistance is 10,000-16,000 ohms, reconnect
ignition coil connector, and perform TEST NS-9A. If resistance is not
10,000-16,000 ohms, replace ignition coil.

TEST NS-2A

CHECKING FUEL SYSTEM

NOTE: For connector terminal identification, see CONNECTOR IDEN-
TIFICATION at beginning of article. For wiring diagram, see appropriate WIRING DIAGRAMS article in ENGINE PERFORMANCE.

1) Turn ignition switch to ON position. Check if vehicle is equipped with
factory theft alarm. If vehicle is equipped with alarm, go to next step. If
vehicle is not equipped with alarm, go to step **3)**.

2) Read theft alarm status using DRB-II. If DRB-II does not display FUEL
ON, perform theft alarm test. See BODY CONTROL COMPUTER article.
Perform VERIFICATION TEST VER-1. If DRB-II displays FUEL ON, go to
next step.

3) Ensure throttle is closed. Using DRB-II, read Throttle Position Sensor
(TPS) voltage. If TPS voltage is more than 1.5 volts, replace TPS.
Perform VERIFICATION TEST VER-1. If voltage is less than 1.5 volts, go
to next step.

4) Disconnect fuel injector 2-pin connector. Place DRB-II in voltmeter
mode. Using DRB-II, actuate fuel system. Probe Dark Green/Black wire
(AN body) or Dark Green/Orange wire (AS body) at fuel injector connector. On all models, go to next step if voltage is more than 10 volts. If voltage is less than 10 volts, repair open in Dark Green/Black or Dark Green/
Orange wire.

**WARNING: High fuel pressure may be present in fuel lines. Open fuel
system with caution. See FUEL PRESSURE RELEASE procedure in
SELF-DIAGNOSTICS INTRODUCTION – GASOLINE article.**

5) Turn ignition switch to OFF position. Reconnect fuel injector 2-pin connector. Install fuel pressure gauge at fuel inlet hose at throttle body.
Ensure fuel tank is at least 1/4 full. Turn ignition switch to ON position.
Using DRB-II, actuate fuel system. Listen for fuel pump operation at fuel
tank.

6) If fuel pump operation cannot be heard, perform TEST NS-7A. If fuel
pump operation can be heard, check fuel pressure. If fuel pressure is
more than 16.5 psi (AN body) or 43 psi (AS body), perform TEST NS-4B.
If fuel pressure is less than 16.5 psi (AN body) or 43 psi (AS body), go to
next step.

7) Check if fuel pressure is less than 12.5 psi (AN body) or 35 psi (AS
body). If fuel pressure is less than 12.5 psi (AN body) or 35 psi (AS body),
perform TEST NS-4A. If fuel pressure is more than 12.5 psi (AN body) or
35 psi (AS body), go to next step.

8) Check for fuel flow at fuel injector area. If fuel flow exists, perform
TEST NS-4C. If fuel flow does not exist and vehicle initially started and
stalled, perform TEST NS-12A. If fuel flow does not exist and vehicle did
not initially start and stall, perform TEST NS-3A.

TEST NS-3A

INSPECTING MECHANICAL SYSTEM

NOTE: For connector terminal identification, see CONNECTOR IDEN-
TIFICATION at beginning of article. For wiring diagram, see appropriate WIRING DIAGRAMS article in ENGINE PERFORMANCE.

1) Turn ignition switch to OFF position. Remove all spark plugs, and
inspect tips for wet fuel. If spark plug tips are wet, replace spark plugs
as necessary. If spark plug tips are not wet, reinstall spark plugs.
Disconnect coolant sensor connector. Connect timing light to engine.
While cranking engine, check ignition timing.

2) If ignition timing is 0-16 degrees, go to step **4)**. If ignition timing is not
0-16 degrees, set basic timing to 12 degrees BTDC. Attempt to start
engine. If engine starts, go to next step. If engine does not start, check

1992 ENGINE PERFORMANCE
Self-Diagnostic Tests – 2.5L TBI (Cont.)

CHRY
1-45

TEST NS-3A (Cont.)

for valve timing, compression or other mechanical failure. Repair as necessary. Perform VERIFICATION TEST VER-1.

3) Check intermediate shaft and valve timing. If engine condition is not okay, repair as necessary; if engine condition is okay, test is complete. Perform VERIFICATION TEST VER-1.

4) If ignition timing is 0-16 degrees in step 2), inspect secondary ignition cables for correct placement. If secondary cables are not positioned correctly, reinstall secondary cables as necessary. Perform VERIFICATION TEST VER-1. If all secondary cables are positioned correctly, go to next step.

5) Turn ignition switch to OFF position. Disconnect Single Board Engine Controller (SBEC). Disconnect Manifold Absolute Pressure (MAP) sensor. Using an external ohmmeter, check resistance of Violet/White wire between terminal No. 6 at SBEC connector and terminal No. 3 at MAP sensor connector. If resistance is less than 10 ohms, go to next step. If resistance is more than 10 ohms, repair open in Violet/White wire. Perform VERIFICATION TEST VER-1.

6) Check valve timing and compression. If valve timing and compression are within specification, replace MAP sensor. Perform VERIFICATION TEST VER-1. If valve timing and compression are not within specification, repair engine as necessary. Perform VERIFICATION TEST VER-1.

TEST NS-4A

CHECKING FUEL DELIVERY

WARNING: High fuel pressure may be present in fuel lines. Open fuel system with caution. See FUEL PRESSURE RELEASE procedure in SELF-DIAGNOSTICS INTRODUCTION – GASOLINE article.

1) Record fuel pressure gauge reading. Turn ignition switch to OFF position. Release fuel pressure. Remove fuel pressure gauge. Install fuel pressure gauge between fuel tank and fuel filter. Reconnect previously disconnected fuel line.

2) With ignition switch in ON position, actuate fuel system using DRB-II. Record fuel pressure gauge reading. Compare reading with previous reading. If fuel pressure is not 10 psi more than previous reading, go to next step. If fuel pressure is 10 psi more than previous reading, go to step 4).

CAUTION: DO NOT allow fuel pressure to exceed 50 psi when squeezing fuel return hose.

3) Gently squeeze fuel return hose while watching fuel pressure gauge. If fuel pressure exceeds 12.5 psi (AN body) or 35 psi (AS body), replace fuel pressure regulator. Perform VERIFICATION TEST VER-1. If fuel pressure does not exceed 12.5 psi (AN body) or 35 psi (AS body), replace fuel pump and filter sock. Perform VERIFICATION TEST VER-1.

4) If fuel pressure is 10 psi more in step 2), check for fuel line restriction between fuel filter and throttle body. Repair as necessary. Perform VERIFICATION TEST VER-1. If restriction does not exist, replace fuel filter. Perform VERIFICATION TEST VER-1.

TEST NS-4B

CHECKING FUEL DELIVERY

WARNING: High fuel pressure may be present in fuel lines. Open fuel system with caution. See FUEL PRESSURE RELEASE procedure in SELF-DIAGNOSTICS INTRODUCTION – GASOLINE article.

1) Turn ignition switch to OFF position. Ensure fuel tank is at least 1/4 full before beginning this test. Relieve system fuel pressure. Remove fuel return hose from throttle body. Connect a 6' fuel hose to fuel return fitting at throttle body.

2) Place other end of hose into an approved 2-gallon gasoline container. Using DRB-II, actuate fuel system. Check fuel pressure. If fuel pressure is more than 16.5 psi (AN body) or 43 psi (AS body), replace fuel pressure regulator. Perform VERIFICATION TEST VER-1. If fuel pressure is less than 16.5 psi (AN body) or 43 psi (AS body), go to next step.

3) Turn ignition switch to OFF position. Reconnect fuel return hose at throttle body. Remove fuel return hose from fuel tank. Connect a 6' hose to disconnected fuel return hose. Place other end of hose into an approved 2-gallon gasoline container.

TEST NS-4B (Cont.)

4) Turn ignition switch to ON position. Using DRB-II, actuate fuel system. Check fuel pressure. If pressure is less than 16.5 psi (AN body) or 43 psi (AS body), replace restricted fuel tank return assembly. Perform VERIFICATION TEST VER-1. If fuel pressure is more than 16.5 psi (AN body) or 43 psi (AS body), repair restricted fuel return line between throttle body and fuel tank. Perform VERIFICATION TEST VER-1.

TEST NS-4C

CHECKING FUEL DELIVERY

NOTE: For connector terminal identification, see CONNECTOR IDENTIFICATION at beginning of article. For wiring diagram, see appropriate WIRING DIAGRAMS article in ENGINE PERFORMANCE.

1) Check if top of fuel pressure regulator is leaking fuel. If top of fuel pressure regulator is leaking, replace fuel pressure regulator. Perform VERIFICATION TEST VER-1. If top of fuel pressure regulator is not leaking, go to next step.

2) Turn ignition switch to OFF position. Remove injector, and inspect injector seals for damage. If seals are damaged, replace fuel injector seals. Perform VERIFICATION TEST VER-1. If seals are not damaged, go to next step.

3) Turn ignition switch to OFF position. Disconnect Single Board Engine Controller (SBEC) connector. Put DRB-II in ohmmeter mode. Probe terminal No. 16 (White/Dark Blue wire) at SBEC connector.

4) If resistance is less than 10 ohms, repair short to ground in White/Dark Blue wire. Perform VERIFICATION TEST VER-1. If resistance is more than 10 ohms, replace fuel injector. Perform VERIFICATION TEST VER-1.

TEST NS-5A

CODE 27, INJECTOR NO. 1 CONTROL CIRCUIT

NOTE: For connector terminal identification, see CONNECTOR IDENTIFICATION at beginning of article. For wiring diagram, see appropriate WIRING DIAGRAMS article in ENGINE PERFORMANCE.

1) Disconnect fuel injector connector at throttle body. Using DRB-II, actuate fuel system. Put DRB-II in voltmeter mode. Probe Dark Green/Black wire (AN body) or Dark Green/Orange wire (AS body).

2) If voltage is less than 10 volts, repair Dark Green/Orange or Dark Green/Black wire between injector and splice. Perform VERIFICATION TEST VER-1. If voltage is more than 10 volts, go to next step.

3) Turn ignition switch to OFF position. Using an external ohmmeter, measure resistance between injector cap terminals on throttle body. If resistance is .9-2.0 ohms, go to next step. If resistance in not .9-2.0 ohms, go to step 6).

4) Disconnect Single Board Engine Controller (SBEC) connector. Put DRB-II in ohmmeter mode. Probe terminal No. 16 (White/Dark Blue) at SBEC connector. If resistance is less than 10 ohms, repair short to ground in White/Dark Blue wire. Perform VERIFICATION TEST VER-1. If resistance is more than 10 ohms, go to next step.

5) Using an external ohmmeter, measure resistance in White/Dark Blue wire between terminal No. 16 at SBEC connector and fuel injector. If resistance is less than 10 ohms, replace SBEC. Perform VERIFICATION TEST VER-1. If resistance is more than 10 ohms, repair open White/Dark Blue wire. Perform VERIFICATION TEST VER-1.

6) If resistance is not .9-2.0 ohms in step 3), gently remove injector cap from injector using 2 screwdrivers. Using an external ohmmeter, measure resistance across injector terminals. If resistance is .9-2.0 ohms, replace injector cap wiring harness assembly. Perform VERIFICATION TEST VER-1. If resistance is not .9-2.0 ohms, replace fuel injector. Perform VERIFICATION TEST VER-1.

TEST NS-6A

CODE 25, AUTOMATIC IDLE SPEED (AIS) MOTOR CIRCUITS

NOTE: For connector terminal identification, see CONNECTOR IDENTIFICATION at beginning of article. For wiring diagram, see appropriate WIRING DIAGRAMS article in ENGINE PERFORMANCE.

CHRY
1-46

1992 ENGINE PERFORMANCE
Self-Diagnostic Tests – 2.5L TBI (Cont.)

TEST NS-6A (Cont.)

1) Disconnect AIS motor connector. Using DRB-II, actuate AIS motor. Put DRB-II in voltmeter mode. Probe Gray/Red wire in AIS motor connector. When normal, voltage will switch from less than one volt to more than 10 volts.

2) If voltage is less than one volt, repair short to ground in Gray/Red wire. Perform VERIFICATION TEST VER-1. If voltage is more than one volt, check if voltage is more than 10 volts. If voltage is more than 10 volts, repair short to voltage in Gray/Red wire. Perform VERIFICATION TEST VER-1. If voltage is less than 10 volts, go to next step.

3) Probe Yellow/Black wire in AIS motor connector. If voltage is less than one volt, repair short to ground in Yellow/Black wire. If voltage is more than one volt, check if voltage is more than 10 volts. If voltage is more than 10 volts, Yellow/Black wire is shorted to Brown/White wire. Repair wiring as necessary. Perform VERIFICATION TEST VER-1. If voltage is less than 10 volts, go to next step.

4) Probe Violet/Black wire in AIS motor connector. If voltage is less than one volt, repair short to ground in Violet/Black wire. Perform VERIFICATION TEST VER-1. If voltage is more than one volt, turn ignition switch to OFF position.

5) Reconnect AIS motor connector. Disconnect Single Board Engine Controller (SBEC) connector. Using an external ohmmeter, check resistance between terminals No. 39 (Gray/Red wire) and 59 (Violet/Black wire). If resistance is less than 10 ohms, Yellow/Black wire is shorted to Gray/Red wire. Repair wiring as necessary. Perform VERIFICATION TEST VER-1. If resistance is more than 10 ohms, go to next step.

6) Check if resistance is less than 75 ohms. If resistance is less than 75 ohms, go to next step. If resistance is more than 75 ohms, check if resistance is more than 120 ohms. If resistance is more than 120 ohms, replace SBEC. Perform VERIFICATION TEST VER-1. If resistance is less than 120 ohms, Brown/White wire is shorted to Violet/Black wire. Repair wiring as necessary. Perform VERIFICATION TEST VER-1.

7) Using an external ohmmeter, check resistance at SBEC connector between terminal No. 60 (Yellow/Black wire) and terminal 59 (Violet/Black wire). If resistance is less than 10 ohms, Yellow/Black wire is shorted to Violet/Black wire. Repair wiring as necessary. Perform VERIFICATION TEST VER-1. If resistance is more than 10 ohms, Gray/Red wire is shorted to Brown/White wire. Repair wiring as necessary. Perform VERIFICATION TEST VER-1.

TEST NS-7A

CHECKING FUEL PUMP (AS BODY)

NOTE: For connector terminal identification, see CONNECTOR IDENTIFICATION at beginning of article. For wiring diagram, see appropriate WIRING DIAGRAMS article in ENGINE PERFORMANCE.

NOTE: On AN body, perform TEST NS-7C.

1) Using DRB-II, stop actuation test. Actuate Auto Shutdown (ASD) relay. Check fuel pump relay to see if relay pulsates with actuation. See Fig. NS-7A. If relay does not pulsate, perform TEST NS-7B. If fuel pump relay pulsates, go to next step.

92C22303

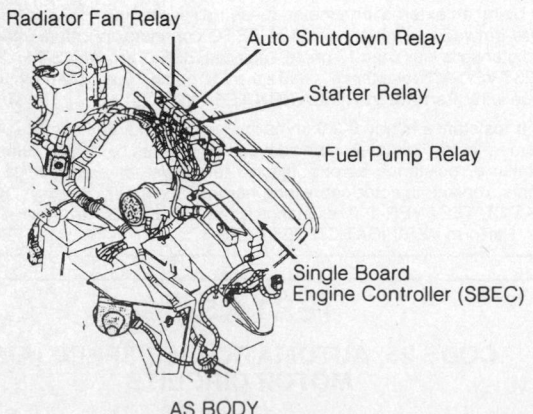

Fig. NS-7A: Locating Relays (AS Body)

TEST NS-7A (Cont.)

2) Using DRB-II, stop actuation test. Disconnect fuel pump relay. Turn ignition switch to ON position. Place DRB-II in voltmeter mode. Probe Red/White wire in fuel pump relay connector. If voltage is less than 10 volts, repair open in Red/White wire. Perform VERIFICATION TEST VER-1. If voltage is more than 10 volts, go to next step.

3) Disconnect fuel pump wiring harness connector. Reconnect fuel pump relay connector. Using DRB-II, actuate fuel system. Place DRB-II in voltmeter mode. Probe terminal No. 1 (Dark Green/Black wire) in fuel pump connector. If voltage is more than 10 volts, go to next step. If voltage is less than 10 volts, go to step 5).

4) Using DRB-II, stop actuation test. Place DRB-II in ohmmeter mode. Probe terminal No. 5 (Black wire) in fuel pump connector. Replace fuel pump if resistance is less than 5 ohms. Perform VERIFICATION TEST VER-1. If resistance is more than 5 ohms, repair open Black wire. Perform VERIFICATION TEST VER-1.

5) If voltage is less than 10 volts at Dark Green/Black wire in step 3), turn ignition switch to OFF position. Disconnect fuel pump relay. Using an external ohmmeter, check resistance of Dark Green/Black wire between fuel pump connector and fuel pump relay connector.

6) If resistance is less than 10 ohms, replace fuel pump relay. Perform VERIFICATION TEST VER-1. If resistance is more than 10 ohms, repair open Dark Green/Black wire. Perform VERIFICATION TEST VER-1.

TEST NS-7B

CHECKING FUEL PUMP (AS BODY)

NOTE: For connector terminal identification, see CONNECTOR IDENTIFICATION at beginning of article. For wiring diagram, see appropriate WIRING DIAGRAMS article in ENGINE PERFORMANCE.

1) Turn ignition switch to OFF position. Disconnect fuel pump relay. See Fig. NS-7A. Put DRB-II in voltmeter mode. Turn ignition switch to ON position. Probe terminal "A" (Dark Blue wire) at relay connector. If voltage is less than 10 volts, repair open in Dark Blue wire. Perform VERIFICATION TEST VER-1. If voltage is more than 10 volts, go to next step.

2) Using an external ohmmeter, check resistance between terminals "A" and "C" at fuel pump relay. If resistance is more than 100 ohms, replace fuel pump relay. Perform VERIFICATION TEST VER-1. If resistance is less than 100 ohms, repair open Dark Blue/Yellow wire. Perform VERIFICATION TEST VER-1.

TEST NS-7C

CHECKING FUEL PUMP (AN BODY)

NOTE: For connector terminal identification, see CONNECTOR IDENTIFICATION at beginning of article. For appropriate wiring diagrams, see WIRING DIAGRAMS article in ENGINE PERFORMANCE.

1) Using DRB-II, actuate fuel system. Check Auto Shutdown (ASD) relay to see if relay pulsates with actuation. See Fig. NS-7C. If ASD relay fails to pulsate with actuation, perform TEST NS-7D. If ASD relay pulsates with actuation, go to next step.

92J04762

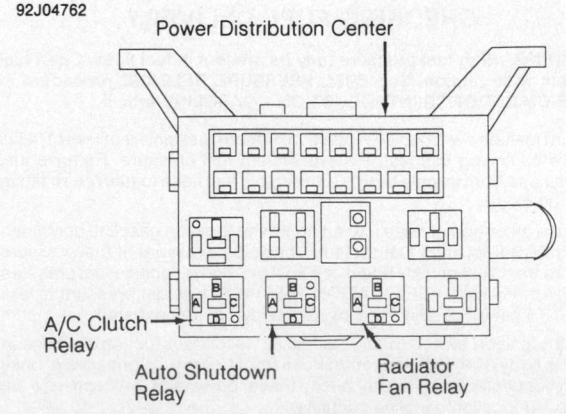

Fig. NS-7C: Locating Relays (AN Body)

1992 ENGINE PERFORMANCE
Self-Diagnostic Tests – 2.5L TBI (Cont.)

CHRY
1-47

TEST NS-7C (Cont.)

2) Using DRB-II, stop actuation test. Disconnect ASD relay. Turn ignition switch to ON position. Put DRB-II in voltmeter mode. Probe terminal "B" (Red/White wire) at ASD relay connector. If voltage is less than 10 volts, repair open Red/White wire. Perform VERIFICATION TEST VER-1. If voltage is more than 10 volts, go to next step.

3) Disconnect fuel pump harness connector, and reconnect ASD relay. Using DRB-II, actuate fuel system. Put DRB-II into voltmeter mode. Probe terminal No. 1 (Dark Green/Black wire) in fuel pump connector. If voltage is less than 10 volts, go to next step. If voltage is more than 10 volts, go to step **6)**.

4) Turn ignition switch to OFF position. Disconnect ASD relay. Using an external ohmmeter, check resistance between terminal No. 1 (Dark Green/Black wire) at fuel pump connector and terminal "D" (Dark Green/Orange wire) at ASD relay.

NOTE: Dark Green/Black wire changes to Dark Green/Orange wire between fuel pump connector and ASD relay connector.

5) If resistance is less than 5 ohms, replace fuel pump relay. Perform VERIFICATION TEST VER-1. If resistance is more than 5 ohms, repair open Dark Green/Black or Dark Green/Orange wire. Perform VERIFICATION TEST VER-1.

6) If voltage is more than 10 volts at Dark Green/Black wire in step **3)**, stop actuation test using DRB-II. Put DRB-II in ohmmeter mode. Probe terminal No. 5 (Black wire) in fuel pump connector. If resistance is less than 5 ohms, replace fuel pump. Perform VERIFICATION TEST VER-1. If resistance is more than 5 ohms, repair open in Black wire. Perform VERIFICATION TEST VER-1.

TEST NS-7D

CHECKING FUEL PUMP (AN BODY)

NOTE: For connector terminal identification, see CONNECTOR IDENTIFICATION at beginning of article. For wiring diagram, see appropriate WIRING DIAGRAMS article in ENGINE PERFORMANCE.

1) Turn ignition switch to OFF position. Disconnect Auto Shutdown (ASD) relay. See Fig. NS-7C. Turn ignition switch to ON position. Probe terminal "A" (Dark Blue) wire at ASD connector. If voltage is less than 10 volts, repair open Dark Blue wire. Perform VERIFICATION TEST VER-1. If voltage is more than 10 volts, go to next step.

2) Using an external ohmmeter, measure resistance between terminals "A" and "C" at ASD relay. If resistance is less than 100 ohms, repair open Dark Blue/Yellow wire. Perform VERIFICATION TEST VER-1. If resistance is more than 100 ohms, replace ASD relay. Perform VERIFICATION TEST VER-1.

TEST NS-8A

REPAIRING NO RESPONSE CONDITION

NOTE: For connector terminal identification, see CONNECTOR IDENTIFICATION at beginning of article. For wiring diagram, see appropriate WIRING DIAGRAMS article in ENGINE PERFORMANCE.

1) Disconnect Throttle Position Sensor (TPS) connector. Turn ignition switch to ON position. Place DRB-II in voltmeter mode. Probe terminal No. 3 (Violet/White wire) at TPS connector. If voltage is less than 6 volts, go to next step. If voltage is more than 6 volts, repair open between terminals No. 5 (Black/White wire) and 11 (Black/Tan wire) or 12 (Black/Tan wire) at Single Board Engine Controller (SBEC). Repair as necessary. Perform VERIFICATION TEST VER-1.

2) If voltage in step **1)** is less than 4.4 volts, go to step **3)**. If voltage is more than 4.4 volts, reconnect TPS connector. Disconnect Manifold Absolute Pressure (MAP) sensor connector. Probe terminal No. 3 (Violet/White wire) at MAP sensor connector. If voltage is more than 4.4 volts, go to NO RESPONSE MESSAGE under DRB-II PROBLEMS & ERROR MESSAGES in SELF-DIAGNOSTICS INTRODUCTION – GASOLINE article. If voltage is less than 4.4 volts, replace TPS sensor. Perform VERIFICATION TEST VER-1.

3) If voltage is less than 4.4 volts at Violet/White wire in step **1)**, disconnect MAP sensor connector. Probe terminal No. 3 (Violet/White wire) at connector. If voltage is more than 4.4 volts, replace MAP sensor. Perform VERIFICATION TEST VER-1. If voltage is less than 4.4 volts, go to next step.

TEST NS-8A (Cont.)

4) Turn ignition switch to OFF position. Disconnect SBEC connector. Place DRB-II in ohmmeter mode. Probe terminal No. 6 (Violet/White) at SBEC connector. If resistance is less than 10 ohms, repair short to ground in Violet/White wire. Perform VERIFICATION TEST VER-1. If resistance is more than 10 ohms, go to next step.

5) Turn ignition switch to ON position. Place DRB-II in voltmeter mode. Probe terminal No. 9 (Dark Blue wire) at SBEC connector. If voltage is less than 10 volts, repair open in Dark Blue wire between SBEC and ignition switch. Perform VERIFICATION TEST VER-1. If voltage is more than 10 volts, go to next step.

6) Probe SBEC connector terminal No. 3 (Red/White wire). If voltage is more than 10 volts, replace SBEC. Perform VERIFICATION TEST VER-1. If voltage is less than 10 volts, put DRB-II in ohmmeter mode. Probe SBEC connector terminal No. 3. If resistance is less than 10 ohms, repair short to ground in Red/White wire between battery and SBEC. Perform VERIFICATION TEST VER-1. If resistance is more than 10 ohms, go to next step.

7) Inspect fused circuit between battery and terminal No. 3 at SBEC connector. If fused circuit is okay, repair open in Red/White wire between terminal No. 3 at SBEC connector and battery. Perform VERIFICATION TEST VER-1. If fused circuit is not okay, disconnect Auto Shutdown (ASD) relay. See Fig. NS-7A or NS-7C. Place DRB-II in ohmmeter mode.

8) Probe Dark Green/Orange wire in ASD relay connector. If resistance is more than 10 ohms, go to step **10)**. If resistance is less than 10 ohms, disconnect ignition coil connector. If resistance is still less than 10 ohms, go to next step. If resistance is now more than 10 ohms, replace ignition coil. Replace fuse or fusible link. Perform VERIFICATION TEST VER-1.

9) Disconnect fuel injector connector at throttle body. If resistance is more than 10 ohms, check if fuel injector cap wire lead is shorted to ground. Replace injector cap wire assembly as necessary. Perform VERIFICATION TEST VER-1. If wire is okay, replace fuel injector. Perform VERIFICATION TEST VER-1. If resistance is less than 10 ohms, repair short in Dark Green/Orange wire. Replace fuse or fusible link. Perform VERIFICATION TEST VER-1.

10) If resistance at Dark Green/Orange wire in step **8)** is more than 10 ohms, reconnect ASD relay. On AN body, disconnect fuel pump connector. Disconnect O₂ sensor connector. Probe terminal "D" (Dark Green/Orange wire) in ASD relay. If resistance is less than 10 ohms, repair short to ground in Dark Green/Orange wire. Replace fuse or fusible link. Perform VERIFICATION TEST VER-1. If resistance is more than 10 ohms, go to step **12)**.

11) On AS bodies, disconnect fuel pump relay. See Fig. NS-7A. Disconnect fuel pump and O₂ sensor connectors. Probe terminal "D" (Dark Green/Black wire) in fuel pump relay connector. If resistance is less than 10 ohms, repair short to ground in Dark Green/Black wire. Replace fuse or fusible link. Perform VERIFICATION TEST VER-1. If resistance is more than 10 ohms, go to next step.

12) On all models, probe Dark Green/Black wire in O₂ sensor connector. If resistance is less than 10 ohms, replace O₂ sensor. Replace fuse or fusible link. Perform VERIFICATION TEST VER-1. If resistance is more than 10 ohms, replace fuel pump. Replace fuse or fusible link. Perform VERIFICATION TEST VER-1.

TEST NS-9A

CODE 11, NO REFERENCE SIGNAL DURING CRANKING

NOTE: For connector terminal identification, see CONNECTOR IDENTIFICATION at beginning of article. For wiring diagram, see appropriate WIRING DIAGRAMS article in ENGINE PERFORMANCE.

CAUTION: When checking for spark, Single Board Engine Controller (SBEC) damage may occur if spark plug cable is held more than 1/4" away from a good ground.

1) Turn ignition switch to OFF position. Disconnect distributor pick-up connector. Disconnect coil wire from distributor. Hold coil wire a maximum of 1/4" away from a good ground. Turn ignition switch to ON position. Connect a jumper wire between terminals No. 2 (Black/Light Blue wire) and 3 (Gray/Black wire) at distributor pick-up connector.

2) Make and break jumper connection while checking for spark at coil wire. If a good spark does not occur, remove jumper wire, and go to next step. If a good spark occurs, perform TEST NS-9B.

CHRY
1-48

1992 ENGINE PERFORMANCE
Self-Diagnostic Tests – 2.5L TBI (Cont.)

TEST NS-9A (Cont.)

3) Connect jumper wire between terminal No. 3 (Gray/Black wire) of distributor pick-up connector and ground. While still holding coil wire a maximum of 1/4" away from a good ground, make and break jumper connection at terminal No. 3 and watch for spark at coil wire. If a good spark does not occur, remove jumper wire, and go to next step. If a good spark occurs, repair open in Black/Light Blue wire. Perform VERIFICATION TEST VER-1.

4) Turn ignition switch to OFF position. Disconnect Single Board Engine Controller (SBEC) connector. Put DRB-II in ohmmeter mode. Probe terminal No. 24 (Gray/Black wire) at SBEC connector. If resistance is less than 10 ohms, repair short to ground in Gray/Black wire. Perform VERIFICATION TEST VER-1. If resistance is more than 10 ohms, go to next step.

5) Using an external ohmmeter, measure resistance of Gray/Black wire between terminal No. 24 at SBEC connector and terminal No. 3 at distributor pick-up connector. If resistance is less than 10 ohms, replace SBEC. Perform VERIFICATION TEST VER-1. If resistance is more than 10 ohms, repair open in Gray/Black wire. Perform VERIFICATION TEST VER-1.

TEST NS-9B

CODE 11, NO REFERENCE SIGNAL DURING CRANKING

NOTE: For connector terminal identification, see CONNECTOR IDENTIFICATION at beginning of article. For wiring diagram, see appropriate WIRING DIAGRAMS article in ENGINE PERFORMANCE.

1) Remove jumper wire. Place DRB-II in voltmeter mode. Probe Orange wire in distributor pick-up connector. If voltage is more than 7 volts, go to next step. If voltage is less than 7 volts, go to step 3).

2) Turn ignition switch to OFF position. Remove distributor cap. Crank engine while watching distributor rotor. If rotor turns, replace distributor plate (Hall Effect pick-up); if distributor rotor does not turn, repair distributor drive system. Perform VERIFICATION TEST VER-1.

3) If voltage is less than 7 volts at Orange wire in step 1), check if voltage is zero volts. If voltage is zero volts, go to step 5). If voltage is more than zero volts, turn ignition switch to OFF position. Disconnect Single Board Engine Controller (SBEC) connector.

4) Using an external ohmmeter, check resistance of Orange wire between terminal No. 7 at SBEC connector and terminal No. 1 at distributor pick-up connector. If resistance is less than 10 ohms, replace SBEC. Perform VERIFICATION TEST VER-1. If resistance is more than 10 ohms, repair open Orange wire. Perform VERIFICATION TEST VER-1.

5) If voltage is zero volts at Orange wire in step 3), turn ignition switch to OFF position. Disconnect SBEC connector. Place DRB-II in ohmmeter mode. Probe terminal No. 7 (Orange wire) of SBEC connector. If resistance is less than 10 ohms, repair short to ground in Orange wire. Disconnect and reconnect battery quick disconnect. Perform VERIFICATION TEST VER-1. If resistance is more than 10 ohms, go to next step.

6) Using an external ohmmeter, check resistance of Orange wire between terminal No. 1 at distributor connector and terminal No. 7 at SBEC connector. If resistance is less than 10 ohms, replace SBEC. Perform VERIFICATION TEST VER-1. If resistance is more than 10 ohms, repair open Orange wire. Perform VERIFICATION TEST VER-1.

TEST NS-10A

CODE 42, AUTO SHUTDOWN (ASD) RELAY CONTROL CIRCUIT

NOTE: For connector terminal identification, see CONNECTOR IDENTIFICATION at beginning of article. For wiring diagram, see appropriate WIRING DIAGRAMS article in ENGINE PERFORMANCE.

1) Turn ignition switch to ON position. Disconnect Auto Shutdown (ASD) relay. See Fig. NS-7A or NS-7C. Place DRB-II in voltmeter mode. Probe terminal "A" (Dark Blue wire) in ASD relay connector. If voltage is less than 10 volts, repair open Dark Blue wire. Perform VERIFICATION TEST VER-1. If voltage is more than 10 volts, go to next step.

2) Using an external ohmmeter, check resistance between ASD relay terminals "A" and "C". If resistance is more than 100 ohms, replace ASD

TEST NS-10A (Cont.)

relay. Perform VERIFICATION TEST VER-1. If resistance is less than 100 ohms, go to next step.

3) Turn ignition switch to OFF position. Disconnect Single Board Engine Controller (SBEC) connector. Using an external ohmmeter, check resistance of Dark Blue/Yellow wire between terminal No. 51 of SBEC and terminal "C" at ASD relay connector.

4) If resistance is less than 10 ohms, replace SBEC. Perform VERIFICATION TEST VER-1. If resistance is more than 10 ohms, repair open Dark Blue/Yellow wire. Perform VERIFICATION TEST VER-1.

TEST NS-11A

CODE 42, AUTO SHUTDOWN (ASD) RELAY CONTROL CIRCUIT

NOTE: For connector terminal identification, see CONNECTOR IDENTIFICATION at beginning of article. For wiring diagram, see appropriate WIRING DIAGRAMS article in ENGINE PERFORMANCE.

1) Disconnect ignition coil connector. Using DRB-II, actuate fuel system. Put DRB-II in voltmeter mode. Probe terminal No. 1 at ignition coil connector. Terminal No. 1 is Dark Green/Black wire on AS body or Dark Green/Orange wire on AN body.

2) If voltage is more than 10 volts, go to step 4). If voltage is less than 10 volts, turn ignition switch to OFF position. Disconnect Single Board Engine Controller (SBEC) connector. Disconnect Auto Shutdown (ASD) relay connector. See Fig. NS-7A or NS-7C.

3) Using an external ohmmeter, measure resistance of Dark Green/Orange wire between terminal "D" at ASD relay connector and terminal No. 57 at SBEC connector. If resistance is more than 10 ohms, repair open Dark Green/Orange wire. Perform VERIFICATION TEST VER-1. If resistance is less than 10 ohms, replace SBEC. Perform VERIFICATION TEST VER-1.

4) If voltage is more than 10 volts in step 2), turn ignition switch to OFF position. Disconnect SBEC connector. Disconnect ASD relay. See Fig. NS-7A or NS-7C. Using an external ohmmeter, measure resistance of Dark Green/Orange wire between terminal No. 57 at SBEC connector and terminal "D" at ASD relay connector. If resistance is more than 10 ohms, repair open Dark Green/Orange wire. Perform VERIFICATION TEST VER-1. If resistance is less than 10 ohms, go to next step.

5) Put DRB-II in voltmeter mode. Probe Red/White wire at ASD connector. If voltage is less than 10 volts, repair open Red/White wire. Perform VERIFICATION TEST VER-1. If voltage is more than 10 volts, replace ASD relay. Perform VERIFICATION TEST VER-1.

TEST NS-12A

CHECKING AUTOMATIC IDLE SPEED (AIS) MOTOR OPERATION

NOTE: For connector terminal identification, see CONNECTOR IDENTIFICATION at beginning of article. For wiring diagram, see appropriate WIRING DIAGRAMS article in ENGINE PERFORMANCE.

1) Turn ignition switch to ON position. Using DRB-II, actuate AIS motor. Disconnect AIS motor connector. Place DRB-II in voltmeter mode. Probe terminal No. 1 (Gray/Red wire) at AIS connector. If voltage at Gray/Red wire is less than one volt, perform TEST NS-12B. If voltage at Gray/Red wire is more than one volt, go to next step.

2) Probe terminal No. 3 (Brown/White wire) at AIS connector. If voltage is less than one volt, perform TEST NS-12C. If voltage is more than one volt, go to next step.

3) Probe Violet/Black wire at AIS connector. If voltage is less than one volt, perform TEST NS-12D. If voltage is more than one volt, go to next step.

4) Probe Yellow/Black wire at AIS connector. If voltage is less than one volt, perform TEST NS-12E. If voltage is more than one volt, go to next step.

5) Remove AIS motor from throttle body. Reconnect AIS motor connector. Actuate AIS motor. If AIS motor tip moves in and out, perform TEST NS-13A. If idle speed motor tip does not move in and out, replace AIS motor. Perform VERIFICATION TEST VER-1.

1992 ENGINE PERFORMANCE
Self-Diagnostic Tests – 2.5L TBI (Cont.)

CHRY
1-49

TEST NS-12B

CHECKING AUTOMATIC IDLE SPEED (AIS) MOTOR OPERATION

NOTE: For connector terminal identification, see CONNECTOR IDENTIFICATION at beginning of article. For wiring diagram, see appropriate WIRING DIAGRAMS article in ENGINE PERFORMANCE.

1) Turn ignition switch to OFF position. Disconnect Single Board Engine Controller (SBEC) connector. Inspect connector. If connector is okay, go to next step. If connector is not okay, repair as necessary. Perform VERIFICATION TEST VER-1.

2) Using an external ohmmeter, check resistance of Gray/Red wire between terminal No. 1 at AIS motor connector and terminal No. 39 at SBEC connector. If resistance is less than 10 ohms, replace SBEC. Perform VERIFICATION TEST VER-1. If resistance is more than 10 ohms, repair open Gray/Red wire. Perform VERIFICATION TEST VER-1.

TEST NS-12C

CHECKING AUTOMATIC IDLE SPEED (AIS) MOTOR OPERATION

NOTE: For connector terminal identification, see CONNECTOR IDENTIFICATION at beginning of article. For wiring diagram, see appropriate WIRING DIAGRAMS article in ENGINE PERFORMANCE.

1) Turn ignition switch to OFF position. Disconnect Single Board Engine Controller (SBEC) connector. Inspect connector. If connector is okay, go to next step. If connector is not okay, repair as necessary. Perform VERIFICATION TEST VER-1.

2) Using an external ohmmeter, check resistance of Brown/White wire between terminal No. 3 at AIS motor connector and terminal No. 40 at SBEC connector. If resistance is less than 10 ohms, replace SBEC. Perform VERIFICATION TEST VER-1. If resistance is more than 10 ohms, repair open Brown/White wire. Perform VERIFICATION TEST VER-1.

TEST NS-12D

CHECKING AUTOMATIC IDLE SPEED (AIS) MOTOR OPERATION

NOTE: For connector terminal identification, see CONNECTOR IDENTIFICATION at beginning of article. For wiring diagram, see appropriate WIRING DIAGRAMS article in ENGINE PERFORMANCE.

1) Turn ignition switch to OFF position. Disconnect Single Board Engine Controller (SBEC) connector. Inspect connector. If connector is okay, go to next step. If connector is not okay, repair as necessary. Perform VERIFICATION TEST VER-1.

2) Using an external ohmmeter, check resistance of Violet/Black wire between terminal No. 4 at AIS motor connector and terminal No. 59 at SBEC connector. If resistance is less than 10 ohms, replace SBEC. Perform VERIFICATION TEST VER-1. If resistance is more than 10 ohms, repair open Violet/Black wire. Perform VERIFICATION TEST VER-1.

TEST NS-12E

CHECKING AUTOMATIC IDLE SPEED (AIS) MOTOR OPERATION

NOTE: For connector terminal identification, see CONNECTOR IDENTIFICATION at beginning of article. For wiring diagram, see appropriate WIRING DIAGRAMS article in ENGINE PERFORMANCE.

1) Turn ignition switch to OFF position. Disconnect Single Board Engine Controller (SBEC) connector. Inspect connector. If connector is okay, go to next step. If connector is not okay, repair as necessary. Perform VERIFICATION TEST VER-1.

2) Using an external ohmmeter, check resistance of Yellow/Black wire between terminal No. 2 at AIS motor connector and terminal No. 60 at SBEC connector. If resistance is less than 10 ohms, replace SBEC. Perform VERIFICATION TEST VER-1. If resistance is more than 10 ohms, repair open Yellow/Black wire. Perform VERIFICATION TEST VER-1.

TEST NS-13A

CORRECTING START & STALL CONDITION

At this point in diagnostic procedure, all engine control systems have been determined to be operating designed and not causing a no-start or start-and-stall problem. Following additional items should be checked as possible causes:
- Check if any MITCHELL® TECHNICAL SERVICE BULLETINS (TSBs) apply to vehicle.
- Check engine compression.
- Check for exhaust system restriction.
- Check camshaft and crankshaft sprockets.
- Check valve timing.
- Check torque converter stall speed.
- Check secondary ignition circuit for abnormal scope pattern.
- Check for fuel contamination.
- Ensure PCV system is functioning properly.

TEST DR-1A

CHECKING SYSTEM FOR FAULTS

NOTE: For connector terminal identification, see CONNECTOR IDENTIFICATION at beginning of article. For wiring diagram, see appropriate WIRING DIAGRAMS article in ENGINE PERFORMANCE. Battery must be fully charged and at rated capacity before performing any driveability test procedure. If vehicle starts and stalls repeatedly, perform TEST NS-2A. If vehicle stalls when A/C is turned on, perform TEST NF-9A.

1) Connect DRB-II to engine diagnostic connector. Turn ignition switch to ON position. Read fault messages. If DRB-II displays fault messages, go to step 5). If DRB-II does not display fault messages, go to next step.

2) Start engine. Allow engine to reach normal operating temperature. Set engine speed manually to 2000 RPM for at least 10 seconds, and return vehicle to idle. On A/T models, go to next step. On M/T models, go to step 4).

3) On A/T models, apply brakes. Shift gear selector through all gears, and return to PARK position. Using DRB-II, read fault messages. If fault messages are displayed, go to step 5). If fault messages are not displayed, go to next step.

4) On all models, check MITCHELL® TECH SERVICE BULLETINS (TSBs) for any pertinent information if DRB-II still displays NO FAULTS. If a TSB exists, perform corrective action. If driveability problem continues after performing TSB procedure or if no TSB information was found, perform TEST NF-1A.

5) If fault message is INTERNAL CONTROLLER FAILURE or CONTROLLER FAILURE, replace Single Board Engine Controller (SBEC). Perform VERIFICATION TEST VER-2. If fault message is not INTERNAL CONTROLLER FAILURE or CONTROLLER FAILURE, go to next step.

NOTE: ENGINE COLD TOO LONG fault message may set erroneously if ambient temperature is extremely cold.

6) If fault message is ENGINE COLD TOO LONG, check engine cooling system. Repair as required. Perform VERIFICATION TEST VER-3. If fault message is not ENGINE COLD TOO LONG, go to next step.

7) Using DRB-II FAULT MESSAGES table, select fault message and corresponding test. Correct all hard fault messages before proceeding to intermittent fault message.

CHRY
1-50

1992 ENGINE PERFORMANCE
Self-Diagnostic Tests – 2.5L TBI (Cont.)

TEST DR-1A (Cont.)

DRB-II FAULT MESSAGES

DRB-II Message	[1] Hard Fault	[2] Intermittent Fault
A/C CLUTCH RELAY CIRCUIT		
AN Body	DR-24A	DR-34A
AS Body	DR-25A	DR-34A
AIS MOTOR CIRCUITS	DR-17A	DR-33A
CHARGE TEMP SENSOR		
VOLTAGE HIGH	DR-13A	DR-32A
CHARGE TEMP SENSOR		
VOLTAGE LOW	DR-14A	DR-32A
CONTROLLER FAILURE EEPROM		
WRITE DENIED	DR-31A	DR-31A
CONTROLLER FAILURE EMR MILES		
NOT STORED	DR-31A	DR-31A
COOLANT SENSOR VOLTAGE		
TOO HIGH	DR-11A	DR-32A
COOLANT SENSOR VOLTAGE		
TOO LOW	DR-12A	DR-32A
EGR SOLENOID CIRCUIT	DR-19A	DR-34A
EGR SYSTEM FAILURE	DR-19A	DR-34A
MAP SENSOR VOLTAGE HIGH	DR-5A	DR-32A
MAP SENSOR VOLTAGE LOW	DR-4A	DR-32A
NO ASD RELAY VOLTAGE SENSE		
AT CONTROLLER	DR-27A	DR-34A
NO CHANGE IN MAP	DR-3A	DR-32B
NO VEHICLE SPEED SIGNAL	DR-6A	DR-6A
O₂ SENSOR SHORTED TO VOLTAGE	DR-8A	DR-32A
O₂ SENSOR STAYS		
ABOVE CENTER	DR-9A	DR-32A
O₂ SENSOR STAYS		
AT CENTER	DR-7A	DR-32A
O₂ SENSOR STAYS		
BELOW CENTER	DR-10A	DR-32A
PURGE SOLENOID CIRCUIT	DR-18A	DR-34A
RADIATOR FAN RELAY CIRCUIT	DR-26A	DR-34A
SLOW CHANGE IN MAP	DR-2A	DR-32B
THROTTLE POSITION SENSOR		
VOLTAGE HIGH	DR-15A	DR-32A
O₂ SENSOR STAYS		
VOLTAGE LOW	DR-16A	DR-32A
TORQUE CONVERTER LOCK-UP		
SOLENOID CHECK	DR-28A	DR-34A

[1] – Key counter is "0".
[2] – Key counter is more than "0".

TEST DR-2A

CODE 13, SLOW CHANGE IN IDLE MAP SIGNAL

NOTE: For connector terminal identification, see CONNECTOR IDENTIFICATION at beginning of article. For wiring diagram, see appropriate WIRING DIAGRAMS article in ENGINE PERFORMANCE.

1) Turn ignition switch to ON position. Using a vacuum "T", install vacuum gauge into vacuum hose at Manifold Absolute Pressure (MAP) sensor. Start engine, and let it idle. Observe vacuum gauge. If vacuum does not exist at idle, repair plugged or restricted vacuum hose to MAP sensor. Perform VERIFICATION TEST VER-2. If vacuum exists at idle, go to next step.

2) Snap throttle open and closed. Observe vacuum gauge. If vacuum gauge does not instantly drop to zero in. Hg and return, repair restricted vacuum hose to MAP sensor. Perform VERIFICATION TEST VER-2. If gauge instantly drops to zero and returns, go to next step.

3) Turn ignition switch to OFF position. Disconnect MAP sensor connector. Inspect connector. If connector is not okay, repair as necessary. Perform VERIFICATION TEST VER-2. If connector is okay, go to next step.

4) Turn ignition switch to ON position. Place DRB-II in voltmeter mode. Probe terminal No. 3 (Violet/White wire) at MAP sensor. If voltage is less than one volt, repair open Violet/White wire. Perform VERIFICATION TEST VER-2. If voltage is more than one volt, replace MAP sensor. Perform VERIFICATION TEST VER-2.

TEST DR-3A

CODE 13, NO CHANGE IN IDLE MAP SIGNAL

Turn ignition switch to ON position. Using a vacuum "T", install vacuum gauge into vacuum hose at Manifold Absolute Pressure (MAP) sensor. Start engine, and let it idle. Observe vacuum gauge. If vacuum does not exist at idle, repair leak in MAP sensor vacuum hose. Perform VERIFICATION TEST VER-2. If vacuum exists at idle, repair restriction in MAP sensor vacuum hose. Perform VERIFICATION TEST VER-2.

TEST DR-4A

CODE 14, MAP SENSOR VOLTAGE TOO LOW

NOTE: For connector terminal identification, see CONNECTOR IDENTIFICATION at beginning of article. For wiring diagram, see appropriate WIRING DIAGRAMS article in ENGINE PERFORMANCE.

1) Turn ignition switch to OFF position. Disconnect Manifold Absolute Pressure (MAP) sensor connector. Turn ignition switch to ON position. Read MAP sensor voltage. If voltage is more than 4.5 volts, replace MAP sensor. Perform VERIFICATION TEST VER-2. If voltage is less than 4.5 volts, go to next step.

2) Turn ignition switch to OFF position. Disconnect Single Board Engine Controller (SBEC). Place DRB-II in ohmmeter mode. Probe Dark Green/Red wire at MAP sensor connector. If resistance is less than 10 ohms, repair short to ground in Dark Green/Red wire. Perform VERIFICATION TEST VER-2. If resistance is more than 10 ohms, replace SBEC. Perform VERIFICATION TEST VER-2.

TEST DR-5A

Code 14, MAP SENSOR VOLTAGE TOO HIGH

NOTE: For connector terminal identification, see CONNECTOR IDENTIFICATION at beginning of article. For wiring diagram, see appropriate WIRING DIAGRAMS article in ENGINE PERFORMANCE.

1) Turn ignition switch to OFF position. Disconnect Manifold Absolute Pressure (MAP) sensor connector. Inspect connector. If connector is okay, go to next step. If connector is not okay, repair as necessary. Perform VERIFICATION TEST VER-2.

2) Connect a jumper wire between Dark Green/Red and Black/Light Blue wires at MAP sensor connector. Turn ignition switch to ON position. Read MAP sensor voltage.

3) If voltage is less than one volt, replace MAP sensor. Perform VERIFICATION TEST VER-2. If voltage is more than one volt, disconnect jumper wire. Reconnect jumper wire between Dark Green/Red wire at MAP sensor connector and ground. If voltage is less than one volt, repair open Black/Light Blue wire. Perform VERIFICATION TEST VER-2. If voltage is more than one volt, go to next step.

4) Disconnect Single Board Engine Controller (SBEC) connector. Inspect connector. If connector is okay, go to next step. If connector is not okay, repair as necessary. Perform VERIFICATION TEST VER-2.

5) Using an external ohmmeter, check resistance of Dark Green/Red wire between terminal No. 1 at SBEC connector and terminal No. 2 at MAP sensor connector. If resistance is more than 10 ohms, repair open Dark Green/Red wire. Perform VERIFICATION TEST VER-2. If resistance is less than 10 ohms, replace SBEC. Perform VERIFICATION TEST VER-2.

TEST DR-6A

CODE 15, NO VEHICLE SPEED SIGNAL

NOTE: For connector terminal identification, see CONNECTOR IDENTIFICATION at beginning of article. For wiring diagram, see appropriate WIRING DIAGRAMS article in ENGINE PERFORMANCE.

1) Turn ignition switch to OFF position. Disconnect distance sensor connector. Connector is located right of starter motor. Inspect connector. If connector is okay, go to next step. If connector is not okay, repair as necessary. Perform VERIFICATION TEST VER-2.

1992 ENGINE PERFORMANCE
Self-Diagnostic Tests – 2.5L TBI (Cont.)

CHRY
1-51

TEST DR-6A (Cont.)

2) Turn ignition switch to ON position. Connect a jumper wire to one terminal of distance sensor connector. Using DRB-II, monitor car speed while tapping other end of jumper wire to remaining distance sensor connector terminal.

3) If DRB-II shows speed to be more than zero, replace distance sensor. Perform VERIFICATION TEST VER-2. If speed is zero, place DRB-II in ohmmeter mode. Probe Black/Light Blue wire at distance sensor connector terminal. If resistance is more than 10 ohms, repair open Black/Light Blue wire. Perform VERIFICATION TEST VER-2. If resistance is less than 10 ohms, go to next step.

4) Turn ignition switch to OFF position. Disconnect Single Board Engine Controller (SBEC). Inspect terminal No. 47 (White/Orange wire) at SBEC connector for damage. If terminal is damaged, repair as necessary. Perform VERIFICATION TEST VER-2. If terminal is okay, go to next step.

5) Turn ignition switch to ON position. Place DRB-II in voltmeter mode. Probe terminal No. 47 (White/Orange wire) of SBEC connector. If voltage is more than 4 volts, go to step 7). If voltage is less than 4 volts, check if speedometer works. If speedometer works, repair open in White/Orange wire between sensor and SBEC. Perform VERIFICATION TEST VER-2. If speedometer does not work, go to next step.

6) Turn ignition switch to OFF position. Place DRB-II in ohmmeter mode. Probe terminal No. 47 of SBEC connector. If resistance is less than 5 ohms, repair short to ground in White/Orange wire. Perform VERIFICATION TEST VER-2. If resistance is more than 5 ohms, repair open White/Orange wire. Perform VERIFICATION TEST VER-2.

7) If voltage is more than 4 volts in White/Orange wire in step 5), probe White/Orange wire at distance sensor connector. Replace SBEC if voltage is more than 4 volts. Perform VERIFICATION TEST VER-2. If voltage is less than 4 volts, repair open in White/Orange wire between distance sensor and SBEC. Perform VERIFICATION TEST VER-2.

TEST DR-7A

CODE 21, OXYGEN (O$_2$) SENSOR SIGNAL STAYS AT CENTER

NOTE: For connector terminal identification, see CONNECTOR IDENTIFICATION at beginning of article. For wiring diagram, see appropriate WIRING DIAGRAMS article in ENGINE PERFORMANCE.

1) Turn ignition switch to OFF position. Disconnect O$_2$ sensor connector. Inspect connector. If connector is okay, go to next step. If connector is not okay, repair as necessary. Perform VERIFICATION TEST VER-2.

2) Turn ignition switch to ON position. Using a jumper wire, connect one end of jumper to Black/Dark Green wire of O$_2$ sensor connector. Connect other end of jumper wire to battery voltage. Read O$_2$ sensor voltage.

3) If voltage is less than one volt, go to step 5). If voltage is more than one volt, disconnect jumper wire. Turn ignition switch to OFF position. Place DRB-II in ohmmeter mode. Probe Black/Light Blue wire in O$_2$ sensor connector, and go to next step.

4) If resistance is more than 10 ohms, repair open Black/Light Blue wire; if resistance is less than 10 ohms, replace O$_2$ sensor. Perform VERIFICATION TEST VER-2.

5) If voltage is less than one volt in Black/Dark Green wire in step 2), disconnect jumper wire. Turn ignition switch to OFF position. Disconnect Single Board Engine Controller (SBEC) connector. Inspect SBEC connector. If connector is okay, go to next step. If connector is not okay, repair as necessary. Perform VERIFICATION TEST VER-2.

6) Using an external ohmmeter, check resistance of Black/Dark Green wire between O$_2$ sensor connector and terminal No. 41 of SBEC connector. If resistance is less than 10 ohms, replace SBEC. Perform VERIFICATION TEST VER-2. If resistance is more than 10 ohms, repair open Black/Dark Green wire. Perform VERIFICATION TEST VER-2.

TEST DR-8A

CODE 21, OXYGEN (O$_2$) SENSOR SHORTED TO VOLTAGE

NOTE: For connector terminal identification, see CONNECTOR IDENTIFICATION at beginning of article. For wiring diagram, see appropriate WIRING DIAGRAMS article in ENGINE PERFORMANCE.

TEST DR-8A (Cont.)

1) Start engine. Allow engine to idle for 2 minutes. Using DRB-II, read O$_2$ sensor voltage. If voltage is more than 1.3 volts, go to step 3). If voltage is less than 1.3 volts, go to next step.

2) Read O$_2$ sensor voltage while wiggling O$_2$ sensor wiring. If voltage is more than 1.3 volts, repair short to voltage in Black/Dark Green wire. Perform VERIFICATION TEST VER-2. If voltage is less than 1.3 volts, replace SBEC. Perform VERIFICATION TEST VER-2.

3) If voltage is more than 1.3 volts in step 1), disconnect O$_2$ sensor connector. If voltage is less than one volt when O$_2$ sensor connector is disconnected, replace O$_2$ sensor. Perform VERIFICATION TEST VER-2. If voltage is more than one volt when O$_2$ sensor connector is disconnected, repair Black/Dark Green wire for short to Dark Green/Black wire.

4) Reconnect O$_2$ sensor connector. Reset adaptive fuel value. Start engine, and let it idle for 2 minutes. Using DRB-II, read O$_2$ sensor value. If O$_2$ sensor switches from rich to lean, test is complete; if O$_2$ sensor does not switch from rich to lean, replace O$_2$ sensor. Perform VERIFICATION TEST VER-2.

TEST DR-9A

CODE 52, OXYGEN (O$_2$) SENSOR SIGNAL STAYS ABOVE CENTER

1) Allow engine to reach normal operating temperature. Turn engine off. Using DRB-II, actuate fuel system test. Inspect fuel injector for leakage. If injector is leaking, replace injector and/or "O" rings as necessary. Perform VERIFICATION TEST VER-2. If fuel injector is not leaking, go to next step.

2) Stop fuel system test. Inspect air cleaner filter and inlet ducts for restrictions. If restrictions exist, clean restricted air inlet system as necessary. Perform VERIFICATION TEST VER-2. If restrictions do not exist, perform TEST NF-13A.

TEST DR-10A

CODE 51, OXYGEN (O$_2$) SENSOR STAYS BELOW CENTER

Code 51 may set for several reasons not related to O$_2$ sensor or O$_2$ sensor circuits. If Code 51 sets, perform TEST NF-1A.

TEST DR-11A

CODE 22, COOLANT SENSOR VOLTAGE TOO HIGH

NOTE: For connector terminal identification, see CONNECTOR IDENTIFICATION at beginning of article. For wiring diagram, see appropriate WIRING DIAGRAMS article in ENGINE PERFORMANCE.

1) Turn ignition switch to OFF position. Disconnect and inspect coolant temperature sensor connector. If connector is okay, go to next step. If connector is not okay, repair connector as necessary. Perform VERIFICATION TEST VER-2.

2) Connect jumper wire between coolant temperature sensor connector terminals. Turn ignition switch to ON position. Read coolant temperature sensor voltage. If voltage is less than one volt, replace coolant temperature sensor. Perform VERIFICATION TEST VER-2. If voltage is more than one volt, go to next step.

3) Remove jumper wire. On AN body, reconnect jumper wire between Tan/White wire at coolant temperature sensor connector and ground. On AS body, reconnect jumper wire between Tan/Black wire at coolant temperature sensor connector and ground. On all models, read coolant temperature sensor voltage.

4) If voltage is less than one volt, repair open in Black/Light Blue wire. Perform VERIFICATION TEST VER-2. If voltage is more than one volt, disconnect and inspect Single Board Engine Controller (SBEC) connector. Repair connector if damaged. Perform VERIFICATION TEST VER-2. If connector is okay, go to next step.

5) On AN body, check resistance of Tan/White wire between coolant temperature sensor connector and terminal No. 2 of SBEC connector

CHRY
1-52

1992 ENGINE PERFORMANCE
Self-Diagnostic Tests – 2.5L TBI (Cont.)

TEST DR-11A (Cont.)

using an external ohmmeter. On AS body, check resistance between Tan/Black wire at coolant temperature sensor connector and terminal No. 2 of SBEC connector using an external ohmmeter.

6) On all models, replace SBEC if resistance is less than 10 ohms. Perform VERIFICATION TEST VER-2. If resistance is more than 10 ohms, repair open Tan/White wire (AN body) or Tan/Black wire (AS body) between coolant temperature sensor connector and SBEC connector terminal No. 2. Perform VERIFICATION TEST VER-2.

TEST DR-12A

CODE 22, COOLANT SENSOR VOLTAGE TOO LOW

NOTE: For connector terminal identification, see CONNECTOR IDENTIFICATION at beginning of article. For wiring diagram, see appropriate WIRING DIAGRAMS article in ENGINE PERFORMANCE.

1) Turn ignition switch to ON position. Using DRB-II, read coolant temperature sensor voltage. Disconnect coolant temperature sensor connector. If voltage changes more than 4 volts, replace coolant temperature sensor. Perform VERIFICATION TEST VER-2. If voltage does not change more than 4 volts, go to next step.

2) Turn ignition switch to OFF position. Disconnect Single Board Engine Controller (SBEC) connector. Place DRB-II in ohmmeter mode. Probe terminal No. 2 (Tan/White wire on AN body or Tan/Black wire on all other models) at SBEC connector. If resistance is less than 10 ohms, repair Tan/White wire (AN body) or Tan/Black wire (AS body) for a short to Black/Light Blue wire or ground. Perform VERIFICATION TEST VER-2. If resistance is more than 10 ohms, replace SBEC. Perform VERIFICATION TEST VER-2.

TEST DR-13A

CODE 23, CHARGE TEMPERATURE SENSOR VOLTAGE HIGH (AN BODY)

NOTE: For connector terminal identification, see CONNECTOR IDENTIFICATION at beginning of article. For wiring diagram, see appropriate WIRING DIAGRAMS article in ENGINE PERFORMANCE.

1) Turn ignition switch to OFF position. Disconnect and inspect throttle body temperature sensor connector. If connector is not okay, repair as necessary. Perform VERIFICATION TEST VER-2. If connector is okay, go to next step.

2) Connect a jumper wire between Black/Red and Black/Light Blue wires at throttle body temperature sensor connector. Using DRB-II, read throttle body temperature voltage. If DRB-II shows less than one volt, replace throttle body temperature sensor. Perform VERIFICATION TEST VER-2. If DRB-II shows more than one volt, go to next step.

3) Disconnect jumper wire from Black/Light Blue wire, and connect it to ground. Using DRB-II, read throttle body temperature voltage. If voltage is less than one volt, repair open Black/Light Blue wire. Perform VERIFICATION TEST VER-2. If voltage is more than one volt, go to next step.

4) Turn ignition switch to OFF position. Disconnect and inspect Single Board Engine Controller (SBEC) connector. If connector is not okay, repair as necessary. Perform VERIFICATION TEST VER-2. If connector is okay, go to next step.

5) Using an external ohmmeter, measure resistance at Black/Red wire between terminal No. 21 at SBEC connector and throttle body temperature sensor connector. If resistance is less than 10 ohms, replace SBEC; if resistance is more than 10 ohms, repair open Black/Red wire. Perform VERIFICATION TEST VER-2.

TEST DR-14A

CODE 23, CHARGE TEMPERATURE SENSOR VOLTAGE LOW (AN BODY)

NOTE: For connector terminal identification, see CONNECTOR IDENTIFICATION at beginning of article. For wiring diagram, see appropriate WIRING DIAGRAMS article in ENGINE PERFORMANCE.

TEST DR-14A (Cont.)

1) Turn ignition switch to ON position. Disconnect throttle body temperature sensor. Using DRB-II, read throttle body temperature sensor voltage. If voltage is more than 4 volts, replace throttle body temperature sensor. Perform VERIFICATION TEST VER-2. If voltage is less than 4 volts, go to next step.

2) Turn ignition switch to OFF position. Disconnect Single Board Engine Controller (SBEC) connector. Put DRB-II in ohmmeter mode. Probe terminal No. 21 (Black/Red wire) of SBEC connector. If resistance is less than 10 ohms, Black/Red wire is shorted to Black/Light Blue wire or ground. Repair as necessary. Perform VERIFICATION TEST VER-2. If resistance is more than 10 ohms, replace SBEC. Perform VERIFICATION TEST VER-2.

TEST DR-15A

CODE 24, THROTTLE POSITION SENSOR (TPS) VOLTAGE HIGH

NOTE: For connector terminal identification, see CONNECTOR IDENTIFICATION at beginning of article. For wiring diagram, see appropriate WIRING DIAGRAMS article in ENGINE PERFORMANCE.

1) Turn ignition switch to OFF position. Disconnect and inspect TPS connector. If connector is okay, go to next step. If connector is not okay, repair connector as necessary. Perform VERIFICATION TEST VER-2.

2) Turn ignition switch to ON position. Connect a jumper wire between TPS connector terminals No. 1 and 2 (Black/Light Blue and Orange/Dark Blue wires). Using DRB-II, read TPS voltage. If voltage is less than one volt, replace TPS. If voltage is more than one volt, go to next step.

3) Remove jumper wire. Reconnect jumper wire between terminal No. 2 (Orange/Dark Blue wire) at TPS connector and ground. Read TPS voltage. If voltage is less than one volt, repair open in Black/Light Blue wire. Perform VERIFICATION TEST VER-2. If voltage is more than one volt, go to next step.

4) Turn ignition switch to OFF position. Disconnect and inspect Single Board Engine Controller (SBEC) connector. Repair connector if damaged. Perform VERIFICATION TEST VER-2. If connector is okay, go to next step.

5) Using an external ohmmeter, check resistance at Orange/Dark Blue wire between terminal No. 2 at TPS connector and terminal No. 22 at SBEC connector. If resistance is less than 10 ohms, replace SBEC. Perform VERIFICATION TEST VER-2. If resistance is more than 10 ohms, repair open in Orange/Dark Blue wire. Perform VERIFICATION TEST VER-2.

TEST DR-16A

CODE 24, THROTTLE POSITION SENSOR (TPS) VOLTAGE LOW

NOTE: For connector terminal identification, see CONNECTOR IDENTIFICATION at beginning of article. For wiring diagram, see appropriate WIRING DIAGRAMS article in ENGINE PERFORMANCE.

1) Turn ignition switch to OFF position. Disconnect TPS connector. Turn ignition switch to ON position. Place DRB-II in voltmeter mode. Probe terminal No. 3 (Violet/White wire) at TPS connector. If voltage is less than one volt, repair open Violet/White wire. If voltage is more than one volt, go to next step.

2) Probe terminal No. 2 (Orange/Dark Blue wire) at TPS connector. If voltage is more than one volt, replace TPS. Perform VERIFICATION TEST VER-2. If voltage is less than one volt, go to next step.

3) Turn ignition switch to OFF position. Disconnect Single Board Engine Controller (SBEC) connector. Place DRB-II in ohmmeter mode. Probe terminal No. 22 (Orange/Dark Blue wire) at SBEC connector. If resistance is less than 10 ohms, repair short to ground in Orange/Dark Blue wire. Perform VERIFICATION TEST VER-2. If resistance is more than 10 ohms, replace SBEC. Perform VERIFICATION TEST VER-2.

1992 ENGINE PERFORMANCE
Self-Diagnostic Tests – 2.5L TBI (Cont.)

CHRY
1-53

TEST DR-17A

CODE 25, AUTOMATIC IDLE SPEED (AIS) MOTOR CIRCUITS

NOTE: For connector terminal identification, see CONNECTOR IDENTIFICATION at beginning of article. For wiring diagram, see appropriate WIRING DIAGRAMS article in ENGINE PERFORMANCE.

1) Disconnect AIS motor connector. Turn ignition switch to ON position. Using DRB-II, actuate AIS motor. Put DRB-II in voltmeter mode. Probe Gray/Red wire in AIS motor connector. When normal, voltage will switch from less than one volt to more than 10 volts.

2) If voltage is less than one volt, repair short to ground in Gray/Red wire. Perform VERIFICATION TEST VER-2. If voltage is more than one volt, check if voltage is more than 10 volts. If voltage is more than 10 volts, repair short to voltage in Gray/Red wire. Perform VERIFICATION TEST VER-2. If voltage is less than 10 volts, go to next step.

3) Probe terminal No. 2 (Yellow/Black wire) in AIS motor connector. If voltage is less than one volt, repair short to ground in Yellow/Black wire. If voltage is more than one volt, check if voltage is more than 10 volts. If voltage is more than 10 volts, repair short to voltage in Yellow/Black wire. Perform VERIFICATION TEST VER-2. If voltage is less than 10 volts, go to next step.

4) Probe terminal No. 3 (Brown/White wire) in AIS motor connector. If voltage is less than one volt, repair short to ground in Brown/White wire. Perform VERIFICATION TEST VER-2. If voltage is more than one volt, go to next step.

5) Probe Violet/Black wire in AIS motor connector. If voltage is less than one volt, repair short to ground in Violet/Black wire. Perform VERIFICATION TEST VER-2. If voltage is more than one volt, turn ignition switch to OFF position. Reconnect AIS motor connector. Disconnect Single Board Engine Controller (SBEC) connector.

6) Check resistance between terminals No. 39 (Gray/Red wire) and 59 (Violet/Black wire) using an external ohmmeter. Replace defective AIS motor if resistance is less than 35 ohms. Perform VERIFICATION TEST VER-2. If resistance is more than 35 ohms, go to next step.

7) Check resistance between terminals No. 40 (Brown/White wire) and 60 (Yellow/Black wire). If resistance is less than 35 ohms, replace defective AIS motor. Perform VERIFICATION TEST VER-2. If resistance is more than 35 ohms, go to next step.

8) Check resistance between terminals No. 39 (Gray/Red wire) and 60 (Yellow/Black wire). If resistance is less than 10 ohms, Yellow/Black wire is shorted to Gray/Red wire. Repair as necessary. Perform VERIFICATION TEST VER-2. If resistance is more than 10 ohms, check if resistance is less than 75 ohms. If resistance is more than 75 ohms, go to next step. If resistance is less than 75 ohms, go to step 10).

9) If resistance is 75-120 ohms, Brown/White wire is shorted to Violet/Black wire. Repair wiring as necessary. Perform VERIFICATION TEST VER-2. If resistance is more than 120 ohms, replace SBEC. Perform VERIFICATION TEST VER-2.

10) If resistance between terminals No. 39 and 60 is less than 75 ohms in step 8), check resistance between terminals No. 59 (Violet/Black wire) and 60 (Yellow/Black wire). If resistance is less than 10 ohms, Yellow/Black wire is shorted to Violet/Black wire. If resistance is more than 10 ohms, Gray/Red wire is shorted to Brown/White wire. Repair wiring as necessary. Perform VERIFICATION TEST VER-2.

TEST DR-18A (Cont.)

92D22304 92E22305

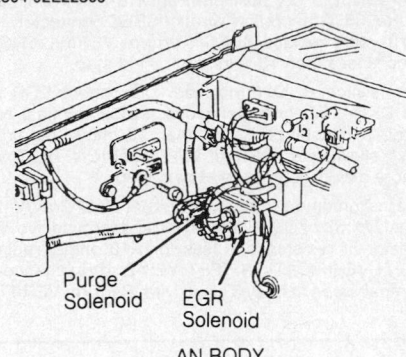

Purge Solenoid   EGR Solenoid

AN BODY

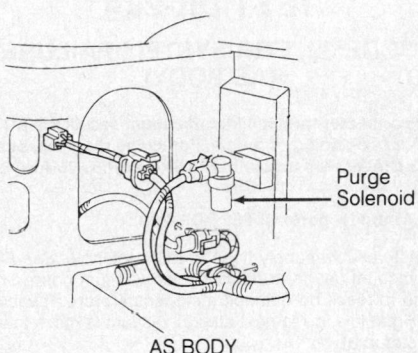

Purge Solenoid

AS BODY

Fig. DR-18A: Locating Purge Solenoid

3) Turn ignition switch to OFF position. Disconnect Single Board Engine Controller (SBEC) connector. Inspect connector. Repair connector if damaged. Perform VERIFICATION TEST VER-2. If connector is okay, go to next step.

4) Place DRB-II in ohmmeter mode. Probe purge solenoid connector terminal No. 2 (Pink/Black wire). If resistance is less than 10 ohms, repair short to ground on Pink/Black wire. Perform VERIFICATION TEST VER-2. If resistance is more than 10 ohms, go to next step.

5) Using an external ohmmeter, check resistance of Pink/Black wire between terminal No. 2 at purge solenoid connector and terminal No. 52 at SBEC connector. If resistance is more than 10 ohms, repair open in Pink/Black wire. Perform VERIFICATION TEST VER-2. If resistance is less than 10 ohms, go to next step.

6) Reconnect purge solenoid connector. Turn ignition switch to ON position. Place DRB-II in voltmeter mode. Probe terminal No. 52 (Pink/Black wire) at SBEC connector. If voltage is more than 10 volts, replace SBEC. Perform VERIFICATION TEST VER-2. If voltage is less than 10 volts, replace purge solenoid. Perform VERIFICATION TEST VER-2.

TEST DR-18A

CODE 31, PURGE SOLENOID CIRCUIT

NOTE: For connector terminal identification, see CONNECTOR IDENTIFICATION at beginning of article. For wiring diagram, see appropriate WIRING DIAGRAMS article in ENGINE PERFORMANCE.

1) Turn ignition switch to OFF position. Disconnect and inspect purge solenoid connector. See Fig. DR-18A. Repair connector as necessary. Perform VERIFICATION TEST VER-2. If connector is okay, go to next step.

2) Turn ignition switch to ON position. Place DRB-II in voltmeter mode. Probe terminal No. 1 (Dark Blue or Dark Blue/White wire) at purge solenoid. If voltage is less than 10 volts, repair open in Dark Blue or Dark Blue/White wire. Perform VERIFICATION TEST VER-2. If voltage is more than 10 volts, go to next step.

TEST DR-19A

CODE 32, EGR SOLENOID CIRCUIT

NOTE: For connector terminal identification, see CONNECTOR IDENTIFICATION at beginning of article. For wiring diagram, see appropriate WIRING DIAGRAMS article in ENGINE PERFORMANCE.

1) Turn ignition switch to OFF position. Disconnect EGR solenoid connector. Inspect connector. If connector is not okay, repair as necessary. Perform VERIFICATION TEST VER-2. If connector is okay, go to next step.

2) Turn ignition switch to ON position. Put DRB-II in voltmeter mode. Probe terminal No. 1 (Dark Blue or Dark Blue/White wire) at EGR solenoid connector. If voltage is less than 10 volts, repair open Dark Blue or Dark Blue/White wire. If voltage is more than 10 volts, go to next step.

3) Turn ignition switch to OFF position. Reconnect EGR solenoid. Disconnect and inspect Single Board Engine Controller (SBEC) connector. If connector is not okay, repair as necessary. Perform VERIFICATION TEST VER-2. If connector is okay, go to next step.

CHRY
1-54

1992 ENGINE PERFORMANCE
Self-Diagnostic Tests – 2.5L TBI (Cont.)

TEST DR-19A (Cont.)

4) Turn ignition switch to ON position. Put DRB-II in voltmeter mode. Probe terminal No. 35 (Gray/Yellow wire) of SBEC connector. If voltage is more than 10 volts, replace SBEC. Perform VERIFICATION TEST VER-2. If voltage is less than 10 volts, go to next step.

5) Turn ignition switch to OFF position. Disconnect EGR solenoid connector. Put DRB-II in ohmmeter mode. Probe terminal No. 35 at SBEC connector. If resistance is less than 10 ohms, repair short to ground in Gray/Yellow wire. Perform VERIFICATION TEST VER-2. If resistance is more than 10 ohms, go to next step.

6) Using an external ohmmeter, measure resistance of Gray/Yellow wire between terminal No. 35 at SBEC connector and terminal No. 2 at EGR solenoid connector. If resistance is less than 10 ohms, replace EGR solenoid. Perform VERIFICATION TEST VER-2. If resistance is more than 10 ohms, repair open in Gray/Yellow wire. Perform VERIFICATION TEST VER-2.

TEST DR-20A
CODE 32, EGR SYSTEM FAILURE (AS BODY)

NOTE: For connector terminal identification, see CONNECTOR IDENTIFICATION at beginning of article. For wiring diagram, see appropriate WIRING DIAGRAMS article in ENGINE PERFORMANCE.

NOTE: On AN body, perform TEST DR-20B.

1) Disconnect vacuum supply hose to EGR solenoid. *See Fig. DR-20A.* Connect a vacuum gauge to disconnected vacuum hose. Start engine. Allow engine to reach normal operating temperature. If vacuum is less than 10 in. Hg at idle, go to next step. If vacuum is more than 10 in. Hg at idle, go to step 3).

92D04764

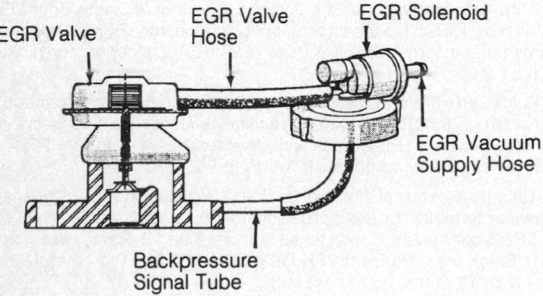

Fig. DR-20A: *Identifying EGR Valve & EGR Solenoid Vacuum Lines (AS Body)*

2) Turn engine off. Disconnect EGR vacuum line at throttle body. Connect vacuum gauge to throttle body nipple. Start engine. Read vacuum gauge at idle. If vacuum is more than 10 in. Hg at idle, repair vacuum leak or restriction in vacuum hose to EGR solenoid. Perform VERIFICATION TEST VER-2. If vacuum is less than 10 in. Hg at idle, repair plugged vacuum nipple at throttle body. Perform VERIFICATION TEST VER-2.

3) If vacuum was more than 10 in. Hg at idle in step 1), turn engine off. Disconnect vacuum gauge. Reconnect vacuum hose to EGR solenoid. Disconnect vacuum hose from EGR valve. Connect vacuum gauge to disconnected hose. Start engine.

4) While reading gauge, momentarily snap throttle open. If vacuum is less than 5 in. Hg, replace EGR valve assembly. Perform VERIFICATION TEST VER-2. If vacuum is more than 5 in Hg, turn ignition switch to OFF position.

5) Disconnect hose from EGR valve backpressure signal tube. *See Fig. DR-20A.* While applying 20-30 psi of air pressure to backpressure signal tube, open and close throttle and listen for tone change. If tone changes, replace EGR valve assembly. Perform VERIFICATION TEST VER-2. If tone does not change, go to next step.

6) Remove vacuum gauge. Cap open nipple on backpressure signal tube. Disconnect vacuum hose to EGR valve. Connect a hand vacuum pump to EGR valve nipple. Start engine.

TEST DR-20A (Cont.)

7) While slowly applying vacuum to EGR valve, listen for engine RPM change. If engine RPM does not change, go to next step. If engine RPM changes, turn ignition switch to OFF position. Apply 10 in. Hg of vacuum and hold for 30 seconds. If vacuum does not hold for 30 seconds, replace EGR valve assembly, Perform VERIFICATION TEST VER-2. If vacuum holds for 30 seconds, perform TEST NF-7A.

8) Remove EGR valve assembly. Check for plugged EGR manifold passages. If manifold passages are plugged, clean passages as necessary. Perform VERIFICATION TEST VER-2. If manifold passages are not plugged, replace EGR valve assembly. Perform VERIFICATION TEST VER-2.

TEST DR-20B
CODE 32, EGR SYSTEM FAILURE (AN BODY)

NOTE: For connector terminal identification, see CONNECTOR IDENTIFICATION at beginning of article. For wiring diagram, see appropriate WIRING DIAGRAMS article in ENGINE PERFORMANCE.

1) Disconnect vacuum supply hose to EGR valve transducer. *See Fig. DR-20B1.* Connect a vacuum gauge to disconnected vacuum hose. Start engine. Allow engine to reach normal operating temperature. While reading gauge, momentarily snap throttle open. If vacuum is less than 5 in. Hg, go to next step. If vacuum is more than 5 in. Hg, go to step 3).

2) Turn engine off. Disconnect EGR vacuum connector at EGR solenoid. *See Fig. DR-20B2.* Connect vacuum gauge to top port of vacuum connector. Start engine. Read vacuum gauge at idle. If vacuum is more than 10 in. Hg at idle, replace EGR solenoid assembly. Perform VERIFICATION TEST VER-2. If vacuum is less than 10 in. Hg at idle, repair plugged vacuum line. Perform VERIFICATION TEST VER-2.

92G04765

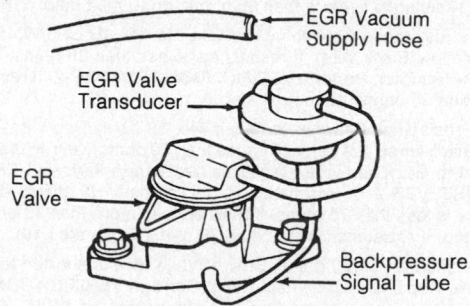

Fig. DR-20B1: *Identifying EGR Valve & EGR Transducer Vacuum Lines (AN Body)*

92I04766

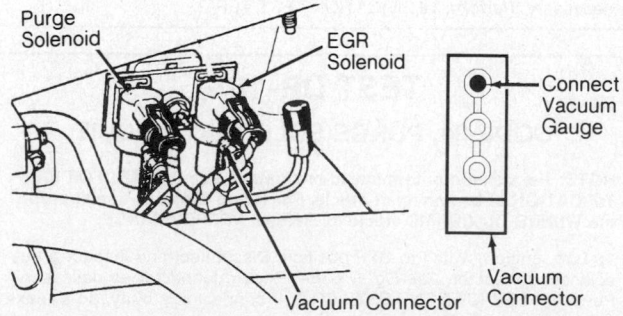

Fig. DR-20B2: *Locating EGR Solenoid & Purge Solenoid (AN Body)*

3) If vacuum was more than 5 in. Hg at idle in step 1), turn engine off. Disconnect vacuum gauge. Reconnect vacuum hose to EGR transducer. Disconnect vacuum hose from EGR valve. Connect vacuum gauge to disconnected hose. Start engine.

1992 ENGINE PERFORMANCE
Self-Diagnostic Tests – 2.5L TBI (Cont.)

CHRY
1-55

TEST DR-20B (Cont.)

4) While reading gauge, momentarily snap throttle open. If vacuum is less than 5 in. Hg, replace EGR valve assembly. Perform VERIFICATION TEST VER-2. If vacuum is more than 5 in. Hg, turn ignition switch to OFF position.

5) Disconnect hose from EGR valve backpressure signal tube. *See Fig. DR-20B1.* While applying 20-30 psi of air pressure to backpressure signal tube, open and close throttle and listen for tone change. If tone changes, replace EGR valve assembly. Perform VERIFICATION TEST VER-2. If tone does not change, go to next step.

6) Remove vacuum gauge. Cap open nipple on backpressure signal tube. Disconnect vacuum hose to EGR valve. Connect a hand vacuum pump to EGR valve nipple. Start engine.

7) While slowly applying vacuum to EGR valve, check for engine RPM change. If engine RPM does not change, go to next step. If engine RPM changes, turn ignition switch to OFF position. Apply 10 in. Hg of vacuum and hold for 30 seconds. If vacuum does not hold for 30 seconds, replace EGR valve assembly, Perform VERIFICATION TEST VER-2. If vacuum holds for 30 seconds, perform TEST NF-7A.

8) Remove EGR valve assembly. Check for plugged EGR manifold passages. If manifold passages are plugged, clean passages as necessary. Perform VERIFICATION TEST VER-2. If manifold passages are not plugged, replace EGR valve assembly. Perform VERIFICATION TEST VER-2.

NOTE: Tests DR-21A through DR-23A apply to passenger cars only. No test procedures are missing.

TEST DR-24A

CODE 33, A/C CLUTCH RELAY CIRCUIT (AN BODY)

NOTE: For connector terminal identification, see CONNECTOR IDENTIFICATION at beginning of article. For wiring diagram, see appropriate WIRING DIAGRAMS article in ENGINE PERFORMANCE.

1) Turn ignition switch to ON position. Press instrument panel A/C button to ON position. Turn A/C blower fan on. With DRB-II, actuate A/C relay. If A/C clutch relay is clicking, perform TEST DR-34A. *See Fig. NS-7.* If A/C clutch relay is not clicking, go to next step.

2) Check if radiator fan is on. If radiator fan is off, perform TEST DR-26A. If radiator fan is on, disconnect A/C clutch relay. Put DRB-II in voltmeter mode. Probe terminal "A" (Light Green wire) in A/C clutch relay. If voltage is not pulsating from 0 to 10 volts, repair open Light Green wire. Perform VERIFICATION TEST VER-2. If voltage pulsates from 0 to 10 volts, go to next step.

3) Turn ignition switch to OFF position. Disconnect and inspect Single Board Engine Controller (SBEC) connector. If connector is not okay, repair as necessary. Perform VERIFICATION TEST VER-2. If connector is okay, go to next step.

4) Put DRB-II in ohmmeter mode. Probe terminal "C" (Dark Blue/Orange wire) of A/C clutch relay connector. If resistance is less than 10 ohms, repair short to ground in Dark Blue/Orange wire. Perform VERIFICATION TEST VER-2. If resistance is more than 10 ohms, go to next step.

5) Using an external ohmmeter, check resistance at Dark Blue/Orange wire between terminal No. 34 at SBEC connector and A/C clutch relay terminal "C". If resistance is more than 10 ohms, repair open Dark Blue/Orange wire. Perform VERIFICATION TEST VER-2. If resistance is less than 10 ohms, go to next step.

6) Connect jumper wire between terminal No. 31 (Dark Blue/Pink wire) at SBEC connector and ground. Turn ignition switch to ON position. Put DRB-II in voltmeter mode. Probe terminal No. 34 (Dark Blue/Orange wire) of SBEC connector. If voltage is more than 10 volts, replace SBEC. Perform VERIFICATION TEST VER-2. If voltage is less than 10 volts, replace A/C clutch relay. Perform VERIFICATION TEST VER-2.

TEST DR-25A

CODE 33, A/C CLUTCH RELAY CIRCUIT (AS BODY)

NOTE: For connector terminal identification, see CONNECTOR IDENTIFICATION at beginning of article. For wiring diagram, see appropriate WIRING DIAGRAMS article in ENGINE PERFORMANCE.

TEST DR-25A (Cont.)

1) Turn ignition switch to ON position. Using DRB-II, actuate A/C clutch relay. If A/C clutch relay is not clicking, go to next step. *See Fig. NS-7A1.* If A/C clutch relay is clicking, perform TEST DR-34A.

2) Put DRB-II in voltmeter mode. Backprobe terminal "A" (Dark Green wire) in A/C clutch relay. If voltage is less than 10 volts, repair open Dark Green wire from radiator fan relay. Perform VERIFICATION TEST VER-2. If voltage is more than 10 volts, go to next step.

3) Turn ignition switch to OFF position. Disconnect and inspect Single Board Engine Controller (SBEC) connector. If connector is not okay, repair as necessary. Perform VERIFICATION TEST VER-2. If connector is okay, go to next step.

4) Turn ignition switch to ON position. With DRB-II in voltmeter mode, probe terminal No. 34 (Dark Blue/Orange wire). Replace SBEC if voltage is more than 10 volts. Perform VERIFICATION TEST VER-2. If voltage is less than 10 volts, go to next step.

5) Turn ignition switch to OFF position. Disconnect and inspect A/C clutch relay connector. If connector is not okay, repair as necessary. Perform VERIFICATION TEST VER-2. If connector is okay, go to next step.

6) Put DRB-II in ohmmeter mode. Probe terminal "C" (Dark Blue/Orange wire) of A/C clutch relay connector. If resistance is less than 10 ohms, repair short to ground in Dark Blue/Orange wire. Perform VERIFICATION TEST VER-2. If resistance is more than 10 ohms, go to next step.

7) Using an external ohmmeter, measure resistance at Dark Blue/Orange wire between terminal No. 34 at SBEC connector and terminal "C" at A/C clutch relay connector. If resistance is less than 10 ohms, replace A/C clutch relay. Perform VERIFICATION TEST VER-2. If resistance is more than 10 ohms, repair open Dark Blue/Orange wire. Perform VERIFICATION TEST VER-2.

TEST DR-26A

CODE 35, RADIATOR FAN RELAY CIRCUIT

NOTE: For connector terminal identification, see CONNECTOR IDENTIFICATION at beginning of article. For wiring diagram, see appropriate WIRING DIAGRAMS article in ENGINE PERFORMANCE.

1) Turn ignition switch to ON position. Using DRB-II, actuate radiator fan relay. If radiator fan relay is not clicking, go to next step. *See Fig. NS-7A or NS-7C.* If radiator fan relay is clicking, perform TEST DR-34A.

2) Put DRB-II in voltmeter mode. Probe terminal "A" at radiator fan relay connector. Terminal "A" is Dark Blue wire on AN body or Dark Blue/Pink wire on AS body. If voltage is less than 10 volts, repair open wire. Perform VERIFICATION TEST VER-2. If voltage is more than 10 volts, go to next step.

3) Turn ignition switch to OFF position. Disconnect and inspect Single Board Engine Controller (SBEC) connector. If connector is okay, go to next step. If connector is not okay, repair as necessary. Perform VERIFICATION TEST VER-2.

4) Turn ignition switch to ON position. With DRB-II still in voltmeter mode, probe terminal No. 31 (Dark Blue/Pink wire) at SBEC connector. If voltage is more than 10 volts, replace SBEC. If voltage is less than 10 volts, go to next step.

5) Turn ignition switch to OFF position. Disconnect and inspect radiator fan relay connector. If connector is not okay, repair as necessary. Perform VERIFICATION TEST VER-2. If connector is okay, go to next step.

6) Place DRB-II in ohmmeter mode. Probe terminal No. 31 (Dark Blue/Pink wire) at SBEC connector. If resistance is less than 10 ohms, repair short to ground in Dark Blue/Pink wire. Perform VERIFICATION TEST VER-2. If resistance is more than 10 ohms, go to next step.

7) Using an external ohmmeter, check resistance at Dark Blue/Pink between terminal "C" at radiator fan relay and terminal No. 31 at SBEC connector. If resistance is more than 10 ohms, repair open Dark Blue/Pink wire. Perform VERIFICATION TEST VER-2. If resistance is less than 10 ohms, replace radiator fan relay.

CHRY
1-56

1992 ENGINE PERFORMANCE
Self-Diagnostic Tests – 2.5L TBI (Cont.)

TEST DR-27A

CODE 42, NO AUTO SHUTDOWN (ASD) RELAY VOLTAGE SENSE AT SBEC

NOTE: For connector terminal identification, see CONNECTOR IDENTIFICATION at beginning of article. For wiring diagram, see appropriate WIRING DIAGRAMS article in ENGINE PERFORMANCE.

1) Turn ignition switch to OFF position. Disconnect ASD relay. See Fig. NS-7A or NS-7C. Disconnect and inspect SBEC connector. If connector is okay, go to next step. If connector is not okay, repair as necessary. Perform VERIFICATION TEST VER-2.

2) Using an external ohmmeter, check resistance at Dark Green/Orange wire between terminal "D" at ASD relay and terminal No. 57 at SBEC connector. If resistance is less than 10 ohms, replace SBEC. Perform VERIFICATION TEST VER-2. If resistance is more than 10 ohms, repair open Dark Green/Orange wire. Perform VERIFICATION TEST VER-2.

TEST DR-28A

CODE 37, TORQUE CONVERTER LOCK-UP SOLENOID CIRCUIT

NOTE: For connector terminal identification, see CONNECTOR IDENTIFICATION at beginning of article. For wiring diagram, see appropriate WIRING DIAGRAMS article in ENGINE PERFORMANCE.

1) Turn ignition switch to OFF position. Disconnect transmission torque converter lock-up solenoid connector. Connector is located below battery. Inspect connector. If connector is okay, go to next step. If connector is not okay, repair as necessary. Perform VERIFICATION TEST VER-2.

2) Turn ignition switch to ON position. Place DRB-II in voltmeter mode. Probe Dark Blue/tracer wire (tracer color may vary) in solenoid connector. If voltage is less than 10 volts, repair open Dark Blue/tracer wire. Perform VERIFICATION TEST VER-2. If voltage is more than 10 volts, go to next step.

3) Turn ignition switch to OFF position. Disconnect Single Board Engine Controller (SBEC) connector. Inspect connector. If connector is okay, go to next step. If connector is not okay, repair as necessary. Perform VERIFICATION TEST VER-2.

4) Place DRB-II in ohmmeter mode. Probe Orange/tracer wire (tracer color may vary) in solenoid connector. If resistance is less than 10 ohms, repair short to ground in Orange/tracer wire. Perform VERIFICATION TEST VER-2. If resistance is more than 10 ohms, go to next step.

5) Using an external ohmmeter, check resistance between Orange/tracer wire at solenoid connector and terminal No. 54 (Orange/tracer wire) at SBEC connector. If resistance is more than 10 ohms, repair open Orange/tracer wire. Perform VERIFICATION TEST VER-2. If resistance is less than 10 ohms, go to next step.

6) Reconnect transmission torque converter lock-up solenoid connector. Turn ignition switch to ON position. Place DRB-II in voltmeter mode. Probe terminal No. 54 of SBEC connector. If voltage is more than 10 volts, replace SBEC. Perform VERIFICATION TEST VER-2. If voltage is less than 10 volts, replace transmission torque converter lock-up solenoid. Perform VERIFICATION TEST VER-2.

NOTE: There is a break in test numbering sequence at this point, skipping Test DR-29A. Break is due to previous chart references to these procedures. No test procedures have been omitted.

TEST DR-30A

CODE 27, INJECTOR CONTROL CIRCUIT

NOTE: For connector terminal identification, see CONNECTOR IDENTIFICATION at beginning of article. For wiring diagram, see appropriate WIRING DIAGRAMS article in ENGINE PERFORMANCE.

1) Turn ignition switch to ON position. Using DRB-II, erase fault codes. Start engine. Using DRB-II, read secondary indicators. Wiggle connector at injector. If fault indicator returns, repair wiring or defective connector at injector. Perform VERIFICATION TEST VER-2. If fault indicator does not return, go to next step.

TEST DR-30A (Cont.)

2) Wiggle harness between injector and Single Board Engine Controller (SBEC). Wait 5 seconds each time before moving to next section of harness. If fault indicator returns, repair harness where wiggling caused indicator to return. Perform VERIFICATION TEST VER-2. If fault indicator does not return, test is complete. Perform VERIFICATION TEST VER-2.

TEST DR-31A

CODE 62, CONTROLLER FAILURE EMR MILES NOT STORED & CODE 63, CONTROLLER FAILURE EEPROM WRITE DENIED

1) Turn ignition switch to ON position. Using DRB-II, perform EMR MEMORY TEST. If DRB-II shows WRITE REFUSED, go to step 3). If DRB-II shows WRITE FAILURE, replace Single Board Engine Controller (SBEC). Perform VERIFICATION TEST VER-2. If DRB-II shows EMR MILEAGE INVALID, update mileage. Retest EMR memory. Perform VERIFICATION TEST VER-2. If DRB-II does not show EMR MILEAGE INVALID, go to next step.

2) Compare EMR mileage stored with instrument panel odometer. If mileage readings are same, retest EMR memory. Perform VERIFICATION TEST VER-2. If mileage readings differ, update mileage. Retest EMR memory. Perform VERIFICATION TEST VER-2.

3) If DRB-II shows WRITE REFUSED in step 1), SBEC was busy. Using DRB-II, perform EMR memory test. Retest EMR memory twice more if necessary. If DRB-II shows WRITE REFUSED again, replace SBEC. Perform VERIFICATION TEST VER-2. If DRB-II does not show WRITE REFUSED again, test is complete. Perform VERIFICATION TEST VER-2.

TEST DR-32A

INTERMITTENT TEST FOR VOLTAGE SENSOR

NOTE: For connector terminal identification, see CONNECTOR IDENTIFICATION at beginning of article. For wiring diagram, see appropriate WIRING DIAGRAMS article in ENGINE PERFORMANCE.

1) If intermittent fault is due to slow change or no change in Manifold Absolute Pressure (MAP) sensor, perform TEST-32B. If intermittent fault is not due to slow change or no change in MAP sensor, start engine. With DRB-II, read suspect circuit voltage. While monitoring voltage, wiggle connector at sensor.

2) If engine stalls or voltage becomes erratic, repair wiring or defective connector at sensor. Perform VERIFICATION TEST VER-2. If engine does not stall and voltage does not become erratic, wiggle harness between sensor and Single Board Engine Controller (SBEC). Wait 5 seconds each time before moving to next section of harness.

3) If engine stalls or voltage becomes erratic, repair harness where wiggling caused erratic reading. Perform VERIFICATION TEST VER-2. If engine does not stall and voltage does not become erratic, test is complete. Perform VERIFICATION TEST VER-2.

TEST DR-32B

INTERMITTENT TEST FOR SLOW CHANGE OR NO CHANGE IN MAP

NOTE: For connector terminal identification, see CONNECTOR IDENTIFICATION at beginning of article. For wiring diagram, see appropriate WIRING DIAGRAMS article in ENGINE PERFORMANCE.

1) Start engine. Using DRB-II, set engine speed to 1400 RPM and read MAP sensor voltage. Wiggle MAP sensor wiring harness while monitoring voltage. If engine stalls or if MAP sensor voltage is erratic, repair wiring or defective connector at MAP sensor. Perform VERIFICATION TEST VER-2. If engine does not stall or MAP sensor voltage is not erratic, go to next step.

1992 ENGINE PERFORMANCE
Self-Diagnostic Tests – 2.5L TBI (Cont.)

CHRY
1-57

TEST DR-32B (Cont.)

2) Turn ignition switch to OFF position. Install a vacuum "T" into MAP sensor vacuum hose. Connect a vacuum gauge. Start engine. Snap throttle open and closed while watching vacuum gauge. If vacuum drops rapidly to zero in. Hg, testing is complete. Perform VERIFICATION TEST VER-2. If vacuum does not drop rapidly to zero in. Hg, repair restricted manifold vacuum supply. Perform VERIFICATION TEST VER-2.

TEST DR-33A

INTERMITTENT TEST FOR AUTOMATIC IDLE SPEED (AIS) MOTOR CIRCUITS

1) Turn ignition switch to ON position. Using DRB-II, erase faults and actuate AIS motor. Read secondary indicators while actuating AIS motor. Wiggle AIS motor connector.

2) If fault indicator returns, repair wiring or connector defect at AIS motor. Perform VERIFICATION TEST VER-2. If fault indicator does not return, wiggle sections of wiring harness between AIS motor and Single Board Engine Controller (SBEC). Wait 5 seconds before moving to next section of wiring harness.

3) If fault indicator returns, repair wiring harness where wiggling caused indicator to return. Perform VERIFICATION TEST VER-2. If fault indicator does not return, testing is complete. Perform VERIFICATION TEST VER-2.

TEST DR-34A

INTERMITTENT TEST FOR RELAYS & SOLENOIDS

NOTE: For connector terminal identification, see CONNECTOR IDENTIFICATION at beginning of article. For wiring diagram, see appropriate WIRING DIAGRAMS article in ENGINE PERFORMANCE.

1) Turn ignition switch to ON position. Using DRB-II, erase faults and actuate intermittent solenoid or relay. Read secondary indicators while actuating. Wiggle connector at intermittent solenoid or relay.

2) If fault indicator returns, repair wiring or connector defect at solenoid or relay. Perform VERIFICATION TEST VER-2. If fault indicator does not return, wiggle sections of wiring harness between solenoid/relay and Single Board Engine Controller (SBEC).

3) Wait 5 seconds before moving to next section of wiring harness. If fault indicator returns, repair wiring harness where wiggling caused fault indicator to return. Perform VERIFICATION TEST VER-2. If fault indicator does not return, testing is complete. Perform VERIFICATION TEST VER-2.

TEST NF-1A

NO FAULT CODE TEST MENU

Check MITCHELL® TECH SERVICE BULLETINS (TSBs) for any pertinent information. If a TSB exists, perform corrective action. If TSB does not exist or if driveability problem still exists, check suspect system and perform indicated test. See NO FAULT CODE TEST SEQUENCE MENU table. If system causing driveability problem is not known, perform TEST NF-2A through TEST NF-13A in sequence until problem is found.

NO FAULT CODE TEST SEQUENCE MENU

Application	Test
Checking Secondary Ignition & Timing	NF-2A
Checking Fuel Pressure	NF-3A
Checking Coolant & TPS Calibrations	NF-4A
Checking MAP Sensor Calibration	NF-5A
Checking Oxygen (O₂) Sensor Switching	NF-6A
Checking Automatic Idle Speed Motor	NF-7A
Checking Park/Neutral Switch (A/T Only)	NF-8A
Checking SBEC Ground & Power Circuits	NF-9A
Checking EGR Valve Operation	NF-10A
Checking Engine Vacuum	NF-11A
Checking Minimum Idle Airflow	NF-12A
Checking Engine Mechanical	NF-13A

TEST NF-2A

CHECKING SECONDARY IGNITION & TIMING

1) Turn engine off. Connect engine analyzer to engine. Start engine, and let it idle. Set scope to read display or parade pattern. Follow equipment manufacturer procedure for pattern analysis. If secondary ignition pattern is not okay, repair indicated component in secondary ignition system. Perform VERIFICATION TEST VER-2. If secondary ignition pattern is okay, go to next step.

2) Disconnect any spark plug wire. Observe secondary kilovolt line. If open circuit secondary voltage is not at least 25 kilovolts, repair indicated component in secondary ignition system. Perform VERIFICATION TEST VER-2. Go to next step if open circuit secondary voltage is at least 25 kilovolts.

3) Reconnect spark plug wire. Ensure engine temperature is more than 180°F (82°C) before proceeding. Disconnect coolant sensor connector. Coolant sensor fault will be set and CHECK ENGINE light will be on. Using a timing light, check ignition timing. If timing is not within 2 degrees of specification, adjust timing. If timing is within 2 degrees of specification, go to next step.

4) Using timing light offset dial, zero timing mark in timing mark window. Remove camshaft timing inspection plug from timing belt cover. Using timing light, check camshaft timing. Camshaft timing index hole should be in center of inspection hole. If camshaft timing index is not in center of inspection hole, adjust or replace timing belt. See 2.2L & 2.5L article in ENGINES. If camshaft timing index is in center of inspection hole, go to next step.

5) Reconnect coolant sensor. Using DRB-II, read spark advance. Increase engine speed to 2000 RPM. If spark advance does not change with increase in RPM, replace Single Board Engine Controller (SBEC). Perform VERIFICATION TEST VER-2. If spark advance changes with increase in RPM, test is complete. Using DRB-II, erase coolant sensor fault.

TEST NF-3A

CHECKING FUEL PRESSURE

WARNING: High fuel pressure may be present in fuel lines. Open fuel system with caution. See FUEL PRESSURE RELEASE procedure in SELF-DIAGNOSTICS INTRODUCTION – GASOLINE article.

1) Relieve fuel pressure. Connect fuel pressure gauge in fuel supply line at throttle body. Turn ignition switch to ON position. Using DRB-II, actuate fuel system test. If fuel pressure is 12-16 psi (AN body) or 35-45 psi (AS body), test is complete. If fuel pressure is not 12-16 psi (AN body) or 35-45 psi (AS body), go to next step.

2) Check if fuel pressure is more than 16 psi (AN body) or 45 psi (AS body). If fuel pressure is more than 16 psi (AN body) or 45 psi (AS body), perform TEST NS-3B. If fuel pressure is less than 16 psi (AN body) or 45 psi (AS body), go to next step.

3) Using DRB-II, stop fuel system actuation test. Turn ignition switch to OFF position. Inspect fuel lines for kinks and restrictions. Repair as necessary. Perform VERIFICATION TEST VER-2. If fuel lines are okay, go to next step.

4) Relieve fuel pressure. Remove fuel pressure gauge from supply line. Install fuel pressure gauge between fuel tank and fuel filter. Turn ignition switch to ON position. Using DRB-II, actuate fuel system test. If fuel pressure is more than 16 psi (AN body) or 35 psi (AS body), replace fuel filter. Perform VERIFICATION TEST VER-2. If fuel pressure is less than 16 psi (AN body) or 35 psi (AS body), go to next step.

CAUTION: DO NOT allow fuel pressure to exceed 50 psi when squeezing fuel return hose.

5) Gently squeeze fuel return hose while observing fuel pressure gauge. If fuel pressure increases, replace fuel pressure regulator. Perform VERIFICATION TEST VER-2. If fuel pressure does not increase, replace fuel pump and sock assembly. Perform VERIFICATION TEST VER-2.

TEST NF-3B

CHECKING FUEL PRESSURE

WARNING: High fuel pressure may be present in fuel lines. Open fuel system with caution. See FUEL PRESSURE RELEASE procedure in SELF-DIAGNOSTICS INTRODUCTION – GASOLINE article.

1992 ENGINE PERFORMANCE
Self-Diagnostic Tests – 2.5L TBI (Cont.)

TEST NF-3B (Cont.)

1) Relieve fuel pressure. Stop fuel system actuation test. Ensure fuel tank is at least 1/2 full before performing following test.

2) Disconnect fuel return line at fuel tank. Connect Fuel Pressure Test Adapter (6541) to fuel return line. Place other end of adapter hose into an approved 2-gallon gasoline can. Turn ignition switch to ON position.

3) Using DRB-II, actuate fuel system test. Observe fuel pressure gauge. If fuel pressure is 12-16 psi (AN body) or 35-45 psi (AS body), repair fuel return line for a restriction at fuel tank. Perform VERIFICATION TEST VER-2. If fuel pressure is not 12-16 psi (AN body) or 35-45 psi (AS body), go to next step.

4) Using DRB-II, stop fuel system actuation test. Relieve fuel pressure. Reconnect fuel return line to fuel tank. Disconnect fuel return line from throttle body. Attach Fuel Pressure Test Adapter (6541) to fuel return line fitting at throttle body. Place other end of adapter hose into an approved 2-gallon gasoline can. Turn ignition switch to ON position.

5) Using DRB-II, actuate fuel system and observe fuel pressure gauge. If fuel pressure is 12-16 psi (AN body) or 35-45 psi (AS body), repair restricted fuel return line to fuel tank; if fuel pressure is not 12-16 psi (AN body) or 35-45 psi (AS body), replace fuel pressure regulator. Perform VERIFICATION TEST VER-2.

TEST NF-4A

CHECKING COOLANT & THROTTLE POSITION SENSOR CALIBRATIONS

1) Start engine. Allow engine to reach normal operating temperature. Using DRB-II, read coolant temperature sensor value. If temperature is 180-250°F (82-121°C), go to next step. If temperature is not 180-250°F (82-121°C), replace coolant temperature sensor. Perform VERIFICATION TEST VER-2.

2) Turn engine off. Turn ignition switch to ON position. Using DRB-II, read TPS voltage with throttle fully closed and against throttle stop. If voltage is not 1.5 volts or less with throttle closed, replace TPS. Perform VERIFICATION TEST VER-2. If voltage is 1.5 volts or more with throttle fully closed, go to next step.

3) Monitor voltage while slowly opening throttle wide open. If voltage change is not a smooth transition, replace TPS. Perform VERIFICATION TEST VER-2. If voltage change is a smooth transition, go to next step.

4) Check if maximum voltage is at least 3.4 volts with throttle wide open. If maximum voltage is not at least 3.4 volts with throttle wide open, replace TPS. Perform VERIFICATION TEST VER-2. If maximum voltage is at least 3.4 volts, go to next step.

5) Start engine, and let it idle. Using DRB-II, read minimum throttle voltage. If voltage is not 0-1.5 volts, replace TPS. Perform VERIFICATION TEST VER-2. If voltage is 0-1.5 volts, test is complete.

TEST NF-5A

CHECKING MAP SENSOR CALIBRATION

1) Turn engine off. Install vacuum "T" in MAP sensor vacuum hose. Install vacuum gauge. Start engine, and let it idle. Using DRB-II, read vacuum gauge. If DRB-II vacuum reading is within one in. Hg of teed-in vacuum gauge, test is complete. If DRB-II vacuum reading is not within one in. Hg of teed-in vacuum gauge, go to next step.

2) Turn engine off. Disconnect vacuum gauge from MAP sensor vacuum hose. Connect an auxiliary vacuum pump to MAP sensor. Apply 5 in. Hg vacuum to MAP sensor. Read and record MAP sensor voltage. Increase vacuum to 20 in. Hg. Read and record MAP sensor voltage. Subtract voltage recorded at 20 in. Hg vacuum from voltage recorded at 5 in. Hg vacuum.

3) If difference is 2.3-2.9 volts, repair restriction in vacuum hose to MAP sensor. Perform VERIFICATION TEST VER-2. If voltage difference is not 2.3-2.9 volts, replace MAP sensor. Perform VERIFICATION TEST VER-2.

TEST NF-6A

CHECKING OXYGEN (O₂) SENSOR SWITCHING

1) Allow engine to reach normal operating temperature. Using DRB-II, read O_2 sensor state. If O_2 sensor state is switching, system is functioning okay. Test is complete. If O_2 sensor state is not switching, check if O_2 sensor is locked on lean. If O_2 sensor is locked on lean, perform TEST NF-6B. If O_2 sensor is not locked on lean, go to next step.

2) Turn engine off. Turn ignition switch to ON position. Using DRB-II, actuate fuel system test. Inspect injector for fuel leakage. If injector is leaking, replace leaking injector and/or "O" rings as necessary. Perform VERIFICATION TEST VER-3. If injector is not leaking, go to next step.

3) Using DRB-II, stop fuel system test. Inspect air cleaner filter and inlet ducts for restrictions. If any restrictions exist, clean restricted air inlet system as necessary. Perform VERIFICATION TEST VER-3. If restrictions do not exist, perform TEST NF-13A.

TEST NF-6B

CHECKING OXYGEN (O₂) SENSOR SWITCHING

NOTE: For connector terminal identification, see CONNECTOR IDENTIFICATION at beginning of article. For wiring diagram, see appropriate WIRING DIAGRAMS article in ENGINE PERFORMANCE.

1) Allow engine to idle. Inspect engine for vacuum leaks. Repair vacuum leaks as required. Perform VERIFICATION TEST VER-2. If no vacuum leaks exist, read O_2 sensor signal voltage using DRB-II.

2) If voltage is more than .1 volt, go to step 4). If voltage is less than .1 volt, turn ignition switch to OFF position. Disconnect O_2 sensor connector and Single Board Engine Controller (SBEC) connector. Place DRB-II in ohmmeter mode. Probe SBEC connector terminal No. 41 (Black/Dark Green wire).

3) If resistance is less than 10 ohms, repair short to ground in Black/Dark Green wire. Perform VERIFICATION TEST VER-2. If resistance is more than 10 ohms, replace O_2 sensor. Perform VERIFICATION TEST VER-2.

4) If O_2 sensor voltage is more than .1 volt in step 2), turn engine off. Replace O_2 sensor. Perform VERIFICATION TEST VER-2. Turn ignition switch to ON position. Using DRB-II, reset adaptive fuel memory. Start engine, and allow it to reach normal operating temperature.

5) Read O_2 sensor state. If O_2 sensor state is switching, repair is complete. Perform VERIFICATION TEST VER-2. If O_2 sensor state is not switching, perform TEST NF-13A.

TEST NF-7A

CHECKING AUTOMATIC IDLE SPEED (AIS) MOTOR OPERATION

NOTE: For connector terminal identification, see CONNECTOR IDENTIFICATION at beginning of article. For wiring diagram, see appropriate WIRING DIAGRAMS article in ENGINE PERFORMANCE.

1) Using DRB-II, set engine speed to 1100 RPM. If engine speed can be set to 1050-1150 RPM, test is complete. If engine speed cannot be set to 1050-1150 RPM, return engine to normal idle speed. Disconnect AIS motor connector.

2) Inspect AIS motor connector. Repair connector if damaged. Perform VERIFICATION TEST VER-2. If connector is okay, place DRB-II in voltmeter mode. Open and close throttle while probing AIS motor connector terminal No. 1 (Gray/Red wire). If voltage is less than one volt, perform TEST NF-7B. If voltage is more than one volt, go to next step.

3) Open and close throttle while probing AIS motor connector terminal No. 2 (Yellow/Black wire). If voltage is less than one volt, perform TEST NF-7B. If voltage is more than one volt, go to next step.

4) Open and close throttle while probing AIS motor connector terminal No. 3 (Brown/White wire). If voltage is less than one volt, perform TEST NF-7B. If voltage is more than one volt, go to next step.

5) Open and close throttle while probing AIS motor connector terminal No. 4 (Violet/Black wire). If voltage is less than one volt, perform TEST NF-7B. If voltage is more than one volt, inspect engine for vacuum leaks. Repair as necessary. Perform VERIFICATION TEST VER-2. If no vacuum leaks exist, replace AIS motor. Perform VERIFICATION TEST VER-2.

1992 ENGINE PERFORMANCE
Self-Diagnostic Tests – 2.5L TBI (Cont.)

CHRY
1-59

TEST NF-7B

CHECKING AUTOMATIC IDLE SPEED (AIS) MOTOR OPERATION

NOTE: For connector terminal identification, see CONNECTOR IDENTIFICATION at beginning of article. For wiring diagram, see appropriate WIRING DIAGRAMS article in ENGINE PERFORMANCE.

1) Turn engine off. Disconnect and inspect Single Board Engine Controller (SBEC) connector. Repair connector if damaged. Perform VERIFICATION TEST VER-2. If connector is okay, go to next step.

2) Using an external ohmmeter, check continuity between AIS motor connector terminal No. 1 (Gray/Red wire) and SBEC connector terminal No. 39 (Gray/Red wire), AIS motor connector terminal No. 2 (Yellow/Black wire) and SBEC connector terminal No. 60 (Yellow/Black wire), AIS motor connector terminal No. 3 (Brown/White wire) and SBEC connector terminal No. 40 (Brown/White wire), AIS motor connector terminal No. 4 (Violet/Black wire) and SBEC connector terminal No. 59 (Violet/Black wire).

3) If resistance is less than 10 ohms for each circuit, replace SBEC. Perform VERIFICATION TEST VER-2. If resistance is more than 10 ohms for any circuit, repair open in that circuit. Perform VERIFICATION TEST VER-2.

TEST NF-8A

CHECKING PARK/NEUTRAL SWITCH

NOTE: For connector terminal identification, see CONNECTOR IDENTIFICATION at beginning of article. For wiring diagram, see appropriate WIRING DIAGRAMS article in ENGINE PERFORMANCE.

1) Using DRB-II, read park/neutral switch input state. While watching DRB-II display, move gear selector in and out of PARK and REVERSE positions. If display shows P/N and D/R, system is functioning correctly. If display does not show P/N and D/R, go to next step.

2) Turn ignition switch to OFF position. Place gear selector in PARK position. Disconnect Single Board Engine Controller (SBEC) connector. Disconnect quick disconnect cable at battery. Place DRB-II in ohmmeter mode. Probe terminal No. 30 (Brown/Yellow wire) of SBEC connector. Watch DRB-II display while moving gear selector in and out of PARK and REVERSE positions.

3) If display switches from less than 5 ohms to more than 5 ohms, replace SBEC. Perform VERIFICATION TEST VER-2. If display does not switch from less than 5 ohms to more than 5 ohms, check if display always stays less than 5 ohms. If display always stays less than 5 ohms, repair short to ground in Brown/Yellow wire. Perform VERIFICATION TEST VER-2. If display does not always stay less than 5 ohms, go to next step.

4) Disconnect park/neutral switch connector. Using an external ohmmeter, check resistance of Brown/Yellow wire between park/neutral switch connector and terminal No. 30 at SBEC connector. If resistance is less than 10 ohms, replace park/neutral switch. Perform VERIFICATION TEST VER-2. If resistance is more than 10 ohms, repair open Brown/Yellow wire. Perform VERIFICATION TEST VER-2.

TEST NF-9A

CHECKING ENGINE CONTROLLER GROUNDS & POWER CIRCUITS

NOTE: For connector terminal identification, see CONNECTOR IDENTIFICATION at beginning of article. For wiring diagram, see appropriate WIRING DIAGRAMS article in ENGINE PERFORMANCE.

1) Turn ignition switch to OFF position. Disconnect and inspect SBEC connector terminals. Repair connector terminals if damaged. Perform VERIFICATION TEST VER-2. If connector terminals are okay, go to next step.

2) Place DRB-II in ohmmeter mode. Probe terminal No. 5 (Black/White wire) of SBEC connector. If resistance is less than one ohm, go to next step. If resistance is more than one ohm, repair open in Black/White wire. Perform VERIFICATION TEST VER-2.

3) Probe terminal No. 11 (Black/Tan wire) at SBEC connector. If resistance is more than one ohm, repair open in Black/Tan wire. Perform

TEST NF-9A (Cont.)

VERIFICATION TEST VER-2. If resistance is less than one ohm, go to next step.

4) Probe terminal No. 12 (Black/Tan wire) at SBEC connector. If resistance is more than one ohm, repair open to ground in Black/Tan wire. Perform VERIFICATION TEST VER-2. If resistance is less than one ohm, go to next step.

5) Place DRB-II in voltmeter mode. Turn ignition switch to ON position. Probe terminal No. 9 (Dark Blue wire) at SBEC connector. If voltage is less than 10 volts, repair open Dark Blue wire. Perform VERIFICATION TEST VER-2. If voltage is more than 10 volts, reconnect SBEC connector. Test is complete.

TEST NF-10A

CHECKING EGR VALVE OPERATION

1) Disconnect vacuum hose to EGR valve solenoid. Connect a vacuum gauge to disconnected vacuum hose. Start engine. If vacuum gauge indicates less than 10 in. Hg at idle, go to next step. If vacuum gauge indicates more than 10 in. Hg at idle, go to step 3).

2) Turn engine off. Disconnect EGR valve vacuum signal hose at throttle body. Connect vacuum gauge to throttle body nipple. Start engine. Read vacuum gauge at idle. If vacuum is more than 10 in. Hg at idle, repair restriction or leak in vacuum line to EGR solenoid. Perform VERIFICATION TEST VER-3. If vacuum is less than 10 in. Hg at idle, repair plugged vacuum nipple at throttle body. Perform VERIFICATION TEST VER-3.

3) If vacuum was more than 10 in. Hg at idle in step 1), turn engine off. Disconnect vacuum gauge. Reconnect vacuum hose to EGR solenoid. Disconnect vacuum hose from EGR valve. Connect vacuum gauge to disconnected hose.

4) Start engine. While watching vacuum gauge, momentarily snap throttle open. If vacuum gauge ever indicates less than 5 in. Hg, go to next step. If vacuum gauge always indicates more than 5 in. Hg, go to step 6).

5) Inspect vacuum hose between EGR transducer and EGR valve for leaks and restrictions. If vacuum hose is okay, replace EGR transducer assembly. Perform VERIFICATION TEST VER-3. If vacuum hose is not okay, repair or replace vacuum hose as necessary.

6) If vacuum gauge always indicates more than 5 in. Hg in step 4), turn ignition switch to OFF position. Disconnect hose to EGR valve backpressure signal tube. Apply 20-30 psi air pressure to nipple on base of EGR valve. While opening and closing throttle, listen for change in air sound.

7) If air sound changes, replace EGR valve assembly. Perform VERIFICATION TEST VER-3. If air sound does not change, remove vacuum pump. Cap open nipple at EGR valve base. Connect vacuum pump to EGR valve. Start engine. While slowly applying vacuum to EGR valve, check for change in engine speed. If engine speed changes, go to next step. If engine speed does not change, go to step 9).

8) Turn ignition switch to OFF position. Apply 10 in. Hg for 30 seconds and hold. If vacuum does not hold for 30 seconds, replace EGR valve assembly. Perform VERIFICATION TEST VER-3. If vacuum holds for 30 seconds, test is complete.

9) If engine speed did not change in step 7), turn engine off. Remove EGR valve assembly. Inspect manifold passages for plugging. Repair as necessary. Perform VERIFICATION TEST VER-3. If manifolds are not plugged, replace EGR valve assembly. Perform VERIFICATION TEST VER-3.

TEST NF-11A

CHECKING ENGINE VACUUM

Connect a vacuum gauge to engine. Start engine, and let it idle. Normal vacuum reading will vary depending on altitude. Observe vacuum gauge reading at idle. If vacuum gauge reading is not steady between 13-22 in. Hg, perform TEST NF-13A. If vacuum gauge reading is steady and within specification, test is complete. Perform VERIFICATION TEST VER-3.

CHRY
1-60

1992 ENGINE PERFORMANCE
Self-Diagnostic Tests – 2.5L TBI (Cont.)

TEST NF-12A

CHECKING MINIMUM IDLE AIRFLOW

1) Turn ignition switch to OFF position. Remove air cleaner assembly, and plug heated air door vacuum hose. Disconnect PCV valve hose from intake manifold nipple. Install Vacuum Fitting (6457) to intake manifold PCV nipple. Start engine. Allow engine to reach normal operating temperature.

2) If vehicle odometer indicates less than 1000 miles, go to next step. If vehicle odometer indicates more than 1000 miles, use DRB-II to read minimum airflow speed. Test is complete if engine speed is 1100-1300 RPM (2.2L) or 1050-1250 RPM (2.5L). If engine speed is not as specified, replace throttle body. Perform VERIFICATION TEST VER-2.

3) Using DRB-II, read minimum airflow speed. Test is complete if engine speed is 700-1300 RPM (2.2L) or 650-1250 RPM (2.5L). Perform VERIFICATION TEST VER-2. If engine speed is not as specified, replace throttle body. Perform VERIFICATION TEST VER-2.

TEST NF-13A

PERFORMING NO FAULT CODE MECHANICAL TEST

At this point in diagnostic test procedure, all engine control systems have been determined to be operating as designed and not causing a driveability problem. Following additional items should be checked as possible causes:

- Check if any MITCHELL® TECH SERVICE BULLETINS (TSBs) apply to vehicle.
- Check engine compression.
- Check for exhaust system restriction.
- Check camshaft and crankshaft sprockets.
- Check valve timing.
- Check torque converter stall speed.
- Check engine vacuum. It must be at least 13 in. Hg in Neutral.
- Check for fuel contamination.
- Ensure PCV system is functioning properly.
- Ensure injector control wire is connected to correct fuel injector and injector is not plugged or restricted.
- Check power booster for internal vacuum leak.

NOTE: If coming to this test from O$_2$ sensor test and rich or lean condition is not corrected after checking items listed below, replace Single Board Engine Controller (SBEC).

TEST VER-1

VERIFICATION TEST VER-1

1) Inspect vehicle to ensure all engine components are connected. Reassemble and reconnect components as necessary. Attempt to start engine. If engine does not start, return to TEST NS-1A.

2) If engine starts, Single Board Engine Controller (SBEC) was changed, and vehicle is equipped with factory theft alarm, start vehicle at least 20 times so alarm system may be activated when desired. Write mileage from odometer to memory location within replacement SBEC. This will enable new SBEC to operate Emission Maintenance Reminder (EMR) light properly. No-start condition is corrected and repair is now complete.

3) If engine starts and SBEC has not been changed, connect DRB-II to engine diagnostic connector, and erase faults. No-start condition has been corrected and fault messages have been erased. Repair is now complete. If repaired fault has reset, check if any MITCHELL® TECH SERVICE BULLETINS (TSBs) apply to vehicle. Return to TEST DR-1A if necessary. If another fault exists, return to TEST DR-1A, and follow path specified by other fault.

TEST VER-2

VERIFICATION TEST VER-2

If TEST VER-3 was performed previously, perform TEST VER-3 again. Inspect vehicle to ensure all engine components are connected. Reassemble and reconnect components as necessary. If another fault was read previously and not corrected, return to TEST DR-1A and follow path specified by other fault.

1) If Single Board Engine Controller (SBEC) was replaced, and vehicle is equipped with a factory theft alarm, start vehicle at least 20 times so alarm system may be activated when desired. Write vehicle mileage from odometer to memory location within replacement SBEC. This will enable new SBEC to operate Emission Maintenance Reminder (EMR) light properly.

2) Connect DRB-II to engine diagnostic connector, and erase faults. Ensure no other fault remains by starting engine and allowing it to reach normal operating temperature.

3) Increase engine speed to 2000 RPM for at least 10 seconds. Allow engine to idle. On A/T models, apply brake and cycle transmission through all gear ranges. Place gear selector in PARK position. On models equipped with air conditioning, turn on air conditioning. Set blower to low speed.

4) On all models, turn engine off. Start engine. Allow engine to idle for at least 2 minutes. Turn engine off. Using DRB-II, read fault messages. If repaired fault resets, repair is not complete.

5) Check all pertinent MITCHELL® TECH SERVICE BULLETINS (TSBs), and return to TEST DR-1A if necessary. If another fault exists, return to TEST DR-1A, and follow path specified by other fault. If no other faults exist, repair is now complete.

TEST VER-3

VERIFICATION TEST VER-3

Inspect vehicle to ensure all engine components are connected. Reassemble and reconnect components as necessary. If another fault was read previously and not corrected, return to TEST DR-1A and follow path specified by other fault. If Single Board Engine Controller (SBEC) has been replaced, perform following:

- If vehicle is equipped with factory theft alarm, start vehicle at least 20 times so alarm system may be activated when desired.
- Write vehicle mileage to memory location within replacement SBEC. This will enable new SBEC to operate Emission Maintenance Reminder (EMR) light properly.
- On all models, connect DRB-II to engine diagnostic connector, and erase faults. Disconnect DRB-II.

To ensure no other fault remains, perform following:

1) On models equipped with A/C, turn A/C on. Set blower to low speed. Drive vehicle for at least 5 minutes and attain a speed of 40 MPH or more. Ensure transmission shifts through all gears.

2) Upon completion of road test, turn engine off. Restart engine, and let it idle for at least 2 minutes. Turn engine off. Connect DRB-II to engine diagnostic connector.

3) Read all fault messages. If repaired fault has reset, repair is not complete. Check all pertinent MITCHELL® TECH SERVICE BULLETINS (TSBs) and return to TEST DR-1A if necessary. If another fault exists, return to TEST DR-1A and follow path specified by other fault. If no other faults exist, repair is now complete.

WARNING: When battery is disconnected, vehicle computer and energy systems may lose memory data. Driveability problems may exist until computer systems have completed a relearn cycle. See COMPUTER RELEARN PROCEDURES article in GENERAL INFORMATION before disconnecting battery.

SELF-DIAGNOSTIC DIRECTORY

SELF-DIAGNOSTIC DIRECTORY

CONNECTOR IDENTIFICATION

CONNECTOR IDENTIFICATION DIRECTORY

Connector	See Fig.
Automatic Idle Speed Motor	2
Coolant Temperature Sensor	3
Distance Sensor	4
Distributor Harness	5
EGR Solenoid	6
Fuel Injector	7
Fuel Injector Harness	8
Fuel Pump Harness	9
Ignition Coil	10
Lock-Up Solenoid	11
MAP Sensor	12
Oxygen (O$_2$) Sensor	13
Purge Solenoid	6
Relays	1
SBEC	14
Throttle Position Sensor	15

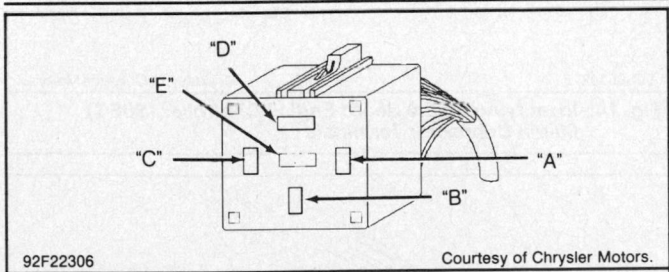

92F22306   Courtesy of Chrysler Motors.

Fig. 1: Identifying A/C Clutch, Auto Shutdown, Fuel Pump & Radiator Fan Relay Connector Terminals

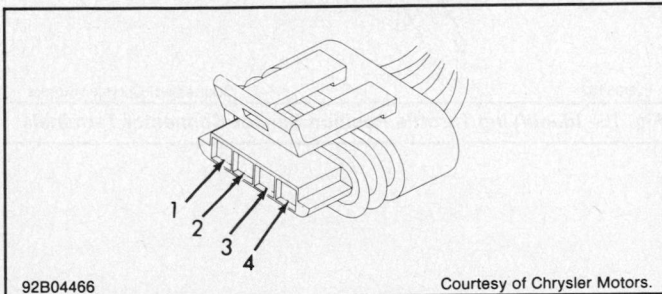

92B04466   Courtesy of Chrysler Motors.

Fig. 2: Identifying Automatic Idle Speed Motor Connector Terminals

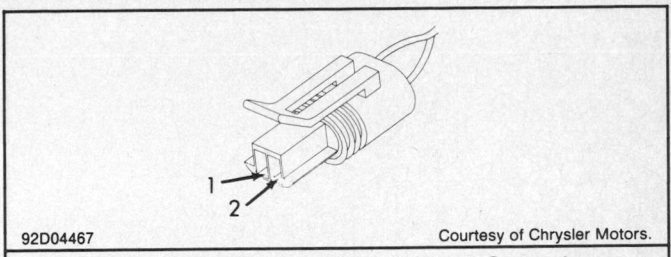

92D04467   Courtesy of Chrysler Motors.

Fig. 3: Identifying Coolant Temperature Sensor Connector Terminals

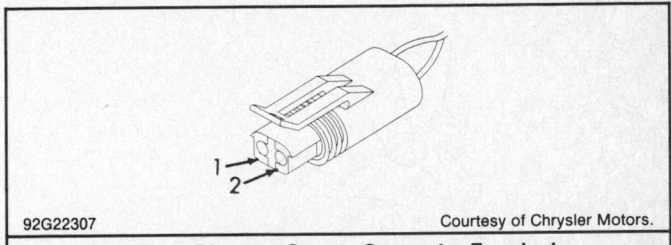

92G22307   Courtesy of Chrysler Motors.

Fig. 4: Identifying Distance Sensor Connector Terminals

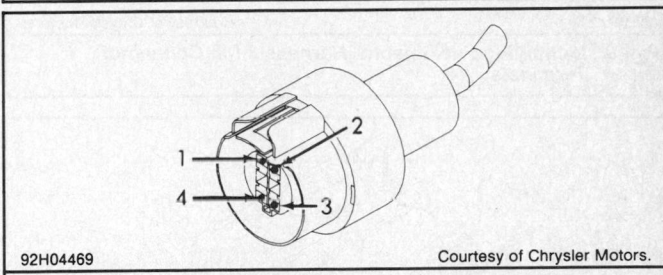

92H04469   Courtesy of Chrysler Motors.

Fig. 5: Identifying Distributor Harness Connector Terminals

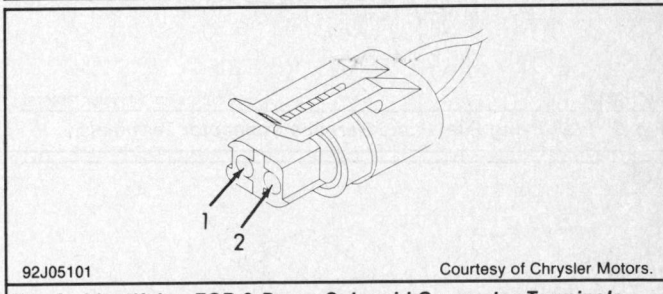

92J05101   Courtesy of Chrysler Motors.

Fig. 6: Identifying EGR & Purge Solenoid Connector Terminals

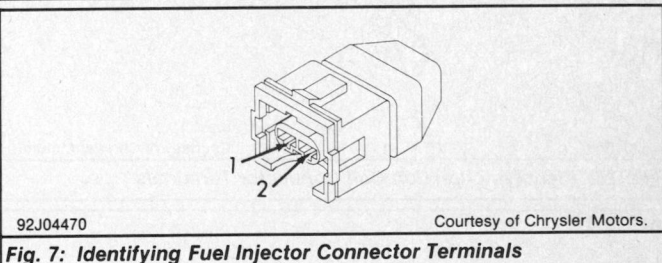

92J04470   Courtesy of Chrysler Motors.

Fig. 7: Identifying Fuel Injector Connector Terminals

CHRY
1-62

1992 ENGINE PERFORMANCE
Self-Diagnostic Tests – 3.0L VIN 3 (Cont.)

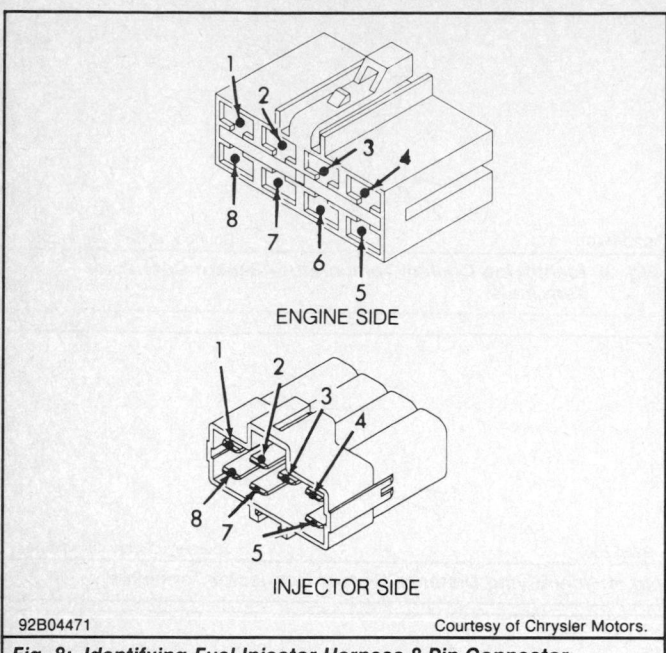

ENGINE SIDE

INJECTOR SIDE

92B04471   Courtesy of Chrysler Motors.

Fig. 8: Identifying Fuel Injector Harness 8-Pin Connector Terminals

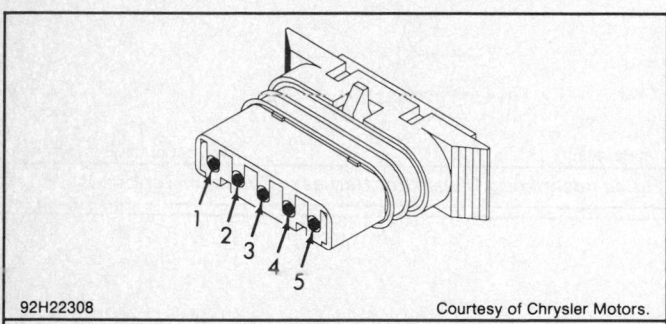

92H22308   Courtesy of Chrysler Motors.

Fig. 9: Identifying Fuel Pump Harness Connector Terminals

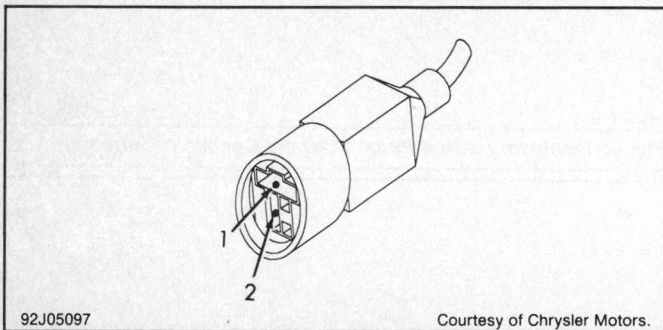

92J05097   Courtesy of Chrysler Motors.

Fig. 10: Identifying Ignition Coil Connector Terminals

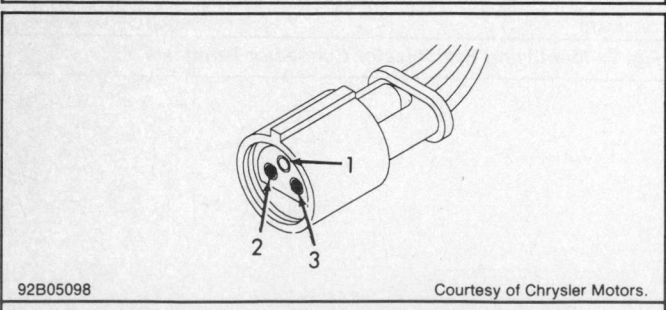

92B05098   Courtesy of Chrysler Motors.

Fig. 11: Identifying Lock-Up Solenoid Connector Terminals

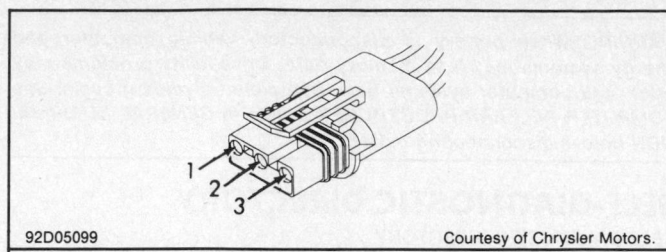

92D05099   Courtesy of Chrysler Motors.

Fig. 12: Identifying MAP Sensor Connector Terminals

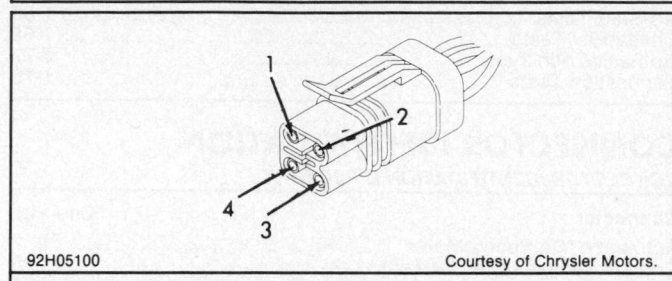

92H05100   Courtesy of Chrysler Motors.

Fig. 13: Identifying Oxygen (O_2) Sensor Connector Terminals

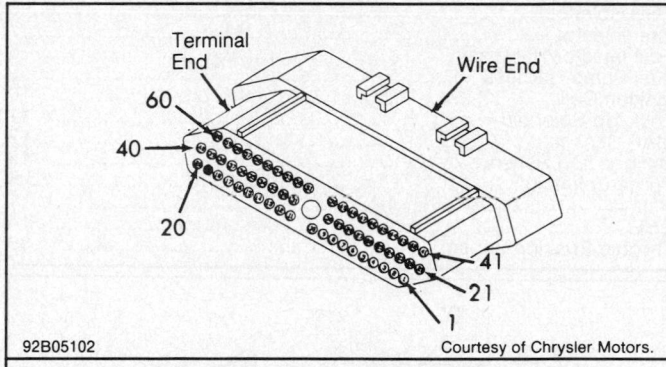

Terminal End

Wire End

92B05102   Courtesy of Chrysler Motors.

Fig. 14: Identifying Single Board Engine Controller (SBEC) 60-Pin Connector Terminals

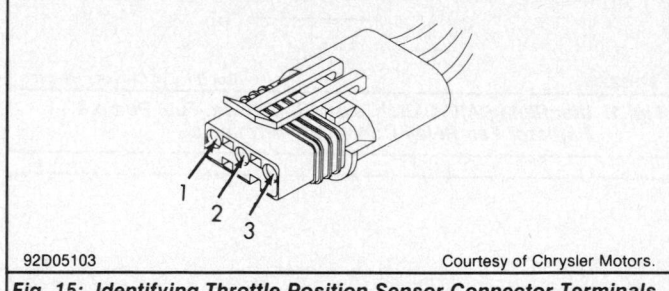

92D05103   Courtesy of Chrysler Motors.

Fig. 15: Identifying Throttle Position Sensor Connector Terminals

1992 ENGINE PERFORMANCE
Self-Diagnostic Tests – 3.0L VIN 3 (Cont.)

CHRY
1-63

SELF-DIAGNOSTIC TESTS

NOTE: In the following self-diagnostic tests, illustrations are courtesy of Chrysler Motors.

TEST NS-1A

CHECKING FOR FAULTS & SPARK

NOTE: For connector terminal identification, see CONNECTOR IDENTIFICATION at beginning of article. For wiring diagram, see appropriate WIRING DIAGRAMS article in ENGINE PERFORMANCE.

1) Ensure battery is fully charged. Disconnect and reconnect battery disconnect cable. Try to start engine by cranking for at least 10 seconds, ensuring ignition switch is turned to OFF position before each attempt to start engine. Turn ignition switch to ON position, and read DRB-II fault messages. See DRB-II FAULT MESSAGES table.

DRB-II FAULT MESSAGES

DRB-II MESSAGE	Test No.
NO RESPONSE	NS-8A
COOLANT VOLTAGE AND TPS VOLTAGE HIGH	1
NO REFERENCE SIGNAL DURING CRANKING	NS-9A
AUTO SHUTDOWN RELAY CONTROL CIRCUIT	NS-10A
NO ASD RELAY VOLTAGE SENSE AT CONTROLLER	NS-11A
INJECTOR CONTROL CIRCUIT	NS-5A
AUTOMATIC IDLE SPEED MOTOR CIRCUITS	NS-6A
INTERNAL CONTROLLER FAILURE	2
CONTROLLER FAILURE SPI COMMUNICATIONS	2

1 - Repair open Black/Light Blue wire at engine controller cavity No. 4. Perform VERIFICATION TEST VER-1.
2 - Replace engine controller. Perform VERIFICATION TEST VER-1

2) If no fault messages are present, turn ignition switch to OFF position. Try to start engine by cranking for at least 10 seconds. Ensure ignition is turned to OFF position before each attempt to start engine.

3) If engine starts and then stalls, perform TEST NS-2A. If engine does not start and stall, turn ignition switch to OFF position. Disconnect any spark plug cable at spark plug. Insert an insulated screwdriver in cable terminal. Hold screwdriver within 1/4" of a good ground.

CAUTION: If spark plug cable is held more than 1/4" away from a good ground, Single Board Engine Controller (SBEC) damage may occur.

4) Watch for spark while cranking engine for 10 seconds. Consider 1-2 sparks as a no-spark condition. If a good spark exists, perform TEST NS-2A. If no spark exists, reconnect spark plug cable. Disconnect coil secondary cable from distributor cap. Hold coil secondary cable within 1/4" of a good ground.

5) Watch for spark while cranking engine for 10 seconds. If a good spark exists, repair secondary ignition (distributor cap, rotor and cables). Perform VERIFICATION TEST VER-1. If a good spark does not exist, remove secondary cable from coil. Using an ohmmeter, check coil secondary cable resistance. If resistance is more than 15,000 ohms, replace coil secondary cable. Perform VERIFICATION TEST VER-1.

6) If resistance is less than 15,000 ohms, remove distributor cap. Crank engine while observing distributor rotor rotation. If rotor does not turn when engine is cranked, repair distributor drive system. Perform VERIFICATION TEST VER-1. If rotor turns when engine is cranked, reinstall distributor cap. Disconnect ignition coil connector. Actuate fuel system using DRB-II.

7) Put DRB-II in voltmeter mode while actuating fuel system. Probe ignition coil connector terminal No. 2 (Dark Green/Black wire). If voltage is less than 10 volts, repair Dark Green/Black wire between ignition coil and Auto Shutdown (ASD) relay splice. Perform VERIFICATION TEST VER-1.

8) If voltage is more than 10 volts, probe ignition coil connector terminal No. 1 (Gray wire). If voltage is more than 10 volts, go to step **11)**. If voltage is less than 10 volts, turn ignition switch to OFF position. Disconnect Single Board Engine Controller (SBEC) 60-pin connector. Put DRB-II in ohmmeter mode. Probe SBEC connector terminal No. 19.

9) If resistance is less than 10 ohms, repair Gray wire for a short to ground. Perform VERIFICATION TEST VER-1. If resistance is more than 10 ohms, go to next step.

TEST NS-1A (Cont.)

10) Using an external ohmmeter, check Gray wire for continuity between SBEC connector terminal No. 19 and ignition coil connector. If resistance is more than 10 ohms, repair Gray wire for an open circuit. Perform VERIFICATION TEST VER-1. If resistance is less than 10 ohms, replace SBEC. Perform VERIFICATION TEST VER-1.

11) If voltage in step **8)** was more than 10 volts, turn ignition switch to OFF position. Using an external ohmmeter, check ignition coil primary circuit resistance. If resistance is not .8-1.3 ohms at 75°F (24°C), replace ignition coil. Perform VERIFICATION TEST VER-1.

12) If resistance is as specified, check ignition coil secondary circuit. If resistance is not 10,000-16,000 ohms, replace ignition coil. Perform VERIFICATION TEST VER-1. If resistance is as specified, reconnect ignition coil connector. Perform TEST NS-9A.

TEST NS-2A

CHECKING FUEL SYSTEM

NOTE: For connector terminal identification, see CONNECTOR IDENTIFICATION at beginning of article. For wiring diagram, see appropriate WIRING DIAGRAMS article in ENGINE PERFORMANCE.

1) Turn ignition switch to ON position. Read Throttle Position Sensor (TPS) voltage. Ensure throttle is at idle position. If voltage is more than 1.5 volts, replace TPS. Perform VERIFICATION TEST VER-1.

2) If voltage is less than 1.5 volts, disconnect fuel injector 8-pin harness connector. *See Fig. NS-2A.* Place DRB-II in voltmeter mode. Actuate fuel system. Probe fuel injector 8-pin harness connector terminal No. 8 (Dark Green/Orange wire).

92F05104

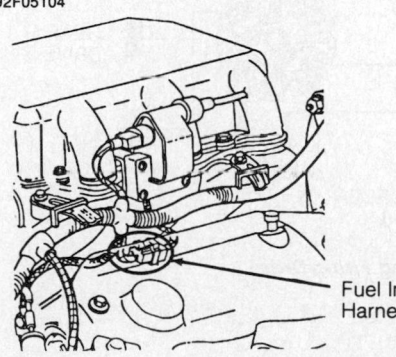

Fig. NS-2A: Locating Fuel Injector 8-Pin Harness Connector

Fuel Injector
Harness 8-Pin Connector

3) If voltage is less than 10 volts, repair open (Dark Green/Orange wire) between fuel injector 8-pin harness connector and harness splice. Perform VERIFICATION TEST VER-1.

WARNING: High fuel pressure may be present in fuel lines. Open fuel system with caution. See FUEL PRESSURE RELEASE procedure in SELF-DIAGNOSTICS INTRODUCTION – GASOLINE article.

4) If voltage is more than 10 volts, turn ignition switch to OFF position. Reconnect fuel injector 8-pin harness connector. Install fuel pressure gauge in fuel rail fitting. Ensure fuel tank is at least 1/4 full. Actuate fuel system using DRB-II. Listen for fuel pump operation at fuel tank.

5) If fuel pump operation cannot be heard, perform TEST NS-7A. If fuel pump operation can be heard, read fuel pressure gauge. If fuel pressure is more than 53 psi, perform TEST NS-4B. If pressure is less than 43 psi, perform TEST NS-4A. If vehicle starts and stalls repeatedly, perform TEST NS-12A. If vehicle does not start and stall repeatedly, perform TEST NS-3A.

CHRY
1-64

1992 ENGINE PERFORMANCE
Self-Diagnostic Tests – 3.0L VIN 3 (Cont.)

TEST NS-3A

INSPECTING MECHANICAL SYSTEM

NOTE: For connector terminal identification, see CONNECTOR IDENTIFICATION at beginning of article. For wiring diagram, see appropriate WIRING DIAGRAMS article in ENGINE PERFORMANCE.

1) Turn ignition switch to OFF position. Remove all spark plugs, and inspect spark plug tips for wet fuel. Dry spark plugs as necessary. Reinstall spark plugs. Check spark plug cables for correct firing order. See Fig. NS-3A. If firing order is incorrect, reconnect spark plug cables in correct firing order. Perform VERIFICATION TEST VER-1.

2) If firing order is correct, disconnect coolant temperature sensor connector. Connect timing light. Check ignition timing while cranking engine. Perform TEST NS-3B if ignition timing is not 0-16 degrees BTDC. If timing is as specified, turn ignition switch to OFF position. Disconnect Single Board Engine Controller (SBEC) and MAP sensor connectors.

3) Using an external ohmmeter, check resistance of Violet/White wire between SBEC connector terminal No. 6 and MAP sensor connector terminal No. 3. If resistance is more than 10 ohms, repair Violet/White wire for an open circuit. If resistance is less than 10 ohms, check valve timing and compression. Repair engine as necessary. Perform VERIFICATION TEST VER-1. If valve timing and compression are okay, replace MAP sensor. Perform VERIFICATION TEST VER-1.

92I05105

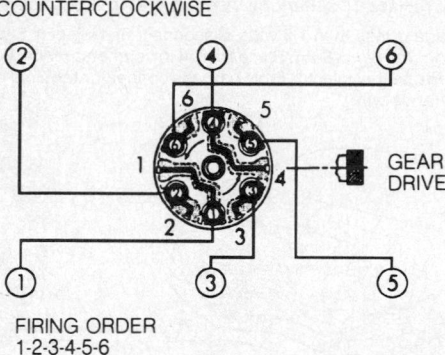

DISTRIBUTOR
ROTATION
COUNTERCLOCKWISE

GEAR
DRIVE

FIRING ORDER
1-2-3-4-5-6

Fig. NS-3A: Checking Firing Order

TEST NS-3B

INSPECTING MECHANICAL SYSTEM

1) Attempt to set basic ignition timing to 10 degrees BTDC. If ignition timing cannot be set, check valve timing, and repair as necessary. Perform VERIFICATION TEST VER-1. If ignition timing can be set to specification, attempt to start engine.

2) If engine will not start, check for valve timing, compression and other mechanical failure. Repair as necessary. Perform VERIFICATION TEST VER-1. If engine starts, check valve timing. If valve timing is correct, test is complete. Perform VERIFICATION TEST VER-1. If valve timing is incorrect, repair as necessary. Perform VERIFICATION TEST VER-1.

TEST NS-4A

CHECKING FUEL DELIVERY

WARNING: High fuel pressure may be present in fuel lines. Open fuel system with caution. See FUEL PRESSURE RELEASE procedure in SELF-DIAGNOSTICS INTRODUCTION – GASOLINE article.

1) Record fuel pressure gauge reading. Turn ignition switch to OFF position. Release fuel pressure. Remove fuel pressure gauge. Install fuel pressure gauge between fuel tank and fuel filter. Reconnect fuel line. With ignition switch in ON position, actuate fuel system using a DRB-II. Record fuel pressure gauge reading.

2) Compare fuel pressure gauge reading with previous reading. If fuel pressure is at least 10 psi more than fuel pressure gauge reading previously recorded, inspect fuel lines between fuel filter and fuel rail for a restriction. If any restrictions exist, repair as necessary. Perform VERIFICATION TEST VER-1. If no restrictions exist, replace fuel filter. Perform VERIFICATION TEST VER-1.

CAUTION: DO NOT allow fuel pressure to exceed 70 psi when squeezing fuel return hose.

3) If fuel pressure was not at least 10 psi more, gently squeeze fuel return hose while watching fuel pressure gauge. If fuel pressure exceeds 43 psi, replace fuel pressure regulator. Perform VERIFICATION TEST VER-1. If pressure does not exceed 43 psi, replace fuel pump and sock filter. Perform VERIFICATION TEST VER-1.

TEST NS-4B

CHECKING FUEL DELIVERY

WARNING: High fuel pressure may be present in fuel lines. Open fuel system with caution. See FUEL PRESSURE RELEASE procedure in SELF-DIAGNOSTICS INTRODUCTION – GASOLINE article.

1) Ensure fuel tank is at least 1/4 full before beginning this test. Release fuel pressure. Remove fuel return hose from fuel rail. Connect a 6' fuel hose to fuel rail return nipple. Place other end of hose into an approved 2-gallon gasoline container. Using DRB-II, actuate fuel system. Read fuel gauge.

2) If fuel pressure is more than 53 psi, replace fuel pressure regulator. Perform VERIFICATION TEST VER-1. If fuel pressure is less than 53 psi, turn ignition switch to OFF position. Reconnect fuel return hose. Remove fuel return hose from fuel tank. Connect a 6' fuel hose to disconnected fuel return hose. Place other end of 6' fuel hose into an approved 2-gallon gasoline container.

3) Turn ignition switch to ON position. Using DRB-II, actuate fuel system. Read fuel pressure gauge. If fuel pressure is less than 53 psi, replace fuel return assembly. Perform VERIFICATION TEST VER-1. If fuel pressure is more than 53 psi, repair restricted fuel return line between fuel rail and fuel tank. Perform VERIFICATION TEST VER-1.

TEST NS-5A

CODE 27, INJECTOR CONTROL CIRCUIT

NOTE: For connector terminal identification, see CONNECTOR IDENTIFICATION at beginning of article. For wiring diagram, see appropriate WIRING DIAGRAMS article in ENGINE PERFORMANCE.

1) Turn ignition switch to OFF position. Disconnect and inspect fuel injector 8-pin harness connector. Repair connector as necessary. Perform VERIFICATION TEST VER-1. If connector is okay, turn ignition switch to ON position. Using DRB-II, actuate fuel system. Place DRB-II in voltmeter mode. Probe fuel injector 8-pin harness connector terminal No. 8 (Dark Green/Orange wire).

2) If voltage is more than 10 volts, repair open Dark Green/Orange wire for an open between ignition coil connector and fuel injector 8-pin harness connector. Perform VERIFICATION TEST VER-1. If voltage is less than 10 volts, repair open in Dark Green/Orange wire between ASD relay and 8-pin connectors. Perform VERIFICATION TEST VER-1.

1992 ENGINE PERFORMANCE
Self-Diagnostic Tests – 3.0L VIN 3 (Cont.)

CHRY
1-65

TEST NS-6A

CODE 25, AUTOMATIC IDLE SPEED (AIS) MOTOR CIRCUITS

NOTE: For connector terminal identification, see CONNECTOR IDENTIFICATION at beginning of article. For wiring diagram, see appropriate WIRING DIAGRAMS article in ENGINE PERFORMANCE.

1) Disconnect Automatic Idle Speed (AIS) motor connector. Turn ignition switch to ON position. Using DRB-II, actuate AIS motor. Place DRB-II in voltmeter mode. Probe AIS motor connector terminal No. 1 (Gray/Red wire). Voltage should switch from less than one volt to more than 10 volts.

2) If voltage stays less than one volt, repair Gray/Red wire for a short to ground. Perform VERIFICATION TEST VER-1. If voltage stays more than 10 volts, repair Gray/Red wire for a short to voltage. Perform VERIFICATION TEST VER-1.

3) If voltage does not stay more than 10 volts, probe AIS motor connector terminal No. 2 (Yellow/Black wire). If voltage stays less than one volt, repair Yellow/Black wire for a short to ground. Perform VERIFICATION TEST VER-1. If voltage stays more than 10 volts, repair Yellow/Black wire for a short to voltage. Perform VERIFICATION TEST VER-1.

4) If voltage does not stay more than 10 volts, probe AIS motor connector terminal No. 3 (Brown/White wire). If voltage stays less than one volt, repair Brown/White wire for short to ground. Perform VERIFICATION TEST VER-1. If voltage stays more than 10 volts, repair Brown/White wire for a short to voltage. Perform VERIFICATION TEST VER-1. If voltage does not stay more than 10 volts, probe AIS motor connector terminal No. 4 (Violet/Black wire).

5) If voltage stays less than one volt, repair Violet/Black wire for a short to ground. Perform VERIFICATION TEST VER-1. If voltage stays more than 10 volts, repair Violet/Black wire for a short to voltage. Perform VERIFICATION TEST VER-1. If voltage does not stay more than 10 volts, turn ignition switch to OFF position. Reconnect AIS motor connector.

6) Disconnect Single Board Engine Controller (SBEC) 60-pin connector. Using an external ohmmeter, check resistance between SBEC connector terminals No. 39 (Gray/Red wire) and 59 (Violet/Black wire). If resistance is less than 35 ohms, replace AIS motor. Perform VERIFICATION TEST VER-1.

7) If resistance is more than 35 ohms, check resistance between SBEC connector terminals No. 40 (Brown/White wire) and 60 (Yellow/Black wire). If resistance is less than 35 ohms, replace AIS motor. Perform VERIFICATION TEST VER-1.

8) If resistance is more than 35 ohms, check resistance between SBEC connector terminals No. 39 (Gray/Red wire) and 60 (Yellow/Black wire). If resistance is less than 10 ohms, repair Yellow/Black wire for a short to Gray/Red wire. Perform VERIFICATION TEST VER-1.

9) If resistance is more than 10 ohms, check if it is more than 75 ohms. If resistance is more than 75 ohms, go to step **11)**. If resistance is less than 75 ohms, check resistance between SBEC connector terminals No. 59 (Violet/Black wire) and 60 (Yellow/Black wire).

10) If resistance is less than 10 ohms, repair Yellow/Black wire for a short to Violet/Black wire; if resistance is more than 10 ohms, repair Gray/Red wire for a short to Brown/White wire. Perform VERIFICATION TEST VER-1.

11) If resistance was more than 75 ohms in step **9)**, check if resistance is less than 120 ohms. If resistance is less than 120 ohms, repair Brown/White wire for a short to Violet/Black wire. Perform VERIFICATION TEST VER-1. If resistance is more than 120 ohms, replace SBEC. Perform VERIFICATION TEST VER-1.

TEST NS-7A

CHECKING FUEL PUMP

NOTE: For connector terminal identification, see CONNECTOR IDENTIFICATION at beginning of article. For wiring diagram, see appropriate WIRING DIAGRAMS article in ENGINE PERFORMANCE.

1) Using DRB-II, actuate Auto Shutdown (ASD) relay. See Fig. NS-7A. Check if fuel pump relay pulsates. If fuel pump relay does not pulsate when ASD relay is actuated, perform TEST NS-7B. If fuel pump relay pulsates, stop ASD actuation. Disconnect fuel pump relay.

TEST NS-7A (Cont.)

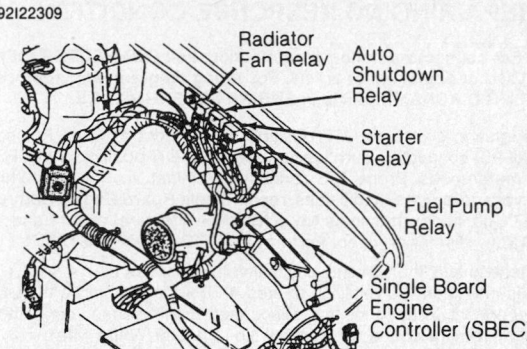

92122309

Radiator Fan Relay — Auto Shutdown Relay — Starter Relay — Fuel Pump Relay — Single Board Engine Controller (SBEC)

Fig. NS-7A: Locating Relays

2) Turn ignition switch to ON position. Place DRB-II in voltmeter mode. Probe fuel pump relay connector terminal "B" (Red/White wire). If voltage is less than 10 volts, repair Red/White wire for an open to splice. Perform VERIFICATION TEST VER-1.

3) If voltage is more than 10 volts, disconnect fuel pump harness connector. Reconnect fuel pump relay. Using DRB-II, actuate fuel system. Place DRB-II in voltmeter mode.

4) Probe fuel pump harness connector terminal No. 1 (Dark Green/Black wire). If voltage is less than 10 volts, go to step **6)**. Stop ASD actuation test if voltage is more than 10 volts.

5) Turn ignition switch to OFF position. Place DRB-II in ohmmeter mode. Probe fuel pump harness connector terminal No. 4 (Black wire). If resistance is more than 5 ohms, repair Black wire for an open to ground. If resistance is less than 5 ohms, replace fuel pump. Perform VERIFICATION TEST VER-1.

6) If voltage was less than 10 volts in step **4)**, turn ignition switch to OFF position. Disconnect fuel pump relay connector. Using an external ohmmeter, check resistance of Dark Green/Black wire between fuel pump harness connector terminal No. 1 and fuel pump relay connector terminal "D".

7) If resistance is less than 10 ohms, replace fuel pump relay. Perform VERIFICATION TEST VER-1. If resistance is more than 10 ohms, repair open Dark Green/Black wire. Perform VERIFICATION TEST VER-1.

TEST NS-7B

CHECKING FUEL PUMP

NOTE: For connector terminal identification, see CONNECTOR IDENTIFICATION at beginning of article. For wiring diagram, see appropriate WIRING DIAGRAMS article in ENGINE PERFORMANCE.

1) Turn ignition switch to OFF position. Disconnect fuel pump relay connector. See Fig. NS-7A. Turn ignition switch to ON position. Probe fuel pump relay connector terminal "A" (Dark Blue wire). If voltage is less than 10 volts, repair Dark Blue wire for an open to splice. Perform VERIFICATION TEST VER-1. If voltage is more than 10 volts, check resistance across terminals of fuel pump relay using an external ohmmeter. See Fig. NS-7B.

2) If resistance is more than 100 ohms, replace fuel pump relay. Perform VERIFICATION TEST VER-1. If resistance is less than 100 ohms, repair open Dark Blue/Yellow wire from fuel pump relay connector to splice. Perform VERIFICATION TEST VER-1.

92E05108

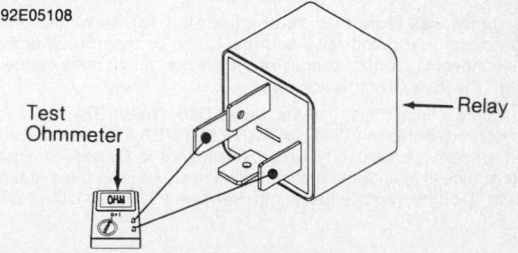

Test Ohmmeter — Relay — OHM

Fig. NS-7B: Testing Relay (Typical)

CHRY
1-66

1992 ENGINE PERFORMANCE
Self-Diagnostic Tests – 3.0L VIN 3 (Cont.)

TEST NS-8A

REPAIRING NO RESPONSE CONDITION

NOTE: For connector terminal identification, see CONNECTOR IDEN-TIFICATION at beginning of article. For wiring diagram, see appropriate WIRING DIAGRAMS article in ENGINE PERFORMANCE.

1) Turn ignition switch to OFF position. Disconnect Throttle Position Sensor (TPS) connector. Turn ignition switch to ON position. Put DRB-II in voltmeter mode. Probe TPS connector terminal No. 1 (Violet/White wire). If voltage is more than 6 volts, repair Single Board Engine Controller (SBEC) connector terminals No. 5 (Black/White wire) and 11 and 12 (Black/Tan wires) for an open. Perform VERIFICATION TEST VER-1.

2) If voltage is less than 6 volts, check if voltage is less than 4.4 volts. If voltage is less than 4.4 volts, go to step **4)**. If voltage is more than 4.4 volts, reconnect TPS connector. Disconnect MAP sensor connector. Probe MAP sensor connector terminal No. 4 (Violet/White wire).

3) If voltage is less than 4.4 volts, replace TPS. Perform VERIFICATION TEST VER-1. If voltage is more than 4.4 volts, see NO RESPONSE MESSAGE under DRB-II PROBLEMS & ERROR MESSAGES in SELF-DIAGNOSTICS INTRODUCTION – GASOLINE article.

4) If voltage was less than 4.4 volts in step **2)**, disconnect MAP sensor connector. Probe TPS connector terminal No. 1 (Violet/White wire). If voltage is more than 4.4 volts, replace MAP sensor. Perform VERIFICATION TEST VER-1. If voltage is less than 4.4 volts, turn ignition switch to OFF position. Disconnect SBEC connector.

5) Put DRB-II in ohmmeter mode. Probe SBEC connector terminal No. 6 (Violet/White wire). If resistance is less than 10 ohms, repair Violet/White wire for short to ground. Perform VERIFICATION TEST VER-1.

6) If resistance is more than 10 ohms, probe SBEC connector terminal No. 9 (Dark Blue wire). If resistance is less than 10 ohms, repair open in Dark Blue wire between SBEC connector terminal No. 9 and ignition switch. Perform VERIFICATION TEST VER-1.

7) If resistance is more than 10 ohms, place DRB-II in voltmeter mode. Probe SBEC connector terminal No. 3 (Red/White wire). If voltage is more than 10 volts, replace SBEC. Perform VERIFICATION TEST VER-1. If voltage is less than 10 volts, place DRB-II in ohmmeter mode. With ignition switch in OFF position, probe SBEC connector terminal No. 3 (Red/White wire).

8) If resistance is less than 10 ohms, repair Red/White wire between battery and SBEC for a short to ground. Perform VERIFICATION TEST VER-1. If resistance is more than 10 ohms, inspect fused circuit between positive battery terminal and SBEC connector terminal No. 3 (Red/White wire).

9) If fused wire is blown, go to next step. If fuse is okay, repair open Red/White wire between SBEC connector terminal No. 3 and positive battery terminal. Perform VERIFICATION TEST VER-1.

10) If fused wire was blown, disconnect Auto Shutdown (ASD) relay connector. Put DRB-II in ohmmeter mode. Probe ASD relay connector terminal "D" (Dark Green/Orange wire).

11) If resistance is more than 10 ohms, go to step **14)**. If resistance is less than 10 ohms, disconnect ignition coil connector. If resistance is more than 10 ohms when ignition coil connector is disconnected, replace ignition coil. Perform VERIFICATION TEST VER-1.

12) If resistance is less than 10 ohms when ignition coil connector is disconnected, disconnect fuel injector harness 8-pin connector. *See Fig. NS-2A.*

13) If resistance is more than 10 ohms when fuel injector harness 8-pin connector is disconnected, repair Dark Green/Orange wire at fuel injector connector for a short to ground. If resistance is less than 10 ohms when fuel injector harness 8-pin connector is disconnected, repair Dark Green/Orange wire at fuel injector harness 8-pin connector for a short to ground.

14) If resistance was more than 10 ohms in step **11)**, reconnect ASD relay. Disconnect fuel pump relay and fuel pump connectors. *See Fig. NS-7A.* Disconnect O₂ sensor connector. Probe fuel pump relay connector terminal "D" (Dark Green/Black wire).

15) If resistance is less than 10 ohms, repair Dark Green/Black wire for a short to ground. Perform VERIFICATION TEST VER-1. If resistance is more than 10 ohms, probe Dark Green/Black wire in O₂ sensor pigtail lead. If resistance is less than 10 ohms, replace O₂ sensor. If resistance is more than 10 ohms, replace fuel pump. Perform VERIFICATION TEST VER-1.

TEST NS-9A

CODE 11, NO REFERENCE SIGNAL DURING CRANKING

NOTE: For connector terminal identification, see CONNECTOR IDEN-TIFICATION at beginning of article. For wiring diagram, see appropriate WIRING DIAGRAMS article in ENGINE PERFORMANCE.

1) If DRB-II displays COOLANT SENSOR VOLTAGE TOO HIGH, repair Black/Light Blue wire for an open between Single Board Engine Controller (SBEC) and splice. Perform VERIFICATION TEST VER-1. If DRB-II does not display COOLANT SENSOR VOLTAGE TOO HIGH, turn ignition switch to OFF position. Disconnect and inspect distributor harness connector. *See Fig. NS-9A.* Repair connector if damaged. Perform VERIFICATION TEST VER-1.

92G05109

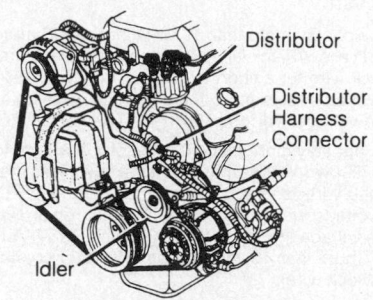

Fig. NS-9A: Locating Distributor Harness Connector

2) If distributor harness connector is okay, disconnect secondary ignition cable from distributor. Place end of ignition cable within 1/4" of a good ground. Connect a jumper wire between distributor harness connector terminals No. 1 (Gray/Black wire) and 4 (Black/Light Blue wire). Turn ignition switch to ON position. While making and breaking jumpered connection, watch for spark at ignition cable.

3) If spark exists, go to TEST NS-9B. If spark does not exist, disconnect jumper wire. Connect jumper wire between distributor harness connector terminal No. 1 (Gray/Black wire) and ground. While making and breaking jumpered connection, watch for spark at ignition cable. If spark exists, repair Black/Light Blue wire for an open circuit between distributor connector and splice. Perform VERIFICATION TEST VER-1.

4) If spark does not exist, turn ignition switch to OFF position. Disconnect and inspect SBEC connector. Repair connector if damaged. Perform VERIFICATION TEST VER-1. If connector is okay, place DRB-II in ohmmeter mode. Probe SBEC connector terminal No. 24 (Gray/Black wire). If resistance is less than 10 ohms, repair Gray/Black wire for short to ground. Perform VERIFICATION TEST VER-1.

5) If resistance is more than 10 ohms, check resistance of Gray/Black wire between SBEC connector terminal No. 24 and distributor harness connector terminal No. 1 using an external ohmmeter. If resistance is less than 10 ohms, replace SBEC. Perform VERIFICATION TEST VER-1. If resistance is more than 10 ohms, repair open in Gray/Black wire. Perform VERIFICATION TEST VER-1.

TEST NS-9B

CODE 11, NO REFERENCE SIGNAL DURING CRANKING

NOTE: For connector terminal identification, see CONNECTOR IDEN-TIFICATION at beginning of article. For wiring diagram, see appropriate WIRING DIAGRAMS article in ENGINE PERFORMANCE.

1) Disconnect jumper wire. Place DRB-II in voltmeter mode. Probe distributor harness connector terminal No. 3 (Orange wire). If voltage is more than 7 volts, turn ignition switch to OFF position. Remove distributor cap. Crank engine while observing distributor rotor.

1992 ENGINE PERFORMANCE
Self-Diagnostic Tests – 3.0L VIN 3 (Cont.)

CHRY
1-67

TEST NS-9B (Cont.)

2) If rotor turns as engine is cranked, replace distributor pick-up. Perform VERIFICATION TEST VER-1. If rotor does not turn as engine is cranked, repair distributor drive system as necessary. Perform VERIFICATION TEST VER-1. If voltage in step **1)** is zero volts, perform TEST NS-9C. If voltage is 0-7 volts, turn ignition switch to OFF position. Disconnect Single Board Engine Controller (SBEC).

3) Place DRB-II in ohmmeter mode. Check resistance of Orange wire between SBEC connector terminal No. 7 and distributor harness connector terminal No. 3. If resistance is more than 10 ohms, repair Orange wire for an open. Perform VERIFICATION TEST VER-1. If resistance is less than 10 ohms, replace distributor pick-up and SBEC. Perform VERIFICATION TEST VER-1.

TEST NS-9C

CODE 11, NO REFERENCE SIGNAL DURING CRANKING

NOTE: For connector terminal identification, see CONNECTOR IDENTIFICATION at beginning of article. For wiring diagram, see appropriate WIRING DIAGRAMS article in ENGINE PERFORMANCE.

1) Turn ignition switch to OFF position. Disconnect Single Board Engine Controller (SBEC) 60-pin connector. Inspect connector. Repair connector if damaged. Perform VERIFICATION TEST VER-1. If connector is okay, place DRB-II in ohmmeter mode. Probe SBEC connector terminal No. 7 (Orange wire). If resistance is less than 10 ohms, repair Orange wire for a short to ground. Perform VERIFICATION TEST VER-1.

2) If resistance is more than 10 ohms, check resistance of Orange wire between SBEC connector terminal No. 7 and distributor harness connector terminal No. 3 using an external ohmmeter. If resistance is less than 10 ohms, replace SBEC. Perform VERIFICATION TEST VER-1. If resistance is more than 10 ohms, repair Orange wire for an open. Perform VERIFICATION TEST VER-1.

TEST NS-10A

CODE 42, AUTO SHUTDOWN (ASD) RELAY CONTROL CIRCUIT

NOTE: For connector terminal identification, see CONNECTOR IDENTIFICATION at beginning of article. For wiring diagram, see appropriate WIRING DIAGRAMS article in ENGINE PERFORMANCE.

1) Turn ignition switch to ON position. Disconnect and inspect Auto Shutdown (ASD) relay connector. See Fig. NS-7A. Repair connector if damaged. Perform VERIFICATION TEST VER-1. If connector is okay, place DRB-II in voltmeter mode. Probe ASD relay connector terminal "A" (Dark Blue wire). If voltage is less than 10 volts, repair open Dark Blue wire from ignition switch. Perform VERIFICATION TEST VER-1.

2) If voltage is more than 10 volts, check resistance across ASD relay terminals using an external ohmmeter. See Fig. NS-7B. If resistance is more than 100 ohms, replace ASD relay. Perform VERIFICATION TEST VER-1. If resistance is less than 100 ohms, turn ignition switch to OFF position. Disconnect and inspect Single Board Engine Controller (SBEC) connector. Repair connector if damaged. Perform VERIFICATION TEST VER-1.

3) If SBEC connector is okay, check resistance of Dark Blue/Yellow wire between SBEC connector terminal No. 51 and ASD relay connector terminal "C". If resistance is less than 10 ohms, replace SBEC. Perform VERIFICATION TEST VER-1. If resistance is more than 10 ohms, repair open in Dark Blue/Yellow wire. Perform VERIFICATION TEST VER-1.

TEST NS-11A

CODE 42, AUTO SHUTDOWN (ASD) RELAY CONTROL CIRCUIT

NOTE: For connector terminal identification, see CONNECTOR IDENTIFICATION at beginning of article. For wiring diagram, see appropriate WIRING DIAGRAMS article in ENGINE PERFORMANCE.

1) Disconnect ignition coil connector. Using DRB-II, actuate fuel system. Place DRB-II in voltmeter mode. Probe Dark Green/Black wire at ignition coil connector terminal No. 2. If voltage is more than 10 volts, go to next step. If voltage is less than 10 volts, go to step **3)**.

2) Turn ignition switch to OFF position. Disconnect Single Board Engine Controller (SBEC) connector. Check resistance of Dark Green/Orange wire between SBEC connector terminal No. 57 and Auto Shutdown (ASD) relay connector terminal "D" using external ohmmeter. See Fig. NS-7A. If resistance is more than 10 ohms, repair open Dark Green/Orange wire between ASD relay terminal "D" and SBEC connector terminal No. 57. Perform VERIFICATION TEST VER-1. If resistance is less than 10 ohms, replace SBEC. Perform VERIFICATION TEST VER-1.

3) If voltage in step **1)** was less than 10 volts, turn ignition switch to OFF position. Disconnect SBEC and ASD relay connectors. Using an external ohmmeter, check resistance of Dark Green/Orange wire between SBEC connector terminal No. 57 and ASD relay terminal "D". If resistance is more than 10 ohms, repair Dark Green/Orange wire for an open circuit between ASD relay terminal "D" and SBEC connector terminal No. 57. If resistance is less than 10 ohms, place DRB-II in voltmeter mode.

4) Probe ASD relay connector terminal "B" (Red/White wire). If voltage is more than 10 volts, replace ASD relay. Perform VERIFICATION TEST VER-1. If voltage is less than 10 volts, repair Red/White wire for an open between ASD relay connector terminal "B" and harness splice.

TEST NS-12A

CHECKING AUTOMATIC IDLE SPEED (AIS) MOTOR OPERATION

NOTE: For connector terminal identification, see CONNECTOR IDENTIFICATION at beginning of article. For wiring diagram, see appropriate WIRING DIAGRAMS article in ENGINE PERFORMANCE.

1) Turn ignition switch to ON position. Using DRB-II, actuate Automatic Idle Speed (AIS) motor. Disconnect AIS motor connector. See Fig. NS-12A. Place DRB-II in voltmeter mode. Probe AIS motor connector terminal No. 1 (Gray/Red wire).

92I05110

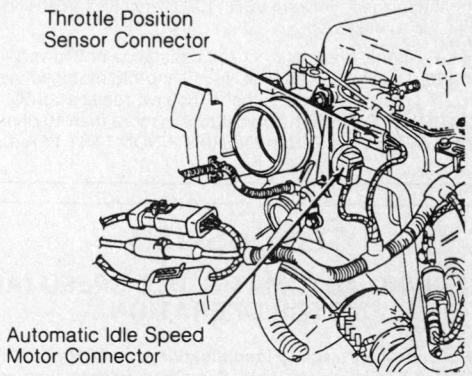

Throttle Position
Sensor Connector

Automatic Idle Speed
Motor Connector

Fig. NS-12A: Locating Automatic Idle Speed (AIS) Motor Connector

2) Perform TEST NS-12B if voltage at Gray/Red wire stays less than one volt. If voltage at Gray/Red wire does not stay less than one volt, probe AIS motor connector terminal No. 3 (Brown/White wire). If voltage at Brown/White wire stays less than one volt, perform TEST NS-12C.

3) If voltage at Brown/White wire does not stay less than one volt, probe AIS motor connector terminal No. 4 (Violet/Black wire). If voltage at Violet/Black wire stays less than one volt, perform TEST NS-12D.

CHRY
1-68

1992 ENGINE PERFORMANCE
Self-Diagnostic Tests – 3.0L VIN 3 (Cont.)

TEST NS-12A (Cont.)

4) If voltage at Violet/Black wire does not stay less than one volt, probe AIS motor connector terminal No. 2 (Yellow/Black wire). If voltage at Yellow/Black wire stays less than one volt, perform TEST NS-12E.

5) If voltage at Yellow/Black wire does not stay less than one volt, turn ignition switch to OFF position. Stop AIS motor actuation. Remove AIS motor from throttle body. Reconnect AIS motor connector with motor off throttle body.

6) Turn ignition switch to ON position. Using DRB-II, actuate AIS motor. If AIS motor tip moves in and out, perform TEST NS-13A. If AIS motor tip does not move in and out, replace AIS motor. Perform VERIFICATION TEST VER-1.

TEST NS-12B

CHECKING AUTOMATIC IDLE SPEED (AIS) MOTOR OPERATION

NOTE: For connector terminal identification, see CONNECTOR IDENTIFICATION at beginning of article. For wiring diagram, see appropriate WIRING DIAGRAMS article in ENGINE PERFORMANCE.

1) Stop AIS motor actuation test. Turn ignition switch to OFF position. Disconnect and inspect Single Board Engine Controller (SBEC). Repair connector if damaged. Perform VERIFICATION TEST VER-1. If connector is okay, go to next step.

2) Using an external ohmmeter, check resistance of Gray/Red wire between SBEC connector terminal No. 39 and AIS motor connector terminal No. 1. If resistance is less than 10 ohms, replace SBEC. Perform VERIFICATION TEST VER-1. If resistance is more than 10 ohms, repair open in Gray/Red wire. Perform VERIFICATION TEST VER-1.

TEST NS-12C

CHECKING AUTOMATIC IDLE SPEED (AIS) MOTOR OPERATION

NOTE: For connector terminal identification, see CONNECTOR IDENTIFICATION at beginning of article. For wiring diagram, see appropriate WIRING DIAGRAMS article in ENGINE PERFORMANCE.

1) Stop AIS motor actuation test. Turn ignition switch to OFF position. Disconnect and inspect Single Board Engine Controller (SBEC). Repair connector if damaged. Perform VERIFICATION TEST VER-1. If connector is okay, go to next step.

2) Using an external ohmmeter, check resistance of Brown/White wire between SBEC connector terminal No. 40 and AIS motor connector terminal No. 3. If resistance is less than 10 ohms, replace SBEC. Perform VERIFICATION TEST VER-1. If resistance is more than 10 ohms, repair open Brown/White wire. Perform VERIFICATION TEST VER-1.

TEST NS-12D

CHECKING AUTOMATIC IDLE SPEED (AIS) MOTOR OPERATION

NOTE: For connector terminal identification, see CONNECTOR IDENTIFICATION at beginning of article. For wiring diagram, see appropriate WIRING DIAGRAMS article in ENGINE PERFORMANCE.

1) Stop AIS motor actuation test. Turn ignition switch to OFF position. Disconnect and inspect Single Board Engine Controller (SBEC). Repair connector if damaged. Perform VERIFICATION TEST VER-1. If connector is okay, go to next step.

2) Using an external ohmmeter, check resistance of Violet/Black wire between SBEC connector terminal No. 59 and AIS motor connector terminal No. 4. If resistance is less than 10 ohms, replace SBEC. Perform VERIFICATION TEST VER-1. If resistance is more than 10 ohms, repair open Violet/Black wire. Perform VERIFICATION TEST VER-1.

TEST NS-12E

CHECKING AUTOMATIC IDLE SPEED (AIS) MOTOR OPERATION

NOTE: For connector terminal identification, see CONNECTOR IDENTIFICATION at beginning of article. For wiring diagram, see appropriate WIRING DIAGRAMS article in ENGINE PERFORMANCE.

1) Stop AIS motor actuation test. Turn ignition switch to OFF position. Disconnect and inspect Single Board Engine Controller (SBEC). Repair connector if damaged. Perform VERIFICATION TEST VER-1. If connector is okay, go to next step.

2) Using an external ohmmeter, check resistance of Yellow/Black wire between SBEC connector terminal No. 60 and AIS motor connector terminal No. 2. If resistance is less than 10 ohms, replace SBEC. Perform VERIFICATION TEST VER-1. If resistance is more than 10 ohms, repair open in Yellow/Black wire. Perform VERIFICATION TEST VER-1.

TEST NS-13A

CORRECTING START & STALL CONDITION

At this point in test procedure, all engine control systems have been determined to be operating as designed and not causing a no-start or start-and-stall problem. Following additional items should be checked as possible causes:

- Check if any MITCHELL® TECH SERVICE BULLETINS (TSBs) apply to vehicle.
- Check engine compression.
- Check for exhaust system restriction.
- Check camshaft and crankshaft sprockets.
- Check valve timing.
- Check torque converter stall speed.
- Check secondary ignition circuit for abnormal scope pattern.
- Check for fuel contamination.
- Ensure PCV system is functioning properly.

TEST DR-1A

CHECKING SYSTEM FOR FAULTS

NOTE: Battery must be fully charged and at rated capacity before performing any driveability test procedure. If vehicle starts and stalls repeatedly, perform TEST NS-2A. If vehicle stalls when A/C is turned on, perform TEST NF-9A.

1) Turn ignition switch to ON position. Connect DRB-II to engine diagnostic connector. Read fault messages. If DRB-II displays fault messages, go to step **5)**. If DRB-II does not display fault messages, go to next step.

2) Start engine. Allow engine to reach normal operating temperature. Set engine speed manually to 2000 RPM for at least 10 seconds, and return vehicle to idle. On A/T models, go to next step. On M/T models, go to step **4)**.

3) On A/T models, apply brakes. Shift gear selector through all gears and return to PARK position. Using DRB-II, read fault messages. If fault messages are displayed, go to step **5)**. If no fault messages are displayed, go to next step.

4) On all models, check MITCHELL® TECH SERVICE BULLETINS (TSBs) for any pertinent information if DRB-II still displays NO FAULTS. If a TSB exists, perform corrective action. If driveability problem continues after performing TSB procedure or if no TSB information is found, perform TEST NF-1A.

NOTE: ENGINE COLD TOO LONG fault message may set erroneously if ambient temperature is extremely cold.

5) If fault message is INTERNAL CONTROLLER FAILURE or CONTROLLER FAILURE, replace Single Board Engine Controller (SBEC). Perform VERIFICATION TEST VER-2. If fault message is ENGINE COLD TOO LONG, check engine cooling system. Repair as required. Perform VERIFICATION TEST VER-3.

1992 ENGINE PERFORMANCE
Self-Diagnostic Tests – 3.0L VIN 3 (Cont.)

CHRY
1-69

TEST DR-1A (Cont.)

6) If fault message is not INTERNAL CONTROLLER FAILURE, CONTROLLER FAILURE or ENGINE COLD TOO LONG, select fault message and corresponding test using DRB-II FAULT MESSAGES table. Correct all hard fault messages before proceeding to intermittent fault message.

DRB-II FAULT MESSAGES

DRB-II Message	[1] Hard Fault	[2] Intermittent Fault
A/C CLUTCH RELAY CIRCUIT	DR-28A	DR-36A
AUTOMATIC IDLE SPEED (AIS) MOTOR CIRCUITS	DR-15A	DR-35A
CONTROLLER FAILURE EEPROM WRITE DENIED	DR-32A	DR-32A
CONTROLLER FAILURE EMR MILES NOT STORED	DR-32A	DR-32A
COOLANT SENSOR VOLTAGE HIGH	DR-11A	DR-33A
COOLANT SENSOR VOLTAGE LOW	DR-12A	DR-33A
EGR SOLENOID CIRCUIT	DR-23A	DR-36A
EGR SYSTEM FAILURE	DR-24A	DR-36A
INJECTOR NO. 1 CONTROL CIRCUIT	DR-16A	DR-37A
INJECTOR NO. 2 CONTROL CIRCUIT	DR-17A	DR-37A
INJECTOR NO. 3 CONTROL CIRCUIT	DR-18A	DR-37A
INJECTOR NO. 4 CONTROL CIRCUIT	DR-19A	DR-37A
INJECTOR NO. 5 CONTROL CIRCUIT	DR-20A	DR-37A
INJECTOR NO. 6 CONTROL CIRCUIT	DR-21A	DR-37A
MAP SENSOR VOLTAGE HIGH	DR-5A	DR-33A
MAP SENSOR VOLTAGE LOW	DR-4A	DR-33A
NO ASD RELAY VOLTAGE SENSE AT CONTROLLER	DR-30A	DR-36A
NO CHANGE IN MAP	DR-3A	DR-33B
NO VEHICLE SPEED SIGNAL	DR-6A	DR-6A
O₂ SENSOR SHORTED TO VOLTAGE	DR-8A	DR-33A
O₂ SENSOR STAYS ABOVE CENTER	DR-9A	DR-33A
O₂ SENSOR STAYS AT CENTER	DR-7A	DR-33
O₂ SENSOR STAYS BELOW CENTER	DR-10A	DR-33A
PURGE SOLENOID CIRCUIT	DR-22A	DR-36A
RADIATOR FAN RELAY CIRCUIT	DR-29A	DR-36A
SLOW CHANGE IN MAP SIGNAL	DR-2A	DR-33B
TORQUE CONVERTER LOCK-UP SOLENOID CIRCUIT	DR-31A	DR-36A
TPS SENSOR VOLTAGE HIGH	DR-13A	DR-33A
TPS SENSOR VOLTAGE LOW	DR-14A	DR-33A

[1] – Key counter is "0".
[2] – Key counter is more than "0".

TEST DR-2A

CODE 13, SLOW CHANGE IN IDLE MAP SIGNAL

NOTE: For connector terminal identification, see CONNECTOR IDENTIFICATION at beginning of article. For wiring diagram, see appropriate WIRING DIAGRAMS article in ENGINE PERFORMANCE.

1) Turn ignition switch to ON position. Install vacuum "T" into Manifold Absolute Pressure (MAP) sensor vacuum hose. Start engine, and let it idle. Observe vacuum gauge. If vacuum does not exist at idle, repair plugged or restricted MAP sensor vacuum hose. Perform VERIFICATION TEST VER-2.

TEST DR-2A (Cont.)

2) If vacuum exists at idle, snap throttle open and closed while observing vacuum gauge. If vacuum gauge does not instantly drop to zero in. Hg and return, repair restricted vacuum hose to MAP sensor. Perform VERIFICATION TEST VER-2.

3) If vacuum gauge instantly drops to zero in. Hg and returns, turn ignition switch to OFF position. Disconnect and inspect MAP sensor electrical connector. Repair as required. Perform VERIFICATION TEST VER-2.

4) If MAP sensor connector is okay, inspect MAP sensor nipple and hose for restrictions. Remove any restrictions, and reconnect vacuum hose. Perform VERIFICATION TEST VER-2. If no restrictions exist, replace MAP sensor. Perform VERIFICATION TEST VER-2.

TEST DR-3A

CORE 13, NO CHANGE IN MAP FROM START TO RUN

NOTE: For connector terminal identification, see CONNECTOR IDENTIFICATION at beginning of article. For wiring diagram, see appropriate WIRING DIAGRAMS article in ENGINE PERFORMANCE.

Turn ignition switch to ON position. Install vacuum "T" into MAP sensor vacuum hose. Start engine, and let it idle. Observe vacuum gauge. If vacuum gauge indicates zero in. Hg at idle, repair leak in MAP sensor vacuum hose. Perform VERIFICATION TEST VER-2. If vacuum is not zero in. Hg at idle, repair restriction in MAP sensor vacuum hose. Perform VERIFICATION TEST VER-2.

TEST DR-4A

CODE 14, MAP VOLTAGE TOO LOW

NOTE: For connector terminal identification, see CONNECTOR IDENTIFICATION at beginning of article. For wiring diagram, see appropriate WIRING DIAGRAMS article in ENGINE PERFORMANCE.

1) Turn ignition switch to OFF position. Disconnect MAP sensor connector. Turn ignition switch to ON position. Read MAP sensor voltage. If MAP sensor voltage is more than 4.5 volts, replace MAP sensor. Perform VERIFICATION TEST VER-2.

2) If MAP sensor voltage is less than 4.5 volts, turn ignition switch to OFF position. Disconnect Single Board Engine Controller (SBEC) 60-pin connector. Place DRB-II in ohmmeter mode. Probe MAP sensor connector terminal No. 2 (Dark Green/Red wire).

3) If resistance is less than 10 ohms, repair Dark Green/Red wire for a short to ground. Perform VERIFICATION TEST VER-2. If resistance is more than 10 ohms, replace SBEC. Perform VERIFICATION TEST VER-2.

TEST DR-5A

CODE 14, MAP SENSOR VOLTAGE TOO HIGH

NOTE: For connector terminal identification, see CONNECTOR IDENTIFICATION at beginning of article. For wiring diagram, see appropriate WIRING DIAGRAMS article in ENGINE PERFORMANCE.

1) Turn ignition switch to OFF position. Disconnect and inspect MAP sensor connector. Repair connector if damaged. Perform VERIFICATION TEST VER-2. If MAP sensor connector is okay, connect a jumper wire between MAP sensor connector terminals No. 1 (Black/Light Blue wire) and 2 (Dark Green/Red wire). Turn ignition switch to ON position. Read MAP sensor voltage.

CHRY
1-70

1992 ENGINE PERFORMANCE
Self-Diagnostic Tests – 3.0L VIN 3 (Cont.)

TEST DR-5A (Cont.)

2) If MAP sensor voltage is less than one volt, replace MAP sensor. Perform VERIFICATION TEST VER-2. If MAP sensor voltage is more than one volt, remove jumper wire. Connect jumper wire between MAP sensor connector terminal No. 2 (Dark Green/Red wire) and ground. If voltage is less than one volt, repair open in Black/Light Blue wire. Perform VERIFICATION TEST VER-2.

3) If voltage is more than one volt, disconnect and inspect Single Board Engine Controller (SBEC) 60-pin connector. Repair connector if damaged. Perform VERIFICATION TEST VER-2. If SBEC connector is okay, go to next step.

4) Using an external ohmmeter, check resistance of Dark Green/Red wire between MAP sensor connector terminal No. 2 and SBEC 60-pin connector terminal No. 1. If resistance is more than 10 ohms, repair open in Dark Green/Red wire. Perform VERIFICATION TEST VER-2. If resistance is less than 10 ohms, replace SBEC. Perform VERIFICATION TEST VER-2.

TEST DR-6A

CODE 15, NO VEHICLE SPEED SIGNAL

NOTE: For connector terminal identification, see CONNECTOR IDENTIFICATION at beginning of article. For wiring diagram, see appropriate WIRING DIAGRAMS article in ENGINE PERFORMANCE.

1) Turn ignition switch to OFF position. Disconnect and inspect distance sensor connector. Repair connector if damaged. Perform VERIFICATION TEST VER-2.

2) If distance sensor connector is okay, turn ignition switch to ON position. Connect jumper wire to one terminal of distance sensor harness connector. Using DRB-II, read distance sensor signal (vehicle speed) while tapping open end of jumper wire to other distance sensor harness connector terminal.

3) If DRB-II shows speed to be more than zero, replace distance sensor. Perform VERIFICATION TEST VER-2. If speed is zero, place DRB-II in ohmmeter mode. Probe distance sensor connector terminal No. 2 (Black/Light Blue wire). If resistance is more than 10 ohms, repair open Black/Light Blue wire. Perform VERIFICATION TEST VER-2.

4) If resistance is less than 10 ohms, turn ignition switch to OFF position. Disconnect Single Board Engine Controller (SBEC) 60-pin connector. Inspect SBEC connector terminal No. 47 (White/Orange wire). Repair terminal if damaged. Perform VERIFICATION TEST VER-2. If terminal is okay, turn ignition switch to ON position.

5) Put DRB-II in voltmeter mode. Probe SBEC connector terminal No. 47 (White/Orange wire). If voltage is more than 4 volts, go to step 7). If voltage is less than 4 volts, check if speedometer works. If speedometer works, repair open in White/Orange wire from distance sensor connector terminal No. 1 to SBEC 60-pin connector terminal No. 47. Perform VERIFICATION TEST VER-2.

6) If speedometer does not work, turn ignition switch to OFF position. Place DRB-II in ohmmeter mode. Probe SBEC 60-pin connector terminal No. 47 (White/Orange wire). If resistance is less than 5 ohms, repair White/Orange wire for a short to ground. Perform VERIFICATION TEST VER-2. If resistance is more than 5 ohms, repair White/Orange wire for an open from distance sensor connector terminal No. 1 to splice. Perform VERIFICATION TEST VER-2.

7) If voltage was more than 4 volts in step 5), probe distance sensor connector terminal No. 1 (White/Orange wire). If voltage is more than 4 volts, replace SBEC. Perform VERIFICATION TEST VER-2. If voltage is less than 4 volts, repair open in White/Orange wire from distance sensor connector terminal No. 1 to SBEC 60-pin connector terminal No. 47. Perform VERIFICATION TEST VER-2.

TEST DR-7A

CODE 21, OXYGEN (O_2) SENSOR SIGNAL STAYS AT CENTER

NOTE: For connector terminal identification, see CONNECTOR IDENTIFICATION at beginning of article. For wiring diagram, see appropriate WIRING DIAGRAMS article in ENGINE PERFORMANCE.

1) Turn ignition switch to OFF position. Disconnect O_2 sensor connector. Inspect connector. Repair connector if damaged. Perform VERIFICATION TEST VER-2. If connector is okay, turn ignition switch to ON position.

2) Connect a jumper wire to O_2 sensor connector terminal No. 2 (Black/Dark Green wire). Connect other end of jumper wire to positive battery terminal. Using DRB-II, read O_2 sensor voltage. If O_2 sensor voltage is less than one volt, go to step 4). If O_2 sensor voltage is more than one volt, disconnect jumper wire. Turn ignition switch to OFF position.

3) Place DRB-II in ohmmeter mode. Probe O_2 sensor connector terminal No. 1 (Black/Light Blue wire). If resistance is more than 10 ohms, repair open in Black/Light Blue wire. Perform VERIFICATION TEST VER-1. If resistance is less than 10 ohms, replace O_2 sensor. Perform VERIFICATION TEST VER-2.

4) If voltage was less than one volt in step 2), disconnect jumper wire. Turn ignition switch to OFF position. Disconnect Single Board Engine Controller (SBEC) 60-pin connector. Inspect connector. Repair connector if damaged. Perform VERIFICATION TEST VER-2. If connector is okay, go to next step.

5) Using an external ohmmeter, test Black/Dark Green wire for resistance between O_2 sensor connector terminal No. 2 and SBEC connector terminal No. 41.

6) If resistance is less than 10 ohms, replace SBEC. Perform VERIFICATION TEST VER-2. If resistance is more than 10 ohms, repair open Black/Dark Green wire. Perform VERIFICATION TEST VER-2.

TEST DR-8A

CODE 21, OXYGEN (O_2) SENSOR SIGNAL SHORTED TO VOLTAGE

NOTE: For connector terminal identification, see CONNECTOR IDENTIFICATION at beginning of article. For wiring diagram, see appropriate WIRING DIAGRAMS article in ENGINE PERFORMANCE.

1) Attempt to start engine. Allow engine to idle for 2 minutes. Read O_2 sensor voltage using DRB-II. If O_2 sensor voltage is more than 1.3 volts, go to step 3). If O_2 sensor voltage is less than 1.3 volts, wiggle O_2 sensor wiring and observe O_2 sensor voltage reading.

2) If voltage is more than 1.3 volts while O_2 sensor wiring is wiggled, repair Black/Dark Green wire for a short to voltage. Perform VERIFICATION TEST VER-2. If voltage is still less than 1.3 volts, replace Single Board Engine Controller (SBEC). Perform VERIFICATION TEST VER-2.

3) If voltage was more than 1.3 volts in step 1), disconnect O_2 sensor connector. If voltage is now less than one volt, replace O_2 sensor. Perform VERIFICATION TEST VER-2.

4) If voltage is still more than one volt, repair Black/Dark Green wire for a short to Dark Green/Black wire. Reconnect O_2 sensor connector. Reset adaptive fuel value. Attempt to start engine. Allow engine to idle for 2 minutes. Read O_2 sensor value.

5) If O_2 sensor switches from rich to lean, repair is complete. Perform VERIFICATION TEST VER-2. If O_2 sensor does not switch from rich to lean, replace O_2 sensor. Perform VERIFICATION TEST VER-2.

1992 ENGINE PERFORMANCE
Self-Diagnostic Tests – 3.0L VIN 3 (Cont.)

CHRY
1-71

TEST DR-9A

CODE 21, OXYGEN (O₂) SENSOR SIGNAL STAYS ABOVE CENTER

1) Allow engine to reach normal operating temperature. Turn engine off. Turn ignition switch to ON position. Allow vehicle to cool for 5 minutes. Remove air inlet hose from air cleaner. While holding throttle wide open, listen for injector leakage.

2) Replace leaking injectors as needed. Perform VERIFICATION TEST VER-2. If no injectors are leaking, inspect air filter and inlet air ducts for restrictions. Clear any restrictions as necessary. Perform VERIFICATION TEST VER-2. If no restrictions exist, perform TEST NF-12A.

TEST DR-10A

CODE 51, OXYGEN (O₂) SENSOR SIGNAL STAYS BELOW CENTER

Code 51 may set for several reasons not related to O₂ sensor or O₂ sensor circuits. If Code 51 sets, perform TEST NF-1A.

TEST DR-11A

CODE 22, COOLANT SENSOR VOLTAGE TOO HIGH

NOTE: For connector terminal identification, see CONNECTOR IDENTIFICATION at beginning of article. For wiring diagram, see appropriate WIRING DIAGRAMS article in ENGINE PERFORMANCE.

1) Turn ignition switch to OFF position. Disconnect coolant temperature sensor connector. Inspect connector. Repair connector if damaged. Perform VERIFICATION TEST VER-2. If connector is okay, connect a jumper wire between coolant temperature sensor connector terminals (Tan/Black and Black/Light Blue wires).

2) Turn ignition switch to ON position. Read coolant temperature sensor voltage. If voltage is less than one volt, replace coolant temperature sensor. Perform VERIFICATION TEST VER-2. If voltage is more than one volt, move jumper wire to coolant temperature sensor connector Tan/Black wire and ground.

3) Read coolant temperature sensor voltage. If voltage is less than one volt, repair open Black/Light Blue wire. Perform VERIFICATION TEST VER-2. If voltage is more than one volt, disconnect Single Board Engine Controller (SBEC). Inspect connector. Repair connector if damaged. Perform VERIFICATION TEST VER-2. If connector is okay, go to next step.

4) Using an external ohmmeter, test Tan/Black wire for resistance between SBEC connector terminal No. 2 and coolant temperature sensor connector. If resistance is less than 10 ohms, replace SBEC. Perform VERIFICATION TEST VER-2. If resistance is more than 10 ohms, repair open Tan/Black wire. Perform VERIFICATION TEST VER-2.

TEST DR-12A

CODE 22, COOLANT SENSOR VOLTAGE TOO LOW

NOTE: For connector terminal identification, see CONNECTOR IDENTIFICATION at beginning of article. For wiring diagram, see appropriate WIRING DIAGRAMS article in ENGINE PERFORMANCE.

1) Turn ignition switch to ON position. Using DRB-II, read coolant temperature sensor voltage. Disconnect coolant temperature sensor connector. If voltage is more than 4 volts, replace coolant temperature sensor. Perform VERIFICATION TEST VER-2. If voltage is not more than 4 volts, turn ignition switch to OFF position.

TEST DR-12A (Cont.)

2) Disconnect Single Board Engine Controller (SBEC) 60-pin connector. Place DRB-II in ohmmeter mode. Probe SBEC connector terminal No. 2 (Tan/Black wire). If resistance is less than 10 ohms, repair Tan/Black wire for a short to Black/Light Blue wire or ground. Perform VERIFICATION TEST VER-2. If resistance is more than 10 ohms, replace SBEC. Perform VERIFICATION TEST VER-2.

TEST DR-13A

CODE 24, THROTTLE POSITION SENSOR (TPS) VOLTAGE HIGH

NOTE: For connector terminal identification, see CONNECTOR IDENTIFICATION at beginning of article. For wiring diagram, see appropriate WIRING DIAGRAMS article in ENGINE PERFORMANCE.

1) Turn ignition switch to OFF position. Disconnect TPS. Inspect connector. Repair connector if damaged. Perform VERIFICATION TEST VER-2. If TPS connector is okay, turn ignition switch to ON position.

2) Connect a jumper wire between TPS connector terminals No. 2 and 3 (Orange/Dark Blue and Black/Light Blue wires). Read TPS voltage. If voltage is less than one volt, replace TPS. Perform VERIFICATION TEST VER-2. If voltage is more than one volt, move jumper wire to Orange/Dark Blue wire and ground.

3) Read TPS voltage. If voltage is less than one volt, repair open in Black/Light Blue wire. Perform VERIFICATION TEST VER-2. If voltage is more than one volt, turn ignition switch to OFF position. Disconnect Single Board Engine Controller (SBEC) 60-pin connector. Inspect connector. Repair connector if damaged. Perform VERIFICATION TEST VER-2. If connector is okay, go to next step.

4) Using an external ohmmeter, test Orange/Dark Blue wire for resistance between SBEC connector terminal No. 22 and throttle position sensor terminal No. 2. If resistance is less than 10 ohms, replace SBEC. Perform VERIFICATION TEST VER-2. If resistance is more than 10 ohms, repair open Orange/Dark Blue wire. Perform VERIFICATION TEST VER-2.

TEST DR-14A

CODE 24, THROTTLE POSITION SENSOR (TPS) VOLTAGE LOW

NOTE: For connector terminal identification, see CONNECTOR IDENTIFICATION at beginning of article. For wiring diagram, see appropriate WIRING DIAGRAMS article in ENGINE PERFORMANCE.

1) Turn ignition switch to OFF position. Disconnect TPS. Turn ignition switch to ON position. Place DRB-II in voltmeter mode. Probe TPS connector terminal No. 1 (Violet/White wire). If voltage is less than one volt, repair open in Violet/White wire. Perform VERIFICATION TEST VER-2.

2) If voltage is more than one volt, probe TPS connector terminal No. 2 (Orange/Dark Blue wire). If voltage is more than one volt, replace TPS. Perform VERIFICATION TEST VER-2. If voltage is less than one volt, turn ignition switch to OFF position. Disconnect Single Board Engine Controller (SBEC) connector.

3) Place DRB-II in ohmmeter mode. Probe terminal No. 22 (Orange/Dark Blue wire) of SBEC connector. If resistance is less than 10 ohms, repair Orange/Dark Blue wire for a short to ground. Perform VERIFICATION TEST VER-2. If resistance is more than 10 ohms, replace SBEC. Perform VERIFICATION TEST VER-2.

CHRY
1-72

1992 ENGINE PERFORMANCE
Self-Diagnostic Tests – 3.0L VIN 3 (Cont.)

TEST DR-15A

CODE 25, AUTOMATIC IDLE SPEED (AIS) MOTOR CIRCUITS

NOTE: For connector terminal identification, see CONNECTOR IDENTIFICATION at beginning of article. For wiring diagram, see appropriate WIRING DIAGRAMS article in ENGINE PERFORMANCE.

1) Disconnect AIS motor connector. Turn ignition switch to ON position. Using DRB-II, actuate AIS motor. Place DRB-II in voltmeter mode. Probe AIS motor connector terminal No. 1 (Gray/Red wire).

2) Under normal conditions, voltage will switch from less than one volt to more than 10 volts. If voltage is less than one volt, repair Gray/Red wire for a short to ground. Perform VERIFICATION TEST VER-2.

3) If voltage is more than one volt, check if voltage is more than 10 volts. If voltage is more than 10 volts, repair Gray/Red wire for a short to voltage. Perform VERIFICATION TEST VER-2.

4) Probe AIS motor connector terminal No. 2 (Yellow/Black wire) if voltage is less than 10 volts. If voltage is less than one volt, repair Yellow/Black wire for a short to ground. Perform VERIFICATION TEST VER-2. If voltage is more than one volt, check if voltage is more than 10 volts.

5) If voltage is more than 10 volts, repair Yellow/Black wire for a short to voltage. Perform VERIFICATION TEST VER-2. If voltage is less than 10 volts, probe AIS connector terminal No. 3 (Brown/White wire). If voltage is less than one volt, repair Brown/White wire for a short to ground. Perform VERIFICATION TEST VER-2.

6) If voltage is more than one volt, check if voltage is more than 10 volts. If voltage is greater than 10 volts, repair Brown/White wire for a short to voltage. Perform VERIFICATION TEST VER-2.

7) If voltage is less than 10 volts, probe AIS connector terminal No. 4 (Violet/Black wire). If voltage is less than one volt, repair Violet/Black wire for short to ground. Perform VERIFICATION TEST VER-2.

8) If voltage is more than one volt, check if voltage is more than 10 volts. If voltage is more than 10 volts, repair Violet/Black wire for a short to voltage. Perform VERIFICATION TEST VER-2.

9) If voltage is less than 10 volts, turn ignition switch to OFF position. Connect AIS motor connector. Disconnect Single Board Engine Controller (SBEC) 60-pin connector.

10) Using an external ohmmeter, check resistance between SBEC connector terminals No. 39 (Gray/Red wire) and 59 (Violet/Black wire). If resistance is less than 35 ohms, replace AIS motor. Perform VERIFICATION TEST VER-2.

11) If resistance is more than 35 ohms, check resistance between SBEC connector terminals No. 40 (Brown/White wire) and 60 (Yellow/Black wire). If resistance is less than 35 ohms, replace AIS motor. Perform VERIFICATION TEST VER-2.

12) If resistance is more than 35 ohms, test resistance between SBEC connector terminals No. 39 (Gray/Red wire) and 60 (Yellow/Black wire). If resistance is less than 10 ohms, repair Yellow/Black wire for a short to Gray/Red wire. Perform VERIFICATION TEST VER-2.

13) If resistance is 10-75 ohms, go to next step. If resistance is 75-120 ohms, repair Brown/White wire for a short to Violet/Black wire. If resistance is more than 120 ohms, replace SBEC.

14) If resistance is 10-75 ohms, check for resistance between SBEC connector terminals No. 59 (Violet/Black wire) and 60 (Yellow/Black wire). If resistance is less than 10 ohms, repair Yellow/Black wire for a short to Violet/Black wire. If resistance is more than 10 ohms, repair Gray/Red wire for a short to Brown/White wire. Perform VERIFICATION TEST VER-2.

TEST DR-16A

CODE 27, INJECTOR NO. 1 CONTROL CIRCUIT

NOTE: For connector terminal identification, see CONNECTOR IDENTIFICATION at beginning of article. For wiring diagram, see appropriate WIRING DIAGRAMS article in ENGINE PERFORMANCE.

1) Turn ignition switch to OFF position. Disconnect fuel injector harness 8-pin connector. See Fig. NS-2A. Using an external ohmmeter, measure resistance between White/Dark Blue and Dark Green/Orange wires on injector side of fuel injector 8-pin connector. If resistance is not 13-16 ohms, go to step 4). If resistance is 13-16 ohms, move ohmmeter lead from Dark Green/Orange wire to a good ground.

2) If resistance is less than 10 ohms, repair White/Dark Blue wire for a short to ground. Perform VERIFICATION TEST VER-2. If resistance is more than 10 ohms, disconnect Single Board Engine Controller (SBEC). Check resistance of White/Dark Blue wire between SBEC connector terminal No. 16 and harness side of 8-pin fuel injector connector terminal No. 4.

3) If resistance is more than 10 ohms, repair White/Dark Blue wire for an open from SBEC connector to fuel injector harness 8-pin connector. Perform VERIFICATION TEST VER-2. If resistance is less than 10 ohms, move one ohmmeter lead to a good ground. If resistance is less than 10 ohms, repair White/Dark Blue wire for a short to ground. Perform VERIFICATION TEST VER-2. If resistance is more than 10 ohms, replace SBEC. Perform VERIFICATION TEST VER-2.

4) If resistance was not 13-16 ohms in step 1), remove intake plenum (if necessary). Reconnect fuel injector harness 8-pin connector. Disconnect fuel injector No. 1 connector. Inspect connector terminals. Repair terminals if damaged. Perform VERIFICATION TEST VER-2.

5) If connector is okay, turn ignition switch to ON position. Actuate fuel injector No. 1 using DRB-II. Place DRB-II in voltmeter mode. Probe fuel injector No. 1 connector terminal No. 2. If voltage is more than 10 volts, repair Dark Green/Orange wire for an open to splice. If voltage is less than 10 volts, go to next step.

6) Using an external ohmmeter, test White/Dark Blue wire for resistance between fuel injector No. 1 connector and injector side of fuel injector harness 8-pin connector. If resistance is more than 10 ohms, repair White/Dark Blue wire for an open. If resistance is less than 10 ohms, replace fuel injector No. 1. Perform VERIFICATION TEST VER-2

TEST DR-17A

CODE 27, INJECTOR NO. 2 CONTROL CIRCUIT

NOTE: For connector terminal identification, see CONNECTOR IDENTIFICATION at beginning of article. For wiring diagram, see appropriate WIRING DIAGRAMS article in ENGINE PERFORMANCE.

1) Turn ignition switch to OFF position. Disconnect fuel injector harness 8-pin connector. See Fig. NS-2A. Using an external ohmmeter, measure resistance between Tan and Dark Green/Orange wires on injector side of fuel injector harness 8-pin connector. If resistance is not 13-16 ohms, go to step 4). If resistance is 13-16 ohms, move ohmmeter lead from Dark Green/Orange wire to a good ground.

2) If resistance is less than 10 ohms, repair Tan wire for a short to ground. Perform VERIFICATION TEST VER-2. If resistance is more than 10 ohms, disconnect Single Board Engine Controller (SBEC). Check resistance of Tan wire between SBEC connector terminal No. 15 and harness side of fuel injector harness 8-pin connector terminal No. 3.

3) If resistance is more than 10 ohms, repair Tan wire for an open from SBEC connector to fuel injector harness 8-pin connector. Perform VERIFICATION TEST VER-2. If resistance is less than 10 ohms, move one ohmmeter lead to a good ground. If resistance is less than 10 ohms, repair Tan wire for a short to ground. Perform VERIFICATION TEST VER-2. If resistance is more than 10 ohms, replace SBEC. Perform VERIFICATION TEST VER-2.

4) If resistance was not 13-16 ohms in step 1), remove intake plenum (if necessary). Reconnect fuel injector 8-pin connector. Disconnect fuel injector No. 2 connector. Inspect all terminals. Repair terminals if damaged. Perform VERIFICATION TEST VER-2.

1992 ENGINE PERFORMANCE
Self-Diagnostic Tests – 3.0L VIN 3 (Cont.)

CHRY
1-73

TEST DR-17A (Cont.)

5) If connector is okay, turn ignition switch to ON position. Actuate fuel injector No. 2. Place DRB-II in voltmeter mode. Probe fuel injector No. 2 connector terminal No. 2. If voltage is more than 10 volts, repair Dark Green/Orange wire for an open to splice. If voltage is less than 10 volts, go to next step.

6) Using an external ohmmeter, Check Tan wire for resistance between fuel injector No. 2 connector and injector side of fuel injector harness 8-pin connector. If resistance is more than 10 ohms, repair Tan wire for an open. Perform VERIFICATION TEST VER-2. If resistance is less than 10 ohms, replace fuel injector No. 2. Perform VERIFICATION TEST VER-2.

TEST DR-18A

CODE 27, INJECTOR NO. 3 CONTROL CIRCUIT

NOTE: For connector terminal identification, see CONNECTOR IDEN-TIFICATION at beginning of article. For wiring diagram, see appropriate WIRING DIAGRAMS article in ENGINE PERFORMANCE.

1) Turn ignition switch to OFF position. Disconnect fuel injector harness 8-pin connector. *See Fig. NS-2A.* Using an external ohmmeter, measure resistance between Yellow/White and Dark Green/Orange wires on injector side of fuel injector harness 8-pin connector. If resistance is not 13-16 ohms, go to step **4)**. If resistance is 13-16 ohms, move ohmmeter lead from Dark Green/Orange wire to a good ground.

2) If resistance is less than 10 ohms, repair Yellow/White wire for short to ground. Perform VERIFICATION TEST VER-2. If resistance is more than 10 ohms, disconnect Single Board Engine Controller (SBEC). Check resistance of Yellow/White wire between SBEC connector terminal No. 14 and harness side of fuel injector 8-pin connector terminal No. 2.

3) If resistance is more than 10 ohms, repair Yellow/White wire for an open from SBEC connector to fuel injector harness 8-pin connector. Perform VERIFICATION TEST VER-2. If resistance is less than 10 ohms, move one ohmmeter lead to a good ground. If resistance is less than 10 ohms, repair Yellow/White wire for a short to ground. Perform VERIFICATION TEST VER-2. If resistance is more than 10 ohms, replace SBEC. Perform VERIFICATION TEST VER-2.

4) If resistance was not 13-16 ohms in step **1)**, remove intake plenum (if necessary). Reconnect fuel injector harness 8-pin connector. Disconnect fuel injector No. 3 connector. Inspect all terminals. Repair terminals if damaged. Perform VERIFICATION TEST VER-2.

5) If connector is okay, turn ignition switch to ON position. Actuate fuel injector No. 3 using DRB-II. Place DRB-II in voltmeter mode. Probe fuel injector No. 3 connector terminal No. 2. If voltage is more than 10 volts, repair Dark Green/Orange wire for an open to splice. If voltage is less than 10 volts, go to next step.

6) Using an external ohmmeter, test Yellow/White wire for resistance between fuel injector No. 3 connector and injector side of fuel injector harness 8-pin connector. If resistance is more than 10 ohms, repair Yellow/White wire for an open; if resistance is less than 10 ohms, replace fuel injector No. 3. Perform VERIFICATION TEST VER-2.

TEST DR-19A

CODE 27, INJECTOR NO. 4 CONTROL CIRCUIT

NOTE: For connector terminal identification, see CONNECTOR IDEN-TIFICATION at beginning of article. For wiring diagram, see appropriate WIRING DIAGRAMS article in ENGINE PERFORMANCE.

1) Turn ignition switch to OFF position. Disconnect fuel injector harness 8-pin connector. *See Fig. NS-2A.* Using an external ohmmeter, measure resistance between Light Blue/Brown and Dark Green/Orange wires on injector side of fuel injector 8-pin connector. If resistance is not 13-16 ohms, go to step **4)**. If resistance is 13-16 ohms, move ohmmeter lead from Light Blue/Brown wire to a good ground.

TEST DR-19A (Cont.)

2) If resistance is less than 10 ohms, repair Light Blue/Brown wire for a short to ground. Perform VERIFICATION TEST VER-2. If resistance is more than 10 ohms, disconnect Single Board Engine Controller (SBEC). Check resistance of Light Blue/Brown wire between SBEC connector terminal No. 13 and harness side of fuel injector harness 8-pin connector terminal No. 1.

3) If resistance is more than 10 ohms, repair Light Blue/Brown wire for an open from SBEC connector to fuel injector harness 8-pin connector. Perform VERIFICATION TEST VER-2. Move one ohmmeter lead to a good ground if resistance is less than 10 ohms. If resistance is still less than 10 ohms, repair Light Blue/Brown wire for a short to ground; if resistance is more than 10 ohms, replace SBEC. Perform VERIFICATION TEST VER-2.

4) If resistance was not 13-16 ohms in step **1)**, remove intake plenum (if necessary). Reconnect fuel injector 8-pin connector. Disconnect fuel injector No. 4 connector. Inspect all terminals. Repair terminals if damaged. Perform VERIFICATION TEST VER-2.

5) If connector is okay, turn ignition switch to ON position. Actuate fuel injector No. 4 using DRB-II. Place DRB-II in voltmeter mode. Probe fuel injector No. 4 connector terminal No. 2. If voltage is more than 10 volts, repair Dark Green/Orange wire for an open to splice. If voltage is less than 10 volts, go to next step.

6) Using an external ohmmeter, test Light Blue/Brown wire for resistance between fuel injector No. 4 connector and injector side of fuel injector harness 8-pin connector. If resistance is more than 10 ohms, repair Light Blue/Brown wire for an open. Perform VERIFICATION TEST VER-2. If resistance is less than 10 ohms, replace fuel injector No. 4. Perform VERIFICATION TEST VER-2.

TEST DR-20A

CODE 27, INJECTOR NO. 5 CONTROL CIRCUIT

NOTE: For connector terminal identification, see CONNECTOR IDEN-TIFICATION at beginning of article. For wiring diagram, see appropriate WIRING DIAGRAMS article in ENGINE PERFORMANCE.

1) Turn ignition switch to OFF position. Disconnect fuel injector harness 8-pin injector harness connector. *See Fig. NS-2A.* Using an external ohmmeter, measure resistance between Gray and Dark Green/Orange wires on injector side of fuel injector harness 8-pin connector. If resistance is not 13-16 ohms, go to step **4)**. If resistance is 13-16 ohms, move ohmmeter lead from Dark Green/Orange wire to a good ground.

2) If resistance is less than 10 ohms, repair Gray wire for a short to ground. Perform VERIFICATION TEST VER-2. If resistance is more than 10 ohms, disconnect Single Board Engine Controller (SBEC). Check resistance of Gray wire between SBEC connector terminal No. 38 and harness side of fuel injector harness 8-pin connector terminal No. 5.

3) If resistance is more than 10 ohms, repair Gray wire for an open from SBEC connector to fuel injector harness 8-pin connector. Perform VERIFICATION TEST VER-2. If resistance is less than 10 ohms, move one ohmmeter lead to a good ground. If resistance is less than 10 ohms, repair Gray wire for a short to ground. Perform VERIFICATION TEST VER-2. If resistance is more than 10 ohms, replace SBEC. Perform VERIFICATION TEST VER-2.

4) If resistance was not 13-16 ohms in step **1)**, remove intake plenum (if necessary). Reconnect fuel injector harness 8-pin connector. Disconnect fuel injector No. 5 connector. Inspect all terminals. Repair terminals if damaged. Perform VERIFICATION TEST VER-2.

5) If connector is okay, turn ignition switch to ON position. Actuate fuel injector No. 5. Place DRB-II in voltmeter mode. Probe fuel injector No. 5 connector terminal No. 2. If voltage is more than 10 volts, repair Dark Green/Orange wire for an open to splice. If voltage is less than 10 volts, go to next step.

6) Using an external ohmmeter, check resistance of Gray wire between fuel injector No. 5 connector and injector side of fuel injector 8-pin connector. If resistance is more than 10 ohms, repair Gray wire for an open. Perform VERIFICATION TEST VER-2. If resistance is less than 10 ohms, replace fuel injector No. 5. Perform VERIFICATION TEST VER-2.

CHRY
1-74

1992 ENGINE PERFORMANCE
Self-Diagnostic Tests – 3.0L VIN 3 (Cont.)

TEST DR-21A

CODE 27, INJECTOR NO. 6 CONTROL CIRCUIT

NOTE: For connector terminal identification, see CONNECTOR IDENTIFICATION at beginning of article. For wiring diagram, see appropriate WIRING DIAGRAMS article in ENGINE PERFORMANCE.

1) Turn ignition switch to OFF position. Disconnect fuel injector harness 8-pin connector. See Fig. NS-2A. Using an external ohmmeter, measure resistance between Brown/Dark Blue and Dark Green/Orange wires on injector side of fuel injector harness 8-pin connector. If resistance is not 13-16 ohms, go to step 4). If resistance is 13-16 ohms, move ohmmeter lead from Dark Green/Orange wire to a good ground.

2) If resistance is less than 10 ohms, repair Brown/Dark Blue wire for a short to ground. Perform VERIFICATION TEST VER-2. If resistance is more than 10 ohms, disconnect Single Board Engine Controller (SBEC). Check resistance of Brown/Dark Blue wire between SBEC connector terminal No. 58 and harness side of fuel injector harness 8-pin connector terminal No. 6.

3) If resistance is more than 10 ohms, repair Brown/Dark Blue wire for an open from SBEC connector to fuel injector harness 8-pin connector. Perform VERIFICATION TEST VER-2. Move one ohmmeter lead to a good ground if resistance is less than 10 ohms. If resistance is less than 10 ohms, repair Brown/Dark Blue wire for a short to ground; if resistance is more than 10 ohms, replace SBEC. Perform VERIFICATION TEST VER-2.

4) If resistance was not 13-16 ohms in step 1), remove intake plenum (if necessary). Reconnect fuel injector harness 8-pin connector. Disconnect fuel injector No. 6 connector. Inspect all terminals. Repair terminals if damaged. Perform VERIFICATION TEST VER-2.

5) If connector is okay, turn ignition switch to ON position. Actuate fuel injector No. 6 using DRB-II. Place DRB-II in voltmeter mode. Probe fuel injector No. 6 connector terminal No. 2. If voltage is more than 10 volts, repair Dark Green/Orange wire for an open to splice. If voltage is less than 10 volts, go to next step.

6) Using an external ohmmeter, test Brown/Dark Blue wire for resistance between fuel injector No. 6 connector and injector side of fuel injector harness 8-pin connector. If resistance is more than 10 ohms, repair Brown/Dark Blue wire for an open. Perform VERIFICATION TEST VER-2. If resistance is less than 10 ohms, replace fuel injector No. 6. Perform VERIFICATION TEST VER-2.

TEST DR-22A

CODE 31, PURGE SOLENOID CIRCUIT

NOTE: For connector terminal identification, see CONNECTOR IDENTIFICATION at beginning of article. For wiring diagram, see appropriate WIRING DIAGRAMS article in ENGINE PERFORMANCE.

1) Turn ignition switch to OFF position. Disconnect and inspect purge solenoid connector. Repair connector if damaged. Perform VERIFICATION TEST VER-2.

2) If connector is okay, turn ignition switch to ON position. Put DRB-II in voltmeter mode. Probe purge solenoid connector Dark Blue or Dark Blue/White wire. If voltage is less than 10 volts, repair open in Dark Blue or Dark Blue/White wire. Perform VERIFICATION TEST VER-2.

3) If voltage is more than 10 volts, turn ignition switch to OFF position. Disconnect SBEC 60-pin connector. Inspect connector. Repair connector if damaged. Perform VERIFICATION TEST VER-2.

4) If connector is okay, place DRB-II in ohmmeter mode. Probe purge solenoid connector terminal No. 2 (Pink/Black wire). If resistance is less than 10 ohms, repair Pink/Black wire for a short to ground. Perform VERIFICATION TEST VER-2. If resistance is more than 10 ohms, go to next step.

5) Using an external ohmmeter, check resistance of Pink/Black wire between purge solenoid connector terminal No. 2 and SBEC connector terminal No. 52. If resistance is more than 10 ohms, repair open in Pink/Black wire. Perform VERIFICATION TEST VER-2. If resistance is less than 10 ohms, reconnect purge solenoid connector.

6) Turn ignition switch to ON position. Place DRB-II in voltmeter mode. Probe SBEC connector terminal No. 52 (Pink/Black wire). If voltage is more than 10 volts, replace SBEC. Perform VERIFICATION TEST VER-2. If voltage is less than 10 volts, replace purge solenoid. Perform VERIFICATION TEST VER-2.

TEST DR-23A

CODE 32, EGR SOLENOID CIRCUIT

NOTE: For connector terminal identification, see CONNECTOR IDENTIFICATION at beginning of article. For wiring diagram, see appropriate WIRING DIAGRAMS article in ENGINE PERFORMANCE.

1) Turn ignition switch to OFF position. Disconnect EGR solenoid connector. Inspect connector. Repair connector if damaged. Perform VERIFICATION TEST VER-2. If EGR solenoid connector is okay, turn ignition switch to ON position. Place DRB-II in voltmeter mode.

2) Probe EGR solenoid connector terminal No. 1 (Dark Blue wire). If voltage is less than 10 volts, repair open Dark Blue wire. Perform VERIFICATION TEST VER-2. If voltage is more than 10 volts, turn ignition switch to OFF position. Reconnect EGR solenoid connector. Disconnect Single Board Engine Controller (SBEC) connector. Inspect connector.

3) Repair connector if damaged. Perform VERIFICATION TEST VER-2. If connector is okay, turn ignition switch to ON position. Place DRB-II in voltmeter mode. Probe SBEC connector terminal No. 35. If voltage is more than 10 volts, replace SBEC. Perform VERIFICATION TEST VER-2.

4) If voltage is less than 10 volts, turn ignition switch to OFF position. Disconnect EGR solenoid connector. Place DRB-II in ohmmeter mode. Probe SBEC connector terminal No. 35. If resistance is less than 10 ohms, repair Gray/Yellow wire for a short to ground. Perform VERIFICATION TEST VER-2. If resistance is more than 10 ohms, go to next step.

5) Using an external ohmmeter, test Gray/Yellow wire for resistance between SBEC connector terminal No. 35 and EGR solenoid connector terminal No. 2. If resistance is less than 10 ohms, replace EGR solenoid; if resistance is more than 10 ohms, repair open in Gray/Yellow wire. Perform VERIFICATION TEST VER-2.

TEST DR-24A

CODE 32, EGR SYSTEM FAILURE

NOTE: For connector terminal identification, see CONNECTOR IDENTIFICATION at beginning of article. For wiring diagram, see appropriate WIRING DIAGRAMS article in ENGINE PERFORMANCE.

1) Disconnect vacuum supply hose to EGR solenoid. Connect a vacuum gauge to disconnected vacuum hose. Start engine. Allow engine to reach normal operating temperature. If vacuum is more than 10 in. Hg at idle, go to step 3). If vacuum is less than 10 in. Hg at idle, turn engine off.

2) Disconnect EGR vacuum signal line at throttle body. Connect a vacuum gauge to throttle body nipple. Attempt to start engine. Read vacuum gauge at idle. If vacuum is more than 10 in. Hg at idle, repair vacuum line to EGR solenoid for a leak or restriction. Perform VERIFICATION TEST VER-2. If vacuum is less than 10 in. Hg at idle, repair plugged vacuum nipple at throttle body. Perform VERIFICATION TEST VER-2.

3) If vacuum was more than 10 in. Hg at idle in step 1), turn engine off. Disconnect vacuum gauge. Reconnect vacuum hose to EGR solenoid.

4) Disconnect vacuum hose from EGR valve. Connect vacuum gauge to disconnected EGR vacuum hose. Attempt to start engine. While reading vacuum gauge, momentarily snap throttle open. If vacuum is not more than 5 in. Hg at any time, replace EGR valve assembly. Perform VERIFICATION TEST VER-2.

5) If vacuum is more than 5 in. Hg at any time, turn ignition switch to OFF position. Disconnect hose to EGR valve backpressure signal tube. Apply 20-30 psi to EGR backpressure signal tube. While opening and closing throttle, listen for a change in air sound. If air sound changes, replace EGR valve assembly. Perform VERIFICATION TEST VER-2.

6) If air sound does not change, remover vacuum gauge. Cap open nipple on backpressure signal tube. Disconnect hose to EGR valve. Connect a hand-held vacuum pump to EGR valve nipple. Start engine. While slowly applying vacuum to EGR valve, listen for a change in engine RPM.

7) If engine RPM does not change, go to next step. If engine RPM changes, turn ignition switch to OFF position. Apply 10 in. Hg of vacuum to EGR backpressure signal tube and hold for 30 seconds. If vacuum does not hold for 30 seconds, replace EGR valve assembly. Perform VERIFICATION TEST VER-2. If vacuum holds for 30 seconds, perform TEST NF-10A.

8) If engine RPM does not change, remove EGR valve assembly. Inspect manifold passages for any plugging. Repair as required. Perform VERIFICATION TEST VER-2. If passages are not plugged, replace EGR valve assembly. Perform VERIFICATION TEST VER-2.

1992 ENGINE PERFORMANCE
Self-Diagnostic Tests – 3.0L VIN 3 (Cont.)

CHRY
1-75

NOTE: Tests DR-25A through DR-27A apply to passenger cars only. No test procedures are missing.

TEST DR-28A

CODE 33, A/C CLUTCH RELAY CIRCUIT

NOTE: For connector terminal identification, see CONNECTOR IDENTIFICATION at beginning of article. For wiring diagram, see appropriate WIRING DIAGRAMS article in ENGINE PERFORMANCE.

1) Turn ignition switch to ON position. Using DRB-II actuate A/C clutch relay. If A/C clutch relay clicks when actuated, perform TEST DR-36A. If A/C clutch relay does not click when actuated, place DRB-II in voltmeter mode. Backprobe A/C clutch relay connector terminal "A" (Dark Blue wire).

2) If voltage is less than 10 volts, repair open Dark Blue wire. Perform VERIFICATION TEST VER-2. If voltage is more than 10 volts, turn ignition switch to OFF position. Disconnect Single Board Engine Controller (SBEC) connector. Inspect connector. Repair connector if damaged. Perform VERIFICATION TEST VER-2.

3) If connector is okay, turn ignition switch to ON position. Probe SBEC connector terminal No. 34 (Dark Blue/Orange wire). If voltage is more than 10 volts, replace SBEC. Perform VERIFICATION TEST VER-2. If voltage is less than 10 volts, turn ignition switch to OFF position.

4) Disconnect A/C clutch relay connector. Inspect connector. Repair connector if damaged. Perform VERIFICATION TEST VER-2. If connector is okay, place DRB-II in ohmmeter mode. Probe A/C clutch relay connector terminal "C" (Dark Blue/Orange wire).

5) If resistance is less than 10 ohms, repair Dark Blue/Orange wire for a short to ground. Perform VERIFICATION TEST VER-2. If resistance is more than 10 ohms, check resistance of Dark Blue/Orange wire between SBEC and A/C clutch relay connector.

6) If resistance is more than 10 ohms, repair open Dark Blue/Orange wire; if resistance is less than 10 ohms, replace A/C clutch relay. Perform VERIFICATION TEST VER-2.

TEST DR-29A

CODE 35, RADIATOR FAN RELAY CIRCUIT

NOTE: For connector terminal identification, see CONNECTOR IDENTIFICATION at beginning of article. For wiring diagram, see appropriate WIRING DIAGRAMS article in ENGINE PERFORMANCE.

1) Turn ignition switch to ON position. Using DRB-II, actuate radiator fan relay. If radiator fan relay clicks when actuated, perform TEST DR-36A. If radiator fan relay does not click when actuated, place DRB-II in voltmeter mode. Probe radiator fan relay connector terminal "A" (Dark Blue/White or White wire).

2) If voltage is less than 10 volts, repair open Dark Blue/White or White wire. Perform VERIFICATION TEST VER-2. If voltage is more than 10 volts, turn ignition switch to OFF position. Disconnect Single Board Engine Controller (SBEC) 60-pin connector. Inspect connector. Repair connector if damaged. Perform VERIFICATION TEST VER-2.

3) If connector is okay, probe SBEC connector terminal No. 31 (Dark Blue/Pink wire). If voltage is more than 10 volts, replace SBEC. Perform VERIFICATION TEST VER-2. If voltage is less than 10 volts, place DRB-II in ohmmeter mode. Disconnect radiator fan relay connector. Inspect connector. Repair connector if damaged. Perform VERIFICATION TEST VER-2.

4) If connector is okay, probe SBEC connector terminal No. 31 (Dark Blue/Pink wire). If resistance is less than 10 ohms, repair Dark Blue/Pink wire for short to ground. Perform VERIFICATION TEST VER-2.

5) If resistance is more than 10 ohms, check resistance of Dark Blue/Pink wire between radiator fan relay and SBEC. If resistance is more than 10 ohms, repair open Dark Blue/Pink wire. Perform VERIFICATION TEST VER-2. If resistance is less than 10 ohms, replace radiator fan relay. Perform VERIFICATION TEST VER-2.

TEST DR-30A

CODE 42, NO AUTO SHUTDOWN RELAY VOLTAGE SENSE AT CONTROLLER

NOTE: For connector terminal identification, see CONNECTOR IDENTIFICATION at beginning of article. For wiring diagram, see appropriate WIRING DIAGRAMS article in ENGINE PERFORMANCE.

1) Turn ignition switch to OFF position. Disconnect ASD relay. Disconnect Single Board Engine Controller (SBEC) connector. Inspect connector. Repair connector if damaged. Perform VERIFICATION TEST VER-2. If connector is okay, go to next step.

2) Using an external ohmmeter, check resistance of Dark Green/Orange wire. If resistance is less than 10 ohms, replace SBEC. Perform VERIFICATION TEST VER-2. If resistance is more than 10 ohms, repair Dark Green/Orange wire for open circuit between SBEC connector and harness splice. Perform VERIFICATION TEST VER-2.

TEST DR-31A

CODE 37, CHECKING TORQUE CONVERTER LOCK-UP SOLENOID CIRCUIT

NOTE: For connector terminal identification, see CONNECTOR IDENTIFICATION at beginning of article. For wiring diagram, see appropriate WIRING DIAGRAMS article in ENGINE PERFORMANCE.

1) Turn ignition switch to OFF position. Disconnect transmission torque converter lock-up solenoid connector. Inspect connector. Repair connector if damaged. Perform VERIFICATION TEST VER-2. If connector is okay, turn ignition switch to ON position.

2) Place DRB-II in voltmeter mode. Probe Dark Blue or Dark Blue/White wire. If voltage is less than 10 volts, repair open Dark Blue/White wire. Perform VERIFICATION TEST VER-2. If voltage is more than 10 volts, turn ignition switch to OFF position.

3) Disconnect Single Board Engine Controller (SBEC) 60-pin connector. Inspect connector. Repair connector if damaged. Perform VERIFICATION TEST VER-2. If connector is okay, place DRB-II in ohmmeter mode. Probe lock-up solenoid connector Orange/Black wire.

4) If resistance is less than 10 ohms, repair Orange/Black wire for a short to ground. Perform VERIFICATION TEST VER-2. If resistance is more than 10 ohms, go to next step.

5) Using an external ohmmeter, check resistance of Orange/Black wire between SBEC and torque converter lock-up solenoid. If resistance is more than 10 ohms, repair open Orange/Black wire. Perform VERIFICATION TEST VER-2.

6) If resistance is less than 10 ohms, reconnect transmission torque converter lock-up solenoid. Turn ignition switch to ON position. Place DRB-II in voltmeter mode. Probe SBEC connector terminal No. 54 (Light Green/White wire).

7) If voltage is more than 10 volts, replace SBEC. Perform VERIFICATION TEST VER-2. If voltage is less than 10 volts, replace transmission torque converter lock-up solenoid. Perform VERIFICATION TEST VER-2.

TEST DR-32A

CODE 62, CONTROLLER FAILURE EMR MILES NOT STORED & CODE 63, CONTROLLER FAILURE EEPROM WRITE DENIED

1) Turn ignition switch to ON position. Using DRB-II, perform EMR memory test. If DRB-II displays WRITE REFUSED, go to step 3). If DRB-II displays WRITE FAILURE, replace Single Board Engine Controller (SBEC). Perform VERIFICATION TEST VER-2. If DRB-II displays EMR MILEAGE INVALID, update mileage, and reset EMR memory. Perform VERIFICATION TEST VER-2.

1992 ENGINE PERFORMANCE
Self-Diagnostic Tests – 3.0L VIN 3 (Cont.)

TEST DR-32A (Cont.)

2) If DRB-II does not show EMR mileage invalid, compare EMR mileage stored with instrument panel odometer. If mileages are same, retest EMR memory. Perform VERIFICATION VER-2. If mileages differ, update mileage, and retest EMR memory. Perform VERIFICATION TEST VER-2.

3) If DRB-II displays WRITE REFUSED in step **1)**, SBEC was busy. Using DRB-II, perform EMR memory test. Retest EMR memory twice more if necessary. If fault WRITE REFUSED returns, replace SBEC. Perform VERIFICATION TEST VER-2. If fault WRITE REFUSED does not return, test is complete. Perform VERIFICATION TEST VER-2.

TEST DR-33A

INTERMITTENT TEST FOR SENSOR VOLTAGE

NOTE: For connector terminal identification, see CONNECTOR IDENTIFICATION at beginning of article. For wiring diagram, see appropriate WIRING DIAGRAMS article in ENGINE PERFORMANCE.

1) If an intermittent sensor fault is detected, turn ignition switch to ON position. Using DRB-II, read suspect circuit voltage. While monitoring voltage, wiggle connector at sensor. If voltage becomes erratic, repair wiring or connector defect at sensor. Perform VERIFICATION TEST VER-2.

2) If voltage does not become erratic, wiggle harness between sensor and Single Board Engine Controller (SBEC). Wait 5 seconds each time before moving to next section of harness.

3) If sensor voltage become erratic, repair harness where wiggling caused erratic reading. Perform VERIFICATION TEST VER-2. If sensor voltage does not become erratic, test is complete. Perform VERIFICATION TEST VER-2.

TEST DR-33B

INTERMITTENT TEST FOR SLOW CHANGE OR NO CHANGE IN MAP

NOTE: For connector terminal identification, see CONNECTOR IDENTIFICATION at beginning of article. For wiring diagram, see appropriate WIRING DIAGRAMS article in ENGINE PERFORMANCE.

1) Attempt to start engine. Using DRB-II, set engine speed to 1400 RPM. With engine speed at 1400 RPM, read MAP sensor voltage. While monitoring voltage, wiggle MAP sensor wiring. If engine stalls or voltage becomes erratic, repair wiring or connector at MAP sensor. Perform VERIFICATION TEST VER-2.

2) If engine stalls or voltage does not become erratic, turn ignition switch to OFF position. Install vacuum "T" into MAP sensor vacuum hose, and connect vacuum gauge. Attempt to start engine.

3) While watching vacuum gauge, snap throttle open and closed. If vacuum drops rapidly to zero in. Hg, test is complete. Perform VERIFICATION TEST VER-2. If vacuum does not drop rapidly to zero in. Hg, repair restricted manifold vacuum supply. Perform VERIFICATION TEST VER-2.

NOTE: There is a break in test numbering sequence at this point, skipping Test DR-34A. Break is due to previous chart references to these procedures. No test procedures have been omitted.

TEST DR-35A

INTERMITTENT TEST FOR AUTOMATIC IDLE SPEED (AIS) MOTOR CIRCUITS

NOTE: For connector terminal identification, see CONNECTOR IDENTIFICATION at beginning of article. For wiring diagram, see appropriate WIRING DIAGRAMS article in ENGINE PERFORMANCE.

1) Turn ignition switch to ON position. Using DRB-II, erase faults. Using DRB-II, actuate AIS motor. While actuating AIS motor, read secondary indicators. Wiggle connector at AIS motor. If fault indicator returns, repair wiring or connector at AIS motor. Perform VERIFICATION TEST VER-2.

2) If fault indicator does not return, wiggle wiring harness between AIS motor and Single Board Engine Controller (SBEC). Wait 5 seconds each time before moving to next section of harness.

3) If fault indicator returns, repair harness where wiggling caused indicator to return. Perform VERIFICATION TEST VER-2. If fault indicator does not return, test is complete. Perform VERIFICATION TEST VER-2.

TEST DR-36A

INTERMITTENT TEST FOR RELAYS & SOLENOIDS

NOTE: For connector terminal identification, see CONNECTOR IDENTIFICATION at beginning of article. For wiring diagram, see appropriate WIRING DIAGRAMS article in ENGINE PERFORMANCE.

1) Turn ignition switch to ON position. Using DRB-II, erase faults and actuate intermittent solenoid or relay. While actuating, read secondary indicators. Wiggle connector at intermittent solenoid or relay.

2) If fault indicator returns, repair wiring or connector defect at solenoid or relay. Perform VERIFICATION TEST VER-2. If fault indicator does not return, wiggle harness between solenoid/relay and Single Board Engine Controller (SBEC). Wait 5 seconds each time before moving to next section of harness.

3) If fault indicator returns, repair harness where wiggling caused indicator to return. Perform VERIFICATION TEST VER-2. If fault indicator does not return, test is complete. Perform VERIFICATION TEST VER-1.

TEST DR-37A

INTERMITTENT INJECTOR CONTROL FAULT

NOTE: For connector terminal identification, see CONNECTOR IDENTIFICATION at beginning of article. For wiring diagram, see appropriate WIRING DIAGRAMS article in ENGINE PERFORMANCE.

1) Using DRB-II, erase fault codes. Attempt to start engine. Select secondary indicators. Wiggle wiring harness from suspect injector to Single Board Engine Controller (SBEC).

2) If fault indicator returns, repair harness where wiggling caused indicator to return. Perform VERIFICATION TEST VER-2. If fault indicator does not return, visually inspect related wiring harness connectors. Look for broken, bent, pushed-out or corroded terminals. Visually inspect related harnesses. Look for chafed, pierced or partially broken wires. Perform VERIFICATION TEST VER-2.

1992 ENGINE PERFORMANCE
Self-Diagnostic Tests – 3.0L VIN 3 (Cont.)

CHRY
1-77

TEST NF-1A

NO FAULT CODE TEST MENU

Check MITCHELL® TECH SERVICE BULLETINS (TSBs) for any pertinent information. If a TSB exists, perform corrective action. If TSB does not exist or if driveability problem still exists, check suspect system and perform indicated test. See NO FAULT CODE TEST SEQUENCE MENU table. If system causing driveability problem is unknown, perform TEST NF-2A through TEST NF-13A in sequence until problem is found.

NO FAULT CODE TEST SEQUENCE MENU

Application	Test
Checking Secondary Ignition & Timing	NF-2A
Checking Fuel Pressure	NF-3A
Checking Coolant & TPS Calibrations	NF-4A
Checking MAP Sensor Calibration	NF-5A
Checking Oxygen (O_2) Sensor Switching	NF-6A
Checking Automatic Idle Speed Motor	NF-7A
Checking Park/Neutral Switch	NF-8A
Checking Engine Controller Grounds	NF-9A
Checking Engine Vacuum	NF-10A
Checking Minimum Idle Airflow	NF-11A
Checking Engine Mechanical	NF-12A

TEST NF-2A

CHECKING SECONDARY IGNITION & TIMING

1) Turn engine off. Connect an engine analyzer to engine. Start engine, and let it idle. Set scope to read display or parade pattern. Follow equipment manufacturer procedure for pattern analysis.

2) If secondary ignition pattern is not okay, repair indicated component in secondary ignition system. Perform VERIFICATION PROCEDURE VER-2. If secondary ignition pattern is okay, disconnect any spark plug wire. Observe secondary kilovolt line.

3) If open circuit secondary voltage is not at least 25 kilovolts, repair indicated component in secondary ignition system. Perform VERIFICATION PROCEDURE VER-2. If open circuit secondary voltage is at least 25 kilovolts, reconnect spark plug wires.

NOTE: When coolant temperature sensor connector is disconnected, coolant sensor fault will set and CHECK ENGINE light will glow.

4) Ensure engine temperature is more than 180°F (82°C) before proceeding. Disconnect coolant temperature sensor connector. Connect timing light. Check ignition timing. If ignition timing is not within 2 degrees of specification, adjust ignition timing to specification. Perform VERIFICATION PROCEDURE VER-2.

5) If ignition timing is within 2 degrees of specification, reconnect coolant temperature sensor connector. Using DRB-II, read spark advance. Increase engine speed to 2000 RPM. If spark advance changes with engine RPM, replace SBEC. Perform VERIFICATION PROCEDURE VER-2. If spark advance does not change with RPM, test is complete. Using DRB-II, erase coolant temperature sensor fault.

TEST NF-3A

CHECKING FUEL PRESSURE

WARNING: High fuel pressure may be present in fuel lines. Open fuel system with caution. See FUEL PRESSURE RELEASE procedure in SELF-DIAGNOSTICS INTRODUCTION – GASOLINE article.

1) Relieve fuel pressure. Connect fuel pressure gauge between fuel supply hose and chassis fuel line. Turn ignition switch to ON position. Using DRB-II, actuate Auto Shutdown (ASD) relay. If fuel pressure is 43-53 psi, fuel pressure is okay. If fuel pressure is not 43-53 psi, record fuel pressure reading. If fuel pressure is more than 53 psi, perform TEST NF-3B.

2) If fuel pressure is less than 53 psi, stop ASD fuel system actuation test. Turn ignition switch to OFF position. Inspect fuel lines for kinked or restricted lines. Repair as necessary. Perform VERIFICATION PROCEDURE VER-2.

TEST NF-3A (Cont.)

3) If lines are not kinked or restricted, remove fuel pressure gauge from fuel supply hose. Reconnect fuel supply hose. Install fuel pressure gauge between fuel tank and fuel filter. Turn ignition switch to ON position. Using DRB-II, actuate ASD relay. If fuel pressure is at least 5 psi more than previously recorded pressure, replace fuel filter. Perform VERIFICATION PROCEDURE VER-2.

4) If fuel pressure is not at least 5 psi more, gently squeeze fuel return hose while observing fuel pressure gauge, ensuring fuel pressure does not exceed 50 psi. If fuel pressure increases, replace fuel pressure regulator. Perform VERIFICATION PROCEDURE VER-2. If fuel pressure does not increase, replace fuel pump and sock assembly. Perform VERIFICATION PROCEDURE VER-2.

TEST NF-3B

CHECKING FUEL PRESSURE

WARNING: High fuel pressure may be present in fuel lines. Open fuel system with caution. See FUEL PRESSURE RELEASE procedure in SELF-DIAGNOSTICS INTRODUCTION – GASOLINE article.

1) Before any repairs or removal of fuel pressure gauge, relieve fuel pressure. Stop ASD fuel system actuation test. Ensure fuel tank is at least 1/2 full before performing following test.

2) Install fuel pressure gauge and adapter between fuel tank and filter at rear of vehicle. Remove fuel return line from fuel pump at fuel tank. Connect Fuel Pressure Test Adapter (6541) to fuel return line. Place other end of adapter hose into an approved 2-gallon gasoline container. Turn ignition switch to ON position.

3) Using DRB-II, actuate ASD fuel system test. Observe fuel pressure gauge. If fuel pressure is 43-53 psi, repair fuel return line for a restriction at fuel tank. Perform VERIFICATION PROCEDURE VER-2.

4) If fuel pressure is not 43-53 psi, stop ASD fuel system actuation test. Relieve fuel pressure. Reconnect fuel return line to fuel tank. Disconnect fuel return line from fuel rail.

5) Attach Fuel Pressure Test Adapter (6541) to fuel return line. Place other end of adapter hose into an approved 2-gallon gasoline can. Turn ignition switch to ON position. Actuate ASD fuel system test. Observe fuel pressure gauge.

6) If fuel pressure is 43-53 psi, repair restricted fuel return line to fuel tank. Perform VERIFICATION PROCEDURE VER-2. If fuel pressure is not 43-53 psi, replace fuel pressure regulator. Perform VERIFICATION PROCEDURE VER-2.

TEST NF-4A

CHECKING COOLANT & THROTTLE POSITION SENSOR CALIBRATIONS

1) Start engine. Allow engine to reach normal operating temperature. Using DRB-II, read coolant temperature sensor value. If temperature is not 180-250°F (82-121°C), replace coolant temperature sensor. Perform VERIFICATION PROCEDURE VER-2.

2) If temperature is 180-250°F (82-121°C), turn engine off. Turn ignition switch to ON position. Using DRB-II, read Throttle Position Sensor (TPS) voltage with throttle fully closed and against throttle stop. Replace TPS if voltage is not 1.5 volts or less with throttle closed. Perform VERIFICATION PROCEDURE VER-2.

3) If voltage is 1.5 volts or less with throttle fully closed, monitor voltage while slowly opening throttle wide open. If voltage change is not a smooth transition, replace throttle position sensor. Perform VERIFICATION PROCEDURE VER-2.

4) If voltage change is a smooth transition, check if maximum voltage is at least 3.4 volts with throttle wide open. If maximum voltage is not at least 3.4 volts with throttle wide open, replace TPS. Perform VERIFICATION PROCEDURE VER-2.

5) If maximum voltage is at least 3.4 volts, start engine, and let it idle. Using DRB-II, read minimum throttle voltage. If voltage is 0-1.5 volts, test is complete. If voltage is not 0-1.5 volts, replace TPS. Perform VERIFICATION PROCEDURE VER-2.

CHRY
1-78

1992 ENGINE PERFORMANCE
Self-Diagnostic Tests – 3.0L VIN 3 (Cont.)

TEST NF-5A

CHECKING MAP SENSOR CALIBRATION

1) Turn engine off. Install vacuum "T" and vacuum gauge in MAP sensor vacuum hose. Start engine, and let it idle. Using DRB-II, read MAP gauge. If vacuum gauge reading is within one in. Hg of MAP gauge reading, test is complete.

2) If reading is not within one in. Hg of MAP gauge reading, turn engine off. Disconnect vacuum gauge from MAP sensor vacuum hose. Connect an auxiliary vacuum pump to MAP sensor. Apply 5 in. Hg to MAP sensor. Read and record MAP sensor voltage. Increase vacuum to 20 in. Hg. Read and record MAP sensor voltage. Subtract voltage recorded at 20 in. Hg from voltage recorded at 5 in. Hg.

3) If difference is 2.3-2.9 volts, repair restriction in vacuum hose to MAP sensor. Perform VERIFICATION PROCEDURE VER-2. If difference is not 2.3-2.9 volts, replace MAP sensor. Perform VERIFICATION PROCEDURE VER-2.

TEST NF-6A

CHECKING OXYGEN (O₂) SENSOR SWITCHING

1) Allow engine to reach normal operating temperature. Using DRB-II, read O_2 sensor state. If O_2 sensor state is switching, system is functioning okay. If O_2 sensor state is not switching, check if O_2 sensor is locked on lean. If O_2 sensor is locked on lean, perform TEST NF-6B. If O_2 sensor is not locked on lean, turn engine off.

2) Let engine cool 5 minutes. Remove and inspect spark plugs for wet tips and fuel fouling. If either condition exists, replace leaking injectors at corresponding cylinders. Perform VERIFICATION PROCEDURE VER-3.

3) If neither condition exists, inspect air cleaner and air inlet ducts for restrictions. Clean restricted air inlet as necessary. Perform VERIFICATION PROCEDURE VER-3. If air inlet is not restricted, perform TEST NF-12A.

TEST NF-6B

CHECKING OXYGEN (O₂) SENSOR SWITCHING

NOTE: For connector terminal identification, see CONNECTOR IDENTIFICATION at beginning of article. For wiring diagram, see appropriate WIRING DIAGRAMS article in ENGINE PERFORMANCE.

1) Allow engine to idle. Inspect engine for vacuum leaks. Repair vacuum leaks as required. Perform VERIFICATION PROCEDURE VER-2. If vacuum leaks do not exist, read O_2 sensor signal voltage using DRB-II.

2) If voltage is more than .1 volt, go to step 4). If voltage is less than .1 volt, turn ignition switch to OFF position. Disconnect O_2 sensor and Single Board Engine Controller (SBEC) connectors. Place DRB-II in ohmmeter mode. Probe SBEC connector terminal No. 41 (Black/Dark Green wire).

3) If resistance is less than 10 ohms, repair Black/Dark Green wire for a short to ground. Perform VERIFICATION PROCEDURE VER-2. If resistance is more than 10 ohms, replace O_2 sensor. Perform VERIFICATION PROCEDURE VER-2.

4) If voltage is more than .1 volt, turn engine off. Replace O_2 sensor. After replacing O_2 sensor, turn ignition switch to ON position. Using DRB-II, reset adaptive fuel memory. Start engine, and allow it to reach normal operating temperature.

5) Read O_2 sensor state. If O_2 sensor state is switching, repair is complete. Perform VERIFICATION PROCEDURE VER-2. If O_2 sensor state is not switching, perform TEST NF-12A.

TEST NF-7A

CHECKING AUTOMATIC IDLE SPEED (AIS) MOTOR OPERATION

NOTE: For connector terminal identification, see CONNECTOR IDENTIFICATION at beginning of article. For wiring diagram, see appropriate WIRING DIAGRAMS article in ENGINE PERFORMANCE.

1) Using DRB-II, set engine speed to 1100 RPM. If engine speed can be set between 1050-1150 RPM, test is complete. If engine speed cannot be set between 1050-1150 RPM, return engine to normal idle speed. Disconnect AIS motor connector.

2) Inspect idle speed motor connector. Repair connector if damaged. Perform VERIFICATION PROCEDURE VER-2. If connector is okay, place DRB-II in voltmeter mode. Open and close throttle while probing AIS motor connector terminal No. 1 (Gray/Red wire). If voltage is less than one volt, perform TEST NF-7B.

3) If voltage is more than one volt, open and close throttle while probing AIS motor connector terminal No. 2 (Yellow/Black wire). If voltage is less than one volt, perform TEST NF-7B. If voltage is more than one volt, open and close throttle while probing terminal No. 3 (Brown/White wire) of AIS motor connector. If voltage is less than one volt, perform TEST NF-7B. If voltage is more than one volt, open and close throttle while probing AIS motor connector terminal No. 4 (Violet/Black wire). If voltage is less than one volt, perform TEST NF-7B.

4) If voltage is more than one volt, inspect engine for vacuum leaks. Repair as required. Perform VERIFICATION PROCEDURE VER-2. If vacuum leaks do not exist, replace AIS motor. Perform VERIFICATION PROCEDURE VER-2.

TEST NF-7B

CHECKING AUTOMATIC IDLE SPEED (AIS) MOTOR OPERATION

NOTE: For connector terminal identification, see CONNECTOR IDENTIFICATION at beginning of article. For wiring diagram, see appropriate WIRING DIAGRAMS article in ENGINE PERFORMANCE.

1) Turn engine off. Disconnect and inspect Single Board Engine Controller (SBEC) connector. Repair connector if damaged. Perform VERIFICATION PROCEDURE VER-2. If connector is okay, go to next step.

2) Using an external ohmmeter, check continuity between AIS motor connector terminal No. 1 (Gray/Red wire) and SBEC connector terminal No. 39 (Gray/Red wire), between AIS motor connector terminal No. 2 (Yellow/Black wire) and SBEC connector terminal No. 60 (Yellow/Black wire), between AIS motor connector terminal No. 3 (Brown/White wire) and SBEC connector terminal No. 40 (Brown/White wire) and between AIS motor connector terminal No. 4 (Violet/Black wire) and SBEC connector terminal No. 59 (Violet/Black wire). If resistance is less than 10 ohms for each circuit, replace SBEC. Perform VERIFICATION PROCEDURE VER-2.

3) If resistance is more than 10 ohms for any circuit, repair that circuit for an open. Perform VERIFICATION PROCEDURE VER-2.

TEST NF-8A

CHECKING PARK/NEUTRAL SWITCH

NOTE: For connector terminal identification, see CONNECTOR IDENTIFICATION at beginning of article. For wiring diagram, see appropriate WIRING DIAGRAMS article in ENGINE PERFORMANCE.

1) Using DRB-II, read park/neutral input state. While moving gear selector in and out of Park and Reverse positions, observe DRB-II display. If DRB-II displays P/N or D/R, test is complete.

2) If DRB-II does not display P/N or D/R, turn ignition switch to OFF position. Put gear selector in Park position. Disconnect Single Board Engine Controller (SBEC) 60-pin connector.

1992 ENGINE PERFORMANCE
Self-Diagnostic Tests – 3.0L VIN 3 (Cont.)

CHRY
1-79

TEST NF-8A (Cont.)

3) Disconnect power disconnect cable at battery. Put DRB-II in ohmmeter mode. Probe SBEC connector terminal No. 30 (Brown/Yellow wire). While moving gear selector in and out of Park and Reverse positions, observe DRB-II display.

4) If DRB-II display switches from less than 5 ohms to more than 5 ohms, replace SBEC. If display does not switch from less than 5 ohms to more than 5 ohms, check if display always stays at less than 5 ohms.

5) If display always stays at less than 5 ohms, repair Brown/Yellow wire for a short to ground. Perform VERIFICATION PROCEDURE VER-2. If display does not always stay at less than 5 ohms, disconnect park/neutral safety switch connector. Using an external ohmmeter, test resistance of park/neutral switch Brown/Yellow wire.

6) If resistance is less than 10 ohms, replace park/neutral safety switch. If resistance is more than 10 ohms, repair open in Brown/Yellow wire. Perform VERIFICATION PROCEDURE VER-2.

TEST NF-9A

CHECKING ENGINE CONTROLLER GROUND & POWER CIRCUITS

NOTE: For connector terminal identification, see CONNECTOR IDENTIFICATION at beginning of article. For wiring diagram, see appropriate WIRING DIAGRAMS article in ENGINE PERFORMANCE.

1) Turn ignition switch to OFF position. Disconnect and inspect SBEC connector terminals. Repair connector terminals if damaged. Perform VERIFICATION PROCEDURE VER-2.

2) If connector terminals are okay, place DRB-II in ohmmeter mode. Probe SBEC connector terminal No. 5 (Black/White wire). If resistance is more than one ohm, repair Black/White wire for an open to ground. Perform VERIFICATION PROCEDURE VER-2. If resistance is less than one ohm, probe terminal No. 11.

3) If resistance is more than one ohm, repair Black/Tan wire for an open to ground. Perform VERIFICATION PROCEDURE VER-2. If resistance is less than one ohm, probe SBEC connector terminal No. 12 (Black/Tan wire). If resistance is more than one ohm, repair Black/Tan wire for an open to ground. Perform VERIFICATION PROCEDURE VER-2.

4) If resistance is less than one ohm, place DRB-II in voltmeter mode. Turn ignition switch to ON position. Probe SBEC connector terminal No. 9 (Dark Blue wire). If voltage is less than 10 volts, repair open Dark Blue wire. Perform VERIFICATION PROCEDURE VER-2. If voltage is more than 10 volts, reconnect SBEC connector. Test is complete.

TEST NF-10A

CHECKING ENGINE VACUUM

NOTE: For connector terminal identification, see CONNECTOR IDENTIFICATION at beginning of article. For wiring diagram, see appropriate WIRING DIAGRAMS article in ENGINE PERFORMANCE.

Connect a vacuum gauge to engine. Start engine, and let it idle. Normal vacuum reading will vary depending on altitude. Observe vacuum gauge at idle. If vacuum gauge reading is not steady between 13-22 in. Hg, perform TEST NF-12A. If vacuum gauge reading is steady and within specification, test is complete.

TEST NF-11A

CHECKING MINIMUM IDLE AIRFLOW

NOTE: For connector terminal identification, see CONNECTOR IDENTIFICATION at beginning of article. For wiring diagram, see appropriate WIRING DIAGRAMS article in ENGINE PERFORMANCE.

1) Turn ignition switch to OFF position. Disconnect Positive Crankcase Ventilation (PCV) valve hose from PCV valve. Plug PCV valve nipple. Disconnect idle purge hose from engine vacuum harness tee.

2) Install Air Metering Fitting (6457) in intake manifold mounted idle purge hose. Start engine. Allow engine to reach normal operating temperature. Read minimum airflow speed using DRB-II. If engine RPM is as specified, test is complete. See MINIMUM IDLE AIRFLOW table.

3) If engine RPM is not as specified, replace throttle body. See MINIMUM IDLE AIRFLOW table. Perform VERIFICATION PROCEDURE VER-2.

MINIMUM IDLE AIRFLOW

Odometer Reading	RPM
Less Than 1000 Miles	750-950
1000 Miles Or More	625-950

TEST NF-12A

PERFORMING NO FAULT CODE MECHANICAL TEST

At this point in start-and-stall test procedure, all engine control systems have been determined to be operating as designed and not causing a no-start or start-and-stall problem. Following additional items should be checked as possible causes:

NOTE: If coming to this test from O_2 sensor test and rich or lean condition is not corrected after checking items listed below, replace Single Board Engine Controller (SBEC).

- Check if any MITCHELL® TECH SERVICE BULLETINS (TSBs) apply to vehicle.
- Check engine compression.
- Check for exhaust system restriction.
- Check camshaft and crankshaft sprockets.
- Check valve timing.
- Check torque converter stall speed.
- Check engine vacuum. It must be at least 13 in. Hg in Neutral.
- Check for fuel contamination.
- Ensure PCV system is functioning properly.
- Ensure injector control wire is connected to correct fuel injector and injector is not plugged or restricted.

TEST VER-1

VERIFICATION TEST VER-1

Inspect vehicle to ensure all engine components are connected. Reassemble and reconnect components as necessary. Attempt to start engine. If engine does not start, return to TEST NS-1A.

If engine starts, Single Board Engine Controller (SBEC) was changed and vehicle is equipped with factory theft alarm, start vehicle at least 20 times so alarm system may be activated when desired. Write EMR mileage into new SBEC. No-start condition is corrected and repair is now complete.

If engine starts and SBEC has not been changed, connect DRB-II to engine diagnostic connector, and erase faults. No-start condition has been corrected and fault messages have been erased. Repair is now complete.

If repaired fault resets, repair is not complete. Check all pertinent MITCHELL® TECH SERVICE BULLETINS (TSBs) and return to TEST DR-1A if necessary. If another fault exists, return to TEST DR-1A and follow path specified by other fault. If other faults do not exist, repair is now complete.

1992 ENGINE PERFORMANCE
Self-Diagnostic Tests – 3.0L VIN 3 (Cont.)

TEST VER-2

VERIFICATION TEST VER-2

If TEST VER-3 was performed previously, perform TEST VER-3 again. Inspect vehicle to ensure all engine components are connected. Reassemble and reconnect components as necessary. If another fault was read previously and not corrected, return to TEST DR-1A and follow path specified by other fault. If Single Board Engine Controller (SBEC) was replaced, perform following:

1) If vehicle is equipped with factory theft alarm, start vehicle at least 20 times so alarm system may be activated as desired. Write EMR mileage into new SBEC. Connect DRB-II to engine diagnostic connector, and erase faults. Ensure no other fault remains by starting engine and allowing it to reach normal operating temperature.

2) Increase engine speed to 2000 RPM for at least 10 seconds. Allow engine to idle. On A/T models, apply brake and cycle transmission through all gear ranges. Place gear selector in PARK position. On vehicles equipped with A/C, turn on A/C. Set blower to low speed.

3) On all models, turn engine off. Start engine. Allow engine to idle for at least 2 minutes. Turn engine off. Using DRB-II, read fault messages. If repaired fault resets, repair is not complete.

4) Check all pertinent MITCHELL® TECH SERVICE BULLETINS (TSBs) and return to TEST DR-1A if necessary. If another fault exists, return to TEST DR-1A and follow path specified by other fault. If other faults do not exist, repair is now complete.

TEST VER-3

VERIFICATION TEST VER-3

Inspect vehicle to ensure all engine components are connected. Reassemble and reconnect components as necessary. If another fault was read previously and not corrected, return to TEST DR-1A and follow path specified by other fault. If SBEC was replaced, perform following:

1) If vehicle is equipped with factory theft alarm, start vehicle at least 20 times so alarm system may be activated when desired. Write EMR mileage into new SBEC. Connect DRB-II to engine diagnostic connector, and erase faults. Disconnect DRB-II. Ensure other faults do not exist.

2) If vehicle is equipped with A/C, turn A/C on. Set blower to low speed. On all models, drive vehicle for at least 5 minutes and attain a speed of at least 40 MPH. Ensure transmission shifts through all gears.

3) Upon completion of road test, turn engine off. Restart engine, and let it idle for at least 2 minutes. Turn engine off. Connect DRB-II to engine diagnostic connector.

4) Read all fault messages. If repaired fault has reset, repair is not complete. Check all pertinent MITCHELL® TECH SERVICE BULLETINS (TSBs). Return to TEST DR-1A if necessary and follow path specified by other fault. If other faults do not exist, repair is now complete.

WARNING: When battery is disconnected, vehicle computer and energy systems may lose memory data. Driveability problems may exist until computer systems have completed a relearn cycle. See COMPUTER RELEARN PROCEDURES article in GENERAL INFORMATION before disconnecting battery.

SELF-DIAGNOSTIC DIRECTORY
SELF-DIAGNOSTIC DIRECTORY

Application	Page
No-Start Tests	1-83
Driveability Tests	1-88
No Fault Code Tests	1-97
Verification Tests	1-100

CONNECTOR IDENTIFICATION
CONNECTOR IDENTIFICATION DIRECTORY

Connector	See Fig.
Automatic Idle Speed (AIS) Motor	1
Camshaft Sensor	2
Coolant Temperature Sensor	3
Crankshaft Sensor	4
Distance Sensor	5
Engine Diagnostic	6
EGR Solenoid	7
Fuel Injector	8
Fuel Pump	9
Ignition Coil	10
Manifold Absolute Pressure (MAP) Sensor	11
Oil Pressure Switch	12
Oxygen (O_2) Sensor	13
Purge Solenoid	14
Relays	
A/C Clutch, A/C Fan, Auto Shutdown, Fuel Pump & Radiator Fan Relays	15
Single Board Engine Controller (SBEC)	16
Throttle Body Charge Temperature Sensor	17
Throttle Position Sensor (TPS)	18
6-Pin Fuel Injector Wiring Harness	19
10-Pin Fuel Injector Wiring Harness	20

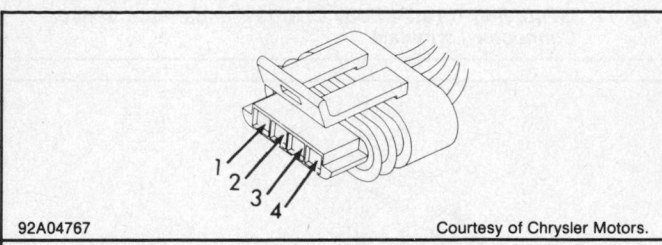

92A04767   Courtesy of Chrysler Motors.

Fig. 1: Identifying Automatic Idle Speed (AIS) Motor Connector Terminals

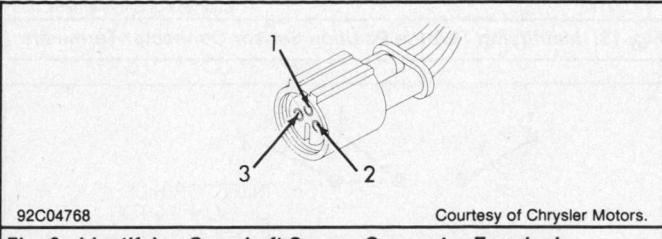

92C04768   Courtesy of Chrysler Motors.

Fig. 2: Identifying Camshaft Sensor Connector Terminals

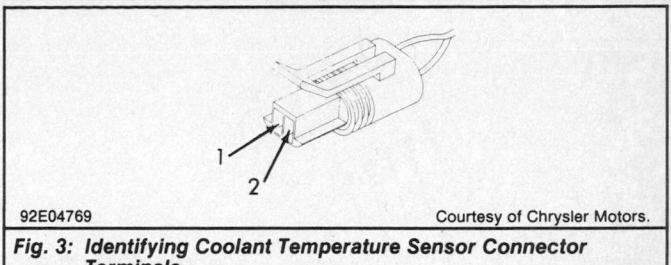

92E04769   Courtesy of Chrysler Motors.

Fig. 3: Identifying Coolant Temperature Sensor Connector Terminals

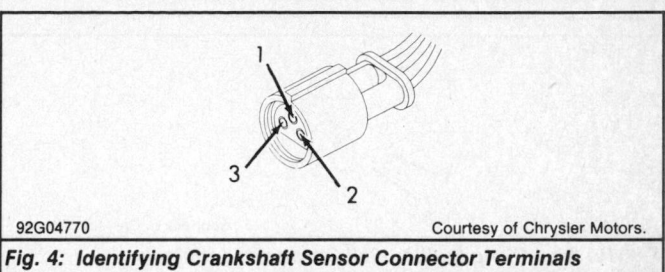

92G04770   Courtesy of Chrysler Motors.

Fig. 4: Identifying Crankshaft Sensor Connector Terminals

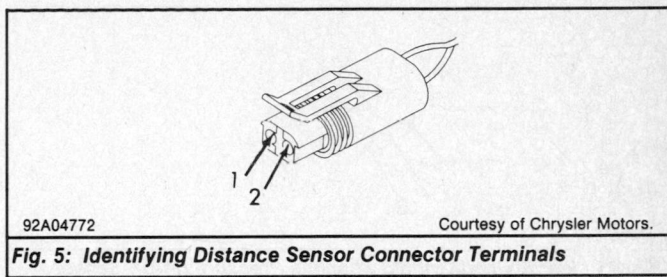

92A04772   Courtesy of Chrysler Motors.

Fig. 5: Identifying Distance Sensor Connector Terminals

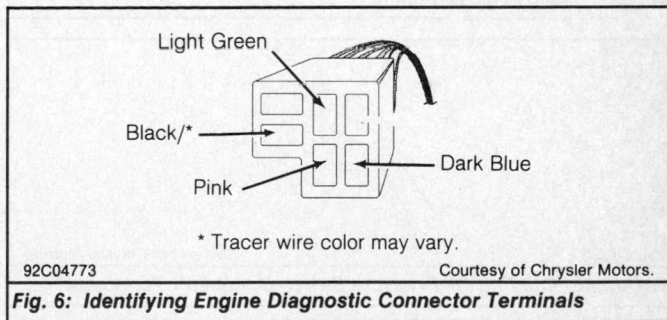

Light Green

Black/*

Pink

Dark Blue

* Tracer wire color may vary.

92C04773   Courtesy of Chrysler Motors.

Fig. 6: Identifying Engine Diagnostic Connector Terminals

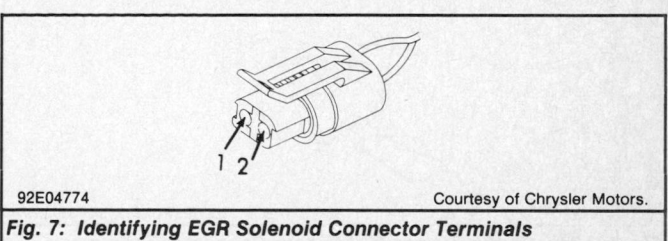

92E04774   Courtesy of Chrysler Motors.

Fig. 7: Identifying EGR Solenoid Connector Terminals

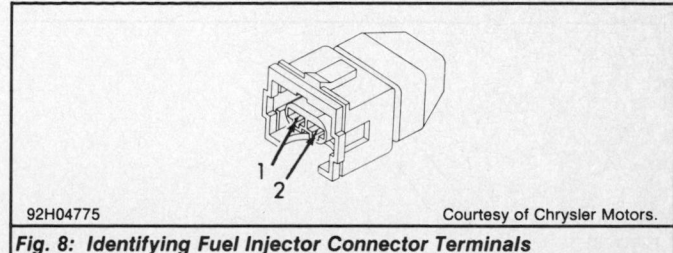

92H04775   Courtesy of Chrysler Motors.

Fig. 8: Identifying Fuel Injector Connector Terminals

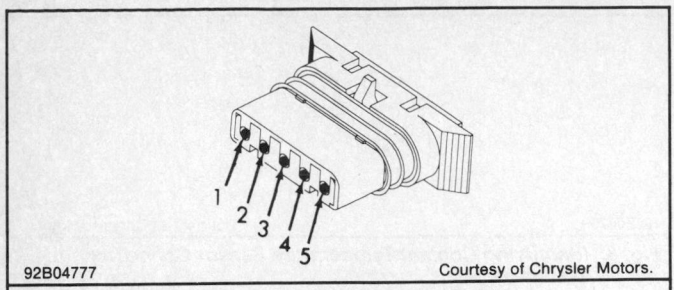

92B04777　　　　　　Courtesy of Chrysler Motors.

Fig. 9: Identifying Fuel Pump Connector Terminals

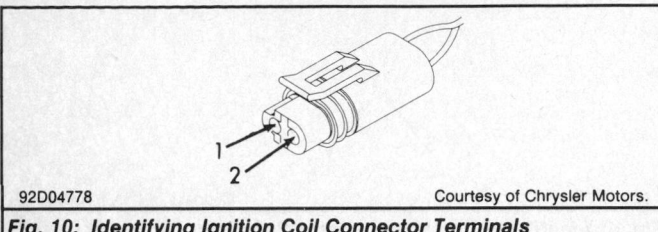

92D04778　　　　　　Courtesy of Chrysler Motors.

Fig. 10: Identifying Ignition Coil Connector Terminals

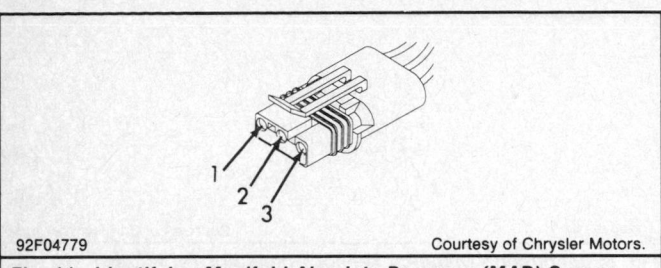

92F04779　　　　　　Courtesy of Chrysler Motors.

Fig. 11: Identifying Manifold Absolute Pressure (MAP) Sensor Connector Terminals

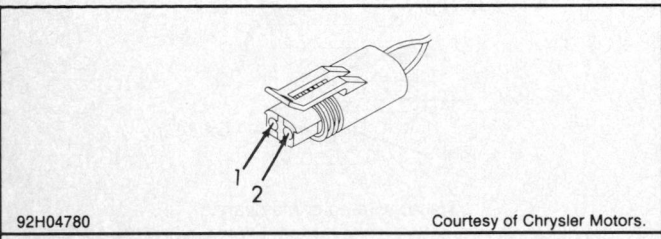

92H04780　　　　　　Courtesy of Chrysler Motors.

Fig. 12: Identifying Oil Pressure Switch Connector Terminals

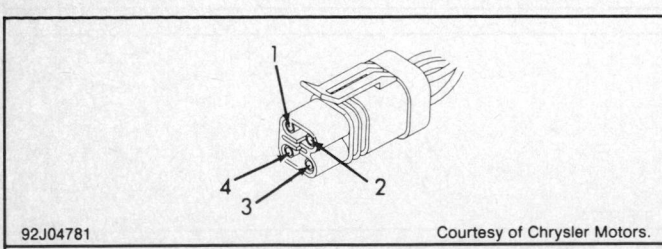

92J04781　　　　　　Courtesy of Chrysler Motors.

Fig. 13: Identifying Oxygen (O₂) Sensor Connector Terminals

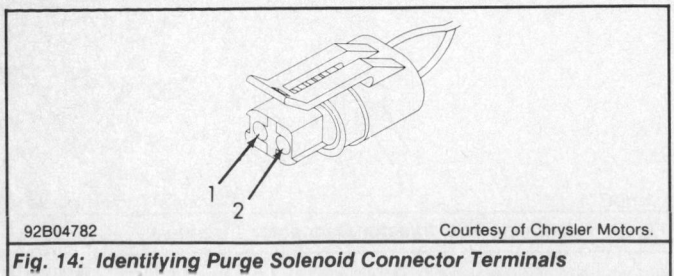

92B04782　　　　　　Courtesy of Chrysler Motors.

Fig. 14: Identifying Purge Solenoid Connector Terminals

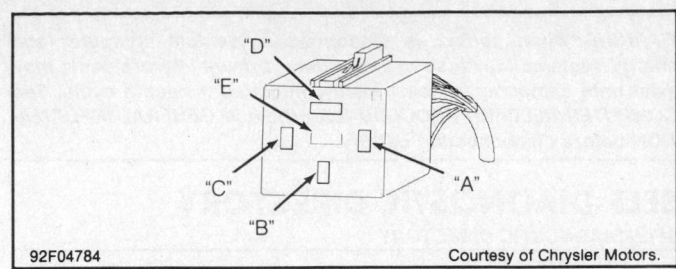

92F04784　　　　　　Courtesy of Chrysler Motors.

Fig. 15: Identifying A/C Clutch, A/C Fan, ASD, Fuel Pump & Radiator Fan Relay Connector Terminals

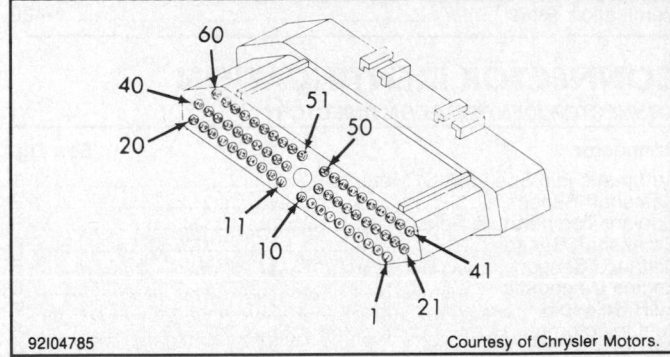

92I04785　　　　　　Courtesy of Chrysler Motors.

Fig. 16: Identifying Single Board Engine Controller (SBEC) Connector Terminals

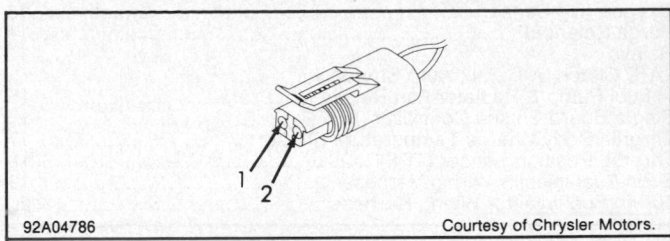

92A04786　　　　　　Courtesy of Chrysler Motors.

Fig. 17: Identifying Throttle Body Charge Temperature Sensor Connector Terminals

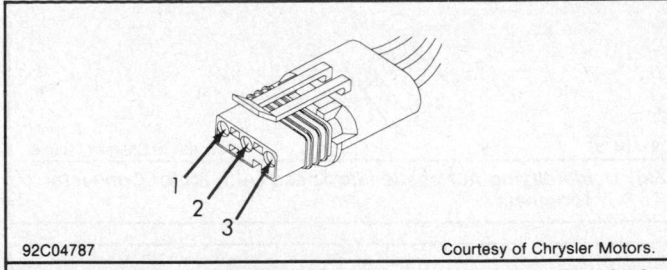

92C04787　　　　　　Courtesy of Chrysler Motors.

Fig. 18: Identifying Throttle Position Sensor Connector Terminals

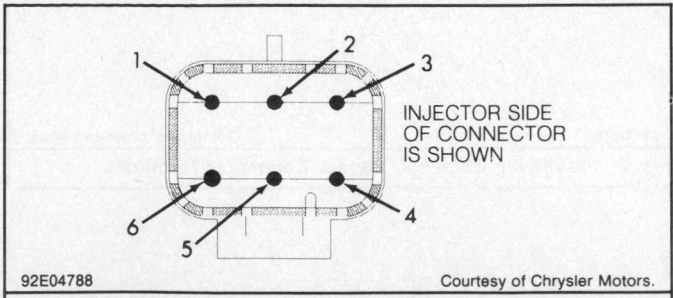

INJECTOR SIDE OF CONNECTOR IS SHOWN

92E04788　　　　　　Courtesy of Chrysler Motors.

Fig. 19: Identifying 6-Pin Injector Wiring Harness Connector Terminals

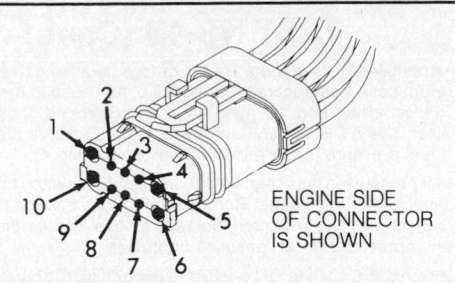

1. Dark Green/Orange Wire
2. Black/Gray Wire
3. Dark Blue/Tan Wire
4. Dark Blue/Gray Wire
5. White/Dark Blue Wire
6. Tan Wire
7. Black/Light Blue Wire
8. Tan/Yellow Wire
9. Orange Wire
10. Yellow/White Wire

ENGINE SIDE
OF CONNECTOR
IS SHOWN

92G04789   Courtesy of Chrysler Motors.

Fig. 20: Identifying 10-Pin Injector Wiring Harness Connector Terminals

SELF-DIAGNOSTIC TESTS

NOTE: In the following self-diagnostic tests, illustrations are courtesy of Chrysler Motors.

TEST NS-1A

CHECKING FOR FAULTS & SPARK

NOTE: For connector terminal identification, see CONNECTOR IDENTIFICATION at beginning of article. For appropriate wiring diagram, see WIRING DIAGRAMS article in ENGINE PERFORMANCE.

1) Ensure battery is fully charged. Disconnect and reconnect battery quick-disconnect cable. Try to start engine by cranking for at least 10 seconds, ensuring ignition switch is turned off before each attempt to start engine. Turn ignition switch to ON position, and read faults using DRB-II. See DRB-II FAULT MESSAGES table.

DRB-II FAULT MESSAGES

DRB-II Message	Test No.
NO RESPONSE	NS-8A
COOLANT VOLTAGE AND TPS VOLTAGE HIGH	[1]
NO REFERENCE SIGNAL DURING CRANKING	NS-9A
AUTO SHUTDOWN RELAY CONTROL CIRCUIT	NS-10A
NO ASD RELAY VOLTAGE SENSE AT CONTROLLER	NS-11A
INJECTOR CONTROL CIRCUIT	NS-5A
IGNITION COIL CKT	NS-5A
AUTOMATIC IDLE SPEED MOTOR CIRCUITS	NS-6A
INTERNAL CONTROLLER FAILURE	[2]
CONTROLLER FAILURE SPI COMMUNICATIONS	[2]

[1] – Repair open Black/Light Blue wire at SBEC connector terminal No. 4. Perform VERIFICATION TEST VER-1.
[2] – Replace SBEC. Perform VERIFICATION TEST VER-1.

2) If no faults are displayed, read Direct Ignition System (DIS) signal status. DO NOT crank engine before reading DIS crankshaft sensor display. If DRB-II displays CRANK ONLY, replace DIS crankshaft sensor. Perform VERIFICATION TEST VER-1.

3) If CAM ONLY is displayed, replace DIS camshaft sensor. Perform VERIFICATION TEST VER-1. If CAM ONLY is not displayed, crank engine. Observe DRB-II display. If CRANK and CAM are not displayed, perform TEST NS-9A.

4) If CRANK and CAM are displayed, try to start engine by cranking engine for at least 10 seconds. Ensure ignition switch is turned to OFF position before each attempt to start engine. If engine starts and then stalls, perform TEST NS-2A. If engine does not start, turn ignition switch to OFF position.

CAUTION: When checking for spark, Single Board Engine Controller (SBEC) damage may occur if spark plug cable is held more than 1/4" away from a good ground.

TEST NS-1A (Cont.)

5) Disconnect any spark plug cable at spark plug. Insert an insulated screwdriver in cable terminal. Hold screwdriver a maximum of 1/4" away from a good ground. Watch for spark while cranking engine for 10 seconds. If a good spark occurs, perform TEST NS-2A. If a good spark does not occur, reconnect spark plug cable. Disconnect another spark plug cable at spark plug, and repeat test.

6) If a good spark occurs, replace spark plug cable which was initially used to test for spark. Perform TEST NS-2A. If a good spark does not occur, perform TEST NS-5A.

TEST NS-2A

CHECKING FUEL SYSTEM

NOTE: For connector terminal identification, see CONNECTOR IDENTIFICATION at beginning of article. For appropriate wiring diagram, see WIRING DIAGRAMS article in ENGINE PERFORMANCE.

1) Turn ignition switch to ON position. Check if vehicle is equipped with factory theft alarm. If vehicle is equipped with factory theft alarm, read theft alarm status using DRB-II.

2) If DRB-II does not display FUEL ON, perform theft alarm test. See BODY CONTROL COMPUTER article. Perform VERIFICATION TEST VER-1. If DRB-II displays FUEL ON, read Throttle Position Sensor (TPS) voltage. If TPS voltage is more than 1.5 volts, replace TPS. Perform VERIFICATION TEST VER-1.

3) If voltage is less than 1.5 volts, disconnect 10-pin fuel injector connector. See Fig. NS-2A. Using DRB-II, actuate fuel system. Place DRB-II in voltmeter mode. Connect voltmeter probe to terminal No. 1 (Dark Green/Orange wire) at 10-pin fuel injector connector (engine side).

92I04790

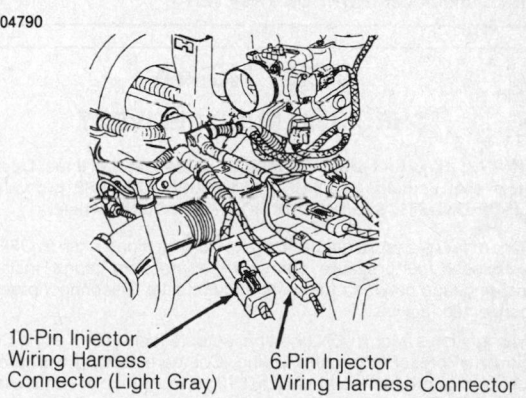

10-Pin Injector
Wiring Harness
Connector (Light Gray)

6-Pin Injector
Wiring Harness Connector

Fig. NS-2A: Locating 6-Pin & 10-Pin Injector Wiring Harness Connectors

4) If voltage is less than 10 volts, repair open in Dark Green/Orange wire. If voltage is more than 10 volts, turn ignition switch to OFF position. Reconnect fuel injector harness connector.

5) Disconnect Manifold Absolute Pressure (MAP) sensor wiring harness connector. Disconnect Single Board Engine Controller (SBEC) 60-pin connector. Using an external ohmmeter, check resistance of Violet/White wire between SBEC connector terminal No. 6 and MAP sensor connector terminal No. 3.

6) If resistance is more than 10 ohms, repair open in Violet/White wire. Perform VERIFICATION TEST VER-1. Reconnect MAP sensor and SBEC connectors if resistance is less than 10 ohms.

WARNING: High fuel pressure may be present in fuel lines. Open fuel system with caution. See FUEL PRESSURE RELEASE procedure in SELF-DIAGNOSTICS INTRODUCTION – GASOLINE article.

7) Install fuel pressure gauge in fuel rail port. Ensure fuel tank is at least 1/4 full. Turn ignition switch to ON position. Using DRB-II, actuate fuel system. Listen for fuel pump operation at fuel tank.

8) If fuel pump operation cannot be heard, perform TEST NS-7A. If fuel pump operation can be heard, read fuel pressure gauge. If fuel pressure is more than 53 psi, perform TEST NS-4B. If pressure is less than 43 psi, perform TEST NS-4A.

9) If vehicle initially started and stalled, perform TEST NS-12A. If vehicle did not initially start and stall, perform TEST NS-3A.

TEST NS-3A

INSPECTING MECHANICAL SYSTEM

NOTE: For connector terminal identification, see CONNECTOR IDENTIFICATION at beginning of article. For appropriate wiring diagram, see WIRING DIAGRAMS article in ENGINE PERFORMANCE.

1) Turn ignition switch to OFF position. Remove all spark plugs. Inspect spark plug tips for fuel. If spark plug tips are wet with fuel, dry and reinstall spark plugs. If spark plug tips are not wet with fuel, reinstall spark plugs.

CAUTION: When checking ignition timing advance, DO NOT crank engine for an extended period of time as damage may occur to starter. Crank engine up to 15 seconds.

2) Using DRB-II, read total advance. Note spark advance while cranking engine. If spark advance is not 0-20 degrees BTDC, replace Single Board Engine Controller (SBEC). Perform VERIFICATION TEST VER-1. If ignition timing advance is 0-20 degrees BTDC, inspect spark plug cables for correct placement.

3) If spark plug cables are not positioned correctly, reinstall spark plug cables as necessary. Perform VERIFICATION TEST VER-1. If all spark plug cables are positioned correctly, go to next step.

4) Turn ignition switch to OFF position. Disconnect SBEC and MAP sensor connectors. Using an external ohmmeter, check resistance at Violet/White wire between SBEC connector terminal No. 6 and MAP sensor connector terminal No. 3. If resistance is more than 10 ohms, repair open Violet/White wire. Perform VERIFICATION TEST VER-1.

5) If resistance is less than 10 ohms, check valve timing and compression. If valve timing and compression are within specifications, replace MAP sensor. Perform VERIFICATION TEST VER-1. If valve timing and compression are not within specifications, repair engine as necessary. Perform VERIFICATION TEST VER-1.

TEST NS-4A

CHECKING FUEL DELIVERY

WARNING: High fuel pressure may be present in fuel lines. Open fuel system with caution. See FUEL PRESSURE RELEASE procedure in SELF-DIAGNOSTICS INTRODUCTION – GASOLINE article.

1) Record fuel pressure gauge reading. Turn ignition switch to OFF position. Release fuel pressure. Remove fuel pressure gauge. Install fuel pressure gauge between fuel tank and fuel filter. Reconnect previously disconnected fuel line.

2) With ignition switch in ON position, actuate fuel system using DRB-II. Record fuel pressure gauge reading. Compare reading with previous reading. If fuel pressure is not at least 10 psi more than previous reading, go to step 4).

3) If fuel pressure is at least 10 psi more than previous reading, check for fuel line restriction between fuel filter and fuel rail. Repair as necessary. Perform VERIFICATION TEST VER-1. If restriction does not exist, replace fuel filter. Perform VERIFICATION TEST VER-1.

CAUTION: DO NOT allow fuel pressure to exceed 70 psi when squeezing fuel return hose.

4) If fuel pressure was not at least 10 psi more in step 2), gently squeeze fuel return hose while watching fuel pressure gauge. If fuel pressure is more than 43 psi, replace fuel pressure regulator. Perform VERIFICATION TEST VER-1. If pressure is less than 43 psi, replace fuel pump and sock filter. Perform VERIFICATION TEST VER-1.

TEST NS-4B

CHECKING FUEL DELIVERY

NOTE: For connector terminal identification, see CONNECTOR IDENTIFICATION at beginning of article. For appropriate wiring diagram, see WIRING DIAGRAMS article in ENGINE PERFORMANCE.

WARNING: High fuel pressure may be present in fuel lines. Open fuel system with caution. See FUEL PRESSURE RELEASE procedure in SELF-DIAGNOSTICS INTRODUCTION – GASOLINE article.

TEST NS-4B (Cont.)

1) Ensure fuel tank is at least 1/4 full before beginning this test. Remove fuel return hose from fuel rail. Connect a 6' fuel hose to fuel rail return fitting. Place other end of hose into an approved 2-gallon gasoline container. Using DRB-II, actuate fuel system. Observe fuel gauge reading. If fuel pressure is more than 53 psi, go to step 4).

2) If fuel pressure is less than 53 psi, turn ignition switch to OFF position. Reconnect fuel return hose. Remove fuel return hose at fuel tank. Connect a 6' hose to disconnected fuel return hose. Place other end of hose into an approved 2-gallon gasoline container.

3) Turn ignition switch to ON position. Using DRB-II, actuate fuel system. Observe fuel gauge pressure reading. If fuel pressure is less than 53 psi, replace fuel tank return assembly. Perform VERIFICATION TEST VER-1. If fuel pressure is more than 53 psi, repair restricted fuel return line between fuel rail and fuel tank. Perform VERIFICATION TEST VER-1.

4) If fuel pressure was more than 53 psi in step 1), turn ignition switch to OFF position. Disconnect fuel pressure damper, and check for a fuel restriction. If restriction exists, replace damper. Perform VERIFICATION TEST VER-1. If no restriction exists, replace fuel pressure regulator. Perform VERIFICATION TEST VER-1.

TEST NS-5A

CODES 27 & 43, INJECTOR CONTROL CIRCUIT OR IGNITION COIL CIRCUIT

NOTE: For connector terminal identification, see CONNECTOR IDENTIFICATION at beginning of article. For appropriate wiring diagram, see WIRING DIAGRAMS article in ENGINE PERFORMANCE.

1) Turn ignition switch to OFF position. Disconnect 10-pin injector wiring harness connector. *See Fig. NS-2A.* Turn ignition switch to ON position. Using DRB-II, actuate fuel system. Place DRB-II in voltmeter mode.

2) Probe terminal No. 1 (Dark Green/Orange wire) of 10-pin connector (engine side). If voltage is less than 10 volts, repair open in Dark Green/Orange wire between Auto Shutdown (ASD) relay and 10-pin injector wiring harness connector. Perform VERIFICATION TEST VER-1.

3) If voltage is more than 10 volts, check if ignition coil circuit fault exists. If ignition coil fault exists, repair open in Dark Green/Orange wire between ignition coil and 10-pin fuel injector connector. Perform VERIFICATION TEST VER-1.

4) If ignition coil fault does not exist, repair open in Dark Green/Orange wire between 10-pin fuel injector harness connector and fuel injectors. Perform VERIFICATION TEST VER-1.

TEST NS-6A

CODE 25, AUTOMATIC IDLE SPEED (AIS) MOTOR CIRCUITS

NOTE: For connector terminal identification, see CONNECTOR IDENTIFICATION at beginning of article. For appropriate wiring diagram, see WIRING DIAGRAMS article in ENGINE PERFORMANCE.

1) Disconnect AIS motor connector. Turn ignition switch to ON position. Using DRB-II, actuate AIS motor. Place DRB-II in voltmeter mode. Probe terminal No. 1 (Gray/Red wire) at AIS motor connector. Voltage should switch from less than one volt to more than 10 volts.

2) If voltage is less than one volt and does not switch, repair short to ground in Gray/Red wire. Perform VERIFICATION TEST VER-1. If voltage is more than one volt and does not switch, check if voltage is more than 10 volts. If voltage is more than 10 volts, repair short to voltage in Gray/Red wire. Perform VERIFICATION TEST VER-1.

3) If voltage is less than 10 volts, probe terminal No. 2 (Yellow/Black wire) at AIS motor connector. If voltage is less than one volt, repair short to ground in Yellow/Black wire. Perform VERIFICATION TEST VER-1. If voltage is more than one volt, check if voltage is more than 10 volts. If voltage stays more than 10 volts, repair Yellow/Black wire for a short to voltage. Perform VERIFICATION TEST VER-1.

4) If voltage does not stay more than 10 volts, probe terminal No. 3 (Brown/White wire) at AIS motor connector. If voltage is less than one volt, repair short to ground in Brown/White wire. Perform VERIFICATION TEST VER-1. If voltage is more than one volt, check if voltage is more than 10 volts. If voltage is more than 10 volts, repair short to voltage in Brown/White wire. Perform VERIFICATION TEST VER-1.

TEST NS-6A (Cont.)

5) If voltage is less than 10 volts, probe terminal No. 4 (Violet/Black wire) at AIS motor connector. If voltage is less than one volt, repair short to ground in Violet/Black wire. Perform VERIFICATION TEST VER-1. If voltage is more than one volt, check if voltage is more than 10 volts. If voltage is more than 10 volts, repair short to voltage in Violet/Black wire. Perform VERIFICATION TEST VER-1.

6) If voltage is less than 10 volts, turn ignition switch to OFF position. Reconnect AIS motor connector. Disconnect Single Board Engine Controller (SBEC) connector. Using an external ohmmeter, check resistance between terminals No. 39 (Gray/Red wire) and 59 (Violet/Black wire) of SBEC connector. If resistance is less than 35 ohms, replace AIS motor. Perform VERIFICATION TEST VER-1. If resistance is more than 35 ohms, check resistance between terminals No. 40 (Brown/White wire) and 60 (Yellow/Black wire) of SBEC connector.

7) If resistance is less than 35 ohms, replace AIS motor. Perform VERIFICATION TEST VER-1. If resistance is more than 35 ohms, check resistance between terminals No. 39 (Gray/Red wire) and 60 (Yellow/Black wire) of SBEC connector. If resistance is less than 10 ohms, Yellow/Black wire is shorted to Gray/Red wire. Repair wiring as necessary. Perform VERIFICATION TEST VER-1.

8) If resistance is more than 10 ohms, check if it is more than 75 ohms. If resistance is more than 75 ohms, go to step **10)**. If resistance is less than 75 ohms, check resistance between terminals No. 59 (Violet/Black wire) and 60 (Yellow/Black wire) of SBEC connector.

9) If resistance is less than 10 ohms, Yellow/Black wire is shorted to Violet/Black wire. Repair wiring as necessary. Perform VERIFICATION TEST VER-1. If resistance is more than 10 ohms, Gray/Red wire is shorted to Brown/White wire. Repair wiring as necessary. Perform VERIFICATION TEST VER-1.

10) If resistance is more than 75 ohms in step **8)**, check if resistance is less than 120 ohms. If resistance is less than 120 ohms, Brown/White wire is shorted to Violet/Black wire. Repair wiring as necessary. Perform VERIFICATION TEST VER-1. If resistance is more than 120 ohms, replace SBEC. Perform VERIFICATION TEST VER-1.

TEST NS-7A

CHECKING FUEL PUMP

NOTE: For connector terminal identification, see CONNECTOR IDENTIFICATION at beginning of article. For appropriate wiring diagram, see WIRING DIAGRAMS article in ENGINE PERFORMANCE.

1) Using DRB-II, actuate Auto Shutdown (ASD) relay. Check if fuel pump relay pulsates. *See Fig. NS-7A.* If fuel pump relay does not pulsate when ASD relay is actuated, perform TEST NS-7B. If fuel pump relay pulsates, turn ignition off. Remove fuel pump relay.

92B22310

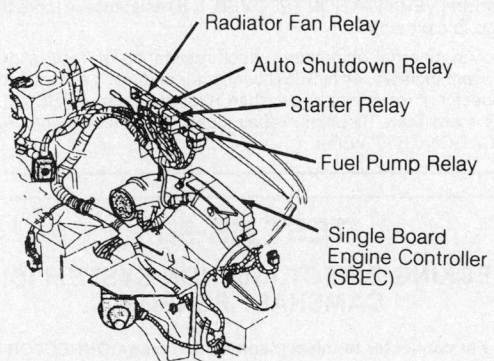

- Radiator Fan Relay
- Auto Shutdown Relay
- Starter Relay
- Fuel Pump Relay
- Single Board Engine Controller (SBEC)

Fig. NS-7A: Locating Relays

2) Turn ignition switch to ON position. Place DRB-II in voltmeter mode. Probe terminal "B" (Red/White wire) at fuel pump relay connector. If voltage is less than 10 volts, repair open Red/White wire. Perform VERIFICATION TEST VER-1.

3) If voltage is more than 10 volts, disconnect fuel pump connector. Reconnect fuel pump relay. Using DRB-II, actuate fuel system. Place DRB-II in voltmeter mode.

TEST NS-7A (Cont.)

4) Probe terminal No. 1 (Dark Green/Black wire) of fuel pump harness connector. If voltage is less than 10 volts, go to step **6)**. If voltage is more than 10 volts, stop fuel system actuation test.

5) Place DRB-II in ohmmeter mode. Probe terminal No. 5 (Black wire) at fuel pump harness connector. Repair open Black wire if resistance is more than 5 ohms. If resistance is less than 5 ohms, replace fuel pump. Perform VERIFICATION TEST VER-1.

6) If voltage is less than 10 volts in step **4)** after probing terminal No. 1 (Dark Green/Black wire) at fuel pump harness connector, turn ignition switch to OFF position. Disconnect fuel pump relay connector. Using an external ohmmeter, check resistance at Dark Green/Black wire between terminal No. 1 at fuel pump harness connector and terminal "D" at fuel pump relay connector.

7) If resistance is less than 10 ohms, replace fuel pump relay. Perform VERIFICATION TEST VER-1. If resistance is more than 10 ohms, repair open Dark Green/Black wire. Perform VERIFICATION TEST VER-1.

TEST NS-7B

CHECKING FUEL PUMP

NOTE: For connector terminal identification, see CONNECTOR IDENTIFICATION at beginning of article. For appropriate wiring diagram, see WIRING DIAGRAMS article in ENGINE PERFORMANCE.

1) Turn ignition switch to OFF position. Disconnect fuel pump relay connector. *See Fig. NS-7A.* Turn ignition switch to ON position. Put DRB-II in voltmeter mode. Probe terminal "A" (Dark Blue wire) at fuel pump relay connector. If voltage is less than 10 volts, repair open Dark Blue wire. Perform VERIFICATION TEST VER-1.

2) If voltage is more than 10 volts, check resistance between terminals "C" and "A" of fuel pump relay using an external ohmmeter. If resistance is more than 100 ohms, replace fuel pump relay. Perform VERIFICATION TEST VER-1. If resistance is less than 100 ohms, repair open in Dark Blue/Yellow wire. Perform VERIFICATION TEST VER-1.

TEST NS-8A

REPAIRING NO RESPONSE CONDITION

NOTE: For connector terminal identification, see CONNECTOR IDENTIFICATION at beginning of article. For appropriate wiring diagram, see WIRING DIAGRAMS article in ENGINE PERFORMANCE.

1) Disconnect Throttle Position Sensor (TPS) connector. Turn ignition switch to ON position. Place DRB-II in voltmeter mode. Probe terminal No. 1 (Violet/White wire) at TPS connector. If voltage is more than 6 volts, repair open in Black/White wire (terminal No. 5) and/or Black/Tan wire (terminals No. 11 and 12) of Single Board Engine Controller (SBEC) connector. Perform VERIFICATION TEST VER-1.

2) If voltage is less than 6 volts, check if it is less than 4.4 volts. If voltage is less than 4.4 volts, go to next step. If voltage is more than 4.4 volts, reconnect TPS connector. Disconnect MAP sensor connector. Probe terminal No. 3 (Violet/White wire) at MAP sensor connector. If voltage is more than 4.4 volts, see NO RESPONSE MESSAGE under DRB-II PROBLEMS & ERROR MESSAGES in SELF-DIAGNOSTICS INTRODUCTION – GASOLINE article. If voltage is less than 4.4 volts, replace TPS. Perform VERIFICATION TEST VER-1.

3) Disconnect MAP sensor connector. Probe terminal No. 3 (Violet/White wire) at TPS connector. If voltage is more than 4.4 volts, replace MAP sensor. Perform VERIFICATION TEST VER-1. If voltage is less than 4.4 volts, turn ignition switch to OFF position. Disconnect SBEC connector.

4) Place DRB-II in ohmmeter mode. Probe terminal No. 6 (Violet/White wire) at SBEC connector. If resistance is less than 10 ohms, repair short to ground in Violet/White wire. Perform VERIFICATION TEST VER-1.

5) If resistance is more than 10 ohms, probe terminal No. 9 (Dark Blue wire) of SBEC connector. If resistance is less than 10 ohms, repair open in Dark Blue wire between terminal No. 9 of SBEC connector and ignition switch. Perform VERIFICATION TEST VER-1.

6) If resistance is more than 10 ohms, place DRB-II in voltmeter mode. Probe terminal No. 3 (Red/White wire) of SBEC connector. If voltage is more than 10 volts, replace SBEC. Perform VERIFICATION TEST VER-1. If voltage is less than 10 volts, place DRB-II in ohmmeter mode. Probe terminal No. 3 (Red/White wire) of SBEC connector. If resistance is less

TEST NS-8A (Cont.)

than 10 ohms, repair short to ground in Red/White wire between battery and SBEC connector. Perform VERIFICATION TEST VER-1.

7) If resistance is more than 10 ohms, inspect fused circuit between battery and terminal No. 3. If fuse or fusible link is okay, repair open in Red/White wire between terminal No. 3 of SBEC connector and battery. Perform VERIFICATION TEST VER-1.

8) If fuse or fusible link is not okay, disconnect Auto Shutdown (ASD) relay connector. *See Fig. NS-7A.* Put DRB-II in ohmmeter mode. Probe ASD relay connector terminal "D" (Dark Green/Orange wire). If resistance is more than 10 ohms, go to step **11)**. If resistance is less than 10 ohms, disconnect ignition coil connector. If resistance is now more than 10 ohms, replace ignition coil. Replace fuse or fusible link. Perform VERIFICATION TEST VER-1.

9) If resistance is still less than 10 ohms, disconnect 10-pin fuel injector connector. *See Fig. NS-2A.* If resistance is now more than 10 ohms, repair short to ground in Dark Green/Orange wire between 10-pin connector and injectors. Replace fuse or fusible link. Perform VERIFICATION TEST VER-1.

10) If resistance is still less than 10 ohms, disconnect 6-pin fuel injector connector. If resistance is now more than 10 ohms, repair short to ground in Dark Green/Orange wire between 6-pin connector and injectors. Replace fuse or fusible link. Perform VERIFICATION TEST VER-1. If resistance is still less than 10 ohms, repair short to ground in Dark Green/Orange wire. Replace fuse or fusible link. Perform VERIFICATION TEST VER-1.

11) If resistance was more than 10 ohms at terminal "D" in step **8)**, reconnect ASD relay. Disconnect fuel pump relay and connector. Disconnect O₂ sensor connector. Probe terminal "D" (Dark Green/Black wire) of fuel pump relay. If resistance is less than 10 ohms, repair short to ground in Dark Green/Black wire. Replace fuse or fusible link. Perform VERIFICATION TEST VER-1.

12) If resistance is more than 10 ohms, probe Dark Green/Black wire of O₂ sensor connector. If resistance is less than 10 ohms, replace O₂ sensor. Replace fuse or fusible link. Perform VERIFICATION TEST VER-1. If resistance is more than 10 ohms, replace fuel pump. Replace fuse or fusible link. Perform VERIFICATION TEST VER-1.

TEST NS-9A

CHECKING DIRECT IGNITION SYSTEM (DIS) SIGNAL STATUS & DIS CRANKSHAFT SENSOR

NOTE: For connector terminal identification, see CONNECTOR IDENTIFICATION at beginning of article. For appropriate wiring diagram, see WIRING DIAGRAMS article in ENGINE PERFORMANCE.

1) Using DRB-II, read DIS signal. If DRB-II displays NO SIGNAL, perform TEST NS-9E. If DRB-II does not display NO SIGNAL, check if DRB-II displays CRANK ONLY.

2) If DRB-II displays CRANK ONLY, perform TEST NS-9C. If DRB-II does not display CRANK ONLY, turn ignition switch to OFF position. Disconnect crankshaft sensor connector. Crankshaft sensor is located on right side of transaxle. Turn ignition switch to ON position. Connect a jumper wire between terminals No. 2 (Black/Light Blue wire) and No. 3 (Gray/Black wire) of crankshaft sensor connector.

3) While making and breaking jumpered connection, read DIS signal using DRB-II. If DRB-II displays CRANK ONLY, perform TEST NS-9B. If DRB-II does not display CRANK ONLY, disconnect jumper wire. Connect jumper wire between terminal No. 3 (Gray/Black wire) and ground.

4) While making and breaking jumpered connection, read DIS signal using DRB-II. If DRB-II displays CRANK ONLY, repair open in Black/Light Blue wire. Perform VERIFICATION TEST VER-1. If DRB-II does not display CRANK ONLY, disconnect jumper wire and turn ignition switch to OFF position. Disconnect Single Board Engine Controller (SBEC) 60-pin connector.

5) Place DRB-II in ohmmeter mode. Probe terminal No. 24 (Gray/Black wire) at SBEC connector. If resistance is less than 10 ohms, repair short to ground in Gray/Black wire. Perform VERIFICATION TEST VER-1. If resistance is more than 10 ohms, go to next step.

6) Using an external ohmmeter, check resistance of Gray/Black wire between terminal No. 24 at SBEC connector and terminal No. 3 at crankshaft sensor connector. If resistance is less than 10 ohms, replace SBEC. Perform VERIFICATION TEST VER-1. If resistance is more than 10 ohms, repair open Gray/Black wire. Perform VERIFICATION TEST VER-1.

TEST NS-9B

CHECKING DIRECT IGNITION SYSTEM (DIS) SIGNAL STATUS & DIS CRANKSHAFT SENSOR

NOTE: For connector terminal identification, see CONNECTOR IDENTIFICATION at beginning of article. For appropriate wiring diagram, see WIRING DIAGRAMS article in ENGINE PERFORMANCE.

1) Place DRB-II in voltmeter mode. Probe terminal No. 1 (Orange wire) at crankshaft sensor connector. If voltage is more than 7 volts, replace DIS crankshaft sensor. Perform VERIFICATION TEST VER-1.

2) If voltage is less than 7 volts, turn ignition switch to OFF position. Disconnect Single Board Engine Controller (SBEC) 60-pin connector. Place DRB-II in ohmmeter mode. Probe terminal No. 7 (Orange wire) at SBEC connector.

3) If resistance is less than 10 ohms, repair short to ground in Orange wire. Perform VERIFICATION TEST VER-1. If resistance is more than 10 ohms, go to next step.

4) Using an external ohmmeter, check resistance at Orange wire between crankshaft sensor connector terminal No. 1 and SBEC connector terminal No. 7. If resistance is less than 10 ohms, replace SBEC. Perform VERIFICATION TEST VER-1. If resistance is more than 10 ohms, repair open in Orange wire. Perform VERIFICATION TEST VER-1.

TEST NS-9C

CHECKING DIRECT IGNITION SYSTEM (DIS) CAMSHAFT SENSOR

NOTE: For connector terminal identification, see CONNECTOR IDENTIFICATION at beginning of article. For appropriate wiring diagram, see WIRING DIAGRAMS article in ENGINE PERFORMANCE.

1) Turn ignition switch to OFF position. Disconnect camshaft sensor connector. Connector is located behind thermostat housing. Turn ignition switch to ON position. Connect jumper wire between DIS camshaft sensor connector terminals No. 2 and 3 (Black/Light Blue and Tan/Yellow wires). While making and breaking jumpered connection, read DIS signal using DRB-II. Perform TEST NS-9D if DRB-II displays CAM ONLY.

2) If DRB-II does not display CAM ONLY, disconnect jumper wire. Connect jumper wire between terminal No. 3 (Tan/Yellow wire) at camshaft sensor connector and ground. While making and breaking jumpered connection, read DIS signal using DRB-II.

3) If DRB-II displays CAM ONLY, repair open in Black/Light Blue wire. Perform VERIFICATION TEST VER-1. If DRB-II does not display CAM ONLY, turn ignition switch to OFF position. Disconnect Single Board Engine Controller (SBEC) connector. Place DRB-II in ohmmeter mode. Probe SBEC connector terminal No. 44 (Tan/Yellow wire).

4) If resistance is less than 10 ohms, repair short to ground in Tan/Yellow wire. Perform VERIFICATION TEST VER-1. If resistance is more than 10 ohms, go to next step.

5) Using an external ohmmeter, check resistance of Tan/Yellow wire between terminals No. 44 at SBEC connector and No. 3 at camshaft sensor connector. If resistance is less than 10 ohms, replace SBEC. If resistance is more than 10 ohms, repair open Tan/Yellow wire. Perform VERIFICATION TEST VER-1.

TEST NS-9D

CHECKING DIRECT IGNITION SYSTEM (DIS) CAMSHAFT SENSOR

NOTE: For connector terminal identification, see CONNECTOR IDENTIFICATION at beginning of article. For appropriate wiring diagram, see WIRING DIAGRAMS article in ENGINE PERFORMANCE.

1) Place DRB-II in voltmeter mode. Probe terminal No. 1 (Orange wire) at camshaft sensor connector. If voltage is more than 7 volts, replace camshaft sensor. Perform VERIFICATION TEST VER-1.

2) If voltage is less than 7 volts, turn ignition switch to OFF position. Disconnect Single Board Engine Controller (SBEC) 60-pin connector. Place DRB-II in ohmmeter mode. Probe terminal No. 7 (Orange wire) at SBEC connector.

TEST NS-9D (Cont.)

3) If resistance is less than 10 ohms, repair short to ground in Orange wire. Perform VERIFICATION TEST VER-1. If resistance is more than 10 ohms, go to next step.

4) Using external ohmmeter, check resistance of Orange wire between camshaft sensor connector terminal No. 1 and SBEC connector terminal No. 7. If resistance is less than 10 ohms, replace SBEC. If resistance is more than 10 ohms, repair open Orange wire. Perform VERIFICATION TEST VER-1.

TEST NS-9E

CHECKING DIRECT IGNITION SYSTEM (DIS) CAMSHAFT & CRANKSHAFT SENSOR CIRCUIT

NOTE: For connector terminal identification, see CONNECTOR IDENTIFICATION at beginning of article. For appropriate wiring diagram, see WIRING DIAGRAMS article in ENGINE PERFORMANCE.

1) Turn ignition switch to OFF position. Disconnect camshaft sensor connector. Connector is located behind thermostat housing. Turn ignition switch to ON position. Place DRB-II in voltmeter mode. Probe terminal No. 1 (Orange wire) of camshaft sensor connector.

2) If voltage is less than 7 volts, perform TEST NS-9F. If voltage is more than 7 volts, turn ignition switch to OFF position. Place DRB-II in ohmmeter mode. Probe terminal No. 2 (Black/Light Blue wire) at camshaft sensor connector.

3) If resistance is more than 10 ohms, repair open in Black/Light Blue wire. Perform VERIFICATION TEST VER-1. If resistance is less than 10 ohms, reconnect camshaft sensor connector. Disconnect crankshaft sensor connector. Crankshaft sensor is located at right side of transaxle. Turn ignition switch to ON position. Place DRB-II in voltmeter mode. Probe crankshaft sensor connector terminal No. 1 (Orange wire).

4) If voltage is more than 7 volts, replace Single Board Engine Controller (SBEC). Perform VERIFICATION TEST VER-1. If voltage is less than 7 volts, replace camshaft sensor. Perform VERIFICATION TEST VER-1.

TEST NS-9F

CHECKING DIRECT IGNITION SYSTEM (DIS) CAMSHAFT & CRANKSHAFT SENSOR CIRCUIT

NOTE: For connector terminal identification, see CONNECTOR IDENTIFICATION at beginning of article. For appropriate wiring diagram, see WIRING DIAGRAMS article in ENGINE PERFORMANCE.

1) Disconnect crankshaft sensor connector. Crankshaft sensor is located at right side of transaxle. Probe terminal No. 1 (Orange wire) at crankshaft sensor connector. If voltage is more than 7 volts, replace crankshaft sensor. Perform VERIFICATION TEST VER-1.

2) If voltage is less than 7 volts, turn ignition switch to OFF position. Disconnect Single Board Engine Connector (SBEC) connector. Place DRB-II in ohmmeter mode. Probe SBEC connector terminal No. 7 (Orange wire). If resistance is less than 7 ohms, repair short to ground in Orange wire. Perform VERIFICATION TEST VER-1. If resistance is more than 10 ohms, go to next step.

3) Using external ohmmeter, check resistance of Orange wire between camshaft sensor connector terminal No. 1 and SBEC connector terminal No. 7. If resistance is less than 10 ohms, replace SBEC. If resistance is more than 10 ohms, repair open Orange wire. Perform VERIFICATION TEST VER-1.

TEST NS-10A

CODE 42, AUTO SHUTDOWN (ASD) RELAY CONTROL CIRCUIT

NOTE: For connector terminal identification, see CONNECTOR IDENTIFICATION at beginning of article. For appropriate wiring diagram, see WIRING DIAGRAMS article in ENGINE PERFORMANCE.

1) Turn ignition switch to ON position. Disconnect ASD relay connector. Place DRB-II in voltmeter mode. Probe terminal "A" (Dark Blue wire) at ASD relay connector. If voltage is less than 10 volts, repair open in Dark Blue wire from ignition switch. Perform VERIFICATION TEST VER-1. If voltage is more than 10 volts, go to next step.

2) Using an external ohmmeter, check resistance between terminals "A" and "C" at ASD relay. If resistance is more than 100 ohms, replace ASD relay. Perform VERIFICATION TEST VER-1. If resistance is less than 100 ohms, turn ignition switch to OFF position.

3) Disconnect Single Board Engine Controller (SBEC) 60-pin connector. Using an external ohmmeter, check resistance of Dark Blue/Yellow wire between terminal No. 51 of SBEC connector and terminal "C" of ASD relay connector.

4) If resistance is less than 10 ohms, replace SBEC. Perform VERIFICATION TEST VER-1. If resistance is more than 10 ohms, repair open in Dark Blue/Yellow wire. Perform VERIFICATION TEST VER-1.

TEST NS-11A

CODE 42, AUTO SHUTDOWN (ASD) RELAY CONTROL CIRCUIT

NOTE: For connector terminal identification, see CONNECTOR IDENTIFICATION at beginning of article. For appropriate wiring diagram, see WIRING DIAGRAMS article in ENGINE PERFORMANCE.

1) Disconnect ASD relay connector. Turn ignition switch to ON position. Place DRB-II in voltmeter mode. Probe ASD relay connector terminal "B" (Red/White wire). If voltage is less than 10 volts, repair open Red/White wire. Perform VERIFICATION TEST VER-1. If voltage is more than 10 volts, probe ASD relay connector terminal "A" (Dark Blue wire).

2) If voltage is less than 10 volts, repair open in Dark Blue wire. Perform VERIFICATION TEST VER-1. If voltage is more than 10 volts, turn ignition switch to OFF position. Disconnect Single Board Engine Controller (SBEC) 60-pin connector.

3) Using an external ohmmeter, check resistance at Dark Green/Orange wire between terminal No. 57 of SBEC connector and terminal "D" of ASD relay connector. If resistance is more than 10 ohms, repair open in Dark Green/Orange wire between ASD relay and SBEC connector. Perform VERIFICATION TEST VER-1.

4) If resistance is less than 10 ohms, check resistance in Dark Blue/Yellow wire between terminal No. 51 of SBEC connector and terminal "C" of ASD connector. If resistance is more than 10 ohms, repair open Dark Blue/Yellow wire. Perform VERIFICATION TEST VER-1. If resistance is less than 10 ohms, reconnect SBEC connector. Substitute ASD relay with a known good relay.

5) Attempt to start vehicle. If vehicle starts, repair is complete. Perform VERIFICATION TEST VER-1. If vehicle does not start, replace SBEC. Perform VERIFICATION TEST VER-1.

TEST NS-12A

CHECKING AUTOMATIC IDLE SPEED (AIS) MOTOR OPERATION

NOTE: For connector terminal identification, see CONNECTOR IDENTIFICATION at beginning of article. For appropriate wiring diagram, see WIRING DIAGRAMS article in ENGINE PERFORMANCE.

1) Turn ignition switch to ON position. Using DRB-II, actuate AIS motor. Disconnect AIS motor connector. Place DRB-II in voltmeter mode. Probe AIS motor connector terminal No. 1 (Gray/Red wire). If voltage is less than one volt, perform TEST NS-12B.

TEST NS-12A (Cont.)

2) If voltage is more than one volt, probe terminal No. 3 (Brown/White wire) at AIS motor connector. If voltage is less than one volt, perform TEST NS-12C. If voltage is more than one volt, probe terminal No. 4 (Violet/Black wire) at AIS motor connector. If voltage is less than one volt, perform TEST NS-12D.

3) If voltage is more than one volt, probe AIS motor connector terminal No. 2 (Yellow/Black wire). If voltage is less than one volt, perform TEST NS-12E. Turn ignition switch to OFF position if voltage is more than one volt.

4) Remove AIS motor from throttle body. Reconnect AIS motor connector. Turn ignition switch to ON position. Using DRB-II, actuate AIS motor. If AIS motor tip moves in and out, perform TEST NS-13A. If AIS motor tip does not move in and out, replace AIS motor. Perform VERIFICATION TEST VER-1.

TEST NS-12B

CHECKING AUTOMATIC IDLE SPEED (AIS) MOTOR OPERATION

NOTE: For connector terminal identification, see CONNECTOR IDENTIFICATION at beginning of article. For appropriate wiring diagram, see WIRING DIAGRAMS article in ENGINE PERFORMANCE.

1) Turn ignition switch to OFF position. Disconnect and inspect Single Board Engine Controller (SBEC) 60-pin connector. Repair connector if damaged. Perform VERIFICATION TEST VER-1. If SBEC connector is okay, go to next step.

2) Using an external ohmmeter, check resistance of Gray/Red wire between terminal No. 1 at AIS motor connector and terminal No. 39 at SBEC connector. If resistance is less than 10 ohms, replace SBEC. Perform VERIFICATION TEST VER-1. If resistance is more than 10 ohms, repair open in Gray/Red wire. Perform VERIFICATION TEST VER-1.

TEST NS-12C

CHECKING AUTOMATIC IDLE SPEED (AIS) MOTOR OPERATION

NOTE: For connector terminal identification, see CONNECTOR IDENTIFICATION at beginning of article. For appropriate wiring diagram, see WIRING DIAGRAMS article in ENGINE PERFORMANCE.

1) Turn ignition switch to OFF position. Disconnect and inspect Single Board Engine Controller (SBEC) 60-pin connector. Repair connector if damaged. Perform VERIFICATION TEST VER-1. If SBEC connector is okay, go to next step.

2) Using an external ohmmeter, check resistance of Brown/White wire between terminal No. 3 at AIS motor connector and terminal No. 40 at SBEC connector. If resistance is less than 10 ohms, replace SBEC. Perform VERIFICATION TEST VER-1. If resistance is more than 10 ohms, repair open in Brown/White wire. Perform VERIFICATION TEST VER-1.

TEST NS-12D

CHECKING AUTOMATIC IDLE SPEED (AIS) MOTOR OPERATION

NOTE: For connector terminal identification, see CONNECTOR IDENTIFICATION at beginning of article. For appropriate wiring diagram, see WIRING DIAGRAMS article in ENGINE PERFORMANCE.

1) Turn ignition switch to OFF position. Disconnect and inspect Single Board Engine Controller (SBEC) 60-pin connector. Repair connector if damaged. Perform VERIFICATION TEST VER-1. If SBEC connector is okay, go to next step.

2) Using an external ohmmeter, check resistance of Violet/Black wire between terminal No. 4 at AIS motor connector and terminal No. 59 at SBEC connector. If resistance is less than 10 ohms, replace SBEC. Perform VERIFICATION TEST VER-1. If resistance is more than 10 ohms, repair open in Violet/Black wire. Perform VERIFICATION TEST VER-1.

TEST NS-12E

CHECKING AUTOMATIC IDLE SPEED (AIS) MOTOR OPERATION

NOTE: For connector terminal identification, see CONNECTOR IDENTIFICATION at beginning of article. For appropriate wiring diagram, see WIRING DIAGRAMS article in ENGINE PERFORMANCE.

1) Turn ignition switch to OFF position. Disconnect and inspect Single Board Engine Controller (SBEC) 60-pin connector. Repair connector if damaged. Perform VERIFICATION TEST VER-1. If SBEC connector is okay, go to next step.

2) Using an external ohmmeter, check resistance of Yellow/Black wire between terminal No. 2 at AIS motor connector and terminal No. 60 at SBEC connector. If resistance is less than 10 ohms, replace SBEC. Perform VERIFICATION TEST VER-1. If resistance is more than 10 ohms, repair open Yellow/Black wire. Perform VERIFICATION TEST VER-1.

TEST NS-13A

CORRECTING START & STALL CONDITION

At this point in diagnostic procedure, all engine control systems have been determined to be operating as designed and not causing a no-start or start-and-stall problem. Following additional items should be checked as possible causes:

- Check if any MITCHELL® TECH SERVICE BULLETINS (TSBs) apply to vehicle.
- Check engine compression.
- Check for exhaust system restriction.
- Check camshaft and crankshaft sprockets.
- Check valve timing.
- Check torque converter stall speed.
- Check secondary ignition circuit for abnormal scope pattern.
- Check for fuel contamination.
- Ensure PCV system is functioning properly.

TEST DR-1A

CHECKING SYSTEM FOR FAULTS

NOTE: For connector terminal identification, see CONNECTOR IDENTIFICATION at beginning of article. For appropriate wiring diagram, see WIRING DIAGRAMS article in ENGINE PERFORMANCE. Battery must be fully charged and at rated capacity before performing any driveability test procedure. If vehicle starts and stalls repeatedly, perform TEST NS-2A. If vehicle stalls when A/C is turned on, perform TEST NF-9A.

1) Connect DRB-II to engine diagnostic connector. Read fault messages. If DRB-II displays fault messages, go to step 5). If DRB-II does not display fault messages, go to next step.

2) Start engine. Allow engine to reach normal operating temperature. Set engine speed manually to 2000 RPM for at least 10 seconds, and return vehicle to idle. On A/T models, go to next step. On M/T models, go to step 4).

3) On A/T models, apply brakes. Shift gear selector through all gears and return to PARK position. Using DRB-II, read fault messages. If no fault messages are displayed, go to next step. If fault messages are displayed, go to step 5).

4) On all models, check MITCHELL® TECH SERVICE BULLETINS (TSBs) for any pertinent information if DRB-II still displays NO FAULTS. If a TSB exists, perform corrective action. If driveability problem continues after performing TSB procedure or if no TSB information was found, perform TEST NF-1A.

5) If fault message is INTERNAL CONTROLLER FAILURE or CONTROLLER FAILURE, replace Single Board Engine Controller (SBEC). Perform VERIFICATION TEST VER-2. If fault message is not INTERNAL CONTROLLER FAILURE or CONTROLLER FAILURE, go to next step.

NOTE: ENGINE COLD TOO LONG fault message may set erroneously if ambient temperature is extremely cold.

TEST DR-1A (Cont.)

6) If fault message is ENGINE COLD TOO LONG, check engine cooling system. Repair cooling system as necessary. Perform VERIFICATION TEST VER-3. If fault message is not ENGINE COLD TOO LONG, go to next step.

7) Using DRB-II FAULT MESSAGES table, select fault message and corresponding test. Correct all hard fault messages before proceeding to intermittent fault message.

DRB-II FAULT MESSAGES

DRB-II Message	[1] Hard Fault	[2] Intermittent Fault
A/C CLUTCH RELAY CIRCUIT	DR-24A	DR-34A
AUTOMATIC IDLE SPEED MOTOR CIRCUITS	DR-14A	DR-32A
CONTROLLER FAILURE EEPROM WRITE DENIED	DR-30A	DR-30A
CONTROLLER FAILURE EMR MILES NOT STORED	DR-30A	DR-30A
COOLANT SENSOR VOLTAGE TOO HIGH	DR-10A	DR-31A
COOLANT SENSOR VOLTAGE TOO LOW	DR-11A	DR-31A
EGR SOLENOID CIRCUIT	DR-22A	DR-34A
EGR SYSTEM FAILURE	DR-23A	DR-34A
IGNITION COIL NO. 1 CONTROL CIRCUIT	DR-27A	DR-36A
IGNITION COIL NO. 2 CONTROL CIRCUIT	DR-28A	DR-36A
IGNITION COIL NO. 3 CONTROL CIRCUIT	DR-29A	DR-36A
INJECTOR NO. 1 CONTROL CIRCUIT	DR-15A	DR-33A
INJECTOR NO. 2 CONTROL CIRCUIT	DR-16A	DR-33A
INJECTOR NO. 3 CONTROL CIRCUIT	DR-17A	DR-33A
INJECTOR NO. 4 CONTROL CIRCUIT	DR-18A	DR-33A
INJECTOR NO. 5 CONTROL CIRCUIT	DR-19A	DR-33A
INJECTOR NO. 6 CONTROL CIRCUIT	DR-20A	DR-33A
MAP SENSOR VOLTAGE HIGH	DR-4A	DR-31A
MAP SENSOR VOLTAGE LOW	DR-3A	DR-31A
NO ASD RELAY VOLTAGE SENSE AT CONTROLLER	DR-26A	DR-35A
NO CHANGE IN MAP	DR-2A	DR-31B
NO VEHICLE SPEED SIGNAL	DR-5A	DR-5A
O₂ SENSOR SHORTED TO VOLTAGE	DR-7A	DR-7A
O₂ SENSOR STAYS ABOVE CENTER	DR-8A	DR-8A
O₂ SENSOR STAYS AT CENTER	DR-6A	DR-6A
O₂ SENSOR STAYS BELOW CENTER	DR-9A	DR-9A
PURGE SOLENOID CIRCUIT	DR-21A	DR-34A
RADIATOR FAN RELAY CIRCUIT	DR-25A	DR-34A
THROTTLE POSITION SENSOR VOLTAGE HIGH	DR-12A	DR-31A
THROTTLE POSITION SENSOR VOLTAGE LOW	DR-13A	DR-31A

[1] – Key counter is "0".
[2] – Key counter is more than "0".

TEST DR-2A

CODE 13, NO CHANGE IN MAP

Turn ignition switch to ON position. Connect a vacuum gauge to a manifold vacuum source. Start engine. Observe vacuum gauge reading, and compare to DRB-II reading. If gauge readings are within one in. Hg of each other, replace MAP sensor. Perform VERIFICATION TEST VER-2. If gauge readings are not within one in. Hg, of each other, perform TEST DR-31A.

TEST DR-3A

CODE 14, MAP SENSOR VOLTAGE TOO LOW

NOTE: For connector terminal identification, see CONNECTOR IDENTIFICATION at beginning of article. For appropriate wiring diagram, see WIRING DIAGRAMS article in ENGINE PERFORMANCE.

1) Turn ignition switch to OFF position. Disconnect MAP sensor connector. Turn ignition switch to ON position. Read MAP sensor voltage. If MAP sensor voltage is more than 4.5 volts, replace MAP sensor. Perform VERIFICATION TEST VER-2.

2) If MAP sensor voltage is less than 4.5 volts, turn ignition switch to OFF position. Disconnect Single Board Engine Controller (SBEC) 60-pin connector. Place DRB-II in ohmmeter mode. Probe terminal No. 2 (Dark Green/Red wire) at MAP sensor connector.

3) If resistance is less than 10 ohms, repair short to ground in Dark Green/Red wire. Perform VERIFICATION TEST VER-2. If resistance is more than 10 ohms, replace SBEC. Perform VERIFICATION TEST VER-2.

TEST DR-4A

CODE 14, MAP SENSOR VOLTAGE TOO HIGH

NOTE: For connector terminal identification, see CONNECTOR IDENTIFICATION at beginning of article. For appropriate wiring diagram, see WIRING DIAGRAMS article in ENGINE PERFORMANCE.

1) Turn ignition switch to OFF position. Disconnect and inspect MAP sensor connector. Repair connector as necessary. Perform VERIFICATION TEST VER-2. If MAP sensor is okay, go to next step.

2) Connect a jumper wire between terminals No. 1 (Black/Light Blue wire) and 2 (Dark Green/Red wire) at MAP sensor connector. Turn ignition switch to ON position. Read MAP sensor voltage. If voltage is less than one volt, replace MAP sensor. Perform VERIFICATION TEST VER-2.

3) If MAP sensor voltage is more than one volt, remove jumper wire. Connect jumper wire between terminal No. 2 (Dark Green/Red wire) at MAP sensor connector and ground. If voltage is less than one volt, repair open in Black/Light Blue wire. Perform VERIFICATION TEST VER-2.

4) If voltage is more than one volt, disconnect Single Board Engine Controller (SBEC) 60-pin connector. Inspect SBEC connector. Repair connector as necessary. Perform VERIFICATION TEST VER-2. If SBEC connector is okay, go to next step.

5) Using an external ohmmeter, check resistance at Dark Green/Red wire between MAP sensor connector terminal No. 2 and SBEC connector terminal No. 1. If resistance is more than 10 ohms, repair open Dark Green/Red wire. Perform VERIFICATION TEST VER-2. If resistance is less than 10 ohms, replace SBEC. Perform VERIFICATION TEST VER-2.

TEST DR-5A

CODE 15, NO VEHICLE SPEED SIGNAL

NOTE: For connector terminal identification, see CONNECTOR IDENTIFICATION at beginning of article. For appropriate wiring diagram, see WIRING DIAGRAMS article in ENGINE PERFORMANCE.

1) Turn ignition switch to OFF position. Disconnect and inspect distance sensor connector. Connector is located at right rear of engine. If connector is not okay, repair as necessary. Perform VERIFICATION TEST VER-2. If connector is okay, go to next step.

2) Turn ignition switch to ON position. Connect a jumper wire to one terminal of distance sensor connector. Monitor car speed while tapping open end of jumper wire to other distance sensor connector terminal.

3) If DRB-II shows car speed to be more than zero, replace distance sensor. Perform VERIFICATION TEST VER-2. If car speed is zero, place DRB-II in ohmmeter mode. Probe terminal No. 2 (Black/Light Blue wire) at distance sensor connector.

4) If resistance is more than 10 ohms, repair open in Black/Light Blue wire. If resistance is less than 10 ohms, turn ignition switch to OFF position. Disconnect Single Board Engine Controller (SBEC) connector.

TEST DR-5A (Cont.)

Inspect terminal No. 47 (White/Orange wire) at SBEC connector. Repair terminal if damaged. Perform VERIFICATION TEST VER-2. If terminal is okay, go to next step.

5) Turn ignition switch to ON position. Place DRB-II in voltmeter mode. Probe terminal No. 47 at SBEC connector. If voltage is more than 4 volts, go to step 7). If voltage is less than 4 volts, check if speedometer works. If speedometer works, repair open in White/Orange wire between distance sensor and SBEC connector. Perform VERIFICATION TEST VER-2.

6) If speedometer does not work, turn ignition switch to OFF position. Place DRB-II in ohmmeter mode. Probe terminal No. 47 at SBEC connector. If resistance is less than 5 ohms, repair short to ground in White/Orange wire. Perform VERIFICATION TEST VER-2. If resistance is more than 5 ohms, repair open White/Orange wire. Perform VERIFICATION TEST VER-2.

7) If voltage at White/Orange wire is more than 4 volts in step 5), probe White/Orange wire at distance sensor connector. Replace SBEC if voltage is more than 4 volts. Perform VERIFICATION TEST VER-2. If voltage is less than 4 volts, repair open in White/Orange wire between distance sensor and SBEC connector. Perform VERIFICATION TEST VER-2.

TEST DR-6A

CODE 21, OXYGEN (O_2) SENSOR SIGNAL STAYS AT CENTER

NOTE: For connector terminal identification, see CONNECTOR IDENTIFICATION at beginning of article. For appropriate wiring diagram, see WIRING DIAGRAMS article in ENGINE PERFORMANCE.

1) Turn ignition switch to OFF position. Disconnect and inspect O_2 sensor connector. Repair connector if damaged. Perform VERIFICATION TEST VER-2. If O_2 sensor connector is okay, go to next step.

2) Turn ignition switch to ON position. Connect a jumper wire to terminal No. 2 (Black/Dark Green wire) at O_2 sensor connector. Connect other end of jumper wire to positive battery terminal. Using DRB-II, read O_2 sensor voltage.

3) If voltage is less than one volt, go to step 5). If voltage is more than one volt, disconnect jumper wire. Turn ignition switch to OFF position. Place DRB-II in ohmmeter mode. Probe terminal No. 1 (Black/Light Blue wire) at O_2 sensor connector.

4) If resistance is more than 10 ohms, repair open Black/Light Blue wire; if resistance is less than 10 ohms, replace O_2 sensor. Perform VERIFICATION TEST VER-2.

5) If voltage is less than one volt in step 3), disconnect jumper wire. Turn ignition switch to OFF position. Disconnect Single Board Engine Controller (SBEC) 60-pin connector, and inspect connector. Repair connector if damaged. Perform VERIFICATION TEST VER-2. If SBEC connector is okay, go to next step.

6) Using an external ohmmeter, check resistance at Black/Dark Green wire between terminal No. 2 at O_2 sensor connector and terminal No. 41 at SBEC connector. If resistance is less than 10 ohms, replace SBEC. If resistance is more than 10 ohms, repair open in Black/Dark Green wire. Perform VERIFICATION TEST VER-2.

TEST DR-7A

CODE 21, OXYGEN (O_2) SENSOR SHORTED TO VOLTAGE

NOTE: For connector terminal identification, see CONNECTOR IDENTIFICATION at beginning of article. For appropriate wiring diagram, see WIRING DIAGRAMS article in ENGINE PERFORMANCE.

1) Start engine, and allow it to idle for 2 minutes. Using DRB-II, read O_2 sensor voltage. If voltage is more than 1.3 volts, go to step 3). If voltage is less than 1.3 volts, read O_2 sensor voltage while wiggling O_2 sensor wiring.

2) If voltage is more than 1.3 volts while O_2 sensor wiring is wiggled, repair short to voltage in Black/Dark Green wire. Perform VERIFICATION TEST VER-2. If voltage stays at less than 1.3 volts while O_2 sensor

TEST DR-7A (Cont.)

wiring is wiggled, replace Single Board Engine Controller (SBEC). Perform VERIFICATION TEST VER-2.

3) If voltage is more than 1.3 volts in step 1), disconnect O_2 sensor connector. If voltage is less than one volt when O_2 sensor connector is disconnected, replace O_2 sensor. Perform VERIFICATION TEST VER-2. If voltage is more than one volt when O_2 sensor connector is disconnected, Black/Dark Green wire is shorted to Dark Green/Black wire. Repair wiring as necessary.

4) Reconnect O_2 sensor connector. Using DRB-II, reset adaptive fuel value. Start engine, and let it idle for 2 minutes. Using DRB-II, read O_2 sensor value. If O_2 sensor switches from rich to lean, test is complete. Perform VERIFICATION TEST VER-2. If O_2 sensor does not switch from rich to lean, replace O_2 sensor. Perform VERIFICATION TEST VER-2.

TEST DR-8A

CODE 52, OXYGEN (O_2) SENSOR SIGNAL STAYS ABOVE CENTER

1) Allow engine to reach normal operating temperature. Turn engine off. Remove upper half of intake manifold (intake plenum). Turn ignition switch to ON position. Using DRB-II, actuate fuel system test. Inspect fuel injectors for leakage. If any injector is leaking, replace leaking injectors and/or "O" rings as necessary. Perform VERIFICATION TEST VER-2.

2) If no injectors leak, stop fuel system test. Inspect air cleaner filter and inlet ducts for restrictions. Clear as necessary. Perform VERIFICATION TEST VER-2. If no restrictions exist, perform TEST NF-13A.

TEST DR-9A

CODE 51, OXYGEN (O_2) SENSOR SIGNAL STAYS BELOW CENTER

Code 51 may set for several reasons not related to O_2 sensor or O_2 sensor circuits. If Code 51 sets, perform TEST NF-1A.

TEST DR-10A

CODE 22, COOLANT SENSOR VOLTAGE TOO HIGH

NOTE: For connector terminal identification, see CONNECTOR IDENTIFICATION at beginning of article. For appropriate wiring diagram, see WIRING DIAGRAMS article in ENGINE PERFORMANCE.

1) Turn ignition switch to OFF position. Disconnect and inspect coolant temperature sensor connector. Repair connector if damage exists. Perform VERIFICATION TEST VER-2. If coolant temperature sensor connector is okay, go to next step.

2) Connect jumper wire between terminals No. 1 (Black/Light Blue wire) and 2 (Tan/Black wire) at coolant temperature sensor connector. Turn ignition switch to ON position. Read coolant temperature sensor voltage. If voltage is less than one volt, replace coolant temperature sensor. Perform VERIFICATION TEST VER-2.

3) If voltage is more than one volt, remove jumper wire. Connect jumper wire between terminal No. 2 (Tan/Black wire) at coolant temperature sensor connector and ground. Read coolant temperature sensor voltage. If voltage is less than one volt, repair open in Black/Light Blue wire. Perform VERIFICATION TEST VER-2.

4) If voltage is more than one volt, disconnect Single Board Engine Controller (SBEC) 60-pin connector, and inspect connector. Repair connector if damaged. Perform VERIFICATION TEST VER-2. If connector is okay, go to next step.

5) Using an external ohmmeter, check resistance of Tan/Black wire between terminal No. 2 at coolant temperature sensor connector and terminal No. 2 at SBEC connector. If resistance is less than 10 ohms, replace SBEC. Perform VERIFICATION TEST VER-2. If resistance is more than 10 ohms, repair open Tan/Black wire. Perform VERIFICATION TEST VER-2.

TEST DR-11A

CODE 22, COOLANT SENSOR VOLTAGE TOO LOW

NOTE: For connector terminal identification, see CONNECTOR IDEN-TIFICATION at beginning of article. For appropriate wiring diagram, see WIRING DIAGRAMS article in ENGINE PERFORMANCE.

1) Turn ignition switch to ON position. Using DRB-II, read coolant temperature sensor voltage. Disconnect coolant temperature sensor connector. If voltage changed by more than 4 volts, replace coolant temperature sensor. Perform VERIFICATION TEST VER-2. If voltage did not change by more than 4 volts, go to next step.

2) Turn ignition switch to OFF position. Disconnect Single Board Engine Controller (SBEC) 60-pin connector. Place DRB-II in ohmmeter mode. Probe terminal No. 2 (Tan/Black wire) at SBEC connector. If resistance is less than 10 ohms, Tan/Black wire is shorted to Black/Light Blue wire or to ground. Repair wiring as necessary. Perform VERIFICATION TEST VER-2. If resistance is more than 10 ohms, replace SBEC. Perform VER-IFICATION TEST VER-2.

TEST DR-12A

CODE 24, THROTTLE POSITION SENSOR (TPS) VOLTAGE HIGH

NOTE: For connector terminal identification, see CONNECTOR IDEN-TIFICATION at beginning of article. For appropriate wiring diagram, see WIRING DIAGRAMS article in ENGINE PERFORMANCE.

1) Turn ignition switch to OFF position. Disconnect and inspect TPS connector. Repair TPS connector if damaged. Perform VERIFICATION TEST VER-2. If TPS connector is okay, go to next step.

2) Turn ignition switch to ON position. Connect jumper wire between TPS connector terminals No. 2 (Orange/Dark Blue wire) and 1 (Black/Light Blue wire). Using DRB-II, read TPS voltage. If voltage is less than one volt, replace TPS.

3) If voltage is more than one volt, remove jumper wire. Connect jumper wire between terminal No. 2 (Orange/Dark Blue wire) at TPS connector and ground. Using DRB-II, read TPS voltage. If voltage is less than one volt, repair open in Black/Light Blue wire. Perform VERIFICATION TEST VER-2.

4) If voltage is more than one volt, turn ignition switch to OFF position. Disconnect Single Board Engine Controller (SBEC) 60-pin connector, and inspect connector. Repair connector if damaged. Perform VERIFI-CATION TEST VER-2. If connector is okay, go to next step.

5) Using an external ohmmeter, check resistance at Orange/Dark Blue wire between terminal No. 2 at TPS connector and terminal No. 22 at SBEC connector. If resistance is less than 10 ohms, replace SBEC. Perform VERIFICATION TEST VER-2. If resistance is more than 10 ohms, repair open in Orange/Dark Blue wire. Perform VERIFICATION TEST VER-2.

TEST DR-13A

CODE 24, THROTTLE POSITION SENSOR (TPS) VOLTAGE LOW

NOTE: For connector terminal identification, see CONNECTOR IDEN-TIFICATION at beginning of article. For appropriate wiring diagram, see WIRING DIAGRAMS article in ENGINE PERFORMANCE.

1) Turn ignition switch to OFF position. Disconnect TPS connector. Turn ignition switch to ON position. Place DRB-II in voltmeter mode. Probe terminal No. 3 (Violet/White wire) at TPS connector.

2) If voltage is less than one volt, repair open in Violet/White wire. Perform VERIFICATION TEST VER-2. If voltage is more than one volt, probe terminal No. 2 (Orange/Dark Blue wire) at TPS connector.

3) If voltage is more than one volt, replace TPS. Perform VERIFICATION TEST VER-2. If voltage is less than one volt, turn ignition switch to OFF position. Disconnect Single Board Engine Controller (SBEC) 60-pin connector. Place DRB-II in ohmmeter mode.

4) Probe terminal No. 22 (Orange/Dark Blue wire) at SBEC connector. If resistance is less than 10 ohms, repair short to ground in Orange/Dark Blue wire. Perform VERIFICATION TEST VER-2. If resistance is more than 10 ohms, replace SBEC. Perform VERIFICATION TEST VER-2.

TEST DR-14A

CODE 25, AUTOMATIC IDLE SPEED (AIS) MOTOR CIRCUITS

NOTE: For connector terminal identification, see CONNECTOR IDEN-TIFICATION at beginning of article. For appropriate wiring diagram, see WIRING DIAGRAMS article in ENGINE PERFORMANCE.

1) Disconnect Automatic Idle Speed (AIS) motor connector. Turn ignition switch to ON position. Using DRB-II, actuate AIS motor. Put DRB-II in voltmeter mode. Probe AIS motor connector terminal No. 1 (Gray/Red wire).

2) Under normal conditions, voltage will switch from less than one volt to more than 10 volts. If voltage is less than one volt, repair short to ground in Gray/Red wire. Perform VERIFICATION TEST VER-2.

3) If voltage is more than one volt, check if voltage is more than 10 volts. If voltage is more than 10 volts, repair short to voltage in Gray/Red wire. Perform VERIFICATION TEST VER-2.

4) If voltage is less than 10 volts, probe terminal No. 2 (Yellow/Black wire) at AIS motor connector. If voltage is less than one volt, repair short to ground in Yellow/Black wire. Perform VERIFICATION TEST VER-2. If voltage is more than one volt, check if voltage is more than 10 volts.

5) If voltage is more than 10 volts, repair short to voltage in Yellow/Black wire. Perform VERIFICATION TEST VER-2. If voltage is less than 10 volts, probe terminal No. 3 (Brown/White wire) at AIS connector. If voltage is less than one volt, repair short to ground in Brown/White wire. Perform VERIFICATION TEST VER-2.

6) If voltage is more than one volt, check if voltage is more than 10 volts. If voltage is more than 10 volts, repair short to voltage in Brown/White wire. Perform VERIFICATION TEST VER-2. If voltage is less than 10 volts, probe No. 4 (Violet/Black wire) at AIS connector terminal. If voltage is less than one volt, repair short to ground in Violet/Black wire. Perform VERIFICATION TEST VER-2.

7) If voltage is more than one volt, check if voltage is more than 10 volts. If voltage is more than 10 volts, repair short to voltage in Violet/Black wire. VERIFICATION TEST VER-2. If voltage is less than 10 volts, turn ignition switch to OFF position. Reconnect AIS motor connector. Discon-nect Single Board Engine Controller (SBEC) 60-pin connector. Using an external ohmmeter, check resistance between terminals No. 39 (Gray/Red wire) and 59 (Violet/Black wire) of SBEC connector. If resistance is less than 35 ohms, replace AIS motor. Perform VERIFICATION TEST VER-2.

8) If resistance is more than 35 ohms, check resistance between termi-nals No. 40 (Brown/White wire) and 60 (Yellow/Black wire) of SBEC con-nector. If resistance is less than 35 ohms, replace AIS motor. Perform VERIFICATION TEST VER-2.

9) If resistance is more than 35 ohms, test resistance between terminals No. 39 (Gray/Red wire) and 60 (Yellow/Black wire) of SBEC connector. If resistance is less than 10 ohms, Yellow/Black wire is shorted to Gray/Red wire. Repair wiring as necessary. Perform VERIFICATION TEST VER-2.

10) If resistance is 10-75 ohms, go to next step. If resistance is 75-120 ohms, Brown/White wire is shorted to Violet/Black wire. Repair wiring as necessary. Perform VERIFICATION TEST VER-2. If resistance is more than 120 ohms, replace SBEC. Perform VERIFICATION TEST VER-2.

11) Check resistance between SBEC connector terminals No. 59 (Violet/Black wire) and 60 (Yellow/Black wire). If resistance is less than 10 ohms, Yellow/Black wire is shorted to Violet/Black wire. Repair wiring as necessary. Perform VERIFICATION TEST VER-2. If resistance is more than 10 ohms, Gray/Red wire is shorted to Brown/White wire. Repair wiring as necessary. Perform VERIFICATION TEST VER-2.

TEST DR-15A

CODE 27, INJECTOR NO. 1 CONTROL CIRCUIT

NOTE: For connector terminal identification, see CONNECTOR IDEN-TIFICATION at beginning of article. For appropriate wiring diagram, see WIRING DIAGRAMS article in ENGINE PERFORMANCE.

1) Turn ignition switch to OFF position. Disconnect 10-pin injector wiring harness connector. See Fig. NS-2A. Using external ohmmeter, measure resistance between terminals No. 1 (White/Dark Blue wire) and 5 (Dark Green/Orange wire) at fuel injector side of connector.

TEST DR-15A (Cont.)

2) If resistance is not 13-16 ohms, go to step **5)**. If resistance is 13-16 ohms, remove ohmmeter lead from terminal No. 5 (Dark Green/Orange wire), and connect it to a good ground. If resistance is less than 10 ohms, repair short to ground in White/Dark Blue wire. Perform VERIFICATION TEST VER-2.

3) If resistance is more than 10 ohms, disconnect Single Board Engine Controller (SBEC) 60-pin connector. Check resistance of White/Dark Blue wire between SBEC connector terminal No. 16 and 10-pin injector harness connector terminal No. 5 (engine side). If resistance is more than 10 ohms, repair open in White/Dark Blue wire between SBEC connector and 10-pin connector. Perform VERIFICATION TEST VER-2.

4) If resistance is less than 10 ohms, remove ohmmeter lead from terminal No. 16 of SBEC connector, and reconnect ohmmeter lead to a good ground. If resistance is less than 10 ohms, repair short to ground in White/Dark Blue wire. Perform VERIFICATION TEST VER-2. If resistance is more than 10 ohms, replace SBEC. Perform VERIFICATION TEST VER-2.

5) If resistance is not 13-16 ohms in step **2)**, reconnect 10-pin injector harness connector. Removal of upper intake manifold (plenum) may be necessary to perform following steps. Disconnect fuel injector No. 1 connector, and inspect terminals.

6) Repair connector terminals as necessary. Perform VERIFICATION TEST VER-2. If connector terminals are okay, turn ignition switch to ON position. Using DRB-II, actuate fuel injector No. 1. Place DRB-II in voltmeter mode. Probe terminal No. 2 (Dark Green/Orange wire) at fuel injector connector.

7) If voltage is less than 10 volts, repair open Dark Green/Orange wire. Perform VERIFICATION TEST VER-2. If voltage is more than 10 volts, turn ignition switch to OFF position. Disconnect 10-pin fuel injector wiring harness connector.

8) Using an external ohmmeter, check resistance of White/Dark Blue wire between fuel injector No. 1 connector and terminal No. 1 at injector side of 10-pin fuel injector wiring harness connector. If resistance is more than 10 ohms, repair open White/Dark Blue wire. Perform VERIFICATION TEST VER-2. If resistance is less than 10 ohms, replace fuel injector. Perform VERIFICATION TEST VER-2.

TEST DR-16A

CODE 27, INJECTOR NO. 2 CONTROL CIRCUIT

NOTE: For connector terminal identification, see CONNECTOR IDENTIFICATION at beginning of article. For appropriate wiring diagram, see WIRING DIAGRAMS article in ENGINE PERFORMANCE.

1) Turn ignition switch to OFF position. Disconnect 10-pin fuel injector wiring harness connector. Using an external ohmmeter, measure resistance between terminals No. 5 (Dark Green/Orange wire) and 10 (Tan wire) at injector side of 10-pin fuel injector harness connector.

2) If resistance is not 13-16 ohms, go to step **5)**. If resistance is 13-16 ohms, remove ohmmeter lead from terminal No. 5 (Dark Green/Orange wire), and reconnect ohmmeter lead to a good ground. If resistance is less than 10 ohms, repair short to ground in Tan wire. Perform VERIFICATION TEST VER-2.

3) If resistance is more than 10 ohms, disconnect Single Board Engine Controller (SBEC) 60-pin connector. Check resistance at Tan wire between terminal No. 15 at SBEC connector and terminal No. 6 at engine side of 10-pin injector wiring harness connector. If resistance is more than 10 ohms, repair open in Tan wire between SBEC connector and 10-pin injector wiring harness connector. Perform VERIFICATION TEST VER-2.

4) If resistance is less than 10 ohms, remove ohmmeter lead from terminal No. 15 at SBEC connector, and reconnect ohmmeter lead to a good ground. If resistance is less than 10 ohms, repair short to ground in Tan wire. Perform VERIFICATION TEST VER-2. If resistance is more than 10 ohms, replace SBEC. Perform VERIFICATION TEST VER-2.

5) If resistance is not 13-16 ohms in step **2)**, reconnect 10-pin fuel injector connector. Removal of upper intake manifold (plenum) may be necessary to perform following steps. Disconnect fuel injector No. 2 connector, and inspect terminals. Repair connector terminals as necessary. Perform VERIFICATION TEST VER-2.

TEST DR-16A (Cont.)

6) If connector terminals are okay, turn ignition switch to ON position. Using DRB-II, actuate fuel injector No. 2. Place DRB-II in voltmeter mode. Probe fuel injector No. 2 connector terminal No. 2 (Dark Green/Orange wire).

7) If voltage is less than 10 volts, repair open Dark Green/Orange wire. Perform VERIFICATION TEST VER-2. If voltage is more than 10 volts, turn ignition switch to OFF position. Disconnect 10-pin fuel injector wiring harness connector.

8) Using an external ohmmeter, check resistance of Tan wire between fuel injector No. 2 connector and terminal No. 10 at injector side of 10-pin fuel injector harness connector. If resistance is more than 10 ohms, repair open Tan wire. Perform VERIFICATION TEST VER-2. If resistance is less than 10 ohms, replace fuel injector. Perform VERIFICATION TEST VER-2.

TEST DR-17A

CODE 27, INJECTOR NO. 3 CONTROL CIRCUIT

NOTE: For connector terminal identification, see CONNECTOR IDENTIFICATION at beginning of article. For appropriate wiring diagram, see WIRING DIAGRAMS article in ENGINE PERFORMANCE.

1) Turn ignition switch to OFF position. Disconnect 10-pin fuel injector wiring harness connector. Using an external ohmmeter, measure resistance between terminals No. 5 (Dark Green/Orange wire) and 6 (Yellow/White wire) at injector side of 10-pin fuel injector harness connector.

2) If resistance is not 13-16 ohms, go to step **5)**. If resistance is 13-16 ohms, remove ohmmeter lead from terminal No. 5 (Dark Green/Orange wire), and reconnect ohmmeter lead to a good ground. If resistance is less than 10 ohms, repair short to ground in Yellow/White wire. Perform VERIFICATION TEST VER-2.

3) If resistance is more than 10 ohms, disconnect Single Board Engine Controller (SBEC) 60-pin connector. Check resistance at Yellow/White wire between terminal No. 14 at SBEC connector and terminal No. 10 at engine side of 10-pin injector wiring harness connector. If resistance is more than 10 ohms, repair open in Yellow/White wire between SBEC connector and 10-pin injector wiring harness connector. Perform VERIFICATION TEST VER-2.

4) If resistance is less than 10 ohms, remove ohmmeter lead from terminal No. 14 of SBEC connector, and reconnect ohmmeter lead to a good ground. If resistance is less than 10 ohms, repair short to ground in Yellow/White wire. Perform VERIFICATION TEST VER-2. If resistance is more than 10 ohms, replace SBEC. Perform VERIFICATION TEST VER-2.

5) If resistance is not 13-16 ohms in step **2)**, reconnect 10-pin fuel injector harness connector. Removal of upper intake manifold (plenum) may be necessary to perform following steps. Disconnect fuel injector No. 3, and inspect connector terminals. Repair connector terminals as necessary. Perform VERIFICATION TEST VER-2.

6) If connector terminals are okay, turn ignition switch to ON position. Using DRB-II, actuate fuel injector No. 3. Place DRB-II in voltmeter mode. Probe fuel injector No. 3 connector terminal No. 2 (Dark Green/Orange wire).

7) If voltage is less than 10 volts, repair open Dark Green/Orange wire. Perform VERIFICATION TEST VER-2. If voltage is more than 10 volts, turn ignition switch to OFF position. Disconnect 10-pin fuel injector wiring harness connector.

8) Using an external ohmmeter, check resistance of Yellow/White wire between fuel injector No. 3 connector and terminal No. 6 at injector side of 10-pin fuel injector harness connector. If resistance is more than 10 ohms, repair open Yellow/White wire. Perform VERIFICATION TEST VER-2. If resistance is less than 10 ohms, replace fuel injector. Perform VERIFICATION TEST VER-2.

TEST DR-18A

CODE 27, INJECTOR NO. 4 CONTROL CIRCUIT

NOTE: For connector terminal identification, see CONNECTOR IDENTIFICATION at beginning of article. For appropriate wiring diagram, see WIRING DIAGRAMS article in ENGINE PERFORMANCE.

1) Turn ignition switch to OFF position. Disconnect 6-pin and 10-pin fuel injector wiring harness connectors. *See Fig. NS-2A.* Using an external ohmmeter, measure resistance between terminal No. 5 (Dark Green/Orange wire) at injector side of 10-pin connector and terminal No. 6 (Light Blue/Brown wire) at 6-pin fuel injector harness connector.

2) If resistance is not 13-16 ohms, go to step **5)**. If resistance is 13-16 ohms, remove ohmmeter lead from terminal No. 5 (Dark Green/Orange wire), and reconnect ohmmeter lead to a good ground. If resistance is less than 10 ohms, repair short to ground in Light Blue/Brown wire. Perform VERIFICATION TEST VER-2.

3) If resistance is more than 10 ohms, disconnect Single Board Engine Controller (SBEC) 60-pin connector. Check resistance at Light Blue/Brown wire between terminal No. 13 at SBEC connector and terminal No. 4 at engine side of 6-pin injector wiring harness connector. If resistance is more than 10 ohms, repair open in Light Blue/Brown wire between SBEC connector and 6-pin injector wiring harness connector. Perform VERIFICATION TEST VER-2.

4) If resistance is less than 10 ohms, remove ohmmeter lead from terminal No. 13 at SBEC connector, and reconnect ohmmeter lead to a good ground. If resistance is less than 10 ohms, repair short to ground in Light Blue/Brown wire. Perform VERIFICATION TEST VER-2. If resistance is more than 10 ohms, replace SBEC. Perform VERIFICATION TEST VER-2.

5) If resistance is not 13-16 ohms in step **2)**, reconnect 6-pin and 10-pin fuel injector harness connectors. Removal of upper intake manifold (plenum) may be necessary to perform following steps. Disconnect fuel injector No. 4 connector, and inspect terminals. Repair connector terminals as necessary. Perform VERIFICATION TEST VER-2.

6) If connector terminals are okay, turn ignition switch to ON position. Using DRB-II, actuate fuel injector No. 4. Place DRB-II in voltmeter mode. Probe fuel injector No. 4 connector terminal No. 2 (Dark Green/Orange wire).

7) If voltage is less than 10 volts, repair open Dark Green/Orange wire. Perform VERIFICATION TEST VER-2. If voltage is more than 10 volts, turn ignition switch to OFF position. Disconnect 6-pin fuel injector wiring harness connector.

8) Using an external ohmmeter, check resistance of Light Blue/Brown wire between fuel injector No. 4 connector and 6-pin fuel injector harness connector terminal No. 6 (injector side). If resistance is more than 10 ohms, repair open Light Blue/Brown wire. Perform VERIFICATION TEST VER-2. If resistance is less than 10 ohms, replace fuel injector. Perform VERIFICATION TEST VER-2.

TEST DR-19A

CODE 27, INJECTOR NO. 5 CONTROL CIRCUIT

NOTE: For connector terminal identification, see CONNECTOR IDENTIFICATION at beginning of article. For appropriate wiring diagram, see WIRING DIAGRAMS article in ENGINE PERFORMANCE.

1) Turn ignition switch to OFF position. Disconnect 6-pin and 10-pin fuel injector wiring harness connectors. *See Fig. NS-2A.* Using an external ohmmeter, measure resistance between terminal No. 5 (Dark Green/Orange wire) at injector side of 10-pin connector and terminal No. 5 (Gray wire) at 6-pin connector.

2) If resistance is not between 13-16 ohms, go to step **5)**. If resistance is between 13-16 ohms, remove ohmmeter lead from terminal No. 5 (Dark Green/Orange wire), and reconnect ohmmeter lead to a good ground. If resistance is less than 10 ohms, repair short to ground in Gray wire. Perform VERIFICATION TEST VER-2.

3) If resistance is more than 10 ohms, disconnect Single Board Engine Controller (SBEC) 60-pin connector. Check resistance at Gray wire between terminal No. 38 of SBEC connector and 6-pin injector wiring harness connector terminal No. 5 (engine side). If resistance is more than 10 ohms, repair open in Gray wire between SBEC connector and 6-pin injector wiring harness connector. Perform VERIFICATION TEST VER-2.

TEST DR-19A (Cont.)

4) If resistance is less than 10 ohms, remove ohmmeter lead from terminal No. 38 of SBEC connector, and reconnect ohmmeter lead to a good ground. If resistance is less than 10 ohms, repair short to ground in Gray wire. Perform VERIFICATION TEST VER-2. If resistance is more than 10 ohms, replace SBEC. Perform VERIFICATION TEST VER-2.

5) If resistance is not 13-16 ohms in step **2)**, reconnect 6-pin and 10-pin fuel injector connectors. Removal of upper intake manifold (plenum) may be necessary to perform following steps. Disconnect fuel injector No. 5 connector, and inspect terminals. Repair connector terminals as necessary. Perform VERIFICATION TEST VER-2.

6) If connector terminals are okay, turn ignition switch to ON position. Using DRB-II, actuate fuel injector No. 5. Place DRB-II in voltmeter mode. Probe fuel injector No. 5 connector terminal No. 2 (Dark Green/Orange wire).

7) If voltage is less than 10 volts, repair open Dark Green/Orange wire. Perform VERIFICATION TEST VER-2. If voltage is more than 10 volts, turn ignition switch to OFF position. Disconnect 6-pin fuel injector wiring harness connector.

8) Using an external ohmmeter, check resistance of Gray wire between fuel injector No. 5 connector and terminal No. 5 at injector side of 6-pin fuel injector harness connector. If resistance is more than 10 ohms, repair open Gray wire. Perform VERIFICATION TEST VER-2. If resistance is less than 10 ohms, replace fuel injector. Perform VERIFICATION TEST VER-2.

TEST DR-20A

CODE 27, INJECTOR NO. 6 CONTROL CIRCUIT

NOTE: For connector terminal identification, see CONNECTOR IDENTIFICATION at beginning of article. For appropriate wiring diagram, see WIRING DIAGRAMS article in ENGINE PERFORMANCE.

1) Turn ignition switch to OFF position. Disconnect 6-pin and 10-pin fuel injector wiring harness connectors. *See Fig. NS-2A.* Using an external ohmmeter, measure resistance between terminal No. 5 (Dark Green/Orange wire) at injector side of 10-pin connector and terminal No. 4 (Brown/Dark Blue wire) at 6-pin connector.

2) If resistance is not 13-16 ohms, go to step **5)**. If resistance is 13-16 ohms, remove ohmmeter lead from terminal No. 5 (Dark Green/Orange wire), and reconnect ohmmeter lead to a good ground. If resistance is less than 10 ohms, repair short to ground in Brown/Dark Blue wire. Perform VERIFICATION TEST VER-2.

3) If resistance is more than 10 ohms, disconnect Single Board Engine Controller (SBEC) 60-pin connector. Check resistance at Brown/Dark Blue wire between SBEC connector terminal No. 58 and 6-pin injector wiring harness connector terminal No. 6 (engine side). If resistance is more than 10 ohms, repair open in Brown/Dark Blue wire between SBEC connector and 6-pin injector wiring harness connector. Perform VERIFICATION TEST VER-2.

4) If resistance is less than 10 ohms, remove ohmmeter lead from SBEC connector terminal No. 58, and reconnect ohmmeter lead to a good ground. If resistance is less than 10 ohms, repair short to ground in Brown/Dark Blue wire. Perform VERIFICATION TEST VER-2. If resistance is more than 10 ohms, replace SBEC. Perform VERIFICATION TEST VER-2.

5) If resistance is not 13-16 ohms in step **2)**, reconnect 6-pin and 10-pin fuel injector harness connectors. Removal of upper intake manifold (plenum) may be necessary to perform following steps. Disconnect fuel injector No. 6, and inspect connector terminals. Repair connector terminals as necessary. Perform VERIFICATION TEST VER-2.

6) If connector terminals are okay, turn ignition switch to ON position. Using DRB-II, actuate fuel injector No. 6. Put DRB-II in voltmeter mode. Probe terminal No. 2 (Dark Green/Orange wire) at fuel injector No. 6 connector.

7) If voltage is less than 10 volts, repair open Dark Green/Orange wire. Perform VERIFICATION TEST VER-2. If voltage is more than 10 volts, turn ignition switch to OFF position. Disconnect 6-pin fuel injector wiring harness connector.

8) Using external ohmmeter, check resistance of Brown/Dark Blue wire between fuel injector No. 6 connector and terminal No. 4 at fuel injector harness connector (injector side). If resistance is more than 10 ohms, repair open Brown/Dark Blue wire. Perform VERIFICATION TEST VER-2. If resistance is less than 10 ohms, replace fuel injector. Perform VERIFICATION TEST VER-2.

TEST DR-21A

CODE 31, PURGE SOLENOID CIRCUIT

NOTE: For connector terminal identification, see CONNECTOR IDENTIFICATION at beginning of article. For appropriate wiring diagram, see WIRING DIAGRAMS article in ENGINE PERFORMANCE.

1) Turn ignition switch to OFF position. Disconnect and inspect purge solenoid connector. Repair connector if damaged. Perform VERIFICATION TEST VER-2. If connector is okay, go to next step.

2) Turn ignition switch to ON position. Place DRB-II in voltmeter mode. Probe purge solenoid connector terminal No. 2 (Dark Blue or Dark Blue/White wire). If voltage is less than 10 volts, repair open in Dark Blue or Dark Blue/White wire. Perform VERIFICATION TEST VER-2.

3) If voltage is more than 10 volts, turn ignition switch to OFF position. Disconnect Single Board Engine Controller (SBEC) 60-pin connector. Inspect connector. Repair connector if damaged. Perform VERIFICATION TEST VER-2. If connector is okay, go to next step.

4) Place DRB-II in ohmmeter mode. Probe purge solenoid connector terminal No. 2 (Pink/Black wire). If resistance is less than 10 ohms, repair short to ground in Pink/Black wire. Perform VERIFICATION TEST VER-2. If resistance is more than 10 ohms, go to next step.

5) Using an external ohmmeter, check resistance of Pink/Black wire between purge solenoid connector terminal No. 2 and SBEC connector terminal No. 52. If resistance is more than 10 ohms, repair open in Pink/Black wire. Perform VERIFICATION TEST VER-2. If resistance is less than 10 ohms, reconnect purge solenoid connector.

6) Turn ignition switch to ON position. Place DRB-II in voltmeter mode. Probe SBEC connector terminal No. 52 (Pink/Black wire). If voltage is more than 10 volts, replace SBEC. Perform VERIFICATION TEST VER-2. If voltage is less than 10 volts, replace purge solenoid. Perform VERIFICATION TEST VER-2.

TEST DR-22A

CODE 32, EGR SOLENOID CIRCUIT

NOTE: For connector terminal identification, see CONNECTOR IDENTIFICATION at beginning of article. For appropriate wiring diagram, see WIRING DIAGRAMS article in ENGINE PERFORMANCE.

1) Turn ignition switch to OFF position. Disconnect and inspect EGR solenoid connector. Repair connector if damaged. Perform VERIFICATION TEST VER-2. If connector is okay, turn ignition switch to ON position. Place DRB-II in voltmeter mode.

2) Probe Dark Blue wire. If voltage is less than 10 volts, repair open Dark Blue wire. Perform VERIFICATION TEST VER-2. If voltage is more than 10 volts, turn ignition switch to OFF position. Reconnect EGR solenoid. Disconnect and inspect Single Board Engine Controller (SBEC) connector.

3) Repair connector if damaged. Perform VERIFICATION TEST VER-2. If connector is okay, turn ignition switch to ON position. Place DRB-II in voltmeter mode. Probe SBEC connector terminal No. 35 (Gray/Yellow wire). If voltage is more than 10 volts, replace SBEC. Perform VERIFICATION TEST VER-2.

4) If voltage is less than 10 volts, turn ignition switch to OFF position. Disconnect EGR solenoid connector. Place DRB-II in ohmmeter mode. Probe SBEC connector terminal No. 35. If resistance is less than 10 ohms, repair short to ground in Gray/Yellow wire. Perform VERIFICATION TEST VER-2. If resistance is more than 10 ohms, go to next step.

5) Using an external ohmmeter, check resistance at Gray/Yellow wire between SBEC connector terminal No. 35 and EGR solenoid terminal No. 2. If resistance is less than 10 ohms, replace EGR solenoid. Perform VERIFICATION TEST VER-2. If resistance is more than 10 ohms, repair open Gray/Yellow wire. Perform VERIFICATION TEST VER-2.

TEST DR-23A

CODE 32, EGR SYSTEM FAILURE

NOTE: For connector terminal identification, see CONNECTOR IDENTIFICATION at beginning of article. For appropriate wiring diagram, see WIRING DIAGRAMS article in ENGINE PERFORMANCE.

1) Disconnect vacuum supply hose from EGR solenoid. *See Fig. DR-23A.* Connect a vacuum gauge to disconnected vacuum hose. Start engine, and allow it to reach normal operating temperature. If vacuum is more than 10 in. Hg at idle, go to step **3)**. If vacuum is less than 10 in. Hg at idle, turn engine off.

92C04792

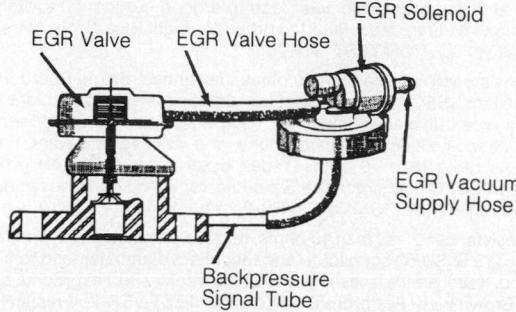

Fig. DR-23A: Identifying EGR Vacuum Hoses

2) Disconnect EGR vacuum signal line at throttle body. Connect a vacuum gauge to throttle body nipple. Start engine, and read vacuum gauge at idle. If vacuum is more than 10 in. Hg at idle, repair vacuum leak or restriction in vacuum line to EGR solenoid. Perform VERIFICATION TEST VER-2. If vacuum is less than 10 in. Hg at idle, repair plugged vacuum nipple at throttle body. Perform VERIFICATION TEST VER-2.

3) Turn engine off. Disconnect vacuum gauge, and reconnect vacuum hose to EGR solenoid. Disconnect vacuum hose from EGR valve, and connect vacuum gauge to disconnected vacuum hose. If vacuum is more than 5 in. Hg, replace EGR valve assembly. Perform VERIFICATION TEST VER-2. If vacuum is less than 5 in. Hg, go to next step.

4) Disconnect vacuum gauge from vacuum hose. Connect vacuum gauge to EGR valve nipple. Start engine. Slowly apply vacuum to EGR valve and listen for engine RPM change. If engine RPM changes, go to next step. If engine RPM does not change, go to step **6)**.

5) Turn ignition switch to OFF position. Apply 10 in. Hg of vacuum and hold for 30 seconds. If vacuum does not hold for 30 seconds, replace EGR valve. Perform VERIFICATION TEST VER-2. If vacuum holds for 30 seconds, EGR system is functioning properly at this time.

6) If engine RPM did not change in step **4)**, remove EGR valve. Check for plugged EGR manifold passages. If manifold passages are plugged, clear passages as necessary. Perform VERIFICATION TEST VER-2. If manifold passages are not plugged, replace EGR valve assembly. Perform VERIFICATION TEST VER-2.

TEST DR-24A

CODE 33, A/C CLUTCH RELAY CIRCUIT

NOTE: For connector terminal identification, see CONNECTOR IDENTIFICATION at beginning of article. For appropriate wiring diagram, see WIRING DIAGRAMS article in ENGINE PERFORMANCE.

1) Turn ignition switch to ON position. Using DRB-II, actuate A/C clutch relay. *See Fig. NS-7A or DR-24A.* If relay is not clicking, go to next step. If relay is clicking, perform TEST DR-34A.

2) Remove A/C clutch relay, and inspect connector. Repair connector if damaged. Perform VERIFICATION TEST VER-2. If connector is okay, substitute A/C relay with a known good relay. Using DRB-II, actuate A/C relay. If relay is clicking, repair is complete. Perform VERIFICATION TEST VER-2. If relay is not clicking, go to next step.

3) Remove substitute relay. Place DRB-II in voltmeter mode. Probe A/C relay connector terminal "A" (Dark Blue wire). If voltage is less than 10 volts, repair open Dark Blue wire. Perform VERIFICATION TEST VER-2. If voltage is more than 10 volts, turn ignition switch to OFF position.

TEST DR-24A (Cont.)

92E04793

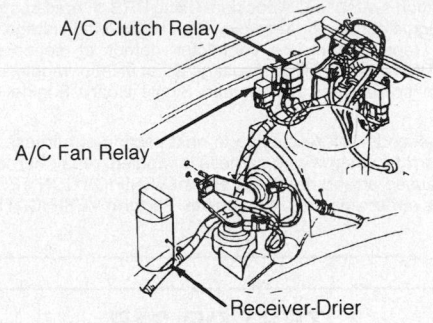

A/C Clutch Relay

A/C Fan Relay

Receiver-Drier

Fig. DR-24A: Locating A/C Relays

4) Disconnect and inspect Single Board Engine Controller (SBEC) connector. Repair connector if damaged. Perform VERIFICATION TEST VER-2. If connector is okay, put DRB-II in ohmmeter mode. Probe A/C clutch relay connector terminal "C". If resistance is less than 10 ohms, repair short to ground in Dark Blue/Orange wire. Perform VERIFICATION TEST VER-2. If resistance is more than 10 ohms, go to next step.

5) Using external ohmmeter, check resistance at Dark Blue/Orange wire between SBEC connector terminal No. 34 and A/C relay connector terminal "C". If resistance is more than 10 ohms, repair open Dark Blue/Orange wire. Perform VERIFICATION TEST VER-2. If resistance is less than 10 ohms, go to next step.

6) Reconnect A/C clutch relay. Turn ignition switch to ON position. Place DRB-II in voltmeter mode. Probe terminal No. 34 (Dark Blue/Orange wire) at SBEC connector. If voltage is more than 10 volts, replace SBEC. Perform VERIFICATION TEST VER-2. If voltage is less than 10 volts, replace A/C clutch relay. Perform VERIFICATION TEST VER-2.

TEST DR-25A

CODE 35, RADIATOR FAN RELAY CIRCUIT

NOTE: For connector terminal identification, see CONNECTOR IDENTIFICATION at beginning of article. For appropriate wiring diagram, see WIRING DIAGRAMS article in ENGINE PERFORMANCE.

1) Turn ignition switch to ON position. Using DRB-II, actuate radiator fan relay. *See Fig. NS-7A.* If relay is clicking, perform TEST DR-34A. If relay is not clicking, place DRB-II in voltmeter mode.

2) Probe terminal "A" (Dark Blue/White wire) at radiator fan relay connector. If voltage is less than 10 volts, repair open Dark Blue/White wire. Perform VERIFICATION TEST VER-2.

3) If voltage is more than 10 volts, turn ignition switch to OFF position. Disconnect Single Board Engine Controller (SBEC) connector. Inspect connector. Repair connector if damaged. Perform VERIFICATION TEST VER-2.

4) If connector is okay, turn ignition switch to ON position. Probe SBEC connector terminal No. 31 (Dark Blue/Pink wire). Replace SBEC if voltage is more than 10 volts. Perform VERIFICATION TEST VER-2. If voltage is less than 10 volts, go to next step.

5) Place DRB-II in ohmmeter mode. Disconnect radiator fan relay, and inspect connector. Repair connector as necessary. Perform VERIFICATION TEST VER-2. If connector is okay, probe SBEC connector terminal No. 31.

6) If resistance is less than 10 ohms, repair short to ground in Dark Blue/Pink wire. Perform VERIFICATION TEST VER-2. If resistance is more than 10 ohms, go to next step.

7) Using an external ohmmeter, check resistance at Dark Blue/Pink wire between SBEC connector terminal No. 31 and radiator fan relay connector terminal "C". If resistance is less than 10 ohms, replace radiator fan relay. Perform VERIFICATION TEST VER-2. If resistance is more than 10 ohms, repair open Dark Blue/Pink wire. Perform VERIFICATION TEST VER-2.

TEST DR-26A

CODE 42, NO AUTO SHUTDOWN (ASD) RELAY VOLTAGE SENSE SBEC

NOTE: For connector terminal identification, see CONNECTOR IDENTIFICATION at beginning of article. For appropriate wiring diagram, see WIRING DIAGRAMS article in ENGINE PERFORMANCE.

1) Turn ignition switch to OFF position. Disconnect Auto Shutdown (ASD) relay. Disconnect Single Board Engine Controller (SBEC) 60-pin connector. Inspect connector terminals. Repair connector terminals if damaged. Perform VERIFICATION TEST VER-2. If connector terminals are okay, go to next step.

2) Using an external ohmmeter, check resistance at Dark Green/Orange wire between SBEC connector terminal No. 57 and ASD relay terminal "D". If resistance is less than 10 ohms, replace SBEC. Perform VERIFICATION TEST VER-2. If resistance is more than 10 ohms, repair open Dark Green/Orange wire. Perform VERIFICATION TEST VER-2.

TEST DR-27A

CODE 43, IGNITION COIL NO. 1 CONTROL CIRCUIT

NOTE: For connector terminal identification, see CONNECTOR IDENTIFICATION at beginning of article. For appropriate wiring diagram, see WIRING DIAGRAMS article in ENGINE PERFORMANCE.

1) Disconnect ignition coil connector. Turn ignition switch to ON position. Using DRB-II, actuate fuel system test. Place DRB-II in voltmeter mode. Probe ignition coil connector terminal No. 2 (Gray wire). If voltage is more than 10 volts, replace ignition coil module. Perform VERIFICATION TEST VER-2.

2) If voltage is less than 10 volts, turn ignition switch to OFF position. Disconnect Single Board Engine Controller (SBEC) 60-pin connector. Inspect connector. Repair connector if damaged. Perform VERIFICATION TEST VER-2. If SBEC connector is okay, place DRB-II in ohmmeter mode. Probe ignition coil connector terminal No. 2 (Gray wire).

3) If resistance is less than 10 ohms, repair short to ground in Gray wire. Perform VERIFICATION TEST VER-2. If resistance is more than 10 ohms, go to next step.

NOTE: Wire color from SBEC connector terminal No. 19 to ignition coil connector terminal No. 2 changes from Gray to Black/Gray.

4) Check resistance between SBEC connector terminal No. 19 (Gray wire) and ignition coil connector terminal No. 2 (Black/Gray wire) using an external ohmmeter.

5) Replace SBEC if resistance is less than 10 ohms. Perform VERIFICATION TEST VER-2. If resistance is more than 10 ohms, repair open in Gray or Black/Gray wire between SBEC connector and ignition coil connector. Perform VERIFICATION TEST VER-2.

TEST DR-28A

CODE 43, IGNITION COIL NO. 2 CONTROL CIRCUIT

NOTE: For connector terminal identification, see CONNECTOR IDENTIFICATION at beginning of article. For appropriate wiring diagram, see WIRING DIAGRAMS article in ENGINE PERFORMANCE.

1) Disconnect ignition coil connector. Turn ignition switch to ON position. Using DRB-II, actuate fuel system. Place DRB-II in voltmeter mode. Probe terminal No. 3 (Dark Blue/Yellow wire) at ignition coil connector. If voltage is more than 10 volts, replace ignition coil module. Perform VERIFICATION TEST VER-2.

2) If voltage is less than 10 volts, turn ignition switch to OFF position. Disconnect and inspect Single Board Engine Controller (SBEC) 60-pin connector. Repair connector if damaged. Perform VERIFICATION TEST VER-2.

1992 ENGINE PERFORMANCE
Self-Diagnostic Tests – 3.3L (Cont.)

TEST DR-28A (Cont.)

3) If connector is okay, place DRB-II in ohmmeter mode. Probe ignition coil connector terminal No. 3 (Dark Blue/Yellow wire). If resistance is less than 10 ohms, repair short to ground in Dark Blue/Yellow wire. Perform VERIFICATION TEST VER-2. If resistance is more than 10 ohms, go to next step.

4) Check resistance of Dark Blue/Yellow wire between SBEC connector terminal No. 17 and ignition coil connector terminal No. 3 using an external ohmmeter. Replace SBEC if resistance is less than 10 ohms. Perform VERIFICATION TEST VER-2. If resistance is more than 10 ohms, repair open in Dark Blue/Yellow wire between ignition coil and SBEC connectors. Perform VERIFICATION TEST VER-2.

TEST DR-29A
CODE 43, IGNITION COIL NO. 3 CONTROL CIRCUIT

NOTE: For connector terminal identification, see CONNECTOR IDENTIFICATION at beginning of article. For appropriate wiring diagram, see WIRING DIAGRAMS article in ENGINE PERFORMANCE.

1) Disconnect ignition coil connector. Turn ignition switch to ON position. Using DRB-II, actuate fuel system. Place DRB-II in voltmeter mode. Probe ignition coil connector terminal No. 1 (Red/Yellow wire). If voltage is more than 10 volts, replace ignition coil module. Perform VERIFICATION TEST VER-2.

2) If voltage is less than 10 volts, turn ignition switch to OFF position. Disconnect and inspect Single Board Engine Controller (SBEC) 60-pin connector. Repair connector if damaged. Perform VERIFICATION TEST VER-2.

3) If connector is okay, put DRB-II in ohmmeter mode. Probe ignition coil connector terminal No. 1 (Red/Yellow wire). If resistance is less than 10 ohms, repair short to ground in Red/Yellow wire. Perform VERIFICATION TEST VER-2. If resistance is more than 10 ohms, go to next step.

4) Check resistance of Red/Yellow wire between SBEC connector terminal No. 18 and ignition coil connector terminal No. 1 using an external ohmmeter. Replace SBEC if resistance is less than 10 ohms. Perform VERIFICATION TEST VER-2. If resistance is more than 10 ohms, repair open in Red/Yellow wire between ignition coil and SBEC connectors. Perform VERIFICATION TEST VER-2.

TEST DR-30A
CODE 53, SBEC FAILURE EEPROM WRITE DENIED

1) Turn ignition switch to ON position. Perform EMR Memory Test using DRB-II. If DRB-II displays WRITE FAILURE, replace Single Board Engine Controller (SBEC). Perform VERIFICATION TEST VER-2.

2) If DRB-II does not display WRITE FAILURE, check if it displays WRITE REFUSED. If DRB-II does not display WRITE REFUSED, go to step 4). If DRB-II displays WRITE REFUSED, SBEC was busy. Perform EMR Memory Test again (twice if necessary).

3) If WRITE REFUSED returns, replace SBEC. Perform VERIFICATION TEST VER-2. If WRITE REFUSED does not return, test is complete. Perform VERIFICATION TEST VER-2.

4) If DRB-II did not display WRITE REFUSED message, check if it displays EMR MILEAGE INVALID. If DRB-II displays EMR MILEAGE INVALID, update EMR mileage, and retest EMR memory. Perform VERIFICATION TEST VER-2.

NOTE: Aftermarket scan tester may not be able to reset EMR mileage. DRB-II may be required for this step.

5) If DRB-II does not display EMR MILEAGE INVALID, compare EMR mileage stored with instrument panel odometer. If mileages are same, retest EMR memory. Perform VERIFICATION TEST VER-2. If mileages differ, update EMR mileage, and retest EMR memory. Perform VERIFICATION TEST VER-2.

TEST DR-31A
INTERMITTENT TEST FOR SENSOR VOLTAGE

1) Turn ignition switch to ON position. Using DRB-II, read suspect circuit voltage. Wiggle connector at sensor while monitoring voltage. If voltage is erratic, repair wiring or connector defect at sensor. Perform VERIFICATION TEST VER-2. If voltage is not erratic, wiggle sections of wiring harness between sensor and Single Board Engine Controller (SBEC).

2) Wait 5 seconds before moving to next section of harness. If sensor voltage is erratic when wiring harness is wiggled, repair harness where wiggling caused erratic reading. Perform VERIFICATION TEST VER-2. If voltage is not erratic, test is complete. Perform VERIFICATION TEST VER-2.

TEST DR-31B
INTERMITTENT TEST FOR SLOW CHANGE OR NO CHANGE IN MAP

NOTE: For connector terminal identification, see CONNECTOR IDENTIFICATION at beginning of article. For appropriate wiring diagram, see WIRING DIAGRAMS article in ENGINE PERFORMANCE.

1) Start engine. Using DRB-II, set engine speed to 1400 RPM and read MAP sensor voltage. Wiggle MAP sensor wiring harness while monitoring voltage.

2) If engine stalls or if MAP sensor voltage is erratic, repair wiring or connector defect at MAP sensor. Perform VERIFICATION TEST VER-2. If engine does not stall or MAP sensor voltage is not erratic, turn ignition switch to OFF position. Install a vacuum "T" into MAP sensor vacuum hose. Connect a vacuum gauge.

3) Start engine. Snap throttle open and closed while watching vacuum gauge. If vacuum drops rapidly to zero in. Hg, test is complete. Perform VERIFICATION TEST VER-2. If vacuum does not drop rapidly to zero in. Hg, remove MAP sensor, and check for vacuum restrictions. Repair restrictions as necessary. If no restrictions exist, replace MAP sensor. Perform VERIFICATION TEST VER-2.

TEST DR-32A
INTERMITTENT TEST FOR AUTOMATIC IDLE SPEED (AIS) MOTOR

1) Turn ignition switch to ON position. Using DRB-II, erase faults and actuate AIS motor. Read secondary indicators while actuating AIS motor. Wiggle AIS motor connector.

2) If fault indicator returns, repair wiring or connector defect at AIS motor. Perform VERIFICATION TEST VER-2. If fault indicator does not return, wiggle sections of wiring harness between AIS motor and Single Board Engine Controller (SBEC). Wait 5 seconds before moving to next section of wiring harness.

3) If fault indicator returns, repair wiring harness where wiggling caused indicator to return. Perform VERIFICATION TEST VER-2. If fault indicator does not return, test is complete. Perform VERIFICATION TEST VER-2.

TEST DR-33A
INTERMITTENT INJECTOR CONTROL FAULT

NOTE: For connector terminal identification, see CONNECTOR IDENTIFICATION at beginning of article. For appropriate wiring diagram, see WIRING DIAGRAMS article in ENGINE PERFORMANCE.

1) Using DRB-II, erase fault codes. Start engine. Select SECONDARY INDICATORS. Wiggle wiring harness from suspect fuel injector to Single Board Engine Controller (SBEC). If fault indicator returns, repair harness where wiggling caused indicator to return. Perform VERIFICATION TEST VER-2.

TEST DR-33A (Cont.)

2) If fault indicator does not return, visually inspect related harness connectors. Look for broken, bent, pushed-out or corroded terminals. Visually inspect related harnesses; look for chafed, pierced or partially broken wire. Repair wiring and/or connectors as necessary. Test is complete. Perform VERIFICATION TEST VER-2.

TEST DR-34A

INTERMITTENT TEST FOR
RELAYS & SOLENOIDS

1) Turn ignition switch to ON position. Using DRB-II, erase faults and actuate suspect solenoid or relay. Read secondary indicators while actuating. Wiggle connector at intermittent solenoid or relay.

2) If fault indicator returns, repair wiring or defective connector at solenoid or relay. Perform VERIFICATION TEST VER-2. If fault indicator does not return, wiggle sections of wiring harness between solenoid/relay and Single Board Engine Controller (SBEC).

3) Wait 5 seconds before moving to next section of wiring harness. If fault indicator returns, repair wiring harness where wiggling caused fault indicator to return. Perform VERIFICATION TEST VER-2. If fault indicator does not return, test is complete. Perform VERIFICATION TEST VER-2.

TEST DR-35A

INTERMITTENT AUTO SHUTDOWN
SENSE CIRCUIT FAULT

1) Turn ignition switch to ON position. Using DRB-II, erase fault codes and select SECONDARY INDICATORS. Actuate ASD relay. Wiggle wires and connectors of ASD circuit.

2) Observe secondary indicators. If ASD fault returns, repair harness or connector where wiggling caused fault indicator to return. Perform VERIFICATION TEST VER-2. If ASD fault does not return, visually inspect related wire harness connectors.

3) Look for broken, bent, pushed-out or corroded terminals. Visually inspect related harnesses; look for chafed, pierced or partially broken wire. Repair wiring and/or connectors as necessary. Test is complete. Perform VERIFICATION TEST VER-2.

TEST DR-36A

INTERMITTENT IGNITION COIL
CONTROL CIRCUIT FAULT

1) Turn ignition switch to ON position. Using DRB-II, erase fault codes. Select SECONDARY INDICATORS. Start engine. Wiggle ignition coil circuit wires and connectors. Observe secondary indicators.

2) If coil control circuit fault returns, repair harness or connector where wiggling caused fault indicator to return. Perform VERIFICATION TEST VER-2. If coil control circuit fault does not return, visually inspect related wire harness connectors.

3) Look for broken, bent, pushed-out or corroded terminals. Visually inspect related harnesses; look for chafed, pierced or partially broken wire. Repair wiring and/or connectors as necessary. Test is complete. Perform VERIFICATION TEST VER-2.

TEST NF-1A

NO FAULT CODE TEST MENU

Check MITCHELL® TECH SERVICE BULLETINS (TSBs) for any pertinent information. If a TSB exists, perform corrective action. If TSB does not exist or if driveability problem still exists, check suspect system and perform indicated test. See NO FAULT CODE TEST MENU table. If system causing driveability problem is not known, perform TEST NF-2A through TEST NF-13A in sequence until problem is found.

TEST NF-1A (Cont.)

NO FAULT CODE TEST MENU

Application	Test
Checking Secondary Ignition & Timing	NF-2A
Checking Fuel Pressure	NF-3A
Checking Coolant & TPS Calibrations	NF-4A
Checking MAP Sensor Calibration	NF-5A
Checking Oxygen (O₂) Sensor Switching	NF-6A
Checking Automatic Idle Speed Motor	NF-7A
Checking Park/Neutral Switch (A/T Only)	NF-8A
Checking SBEC Ground	NF-9A
Checking EGR Operation	NF-10A
Checking Engine Vacuum	NF-11A
Checking Minimum Idle Airflow	NF-12A
Checking Engine Mechanical	NF-13A

TEST NF-2A

CHECKING SECONDARY IGNITION & TIMING

1) Turn engine off. Connect engine analyzer to engine. Start engine, and let it idle. Set scope to read display or parade pattern. Follow equipment manufacturer procedure for pattern analysis.

2) If secondary ignition pattern is not okay, repair indicated component in secondary ignition system. Perform VERIFICATION TEST VER-2. If secondary ignition pattern is okay, remove all lower spark plug wires individually from coil pack. Observe secondary kilovolt line.

3) If open circuit secondary voltage is less than 25 kilovolts, replace ignition coil module. Perform VERIFICATION TEST VER-2. If open circuit secondary voltage is at least 25 kilovolts, reinstall spark plug wire.

4) Ensure engine temperature is more than 180°F (82°C) before proceeding. Using DRB-II, read spark advance. Increase engine speed to 2000 RPM. If spark advance does not change with increase in RPM, replace Single Board Engine Controller (SBEC). Perform VERIFICATION TEST VER-2. If spark advance changes with increase in RPM, test is complete.

TEST NF-3A

CHECKING FUEL PRESSURE

WARNING: High fuel pressure may be present in fuel lines. Open fuel system with caution. See FUEL PRESSURE RELEASE procedure in SELF-DIAGNOSTICS INTRODUCTION – GASOLINE article.

1) Relieve fuel pressure. Connect fuel pressure gauge to fuel rail service port. Turn ignition switch to ON position. Using DRB-II, actuate fuel system test. If fuel pressure is 43-53 psi, test is complete. If fuel pressure is not 43-53 psi, record fuel pressure reading. If pressure is more than 53 psi, perform TEST NF-3B.

2) If fuel pressure is less than 53 psi, stop fuel system actuation test. Turn ignition switch to OFF position. Inspect fuel lines for kinked or restricted lines. Repair fuel lines as necessary. Perform VERIFICATION TEST VER-2.

3) If no kinked or restricted lines exist, release fuel pressure. Remove fuel pressure gauge from fuel rail. Install fuel pressure gauge between fuel tank and fuel filter. Turn ignition switch to ON position. Actuate ASD relay using DRB-II. If fuel pressure is at least 5 psi more than previously recorded pressure, replace fuel filter. Perform VERIFICATION TEST VER-2.

CAUTION: DO NOT allow fuel pressure to exceed 70 psi when squeezing fuel return hose.

4) If fuel pressure is not at least 5 psi more than previous reading, gently squeeze fuel return hose while observing fuel pressure gauge, ensuring fuel pressure does not exceed 70 psi. If fuel pressure increases, replace fuel pressure regulator. Perform VERIFICATION TEST VER-2. If fuel pressure does not increase, replace fuel pump and sock assembly. Perform VERIFICATION TEST VER-2.

TEST NF-3B

CHECKING FUEL PRESSURE

WARNING: High fuel pressure may be present in fuel lines. Open fuel system with caution. See FUEL PRESSURE RELEASE procedure in SELF-DIAGNOSTICS INTRODUCTION – GASOLINE article.

1) Relieve fuel pressure. Using DRB-II, stop fuel system actuation test. Ensure fuel tank is at least 1/2 full before performing following test. Install fuel pressure gauge and adapter between fuel tank and filter at rear of vehicle.

2) Remove fuel return line from fuel tank. Connect Fuel Pressure Test Adapter (6541) to fuel return line. Place other end of adapter hose into an approved 2-gallon gasoline can. Turn ignition switch to ON position.

3) Using DRB-II, actuate fuel system test. Observe fuel pressure gauge. If fuel pressure is 43-53 psi, repair fuel return line for a restriction at fuel tank. Perform VERIFICATION TEST VER-2.

4) If fuel pressure is not 43-53 psi, stop fuel system actuation test. Relieve fuel pressure. Reconnect fuel return line to fuel tank. Disconnect fuel return line from fuel rail.

5) Attach Fuel Pressure Test Adapter (6541) to fuel return line nipple at fuel rail. Place other end of adapter hose into an approved 2-gallon gasoline can. Turn ignition switch to ON position. Actuate fuel system test. Observe fuel pressure gauge.

6) If fuel pressure is 43-53 psi, repair restricted fuel return line to fuel tank. Perform VERIFICATION TEST VER-2. If fuel pressure is not 43-53 psi, inspect fuel pressure damper line for restrictions.

7) If restriction exists, replace fuel pressure damper line. Perform VERIFICATION TEST VER-2. If no restriction exists, replace fuel pressure regulator. Perform VERIFICATION TEST VER-2.

TEST NF-4A

CHECKING COOLANT SENSOR & THROTTLE POSITION SENSOR (TPS) CALIBRATIONS

1) Start engine. Allow engine to reach normal operating temperature. Using DRB-II, read coolant temperature sensor value. If temperature is 180-250°F (82-121°C), go to next step. If temperature is not 180-250°F (82-121°C), replace coolant temperature sensor. Perform VERIFICATION TEST VER-2.

2) Turn engine off. Turn ignition switch to ON position. Using DRB-II, read TPS voltage with throttle fully closed and against throttle stop. If voltage is not 1.5 volts or less with throttle closed, replace TPS. Perform VERIFICATION TEST VER-2. If voltage is 1.5 volts or more with throttle fully closed, go to next step.

3) Monitor voltage while slowly opening throttle wide open. If voltage change is not a smooth transition, replace TPS. Perform VERIFICATION TEST VER-2. If voltage change is a smooth transition, go to next step.

4) Check if maximum voltage is at least 3.4 volts with throttle wide open. If maximum voltage is not at least 3.4 volts with throttle wide open, replace TPS. Perform VERIFICATION TEST VER-2. If maximum voltage is at least 3.4 volts, go to next step.

5) Start engine, and let it idle. Using DRB-II, read minimum throttle voltage. If voltage is not 0-1.5 volts, replace TPS. Perform VERIFICATION TEST VER-2. If voltage is 0-1.5 volts, test is complete.

TEST NF-5A

CHECKING MANIFOLD ABSOLUTE PRESSURE (MAP) SENSOR CALIBRATION

1) Turn engine off. Install vacuum "T" in MAP sensor vacuum hose. Install vacuum gauge. Start engine, and let it idle. Using DRB-II, read vacuum gauge. If DRB-II vacuum reading is within one in. Hg of vacuum gauge reading, test is complete. If DRB-II vacuum reading is not within one in. Hg of vacuum gauge reading, go to next step.

2) Turn engine off. Disconnect vacuum gauge from MAP sensor vacuum hose. Connect an auxiliary vacuum pump to MAP sensor. Apply 5 in. Hg vacuum to MAP sensor. Read and record MAP sensor voltage. Increase vacuum to 20 in. Hg. Read and record MAP sensor voltage. Subtract

TEST NF-5A (Cont.)

voltage recorded at 20 in. Hg vacuum from voltage recorded at 5 in. Hg vacuum.

3) If difference is 2.3-2.9 volts, repair restriction in vacuum hose to MAP sensor. Perform VERIFICATION TEST VER-2. If voltage difference is not 2.3-2.9 volts, replace MAP sensor. Perform VERIFICATION TEST VER-2.

TEST NF-6A

CHECKING OXYGEN (O₂) SENSOR SWITCHING

1) Allow engine to reach normal operating temperature. Using DRB-II, read O_2 sensor state. If O_2 sensor state is switching, system is functioning okay. Test is complete. If O_2 sensor state is not switching, check if O_2 sensor is locked on lean. If O_2 sensor is locked on lean, perform TEST NF-6B. If O_2 sensor is not locked on lean, go to next step.

2) Turn engine off. Remove upper intake manifold (intake plenum). Refer to 3.3L V6 article in ENGINES. Turn ignition switch to ON position. Using DRB-II, actuate fuel system test. Inspect injectors for fuel leakage. If any injectors are leaking, replace leaking injectors and/or "O" rings as necessary. Perform VERIFICATION TEST VER-3. If injectors are not leaking, go to next step.

3) Using DRB-II, stop fuel system test. Turn ignition switch to OFF position. Install upper intake manifold. Inspect air cleaner filter and inlet ducts for restrictions. If any restrictions exist, clear restricted air inlet system as necessary. Perform VERIFICATION TEST VER-3. If restrictions do not exist, perform TEST NF-13A.

TEST NF-6B

CHECKING OXYGEN (O₂) SENSOR SWITCHING

NOTE: For connector terminal identification, see CONNECTOR IDENTIFICATION at beginning of article. For appropriate wiring diagram, see WIRING DIAGRAMS article in ENGINE PERFORMANCE.

1) Allow engine to idle. Inspect engine for vacuum leaks. Repair vacuum leaks as necessary. Perform VERIFICATION TEST VER-2. If no vacuum leaks exist, read O_2 sensor signal voltage using DRB-II.

2) If voltage is more than .1 volt, go to step 4). If voltage is less than .1 volt, turn ignition switch to OFF position. Disconnect O_2 sensor connector and Single Board Engine Controller (SBEC) connector. Put DRB-II in ohmmeter mode. Probe SBEC connector terminal No. 41 (Black/Dark Green wire).

3) If resistance is less than 10 ohms, repair short to ground in Black/Dark Green wire. Perform VERIFICATION TEST VER-2. If resistance is more than 10 ohms, replace O_2 sensor. Perform VERIFICATION TEST VER-2.

4) If O_2 sensor voltage is more than .1 volt in step 2), turn engine off. Replace O_2 sensor. Perform VERIFICATION TEST VER-2. Turn ignition switch to ON position. Using DRB-II, reset adaptive fuel memory. Start engine, and allow it to reach normal operating temperature.

5) Read O_2 sensor state. If O_2 sensor state is switching, repair is complete. Perform VERIFICATION TEST VER-2. If O_2 sensor state is not switching, perform TEST NF-13A.

TEST NF-7A

CHECKING AUTOMATIC IDLE SPEED (AIS) MOTOR OPERATION

NOTE: For connector terminal identification, see CONNECTOR IDENTIFICATION at beginning of article. For appropriate wiring diagram, see WIRING DIAGRAMS article in ENGINE PERFORMANCE.

1) Using DRB-II, set engine speed to 1100 RPM. If engine speed can be set to 1050-1150 RPM, test is complete. If engine speed cannot be set to 1050-1150 RPM, return engine to normal idle speed. Disconnect AIS motor connector.

TEST NF-7A (Cont.)

2) Inspect idle speed motor connector. Repair connector if damaged. Perform VERIFICATION TEST VER-2. If connector is okay, place DRB-II in voltmeter mode. Open and close throttle while probing AIS motor connector terminal No. 1 (Gray/Red wire). If voltage is less than one volt, perform TEST NF-7B. If voltage is more than one volt, go to next step.

3) Open and close throttle while probing AIS motor connector terminal No. 2 (Yellow/Black wire). If voltage is less than one volt, perform TEST NF-7B. If voltage is more than one volt, go to next step.

4) Open and close throttle while probing AIS motor connector terminal No. 3 (Brown/White wire). If voltage is less than one volt, perform TEST NF-7B. If voltage is more than one volt, go to next step.

5) Open and close throttle while probing AIS motor connector terminal No. 4 (Violet/Black wire). If voltage is less than one volt, perform TEST NF-7B. If voltage is more than one volt, inspect engine for vacuum leaks. Repair as necessary. Perform VERIFICATION TEST VER-2. If no vacuum leaks exist, replace AIS motor. Perform VERIFICATION TEST VER-2.

TEST NF-7B

CHECKING AUTOMATIC IDLE SPEED (AIS) MOTOR OPERATION

NOTE: For connector terminal identification, see CONNECTOR IDENTIFICATION at beginning of article. For appropriate wiring diagram, see WIRING DIAGRAMS article in ENGINE PERFORMANCE.

1) Turn engine off. Disconnect and inspect Single Board Engine Controller (SBEC) connector. Repair connector if damaged. Perform VERIFICATION TEST VER-2. If connector is okay, go to next step.

2) Using an external ohmmeter, check continuity between AIS motor connector terminal No. 1 (Gray/Red wire) and SBEC connector terminal No. 39 (Gray/Red wire), AIS motor connector terminal No. 2 (Yellow/Black wire) and SBEC connector terminal No. 60 (Yellow/Black wire), AIS motor connector terminal No. 3 (Brown/White wire) and SBEC connector terminal No. 40 (Brown/White wire), and AIS motor connector terminal No. 4 (Violet/Black wire) and SBEC connector terminal No. 59 (Violet/Black wire).

3) If resistance is less than 10 ohms for each circuit, replace SBEC. Perform VERIFICATION TEST VER-2. If resistance is more than 10 ohms for any circuit, repair open in that circuit. Perform VERIFICATION TEST VER-2.

TEST NF-8A

CHECKING PARK/NEUTRAL SWITCH INPUT

NOTE: For connector terminal identification, see CONNECTOR IDENTIFICATION at beginning of article. For appropriate wiring diagram, see WIRING DIAGRAMS article in ENGINE PERFORMANCE.

1) Using DRB-II, read park/neutral switch input state. While watching DRB-II display, move gear selector in and out of Park and Reverse positions. If display shows P/N and D/R, system is functioning correctly. If display does not show P/N and D/R, go to next step.

2) Turn ignition switch to OFF position. Place gear selector in Park position. Disconnect Single Board Engine Controller (SBEC) connector. Disconnect quick-disconnect cable at battery. Place DRB-II in ohmmeter mode. Probe terminal No. 30 (Brown Yellow wire) in SBEC connector. Watch DRB-II display while moving gear selector in and out of Park and Reverse positions.

3) If display switches from less than 5 ohms to more than 5 ohms, replace SBEC. Perform VERIFICATION TEST VER-2. If display does not switch from less than 5 ohms to more than 5 ohms, check if display always stays less than 5 ohms. If display always stays less than 5 ohms, repair short to ground in Brown/Yellow wire. Perform VERIFICATION TEST VER-2. If display does not always stay less than 5 ohms, go to next step.

4) Disconnect park/neutral switch connector. Using external ohmmeter, check resistance of Brown/Yellow wire between park/neutral switch connector and SBEC connector terminal No. 30. If resistance is less than 10 ohms, replace park/neutral switch. Perform VERIFICATION TEST VER-2. If resistance is more than 10 ohms, repair open Brown/Yellow wire. Perform VERIFICATION TEST VER-2.

TEST NF-9A

CHECKING ENGINE CONTROLLER GROUND & POWER CIRCUITS

NOTE: For connector terminal identification, see CONNECTOR IDENTIFICATION at beginning of article. For appropriate wiring diagram, see WIRING DIAGRAMS article in ENGINE PERFORMANCE.

1) Turn ignition switch to OFF position. Disconnect and inspect SBEC connector terminals. Repair connector terminals if damaged. Perform VERIFICATION TEST VER-2. If connector terminals are okay, go to next step.

2) Put DRB-II in ohmmeter mode. Probe SBEC connector terminal No. 5 (Black/White wire). If resistance is more than one ohm, repair open in Black/White wire. Perform VERIFICATION TEST VER-2. If resistance is less than one ohm, go to next step.

3) Probe SBEC connector terminal No. 11 (Black/Tan wire). If resistance is more than one ohm, repair open in Black/Tan wire. Perform VERIFICATION TEST VER-2. If resistance is less than one ohm, go to next step.

4) Probe SBEC connector terminal No. 12 (Black/Tan wire). If resistance is more than one ohm, repair open in Black/Tan wire. Perform VERIFICATION TEST VER-2. If resistance is less than one ohm, go to next step.

5) Place DRB-II in voltmeter mode. Turn ignition switch to ON position. Probe SBEC connector terminal No. 9 (Dark Blue wire). If voltage is less than 10 volts, repair open Dark Blue wire. Perform VERIFICATION TEST VER-2. If voltage is more than 10 volts, reconnect SBEC connector. Test is complete.

TEST NF-10A

CHECKING EGR OPERATION (FEDERAL EMISSIONS)

1) Check if vehicle is equipped with an EGR valve. If vehicle is not equipped with an EGR valve, test is complete. If vehicle is equipped with EGR valve, check if vehicle has California emissions. See emissions decal in engine compartment. If vehicle is not equipped with California emissions, go to next step. If vehicle is equipped with California emissions, test is complete.

2) Disconnect vacuum hose from EGR solenoid. See Fig. DR-23A. Connect vacuum gauge to disconnected vacuum hose. Start engine. If vacuum is more than 10 in. Hg at idle, go to step 4). If less than 10 in. Hg at idle, turn engine off.

3) Disconnect EGR vacuum supply hose at throttle body. Connect a vacuum gauge to throttle body nipple. Start engine. Read vacuum gauge at idle. If vacuum is more than 10 in. Hg at idle, repair restriction or leak in vacuum line to EGR solenoid. Perform VERIFICATION TEST VER-2. If vacuum is less than 10 in. Hg at idle, repair plugged vacuum nipple at throttle body. Perform VERIFICATION TEST VER-2.

4) Stop engine. Disconnect vacuum gauge, and reconnect vacuum hose to EGR solenoid. Disconnect vacuum hose from EGR valve, and connect vacuum gauge to disconnected hose. Start engine.

5) Momentarily snap throttle open while watching gauge. If vacuum is ever less than 5 in. Hg, replace EGR valve assembly. Perform VERIFICATION TEST VER-2. If vacuum is always more than 5 in. Hg, go to next step.

6) Turn ignition switch to OFF position. Disconnect hose to EGR valve backpressure signal tube. Adjust a shop air hose at 20-30 psi. Connect shop air to nipple on base of EGR valve. Listen for a tone change while opening and closing throttle.

7) If tone changes, replace EGR valve assembly. Perform VERIFICATION TEST VER-2. If tone does not change, remove vacuum gauge. Cap open nipple at EGR valve base. Connect hand vacuum pump to EGR valve. Start engine.

8) Listen for engine RPM change while slowly applying vacuum to EGR valve. If engine RPM does not change, go to step 9). If engine RPM changes, turn ignition switch to OFF position. Apply 10 in. Hg vacuum and hold for 30 seconds. If vacuum holds for 30 seconds, test is complete. If vacuum does not hold for 30 seconds, replace EGR valve assembly. Perform VERIFICATION TEST VER-2.

9) Remove EGR valve assembly. Check for plugged manifold passages. Clear manifold passages as necessary. Perform VERIFICATION TEST VER-2. If passages are not plugged, replace EGR valve assembly. Perform VERIFICATION TEST VER-2.

TEST NF-11A

CHECKING ENGINE VACUUM

Connect a vacuum gauge to engine. Start engine, and let it idle. Normal vacuum reading will vary depending on altitude. Observe vacuum gauge at idle. If vacuum gauge reading is not steady 13-22 in. Hg, perform TEST NF-13A. If vacuum gauge reading is steady and within specification, test is complete. Perform VERIFICATION TEST VER-3.

TEST NF-12A

CHECKING MINIMUM IDLE AIRFLOW

1) Turn ignition switch to OFF position. Disconnect PCV valve hose from intake manifold nipple. Install Vacuum Fitting (6457) to intake manifold PCV nipple. Start engine. Allow engine to reach normal operating temperature.

2) Disconnect 3/16" idle purge hose from throttle body, and cap nipple. Start engine. Allow engine to reach normal operating temperature. If vehicle odometer indicates less than 1000 miles, go to step **4)**.

3) If vehicle odometer indicates more than 1000 miles, read minimum airflow speed using DRB-II. If engine speed is 700-950 RPM, test is complete. If engine speed is not as specified, replace throttle body. Perform VERIFICATION TEST VER-2.

4) Using DRB-II, read minimum airflow speed. If engine speed is 650-950 RPM, test is complete. Perform VERIFICATION TEST VER-2. If engine speed is not as specified, replace throttle body. Perform VERIFICATION TEST VER-2.

TEST NF-13A

PERFORMING NO FAULT CODE MECHANICAL TEST

At this point in diagnostic test procedure, all engine control systems have been determined to be operating as designed and not causing a driveability problem. Following additional items should be checked as possible causes:

NOTE: If coming to this test from O_2 sensor test and rich or lean condition is not corrected after checking items listed below, replace Single Board Engine Controller (SBEC).

- Check if any MITCHELL® TECH SERVICE BULLETINS (TSBs) apply to vehicle.
- Check engine compression.
- Check for exhaust system restriction.
- Check camshaft and crankshaft sprockets.
- Check valve timing.
- Check torque converter stall speed.
- Check engine vacuum. It must be at least 13 in. Hg in Neutral.
- Check for fuel contamination.
- Ensure PCV system is functioning properly.
- Ensure injector control wire is connected to correct fuel injector and injector is not plugged or restricted.
- Check power booster for internal vacuum leak.

TEST VER-1

VERIFICATION TEST VER-1

Inspect vehicle to ensure all engine components are connected. Reassemble and reconnect components as necessary. Attempt to start engine. If engine does not start, return to TEST NS-1A.

If engine starts, Single Board Engine Controller (SBEC) was changed and vehicle is equipped with factory theft alarm, start vehicle at least 20 times so alarm system may be activated when desired. On AS body, write vehicle mileage from its odometer to memory location within replacement SBEC. This will enable new SBEC to operate Emission Maintenance Reminder (EMR) light properly. On all models, no-start condition is corrected and repair is now complete.

TEST VER-1 (Cont.)

If engine starts and SBEC has not been changed, connect DRB-II to engine diagnostic connector, and erase faults. No-start condition has been corrected and fault messages have been erased. Repair is now complete. If repaired fault has reset, check if any MITCHELL® TECH SERVICE BULLETINS (TSBs) apply to vehicle. Return to TEST DR-1A if necessary. If another fault exists, return to TEST DR-1A and follow path specified by other fault.

TEST VER-2

VERIFICATION TEST VER-2

If TEST VER-3 was performed previously, perform TEST VER-3 again. Inspect vehicle to ensure all engine components are connected. Reassemble and reconnect components as necessary. If another fault was read previously and not corrected, return to TEST DR-1A and follow path specified by other fault. If Single Board Engine Controller (SBEC) was replaced, perform following:

1) If vehicle is equipped with factory theft alarm, start vehicle at least 20 times so alarm system may be activated when desired. Write vehicle mileage from its odometer to memory location within replacement SBEC. This will enable new SBEC to operate Emission Maintenance Reminder (EMR) light properly.

2) Connect DRB-II to engine diagnostic connector, and erase faults. Ensure no other fault remains by starting engine and allowing it to reach normal operating temperature.

3) Increase engine speed to 2000 RPM for at least 10 seconds. Allow engine to idle. On A/T models, apply brake and cycle transmission through all gear ranges. Place gear selector in Park position. If vehicle is equipped with A/C, turn on A/C. Set blower to low speed.

4) On all models, turn engine off. Start engine. Allow engine to idle for at least 2 minutes. Turn engine off. Using DRB-II, read fault messages. If repaired fault resets, repair is not complete.

5) Check all pertinent MITCHELL® TECH SERVICE BULLETINS (TSBs), and return to TEST DR-1A if necessary. If another fault exists, return to TEST DR-1A and follow path specified by other fault. If no other faults exist, repair is now complete.

TEST VER-3

VERIFICATION TEST VER-3

Inspect vehicle to ensure all engine components are connected. Reassemble and reconnect components as necessary. If another fault was read previously and not corrected, return to TEST DR-1A and follow path specified by other fault. If Single Board Engine Controller (SBEC) has been replaced, perform following:

- If vehicle is equipped with factory theft alarm, start vehicle at least 20 times so alarm system may be activated when desired.
- Write vehicle odometer mileage to memory location within replacement SBEC. This will enable new SBEC to operate Emission Maintenance Reminder (EMR) light properly.
- Connect DRB-II to engine diagnostic connector, and erase faults. Disconnect DRB-II.

To ensure no other fault remains, perform following:

1) If vehicle is equipped with A/C, turn A/C on. Set blower to low speed. On all models, drive vehicle for at least 5 minutes and attain a speed of at least 40 MPH. Ensure transmission shifts through all gears.

2) Upon completion of road test, turn engine off. Restart engine, and let it idle for at least 2 minutes. Turn engine off. Connect DRB-II to engine diagnostic connector.

3) Read all fault messages. If repaired fault has reset, repair is not complete. Check all pertinent MITCHELL® TECH SERVICE BULLETINS (TSBs), and return to TEST DR-1A if necessary. If another fault exists, return to TEST DR-1A and follow path specified by other fault. If no other faults exist, repair is now complete.

WARNING: *When battery is disconnected, vehicle computer and energy systems may lose memory data. Driveability problems may exist until computer systems have completed a relearn cycle. See COMPUTER RELEARN PROCEDURES article in GENERAL INFORMATION before disconnecting battery.*

SELF-DIAGNOSTIC DIRECTORY

SELF-DIAGNOSTIC DIRECTORY

CONNECTOR IDENTIFICATION

CONNECTOR IDENTIFICATION DIRECTORY

Connector	See Fig.
Automatic Idle Speed (AIS) Motor	1
Coolant Temperature Sensor	2
Crank Position Sensor	3
Distance Sensor	4
Distributor Pick-Up	5
EGR Solenoid	6
Engine Controller	7
Engine Diagnostic	8
Fuel Injector	9
Ignition Coil	10
Manifold Absolute Pressure (MAP) Sensor	11
Oil Pressure Switch	12
Oxygen (O₂) Sensor	13
Purge Solenoid	14
Relays	
AB & AD Bodies	
A/C Clutch, Auto Shutdown, Fuel Pump & Part Throttle Unlock Relays	15
AN Body	
A/C Clutch, Auto Shutdown, Fuel Pump & Starter Relays	16
Throttle Body Charge Temperature Sensor	17
Throttle Position Sensor (TPS)	18

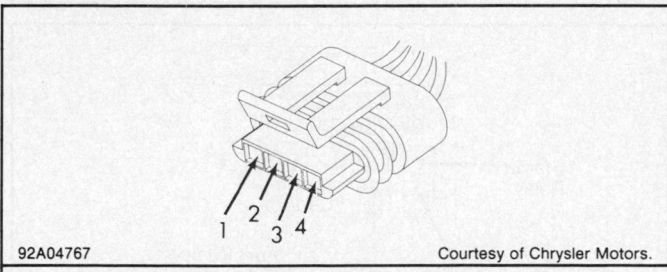

92A04767   Courtesy of Chrysler Motors.

Fig. 1: Identifying Automatic Idle Speed (AIS) Motor Connector Terminals

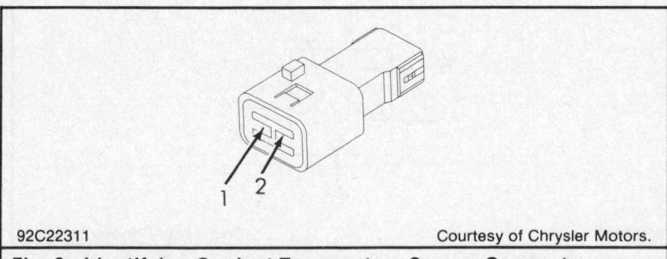

92C22311   Courtesy of Chrysler Motors.

Fig. 2: Identifying Coolant Temperature Sensor Connector Terminals

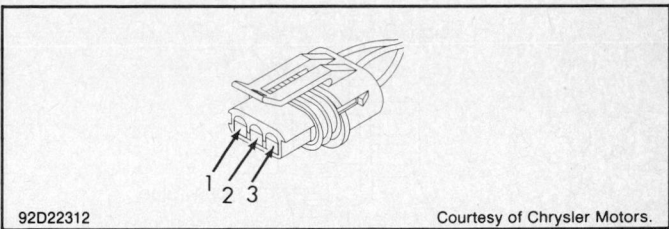

92D22312   Courtesy of Chrysler Motors.

Fig. 3: Identifying Crank Position Sensor Connector Terminals

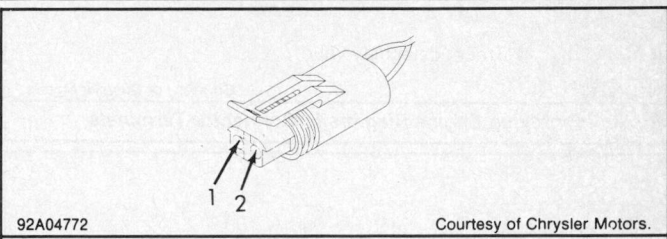

92A04772   Courtesy of Chrysler Motors.

Fig. 4: Identifying Distance Sensor Connector Terminals

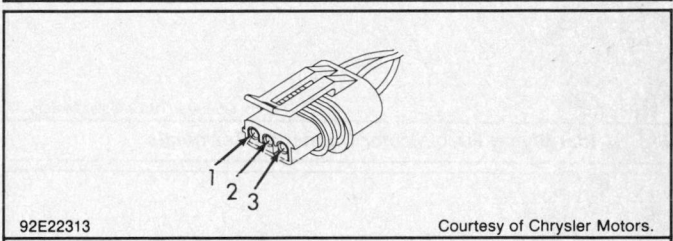

92E22313   Courtesy of Chrysler Motors.

Fig. 5: Identifying Distributor Pick-Up Connector Terminals

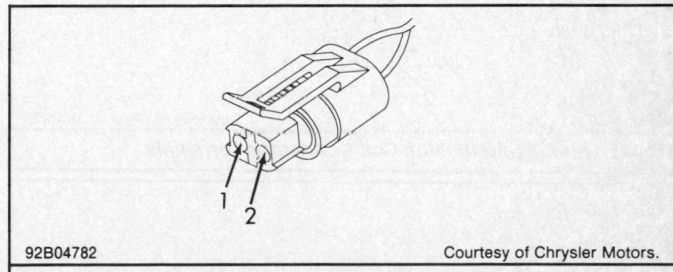

92B04782   Courtesy of Chrysler Motors.

Fig. 6: Identifying EGR Solenoid Connector Terminals

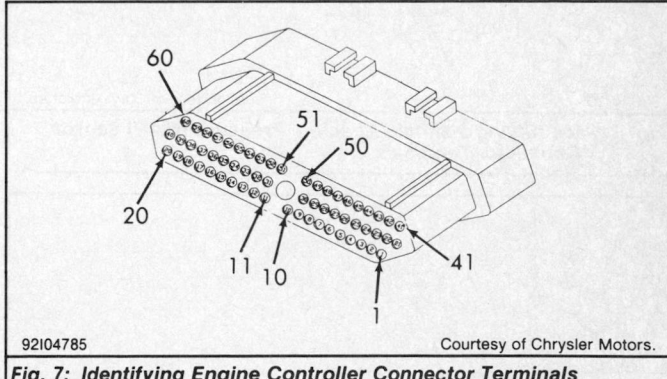

92I04785   Courtesy of Chrysler Motors.

Fig. 7: Identifying Engine Controller Connector Terminals

1992 ENGINE PERFORMANCE
Self-Diagnostic Tests – 3.9L & 5.2L (Cont.)

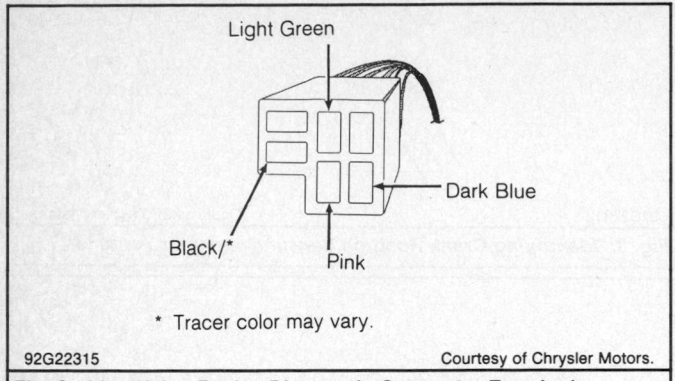

Light Green

Dark Blue

Black/*

Pink

* Tracer color may vary.

92G22315   Courtesy of Chrysler Motors.

Fig. 8: Identifying Engine Diagnostic Connector Terminals

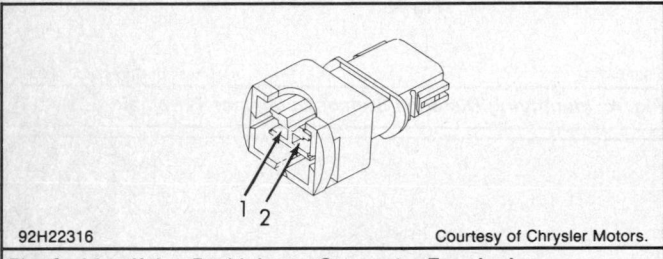

1
2

92H22316   Courtesy of Chrysler Motors.

Fig. 9: Identifying Fuel Injector Connector Terminals

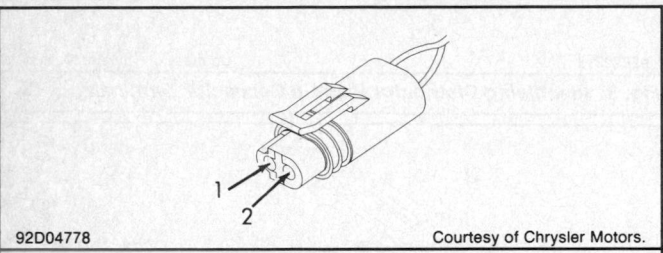

1
2

92D04778   Courtesy of Chrysler Motors.

Fig. 10: Identifying Ignition Coil Connector Terminals

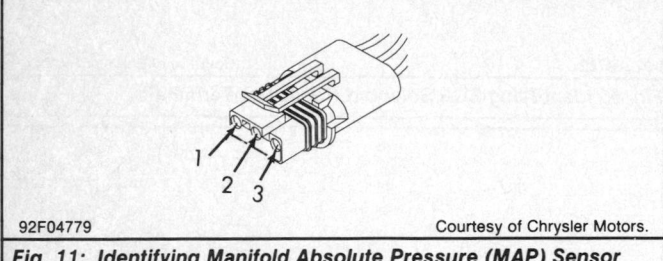

1
2 3

92F04779   Courtesy of Chrysler Motors.

Fig. 11: Identifying Manifold Absolute Pressure (MAP) Sensor Connector Terminals

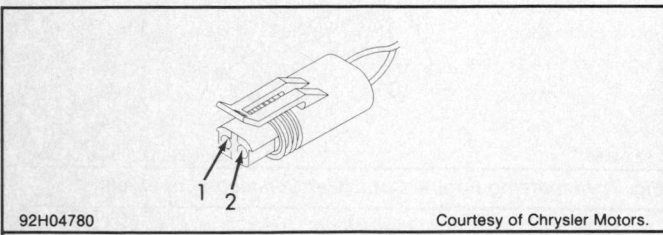

1
2

92H04780   Courtesy of Chrysler Motors.

Fig. 12: Identifying Oil Pressure Switch Connector Terminals

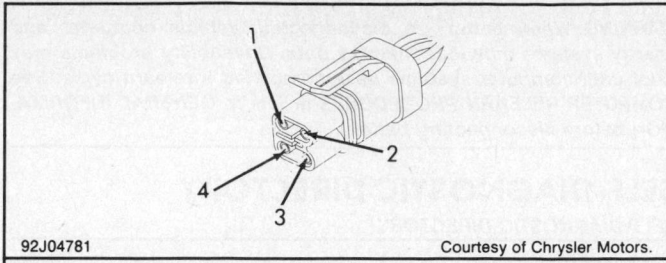

1
2
4
3

92J04781   Courtesy of Chrysler Motors.

Fig. 13: Identifying Oxygen (O$_2$) Sensor Connector Terminals

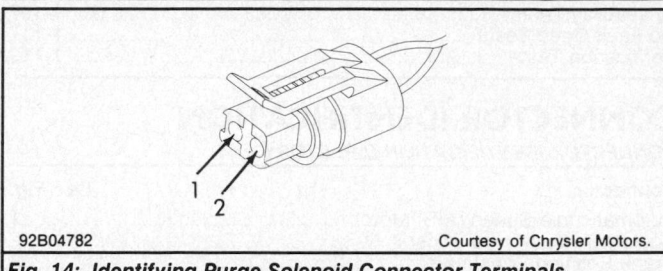

1
2

92B04782   Courtesy of Chrysler Motors.

Fig. 14: Identifying Purge Solenoid Connector Terminals

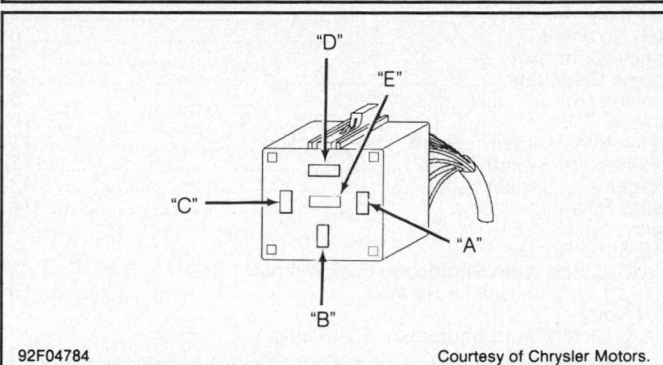

"D"
"E"
"C"
"A"
"B"

92F04784   Courtesy of Chrysler Motors.

Fig. 15: Identifying A/C Clutch, ASD, Fuel Pump & Part Throttle Unlock Relay Connector Terminals (AB & AD Bodies)

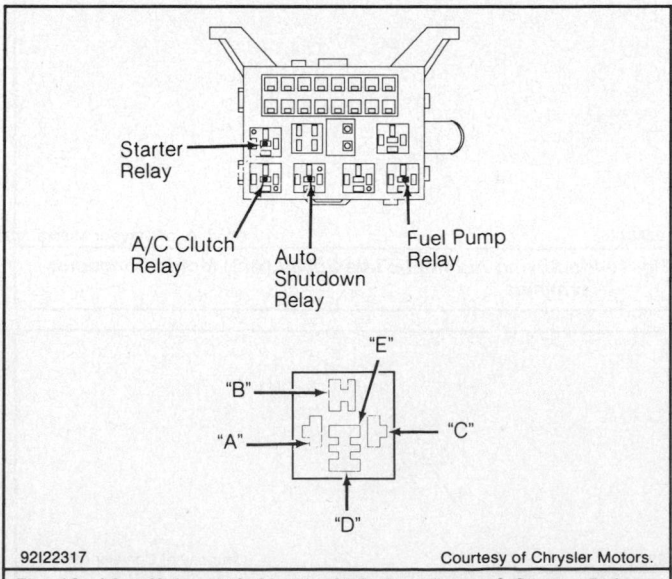

Starter Relay

A/C Clutch Relay

Auto Shutdown Relay

Fuel Pump Relay

"E"
"B"
"A"
"C"
"D"

92I22317   Courtesy of Chrysler Motors.

Fig. 16: Identifying A/C Clutch, ASD, Fuel Pump & Starter Relay Connector Terminals (AN Body)

1992 ENGINE PERFORMANCE
Self-Diagnostic Tests – 3.9L & 5.2L (Cont.)

CHRY
1-103

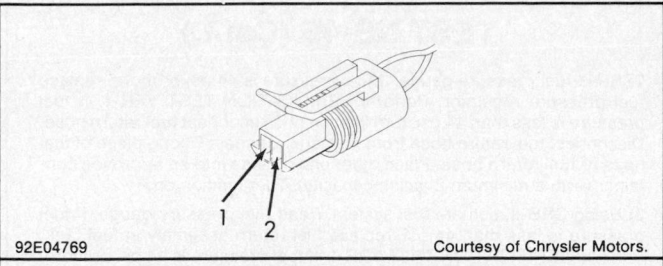

92E04769   Courtesy of Chrysler Motors.

Fig. 17: Identifying Throttle Body Charge Temperature Sensor Connector Terminals

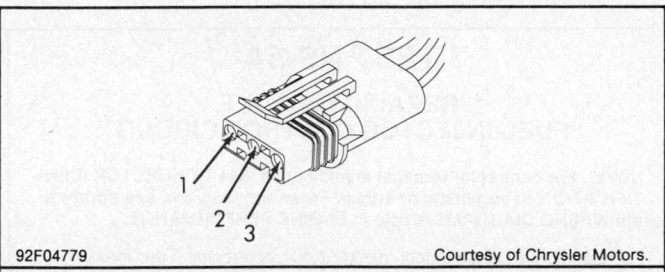

92F04779   Courtesy of Chrysler Motors.

Fig. 18: Identifying Throttle Position Sensor Connector Terminals

SELF-DIAGNOSTIC TESTS

NOTE: In the following self-diagnostic tests, illustrations are courtesy of Chrysler Motors.

TEST NS-1A

QUALIFYING NO START CONDITION

NOTE: For connector terminal identification, see CONNECTOR IDEN-TIFICATION at beginning of article. For wiring diagram, see appropriate WIRING DIAGRAMS article in ENGINE PERFORMANCE.

1) Perform visual inspection of vehicle. See VISUAL INSPECTION in SELF-DIAGNOSTICS INTRODUCTION – GASOLINE. Ensure battery is fully charged. Disconnect and reconnect battery quick-disconnect. Try to start engine by cranking for at least 10 seconds. Ensure key is turned off before each attempt to start engine. Turn ignition on. Using DRB-II, read faults.

2) If DRB-II displays a fault, perform appropriate test. See DRB-II FAULT MESSAGES table. If DRB-II does not display any fault codes, go to step 3).

DRB-II FAULT MESSAGES

DRB-II Message	Test No.
NO RESPONSE	NS-8A
COOLANT VOLTAGE & TPS VOLTAGE HIGH	[1]
NO REFERENCE SIGNAL DURING CRANKING	NS-9A
AUTO SHUTDOWN RELAY CONTROL CIRCUIT	NS-10A
NO ASD RELAY VOLTAGE SENSE AT CONTROLLER	NS-11A
INJECTOR CONTROL CIRCUIT FAULT	NS-5A
AUTOMATIC IDLE SPEED MOTOR CIRCUITS	NS-6A
NO SYNC PICK-UP SIGNAL	NS-9B
INTERNAL CONTROLLER FAILURE or CONTROLLER FAILURE SPI COMMUNICATIONS	[2]

[1] – Repair Black/Light Blue wire for an open circuit to engine controller terminal No. 4.
[2] – Replace engine controller. Perform VERIFICATION TEST VER-1.

3) Try to start engine by cranking for at least 10 seconds. Ensure key is turned off before each attempt to start engine. If engine starts and stalls, perform TEST NS-2A. If engine does not start and stall, turn ignition off. Disconnect any spark plug wire from spark plug.

4) Insert an insulated screwdriver in cable terminal. Hold screwdriver a maximum of 1/4" away from a good ground. Watch for spark while cranking engine for 10 seconds. Consider 1-2 sparks as a no-spark condition. If a good spark occurs, perform TEST NS-2A.

TEST NS-1A (Cont.)

5) If a good spark does not occur, reconnect spark plug cable. Disconnect coil secondary wire from distributor. Hold coil wire a maximum of 1/4" away from a good ground. Watch for spark while cranking engine for 10 seconds. If there is good spark, repair secondary ignition system (distributor cap, rotor or spark plug wires). Perform VERIFICATION TEST VER-1.

6) If a good spark does not occur, turn ignition off. Remove coil secondary wire. Using a DVOM, measure coil secondary wire resistance. If resistance is greater than 15 k/ohms, replace coil secondary wire. Perform VERIFICATION TEST VER-1. If resistance is 15 k/ohms or less, remove distributor cap. Watch for rotor to turn while cranking engine. If rotor does not turn, repair distributor drive system. Perform VERIFICATION TEST VER-1.

7) If rotor turned, reinstall distributor cap. Reconnect coil secondary wire. Disconnect ignition coil connector. Using DRB-II, actuate fuel system. With fuel system actuating, put DRB-II in voltmeter mode. Probe Dark Green/Orange wire in ignition coil harness connector. If voltage is not greater than 10 volts, repair Dark Green/Orange wire between coil and ASD relay splice. Perform VERIFICATION TEST VER-1.

8) If voltage is 10 volts or more, probe Gray wire (Black/Gray wire on Dakota) in ignition coil harness connector. If voltage is greater than 10 volts, go to step **11)**. If voltage is 10 volts or less, turn ignition off. Disconnect engine controller connector. Place DRB-II in ohmmeter mode. Probe Gray wire (Black/Gray wire on Dakota) in engine controller connector terminal No. 19.

9) If resistance is less than 10 ohms, repair Gray wire (Black/Gray wire on Dakota) for a short to ground. Perform VERIFICATION TEST VER-1. If resistance is 10 ohms or more, check resistance of Gray wire (Black/Gray wire on Dakota) between coil harness connector and engine controller connector terminal No. 19 using a DVOM.

10) If resistance is greater than 10 ohms, repair open Gray wire (Black/Gray wire on Dakota). Perform VERIFICATION TEST VER-1. If resistance is 10 ohms or less, replace engine controller. Perform VERIFICATION TEST VER-1.

11) Turn ignition off. Using a DVOM, check ignition coil primary circuit resistance. If resistance is not .8-1.3 ohms at 75°F (24°C), replace ignition coil. Perform VERIFICATION TEST VER-1.

12) If resistance is .8-1.3 ohms at 75°F (24°C), check ignition coil secondary circuit resistance. If resistance is not 10-16 k/ohms, replace ignition coil. Perform VERIFICATION TEST VER-1. If resistance is 10-16 k/ohms, reconnect ignition coil connector. Perform TEST NS-9A.

TEST NS-2A

INSPECTING FUEL SYSTEM

NOTE: For connector terminal identification, see CONNECTOR IDEN-TIFICATION at beginning of article. For wiring diagram, see appropriate WIRING DIAGRAMS article in ENGINE PERFORMANCE.

1) Ensure throttle is at idle position. Using DRB-II, read TPS sensor voltage. If voltage is more than 1.5 volts, replace throttle position sensor. Perform VERIFICATION TEST VER-1. If voltage is 1.5 volts or less, disconnect fuel injector No. 1 harness connector.

2) Place DRB-II in voltmeter mode. Using DRB-II, actuate fuel system. Probe Dark Green/Orange wire. If voltage is 10 volts or less, repair Dark Green/Orange wire between injector connector and harness splice. Perform VERIFICATION TEST VER-1. If voltage is more than 10 volts, turn ignition off.

WARNING: Fuel system must be opened and may be under high pressure.

3) Install fuel pressure gauge in fuel supply line at fitting, near throttle body. Ensure fuel tank is at least 1/4 full. Turn ignition on. Using DRB-II, actuate fuel system. Listen for fuel pump operation at fuel tank. If fuel pump operation cannot be heard, go to TEST NS-7A.

4) If fuel pump operation can be heard, read fuel pressure gauge. If fuel pressure is more than 44 psi, perform TEST NS-4B. If fuel pressure is 33-44 psi and vehicle initially started and stalled repeatedly, perform TEST NS-12A. If fuel pressure is 33-44 psi and vehicle did not initially start and stall repeatedly, perform TEST NS-3A. If fuel pressure is less than 34 psi, perform TEST-4A.

CHRY
1-104

1992 ENGINE PERFORMANCE
Self-Diagnostic Tests – 3.9L & 5.2L (Cont.)

TEST NS-3A

INSPECTING MECHANICAL SYSTEM

NOTE: For connector terminal identification, see CONNECTOR IDENTIFICATION at beginning of article. For wiring diagram, see appropriate WIRING DIAGRAMS article in ENGINE PERFORMANCE.

1) Turn ignition off. Check spark plug wires for proper firing order. If firing order is not correct, reconnect wires in correct firing order. Perform VERIFICATION TEST VER-1. If firing order is correct, remove all spark plugs and inspect tips for fuel. Clean spark plugs as necessary. Reinstall spark plugs. Connect timing light to engine.

NOTE: DO NOT crank engine for more than 15 seconds. Starter may be damaged if engine is cranked for an extended period of time.

2) Check ignition timing while cranking engine. If ignition timing is 0-16 degrees BTDC, go to step **4)**. If timing is not 0-16 degrees BTDC, set base timing to 10 degrees BTDC. Try to start engine. If engine does not start, repair problem with valve timing, compression or other mechanical problem. Perform VERIFICATION TEST VER-1.

3) If engine starts, check distributor drive system and engine compression. If distributor drive system and engine compression are okay, repair is complete. Perform VERIFICATION TEST VER-1. If distributor drive system and engine compression are not okay, repair as necessary. Perform VERIFICATION TEST VER-1.

4) Turn ignition off. Disconnect and inspect engine controller connector. Repair connector as necessary. Perform VERIFICATION TEST VER-1. If connector is okay, disconnect and inspect MAP sensor connector. Repair connector as necessary. Perform VERIFICATION TEST VER-1. If connector is okay, check resistance of Violet/White wire between MAP sensor and engine controller connectors using a DVOM.

5) If resistance is 10 ohms or more, repair open Violet/White wire. If resistance is less than 10 ohms, check valve timing and engine compression. If valve timing and engine compression are okay, replace MAP sensor. Perform VERIFICATION TEST VER-1. If valve timing and engine compression are not okay, repair engine as necessary. Perform VERIFICATION TEST VER-1.

TEST NS-4A

CORRECTING FUEL DELIVERY

WARNING: Fuel system must be opened and may be under high pressure.

1) Record fuel pressure gauge reading. Turn ignition off. Remove fuel pressure gauge. Install fuel pressure gauge in fuel line between fuel tank and fuel filter. Turn ignition on. Using DRB-II, actuate fuel system. Record fuel pressure gauge reading.

2) Compare 2 fuel pressure gauge readings. If fuel pressure is not at least 10 psi more, go to step **3)**. If fuel pressure is at least 10 psi more, inspect fuel lines between fuel filter and fuel rail for a restriction. Repair restriction as necessary. Perform VERIFICATION TEST VER-1. If fuel lines are okay, replace fuel filter. Perform VERIFICATION TEST VER-1.

CAUTION: DO NOT allow fuel pressure to exceed 70 psi.

3) Watch fuel pressure gauge while gently squeezing fuel return hose. If fuel pressure is greater than 34 psi, replace fuel pressure regulator. Perform VERIFICATION TEST VER-1. If fuel pressure is 34 psi or less, replace fuel pump and filter sock assembly. Perform VERIFICATION TEST VER-1.

TEST NS-4B

CORRECTING FUEL DELIVERY

WARNING: Fuel system must be opened and may be under high pressure.

1) Ensure fuel tank is at least 1/4 full. Relieve fuel system pressure. Remove fuel return hose from fuel rail. Connect 6' long piece of fuel hose to fuel rail return pipe. Place other end of hose into an approved container (with a minimum 2 gallon capacity). Turn ignition on. Using DRB-II, actuate fuel system.

TEST NS-4B (Cont.)

2) Read fuel pressure gauge. If fuel pressure is 44 psi or more, replace fuel pressure regulator. Perform VERIFICATION TEST VER-1. If fuel pressure is less than 44 psi, turn ignition off. Reconnect fuel return hose. Disconnect fuel return hose from fuel tank. Connect 6' long piece of fuel hose to fuel return hose. Place other end of hose into an approved container (with a minimum 2 gallon capacity). Turn ignition on.

3) Using DRB-II, actuate fuel system. Read fuel pressure gauge. If fuel pressure is less than 44 psi, replace fuel return assembly in fuel tank. Perform VERIFICATION TEST VER-1. If fuel pressure is 44 psi or more, repair restricted fuel return line between fuel rail and fuel tank. Perform VERIFICATION TEST VER-1.

TEST NS-5A

REPAIRING FAULT
"FUEL INJECTOR CONTROL CIRCUIT"

NOTE: For connector terminal identification, see CONNECTOR IDENTIFICATION at beginning of article. For wiring diagram, see appropriate WIRING DIAGRAMS article in ENGINE PERFORMANCE.

Turn ignition off. Disconnect injector No. 1 connector. Turn ignition on. Using DRB-II, actuate fuel system. Place DRB-II in voltmeter mode. Probe Dark Green/Orange wire in injector connector. If voltage is less than 10 volts, repair open Dark Green/Orange wire. Perform VERIFICATION TEST VER-1. If voltage is 10 volts or more, replace engine controller. Perform VERIFICATION TEST VER-1.

TEST NS-6A

REPAIRING FAULT
"AUTOMATIC IDLE SPEED MOTOR CIRCUITS"

NOTE: For connector terminal identification, see CONNECTOR IDENTIFICATION at beginning of article. For wiring diagram, see appropriate WIRING DIAGRAMS article in ENGINE PERFORMANCE.

1) Disconnect Automatic Idle Speed (AIS) motor connector. Turn ignition on. Using DRB-II, actuate AIS motor. Place DRB-II in voltmeter mode. Probe Gray/Red wire in AIS motor harness connector. When normal, voltage will switch from less than one volt to more than 10 volts. If voltage stayed less than one volt, repair Gray/Red wire for a short to ground. Perform VERIFICATION TEST VER-1.

2) If voltage stayed more than 10 volts, repair Gray/Red wire for a short to voltage. Perform VERIFICATION TEST VER-1. If voltage did not stay less than one volt or greater than 10 volts, probe Yellow/Black wire in AIS motor harness connector. If voltage stayed less than one volt, repair Yellow/Black wire for a short to ground. Perform VERIFICATION TEST VER-1.

3) If voltage stayed more than 10 volts, repair Yellow/Black wire for a short to voltage. Perform VERIFICATION TEST VER-1. If voltage did not stay less than one volt or more than 10 volts, probe Brown/White wire in AIS motor harness connector. If voltage stayed less than one volt, repair Brown/White wire for a short to ground. Perform VERIFICATION TEST VER-1.

4) If voltage stayed more than 10 volts, repair Brown/White wire for a short to voltage. Perform VERIFICATION TEST VER-1. If voltage did not stay less than one volt or more than 10 volts, probe Violet/Black wire in AIS motor harness connector. If voltage stayed less than one volt, repair Violet/Black wire for a short to ground. Perform VERIFICATION TEST VER-1.

5) If voltage stayed more than 10 volts, repair Violet/Black wire for a short to voltage. Perform VERIFICATION TEST VER-1. If voltage did not stay less than one volt or more than 10 volts, turn ignition off. Disconnect engine controller 60-pin connector. Using a DVOM, measure resistance between engine controller connector cavities No. 39 and 59.

6) If resistance is less than 35 ohms, replace AIS motor. Perform VERIFICATION TEST VER-1. If resistance is 35 ohms or more, check resistance between terminals No. 39 and 60. If resistance is less than 10 ohms, repair Yellow/Black wire for a short to Gray/Red wire. Perform VERIFICATION TEST VER-1.

1992 ENGINE PERFORMANCE
Self-Diagnostic Tests – 3.9L & 5.2L (Cont.)

CHRY
1-105

TEST NS-6A (Cont.)

7) If resistance is 75-120 ohms, repair Brown/White wire for a short to Violet/Black wire. Perform VERIFICATION TEST VER-1. If resistance is 120 ohms or more, replace engine controller. Perform VERIFICATION TEST VER-1. If resistance is 10-75 ohms, check resistance between cavities No. 59 and 60.

8) If resistance is less than 10 ohms, repair Yellow/Black wire for a short to Violet/Black wire. Perform VERIFICATION TEST VER-1. If resistance is less 10 ohms or more, repair Gray/Red wire for a short to Brown/White wire. Perform VERIFICATION TEST VER-1.

TEST NS-7A

INSPECTING FUEL PUMP

NOTE: For connector terminal identification, see CONNECTOR IDENTIFICATION at beginning of article. For wiring diagram, see appropriate WIRING DIAGRAMS article in ENGINE PERFORMANCE.

1) Using DRB-II, stop actuation test. Using DRB-II, actuate ASD relay. Touch fuel pump relay to check for operation. If fuel pump relay does not pulsate, perform TEST-7B. If fuel pump relay pulsates, stop actuation test. Disconnect fuel pump relay. Turn ignition on. Place DRB-II in voltmeter mode. Probe Red wire (Red/White wire on Dakota) in fuel pump relay connector terminal "B".

2) If voltage is 10 volts or less, repair Red wire (Red/White wire on Dakota) for an open to splice. Perform VERIFICATION TEST VER-1. If voltage is greater than 10 volts, disconnect fuel pump harness connector. Reconnect fuel pump relay. Using DRB-II, actuate fuel system. Place DRB-II in voltmeter mode. Probe Dark Green/Black wire in fuel pump connector.

3) If voltage is more than 10 volts, go to step 4). If voltage is 10 volts or less, turn ignition off. Disconnect fuel pump relay. Check resistance of Dark Green/Black wire between fuel pump and fuel pump relay connectors using a DVOM. If resistance is less than 10 ohms, replace fuel pump relay. Perform VERIFICATION TEST VER-1. If resistance is 10 ohms or more, repair open Dark Green/Black wire. Perform VERIFICATION TEST VER-1.

4) If voltage is 10 volts or less in step 3), put DRB-II in ohmmeter mode. Probe Black wire in fuel pump connector. If resistance is less than 5 ohms, replace fuel pump. Perform VERIFICATION TEST VER-1. If resistance is 5 ohms or more, repair Black wire for an open to ground. Perform VERIFICATION TEST VER-1.

TEST NS-7B

INSPECTING FUEL PUMP

NOTE: For connector terminal identification, see CONNECTOR IDENTIFICATION at beginning of article. For wiring diagram, see appropriate WIRING DIAGRAMS article in ENGINE PERFORMANCE.

Turn ignition off. Disconnect fuel pump relay. Turn ignition on. Probe Dark Blue wire. If voltage is 10 volts or less, repair Dark Blue wire for an open to splice. Perform VERIFICATION TEST VER-1. If voltage is more than 10 volts, measure resistance across fuel pump relay terminals using a DVOM. If resistance is 100 ohms or more, replace fuel pump relay. Perform VERIFICATION TEST VER-1. If resistance is less than 100 ohms, repair open Dark Blue/Yellow wire between fuel pump relay connector and splice. Perform VERIFICATION TEST VER-1.

TEST NS-8A

REPAIRING NO RESPONSE CONDITION

NOTE: For connector terminal identification, see CONNECTOR IDENTIFICATION at beginning of article. For wiring diagram, see appropriate WIRING DIAGRAMS article in ENGINE PERFORMANCE.

1) Turn ignition off. Disconnect Throttle Position Sensor (TPS) and inspect connector. Repair connector as necessary. Perform VERIFICATION TEST VER-1. If connector is okay, turn ignition on. Place DRB-II in

TEST NS-8A (Cont.)

voltmeter mode. Probe Violet/White wire in TPS harness connector. If voltage is more than 6 volts, repair open to ground in Black/White wire (terminal No. 5) or Black/Tan wire (terminals No. 11 and 12) of engine controller connector. Perform VERIFICATION TEST VER-1.

2) If voltage is less than 4.4 volts, go to next step. If voltage is 4.4-6.0 volts, reconnect TPS connector. Disconnect and inspect MAP sensor connector. Repair connector as necessary. Perform VERIFICATION TEST VER-1. If connector is okay, probe Violet/White wire at MAP sensor connector. If voltage is more than 4.4 volts, see NO RESPONSE MESSAGE under DRB-II PROBLEMS & ERROR MESSAGES in SELF-DIAGNOSTICS INTRODUCTION – GASOLINE. If voltage is 4.4 volts or less, replace TPS. Perform VERIFICATION TEST VER-1.

3) Turn ignition off. Disconnect MAP sensor connector. Turn ignition on. Probe Violet/White wire at TPS connector. If voltage is more than 4.4 volts, replace MAP sensor. Perform VERIFICATION TEST VER-1. If voltage is 4.4 volts or less, turn ignition off. Disconnect and inspect engine controller connector. Repair connector as necessary. Perform VERIFICATION TEST VER-1.

4) Place DRB-II in ohmmeter mode. Probe engine controller connector terminal No. 6 (Violet/White wire). If resistance is less than 10 ohms, repair short to ground in Violet/White wire. Perform VERIFICATION TEST VER-1.

5) If resistance is 10 ohms or more, turn ignition on. Place DRB-II in voltmeter mode. Probe engine controller connector terminal No. 9 (Dark Blue wire). If voltage is 10 volts or less, repair open in Dark Blue wire between engine controller connector terminal No. 9 and ignition switch. Perform VERIFICATION TEST VER-1.

6) If voltage is more than 10 volts, probe engine controller connector terminal No. 3 (Red/White wire on Dakota, Red wire on all others). If voltage is more than 10 volts, replace engine controller. Perform VERIFICATION TEST VER-1. If voltage is 10 volts or less, inspect fusible link (fuse on Dakota) between battery and terminal No. 3. If fuse or fusible link is okay, repair open in Red wire (Red/White wire on Dakota) between engine controller connector terminal No. 3 and battery. Perform VERIFICATION TEST VER-1.

7) If fuse or fusible link is not okay, put DRB-II in ohmmeter mode. Probe engine controller connector terminal No. 3. If resistance is less than 10 ohms, repair Red wire (Red/White wire on Dakota) for a short to ground. Replace fusible link (fuse on Dakota). Perform VERIFICATION TEST VER-1.

8) If resistance is 10 ohms or more, disconnect and inspect Auto Shutdown (ASD) relay connector. Repair connector as necessary. Replace fusible link (fuse on Dakota). Probe Dark Green/Orange wire in ASD relay connector. If resistance is 10 ohms or more, go to step 11).

9) If resistance is less than 10 ohms, disconnect and inspect ignition coil connector. Repair connector as necessary. Replace fusible link (fuse on Dakota). Probe Dark Green/Orange wire in ASD relay connector. If resistance is 10 ohms or more, replace ignition coil. Replace fuse or fusible link. Perform VERIFICATION TEST VER-1.

10) If resistance is less than 10 ohms, repair short to ground in Dark Green/Orange wire. Replace fusible link (fuse on Dakota). Perform VERIFICATION TEST VER-1.

11) If resistance is 10 ohms or more in step 8), reconnect ASD relay. Disconnect and inspect fuel pump relay connector. Repair connector as necessary. Replace fusible link (fuse on Dakota). Disconnect and inspect fuel pump connector. Repair connector as necessary. Replace fusible link (fuse on Dakota).

12) Disconnect and inspect O2 sensor connector. Repair connector as necessary. Replace fusible link (fuse on Dakota). Probe Dark Green/Black wire in fuel pump relay connector. If resistance is less than 10 ohms, repair short to ground in Dark Green/Black wire. Replace fusible link (fuse on Dakota). Perform VERIFICATION TEST VER-1. If resistance is 10 ohms or more, replace fuel pump. Replace fuse or fusible link. Perform VERIFICATION TEST VER-1.

1992 ENGINE PERFORMANCE
Self-Diagnostic Tests – 3.9L & 5.2L (Cont.)

TEST NS-9A

REPAIRING FAULT
"NO REFERENCE SIGNAL DURING CRANKING"

NOTE: For connector terminal identification, see CONNECTOR IDENTIFICATION at beginning of article. For wiring diagram, see appropriate WIRING DIAGRAMS article in ENGINE PERFORMANCE.

1) Disconnect crank position sensor. Turn ignition on. Place DRB-II in voltmeter mode. Probe Gray/Black wire in crank position sensor connector. If voltage is greater than 4.5 volts, go to step 4). Turn ignition off. Disconnect engine controller 60-pin connector. Place DRB-II in ohmmeter mode.

2) Probe engine controller connector terminal No. 24 (Gray/Black wire). If resistance is less than 10 ohms, repair Gray/Black wire for a short to ground. Perform VERIFICATION TEST VER-1. If resistance is 10 ohms or more, check continuity of Gray/Black wire between engine controller and crank position sensor connectors.

3) If resistance is less than 10 ohms, replace engine controller. Perform VERIFICATION TEST VER-1. If resistance is 10 ohms or more, repair open Gray/Black wire. Perform VERIFICATION TEST VER-1.

4) If voltage is greater than 4.5 volts in step 1), probe Orange wire in crank position sensor connector. If voltage is 7.5 volts or less, go to step 6). If voltage is greater than 7.5 volts, turn ignition off. Place DRB-II in ohmmeter mode.

5) Probe Black/Light Blue wire in crank position sensor connector. If resistance is less than 10 ohms, replace crank position sensor. Perform VERIFICATION TEST VER-1. If resistance is 10 ohms or more, repair Black/Light Blue wire for an open to splice. Perform VERIFICATION TEST VER-1.

6) If voltage in step 4) is 7.5 volts or less, turn ignition off. Disconnect engine controller connector. Place DRB-II in ohmmeter mode. Probe engine controller connector terminal No. 7. If resistance is less than 10 ohms, repair Orange wire for a short to ground. Disconnect battery quick disconnect. Reconnect battery quick disconnect. Perform VERIFICATION TEST VER-1.

7) If resistance is 10 ohms or more, check Orange wire for continuity between engine controller and crank position sensor connectors using a DVOM. If resistance is less than 10 ohms, replace engine controller. Perform VERIFICATION TEST VER-1. If resistance is 10 ohms or more, repair Orange wire. Perform VERIFICATION TEST VER-1.

TEST NS-9B

REPAIRING FAULT "NO SYNC PICK-UP SIGNAL"

NOTE: For connector terminal identification, see CONNECTOR IDENTIFICATION at beginning of article. For wiring diagram, see appropriate WIRING DIAGRAMS article in ENGINE PERFORMANCE.

1) Ensure distributor shaft turns when engine is cranked. If shaft does not turn, repair as necessary. If shaft turns, disconnect distributor sync pick-up sensor. Turn ignition on. Place DRB-II in voltmeter mode. Probe Tan/Yellow wire in distributor sync pick-up connector. If voltage is more than 4.5 volts, go to step 4).

2) If voltage is 4.5 volts or less, turn ignition off. Disconnect engine controller connector. Place DRB-II in ohmmeter mode. Probe engine controller connector terminal No. 44. If resistance is less than 10 ohms, repair Tan/Yellow wire for a short to ground. Perform VERIFICATION TEST VER-1.

3) If resistance is 10 ohms or more, check Tan/Yellow wire for continuity between engine controller and distributor sync pick-up connectors using a DVOM. If resistance is less than 10 ohms, replace engine controller. Perform VERIFICATION TEST VER-1. If resistance is 10 ohms or more, repair open Tan/Yellow wire. Perform VERIFICATION TEST VER-1.

4) If voltage is more than 4.5 volts in step 1), probe Orange wire in distributor sync pick-up connector. If voltage is 7.5 volts or less, go to step 6). If voltage is greater than 7.5 volts, turn ignition off. Place DRB-II in ohmmeter mode.

5) Probe Black/Light Blue wire in distributor sync pick-up connector. If resistance is less than 10 ohms, replace distributor sync pick-up. Perform VERIFICATION TEST VER-1. If resistance is 10 ohms or more, repair Black/Light Blue wire for an open to splice. Perform VERIFICATION TEST VER-1.

TEST NS-9B (Cont.)

6) If voltage is 7.5 volts or less in step 4), turn ignition off. Disconnect engine controller connector. Check Orange wire for continuity between engine controller and distributor sync pick-up connectors using a DVOM. If resistance is less than 10 ohms, replace engine controller. Perform VERIFICATION TEST VER-1. If resistance is 10 ohms or more, repair open Orange wire. Perform VERIFICATION TEST VER-1.

TEST NS-10A

REPAIRING FAULT
"AUTO SHUTDOWN RELAY (ASD) CONTROL CIRCUIT"

NOTE: For connector terminal identification, see CONNECTOR IDENTIFICATION at beginning of article. For wiring diagram, see appropriate WIRING DIAGRAMS article in ENGINE PERFORMANCE.

1) Turn ignition on. Disconnect ASD relay connector. Place DRB-II in voltmeter mode. Probe Dark Blue wire in ASD relay connector. If voltage is 10 volts or less, repair open in Dark Blue wire from ignition switch. Perform VERIFICATION TEST VER-1. If voltage is more than 10 volts, go to next step.

2) Check resistance between terminals "A" and "C" at ASD relay using a DVOM. If resistance is 100 ohms or more, replace ASD relay. Perform VERIFICATION TEST VER-1. If resistance is less than 100 ohms, turn ignition off.

3) Disconnect engine controller 60-pin connector. Check resistance of Dark Blue/Yellow wire between engine controller connector terminal No. 51 and ASD relay connector terminal "C".

4) If resistance is less than 10 ohms, replace engine controller. Perform VERIFICATION TEST VER-1. If resistance is 10 ohms or more, repair open in Dark Blue/Yellow wire. Perform VERIFICATION TEST VER-1.

TEST NS-11A

REPAIRING FAULT
"NO ASD RELAY VOLTAGE SENSE AT CONTROLLER"

NOTE: For connector terminal identification, see CONNECTOR IDENTIFICATION at beginning of article. For wiring diagram, see appropriate WIRING DIAGRAMS article in ENGINE PERFORMANCE.

1) Disconnect ASD relay. Turn ignition on. Place DRB-II in voltmeter mode. Probe ASD relay connector terminal "B". If voltage is 10 volts or less, repair open Red wire (Red/White wire on Dakota) to splice. Perform VERIFICATION TEST VER-1. If voltage is more than 10 volts, probe Dark Blue wire in ASD relay connector. If voltage is 10 volts or less, repair open Dark Blue wire between ASD relay connector and ignition switch. Perform VERIFICATION TEST VER-1.

2) If voltage is more than 10 volts, turn ignition off. Disconnect engine controller connector. Check for continuity in Dark Green/Orange wire between engine controller and ASD relay connectors using a DVOM. If resistance is 10 ohms or more, repair open Dark Green/Orange wire between ASD relay and engine controller. Perform VERIFICATION TEST VER-1.

3) If resistance is less than 10 ohms, check resistance of Dark Blue/Yellow wire between engine controller and ASD relay connectors. If resistance is 10 ohms or more, repair open Dark Blue/Yellow wire between ASD relay and engine controller connector terminal No. 51. Perform VERIFICATION TEST VER-1.

4) If resistance is less than 10 ohms, reconnect engine controller connector. Substitute a known good relay for ASD relay. DO NOT use fuel pump relay. Try to start engine. If engine started, repair is complete. Perform VERIFICATION TEST VER-1. If engine did not start, replace engine controller. Perform VERIFICATION TEST VER-1.

1992 ENGINE PERFORMANCE
Self-Diagnostic Tests – 3.9L & 5.2L (Cont.)

CHRY
1-107

TEST NS-12A

CHECKING AUTOMATIC IDLE SPEED (AIS) MOTOR OPERATION

NOTE: For connector terminal identification, see CONNECTOR IDENTIFICATION at beginning of article. For wiring diagram, see appropriate WIRING DIAGRAMS article in ENGINE PERFORMANCE.

1) Using DRB-II, stop fuel system test. Turn ignition off. Disconnect AIS motor connector. Turn ignition on. Using DRB-II, actuate AIS motor. Place DRB-II in voltmeter mode. Probe AIS motor connector Gray/Red wire. Voltage should cycle from less than one volt to greater than 10 volts. If voltage stays less than one volt, perform TEST NS-12B.

2) If voltage does not stay less one volt, probe Brown/White wire at AIS motor connector. If voltage stays less than one volt, perform TEST NS-12C. If voltage does not stay less than one volt, probe Violet/Black wire at AIS motor connector. If voltage stays less than one volt, perform TEST NS-12D.

3) If voltage does not stay less than one volt, probe AIS motor connector Yellow/Black wire. If voltage stays less than one volt, perform TEST NS-12E. If voltage did not stay less than one volt, stop AIS motor test. Turn ignition off.

4) Remove AIS motor from throttle body. Reconnect AIS motor connector. Turn ignition on. Using DRB-II, actuate AIS motor. If AIS motor tip moves in and out, perform TEST NS-13A. If AIS motor tip does not move in and out, replace AIS motor. Perform VERIFICATION TEST VER-1.

TEST NS-12B

CHECKING AUTOMATIC IDLE SPEED (AIS) MOTOR OPERATION

NOTE: For connector terminal identification, see CONNECTOR IDENTIFICATION at beginning of article. For wiring diagram, see appropriate WIRING DIAGRAMS article in ENGINE PERFORMANCE.

Using DRB-II, stop AIS motor test. Turn ignition off. Disconnect and inspect engine controller 60-pin connector. Repair connector as necessary. Perform VERIFICATION TEST VER-1. If connector is okay, check resistance of Gray/Red wire between AIS motor connector and engine controller connector terminal No. 39 using a DVOM. If resistance is less than 10 ohms, replace engine controller. Perform VERIFICATION TEST VER-1. If resistance is 10 ohms or more, repair open in Gray/Red wire. Perform VERIFICATION TEST VER-1.

TEST NS-12C

CHECKING AUTOMATIC IDLE SPEED (AIS) MOTOR OPERATION

NOTE: For connector terminal identification, see CONNECTOR IDENTIFICATION at beginning of article. For wiring diagram, see appropriate WIRING DIAGRAMS article in ENGINE PERFORMANCE.

Using DRB-II, stop AIS motor test. Turn ignition off. Disconnect and inspect engine controller 60-pin connector. Repair connector as necessary. Perform VERIFICATION TEST VER-1. If connector is okay, check resistance of Brown/White wire between AIS motor connector and engine controller connector terminal No. 40 using a DVOM. If resistance is less than 10 ohms, replace engine controller. Perform VERIFICATION TEST VER-1. If resistance is 10 ohms or more, repair open in Brown/White wire. Perform VERIFICATION TEST VER-1.

TEST NS-12D

CHECKING AUTOMATIC IDLE SPEED (AIS) MOTOR OPERATION

NOTE: For connector terminal identification, see CONNECTOR IDENTIFICATION at beginning of article. For wiring diagram, see appropriate WIRING DIAGRAMS article in ENGINE PERFORMANCE.

Using DRB-II, stop AIS motor test. Turn ignition off. Disconnect and inspect engine controller 60-pin connector. Repair connector as necessary. Perform VERIFICATION TEST VER-1. If connector is okay, check resistance of Violet/Black wire between AIS motor connector and engine controller connector terminal No. 59 using a DVOM. If resistance is less than 10 ohms, replace engine controller. Perform VERIFICATION TEST VER-1. If resistance is 10 ohms or more, repair open in Violet/Black wire. Perform VERIFICATION TEST VER-1.

TEST NS-12E

CHECKING AUTOMATIC IDLE SPEED (AIS) MOTOR OPERATION

NOTE: For connector terminal identification, see CONNECTOR IDENTIFICATION at beginning of article. For wiring diagram, see appropriate WIRING DIAGRAMS article in ENGINE PERFORMANCE.

Using DRB-II, stop AIS motor test. Turn ignition off. Disconnect and inspect engine controller 60-pin connector. Repair connector as necessary. Perform VERIFICATION TEST VER-1. If connector is okay, check resistance of Yellow/Black wire between AIS motor connector and engine controller connector terminal No. 60. If resistance is less than 10 ohms, replace engine controller. Perform VERIFICATION TEST VER-1. If resistance is 10 ohms or more, repair open Yellow/Black wire. Perform VERIFICATION TEST VER-1.

TEST NS-13A

CORRECTING START & STALL CONDITION

At this point in diagnostic procedure, all engine control systems have been determined to be operating as designed and are not the cause of the no-start or start-and-stall problem. Following additional items should be checked as possible causes:
- Check if any MITCHELL® TECHNICAL SERVICE BULLETINS (TSBs) apply to vehicle.
- Check engine valve timing.
- Check engine compression.
- Check for exhaust system restriction.
- Ensure PCV system is functioning properly.
- Check camshaft and crankshaft sprockets.
- Check torque converter stall speed.
- Check for fuel contamination.
- Check secondary ignition circuit for abnormal scope pattern.

TEST DR-1A

CHECKING SYSTEM FOR FAULTS

NOTE: For connector terminal identification, see CONNECTOR IDENTIFICATION at beginning of article. For wiring diagram, see appropriate WIRING DIAGRAMS article in ENGINE PERFORMANCE. Battery must be fully charged and at rated capacity before performing any driveability test procedure. If vehicle starts and stalls repeatedly, perform TEST NS-2A. If vehicle stalls when A/C is turned on, perform TEST NF-9A.

1) Connect DRB-II to engine diagnostic connector. Read fault messages. If DRB-II displays fault messages, go to step 5). If DRB-II does not display fault messages, go to next step.

2) Start engine. Allow engine to reach normal operating temperature. Set engine speed manually to 2000 RPM for at least 10 seconds, and return vehicle to idle. On A/T models, go to next step. On M/T models, go to step 4).

1992 ENGINE PERFORMANCE
Self-Diagnostic Tests – 3.9L & 5.2L (Cont.)

TEST DR-1A (Cont.)

3) On A/T models, apply brakes. Shift gear selector through all gears and return to PARK position. Using DRB-II, read fault messages. If no fault messages are displayed, go to next step. If fault messages are displayed, go to step **5)**.

4) On all models, check MITCHELL® TECHNICAL SERVICE BULLETINS (TSBs) for any pertinent information if DRB-II still displays NO FAULTS. If a TSB exists, perform corrective action. If driveability problem continues after performing TSB procedure or if no TSB information was found, perform TEST NF-1A.

5) If fault message is INTERNAL CONTROLLER FAILURE or CONTROLLER FAILURE, replace Single Board Engine Controller (SBEC). Perform VERIFICATION TEST VER-2. If fault message is not INTERNAL CONTROLLER FAILURE or CONTROLLER FAILURE, go to next step.

NOTE: ENGINE COLD TOO LONG fault message may set erroneously if ambient temperature is extremely cold.

6) If fault message is ENGINE COLD TOO LONG, check engine cooling system. Repair cooling system as necessary. Perform VERIFICATION TEST VER-3. If fault message is not ENGINE COLD TOO LONG, go to next step.

7) Using DRB-II FAULT MESSAGES table, select fault message and corresponding test. Correct all hard fault messages before proceeding to intermittent fault message.

NOTE: A false fault code may set if vehicle being tested is not equipped with these options.

DRB-II FAULT MESSAGES

DRB-II Message	[1] Hard Fault	[2] Intermittent Fault
A/C CLUTCH RELAY CIRCUIT	DR-29A	DR-38A
AUTOMATIC IDLE SPEED MOTOR CIRCUITS	DR-15A	DR-36A
CHARGE TEMP VOLTAGE HIGH	DR-25A	DR-35A
CHARGE TEMP VOLTAGE LOW	DR-26A	DR-35A
CONTROLLER FAILURE EEPROM WRITE DENIED	DR-34A	DR-34A
CONTROLLER FAILURE EMR MILES NOT STORED	DR-34A	DR-34A
COOLANT SENSOR VOLTAGE HIGH	DR-11A	DR-35A
COOLANT SENSOR VOLTAGE LOW	DR-12A	DR-35A
EGR SOLENOID CIRCUIT	DR-27A	DR-38A
EGR SYSTEM FAILURE	DR-28A	DR-28A
INJECTOR NO. 1 CONTROL CIRCUIT	DR-16A	DR-37A
INJECTOR NO. 2 CONTROL CIRCUIT	DR-17A	DR-37A
INJECTOR NO. 3 CONTROL CIRCUIT	DR-18A	DR-37A
INJECTOR NO. 4 CONTROL CIRCUIT	DR-19A	DR-37A
INJECTOR NO. 5 CONTROL CIRCUIT	DR-20A	DR-37A
INJECTOR NO. 6 CONTROL CIRCUIT	DR-21A	DR-37A
INJECTOR NO. 7 CONTROL CIRCUIT (5.2L)	DR-22A	DR-37A
INJECTOR NO. 8 CONTROL CIRCUIT (5.2L)	DR-23A	DR-37A
MAP SENSOR VOLTAGE HIGH	DR-5A	DR-35A
MAP SENSOR VOLTAGE LOW	DR-4A	DR-35A
NO ASD RELAY VOLTAGE SENSE AT CONTROLLER	DR-33A	DR-39A
NO CHANGE IN MAP	DR-3A	DR-35B
NO VEHICLE SPEED SIGNAL	DR-6A	DR-6A
OVERDRIVE SOLENOID CIRCUIT [3] W/LOCK-UP	DR-32A	DR-32A
W/O LOCK-UP	DR-31A	DR-31A
O₂ SENSOR SHORTED TO VOLTAGE	DR-8A	DR-35A

TEST DR-1A (Cont.)

DRB-II FAULT MESSAGES (Cont.)

DRB-II Message	[1] Hard Fault	[2] Intermittent Fault
O₂ SENSOR STAYS ABOVE CENTER	DR-9A	DR-35A
O₂ SENSOR STAYS AT CENTER	DR-7A	DR-35A
O₂ SENSOR STAYS BELOW CENTER	DR-10A	DR-35A
PURGE SOLENOID CIRCUIT	DR-24A	DR-38A
SLOW CHANGE IN IDLE MAP SIGNAL	DR-2A	DR-35B
THROTTLE POSITION SENSOR VOLTAGE HIGH	DR-13A	DR-35A
THROTTLE POSITION SENSOR VOLTAGE LOW	DR-14A	DR-35A
TORQUE CONVERTER LOCK-UP SOLENOID CIRCUIT [3]	DR-30A	DR-38A

[1] – Key counter is "0".
[2] – Key counter is more than "0".
[3] – Possible combinations of A/T Part Throttle Unlock (PTU) and Overdrive Solenoid:
  • 4-speed w/OD: 2-wire connector at trans.
  • 4-speed w/OD and PTU: 3-wire connector at trans.
  • 3-speed w/PTU: 1-wire connector at trans.
  • 3-speed w/o PTU: no connector at trans.

TEST DR-2A

CODE 13, SLOW CHANGE IN IDLE MAP SIGNAL

NOTE: For connector terminal identification, see CONNECTOR IDENTIFICATION at beginning of article. For wiring diagram, see appropriate WIRING DIAGRAMS article in ENGINE PERFORMANCE.

1) Turn ignition off. Tee a vacuum gauge into a vacuum source at intake manifold. Start engine. Using DRB-II, read MAP sensor vacuum. Compare DRB-II reading to vacuum gauge. If gauge readings are within one in. Hg of each other, perform TEST DR-35A. If gauge readings are not within one in. Hg of each other, turn ignition off. Disconnect MAP sensor electrical connector. Repair connector as necessary. Perform VERIFICATION TEST VER-2.

2) If connector is okay, turn ignition on. Place DRB-II in voltmeter mode. Probe Violet/White wire. If voltage is less than one volt, repair open Violet/White wire. Perform VERIFICATION TEST VER-2. If voltage is one volt or more, replace MAP sensor. Perform VERIFICATION TEST VER-2.

TEST DR-3A

CODE 13, NO CHANGE IN MAP FROM START TO RUN

Turn ignition on. Tee a vacuum gauge into a vacuum source at intake manifold. Start engine. While at idle, read vacuum gauge. If reading is zero in. Hg at idle, repair leak in vacuum hose to MAP sensor. Perform VERIFICATION TEST VER-2. If reading is not zero in. Hg, repair restriction in vacuum supply hose to MAP sensor. Perform VERIFICATION TEST VER-2.

TEST DR-4A

CODE 14, MAP VOLTAGE TOO LOW

NOTE: For connector terminal identification, see CONNECTOR IDENTIFICATION at beginning of article. For wiring diagram, see appropriate WIRING DIAGRAMS article in ENGINE PERFORMANCE.

1) Turn ignition off. Disconnect and inspect MAP sensor connector. Repair connector as necessary. Perform VERIFICATION TEST VER-2. Turn ignition on. Read MAP sensor voltage. If MAP sensor voltage is more than 4.5 volts, replace MAP sensor. Perform VERIFICATION TEST VER-2.

1992 ENGINE PERFORMANCE
Self-Diagnostic Tests – 3.9L & 5.2L (Cont.)

CHRY
1-109

TEST DR-4A (Cont.)

2) If MAP sensor voltage is 4.5 volts or less, turn ignition off. Disconnect engine controller 60-pin connector. Place DRB-II in ohmmeter mode. Probe Dark Green/Red wire at MAP sensor connector.

3) If resistance is less than 10 ohms, repair short to ground in Dark Green/Red wire. Perform VERIFICATION TEST VER-2. If resistance 10 ohms or more, replace engine controller. Perform VERIFICATION TEST VER-2.

TEST DR-5A

CODE 14, MAP VOLTAGE TOO HIGH

NOTE: For connector terminal identification, see CONNECTOR IDEN-TIFICATION at beginning of article. For wiring diagram, see appropriate WIRING DIAGRAMS article in ENGINE PERFORMANCE.

1) Turn ignition off. Disconnect and inspect MAP sensor connector. Repair connector as necessary. Perform VERIFICATION TEST VER-2. If MAP sensor connector is okay, go to next step.

2) Connect a jumper wire between Black/Light Blue wire and Dark Green/Red wire at MAP sensor connector. Turn ignition on. Read MAP sensor voltage. If voltage is less than one volt, replace MAP sensor. Perform VERIFICATION TEST VER-2.

3) If MAP sensor voltage is one volt or more, remove jumper wire. Connect jumper wire between Dark Green/Red wire at MAP sensor connector and ground. If voltage is less than one volt, repair open in Black/Light Blue wire. Perform VERIFICATION TEST VER-2.

4) If voltage is one volt or more, disconnect and inspect engine controller 60-pin connector. Repair connector as necessary. Perform VERIFICA-TION TEST VER-2. If engine controller connector is okay, go to next step.

5) Using an external ohmmeter, check resistance of Dark Green/Red wire between MAP sensor connector and engine controller connector terminal No. 1. If resistance is 10 ohms or more, repair open Dark Green/Red wire. Perform VERIFICATION TEST VER-2. If resistance is less than 10 ohms, replace engine controller. Perform VERIFICATION TEST VER-2.

TEST DR-6A

CODE 15, NO VEHICLE SPEED SIGNAL

NOTE: For connector terminal identification, see CONNECTOR IDEN-TIFICATION at beginning of article. For wiring diagram, see appropriate WIRING DIAGRAMS article in ENGINE PERFORMANCE.

1) Turn ignition off. Disconnect and inspect distance sensor connector. Repair connector as necessary. Perform VERIFICATION TEST VER-2. If connector is okay, go to next step.

2) Turn ignition on. Connect a jumper wire to one terminal of distance sensor connector. Monitor vehicle speed on DRB-II while tapping open end of jumper wire to other distance sensor harness connector terminal.

3) If DRB-II shows vehicle speed to be more than zero MPH, replace distance sensor. Perform VERIFICATION TEST VER-2. If vehicle speed is zero, place DRB-II in ohmmeter mode. Probe Black/Light Blue wire at distance sensor connector.

4) If resistance is 10 ohms or more, repair open in Black/Light Blue wire. Perform VERIFICATION TEST VER-2. If resistance is less than 10 ohms, turn ignition off. Disconnect and inspect engine controller connector. Repair connector if damaged. Perform VERIFICATION TEST VER-2. If terminal is okay, go to next step.

5) On Dakota models, go to TEST DR-6B. On all other models, turn ignition on. Place DRB-II in voltmeter mode. Probe terminal No. 47 at engine controller connector. If voltage is more than 4 volts, go to step 7). If voltage is 4 volts or less, check if speedometer works. If speedometer works, repair open in White/Orange wire between distance sensor and engine controller connector. Perform VERIFICATION TEST VER-2.

TEST DR-6A (Cont.)

6) If speedometer does not work, turn ignition off. Place DRB-II in ohm-meter mode. Probe terminal No. 47 at engine controller connector. If resistance is less than 5 ohms, repair short to ground in White/Orange wire. Perform VERIFICATION TEST VER-2. If resistance is 5 ohms or more, repair open White/Orange wire between sensor and splice. Perform VERIFICATION TEST VER-2.

7) If voltage at White/Orange wire is more than 4 volts in step 5), probe White/Orange wire at distance sensor connector. Replace engine controller if voltage is more than 4 volts. Perform VERIFICATION TEST VER-2. If voltage is 4 volts or less, repair open in White/Orange wire between distance sensor and engine controller connector. Perform VERIFICATION TEST VER-2.

TEST DR-6B

CODE 15, NO VEHICLE SPEED SIGNAL

NOTE: For connector terminal identification, see CONNECTOR IDEN-TIFICATION at beginning of article. For wiring diagram, see appropriate WIRING DIAGRAMS article in ENGINE PERFORMANCE.

1) Place DRB-II in ohmmeter mode. Probe terminal No. 47 at engine controller connector. If resistance is less than 10 ohms, repair short to ground in White/Orange wire. Perform VERIFICATION TEST VER-2. If resistance is 10 ohms or more, check resistance of White/Orange wire between engine controller connector terminal No. 47 and distance sensor connector using a DVOM.

2) If resistance is less than 10 ohms, replace engine controller. Perform VERIFICATION TEST VER-2. If resistance is 10 ohms or less, repair open in White/Orange wire between distance sensor and engine controller connector. Perform VERIFICATION TEST VER-2.

TEST DR-7A

CODE 21, OXYGEN (O₂) SIGNAL STAYS AT CENTER

NOTE: For connector terminal identification, see CONNECTOR IDEN-TIFICATION at beginning of article. For wiring diagram, see appropriate WIRING DIAGRAMS article in ENGINE PERFORMANCE.

1) Turn ignition off. Disconnect and inspect O_2 sensor connector. Repair connector if damaged. Perform VERIFICATION TEST VER-2. If O_2 sensor connector is okay, turn ignition on. Connect a jumper wire to Black/Dark Green wire at O_2 sensor connector. DO NOT connect jumper wire to Dark Green/Black wire in O_2 sensor connector.

2) Connect other end of jumper wire to positive battery terminal. Using DRB-II, read O_2 sensor voltage. If voltage is less than one volt, go to next step. If voltage is one volt or more, disconnect jumper wire. Turn ignition off. Place DRB-II in ohmmeter mode. Probe Black/Light Blue wire at O_2 sensor connector. If resistance is 10 ohms or more, repair open Black/Light Blue wire. Perform VERIFICATION TEST VER-2. If resistance is less than 10 ohms, replace O_2 sensor. Perform VERIFICATION TEST VER-2.

3) If voltage is less than one volt in step 2), disconnect jumper wire. Turn ignition off. Disconnect and inspect engine controller 60-pin connector. Repair connector if damaged. Perform VERIFICATION TEST VER-2. If engine controller connector is okay, go to next step.

4) Using a DVOM, check resistance of Black/Dark Green wire between O_2 sensor connector and engine controller connector terminal No. 41. If resistance is less than 10 ohms, replace engine controller. Perform VER-IFICATION TEST VER-2. If resistance is 10 ohms or more, repair open in Black/Dark Green wire. Perform VERIFICATION TEST VER-2.

1992 ENGINE PERFORMANCE
Self-Diagnostic Tests – 3.9L & 5.2L (Cont.)

TEST DR-8A

CODE 21, OXYGEN (O₂) SIGNAL SHORTED TO VOLTAGE

NOTE: For connector terminal identification, see CONNECTOR IDENTIFICATION at beginning of article. For wiring diagram, see appropriate WIRING DIAGRAMS article in ENGINE PERFORMANCE.

1) Start engine, and allow it to idle for 2 minutes. Using DRB-II, read O₂ sensor voltage. If voltage is more than 1.3 volts, go to step **3)**. If voltage is 1.3 volts or less, read O₂ sensor voltage while wiggling O₂ sensor wiring.

2) If voltage is more than 1.3 volts while O₂ sensor wiring is wiggled, repair short to voltage in Black/Dark Green wire. Perform VERIFICATION TEST VER-2. If voltage stays less than 1.3 volts while O₂ sensor wiring is wiggled, replace engine controller. Perform VERIFICATION TEST VER-2.

3) If voltage is more than 1.3 volts in step **1)**, disconnect O₂ sensor connector. If voltage is less than one volt when O₂ sensor connector is disconnected, replace O₂ sensor. Perform VERIFICATION TEST VER-2. If voltage is more than one volt when O₂ sensor connector is disconnected, repair Black/Dark Green wire for a short to Dark Green/Black wire.

4) Reconnect O₂ sensor connector. Using DRB-II, reset adaptive fuel value. Start engine, and let it idle for 2 minutes. Using DRB-II, read O₂ sensor value. If O₂ sensor switches from rich to lean, test is complete. Perform VERIFICATION TEST VER-2. If O₂ sensor does not switch from rich to lean, replace O₂ sensor. Perform VERIFICATION TEST VER-2.

TEST DR-9A

CODE 52, OXYGEN (O₂) SIGNAL STAYS ABOVE CENTER

1) Start engine. Allow engine to reach normal operating temperature. Turn engine off. Allow engine to "hot soak" for 5 minutes. Remove spark plugs, keeping them in order according to cylinder. Inspect spark plugs for wet tips or fuel fouling. If any spark plugs are wet or fuel fouled, replace leaking injectors and/or "O" rings at corresponding cylinder(s). Perform VERIFICATION TEST VER-2.

2) If spark plugs are wet or fuel fouled, inspect air cleaner filter and inlet ducts for restrictions. Clean as necessary. Perform VERIFICATION TEST VER-2. If no restrictions exist, perform TEST NF-1A.

TEST DR-10A

CODE 51, OXYGEN (O₂) SIGNAL STAYS BELOW CENTER

Code 51 may set for several reasons not related to O₂ sensor or O₂ sensor circuits. If Code 51 sets, perform TEST NF-1A.

TEST DR-11A

CODE 22, COOLANT SENSOR VOLTAGE TOO HIGH

NOTE: For connector terminal identification, see CONNECTOR IDENTIFICATION at beginning of article. For wiring diagram, see appropriate WIRING DIAGRAMS article in ENGINE PERFORMANCE.

1) Turn ignition off. Disconnect and inspect coolant temperature sensor connector. Repair connector if damaged. Perform VERIFICATION TEST VER-2. If coolant temperature sensor connector is okay, go to next step.

2) Connect jumper wire between Black/Light Blue and Tan/Black wires at coolant temperature sensor connector. Turn ignition on. Using DRB-II, read coolant temperature sensor voltage. If voltage is less than one volt, replace coolant temperature sensor. Perform VERIFICATION TEST VER-2.

TEST DR-11A (Cont.)

3) If voltage is one volt or more, remove jumper wire. Connect jumper wire between Tan/Black wire at coolant temperature sensor connector and ground. Using DRB-II, read coolant temperature sensor voltage. If voltage is less than one volt, repair open in Black/Light Blue wire. Perform VERIFICATION TEST VER-2.

4) If voltage is one volt or more, disconnect and inspect engine controller 60-pin connector. Repair connector if damaged. Perform VERIFICATION TEST VER-2. If connector is okay, go to next step.

5) Using a DVOM, check resistance of Tan/Black wire between coolant temperature sensor connector and engine controller connector terminal No. 2. If resistance is less than 10 ohms, replace engine controller. Perform VERIFICATION TEST VER-2. If resistance is 10 ohms or more, repair open Tan/Black wire. Perform VERIFICATION TEST VER-2.

TEST DR-12A

CODE 22, COOLANT SENSOR VOLTAGE TOO LOW

NOTE: For connector terminal identification, see CONNECTOR IDENTIFICATION at beginning of article. For wiring diagram, see appropriate WIRING DIAGRAMS article in ENGINE PERFORMANCE.

1) Turn ignition on. Using DRB-II, read coolant temperature sensor voltage. Disconnect coolant temperature sensor connector. If voltage changed by more than 4 volts when sensor was disconnected, replace coolant temperature sensor. Perform VERIFICATION TEST VER-2. If voltage did not change by more than 4 volts when sensor was disconnected, turn ignition off.

2) Disconnect and inspect engine controller 60-pin connector. Repair connector if damaged. Perform VERIFICATION TEST VER-2. Place DRB-II in ohmmeter mode. Probe engine controller connector terminal No. 2 (Tan/Black wire). If resistance is less than 10 ohms, repair Tan/Black wire for short to Black/Light Blue wire or ground. Perform VERIFICATION TEST VER-2. If resistance is 10 ohms or more, replace engine controller. Perform VERIFICATION TEST VER-2.

TEST DR-13A

CODE 24, THROTTLE POSITION SENSOR (TPS) VOLTAGE HIGH

NOTE: For connector terminal identification, see CONNECTOR IDENTIFICATION at beginning of article. For wiring diagram, see appropriate WIRING DIAGRAMS article in ENGINE PERFORMANCE.

1) Turn ignition off. Disconnect and inspect TPS connector. Repair TPS connector if damaged. Perform VERIFICATION TEST VER-2. If TPS connector is okay, go to next step.

2) Turn ignition on. Connect jumper wire between Orange/Dark Blue wire and Black/Light Blue wire at TPS connector. Using DRB-II, read TPS voltage. If voltage is less than one volt, replace TPS. Perform VERIFICATION TEST VER-2.

3) If voltage is one volt or more, remove jumper wire. Connect jumper wire between Orange/Dark Blue wire at TPS connector and ground. Using DRB-II, read TPS voltage. If voltage is less than one volt, repair open in Black/Light Blue wire. Perform VERIFICATION TEST VER-2.

4) If voltage is one volt or more, turn ignition off. Disconnect and inspect engine controller 60-pin connector. Repair connector if damaged. Perform VERIFICATION TEST VER-2. If connector is okay, go to next step.

5) Using a DVOM, check resistance of Orange/Dark Blue wire between TPS connector and engine controller connector terminal No. 22. If resistance is less than 10 ohms, replace engine controller. Perform VERIFICATION TEST VER-2. If resistance is 10 ohms or more, repair open in Orange/Dark Blue wire. Perform VERIFICATION TEST VER-2.

1992 ENGINE PERFORMANCE
Self-Diagnostic Tests – 3.9L & 5.2L (Cont.)

CHRY
1-111

TEST DR-14A

CODE 24, THROTTLE POSITION SENSOR (TPS) VOLTAGE LOW

NOTE: For connector terminal identification, see CONNECTOR IDENTIFICATION at beginning of article. For wiring diagram, see appropriate WIRING DIAGRAMS article in ENGINE PERFORMANCE.

1) Turn ignition off. Disconnect TPS connector. Turn ignition on. Place DRB-II in voltmeter mode. Probe Violet/White wire at TPS connector. If voltage is less than one volt, go to step **4)**.

2) If voltage is one volt or more, probe Orange/Dark Blue wire at TPS connector. If voltage is one volt or more, replace TPS. Perform VERIFICATION TEST VER-2. If voltage is less than one volt, turn ignition off. Disconnect engine controller 60-pin connector.

3) Place DRB-II in ohmmeter mode. Probe terminal No. 22 (Orange/Dark Blue wire) at engine controller connector. If resistance is less than 10 ohms, repair short to ground in Orange/Dark Blue wire. Perform VERIFICATION TEST VER-2. If resistance is 10 ohms or more, replace engine controller. Perform VERIFICATION TEST VER-2.

4) If voltage is less than one volt in step **1)**, turn ignition off. Place DRB-II in ohmmeter mode. Probe Violet/White wire. If resistance is less than 10 ohms, repair Violet/White wire for a short to ground. Perform VERIFICATION TEST VER-2. If resistance is 10 ohms or more, disconnect and inspect engine controller connector. Repair connector if damaged. Perform VERIFICATION TEST VER-2.

5) If connector is okay, check resistance of Violet/White wire between TPS connector and engine controller connector terminal No. 6 using a DVOM. If resistance is less than 10 ohms, replace engine controller. Perform VERIFICATION TEST VER-2. If resistance is 10 ohms or more, repair open Violet/White wire. Perform VERIFICATION TEST VER-2.

TEST DR-15A

CODE 25, AUTOMATIC IDLE SPEED (AIS) MOTOR CIRCUITS

NOTE: For connector terminal identification, see CONNECTOR IDENTIFICATION at beginning of article. For wiring diagram, see appropriate WIRING DIAGRAMS article in ENGINE PERFORMANCE.

1) Disconnect Automatic Idle Speed (AIS) motor connector. Turn ignition on. Using DRB-II, actuate AIS motor. Put DRB-II in voltmeter mode. Probe AIS motor connector Gray/Red wire.

2) Under normal conditions, voltage will switch from less than one volt to more than 10 volts. If voltage stays less than one volt, repair short to ground in Gray/Red wire. Perform VERIFICATION TEST VER-2.

3) If voltage stayed more than 10 volts, repair short to voltage in Gray/Red wire. Perform VERIFICATION TEST VER-2. If voltage did not stay less than one volt or more than 10 volts, probe Yellow/Black wire at AIS motor connector. If voltage stays less than one volt, repair short to ground in Yellow/Black wire. Perform VERIFICATION TEST VER-2.

4) If voltage stays more than 10 volts, repair short to voltage in Yellow/Black wire. Perform VERIFICATION TEST VER-2. If voltage does not stay less than one volt or more than 10 volts, probe Brown/White wire at AIS connector. If voltage stays less than one volt, repair short to ground in Brown/White wire. Perform VERIFICATION TEST VER-2.

5) If voltage stays more than 10 volts, repair short to voltage in Brown/White wire. Perform VERIFICATION TEST VER-2. If voltage does not stay less than one volt or more than 10 volts, probe Violet/Black wire at AIS connector terminal. If voltage stays less than one volt, repair short to ground in Violet/Black wire. Perform VERIFICATION TEST VER-2.

6) If voltage stays more than 10 volts, repair short to voltage in Violet/Black wire. VERIFICATION TEST VER-2. If voltage does not stay less than one volt or more than 10 volts, turn ignition off. Reconnect AIS motor connector.

7) Disconnect engine controller 60-pin connector. Using a DVOM, check resistance between terminals No. 39 (Gray/Red wire) and 59 (Violet/Black wire) of engine controller connector. If resistance is less than 35 ohms, replace AIS motor. Perform VERIFICATION TEST VER-2.

8) If resistance is 35 ohms or more, check resistance between terminals No. 40 (Brown/White wire) and 60 (Yellow/Black wire) of engine controller connector. If resistance is less than 35 ohms, replace AIS motor. Perform VERIFICATION TEST VER-2.

TEST DR-15A (Cont.)

9) If resistance is 35 ohms or more, check resistance between engine controller connector terminals No. 39 (Gray/Red wire) and 60 (Yellow/Black wire). If resistance is less than 10 ohms, repair Yellow/Black wire for a short to Gray/Red wire. Perform VERIFICATION TEST VER-2.

10) If resistance is 10-75 ohms, go to next step. If resistance is 75-120 ohms, repair Brown/White wire for a short to Violet/Black wire. Perform VERIFICATION TEST VER-2. If resistance is more than 120 ohms, replace engine controller. Perform VERIFICATION TEST VER-2.

11) If resistance is 10-75 ohms in step **10)**, check resistance between engine controller connector terminals No. 59 (Violet/Black wire) and 60 (Yellow/Black wire). If resistance is less than 10 ohms, repair Yellow/Black wire for a short to Violet/Black wire. Perform VERIFICATION TEST VER-2. If resistance is 10 ohms or more, repair Gray/Red wire for a short to Brown/White wire. Perform VERIFICATION TEST VER-2.

TEST DR-16A

CODE 27, INJECTOR NO. 1 CONTROL CIRCUIT

NOTE: For connector terminal identification, see CONNECTOR IDENTIFICATION at beginning of article. For wiring diagram, see appropriate WIRING DIAGRAMS article in ENGINE PERFORMANCE.

1) Turn ignition off. Disconnect and inspect fuel injector No. 1 connector. Repair connector if damaged. Perform VERIFICATION TEST VER-2. If connector is okay, measure fuel injector resistance using a DVOM.

2) If resistance is not 13-16 ohms, replace injector. Perform VERIFICATION TEST VER-2. If resistance is 13-16 ohms, disconnect DVOM. Turn ignition on. Put DRB-II in voltmeter mode. Probe Dark Green/Orange wire at injector No. 1 connector. If voltage is 10 volts or less, repair open Dark Green/Orange wire between injector connector and harness splice. Perform VERIFICATION TEST VER-2.

3) If voltage is more than 10 volts, turn ignition off. Disconnect and inspect engine controller 60-pin connector. Repair connector if damaged. Perform VERIFICATION TEST VER-2. If connector is okay, place DRB-II in ohmmeter mode. Check resistance of engine controller connector terminal No. 16 (White/Dark Blue wire). If resistance is less than 10 ohms, repair White/Dark Blue wire for a short to ground. Perform VERIFICATION TEST VER-2.

4) If resistance is 10 ohms or more, check resistance of White/Dark Blue wire between fuel injector No. 1 connector and engine controller connector terminal No. 16 using a DVOM. If resistance is 10 ohms or more, repair open White/Dark Blue wire. Perform VERIFICATION TEST VER-2. If resistance is less than 10 ohms, replace engine controller. Perform VERIFICATION TEST VER-2.

TEST DR-17A

CODE 27, INJECTOR NO. 2 CONTROL CIRCUIT

NOTE: For connector terminal identification, see CONNECTOR IDENTIFICATION at beginning of article. For wiring diagram, see appropriate WIRING DIAGRAMS article in ENGINE PERFORMANCE.

1) Turn ignition off. Disconnect and inspect fuel injector No. 2 connector. Repair connector if damaged. Perform VERIFICATION TEST VER-2. If connector is okay, measure fuel injector resistance using a DVOM.

2) If resistance is not 13-16 ohms, replace injector. Perform VERIFICATION TEST VER-2. If resistance is 13-16 ohms, disconnect DVOM. Turn ignition on. Put DRB-II in voltmeter mode. Probe Dark Green/Orange wire at injector No. 2 connector. If voltage is 10 volts or less, repair open Dark Green/Orange wire between injector connector and harness splice. Perform VERIFICATION TEST VER-2.

3) If voltage is more than 10 volts, turn ignition off. Disconnect and inspect engine controller 60-pin connector. Repair connector if damaged. Perform VERIFICATION TEST VER-2. If connector is okay, place DRB-II in ohmmeter mode. Check resistance of engine controller connector terminal No. 15 (Tan wire). If resistance is less than 10 ohms, repair Tan wire for a short to ground. Perform VERIFICATION TEST VER-2.

CHRY
1-112

1992 ENGINE PERFORMANCE
Self-Diagnostic Tests – 3.9L & 5.2L (Cont.)

TEST DR-17A (Cont.)

4) If resistance is 10 ohms or more, check resistance of Tan wire between fuel injector No. 2 connector and engine controller connector terminal No. 15 using a DVOM. If resistance is 10 ohms or more, repair open Tan wire. Perform VERIFICATION TEST VER-2. If resistance is less than 10 ohms, replace engine controller. Perform VERIFICATION TEST VER-2.

TEST DR-18A
CODE 27, INJECTOR NO. 3 CONTROL CIRCUIT

NOTE: For connector terminal identification, see CONNECTOR IDEN-TIFICATION at beginning of article. For wiring diagram, see appropriate WIRING DIAGRAMS article in ENGINE PERFORMANCE.

1) Turn ignition off. Disconnect and inspect fuel injector No. 3 connector. Repair connector if damaged. Perform VERIFICATION TEST VER-2. If connector is okay, measure fuel injector resistance using a DVOM.

2) If resistance is not 13-16 ohms, replace injector. Perform VERIFICA-TION TEST VER-2. If resistance is 13-16 ohms, disconnect DVOM. Turn ignition on. Put DRB-II in voltmeter mode. Probe Dark Green/Orange wire at injector No. 3 connector. If voltage is 10 volts or less, repair open Dark Green/Orange wire between injector connector and harness splice. Perform VERIFICATION TEST VER-2.

3) If voltage is more than 10 volts, turn ignition off. Disconnect and inspect engine controller 60-pin connector. Repair connector if damaged. Perform VERIFICATION TEST VER-2. If connector is okay, place DRB-II in ohmmeter mode. Check resistance of engine controller connector terminal No. 14 (Yellow/White wire). If resistance is less than 10 ohms, repair Yellow/White wire for a short to ground. Perform VER-IFICATION TEST VER-2.

4) If resistance is 10 ohms or more, check resistance of Yellow/White wire between fuel injector No. 3 connector and engine controller connector terminal No. 14 using a DVOM. If resistance is 10 ohms or more, repair open Yellow/White wire. Perform VERIFICATION TEST VER-2. If resistance is less than 10 ohms, replace engine controller. Perform VER-IFICATION TEST VER-2.

TEST DR-19A
CODE 27, INJECTOR NO. 4 CONTROL CIRCUIT

NOTE: For connector terminal identification, see CONNECTOR IDEN-TIFICATION at beginning of article. For wiring diagram, see appropriate WIRING DIAGRAMS article in ENGINE PERFORMANCE.

1) Turn ignition off. Disconnect and inspect fuel injector No. 4 connector. Repair connector if damaged. Perform VERIFICATION TEST VER-2. If connector is okay, measure fuel injector resistance using a DVOM.

2) If resistance is not 13-16 ohms, replace injector. Perform VERIFICA-TION TEST VER-2. If resistance is 13-16 ohms, disconnect DVOM. Turn ignition on. Put DRB-II in voltmeter mode. Probe Dark Green/Orange wire at injector No. 4 connector. If voltage is 10 volts or less, repair open Dark Green/Orange wire between injector connector and harness splice. Perform VERIFICATION TEST VER-2.

3) If voltage is more than 10 volts, turn ignition off. Disconnect and inspect engine controller 60-pin connector. Repair connector if damaged. Perform VERIFICATION TEST VER-2. If connector is okay, place DRB-II in ohmmeter mode. Check resistance of engine controller connector terminal No. 13 (Light Blue/Brown wire). If resistance is less than 10 ohms, repair Light Blue/Brown wire for a short to ground. Perform VERIFICATION TEST VER-2.

4) If resistance is 10 ohms or more, check resistance of Light Blue/Brown wire between fuel injector No. 4 connector and engine controller connector terminal No. 13 using a DVOM. If resistance is 10 ohms or more, repair open Light Blue/Brown wire. Perform VERIFICATION TEST VER-2. If resistance is less than 10 ohms, replace engine controller. Per-form VERIFICATION TEST VER-2.

TEST DR-20A
CODE 27, INJECTOR NO. 5 CONTROL CIRCUIT

NOTE: For connector terminal identification, see CONNECTOR IDEN-TIFICATION at beginning of article. For wiring diagram, see appropriate WIRING DIAGRAMS article in ENGINE PERFORMANCE.

1) Turn ignition off. Disconnect and inspect fuel injector No. 5 connector. Repair connector if damaged. Perform VERIFICATION TEST VER-2. If connector is okay, measure fuel injector resistance using a DVOM.

2) If resistance is not 13-16 ohms, replace injector. Perform VERIFICA-TION TEST VER-2. If resistance is 13-16 ohms, disconnect DVOM. Turn ignition on. Put DRB-II in voltmeter mode. Probe Dark Green/Orange wire at injector No. 5 connector. If voltage is 10 volts or less, repair open Dark Green/Orange wire between injector connector and harness splice. Perform VERIFICATION TEST VER-2.

3) If voltage is more than 10 volts, turn ignition off. Disconnect and inspect engine controller 60-pin connector. Repair connector if dam-aged. Perform VERIFICATION TEST VER-2. If connector is okay, place DRB-II in ohmmeter mode. Check resistance of engine controller connector terminal No. 38 (Pink/Black wire). If resistance is less than 10 ohms, repair Pink/Black wire for a short to ground. Perform VERIFICA-TION TEST VER-2.

4) If resistance is 10 ohms or more, check resistance of Pink/Black wire between fuel injector No. 5 connector and engine controller connector terminal No. 38 using a DVOM. If resistance is 10 ohms or more, repair open Pink/Black wire. Perform VERIFICATION TEST VER-2. If resis-tance is less than 10 ohms, replace engine controller. Perform VERIFICATION TEST VER-2.

TEST DR-21A
CODE 27, INJECTOR NO. 6 CONTROL CIRCUIT

NOTE: For connector terminal identification, see CONNECTOR IDEN-TIFICATION at beginning of article. For wiring diagram, see appropriate WIRING DIAGRAMS article in ENGINE PERFORMANCE.

1) Turn ignition off. Disconnect and inspect fuel injector No. 6 connector. Repair connector if damaged. Perform VERIFICATION TEST VER-2. If connector is okay, measure fuel injector resistance using a DVOM.

2) If resistance is not 13-16 ohms, replace injector. Perform VERIFICA-TION TEST VER-2. If resistance is 13-16 ohms, disconnect DVOM. Turn ignition on. Put DRB-II in voltmeter mode. Probe Dark Green/Orange wire at injector No. 6 connector. If voltage is 10 volts or less, repair open Dark Green/Orange wire between injector connector and harness splice. Perform VERIFICATION TEST VER-2.

3) If voltage is more than 10 volts, turn ignition off. Disconnect and inspect engine controller 60-pin connector. Repair connector if dam-aged. Perform VERIFICATION TEST VER-2. If connector is okay, place DRB-II in ohmmeter mode. Check resistance of engine controller connector terminal No. 58 (Light Green/Black wire). If resistance is less than 10 ohms, repair Light Green/Black wire for a short to ground. Per-form VERIFICATION TEST VER-2.

4) If resistance is 10 ohms or more, check resistance of Light Green/Black wire between fuel injector No. 6 connector and engine controller connector terminal No. 58 using a DVOM. If resistance is 10 ohms or more, repair open Light Green/Black wire. Perform VERIFICATION TEST VER-2. If resistance is less than 10 ohms, replace engine control-ler. Perform VERIFICATION TEST VER-2.

TEST DR-22A
CODE 27, INJECTOR NO. 7 CONTROL CIRCUIT

NOTE: For connector terminal identification, see CONNECTOR IDEN-TIFICATION at beginning of article. For wiring diagram, see appropri-ate WIRING DIAGRAMS article in ENGINE PERFORMANCE.

1) Turn ignition off. Disconnect and inspect fuel injector No. 7 connector. Repair connector if damaged. Perform VERIFICATION TEST VER-2. If connector is okay, measure fuel injector resistance using a DVOM.

1992 ENGINE PERFORMANCE
Self-Diagnostic Tests – 3.9L & 5.2L (Cont.)

CHRY
1-113

TEST DR-22A (Cont.)

2) If resistance is not 13-16 ohms, replace injector. Perform VERIFICATION TEST VER-2. If resistance is 13-16 ohms, disconnect DVOM. Turn ignition on. Put DRB-II in voltmeter mode. Probe Dark Green/Orange wire at injector No. 7 connector. If voltage is 10 volts or less, repair open Dark Green/Orange wire between injector connector and harness splice. Perform VERIFICATION TEST VER-2.

3) If voltage is more than 10 volts, turn ignition off. Disconnect and inspect engine controller 60-pin connector. Repair connector if damaged. Perform VERIFICATION TEST VER-2. If connector is okay, place DRB-II in ohmmeter mode. Check resistance of engine controller connector terminal No. 17 (Dark Blue/Tan wire). If resistance is less than 10 ohms, repair Dark Blue/Tan wire for a short to ground. Perform VERIFICATION TEST VER-2.

4) If resistance is 10 ohms or more, check resistance of Dark Blue/Tan wire between fuel injector No. 7 connector and engine controller connector terminal No. 17 using a DVOM. If resistance is 10 ohms or more, repair open Dark Blue/Tan wire. Perform VERIFICATION TEST VER-2. If resistance is less than 10 ohms, replace engine controller. Perform VERIFICATION TEST VER-2.

TEST DR-23A

CODE 27, INJECTOR NO. 8 CONTROL CIRCUIT

NOTE: For connector terminal identification, see CONNECTOR IDENTIFICATION at beginning of article. For wiring diagram, see appropriate WIRING DIAGRAMS article in ENGINE PERFORMANCE.

1) Turn ignition off. Disconnect and inspect fuel injector No. 8 connector. Repair connector if damaged. Perform VERIFICATION TEST VER-2. If connector is okay, measure fuel injector resistance using a DVOM.

2) If resistance is not 13-16 ohms, replace injector. Perform VERIFICATION TEST VER-2. If resistance is 13-16 ohms, disconnect DVOM. Turn ignition on. Put DRB-II in voltmeter mode. If vehicle is a Pickup or Ramcharger, go to TEST DR-23B. On all other models, probe Dark Green/Orange wire at injector No. 8 connector. If voltage is 10 volts or less, repair open Dark Green/Orange wire between injector connector and harness splice. Perform VERIFICATION TEST VER-2.

3) If voltage is more than 10 volts, turn ignition off. Disconnect and inspect engine controller 60-pin connector. Repair connector if damaged. Perform VERIFICATION TEST VER-2. If connector is okay, place DRB-II in ohmmeter mode. Check resistance of engine controller connector terminal No. 18 (Dark Blue/Gray wire). If resistance is less than 10 ohms, repair Dark Blue/Gray wire for a short to ground. Perform VERIFICATION TEST VER-2.

4) If resistance is 10 ohms or more, check resistance of Dark Blue/Gray wire between fuel injector No. 8 connector and engine controller connector terminal No. 18 using a DVOM. If resistance is 10 ohms or more, repair open Dark Blue/Gray wire. Perform VERIFICATION TEST VER-2. If resistance is less than 10 ohms, replace engine controller. Perform VERIFICATION TEST VER-2.

TEST DR-23B

CODE 27, INJECTOR NO. 8 CONTROL CIRCUIT

NOTE: For connector terminal identification, see CONNECTOR IDENTIFICATION at beginning of article. For wiring diagram, see appropriate WIRING DIAGRAMS article in ENGINE PERFORMANCE.

1) Probe Dark Green/Orange wire at injector No. 8 connector. If voltage is 10 volts or less, repair open Dark Green/Orange wire between injector connector and harness splice. Perform VERIFICATION TEST VER-2. If voltage is more than 10 volts, turn ignition off.

2) Disconnect and inspect engine controller 60-pin connector. Repair connector if damaged. Perform VERIFICATION TEST VER-2. If connector is okay, place DRB-II in ohmmeter mode. Check resistance of engine controller connector terminal No. 18 (Red/Yellow wire). If resistance is less than 10 ohms, repair Red/Yellow wire for a short to ground. Perform VERIFICATION TEST VER-2.

3) If resistance is 10 ohms or more, check resistance of Red/Yellow wire between fuel injector No. 8 connector and engine controller connector terminal No. 18 using a DVOM. If resistance is 10 ohms or more, repair open Red/Yellow wire. Perform VERIFICATION TEST VER-2. If resistance is less than 10 ohms, replace engine controller. Perform VERIFICATION TEST VER-2.

TEST DR-24A

CODE 31, PURGE SOLENOID CIRCUIT

NOTE: For connector terminal identification, see CONNECTOR IDENTIFICATION at beginning of article. For wiring diagram, see appropriate WIRING DIAGRAMS article in ENGINE PERFORMANCE.

1) Turn ignition off. Disconnect and inspect purge solenoid connector. Repair connector if damaged. Perform VERIFICATION TEST VER-2. If connector is okay, turn ignition on. Place DRB-II in voltmeter mode. Probe purge solenoid connector Dark Blue wire. If voltage is 10 volts or less, repair open in Dark Blue wire. Perform VERIFICATION TEST VER-2.

2) If voltage is more than 10 volts, turn ignition off. Disconnect and inspect engine controller 60-pin connector. Repair connector if damaged. Perform VERIFICATION TEST VER-2. If connector is okay, place DRB-II in ohmmeter mode. Probe engine controller connector terminal No. 52 (Pink/Black wire). If resistance is less than 10 ohms, repair short to ground in Pink/Black wire. Perform VERIFICATION TEST VER-2.

3) If resistance is 10 ohms or more, check resistance of Pink/Black wire between purge solenoid connector and engine controller connector terminal No. 52 using a DVOM. If resistance is 10 ohms or more, repair open in Pink/Black wire. Perform VERIFICATION TEST VER-2. If resistance is less than 10 ohms, reconnect purge solenoid connector.

4) Turn ignition on. Place DRB-II in voltmeter mode. Probe engine controller connector terminal No. 52 (Pink/Black wire). If voltage is more than 10 volts, replace engine controller. Perform VERIFICATION TEST VER-2. If voltage is 10 volts or less, replace purge solenoid. Perform VERIFICATION TEST VER-2.

TEST DR-25A

CODE 23, CHARGE TEMPERATURE SENSOR HIGH

NOTE: For connector terminal identification, see CONNECTOR IDENTIFICATION at beginning of article. For wiring diagram, see appropriate WIRING DIAGRAMS article in ENGINE PERFORMANCE.

1) Turn ignition on. Using DRB-II, select charge temperature sensor voltage. Disconnect charge temperature sensor. Connect a jumper wire across sensor harness connector. Read sensor voltage. If voltage is less than one volt, replace charge temperature sensor. Perform VERIFICATION TEST VER-2.

2) If voltage is one volt or more, disconnect jumper wire. Reconnect jumper wire between charge temperature sensor connector Black/Red wire and ground. Read sensor voltage. If voltage is less than one volt, repair Black/Light Blue wire for an open circuit to splice. Perform VERIFICATION TEST VER-2.

3) If voltage is one volt or more, turn ignition off. Disconnect and inspect engine controller connector. Repair connector if damaged. Perform VERIFICATION TEST VER-2. If connector is okay, check resistance of Black/Red wire between engine controller connector terminal No. 21 and charge temperature sensor connector using a DVOM.

4) If resistance is less than 10 ohms, replace engine controller. Perform VERIFICATION TEST VER-2. If resistance is 10 ohms or more, repair open Black/Red wire. Perform VERIFICATION TEST VER-2.

TEST DR-26A

CODE 23, CHARGE TEMPERATURE SENSOR LOW

NOTE: For connector terminal identification, see CONNECTOR IDENTIFICATION at beginning of article. For wiring diagram, see appropriate WIRING DIAGRAMS article in ENGINE PERFORMANCE.

1) Turn ignition on. Using DRB-II, select charge temperature sensor voltage. Disconnect charge temperature sensor. Read sensor voltage. If voltage is more than 4 volts, replace charge temperature sensor. Perform VERIFICATION TEST VER-2. If voltage is 4 volts or less, turn ignition off. Disconnect and inspect engine controller connector.

1992 ENGINE PERFORMANCE
Self-Diagnostic Tests – 3.9L & 5.2L (Cont.)

TEST DR-26A (Cont.)

2) Repair connector if damaged. Perform VERIFICATION TEST VER-2. If connector is okay, place DRB-II in ohmmeter mode. Probe engine controller connector terminal No. 21 (Black/Red wire). If resistance is 10 ohms or more, replace engine controller. Perform VERIFICATION TEST VER-2. If resistance is less than 10 ohms, repair short to ground in Black/Red wire. Perform VERIFICATION TEST VER-2.

TEST DR-27A
CODE 32, EGR SOLENOID CIRCUIT

NOTE: For connector terminal identification, see CONNECTOR IDENTIFICATION at beginning of article. For wiring diagram, see appropriate WIRING DIAGRAMS article in ENGINE PERFORMANCE.

1) Turn ignition off. On all models except Dakota, go to TEST DR-27B. On Dakota models, disconnect and inspect EGR solenoid connector. Repair connector if damaged. Perform VERIFICATION TEST VER-2. If connector is okay, turn ignition on. Place DRB-II in voltmeter mode.

2) Probe Dark Blue wire. If voltage is 10 volts or less, repair open Dark Blue wire. Perform VERIFICATION TEST VER-2. If voltage is more than 10 volts, turn ignition off. Reconnect EGR solenoid. Disconnect and inspect engine controller connector. Repair connector if damaged. Perform VERIFICATION TEST VER-2.

3) If connector is okay, turn ignition on. Place DRB-II in voltmeter mode. Probe engine controller connector terminal No. 35 (Gray/Yellow wire). If voltage is more than 10 volts, replace engine controller. Perform VERIFICATION TEST VER-2.

4) If voltage is 10 volts or less, turn ignition off. Disconnect EGR solenoid connector. Place DRB-II in ohmmeter mode. Probe engine controller connector terminal No. 35 (Gray/Yellow wire). If resistance is less than 10 ohms, repair short to ground in Gray/Yellow wire. Perform VERIFICATION TEST VER-2. If resistance is more than 10 ohms, go to next step.

5) Using a DVOM, check resistance of Gray/Yellow wire between engine controller connector terminal No. 35 and EGR solenoid connector. If resistance is less than 10 ohms, replace EGR solenoid. Perform VERIFICATION TEST VER-2. If resistance is more than 10 ohms, repair open Gray/Yellow wire. Perform VERIFICATION TEST VER-2.

TEST DR-27B
CODE 32, EGR SOLENOID CIRCUIT

NOTE: For connector terminal identification, see CONNECTOR IDENTIFICATION at beginning of article. For wiring diagram, see appropriate WIRING DIAGRAMS article in ENGINE PERFORMANCE.

1) Turn ignition off. Disconnect and inspect EGR solenoid connector. Repair connector if damaged. Perform VERIFICATION TEST VER-2. If connector is okay, measure solenoid resistance using a DVOM. If resistance is not 20-50 ohms, replace EGR solenoid. If resistance is 20-50 ohms, turn ignition on. Place DRB-II in voltmeter mode.

2) Probe Dark Green/Orange wire. If voltage is 10 volts or less, repair Dark Green/Orange wire for an open circuit to splice. Perform VERIFICATION TEST VER-2. If voltage is more than 10 volts, turn ignition off. Disconnect and inspect engine controller connector. Repair connector if damaged. Perform VERIFICATION TEST VER-2.

3) If connector is okay, place DRB-II in ohmmeter mode. Probe engine controller connector terminal No. 35 (Gray/Yellow wire). If resistance is less than 10 ohms, repair short to ground in Gray/Yellow wire. Perform VERIFICATION TEST VER-2. If resistance is more than 10 ohms, go to next step.

4) Using an external ohmmeter, check resistance of Gray/Yellow wire between engine controller connector terminal No. 35 and EGR solenoid connector. If resistance is less than 10 ohms, replace engine controller. Perform VERIFICATION TEST VER-2. If resistance is more than 10 ohms, repair open Gray/Yellow wire. Perform VERIFICATION TEST VER-2.

TEST DR-28A
CODE 32, EGR SYSTEM FAILURE

NOTE: For connector terminal identification, see CONNECTOR IDENTIFICATION at beginning of article. For wiring diagram, see appropriate WIRING DIAGRAMS article in ENGINE PERFORMANCE.

1) Disconnect vacuum supply hose from EGR solenoid. Connect a vacuum gauge to disconnected vacuum hose. Start engine, and allow it to reach normal operating temperature. If vacuum is more than 10 in. Hg at idle, go to step 3). If vacuum is 10 in. Hg or less at idle, turn engine off.

2) Disconnect EGR vacuum signal line at intake manifold. Connect a vacuum gauge to manifold nipple. Start engine, and read vacuum gauge at idle. If vacuum is more than 10 in. Hg at idle, repair vacuum leak or restriction in vacuum line to EGR solenoid. Perform VERIFICATION TEST VER-2. If vacuum is 10 in. Hg or less at idle, repair plugged vacuum nipple at manifold. Perform VERIFICATION TEST VER-2.

3) Turn engine off. Disconnect vacuum gauge, and reconnect supply vacuum hose to EGR solenoid. Disconnect vacuum hose from EGR valve. Connect vacuum gauge to disconnected vacuum hose. Start engine. While reading vacuum gauge, momentarily snap throttle open. If vacuum is not more than 5 in. Hg at any time, replace EGR valve assembly. Perform VERIFICATION TEST VER-2. If vacuum is 5 in. Hg or more at any time, go to next step.

4) Disconnect vacuum gauge from vacuum hose. Connect vacuum pump to EGR valve nipple. Start engine. Slowly apply vacuum to EGR valve and listen for engine RPM change. If engine RPM does not change, go to step 6). If engine RPM changes, go to next step.

5) Turn ignition off. Apply 10 in. Hg of vacuum and hold for 30 seconds. If vacuum does not hold for 30 seconds, replace EGR valve assembly. Perform VERIFICATION TEST VER-2. If vacuum holds for 30 seconds, EGR system is functioning properly at this time. If driveability problem is still present, go to TEST NF-1A. If driveability problem is no longer present, test is complete. Perform VERIFICATION TEST VER-2.

6) If engine RPM did not change in step 4), remove EGR valve assembly. Check for plugged EGR manifold passages. If manifold passages are plugged, clear passages as necessary. Perform VERIFICATION TEST VER-2. If manifold passages are not plugged, replace EGR valve assembly. Perform VERIFICATION TEST VER-2.

TEST DR-29A
CODE 33, A/C CLUTCH RELAY CIRCUIT

NOTE: For connector terminal identification, see CONNECTOR IDENTIFICATION at beginning of article. For wiring diagram, see appropriate WIRING DIAGRAMS article in ENGINE PERFORMANCE.

1) Turn ignition on. Using DRB-II, actuate A/C clutch relay. If relay is clicking, perform TEST DR-34A. If relay is not clicking, remove A/C clutch relay, and inspect connector. Repair connector if damaged. Perform VERIFICATION TEST VER-2. If connector is okay, substitute A/C relay with a known good relay. Using DRB-II, actuate A/C relay. If relay is clicking, repair is complete. Perform VERIFICATION TEST VER-2.

2) If relay is not clicking, remove substitute relay. Place DRB-II in voltmeter mode. Probe A/C relay connector terminal "A" (Light Green wire on Dakota, Dark Blue wire on all other models). If voltage is 10 volts or less, repair open Light Green or Dark Blue wire. Perform VERIFICATION TEST VER-2. If voltage is more than 10 volts, turn ignition off.

3) Disconnect and inspect engine controller connector. Repair connector if damaged. Perform VERIFICATION TEST VER-2. If connector is okay, put DRB-II in ohmmeter mode. Probe A/C clutch relay connector terminal "C" (Dark Blue/Orange wire). If resistance is less than 10 ohms, repair short to ground in Dark Blue/Orange wire. Perform VERIFICATION TEST VER-2. If resistance is 10 ohms or more, go to next step.

4) Using a DVOM, check resistance of Dark Blue/Orange wire between engine controller connector terminal No. 34 and A/C relay connector terminal "C". If resistance is 10 ohms or more, repair open Dark Blue/Orange wire. Perform VERIFICATION TEST VER-2. If resistance is less than 10 ohms, go to next step.

5) Reconnect A/C clutch relay. Turn ignition on. Place DRB-II in voltmeter mode. Probe terminal No. 34 (Dark Blue/Orange wire) in engine controller connector. If voltage is more than 10 volts, replace engine controller. Perform VERIFICATION TEST VER-2. If voltage is 10 volts or less, replace A/C clutch relay. Perform VERIFICATION TEST VER-2.

1992 ENGINE PERFORMANCE
Self-Diagnostic Tests – 3.9L & 5.2L (Cont.)

CHRY
1-115

TEST DR-30A

CODE 37, TORQUE CONVERTER LOCK-UP CIRCUIT

NOTE: For connector terminal identification, see CONNECTOR IDENTIFICATION at beginning of article. For wiring diagram, see appropriate WIRING DIAGRAMS article in ENGINE PERFORMANCE.

1) If vehicle is also equipped with overdrive, go to TEST DR-30B. Turn ignition off. Disconnect Part Throttle Unlock (PTU) relay. Inspect PTU connector. Repair connector if damaged. Perform VERIFICATION TEST VER-2. If connector is okay, turn ignition on. Place DRB-II in voltmeter mode. Probe PTU relay connector terminal "A" (Dark Blue wire).

2) If voltage is 10 volts or less, repair open Dark Blue wire between relay and splice. Perform VERIFICATION TEST VER-2. If voltage is more than 10 volts, turn ignition off. Disconnect and inspect engine controller connector. Repair connector if damaged. Perform VERIFICATION TEST VER-2. If connector is okay, place DRB-II in ohmmeter mode.

3) Probe engine controller connector terminal No. 54 (Orange/Black wire). If resistance is less than 10 ohms, repair Orange/Black wire for a short to ground. Perform VERIFICATION TEST VER-2. If resistance is 10 ohms or more, check resistance of Orange/Black wire between engine controller and PTU relay connectors using a DVOM.

4) If resistance is 10 ohms or more, repair open Orange/Black wire. Perform VERIFICATION TEST VER-2. If resistance is less than 10 ohms, reconnect PTU relay. Turn ignition on. Place DRB-II in voltmeter mode. Probe terminal No. 54 (Orange/Black wire) in engine controller connector. If voltage is more than 10 volts, replace engine controller. Perform VERIFICATION TEST VER-2. If voltage is 10 volts or less, replace PTU relay. Perform VERIFICATION TEST VER-2.

TEST DR-30B

CODE 37, TORQUE CONVERTER LOCK-UP CIRCUIT

NOTE: For connector terminal identification, see CONNECTOR IDENTIFICATION at beginning of article. For wiring diagram, see appropriate WIRING DIAGRAMS article in ENGINE PERFORMANCE.

1) Turn ignition off. Disconnect and inspect PTU/overdrive solenoid connector. Repair connector if damaged. Perform VERIFICATION TEST VER-2. If connector is okay, turn ignition on. Place DRB-II in voltmeter mode. Probe Dark Blue wire in transmission solenoid connector. If voltage is 10 volts or less, repair open Dark Blue wire. Perform VERIFICATION TEST VER-2.

2) If voltage is more than 10 volts, turn ignition off. Disconnect and inspect engine controller connector. Repair connector if damaged. Perform VERIFICATION TEST VER-2. If connector is okay, place DRB-II in ohmmeter mode.

3) Probe engine controller connector terminal No. 54 (Orange/Black wire). If resistance is 10 ohms or more, repair open Orange/Black wire. Perform VERIFICATION TEST VER-2. If resistance is less than 10 ohms, reconnect solenoid connector.

4) Turn ignition on. Place DRB-II in voltmeter mode. Probe terminal No. 54 (Orange/Black wire) in engine controller connector. If voltage is more than 10 volts, replace engine controller. Perform VERIFICATION TEST VER-2. If voltage is 10 volts or less, replace PTU solenoid. Perform VERIFICATION TEST VER-2.

TEST DR-31A

CODE 45, OVERDRIVE SOLENOID CIRCUIT (WITHOUT LOCK-UP)

NOTE: For connector terminal identification, see CONNECTOR IDENTIFICATION at beginning of article. For wiring diagram, see appropriate WIRING DIAGRAMS article in ENGINE PERFORMANCE.

1) Turn ignition off. Disconnect and inspect overdrive solenoid connector. Repair connector if damaged. Perform VERIFICATION TEST VER-2. If connector is okay, turn ignition on. Place DRB-II in voltmeter mode. Probe Dark Blue wire in transmission overdrive solenoid connector. If voltage is 10 volts or less, repair open Dark Blue wire. Perform VERIFICATION TEST VER-2.

TEST DR-31A (Cont.)

2) If voltage is more than 10 volts, turn ignition off. Disconnect and inspect engine controller connector. Repair connector if damaged. Perform VERIFICATION TEST VER-2. If connector is okay, place DRB-II in ohmmeter mode. Probe engine controller connector terminal No. 55 (Brown wire on Pickup and Ramcharger, Orange/White wire on Van).

3) If resistance is less than 10 ohms, repair Brown wire (Orange/White wire on Van) for a short to ground. Perform VERIFICATION TEST VER-2. If resistance is 10 ohms or more, check resistance of Brown wire (Orange/White wire on Van) between engine controller and solenoid connectors using a DVOM. If resistance is 10 ohms or more, repair open Brown wire (Orange/White wire on Van). Perform VERIFICATION TEST VER-2.

4) If resistance is less than 10 ohms, reconnect solenoid connector. Turn ignition on. Place DRB-II in voltmeter mode. Probe terminal No. 55 (Brown wire on Pickup and Ramcharger, Orange/White wire on Van) in engine controller connector. If voltage is more than 10 volts, replace engine controller. Perform VERIFICATION TEST VER-2. If voltage is 10 volts or less, replace overdrive solenoid. Perform VERIFICATION TEST VER-2.

TEST DR-32A

CODE 45, OVERDRIVE SOLENOID CIRCUIT (WITH LOCK-UP)

NOTE: For connector terminal identification, see CONNECTOR IDENTIFICATION at beginning of article. For wiring diagram, see appropriate WIRING DIAGRAMS article in ENGINE PERFORMANCE.

1) Turn ignition off. Disconnect and inspect PTU/overdrive solenoid connector. Repair connector if damaged. Perform VERIFICATION TEST VER-2. If connector is okay, turn ignition on. Place DRB-II in voltmeter mode. Probe Dark Blue wire in transmission solenoid connector. If voltage is 10 volts or less, repair open Dark Blue wire. Perform VERIFICATION TEST VER-2.

2) If voltage is more than 10 volts, turn ignition off. Disconnect and inspect engine controller connector. Repair connector if damaged. Perform VERIFICATION TEST VER-2. If connector is okay, place DRB-II in ohmmeter mode. Probe engine controller connector terminal No. 55 (Orange/Light Green wire on Dakota, Brown wire on Pickup and Ramcharger, Orange/White wire on Van).

3) If resistance is less than 10 ohms, repair Brown wire (Orange/Light Green wire on Dakota, Orange/White wire on Van) for a short to ground. Perform VERIFICATION TEST VER-2. If resistance is 10 ohms or more, check resistance of Brown wire (Orange/Light Green wire on Dakota, Orange/White wire on Van) between engine controller and solenoid connectors using a DVOM. If resistance is 10 ohms or more, repair open Brown wire (Orange/Light Green wire on Dakota, Orange/White wire on Van). Perform VERIFICATION TEST VER-2.

4) If resistance is less than 10 ohms, reconnect solenoid connector. Turn ignition on. Place DRB-II in voltmeter mode. Probe terminal No. 55 (Orange/Light Green wire on Dakota, Brown wire on Pickup and Ramcharger, Orange/White wire on Van) in engine controller connector. If voltage is more than 10 volts, replace engine controller. Perform VERIFICATION TEST VER-2. If voltage is 10 volts or less, replace PTU/overdrive solenoid. Perform VERIFICATION TEST VER-2.

TEST DR-33A

CODE 42, NO AUTO SHUTDOWN (ASD) RELAY VOLTAGE SENSE AT ENGINE CONTROLLER

NOTE: For connector terminal identification, see CONNECTOR IDENTIFICATION at beginning of article. For wiring diagram, see appropriate WIRING DIAGRAMS article in ENGINE PERFORMANCE.

1) Turn ignition off. Disconnect Auto Shutdown (ASD) relay. Disconnect and inspect engine controller 60-pin connector. Repair connector terminals if damaged. Perform VERIFICATION TEST VER-2. If connector terminals are okay, go to next step.

2) Using a DVOM, check resistance at Dark Green/Orange wire between engine controller connector terminal No. 57 and ASD relay terminal "D". If resistance is less than 10 ohms, replace engine controller. Perform VERIFICATION TEST VER-2. If resistance is 10 ohms or more, repair open Dark Green/Orange wire. Perform VERIFICATION TEST VER-2.

CHRY
1-116

1992 ENGINE PERFORMANCE
Self-Diagnostic Tests – 3.9L & 5.2L (Cont.)

TEST DR-34A

CODE 62, CONTROLLER FAILURE EMR MILES NOT STORED OR
CODE 63, CONTROLLER FAILURE EEPROM WRITE DENIED

NOTE: Aftermarket scan testers may not be able to reset EMR mileage. DRB-II may be required for this test.

1) Turn ignition on. Perform EMR Memory Check Test using DRB-II. If DRB-II displays WRITE FAILURE, replace engine controller. Perform VERIFICATION TEST VER-2. If DRB-II displays WRITE REFUSED, go to step 3). If DRB-II displays EMR MILEAGE INVALID, update mileage and retest EMR mileage. Perform VERIFICATION TEST VER-2.

2) If DRB-II does not display WRITE FAILURE, WRITE REFUSED or EMR MILEAGE INVALID, compare EMR mileage stored with instrument panel odometer. If mileage is the same, retest EMR memory. Perform VERIFICATION TEST VER-2. If mileage is not the same, update mileage and retest EMR mileage. Perform VERIFICATION TEST VER-2.

3) Engine controller was busy. Perform EMR Memory Check Test using DRB-II. Retest EMR memory 2 or more times if necessary. If WRITE REFUSED fault returns, replace engine controller. Perform VERIFICATION TEST VER-2. If WRITE REFUSED fault does not return, test is complete. Perform VERIFICATION TEST VER-2.

TEST DR-35A

INTERMITTENT TEST FOR SENSOR VOLTAGE

1) If intermittent fault is SLOW CHANGE OR NO CHANGE IN MAP, perform TEST DR-35B. If intermittent fault was not SLOW CHANGE OR NO CHANGE IN MAP, start engine. Using DRB-II, read suspect sensor circuit voltage. While monitoring voltage, wiggle sensor connector and wiring. If engine stalls or voltage becomes erratic, repair wiring or connector problem at sensor. Perform VERIFICATION TEST VER-2.

2) If engine does not stall or voltage does not become erratic, wiggle sections of wiring harness between sensor and engine controller. Wait 5 seconds before moving to next section of harness. If engine stalls or sensor voltage is erratic when wiring harness is wiggled, repair harness where wiggling caused erratic reading. Perform VERIFICATION TEST VER-2. If engine does not stall or voltage is not erratic, test is complete. Perform VERIFICATION TEST VER-2.

TEST DR-35B

INTERMITTENT TEST FOR SLOW CHANGE OR NO CHANGE IN MAP

NOTE: For connector terminal identification, see CONNECTOR IDENTIFICATION at beginning of article. For wiring diagram, see appropriate WIRING DIAGRAMS article in ENGINE PERFORMANCE.

1) Start engine. Using DRB-II, set engine speed to 1400 RPM and read MAP sensor voltage. Wiggle MAP sensor wiring harness while monitoring voltage. If engine stalls or if MAP sensor voltage is erratic, repair wiring or connector defect at MAP sensor. Perform VERIFICATION TEST VER-2.

2) If engine does not stall or MAP sensor voltage is not erratic, turn ignition off. Install a vacuum "T" into MAP sensor vacuum hose. Connect a vacuum gauge. Start engine. Snap throttle open and closed while watching vacuum gauge.

3) If vacuum drops rapidly to zero in. Hg, test is complete. Perform VERIFICATION TEST VER-2. If vacuum does not drop rapidly to zero in. Hg, remove MAP sensor and check for vacuum restrictions. Repair restrictions as necessary. Perform VERIFICATION TEST VER-2. If no restrictions exist, replace MAP sensor. Perform VERIFICATION TEST VER-2.

TEST DR-36A

INTERMITTENT TEST FOR AUTOMATIC IDLE SPEED (AIS) MOTOR

1) Turn ignition on. Using DRB-II, erase faults and actuate AIS motor. Read secondary indicators while actuating AIS motor. Wiggle AIS motor connector. If fault indicator returns, repair wiring or connector problem at AIS motor. Perform VERIFICATION TEST VER-2.

2) If fault indicator does not return, wiggle sections of wiring harness between AIS motor and engine controller. Wait 5 seconds before moving to next section of wiring harness.

3) If fault indicator returns, repair wiring harness where wiggling caused indicator to return. Perform VERIFICATION TEST VER-2. If fault indicator does not return, test is complete. Perform VERIFICATION TEST VER-2.

TEST DR-37A

INTERMITTENT INJECTOR CONTROL FAULT

NOTE: For connector terminal identification, see CONNECTOR IDENTIFICATION at beginning of article. For wiring diagram, see appropriate WIRING DIAGRAMS article in ENGINE PERFORMANCE.

1) Using DRB-II, erase fault codes. Start engine. Using DRB-II, select SECONDARY INDICATORS. Wiggle wiring harness from suspect fuel injector to engine controller. If fault indicator returns, repair harness where wiggling caused indicator to return. Perform VERIFICATION TEST VER-2.

2) If fault indicator does not return, visually inspect related harness connectors. Look for broken, bent, pushed-out or corroded terminals. Visually inspect related harnesses. Look for chafed, pierced or partially broken wire. Repair wiring and/or connectors as necessary. Test is complete. Perform VERIFICATION TEST VER-2.

TEST DR-38A

INTERMITTENT TEST FOR RELAYS & SOLENOIDS

1) Turn ignition on. Using DRB-II, erase faults and actuate suspect solenoid or relay. Read secondary indicators while actuating solenoid or relay. Wiggle connector at intermittent solenoid or relay.

2) If fault indicator returns, repair wiring or defective connector at solenoid or relay. Perform VERIFICATION TEST VER-2. If fault indicator does not return, wiggle sections of wiring harness between solenoid or relay and engine controller. Wait 5 seconds before moving to next section of wiring harness.

3) If fault indicator returns, repair wiring harness where wiggling caused fault indicator to return. Perform VERIFICATION TEST VER-2. If fault indicator does not return, test is complete. Perform VERIFICATION TEST VER-2.

TEST DR-39A

INTERMITTENT AUTO SHUTDOWN SENSE CIRCUIT FAULT

1) Turn ignition on. Using DRB-II, erase fault codes and select ACTUATE ASD RELAY. Using DRB-II, select SECONDARY INDICATORS. Observe secondary indicators while wiggling wires and connectors of ASD circuit. If ASD fault returns, repair harness or connector where wiggling caused fault indicator to return. Perform VERIFICATION TEST VER-2.

2) If ASD fault does not return, visually inspect related wire harness connectors. Look for broken, bent, pushed-out or corroded terminals. Visually inspect related harnesses. Look for chafed, pierced or partially broken wire. Repair wiring and/or connectors as necessary. Test is complete. Perform VERIFICATION TEST VER-2.

1992 ENGINE PERFORMANCE
Self-Diagnostic Tests – 3.9L & 5.2L (Cont.)

CHRY
1-117

TEST NF-1A

NO FAULT CODE TEST MENU

Check MITCHELL® TECHNICAL SERVICE BULLETINS (TSBs) for any pertinent information. If a TSB exists, perform corrective action. If TSB does not exist or if driveability problem still exists after performing TSB, check suspect system and perform indicated test. See NO FAULT CODE TEST MENU table. If system causing driveability problem is not known, perform TEST NF-2A through TEST NF-12A in sequence until problem is found.

NO FAULT CODE TEST MENU

Application	Test
Checking Automatic Idle Speed Motor	NF-7A
Checking Coolant Sensor & TPS Calibrations	NF-4A
Checking EGR Operation	NF-10A
Checking Engine Controller Grounds	NF-9A
Checking Engine Mechanical	NF-12A
Checking Engine Vacuum	NF-11A
Checking Fuel Pressure	NF-3A
Checking MAP Sensor Calibration	NF-5A
Checking Oxygen (O_2) Sensor Switching	NF-6A
Checking Park/Neutral Switch (A/T Only)	NF-8A
Checking Secondary Ignition & Timing	NF-2A

TEST NF-2A

CHECKING SECONDARY IGNITION & TIMING

1) Turn engine off. Connect engine analyzer to engine. Start engine and let it idle. Set scope to read display or parade pattern. Follow equipment manufacturer's procedure for pattern analysis.

2) If secondary ignition pattern is not okay, repair indicated component in secondary ignition system. Perform VERIFICATION TEST VER-2. If secondary ignition pattern is okay, disconnect any spark plug wire. Observe secondary kilovolt line.

3) If open circuit secondary voltage is less than 25 kilovolts, replace ignition coil. Perform VERIFICATION TEST VER-2. If open circuit secondary voltage is at least 25 kilovolts, reinstall spark plug wire. Ensure engine temperature is more than 180°F (82°C) before proceeding. Disconnect coolant sensor connector. Coolant sensor fault should set and check engine light should turn on.

4) Connect timing light and check ignition timing. If timing is not within 2 degrees of specification, replace engine controller. Perform VERIFICATION TEST VER-2. Reconnect coolant sensor connector. Using DRB-II, read spark advance. Increase engine speed to 2000 RPM. If spark advance does not change with increase in RPM, replace engine controller. Perform VERIFICATION TEST VER-2. If spark advance changes with increase in RPM, test is complete.

TEST NF-3A

CHECKING FUEL PRESSURE

WARNING: High fuel pressure may be present in fuel lines. Open fuel system with caution. See FUEL PRESSURE RELEASE procedure in SELF-DIAGNOSTICS INTRODUCTION – GASOLINE article.

1) Relieve fuel pressure. Connect fuel pressure gauge to fuel rail fitting. Turn ignition on. Using DRB-II, actuate ASD fuel system test. If fuel pressure is 35-43 psi, test is complete. If fuel pressure is not 35-43 psi, record fuel pressure reading. If pressure is more than 43 psi, perform TEST NF-3B.

2) If fuel pressure is less than 35 psi, stop ASD fuel system actuation test. Turn ignition off. Inspect fuel lines for kinks or restrictions. Repair fuel lines as necessary. Perform VERIFICATION TEST VER-2. If lines are not kinked or restricted, release fuel pressure. Remove fuel pressure gauge from fuel rail.

3) Install fuel pressure gauge between fuel tank and fuel filter. Turn ignition on. Actuate ASD fuel system test using DRB-II. If fuel pressure is at least 5 psi more than previously recorded pressure, replace fuel filter. Perform VERIFICATION TEST VER-2.

TEST NF-3A (Cont.)

CAUTION: DO NOT allow fuel pressure to exceed 50 psi when squeezing fuel return hose.

4) If fuel pressure did not increase at least 5 psi more than previous reading, gently squeeze fuel return hose while observing fuel pressure gauge, ensuring fuel pressure does not exceed 50 psi. If fuel pressure increases, replace fuel pressure regulator. Perform VERIFICATION TEST VER-2. If fuel pressure does not increase, replace fuel pump and sock assembly. Perform VERIFICATION TEST VER-2.

TEST NF-3B

CHECKING FUEL PRESSURE

WARNING: High fuel pressure may be present in fuel lines. Open fuel system with caution. See FUEL PRESSURE RELEASE procedure in SELF-DIAGNOSTICS INTRODUCTION – GASOLINE article.

1) Using DRB-II, stop fuel system actuation test. Relieve fuel pressure. Ensure fuel tank is at least 1/2 full before performing following test. Remove fuel return line from fuel pump at fuel tank. Connect Fuel Pressure Test Adapter (6541) to fuel return line. Place other end of adapter hose into an approved 2-gallon gasoline can.

2) Turn ignition on. Using DRB-II, actuate ASD fuel system test. Observe fuel pressure gauge. If fuel pressure is 35-43 psi, repair fuel return line for a restriction at fuel tank. Perform VERIFICATION TEST VER-2. If fuel pressure is not 35-43 psi, stop ASD fuel system actuation test. Relieve fuel pressure. Reconnect fuel return line to fuel tank. Disconnect fuel return line from fuel rail.

3) Attach Fuel Pressure Test Adapter (6541) to fuel return line nipple at fuel rail. Place other end of adapter hose into an approved 2-gallon gasoline can. Turn ignition on. Actuate ASD fuel system test. Observe fuel pressure gauge.

4) If fuel pressure is 35-43 psi, repair restricted fuel return line to fuel tank. Perform VERIFICATION TEST VER-2. If fuel pressure is not 35-43 psi, inspect fuel pressure damper line for restrictions. If restriction exists, replace fuel pressure damper line. Perform VERIFICATION TEST VER-2. If no restriction exists, replace fuel pressure regulator. Perform VERIFICATION TEST VER-2.

TEST NF-4A

CHECKING COOLANT SENSOR & THROTTLE POSITION SENSOR (TPS) CALIBRATIONS

1) Start engine. Allow engine to reach normal operating temperature. Using DRB-II, read coolant temperature sensor value. If temperature is not 180-220°F (82-104°C), replace coolant temperature sensor. Perform VERIFICATION TEST VER-2. If temperature is 180-220°F (82-104°C), turn engine off.

2) Turn ignition on. Using DRB-II, read TPS voltage with throttle fully closed and against throttle stop. If voltage is 1.5 volts or more with throttle closed, replace TPS. Perform VERIFICATION TEST VER-2. If voltage is less than 1.5 volts with throttle fully closed, monitor TPS voltage while slowly opening throttle to wide open position.

3) If voltage change is not a smooth transition, replace TPS. Perform VERIFICATION TEST VER-2. If voltage change is a smooth transition, check if maximum voltage is at least 3.4 volts with throttle wide open. If maximum voltage is not at least 3.4 volts with throttle wide open, replace TPS. Perform VERIFICATION TEST VER-2. If maximum voltage is at least 3.4 volts, go to next step.

4) Start engine, and let it idle. Using DRB-II, read minimum throttle voltage. If voltage is not 0-1.5 volts, replace TPS. Perform VERIFICATION TEST VER-2. If voltage is 0-1.5 volts, test is complete.

CHRY
1-118

1992 ENGINE PERFORMANCE
Self-Diagnostic Tests – 3.9L & 5.2L (Cont.)

TEST NF-5A

CHECKING MANIFOLD ABSOLUTE PRESSURE (MAP) SENSOR CALIBRATION

1) Turn engine off. Install vacuum "T" in MAP sensor vacuum hose. Install vacuum gauge. Start engine, and let it idle. Using DRB-II, read vacuum gauge. If DRB-II vacuum reading is within one in. Hg of vacuum gauge reading, test is complete. If DRB-II vacuum reading is not within one in. Hg of vacuum gauge reading, go to next step.

2) Turn engine off. Remove MAP sensor from throttle body. Leave MAP sensor connected to wiring harness. Disconnect vacuum gauge from MAP sensor vacuum hose. Connect an auxiliary vacuum pump to MAP sensor. Apply 5 in. Hg vacuum to MAP sensor. Read and record MAP sensor voltage. Increase vacuum to 20 in. Hg. Read and record MAP sensor voltage. Subtract voltage recorded at 20 in. Hg vacuum from voltage recorded at 5 in. Hg vacuum.

3) If difference is 2.3-2.9 volts, repair restriction in vacuum hose to MAP sensor. Perform VERIFICATION TEST VER-2. If voltage difference is not 2.3-2.9 volts, replace MAP sensor. Perform VERIFICATION TEST VER-2.

TEST NF-6A

CHECKING OXYGEN (O₂) SENSOR SWITCHING

1) Allow engine to reach normal operating temperature. Using DRB-II, read O₂ sensor state. If O₂ sensor state is switching, system is functioning okay. Test is complete. If O₂ sensor state is not switching, check if O₂ sensor is locked on lean. If O₂ sensor is locked on lean, perform TEST NF-6B. If O₂ sensor is not locked on lean, go to next step.

2) Turn engine off. Allow vehicle to hot soak for 5 minutes. Remove and inspect spark plugs. Keep spark plugs in order for reinstallation. If any spark plugs are wet or fuel fouled, replace leaking injectors at corresponding cylinders. Perform VERIFICATION TEST VER-3.

3) If spark plugs are not wet or fuel fouled, inspect air filter and inlet ducts for restrictions. If any restrictions exist, replace air filter or repair air inlet system as necessary. Perform VERIFICATION TEST VER-3. If there are no restrictions, perform TEST NF-12A.

TEST NF-6B

CHECKING OXYGEN (O₂) SENSOR (LOCKED LEAN)

NOTE: For connector terminal identification, see CONNECTOR IDENTIFICATION at beginning of article. For wiring diagram, see appropriate WIRING DIAGRAMS article in ENGINE PERFORMANCE.

1) Allow engine to idle. Inspect engine for vacuum leaks. Repair vacuum leaks as necessary. Perform VERIFICATION TEST VER-2. If there are no vacuum leaks, read O₂ sensor signal voltage using DRB-II. If voltage is .1 volt or more, go to step **3)**. If voltage is less than .1 volt, turn ignition off. Disconnect O₂ sensor and engine controller connectors.

2) Put DRB-II in ohmmeter mode. Probe engine controller connector terminal No. 41 (Black/Dark Green wire). If resistance is less than 10 ohms, repair short to ground in Black/Dark Green wire. Perform VERIFICATION TEST VER-2. If resistance is 10 ohms or more, replace O₂ sensor. Perform VERIFICATION TEST VER-2.

3) If O₂ sensor voltage is .1 volt or more in step **1)**, turn engine off. Replace O₂ sensor. Perform VERIFICATION TEST VER-2. Turn ignition on. Using DRB-II, reset adaptive fuel memory. Start engine, and allow it to reach normal operating temperature.

4) Using DRB-II, read O₂ sensor state. If O₂ sensor state is switching, repair is complete. Perform VERIFICATION TEST VER-2. If O₂ sensor state is not switching, perform TEST NF-12A.

TEST NF-7A

CHECKING AUTOMATIC IDLE SPEED (AIS) MOTOR OPERATION

NOTE: For connector terminal identification, see CONNECTOR IDENTIFICATION at beginning of article. For wiring diagram, see appropriate WIRING DIAGRAMS article in ENGINE PERFORMANCE.

1) Using DRB-II, set engine speed to 1100 RPM. If engine speed can be set to 1050-1150 RPM, test is complete. If engine speed cannot be set to 1050-1150 RPM, return engine to normal idle speed. Disconnect and inspect AIS motor connector. Repair connector if damaged. Perform VERIFICATION TEST VER-2.

2) If connector is okay, place DRB-II in voltmeter mode. Open and close throttle while probing AIS motor connector Gray/Red wire. If voltage stays less than one volt, perform TEST NF-7B. If voltage does not stay less than one volt, go to next step.

3) Open and close throttle while probing AIS motor connector Yellow/Black wire. If voltage stays less than one volt, perform TEST NF-7B. If voltage does not stay less than one volt, go to next step.

4) Open and close throttle while probing AIS motor connector Brown/White wire. If voltage stays less than one volt, perform TEST NF-7B. If voltage does not stay less than one volt, go to next step.

5) Open and close throttle while probing AIS motor connector Violet/Black wire. If voltage stays less than one volt, perform TEST NF-7B. If voltage does not stay less than one volt, inspect engine for vacuum leaks. Repair as necessary. Perform VERIFICATION TEST VER-2. If no vacuum leaks exist, replace AIS motor. Perform VERIFICATION TEST VER-2.

TEST NF-7B

CHECKING AUTOMATIC IDLE SPEED (AIS) MOTOR OPERATION

NOTE: For connector terminal identification, see CONNECTOR IDENTIFICATION at beginning of article. For wiring diagram, see appropriate WIRING DIAGRAMS article in ENGINE PERFORMANCE.

1) Turn engine off. Disconnect and inspect engine controller connector. Repair connector if damaged. Perform VERIFICATION TEST VER-2.

2) If connector is okay, check continuity of Gray/Red wire between AIS motor connector and engine controller connector terminal No. 39, Black/Yellow wire between AIS motor connector and engine controller connector terminal No. 60, Brown/White wire between AIS motor connector and engine controller connector terminal No. 40, and Violet/Black wire between AIS motor connector and engine controller connector terminal No. 59.

3) If resistance is less than 10 ohms for each circuit, replace engine controller. Perform VERIFICATION TEST VER-2. If resistance is more than 10 ohms for any circuit, repair open in that circuit. Perform VERIFICATION TEST VER-2.

TEST NF-8A

CHECKING PARK/NEUTRAL SWITCH INPUT (A/T ONLY)

NOTE: For connector terminal identification, see CONNECTOR IDENTIFICATION at beginning of article. For wiring diagram, see appropriate WIRING DIAGRAMS article in ENGINE PERFORMANCE.

1) Using DRB-II, read park/neutral switch input state. While watching DRB-II display, move gear selector in and out of Park and Reverse positions. If display shows P/N and D/R, system is functioning correctly. If display does not show P/N and D/R, go to next step.

2) Turn ignition off. Place gear selector in Park position. Disconnect engine controller connector. Disconnect starter relay connector. Place DRB-II in ohmmeter mode. Probe terminal No. 30 (Brown/Yellow wire) in engine controller connector. Watch DRB-II display while moving gear selector in and out of Park and Reverse positions.

1992 ENGINE PERFORMANCE
Self-Diagnostic Tests – 3.9L & 5.2L (Cont.)

CHRY
1-119

TEST NF-8A (Cont.)

3) If display switches from less than 5 ohms to more than 5 ohms, replace engine controller. Perform VERIFICATION TEST VER-2. If display always stays less than 5 ohms, repair short to ground in Brown/Yellow wire. Perform VERIFICATION TEST VER-2. If display does not always stay less than 5 ohms, disconnect park/neutral switch connector.

4) Using a DVOM, check resistance of Brown/Yellow wire between park/neutral switch connector and engine controller connector terminal No. 30. If resistance is less than 10 ohms, replace park/neutral switch. Perform VERIFICATION TEST VER-2. If resistance is 10 ohms or more, repair open Brown/Yellow wire. Perform VERIFICATION TEST VER-2.

TEST NF-9A

CHECKING ENGINE CONTROLLER GROUND & POWER CIRCUITS

NOTE: For connector terminal identification, see CONNECTOR IDENTIFICATION at beginning of article. For wiring diagram, see appropriate WIRING DIAGRAMS article in ENGINE PERFORMANCE.

1) Turn ignition off. Disconnect and inspect engine controller connector. Repair connector if damaged. Perform VERIFICATION TEST VER-2. If connector terminals are okay, place DRB-II in ohmmeter mode. Probe engine controller connector terminal No. 5 (Black/White wire). If resistance is one ohm or more, repair open in Black/White wire. Perform VERIFICATION TEST VER-2.

2) If resistance is less than one ohm, go to next step. Probe engine controller connector terminal No. 11 (Black/Tan wire). If resistance is one ohm or more, repair open in Black/Tan wire. Perform VERIFICATION TEST VER-2. If resistance is less than one ohm, go to next step.

3) Probe engine controller connector terminal No. 12 (Black/Tan wire). If resistance is one ohm or more, repair open in Black/Tan wire. Perform VERIFICATION TEST VER-2. If resistance is less than one ohm, place DRB-II in voltmeter mode. Turn ignition on.

4) Probe engine controller connector terminal No. 9 (Dark Blue wire). If voltage is 10 volts or less, repair open Dark Blue wire. Perform VERIFICATION TEST VER-2. If voltage is more than 10 volts, reconnect SBEC connector. Test is complete.

TEST NF-10A

CHECKING EGR VALVE OPERATION

1) Disconnect vacuum hose from EGR solenoid. Connect vacuum gauge to disconnected vacuum hose. Start engine. If vacuum is more than 10 in. Hg at idle, go to step **3)**. If vacuum is 10 in. Hg or less at idle, turn engine off.

2) Disconnect EGR vacuum supply hose at intake manifold. Connect a vacuum gauge to intake manifold nipple. Start engine. Read vacuum gauge at idle. If vacuum is more than 10 in. Hg at idle, repair restriction or leak in vacuum line to EGR solenoid. Perform VERIFICATION TEST VER-2. If vacuum is 10 in. Hg or less at idle, repair plugged vacuum nipple at throttle body. Perform VERIFICATION TEST VER-2.

3) Stop engine. Disconnect vacuum gauge. Reconnect vacuum hose to EGR solenoid. Disconnect vacuum hose from EGR valve. Connect vacuum gauge to disconnected hose. Start engine. Momentarily snap throttle open while watching gauge. If vacuum is not more than 5 in. Hg at any time, replace EGR valve assembly. Perform VERIFICATION TEST VER-2. If vacuum is more than 5 in. Hg at any time, go to next step.

4) Turn ignition off. Disconnect vacuum gauge. Reconnect vacuum hose to EGR solenoid. Disconnect vacuum hose from EGR valve. Connect vacuum gauge to hose. Start engine. Momentarily snap throttle open while watching gauge. If vacuum is not more than 5 in. Hg at any time, replace EGR valve assembly. Perform VERIFICATION TEST VER-2.

5) If vacuum is more than 5 in. Hg at any time, turn ignition off. Disconnect vacuum hose to EGR valve backpressure signal tube. Adjust a shop air hose at 20-30 psi. Connect shop air to nipple on base of EGR valve. Listen for a tone change while opening and closing throttle.

6) If tone changes, replace EGR valve assembly. Perform VERIFICATION TEST VER-2. If tone does not change, remove vacuum gauge. Cap open nipple at EGR valve base. Connect hand vacuum pump to EGR valve. Start engine. Listen for engine RPM change while slowly applying vacuum to EGR valve. If engine RPM does not change, go to step **8)**.

TEST NF-10A (Cont.)

7) If engine RPM changes, turn ignition off. Apply 10 in. Hg vacuum and hold for 30 seconds. If vacuum holds for 30 seconds, test is complete. If vacuum does not hold for 30 seconds, replace EGR valve assembly. Perform VERIFICATION TEST VER-2.

8) Remove EGR valve assembly. Check for plugged manifold passages. Clear manifold passages as necessary. Perform VERIFICATION TEST VER-2. If passages are not plugged, replace EGR valve assembly. Perform VERIFICATION TEST VER-2.

TEST NF-11A

CHECKING ENGINE VACUUM

Connect a vacuum gauge to engine. Start engine, and let it idle. Normal vacuum reading will vary depending on altitude. Observe vacuum gauge at idle. If vacuum gauge reading is not steady 13-22 in. Hg, perform TEST NF-12A. If vacuum gauge reading is steady and within specification, test is complete. Perform VERIFICATION PROCEDURE VER-2.

TEST NF-12A

PERFORMING NO FAULT CODE MECHANICAL TEST

At this point in diagnostic test procedure, all engine control systems have been determined to be operating as designed and not causing a driveability problem. Following additional items should be checked as possible causes:

NOTE: If coming to this test from O$_2$ sensor test and rich or lean condition is not corrected after checking the following items, replace engine controller.

- Check if any MITCHELL® TECHNICAL SERVICE BULLETINS (TSBs) apply to vehicle.
- Check engine vacuum. It must be at least 13 in. Hg in Neutral.
- Check valve timing.
- Check engine compression.
- Check for exhaust system restriction.
- Ensure PCV system is functioning properly.
- Check camshaft and crankshaft sprockets.
- Check torque converter stall speed.
- Check power brake booster for internal vacuum leak.
- Check for fuel contamination.
- Ensure injector control wire is connected to correct fuel injector and injector is not plugged or restricted.

TEST VER-1

VERIFICATION TEST VER-1

1) Inspect vehicle to ensure all engine components are connected. Reassemble and reconnect components as necessary. Attempt to start engine. If engine does not start, return to TEST NS-1A.

2) If engine starts, engine controller was changed and vehicle is equipped with factory theft alarm, start vehicle at least 20 times so alarm system may be activated when desired. Write vehicle mileage from its odometer to memory location within replacement engine controller. This will enable new engine controller to operate Emission Maintenance Reminder (EMR) light properly. On all models, no-start condition is corrected and repair is now complete.

3) If engine starts and engine controller has not been changed, connect DRB-II to engine diagnostic connector, and erase faults. No-start condition has been corrected and fault messages have been erased. Repair is now complete. If repaired fault has reset, check if any MITCHELL® TECHNICAL SERVICE BULLETINS (TSBs) apply to vehicle. Return to TEST DR-1A if necessary. If another fault exists, return to TEST DR-1A and follow path specified by other fault.

CHRY
1-120

1992 ENGINE PERFORMANCE
Self-Diagnostic Tests – 3.9L & 5.2L (Cont.)

TEST VER-2

VERIFICATION TEST VER-2

If VERIFICATION TEST VER-3 was performed previously, perform VERIFICATION TEST VER-3 again. Inspect vehicle to ensure all engine components are connected. Reassemble and reconnect components as necessary. If another fault was read previously and not corrected, return to TEST DR-1A and follow path specified by other fault. If engine controller was replaced, perform following:

1) If vehicle is equipped with factory theft alarm, start vehicle at least 20 times so alarm system may be activated when desired. Write vehicle mileage from its odometer to memory location within replacement engine controller. This will enable new engine controller to operate Emission Maintenance Reminder (EMR) light properly.

2) Connect DRB-II to engine diagnostic connector, and erase faults. Start engine and allow it to reach normal operating temperature. Increase engine speed to 2000 RPM for at least 10 seconds. Allow engine to idle. On A/T models, apply brake and cycle transmission through all gear ranges. Place gear selector in Park position. If vehicle is equipped with A/C, turn on A/C. Set blower to low speed.

3) On all models, turn engine off. Start engine. Allow engine to idle for at least 2 minutes. Turn engine off. Using DRB-II, read fault messages. If repaired fault resets, repair is not complete. Check all pertinent MITCHELL® TECHNICAL SERVICE BULLETINS (TSBs), and return to TEST DR-1A if necessary. If another fault exists, return to TEST DR-1A and follow path specified by other fault. If no other faults exist, repair is now complete.

TEST VER-3

VERIFICATION TEST VER-3

Inspect vehicle to ensure all engine components are connected. Reassemble and reconnect components as necessary. If another fault was read previously and not corrected, return to TEST DR-1A and follow path specified by other fault. If engine controller has been replaced, perform following:

- If vehicle is equipped with factory theft alarm, start vehicle at least 20 times so alarm system may be activated when desired.
- Write vehicle odometer mileage to memory location within replacement engine controller. This will enable new engine controller to operate Emission Maintenance Reminder (EMR) light properly.
- Connect DRB-II to engine diagnostic connector, and erase faults. Disconnect DRB-II.

To ensure no other fault remains, perform following:

1) If vehicle is equipped with A/C, turn A/C on. Set blower to low speed. On all models, drive vehicle for at least 5 minutes and attain a speed of at least 40 MPH. Ensure transmission shifts through all gears. Upon completion of road test, turn engine off. Restart engine, and let it idle for at least 2 minutes.

2) Turn engine off. Connect DRB-II to engine diagnostic connector. Read all fault messages. If repaired fault has reset, repair is not complete. Check all pertinent MITCHELL® TECHNICAL SERVICE BULLETINS (TSBs), and return to TEST DR-1A if necessary. If another fault exists, return to TEST DR-1A and follow path specified by other fault. If no other faults exist, repair is now complete.

WARNING: *When battery is disconnected, vehicle computer and energy systems may lose memory data. Driveability problems may exist until computer systems have completed a relearn cycle. See COMPUTER RELEARN PROCEDURES article in GENERAL INFORMATION before disconnecting battery.*

SELF-DIAGNOSTIC DIRECTORY

SELF-DIAGNOSTIC DIRECTORY

CONNECTOR IDENTIFICATION

CONNECTOR IDENTIFICATION DIRECTORY

Connector	See Fig.
Air Switching Solenoid	1
Automatic Idle Speed (AIS) Motor	2
Coolant Temperature Sensor	3
Distance Sensor	4
Distributor Pick-Up	5
Engine Controller	6
Engine Diagnostic	7
EGR Solenoid	8
Fuel Injector	9
Manifold Absolute Pressure (MAP) Sensor	10
Oil Pressure Switch	11
Oxygen (O₂) Sensor	12
Part Throttle Unlock (PTU) Solenoid	13
Purge Solenoid	14
Relays	
A/C Clutch, Auto Shutdown &	
Part Throttle Unlock (PTU) Relays	15
Throttle Body Temperature Sensor	16
Throttle Position Sensor (TPS)	17

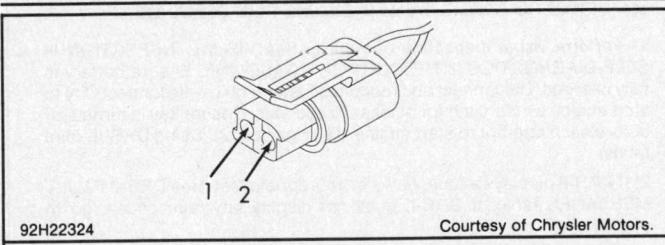

92H22324   Courtesy of Chrysler Motors.

Fig. 1: Identifying Air Switching Solenoid Connector Terminals

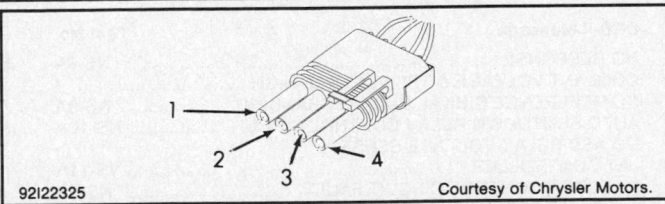

92I22325   Courtesy of Chrysler Motors.

Fig. 2: Identifying Automatic Idle Speed (AIS) Motor Connector Terminals

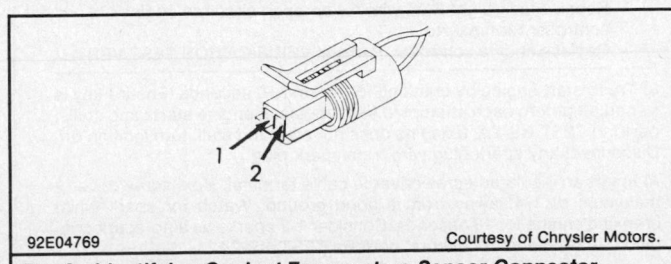

92E04769   Courtesy of Chrysler Motors.

Fig. 3: Identifying Coolant Temperature Sensor Connector Terminals

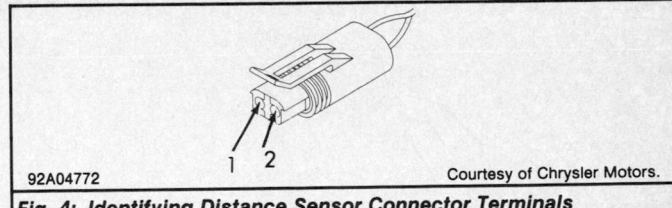

92A04772   Courtesy of Chrysler Motors.

Fig. 4: Identifying Distance Sensor Connector Terminals

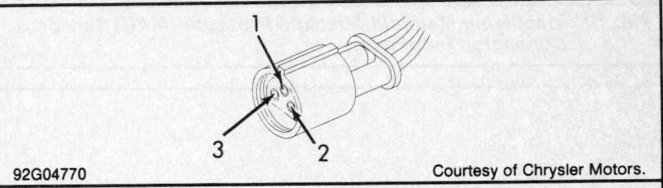

92G04770   Courtesy of Chrysler Motors.

Fig. 5: Identifying Distributor Pick-Up Connector Terminals

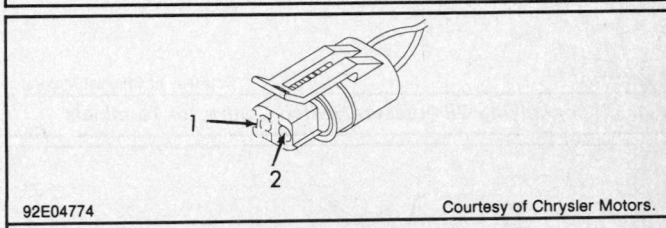

92E04774   Courtesy of Chrysler Motors.

Fig. 6: Identifying EGR Solenoid Connector Terminals

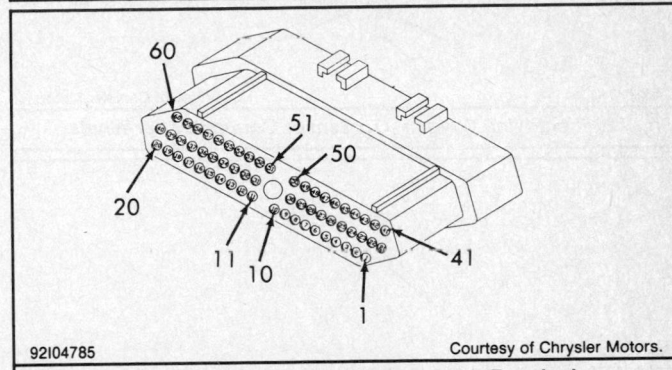

92I04785   Courtesy of Chrysler Motors.

Fig. 7: Identifying Engine Controller Connector Terminals

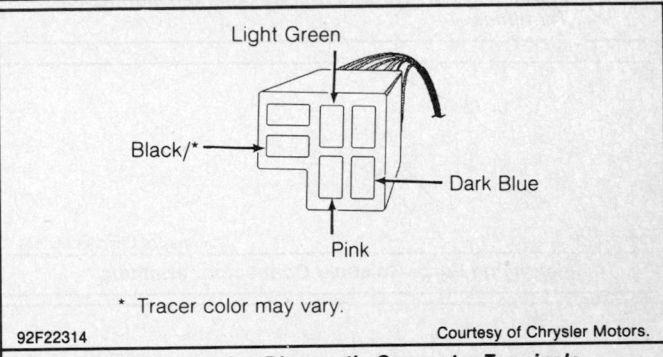

Light Green

Black/*

Dark Blue

Pink

* Tracer color may vary.

92F22314   Courtesy of Chrysler Motors.

Fig. 8: Identifying Engine Diagnostic Connector Terminals

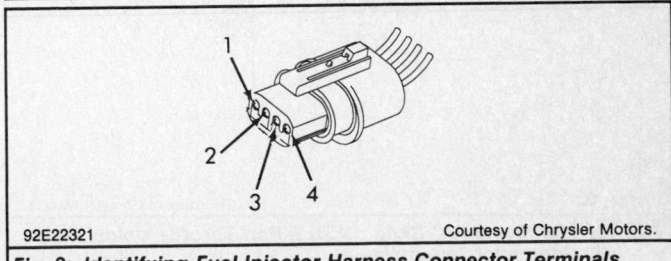

92E22321   Courtesy of Chrysler Motors.

Fig. 9: Identifying Fuel Injector Harness Connector Terminals

CHRY
1-122

1992 ENGINE PERFORMANCE
Self-Diagnostic Tests – 5.9L Gasoline (Cont.)

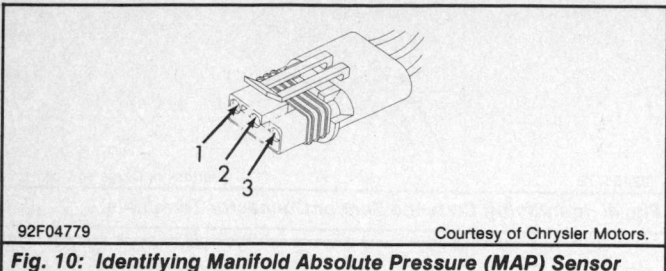

92F04779   Courtesy of Chrysler Motors.

Fig. 10: Identifying Manifold Absolute Pressure (MAP) Sensor Connector Terminals

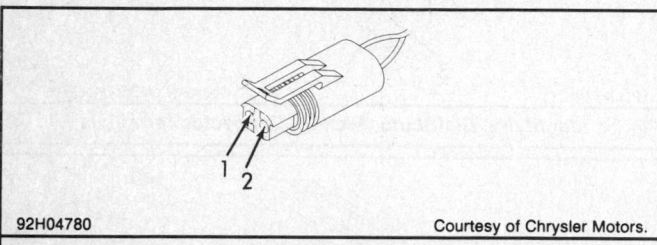

92H04780   Courtesy of Chrysler Motors.

Fig. 11: Identifying Oil Pressure Switch Connector Terminals

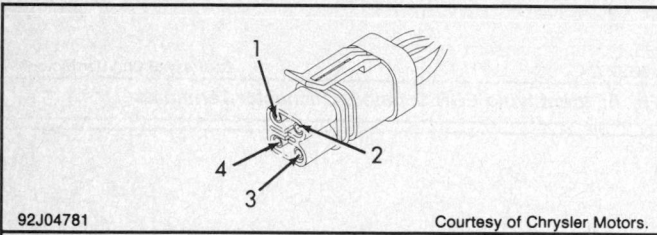

92J04781   Courtesy of Chrysler Motors.

Fig. 12: Identifying Oxygen (O₂) Sensor Connector Terminals

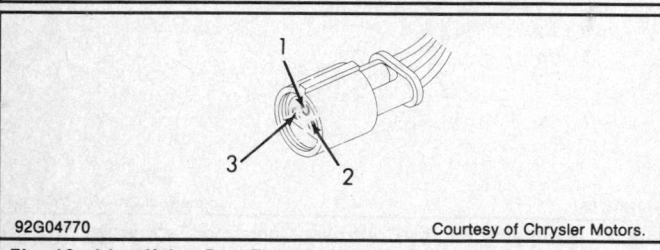

92G04770   Courtesy of Chrysler Motors.

Fig. 13: Identifying Part Throttle Unlock Solenoid Connector Terminals

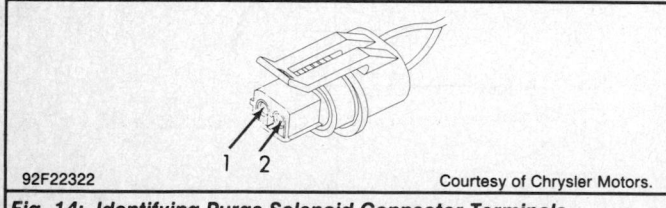

92F22322   Courtesy of Chrysler Motors.

Fig. 14: Identifying Purge Solenoid Connector Terminals

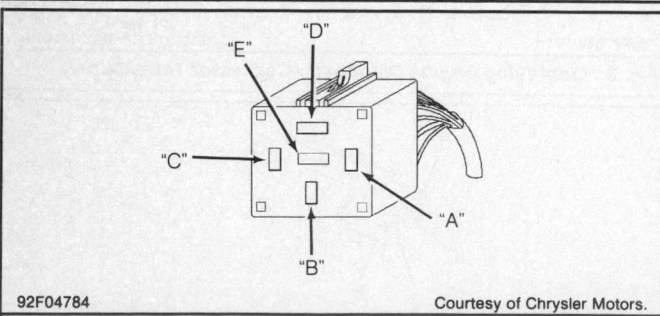

92F04784   Courtesy of Chrysler Motors.

Fig. 15: Identifying A/C Clutch, ASD & Part Throttle Unlock Relay Connector Terminals

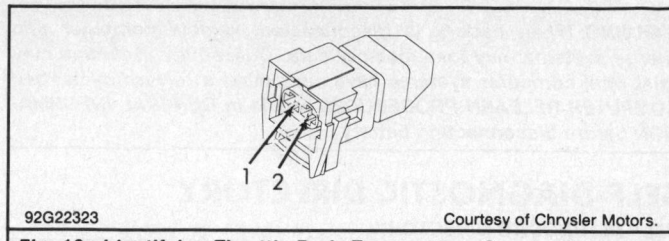

92G22323   Courtesy of Chrysler Motors.

Fig. 16: Identifying Throttle Body Temperature Sensor Connector Terminals

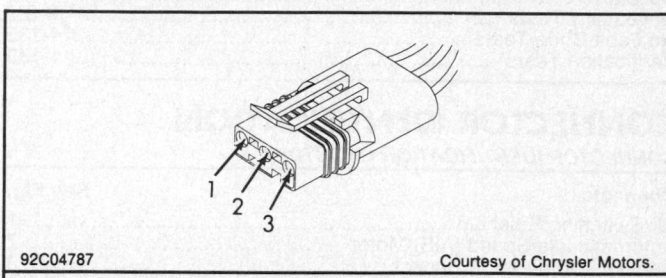

92C04787   Courtesy of Chrysler Motors.

Fig. 17: Identifying Throttle Position Sensor Connector Terminals

SELF-DIAGNOSTIC TESTS

NOTE: In the following self-diagnostic tests, illustrations are courtesy of Chrysler Motors.

TEST NS-1A
QUALIFYING NO START CONDITION

NOTE: For connector terminal identification, see CONNECTOR IDENTIFICATION at beginning of article. For wiring diagram, see appropriate WIRING DIAGRAMS article in ENGINE PERFORMANCE.

1) Perform visual inspection of vehicle. See VISUAL INSPECTION in SELF-DIAGNOSTICS INTRODUCTION – GASOLINE. Ensure battery is fully charged. Disconnect and reconnect battery quick-disconnect. Try to start engine by cranking for at least 10 seconds. Ensure key is turned off before each attempt to start engine. Turn ignition on. Using DRB-II, read faults.

2) If DRB-II displays a fault, perform appropriate test. See DRB-II FAULT MESSAGES table. If DRB-II does not display any fault codes, go to step 3).

DRB-II FAULT MESSAGES

DRB-II Message	Test No.
NO RESPONSE	NS-8A
COOLANT VOLTAGE & TPS VOLTAGE HIGH	¹
NO REFERENCE SIGNAL DURING CRANKING	NS-9A
AUTO SHUTDOWN RELAY CONTROL CIRCUIT	NS-10A
NO ASD RELAY VOLTAGE SENSE AT CONTROLLER	NS-11A
INJECTOR CONTROL CIRCUIT FAULT	NS-5A
AUTOMATIC IDLE SPEED MOTOR CIRCUITS	NS-6A
INTERNAL CONTROLLER FAILURE or CONTROLLER FAILURE SPI COMMUNICATIONS	²

¹ – Repair Black/Light Blue wire for an open circuit to engine controller terminal No. 4.
² – Replace engine controller. Perform VERIFICATION TEST VER-1.

3) Try to start engine by cranking for at least 10 seconds. Ensure key is turned off before each attempt to start engine. If engine starts and stalls, perform TEST NS-2A. If engine does not start and stall, turn ignition off. Disconnect any spark plug wire from spark plug.

4) Insert an insulated screwdriver in cable terminal. Hold screwdriver a maximum of 1/4" away from a good ground. Watch for spark while cranking engine for 10 seconds. Consider 1-2 sparks as a no-spark condition. If a good spark occurs, perform TEST NS-2A.

1992 ENGINE PERFORMANCE
Self-Diagnostic Tests – 5.9L Gasoline (Cont.)

CHRY
1-123

TEST NS-1A (Cont.)

5) If a good spark does not occur, reconnect spark plug cable. Disconnect coil secondary wire from distributor. Hold coil wire a maximum of 1/4" away from a good ground. Watch for spark while cranking engine for 10 seconds. If there is good spark, repair secondary ignition system (distributor cap, rotor or spark plug wires). Perform VERIFICATION TEST VER-1.

6) If a good spark does not occur, turn ignition off. Remove coil secondary wire. Using a DVOM, measure coil secondary wire resistance. If resistance is greater than 15 k/ohms, replace coil secondary wire. Perform VERIFICATION TEST VER-1. If resistance is 15 k/ohms or less, remove distributor cap. Watch for rotor to turn while cranking engine. If rotor does not turn, repair distributor drive system. Perform VERIFICATION TEST VER-1.

7) If rotor turned, reinstall distributor cap. Reconnect coil secondary wire. Disconnect Dark Green/Orange wire (Gray wire on Van) at ignition coil positive (+) terminal. Using DRB-II, actuate ASD fuel system. With fuel system actuating, put DRB-II in voltmeter mode. Probe Dark Green/Orange wire (Gray wire on Van) to ignition coil. If voltage is 10 volts or less, stop actuation test. Perform TEST NS-11A.

8) If voltage is more than 10 volts, stop actuation test. Disconnect Gray wire (Black/Gray wire on Van) from ignition coil negative (–) terminal. Probe Gray wire (Black/Gray wire on Van) at ignition coil. If voltage is 10 volts or less, go to step **10)**. If voltage is more than 10 volts, turn ignition off.

9) Check ignition coil primary resistance using a DVOM. If resistance is not 1.0-1.9 ohms at 70°F (21°C), replace ignition coil. Perform VERIFICATION TEST VER-1. If resistance is not 1.0-1.9 ohms at 70°F (21°C), check ignition coil secondary resistance. If resistance is not 9.4-19.0 k/ohms, replace ignition coil. Perform VERIFICATION TEST VER-1. If resistance is 9.4-19.0 k/ohms, reconnect ignition coil.

10) Turn ignition off. Disconnect and inspect engine controller connector. Repair connector if damaged. Perform VERIFICATION TEST VER-1. Place DRB-II in ohmmeter mode. Probe Gray wire (Black/Gray wire on Van) in engine controller connector terminal No. 19.

11) If resistance is less than 10 ohms, repair Gray wire (Black/Gray wire on Van) for a short to ground. Perform VERIFICATION TEST VER-1. If resistance is 10 ohms or more, check resistance of Gray wire (Black/Gray wire on Van) between coil connector and engine controller connector terminal No. 19 using a DVOM.

12) If resistance is more than 10 ohms, repair open Gray wire (Black/Gray wire on Van). Perform VERIFICATION TEST VER-1. If resistance is 10 ohms or less, replace engine controller. Perform VERIFICATION TEST VER-1.

TEST NS-2A

INSPECTING FUEL SYSTEM

NOTE: For connector terminal identification, see CONNECTOR IDENTIFICATION at beginning of article. For wiring diagram, see appropriate WIRING DIAGRAMS article in ENGINE PERFORMANCE.

1) Ensure throttle is at idle position. Using DRB-II, read TPS sensor voltage. If voltage is more than 1.5 volts, replace throttle position sensor. Perform VERIFICATION TEST VER-1. If voltage is 1.5 volts or less, disconnect fuel injector connector.

2) Place DRB-II in voltmeter mode. Using DRB-II, actuate ASD fuel system. Probe Dark Green/Orange wires (Dark Green/Black wires on Van). If voltage is 10 volts or less on both wires, repair Dark Green/Orange wire (Dark Green/Black wire on Van) between injector connector and harness splice. Perform VERIFICATION TEST VER-1. If voltage is more than 10 volts on both wires, turn ignition off.

WARNING: Fuel system must be opened and may be under high pressure.

3) Install fuel pressure gauge in fuel supply line, near throttle body. Ensure fuel tank is at least 1/4 full. Reconnect injector connector. Turn ignition on. Using DRB-II, actuate ASD fuel system. Listen for fuel pump operation at fuel tank. If fuel pump operation cannot be heard, go to TEST NS-7A.

TEST NS-2A (Cont.)

4) If fuel pump operation can be heard, read fuel pressure gauge. If fuel pressure is more than 16.5 psi, perform TEST NS-4B. If fuel pressure is less than 12.5 psi, perform TEST NS-4A. If fuel pressure is 12.5-16.5 psi, look for fuel flow at fuel injector area. If fuel flow exists, perform TEST NS-4C. If vehicle starts and stalls repeatedly, perform TEST NS-12A. If vehicle does not start and stall repeatedly, stop actuator test. Perform TEST NS-3A.

TEST NS-3A

INSPECTING MECHANICAL SYSTEM

NOTE: For connector terminal identification, see CONNECTOR IDENTIFICATION at beginning of article. For wiring diagram, see appropriate WIRING DIAGRAMS article in ENGINE PERFORMANCE.

1) Turn ignition off. Check spark plug wires for proper firing order. If firing order is not correct, reconnect wires in correct firing order. Perform VERIFICATION TEST VER-1. If firing order is correct, remove all spark plugs and inspect tips for fuel. Clean spark plugs as necessary. Reinstall spark plugs. Connect timing light to engine.

NOTE: DO NOT crank engine for more than 15 seconds. Starter may be damaged if engine is cranked for an extended period of time.

2) Check ignition timing while cranking engine. If ignition timing is 0-16 degrees BTDC, go to step **4)**. If timing is not 0-16 degrees BTDC, set base timing to 10 degrees BTDC. Try to start engine. If engine does not start, repair problem with valve timing, compression or other mechanical problem. Perform VERIFICATION TEST VER-1.

3) If engine starts, check distributor drive system and engine compression. If distributor drive system and engine compression are okay, repair is complete. Perform VERIFICATION TEST VER-1. If distributor drive system and engine compression are not okay, repair as necessary. Perform VERIFICATION TEST VER-1.

4) Turn ignition off. Disconnect and inspect engine controller connector. Repair connector as necessary. Perform VERIFICATION TEST VER-1. If connector is okay, disconnect and inspect MAP sensor connector. Repair connector as necessary. Perform VERIFICATION TEST VER-1. If connector is okay, check resistance of Violet/White wire between MAP sensor and engine controller connectors using a DVOM.

5) If resistance is 10 ohms or more, repair open Violet/White wire. Perform VERIFICATION TEST VER-1. If resistance is less than 10 ohms, check valve timing and engine compression. If valve timing and engine compression are okay, replace MAP sensor. Perform VERIFICATION TEST VER-1. If valve timing and engine compression are not okay, repair engine as necessary. Perform VERIFICATION TEST VER-1.

TEST NS-4A

CORRECTING FUEL DELIVERY

WARNING: Fuel system must be opened and may be under high pressure.

1) Record fuel pressure gauge reading. Turn ignition off. Remove fuel pressure gauge and reconnect fuel line. Install fuel pressure gauge in fuel line between fuel tank and fuel filter. Turn ignition on. Using DRB-II, actuate ASD fuel system. Record fuel pressure gauge reading.

2) Compare 2 fuel pressure gauge readings. If fuel pressure is not at least 10 psi more, go to step **4)**. If fuel pressure is at least 10 psi more, inspect fuel lines between fuel filter and fuel rail for a restriction. Repair restriction as necessary. Perform VERIFICATION TEST VER-1. If fuel lines are okay, replace fuel filter. Perform VERIFICATION TEST VER-1.

CAUTION: DO NOT allow fuel pressure to exceed 70 psi.

3) Watch fuel pressure gauge while gently squeezing fuel return hose. If fuel pressure is greater than 12.5 psi, replace fuel pressure regulator. Perform VERIFICATION TEST VER-1. If fuel pressure is 12.5 psi or less, replace fuel pump and filter sock assembly. Perform VERIFICATION TEST VER-1.

4) Inspect fuel lines between fuel filter and throttle body for restriction. If lines are restricted, repair lines as necessary. Perform VERIFICATION TEST VER-1. If lines are not restricted, replace fuel filter. Perform VERIFICATION TEST VER-1.

CHRY
1-124

1992 ENGINE PERFORMANCE
Self-Diagnostic Tests – 5.9L Gasoline (Cont.)

TEST NS-4B

CORRECTING FUEL DELIVERY

WARNING: Fuel system must be opened and may be under high pressure.

1) Ensure fuel tank is at least 1/4 full. Relieve fuel system pressure. Remove fuel return hose from throttle body. Connect 6' long piece of fuel hose to throttle body. Place other end of hose into an approved container (with a minimum 2 gallon capacity). Turn ignition on. Using DRB-II, actuate ASD fuel system.

2) Read fuel pressure gauge. If fuel pressure is 16.5 psi or more, replace fuel pressure regulator. Perform VERIFICATION TEST VER-1. If fuel pressure is less than 16.5 psi, turn ignition off. Reconnect fuel return hose. Disconnect fuel return hose from fuel tank. Connect 6' long piece of fuel hose to fuel return hose. Place other end of hose into an approved container (with a minimum 2 gallon capacity). Turn ignition on.

3) Using DRB-II, actuate ASD fuel system. Read fuel pressure gauge. If fuel pressure is less than 16.5 psi, replace fuel return assembly in fuel tank. Perform VERIFICATION TEST VER-1. If fuel pressure is 16.5 psi or more, repair restricted fuel return line between fuel rail and fuel tank. Perform VERIFICATION TEST VER-1.

TEST NS-4C

CORRECTING FUEL DELIVERY

WARNING: Fuel system must be opened and may be under high pressure.

Relieve fuel system pressure. Remove leaking fuel injector from throttle body. Inspect injector seals for damage. If seals are damaged, replace seals as necessary. Perform VERIFICATION TEST VER-1. If seals are not damaged, replace fuel injector. Perform VERIFICATION TEST VER-1.

TEST NS-5A

REPAIRING FAULT
"FUEL INJECTOR CONTROL CIRCUIT"

NOTE: For connector terminal identification, see CONNECTOR IDENTIFICATION at beginning of article. For wiring diagram, see appropriate WIRING DIAGRAMS article in ENGINE PERFORMANCE.

1) Turn ignition off. Disconnect injector harness 4-pin connector at throttle body. Turn ignition on. Using DRB-II, actuate ASD fuel system. Place DRB-II in voltmeter mode. Probe Dark Green/Orange wire (Dark Green/Black on Van) in injector harness connector terminal No. 1.

2) If voltage is 10 volts or less, repair open Dark Green/Orange wire (Dark Green/Black wire on Van). Perform VERIFICATION TEST VER-1. If voltage is more than 10 volts, probe Dark Green/Orange wire (Dark Green/Black on Van) in injector harness connector terminal No. 4. If voltage is 10 volts or less, repair open Dark Green/Orange wire (Dark Green/Black wire on Van). Perform VERIFICATION TEST VER-1.

3) If voltage is more than 10 volts, turn ignition off. Disconnect engine controller connector. Place DRB-II in ohmmeter mode. Probe engine controller connector terminal No. 16 (White/Dark Blue wire). If resistance is less than 10 ohms, repair short to ground in White/Dark Blue wire. Perform VERIFICATION TEST VER-1.

4) If resistance is 10 ohms or more, probe engine controller connector terminal No. 15 (Tan wire). If resistance is less than 10 ohms, repair short to ground in Tan wire. Perform VERIFICATION TEST VER-1. If resistance is 10 ohms or more, check resistance of White/Dark Blue wire between injector harness connector and engine controller connector terminal No. 16 using a DVOM.

5) If resistance is 10 ohms or more, repair open White/Dark Blue wire. Perform VERIFICATION TEST VER-1. If resistance is less than 10 ohms, check resistance of Tan wire between injector harness connector and engine controller connector terminal No. 15. If resistance is 10 ohms or more, repair open Tan wire. Perform VERIFICATION TEST VER-1.

TEST NS-5A (Cont.)

WARNING: Fuel system must be opened and may be under high pressure.

6) If resistance is less than 10 ohms, relieve fuel system pressure. Disconnect injector caps. Inspect injector caps and terminals. Repair caps and terminals if damaged. Perform VERIFICATION TEST VER-1. If caps and terminals are okay, check resistance of injector harness on throttle body using a DVOM.

7) If resistance of each wire is 10 ohms or less, replace engine controller. Perform VERIFICATION TEST VER-1. If resistance of any wire is more than 10 ohms, replace caps and wiring harness assembly. Perform VERIFICATION TEST VER-1.

TEST NS-6A

REPAIRING FAULT
"AUTOMATIC IDLE SPEED MOTOR CIRCUITS"

NOTE: For connector terminal identification, see CONNECTOR IDENTIFICATION at beginning of article. For wiring diagram, see appropriate WIRING DIAGRAMS article in ENGINE PERFORMANCE.

1) Turn ignition off. Disconnect Automatic Idle Speed (AIS) motor connector. Turn ignition on. Using DRB-II, actuate AIS motor. Check for voltage between Yellow/Black wire (Gray/Red wire on Van) and Brown/White wire in AIS motor harness connector using a DVOM. If voltage pulsates, replace AIS motor. Perform VERIFICATION TEST VER-1.

2) If voltage does not pulsate, turn ignition off. Disconnect engine controller 60-pin connector. Place DRB-II in ohmmeter mode. Probe engine controller connector terminal No. 40 (Brown/White wire). If resistance is less than 10 ohms, repair Brown/White wire for a short to ground. Perform VERIFICATION TEST VER-1. If resistance is 10 ohms or more, probe engine controller connector terminal No. 60 (Yellow/Black wire on Pickup and Ramcharger, Gray/Red wire on Van).

3) If resistance is less than 10 ohms, repair Yellow/Black wire (Gray/Red wire on Van) for a short to ground. Perform VERIFICATION TEST VER-1. If resistance is 10 ohms or more, check resistance of Brown/White wire between AIS motor connector and engine controller connector terminal No. 40. If resistance is 10 ohms or more, repair open Brown/White wire. Perform VERIFICATION TEST VER-1.

4) If resistance is less than 10 ohms, check resistance of Yellow/Black wire (Gray/Red wire on Van) between AIS motor connector and engine controller connector terminal No. 60 using a DVOM. If resistance is less than 10 ohms, replace engine controller. Perform VERIFICATION TEST VER-1. If resistance is 10 ohms or more, repair open Yellow/Black wire (Gray/Red wire on Van). Perform VERIFICATION TEST VER-1.

TEST NS-7A

INSPECTING FUEL PUMP

NOTE: For connector terminal identification, see CONNECTOR IDENTIFICATION at beginning of article. For wiring diagram, see appropriate WIRING DIAGRAMS article in ENGINE PERFORMANCE.

1) Using DRB-II, actuate ASD fuel system. Touch ASD relay. If ASD relay does not click, perform TEST NS-7B. If ASD relay clicks, stop actuation test. Disconnect ASD relay. Turn ignition on. Place DRB-II in voltmeter mode. Probe Red wire in ASD relay connector terminal "B".

2) If voltage is 10 volts or less, repair Red wire for an open to splice. Perform VERIFICATION TEST VER-1. If voltage is greater than 10 volts, disconnect fuel pump harness connector. Reconnect ASD relay. Using DRB-II, actuate ASD fuel system. Place DRB-II in voltmeter mode. Probe Dark Green/Black wire (Dark Green/Orange wire on Pickup and Ramcharger) in fuel pump connector.

3) If voltage is more than 10 volts, go to step 4). If voltage is 10 volts or less, turn ignition off. Disconnect ASD relay. Check resistance of Dark Green/Black wire (Dark Green/Orange wire on Pickup and Ramcharger) between fuel pump and fuel pump relay connectors using a DVOM. If

1992 ENGINE PERFORMANCE
Self-Diagnostic Tests – 5.9L Gasoline (Cont.)

CHRY
1-125

TEST NS-7A (Cont.)

resistance is less than 10 ohms, replace ASD relay. Perform VERIFICATION TEST VER-1. If resistance is 10 ohms or more, repair open Dark Green/Black wire (Dark Green/Orange wire on Pickup and Ramcharger). Perform VERIFICATION TEST VER-1.

4) If voltage is 10 volts or less in step 3), put DRB-II in ohmmeter mode. Probe Black wire in fuel pump connector. If resistance is less than 5 ohms, replace fuel pump. Perform VERIFICATION TEST VER-1. If resistance is 5 ohms or more, repair Black wire for an open to ground. Perform VERIFICATION TEST VER-1.

TEST NS-7B

INSPECTING FUEL PUMP

NOTE: For connector terminal identification, see CONNECTOR IDENTIFICATION at beginning of article. For wiring diagram, see appropriate WIRING DIAGRAMS article in ENGINE PERFORMANCE.

Turn ignition off. Disconnect ASD relay. Turn ignition on. Probe Dark Blue wire. If voltage is 10 volts or less, repair Dark Blue wire for an open to ignition switch. Perform VERIFICATION TEST VER-1. If voltage is more than 10 volts, measure resistance across ASD relay terminals using a DVOM. If resistance is 100 ohms or more, replace ASD relay. Perform VERIFICATION TEST VER-1. If resistance is less than 100 ohms, repair open Dark Blue/Yellow wire between fuel pump relay and engine controller connectors. Perform VERIFICATION TEST VER-1.

TEST NS-8A

REPAIRING NO RESPONSE CONDITION

NOTE: For connector terminal identification, see CONNECTOR IDENTIFICATION at beginning of article. For wiring diagram, see appropriate WIRING DIAGRAMS article in ENGINE PERFORMANCE.

1) Turn ignition off. Disconnect Throttle Position Sensor (TPS) and inspect connector. Repair connector as necessary. Perform VERIFICATION TEST VER-1. If connector is okay, turn ignition on. Place DRB-II in voltmeter mode. Probe Violet/White wire in TPS harness connector. If voltage is more than 6 volts, repair open in Black/White wire (terminal No. 5) and Black/Tan wire (terminals No. 11 and 12) of engine controller connector. Perform VERIFICATION TEST VER-1.

2) If voltage is less than 4.4 volts, go to next step. If voltage is 4.4-6 volts, reconnect TPS connector. Disconnect and inspect MAP sensor connector. Repair connector as necessary. Probe Violet/White wire at MAP sensor connector. If voltage is more than 4.4 volts, see NO RESPONSE MESSAGE under DRB-II PROBLEMS & ERROR MESSAGES in SELF-DIAGNOSTICS INTRODUCTION – GASOLINE. If voltage is 4.4 volts or less, replace TPS. Perform VERIFICATION TEST VER-1.

3) Turn ignition off. Disconnect and inspect MAP sensor connector. Repair connector as necessary. Probe Violet/White wire at TPS connector. If voltage is more than 4.4 volts, replace MAP sensor. Perform VERIFICATION TEST VER-1. If voltage is 4.4 volts or less, turn ignition off. Disconnect and inspect engine controller connector. Repair connector as necessary.

4) Place DRB-II in ohmmeter mode. Probe engine controller connector terminal No. 6 (Violet/White wire). If resistance is less than 10 ohms, repair short to ground in Violet/White wire. Perform VERIFICATION TEST VER-1.

5) If resistance is 10 ohms or more, turn ignition on. Place DRB-II in voltmeter mode. Probe engine controller connector terminal No. 9 (Dark Blue wire). If voltage is 10 volts or less, repair open in Dark Blue wire between engine controller connector terminal No. 9 and ignition switch. Perform VERIFICATION TEST VER-1.

6) If voltage is more than 10 volts, probe engine controller connector terminal No. 3 (Red wire). If voltage is more than 10 volts, replace engine controller. Perform VERIFICATION TEST VER-1. If voltage is 10 volts or less, perform TEST NS-8B.

TEST NS-8B

REPAIRING NO RESPONSE CONDITION

NOTE: For connector terminal identification, see CONNECTOR IDENTIFICATION at beginning of article. For wiring diagram, see appropriate WIRING DIAGRAMS article in ENGINE PERFORMANCE.

1) Gain access to fusible link in left rear corner of engine compartment. Inspect fusible link between battery and engine controller connector terminal No. 3. If fusible link is open, perform TEST NS-8C.

2) If fusible link is okay, disconnect and inspect battery quick-disconnect connector. Repair connector if damaged. Perform VERIFICATION TEST VER-1. If connector is okay, repair open in Red wire between engine controller connector terminal No. 3 and battery. Perform VERIFICATION TEST VER-1.

TEST NS-8C

REPAIRING NO RESPONSE CONDITION

NOTE: For connector terminal identification, see CONNECTOR IDENTIFICATION at beginning of article. For wiring diagram, see appropriate WIRING DIAGRAMS article in ENGINE PERFORMANCE.

1) Disconnect and inspect ASD relay connector. Repair connector if damaged. Replace fusible link. Perform VERIFICATION TEST VER-1. If connector is okay, place DRB-II in ohmmeter mode. Probe engine controller connector terminal No. 3 (Red wire).

2) If resistance is less than 10 ohms, repair Red wire for a short to ground. Replace fusible link. Perform VERIFICATION TEST VER-1. If resistance is 10 ohms or more, disconnect and inspect O2 sensor connector. Repair connector as necessary. Replace fusible link. Perform VERIFICATION TEST VER-1. If connector is okay, probe Dark Green/Orange wire in ASD relay connector. If resistance is 10 ohms or more, replace O2 sensor and fusible link. Perform VERIFICATION TEST VER-1.

3) If resistance is less than 10 ohms, disconnect wire to positive (+) ignition coil terminal. Probe Dark Green/Orange wire in ASD relay connector. If resistance is 10 ohms or more, replace ignition coil and fusible link. Perform VERIFICATION TEST VER-1. If resistance is less than 10 ohms, disconnect and inspect fuel pump connector. Repair connector if damaged. Replace fusible link. Perform VERIFICATION TEST VER-1.

4) If connector is okay, probe Dark Green/Orange wire in ASD relay connector. If resistance is 10 ohms or more, replace fuel pump and fusible link. Perform VERIFICATION TEST VER-1. If resistance is less than 10 ohms, disconnect and inspect injector 4-pin connector at throttle body. Repair connector if damaged. Perform VERIFICATION TEST VER-1.

5) Probe Dark Green/Orange wire in ASD relay connector. If resistance is less than 10 ohms, repair short to ground in Dark Green/Orange wire. Replace fusible link. Perform VERIFICATION TEST VER-1. If resistance is 10 ohms or more, replace fuel injector caps and harness. Replace fusible link. Perform VERIFICATION TEST VER-1.

TEST NS-9A

REPAIRING FAULT
"NO REFERENCE SIGNAL DURING CRANKING"

NOTE: For connector terminal identification, see CONNECTOR IDENTIFICATION at beginning of article. For wiring diagram, see appropriate WIRING DIAGRAMS article in ENGINE PERFORMANCE.

1) Ensure distributor turns as engine is cranked. If rotor does not turn as engine is cranked, repair engine as necessary. Perform VERIFICATION TEST VER-1. If rotor turns, turn ignition off. Disconnect distributor connector. Place DRB-II in ohmmeter mode. Probe Black/Light Blue wire in distributor harness connector.

2) If resistance is 10 ohms or more, repair open Black/Light Blue wire. Perform VERIFICATION TEST VER-1. If resistance is less than 10 ohms, turn ignition on. Place DRB-II in voltmeter mode. Probe Orange wire in distributor harness connector. If voltage is 7.5 volts or less, go to step 4). If voltage is more than 7.5 volts, probe Gray/Black wire in distributor harness connector. If voltage is 4.5 volts or less, perform TEST NS-9B.

CHRY
1-126

1992 ENGINE PERFORMANCE
Self-Diagnostic Tests – 5.9L Gasoline (Cont.)

TEST NS-9A (Cont.)

3) If voltage is more than 4.5 volts, reconnect distributor connector. While cranking engine, read RPM using DRB-II. If DRB-II displays less than 10 RPM, replace distributor pick-up. If DRB-II displays 10 RPM or more, replace engine controller.

4) Turn ignition off. Disconnect and inspect engine controller 60-pin connector. Place DRB-II in ohmmeter mode. Probe engine controller connector terminal No. 7 (Orange wire). If resistance is less than 10 ohms, repair Orange wire for a short to ground. Perform VERIFICATION TEST VER-1.

5) If resistance is 10 ohms or more, check continuity of Orange wire between engine controller and distributor connectors. If resistance is less than 10 ohms, replace engine controller. Perform VERIFICATION TEST VER-1. If resistance is 10 ohms or more, repair open Orange wire. Perform VERIFICATION TEST VER-1.

TEST NS-9B

REPAIRING FAULT
"NO REFERENCE SIGNAL DURING CRANKING"

NOTE: For connector terminal identification, see CONNECTOR IDENTIFICATION at beginning of article. For wiring diagram, see appropriate WIRING DIAGRAMS article in ENGINE PERFORMANCE.

1) Turn ignition off. Disconnect and inspect engine controller connector. Repair connector if damaged. Perform VERIFICATION TEST VER-1. If connector is okay, place DRB-II in ohmmeter mode. Probe engine controller connector terminal No. 24 (Gray/Black wire). If resistance is less than 10 ohms, repair Gray/Black wire for a short to ground. Perform VERIFICATION TEST VER-1.

2) If resistance is 10 ohms or more, check resistance of Gray/Black wire between distributor connector and engine controller connector terminal No. 24 using a DVOM. If resistance is less than 10 ohms, replace engine controller. Perform VERIFICATION TEST VER-1. If resistance is 10 ohms or more, repair open Gray/Black wire. Perform VERIFICATION TEST VER-1.

TEST NS-10A

REPAIRING FAULT "AUTO SHUTDOWN (ASD) RELAY CONTROL CIRCUIT"

NOTE: For connector terminal identification, see CONNECTOR IDENTIFICATION at beginning of article. For wiring diagram, see appropriate WIRING DIAGRAMS article in ENGINE PERFORMANCE.

1) Turn ignition on. Disconnect ASD relay connector. Place DRB-II in voltmeter mode. Probe Dark Blue wire in ASD relay connector. If voltage is 10 volts or less, repair open in Dark Blue wire from ignition switch. Perform VERIFICATION TEST VER-1. If voltage is more than 10 volts, go to next step.

2) Check resistance between terminals "A" and "C" at ASD relay using a DVOM. If resistance is 100 ohms or more, replace ASD relay. Perform VERIFICATION TEST VER-1. If resistance is less than 100 ohms, turn ignition off.

3) Disconnect engine controller 60-pin connector. Check resistance of Dark Blue/Yellow wire between engine controller connector terminal No. 51 and ASD relay connector terminal "C".

4) If resistance is less than 10 ohms, replace engine controller. Perform VERIFICATION TEST VER-1. If resistance is 10 ohms or more, repair open in Dark Blue/Yellow wire. Perform VERIFICATION TEST VER-1.

TEST NS-11A

REPAIRING FAULT "NO ASD RELAY VOLTAGE SENSE AT CONTROLLER"

NOTE: For connector terminal identification, see CONNECTOR IDENTIFICATION at beginning of article. For wiring diagram, see appropriate WIRING DIAGRAMS article in ENGINE PERFORMANCE.

1) Disconnect ASD relay. Turn ignition on. Place DRB-II in voltmeter mode. Probe ASD relay connector terminal "B" (Red wire). If voltage is 10 volts or less, repair open Red wire to splice. Perform VERIFICATION TEST VER-1. If voltage is more than 10 volts, probe Dark Blue wire in ASD relay connector. If voltage is 10 volts or less, repair open Dark Blue wire between ASD relay connector and ignition switch. Perform VERIFICATION TEST VER-1.

NOTE: In the following step, Dark Green/Orange wire at ASD relay changes to Dark Green/Black wire at splice (to engine controller terminal No. 8) on Van models.

2) If voltage is more than 10 volts, turn ignition off. Disconnect engine controller connector. Check for continuity in Dark Green/Orange wire between engine controller terminal No. 8 and ASD relay connectors using a DVOM. If resistance is 10 ohms or more, repair open Dark Green/Orange wire between ASD relay and engine controller. Perform VERIFICATION TEST VER-1.

3) If resistance is less than 10 ohms, reconnect engine controller connector. Substitute a known good relay for ASD relay. Try to start engine. If engine starts, repair is complete. Perform VERIFICATION TEST VER-1. If engine does not start, replace engine controller. Perform VERIFICATION TEST VER-1.

TEST NS-12A

CHECKING AUTOMATIC IDLE SPEED (AIS) MOTOR OPERATION

NOTE: For connector terminal identification, see CONNECTOR IDENTIFICATION at beginning of article. For wiring diagram, see appropriate WIRING DIAGRAMS article in ENGINE PERFORMANCE.

1) Using DRB-II, stop fuel system test. Using DRB-II, actuate AIS motor. Monitor highest and lowest TPS voltage readings on DRB-II. If difference between highest and lowest readings is more than .15 volt, perform TEST NS-13A. If TPS voltage reading difference is .15 volt or less, stop AIS motor test using DRB-II. Turn ignition off.

2) Disconnect and inspect AIS motor connector. Repair connector if damaged. Perform VERIFICATION TEST VER-1. If connector is okay, turn ignition on. Using DRB-II, actuate AIS motor. Check for voltage between AIS motor connector Brown/White wire and Yellow/Black wire (Gray/Red wire on Van). If voltage is pulsating, replace AIS motor. Perform VERIFICATION TEST VER-1.

3) If voltage is not pulsating, stop AIS motor test. Turn ignition off. Disconnect and inspect engine controller connector. Repair connector if damaged. Perform VERIFICATION TEST VER-1. If connector is okay, place DRB-II in ohmmeter mode. Probe Brown/White wire in engine controller connector terminal No. 40. If resistance is less than 10 ohms, repair Brown/White wire for a short to ground. Perform VERIFICATION TEST VER-1.

4) If resistance is 10 ohms or more, probe engine controller connector terminal No. 60 (Yellow/Black wire on Pickup and Ramcharger, Gray/Red wire on Van). If resistance is less than 10 ohms, repair Yellow/Black wire (Gray/Red wire on Van) for a short to ground. Perform VERIFICATION TEST VER-1. If resistance is more than 10 ohms, check resistance of Brown/White wire between AIS motor connector and engine controller connector terminal No. 40.

5) If resistance is 10 ohms or more, repair Brown/White wire between AIS motor and engine controller connectors. Perform VERIFICATION TEST VER-1. If resistance is less than 10 ohms, replace engine controller. Perform VERIFICATION TEST VER-1.

1992 ENGINE PERFORMANCE
Self-Diagnostic Tests – 5.9L Gasoline (Cont.)

CHRY
1-127

TEST NS-13A

CORRECTING START & STALL CONDITION

At this point in diagnostic procedure, all engine control systems have been determined to be operating as designed and are not the cause of the no-start or start-and-stall problem. Following additional items should be checked as possible causes:

- Check if any MITCHELL® TECHNICAL SERVICE BULLETINS (TSBs) apply to vehicle.
- Check engine valve timing.
- Check engine compression.
- Check for exhaust system restriction.
- Ensure PCV system is functioning properly.
- Check camshaft and crankshaft sprockets.
- Check torque converter stall speed.
- Check for fuel contamination.
- Check secondary ignition circuit for abnormal scope pattern.

TEST DR-1A

CHECKING SYSTEM FOR FAULTS

NOTE: For connector terminal identification, see CONNECTOR IDENTIFICATION at beginning of article. For wiring diagram, see appropriate WIRING DIAGRAMS article in ENGINE PERFORMANCE. Battery must be fully charged and at rated capacity before performing any driveability test procedure. If vehicle starts and stalls repeatedly, perform TEST NS-2A. If vehicle stalls when A/C is turned on, perform TEST NF-13A.

1) Turn ignition on. Connect DRB-II to engine diagnostic connector. Read fault messages. If DRB-II displays fault messages, go to step 4). If DRB-II does not display fault messages, start engine. Allow engine to reach normal operating temperature. Set engine speed manually to 2000 RPM for at least 10 seconds, and return engine to idle.

2) On A/T models, apply brakes. Shift gear selector through all gears and return to PARK position. Using DRB-II, read fault messages. If no fault messages are displayed, go to next step. If fault messages are displayed, go to step 4).

3) On all models, check MITCHELL® TECHNICAL SERVICE BULLETINS (TSBs) for any pertinent information if DRB-II still displays NO FAULTS. If a TSB exists, perform corrective action. If driveability problem continues after performing TSB procedure or if no TSB information was found, perform TEST NF-1A.

4) If fault message is INTERNAL CONTROLLER FAILURE or CONTROLLER FAILURE, replace Single Board Engine Controller (SBEC). Perform VERIFICATION TEST VER-2. If fault message is not INTERNAL CONTROLLER FAILURE or CONTROLLER FAILURE, go to next step.

NOTE: ENGINE COLD TOO LONG fault message may set erroneously if ambient temperature is extremely cold.

5) If fault message is ENGINE COLD TOO LONG, check engine cooling system. Repair cooling system as necessary. Perform VERIFICATION TEST VER-3. If fault message is not ENGINE COLD TOO LONG, go to next step.

6) Using DRB-II FAULT MESSAGES table, select fault message and corresponding test. Correct all hard fault messages before proceeding to intermittent fault message.

NOTE: A false fault code may set if vehicle being tested is not equipped with these options.

DRB-II FAULT MESSAGES

DRB-II Message	[1] Hard Fault	[2] Intermittent Fault
A/C CLUTCH RELAY CIRCUIT	DR-23A	DR-33A
AUTOMATIC IDLE SPEED MOTOR CIRCUITS	DR-17A	DR-31A
AIR SWITCHING SOLENOID CIRCUIT	DR-28A	DR-33A
CONTROLLER FAILURE EEPROM WRITE DENIED	DR-29A	DR-29A
CONTROLLER FAILURE EMR MILES NOT STORED	DR-29A	DR-29A

TEST DR-1A (Cont.)

DRB-II FAULT MESSAGES (Cont.)

DRB-II Message	[1] Hard Fault	[2] Intermittent Fault
COOLANT SENSOR VOLTAGE HIGH	DR-11A	DR-30A
COOLANT SENSOR VOLTAGE LOW	DR-12A	DR-30A
EGR SOLENOID CIRCUIT	DR-21A	DR-33A
EGR SYSTEM FAILURE	DR-22A	DR-22A
IDLE SWITCH SHORTED LOW	DR-17A	DR-17A
IDLE SWITCH OPEN CIRCUIT	DR-17A	DR-17A
INJECTOR NO. 1 CONTROL CIRCUIT [3]	DR-18A	DR-32A
INJECTOR NO. 2 CONTROL CIRCUIT	DR-19A	DR-32A
MAP SENSOR VOLTAGE HIGH	DR-5A	DR-30A
MAP SENSOR VOLTAGE LOW	DR-4A	DR-30A
NO ASD RELAY VOLTAGE SENSE AT CONTROLLER	DR-27A	DR-34A
NO CHANGE IN MAP	DR-3A	DR-30B
NO VEHICLE SPEED SIGNAL	DR-6A	DR-6A
OVERDRIVE SOLENOID CIRCUIT [3] W/LOCK-UP	DR-26A	DR-26A
W/O LOCK-UP	DR-25A	DR-25A
O₂ SENSOR SHORTED TO VOLTAGE	DR-8A	DR-30A
O₂ SENSOR STAYS ABOVE CENTER	DR-9A	DR-30A
O₂ SENSOR STAYS AT CENTER	DR-7A	DR-30A
O₂ SENSOR STAYS BELOW CENTER	DR-10A	DR-30A
PURGE SOLENOID CIRCUIT	DR-20A	DR-33A
SLOW CHANGE IN IDLE MAP SIGNAL	DR-2A	DR-30B
THROTTLE BODY TEMP VOLTAGE HIGH	DR-15A	DR-30A
THROTTLE BODY TEMP VOLTAGE LOW	DR-16A	DR-30A
THROTTLE POSITION SENSOR VOLTAGE HIGH	DR-13A	DR-30A
THROTTLE POSITION SENSOR VOLTAGE LOW	DR-14A	DR-30A
TORQUE CONVERTER LOCK-UP SOLENOID CIRCUIT [3]	DR-24A	DR-33A

[1] – Key counter is "0".
[2] – Key counter is more than "0".
[3] – Possible combinations of A/T Part Throttle Unlock (PTU) and Overdrive Solenoid:
- 4-speed w/OD: 2-wire connector at trans.
- 4-speed w/OD and PTU: 3-wire connector at trans.
- 3-speed w/PTU: 1-wire connector at trans.
- 3-speed w/o PTU: no connector at trans.

TEST DR-2A

CODE 13, SLOW CHANGE IN IDLE MAP SIGNAL

NOTE: For connector terminal identification, see CONNECTOR IDENTIFICATION at beginning of article. For wiring diagram, see appropriate WIRING DIAGRAMS article in ENGINE PERFORMANCE.

1) Turn ignition off. Tee a vacuum gauge into vacuum hose to MAP sensor. Start engine. Observe vacuum gauge reading. If vacuum reading is zero in. Hg at idle, repair plugged or restricted hose to MAP sensor. Perform VERIFICATION TEST VER-2. If vacuum reading is not zero in. Hg at idle, snap throttle open and closed while observing vacuum gauge.

2) If vacuum gauge does not instantly drop to zero and return, repair restricted vacuum hose to MAP sensor. Perform VERIFICATION TEST VER-2. If vacuum reading instantly drops to zero and returns, turn ignition off. Disconnect and inspect MAP sensor connector. Repair connector if damaged. Perform VERIFICATION TEST VER-2.

3) If connector is okay, turn ignition on. Place DRB-II in voltmeter mode. Probe Violet/White wire. If voltage is less than one volt, repair open Violet/White wire. Perform VERIFICATION TEST VER-2. If voltage is one volt or more, replace MAP sensor. Perform VERIFICATION TEST VER-2.

CHRY
1-128

1992 ENGINE PERFORMANCE
Self-Diagnostic Tests – 5.9L Gasoline (Cont.)

TEST DR-3A

CODE 13, NO CHANGE IN MAP FROM START TO RUN

Turn ignition on. Tee a vacuum gauge into MAP sensor vacuum hose. Start engine. While at idle, read vacuum gauge. If reading is zero in. Hg at idle, repair leak in vacuum hose to MAP sensor. Perform VERIFICATION TEST VER-2. If reading is not zero in. Hg, repair restriction in vacuum supply hose to MAP sensor. Perform VERIFICATION TEST VER-2.

TEST DR-4A

CODE 14, MAP VOLTAGE TOO LOW

NOTE: For connector terminal identification, see CONNECTOR IDENTIFICATION at beginning of article. For wiring diagram, see appropriate WIRING DIAGRAMS article in ENGINE PERFORMANCE.

1) Turn ignition off. Disconnect and inspect MAP sensor connector. Repair connector as necessary. Perform VERIFICATION TEST VER-2. Turn ignition on. Read MAP sensor voltage. If MAP sensor voltage is more than 4.5 volts, replace MAP sensor. Perform VERIFICATION TEST VER-2.

2) If MAP sensor voltage is 4.5 volts or less, turn ignition off. Disconnect engine controller 60-pin connector. Place DRB-II in ohmmeter mode. Probe Dark Green/Red wire at MAP sensor connector.

3) If resistance is less than 10 ohms, repair short to ground in Dark Green/Red wire. Perform VERIFICATION TEST VER-2. If resistance 10 ohms or more, replace engine controller. Perform VERIFICATION TEST VER-2.

TEST DR-5A

CODE 14, MAP VOLTAGE TOO HIGH

NOTE: For connector terminal identification, see CONNECTOR IDENTIFICATION at beginning of article. For wiring diagram, see appropriate WIRING DIAGRAMS article in ENGINE PERFORMANCE.

1) Turn ignition off. Disconnect and inspect MAP sensor connector. Repair connector as necessary. Perform VERIFICATION TEST VER-2. If MAP sensor connector is okay, go to next step.

2) Connect a jumper wire between Black/Light Blue wire and Dark Green/Red wire at MAP sensor connector. Turn ignition on. Read MAP sensor voltage. If voltage is less than one volt, replace MAP sensor. Perform VERIFICATION TEST VER-2.

3) If MAP sensor voltage is one volt or more, remove jumper wire. Connect jumper wire between Dark Green/Red wire at MAP sensor connector and ground. If voltage is less than one volt, repair open in Black/Light Blue wire. Perform VERIFICATION TEST VER-2.

4) If voltage is one volt or more, disconnect and inspect engine controller 60-pin connector. Repair connector if damaged. Perform VERIFICATION TEST VER-2. If engine controller connector is okay, go to next step.

5) Using an external ohmmeter, check resistance of Dark Green/Red wire between MAP sensor connector and engine controller connector terminal No. 1. If resistance is 10 ohms or more, repair open Dark Green/Red wire. Perform VERIFICATION TEST VER-2. If resistance is less than 10 ohms, replace engine controller. Perform VERIFICATION TEST VER-2.

TEST DR-6A

CODE 15, NO VEHICLE SPEED SIGNAL

NOTE: For connector terminal identification, see CONNECTOR IDENTIFICATION at beginning of article. For wiring diagram, see appropriate WIRING DIAGRAMS article in ENGINE PERFORMANCE.

1) Turn ignition off. Disconnect and inspect distance sensor connector. Repair connector if damaged. Perform VERIFICATION TEST VER-2. If connector is okay, go to next step.

2) Turn ignition on. Connect a jumper wire to one terminal of distance sensor connector. Monitor vehicle speed on DRB-II while tapping open end of jumper wire to other distance sensor harness connector terminal.

3) If DRB-II shows vehicle speed to be more than zero MPH, replace distance sensor. Perform VERIFICATION TEST VER-2. If vehicle speed is zero, place DRB-II in ohmmeter mode. Probe Black/Light Blue wire at distance sensor connector.

4) If resistance is 10 ohms or more, repair open in Black/Light Blue wire. Perform VERIFICATION TEST VER-2. If resistance is less than 10 ohms, turn ignition off. Disconnect and inspect engine controller connector. Repair connector if damaged. Perform VERIFICATION TEST VER-2. If connector is okay, go to next step.

5) Turn ignition on. Place DRB-II in voltmeter mode. Probe terminal No. 47 (White/Orange wire) at engine controller connector. If voltage is more than 4 volts, go to step 7). If voltage is 4 volts or less, check if speedometer works. If speedometer works, repair open in White/Orange wire between distance sensor and engine controller connector. Perform VERIFICATION TEST VER-2.

6) If speedometer does not work, turn ignition off. Place DRB-II in ohmmeter mode. Probe terminal No. 47 at engine controller connector. If resistance is less than 5 ohms, repair short to ground in White/Orange wire. Perform VERIFICATION TEST VER-2. If resistance is 5 ohms or more, repair open White/Orange wire between sensor and splice. Perform VERIFICATION TEST VER-2.

7) If voltage at White/Orange wire is more than 4 volts in step 5), probe White/Orange wire at distance sensor connector. If voltage is more than 4 volts, replace engine controller. Perform VERIFICATION TEST VER-2. If voltage is 4 volts or less, repair open in White/Orange wire between distance sensor and engine controller connectors. Perform VERIFICATION TEST VER-2.

TEST DR-7A

CODE 21, OXYGEN (O₂) SIGNAL STAYS AT CENTER

NOTE: For connector terminal identification, see CONNECTOR IDENTIFICATION at beginning of article. For wiring diagram, see appropriate WIRING DIAGRAMS article in ENGINE PERFORMANCE.

1) Turn ignition off. Disconnect and inspect O_2 sensor connector. Repair connector if damaged. Perform VERIFICATION TEST VER-2. If O_2 sensor connector is okay, turn ignition on. Connect a jumper wire to Black/Dark Green wire at O_2 sensor connector. DO NOT connect jumper wire to Dark Green/Black wire in O_2 sensor connector.

2) Connect other end of jumper wire to positive battery terminal. Using DRB-II, read O_2 sensor voltage. If voltage is less than one volt, go to next step. If voltage is one volt or more, disconnect jumper wire. Turn ignition off. Place DRB-II in ohmmeter mode. Probe Black/Light Blue wire at O_2 sensor connector. If resistance is 10 ohms or more, repair open Black/Light Blue wire. Perform VERIFICATION TEST VER-2. If resistance is less than 10 ohms, replace O_2 sensor. Perform VERIFICATION TEST VER-2.

3) If voltage is less than one volt in step 2), disconnect jumper wire. Turn ignition off. Disconnect and inspect engine controller connector. Repair connector if damaged. Perform VERIFICATION TEST VER-2. If engine controller connector is okay, go to next step.

4) Using a DVOM, check resistance of Black/Dark Green wire between O_2 sensor connector and engine controller connector terminal No. 41. If resistance is less than 10 ohms, replace engine controller. Perform VERIFICATION TEST VER-2. If resistance is 10 ohms or more, repair open in Black/Dark Green wire. Perform VERIFICATION TEST VER-2.

1992 ENGINE PERFORMANCE
Self-Diagnostic Tests – 5.9L Gasoline (Cont.)

CHRY
1-129

TEST DR-8A

CODE 21, OXYGEN (O₂) SIGNAL SHORTED TO VOLTAGE

NOTE: For connector terminal identification, see CONNECTOR IDENTIFICATION at beginning of article. For wiring diagram, see appropriate WIRING DIAGRAMS article in ENGINE PERFORMANCE.

1) Start engine, and allow it to idle for 2 minutes. Using DRB-II, read O₂ sensor voltage. If voltage is more than 1.3 volts, go to step **3)**. If voltage is 1.3 volts or less, read O₂ sensor voltage while wiggling O₂ sensor wiring.

2) If voltage is more than 1.3 volts while O₂ sensor wiring is wiggled, repair short to voltage in Black/Dark Green wire. Perform VERIFICATION TEST VER-2. If voltage stays less than 1.3 volts while O₂ sensor wiring is wiggled, replace engine controller. Perform VERIFICATION TEST VER-2.

3) If voltage is more than 1.3 volts in step **1)**, disconnect O₂ sensor connector. If voltage is less than one volt when O₂ sensor connector is disconnected, replace O₂ sensor. Perform VERIFICATION TEST VER-2. If voltage is more than one volt when O₂ sensor connector is disconnected, repair Black/Dark Green wire for a short to Dark Green/Black wire.

4) Reconnect O₂ sensor connector. Using DRB-II, reset adaptive fuel value. Start engine, and let it idle for 2 minutes. Using DRB-II, read O₂ sensor value. If O₂ sensor switches from rich to lean, test is complete. Perform VERIFICATION TEST VER-2. If O₂ sensor does not switch from rich to lean, replace O₂ sensor. Perform VERIFICATION TEST VER-2.

TEST DR-9A

CODE 52, OXYGEN (O₂) SIGNAL STAYS ABOVE CENTER

1) Start engine. Allow engine to reach normal operating temperature. Turn engine off. Turn ignition on. Using DRB-II, actuate ASD fuel system. Inspect injectors for fuel leakage. If injectors are leaking, replace leaking injectors or "O" rings. Perform VERIFICATION TEST VER-2.

2) If injectors are not leaking, stop ASD fuel system actuation. Inspect air cleaner filter and inlet ducts for restrictions. Clean as necessary. Perform VERIFICATION TEST VER-2. If no restrictions exist, perform TEST NF-13A.

TEST DR-10A

CODE 51, OXYGEN (O₂) SIGNAL STAYS BELOW CENTER

Code 51 may set for several reasons not related to O₂ sensor or O₂ sensor circuits. If Code 51 sets, perform TEST NF-1A.

TEST DR-11A

CODE 22, COOLANT SENSOR VOLTAGE TOO HIGH

NOTE: For connector terminal identification, see CONNECTOR IDENTIFICATION at beginning of article. For wiring diagram, see appropriate WIRING DIAGRAMS article in ENGINE PERFORMANCE.

1) Turn ignition off. Disconnect and inspect coolant temperature sensor connector. Repair connector if damaged. Perform VERIFICATION TEST VER-2. If coolant temperature sensor connector is okay, go to next step.

2) Connect jumper wire between Black/Light Blue and Tan/Black wires at coolant temperature sensor connector. Turn ignition on. Using DRB-II, read coolant temperature sensor voltage. If voltage is less than one volt, replace coolant temperature sensor. Perform VERIFICATION TEST VER-2.

TEST DR-11A (Cont.)

3) If voltage is one volt or more, remove jumper wire. Connect jumper wire between Tan/Black wire at coolant temperature sensor connector and ground. Using DRB-II, read coolant temperature sensor voltage. If voltage is less than one volt, repair open in Black/Light Blue wire. Perform VERIFICATION TEST VER-2.

4) If voltage is one volt or more, disconnect and inspect engine controller 60-pin connector. Repair connector if damaged. Perform VERIFICATION TEST VER-2. If connector is okay, go to next step.

5) Using a DVOM, check resistance of Tan/Black wire between coolant temperature sensor connector and engine controller connector terminal No. 2. If resistance is less than 10 ohms, replace engine controller. Perform VERIFICATION TEST VER-2. If resistance is 10 ohms or more, repair open Tan/Black wire. Perform VERIFICATION TEST VER-2.

TEST DR-12A

CODE 22, COOLANT SENSOR VOLTAGE TOO LOW

NOTE: For connector terminal identification, see CONNECTOR IDENTIFICATION at beginning of article. For wiring diagram, see appropriate WIRING DIAGRAMS article in ENGINE PERFORMANCE.

1) Turn ignition on. Using DRB-II, read coolant temperature sensor voltage. Disconnect coolant temperature sensor connector. If voltage changed to more than 4 volts when sensor was disconnected, replace coolant temperature sensor. Perform VERIFICATION TEST VER-2. If voltage did not change to more than 4 volts when sensor was disconnected, turn ignition off.

2) Disconnect and inspect engine controller 60-pin connector. Repair connector if damaged. Perform VERIFICATION TEST VER-2. Place DRB-II in ohmmeter mode. Probe engine controller connector terminal No. 2 (Tan/Black wire). If resistance is less than 10 ohms, repair Tan/Black wire for short to Black/Light Blue wire or ground. Perform VERIFICATION TEST VER-2. If resistance is 10 ohms or more, replace engine controller. Perform VERIFICATION TEST VER-2.

TEST DR-13A

CODE 24, THROTTLE POSITION SENSOR (TPS) VOLTAGE HIGH

NOTE: For connector terminal identification, see CONNECTOR IDENTIFICATION at beginning of article. For wiring diagram, see appropriate WIRING DIAGRAMS article in ENGINE PERFORMANCE.

1) Turn ignition off. Disconnect and inspect TPS connector. Repair TPS connector if damaged. Perform VERIFICATION TEST VER-2. If TPS connector is okay, go to next step.

2) Turn ignition on. Connect jumper wire between Orange/Dark Blue wire and Black/Light Blue wire at TPS connector. Using DRB-II, read TPS voltage. If voltage is less than one volt, replace TPS. Perform VERIFICATION TEST VER-2.

3) If voltage is one volt or more, remove jumper wire. Connect jumper wire between Orange/Dark Blue wire at TPS connector and ground. Using DRB-II, read TPS voltage. If voltage is less than one volt, repair open in Black/Light Blue wire. Perform VERIFICATION TEST VER-2.

4) If voltage is one volt or more, turn ignition off. Disconnect and inspect engine controller 60-pin connector. Repair connector if damaged. Perform VERIFICATION TEST VER-2. If connector is okay, go to next step.

5) Using a DVOM, check resistance of Orange/Dark Blue wire between TPS connector and engine controller connector terminal No. 22. If resistance is less than 10 ohms, replace engine controller. Perform VERIFICATION TEST VER-2. If resistance is 10 ohms or more, repair open in Orange/Dark Blue wire. Perform VERIFICATION TEST VER-2.

CHRY
1-130

1992 ENGINE PERFORMANCE
Self-Diagnostic Tests – 5.9L Gasoline (Cont.)

TEST DR-14A

CODE 24, THROTTLE POSITION SENSOR (TPS) VOLTAGE LOW

NOTE: For connector terminal identification, see CONNECTOR IDENTIFICATION at beginning of article. For wiring diagram, see appropriate WIRING DIAGRAMS article in ENGINE PERFORMANCE.

1) Turn ignition off. Disconnect TPS connector. Turn ignition on. Place DRB-II in voltmeter mode. Probe Violet/White wire at TPS connector. If voltage is less than one volt, go to step 4).

2) If voltage is one volt or more, probe Orange/Dark Blue wire at TPS connector. If voltage is one volt or more, replace TPS. Perform VERIFICATION TEST VER-2. If voltage is less than one volt, turn ignition off. Disconnect engine controller connector.

3) Place DRB-II in ohmmeter mode. Probe terminal No. 22 (Orange/Dark Blue wire) at engine controller connector. If resistance is less than 10 ohms, repair short to ground in Orange/Dark Blue wire. Perform VERIFICATION TEST VER-2. If resistance is 10 ohms or more, replace engine controller. Perform VERIFICATION TEST VER-2.

4) If voltage is less than one volt in step 1), turn ignition off. Place DRB-II in ohmmeter mode. Probe Violet/White wire. If resistance is less than 10 ohms, repair Violet/White wire for a short to ground. Perform VERIFICATION TEST VER-2. If resistance is 10 ohms or more, disconnect and inspect engine controller connector. Repair connector if damaged. Perform VERIFICATION TEST VER-2.

5) If connector is okay, check resistance of Violet/White wire between TPS connector and engine controller connector terminal No. 6 using a DVOM. If resistance is less than 10 ohms, replace engine controller. Perform VERIFICATION TEST VER-2. If resistance is 10 ohms or more, repair open Violet/White wire. Perform VERIFICATION TEST VER-2.

TEST DR-15A

CODE 23, THROTTLE BODY TEMP VOLTAGE HIGH

NOTE: For connector terminal identification, see CONNECTOR IDENTIFICATION at beginning of article. For wiring diagram, see appropriate WIRING DIAGRAMS article in ENGINE PERFORMANCE.

1) Turn ignition on. Using DRB-II, select throttle body temperature voltage. Disconnect throttle body temperature sensor. Connect a jumper wire across sensor connector terminals. Read sensor voltage. If voltage is less than one volt, replace throttle body temperature sensor. Perform VERIFICATION TEST VER-2. If voltage is one volt or more, disconnect jumper wire.

2) Connect jumper wire between Black/Red wire at throttle body temperature sensor connector terminal and ground. Read sensor voltage. If voltage is less than one volt, repair Black/Red wire for an open circuit to splice. Perform VERIFICATION TEST VER-2. If voltage is one volt or more, turn ignition off. Disconnect and inspect engine controller connector. Repair connector if damaged. Perform VERIFICATION TEST VER-2.

3) If connector is okay, check resistance of Black/Red wire between throttle body temperature sensor and engine controller connector terminal No. 21. If resistance is less than 10 ohms, replace engine controller. Perform VERIFICATION TEST VER-2. If resistance is 10 ohms or more, repair open Black/Red wire. Perform VERIFICATION TEST VER-2.

TEST DR-16A

CODE 23, THROTTLE BODY TEMP VOLTAGE LOW

NOTE: For connector terminal identification, see CONNECTOR IDENTIFICATION at beginning of article. For wiring diagram, see appropriate WIRING DIAGRAMS article in ENGINE PERFORMANCE.

1) Turn ignition on. Using DRB-II, select throttle body temperature voltage. Disconnect throttle body temperature sensor. Read sensor voltage. If voltage is more than 4 volts, replace throttle body temperature sensor. Perform VERIFICATION TEST VER-2. If voltage is 4 volts or less, turn ignition off.

TEST DR-16A (Cont.)

2) Disconnect and inspect engine controller connector. Repair connector if damaged. Perform VERIFICATION TEST VER-2. If connector is okay, place DRB-II in ohmmeter mode. Probe engine controller connector terminal No. 21 (Black/Red wire). If resistance is less than 10 ohms, replace engine controller. Perform VERIFICATION TEST VER-2. If resistance is 10 ohms or more, repair Black/Red wire for a short to ground. Perform VERIFICATION TEST VER-2.

TEST DR-17A

CODE 25, AUTOMATIC IDLE SPEED (AIS) MOTOR CIRCUITS

NOTE: For connector terminal identification, see CONNECTOR IDENTIFICATION at beginning of article. For wiring diagram, see appropriate WIRING DIAGRAMS article in ENGINE PERFORMANCE.

1) Turn ignition on. Using DRB-II, read faults. If DRB-II does not display AIS MOTOR FAULT, go to TEST DR-17B. If DRB-II displays AIS MOTOR FAULT, disconnect Automatic Idle Speed (AIS) motor connector. Using DRB-II, actuate AIS motor. Put DRB-II in voltmeter mode. Probe AIS motor connector Yellow/Black wire (Gray/Red wire on Van).

2) When normal, voltage should switch from less than one volt to more than 10 volts. If voltage stays less than one volt, repair short to ground in Yellow/Black wire (Gray/Red wire on Van). Perform VERIFICATION TEST VER-2.

3) If voltage does not stay less than one volt, probe Brown/White wire at AIS motor connector. If voltage stays less than one volt, repair short to ground in Brown/White wire. Perform VERIFICATION TEST VER-2. If voltage does not stay less than 10 volts, check for voltage between Yellow/Black wire (Gray/Red wire on Van) and Brown/White wire.

4) If voltage is pulsating, repair Yellow/Black wire (Gray/Red wire on Van) for a short to Brown/White wire. Perform VERIFIFCATION TEST VER-2. If voltage is not pulsating, replace AIS motor. Perform VERIFICATION TEST VER-2.

TEST DR-17B

CODE 35, IDLE SWITCH OPEN CIRCUIT

NOTE: For connector terminal identification, see CONNECTOR IDENTIFICATION at beginning of article. For wiring diagram, see appropriate WIRING DIAGRAMS article in ENGINE PERFORMANCE.

1) If DRB-II does not display IDLE SWITCH OPEN CKT, go to TEST DR-17C. If DRB-II displays IDLE SWITCH OPEN CKT, inspect throttle linkage for proper adjustment. Adjust linkage as required. Perform VERIFICATION TEST VER-2. If linkage adjustment is okay, disconnect Automatic Idle Speed (AIS) motor connector.

2) Connect a jumper wire between Violet wire and ground. Using DRB-II, read idle switch status. If DRB-II does not display SWITCH CLOSED, go to step 4). If DRB-II displays SWITCH CLOSED, connect jumper wire between Violet and Black/White wires in AIS motor connector.

3) Using DRB-II, read idle switch status. If DRB-II displays SWITCH CLOSED, replace AIS motor. Perform VERIFICATION TEST VER-2. If DRB-II does not display SWITCH CLOSED, repair Black/White wire for an open to ground or engine controller connector terminal No. 5.

4) Turn ignition off. Disconnect engine controller connector. Check resistance of Violet wire between engine controller connector terminal No. 28 and AIS motor connector using a DVOM. If resistance is less than 5 ohms, replace engine controller. Perform VERIFICATION TEST VER-2. If resistance is 5 ohms or more, repair open Violet wire. Perform VERIFICATION TEST VER-2.

1992 ENGINE PERFORMANCE
Self-Diagnostic Tests – 5.9L Gasoline (Cont.)

CHRY
1-131

TEST DR-17C

CODE 35, IDLE SWITCH SHORTED LOW

NOTE: For connector terminal identification, see CONNECTOR IDEN-TIFICATION at beginning of article. For wiring diagram, see appropriate WIRING DIAGRAMS article in ENGINE PERFORMANCE.

1) Turn ignition on. Using DRB-II, read idle switch status. While observing DRB-II, manually open and close throttle. If switch state changes from closed to open, go to step 3). If switch status does not change from closed to open, disconnect AIS motor. If switch status changes from closed to open, replace AIS motor. Perform VERIFICATION TEST VER-2.

2) If switch state does not change from closed to open, turn ignition off. Disconnect engine controller connector. Place DRB-II in ohmmeter mode. Probe terminal No. 28 (Violet wire) in engine controller connector. If resistance is less than 5 ohms, repair Violet wire for a short to ground. Perform VERIFICATION TEST VER-2. If resistance is 5 ohms or more, replace engine controller. Perform VERIFICATION TEST VER-2.

3) While wiggling wiring to AIS motor, observe DRB-II display. If display changed from closed to open, repair Violet wire for a short to ground. Perform VERIFICATION TEST VER-2. If display does not change from closed to open, test is complete. Perform VERIFICATION TEST VER-2.

TEST DR-18A

CODE 27, INJECTOR NO. 1 CONTROL CIRCUIT

NOTE: For connector terminal identification, see CONNECTOR IDEN-TIFICATION at beginning of article. For wiring diagram, see appropriate WIRING DIAGRAMS article in ENGINE PERFORMANCE.

1) Turn ignition off. Disconnect 4-pin injector harness connector. Turn ignition on. Using DRB-II, actuate ASD fuel system test. Place DRB-II in voltmeter mode. Probe Dark Green/Orange wire in injector harness connector terminal No. 4. If voltage is 10 volts or less, repair Dark Green/Orange wire for an open to splice. Perform VERIFICATION TEST VER-2.

2) If voltage is more than 10 volts, measure resistance between terminals No. 3 and 4 (White/Dark Blue and Dark Green/Orange wires) in throttle body connector using a DVOM. If resistance is 5 ohms or more, go to TEST DR-18B. If resistance is less than 5 ohms, connect DVOM between White/Dark Blue wire and ground. If resistance is less than 10 ohms, replace injector harness. Perform VERIFICATION TEST VER-2.

3) If resistance is 10 ohms or more, disconnect and inspect engine controller connector. Repair connector if damaged. Perform VERIFICATION TEST VER-2. If connector is okay, check resistance of White/Dark Blue wire between engine controller connector terminal No. 16 and throttle body connector using a DVOM. If resistance is 10 ohms or more, repair White/Dark Blue wire for an open between engine controller and throttle body connectors. Perform VERIFICATION TEST VER-2.

4) If resistance is less than 10 ohms, place DRB-II in ohmmeter mode. Probe engine controller connector terminal No. 16 (White/Dark Blue wire). If resistance is less than 10 ohms, repair White/Dark Blue wire for a short to ground. Perform VERIFICATION TEST VER-2. If resistance is 10 ohms or more, replace engine controller. Perform VERIFICATION TEST VER-2.

TEST DR-18B

CODE 27, INJECTOR NO. 1 CONTROL CIRCUIT

Disconnect and inspect injector No. 1 connector. Repair connector if damaged. Perform VERIFICATION TEST VER-2. If connector is okay, measure injector resistance using a DVOM. If resistance is less than 5 ohms, replace injector harness. Perform VERIFICATION TEST VER-2. If resistance is 5 ohms or more, replace injector. Perform VERIFICATION TEST VER-2.

TEST DR-19A

CODE 27, INJECTOR NO. 2 CONTROL CIRCUIT

NOTE: For connector terminal identification, see CONNECTOR IDEN-TIFICATION at beginning of article. For wiring diagram, see appropriate WIRING DIAGRAMS article in ENGINE PERFORMANCE.

1) Turn ignition off. Disconnect 4-pin injector harness connector. Turn ignition on. Using DRB-II, actuate ASD fuel system test. Place DRB-II in voltmeter mode. Probe Dark Green/Orange wire in injector harness connector terminal No. 1. If voltage is 10 volts or less, repair Dark Green/Orange wire for an open to splice. Perform VERIFICATION TEST VER-2.

2) If voltage is more than 10 volts, measure resistance between terminals No. 1 and 2 (Dark Green/Orange and Tan wires) in throttle body connector using a DVOM. If resistance is 5 ohms or more, go to TEST DR-18B. If resistance is less than 5 ohms, connect DVOM between Tan wire and ground. If resistance is less than 10 ohms, replace injector harness. Perform VERIFICATION TEST VER-2.

3) If resistance is 10 ohms or more, disconnect and inspect engine controller connector. Repair connector if damaged. Perform VERIFICATION TEST VER-2. If connector is okay, check resistance of Tan wire between engine controller connector terminal No. 15 and throttle body connector using a DVOM. If resistance is 10 ohms or more, repair Tan wire for an open between engine controller and throttle body connectors. Perform VERIFICATION TEST VER-2.

4) If resistance is less than 10 ohms, place DRB-II in ohmmeter mode. Probe engine controller connector terminal No. 15 (Tan wire). If resistance is less than 10 ohms, repair Tan wire for a short to ground. Perform VERIFICATION TEST VER-2. If resistance is 10 ohms or more, replace engine controller. Perform VERIFICATION TEST VER-2.

TEST DR-19B

CODE 27, INJECTOR NO. 2 CONTROL CIRCUIT

Disconnect and inspect injector No. 2 connector. Repair connector if damaged. Perform VERIFICATION TEST VER-2. If connector is okay, measure injector resistance using a DVOM. If resistance is less than 5 ohms, replace injector harness. Perform VERIFICATION TEST VER-2. If resistance is 5 ohms or more, replace injector. Perform VERIFICATION TEST VER-2.

TEST DR-20A

CODE 31, PURGE SOLENOID CIRCUIT

NOTE: For connector terminal identification, see CONNECTOR IDEN-TIFICATION at beginning of article. For wiring diagram, see appropriate WIRING DIAGRAMS article in ENGINE PERFORMANCE.

1) Turn ignition off. Disconnect and inspect purge solenoid connector. Repair connector if damaged. Perform VERIFICATION TEST VER-2. If connector is okay, turn ignition on. Place DRB-II in voltmeter mode. Probe purge solenoid connector Dark Blue wire. If voltage is 10 volts or less, repair open in Dark Blue wire. Perform VERIFICATION TEST VER-2.

2) If voltage is more than 10 volts, turn ignition off. Disconnect and inspect engine controller 60-pin connector. Repair connector if damaged. Perform VERIFICATION TEST VER-2. If connector is okay, place DRB-II in ohmmeter mode. Probe engine controller connector terminal No. 52 (Pink/Black wire). If resistance is less than 10 ohms, repair short to ground in Pink/Black wire. Perform VERIFICATION TEST VER-2.

3) If resistance is 10 ohms or more, check resistance of Pink/Black wire between purge solenoid connector and engine controller connector terminal No. 52 using a DVOM. If resistance is 10 ohms or more, repair open in Pink/Black wire. Perform VERIFICATION TEST VER-2. If resistance is less than 10 ohms, reconnect purge solenoid connector.

4) Turn ignition on. Place DRB-II in voltmeter mode. Probe engine controller connector terminal No. 52 (Pink/Black wire). If voltage is more than 10 volts, replace engine controller. Perform VERIFICATION TEST VER-2. If voltage is 10 volts or less, replace purge solenoid. Perform VERIFICATION TEST VER-2.

CHRY
1-132

1992 ENGINE PERFORMANCE
Self-Diagnostic Tests – 5.9L Gasoline (Cont.)

TEST DR-21A

CODE 32, EGR SOLENOID CIRCUIT

NOTE: For connector terminal identification, see CONNECTOR IDEN-TIFICATION at beginning of article. For wiring diagram, see appropriate WIRING DIAGRAMS article in ENGINE PERFORMANCE.

1) Turn ignition off. Disconnect and inspect EGR solenoid connector. Repair connector if damaged. Perform VERIFICATION TEST VER-2. If connector is okay, turn ignition on. Place DRB-II in voltmeter mode.

2) Probe Dark Blue wire. If voltage is 10 volts or less, repair open Dark Blue wire. Perform VERIFICATION TEST VER-2. If voltage is more than 10 volts, turn ignition off. Reconnect EGR solenoid. Disconnect and inspect engine controller connector. Repair connector if damaged. Perform VERIFICATION TEST VER-2.

3) If connector is okay, turn ignition on. Place DRB-II in voltmeter mode. Probe engine controller connector terminal No. 35 (Gray/Yellow wire). If voltage is more than 10 volts, replace engine controller. Perform VERIFI-CATION TEST VER-2.

4) If voltage is 10 volts or less, turn ignition off. Disconnect EGR solenoid connector. Place DRB-II in ohmmeter mode. Probe engine controller connector terminal No. 35 (Gray/Yellow wire). If resistance is less than 10 ohms, repair short to ground in Gray/Yellow wire. Perform VERIFICA-TION TEST VER-2. If resistance is more than 10 ohms, go to next step.

5) Using a DVOM, check resistance of Gray/Yellow wire between engine controller connector terminal No. 35 and EGR solenoid connector. If resistance is less than 10 ohms, replace EGR solenoid. Perform VERIFI-CATION TEST VER-2. If resistance is more than 10 ohms, repair open Gray/Yellow wire. Perform VERIFICATION TEST VER-2.

TEST DR-22A

CODE 32, EGR SYSTEM FAILURE

NOTE: For connector terminal identification, see CONNECTOR IDEN-TIFICATION at beginning of article. For wiring diagram, see appropriate WIRING DIAGRAMS article in ENGINE PERFORMANCE.

1) Disconnect vacuum supply hose from EGR solenoid. Connect a vacuum gauge to disconnected vacuum hose. Start engine, and allow it to reach normal operating temperature. If vacuum is more than 10 in. Hg at idle, go to step 2). If vacuum is 10 in. Hg or less at idle, repair vacuum line to EGR solenoid for a leak or restriction. Perform VERIFICATION TEST VER-2.

2) Turn engine off. Disconnect vacuum gauge. Reconnect vacuum supply hose to EGR solenoid. Disconnect vacuum hose from EGR valve. Connect vacuum gauge to disconnected vacuum hose. Start engine. While reading vacuum gauge, momentarily snap throttle open. If vacuum is not more than 5 in. Hg at any time, replace EGR valve assembly. Perform VERIFICATION TEST VER-2. If vacuum is 5 in. Hg or less, go to next step.

3) Disconnect vacuum gauge from vacuum hose. Connect vacuum pump to EGR valve nipple. Start engine. Slowly apply vacuum to EGR valve and listen for engine RPM change. If engine RPM does not change, go to step 5). If engine RPM changes, go to next step.

4) Turn ignition off. Apply 10 in. Hg of vacuum and hold for 30 seconds. If vacuum does not hold for 30 seconds, replace EGR valve assembly. Perform VERIFICATION TEST VER-2. If vacuum holds for 30 seconds, EGR system is functioning properly at this time. If driveability problem is still present, go to TEST NF-1A. If driveability problem is no longer present, test is complete. Perform VERIFICATION TEST VER-2.

5) If engine RPM did not change in step 3), remove EGR valve assembly. Check for plugged EGR manifold passages. If manifold passages are plugged, clear passages as necessary. Perform VERIFICATION TEST VER-2. If manifold passages are not plugged, replace EGR valve assembly. Perform VERIFICATION TEST VER-2.

TEST DR-23A

CODE 33, A/C CLUTCH RELAY CIRCUIT

NOTE: For connector terminal identification, see CONNECTOR IDEN-TIFICATION at beginning of article. For wiring diagram, see appropriate WIRING DIAGRAMS article in ENGINE PERFORMANCE.

1) Turn ignition on. Using DRB-II, actuate A/C clutch relay. If relay is clicking, perform TEST DR-32A. If relay is not clicking, remove A/C clutch relay and inspect connector. Repair connector if damaged. Perform VERIFICATION TEST VER-2. If connector is okay, substitute A/C relay with a known good relay. Using DRB-II, actuate A/C relay. If relay is clicking, repair is complete. Perform VERIFICATION TEST VER-2.

2) If relay is not clicking, remove substitute relay. Place DRB-II in voltmeter mode. Probe A/C relay connector terminal "A" (Dark Blue wire). If voltage is 10 volts or less, repair open Dark Blue wire. Perform VERIFI-CATION TEST VER-2. If voltage is more than 10 volts, turn ignition off.

3) Disconnect and inspect engine controller connector. Repair connector if damaged. Perform VERIFICATION TEST VER-2. If connector is okay, put DRB-II in ohmmeter mode. Probe engine controller connector terminal No. 34 (Dark Blue/Orange wire). If resistance is less than 10 ohms, repair short to ground in Dark Blue/Orange wire. Perform VERIFICA-TION TEST VER-2. If resistance is 10 ohms or more, go to next step.

4) Using a DVOM, check resistance of Dark Blue/Orange wire between engine controller connector terminal No. 34 and A/C relay connector terminal "C". If resistance is 10 ohms or more, repair open Dark Blue/Orange wire. Perform VERIFICATION TEST VER-2. If resistance is less than 10 ohms, go to next step.

5) Reconnect A/C clutch relay. Turn ignition on. Place DRB-II in voltmeter mode. Probe terminal No. 34 (Dark Blue/Orange wire) in engine controller connector. If voltage is more than 10 volts, replace engine controller. Perform VERIFICATION TEST VER-2. If voltage is 10 volts or less, replace A/C clutch relay. Perform VERIFICATION TEST VER-2.

TEST DR-24A

CODE 37, TORQUE CONVERTER LOCK-UP CIRCUIT

NOTE: For connector terminal identification, see CONNECTOR IDEN-TIFICATION at beginning of article. For wiring diagram, see appropriate WIRING DIAGRAMS article in ENGINE PERFORMANCE.

1) If vehicle is also equipped with overdrive, go to TEST DR-24B. Turn ignition off. Disconnect Part Throttle Unlock (PTU) relay. Inspect PTU connector. Repair connector if damaged. Perform VERIFICATION TEST VER-2. If connector is okay, turn ignition on. Place DRB-II in voltmeter mode. Probe PTU relay connector terminal "A" (Dark Blue wire).

2) If voltage is 10 volts or less, repair open Dark Blue wire between relay and splice. Perform VERIFICATION TEST VER-2. If voltage is more than 10 volts, probe Dark Blue wire in relay connector terminal "B". If voltage is 10 volts or less, repair open Dark Blue wire between relay and splice. Perform VERIFICATION TEST VER-2.

3) If voltage is more than 10 volts, turn ignition off. Disconnect and inspect engine controller connector. Repair connector if damaged. Perform VERIFICATION TEST VER-2. If connector is okay, place DRB-II in ohmmeter mode. Probe engine controller connector terminal No. 54 (Orange/Black wire). If resistance is less than 10 ohms, repair Orange/Black wire for a short to ground. Perform VERIFICATION TEST VER-2.

4) If resistance is 10 ohms or more, check resistance of Orange/Black wire between engine controller and PTU relay connectors using a DVOM. If resistance is 10 ohms or more, repair open Orange/Black wire. Perform VERIFICATION TEST VER-2. If resistance is less than 10 ohms, reconnect PTU relay. Turn ignition on. Place DRB-II in voltmeter mode.

5) Probe terminal No. 54 (Orange/Black wire) in engine controller connector. If voltage is more than 10 volts, replace engine controller. Perform VERIFICATION TEST VER-2. If voltage is 10 volts or less, replace PTU relay. Perform VERIFICATION TEST VER-2.

1992 ENGINE PERFORMANCE
Self-Diagnostic Tests – 5.9L Gasoline (Cont.)

CHRY
1-133

TEST DR-24B

CODE 37, TORQUE CONVERTER LOCK-UP CIRCUIT

NOTE: For connector terminal identification, see CONNECTOR IDENTIFICATION at beginning of article. For wiring diagram, see appropriate WIRING DIAGRAMS article in ENGINE PERFORMANCE.

1) Turn ignition off. Disconnect and inspect PTU/overdrive solenoid connector. Repair connector if damaged. Perform VERIFICATION TEST VER-2. If connector is okay, turn ignition on. Place DRB-II in voltmeter mode. Probe Dark Blue wire in transmission solenoid connector. If voltage is 10 volts or less, repair open Dark Blue wire. Perform VERIFICATION TEST VER-2.

2) If voltage is more than 10 volts, turn ignition off. Disconnect and inspect engine controller connector. Repair connector if damaged. Perform VERIFICATION TEST VER-2. If connector is okay, place DRB-II in ohmmeter mode.

3) Probe engine controller connector terminal No. 54 (Orange/Black wire). If resistance is 10 ohms or more, repair open Orange/Black wire. Perform VERIFICATION TEST VER-2. If resistance is less than 10 ohms, reconnect solenoid connector.

4) Turn ignition on. Place DRB-II in voltmeter mode. Probe terminal No. 54 (Orange/Black wire) in engine controller connector. If voltage is more than 10 volts, replace engine controller. Perform VERIFICATION TEST VER-2. If voltage is 10 volts or less, replace PTU solenoid. Perform VERIFICATION TEST VER-2.

TEST DR-25A

CODE 45, OVERDRIVE SOLENOID CIRCUIT (WITHOUT LOCK-UP)

NOTE: For connector terminal identification, see CONNECTOR IDENTIFICATION at beginning of article. For wiring diagram, see appropriate WIRING DIAGRAMS article in ENGINE PERFORMANCE.

1) Turn ignition off. Disconnect and inspect overdrive solenoid connector. Repair connector if damaged. Perform VERIFICATION TEST VER-2. If connector is okay, turn ignition on. Place DRB-II in voltmeter mode. Probe Dark Blue wire in transmission overdrive solenoid connector. If voltage is 10 volts or less, repair open Dark Blue wire. Perform VERIFICATION TEST VER-2.

2) If voltage is more than 10 volts, turn ignition off. Disconnect and inspect engine controller connector. Repair connector if damaged. Perform VERIFICATION TEST VER-2. If connector is okay, place DRB-II in ohmmeter mode. Probe engine controller connector terminal No. 55 (Brown wire on Pickup and Ramcharger, Orange/White wire on Van).

3) If resistance is less than 10 ohms, repair Brown wire (Orange/White wire on Van) for a short to ground. Perform VERIFICATION TEST VER-2. If resistance is 10 ohms or more, check resistance of Brown wire (Orange/White wire on Van) between engine controller and solenoid connectors using a DVOM. If resistance is 10 ohms or more, repair open Brown wire (Orange/White wire on Van). Perform VERIFICATION TEST VER-2.

4) If resistance is less than 10 ohms, reconnect solenoid connector. Turn ignition on. Place DRB-II in voltmeter mode. Probe terminal No. 55 (Brown wire on Pickup and Ramcharger, Orange/White wire on Van) in engine controller connector. If voltage is more than 10 volts, replace engine controller. Perform VERIFICATION TEST VER-2. If voltage is 10 volts or less, replace overdrive solenoid. Perform VERIFICATION TEST VER-2.

TEST DR-26A

CODE 45, OVERDRIVE SOLENOID CIRCUIT (WITH LOCK-UP)

NOTE: For connector terminal identification, see CONNECTOR IDENTIFICATION at beginning of article. For wiring diagram, see appropriate WIRING DIAGRAMS article in ENGINE PERFORMANCE.

TEST DR-26A (Cont.)

1) Turn ignition off. Disconnect and inspect PTU/overdrive solenoid connector. Repair connector if damaged. Perform VERIFICATION TEST VER-2. If connector is okay, turn ignition on. Place DRB-II in voltmeter mode. Probe Dark Blue wire in transmission solenoid connector. If voltage is 10 volts or less, repair open Dark Blue wire. Perform VERIFICATION TEST VER-2.

2) If voltage is more than 10 volts, turn ignition off. Disconnect and inspect engine controller connector. Repair connector if damaged. Perform VERIFICATION TEST VER-2. If connector is okay, place DRB-II in ohmmeter mode. Probe engine controller connector terminal No. 55 (Brown wire on Pickup and Ramcharger, Orange/White wire on Van).

3) If resistance is less than 10 ohms, repair Brown wire (Orange/White wire on Van) for a short to ground. Perform VERIFICATION TEST VER-2. If resistance is 10 ohms or more, check resistance of Brown wire (Orange/White wire on Van) between engine controller and solenoid connectors using a DVOM. If resistance is 10 ohms or more, repair open Brown wire (Orange/White wire on Van). Perform VERIFICATION TEST VER-2.

4) If resistance is less than 10 ohms, reconnect solenoid connector. Turn ignition on. Place DRB-II in voltmeter mode. Probe terminal No. 55 (Brown wire on Pickup and Ramcharger, Orange/White wire on Van) in engine controller connector. If voltage is more than 10 volts, replace engine controller. Perform VERIFICATION TEST VER-2. If voltage is 10 volts or less, replace PTU/overdrive solenoid. Perform VERIFICATION TEST VER-2.

TEST DR-27A

CODE 42, NO AUTO SHUTDOWN (ASD) RELAY VOLTAGE SENSE AT ENGINE CONTROLLER

NOTE: For connector terminal identification, see CONNECTOR IDENTIFICATION at beginning of article. For wiring diagram, see appropriate WIRING DIAGRAMS article in ENGINE PERFORMANCE.

1) Turn ignition off. Disconnect Auto Shutdown (ASD) relay. Disconnect and inspect engine controller 60-pin connector. Repair connector terminals if damaged. Perform VERIFICATION TEST VER-2. If connector terminals are okay, go to next step.

2) Using a DVOM, check resistance at Dark Green/Orange wire between engine controller connector terminal No. 8 and ASD relay terminal "D". If resistance is less than 10 ohms, replace engine controller. Perform VERIFICATION TEST VER-2. If resistance is 10 ohms or more, repair Dark Green/Orange wire for open to harness splice. Perform VERIFICATION TEST VER-2.

TEST DR-28A

CODE 36, AIR SWITCHING SOLENOID CIRCUIT

NOTE: For connector terminal identification, see CONNECTOR IDENTIFICATION at beginning of article. For wiring diagram, see appropriate WIRING DIAGRAMS article in ENGINE PERFORMANCE.

1) Turn ignition off. Disconnect and inspect air switching solenoid connector. Repair connector if damaged. Perform VERIFICATION TEST VER-2. If connector is okay, turn ignition on. Place DRB-II in voltmeter mode. Probe Dark Blue wire in air switching solenoid connector. If voltage is 10 volts or less, repair open Dark Blue wire. Perform VERIFICATION TEST VER-2.

2) If voltage is more than 10 volts, turn ignition off. Disconnect and inspect engine controller 60-pin connector. Repair connector terminals if damaged. Perform VERIFICATION TEST VER-2. If connector terminals are okay, place DRB-II in ohmmeter mode. Probe engine controller connector terminal No. 36 (Black/Orange wire). If resistance is less than 10 ohms, repair Black/Orange wire for a short to ground. Perform VERIFICATION TEST VER-2.

CHRY
1-134

1992 ENGINE PERFORMANCE
Self-Diagnostic Tests – 5.9L Gasoline (Cont.)

TEST DR-28A (Cont.)

3) If resistance is 10 ohms or more, check resistance of Black/Orange wire between engine controller connector terminal No. 36 and air switching solenoid connector using a DVOM. If resistance is 10 ohms or more, repair open Black/Orange wire. Perform VERIFICATION TEST VER-2. If resistance is less than 10 ohms, reconnect air switching solenoid connector. Turn ignition on. Place DRB-II in voltmeter mode.

4) Probe engine controller connector terminal No. 36 (Black/Orange wire). If voltage is more than 10 volts, replace engine controller. Perform VERIFICATION TEST VER-2. If voltage is 10 volts or less, replace air switching solenoid. Perform VERIFICATION TEST VER-2.

TEST DR-29A

CODE 62, CONTROLLER FAILURE EMR MILES NOT STORED OR
CODE 63, CONTROLLER FAILURE EEPROM WRITE DENIED

NOTE: Aftermarket scan testers may not be able to reset EMR mileage. DRB-II may be required for this test.

1) Turn ignition on. Perform EMR Memory Check Test using DRB-II. If DRB-II displays WRITE FAILURE, replace engine controller. Perform VERIFICATION TEST VER-2. If DRB-II displays WRITE REFUSED, go to step 3). If DRB-II displays EMR MILEAGE INVALID, update mileage and retest EMR mileage. Perform VERIFICATION TEST VER-2.

2) If DRB-II does not display WRITE FAILURE, WRITE REFUSED or EMR MILEAGE INVALID, compare EMR mileage stored with instrument panel odometer. If mileage is the same, retest EMR memory. Perform VERIFICATION TEST VER-2. If mileage is not the same, update mileage and retest EMR mileage. Perform VERIFICATION TEST VER-2.

3) If DRB-II displayed WRITE REFUSED in step 1), engine controller was busy. Perform EMR Memory Check Test using DRB-II. Retest EMR memory 2 or more times if necessary. If WRITE REFUSED fault returns, replace engine controller. Perform VERIFICATION TEST VER-2. If WRITE REFUSED fault does not return, test is complete. Perform VERIFICATION TEST VER-2.

TEST DR-30A

INTERMITTENT SENSOR VOLTAGE FAULT

1) If intermittent fault is SLOW CHANGE OR NO CHANGE IN MAP, perform TEST DR-30B. If intermittent fault was not SLOW CHANGE OR NO CHANGE IN MAP, start engine. Using DRB-II, read suspect sensor circuit voltage. While monitoring voltage, wiggle suspect sensor connector and wiring. If engine stalls or voltage becomes erratic, repair wiring or connector problem at sensor. Perform VERIFICATION TEST VER-2.

2) If engine does not stall or voltage does not become erratic, wiggle sections of wiring harness between sensor and engine controller. Wait 5 seconds before moving to next section of harness. If engine stalls or sensor voltage is erratic when wiring harness is wiggled, repair harness where wiggling caused erratic reading. Perform VERIFICATION TEST VER-2. If engine does not stall or voltage is not erratic, test is complete. Perform VERIFICATION TEST VER-2.

TEST DR-30B

INTERMITTENT SENSOR VOLTAGE FAULT

NOTE: For connector terminal identification, see CONNECTOR IDENTIFICATION at beginning of article. For wiring diagram, see appropriate WIRING DIAGRAMS article in ENGINE PERFORMANCE.

1) Start engine. Using DRB-II, set engine speed to 1400 RPM and read MAP sensor voltage. Wiggle MAP sensor wiring harness while monitoring voltage. If engine stalls or if MAP sensor voltage is erratic, repair wiring or connector defect at MAP sensor. Perform VERIFICATION TEST VER-2.

TEST DR-30B (Cont.)

2) If engine does not stall or MAP sensor voltage is not erratic, turn ignition off. Install a vacuum "T" into MAP sensor vacuum hose. Connect a vacuum gauge. Start engine. Snap throttle open and closed while watching vacuum gauge.

3) If vacuum drops rapidly to zero in. Hg, test is complete. Perform VERIFICATION TEST VER-2. If vacuum does not drop rapidly to zero in. Hg, remove MAP sensor and check for vacuum restrictions. Repair restrictions as necessary. Perform VERIFICATION TEST VER-2. If no restrictions exist, replace MAP sensor. Perform VERIFICATION TEST VER-2.

TEST DR-31A

INTERMITTENT TEST FOR AUTOMATIC IDLE SPEED (AIS) MOTOR

1) Turn ignition on. Using DRB-II, erase faults and actuate AIS motor. Read secondary indicators while actuating AIS motor. Wiggle AIS motor connector. If fault indicator returns, repair wiring or connector problem at AIS motor. Perform VERIFICATION TEST VER-2.

2) If fault indicator does not return, wiggle sections of wiring harness between AIS motor and engine controller. Wait 5 seconds before moving to next section of wiring harness.

3) If fault indicator returns, repair wiring harness where wiggling caused indicator to return. Perform VERIFICATION TEST VER-2. If fault indicator does not return, test is complete. Perform VERIFICATION TEST VER-2.

TEST DR-32A

INTERMITTENT INJECTOR CONTROL FAULT

NOTE: For connector terminal identification, see CONNECTOR IDENTIFICATION at beginning of article. For wiring diagram, see appropriate WIRING DIAGRAMS article in ENGINE PERFORMANCE.

1) Using DRB-II, erase fault codes. Start engine. Using DRB-II, select SECONDARY INDICATORS. Wiggle wiring harness from suspect fuel injector to engine controller. If fault indicator returns, repair harness where wiggling caused indicator to return. Perform VERIFICATION TEST VER-2.

2) If fault indicator does not return, visually inspect related harness connectors. Look for broken, bent, pushed-out or corroded terminals. Visually inspect related harnesses. Look for chafed, pierced or partially broken wire. Repair wiring and/or connectors as necessary. Test is complete. Perform VERIFICATION TEST VER-2.

TEST DR-33A

INTERMITTENT TEST FOR RELAYS & SOLENOIDS

1) Turn ignition on. Using DRB-II, erase faults and actuate suspect solenoid or relay. Read secondary indicators while actuating solenoid or relay. Wiggle connector at intermittent solenoid or relay.

2) If fault indicator returns, repair wiring or defective connector at solenoid or relay. Perform VERIFICATION TEST VER-2. If fault indicator does not return, wiggle sections of wiring harness between solenoid or relay and engine controller. Wait 5 seconds before moving to next section of wiring harness.

3) If fault indicator returns, repair wiring harness where wiggling caused fault indicator to return. Perform VERIFICATION TEST VER-2. If fault indicator does not return, test is complete. Perform VERIFICATION TEST VER-2.

1992 ENGINE PERFORMANCE
Self-Diagnostic Tests – 5.9L Gasoline (Cont.)

CHRY
1-135

TEST DR-34A

INTERMITTENT AUTO SHUTDOWN SENSE CIRCUIT FAULT

1) Turn ignition on. Using DRB-II, erase fault codes and select ACTUATE ASD RELAY. Using DRB-II, select SECONDARY INDICATORS. Observe secondary indicators while wiggling wires and connectors of ASD circuit. If ASD fault returns, repair harness or connector where wiggling caused fault indicator to return. Perform VERIFICATION TEST VER-2.

2) If ASD fault does not return, visually inspect related wire harness connectors. Look for broken, bent, pushed-out or corroded terminals. Visually inspect related harnesses. Look for chafed, pierced or partially broken wire. Repair wiring and/or connectors as necessary. Test is complete. Perform VERIFICATION TEST VER-2.

TEST NF-1A

NO FAULT CODE TEST MENU

Check MITCHELL® TECHNICAL SERVICE BULLETINS (TSBs) for any pertinent information. If a TSB exists, perform corrective action. If TSB does not exist or if driveability problem still exists after performing TSB, check suspect system and perform indicated test. See NO FAULT CODE TEST MENU table. If system causing driveability problem is not known, perform TEST NF-2A through TEST NF-16A in sequence until problem is found.

NO FAULT CODE TEST MENU

Application	Test
Checking Air Pump Switching	NF-10A
Checking Closed Throttle Switch	NF-6A
Checking Coolant Sensor & TPS Calibrations	NF-4A
Checking EGR Valve Operation	NF-9A
Checking Engine Controller Grounds	NF-13A
Checking Engine Mechanical	NF-16A
Checking Engine Vacuum	NF-14A
Checking Fuel Pressure	NF-3A
Checking Idle Speed Motor Operation	NF-7A
Checking MAP Sensor Calibration	NF-5A
Checking Maximum Airflow	NF-15A
Checking Oxygen (O_2) Sensor Switching	NF-11A
Checking Park/Neutral Switch (A/T Only)	NF-12A
Checking Secondary Ignition & Timing	NF-2A
Checking Solenoid Operation	NF-8A

TEST NF-2A

CHECKING SECONDARY IGNITION & TIMING

1) Turn engine off. Connect engine analyzer to engine. Start engine and let it idle. Set scope to read display or parade pattern. Follow equipment manufacturer's procedure for pattern analysis.

2) If secondary ignition pattern is not okay, repair indicated component in secondary ignition system. Perform VERIFICATION TEST VER-2. If secondary ignition pattern is okay, disconnect any spark plug wire. Observe secondary kilovolt line.

3) If open circuit secondary voltage is less than 25 kilovolts, replace ignition coil. Perform VERIFICATION TEST VER-2. If open circuit secondary voltage is at least 25 kilovolts, reinstall spark plug wire. Ensure engine temperature is more than 180°F (82°C) before proceeding. Disconnect coolant sensor connector. Coolant sensor fault should set and check engine light should turn on.

4) Connect timing light and check ignition timing. If timing is not within 2 degrees of specification, adjust ignition timing to specification. Perform VERIFICATION TEST VER-2. Reconnect coolant sensor connector. Using DRB-II, read spark advance. Increase engine speed to 2000 RPM. If spark advance does not change with increase in RPM, replace engine controller. Perform VERIFICATION TEST VER-2. If spark advance changes with increase in RPM, test is complete.

TEST NF-3A

CHECKING FUEL PRESSURE

WARNING: High fuel pressure may be present in fuel lines. Open fuel system with caution. See FUEL PRESSURE RELEASE procedure in SELF-DIAGNOSTICS INTRODUCTION – GASOLINE article.

1) Relieve fuel pressure. Connect fuel pressure gauge in line to throttle body. Turn ignition on. Using DRB-II, actuate ASD fuel system test. If fuel pressure is 12-16 psi, test is complete. If fuel pressure is not 12-16 psi, record fuel pressure reading. If pressure is more than 16 psi, perform TEST NF-3B.

2) If fuel pressure is less than 12 psi, stop ASD fuel system actuation test. Turn ignition off. Inspect fuel lines for kinks or restrictions. Repair fuel lines as necessary. Perform VERIFICATION TEST VER-2. If lines are not kinked or restricted, release fuel pressure. Remove fuel pressure gauge.

3) Install fuel pressure gauge between fuel tank and fuel filter. Turn ignition on. Actuate ASD fuel system test using DRB-II. If fuel pressure is more than 12 psi, replace fuel filter. Perform VERIFICATION TEST VER-2.

CAUTION: DO NOT allow fuel pressure to exceed 20 psi when squeezing fuel return hose.

4) If fuel pressure is not at least 12 psi, gently squeeze fuel return hose while observing fuel pressure gauge, ensuring fuel pressure does not exceed 20 psi. If fuel pressure increases, replace fuel pressure regulator. Perform VERIFICATION TEST VER-2. If fuel pressure does not increase, replace fuel pump and sock assembly. Perform VERIFICATION TEST VER-2.

TEST NF-3B

CHECKING FUEL PRESSURE

WARNING: High fuel pressure may be present in fuel lines. Open fuel system with caution. See FUEL PRESSURE RELEASE procedure in SELF-DIAGNOSTICS INTRODUCTION – GASOLINE article.

1) Using DRB-II, stop fuel system actuation test. Relieve fuel pressure. Ensure fuel tank is at least 1/2 full before performing following test. Remove fuel return line from fuel pump at fuel tank. Connect a 6' piece of fuel hose to fuel return line. Place other end of hose into an approved 2-gallon gasoline can.

2) Turn ignition on. Using DRB-II, actuate ASD fuel system test. Observe fuel pressure gauge. If fuel pressure is 12-16 psi, repair fuel return line for a restriction at fuel tank. Perform VERIFICATION TEST VER-2. If fuel pressure is not 12-16 psi, stop ASD fuel system actuation test. Relieve fuel pressure.

3) Reconnect fuel return line to fuel tank. Disconnect fuel return line from throttle body. Attach 6' piece of fuel hose to fitting on throttle body. Place other end of hose into an approved 2-gallon gasoline can. Turn ignition on. Actuate ASD fuel system test. Observe fuel pressure gauge.

4) If fuel pressure is 12-16 psi, repair restricted fuel return line to fuel tank. Perform VERIFICATION TEST VER-2. If fuel pressure is not 12-16 psi, replace fuel pressure regulator. Perform VERIFICATION TEST VER-2.

TEST NF-4A

CHECKING COOLANT SENSOR & THROTTLE POSITION SENSOR (TPS) CALIBRATIONS

1) Start engine. Allow engine to reach normal operating temperature. Using DRB-II, read coolant temperature sensor value. If temperature is not 180-220°F (82-104°C), replace coolant temperature sensor. Perform VERIFICATION TEST VER-2. If temperature is 180-220°F (82-104°C), turn engine off.

2) Turn ignition on. Using DRB-II, read TPS voltage with throttle fully closed and against throttle stop. If voltage is 1.5 volts or more with throttle closed, replace TPS. Perform VERIFICATION TEST VER-2. If voltage is less than 1.5 volts with throttle fully closed, monitor TPS voltage while slowly opening throttle to wide open position.

1992 ENGINE PERFORMANCE
Self-Diagnostic Tests – 5.9L Gasoline (Cont.)

TEST NF-4A (Cont.)

3) If voltage change is not a smooth transition, replace TPS. Perform VERIFICATION TEST VER-2. If voltage change is a smooth transition, check if maximum voltage is at least 3.4 volts with throttle wide open. If maximum voltage is not at least 3.4 volts with throttle wide open, replace TPS. Perform VERIFICATION TEST VER-2.

4) If maximum voltage is at least 3.4 volts, read minimum throttle voltage using DRB-II. If voltage is not 0-1.5 volts, replace TPS. Perform VERIFICATION TEST VER-2. If voltage is 0-1.5 volts, test is complete.

TEST NF-5A

CHECKING MANIFOLD ABSOLUTE PRESSURE (MAP) SENSOR CALIBRATION

1) Turn engine off. Install vacuum "T" in MAP sensor vacuum hose. Install vacuum gauge. Start engine, and let it idle. Using DRB-II, read vacuum gauge. If DRB-II vacuum reading is within one in. Hg of vacuum gauge reading, test is complete. If DRB-II vacuum reading is not within one in. Hg of vacuum gauge reading, go to next step.

2) Turn engine off. Using DRB-II, read MAP sensor voltage. Disconnect vacuum gauge from MAP sensor. Connect an auxiliary vacuum pump to MAP sensor. Apply 5 in. Hg vacuum to MAP sensor. Read and record MAP sensor voltage. Increase vacuum to 20 in. Hg. Read and record MAP sensor voltage. Subtract voltage recorded at 20 in. Hg vacuum from voltage recorded at 5 in. Hg vacuum.

3) If difference is 2.3-2.9 volts, repair restriction in vacuum hose to MAP sensor. Perform VERIFICATION TEST VER-2. If voltage difference is not 2.3-2.9 volts, replace MAP sensor. Perform VERIFICATION TEST VER-2.

TEST NF-6A

CHECKING CLOSED THROTTLE SWITCH

NOTE: For connector terminal identification, see CONNECTOR IDENTIFICATION at beginning of article. For wiring diagram, see appropriate WIRING DIAGRAMS article in ENGINE PERFORMANCE.

1) Using DRB-II, read throttle switch. Open and close throttle. If display changed between open and closed, test passed. If display did not change between open and closed, turn ignition off. Disconnect engine controller connector. Close throttle. Place DRB-II in ohmmeter mode. Probe engine controller connector terminal No. 28 (Violet wire). If resistance is less than 10 ohms, perform TEST NF-6B.

2) If resistance is 10 ohms or more, disconnect AIS motor connector. Place DRB-II in ohmmeter mode. Probe Black/White wire in AIS motor connector. If resistance is 10 ohms or more, repair open Black/White wire. Perform VERIFICATION TEST VER-2. If resistance is less than 10 ohms, connect a jumper wire between AIS motor connector Black/White and Violet wires.

3) If resistance is less than 10 ohms, replace AIS motor. Perform VERIFICATION TEST VER-2. If resistance is 10 ohms or more, repair open Violet wire.

TEST NF-6B

CHECKING CLOSED THROTTLE SWITCH

NOTE: For connector terminal identification, see CONNECTOR IDENTIFICATION at beginning of article. For wiring diagram, see appropriate WIRING DIAGRAMS article in ENGINE PERFORMANCE.

While probing engine controller connector terminal No. 28 (Violet wire), hold throttle open. If resistance is 10 ohms or more, replace engine controller. Perform VERIFICATION TEST VER-2. If resistance is less than 10 ohms, disconnect AIS motor connector. Probe engine controller connector terminal No. 28. If resistance is less than 10 ohms, repair Violet wire for a short. Perform VERIFICATION TEST VER-2. If resistance is 10 ohms or more, replace AIS motor. Perform VERIFICATION TEST VER-2.

TEST NF-7A

CHECKING IDLE SPEED ACTUATION OPERATION

NOTE: For connector terminal identification, see CONNECTOR IDENTIFICATION at beginning of article. For wiring diagram, see appropriate WIRING DIAGRAMS article in ENGINE PERFORMANCE.

1) Turn ignition on. Using DRB-II, actuate AIS motor. If actuator extends and retracts, test passed. If actuator does not extend and retract, disconnect AIS motor connector while actuating AIS motor. Check for voltage between Brown/White and Yellow/Black wire (Gray/Red wire on Van) using a DVOM.

2) If voltage is pulsating, replace AIS motor. Perform VERIFICATION TEST VER-2. If voltage is not pulsating, turn ignition off. Disconnect engine controller connector. Using a DVOM, check resistance of Yellow/Black wire (Gray/Red wire on Van). If resistance is 10 ohms or more, repair open Yellow/Black wire (Gray/Red wire on Van). Perform VERIFICATION TEST VER-2.

3) If resistance is less than 10 ohms, check resistance of Brown/White wire between engine controller connector terminal No. 40 and AIS motor connector. If resistance is less than 10 ohms, replace engine controller. Perform VERIFICATION TEST VER-2. If resistance is 10 ohms or more, repair open Brown/White wire. Perform VERIFICATION TEST VER-2.

TEST NF-8A

CHECKING SOLENOID OPERATION

NOTE: For connector terminal identification, see CONNECTOR IDENTIFICATION at beginning of article. For wiring diagram, see appropriate WIRING DIAGRAMS article in ENGINE PERFORMANCE.

1) Actuate air switching solenoid. Check air switching solenoid operation by touching top of solenoid. If air switching solenoid is not operating, replace air switching solenoid. Perform VERIFICATION TEST VER-2. If air switching solenoid is operating, actuate purge solenoid. Check purge solenoid operation by touching top of solenoid. If purge solenoid is not operating, replace purge solenoid. Perform VERIFICATION TEST VER-2.

NOTE: If vehicle is not equipped with EGR solenoid, test is complete.

2) If purge solenoid is operating, actuate EGR solenoid (if equipped). Check EGR solenoid operation by touching top of solenoid. If EGR solenoid is not operating, replace EGR solenoid. Perform VERIFICATION TEST VER-2. If EGR solenoid is operating, test is complete.

TEST NF-9A

CHECKING EGR VALVE OPERATION

1) Disconnect vacuum hose to EGR backpressure transducer. Connect vacuum gauge to disconnected vacuum hose. Start engine. Disconnect AIS motor. While observing vacuum gauge, snap throttle open and closed. If vacuum is more than 5 in. Hg at any time, go to step 3). If vacuum is not more than 5 in. Hg at any time, turn ignition off.

2) Disconnect vacuum hose connector at EGR solenoid. Connect vacuum gauge to top port in vacuum hose connector. Start engine. Read vacuum gauge at idle. If vacuum is 10 in. Hg or less at idle, repair vacuum hose between EGR solenoid and manifold vacuum source. Perform VERIFICATION TEST VER-2. If vacuum is more than 10 in. Hg at idle, replace EGR solenoid. Perform VERIFICATION TEST VER-2.

3) If vacuum is more than 5 in. Hg in step 1), turn ignition off. Disconnect vacuum gauge from EGR vacuum supply hose. Reconnect EGR vacuum supply hose to backpressure transducer. Disconnect vacuum hose from EGR valve. Connect vacuum gauge to disconnected hose. Start engine. While reading vacuum gauge, snap throttle open and closed. If vacuum is not more than 5 in. Hg at any time, replace EGR valve assembly. Perform VERIFICATION TEST VER-2.

1992 ENGINE PERFORMANCE
Self-Diagnostic Tests – 5.9L Gasoline (Cont.)

CHRY
1-137

TEST NF-9A (Cont.)

4) If vacuum reading is more than 5 in. Hg at any time, turn ignition off. Disconnect vacuum hose to EGR backpressure signal tube. Adjust shop air supply hose to 20 psi. Connect shop air to backpressure signal tube nipple. While opening and closing throttle, listen for a tone change. If the tone changes, replace EGR valve assembly. Perform VERIFICATION TEST VER-2.

5) If tone does not change, disconnect vacuum gauge. Cap open backpressure signal tube nipple. Connect vacuum pump to EGR valve. Start engine. While slowly applying vacuum to EGR valve, listen for an engine RPM change. If engine RPM changes, go to step 7).

6) If engine RPM did not change, turn ignition off. Apply 10 in. Hg vacuum and hold for 30 seconds. If vacuum does not hold for 30 seconds, replace EGR valve assembly. Perform VERIFICATION TEST VER-2. If vacuum holds for 30 seconds, test is complete.

7) Remove EGR valve. Inspect manifold passages for plugging. Clean passages if plugged. Perform VERIFICATION TEST VER-2. If passages are not plugged, replace EGR valve assembly. Perform VERIFICATION TEST VER-2.

TEST NF-10A

CHECKING AIR PUMP SWITCHING

1) Disconnect upstream and downstream air switching valve hoses. Disconnect and plug vacuum hose from air switching hose. Start engine. Check air switching valve port for airflow. If air is flowing at downstream port only, go to step 3).

2) If air is not flowing at downstream port only, check if air is flowing at upstream port. If air is flowing at upstream port, replace air switching valve. Perform VERIFICATION TEST VER-2. If air is not flowing at upstream port, replace air pump. Perform VERIFICATION TEST VER-2.

3) Connect vacuum pump to air switching valve. Apply 16 in. Hg vacuum to air switching valve. Check airflow at downstream port. If air is flowing at downstream port, replace air switching valve. Perform VERIFICATION TEST VER-2. If air is not flowing at downstream port, connect a vacuum gauge to control valve vacuum hose.

4) If vacuum reading is more than 10 in. Hg vacuum, go to next step. If vacuum reading is 10 in. Hg vacuum or less, check vacuum hose to air switching valve for leaks or restrictions. Repair vacuum hose as necessary. Perform VERIFICATION TEST VER-2. If vacuum hose is okay, replace air switching solenoid.

5) Raise engine speed to 1500 RPM. If vacuum reading is zero in. Hg, test passed. If vacuum reading is not zero in. Hg, check air switching solenoid supply hoses and bleed hose for restrictions. Repair vacuum hose as necessary. Perform VERIFICATION TEST VER-2. If vacuum hose is okay, replace air switching solenoid. Perform VERIFICATION TEST VER-2.

TEST NF-11A

CHECKING OXYGEN (O_2) SENSOR SWITCHING

1) Allow engine to reach normal operating temperature. Using DRB-II, read O_2 sensor state. Raise engine speed to 1500 RPM. If O_2 sensor state is switching, test is complete. If O_2 sensor state is not switching, check if O_2 sensor is locked on lean. If O_2 sensor is locked on lean, perform TEST NF-11B. If O_2 sensor is not locked on lean, go to next step.

2) Turn engine off. Turn ignition on. Actuate ASD fuel system test. Inspect injectors for leakage, replace leaking injectors or "O" rings as necessary. Perform VERIFICATION TEST VER-3. If injectors are not leaking, stop ASD fuel system actuation test.

3) Inspect air filter and inlet ducts for restrictions. If any restrictions exist, replace air filter or repair air inlet system as necessary. Perform VERIFICATION TEST VER-3. If there are no restrictions, perform TEST NF-16A.

TEST NF-11B

CHECKING OXYGEN (O_2) SENSOR (LOCKED LEAN)

NOTE: For connector terminal identification, see CONNECTOR IDENTIFICATION at beginning of article. For wiring diagram, see appropriate WIRING DIAGRAMS article in ENGINE PERFORMANCE.

1) Allow engine to idle. Inspect engine for vacuum leaks. Repair vacuum leaks as necessary. Perform VERIFICATION TEST VER-3. If there are no vacuum leaks, read O_2 sensor signal voltage using DRB-II. If voltage is .1 volt or more, go to step 3). If voltage is less than .1 volt, turn ignition off. Disconnect O_2 sensor and engine controller connectors.

2) Put DRB-II in ohmmeter mode. Probe engine controller connector terminal No. 41 (Black/Dark Green wire). If resistance is less than 10 ohms, repair short to ground in Black/Dark Green wire. Perform VERIFICATION TEST VER-3. If resistance is 10 ohms or more, replace O_2 sensor. Perform VERIFICATION TEST VER-3.

3) If O_2 sensor voltage is .1 volt or more in step 1), turn engine off. Replace O_2 sensor. Turn ignition on. Using DRB-II, reset adaptive fuel memory. Start engine and allow it to reach normal operating temperature. Using DRB-II, read O_2 sensor state. Raise engine speed to 1500 RPM. If O_2 sensor state is switching, test is complete. Perform VERIFICATION TEST VER-3. If O_2 sensor state is not switching, perform TEST NF-16A.

TEST NF-12A

CHECKING PARK/NEUTRAL SWITCH INPUT (A/T ONLY)

NOTE: For connector terminal identification, see CONNECTOR IDENTIFICATION at beginning of article. For wiring diagram, see appropriate WIRING DIAGRAMS article in ENGINE PERFORMANCE.

1) Using DRB-II, read park/neutral switch input state. While watching DRB-II display, move gear selector in and out of Park and Reverse positions. If display shows P/N and D/R, system is functioning correctly. If display does not show P/N and D/R, go to next step.

2) Turn ignition off. Place gear selector in Park position. Disconnect engine controller connector. Disconnect starter relay connector. Place DRB-II in ohmmeter mode. Probe terminal No. 30 (Brown/Yellow wire) in engine controller connector. Watch DRB-II display while moving gear selector in and out of Park and Reverse positions.

3) If display switches from less than 5 ohms to more than 5 ohms, replace ignition switch. Perform VERIFICATION TEST VER-2. If display stays less than 5 ohms, repair short to ground in Brown/Yellow wire. Perform VERIFICATION TEST VER-2. If display does not always stay less than 5 ohms, disconnect park/neutral switch connector.

4) Using a DVOM, check resistance of Brown/Yellow wire between park/neutral switch connector and engine controller connector terminal No. 30. If resistance is less than 10 ohms, replace park/neutral switch. Perform VERIFICATION TEST VER-2. If resistance is 10 ohms or more, repair open Brown/Yellow wire. Perform VERIFICATION TEST VER-2.

TEST NF-13A

CHECKING ENGINE CONTROLLER GROUND & POWER CIRCUITS

NOTE: For connector terminal identification, see CONNECTOR IDENTIFICATION at beginning of article. For wiring diagram, see appropriate WIRING DIAGRAMS article in ENGINE PERFORMANCE.

1) Turn ignition off. Disconnect and inspect engine controller connector. Repair connector if damaged. Perform VERIFICATION TEST VER-2. If connector terminals are okay, place DRB-II in ohmmeter mode. Probe engine controller connector terminal No. 5 (Black/White wire). If resistance is one ohm or more, repair open in Black/White wire. Perform VERIFICATION TEST VER-2.

CHRY
1-138

1992 ENGINE PERFORMANCE
Self-Diagnostic Tests – 5.9L Gasoline (Cont.)

TEST NF-13A (Cont.)

2) If resistance is less than one ohm, go to next step. Probe engine controller connector terminal No. 11 (Black/Tan wire on Pickup and Ramcharger, Light Blue/Red wire on Van). If resistance is one ohm or more, repair open in Black/Tan wire (Light Blue/Red wire on Van). Perform VERIFICATION TEST VER-2. If resistance is less than one ohm, go to next step.

3) Probe engine controller connector terminal No. 12 (Black/Tan wire on Pickup and Ramcharger, Light Blue/Red wire on Van). If resistance is one ohm or more, repair open in Black/Tan wire (Light Blue/Red wire on Van). Perform VERIFICATION TEST VER-2. If resistance is less than one ohm, place DRB-II in voltmeter mode. Turn ignition on.

4) Probe engine controller connector terminal No. 9 (Dark Blue wire). If voltage is 10 volts or less, repair open Dark Blue wire. Perform VERIFICATION TEST VER-2. If voltage is more than 10 volts, reconnect SBEC connector. Test is complete.

TEST NF-14A

CHECKING ENGINE VACUUM

Connect a vacuum gauge to engine. Start engine, and let it idle. Normal vacuum reading will vary depending on altitude. Observe vacuum gauge at idle. If vacuum gauge reading is not steady 13-22 in. Hg vacuum, perform TEST NF-16A. If vacuum gauge reading is steady 13-22 in. Hg vacuum, perform TEST NF-15A.

TEST NF-15A

CHECKING MAXIMUM AIRFLOW

Turn ignition off. Disconnect AIS motor and coolant temperature sensor connectors. Start engine. Using DRB-II, read RPM value. Engine speed should be 2700-2900 RPM (2600-2900 RPM if odometer reading is less than 1000 miles). If RPM is as specified, test is complete. If RPM is not as specified, adjust engine speed to 2750-2850 RPM (2650-2750 if odometer reading is less than 1000 miles) by turning adjusting screw on ISC motor.

TEST NF-16A

PERFORMING NO FAULT CODE MECHANICAL TEST

At this point in diagnostic test procedure, all engine control systems have been determined to be operating as designed and not causing a driveability problem. Following additional items should be checked as possible causes:

NOTE: If coming to this test from O₂ sensor test and rich or lean condition is not corrected after checking the following items, replace engine controller.

* Check if any MITCHELL® TECHNICAL SERVICE BULLETINS (TSBs) apply to vehicle.
* Check engine vacuum. It must be at least 13 in. Hg in Neutral.
* Check valve timing.
* Check engine compression.
* Check for exhaust system restriction.
* Ensure PCV system is functioning properly.
* Check camshaft and crankshaft sprockets.
* Check torque converter stall speed.
* Check power brake booster for internal vacuum leak.
* Check for fuel contamination.
* Ensure injector control wire is connected to correct fuel injector and injector is not plugged or restricted.

TEST VER-1

VERIFICATION TEST VER-1

1) Inspect vehicle to ensure all engine components are connected. Reassemble and reconnect components as necessary. Attempt to start engine. If engine does not start, return to TEST NS-1A.

2) If engine starts and engine controller was changed, write vehicle mileage from its odometer to memory location within replacement engine controller. This will enable new engine controller to operate Emission Maintenance Reminder (EMR) light properly. On all models, no-start condition is corrected and repair is now complete.

3) If engine starts and engine controller has not been changed, connect DRB-II to engine diagnostic connector, and erase faults. No-start condition has been corrected and fault messages have been erased. Repair is now complete.

TEST VER-2

VERIFICATION TEST VER-2

If VERIFICATION TEST VER-3 was performed previously, perform VERIFICATION TEST VER-3 again. Inspect vehicle to ensure all engine components are connected. Reassemble and reconnect components as necessary. If another fault was read previously and not corrected, return to TEST DR-1A and follow path specified by other fault. If engine controller was replaced, perform following:

1) Write vehicle mileage from its odometer to memory location within replacement engine controller. This will enable new engine controller to operate Emission Maintenance Reminder (EMR) light properly. Connect DRB-II to engine diagnostic connector, and erase faults. Disconnect DRB-II.

2) Start engine and allow it to reach normal operating temperature. Raise engine speed to 2000 RPM for at least 10 seconds. Allow engine to idle. On A/T models, apply brake and cycle transmission through all gear ranges. Place gear selector in Park position. If vehicle is equipped with A/C, turn on A/C. Set blower to low speed.

3) On all models, turn engine off. Start engine. Allow engine to idle for at least 2 minutes. Turn engine off. Using DRB-II, read fault messages. If repaired fault resets, repair is not complete. Check all pertinent MITCHELL® TECHNICAL SERVICE BULLETINS (TSBs), and return to TEST DR-1A if necessary. If another fault exists, return to TEST DR-1A and follow path specified by other fault. If no other faults exist, repair is now complete.

TEST VER-3

VERIFICATION TEST VER-3

Inspect vehicle to ensure all engine components are connected. Reassemble and reconnect components as necessary. If another fault was read previously and not corrected, return to TEST DR-1A and follow path specified by other fault. If engine controller has been replaced, perform following:

* Write vehicle odometer mileage to memory location within replacement engine controller. This will enable new engine controller to operate Emission Maintenance Reminder (EMR) light properly.
* Connect DRB-II to engine diagnostic connector, and erase faults. Disconnect DRB-II.

To ensure no other fault remains, perform following:

1) If vehicle is equipped with A/C, turn A/C on. Set blower to low speed. On all models, drive vehicle for at least 5 minutes and attain a speed of at least 40 MPH. Ensure transmission shifts through all gears. Upon completion of road test, turn engine off. Restart engine, and let it idle for at least 2 minutes.

2) Turn engine off. Connect DRB-II to engine diagnostic connector. Read all fault messages. If repaired fault has reset, repair is not complete. Check all pertinent MITCHELL® TECHNICAL SERVICE BULLETINS (TSBs), and return to TEST DR-1A if necessary. If another fault exists, return to TEST DR-1A and follow path specified by other fault. If no other faults exist, repair is now complete.

Pickup

INTRODUCTION

If no faults were found while performing BASIC DIAGNOSTIC PROCEDURES – DIESEL article, proceed with self-diagnostics. If no fault codes are present after entering self-diagnostics, proceed to TROUBLE SHOOTING – NO CODES – DIESEL article for diagnosis by symptom (i.e. ROUGH IDLE, NO START, etc.).

SELF-DIAGNOSTIC SYSTEM

WARNING: When battery is disconnected, vehicle computer and memory systems may lose memory data. Driveability problems may exist until computer systems have completed a relearn cycle. See COMPUTER RELEARN PROCEDURES article in GENERAL INFORMATION before disconnecting battery.

SYSTEM DIAGNOSIS

The self-diagnostic capabilities of this system, if properly utilized, can simplify testing. The Single-Board Engine Controller (SBEC) monitors several different engine control system circuits.

If a problem is sensed with a monitored circuit, a fault code is stored in the SBEC, the CHECK ENGINE light illuminates, and SBEC enters limp-in mode. In limp-in mode, SBEC compensates for component failure by substituting information from other sources. This allows vehicle operation until repairs can be made.

Once fault codes are known, refer to FAULT CODES table in this article to determine the questionable circuit. Test circuits and repair or replace components as required. If problem is repaired or ceases to exist, the SBEC cancels that fault code after approximately 50 ignition on-off cycles. To clear fault codes, see CLEARING FAULT CODES in this article.

A fault code does not condemn a specific component. Component is not necessarily the reason for failure. Fault codes pinpoint probable malfunctioning circuits.

Hard Failures – Hard failures cause CHECK ENGINE light to illuminate and remain on until the malfunction is repaired. If light comes on and remains on (light may flash) during vehicle operation, cause of malfunction must be determined using diagnostic (code) charts. If a sensor fails, SBEC will use a substitute value in its calculations, allowing engine operation in limp-in mode. In this condition, vehicle will run but driveability may be poor.

NOTE: A start counter (key counter) appears at bottom of fault message on DRB-II to show number of engine starts since fault code last occurred. This helps determine if fault is intermittent. As an example, if DRB-II displays 0 STARTS SINCE ERS, it indicates zero engine starts since fault occurred, and fault code is a hard failure. If start counter (key counter) shows more than zero engine starts since fault last occurred, then fault code is an intermittent failure.

Intermittent Failures – Intermittent failures may cause CHECK ENGINE light to flicker or illuminate and go out after the intermittent fault goes away. However, the corresponding fault code will be retained in SBEC memory.

If related fault does not reoccur within a certain time frame, fault code will be erased from SBEC memory. Intermittent failures can be caused by a defective sensor, connector, or wiring-related problems. See INTERMITTENTS in TROUBLE SHOOTING – NO CODES – DIESEL article.

SERVICE PRECAUTIONS

Before proceeding with diagnosis, the following precautions must be followed:

- Vehicle must have a fully charged battery, and functional charging system.
- Probe SBEC connector from pin side. DO NOT backprobe SBEC connector.

- DO NOT cause short circuits when performing electrical tests. This will set additional fault codes, making diagnosis of original problem more difficult.
- DO NOT use a test light instead of a voltmeter.
- Always repair lowest fault code number (CHECK ENGINE light) or first fault displayed (DRB-II) first.
- Always perform VERIFICATION TEST VER-1 after repairs.
- Always disconnect DRB-II after use.
- Always disconnect DRB-II before charging battery.

CAUTION: DRB-II will be damaged if connected to vehicle while battery is being recharged.

VISUAL INSPECTION

Most driveability problems in engine control system result from faulty wiring, poor electrical connections or leaking air and vacuum hose connections. To avoid unnecessary component testing, perform a visual inspection before beginning self-diagnostic tests.

DIAGNOSTIC PROCEDURES

To obtain fault codes, see ENTERING ON-BOARD DIAGNOSTICS. If fault codes are not present and/or Diagnostic Readout Box II (DRB-II) is used, proceed to one of following tests.

- Go to TEST DR-1A (DRIVEABILITY TEST 1A) if engine runs but has performance problems. Perform VERIFICATION TEST VER-1 after repairs. Ensure self-diagnostic tests apply to engine being tested. See SELF-DIAGNOSTICS DIRECTORY table under SELF-DIAGNOSTIC SYSTEM.
- Go to TEST NF-1A (NO FAULT CODE TEST 1A) if a driveability problem exits and no fault codes are present. Perform VERIFICATION TEST VER-1 after repairs. Ensure self-diagnostic tests apply to engine being tested. See SELF-DIAGNOSTICS DIRECTORY table under SELF-DIAGNOSTIC SYSTEM.

NOTE: When using diagnostic tests, DO NOT skip any steps in chart or incorrect diagnosis may result.

ENTERING ON-BOARD DIAGNOSTICS

NOTE: Although other scan testers are available, manufacturer recommends using DRB-II (Diagnostic Readout Box-II) to diagnose the system. CHECK ENGINE light function can be used but has limited diagnostic usage.

CHECK ENGINE Light Diagnostic Mode – 1) Start engine (if possible). Move transmission shift lever through all gear positions, ending in Park. Turn A/C switch on, then off (if equipped).
2) Turn engine off. Without starting engine again, turn ignition on, off, on, off, and on. Record 2-digit fault codes as displayed by the flashing CHECK ENGINE light.
3) For example, Code 23 is displayed as flash, flash, 4-second pause, flash, flash, flash. After a slightly longer pause, other codes stored are displayed in numerical order.
4) Once CHECK ENGINE light begins to flash fault codes, it cannot be stopped. If you lose count, it will be necessary to start over. Code 55 indicates end of fault code display.
5) Refer to FAULT CODES table to translate fault code number to a system fault description (display on DRB-II). Once fault code description is obtained, refer to TEST DR-1A (DRIVEABILITY TEST 1A) for additional testing procedures.
6) Select fault message and corresponding test from table, and proceed to appropriate test. Test procedure may vary depending whether fault code is a hard or intermittent failure.

1992 ENGINE PERFORMANCE
Self-Diagnostics – Diesel (Cont.)

NOTE: When using diagnostic tests, DO NOT skip any steps in chart or incorrect diagnosis may result.

NOTE: DRB-II can also be used to: display state or values of sensors, inputs/outputs and components; allow various outputs such as valves and hydraulics to be tested; and reset Emission Maintenance Reminder (EMR) functions. See OPERATING MODES and EMISSION MAINTENANCE REMINDER (EMR) MILEAGE TRANSFER.

DRB-II Diagnostic Mode – 1) Turn ignition off. Attach DRB-II Tester (C-4805) to diagnostic connector. See Fig. 1.

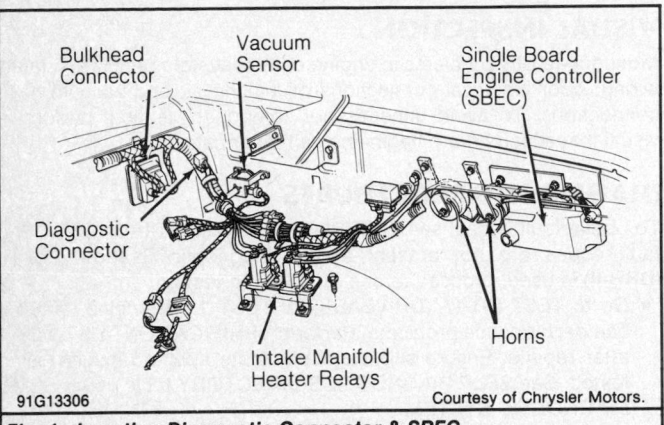

Bulkhead Connector
Vacuum Sensor
Single Board Engine Controller (SBEC)
Diagnostic Connector
Intake Manifold Heater Relays
Horns

91G13306
Courtesy of Chrysler Motors.

Fig. 1: Locating Diagnostic Connector & SBEC

2) Start engine (if possible). Move transmission shift lever through all positions, ending in Park. Turn A/C switch on, then off (if equipped). Turn engine off. Without starting engine again, turn ignition on. DO NOT touch keypad on DRB-II during power-up sequence, or an error will result. The copyright date and diagnostic program will be displayed briefly.

3) If DRB-II screen is blank, or if an error message appears, proceed to DRB-II PROBLEMS & ERROR MESSAGES in this article. The following are possible error messages that may appear: BAD FRAMING, BAD OP CODE, CARTRIDGE ERROR, COMMAND REJECTED, HIGH BATTERY, KEYPAD TEST FAILURE, LOW BATTERY, NO RESPONSE or RAM TEST FAILURE.

4) After a few seconds, display will change to read as follows: DRB-II, 1) VEHICLES TESTED, or 2) HOW TO USE, 3) CONFIGURE, and 4) SELECT SYSTEM.

5) Select No. 4 (SELECT SYSTEM) to enter the diagnostic system. Display will read as follows: SELECT SYSTEM, 1) ENGINE, 2) TRANSMISSION, 3) BODY. Press the down arrow UP TO 5 times to view rest of menu. Display will change to read as follows: SELECT SYSTEM, 4) SUSPENSION 5) ABS, 6) PASSIVE REST. and will scroll to 7) THEFT ALARM and 8) SYSTEM MONITORS.

6) Select No. 1 (ENGINE) to enter the engine system part of the DRB-II program. Display will change to read as follows: 1992 5.9, XXXX EMISSIONS, AUTOMATIC TRANS, SBEC XX,#XXXX.

NOTE: Display may vary slightly depending on engine package being diagnosed.

7) After a few seconds, display will change to read as follows: AIR COND, 1) WITH A/C, and 2) WITHOUT A/C. Press ENTER button to change display immediately. Select No. 1 or No. 2 as appropriate for vehicle being tested.

8) Display will now read as follows: ENGINE SYSTEM, 1) FUEL/IGNITION, 2) CHARGING, and 3) SPEED CONTROL. Select No. 1 (FUEL/IGNITION) to bring up menu of test categories for the fuel/ignition system. Display will change to read as follows: FUEL/IGN MENU, 1) SYSTEM TEST and 2) READ FAULTS.

9) Press the down arrow 3 times to view rest of menu. Display will read as follows: FUEL/IGN MENU, 3) STATE DISPLAY, 4) ACTUATOR TEST, and 5) ADJUSTMENTS. To read fault codes, select No. 2 (READ FAULTS).

FAULT CODES

FAULT CODES

Code	Display On DRB-II [1]	Fault Condition
11	NO REFERENCE SIGNAL DURING CRANKING	No Reference Signal From Crankshaft Position Sensor Picked Up During Cranking.
15	NO VEHICLE SPEED SIGNAL	No Distance Sensor Signal Detected With Road Load Conditions.
22	COOLANT SENSOR VOLTAGE TOO LOW	Coolant Temperature Sensor Input Less Than Minimum Acceptable Voltage.
	COOLANT SENSOR VOLTAGE TOO HIGH	Coolant Temperature Sensor Input More Than Maximum Acceptable Voltage.
23	CHARGE TEMP VOLT LOW	Charge Temperature Sensor Input Less Than Minimum Acceptable Voltage.
	CHARGE TEMP VOLT HI	Charge Temperature Sensor Input More Than Maximum Acceptable Voltage.
24 [2]	TPS VOLTAGE LOW	TPS Sensor Input Less Than Minimum Acceptable Voltage.
	TPS VOLTAGE HIGH	TPS Sensor Input More Than Maximum Acceptable Voltage.
33	A/C CLUTCH RELAY CKT	Open Or Shorted Condition Detected In A/C Clutch Relay Circuit.
34	S/C SOLENOIDS CKT	Open Or Shorted Condition Detected In Speed Control (S/C) Vacuum Or Vent Solenoid Circuits.
41 [2]	ALTERNATOR FIELD CKT	An Open Or Shorted Condition Detected In Alternator Field Circuit.
42	ASD RELAY CIRCUIT	An Open Or Shorted Condition Detected In ASD Relay Circuit.
	NO ASD RELAY VOLTAGE SENSED AT SBEC	No ASD Relay Voltage Sensed When ASD Relay Is Energized.
45 [2]	OVERDRIVE SOLENOID	An Open Or Shorted Condition Detected In Overdrive Solenoid Circuit.
46 [3]	CHARGING VOLTAGE TOO HIGH	Battery Voltage Sense Input More Than Target Charging Voltage During Engine Operation.
47 [3]	CHARGING VOLTAGE TOO LOW	Battery Voltage Sense Input Less Than Target Charging Voltage During Engine Operation And No Significant Change In Voltage Detected During Active Test Of Alternator Output.
62	EMR MILES NOT STORED	Unsuccessful Attempt To Update EMR Mileage In SBEC EEPROM
63	SBEC FAILURE EEPROM WRITE DENIED	Unsuccessful Attempt To Write To An EEPROM Location By SBEC.

[1] – Actual message displayed on DRB-II may vary between vehicles.
[2] – Automatic transmission only.
[3] – If code is displayed, charging system malfunction exists. See appropriate ALTERNATORS & REGULATORS article in ELECTRICAL.

10) If no fault code exists, display will read as follows: NO FAULTS DETECTED. If fault codes exist, display will show number of faults detected, such as 1 of 3 faults, and fault message. This is fault counter. Below fault message, start counter (key counter) will list number of starts since fault code was set.

11) Start counter (key counter) helps to determine if fault is intermittent. As an example, if DRB-II displays 0 STARTS SINCE ERS, zero engine starts have occurred since fault occurred and fault code is a hard failure. If start counter (key counter) on DRB-II shows more than zero engine starts since fault last occurred, fault code is an intermittent failure.

12) If more than one fault code exists, press down arrow to display next fault code. All fault codes must be read before fault codes can be erased. Once fault codes are obtained, refer to TEST DR-1A (DRIVEABILITY TEST 1A).

NOTE: When using diagnostic tests, DO NOT skip any steps in chart or incorrect diagnosis may result.

CLEARING FAULT CODES

NOTE: Place DRB-II in FUEL/IGN MENU to erase fault codes. This menu is obtained when retrieving fault codes. See DRB-II DIAGNOSTIC MODE under ENTERING ON-BOARD DIAGNOSTICS.

1) Once fault codes have been read and DRB-II is in FUEL/IGN MENU, press the down arrow. Display will read as follows: ERASE FAULTS, 1) DON'T ERASE, and 2) ERASE. Press the down arrow.

2) Display will ask you if you are sure you want to erase fault codes. Press ENTER button to erase fault codes. DRB-II will display FAULTS ERASED message.

NOTE: ERASE FAULTS option is also available in ADJUSTMENTS MENU.

OPERATING MODES

SYSTEM TEST MODE

This mode is not available in the engine diagnostics program.

READ FAULTS MODE

This mode allows user to read and erase fault codes. A fault counter will appear along with fault displayed. As an example, DRB-II will display 1 OF 2 FAULTS. SBEC will store up to 8 fault messages. Faults are numbered in reverse order of setting. The most recent fault to occur will be displayed first. Vehicles without air conditioning will always have A/C CLUTCH RELAY CKT (circuit) stored in memory. This fault will always be displayed first if vehicle is not equipped with A/C. If no fault messages are stored, DRB-II will display NO FAULTS DETECTED and start counter will show 0 STARTS SINCE ERS (erased).

A start counter will appear below DRB-II fault counter display. Start counter counts the number of times vehicle is started since faults were last set or erased or battery was disconnected. This helps determine if fault is intermittent. Memory space limits start counter to first 3 faults. Start counter of zero equals a hard fault. Start counter of more than zero indicates an intermittent fault. Start counter will count up to 255 starts. If no fault messages are stored, DRB-II will display NO FAULTS DETECTED and start counter will show 0 STARTS SINCE ERS (erased).

STATE DISPLAY MODE

The SBEC can only recognize high and low states on switch circuits. SBEC cannot tell the difference between switch position versus an open or short circuit, or a defective switch.

If a change is noted, it is assumed entire switch circuit to the SBEC is operating correctly. The following information can be selected from the state display mode: module, sensors, inputs/outputs, monitors, and custom displays.

Module Info – When module information is selected from STATE DISPLAY mode, information about the SBEC, such as, engine application, transmission application and identification number can be obtained. Information can be used to verify proper SBEC application.

Sensors – When sensor information is selected from STATE DISPLAY mode, information is provided about engine operation through various sensors and engine controls. The following information may be displayed.

* Charge Temperature
* Charge Temperature Sensor Voltage
* Coolant Temperature
* Coolant Temperature Sensor Voltage
* Engine Speed
* Minimum Throttle Position Sensor Voltage
* Throttle Position Sensor Voltage
* Vehicle Speed
* Water/Fuel Voltage Reading

Inputs/Outputs – When input/output information is selected from state display mode, information is provided about component operation through various lights, relays, solenoids and switches. The following information may be displayed.

* A/C Clutch Relay
* A/C Switch
* Auto Shutdown (ASD) Relay
* Brake Switch
* CHECK ENGINE Light
* Intake Manifold Heater Relay No. 1
* Intake Manifold Heater Relay No. 2
* Overdrive Override Light
* Overdrive Override Switch
* Overdrive Solenoid
* Park Neutral Switch (A/T Models)
* Transmission Coolant Temperature Switch
* WAIT-TO-START Light
* WATER-IN-FUEL Light

Monitors – **1)** When monitors information is selected from state display mode, information is provided about component operation. The interrogators choice is for use during the engineering process. This mode is not available in the engine diagnostics program.

2) SEC (Secondary) Indicators mode allows user to display inputs and outputs which are not within optimum parameters but have not yet become faults. Secondary indicators are monitored by the DRB-II at all times after engine is selected in SELECT SYSTEM menu and may be viewed live or recorded.

3) When a secondary indicator is generated, DRB-II will emit 5 short beeps. If a secondary indicator becomes a hard fault, DRB-II Red LED (light emitting diode) will glow.

4) If no secondary indicators are being generated, SEC INDICATORS screen will indicate as such if LIVE is chosen. If RECORDED is chosen, first secondary indicator displayed is oldest. Subsequent indicators are displayed in ascending order. XX INDICATORS RECORDED screen is displayed after newest indicator is displayed.

Custom Displays – This mode allows the user to customize DRB-II display. The user can select up to 4 different displays which can be shown on a single screen. Any item from inputs/output list, sensor list or actuator list can be selected from the custom display. Once selected, custom display will be retained in memory until changed. Up to 2 custom display screens can be customized by user.

ACTUATOR TEST MODE

Actuator test mode is used to check operation of output circuits of devices the SBEC cannot recognize. The following can be activated in actuator test mode to ensure component operation: relays, solenoids and various components. The following are information or components that may be accessed through actuator test mode.

* A/C Clutch Relay
* All Solenoid/Relays
* ASD (Alternator Field)
* ASD (Auto Shutdown) Relay
* ASD (Auto Shutdown) System
* Intake Manifold Heater Relay No. 1

- Intake Manifold Heater Relay No. 2
- Overdrive Solenoid
- Stop All Tests
- Tachometer Output

ADJUSTMENTS MODE

Erase Faults – This mode erases fault messages which are stored in SBEC memory. Once this mode is selected, DRB-II displays ARE YOU SURE?. If fault erasure is not desired, press ATM key. If fault erasure is desired, press ENTER key; all faults and secondary indicators will be erased.

Reset Memory – This mode provides a sub-menu listing resettable memories. As vehicle is operated, SBEC learns minimum throttle position sensor signal voltage to compensate for different engine operating conditions. Following mode can be accessed from RESET MEMORY menu: MINIMUM TPS. For additional information about function of this mode, see DRB-II manufacturer's manual.

Reset EMR Light – This mode allows user to reset EMR light.

EMR Memory Check – This mode allows user to check and, if necessary, correct mileage stored in SBEC. See EMISSION MAINTENANCE REMINDER (EMR) MILEAGE TRANSFER.

DRB-II VOLT/OHMMETER

1) To access volt/ohmmeter mode of DRB-II, connect Red volt/ohmmeter test lead to Red port, located on right top side of DRB-II.

NOTE: Because DRB-II is grounded through engine diagnostic connector, only one volt/ohmmeter test lead is required when using volt/ohmmeter option. DRB-II volt/ohmmeter should only be used when self-diagnostic tests require the use of this option.

2) To access voltmeter, press VOLT/OHM key once. DRB-II is now in voltmeter mode. Touch test probe to connector or wire to be measured. Read voltage on DRB-II display. When voltage testing is complete, press VOLT/OHM key 3 times to exit voltmeter mode.

3) To access ohmmeter, press VOLT/OHM key twice. DRB-II is now in ohmmeter mode. Touch test probe to connector or wire to be measured. Read resistance to circuit ground on DRB-II display. When resistance testing is complete, press VOLT/OHM key twice to exit ohmmeter mode.

DRB-II Continuity Meter Mode – Press VOLT/OHM key 3 times. Display will read NO CONTINUITY. Touch test probe to connector or wire to be measured. Read continuity on DRB-II display. When continuity testing is complete, press VOLT/OHM key once to exit continuity meter mode.

DRB-II PROBLEMS & ERROR MESSAGES

Blank Message Screen – 1) Connect DRB-II to a different vehicle. If message screen is still blank, DRB-II or cable adapter are faulty. Substitute to find faulty component.

2) If message screen is not blank, DRB-II and cable adapter are functioning properly. Inspect diagnostic connector for proper wire placement, damaged terminals and pushed-out pins. Repair as necessary.

3) If engine diagnostic connector is okay, check for continuity between Black/tracer wire (tracer color may vary) and ground at engine diagnostic connector using an ohmmeter. If continuity does not exist, repair open in Black/tracer wire.

NO RESPONSE Message – 1) Connect DRB-II to another vehicle. If DRB-II displays NO RESPONSE message again, DRB-II or cable adapter are faulty. Substitute to find faulty component. If message screen does not display NO RESPONSE, DRB-II and cable adapter are functioning properly. Go to next step.

2) Turn ignition off. Disconnect DRB-II. Using an ohmmeter, check Pink wire for continuity between SBEC connector terminal No. 25 and engine diagnostic connector. If continuity does not exist, repair open in Pink wire.

3) If continuity exists, check Light Green wire for continuity between SBEC connector terminal No. 45 and engine diagnostic connector. If continuity does not exist, repair open in Light Green wire.

RAM TEST FAILURE Message – Replace DRB-II.

CARTRIDGE ERROR Or ROM CHECKSUM FAILURE Message – Replace DRB-II cartridge.

KEYPAD TEST FAILURE Message – Ensure ignition is off. DO NOT touch keypad on DRB-II. Turn ignition on. If DRB-II displays KEYPAD TEST FAILURE message, replace DRB-II, and proceed with diagnostics. If KEYPAD TEST FAILURE message is not displayed, proceed with diagnostics.

NOTE: HIGH BATTERY or LOW BATTERY message may not be displayed on all models.

HIGH BATTERY Or LOW BATTERY Message – If message is displayed, connect DRB-II to a different vehicle. If message is still present, DRB-II or adapter cable are faulty. Substitute components as needed. If DRB-II and adapter cable are okay, check charging system.

EMISSION MAINTENANCE REMINDER (EMR) MILEAGE TRANSFER

1) When SBEC is replaced, vehicle mileage must be copied from odometer to replacement SBEC memory. Transfer of vehicle mileage will enable new SBEC to operate EMR light properly.

2) Using DRB-II, enter FUEL/IGN MENU. See ENTERING ON-BOARD DIAGNOSTICS. At FUEL/IGN menu, press "5" (ADJUSTMENTS) key. Press ENTER key. At ADJUSTMENTS menu, press "4" (EMR MEMORY CHECK) key. Press ENTER key. DRB-II will display EMR MEMORY CHECK ARE YOU SURE? ENTER TO CONTINUE.

3) Press ENTER key. DRB-II will display IS INSTRUMENT PANEL MILEAGE BETWEEN XXXX AND XXXXX? If vehicle mileage is within specification, EMR memory check is complete. Press YES key. If vehicle mileage is not within specification, go to next step.

4) Press NO key. DRB-II will display ENTER MILEAGE SHOWN ON INSTRUMENT PANEL, USE ENTER KEY TO END. Enter vehicle mileage. DO NOT enter tenths. When correct vehicle mileage is entered, press ENTER key.

5) DRB-II will ask for verification of mileage entry. If mileage entry was accurate, press ENTER key. DRB-II will display EMR MEMORY CHECK TEST COMPLETE. Vehicle must travel at least 8 miles for reset to occur.

SELF-DIAGNOSTIC DIRECTORY

SELF-DIAGNOSTIC DIRECTORY

CONNECTOR IDENTIFICATION

CONNECTOR IDENTIFICATION DIRECTORY

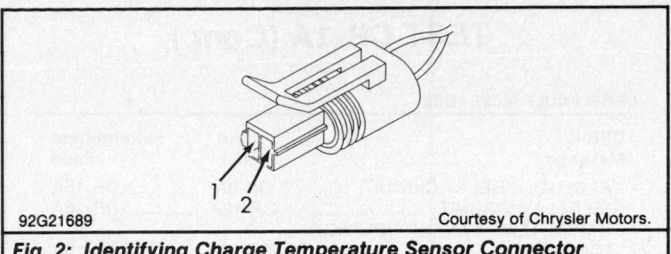

92G21689   Courtesy of Chrysler Motors.

Fig. 2: Identifying Charge Temperature Sensor Connector Terminals

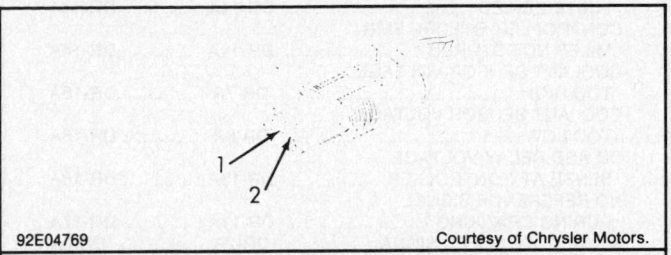

92E04769   Courtesy of Chrysler Motors.

Fig. 3: Identifying Coolant Temperature Sensor & Transmission Thermoswitch Connector Terminals

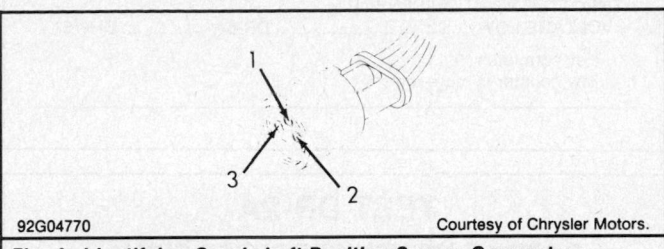

92G04770   Courtesy of Chrysler Motors.

Fig. 4: Identifying Crankshaft Position Sensor Connector Terminals

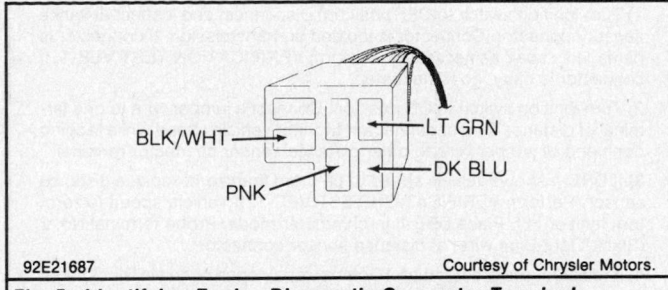

92E21687   Courtesy of Chrysler Motors.

Fig. 5: Identifying Engine Diagnostic Connector Terminals

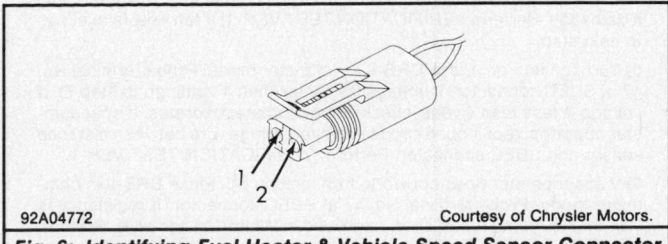

92A04772   Courtesy of Chrysler Motors.

Fig. 6: Identifying Fuel Heater & Vehicle Speed Sensor Connector Terminals

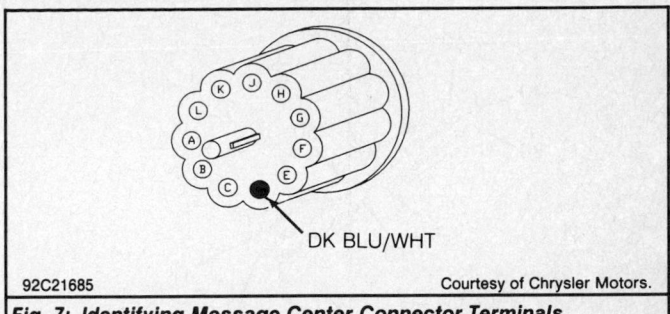

DK BLU/WHT

92C21685   Courtesy of Chrysler Motors.

Fig. 7: Identifying Message Center Connector Terminals

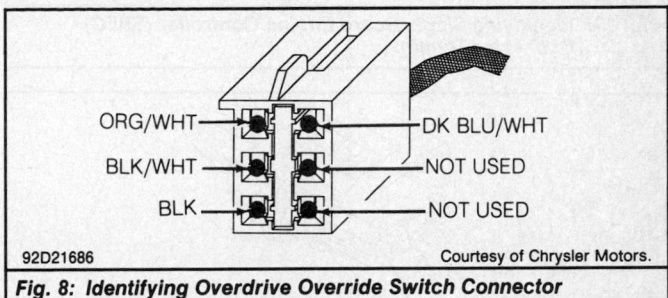

ORG/WHT — — DK BLU/WHT
BLK/WHT — — NOT USED
BLK — — NOT USED

92D21686   Courtesy of Chrysler Motors.

Fig. 8: Identifying Overdrive Override Switch Connector Terminals

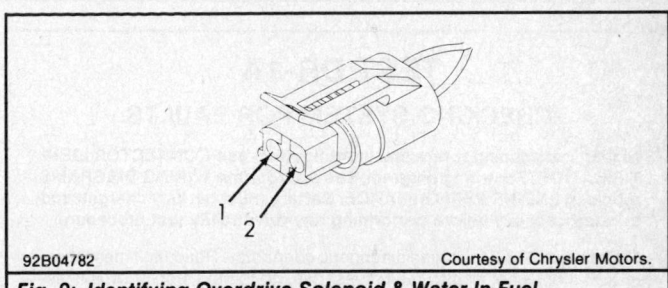

92B04782   Courtesy of Chrysler Motors.

Fig. 9: Identifying Overdrive Solenoid & Water-In-Fuel Sensor Connector Terminals

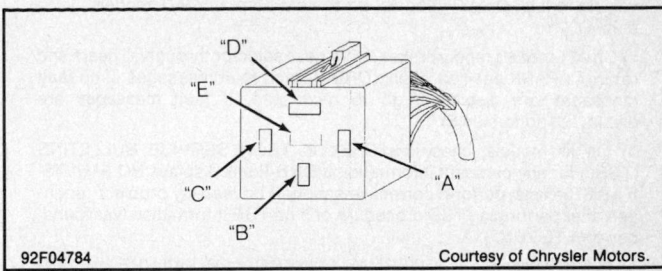

"D"
"E"
"C"
"B"
"A"

92F04784   Courtesy of Chrysler Motors.

Fig. 10: Identifying A/C Clutch & ASD Relay Connector Terminals

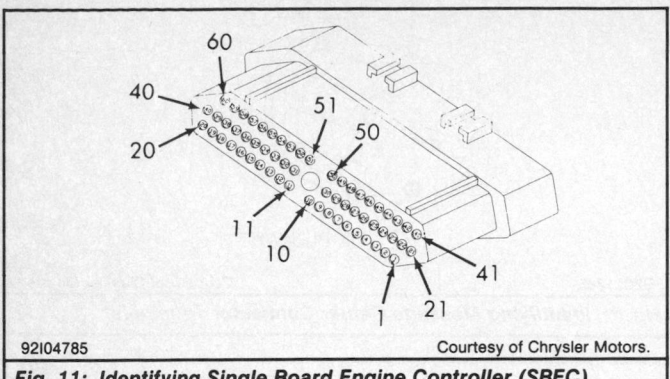

92I04785   Courtesy of Chrysler Motors.

Fig. 11: Identifying Single Board Engine Controller (SBEC) Connector Terminals

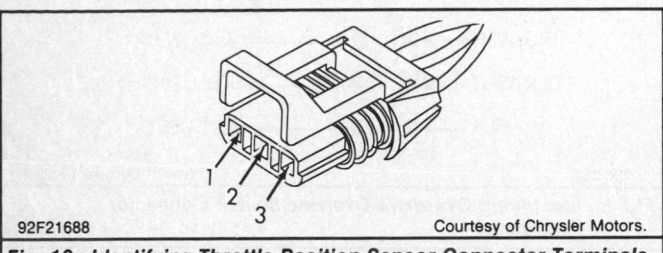

92F21688   Courtesy of Chrysler Motors.

Fig. 12: Identifying Throttle Position Sensor Connector Terminals

TEST DR-1A
CHECKING SYSTEM FOR FAULTS

NOTE: For connector terminal identification, see CONNECTOR IDEN-TIFICATION. For wiring diagram, see appropriate WIRING DIAGRAMS article in ENGINE PERFORMANCE. Battery must be fully charged and at rated capacity before performing any driveability test procedure.

1) Connect DRB-II to engine diagnostic connector. Read fault messages. If DRB-II does not display fault messages, go to next step. If DRB-II displays fault messages, go to step **5)**.

2) Start engine. Allow engine to reach normal operating temperature. Set engine speed manually to 2000 RPM for at least 10 seconds, and return vehicle to idle. On A/T models, go to next step. On M/T models, go to step **4)**.

3) On A/T models, apply brakes. Shift gear selector through all gears and return to PARK position. Using DRB-II, read fault messages. If no fault messages are displayed, go to next step. If fault messages are displayed, go to step **5)**.

4) On all models, check MITCHELL® TECH SERVICE BULLETINS (TSBs) for any pertinent information if DRB-II still displays NO FAULTS. If a TSB exists, perform corrective action. If driveability problem continues after performing TSB procedure or if no TSB information was found, perform TEST NF-1A.

5) If fault message is INTERNAL CONTROLLER FAILURE or CON-TROLLER FAILURE, replace Single Board Engine Controller (SBEC). Perform VERIFICATION TEST VER-1. If fault message is not INTERNAL CONTROLLER FAILURE or CONTROLLER FAILURE, go to next step.

6) Using DRB-II FAULT MESSAGES table, select fault message and corresponding test. Correct all hard fault messages before proceeding to intermittent fault message.

TEST DR-1A (Cont.)

DRB-II FAULT MESSAGES

DRB-II Message	[1] Hard Fault	[2] Intermittent Fault
A/C CLUTCH RELAY CIRCUIT	DR-9A	DR-16A
ASD RELAY CIRCUIT	DR-12A	DR-16A
CHARGE TEMP SENSOR VOLTAGE TOO HIGH	DR-3A	DR-15A
CHARGE TEMP SENSOR VOLTAGE TOO LOW	DR-4A	DR-15A
CONTROLLER FAILURE EEPROM WRITE DENIED	DR-14A	DR-14A
CONTROLLER FAILURE EMR MILES NOT STORED	DR-14A	DR-14A
COOLANT SENSOR VOLTAGE TOO HIGH	DR-7A	DR-15A
COOLANT SENSOR VOLTAGE TOO LOW	DR-8A	DR-15A
NO ASD RELAY VOLTAGE SENSE AT CONTROLLER	DR-13A	DR-18A
NO REFERENCE SIGNAL DURING CRANKING	DR-11A	DR-17A
NO VEHICLE SPEED SIGNAL	DR-2A	DR-2A
OVERDRIVE SOLENOID CIRCUIT	DR-10A	DR-16A
SENSOR GROUND TEST	DR-5B	DR-5B
THROTTLE POSITION SENSOR VOLTAGE HIGH	DR-5A	DR-15A
THROTTLE POSITION SENSOR VOLTAGE LOW	DR-6A	DR-15A

[1] – Key counter is "0".
[2] – Key counter is more than "0".

TEST DR-2A
CODE 15, NO VEHICLE SPEED SIGNAL

NOTE: For wiring diagram, see appropriate WIRING DIAGRAMS article in ENGINE PERFORMANCE.

1) Turn ignition switch to OFF position. Disconnect and inspect distance sensor connector. Connector is located on transmission. If connector is damaged, repair as necessary. Perform VERIFICATION TEST VER-1. If connector is okay, go to next step.

2) Turn ignition switch to ON position. Connect a jumper wire to one terminal of distance sensor connector. Monitor vehicle speed while tapping open end of jumper wire to other distance sensor connector terminal.

3) If DRB-II shows vehicle speed to be more than zero, replace distance sensor. Perform VERIFICATION TEST VER-1. If vehicle speed is zero, turn ignition off. Place DRB-II in ohmmeter mode. Probe terminal No. 2 (Black/Light Blue wire) at distance sensor connector.

4) If resistance is greater than 10 ohms, repair open circuit in Black/Light Blue wire. If resistance is less than 10 ohms, ensure ignition is off. Disconnect Single Board Engine Controller (SBEC) connector. Inspect terminal No. 47 (White/Orange wire) at SBEC connector. Repair terminal if damaged. Perform VERIFICATION TEST VER-1. If terminal is okay, go to next step.

5) Turn ignition on. Place DRB-II in voltmeter mode. Probe terminal No. 47 at SBEC connector. If voltage is greater than 4 volts, go to step **7)**. If voltage is less than 4 volts, check if speedometer operates. If speedometer operates, repair open circuit in White/Orange wire between distance sensor and SBEC connector. Perform VERIFICATION TEST VER-1.

6) If speedometer does not work, turn ignition off. Place DRB-II in ohmmeter mode. Probe terminal No. 47 at SBEC connector. If resistance is less than 5 ohms, repair short to ground in White/Orange wire. Perform VERIFICATION TEST VER-1. If resistance is greater than 5 ohms, repair open White/Orange wire. Perform VERIFICATION TEST VER-1.

7) If voltage at White/Orange wire is greater than 4 volts in step **5)**, probe White/Orange wire at distance sensor connector. Replace SBEC if voltage is greater than 4 volts. Perform VERIFICATION TEST VER-1. If voltage is less than 4 volts, repair open in White/Orange wire between distance sensor and SBEC connector. Perform VERIFICATION TEST VER-1.

TEST DR-3A

CODE 23, CHARGE TEMPERATURE SENSOR VOLTAGE TOO HIGH

NOTE: For connector terminal identification, see CONNECTOR IDEN-TIFICATION. For wiring diagram, see appropriate WIRING DIAGRAMS article in ENGINE PERFORMANCE.

1) Turn ignition on. Using DRB-II, select charge temperature sensor volt-age. Connect a jumper wire across charge temperature sensor connec-tor. Read sensor voltage. If voltage reading is greater than one volt, go to next step. If voltage reading is less than one volt, replace charge tem-perature sensor. Perform VERIFICATION TEST VER-1.

2) Move jumper wire so that terminal No. 2 (Black/Red) wire is connected to chassis ground. Read sensor voltage. If voltage reading is greater than one volt, go to next step. If voltage reading is less than one volt, repair open circuit in Black/Red wire. Perform VERIFICATION TEST VER-1.

3) Turn ignition off. Disconnect SBEC 60-pin connector and inspect con-nector. Repair as necessary. Using an external ohmmeter, check for resistance between charge temperature sensor terminal No. 2 (Black/Red wire) and SBEC connector pin No. 21.

4) If resistance reading is less than 10 ohms, replace SBEC. Perform VERIFICATION TEST VER-1. If resistance reading is greater than 10 ohms, repair open circuit in Black/Red wire between charge temperature sensor connector and SBEC 60-pin connector. Perform VERIFICATION TEST VER-1.

TEST DR-4A

CODE 23, CHARGE TEMPERATURE SENSOR VOLTAGE TOO LOW

NOTE: For connector terminal identification, see CONNECTOR IDEN-TIFICATION. For wiring diagram, see appropriate WIRING DIAGRAMS article in ENGINE PERFORMANCE.

1) Turn ignition on. Using DRB-II, select charge temperature sensor volt-age. Disconnect charge temperature sensor harness connector. If charge temperature sensor voltage reading is greater than 4 volts, replace sensor. Perform VERIFICATION TEST VER-1.

2) If charge temperature sensor voltage reading is less than 4 volts, turn ignition off and disconnect SBEC 60-pin connector. Inspect SBEC connector, and repair as necessary. Place DRB-II in ohmmeter mode.

3) Probe SBEC 60-pin connector cavity No. 21 (Black/Red wire). If resis-tance is greater than 10 ohms, repair short to ground in Black/Red wire. Perform VERIFICATION TEST VER-1. If resistance is less than 10 ohms, replace SBEC. Perform VERIFICATION TEST VER-1.

TEST DR-5A

CODE 23, THROTTLE POSITION SENSOR VOLTAGE HIGH

NOTE: For connector terminal identification, see CONNECTOR IDEN-TIFICATION. For wiring diagram, see appropriate WIRING DIAGRAMS article in ENGINE PERFORMANCE.

1) Turn ignition off. Disconnect and inspect TPS connector. Repair TPS connector if damaged. Perform VERIFICATION TEST VER-1. If TPS con-nector is okay, go to next step.

2) Turn ignition on. Connect jumper wire between TPS connector termi-nals No. 1 (Black/Light Blue wire) and No. 2 (Orange/Dark Blue wire). Using DRB-II, read TPS voltage. If voltage is less than one volt, adjust or replace TPS. For TPS adjustment procedure, See ON-VEHICLE ADJUSTMENTS – DIESEL article.

3) If voltage is greater than one volt, remove jumper wire. Connect jump-er wire between terminal No. 2 (Orange/Dark Blue wire) at TPS connec-tor and chassis ground. Using DRB-II, read TPS voltage. If voltage reading is greater than one volt, perform TEST DR-5B.

TEST DR-5A (Cont.)

4) If voltage is less than one volt, turn ignition off. Disconnect and inspect Single Board Engine Controller (SBEC) 60-pin connector. Repair connector if damaged. If connector is okay, check for continuity between TPS connector pin No. 2 (Orange/Dark Blue wire) and SBEC connector pin No. 22.

5) If resistance is less than 10 ohms, replace SBEC. Perform VERIFICA-TION TEST VER-1. If resistance is greater than 10 ohms, repair open in Orange/Dark Blue wire. Perform VERIFICATION TEST VER-1.

TEST DR-5B

SENSOR GROUND TEST

1) Turn ignition off. Disconnect SBEC connector and inspect for damage. Repair as necessary. If SBEC connector is okay, disconnect TPS connector and inspect for damage. Repair as necessary.

2) Using an external ohmmeter, check for continuity between TPS con-nector pin No. 1 (Black/Light Blue wire) and SBEC connector pin No. 4. If resistance reading is less than 10 ohms, replace SBEC. Perform VER-IFICATION TEST VER-1.

3) If resistance reading is greater than 10 ohms, repair open circuit in Black/Light Blue wire between TPS and SBEC. Perform VERIFICATION TEST VER-1.

TEST DR-6A

CODE 23, THROTTLE POSITION SENSOR VOLTAGE LOW

NOTE: For connector terminal identification, see CONNECTOR IDEN-TIFICATION. For wiring diagram, see appropriate WIRING DIAGRAMS article in ENGINE PERFORMANCE.

1) Turn ignition off. Disconnect TPS connector. Turn ignition on. Place DRB-II in voltmeter mode. Probe terminal No. 1 (Violet/White wire) at TPS connector.

2) If voltage is greater than 4.5 volts, perform TEST DR-6B. If voltage reading is less than 4.5 volts, turn ignition off. Disconnect SBEC connec-tor. Inspect connector and repair as necessary. Place DRB-II in ohmme-ter mode.

3) Probe TPS connector terminal No. 3 (Violet/White wire). If resistance reading is greater than 10 ohms, repair short to ground in Violet/White wire. If resistance reading is less than 10 ohms replace SBEC. Perform VERIFICATION TEST VER-1.

TEST DR-6B

CODE 23, THROTTLE POSITION SENSOR VOLTAGE LOW

1) Probe terminal No. 2 (Orange/Dark Blue wire) at TPS connector. If voltage is greater than 4 volts, replace TPS. If voltage reading is less than 4 volts, turn ignition off.

2) Disconnect Single Board Engine Controller (SBEC) 60-pin connector. Place DRB-II in ohmmeter mode. Probe terminal No. 22 (Orange/Dark Blue wire) at SBEC connector.

3) If resistance is less than 10 ohms, repair short to ground in Orange/Dark Blue wire. Perform VERIFICATION TEST VER-1. If resistance is more than 10 ohms, replace SBEC. Perform VERIFICATION TEST VER-1.

TEST DR-7A

CODE 22, COOLANT SENSOR VOLTAGE TOO HIGH

NOTE: For connector terminal identification, see CONNECTOR IDENTIFICATION. For wiring diagram, see appropriate WIRING DIAGRAMS article in ENGINE PERFORMANCE.

1) Turn ignition off. Disconnect and inspect coolant temperature sensor connector. Repair connector if damage exists. Perform VERIFICATION TEST VER-1. If coolant temperature sensor connector is okay, go to next step.

2) Connect jumper wire between terminals No. 1 (Tan/Black wire) and No. 2 (Black/Light Blue wire) at coolant temperature sensor connector. Turn ignition on. Read coolant temperature sensor voltage on DRB-II display. If voltage is less than one volt, replace coolant temperature sensor. Perform VERIFICATION TEST VER-1.

3) If voltage is greater than one volt, remove jumper wire. Connect jumper wire between terminal No. 1 (Tan/Black wire) at coolant temperature sensor connector and chassis ground. Read coolant temperature sensor voltage. If voltage is less than one volt, repair open in Black/Light Blue wire. Perform VERIFICATION TEST VER-1.

4) If voltage is greater than one volt, disconnect and inspect Single Board Engine Controller (SBEC) 60-pin connector. Repair connector if damaged. Perform VERIFICATION TEST VER-1. If connector is okay, go to next step.

5) Using an external ohmmeter, check resistance of Tan/Black wire between coolant temperature sensor terminal No. 2 and terminal No. 2 at SBEC connector. If resistance is less than 10 ohms, replace SBEC. Perform VERIFICATION TEST VER-1. If resistance is greater than 10 ohms, repair open circuit in Tan/Black wire. Perform VERIFICATION TEST VER-1.

TEST DR-8A

CODE 22, COOLANT SENSOR VOLTAGE TOO LOW

NOTE: For connector terminal identification, see CONNECTOR IDENTIFICATION. For wiring diagram, see appropriate WIRING DIAGRAMS article in ENGINE PERFORMANCE.

1) Turn ignition on. Using DRB-II, read coolant temperature sensor voltage. Disconnect coolant temperature sensor connector. If voltage changed by more than 4 volts, replace coolant temperature sensor. Perform VERIFICATION TEST VER-1. If voltage did not change by more than 4 volts, go to next step.

2) Turn ignition off. Disconnect Single Board Engine Controller (SBEC) 60-pin connector. Place DRB-II in ohmmeter mode. Probe terminal No. 2 (Tan/Black wire) at SBEC connector. If resistance is less than 10 ohms, Tan/Black wire is shorted to Black/Light Blue wire or to ground. Repair wiring as necessary. Perform VERIFICATION TEST VER-1. If resistance is greater than 10 ohms, replace SBEC. Perform VERIFICATION TEST VER-1.

TEST DR-9A

CODE 33, A/C CLUTCH RELAY CIRCUIT

NOTE: For connector terminal identification, see CONNECTOR IDENTIFICATION. For wiring diagram, see appropriate WIRING DIAGRAMS article in ENGINE PERFORMANCE.

1) Turn ignition switch to ON position. Using DRB-II, actuate A/C clutch relay. If relay is not clicking, go to next step. If relay is clicking, perform TEST DR-16A.

2) Remove A/C clutch relay, and inspect connector. Repair connector if damaged. Perform VERIFICATION TEST VER-1. If connector is okay, substitute known good A/C relay. Using DRB-II, actuate A/C relay. If relay is clicking, repair is complete. Perform VERIFICATION TEST VER-1. If relay is not clicking, go to next step.

TEST DR-9A (Cont.)

3) Remove substitute relay. Place DRB-II in voltmeter mode. Probe A/C relay connector terminal "A" (Dark Blue wire). If voltage is less than 10 volts, repair open circuit in Dark Blue wire. Perform VERIFICATION TEST VER-1. If voltage is greater than 10 volts, turn ignition off.

4) Disconnect and inspect Single Board Engine Controller (SBEC) connector. Repair connector if damaged. Perform VERIFICATION TEST VER-1. If connector is okay, put DRB-II in ohmmeter mode. Probe A/C clutch relay connector terminal "C" (Dark Blue/Orange wire). If resistance is less than 10 ohms, repair short to ground in Dark Blue/Orange wire. Perform VERIFICATION TEST VER-1. If resistance is greater than 10 ohms, go to next step.

5) Using external ohmmeter, check resistance at Dark Blue/Orange wire between SBEC connector terminal No. 34 and A/C relay connector terminal "C". If resistance is greater than 10 ohms, repair open Dark Blue/Orange wire. Perform VERIFICATION TEST VER-1. If resistance is less than 10 ohms, go to next step.

6) Reconnect A/C clutch relay. Turn ignition on. Place DRB-II in voltmeter mode. Probe SBEC connector terminal No. 34 (Dark Blue/Orange wire). If voltage is greater than 10 volts, replace SBEC; if voltage is less than 10 volts, replace A/C clutch relay. Perform VERIFICATION TEST VER-1.

TEST DR-10A

CODE 45, OVERDRIVE SOLENOID CIRCUIT

NOTE: For connector terminal identification, see CONNECTOR IDENTIFICATION. For wiring diagram, see appropriate WIRING DIAGRAMS article in ENGINE PERFORMANCE.

1) Turn ignition off. Disconnect overdrive solenoid connector located on transmission. Inspect connector and repair as necessary. Turn ignition on. Place DRB-II in voltmeter mode. Probe overdrive solenoid connector terminal No. 2 (Dark Blue wire).

2) If voltage reading is less than 10 volts, repair open in Dark Blue wire. Perform VERIFICATION TEST VER-1. If voltage reading is greater than 10 volts, turn ignition off and disconnect SBEC 60-pin connector. Inspect connector and repair as necessary.

3) Place DRB-II in ohmmeter mode. Probe SBEC connector cavity No. 55 (Orange/Light Green wire). If resistance reading is greater than 10 ohms, go to next step. If resistance reading is less than 10 ohms, repair short to ground in Orange/Light Green wire. Perform VERIFICATION TEST VER-1.

4) Using an external ohmmeter, check resistance in Orange/Light Green wire between overdrive solenoid connector and SBEC connector cavity No. 55. If resistance reading is less than 10 ohms, go to next step. If resistance reading is greater than 10 ohms, repair open circuit in Orange/Light Green wire. Perform VERIFICATION TEST VER-1.

5) Reconnect overdrive solenoid connector. Turn ignition on. Place DRB-II in voltmeter mode. Probe SBEC cavity No. 55 (Orange/Light Green wire). If voltage reading is less than 10 volts, replace overdrive solenoid. Perform VERIFICATION TEST VER-1. If voltage reading is greater than 10 volts, replace SBEC. Perform VERIFICATION TEST VER-1.

TEST DR-11A

CODE 33, NO REFERENCE SIGNAL DURING CRANKING

NOTE: For connector terminal identification, see CONNECTOR IDENTIFICATION. For wiring diagram, see appropriate WIRING DIAGRAMS article in ENGINE PERFORMANCE.

1) Disconnect crank position sensor and turn ignition on. Place DRB-II in voltmeter mode. Probe crank position sensor connector terminal No. 1 (Tan/Yellow wire). If voltage reading is less than 7 volts, go to next step. If voltage reading is greater than 7 volts, go to step 6).

2) Turn ignition off. Disconnect SBEC 60-pin connector. Inspect connector and repair as necessary. Place DRB-II in ohmmeter mode. Probe crank position sensor connector terminal No. 1 (Tan/Yellow wire).

TEST DR-11A (Cont.)

3) If resistance reading is greater than 5 ohms, go to next step. If resistance reading is less than 5 ohms, repair short to ground in Tan/Yellow wire. Perform VERIFICATION TEST VER-1.

4) Using an external ohmmeter, check for resistance in Tan/Yellow wire between Crank position sensor and SBEC connector cavity No. 7. If resistance reading is greater than 5 ohms, repair open circuit in Tan/Yellow wire. Perform VERIFICATION TEST VER-1.

5) If resistance reading is less than 5 ohms, replace SBEC. Perform VERIFICATION TEST VER-1.

6) Probe crank position sensor connector terminal No. 3 (Gray/Black wire). If voltage reading is less than 4.5 volts, go to next step. If voltage reading is greater than 4.5 volts, go to step **11)**.

7) Turn ignition off. Disconnect SBEC 60-pin connector. Inspect connector and repair as necessary. Place DRB-II in ohmmeter mode. Probe crank position sensor connector terminal No. 3 (Gray/Black wire).

8) If resistance reading is greater than 5 ohms, go to next step. If resistance reading is less than 5 ohms, repair short to ground in Gray/Black wire. Perform VERIFICATION TEST VER-1.

9) Using an external ohmmeter, check for resistance in Gray/Black wire between crank position sensor and SBEC connector cavity No. 24. If resistance reading is greater than 5 ohms, repair open circuit in Gray/Black wire. Perform VERIFICATION TEST VER-1.

10) If resistance reading is less than 5 ohms, replace SBEC. Perform VERIFICATION TEST VER-1.

11) Turn Ignition off. Place DRB-II in ohmmeter mode. Probe crank position sensor terminal No. 2 (Black/Light Blue wire). If resistance reading is greater than 5 ohms, go to next step. If resistance reading is less than 5 ohms, go to step **14)**.

12) Disconnect SBEC 60-pin connector. Using an external ohmmeter, check resistance between crank position sensor terminal No. 2 (Black/Light Blue wire) and SBEC connector cavity No. 4.

13) If resistance reading is greater than 5 ohms, repair open circuit in Black/Light Blue wire. Perform VERIFICATION TEST VER-1. If resistance reading is less than 5 ohms, replace SBEC. Perform VERIFICATION TEST VER-1.

14) Turn ignition on. Connect one end of a jumper wire to crank position sensor terminal No. 3 (Gray/Black wire). Place DRB-II in RPM mode. While observing DRB-II display, tap other end of jumper wire to chassis ground.

15) If RPM reading is 10 RPM, replace crank position sensor. Perform VERIFICATION TEST VER-1. If RPM reading is not 10 RPM, replace SBEC. Perform VERIFICATION TEST VER-1.

TEST DR-12A

CODE 42, ASD RELAY CIRCUIT

NOTE: For connector terminal identification, see CONNECTOR IDENTIFICATION. For wiring diagram, see appropriate WIRING DIAGRAMS article in ENGINE PERFORMANCE.

1) Turn ignition on. Using DRB-II, actuate ASD relay. If relay is making a "clicking" sound perform TEST DR-16A. If relay is not making a "clicking" sound, remove ASD relay. Inspect relay connector and repair as necessary. Perform VERIFICATION TEST VER-1.

NOTE: DO NOT turn off relay actuation.

2) If relay connector is okay, substitute known good relay. If new relay is "clicking", repair is complete. Perform VERIFICATION TEST VER-1. If relay is not "clicking", remove relay. Place DRB-II in voltmeter mode.

3) Probe cavity "A" (Dark Blue wire) of ASD relay connector. If voltage reading is greater than 10 volts, go to next step. If voltage reading is less than 10 volts, repair open circuit in Dark Blue wire. Perform VERIFICATION TEST VER-1.

4) Turn ignition off. Disconnect SBEC 60-pin connector. Inspect connector and repair as necessary. Place DRB-II in ohmmeter mode. Probe cavity "C" (Dark Blue/Yellow wire) of ASD relay connector.

5) If resistance reading is greater than 10 ohms, go to next step. If resistance reading is less than 10 ohms, repair open circuit in Dark Blue/Yellow wire. Perform VERIFICATION TEST VER-1.

TEST DR-12A (Cont.)

6) Using an external ohmmeter, check resistance in Dark Blue/Yellow wire between ASD relay connector and SBEC connector cavity No. 51. If resistance reading is less than 10 ohms, go to next step. If resistance reading is greater than 10 ohms, repair open circuit in Dark Blue/Yellow wire. Perform VERIFICATION TEST VER-1.

7) Reconnect ASD relay. Turn ignition on. Place DRB-II in voltmeter mode. Probe cavity No. 51 of SBEC 60-pin connector. If voltage reading is less than 10 volts, replace ASD relay. Perform VERIFICATION TEST VER-1. If voltage reading is greater than 10 volts, replace SBEC. Perform VERIFICATION TEST VER-1.

TEST DR-13A

CODE 42, NO ASD RELAY VOLTAGE SENSE AT CONTROLLER

NOTE: For connector terminal identification, see CONNECTOR IDENTIFICATION. For wiring diagram, see appropriate WIRING DIAGRAMS article in ENGINE PERFORMANCE.

1) Turn ignition off. Disconnect Auto Shutdown (ASD) relay. Disconnect Single Board Engine Controller (SBEC) 60-pin connector. Inspect connector terminals. Repair connector terminals if damaged. Perform VERIFICATION TEST VER-1. If connector terminals are okay, go to next step.

2) Using an external ohmmeter, check resistance at Dark Green/Orange wire between SBEC connector terminal No. 57 and ASD relay terminal "D". If resistance is less than 10 ohms, replace SBEC. Perform VERIFICATION TEST VER-1. If resistance is greater than 10 ohms, repair open Dark Green/Orange wire. Perform VERIFICATION TEST VER-1.

TEST DR-14A

CODE 62 & 63, CONTROLLER FAILURE EMR MILES NOT STORED & CONTROLLER FAILURE EEPROM WRITE DENIED

1) Turn ignition switch to ON position. Perform EMR Memory Test using DRB-II. If DRB-II displays WRITE FAILURE, replace Single Board Engine Controller (SBEC). Perform VERIFICATION TEST VER-1.

2) If DRB-II displays WRITE REFUSED, SBEC was busy. Perform EMR Memory Test again (twice if necessary). Go to next step. If EMR MILEAGE INVALID message is displayed, go to step **4)**.

3) If WRITE REFUSED message returns, replace SBEC. Perform VERIFICATION TEST VER-1. If WRITE REFUSED does not return, test is complete. Perform VERIFICATION TEST VER-1.

NOTE: Aftermarket scan tester may not be able to update EMR mileage. DRB-II may be required for this step.

4) Update EMR mileage, and retest EMR memory. Perform VERIFICATION TEST VER-1. If DRB-II does not display EMR MILEAGE INVALID, compare EMR mileage stored with instrument panel odometer. Go to next step.

5) If mileage readings are same, retest EMR memory. Perform VERIFICATION TEST VER-1. If mileage readings differ, update EMR mileage, and retest EMR memory. Perform VERIFICATION TEST VER-1.

TEST DR-15A

INTERMITTENT SENSOR VOLTAGE FAULT

1) Erase fault codes. Turn ignition on, and read voltage in affected circuit using DRB-II. While observing DRB-II display, wiggle sensor connector. If voltage reading changes, repair wiring or connector. If voltage reading does not change, go to next step.

2) Wiggle wiring harness between affected sensor and SBEC, beginning with section of harness closest to sensor. See appropriate WIRING DIAGRAMS article in ENGINE PERFORMANCE. Wait at least 5 seconds before moving to next section of harness. If voltage reading changes, repair harness at point that caused voltage change.

3) If voltage reading does not change, problem is not in wiring. Replace suspect sensor with known good unit, and road test vehicle. If condition does not return, test is complete. If condition returns, replace SBEC. Perform VERIFICATION TEST VER-1.

TEST DR-16A

INTERMITTENT TEST FOR SOLENOIDS & RELAYS

1) Turn ignition on. Erase fault codes. Using DRB-II actuate the suspect solenoid or relay. While actuating, read secondary indicators. See STATE DISPLAY MODE under OPERATING MODES.

2) Wiggle connector at affected component while observing DRB-II display. If secondary indicator returns, repair wiring or harness connector. Perform VERIFICATION TEST VER-1.

3) If secondary indicator does not return, wiggle wiring harness between affected component and SBEC, beginning with section of harness closest to component. See appropriate WIRING DIAGRAMS article in ENGINE PERFORMANCE. Wait at least 5 seconds before moving to next section of harness.

4) If secondary indicator returns, repair harness at point that caused voltage change. If secondary indicator does not return, replace suspect component and road test vehicle while observing secondary indicators.

5) If secondary indicators do not change, test is complete. Perform VERIFICATION TEST VER-1. If condition returns, replace SBEC. Perform VERIFICATION TEST VER-1.

TEST DR-17A

INTERMITTENT NO REFERENCE SIGNAL PICK-UP FAULT

1) Turn ignition on. Erase fault codes. Start engine and allow to idle. Using DRB-II read engine RPM. While observing DRB-II display, wiggle crank position sensor harness connector.

2) If RPM display becomes erratic, repair crank position sensor wiring or harness connector. If RPM reading remains steady, wiggle harness between crank position sensor and SBEC. Wait at least 5 seconds before moving to next section of harness. If RPM reading becomes erratic, repair harness at point that caused RPM change.

3) If RPM reading does not change, problem is not in wiring. Replace crank position sensor with known good unit and road test vehicle. If condition does not return, test is complete. If condition returns, replace SBEC. Perform VERIFICATION TEST VER-1.

TEST DR-18A

INTERMITTENT NO ASD VOLTAGE SENSE AT CONTROLLER FAULT

1) Turn ignition on. Erase fault codes. Using DRB-II, actuate ASD relay. With ASD relay actuating, select secondary indicators. See STATE DISPLAY MODE under OPERATING MODES.

2) Wiggle ASD wiring and harness connectors while observing secondary indicators. If fault code returns, repair harness at point that caused fault code to return. Perform VERIFICATION TEST VER-1.

3) If fault code does not return, visually inspect connectors for broken, bent, pushed out or corroded terminals. Inspect related harnesses for chafed, pierced, or partially broken wires. Repair as necessary. Perform VERIFICATION TEST VER-1.

TEST NF-1A

NO FAULT CODE TEST MENU

Check MITCHELL® TECH SERVICE BULLETINS (TSBs) for any pertinent information. If a TSB exists, perform corrective action. If TSB does not exist or if driveability problem still exists, check suspect system and perform indicated test. See NO FAULT CODE TEST MENU table. If system causing driveability problem is not known, perform TEST NF-2A through TEST NF-7A in sequence until problem is found.

NOTE: Components listed below that provide an input to SBEC are being checked for a condition that WILL NOT set a fault code, but cause a driveability condition.

NO FAULT CODE TEST MENU

Application	Test
Checking Transmission Overdrive Circuit [1]	NF-2A
Checking Air Intake Heater No.1	NF-3A
Checking Air Intake Heater No.2	NF-4A
Checking WAIT-TO-START Light	NF-5A
Checking WATER-IN-FUEL Light	NF-6A
Checking Engine Mechanical	NF-7A

[1] – A/T models only.

TEST NF-2A

CHECKING TRANSMISSION OVERDRIVE CIRCUIT

NOTE: For connector terminal identification, see CONNECTOR IDENTIFICATION. For wiring diagram, see appropriate WIRING DIAGRAMS article in ENGINE PERFORMANCE.

1) If vehicle fails to go into overdrive, perform TEST NF-2B. If vehicle does go into overdrive, ensure coolant temperature is greater than 60°F (16°C) before proceeding. Using DRB-II, read overdrive switch state. See STATE DISPLAY MODE under OPERATING MODES.

2) Turn overdrive switch on and off while observing DRB-II display. If overdrive switch state changes between on and off, repair transmission as necessary. If overdrive switch state does not change between on and off, go to next step.

3) Turn ignition off. Disconnect SBEC 60-pin connector. Place DRB-II in ohmmeter mode. Probe SBEC connector cavity No. 10 (Orange/White wire). Turn overdrive switch on and off while observing DRB-II display. If overdrive switch state changes between on and off, replace SBEC. Perform VERIFICATION TEST VER-1.

4) If overdrive switch state does not change between on and off, disconnect overdrive switch harness connector. Using an external ohmmeter, check resistance in Orange/White wire between overdrive switch connector and SBEC connector.

TEST NF-2A (Cont.)

5) If resistance reading is greater than 10 ohms, repair open circuit in Orange/White wire. If resistance reading is less than 10 ohms, probe Black wire in overdrive switch connector with DRB-II in ohmmeter mode.

6) If resistance reading is greater than 10 ohms, repair open circuit or poor ground connection in Black wire. Perform VERIFICATION TEST VER-1. If resistance reading is less than 10 ohms, replace overdrive switch. Perform VERIFICATION TEST VER-1.

TEST NF-2B

CHECKING OVERDRIVE CIRCUIT (NO OVERDRIVE)

NOTE: For connector terminal identification, see CONNECTOR IDEN-TIFICATION. For wiring diagram, see appropriate WIRING DIAGRAMS article in ENGINE PERFORMANCE.

1) Using DRB-II, ensure coolant temperature is greater than 65°F (18°C). If coolant temperature does not read above 65°F (18°C), replace coolant temperature sensor and retest vehicle for overdrive operation. Perform VERIFICATION TEST VER-1.

2) If coolant temperature reads okay, read TPS voltage using DRB-II. If TPS voltage is not between .98 and 1.2 volts, adjust or replace TPS and retest vehicle for overdrive operation. Perform VERIFICATION TEST VER-1.

3) If TPS voltage is as specified, read overdrive switch state using DRB-II. See STATE DISPLAY MODE under OPERATING MODES. Turn overdrive switch on and off while observing DRB-II display. If overdrive switch state changes between on and off, repair transmission as necessary. If overdrive switch state does not change between on and off, go to next step.

4) Turn ignition off. Disconnect SBEC 60-pin connector. Place DRB-II in ohmmeter mode. Probe SBEC connector cavity No. 10 (Orange/White wire). Turn overdrive switch on and off while observing DRB-II. If DRB-II resistance reading switches between less than 5 ohms and greater than 5 ohms, replace SBEC. Perform VERIFICATION TEST VER-1.

5) If DRB-II display did not change as specified, disconnect overdrive switch harness connector. Using DRB-II in ohmmeter mode, probe cavity No. 10 (Orange/White wire).

6) If resistance reading is less than 10 ohms, repair short to ground in Orange/White wire. Perform VERIFICATION TEST VER-1. If resistance reading is greater than 10 ohms, replace overdrive switch. Perform VERIFICATION TEST VER-1.

TEST NF-3A

CHECKING AIR INTAKE HEATER NO. 1

NOTE: For connector terminal identification, see CONNECTOR IDEN-TIFICATION. For wiring diagram, see appropriate WIRING DIAGRAMS article in ENGINE PERFORMANCE.

NOTE: If vehicle is hard to start or blows black smoke on start-up, test does not apply.

1) Using DRB-II, actuate air intake heater No. 1. See ENTERING ON-BOARD DIAGNOSTICS under SELF-DIAGNOSTIC SYSTEM. While actuating heater, place DRB-II in voltmeter mode. Probe positive battery cable. If voltage reading drops at least .5 volt when heater actuates, system is operating properly.

2) If voltage reading did not drop, listen for "clicking" noise from air intake heater relay No. 1. Relay No. 1 is forward most of 2 air intake heater relays mounted on left front fender. If relay is not "clicking", go to next step. If relay is "clicking", perform TEST NF-3B.

3) Place DRB-II in voltmeter mode. Probe Dark Blue wire at heater relay No. 1. If voltage reading is greater than 10 volts, go to next step. If voltage reading is less than 10 volts, repair open circuit in Dark Blue wire between heater relay and ignition switch. Perform VERIFICATION TEST VER-1.

TEST NF-3A (Cont.)

4) Reconnect Dark Blue wire connector to heater relay No. 1. Disconnect Yellow/Black wire connector from heater relay No. 1 ground control terminal. Connect one end of a jumper wire to ground control terminal and touch other end of jumper to chassis ground.

CAUTION: DO NOT ground jumper wire for more than 5 seconds.

5) If heater relay No. 1 now operates, go to next step. If relay did not operate, replace relay. Perform VERIFICATION TEST VER-1.

6) Turn ignition off. Disconnect SBEC 60-pin connector. Using an external ohmmeter, check resistance between Yellow/Black wire terminal and SBEC connector cavity No. 16. If resistance reading is less than 10 ohms, go to next step. If resistance reading is greater than 10 ohms, replace SBEC. Perform VERIFICATION TEST VER-1.

7) Place DRB-II in ohmmeter mode. Probe Yellow/Black wire connector. If resistance reading is less than 10 ohms, repair short to ground in Yellow/Black wire. Perform VERIFICATION TEST VER-1. If resistance reading is greater than 10 ohms, replace SBEC. Perform VERIFICATION TEST VER-1.

TEST NF-3B

CHECKING AIR INTAKE HEATER NO. 1

NOTE: For connector terminal identification, see CONNECTOR IDEN-TIFICATION. For wiring diagram, see appropriate WIRING DIAGRAMS article in ENGINE PERFORMANCE.

1) Place DRB-II in voltmeter mode. Check for voltage at both Black wires on heater relay No. 1. If voltage reading is greater than 10 volts at either wires, go to next step. If voltage reading is not as specified, repair open circuit in Black wire between heater relay and battery. Perform VERIFICATION TEST VER-1.

2) Using DRB-II, actuate heater relay No. 1. Using DRB-II in voltmeter mode, probe both Black wires at heater block. If voltage reading is greater than 10 volts at either wire, go to next step. If voltage reading is not as specified, repair open circuit between heater relay No. 1 and heater block. Perform VERIFICATION TEST VER-1.

3) Turn ignition off. Place DRB-II in ohmmeter mode. Check air intake heater block ground wire. If resistance reading is greater than 10 ohms, repair open circuit in Black wire. Perform VERIFICATION TEST VER-1. If resistance reading is not as specified, replace air intake heater.

TEST NF-4A

CHECKING AIR INTAKE HEATER NO. 2

NOTE: For connector terminal identification, see CONNECTOR IDEN-TIFICATION. For wiring diagram, see appropriate WIRING DIAGRAMS article in ENGINE PERFORMANCE.

NOTE: If vehicle is hard to start or blows black smoke on start-up, test does not apply.

1) Using DRB-II, actuate air intake heater No. 2. See ENTERING ON-BOARD DIAGNOSTICS under SELF-DIAGNOSTIC SYSTEM. While actuating heater, place DRB-II in voltmeter mode. Probe positive battery cable. If voltage reading drops at least .5 volt when heater actuates, system is operating properly.

2) If voltage reading did not drop, listen for "clicking" noise from air intake heater relay No. 2. Relay No. 2 is rearward most of 2 air intake heater relays mounted on left front fender. If relay is "clicking", perform TEST NF-4B.

3) Place DRB-II in voltmeter mode. Probe Dark Blue wire at heater relay No. 1. If voltage reading is greater than 10 volts, go to next step. If voltage reading is less than 10 volts, repair open circuit in Dark Blue wire between heater relay and ignition switch. Perform VERIFICATION TEST VER-1.

TEST NF-4A (Cont.)

4) Reconnect Dark Blue wire connector to heater relay No. 1. Disconnect Orange/Black wire connector from heater relay No. 1 ground control terminal. Connect one end of a jumper wire to ground control terminal and touch other end of jumper to chassis ground.

CAUTION: DO NOT ground jumper wire for more than 5 seconds.

5) If heater relay No. 1 now operates, go to next step. If relay did not operate, replace relay. Perform VERIFICATION TEST VER-1.

6) Turn ignition off. Disconnect SBEC 60-pin connector. Using an external ohmmeter, check resistance between Orange/Black wire terminal and SBEC connector cavity No. 15. If resistance reading is less than 10 ohms, go to next step. If resistance reading is greater than 10 ohms, replace SBEC. Perform VERIFICATION TEST VER-1.

7) Place DRB-II in ohmmeter mode. Probe Orange/Black wire connector. If resistance reading is less than 10 ohms, repair short to ground in Orange/Black wire. Perform VERIFICATION TEST VER-1. If resistance reading is greater than 10 ohms, replace SBEC. Perform VERIFICATION TEST VER-1.

TEST NF-4B

CHECKING AIR INTAKE HEATER NO. 2

NOTE: For connector terminal identification, see CONNECTOR IDENTIFICATION. For wiring diagram, see appropriate WIRING DIAGRAMS article in ENGINE PERFORMANCE.

1) Place DRB-II in voltmeter mode. Check for voltage at both Black wires on heater relay No. 2. If voltage reading is greater than 10 volts at either wires, go to next step. If voltage reading is not as specified, repair open circuit in Black wire between heater relay and battery. Perform VERIFICATION TEST VER-1.

2) Using DRB-II, actuate heater relay No. 2. Using DRB-II in voltmeter mode, probe both Black wires at heater block. If voltage reading is greater than 10 volts at either wire, go to next step. If voltage reading is not as specified, repair open circuit between heater relay No. 2 and heater block. Perform VERIFICATION TEST VER-1.

3) Turn ignition off. Place DRB-II in ohmmeter mode. Check air intake heater block ground wire. If resistance reading is greater than 10 ohms, repair open circuit in Black wire. Perform VERIFICATION TEST VER-1. If resistance reading is not as specified, replace air intake heater.

TEST NF-5A

CHECKING WAIT-TO-START LIGHT

NOTE: For connector terminal identification, see CONNECTOR IDENTIFICATION. For wiring diagram, see appropriate WIRING DIAGRAMS article in ENGINE PERFORMANCE.

1) Turn ignition off. Disconnect SBEC 60-pin connector. Turn ignition on. Place DRB-II in voltmeter mode. Probe SBEC connector cavity No. 56 (Dark Green/White wire). If voltage reading is less than 10 volts, go to next step. If voltage reading is greater than 10 volts, replace SBEC. Perform VERIFICATION TEST VER-1.

2) Remove WAIT-TO-START light bulb and inspect bulb. If bulb is burnt out, replace bulb. Perform VERIFICATION TEST VER-1. If bulb is okay, reinstall bulb. Backprobe Dark Blue/White wire at message center connector. If voltage reading is greater than 10 volts, go to next step. If voltage reading is less than 10 volts, repair open circuit in Dark Blue/White wire. Perform VERIFICATION TEST VER-1.

3) Connect a jumper wire between message center cavity "F" (Dark Green/White wire) and chassis ground. If WAIT-TO-START light illuminates, repair open circuit in Dark Green/White wire. Perform VERIFICATION TEST VER-1. If WAIT-TO-START light does not illuminate, replace message center printed circuit assembly. Perform VERIFICATION TEST VER-1.

TEST NF-6A

CHECKING WATER-IN-FUEL LIGHT

NOTE: For connector terminal identification, see CONNECTOR IDENTIFICATION. For wiring diagram, see appropriate WIRING DIAGRAMS article in ENGINE PERFORMANCE.

1) Disconnect WATER-IN-FUEL sensor connector. Connect a jumper wire between WATER-IN-FUEL sensor connector terminal No. 2 (White/Black wire) and chassis ground. Turn ignition off then on. If WATER-IN-FUEL light is illuminated perform TEST NF-6B. If WATER-IN-FUEL light is not illuminated go to next step.

2) Turn ignition off. Disconnect SBEC 60-pin connector. Inspect connector and repair as required. Using an external ohmmeter, check resistance in White/Black wire between WATER-IN-FUEL sensor connector and SBEC connector cavity No. 1.

3) If resistance reading is less than 10 ohms, go to next step. If resistance reading is greater than 10 ohms, repair open circuit in White/Black wire. Perform VERIFICATION TEST VER-1.

4) Turn ignition on. Place DRB-II in voltmeter mode. Probe SBEC connector cavity No. 54 (Black/Pink wire). If the voltage reading is less than 10 volts, go to next step. If voltage reading is greater than 10 volts, replace SBEC. Perform VERIFICATION TEST VER-1.

5) Remove WATER-IN-FUEL light bulb and inspect bulb. If bulb is burnt out, replace bulb. Perform VERIFICATION TEST VER-1. If bulb is okay, reinstall bulb. Backprobe Dark Blue/White wire at message center connector. If voltage reading is greater than 10 volts, go to next step. If voltage reading is less than 10 volts, repair open circuit in Dark Blue/White wire. Perform VERIFICATION TEST VER-1.

6) Connect a jumper wire between message center cavity "H" (Black/Pink wire) and chassis ground. If WATER-IN-FUEL light illuminates, repair open circuit in Black/Pink wire. Perform VERIFICATION TEST VER-1. If WATER-IN-FUEL light does not illuminate, replace message center printed circuit assembly. Perform VERIFICATION TEST VER-1.

TEST NF-6B

CHECKING WATER-IN-FUEL LIGHT

NOTE: For connector terminal identification, see CONNECTOR IDENTIFICATION. For wiring diagram, see appropriate WIRING DIAGRAMS article in ENGINE PERFORMANCE.

1) Turn ignition off. Place DRB-II in ohmmeter mode. Probe WATER-IN-FUEL connector terminal No. 1 (Black/Light Blue wire).

2) If resistance reading is greater than 10 ohms, repair open circuit in Black/Light Blue wire. Perform VERIFICATION TEST VER-1. If resistance reading is less than 10 ohms, replace WATER-IN-FUEL sensor. Perform VERIFICATION TEST VER-1.

TEST NF-7A

PERFORMING NO FAULT CODE MECHANICAL TEST

At this point in diagnostic test procedure, all engine control systems have been determined to be operating as designed and not causing a driveability problem. Following additional items should be checked as possible causes:

- Check if any MITCHELL® TECH SERVICE BULLETINS (TSBs) apply to vehicle.
- Check for fuel injection pump malfunction.
- Check fuel injection pump timing.
- Check for air in fuel system.
- Check for restricted or damaged fuel injector.
- Check for fuel contamination.
- Check for restricted fuel filter.
- Check for leaking or damaged fuel lines.
- Check for empty fuel tank or blocked tank vent.
- Check for clogged air filter.
- Check for blocked or leaking intercooler.
- Check engine compression.
- Check for misadjusted low idle.
- Check for throttle lever not reaching full throttle position.
- Check torque converter stall speed.

TEST VER-1

VERIFICATION TEST VER-1

1) Ensure all engine components are connected. Erase fault codes. Disconnect DRB-II and road test vehicle. Check for driveability problem or CHECK ENGINE LIGHT coming on.

2) Complete road test and reconnect DRB-II. Check for fault codes. If repaired fault code has reset, repair is not complete, return to TEST DR-1A. If a new fault code has set, return to TEST DR-1A. If no fault codes have set and no driveability problems are evident, repair is complete.

RWD Van

INTRODUCTION

If no faults were found while performing BASIC DIAGNOSTIC PROCEDURES, proceed with self-diagnostics. If no fault codes or only pass codes are present after entering self-diagnostics, proceed to TROUBLE SHOOTING – NO CODES – CNG article for diagnosis by symptom (i.e., ROUGH IDLE, NO START, etc.).

FUEL PRESSURE RELEASE

WARNING: ALWAYS relieve fuel pressure before attempting to open system for testing or component replacement. High fuel pressure may be present in fuel lines and component parts. DO NOT allow fuel to flow onto engine or electrical parts while testing fuel system components.

Fuel System Purging – Before any part of Compressed Natural Gas (CNG) fuel system is opened for repair, system must be purged of all natural gas.

The fuel system must first be purged of natural gas if any of the following components are to be removed or repaired.

- Fuel Tube Or Fuel Tube Fitting
- Fuel Injector Rail Assembly
- Fuel Temperature Sensor
- Fuel Low-Pressure Sensor
- Fuel Gauge Pressure Sensor
- Fuel Fill Receptacle
- Fuel Cylinder
- Manual Shutoff Valve
- Fuel Filter
- Fuel Injectors
- Low-Pressure Fuel Shutoff Solenoid
- Fuel Pressure Regulator
- Fill Check Valves
- High-Pressure Fuel Shutoff Solenoid

Fuel Tube Purging – 1) Close control valve (clockwise) on side mounted fuel cylinder. Close control valves (clockwise) on both of rear mounted fuel cylinders. Open manual shutoff valve.
2) Start and operate engine until it runs out of fuel. Attempt 3 more engine starts. If check valve or fuel fill receptacle is to be serviced, slowly loosen inlet side of fuel fill tube fitting at check valve. It is normal for approximately 25 psi of natural gas pressure to flow from loosened fitting.
At this point, all fuel tubes are purged of natural gas between fuel cylinders and engine. It is now OK to open fuel system for repair.
Fuel Cylinder Purging – 1) Open manual shutoff valve. Open only the fuel control valve(s) (counterclockwise) on the fuel cylinder(s) to be serviced. Close all other control valve(s) (clockwise) on fuel cylinder(s) not being serviced.
2) Start and operate engine until it runs out of fuel. Attempt 3 more engine starts. At this point, all fuel tubes and opened cylinders are purged of natural gas between fuel cylinders and engine. It is now OK to open fuel system for repair.

SELF-DIAGNOSTIC SYSTEM

WARNING: When battery is disconnected, vehicle computer and memory systems may lose memory data. Driveability problems may exist until computer systems have completed a relearn cycle. See COMPUTER RELEARN PROCEDURES article in GENERAL INFORMATION before disconnecting battery.

SYSTEM DIAGNOSTICS

The self-diagnostic capabilities of this system, if properly utilized, can simplify testing. The Powertrain Control Module (PCM) monitors several different engine control system circuits.

If a problem is sensed with a monitored circuit, PCM memory stores a fault code, the CHECK ENGINE light glows and PCM enters limp-in mode. In limp-in mode, PCM compensates for component failure by substituting information from other sources. This allows vehicle operation until repairs can be made.

Once codes are known, see FAULT CODES table to determine the questionable circuit. Test circuits and repair or replace components as required. If problem is repaired or ceases to exist, the PCM cancels fault code after 50 ignition on/off cycles. To clear codes, see CLEARING FAULT CODES.

A specific fault code results from a particular system failure. A fault code does not condemn a specific component. Component is not necessarily the reason for failure. Fault codes only call out a probable malfunction area.

Hard Failures – Hard failures cause CHECK ENGINE light to glow and remain on until the malfunction is repaired. If light comes on and remains on (light may flash) during vehicle operation, cause of malfunction must be determined using self-diagnostic tests. If a sensor fails, PCM will use a substitute value in its calculations, allowing engine to operate in limp-in mode. In this condition, vehicle will run, but driveability may be poor. DRB-II will display key counter as zero.

Intermittent Failures – Intermittent failures may cause CHECK ENGINE light to flicker or stay on until the intermittent fault goes away. However, the corresponding fault code will be retained in PCM memory. If related fault does not reoccur within a certain time frame, related fault code will be erased from PCM memory. Intermittent failures can be caused by a faulty sensor, bad connector or wiring related problems. DRB-II will display key counter as one or more. See TEST NF-1A in SELF-DIAGNOSTICS – GASOLINE article or INTERMITTENTS in TROUBLE SHOOTING – NO CODES – CNG article.

SERVICE PRECAUTIONS

Before proceeding with diagnosis, the following precautions must be followed:
- ALWAYS purge fuel system pressure before disconnecting any fuel injection-related component. DO NOT allow fuel to contact engine or electrical components. See FUEL PRESSURE RELEASE.
- When battery is disconnected, vehicle computer and memory systems may lose memory data. Driveability problems may exist until computer systems have completed a relearn cycle. See COMPUTER RELEARN PROCEDURES article in GENERAL INFORMATION before disconnecting battery.
- Vehicle must have a fully charged battery and functional charging system.
- Probe PCM 60-pin connector from pin side. DO NOT backprobe PCM connector.
- DO NOT cause short circuits when performing electrical tests. This will set additional fault codes, making diagnosis of original problem more difficult.
- DO NOT use a test light instead of a voltmeter.
- When checking for spark, ensure coil wire is no more than 1/4" from ground. If coil wire is more than 1/4" from ground, damage to vehicle electronics and/or PCM may result.
- DO NOT prolong testing of fuel injectors or engine may hydrostatically (liquid) lock.
- Always repair lowest fault code number (CHECK ENGINE light) or first fault displayed (DRB-II) first.
- Always perform verification procedure test after repairs are made.
- Always disconnect DRB-II after use.
- Always disconnect DRB-II before charging battery.

VISUAL INSPECTION

Most driveability problems in the engine control system result from faulty wiring, poor electrical connections or leaking air and vacuum hose connections. To avoid unnecessary component testing, perform a visual inspection before beginning self-diagnostic tests.

DIAGNOSTIC PROCEDURE

NOTE: DO NOT skip any steps in self-diagnostic tests or incorrect diagnosis may result.

Always perform a visual inspection before attempting to diagnose engine control system problems. See VISUAL INSPECTION. Enter on-board diagnostics, and retrieve fault codes. See ENTERING ON-BOARD DIAGNOSTICS. If fault codes are not present and/or DRB-II (Diagnostic Readout Box II) is used, proceed to one of following tests:

- Go to TEST NS-1A (NO-START TEST 1A) in SELF-DIAGNOSTIC TESTS – 3.9L & 5.2L article if a no-start condition exists or engine stalls after start-up. Perform indicated VERIFICATION TEST after repairs have been made. Ensure self-diagnostic tests apply to engine being tested. See SELF-DIAGNOSTICS DIRECTORY table under SELF-DIAGNOSTIC SYSTEM.

- Go to TEST DR-1A (DRIVEABILITY TEST 1A) in SELF-DIAGNOSTIC TESTS – 3.9L & 5.2L article if engine runs but has performance problems. Perform indicated VERIFICATION TEST after repairs have been made. Ensure self-diagnostic tests apply to engine being tested. See SELF-DIAGNOSTIC SYSTEM.

- Go to TEST NF-1A (NO FAULT CODE TEST 1A) in SELF-DIAGNOSTIC TESTS – 3.9L & 5.2L article if a driveability problem exits and no fault codes are present. Perform indicated VERIFICATION TEST after repairs have been made. Ensure self-diagnostic tests apply to engine being tested. See SELF-DIAGNOSTICS DIRECTORY table under SELF-DIAGNOSTIC SYSTEM.

ENTERING ON-BOARD DIAGNOSTICS

NOTE: Although other scan testers are available, manufacturer recommends using DRB-II (Diagnostic Readout Box-II) to diagnose the system. CHECK ENGINE light function can be used but has limited diagnostic usage.

CHECK ENGINE Light Diagnostic Mode – 1) Start engine (if possible). Move transmission shift lever through all positions, ending in PARK. Turn A/C switch on and then off (if equipped).
2) Turn engine off. Without starting engine again, turn ignition on, off, on, off and on. Record 2-digit fault codes as displayed by flashing CHECK ENGINE light.

3) For example, Code 23 is displayed as flash, flash, 4-second pause, flash, flash, flash. After a slightly longer pause, other codes stored are displayed in numerical order.
4) When CHECK ENGINE light begins to flash fault codes, it cannot be stopped. Start over if count is lost. Code 55 indicates end of fault code display. Refer to FAULT CODES table to translate trouble code number to a system fault description (DRB-II display).
5) Once trouble area is identified, refer to appropriate TEST NS-1A (NO-START TEST 1A) or TEST DR-1A (DRIVEABILITY TEST 1A) to diagnose problem. Use self-diagnostic test titles to find appropriate test.
6) As an example, a 5.2L engine starts and runs but has a driveability problem. CHECK ENGINE light indicates a Code 14. Refer to FAULT CODES table to translate trouble code number to a system fault description (DRB-II display).
7) When system fault description (DRB-II display) is obtained, refer to appropriate TEST DR-1A (DRIVEABILITY TEST DR-1A) since vehicle has a driveability problem. Select fault message and corresponding test from table, and proceed to appropriate test. To clear fault codes, see CLEARING FAULT CODES.

DRB-II Diagnostic Mode – 1) Turn ignition off. Connect DRB-II to engine diagnostic connector. Engine diagnostic connector is located in engine compartment, near PCM.
2) Start engine (if possible). With foot on brake, move transmission shift lever through all positions, ending in PARK. Turn A/C switch on and then off (if equipped).
3) Turn engine off. Without starting engine again, turn ignition on. Enter FUEL/IGN MENU. To enter FUEL/IGN MENU, see FUEL/IGN MENU under DRB-II TEST FUNCTIONS. At FUEL/IGN MENU, press "2" (READ FAULTS) key. Press ENTER key. After fault codes are accessed, see appropriate TEST NS-1A (NO-START TEST 1A) or TEST DR-1A (DRIVEABILITY TEST 1A) to diagnose problem.
4) To erase fault codes while in this mode, press ATM key. At DRB-II display, press "2" (ERASE) key. DRB-II will display ERASE FAULTS ARE YOU SURE? (ENTER TO ERASE). Press ENTER key.
5) When DRB-II is finished erasing fault codes, it will display FAULTS ERASED. This display will remain until ATM key is pressed. After ATM key is pressed, display will return to FUEL/IGN MENU screen.

NOTE: Diagnostic procedures for all fault codes except Codes 23 and 64 are as for gasoline vehicles. See SELF-DIAGNOSTIC TESTS – 3.9L & 5.2L article. To diagnose Code 64, see CNG TROUBLE CODE 64 at end of this article. No information is available for diagnosing Code 23.

FAULT CODES

Code	Display On DRB-II [1]	Fault Condition
11	NO REFERENCE SIGNAL DURING CRANKING	No Distributor Reference Signal Detected During Cranking.
13	SLOW CHANGE IN IDLE MAP SIGNAL	MAP Output Change Is Slower And/Or Smaller Than Expected.
	NO CHANGE IN MAP FROM START TO RUN	No Difference Recognized Between MAP Reading And Barometric (Atmospheric) Pressure Reading At Start-Up.
14	MAP VOLTAGE TOO LOW	MAP Sensor Input Less Than Minimum Acceptable Voltage.
	MAP VOLTAGE TOO HIGH	MAP Sensor Input More Than Maximum Acceptable Voltage.
15	NO VEHICLE SPEED SIGNAL	No Distance Sensor Signal Detected During Road Load Conditions.
17	ENGINE COLD TOO LONG	Coolant Temperature Stays Less Than Normal Operating Temperature During Vehicle Operation.
21	O₂ SIGNAL STAYS AT CENTER	No Rich Or Lean Signal Is Detected From O₂ Sensor Input.
	O₂ SIGNAL SHORTED TO VOLTAGE	O₂ Sensor Input Voltage Maintained At More Than Normal Operating Range.
22	COOLANT SENSOR VOLTAGE TOO LOW	Coolant Temperature Sensor Input Less Than Minimum Acceptable Voltage.
	COOLANT SENSOR VOLTAGE TOO HIGH	Coolant Temperature Sensor Input More Than Maximum Acceptable Voltage.
23 [2]	MANIFOLD AIR TEMP SENSOR VOLTAGE LOW	Intake Manifold Air Temperature Input Less Than Minimum Acceptable Voltage.
	MANIFOLD AIR TEMP SENSOR VOLTAGE LOW	Intake Manifold Air Temperature More Than Maximum Acceptable Voltage.
24	TPS VOLTAGE LOW	TPS Sensor Input Less Than Minimum Acceptable Voltage.
	TPS VOLTAGE HIGH	TPS Sensor Input More Than Maximum Acceptable Voltage.
25	AIS MOTOR CIRCUITS	Open Or Shorted Condition Detected In One Or More Auto Idle Speed (AIS) Control Circuits.

[1] – Actual message displayed on DRB-II may vary between vehicles.
[2] – Diagnostic information is not available for Code 23.

FAULT CODES (Cont.)

Code	Display On DRB-II [1]	Fault Condition
32	EGR SOLENOID CIRCUIT	Open Or Shorted Condition Is Detected In EGR Solenoid Circuit.
	EGR SYSTEM FAILURE	PCM Did Not Detect Required Air/Fuel Change During Diagnostic Test.
33	A/C CLUTCH RELAY CKT	Open Or Shorted Condition Detected In A/C Clutch Relay Circuit.
34	S/C SOLENOIDS CKT	Open Or Shorted Condition Detected In Speed Control (S/C) Vacuum Or Vent Solenoid Circuits.
37	TORQUE CONVERTER LOCK-UP SOLENOID CIRCUIT	An Open Or Shorted Condition Detected In Torque Converter Lock-Up Solenoid Circuit.
41 [3]	ALTERNATOR FIELD NOT SWITCHING PROPERLY	Alternator Field Not Switching Properly.
42	ASD RELAY CONTROL CIRCUIT	An Open Or Shorted Condition Detected In ASD Relay Circuit.
	NO ASD RELAY VOLTAGE SENSED AT CONTROLLER	No ASD Relay Voltage Sensed When ASD Relay Is Energized.
44 [3]	BATTERY TEMP VOLTAGE	An Open Or Shorted Condition Exists In Coolant Temperature Sensor Circuit Or In PCM Battery Temperature Voltage Circuit.
45	OVERDRIVE SOLENOID	Open Or Short Detected In Overdrive Solenoid Circuit.
46 [3]	CHARGING VOLTAGE TOO HIGH	Charging System Voltage Too High.
47 [3]	CHARGING VOLTAGE TOO LOW	Charging System Voltage Too Low.
51	O_2 SIGNAL STAYS BELOW CENTER (LEAN)	O_2 Sensor Input Indicates Lean Air/Fuel Ratio During Engine Operation.
	ADDITIVE ADAPTIVE MEMORY AT RICH LIMIT	Additive Adaptive Memory At Rich Limit.
52	O_2 SIGNAL STAYS ABOVE CENTER (RICH)	O_2 Sensor Input Indicates Rich Air/Fuel Ratio During Engine Operation.
	ADDITIVE ADAPTIVE MEMORY AT LEAN LIMIT	Additive Adaptive Memory At Lean Limit.
53	INTERNAL CONTROLLER FAILURE	Internal Failure In Engine Controller.
54	NO SYNC PICK-UP SIGNAL	No Fuel Sync Signal Detected During Engine Rotation.
55	[4]	Completion Of Fault Code Display By CHECK ENGINE Light.
62	CONTROLLER FAILURE EMR MILES NOT STORED	Unsuccessful Attempt To Update EMR Mileage In PCM.
63	CONTROLLER FAILURE EEPROM WRITE DENIED	Unsuccessful Attempt To Write To An EEPROM Location By PCM.
64 [5]	FUEL TEMPERATURE SENSE TOO LOW	Fuel Temperature Sensor Input Less Than Minimum Acceptable Voltage.
	FUEL TEMPERATURE SENSE TOO HIGH	Fuel Temperature Sensor Input More Than Maximum Acceptable Voltage.
	FUEL PRESSURE TOO LOW	Fuel Pressure Sensor Input Less Than Minimum Acceptable Voltage.
	FUEL PRESSURE TOO HIGH	Fuel Pressure Sensor Input More Than Maximum Acceptable Voltage.

[1] – Actual message displayed on DRB-II may vary between vehicles.
[3] – If code is displayed, charging system malfunction exists. See appropriate ALTERNATORS & REGULATORS article in ELECTRICAL.
[4] – No display on DRB-II.
[5] – See CNG TROUBLE CODE 64 at end of article. For other codes, see SELF-DIAGNOSTIC TESTS – 3.9L & 5.2L article.

CLEARING FAULT CODES

NOTE: Fault codes can also be cleared in READ FAULTS mode of DRB-II. To ensure all faults are read, use READ FAULTS mode to erase fault codes. See DRB-II DIAGNOSTIC MODE under ENTERING ON-BOARD DIAGNOSTICS.

1) If DRB-II is not available, go to step 3). If DRB-II is available, enter FUEL/IGN MENU. See FUEL/IGN MENU under DRB-II TEST FUNCTIONS. At FUEL/IGN MENU, press "5" (ADJUSTMENTS) key. Press ENTER key. At ADJUSTMENTS menu, press "1" (ERASE FAULTS) key. Press ENTER key.
2) DRB-II will display ERASE FAULTS ARE YOU SURE? (ENTER TO ERASE). Press ENTER key. When DRB-II is finished erasing fault codes, screen will display FAULTS ERASED.
3) If DRB-II is not available, fault codes may be cleared by disconnecting negative battery cable for at least 15 seconds, allowing PCM to clear fault codes.

SUMMARY

If no hard fault codes (or only pass codes) are present, driveability symptoms exist or intermittent codes exist, proceed to appropriate TROUBLE SHOOTING – NO CODES article for diagnosis by symptom (i.e., ROUGH IDLE, NO START, etc.) or intermittent diagnostic procedures.

DRB-II TEST FUNCTIONS

WARNING: When battery is disconnected, vehicle computer and memory systems may lose memory data. Driveability problems may exist until computer systems have completed a relearn cycle. See COMPUTER RELEARN PROCEDURES article in GENERAL INFORMATION before disconnecting battery.

FUEL/IGN MENU

NOTE: DO NOT touch DRB-II keypad during DRB-II power-up sequence or an error message will result.

1) In order to perform self-diagnostic tests using DRB-II, DRB-II must be in the FUEL/IGN MENU. At the FUEL/IGN MENU, fault codes and DRB-II test functions can be accessed.
2) To reach FUEL/IGN MENU, turn ignition off. Connect DRB-II to engine diagnostic connector, located in engine compartment, near PCM. Turn ignition switch to RUN position.
3) All DRB-II character positions will glow and copyright information will appear on screen for a few seconds. If screen is blank or any error messages appear, see DRB-II PROBLEMS & ERROR MESSAGES.
4) After a few seconds, DRB-II menu will appear. At DRB-II menu, press "4" (SELECT SYSTEM) key. Press ENTER key. At SELECT SYSTEM menu, press "1" (ENGINE) key. Press ENTER key. DRB-II screen will indicate engine year, size, type of transmission and PCM part number.
5) After a few seconds, AIR COND menu will appear. Press "1" (WITH A/C) or "2" (WITHOUT A/C). DRB-II display will change to ENGINE SYSTEMS menu. At ENGINE SYSTEMS menu, press "1" (FUEL/IGNITION) key. Press ENTER key.
6) Display will change to FUEL/IGN MENU. At FUEL/IGN MENU of engine diagnostic program, specific test functions programmed into DRB-II can be performed. The following DRB-II modes can be accessed: SYSTEM TESTS, READ FAULTS, STATE DISPLAY, ACTUATOR TESTS and ADJUSTMENTS.

SYSTEM TESTS Mode – This mode is not available in the engine diagnostics program.

READ FAULTS Mode – This mode allows user to read and erase fault codes. A fault counter will appear along with fault displayed. As an example, DRB-II will display 1 OF 2 FAULTS. PCM will store up to

8 fault messages. Faults are numbered in reverse order of setting. The most recent fault to occur will be displayed first. Vehicles without air conditioning will always have A/C CLUTCH RELAY CKT (circuit) stored in memory. This fault will always be displayed first if vehicle is not equipped with A/C. If no fault messages are stored, DRB-II will display NO FAULTS DETECTED and start counter will show 0 STARTS SINCE ERS (erased).

A start counter will appear below DRB-II fault counter display. Start counter counts the number of times vehicle is started since faults were last set or erased or battery was disconnected. This helps determine if fault is intermittent. Memory space limits start counter to first 3 faults. Start counter of zero equals a hard fault. Start counter of more than zero indicates an intermittent fault. Start counter will count up to 255 starts. If no fault messages are stored, DRB-II will display NO FAULTS DETECTED and start counter will show 0 STARTS SINCE ERS (erased).

STATE DISPLAY Mode – This mode provides access to FUEL/IGN STATE menu. FUEL/IGN STATE menu permits viewing groups of data regarding the PCM, sensor and switch inputs, controlled outputs, and predetermined or user selectable groups of data. The following modes can be accessed from the FUEL/IGN STATE menu: MODULE INFO, SENSORS, INPUTS/OUTPUTS, MONITORS and CUSTOM DISPLAYS. For information about the function of these modes, see FUEL/IGN STATE MENU.

ACTUATOR TESTS Mode – This mode allows the user to check for proper operation of output circuits or devices which the PCM cannot internally recognize. DRB-II allows PCM to activate these outputs or devices, allowing an observer to verify proper operation.

Most of the tests available in this mode provide an audible or visual indication of device operation (click of relay contacts, spray fuel, etc.). With the exception of an intermittent condition, if a device functions properly during its test, the device, wiring and its driver circuit are presumably functioning properly.

ADJUSTMENTS Mode – This mode allows the opportunity to make adjustments to PCM memory. The following modes can be accessed from the ADJUSTMENTS menu: ERASE FAULTS, RESET MEMORY and EMR MEMORY CHECK. For information about the function of these modes, see ADJUSTMENTS MENU.

ADJUSTMENTS MENU

ERASE FAULTS Mode – This mode erases fault messages which are stored in PCM memory. Once this mode is selected, DRB-II displays ARE YOU SURE?. If fault erasure is not desired, press ATM key. If fault erasure is desired, press ENTER key. All faults and secondary indicators will be erased.

RESET MEMORY Mode – This mode provides a sub-menu listing resettable memories. As vehicle is operated, PCM learns to adjust fuel delivery, automatic idle speed motor position and minimum throttle position sensor signal voltage to compensate for different engine operating conditions. The following modes can be accessed from the RESET MEMORY menu: ADAPTIVE FUEL, AIS COUNTER, MINIMUM TPS and ALL VALUES. For additional information about the function of these modes, see RESET MEMORY MENU.

EMR MEMORY CHECK Mode – This mode allows the user to check and correct mileage stored in PCM (if necessary). See EMISSION MAINTENANCE REMINDER (EMR) MILEAGE TRANSFER.

FUEL/IGN STATE MENU

MODULE INFO Mode – Mode displays model year, engine displacement, emission type, transmission type and PCM part number.

SENSORS Mode – This mode provides a list of sensors and their input value to PCM.

INPUTS/OUTPUTS Mode – This mode provides a list of input switch and output device circuits and status.

MONITORS Mode – This mode provides access to MONITORS menu. MONITORS menu displays up to 12 inputs and outputs relating to a specific area of fuel and ignition system performance. Following modes can be accessed from MONITORS menu: FUEL CONTROL, ADVANCE, RPM, ADAPTIVE MEM, NO START, INTERROGATOR

and SEC INDICATORS. For additional information about function of these modes, see MONITORS MENU.

CUSTOM DISPLAYS Mode – This mode allows user to customize DRB-II display. User can select up to 4 different displays which can be shown on a single screen. Any item from inputs/output list, sensor list or actuator list can be selected from custom display. Once selected, custom display will be retained in memory until changed. Up to 2 custom display screens can be customized by user.

MONITORS MENU

FUEL CONTROL Mode – This mode allows the user to display inputs and outputs which affect fuel delivery.

ADVANCE Mode – This mode allows the user to display inputs and outputs which affect ignition timing advance.

RPM Mode – This mode allows the user to display inputs and outputs which affect engine speed.

ADAPTIVE MEM Mode – This mode allows the user to display inputs and outputs which affect adaptive memory. As a vehicle is operated, PCM learns to adjust fuel delivery, automatic idle speed motor position and minimum throttle position sensor signal voltage to compensate for different engine operating conditions.

NO START Mode – This mode allows user to display inputs and outputs which affect engine starting.

INTERROGATOR Mode – This mode displays selectable inputs and outputs for use during the engineering process. This mode is not available in the engine diagnostics program.

SEC INDICATORS Mode – This mode allows user to display inputs and outputs which are not within optimum parameters but have not yet become faults. Secondary indicators are monitored by the DRB-II at all times after engine is selected in SELECT SYSTEM menu. When a secondary indicator is generated, DRB-II will emit 5 short beeps. If a secondary indicator becomes a hard fault, DRB-II Red LED (light emitting diode) will glow.

RESET MEMORY MENU

ADAPTIVE FUEL Mode – This mode allows the user to erase PCM memory of learned fuel delivery. As a vehicle is operated, PCM learns to adjust fuel delivery, automatic idle speed motor position and minimum throttle position sensor signal voltage to compensate for different engine operating conditions.

AIS COUNTER Mode – This mode allows the user to erase PCM memory of start-up Automatic Idle Speed (AIS) motor steps.

MINIMUM TPS Mode – This mode allows the user to erase PCM memory of lowest Throttle Position Sensor (TPS) voltage.

ALL VALUES Mode – This mode allows the user to erase PCM memory of adaptive fuel delivery, automatic idle speed motor position and minimum throttle position sensor signal voltage.

DRB-II VOLT/OHMMETER

1) To access volt/ohmmeter mode of DRB-II, connect Red volt/ohmmeter test lead to Red port, located on right top side of DRB-II.

NOTE: Because DRB-II is grounded through engine diagnostic connector, only one volt/ohmmeter test lead is required when using volt/ohmmeter option. DRB-II volt/ohmmeter should only be used when self-diagnostic tests require the use of this option.

2) To access voltmeter, press VOLT/OHM key once. DRB-II is now in voltmeter mode. Touch test probe to connector or wire to be measured. Read voltage on DRB-II display. When voltage testing is complete, press VOLT/OHM key 3 times to exit voltmeter mode.

3) To access ohmmeter, press VOLT/OHM key twice. DRB-II is now in ohmmeter mode. Touch test probe to connector or wire to be measured. Read resistance to circuit ground on DRB-II display. When resistance testing is complete, press VOLT/OHM key twice to exit ohmmeter mode.

DRB-II Continuity Meter Mode – Press VOLT/OHM key 3 times. Display will read NO CONTINUITY. Touch test probe to connector or wire to be measured. Read continuity on DRB-II display. When continuity testing is complete, press VOLT/OHM key once to exit continuity meter mode.

DRB-II PROBLEMS & ERROR MESSAGES

Blank Message Screen – **1)** Connect DRB-II to a different vehicle. If message screen is still blank, DRB-II or cable adapter is faulty. Substitute to find faulty component.

2) If message screen is not blank, DRB-II and cable adapter are functioning properly. Inspect diagnostic connector for proper wire placement, damaged terminals and pushed-out pins. Repair as necessary.

3) If engine diagnostic connector is okay, check for continuity between Black/tracer wire (tracer color may vary) and ground at engine diagnostic connector using an ohmmeter. If continuity does not exist, repair open in Black/tracer wire.

NO RESPONSE Message – **1)** Connect DRB-II to another vehicle. If DRB-II displays NO RESPONSE message again, DRB-II or cable adapter are faulty. Substitute to find faulty component. If message screen does not display NO RESPONSE, DRB-II and cable adapter are functioning properly. Go to next step.

2) Turn ignition off. Disconnect DRB-II. Using an ohmmeter, check Pink wire for continuity between PCM connector terminal No. 25 and engine diagnostic connector. Check Pink wire for a short to ground. If continuity does not exist or wire is shorted to ground, repair open/shorted in Pink wire.

3) If continuity exists and wire is not shorted to ground, check Light Green wire for continuity between PCM connector terminal No. 45 and engine diagnostic connector. Check Light Green wire for a short to ground. If continuity does not exist or wire is shorted to ground, repair open/shorted in Light Green wire. If all systems check okay, replace PCM. Reset EMR mileage.

Other Failure Messages – If BAD FRAMING, CARTRIDGE ERROR, LOW BATTERY, BAD OP CODE, HIGH BATTERY, RAM TEST FAILURE, COMMAND REJECTED or KEYPAD TEST FAILURE Message is displayed, see BODY CONTROL COMPUTER – VEHICLE COMMUNICATIONS article.

EMISSION MAINTENANCE REMINDER (EMR) MILEAGE TRANSFER

1) When PCM is replaced, vehicle mileage must be copied from odometer to replacement PCM memory. Transfer of vehicle mileage will enable new PCM to operate EMR light properly.

2) Using DRB-II, enter FUEL/IGN MENU. See DRB-II TEST FUNCTIONS. At FUEL/IGN menu, press "5" (ADJUSTMENTS) key. Press ENTER key. At ADJUSTMENTS menu, press "3" (EMR MEMORY CHECK) key. Press ENTER key. DRB-II will display EMR MEMORY CHECK ARE YOU SURE? ENTER TO CONTINUE.

3) Press ENTER key. DRB-II will display IS INSTRUMENT PANEL MILEAGE BETWEEN XXXXX AND XXXXX? If vehicle mileage is within specification, EMR memory check is complete. Press YES key. If vehicle mileage is not within specification, go to next step.

4) Press NO key. DRB-II will display ENTER MILEAGE SHOWN ON INSTRUMENT PANEL, USE ENTER KEY TO END. Enter vehicle mileage. DO NOT enter tenths. When correct vehicle mileage is entered, press ENTER key.

5) DRB-II will ask for verification of mileage entry. If mileage entry was accurate, press ENTER key. DRB-II will display EMR MEMORY CHECK TEST COMPLETE. Vehicle must travel at least 8 miles for reset to occur.

CONNECTOR IDENTIFICATION
Connector Identification

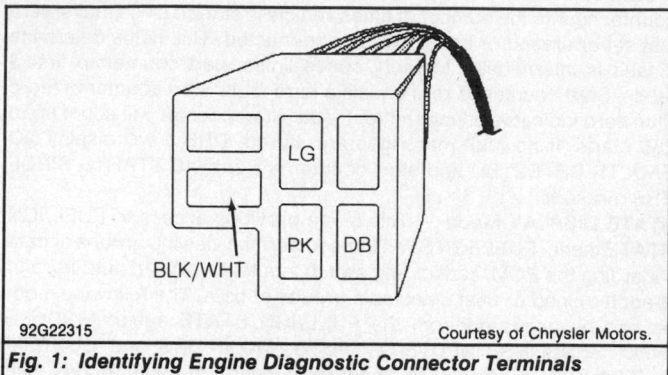

92G22315   Courtesy of Chrysler Motors.
Fig. 1: Identifying Engine Diagnostic Connector Terminals

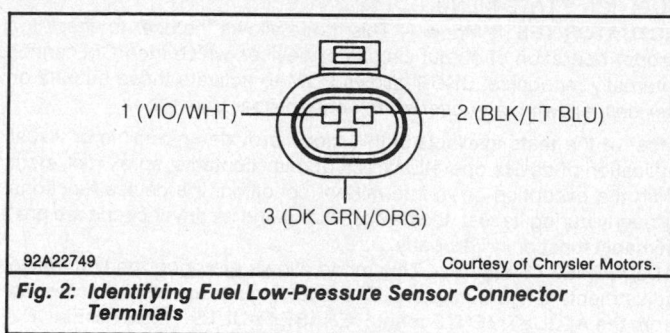

92A22749   Courtesy of Chrysler Motors.
Fig. 2: Identifying Fuel Low-Pressure Sensor Connector Terminals

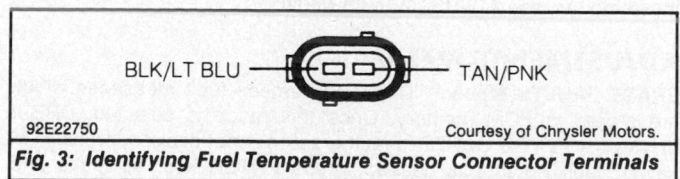

92E22750   Courtesy of Chrysler Motors.
Fig. 3: Identifying Fuel Temperature Sensor Connector Terminals

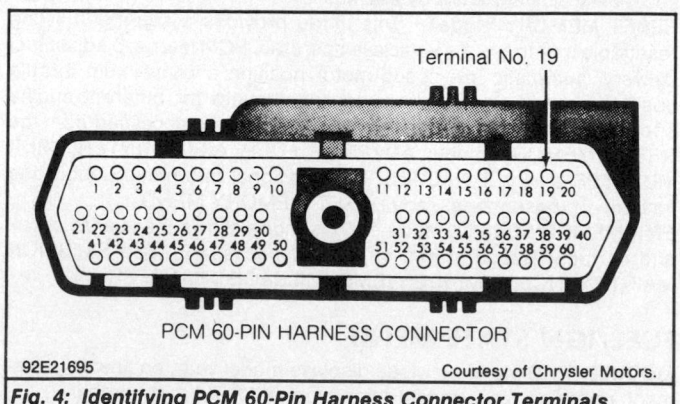

92E21695   Courtesy of Chrysler Motors.
Fig. 4: Identifying PCM 60-Pin Harness Connector Terminals

CNG TROUBLE CODE 64

FUEL TEMPERATURE SENSE HIGH OR LOW

NOTE: For connector terminal identification, see CONNECTOR IDEN-TIFICATION. For wiring diagram, see appropriate WIRING DIAGRAMS article in ENGINE PERFORMANCE.

1) Turn ignition off. Disconnect and inspect fuel temperature sensor connector. If connector is okay, go to next step. If connector is not okay, repair connector as necessary. Perform VERIFICATION TEST.
2) Using an ohmmeter, connect leads across fuel temperature sensor terminals. If ohmmeter reading is some resistance other than infinity, go to next step. If ohmmeter reading is infinity, replace fuel tempera-ture sensor.

WARNING: Relieve fuel pressure prior to replacing sensor. See FUEL PRESSURE RELEASE.

3) Disconnect PCM 60-pin connector. Check resistance between Tan/Pink wire at fuel temperature sensor connector and cavity No. 42 in PCM 60-pin connector. If resistance reading is less than 10 ohms, go to next step. If resistance is greater than 10 ohms, repair open circuit in Tan/Pink wire.
4) Check resistance in Tan/Pink wire between Fuel Temperature sen-sor and chassis ground. If resistance reading is greater than 10 ohms, go to next step. If resistance is less than 10 ohms, repair short to ground.
5) Check resistance between Black/Light Blue at fuel temperature sensor connector and cavity No. 4 in PCM 60-pin connector. If resis-tance reading is less than 10 ohms, go to next step. If resistance is greater than 10 ohms, repair open circuit in Black/Light Blue.
6) Check resistance in Black/Light Blue wire between Fuel Tempera-ture sensor and chassis ground. If resistance is less than 10 ohms, repair short to ground. If resistance reading is greater than 10 ohms, replace PCM. Perform VERIFICATION TEST.

FUEL PRESSURE SENSE HIGH OR LOW

NOTE: For connector terminal identification, see CONNECTOR IDEN-TIFICATION. For wiring diagram, see appropriate WIRING DIAGRAMS article in ENGINE PERFORMANCE.

1) Turn ignition off. Disconnect and inspect fuel low-pressure sensor connector. If connector is okay, go to next step. If connector is not okay, repair connector as necessary. Perform VERIFICATION TEST.
2) Using an ohmmeter, connect leads across fuel low-pressure sensor terminals No. 1 and 3. *See Fig. 2.* If ohmmeter reading is some resis-tance other than infinity, go to next step. If ohmmeter reading is infin-ity, replace fuel low-pressure sensor.
3) Disconnect PCM 60-pin connector. Check resistance in Violet/White wire between fuel low-pressure sensor connector and cavity No. 6 in PCM 60-pin connector. Check resistance in Dark Green/Orange wire between fuel low-pressure sensor connector and cavity No. 23 in PCM 60-pin connector.
4) If resistance reading is less than 10 ohms in both wires, go to next step. If resistance reading is greater than 10 ohms in either wire, repair open circuit in affected wire.
5) Check resistance in Violet/White wire and Dark Green/Orange wire between fuel low-pressure sensor and chassis ground. If resistance reading in both wires is greater than 10 ohms, go to next step. If resis-tance reading is less than 10 ohms in either wire, repair short to ground in affected wire.
6) Check resistance in Black/Light blue wire between fuel low-pressure sensor and cavity No. 4 of PCM 60-pin connector. If resistance is less than 10 ohms, go to next step. If resistance is great-er than 10 ohms, repair open circuit in Black/Light Blue wire.
7) Check resistance between chassis ground and Black/Light Blue wire in fuel low-pressure sensor connector. If resistance is less than 10 ohms, repair short to ground in Black/Light Blue wire. If resistance reading is greater than 10 ohms, replace PCM. Perform VERIFICA-TION TEST.

VERIFICATION TEST

Inspect vehicle to ensure all engine components are connected. Reas-semble and reconnect components as necessary. If another fault was read previously and not corrected, go to TEST DR-1A in SELF-DIAG-NOSTIC TESTS – 3.9L & 5.2L article. Follow path specified by other fault. If Powertrain Control Module (PCM) has been replaced:
* Write vehicle mileage to memory location within replacement SBEC. This will enable new SBEC to operate Emission Mainte-nance Reminder (EMR) light properly.
* Connect DRB-II to engine diagnostic connector, and erase faults. Disconnect DRB-II.
To ensure no other fault remains:
1) On models equipped with A/C, turn A/C on. Set blower to low speed. Drive vehicle for at least 5 minutes and attain a speed of 40 MPH or more. Ensure transmission shifts through all gears.
2) Upon completion of road test, turn engine off. Restart engine, and let it idle for at least 2 minutes. Turn engine off. Connect DRB-II to engine diagnostic connector.
3) Read all fault messages. If repaired fault has reset, repair is not complete. Check all pertinent MITCHELL® TECH SERVICE BUL-LETINS (TSBs) and return to TEST DR-1A in SELF-DIAGNOSTIC TESTS – 3.9L & 5.2L article if necessary. If another fault exists, return to TEST DR-1A in SELF-DIAGNOSTIC TESTS – 3.9L & 5.2L article. Follow path specified by other fault. If no other faults exist, repair is now complete.

1992 ENGINE PERFORMANCE
Body Control Computer Introduction

Caravan, Town & Country, Voyager

DESCRIPTION

The body control computer system consists of a combination of modules that communicate over the Chrysler Collision Detection (CCD) bus system. Through the CCD bus, information related to the operation of vehicle components and circuits is relayed to the appropriate system module(s). Each module receives the same component information. This reduces the complexity of vehicle wiring and size of wiring harness.

The following body control computer systems are covered in this article: electronic instrument cluster, electro/mechanical instrument cluster, automatic door locks, compass/mini-trip module, illuminated entry, headlights, and intermittent wipers. System failures within these systems can be diagnosed via the CCD bus diagnostic connector using Chrysler Diagnostic Readout Box II (DRB-II) tester.

OPERATION

Diagnostic test procedures are designed to detect system faults as quickly as possible. Body and chassis fault codes are accessed through CCD bus diagnostic connector. CCD bus diagnostic connector is located under left side of dash. *See Fig. 1.* DRB-II tester is used to access information from CCD bus.

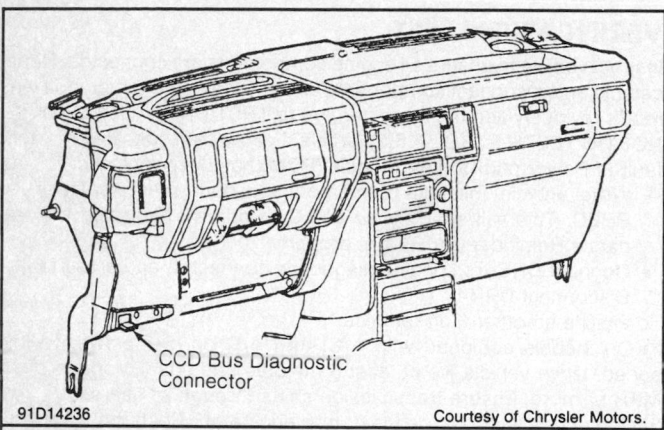

91D14236   Courtesy of Chrysler Motors.

Fig. 1: Locating CCD Bus Diagnostic Connector (Typical)

BODY CONTROL COMPUTER

The body control computer, sometimes referred to as body controller, is located under left side of instrument panel. Body control computer stores odometer information for electronic instrument cluster and electro/mechanical instrument cluster display and provides power and ground for a variety of systems. Systems are monitored by body control computer through voltage drops.

CCD BUS

The CCD bus is a twisted pair of wires traveling from module to module receiving and delivering coded information. The code identifies the message and its importance. When multiple messages attempt to access CCD bus at once, code assigns priority ranking.

The 2 twisted wires used by the CCD bus system are called Bus "+" and Bus "–". Both wires carry approximately 2.5 volts.

SELF-DIAGNOSTIC SYSTEM

Use diagnostic tests listed in BODY CONTROL COMPUTER DIRECTORY table when using DRB-II.

BODY CONTROL COMPUTER DIRECTORY

PRETEST INSPECTION

Before diagnosis, following precautions must be followed:
- Vehicle must have a fully charged battery and functional charging system.
- Always start at TEST 1A: IDENTIFYING VEHICLE EQUIPMENT & SYSTEM PROBLEMS. Starting with any other test may result in incorrect results.
- Only perform test steps indicated. It is NOT necessary to perform all steps in a test.
- VEHICLE COMMUNICATIONS tests should only be used when instructed to do so by another test. Always start at TEST 1A: BLANK DRB-II MESSAGE SCREEN.
- Always perform appropriate VERIFICATION TEST after repairs are completed.
- At end of each test step, reconnect all wires and install any components removed for testing.
- Use extreme care when connecting or disconnecting wiring during testing to prevent accidental grounding or shorting.
- DO NOT use a test light in place of a voltmeter.
- Always disconnect DRB-II after use.
- Always disconnect DRB-II before charging battery.

DIAGNOSTIC PROCEDURE

NOTE: Before proceeding with diagnosis, certain precautions must be followed. See PRETEST INSPECTION under SELF-DIAGNOSTIC SYSTEM.

Diagnostic test procedures are designed to detect system faults as quickly as possible. Body fault codes are accessed through CCD bus diagnostic connector. *See Fig. 1.* DRB-II tester is used to access information from CCD bus diagnostic connector.

DRB-II tester, jumper wires and volt/ohmmeter will be needed for testing. Proceed to TEST 1A: IDENTIFYING VEHICLE EQUIPMENT & SYSTEM PROBLEMS. Ensure self-diagnostic tests apply to vehicle being tested. See BODY CONTROL COMPUTER DIRECTORY table under SELF-DIAGNOSTIC SYSTEM. When system problem is identified according to customer complaint, perform indicated diagnostic test.

DRB-II KEY FUNCTIONS

YES or Down Arrow & NO or Up Arrow – Keys will move lines on screen up or down, allowing technician to choose an item or scroll through all selections available.
ATM Key – Key will return technician to previous screen.
ENTER Key – Allows technician to select a test or display. The flashing arrow must be on the display user wishes to select. Pressing the ENTER key in the sensor state will cause display to change from a 3-line display to a 1-line display.
F3 Key – Key is used to display a help screen. This key may be used at any time.
READ/HOLD Key – Key is used to freeze any sensor display.
MODE & ATM Keys – Pressing MODE and ATM keys at same time will cause DRB-II to reset to copyright screen.

ENTERING ON-BOARD DIAGNOSTICS

1) Before entering on-board diagnostics, refer to PRETEST INSPECTION. Turn ignition off. Attach appropriate cartridge to DRB-II. Connect DRB-II to CCD bus diagnostic connector. *See Fig. 1.*
2) Turn all accessories off. Turn ignition on. All character positions will glow and copyright information will appear on DRB-II screen for a few seconds. Display will then change to DRB-II menu.
3) If DRB-II displays an error message or screen is blank, refer to VEHICLE COMMUNICATIONS tests. See BODY CONTROL COMPUTER DIRECTORY table. Always start at TEST 1A: BLANK DRB-II MESSAGE SCREEN
4) Following DRB-II modes are accessible from DRB-II menu: VEHICLES TESTED, HOW TO USE, CONFIGURE and SELECT SYSTEM.

VEHICLES TESTED Mode – At DRB-II menu, press "1" (VEHICLES TESTED) key. Press ENTER key. At VEHICLES TESTED, DRB-II will display vehicles supported by cartridge used. This screen will display for 5 seconds and return to DRB-II menu. To return to menu sooner, press ATM key.

HOW TO USE Mode – At DRB-II menu, press "2" (HOW TO USE) key. Press ENTER key. DRB-II will display instructions for use of DRB-II for cartridge being used.

CONFIGURE Mode – At DRB-II menu, press "3" (CONFIGURE) key. Press ENTER key. At CONFIGURE menu, technician can customize DRB-II display. For example, if metric system is more useful, select METRIC from appropriate menu. All selections made under CONFIGURE option remain active until user changes selection.

SELECT SYSTEM Mode – 1) This mode enables the technician to select system to be diagnosed. At DRB-II menu, press "4" (SELECT SYSTEM) key. Press ENTER key. DRB-II will display SELECT SYSTEM menu.

2) At SELECT SYSTEM menu, press "3" (BODY) key. Press ENTER key. DRB-II should display BUS TEST IN PROGRESS and BUS OPERATIONAL. After a few seconds, display should change to BODY STYLE menu.

3) If a bus failure message appears during BUS TEST IN PROGRESS, proceed to VEHICLE COMMUNICATIONS tests. See BODY CONTROL COMPUTER DIRECTORY table. Always start at TEST 1A: BLANK DRB-II MESSAGE SCREEN. At BODY STYLE menu, select appropriate body style for vehicle being worked on. DRB-II will display SELECT MODULE MENU.

SELECT MODULE MENU – Menu will display body control systems available for technician to diagnose. Select appropriate body system to be tested. DRB-II will then display a menu for specific system being tested. Following functions are accessible from each system menu:

- **System Tests** – This function allows technician to determine whether Single Board Engine Controller (SBEC) is active over CCD bus.
- **Read Faults** – This functions allows technician to read faults. If no faults exist, NO FAULTS DETECTED will be displayed. If faults exist, DRB-II will display number of faults, fault code and message.
- **State Display** – This functions allows technician to read states or values of a variety of sensors, inputs/outputs and components.
- **Actuator Tests** – This function allows technician to activate various outputs, motors and relays to test their operation.
- **Adjustments** – This function allows the technician to change vehicle theft alarm system mode from disarmed to armed, or to put alarm system in self-diagnostics mode. Adjustments function is not available for testing of other body control modules.

DRB-II Volt-Ohmmeter Mode – 1) To access volt-ohmmeter mode of DRB-II, connect Red volt-ohmmeter test lead to Red port, located on right top side of DRB-II.

NOTE: Because DRB-II is grounded through engine diagnostic connector, only one volt-ohmmeter test lead is required when using volt-ohmmeter option. DRB-II volt-ohmmeter should only be used when self-diagnostic tests require this option.

---

2) To access voltmeter, press VOLT/OHM key once. DRB-II is now in voltmeter mode. Touch test probe to connector or wire to be measured. Read voltage on DRB-II display. When voltage testing is complete, press VOLT/OHM key 3 times to exit voltmeter mode.

3) To access ohmmeter, press VOLT/OHM key twice. DRB-II is now in ohmmeter mode. Touch test probe to connector or wire to be measured. Read resistance to circuit ground on DRB-II display. When resistance testing is complete, press VOLT/OHM key twice to exit ohmmeter mode.

DRB-II Continuity Meter Mode – Press VOLT/OHM key 3 times. Display will read NO CONTINUITY. Touch test probe to connector or wire to be measured. Read continuity on DRB-II display. When continuity testing is complete, press VOLT/OHM key once to exit continuity meter mode.

ELECTRONIC INSTRUMENT CLUSTER (EIC) ACTUATOR TESTS

After ACTUATOR TESTS is selected from ELEC CLUSTER menu, display will change to ACTUATOR TEST and tests available for technician to diagnose. Select appropriate test. DRB-II will then display a menu for specific test and ACTUATING/COMPLETED. To determine whether or not any of these tests pass or fail, observe EIC display as test is being actuated. Following tests can be accessed from menu:

- **INTERNAL CHECK** – This tests the internal functions of EIC. This test also displays any fault codes present.
- **ALL SEGMENTS ON** – This test turns on all segments of EIC and then turns them off. If all segments do not glow and then turn off, test is failed.
- **SEQUENTIAL SEGMENTS TEST** – This test illuminates all vacuum fluorescent bars on all gauges in EIC and then turns them off. If any bar fails to glow, test is failed.
- **SEQUENTIAL LEGENDS TEST** – This test illuminates all legends in EIC individually and then turns them off. If any legend fails to glow or if 2 legends are illuminated together, test is failed.
- **SEQUENTIAL LAMP CHECK** – This test illuminates following lights in EIC display individually and then turns them off: WASHER FLUID, DOOR/DECK, CHECK ENGINE, SEAT BELT, BRAKE and CHECK GAGES. If any light does not glow and then turn off, test is failed.

DRB-II PROBLEMS & ERROR MESSAGES

If a problem exists with the operation of DRB-II, DRB-II displays a blank screen, CCD bus failure message or NO RESPONSE, RAM TEST FAILURE, CARTRIDGE ERROR, KEYPAD TEST FAILURE, HIGH BATTERY or LOW BATTERY error message appears, refer to VEHICLE COMMUNICATIONS tests. See BODY CONTROL COMPUTER DIRECTORY table. Always start at TEST 1A: BLANK DRB-II MESSAGE SCREEN.

CONNECTOR IDENTIFICATION

CONNECTOR IDENTIFICATION DIRECTORY

Connector	See Fig.
Body Control Computer	
Blue	2
Natural	3
CCD Bus Diagnostic	4
Compass/Mini-Trip Module	5
Diode Assembly	6
Front & Side Door Jamb Switch	8
Fuel Pump/Sending Unit	7
Instrument Cluster	9
Ignition Key-In-Ignition	10
Left Pod Switch Assembly	11
Left Pod Switch Connectors	
Blue & Gray	12
Black	13
Liftgate Switch	14
Multifunction Switch	15
Power Distribution Center Relay	16
Single Board Engine Controller (SBEC)	17

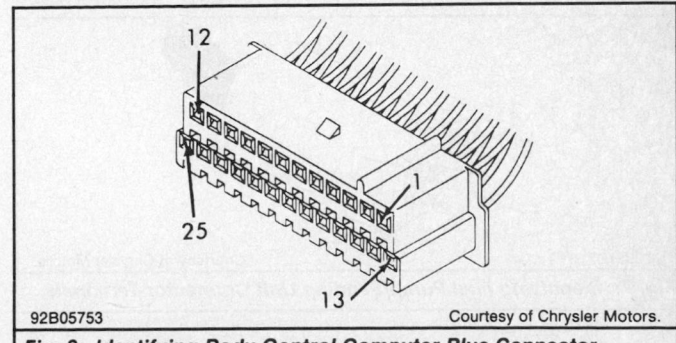

92B05753   Courtesy of Chrysler Motors.

Fig. 2: Identifying Body Control Computer Blue Connector Terminals

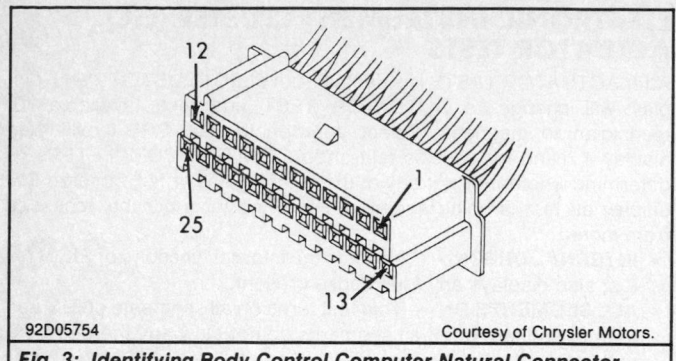

92D05754   Courtesy of Chrysler Motors.

Fig. 3: **Identifying Body Control Computer Natural Connector Terminals**

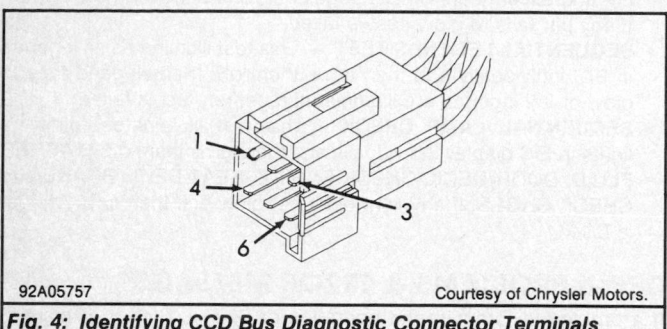

92A05757   Courtesy of Chrysler Motors.

Fig. 4: **Identifying CCD Bus Diagnostic Connector Terminals**

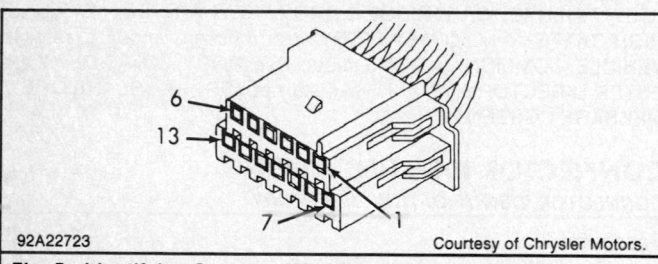

92A22723   Courtesy of Chrysler Motors.

Fig. 5: **Identifying Compass/Mini-Trip Module Connector Terminals**

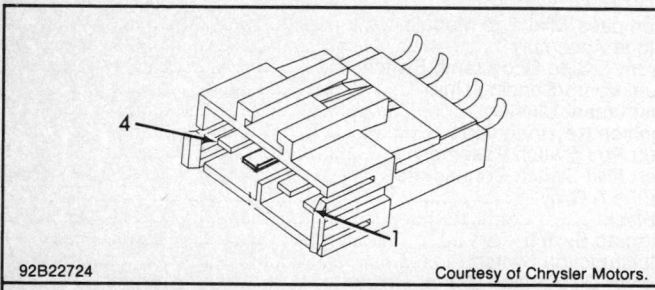

92B22724   Courtesy of Chrysler Motors.

Fig. 6: **Identifying Diode Assembly Connector Terminals**

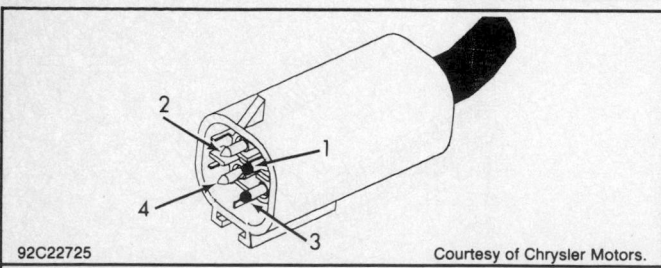

92C22725   Courtesy of Chrysler Motors.

Fig. 7: **Identifying Fuel Pump/Sending Unit Connector Terminals**

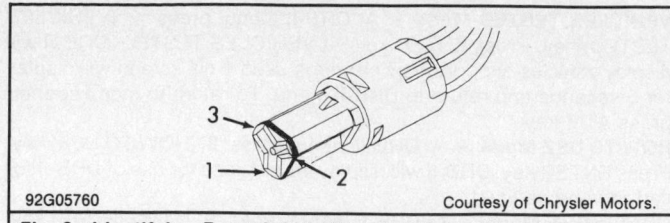

92G05760   Courtesy of Chrysler Motors.

Fig. 8: **Identifying Front & Side Door Jamb Switch Connector Terminals**

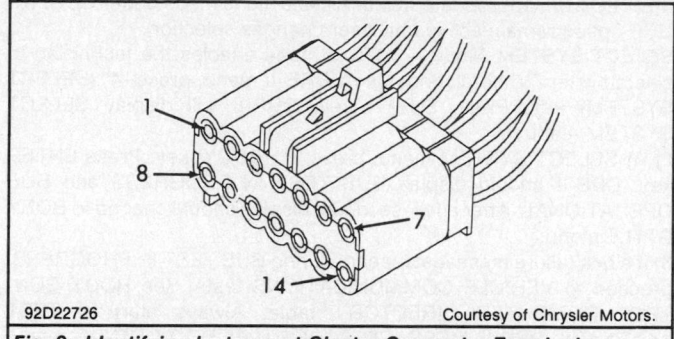

92D22726   Courtesy of Chrysler Motors.

Fig. 9: **Identifying Instrument Cluster Connector Terminals**

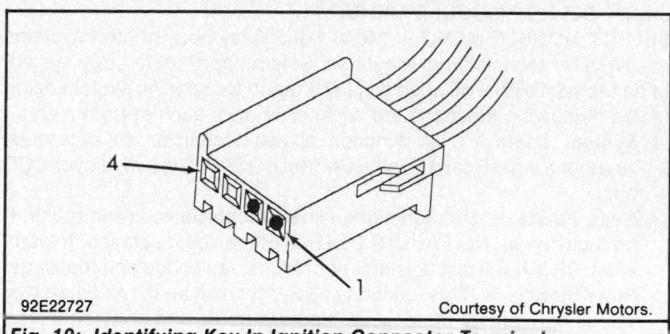

92E22727   Courtesy of Chrysler Motors.

Fig. 10: **Identifying Key-In-Ignition Connector Terminals**

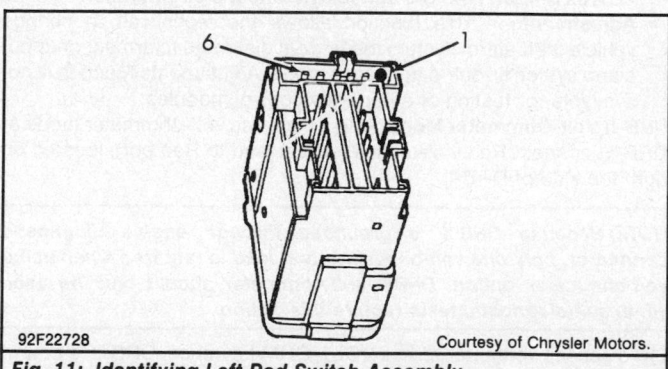

92F22728   Courtesy of Chrysler Motors.

Fig. 11: **Identifying Left Pod Switch Assembly Connector Terminals**

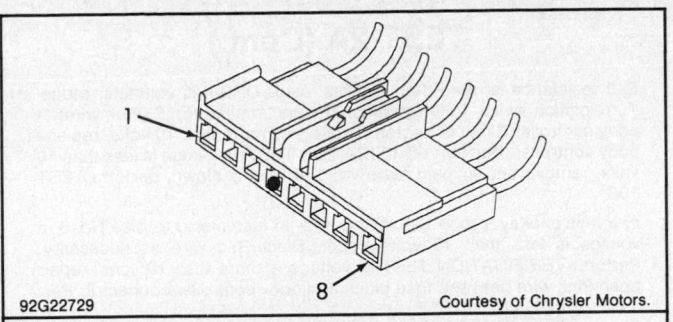

Fig. 12: *Identifying Left Pod Switch Connector Terminals (Blue & Gray Connectors)*

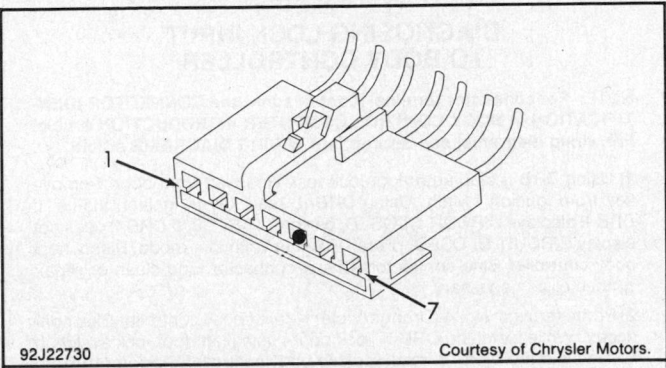

Fig. 13: *Identifying Left Pod Switch Connector Terminals (Black Connector)*

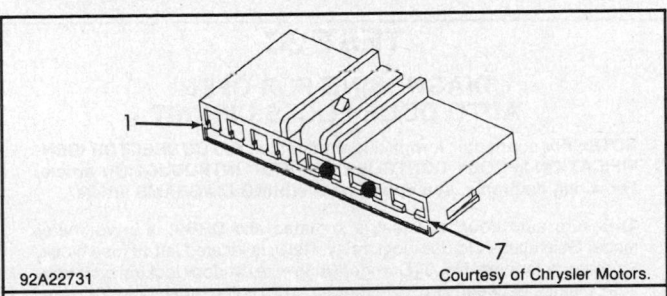

Fig. 14: *Identifying Liftgate Switch Connector Terminals*

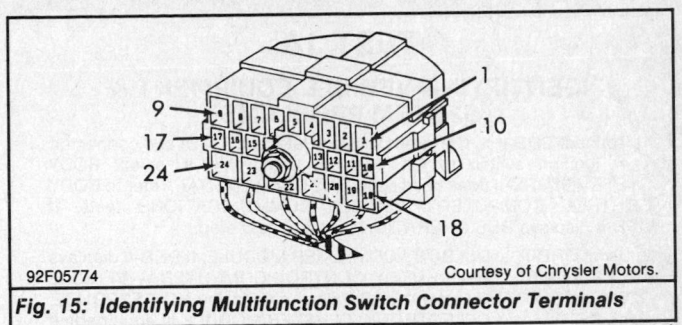

Fig. 15: *Identifying Multifunction Switch Connector Terminals*

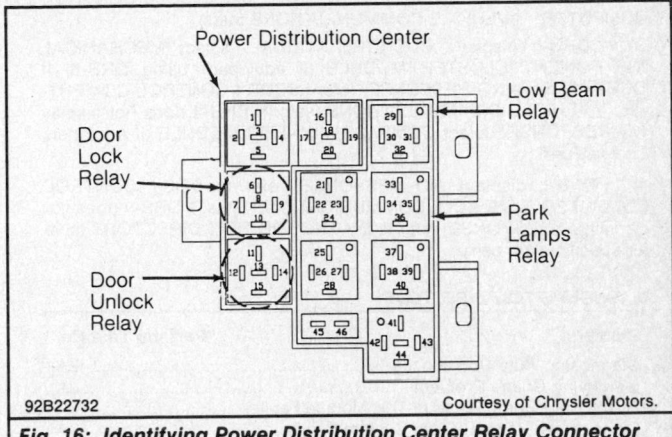

Fig. 16: *Identifying Power Distribution Center Relay Connector Terminals*

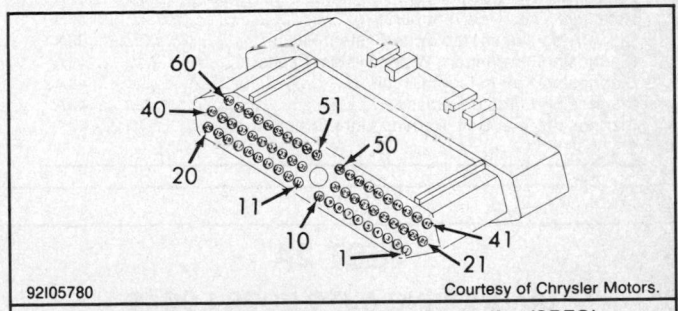

Fig. 17: *Identifying Single Board Engine Controller (SBEC) Connector Terminals*

WIRING DIAGRAMS

For wiring diagram, see appropriate WIRING DIAGRAMS article in ENGINE PERFORMANCE.

1992 ENGINE PERFORMANCE
Body Control Computer Tests

TEST 1A

IDENTIFYING VEHICLE EQUIPMENT & SYSTEM PROBLEMS

1) Connect DRB-II to Chrysler Collision Detection (CCD) bus connector. Turn ignition switch to ON position. Using DRB-II, select BODY SYSTEM. If DRB-II does not display BUS OPERATIONAL, refer to BODY CONTROL COMPUTER – VEHICLE COMMUNICATIONS tests. If DRB-II displays BUS OPERATIONAL, go to next step.

2) Using DRB-II, select BODY COMPUTER MODULE. If DRB-II displays NO RESPONSE, refer to BODY CONTROL COMPUTER – VEHICLE COMMUNICATIONS tests. If DRB-II does not display NO RESPONSE, using DRB-II, select ELECTRONIC CLUSTER MODULE (if equipped). If DRB-II does not display BUS OPERATIONAL, refer to BODY CONTROL COMPUTER – VEHICLE COMMUNICATIONS tests.

3) If DRB-II displays BUS OPERATIONAL, select MECHANICAL INSTRUMENT CLUSTER MODULE (if equipped) using DRB-II. If DRB-II displays NO RESPONSE, refer to BODY CONTROL COMPUTER – VEHICLE COMMUNICATIONS tests. If DRB-II does not display NO RESPONSE, select COMPASS/MINI-TRIP MODULE (if equipped) using DRB-II.

4) If DRB-II displays NO RESPONSE, refer to BODY CONTROL COMPUTER – VEHICLE COMMUNICATIONS tests. If DRB-II does not display NO RESPONSE, refer to DIAGNOSTIC TEST DIRECTORY table for specific diagnosis.

DIAGNOSTIC TEST DIRECTORY

Problem	Perform Test No.
Diagnosing Auto Door Locks	2A
Identifying Chime Problem	5A
Diagnosing Compass/Mini-Trip Module Faults	6A
Diagnosing Courtesy Light System Faults	10A
Electronic Instrument Cluster Diagnostics	22A
Electro/Mechanical Instrument Cluster Diagnostics	29A
Headlights Will Not Turn Off	37A
Headlight Time Delay Inoperative	37B
Diagnosing Illuminated Entry System Faults	38A
Diagnosing Intermittent Wiper System Faults	41A
Diagnosing Key-In Light Circuit	44A
Diagnosing Liftgate Release	45A
Diagnosing Seat Belt Warning Light Circuit	47A

TEST 2A

DIAGNOSING AUTO DOOR LOCKS

NOTE: For connector terminal identification, see CONNECTOR IDENTIFICATION in BODY CONTROL COMPUTER INTRODUCTION article. For wiring diagrams, see appropriate WIRING DIAGRAMS article.

1) Check if problem is with side door memory lock only. If problem is with side door memory lock only, perform TEST 3A. If problem is other than side door memory lock, go to next step.

NOTE: Ensure left front door is open and key is removed from ignition switch.

2) Depress power door lock switch to LOCK position. If doors lock, perform TEST 4A. If doors do not lock, turn ignition switch to ON position. Using DRB-II, actuate auto door lock test. If doors lock, perform TEST 2B. If doors do not lock, gain access to body controller. Body controller is located under left side of instrument panel.

3) Place DRB-II in voltmeter mode. With actuation test still running, backprobe terminal No. 21 (Orange/White wire) of body controller Blue connector. If voltage pulsates between zero and more than 10 volts, perform TEST 2C. If voltage does not pulsate between zero and more than 10 volts, using DRB-II, stop auto door lock test.

4) Turn ignition switch to OFF position. Remove lock relay from relay center. Disconnect body controller Blue connector. Check connector, and clean or repair connector as necessary. Place DRB-II in ohmmeter mode. Probe terminal No. 21 (Orange/White wire) of body controller Blue connector. If resistance is less than 5 ohms, repair short to ground in Orange/White wire. Perform VERIFICATION TEST.

TEST 2A (Cont.)

5) If resistance is more than 5 ohms, place DRB-II in voltmeter mode. Turn ignition switch to ON position. Probe terminal No. 8 (Pink wire) of body controller Blue connector. If voltage is more than 10 volts, replace body controller. Perform VERIFICATION TEST. If voltage is less than 10 volts, remove and inspect fuse No. 3. If fuse is blown, perform TEST 10C.

6) If fuse is okay, probe Black/Red wire (in fuse block) to fuse No. 3. If voltage is less than 10 volts, repair Black/Red wire as necessary. Perform VERIFICATION TEST. If voltage is more than 10 volts, repair open Pink wire between fuse block and body controller connector. Perform VERIFICATION TEST.

TEST 2B

DIAGNOSING LOCK INPUT TO BODY CONTROLLER

NOTE: For connector terminal identification, see CONNECTOR IDENTIFICATION in BODY CONTROL COMPUTER INTRODUCTION article. For wiring diagrams, see appropriate WIRING DIAGRAMS article.

1) Using DRB-II stop auto door lock test. Open left front door. Remove key from ignition switch. Using DRB-II, read key in ignition status. If DRB-II displays CIRCUIT CLOSED, perform TEST 5B. If DRB-II does not display CIRCUIT CLOSED, place DRB-II in voltmeter mode. Disconnect body controller Blue connector. Check connector, and clean or repair connector as necessary.

2) Probe terminal No. 4 (Orange/Violet wire) of body controller Blue connector. While watching DRB-II, lock doors using left door lock switch. If voltage is more than 10 volts, replace body controller. Perform VERIFICATION TEST. If voltage is less than 10 volts, repair Orange/Violet wire as necessary. Perform VERIFICATION TEST.

TEST 2C

DIAGNOSING FOR OPEN AUTO DOOR LOCKS CIRCUIT

NOTE: For connector terminal identification, see CONNECTOR IDENTIFICATION in BODY CONTROL COMPUTER INTRODUCTION article. For wiring diagrams, see appropriate WIRING DIAGRAMS article.

1) Ensure auto door lock test is actuated and DRB-II is in voltmeter mode. Gain access to door lock relay. Relay is located left of fuse block. Backprobe terminal No. 9 (Orange/White wire) at door lock relay. If voltage pulsates between zero and more than 10 volts, repair open Orange/White. Perform VERIFICATION TEST.

2) If voltage does not pulsate between zero and more than 10 volts, backprobe terminal No. 6 (Orange/Black wire) at door lock relay. If voltage pulsates between zero and more than 10 volts, go to next step. If voltage does not pulsate between zero and more than 10 volts, go to step **5)**.

3) Backprobe terminal No. 11 (Pink/Black wire) at door unlock relay. If voltage pulsates between zero and above 10 volts, repair open in Pink/Black wire. Perform VERIFICATION TEST. If voltage does not pulsate between zero and above 10 volts, using DRB-II, stop auto door lock test.

4) Turn ignition switch to OFF position. Put DRB-II in ohmmeter mode. Remove door lock and unlock relays. Probe terminal No. 13 (Black wire) at door unlock relay connector. If resistance is more than 5 ohms, repair open Black wire. Perform VERIFICATION TEST. If resistance is less than 5 ohms, replace door unlock relay. Perform VERIFICATION TEST.

5) If voltage does not pulsate between zero and more than 10 volts in step **2)**, stop auto door lock actuation test using DRB-II. Backprobe terminal No. 10 (Red wire) at door lock relay. If voltage less than 10 volts, repair Red wire as necessary. Perform VERIFICATION TEST. If voltage is more than 10 volts, turn ignition switch to OFF position. Place DRB-II in ohmmeter mode. Remove lock, and unlock relays.

6) Probe terminal No. 7 (Black wire) at door lock relay connector. If resistance is more than 5 ohms, repair open Black wire. Perform VERIFICATION TEST. If resistance is less than 5 ohms, probe terminal No. 6 (Orange/Black wire) at door lock relay connector.

7) If resistance is more than 5 ohms, replace lock relay. Perform VERIFICATION TEST. If resistance is less than 5 ohms, repair short to ground in Orange/Black wire. Perform VERIFICATION TEST.

TEST 3A

DIAGNOSING FOR SIDE DOOR MEMORY LOCK

NOTE: For connector terminal identification, see CONNECTOR IDENTIFICATION in BODY CONTROL COMPUTER INTRODUCTION article. For wiring diagrams, see appropriate WIRING DIAGRAMS article.

1) Ensure all doors are closed. Using DRB-II, read side door ajar switch status. If DRB-II does not display CIRCUIT CLOSED, go to step 4). If DRB-II displays CIRCUIT CLOSED, disconnect side door ajar switch. If DRB-II does not display CIRCUIT CLOSED, replace door ajar switch. Perform VERIFICATION TEST.

2) If DRB-II displays CIRCUIT CLOSED, turn ignition switch to OFF position. Disconnect body controller Natural connector. Check connector, and clean or repair connector as necessary. Place DRB-II in ohmmeter mode. Probe terminal No. 14 (Tan/Yellow wire) of body controller Natural connector.

3) If resistance is more than 5 ohms, replace body controller. Perform VERIFICATION TEST. If resistance is less than 5 ohms, repair short to ground in Tan/Yellow wire. Perform VERIFICATION TEST.

4) If DRB-II does not display CIRCUIT CLOSED In step 1), lock doors using left door lock switch. If side door does not lock, repair or replace side door motor and/or wiring. If side door locks, open side door. Using DRB-II, read side door ajar switch status. If DRB-II displays CIRCUIT CLOSED, replace body controller. Perform VERIFICATION TEST.

5) If DRB-II does not display CIRCUIT CLOSED, disconnect side door ajar switch. Connect a jumper wire between Tan/Yellow and Black wires of side door switch connector. If DRB-II displays CIRCUIT CLOSED, replace side door ajar switch. Perform VERIFICATION TEST. If DRB-II does not display CIRCUIT CLOSED, disconnect jumper wire.

6) Connect a jumper wire between Tan/Yellow wire of side door switch connector and ground. If DRB-II displays CIRCUIT CLOSED, repair open in Black wire. Perform VERIFICATION TEST. If DRB-II does not display CIRCUIT CLOSED, access body controller. Body controller is located under left side of instrument panel.

7) Connect a jumper wire between terminal No. 14 (Tan/Yellow wire) at wiring harness side of body controller Natural connector and ground. If DRB-II displays CIRCUIT CLOSED, repair open Tan/Yellow wire. Perform VERIFICATION TEST. If DRB-II does not display CIRCUIT CLOSED, replace body controller. Perform VERIFICATION TEST.

TEST 4A

IDENTIFYING DOOR AJAR FAULTS

NOTE: For connector terminal identification, see CONNECTOR IDENTIFICATION in BODY CONTROL COMPUTER INTRODUCTION article. For wiring diagrams, see appropriate WIRING DIAGRAMS article.

1) Close all doors. Using DRB-II, read left front door ajar switch status. If DRB-II displays CIRCUIT CLOSED, perform TEST 18A. If DRB-II does not display CIRCUIT CLOSED, using DRB-II, read right front door ajar switch status.

2) If DRB-II displays CIRCUIT CLOSED, perform TEST 19A. If DRB-II does not display CIRCUIT CLOSED, read side door ajar switch status using DRB-II. If DRB-II displays CIRCUIT CLOSED, perform TEST 20A. If DRB-II does not display CIRCUIT CLOSED, using DRB-II, read left front door ajar switch status.

3) If DRB-II displays CIRCUIT CLOSED, perform TEST 44C. If DRB-II does not display CIRCUIT CLOSED, system is operating properly. Recheck customer complaint.

TEST 5A

IDENTIFYING CHIME PROBLEM

NOTE: For connector terminal identification, see CONNECTOR IDENTIFICATION in BODY CONTROL COMPUTER INTRODUCTION article. For wiring diagrams, see appropriate WIRING DIAGRAMS article.

TEST 5A (Cont.)

1) Close all doors. If a speedometer problem exists, perform TEST 24A for Electronic Cluster or TEST 30A for Electro/Mechanical Cluster. If no speedometer problem exists, turn ignition switch to ON position. Using DRB-II actuate chime test.

2) If chime does not sound, replace body controller. Perform VERIFICATION TEST. If chime sounds, stop chime test using DRB-II. Open left front door. Turn ignition switch to OFF position, remove key from ignition switch and then wait 30 seconds. Using DRB-II, read key-in-ignition switch status.

3) If DRB-II displays NO RESPONSE, perform TEST 44C. If DRB-II displays CIRCUIT CLOSED, perform TEST 5B. If DRB-II does not display NO RESPONSE or CIRCUIT CLOSED, place key in ignition switch. If chime does not sound, perform TEST 5B. If chime sounds, turn ignition switch to ON position.

4) Check turn signals for proper operation. If turn signals do not operate properly, repair turn signal circuit as necessary. If turn signals operate properly, turn left signal on. Using DRB-II, read left turn signal status. If DRB-II does not display OPEN and then CLOSE, perform TEST 5C.

5) If DRB-II displays OPEN and then CLOSE, turn right turn signal on. Using DRB-II, read right turn signal status. If DRB-II does not display OPEN and then CLOSE, perform TEST 5D. If DRB-II displays OPEN and then CLOSE, perform TEST 28A.

TEST 5B

DIAGNOSING KEY IN IGNITION CIRCUIT

NOTE: For connector terminal identification, see CONNECTOR IDENTIFICATION in BODY CONTROL COMPUTER INTRODUCTION article. For wiring diagrams, see appropriate WIRING DIAGRAMS article.

1) Turn ignition switch to ON position. Using DRB-II, read key-in-ignition switch status. If DRB-II displays CIRCUIT CLOSED, go to step 5). If DRB-II does not display CIRCUIT CLOSED, turn ignition switch to OFF position. Disconnect key-in-ignition connector. See Fig. 5B. Check connector, and clean or repair connector as necessary.

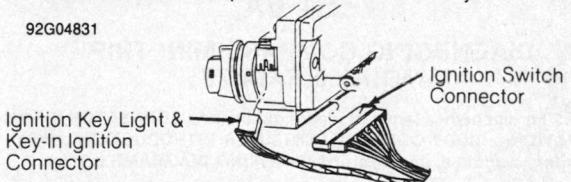

92G04831

Ignition Key Light & Key-In Ignition Connector

Ignition Switch Connector

Fig. 5B: Locating Ignition Key Light & Key-In-Ignition Connector

2) Connect a jumper wire between terminals No. 1 (Light Blue wire) and No. 2 (Black wires) of key-in-ignition connector. Ensure driver's door is open. If DRB-II displays CIRCUIT CLOSED, replace key in ignition switch. Perform VERIFICATION TEST. If DRB-II does not display CIRCUIT CLOSED, disconnect jumper wire.

3) Connect a jumper wire between terminal No. 2 (Light Blue wire) and ground. If DRB-II displays CIRCUIT CLOSED, repair open Black wire. Perform VERIFICATION TEST. If DRB-II does not display CIRCUIT CLOSED, disconnect jumper wire. Access body controller. Body controller is located under left side of instrument panel.

4) Connect jumper wire between terminal No. 2 (Light Blue wire) at wiring harness side of body controller Blue connector and ground. If DRB-II displays CIRCUIT CLOSED, repair open Light Blue wire. Perform VERIFICATION TEST. If DRB-II does not display CIRCUIT CLOSED, replace body controller. Perform VERIFICATION TEST.

5) If DRB-II displays CIRCUIT CLOSED in step 1), ensure left front door is open, remove key from ignition switch. If DRB-II displays CIRCUIT OPEN, retest system. Perform VERIFICATION TEST. If DRB-II does not display CIRCUIT OPEN, disconnect key-in-ignition connector. See Fig. 5B. Check connector, and clean or repair connector as necessary.

6) If DRB-II does not display CIRCUIT CLOSED, replace key in ignition switch. Perform VERIFICATION TEST. If DRB-II displays CIRCUIT CLOSED, disconnect body controller Blue connector. Check connector, and clean or repair connector as necessary.

7) Place DRB-II in ohmmeter mode. Probe terminal No. 2 (Light Blue wire) of body controller Blue connector. If resistance is less than 5 ohms, repair short to ground in Light Blue wire. Perform VERIFICATION TEST. If resistance is more than 5 ohms, replace body controller. Perform VERIFICATION TEST.

TEST 5C

DIAGNOSING TURN SIGNAL INPUT TO BODY CONTROLLER FOR CHIME FUNCTION

NOTE: For connector terminal identification, see CONNECTOR IDENTIFICATION in BODY CONTROL COMPUTER INTRODUCTION article. For wiring diagrams, see appropriate WIRING DIAGRAMS article.

1) Disconnect body controller Blue connector. Body controller is located under left side of instrument panel. Check connector, and clean or repair connector as necessary. Turn left turn signal on.

2) Put DRB-II in voltmeter mode. Probe terminal No. 15 (Light Green wire) of body controller Blue connector. If voltage pulsates between zero and more than 10 volts, replace body controller. Perform VERIFICATION TEST. If voltage does not pulsate between zero and more than 10 volts, repair open Light Green wire. Perform VERIFICATION TEST.

TEST 5D

DIAGNOSING TURN SIGNAL INPUT TO BODY CONTROLLER FOR CHIME FUNCTION

NOTE: For connector terminal identification, see CONNECTOR IDENTIFICATION in BODY CONTROL COMPUTER INTRODUCTION article. For wiring diagrams, see appropriate WIRING DIAGRAMS article.

1) Disconnect body controller Natural connector. Body controller is located under left side of instrument panel. Check connector, and clean or repair connector as necessary. Turn right turn signal on.

2) Place DRB-II in voltmeter mode. Probe terminal No. 7 (Tan wire) of body controller Natural connector. If voltage pulsates between zero and more than 10 volts, replace body controller. Perform VERIFICATION TEST. If voltage does not pulsate between zero and more than 10 volts, repair open Tan wire. Perform VERIFICATION TEST.

TEST 6A

DIAGNOSING COMPASS/MINI-TRIP MODULE FAULTS

NOTE: For connector terminal identification, see CONNECTOR IDENTIFICATION in BODY CONTROL COMPUTER INTRODUCTION article. For wiring diagrams, see appropriate WIRING DIAGRAMS article.

1) Turn ignition switch to ON position. If compass/mini-trip screen is blank, perform TEST 6B. If compass/mini-trip screen displays "OC" or "SC", perform TEST 7A. If compass/mini-trip screen does not display- "OC" or "SC", actuate field strength test using DRB-II.

NOTE: On compass/mini-trip screen, number 8 normally follows a letter; however, a reading can be 0-15.

2) If compass/mini-trip screen does not display "N8", "W8" and then "D1", replace compass/mini-trip module. Perform VERIFICATION TEST. If compass/mini-trip screen displays "N8", "W8" and then "D1", actuate internal test using DRB-II.

3) If compass/mini-trip screen does not display a blank screen and then "2", replace compass/mini-trip module. Perform VERIFICATION TEST. If compass/mini-trip screen displays a blank screen and then "D2", actuate "VF" display test using DRB-II.

4) All compass/mini-trip screen segments should light and then "D3" should be displayed. If compass/mini-trip does not function as specified, replace compass/mini-trip module. Perform VERIFICATION TEST. If all compass/mini-trip screen segments light and then "D3" is displayed, read compass/mini-trip faults using DRB-II.

5) If any fault messages exist, replace compass/mini-trip module. Perform VERIFICATION TEST. If no fault messages exist, check for a compass/mini-trip illumination problem. If a problem exists, perform TEST 28A. If a problem with compass/mini-trip illumination does not exist, check if ECO (average MPG) is inoperative or wrong. If a problem exists with ECO (average MPG), perform TEST 8A.

TEST 6A (Cont)

6) If no problems exist with ECO (average MPG), check if ECO (MPG) is inoperative or wrong. If a problem exists with ECO (MPG), perform TEST 8A. If no problems exist with ECO (MPG), check if "ET" (elapsed time) is inoperative. If a problem exists with "ET", perform TEST 9A. If no problems exist with "ET", check if trip odometer is inoperative or wrong.

7) If a problem exists with trip odometer, replace compass/mini-trip module. Perform VERIFICATION TEST. If no problems exist with trip odometer, perform TEST 36A. TEST 36A is for inoperative or inaccurate DTE (distance to empty) only.

TEST 6B

DIAGNOSING BLANK SCREEN COMPASS/MINI-TRIP MODULE

NOTE: For connector terminal identification, see CONNECTOR IDENTIFICATION in BODY CONTROL COMPUTER INTRODUCTION article. For wiring diagrams, see appropriate WIRING DIAGRAMS article.

1) Press step button one time. If compass/mini-trip screen is not blank, restart TEST 6A. If compass/mini-trip screen is still blank, gain access to compass/mini-trip module connector. Place DRB-II in voltmeter mode. Backprobe terminal No. 7 (Tan wire) of compass/mini-trip module connector.

2) If voltage is less than 10 volts, go to step 4). If voltage is more than 10 volts, turn ignition switch to OFF position. Disconnect compass/mini-trip module connector. Check connector, and clean or repair connector as necessary. Put DRB-II in ohmmeter mode.

3) Probe terminal No. 5 (Black/Light Green wire) of compass/mini-trip module connector. If resistance is more than 5 ohms, repair open Black/Light Green wire. Perform VERIFICATION TEST. If resistance is less than 5 ohms, perform TEST 6C.

4) If voltage is less than 10 volts in step 2), remove circuit breaker No. 25 from fuse panel. Probe Black/White wire (in fuse block) to circuit breaker No. 25. If voltage is more than 10 volts, go to step 7). If voltage is less than 10 volts, access ignition switch.

5) Backprobe terminal No. 6 (Black/White wire) at ignition switch connector. If voltage is more than 10 volts, repair open in Black/White wire between ignition switch and fuse block. Perform VERIFICATION TEST. If voltage is less than 10 volts, backprobe terminal No. 7 (Red wire) at ignition switch connector.

6) If voltage is more than 10 volts, replace ignition switch. Perform VERIFICATION TEST. If voltage is less than 10 volts, repair open Red wire. Perform VERIFICATION TEST.

7) If voltage is more than 10 volts in step 2), place DRB-II in ohmmeter mode. Probe Tan wire (in fuse block) to No. 25 circuit breaker. If resistance is less than 5 ohms, repair short to ground in Tan wire. Perform VERIFICATION TEST. If resistance is more than 5 ohms, replace circuit breaker. Perform VERIFICATION TEST.

TEST 6C

DIAGNOSING BLANK SCREEN/BUTTONS ON COMPASS/MINI-TRIP MODULE

NOTE: For connector terminal identification, see CONNECTOR IDENTIFICATION in BODY CONTROL COMPUTER INTRODUCTION article. For wiring diagrams, see appropriate WIRING DIAGRAMS article.

1) Reconnect compass/mini-trip module. Turn ignition switch to ON position. Disconnect compass/mini-trip module 5-pin connector. See Fig. 6C. Check connector, and clean or repair connector as necessary. Momentarily connect a jumper wire between terminals No. 1 and 2.

TEST 6C (Cont.)

2) If compass/mini-trip screen is still blank, replace compass/mini-trip module. Perform VERIFICATION TEST. If compass/mini-trip screen is not blank, replace step US/M button assembly. Perform VERIFICATION TEST.

92C22733

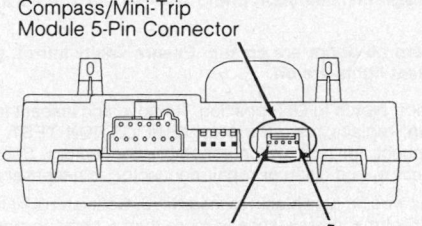

Compass/Mini-Trip
Module 5-Pin Connector

1   5

Fig. 6C: Locating & Identifying Compass/Mini-Trip Module 5-Pin Connector Terminals

TEST 7A

DIAGNOSING EXTERNAL TEMPERATURE SENSOR

NOTE: For connector terminal identification, see CONNECTOR IDENTIFICATION in BODY CONTROL COMPUTER INTRODUCTION article. For wiring diagrams, see appropriate WIRING DIAGRAMS article.

1) If compass/mini-trip screen displays "OC", go to step **5)**. If compass/mini-trip screen does not display "OC", turn ignition switch to OFF position. Disconnect external temperature sensor. *See Fig. 7A.* Check connector, and clean or repair connector as necessary. Turn ignition switch to ON position. If compass/mini-trip screen displays "OC", replace external temperature sensor. Perform VERIFICATION TEST.

92D22734

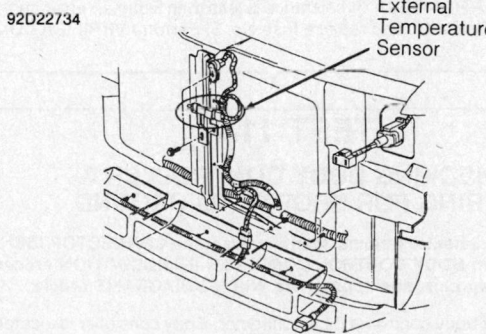

External
Temperature
Sensor

Fig. 7A: Locating External Temperature Sensor

2) If compass/mini-trip screen does not display "OC", remove compass/mini-trip module. Check connector, and clean or repair connector as necessary. Turn ignition switch to OFF position. Put DRB-II in ohmmeter mode. Probe terminal No. 9 (Violet/Light Green wire) of compass/mini-trip module connector.

3) If resistance is less than 5 ohms, repair short to ground in Violet/Light Green wire. Perform VERIFICATION TEST. If resistance is more than 5 ohms, using a external ohmmeter, check resistance between terminals No. 9 (Violet/Light Green wire) and No. 10 (Black/Light Blue wire).

4) If resistance is less than 5 ohms, repair Violet/Light Green for a short to Black/Light Blue wire. Perform VERIFICATION TEST. If resistance is more than 5 ohms, replace compass/mini-trip module. Perform VERIFICATION TEST.

5) If compass/mini-trip screen displays "OC" in step **1)**, turn ignition switch to OFF position. Disconnect external temperature sensor. Check connector, and clean or repair connector as necessary. Connect a jumper wire between Violet/Light Green and Black Light Blue wires of external temperature sensor connector. Turn ignition switch to ON position.

6) If compass/mini-trip screen displays "SC", replace external temperature sensor. Perform VERIFICATION TEST. If compass/mini-trip screen does not display "SC", turn ignition switch to OFF position. Connect a jumper wire between Violet/Light Green and Black/Light Blue wires of external temperature sensor connector and ground.

TEST 7A (Cont.)

7) Disconnect compass/mini-trip module. Check connector condition and clean or repair connector as necessary. Put DRB-II in ohmmeter mode. Probe terminal No. 9 (Violet/Light Green wire) of compass/mini-trip module connector. If resistance is more than 5 ohms, repair open Violet/Light Green wire. Perform VERIFICATION TEST.

8) If resistance is less than 5 ohms, with jumper wire is still connected, probe terminal No. 10 (Black/Light Blue wire) of compass/mini-trip module connector. If resistance is more than 5 ohms, repair open Black/Light Blue wire. Perform VERIFICATION TEST. If resistance is less than 5 ohms, replace compass/mini-trip module. Perform VERIFICATION TEST.

TEST 8A

DIAGNOSING ECO (MPG) FUNCTION-COMPASS/MINI-TRIP MODULE

NOTE: For connector terminal identification, see CONNECTOR IDENTIFICATION in BODY CONTROL COMPUTER INTRODUCTION article. For wiring diagrams, see appropriate WIRING DIAGRAMS article.

1) Ensure no speed sensor faults are present before proceeding. See appropriate SELF-DIAGNOSTICS article. If no speed sensor faults are present, turn ignition switch to ON position. Using DRB-II, read engine controller status.

2) If DRB-II does not display ACTIVE ON BUS, refer to BODY CONTROL COMPUTER – VEHICLE COMMUNICATIONS tests. If DRB-II displays ACTIVE ON BUS, replace body controller. Perform VERIFICATION TEST.

TEST 9A

DIAGNOSING ESTIMATED TIME (ET) FUNCTION-COMPASS/MINI-TRIP MODULE

NOTE: For connector terminal identification, see CONNECTOR IDENTIFICATION in BODY CONTROL COMPUTER INTRODUCTION article. For wiring diagrams, see appropriate WIRING DIAGRAMS article.

1) Turn ignition switch to OFF position. Disconnect body controller Blue connector. Body controller is located under left side of instrument panel. Check connector, and clean or repair connector as necessary. Turn ignition switch to ON position. Put DRB-II in voltmeter mode.

2) Probe terminal No. 6 (Dark Blue/White wire) of body controller Blue connector. If voltage is more than 10 volts, replace body controller. Perform VERIFICATION TEST. If voltage is less than 10 volts, repair open Dark Blue/White wire. Perform VERIFICATION TEST.

TEST 10A

DIAGNOSING LEFT POD SWITCH & POWER SUPPLY

NOTE: For connector terminal identification, see CONNECTOR IDENTIFICATION in BODY CONTROL COMPUTER INTRODUCTION article. For wiring diagrams, see appropriate WIRING DIAGRAMS article.

NOTE: All except liftgate lights operate by front doors and pod switch. Forward rear dome and overhead lights (if equipped) operate by side door. Liftgate and rear dome lights (if equipped) operate by opening liftgate.

1) While observing all courtesy lights, open and close every door. If any light is on when it is supposed to be off, replace diode assembly. Diode assembly is located behind trim panel at left rear quarterpanel. Perform VERIFICATION TEST.

2) When opening doors, if all lights function as properly, move dimmer control lever to center position. Close all doors. If a problem exists with rear dome light or liftgate lights only, perform TEST 16A. If a problem with rear dome light or liftgate lights only does not exist, turn courtesy lights on by opening left front door.

TEST 10A (Cont.)

3) Observe all courtesy lights except liftgate and rear dome lights. If there is only one inoperative bulb, perform TEST 10B. If all bulbs function properly, turn ignition switch to ON position. Close all doors. If any courtesy lights stay on, perform TEST 11A.

4) If no courtesy lights stay on, actuate courtesy lights test using DRB-II. Observe all courtesy lights during this test. If any courtesy lights are on, perform TEST 12A. If no courtesy lights are on, using DRB-II, stop courtesy lights test.

5) Remove and inspect fuse No. 3 in fuse block. If fuse is blown, perform Test 10C. If fuse is okay, reinstall fuse. Put DRB-II in voltmeter mode. Probe Black/Red wire (in fuse block) to fuse No. 3. Repair open Black/Red wire if voltage is less than 10 volts. Perform VERIFICATION TEST.

6) If voltage is more than 10 volts, access left pod switch assembly. See Fig. 10A. Disconnect left pod switch Black connector. Check connector, and clean or repair connector as necessary.

NOTE: Ensure fuse No. 3 is installed.

7) Place DRB-II in voltmeter mode. Probe terminal No. 4 (Pink wire) of left pod switch Black connector. If voltage is less than 10 volts, repair open Pink wire. Perform VERIFICATION TEST. If voltage is more than 10 volts, probe terminal No. 5 (Pink/Light Blue wire) of left pod switch Black connector.

8) If voltage is less than 10 volts, replace left pod switch. Perform VERIFICATION TEST. If voltage is more than 10 volts, repair open Pink/Light Blue wire. Perform VERIFICATION TEST.

92E22735

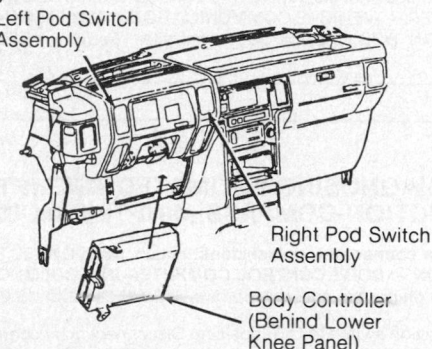

Left Pod Switch Assembly

Right Pod Switch Assembly

Body Controller (Behind Lower Knee Panel)

Fig. 10A: Locating Pod Switch Assemblies

TEST 10B

CHECKING POWER & GROUND SUPPLY

NOTE: For connector terminal identification, see CONNECTOR IDENTIFICATION in BODY CONTROL COMPUTER INTRODUCTION article. For wiring diagrams, see appropriate WIRING DIAGRAMS article.

1) Remove inoperative bulb. If bulb is open, replace bulb. Perform VERIFICATION TEST. If bulb is okay, disconnect inoperative light assembly. Turn ignition switch to OFF position. Place DRB-II in ohmmeter mode. Probe Yellow wire in inoperative light assembly.

2) If resistance is less than 5 ohms, repair open in Pink/Light Blue wire between inoperative light assembly and left pod switch. Perform VERIFICATION TEST. If resistance is more than 5 ohms and inoperative light is not front dome light assembly, repair open in ground wire. Perform VERIFICATION TEST.

3) If resistance is more than 5 ohms and inoperative light is front dome light assembly, reconnect inoperative light assembly. Reinstall inoperative bulb. Access diode assembly. Diode assembly is located behind trim panel at left rear quarterpanel.

4) Connect a jumper wire between Yellow wire of diode assembly connector and ground. Check front dome light. If front dome light is off, repair open Yellow wire. Perform VERIFICATION TEST. If front dome light Is on, replace diode assembly. Perform VERIFICATION TEST.

TEST 10C

CHECKING WIRING & BODY CONTROLLER FOR SHORTS

NOTE: For connector terminal identification, see CONNECTOR IDENTIFICATION in BODY CONTROL COMPUTER INTRODUCTION article. For wiring diagrams, see appropriate WIRING DIAGRAMS article.

NOTE: Ensure all doors are closed. Ensure vanity mirror, glove box and under seat lights are off.

1) Turn ignition switch to OFF position. Remove and inspect fuse No. 3. If fuse blown, replace fuse. Perform VERIFICATION TEST. If fuse is okay, disconnect left pod switch assembly connectors. See Fig. 10A. Check connector, and clean or repair connector as necessary.

2) Probe Pink wire (in fuse block) to fuse No. 3. Go to step 4) if resistance is less than 5 ohms. If resistance is more than 5 ohms, probe terminal No. 5 (Pink/Light Blue wire) of left pod switch Black connector.

3) If resistance is less than 5 ohms, repair short to ground in Pink/Light Blue wire and replace fuse No. 3. Perform VERIFICATION TEST. If resistance is more than 5 ohms, replace left pod switch and fuse No. 3. Perform VERIFICATION TEST.

4) If resistance is less than 5 ohms in step 2), disconnect body controller Blue connector. Body controller is located under left side of instrument panel. Check connector, and clean or repair connector as necessary. Probe Pink wire (in fuse block) to fuse No. 3.

5) If resistance is more than 5 ohms, replace body controller and fuse No. 3. Perform VERIFICATION TEST. If resistance is less than 5 ohms, disconnect instrument cluster connector. Check connector condition and clean or repair connector as necessary. Probe Pink wire (in fuse block) to fuse No. 3.

6) If resistance is more than 5 ohms, repair or replace instrument cluster, and replace fuse No. 3. Perform VERIFICATION TEST. If resistance is less than 5 ohms, disconnect radio connector. Probe Pink wire (in fuse block) to fuse No. 3.

7) If resistance is more than 5 ohms, replace radio and fuse No. 3. Perform VERIFICATION TEST. If resistance is less than 5 ohms, repair short to ground in Pink wire, and replace fuse No. 3. Perform VERIFICATION TEST.

TEST 11A

CHECKING BODY CONTROLLER & WIRING FOR SHORTS TO GROUND

NOTE: For connector terminal identification, see CONNECTOR IDENTIFICATION in BODY CONTROL COMPUTER INTRODUCTION article. For wiring diagrams, see appropriate WIRING DIAGRAMS article.

1) Disconnect body controller Blue connector. Body controller is located under left side of instrument panel. Check connector, and clean or repair connector as necessary.

2) If courtesy lights are off, replace body controller. Perform VERIFICATION TEST. If courtesy lights are on, disconnect left pod switch assembly. See Fig. 10A. Check connector, and clean or repair connector as necessary.

3) Connect a jumper wire between terminals No. 4 (Pink wire) and No. 5 (Pink/Light Blue wire) of left pod switch assembly connector. If courtesy lights are off, replace left pod switch. Perform VERIFICATION TEST. If courtesy lights are on, repair short to ground in Yellow/Dark Green wire. Perform VERIFICATION TEST.

TEST 12A

CHECKING LEFT FRONT DOOR JAMB SWITCH & RELATED WIRING FOR OPEN

NOTE: For connector terminal identification, see CONNECTOR IDENTIFICATION in BODY CONTROL COMPUTER INTRODUCTION article. For wiring diagrams, see appropriate WIRING DIAGRAMS article.

1) Using DRB-II, stop courtesy lights test. If all courtesy lights did not come on while test was running, perform TEST 12B. If all courtesy lights were on while test was running, open left front door.

TEST 12A (Cont.)

NOTE: All except liftgate lights should operate by left front door

2) If courtesy lights are on, perform TEST 13A. If courtesy lights are off, disconnect left front door jamb switch connector. Check connector, and clean or repair connector as necessary. Connect a jumper wire between Yellow and Black wires of left front door jamb switch connector.

3) If courtesy lights are on, replace left front door jamb switch. Perform VERIFICATION TEST. If courtesy lights are off, disconnect jumper wire. Connect a jumper wire between Yellow wire of left front door switch connector and ground.

4) If courtesy lights are on, repair Black wire for an open to ground. Perform VERIFICATION TEST. If courtesy lights are off, repair open in Yellow wire to left front door jamb switch. Perform VERIFICATION TEST.

TEST 12B

CHECKING GROUND SUPPLY & DIODE ASSEMBLY FOR OPEN

NOTE: For connector terminal identification, see CONNECTOR IDENTIFICATION in BODY CONTROL COMPUTER INTRODUCTION article. For wiring diagrams, see appropriate WIRING DIAGRAMS article.

1) Disconnect diode assembly connector. Diode assembly is located behind trim panel at left rear quarterpanel. Check connector, and clean or repair connector as necessary. Ensure all doors are closed. Connect a jumper wire between terminal No. 1 (Yellow/Dark Green wire) of diode assembly connector and ground.

2) If right and left front door courtesy lights are off, repair open Yellow/Dark Green wire. Perform VERIFICATION TEST. If right and left front door courtesy lights are on, disconnect jumper wire.

NOTE: Continue with this test only if a problem exists with rear overhead lights.

3) Connect a jumper wire between terminal No. 3 (Yellow wire) of diode assembly connector and ground. Check rear overhead lights. If rear overhead lights are off, repair open Yellow wire. Perform VERIFICATION TEST. If rear overhead lights are on, replace diode assembly. Perform VERIFICATION TEST.

TEST 13A

CHECKING RIGHT FRONT DOOR JAMB SWITCH & RELATED WIRING FOR OPEN

NOTE: For connector terminal identification, see CONNECTOR IDENTIFICATION in BODY CONTROL COMPUTER INTRODUCTION article. For wiring diagrams, see appropriate WIRING DIAGRAMS article.

NOTE: All except liftgate lights should operate from right front door.

1) Close left front door. Open right front door. If courtesy lights are on, perform TEST 14A. If courtesy lights are off, disconnect right front door jamb switch connector. Check connector condition and clean or repair connector as necessary. Connect a jumper wire between Yellow and Black wires of right front door jamb switch connector.

2) If courtesy lights are on, replace right front door jamb switch. Perform VERIFICATION TEST. If courtesy lights are off, disconnect jumper wire. Connect a jumper wire between Yellow wire of right front door jamb switch connector and ground.

3) If courtesy lights are on, repair open Black wire. Perform VERIFICATION TEST. If courtesy lights are off, repair open Yellow wire to right front door jamb switch. Perform VERIFICATION TEST.

TEST 14A

CHECKING SIDE DOOR JAMB SWITCH & RELATED WIRING FOR OPEN

NOTE: For connector terminal identification, see CONNECTOR IDENTIFICATION in BODY CONTROL COMPUTER INTRODUCTION article. For wiring diagrams, see appropriate WIRING DIAGRAMS article.

TEST 14A (Cont.)

NOTE: Front rear dome and overhead lights (if equipped) operate by side door.

1) Close right front door. Open side door. If courtesy lights are on, perform TEST 15A. If courtesy lights are off, disconnect side door jamb switch connector. Check connector, and clean or repair connector as necessary.

2) Connect a jumper wire between Yellow wire of side door jamb switch connector and ground. All courtesy lights should be on except front door and liftgate lights. If courtesy lights are off, repair open Yellow wire. Perform VERIFICATION TEST. If courtesy lights are on, replace side door jamb switch. Perform VERIFICATION TEST.

TEST 15A

CHECKING LEFT POD SWITCH FOR OPEN

NOTE: For connector terminal identification, see CONNECTOR IDENTIFICATION in BODY CONTROL COMPUTER INTRODUCTION article. For wiring diagrams, see appropriate WIRING DIAGRAMS article.

NOTE: This test is only for inoperative courtesy lights controlled by left pod switch.

1) Close side door. Turn courtesy lights on by sliding left pod switch. If courtesy lights are on, system is operational. Perform VERIFICATION TEST. If courtesy lights are off, disconnect left pod switch assembly Black connector. Check connector condition and clean or repair connector as necessary.

2) Put DRB-II in ohmmeter mode. Probe terminal No. 6 (Black wire) of left pod switch Black connector. If resistance is more than 5 ohms, repair open Black wire. Perform VERIFICATION TEST. If resistance is less than 5 ohms, connect a jumper wire between terminals No. 2 (Yellow wire) and No. 6 (Black wire) of left pod switch Black connector.

3) Also connect a jumper wire between terminals No. 4 (Pink wire) and No. 5 (Pink/Light Blue wire) of left pod switch Black connector. If courtesy lights are on, replace left pod switch. Perform VERIFICATION TEST. If courtesy lights are off, repair open Yellow wire. Perform VERIFICATION TEST.

TEST 16A

REPAIRING FAULTY REAR DOME & LIFTGATE LAMPS

NOTE: For connector terminal identification, see CONNECTOR IDENTIFICATION in BODY CONTROL COMPUTER INTRODUCTION article. For wiring diagrams, see appropriate WIRING DIAGRAMS article.

1) Ensure liftgate is closed. If vehicle is not equipped with liftgate lights, perform TEST 17A. If vehicle is equipped with liftgate lights, check rear dome light.

NOTE: Liftgate lights are supposed to come on only by opening liftgate.

2) If rear dome light is the only light staying on, repair short to ground in Yellow/Black wire. Perform VERIFICATION TEST. If both liftgate lights and rear dome light are staying on, perform TEST 16B. If both liftgate lights and rear dome light are not staying on, open liftgate.

3) Observe liftgate lights and rear dome light. If both liftgate lights and rear dome light are on, system is operational. Perform VERIFICATION TEST. If both liftgate lights are off, perform TEST 16C. If both liftgate lights are on, place DRB-II in ohmmeter mode.

4) Disconnect diode assembly. Diode assembly is located behind trim panel at left rear quarter panel. Check connector condition and clean or repair connector as necessary. Probe terminal No. 4 (Yellow/Red wire) of diode assembly connector. If resistance is more than 5 ohms, repair open Yellow/Red wire. Perform VERIFICATION TEST.

TEST 16A (Cont.)

5) If resistance is less than 5 ohms, connect a jumper wire between terminal No. 2 (Yellow/Black) of diode assembly connector and ground. If rear dome light is on, replace diode assembly. Perform VERIFICATION TEST. If rear dome light is off, access rear dome light assembly.

6) Inspect bulb. If bulb is open, replace bulb. Perform VERIFICATION TEST. If bulb is okay, connect a jumper wire between Yellow/Black wire of rear dome light assembly and ground.

NOTE: Ensure rear dome light connector is still connected.

7) If rear dome light is on, repair open Yellow/Black wire. Perform VERIFICATION TEST. If rear dome light is off, repair open in Pink/Light Blue wire between left pod switch and rear dome light assembly. Perform VERIFICATION TEST.

TEST 16B

CHECKING LIFTGATE LATCH SWITCH & RELATED WIRING FOR SHORTS

NOTE: For connector terminal identification, see CONNECTOR IDENTIFICATION in BODY CONTROL COMPUTER INTRODUCTION article. For wiring diagrams, see appropriate WIRING DIAGRAMS article.

Open liftgate. Disconnect liftgate latch switch connector. Connector is located at bottom of liftgate behind trim panel. Check connector condition and clean or repair connector as necessary. If liftgate and rear dome lights go off, replace liftgate latch switch. Perform VERIFICATION TEST. If liftgate and rear dome lights stay on, repair short to ground in Yellow/Red wire. Perform VERIFICATION TEST.

TEST 16C

CHECKING LIFTGATE LATCH SWITCH & RELATED WIRING FOR OPEN

NOTE: For connector terminal identification, see CONNECTOR IDENTIFICATION in BODY CONTROL COMPUTER INTRODUCTION article. For wiring diagrams, see appropriate WIRING DIAGRAMS article.

1) Disconnect liftgate latch switch connector. Connector is located at bottom of liftgate behind trim panel. Check connector condition and clean or repair connector as necessary. Connect a jumper wire between Yellow wire of liftgate ajar switch connector and ground. If both liftgate lights are on, replace liftgate latch switch. Perform VERIFICATION TEST.

2) If both liftgate lights did not come on, access right and left liftgate light assemblies. Inspect bulbs. Replace bulbs as necessary. If bulbs are okay, disconnect right liftgate light connector. Connector is located behind trim panel on right side of liftgate. Check connector, and clean or repair connector as necessary.

3) Place DRB-II in ohmmeter mode. Ensure jumper wire is still connected to liftgate latch switch connector. Probe Yellow wire in right liftgate light connector. If resistance is more than 5 ohms, repair open Yellow wire. Perform VERIFICATION TEST. If resistance is less than 5 ohms, disconnect left liftgate light assembly. Connector is located behind trim panel on left side of liftgate.

4) Check connector, and clean or repair connector as necessary. Probe Yellow wire in left liftgate light connector. If resistance is more than 5 ohms, repair open Yellow wire. Perform VERIFICATION TEST. If resistance is less than 5 ohms, repair open in Pink/Light Blue wire between left pod switch and left liftgate light connector. Perform VERIFICATION TEST.

TEST 17A

CHECKING DIODE ASSEMBLY & LIFTGATE LAMPS WIRING

NOTE: For connector terminal identification, see CONNECTOR IDENTIFICATION in BODY CONTROL COMPUTER INTRODUCTION article. For wiring diagrams, see appropriate WIRING DIAGRAMS article.

TEST 17A (Cont.)

1) If rear dome light is off, go to step **3)**. If rear dome light is staying on, disconnect diode assembly. Diode assembly is located behind trim panel at left rear quarterpanel. Check connector, and clean or repair connector as necessary. If rear dome light still on, repair short to ground in Yellow/Black wire. Perform VERIFICATION TEST.

2) If rear dome light is off, place DRB-II in ohmmeter mode. Probe terminal No. 4 (Yellow/Red wire) of diode assembly connector. If resistance is less than 5 ohms, repair short to ground in Yellow/Red wire. Perform VERIFICATION TEST. If resistance is more than 5 ohms, replace diode assembly. Perform VERIFICATION TEST.

3) If rear dome light is off in step **1)**, open liftgate. If rear dome light is on, system is operational. Perform VERIFICATION TEST. If rear dome light is off, gain access to rear dome light assembly. Inspect bulb. If bulb is open, replace bulb. Perform VERIFICATION TEST.

4) If bulb is not open, connect a jumper wire between Yellow/Black wire of rear dome light assembly and ground. Ensure rear dome light connector is still connected. If rear dome light is off, repair open Pink/Light Blue wire. Perform VERIFICATION TEST.

5) If rear dome light is on, disconnect jumper wire. Gain access to diode assembly. Disconnect diode assembly. Diode assembly is located behind trim panel at left rear quarter panel. Check connector condition and clean or repair connector as necessary. Connect a jumper wire between terminal No. 2 (Yellow/Black wire) of diode assembly connector and ground.

6) If rear dome light is off, repair open Yellow/Black wire. Perform VERIFICATION TEST. If rear dome light is on. Disconnect jumper wire. Connect a jumper wire between terminal No. 4 (Yellow/Red wire) of diode assembly connector and ground.

7) If rear dome light is off, replace diode assembly. Perform VERIFICATION TEST. If rear dome light is on, disconnect jumper wire. Access liftgate latch switch. Connector is located at bottom of liftgate behind trim panel. Disconnect connector. Check connector, and clean or repair connector as necessary.

8) Connect a jumper wire between Yellow wire of liftgate switch connector and ground. If rear dome light is off, repair open Yellow/Red wire. Perform VERIFICATION TEST. If rear dome light is on, replace liftgate latch switch. Perform VERIFICATION TEST.

TEST 18A

DIAGNOSING DOOR AJAR CIRCUIT (LEFT FRONT DOOR)

NOTE: For connector terminal identification, see CONNECTOR IDENTIFICATION in BODY CONTROL COMPUTER INTRODUCTION article. For wiring diagrams, see appropriate WIRING DIAGRAMS article.

1) Close all doors. Turn ignition switch to ON position. Using DRB-II, read left front door ajar switch status. If DRB-II displays CIRCUIT CLOSED, go to step **6)**. If DRB-II does not display CIRCUIT CLOSED, open left front door.

2) If DRB-II displays CIRCUIT CLOSED, retest system. Perform VERIFICATION TEST. If DRB-II does not display CIRCUIT CLOSED, disconnect left front door ajar switch connector. Connector is located at lower left "B" pillar. Check connector, and clean or repair connector as necessary.

3) Connect a jumper wire between Tan wire of left front door ajar switch connector and ground. If DRB-II displays CIRCUIT CLOSED, replace left front door ajar switch. Perform VERIFICATION TEST.

4) If DRB-II does not display CIRCUIT CLOSED, gain access to body controller. Body controller is located under left side of instrument panel. Connect a jumper wire between terminal No. 1 (Tan wire) at wiring harness side of body controller Blue connector and ground.

5) If DRB-II displays CIRCUIT CLOSED, repair open Tan wire. Perform VERIFICATION TEST. If DRB-II does not display CIRCUIT CLOSED, replace body controller. Perform VERIFICATION TEST.

6) If DRB-II displays CIRCUIT CLOSED in step **1)**, disconnect left front door ajar switch connector. Connector is located at lower left "B" pillar. Check connector, and clean or repair as necessary. Turn ignition switch to OFF position.

7) Disconnect body controller Blue connector. Body controller is located under left side of instrument panel. Check connector, and clean or repair connector as necessary. Put DRB-II in ohmmeter mode. Probe terminal No. 1 (Tan wire) of body controller Blue connector.

TEST 18A (Cont.)

8) If resistance is less than 5 ohms, repair short to ground in Tan wire. Perform VERIFICATION TEST. If resistance is more than 5 ohms, replace body controller. Perform VERIFICATION TEST.

TEST 19A

DIAGNOSING DOOR AJAR CIRCUIT (RIGHT FRONT DOOR)

NOTE: For connector terminal identification, see CONNECTOR IDENTIFICATION in BODY CONTROL COMPUTER INTRODUCTION article. For wiring diagrams, see appropriate WIRING DIAGRAMS article.

1) Close all doors. Turn ignition switch to ON position. Using DRB-II, read right front door ajar switch status. If DRB-II displays CIRCUIT CLOSED, go to step 5). If DRB-II does not display CIRCUIT CLOSED, open right front door. If DRB-II displays CIRCUIT CLOSED, retest system. Perform VERIFICATION TEST.

2) If DRB-II does not display CIRCUIT CLOSED, disconnect right front door ajar switch connector. Connector is located at lower right "B" pillar. Check connector, and clean or repair connector as necessary. Connect a jumper wire between Tan/Red wire of right front door ajar switch connector and ground.

3) If DRB-II displays CIRCUIT CLOSED, replace right front door ajar switch. Perform VERIFICATION TEST. If DRB-II does not display CIRCUIT CLOSED, access body controller. Body controller is located under left side of instrument panel. Connect a jumper wire between terminal No. 1 (Tan/Red wire) at wiring harness side of body controller Natural connector and ground.

4) If DRB-II displays CIRCUIT CLOSED, repair open Tan/Red wire, Perform VERIFICATION TEST. If DRB-II does not display CIRCUIT CLOSED, replace body controller. Perform VERIFICATION TEST.

5) If DRB-II displays CIRCUIT CLOSED in step 1), disconnect right front door ajar switch connector. Connector is located at lower right "B" pillar. Check connector, and clean or repair connector as necessary.

6) If DRB-II does not display CIRCUIT CLOSED, replace right front door ajar switch. Perform VERIFICATION TEST. If DRB-II displays CIRCUIT CLOSED, turn ignition switch to OFF position. Disconnect body controller Natural connector. Body controller is located under left side of instrument panel.

7) Check connector, and clean or repair connector as necessary. Put DRB-II in ohmmeter mode. Probe terminal No. 1 (Tan/Red wire) of body controller Natural connector. If resistance is less than 5 ohms, repair short to ground in Tan/Red wire. Perform VERIFICATION TEST. If resistance is more than 5 ohms, replace body controller. Perform VERIFICATION TEST.

TEST 20A

DIAGNOSING DOOR AJAR CIRCUIT (SIDE DOOR)

NOTE: For connector terminal identification, see CONNECTOR IDENTIFICATION in BODY CONTROL COMPUTER INTRODUCTION article. For wiring diagrams, see appropriate WIRING DIAGRAMS article.

1) Close all doors. Turn ignition switch to ON position. Using DRB-II, read side door ajar switch status. If DRB-II displays CIRCUIT CLOSED, go to step 5). If DRB-II does not display CIRCUIT CLOSED, open side door. If DRB-II displays CIRCUIT CLOSED, retest system. Perform VERIFICATION TEST.

2) If DRB-II does not display CIRCUIT CLOSED, disconnect side door ajar switch connector. Check connector, and clean or repair connector as necessary. Connect a jumper wire between Tan/Yellow and Black wires of side door ajar switch connector. If DRB-II displays CIRCUIT CLOSED, replace side door ajar switch. Perform VERIFICATION TEST.

3) If DRB-II does not display CIRCUIT CLOSED, remove jumper wire. Connect a jumper wire between Tan/Yellow wire of side door ajar switch connector and ground. If DRB-II displays CIRCUIT CLOSED, repair open Black wire. Perform VERIFICATION TEST. If DRB-II does not display CIRCUIT CLOSED, access body controller.

TEST 20A (Cont.)

4) Body controller is located under left side of instrument panel. Connect a jumper wire between terminal No. 14 (Tan/Yellow wire) at wiring harness side of body controller Natural connector and ground. Repair open Tan/Yellow wire if DRB-II displays CIRCUIT CLOSED. Perform VERIFICATION TEST. If DRB-II does not display CIRCUIT CLOSED, replace body controller. Perform VERIFICATION TEST.

5) If DRB-II displays CIRCUIT CLOSED in step 1), disconnect side door ajar switch connector. Check connector, and clean or repair connector as necessary. If DRB-II does not display CIRCUIT CLOSED, replace side door ajar switch. Perform VERIFICATION TEST.

6) If DRB-II displays CIRCUIT CLOSED, turn ignition switch to OFF position. Disconnect body controller Natural connector. Body controller is located under left side of instrument panel. Check connector, and clean or repair connector as necessary.

7) Put DRB-II in ohmmeter mode. Probe terminal No. 14 (Tan/Yellow wire) of body controller Natural connector. If resistance is less than 5 ohms, repair short to ground in Tan/Yellow wire. Perform VERIFICATION TEST. If resistance is more than 5 ohms, replace body controller. Perform VERIFICATION TEST.

TEST 21A

DIAGNOSING DOOR AJAR CIRCUIT (LIFTGATE)

NOTE: For connector terminal identification, see CONNECTOR IDENTIFICATION in BODY CONTROL COMPUTER INTRODUCTION article. For wiring diagrams, see appropriate WIRING DIAGRAMS article.

1) Close liftgate Turn ignition switch to ON position. Using DRB-II, read liftgate ajar switch status. If DRB-II displays CIRCUIT CLOSED, go to step 5). If DRB-II does not display CIRCUIT CLOSED, open liftgate. If DRB-II displays CIRCUIT CLOSED, retest system. Perform VERIFICATION TEST.

2) If DRB-II does not display CIRCUIT CLOSED, disconnect liftgate ajar switch connector. Connector is located at bottom of liftgate behind trim panel. Check connector, and clean or repair connector as necessary. Connect a jumper wire between Tan/Black wire of liftgate ajar switch connector and ground.

3) If DRB-II displays CIRCUIT CLOSED, replace liftgate ajar switch. Perform VERIFICATION TEST. If DRB-II does not display CIRCUIT CLOSED, access body controller. Body controller is located under left side of instrument panel.

4) Connect a jumper wire between terminal No. 2 (Tan/Black wire) of body controller Natural connector and ground. If DRB-II displays CIRCUIT CLOSED, repair open Tan/Black wire. Perform VERIFICATION TEST. If DRB-II does not display CIRCUIT CLOSED, replace body controller. Perform VERIFICATION TEST.

5) If DRB-II displays CIRCUIT CLOSED in step 1), disconnect liftgate ajar switch connector. Connector is located at bottom of liftgate behind trim panel. Check connector, and clean or repair connector as necessary. If DRB-II does not display CIRCUIT CLOSED, replace liftgate ajar switch. Perform VERIFICATION TEST.

6) If DRB-II displays CIRCUIT CLOSED, turn ignition switch to OFF position. Disconnect body controller Natural connector. Body controller is located under left side of instrument panel. Check connector, and clean or repair connector as necessary.

7) Put DRB-II in ohmmeter mode. Probe terminal No. 2 (Tan/Black wire) of body controller Natural connector. If resistance is less than 5 ohms, repair short to ground in Tan/Black wire. Perform VERIFICATION TEST. If resistance is more than 5 ohms, replace body controller. Perform VERIFICATION TEST.

TEST 22A

ELECTRONIC INSTRUMENT CLUSTER DIAGNOSTICS

NOTE: For connector terminal identification, see CONNECTOR IDENTIFICATION in BODY CONTROL COMPUTER INTRODUCTION article. For wiring diagrams, see appropriate WIRING DIAGRAMS article.

1992 ENGINE PERFORMANCE
Body Control Computer Tests (Cont.)

TEST 22A (Cont.)

1) Using DRB-II, select module electronic cluster. If DRB-II displays NO RESPONSE, refer to BODY CONTROL COMPUTER – VEHICLE COMMUNICATIONS tests. Always start with TEST 1A. If DRB-II does not display NO RESPONSE, turn ignition switch to ON position. If instrument cluster display is blank, replace electronic instrument cluster. Perform VERIFICATION TEST.

2) If cluster display is not blank, close all doors. Turn ignition switch to OFF position. Wait one minute, then open left front door. If electronic instrument cluster does not glow, perform TEST 22B.

3) If electronic cluster glows, read electronic instrument cluster faults using DRB-II. If DRB-II displays any fault codes, perform TEST 23A. If DRB-II does not display any fault codes, perform TEST 24A.

TEST 22B

REPAIRING ELECTRONIC INSTRUMENT CLUSTER (POWER UP UPON ENTRY)

NOTE: For connector terminal identification, see CONNECTOR IDENTIFICATION in BODY CONTROL COMPUTER INTRODUCTION article. For wiring diagrams, see appropriate WIRING DIAGRAMS article.

1) Turn ignition switch to ON position. Close left front door. Read left front door jamb switch status using DRB-II. If DRB-II displays CIRCUIT OPEN, go to step 5). If DRB-II does not display CIRCUIT OPEN, disconnect left front door jamb switch.

2) Check connector, and clean or repair connector as necessary. If DRB-II displays CIRCUIT OPEN, replace left front door jamb switch. Perform VERIFICATION TEST. If DRB-II does not display CIRCUIT OPEN, turn ignition switch to OFF position. Disconnect body controller Blue connector.

3) Body controller is located under left side of instrument panel. Check connector, and clean or repair connector as necessary. Put DRB-II in ohmmeter mode. Probe terminal No. 13 (Black/Light Blue wire) at body controller Blue connector.

4) If resistance is less than 5 ohms, repair short to ground in Black/Light Blue wire. Perform VERIFICATION TEST. If resistance is more than 5 ohms, replace body controller. Perform VERIFICATION TEST.

5) If DRB-II displays CIRCUIT OPEN in step 1), open left front door. If DRB-II displays CIRCUIT CLOSED, replace body controller. Perform VERIFICATION TEST. If DRB-II does not display CIRCUIT CLOSED, disconnect left front door jamb switch. Check connector, and clean or repair connector as necessary.

6) Connect a jumper wire between Black/Light Blue and Black wires of left front door jamb switch connector. If DRB-II displays CIRCUIT CLOSED, replace left front door jamb switch. Perform VERIFICATION TEST. If DRB-II does not display CIRCUIT CLOSED, connect a jumper wire between terminal Black/Light Blue wire of left front door jamb switch connector and ground.

7) If DRB-II displays CIRCUIT CLOSED, repair open Black wire. Perform VERIFICATION TEST. If DRB-II does not display CIRCUIT CLOSED, disconnect jumper wire. Access body controller. Body controller is located under left side of instrument panel.

8) Connect a jumper wire between terminal No. 13 (Black/Light Blue wire) at wiring harness side of body controller Blue connector and ground. If DRB-II displays CIRCUIT CLOSED, repair open Black/Light Blue wire. Perform VERIFICATION TEST. If DRB-II does not display CIRCUIT CLOSED, replace body controller. Perform VERIFICATION TEST.

TEST 23A

ELECTRONIC INSTRUMENT CLUSTER FAULT CODES

Identify fault codes and perform test and repair as necessary. See ELECTRONIC CLUSTER FAULT CODES table.

ELECTRONIC CLUSTER FAULT CODES

Code	Description
01	NO BUS ACTIVITY [1]
02	NO MESSAGE FROM BODY CONTROLLER [1]
04	NO MESSAGES FROM ENGINE CONTROLLER [1]
08	BUS LOOP FAILURE MESSAGE [2]
10	DISPLAY DRIVER [2]
20	MICROCOMPUTER INTERNAL FAILURE [2]
40	POWER SUPPLY SHORT CIRCUIT [2]
80	BODY COMPUTER ODOMETER FAILURE [3]

[1] – Refer to BODY CONTROL COMPUTER – VEHICLE COMMUNICATIONS tests. Always start with TEST 1A.
[2] – Replace electronic instrument cluster. After repair is made, perform VERIFICATION TEST.
[3] – Replace body controller. After repair is made, perform VERIFICATION TEST.

TEST 24A

ELECTRONIC INSTRUMENT CLUSTER PROBLEMS NOT IDENTIFIED BY FAULT CODES

1) If no fault codes are displayed, identify fault area of electronic instrument cluster and perform test as specified. See ELECTRONIC INSTRUMENT CLUSTER PROBLEMS table.

ELECTRONIC INSTRUMENT CLUSTER PROBLEMS

Problem	Test No.
Defective Cluster Illumination	28A
Defective Gauges	25A
Defective Odometer	24B
Defective Warning Lights	27A

NOTE: If any legends fail to light or 2 legends light together during electronic cluster sequential legends test, test is failed.

2) If no speedometer problem exists, perform TEST 24C. If a speedometer problem exists, actuate electronic cluster sequential legends test using DRB-II. If test is passed, replace electronic instrument cluster. Perform VERIFICATION TEST. If test is failed, check for engine diagnostic codes. See appropriate SELF-DIAGNOSTICS article.

TEST 24B

ELECTRONIC INSTRUMENT CLUSTER ODOMETER PROBLEM

NOTE: If any legends fail to glow or 2 legends glow together during electronic cluster sequential legends test, test is failed.

Using DRB-II, actuate electronic instrument cluster sequential legends test. If test is failed, replace electronic instrument cluster. Perform VERIFICATION TEST. If test is passed, replace body controller. Perform VERIFICATION TEST.

TEST 24C

ELECTRONIC INSTRUMENT CLUSTER SWITCH TEST

1) Press TRIP button on electronic instrument cluster and read DRB-II status. If DRB-II displays CIRCUIT CLOSED, replace electronic instrument cluster. Perform VERIFICATION TEST. If DRB-II does not display CIRCUIT CLOSED, press RESET button on electronic instrument cluster and read DRB-II status.

2) If DRB-II does not display CIRCUIT CLOSED, replace electronic instrument cluster. Perform VERIFICATION TEST. If DRB-II displays CIRCUIT CLOSED, press US/METRIC button on electronic instrument cluster and read DRB-II status.

3) If DRB-II displays CIRCUIT CLOSED, retest system. Perform VERIFICATION TEST. If DRB-II does not display CIRCUIT CLOSED, replace electronic instrument cluster. Perform VERIFICATION TEST.

TEST 25A

IDENTIFYING DEFECTIVE GAUGE

1) Using DRB-II, actuate electronic instrument cluster sequential segment test. This test should cause all vacuum florescent bars on gauges to glow. If any bar does not glow or 2 bars glow together, test is failed.

2) If test is failed, replace electronic instrument cluster. Perform VERIFICATION TEST. If test is passed, check temperature gauge operation. If temperature gauge is not operating correctly, perform TEST 26A. If temperature gauge is operating correctly, check fuel gauge operation.

3) If fuel gauge is not operating correctly, perform TEST 36A. If fuel gauge is operating correctly, check oil gauge operation. If oil gauge is not operating correctly, perform TEST 46A.

4) If oil gauge is operating correctly, check voltage gauge. If voltage gauge is not operating correctly, check charging system. If voltage gauge is operating correctly, test is complete. Perform VERIFICATION TEST.

TEST 26A

TEMPERATURE GAUGE PROBLEM

NOTE: For connector terminal identification, see CONNECTOR IDENTIFICATION in BODY CONTROL COMPUTER INTRODUCTION article. For wiring diagrams, see appropriate WIRING DIAGRAMS article.

1) Check cooling system. If cooling system is not operating correctly, repair cooling system as necessary. If cooling system is operating correctly, stop sequential segments test using DRB-II. Turn ignition switch to ON position.

2) Using DRB-II, read engine temperature sensor voltage. If DRB-II displays less than 10 volts, go to step 5). If DRB-II displays more than 10 volts, disconnect engine temperature sensor connector. Check connector, and clean or repair connector as necessary.

3) Connect a jumper wire between Violet/Yellow wire of engine temperature sensor connector and ground. If DRB-II displays less than one volt, replace engine temperature sensor. Perform VERIFICATION TEST. If DRB-II displays more than one volt, access body controller.

4) Body controller is located under left side of instrument panel. Connect a jumper wire between terminal No. 24 (Violet/Yellow wire) at wiring harness side of body controller Natural connector and ground. If DRB-II displays less than one volt, repair open Violet/Yellow wire. Perform VERIFICATION TEST. If DRB-II displays more than one volt, replace body controller. Perform VERIFICATION TEST.

5) If DRB-II displays less than 10 volts in step 2), disconnect engine temperature sensor connector. Check connector, and clean or repair connector as necessary. If DRB-II displays more than 10 volts, replace engine temperature sensor. Perform VERIFICATION TEST.

6) If DRB-II displays less than 10 volts, turn ignition switch to OFF position. Disconnect body controller Blue connector. Body controller is located under left side of instrument panel. Check connector, and clean or repair connector as necessary. Put DRB-II in voltmeter mode.

TEST 26A (Cont.)

7) Turn ignition switch to ON position. Probe terminal No. 6 (Dark Blue/White wire) of body controller Blue connector. If voltage is less than 10 volts, repair open Dark Blue/White wire. Perform VERIFICATION TEST. If voltage is more than 10 volts, turn ignition switch to OFF position.

8) Put DRB-II in ohmmeter mode. Probe Violet/Yellow wire of engine temperature sensor connector. If resistance is less than 5 ohms, repair short to ground in Violet/Yellow wire. Perform VERIFICATION TEST. If resistance is more than 5 ohms, replace body controller. Perform VERIFICATION TEST.

TEST 27A

FAULTY WARNING LIGHT

1) Ensure parking brake is off. Close all doors, and start engine. Check oil pressure and engine temperature gauges operation. If gauges are not operating correctly, perform TEST 25A. If gauges are operating correctly, turn engine off.

2) Turn ignition switch to ON position. Using DRB-II, actuate sequential light test. Sequential light test should individually turn every warning light on and then off.

3) If test did not sequentially illuminate all 6 warning lights, remove and inspect any inoperative warning light bulbs from electronic instrument cluster. If bulb is defective, replace bulb. Perform VERIFICATION TEST. If bulb is okay, replace electronic instrument cluster. Perform VERIFICATION TEST.

4) If test did sequentially illuminate all 6 warning lights, determine which warning light circuit is not operating correctly. Perform test as specified. See DEFECTIVE WARNING LIGHTS DIRECTORY table.

DEFECTIVE WARNING LIGHTS DIRECTORY

Defective Warning Light	Test No.
CHECK ENGINE	1
Check Gauges	1
Left Front Door	18A
Liftgate	21A
Right Front Door	19A
Side Door	20A
Washer Fluid	48A

1 – See appropriate SELF-DIAGNOSTICS article.

TEST 28A

ELECTRONIC CLUSTER OR COMPASS/ MINI-TRIP ILLUMINATION TEST

NOTE: For connector terminal identification, see CONNECTOR IDENTIFICATION in BODY CONTROL COMPUTER INTRODUCTION article. For wiring diagrams, see appropriate WIRING DIAGRAMS article.

1) Ensure park light switch is ON. If park lights do not turn ON, perform TEST 28B. If park lights turn ON, read panel light sensor voltage while moving dimmer control lever from LOW to HIGH position and using DRB-II.

2) If DRB-II display changes from one to 5 volts, perform TEST 28C. If DRB-II display does not change from one to 5 volts, using DRB-II, read panel light sensor voltage. If voltage is more than 4 volts, perform TEST 28F. If voltage is less than 4 volts, inspect fuse No. 9 in fuse block.

3) If fuse is okay, repair short to ground in Orange/Black wire. Perform VERIFICATION TEST. If fuse is blown, turn ignition switch to OFF position. Place DRB-II in ohmmeter mode. Disconnect body Natural connector. Body controller is located under left side of instrument panel. Check connector, and clean or repair connector as necessary.

4) Probe Tan wire (in fuse block) to fuse No. 9. Repair short to ground in Tan wire if resistance is less than 5 ohms. Perform VERIFICATION TEST. If resistance is more than 5 ohms, replace fuse. Perform VERIFICATION TEST.

TEST 28B

ELECTRONIC INSTRUMENT CLUSTER OR COMPASS/MINI-TRIP ILLUMINATION TEST

NOTE: For connector terminal identification, see CONNECTOR IDENTIFICATION in BODY CONTROL COMPUTER INTRODUCTION article. For wiring diagrams, see appropriate WIRING DIAGRAMS article.

1) Access left switch pod assembly. *See Fig. 10A.* Place DRB-II in voltmeter mode. Disconnect left switch pod Blue connector. Check connector, and clean or repair connector as necessary. Probe terminal No. 4 (Brown/Orange wire) of left switch pod Blue connector.

2) If voltage is more than 10 volts, replace left switch pod. Perform VERIFICATION TEST. If voltage is less than 10 volts, inspect fuse No. 22 in fuse block. If fuse is blown, perform TEST 28E. If fuse is okay, probe Red/Black wire (in fuse block) to fuse No. 22. If voltage is less than 10 volts, repair open Red/Black wire. Perform VERIFICATION TEST.

3) If voltage is more than 10 volts, remove park light relay from power distribution center. Check connector, and clean or repair connector as necessary. Reinstall fuse No. 22. Using an external ohmmeter, check resistance of Brown/Orange wire between terminal No. 4 of left pod switch connector and park light relay connector.

4) If resistance is more than 5 ohms, repair open Brown/Orange wire. Perform VERIFICATION TEST. If resistance is less than 5 ohms, place DRB-II in voltmeter mode. Probe Pink/Red wire of park light relay connector. If voltage is less than 10 volts, repair open Pink/Red wire between fuse and relay connector. Perform VERIFICATION TEST.

5) If voltage is more than 10 volts, probe Pink/Red wire of park light relay connector. If voltage is less than 10 volts, repair open Pink/Red wire. Perform VERIFICATION TEST. If voltage is more than 10 volts, connect a jumper wire between Pink/Red and Black/Yellow of park light relay connector.

6) If instrument cluster glows, replace park light relay. Perform VERIFICATION TEST. If instrument cluster does not glow, inspect fuse No. 9. If fuse is okay, perform TEST 28G. If fuse is blown, place DRB-II in ohmmeter mode. Probe Tan wire (in fuse block) to fuse No. 9.

7) If resistance is more than 5 ohms, replace fuse No. 9. Perform VERIFICATION TEST. If resistance is less than 5 ohms, disconnect body controller Natural connector. Body controller is located under left side of instrument panel. Check connector, and clean or repair connector as necessary.

8) Probe terminal No. 8 (Tan wire) of body controller Natural connector. If resistance is less than 5 ohms, repair short to ground in Tan wire and replace fuse No. 9. Perform VERIFICATION TEST. If resistance is more than 5 ohms, replace body controller and fuse No. 9. Perform VERIFICATION TEST.

TEST 28C

ELECTRONIC INSTRUMENT CLUSTER OR COMPASS/MINI-TRIP ILLUMINATION TEST

NOTE: For connector terminal identification, see CONNECTOR IDENTIFICATION in BODY CONTROL COMPUTER INTRODUCTION article. For wiring diagrams, see appropriate WIRING DIAGRAMS article.

1) Turn ignition switch to ON position. If there is a problem with electronic instrument cluster illumination only, perform TEST 28D. If there is a problem with compass/mini-trip illumination only, replace compass/mini-trip module. Perform VERIFICATION TEST.

2) If a problem exists with Mechanical Instrument Cluster (MIC) illumination only, replace MIC. Perform VERIFICATION TEST. If no problem with MIC illumination exists, replace body controller. Perform VERIFICATION TEST.

TEST 28D

ELECTRONIC INSTRUMENT CLUSTER OR COMPASS/MINI-TRIP ILLUMINATION TEST

NOTE: For connector terminal identification, see CONNECTOR IDENTIFICATION in BODY CONTROL COMPUTER INTRODUCTION article. For wiring diagrams, see appropriate WIRING DIAGRAMS article.

TEST 28D (Cont.)

1) Disconnect left pod switch Black connector. *See Fig. 10A.* Check connector condition and clean or repair connector as necessary. Place DRB-II in ohmmeter mode. Probe terminal No. 3 (Yellow/Black wire) of left pod switch Black connector. If resistance is more than 10 ohms, replace electronic instrument cluster.

2) If resistance is less than 10 ohms, disconnect body controller Blue connector. Body controller is located under left side of instrument panel. Check connector, and clean or repair connector as necessary. Probe terminal No. 3 (Yellow/Black wire) of body controller Blue connector.

3) If resistance is less than 10 ohms, repair short to ground in Yellow/Black wire. Perform VERIFICATION TEST. If resistance is more than 10 ohms, replace body controller. Perform VERIFICATION TEST.

TEST 28E

ELECTRONIC INSTRUMENT CLUSTER OR COMPASS/MINI-TRIP ILLUMINATION TEST

NOTE: For connector terminal identification, see CONNECTOR IDENTIFICATION in BODY CONTROL COMPUTER INTRODUCTION article. For wiring diagrams, see appropriate WIRING DIAGRAMS article.

1) Turn ignition switch to OFF position. Disconnect left pod switch. *See Fig. 10A.* Remove park light relay from power distribution center. Remove fuse No. 9 from fuse block. Place DRB-II in ohmmeter mode. Probe Black/Yellow wire of park light relay connector.

2) If resistance is less than 5 ohms, repair short to ground in Black/Yellow wire and replace fuse No. 22. Perform VERIFICATION TEST. If resistance is more than 5 ohms, probe Brown/Orange wire of park light relay connector.

3) If resistance is less than 5 ohms, repair short to ground in Brown/Orange wire and replace fuse No. 22. Perform VERIFICATION TEST. If resistance is more than 5 ohms, probe Pink/Red wire of park light relay connector.

4) If resistance is less than 5 ohms, repair short to ground in Pink/Red wire and replace fuse No. 22. If resistance is more than 5 ohms, replace fuse No. 22. Perform VERIFICATION TEST.

TEST 28F

ELECTRONIC INSTRUMENT CLUSTER OR COMPASS/MINI-TRIP ILLUMINATION TEST

NOTE: For connector terminal identification, see CONNECTOR IDENTIFICATION in BODY CONTROL COMPUTER INTRODUCTION article. For wiring diagrams, see appropriate WIRING DIAGRAMS article.

1) Turn ignition switch to OFF position. Disconnect left switch pod Black connector. Check connector, and clean or repair connector as necessary. Disconnect body controller Natural connector. Body controller is located under left side of instrument panel. Check connector, and clean or repair connector as necessary.

2) Using an external ohmmeter, check resistance of Orange/Black wire between terminals No. 1 of left pod switch Black connector and No. 10 of body controller Natural connector. If resistance is more than 5 ohms, repair open Orange/Black wire. Perform VERIFICATION TEST.

3) If resistance is less than 5 ohms, disconnect left pod switch Gray connector. Check connector condition and clean or repair connector as necessary. Probe terminal No. 1 (Black wire) of left pod switch Gray connector. If resistance is more than 10 ohms, repair open Black wire. Perform VERIFICATION TEST.

4) If resistance is less 10 ohms, probe terminal No. 5 (Black wire) of left pod switch Black connector. If resistance is more than 10 ohms, repair open Black wire. Perform VERIFICATION TEST. If resistance is less than 10 ohms, replace body controller. Perform VERIFICATION TEST.

TEST 28G

ELECTRONIC INSTRUMENT CLUSTER OR COMPASS/MINI-TRIP ILLUMINATION TEST

NOTE: For connector terminal identification, see CONNECTOR IDENTIFICATION in BODY CONTROL COMPUTER INTRODUCTION article. For wiring diagrams, see appropriate WIRING DIAGRAMS article.

1) Turn ignition switch to OFF position. Put DRB-II in ohmmeter mode. Probe Black/Yellow wire (in fuse block) to fuse No. 9. If voltage is more than 10 volts, go to step 4). If voltage is less than 10 volts, disconnect body controller Natural connector. Body controller is located under left side of instrument panel.

2) Check connector, and clean or repair connector as necessary. Using an external ohmmeter, check resistance of Tan wire between fuse No. 9 (in fuse block) and terminal No. 8 of body controller Natural connector. If resistance is more than 5 ohms, repair open Tan wire. Perform VERIFICATION TEST.

3) If resistance is less than 5 ohms, connect a jumper wire between Pink/Red and Black/Yellow wires at park light relay connector. Check park lights. If park lights are off, repair open Black/Yellow wire. Perform VERIFICATION TEST. If park lights are on, replace park light relay. Perform VERIFICATION TEST.

4) If voltage is more than 10 volts in step 1), turn ignition switch to OFF position. Disconnect left pod switch Blue and Black connectors. Check connectors, and clean or repair connectors as necessary. Place DRB-II in ohmmeter mode. Probe terminal No. 1 of left pod switch.

5) Move dimmer switch from low to high position. If resistance does not change from 1000 to 10,000 ohms, replace left switch pod. Perform VERIFICATION TEST. If resistance change from 1000 to 10,000 ohms, replace body controller. Perform VERIFICATION TEST.

TEST 29A

ELECTRO/MECHANICAL INSTRUMENT CLUSTER DIAGNOSTICS

NOTE: For connector terminal identification, see CONNECTOR IDENTIFICATION in BODY CONTROL COMPUTER INTRODUCTION article. For wiring diagrams, see appropriate WIRING DIAGRAMS article.

NOTE: These test procedures cover both base and premium Mechanical instrument cluster (MIC).

1) Using DRB-II, select module MIC cluster. If DRB-II displays NO RESPONSE, refer to BODY CONTROL COMPUTER – VEHICLE COMMUNICATIONS tests. If DRB-II does not display NO RESPONSE, using DRB-II, read instrument cluster I.D. switch status.

2) If DRB-II displays EIC, go to next step. If DRB-II does not display EIC, identify instrument cluster problem and perform test as specified. See INSTRUMENT CLUSTER PROBLEM DIRECTORY table.

INSTRUMENT CLUSTER PROBLEM DIRECTORY

Problem	Test No.
Defective Gauges	30A
Defective Odometer	31A
Defective Warning Lights	32A
Improper Cluster Illumination	28A

3) Turn ignition switch to OFF position. Disconnect instrument cluster connector. Check connector, and clean or repair connector as necessary. Turn ignition switch to ON position. Connect a jumper wire between terminal No. 3 (Orange/Dark Blue wire) of instrument cluster connector and ground.

4) Using DRB-II, read cluster ID switch status. If DRB-II does not display EIC, replace MIC. Perform VERIFICATION TEST. If DRB-II displays EIC, access body controller. Body controller is located under left side of instrument panel.

5) Connect a jumper wire between terminal No. 5 (Orange/Dark Blue wire) at wiring harness side of body controller Natural connector and ground. If DRB-II does not display EIC, repair open Orange/Dark Blue or Light Blue wire. Perform VERIFICATION TEST. If DRB-II displays EIC, replace body controller. Perform VERIFICATION TEST.

TEST 30A

IDENTIFYING FAULTY GAUGE ON ELECTRO/MECHANICAL INSTRUMENT CLUSTER

NOTE: For connector terminal identification, see CONNECTOR IDENTIFICATION in BODY CONTROL COMPUTER INTRODUCTION article. For wiring diagrams, see appropriate WIRING DIAGRAMS article.

1) Using DRB-II actuate the faulty gauge in electro/mechanical cluster. This should actuate gauge from LO to HI and then return it to its original position. If more than one gauge actuated, perform TEST 30C. If more than one gauge did not actuate, check if actuator test passed.

2) If actuator test did not pass, perform TEST 30B. If actuator test passed, check fuel gauge operation. If fuel gauge is not functioning properly, perform TEST 36A. If fuel gauge is functioning properly, check temperature gauge operation.

3) If temperature gauge is not functioning properly, perform TEST 35A. If temperature gauge is functioning properly check speedometer and tachometer operation. If either speedometer or tachometer is not functioning correctly, repair as necessary.

TEST 30B

REPAIRING FAULTY GAUGE ON ELECTRO/MECHANICAL INSTRUMENT CLUSTER

NOTE: For connector terminal identification, see CONNECTOR IDENTIFICATION in BODY CONTROL COMPUTER INTRODUCTION article. For wiring diagrams, see appropriate WIRING DIAGRAMS article.

1) Turn ignition switch to OFF position. Disconnect Mechanical Instrument Cluster (MIC) connector. Check connector, and clean or repair connector as necessary. Put DRB-II in ohmmeter mode. Probe terminal No. 7 (Black/Light Green wire) of MIC connector.

2) If resistance is more than 5 ohms, repair open Black/Light Green wire. Perform VERIFICATION TEST. If resistance is less than 5 ohms, remove faulty gauge. Inspect printed circuit board. If circuit board is not okay, repair or replace circuit board as necessary. Perform VERIFICATION TEST. If circuit board is okay, replace gauge. Perform VERIFICATION TEST.

TEST 30C

REPAIRING FAULTY INSTRUMENT CLUSTER

NOTE: For connector terminal identification, see CONNECTOR IDENTIFICATION in BODY CONTROL COMPUTER INTRODUCTION article. For wiring diagrams, see appropriate WIRING DIAGRAMS article.

1) Turn ignition switch to OFF position. Disconnect body controller Natural connector. Body controller is located under left side of instrument panel. Check connector, and clean or repair connector as necessary. Disconnect Mechanical Instrument Cluster (MIC) connector.

2) Check connector, and clean or repair connector as necessary. Using an external ohmmeter, check resistance of Orange/Dark Blue wire between terminals No. 5 of body controller Natural connector and No. 3 of MIC connector. If resistance is more than 5 ohms, repair open Orange/Dark Blue wire. Perform VERIFICATION TEST.

3) If resistance is less than 5 ohms, check resistance of Light Blue wire between terminals No. 6 of body controller Natural connector and No. 5 of MIC connector. If resistance is more than 5 ohms, repair open Light Blue wire. Perform VERIFICATION TEST. If resistance is less than 5 ohms, replace body controller. Perform VERIFICATION TEST.

TEST 31A

ELECTRO/MECHANICAL INSTRUMENT CLUSTER ODOMETER FAILURE

NOTE: For connector terminal identification, see CONNECTOR IDENTIFICATION in BODY CONTROL COMPUTER INTRODUCTION article. For wiring diagrams, see appropriate WIRING DIAGRAMS article.

TEST 31A (Cont.)

1) Using DRB-II, select body controller module. If DRB-II displays NO RESPONSE, refer to BODY CONTROL COMPUTER – VEHICLE COMMUNICATIONS. If DRB-II does not display NO RESPONSE, read electronic instrument cluster faults using DRB-II.

2) If fault 08 (odometer test failure) exists, replace body controller. Perform VERIFICATION TEST. If fault 08 does not exist, turn ignition switch to OFF position. Disconnect Mechanical Instrument Cluster (MIC) connector. Check connector, and clean or repair connector as necessary.

3) Check if odometer is original equipment. If odometer assembly has not previously been replaced, replace odometer assembly. Perform VERIFICATION TEST. If odometer assembly has been replaced previously, replace printed circuit board. Perform VERIFICATION TEST.

TEST 32A

IDENTIFYING FAULTY WARNING LIGHT ON PREMIUM ELECTRO/MECHANICAL INSTRUMENT CLUSTER

NOTE: For connector terminal identification, see CONNECTOR IDENTIFICATION in BODY CONTROL COMPUTER INTRODUCTION article. For wiring diagrams, see appropriate WIRING DIAGRAMS article.

NOTE: A base Mechanical Instrument Cluster (MIC) has only 3 gauges.

1) If vehicle is equipped with a base MIC, perform TEST 32B. If vehicle is equipped with a premium instrument cluster, check if an instrument cluster gauge problem exists. If a coolant temperature gauge, oil pressure gauge or voltage gauge problem exists, perform TEST 30A. If gauges are functioning properly, actuate sequential light test using DRB-II.

2) If sequential light test did not pass, perform TEST 32C. If sequential light test passed, identify faulty warning light and perform test as indicated. See WARNING LIGHT TEST DIRECTORY.

WARNING LIGHT TEST DIRECTORY

Defective Warning Light	Test No.
CHECK ENGINE	[1]
Check Gauges	[1]
Door Ajar	33A
Liftgate Ajar	21A
Low Fuel	36A
Low Washer Fluid	48A

[1] – See appropriate SELF-DIAGNOSTICS article.

TEST 32B

IDENTIFYING FAULTY WARNING LIGHT ON BASE ELECTRO/MECHANICAL INSTRUMENT CLUSTER

NOTE: For connector terminal identification, see CONNECTOR IDENTIFICATION in BODY CONTROL COMPUTER INTRODUCTION article. For wiring diagrams, see appropriate WIRING DIAGRAMS article.

1) While observing oil warning light, start engine. If oil light stays on, perform TEST 46A. If oil warning light stays off, perform TEST 32C. If oil warning light comes on and then goes out when engine starts, check if a coolant temperature or voltage problem exists. If a problem exists, repair cooling system or charging circuit as necessary.

2) If coolant system and charging circuit are okay, using DRB-II, actuate sequential light test. If sequential light test did not pass, perform TEST 32C. If sequential light test passed, identify faulty warning light and perform test as indicated. See WARNING LIGHT TEST DIRECTORY.

TEST 32B (Cont.)

WARNING LIGHT TEST DIRECTORY

Defective Warning Light	Test No.
CHECK ENGINE	[1]
Check Gauges	[1]
Door Ajar	33A
Liftgate Ajar	21A
Low Fuel	36A
Low Washer Fluid	48A
Voltage (Battery Symbol)	34A

[1] – See appropriate SELF-DIAGNOSTICS article.

TEST 32C

REPAIRING FAULTY WARNING LIGHT CONDITION

NOTE: For connector terminal identification, see CONNECTOR IDENTIFICATION in BODY CONTROL COMPUTER INTRODUCTION article. For wiring diagrams, see appropriate WIRING DIAGRAMS article.

1) Turn ignition switch to OFF position. Disconnect Mechanical Instrument Cluster (MIC) connector. Check connector, and clean or repair connector as necessary. Remove inoperative warning light bulb. Inspect bulb. Replace bulb as necessary. Perform VERIFICATION TEST.

2) If bulb is okay, inspect printed circuit board. Repair or replace circuit board as necessary. Perform VERIFICATION TEST. If circuit board is okay, replace MIC printed circuit board. Perform VERIFICATION TEST.

TEST 33A

REPAIRING DOOR AJAR WARNING LIGHT

NOTE: For connector terminal identification, see CONNECTOR IDENTIFICATION in BODY CONTROL COMPUTER INTRODUCTION article. For wiring diagrams, see appropriate WIRING DIAGRAMS article.

1) Close all doors. Using DRB-II, read left front door ajar switch status. If DRB-II displays CIRCUIT CLOSED, perform TEST 18A. If DRB-II does not display CIRCUIT CLOSED, open left front door. If DRB-II does not display CIRCUIT CLOSED, perform TEST 18A.

2) If DRB-II displays CIRCUIT CLOSED, using DRB-II, read right front door ajar switch status. If DRB-II displays CIRCUIT CLOSED, perform TEST 19A. If DRB-II does not display CIRCUIT CLOSED, open right front door. If DRB-II does not display CIRCUIT CLOSED, perform TEST 19A.

3) If DRB-II displays CIRCUIT CLOSED, read side door ajar switch status using DRB-II. If DRB-II displays or does not display CIRCUIT CLOSED, perform TEST 20A.

TEST 34A

REPAIRING VOLTAGE GAUGE OR VOLTAGE LIGHT PROBLEM

NOTE: For connector terminal identification, see CONNECTOR IDENTIFICATION in BODY CONTROL COMPUTER INTRODUCTION article. For wiring diagrams, see appropriate WIRING DIAGRAMS article.

1) Turn ignition switch to OFF position. Disconnect body controller Blue connector. Body controller is located under left side of instrument panel. Check connector, and clean or repair connector as necessary.

2) Put DRB-II in voltmeter mode. Probe terminal No. 8 (Pink wire) of body controller Blue connector. If voltage is less than 10 volts, perform TEST 10A. If voltage is more than 10 volts, replace body controller. Perform VERIFICATION TEST.

TEST 35A

REPAIRING TEMPERATURE GAUGE PROBLEM

NOTE: For connector terminal identification, see CONNECTOR IDEN-TIFICATION in BODY CONTROL COMPUTER INTRODUCTION article. For wiring diagrams, see appropriate WIRING DIAGRAMS article.

NOTE: Ensure engine cooling system is operating properly.

1) If cooling system not operating properly, repair cooling system as necessary. Perform VERIFICATION TEST. If cooling system is operating properly, stop actuator test using DRB-II. Using DRB-II, read engine temperature sensor voltage. If voltage is less than 10 volts, go to step 5).

2) If voltage is more than 10 volts, disconnect engine temperature sensor connector. Check connector, and clean or repair connector as necessary. Connect a jumper wire between Violet/Yellow wire of engine temperature sensor connector and ground. Using DRB-II, read engine temperature sensor voltage.

3) If voltage is less than one volt, replace engine temperature sensor. Perform VERIFICATION TEST. If voltage is more than one volt, gain access to body controller. Body controller is located under left side of instrument panel. Connect a jumper wire between terminal No. 24 (Violet/Yellow wire) of body controller Natural connector and ground.

4) If DRB-II displays less than one volt, repair open Violet/Yellow wire. Perform VERIFICATION TEST. If DRB-II displays more than one volt, disconnect body controller Natural connector. Check connector, and clean or repair connector as necessary and replace body controller. Perform VERIFICATION TEST.

5) If voltage is less than 10 volts in step 1), disconnect engine temperature sensor connector. Using DRB-II, read engine temperature sensor voltage. If voltage is more than 10 volts, replace engine temperature sensor. Perform VERIFICATION TEST. If voltage is less than 10 volts, turn ignition switch to OFF position.

6) Disconnect body controller Blue connector. Body controller is located under left side of instrument panel. Check connector, and clean or repair connector as necessary. Turn ignition switch to ON position. Put DRB-II in voltmeter mode.

7) Probe terminal No. 6 (Dark Blue/White wire) of body controller Blue connector. If voltage is less than 10 volts, repair open Dark Blue/White wire. Perform VERIFICATION TEST. If voltage is more than 10 volts, turn ignition switch to OFF position. Put DRB-II in ohmmeter mode.

8) Probe Violet/Yellow wire of temperature sensor connector. If resistance is more than 5 ohms, replace body controller. Perform VERIFICATION TEST. If resistance is less than 5 ohms, repair short to ground in Violet/Yellow wire. Perform VERIFICATION TEST.

TEST 36A

REPAIRING FUEL LEVEL PROBLEM

NOTE: For connector terminal identification, see CONNECTOR IDEN-TIFICATION in BODY CONTROL COMPUTER INTRODUCTION article. For wiring diagrams, see appropriate WIRING DIAGRAMS article.

1) Using DRB-II, stop actuator test. Disconnect fuel pump/sending unit harness connector. Connector is located underneath vehicle along frame rail. Check connector, and clean or repair connector as necessary. Using DRB-II, read fuel level sensor voltage.

2) If voltage is more than 8 volts, go to step 5). If voltage is less than 8 volts, turn ignition switch to OFF position. Disconnect body controller Blue connector. Check connector, and clean or repair connector as necessary.

3) Turn ignition switch to ON position. Put DRB-II in voltmeter mode. Probe terminal No. 6 (Dark Blue/White wire) of body controller Blue connector. If voltage is less than 10 volts, repair open Dark Blue/White wire. Perform VERIFICATION TEST. If voltage is more than 10 volts, turn ignition switch to OFF position.

4) Put DRB-II in ohmmeter mode. Probe terminal No. 18 (Dark Blue wire) of body controller Blue connector. If resistance is less than 5 ohms, repair short to ground in Dark Blue wire. Perform VERIFICATION TEST. If resistance is more than 5 ohms, replace body controller. Perform VER-IFICATION TEST.

5) If voltage is more than 8 volts in step 2), connect a jumper wire between Dark Blue and Black wires of fuel pump/sending unit connector. Using DRB-II, read fuel level sensor voltage. If DRB-II displays 0.0 VOLTS, replace fuel level sensor. Perform VERIFICATION TEST.

TEST 36A (Cont.)

6) If DRB-II does not display 0.0 VOLTS, disconnect jumper wire. Connect a jumper wire between Dark Blue wire of fuel pump/sending unit connector and ground. If DRB-II displays 0.0 VOLTS, repair open Black wire. Perform VERIFICATION TEST. If DRB-II does not display 0.0 VOLTS, disconnect jumper wire. Access body controller.

7) Body controller is located under left side of instrument panel. Connect a jumper wire between terminal No. 18 (Dark Blue wire) at wiring harness side of body controller Blue connector and ground. If DRB-II displays 0.0 VOLTS, repair open Dark Blue wire. Perform VERIFICATION TEST. If DRB-II does not display 0.0 VOLTS, turn ignition switch to OFF position. Disconnect body controller. Check connectors, and clean or repair connectors as necessary. Replace body controller. Perform VERIFICATION TEST.

TEST 37A

HEADLIGHTS WILL NOT TURN OFF

NOTE: For connector terminal identification, see CONNECTOR IDEN-TIFICATION in BODY CONTROL COMPUTER INTRODUCTION article. For wiring diagrams, see appropriate WIRING DIAGRAMS article.

1) Ensure headlight switch is off. Disconnect body controller Natural connector. Body controller is located under left side of instrument panel. Check connector, and clean or repair connector as necessary. If headlights go off, replace body controller. Perform VERIFICATION TEST.

2) If headlights are still on, remove headlight low beam relay from power distribution center. If headlights are still on, repair wiring as necessary. If headlights go off, place DRB-II in ohmmeter mode.

3) Probe Orange/White wire of low beam relay connector. If resistance is more than 5 ohms, replace headlight low beam relay. Perform VERIFI-CATION TEST. If resistance is less than 5 ohms, disconnect left pod switch assembly. See Fig. 10A. Check connector, and clean or repair connector as necessary.

4) Probe Orange/White wire of low beam relay connector. If resistance is less than 5 ohms, repair short to ground in Orange/White wire. Perform VERIFICATION TEST. If resistance is more than 5 ohms, replace left pod switch assembly. Perform VERIFICATION TEST.

TEST 37B

HEADLIGHT TIME DELAY INOPERATIVE

NOTE: For connector terminal identification, see CONNECTOR IDEN-TIFICATION in BODY CONTROL COMPUTER INTRODUCTION article. For wiring diagrams, see appropriate WIRING DIAGRAMS article.

NOTE: This test is for vehicles equipped with compass/mini-trip com-puter.

1) Turn ignition switch to ON position. Turn headlight switch to low beam position. If park and headlights do not operate properly by headlight switch, check headlight switch circuit and repair as necessary. If vehicle has an illumination problem, perform TEST 28A.

2) If vehicle does not have an illumination problem, turn headlight switch to OFF position. Turn ignition switch to OFF position. Disconnect body controller Natural connector. Body controller is located under left side of instrument panel. Check connector, and clean or repair connector as necessary.

3) Connect a jumper wire between terminal No. 20 (Orange/White wire) of body controller Natural connector and ground. Check headlights. If headlights are off, repair open Orange/White wire. Perform VERIFICA-TION TEST. If headlights are on, replace body controller. Perform VER-IFICATION TEST.

TEST 38A

DIAGNOSING GROUND SUPPLY & LEFT FRONT DOOR ILLUMINATED ENTRY CIRCUIT

NOTE: For connector terminal identification, see CONNECTOR IDEN-TIFICATION in BODY CONTROL COMPUTER INTRODUCTION article. For wiring diagrams, see appropriate WIRING DIAGRAMS article.

1992 ENGINE PERFORMANCE
Body Control Computer Tests (Cont.)

TEST 38A (Cont.)

NOTE: Liftgate lights are not a part of this system.

1) Move dimmer control lever to center position. Turn courtesy lights on by opening left front door. If courtesy lights are off, perform TEST 10A. If only one light is inoperative, perform TEST 40A. If courtesy lights are on, lower left front window.

2) Close all doors. Manually lock left front door. Turn ignition switch to OFF position. Wait 30 seconds. Using DRB-II, actuate illuminated entry system by lifting left front door handle. If courtesy lights are on, perform TEST 39A. If lights are off, disconnect body controller Blue connector.

3) Body controller is located under left side of instrument panel. Check connector, and clean or repair connector as necessary. Remove left front door panel and disconnect illuminated entry switch Black connector. Using an external ohmmeter while lifting left front door handle, check resistance between terminal No. 16 (White wire) of body controller Blue connector and Gray wire at wiring harness side of illuminated entry switch Black connector.

4) If resistance is more than 5 ohms, perform TEST 38B. If resistance is less than 5 ohms, reconnect body controller connector. Close all doors. Connect a jumper wire between terminal No. 25 (Yellow wire) at wiring harness side of body controller Blue connector and ground.

5) Check courtesy lights. If courtesy lights are off, repair open Yellow wire. Perform VERIFICATION TEST. If courtesy lights are on, disconnect jumper wire. Disconnect illuminated entry switch Black connector. Check connector, and clean or repair connector as necessary.

6) Using an external ohmmeter, check resistance between White and Gray wires of illuminated entry switch Black connector. If resistance is less than 5 ohms, replace left front door illuminated entry switch. Perform VERIFICATION TEST. If resistance is more than 5 ohms, remove right front door panel.

7) Disconnect illuminated entry switch connector. Check connector, and clean or repair connector as necessary. Disconnect body controller Blue connector. Body controller is located under left side of instrument panel. Check connector, and clean or repair connector as necessary.

8) Manually lock right front door. Using an external ohmmeter while lifting right front door handle, check resistance between terminal No. 16 (White wire) at wiring harness side of body controller Blue connector and Gray wire of illuminated entry switch connector.

9) If resistance is more than 5 ohms, replace right front door illuminated entry switch. Perform VERIFICATION TEST. If resistance is less than 5 ohms, place DRB-II in ohmmeter mode. Probe terminal No. 16 (White wire) of body controller Blue connector.

10) If resistance is more than 5 ohms, perform TEST 38C. If resistance is less than 5 ohms, repair short to ground in White wire. Perform VERIFICATION TEST.

TEST 38B

DIAGNOSING LEFT FRONT DOOR ILLUMINATED ENTRY CIRCUIT

NOTE: For connector terminal identification, see CONNECTOR IDENTIFICATION in BODY CONTROL COMPUTER INTRODUCTION article. For wiring diagrams, see appropriate WIRING DIAGRAMS article.

1) With left front door panel removed, disconnect illuminated entry switch Black connector. Check connector, and clean or repair connector as necessary. Reconnect body controller Blue connector. Connect a jumper wire between White and Black wires of illuminated entry switch connector.

2) Check courtesy lights. If courtesy lights are on, replace left front door illuminated entry switch. Perform VERIFICATION TEST. If courtesy lights are off, disconnect jumper wire. Connect a jumper wire between White wire of illuminated entry switch connector and ground.

3) Check courtesy lights. If courtesy lights are on, repair open Black wire. Perform VERIFICATION TEST. If courtesy lights are off, repair open White wire. Perform VERIFICATION TEST.

TEST 38C

TESTING POWER SUPPLY TO BODY CONTROLLER

NOTE: For connector terminal identification, see CONNECTOR IDENTIFICATION in BODY CONTROL COMPUTER INTRODUCTION article. For wiring diagrams, see appropriate WIRING DIAGRAMS article.

Place DRB-II in voltmeter mode. Probe terminal No. 8 (Pink wire) of body controller Blue connector. If voltage is more than 10 volts, replace body controller. Perform VERIFICATION TEST. If voltage is less than 10 volts, repair open Pink wire. Perform VERIFICATION TEST.

TEST 39A

DIAGNOSING RIGHT FRONT DOOR ILLUMINATED ENTRY CIRCUIT

NOTE: For connector terminal identification, see CONNECTOR IDENTIFICATION in BODY CONTROL COMPUTER INTRODUCTION article. For wiring diagrams, see appropriate WIRING DIAGRAMS article.

1) Lower right front window. Close all doors. Manually lock right front door. Turn ignition switch to OFF position. Wait 30 seconds. Using DRB-II, actuate illuminated entry system by lifting right front door handle. If courtesy lights are on, system is functioning properly. Retest system.

2) If courtesy lights are off, remove right front door panel and disconnect illuminated entry switch Black connector. Check connector, and clean or repair connector as necessary. Connect a jumper wire between White and Black wires of illuminated entry switch connector.

3) Check courtesy lights. If courtesy lights are on, replace right front door illuminated entry switch. Perform VERIFICATION TEST. If courtesy lights are off, disconnect jumper wire. Connect a jumper wire between White wire of illuminated entry switch and ground.

4) Check courtesy lights. If courtesy lights are on, repair open Black wire. Perform VERIFICATION TEST. If courtesy lights did are off, repair open White wire. Perform VERIFICATION TEST.

TEST 40A

CHECKING DIODE ASSEMBLY & POWER SUPPLY

NOTE: For connector terminal identification, see CONNECTOR IDENTIFICATION in BODY CONTROL COMPUTER INTRODUCTION article. For wiring diagrams, see appropriate WIRING DIAGRAMS article.

1) Inspect inoperative courtesy light bulb. Replace bulb as necessary. Perform VERIFICATION TEST. If bulb is okay, disconnect inoperative light assembly. Check connectors, and clean or repair connectors as necessary. Place DRB-II in ohmmeter mode.

NOTE: Ensure left front door is still open.

2) Probe Yellow/tracer wire (color of tracer may vary) in inoperative light connector. If resistance is more than 5 ohms, repair open Yellow/tracer wire (color of tracer may vary). Perform VERIFICATION TEST. If resistance is less than 5 ohms, check if rear dome light is the only inoperative light. If rear dome light is not the only light that is inoperative, repair open in Pink/Light Blue wire. Perform VERIFICATION TEST.

3) If rear dome light is the only inoperative light, access diode assembly. Diode assembly is located behind trim panel at left rear quarterpanel. Connect a jumper wire between Yellow/Black wire of diode assembly connector and ground.

4) Check rear dome light. If rear dome light is off, repair open in Yellow/Black wire between diode assembly connector and rear dome light. Perform VERIFICATION TEST. If rear dome light is on, replace diode assembly. Perform VERIFICATION TEST.

TEST 41A

IDENTIFYING INTERMITTENT WIPER PROBLEM

NOTE: For connector terminal identification, see CONNECTOR IDENTIFICATION in BODY CONTROL COMPUTER INTRODUCTION article. For wiring diagrams, see appropriate WIRING DIAGRAMS article.

TEST 41A (Cont.)

1) Turn ignition switch to ON position. Operate front wipers in all modes. If a problem exists with low or high speed wiper functions, see WIPER/WASHER SYSTEMS article in SAFETY EQUIPMENT. If wipers operate in intermittent (delay) mode, perform TEST 42A.

2) If wipers operate in all intermittent ranges, perform TEST 42A. If washer pump does not operate, perform TEST 43A. If washer pump operates, turn wiper switch to intermittent (delay) position. Actuate wiper motor test using DRB-II. If wiper motor operates, perform TEST 41B.

3) If wiper motor does not operate, using DRB-II, stop wiper motor test. Turn ignition switch to ON position. Remove and inspect fuse No. 5 from fuse block. If fuse is blown, perform TEST 41C. If fuse is okay, place DRB-II in voltmeter mode. Probe Black/White wire (in fuse block) to fuse No. 5.

4) If voltage is less than 10 volts, repair open Black/White wire between fuse No. 5 and ignition switch. Perform VERIFICATION TEST. If voltage is more than 10 volts, replace fuse No. 5. Disconnect body controller Blue connector. Body controller is located under left side of instrument panel. Check connector, and clean or repair connector as necessary.

5) Probe terminal No. 11 (Dark Blue wire) of body controller Blue connector. If voltage is less than 10 volts, repair open Dark Blue wire between fuse No. 5 and Blue connector. Perform VERIFICATION TEST. If voltage is more than 10 volts, turn ignition switch to OFF position.

6) Access multifunction switch Black connector. Check connector, and clean or repair connector as necessary. Probe terminal No. 4 (Dark Blue wire) of multifunction switch Black connector. If voltage is less than 10 volts, repair open Dark Blue wire between fuse No. 5 and multifunction switch connector. Perform VERIFICATION TEST.

7) If voltage is more than 10 volts, disconnect wiper motor connector. Check connector condition and clean or repair connector as necessary. Probe Dark Blue wire of wiper motor connector. If voltage is less than 10 volts, repair open Dark Blue wire between fuse No. 5 and wiper motor connector. Perform VERIFICATION TEST.

8) If voltage is more than 10 volts, place DRB-II in ohmmeter mode. Probe Black wire of multifunction switch connector. If resistance is more than 5 ohms, repair open Black wire. Perform VERIFICATION TEST. If resistance is less than 5 ohms, probe Dark Green wire at wiper motor connector.

9) If resistance is more than 5 ohms, repair open Dark Green wire. Perform VERIFICATION TEST. If resistance is less than 5 ohms, replace wiper motor. Perform VERIFICATION TEST.

TEST 41B
CHECKING CONTROLLER & WIPER SWITCH

NOTE: For connector terminal identification, see CONNECTOR IDENTIFICATION in BODY CONTROL COMPUTER INTRODUCTION article. For wiring diagrams, see appropriate WIRING DIAGRAMS article.

1) Using DRB-II, stop wiper motor actuation test. Gain access to multifunction switch connector. Ensure wiper switch is still in delay position. Put DRB-II in voltmeter mode. Backprobe terminal No. 1 (Dark Green/Yellow wire) of multifunction switch connector. While rotating wiper switch from low to high, read voltage.

2) If voltage changes from one to 12 volts, replace body controller. Perform VERIFICATION TEST. If voltage does not change from one to 12 volts, turn ignition switch to OFF position. Disconnect body controller Blue connector. Body controller is located under left side of instrument panel. Check connector, and clean or repair connector as necessary.

3) Put DRB-II in ohmmeter mode. Probe terminal No. 1 (Dark Green/Yellow wire) of multifunction switch connector. Rotate wiper switch from low to high. If DRB-II displays a change from 40/k ohms to 350/k ohms, replace body controller. Perform VERIFICATION TEST.

4) If DRB-II does not display a change from 40/k ohms to 350/k ohms, disconnect multifunction switch connector. Check connector, and clean or repair connector as necessary. Probe terminal No. 17 (Dark Green/Yellow wire) of body controller Blue connector. If resistance is more than 5 ohms, repair open Dark Green/Yellow wire. Perform VERIFICATION TEST. If resistance is less than 5 ohms, replace multifunction switch module. Perform VERIFICATION TEST.

TEST 41C
CHECKING POWER & GROUND SUPPLY

NOTE: For connector terminal identification, see CONNECTOR IDENTIFICATION in BODY CONTROL COMPUTER INTRODUCTION article. For wiring diagrams, see appropriate WIRING DIAGRAMS article.

1) Disconnect multifunction switch connector. Check connector condition and clean or repair connector as necessary. Disconnect body controller Blue connector. Body controller is located under left side of instrument panel. Check connector, and clean or repair connector as necessary.

2) Disconnect wiper motor connector. Check connector condition and clean or repair connector as necessary. Probe Dark Blue wire (in fuse block) to fuse No. 5. If resistance is less than 5 ohms, repair short to ground in Dark Blue wire. Replace fuse No. 5. Perform VERIFICATION TEST. If resistance is more than 5 ohms, reconnect multifunction switch connector.

3) Probe Dark Blue wire (in fuse block) to fuse No. 5. If resistance is less than 5 ohms, replace multifunction switch. Replace fuse No. 5. Perform VERIFICATION TEST. If resistance is more than 5 ohms, reconnect body controller Blue connector. Probe Dark Blue wire (in fuse block) to fuse No. 5.

4) If resistance is less than 5 ohms, replace body controller. Replace fuse No. 5. Perform VERIFICATION TEST. If resistance is more than 5 ohms, reconnect wiper motor connector. Probe Dark Blue wire (in fuse block) to fuse No. 5. If resistance is less than 5 ohms, replace wiper motor and fuse No. 5. Perform VERIFICATION TEST. If resistance is more than 5 ohms, replace fuse No. 5. Perform VERIFICATION TEST.

TEST 42A
CHECKING POWER & GROUND SUPPLY

NOTE: For connector terminal identification, see CONNECTOR IDENTIFICATION in BODY CONTROL COMPUTER INTRODUCTION article. For wiring diagrams, see appropriate WIRING DIAGRAMS article.

1) Turn wiper switch off. If wipers park properly, perform TEST 43A. If wipers do not park properly, place DRB-II in voltmeter mode. Disconnect wiper motor connector. Check connector, and clean or repair connector as necessary.

2) Turn wiper switch ON. Probe Dark Green wire at wiper motor connector. Voltage should change from zero to 12 volts. If DRB-II does not display 0-12 volts during sweep, replace wiper motor. Perform VERIFICATION TEST. If DRB-II displays 0-12 volts during sweep, turn ignition switch to OFF position.

3) Disconnect body controller Blue connector. Body controller is located under left side of instrument panel. Check connector, and clean or repair connector as necessary. Disconnect wiper motor connector. Check connector, and clean or repair connector as necessary.

4) Using an external ohmmeter, check resistance between terminal No. 12 (Dark Green/White wire) of body controller Blue connector and Dark Green wire of wiper motor connector. If resistance is more than 5 ohms, replace body controller. Perform VERIFICATION TEST.

5) If resistance is less than 5 ohms, place DRB-II in ohmmeter mode. Probe terminal No. 10 (Dark Green/White wire) of body controller Blue connector. If resistance is more than 5 ohms, repair open Dark Green/White or Dark Green wire. Perform VERIFICATION TEST.

6) If resistance is less than 5 ohms, probe terminal No. 17 (Black wire) of multifunction switch connector. If resistance is more than 5 ohms, repair open Black wire. Perform VERIFICATION TEST. If resistance is less than 5 ohms, replace multifunction switch module. Perform VERIFICATION TEST.

TEST 43A
CHECKING WASHER PUMP OPERATION

NOTE: For connector terminal identification, see CONNECTOR IDENTIFICATION in BODY CONTROL COMPUTER INTRODUCTION article. For wiring diagrams, see appropriate WIRING DIAGRAMS article.

TEST 43A (Cont.)

1) Access multifunction switch connector. Place DRB-II in voltmeter mode. Backprobe terminal No. 3 (Brown wire) of multifunction switch connector. Push washer button on stalk switch. While holding washer button in, observe voltage. If voltage is more than 10 volts, go to step **3)**.

2) If voltage is less than 10 volts, probe terminal No. 4 (Dark Blue wire) of multifunction switch connector. If voltage is more than 10 volts, replace multifunction switch. Perform VERIFICATION TEST. If voltage is less than 10 volts, remove and inspect fuse No. 5 from fuse block. If fuse is blown, replace fuse No. 5. Perform VERIFICATION TEST. If fuse is okay, go to next step.

3) If voltage was more than 10 volts in step **1)** or fuse is okay in step **2)**, disconnect washer pump connector. Check connector, and clean or repair connector as necessary. Probe Brown wire of washer pump connector. While pushing washer button in, observe DRB-II display, If voltage is less than 10 volts, repair open Brown wire between washer motor connector and multifunction switch connector. Perform VERIFICATION TEST.

4) If voltage is more than 10 volts, disconnect multifunction switch connector. Check connector, and clean or repair connector as necessary. Using an external ohmmeter, probe Dark Blue wire between fuse No. 5 in fuse block and multifunction switch connector.

5) If resistance is more than 5 ohms, repair open Dark Blue wire between fuse block and multifunction switch connector. Perform VERIFICATION TEST. If resistance is less than 5 ohms, replace washer pump. Perform VERIFICATION TEST.

TEST 44A

DIAGNOSING KEY-IN LIGHT CIRCUIT

NOTE: For connector terminal identification, see CONNECTOR IDENTIFICATION in BODY CONTROL COMPUTER INTRODUCTION article. For wiring diagrams, see appropriate WIRING DIAGRAMS article.

1) Check courtesy lights. If courtesy lights are inoperative, perform TEST 10A. If courtesy lights are functioning properly, ensure all doors are closed. Turn ignition switch to OFF position. Wait one minute. Ensure dimmer control lever is in center position.

2) If key light is on constantly, perform TEST 44B. If key light is not on constantly, turn ignition switch to ON position. Using DRB-II, actuate key in light test. If key light flashes off then on, perform TEST 44C. If key light does not flash off then on, using DRB-II, stop key light test.

3) Disconnect key ignition switch connector. *See Fig. 5B*. Check connector, and clean or repair connector as necessary. Place DRB-II in voltmeter mode. Probe Pink/Light Blue wire of key-in light connector. If voltage is less than 10 volts, repair open Pink/Light Blue wire. Perform VERIFICATION TEST.

4) If voltage is more than 10 volts, remove key light bulb. Inspect bulb and socket. If bulb and socket are not okay, repair replace as necessary. Perform VERIFICATION TEST. If bulb and socket are okay, reconnect key-in light connector.

5) Access body controller. Body controller is located under left side of instrument panel. Ensure DRB-II is in voltmeter mode. Probe terminal No. 22 (Yellow/Red wire) of body controller Blue connector. If voltage is less than 10 volts, repair open Yellow/Red wire. Perform VERIFICATION TEST. If voltage is more than 10 volts, replace body controller. Perform VERIFICATION TEST.

TEST 44B

CHECKING FOR KEY-IN LIGHT SHORT

NOTE: For connector terminal identification, see CONNECTOR IDENTIFICATION in BODY CONTROL COMPUTER INTRODUCTION article. For wiring diagrams, see appropriate WIRING DIAGRAMS article.

Disconnect body controller. Body controller is located under left side of instrument panel. Check connector, and clean or repair connector as necessary. If key light goes out, perform TEST 44C. If key light does not go out, repair short to ground in Yellow/Red wire. Perform VERIFICATION TEST.

TEST 44C

DIAGNOSING DOOR JAMB CIRCUIT FOR IGNITION KEY LIGHT

NOTE: For connector terminal identification, see CONNECTOR IDENTIFICATION in BODY CONTROL COMPUTER INTRODUCTION article. For wiring diagrams, see appropriate WIRING DIAGRAMS article.

NOTE: Ensure all doors are closed.

1) Using DRB-II, read left front door jamb switch status. If DRB-II displays CIRCUIT OPEN, go to step **4)**. If DRB-II does not display CIRCUIT OPEN, disconnect left front door jamb switch. Check connector condition and clean or repair connector as necessary. If DRB-II displays CIRCUIT OPEN, replace left front door jamb switch. Perform VERIFICATION TEST.

2) If DRB-II does not display CIRCUIT OPEN, turn ignition switch to OFF position. Disconnect body controller Blue connector. Body controller is located under left side of instrument panel. Check connector, and clean or repair connector as necessary.

3) Probe terminal No. 13 (Black/Light Blue) of body controller Blue connector. If resistance is less than 10 ohms, repair short to ground in Black/Light Blue wire. Perform VERIFICATION TEST. If resistance is more than 10 ohms, replace body controller. Perform VERIFICATION TEST.

4) If DRB-II displays CIRCUIT OPEN in step **1)**, disconnect left front door jamb switch. Check connector, and clean or repair connector as necessary. Connect a jumper wire between Black and Black/light Blue wires of left front door jamb switch connector. If DRB-II displays CIRCUIT CLOSED, replace left front door switch.

5) If DRB-II does not display CIRCUIT CLOSED, disconnect jumper wire. Connect a jumper wire between Black/Light Blue wire of left front door switch connector and ground. If DRB-II displays CIRCUIT CLOSED, repair open Black wire. Perform VERIFICATION TEST. If DRB-II does not display CIRCUIT CLOSED, disconnect jumper wire.

6) Access body controller. Body controller is located under left side of instrument panel. Connect a jumper wire between terminal No. 13 (Black/Light Blue wire) at wiring harness side of body controller Blue connector and ground.

7) If DRB-II displays CIRCUIT CLOSED, repair open Black/Light Blue wire. Perform VERIFICATION TEST. If DRB-II does not display CIRCUIT CLOSED, replace body controller. Perform VERIFICATION TEST.

TEST 45A

DIAGNOSING LIFTGATE RELEASE

NOTE: For connector terminal identification, see CONNECTOR IDENTIFICATION in BODY CONTROL COMPUTER INTRODUCTION article. For wiring diagrams, see appropriate WIRING DIAGRAMS article.

NOTE: Ensure liftgate mechanical linkage is operating properly before proceeding with test.

1) Press liftgate release button. If liftgate opens, perform TEST 45B. If liftgate does not open, remove and inspect fuse No. 3 from fuse block. If fuse is blown, repair short to ground in Pink wire between fuse No. 3 and body controller connector. Replace fuse No. 3. Perform VERIFICATION TEST.

2) If fuse is okay, reinstall fuse No. 3. Disconnect body controller Blue connector. Body controller is located under left side of instrument panel. Check connector, and clean or repair connector as necessary. Put DRB-II in voltmeter mode. Probe terminal No. 8 (Pink wire) of body controller Blue connector.

3) If voltage is more than 10 volts, perform TEST 45C. If voltage is less than 10 volts, remove fuse No. 3. Using an external ohmmeter, check resistance of Pink wire between terminal No. 8 of body controller Blue connector and connector to fuse No. 3. in fuse block. If resistance is more than 5 ohms, repair open Pink wire. Perform VERIFICATION TEST. If resistance is less than 5 ohms, short to ground in Pink wire. Perform VERIFICATION TEST.

TEST 45B

DIAGNOSING LIFTGATE RELEASE

NOTE: For connector terminal identification, see CONNECTOR IDEN-TIFICATION in BODY CONTROL COMPUTER INTRODUCTION article. For wiring diagrams, see appropriate WIRING DIAGRAMS article.

1) Turn ignition switch to ON position with engine off. Set parking brake. Place transmission gear selector in REVERSE or DRIVE position. Press liftgate switch. If liftgate solenoid did not actuate, liftgate system is functioning properly.

2) If liftgate solenoid actuated, disconnect body controller Blue connector. Body controller is located under left side of instrument panel. Check connector, and clean or repair connector as necessary. Press liftgate switch. If liftgate solenoid actuated, repair short to ground in Brown/Light Blue wire between body controller Blue connector and liftgate switch. Perform VERIFICATION TEST.

3) If liftgate solenoid did not actuate, shift lever may be misaligned. If vehicle is equipped with a A604/30TH transmission, check shift lever alignment and adjust as necessary. Perform VERIFICATION TEST. If vehicle is not equipped with a A604/30TH transmission, verify shift indicator alignment using DRB-II. Align shifter as necessary. Perform VER-IFICATION TEST.

TEST 45C

DIAGNOSING LIFTGATE RELEASE

NOTE: For connector terminal identification, see CONNECTOR IDEN-TIFICATION in BODY CONTROL COMPUTER INTRODUCTION article. For wiring diagrams, see appropriate WIRING DIAGRAMS article.

1) Reconnect body controller connector. Connect a jumper wire between terminal No. 9 (Brown/Light Blue wire) at wiring harness side of body controller Blue connector and ground. Press liftgate switch. If liftgate solenoid actuated, replace body controller. Perform VERIFICATION TEST.

2) If liftgate solenoid did not actuate, disconnect liftgate switch connector. Check connector, and clean or repair connector as necessary. Using an external ohmmeter, check resistance of Brown/Light Blue wire between terminals No. 1 of liftgate switch connector and No. 9 of body controller Blue connector.

3) If resistance is more than 5 ohms, repair open Brown/Light Blue wire. Perform VERIFICATION TEST. If resistance is less than 5 ohms, put DRB-II in voltmeter mode. Probe terminal No. 6 (Black/Red wire) of lift-gate switch connector. If voltage is less than 10 volts, repair Black/Red wire as necessary.

4) If voltage is more than 10 volts, reconnect liftgate switch connector. While pressing liftgate switch, probe terminal No. 5 (Light Green/Black wire) of liftgate switch connector. If voltage is less than 10 volts, replace liftgate switch. Perform VERIFICATION TEST.

5) If voltage is more than 10 volts, connect a jumper wire between terminals No. 5 (Light Green/Black wire) and No. 6 (Black/Red wire) of liftgate switch connector. Disconnect liftgate release solenoid connector. Connector is located at bottom of liftgate behind trim panel. Check connector, and clean or repair connector as necessary.

6) Connect a jumper wire between liftgate solenoid body and ground. If liftgate solenoid actuate, repair liftgate release solenoid connector and ground. If liftgate solenoid actuated, clean or repair release solenoid ground as necessary. If liftgate solenoid did not actuate, replace liftgate solenoid.

TEST 46A

OIL PRESSURE SENSOR CIRCUIT

NOTE: For connector terminal identification, see CONNECTOR IDEN-TIFICATION in BODY CONTROL COMPUTER INTRODUCTION article. For wiring diagrams, see appropriate WIRING DIAGRAMS article.

1) Check engine oil level, and top it off as necessary. If oil level is okay, using DRB-II stop electronic instrument cluster sequential segment test. Remove oil pressure sending unit, and connect an oil pressure gauge in its place. Start engine.

TEST 46A (Cont.)

2) Allow engine to reach normal operating temperature and check oil pressure reading. If oil pressure is less than 5 psi (.4 kg/cm²) at idle, check engine condition. See appropriate article in ENGINES. If oil pressure is more than 5 psi (.4 kg/cm²) at idle, turn ignition switch to OFF position.

3) Remove oil pressure test gauge. Reinstall oil pressure sending unit. Check oil pressure sending unit connector condition and clean or repair connector as necessary. Reconnect oil pressure sending unit connector. Start engine. If instrument cluster is not equipped with an oil gauge, perform TEST 46B.

4) If instrument panel is equipped with an oil pressure gauge, observe gauge. If oil gauge indicates zero oil pressure, perform TEST 46C. If oil gauge indicates more than zero oil pressure, check if oil pressure gauge indicates maximum oil pressure. If oil pressure gauge indicates maximum oil pressure, go to step 7).

5) If oil pressure gauge indicates less than maximum oil pressure, turn ignition switch to OFF position. Disconnect electronic instrument cluster connector. Check connector, and clean or repair connector as necessary. Disconnect oil pressure sending unit.

6) Using an external ohmmeter, check resistance at Gray wire between terminal No. 8 of electronic instrument cluster connector and terminal No. 2 of oil pressure sending unit connector. If resistance is less than 5 ohms, replace oil pressure sending unit. Perform VERIFICATION TEST. If resistance is more than 5 ohms, repair open Gray wire. Perform VER-IFICATION TEST.

7) If oil pressure gauge indicates maximum oil pressure in step 4), turn ignition switch to OFF position. Disconnect oil pressure sending unit connector. Turn ignition switch to ON position. Using DRB-II, read oil pressure sending unit voltage. If DRB-II displays more than 8 volts, replace oil pressure sending unit. Perform VERIFICATION TEST.

8) If DRB-II displays less than 8 volts, turn ignition switch to OFF position. Disconnect body controller Blue connector. Body controller is located under left side of instrument panel. Check connector, and clean or repair connector as necessary. Put DRB-II in voltmeter mode.

9) Turn ignition switch to ON position. Probe terminal No. 6 (Dark Blue/White wire) of body controller Blue connector. If voltage is less than 10 volts, repair open Dark Blue/White wire. Perform VERIFICATION TEST. If voltage is more than 10 volts, turn ignition switch to OFF position.

10) Put DRB-II in ohmmeter mode. Probe terminal No. 1 (Gray/Yellow wire) of pressure sending unit connector. If resistance is more than 5 ohms, replace body controller. Perform VERIFICATION TEST. If resistance is less than 5 ohms, repair short to ground in Gray/Yellow wire. Perform VERIFICATION TEST.

TEST 46B

OIL PRESSURE SENSOR CIRCUIT

NOTE: For connector terminal identification, see CONNECTOR IDEN-TIFICATION in BODY CONTROL COMPUTER INTRODUCTION article. For wiring diagrams, see appropriate WIRING DIAGRAMS article.

NOTE: This test is for vehicles equipped with a base instrument cluster (without oil gauge).

Ensure engine is still running. Disconnect oil pressure sending unit connector. Check connector, and clean or repair connector as necessary. Check instrument cluster oil warning light. If oil warning light is off, replace oil pressure sending unit. Perform VERIFICATION TEST. If oil warning light is on, repair short to ground in Gray wire. Perform VERIFI-CATION TEST.

TEST 46C

OIL PRESSURE SENSOR CIRCUIT

NOTE: For connector terminal identification, see CONNECTOR IDEN-TIFICATION in BODY CONTROL COMPUTER INTRODUCTION article. For wiring diagrams, see appropriate WIRING DIAGRAMS article.

TEST 46C (Cont.)

NOTE: This test is for vehicles equipped with an electronic instrument cluster.

1) Observe electronic instrument cluster. If oil warning indicator (oil can symbol) is flashing, go to step **5)**. If oil warning indicator is not flashing, turn engine off. Turn ignition switch to ON position. Disconnect oil pressure sending unit connector. Connect a jumper wire between terminal No. 1 (Gray/Yellow wire) of oil pressure sending unit connector and ground.

2) Using DRB-II, read oil pressure sending unit voltage. If DRB-II displays less than one volt, replace oil pressure sending unit. Perform VERIFICATION TEST. If DRB-II displays more than one volt, turn ignition switch to OFF position. Disconnect body controller Blue connector. Body controller is located under left side of instrument panel.

3) Check connector, and clean or repair connector as necessary. Reconnect body controller Blue connector. Connect a jumper wire between terminal No. 11 (Gray/Yellow wire) at wiring harness side of body controller Blue connector and ground. Turn ignition switch to ON position.

4) If DRB-II displays less than one volt, repair open Gray/Yellow wire. Perform VERIFICATION TEST. If DRB-II displays more than one volt, replace body controller. Perform VERIFICATION TEST.

5) If oil warning indicator (oil can symbol) is flashing in step **1)**, turn engine off. Turn ignition switch to ON position. Disconnect oil pressure sending unit connector. Observe electronic instrument cluster. If oil warning indicator (oil can symbol) is not flashing, replace oil pressure sending unit. Perform VERIFICATION TEST.

6) If oil warning indicator is flashing, turn ignition switch to OFF position. Disconnect electronic instrument cluster connector. Check connector, and clean or repair connector as necessary. Put DRB-II in ohmmeter mode.

7) Probe terminal No. 2 (Gray wire) of oil pressure sending unit connector. If resistance is more than 5 ohms, replace electronic instrument cluster. Perform VERIFICATION TEST. If resistance is less than 5 ohms, repair short to ground in Gray wire. Perform VERIFICATION TEST.

TEST 47A

DIAGNOSING SEAT BELT
WARNING LIGHT CIRCUIT

NOTE: For connector terminal identification, see CONNECTOR IDENTIFICATION in BODY CONTROL COMPUTER INTRODUCTION article. For wiring diagrams, see appropriate WIRING DIAGRAMS article.

1) Turn ignition switch to ON position. If seat belt warning light is on constantly, perform TEST 47B. If seat belt warning light is not on constantly, ensure left front seat belt is not fastened. Using DRB-II, read left seat belt switch status. If DRB-II does not display CIRCUIT CLOSED, perform TEST 47C.

2) If DRB-II displays CIRCUIT CLOSED, fasten left front seat belt. If DRB-II does not display CIRCUIT OPEN, perform TEST 47D. If DRB-II displays CIRCUIT OPEN, actuate seat belt warning light test using DRB-II. If seat belt warning light flashes, retest system. Perform VERIFICATION TEST. If seat belt warning light does not flash, turn ignition switch to OFF position.

3) Disconnect body controller Blue connector. Body controller is located under left side of instrument panel. Check connector, and clean or repair connector as necessary. Turn ignition switch to ON position. Put DRB-II in voltmeter mode.

4) Probe terminal No. 23 (Dark Blue/Red wire) of body controller Blue connector. If voltage is less than 10 volts, replace body controller. Perform VERIFICATION TEST. If voltage is more than 10 volts, remove and inspect fuse No. 15 from fuse block. If fuse is blown, go to step **8)**. If fuse is okay, turn ignition switch to ON position.

5) Probe Dark Blue wire (in fuse block) to fuse No. 15. If voltage is less than 10 volts, repair open Dark Blue wire between fuse No. 15 and ignition switch. Perform VERIFICATION TEST. If voltage is more than 10 volts, remove driver warning light assembly from instrument cluster.

TEST 47A (Cont.)

6) Remove and inspect seat belt warning light bulb. If bulb is open, repair open Dark Blue wire. Perform VERIFICATION TEST. If bulb is okay, using an external ohmmeter, check resistance of Dark Blue/Red wire between body controller Blue connector and seat belt warning light bulb.

7) If resistance is more than 5 ohms, repair open in Dark Blue/Red wire between body controller connector and seat belt warning light. Perform VERIFICATION TEST. If resistance is less than 5 ohms, repair open in Dark Blue/White wire between fuse No. 15 and seat belt warning light. Perform VERIFICATION TEST.

8) If fuse is blown in step **4)**, put DRB-II in ohmmeter mode. Probe Dark Blue/White wire (in fuse block) to fuse No. 15. If resistance is less than 5 ohms, repair short to ground in Dark Blue/White wire. Perform VERIFICATION TEST. If resistance is more than 5 ohms, probe Dark Blue wire (in fuse block) to fuse No. 15.

9) If resistance is less than 5 ohms, repair short to ground in Dark Blue wire. Perform VERIFICATION TEST. If resistance is more than 5 ohms, remove driver warning light assembly from instrument cluster. Remove seat belt warning light bulb.

10) Probe terminal No. 23 (Dark Blue/Red wire) of body controller Blue connector. If resistance is less than 5 ohms, repair short to ground in Dark Blue/Red wire. Perform VERIFICATION TEST. If resistance is more than 5 ohms, replace fuse No. 15. Perform VERIFICATION TEST.

TEST 47B

CHECKING FOR SHORT IN SEAT
BELT WARNING LIGHT CIRCUIT

NOTE: For connector terminal identification, see CONNECTOR IDENTIFICATION in BODY CONTROL COMPUTER INTRODUCTION article. For wiring diagrams, see appropriate WIRING DIAGRAMS article.

1) Turn ignition switch to OFF position. Disconnect body controller Blue connector. Body controller is located under left side of instrument panel. Check connector, and clean or repair connector as necessary.

2) Turn ignition switch to ON position. If seat belt warning light is off, replace body controller. Perform VERIFICATION TEST. If seat belt warning light is on, repair short to ground in Dark Blue/Red wire. Perform VERIFICATION TEST.

TEST 47C

CHECKING FOR OPEN IN SEAT
BELT SWITCH CIRCUIT

NOTE: For connector terminal identification, see CONNECTOR IDENTIFICATION in BODY CONTROL COMPUTER INTRODUCTION article. For wiring diagrams, see appropriate WIRING DIAGRAMS article.

1) Disconnect left front seat belt switch connector. Connector is located under left front seat. Connect a jumper wire between Light Green/Red and Black wires of seat belt switch connector. If DRB-II displays CIRCUIT CLOSED, replace left front seat belt switch. Perform VERIFICATION TEST. If DRB-II does not display CIRCUIT CLOSED, disconnect jumper wire.

2) Connect a jumper wire between Light Green/Red wire of seat belt switch connector and ground. If DRB-II displays CIRCUIT CLOSED, repair open Light Green/Red wire. Perform VERIFICATION TEST. If DRB-II does not display CIRCUIT CLOSED, replace body controller. Perform VERIFICATION TEST.

TEST 47D

CHECKING FOR SHORT IN SEAT
BELT SWITCH CIRCUIT

NOTE: For connector terminal identification, see CONNECTOR IDENTIFICATION in BODY CONTROL COMPUTER INTRODUCTION article. For wiring diagrams, see appropriate WIRING DIAGRAMS article.

TEST 47D (Cont.)

1) Disconnect left front seat belt switch connector. Connector is located under left front seat. If DRB-II does not display CIRCUIT CLOSED, replace left front seat belt switch. Perform VERIFICATION TEST. If DRB-II displays CIRCUIT CLOSED, turn ignition switch to OFF position.

2) Disconnect body controller Blue connector. Body controller is located under left side of instrument panel. Check connector, and clean or repair connector as necessary. Put DRB-II in ohmmeter mode. Probe terminal No. 14 (Light Green/Red wire) of body controller Blue connector.

3) If resistance is more than 5 ohms, replace body controller. Perform VERIFICATION TEST. If resistance is less than 5 ohms, repair short to ground in Light Green/Red wire. Perform VERIFICATION TEST.

TEST 48A

REPAIRING FAULTY WASHER
FLUID LEVEL SWITCH

NOTE: For connector terminal identification, see CONNECTOR IDEN-TIFICATION in BODY CONTROL COMPUTER INTRODUCTION article. For wiring diagrams, see appropriate WIRING DIAGRAMS article.

1) Check washer fluid level. If washer fluid is not full, add fluid as necessary. Perform VERIFICATION TEST. If washer fluid is full, using DRB-II, read washer fluid switch status. If DRB-II displays CIRCUIT OPEN, go to step 4). If DRB-II does not display CIRCUIT OPEN, disconnect washer fluid level switch connector.

2) If DRB-II displays CIRCUIT OPEN, replace washer fluid level switch. Perform VERIFICATION TEST. If DRB-II does not display CIRCUIT OPEN, turn ignition switch to OFF position. Disconnect body controller Natural connector. Body controller is located under left side of instrument panel.

3) Check connector, and clean or repair connector as necessary. Place DRB-II in ohmmeter mode. Probe terminal No. 19 (Black/Tan wire) of body controller Natural connector. If resistance is less than 5 ohms, repair short to ground in Black/Tan wire. Perform VERIFICATION TEST. If resistance is more than 5 ohms, replace body controller. Perform VER-IFICATION TEST.

4) If DRB-II displays OPEN CIRCUIT in step 1), disconnect washer fluid level switch connector. Connect a jumper wire between Black/Tan and Black wires of washer fluid level switch connector. If DRB-II displays CIRCUIT CLOSED, replace washer fluid level switch. Perform VERIFI-CATION TEST. If DRB-II does not display CIRCUIT CLOSED, disconnect jumper wire.

5) Connect a jumper wire between Black/Tan wire of washer fluid level switch connector and ground. If DRB-II displays CIRCUIT CLOSED, repair open Black wire. Perform VERIFICATION TEST. If DRB-II does not display CIRCUIT CLOSED, access body controller.

6) Body controller is located under left side of instrument panel. Connect a jumper wire between terminal No. 19 (Black/Tan wire) at body controller Natural connector and ground. If DRB-II displays CIRCUIT CLOSED, repair open Black/Tan wire. Perform VERIFICATION TEST. If DRB-II does not display CIRCUIT CLOSED, replace body controller. Perform VERIFICATION TEST.

VERIFICATION TEST

VERIFICATION OF REPAIRS

Inspect vehicle to ensure all engine components are connected. Reassemble and reconnect components as necessary. Ensure all repairs have been made. Actuate system that was not operational. If system operates properly, repair is complete. If system does not operate properly, perform TEST 1A: IDENTIFYING VEHICLE EQUIPMENT & SYSTEM PROBLEMS.

TEST 1A

BLANK DRB-II MESSAGE SCREEN

NOTE: For connector terminal identification, see CONNECTOR IDENTIFICATION in BODY CONTROL COMPUTER INTRODUCTION article. For wiring diagrams, see appropriate WIRING DIAGRAMS article.

1) Disconnect DRB-II. Using an external voltmeter, check voltage at terminal No. 5 (Red wire) at Chrysler Collision Detection (CCD) bus diagnostic connector. Connector is located underneath dash at left side of steering column. If voltage is more than 10 volts, perform TEST 1B. If voltage is less than 10 volts, go to next step.

2) Remove fuse No. 23 from fuse block. Inspect fuse. If fuse is blown, go to next step. If fuse is not blown, using an external voltmeter, check voltage available to fuse that was removed. If voltage is more than 10 volts, repair open wire between fuse block and CCD bus diagnostic connector. Perform VERIFICATION TEST. If voltage is less than 10 volts, repair open wire to fuse block. Perform VERIFICATION TEST.

3) Using an external ohmmeter, check resistance between fuse output terminal (at fuse block) and ground. If resistance is less than 5 ohms, repair short to ground in wiring. Perform VERIFICATION TEST. If resistance is more than 5 ohms, replace blown fuse. Perform VERIFICATION TEST.

TEST 1B

BLANK DRB-II MESSAGE SCREEN

NOTE: For connector terminal identification, see CONNECTOR IDENTIFICATION in BODY CONTROL COMPUTER INTRODUCTION article. For wiring diagrams, see appropriate WIRING DIAGRAMS article.

1) Using external ohmmeter, check resistance between terminal No. 3 (Black/Light Green wire) at CCD bus diagnostic connector and ground. If resistance is more than 5 ohms, repair open in wiring to terminal No. 3. Perform VERIFICATION TEST.

2) If resistance is less than 5 ohms, test DRB-II. Refer to TEST 5A. If DRB-II is good, replace DRB-II adapter cable. Perform VERIFICATION TEST. If DRB-II is defective, replace DRB-II. Perform VERIFICATION TEST.

TEST 2A

RAM TEST ERROR

If DRB-II does not display RAM FAILURE, return to test that sent you here. If DRB-II displays RAM FAILURE, reboot DRB-II by reinstalling DRB-II cartridge. If DRB-II does not display RAM FAILURE, return to test that sent you here. If DRB-II displays RAM FAILURE, replace DRB-II cartridge.

TEST 3A

ROM CHECKSUM ERROR

If DRB-II does not display ROM FAILURE, return to test that sent you here. If DRB-II displays ROM FAILURE, reboot DRB-II by reinstalling DRB-II cartridge. If DRB-II does not display ROM FAILURE, return to test that sent you here. If DRB-II displays ROM FAILURE, replace DRB-II.

TEST 4A

KEYPAD TEST FAILURE MESSAGE

NOTE: DO NOT touch DRB-II keypad during following test.

If DRB-II does not display KEYPAD TEST FAILURE, return to test that sent you here. If DRB-II displays KEYPAD TEST FAILURE, reboot DRB-II by reinstalling DRB-II cartridge. If DRB-II does not display KEYPAD TEST FAILURE, return to test that sent you here. If DRB-II displays KEYPAD TEST FAILURE, replace DRB-II.

TEST 5A

TESTING DRB-II

Although only manufacturer is equipped to physically test DRB-II, you should be able to determine state of your DRB-II by using following substitution techniques and process of elimination.

1) Turn ignition switch to OFF position. Disconnect DRB-II adapter cable and DRB-II cartridge. Locate a second vehicle with identical equipment to original vehicle. Connect DRB-II assembly to second vehicle, and turn ignition switch to ON position. Use DRB-II as it was used on first vehicle. If DRB-II results are not as before, problem is not DRB-II. Return to test that sent you here.

2) If same problem still exists as before substituting vehicles, DRB-II has a defective adapter cable or DRB-II cartridge. If a second DRB-II cartridge for the same vehicle is available, try substituting DRB-II cartridge. If DRB-II now functions correctly, original DRB-II cartridge is defective. Use good DRB-II cartridge, and return to test that sent you here.

3) If DRB-II still does not function correctly, substitute a second DRB-II adapter cable. If a second DRB-II adapter cable of same type is not available, use a SCI or CCD adapter cable. If DRB-II now functions correctly, DRB-II has a defective adapter cable. Use good adapter cable, and return to test that sent you here.

4) If DRB-II still does not work, substitute a second DRB-II. If a second DRB-II is not available, send DRB-II in for repair. If DRB-II now functions correctly, original DRB-II is defective. Use good DRB-II, and return to test that sent you here.

TEST 6A

NOTE: TEST 6A does not apply to Caravan, Town & Country or Voyager.

TEST 7A

BUS FAILURE MESSAGES

Select error message and corresponding test from BUS FAILURE MESSAGES table. Proceed to indicated test. Each specific error message is diagnosed by following a specific testing sequence. Performing all tests is not necessary to diagnose an individual error message.

BUS FAILURE MESSAGES

Message	Test No.
BUS BIAS LEVEL TO HIGH	14A
BUS BIAS LEVEL TOO LOW	13A
BUS (+) OPEN	16A
BUS (-) OPEN	17A
BUS (+) & (-) OPEN	18A
BUS (+) & BUS (-) SHORTED TOGETHER	11A
SHORT TO BATTERY	8A
SHORT TO GROUND	10A
SHORT TO 5 VOLTS	9A
NO BUS BIAS	15A
NOT RECEIVING BUS MESSAGES CORRECTLY	19A
NO TERMINATION	12A

TEST 8A

SHORT TO BATTERY ON BUS

NOTE: For connector terminal identification, see CONNECTOR IDENTIFICATION in BODY CONTROL COMPUTER INTRODUCTION article. For wiring diagrams, see appropriate WIRING DIAGRAMS article.

CAUTION: Always turn ignition switch to OFF position before disconnecting or connecting any module connector.

1) Using DRB-II, indicate whether a module is present or not. Disconnect Electronic Automatic Transaxle (EATX) controller connector. Connector

TEST 8A (Cont.)

is located on firewall on right side of engine compartment. Check connector, and clean or repair connector as necessary. If DRB-II does not display SHORT TO BATTERY, replace EATX controller. Perform VERIFICATION TEST. If DRB-II displays SHORT TO BATTERY, disconnect Single Board Engine Controller (SBEC) connector. Connector is located in engine compartment. Check connector, and clean or repair connector as necessary.

2) If DRB-II does not display SHORT TO BATTERY, replace SBEC. Perform VERIFICATION TEST. If DRB-II displays SHORT TO BATTERY, connect a jumper wire between body controller case and ground. Body controller is located under left side of instrument panel. If DRB-II does not display SHORT TO BATTERY, repair open Black/Light Green wire between terminal No. 19 of body controller Blue connector and ground.

3) If DRB-II displays SHORT TO BATTERY, disconnect body controller Blue connector. Body controller is located under left side of instrument panel. DRB-II. If DRB-II does not display SHORT TO BATTERY, replace body controller. Perform VERIFICATION TEST. If DRB-II displays SHORT TO BATTERY, disconnect instrument cluster 14-pin connector.

4) If DRB-II does not display SHORT TO BATTERY, perform TEST 8B. If DRB-II displays SHORT TO BATTERY, disconnect compass/mini-trip module connector. Connector is located in overhead console. Check connector, and clean or repair connector as necessary. If DRB-II does not display SHORT TO BATTERY, perform TEST 8C.

5) If DRB-II displays SHORT TO BATTERY, disconnect DRB-II. Using an external voltmeter, measure voltage between terminal No. 1 (Violet/Brown wire) of CCD bus connector and ground. If voltage is more than 10 volts, repair short to voltage in Violet/Brown wire. Perform VERIFICATION TEST. If voltage is less than 10 volts, repair short to voltage in White/Black wire. Perform VERIFICATION TEST.

TEST 8B

SHORT TO BATTERY ON BUS

NOTE: For connector terminal identification, see CONNECTOR IDENTIFICATION in BODY CONTROL COMPUTER INTRODUCTION article. For wiring diagrams, see appropriate WIRING DIAGRAMS article.

Turn ignition switch to OFF position. Put DRB-II in ohmmeter mode. Probe terminal No. 7 (Black/Light Green wire) of instrument cluster connector. If resistance is less than 5 ohms, replace electronic instrument cluster. Perform VERIFICATION TEST. If resistance is more than 5 ohms, repair open Black/Green wire. Perform VERIFICATION TEST.

TEST 8C

SHORT TO BATTERY ON BUS

NOTE: For connector terminal identification, see CONNECTOR IDENTIFICATION in BODY CONTROL COMPUTER INTRODUCTION article. For wiring diagrams, see appropriate WIRING DIAGRAMS article.

Turn ignition switch to OFF position. Probe terminal No. 5 (Black/Light Green wire) of compass/mini-trip module connector. If resistance is less than 5 ohms, replace compass/mini-trip module. Perform VERIFICATION TEST. If resistance is more than 5 ohms, repair open Black/Green wire. Perform VERIFICATION TEST.

TEST 9A

SHORT TO 5 VOLTS ON BUS

NOTE: For connector terminal identification, see CONNECTOR IDENTIFICATION in BODY CONTROL COMPUTER INTRODUCTION article. For wiring diagrams, see appropriate WIRING DIAGRAMS article.

CAUTION: Always turn ignition switch to OFF position before disconnecting or connecting any module connector.

1) Using DRB-II, indicate whether a module is present or not. Disconnect Electronic Automatic Transaxle (EATX) controller connector. Connector is located on firewall on right side of engine compartment. Check

TEST 9A (Cont.)

connector, and clean or repair connector as necessary. If DRB-II does not display SHORT TO 5 VOLTS, replace EATX controller. Perform VERIFICATION TEST. If DRB-II displays SHORT TO 5 VOLTS, disconnect Single Board Engine Controller (SBEC) connector.

2) Check connector, and clean or repair connector as necessary. Using an external ohmmeter, check resistance between terminals No. 6 (Violet/White wire) and No. 26 (Violet/Brown wire) at SBEC connector. If resistance is less than 1000 ohms, repair short in Violet/Brown and Violet/White wires. Perform VERIFICATION TEST.

3) If resistance is more than 1000 ohms, check resistance between terminals No. 46 (White/Black wire) and No. 6 (Violet/White wire) of SBEC connector. If resistance is less than 1000 ohms, repair short in White/Black and Violet/Black wires. Perform VERIFICATION TEST.

4) If resistance is more than 1000 ohms, turn ignition switch to ON position with engine off. If DRB-II does not display SHORT TO 5 VOLTS, replace SBEC. Perform VERIFICATION TEST. If DRB-II displays SHORT TO 5 VOLTS, disconnect compass/mini-trip module connector (if equipped). Connector is located in overhead console.

5) If DRB-II does not display SHORT TO 5 VOLTS, replace compass/mini-trip module. If DRB-II displays SHORT TO 5 VOLTS, disconnect body controller Blue connector. Body controller is located under left side of instrument panel.

6) If DRB-II does not display SHORT TO 5 VOLTS, replace body controller. Perform VERIFICATION TEST. If DRB-II displays SHORT TO 5 VOLTS, replace instrument cluster. Perform VERIFICATION TEST.

TEST 10A

SHORT TO GROUND ON BUS

NOTE: For connector terminal identification, see CONNECTOR IDENTIFICATION in BODY CONTROL COMPUTER INTRODUCTION article. For wiring diagrams, see appropriate WIRING DIAGRAMS article.

CAUTION: Always turn ignition switch to OFF position before disconnecting or connecting any module connector.

1) Using DRB-II, indicate whether a module is present. Disconnect Electronic Automatic Transaxle (EATX) controller connector. Connector is located on firewall on right side of engine compartment. Check connector, and clean or repair connector as necessary.

2) If DRB-II does not display SHORT TO GROUND, replace EATX controller. Perform VERIFICATION TEST. If DRB-II displays SHORT TO GROUND, disconnect Single Board Engine Controller (SBEC) connector. Check connector, and clean or repair connector as necessary.

3) If DRB-II does not display SHORT TO GROUND, replace SBEC. Perform VERIFICATION TEST. If DRB-II displays SHORT TO GROUND, disconnect body controller Blue connector. Body controller is located under left side of instrument panel. If DRB-II does not display SHORT TO GROUND, replace body controller. Perform VERIFICATION TEST.

4) If DRB-II displays SHORT TO GROUND, disconnect compass/mini-trip module connector (if equipped). Connector is located in overhead console. Check connector condition and clean or repair connector as necessary. If DRB-II does not display SHORT TO GROUND, replace compass/mini-trip module. Perform VERIFICATION TEST.

5) If DRB-II displays SHORT TO GROUND, disconnect DRB-II. Using an external ohmmeter, check resistance between terminal No. 1 (Violet/Brown wire) of CCD bus diagnostic connector and ground. If resistance is less than 5 ohms, repair short to ground in Violet/Brown wire. Perform VERIFICATION TEST. If resistance is more than 5 ohms, repair short to ground in White/Black wire. Perform VERIFICATION TEST.

TEST 11A

BUS (+) & (-) SHORTED TOGETHER ON BUS

NOTE: For connector terminal identification, see CONNECTOR IDENTIFICATION in BODY CONTROL COMPUTER INTRODUCTION article. For wiring diagrams, see appropriate WIRING DIAGRAMS article.

CAUTION: Always turn ignition switch to OFF position before disconnecting or connecting any module connector.

TEST 11A (Cont.)

NOTE: A common cause of this message is a low battery condition

1) Using DRB-II, indicate whether a module is present. Disconnect Electronic Automatic Transaxle (EATX) controller connector. Connector is located on firewall on right side of engine compartment. Check connector, and clean or repair connector as necessary. If DRB-II does not display BUS (+) and BUS (-) SHORTED TOGETHER, replace EATX controller. Perform VERIFICATION TEST. If DRB-II displays BUS (+) and BUS (-) SHORTED TOGETHER, disconnect Single Board Engine Controller (SBEC) connector.

2) If DRB-II does not display BUS (+) and BUS (-) SHORTED TOGETHER, replace SBEC. Perform VERIFICATION TEST. If DRB-II displays BUS (+) and BUS (-) SHORTED TOGETHER, disconnect body controller Blue connector. Body controller is located under left side of instrument panel. If DRB-II does not display BUS (+) and BUS (-) SHORTED TOGETHER, replace body controller. Perform VERIFICATION TEST.

3) If DRB-II displays BUS (+) and BUS (-) SHORTED TOGETHER, disconnect compass/mini-trip module connector (if equipped). Connector is located in overhead console. If DRB-II does not display BUS (+) and BUS (-) SHORTED TOGETHER, replace compass/mini-trip module. Perform VERIFICATION TEST.

4) If DRB-II displays BUS (+) and BUS (-) SHORTED TOGETHER, disconnect instrument cluster. Check connector condition and clean or repair connector as necessary. If DRB-II does not display BUS (+) and BUS (-) SHORTED TOGETHER, replace instrument cluster. Perform VERIFICATION TEST. If DRB-II displays BUS (+) and BUS (-) SHORTED TOGETHER, disconnect DRB-II.

5) Using external ohmmeter, check resistance between terminals No. 1 (Violet/Brown wire) and No. 6 (White/Black wire) of CCD bus diagnostic connector. If resistance is less than 20 ohms, repair short between Violet/Black and White/Black wires. Perform VERIFICATION TEST. If resistance is more than 20 ohms, test DRB-II. Refer to TEST 5A.

TEST 12A

NO TERMINATION ON BUS

NOTE: For connector terminal identification, see CONNECTOR IDENTIFICATION in BODY CONTROL COMPUTER INTRODUCTION article. For wiring diagrams, see appropriate WIRING DIAGRAMS article.

1) Turn ignition switch to OFF position. Disconnect body controller Blue connector. Body controller is located under left side of instrument panel. Check connector, and clean or repair connector as necessary.

2) Using an external ohmmeter, check resistance between terminals No. 7 and 20 at body controller. If resistance is not 100-140 ohms, replace body controller and go to next step. If resistance is 100-140 ohms, go to next step.

3) Check resistance at Violet/Brown wire between terminal No. 7 of body controller Blue connector and terminal No. 1 at CCD bus diagnostic connector. If resistance is more than 5 ohms, repair open Violet/Brown wire and go to next step. If resistance is less than 5 ohms, go to next step.

4) Check resistance of White/Black wire between terminal No. 20 of body controller Blue connector and terminal No. 6 at CCD bus diagnostic connector. If resistance is more than 5 ohms, repair open White/Black wire to Violet/Brown wire and go to next step. If resistance is less than 5 ohms, go to next step.

5) Disconnect Single Board Engine Controller (SBEC) connector. Check connector, and clean or repair connector as necessary. Using an external ohmmeter, check resistance between terminals No. 26 and 46 at SBEC. If resistance is not 100-140 ohms, replace SBEC and go to next step. If resistance is 100-140 ohms, go to next step.

6) Check resistance at Violet/Brown wire between terminal No. 1 at CCD bus diagnostic connector and terminal No. 26 at SBEC connector. If resistance is more than 5 ohms, repair open Violet/Brown wire and go to next step. If resistance is less than 5 ohms, go to next step.

7) Check resistance at White/Black wire between terminal No. 6 at CCD bus diagnostic connector and terminal No. 20 at body controller Blue connector. If resistance is more than 5 ohms, repair open White/Black wire and go to next step. If resistance is less than 5 ohms, go to next step.

8) Test DRB-II. Refer to TEST 5A. Replace DRB-II and/or adapter cable as necessary. Perform VERIFICATION TEST. If DRB-II is good, perform TEST 20A.

TEST 13A

BUS BIAS LEVEL TOO LOW ON BUS

NOTE: For connector terminal identification, see CONNECTOR IDENTIFICATION in BODY CONTROL COMPUTER INTRODUCTION article. For wiring diagrams, see appropriate WIRING DIAGRAMS article.

NOTE: A common cause of this failure is ignition switch in OFF position.

1) If ignition switch was in OFF position when performing TEST 7A, turn ignition switch to ON position with engine off. Perform VERIFICATION TEST. If ignition switch was not in OFF position when performing TEST 7A, check if battery is fully charged. If battery is not fully charged, charge battery. Perform VERIFICATION TEST.

2) If battery is fully charged, disconnect DRB-II. Using an external voltmeter, check voltage at terminal No. 1 (Violet/Brown wire) at CCD bus diagnostic connector. If voltage is not 2.1-2.7 volts, go to step 4).

3) If voltage is 2.1-2.7 volts, check voltage at terminal No. 6 (White/Black wire) at CCD bus diagnostic connector. If voltage is not 2.1-2.7 volts, perform TEST 13B. If voltage is 2.1-2.7 volts, test DRB-II. Refer to TEST 5A. Perform VERIFICATION TEST.

4) If voltage at Violet/Brown wire is not 2.1-2.7 volts in step 2), turn ignition switch to OFF position. Disconnect body controller Blue connector. Body controller is located under left side of instrument panel. Check connector, and clean or repair connector as necessary. Using an external ohmmeter, check resistance between terminals No. 7 and 20 at body controller.

5) If resistance is not 100-140 ohms, replace body controller. Perform VERIFICATION TEST. If resistance is 100-140 ohms, check resistance at Violet/Brown wire between terminal No. 1 at CCD bus diagnostic connector and terminal No. 7 at body controller Blue connector. If resistance is more than 5 ohms, repair open Violet/Brown. Perform VERIFICATION TEST. If resistance is less that 5 ohms, go to next step.

6) Disconnect Single Board Engine Controller (SBEC) connector. Check connector, and clean or repair connector as necessary. Check resistance between terminals No. 26 and 46 of SBEC. If resistance is not 100-140 ohms, replace SBEC. Perform VERIFICATION TEST.

7) If resistance is 100-140 ohms, check resistance at Violet/Brown wire between terminal No. 1 at CCD bus diagnostic connector and terminal No. 26 at SBEC connector. If resistance is more than 5 ohms, perform TEST 20A. If resistance is less than 5 ohms, repair open Violet/Brown wire. Perform VERIFICATION TEST.

TEST 13B

BUS BIAS LEVEL TOO LOW ON BUS

NOTE: For connector terminal identification, see CONNECTOR IDENTIFICATION in BODY CONTROL COMPUTER INTRODUCTION article. For wiring diagrams, see appropriate WIRING DIAGRAMS article.

1) Turn ignition switch to OFF position. Disconnect body controller Blue connector. Body controller is located under left side of instrument panel. Check connector, and clean or repair connector as necessary. Using an external ohmmeter, check resistance between terminals No. 7 and 20 of body controller. If resistance is not 100-140 ohms, replace body controller. Perform VERIFICATION TEST.

2) If resistance is 100-140 ohms, check resistance at White/Black wire between terminal No. 6 at CCD bus diagnostic connector and terminal No. 20 at body controller Blue connector. If resistance is more than 5 ohms, repair open White/Black wire. Perform VERIFICATION TEST. If resistance is less than 5 ohms, go to next step.

3) Disconnect Single Board Engine Controller (SBEC) connector. Check connector, and clean or repair connector as necessary. Using an external ohmmeter, check resistance between terminals No. 26 and 46 at SBEC. If resistance is not 100-140 ohms, replace SBEC. Perform VERIFICATION TEST.

4) If resistance is 100-140 ohms, check resistance at White/Black wire between terminal No. 6 at CCD bus diagnostic connector and terminal No. 46 at SBEC connector. If resistance is more than 5 ohms, repair open White/Black wire. Perform VERIFICATION TEST. If resistance is less than 5 ohms, perform TEST 20A.

TEST 14A

BUS BIAS LEVEL TOO HIGH ON BUS

**NOTE: For connector terminal identification, see CONNECTOR IDEN-
TIFICATION in BODY CONTROL COMPUTER INTRODUCTION article.
For wiring diagrams, see appropriate WIRING DIAGRAMS article.**

1) Turn ignition switch to ON position with engine off. Disconnect DRB-
II. Using an external voltmeter, check voltage at terminal No. 1 (Violet/
Brown wire) of CCD bus diagnostic connector. If voltage is not 2.1-2.7
volts, go to step **3)**.

2) If voltage is 2.1-2.7 volts, check voltage at terminal No. 6 (White/Black
wire) at CCD bus diagnostic connector. If voltage is not 2.1-2.7 volts, perform TEST 14B. If voltage is 2.1-2.7 volts, test DRB-II. Perform TEST 5A.
Perform VERIFICATION TEST.

3) If voltage at Violet/Brown wire is not 2.1-2.7 volts in step **1)**, turn ignition switch to OFF position. Disconnect body controller Blue connector.
Body controller is located under left side of instrument panel. Check connector, and clean or repair connector as necessary.

4) Using an external ohmmeter, check resistance between terminals No.
7 and 20 at body controller. If resistance is not 100-140 ohms, replace
body controller. Perform VERIFICATION TEST. If resistance is 100-140
ohms, go to next step.

5) Check resistance at Violet/Brown wire between terminal No. 1 at CCD
bus diagnostic connector and terminal No. 7 at body controller connector. If resistance is more than 5 ohms, repair open Violet/Brown wire.
Perform VERIFICATION TEST. If resistance is less than 5 ohms, go to
next step.

6) Disconnect Single Board Engine Controller (SBEC) connector. Check
connector, and clean or repair connector as necessary. Check resistance between terminals No. 26 and 46 of SBEC. If resistance is not 100-
140 ohms, replace SBEC. Perform VERIFICATION TEST.

7) If resistance is 100-140 ohms, check resistance at Violet/Brown wire
between terminal No. 1 at CCD bus diagnostic connector and terminal
No. 26 at SBEC connector. If resistance is more than 5 ohms, perform
TEST 20A. If resistance is less than 5 ohms, repair open Violet/Brown
wire. Perform VERIFICATION TEST.

TEST 14B

BUS BIAS LEVEL TOO HIGH ON BUS

**NOTE: For connector terminal identification, see CONNECTOR IDEN-
TIFICATION in BODY CONTROL COMPUTER INTRODUCTION article.
For wiring diagrams, see appropriate WIRING DIAGRAMS article.**

1) Turn ignition switch to OFF position. Disconnect body controller Blue
connector. Body controller is located under left side of instrument panel.
Check connector, and clean or repair connector as necessary. Using an
external ohmmeter, check resistance between terminals No. 7 and 20 at
body controller.

2) If resistance is not 100-140 ohms, replace body controller. Perform
VERIFICATION TEST. If resistance is 100-140 ohms, check resistance
at White/Black wire between terminal No. 6 at CCD bus diagnostic connector and terminal No. 20 at body controller Blue connector. If
resistance is more than 5 ohms, repair open White/Black wire. Perform
VERIFICATION TEST. If resistance is less than 5 ohms, go to next step.

3) Disconnect Single Board Engine Controller (SBEC) connector. Check
connector condition and clean or repair connector as necessary. Using
an external ohmmeter, check resistance between terminals No. 26 and
46 at SBEC. If resistance is not 100-140 ohms, replace SBEC. Perform
VERIFICATION TEST.

4) If resistance is 100-140 ohms, check resistance at White/Black wire
between terminal No. 6 at CCD bus diagnostic connector and terminal
No. 46 at SBEC connector. If resistance is more than 5 ohms, repair
open White/Black wire. Perform VERIFICATION TEST. If resistance is
less than 5 ohms, perform TEST 20A.

TEST 15A

NO BUS BIAS ON BUS

**NOTE: For connector terminal identification, see CONNECTOR IDEN-
TIFICATION in BODY CONTROL COMPUTER INTRODUCTION article.
For wiring diagrams, see appropriate WIRING DIAGRAMS article.**

TEST 15A (Cont.)

1) If DRB-II is not connected to correct diagnostic connector, connect
DRB-II to CCD bus diagnostic connector. Perform VERIFICATION TEST.
If DRB-II is connected to CCD bus diagnostic connector, turn ignition
switch to OFF position. Disconnect body controller Blue connector.
Body controller is located under left side of instrument panel. Check con-
nector, and clean or repair connector as necessary.

2) Using external ohmmeter, check resistance between terminals No. 7
and 20 at body controller. If resistance is not 100-140 ohms, replace
body controller. Perform VERIFICATION TEST. If resistance is 100-140
ohms, go to next step.

3) Check resistance at Violet/Brown wire between terminal No. 1 at CCD
bus diagnostic connector and terminal No. 7 at body controller Blue connector. If resistance is more than 5 ohms, repair open Violet/Brown wire
and go to next step. If resistance is less than 5 ohms, go to next step.

4) Check resistance of White/Black wire between terminal No. 6 at CCD
bus diagnostic connector and terminal No. 20 at body controller Blue
connector. If resistance is more than 5 ohms, repair open White/Black
wire. Perform VERIFICATION TEST. If resistance is less than 5 ohms, go
to next step.

5) Disconnect Single Board Engine Controller (SBEC) connector. Check
connector, and repair or replace connector as necessary. Using an
external ohmmeter, check resistance between terminals No. 26 and 46
at SBEC.

6) If resistance is not 100-140 ohms, replace SBEC. Perform VERIFICA-
TION TEST. If resistance is 100-140 ohms, check resistance at Violet/
Brown wire between terminal No. 1 at CCD bus diagnostic connector
and terminal No. 26 at SBEC connector. If resistance is more than 5
ohms, repair open Violet/Brown wire and go to next step. If resistance
is less than 5 ohms, go to next step.

7) Check resistance at White/Black wire between terminal No. 6 at CCD
bus diagnostic connector and terminal No. 46 at SBEC connector. If
resistance is more than 5 ohms, repair open White/Black wire. Perform
VERIFICATION TEST. If resistance is less than 5 ohms, test DRB-II. Refer to TEST 5A.

8) Replace DRB-II and/or adapter cable as necessary. Perform VERIFI-
CATION TEST. If DRB-II and adapter cable are good, perform TEST
20A.

TEST 16A

BUS (+) OPEN ON BUS

**NOTE: For connector terminal identification, see CONNECTOR IDEN-
TIFICATION in BODY CONTROL COMPUTER INTRODUCTION article.
For wiring diagrams, see appropriate WIRING DIAGRAMS article.**

1) If DRB-II is not connected to correct diagnostic connector, connect
DRB-II to CCD bus diagnostic connector. Perform VERIFICATION TEST.
If DRB-II is connected to CCD bus diagnostic connector, turn ignition
switch to OFF position. Disconnect body controller Blue connector.
Body controller is located under left side of instrument panel. Check con-
nector, and clean or repair connector as necessary.

2) Using external ohmmeter, check resistance between terminals No. 7
and 20 at body controller. If resistance is not 100-140 ohms, replace
body controller. Perform VERIFICATION TEST. If resistance is 100-140
ohms, check resistance at Violet/Brown wire between terminal No. 1 at
CCD bus diagnostic connector and terminal No. 7 at body controller Blue
connector. If resistance is more than 5 ohms, repair open Violet/Brown
wire and go to next step. If resistance is less than 5 ohms, go to next
step.

3) Using an external ohmmeter, check resistance of Violet/Black wire
between terminals No. 7 of body controller Blue connector and No. 1 of
CCD bus diagnostic connector. If resistance is more than 5 ohms, repair
open Violet/Black wire and go to next step. If resistance is less than 5
ohms, go to next step.

4) Check resistance of White/Black wire between terminals No. 6 at CCD
bus diagnostic connector and No. 20 at body controller Blue connector.
If resistance is more than 5 ohms, repair open White/Black wire. Perform
VERIFICATION TEST. If resistance is less than 5 ohms, go to next step.

5) Disconnect Single Board Engine Controller (SBEC) connector. Check
connector, and clean or repair connector as necessary. Using an external ohmmeter, check resistance between terminals No. 26 and 46 at
SBEC.

TEST 16A (Cont.)

6) If resistance is not 100-140 ohms, replace SBEC. Perform VERIFICATION TEST. If resistance is 100-140 ohms, check resistance at Violet/Brown wire between terminal No. 1 at CCD bus diagnostic connector and terminal No. 26 at SBEC connector. If resistance is more than 5 ohms, repair open Violet/Brown wire and go to next step. If resistance is less than 5 ohms, go to next step.

7) Check resistance at White/Black wire between terminals No. 6 at CCD bus diagnostic connector and No. 46 at SBEC connector. If resistance is more than 5 ohms, repair open White/Black wire. Perform VERIFICATION TEST. If resistance is less than 5 ohms, test DRB-II. Refer to TEST 5A.

8) If DRB-II and/or adapter cable is defective, replace DRB-II or adapter cable as necessary. Perform VERIFICATION TEST. If DRB-II and adapter cable are good, perform TEST 20A.

TEST 17A

BUS (-) OPEN ON BUS

NOTE: For connector terminal identification, see CONNECTOR IDENTIFICATION in BODY CONTROL COMPUTER INTRODUCTION article. For wiring diagrams, see appropriate WIRING DIAGRAMS article.

1) If DRB-II is not connected to correct diagnostic connector, connect DRB-II to CCD bus diagnostic connector. Perform VERIFICATION TEST. If DRB-II is connected to CCD bus diagnostic connector, turn ignition switch to OFF position. Disconnect body controller Blue connector. Body controller is located under left side of instrument panel. Check connector, and clean or repair connector as necessary.

2) Using external ohmmeter, check resistance between terminals No. 7 and 20 at body controller. If resistance is not 100-140 ohms, replace body controller. Perform VERIFICATION TEST. If resistance is 100-140 ohms, check resistance at Violet/Brown wire between terminals No. 1 at CCD bus diagnostic connector and No. 7 at body controller Blue connector. If resistance is more than 5 ohms, repair open Violet/Brown wire and go to next step. If resistance is less than 5 ohms, go to next step.

3) Check resistance of White/Black wire between terminals No. 6 at CCD bus diagnostic connector and No. 20 at body controller Blue connector. If resistance is more than 5 ohms, repair open White/Black wire. Perform VERIFICATION TEST. If resistance is less than 5 ohms, go to next step.

4) Disconnect Single Board Engine Controller (SBEC) connector. Check connector condition and clean or repair connector as necessary. Using external ohmmeter, check resistance between terminals No. 26 and 46 at SBEC. If resistance is not 100-140 ohms, replace SBEC. Perform VERIFICATION TEST. If resistance is 100-140 ohms, go to next step.

5) Check resistance at Violet/Brown wire between terminal No. 1 at CCD bus diagnostic connector and terminal No. 26 at SBEC connector. If resistance is more than 5 ohms, repair open Violet/Brown wire and go to next step. If resistance is less than 5 ohms, go to next step.

6) Check resistance at White/Black wire between terminal No. 6 at CCD bus diagnostic connector and terminal No. 46 at SBEC connector. If resistance is more than 5 ohms, repair open White/Black wire. Perform VERIFICATION TEST. If resistance is less than 5 ohms, test DRB-II. Refer to TEST 5A.

7) Replace DRB-II and/or adapter cable as necessary. Perform VERIFICATION TEST. If DRB-II and adapter cable are good, perform TEST 20A.

TEST 18A

BUS (+) & BUS (-) OPEN ON BUS

NOTE: For connector terminal identification, see CONNECTOR IDENTIFICATION in BODY CONTROL COMPUTER INTRODUCTION article. For wiring diagrams, see appropriate WIRING DIAGRAMS article.

1) If DRB-II is not connected to correct diagnostic connector, connect DRB-II to CCD bus diagnostic connector. Perform VERIFICATION TEST. If DRB-II is connected to CCD bus diagnostic connector, turn ignition switch to OFF position. Disconnect body controller Blue connector. Body controller is located under left side of instrument panel. Check connector, and clean or repair connector as necessary.

TEST 18A (Cont.)

2) Using external ohmmeter, check resistance between terminals No. 7 and 20 at body controller. If resistance is not 100-140 ohms, replace body controller. Perform VERIFICATION TEST. If resistance is 100-140 ohms, check resistance at Violet/Brown wire between terminals No. 1 at CCD bus diagnostic connector and No. 7 at body controller Blue connector. If resistance is more than 5 ohms, repair open Violet/Brown wire and go to next step. If resistance is less than 5 ohms, go to next step.

3) Check resistance of White/Black wire between terminals No. 6 at CCD bus diagnostic connector and No. 20 at body controller Blue connector. If resistance is more than 5 ohms, repair open White/Black wire. Perform VERIFICATION TEST. If resistance is less than 5 ohms, go to next step.

4) Disconnect Single Board Engine Controller (SBEC) connector. Check connector, and clean or repair connector as necessary. Using an external ohmmeter, check resistance between terminals No. 26 and 46 at SBEC. If resistance is not 100-140 ohms, replace SBEC. Perform VERIFICATION TEST. If resistance is 100-140 ohms, go to next step.

5) Check resistance at Violet/Brown wire between terminal No. 1 at CCD bus diagnostic connector and terminal No. 26 at SBEC connector. If resistance is more than 5 ohms, repair open Violet/Brown wire and go to next step. If resistance is less than 5 ohms, go to next step.

6) Check resistance at White/Black wire between terminal No. 6 at CCD bus diagnostic connector and terminal No. 46 at SBEC connector. If resistance is more than 5 ohms, repair open White/Black wire. Perform VERIFICATION TEST. If resistance is less than 5 ohms, test DRB-II. Refer to TEST 5A.

7) Replace DRB-II and/or adapter cable as necessary. Perform VERIFICATION TEST. If DRB-II and adapter cable are good, perform TEST 20A.

TEST 19A

NOT RECEIVING BUS MESSAGES CORRECTLY ON BUS

NOTE: For connector terminal identification, see CONNECTOR IDENTIFICATION in BODY CONTROL COMPUTER INTRODUCTION article. For wiring diagrams, see appropriate WIRING DIAGRAMS article.

1) If DRB-II is not connected to correct diagnostic connector, connect DRB-II to CCD bus diagnostic connector. Perform VERIFICATION TEST. If DRB-II is connected to CCD bus diagnostic connector, turn ignition switch to OFF position. Disconnect instrument cluster connector. Check connector, and clean or repair connector as necessary.

2) Using an external ohmmeter, check resistance of White/Black wire between terminals No. 6 of CCD bus diagnostic connector and No. 9 at instrument cluster connector. If resistance more than 5 ohms, repair open White/Black wire. Perform VERIFICATION TEST.

3) If resistance is less than less 5 ohms, reconnect instrument cluster connector. Turn ignition switch to ON position. If DRB-II displays NOT RECEIVING BUS MESSAGES CORRECTLY, replace instrument cluster. Perform VERIFICATION TEST. If DRB-II does not display NOT RECEIVING BUS MESSAGES CORRECTLY, perform TEST 20A.

TEST 20A

NO RESPONSE MESSAGES

NOTE: For connector terminal identification, see CONNECTOR IDENTIFICATION in BODY CONTROL COMPUTER INTRODUCTION article. For wiring diagrams, see appropriate WIRING DIAGRAMS article.

Three ways exist to get to this test:
1) DRB-II is currently connected to CCD bus diagnostic connector and you have selected ENGINE from main menu. Perform VERIFICATION TEST.
2) A self-diagnostic test brought you here.
3) DRB-II displayed NO RESPONSE message when an attempt was made to read information from a module. Perform VERIFICATION TEST.

NOTE: Monitoring SBEC for an ACTIVE ON BUS message is only possible at CCD bus diagnostics connector. Monitor SBEC for a NO RESPONSE message by selecting SYSTEM TEST under any module test selection menu.

TEST 20A (Cont.)

If step **1)** is reason you came to this test, select either an appropriate selection from DRB-II menu (BODY, ABS OR TRANSMISSION) or, if you want to perform engine tests, connect DRB-II to engine diagnostic connector located in engine compartment.

If step **2)** is reason you came to this test, verify all modules on vehicle are accessible. Perform tests as necessary. See NO RESPONSE MESSAGE table.

NO RESPONSE MESSAGE

Module	Test No.
Body Controller	23A
Compass/Mini-Trip Module	22A
Electronic Instrument Cluster	21A
Single Board Engine Controller	24A

If step **3)** is reason you came to this test, perform test as necessary in order that they appear. See NO RESPONSE MESSAGE table. DRB-II will also show a NO RESPONSE message if you try to access a module that is not on vehicle.

TEST 21A

TESTING ELECTRONIC INSTRUMENT CLUSTER FOR NO RESPONSE

NOTE: For connector terminal identification, see CONNECTOR IDENTIFICATION in BODY CONTROL COMPUTER INTRODUCTION article. For wiring diagrams, see appropriate WIRING DIAGRAMS article.

1) Turn ignition switch to OFF position. Disconnect electronic instrument cluster connector. Check connector, and clean or repair connector as necessary. Disconnect DRB-II. Using an external ohmmeter, check resistance of Violet/Brown wire between terminal No. 1 at CCD bus diagnostic connector and terminal No 10 at instrument cluster connector.

2) If resistance is more than 5 ohms, repair open Violet/Brown wire. Perform VERIFICATION TEST. If resistance is less than 5 ohms, check resistance at White/Black wire between terminal No. 6 at CCD bus diagnostic connector and terminal No. 9 at instrument cluster connector. If resistance is more than 5 ohms, repair open White/Black wire. Perform VERIFICATION TEST.

3) If resistance is less than 5 ohms, reconnect DRB-II. Put DRB-II in ohmmeter mode. Probe terminal No. 7 (Black/Light Green wire) at instrument cluster connector. If resistance is more than 5 ohms, repair open Black/Light Green wire. Perform VERIFICATION TEST.

4) If resistance is less than 5 ohms, turn ignition switch to ON position. Put DRB-II in voltmeter mode. Probe terminal No. 11 (Dark Blue/White wire) at instrument cluster connector. If voltage is more than 10 volts, perform TEST 21B.

5) If voltage is less than 10 volts, remove and inspect fuse No. 15 from fuse block. If fuse is blown, go to next step. If fuse is okay, probe input terminal to fuse No. 15 (Dark Blue wire) in fuse block. If voltage is more than 10 volts, repair open Dark Blue/White wire between fuse block and instrument cluster connector. Perform VERIFICATION TEST. If voltage is less than 10 volts, repair open Dark Blue wire to fuse block. Perform VERIFICATION TEST.

6) Turn ignition switch to OFF position. Replace fuse No. 15. Disconnect body controller Blue connector. Body controller is located under left side of instrument panel. Check connector condition and clean or repair connector as necessary. Disconnect warning indicator module connector. Module is located above instrument cluster. Check connector, and clean or repair connector as necessary.

7) Turn ignition switch to ON position. Remove and inspect fuse No. 15. If fuse is blown, repair short to ground in Dark Blue/White wire. After repair is completed, perform TEST 21B. If fuse is okay, turn ignition switch to OFF position. Reconnect warning indicator module connector. Turn ignition switch to ON position.

8) Remove and recheck fuse No. 15. If fuse is blown, replace warning indicator module. After repair is completed, perform TEST 21B. If fuse is okay, turn ignition switch to OFF position. Reconnect instrument cluster connector. Turn ignition switch to ON position. Remove and recheck fuse No. 15. If fuse is blown, replace instrument cluster. After repair is completed, perform TEST 21B. If fuse is okay, turn ignition switch to OFF position.

TEST 21A (Cont.)

9) Reconnect body controller Blue connector. Turn ignition switch to ON position. Remove and recheck fuse No. 15. If fuse is blown, replace body controller. After repair is completed, perform TEST 21B. If fuse is okay, perform TEST 21B.

TEST 21B

TESTING ELECTRONIC INSTRUMENT CLUSTER FOR NO RESPONSE

NOTE: For connector terminal identification, see CONNECTOR IDENTIFICATION in BODY CONTROL COMPUTER INTRODUCTION article. For wiring diagrams, see appropriate WIRING DIAGRAMS article.

1) Probe terminal No. 2 (Pink wire) of instrument cluster connector. If voltage is more than 10 volts, replace instrument cluster (if not already replaced). Perform VERIFICATION TEST. If voltage is less than 10 volts, replace and inspect fuse No. 3 from fuse block. If fuse is blown, go to step **3)**.

2) If fuse is okay, probe output terminal (in fuse block) from fuse No. 3. If voltage is more than 10 volts, repair open Pink wire between fuse block and instrument cluster connector. Perform VERIFICATION TEST. If voltage is less than 10 volts, repair open Black/Red wire to fuse block. Perform VERIFICATION TEST.

NOTE: Ensure trunk, hood and all doors are closed. Tape glove box light switch closed or disconnect switch.

3) If fuse No. 3 is blown in step **1)**, put DRB-II in ohmmeter mode. Probe output terminal (in fuse block) from fuse No. 3. If resistance is more than 5 ohms, go to step **5)**. If resistance is less than 5 ohms, disconnect body controller Blue connector. Body controller is located under left side of instrument panel. Check connector, and clean or repair connector as necessary.

4) Reprobe output terminal from fuse No. 13. If resistance is more than 5 ohms, replace body controller. Perform VERIFICATION TEST. If resistance is less than 5 ohms, repair short to ground in fuse No. 3 output circuit. Perform VERIFICATION TEST.

5) If resistance is more than 5 ohms at fuse No. 3 output terminal in step **3)**, reconnect electronic instrument cluster connector. Probe output terminal (in fuse block) from fuse No. 3. If resistance is more than 5 ohms, replace fuse No. 3. Perform VERIFICATION TEST. If resistance is less than 5 ohms, replace instrument cluster. Perform VERIFICATION TEST.

TEST 22A

TESTING COMPASS/MINI-TRIP MODULE FOR NO RESPONSE

NOTE: For connector terminal identification, see CONNECTOR IDENTIFICATION in BODY CONTROL COMPUTER INTRODUCTION article. For wiring diagrams, see appropriate WIRING DIAGRAMS article.

1) Turn ignition switch to OFF position. Disconnect compass/mini-trip module connector. Connector is located behind overhead console. Check connector, and clean or repair connector as necessary. Disconnect DRB-II. Using an external ohmmeter, check resistance at Violet/Brown wire between terminals No. 1 at CCD bus diagnostic connector and No. 9 at compass/mini-trip module connector.

2) If resistance is more than 5 ohms, repair open Violet/Brown wire. Perform VERIFICATION TEST. If resistance is less than 5 ohms, check resistance at White/Black wire between terminals No. 6 at CCD bus diagnostic connector and No. 11 at compass/mini-trip module connector.

3) If resistance is more than 5 ohms, repair open White/Black wire. Perform VERIFICATION TEST. If resistance is less than 5 ohms, reconnect DRB-II. Put DRB-II in voltmeter mode. Turn ignition switch to ON position. Probe terminal No. 7 (Tan wire) at compass/mini-trip module connector. If voltage is more than 10 volts, replace compass/temperature module. Perform VERIFICATION TEST.

4) If voltage is less than 10 volts, remove circuit breaker No. 25 from fuse block. Using an external ohmmeter, check resistance of circuit breaker. If resistance is less than 5 ohms, go to step **7)**. If resistance is more than 5 ohms, put DRB-II in ohmmeter mode.

TEST 22A (Cont.)

5) Probe output terminal (in fuse block) from circuit breaker No. 25. If resistance is less than 5 ohms, repair short to ground in Tan wire and replace circuit breaker No. 25. Perform VERIFICATION TEST. If resistance is more than 5 ohms, reconnect compass/mini-trip module connector.

6) Probe output terminal (in fuse block) from circuit breaker No. 25. If resistance is less than 5 ohms, replace compass/mini-trip module and circuit breaker No. 25. Perform VERIFICATION TEST. If resistance is more than 5 ohms, replace circuit breaker No. 25. Perform VERIFICATION TEST.

7) If resistance is less than 5 ohms in step **4)**, probe input terminal (in fuse block) to circuit breaker No. 25. If voltage is less than 10 volts, repair open in wire between fuse block and compass/mini-trip module connector. Perform VERIFICATION TEST. If voltage is more than 10 volts, repair open in Black/White wire to fuse block. Perform VERIFICATION TEST.

TEST 23A

TESTING BODY CONTROLLER FOR NO RESPONSE

NOTE: For connector terminal identification, see CONNECTOR IDENTIFICATION in BODY CONTROL COMPUTER INTRODUCTION article. For wiring diagrams, see appropriate WIRING DIAGRAMS article.

1) Turn ignition switch to OFF position. Disconnect body controller Blue connector. Body controller is located under left side of instrument panel. Check connector, and clean or repair connector as necessary. Using an external ohmmeter, check resistance of Violet/Brown wire between terminals No. 1 at CCD bus diagnostic connector and No. 7 at body controller Blue connector.

2) If resistance is more than 5 ohms, repair open Violet/Brown wire. Perform VERIFICATION TEST. If resistance is less than 5 ohms, check resistance at White/Black wire between terminals No. 6 at CCD bus diagnostic connector and No. 20 at body controller Blue connector.

3) If resistance is more than 5 ohms, repair open White/Black wire. Perform VERIFICATION TEST. If resistance is less than 5 ohms, Reconnect DRB-II. Put DRB-II in ohmmeter mode. Probe terminal No. 19 (Black/Light Green wire) at body controller Blue connector.

4) If resistance is more than 5 ohms, repair open Black/Light Green wire. Perform VERIFICATION TEST. If resistance is less than 5 ohms, put DRB-II in voltmeter mode. Turn ignition switch to ON position. Probe terminal No. 6 (Dark Blue/White wire) at body controller Blue connector.

5) If voltage is more than 10 volts, perform TEST 23B. If voltage is less than 10 volts, remove and inspect fuse No. 15 from fuse block. If fuse is blown, go to next step. If fuse is okay, probe voltage input terminal to fuse No. 15. If voltage is more than 10 volts, repair open Dark Blue/White wire between fuse block and body controller Blue connector. After repair, perform TEST 23B.

6) Turn ignition switch to OFF position. Disconnect instrument cluster connector. Check connector condition and clean or repair as necessary. Disconnect warning indicator module connector. Warning module is located above instrument cluster. Turn ignition switch to ON position.

7) Remove and recheck fuse No. 15. If fuse is blown repair short to ground in Dark Blue/White wire. After repair is completed, perform TEST 23B. If fuse is okay, turn ignition switch to OFF position. Reconnect warning indictor module connector. Turn ignition switch to ON position. Remove and recheck fuse No. 15. If use is blown, replace body controller. After repair is completed, perform TEST 23B. If fuse is okay, perform TEST 23B.

TEST 23B

TESTING BODY CONTROLLER FOR NO RESPONSE

NOTE: For connector terminal identification, see CONNECTOR IDENTIFICATION in BODY CONTROL COMPUTER INTRODUCTION article. For wiring diagrams, see appropriate WIRING DIAGRAMS article.

TEST 23B (Cont.)

1) Probe terminal No. 8 (Pink wire) of body controller Blue connector. If voltage is more than 10 volts, replace body controller (if not already replaced). Perform VERIFICATION TEST. If voltage is less than 10 volts, remove and inspect fuse No. 3 from fuse block.

2) If fuse is blown, go to next step. If fuse is okay, probe output terminal (at fuse block) from fuse No. 3. If voltage is more than 10 volts, repair open Pink wire between fuse block and body controller Blue connector. Perform VERIFICATION TEST. If voltage is less than 10 volts, repair open Black/Red wire to fuse block. Perform VERIFICATION TEST.

NOTE: Ensure, trunk, hood and all doors are closed. Tape glove box light switch closed or disconnect switch.

3) Put DRB-II in ohmmeter mode. Probe output terminal (in fuse block) from fuse No. 3. If resistance is more than 5 ohms, go to step **5)**. If resistance is less than 5 ohms, disconnect instrument cluster connector. Check connector, and clean or repair connector as necessary.

4) Reprobe output terminal from fuse No. 13. If resistance is more than 5 ohms, replace instrument cluster. Perform VERIFICATION TEST. If resistance is less than 5 ohms, repair short to ground in fuse No. 3 output circuit. Perform VERIFICATION TEST.

5) If more than 5 ohms exist at fuse No. 3 output terminal in step **3)**, reconnect body controller Blue connector. Probe output terminal (in fuse block) from fuse No. 3. If resistance is more than 5 ohms, replace fuse No. 3. Perform VERIFICATION TEST. If resistance is less than 5 ohms, replace body controller. Perform VERIFICATION TEST.

TEST 24A

TESTING SINGLE BOARD ENGINE CONTROLLER (SBEC) FOR NO RESPONSE

NOTE: For connector terminal identification, see CONNECTOR IDENTIFICATION in BODY CONTROL COMPUTER INTRODUCTION article. For wiring diagrams, see appropriate WIRING DIAGRAMS article.

1) Disconnect SBEC connector. Check connector condition and clean or repair connector as necessary. Using an external ohmmeter, check resistance between terminals No. 26 and 46 at SBEC. If resistance is not 100-140 ohms, replace SBEC. Perform VERIFICATION TEST.

2) If resistance is 100-140 ohms, check resistance at Violet/Brown wire between terminal No. 1 at CCD bus diagnostic connector and terminal No. 26 at SBEC connector. If resistance is more than 5 ohms, repair open Violet/Brown wire. Perform VERIFICATION TEST.

3) If resistance is less than 5 ohms, check resistance at White/Black wire between terminal No. 6 at CCD bus diagnostic connector and terminal No. 46 at SBEC connector. If resistance is more than 5 ohms, repair open White/Black wire. Perform VERIFICATION TEST. If resistance is less than 5 ohms, replace SBEC. Perform VERIFICATION TEST.

VERIFICATION TEST

1) Reconnect all components and connectors that have been disconnected. Connect DRB-II if it is not already disconnected. Turn ignition switch to ON position with engine off. If DRB-II display is blank, perform TEST 1A.

2) If DRB-II displays a bus failure message, perform bus failure message test. See TEST 7A. If DRB-II displays NO RESPONSE for any vehicle equipped module, perform NO RESPONSE test. See TEST 20A.

3) If DRB-II does not display NO RESPONSE for any vehicle equipped module, check vehicle for original customer complaint. If original complaint is present, retest system. If original complaint is not present, repair is complete.

**Caravan, Dakota, Pickup, Ramcharger
RWD Van, Town & Country, Voyager**

WARNING: When battery is disconnected, vehicle computer and memory systems may lose memory data. Driveability problems may exist until computer systems have completed a relearn cycle. See COMPUTER RELEARN PROCEDURES article in GENERAL INFORMATION before disconnecting battery.

INTRODUCTION

Before diagnosing symptoms or intermittent faults, perform steps in appropriate BASIC DIAGNOSTIC PROCEDURES and SELF-DIAGNOSTICS (if applicable) articles. Use this article to diagnose driveability problems that exist when a hard fault code is not present.

NOTE: Some driveability problems may have been corrected by manufacturer with a revised computer calibration chip or control unit. Check with manufacturer for latest chip or control unit application.

Symptom checks can direct the technician to malfunctioning components for further diagnosis. A symptom should lead to a specific component, system test or adjustment specification.

Use intermittent test procedures to locate driveability problems that do not occur while the vehicle is tested. These problems may noticeably affect driveability or cause CHECK ENGINE light to glow. Also use these test procedures if a soft (intermittent) trouble code was present but no problem is found during self-diagnostic testing.

NOTE: For specific testing procedures, see appropriate SYSTEM & COMPONENT TESTING article. For specifications, see appropriate ON-VEHICLE ADJUSTMENTS or SERVICE & ADJUSTMENT SPECIFICATIONS article.

SYMPTOMS

SYMPTOM DIAGNOSIS

Symptom checks cannot be used properly unless problem occurs while vehicle is tested. To reduce diagnostic time, verify customer's complaint, ensure steps in appropriate BASIC DIAGNOSTIC PROCEDURES and SELF-DIAGNOSTICS (if applicable) articles are performed and visually inspect all systems before diagnosing a symptom. Symptoms available for diagnosis include the following.

- No Start – Cold Engine
- No Start – Warm Engine
- Starts But Stalls
- Hard To Start – Cold Engine
- Erratic Idle – Warm-Up
- Engine Surges
- Backfiring
- Incorrect Idle Speed
- Hesitation – Acceleration
- Hesitation – Coasting
- Knocking
- Engine Misfire – All Conditions
- Insufficient Engine Power
- Poor Fuel Economy
- Excessive HC & NOx

NO START – COLD ENGINE

- Ensure battery is fully charged.
- Check for contaminated fuel.
- Check spark plugs.
- Check fuel pump fuse(s).
- Check in-line fuse to control unit (if applicable).
- Ensure ignition timing and fuel pressure are correct.
- Check fuel injectors.
- Ensure timing belt is not broken (if applicable).
- Ensure ignition coil resistance is correct.

- Ensure rotor, distributor and spark plug wires are okay.
- Check ignition control unit.
- Check coolant temperature sensor and connector.
- Check throttle switch and connector (if applicable).
- Check engine speed sensor.
- Check airflow sensor.

NO START – WARM ENGINE

- Ensure fuel pressure is correct.
- Check for gasoline in oil.
- Ensure fuel injectors are not leaking.
- Check ignition and sensor wires for proper connection.
- Ensure spark plugs are not fouled.
- Check ignition and coil circuit.
- Check engine speed sensor.
- Check throttle switch and connector (if applicable).

STARTS BUT STALLS

- Check coolant temperature sensor.
- Check ignition and sensor wires for proper connection.
- Check fuel injectors.
- Check throttle switch and connector (if applicable).
- Check engine speed sensor.

HARD TO START – COLD ENGINE

- Check spark plugs.
- Check distributor (if applicable).
- Ensure fuel pressure is correct.
- Check ignition timing.
- Check throttle switch and connector (if applicable).

ERRATIC IDLE – WARM-UP

- Check throttle switch and connection (if applicable).
- Check coolant temperature sensor and connection.
- Check air temperature sensor (if applicable).
- Ensure spark plugs are not fouled.
- Check ignition and sensor wires for proper connection.
- Check distributor (if applicable).
- Check ignition and coil circuit.
- Check intake system.
- Check engine speed sensor.
- Check throttle switch and connector (if applicable).
- Check MAP sensor (if applicable).

ENGINE SURGES

- Check ignition and fuel system.
- Check for vacuum leaks.
- Check EGR system.

BACKFIRING

- Ensure ignition timing is correct.
- Ensure timing belt/chain has not jumped.
- Check distributor (if applicable).
- Check for gasoline in oil.
- Ensure fuel injectors are not leaking.
- Check spark plugs.
- Check ignition and coil circuit.
- Check engine speed sensor.
- Check throttle switch and connector.
- Check exhaust system.

INCORRECT IDLE SPEED

- Check fuel injectors.
- Check intake system for leaks.
- Check coolant temperature sensor.
- Check throttle switch and connector (if applicable).
- Check distributor (if applicable).

1992 ENGINE PERFORMANCE
Trouble Shooting – No Codes – Gasoline (Cont.)

HESITATION – ACCELERATION
- Check ignition and sensor wires for proper connection.
- Check distributor cap for moisture and carbon tracking.
- Ensure spark plug wires are okay.
- Ensure spark plugs are not fouled.
- Check MAP sensor (if applicable).
- Check throttle switch and connector (if applicable).
- Check ignition and coil circuit.
- Check engine speed sensor.

HESITATION – COASTING
- Check fuel injectors.
- Check ignition and sensor wires for proper connection.
- Check throttle switch and connector.
- Check engine speed sensor.
- Check for gasoline in oil.

KNOCKING
- Check ignition and coil circuit.
- Check for defect in throttle body power system.
- Check for restrictions at throttle body air inlet.
- Check EGR system.
- Ensure spark plugs fire.
- Check knock sensor (if applicable).
- Check throttle switch and connector (if applicable).
- Check engine speed sensor.
- Check MAP sensor (if applicable).

ENGINE MISFIRE – ALL CONDITIONS
- Check fuel injectors.
- Check ignition and sensor wires for proper connection.
- Check ignition and coil circuit.
- Check for gasoline in oil.
- Check intake and exhaust system.
- Check throttle switch and connector (if applicable).
- Check for vacuum leaks.
- Check engine speed sensor.
- Check MAP sensor (if applicable).

INSUFFICIENT ENGINE POWER
- Check fuel injectors.
- Check for air inlet restriction.
- Ensure fuel pressure is correct.
- Check airflow sensor.
- Check for restricted exhaust.
- Check coolant temperature sensor.
- Check air temperature sensor (if applicable).
- Check throttle switch and connector (if applicable).
- Check ignition and coil circuit.
- Check MAP sensor (if applicable).
- Check engine speed sensor.
- Check intake and exhaust system.
- Check EGR system.

POOR FUEL ECONOMY
- Check for leaky fuel injectors.
- Ensure spark plugs are not fouled.
- Check for faulty oxygen sensor.
- Check throttle switch and connector.
- Check for poor wire connections.
- Check engine speed sensor.
- Check for gasoline in oil.
- Check MAP sensor (if applicable).

EXCESSIVE HC & NOx
- Check for gasoline in oil.
- Check for leaky fuel injectors.
- Check for faulty oxygen sensor.
- Check ignition and sensor wires for poor connection.
- Check engine speed sensor.
- Check throttle switch and connector (if applicable).
- Check for vacuum leaks.

INTERMITTENTS

INTERMITTENT PROBLEM DIAGNOSIS

Intermittent fault testing requires duplicating circuit or component failure to identify problem. These procedures may lead to computer setting a fault code (on some systems) which may help in diagnosis.

If problem vehicle does not produce fault codes, monitor voltage or resistance values using a digital volt-ohmmeter (DVOM) while attempting to reproduce conditions causing intermittent fault. A status change on DVOM indicates a fault has been located.

Use a DVOM to pinpoint faults. When monitoring voltage, ensure ignition switch is in ON position or engine is running. Ensure ignition switch is in OFF position or negative battery cable is disconnected when monitoring circuit resistance. Status changes on DVOM during test procedures indicate area of fault.

TEST PROCEDURES

Following methods may reproduce conditions which create an intermittent fault which may be identified during testing:
- Lightly vibrate component.
- Heat component.
- Wiggle or bend wiring harness.
- Spray component with water.
- Remove/apply vacuum source.

Monitor circuit/component voltage or resistance while simulating intermittent fault. If engine is running, monitor for self-diagnostic codes. Use test results to identify a faulty component or area to be closely inspected for problem.

Pickup

INTRODUCTION

Before diagnosing symptoms, perform steps in BASIC DIAGNOSTIC PROCEDURES – DIESEL and SELF-DIAGNOSTICS – DIESEL articles. Use this article to diagnose driveability problems existing when a trouble code is not present.

NOTE: Some driveability problems may have been corrected by manufacturer with a revised computer control unit. Check with manufacturer for latest computer application.

Symptom checks can direct the technician to malfunctioning component(s) for further diagnosis. A symptom should lead to a specific component, system test or an adjustment.

Use intermittent test procedures to locate driveability problems that DO NOT occur when the vehicle is tested. Also use these test procedures if a soft (intermittent) trouble code was present, but no problem is found during self-diagnostic testing.

NOTE: For specific testing procedures, refer to SYSTEM & COMPONENT TESTING – DIESEL article. For specifications, see ON-VEHICLE ADJUSTMENTS – DIESEL or SERVICE & ADJUSTMENT SPECIFICATIONS – DIESEL article.

SYMPTOMS

SYMPTOM DIAGNOSIS

Symptom checks cannot be used properly unless problem occurs while vehicle is being tested. Reduce diagnostic time by ensuring steps in BASIC DIAGNOSTIC PROCEDURES – DIESEL and SELF-DIAGNOSTICS – DIESEL articles are performed before diagnosing a symptom. On all models, symptoms available for diagnosis include these symptoms.

- Engine Hard To Start
- Engine Surges At Idle
- Engine Has Rough Idle When Warm
- Engine Misfiring Under Load
- Engine Has Low Power
- Excessive Fuel Consumption
- Engine Will Not Shut Off
- White Or Blue Exhaust Smoke
- Incorrect Idle Speed
- Engine Speed Will Not Increase
- Fuel Injection Pump Runs Hot

ENGINE HARD TO START

- Air In Fuel System
- Clogged Fuel Filter
- Poor Fuel Quality
- Electrical Shutoff Solenoid Not Operating
- Fuel Tank Empty Or Fuel Tank Vent Blocked
- Restricted, Blocked Or Leaking Fuel Injection Or Supply Lines
- Incorrect Timing Or Defective Fuel Injection Pump
- Malfunctioning Intake Manifold Heater System
- Malfunctioning KSB Valve
- Low Or Uneven Engine Compression
- Injection Sequence Does Not Correspond With Firing Order
- Restricted Or Damaged Air Filter

ENGINE SURGES AT IDLE

- Air In Fuel System
- Fuel Tank Empty Or Fuel Tank Vent Blocked
- Low Idle Speed
- Incorrect Timing Or Defective Fuel Injection Pump

ENGINE HAS ROUGH IDLE WHEN WARM

- Air In Fuel System
- Poor Fuel Quality
- Low Idle Speed
- Restricted Or Damaged Fuel Injector
- Injection Sequence Does Not Correspond With Firing Order
- Low Or Uneven Engine Compression
- Incorrect Timing Or Defective Fuel Injection Pump

ENGINE MISFIRING UNDER LOAD

- Air In Fuel System
- Poor Fuel Quality
- Fuel Tank Empty Or Fuel Tank Vent Blocked
- Clogged Or Defective Fuel Filter
- Restricted, Blocked Or Leaking Fuel Injection Or Supply Lines
- Incorrect Timing Or Defective Fuel Injection Pump
- Restricted Or Damaged Fuel Injector
- Restricted Or Damaged Air Filter

ENGINE HAS LOW POWER

- Air In Fuel System
- Poor Fuel Quality
- Fuel Tank Empty Or Fuel Tank Vent Blocked
- Fuel Control Lever Not Obtaining Full Throttle
- Clogged Or Defective Fuel Filter
- Clogged Or Leaking Intercooler
- Restricted, Blocked Or Leaking Fuel Injection Or Supply Lines
- Improper Fuel Line Banjo Bolts At Fuel Injection Pump
- Incorrect Timing Or Defective Fuel Injection Pump
- Restricted Or Damaged Fuel Injector
- Restricted Or Damaged Air Filter
- Turbocharger Boost Control Line Broken Or Leaking
- Low Manifold Pressure
- Injection Sequence Does Not Correspond With Firing Order
- Low Or Uneven Engine Compression

EXCESSIVE FUEL CONSUMPTION

- Poor Fuel Quality
- Incorrect Timing Or Defective Fuel Injection Pump
- Damaged Fuel Injector
- Restricted Or Damaged Air Filter
- Injection Sequence Does Not Correspond With Firing Order
- Clogged Or Leaking Intercooler
- Improper Idle Speed
- Malfunctioning KSB Valve

ENGINE WILL NOT SHUT OFF

- Electrical Shutoff Solenoid Not Operating
- Voltage Always Exists At Electrical Shutoff Solenoid

WHITE OR BLUE EXHAUST SMOKE

- Air In Fuel System
- Poor Fuel Quality
- Clogged Or Defective Fuel Filter
- Restricted Or Blocked Fuel Injection Or Supply Lines
- Improper Fuel Line Banjo Bolts At Fuel Injection Pump
- Incorrect Timing Or Defective Fuel Injection Pump

INCORRECT IDLE SPEED

- Improper Idle Speed Adjustment
- Defective Fuel Injection Pump

ENGINE SPEED WILL NOT INCREASE

- Air In Fuel System
- Poor Fuel Quality
- Fuel Tank Empty Or Fuel Tank Vent Blocked
- Fuel Control Lever Not Obtaining Full Throttle
- Clogged Or Defective Fuel Filter
- Clogged Or Leaking Intercooler
- Restricted, Blocked Or Leaking Fuel Injection Or Lines
- Incorrect Timing Or Defective Fuel Injection Pump
- Improper Fuel Line Banjo Bolts At Fuel Injection Pump
- Low Or Uneven Engine Compression

FUEL INJECTION PUMP RUNS HOT

- Fuel Injection Pump Return Line Restricted

INTERMITTENTS

INTERMITTENT PROBLEM DIAGNOSIS

Intermittent fault testing requires duplicating circuit or component failure to identify problem. These procedures may lead to computer setting a fault code which may help in diagnosis.

If problem vehicle does not produce fault codes, monitor voltage or resistance values using a digital volt-ohmmeter (DVOM) while attempting to reproduce conditions causing intermittent fault. A status change on DVOM indicates a fault has been located.

Use a DVOM to pinpoint faults. When monitoring voltage, ensure ignition switch is in ON position or engine is running. Ensure ignition switch is in OFF position or negative battery cable is disconnected when monitoring circuit resistance. Status changes on DVOM during test procedures indicate area of fault.

TEST PROCEDURES

Intermittent Simulation – To reproduce conditions creating an intermittent fault, use following methods:

- Lightly vibrate component.
- Heat component.
- Wiggle or bend wiring harness.
- Spray component with water.
- Remove/apply vacuum source.

Monitor circuit/component voltage or resistance while simulating intermittent. If engine is running, monitor for self-diagnostic codes. Use test results to identify a faulty component or circuit.

RWD Van

INTRODUCTION

Before diagnosing symptoms or intermittent faults, perform steps in BASIC DIAGNOSTIC PROCEDURES – CNG and SELF-DIAGNOSTICS – CNG (if applicable) articles. Use this article to diagnose driveability problems that exist when a hard fault code is not present.

NOTE: Some driveability problems may have been corrected by manufacturer with a revised computer control unit. Check with manufacturer for latest computer application.

Symptom checks can direct the technician to malfunctioning components for further diagnosis. A symptom should lead to a specific component, system test or an adjustment.

Use intermittent test procedures to locate driveability problems that do not occur when the vehicle is tested. Also use these test procedures if a soft (intermittent) trouble code was present but no problem is found during self-diagnostic testing.

NOTE: For specific testing procedures, see SYSTEM & COMPONENT TESTING – CNG article. For specifications, see ON-VEHICLE ADJUSTMENTS – CNG or SERVICE & ADJUSTMENT SPECIFICATIONS – CNG article.

SYMPTOMS

SYMPTOM DIAGNOSIS

Symptom checks cannot be used properly unless problem occurs while vehicle is tested. To reduce diagnostic time, ensure steps in BASIC DIAGNOSTIC PROCEDURES – CNG and SELF-DIAGNOSTICS – CNG (if applicable) articles are performed before diagnosing a symptom. Symptoms available for diagnosis include these symptoms.

- No Start – Cold Engine
- No Start – Warm Engine
- Starts But Stalls
- Hard To Start – Cold Engine
- Erratic Idle – Warm-Up
- Engine Surges
- Backfiring
- Incorrect Idle Speed
- Hesitation – Acceleration
- Hesitation – Coasting
- Knocking
- Engine Misfire – All Conditions
- Insufficient Engine Power
- Poor Fuel Economy
- Excessive HC & NOx

NO START – COLD ENGINE

- Ensure battery is fully charged.
- Check manual shutoff valve.
- Check high-pressure and low-pressure fuel shutoff solenoids.
- Check fuel shutoff solenoid relay.
- Check spark plugs.
- Check in-line fuse to control unit.
- Ensure ignition timing and fuel pressure are correct.
- Check fuel injectors.
- Check fuel injector driver module.
- Ensure ignition coil resistance is correct.
- Ensure rotor, distributor and spark plug wires are okay.
- Check ignition control unit.
- Check coolant temperature sensor and connector.
- Check crankshaft position sensor.

NO START – WARM ENGINE

- Ensure fuel pressure is correct.
- Ensure fuel injectors are not leaking.

- Check ignition and sensor wires for proper connection.
- Ensure spark plugs are not fouled.
- Check ignition and coil circuit.
- Check crankshaft position sensor.

STARTS BUT STALLS

- Check coolant temperature sensor.
- Check fuel temperature sensor.
- Ensure all fuel cylinder control valves are open.
- Check ignition and sensor wires for proper connection.
- Check fuel injectors.
- Check crankshaft position sensor.

HARD TO START – COLD ENGINE

- Check spark plugs.
- Check distributor.
- Ensure fuel pressure is correct.
- Check ignition timing.

ERRATIC IDLE – WARM-UP

- Check coolant temperature sensor and connection.
- Check charge air temperature sensor.
- Check fuel temperature sensor.
- Check fuel low-pressure sensor.
- Ensure spark plugs are not fouled.
- Check ignition and sensor wires for proper connection.
- Check distributor.
- Check ignition and coil circuit.
- Check intake system.
- Check crankshaft position sensor.
- Check MAP sensor

ENGINE SURGES

- Check ignition and fuel system.
- Check fuel temperature sensor.
- Check fuel low-pressure sensor.
- Check for vacuum leaks.
- Ensure fuel pressure is correct.
- Check EGR system.

BACKFIRING

- Ensure ignition timing is correct.
- Ensure timing chain has not jumped.
- Check distributor.
- Ensure fuel injectors are not leaking.
- Check spark plugs.
- Check ignition and coil circuit.
- Check crankshaft position sensor.
- Check exhaust system.

INCORRECT IDLE SPEED

- Check fuel injectors.
- Check intake system for leaks.
- Check coolant temperature sensor.
- Check distributor.

HESITATION – ACCELERATION

- Check ignition and sensor wires for proper connection.
- Check distributor cap for moisture and carbon tracking.
- Ensure spark plug wires are okay.
- Ensure spark plugs are not fouled.
- Check MAP sensor.
- Check oxygen sensor.
- Check fuel temperature sensor.
- Check fuel pressure regulator.
- Ensure all fuel cylinder control valves are open.
- Check ignition and coil circuit.
- Check crankshaft position sensor.

HESITATION – COASTING
- Check fuel injectors.
- Check ignition and sensor wires for proper connection.
- Check crankshaft position sensor.
- Check MAP sensor.

KNOCKING
- Check ignition and coil circuit.
- Check for defect in throttle body power system.
- Check for restrictions at throttle body air inlet.
- Check EGR system.
- Ensure spark plugs fire.
- Check crankshaft position sensor.
- Check MAP sensor.

ENGINE MISFIRE – ALL CONDITIONS
- Check fuel injectors.
- Check ignition and sensor wires for proper connection.
- Check ignition and coil circuit.
- Check intake and exhaust system.
- Check for vacuum leaks.
- Check crankshaft position sensor.
- Check MAP sensor.

INSUFFICIENT ENGINE POWER
- Check fuel injectors.
- Check for air inlet restriction.
- Ensure fuel pressure is correct.
- Check for restricted exhaust.
- Check for restricted fuel filter.
- Check for restricted air filter.
- Check coolant temperature sensor.
- Check fuel temperature sensor.
- Check fuel low-pressure sensor.
- Check charge air temperature sensor.
- Check ignition and coil circuit.
- Check MAP sensor.
- Check oxygen sensor.
- Check crankshaft position sensor.
- Check intake and exhaust system.
- Check EGR system.

POOR FUEL ECONOMY
- Check for leaky fuel injectors.
- Check fuel pressure regulator.
- Ensure spark plugs are not fouled.
- Check for faulty oxygen sensor.
- Check for poor wire connections.
- Check crankshaft position sensor.
- Check MAP sensor.

EXCESSIVE HC & NOx
- Check for leaky fuel injectors.
- Ensure fuel pressure is correct.
- Check for faulty oxygen sensor.
- Check ignition and sensor wires for poor connection.
- Check crankshaft position sensor.
- Check for vacuum leaks.

INTERMITTENTS
INTERMITTENT PROBLEM DIAGNOSIS
Intermittent fault testing requires duplicating circuit or component failure to identify problem. These procedures may lead to computer setting a fault code (on some systems) which may help in diagnosis.

If problem vehicle does not produce fault codes, monitor voltage or resistance values using a digital volt-ohmmeter (DVOM) while attempting to reproduce conditions causing intermittent fault. A status change on DVOM indicates a fault has been located.

CAUTION: DO NOT use a test light on computer controlled circuits.

Use a DVOM to pinpoint faults. When monitoring voltage, ensure ignition switch is in ON position or engine is running. Ensure ignition switch is in OFF position or negative battery cable is disconnected when monitoring circuit resistance. Status changes on DVOM during test procedures indicate area of fault.

TEST PROCEDURES
Intermittent Simulation – To reproduce conditions creating an intermittent fault, use following methods:
- Lightly vibrate component.
- Heat component.
- Wiggle or bend wiring harness.
- Spray component with water.
- Remove/apply vacuum source.

Monitor circuit/component voltage or resistance while simulating intermittent. If engine is running, monitor for self-diagnostic codes. Use test results to identify a faulty component or circuit.

Caravan, Dakota, Pickup, Ramcharger, RWD Van, Town & Country, Voyager

NOTE: Testing procedures not covered in this article require a Chrysler Diagnostic Readout Box II (DRB-II). See appropriate SELF-DIAGNOSTICS article.

INTRODUCTION

Before testing individual components or systems, perform procedures in appropriate BASIC DIAGNOSTIC PROCEDURES article. Since many computer controlled and monitored components set a trouble code if they malfunction, also perform procedures in appropriate SELF-DIAGNOSTICS article.

NOTE: Testing of individual components does not isolate possible shorts or opens in wiring harness of electronically controlled systems. Perform all voltage tests using a Digital Volt-Ohmmeter (DVOM) with a minimum 10-megohm input impedance unless otherwise instructed in procedure. Use an ohmmeter to isolate wiring harness shorts or opens.

COMPUTERIZED ENGINE CONTROLS

SINGLE BOARD ENGINE CONTROLLER (SBEC)

Harness Check – **1)** If SBEC is found to be faulty during SELF-DIAGNOSTICS testing, perform following steps to confirm diagnosis. Most components are incorrectly diagnosed due to faulty electrical connectors or poor connections between component and vehicle. Sometimes, simply disconnecting and connecting an electrical component will provide a good electrical connection.
2) Before replacing an SBEC, check all components in suspected circuit. If components are okay, carefully disconnect SBEC from vehicle harness.
3) Inspect SBEC harness connector and SBEC contact pins for corrosion, bent pins, missing pins, spread cavities and broken wires. Clean, repair or replace connector as necessary.
4) Connect SBEC harness connector to SBEC, and retest system using Diagnostic Readout Box (DRB-II) or similar scan tool. See appropriate SELF-DIAGNOSTICS article. If vehicle does not pass test and fails with same message, replace SBEC.

ENGINE SENSORS & SWITCHES

Air Temperature Sensor – See THERMOSTATIC AIR CLEANER under EMISSION SYSTEMS & SUB-SYSTEMS.
Charge Air Temperature Sensor (CAS) – Sensor is mounted in intake manifold, under throttle cable bracket at throttle body. With key off, disconnect wire connector from sensor. Connect ohmmeter between sensor terminals. See TEMPERATURE SENSOR RESISTANCE table. If readings are not within specification, replace CAS sensor.
Coolant Temperature Sensor (CTS) – Sensor is mounted in intake manifold, next to thermostat housing. With key off, disconnect wire connector from sensor. Connect ohmmeter between sensor terminals. See TEMPERATURE SENSOR RESISTANCE table. If ohmmeter readfings are not within specification, replace CTS.
Crankshaft Position Sensor (CPS) – CPS is bolted to cylinder block near rear of right cylinder head. Disconnect CPS connector from main wiring harness. Measure resistance across CPS wiring connector terminals "A" and "B". *See Fig. 1.* Replace CPS if any resistance exists.

TEMPERATURE SENSOR RESISTANCE

Temperature	Ohms
–4°F (–20°C)	85,850-108,390
14°F (–10°C)	49,250-61,430
32°F (0°C)	29,330-35,990
50°F (10°C)	17,990-21,810
68°F (20°C)	11,370-13,610
77°F (25°C)	9120-10,880
86°F (30°C)	7370-8750
104°F (40°C)	4900-5750
122°F (50°C)	3330-3880
140°F (60°C)	2310-2670
158°F (70°C)	1630-1870
176°F (80°C)	1170-1340
194°F (90°C)	860-970
212°F (100°C)	640-720
230°F (110°C)	480-540
248°F (120°C)	370-410

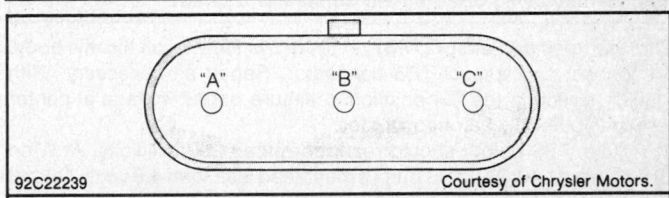

92C22239   Courtesy of Chrysler Motors.

Fig. 1: Identifying Crankshaft Position Sensor (CPS) Connector Terminals

Idle Position Switch – **1)** Idle position switch is located on throttle body. Disconnect idle position switch connector. Using an ohmmeter, check continuity between switch terminal and ground.
2) With accelerator pedal depressed, continuity should not exist. With accelerator pedal released, continuity should exist. Replace idle position switch if it does not test as specified.
Manifold Absolute Pressure (MAP) Sensor – **1)** MAP sensor is connected to side of throttle body by a rubber fitting. Inspect rubber fitting, and repair as needed.

NOTE: MAP sensor test must be performed with wiring connector connected.

2) Measure MAP sensor output voltage at connector center terminal. With ignition switch in ON position, output voltage should be 4.0-5.0 volts. With ignition switch in RUN position, voltage should be 1.5-2.1 volts. Replace MAP sensor if it does not test as specified.
Oxygen (O₂) Sensor – Oxygen sensor is located at outlet of exhaust manifold. Warm engine until coolant temperature reaches 185-205°F (85-95°C). Disconnect oxygen sensor connector, and connect a voltmeter to connector. With engine speed more than 1300 RPM, measure oxygen sensor output voltage. Voltage should be **.6-1.0 volt**. If voltage is not within specification, replace oxygen sensor.
Park/Neutral Switch – **1)** Park/neutral switch is located on transmission. Turn ignition off. Put shift selector in PARK position. Disconnect SBEC connector. Disconnect starter relay connector (located in engine compartment).
2) Using an ohmmeter, backprobe cavity No. 30 in SBEC connector while moving shift selector in and out of PARK and REVERSE positions. *See Fig. 2.* If reading varies from less than 5 ohms to more than 5 ohms, replace ignition switch. If reading is always less than 5 ohms, check Brown/Yellow wire for short to ground.
3) If reading is always more than 5 ohms, disconnect park/neutral switch connector. Check resistance in Brown/Yellow wire. If resistance is less than 10 ohms, replace park/neutral switch. If resistance is more than 10 ohms, check Brown/Yellow wire for open.

1992 ENGINE PERFORMANCE
System & Component Testing – Gasoline (Cont.)

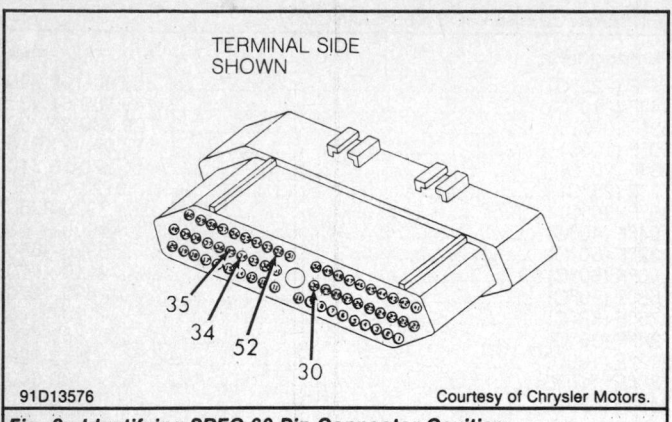

TERMINAL SIDE
SHOWN

35
34 52
30

91D13576   Courtesy of Chrysler Motors.

Fig. 2: Identifying SBEC 60-Pin Connector Cavities

Throttle Position Sensor (TPS) – 1) TPS is located on throttle body. Disconnect and inspect TPS connector. Repair as necessary. With ignition switch in the ON position, measure output voltage at center terminal (output) wire of connector.
2) At idle, TPS output should read more than 200 millivolts. At Wide Open Throttle (WOT), TPS output must read less than 4.8 volts. Output voltage should increase gradually as throttle is increased from idle to WOT. If voltage readings are not within specification, replace TPS.
Vehicle Speed Sensor (VSS) – VSS is located on transmission extension housing on 2WD models. VSS is located on transfer case on 4WD models. For VSS testing, see appropriate SELF-DIAGNOSTICS article.

MODULES, MOTORS, RELAYS & SOLENOIDS

MODULES

Ignition Module – See appropriate BASIC DIAGNOSTIC PROCEDURES article.

MOTORS

Idle Speed Control (ISC) Motor – See appropriate SELF-DIAGNOSTICS article.

RELAYS

Auto Shutdown (ASD) Relay – 1) ASD relay is located in engine compartment. Relay terminal numbers are stamped on bottom of relay. Relay must be disconnected for testing. If any of following resistance and continuity tests fail, replace relay.
2) Using an ohmmeter, measure resistance between terminals No. 85 and 86. Resistance should be **70-80 ohms**.
3) Connect ohmmeter between terminals No. 87A and 30. Continuity should exist. Connect ohmmeter between terminals No. 87 and 30. Continuity should not exist.
4) Using a pair of jumper wires, connect a jumper wire between terminal No. 85 and battery ground. Connect other jumper wire to battery positive terminal, but DO NOT connect to relay yet.

CAUTION: DO NOT allow ohmmeter to contact terminal No. 85 or 86 during following test. Damage to ohmmeter may result.

5) Attach other jumper wire to relay terminal No. 86 to activate relay. Continuity should exist between terminals No. 87 and 30, but not between terminals No. 87A and 30. Disconnect jumper wires from battery and relay.
Torque Converter Lock-Up Relay – See TRANSMISSION under MISCELLANEOUS CONTROLS.

SOLENOIDS

EGR Solenoid – See EMISSION SYSTEMS & SUB-SYSTEMS.
Torque Converter Lock-Up Solenoid – See TRANSMISSION under MISCELLANEOUS CONTROLS.

FUEL SYSTEM

FUEL DELIVERY

NOTE: For fuel system pressure testing, see appropriate BASIC DIAGNOSTIC PROCEDURES article.

FUEL CONTROL

Fuel Injector – Disconnect fuel injector connector. Using a DVOM in ohmmeter position, test between pins of injector for resistance. If resistance is less than 10 ohms, replace throttle body injector wiring. If resistance is more than 10 ohms, replace fuel injector.

IDLE CONTROL SYSTEM

Idle Speed Control (ISC) Motor – See appropriate SELF-DIAGNOSTICS article.

IGNITION SYSTEM

NOTE: For basic ignition checks, see appropriate BASIC DIAGNOSTIC PROCEDURES article.

EMISSION SYSTEMS & SUB-SYSTEMS

NOTE: To locate emission components, refer to emission control information label in engine compartment.

AIR INJECTION

No Air Supply – 1) Start engine, and raise engine speed to 1500 RPM. Check air supply at rubber hoses. If air supply increases with RPM, air pump operation is okay. If air pump is okay, check for leakage at hoses and fittings. Repair or replace as necessary.
2) If hoses are okay, check diverter valve for leakage. If air is expelled through diverter exhaust with vehicle at idle, replace diverter valve. If diverter valve is okay, remove check valve. Blow air through check valve in direction of air pump. Air should not pass through. Blow air through opposite direction. Air should pass freely.

CAUTION: DO NOT pry on air pump to adjust belt tension; housing may collapse.

Air Supply Pump – Check and adjust belt tension (if necessary). Disconnect air supply hose from by-pass control valve. Start engine. Pump is operating correctly if airflow is felt at pump outlet and airflow increases as engine speed increases. If pump does not operate as specified, replace pump.

EXHAUST GAS RECIRCULATION (EGR)

NOTE: To ensure proper EGR system operation all passages and moving parts must be free from restrictive deposits. Clean or replace components as necessary.

EGR System Operation Check – 1) Warm engine to operating temperature. Attach a tachometer to engine. Run engine at idle in Neutral an additional 70 seconds.
2) Accelerate engine speed abruptly to 2000-3000 RPM, and check EGR valve stem for movement. Repeat test to confirm stem movement, indicating EGR control system is functioning correctly. If

EGR valve stem does not move, connect external vacuum source and recheck EGR valve stem for movement. If EGR operates normally on external vacuum source, go to step **6)**.

3) If EGR valve stem does not move, check for cracked, leaking, disconnected or plugged vacuum hoses. Verify correct hose routing. Disconnect hose harness from EGR valve/transducer, and connect a vacuum pump to harness.

4) Start engine, and raise engine speed to 2000 RPM and hold. Apply 10 in. Hg. vacuum to EGR while checking for EGR valve movement. If no movement occurs, replace EGR valve/transducer assembly.

5) If valve opens approximately 1/8" (3 mm), hold vacuum constant and check for valve diaphragm leakage. Valve should remain open for at least 30 seconds. If leakage occurs, replace valve/transducer assembly. If valve is okay, check control system.

6) If EGR valve stem does not move in step **2)** but operates normally on external vacuum source, remove throttle body and check port in throttle bore for blockage. Use a solvent to remove deposits, and check flow using light air pressure. Normal operation should be restored.

7) If engine will not idle correctly or stalls, check for leaking EGR valve. With engine running, remove vacuum hose from EGR valve. If removing vacuum hose does not correct rough idle, remove EGR valve/transducer assembly. Check valve for proper seating. Replace assembly as necessary.

8) Also check EGR-to-intake manifold tube for leak. Remove tube and inspect gasket. Tube end should be uniformly indented on gasket, without signs of leakage. If leakage is not evident, replace gaskets and tighten flange nuts to **17 ft. lbs. (23 N.m)**. If leak persists, replace EGR tube and gaskets.

NOTE: DO NOT use drills or wires to clean passages for EGR control system. Calibration of precision orifices could be altered, resulting in unsatisfactory vehicle operation.

EGR Solenoid – **1)** EGR solenoid is located in engine compartment. With ignition switch in OFF position, disconnect and inspect solenoid connector. Repair as necessary. If connector is okay, turn ignition switch to ON position.

2) Using a DVOM in voltmeter mode, backprobe Dark Brown wire. If voltage is less than 10 volts, check for open in Dark Brown wire. If voltage is more than 10 volts, turn ignition switch to OFF position. Connect EGR solenoid connector. Disconnect and inspect SBEC connector. Repair as necessary.

3) Turn ignition switch to ON position. With DVOM in voltmeter mode, backprobe SBEC cavity No. 35. *See Fig. 2.* If voltage is more than 10 volts, replace SBEC. If voltage is less than 10 volts, turn ignition switch to OFF position. Disconnect EGR solenoid connector.

4) Using an ohmmeter, backprobe cavity No. 35 on SBEC. If resistance is less than 10 ohms, check Gray/Yellow wire for short to ground. If resistance is more than 10 volts, test resistance in Gray/Yellow wire. If resistance is less than 10 ohms, replace EGR solenoid. If resistance is more than 10 ohms, check Gray/Yellow wire for open.

FUEL EVAPORATION

EVAP Canister – EVAP canister is located in engine compartment. Canister has no moving parts. Check for loose, missing, cracked or broken connections and parts. Repair or replace as necessary. No liquid should be in canister.

EVAP Solenoid – **1)** EVAP solenoid is located in engine compartment. Turn ignition switch to OFF position. Disconnect and inspect solenoid connector. Repair as necessary.

2) Turn ignition switch to ON position. Using DVOM in voltmeter mode, backprobe Dark Brown wire at connector. If voltage is less than 10 volts, check for open in Dark Brown wire. If voltage is more than 10 volts, turn ignition switch to OFF position. Connect solenoid connector. Disconnect and inspect SBEC connector. Repair as necessary.

3) Turn ignition switch to ON position. With DVOM in voltage mode, backprobe cavity No. 52 on SBEC connector. *See Fig. 2.* If voltage is more than 10 volts, replace SBEC. If voltage is less than 10 volts, turn

ignition switch to OFF position. Disconnect solenoid connector. Using an ohmmeter, backprobe cavity No. 52 on SBEC connector.

4) If resistance is less than 10 ohms, check Pink/Black wire for short to ground. If resistance is more than 10 ohms, test Pink/Black wire for resistance. If resistance is less than 10 ohms, replace EVAP solenoid. If resistance is more than 10 ohms, check Pink/Black wire for open.

POSITIVE CRANKCASE VENTILATION (PCV)

PCV Valve – **1)** With engine running at curb idle, remove PCV valve from grommet. If valve is functioning properly, a hissing sound will be heard as air passes through valve.

2) With engine running, place finger over valve inlet. Strong vacuum should be felt at valve inlet. Stop engine. Remove and shake PCV valve to ensure a metallic clicking noise can be heard, indicating valve is free. Reinstall PCV valve.

3) Remove crankcase ventilation filter or oil filler cap from valve cover. Hold a piece of stiff paper over opening. After allowing about one minute for crankcase pressure stabilization, paper should be drawn against opening.

4) If paper is held against opening, performance is okay. If paper is not held against opening, replace PCV valve and retest. If performance does not improve, inspect system for restrictions and clean as necessary.

THERMOSTATIC AIR CLEANER

NOTE: With engine cold, heat control door in air cleaner snorkel should be closed. With engine running at normal operating temperature, door should be open.

Air Temperature Sensor – Ensure all vacuum hoses are in good condition. Using external vacuum source, apply 20 in. Hg vacuum to air temperature sensor. Door should be in open position. If door is not open, check vacuum diaphragm for leaks and restrictions. If diaphragm is okay but proper temperature is not maintained, replace temperature sensor.

Air Control Door – Apply 20 in. Hg vacuum to diaphragm. Diaphragm should not bleed down more than 10 in. Hg in 5 minutes. Door should not lift off bottom at less than 2 in. Hg. Door should be fully open at no more than 4 in. Hg. If vacuum diaphragm does not operate properly, replace vacuum diaphragm and repeat test.

MISCELLANEOUS CONTROLS

NOTE: Although some controlled devices listed here are not technically engine performance components, they can affect driveability if they malfunction.

A/C CLUTCH RELAY

A/C Clutch Relay (Except Dakota) – **1)** A/C clutch relay is located in engine compartment. Turn ignition switch to ON position. Using a DVOM in voltmeter mode, backprobe Dark Blue/Orange wire at A/C clutch relay. *See Fig. 3.* If voltage is more than 10 volts, see appropriate SELF-DIAGNOSTICS article. If voltage is less than 10 volts, turn ignition switch to OFF position. Disconnect and inspect clutch relay connector. Repair as necessary.

2) If connector is okay, backprobe Light Green wire in clutch relay connector. If voltage is less than 10 volts, check for open in Light Green wire. If voltage is more than 10 volts, using an ohmmeter, backprobe Dark Blue/Orange wire in clutch relay connector. If resistance is less than 10 volts, check Dark Blue/Orange wire for short to ground. If resistance is more than 10 volts, replace A/C clutch relay.

A/C Clutch Relay (Dakota) – **1)** A/C clutch relay is located at power distribution center in engine compartment. Turn ignition switch to ON position. Actuate A/C switch on dash panel. If A/C clutch relay clicks, see appropriate SELF-DIAGNOSTICS article.

2) If A/C clutch relay does not click, disconnect and inspect clutch relay connector. Repair as necessary. If connector is okay, replace

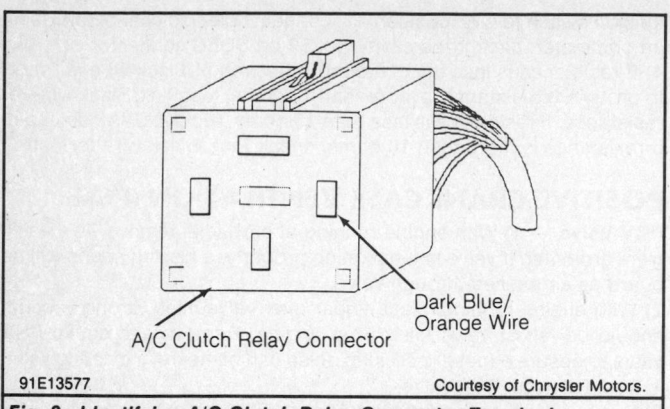

91E13577   Courtesy of Chrysler Motors.

Fig. 3: Identifying A/C Clutch Relay Connector Terminals

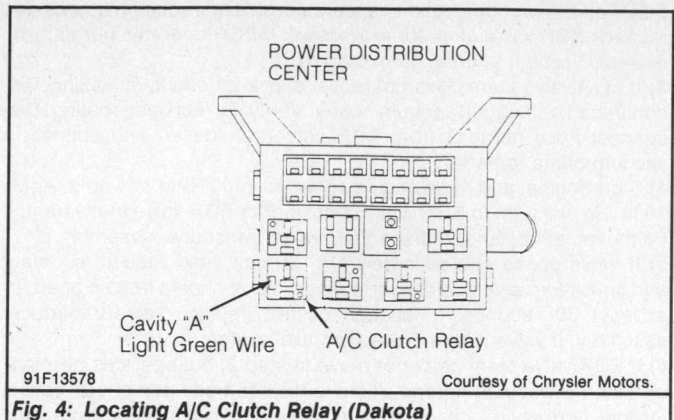

91F13578   Courtesy of Chrysler Motors.

Fig. 4: Locating A/C Clutch Relay (Dakota)

clutch relay. Actuate A/C switch on dash. If clutch relay clicks, repair is complete. If clutch relay does not click, remove clutch relay.

3) Using DVOM in voltage mode, backprobe cavity "A" in relay connector. See Fig. 4. If voltage is less than 10 volts, check for open in Light Green wire. If voltage is more than 10 volts, turn ignition switch to OFF position.

4) Reconnect A/C clutch relay. Disconnect and inspect SBEC connector. Repair as necessary. If connector is okay, turn ignition switch to ON position. Using DVOM in voltage mode, backprobe cavity No. 34 on SBEC connector. See Fig. 2. If voltage is more than 10 volts, replace SBEC. If voltage is less than 10 volts, check for open in Dark Blue/Orange wire.

TRANSMISSION

Torque Converter Lock-Up Relay – 1) Torque converter lock-up relay is located in engine compartment. Turn ignition switch to ON position. Using a DVOM in voltmeter mode, backprobe Orange/Black wire at relay. If voltage is more than 10 volts, see appropriate SELF-DIAGNOSTICS article. If voltage is less than 10 volts, disconnect and inspect relay connector. Repair as necessary.

2) If connector is okay, backprobe Dark Blue wire at relay. If voltage is more than 10 volts, replace lock-up relay. If voltage is less than 10 volts, repair open in Dark Blue wire.

Torque Converter Lock-Up Solenoid – 1) Lock-up solenoid is located on left side of transmission. Turn ignition switch to OFF position. Disconnect solenoid connector from transmission. Inspect connector, and repair as necessary.

2) If connector is okay, turn ignition switch to ON position. Using DVOM in voltage mode, backprobe Dark Blue wire on connector. If voltage is less than 10 volts, check for open Dark Blue wire. If voltage is more than 10 volts, see appropriate SELF-DIAGNOSTICS article.

Pickup

INTRODUCTION

Before testing separate components or systems, perform procedures in appropriate BASIC DIAGNOSTIC PROCEDURES article. Since many computer-controlled and monitored components set a trouble code if they malfunction, also perform procedures in appropriate SELF-DIAGNOSTICS article.

NOTE: Testing individual components does not isolate shorts or opens. Perform all voltage tests using a Digital Volt-Ohmmeter (DVOM) with a minimum 10-megohm input impedance, unless otherwise instructed in test procedure. Use ohmmeter to isolate wiring harness shorts or opens.

AIR INDUCTION SYSTEMS

TURBOCHARGERS

NOTE: Items listed in INITIAL CHECKS can cause excessive smoke, low manifold pressure and loss of power.

Initial Checks – **1)** Check air intake for clogged air cleaner. Check for loose connections and cracks on suction (intake) side of turbocharger. Check for damage to compressor blades causing an imbalance and resulting in bearing failure.

2) Check for air leaks at intercooler and intercooler ducts from turbocharger to intercooler and from intercooler to air inlet on intake manifold cover. Use soapy solution to check for pressurized air leaks at intake manifold cover, crossover tube, intercooler and connections.

3) Check for exhaust leaks at exhaust manifold and turbocharger. Check for exhaust pipe restrictions and restricted or damaged turbocharger oil return line.

4) To verify a bearing failure or damaged compressor, remove intake and exhaust piping, and check for compressor or turbine wheel-to-housing contact. Compressor or turbine wheel must rotate freely. Measure shaft end play and radial clearance. See SHAFT END PLAY & RADIAL CLEARANCE.

Boost Pressure – Boost pressure testing information is not available from manufacturer.

Shaft End Play & Radial Clearance – Shaft end play and radial clearance can be checked to determine if turbocharger repairs are required. Using a dial indicator, check shaft end play and radial clearance. *See Fig. 1.* Turbocharger must be repaired if clearances are not within specification. See TURBOCHARGER SPECIFICATIONS table.

TURBOCHARGER SPECIFICATIONS

Application	In. (mm)
Shaft Clearances	
End Play	1
Radial Clearance	.012-.018 (.30-.46)
Turbine Shaft Minimum O.D.	.432 (10.97)

¹ – On turbochargers with serial No. 840637 and earlier, end play should be .004-.006" (.10-.15 mm). On turbochargers with serial No. 840638 and later, end play should be .001-.003" (.03-.08 mm).

COMPUTERIZED ENGINE CONTROLS

SINGLE BOARD ENGINE CONTROLLER (SBEC)

SBEC is located on left front corner of engine compartment, near horns on left fender.

Harness Check – **1)** If SBEC is found to be faulty during SELF-DIAGNOSTICS testing, perform following steps to confirm diagnosis. Most components are incorrectly diagnosed due to faulty electrical connectors or poor connections between component and vehicle. Sometimes simply disconnecting and connecting an electrical component will provide a good electrical connection.

2) Before replacing an SBEC, check all components in suspected circuit. If components are okay, carefully disconnect SBEC from vehicle harness.

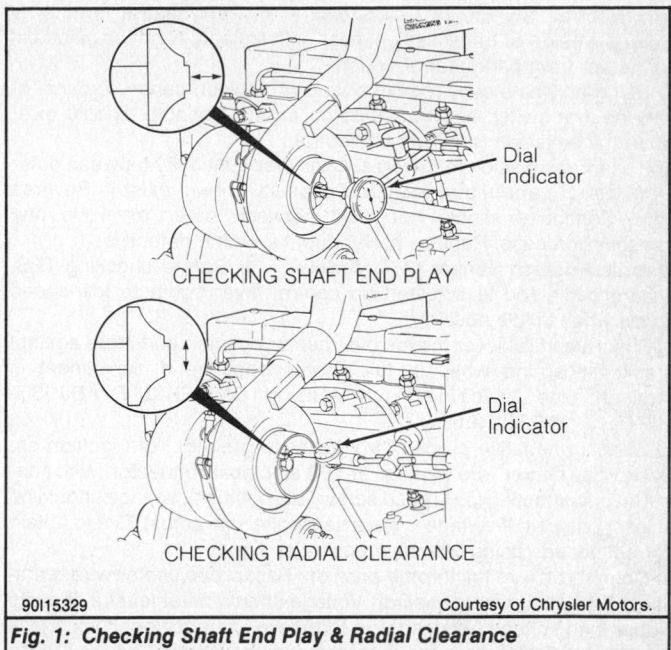

CHECKING SHAFT END PLAY

Dial Indicator

Dial Indicator

CHECKING RADIAL CLEARANCE

90I15329   Courtesy of Chrysler Motors.

Fig. 1: Checking Shaft End Play & Radial Clearance

3) Inspect SBEC harness connector and SBEC contact pins for corrosion. Clean harness connector and SBEC contact pins with contact cleaner.

4) Inspect SBEC harness connector for bent pins, missing pins and broken wires. Repair or replace as necessary.

5) Using an ohmmeter, check for continuity between chassis ground and SBEC harness connector pins No. 5, 11 and 12. If continuity does not exist on all pins, repair open circuit in affected wire. See appropriate WIRING DIAGRAMS article.

6) Connect negative voltmeter lead to chassis ground and positive lead to pin No. 57. If battery voltage does not exist, repair open circuit between SBEC and battery.

7) Turn ignition on. Connect negative voltmeter lead to chassis ground and positive lead to pin No. 9. If battery voltage does not exist, repair open circuit between SBEC and ignition switch. See appropriate WIRING DIAGRAMS article.

8) Connect SBEC harness connector to SBEC, and retest system using Diagnostic Readout Box (DRB-II) or similar scan tool. See SELF-DIAGNOSTICS – DIESEL article. If vehicle does not pass test and fails with same message, replace SBEC.

ENGINE SENSORS & SWITCHES

Air Temperature Switch – **1)** Air temperature switch is located in intake manifold cover. *See Fig. 5.* Air temperature switch is used for controlling KSB valve.

2) Air temperature switch is open when intake manifold air temperature is more than 60°F (16°C) and fully closed when temperature is less than 54°F (12°C). When air temperature switch is closed, voltage is applied to KSB valve. No other information is available from manufacturer.

Charge Air Temperature Sensor – See CHARGE AIR TEMPERATURE SENSOR under INTAKE MANIFOLD HEATER SYSTEM under EMISSION SYSTEMS & SUB-SYSTEMS.

Coolant Temperature Switch (A/T Models) – **1)** Coolant temperature switch is located in cylinder head, below intake manifold, near air temperature switch. *See Fig. 5.* Coolant temperature switch opens when coolant temperature is less than 60°F (16°C).

2) When coolant temperature switch opens, transmission will not shift into Overdrive. Transmission will downshift if it is in Overdrive when coolant temperature switch opens.

Crankshaft Position Sensor – Crankshaft position sensor, located on front of engine, generates engine RPM signal to SBEC. See SELF-DIAGNOSTICS – DIESEL article.

Park/Neutral Switch (A/T Models) – 1) Park/neutral switch is located on side of transmission, near shift linkage. Remove electrical connector from park/neutral switch.

2) Using an ohmmeter, check continuity between center terminal of park/neutral switch and transmission case. Continuity should exist when transmission is in Park or Neutral.

3) Place transmission in Reverse. Check for continuity between outer terminals of park/neutral switch. Continuity should exist in Reverse only. Continuity should not exist between outer terminals and transmission case. Replace park/neutral switch if defective.

Throttle Position Sensor (A/T Models) – 1) Before checking TPS, ensure cable rod is adjusted so control lever contacts low-speed screw when in idle position.

2) Ensure control lever moves over center position and rests against breakover spring when in full throttle position. If adjustment is required, see THROTTLE LINKAGE in ON-VEHICLE ADJUSTMENTS – DIESEL article.

3) Connect negative probe of voltmeter to ground. Turn ignition on. Backprobe center wire terminal at TPS electrical connector. With control lever contacting low-speed screw (idle position), voltage should be at least one volt. If voltage is not at least one volt, adjust TPS to obtain correct voltage using 10-mm wrench. *See Fig. 2.*

4) Open throttle to full throttle position. Backprobe center wire terminal at TPS electrical connector. Voltage should be at least 2.25 volts higher than voltage obtained with throttle in idle position. If voltage is not at least 2.25 volts more than idle position voltage, adjust TPS to obtain correct voltage. Replace TPS if it cannot be adjusted.

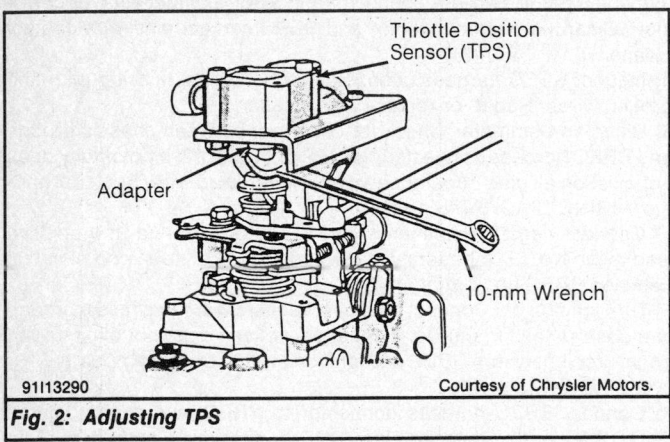

Fig. 2: *Adjusting TPS*

Water-In-Fuel Sensor – See SELF-DIAGNOSTICS – DIESEL article.

Vehicle Speed Sensor – 1) Disconnect vehicle speed sensor harness connector, and remove sensor. DO NOT lose rubber seal on sensor harness connector. Using an analog ohmmeter, connect ohmmeter leads across sensor terminals.

2) Slowly rotate sensor shaft while observing ohmmeter. Ohmmeter needle should jump between zero and infinity readings 8 times for each complete sensor shaft revolution. If sensor does not operate as specified, replace sensor.

NOTE: Ensure rubber seal on vehicle speed sensor harness connector is not missing or damaged. Water and road dirt in sensor connection will cause a false trouble code to be set.

RELAYS & SOLENOIDS

RELAYS

A/C Clutch Relay – 1) A/C clutch relay is located in engine compartment. Turn ignition switch to ON position. Using a DVOM in voltmeter mode, backprobe Dark Brown/Orange wire at A/C clutch relay. If voltage is greater than 10 volts, see SELF-DIAGNOSTICS – DIESEL article. If voltage is less than 10 volts, turn ignition switch to OFF position. Disconnect and inspect clutch relay connector. Repair as necessary.

2) If connector is okay, backprobe Dark Brown wire in clutch relay connector. If voltage is less than 10 volts, check for open in Dark Brown wire. If voltage is more than 10 volts, using an ohmmeter, backprobe Dark Brown/Orange wire in clutch relay connector. If resistance is less than 10 volts, check Dark Brown/Orange wire for short to ground. If resistance is more than 10 volts, replace A/C clutch relay.

Auto Shutdown (ASD) Relay – See SELF-DIAGNOSTICS – DIESEL article.

Intake Manifold Heater Relays – 1) Intake manifold heater relays are mounted on inner wheelwell. *See Fig. 3.* Intake manifold heater relays are energized by SBEC depending on intake manifold air temperature monitored by charge air temperature sensor.

2) Intake manifold heater relays are not energized during engine cranking. A clicking sound will be heard when relays are energized. See SELF-DIAGNOSTICS – DIESEL article.

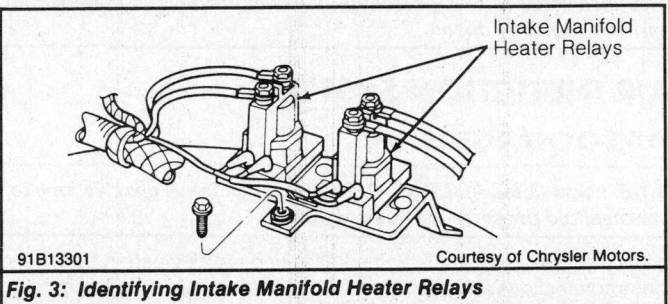

Fig. 3: *Identifying Intake Manifold Heater Relays*

CAUTION: Intake manifold heater relays should not be cycled (ignition turned off and then on) more than once within 15 minutes. Wait 15 minutes before turning ignition on.

SOLENOIDS

KSB Solenoid – 1) KSB solenoid is located on fuel injection pump. *See Fig. 4.* Power is provided to KSB solenoid from SBEC through an air temperature switch located on intake manifold cover. *See Fig. 5.*

2) Air temperature switch is open when intake manifold air temperature is greater than 60°F (16°C). KSB valve should "click" when 10 volts is applied to KSB valve and air temperature switch is fully closed.

CAUTION: DO NOT apply 12 volts to KSB valve. Wiring circuit contains a 3-ohm resistor to decrease voltage to KSB valve to 10 volts.

3) Using a DVOM in voltmeter mode, backprobe White wire at solenoid. If voltage is greater than 10 volts, in-line resistor is damaged. Replace resistor and KSB solenoid. If voltage is less than 10 volts, repair open circuit between KSB solenoid and SBEC pin No. 9. See appropriate WIRING DIAGRAMS article in ENGINE PERFORMANCE.

Overdrive Solenoid – See SELF-DIAGNOSTICS – DIESEL article.

FUEL SYSTEM

FUEL DELIVERY

Fuel Heater – 1) Fuel heater is located between fuel/water separator filter and filter adapter on cylinder head. *See Fig. 4.* Voltage to operate fuel heater is provided from ignition switch.

2) At least 7 volts are required for fuel heater operation. Fuel heater will operate when temperature is approximately 43°F (6°C) and shut off at about 53°F (13°C). Fuel heater resistance is **2.5-3.0 ohms.** No other information is available from manufacturer.

Fuel Lift Pump – 1) Fuel lift pump is located on left rear side of engine. *See Fig. 4.* To check lift pump vacuum, disconnect fuel supply line at fuel lift pump. Install vacuum gauge on a fitting between fuel supply line and fuel lift pump.

2) Operate engine at approximately 1500 RPM for 30 seconds, and note vacuum reading. If vacuum reading exceeds 3.75 in. Hg, check for restriction in fuel/water separator filter or fuel supply line.

CAUTION: Defective fuel lift pump can create low engine power and long cranking periods. Hand lever must be in upward position to provide proper engine operation.

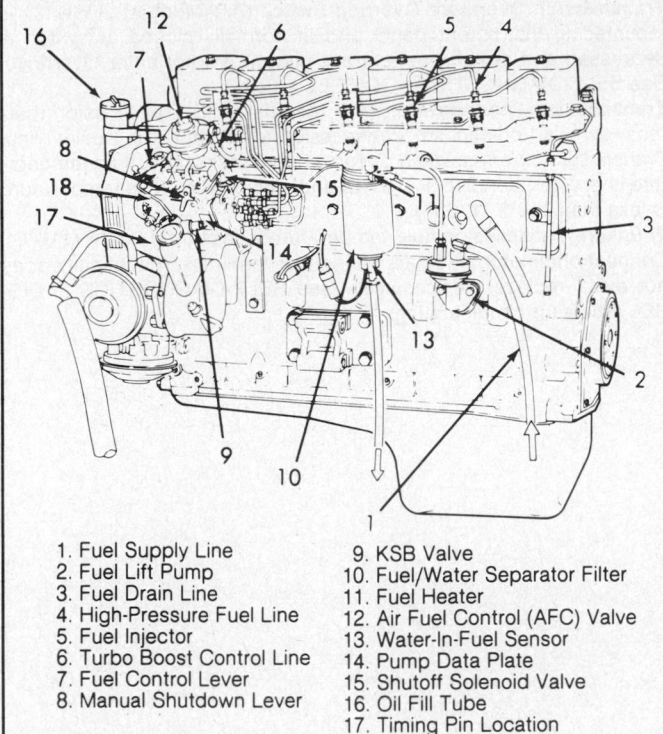

1. Fuel Supply Line
2. Fuel Lift Pump
3. Fuel Drain Line
4. High-Pressure Fuel Line
5. Fuel Injector
6. Turbo Boost Control Line
7. Fuel Control Lever
8. Manual Shutdown Lever
9. KSB Valve
10. Fuel/Water Separator Filter
11. Fuel Heater
12. Air Fuel Control (AFC) Valve
13. Water-In-Fuel Sensor
14. Pump Data Plate
15. Shutoff Solenoid Valve
16. Oil Fill Tube
17. Timing Pin Location
18. Fuel Injection Pump

91F13305   Courtesy of Chrysler Motors.

Fig. 4: Identifying Fuel System Components

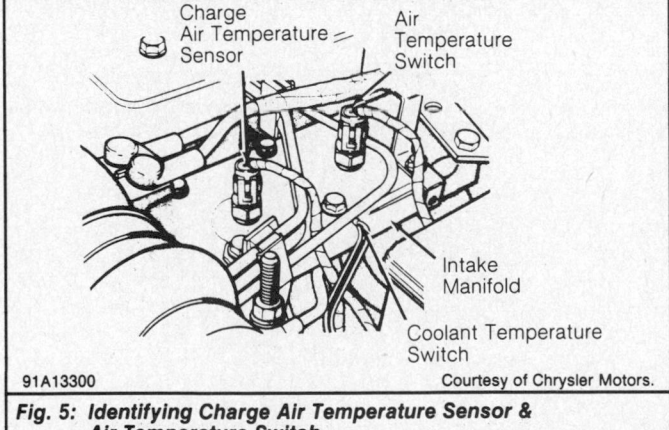

91A13300   Courtesy of Chrysler Motors.

Fig. 5: Identifying Charge Air Temperature Sensor & Air Temperature Switch

3) Check fuel lift pump output pressure and volume at cranking speed. Replace fuel lift pump if not within specification. See FUEL LIFT PUMP SPECIFICATIONS table.

FUEL LIFT PUMP SPECIFICATIONS

Application	Output
Pump Pressure	3 psi Minimum (.2 kg/cm²)
Volume Within 30 Seconds	.7 Qts. (.6L)

FUEL CONTROL

Fuel Injector – 1) To determine which fuel injector is defective, operate engine and loosen high-pressure fuel line nut at fuel injector.

CAUTION: Carefully loosen high-pressure fuel line nut. Fuel is under excessive pressure and will spray out around fuel line nut.

2) Listen for a change in engine RPM. If engine RPM decreases, fuel injector is operating properly. If engine RPM stays the same, fuel injector or engine components are defective. Ensure all high-pressure fuel line nuts are tightened to **18 ft. lbs. (24 N.m)**.
Shutoff Solenoid Valve – 1) Shutoff solenoid valve is located on rear side of fuel injection pump. *See Fig. 4.* Using a voltmeter, ensure at least 10 volts exist at shutoff solenoid valve. If at least 10 volts exist, remove shutoff solenoid valve from fuel injection pump.

CAUTION: DO NOT attach power supply to shutoff solenoid valve with plunger removed; otherwise, valve assembly will be damaged.

2) Remove plunger and spring from fuel injection pump. Reinstall shutoff solenoid valve with electrical connector disconnected. If engine starts, replace shutoff solenoid valve.

NOTE: Engine must be shut off using manual shutdown lever when plunger and spring are removed. See Fig. 4.

3) If engine does not start, shutoff solenoid valve is not problem; fuel system or engine should be checked for proper operation. Reinstall plunger, spring and shutoff solenoid valve. Tighten shutoff solenoid valve to **32 ft. lbs. (43 N.m)**.

EMISSION SYSTEMS & SUB-SYSTEMS

INTAKE MANIFOLD HEATER SYSTEM

NOTE: Intake manifold heater will operate when intake manifold air temperature is less than 59°F (15°C).

Charge Air Temperature Sensor – Charge air temperature sensor is located in intake manifold cover. *See Fig. 5.* Charge air temperature sensor monitors intake manifold air temperature and sends signal to SBEC. SBEC controls intake manifold heater. See SELF-DIAGNOSTICS – DIESEL article.
Intake Manifold Heater – 1) Disconnect electrical leads from intake manifold heater. Intake manifold heater is located between air inlet housing and intake manifold. Isolate electrical leads from contacting other components.
2) Using ohmmeter, measure continuity to ground from each terminal on intake manifold heater. Replace intake manifold heater if continuity exists.

CAUTION: Intake manifold heater relays should not be cycled (ignition turned off and then on) more than once within 15 minutes. Wait 15 minutes before turning ignition on.

NOTE: If intake manifold air temperature is less than 59°F (15°C) during preheat/postheat cycle, intake manifold heater will preheat before engine starts. For normal preheat/postheat cycle operating ranges, see HEAT CYCLE SPECIFICATIONS table.

Preheat/Postheat Cycle – 1) With intake manifold air temperature less than 60°F (16°C), turn ignition on. WAIT-TO-START light on message center in cab should come on. A "click" sound should be heard at intake heater relays, indicating preheat cycle.
2) Using voltmeter, check for battery voltage at both terminals on intake manifold heater. Intake manifold heater is located between air inlet housing and intake manifold.
3) Voltage should exist at intake manifold heater terminals for 10-20 seconds. Preheat cycle should operate for specified amount of time depending on intake manifold temperature. See HEAT CYCLE SPECIFICATIONS table.

1992 ENGINE PERFORMANCE
System & Component Testing – Diesel (Cont.)

HEAT CYCLE SPECIFICATIONS

Intake Manifold Air Temperature	Preheat Cycle With Ignition On Engine Off	Postheat Cycle With Ignition On Engine On
Above 59°F (15°C)	0.0 Seconds	No
18°F (-8°C) To 59°F (15°C)	10.0 Seconds	Yes
1°F (-17°C) To 16°F (-9°C)	15.0 Seconds	Yes
-15°F (-26°C) To 0°F (-18°C)	17.5 Seconds	Yes
Below -15°F (-26°C)	20.0 Seconds	Yes

MISCELLANEOUS CONTROLS

NOTE: Although some controlled devices listed here are not technically engine performance components, they can affect driveability if they malfunction.

Transmission Overdrive Override Switch (A/T Models) – Switch is mounted in instrument panel and is normally closed. If switch is depressed and switch opens, transmission will not enter Overdrive. See SELF-DIAGNOSTICS – DIESEL article.

Transmission Thermoswitch (A/T Models) – 1) Transmission thermoswitch is located in transmission-to-radiator oil cooler line. Transmission thermoswitch opens when transmission fluid temperature is greater than 273°F (134°C) and closes when fluid temperature is less than 240°F (116°C).

2) Ensure transmission fluid temperature is less than 240°F (116°C). Connect ohmmeter leads across sensor terminals. If continuity does not exist, replace thermoswitch. See SELF-DIAGNOSTICS – DIESEL article for circuit testing.

RWD Van

NOTE: Testing procedures not covered in this article require a Chrysler Diagnostic Readout Box-II (DRB-II). See appropriate SELF-DIAGNOSTICS article.

INTRODUCTION

Before testing individual components or systems, perform procedures in BASIC DIAGNOSTIC PROCEDURES – CNG article. Since many computer controlled and monitored components set a trouble code if they malfunction, also perform procedures in appropriate SELF-DIAGNOSTICS article.

NOTE: Testing of individual components does not isolate possible shorts or opens in the wiring harness of electronically controlled systems. Perform all voltage tests with a Digital Volt-Ohmmeter (DVOM) with a minimum 10-megohm input impedance, unless stated otherwise in procedure. Use an ohmmeter to isolate wiring harness shorts or opens.

COMPUTERIZED ENGINE CONTROLS

POWERTRAIN CONTROL MODULE (PCM)

Harness Check – 1) If during self-diagnostics testing, PCM is found to be faulty, perform the following steps to confirm diagnosis. Most components are incorrectly diagnosed due to faulty electrical connectors or poor connections between component and vehicle. Sometimes, simply disconnecting and connecting an electrical component will provide a good electrical connection.

2) Before replacing PCM, check all components in suspected circuit. If components are okay, carefully disconnect PCM from vehicle harness.

3) Inspect PCM harness connector and PCM contact pins for corrosion. Clean harness connector and PCM contact pins with contact cleaner.

4) Inspect PCM harness connector for bent pins, missing pins and broken wires. Repair or replace as necessary.

5) Connect PCM harness connector to PCM, and retest system with Diagnostic Readout Box (DRB-II) or similar scan tool. See appropriate SELF-DIAGNOSTICS article. If vehicle does not pass test and fails with the same message, replace PCM.

ENGINE SENSORS & SWITCHES

Charge Air Temperature Sensor – Sensor is mounted in intake manifold, next to throttle body. With key off, disconnect wire connector from sensor. Connect ohmmeter between sensor terminals. See TEMPERATURE SENSOR RESISTANCE (OHMS) table. If ohmmeter readings are not within specification, replace sensor.

Coolant Temperature Sensor (CTS) – Sensor is mounted in intake manifold, next to thermostat housing. With key off, disconnect wire connector from sensor. Connect ohmmeter between sensor terminals. See TEMPERATURE SENSOR RESISTANCE (OHMS) table. If ohmmeter readings are not within specification, replace CTS.

TEMPERATURE SENSOR RESISTANCE (OHMS)

Temperature	Resistance
-4°F (-20°C)	85,850-108,390
14°F (-10°C)	49,250-61,430
32°F (0°C)	29,330-35,990
50°F (10°C)	17,990-21,810
68°F (20°C)	11,370-13,610
77°F (25°C)	9120-10,880
86°F (30°C)	7370-8750
104°F (40°C)	4900-5750
122°F (50°C)	3330-3880
140°F (60°C)	2310-2670
158°F (70°C)	1630-1870
176°F (80°C)	1170-1340
194°F (90°C)	860-970
212°F (100°C)	640-720
230°F (110°C)	480-540
248°F (120°C)	370-410

Fuel Temperature Sensor – Sensor is mounted in fuel rail mounting block. With key off, disconnect wire connector from sensor. Connect ohmmeter between sensor terminals. See TEMPERATURE SENSOR RESISTANCE (OHMS) table. If ohmmeter readings are not within specification, replace sensor.

Oxygen Sensor – Oxygen sensor is located at outlet of exhaust manifold. Warm engine until coolant temperature reaches 185-205°F (85-95°C). Disconnect oxygen sensor connector and connect a voltmeter to connector. With engine speed more than 1300 RPM, measure oxygen sensor output voltage. Output voltage should be .6-1.0 volt. If output voltage is not within specification, replace oxygen sensor.

Park/Neutral Switch – 1) Park/Neutral switch is located on transmission. Turn ignition off. Put shift selector in Park position. Disconnect PCM connector. Disconnect starter relay connector (located in engine compartment).

2) Using an ohmmeter, backprobe cavity No. 30 in PCM connector while moving shift selector in and out of Park and Reverse. See Fig. 1. If ohmmeter reading varies from less than 5 ohms to more than 5 ohms, replace ignition switch. If ohmmeter reading is less than 5 ohms at all times, check Brown/Yellow wire for short to ground.

3) If resistance reading is greater than 5 ohms at all times, disconnect Park/Neutral switch connector. Check resistance in Brown/Yellow wire. If resistance is less than 10 ohms, replace Park/Neutral switch. If resistance is greater than 10 ohms, check Brown/Yellow wire for open.

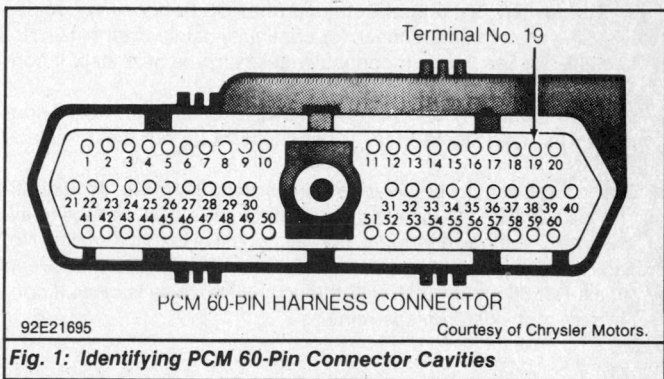

Fig. 1: Identifying PCM 60-Pin Connector Cavities

Throttle Position Sensor (TPS) – 1) TPS is located on throttle body. Disconnect and inspect TPS connector. Repair as necessary. Measure resistance between TPS terminals No. 3 (sensor ground) and No. 1 (sensor power).

2) Resistance should be approximately 3500-6500 ohms. If resistance is not within specification, replace TPS. If resistance is within specification, go to next step.

3) Connect an ohmmeter between terminals No. 3 (sensor ground) and No. 2 (sensor output). Operate throttle valve slowly from idle position to fully open position. Resistance should change smoothly in proportion to throttle valve opening angle. Replace TPS if it does not test as specified.

MODULES, MOTORS, RELAYS & SOLENOIDS

MODULES

Fuel Injector Driver Module – Fuel injector driver module is located on firewall near PCM. For no-start testing, see FUEL SYSTEM in BASIC DIAGNOSTIC PROCEDURES – CNG article.

MOTORS

NOTE: To test automatic idle speed motor circuitry, see appropriate SELF-DIAGNOSTICS article.

Automatic Idle Speed (AIS) Motor – 1) Set parking brake and block drive wheels. Remove engine cover. With ignition off, disconnect AIS motor harness connector. Connect AIS Motor Exerciser (7558) to AIS motor and to vehicle battery.

2) Start engine and observe exerciser indicator light. If indicator light is flashing, AIS motor is receiving voltage pulses from the PCM. Place exerciser switch in HIGH position. Engine speed should increase.

3) Place exerciser switch in LOW position. Engine speed should decrease. If engine speed changes as specified, AIS is functioning properly. If engine speed does not change as specified, shut engine off.

4) Remove AIS motor from throttle body. With ignition off, cycle exerciser switch between HIGH and LOW position while observing AIS motor pintle. If pintle moves in and out, motor is functioning properly. Check AIS motor bore for blockage and clean as necessary. If pintle does not function as specified, replace AIS motor.

CAUTION: When testing AIS motor removed from throttle body, DO NOT allow pintle to extend more than .250" (6.35 mm) or pintle may separate from motor. If pintle separates, AIS MUST be replaced. Return engine to idle speed before removing exerciser.

RELAYS

NOTE: If ASD relay is suspected of causing a fuel or ignition system malfunction, it will be necessary to use Diagnostic Readout Box (DRB-II) to diagnose ASD relay. See appropriate SELF-DIAGNOSTICS article. Perform NO-START TEST NS-1A or DRIVEABILITY TEST DR-1A test if fault code is present. If no fault code is present, perform NO-FAULT TEST NF-1A.

Auto Shutdown (ASD) & Fuel Solenoid Shut-Off Relay – 1) Remove relay. Using an ohmmeter, check for continuity between terminals No. 85 and No. 86. *See Fig. 2.* If continuity exists, go to next step. If continuity does not exist, replace relay.

2) Check for continuity between terminals No. 30 and No. 87A. If continuity exists, go to next step. If continuity does not exist, replace relay.

3) Check for continuity between terminals No. 30 and No. 87. If continuity does not exist, go to next step. If continuity exists, replace relay.

4) Using a 12-volt power supply, connect positive lead to terminal No. 85 and negative lead to terminal No. 86. Check for continuity between terminals No. 30 and No. 87. If continuity exists, relay is okay. If continuity does not exist, replace relay.

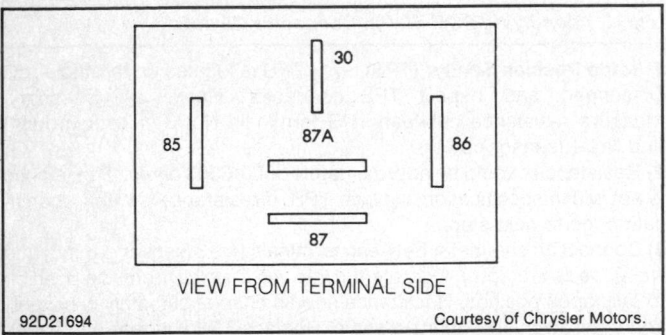

VIEW FROM TERMINAL SIDE

92D21694   Courtesy of Chrysler Motors.

Fig. 2: Identifying Auto Shutdown (ASD) & Fuel Solenoid Shut-Off Relay Terminals

SOLENOIDS

EGR Solenoid – See EMISSION SYSTEMS & SUB-SYSTEMS.
High-Pressure Fuel Shut-Off Solenoid – 1) Purge fuel system. See FUEL PRESSURE in BASIC DIAGNOSTIC PROCEDURES – CNG article. Disconnect solenoid harness connector.

2) Using jumper wires, connect one terminal of high-pressure fuel shut-off solenoid to a 12-volt power source. Connect another jumper wire to the other solenoid terminal.

CAUTION: Use jumper wires made from 18-gauge or smaller wire.

3) Momentarily touch other end of second jumper wire to chassis ground. Solenoid should "click". If solenoid does not operate as specified, replace fuel pressure regulator.

Lock-Up Solenoid – See MISCELLANEOUS CONTROLS.
Low-Pressure Fuel Shut-Off Solenoid – 1) Purge fuel system. See FUEL PRESSURE in BASIC DIAGNOSTIC PROCEDURES – CNG article. Disconnect solenoid harness connector.

2) Using jumper wires, connect one terminal of low-pressure fuel shut-off solenoid to a 12-volt power source. Connect another jumper wire to the other solenoid terminal.

CAUTION: Use jumper wires made from 18-gauge or smaller wire.

3) Momentarily touch other end of second jumper wire to chassis ground. Solenoid should "click". If solenoid does not operate as specified, replace low-pressure fuel shut-off solenoid.

Overdrive Lock-Out Solenoid – See MISCELLANEOUS CONTROLS.

FUEL SYSTEM
FUEL DELIVERY

NOTE: For fuel system pressure testing, see appropriate BASIC DIAGNOSTIC PROCEDURES article.

FUEL CONTROL

Fuel Injector – Disconnect fuel injector connector. Using a DVOM in ohmmeter position, test between pins of injector for resistance. If resistance is NOT 1.1-2.1 ohms, replace fuel injector.
Fuel Pressure Regulator – See appropriate BASIC DIAGNOSTIC PROCEDURES article.

IGNITION SYSTEM

NOTE: For basic ignition checks, see BASIC DIAGNOSTIC PROCEDURES – CNG article.

EMISSION SYSTEMS & SUB-SYSTEMS

NOTE: To locate emission components, refer to emission control information label in engine compartment.

EXHAUST GAS RECIRCULATION (EGR)

NOTE: To ensure proper EGR system operation, all passages and moving parts must be free from restrictive deposits. Clean or replace components as necessary.

EGR System Operation Check – 1) Warm engine to operating temperature. Attach a tachometer to engine. Run engine at idle in Neutral an additional 70 seconds.

2) Accelerate the engine abruptly to 2000-3000 RPM and check EGR valve stem for movement. Repeat test to confirm stem movement, indicating EGR control system is functioning correctly.

3) If EGR valve stem does not move, check for cracked, leaking, disconnected or plugged vacuum hoses. Verify correct hose routing. Disconnect hose harness from EGR valve/transducer, and connect a vacuum pump to harness.

4) Start engine and raise engine speed to 2000 RPM and hold. Apply 10 In. Hg. vacuum to EGR, while checking for EGR valve movement. If no movement occurs, replace EGR valve/transducer assembly.

5) If valve opens approximately 1/8", hold vacuum constant and check for valve diaphragm leakage. Valve should remain open for at least 30 seconds. If leakage occurs, replace valve/transducer assembly. If valve is okay, check control system.

6) If EGR valve stem did not move in step **2)**, but operates normally on external vacuum source, remove throttle body and check port in throttle bore for blockage. Use a solvent to remove deposits and check flow with light air pressure. Normal operation should be restored.

7) If engine will not idle correctly or stalls, check for leaking EGR valve. With engine running, remove vacuum hose from EGR valve. If removing the vacuum hose does not correct rough idle, remove EGR valve/transducer assembly. Check valve for proper seating. Replace assembly as necessary.

8) Also check EGR-to-intake manifold tube for leak. Remove tube and inspect gasket. Tube end should be uniformly indented on gasket, without signs of leakage. If there are signs of leakage, replace gaskets and tighten flange nuts to **17 ft. lbs. (23 N.m)**. If leak persists, replace EGR tube and gaskets.

NOTE: DO NOT use drills or wires to clean passages for EGR control system. Calibration of precision orifices could be altered, resulting in unsatisfactory vehicle operation.

EGR Solenoid – 1) EGR solenoid is located on EGR transducer. With ignition switch in OFF position, disconnect and inspect solenoid connector. Repair as necessary. If connector is okay, go to next step.
2) Using an ohmmeter, check resistance across solenoid terminals. If resistance is NOT 20-50 ohms, replace solenoid. If solenoid is okay, test EGR solenoid system. See appropriate SELF-DIAGNOSTICS article.

POSITIVE CRANKCASE VENTILATION (PCV)

PCV Valve – 1) With engine running at curb idle, remove PCV valve from grommet. If valve is functioning properly, a hissing sound will be heard as air passes through valve.
2) With engine running, place finger over valve inlet. Strong vacuum should be felt at valve inlet. Stop engine. Remove and shake PCV valve to ensure a metallic clicking noise can be heard, indicating valve is free. Reinstall PCV valve.
3) Remove the crankcase ventilation filter or oil filler cap from the valve cover. Hold a piece of stiff paper over the opening. After allowing about one minute for crankcase pressure stabilization, the paper should be drawn against opening.
4) If paper is held against opening, performance is okay. If not, replace PCV valve and retest. If performance does not improve, inspect system for restrictions, and clean as necessary.

MISCELLANEOUS CONTROLS

NOTE: Although some of the controlled devices listed here are not technically engine performance components, they can affect driveability if they malfunction.

A/C Clutch Relay – 1) A/C clutch relay is located in engine compartment. Using a DVOM, backprobe Red/Light Green wire at relay connector. If voltmeter reading is greater than 10 volts, go to next step. If voltmeter reading is less than 10 volts, repair open circuit between A/C clutch relay and battery.
2) Turn ignition on. Using voltmeter, backprobe Dark Blue/Orange wire at A/C clutch relay. If voltage is greater than 10 volts, see appropriate SELF-DIAGNOSTICS article. If voltage reading is less than 10 volts, backprobe Dark Blue wire in relay connector.
3) If voltage reading is greater than 10 volts, replace relay. If voltage reading is less than 10 volts, repair open circuit between A/C clutch relay and ignition switch.
4) Using a jumper wire, connect Dark Blue/Orange wire to chassis ground. Relay should "click". If relay does not operate as specified, replace relay. If relay operates as specified, relay is okay.

TRANSMISSION

Lock-Up Solenoid – 1) Lock-up solenoid is located on left side of transmission. Turn ignition off. Disconnect solenoid connector from transmission. Inspect connector and repair as necessary.
2) If connector is okay, turn ignition on. Using a DVOM, check for voltage on Dark Blue wire in connector. If voltage is less than 10 volts, repair open circuit in Dark Blue wire between solenoid connector and ignition switch. If voltage is greater than 10 volts, see appropriate SELF-DIAGNOSTICS article.
Overdrive Lock-Out Solenoid – 1) Lock-up solenoid is located on left side of transmission. Turn ignition off. Disconnect solenoid connector from transmission. Inspect connector and repair as necessary.
2) If connector is okay, turn ignition on. Using a DVOM, check for voltage on Dark Blue wire in connector. If voltage is less than 10 volts, repair open circuit in Dark Blue wire between solenoid connector and ignition switch. If voltage is greater than 10 volts, see appropriate SELF-DIAGNOSTICS article.

1992 ENGINE PERFORMANCE
Wiring Diagrams – Gasoline & Diesel

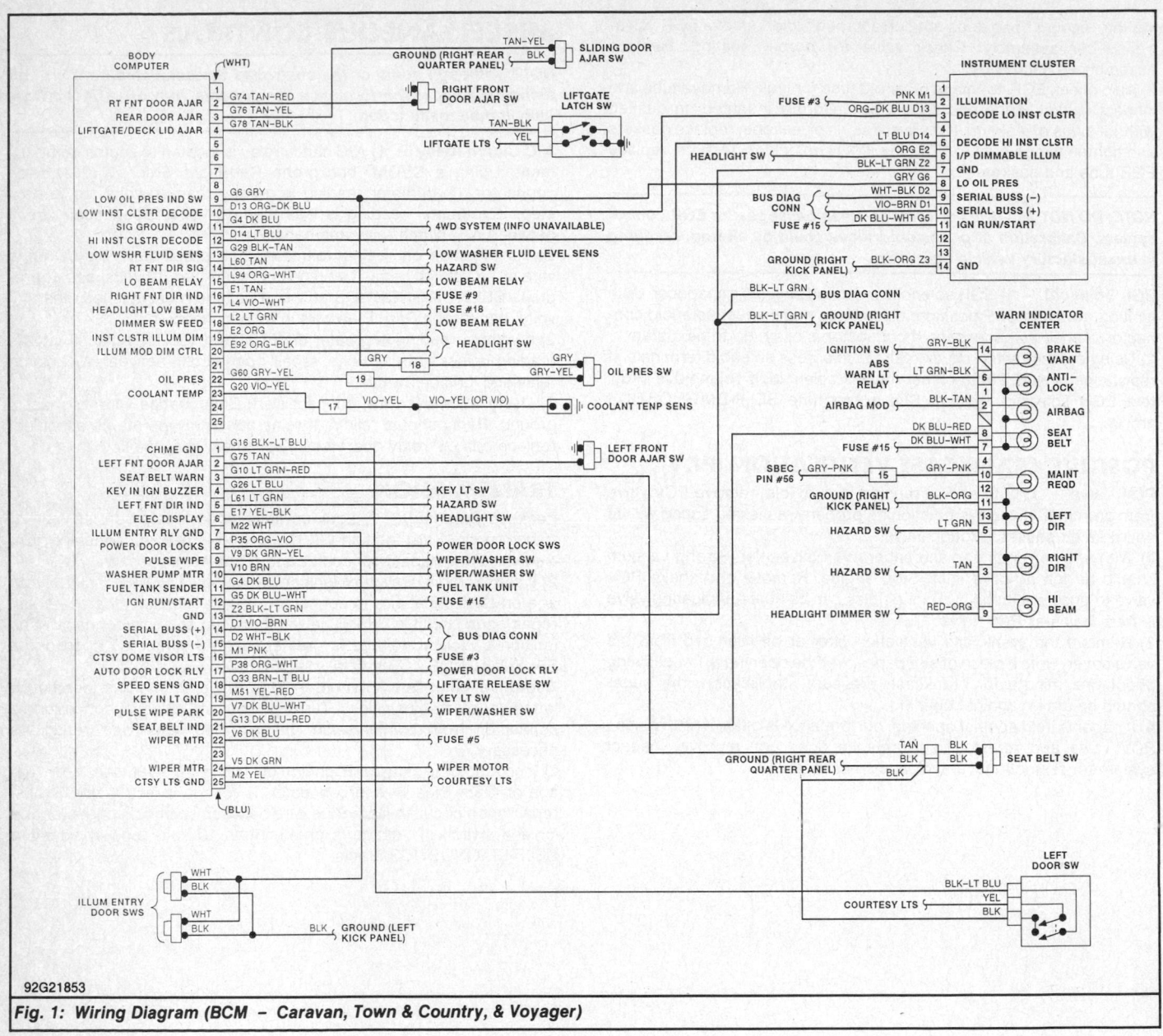

92G21853

Fig. 1: Wiring Diagram (BCM – Caravan, Town & Country, & Voyager)

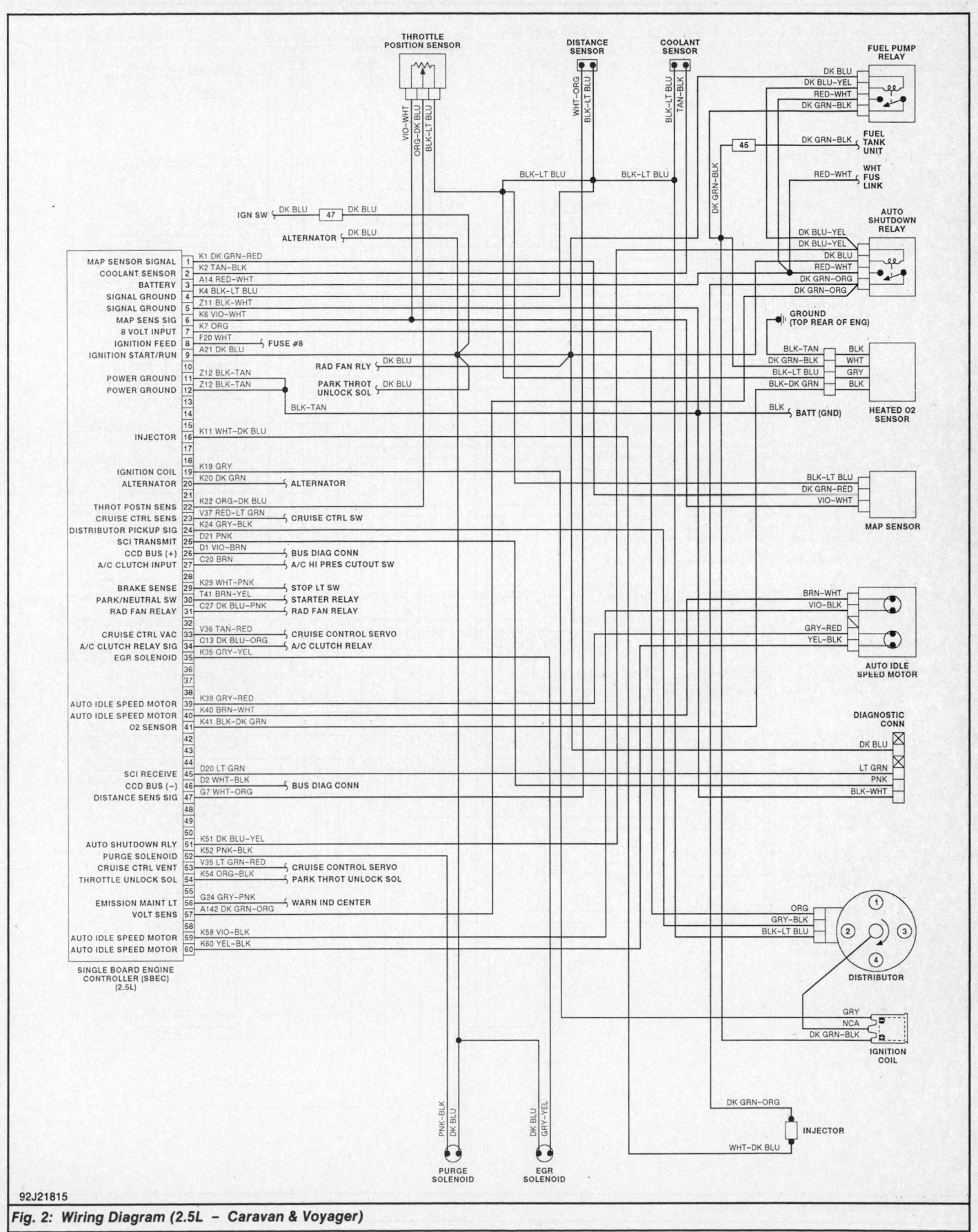

92J21815

Fig. 2: Wiring Diagram (2.5L – Caravan & Voyager)

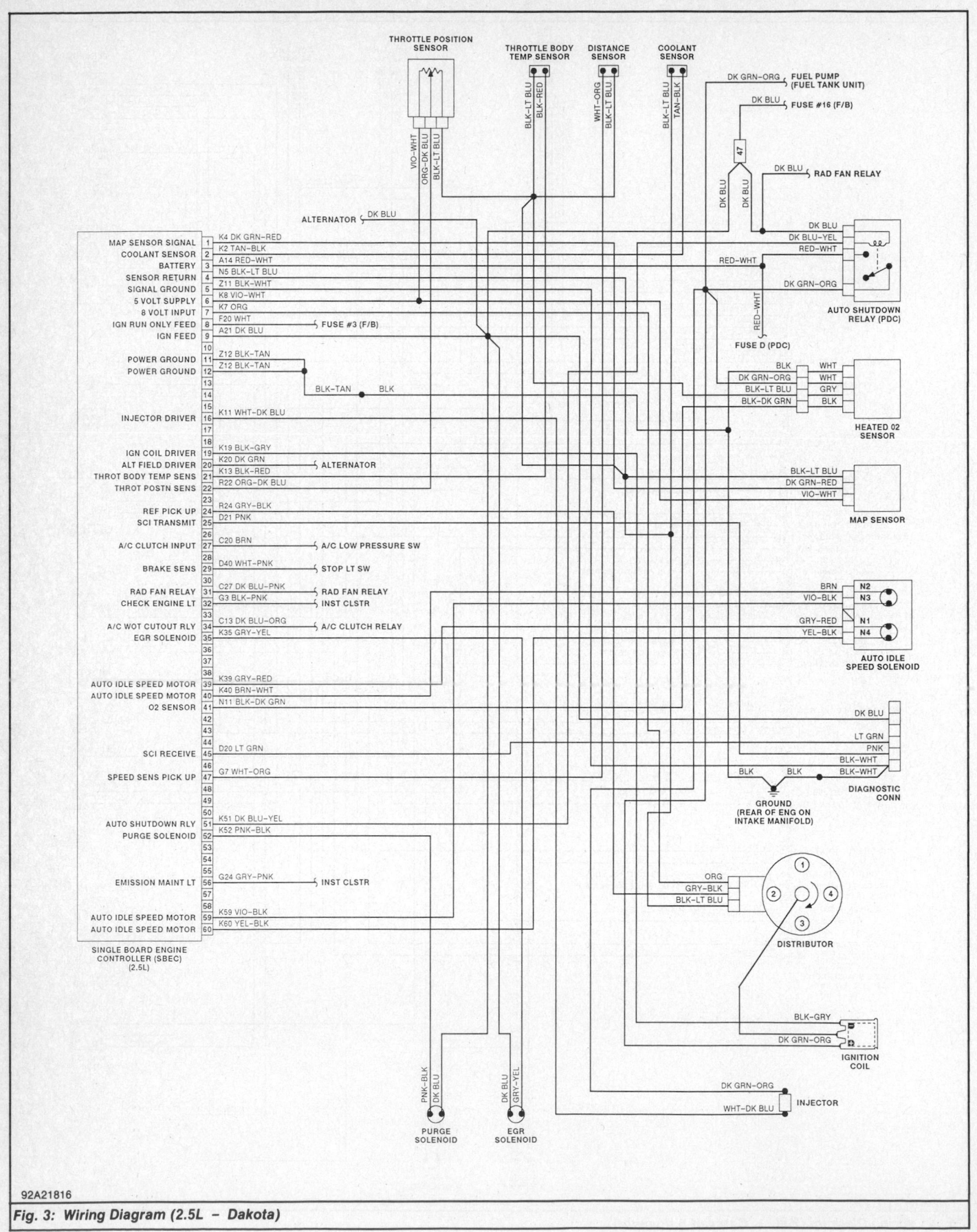

92A21816

Fig. 3: Wiring Diagram (2.5L – Dakota)

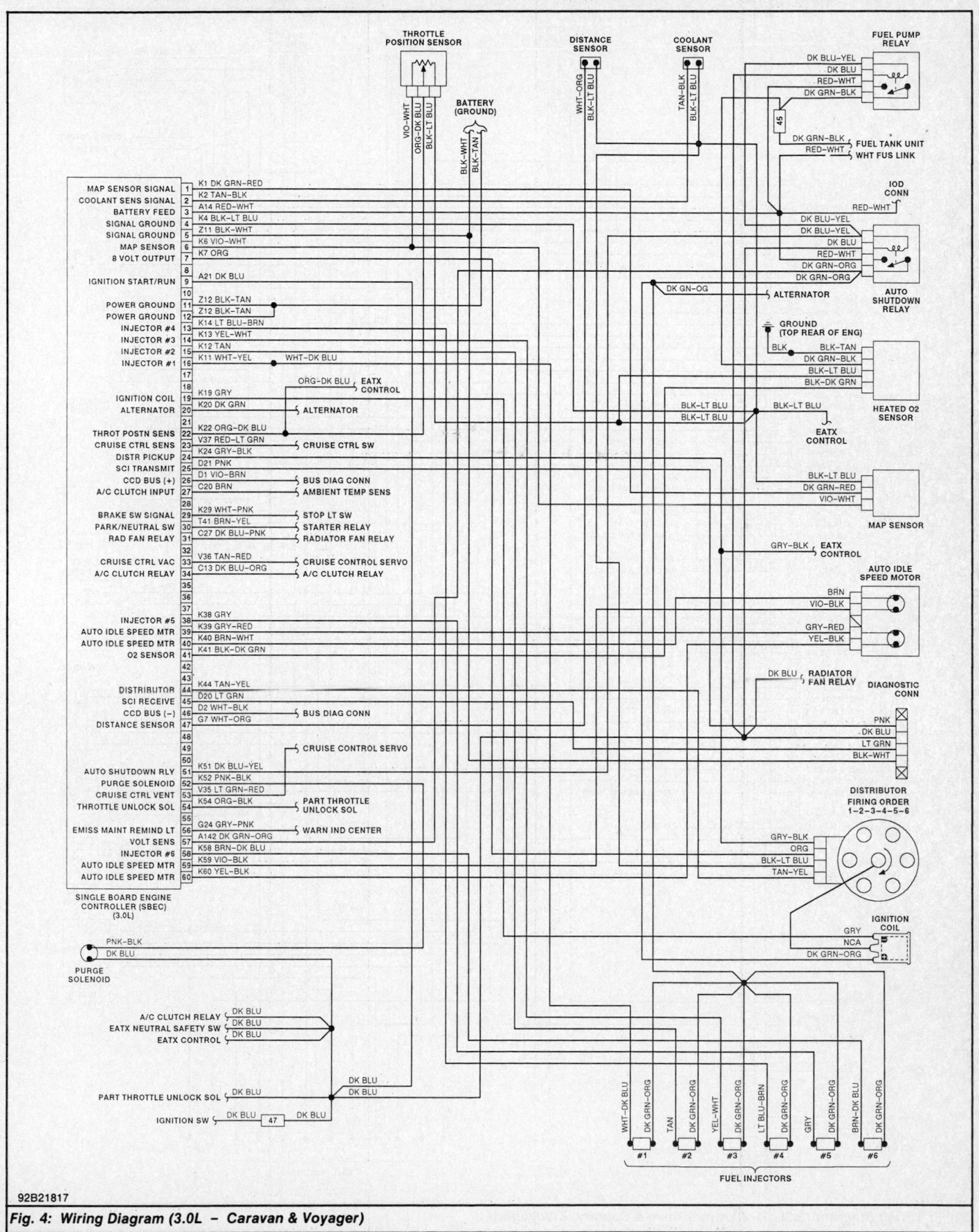

Fig. 4: Wiring Diagram (3.0L – Caravan & Voyager)

92B21817

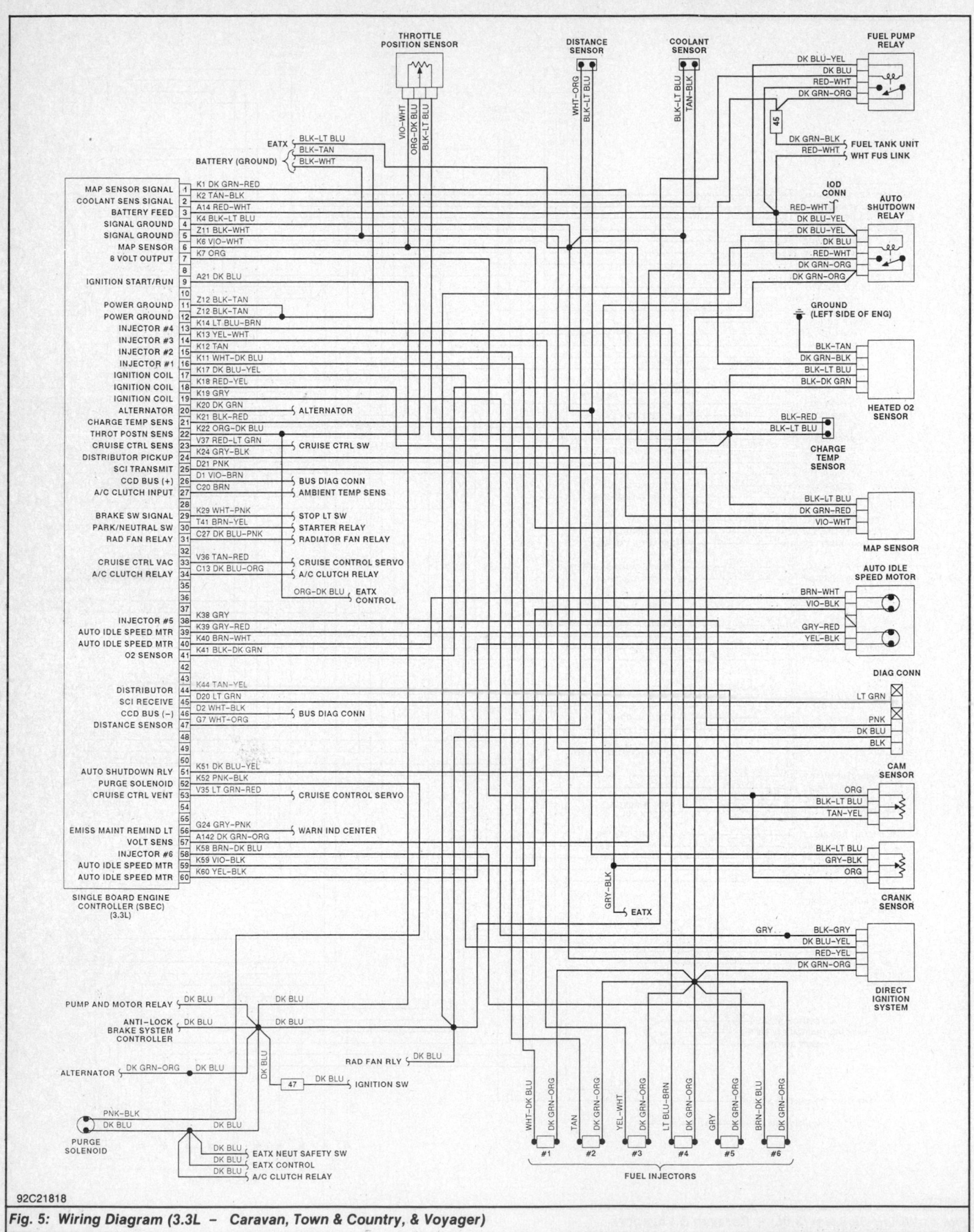

92C21818

Fig. 5: Wiring Diagram (3.3L – Caravan, Town & Country, & Voyager)

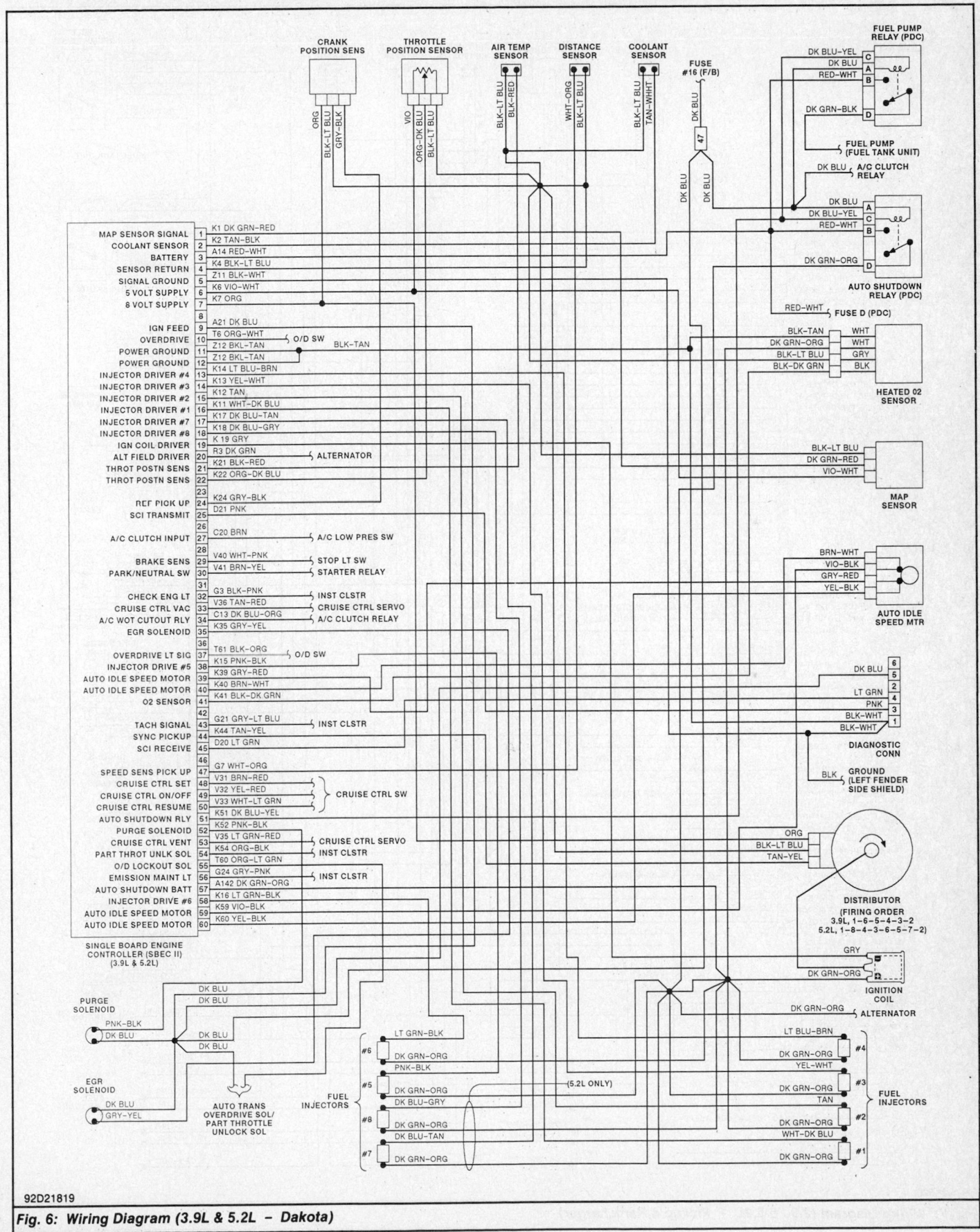

Fig. 6: Wiring Diagram (3.9L & 5.2L - Dakota)

92D21819

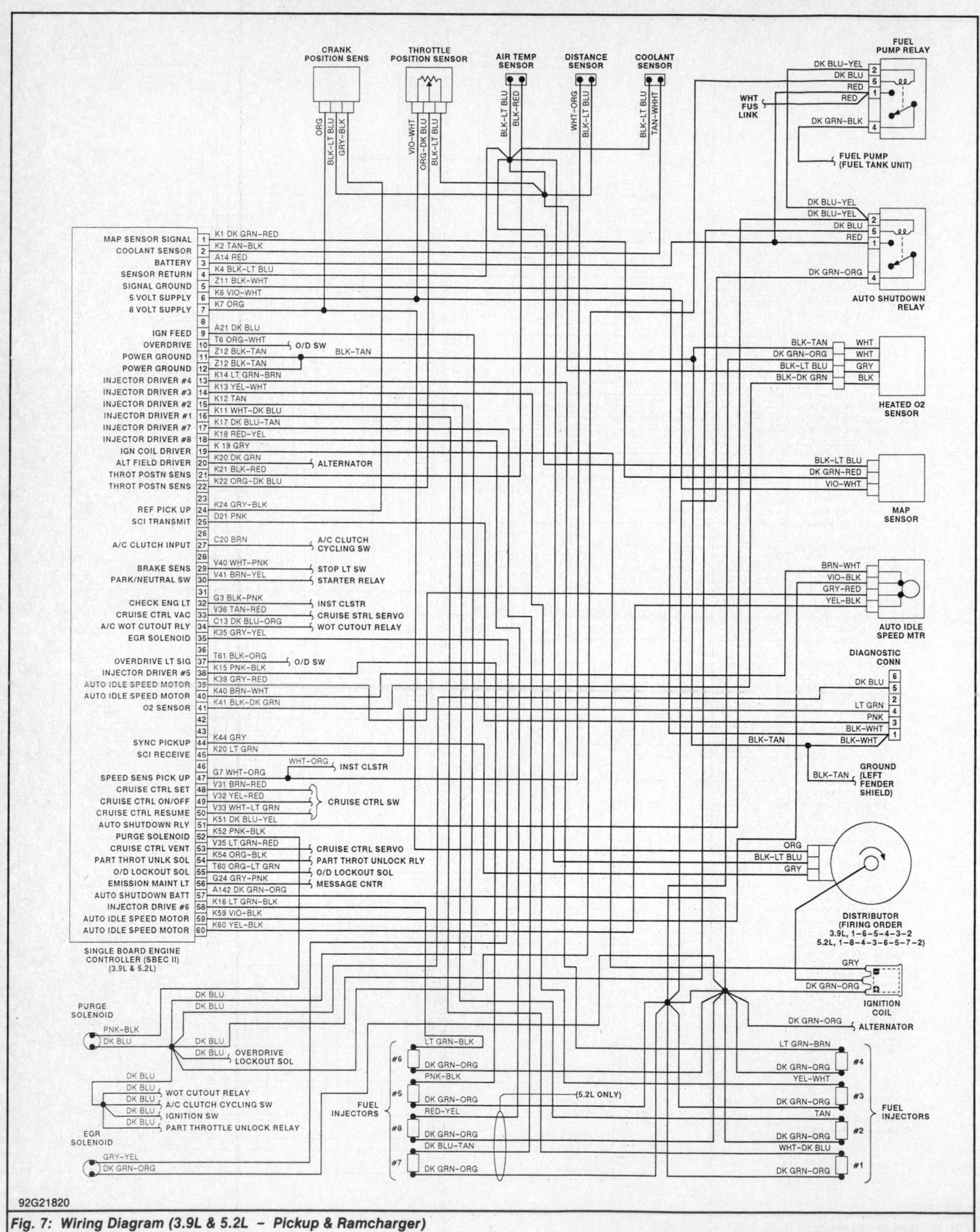

Fig. 7: Wiring Diagram (3.9L & 5.2L – Pickup & Ramcharger)

92G21820

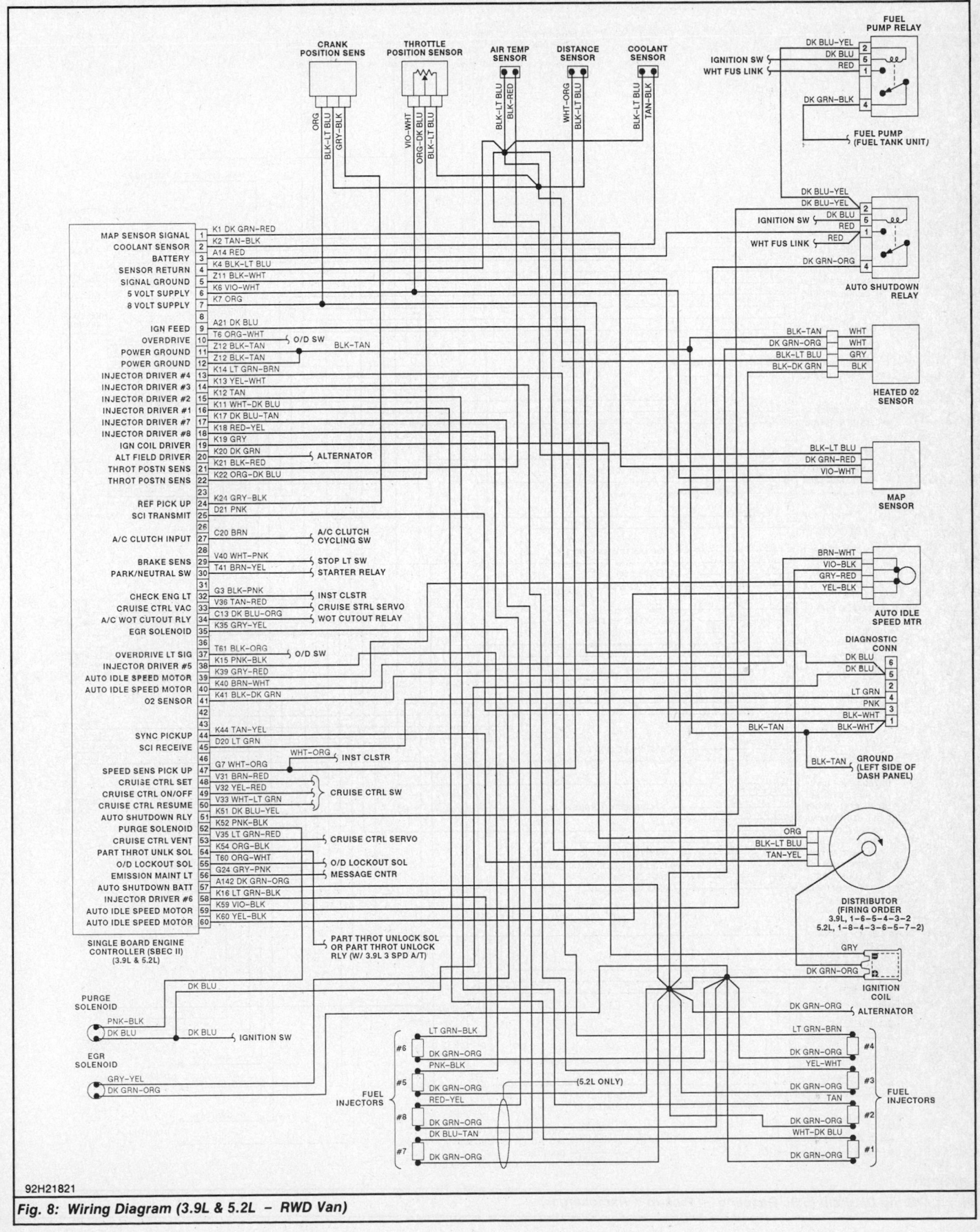

Fig. 8: Wiring Diagram (3.9L & 5.2L – RWD Van)

92H21821

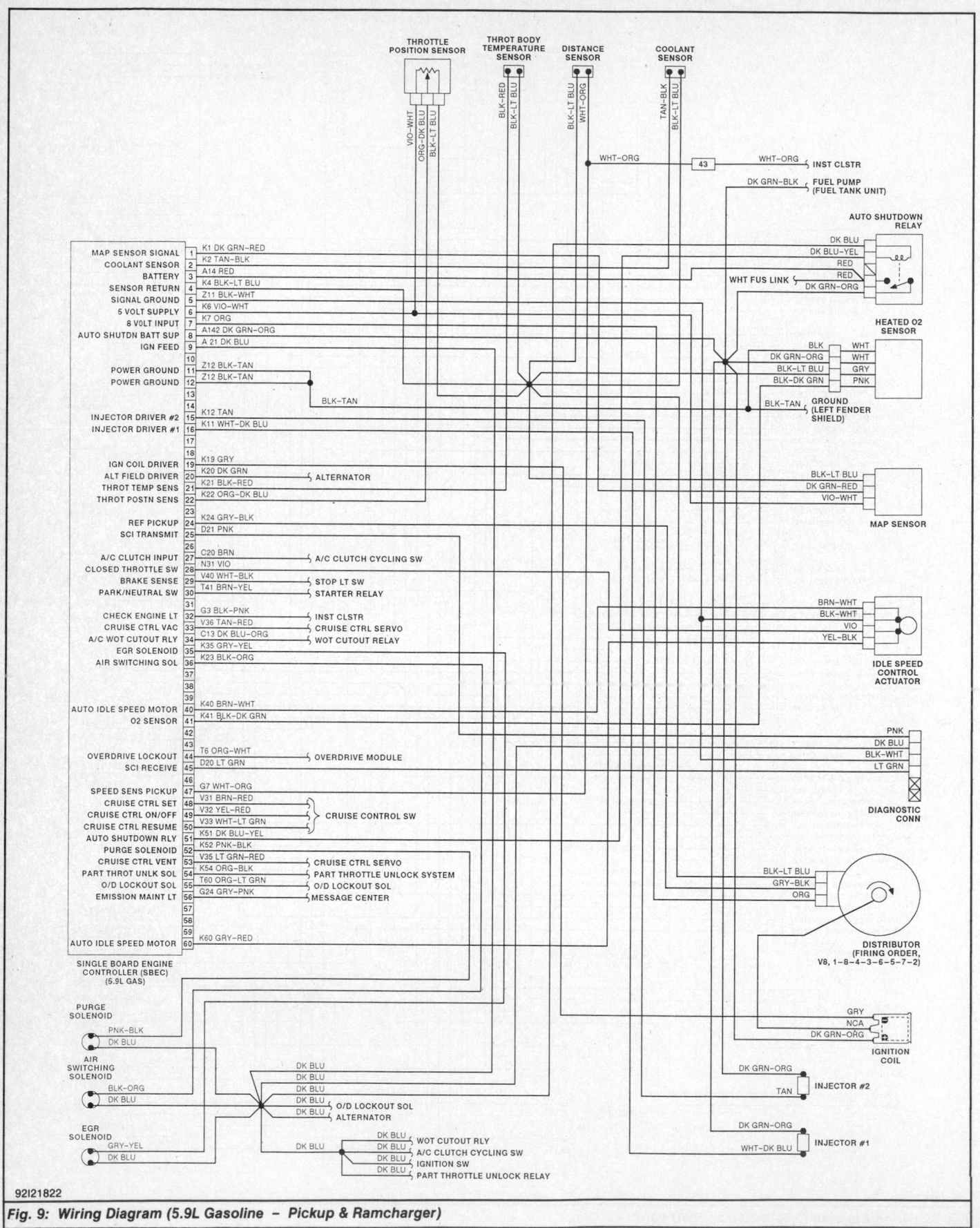

Fig. 9: Wiring Diagram (5.9L Gasoline – Pickup & Ramcharger)

92121822

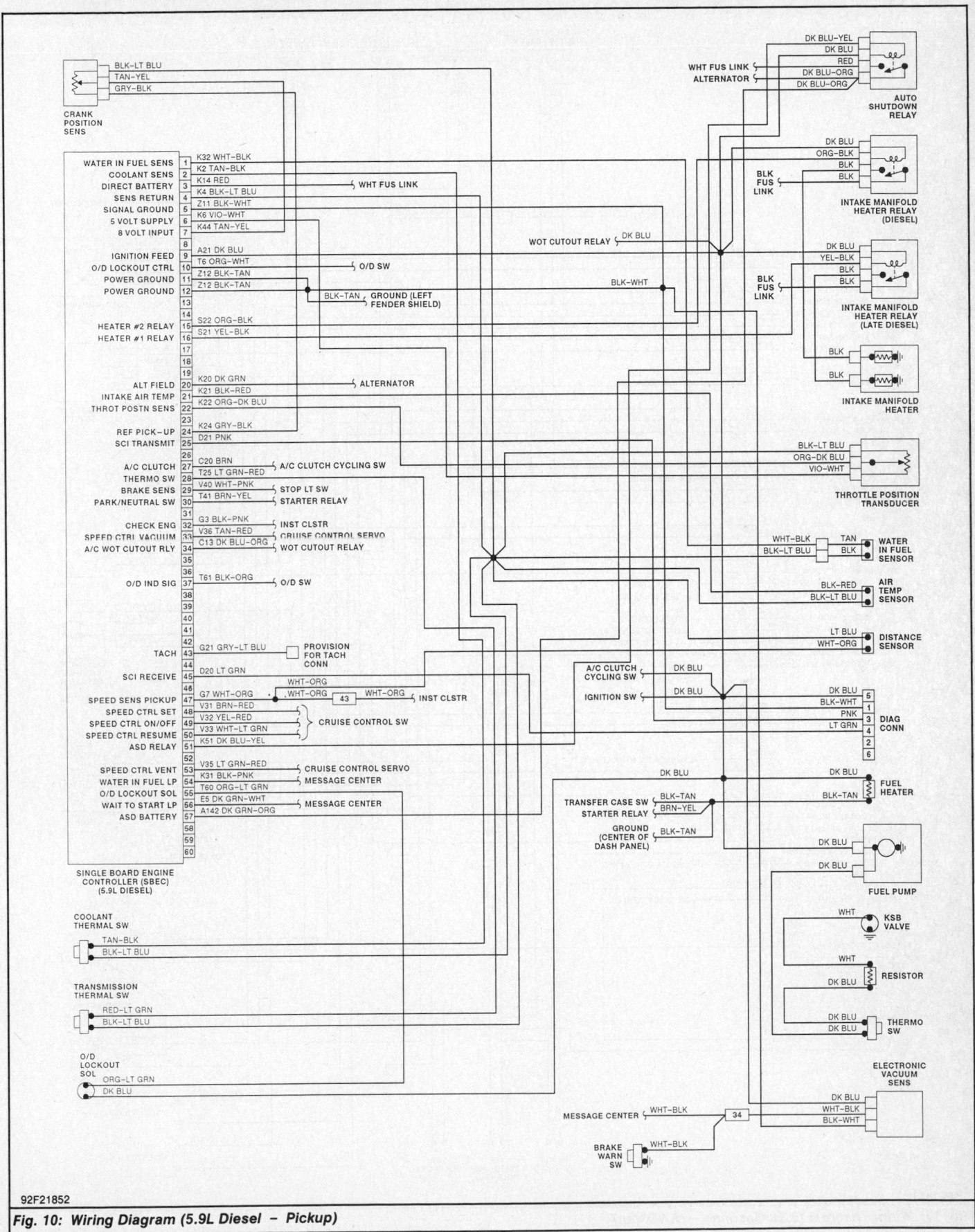

Fig. 10: Wiring Diagram (5.9L Diesel - Pickup)

92F21852

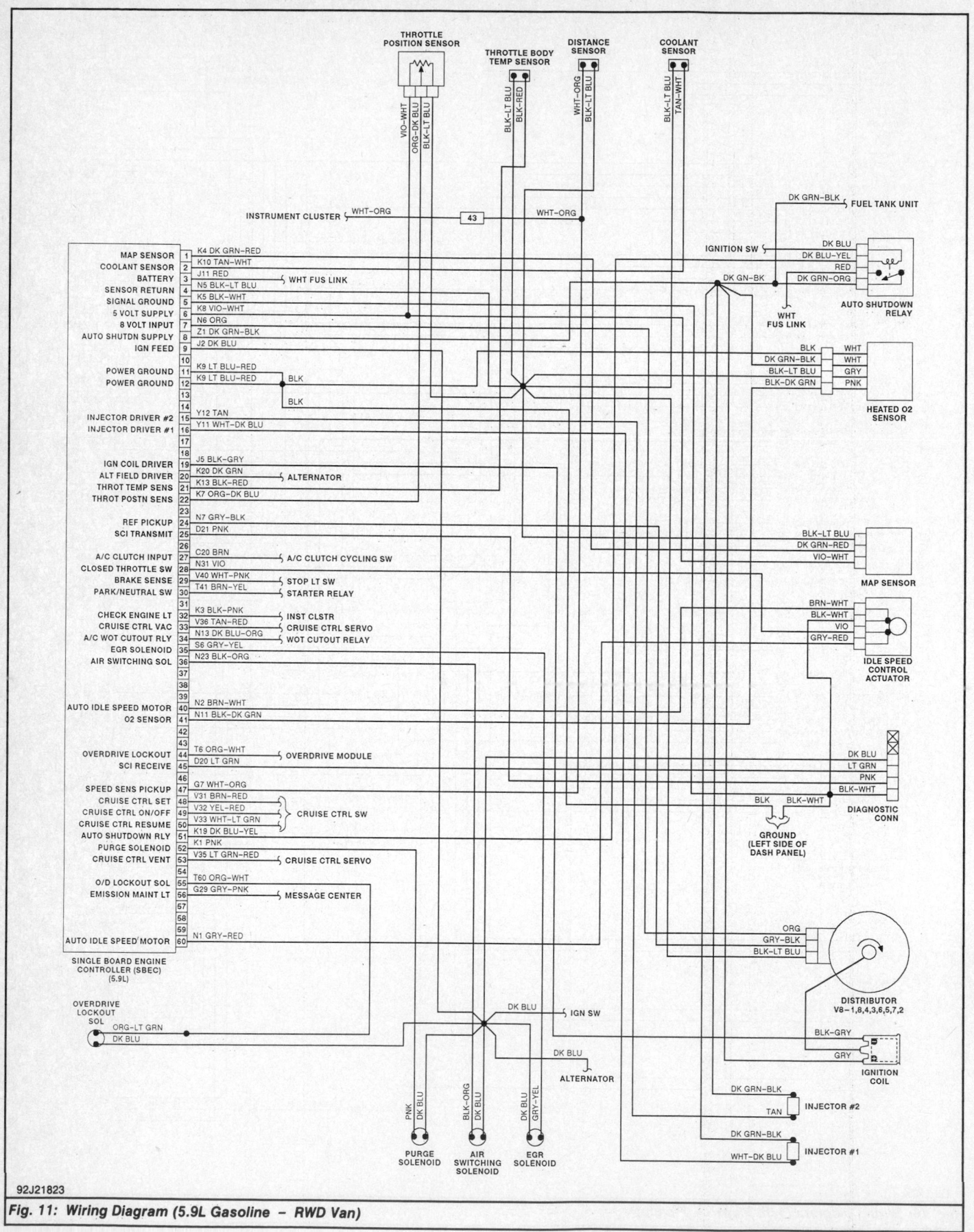

Fig. 11: Wiring Diagram (5.9L Gasoline – RWD Van)

92J21823

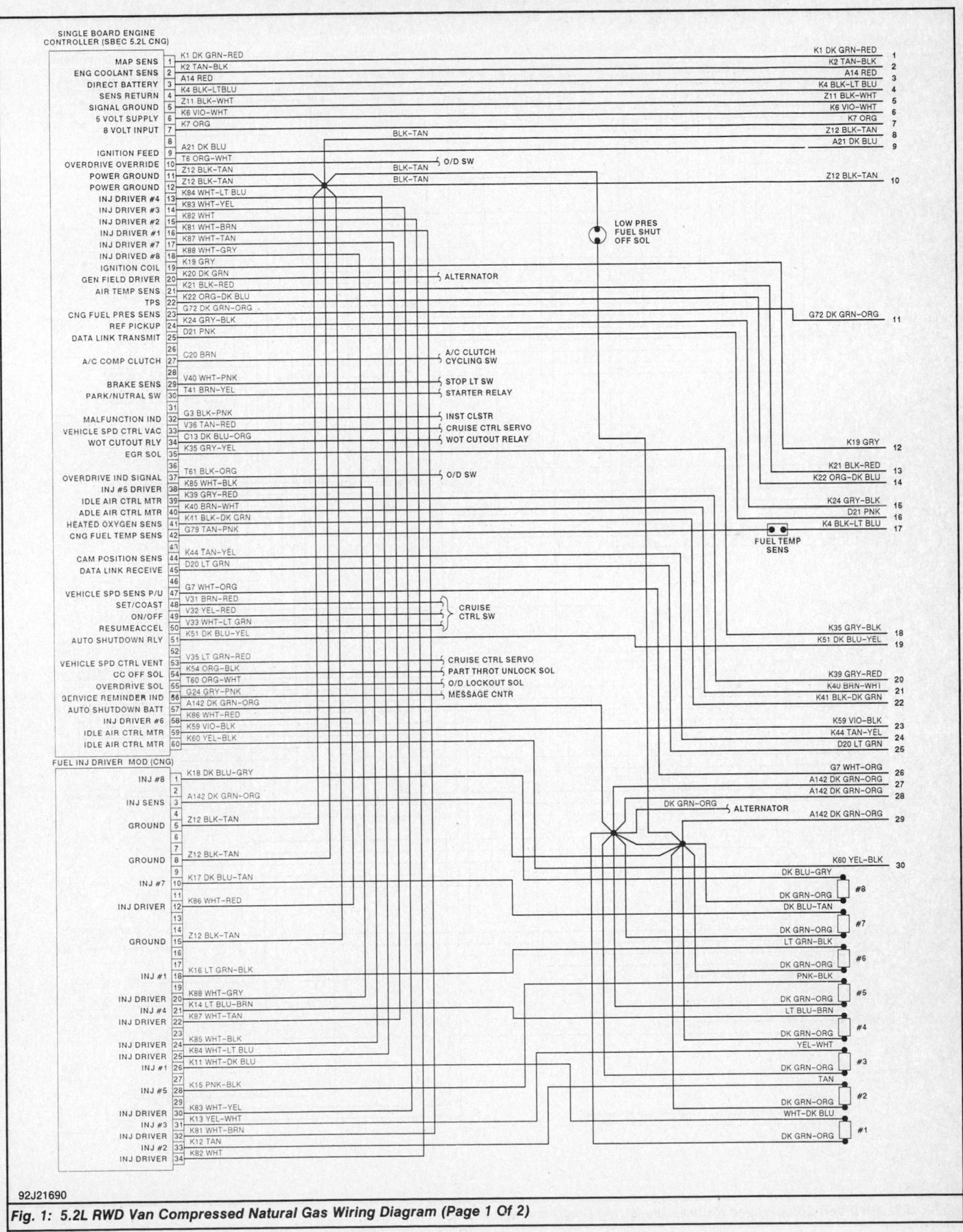

92J21690

Fig. 1: 5.2L RWD Van Compressed Natural Gas Wiring Diagram (Page 1 Of 2)

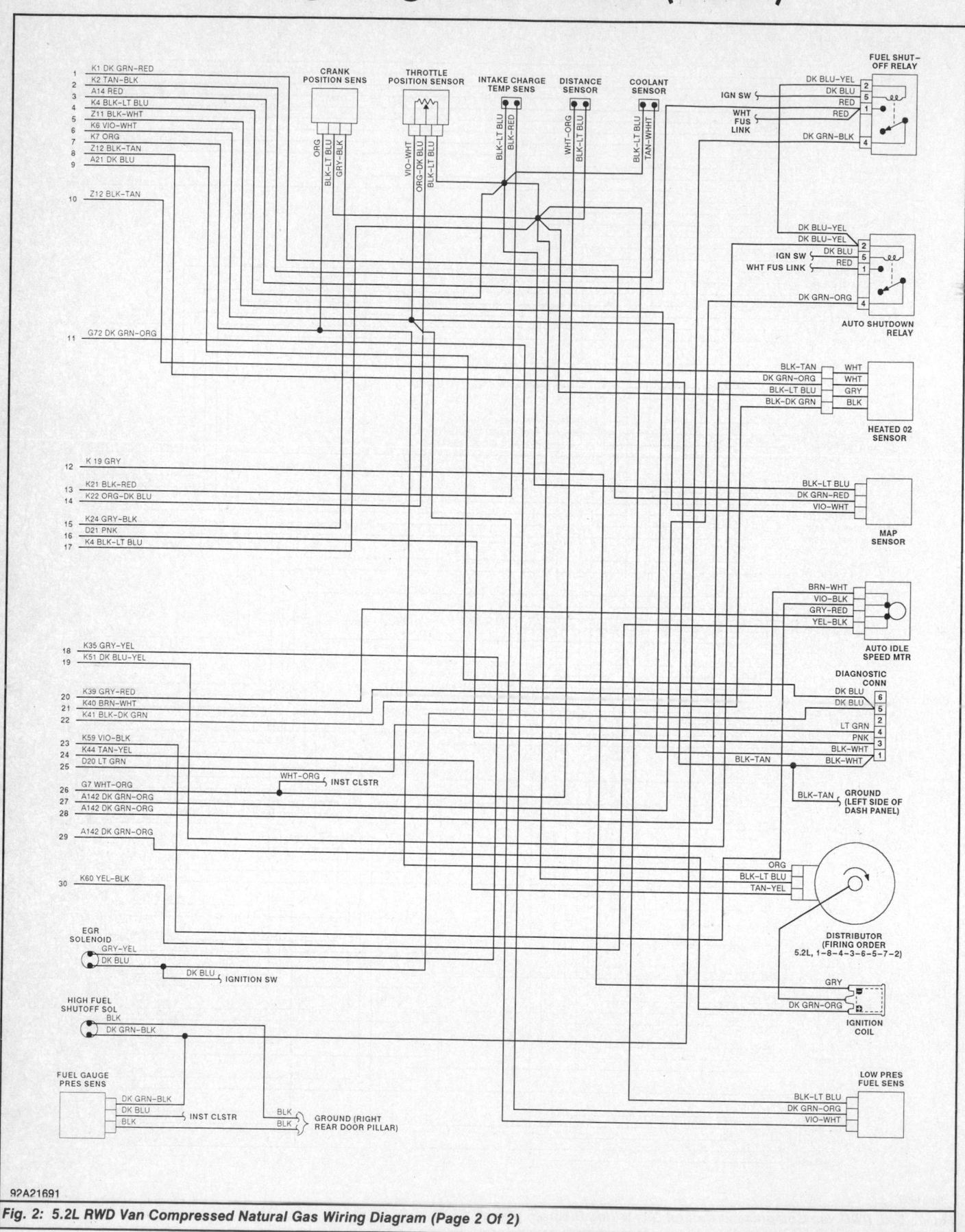

92A21691

Fig. 2: 5.2L RWD Van Compressed Natural Gas Wiring Diagram (Page 2 Of 2)

1992 ENGINE PERFORMANCE
Vacuum Diagrams – Gasoline

Caravan, Dakota, Pickup, Ramcharger, RWD Van, Town & Country, Voyager

INTRODUCTION

This article contains underhood views or schematics of vacuum hose routing. Use these vacuum diagrams during visual inspection in appropriate BASIC DIAGNOSTIC PROCEDURES article. This will assist in identifying improperly routed vacuum hoses, which cause driveability and/or computer-indicated malfunctions.

NOTE: Always refer to Emission Control Label in engine compartment before attempting service. If manual and label differ, always use emission label specifications.

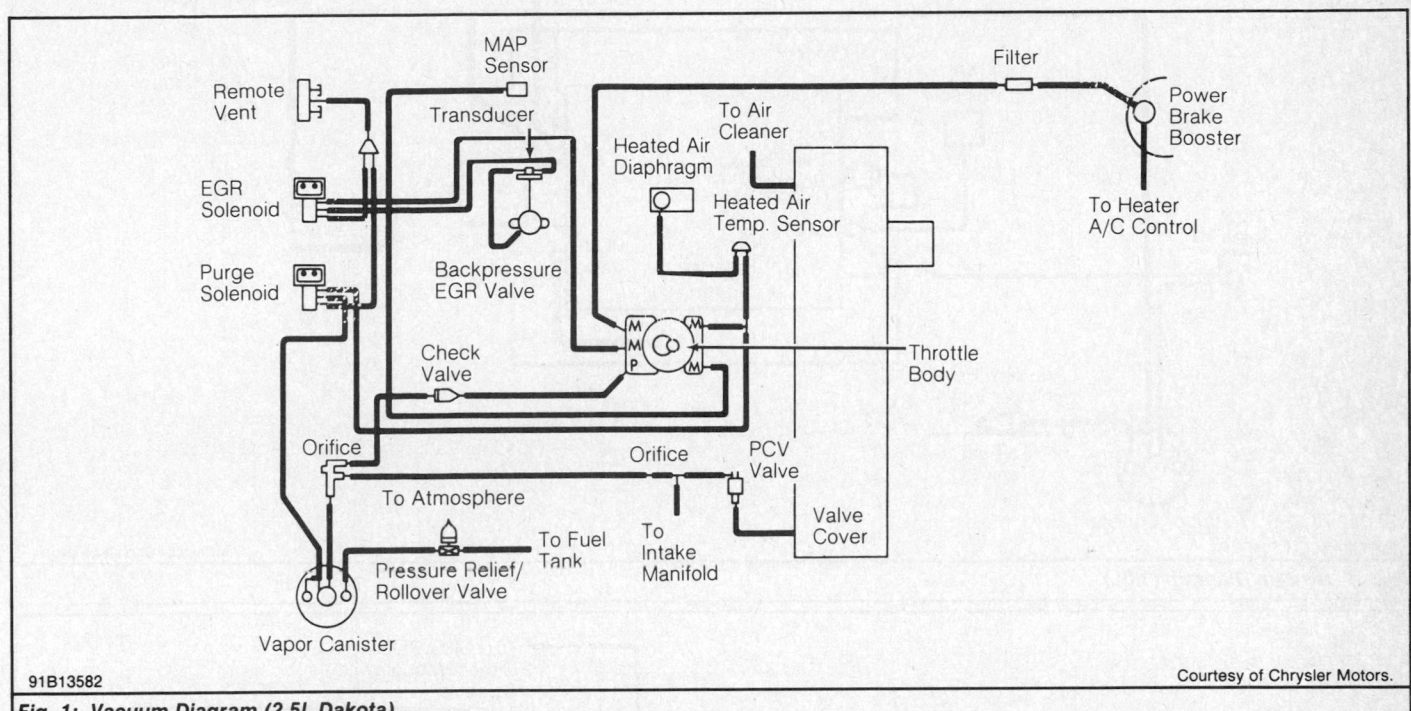

Courtesy of Chrysler Motors.

Fig. 1: Vacuum Diagram (2.5L Dakota)

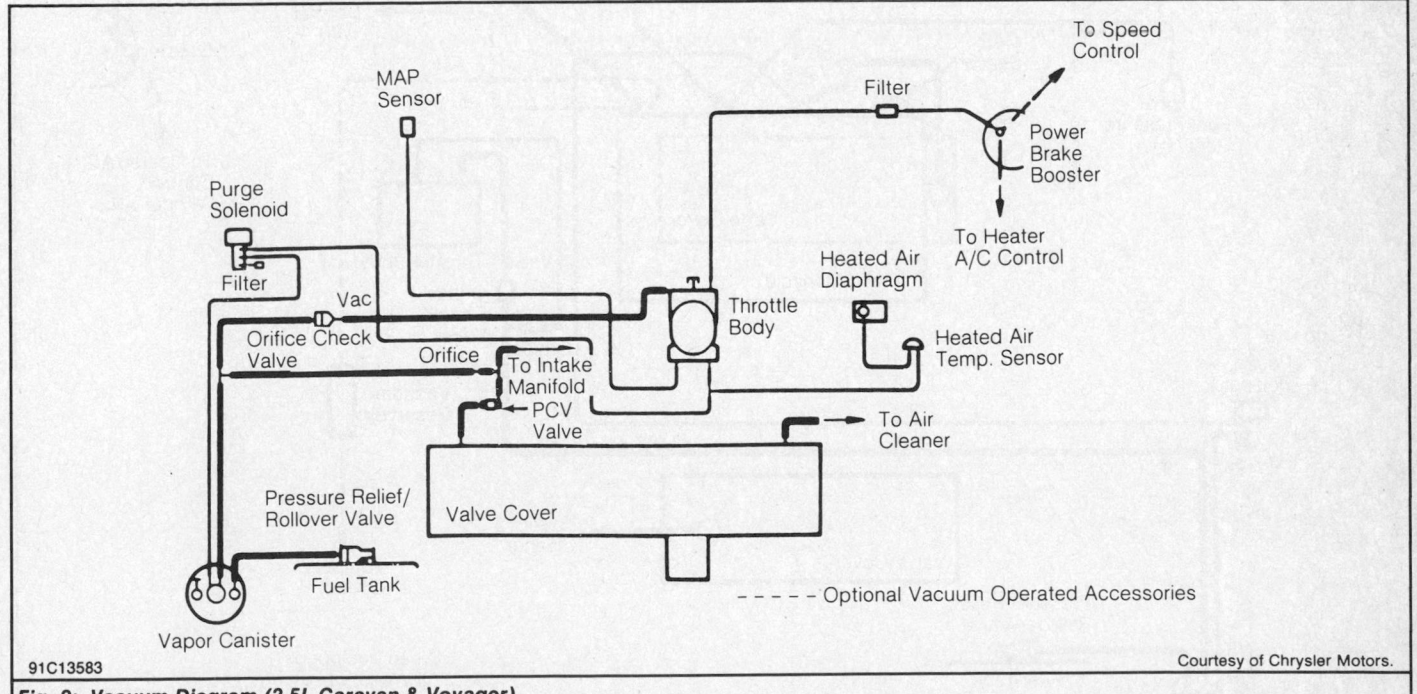

Courtesy of Chrysler Motors.

Fig. 2: Vacuum Diagram (2.5L Caravan & Voyager)

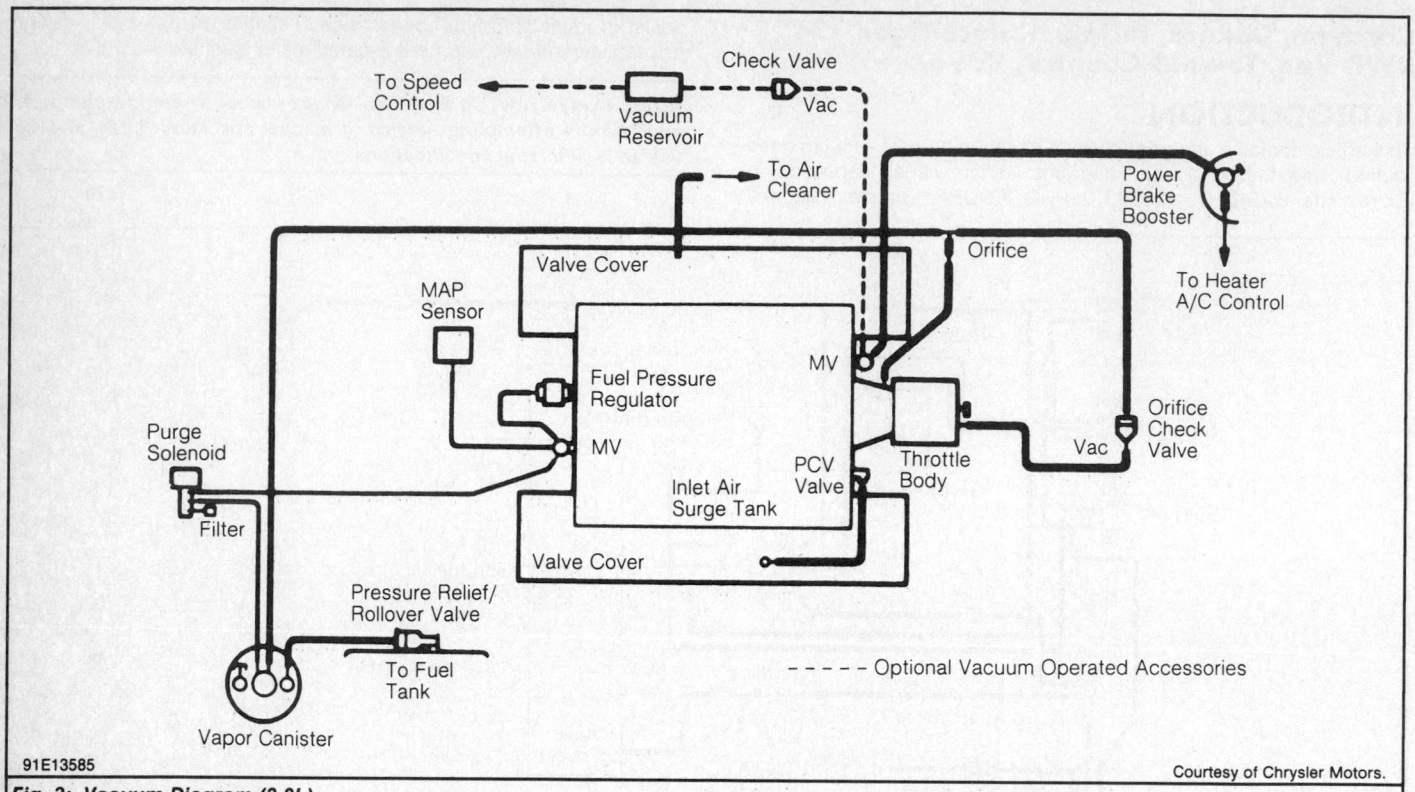

Fig. 3: Vacuum Diagram (3.0L)

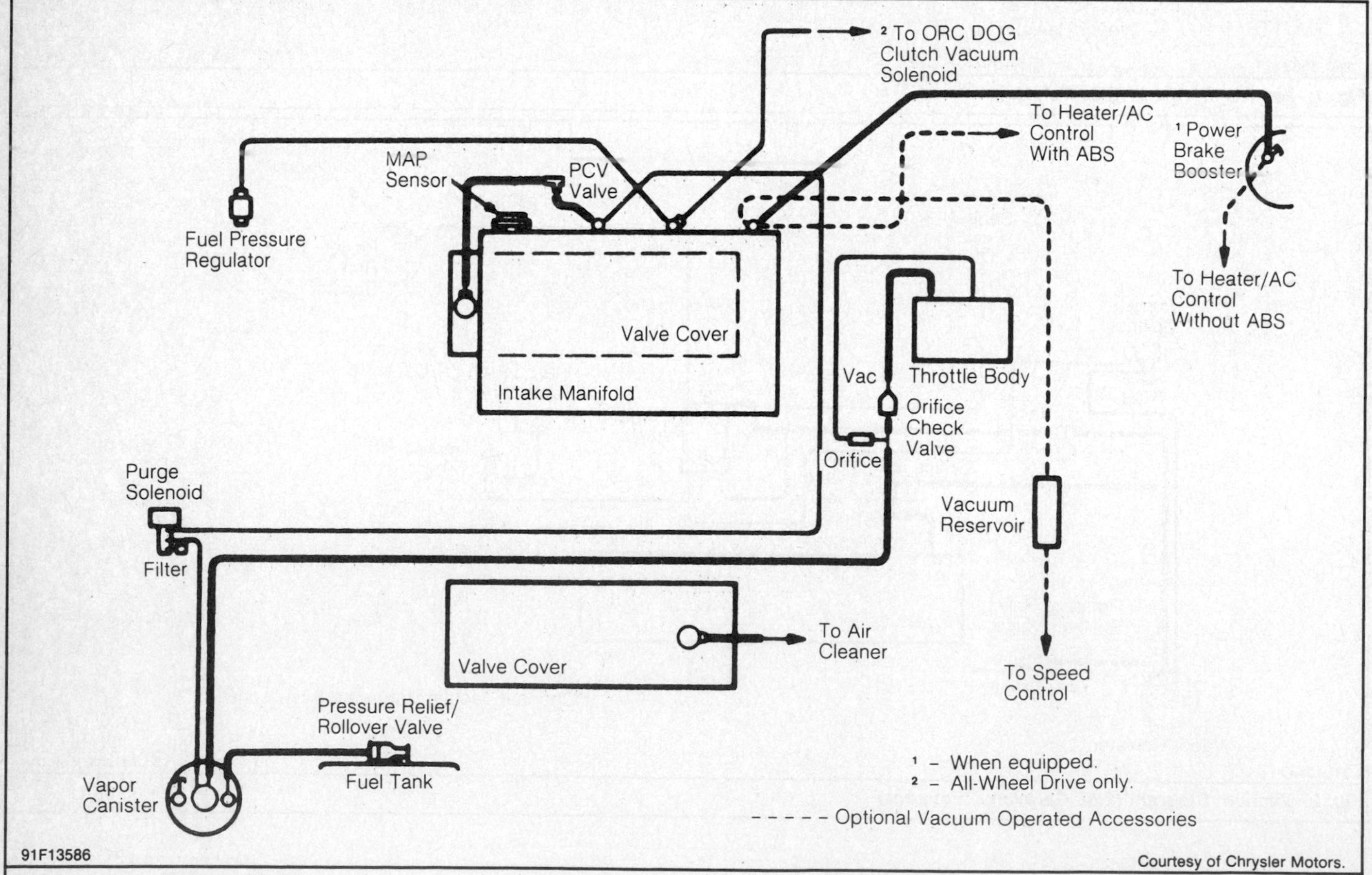

91E13585

Courtesy of Chrysler Motors.

Fig. 4: Vacuum Diagram (3.3L)

91F13586

Courtesy of Chrysler Motors.

1992 ENGINE PERFORMANCE
Vacuum Diagrams – Gasoline (Cont.)

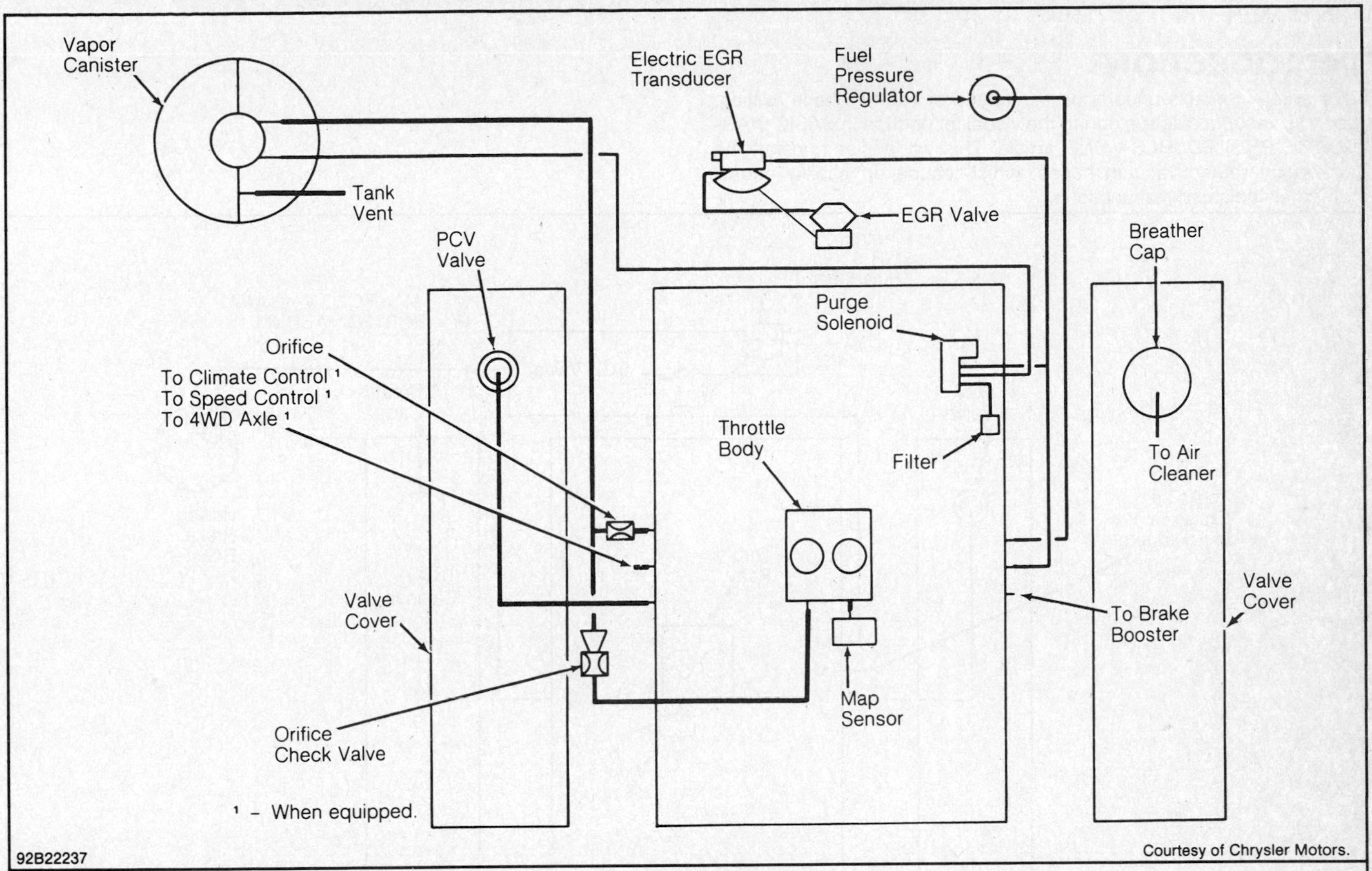

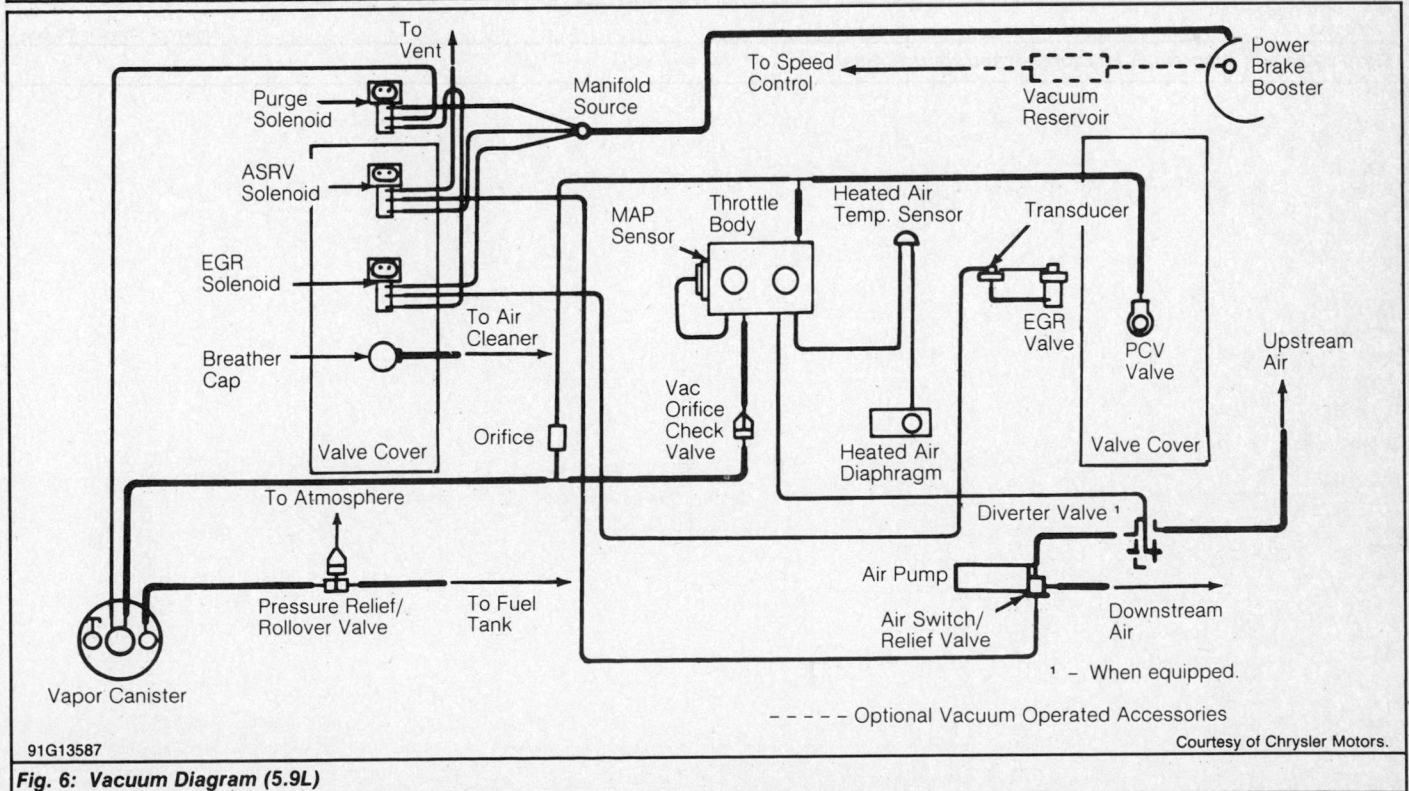

Fig. 5: Vacuum Diagram (3.9L & 5.2L)

Fig. 6: Vacuum Diagram (5.9L)

1992 ENGINE PERFORMANCE
Vacuum Diagram – CNG

RWD Van

INTRODUCTION

This article contains underhood schematic of vacuum hose routing. Use this vacuum diagram during the visual inspection in BASIC DIAGNOSTIC PROCEDURES – CNG article. This will assist in identifying improperly routed vacuum hoses, which cause driveability and/or computer-indicated malfunctions.

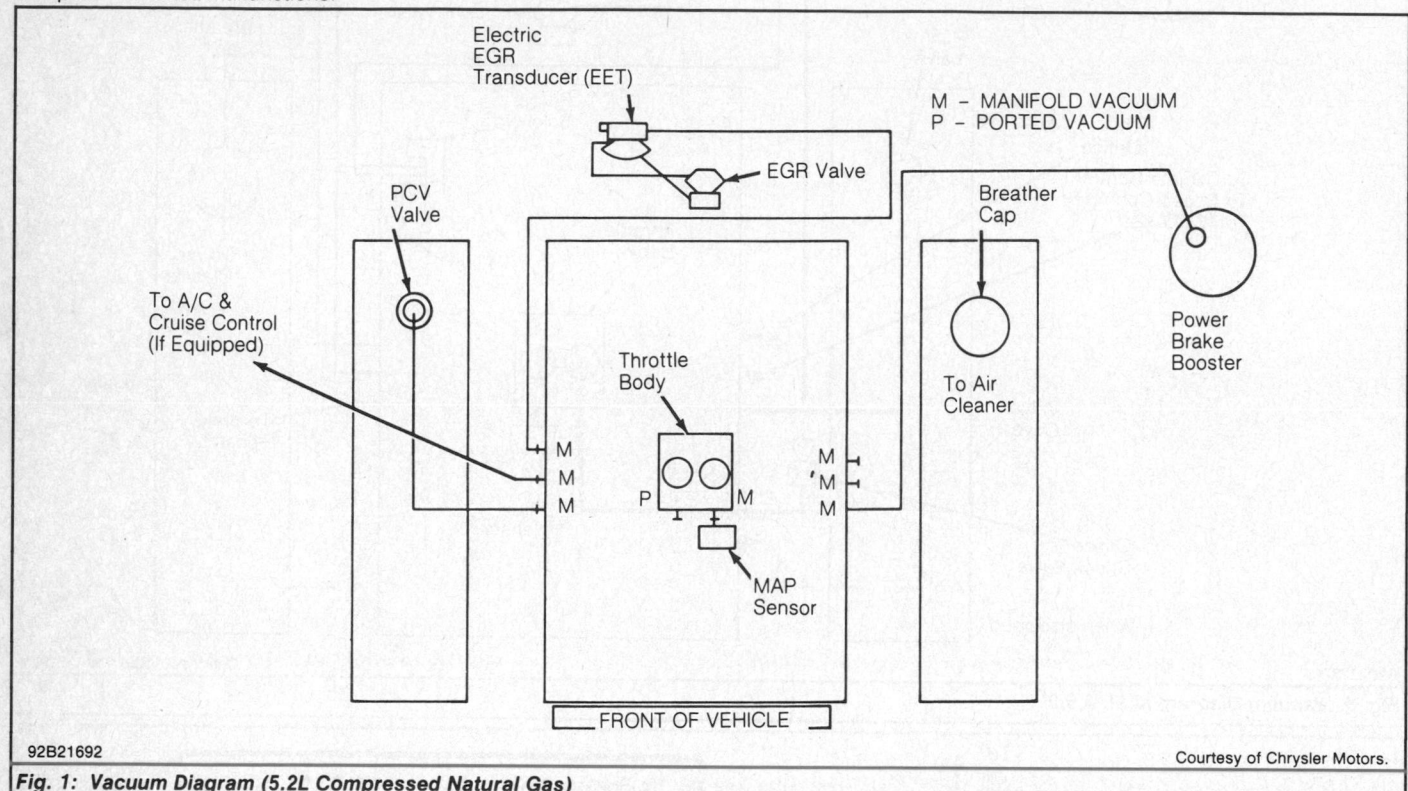

92B21692

Courtesy of Chrysler Motors.

Fig. 1: Vacuum Diagram (5.2L Compressed Natural Gas)

Caravan, Dakota, Pickup, Ramcharger, RWD Van, Town & Country, Voyager

WARNING: When battery is disconnected, vehicle computer and memory systems may lose memory data. Driveability problems may exist until computer systems have completed a relearn cycle. See COMPUTER RELEARN PROCEDURES article in GENERAL INFORMATION before disconnecting battery.

INTRODUCTION

Removal, overhaul and installation procedures (when provided by manufacturer) are covered in this article. If component removal and installation is basically an unbolt and bolt-on procedure, only a torque specification may be provided.

IGNITION SYSTEM

DISTRIBUTOR (3.0L OPTICAL)

Removal – 1) Disconnect distributor lead wire at wiring harness connector. Loosen distributor cap retaining screws. *See Fig. 1.* Lift off distributor cap.

2) Rotate engine crankshaft until distributor rotor is pointing toward intake plenum. Scribe a mark on plenum, as reference, to indicate rotor position when reinstalling distributor. Remove distributor hold-down nut. Carefully lift distributor from engine.

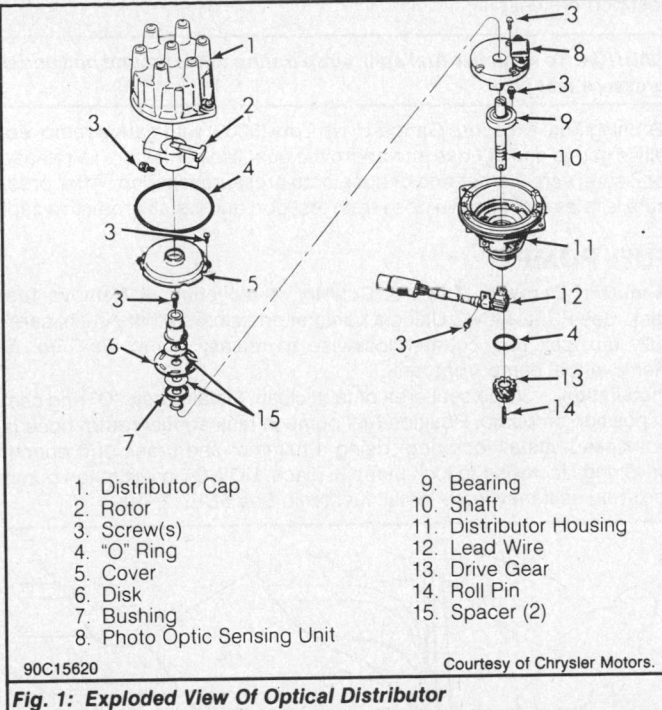

1. Distributor Cap
2. Rotor
3. Screw(s)
4. "O" Ring
5. Cover
6. Disk
7. Bushing
8. Photo Optic Sensing Unit
9. Bearing
10. Shaft
11. Distributor Housing
12. Lead Wire
13. Drive Gear
14. Roll Pin
15. Spacer (2)

90C15620   Courtesy of Chrysler Motors.

Fig. 1: Exploded View Of Optical Distributor

Installation – 1) Position distributor in engine. Ensure "O" ring is properly seated on distributor. Replace "O" ring if it is cracked or nicked.

2) Carefully engage distributor drive with camshaft drive so, when distributor is installed properly, rotor aligns with reference mark on intake plenum.

3) Install distributor cap. Check all high tension wires for good connections. Install and finger-tighten hold-down nut. Connect distributor lead wire at wiring harness connector. Set ignition timing.

HALL EFFECT SWITCH

Removal & Installation (2.5L, 3.9L, 5.2L & 5.9L) – 1) Disconnect distributor pick-up lead wire at wiring harness connectors. Remove splash shield retaining screws, and remove splash shield (if equipped).

2) Loosen distributor cap retaining screws or unfasten distributor cap retaining clips. Remove distributor cap. Scribe a mark on edge of distributor housing to indicate position of rotor as reinstallation reference.

3) Remove ignition rotor from distributor shaft. On 3.9L, 5.2L and 5.9L, remove Hall Effect pick-up attaching screws on opposite sides of distributor housing.

4) On all models, carefully lift Hall Effect pick-up assembly from distributor housing. *See Fig. 2.* To install, reverse removal procedure.

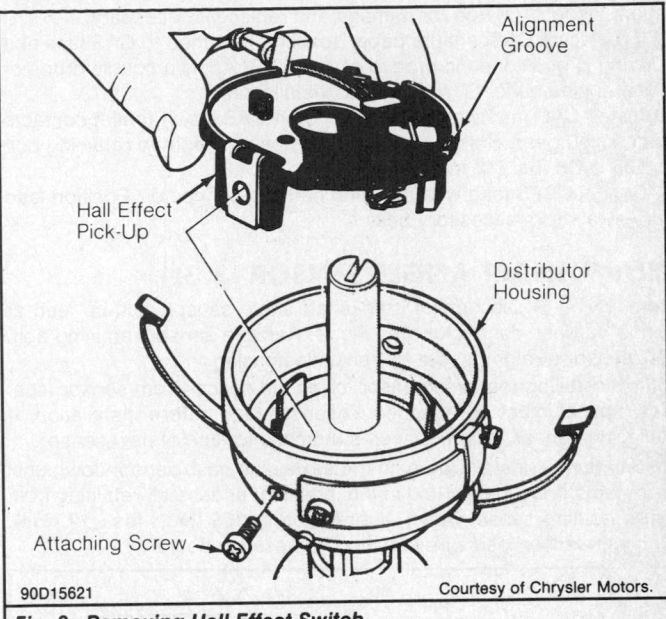

Alignment Groove
Hall Effect Pick-Up
Distributor Housing
Attaching Screw

90D15621   Courtesy of Chrysler Motors.

Fig. 2: Removing Hall Effect Switch (3.9L, 5.2L & 5.9L Shown; 2.5L Is Similar)

IGNITION COIL (3.3L DIS)

Removal & Installation – Remove spark plug cables from coil. Remove electrical connector and ignition coil fasteners. *See Fig. 3.* To install, reverse removal procedure. Tighten fasteners to **105 INCH lbs. (12 N.m).**

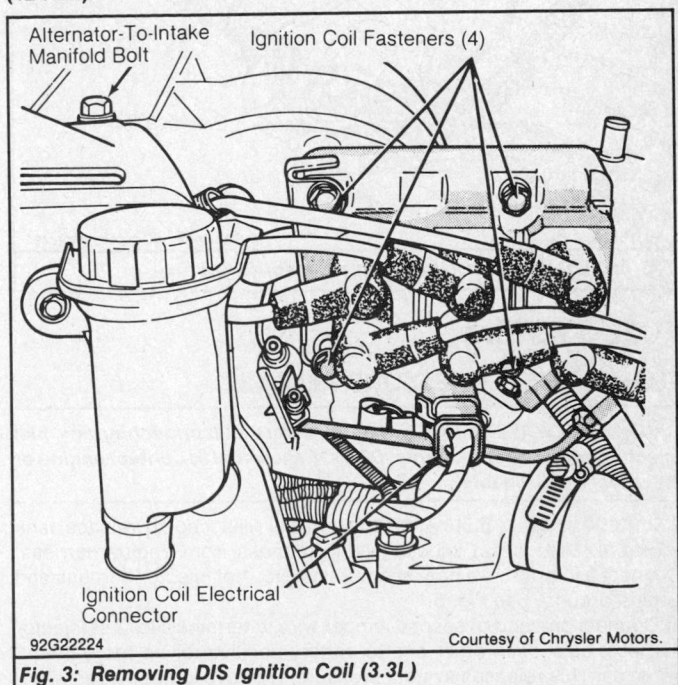

Alternator-To-Intake Manifold Bolt
Ignition Coil Fasteners (4)
Ignition Coil Electrical Connector

92G22224   Courtesy of Chrysler Motors.

Fig. 3: Removing DIS Ignition Coil (3.3L)

CAMSHAFT ANGLE SENSOR (3.3L)

Removal – **1)** Disconnect Camshaft Angle Sensor (CAS) lead at wiring harness connector. Loosen CAS retaining bolt far enough to allow slot in CAS to slide past bolt.

2) Pull CAS up out of chain case cover. DO NOT pull on CAS lead. Removal effort will be great due to "O" ring seal on CAS. A light tap to top of CAS before removal may reduce effort.

Installation – **1)** If reinstalling removed CAS, clean off old spacer from CAS face. A new spacer must be attached to face before installation. Inspect "O" ring for damage and replace if necessary.

2) If replacing CAS, ensure paper spacer is attached to CAS face and "O" ring is positioned in groove of new CAS. Apply a couple drops of clean engine oil to "O" ring prior to installation.

3) Install CAS in chain case cover. Push CAS down until it contacts cam timing gear. Hold CAS in this position, and tighten retaining bolt to **105 INCH lbs. (12 N.m).**

4) Connect CAS lead wire at wiring harness connector. Position lead wire away from accessory belt.

CRANKSHAFT ANGLE SENSOR (3.3L)

Removal – **1)** Disconnect crankshaft angle sensor pick-up lead at wiring harness connector. *See Fig. 4.* Remove sensor retaining bolt. Pull sensor straight up out of transaxle housing.

2) If reinstalling removed sensor, clean old spacer from sensor face. New spacer must be attached to sensor face before installation. If replacing sensor, paper spacer is attached to face of new sensor.

Installation – Install sensor in transaxle, and push sensor down until it contacts drive plate. Hold in this position, and install retaining bolt. While holding sensor down, tighten bolt to **105 INCH lbs. (12 N.m).** Connect sensor lead wire to wiring harness connector.

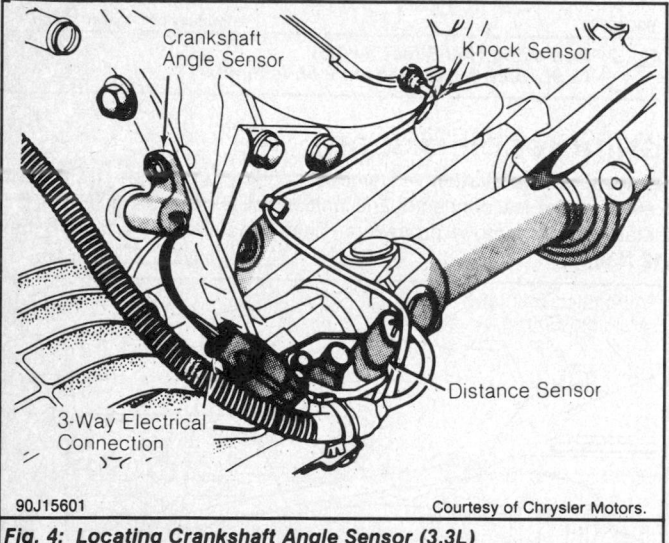

Fig. 4: Locating Crankshaft Angle Sensor (3.3L)

FUEL SYSTEM

FUEL SYSTEM PRESSURE RELEASE

CAUTION: ALWAYS relieve pressure before disconnecting any fuel injection-related components. DO NOT allow fuel to contact engine or electrical components.

2.5L, 3.0L, 3.3L & 5.9L – **1)** Loosen fuel filler cap to release tank pressure. Disconnect injector wiring harness from engine harness. Connect a jumper wire between terminal No. 1 of injector harness and engine ground. *See Fig. 5.*

2) Connect one end of second jumper wire to terminal No. 2 of injector harness, and touch other end to battery positive for no more than 5 seconds. This releases system pressure. Remove jumper wires. Continue fuel system service.

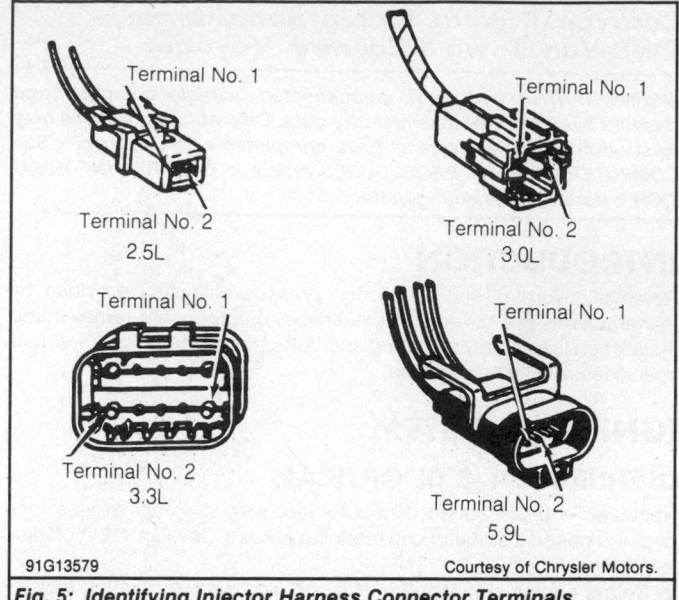

Fig. 5: Identifying Injector Harness Connector Terminals

3.9L & 5.2L – **1)** Disconnect negative battery cable. Loosen fuel filler cap to release tank pressure. Remove protective cap from pressure test port on fuel rail.

CAUTION: To minimize fuel spill, wrap a shop towel around and under pressure test port.

2) Using Fuel Pressure Gauge/Hose Tool (5069) with gauge removed, place gauge end of hose into approved gasoline container. To release pressure, screw other end of hose onto pressure test port. After pressure is released, remove hose from test port and install protective cap.

FUEL PUMP

Removal (Caravan, Town & Country, & Voyager) – Remove fuel tank. See FUEL TANK. Using a hammer and a brass drift punch, carefully tap lock ring counterclockwise to release pump. *See Fig. 6.* Remove fuel pump from tank.

Installation – Wipe seal area of tank clean. Install a new "O" ring seal in position on pump. Position fuel pump in tank so fuel return hose is not kinked. Install lock ring. Using a hammer and brass drift punch, drive ring clockwise to lock pump in place. DO NOT overtighten pump lock ring as it may leak. Install fuel tank. See FUEL TANK.

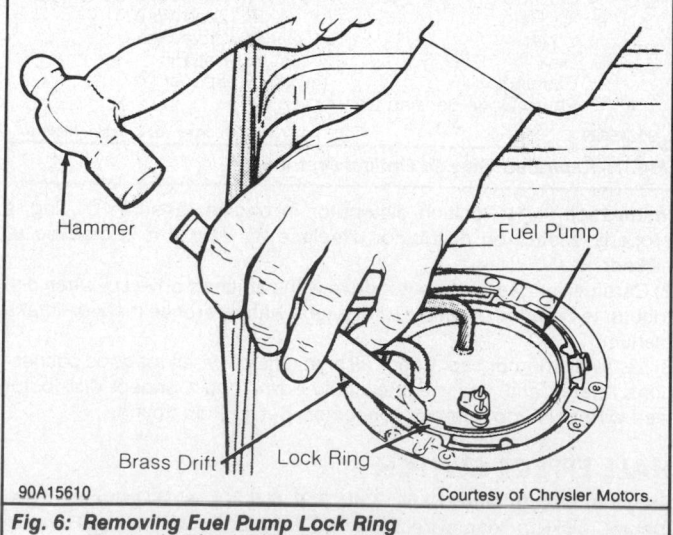

Fig. 6: Removing Fuel Pump Lock Ring (Caravan, Town & Country, & Voyager)

FUEL PUMP MODULE

Removal (Caravan, Town & Country, & Voyager – 4WD) – Release fuel system pressure. See FUEL SYSTEM PRESSURE RELEASE. Disconnect negative battery cable. Remove fuel tank. See FUEL TANK. Unclip fuel vapor hose and fuel drain hose from fuel tank. *See Fig. 7.* Remove fuel pump module retaining clamp. Remove fuel pump module.

Installation – Wipe seal area of tank clean, and place new seal in position on pump. Position fuel pump module so arrow on edge of module is between 2 lines on fuel tank. Compress fuel pump module, and install retaining clamp. Tighten clamp to **40 INCH lbs. (4.5 N.m)**. Install fuel tank. See FUEL TANK.

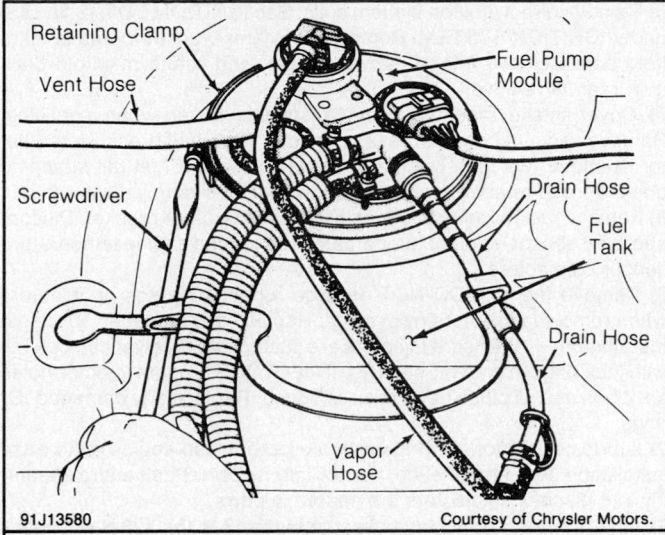

91J13580   Courtesy of Chrysler Motors.

*Fig. 7: Servicing Fuel Pump Module
(Caravan, Town & Country, & Voyager – 4WD)*

Removal (Dakota, Pickup, Ramcharger & RWD Van) – Release fuel system pressure. See FUEL SYSTEM PRESSURE RELEASE. Disconnect negative battery cable. Remove fuel tank. See FUEL TANK. Remove fuel pump module lock nut. Lock nut is threaded onto fuel tank. *See Fig. 8.* Fuel pump module will spring up from its position when lock nut is removed. Remove module from tank.

Installation – Install fuel pump module into fuel tank. Push module down, and install lock nut. Install fuel tank. See FUEL TANK.

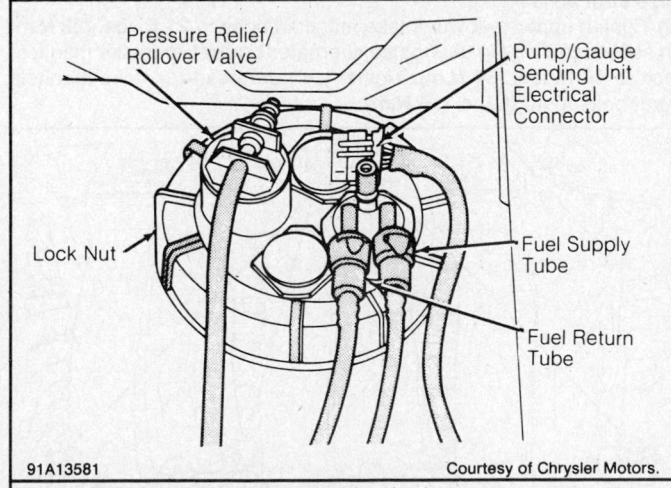

91A13581   Courtesy of Chrysler Motors.

*Fig. 8: Servicing Fuel Pump Module
(Dakota, Pickup, Ramcharger & RWD Van)*

FUEL TANK

Draining Fuel Tank (Caravan, Town & Country, & Voyager) – 1) Remove fuel filler cap to release fuel tank pressure. Release fuel system pressure. See FUEL SYSTEM PRESSURE RELEASE. Disconnect negative battery cable. Raise vehicle on hoist.

2) Remove drain tube rubber cap located on left frame rail, and connect either a portable holding tank or a siphon hose to drain tube. Drain fuel into an appropriate gasoline safety container.

Removal – 1) Disconnect negative battery cable. Remove fuel tank filler cap to release any tank pressure. Drain fuel tank into a suitable holding tank. See DRAINING FUEL TANK (CARAVAN, TOWN & COUNTRY, & VOYAGER). Position vehicle on hoist. Remove screws holding filler tube to inner and outer quarterpanels.

2) Raise vehicle on hoist. Disconnect all wiring and lines from tank. Use a transmission jack to support fuel tank, and remove bolts from fuel tank straps. Lower tank slightly and carefully work filler tube from tank. Lower fuel tank. Disconnect vapor separator rollover valve hose, and remove fuel tank from vehicle.

Installation – 1) Place fuel tank on top of transmission jack. Connect vapor separator rollover valve hose. Raise tank into position, and carefully work filler tube into tank. Transmission fluid may be used to lubricate tube as an aid in assembly.

CAUTION: Ensure vapor vent hose is clipped to tank and is not pinched between tank and floor pan during installation. Ensure straps are not twisted or bent before and after tightening strap nuts.

---

2) Install strap bolts, and tighten to **40 ft. lbs. (54 N.m)**. Remove transmission jack. Connect lines, drain tube cap and wiring connector. Use new hose clamps, and tighten to **10 INCH lbs. (1 N.m)**.

3) Install filler tube and tighten filler tube-to-inner and outer quarterpanel screws to **17 INCH lbs. (1.9 N.m)**. On affected models, install gasket between filler tube and inner quarterpanel before installing mounting screws.

4) Replace cap on drain tube using new hose clamp. Fill fuel tank, and replace filler cap. Connect negative battery cable. Check for proper operation.

Draining Fuel Tank (Dakota, Pickup, Ramcharger & RWD Van) – 1) Remove fuel filler cap to release fuel tank pressure. Release fuel system pressure. See FUEL SYSTEM PRESSURE RELEASE. Disconnect negative battery cable. Raise vehicle on hoist.

2) Drain fuel into an appropriate gasoline safety container. If fuel pump operates, fuel can be drained through fuel supply hose. If fuel pump does not operate but fuel level in tank is below fuel filler hose, fuel can be siphoned through fuel filler hose. Disconnect hose from filler neck. If fuel tank is full and fuel pump does not operate, drain fuel from filler neck.

3) To drain fuel tank from filler neck, support fuel tank using transmission jack. Loosen fuel tank mounting straps with passenger-side strap loosened more than driver-side strap. Lower tank slightly. Loosen filler neck to filler hose clamp. Slide clamp back on hose. To minimize fuel spill, wrap shop towels around filler hose. Disconnect filler hose from filler neck. Drain fuel tank through filler hose.

Removal – 1) Disconnect negative battery cable. Remove fuel tank filler cap to release fuel tank pressure. Drain fuel tank into a suitable holding tank. See DRAINING FUEL TANK (DAKOTA, PICKUP, RAMCHARGER & RWD VAN). Raise vehicle on hoist. Disconnect all vent hoses and filler hose.

2) Place a transmission jack under center of fuel tank, and apply slight pressure. Remove fuel tank retaining straps. Lower tank on transmission jack far enough to access fuel pump module connectors.

3) Disconnect fuel tubes and fuel gauge sending unit connections from fuel pump module. Remove ground strap (if equipped). Remove fuel tank.

Installation – 1) Place fuel tank on top of transmission jack, and raise it high enough to connect fuel tubes and fuel gauge wire to fuel pump module. Connect fuel tubes and fuel gauge wire to fuel pump module.

2) Raise tank into position. Install ground strap (if equipped). Install fuel tank mounting straps. On Ramcharger, connect and tighten nuts to end of threads on "J" bolts. On all other models, tighten mounting straps to **35 ft. lbs. (47 N.m)**. On all models, remove transmission jack.

3) Connect vent hoses, filler tube and drain tube cap. Install new hose clamps, and tighten clamps securely. Connect fuel line if disconnected earlier. Refill tank, and inspect all hoses and lines for leaks. Reconnect negative battery cable. Pressurize system, and check for leaks.

FUEL INJECTOR RAILS (PFI)

Removal (3.0L) – 1) Release fuel system pressure. See FUEL SYSTEM PRESSURE RELEASE. Disconnect negative battery cable.

2) Remove air cleaner-to-throttle body hose. Remove throttle cable and transaxle kickdown linkage (if equipped). Remove wiring connectors for automatic idle speed motor and throttle position sensor from throttle body.

3) Remove vacuum/vapor harness from throttle body. Remove brake booster hose from air intake plenum. Remove ignition coil from air intake plenum. Disconnect coolant temperature sensor.

4) Remove vacuum connections from air intake plenum vacuum connector. Remove fuel hoses from fuel rail. Remove fasteners attaching air intake plenum to intake manifold. Remove air intake plenum.

5) Cover intake manifold using suitable cover when servicing. Remove vacuum hoses from fuel rail. Disconnect fuel injector wiring harness from engine wiring harness.

6) Remove fuel pressure regulator attaching bolts. Remove regulator from rail. Remove fuel rail attaching bolts and lift fuel rail assembly from intake manifold.

CAUTION: Carefully remove fuel injectors and fuel pressure regulator. DO NOT damage rubber "O" rings.

Installation – 1) Ensure injectors are seated into receiver cups on rail with lock rings in place. See FUEL INJECTORS. Ensure injector holes are clean and all plugs have been removed.

2) Lubricate injector "O" rings with a drop of clean engine oil to ease installation. Push tip of each injector into its port. Push entire assembly into place until injectors are seated in ports.

3) Install 3 fuel rail attaching bolts, and tighten to **10 ft. lbs. (14 N.m)**. Lubricate fuel pressure regulator "O" ring with a drop of clean engine oil. Install fuel pressure regulator onto fuel rail.

4) Install fuel pressure regulator attaching bolts, and tighten bolts to **77 INCH lbs. (8.7 N.m)**. Install fuel supply and return tube hold-down bolt. Install vacuum crossover tube hold-down bolt. Tighten both bolts to **95 INCH lbs. (11 N.m)**.

5) Tighten pressure regulator hose clamps to **10 INCH lbs. (1 N.m)**. Connect fuel injector wiring harness to engine wiring harness. Connect vacuum harness to fuel rail assembly. Remove covering from lower intake manifold. Clean manifold surface.

6) Place intake manifold gaskets with beaded sealer up on lower manifold. Place air intake plenum in position. Loosely install ignition coil to intake manifold. Install manifold attaching fasteners.

7) Tighten 8 manifold fasteners to **10 ft. lbs. (14 N.m)**. Tighten 2 ignition coil fasteners to **95 INCH lbs. (11 N.m)**. Connect fuel line to fuel rail. Tighten hose clamps to **10 INCH lbs. (1 N.m)**.

8) Connect vacuum harness to air intake plenum and fuel pressure regulator. Reconnect coolant temperature sensor electrical connector. Connect brake booster supply hose to intake plenum.

9) Reconnect automatic idle speed motor and throttle position sensor wiring connectors. Connect vacuum/vapor hose harness to throttle body.

10) Install throttle cable and transaxle kickdown linkage (if equipped). Install air inlet hose assembly. Connect negative battery cable. Pressure test system for leaks.

Removal (3.3L) – 1) Release fuel system pressure. See FUEL SYSTEM PRESSURE RELEASE. Disconnect negative battery cable.

2) Remove air cleaner-to-throttle body hose. Remove throttle cable. Remove wiring harness from throttle cable bracket and intake manifold water tube. Remove wiring connectors for automatic idle speed motor and throttle position sensor from throttle body.

3) Remove vacuum hose harness from throttle body. Remove PCV and brake booster hoses from air intake plenum. Remove EGR tube flange from intake plenum. Disconnect charge temperature sensor.

4) Remove vacuum harness connections from air intake plenum. Remove cylinder head-to-intake plenum strut. Disconnect MAP sensor and oxygen sensor electrical connectors.

5) Remove engine-mounted ground strap. Remove fuel hose quick-connect fitting from fuel rail by pushing in on plastic ring located on end of fittings. Gently pull fittings from fuel rail.

CAUTION: To minimize fuel spill, wrap a shop towel around and under fuel rail fittings.

---

6) Remove direct ignition system coils. See IGNITION COIL (3.3L DIS) under IGNITION SYSTEM. Remove alternator bracket-to-intake manifold bolt. Remove intake manifold bolts, and rotate manifold back over rear valve cover.

7) Cover intake manifold using a suitable cover when servicing. Remove vacuum hose harness connector from fuel pressure regulator. Remove fuel tube retainer bracket screw and fuel rail attaching bolts. Spread retainer bracket to allow fuel tube removal clearance.

8) Remove fuel rail injector wiring clip from alternator bracket. Disconnect cam sensor, coolant temperature sensor and engine temperature sensor connectors.

9) Remove fuel rail. DO NOT damage rubber "O" rings on injectors when removing injectors from ports. Replace any damaged "O" rings.

Installation – 1) Ensure injectors are seated into receiver cups on rail with lock rings in place. See FUEL INJECTORS. Ensure injector holes are clean and all plugs have been removed. Replace any damaged "O" rings.

2) Lubricate injector "O" rings with a drop of clean engine oil to ease installation. Push tip of each injector into its port. Push entire assembly into place until injectors are seated in ports.

3) Install 4 fuel rail attaching bolts; tighten to **17 ft. lbs. (23 N.m)**. Install fuel tube retaining bracket screw, and tighten to **35 INCH lbs. (4 N.m)**. Reconnect cam sensor, coolant temperature sensor and engine temperature sensor.

4) Reconnect fuel injector wiring harness to engine harness. Install fuel injector wiring harness wiring clips on alternator bracket and intake manifold water tube. Connect fuel pressure regulator vacuum hose. Remove covering on lower intake manifold, and clean manifold surface.

5) Place intake manifold gasket on lower manifold. Put upper manifold into place, and install bolts finger tight. Install and finger-tighten alternator bracket-to-intake manifold bolt and cylinder head-to-intake manifold strut bolts.

6) Tighten upper-to-lower intake manifold bolts to **21 ft. lbs. (28 N.m)** in sequence. *See Fig. 9.* Tighten alternator bracket-to-intake manifold bolt to **40 ft. lbs. (54 N.m)**. Tighten cylinder head-to-intake manifold strut bolts to **40 ft. lbs. (54 N.m)**.

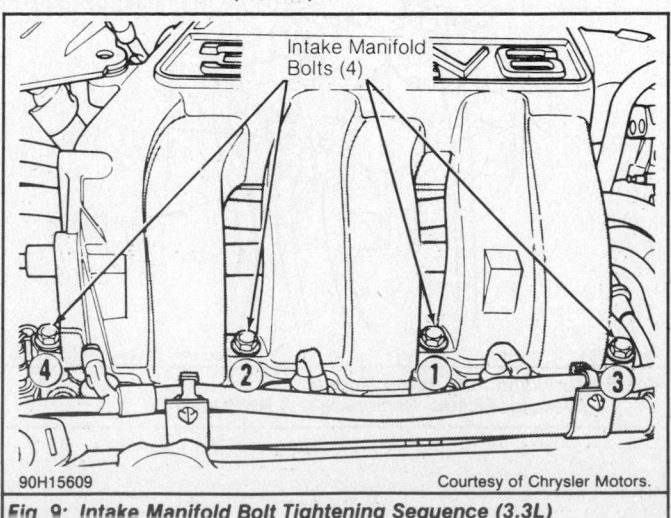

90H15609   Courtesy of Chrysler Motors.

Fig. 9: Intake Manifold Bolt Tightening Sequence (3.3L)

7) Install ground strap. Reconnect MAP sensor, oxygen sensor and charge temperature sensor electrical connectors. Connect vacuum hose harness to intake plenum.

8) Connect PCV system. Using a new gasket, connect EGR tube flange to intake manifold and tighten to **17 ft. lbs. (23 N.m)**.

9) Clip wiring harness into hole in throttle cable bracket. Connect wiring connectors to throttle position sensor and automatic idle speed motor. Connect vacuum harness to throttle body.

10) Install direct ignition system coils. See IGNITION COIL under IGNITION SYSTEM. Tighten fasteners to **105 INCH lbs. (12 N.m)**. Install fuel hose quick-connect fittings to fuel rail. Push each fitting onto rail until it clicks into place. Fuel supply fitting is 5/16" and fuel return fitting is 1/4".

11) Install throttle cable. Install air cleaner and hose assembly. Connect negative battery cable. Pressure test system for leaks.

Removal (3.9L & 5.2L) – 1) Release fuel system pressure. See FUEL SYSTEM PRESSURE RELEASE. Disconnect negative battery cable. Remove air cleaner. Remove throttle body from intake manifold. Remove air conditioning compressor-to-intake manifold support bracket (if equipped).

2) Disconnect fuel injector wiring connectors (injector connectors are numerically tagged for installation reference). Remove vacuum line from fuel pressure regulator.

3) On 3.9L, disconnect intake manifold charge air temperature sensor connector. DO NOT remove sensor.

4) On all models, remove EVAP canister purge solenoid/bracket assembly from intake manifold. Disconnect 2 rear fuel rail fuel lines, and remove remaining fuel rail mounting bolts.

5) Gently rock and pull on left fuel rail and then right fuel rail until injectors start to clear intake manifold. Repeat procedure until injectors clear intake manifold, and remove fuel rail with injectors attached. Remove injector-to-fuel rail clips. *See Fig. 12.*

Installation – 1) Lubricate injector "O" rings with a drop of clean engine oil. Install injectors and clips into fuel rail receiver cups. Ensure injectors and clips are fully seated. Position fuel rail/injector assembly on intake manifold openings. Using care not to tear "O" rings, guide each injector into intake manifold. Push right and then left fuel rail down until injectors are bottomed on injector shoulder.

2) To complete installation, reverse removal procedure. Connect negative battery cable, and check for leaks.

FUEL INJECTORS

Removal (2.5L) – 1) Remove air cleaner assembly. Release fuel system pressure. See FUEL SYSTEM PRESSURE RELEASE. Disconnect negative battery cable. Remove injector hold-down clamp Torx screw.

2) With 2 small screwdrivers, lift top off injector using slots provided. *See Fig. 10.* Using a small screwdriver placed in hole in front of electrical connector, gently pry injector from pod. Ensure lower "O" ring has been removed from pod.

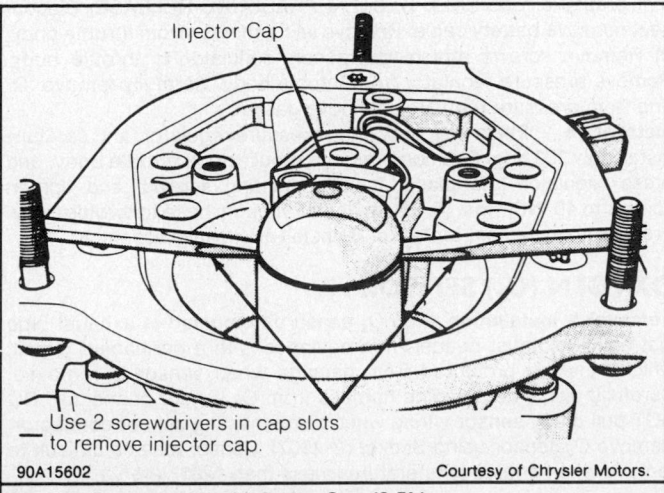

Use 2 screwdrivers in cap slots to remove injector cap.

90A15602   Courtesy of Chrysler Motors.

Fig. 10: Removing Fuel Injector Cap (2.5L)

Installation – 1) Place a new "O" ring on injector cap. New injector has new upper and lower "O" ring already installed. Apply a light coating of clean engine oil on "O" rings.

2) Place assembly in pod, and align injector wiring terminals with injector cap fastener hole. *See Fig. 11.* Install injector cap with locating notch aligned with locating lobe on injector.

3) Push down on cap to ensure good seal. Rotate cap and injector to line up attachment hole. Install Torx screw; tighten to **35-45 INCH lbs. (4-5 N.m)**. Reconnect negative battery cable. Pressure test system for leaks. Reinstall air cleaner assembly.

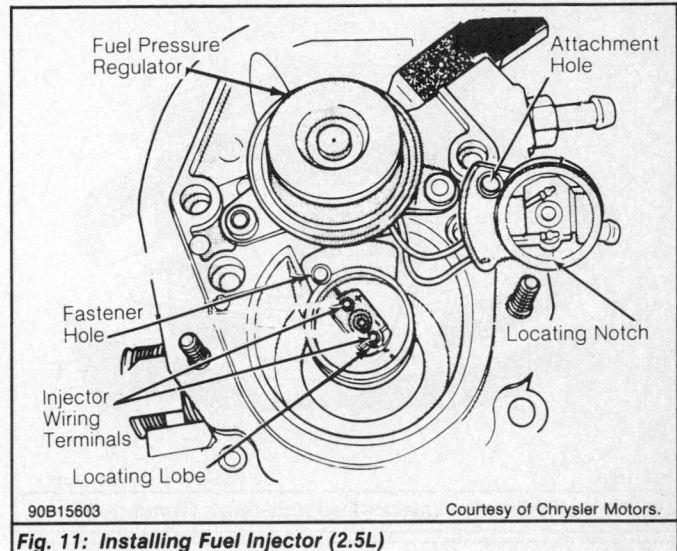

90B15603   Courtesy of Chrysler Motors.

Fig. 11: Installing Fuel Injector (2.5L)

Removal (3.0L, 3.3L, 3.9L & 5.2L) – 1) Remove fuel rail. See FUEL INJECTOR RAILS (PFI). Disconnect injector wiring connector from injector. Position fuel rail assembly so injectors are accessible.

2) Rotate and pull injector out of fuel rail (clip will remain on injector). *See Fig. 12.* Inspect injector "O" ring and clip for damage. Replace "O" ring if it is damaged. If injector is to be reused, install a protective cap on injector tip to prevent damage. Replace clip if it is damaged. Repeat for remaining injectors.

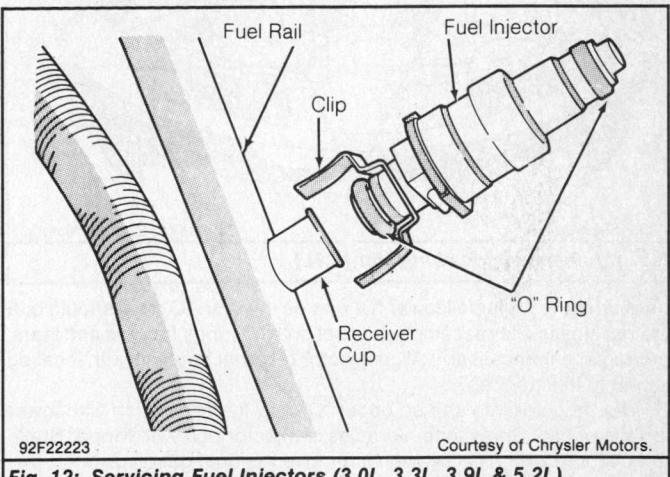

92F22223   Courtesy of Chrysler Motors.

Fig. 12: Servicing Fuel Injectors (3.0L, 3.3L, 3.9L & 5.2L)

Installation – 1) Lubricate "O" ring of each injector with a drop of clean engine oil to aid in installation. Install injector top end into fuel rail receiver cup. Be careful not to damage "O" ring during installation.

2) Repeat for remaining injectors. Install wiring harness to injectors. Fasten wiring harness into wiring clips (if equipped).

Removal (5.9L) – 1) Remove air cleaner assembly. Release fuel system pressure. See FUEL SYSTEM PRESSURE RELEASE. Disconnect negative battery cable. Remove injector hold-down clamp Torx screw. *See Fig. 13.*

CAUTION: DO NOT damage loose spacer under clamp.

2) Using a small screwdriver and area in front of hold-down clamp for leverage, lift caps off injectors. Using a small screwdriver placed in hole in front of electrical connector, gently pry injectors from pods. *See Fig. 14.* Ensure each injector lower "O" ring has been removed from pod.

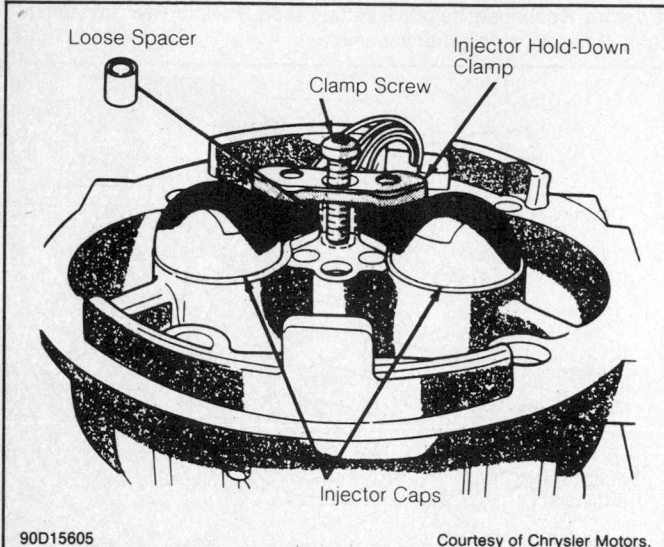

90D15605   Courtesy of Chrysler Motors.

Fig. 13: *Removing Fuel Injector Cap Hold-Down Clamp (5.9L)*

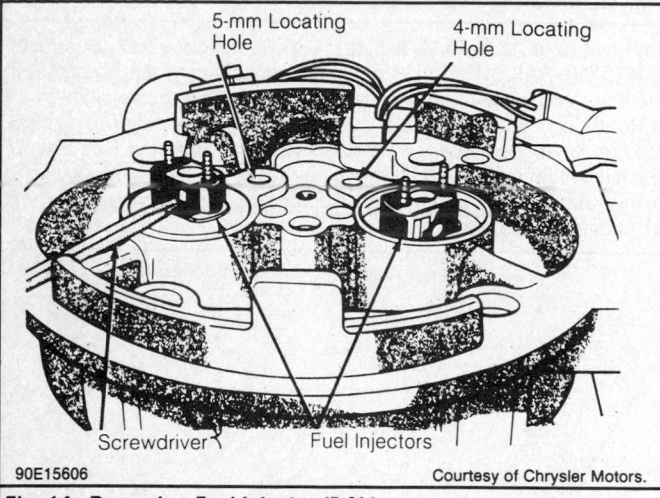

90E15606   Courtesy of Chrysler Motors.

Fig. 14: *Removing Fuel Injector (5.9L)*

Installation – 1) Install lower "O" ring on injector. "O" ring should butt against plastic filter assembly. Inspect both "O" rings for cuts and tears, and replace if necessary. Align injector terminal housing with locating socket in injector cap.

2) Press injector into cap so upper "O" ring flange is flush with lower surface of cap. Spray inner surfaces of injector pod with Mopar Brake and Carburetor Parts Cleaner to remove residual gasoline.

3) Lightly lubricate upper and lower "O" rings with petroleum jelly. Place injector and cap in injector pod, and align cap locating pin with locating hole in casting. *See Fig. 14.*

CAUTION: Passenger-side cap locating pin is 5 mm in diameter and will only fit in passenger-side locating hole. Driver-side locating pin is 4 mm in diameter.

4) Repeat steps 1)–3) for other injector and cap. Press firmly on injector caps until flush with casting surface. Place injector hold-down

clamp with spacer on rear portion of caps, aligning holes in clamp with pins on caps. Install clamp screw. Ensure spacer is in place.

CAUTION: "O" ring may cause caps to lift up; press firmly on both caps with one hand to ensure caps are flush while installing clamp screw.

5) Tighten screw to **35 INCH lbs. (4 N.m)**. Connect negative battery cable. Pressure test system for leaks. Reinstall air cleaner assembly.

FUEL PRESSURE REGULATOR

Removal & Installation (3.0L, 3.3L, 3.9L & 5.2L) – See FUEL INJECTOR RAILS (PFI).

Removal (2.5L) – Release fuel system pressure. See FUEL SYSTEM PRESSURE RELEASE. Disconnect negative battery cable. Remove fuel pressure regulator vacuum connector. Remove regulator retainer screw. Remove fuel pressure regulator retainer. Remove fuel pressure regulator.

Installation – 1) Ensure fuel pressure regulator has 2 plastic spacers. Ensure fuel rail has 2 "O" rings installed in fuel pressure regulator cavity. *See Fig. 15.* Lubricate "O" rings with clean engine oil. Insert fuel pressure regulator into fuel rail. Install fuel pressure regulator retainer.

2) Install retainer screw. Tighten to **50 INCH lbs. (5.6 N.m)**. Connect fuel pressure regulator vacuum connection. Pressure test system for leaks.

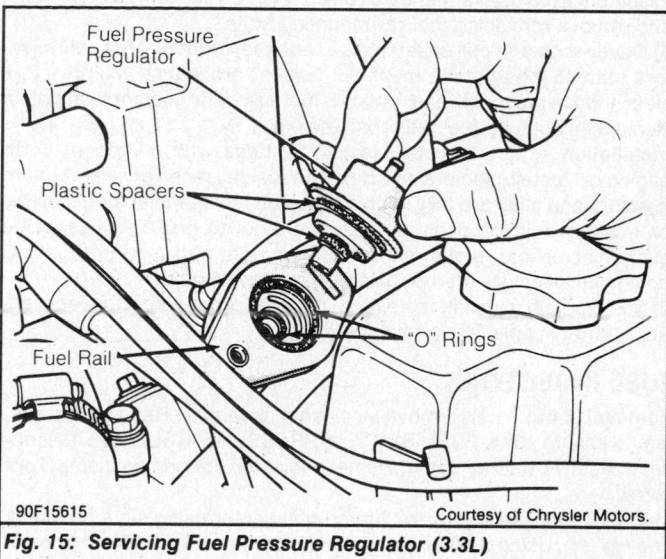

90F15615   Courtesy of Chrysler Motors.

Fig. 15: *Servicing Fuel Pressure Regulator (3.3L)*

Removal (5.9L) – 1) Remove air cleaner assembly. Release fuel system pressure. See FUEL SYSTEM PRESSURE RELEASE. Disconnect negative battery cable. Remove vacuum hose from throttle body.

2) Remove screws attaching pressure regulator to throttle body. Remove pressure regulator from throttle body. Carefully remove "O" ring from pressure regulator. Remove gasket.

Installation – Place new gasket on pressure regulator, and carefully install new "O" ring. Position pressure regulator on throttle body, and press regulator into place. Install mounting screws, and tighten screws to **40 INCH lbs. (4.5 N.m)**. Install vacuum hose to throttle body. Pressure test system for leaks. Reinstall air cleaner assembly.

OXYGEN (O₂) SENSOR

Removal & Installation – 1) O_2 sensor is mounted in exhaust pipe just below exhaust header. It is equipped with a permanent pigtail, which must be protected from damage when sensor is removed. Carefully disconnect engine harness from O_2 sensor connector. DO NOT pull on O_2 sensor wiring when disconnecting sensor connector. Remove O_2 sensor using Socket (C-4907). Sensor may be difficult to remove when engine temperature is less than 120°F (48°C).

2) Ensure sensor is free of contaminants; avoid using cleaning solvents. Use an 18 mm x 1.5 x 6E tap to clean threads in exhaust manifold. If installing original sensor, sensor threads must be coated with anti-seize compound. New O_2 sensors are packaged with compound already on threads. Tighten sensor to **20 ft. lbs. (27 N.m)**.

THROTTLE BODY

Removal & Installation (PFI) – 1) Disconnect negative battery cable. Remove air cleaner-to-throttle body hose and clamp.
2) Remove throttle cable, speed control cables and transaxle linkage (if equipped). Disconnect wiring connectors for automatic idle speed motor and throttle position sensor. Disconnect vacuum hoses from throttle body.
3) Remove throttle body-to-intake manifold attaching nuts. Remove throttle body and gasket. To install, reverse removal procedure. Tighten throttle body attaching nuts to **19 ft. lbs (26 N.m)**.
Removal (TBI) – 1) Remove air cleaner. Release fuel system pressure. See FUEL SYSTEM PRESSURE RELEASE. Disconnect negative battery cable. Disconnect vacuum hoses and electrical connectors from throttle body.
2) Remove throttle cable, speed control cable and transmission kickdown cables (if equipped). Remove throttle return spring. Remove fuel intake and return hoses.
3) Remove throttle body mounting screws, and lift throttle body from vehicle. Remove throttle body gasket from intake manifold.
Installation – 1) Using a new gasket, install throttle body and tighten mounting screws to **15 ft. lbs. (20 N.m)**. Install fuel intake and return hoses using new original-equipment type clamps.
2) Install throttle return spring. Install throttle cable. Install speed control and transmission kickdown cables (if equipped). Install wiring connectors and vacuum hoses. Install air cleaner. Reconnect negative battery cable.

THROTTLE POSITION SENSOR (TPS)

Removal – Disconnect negative battery cable. Remove air cleaner (if necessary). Disconnect TPS electrical connector. Remove TPS mounting screws. Lift TPS off throttle shaft.
Installation – Install TPS on throttle body. Tighten mounting screws. See TORQUE SPECIFICATIONS table. Connect TPS electrical connector. Install air cleaner (if removed). Connect negative battery cable.

THROTTLE TEMPERATURE SENSOR

Removal (5.9L) – Remove air cleaner. Disconnect throttle body temperature sensor electrical connector. Remove sensor.
Installation – Apply heat transfer compound (provided with new sensor) to tip of new sensor. Install sensor, and tighten it to **110 INCH lbs. (12 N.m)**.

TORQUE SPECIFICATIONS

TORQUE SPECIFICATIONS

Application	Ft. Lbs. (N.m)
Alternator Bracket-To-Intake Manifold Bolt	40 (54)
Cylinder Head-To-Intake Manifold Strut Bolts	40 (54)
EGR Tube Flange-To-Manifold	17 (23)
Fuel Rail Attaching Bolts	
3.0L	10 (14)
3.3L	17 (23)
Fuel Tank Attaching Bolts	
Caravan, Town & Country, & Voyager	40 (54)
Fuel Tank Attaching Nuts	
Dakota, Pickup & RWD Van	35 (47)
Intake Manifold Bolts (3.3L)	21 (28)
Oxygen Sensor	
3.9L & 5.2L	22 (30)
5.9L	20 (27)
Manifold Fasteners	10 (14)
Throttle Body Mounting Nuts	
3.0L & 3.3L	19 (26)
2.5L & 5.9L	15 (20)
3.9L & 5.2L	17 (23)

	INCH Lbs. (N.m)
Camshaft Angle Sensor Bolt	105 (12.0)
Crankshaft Timing Sensor Bolt	105 (12.0)
Crossover Tube Hold-Down Bolt	95 (11.0)
Fuel Injector Torx Screws (2.5L)	35-45 (4.0-5.0)
Fuel Pressure Regulator Attaching Bolts	
2.5L	40 (5.0)
3.3L	60 (7.0)
5.9L	40 (5.0)
Fuel Pressure Regulator Retaining Screw (3.0L)	90 (10.0)
Fuel Pump Module Retaining Clamp	40 (5.0)
Ignition Coil Fasteners	
3.0L	95 (11.0)
3.3L	105 (12.0)
Throttle Body Temperature Sensor	105 (12.0)
Throttle Position Sensor Screws	
2.5L	20 (2.3)
3.0L & 3.3L	17 (2.0)
3.9L & 5.2L	60 (7.0)
5.9L	27 (3.0)

1992 ENGINE PERFORMANCE
Removal, Overhaul & Installation – Diesel

Pickup

INTRODUCTION

WARNING: When battery is disconnected, vehicle computer and memory systems may lose memory data. Driveability problems may exist until computer systems have completed a relearn cycle. See COMPUTER RELEARN PROCEDURES article in GENERAL INFORMATION before disconnecting battery.

Removal, overhaul and installation procedures are covered in this article. If component removal and installation is primarily an unbolt and bolt-on procedure, only a torque specification may be furnished.

AIR INDUCTION SYSTEM

TURBOCHARGER ASSEMBLY

Removal – 1) Disconnect negative battery cable. Remove air intake piping and exhaust pipe at turbocharger. Remove intercooler inlet duct from turbocharger. *See Fig. 4.*
2) Remove and plug turbocharger oil lines. Remove turbocharger retaining nuts and turbocharger. Plug all air intake and oil line openings.

NOTE: Compressor and turbine assembly is a balanced unit. If compressor or turbine wheel is damaged during disassembly, turbine shaft and wheel and compressor wheel MUST be replaced as an assembly.

Disassembly – 1) Place reference mark on turbine housing, bearing housing and compressor housing for reassembly reference. Clamp turbocharger housing in soft-jawed vise. Remove "V" band clamp. *See Fig. 1.* Remove compressor housing and seal ring.

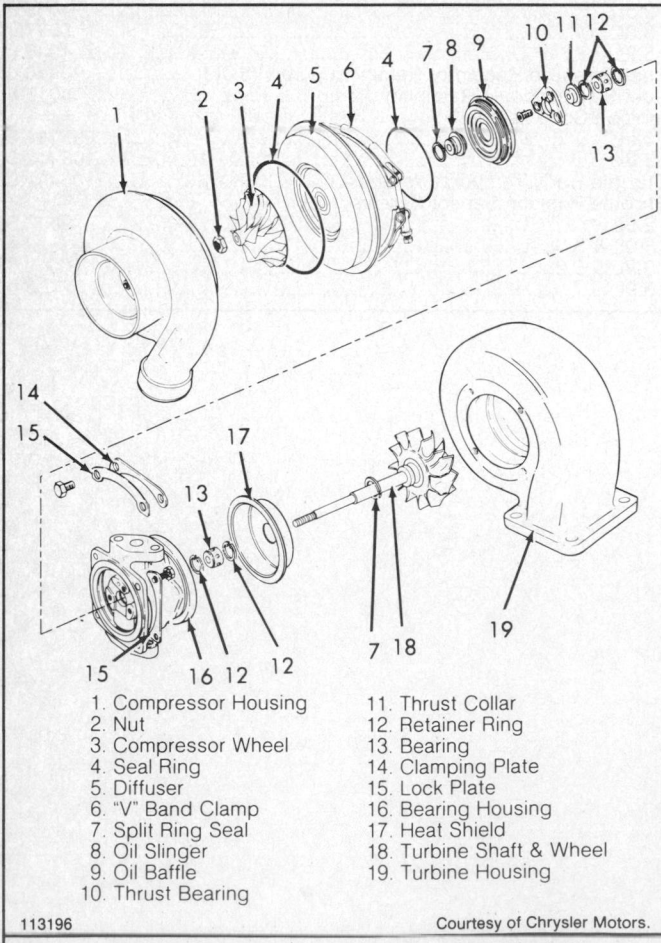

113196   Courtesy of Chrysler Motors.

1. Compressor Housing
2. Nut
3. Compressor Wheel
4. Seal Ring
5. Diffuser
6. "V" Band Clamp
7. Split Ring Seal
8. Oil Slinger
9. Oil Baffle
10. Thrust Bearing
11. Thrust Collar
12. Retainer Ring
13. Bearing
14. Clamping Plate
15. Lock Plate
16. Bearing Housing
17. Heat Shield
18. Turbine Shaft & Wheel
19. Turbine Housing

Fig. 1: *Exploded View Of Turbocharger Assembly (Typical)*

CAUTION: Turbine shaft and nut have left-hand threads.

2) Hold turbine shaft and wheel from turning while removing compressor wheel nut. Note alignment marks on turbine shaft and compressor wheel. *See Fig. 2.*
3) Remove left-hand thread retaining nut and compressor wheel. Bend out diffuser retaining bolt lock plates, and remove bolts. Remove diffuser and seal ring. Note alignment marks on oil slinger and turbine shaft. *See Fig. 2.* Remove oil slinger and split ring seal. Remove oil baffle.
4) Remove thrust bearing. Note alignment marks on thrust collar and turbine shaft. *See Fig. 2.* Remove thrust collar. Inspect thrust collar for wear. Thrust bearing must be replaced and cannot be reused. Remove turbine housing, lock plates and clamping plates.
5) Remove bearing housing from turbine housing. Remove turbine shaft and wheel along with heat shield from bearing housing. Remove split ring seals from shaft.
6) Remove outer retainer rings from bearing housing, and remove bearings. Remove inner retainer rings from bearing housing.

Cleaning & Inspection – 1) Using nylon brush and solvent, clean all components. Clean carbon from turbine housing. Turbine shaft and wheel bearing surfaces can be polished using crocus cloth and kerosene.

CAUTION: DO NOT bead blast components or use wire brush to clean compressor wheel.

2) Inspect compressor housing and compressor wheel for contact. Inspect oil slinger and diffuser for cracks. Inspect thrust collar for wear. Inspect turbine shaft and wheel for cracks or damaged blades.
3) Measure O.D. of turbine shaft. Turbine shaft and wheel and compressor wheel must be replaced as an assembly if not within specification. See TURBOCHARGER SPECIFICATIONS table. Replace damaged components.

TURBOCHARGER SPECIFICATIONS

Application	In. (mm)
Turbine Shaft Clearances	
End Play	[1]
Radial Clearance	.012-.018 (.30-.46)
Turbine Shaft Minimum O.D.	.432 (10.97)

[1] – On turbochargers with serial No. 840637 and earlier, end play should be .004-.006" (.10-.15 mm). On turbochargers with serial No. 840638 and later, end play should be .001-.003" (.03-.08 mm).

CAUTION: During reassembly, thrust bearing, all split ring seals, seal rings, retainer rings and bearings MUST be replaced. DO NOT reuse these components.

Reassembly – 1) Install split ring seal on turbine shaft, and lubricate with oil. Install heat shield. Place turbine shaft and wheel in socket, and clamp in soft-jawed vise. Install inner retainer rings in bearing housing with chamfered edge toward bearing.

CAUTION: Inner and outer bearing retainer rings must be installed with chamfered edge toward bearing. Rotate bearing housing during installation on turbine shaft to seat split ring seals.

2) Lubricate bearings with oil and install. Install outer retainer rings with chamfered edge toward bearing. Install bearing housing over turbine shaft and wheel. Rotate bearing housing during installation to seat split ring seals.
3) Install thrust collar. Ensure alignment marks on thrust collar and turbine shaft are aligned. *See Fig. 2.* Place reference mark on thrust collar so alignment can be verified with thrust bearing installed.
4) Lubricate thrust bearing with oil, and install bearing. Tighten retaining bolts to specification. See TORQUE SPECIFICATIONS table at end of article. Install oil baffle. Ensure thrust collar is aligned with turbine shaft. Install split ring seal on oil slinger.

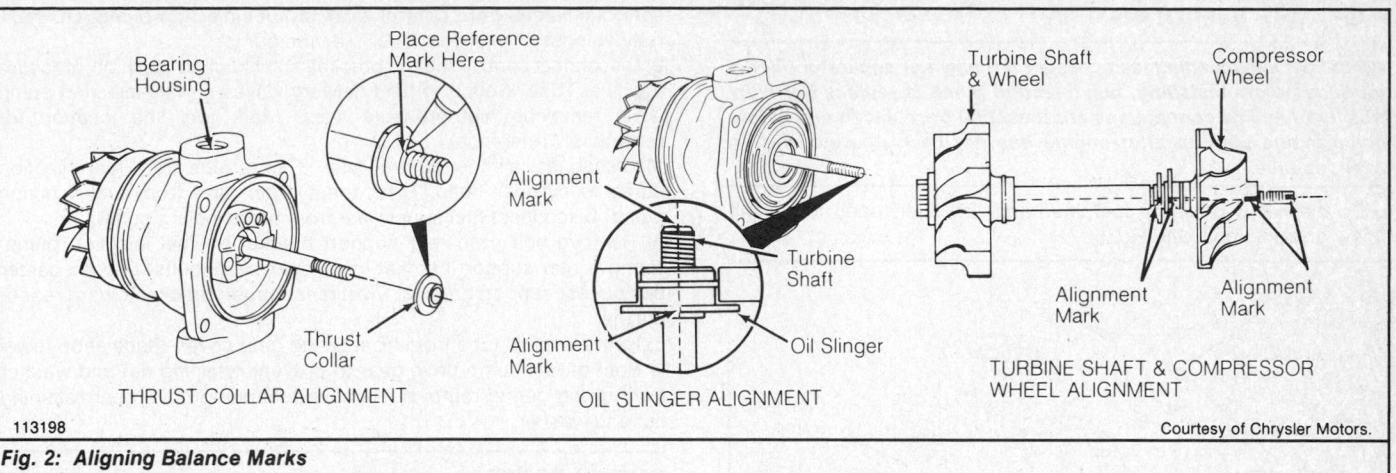

THRUST COLLAR ALIGNMENT

OIL SLINGER ALIGNMENT

TURBINE SHAFT & COMPRESSOR WHEEL ALIGNMENT

Courtesy of Chrysler Motors.

113198

Fig. 2: Aligning Balance Marks

5) Note alignment mark on oil slinger. Place alignment mark on shaft end of oil slinger to verify alignment once installed. Lubricate oil slinger and install in diffuser.

CAUTION: Ensure bearing housing DOES NOT rotate during compressor wheel installation.

6) Install seal ring in diffuser. Install diffuser. Ensure alignment mark on oil slinger is aligned with turbine shaft. *See Fig. 2.* Install compressor wheel. Ensure alignment mark on compressor wheel aligns with mark on turbine shaft.

7) Install left-hand nut on shaft, and tighten nut to specification. See TORQUE SPECIFICATIONS table. Install bearing housing assembly in turbine housing with reference marks aligned.

8) Apply anti-seize compound to all bolts. Install clamp plate, lock plates and bolts to retain bearing housing. Tighten bolts to specification. See TORQUE SPECIFICATIONS table.

9) Install lock plates and bolts to retain diffuser on bearing housing. Tighten bolts to specification, and bend over lock tabs. See TORQUE SPECIFICATIONS table.

10) Using dial indicator, check shaft end play and radial clearance. *See Fig. 3.* Clearance should be within specification. See TURBOCHARGER SPECIFICATIONS table. Install seal ring and compressor housing. Ensure reference mark is aligned on compressor housing and bearing housing.

11) Install "V" band clamp. Apply anti-seize compound to "V" band bolt threads. Install nut, and tighten to specification. Tap on "V" band clamp in 4 equal areas, and retighten nut to specification. See TORQUE SPECIFICATIONS table.

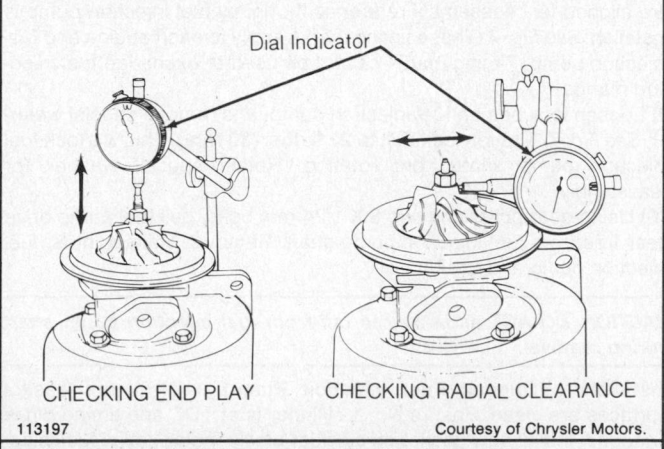

CHECKING END PLAY

CHECKING RADIAL CLEARANCE

Courtesy of Chrysler Motors.

113197

Fig. 3: Checking Shaft End Play & Radial Clearance

Installation – To install, reverse removal procedure using new gaskets. Coat all bolts and studs with anti-seize compound. Install oil drain tube on turbocharger. Pour 3 ozs. (60 cc) of clean oil in oil inlet

while spinning turbocharger. Install remaining components, and tighten fasteners to specification. See TORQUE SPECIFICATIONS table at end of article.

INTERCOOLER

Removal – **1)** Remove grille. Remove front support bracket, located above center of intercooler. On A/C-equipped models, discharge A/C system using approved refrigerant recovery/recycling equipment.

2) Remove bolt from center of sealing plate on A/C lines at the condenser. Remove condenser-to-intercooler retaining nuts. Lift condenser and sealing plate from intercooler. Plug all A/C lines to prevent contamination.

3) Remove intercooler inlet and outlet ducts. *See Fig. 4.* Remove intercooler retaining bolts. Pivot intercooler forward and upward to remove.

Installation – To install, reverse removal procedure. Tighten bolts/nuts to specification. See TORQUE SPECIFICATIONS table at end of article. Evacuate and recharge A/C system (if equipped).

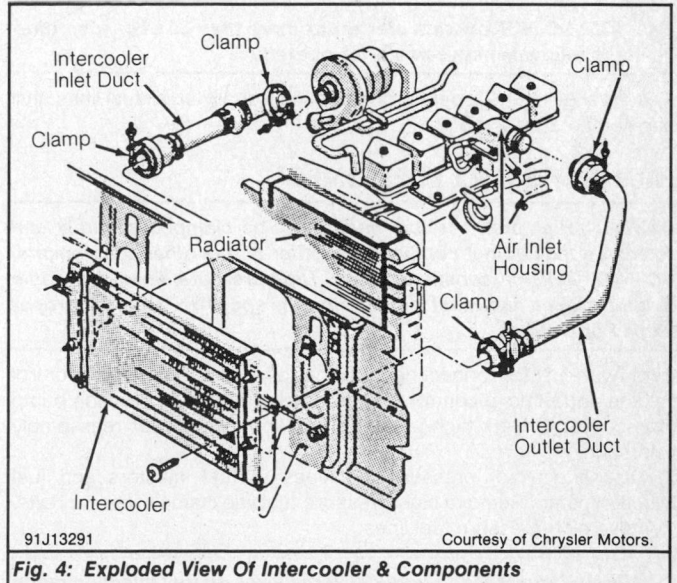

91J13291

Courtesy of Chrysler Motors.

Fig. 4: Exploded View Of Intercooler & Components

FUEL SYSTEM

WARNING: DO NOT bleed fuel lines on a hot engine as high exhaust temperatures could cause a fire. Carefully bleed fuel lines as fuel exists under extremely high pressure and could penetrate skin.

FUEL LINE BLEEDING

NOTE: *Fuel line bleeding is necessary if fuel/water separator filter is not filled before installing, fuel injection pump is replaced or high-pressure fuel line connections are loosened or replaced and before initial engine start-up after engine has not been operated for an extended time.*

1) To bleed low-pressure fuel lines and fuel filter, open fuel bleed screw on banjo bolt. *See Fig. 5.*

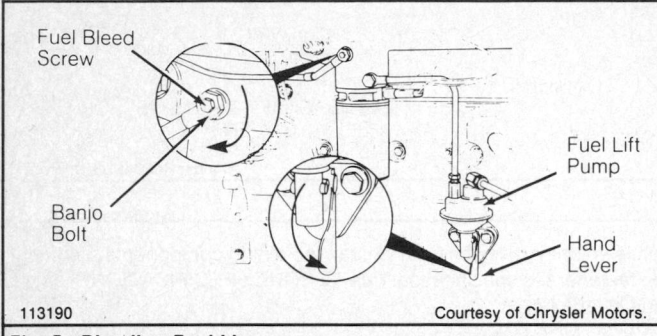

113190   Courtesy of Chrysler Motors.

Fig. 5: Bleeding Fuel Lines

2) Operate hand lever on fuel lift pump until steady stream flows from fuel bleed screw. Tighten fuel bleed screw to **72 INCH lbs. (8 N.m)**. If hand lever feels like pump is not operating, rotate engine 90 degrees and repeat procedure. Position hand lever in upward position once fuel line is bled.

CAUTION: Fuel lift pump hand lever must be in upward position once fuel lines are bled to provide proper engine operation.

3) To bleed high-pressure fuel lines, carefully loosen high-pressure fuel line nut at fuel injector. Operate starter until fuel flows steadily, and tighten high-pressure fuel line nut to specification. See TORQUE SPECIFICATIONS table at end of article.

CAUTION: DO NOT operate starter for more than 30 seconds. Allow 2-minute intervals between starter operations.

4) Start engine, and repeat procedure individually on all fuel lines until engine operates smoothly.

HIGH-PRESSURE FUEL LINES

CAUTION: High-pressure fuel lines must be clamped securely and routed so they do not contact each other or any other components. DO NOT weld or substitute lines. High-pressure lines are same length; proper line must be installed in specified area for proper engine operation.

Removal – 1) Disconnect negative battery cable. Disconnect control linkage and remove control linkage bracket from fuel injection pump (if necessary). Mark high-pressure fuel line location for reassembly reference.
2) Disconnect high-pressure fuel lines at fuel injectors and fuel injection pump. Remove high-pressure fuel line clamp retaining bolts. Remove high-pressure fuel lines.

CAUTION: Use wrench to hold delivery valves on fuel injection pump while removing high-pressure lines. Mark fuel line location before removing.

Installation – To install, reverse removal procedure. Bleed high-pressure fuel lines. See FUEL LINE BLEEDING under FUEL SYSTEM.

FUEL INJECTION PUMP

Removal – 1) Disconnect negative battery cable. Disconnect necessary electrical connections at fuel injection pump. Disconnect

control linkages from control lever on fuel injection pump. DO NOT remove control lever from fuel injection pump.
2) Disconnect control linkage bracket. Remove and cap high-pressure fuel lines. Use wrench to hold delivery valves on fuel injection pump while removing high-pressure lines. Mark fuel line location for reassembly reference.
3) Disconnect air fuel control tube. This is tube from fuel injection pump to cylinder head. Disconnect drain tube from fuel injection pump. Disconnect fuel supply line from fuel injection pump.
4) Remove bolt from rear support bracket on fuel injection pump. Remove rear support bracket-to-cylinder block bolts. Loosen center bolt on rear support bracket. Pivot rear support bracket toward rear of engine.
5) Remove oil fill tube from front timing gear cover. Place shop towel in front of fuel pump drive gear to prevent retaining nut and washer from falling during removal. Remove fuel pump drive gear retaining nut and washer.

CAUTION: DO NOT allow fuel pump drive gear retaining nut or washer to fall into front timing gear cover.

6) Rotate engine clockwise so No. 1 cylinder is at TDC of compression stroke. Engine can be rotated by removing dust cover from transmission adapter plate and installing Engine Barring Tool (3377462) in transmission adapter plate. *See Fig. 6.*

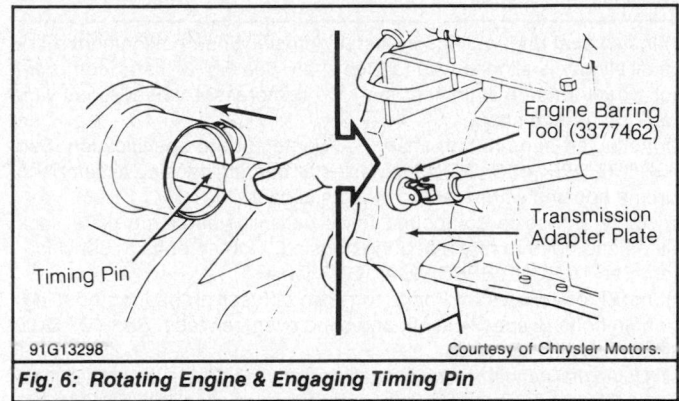

91G13298   Courtesy of Chrysler Motors.

Fig. 6: Rotating Engine & Engaging Timing Pin

7) When No. 1 cylinder is at TDC, key of fuel injection pump shaft should be pointing toward bottom of engine. Ensure timing pin will engage. *See Fig. 6.* Timing pin is located below fuel injection pump.

CAUTION: Carefully engage timing pin to avoid breaking tip of timing pin. DO NOT rotate engine with timing pin engaged.

8) Note if timing marks on fuel injection pump flange and gear housing are aligned for reassembly reference if original fuel injection pump is installed. *See Fig. 7.* These timing marks apply to each engine and fuel injection pump. Timing marks cannot be used to exchange fuel injection pumps.
9) Loosen lock bolt on fuel injection pump, and remove special washer. *See Fig. 7.* Tighten lock bolt to **22 ft. lbs. (30 N.m)**. This will lock fuel injection pump shaft from rotating. Retain special washer for reassembly.
10) Using gear puller and two 8 X 1.24-mm bolts, pull fuel pump drive gear free from fuel injection pump shaft. Remove retaining nuts, fuel injection pump and gasket.

CAUTION: DO NOT allow key to fall from fuel injection pump shaft during removal.

Installation (Original Fuel Injection Pump) – 1) Ensure gasket surfaces are clean. Ensure No. 1 cylinder is at TDC and timing pin is engaged. Install new gasket on cylinder block. Install key in fuel injection pump shaft and install fuel injection pump. DO NOT allow key to drop from fuel injection pump shaft.

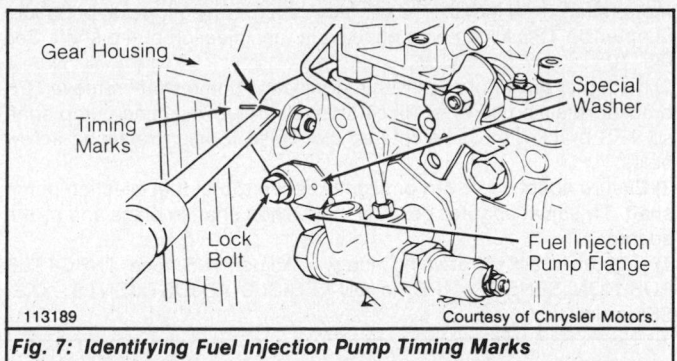

Fig. 7: Identifying Fuel Injection Pump Timing Marks

CAUTION: DO NOT allow key to fall from fuel injection pump shaft during installation.

2) Install mounting nuts. DO NOT tighten nuts yet. Fuel injection pump must be free to rotate in slots. Install fuel pump drive gear retaining nut and washer. Tighten retaining nut to **11-15 ft. lbs. (15-20 N.m)**.
3) If fuel injection pump timing marks on fuel injection pump flange and gear housing were aligned at removal, fuel injection pump timing does not require adjustment. If marks were not aligned, check fuel injection pump timing. See FUEL INJECTION PUMP TIMING in ON-VEHICLE ADJUSTMENTS – DIESEL article.
4) If timing marks were aligned at removal, rotate fuel injection pump to align timing marks. Tighten mounting nuts to **18 ft. lbs. (24 N.m)**. Loosen lock bolt, and install special washer under lock bolt. Tighten lock bolt to **10 ft. lbs. (14 N.m)**. Tighten fuel pump drive gear nut to specification. See TORQUE SPECIFICATIONS table at end of article.
5) Disengage timing pin if not previously disengaged. To install remaining components, reverse removal procedure. Loosely install all bolts in rear support bracket.
6) Tighten rear support bracket bolts to vacuum pump, cylinder block and then to fuel injection pump. Tighten bolts to specification. See TORQUE SPECIFICATIONS table.
7) Install and bleed fuel lines. See FUEL LINE BLEEDING under FUEL SYSTEM. Ensure cable rod is adjusted so control lever contacts low-speed screw when in idle position. Cable rod is located between control linkage and control lever on fuel injection pump.
8) Ensure control lever on fuel injection pump moves over center position and rests against breakover spring (located in center of control lever) when in full throttle position.
Installation (New Or Rebuilt Fuel Injection Pump) – 1) Ensure gasket surfaces are clean. Ensure No. 1 cylinder is at TDC and timing pin is engaged. Install new gasket on cylinder block. Install key in fuel injection pump shaft, and install fuel injection pump.

CAUTION: DO NOT allow key to fall from fuel injection pump shaft during installation.

2) Install mounting nuts. DO NOT tighten nuts yet. Fuel injection pump must be free to rotate in slots. Install fuel pump drive gear retaining nut and washer. Tighten nut to **11-15 ft. lbs. (15-20 N.m)**.
3) Rotate fuel injection pump toward cylinder head to take up gear lash. Check fuel injection pump timing. See FUEL INJECTION PUMP TIMING in ON-VEHICLE ADJUSTMENTS – DIESEL article.

CAUTION: Ensure lock bolt is loosened and special washer is installed under lock bolt. Tighten lock bolt to 10 ft. lbs. (14 N.m).

4) Once correct timing is obtained and mounting nuts are tightened, place timing mark on fuel injection pump flange to align with mark on gear housing. *See Fig. 7.*
5) Disengage timing pin if it was not previously disengaged. To install remaining components, reverse removal procedure. Install all bolts in rear support.
6) Tighten rear support bracket bolts to vacuum pump, cylinder block and then to fuel injection pump. Tighten bolts to specification. See TORQUE SPECIFICATIONS table at end of article.

7) Install and bleed fuel lines. See FUEL LINE BLEEDING under FUEL SYSTEM. Ensure ensure cable rod is adjusted so control lever contacts low-speed screw when in idle position. Cable rod is located between control linkage and control lever on fuel injection pump.
8) Ensure control lever on fuel injection pump moves over center position and rests against breakover spring (located in center of control lever) when in full throttle position.

FUEL LIFT PUMP

Removal & Installation – 1) Disconnect negative battery cable. Disconnect fuel lines at fuel lift pump. Remove retaining bolts, fuel lift pump and gasket.
2) To install, reverse removal procedure using new pump mounting gasket and fuel line banjo bolt sealing washers. Bleed low-pressure fuel lines. See FUEL LINE BLEEDING under FUEL SYSTEM.

FUEL HEATER

Removal – 1) Fuel heater is located between fuel/water separator filter and filter adapter on cylinder head. Ensure area around fuel heater is clean.
2) Disconnect water-in-fuel sensor electrical connection at bottom of fuel/water separator filter. Remove fuel/water separator filter. Disconnect electrical connection at fuel heater. Remove retaining adapter from center of fuel heater. Remove fuel heater and seal rings.
Installation – 1) To install, reverse removal procedure using new seal rings. Tighten retaining adapter to specification. See TORQUE SPECIFICATIONS table at end of article.
2) If water-in-fuel sensor is removed from fuel/water separator, coat water-in-fuel sensor sealing surface with engine oil before installing on fuel/water separator filter.
3) Ensure fuel/water separator filter is full of diesel fuel and sealing surface is coated with engine oil before installing. Tighten fuel/water separator filter 1/2 turn after it contacts fuel heater.

FUEL INJECTOR

Removal – 1) Disconnect negative battery cable. Remove throttle linkage and bracket. Remove high-pressure fuel lines, and mark location for reassembly reference. Remove fuel drain lines from fuel injectors, and plug all fuel openings.
2) Clean around fuel injector. Hold fuel injector body using wrench while loosening hold-down nut. Using Fuel Injector Puller (3823276), pull fuel injectors from cylinder head. Remove sealing ring (located below fuel injector) from cylinder head.
Installation – 1) Install new sealing ring on fuel injector. Coat fuel injector retaining nut and top of fuel injector body with anti-seize compound. Install fuel injector in original position.
2) Ensure protrusion side of fuel injector aligns with notch area of cylinder head. Tighten fuel injector retaining nut to specification. See TORQUE SPECIFICATIONS table at end of article. Once fuel injector retaining nut is tightened, push "O" ring on top of fuel injector into groove.

CAUTION: Ensure protruding side of fuel injector aligns with notch area of cylinder head.

3) To install remaining components, reverse removal procedure using new sealing washers. Install and bleed high-pressure fuel lines. See FUEL LINE BLEEDING under FUEL SYSTEM.

INTAKE MANIFOLD HEATER

Removal & Installation – 1) Disconnect negative battery cable. Intake manifold heater is located between air inlet housing and intake manifold cover. Disconnect intercooler outlet duct from air inlet housing. *See Fig. 4.*
2) Remove high-pressure fuel lines (if necessary). Hold delivery valves on fuel injection pump using wrench while removing high-pressure lines. Mark fuel line location for reassembly reference.
3) Disconnect intake manifold heater electrical connector. Disconnect fuel heater ground wire (located above fuel filter) from intake manifold

cover. Remove retaining bolts, air inlet housing and gasket. Remove intake manifold heater and gasket.

4) To install, reverse removal procedure. Tighten fasteners to specification. See TORQUE SPECIFICATIONS table at end of article. Install and bleed high-pressure fuel lines (if removed). See FUEL LINE BLEEDING under FUEL SYSTEM.

INTAKE MANIFOLD HEATER RELAYS

Removal & Installation – Disconnect negative battery cable. Disconnect electrical connections for intake manifold heater relays, located on inner fenderwell. *See Fig. 8.* Remove retaining bolts and intake manifold heater relays. To install, reverse removal procedure.

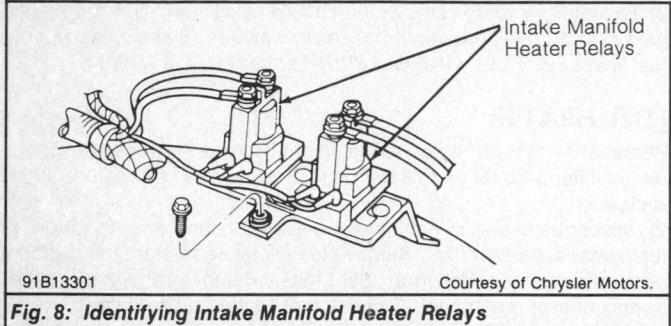

91B13301   Courtesy of Chrysler Motors.

Fig. 8: Identifying Intake Manifold Heater Relays

SHUTOFF SOLENOID VALVE

CAUTION: DO NOT allow plunger and spring to fall in fuel injection pump while servicing shutoff solenoid valve.

Removal & Installation – 1) Disconnect wire from shutoff solenoid valve, located on rear of fuel injection pump. Ensure area around shutoff solenoid valve is clean. Remove shutoff solenoid valve, plunger and spring.

2) To install, reverse removal procedure using new "O" ring. Tighten shutoff solenoid valve to specification. See TORQUE SPECIFICATIONS table at end of article.

CHARGE AIR TEMPERATURE SENSOR & AIR TEMPERATURE SWITCH

Removal & Installation – Charge air temperature sensor and air temperature switch are located in intake manifold cover. *See Fig. 9.*

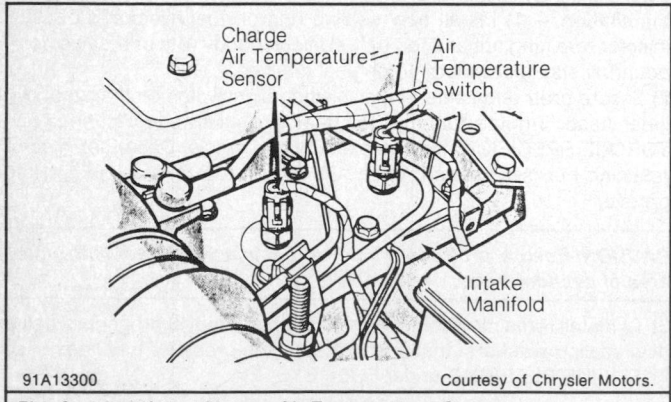

91A13300   Courtesy of Chrysler Motors.

Fig. 9: Identifying Charge Air Temperature Sensor & Air Temperature Switch

THROTTLE POSITION SENSOR (TPS)

Removal – TPS is located above control lever on fuel injection pump. *See Fig. 10.* Disconnect electrical connector at TPS. Remove TPS retaining screws. Lift TPS straight upward from fuel injection pump.

Installation – 1) Install TPS in bracket on fuel injection pump. Ensure adapter on TPS aligns with opening in fuel injection pump shaft. *See Fig. 10.*

2) If adapter does not align with fuel injection pump shaft, remove TPS bracket retaining screws. Place adapter on fuel injection pump shaft so TPS bracket must be rotated clockwise to align retaining screw holes.

3) Ensure adapter is even or slightly above top of fuel injection pump shaft. To adjust adapter position, hold nylon shaft in place and rotate adapter.

4) Tighten bracket retaining screws. Adjust TPS. See THROTTLE POSITION SENSOR (TPS) in ON-VEHICLE ADJUSTMENTS – DIESEL article.

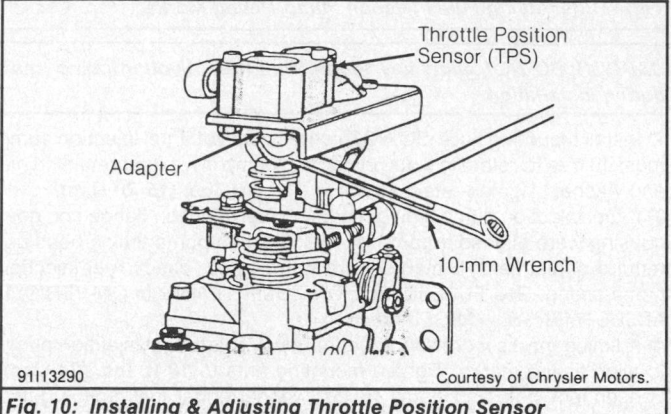

91I13290   Courtesy of Chrysler Motors.

Fig. 10: Installing & Adjusting Throttle Position Sensor

WATER-IN-FUEL SENSOR

Removal & Installation – 1) Disconnect water-in-fuel sensor electrical connection at bottom of fuel/water separator filter. Remove fuel/water separator filter and drain fuel. Unscrew water-in-fuel sensor from bottom of fuel/water separator filter.

2) To install, reverse removal procedure using new "O" rings. Lubricate "O" rings and fuel/water separator filter sealing surface with engine oil before installing. Only hand tighten water-in-fuel sensor. Fill fuel/water separator filter with diesel fuel and install. Tighten fuel/water separator filter 1/2 turn after it contacts sealing surface of fuel heater.

FUEL/WATER SEPARATOR FILTER

Removal – 1) Disconnect water-in-fuel sensor electrical connection at bottom of fuel/water separator filter. Remove fuel/water separator filter. Ensure electrical connection on fuel heater (located above filter) is not rotated against cylinder block when removing fuel/water separator filter.

2) Remove square cut "O" ring from fuel/water separator filter-to-fuel heater contact area. Drain fuel/water separator filter. Unscrew water-in-fuel sensor from bottom of filter.

Installation – 1) To install, reverse removal procedure using new "O" rings. Lubricate "O" rings and fuel/water separator filter sealing surface with engine oil before installing.

2) Reinstall water-in-fuel sensor in bottom of fuel/water separator filter. Hand-tighten water-in-fuel sensor ONLY. Fill fuel/water separator filter with diesel fuel before installing.

3) Tighten fuel/water separator filter 1/2 turn after it contacts sealing surface of fuel heater.

TORQUE SPECIFICATIONS

TORQUE SPECIFICATIONS

Application	Ft. Lbs. (N.m)
Air Crossover Tube Bolt	18 (24)
Air Inlet Housing Bolt	18 (24)
Fuel Heater Retaining Adapter	24 (33)
Fuel Injector Retaining Nut	44 (60)
Fuel Lift Pump Bolt	18 (24)
Fuel Line Banjo Bolt	
At Cylinder Head	18 (24)
At Fuel Pump	24 (33)
Fuel Pump Drive Gear Nut	48 (65)
Fuel Pump Mounting Nut	18 (24)
Fuel Pump Rear Support Bracket Bolt	18 (24)
High-Pressure Fuel Line Nut	18 (24)
Shutoff Solenoid Valve	32 (43)
Thermistor	18 (24)
Turbocharger Mounting Nut	24 (33)
Turbocharger Oil Lines	
Drain Line	18 (24)
Supply Line	11 (15)

Application	INCH Lbs. (N.m)
Air Crossover Clamp	44 (5)
Air Intake Pipe-To-Turbocharger Clamp Nut	72 (8)
Bearing Housing-To-Diffuser Bolt	50 (6)
Bearing Housing-To-Turbine Housing Bolt	100 (11)
Exhaust Pipe-To-Turbocharger Clamp Nut	72 (8)
Fuel Bleed Screw	72 (8)
Fuel Injector Fuel Line Banjo Bolt	72 (8)
Fuel Pump Turbocharger Boost Line Banjo Bolt	108 (12)
Intercooler Inlet & Outlet Duct Clamp Nut	72 (8)
Intercooler Retaining Bolt	17 (2)
Thrust Bearing Bolt	40 (4)
Turbine Shaft Nut [1]	129 (14)
"V" Clamp Nut [2]	72 (8)

[1] – Nut is left-hand thread.
[2] – Apply anti-seize compound to threads. Tighten nut to specification. Tap equally on "V" clamp in 4 places, and then retighten nut to specification.

1992 ENGINE PERFORMANCE
Removal, Overhaul & Installation – CNG

RWD Van

INTRODUCTION

Removal, overhaul and installation procedures (when given by manufacturer) are covered in this article. If component removal and installation is primarily an unbolt and bolt-on procedure, only a torque specification may be provided.

IGNITION SYSTEM

NOTE: For servicing information on this system, see REMOVAL, OVERHAUL & INSTALLATION – GASOLINE article.

FUEL SYSTEM

SAFETY PRECAUTIONS

WARNING: Before servicing any fuel system component, see COMPRESSED NATURAL GAS SAFETY PRECAUTIONS article in GENERAL INFORMATION.

CAUTION: After repairs to fuel system have been completed, a go/no-go gauge MUST be used to check fuel tube high-pressure fittings. These high-pressure fittings are located only on high-pressure side of fuel system. See FUEL TUBES & FITTINGS.

FUEL SYSTEM PRESSURE RELEASE

WARNING: Always relieve fuel pressure before trying to open system for testing or component replacement. High fuel pressure may exist in fuel lines and component parts. DO NOT allow fuel to flow onto engine or electrical parts while testing fuel system components.

Fuel System Purging – Before any part of compressed natural gas (CNG) fuel system is opened for repair, system must be purged of all natural gas.

Fuel system must first be purged of natural gas if any of following components are to be removed or repaired.
- Fuel Tube Or Fuel Tube Fitting
- Fuel Injector Rail Assembly
- Fuel Temperature Sensor
- Fuel Low-Pressure Sensor
- Fuel Gauge Pressure Sensor
- Fuel Fill Receptacle
- Fuel Cylinder
- Manual Shutoff Valve
- Fuel Filter
- Fuel Injectors
- Low-Pressure Fuel Shutoff Solenoid
- Fuel Pressure Regulator
- Fuel Fill Check Valves
- High-Pressure Fuel Shutoff Solenoid

Fuel Tube Purging – **1)** Close control valve (clockwise) on side mounted fuel cylinder. Close control valves (clockwise) on both of rear mounted fuel cylinders. Open manual shutoff valve.

2) Start engine, and operate it until it runs out of fuel. Attempt 3 more engine starts. If check valve or fuel fill receptacle is to be serviced, slowly loosen inlet side of fuel fill tube fitting at check valve. About 25 psi of natural gas pressure may flow from loosened fitting. All fuel tubes are now purged of natural gas between fuel cylinders and engine; fuel system may be opened for repair.

Fuel Cylinder Purging – **1)** Open manual shutoff valve. Open fuel control valves (counterclockwise) only on fuel cylinders to be serviced. Close all control valves (clockwise) on fuel cylinders not being serviced.

2) Start engine, and operate it until it runs out of fuel. Attempt 3 more engine starts. All fuel tubes and opened cylinders are now purged of natural gas between fuel cylinders and engine; fuel system may be opened for repair.

NOTE: Although fuel tubes and opened fuel cylinders are now purged of gas, fuel cylinders (with valves still closed) are still under high-pressure. DO NOT open closed valves until all high-pressure components have been resealed.

FUEL TUBES & FITTINGS

Service Precautions – Due to high-pressure requirements of CNG system, stainless steel, double-ferrule, compression-type fuel tube fittings are used. Following precautions should be observed when servicing these fuel tubes:
- Use only OE standard replacement parts.
- DO NOT allow fuel tube ends to become scratched. Leaks will occur.
- Check and remove burrs from end of fuel tubes.
- DO NOT attempt to loosen or tighten a fitting with fuel system under pressure.
- NEVER attempt to force fuel tube into fitting or ferrule. Tubes should fit easily.
- Fuel tubes are under EXTREME high pressure. DO NOT substitute tubes made of any other material other than OE equipment.
- ALWAYS use a back-up wrench when loosening or tightening fuel fittings to prevent fuel tube from twisting.
- Two sizes of fuel tubes are used, 1/4" and 3/8". ALWAYS use proper size.

Removal (Double-Ferrel Type Fittings) – See SAFETY PRECAUTIONS. Use a back-up wrench to loosen fittings to prevent fuel tube from twisting.

Installation (New Fittings) – **1)** See SAFETY PRECAUTIONS. Install tube into fitting assembly. *See Fig. 1.* Tighten fitting finger tight. Scribe a mark at 6 o'clock position on fitting. *See Fig. 2.*

2) Using a wrench and a back-up wrench, tighten fitting 1 1/4 turn. Scribe mark should be at 9 o'clock position. *See Fig. 2.* Check fitting using go/no-go gauge. *See Fig. 3.* Fitting is properly tightened if go/no-go gauge does not fit between fitting and fitting body.

CAUTION: DO NOT install go/no-go gauge to fitting while tightening; use gauge only as a check.

3) If go/no-go gauge fits between fitting and fitting body after tightening fitting 1 1/4 turns, slowly continue to tighten fitting in small increments until gauge no longer fits. DO NOT overtighten fitting.

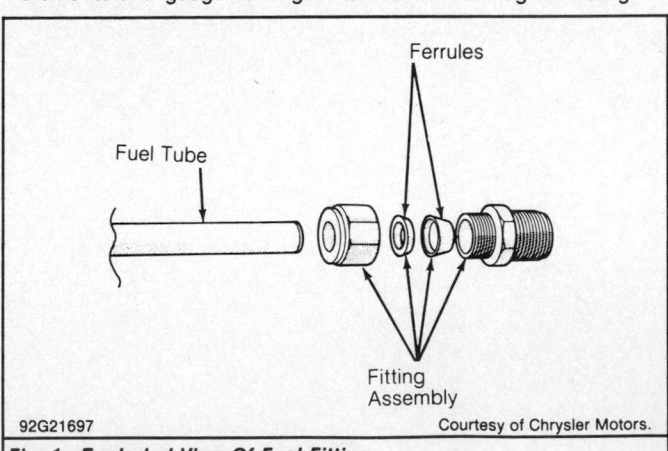

Fig. 1: Exploded View Of Fuel Fitting

Installation (Used Fittings) – **1)** Install tube with pre-swaged, collapsed ferrule into fitting body until ferrule seats. Tighten fitting by hand. Using a wrench and a back-up wrench, tighten fitting until increase in resistance is felt.

2) Slowly tighten fitting an additional 1/12 turn. DO NOT overtighten fitting. Check fitting using go/no-go gauge. If go/no-go gauge still fits between fitting and fitting body, replace fitting.

Removal (High-Pressure "O" Ring Type Fittings) – **1)** Certain fuel fittings use "O" rings. See "O" RING TYPE PRESSURE FITTINGS table. See Fig. 4.

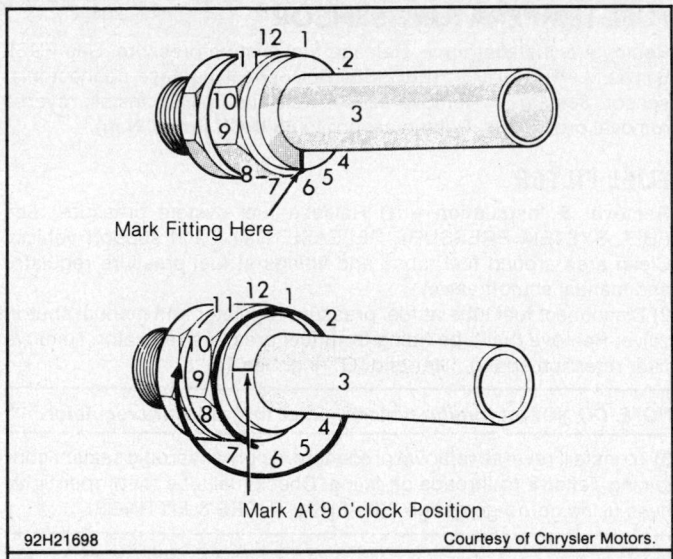

Mark Fitting Here

Mark At 9 o'clock Position

92H21698   Courtesy of Chrysler Motors.

Fig. 2: Tightening Fuel Fitting

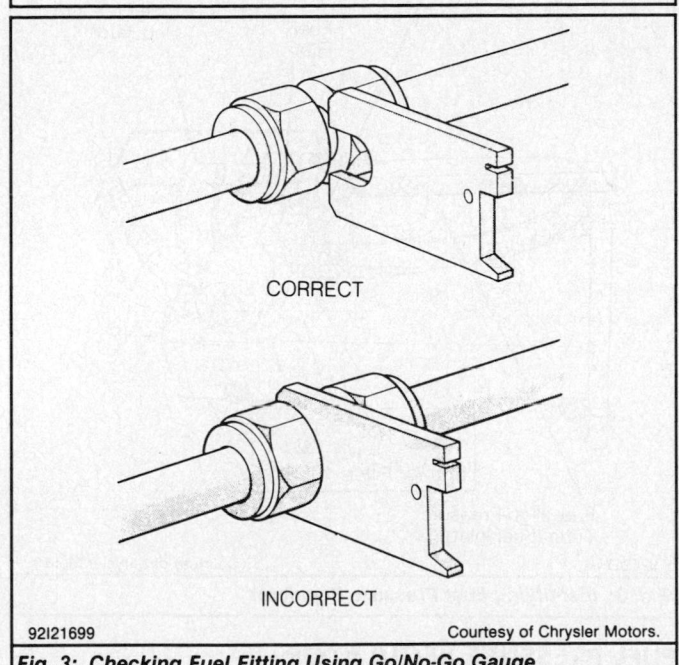

CORRECT

INCORRECT

92I21699   Courtesy of Chrysler Motors.

Fig. 3: Checking Fuel Fitting Using Go/No-Go Gauge

2) When removing 90-degree type fittings, loosen lock nut first to prevent "O" ring damage. *See Fig. 5.*

"O" RING TYPE PRESSURE FITTINGS

Application	Type
Main Fuel Tube	
Rear Cylinder	90-Degree
Side Cylinder	Straight
Rear Cylinder Joining Tube	Straight

Installation – 1) On 90-degree fittings, back off lock nut as far as possible. Thread fitting into port until back-up washer contacts port face. *See Fig. 5.*

2) Rotate fitting to desired position. DO NOT unscrew fitting more than one full turn. Hold fitting in position, and tighten lock nut to **16 ft. lbs. (22 N.m)**. On straight fittings, tighten fitting to **21 ft. lbs. (28 N.m)**

FUEL INJECTOR

Removal & Installation – 1) Release fuel system pressure. See FUEL SYSTEM PRESSURE RELEASE. Disconnect fuel injector harness connector. Using slimline wrench, remove injector from fuel block.

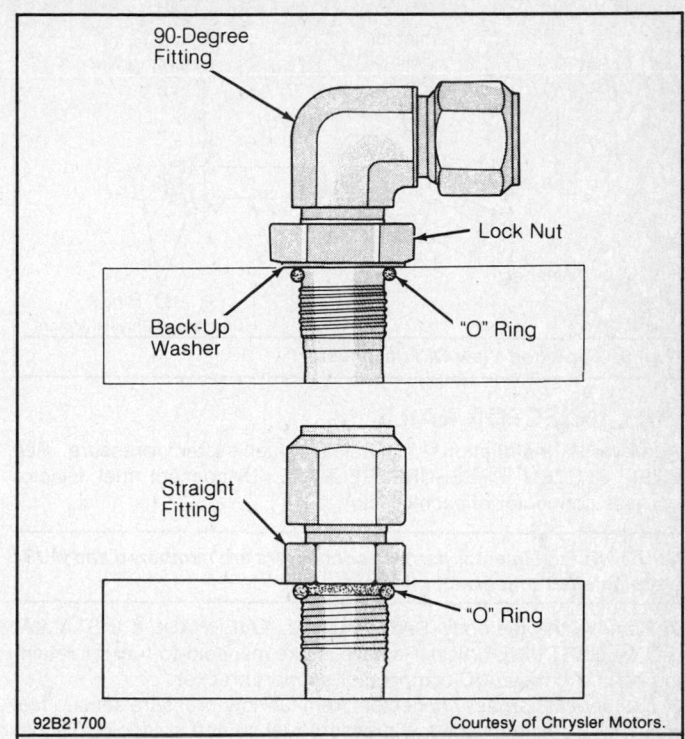

90-Degree Fitting

Lock Nut

Back-Up Washer

"O" Ring

Straight Fitting

"O" Ring

92B21700   Courtesy of Chrysler Motors.

Fig. 4: Identifying "O" Ring Type High-Pressure Fittings

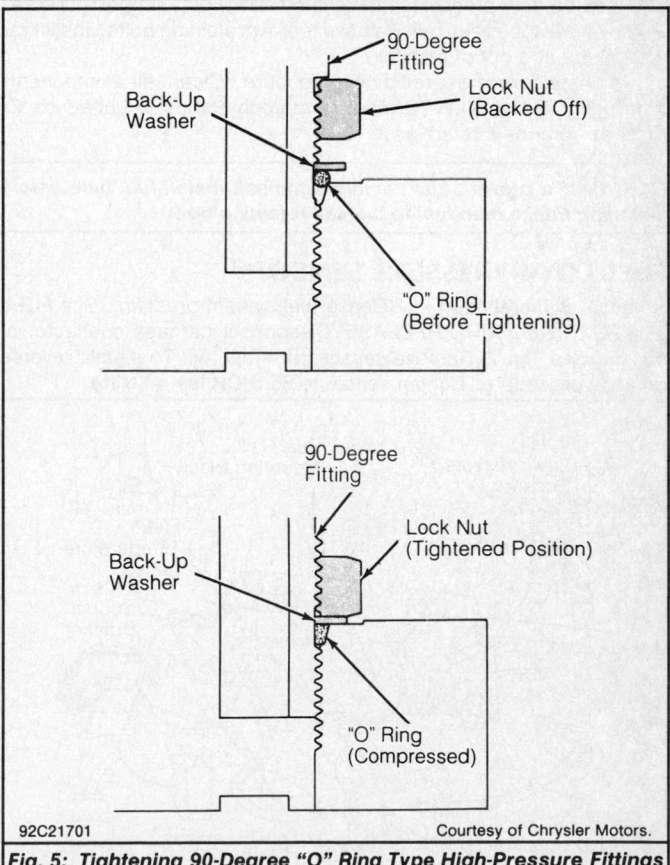

90-Degree Fitting

Back-Up Washer

Lock Nut (Backed Off)

"O" Ring (Before Tightening)

90-Degree Fitting

Lock Nut (Tightened Position)

Back-Up Washer

"O" Ring (Compressed)

92C21701   Courtesy of Chrysler Motors.

Fig. 5: Tightening 90-Degree "O" Ring Type High-Pressure Fittings

2) To install, reverse removal procedure. Apply Parker O-Lube® to 2 NEW "O" rings. Install "O" rings on injector. *See Fig. 6.* Tighten injector to **12 ft. lbs. (16 N.m)**.

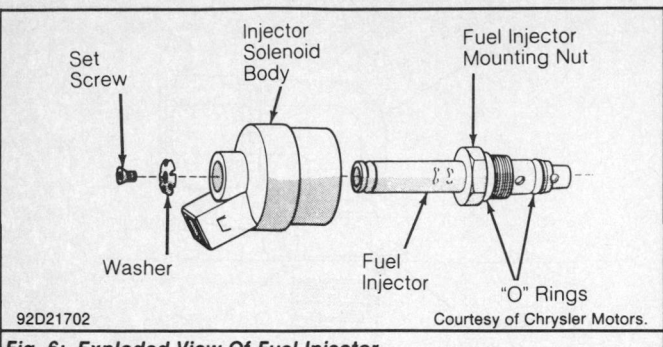

92D21702   Courtesy of Chrysler Motors.

Fig. 6: Exploded View Of Fuel Injector

FUEL INJECTOR RAILS

Removal & Installation – 1) Release fuel system pressure. See FUEL SYSTEM PRESSURE RELEASE. Disconnect fuel injector harness connector at each injector.

CAUTION: Fuel injector harness connectors are numbered and MUST be reinstalled on correct injector.

2) Remove throttle body. See REMOVAL, OVERHAUL & INSTALLATION – GASOLINE article. Remove intake manifold-to-fuel rail retaining bolts. Remove A/C compressor support bracket.
3) Disconnect harness connectors from fuel low-pressure sensor, fuel temperature sensor and low-pressure fuel shutoff solenoid. Disconnect fuel tube from low-pressure fuel shutoff solenoid.
4) Remove low-pressure fuel shutoff solenoid support bracket. Remove fuel tube from rail. Remove fuel rail retaining bolts, and lift rail straight up and out of manifold.
5) To install, reverse removal procedure. Clean all components thoroughly. Install NEW "O" rings, and apply Parker O-Lube® to "O" rings as components are assembled.

CAUTION: To prevent fuel rail misalignment, install fuel tube before installing intake manifold-to-fuel rail retaining bolts.

FUEL LOW-PRESSURE SENSOR

Removal & Installation – Release fuel system pressure. See FUEL SYSTEM PRESSURE RELEASE. Disconnect harness connector at sensor. *See Fig. 7.* Remove sensor from fuel rail. To install, reverse removal procedure. Tighten sensor to **65 INCH lbs. (7 N.m).**

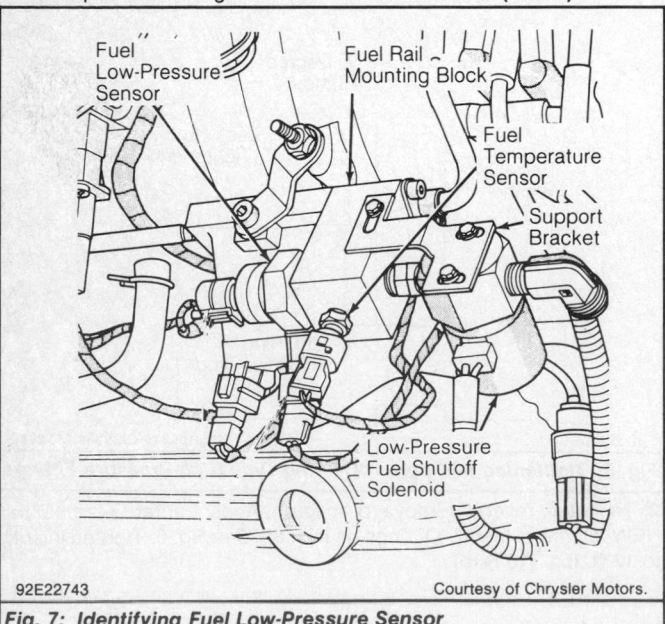

92E22743   Courtesy of Chrysler Motors.

Fig. 7: Identifying Fuel Low-Pressure Sensor

FUEL TEMPERATURE SENSOR

Removal & Installation – Release fuel system pressure. See FUEL SYSTEM PRESSURE RELEASE. Disconnect harness connector at sensor. *See Fig. 7.* Remove sensor from fuel rail. To install, reverse removal procedure. Tighten sensor to **65 INCH lbs. (7 N.m).**

FUEL FILTER

Removal & Installation – 1) Release fuel system pressure. See FUEL SYSTEM PRESSURE RELEASE. Raise and support vehicle. Clean area around fuel tubes and fittings at fuel pressure regulator and manual shutoff valve.
2) Disconnect fuel tube at fuel pressure regulator and manual shutoff valve. Remove fuel tube fitting from fuel pressure regulator. Remove filter retention spring, filter and "O" ring. *See Fig. 8.*

NOTE: DO NOT let foreign material enter fuel pressure regulator.

3) To install, reverse removal procedure. Apply anaerobic sealant containing Teflon® to threads on fitting. Check fuel tube for proper tightness using go/no-go gauge. See FUEL TUBES & FITTINGS.

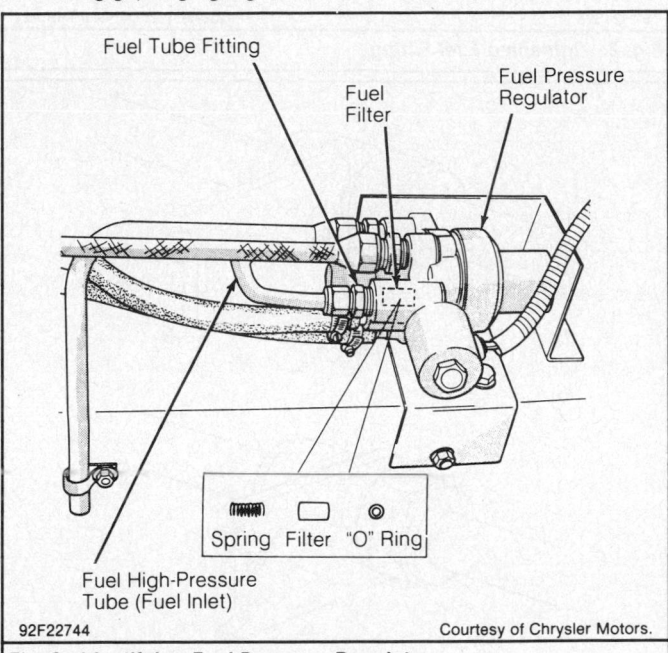

92F22744   Courtesy of Chrysler Motors.

Fig. 8: Identifying Fuel Pressure Regulator

FUEL PRESSURE REGULATOR

Removal & Installation – 1) Release fuel system pressure. See FUEL SYSTEM PRESSURE RELEASE. Drain a small amount of coolant from radiator. Raise and support vehicle.
2) Place a drain pan under fuel pressure regulator, and disconnect coolant hoses. Disconnect regulator harness connector. Clean area around fuel tubes and fittings. Disconnect fuel tubes. Remove 4 regulator-to-frame rail mounting bolts, and remove regulator.
3) To install, reverse removal procedure. Tighten regulator-to-frame rail mounting bolts to **100 INCH lbs. (11 N.m).** Connect fuel tubes, and check for tightness using go/no-go gauge. See FUEL TUBES & FITTINGS.

LOW-PRESSURE FUEL SHUTOFF SOLENOID

Removal & Installation – 1) Release fuel system pressure. See FUEL SYSTEM PRESSURE RELEASE. Remove distributor cap, and position it aside. Remove fuel tube from low-pressure fuel shutoff solenoid.
2) Remove solenoid support bracket bolts and bracket. *See Fig. 7.* Unscrew solenoid from fuel rail mounting block.

3) To install, reverse removal procedure. Tighten solenoid support bracket bolts to **80 INCH lbs. (9 N.m)**. Apply Parker O-Lube® to NEW "O" rings, and install "O" rings on fuel tube.

HIGH-PRESSURE FUEL SHUTOFF SOLENOID

High-pressure fuel shutoff solenoid is integral to fuel pressure regulator. If solenoid is defective, fuel pressure regulator must be replaced. See FUEL PRESSURE REGULATOR.

MANUAL SHUTOFF VALVE

Removal & Installation – 1) Manual shutoff valve is located in front of right rear wheel. Release fuel pressure. See FUEL SYSTEM PRESSURE RELEASE. Raise and support vehicle. Remove rubber shield around valve.

2) Clean area around fuel tube fittings, and disconnect fuel tubes. Remove manual shutoff valve handle. Remove valve mounting bracket retaining bolts, and remove valve assembly. Remove valve from mounting bracket.

3) Install valve mounting bracket and valve assembly to frame rail. Tighten mounting bracket retaining bolts to **100 INCH lbs. (11 N.m)**. Apply thread locking compound to valve mounting nut, and tighten nut to **16 ft. lbs. (22 N.m)**. Check fuel tubes for proper tightness using go/no-go gauge. See FUEL TUBES & FITTINGS.

4) Install valve handle, and tighten set screw to **15 INCH lbs. (1.5 N.m)**. Check tubes and fittings for leaks. To complete installation, reverse removal procedure.

FUEL FILL CHECK VALVES

NOTE: CNG vehicles use 2 fuel fill check valves. One check valve is located on frame rail near top of left rear shock absorber. Other check valve is integral to fuel fill receptacle. If this check valve is defective, fuel fill receptacle MUST be replaced. See FUEL FILL RECEPTACLE.

Removal & Installation (Frame-Mounted Check Valve) – 1) Release fuel system pressure. See FUEL SYSTEM PRESSURE RELEASE. Raise and support vehicle.

2) Disconnect fuel tube fittings from either end of check valve. *See Fig. 9*. Note direction of valve mounting, and remove check valve. To install, reverse removal procedure. Check fuel tube fittings for proper tightness using go/no-go gauge. See FUEL TUBES & FITTINGS.

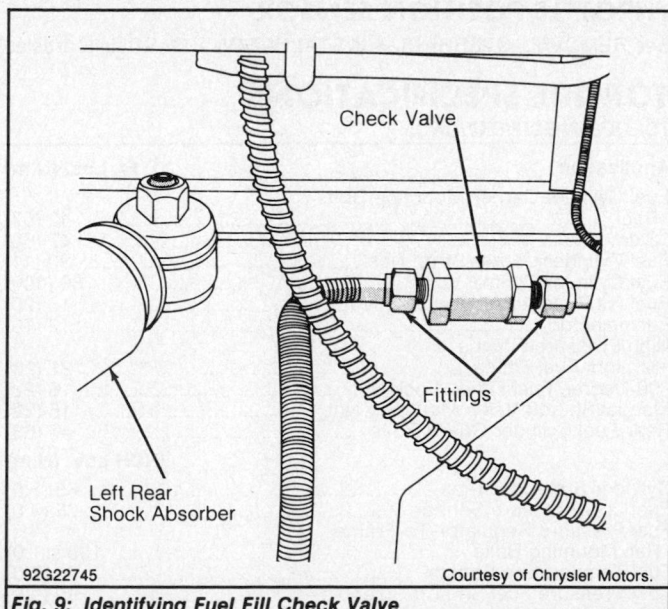

92G22745   Courtesy of Chrysler Motors.
Fig. 9: Identifying Fuel Fill Check Valve

FUEL FILL RECEPTACLE

Removal & Installation – 1) Release fuel system pressure. See FUEL SYSTEM PRESSURE RELEASE. Remove rubber shield located behind left rear wheel.

2) Disconnect fuel tube from fuel fill receptacle. Remove receptacle mounting nut. Remove receptacle.

3) Install receptacle in mounting bracket. Apply thread locking compound to receptacle threads, and install mounting nut. Tighten nut to **15 ft. lbs. (20 N.m)**. Connect fuel tube. Check fuel tube for proper tightness using go/no-go gauge. See FUEL TUBES & FITTINGS.

FUEL CYLINDER CONTROL VALVE

Removal (Side Cylinder) – 1) Release fuel system pressure. See FUEL SYSTEM PRESSURE RELEASE. Ensure side cylinder is empty. Raise and support vehicle.

2) Remove cylinder guard. Clean area around fuel tube fitting, and disconnect fuel tube. *See Fig. 10*. Disconnect fuel gauge pressure sensor harness connector. Remove fuel cylinder control valve.

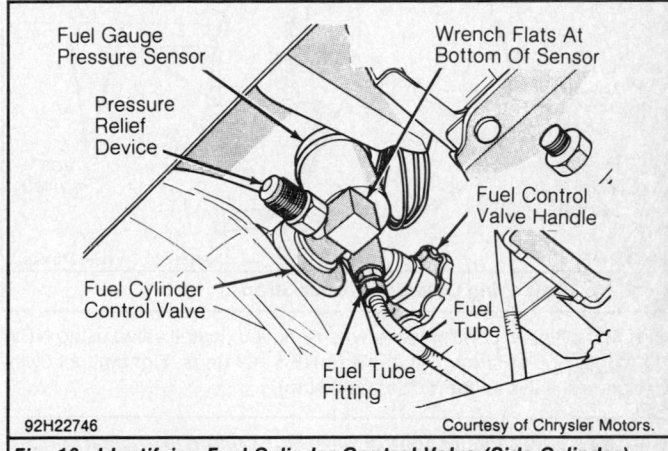

92H22746   Courtesy of Chrysler Motors.
Fig. 10: Identifying Fuel Cylinder Control Valve (Side Cylinder)

Installation – 1) Apply Parker O-Lube® to NEW "O" ring, and install "O" ring on fuel cylinder control valve. Install control valve, and tighten to **80 ft. lbs. (100 N.m)**.

2) Loosen cylinder strap, and rotate cylinder until control valve is in horizontal position. Tighten cylinder strap bolts to **30 ft. lbs. (40 N.m)**.

3) Apply Parker O-Lube® to NEW "O" ring, and install "O" ring on fuel gauge pressure sensor. Install pressure sensor and sensor harness connector.

4) Connect fuel tube, and check for proper tightness using go/no-go gauge. See FUEL TUBES & FITTINGS. Install cylinder guard, and tighten bolts to **32 INCH lbs. (4 N.m)**.

Removal & Installation (Rear Cylinder) – Rear fuel cylinder control valve removal requires rear cylinder removal. See FUEL CYLINDERS.

FUEL CYLINDERS

NOTE: U.S. Department of Transportation (DOT) requires fuel cylinders be retested every three years from date of manufacture. Fuel cylinders expire and must be removed from service 15 years from date of manufacture. A label affixed to fuel filler door states first cylinder retest date and cylinder expiration date.

WARNING: Fuel cylinders MUST be empty before removal.

Removal (Side Cylinder) – 1) Release fuel system pressure. See FUEL SYSTEM PRESSURE RELEASE. Raise and support vehicle. Remove 5 heat shield mounting bolts. Remove heat shield. Remove 3 bolts securing cylinder guard and remove guard.

2) Clean area around fuel tube connection. Disconnect fuel tube. Disconnect fuel gauge pressure sensor harness connector. *See Fig. 10*. Lower vehicle. Remove second seat. Move carpet to expose 2 cylinder carrier mounting bolts. Remove bolts.

3) Raise vehicle. Support fuel cylinder/cylinder carrier assembly using a suitable jack. Remove 2 cylinder carrier mounting bolts at frame rail. Lower cylinder from vehicle. If cylinder carrier assembly is being held in place by adhesive, gently pry assembly loose using a wide-blade screwdriver.

4) Mark cylinder-to-cylinder carrier position for reassembly reference. Remover carrier strap nuts and remove cylinder from carrier. If cylinder is being replaced, remove fuel cylinder control valve.

Installation – 1) Position cylinder in carrier. Install cylinder carrier straps in parallel position. *See Fig. 11.* Tighten cylinder carrier strap nuts to **30 ft. lbs. (41 N.m).**

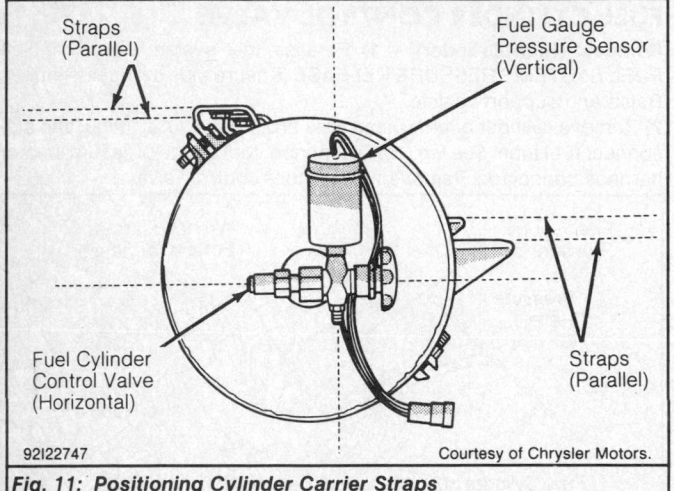

Fig. 11: *Positioning Cylinder Carrier Straps*

2) If fuel cylinder control valve was removed, install valve using NEW "O" rings. Apply Parker O-Lube® to NEW "O" rings. Tighten fuel cylinder control valve to **80 ft. lbs. (100 N.m).**

CAUTION: Fuel cylinder control valve MUST return to original horizontal position. Loosen and reposition fuel cylinder in carrier as necessary.

---

3) Apply sealant around 2 carrier mounting bolt holes, and lift fuel cylinder/cylinder carrier assembly into place. Install 2 carrier mounting bolts at frame rail, but DO NOT tighten. From inside vehicle, install carrier mounting bolts and tighten to **47 ft. lbs. (63 N.m).**

4) Install carpeting and second seat. Tighten carrier mounting bolts at frame rail to **47 ft. lbs. (63 N.m).** Connect fuel tube and check for proper tightness using go/no-go gauge. See FUEL TUBES & FITTINGS. Connect fuel gauge pressure sensor harness connector.

5) Apply thread locking compound to fuel control valve guard mounting bolts. Install guard, and tighten bolts to **32 INCH lbs. (3 N.m).** Install heat shield, and tighten bolts to **32 INCH lbs. (3 N.m).**

Removal (Rear Cylinder) – 1) Release fuel system pressure. See FUEL SYSTEM PRESSURE RELEASE. Ensure rear cylinders are empty. Raise and support vehicle.

2) Remove cylinder guard. Remove main fuel tube. *See Fig. 12.* Lower vehicle. Remove spare tire, jack and rear seat. Move carpeting to expose 8 fuel cylinder carrier mounting bolts. Remove mounting bolts.

3) Raise vehicle. Support fuel cylinder/cylinder carrier assembly with a suitable jack. Remove 2 cylinder support strap nuts. Lower cylinder/cylinder carrier assembly from vehicle. Remove joining fuel tube. *See Fig. 12.*

4) Mark cylinder-to-cylinder carrier position for reassembly reference. Remover carrier strap nuts, and remove cylinders from carrier. Remove fuel cylinder control valve and rubber isolator from cylinders to be replaced.

Installation – 1) Position cylinders in carrier. Install rubber isolators and straps. Tighten cylinder carrier strap nuts to **30 ft. lbs. (41 N.m).** If fuel cylinder control valves were removed, install valves using NEW "O" rings. Apply Parker O-Lube® to NEW "O" rings.

2) Tighten fuel cylinder control valves to **80 ft. lbs. (100 N.m).** Install joining fuel tube, and check for proper tightness using go/no-go gauge. See FUEL TUBES & FITTINGS.

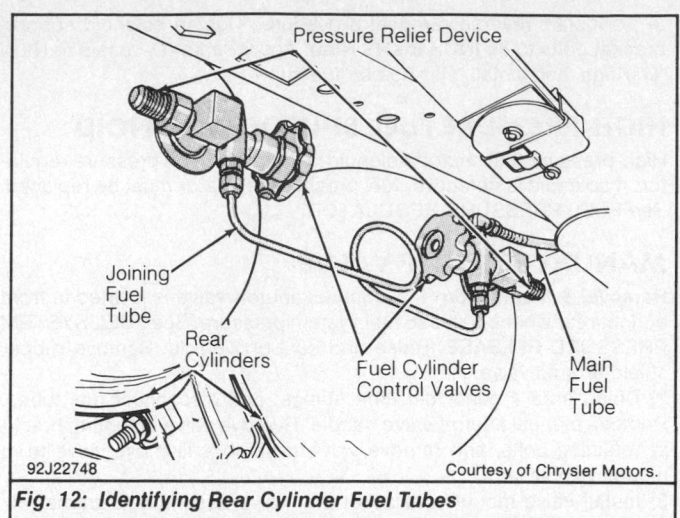

Fig. 12: *Identifying Rear Cylinder Fuel Tubes*

CAUTION: Fuel cylinder control valves MUST return to original horizontal position. Loosen and reposition fuel cylinder in carrier as necessary.

---

3) Apply sealant around 8 carrier mounting bolt holes and lift fuel cylinder/cylinder carrier assembly into place. From inside vehicle, install carrier mounting bolts and tighten to **42 ft. lbs. (57 N.m).** Tighten bolts in a crisscross pattern to prevent distortion of floor pan.

4) Install spare tire, jack and rear seat. Install cylinder support straps, and tighten nuts to **65 INCH lbs. (7 N.m).** Install main fuel tube, and check for proper tightness using go/no-go gauge. See FUEL TUBES & FITTINGS.

5) Install cylinder guard, and tighten bolts to **47 ft. lbs. (63 N.m).** Fill fuel system, and check for leaks.

OXYGEN (O₂) SENSOR
See REMOVAL, OVERHAUL & INSTALLATION – GASOLINE article.

THROTTLE BODY
See REMOVAL, OVERHAUL & INSTALLATION – GASOLINE article.

THROTTLE POSITION SENSOR
See REMOVAL, OVERHAUL & INSTALLATION – GASOLINE article.

TORQUE SPECIFICATIONS
TORQUE SPECIFICATIONS

Application	Ft. Lbs. (N.m)
Fuel Cylinder Carrier Mounting Bolts	
Rear	42 (57)
Side	47 (63)
Fuel Cylinder Carrier Strap Nut	30 (41)
Fuel Cylinder Control Valve	80 (100)
Fuel Fill Receptacle Mounting Nut	15 (20)
Fuel Injector	12 (16)
High Pressure Fittings	
Straight Fuel Fitting	21 (28)
90-Degree Fuel Fitting Lock Nut	16 (22)
Manual Shutoff Valve Mounting Nut	16 (22)
Rear Fuel Cylinder Guard Bolts	47 (63)

	INCH Lbs. (N.m)
Cylinder Support Straps	65 (7.0)
Fuel Low-Pressure Sensor	65 (7.0)
Fuel Pressure Regulator-To-Frame	
Rail Mounting Bolts	100 (11.0)
Fuel Temperature Sensor	65 (7.0)
Low-Pressure Fuel Shutoff Solenoid	80 (9.0)
Manual Shutoff Valve Mounting	
Bracket Retaining Bolts	100 (11.0)
Manual Shutoff Valve Handle Set Screw	15 (1.5)
Side Fuel Cylinder Guard Bolts	32 (3.0)
Side Fuel Cylinder Heat Shield	32 (3.0)

Caravan, Dakota, Pickup, Ramcharger, RWD Van, Town & Country, Voyager

DESCRIPTION

Chrysler Motors light trucks use either a Bosch or a Denso alternator. The alternator consists of a rotor, stator, rectifiers, front and rear covers and drive pulley. Voltage regulation is controlled by the Single Board Engine Controller (SBEC) on all models except diesel. On diesel models, voltage regulation is controlled by a transistorized voltage regulator.

ALTERNATOR APPLICATION

Application	[1] Case Number	Pulley Grooves
Caravan, Town & Country, Voyager		
2.5L		
Bosch 84-Amp	4557431	4
Denso 86-Amp	5234031	4
Denso 98-Amp	5234208	4
3.0L & 3.3L		
Denso 90-Amp	5234032	6
Denso 102-Amp	5234033	6
Dakota		
2.5L		
Denso 75-Amp	4557301	4
Denso 90-Amp	5234026	4
Denso 120-Amp	5234027	4
3.9L & 5.2L		
Denso 75-Amp	53008646	7
Denso 90-Amp	53008647	7
Denso 120-Amp	53008651	7
Pickup, Ramcharger & RWD Van		
3.9L & 5.2L		
Denso 75-Amp	53008646	7
Denso 90-Amp	53008647	7
Denso 120-Amp	53008651	7
5.9L		
Denso 75-Amp	5234026	2
Denso 90-Amp	5234028	2
Denso 120-Amp	5234199	2

[1] – Located on tag on bottom of alternator case.

OPERATION

The SBEC monitors critical input to control fuel injection, ignition, emission and other engine management functions. The SBEC has also been programmed to monitor several charging system related circuits:

- Battery feed to SBEC
- Alternator field control
- Battery charging voltage (high and low)

If a problem is sensed in a monitored circuit, a fault code is stored in the SBEC's memory and the CHECK ENGINE light will be turned on (with a few exceptions). Fault codes can be read using the CHECK ENGINE light or with the Chrysler Diagnostic Readout Box-II (DRB-II).

NOTE: Fault codes remain in memory for 50 engine starts. Fault is erased from memory if failure does not reoccur .

For certain fault codes, CHECK ENGINE light will illuminate and engine controller will enter limp-in mode. In limp-in mode, engine controller attempts to compensate for particular component failure by substituting information from other sources. This allows vehicle operation until proper repairs are made.

ADJUSTMENTS

BELT TENSION

	New Belt	[1] Used Belt
Application	Lbs. (kg)	Lbs. (kg)
Caravan, Town & Country, Voyager		
2.5L	125 (57)	80 (36)
3.0L	[2]	[2]
3.3L	[2]	[2]
Dakota		
2.5L	160 (73)	80 (36)
3.9L	[2]	[2]
5.2L	[2]	[2]
Pickup & Ramcharger		
3.9L & 5.2L	[2]	[2]
5.9L		
Gas	100-140 (45-64)	60-90 (27-41)
Diesel	[2]	[2]
RWD Van [3]		
3.9L & 5.2L	[2]	[2]
5.9L	100-140 (45-64)	60-90 (27-41)

[1] – Any belt operated for 15 minutes.
[2] – Dynamic tensioner used, no adjustment is required.

TROUBLE SHOOTING

INITIAL CHECKS

Before proceeding with charging system diagnosis, ensure:

- Battery is fully charged and in good condition
- Battery cables are in good condition with connections clean and secure
- Alternator belt is in good condition and properly tightened
- Alternator and SBEC wiring harness connections are clean and tight
- Engine ground strap is in place

UNSTEADY OR LOW CHARGING

Check for loose alternator belt, charging resistance too high, defective alternator, loose alternator ground wire or corroded battery terminals.

OVERCHARGING

Check for grounded alternator field wiring or faulty alternator.

NOISY ALTERNATOR

Check for worn alternator bearings or loose alternator mounting.

SELF-DIAGNOSTIC SYSTEM

SYSTEM DIAGNOSIS

The self-diagnostic capabilities of this system, if properly used, can simplify testing. SBEC monitors several different engine control system circuits.

If a problem is sensed with a monitored circuit, a fault code is stored in SBEC, CHECK ENGINE light illuminates and SBEC enters limp-in mode. In limp-in mode, SBEC compensates for component failure by substituting information from other sources. This allows vehicle operation until repairs can be made.

Once codes are known, refer to CHARGING SYSTEM FAULT CODES table to determine the questionable circuit. Test circuits and repair or replace components as required. If problem is repaired or ceases to exist, SBEC cancels that fault code after 50 ignition on/off cycles. To clear codes, refer to ERASING FAULT CODES under ENTERING ON-BOARD DIAGNOSTICS.

A specific fault code results from a particular system failure. Components in that system are NOT necessarily the reason for that failure. The fault code does not condemn a specific component, it calls out a CIRCUIT malfunction.

Hard Failures – Hard failures cause CHECK ENGINE light to illuminate and remain on until malfunction is repaired. If light comes on and remains on (light may flash) during vehicle operation, cause of malfunction must be determined using diagnostic (code) charts. If a sensor fails, SBEC will use a substitute value in its calculations, allowing engine operation in limp-in mode. In this condition, vehicle will run, but driveability may be poor.

Intermittent Failures – Intermittent failures may cause CHECK ENGINE light to flicker or stay on until intermittent fault goes away. The corresponding trouble code will be retained in SBEC memory, however. If fault does not reoccur within a certain time frame, corresponding trouble code will be erased from SBEC memory. Intermittent failures can be caused by faulty sensor, bad connector or wiring related problems. See INTERMITTENTS in appropriate TROUBLE SHOOTING – NO CODES article in ENGINE PERFORMANCE.

DIAGNOSTIC PROCEDURE

Refer to ENTERING ON-BOARD DIAGNOSTICS to retrieve fault codes. If fault codes are NOT present and/or DRB-II (Diagnostic Readout Box-II) is used, proceed to TEST CH-1, BATTERY TEST.

NOTE: When using trouble shooting charts for diagnosis, DO NOT skip any steps in chart or incorrect diagnosis may result.

Before proceeding with diagnosis, the following precautions must be followed:

- Vehicle must have a fully charged battery and functional charging system. See TROUBLE SHOOTING and ON-VEHICLE TESTING.
- Probe SBEC connector from pin side. DO NOT backprobe SBEC connector.
- DO NOT cause short circuits when performing electrical tests. This will set additional fault codes, making diagnosis of original problem more difficult.
- DO NOT use a test light in place of a voltmeter.
- Always repair lowest fault code number (CHECK ENGINE light) or first fault displayed (DRB-II) first.
- Always perform verification procedure test after repairs are made.
- Always disconnect DRB-II after use.
- Always disconnect DRB-II before charging battery.

ENTERING ON-BOARD DIAGNOSTICS

CAUTION: Before entering on-board diagnostics, check charging system for other problems. See INITIAL CHECKS under TROUBLE SHOOTING. DO NOT connect DRB-II to vehicle with battery charger connected, as damage to DRB-II may result.

Reading Trouble Codes – Trouble codes may be read by using CHECK ENGINE light on instrument panel or with DRB-II. See CHECK ENGINE LIGHT DIAGNOSTIC MODE and DIAGNOSIS USING DRB-II. A more complete diagnosis is possible using DRB-II.

NOTE: SBEC CANNOT diagnose every charging system problem. If a fault still exists after performing self-diagnostic procedures, proceed to ON-VEHICLE TESTING.

Trouble Code Explanation – 1) See CHARGING SYSTEM FAULT CODES table for charging-related faults.

2) Code 12 will set if battery feed to SBEC has been disconnected within last 50-100 starts. SBEC monitors this circuit whenever ignition is on.

3) Code 41 will set if alternator field control fails to switch properly. SBEC monitors this circuit whenever ignition is on.

4) If battery temperature sense voltage goes out of range, Code 44 will be set in memory. SBEC monitors this circuit any time ignition is on.

5) If battery sense voltage is more than one volt above desired control voltage for more than 20 seconds, a Code 46 will be set in memory. SBEC monitors this signal whenever engine is running.

6) If battery sense voltage is more than one volt below desired control voltage for more than 20 seconds and no significant change in voltage is detected during active test of alternator, Code 47 will be set. SBEC monitors this signal whenever engine speed is more than 1500 RPM.

CHARGING SYSTEM FAULT CODES

Code	Circuit	CHECK ENGINE Light On?
12	Battery Feed To SBEC	No
41 [1]	Alternator Field Control	Yes
44 [1]	[2] Battery Temp. Sensor	Yes
46 [1]	High Battery Voltage	Yes
47 [1]	Low Battery Voltage	No
55	End Of Diagnostic Mode	No

[1] – This code will cause limp-in mode.
[2] – Sensor inside SBEC. If failed, replace SBEC.

NOTE: Only charging system-related codes are listed here. For engine-related codes, see appropriate SELF-DIAGNOSTICS article in ENGINE PERFORMANCE.

CHECK ENGINE Light Diagnostic Mode – 1) Start engine (if possible). On models equipped with automatic transmission, place foot on brake and cycle transmission shift lever through all positions, ending in Park. On all models, turn A/C switch on and then off (if equipped).

2) Turn engine off. Without starting engine again, turn ignition on, off, on, off and on. CHECK ENGINE light will come on for 2 seconds as a bulb check, followed by fault codes. Record 2-digit fault codes as displayed by flashing CHECK ENGINE light.

3) For example, Code 23 is displayed as flash, flash, 4 second pause, then flash, flash, flash. After a slightly longer pause, any other codes stored are displayed in numerical order.

4) Once check engine light begins to flash fault codes, it cannot be stopped. Go to step 1) to enter diagnostic mode again. Code 55 indicates end of fault code display. For more information on vehicle self-diagnostics, see appropriate SELF-DIAGNOSTICS article in ENGINE PERFORMANCE.

5) Refer to CHARGING SYSTEM FAULT CODES table to translate trouble code number to a system fault description (DRB-II display). Once trouble area is identified, refer to appropriate charging system test procedures.

NOTE: CHECK ENGINE light CANNOT be used to perform actuation test mode, sensor test modes or engine running test. Fault codes can only be erased using DRB-II. Fault codes will be erased from SBEC memory after 50 key starts if fault does not reoccur.

Diagnosis Using DRB-II – DRB-II is used as part of a charging system diagnostic procedure. Perform tests CH-1, BATTERY TEST through CH-VER, CHARGING VERIFICATION.

DRB-II Diagnostic Mode – 1) Turn ignition off. Attach DRB-II to engine diagnostic connector. Connector is located in engine compartment, near SBEC.

2) Start engine (if possible). On models equipped with automatic transmission, place foot on brake pedal and cycle transmission shift lever through all positions, ending in Park. On all models, turn A/C switch on and then off (if equipped).

3) Turn engine off. Without starting engine again, turn ignition on. Enter CHARGING MENU. To enter CHARGING MENU, see DRB-II TEST FUNCTIONS. At CHARGING MENU, press "2" (READ FAULTS) key. Press ENTER key. After fault codes are accessed, refer to TEST CH-1, BATTERY TEST under ON-VEHICLE TESTING.

Erasing Fault Codes – 1) To erase faults, press ATM key. At DRB-II display, press "2" (ERASE) key. DRB-II will display ERASE FAULTS ARE YOU SURE? (ENTER TO ERASE). Press ENTER key.

2) When DRB-II is finished erasing fault codes, it will display FAULTS ERASED. This display will remain until ATM key is pressed. After ATM key is pressed, display will return to CHARGING MENU screen.

DRB-II TEST FUNCTIONS

NOTE: DO NOT touch DRB-II keypad during DRB-II power-up sequence, or an error message will result.

1) To perform diagnostic tests using DRB-II, DRB-II must be in CHARGING MENU. At CHARGING MENU, fault codes and DRB-II test functions can be accessed.

2) To reach CHARGING MENU, turn ignition off. Attach DRB-II to engine diagnostic connector. Connector is located in engine compartment, near SBEC. Turn ignition switch to RUN position.

3) All DRB-II character positions will illuminate and copyright information will appear on screen for several seconds. If DRB-II screen is blank or any error messages appear, see DRB-II PROBLEMS & ERROR MESSAGES.

4) After several seconds DRB-II menu will appear. At DRB-II menu, press "4" (SELECT SYSTEM) key. Press ENTER key. At SELECT SYSTEM menu, press "1" (ENGINE) key. Press ENTER key. DRB-II menu will appear, indicating engine year and size, type of transmission and SBEC part number.

5) After several seconds AIR COND menu will appear. Press "1" (WITH A/C) or press "2" (WITHOUT A/C). DRB-II display will change to ENGINE SYSTEMS menu. At ENGINE SYSTEMS menu, press "2" (CHARGING) key. Press ENTER key.

6) Display will change to CHARGING MENU. At CHARGING menu of engine diagnostic program, specific test functions programmed into DRB-II can be performed. The following DRB-II modes can be accessed: SYSTEM TEST, READ FAULTS, STATE DISPLAYS, ACTUATOR TEST and ADJUSTMENTS.

SYSTEM TEST Mode – This function is not available in engine diagnostics program.

READ FAULTS Mode – 1) This function allows user to read and erase fault codes. A fault counter will appear along with fault displayed on DRB-II. As an example, DRB-II will display 1 OF 2 FAULTS. SBEC will store up to 8 fault messages. Faults are numbered in reverse order of setting. The most recent fault to occur will appear first. Vehicles without A/C will always have A/C CLUTCH RELAY CKT (circuit) stored in memory. This fault will always appear first if vehicle is not equipped with A/C. If no fault messages are stored, DRB-II will display NO FAULTS DETECTED and start counter will show 0 STARTS SINCE ERS.

2) A start counter will appear below DRB-II fault counter display. Start counter tracks the number of times vehicle is started since faults were last set, erased, or battery was disconnected. This helps determine if fault is intermittent. Memory space limits start counter to first 3 faults. Start counter of zero equals a hard fault. Start counter of more than zero indicates an intermittent fault. Start counter will count up to 255 starts. If no fault messages are stored, DRB-II will display NO FAULTS DETECTED and start counter will show 0 STARTS SINCE ERS.

STATE DISPLAYS Mode – 1) This function allows user to read states or values of a variety of sensors, inputs/outputs and components.

2) The SBEC can only recognize high and low states on switch circuits. SBEC cannot differentiate between an open or short circuit or a defective switch. If DRB-II displays a change between INPUT HIGH and INPUT LOW, it can be assumed that the entire switch circuit to the SBEC is functioning.

ACTUATOR TEST Mode – 1) This function allows the user to check for proper operation of output circuits or devices, which the SBEC cannot internally recognize. DRB-II allows SBEC to activate these outputs or devices, allowing an observer to verify proper operation.

2) Most of the tests available in this mode provide an audible or visual indication of device operation (click of relay contacts, fuel spray, etc.). With the exception of an intermittent condition, if a device functions properly during its test, it can be assumed that the device, wiring and its driver circuit are functioning properly.

ADJUSTMENTS Mode – This function allows the user to erase fault codes. Function also allows user to reset Emission Maintenance Reminder (EMR) light and mileage (trucks only).

DRB-II Volt/Ohmmeter Mode – 1) To access volt/ohmmeter mode of DRB-II, connect Red volt/ohmmeter test lead to Red port, located on right-top side of DRB-II.

NOTE: Because DRB-II is grounded through engine diagnostic connector, only one volt/ohmmeter test lead is required when using volt/ohmmeter option. DRB-II volt/ohmmeter should only be used when diagnostic procedures require the use of this option.

2) To access voltmeter, press VOLT/OHM key once. DRB-II is now in voltmeter mode. Touch test probe to connector or wire to be measured. Read voltage on DRB-II display. When voltage testing is complete, press VOLT/OHM key 3 times to exit voltmeter mode.

3) To access ohmmeter, press VOLT/OHM key twice. DRB-II is now in ohmmeter mode. Touch test probe to connector or wire to be measured. Read resistance to circuit ground on DRB-II display. When resistance testing is complete, press VOLT/OHM key twice to exit ohmmeter mode.

DRB-II Continuity Meter Mode – Press VOLT/OHM key 3 times. Display will read NO CONTINUITY. Touch test probe to connector or wire to be measured. Read continuity on DRB-II display. When continuity testing is complete, press VOLT/OHM key once to exit continuity meter mode.

VEHICLES TESTED Mode – 1) Mode is used to show what vehicles are covered by DRB-II cartridge. To access vehicles tested mode, turn ignition off. Attach DRB-II to engine diagnostic connector. Connector is located in engine compartment, near SBEC.

2) Turn ignition switch to RUN position. All DRB-II character positions will illuminate and copyright information will appear on screen. After several seconds DRB-II menu will appear.

3) At DRB-II menu, press "1" (VEHICLES TESTED) key. Press ENTER key. DRB-II will display vehicles covered by cartridge. Screen will display for 5 seconds and return to DRB-II menu.

HOW TO USE Mode – Enter DRB-II menu display. Refer to steps **1)** and **2)** under VEHICLES TESTED MODE. At DRB-II menu, press "2" (HOW TO USE) key. Press ENTER key. A series of screens will be displayed explaining the use of DRB-II keys used to move through engine diagnostic program.

CONFIGURE Mode – 1) Configure option allows user to customize DRB-II display. For example, if metric system is more useful to use, simply select METRIC from the appropriate menu.

2) All selections made under CONFIGURE option remain active until user changes selection. To enter configure mode, enter DRB-II menu display. Refer to steps **1)** and **2)** under VEHICLES TESTED MODE. At DRB-II menu, press "3" (CONFIGURE) key. Press ENTER key. DRB-II will display CONFIGURE menu.

DRB-II PROBLEMS & ERROR MESSAGES

Blank Message Screen – 1) Connect DRB-II to a different vehicle. If message screen is still blank, DRB-II or cable adapter is faulty. Substitute to find faulty component.

2) If message screen is not blank, DRB-II and cable adapter are functioning properly. Inspect diagnostic connector for proper wire placement, damaged terminals or pushed out pins. Repair as necessary.

3) If diagnostic connector is okay, using an ohmmeter, check resistance between Black/White or Black/Yellow wire and ground at engine diagnostic connector. If resistance is greater than 10 ohms, repair open in Black/White or Black/Yellow wire.

NO RESPONSE Message – 1) Connect DRB-II to another vehicle. If DRB-II displays NO RESPONSE message again, DRB-II or cable adapter is faulty. Substitute to find faulty component. If message screen does not display NO RESPONSE, DRB-II and cable adapter are functioning properly. Go to next step.

2) Turn ignition off. Disconnect DRB-II. Using an ohmmeter, check Pink or Black/Red wire for resistance between SBEC and engine diagnostic connectors. If resistance is more than 10 ohms, repair open in Pink or Black/Red wire.

3) If resistance is less than 10 ohms, check Light Green/Orange or Black/Pink wire for resistance between SBEC and engine diagnostic connectors. If resistance is more than 10 ohms, repair open in Light Green/Orange or Black/Pink wire.

RAM TEST FAILURE Message – Replace DRB-II.

CARTRIDGE ERROR Message – Replace DRB-II cartridge.

KEY PAD TEST FAILURE Message – Power up DRB-II again with fingers off keypad. If error message returns, replace DRB-II.

HIGH OR LOW BATTERY Message – Correct condition of vehicle battery and reconnect DRB-II.

NOTE: For more information on SBEC diagnostic capabilities and using DRB-II, see appropriate SELF-DIAGNOSTICS article in ENGINE PERFORMANCE.

ON-VEHICLE TESTING

NOTE: ALTERNATOR OUTPUT WIRE RESISTANCE TEST will show amount of voltage drop across alternator output wire between alternator BAT terminal and positive battery post.

WARNING: When battery is disconnected, vehicle computer and memory systems may lose memory data. Driveability problems may exist until computer systems have completed a relearn cycle. See COMPUTER RELEARN PROCEDURES article in GENERAL INFORMATION before disconnecting battery.

ALTERNATOR OUTPUT WIRE RESISTANCE TEST

1) Charge battery as necessary. Turn ignition off. Disconnect negative battery cable. Disconnect alternator output wire from alternator BAT terminal.

2) Using a 0-150-ampere scale DC ammeter, connect positive ammeter lead to alternator BAT terminal and negative lead to disconnected alternator output wire. *See Figs. 1 and 2.*

3) Using a voltmeter (0-18 volts minimum), connect positive voltmeter lead to disconnected alternator output wire and negative lead to positive battery cable.

CAUTION: Alternator has 2 field terminals. One field terminal has Dark Green wire and other field terminal has Dark Blue wire. DO NOT connect jumper wire to alternator field terminal Dark Blue wire.

4) On Caravan, Town & Country and Voyager, remove air hose between SBEC and air cleaner. On all models, connect one end of jumper wire to ground and other end to alternator field terminal Dark Green wire on rear side of alternator.

5) Connect engine tachometer and reconnect negative battery cable. Connect carbon pile rheostat between battery terminals. Ensure carbon pile is in OFF position before connecting leads.

6) Start engine. Reduce engine speed to idle. Adjust engine speed and carbon pile to maintain 20 amps flowing in circuit. Observe voltmeter reading. Voltage drop should be .5 volt or less.

7) If voltage drop is more than .5 volt, inspect, clean and tighten all connections between alternator BAT terminal and positive battery post. Voltage drop test may be performed at each connection to locate connection with excessive resistance. If resistance tests satisfactorily, reduce engine speed, turn off carbon pile and ignition switch.

8) Disconnect negative battery cable. Remove test ammeter, voltmeter, carbon pile and tachometer. Remove jumper wire between alternator Dark Green field wire and ground. Connect alternator output wire to alternator BAT terminal. Reconnect negative battery cable and hose between SBEC and air cleaner.

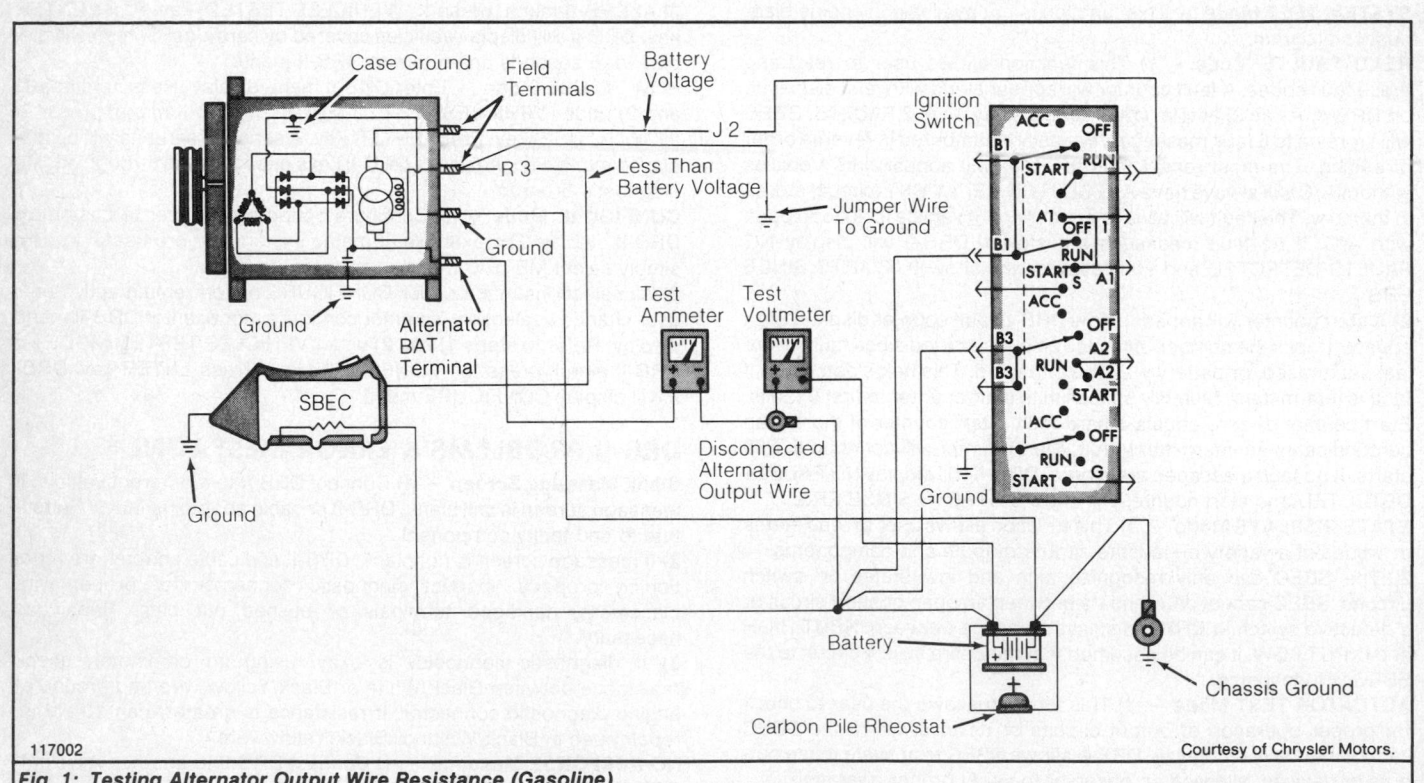

117002

Courtesy of Chrysler Motors.

Fig. 1: Testing Alternator Output Wire Resistance (Gasoline)

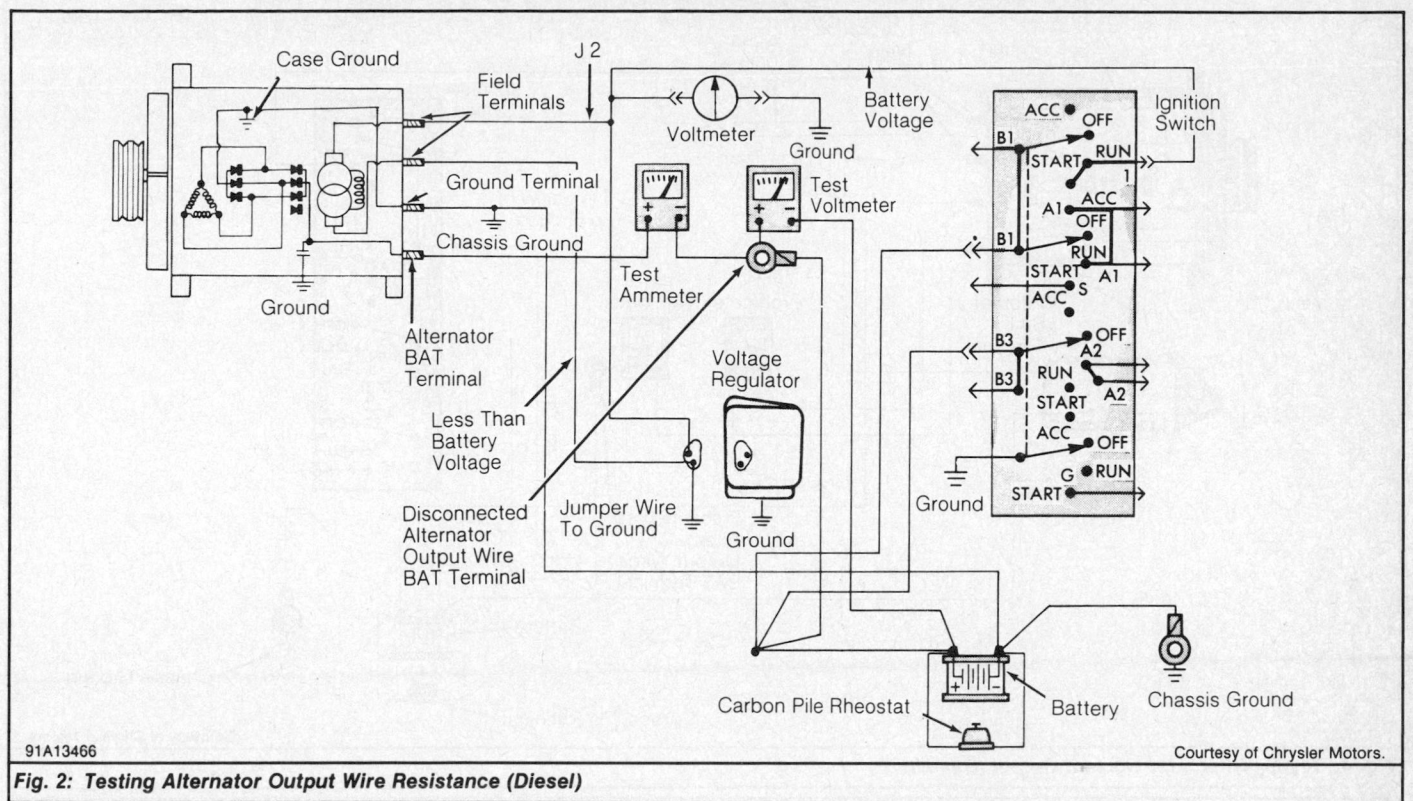

91A13466   Courtesy of Chrysler Motors.

Fig. 2: Testing Alternator Output Wire Resistance (Diesel)

CURRENT OUTPUT TEST

NOTE: CURRENT OUTPUT TEST determines if alternator is capable of delivering its rated current output.

1) Charge battery as necessary. Disconnect negative battery cable. Disconnect alternator output wire at alternator BAT terminal. *See Fig. 3.* Using a 0-150-ampere scale DC ammeter, connect positive ammeter lead to alternator BAT terminal and negative lead to disconnected alternator output wire. *See Figs. 4 and 5.*
2) Using a voltmeter (0-18 volts range minimum), connect positive voltmeter lead to disconnected alternator BAT terminal and negative lead to good ground.
3) Connect engine tachometer and reconnect negative battery cable. Connect carbon pile rheostat between battery terminals. Ensure carbon pile is in OFF position before connecting leads.

CAUTION: Alternator has 2 field terminals. One field terminal has Dark Green wire and other field terminal has Dark Blue wire. DO NOT connect jumper wire to alternator field terminal Dark Blue wire.

4) On Caravan, Town & Country and Voyager, remove air hose between SBEC and air cleaner. On all models, connect one end of jumper wire to ground and other end to alternator field terminal Dark Green wire on back of alternator.
5) Start engine and reduce engine speed to idle. Adjust carbon pile and engine speed in increments until engine speed is 1250 RPM and voltmeter reads 15 volts. DO NOT allow voltage to read more than 16 volts.

6) Ammeter should read within specification. See ALTERNATOR MINIMUM OUTPUT table. If alternator amperage reads less than specified and alternator output wire resistance is not excessive, replace alternator. After CURRENT OUTPUT TEST is completed, reduce engine speed, turn off carbon pile and ignition switch.
7) Disconnect negative battery cable. Remove test ammeter, voltmeter, tachometer and carbon pile. Remove jumper wire between alternator field terminal Dark Green wire and ground. Reconnect alternator output wire to alternator BAT terminal. Reconnect negative battery cable and hose between SBEC and air cleaner.

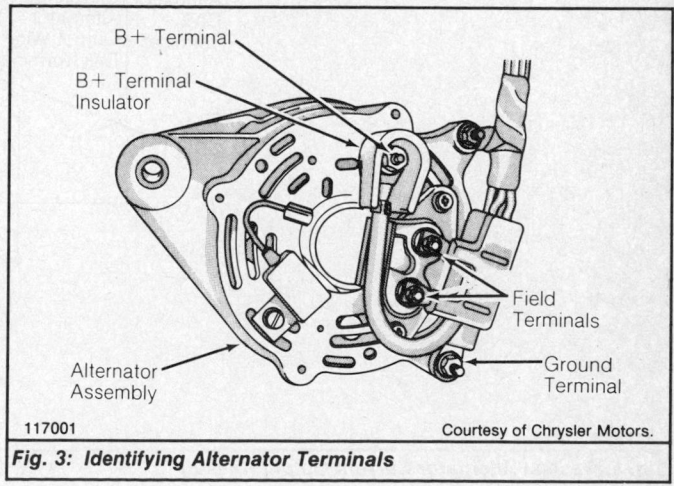

117001   Courtesy of Chrysler Motors.

Fig. 3: Identifying Alternator Terminals

1992 ELECTRICAL
Alternators & Regulators (Cont.)

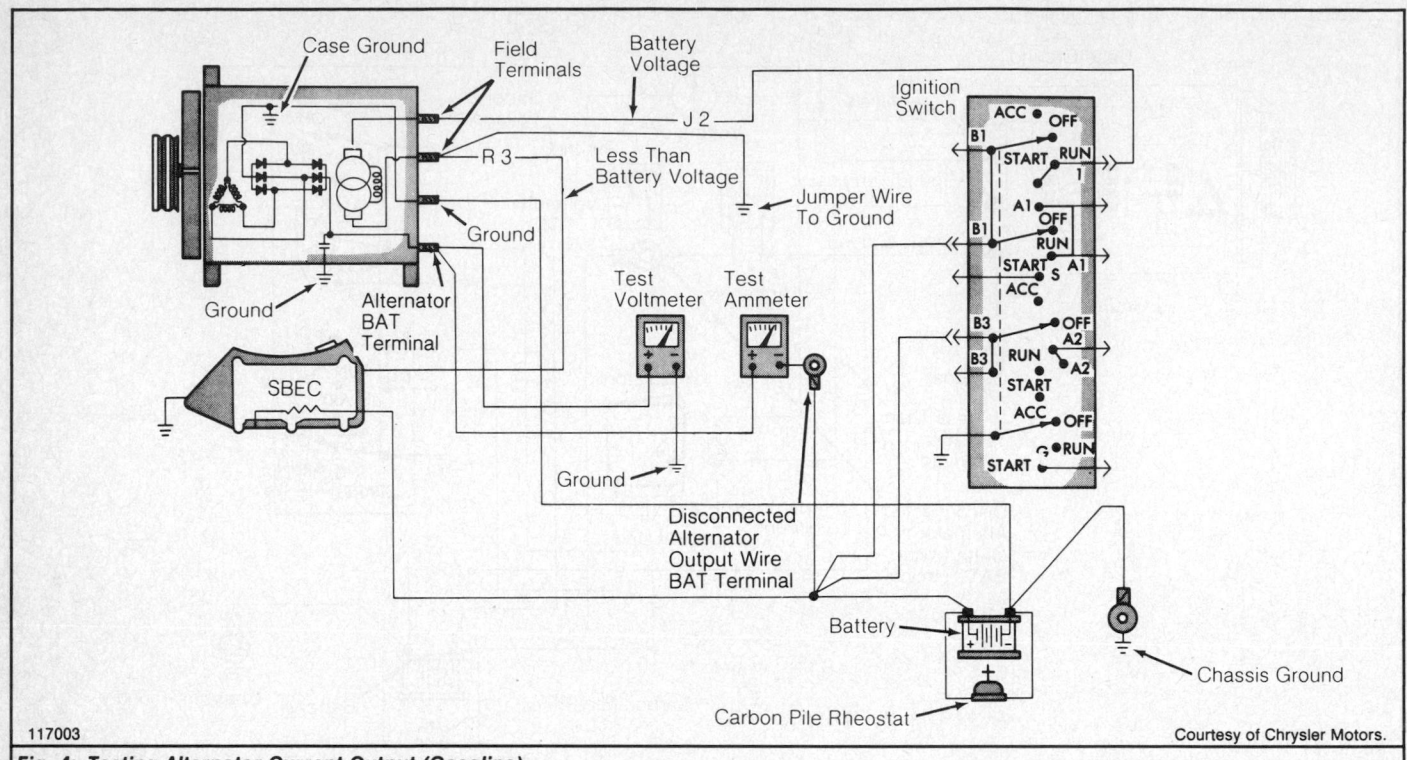

117003

Courtesy of Chrysler Motors.

Fig. 4: Testing Alternator Current Output (Gasoline)

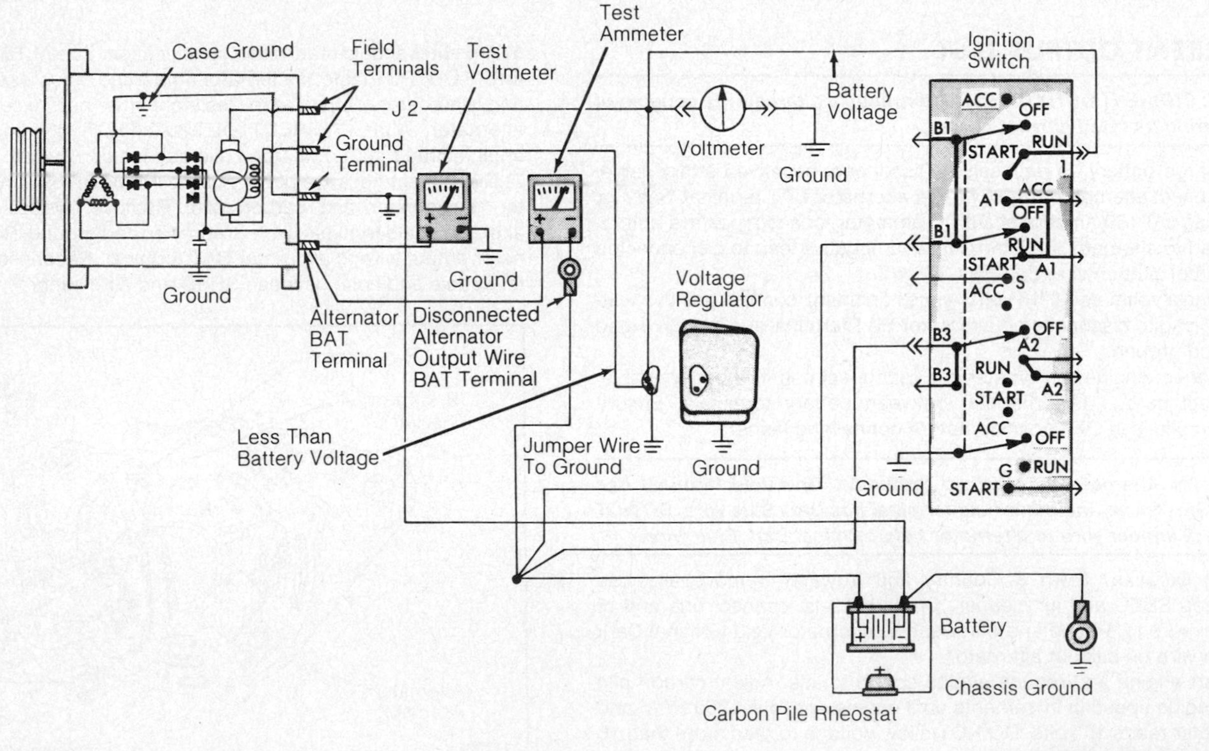

91B13467

Courtesy of Chrysler Motors.

Fig. 5: Testing Alternator Current Output (Diesel)

ALTERNATOR MINIMUM OUTPUT

Application	[1] Case Number	[2] Minimum Amperage
Caravan, Town & Country, Voyager		
Bosch 90 Amp	4557431	84
	5234231	88
Denso 90 Amp	5234031	86
	5234032	90
Denso 120 Amp	5234208	98
	5234033	102
Dakota		
Bosch 90 Amp	5234231	90
	5235028	90
Denso 75 Amp	4557301	75
	5234026	75
	5234027	75
Denso 90 Amp	5234031	90
	5234028	90
	5234032	90
Denso 120 Amp	5234199	90
	5234208	120
	5234033	120
Pickup & Ramcharger		
Bosch 90 Amp	5235028	90
Denso 75 Amp	5234026	75
Denso 90 Amp	5234028	90
Denso 120 Amp	5234199	120
	5234374	120
RWD Van		
Denso 75 Amp	5234026	75
Denso 90 Amp	5234028	90
Denso 120 Amp	5234199	120

[1] – Located on tag on bottom of alternator case.
[2] – Full-fielded at 1250 RPM.

VOLTAGE REGULATOR TEST (DIESEL)

1) Charge battery as necessary. Turn ignition off. Using a voltmeter with a minimum of a 0-18 volt scale, connect positive lead to positive battery post. Connect voltmeter negative lead to chassis ground. Connect a tachometer to engine See Fig. 6.
2) Start engine and adjust idle to 1250 RPM. Turn all lights and accessories off. Observe voltmeter readings. Voltage regulator is working properly if voltage readings are within specification. See VOLTAGE REGULATOR SPECIFICATIONS table.
3) If voltage is out of range, or is fluctuating, check the following:
• Voltage regulator is properly grounded
• Voltage regulator terminals are not spread causing an open
• Battery voltage is present at both terminals with ignition on
4) If voltage regulator ground connection and wiring check okay, replace regulator.

VOLTAGE REGULATOR SPECIFICATIONS

Temperature [1]	Volts
20° (-30°C)	14.6-15.8
80° (27°C)	13.9-14.4
140° (60°C)	13.0-13.7
Above 140° (60°)	Less than 13.7

[1] – Ambient at voltage regulator.

TEST CH-1, BATTERY TEST

NOTE: Perform visual check before proceeding.

CAUTION: If battery shows signs of freezing or leakage, battery posts are loose or battery has low electrolyte level, DO NOT test.

1) If battery has a built-in hydrometer, go to step **2)**. Turn ignition and all accessories off. Using a voltmeter, check battery voltage across battery posts. If voltage is 12.3 volts or more, go to step **3)**. If voltage is less than 12.3 volts, charge battery and go to step **3)**.

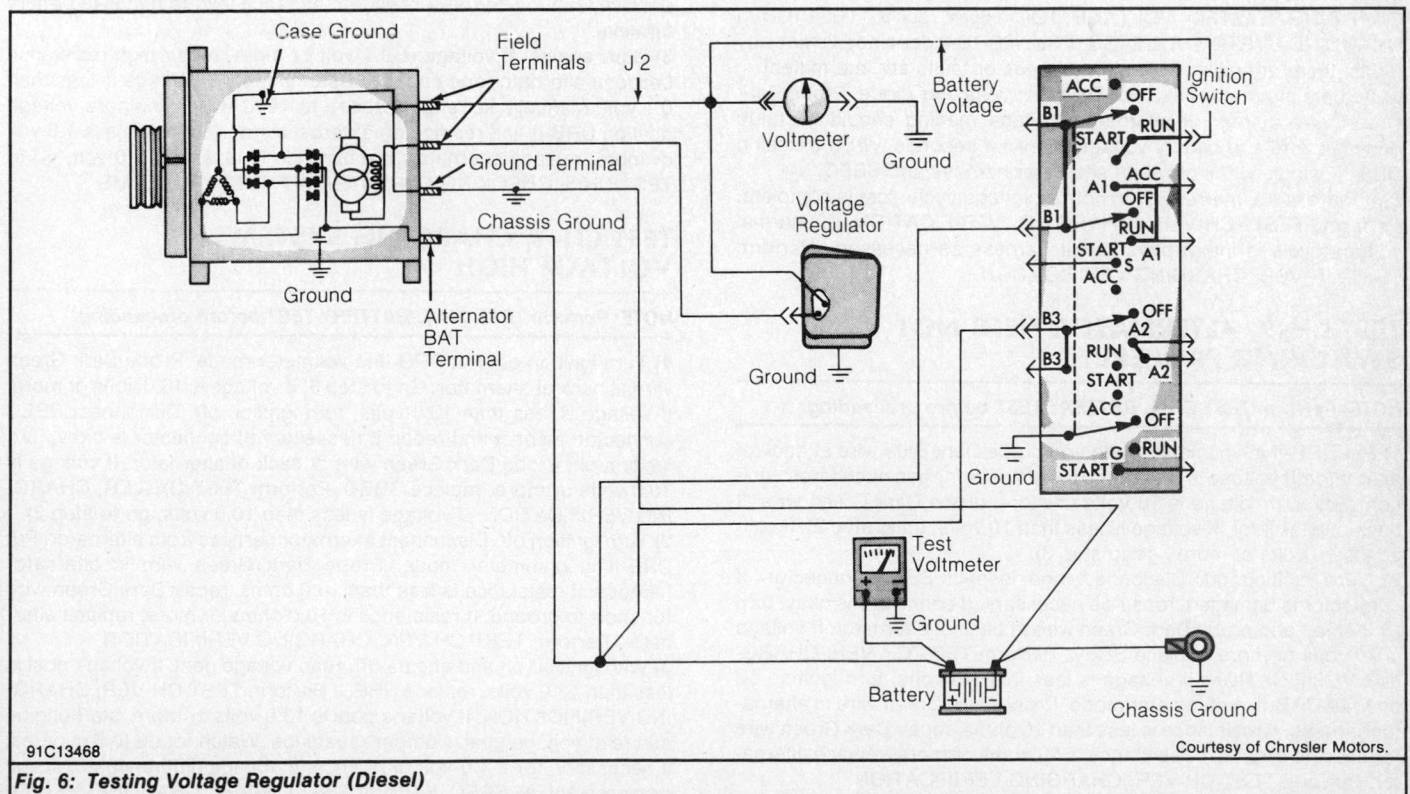

91C13468   Courtesy of Chrysler Motors.

Fig. 6: Testing Voltage Regulator (Diesel)

2) If battery hydrometer is Green, go to step **3)**. If battery hydrometer is Yellow or a bright color, replace battery and perform TEST CH-VER, CHARGING VERIFICATION. If battery hydrometer is dark in color, charge battery and go to step **3)**.

3) Disconnect battery cables and check terminals and posts. Clean terminals and posts as necessary and retest. Connect a load tester to battery posts. Apply 300-amp load for 15 seconds. Wait 15 seconds to allow battery to stabilize. Apply a load equal to 50 percent of battery cold cranking rating for 15 seconds and record minimum voltage reading.

4) Determine battery operating temperature and check battery minimum voltage specification. See MINIMUM VOLTAGE SPECIFICATIONS table. If voltage is not to specification, replace battery and perform TEST CH-VER, CHARGING VERIFICATION. If voltage reading is to specification, go to step **5)**.

MINIMUM VOLTAGE SPECIFICATIONS

Battery Temperature	Minimum Volts
70°F (21°C) Or More	9.6
60°F (16°C)	9.5
50°F (12°C)	9.4
40°F (4°C)	9.3
30°F (-1°C)	9.1
20°F (-7°C)	8.9
10°F (-12°C)	8.7
0°F (-18°C)	8.5

5) Reconnect battery cables. Inspect alternator belt tension and condition. Replace belt as necessary. Start engine. Set engine speed to 2000 RPM for 30 seconds. Turn ignition off. Connect DRB-II. Turn ignition on with engine off. Read faults.

6) If DRB-II displays BATTERY TEMP SENSOR OUT OF LIMIT, replace SBEC and perform TEST CH-VER, CHARGING VERIFICATION. If DRB-II displays ALTERNATOR FIELD NOT SWITCHING PROPERLY, go to TEST CH-2, ALTERNATOR FIELD NOT SWITCHING PROPERLY. If DRB-II does not display either message, go to next step.

7) If DRB-II displays CHARGING SYSTEM VOLTAGE TOO LOW, go to TEST CH-3, CHARGING SYSTEM VOLTAGE LOW. If DRB-II displays CHARGING SYSTEM VOLTAGE TOO HIGH, go to TEST CH-4, CHARGING SYSTEM VOLTAGE HIGH. If DRB-II does not display any faults, there are either no fault messages or faults are intermittent.

8) Actuate alternator field. Put DRB-II in voltmeter mode. Probe Dark Green wire at rear of alternator. Voltage reading should fluctuate between zero and battery voltage every 1.4 seconds. While watching DRB-II, wiggle wires between alternator harness and SBEC.

9) If there is no interruption in normal voltage cycle, test is complete. Perform TEST CH-VER, CHARGING VERIFICATION. If normal voltage cycle is interrupted, repair harness as necessary. Perform TEST CH-VER, CHARGING VERIFICATION.

TEST CH-2, ALTERNATOR FIELD NOT SWITCHING PROPERLY

NOTE: Perform TEST CH-1, BATTERY TEST before proceeding.

1) Put DRB-II in voltmeter mode and probe Dark Blue wire at back of alternator. If voltage is less than 10 volts, repair open circuit from ignition switch. If voltage is 10 volts or more, probe Dark Green wire at back of alternator. If voltage is less than 10 volts, go to step **2)**. If voltage is 10 volts or more , go to step **3)**.

2) Turn ignition off. Disconnect and inspect SBEC connector. If connector is damaged, repair as necessary. If connector is okay, turn ignition on and probe Dark Green wire at back of alternator. If voltage is 10 volts or more, replace SBEC. Perform TEST CH-VER, CHARGING VERIFICATION. If voltage is less than 10 volts, turn ignition off and put DRB-II in ohmmeter mode. Probe Dark Green wire in alternator harness. If resistance is less than 10 ohms, repair Dark Green wire for short to ground. If resistance is 10 ohms or more, replace alternator. Perform TEST CH-VER, CHARGING VERIFICATION.

3) Turn ignition off. Disconnect and inspect SBEC connector. If connector is damaged, repair as necessary. If connector is okay, turn ignition on and put DRB-II in voltmeter mode. Probe cavity No. 20. *See Fig. 7.* If voltage is 10 volts or more, replace SBEC. Perform TEST CH-VER, CHARGING VERIFICATION. If voltage is less than 10 volts, repair open circuit in Dark Green wire. Perform TEST CH-VER, CHARGING VERIFICATION.

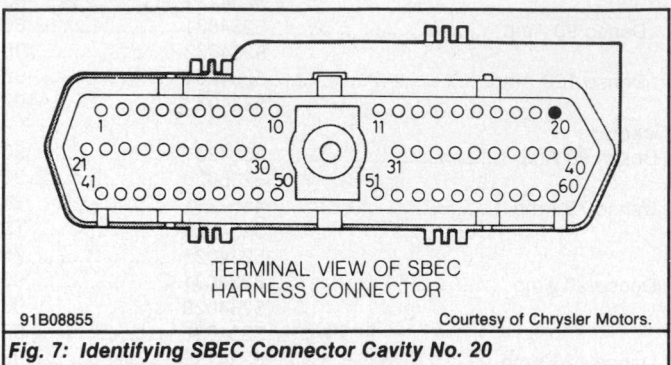

TERMINAL VIEW OF SBEC
HARNESS CONNECTOR

91B08855   Courtesy of Chrysler Motors.

Fig. 7: Identifying SBEC Connector Cavity No. 20

TEST CH-3, CHARGING SYSTEM VOLTAGE LOW

NOTE: Perform TEST CH-1, BATTERY TEST before proceeding.

1) Read voltage goal. If voltage goal is 15.1 volts or more, replace SBEC. If voltage goal is less than 15.1 volts, use an external voltmeter and connect positive lead to alternator BAT (B+) and negative lead to battery positive terminal.

CAUTION: Ensure all wires are clear of moving parts.

2) Start engine. If voltage is 0.4 volt or more, repair Black or Red wire for high resistance between alternator and battery. If voltage is less than 0.4 volt, turn ignition off. Using an external voltmeter, connect positive lead to alternator case and negative lead to negative battery terminal.

3) Start engine. If voltage is 0.1 volt or more, repair high resistance between alternator and negative battery cable. If voltage is less than 0.1 volt, manually set engine speed to 1600 RPM. Compare voltage goal on DRB-II and reading on external meter. If difference is 1.0 volt or more, replace alternator. If difference is less than 1.0 volt, go to TEST CH-5, CHECKING FOR INTERMITTENT PROBLEMS.

TEST CH-4, CHARGING SYSTEM VOLTAGE HIGH

NOTE: Perform TEST CH-1, BATTERY TEST before proceeding.

1) Turn ignition on. Put DRB-II in voltmeter mode. Probe Dark Green wire at back of alternator. Go to step **3)** if voltage is 10.0 volts or more. If voltage is less than 10.0 volts, turn ignition off. Disconnect SBEC connector; inspect and repair if necessary. If connector is okay, turn ignition on. Probe Dark Green wire at back of alternator. If voltage is 10.0 volts or more, replace SBEC. Perform TEST CH-VER, CHARGING VERIFICATION. If voltage is less than 10.0 volts, go to step **2)**.

2) Turn ignition off. Disconnect alternator harness from alternator. Put DRB-II in ohmmeter mode. Probe Dark Green wire in alternator harness. If resistance is less than 10.0 ohms, repair Dark Green wire for short to ground. If resistance is 10.0 ohms or more, replace alternator. Perform TEST CH-VER, CHARGING VERIFICATION.

3) With ignition on and engine off, read voltage goal. If voltage goal is less than 13.0 volts, replace SBEC. Perform TEST CH-VER, CHARGING VERIFICATION. If voltage goal is 13.0 volts or more, start engine and read voltage goal. Compare readings. Watch for up to 5 minutes, if necessary, for a 1.0-volt difference. If voltage difference is 1.0 volt or more, replace SBEC. Perform TEST CH-VER, CHARGING VERIFICATION. If voltage difference is less than 1.0 volt, go to TEST CH-5, CHECKING FOR INTERMITTENT PROBLEMS.

TEST CH-5, CHECKING FOR INTERMITTENT PROBLEMS

NOTE: Perform TEST CH-4, CHARGING SYSTEM VOLTAGE HIGH before proceeding.

1) Actuate alternator field. Put DRB-II in voltmeter mode. Probe Dark Green wire at back of alternator.

NOTE: Voltage should cycle from zero to battery voltage every 1.4 seconds.

2) While watching DRB-II, wiggle wires between alternator and SBEC. If there is any interruption in voltage cycle, repair wire at interruption point in cycle. If there is no interruption of voltage cycle, test is complete. Perform TEST CH-VER, CHARGING VERIFICATION.

TEST CH-VER, CHARGING VERIFICATION

1) Inspect and ensure all engine components are connected.
2) If SBEC has been changed and if vehicle is equipped with a factory theft alarm, start vehicle at least 20 times so alarm will activate when desired. If vehicle is a minivan or truck body, write Emission Maintenance Reminder (EMR) mileage into new SBEC.
3) Connect DRB-II to engine diagnostic and erase faults.
4) Ensure no other charging system problems remain by doing the following:

- Start engine.
- Raise engine speed to 2000 RPM for at least 30 seconds.
- Allow engine to idle.
- Turn engine off.
- Turn ignition on.
- With DRB-II, read fault messages.

5) If repaired fault has reset, repair is incomplete. Check all pertinent MITCHELL® TECHNICAL SERVICE BULLETINS and return to TEST CH-1, BATTERY TEST if necessary. If there are no other faults, repair is complete.

BENCH TESTING

NOTE: Alternators are non-serviceable and must be replaced as complete units.

TORQUE SPECIFICATIONS

TORQUE SPECIFICATIONS

Application	Ft. Lbs. (N.m)
Alternator Mounting Bolts	
2.5L	40 (54)
3.0L	
Upper	18 (24)
Lower	21 (28)
3.3L	40 (54)
3.9L & 5.2L	30 (41)
5.9L	
Gas	[1]
Diesel	
Upper	18 (24)
Lower	32 (43)

[1] - Information not available from manufacturer.

Caravan, Dakota, Pickup, Ramcharger, RWD Van, Town & Country, Voyager

DESCRIPTION

Bosch starter is a permanent magnet motor design. A planetary gear system between the armature and pinion shaft makes it possible to increase torque and reduce starter size. The planetary gear drive is splined to both the armature shaft and overrunning clutch. Starter torque is transmitted to the overrunning clutch pinion through the planetary gears which provide higher rotational speeds. Starter has serviceable solenoid and gear and clutch assembly.

Nippondenso starter is a 4-field, 4-brush 12-volt motor with a solenoid mounted within the housing. The unit has a 2-to-1 reduction gear set in a die cast aluminum housing. Starter has serviceable gear and clutch assembly only. If starter solenoid fails, entire starter motor must be replaced.

STARTER APPLICATIONS

Model	Type
Caravan, Town & Country & Voyager	
2.5L	Bosch
3.0L	[1]
3.3L	Nippondenso
Dakota	
2.5L	Bosch
3.9L & 5.2L	Nippondenso
Pickup & Ramcharger	
3.9L, 5.2L, 5.9L & 5.9L Diesel	Nippondenso
RWD Van	
3.9L, 5.2L & 5.9L	Nippondenso

[1] – May be equipped with either Bosch or Nippondenso starter.

TROUBLE SHOOTING

STARTER DOES NOT CRANK OR CRANKS SLOWLY

1) Ensure battery is fully charged. Turn on headlights. Crank engine using ignition key. If starter fails to crank or cranks slowly then stops and headlights dim way down, proceed to AMPERAGE DRAW TEST under ON-VEHICLE TESTING.

2) If starter fails to crank or cranks slowly and headlights dim slightly, proceed to STARTER RESISTANCE TEST under ON-VEHICLE TESTING. If starter fails to crank engine and headlights do not dim, proceed to RELAY TEST under ON-VEHICLE TESTING.

ON-VEHICLE TESTING

AMPERAGE DRAW TEST

NOTE: Ensure battery is fully charged and terminals are clean and tight. Perform a battery load test before proceeding.

1) Using an inductive volt/ammeter type battery tester, clamp ammeter probe to positive battery cable. Connect positive voltmeter lead to positive battery post and negative voltmeter lead to negative battery post. On 3.3L engine, disconnect coil pack harness connector. On 5.9L diesel engine, disconnect both wires at fuel solenoid on injection pump. On all other models, disconnect coil wire from distributor cap and attach to ground.

2) Ensure all vehicle accessories are off and transmission is in Neutral or Park. Crank engine using ignition key and observe exact reading on volt/ammeter. Readings should be as specified. See STARTER SPECIFICATIONS table.

3) If amperage is greater than specified or voltage is less than specified, check and repair wiring between battery and starter. If wiring is okay, turn engine by hand and check for ease of turning. If engine turns okay, proceed to STARTER RESISTANCE TEST.

STARTER RESISTANCE TEST

1) Using a voltmeter that will indicate tenths of a volt, perform the following voltage drop tests. Crank engine and observe voltmeter readings with voltmeter connected at following locations:
- Positive lead to battery positive post and negative lead to battery terminal on starter.
- Positive lead to starter housing and negative lead to negative post on battery.
- Positive lead to battery negative post and negative lead to battery cable engine ground connection.

2) If voltage reading is greater than .2 volt at any connection, repair or replace wiring, or repair starter-to-engine ground. If voltage readings are less than .2 volt at all connections, proceed to step **3)**.

3) Connect voltmeter at following locations and observe readings:
- Positive lead to battery positive post and negative lead to positive cable clamp.
- Positive lead to battery negative post and negative lead to negative cable clamp.

If either reading is greater than zero, repair or replace battery cables. If both readings are zero, proceed to step **4)**.

4) Connect positive voltmeter lead to battery positive post and negative lead to starter solenoid battery terminal. If voltage reading is greater than .3 volt, repair or replace cable between starter and battery. If voltage reading is less than .3 volt, starter circuitry is okay and test is complete. Repair or replace starter.

RELAY TEST

1) On automatic transmission/transaxle vehicles, put gear selector in Neutral or Park. On manual transmission/transaxle vehicles, put gear selector in Neutral. Set parking brake and block wheels. DO NOT remove relay connector. Using a 12-volt test light, check for power between starter relay battery terminal and ground. If power does not exist, repair wiring. If power exists, proceed to step **2)**.

2) Using test light, check for power at ignition terminal on starter relay while an assistant holds key in START position. If power does not exist, repair wiring between ignition switch and starter relay. If power exists, proceed to step **3)**.

3) Reconnect jumper wire between battery and ignition terminals. Connect a second jumper wire between starter relay ground terminal and chassis ground. If engine cranks, starter relay is good. Check and repair poor ground connection between relay housing and mounting surface. On models with automatic transmission, inspect neutral safety switch for malfunction and transmission linkage for improper adjustment.

SOLENOID TEST

1) Connect a heavy jumper wire between battery and starter solenoid terminals on starter relay. If engine cranks, solenoid is okay. Proceed to RELAY TEST.

2) If engine does not crank, check and repair wiring between starter relay and starter. Repeat test. If engine still fails to crank, repair or replace starter.

BENCH TESTING

CAUTION: Starters are extremely sensitive to hammering, shocks and external pressure. DO NOT clamp starter in a vise by field housing. Starter can be clamped in vise by mounting flange.

INSPECTION

1) Check pinion gear for freedom of movement by turning it on shaft. Check armature for freedom of movement by prying on pinion gear to engage it with shaft.

2) If gear and armature do not rotate freely, starter should be disassembled. If pinion gear and armature rotate freely, proceed to NO-LOAD TEST.

3) No rotation and high current draw indicate that bearings are seized or connecting terminal or armature windings are shorted to ground.

4) No rotation or current flow indicate one or both of the following:

- Open armature windings (inspect commutator for burned commutator bars after disassembly).
- Broken brush springs, worn brushes, protruding insulation between commutator bars, or other causes that could prevent good contact between brushes and commutator.

NO-LOAD TEST

1) Mount starter in soft-jawed vise by mounting flange. Install voltmeter between solenoid terminal and starter frame.

2) Connect a switch, ammeter and fully charged battery in series with starter motor. Ensure switch is in OPEN position prior to connecting battery.

3) Close switch and note voltage and amperage. Reading should be within specification. See STARTER SPECIFICATIONS table at end of article.

4) Disconnect electrical connections with switch in OPEN position only. Repair or replace starter if not within specification.

CAUTION: DO NOT operate starter for more than 30 seconds at a time without allowing starter to cool for at least 2 minutes.

OVERHAUL

STARTER GEAR AND CLUTCH

Bosch – Remove starter. Remove 2 starter solenoid field terminal nuts. Remove 3 solenoid mounting screws and remove solenoid. Remove 2 through bolts securing starter drive end housing to motor housing. Remove rubber seal and pull gear and clutch assembly from drive housing. To install, reverse removal procedure.

Nippondenso – Remove starter. Remove 2 gear housing attaching screws and separate gear housing from solenoid housing. Remove pinion gear, pinion gear bearing, and drive gear from gear housing. Remove starter gear and clutch assembly from solenoid housing. Clean and lubricate pinion gear, bearing and drive gear and reinstall in gear housing. Install starter gear and clutch assembly in solenoid. To install starter, reverse removal procedure.

STARTER SPECIFICATIONS

STARTER SPECIFICATIONS

Application	Specification
Cranking Amps [1]	
Gas	150-220 Amps
Diesel	450-550 Amps
Cranking Voltage	
Gas	7.5 Volts
Diesel	8 Volts
No-Load Test	
Amperage	
2.5L	69 @ 3447 RPM
3.0L	73 @ 3473 RPM
3.3L, 3.9L, 5.2L & 5.9L (Gas)	@ 3601 RPM
5.9L (Diesel)	220 @ 4200 RPM
Voltage	
Gas & Diesel	11 Volts

[1] – Engine at full operating temperature.

TORQUE SPECIFICATIONS

TORQUE SPECIFICATIONS

Application	Ft. Lbs. (N.m)
Mounting Bolts	
2.5L, 3.0L & 3.8L	40 (54)
3.9L, 5.2L & 5.9L (Gas)	50 (68)
5.9L (Diesel)	32 (43)

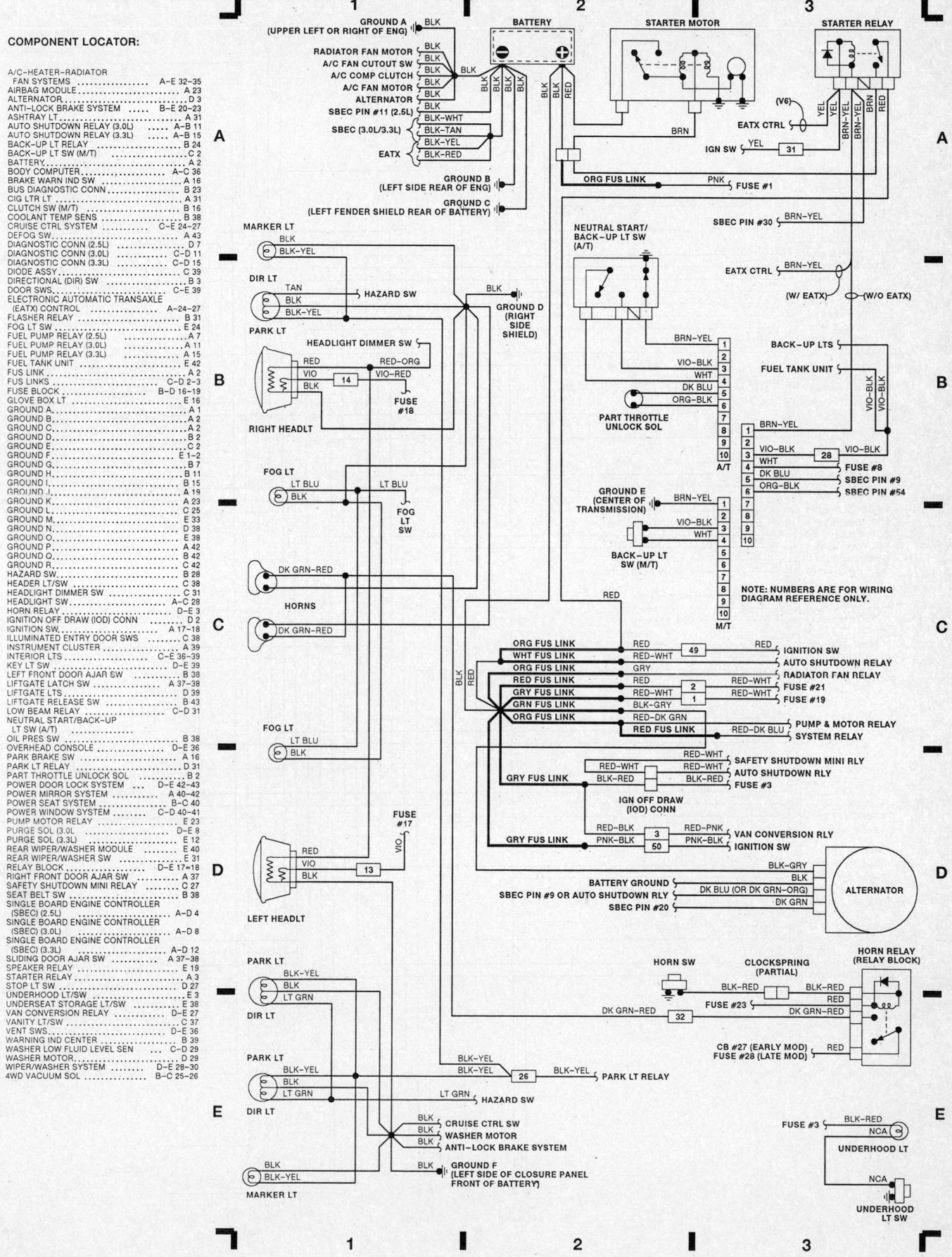

COMPONENT LOCATOR:

1992 WIRING DIAGRAMS
Caravan, Town & Country, & Voyager (Cont.)

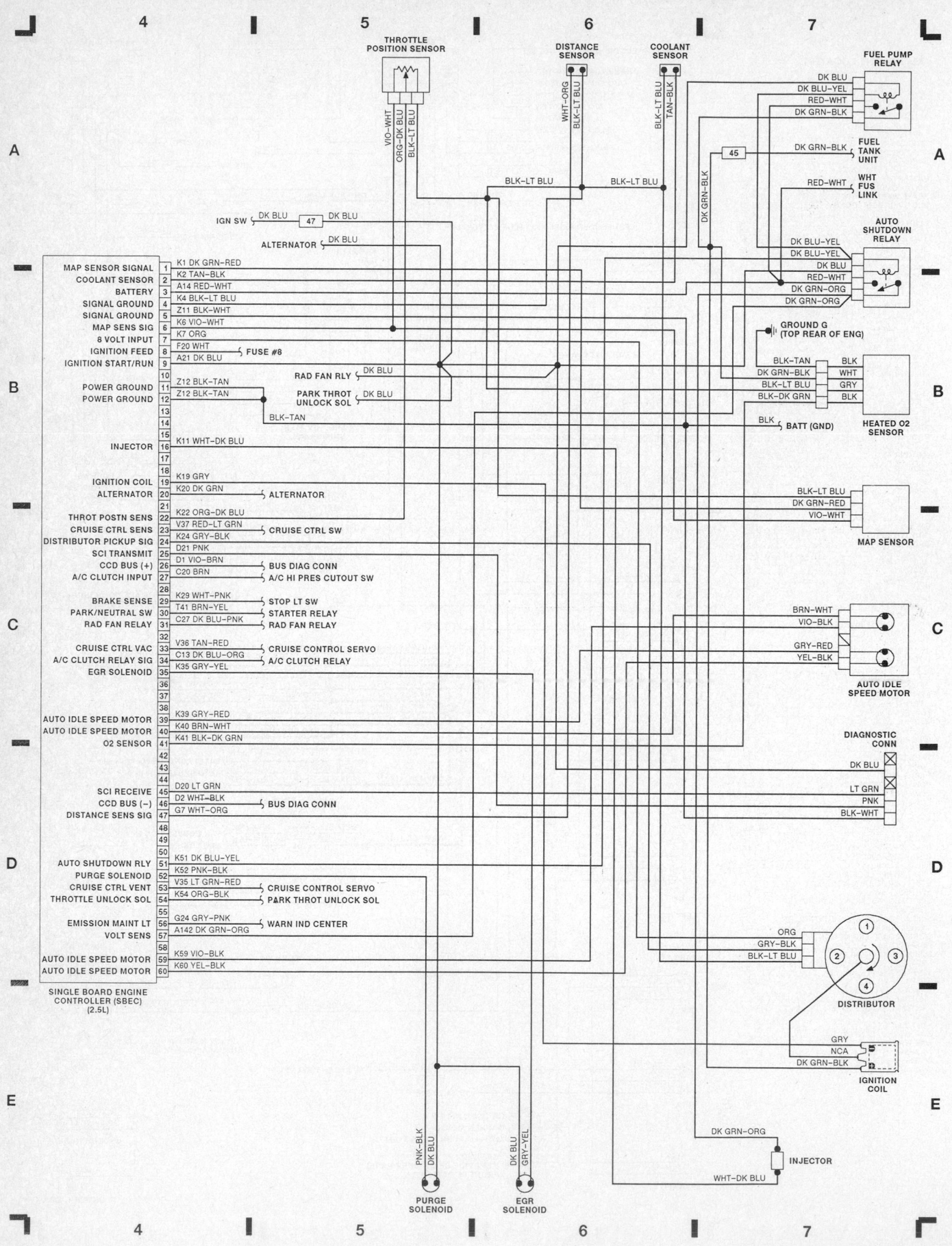

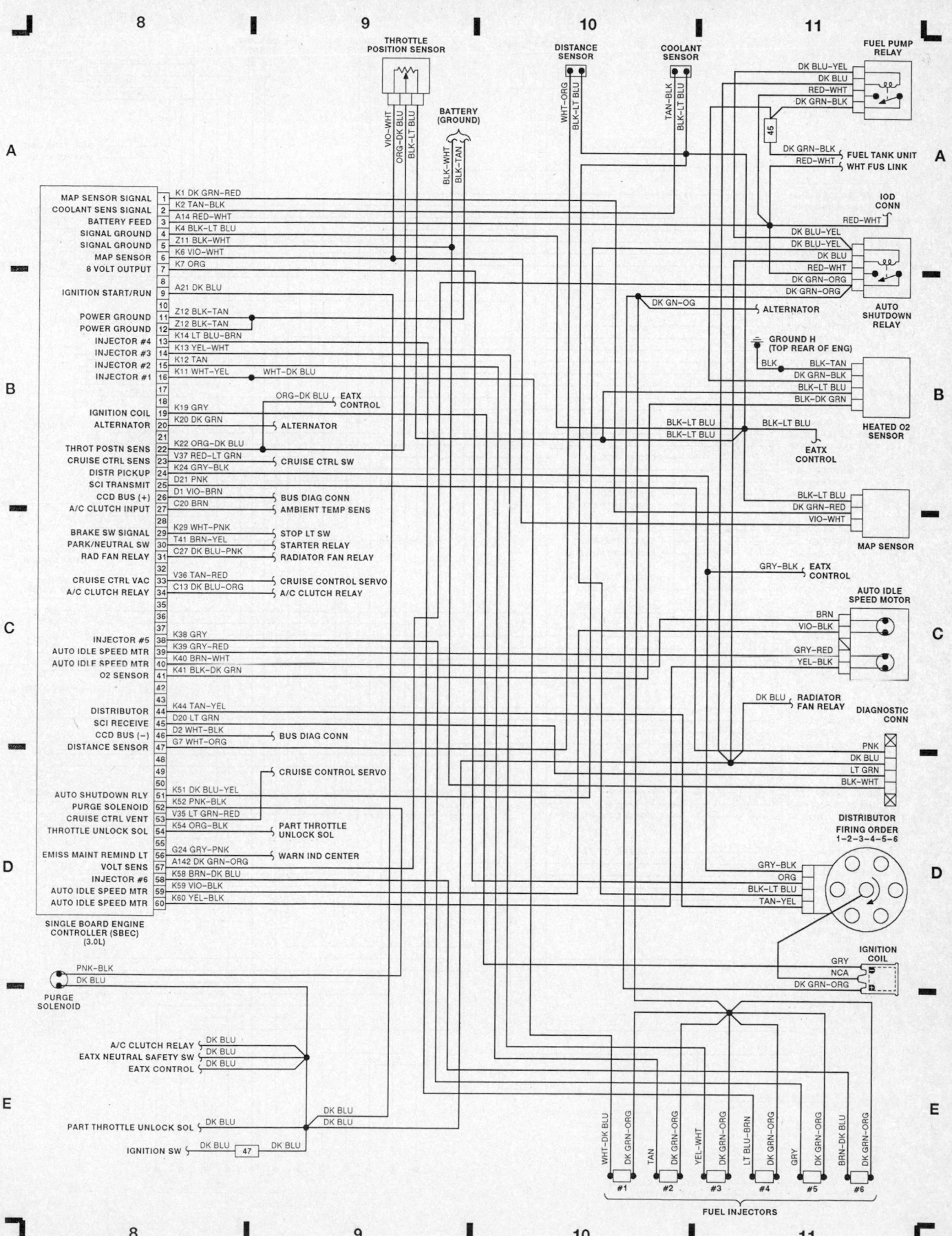

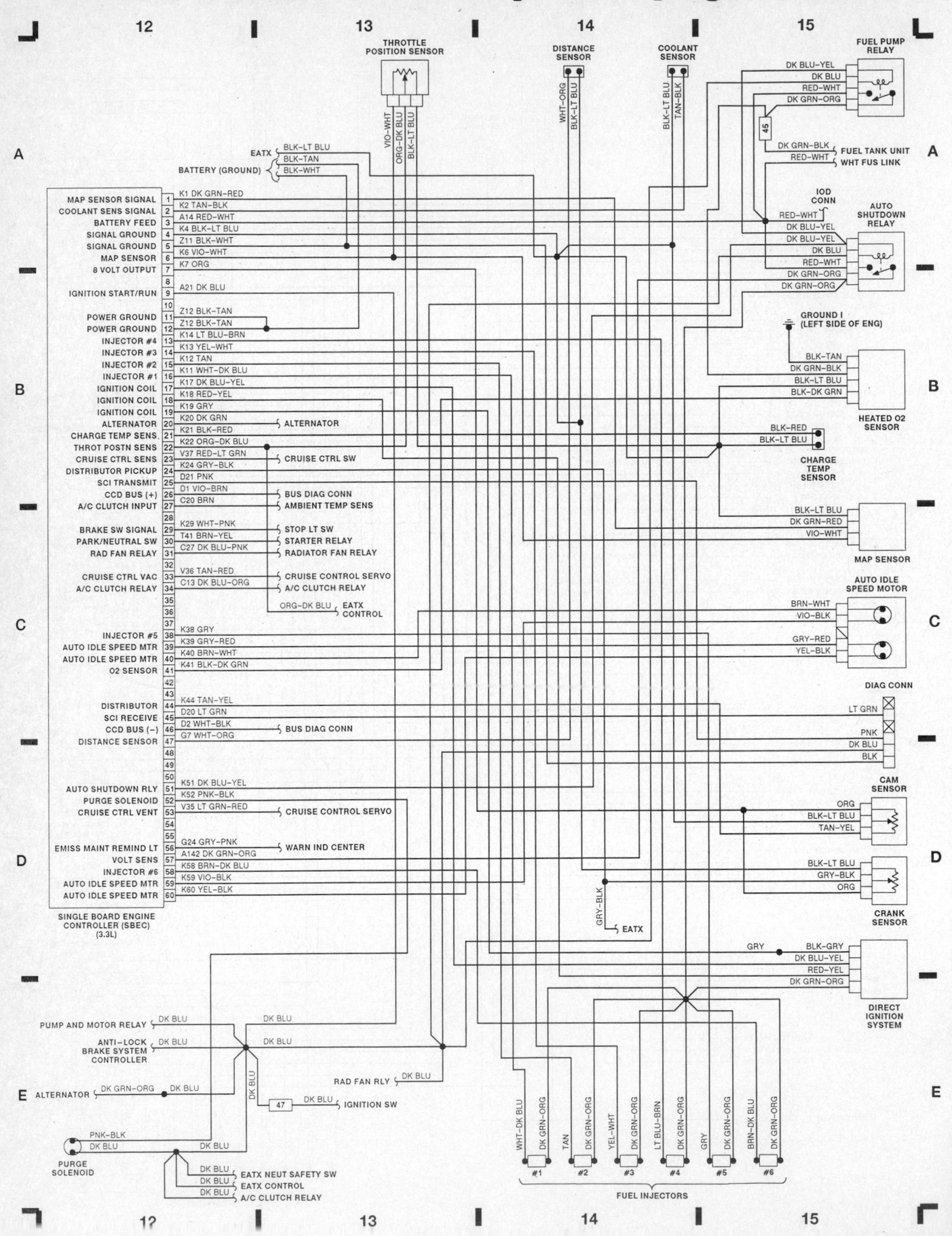

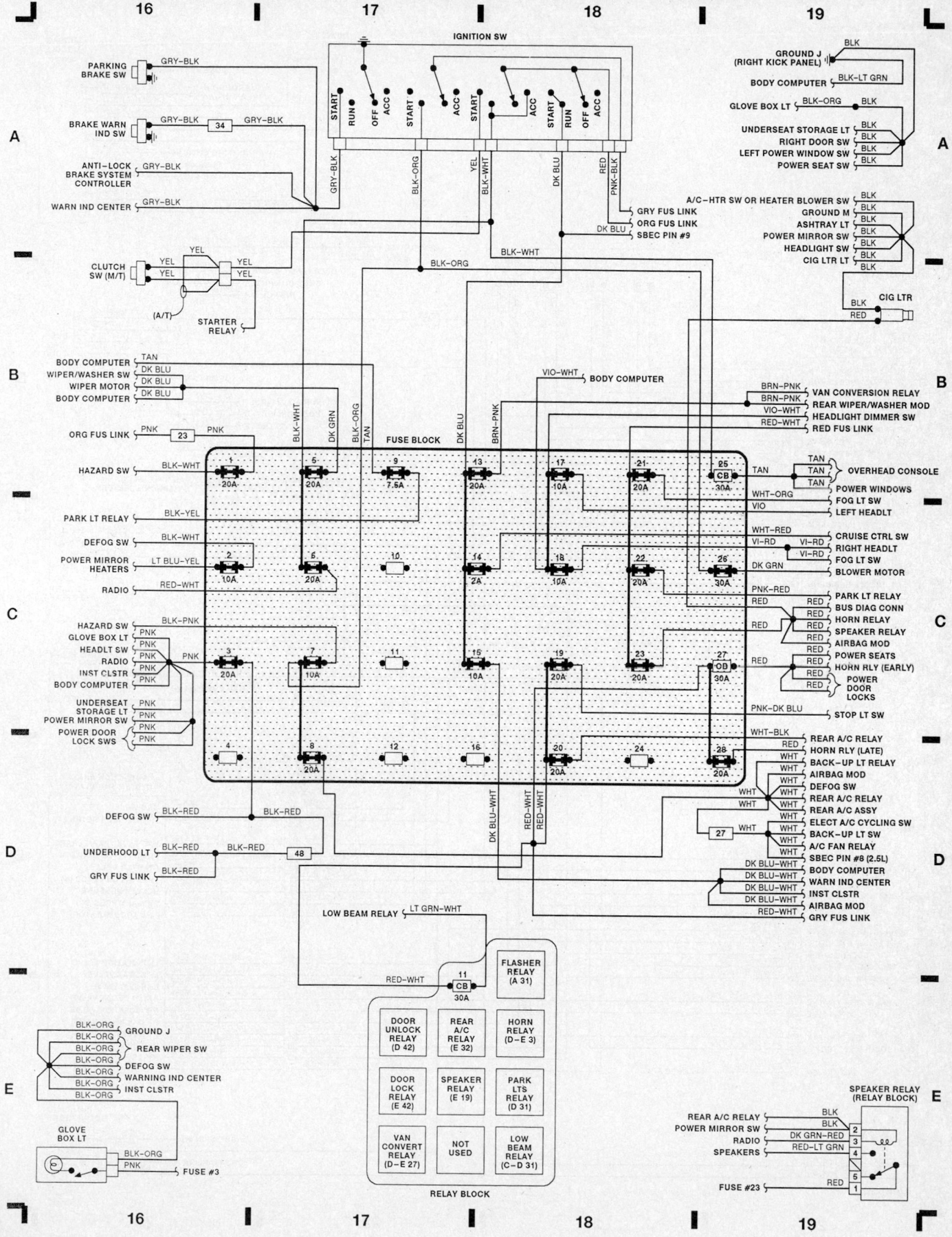

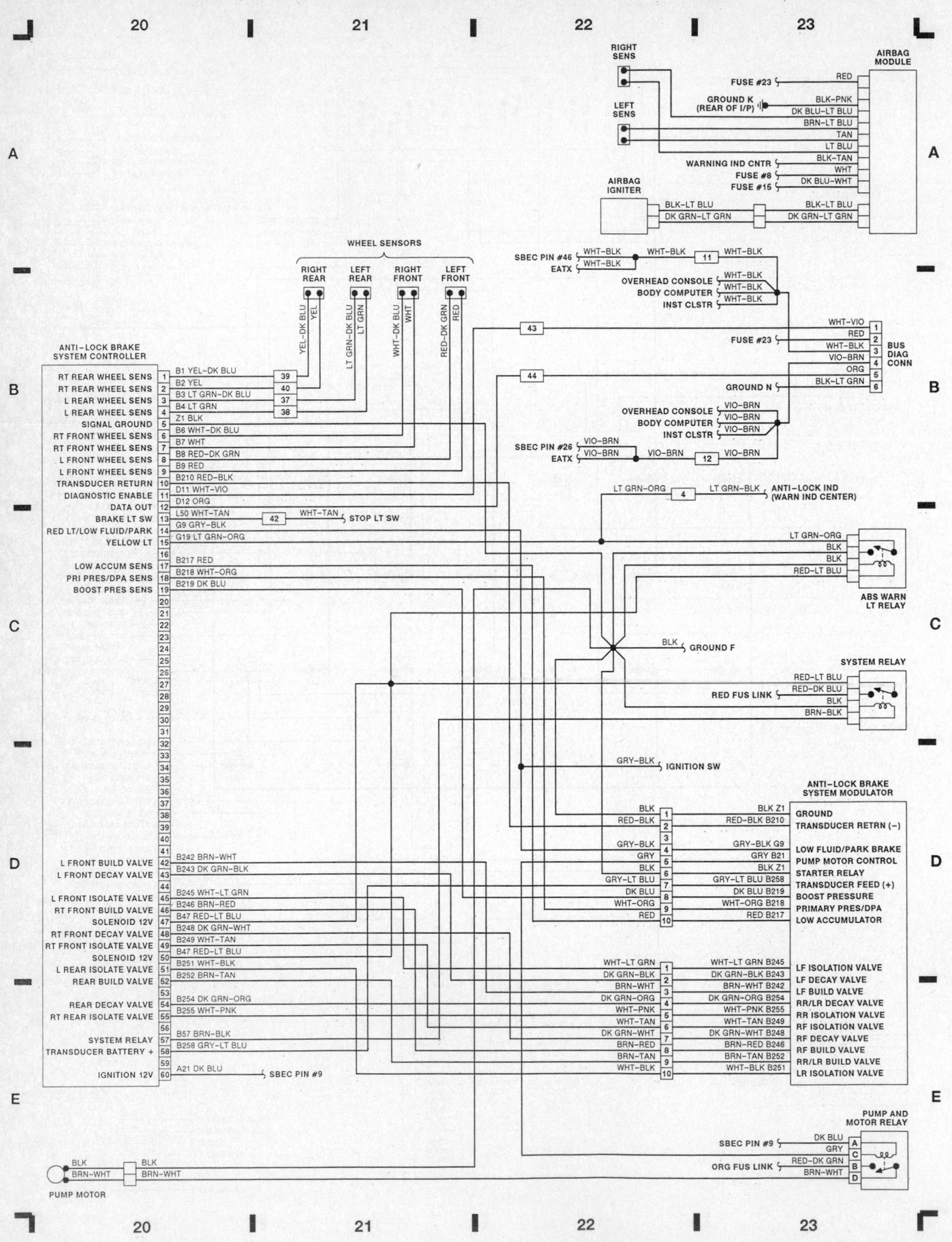

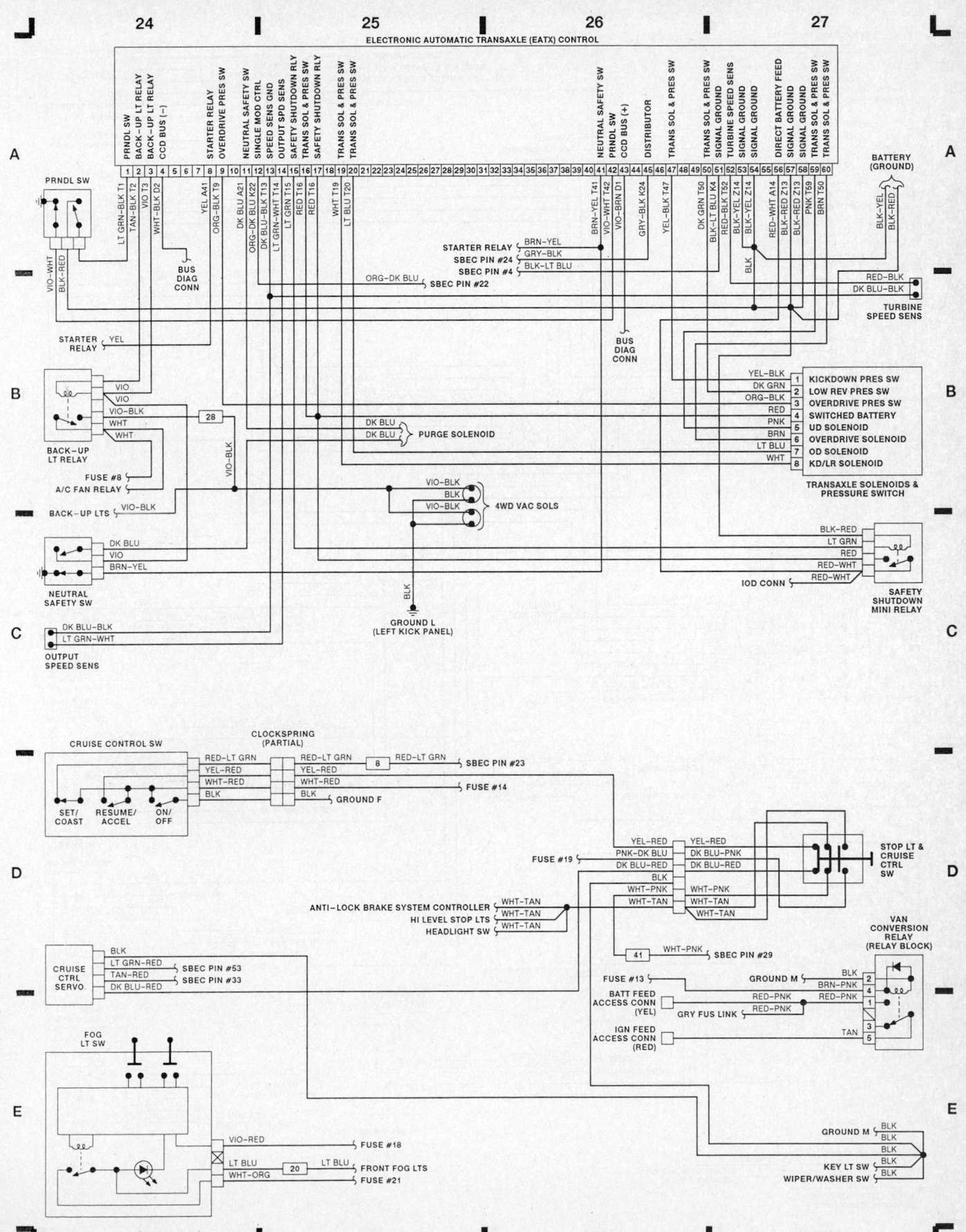

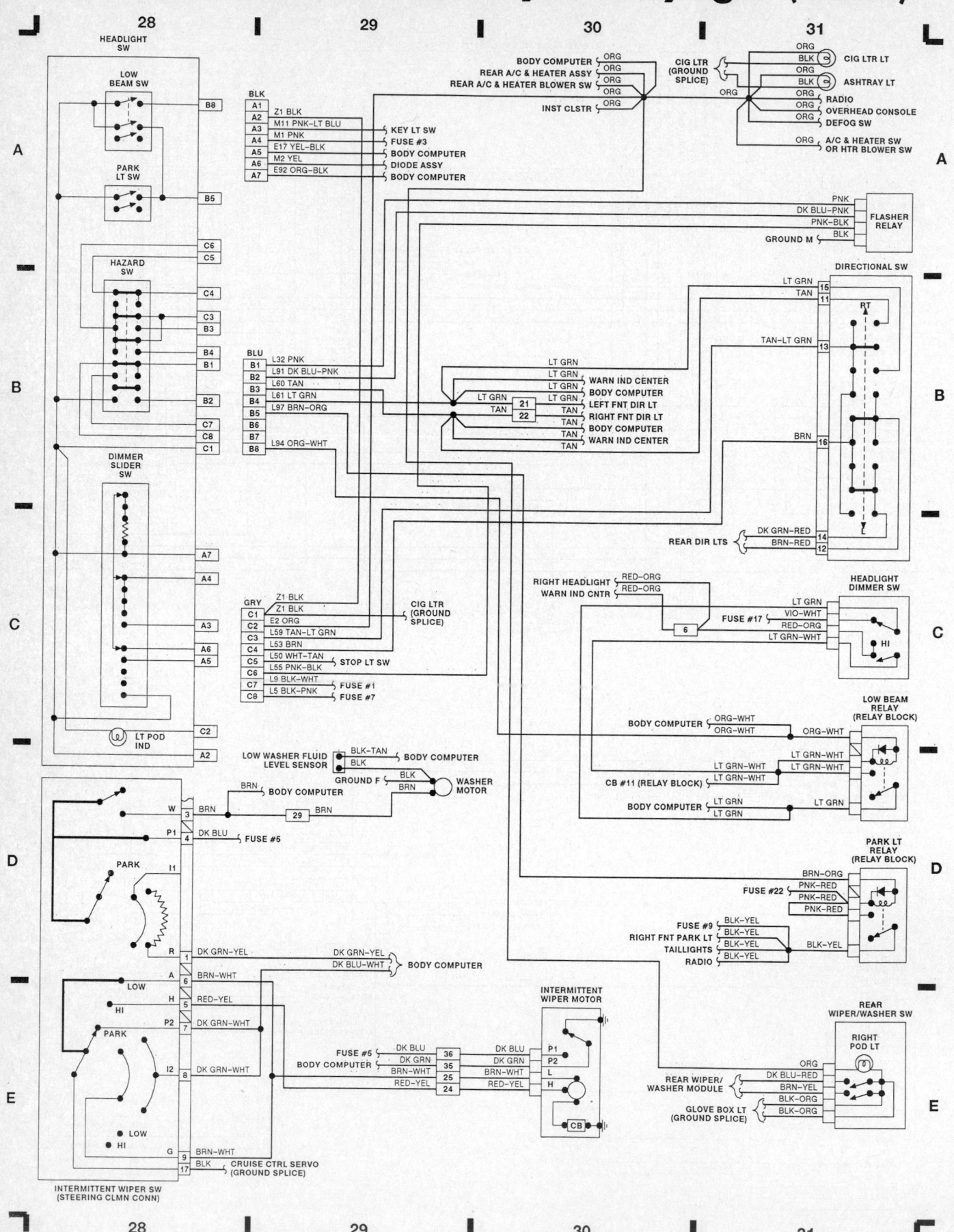

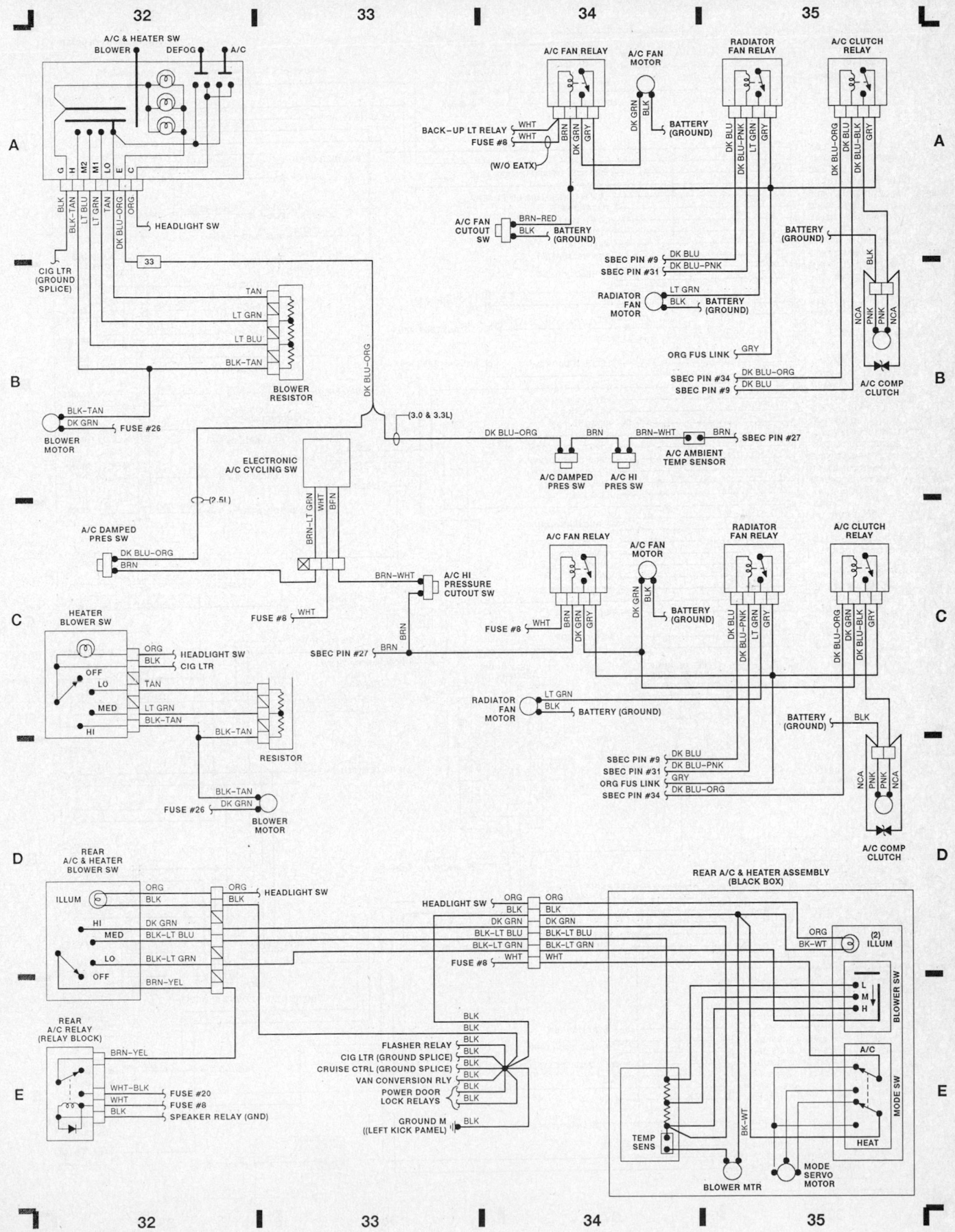

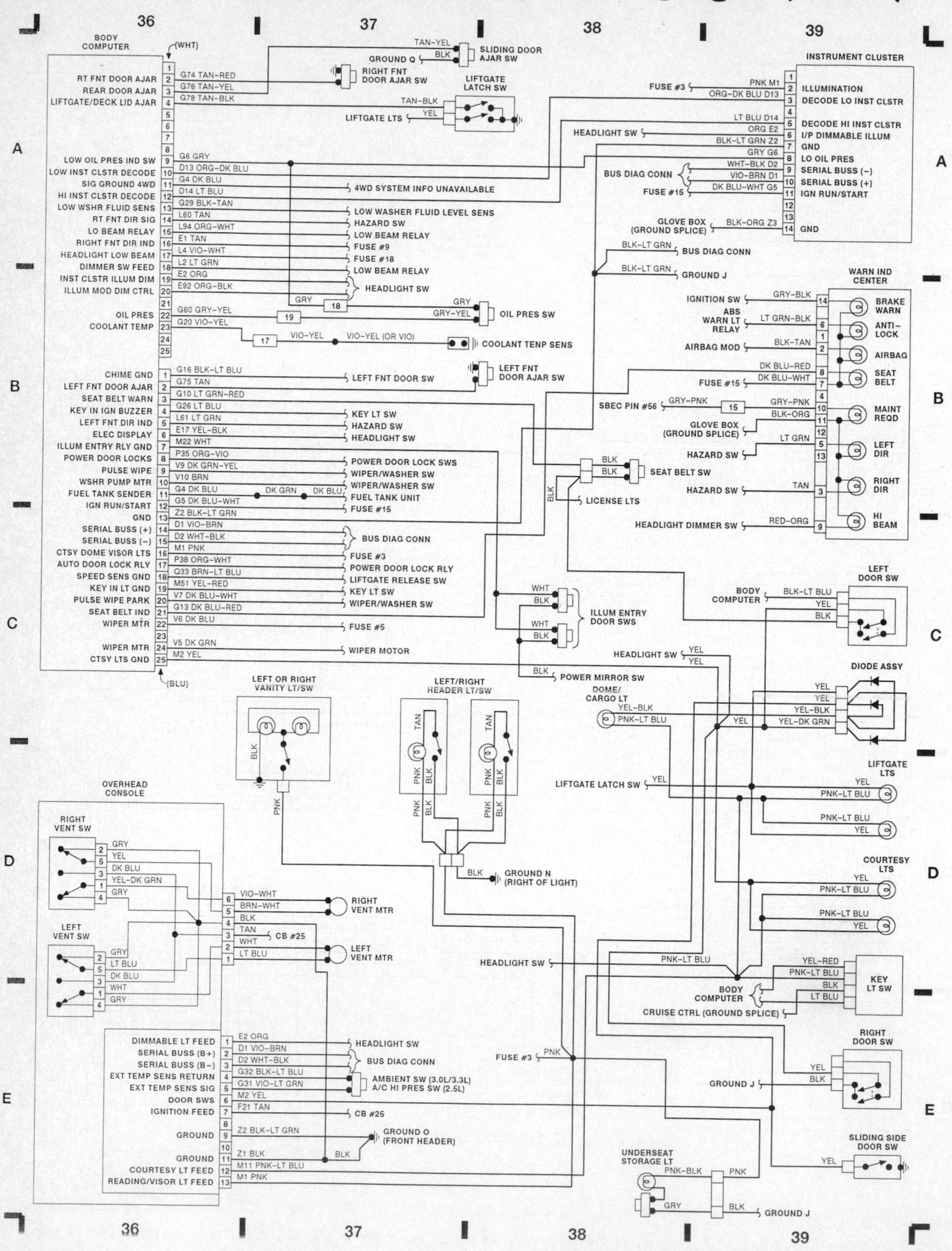

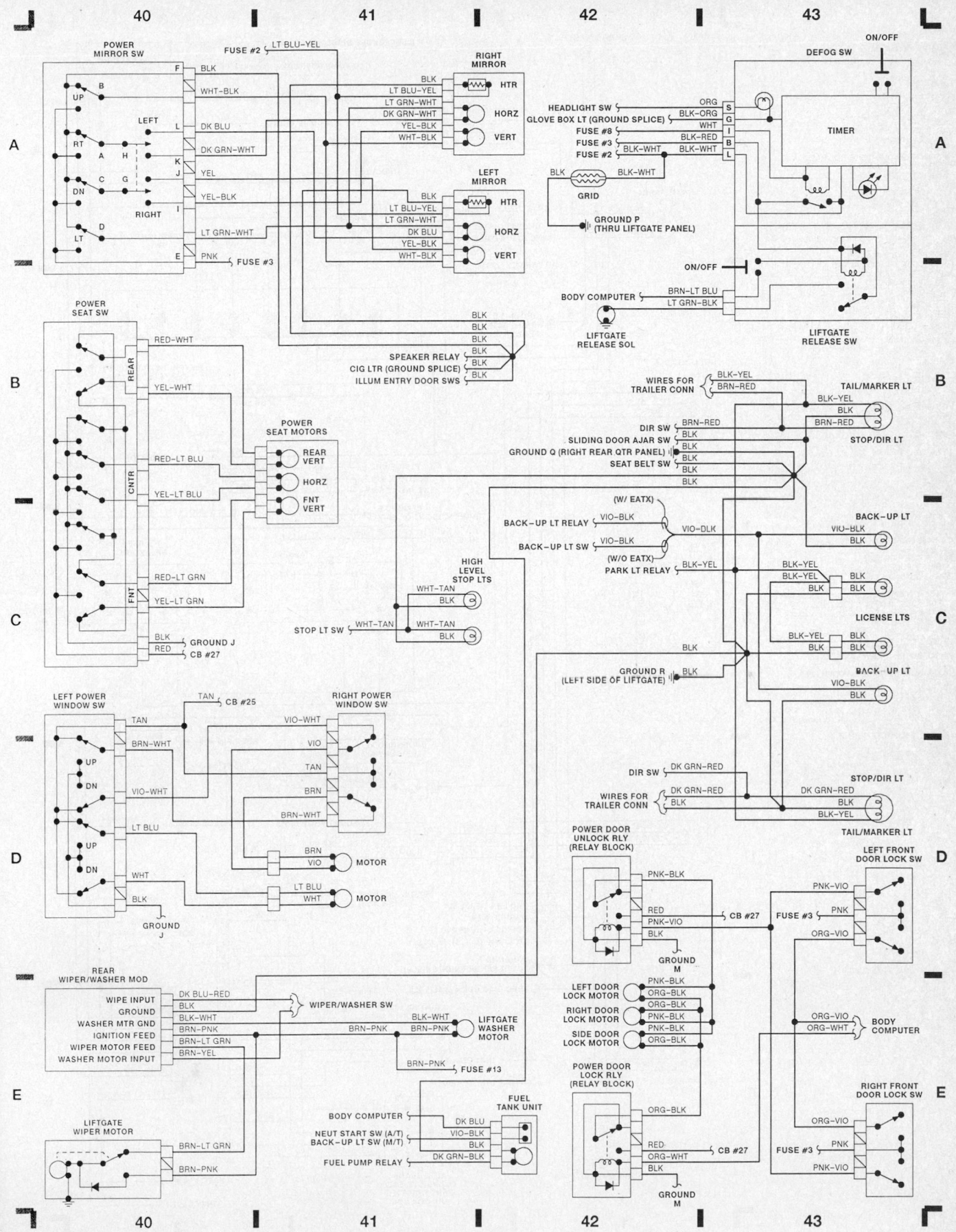

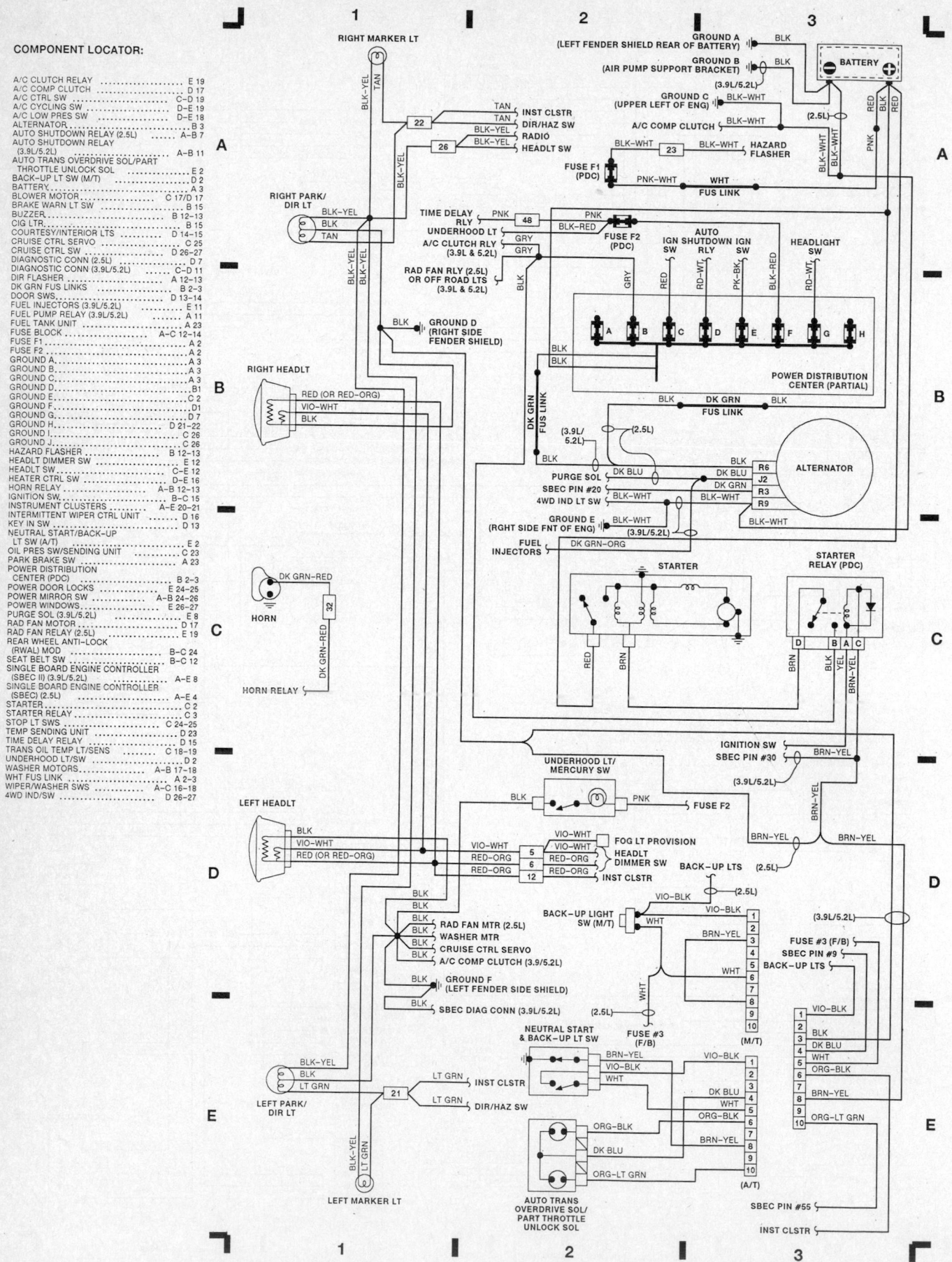

COMPONENT LOCATOR:

A/C CLUTCH RELAY .... E 19
A/C COMP CLUTCH .... D 17
A/C CTRL SW .... C-D 19
A/C CYCLING SW .... D-E 19
A/C LOW PRES SW .... D-E 18
ALTERNATOR .... B 3
AUTO SHUTDOWN RELAY (2.5L) .... A-B 7
AUTO SHUTDOWN RELAY
   (3.9L/5.2L) .... A-B 11
AUTO TRANS OVERDRIVE SOL/PART
   THROTTLE UNLOCK SOL .... E 2
BACK-UP LT SW (M/T) .... D 2
BATTERY .... A 3
BLOWER MOTOR .... C 17/D 17
BRAKE WARN LT SW .... B 15
BUZZER .... B 12-13
CIG LTR .... B 15
COURTESY/INTERIOR LTS .... D 14-15
CRUISE CTRL SERVO .... C 25
CRUISE CTRL SW .... D 26-27
DIAGNOSTIC CONN (2.5L) .... D 7
DIAGNOSTIC CONN (3.9L/5.2L) .... C-D 11
DIR FLASHER .... A 12-13
DK GRN FUS LINKS .... B 2-3
DOOR SWS. ....
FUEL INJECTORS (3.9L/5.2L) ..... E 11
FUEL PUMP RELAY (3.9L/5.2L) .... A 11
FUEL TANK UNIT .... A 23
FUSE BLOCK .... A-C 12-14
FUSE F1 .... A 2
FUSE F2 .... A 2
GROUND A .... A 3
GROUND B .... A 3
GROUND C .... A 3
GROUND D B1
GROUND E .... C 2
GROUND F D1
GROUND G .... D 7
GROUND H .... D 21-22
GROUND I .... C 26
GROUND J .... C 26
HAZARD FLASHER .... B 12-13
HEADLT DIMMER SW .... E 12
HEADLT SW .... C-E 12
HEATER CTRL SW .... D-E 16
HORN RELAY .... A-B 12-13
IGNITION SW. .... B-C 15
INSTRUMENT CLUSTERS .... A-E 20-21
INTERMITTENT WIPER CTRL UNIT ... D 16
KEY IN SW .... D 13
NEUTRAL START/BACK-UP
   LT SW (A/T) .... E 2
OIL PRES SW/SENDING UNIT .... C 23
PARK BRAKE SW .... A 23
POWER DISTRIBUTION
   CENTER (PDC) .... B 2-3
POWER DOOR LOCKS .... E 24-25
POWER MIRROR SW .... A-B 24-26
POWER WINDOWS .... E 26-27
PURGE SOL (3.9L/5.2L) .... E 8
RAD FAN MOTOR .... D 17
RAD FAN RELAY (2.5L) .... E 19
REAR WHEEL ANTI-LOCK
   (RWAL) MOD .... B-C 24
SEAT BELT SW .... B-C 12
SINGLE BOARD ENGINE CONTROLLER
   (SBEC II) (3.9L/5.2L) .... A-E 8
SINGLE BOARD ENGINE CONTROLLER
   (SBEC) (2.5L) .... A-E 4
STARTER .... C 2
STARTER RELAY .... C 3
STOP LT SWS .... C 24-25
TEMP SENDING UNIT .... D 23
TIME DELAY RELAY .... D 15
TRANS OIL TEMP LT/SENS .... C 18-19
UNDERHOOD LT/SW .... D 2
WASHER MOTORS .... A-B 17-18
WHT FUS LINK .... A 2-3
WIPER/WASHER SWS .... A-C 16-18
4WD IND/SW .... D 26-27

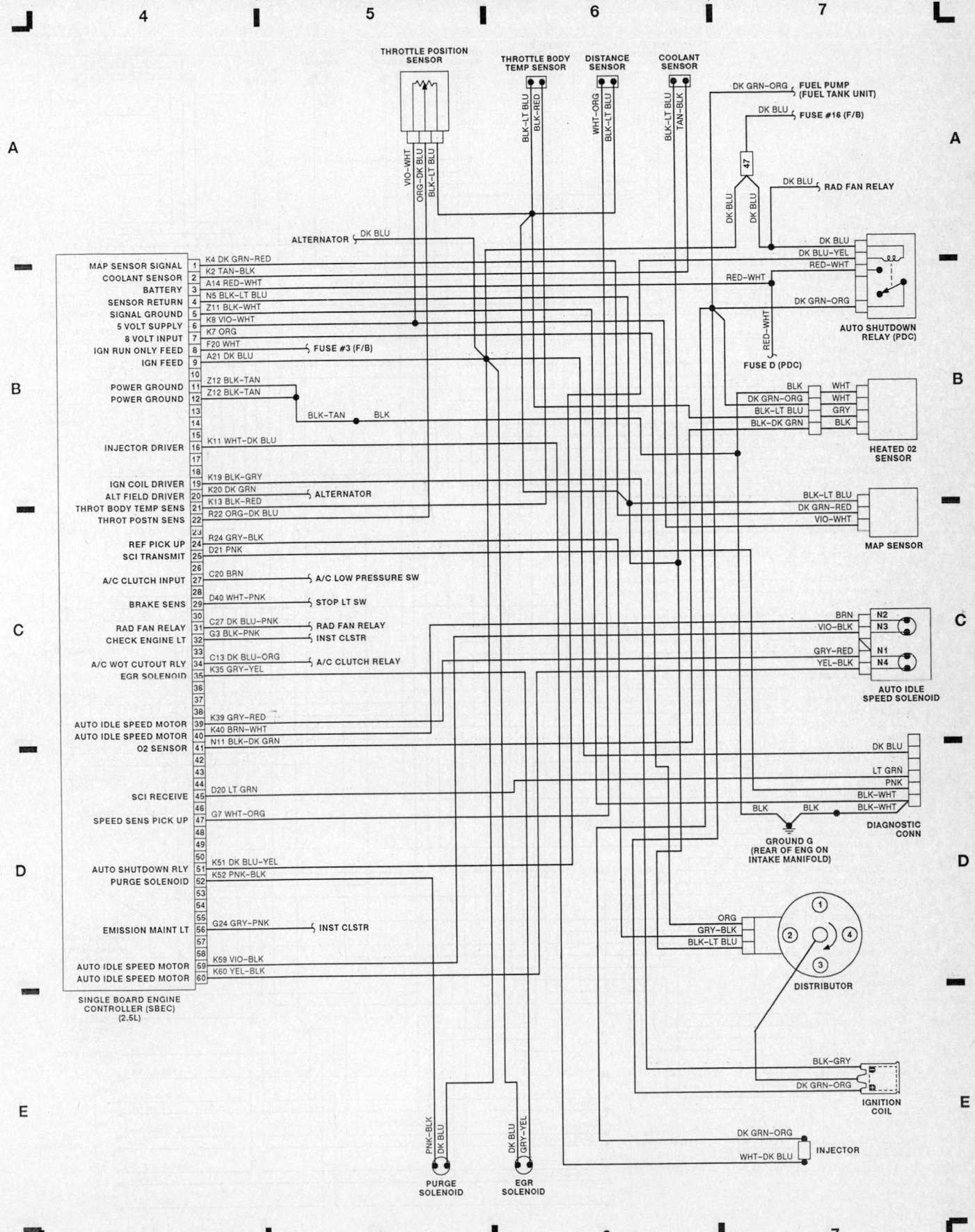

SINGLE BOARD ENGINE
CONTROLLER (SBEC)
(2.5L)

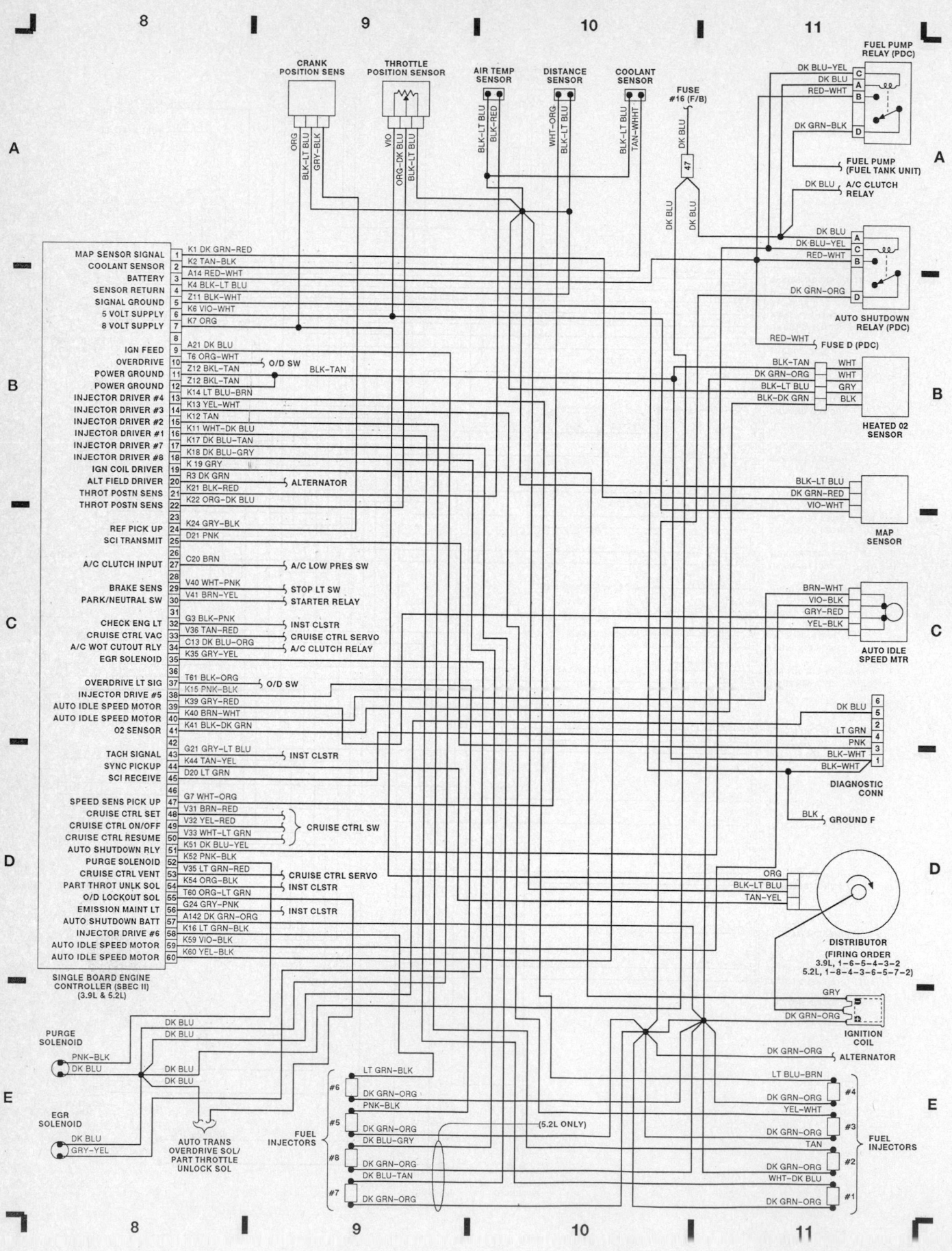

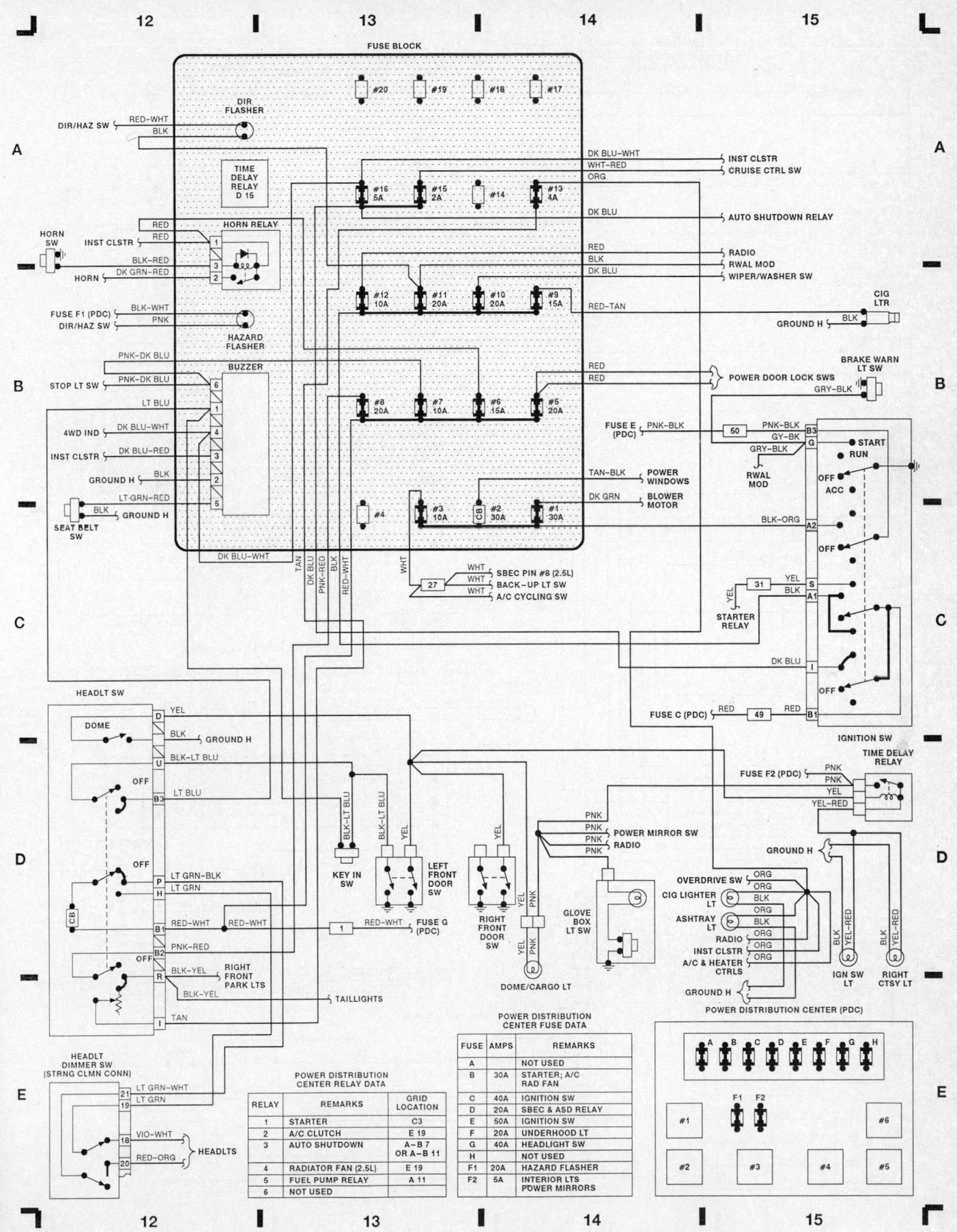

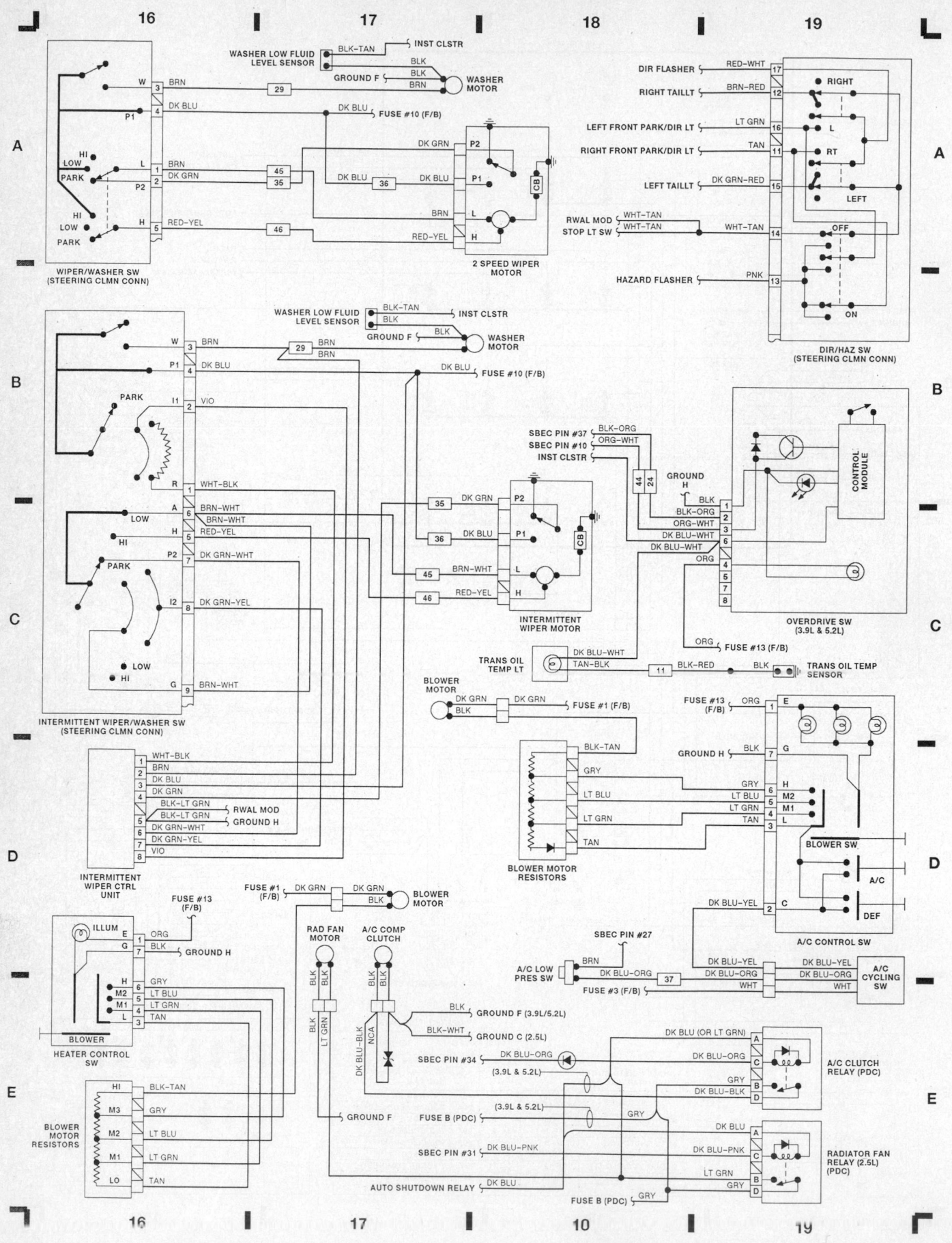

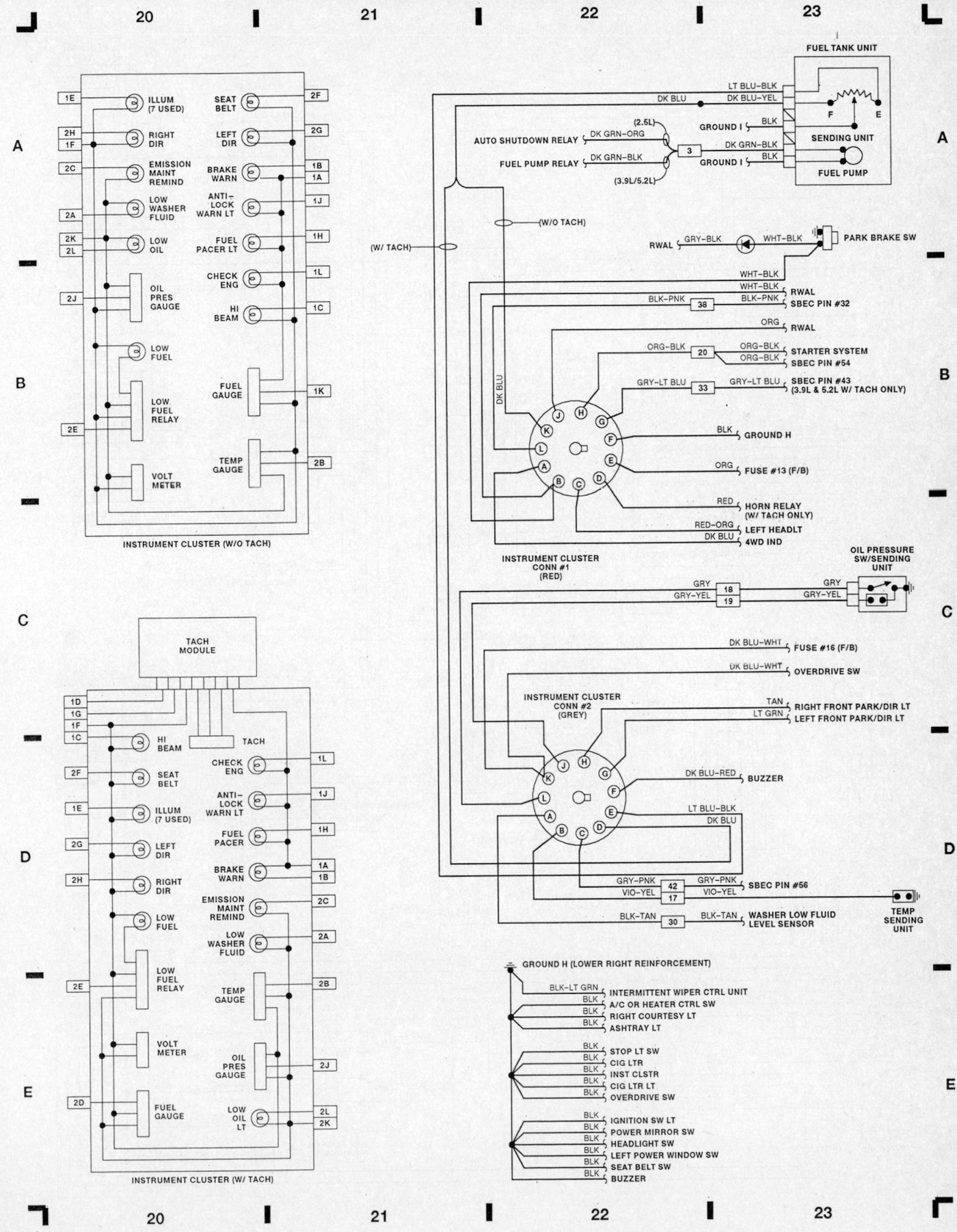

INSTRUMENT CLUSTER (W/O TACH)

TACH MODULE

INSTRUMENT CLUSTER (W/ TACH)

FUEL TANK UNIT

AUTO SHUTDOWN RELAY

FUEL PUMP RELAY

SENDING UNIT

FUEL PUMP

PARK BRAKE SW

INSTRUMENT CLUSTER CONN #1 (RED)

OIL PRESSURE SW/SENDING UNIT

INSTRUMENT CLUSTER CONN #2 (GREY)

TEMP SENDING UNIT

GROUND H (LOWER RIGHT REINFORCEMENT)

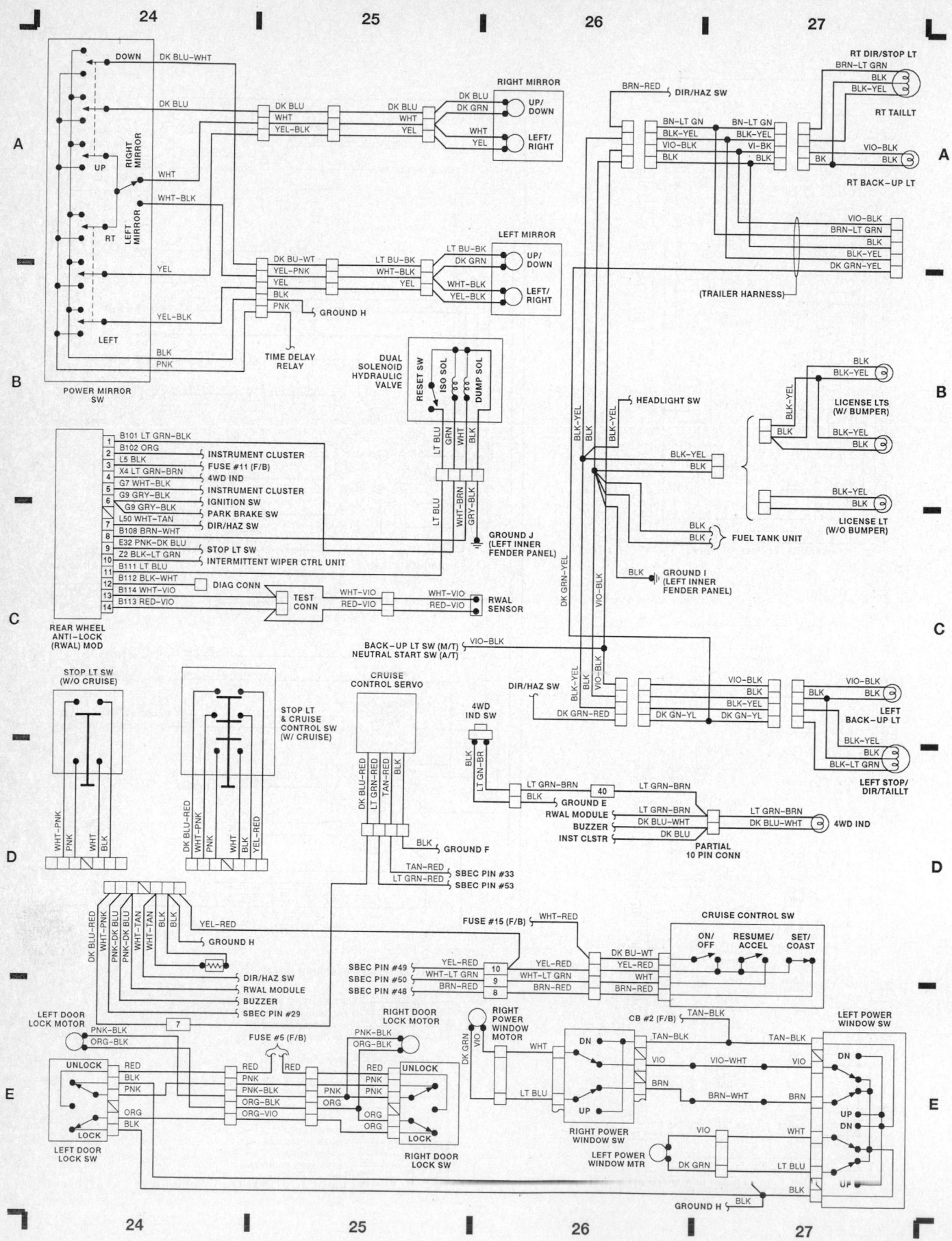

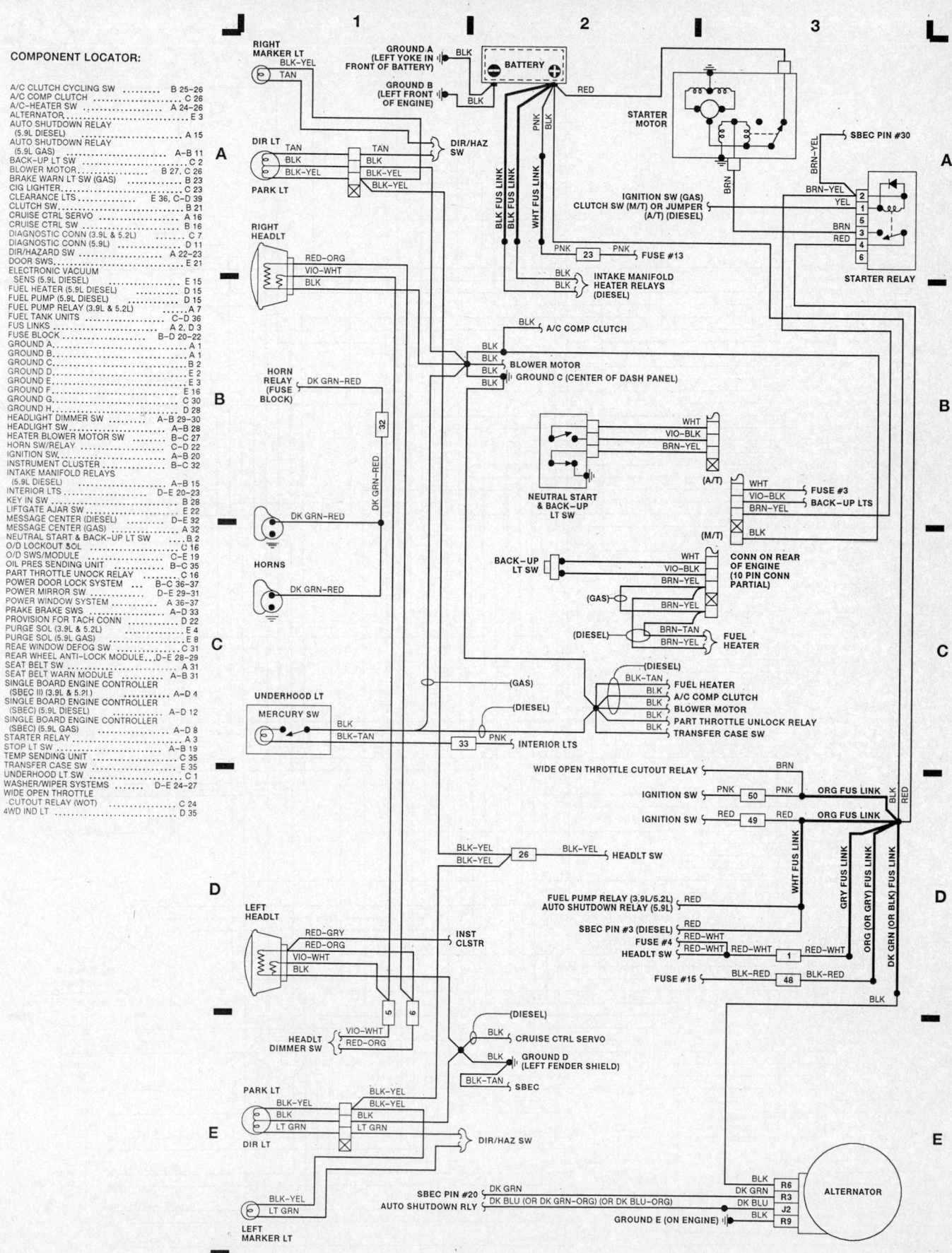

COMPONENT LOCATOR:

A/C CLUTCH CYCLING SW .... B 25–26
A/C COMP CLUTCH .... C 26
A/C–HEATER SW .... A 24–26
ALTERNATOR .... E 3
AUTO SHUTDOWN RELAY
(5.9L DIESEL) .... A 15
AUTO SHUTDOWN RELAY
(5.9L GAS) .... A–B 11
BACK–UP LT SW .... C 2
BLOWER MOTOR .... B 27, C 26
BRAKE WARN LT SW (GAS) ...... B 23
CIG LIGHTER .... C 23
CLEARANCE LTS .... E 36, C–D 39
CLUTCH SW. .... B 21
CRUISE CTRL SERVO .... A 16
CRUISE CTRL SW .... B 16
DIAGNOSTIC CONN (3.9L & 5.2L) .. C 7
DIAGNOSTIC CONN (5.9L) .... D 11
DIR/HAZARD SW .... A 22–23
DOOR SWS. .... E 21
ELECTRONIC VACUUM
SENS (5.9L DIESEL) .... E 15
FUEL HEATER (5.9L DIESEL) ..... D 15
FUEL PUMP (5.9L DIESEL) .... D 15
FUEL PUMP RELAY (3.9L & 5.2L) .. A 7
FUEL TANK UNITS .... C–D 36
FUS LINKS .... A 2, D 3
FUSE BLOCK .... B–D 20–22
GROUND A .... A 1
GROUND B .... A 1
GROUND C .... B 2
GROUND D .... E 2
GROUND E .... E 3
GROUND F .... E 16
GROUND G .... C 30
GROUND H .... D 28
HEADLIGHT DIMMER SW .... A–B 29–30
HEADLIGHT SW. .... A–B 28
HEATER BLOWER MOTOR SW .. B–C 27
HORN SW/RELAY .... C–D 22
IGNITION SW. .... A–B 20
INSTRUMENT CLUSTER ...... B–C 32
INTAKE MANIFOLD RELAYS
(5.9L DIESEL) .... A–B 15
INTERIOR LTS .... D–E 20–23
KEY IN SW .... B 28
LIFTGATE AJAR SW .... E 22
MESSAGE CENTER (DIESEL) .. D–E 32
MESSAGE CENTER (GAS) .... A 32
NEUTRAL START & BACK–UP LT SW . B 2
O/D LOCKOUT SOL .... C 16
O/D SWS/MODULE .... C–E 19
OIL PRES SENDING UNIT ..... B–C 35
PART THROTTLE UNOCK RELAY .. C 16
POWER DOOR LOCK SYSTEM . B–C 36–37
POWER MIRROR SW .... D–E 29–31
POWER WINDOW SYSTEM ..... A 36–37
PRAKE BRAKE SWS .... A–D 33
PROVISION FOR TACH CONN ...... D 22
PURGE SOL (3.9L & 5.2L) .... E 4
PURGE SOL (5.9L GAS) .... E 8
REAE WINDOW DEFOG SW .... C 31
REAR WHEEL ANTI–LOCK MODULE . D–E 28–29
SEAT BELT SW .... A 31
SEAT BELT WARN MODULE .... A 31
SINGLE BOARD ENGINE CONTROLLER
(SBEC II) (3.9L & 5.2l) ...... A–D 5
SINGLE BOARD ENGINE CONTROLLER
(SBEC) (5.9L DIESEL) ...... A–D 12
SINGLE BOARD ENGINE CONTROLLER
(SBEC) (5.9L GAS) .... A–D 8
STARTER RELAY .... A 3
STOP LT SW .... A–B 19
TEMP SENDING UNIT .... C 35
TRANSFER CASE SW .... E 35
UNDERHOOD LT .... C 1
WASHER/WIPER SYSTEMS ... D–E 24–27
WIDE OPEN THROTTLE
CUTOUT RELAY (WOT) .... C 24
4WD IND LT .... D 35

1992 WIRING DIAGRAMS
Pickup & Ramcharger (Cont.)

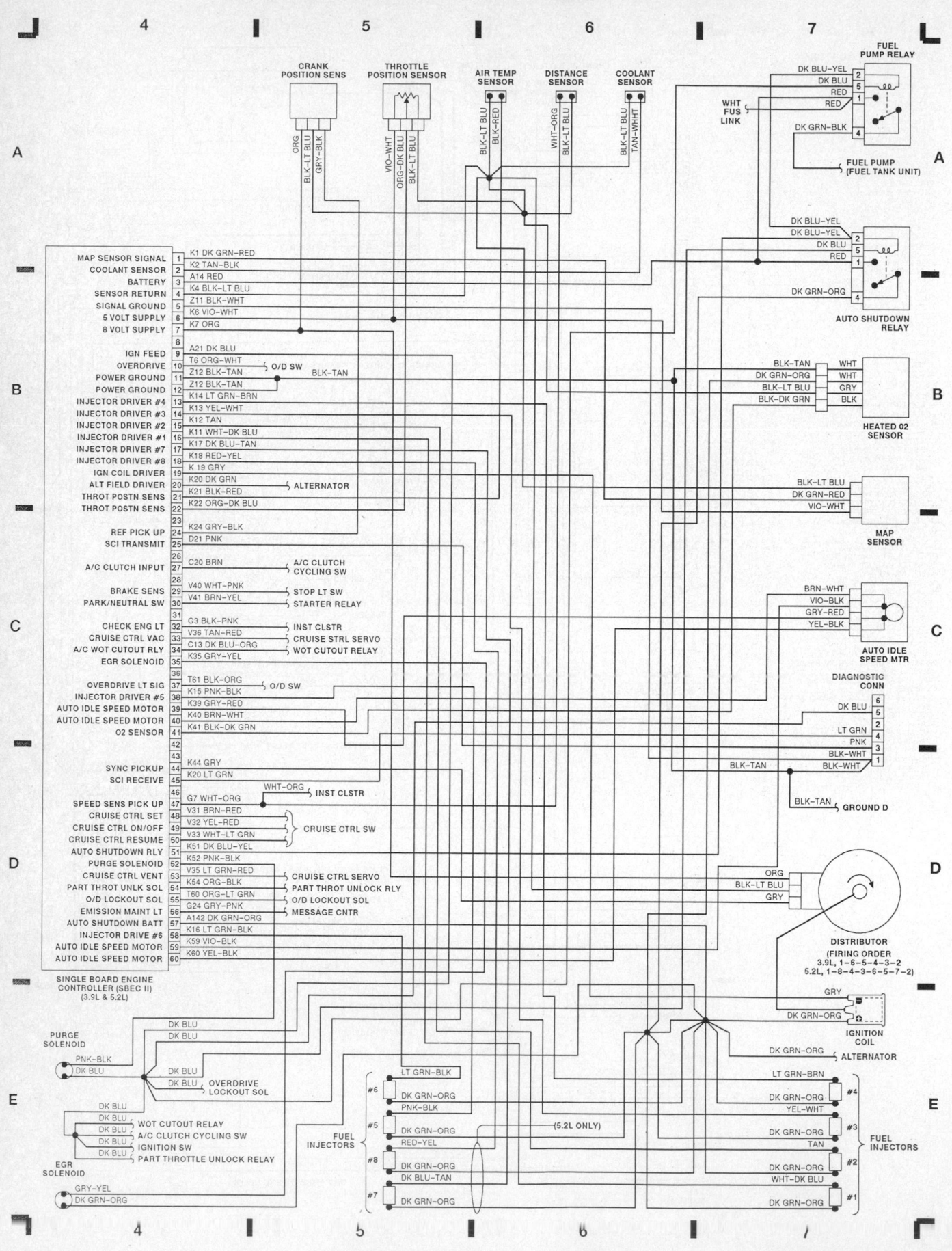

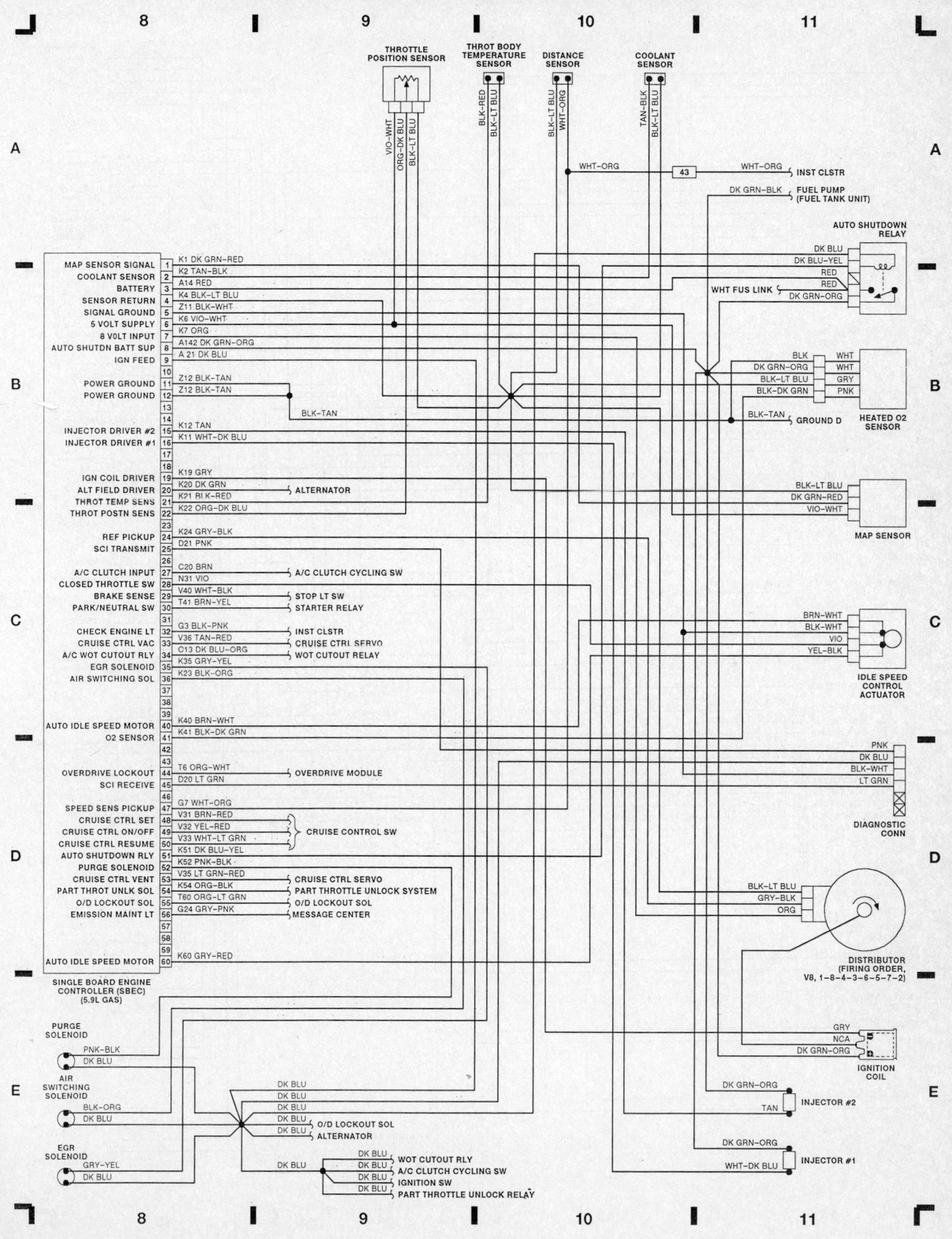

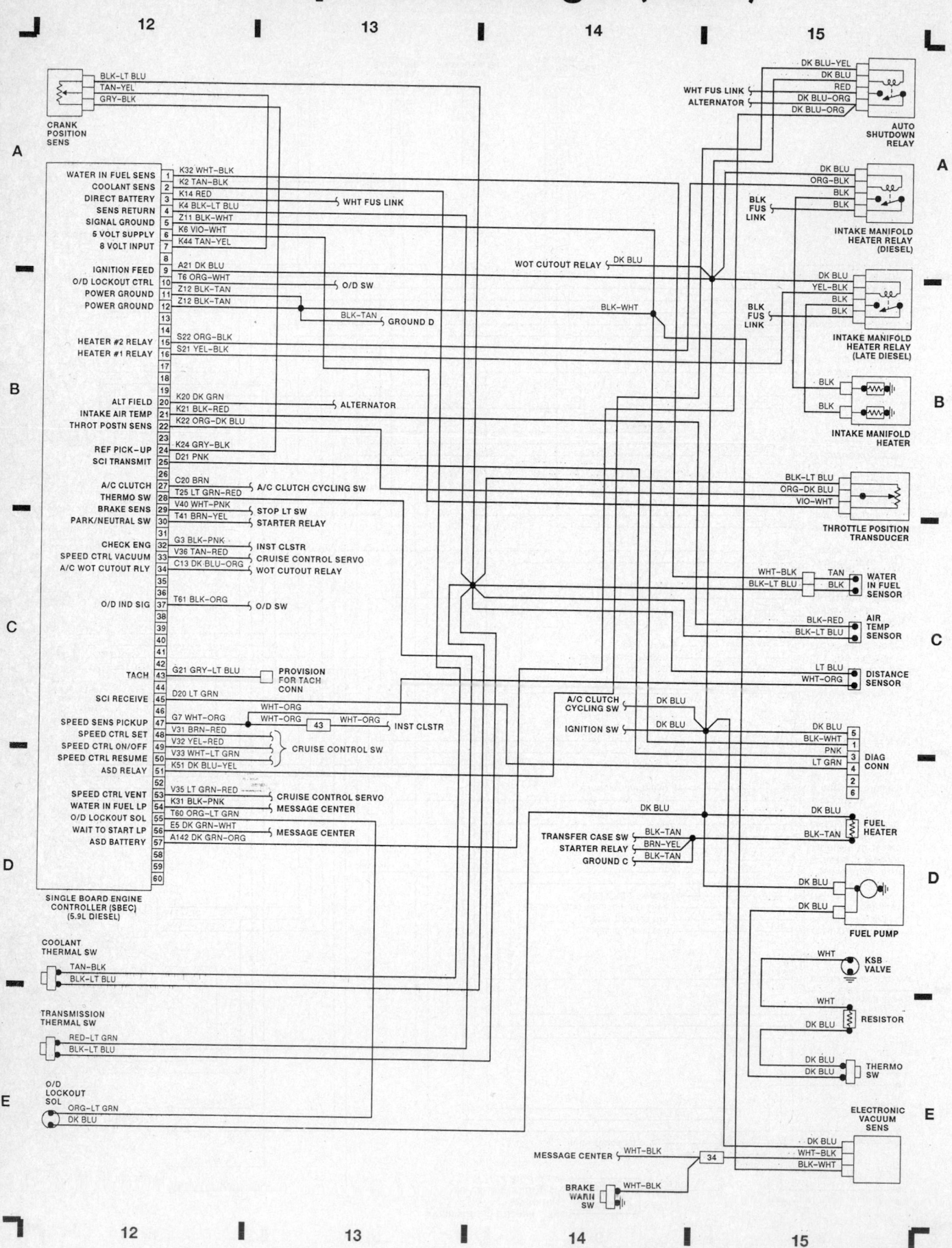

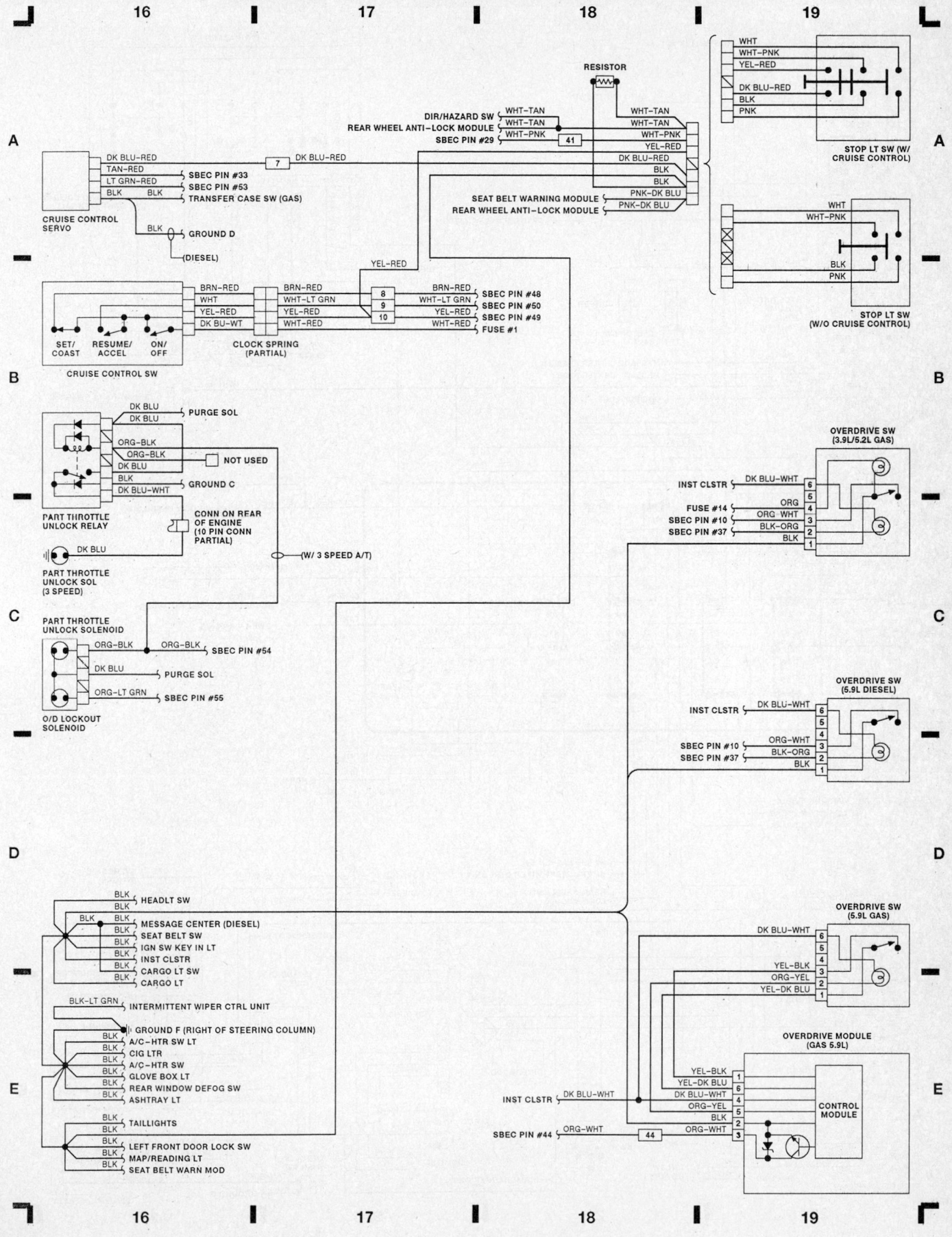

1992 WIRING DIAGRAMS
Pickup & Ramcharger (Cont.)

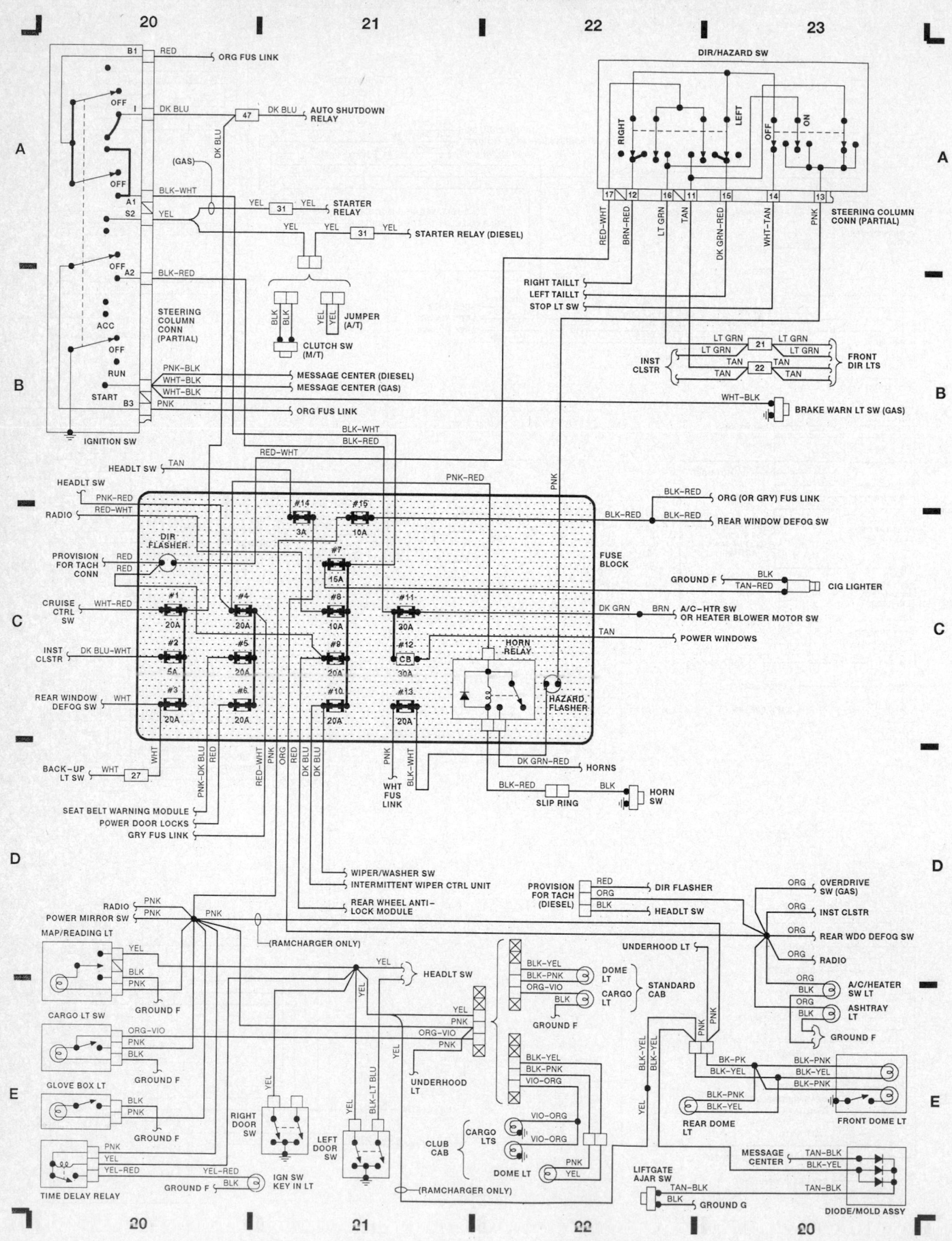

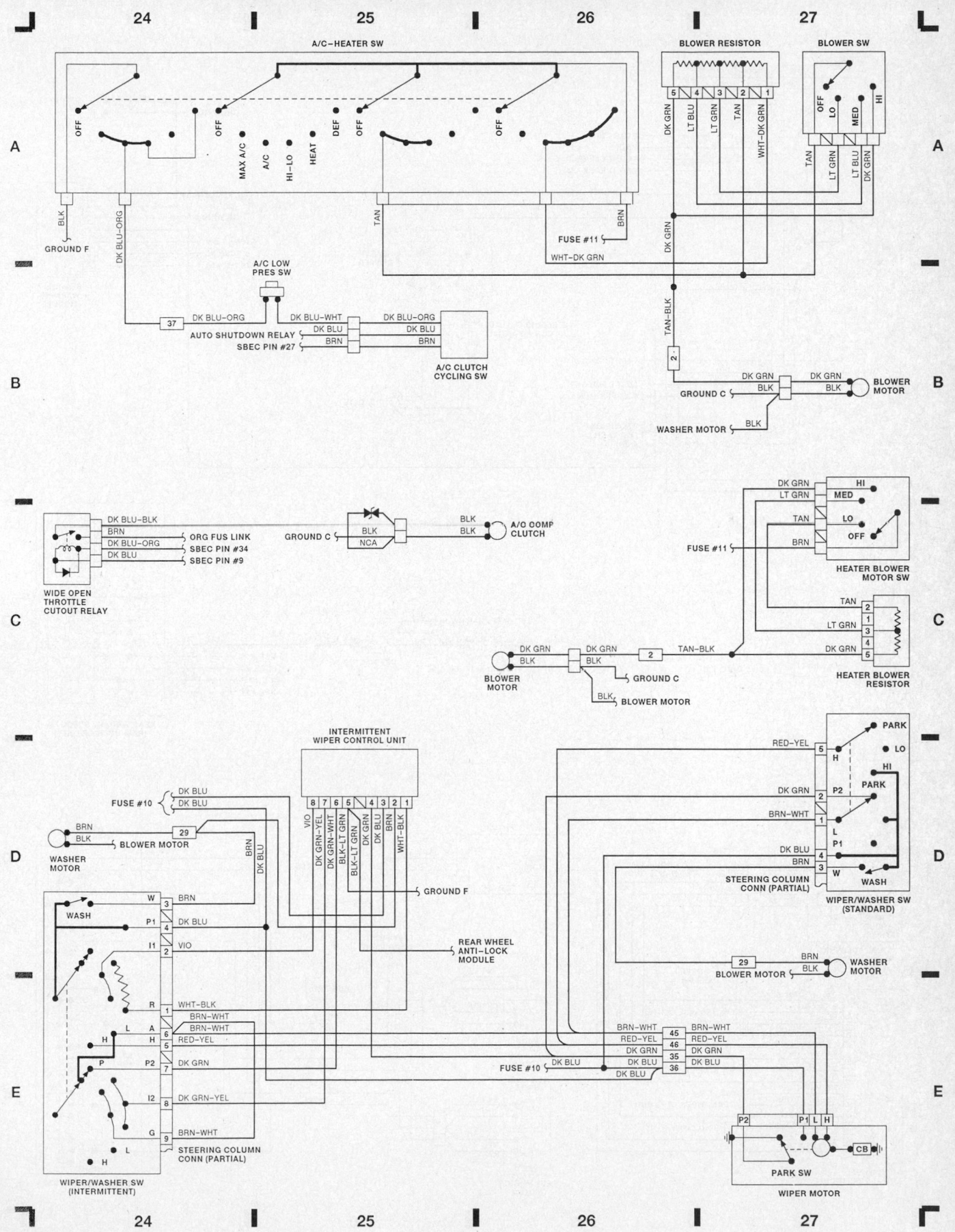

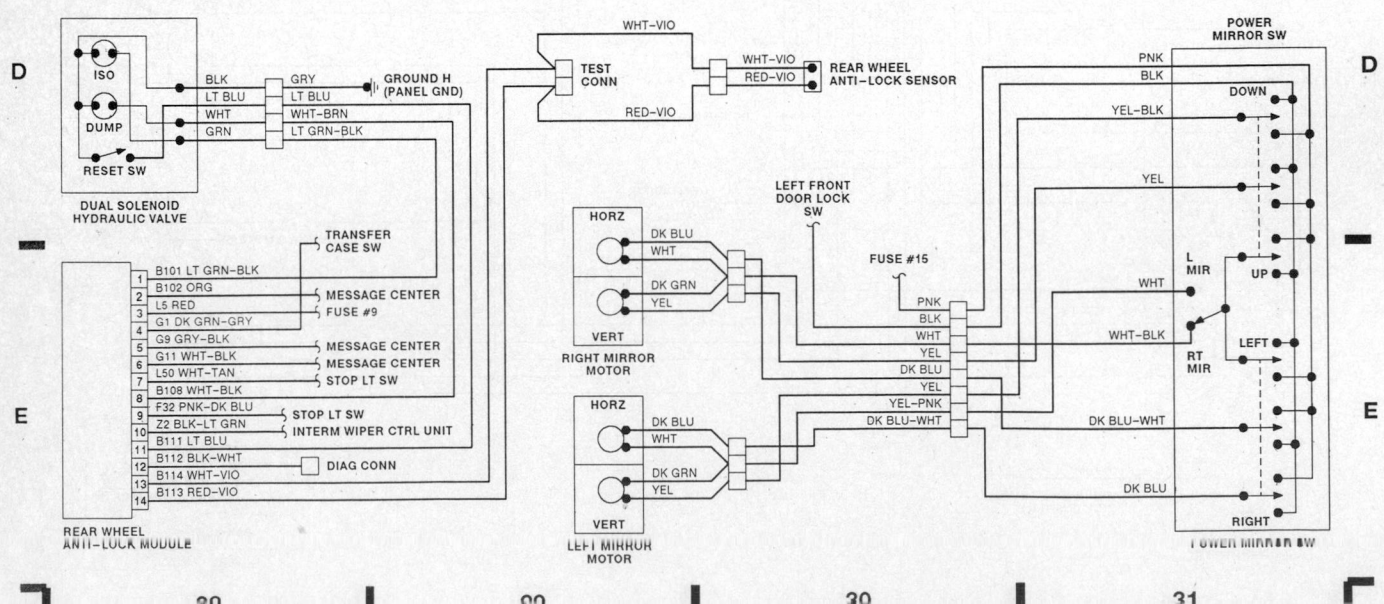

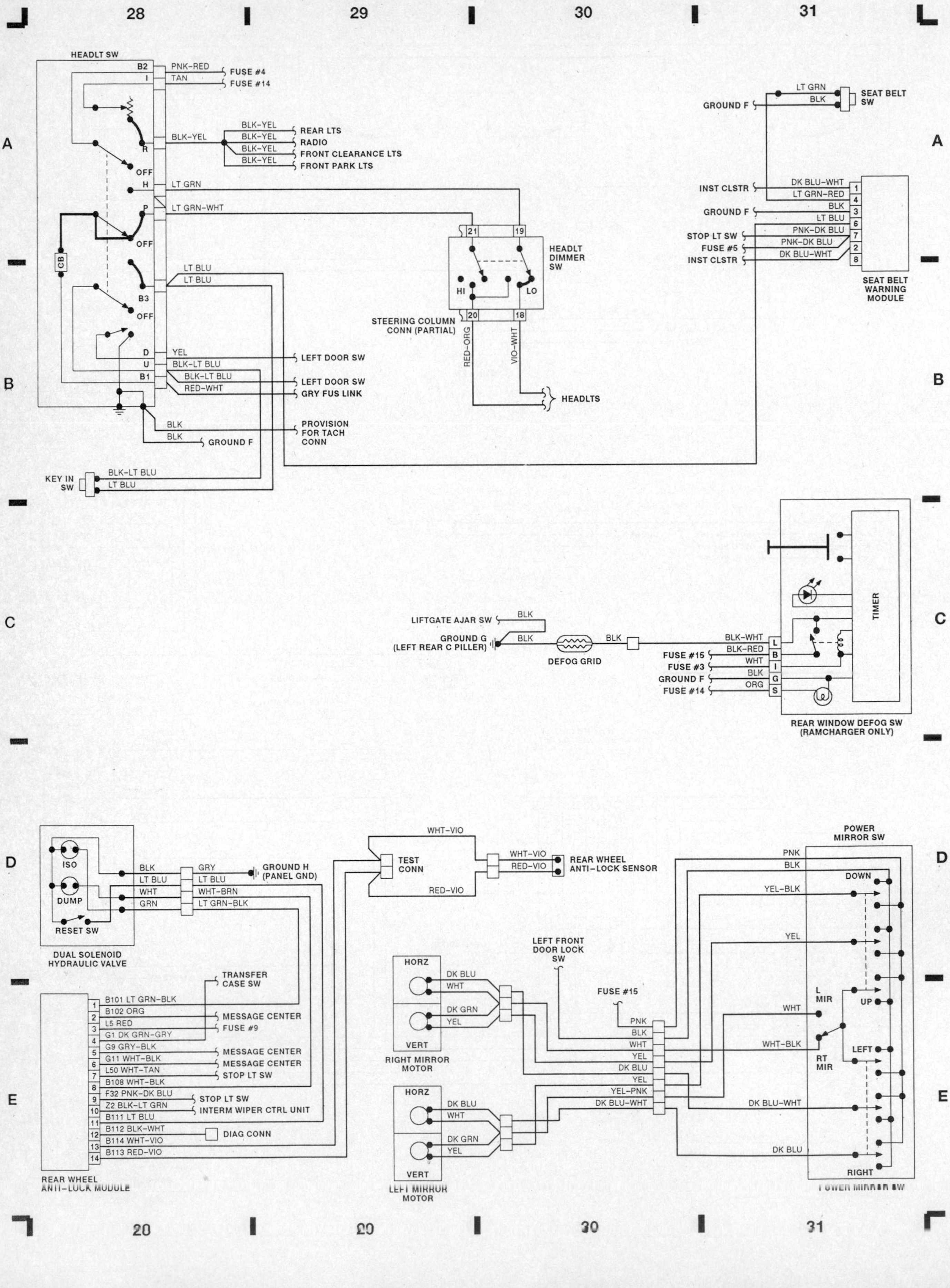

1992 WIRING DIAGRAMS
Pickup & Ramcharger (Cont.)

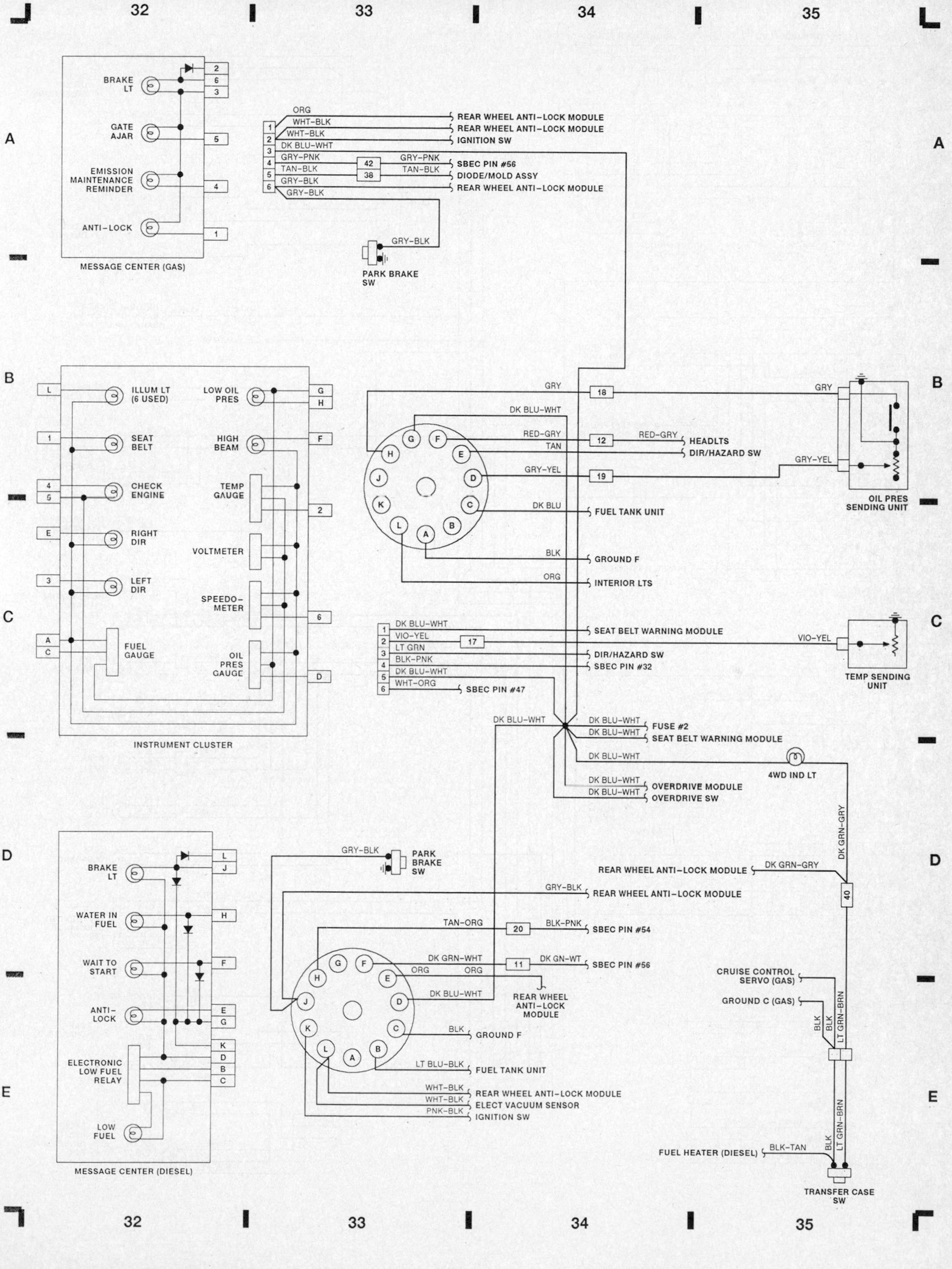

1992 WIRING DIAGRAMS
Pickup & Ramcharger (Cont.)

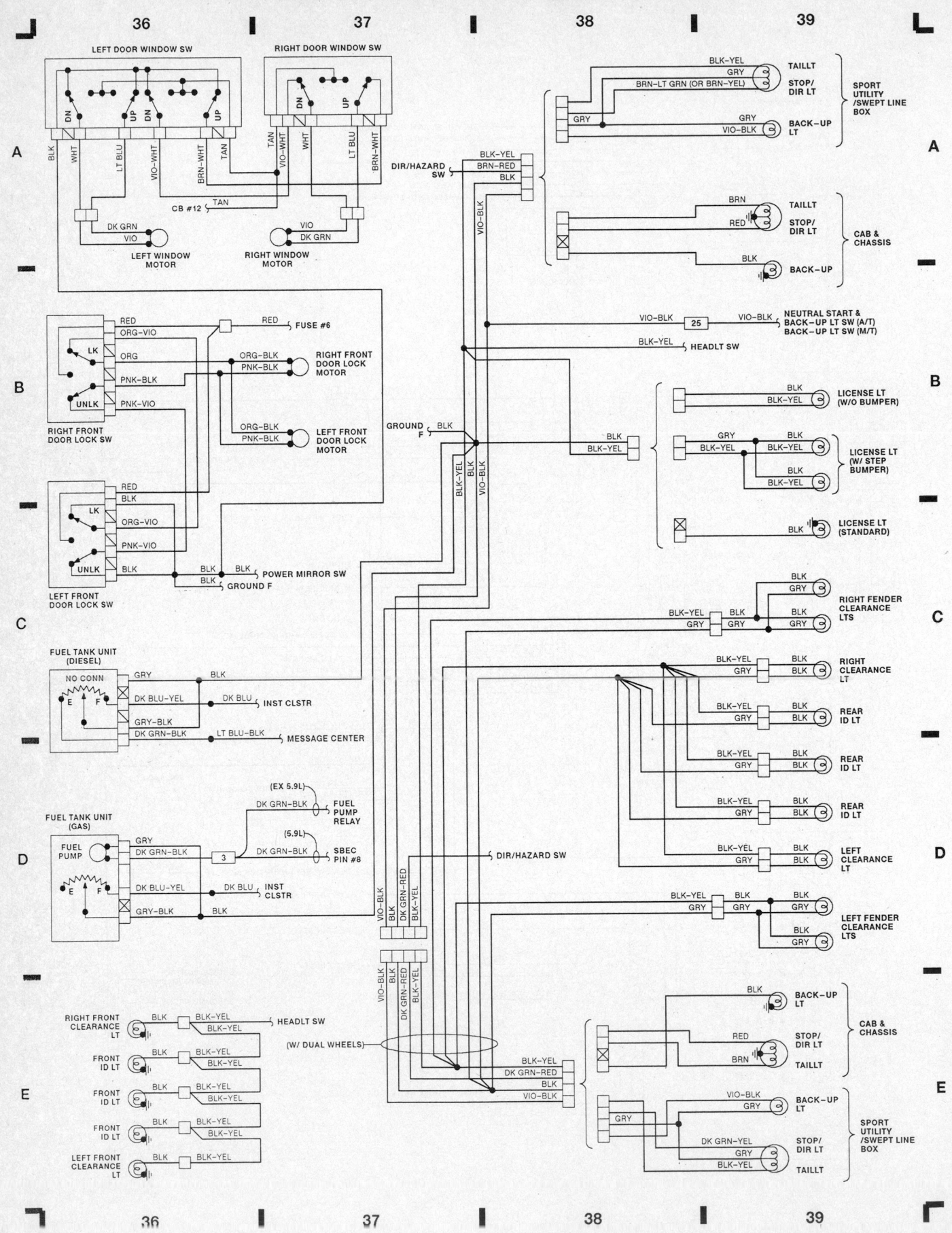

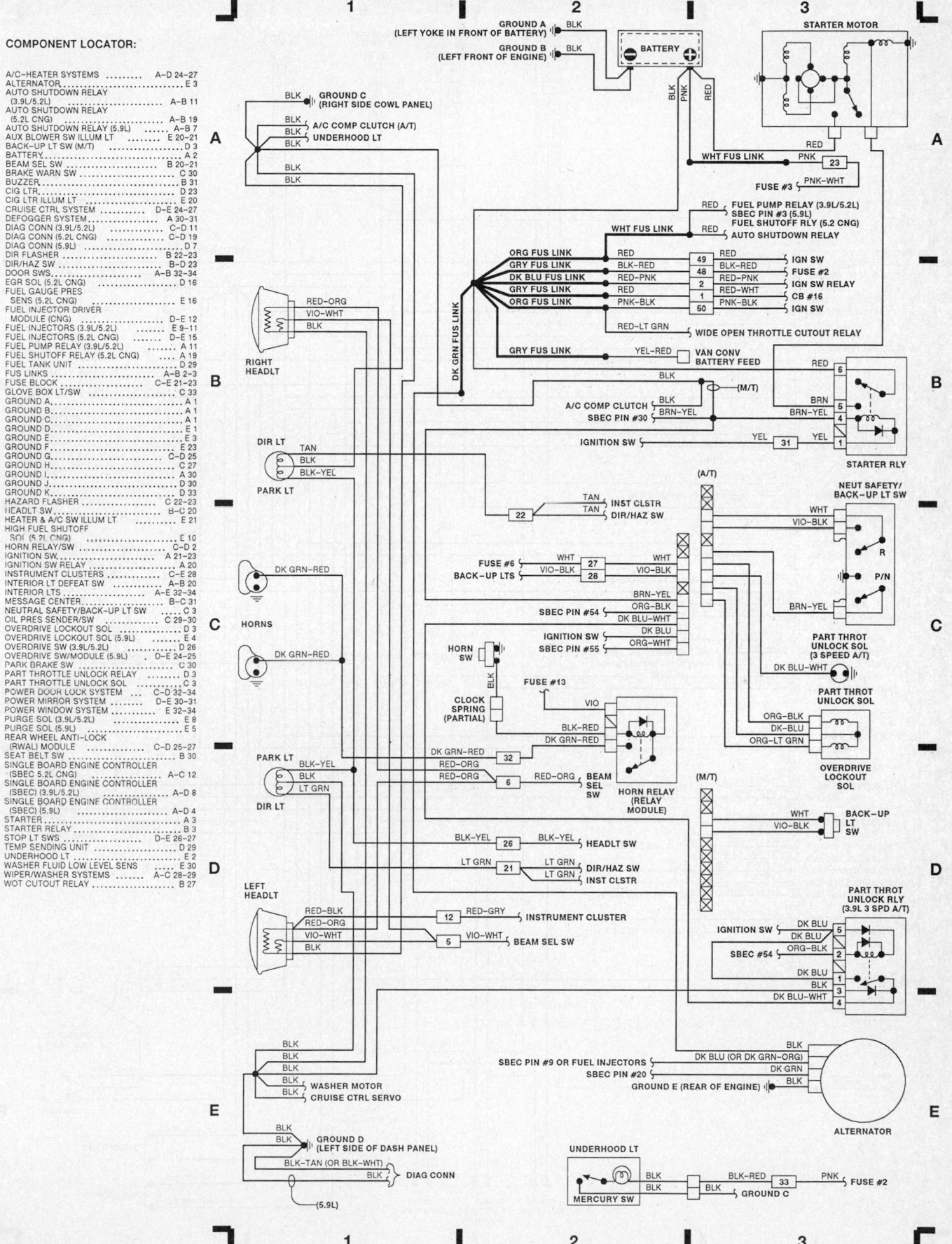

COMPONENT LOCATOR:

A/C-HEATER SYSTEMS .... A-D 24-27
ALTERNATOR .... E 3
AUTO SHUTDOWN RELAY
(3.9L/5.2L) .... A-B 11
AUTO SHUTDOWN RELAY
(5.2L CNG) .... A-B 19
AUTO SHUTDOWN RELAY (5.9L) .. A-B 7
AUX BLOWER SW ILLUM LT ...... E 20-21
BACK-UP LT SW (M/T) .... D 3
BATTERY .... A 2
BEAM SEL SW .... B 20-21
BRAKE WARN SW .... C 30
BUZZER .... B 31
CIG LTR. .... D 23
CIG LTR ILLUM LT .... E 20
CRUISE CTRL SYSTEM .... D-E 24-27
DEFOGGER SYSTEM .... A 30-31
DIAG CONN (3.9L/5.2L) .... C-D 11
DIAG CONN (5.2L CNG) .... C-D 19
DIAG CONN (5.9L) .... D 7
DIR FLASHER .... B 22-23
DIR/HAZ SW .... B-D 23
DOOR SWS. .... A-B 32-34
EGR SOL (5.2L CNG) .... D 16
FUEL GAUGE PRES
SENS (5.2L CNG) .... E 16
FUEL INJECTOR DRIVER
MODULE (CNG) .... D-E 12
FUEL INJECTORS (3.9L/5.2L) .... E 9-11
FUEL INJECTORS (5.2L CNG) .... D-E 15
FUEL PUMP RELAY (3.9L/5.2L) ... A 11
FUEL SHUTOFF RELAY (5.2L CNG) . A 19
FUEL TANK UNIT .... D 29
FUS LINKS .... A-B 2-3
FUSE BLOCK .... C-E 21-23
GLOVE BOX LT/SW .... C 33
GROUND A .... A 1
GROUND B .... A 1
GROUND C .... A 1
GROUND D .... E 1
GROUND E .... E 3
GROUND F .... E 23
GROUND G .... C-D 25
GROUND H .... C 27
GROUND I .... A 30
GROUND J .... D 30
GROUND K .... D 33
HAZARD FLASHER .... C 22-23
HEADLT SW .... B-C 20
HEATER & A/C SW ILLUM LT .... E 21
HIGH FUEL SHUTOFF
SOL (5.2L CNG) .... E 10
HORN RELAY/SW .... C-D 2
IGNITION SW .... A 21-23
IGNITION SW RELAY .... A 20
INSTRUMENT CLUSTERS .... C-E 28
INTERIOR LT DEFEAT SW .... A-B 20
INTERIOR LTS .... A-E 32-34
MESSAGE CENTER .... B-C 31
NEUTRAL SAFETY/BACK-UP LT SW .. C 3
OIL PRES SENDER/SW .... C 29-30
OVERDRIVE LOCKOUT SOL ..... D 3
OVERDRIVE LOCKOUT SOL (5.9L) . E 4
OVERDRIVE SW (3.9L/5.2L) ..... D 26
OVERDRIVE SW/MODULE (5.9L) .. D-E 24-25
PARK BRAKE SW .... C 30
PART THROTTLE UNLOCK RELAY .. D 3
PART THROTTLE UNLOCK SOL ... C 3
POWER DOOR LOCK SYSTEM ... C-D 32-34
POWER MIRROR SYSTEM ...... D-E 30-31
POWER WINDOW SYSTEM ...... E 32-34
PURGE SOL (3.9L/5.2L) .... E 8
PURGE SOL (5.9L) .... E 5
REAR WHEEL ANTI-LOCK
(RWAL) MODULE .... C-D 25-27
SEAT BELT SW .... B 30
SINGLE BOARD ENGINE CONTROLLER
(SBEC 5.2L CNG) .... A-C 12
SINGLE BOARD ENGINE CONTROLLER
(SBEC) (3.9L/5.2L) .... A-D 8
SINGLE BOARD ENGINE CONTROLLER
(SBEC) (5.9L) .... A-D 4
STARTER .... A 3
STARTER RELAY .... B 3
STOP LT SWS .... D-E 26-27
TEMP SENDING UNIT .... D 29
UNDERHOOD LT .... E 2
WASHER FLUID LOW LEVEL SENS . E 30
WIPER/WASHER SYSTEMS ...... A-C 28-29
WOT CUTOUT RELAY .... B 27

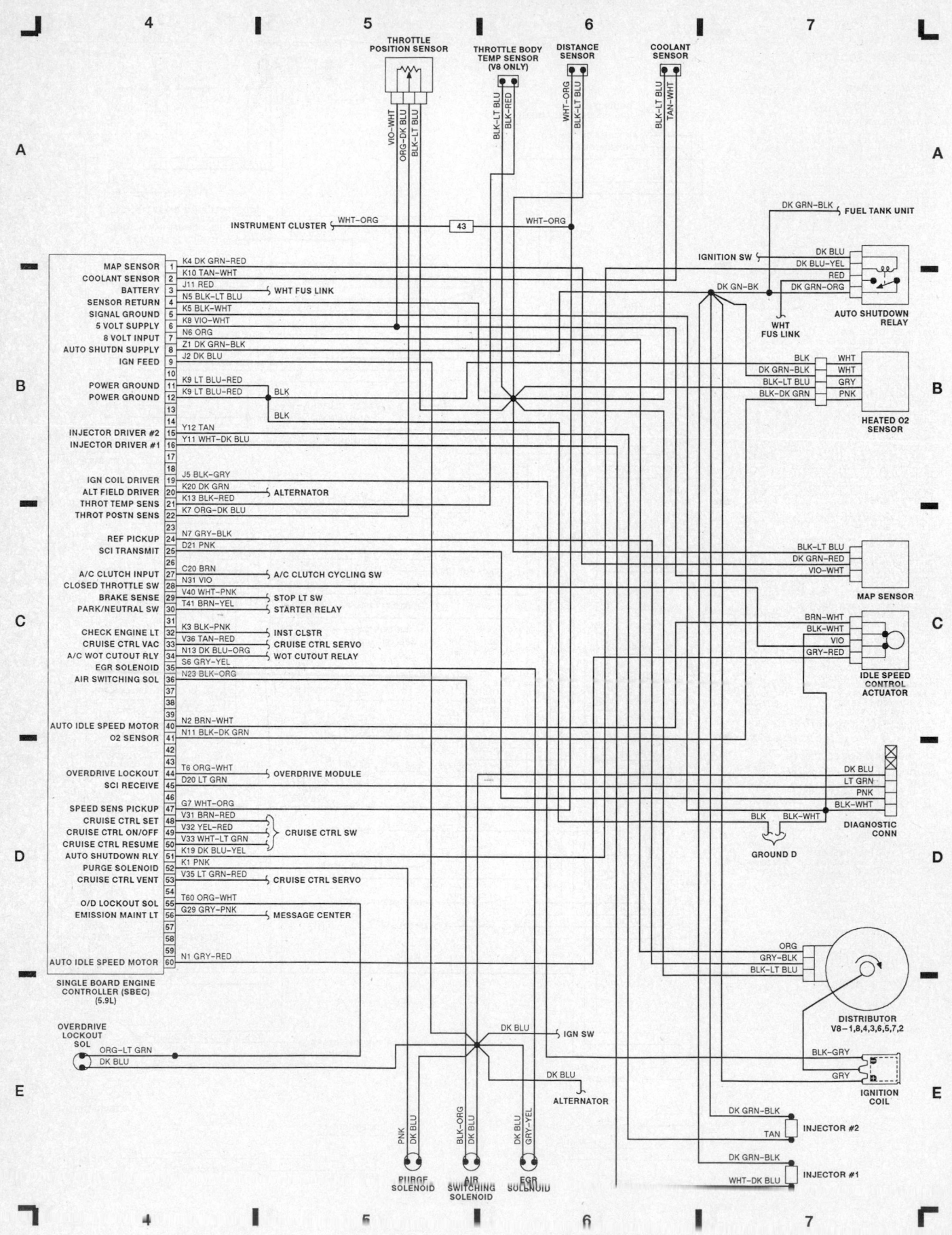

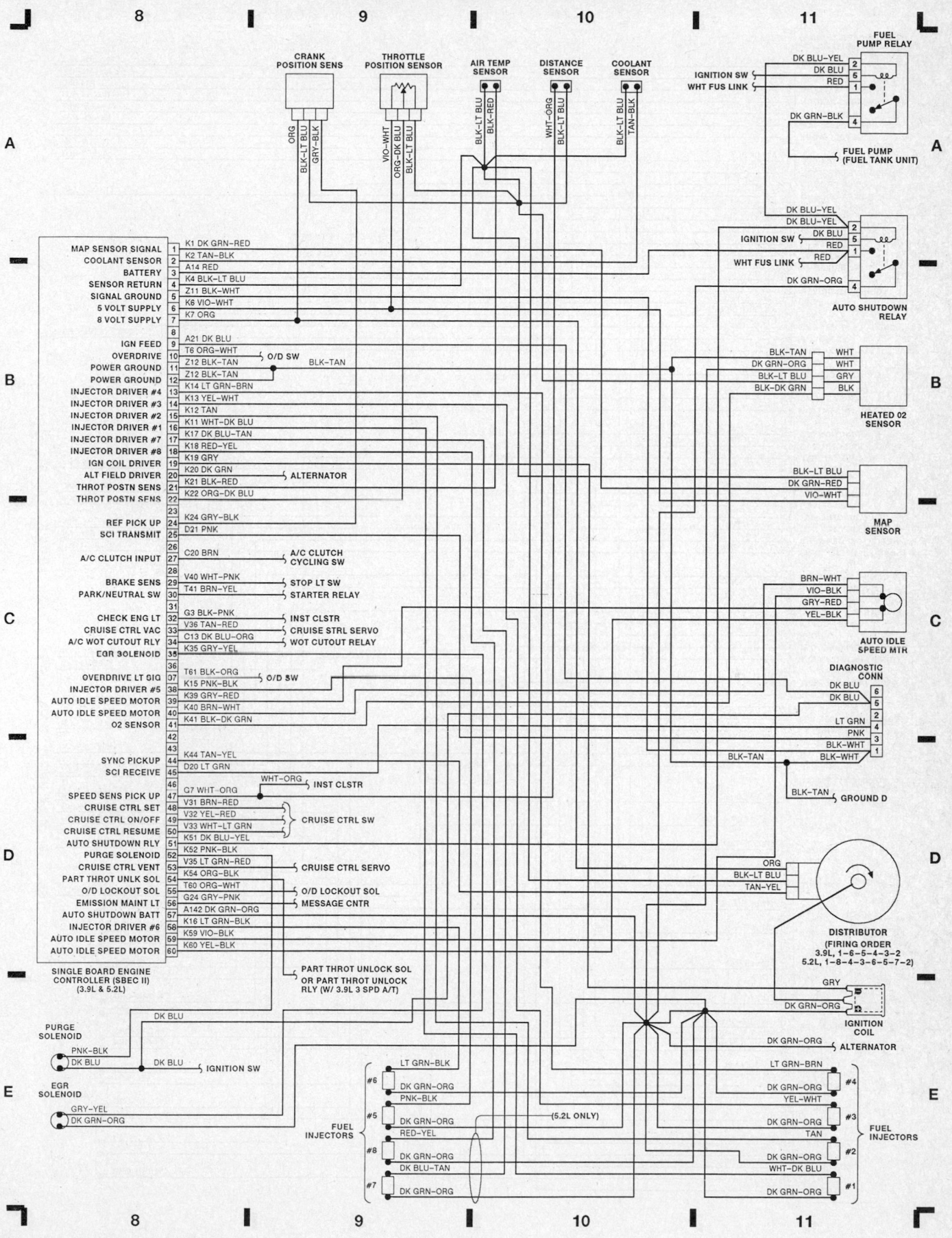

1992 WIRING DIAGRAMS
RWD Van (Cont.)

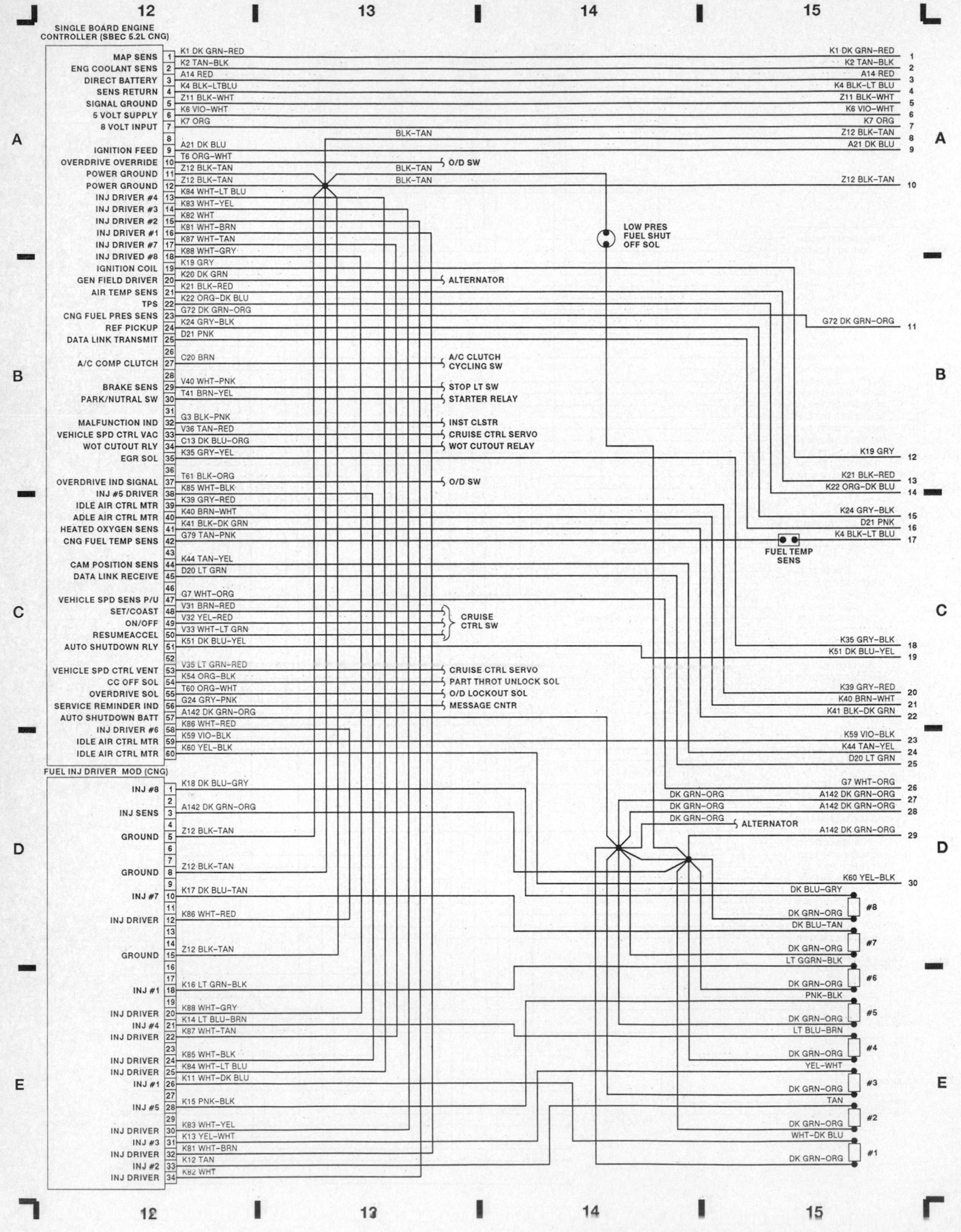

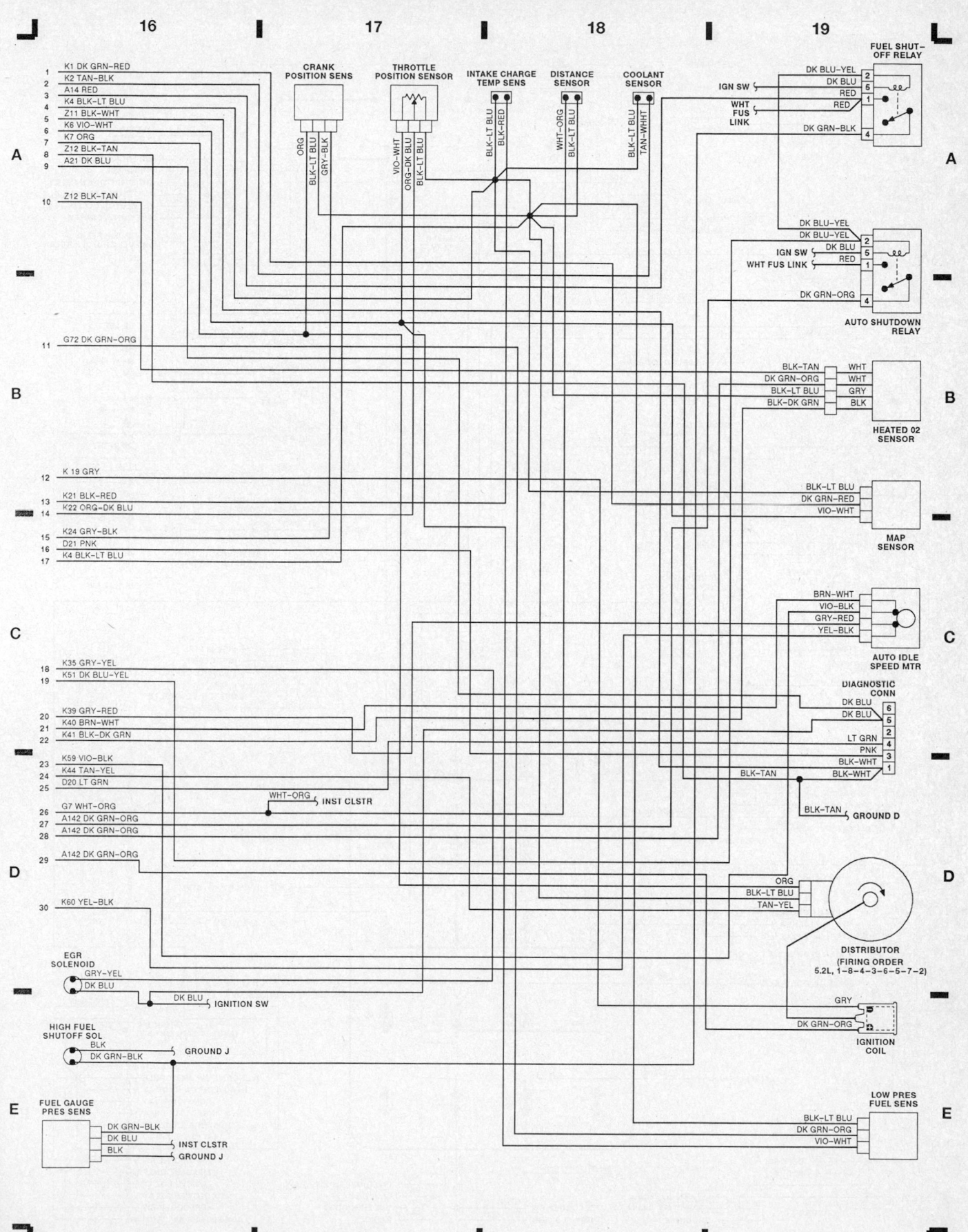

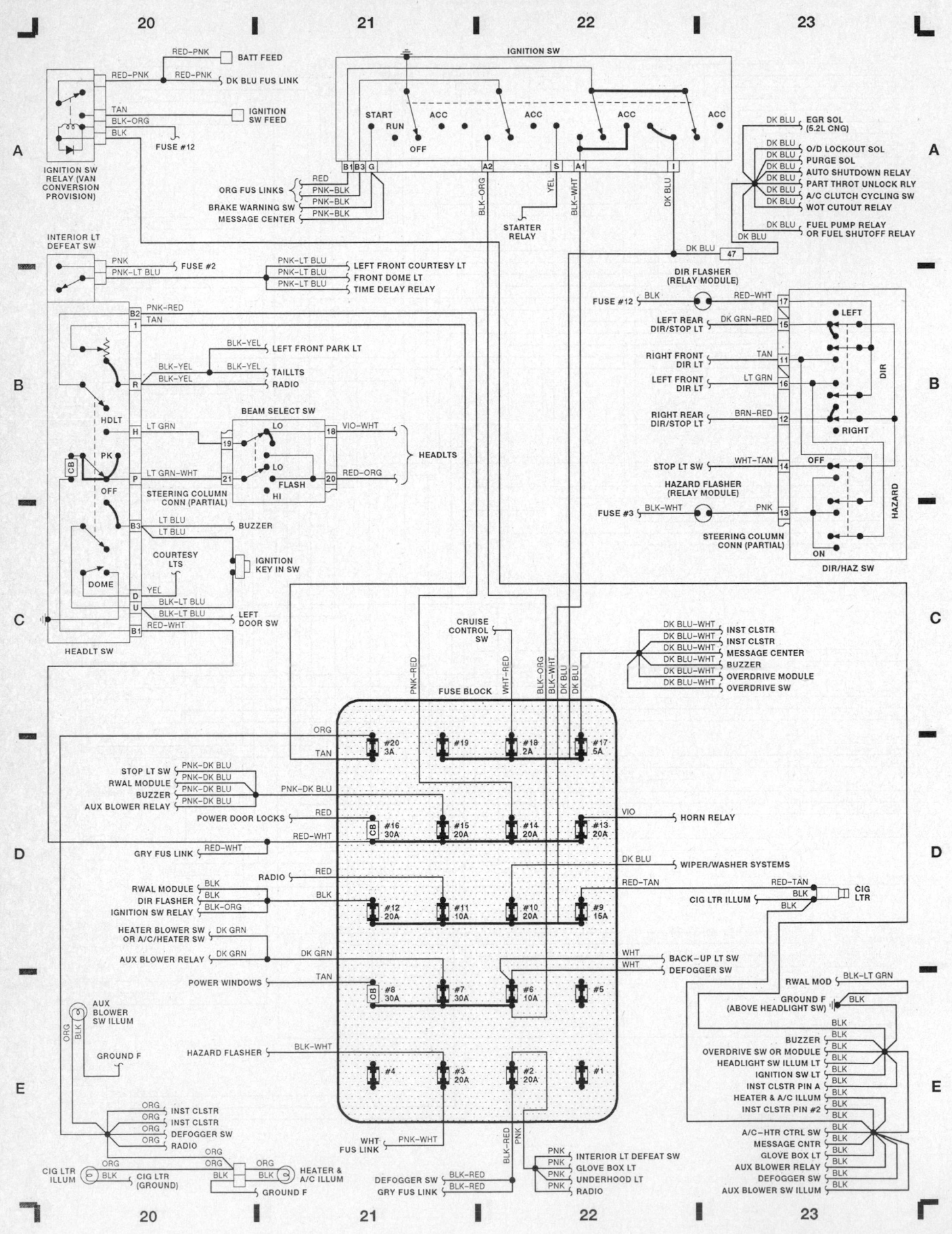

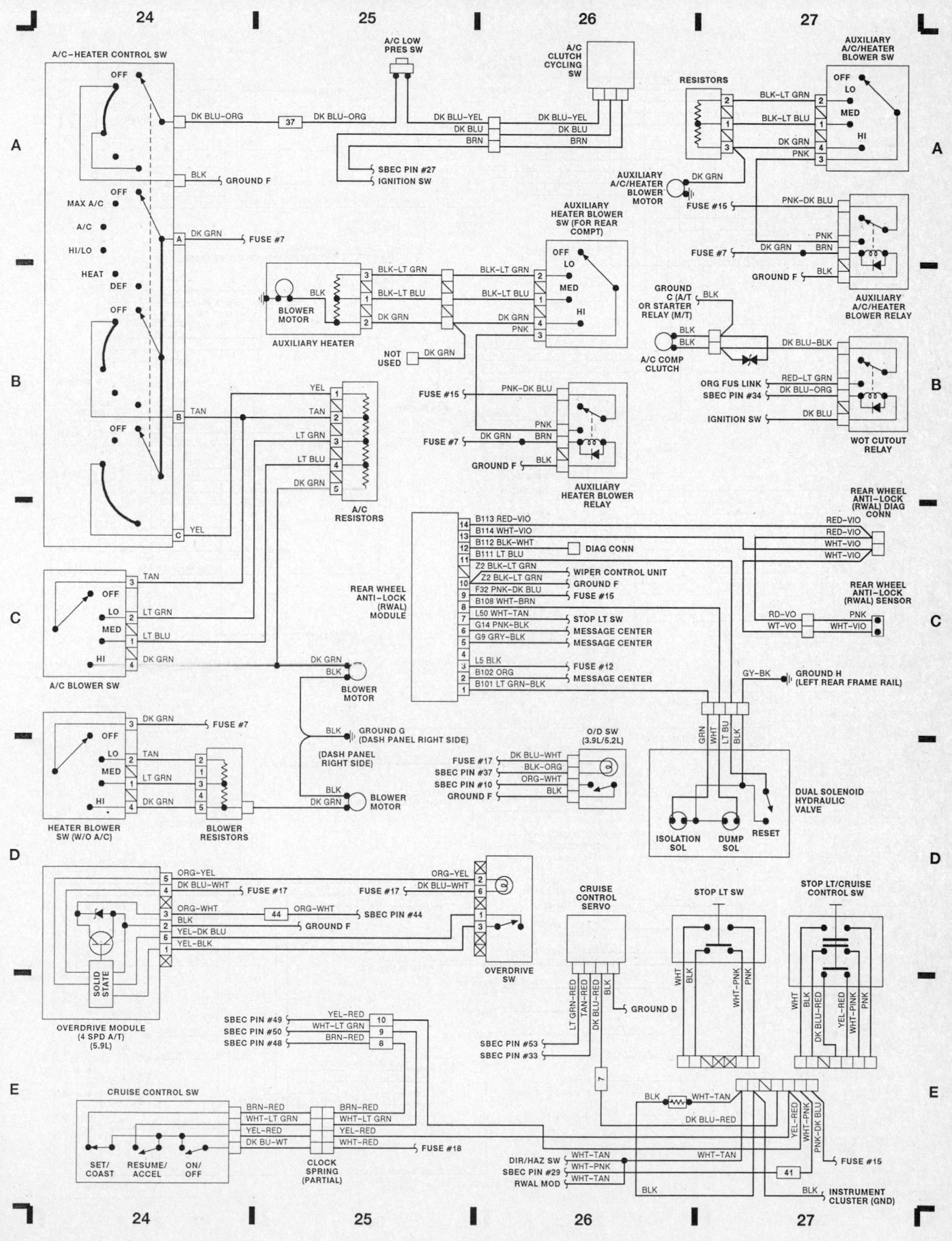

1992 WIRING DIAGRAMS
RWD Van (Cont.)

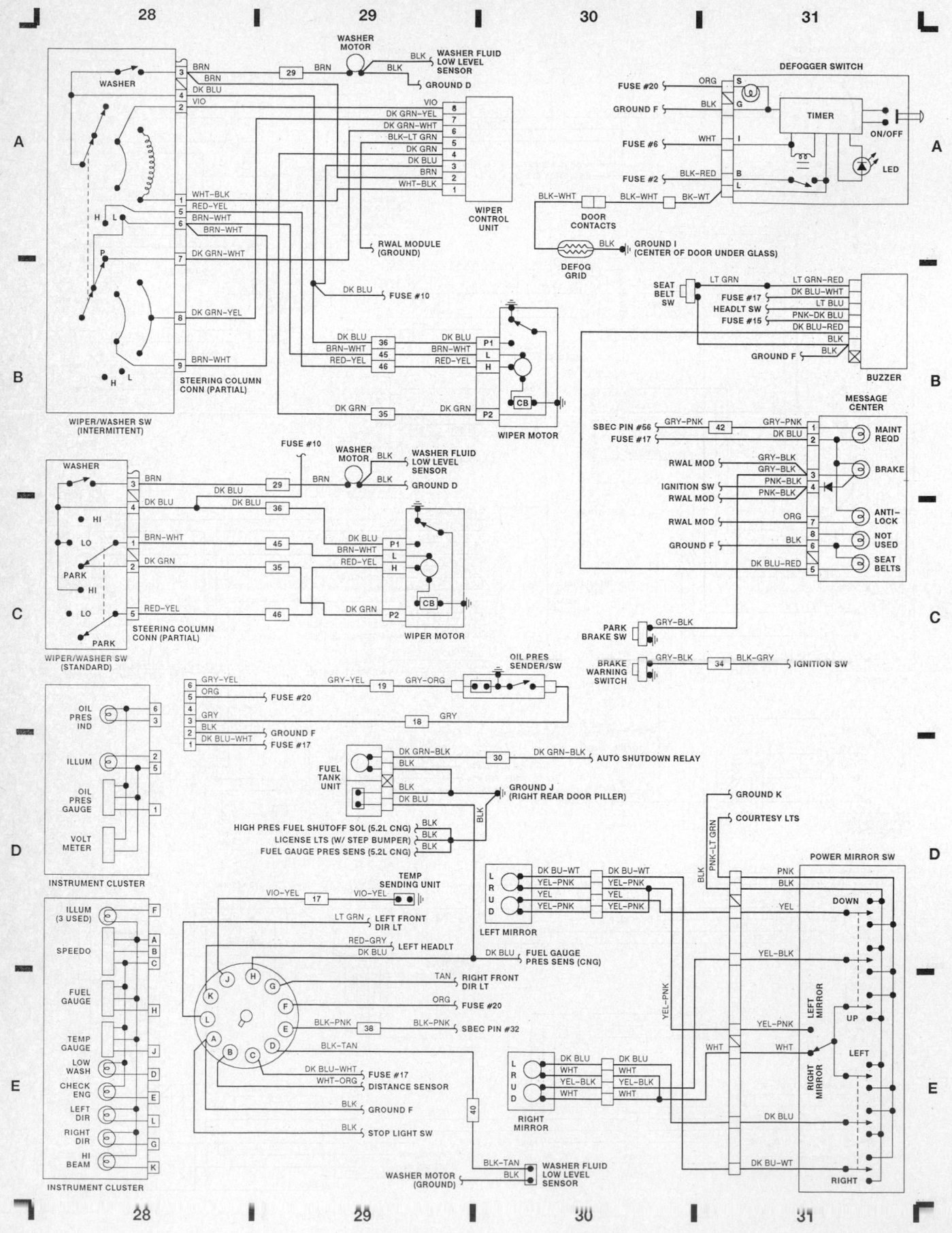

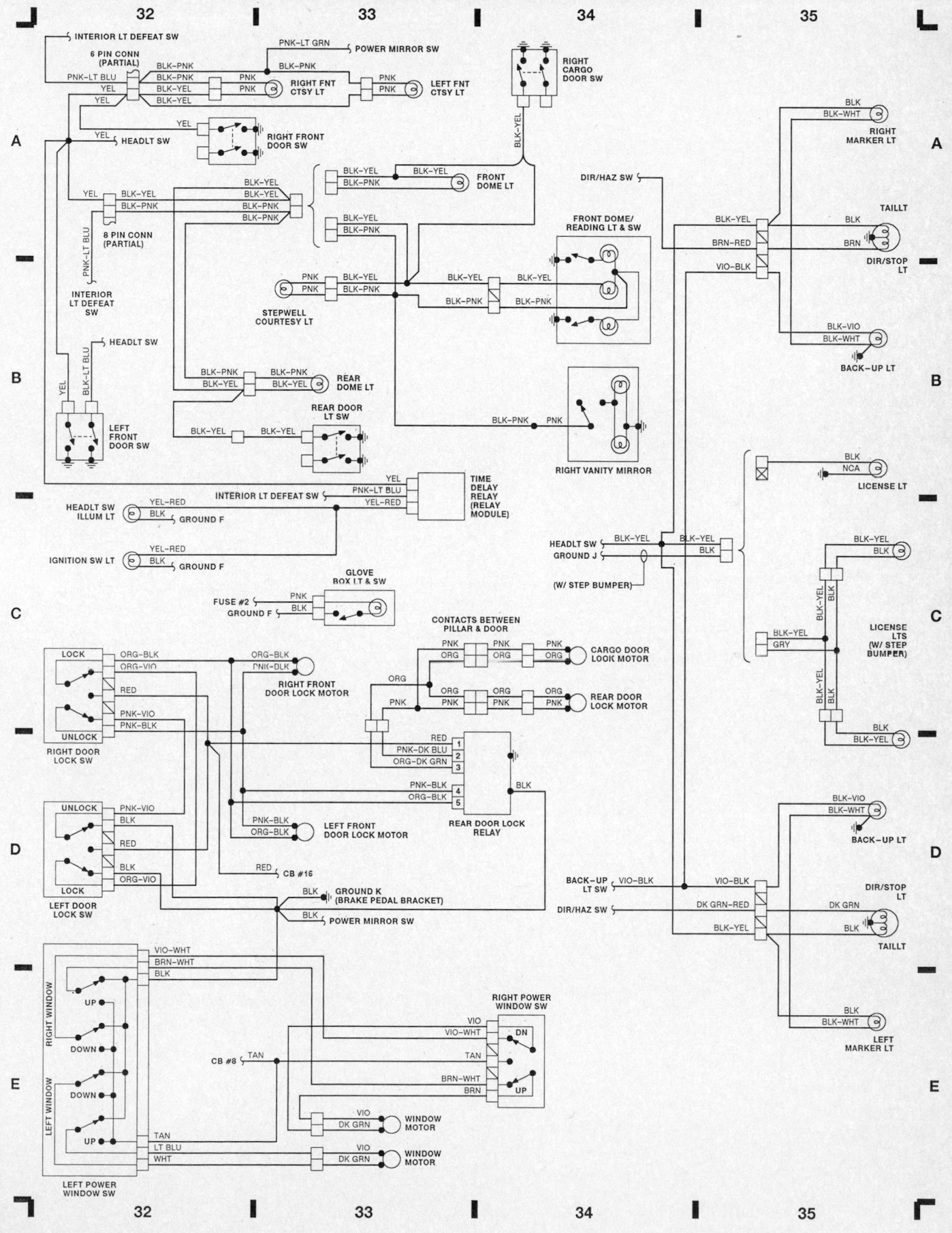

Caravan, Town & Country, Voyager

WARNING: To avoid injury from accidental air bag deployment, read and carefully follow all WARNINGS and SERVICE PRECAUTIONS.

NOTE: For information on air bag DIAGNOSIS & TESTING PROCEDURES, see MITCHELL® AIR BAG SERVICE & REPAIR MANUAL, DOMESTIC & IMPORTED MODELS.

DESCRIPTION & OPERATION

Air Bag Restraint System (ABRS) is a supplemental restraint system, designed to work in conjunction with seat belts. ABRS increases driver protection from serious injury during a front-end collision. Air bag, stored in a module in steering wheel hub, begins to inflate in 1/10 of a second when impact sensors close, creating a cushion of air between driver and steering wheel.

System consists of AIR BAG light, clockspring, air bag module, Air Bag System Diagnostic Module (ASDM) and 3 impact sensors. *See Fig. 1.* ASDM contains one impact sensor, called a safing sensor. ASDM monitors system, stores fault codes and provides information to AIR BAG light and diagnostic connector. A fault code is stored when AIR BAG light is activated for more than 12 seconds.

During a front-end collision, impact sensors receive impact force and complete a circuit through ASDM and clockspring to air bag module on steering wheel. An inflator, located inside air bag module, uses electrical current to quickly produce a large quantity of non-toxic nitrogen gas, which inflates air bag.

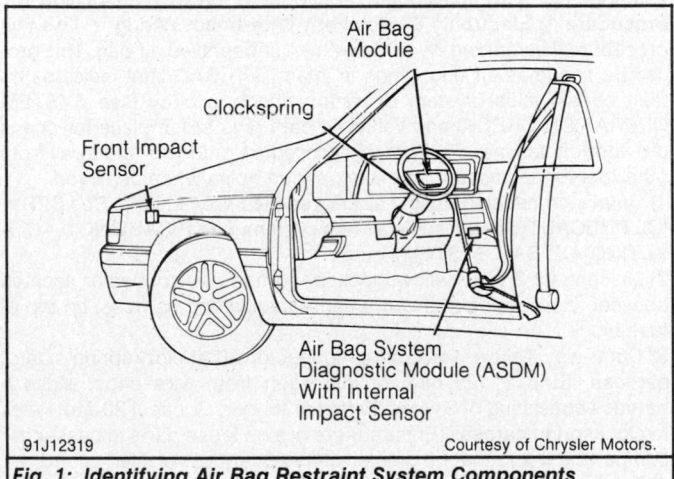

91J12319   Courtesy of Chrysler Motors.

Fig. 1: Identifying Air Bag Restraint System Components

AIR BAG LIGHT

Whenever ignition switch is in RUN or START position, AIR BAG light on instrument panel will illuminate for 6-8 seconds and then turn off, indicating ASDM has checked system and found it free of problems. If air bag light illuminates for 12 seconds or more, stays on constantly or does not come on, a system malfunction exists.

AIR BAG MODULE

Air bag module is mounted on front face of steering wheel. *See Figs. 1 and 3.* Module's inflator assembly produces non-toxic nitrogen gas to fill air bag. When a small amount of current from ASDM is applied, ignitor assembly (also known as squib or initiator) starts a thermal reaction that spreads an ignitor charge.

Surrounding ignitor charge is a pellet-filled area, which produces non-toxic nitrogen gas. Gas pressure builds and discharges from inflator through a diffuser and screen assembly, forcing steering wheel cover to burst along its seams until air bag is fully inflated. Once air bag is fully inflated, gas escapes air bag through vents at back, toward instrument panel.

AIR BAG SYSTEM
DIAGNOSTIC MODULE (ASDM)

ASDM is located behind center console, at center of instrument panel. *See Fig. 2.* ASDM stores fault codes and provides system information to AIR BAG light and diagnostic connector. A fault code is stored whenever AIR BAG light stays on, or if light is activated for 12 seconds or more. Safing sensor is an integral part of ASDM.

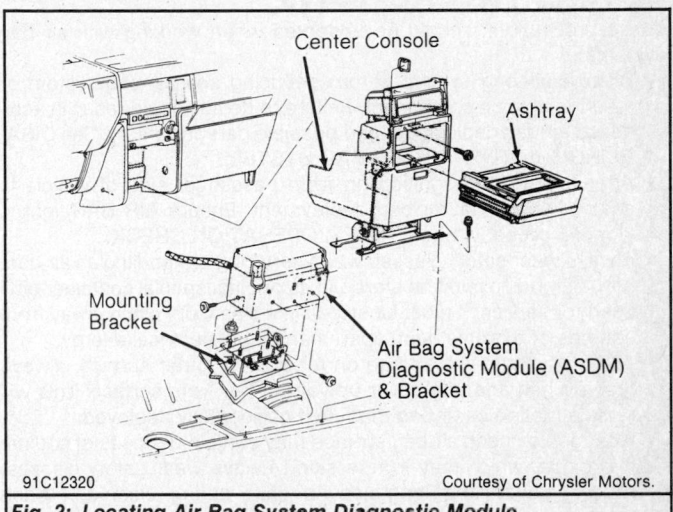

91C12320   Courtesy of Chrysler Motors.

Fig. 2: Locating Air Bag System Diagnostic Module

CLOCKSPRING

Clockspring connects air bag module to steering column wiring, completing ABRS circuit. *See Fig. 3.* Inside clockspring is a flat, ribbon-like tape of conductive material, which winds and unwinds with steering wheel movement. Clockspring is most fragile part in system. Clockspring must be centered properly to allow 1 1/2 steering wheel turns in either direction. If clockspring is not centered properly, it can break from stretching or fatigue.

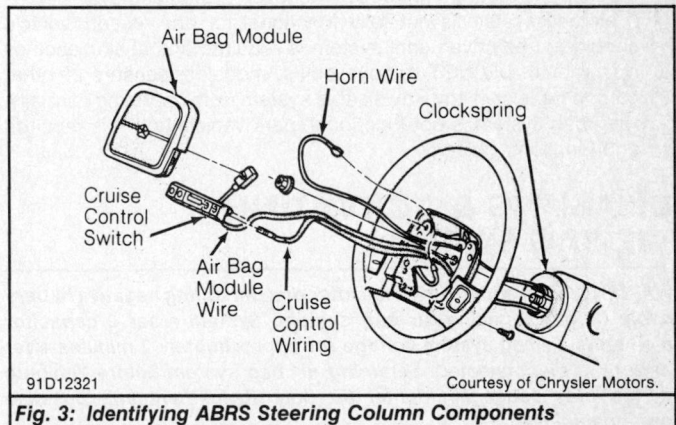

91D12321   Courtesy of Chrysler Motors.

Fig. 3: Identifying ABRS Steering Column Components

IMPACT SENSORS

Three impact sensors are used. One sensor (safing sensor) is located inside ASDM. Two impact sensors are mounted on left and right radiator closure panels. Impact sensors are inertia switches, which complete an electrical circuit when impact provides sufficient "G" force. Sensors close during crashes equivalent to a 14-MPH or more front-end collision. For air bag to deploy, safing sensor and at least one impact sensor must activate simultaneously.

SYSTEM OPERATION CHECK

WARNING: After repairs, turn ignition on from passenger side of vehicle in case of accidental air bag deployment.

Turn ignition on and observe AIR BAG light. If system is functioning properly, AIR BAG light will illuminate for 6-8 seconds, then go out. If AIR BAG light either fails to illuminate or comes on and stays on, a system malfunction exists. For information on air bag DIAGNOSIS & TESTING PROCEDURES, see MITCHELL® AIR BAG SERVICE & REPAIR MANUAL, DOMESTIC & IMPORTED MODELS.

SERVICE PRECAUTIONS

These precautions should be observed when working with air bag systems:

- Disable air bag system before servicing any air bag system or steering column component. Failure to do this could result in accidental air bag deployment and possible personal injury. See DISABLING & ACTIVATING AIR BAG SYSTEM.
- After repairs, turn ignition on from passenger side of vehicle in case of accidental air bag deployment. Ensure AIR BAG light is working properly. See SYSTEM OPERATION CHECK.
- Always wear safety glasses when servicing or handling an air bag.
- Air bag module must be stored in its original special container until used for service. It must be stored in a clean, dry place, away from sources of extreme heat, sparks and high electrical energy.
- When placing a live air bag on a bench or other surface, always face air bag and trim cover upward, away from surface. This will reduce motion of air bag module if accidentally deployed.
- After deployment, air bag surface may contain deposits of sodium hydroxide, which may irritate skin. Always wear safety glasses, rubber gloves and long-sleeved shirt during clean-up. Wash hands, using mild soap and water. Follow correct disposal procedures. See DISPOSAL PROCEDURES.
- Because of critical system operating requirements, DO NOT attempt to service any air bag components. Replace component if defective.
- NEVER allow electrical sources, including electrical test equipment, near inflator on back of air bag module.
- When carrying a live air bag module, trim cover should be pointed away from your body to minimize injury in case of accidental deployment.
- Clockspring must be replaced whenever air bag deploys.
- If air bag system is not fully functional for any reason, vehicle should not be driven until system is repaired and again becomes operational. DO NOT remove bulbs, modules, sensors or other components or in any way disable system from operating normally. If air bag system is not functional, park vehicle until it is repaired and functions properly.

DISABLING & ACTIVATING AIR BAG SYSTEM

WARNING: Wait about 2 minutes after disconnecting negative battery cable before servicing air bag system. System reserve capacitor maintains air bag system voltage for approximately 2 minutes after battery is disconnected. Servicing air bag system before 2-minute period may cause accidental air bag deployment and possible personal injury.

Disabling & Activating System For Repairs – To disable system for repairs, turn ignition off. Disconnect negative battery cable, and tape cable end. Before activating system, see SYSTEM OPERATION CHECK. To activate system, reconnect negative battery cable.

NOTE: Complete system deactivation should be performed only when ABRS is not functioning properly and vehicle needs to be driven.

Complete System Deactivation – **1)** Disconnect negative battery cable, and tape cable end. Disconnect 2-way Yellow clockspring harness connector, located between clockspring and instrument panel wiring harness, on top of fuse block.

2) Clockspring connector may also be disconnected at ASDM. Reconnect battery, and drive vehicle to repair area. Disconnect negative battery cable, and tape cable end.

3) Reconnect clockspring connector. Reconnect negative battery cable. Repair as required.

DISPOSAL PROCEDURES

WARNING: Vehicle interior will contain sodium hydroxide powder, a by-product of air bag deployment. Since powder can irritate skin, eyes, nose, or throat, be sure to wear safety glasses, rubber gloves and long-sleeved shirt during clean-up.

DEPLOYED AIR BAG

1) Begin clean-up by putting tape over air bag exhaust vent, so no additional powder will escape into vehicle interior. Using a vacuum cleaner, remove residual powder from A/C-heater outlets and vehicle interior.

2) Turn blower motor on low speed for a few minutes and exit vehicle. Turn blower off. Vacuum additional powder expelled from plenum. Vacuum interior again to recover all powder. Avoid kneeling or sitting on uncleaned surfaces. Dispose of deployed air bag as any part.

UNDEPLOYED AIR BAG

WARNING: Failure to follow service precautions may result in air bag deployment and personal injury. See SERVICE PRECAUTIONS.

In some accidents, such as side or rear-end collisions, air bag may not deploy. If damage results in scrapping vehicle or selling it for junk, air bag must be deployed. Air bag module should never be sold as a used component. Follow appropriate procedure for deployment of air bags.

Procedure 1: Electronic Deployment With Intact Wiring – Use this procedure if scrapping a vehicle with an undeployed air bag. This procedure assumes air bag wiring is intact: AIR BAG light indicates no fault codes, initial system operation check is okay (see SYSTEM OPERATION CHECK) and vehicle's battery is still in place (or one is provided for testing). Perform this procedure outdoors and away from other personnel, as air bag makes a loud noise when deployed.

1) Before proceeding, follow air bag service precautions. See SERVICE PRECAUTIONS. Disable air bag system. See DISABLING & ACTIVATING AIR BAG SYSTEM.

2) Disconnect 2-way Yellow clockspring harness connector, located between clockspring and instrument panel wiring harness, on top of fuse block.

3) Cut 2-way Yellow clockspring connector off at clockspring side of harness. Strip 1" (25 mm) of insulation from wire ends. Make a harness consisting of 2 wires 20 feet or longer. Connect 20-foot wires to clockspring harness. Ensure there are no loose parts in passenger compartment and that no one is within 20 feet of vehicle.

4) Stay at least 20 feet away from vehicle. Connect other 2 ends of 20-foot wires to terminals of a 12-volt battery. When deployment is achieved, loud bang will be heard and air bag will inflate. After air bag module deploys, allow air bag module to cool and dust settle before approaching vehicle. If air bag fails to deploy, go to PROCEDURE 2.

Procedure 2: Remote Deployment Of Air Bag – Use this procedure if scrapping a vehicle with live air bag, but a problem in electrical system prevents deployment with air bag still installed in vehicle. Also use this procedure if PROCEDURE 1 was unsuccessful.

WARNING: Perform remote deployment outdoors. NEVER attempt to deploy air bag module inside a building, within 20 feet of personnel, or with air bag module trim cover facing downward.

1) Before proceeding, follow air bag service precautions. See SERVICE PRECAUTIONS. Disable air bag system. See DISABLING & ACTIVATING AIR BAG SYSTEM. Remove air bag module. See AIR BAG MODULE & STEERING WHEEL under REMOVAL & INSTALLATION.

2) Cut pigtail wiring harness between clockspring and air bag as close to clockspring housing as possible. Reconnect other end of pigtail harness back into air bag module.

3) Strip 1" (25 mm) of insulation from cut ends of harness. Position air bag module with trim cover facing upward. Connect two 20-foot wires to end of harness wires. Move 20 feet away. Connect other end of 20 foot wires to terminals of a 12-volt battery. After air bag module deploys, let air bag module cool and dust settle before approaching.

REMOVAL & INSTALLATION

WARNING: Failure to follow air bag service precautions may result in air bag deployment and personal injury. See SERVICE PRECAUTIONS. Always use NEW parts and correct part number for vehicle being worked on. After component replacement, always perform a system operation check to ensure proper system operation. See SYSTEM OPERATION CHECK.

LEFT & RIGHT IMPACT SENSORS

CAUTION: Always replace impact sensors if faulty. NEVER repair or disassemble impact sensors. Handle impact sensors carefully. Replace impact sensors if they are dented, cracked, deformed rusted, or after air bag has deployed.

Removal – **1)** Before proceeding, follow air bag service precautions. See SERVICE PRECAUTIONS. Disable air bag system. See DISABLING & ACTIVATING AIR BAG SYSTEM.
2) Impact sensors are mounted on left and right side of radiator closure panels. *See Fig. 1.* Disconnect impact sensor electrical connector. Remove impact sensor-to-radiator closure panel retaining screws. Remove impact sensor.
Installation – **1)** Mount impact sensor with arrow pointing toward front of vehicle, on engine side of radiator closure panel. Install NEW screws and tighten to specification. See TORQUE SPECIFICATIONS table at end of article. Use only screws supplied with new impact sensor.
2) Install electrical connector on impact sensor, ensuring locking tab is engaged. Before activating system, see SYSTEM OPERATION CHECK. Connect negative battery cable. Check AIR BAG indicator light to ensure system is functioning properly.

AIR BAG SYSTEM DIAGNOSTIC MODULE (ASDM)

WARNING: ASDM contains safing sensor which enables ABRS system to activate air bag. To avoid accidental air bag deployment, NEVER connect ASDM electrically to system unless it is bolted to vehicle.

Removal – **1)** Before proceeding, follow air bag service precautions. See SERVICE PRECAUTIONS. Disable air bag system. See DISABLING & ACTIVATING AIR BAG SYSTEM.
2) ASDM is located behind center console, at center of instrument panel. *See Fig. 2.* Remove forward console or cover as necessary. Remove ASDM module and bracket mounting screws. Carefully lift module up and rearward. Disconnect wiring at ASDM, and remove ASDM module.
Installation – **1)** Install ASDM module with arrow pointing toward front of vehicle. Install electrical connectors, ensuring connectors are locked into position. Place ASDM module and bracket on lower mounting bracket, using locating tab to position ASDM module.
2) Install ASDM module and bracket with new screws and tighten to specification. See TORQUE SPECIFICATIONS table at end of article. Use only screws supplied with new ASDM module. Before activating system, see SYSTEM OPERATION CHECK. Check AIR BAG indicator light to ensure system is functioning properly.

AIR BAG MODULE & STEERING WHEEL

NOTE: Clockspring must be replaced whenever replacing a deployed air bag. See CLOCKSPRING under REMOVAL & INSTALLATION.

Removal – **1)** Before proceeding, follow air bag service precautions. See SERVICE PRECAUTIONS. Disable air bag system. See DISABLING & ACTIVATING AIR BAG SYSTEM.

CAUTION: Failure to position wheels in straight-ahead position with steering wheel locked when removing steering wheel could damage clockspring and/or require clockspring to be readjusted.

2) Air bag module is mounted on face of steering wheel. *See Figs. 1 and 3.* Ensure wheels are in straight-ahead position and steering wheel is locked. Remove air bag module-to-steering wheel nuts from back side of steering wheel.
3) Lift air bag module and disconnect electrical connector. Remove cruise control switch and connectors (if equipped) or cover.
4) Remove steering wheel retaining nut. Using Puller (C-3428B), remove steering wheel. Self-centering clockspring will automatically lock in place when steering wheel is removed.
Installation – **1)** If replacing a deployed air bag module, clockspring must be replaced. See CLOCKSPRING under REMOVAL & INSTALLATION. Position steering wheel on column. Ensure flats, on steering wheel hub, fit formations on inside of clockspring.
2) Pull air bag module wire and cruise control switch wire (if equipped) through larger bottom hole and horn wire through small upper hole in steering wheel.
3) Install steering wheel retaining nut and tighten to specification. See TORQUE SPECIFICATIONS table at end of article. Connect horn and cruise control wiring.
4) Attach cruise control switch to steering wheel (if equipped). Connect air bag wire connector to air bag module, and secure air bag module to steering wheel.
5) Tighten air bag module-to-steering wheel nuts to specification. See TORQUE SPECIFICATIONS table at end of article. Before activating system, see SYSTEM OPERATION CHECK. Check AIR BAG indicator light to ensure system is functioning properly.

CLOCKSPRING

CAUTION: Failure to position wheels in straight-ahead position with steering wheel locked when removing steering wheel could damage clockspring and/or require clockspring readjustment.

NOTE: Clockspring is self-centering and will automatically lock in centered position when steering wheel is removed. Adjustment is only required if centering position is disturbed.

Removal – **1)** If replacing a deployed air bag, clockspring must be replaced. Before proceeding, follow air bag service precautions. See SERVICE PRECAUTIONS. Disable air bag system. See DISABLING & ACTIVATING AIR BAG SYSTEM.
2) Clockspring is located behind steering wheel. *See Figs. 1, 3 and 4.* Remove air bag module and steering wheel. See AIR BAG MODULE & STEERING WHEEL under REMOVAL & INSTALLATION. When steering wheel is removed, self-centering clockspring will automatically lock in place.
3) Remove upper and lower steering column shrouds to gain access to clockspring wiring.
4) Disconnect 2-way Yellow clockspring harness connector between clockspring and instrument panel wiring harness, on top of fuse block.
5) Remove clockspring by releasing 2 tabs on side of clockspring. *See Fig. 4.* Clocksprings CANNOT be repaired and must be replaced if faulty.
Installation – **1)** Snap clockspring onto steering column. Adjust clockspring if centering adjustment is disturbed. See CLOCKSPRING CENTERING under ADJUSTMENTS before installing steering wheel. Connect clockspring wiring connectors. Install steering column covers.
2) Install steering wheel. Ensure flats, on steering wheel hub, fit formations on inside of clockspring. Pull horn wire through small upper hole and air bag module and cruise control wires (if equipped) through larger bottom hole in steering wheel. *See Fig. 4.*
3) Tighten retaining nut to specification. See TORQUE SPECIFICATIONS table at end of article.
4) Install electrical connectors on horn and cruise control wires (if equipped). Connect air bag module wire to air bag module, ensuring

latching arms on connector are visible on top of connector housing. Tighten nuts to specification. See TORQUE SPECIFICATIONS table at end of article.

5) Before activating system, see SYSTEM OPERATION CHECK. Check AIR BAG indicator light to ensure system is functioning properly.

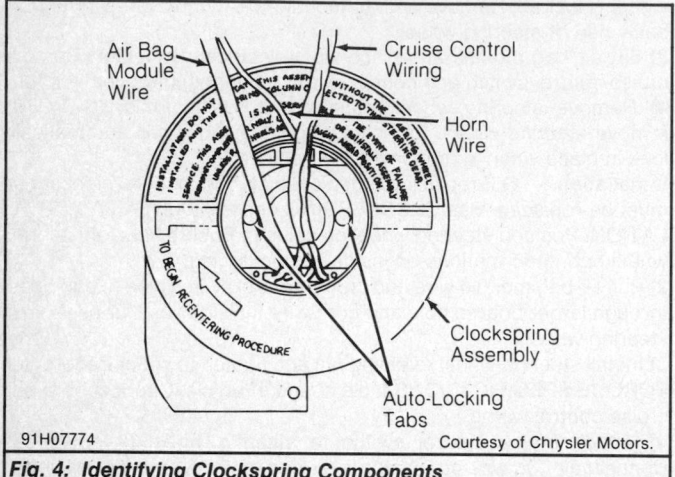

91H07774   Courtesy of Chrysler Motors.

Fig. 4: Identifying Clockspring Components

ADJUSTMENTS

CLOCKSPRING CENTERING

CAUTION: If rotating part of clockspring is not positioned properly with steering column and front wheels, clockspring failure may result. Following procedure must be used to center clockspring.

1) Before proceeding, follow air bag service precautions. See SERVICE PRECAUTIONS. Disable air bag system. See DISABLING & ACTIVATING AIR BAG SYSTEM.

2) Place front wheels in straight-ahead position. Remove air bag module and steering wheel. See AIR BAG MODULE & STEERING WHEEL under REMOVAL & INSTALLATION. Depress 2 plastic auto-locking tabs. *See Fig. 4.* Rotate clockspring rotor in clockwise direction to end of its travel.

3) From end of its travel, rotate rotor 2 1/2 turns in counterclockwise direction. Horn wire should end up at top and air bag module wire at bottom. *See Fig. 4.*

4) Install steering wheel and air bag module. Tighten retaining nuts to specification. See TORQUE SPECIFICATIONS table. Check AIR BAG indicator light to ensure system is functioning properly. See SYSTEM OPERATION CHECK.

TORQUE SPECIFICATIONS
TORQUE SPECIFICATIONS

Application	Ft. Lbs. (N.m)
Steering Wheel Nut	45 (61)

	INCH Lbs. (N.m)
Air Bag Diagnostic Module Screw	35 (4)
Air Bag Module Nut	80-100 (9-11)
Impact Sensor Screw	40-60 (4.5-7.0)

Caravan, Dakota, Pickup, Ramcharger, RWD Van, Town & Country, Voyager

WARNING: If vehicle is equipped with air bag, air bag MUST be deactivated before servicing cruise control components on or around steering column. See AIR BAG RESTRAINT SYSTEM article in SAFETY EQUIPMENT.

DESCRIPTION

The cruise control system is electronically controlled and vacuum operated. The electronic control is integrated into the Single Board Engine Controller (SBEC). System consists of SBEC, servo, cruise control switch panel, vacuum reservoir, distance (speed) sensor, brakelight switch and park/neutral switch (A/T models). System controls are located on the steering wheel and consist of on/off, resume/accel and set/decel or set/coast buttons.

OPERATION

SYSTEM CONTROLS

To Set Speed Control – Press on/off button to turn cruise control on. Accelerate to desired speed (at least 35 MPH), and depress set/decel or set/coast button. Vehicle speed will be maintained.

To Disengage Speed Control – Depress brake pedal or clutch pedal. The on/off button may also be used, but set speed will be erased from memory. If clutch pedal is used to disengage cruise control, engine speed will increase before cruise control cuts out.

To Resume Previous Speed – If set speed has not been erased from memory and vehicle speed is more than 30 MPH, press resume/accel button.

To Increase Speed – With cruise control system on, increase set speed by pressing and releasing resume/accel button within one second. Each press and release of button will cause an increase of 2 MPH. For example, 3 presses would result in a speed increase of 6 MPH. To increase speed gradually, hold resume/accel button down until desire speed is reached. When button is released, new set speed will be maintained.

To Decrease Speed – With cruise control system on, decrease set speed by pressing set/decel or set/coast button. Vehicle speed will gradually decrease. Releasing button will set a new set speed as long as vehicle speed is still more than 35 MPH.

NOTE: Speed control system will automatically disengage when vehicle speed decreases to less than 35 MPH or increases to more than 85 MPH.

SELF-DIAGNOSTIC SYSTEM

SYSTEM DIAGNOSTICS

Self-diagnostic capabilities of this system, if used properly, can simplify testing. Cruise control system is monitored by Single Board Engine Controller (SBEC).

If a problem is sensed with a monitored circuit, a fault code is stored in SBEC. Once codes are known, refer to FAULT CODES to determine questionable circuit. Test circuits and repair or replace components as required. If problem is repaired or ceases to exist, the SBEC cancels that fault code after 50 ignition on/off cycles. To clear codes, refer to CLEARING FAULT CODES.

A specific fault code results from a particular system failure, but is not necessarily reason for failure. Fault code does not condemn a specific component, but calls out a probable malfunction area.

SERVICE PRECAUTIONS

Before proceeding with diagnosis, follow these precautions:
- Vehicle must have a fully charged battery and functional charging system.

- Probe SBEC 60-pin connector from pin side. DO NOT backprobe SBEC connector.
- DO NOT cause short circuits when performing electrical tests. This will set additional fault codes, making diagnosis of original problem more difficult.
- Always repair lowest fault code number (CHECK ENGINE light) or first fault displayed (DRB-II) first.
- Always perform VERIFICATION TEST SP-VER under SELF-DIAGNOSTIC TESTS after repairs are made.

VISUAL INSPECTION

Always perform a visual inspection before attempting to diagnose cruise control system problems. A visual inspection may quickly identify cause of a malfunction and eliminate the need for diagnostic testing. A thorough visual inspection includes checking for disconnected or faulty wiring harness connectors, leaking or misrouted vacuum hoses, corroded battery terminals and bare wires.

DIAGNOSTIC PROCEDURE

NOTE: When using self-diagnostic tests for diagnosis, DO NOT skip any steps or incorrect diagnosis may result. Always start with TEST SP-1A under SELF-DIAGNOSTIC TESTS.

Perform a visual inspection before attempting to diagnose engine control system problems. See VISUAL INSPECTION. Enter on-board diagnostics, and retrieve fault codes. See ENTERING ON-BOARD DIAGNOSTICS. If fault codes are not present and/or DRB-II (Diagnostic Readout Box II) is used, proceed to TEST SP-1A under SELF-DIAGNOSTIC TESTS.

ENTERING ON-BOARD DIAGNOSTICS

NOTE: Although other scan testers are available, manufacturer recommends using DRB-II (Diagnostic Readout Box II) to diagnose system. CHECK ENGINE light function can be used but has limited diagnostic usage.

CHECK ENGINE Light Diagnostic Mode – 1) With key inserted in ignition switch, cycle ignition switch to ON position 3 times. On third cycle, leave ignition switch in ON position. Record 2-digit fault codes as displayed by flashing CHECK ENGINE light.

2) For example, Code 34 is displayed as a series of 3 flashes in rapid succession, a 4-second pause, then 4 flashes in rapid succession. After a slightly longer pause, other codes stored are displayed in numerical order.

3) When CHECK ENGINE light begins to flash fault codes, it cannot be stopped. If you lose count, it will be necessary to start over. Code 55 indicates end of fault code display.

4) Refer to FAULT CODES to translate trouble code number to a system fault description (DRB-II display). Once trouble area is identified, refer to TEST SP-1A under SELF-DIAGNOSTIC TESTS to diagnose problem.

NOTE: If codes exist that are not related to cruise control system, see appropriate SELF-DIAGNOSTICS article in ENGINE PERFORMANCE.

DRB-II Diagnostic Mode – 1) Connect DRB-II to engine diagnostic connector. Connector is located in engine compartment, near SBEC. Start engine. Turn ignition switch to ON position. Enter SPEED CONTROL MENU. To enter SPEED CONTROL MENU, see DRB-II TEST FUNCTIONS.

2) At SPEED CONTROL MENU, press "2" (READ FAULTS) key. Press ENTER key. After fault codes are accessed, refer to TEST SP-1A to diagnose problem. If no fault codes are present, see TROUBLE SHOOTING.

3) To erase fault codes while in this option, press ATM key. Press "2" (ERASE) key at DRB-II display. DRB-II will display ERASE FAULTS ARE YOU SURE? (ENTER TO ERASE). Press ENTER key.

4) When DRB-II is finished erasing fault codes, it will display FAULTS ERASED. This display will remain until ATM key is pressed. After ATM key is pressed, display will return to SPEED CONTROL MENU screen.

FAULT CODES
FAULT CODES

Code	Display On DRB-II	Fault Condition
15	NO VEHICLE SPEED SIGNAL	No Vehicle Distance (Speed) Sensor Signal Detected During Road Load Conditions.
34	SPEED CONTROL SOLENOID CIRCUITS	An Open Or Shorted Condition Detected In Cruise Control Vacuum Or Vent Solenoid Circuits.
77	SPEED CONTROL POWER RELAY CIRCUIT	An Open Or Shorted Condition Detected In Cruise Control Power Relay Circuit.

CLEARING FAULT CODES

NOTE: Fault codes can also be cleared in READ FAULTS option of DRB-II. To ensure that all faults are read, use READ FAULTS option to erase fault codes. See DRB-II DIAGNOSTIC MODE under ENTERING ON-BOARD DIAGNOSTICS.

1) If DRB-II is not available, go to step **3)**. If DRB-II is available, enter SPEED CONTROL MENU. See DRB-II TEST FUNCTIONS. At SPEED CONTROL menu, press "5" (ADJUSTMENTS) key. Press ENTER key. At ADJUSTMENTS menu, press "1" (ERASE FAULTS) key. Press ENTER key.
2) DRB-II will display ERASE FAULTS ARE YOU SURE? (ENTER TO ERASE). Press ENTER key. When DRB-II is finished erasing fault codes, screen will display FAULTS ERASED.
3) If DRB-II is not available, fault codes may be cleared by disconnecting negative battery cable for at least 15 seconds, allowing SBEC to clear fault codes.

DRB-II TEST FUNCTIONS
SPEED CONTROL MENU

1) To perform cruise control system tests using DRB-II, DRB-II must be in SPEED CONTROL MENU. At SPEED CONTROL MENU, fault codes and DRB-II test functions can be accessed.
2) To reach SPEED CONTROL MENU, turn ignition off and connect DRB-II to engine diagnostic connector. Connector is located in engine compartment, near SBEC. Turn ignition switch to RUN position.

NOTE: DO NOT touch DRB-II keypad during DRB-II power-up sequence or an error message will result.

3) All DRB-II character positions will glow and copyright information will appear on screen for a few seconds. If DRB-II screen is blank or any error messages appear, refer to DRB-II PROBLEMS & ERROR MESSAGES under DRB-II TEST FUNCTIONS in appropriate SELF-DIAGNOSTICS article in ENGINE PERFORMANCE.
4) After a few seconds DRB-II menu will appear. At DRB-II menu, press "4" (SELECT SYSTEM) key. Press ENTER key. At SELECT SYSTEM menu, press "1" (ENGINE) key. Press ENTER key. DRB-II menu will appear indicating engine year, size, type of transmission and SBEC part number.
5) After a few seconds AIR COND menu will appear. Press "1" (WITH A/C) or press "2" (WITHOUT A/C). DRB-II display will change to ENGINE SYSTEMS menu. At ENGINE SYSTEMS menu, press "3" (SPEED CONTROL) key. Press ENTER key.
6) Display will change to SPEED CONTROL. At SPEED CONTROL MENU, specific test functions programmed into DRB-II can be performed. Following DRB-II modes can be accessed: SYSTEM TEST, READ FAULTS, STATE DISPLAYS, ACTUATOR TEST and ADJUSTMENTS.

NOTE: For more information on DRB-II test functions, see DRB-II TEST FUNCTIONS in appropriate SELF-DIAGNOSTICS article in ENGINE PERFORMANCE.

TROUBLE SHOOTING

NO CRUISE CONTROL WHEN SET BUTTON IS PRESSED & RELEASED
Fuse blown. No vacuum at servo. Speed control cable is disconnected. Brakelight switch out of adjustment. Faulty electrical circuit. Faulty neutral safety switch input to SBEC. Defective servo. Faulty SBEC.

CRUISE CONTROL ENGAGES WITHOUT ACTUATING CRUISE SET BUTTON
Faulty electrical circuit or control switch. Defective servo.

CRUISE CONTROL ENGAGES WHEN ENGINE IS STARTED
Faulty electrical circuit. Defective servo.

ERRATIC SPEED OR ENGINE SHUTS OFF
Poor engine performance (surge). Defective distance (speed) sensor. Vacuum leak. Faulty servo. Faulty SBEC.

CRUISE CONTROL DISENGAGES ON ROUGH ROAD
Brakelight switch out of adjustment. Faulty electrical circuit.

ENGINE DOES NOT RETURN TO NORMAL IDLE
Kinked or damaged cruise control cable. Faulty throttle linkage.

NO RESUME WHEN RESUME BUTTON IS PRESSED
Defective switch. Faulty electrical circuit.

CRUISE CONTROL DOES NOT DISENGAGE WITH BRAKE PEDAL DEPRESSED
Defective or improperly adjusted brakelight switch. Speed control cable is kinked or damaged. Faulty electrical circuit.

TESTING (WITHOUT DRB-II)
BRAKELIGHT SWITCH
Disconnect brakelight switch 6-pin connector. Using an ohmmeter, check for continuity at switch side of connector terminals. See TESTING BRAKELIGHT SWITCH table. If continuity is not as specified, check brakelight switch adjustment. If switch adjustment is okay, replace defective brakelight switch.

TESTING BRAKELIGHT SWITCH

Brake Pedal Position	Check Between Terminals No.	Continuity
Released	1 & 4	Yes
	3 & 6	Yes
	2 & 5	No
Depressed	1 & 4	No
	3 & 6	No
	2 & 5	Yes

CRUISE CONTROL CIRCUIT

1) Disconnect Single Board Engine Controller (SBEC) 60-pin connector. Connect negative lead of voltmeter to a good chassis ground near SBEC. Turn ignition switch to ON position. Depress and hold cruise control switch in OFF position.

2) Touch positive lead of voltmeter to terminal No. 53 (Light Green/Red wire) at SBEC connector. Voltage should be zero volts with cruise control switch in OFF position and battery voltage with cruise control switch in ON position. If voltage is not as specified, repair Light Green/Red wire as necessary. If voltage is as specified, go to next step.

3) Measure voltage at terminal No. 33 (Tan/Red wire) at SBEC connector. Voltage should be zero volts with cruise control switch off and battery voltage with cruise control switch on. If voltage is not as specified, repair Tan/Red wire as necessary. If voltage is as specified, go to next step.

4) Measure voltage at terminal No. 48 (Brown/Red wire) at SBEC connector with switch in specified position. Voltage reading should be as follows:

- Zero volts with cruise control switch off.
- Battery voltage with cruise control switch on.
- Pressing cruise control set button should cause voltage to change from battery voltage to zero volts.

If voltage is as specified, go to next step. If voltage is not as specified, check cruise control switch. See CRUISE CONTROL SWITCH under TESTING (WITHOUT DRB-II). If cruise control switch is defective, replace switch. If cruise control switch is okay, repair Brown/Red wire as necessary.

5) Measure voltage at terminal No. 50 (White/Light Green wire) at SBEC connector. Voltage should be zero volts with cruise control switch in OFF or ON positions. With cruise control switch on, depress resume button.

6) Voltage at terminal No. 50 should change from zero volts to battery voltage. If voltage is as specified, go to next step. If voltage is not as specified, check cruise control switch. See CRUISE CONTROL SWITCH under TESTING (WITHOUT DRB-II). Replace cruise control switch, if defective. If cruise control switch is okay, repair White/Light Green wire as necessary.

7) Measure voltage at terminal No. 49 (Yellow/Red wire) at SBEC connector. Voltage should be zero volts with cruise control switch off and battery voltage with cruise control switch on. If voltage is as specified, go to next step. If voltage is not as specified, repair Yellow/Red wire as necessary.

8) While depressing brake pedal, using an ohmmeter, check resistance between terminal No. 29 (White/Pink wire) at SBEC connector and ground. If continuity exists, go to step **10)**. If no continuity exists, check continuity at White/Pink wire between terminals No. 29 at SBEC connector and No. 1 at brakelight switch. If no continuity exists, repair open in White/Pink wire. If continuity exists, go to next step.

9) Test brakelight switch. See BRAKELIGHT SWITCH under TESTING (WITHOUT DRB-II). Replace brakelight switch if it is defective. If brakelight switch is okay, check continuity at Black wire between terminal No. 2 at brakelight switch and ground. If continuity exists, go to next step. If no continuity exists, repair open Black wire.

10) Using an external ohmmeter, check resistance between ground and terminal No. 30 (Brown/Yellow wire) at SBEC connector. With transmission in Drive, no continuity should exist. With transmission in Neutral or Park, continuity should exist. If results are as specified, test is complete. If test results are not as specified, check neutral safety switch and/or back-up switch.

CRUISE CONTROL SERVO

1) Turn ignition switch to ON position. Disconnect servo 4-pin connector. Using a voltmeter, measure voltage at terminal No. 2 (Dark Blue/Red wire) at servo connector. If battery voltage is not present, go to next step. If battery voltage is present, go to step **7)**.

2) Disconnect brakelight switch 6-pin connector. Measure voltage at terminal No. 6 (Dark Blue/Red wire). If battery voltage is not present, go to next step. If battery voltage is present, test brakelight switch. See BRAKELIGHT SWITCH under TESTING (WITHOUT DRB-II). Replace brakelight switch if it is defective. If brakelight switch is okay, repair Dark Blue/Red wire as necessary.

3) Access cruise control switch. See Fig. 1. Disconnect cruise control 4-pin connector. Measure voltage at terminal No. 1 (Yellow/Red wire) at cruise control connector.

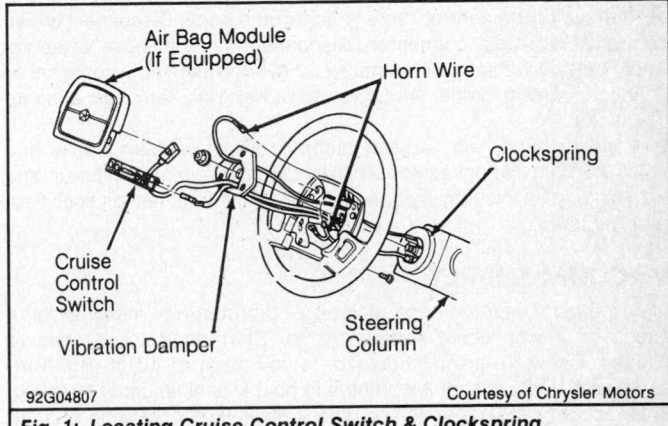

92G04807   Courtesy of Chrysler Motors

Fig. 1: Locating Cruise Control Switch & Clockspring Connectors

4) If battery voltage is not present, go to step **6)**. If battery voltage is present, test cruise control switch. See CRUISE CONTROL SWITCH under TESTING (WITHOUT DRB-II). Replace cruise control switch, if defective. If cruise control switch is okay, check for continuity across clockspring.

5) If no continuity exists across clockspring, replace clockspring. If continuity exists across clockspring, repair Yellow/Red wire between clockspring and brakelight switch.

6) If battery voltage is not present in step **4)**, measure voltage at input side of cruise control fuse. If battery voltage is not present, repair open in wire between ignition switch and cruise control fuse. If battery voltage is present, check cruise control fuse. Replace fuse if blown. If fuse is okay, repair wire between fuse and clockspring.

7) If battery voltage is present in step **1)**, connect a jumper wire between terminal No. 2 (Dark Blue/Red wire) at cruise control servo connector and terminal No. 2 at cruise control servo.

8) With jumper wire connected, battery voltage should be present at remaining 3 terminals at servo. If battery voltage is present at remaining 3 terminals of servo, go to next step. If battery voltage is not present at remaining 3 terminals of servo, replace servo.

9) Using an ohmmeter, check for continuity between terminal No. 1 (Black wire) at servo connector and ground. If no continuity exists, repair open in Black wire. If continuity exists, test is complete.

CRUISE CONTROL SWITCH

Remove cruise control switch. Using an ohmmeter, check cruise control switch. If cruise control switch does not test as specified, replace switch. See TESTING CRUISE CONTROL SWITCH table.

TESTING CRUISE CONTROL SWITCH

Switch Position	Check Between Terminals No.	Ohms
OFF	3 & 4	5890-6510
OFF	1 & 3	[1]
ON	1 & 4	5890-6510
ON	1 & 3	[2]
ON/SET	3 & 4	1020-1130
ON/RESUME	3 & 4	2040-2260

[1] – Continuity should not exist.
[2] – Continuity should exist.

SERVO VACUUM TEST

1) Remove cruise control cable from throttle body. Disconnect cruise control servo 4-pin connector. Disconnect vacuum hose at servo. Apply battery voltage to terminal No. 2 (Dark Blue/Red wire) at servo connector. Using jumper wire, ground remaining 3 terminals at servo connector.
2) Connect hand held vacuum pump to servo vacuum nipple, and apply 10-15 in. Hg of vacuum. Cruise control cable should pull in and hold as long as vacuum is applied. If servo does not test as specified, replace servo.

VACUUM SUPPLY

1) Disconnect vacuum hose at cruise control servo. Install vacuum gauge to disconnected vacuum hose. Start engine and observe gauge. Vacuum reading should be a minimum of 10 in. Hg. Turn engine off. Vacuum should continue to hold at a minimum of 10 in. Hg.
2) If vacuum is not as specified, check for kinked or leaking vacuum lines, defective check valve, defective vacuum reservoir and/or poor engine performance. If no problems are found, check servo. See CRUISE CONTROL SERVO under TESTING (WITHOUT DRB-II).

REMOVAL & INSTALLATION

WARNING: If vehicle is equipped with air bag, air bag MUST be deactivated before servicing cruise control components on or around steering column. See AIR BAG RESTRAINT SYSTEM article in SAFETY EQUIPMENT.

CRUISE CONTROL SERVO

Removal – Remove cruise control cable mounting bracket from servo. Remove servo mounting bracket from battery tray. Disconnect wiring harness connector and vacuum hose from servo. Pull cable away from servo to expose retaining clip. Remove retaining clip and cable. Remove servo.

Installation – With throttle in full open position, align hole in cruise control cable sleeve with hole in servo pin. Install retaining clip. To complete installation, reverse removal procedure.

CRUISE CONTROL SWITCH

Removal & Installation – Turn ignition switch to OFF position. Remove 2 screws from back of steering wheel. Rock switch back and forth to remove it from steering wheel. Disconnect cruise control switch connector. To install switch, reverse removal procedure.

CONNECTOR IDENTIFICATION
CONNECTOR IDENTIFICATION DIRECTORY

Connector	See Fig.
Brakelight Switch	2
Clockspring	3
Cruise Control Relay	4
Cruise Control Servo	5
Cruise Control Switch	6
Distance Sensor	7
Single Board Engine Controller (SBEC)	8

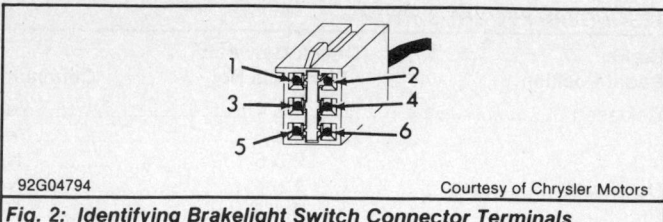

92G04794   Courtesy of Chrysler Motors

Fig. 2: Identifying Brakelight Switch Connector Terminals

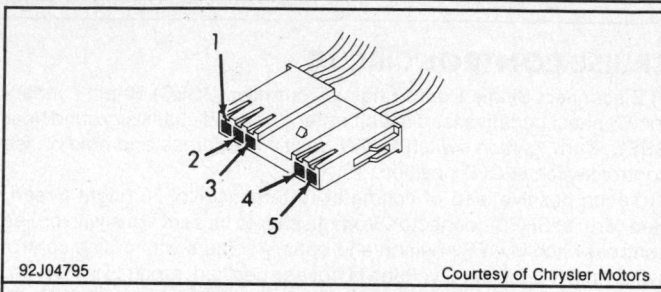

92J04795   Courtesy of Chrysler Motors

Fig. 3: Identifying Clockspring Connector Terminals

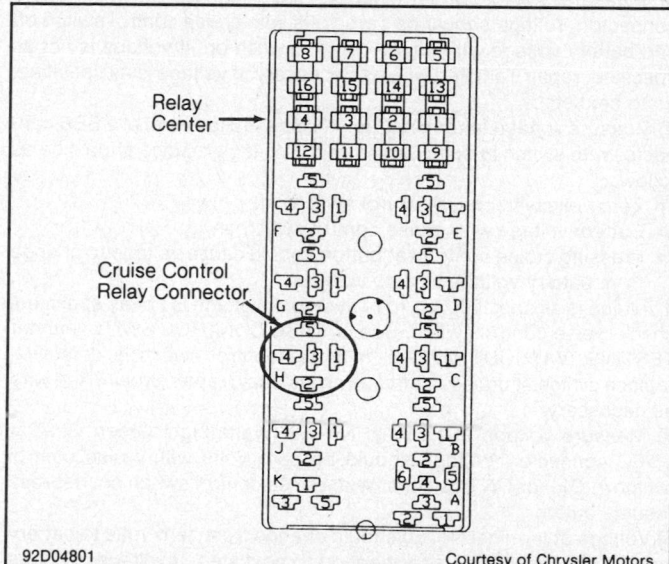

Relay Center

Cruise Control Relay Connector

92D04801   Courtesy of Chrysler Motors

Fig. 4: Identifying Cruise Control Relay Connector Terminals

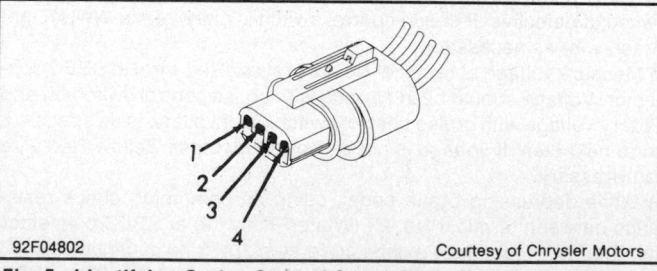

92F04802   Courtesy of Chrysler Motors

Fig. 5: Identifying Cruise Control Servo Connector Terminals

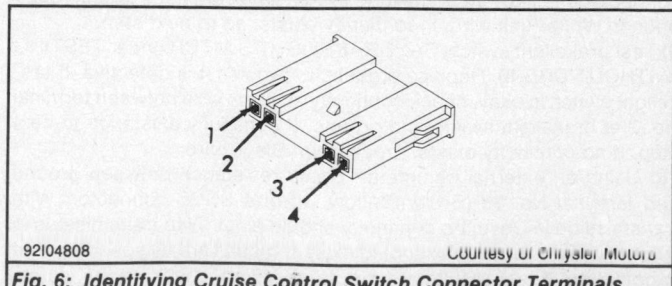

92I04808   Courtesy of Chrysler Motors

Fig. 6: Identifying Cruise Control Switch Connector Terminals

1991 SAFETY EQUIPMENT
Cruise Control Systems (Cont.)

1
2

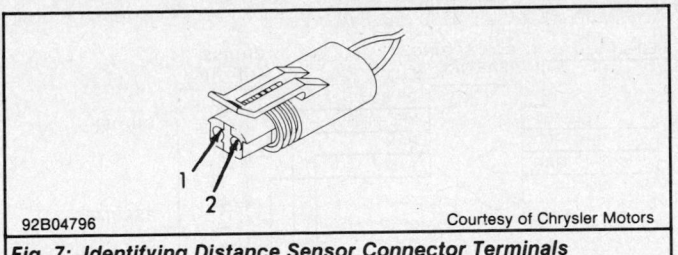

92B04796 Courtesy of Chrysler Motors

Fig. 7: Identifying Distance Sensor Connector Terminals

60
40
51
50
20
41
11
10
21
1

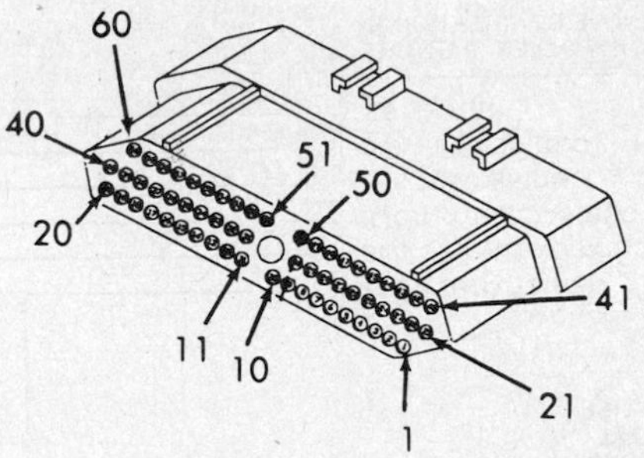

92B04800 Courtesy of Chrysler Motors

Fig. 8: Identifying Single Board Engine Controller (SBEC) Connector Terminals

WIRING DIAGRAMS

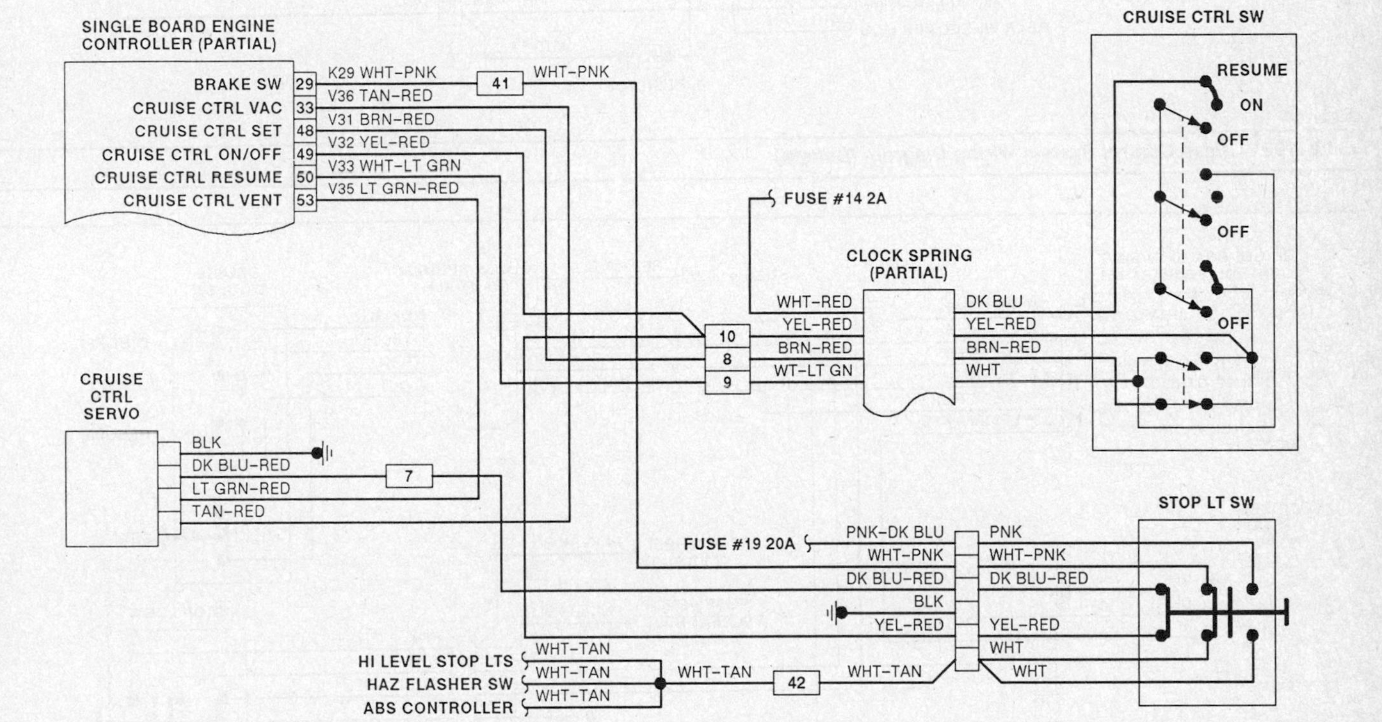

SINGLE BOARD ENGINE CONTROLLER (PARTIAL)
BRAKE SW 29
CRUISE CTRL VAC 33
CRUISE CTRL SET 48
CRUISE CTRL ON/OFF 49
CRUISE CTRL RESUME 50
CRUISE CTRL VENT 53
K29 WHT-PNK
V36 TAN-RED
V31 BRN-RED
V32 YEL-RED
V33 WHT-LT GRN
V35 LT GRN-RED
41
WHT-PNK
CRUISE CTRL SW
RESUME
ON
OFF
OFF
OFF
FUSE #14 2A
CLOCK SPRING (PARTIAL)
WHT-RED
YEL-RED
BRN-RED
WT-LT GN
10
8
9
DK BLU
YEL-RED
BRN-RED
WHT
CRUISE CTRL SERVO
BLK
DK BLU-RED
LT GRN-RED
TAN-RED
7
STOP LT SW
FUSE #19 20A
PNK-DK BLU
WHT-PNK
DK BLU-RED
BLK
YEL-RED
PNK
WHT-PNK
DK BLU-RED
YEL-RED
WHT
WHT
HI LEVEL STOP LTS
HAZ FLASHER SW
ABS CONTROLLER
WHT-TAN
WHT-TAN
WHT-TAN
WHT-TAN
42
WHT-TAN

92I04813

Fig. 9: 1991 Cruise Control System Wiring Diagram (Caravan, Town & Country, & Voyager)

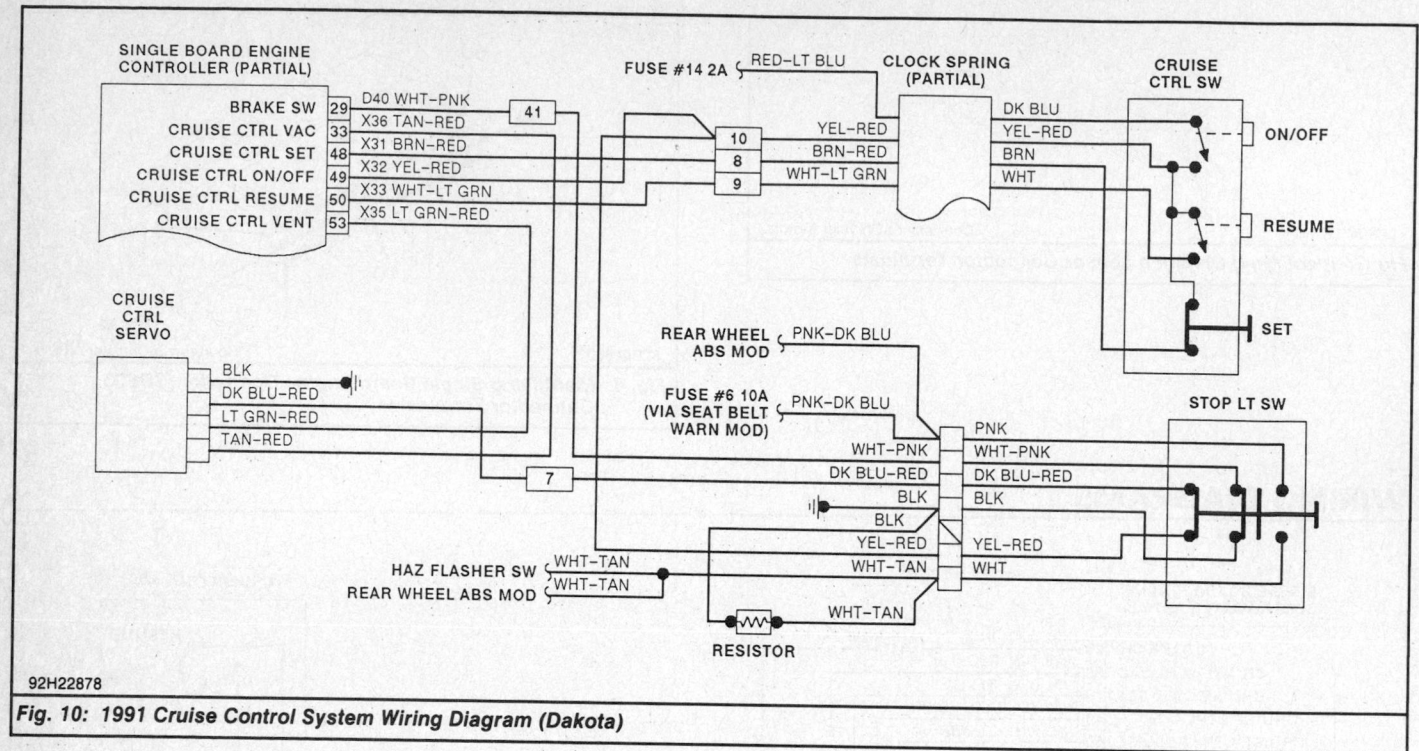

Fig. 10: 1991 Cruise Control System Wiring Diagram (Dakota)

92H22878

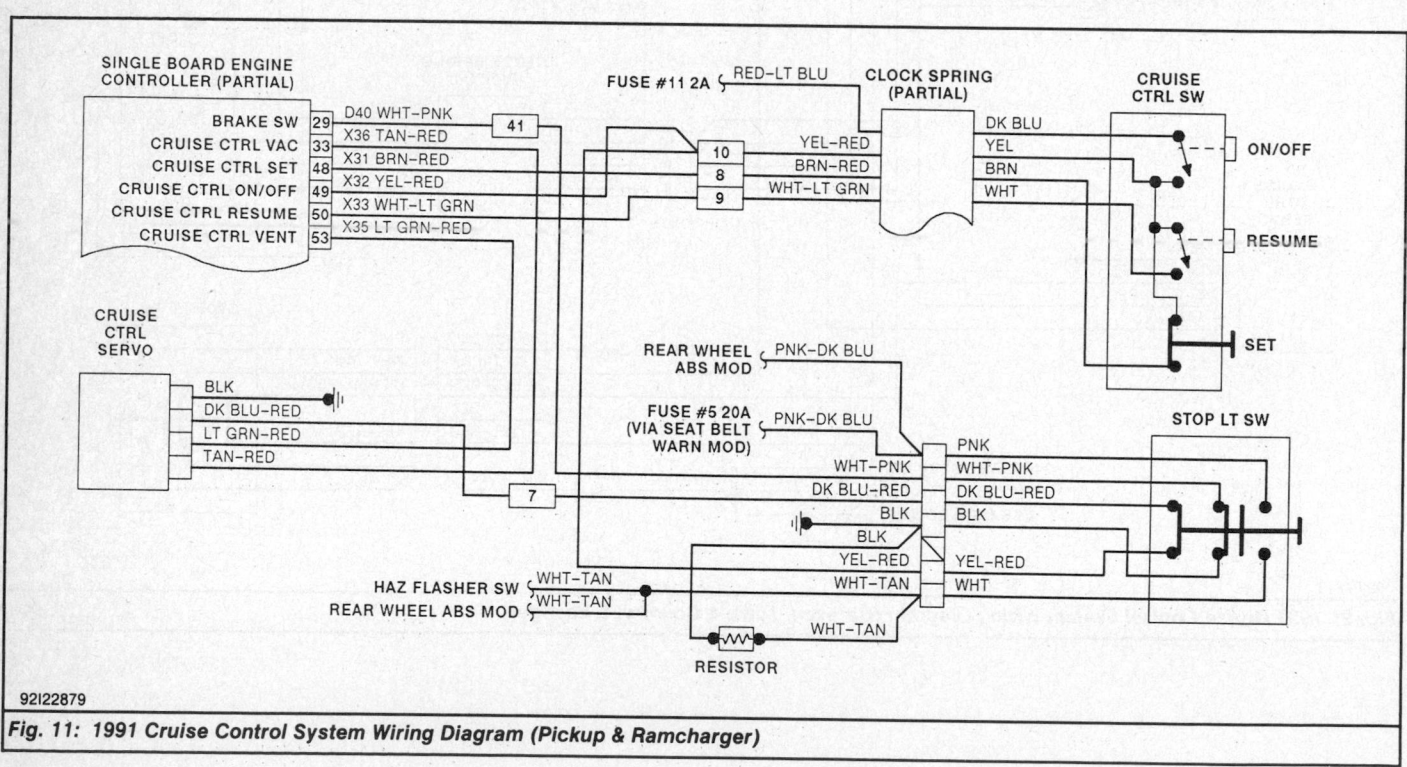

Fig. 11: 1991 Cruise Control System Wiring Diagram (Pickup & Ramcharger)

92I22879

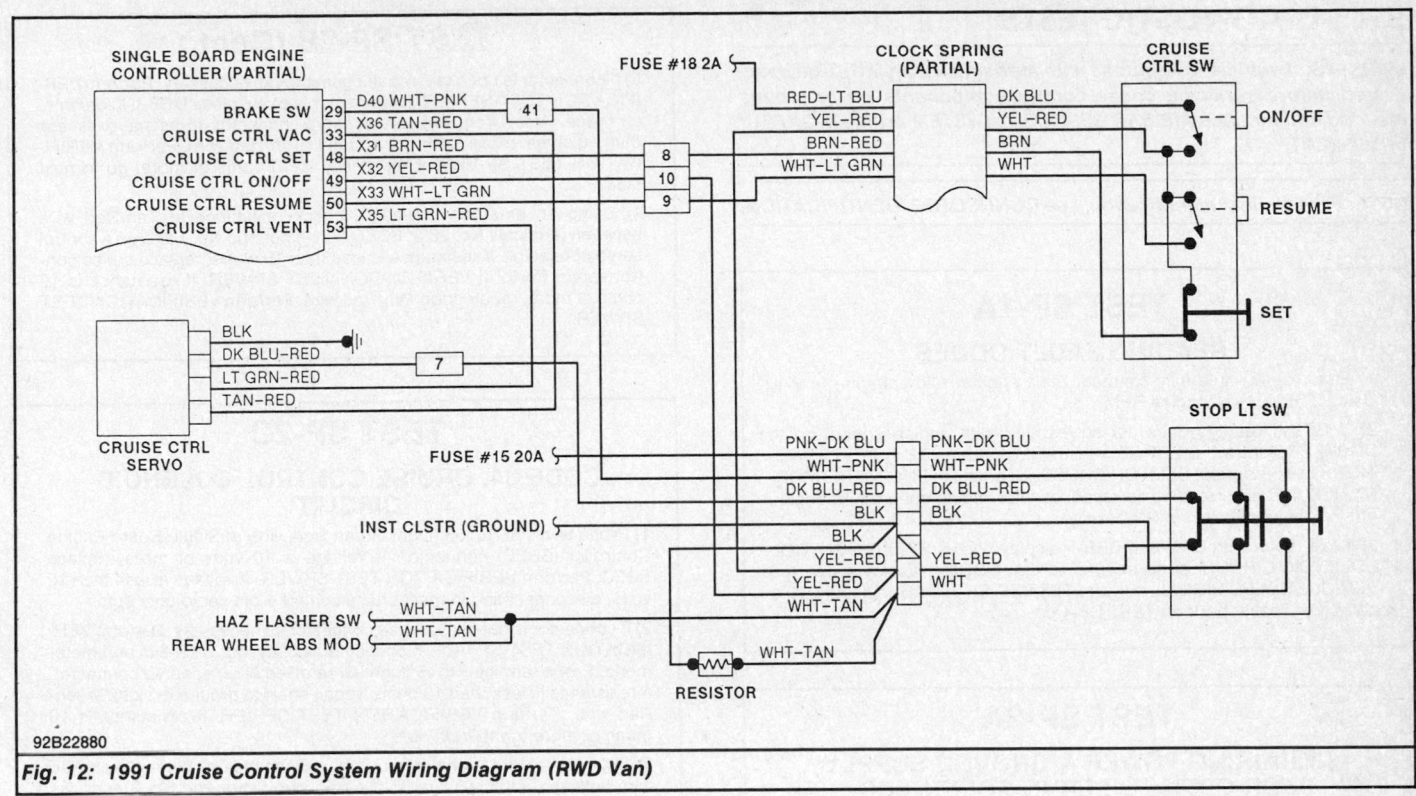

Fig. 12: 1991 Cruise Control System Wiring Diagram (RWD Van)

92B22880

1991 SAFETY EQUIPMENT
Cruise Control Systems (Cont.)

SELF-DIAGNOSTIC TESTS

WARNING: If vehicle is equipped with air bag, air bag MUST be deactivated before servicing cruise control components on or around steering column. See AIR BAG RESTRAINT SYSTEM article in SAFETY EQUIPMENT.

NOTE: For terminal identification, see CONNECTOR IDENTIFICATION.

TEST SP-1A

READING FAULT CODES

1) Ensure battery is fully charged. Start engine. Allow engine to idle. Using DRB-II, read engine RPM.

2) If DRB-II reading does not correspond with engine speed, go to DRB-II PROBLEMS & ERROR MESSAGES under DRB-II TEST FUNCTIONS in appropriate SELF-DIAGNOSTICS article in ENGINE PERFORMANCE. If DRB-II reading corresponds with engine speed, turn engine off. Put ignition switch in ON position.

3) Read faults with DRB-II. If DRB-II display shows SPEED CONTROL SOLENOID CIRCUIT, perform TEST SP-2A. If DRB-II display shows NO VEHICLE SPEED SIGNAL, perform TEST SP-3A. If DRB-II display does not show a fault, perform TEST SP-4A.

TEST SP-2A

REPAIRING POWER & GROUND SUPPLY FOR OPEN TO SERVO SOLENOIDS

1) While listening to cruise control servo, cycle cruise control on/off switch. If cruise control servo clicks when cycling on/off switch, perform TEST SP-2B. If cruise control servo does not click when cycling on/off switch, disconnect cruise control servo 4-pin connector.

2) Inspect connector. If connector is not okay, repair connector as necessary. Perform VERIFICATION TEST SP-VER. If connector is okay, put cruise control on/off switch in ON position. Place DRB-II in voltmeter mode.

3) Ensure brake pedal is not depressed. Probe Dark Blue/Red wire at cruise control servo connector. If voltage is 10 volts or more, go to next step. If voltage is less than 10 volts, go to step 5).

4) Place DRB-II in ohmmeter mode. Probe terminal No. 1 (Black wire) at cruise control servo connector. If resistance is 10 ohms or more, replace cruise control servo. If resistance is less than 10 ohms, repair short to ground in Black wire. Perform VERIFICATION TEST SP-VER.

5) If voltage is less than 10 volts at Dark Blue/Red wire in step 3), ensure brake pedal is not depressed. Backprobe Dark Blue/Red wire at brakelight switch connector. If voltage is 10 volts or more, repair open in Dark Blue/Red wire. Perform VERIFICATION TEST SP-VER. If voltage is less than 10 volts, go to next step.

6) Backprobe Yellow/Red wire at brakelight switch connector. If voltage is 10 volts or more, adjust or replace brakelight switch as necessary. Perform VERIFICATION TEST SP-VER. If voltage is less than 10 volts, repair open in Yellow/Red wire. Perform VERIFICATION TEST SP-VER.

TEST SP-2B

CODE 34, CRUISE CONTROL VACUUM SOLENOID CONTROL CIRCUIT

1) Turn ignition switch to OFF position. Disconnect and inspect Single Board Engine Controller (SBEC) connector. If connector is not okay, repair connector as necessary. Perform VERIFICATION TEST SP-VER. If connector is okay, turn ignition switch to ON position.

2) Put cruise control on/off switch in ON position. Place DRB-II in voltmeter mode. Probe terminal No. 33 (Tan/Red wire) at SBEC connector. If voltage is 10 volts or more, perform TEST SP-2C. If voltage is less than 10 volts, disconnect cruise control servo connector. Inspect connector.

TEST SP-2B (Cont.)

3) If connector is not okay, repair connector as necessary. Perform VERIFICATION TEST SP-VER. If connector is okay, place DRB-II in ohmmeter mode. Probe Tan/Red wire in servo connector. If resistance is less than 10 ohms, repair short to ground in Tan/Red wire. Perform VERIFICATION TEST SP-VER. If resistance is 10 ohms or more, go to next step.

4) Using an external ohmmeter, check resistance at Tan/Red wire between terminals No. 33 at SBEC connector and No. 4 at cruise control servo connector. If resistance is less than 10 ohms, replace cruise control servo. Perform VERIFICATION TEST SP-VER. If resistance is 10 ohms or more, repair open Tan/Red wire. Perform VERIFICATION TEST SP-VER.

TEST SP-2C

CODE 34, CRUISE CONTROL SOLENOID CIRCUIT

1) Probe terminal No. 53 (Light Green/Red wire) at Single Board Engine Controller (SBEC) connector. If voltage is 10 volts or more, replace SBEC. Perform VERIFICATION TEST SP-VER. If voltage is less than 10 volts, disconnect and inspect cruise control 4-pin servo connector.

2) If connector is not okay, repair connector as necessary. Perform VERIFICATION TEST SP-VER. If connector is okay, put DRB-II in ohmmeter mode. Probe terminal No. 3 (Light Green/Red wire) at servo connector. If resistance is less than 10 ohms, repair short to ground in Light Green/Red wire. Perform VERIFICATION TEST SP-VER. If resistance is 10 ohms or more, go to next step.

3) Using an external ohmmeter, check resistance at Light Green/Red wire between terminals No. 53 at SBEC connector and No. 3 at cruise control servo connector. If resistance is less than 10 ohms, replace cruise control servo. Perform VERIFICATION TEST SP-VER. If resistance is 10 ohms or more, repair open Light Green/Red wire. Perform VERIFICATION TEST SP-VER.

TEST SP-3A

CODE 15, NO VEHICLE SPEED SIGNAL

1) Turn ignition switch to OFF position. Disconnect vehicle distance sensor connector. Inspect connector. If connector is not okay, repair connector as necessary. Perform VERIFICATION TEST SP-VER.

2) If connector is okay, turn ignition switch to ON position. Connect a jumper wire to either distance sensor connector terminal. Using DRB-II, monitor car speed while tapping open end of jumper wire to other distance sensor connector terminal.

3) If DRB-II display shows car speed to be more than zero, replace distance sensor. Perform VERIFICATION TEST SP-VER. If vehicle speed is zero, put DRB-II in voltmeter mode. Probe terminal No. 1 (White/Orange wire) at distance sensor connector.

4) If voltage is less than 4 volts, go to next step. If voltage is 4 volts or more, turn ignition switch to OFF position. Put DRB-II in ohmmeter mode. Probe terminal No. 2 (Black/Light Blue wire) at distance sensor. If resistance is less than 10 ohms, replace SBEC. If resistance is 10 ohms or more, repair open Black/Light Blue wire.

5) Turn ignition switch to OFF position. Place DRB-II in ohmmeter mode. Probe terminal No. 1 (White/Orange wire) at distance sensor connector. If resistance is 10 ohms or more, perform TEST SP-3B. If resistance is less than 10 ohms, disconnect instrument panel 50-pin connector at firewall. Probe terminal No. 1 (White/Orange wire) at distance sensor connector.

6) If resistance is less than 10 ohms, repair White/Orange wire for a short to ground in engine wiring harness. Perform VERIFICATION TEST SP-VER. If resistance is 10 ohms or more, repair open White/Orange wire. Perform VERIFICATION TEST SP-VER.

TEST SP-3B

CODE 15, NO VEHICLE SPEED SIGNAL

1) Disconnect Single Board Engine Controller (SBEC) connector. Inspect connector. If connector is not okay, repair connector as necessary. Perform VERIFICATION TEST SP-VER. If connector is okay, go to next step.

2) Using an external ohmmeter, check resistance at White/Orange wire between terminals No. 47 at SBEC connector and No. 1 at distance sensor connector. If resistance is less than 10 ohms, replace SBEC. Perform VERIFICATION TEST SP-VER. If resistance is 10 ohms or more, repair open White/Orange wire. Perform VERIFICATION TEST SP-VER.

TEST SP-4A

TESTING CRUISE CONTROL SWITCHES

1) Using DRB-II, read inputs monitor. While watching ON/OFF input, cycle on/off switch several times. If DRB-II display does not correspond with switch position, perform TEST SP-5A.

2) If DRB-II display does correspond with switch position, place cruise control on/off switch in ON position. While watching RESUME input, cycle resume switch several times. If DRB-II display does not correspond with switch position, perform TEST SP-7A. If DRB-II display corresponds with switch position, go to next step.

3) While watching SET input on DRB-II display, cycle set switch several times. If DRB-II display does not correspond with switch position, perform TEST SP-9A. If DRB-II display corresponds with switch position, cycle brake pedal several times, while watching BRAKE input display.

4) If DRB-II display does not correspond with brake pedal position, perform TEST SP-11A. If DRB-II display corresponds with brake pedal position, check if vehicle is equipped with a manual transmission. If vehicle is equipped with manual transmission, perform TEST SP-13A. If vehicle is not equipped with manual transmission, go to next step.

5) With ignition switch in ON position and engine not running, cycle gear lever several times between "P", "R", "N" and "D", while watching PARK/NEUTRAL input. If DRB-II display does not correspond with selector position, perform TEST SP-12A. If DRB-II display corresponds with selector position, perform TEST SP-13A.

TEST SP-5A

TESTING CRUISE CONTROL ON/OFF SWITCH

1) Turn ignition switch to ON position. Place DRB-II in voltmeter mode. Probe both sides of cruise control fuse. If voltage at both sides of fuse is 10 volts or more, go to step **4)**.

2) If voltage is 10 volts or more at input side of fuse only, go to next step. If voltage is less than 10 volts at input side of fuse, repair open in Dark Blue wire between ignition switch and speed control fuse. Perform VERIFICATION TEST SP-VER.

3) Put cruise control on/off switch in OFF position. Replace speed control fuse. Probe end of fuse (White/Red wire at output side) that had less than 10 volts. If voltage is less than 10 volts, repair short to ground in White/Red wire. Perform VERIFICATION TEST SP-VER. If voltage is 10 volts or more at White/Red wire, perform TEST SP-5B.

4) If voltage at both sides of fuse is 10 volts or more in step **1)**, disconnect cruise control switch connector. Put DRB-II in voltmeter mode. Probe terminal No. 1 (Dark Blue wire) at cruise control switch connector. If voltage is less than 10 volts, repair open Dark Blue wire. Perform VERIFICATION TEST SP-VER.

5) If voltage is 10 volts or more, turn ignition switch to OFF position. Disconnect Single Board Engine Controller (SBEC) connector. Inspect connector. If connector is not okay, repair connector as necessary. Perform VERIFICATION TEST SP-VER. If connector is okay, go to next step.

6) Using an external ohmmeter, check resistance at Yellow/Red wire between terminal No. 49 at SBEC connector and No. 2 at cruise control switch connector. If resistance is 10 ohms or more, repair open Yellow/Red wire. Perform VERIFICATION TEST SP-VER. If resistance is less than 10 ohms, reconnect cruise control switch connector.

7) Put cruise control on/off switch in ON position. Turn ignition switch to ON position. Put DRB-II in voltmeter mode. Probe terminal No. 49 (Yellow/Red wire) at SBEC connector. If voltage is 10 volts or more, replace SBEC. Perform VERIFICATION TEST SP-VER. If voltage is less than 10 volts, replace cruise control switch. Perform VERIFICATION TEST SP-VER.

TEST SP-5B

CHECKING CRUISE CONTROL ON/OFF SWITCH

With cruise control on/off switch in ON position, probe White/Red wire at end of fuse (output side) that had less than 10 volts. If voltage is 10 volts or more, repair is complete or a intermittent short to ground exists. Perform VERIFICATION TEST SP-VER. If voltage is less than 10 volts, repair White/Red wire for short to ground. Perform VERIFICATION TEST SP-VER.

TEST SP-6A

NOTE: Test SP-6A applies to Jeep models only. No test procedures are missing.

TEST SP-7A

TESTING CRUISE CONTROL RESUME SWITCH

1) Turn ignition switch to OFF position. Disconnect Single Board Engine Controller (SBEC) connector. Inspect connector. If connector is not okay, repair connector as necessary. Perform VERIFICATION TEST SP-VER. If connector is okay, disconnect cruise control switch connector.

2) Using an external ohmmeter, check resistance at White/Light Green wire between terminal No. 50 at SBEC connector and terminal No. 3 at cruise control switch connector.

3) If resistance is 10 ohms or more, repair open in White/Light Green wire. Perform VERIFICATION TEST SP-VER. If resistance is less than 10 ohms, reconnect cruise control switch connector. Put cruise control on/off switch in ON position. Turn ignition switch to ON position. Put DRB-II in voltmeter mode.

4) Hold RESUME button down and probe terminal No. 50 (White/Light Green wire) at SBEC connector. If voltage is 10 volts or more, replace SBEC; if voltage is less than 10 volts, replace cruise control switch. Perform VERIFICATION TEST SP-VER.

TEST SP-8A

NOTE: Test SP-8A applies to Jeep models only. No test procedures are missing.

TEST SP-9A

TESTING CRUISE CONTROL SET SWITCH

1) Turn ignition switch to OFF position. Disconnect Single Board Engine Controller (SBEC). Inspect connector. If connector is not okay, repair connector as necessary. Perform VERIFICATION TEST SP-VER.

2) If connector is okay, disconnect cruise control switch connector. Inspect connector. If connector is not okay, repair connector as necessary. Perform VERIFICATION TEST SP-VER. If connector is okay, go to next step.

3) Using an external ohmmeter, check resistance at Brown/Red wire between terminal No. 48 at SBEC connector and terminal No. 4 at cruise control switch connector. If resistance is 10 ohms or more, repair open Brown/Red wire. Perform VERIFICATION TEST SP-VER.

4) If resistance is less than 10 ohms, reconnect cruise control switch connector. Put cruise control on/off switch in ON position. Turn ignition switch to ON position. Place DRB-II in voltmeter mode. Probe SBEC connector terminal No. 48 (Brown/Red wire). If voltage is less than 10 volts, replace cruise control switch. Perform VERIFICATION TEST SP-VER.

5) If voltage is 10 volts or more, hold down set button and probe terminal No. 48 at SBEC connector. If voltage is less than 10 volts, replace SBEC. Perform VERIFICATION TEST SP-VER. If voltage is 10 volts or more, replace cruise control switch. Perform VERIFICATION TEST SP-VER.

TEST SP-10A

NOTE: Test SP-10A applies to Jeep models only. No test procedures are missing.

TEST SP-11A

CHECKING BRAKELIGHT SWITCH CIRCUITS FOR OPENS

1) If DRB-II display always shows RE, perform TEST SP-11B. If DRB-II does not always show RE, disconnect brakelight switch connector. Inspect connector. If connector is not okay, repair connector as necessary. Perform VERIFICATION TEST SP-VER.

2) If connector is okay, connect a jumper wire between terminals No. 1 (White/Pink wire) and No. 2 (Black wire) at brakelight switch connector. Using DRB-II, read inputs monitor. if DRB-II display does not show RE, go to step 4).

3) If DRB-II display shows RE, check brakelight switch adjustment. If brakelight switch is adjusted correctly, replace brakelight switch; if brakelight switch is not adjusted correctly, adjust brakelight switch. Perform VERIFICATION TEST SP-VER.

4) If DRB-II display does not show RE in step 2), connect jumper wire between terminal No. 1 (White/Pink wire) and ground. Using DRB-II, read inputs monitor. If DRB-II display shows RE, repair open in Black wire.

5) If DRB-II does not show RE, turn ignition switch to OFF position. Remove jumper wire. Disconnect Single Board Engine Controller (SBEC) connector. Inspect connector. If connector is not okay, repair connector as necessary. Perform VERIFICATION TEST SP-VER.

6) If connector is okay, use an external ohmmeter to check resistance of White/Pink wire between terminals No. 29 at SBEC connector and No. 1 at brakelight switch connector. If resistance is 10 ohms or more, repair open White/Pink wire. Perform VERIFICATION TEST SP-VER. If resistance is less than 10 ohms, replace SBEC. Perform VERIFICATION TEST SP-VER.

TEST SP-11B

CHECKING BRAKELIGHT SWITCH CIRCUITS FOR SHORTS

1) Disconnect brakelight switch connector. Using DRB-II, read inputs monitor. If DRB-II display shows PR, go to step 3). If DRB-II display does not show PR, turn ignition switch to OFF position. Disconnect Single Board Engine Controller (SBEC) connector. Place DRB-II in ohmmeter mode. Probe terminal No. 29 (White/Pink wire) at SBEC connector.

2) If resistance is less than 10 ohms, repair short to ground in White/Pink wire. Perform VERIFICATION TEST SP-VER. If resistance is 10 ohms or more, replace SBEC. Perform VERIFICATION TEST SP-VER.

3) If DRB-II display shows PR in step 1), check brakelight switch adjustment. If brakelight switch is adjusted correctly, replace brakelight switch; if brakelight switch is not adjusted correctly, adjust brakelight switch. Perform VERIFICATION TEST SP-VER.

TEST SP-12A

CHECKING PARK/NEUTRAL SAFETY SWITCH

1) Disconnect park/neutral safety switch connector at transmission. Inspect connector. If connector is not okay, repair connector as necessary. Perform VERIFICATION TEST SP-VER. If connector is okay, using DRB-II read inputs monitor.

2) If DRB-II display shows D/R, replace park/neutral safety switch. Perform VERIFICATION TEST SP-VER. If DRB-II display does not show D/R, turn ignition switch to OFF position. Disconnect and inspect Single Board Engine Controller (SBEC) connector. If connector is not okay, repair connector as necessary. Perform VERIFICATION TEST SP-VER.

3) If connector is okay, place DRB-II in ohmmeter mode. Probe terminal No. 30 (Brown/Yellow wire) at SBEC connector. If resistance is less than 10 ohms, repair short to ground in Brown/Yellow wire. Perform VERIFICATION TEST SP-VER. If resistance is 10 ohms or more, replace SBEC. Perform VERIFICATION TEST SP-VER.

TEST SP-13A

CHECKING CRUISE CONTROL SERVO OPERATION

1) Disconnect and inspect 4-pin cruise control servo connector. If connector is not okay, repair as necessary. Perform VERIFICATION TEST SP-VER. If connector is okay, place DRB-II in ohmmeter mode. Probe terminal No. 1 (Black wire) at cruise control servo connector.

2) If resistance is 10 ohms or more, repair open Black wire. Perform VERIFICATION TEST SP-VER. If resistance is less than 10 ohms, reconnect cruise control servo connector. Check if vehicle is equipped with a vacuum reservoir. If vehicle is equipped with vacuum reservoir, perform TEST SP-13B.

3) If vehicle is not equipped with a vacuum reservoir, disconnect cruise control servo vacuum hose. Using an alternative source of constant vacuum supply, connect a vacuum supply hose to servo. Using DRB-II, actuate servo solenoids. If throttle fully opens and closes, perform TEST SP-14A.

4) If throttle does not fully open and close, stop actuation test using DRB-II. Inspect cruise control servo cable condition. If cruise control servo cable okay, replace cruise control servo. Perform VERIFICATION TEST SP-VER. If cruise control servo cable is not okay, repair cable as necessary. Perform VERIFICATION TEST SP-VER.

TEST SP-13B

CHECKING CRUISE CONTROL SERVO OPERATION

1) Start engine. Turn engine off. Turn ignition switch to ON position. Using DRB-II, actuate servo solenoids. If throttle fully opens and closes, perform TEST SP-14A. If throttle does not fully open and close, stop actuation test using DRB-II.

2) Disconnect vacuum hose at cruise control servo. Using an alternative source of constant vacuum supply, connect a vacuum supply hose to servo. Using DRB-II, actuate servo solenoids. If throttle fully opens and closes, repair vacuum leak or restriction between servo and vacuum source. Perform VERIFICATION TEST SP-VER.

3) If throttle does not fully open and close, using DRB-II, stop actuation test. Inspect cruise control servo cable condition. If cruise control servo cable is okay, replace cruise control servo. Perform VERIFICATION TEST SP-VER. If cruise control servo cable is not okay, repair cable as necessary. Perform VERIFICATION TEST SP-VER.

TEST SP-14A

CHECKING FOR INTERMITTENT FAULTS

1) Reconnect and reassemble all previously tested components. Connect DRB-II to engine diagnostic connector so DRB-II display can be seen from driver-side seat. Road test vehicle. Using DRB-II, read cutout monitor on DRB-II display. If DRB-II display shows erratic vehicle speed, replace distance sensor. Perform VERIFICATION TEST SP-VER.

2) If DRB-II display does not show erratic vehicle speed, put cruise control on/off switch in ON position. With vehicle speed at least 35 MPH, depress and release cruise control set switch. If DRB-II display shows S/C DENIED, see appropriate DENIED MESSAGE in DRB-II INTERMITTENT FAULT MESSAGES table and correct problem as necessary.

DRB-II INTERMITTENT FAULT MESSAGES

Denied Message	Problem To Correct
BRAKE	Open Circuit At Terminal No. 29 At SBEC
CLUTCH	RPM/Vehicle Speed Ratio Is Not Constant
ON/OFF	Lack Of Voltage At Terminal No. 49 At SBEC
P/N	Ground Exists At Terminal No. 30 At SBEC
RPM/SPD	RPM/Speed Ratio Is Not Constant
SPEED	Vehicle Speed As Read By Distance Sensor Is Less Than 35 MPH
RPM	Engine RPM Is Excessively High
SOL/FLT	Fault In Servo Vent Or Vacuum Solenoid Circuit That Is Either Maturing Or Set

TEST SP-14A (Cont.)

3) If DRB-II display shows S/C ALLOWED and cruise control is operative, perform following:
- Check for cruise control disengagement without driver command by driving vehicle under various road conditions.
- If cruise control disengages without driver command, read cutout monitor S/C DENIED message on DRB-II display. See appropriate DENIED MESSAGE in DRB-II INTERMITTENT FAULT MESSAGES table and repair as necessary.
- If cruise control does not disengage without driver command, read DRB-II cutout monitor display. Compare GOAL value with SPEED value. If the 2 values are not within 2 MPH of each other, replace SBEC.

VERIFICATION TEST SP-VER
CRUISE CONTROL VERIFICATION

Reconnect and reassemble all previously tested components. If Single Board Engine Controller has been changed, perform following:
- If vehicle is equipped with factory theft alarm, start vehicle at least 20 times so alarm system may be activated when desired.
- Write vehicle odometer mileage to memory location within replacement SBEC. This will enable new SBEC to operate Emission Maintenance Reminder (EMR) light properly. See EMISSION MAINTENANCE REMINDER (EMR) MILEAGE TRANSFER under DRB-II TEST FUNCTIONS in appropriate SELF-DIAGNOSTICS article in ENGINE PERFORMANCE.
- Connect DRB-II to engine diagnostic connector and erase faults.

To ensure no other faults remain, perform following:

1) Road test vehicle at a speed greater than 35 MPH. Put cruise control on/off switch in ON position. Depress and release set switch. If cruise control did not engage, repair is not complete. Check all pertinent MITCHELL® TECH SERVICE BULLETINS (TSBs) and return to TEST SP-1A if necessary.

2) Depress and release resume/accel switch. If vehicle speed did not increase by 2 MPH, repair is not complete. Check all pertinent MITCHELL® TECH SERVICE BULLETINS (TSBs) and return to TEST SP-1A if necessary.

3) Depress and release brake pedal. If cruise control did not disengage, repair is not complete. Check all pertinent MITCHELL® TECH SERVICE BULLETINS (TSBs) and return to TEST SP-1A if necessary.

4) Bring vehicle speed back up to 35 MPH. Depress resume/accel switch. If cruise control did not resume the previously set speed, repair is not complete. Check all pertinent MITCHELL® TECH SERVICE BULLETINS (TSBs) and return to TEST SP-1A if necessary.

5) Hold down set switch. If vehicle did not decelerate, repair is not complete. Check all pertinent MITCHELL® TECH SERVICE BULLETINS (TSBs) and return to TEST SP-1A if necessary.

6) Ensure vehicle speed is greater than 35 MPH and release set switch. If vehicle did not adjust and set to new vehicle speed, repair is not complete. Check all pertinent MITCHELL® TECH SERVICE BULLETINS (TSBs) and return to TEST SP-1A if necessary.

7) Turn on/off switch to OFF position. If cruise control did not disengage, repair is not complete. Check all pertinent MITCHELL® TECH SERVICE BULLETINS (TSBs) and return to TEST SP-1A if necessary. If vehicle successfully passed all previous tests, cruise control system is now functioning correctly. Repair is complete.

1992 SAFETY EQUIPMENT
Cruise Control Systems

Caravan, Dakota, Pickup, Ramcharger, RWD Van, Town & Country, Voyager

DESCRIPTION

The cruise control system is electronically controlled and vacuum operated. The electronic control is integrated into the Single Board Engine Controller (SBEC). System consists of the following components: SBEC, servo, cruise control switch panel, vacuum reservoir, distance sensor, brake switch and Park/Neutral switch (automatic transmission). System controls are located on the steering wheel and consist of ON/OFF, RESUME/ACCEL, and SET/DECEL or SET/COAST buttons.

OPERATION

SYSTEM CONTROLS

To Set Cruise Control – Press ON/OFF button to turn cruise control system on. Accelerate to desired speed (minimum of 35 MPH) and press SET/DECEL or SET/COAST button. Vehicle speed will be maintained.

To Disengage Cruise Control – Press brake pedal or clutch pedal. The ON/OFF button may also be used, but set speed will be erased from memory. If clutch pedal is used to disengage cruise control, engine speed will increase before cruise control cuts out.

To Resume Previous Speed – If set speed has not been erased from memory and vehicle speed is more than 30 MPH, press RESUME/ACCEL button.

To Increase Speed – With cruise control system on, increase set speed by rapidly pressing and releasing RESUME/ACCEL button. Each pressing of button will cause a speed increase of 2 MPH. For example, 3 presses would result in an increased speed of 6 MPH. To increase speed gradually, hold RESUME/ACCEL button down until desired speed is reached. When button is released, new set speed will be maintained.

To Decrease Speed – With cruise control system on, decrease set speed by pressing SET/DECEL or SET/COAST button. Vehicle speed will gradually decrease. Releasing button will set a new speed as long as vehicle speed is still more than 35 MPH.

NOTE: Cruise control system will automatically disengage when vehicle speed drops to less than 35 MPH or rises to more than 85 MPH.

SELF-DIAGNOSTIC SYSTEM

SYSTEM DIAGNOSTICS

The self-diagnostic capabilities of this system, if properly utilized, can simplify testing. Cruise control system is monitored by Single Board Engine Controller (SBEC).

If a problem is sensed with a monitored circuit, a fault code is stored in SBEC. Once codes are known, refer to FAULT CODES table to determine questionable circuit. Test circuits and repair or replace components as required. If problem is repaired or ceases to exist, SBEC cancels that fault code after 50 ignition on/off cycles. To clear codes, refer to CLEARING FAULT CODES.

A specific fault code results from a particular system failure. It is NOT necessarily the reason for that failure. Fault code does not condemn a specific component. Fault code calls out a probable malfunction area.

SERVICE PRECAUTIONS

Before proceeding with diagnosis, the following precautions must be observed:
- Vehicle must have a fully charged battery and functional charging system.
- Probe SBEC 60-pin connector from pin side. DO NOT backprobe SBEC connector.

- DO NOT cause short circuits when performing electrical tests. This will set additional fault codes, making diagnosis of original problem more difficult.
- Always repair lowest fault code number (CHECK ENGINE light) or first fault displayed (DRB-II) before repairing others.
- Always perform VERIFICATION TEST SP-VER after repairs are made.

VISUAL INSPECTION

Perform a visual inspection before attempting to diagnose cruise control system problems. A visual inspection may quickly identify cause of a malfunction and eliminate need for diagnostic testing. A thorough visual inspection includes checking for disconnected or faulty wiring harness connectors, leaking or misrouted vacuum hoses, corroded battery terminals or bare wires.

DIAGNOSTIC PROCEDURE

NOTE: When using self-diagnostic tests for diagnosis, DO NOT skip any steps or incorrect diagnosis may result. Always start with TEST SP-1A.

Perform a visual inspection before attempting to diagnose engine control system problems. See VISUAL INSPECTION. Enter on-board diagnostics and retrieve fault codes. See ENTERING ON-BOARD DIAGNOSTICS. If fault codes are NOT present and/or DRB-II (Diagnostic Readout Box II) is used, proceed to TEST SP-1A.

ENTERING ON-BOARD DIAGNOSTICS

NOTE: Although other scan testers are available, manufacturer recommends using DRB-II (Diagnostic Readout Box-II) to diagnose system. CHECK ENGINE light function can be used but has limited diagnostic abilities.

CHECK ENGINE Light Diagnostic Mode – 1) With key inserted in ignition switch, cycle ignition switch to ON position 3 times. On third cycle, leave ignition switch in ON position. Record 2-digit fault codes as displayed by flashing CHECK ENGINE light.
2) For example, Code 34 is displayed as a series of 3 flashes in rapid succession, followed by a 4-second pause, then 4 flashes in rapid succession. After a slightly longer pause, other stored codes are displayed in numerical order.
3) When CHECK ENGINE light begins to flash fault codes, it cannot be stopped. If you lose count, it will be necessary to start over. Code 55 indicates end of fault code display.
4) Refer to FAULT CODES table to translate trouble code number to a system fault description (DRB-II display). Once trouble area is identified, refer to TEST SP-1A to diagnose problem.

NOTE: If fault code exists that is not related to cruise control system, see appropriate SELF-DIAGNOSTICS article in ENGINE PERFORMANCE.

DRB-II Diagnostic Mode – 1) Connect DRB-II to engine diagnostic connector. Connector is located in engine compartment, near SBEC. Start engine. Turn ignition switch to ON position. Enter SPEED CONTROL MENU. To enter SPEED CONTROL MENU, see DRB-II TEST FUNCTIONS.
2) At SPEED CONTROL MENU, press "2" (READ FAULTS) key. Press ENTER key. After fault codes are accessed, refer to TEST SP-1A to diagnose problem. If no fault codes are present, see TROUBLE SHOOTING.
3) To erase fault codes while in this option, press ATM key. At DRB-II display, press "2" (ERASE) key. DRB-II will display ERASE FAULTS ARE YOU SURE? (ENTER TO ERASE). Press ENTER key.
4) When DRB-II is finished erasing fault codes, it will display FAULTS ERASED, This display will remain until ATM key is pressed. After ATM key is pressed, display will return to SPEED CONTROL MENU screen.

FAULT CODES
FAULT CODES

Code	Display On DRB-II	Fault Condition
15	NO VEHICLE SPEED SIGNAL	No Vehicle Distance (Speed) Sensor Signal Detected During Road Load Conditions
34	SPEED CONTROL SOLENOID CIRCUITS	An Open Or Shorted Condition Detected In Cruise Control Vacuum Or Vent Solenoid Circuits
77	SPEED CONTROL POWER RELAY CIRCUIT	An Open Or Shorted Condition Detected In Cruise Control Power Relay Circuit

CLEARING FAULT CODES

NOTE: Fault codes can also be cleared in READ FAULTS option of DRB-II. To ensure that all faults are read, it is advisable to use READ FAULTS option to erase fault codes. See DRB-II DIAGNOSTIC MODE under ENTERING ON-BOARD DIAGNOSTICS.

1) If DRB-II is not available, go to step 3). If DRB-II is available, enter SPEED CONTROL MENU. See DRB-II TEST FUNCTIONS. At SPEED CONTROL menu, press "5" (ADJUSTMENTS) key. Press ENTER key. At ADJUSTMENTS menu, press "1" (ERASE FAULTS) key. Press ENTER key.
2) DRB-II will display ERASE FAULTS ARE YOU SURE? (ENTER TO ERASE). Press ENTER key. When DRB-II is finished erasing fault codes, screen will display FAULTS ERASED.
3) If DRB-II is not available, fault codes may be cleared by disconnecting negative battery cable for at least 15 seconds, allowing SBEC to clear fault codes.

DRB-II TEST FUNCTIONS

SPEED CONTROL MENU

1) In order to perform cruise control system tests using DRB-II, DRB-II must be in SPEED CONTROL MENU. At SPEED CONTROL MENU, fault codes and DRB-II test functions can be accessed.
2) To reach SPEED CONTROL MENU, turn ignition off. Connect DRB-II to engine diagnostic connector. Connector is located in engine compartment, near SBEC. Turn ignition switch to RUN position.

NOTE: DO NOT touch DRB-II keypad during DRB-II power-up sequence or an error message will result.

3) All DRB-II character positions will illuminate and copyright information will appear on screen for a few seconds. If DRB-II screen is blank or any error messages appear, refer to DRB-II PROBLEMS & ERROR MESSAGES. See appropriate SELF-DIAGNOSTICS article in ENGINE PERFORMANCE.
4) After a few seconds DRB-II menu will appear. At DRB-II menu, press "4" (SELECT SYSTEM) key. Press ENTER key. At SELECT SYSTEM menu, press "1" (ENGINE) key. Press ENTER key. DRB-II menu will appear indicating engine year, size, type of transmission and SBEC part number.
5) After a few seconds AIR COND menu will appear. Press "1" (WITH A/C) or press "2" (WITHOUT A/C). DRB-II display will change to ENGINE SYSTEMS menu. At ENGINE SYSTEMS menu, press "3" (SPEED CONTROL) key. Press ENTER key.
6) Display will change to SPEED CONTROL. At SPEED CONTROL MENU, specific test functions programmed into DRB-II can be performed. The following DRB-II modes can be accessed: SYSTEM TEST, READ FAULTS, STATE DISPLAYS, ACTUATOR TEST and ADJUSTMENTS.

NOTE: For more information on DRB-II test functions, see appropriate SELF-DIAGNOSTICS article in ENGINE PERFORMANCE.

TROUBLE SHOOTING

NO CRUISE CONTROL WHEN SET BUTTON IS PRESSED & RELEASED

Check for blown fuse, no vacuum at servo and/or defective servo, disconnected speed control cable, brake switch out of adjustment, faulty electrical circuit, faulty neutral safety switch input to SBEC and/or faulty SBEC.

CRUISE CONTROL ENGAGES WITHOUT ACTUATING CRUISE SET BUTTON

Check for defective servo, faulty electrical circuit or control switch.

CRUISE CONTROL ENGAGES WHEN ENGINE IS STARTED

Check for defective servo, faulty electrical circuit.

ERRATIC SPEED OR ENGINE SHUTS OFF

Check for poor engine performance (surge), defective distance (speed) sensor, vacuum leak, faulty servo or SBEC.

CRUISE CONTROL DISENGAGES ON ROUGH ROAD

Check for brake switch out of adjustment, faulty electrical circuit.

ENGINE DOES NOT RETURN TO NORMAL IDLE

Check for kinked and/or damaged cruise control cable, faulty throttle linkage.

NO RESUME WHEN RESUME BUTTON IS PRESSED

Check for defective switch, faulty electrical circuit.

CRUISE CONTROL DOES NOT DISENGAGE WITH BRAKE PEDAL DEPRESSED

Check for defective or improperly adjusted brake switch, kinked and/or damaged speed control cable, faulty electrical circuit.

WARNING: If vehicle is equipped with air bag, air bag MUST be deactivated before servicing cruise control components on or around steering column. See AIR BAG RESTRAINT SYSTEM article in SAFETY EQUIPMENT.

TESTING (WITHOUT DRB-II)

BRAKE SWITCH

Disconnect brake switch 6-pin connector. Using an ohmmeter, check for continuity at switch side of connector terminals. See TESTING BRAKE SWITCH table. If continuity is not as specified, check brake switch adjustment. If switch adjustment is okay, replace defective brake switch.

TESTING BRAKE SWITCH

Brake Pedal Position	Check Between Terminals No.	Continuity
Released	1 & 4	Yes
	3 & 6	Yes
	2 & 5	No
Depressed	1 & 4	No
	3 & 6	No
	2 & 5	Yes

CRUISE CONTROL CIRCUIT

1) Disconnect Single Board Engine Controller (SBEC) 60-pin connector. Access cruise control switch. *See Fig. SP-2A.* Disconnect cruise control 4-pin connector. Using an ohmmeter, check resistance between terminal No. 4 (Brown/Red wire) at cruise control connector and terminal No. 23 (Red/Light Green wire) at SBEC connector.

2) If no continuity exists, repair open in Brown/Red and Red/Light Green wire between SBEC and cruise control connectors. If continuity exists, test cruise control switch. See CRUISE CONTROL SWITCH under TESTING (WITHOUT DRB-II).

3) Replace cruise control switch, if defective. If cruise control switch is okay, reconnect cruise control 4-pin connector. Connect negative lead of voltmeter to a good chassis ground near SBEC. Put cruise control switch in ON position. Measure voltage at terminal No. 53 (Light Green/Red wire) at SBEC connector. If battery voltage is not present, repair open in Light Green/Red wire.

4) If battery voltage is present, measure voltage at terminal No. 33 (Tan/Red wire) at SBEC connector. If battery voltage is not present, repair open in Tan/Red wire. If battery voltage is present, using an ohmmeter, connect one lead to good chassis ground. Connect remaining lead of ohmmeter to terminal No. 29 (White/Pink wire) at SBEC connector.

5) Depress brake pedal. If continuity exists, go to step **7)**. If no continuity exists, check continuity at White/Pink wire between terminal No. 29 at SBEC connector and terminal No. 1 at brake switch. If no continuity exists, repair open in White/Pink wire. If continuity exists, go to next step.

6) Test brake switch. See BRAKE SWITCH under TESTING (WITHOUT DRB-II). Replace brake switch, if defective. If brake switch is okay, check continuity at Black wire between terminal No. 2 at brake switch and ground. If continuity exists, go to next step. If no continuity exists, repair open in Black wire.

7) Connect one lead of ohmmeter to good chassis ground. Touch other lead of ohmmeter to terminal No. 30 (Brown/Yellow wire) at SBEC connector. With transmission in Drive, no continuity should exist. With transmission in Neutral or Park, continuity should exist. If results are as specified, test is complete. If test results are not as specified, check neutral safety switch and/or back-up switch.

CRUISE CONTROL SERVO

1) Turn ignition switch to ON position. Using a voltmeter, connect negative lead to a good chassis ground. Disconnect servo 4-pin connector. Measure voltage at terminal No. 2 (Dark Blue/Red wire) at servo connector. If battery voltage is not present, go to next step. If battery voltage is present, go to step **7)**.

2) Disconnect brake switch 6-pin connector. Measure voltage at terminal No. 6 (Dark Blue/Red wire). If battery voltage is present, test brake switch. Replace brake switch, if defective. If brake switch is okay, repair Dark Blue/Red wire as necessary. See BRAKE SWITCH under TESTING (WITHOUT DRB-II). If battery voltage is not present, go to next step.

3) Gain access to cruise control switch. *See Fig. SP-2A.* Disconnect cruise control 4-pin connector. Measure voltage at terminal No. 1 (Yellow/Red wire) at cruise control connector.

4) If battery voltage is not present, go to step **6)**. If battery voltage is present, test cruise control switch. See CRUISE CONTROL SWITCH. Replace cruise control switch, if defective. If cruise control switch is okay, check for continuity across clockspring. *See Fig. SP-2A.*

5) If no continuity exists across clockspring, replace clockspring. If continuity exists across clockspring, repair Yellow/Red wire between clockspring and brake switch.

6) If battery voltage is not present in step **4)**, measure voltage at input side of cruise control fuse. If battery voltage is not present, repair open in wire between ignition switch and cruise control fuse. If battery voltage is present, check cruise control fuse. Replace fuse if blown. If fuse is okay, repair wire between fuse and clockspring.

7) If battery voltage is present in step **1)**, connect a jumper wire between terminal No. 2 (Dark Blue/Red wire) at cruise control servo connector and terminal No. 2 at cruise control servo.

8) With jumper wire connected, battery voltage should be present at servo's 3 remaining terminals. If battery voltage is present at servo's 3 remaining terminals, go to next step. If battery voltage is not present at servo's 3 remaining terminals, replace servo.

9) Using an ohmmeter, connect one lead to good chassis ground. Connect remaining lead to terminal No. 1 (Black wire) at servo connector. If no continuity exists, repair open in Black wire. If continuity exists, test is complete.

CRUISE CONTROL SWITCH

Access cruise control switch. *See Fig. SP-2A.* Disconnect cruise control 4-pin connector. Using an ohmmeter, check cruise control switch. If cruise control switch does not test as specified, replace switch. See TESTING CRUISE CONTROL SWITCH table.

TESTING CRUISE CONTROL SWITCH

Switch Position	Check Between Terminals No.	Ohms
OFF	3 & 4	5890-6510
OFF	1 & 3	[1]
ON	1 & 4	5890-6510
ON	1 & 3	[2]
ON/SET	3 & 4	1020-1130
ON/RESUME	3 & 4	2040-2260

[1] – No continuity should exist.
[2] – Continuity should exist.

SERVO VACUUM TEST

1) Remove cruise control cable from throttle body. Disconnect cruise control 4-pin servo connector. Disconnect vacuum hose at servo. Apply battery voltage to terminal No. 2 (Dark Blue/Red wire) at servo connector. Using jumper wire, ground remaining 3 terminals at servo connector.

2) Connect hand held vacuum pump to servo vacuum nipple. Apply 10-15 in. Hg of vacuum. Cruise control cable should retract and maintain position as long as vacuum is applied. If servo does not test as specified, replace servo.

VACUUM SUPPLY

1) Disconnect vacuum hose at cruise control servo. Install vacuum gauge to disconnected vacuum hose. Start engine and observe gauge. Vacuum reading should be a minimum of 10 in. Hg. Turn engine off. Vacuum should continue to hold at a minimum of 10 in. Hg.

2) If vacuum is not as specified, check for kinked or leaking vacuum lines, defective check valve, defective vacuum reservoir and/or poor engine performance. If no problems are found, check servo. See CRUISE CONTROL SERVO under TESTING (WITHOUT DRB-II).

REMOVAL & INSTALLATION

WARNING: If vehicle is equipped with air bag, air bag MUST be deactivated before servicing cruise control components on or around steering column. See AIR BAG RESTRAINT SYSTEM article in SAFETY EQUIPMENT.

CRUISE CONTROL SERVO

Removal – Remove cruise control cable mounting bracket from servo. Remove servo mounting bracket. Disconnect wiring harness connector and vacuum hose from servo. Pull cable away from servo to expose retaining clip. Remove retaining clip and cable. Remove servo.
Installation – With throttle in full open position, align hole in cruise control cable sleeve with hole in servo pin. Install retaining clip. To complete installation, reverse removal procedure.

CRUISE CONTROL SWITCH

Removal & Installation – Turn ignition switch to OFF position. Remove 2 screws from back of steering wheel. Rock switch back and forth and remove switch from steering wheel. Disconnect cruise control switch connector. To install switch, reverse removal procedure.

CONNECTOR IDENTIFICATION

CONNECTOR IDENTIFICATION DIRECTORY

Connector	See Fig.
Brake Switch	1
Clockspring	2
Cruise Control Relay	3
Cruise Control Servo	4
Cruise Control Switch	
Except AD & AN With Sport Wheel	5
AD & AN Bodies With Sport Wheel	6
Distance Sensor	7
Engine Diagnostic Connector	8
Single Board Engine Controller (SBEC)	9
Park/Neutral Safety Switch	10

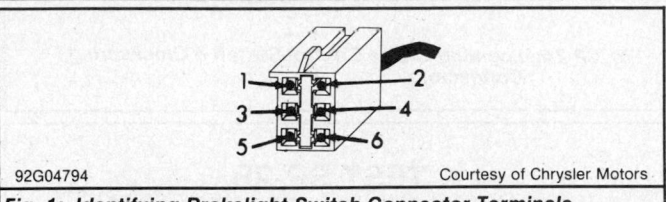

92G04794   Courtesy of Chrysler Motors

Fig. 1: Identifying Brakelight Switch Connector Terminals

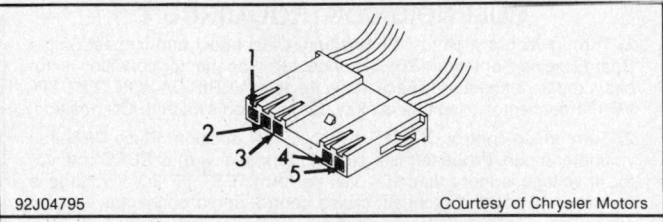

92J04795   Courtesy of Chrysler Motors

Fig. 2: Identifying Clockspring Connector Terminals

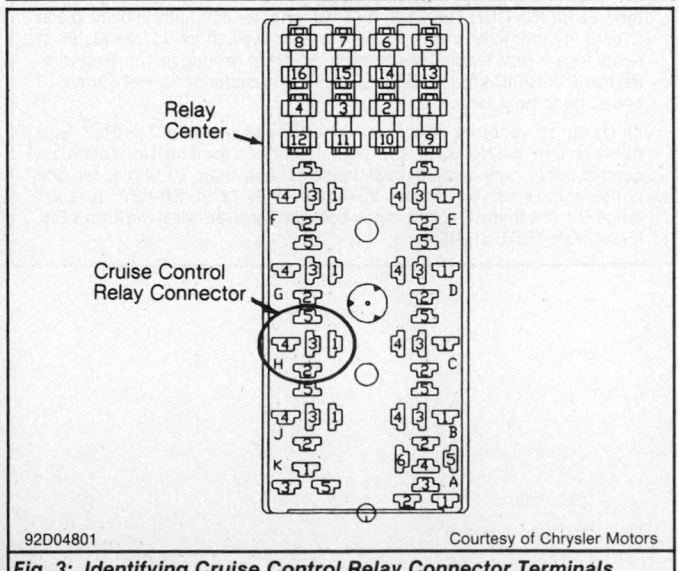

92D04801   Courtesy of Chrysler Motors

Fig. 3: Identifying Cruise Control Relay Connector Terminals

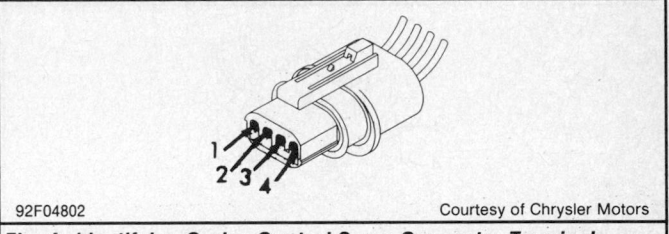

92F04802   Courtesy of Chrysler Motors

Fig. 4: Identifying Cruise Control Servo Connector Terminals

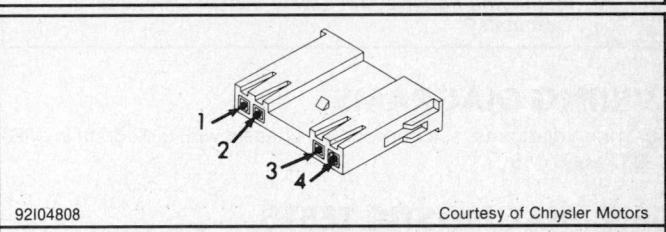

92I04808   Courtesy of Chrysler Motors

Fig. 5: Identifying Cruise Control Switch Connector Terminals (Except AD & AN With Sport Wheel)

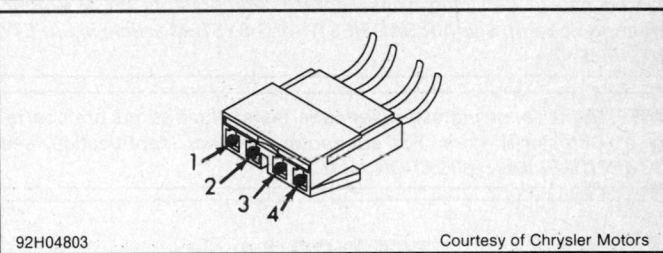

92H04803   Courtesy of Chrysler Motors

Fig. 6: Identifying Cruise Control Switch Connector Terminals (AD & AN With Sport Wheel)

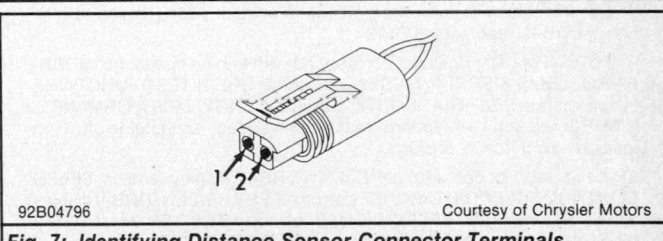

92B04796   Courtesy of Chrysler Motors

Fig. 7: Identifying Distance Sensor Connector Terminals

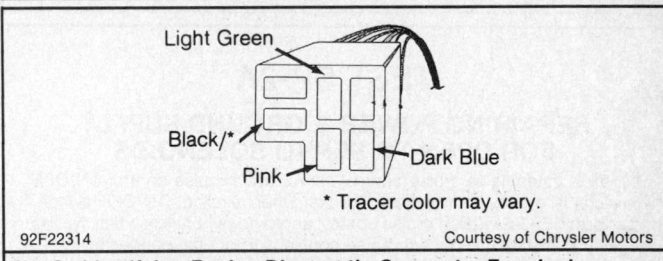

92F22314   Courtesy of Chrysler Motors

Fig. 8: Identifying Engine Diagnostic Connector Terminals

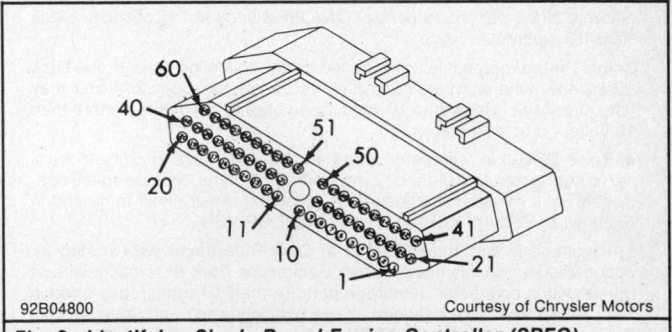

92B04800   Courtesy of Chrysler Motors

Fig. 9: Identifying Single Board Engine Controller (SBEC) Connector Terminals

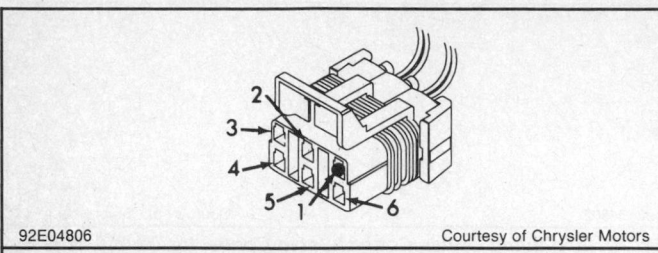

92E04806   Courtesy of Chrysler Motors

Fig. 10: Identifying Park/Neutral Safety Switch Connector Terminals

WIRING DIAGRAMS

For wiring diagrams, see appropriate chassis wiring diagram in WIRING DIAGRAMS.

SELF-DIAGNOSTIC TESTS

WARNING: If vehicle is equipped with air bag, air bag MUST be deactivated before servicing cruise control components on or around steering column. See AIR BAG RESTRAINT SYSTEM article in SAFETY EQUIPMENT.

NOTE: In the following self-diagnostic tests, illustrations are courtesy of Chrysler Motors. For connector terminal identification, see CONNECTOR IDENTIFICATION table.

TEST SP-1A
READING FAULT CODES

1) Ensure battery is fully charged. Start engine. Allow engine to idle. Using DRB-II, read engine RPM.

2) If DRB-II reading does not correspond with engine speed, go to DRB-II PROBLEMS & ERROR MESSAGES under DRB-II TEST FUNCTIONS in appropriate SELF-DIAGNOSTICS article in ENGINE PERFORMANCE. If DRB-II reading corresponds with engine speed, turn engine off. Turn ignition switch to ON position.

3) Read fault codes with DRB-II. If DRB-II display shows SPEED CONTROL SOLENOID CIRCUIT, perform TEST SP-2A. If DRB-II display shows NO VEHICLE SPEED SIGNAL, perform TEST SP-3A. If DRB-II display does not show a fault code, perform TEST SP-4A.

TEST SP-2A
REPAIRING POWER & GROUND SUPPLY FOR OPEN TO SERVO SOLENOIDS

1) While listening to cruise control servo, cycle cruise control ON/OFF switch. If cruise control servo clicks when cycling ON/OFF switch, perform TEST SP-2B. If cruise control servo does not click when cycling ON/OFF switch, disconnect cruise control servo 4-pin connector.

2) Inspect connector. If connector condition is not okay, repair connector as necessary. Perform VERIFICATION TEST SP-VER. If connector condition is okay, put cruise control ON/OFF switch in ON position. Place DRB-II in voltmeter mode.

3) Ensure brake pedal is not pressed during following step. Probe Dark Blue/tracer wire at cruise control servo connector. Color of tracer may vary. If voltage is less than 10 volts, go to step **5)**. If voltage is more than 10 volts, go to next step.

4) Place DRB-II in ohmmeter mode. Probe Black wire at cruise control servo connector. If resistance is more than 10 ohms, replace cruise control servo. If resistance is less than 10 ohms, repair short to ground in Black wire. Perform VERIFICATION TEST SP-VER.

5) If voltage is less than 10 volts at Dark Blue/tracer wire in step **3)**, ensure brake pedal is not pressed. Backprobe Dark Blue/tracer wire at brake switch connector. If voltage is more than 10 volts, repair open in Dark Blue/tracer wire between cruise control switch and brake switch. Perform VERIFICATION TEST SP-VER.

TEST SP-2A (Cont.)

6) If voltage is less than 10 volts, backprobe Yellow/Red wire at brake switch connector. If voltage is more than 10 volts, adjust or replace brake switch as necessary. Perform VERIFICATION TEST SP-VER. If voltage is less than 10 volts, go to next step.

7) If vehicle is not an AS body, repair open in Yellow/Red wire to brake switch connector. Perform VERIFICATION TEST SP-VER. If vehicle is an AS body, access cruise control switch connector. *See Fig. SP-2A.* Backprobe White wire at switch connector. If voltage is less than 10 volts, replace cruise control switch. Perform VERIFICATION TEST SP-VER.

8) If voltage is more than 10 volts, gain access to clockspring 5-pin connector. *See Fig. SP-2A.* Backprobe Yellow/Red wire at clockspring 5-pin connector. If voltage is less than 10 volts, replace clockspring assembly. See AIR BAG RESTRAINT SYSTEM article in SAFETY EQUIPMENT. Perform VERIFICATION TEST SP-VER. If voltage is more than 10 volts, repair open in Yellow/Red wire to brake switch connector. Perform VERIFICATION TEST SP-VER.

92G04807

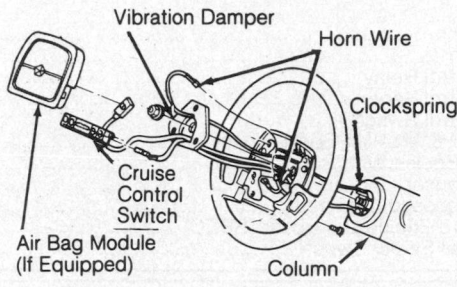

Fig. SP-2A: Locating Cruise Control Switch & Clockspring Connectors

TEST SP-2B
CODE 34, CRUISE CONTROL VACUUM SOLENOID CONTROL CIRCUIT

1) Turn ignition switch to OFF position. Disconnect and inspect Single Board Engine Controller (SBEC) connector. If connector condition is not okay, repair connector as necessary. Perform VERIFICATION TEST SP-VER. If connector condition is okay, turn ignition switch to ON position.

2) Turn cruise control ON/OFF switch to ON position. Place DRB-II in voltmeter mode. Probe terminal No. 33 (Tan/Red wire) at SBEC connector. If voltage is more than 10 volts, perform TEST SP-2C. If voltage is less than 10 volts, disconnect cruise control servo connector. Inspect connector.

3) If connector condition is not okay, repair connector as necessary. Perform VERIFICATION TEST SP-VER. If connector condition is okay, place DRB-II in ohmmeter mode. Probe Tan/Red wire in servo connector. If resistance is less than 10 ohms, repair short to ground in Tan/Red wire. Perform VERIFICATION TEST SP-VER. If resistance is more than 10 ohms, go to next step.

4) Using an external ohmmeter, check resistance at Tan/Red wire between terminal No. 33 at SBEC connector and terminal No. 4 at cruise control servo connector. If resistance is less than 10 ohms, replace cruise control servo. Perform VERIFICATION TEST SP-VER. If resistance is more than 10 ohms, repair open in Tan/Red wire. Perform VERIFICATION TEST SP-VER.

TEST SP-2C

CODE 34, CRUISE CONTROL VENT SOLENOID CONTROL CIRCUIT

1) Probe terminal No. 53 (Light Green/Red wire) at Single Board Engine Controller (SBEC) connector. If voltage is more than 10 volts, replace SBEC. Perform VERIFICATION TEST SP-VER. If voltage is less than 10 volts, disconnect and inspect cruise control 4-pin servo connector.

2) If connector condition is not okay, repair connector as necessary. Perform VERIFICATION TEST SP-VER. If connector condition is okay, put DRB-II in ohmmeter mode. Probe terminal No. 3 (Light Green/Red wire) at servo connector. If resistance is less than 10 ohms, repair short to ground in Light Green/Red wire. Perform VERIFICATION TEST SP-VER. If resistance is more than 10 ohms, go to next step.

3) Using an external ohmmeter, check resistance at Light Green/Red wire between terminals No. 53 at SBEC connector and No. 3 at cruise control servo connector. If resistance is less than 10 ohms, replace cruise control servo. Perform VERIFICATION TEST SP-VER. If resistance is more than 10 ohms, repair open in Light Green/Red wire. Perform VERIFICATION TEST SP-VER.

TEST SP-3A

CODE 15, NO VEHICLE SPEED SIGNAL

1) Turn ignition switch to OFF position. Disconnect vehicle distance sensor connector. Inspect connector. If connector condition is not okay, repair connector as necessary. Perform VERIFICATION TEST SP-VER.

2) If connector is okay, turn ignition switch to ON position. Connect a jumper wire to one terminal of distance sensor connector. Using DRB-II, monitor car speed while tapping open end of jumper wire to other distance sensor connector terminal.

3) If DRB-II display shows car speed to be more than zero, replace distance sensor. Perform VERIFICATION TEST SP-VER. If car speed is zero, turn ignition switch to OFF position. Place DRB-II in ohmmeter mode. Probe Black/Light Blue wire at distance sensor connector.

4) If resistance is more than 10 ohms, repair open in Black/Light Blue wire. Perform VERIFICATION TEST SP-VER. If resistance is less than 10 ohms, disconnect Single Board Engine Controller (SBEC) connector. Inspect connector. If connector condition is not okay, repair connector as necessary. Perform VERIFICATION TEST SP-VER.

5) If connector is okay, check if vehicle is an AN body. If vehicle is an AN body, perform TEST SP-3C. On all other models, turn ignition switch to ON position. Put DRB-II in voltmeter mode. Probe terminal No. 47 (White/Orange wire) at SBEC connector.

6) If voltage is more than 4 volts, go to step 8). If voltage is less than 4 volts, check if speedometer works. If speedometer works, repair open in White/Orange wire between distance sensor connector and SBEC connector. Perform VERIFICATION TEST SP-VER.

7) If speedometer does not work, turn ignition switch to OFF position. Place DRB-II in ohmmeter mode. Probe terminal No. 47 (White/Orange wire) at SBEC connector. If resistance is less than 10 ohms, repair short to ground in White/Orange wire. Perform VERIFICATION TEST SP-VER. If resistance is more than 10 ohms, repair open in White/Orange wire. Perform VERIFICATION TEST SP-VER.

8) If voltage at White/Orange wire is more than 4 volts in step 6), probe White/Orange wire at distance sensor connector. If voltage is more than 4 volts, replace SBEC. Perform VERIFICATION TEST SP-VER.

9) If voltage is less than 4 volts, repair open in White or White/Orange wire between distance sensor and SBEC connector. Perform VERIFICATION TEST SP-VER.

TEST SP-3B

NOTE: Test SP-3B applies to passenger car models only. No test procedures are missing.

TEST SP-3C

CODE 15, NO VEHICLE SPEED SIGNAL (AN BODY)

1) Place DRB-II in ohmmeter mode. Probe terminal No. 47 (White/Orange wire) at Single Board Engine Controller (SBEC) connector. If resistance is less than 10 ohms, repair short to ground in White/Orange wire. Perform VERIFICATION TEST SP-VER. If resistance is more than 10 ohms, go to next step.

2) Using an external ohmmeter, check resistance at White/Orange wire between terminal No. 47 at SBEC connector and terminal No. 1 (White/Orange wire) at distance sensor connector.

3) If resistance is more than 10 ohms, repair open in White/Orange wire. Perform VERIFICATION TEST SP-VER. If resistance is less than 10 ohms, replace SBEC. Perform VERIFICATION TEST SP-VER.

TEST SP-4A

CHECKING CRUISE CONTROL SWITCHES

1) Using DRB-II, read inputs monitor. While watching ON/OFF input, cycle ON/OFF switch several times. If DRB-II display does not correspond with switch position, perform TEST SP-5A.

2) If DRB-II display does correspond with switch position, place cruise control ON/OFF switch in ON position. While watching RESUME input, cycle RESUME switch several times. If DRB-II display does not correspond with switch position, perform TEST SP-6A. If DRB-II display does correspond with switch position, go to next step.

3) While watching SET input, cycle SET switch several times. If DRB-II display does not correspond with switch position, perform TEST SP-7A. If DRB-II display does correspond with switch position, cycle brake pedal several times, while watching BRAKE input.

4) If DRB-II display does not correspond with brake pedal position, perform TEST SP-11A. If DRB-II display does correspond with brake pedal position, check if vehicle is equipped with a manual transmission. If vehicle is equipped with manual transmission, perform TEST SP-12A. If vehicle is not equipped with manual transmission, go to next step.

5) With ignition switch in ON position and engine not running, cycle gear lever several times between "P", "R", "N" and "D", while watching PARK/NEUTRAL input. If DRB-II display does not correspond with selector position, perform TEST SP-13A. If DRB-II display does correspond with selector position, perform TEST SP-12A.

TEST SP-5A

CHECKING CRUISE CONTROL ON/OFF SWITCH CIRCUITS

1) Place DRB-II in voltmeter mode. Probe both sides of cruise control fuse. If voltage input side of fuse is less than 10 volts, repair open in Dark Blue or Orange/Black wire to cruise control fuse. Perform VERIFICATION TEST SP-VER. If voltage input side of fuse is more than 10 volts, go to next step.

2) If vehicle is an AS body, perform TEST SP-9A. On all other models, inspect cruise control fuse. If fuse is not blown, go to step 4).

3) If fuse is blown, disconnect cruise control switch. Inspect connector. If connector condition is not okay, repair connector as necessary and replace fuse. Perform VERIFICATION TEST SP-VER. If connector condition is okay, perform TEST SP-5B.

4) If fuse is not blown in step 2), backprobe Dark Blue/tracer wire in cruise control switch connector. Color of tracer may vary. If voltage is less than 10 volts, perform TEST SP-5D. If voltage is more than 10 volts, turn cruise control switch to ON position.

5) Backprobe Yellow/Red wire at cruise control switch connector. If voltage is less than 10 volts, replace cruise control switch. Perform VERIFICATION TEST SP-VER. If voltage is more than 10 volts, turn ignition switch to OFF position. Disconnect Single Board Engine Controller (SBEC) connector. Inspect connector. If connector condition is not okay, repair connector as necessary. Perform VERIFICATION TEST SP-VER.

6) If connector condition is okay, turn ignition switch to ON position. Ensure cruise control switch is still in ON position. Probe terminal No. 49 (Yellow/Red wire) at SBEC connector. If voltage is less than 10 volts, repair open in Yellow/Red wire. Perform VERIFICATION TEST SP-VER. If voltage is more than 10 volts, replace SBEC. Perform VERIFICATION TEST SP-VER.

TEST SP-5B

REPAIRING CRUISE CONTROL SWITCH CIRCUITS FOR A SHORT TO GROUND

1) Place DRB-II in ohmmeter mode. Probe Dark Blue/tracer wire in cruise control switch connector. Color of tracer may vary. If resistance is less than 10 ohms, perform TEST SP-5C. If resistance is more than 10 ohms, turn ignition switch to OFF position.

2) Disconnect Single Board Engine Controller (SBEC) connector. Inspect connector. If connector condition is not okay, repair connector as necessary. Replace cruise control fuse. Perform VERIFICATION TEST SP-VER. If connector condition is okay, probe terminal No. 48 (Brown/Red wire) at SBEC connector.

3) If resistance is less than 10 ohms, repair short to ground in Brown/Red wire. Replace cruise control fuse. Perform VERIFICATION TEST SP-VER. If resistance is more than 10 ohms, probe terminal No. 50 (White/Light Green) wire at SBEC connector. If resistance is less than 10 ohms, repair short to ground in White/Light Green wire. Replace cruise control fuse. Perform VERIFICATION TEST SP-VER.

4) If resistance is more than 10 ohms, probe terminal No. 49 (Yellow/Red wire) at SBEC connector. If resistance is more than 10 ohms, replace SBEC. Replace cruise control fuse. Perform VERIFICATION TEST SP-VER. If resistance is less than 10 ohms, disconnect brake switch connector.

5) Inspect connector. If connector condition is not okay, repair connector as necessary. Replace cruise control fuse. Perform VERIFICATION TEST SP-VER. If connector condition is okay, probe terminal No. 49 (Yellow/Red wire) at SBEC connector. If resistance is less than 10 ohms, repair short to ground in Yellow/Red wire. Replace cruise control fuse. Perform VERIFICATION TEST SP-VER.

6) If resistance is more than 10 ohms, probe Dark Blue/tracer wire at brake switch connector. Color of tracer may vary. If resistance is more than 10 ohms, replace brake switch. Replace cruise control fuse. Perform VERIFICATION TEST SP-VER. If resistance is less than 10 ohms, disconnect cruise control servo.

7) Inspect connector. If connector condition is not okay, repair connector as necessary. Replace cruise control fuse. Perform VERIFICATION TEST SP-VER. If connector condition is okay, probe Dark Blue/tracer wire at brake switch connector. If resistance is more than 10 ohms, replace cruise control servo. Replace cruise control fuse. Perform VERIFICATION TEST SP-VER.

8) If resistance is less than 10 ohms, repair short to ground in Dark Blue/tracer wire. Replace cruise control fuse. Perform VERIFICATION TEST SP-VER.

TEST SP-5C

CHECKING SWITCH WIRING FOR SHORT TO GROUND

1) Disconnect clockspring 5-pin connector. See Fig. SP-2A. Inspect connector. If connector condition is not okay, repair connector as necessary. Replace cruise control fuse. Perform VERIFICATION TEST SP-VER.

2) If connector condition is okay, probe terminal No. 3 (White/Red wire) at clockspring connector. If resistance is less than 10 ohms, repair short to ground in White/Red wire. Replace cruise control fuse. Perform VERIFICATION TEST SP-VER.

3) If resistance is more than 10 ohms, replace clockspring assembly. Replace cruise control fuse. Perform VERIFICATION TEST SP-VER.

TEST SP-5D

CHECKING SWITCH WIRING FOR OPEN CIRCUIT

1) Disconnect clockspring 5-pin connector. See Fig. SP-2A. Inspect connector. If connector condition is not okay, repair connector as necessary. Perform VERIFICATION TEST SP-VER. If connector condition is okay, place DRB-II in voltmeter mode. Probe terminal No. 3 (White/Red wire) in clockspring 5-pin connector.

2) If voltage is more than 10 volts, replace clockspring assembly. Perform VERIFICATION TEST SP-VER. If voltage is less than 10 volts, repair White/Red wire for an open to fuse panel. Perform VERIFICATION TEST SP-VER.

TEST SP-6A

CHECKING CRUISE CONTROL RESUME SWITCH CIRCUIT

1) Turn ignition switch to OFF position. If vehicle is an AS body, perform TEST SP-6B. On all other models, disconnect Single Board Engine Controller (SBEC) connector. Inspect connector. If connector condition is not okay, repair connector as necessary. Perform VERIFICATION TEST SP-VER.

2) If connector condition is okay, turn ignition switch to ON position. Place DRB-II in voltmeter mode. Probe terminal No. 50 (White/Light Green wire) at SBEC connector. If voltage is more than 10 volts, replace cruise control switch. Perform VERIFICATION TEST SP-VER. If voltage is less than 10 volts, go to next step.

3) Access cruise control switch connector. See Fig. SP-2A. Hold RESUME switch down and backprobe White wire at cruise control switch connector. If voltage is less than 10 volts, replace cruise control switch. Perform VERIFICATION TEST SP-VER. If voltage is more than 10 volts, access clockspring connector.

4) Continue to hold RESUME switch down and backprobe White/Light Green wire at clockspring connector. If voltage is less than 10 volts, replace clockspring assembly. Perform VERIFICATION TEST SP-VER. If voltage is more than 10 volts, go to next step.

5) Continue to hold RESUME switch down and probe terminal No. 50 (White/Light Green wire) at SBEC connector. If voltage is less than 10 volts, repair open in White/Light Green wire. Perform VERIFICATION TEST SP-VER. If voltage is more than 10 volts, replace SBEC. Perform VERIFICATION TEST SP-VER.

TEST SP-6B

CHECKING CRUISE CONTROL RESUME SWITCH CIRCUIT (AS BODY)

1) Disconnect and inspect cruise control switch connector. If connector condition is not okay, repair connector as necessary. Perform VERIFICATION TEST SP-VER. If connector condition is okay, go to next step.

2) With cruise control ON/OFF switch still in ON position, hold cruise control RESUME switch down. Using an external ohmmeter, check resistance between terminals No. 1 and 4 at cruise control switch. See Fig. SP-6B.

3) If resistance is not 2040-2260 ohms, replace cruise control switch. Perform VERIFICATION TEST SP-VER. If resistance is 2040-2260 ohms, replace Single Board Engine Controller (SBEC). Perform VERIFICATION TEST SP-VER.

92E04811

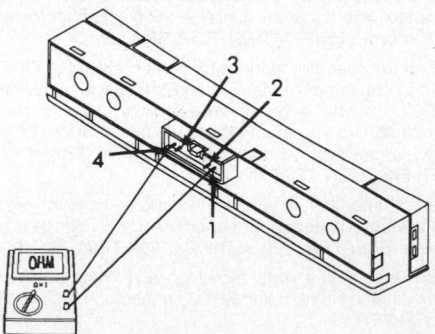

Fig. SP-6B: Testing Cruise Control Switch (AS Body)

TEST SP-7A

CHECKING CRUISE CONTROL SET SWITCH CIRCUIT

1) Turn ignition switch to OFF position. If vehicle is an AS body, perform TEST SP-7B. On all other models, disconnect Single Board Engine Controller (SBEC).

2) Inspect connector. If connector condition is not okay, repair connector as necessary. Perform VERIFICATION TEST SP-VER. If connector condition is okay, turn ignition switch to ON position. Place DRB-II in voltmeter mode. Access cruise control switch connector. See Fig. SP-2A.

3) Backprobe Brown/Red wire at cruise control switch connector. If voltage is less than 10 volts, replace cruise control switch. Perform VERIFICATION TEST SP-VER. If voltage is more than 10 volts, probe terminal No. 48 (Brown/Red wire) at SBEC connector.

4) If voltage is less than 10 volts, repair open in Brown/Red wire. Perform VERIFICATION TEST SP-VER. If voltage is more than 10 volts, hold SET switch down and probe terminal No. 48 (Brown/Red wire) at SBEC connector.

5) If voltage is more than 10 volts, replace cruise control switch. Perform VERIFICATION TEST SP-VER. If voltage is less than 10 volts, replace SBEC. Perform VERIFICATION TEST SP-VER.

TEST SP-7B

CHECKING CRUISE CONTROL SET SWITCH CIRCUIT (AS BODY)

1) Disconnect and inspect cruise control switch connector. If connector condition is not okay, repair connector as necessary. Perform VERIFICATION TEST SP-VER. If connector condition is okay, go to next step.

2) With cruise control ON/OFF switch still in ON position, hold cruise control SET switch down. Using an external ohmmeter, check resistance between terminals No. 1 and 4 at cruise control switch. See Fig. SP-6B.

3) If resistance is not 1020-1130 ohms, replace cruise control switch. Perform VERIFICATION TEST SP-VER. If resistance is 1020-1130 ohms, replace SBEC. Perform VERIFICATION TEST SP-VER.

TEST SP-8A

NOTE: Test SP-8A applies to Jeep models only. No test procedures are missing.

TEST SP-9A

TESTING CRUISE CONTROL SWITCH CIRCUITS

1) Inspect cruise control fuse. If fuse is okay, go to step 4). If fuse is blown, disconnect and inspect cruise control switch connector. If connector condition is not okay, repair connector as necessary and replace cruise control fuse. Perform VERIFICATION TEST SP-VER. If connector condition is okay, place DRB-II in ohmmeter mode. Probe terminal No. 1 (Yellow/Red wire) at cruise control switch connector.

2) If resistance is more than 10 ohms, perform TEST SP-10A. If resistance is less than 10 ohms, disconnect clockspring 5-pin connector. See Fig. SP-2A. Inspect connector. If connector condition is not okay, repair connector as necessary. Replace cruise control fuse. Perform VERIFICATION TEST SP-VER.

3) If connector condition is okay, probe terminal No. 5 (White/Red wire) at clockspring connector. If resistance is more than 10 ohms, replace clockspring. Replace cruise control fuse. Perform VERIFICATION TEST SP-VER. If resistance is less than 10 ohms, repair short to ground in White/Red wire. Replace cruise control fuse. Perform VERIFICATION TEST SP-VER.

4) If fuse is not blown in step 1), backprobe Yellow/Red wire at cruise control switch connector. If voltage is less than 10 volts, go to step 8). If voltage is more than 10 volts, turn ignition switch to OFF position. Disconnect Single Board Engine Controller (SBEC) connector. If connector condition is not okay, repair connector as necessary. If connector condition is okay, turn ignition switch to ON position.

TEST SP-9A (Cont.)

5) Place cruise control switch in ON position. Backprobe Brown/Red wire at cruise control switch connector. If voltage is less than 10 volts, perform TEST SP-9B. If voltage is more than 10 volts, probe terminal No. 23 (Red/Light Green wire) at SBEC connector. If voltage is less than 10 volts, perform TEST SP-9C. If voltage is more than 10 volts, disconnect cruise control switch.

6) Inspect connector. If connector condition is not okay, repair connector as necessary. Perform VERIFICATION TEST SP-VER. If connector condition is okay, using an external ohmmeter, check resistance between terminals No. 1 and 4 at cruise control switch connector. See Fig. SP-6B.

7) If resistance is not 5890-6510 ohms, replace cruise control switch. Perform VERIFICATION TEST SP-VER. If resistance is 5890-6510 ohms, replace SBEC. Perform VERIFICATION TEST SP-VER.

8) If voltage is less than 10 volts at Yellow/Red wire in step 4), backprobe terminal No. 1 (White/Red wire) at clockspring connector. If voltage is more than 10 volts, replace clockspring. Perform VERIFICATION TEST SP-VER. If voltage is less than 10 volts, repair White/Red wire for an open to fuse panel. Perform VERIFICATION TEST SP-VER.

TEST SP-9B

TESTING CLOCKSPRING CIRCUIT FOR SHORTS

1) Disconnect and inspect cruise control switch. If connector condition is not okay, repair connector as necessary. Perform VERIFICATION TEST SP-VER. If connector condition is okay, place DRB-II in ohmmeter mode. Probe terminal No. 23 (Red/Light Green wire) at Single Board Engine Controller (SBEC) connector.

2) If resistance is more than 10 ohms, replace cruise control switch. Perform VERIFICATION TEST SP-VER. If resistance is less than 10 ohms, disconnect clockspring 5-pin connector. See Fig. SP-2A. Inspect connector. If connector condition is not okay, repair connector as necessary. Perform VERIFICATION TEST SP-VER.

3) If connector condition is okay, probe terminal No. 23 (Red/Light Green wire) at SBEC connector. If resistance is more than 10 ohms, replace clockspring. Perform VERIFICATION TEST SP-VER. If resistance is less than 10 ohms, repair short to ground in Red/Light Green wire. Perform VERIFICATION TEST SP-VER.

TEST SP-9C

TESTING CLOCKSPRING CIRCUIT FOR OPEN

Backprobe Red/Light Green wire at clockspring 5-pin connector. If voltage is less than 10 volts, replace clockspring. Perform VERIFICATION TEST SP-VER. If voltage is more than 10 volts, repair open in Red/Light Green wire. Perform VERIFICATION TEST SP-VER.

TEST SP-10A

REPAIRING CRUISE CONTROL SWITCH CIRCUITS FOR SHORT TO GROUND

1) Disconnect and inspect cruise control servo connector. If connector condition is not okay, repair connector as necessary. Replace cruise control fuse. Perform VERIFICATION TEST SP-VER. If connector condition is okay, probe terminal No. 3 (White wire) at cruise control switch connector.

2) If resistance is more than 10 ohms, replace cruise control servo and cruise control fuse. Perform VERIFICATION TEST SP-VER. If resistance is less than 10 ohms, disconnect brake switch connector. Inspect connector. If connector condition is not okay, repair connector as necessary. Replace cruise control fuse. Perform VERIFICATION TEST SP-VER.

3) If connector condition is okay, probe terminal No. 3 (White wire) at cruise control switch connector. If resistance is less than 10 ohms, go to step 5). If resistance is more than 10 ohms, probe terminal No. 6 (Dark Blue/Red wire) at brake switch connector.

TEST SP-10A (Cont.)

4) If resistance is less than 10 ohms, repair short to ground in Dark Blue/Red wire. Replace cruise control fuse. Perform VERIFICATION TEST SP-VER. If resistance is more than 10 ohms, replace brake switch and cruise control fuse. Perform VERIFICATION TEST SP-VER.

5) If resistance at White wire is less than 10 ohms in step **3)**, disconnect clockspring 5-pin connector. *See Fig. SP-2A.* Inspect connector. If connector condition is not okay, repair connector as necessary. Replace cruise control fuse. Perform VERIFICATION TEST SP-VER.

6) If connector condition is okay, probe terminal No. 5 (Yellow/Red wire) at brake switch connector. If resistance is more than 10 ohms, replace clockspring assembly and cruise control fuse. Perform VERIFICATION TEST SP-VER. If resistance is less than 10 ohms, repair short to ground in Yellow/Red wire. Replace cruise control fuse. Perform VERIFICATION TEST SP-VER.

TEST SP-11A

CHECKING BRAKE SWITCH CIRCUITS FOR OPEN

1) If DRB-II display shows RELEASED at all times, perform TEST SP-11B. If DRB-II does not show RELEASED at all times, disconnect brake switch connector. Inspect connector. If connector condition is not okay, repair connector as necessary. Perform VERIFICATION TEST SP-VER.

2) If connector condition is okay, connect a jumper wire between terminal No. 1 (White/Pink wire) and terminal No. 2 (Black wire) at brake switch connector. Using DRB-II, read inputs monitor. if DRB-II display does not show RELEASED, go to step **4)**.

3) If DRB-II display shows RELEASED, check brake switch adjustment. If brake switch is adjusted correctly, replace brake switch. Perform VERIFICATION TEST SP-VER. If brake switch is not adjusted correctly, adjust brake switch. Perform VERIFICATION TEST SP-VER.

4) If DRB-II display does not show RELEASED in step **2)**, connect jumper wire between terminal No. 1 (White/Pink wire) and ground. Using DRB-II, read inputs monitor.

5) If DRB-II display shows RELEASED, repair open in Black wire. If DRB-II does not show RELEASED, turn ignition switch to OFF position. Remove jumper wire. Disconnect Single Board Engine Controller (SBEC) connector. Inspect connector. If connector condition is not okay, repair connector as necessary. Perform VERIFICATION TEST SP-VER.

6) If connector condition is okay, using an external ohmmeter, check resistance between terminal No. 1 (White/Pink wire) and terminal No. 29 at SBEC connector. If resistance is more than 10 ohms, repair open in White/Pink wire. Perform VERIFICATION TEST SP-VER. If resistance is less than 10 ohms, replace SBEC. Perform VERIFICATION TEST SP-VER.

TEST SP-11B

CHECKING BRAKE SWITCH CIRCUITS FOR SHORTS

1) Disconnect brake switch connector. Using DRB-II, read inputs monitor. If DRB-II display shows PRESSED, go to step **3)**. If DRB-II display does not show PRESSED, turn ignition switch to OFF position. Disconnect Single Board Engine Controller (SBEC) connector. Place DRB-II in ohmmeter mode. Probe terminal No. 29 (White/Pink wire).

2) If resistance is less than 10 ohms, repair short to ground in White/Pink wire. Perform VERIFICATION TEST SP-VER. If resistance is more than 10 ohms, replace SBEC. Perform VERIFICATION TEST SP-VER.

3) If DRB-II display shows PRESSED in step **1)**, check brake switch adjustment. If brake switch is adjusted correctly, replace brake switch. Perform VERIFICATION TEST SP-VER. If brake switch is not adjusted correctly, adjust brake switch. Perform VERIFICATION TEST SP-VER.

TEST SP-12A

CHECKING CRUISE CONTROL SERVO OPERATION

1) Disconnect and inspect 4-pin cruise control servo connector. If connector condition is not okay, repair connector as necessary. Perform VERIFICATION TEST SP-VER. If connector condition is okay, place DRB-II in ohmmeter mode. Probe terminal No. 1 (Black wire) at cruise control servo connector.

2) If resistance is more than 10 ohms, repair open Black wire. Perform VERIFICATION TEST SP-VER. If resistance is less than 10 ohms, reconnect cruise control servo connector. Check if vehicle is equipped with a vacuum reservoir. If vehicle is equipped with vacuum reservoir, perform TEST SP-12B.

3) If vehicle is not equipped with a vacuum reservoir, disconnect cruise control servo vacuum hose. Connect vacuum gauge to disconnected servo vacuum hose. Start engine. If gauge does not show a minimum of 10 in. Hg of vacuum, repair vacuum leak or restriction between servo and vacuum source. Perform VERIFICATION TEST SP-VER.

4) If gauge does show a minimum of 10 in. Hg of vacuum, turn engine off. Turn ignition switch to ON position. Using an alternative source of constant vacuum supply, connect a vacuum supply hose to servo. Using DRB-II, actuate servo solenoids. If throttle fully opens and closes, perform TEST SP-14A.

5) If throttle does not fully open and close, using DRB-II, stop actuation test. Inspect cruise control servo cable condition. If cruise control servo cable condition is okay, replace cruise control servo. Perform VERIFICATION TEST SP-VER. If cruise control servo cable condition is not okay, repair cable as necessary. Perform VERIFICATION TEST SP-VER.

TEST SP-12B

CHECKING VACUUM TO CRUISE CONTROL SERVO

1) Start engine. Turn engine off. Turn ignition switch to ON position. Using DRB-II, actuate servo solenoids. If throttle fully opens and closes, perform TEST SP-14A. If throttle does not fully open and close, using DRB-II, stop actuation test.

2) Disconnect vacuum hose at cruise control servo. Using an alternative source of constant vacuum supply, connect a vacuum supply hose to servo. Using DRB-II, actuate servo solenoids. If throttle fully opens and closes, repair vacuum leak or restriction between servo and vacuum source. Perform VERIFICATION TEST SP-VER.

3) If throttle does not fully open and close, using DRB-II, stop actuation test. Inspect cruise control servo cable condition. If cruise control servo cable condition is okay, replace cruise control servo. Perform VERIFICATION TEST SP-VER. If cruise control servo cable condition is not okay, repair cable as necessary. Perform VERIFICATION TEST SP-VER.

TEST SP-13A

CHECKING PARK/NEUTRAL SAFETY SWITCH

1) Disconnect Park/Neutral safety switch connector at transmission. Inspect connector. If connector condition is not okay, repair connector as necessary. Perform VERIFICATION TEST SP-VER. If connector condition is okay, using DRB-II read inputs monitor.

2) If DRB-II display shows D/R, replace Park/Neutral safety switch. Perform VERIFICATION TEST SP-VER. If DRB-II display does not show D/R, turn ignition switch to OFF position. Disconnect and inspect Single Board Engine Controller (SBEC) connector. If connector condition is not okay, repair connector as necessary. Perform VERIFICATION TEST SP-VER.

3) If connector condition is okay, place DRB-II in ohmmeter mode. Probe terminal No. 30 (Brown/tracer wire). Color of tracer may vary. If resistance is less than 10 ohms, repair short to ground in Brown/tracer wire. Perform VERIFICATION TEST SP-VER. If resistance is more than 10 ohms, replace SBEC. Perform VERIFICATION TEST SP-VER.

TEST SP-14A

CHECKING FOR INTERMITTENT FAULTS

1) Reconnect and reassemble all previously tested components. Connect DRB-II to engine diagnostic connector so DRB-II display can be seen from driver's seat. Road test vehicle. Using DRB-II, read cutout monitor on DRB-II display. If DRB-II display shows erratic vehicle speed, replace distance sensor. Perform VERIFICATION TEST SP-VER.

2) If DRB-II display does not show erratic vehicle speed, put cruise control ON/OFF switch in ON position. With vehicle speed at a minimum of 35 MPH, press and release cruise control set switch. If DRB-II display shows S/C DENIED, see appropriate DENIED MESSAGE in DRB-II INTERMITTENT FAULT MESSAGES table and correct problem as necessary.

DRB-II INTERMITTENT FAULT MESSAGES

Denied Message	Problem To Correct
BRAKE	Open Circuit At Terminal No. 29 At SBEC
CLUTCH	RPM/Vehicle Speed Ratio Is Not Constant
ON/OFF	Lack Of Voltage At Terminal No. 23 Or No. 49 At SBEC
P/N	Ground Exists At Terminal No. 30 At SBEC
RPM/SPD	RPM/Speed Ratio Is Not Constant
SPEED	Vehicle Speed As Read By Distance Sensor Is Less Than 35 MPH
RPM	Engine RPM Is Excessively High
SOL/FLT	Fault In Servo Vent Or Vacuum Solenoid Circuit That Is Either Maturing Or Set

3) If DRB-II display shows S/C ALLOWED and cruise control is operative, perform the following:

- Check for cruise control disengagement without driver command by driving vehicle under various road conditions.
- If cruise control disengages without driver command, read cutout monitor S/C DENIED message on DRB-II display. See appropriate DENIED MESSAGE in DRB-II INTERMITTENT FAULT MESSAGES table and repair as necessary.
- If cruise control does not disengage without driver command, read cutout monitor on DRB-II display. Compare GOAL value with SPEED value. If 2 values are not within 2 MPH of each other, replace SBEC.

VERIFICATION TEST SP-VER

CRUISE CONTROL VERIFICATION

Reconnect and reassemble all previously tested components. If Single Board Engine Controller (SBEC) has been changed, perform the following:

- If vehicle is equipped with factory theft alarm, start vehicle at least 20 times so alarm system may be activated when desired.
- Write vehicle's odometer mileage to memory location within replacement SBEC. This will enable new SBEC to operate Emission Maintenance Reminder (EMR) light properly. See MAINTENANCE REMINDER (EMR) MILEAGE TRANSFER under SELF-DIAGNOSTIC SYSTEM in appropriate SELF-DIAGNOSTICS article in ENGINE PERFORMANCE.
- Connect DRB-II to engine diagnostic connector and erase faults.

To ensure no other fault remains, perform the following:

1) Road test vehicle at a speed above 35 MPH. Put cruise control ON/OFF switch in ON position. Press and release set switch. If cruise control did not engage, repair is not complete. Check all pertinent MITCHELL® TECH SERVICE BULLETINS (TSBs) and return to TEST SP-1A, if necessary.

2) Press and release RESUME/ACCEL switch. If vehicle speed did not increase by 2 MPH, repair is not complete. Check all pertinent MITCHELL® TECH SERVICE BULLETINS (TSBs) and return to TEST SP-1A, if necessary.

3) Press and release brake pedal. If cruise control did not disengage, repair is not complete. Check all pertinent MITCHELL® TECH SERVICE BULLETINS (TSBs) and return to TEST SP-1A, if necessary.

4) Bring vehicle speed back up to 35 MPH. Press RESUME/ACCEL switch. If cruise control did not resume previously set speed, repair is not complete. Check all pertinent MITCHELL® TECH SERVICE BULLETINS (TSBs) and return to TEST SP-1A, if necessary.

5) Hold down set switch. If vehicle did not decelerate, repair is not complete. Check all pertinent MITCHELL® TECH SERVICE BULLETINS (TSBs) and return to TEST SP-1A, if necessary.

6) Ensure vehicle speed is greater than 35 MPH and release SET switch. If vehicle did not adjust to new vehicle speed, repair is not complete. Check all pertinent MITCHELL® TECH SERVICE BULLETINS (TSBs) and return to TEST SP-1A, if necessary.

7) Turn ON/OFF switch to OFF position. If cruise control did not disengage, repair is not complete. Check all pertinent MITCHELL® TECH SERVICE BULLETINS (TSBs) and return to TEST SP-1A, if necessary.

8) If vehicle successfully passed all previous tests, cruise control system is now functioning correctly. Repair is complete.

1992 SAFETY EQUIPMENT
Rear Window Defogger

Caravan, Ramcharger, RWD Van, Town & Country, Voyager

DESCRIPTION & OPERATION

Heated rear window defogger system, consisting of a window with 2 vertical bus bars electrically connected to a set of grid lines baked on inside surface of glass, is available on single rear door wagons and vans. A fusible link protects rear grid and a fuse protects relay control circuit.

When control switch is in ON position, current is directed to grid. Actuating control switch energizes relay circuit. Relay circuit will remain energized for approximately 10 minutes or until ignition is turned off. Relay is integral in control switch/timer relay module. An indicator light on module indicates when system is operating.

TROUBLE SHOOTING

Ensure ignition switch is in ON position. Ensure defogger pigtail is connected to wiring harness and ground is secure. Ensure fuse is okay and all wiring and relay connectors are securely attached. If all conditions are okay, one or more of following conditions exist.
- Defective control switch
- Defective control switch relay
- Broken grid line(s)
- Loose connector(s)

To test above components, proceed to individual tests under TESTING.

TESTING

SYSTEM TEST

1) Turn ignition on and place control switch in ON position. Vehicle ammeter (voltmeter on Caravan, Town & Country and Voyager) should indicate current draw. If vehicle is not equipped with an ammeter, defogger operation can be checked by feeling glass. Glass should be warm in 3-4 minutes.

2) Connect a DC voltmeter between right and left vertical grids. It should indicate 10-14 volts. If no current draw is indicated, ensure power feed wire is connected to rear window grid. Ensure ground wire is properly grounded.

3) If turning control switch produces severe ammeter (voltmeter) deflections, check system for short circuit. If system operation has been verified, but indicator bulb does not light, check and replace bulb.

CONTROL SWITCH/TIMER RELAY MODULE TEST

1) Remove switch assembly, leaving harness connected. Turn ignition on. Using a voltmeter, backprobe connector and check voltage at terminals No. 1, 2 and 4. Terminals No. 2 and 4 should have battery voltage. Terminal No. 1 should have zero volts. If readings are not as specified, go to next step. If readings are as specified, go to step **3)**.

2) If voltage does not exist at terminals No. 2 and 4, check for wiring problems, burned-out fusible links and inoperative circuit breaker. If terminal No. 1 reads more than zero volts, turn ignition off and recheck terminal. If voltage reading is still more than zero, replace module.

3) Turn defogger on. Check for voltage at terminal No. 1. Voltage should read battery voltage for about 10 minutes and then drop to zero. Indicator light should glow and remain on for about 10 minutes when defogger is turned on. If indicator light fails to glow or voltage reading is not as specified, replace module.

GRID FILAMENT TEST

1) Using a voltmeter with a 0-15 volt range, contact bus bar connecting grid lines on passenger-side of glass with negative lead of voltmeter. Contact driver-side bus bar with positive lead. *See Fig. 2.*

2) Turn ignition and control switches to ON position. Reading should be 10-14 volts. Lower voltage indicates a poor ground. Attach negative voltmeter lead to ground. Voltage reading should not vary.

3) Contact negative lead to passenger-side bus bar. Probe each grid line at midpoint with positive lead. A 6-volt reading indicates line is

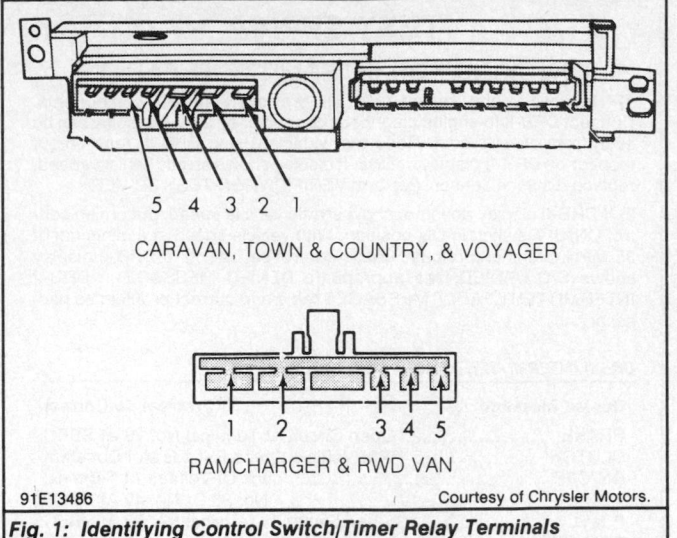

CARAVAN, TOWN & COUNTRY, & VOYAGER

RAMCHARGER & RWD VAN

91E13486   Courtesy of Chrysler Motors.

Fig. 1: *Identifying Control Switch/Timer Relay Terminals*

good. A zero volt reading indicates a break between midpoint and driver-side bus bar line.

4) A 10-14 volt reading indicates a break between midpoint and passenger-side bus bar line. Move positive lead toward break; voltage will change when break is crossed.

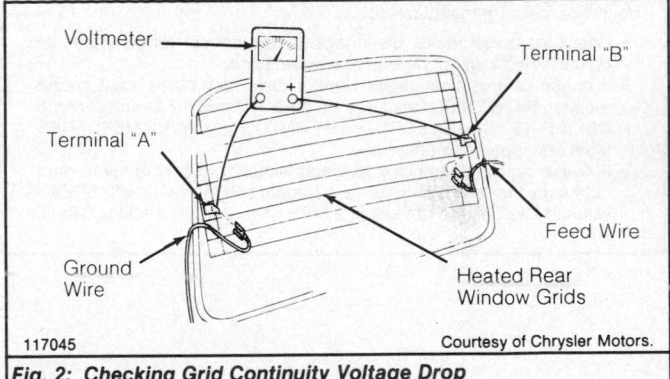

117045   Courtesy of Chrysler Motors.

Fig. 2: *Checking Grid Continuity Voltage Drop*

ON-VEHICLE SERVICE

GRID FILAMENT REPAIR

1) Gently clean repair area using fine steel wool. Finish cleaning repair area using alcohol or similar solvent. Using Mopar Repair Kit (3744970) for grids and Mopar Repair Kit (4267922) for terminals, prepare conductive epoxy.

2) For grid line repair, mask damaged area using tape. *See Fig. 3.* Apply conductive epoxy over damaged area overlapping both ends of break. Allow epoxy to dry for 24 hours at room temperature, or use heat gun for 15 minutes.

3) For grid terminal repair, apply conductive epoxy over damaged area overlapping both ends of terminal break. Position terminal in desired location and secure to prevent from falling. Allow epoxy to dry for 24 hours at room temperature or use heat gun for 15 minutes.

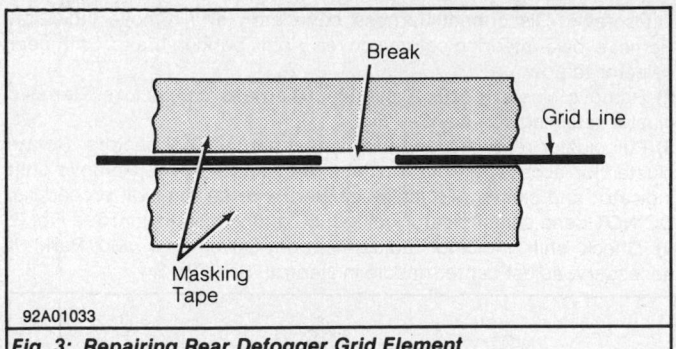

Fig. 3: Repairing Rear Defogger Grid Element

REMOVAL & INSTALLATION

WARNING: When battery is disconnected, vehicle computer and memory systems may lose memory data. Driveability problems may exist until computer systems have completed a relearn cycle. See COMPUTER RELEARN PROCEDURES article in GENERAL INFORMATION before disconnecting battery.

DEFOGGER SWITCH/TIMER RELAY MODULE

Removal & Installation (Caravan, Town & Country, & Voyager) – Rear window defogger switch/timer relay module is an integral part of Accessory Switch Carrier (ASC). Using a trim stick, remove center bezel from instrument panel. Remove ASC from panel. Disconnect wire connectors and lamp. To install, reverse removal procedure.

Removal & Installation (Ramcharger & RWD Van) – Defogger switch, timer and relay are integrated in switch assembly. Disconnect and isolate negative battery cable. Remove 2 heater control bezel mounting screws. Squeeze defogger switch retaining tangs and pull switch from rear of bezel. Remove connector from switch. To install, reverse removal procedure.

WIRING DIAGRAMS

See appropriate chassis wiring diagram in WIRING DIAGRAMS.

Caravan, Town & Country, Voyager

WARNING: On vehicles equipped with Air Bag Restraint System (ABRS), see SERVICE PRECAUTIONS in AIR BAG RESTRAINT SYSTEM article before working around steering column switches (air bag could deploy).

DESCRIPTION & OPERATION

Vehicles are equipped with either an analog or electronic instrument cluster. The body control computer, which receives input from various sensors, sends display information to the cluster.

On analog clusters, this information is used to drive the magnetic gauges. Cluster also incorporates warning lights for low fuel, check gauges, door ajar, low washer fluid, check engine and liftgate ajar. Non-gauge equipped models also have warning lights for low oil pressure and charging system malfunction.

Electronic cluster uses analog bar gauge displays for oil pressure, coolant temperature, charging voltage, engine RPM and fuel level. Cluster also contains LED message center for door ajar, liftgate ajar and low washer fluid. Odometer mileage memory is in the body control computer, not in the cluster.

MAINTENANCE REMINDER LIGHT

For information about maintenance reminder lights, see MAINTENANCE REMINDER LIGHTS article in GENERAL INFORMATION.

TESTING

NOTE: Analog and electronic instrument clusters are controlled by body control computer. For testing of analog and electronic instrument clusters, see BODY CONTROL COMPUTER INTRODUCTION article in ENGINE PERFORMANCE.

REMOVAL & INSTALLATION

WARNING: On vehicles equipped with Air Bag Restraint System (ABRS), see SERVICE PRECAUTIONS in AIR BAG RESTRAINT SYSTEM article before working around steering column switches (air bag could deploy).

CAUTION: When battery is disconnected, vehicle computer and memory systems may lose memory data. Driveability problems may exist until computer systems have completed a relearn cycle. See COMPUTER RELEARN PROCEDURES article in GENERAL INFORMATION before disconnecting battery.

NOTE: Disconnect negative battery cable before servicing instrument panel, cluster or gauges.

INSTRUMENT CLUSTER

Removal & Installation – 1) Using a flat-blade screwdriver, pry up and remove warning indicator grille. Remove warning indicator retain-

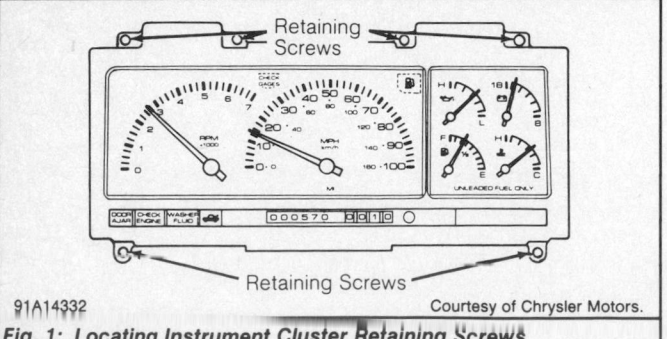

Fig. 1: Locating Instrument Cluster Retaining Screws

91A14332   Courtesy of Chrysler Motors.

ing screws. Disconnect harness connector, and remove indicator. Remove lower steering column cover. Apply parking brake. Shift gear selector to Low.

2) Remove cluster bezel. Disconnect harness connectors. Remove cluster retaining screws. *See Fig. 1.*

3) Pull cluster rearward and disconnect harness connectors. Rotate cluster for access to shift indicator retaining screws. Remove shift indicator and cluster. To install cluster, reverse removal procedure. DO NOT bend shift indicator guide tube during installation. *See Fig. 2.*

4) Check shift indicator adjustment in Drive, Low and Park. If necessary, adjust center needle in Neutral. *See Fig. 3.*

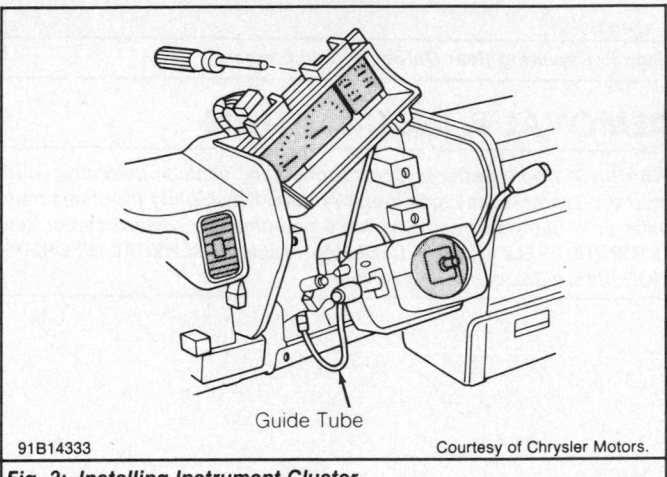

Guide Tube

91B14333   Courtesy of Chrysler Motors.

Fig. 2: Installing Instrument Cluster

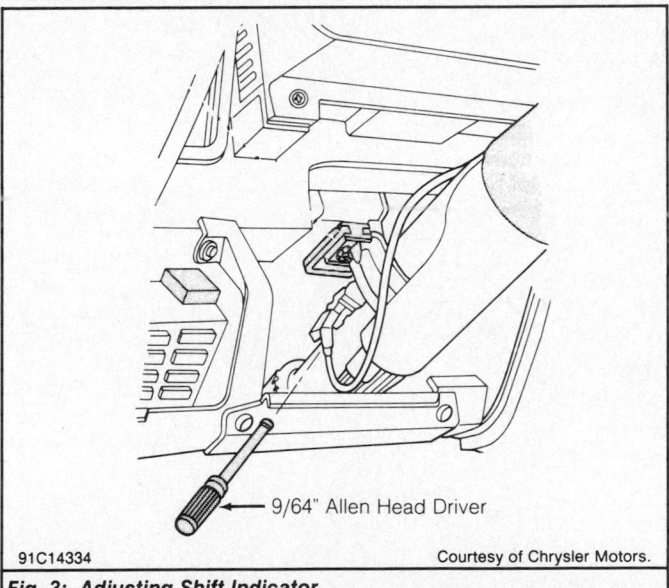

9/64" Allen Head Driver

91C14334   Courtesy of Chrysler Motors.

Fig. 3: Adjusting Shift Indicator

GAUGES

Removal & Installation – 1) Using a flat-blade screwdriver, pry up and remove warning indicator grille. Remove warning indicator retaining screws. Disconnect harness connector, and remove indicator. Remove lower steering column cover. Apply parking brake. Shift gear selector to Low.

2) Remove cluster bezel. Disconnect harness connectors. Remove cluster lens. Remove gauge attaching screws. Pull gauge straight out so as not to damage gauge pins. To install gauge, reverse removal procedure.

WIRING DIAGRAMS

See appropriate chassis wiring diagram in WIRING DIAGRAMS.

Dakota, Pickup, Ramcharger, RWD Van

WARNING: When battery is disconnected, vehicle computer and memory systems may lose memory data. Driveability problems may exist until computer systems have completed a relearn cycle. See COMPUTER RELEARN PROCEDURES article in GENERAL INFORMATION before disconnecting battery.

DESCRIPTION & OPERATION

Analog instrument panel includes either warning lights or electromagnetic type gauges. Varying resistance from sending units control oil and temperature gauge readings. Voltmeter is controlled directly from charging circuit. Speedometer (except Dakota) is electric stepper motor-type and is controlled by vehicle speed sensor. Dakota models are equipped with a cable-driven speedometer.

Brake warning light activates when ignition is on and parking brake is applied. Warning light also activates if brake hydraulic system failure occurs during service brake application. Brake warning light bulb test occurs when ignition switch is in START position.

Oil pressure warning light illuminates when engine oil pressure is not sufficient to open oil pressure sending unit switch. Oil pressure warning light bulb test occurs with ignition switch in RUN position.

MAINTENANCE REMINDER LIGHT

For information about maintenance reminder lights, see MAINTENANCE REMINDER LIGHTS article in GENERAL INFORMATION.

TESTING

WARNING: RWD vans powered by compressed natural gas use a fuel gauge pressure sensor to drive fuel gauge. Fuel system MUST be purged before removing pressure sensor. See COMPRESSED NATURAL GAS SAFETY PRECAUTIONS article in GENERAL INFORMATION.

COMPRESSED NATURAL GAS FUEL SYSTEM PURGING

Fuel Tube Purging – 1) Close control valve (clockwise) on side mounted fuel cylinder. Close control valves (clockwise) on both rear mounted fuel cylinders. Open manual shutoff valve.
2) Start and operate engine until it runs out of fuel. Attempt 3 more engine starts. If check valve or fuel fill receptacle is to be serviced, slowly loosen inlet side of fuel fill tube fitting at check valve. It is normal for approximately 25 psi (1.76 kg/cm²) of natural gas pressure to flow from loosened fitting.

At this point, all fuel tubes are purged of natural gas between fuel cylinders and engine. It is now okay to open fuel system.

FUEL GAUGE & FUEL TANK SENDING UNIT

NOTE: DO NOT leave sending unit lead grounded for extended periods; gauge damage will result.

Dakota – 1) Test fuel gauge and wiring by grounding fuel tank sending unit lead. Turn ignition on, and note gauge reading. DO NOT leave sending unit lead grounded for extended periods; gauge damage will result.
2) If gauge indicates maximum reading, wiring and fuel gauge are operating properly. Go to step **4)**. If gauge does not indicate maximum reading, remove gauge. Using a voltmeter, check for battery voltage between B+ pin and ground pin. *See Fig. 1.*
3) If voltage reading is not as specified, check wiring connections and instrument panel printed circuit board continuity. If wiring and circuit board test okay, replace fuel gauge.
4) If gauge indicates maximum reading in step **2)**, remove fuel tank sending unit. Connect a jumper wire between sending unit body and chassis ground. Install sending unit harness connector. Move float

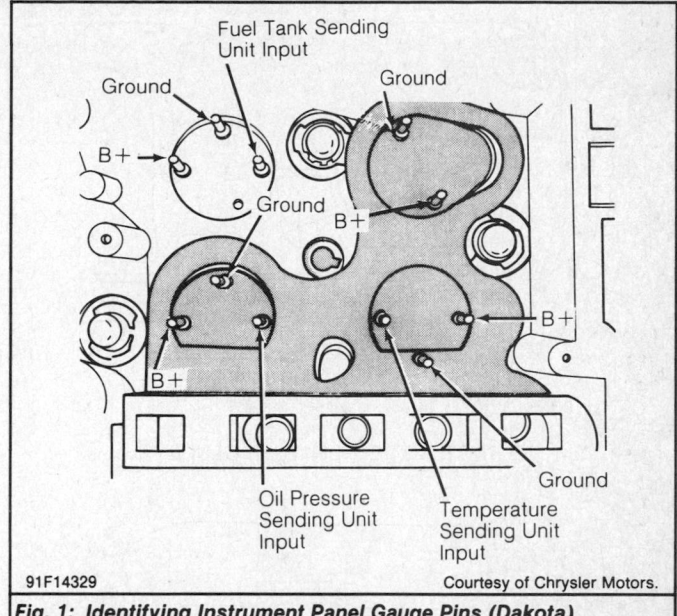

Fuel Tank Sending Unit Input

Ground

Ground

B+

Ground

B+

B+

B+

Ground

Oil Pressure Sending Unit Input

Temperature Sending Unit Input

91F14329

Courtesy of Chrysler Motors.

Fig. 1: Identifying Instrument Panel Gauge Pins (Dakota)

arm to FULL, then EMPTY position. Note fuel gauge readings at each float arm position. Allow at least 2 minutes at each test point for gauge to stabilize.
5) If no reading or improper reading is obtained at either test position, replace sending unit. If sending unit tests okay, check for damaged ground wire or poor connection. Ensure float assembly does not bind in fuel tank and tank is not damaged. Repair as required.
Pickup, Ramcharger & RWD Van – 1) Disconnect wire from fuel tank sending unit. Attach wire to known good sending unit. Install jumper wire between sending unit body and chassis ground.
2) Turn ignition switch to ON position. Move sending unit float arm to EMPTY position, and note fuel gauge reading. Gauge should read EMPTY plus one pointer width or minus 2 pointer widths. Allow at least 2 minutes for gauge to stabilize.
3) Move float arm to FULL position. Gauge should read FULL plus 2 pointer widths or minus one pointer width. Allow at least 2 minutes for gauge to stabilize. If correct reading is obtained, go to step **5)**. If correct reading is not obtained, remove gauge. Using a voltmeter, check for battery voltage between B+ pin and ground pin. *See Figs. 2 and 3.*
4) If voltage reading is not as specified, check wiring connections and instrument panel printed circuit board continuity. If wiring and circuit board test okay, replace fuel gauge.
5) Remove fuel tank sending unit. Install sending unit harness connector. Move float arm to FULL, then EMPTY positions. Note fuel gauge readings at each float arm position. Allow at least 2 minutes at each test point for gauge to stabilize.
6) If no reading or improper reading is obtained at either test position, replace sending unit. If sending unit tests okay, check for poor ground or damaged ground wire. Ensure float assembly does not bind in fuel tank and tank is not damaged. Repair as required.

PRINTED CIRCUIT BOARDS

Perform visual inspection of circuit boards for cracks or damaged circuits. If no visual damage is evident, use an ohmmeter or a test light to check each circuit for continuity. If an open circuit exists, replace circuit board.

TEMPERATURE & OIL PRESSURE GAUGES

Temperature Gauge – 1) Test temperature gauge and wiring by grounding temperature sending unit lead. Turn ignition on, and note gauge reading. DO NOT leave sending unit lead grounded for extended periods; gauge damage will result.

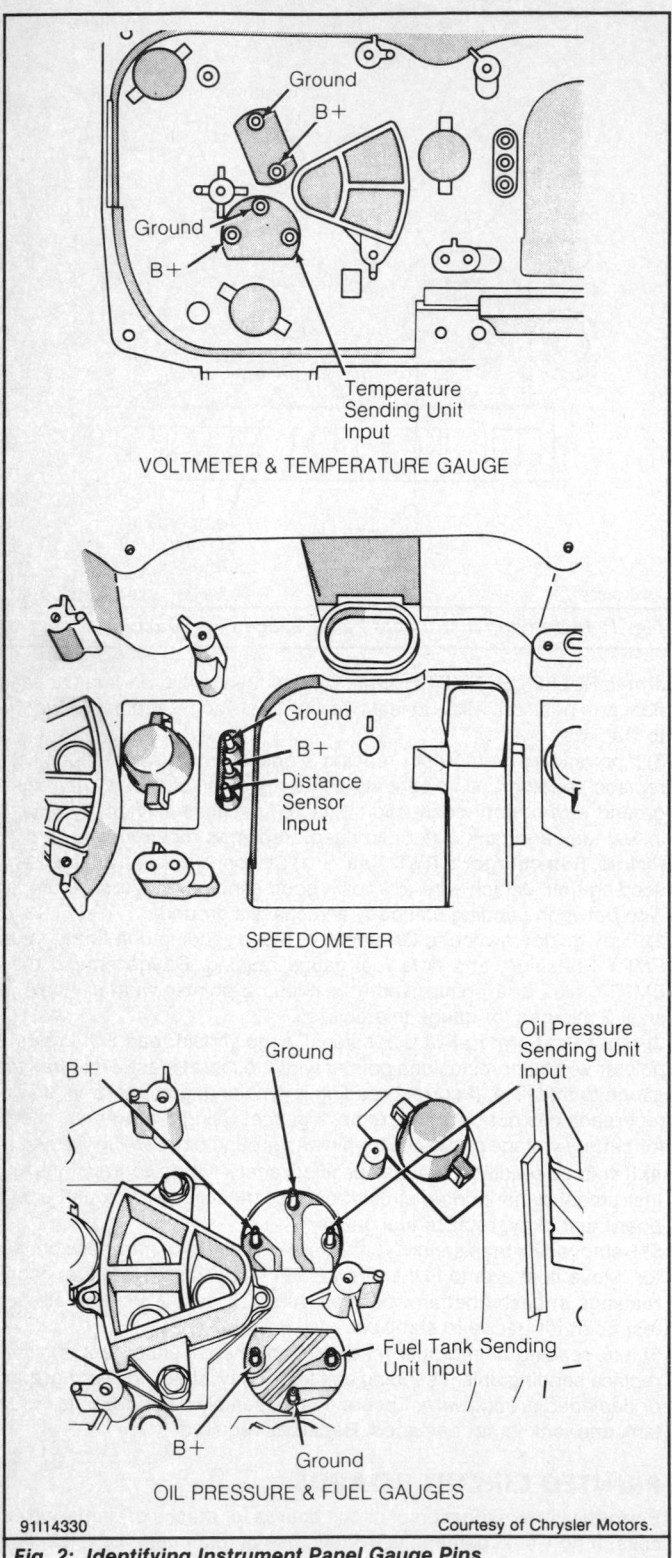

Fig. 2: Identifying Instrument Panel Gauge Pins (Pickup & Ramcharger)

91I14330   Courtesy of Chrysler Motors.

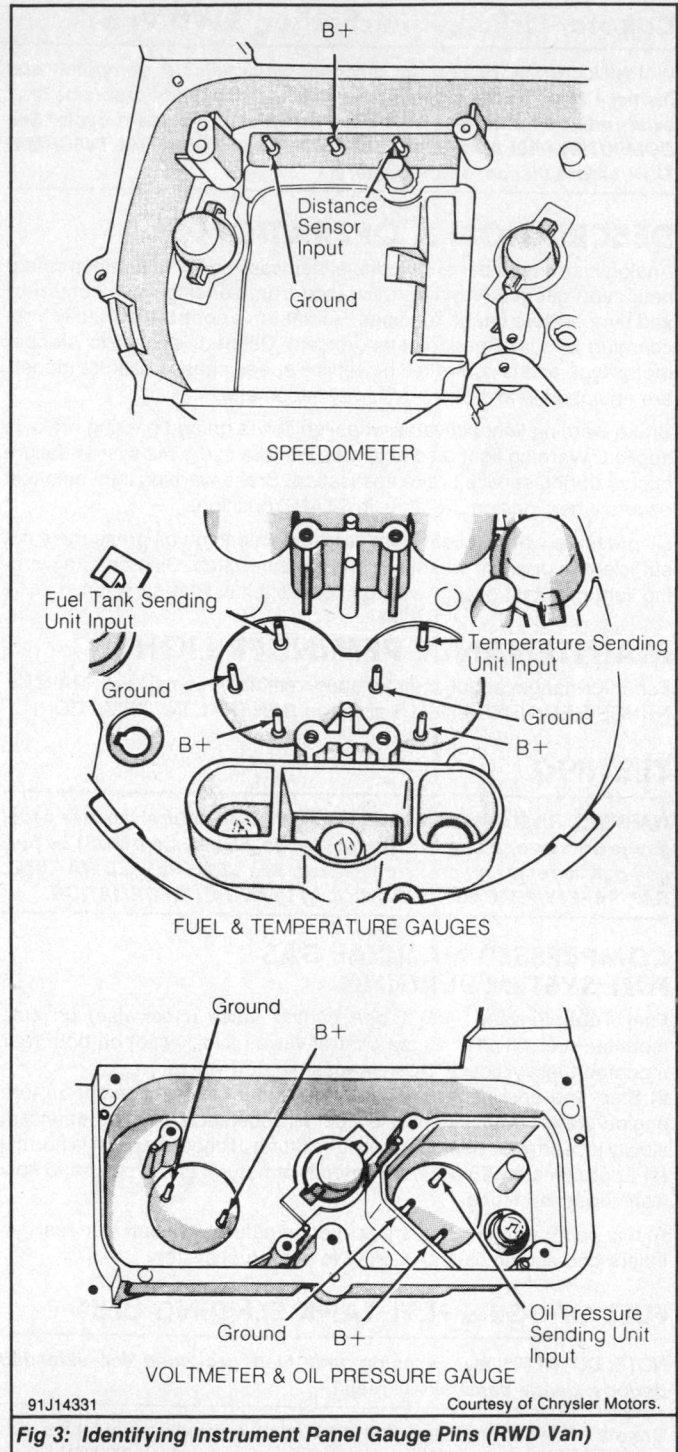

Fig 3: Identifying Instrument Panel Gauge Pins (RWD Van)

91J14331   Courtesy of Chrysler Motors.

2) If gauge indicates maximum reading, wiring and temperature gauge are operating properly. Go to step 4). If gauge does not indicate maximum reading, remove gauge. See GAUGES under REMOVAL & INSTALLATION. Using a voltmeter, check for battery voltage between B+ pin and ground pin. See Figs. 1-3.

3) If voltage reading is not as specified, check wiring connections and instrument panel printed circuit board continuity. If wiring and circuit board test okay, replace temperature gauge.

4) If gauge indicates maximum reading in step 2), disconnect temperature sending unit harness connector. Using an ohmmeter, test resistance between sending unit terminal and engine block. If resistance reading is zero or infinity, replace sending unit. If resistance reading is between zero and infinity and gauge does not read correctly, sending unit may be faulty. Compare with known good unit. Replace as required.

Oil Pressure Gauge – 1) Test oil pressure gauge and wiring by grounding oil pressure sending unit lead. Turn ignition on, and note gauge reading. DO NOT leave sending unit lead grounded for extended periods; gauge damage will result.

2) If gauge indicates maximum reading, wiring and oil pressure gauge are operating properly. Go to step **4)**. If gauge does not indicate maximum reading, remove gauge. Using a voltmeter, check for battery voltage between B+ pin and ground pin. *See Figs. 1-3.*

3) If voltage reading is not as specified, check wiring connections and instrument panel printed circuit board continuity. If wiring and circuit board test okay, replace oil pressure gauge.

4) If gauge indicates maximum reading in step **2)**, disconnect oil pressure sending unit harness connector. Using an ohmmeter, test resistance between sending unit terminal and engine block. If resistance reading is zero or infinity, replace sending unit. If resistance reading is between zero and infinity and gauge does not read correctly, sending unit may be faulty. Replace as required.

5) Oil pressure should be checked with a mechanical gauge to ensure correct oil pressure is available. If correct oil pressure is available and correct gauge reading was obtained in step **1)**, replace sending unit. If correct oil pressure is not available, repair engine.

VOLTMETER

1) Remove voltmeter gauge and seat belt indicator (if equipped). Using a voltmeter, connect positive lead to "B+" terminal and negative lead to chassis ground. *See Figs. 1-3.*

2) Turn ignition on, and note reading. If voltage reading obtained is battery voltage, replace voltmeter gauge. If voltage reading is less than battery voltage, check wiring and printed circuit board for continuity.

OIL PRESSURE WARNING LIGHT

1) Turn ignition on. If warning light does not glow, check fuse. If fuse is blown, replace fuse, and retest. If fuse is okay, go to step **3)**. If light glows, start engine.

2) If light remains on, immediately turn engine off. Check oil pressure using mechanical gauge. If pressure reading is correct, check wiring for short to ground. If wiring tests okay, replace oil pressure switch.

3) If fuse is okay in step **1)**, remove molded or single lead connector at oil pressure switch. Ground oil pressure signal wire (center terminal on 3-wire molded connector).

4) If warning light glows, replace oil pressure switch. If warning light does not glow, check bulb, socket, wiring and connections. Repair as required.

BRAKE WARNING LIGHT

1) Turn ignition on. Apply parking brake. If brake warning light glows, go to step **3)**. If brake warning light does not glow, check fuse. If fuse is blown, replace fuse, and retest. If fuse is okay, go to next step.

2) Using a test light, check for power at parking brake switch. If power does not exist, repair open circuit between fuse block and parking brake switch. If power exists, replace switch.

3) If brake warning light glows in step **1)**, raise and support vehicle. Have an assistant depress brake pedal and observe warning light. Open bleeder screw on wheel cylinder. Brake pedal should fall to floor and warning light should glow. If warning light glows, test is complete. If warning light does not glow, go to next step.

4) Inspect bulb, socket, wiring and brake warning light switch on proportioning valve. Repair as required. Check master cylinder reservoir, and add fluid if necessary.

REMOVAL & INSTALLATION

NOTE: Disconnect negative battery cable before servicing instrument panel, cluster or gauges.

WARNING: When battery is disconnected, vehicle computer and memory systems may lose memory data. Driveability problems may exist until computer systems have completed a relearn cycle. See COMPUTER RELEARN PROCEDURES article in GENERAL INFORMATION before disconnecting battery.

INSTRUMENT CLUSTER

Removal & Installation (Dakota) – 1) Remove silencer pad (if equipped). Remove steering column cover. Remove cluster bezel. *See Fig. 4.* On A/T equipped vehicles, place shift lever in "D" position. Remove gearshift indicator cable retaining clip at steering column, and disconnect indicator cable.

2) Remove instrument cluster retaining screws. Move cluster rearward. Disconnect speedometer cable and cluster wiring. Remove cluster assembly. To install cluster, reverse removal procedure.

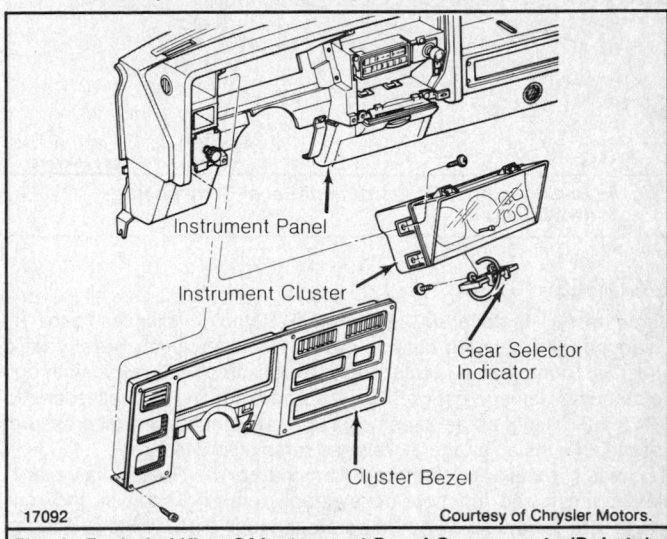

17092   Courtesy of Chrysler Motors.

Fig. 4: Exploded View Of Instrument Panel Components (Dakota)

Removal & Installation (Pickup & Ramcharger) – 1) Tape or cover steering column to protect paint. Remove bezel. Remove 4 steering column lower cover retaining screws. Spread upper steering column cover from locking tangs, and slide cover downward. Disconnect shift actuator cable from steering column.

2) Loosen heater and A/C control assembly. Pull control assembly rearward to clear forward mount on instrument cluster housing. Remove 6 cluster retaining screws. Remove instrument cluster. *See Fig. 5.* To install cluster, reverse removal procedure.

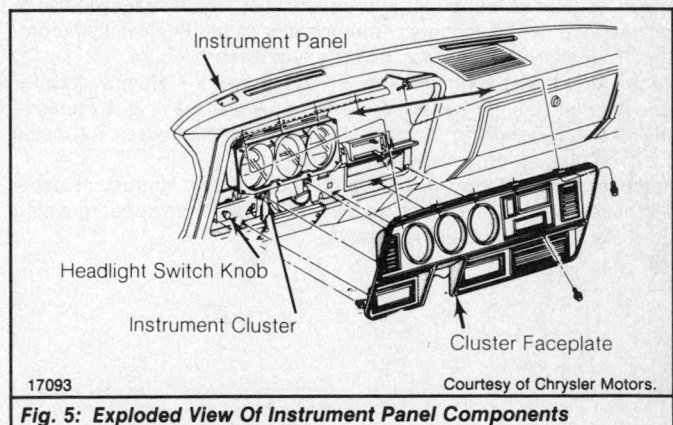

17093   Courtesy of Chrysler Motors.

Fig. 5: Exploded View Of Instrument Panel Components (Pickup & Ramcharger)

Removal & Installation (RWD Van) – 1) Remove instrument cluster hood and bezel assembly retaining screws. *See Fig. 6.* Pull bezel from upper retaining clips. Remove cluster retaining screws. Disconnect message center connector.

2) Disconnect gearshift indicator cable from column. Remove connectors from printed circuit board. Remove instrument cluster assembly. To install, reverse removal procedure.

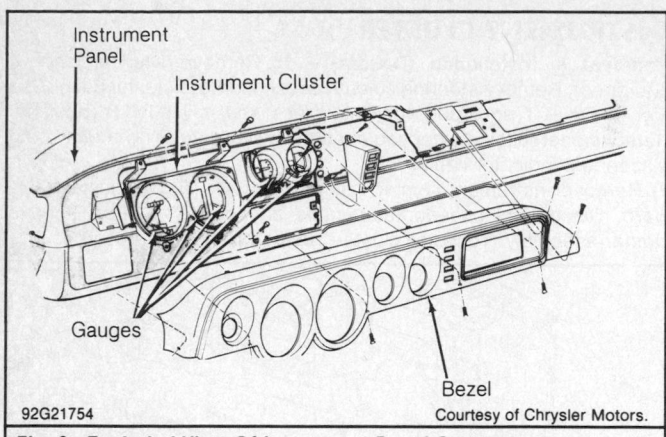

Fig. 6: Exploded View Of Instrument Panel Components (RWD Van)

92G21754 — Courtesy of Chrysler Motors.

GAUGES

Removal & Installation (Dakota) – Remove silencer pad (if equipped) and steering column cover. Remove cluster bezel, mask and lens. Remove gauge retaining screws, and pull gauge straight out so as not to damage gauge pins. On some models, it is necessary to remove 2 gauges as an assembly (such as temperature/oil pressure gauges). To install gauge(s), reverse removal procedure.

Removal & Installation (Pickup & Ramcharger) – Remove faceplate, cluster mask and lens. Remove gauge retaining screws, and pull gauge straight out so as not to damage gauge pins. To install gauge, reverse removal procedure.

Removal & Installation (RWD Van) – **1)** Remove instrument panel hood and bezel retaining screws. Pull bezel from upper retaining clips.

2) Remove lens retaining screws, and remove lens and shroud. Remove mask. Remove gauge retaining screws, and pull gauge straight out so as not to damage gauge pins. To install gauge, reverse removal procedure.

SPEEDOMETER

Removal & Installation (Dakota) – Remove cluster bezel and mask. *See Fig. 4.* Remove speedometer retaining screws. Move speedometer rearward, and disconnect speedometer cable. Remove speedometer. To install speedometer, reverse removal procedure.

Removal & Installation (Pickup & Ramcharger) – Remove cluster faceplate and cluster assembly. Remove cluster mask lens. Remove speedometer retaining screws. Remove speedometer. To install speedometer, reverse removal procedure.

Removal & Installation (RWD Van) – **1)** Remove instrument panel and bezel assembly retaining screws. Pull bezel from upper retaining clips. Remove lens retaining screws.

2) Remove lens and shroud. Remove mask and speedometer retaining screws. To install speedometer, reverse removal procedure.

PRINTED CIRCUIT BOARDS

NOTE: DO NOT overtighten printed circuit board retaining screws.

Removal & Installation (Dakota) – Remove instrument cluster. Disconnect low fuel relay. Remove light sockets. Remove printed circuit retaining screws. Remove printed circuit board. To install, reverse removal procedure.

Removal & Installation (RWD Van) – **1)** Remove instrument cluster. Remove lens and shroud retaining screws. Remove lens and shroud. Remove voltage limiter and light socket assemblies. Remove all gauges. Speedometer does not require removal.

2) Remove circuit board retaining screws, and remove circuit board. To install circuit board, reverse removal procedure.

Removal & Installation (Pickup & Ramcharger) – **1)** Remove instrument cluster mask and lens. Remove instrument cluster. Remove voltmeter, and fuel, temperature and oil gauges. Remove speedometer.

2) Remove light socket assemblies. Rotate light sockets counterclockwise to remove. Remove circuit board retaining screws, and remove circuit board. To install circuit board, reverse removal procedure.

HEADLIGHT SWITCH

Removal & Installation (Dakota) – **1)** Remove silencer pad (if equipped). Remove steering column cover and cluster bezel. Remove headlight bezel retaining screws. Move headlight switch rearward, and disconnect wiring.

2) Pull headlight knob outward. Push release button on right side of switch inward and pull knob outward. Remove retaining spanner nut. Remove headlight switch. To install switch, reverse removal procedure.

Removal & Installation (Pickup & Ramcharger) – **1)** Remove cluster faceplate. From under instrument panel, depress release button located on bottom of switch. Pull knob and stem from front panel.

2) Remove power mirror switch knob. Remove bezel. Remove switch retaining spanner nut. Lower switch down far enough to disconnect wiring harness. Remove switch. To install switch, reverse removal procedure.

Removal & Installation (RWD Van) – **1)** From under instrument panel, depress stem locking button located on bottom of switch. Pull knob and stem from switch while locking button is depressed.

2) Remove instrument panel hood and bezel assembly. Remove switch bezel attaching screws. Remove headlight switch retaining nut. Remove switch, and disconnect wiring harness. To install switch, reverse removal procedure.

Caravan, Dakota, Pickup, Ramcharger, RWD Van, Town & Country, Voyager

DESCRIPTION

Outside power rear view mirrors consist of door-mounted mirrors with internal motor drive and backing plate. Mirrors are controlled by a single toggle switch assembly. Mirror motors are integral with mirror assemblies and cannot be serviced separately.

TESTING

MOTOR TEST

Remove power mirror switch from mounting position. See MIRROR SWITCH under REMOVAL & INSTALLATION. Remove wiring harness at switch connector. Connect one jumper wire to a 12-volt source and another jumper wire to ground. Perform tests as outlined. See Fig. 1 or 2. If results are not as specified, check for broken or shorted circuit. Repair or replace as necessary.

MIRROR SWITCH TEST

Remove switch, and disconnect wiring connector. See MIRROR SWITCH under REMOVAL & INSTALLATION. Using an ohmmeter, check for continuity between switch terminals. See Fig. 3, 4, 5 or 6. If ohmmeter readings are not as specified, replace switch.

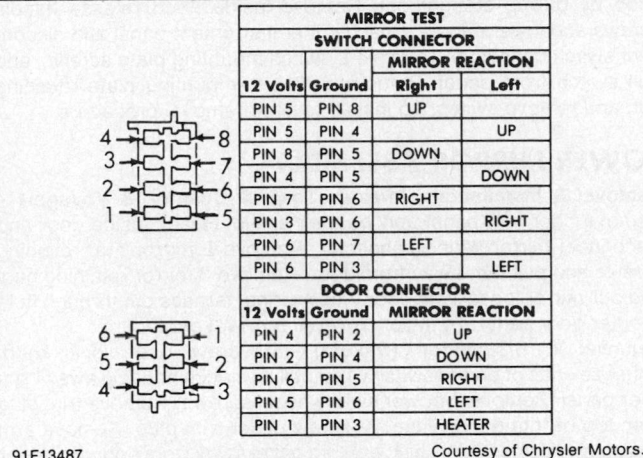

Fig. 1: Mirror Test Chart
(Caravan, Town & Country, & Voyager)

SWITCH CONNECTOR			
		MIRROR REACTION	
12 Volts	**Ground**	**Right**	**Left**
PIN 5	PIN 8	UP	
PIN 5	PIN 4		UP
PIN 8	PIN 5	DOWN	
PIN 4	PIN 5		DOWN
PIN 7	PIN 6	RIGHT	
PIN 3	PIN 6		RIGHT
PIN 6	PIN 7	LEFT	
PIN 6	PIN 3		LEFT

DOOR CONNECTOR		
12 Volts	**Ground**	**MIRROR REACTION**
PIN 4	PIN 2	UP
PIN 2	PIN 4	DOWN
PIN 6	PIN 5	RIGHT
PIN 5	PIN 6	LEFT
PIN 1	PIN 3	HEATER

91F13487   Courtesy of Chrysler Motors.

Fig. 2: Mirror Test Charts
(Dakota, Pickup, Ramcharger & RWD Van)

DAKOTA

12 Volts	Ground	MIRROR REACTION	
		Right	**Left**
DB	WT	UP	
DB/WT	YL/PK		UP
WT	DB	DOWN	
YL/PK	DB/WT		DOWN
YL/BK	WT	RIGHT	
YL	YL/PK		RIGHT
WT	YL/BK	LEFT	
YL/PK	YL		LEFT

PICKUP & RAMCHARGER

12 Volts	Ground	MIRROR REACTION	
		Right	**Left**
YL/BK	WT/BK	UP	
YL	WT		UP
WT/BK	YL/BK	DOWN	
WT	YL		DOWN
WT/BK	DB/WT	RIGHT	
WT	DB		RIGHT
DB/WT	WT/BK	LEFT	
DB	WT		LEFT

RWD VAN

12 Volts	Ground	MIRROR REACTION	
		Right	**Left**
YL/BK	WT	UP	
YL	YL/PK		UP
WT	YL/BK	DOWN	
YL/PK	YL		DOWN
WT	DB	RIGHT	
YL/PK	DB/WT		RIGHT
DB	WT	LEFT	
DB/WT	YL/PK		LEFT

92C21750   Courtesy of Chrysler Motors.

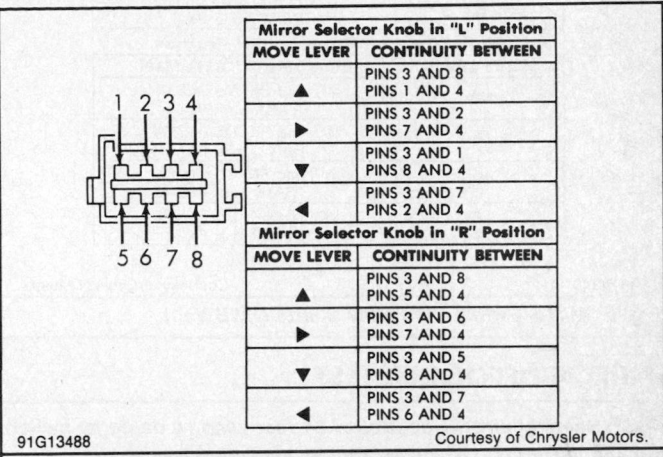

Fig. 3: Mirror Switch Continuity Charts
(Caravan, Town & Country, & Voyager)

Mirror Selector Knob in "L" Position		
MOVE LEVER	**CONTINUITY BETWEEN**	
▲	PINS 3 AND 8	PINS 1 AND 4
▶	PINS 3 AND 2	PINS 7 AND 4
▼	PINS 3 AND 1	PINS 8 AND 4
◀	PINS 3 AND 7	PINS 3 AND 4

Mirror Selector Knob in "R" Position		
MOVE LEVER	**CONTINUITY BETWEEN**	
▲	PINS 3 AND 8	PINS 5 AND 4
▶	PINS 3 AND 6	PINS 7 AND 4
▼	PINS 3 AND 5	PINS 8 AND 4
◀	PINS 3 AND 7	PINS 6 AND 4

91G13488   Courtesy of Chrysler Motors.

Fig. 4: Mirror Switch Continuity Charts (Dakota)

Mirror Selector Knob in "L" Position	
MOVE LEVER	**CONTINUITY BETWEEN**
⬆	BK and WT/BK, PK and DB/WT, PK and DB
➡	BK and WT/BK, PK and YL, PK and YL/BK
⬇	PK and WT/BK, BK and DB/WT, BK and DB
⬅	PK and WT/BK, BK and YL, BK and YL/BK

Mirror Selector Knob in "R" Position	
MOVE LEVER	**CONTINUITY BETWEEN**
⬆	BK and WT, PK and DB/WT, PK and DB
➡	BK and WT, PK and YL, PK and YL/BK
⬇	PK and WT, BK and DB/WT, BK and DB
⬅	PK and WT, BK and YL, BK and YL/BK

92D21751   Courtesy of Chrysler Motors.

Fig. 5: Mirror Switch Continuity Charts
(Pickup & Ramcharger)

MIRROR SELECTOR KNOB IN "L" POSITION	
Move Lever	**Continuity Between**
⬆	WT and BK YL and PK and YL/BK and PK
➡	WT and PK, DB/WT and BK and DB & BK
⬇	YL/BK and BK, YL and BK WT and PK
⬅	WT and BK, DB/WT and PK DB and PK

MIRROR SELECTOR KNOB IN "R" POSITION	
Move Lever	**Continuity Between**
⬆	WT/BK and BK, YL and PK YL/BK and PK
➡	WT/BK and PK, DB and BK DB/WT and BK
⬇	WT and PK, YL and BK YL/BK and PK
⬅	WT/BK and BK, DB and BK DB/WT and PK

92D22239   Courtesy of Chrysler Motors.

Mirror Selector Knob in "L" Position	
MOVE LEVER	CONTINUITY BETWEEN
▲	YL/BK and PK, YL/PK and BK YL and PK
►	YL/PK and PK, DB and BK DB/WT and BK
▼	YL/PK and PK, YL and BK YL/BK and BK
◄	YL/PK and BK, DB and PK DB/WT and PK
Mirror Selector Knob in "R" Position	
MOVE LEVER	CONTINUITY BETWEEN
▲	WT and BK, YL and PK YL/BK and PK
►	WT and PK, DB and BK DB/WT and BK
▼	WT and PK, YL and BK YL/BK and BK
◄	WT and BK, DB and PK DB/WT and PK

92G22240   Courtesy of Chrysler Motors.

Fig. 6: Mirror Switch Continuity Charts (RWD Van)

MIRROR DEFOGGER TEST

NOTE: *Heated mirror is controlled by rear window defogger switch. Heated mirror is on whenever rear window defogger is on.*

Caravan, Town & Country, & Voyager – **1)** Mirror should be warm to touch with rear window defogger activated. If mirror is not warm to touch, check fuses and test voltage at rear window defogger switch. If voltage does not exist, repair wire. See REAR WINDOW DEFOGGER article.

2) Apply voltage to Light Blue wire to heated mirror, and ground Black wire to heated mirror. Mirror should become warm to touch. If mirror is not warm to touch, remove mirror and test wires for continuity. If no continuity exists, repair wires. If wires are okay, replace mirror. To test defogger switch, see REAR WINDOW DEFOGGER article.

REMOVAL & INSTALLATION

WARNING: *When battery is disconnected, vehicle computer and memory systems may lose memory data. Driveability problems may exist until computer systems have completed a relearn cycle. See COMPUTER RELEARN PROCEDURES article in GENERAL INFORMATION before disconnecting battery.*

MIRROR SWITCH

Removal & Installation (Caravan, Town & Country, & Voyager) – Remove driver-side door mirror switch bezel from armrest. Disconnect wiring connector. Remove switch from bezel. To install, reverse removal procedure.

Removal & Installation (Dakota) – **1)** Remove 3 steering column cover and 10 instrument cluster bezel screws. Remove cover and cluster bezel. Remove 5 headlight and accessory switch bezel screws. Disconnect wiring connectors.

2) Remove power mirror switch knob by pulling straight back from switch. Remove 2 switch mounting plate screws on back of switch bezel. Remove switch-to-mounting plate retaining ring. Remove switch. To install, reverse removal procedure.

Removal & Installation (Pickup & Ramcharger) – **1)** Remove 2 mirror lamp screws. Remove 6 bezel-to-instrument panel screws. Ensure screw below heater control is removed. Place column shift lever in "1" position. Remove bezel by pulling top edge rearward. Disengage bezel attaching clips, and remove bezel.

2) Remove bulb socket (if equipped). Disconnect message center wires. Remove instrument panel cluster assembly. Remove headlight switch knob by reaching under instrument panel and pressing button on side of instrument panel while pulling stem out. Remove switch bezel retaining screws and pull bezel out of instrument panel.

3) Pull harness out through opening in instrument panel and disconnect mirror switch connector. Remove 2 switch mounting plate-to-bezel retaining screws. Remove switch-to-mounting plate nut. Remove switch. To install, reverse removal procedure.

Removal & Installation (RWD Van) – Disconnect battery. Remove instrument panel lower steering column cover. Remove mirror control knob by pulling straight out. Remove inside hood release handle screws and lower handle. Reach under instrument panel and disconnect switch connector. Remove 2 switch mounting plate screws, and pull switch from panel. Remove switch-to-mounting plate retaining nut, and remove switch. To install, reverse removal procedure.

POWER MIRROR ASSEMBLY

Removal & Installation (Caravan, Town & Country, & Voyager) – Remove door trim panel and weather shield. Reach inside door and disconnect mirror wiring connector. Remove 2 mirror trim retaining screws and pull trim away from door. Remove 3 mirror retaining nuts and pull mirror loose from door. Feed wiring harness out through hole in outer door panel. To install, reverse removal procedure.

Removal & Installation (Dakota) – Unscrew door lock knob. Squeeze ends of power switch while pulling switch housing away from door panel. Remove 2 power switch bezel screws. Remove trim plug from top of trim panel. Remove screw under trim plug. Remove arm rest screw. Using a trim stick, pry trim panel away from door. Roll door watershield away from lower rear corner of door to expose panel access. Reach inside door and disconnect mirror wiring connector. Remove 3 mirror retaining nuts and pull mirror loose from door. Feed wiring harness out through hole in outer door panel. To install, reverse removal procedure.

Removal & Installation (Pickup, Ramcharger & RWD Van) – **1)** Remove remote control handle. Remove power window/lock switch by inserting blade screwdriver into switch housing forward notch, and depressing locking tab. Pull switch bezel out and forward to remove from door panel. Remove 2 screws from bottom (front and rear) of trim panel. Remove screw behind remote handle. Using trim stick, pry trim panel away from door. Roll door watershield away from lower rear corner of door to expose panel access. Reach inside door and disconnect mirror wiring connector.

NOTE: *Spray silicone on mounting bracket cover grommet to prevent grommet from coming off when cover is moved up on mirror stem.*

2) Remove mirror mounting bracket cover and slide up on mirror stem. Remove mirror mounting bracket nuts. Pull mirror loose from door and feed wiring harness out through hole in outer door panel. To install, reverse removal procedure.

WIRING DIAGRAMS

See appropriate chassis wiring diagram in WIRING DIAGRAMS.

Caravan, Dakota, Pickup, Ramcharger, RWD Van, Town & Country, Voyager

WARNING: On vehicles equipped with Air Bag Restraint System (ABRS), see SERVICE PRECAUTIONS in AIR BAG RESTRAINT SYSTEM article before working around steering column switches (air bag could deploy).

DESCRIPTION

Turn signal, hazard flasher, headlight beam selector, headlight optical horn, windshield wipe, pulse wipe and windshield wash systems use a common switch assembly (multifunction switch), mounted within upper steering column housing.

Ignition switch and lock cylinder are incorporated into an assembly attached to side of steering column. Lock cylinder can be serviced as a separate unit, but requires removal of ignition switch assembly.

DISABLING & ACTIVATING AIR BAG SYSTEM

WARNING: When battery is disconnected, vehicle computer and memory systems may lose memory data. Driveability problems may exist until computer systems have completed a relearn cycle. See COMPUTER RELEARN PROCEDURES article in GENERAL INFORMATION before disconnecting battery.

WARNING: Wait about 2 minutes after disconnecting negative battery cable before servicing air bag system. System reserve capacitor maintains air bag system voltage for about 2 minutes after battery is disconnected. Servicing air bag system before 2 minutes may cause accidental air bag deployment and possible personal injury.

Disabling & Activating System For Repairs – To disable system for repairs, turn ignition switch to OFF position. Disconnect and isolate negative battery cable. To activate system, reconnect negative battery cable.

NOTE: Complete system deactivation should be performed only if ABRS is not functioning properly and vehicle must be driven.

Complete System Deactivation – **1)** Disconnect and isolate negative battery cable. Disconnect 2-pin Yellow clockspring harness connector, located between clockspring and instrument panel wiring harness, on top of fuse block.
2) Clockspring connector may also be disconnected at Air Bag System Diagnostic Module (ASDM). Reconnect battery, and drive vehicle to repair area. Disconnect and isolate negative battery cable.

TROUBLE SHOOTING

Hazard Flashers Inoperative – Blown fuse. Faulty hazard flasher. Open circuit in feed wire to hazard switch. Faulty turn signal/hazard switch. Open or grounded circuit in wiring to external lights.
Indicator Light Inoperative, External Lights Okay – Burned-out indicator bulb in instrument cluster.
Indicator Light Okay, External Lights Inoperative – Open circuit in wire to external light(s).
Indicator Light Okay, External Lights Glow Dimly Or Do Not Flash – Loose or corroded external light connections. Poor ground circuit at external light(s).
Turn Signals Do Not Cancel After Turn – Broken canceling finger on turn signal switch. Improperly aligned canceling cam. Broken or loose canceling cam.
Turn Signals Inoperative (Both Sides) – Blown fuse. Faulty turn signal flasher. Loose bulkhead connector. Loose or faulty rear wiring harness or terminals. Open circuit to turn signal flasher. Open circuit in feed wire to turn signal switch. Faulty switch connections. Open or grounded circuit in wiring to external lights.

Turn Signal Inoperative (One Side) – Faulty external bulb. Poor ground at external light. Open circuit in wiring to external light(s). Faulty turn signal/hazard switch.

TESTING

WARNING: When battery is disconnected, vehicle computer and memory systems may lose memory data. Driveability problems may exist until computer systems have completed a relearn cycle. See COMPUTER RELEARN PROCEDURES article in GENERAL INFORMATION before disconnecting battery.

HORN

Horns Will Not Sound – **1)** Check for blown horn fuse. If fuse is okay, go to step **2)**. If fuse is blown, replace it and ensure horn is functioning. If horn sounds and new fuse does not blow, repair is completed. If horns fail to sound and new fuse does not blow, go to step **2)**. If horn fails to sound and new fuse blows, check for faulty wiring between fuse terminal and horn, and check for short circuit in horn.
2) If fuse is okay in step **1)**, unplug wire connector at horn. Using a test light, connect one lead to wire connector and other lead to ground. Depress horn switch. If test light glows, horn is ungrounded or faulty, go to next step. If test light does not glow, go to step **4)**.

NOTE: Ground can be checked by connecting jumper wire between horn bracket (scratch through paint) and negative battery terminal.

3) Connect jumper wire to horn bracket. Reconnect horn connector. If horn fails to sound with jumper wire and horn connector connected, replace horn.
4) If test light fails to glow in step **2)**, check for defective horn relay by substituting another relay. If test light glows when horn switch is depressed, original relay is defective. If test light fails to glow with substitute relay, go to next step.
5) Disconnect relay. Connect jumper wire between battery terminal and horn terminal on relay terminal board. *See Fig. 1.* If test light fails to glow, check for open circuit between horn fuse and horn terminal on relay terminal board. Also check for open circuit between relay terminal board and horn terminals. If test light glows, fault exists in horn switch or open circuit in wiring between relay terminal and horn switch.

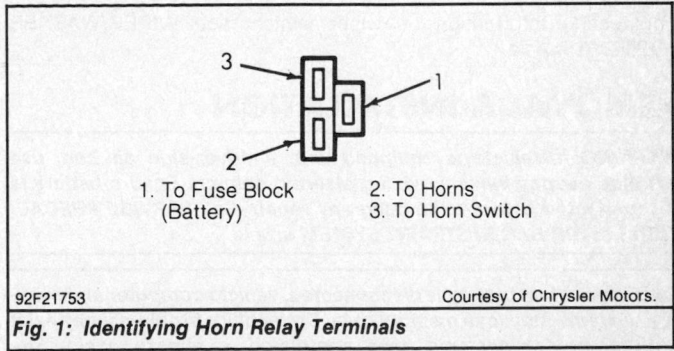

| 1. To Fuse Block (Battery) | 2. To Horns |
| | 3. To Horn Switch |

92F21753   Courtesy of Chrysler Motors.

Fig. 1: Identifying Horn Relay Terminals

CAUTION: Continuous sounding of horns may cause relay to fail.

Horns Sound Continuously – **1)** If horns sound continuously, disconnect horn relay. Plug in another relay. If horn stops blowing, repair is completed. If horn continues to sound, go to next step.
2) Using a voltmeter, connect one lead to battery terminal on relay board. Connect other lead to switch terminal. *See Fig. 1.*

NOTE: Voltmeter will register battery voltage when wire to horn is shorted to ground or horn switch is defective.

3) Remove steering wheel horn pad, and disconnect horn switch wire. See HORN PAD under REMOVAL & INSTALLATION. Repeat step **2)**. If test light glows, repair short in horn switch wire. If test light does not glow, replace horn switch.

Horns Sound Intermittently – Check horn switch or wire to horn switch for grounding out.

MULTIFUNCTION SWITCH TEST

Disconnect and isolate negative battery cable. Remove multifunction switch. See MULTIFUNCTION SWITCH under REMOVAL & INSTALLATION. Use an ohmmeter to check continuity between switch terminals. *See Fig. 2.* See MULTIFUNCTION SWITCH CONTINUITY table. If continuity is not as specified, replace multifunction switch.

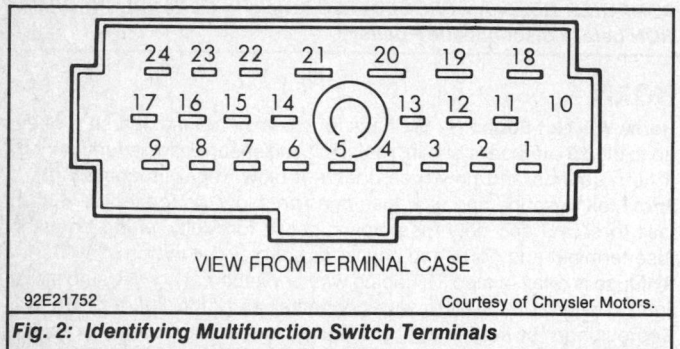

VIEW FROM TERMINAL CASE

92E21752   Courtesy of Chrysler Motors.

Fig. 2: Identifying Multifunction Switch Terminals

MULTIFUNCTION SWITCH CONTINUITY

Switch Position	Terminals No.
Caravan, Town & Country, & Voyager	
Turn Signal	
Neutral	12, 14 & 16
Left	12 & 16; 13, 14 & 15
Right	14 & 16; 11, 12 & 13
Dakota, Pickup, Ramcharger & RWD Van	
With Optional Corner Lights	
Turn Signal/Hazard Warning	
Left/Off	22 & 23
Right/Off	23 & 24
Without Optional Corner Lights	
Turn Signal/Hazard Warning	
Neutral/Off	12, 14 & 15
Left/Off	12 & 14; 15, 16 & 17
Right/Off	14 & 15; 11, 12 & 17
Neutral/On	11, 12, 13, 15 & 16

WIPER SWITCH TEST

For testing information on wiper switch, see WIPER/WASHER SYSTEMS article.

REMOVAL & INSTALLATION

WARNING: If vehicle is equipped with a driver-side air bag, use extreme caution while servicing steering column. Ensure battery is disconnected before attempting any repair. See SERVICE PRECAUTIONS in AIR BAG RESTRAINT SYSTEM article.

CAUTION: When battery is disconnected, vehicle computer and memory systems may lose memory data. Driveability problems may exist until computer systems have completed a relearn cycle. See COMPUTER RELEARN PROCEDURES article in GENERAL INFORMATION before disconnecting battery.

HORN PAD

Removal & Installation (Caravan, Town & Country, & Voyager) –
1) Disconnect and isolate negative battery cable. Remove air bag retaining nuts from back of steering wheel, and remove air bag module. Place air bag module face up on a clean level surface. Disconnect air bag initiator harness connector.
2) Remove horn switch retaining screws, and remove switch. To install pad, reverse removal procedure.

Removal & Installation (Dakota, Pickup, Ramcharger & RWD Van) – Remove horn pad mounting screws located on underside of steering wheel. Pull pad from wheel, and disconnect harness connector(s). Remove pad. To install pad, reverse removal procedure.

MULTIFUNCTION SWITCH

Removal & Installation – Disconnect and isolate negative battery cable. On tilt columns, remove tilt lever. On all models, remove upper and lower steering column covers. Remove (tamperproof Torx) mounting screws. Pull switch away from column, and loosen connector screw (screw remains in connector). Remove switch. To install switch, reverse removal procedure.

IGNITION SWITCH & LOCK CYLINDER

CAUTION: Special care must be taken to avoid bumping, jolting or hammering on steering shaft and gearshift tube.

Ignition Switch (Removal & Installation) – Disconnect and isolate negative battery cable. On tilt columns, remove tilt lever. On all models, remove upper and lower steering column covers. Remove 3 (tamperproof Torx) mounting screws. *See Fig. 3.* Gently pull switch away from column. Release connector locks on ignition, Key In switch and Halo light connectors, and remove switch from connectors. To install switch, reverse removal procedure.

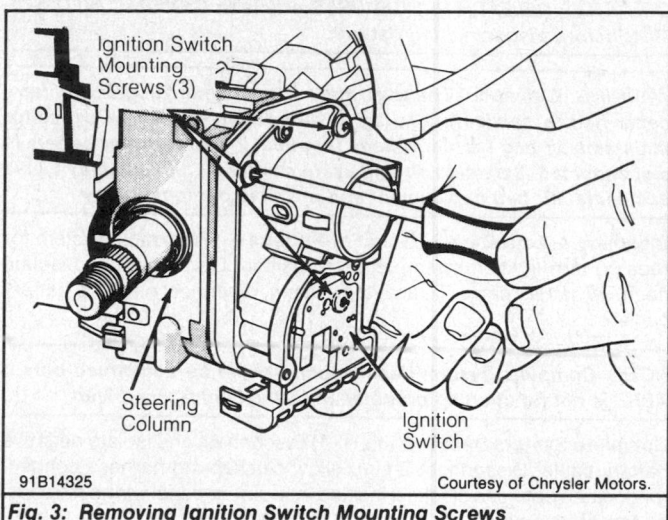

Ignition Switch Mounting Screws (3)

Steering Column

Ignition Switch

91B14325   Courtesy of Chrysler Motors.

Fig. 3: Removing Ignition Switch Mounting Screws

Lock Cylinder (Removal) – Remove ignition switch. With key inserted and ignition switch in LOCK position, depress lock cylinder retaining pin using a small screwdriver. *See Fig. 4.* Rotate cylinder to OFF position. Lock cylinder should now be unseated from ignition switch assembly. Rotate cylinder back to LOCK position, and remove key. Remove lock cylinder.
Installation – 1) Install electrical connectors on switch assembly. Position park lock slider linkage in mid-travel. *See Fig. 5.*

NOTE: On column shift vehicles, shifter must be in PARK position. Ignition switch must be in LOCK position (column lock flag parallel with ignition switch terminals). See Fig. 6.

2) Mount ignition switch to column. Tighten mounting screws to **17 INCH lbs. (2 N.m).** Install upper and lower steering column covers. Install tilt lever (if equipped). Reconnect negative battery cable.
3) With lock cylinder and ignition switch in LOCK position, insert lock cylinder into switch assembly until it bottoms. Insert key. Gently push in on key while rotating key clockwise to end of travel. Check for proper operation of ignition switch in all positions.

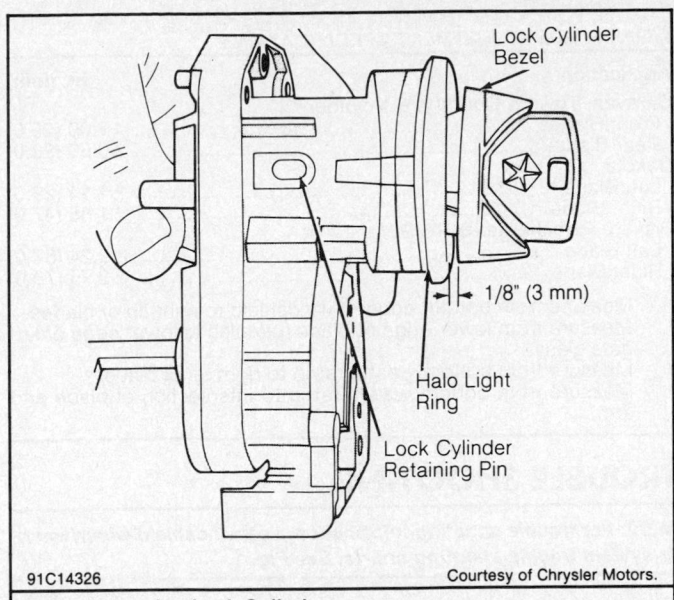

Lock Cylinder
Bezel

1/8" (3 mm)

Halo Light
Ring

Lock Cylinder
Retaining Pin

91C14326   Courtesy of Chrysler Motors.

Fig. 4: Removing Lock Cylinder

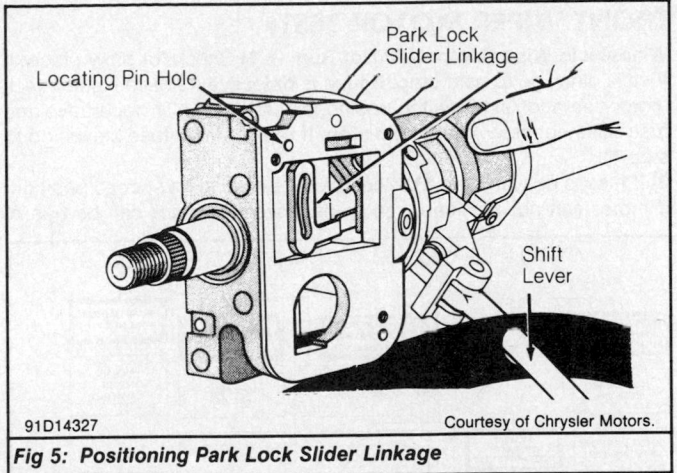

Locating Pin Hole

Park Lock
Slider Linkage

Shift
Lever

91D14327   Courtesy of Chrysler Motors.

Fig 5: Positioning Park Lock Slider Linkage

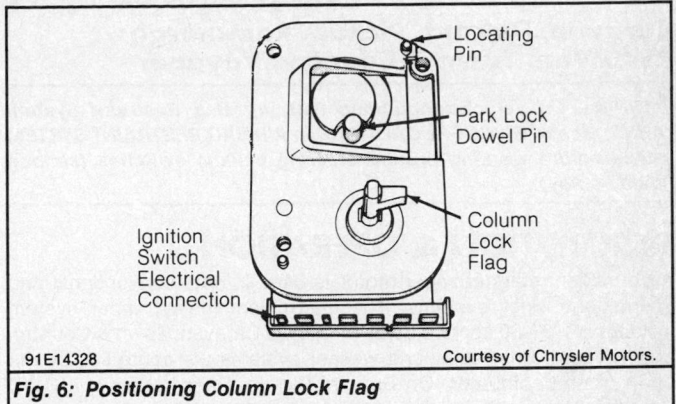

Locating
Pin

Park Lock
Dowel Pin

Column
Lock
Flag

Ignition
Switch
Electrical
Connection

91E14328   Courtesy of Chrysler Motors.

Fig. 6: Positioning Column Lock Flag

WIRING DIAGRAMS

See appropriate chassis wiring diagram in WIRING DIAGRAMS.

TORQUE SPECIFICATIONS

TORQUE SPECIFICATIONS

Application	INCH. Lbs. (N.m)
Air Bag Retaining Nuts	80-100 (9-11)
Ignition Switch Mounting Screws	17 (2)

1992 SAFETY EQUIPMENT
Wiper/Washer Systems

**Caravan, Dakota, Pickup, Ramcharger
RWD Van, Town & Country, Voyager**

WARNING: On vehicles equipped with Air Bag Restraint System (ABRS), see SERVICE PRECAUTIONS in AIR BAG RESTRAINT SYSTEM article before working around steering column switches (air bag could deploy).

DESCRIPTION & OPERATION

A permanent magnet wiper motor is used in both conventional and intermittent wiper systems. The intermittent (delay) wiper system includes a 1/2 - 30 second delay mode. On Caravan, Town & Country, and Voyager, front delay and washer systems are controlled by the body control computer. On Dakota, Pickup, Ramcharger and RWD Van, delay system is controlled by an intermittent Wiper Control Module (WCM).

Washer system consists of an electric pump, sealed motor, reservoir, rubber hoses and nozzles.

Caravan, Town & Country and Voyager models are also equipped with a rear wiper/washer system controlled by an intermittent wipe module.

ADJUSTMENTS

WIPER BLADES

With wiper arms removed, cycle wiper motor into PARK position. Mount arms on pivot shafts. See WIPER BLADE ADJUSTMENT SPECIFICATIONS table. Operate wiper blades, and check whether they return to specified distance. If wiper blades do not return to this position, check linkage and pivot assembly for wear and binding.

WIPER BLADE ADJUSTMENT SPECIFICATIONS

Application	In. (mm)
Caravan, Town & Country, & Voyager	
Front Blades	[1] 1.00 (25.0)
Rear Blade	[2] 3.50 (90.0)
Dakota	
Left Blade	[3] 1.14 (29.0)
Right Blade	[3] 1.85 (47.0)
Pickup, Ramcharger & RWD Van	
Left Blade	[4] 2.24 (57.0)
Right Blade	[4] 2.75 (70.0)

[1] – Measure from bottom edge of windshield to right tip of blades.
[2] – Measure from lower edge of blade (parallel) to lower edge of lift-gate glass.
[3] – Measure from bottom weatherstrip to right tip of blade.
[4] – Measure from bottom weatherstrip to intersection of blade and arm.

TROUBLE SHOOTING

NOTE: For trouble shooting information, see windshield wiper/washer system trouble shooting charts. See Fig. 1.

TESTING

FRONT WIPER MOTOR TEST

Windshield Wiper Motor Will Not Run – 1) Check for blown fuse. If fuse is okay, go to next step. If fuse is defective, replace it and check motor operation in all switch positions. If motor is still inoperative and fuse does not blow, go to next step. If replacement fuse blows, go to step **4)**.

2) If fuse is okay in step **1)**, place panel switch in low-speed position. If motor can not be heard, go to next step. If motor can be heard,

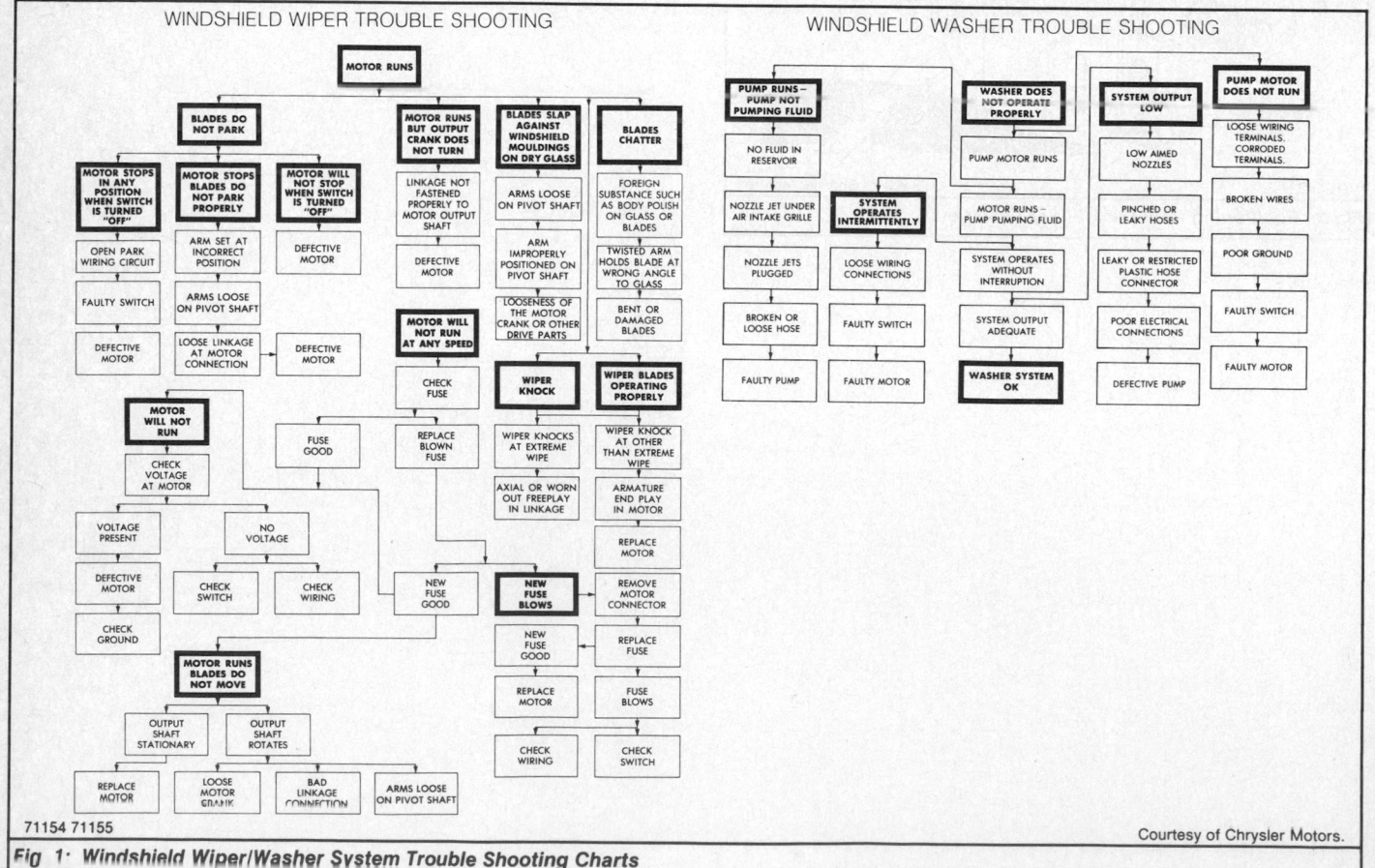

Fig 1: Windshield Wiper/Washer System Trouble Shooting Charts

71154 71155

Courtesy of Chrysler Motors.

check motor output shaft. If shaft is not turning, replace motor assembly. If shaft is turning, check drive link to output shaft for worn or disconnected components.

3) If motor can not be heard in step **2)**, connect a voltmeter between motor terminal "L" and ground strap. *See Fig. 2.* If battery voltage does not exist, move voltmeter negative probe from ground strap to battery negative terminal. If battery voltage still does not exist, fault is open circuit in wiring harness or switch. If battery voltage exists, check for open ground circuit. Ensure motor assembly mount is free of paint, and mounting bolts are tight. If a small voltage increase exists, replace motor assembly.

4) If fuse blows in step **1)**, disconnect motor wiring harness connector and replace fuse. If fuse blows again, repair switch or wiring as needed. If fuse does not blow, replace motor assembly.

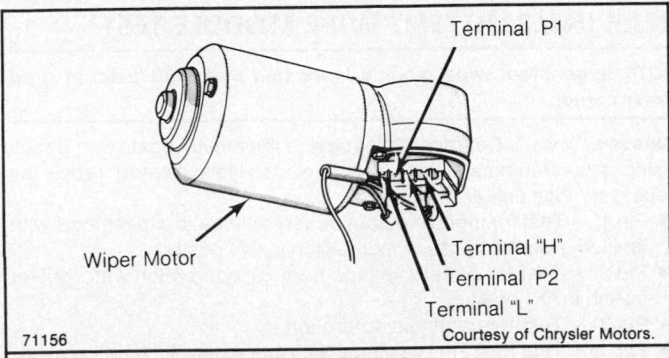

Terminal P1

Wiper Motor

Terminal "H"
Terminal P2
Terminal "L"

71156

Courtesy of Chrysler Motors.

Fig. 2: Identifying Wiper Motor Terminals

Windshield Wiper Motor Slow At All Speeds – **1)** Disconnect wiring harness at motor. Remove wiper arms and blades. Connect ammeter between battery and terminal "L" on motor. *See Fig. 2.* If motor runs and average ammeter reading is more than 6 amps, go to next step. If reading is less than 6 amps, go to step **3)**.

2) Disconnect drive link from motor. If motor now runs and draws less than 3 amps, check wiper linkage and pivots for binding condition. Repair or replace linkage components as necessary. If motor continues to draw more than 3 amps, replace motor.

3) Check motor wiring harness for short between high and low speed wires using following procedure:

- Connect voltmeter or test light to motor ground strap.
- Set wiper switch to LOW position.
- Connect other lead of voltmeter or test light to terminal "H" of wiring harness. *See Fig. 2.* If voltage is present or test light glows, short exists in wiring or wiper switch. If voltage is not present or test light does not glow, continue with procedure.
- Set wiper switch to HIGH position.
- Move voltmeter or test light lead from terminal "H" to terminal "L" of wiring harness. If voltage is present or test light glows, short exists in wiring or wiper switch.
- Repair wiring or replace wiper switch as needed.

Windshield Wiper Motor Runs In LOW Position Only – Place switch in HIGH position, and connect test light or voltmeter between terminal "H" and ground. If test light does not glow or voltage is not present, an open exists in wiring or switch. If test light glows or voltage exists, replace motor.

Windshield Wiper Motor Runs In HIGH Position Only – Place switch in LOW position, and connect test light or voltmeter between terminal "L" and ground. If test light does not glow or voltage is not present, an open exists in wiring or switch. If test light glows or voltage is present, replace motor.

Windshield Wiper Motor Runs With Switch In OFF Or PARK Position – Remove wiring harness, and connect a jumper wire from terminal P2 to terminal "L". Connect another jumper wire from terminal P1 to battery. *See Fig. 2.* If wiper motor runs to PARK position and stops, instrument panel switch is defective. If motor continues to run and does not park, replace motor.

Windshield Wiper Motor Will Not Park When Switch Is In OFF Position – **1)** Remove wiper motor wiring connector, and clean terminals. Reconnect connector, and test motor. If problem continues, place switch in OFF position and go to next step.

2) Disconnect wiper motor wiring connector. Connect a voltmeter or test light to motor ground. Connect other lead to terminal P1 of wiring connector. If voltage is not present or test light does not glow, check for an open circuit in wiring harness or wiper control switch.

3) If voltage is present or test light glows, connect an ohmmeter between terminals "L" and P2. *See Fig. 2.* If continuity exists, motor is faulty. If continuity does not exist, open circuit is present in wiper control switch or wiring harness.

FRONT DELAY WIPER MOTOR TEST (CARAVAN, TOWN & COUNTRY, & VOYAGER)

NOTE: Wiper/washer system is controlled by body control computer. Test procedure requires DRB-II tester.

Intermittent (delay) wipe and standard motors are identical. See FRONT WIPER MOTOR TEST under TESTING for diagnosing system problems not involving delay function. If problem occurs only in DELAY mode, perform following tests.

Excessive Delay Or Inadequate Variation In Delay – **1)** Variations in delay should be as follows:

- Minimum delay (control to extreme counterclockwise position before first detente) 1/2 to 2 seconds.
- Maximum delay (control to extreme clockwise position before OFF position) 10 to 30 seconds.

2) If excessive delay or no variations in delay exists, see FRONT WIPER/WASHER SWITCH TEST under TESTING. If delay is not within specification, replace body control computer.

Wipers Run Continuously In DELAY Mode While Wash Is Operated But No Extra Wipe When Wash Is Released – If this condition exists, replace body control computer.

Wipers Start Erratically During Delay Mode – **1)** Ensure ground connection at instrument panel is good, tight and free of paint. Ensure motor ground strap makes good contact and mounting bolts are tight.

2) Ensure intermittent wipe control unit and wiper switch wiring ground connections are tight. If all conditions above are okay and problem continues, replace body control computer. See BODY CONTROL COMPUTER INTRODUCTION article in ENGINE PERFORMANCE.

FRONT DELAY WIPER MOTOR TEST (DAKOTA, PICKUP, RAMCHARGER & RWD VAN)

Intermittent (delay) wipe and standard motors are identical. See FRONT WIPER MOTOR TEST under TESTING for diagnosing system problems not involving delay function. If problem occurs only in DELAY mode, tests require removing intermittent Wiper Control Module (WCM). For module location, see WIPER CONTROL MODULE LOCATION table.

WIPER CONTROL MODULE LOCATION

Application	Location
Dakota	Bracket To Right Of Lower Steering Column
Pickup & Ramcharger	On Left Side Of Steering Column Support Bracket
RWD Van	Bracket Behind Radio

Excessive Delay Or Inadequate Variation In Delay – **1)** Variations in delay should be as follows:

- Minimum delay (control to extreme counterclockwise position before first detente) 1/2 to 2 seconds.
- Maximum delay (control to extreme clockwise position before OFF position) 10 to 30 seconds.

2) If excessive delay or no variations in delay exists, see FRONT WASHER/WIPER SWITCH TEST under TESTING.

Wipers Run Continuously In DELAY Mode While Wash Is Operated But No Extra Wipe When Wash Is Released – If this condition exists, replace control unit.

Wipers Start Erratically During Delay Mode – **1)** Ensure ground connection at instrument panel is good, tight and free of paint. Ensure motor ground strap makes good contact and mounting bolts are tight.

2) Ensure intermittent wipe control unit and wiper switch wiring ground connections are tight. If all conditions above are okay and problem continues, replace control unit.

1992 SAFETY EQUIPMENT
Wiper/Washer Systems (Cont.)

FRONT WIPER/WASHER SWITCH TEST

CAUTION: On vehicles equipped with Air Bag Restraint System (ABRS), see SERVICE PRECAUTIONS in AIR BAG RESTRAINT SYSTEM article before working around steering column switches (air bag could deploy).

NOTE: Wiper/washer switch is part of multifunction steering column switch. If wiper/washer switch fails, entire multifunction switch must be replaced.

Caravan, Town & Country, & Voyager – Disconnect wiper/washer switch connector. Using ohmmeter, test for continuity between terminals indicated in windshield wiper/washer continuity chart. *See Fig. 3.* Wiper/washer system is controlled by body control computer. For additional wiper/washer switch testing, see BODY CONTROL COMPUTER INTRODUCTION article in ENGINE PERFORMANCE.

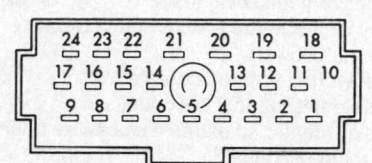

WINDSHIELD WIPER/WASHER SWITCH PINS

TWO SPEED WIPER SWITCH CONTINUITY CHART	
SWITCH POSITION	CONTINUITY BETWEEN
OFF & PARK	PIN 1 & PIN 2
LOW	PIN 1 & PIN 4
HIGH	PIN 4 & PIN 5
WASH	PIN 3 & PIN 4

SWITCH POSITION	CONTINUITY BETWEEN
OFF	PIN 6 AND PIN 7
DELAY	PIN 8 AND PIN 9 PIN 2 AND PIN 4 PIN 1 AND PIN 2 PIN 1 AND PIN 4
LOW	PIN 4 AND PIN 6
HIGH	PIN 4 AND PIN 5
WASH	PIN 3 AND PIN 4

*RESISTANCE AT MAXIMUM DELAY POSITION SHOULD BE BETWEEN 270,000 OHMS AND 330,000 OHMS.
*RESISTANCE AT MINIMUM DELAY POSITION SHOULD BE ZERO WITH OHMMETER SET ON HIGH OHM SCALE.

91A14324   Courtesy of Chrysler Motors.

Fig. 3: Windshield Wiper/Washer Switch Continuity Test Charts

Dakota, Pickup, Ramcharger & RWD Van – Disconnect wiper/washer switch connector. Using an ohmmeter, test for continuity between switch terminals as indicated in windshield wiper/washer continuity chart. *See Fig. 3.* If continuity is not as specified in any test, replace switch.

FRONT WASHER MOTOR TEST

NOTE: If a windshield washer malfunction occurs, ensure washer wiring harness is properly connected before proceeding with diagnosis or repair procedures.

For windshield washer diagnosis, see windshield wiper/washer system trouble shooting charts. *See Fig. 1.*

REAR WIPER MOTOR TEST

Caravan, Town & Country, & Voyager – 1) Disconnect feed wire connector from wiper motor. With ignition switch in ON position, check for battery voltage at Blue wire. If battery voltage does not exist, check fuse, rear wiper switch and wiring. If battery voltage exists, replace rear wiper motor.
2) With ignition switch and rear wiper switch both in ON position, check for battery voltage at Blue and Brown wires. If battery voltage does not exist, check fuse, rear wiper switch and wiring. If battery voltage exists, replace rear wiper motor.
3) With ignition switch in ON position and rear wiper switch in OFF position, check for battery voltage between Blue and Brown wires. If battery voltage does not exist, check ground wire to rear wiper switch.

REAR INTERMITTENT WIPE MODULE TEST

NOTE: Intermittent wipe module is located inside lift gate, at right lower corner.

Caravan, Town & Country, & Voyager – Remove liftgate trim panel. Using a volt/ohmmeter, test each pin as follows and repair as necessary. *See Fig. 4*:
* Pin 1 – Test for module output battery voltage to wiper motor with ignition switch and rear wiper switch in ON position.
* Pin 2 – Test for battery voltage from ignition switch with ignition switch in ON position.
* Pin 3 – Test for continuity to ground.
* Pin 4 – Test for battery voltage with ignition switch and rear window washer switch in ON position.
* Pin 5 – Test for continuity to ground with ignition switch and wiper switch in On position (intermittent mode will have an 8-second delay between wipes).
* Pin 6 – Test for continuity to ground with ignition switch and washer switch in ON position.

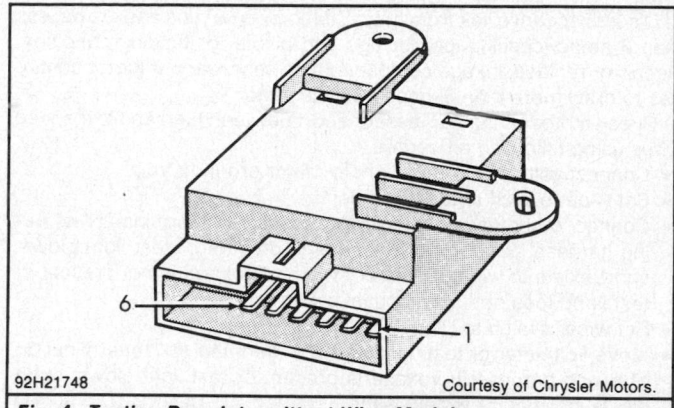

92H21748   Courtesy of Chrysler Motors.

Fig. 4: Testing Rear Intermittent Wipe Module (Caravan, Town & Country, & Voyager)

REAR WIPER/WASHER CONTROL POD SWITCH TEST

Caravan, Town & Country, & Voyager – Disconnect rear wiper/washer pod switch connector. Using an ohmmeter, test for continuity between switch terminals as indicated in continuity chart. See REAR WIPER/WASHER POD SWITCH CONTINUITY table. *See Fig. 5.* If continuity is not as specified in any test, replace switch.

REAR WIPER/WASHER POD SWITCH CONTINUITY

Switch Position	Terminals
Wiper ON	B2 & B5
Washer ON	B3 & B4

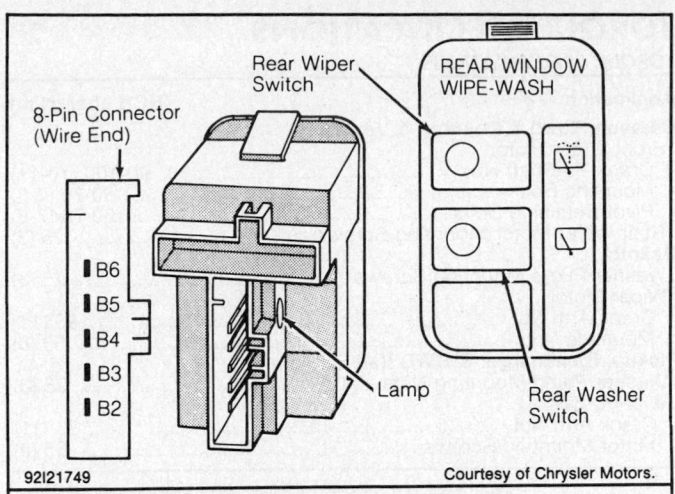

Fig. 5: Identifying Rear Wiper/Washer Pod Switch (Caravan, Town & Country, & Voyager)

VERIFICATION TEST

Reconnect all components. Actuate wiper/washer system and ensure all modes operate correctly. If system operates okay, repair is complete. If system is still inoperative, return to start of testing.

REMOVAL & INSTALLATION

WARNING: On vehicles equipped with Air Bag Restraint System (ABRS), see SERVICE PRECAUTIONS in AIR BAG RESTRAINT SYSTEM article before working around steering column switches (air bag could deploy).

CAUTION: When battery is disconnected, vehicle computer and memory systems may lose memory data. Driveability problems may exist until computer systems have completed a relearn cycle. See COMPUTER RELEARN PROCEDURES article in GENERAL INFORMATION before disconnecting battery.

FRONT WIPER MOTOR

Removal & Installation (Caravan, Town & Country, & Voyager) – 1) Disconnect negative battery cable. With wipers in PARK position, remove wiper arms. Open hood, and remove cowl top plenum grille. Disconnect washer hoses from connectors.
2) Remove cowl plenum chamber plastic screen. Remove hose connectors and wiper pivot retaining bolts. Push pivots down into plenum chamber. Remove nut from wiper motor output shaft, and remove linkage assembly.
3) Disconnect wiper motor wiring harness. Remove mounting bolt and nuts from wiper motor. Remove wiper motor. Clamp motor crank in a vise and remove nut from end of motor shaft. Be careful NOT to rotate motor from PARK position.
4) Remove crank from motor. To install, reverse removal procedure. Tighten bolts and nuts to specification. See TORQUE SPECIFICATIONS table at end of article. Install wiper arms. See WIPER BLADES under ADJUSTMENTS.
Removal & Installation (Dakota) – 1) Disconnect negative battery cable. Disconnect wiper motor wiring connector. Remove 3 motor mounting nuts. Remove wiper arms. Remove cowl screen. Hold drive crank using a wrench, and remove crank nut.
2) Remove drive crank. Remove wiper motor. To install, reverse removal procedure. Tighten nuts to specification. See TORQUE SPECIFICATIONS table at end of article. Install wiper arms. See WIPER BLADES under ADJUSTMENTS.
Removal & Installation (Pickup, Ramcharger & RWD Van) – 1) Disconnect battery negative cable. Disconnect wiper motor wiring connector. Remove wiper motor mounting screws. Lower motor far

enough to gain access to crank arm-to-drive link retainer bushing. Remove crank arm by prying retainer bushing from crank arm pin.
2) Remove wiper motor. Remove crank arm-to-motor drive shaft nut. Remove crank arm from motor. To install, reverse removal procedure. Tighten nuts and screws to specification. See TORQUE SPECIFICATIONS table at end of article. Install wiper arms. See WIPER BLADES under ADJUSTMENTS.

FRONT WIPER/WASHER SWITCH

WARNING: On vehicles equipped with Air Bag Restraint System (ABRS), see SERVICE PRECAUTIONS in AIR BAG RESTRAINT SYSTEM article before working around steering column switches (air bag could deploy).

NOTE: Wiper/washer switch is part of multifunction steering column switch. If wiper/Washer switch fails, entire multifunction switch must be replaced.

Removal & Installation – Disconnect negative battery cable. Remove tilt lever (if equipped). Remove upper and lower column covers to access switch connector. Remove switch connector. Remove multifunction switch tamperproof mounting screws. Gently pull switch away from column, and loosen connector screw (screw remains in connector). Remove multifunction switch. To install, reverse removal procedure. Tighten retaining screws to **17 INCH. lbs. (2 N.m)**. Ensure switch is functioning properly.

FRONT WASHER MOTOR

Removal & Installation (Caravan, Town & Country, & Voyager) – 1) Drain fluid from reservoir. Remove reservoir mounting screws, reservoir and pump assembly. Disconnect electrical lead and rubber hose from bottom of pump. Disconnect fluid level sensor (if equipped).
2) Note position of pump. Loosen pump filter and nut by reaching through reservoir neck using an extension and deep socket. Disconnect outside portion of pump. Remove inner and outer portions of pump and remove pump. To install, reverse removal procedure.
Removal & Installation (Dakota) – 1) Drain fluid from reservoir. Remove reservoir mounting screws, reservoir and pump assembly.
2) Disconnect electrical lead and rubber hose from bottom of pump. Pry pump away from reservoir, being careful not to puncture reservoir. Remove and discard grommet. To install, reverse removal procedure.
Removal & Installation (Pickup, Ramcharger & RWD Van) – 1) Remove reservoir mounting screws, reservoir and pump assembly. Drain fluid from reservoir. Disconnect electrical lead and rubber hose from bottom of pump.
2) Using an extension and deep socket, remove pump mounting nut and plastic washer through reservoir neck. Remove pump and rubber grommet from reservoir. DO NOT reuse rubber grommet. To install, reverse removal procedure.

REAR WIPER MOTOR

Removal (Caravan, Town & Country, & Voyager) – Disconnect negative battery cable. Lift and remove wiper arm from output shaft. Raise liftgate. Remove liftgate trim panel. Remove 5 rear wiper motor mounting screws. Disconnect wiring harness from rear wiper motor. Remove rear wiper motor.
Installation – To install, reverse removal procedure. Mount rear wiper arm. Ensure wiper blade is parallel to lower edge of liftgate glass. See WIPER BLADES under ADJUSTMENTS.

REAR WASHER PUMP/RESERVOIR ASSEMBLY

Removal & Installation (Caravan, Town & Country, & Voyager) – 1) Unlock and open liftgate. Remove 2 left side rear trim panel and reservoir mounting screws. Disconnect wiring harness from washer pump. Disconnect washer hose from reservoir, and block outlet to prevent fluid from running out. Remove one upper reservoir mounting screw. Remove reservoir and pump assembly through access hole.

2) Work filler tube off reservoir and empty reservoir. Loosen pump filter and nut through reservoir neck. Disconnect outside portion of pump. Remove inner and outer portions of pump and remove pump. To install, reverse removal procedure.

REAR WIPER/WASHER POD SWITCH

Removal & Installation – Using a flat blade tool, remove warning indicator grille by prying up. Remove 3 screws from warning indicator module assembly. Tilt column down if possible. Remove 8 screws retaining cluster bezel to instrument panel. Pull cluster out to access switch snap fingers. Depress snap fingers and push switch out of bezel. Remove harness connector. Remove lamp. To install switch, reverse removal procedure. Verify switch function.

OVERHAUL

WIPER MOTORS

Windshield and rear wiper motors are serviced as complete units. If either motor is defective, replace assembly.

TORQUE SPECIFICATIONS
TORQUE SPECIFICATIONS

Application	INCH Lbs. (N.m)
Caravan, Town & Country, & Voyager	
Front Wiper Motor	
Crank-To-Shaft Nut	90-100 (10-11)
Mounting Bolts	60-70 (7-8)
Pivot Retaining Bolts	60-70 (7-8)
Rear Wiper Motor Mounting Screws	25 (3)
Dakota	
Washer Pump Mounting Screws	25 (3)
Wiper Motor	
Crank Arm Nut	95 (11)
Mounting Nuts	65 (8)
Pickup, Ramcharger & RWD Van	
Washer Pump Mounting Nuts	25 (3)
Wiper Motor	
Crank Arm Nut	95 (11)
Motor Mounting Screws	65 (8)

WIRING DIAGRAMS

See appropriate chassis wiring diagram in WIRING DIAGRAMS.

1992 ENGINES
2.5L 4-Cylinder

Caravan, Dakota, Voyager

NOTE: For repair procedures not covered in this article, see ENGINE OVERHAUL PROCEDURES article in GENERAL INFORMATION.

ENGINE IDENTIFICATION

Engine may be identified by eighth character of Vehicle Identification Number (VIN) stamped on a plate on top of instrument panel, at lower left corner of windshield.

ENGINE IDENTIFICATION CODE

Engine	Code
2.5L TBI	K

SPECIAL ENGINE MARKS

Information identifying undersize and oversize components will be found at various locations on engine and is decoded as follows:
- Oversize camshaft journals are indicated by Green camshaft bearing caps and "O/S J" stamped behind oil gallery plug on rear of cylinder head.
- Green camshaft with "O/S J" stamped on end of camshaft indicates oversize camshaft journal diameter.

ADJUSTMENTS

VALVE CLEARANCE ADJUSTMENT

Hydraulic lash adjusters are used. No valve adjustment is required.

DRY LASH

NOTE: Dry lash should be checked whenever valve components are serviced.

1) Dry lash is amount of clearance between camshaft base circle and rocker arm pad. Lash adjuster must be completely collapsed and free of oil when checking clearance.
2) Remove retainer cap from lash adjuster. Disassemble and drain oil. Install lash adjuster completely collapsed. Using feeler gauge, measure clearance between camshaft base circle and rocker arm pad.
3) Clearance should be .024-.060" (.61-1.52 mm). If clearance is not within specification, check for wear on related parts and replace as necessary. Fill lash adjuster with engine oil. Reassemble using NEW retainer cap. Allow 10 minutes for lash adjuster to bleed down before rotating camshaft.

REMOVAL & INSTALLATION

NOTE: For reassembly reference, label all electrical connectors, vacuum hoses and fuel lines before removal. Also place mating marks on engine hood and other major assemblies before removal.

WARNING: When battery is disconnected, vehicle computer and memory systems may lose memory data. Driveability problems may exist until computer systems have completed a relearn cycle. See COMPUTER RELEARN PROCEDURES article in GENERAL INFORMATION before disconnecting battery.

FUEL PRESSURE RELEASE

CAUTION: Fuel system is under pressure. Pressure must be released before servicing fuel system components.

1) Loosen fuel tank cap to release pressure. Disconnect injector wiring harness from engine wiring harness. Connect jumper wire from terminal No. 1 of injector harness to ground. See Fig. 1.
2) Connect another jumper wire to terminal No. 2 of injector harness. Touch jumper wire to positive battery terminal for no more than 5 seconds to release fuel pressure. Remove jumper wires, and reconnect wiring harness.

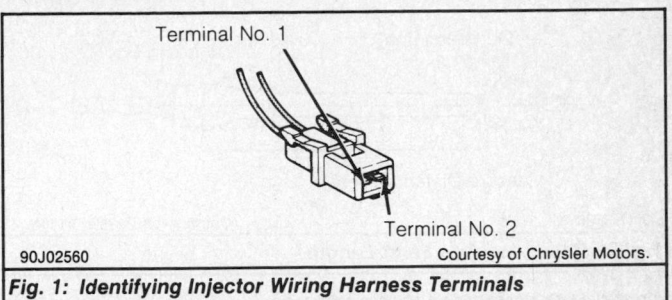

Fig. 1: Identifying Injector Wiring Harness Terminals

COOLING SYSTEM BLEEDING

Remove vent plug from top of thermostat housing. Fill cooling system. Allow air to bleed from cooling system. Install vent plug once coolant reaches thermostat housing level. Tighten vent plug to specification. See TORQUE SPECIFICATIONS table at end of article. Finish filling cooling system.

ENGINE

NOTE: Remove engine with transaxle or transmission remaining in vehicle.

Removal (Caravan & Voyager) – 1) Release fuel pressure. See FUEL PRESSURE RELEASE under REMOVAL & INSTALLATION. Disconnect battery. Scribe hood hinge location on hood for reassembly. Remove hood. Drain cooling system. Disconnect necessary coolant hoses, fuel lines, electrical connections and vacuum hoses.
2) Remove radiator, shroud and fan. Remove air cleaner with hoses. Remove A/C compressor and power steering pump with hoses attached and set aside (if equipped).
3) Remove oil filter, alternator and starter. Disconnect accelerator cable. Remove alternator. Remove transaxle lower case cover. Disconnect exhaust pipe at manifold.
4) Mark flexplate to torque converter for installation reference. Remove torque converter-to-flexplate bolts. Attach "C" clamp to bottom front edge of torque converter housing to secure torque converter.
5) Support transaxle, and attach lifting hoist to engine. Remove right inner splash shield. Disconnect ground strap. To lower engine from engine compartment, separate right (timing belt side) mount bracket from bracket at front of cylinder block. To raise engine from engine compartment, remove long through bolt from right (timing belt side) mount bracket. Separate insulator from right side rail.

CAUTION: If removing insulator from right side rail, mark insulator-to-side rail position for reassembly reference. Insulator must be installed in original position.

6) Remove transaxle-to-cylinder block bolts. Remove front engine mount bolt. Remove insulator through bolt of left mount from inside fenderwell. Insulator bracket-to-transaxle bolts may be removed instead of through bolt. Remove engine from vehicle.
Installation – 1) To install, reverse removal procedure. DO NOT tighten engine mount bolts until all bolts are installed. If vertical bolts on right or left upper mount on frame rail were loosened, axle shaft length must be checked.
2) To determine axle shaft length, measure distance between inner edge of outboard boot and inner edge of inboard boot at 6 o'clock position. See Fig. 2.
3) Slide engine in slots on engine mounts so axle shaft length is within specification. See AXLE SHAFT LENGTH SPECIFICATIONS table. Tighten all mounting bolts to specification once correct axle length is obtained. See TORQUE SPECIFICATIONS table at end of article.

CAUTION: Tighten vertical bolt in right (timing belt side) mount bracket before tightening long through bolt.

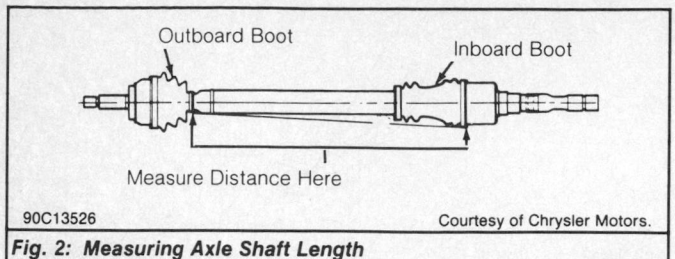

90C13526   Courtesy of Chrysler Motors.

Fig. 2: Measuring Axle Shaft Length

AXLE SHAFT LENGTH SPECIFICATIONS

Application	In. (mm)
Right Axle Shaft	20.5-20.9 (521-531)
Left Axle Shaft	9.0-9.4 (229-239)

4) Ensure reference mark is aligned on torque converter and flexplate. Fill and bleed cooling system. See COOLING SYSTEM BLEEDING under REMOVAL & INSTALLATION.

CAUTION: Fuel system is under pressure. Pressure must be released before disconnecting fuel system components.

Removal (Dakota) – 1) Release fuel pressure. See FUEL PRESSURE RELEASE under REMOVAL & INSTALLATION. Remove battery and air cleaner. Scribe hood hinge location on hood for reassembly reference. Remove hood. Drain cooling system. Disconnect necessary coolant hoses, fuel lines, electrical connections and vacuum hoses.

2) Remove radiator and shroud. Discharge A/C system, and remove necessary A/C hoses. Plug A/C hoses to prevent contamination. Remove throttle body and linkage. Disconnect power steering hoses.

3) Remove starter, alternator, charcoal canister and horns. Raise and support vehicle. Disconnect exhaust pipe at manifold. Remove engine mount bolts. Install lifting fixture. Raise engine until front engine insulators clear crossmember retaining brackets. Support transmission using floor jack.

4) Disconnect clutch release assembly. Remove transmission-to-clutch housing bolts. Move engine forward until transmission shaft clears clutch disc. Lift engine from vehicle.

Installation – To install, reverse removal procedure. Tighten bolts to specification. See TORQUE SPECIFICATIONS table at end of article. Fill and bleed cooling system. See COOLING SYSTEM BLEEDING under REMOVAL & INSTALLATION.

INTAKE & EXHAUST MANIFOLDS

NOTE: Exhaust and intake manifolds use a one-piece mounting gasket. Both manifolds must be removed to perform service on either manifold.

Removal (Caravan & Voyager) – 1) Release fuel pressure. See FUEL PRESSURE RELEASE under REMOVAL & INSTALLATION. Disconnect negative battery cable. Drain cooling system. Remove air cleaner. Disconnect necessary wiring, fuel lines and linkage at throttle body.

2) Remove drive belt from power steering. Remove brake booster vacuum hose from intake manifold. Disconnect EGR tube from intake manifold. Disconnect coolant hoses from coolant crossover.

3) Raise and support vehicle. Disconnect exhaust pipe from exhaust manifold. Remove power steering pump with hoses attached, and secure it aside. Remove intake manifold bolts.

4) Lower vehicle. Remove exhaust manifold nuts. Remove intake and exhaust manifolds.

Inspection – Check manifold gasket surface for warpage. Repair or replace manifold if warpage is greater than .006" (.15 mm) per 12" (305 mm).

Installation – 1) To install, reverse removal procedure. Steel manifold gasket must be coated with gasket sealant on manifold side. If composition gasket is used, DO NOT use sealant.

2) Tighten bolts or nuts to specification starting at center and working outward in both directions. See TORQUE SPECIFICATIONS table at end of article.

3) Fill and bleed cooling system. See COOLING SYSTEM BLEEDING under REMOVAL & INSTALLATION.

Removal (Dakota) – 1) Release fuel pressure. See FUEL PRESSURE RELEASE under REMOVAL & INSTALLATION. Disconnect negative battery cable. Drain cooling system. Remove air cleaner. Disconnect necessary wiring, fuel lines and linkage at throttle body.

2) Remove throttle body. Remove power steering and air pump support bracket. Remove brake booster vacuum hose from intake manifold. Remove diverter valve assembly. Disconnect air injection tube from exhaust manifold. Disconnect coolant hoses from coolant crossover.

3) Raise and support vehicle. Remove EGR tube. Disconnect exhaust pipe from exhaust manifold. Remove intake manifold bolts. Lower vehicle. Remove exhaust manifold nuts. Remove intake and exhaust manifolds.

Inspection – Check manifold gasket surface for warpage. Repair or replace manifold if warpage is greater than .006" (.15 mm) per 12" (305 mm).

Installation – 1) To install, reverse removal procedure. Install new manifold gaskets; coat gaskets with gasket sealant on manifold side. If composition gasket is used, DO NOT use sealant.

2) Tighten bolts or nuts to specification starting at center and working outward in both directions. See TORQUE SPECIFICATIONS table at end of article.

3) Fill and bleed cooling system. See COOLING SYSTEM BLEEDING under REMOVAL & INSTALLATION.

CYLINDER HEAD

NOTE: Camshaft sprocket must be separated from camshaft when removing and installing camshaft or cylinder head. To maintain camshaft, intermediate shaft and crankshaft timing during service procedures, timing belt must remain installed on camshaft sprocket while assembly is suspended under a continuous light tension. See Fig. 3.

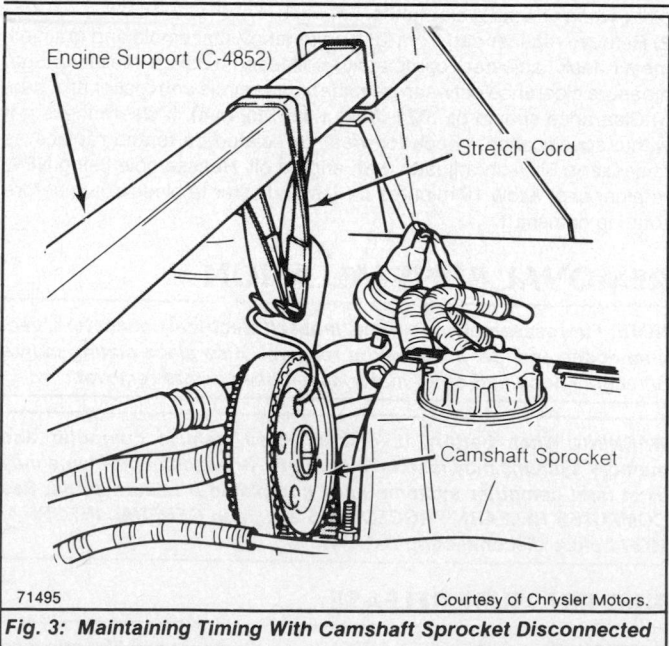

71495   Courtesy of Chrysler Motors.

Fig. 3: Maintaining Timing With Camshaft Sprocket Disconnected

Removal – 1) Release fuel pressure. See FUEL PRESSURE RELEASE under REMOVAL & INSTALLATION. Disconnect negative battery cable. Drain cooling system.

2) Remove air cleaner. Disconnect necessary vacuum hoses, linkages, coolant hoses and electrical connections. On Caravan and Voyager, remove power steering pump and secure it aside.

3) On all models, disconnect exhaust pipe from exhaust manifold. Disconnect dipstick tube from thermostat housing, and rotate bracket from stud. Remove all drive belts. On A/C-equipped models, remove A/C compressor with lines connected and secure aside.

4) On all models, remove alternator pivot bolt. Disconnect wiring, and remove alternator. Remove A/C compressor idler pulley (if equipped). Remove side mounting bolts No. 1, 4, 5, 6 and 7 from solid mount A/C compressor bracket. *See Fig. 4.*

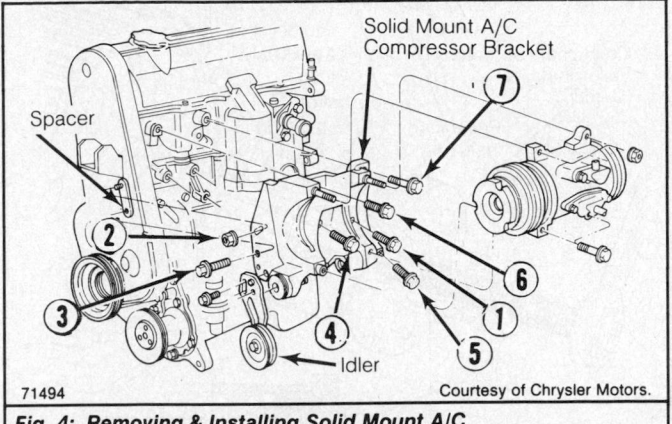

Fig. 4: Removing & Installing Solid Mount A/C Compressor Bracket

71494   Courtesy of Chrysler Motors.

5) Remove front mounting nut No. 2, and remove (or loosen) front bolt No. 3. Coolant will leak from bolt hole. Rotate solid mount A/C compressor bracket away from engine, and slide on stud (No. 2 mounting stud) until free.

6) Front mounting bolt and spacer will be removed with bracket. Remove upper timing belt cover. Using Sprocket Holder (C-4687) and Adapter (C-4687-1), hold camshaft sprocket and remove sprocket bolt. *See Fig. 5.*

7) Remove camshaft sprocket, maintaining camshaft, intermediate shaft and crankshaft timing with timing belt. If necessary, remove timing belt. See TIMING BELT under REMOVAL & INSTALLATION.

8) Remove valve cover and curtain (if equipped). *See Fig. 7.* Remove cylinder head bolts in proper sequence. *See Fig. 6.* Remove cylinder head and gasket.

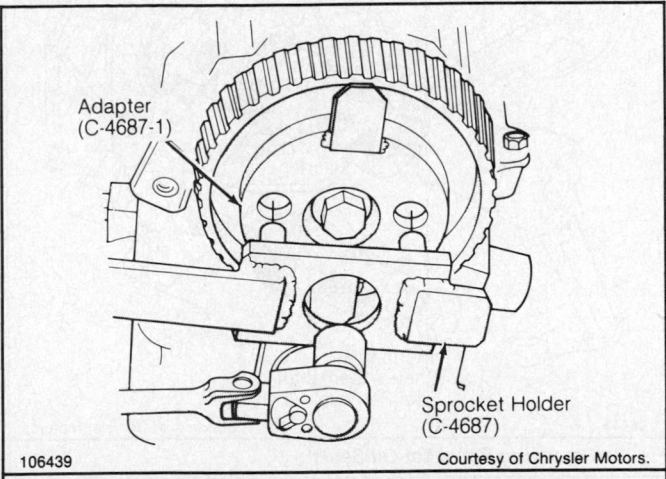

Fig. 5: Removing Camshaft Or Intermediate Shaft Sprocket

106439   Courtesy of Chrysler Motors.

Inspection – Check cylinder head warpage. Warpage must not exceed specification. See CYLINDER HEAD table under ENGINE SPECIFICATIONS at end of article. If cylinder head or camshaft is serviced, ensure oversized camshaft is used in cylinder head with oversized bores. See SPECIAL ENGINE MARKS.

CAUTION: Use proper cylinder head bolts when installing cylinder head. Cylinder head bolt diameter is 11 mm and is identified by "11" on bolt head. Ten-mm bolts will thread into 11-mm bolt hole, but cylinder block threads will be stripped.

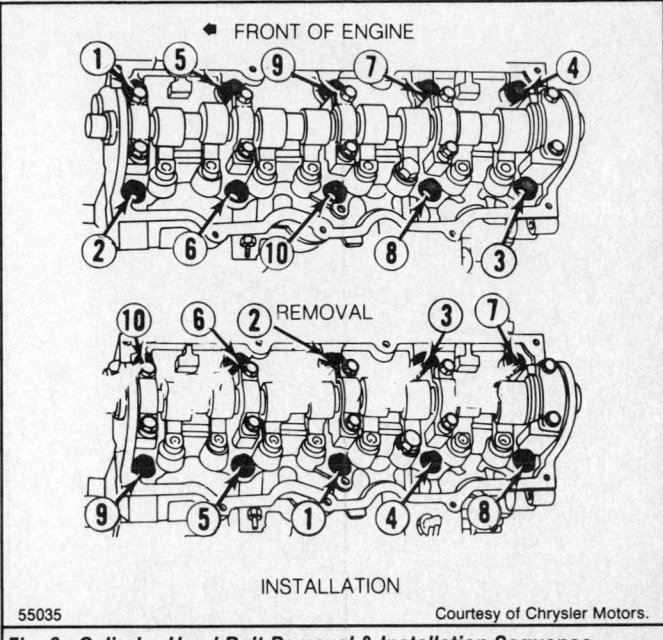

Fig. 6: Cylinder Head Bolt Removal & Installation Sequence

55035   Courtesy of Chrysler Motors.

Installation – 1) Hold a straightedge across threads of cylinder head bolts. Ensure cylinder head bolt threads contact straightedge in all areas. If threads fail to contact straightedge, cylinder head bolts are stretched and must be replaced.

2) To install cylinder head, reverse removal procedure. Tighten cylinder head bolts to specification in proper sequence. *See Fig. 6.* See TORQUE SPECIFICATIONS table at end of article.

NOTE: Cylinder head bolt torque should be greater than 90 ft. lbs. (122 N.m) after 1/4 turn. If torque is not as specified, replace cylinder head bolt.

---

3) Adjust timing belt (if removed). See TIMING BELT under REMOVAL & INSTALLATION. Install curtain, manifold side first, with cutouts over camshaft towers and touching cylinder head.

4) Press opposite (distributor) side into position below cylinder head rail. Curtain is retained in its location by bumpers. *See Fig. 7.*

5) When installing solid mount A/C compressor bracket, note bolt identification. *See Fig. 4.* Tighten bolts in following order.

- Bolt No. 1 – 30 INCH lbs. (3.3 N.m)
- Bolts No. 2 and 3 – 40 ft. lbs. (54 N.m)
- Bolts No. 1, 4 and 5 – 40 ft. lbs. (54 N.m)
- Bolts No. 6 and 7 – 40 ft. lbs. (54 N.m)

6) Fill and bleed cooling system. See COOLING SYSTEM BLEEDING under REMOVAL & INSTALLATION.

CAMSHAFT, CRANKSHAFT OR INTERMEDIATE SHAFT SPROCKET OIL SEAL

Removal – 1) Remove timing belt. See TIMING BELT under REMOVAL & INSTALLATION. For crankshaft sprocket seal replacement, remove crankshaft sprocket retaining bolt. Using Crankshaft Sprocket Puller/Installer (C-4685) and puller insert, remove crankshaft sprocket. *See Fig. 8.*

2) To remove camshaft or intermediate shaft sprockets, use Sprocket Holder (C-4687) and Adapter (C-4687-1) to hold sprocket and remove sprocket bolt. *See Fig. 5.* Note direction of sprocket offset for reassembly reference. Remove sprocket.

3) Using Crankshaft Sprocket Seal Remover (C-6341) or Intermediate Shaft/Camshaft Seal Remover (C-4679), remove sprocket oil seals. *See Fig. 9.*

Installation – 1) Using Crankshaft Seal Installer (C-6342) or Intermediate Shaft/Camshaft Seal Installer (C-4680), install seal until seal is even with surface. *See Figs. 10 and 11.*

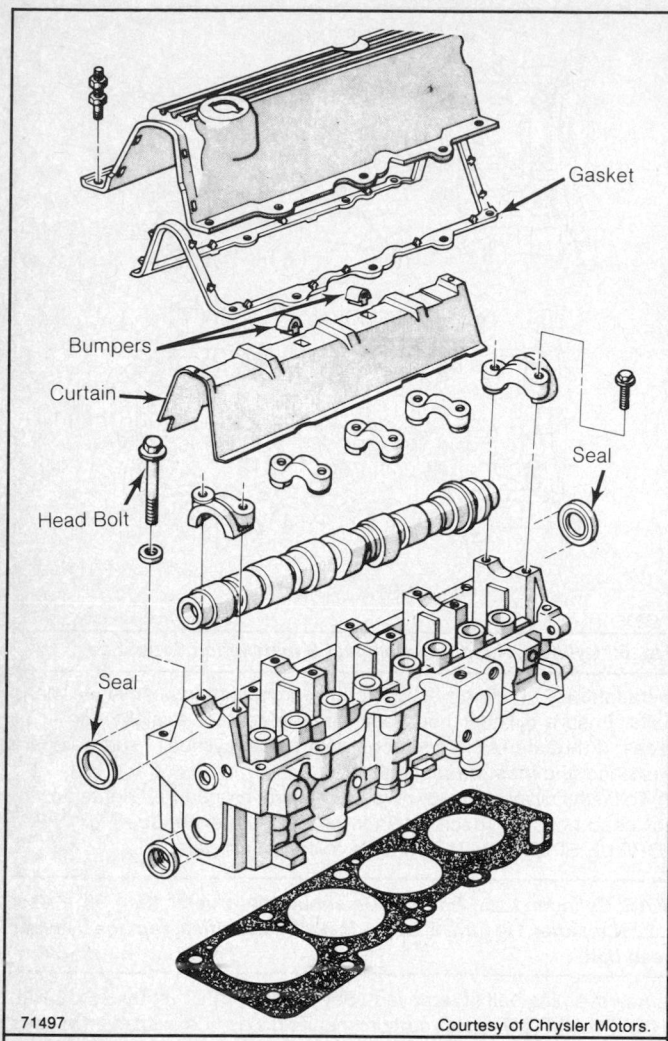

Fig. 7: Exploded View Of Cylinder Head & Valve Assembly

2) Using crankshaft sprocket puller/installer and thrust bearing, install crankshaft sprocket. *See Fig. 8.* To install remaining components, reverse removal procedure. Ensure all timing marks are aligned during timing belt installation.

TIMING BELT

Removal – 1) Disconnect negative battery cable. On Caravan and Voyager, remove right inner splash shield. On all models, remove accessory drive belts.

2) Remove water pump and crankshaft pulleys. Remove upper and lower timing belt covers. *See Fig. 12.* Support engine using a floor jack.

3) Remove right engine mount bolt, and raise engine slightly. Loosen timing belt tensioner bolt. Rotate hex area on timing belt tensioner, and remove timing belt.

CAUTION: If timing belt is to be reused, mark timing belt for direction of rotation for reassembly reference.

Installation – 1) Remove spark plugs. Place No. 1 cylinder at TDC. Align timing marks on crankshaft and intermediate shaft sprockets. *See Fig. 13.* Rotate camshaft sprocket until 2 holes on sprocket hub align with camshaft bearing cap-to-cylinder head parting line. Small hole on camshaft sprocket must be at 12 o'clock position.

2) Install timing belt. Ensure timing belt is installed in original direction of rotation. Install Timing Belt Tensioner Wrench (C-4703) horizontally an large hex of timing belt tensioner.

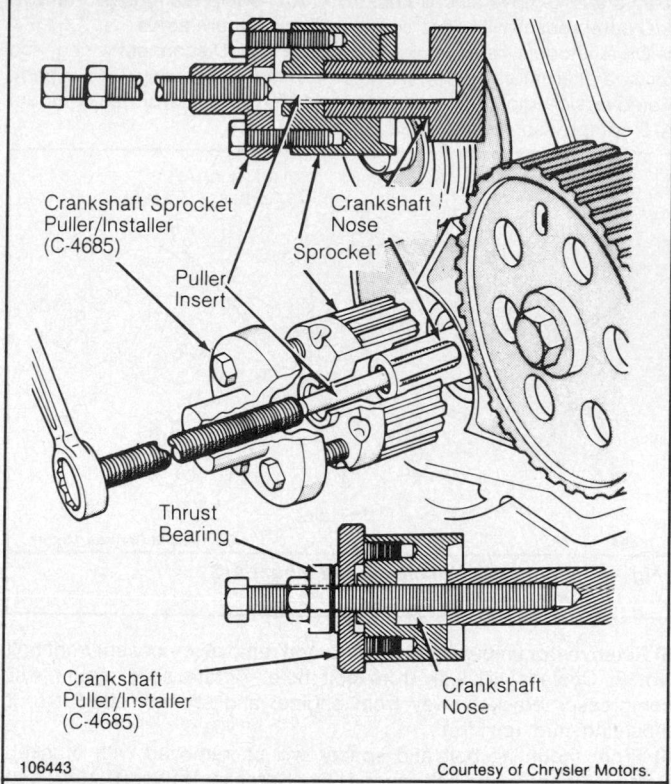

Fig. 8: Removing & Installing Crankshaft Sprocket

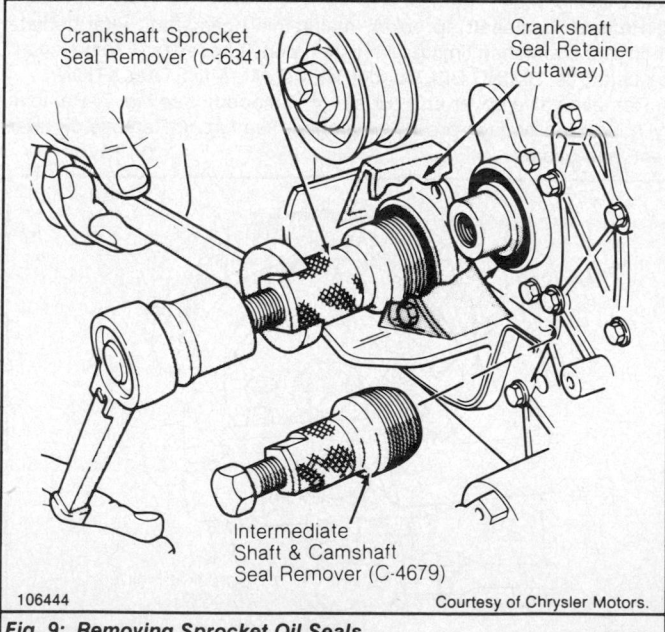

Fig. 9: Removing Sprocket Oil Seals

3) Loosen timing belt tensioner bolt (if necessary) to reset timing belt tensioner to within a 15-degree axis of timing belt tensioner wrench horizontal position. *See Fig. 14.*

4) Rotate crankshaft clockwise 2 complete revolutions to TDC. Tighten timing belt tensioner bolt to specification while holding timing belt tensioner wrench in position. See TORQUE SPECIFICATIONS table at end of article.

5) Ensure all timing marks align. To install remaining components, reverse removal procedure.

CAUTION: DO NOT rotate crankshaft counterclockwise or rotate engine using camshaft or intermediate shaft sprocket bolts.

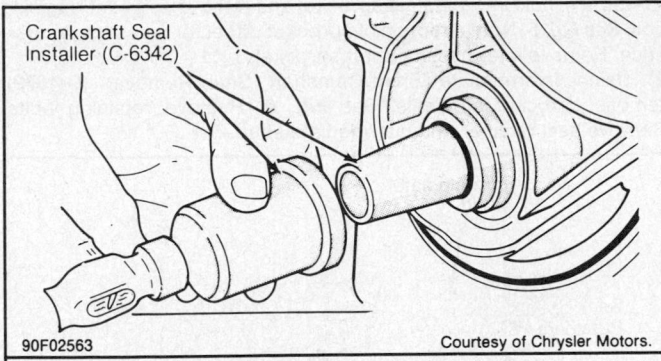

Fig. 10: Installing Crankshaft Sprocket Oil Seal

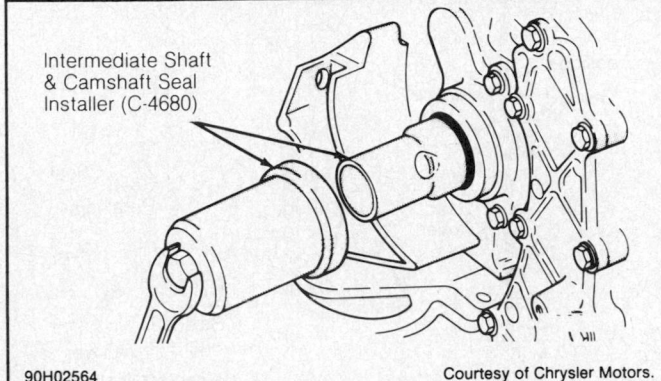

Fig. 11: Installing Intermediate Or Camshaft Sprocket Oil Seal

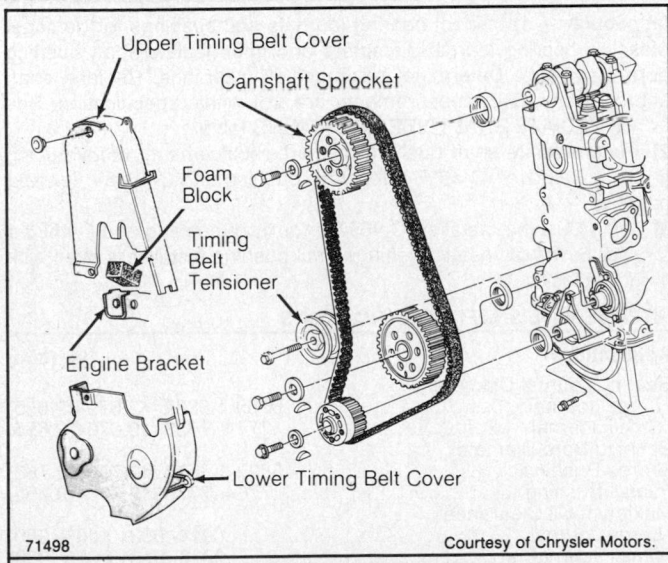

Fig. 12: Exploded View Of Timing Belt & Components

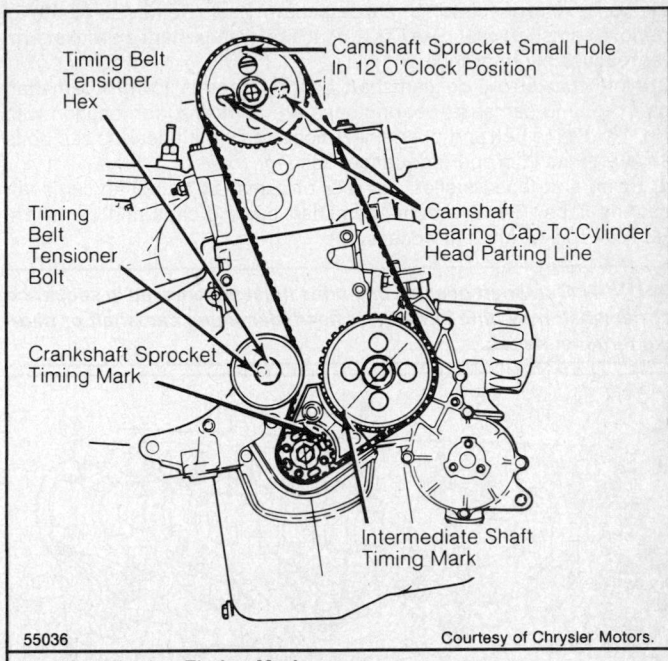

Fig. 13: Aligning Timing Marks

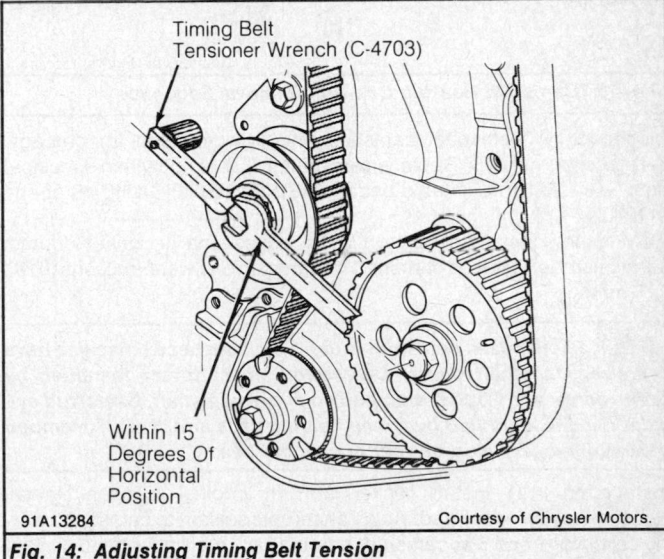

Fig. 14: Adjusting Timing Belt Tension

Fig. 21. Clearance must be at least **.050" (1.27 mm)**. If insufficient clearance exists, grind rocker arm ears to correct clearance. Install valve cover.

CAUTION: Ensure valve spring retainer locks are fully seated after servicing rocker arms.

CAMSHAFT

NOTE: Camshaft can be removed while supporting camshaft sprocket in timing belt, with tension applied to timing belt. See Fig. 3. If camshaft sprocket cannot be supported, timing belt must be removed.

Removal – 1) Remove timing belt if camshaft sprocket cannot be supported. See TIMING BELT under REMOVAL & INSTALLATION. Remove valve cover and curtain. If camshaft sprocket is to be removed, use Sprocket Holder (C-4687) and Adapter (C-4687-1) to hold camshaft sprocket and remove sprocket bolt. *See Fig. 5.* Remove camshaft sprocket. Support timing belt and camshaft sprocket. *See Fig. 3.*

ROCKER ARM & LASH ADJUSTER

Removal — Remove valve cover. Rotate camshaft until base circle contacts rocker arm. Using Spring Compressor (C-4682), compress valve spring. Note location of rocker arm and lash adjuster for reassembly reference. Remove rocker arm and lash adjuster.

NOTE: If rocker arm or camshaft are changed, check dry lash to ensure proper clearance. See DRY LASH under ADJUSTMENTS.

Installation – 1) To install, reverse removal procedure. Ensure lash adjusters are at least partially full of oil before installing. Little or no plunger travel should exist when lash adjuster is depressed.
2) Ensure components are installed in original locations. Check clearance between rocker arm ear and valve spring retainer. *See*

2) Using Intermediate Shaft/Camshaft Seal Remover (C-4679), remove camshaft seal. *See Fig. 9.* Place reference mark on rocker arm for reassembly reference.

3) Note that arrow on camshaft bearing caps is toward camshaft sprocket and camshaft bearing caps are numbered for location with No. 1 at timing belt end of engine. Loosen camshaft bearing cap bolts several turns in proper sequence. *See Fig. 15.*

4) Using soft-faced mallet, tap rear of camshaft to loosen camshaft bearing caps. Remove bolts, camshaft bearing caps and camshaft. Remove rocker arms (if necessary).

CAUTION: Camshaft bearing cap bolts must be removed in sequence or camshaft may bind in cylinder head, damaging camshaft or bearing thrust surfaces.

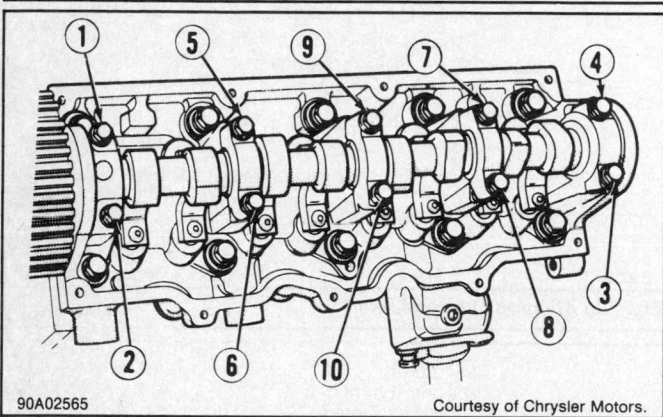

90A02565   Courtesy of Chrysler Motors.

Fig. 15: Camshaft Bearing Cap Bolt Removal Sequence

Inspection – 1) Inspect camshaft and cylinder head for damage. Measure journal O.D. Replace camshaft if O.D. is not within specification. See CAMSHAFT table under ENGINE SPECIFICATIONS at end of article.

2) Measure camshaft lobe on outer edges and in rocker contact surface areas. Replace camshaft if camshaft lobe wear exceeds .010" (.25 mm).

NOTE: If an oversized camshaft is used, cylinder head must also have oversized camshaft bores. Oversized camshafts are identified by Green barrel and "O/S J" stamped on end of camshaft. Oversized cylinder head is identified by Green bearing caps and "O/S J" stamped behind oil gallery plug on rear of cylinder head.

Installation – 1) Install rocker arm in original location. Install camshaft on cylinder head. Apply anaerobic sealant to camshaft bearing caps No. 1 and 5 at camshaft bearing cap-to-cylinder head surfaces. Install No. 1 camshaft bearing cap at timing belt end and No. 5 at rear of cylinder head.

2) Ensure arrows on camshaft bearing caps No. 1, 2, 3 and 4 point toward timing belt. Install bolts, and tighten alternately, working outward from middle, to specification. See TORQUE SPECIFICATIONS table at end of article.

3) Check camshaft end play. If end play exceeds specification, replace camshaft and/or cylinder head. See CAMSHAFT table under ENGINE SPECIFICATIONS at end of article.

4) Coat camshaft oil seal lip with oil. Using Intermediate Shaft/Camshaft Seal Installer (C-4680), install camshaft oil seal even with camshaft bearing cap. To install remaining components, reverse removal procedure. Tighten bolts to specification. See TORQUE SPECIFICATIONS table.

INTERMEDIATE SHAFT

CAUTION: Remove oil pump and distributor before removing intermediate shaft.

Removal – 1) Remove timing belt. See TIMING BELT under REMOVAL & INSTALLATION. Using Sprocket Holder (C-4687) and Adapter

(C-4687-1), hold intermediate sprocket and remove sprocket retaining bolt. *See Fig. 5.* Note direction of sprocket offset for reassembly reference. Remove intermediate shaft sprocket.

2) Using Intermediate Shaft/Camshaft Seal Remover (C-4679), remove sprocket oil seals. *See Fig. 9.* Remove retaining bolts. Remove seal retainer and intermediate shaft. *See Fig. 16.*

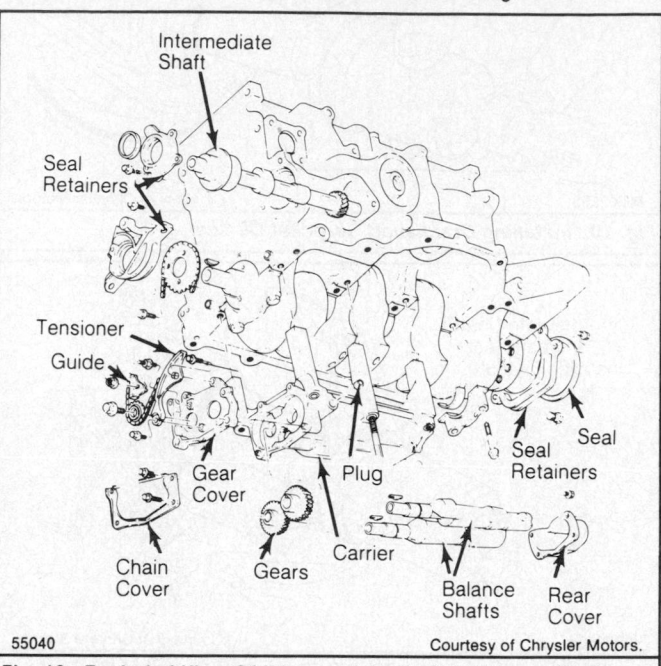

55040   Courtesy of Chrysler Motors.

Fig. 16: Exploded View Of Intermediate Shaft & Balance Shafts

Inspection – 1) Inspect bearing journals and bushings for damage. Measure bearing journal diameters and intermediate shaft bushing bore diameters. Determine maximum oil clearance. Replace shaft and/or bushings if measurements are not within specification. See INTERMEDIATE SHAFT SPECIFICATIONS table.

2) If intermediate shaft bushings require replacement, remove using Bushing Remover (C-4697-2 for front bushing and C-4686-2 for rear bushing).

3) Using Bushing Installer (C-4697-1 for front bushing and C-4686-1 for rear bushing), install bushings until bushing installer is even with cylinder block.

INTERMEDIATE SHAFT SPECIFICATIONS

Application	In. (mm)
Bearing Journal Diameter	
Large Journal	1.6799-1.6809 (42.670-42.695)
Small Journal	.7744-.7753 (19.670-19.695)
Bushing Bore Diameter	
Large Bushing	1.6823-1.6830 (42.730-42.750)
Small Bushing	.7764-.7776 (19.720-19.750)
Maximum Oil Clearance	
Large Journal	.0014-.0031 (.035-.080)
Small Journal	.0010-.0031 (.025-.080)

Installation – 1) To install, reverse removal procedure. Lubricate distributor drive gear before installing. Apply a 1/16" bead of anaerobic gasket sealant on seal retainer before installing.

2) Install seal retainer, and tighten bolts to specification. See TORQUE SPECIFICATIONS table at end of article. Using Intermediate Shaft/Camshaft Seal Installer (C-4680), install seal until even with surface. *See Fig. 11.* To complete installation, reverse removal procedure.

BALANCE SHAFTS

NOTE: Balance shafts are used on Caravan and Voyager only.

Removal & Installation (Gears & Shafts) – 1) Remove oil pan and oil pick-up. See OIL PAN under REMOVAL & INSTALLATION. Remove timing belt. See TIMING BELT under REMOVAL & INSTALLATION.

2) Remove crankshaft sprocket bolt. Using Crankshaft Sprocket Puller/Installer (C-4685) and puller insert, remove crankshaft sprocket. *See Fig. 8.* Remove crankshaft seal retainer.

3) Remove chain cover, guide and tensioner. *See Fig. 16.* Remove balance shaft chain sprocket bolts and crankshaft balance shaft chain sprocket Torx bolts. Remove chain and sprocket assembly. Remove gear cover retaining stud.

4) Remove gear cover and balance shaft gears. Remove rear cover, and remove balance shafts from carrier.

5) To install, reverse removal procedure. Ensure correct timing of balance shafts and crankshaft. See ALIGNING BALANCE SHAFTS.

Removal (Carrier Assembly & Balance Shafts) – 1) Following components will remain intact during carrier assembly removal: gear cover, gears, balance shafts and rear cover.

2) Remove oil pan and oil pick-up. See OIL PAN under REMOVAL & INSTALLATION. Remove timing belt. See TIMING BELT under REMOVAL & INSTALLATION.

3) Remove crankshaft sprocket bolt. Using Crankshaft Sprocket Puller/Installer (C-4685) and puller insert, remove crankshaft sprocket. *See Fig. 8.* Remove crankshaft seal retainer.

4) Remove chain cover. Remove balance shaft sprocket bolt. Loosen tensioner pivot and adjusting bolts. Move chain-driven balance shaft inboard through chain sprocket. Sprocket should remain hanging in lower chain loop. Remove carrier-to-cylinder block bolts, and remove carrier assembly.

Installation – To install, reverse removal procedure. Ensure correct timing of balance shafts. See ALIGNING BALANCE SHAFTS.

Aligning Balance Shafts – 1) With balance shafts installed in carrier, position carrier (if removed) on cylinder block, and install carrier bolts. Tighten bolts to specification. See TORQUE SPECIFICATIONS table at end of article.

2) Rotate both balance shafts until shaft keyways are facing upward (parallel to vertical center line of engine). Install short hub gear on sprocket-driven shaft. Install long hub gear on gear-driven shaft. After installing, ensure balance shaft keyways remain facing upward when alignment marks are together. *See Fig. 17.*

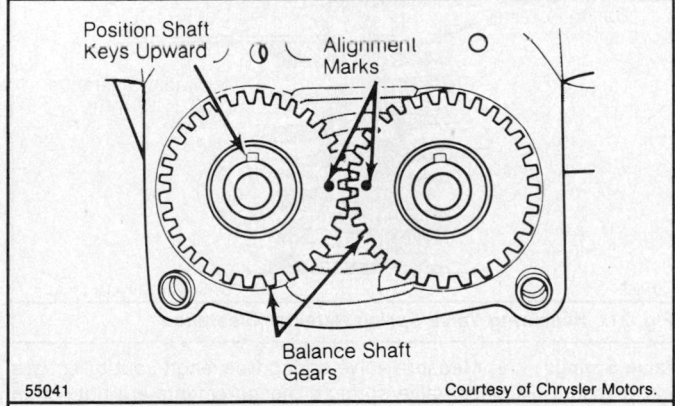

Fig. 17: Aligning Balance Shafts

3) Install gear cover, and tighten double-ended stud to specification. Install crankshaft balance shaft chain sprocket. Tighten bolt to specification. See TORQUE SPECIFICATIONS table. Rotate crankshaft until No. 1 cylinder is at TDC. Ensure crankshaft sprocket timing mark aligns with No. 1 main bearing cap parting line. *See Fig. 18.*

4) Install chain over crankshaft sprocket, with upper nickel-plated link of chain aligned with timing mark on crankshaft sprocket. *See Fig. 18.*

5) Install balance shaft chain (lower) sprocket into timing chain, with timing mark (Yellow dot) of sprocket aligned with lower nickel-plated link on chain. *See Fig. 18.*

NOTE: Upper and lower nickel-plated chain links should align with timing marks of upper and lower chain sprockets respectively.

6) With balance shaft keyways at 12 o'clock position, install balance shaft chain sprocket on nose of left balance shaft. Balance shaft may have to be pushed slightly inward to allow for clearance.

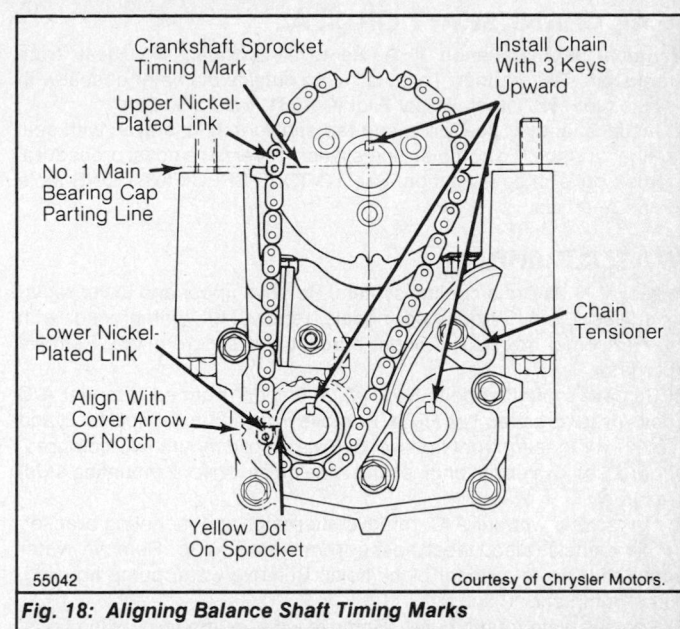

Fig. 18: Aligning Balance Shaft Timing Marks

NOTE: Balance shaft timing is correctly set when timing mark (Yellow dot) on balance shaft chain (lower) sprocket and lower nickel-plated chain link are aligned with cover arrow or notch. See Fig. 18.

7) Install sprocket retaining bolts, and tighten to specification. See TORQUE SPECIFICATIONS table. Adjust chain tension. See CHAIN TENSIONING.

Chain Tensioning – 1) Loosely install chain tensioner. Install guide on double-ended stud on gear cover. Ensure guide tab on guide engages with slot in gear cover.

2) Install guide retaining nut; tighten it to specification. See TORQUE SPECIFICATIONS table at end of article. Install a .039" (.99 mm) thick by 2.75" (69.8 mm) long shim between chain tensioner and chain.

3) Push chain tensioner and shim against chain. Apply firm pressure directly behind chain tensioner adjusting slot to take up all slack. *See Fig. 19.*

4) With pressure applied on chain tensioner, tighten chain tensioner adjusting bolt and then pivot bolt to specification. See TORQUE SPECIFICATIONS table. *See Fig. 19.* Remove shim. Install chain cover. Tighten bolts to specification. See TORQUE SPECIFICATIONS table.

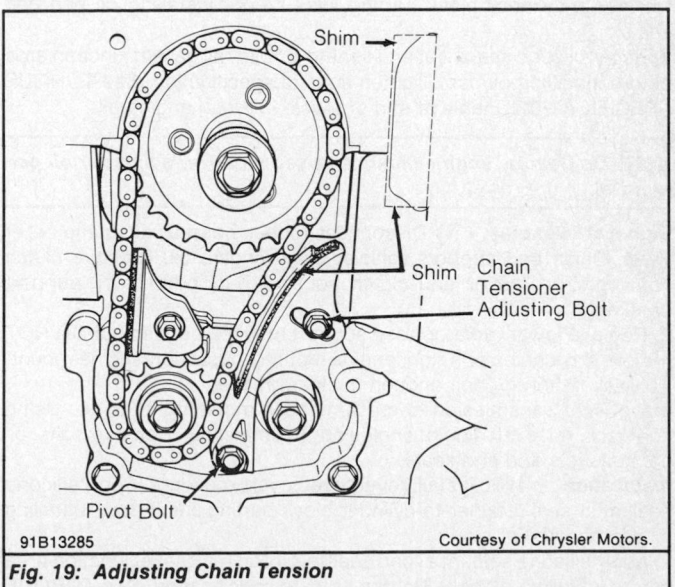

Fig. 19: Adjusting Chain Tension

REAR CRANKSHAFT OIL SEAL

Removal & Installation – 1) Remove flywheel. Pry seal from crankshaft seal retainer. To install, coat outside diameter of seal with Loctite (4057987). Install Seal Pilot (C-4681) on crankshaft.

2) Install seal over seal pilot, and tap seal in until it is even with seal retainer surface. To complete installation, reverse removal procedure. Tighten bolts to specification. See TORQUE SPECIFICATIONS table at end of article.

WATER PUMP

Removal – 1) Drain cooling system. Remove upper and lower radiator hoses. On A/C-equipped models, remove A/C compressor with lines attached from solid mount bracket and secure aside. Remove alternator.

2) Remove mounting bolts No. 1, 4, 5, 6 and 7 from solid mount A/C compressor bracket. See Fig. 4. Remove front mounting nut No. 2, and remove (or loosen) front bolt No. 3. Rotate solid mount A/C compressor bracket away from engine, and slide on stud (No. 2 mounting stud) until free.

3) On models without A/C, remove alternator and mounting bracket. On all models, disconnect hoses from water pump. Remove water pump housing-to-cylinder block bolts. Remove water pump housing, water pump and "O" ring.

4) Remove water pump pulley. Remove water pump-to-housing bolts. Separate water pump from housing. Remove "O" ring from housing groove.

Installation – 1) Install water pump on housing using a new gasket and "O" ring. Tighten retaining bolts to specification. See TORQUE SPECIFICATIONS table at end of article. Install new "O" ring in housing groove.

2) Install water pump pulley. Ensure pump rotates freely. Install water pump and housing on engine, and tighten bolts to specification. See TORQUE SPECIFICATIONS table. When installing solid mount A/C compressor bracket, tighten bolts in following order.

- Bolt No. 1 – 30 INCH lbs. (3.3 N.m)
- Bolts No. 2 and 3 – 40 ft. lbs. (54 N.m)
- Bolts No. 1, 4 and 5 – 40 ft. lbs. (54 N.m)
- Bolts No. 6 and 7 – 40 ft. lbs. (54 N.m)

3) Fill cooling system. See COOLING SYSTEM BLEEDING under REMOVAL & INSTALLATION.

OIL PAN

Removal & Installation (Caravan & Voyager) – 1) Drain engine oil. Remove retaining bolts, oil pan, gaskets and end seals.

2) To install, reverse removal procedure. Apply silicone sealant at seal retainer-to-cylinder block parting lines before installing oil pan end seals.

3) Apply silicone sealant at end seal-to-oil pan rail gasket junction area before installing oil pan. Tighten bolts to specification. See TORQUE SPECIFICATIONS table at end of article. Fill with engine oil.

NOTE: On Dakota, engine must be raised on driver's side for oil pan removal.

Removal (Dakota) – 1) Disconnect rubber hose at air pump relief valve. Raise and support vehicle. Drain engine oil. Remove clutch housing lower cover and clutch housing-to-cylinder block support brackets.

2) Remove lower radiator hose support bracket. Loosen but DO NOT remove through bolt on right engine mount. Loosen left engine mount-to-bracket through bolt enough to clear bracket.

3) Loosen transmission-to-crossmember mounting bracket. Using floor jack, raise left side of engine approximately 2". Remove bolts, oil pan, gaskets and end seals.

Installation – 1) To install, reverse removal procedure. Apply silicone sealant at seal retainer-to-cylinder block parting line before installing oil pan end seals.

2) Apply silicone sealant at end seal-to-oil pan rail gasket junction area before installing oil pan. Tighten bolts to specification. See TORQUE SPECIFICATIONS table at end of article. Fill with engine oil.

OVERHAUL

CYLINDER HEAD

Cylinder Head – 1) Check cylinder head warpage. Warpage must not exceed specification. See CYLINDER HEAD table under ENGINE SPECIFICATIONS at end of article.

2) If cylinder head or camshaft is serviced, ensure oversized camshaft is used in cylinder head with oversized bores. See SPECIAL ENGINE MARKS.

3) After grinding valves or valve seats, install valve into cylinder. Measure valve stem installed height from spring seat of cylinder head to tip of valve. See Fig. 20. Distance should be **1.960-2.009"** **(49.78-51.03 mm)**. Grind valve tip if necessary.

CAUTION: If valve tip is ground more than .020" (.51 mm), check clearance between rocker arm ear and valve spring retainer. See Fig. 21. Clearance must be at least .050" (1.27 mm). If clearance is insufficient, grind rocker arm ears to obtain correct clearance.

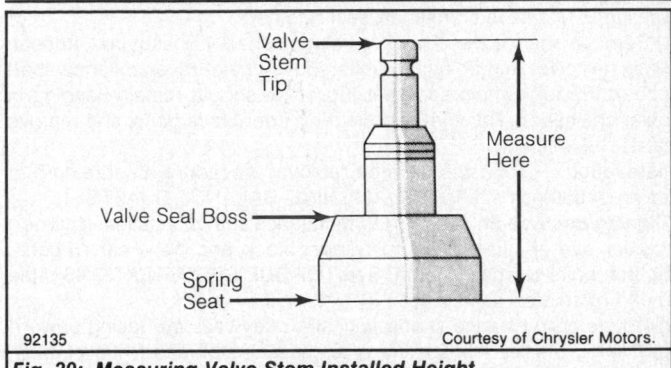

92135   Courtesy of Chrysler Motors.
Fig. 20: Measuring Valve Stem Installed Height

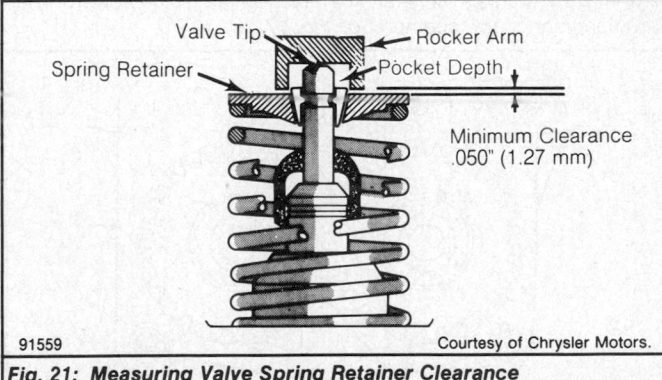

91559   Courtesy of Chrysler Motors.
Fig. 21: Measuring Valve Spring Retainer Clearance

Valve Springs – 1) Measure valve spring free length, out-of-square and pressure. Replace valve spring if measurements are not within specification. See VALVES & VALVE SPRINGS table under ENGINE SPECIFICATIONS at end of article.

2) Measure valve spring installed height from lower edge of valve spring to upper edge. DO NOT include spring seat or retainer flange. Ensure valve spring installed height is within specification. See VALVES & VALVE SPRINGS table. If valve spring installed height is not within specification, add an additional spring seat.

Valve Stem Oil Seals – Oversize valve stem seals must be used with oversize valves. Ensure lower edge of valve stem oil seal is against valve guide after installation.

Valve Guides — 1) Check valve stem oil clearance. Ensure valve stem diameter is within specification. Valve guide must be reamed for oversize valve stem if clearance exceeds specification. See CYLINDER HEAD table under ENGINE SPECIFICATIONS at end of article.

2) Valves are available with oversize valve stems of .006" (.15 mm), .016" (.40 mm) and .031" (.80 mm). Replace cylinder head if valve guide cannot be reamed using a .031" (.80 mm) reamer or if valve guide is loose.

NOTE: DO NOT ream valve guides from standard to maximum oversize in one step. Ream valve guides to oversize in gradual steps so valve guides are reamed in relation to valve seat.

Valve Seats — 1) Ensure valve seat angle, seat width and seat runout are within specification. See CYLINDER HEAD table under ENGINE SPECIFICATIONS at end of article.

2) If valve face and/or valve seats have been ground, measure valve stem installed height from spring seat of cylinder head to tip of valve. *See Fig. 20.* Distance should be **1.960-2.009" (49.78-51.03 mm)**. Grind valve tip if necessary.

Valves – 1) Check head diameter, valve margin and stem diameter. Replace valve if measurements are not within specification. See VALVES & VALVE SPRINGS table under ENGINE SPECIFICATIONS at end of article.

2) After grinding valves, install valve into cylinder and measure valve stem installed height from spring seat of cylinder head to tip of valve. *See Fig. 20.* Distance should be **1.960-2.009" (49.78-51.03 mm)**. Grind valve tip if necessary.

CAUTION: If valve tip is ground more than .020" (.51 mm), check clearance between rocker arm ear and valve spring retainer. See Fig. 21. Clearance must be at least .050" (1.27 mm). If clearance is insufficient, grind rocker arm ears to obtain correct clearance.

3) Valves are available with oversize valve stems of .006" (.15 mm), .016" (.40 mm) and .031" (.80 mm). Valve tip diameter should be no less than .275" (6.99 mm) after grinding. If necessary, tip chamfer should be reground to prevent seal damage when valve is installed.

Seat Correction Angles – After grinding, if seat width is too wide, use a 15-degree or 65-degree stone to alter seat width. A 15-degree stone will lower valve seat and a 65-degree stone will raise valve seat.

VALVE TRAIN

Rocker Arm – Replace rocker arms if damaged.

Lash Adjusters – 1) No adjustment is required on lash adjusters. If lash adjuster is disassembled for cleaning purposes, reassemble using NEW cap.

2) Ensure lash adjusters are partially full of oil before installing. Little or no plunger travel should exist when lash adjuster is depressed.

NOTE: Always service lash adjusters as complete assemblies. Lash adjuster internal components are not interchangeable.

CYLINDER BLOCK ASSEMBLY

Piston & Rod Assembly – Valve clearance cutout(s) on top of piston should face manifold side of engine. Oiling hole on connecting rod must face toward front (timing belt end) of engine. *See Fig. 22.*

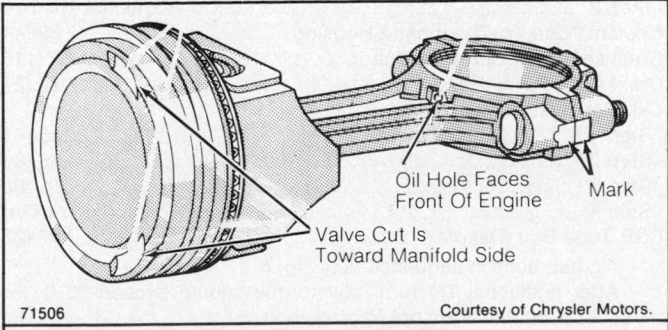

Oil Hole Faces Front Of Engine

Mark

Valve Cut Is Toward Manifold Side

71506   Courtesy of Chrysler Motors.

Fig. 22: Installing Piston On Connecting Rod

Fitting Pistons – Measure piston diameter at 1.87" (47.4 mm) below top of piston, at 90-degree angle to piston pin. Measure cylinder bore diameter at center of cylinder bore. Ensure piston diameter and piston clearance are within specification. See PISTONS, PINS & RINGS table under ENGINE SPECIFICATIONS at end of article.

Piston Rings – Ensure ring end gap and side clearances are within specification. See PISTON, PINS & RINGS table under ENGINE SPECIFICATIONS at end of article. Ensure piston ring end gaps are properly positioned. *See Fig. 23.*

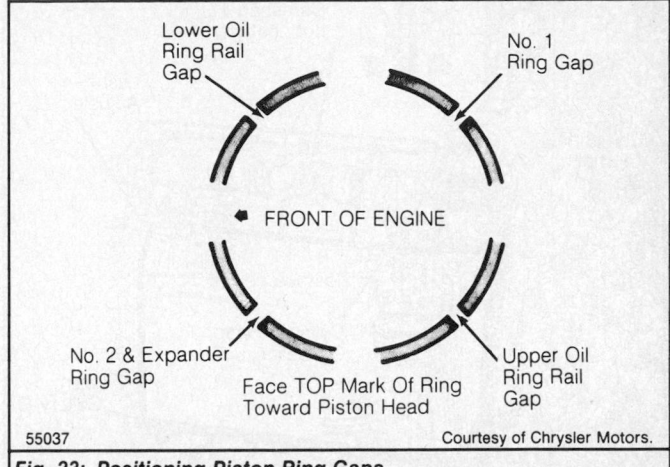

Lower Oil Ring Rail Gap

No. 1 Ring Gap

FRONT OF ENGINE

No. 2 & Expander Ring Gap

Upper Oil Ring Rail Gap

Face TOP Mark Of Ring Toward Piston Head

55037   Courtesy of Chrysler Motors.

Fig. 23: Positioning Piston Ring Gaps

Rod Bearings – 1) Before installing connecting rod bearings, hold a straightedge across connecting rod bolt threads. Ensure threads contact straightedge in all areas. If threads fail to contact straightedge, rod bolts are stretched and must be replaced.

2) Lightly coat rod bolts with engine oil before installing nuts. Ensure connecting rod is installed so oiling hole on connecting rod faces toward front (timing belt end) of engine. *See Fig. 22.*

3) Tighten connecting rod nuts to specification. See TORQUE SPECIFICATIONS table at end of article. Ensure bearing oil clearance and side play are within specification. See CRANKSHAFT, MAIN & CONNECTING ROD BEARINGS and CONNECTING RODS tables under ENGINE SPECIFICATIONS at end of article.

Crankshaft & Main Bearings – 1) Main bearing caps are numbered with No. 1 at timing belt end and No. 5 at flywheel end. Arrow on main bearing cap must point toward timing belt end of engine.

2) Before installing main bearings, hold a straightedge across threads of main bearing cap bolts. Ensure threads contact straightedge in all areas. If threads fail to contact straightedge, bolts are stretched and must be replaced.

3) Lightly coat bolt threads with engine oil before installing. Tighten main bearing cap bolts to specification. See TORQUE SPECIFICATIONS table at end of article.

4) Ensure main bearing oil clearance and crankshaft end play are within specification. See CRANKSHAFT, MAIN & CONNECTING ROD BEARINGS table under ENGINE SPECIFICATIONS at end of article. Replace thrust bearing if end play is not within specification.

Thrust Bearing – Thrust bearing is located on No. 3 main bearing. Replace thrust bearing if crankshaft end play is not within specification. See CRANKSHAFT, MAIN & CONNECTING ROD BEARINGS table under ENGINE SPECIFICATIONS at end of article.

Cylinder Block – 1) Using a feeler gauge and straightedge, check cylinder block head surface for warpage. Measure cylinder bore, taper and out-of-round. Measure at .375" (9.52 mm) below top surface of cylinder bore, middle of bore and .375" (9.52 mm) from bottom of cylinder bore.

2) Repair or replace cylinder block if measurements are not within specification. See CYLINDER BLOCK table under ENGINE SPECIFICATIONS at end of article.

ENGINE OILING

ENGINE LUBRICATION SYSTEM

A crankshaft-driven oil pump provides pressurized lubrication to main oil gallery. *See Fig. 24.*

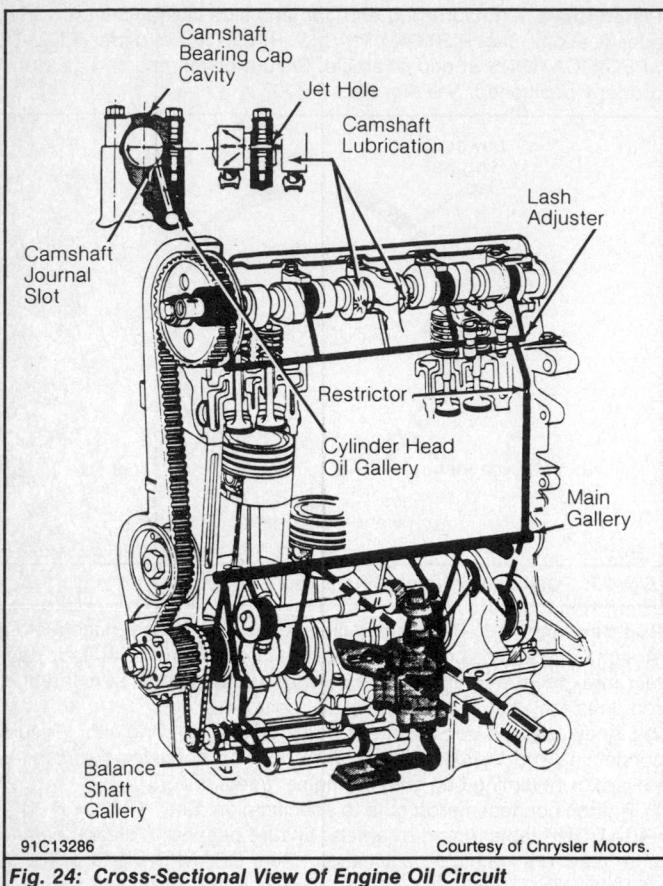

Fig. 24: Cross-Sectional View Of Engine Oil Circuit

Crankcase Capacity – Oil capacity with oil filter is 4.5 qts. (4.2L).
Oil Pressure – Oil pressure should be **4 psi (.28 kg/cm²)** at curb idle and **25-80 psi (1.75-5.6 kg/cm²)** at 3000 RPM with engine at normal operating temperature.

OIL PUMP

Removal & Disassembly – **1)** Remove oil pan. See OIL PAN under REMOVAL & INSTALLATION. Remove oil pick-up tube-to-oil pump bolt. Remove pick-up tube and "O" ring. Remove oil pump-to-cylinder block bolts. Remove oil pump.

2) Remove pump cover-to-pump housing bolts. Remove pump cover. Note direction of rotor installation. Remove inner and outer rotors. See Fig. 25. Remove pin, cap, spring and pressure relief valve from oil pump housing. Clean all components in solvent, and blow dry using compressed air.

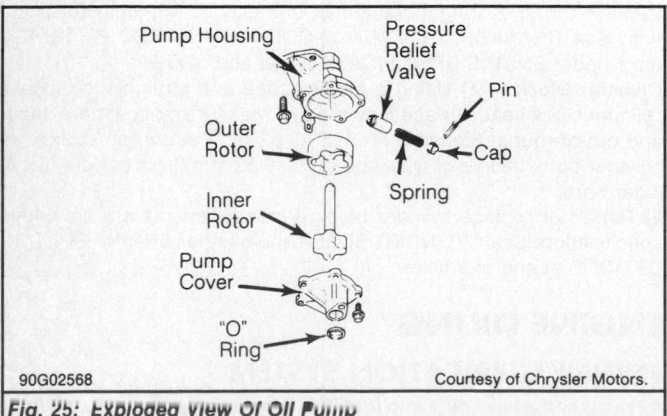

Fig. 25: Exploded View Of Oil Pump

Inspection – **1)** Install inner rotor (drive gear) and outer rotor (driven gear) into pump housing. Place straightedge across pump housing

and both gears. Using feeler gauge, check rotor-to-housing clearance between rotor and straightedge.

2) With rotors installed, check outer rotor-to-inner rotor clearance. Check outer rotor-to-housing clearance. Remove rotors. Measure outer rotor O.D. and thickness. Measure inner rotor thickness. Check pump cover flatness.

3) Measure free length of pressure relief valve spring. Using spring pressure tester, check pressure of pressure relief valve spring. Replace oil pump assembly if measurements are not within specification. See OIL PUMP SPECIFICATIONS table.

OIL PUMP SPECIFICATIONS

Application	Specification
Inner Rotor Thickness	.9435" (23.965 mm)
Outer Rotor O.D.	2.469" (62.71 mm)
Outer Rotor Thickness	.9435" (23.965 mm)
Outer Rotor-To-Housing Clearance [1]	.014" (.35 mm)
Outer Rotor-To-Inner Rotor Clearance	.008" (.20 mm)
Pressure Relief Valve Spring	
Free Length	1.95" (49.5 mm)
Pressure	20 Lbs. @ 1.34" (9 kg @ 34.0 mm
Pump Cover Flatness	.003" (.07 mm)
Rotor-To-Housing Clearance [2]	.0010-.0035" (.025-.088 mm)

[1] – Measured by inserting feeler gauge between outer rotor and housing.
[2] – Measured by placing straightedge across pump housing.

Reassembly & Installation – **1)** To reassemble, reverse disassembly procedure. Install outer rotor in pump housing, with large chamfered edge toward pump housing.

2) To install, apply Loctite Sealer (515) to oil pump housing-to-cylinder block surface. Align slot in oil pump drive gear. Install oil pump. Rotate pump back and forth to ensure proper seating while tightening retaining bolts to specification. See TORQUE SPECIFICATIONS table at end of article.

3) Install new "O" ring on pick-up tube. To install remaining components, reverse removal procedure.

TORQUE SPECIFICATIONS

TORQUE SPECIFICATIONS

Application	Ft. Lbs. (N.m)
Balance Shaft Carrier-To-Cylinder Block Bolt	40 (54)
Balance Shaft Chain Sprocket Bolt	21 (29)
Balance Shaft Sprocket-To-Crankshaft Bolt	11 (15)
Camshaft Bearing Cap Bolt	18 (24)
Camshaft Sprocket Bolt	65 (88)
Clutch Housing-To-Cylinder Block	
Support Bracket Bolt (Dakota)	70 (95)
Connecting Rod Cap Nut	
Step 1	40 (54)
Step 2	Additional 1/4 Turn
Coolant Tube-To-Thermostat Housing	30 (41)
Crankshaft Belt Sprocket Bolt	85 (115)
Crankshaft Pulley Bolt	20 (27)
Cylinder Head Bolt [1]	
Step 1	45 (61)
Step 2	65 (88)
Step 3	65 (88)
Step 4	[2] Additional 1/4 Turn
EGR Tube Bolt (Dakota)	17 (23)

[1] – Tighten bolts in sequence. See Fig. 6.
[2] – After additional 1/4 turn, bolt torque should exceed 90 ft. lbs. (122 N.m). If it does not, replace bolt.
[3] – See Fig. 4 for bolt identification. Tighten bolts in sequence.
  - Bolt No. 1 to 30 INCH lbs. (3.3 N.m)
  - Bolts No. 2 & 3 to 40 ft. lbs. (54 N.m)
  - Bolts No. 1, 4 & 5 to 40 ft. lbs. (54 N.m)
  - Bolts No. 6 & 7 to 40 ft. lbs. (54 N.m)
[4] – Tighten 8-mm bolts to 17 ft. lbs. (23 N.m) and 6-mm bolts to 105 INCH lbs. (12 N.m).

TORQUE SPECIFICATIONS (Cont.)

Application	Ft. Lbs. (N.m)
Engine Mount Through Bolt (Dakota)	50 (68)
Exhaust Manifold Nut	17 (23)
Flywheel Bolt	70 (95)
Front Mount Through Bolt (Caravan & Voyager)	50 (68)
Front Mount-To-Cylinder Block Bolt	
Caravan & Voyager	75 (102)
Fuel Rail Bolt	21 (29)
Insulator-To-Side Rail Bolt (Caravan & Voyager)	27 (37)
Intake Manifold Bolt	17 (23)
Intermediate Shaft Sprocket Bolt	65 (88)
Main Bearing Cap Bolt	
Step 1	30 (41)
Step 2	Additional 1/4 Turn
Oil Pump Pick-Up Tube Bolt	21 (29)
Oil Pump-To-Cylinder Block Bolt	17 (23)
Right (Timing Belt Side) Mount Through Bolt	
Caravan & Voyager	100 (136)
Right (Timing Belt Side) Mount Vertical Bolt	
Caravan & Voyager	75 (102)
Solid Mount A/C Compressor Bracket	3
Throttle Body Bolt	17 (23)
Timing Belt Tensioner Bolt	45 (61)
Torque Converter-To-Flexplate Bolt	
Caravan & Voyager	40 (54)
Transaxle-To-Cylinder Block Bolt	
Caravan & Voyager	70 (95)
Transmission-To-Clutch Housing Bolt (Dakota)	30 (41)
Water Pump Housing Bolt	
Lower	40 (54)
Upper	21 (29)
Vent Plug	15 (20)

	INCH Lbs. (N.m)
Balance Shaft Chain Guide Nut	105 (12)
Balance Shaft Chain Pivot & Tensioner Bolt	105 (12)
Balance Shaft Cover Bolt	105 (12)
Crankshaft Balance Shaft	
Chain Sprocket Torx Bolt	130 (15)
Crankshaft Front & Rear Seal Retainer Bolt	105 (12)
Fuel Pressure Regulator Nut	65 (7)
Gear Cover Stud/Bolt	105 (12)
Intermediate Shaft Seal Retainer Bolt	105 (12)
Oil Pan Bolt	4
Oil Pump Cover Bolt	105 (12)
Timing Belt Cover Bolt	40 (5)
Valve Cover Bolt	105 (12)
Water Pump Pulley Bolt	105 (12)
Water Pump-To-Housing Bolt	105 (12)

1 – Tighten bolts in sequence. See Fig. 6.
2 – After additional 1/4 turn, bolt torque should exceed 90 ft. lbs. (122 N.m). If it does not, replace bolt.
3 – See Fig. 4 for bolt identification. Tighten bolts in sequence.
   • Bolt No. 1 to 30 INCH lbs. (3.3 N.m)
   • Bolts No. 2 & 3 to 40 ft. lbs. (54 N.m)
   • Bolts No. 1, 4 & 5 to 40 ft. lbs. (54 N.m)
   • Bolts No. 6 & 7 to 40 ft. lbs. (54 N.m)
4 – Tighten 8-mm bolts to 17 ft. lbs. (23 N.m) and 6-mm bolts to 105 INCH lbs. (12 N.m).

ENGINE SPECIFICATIONS

GENERAL SPECIFICATIONS

Application	Specification
Displacement	153 Cu. In. (2.5L)
Bore	3.44" (87.4 mm)
Stroke	4.09" (103.8 mm)
Compression Ratio	8.9:1
Fuel System	TBI
Horsepower @ RPM	
Caravan & Voyager	100 @ 4800
Dakota	117 @ 5250
Torque Ft. Lbs. @ RPM	
Caravan & Voyager	135 @ 2800
Dakota	139 @ 3500

CRANKSHAFT, MAIN & CONNECTING ROD BEARINGS

Application	In. (mm)
Crankshaft End Play	
Standard	.002-.007 (.05-.18)
Wear Limit	.014 (.36)
Main Bearings	
Journal Diameter	2.362-2.363 (59.99-60.02)
Journal Out-Of-Round	.0003 (.008)
Journal Taper	.0003 (.008)
Oil Clearance	
Caravan & Voyager	
Standard	.0004-.0028 (.010-.071)
Wear Limit	.004 (.10)
Dakota	
Standard	.0003-.0031 (.008-.079)
Wear Limit	.004 (.10)
Connecting Rod Bearings	
Journal Diameter	1.968-1.969 (49.99-50.01)
Journal Out-Of-Round	.0003 (.008)
Journal Taper	.0003 (.008)
Oil Clearance	
Standard	.0008-.0034 (.020-.086)
Wear Limit	.004 (.10)

CONNECTING RODS

Application	In. (mm)
Maximum Bend	.003 (.08)
Maximum Twist	.003 (.08)
Side Play	.005-.013 (.13-.33)

1992 ENGINES
2.5L 4-Cylinder (Cont.)

PISTONS, PINS & RINGS

Application	In. (mm)
Pistons	
Clearance	
Standard	.0010-.0020 (.025-.051)
Wear Limit	.0027 (.069)
Diameter	3.442-3.444 (87.43-87.48)
Rings	
No. 1	
End Gap	
Standard	.010-.020 (.25-.51)
Wear Limit	.039 (.99)
Side Clearance	
Standard	.0015-.0031 (.038-.079)
Wear Limit	.004 (.10)
No. 2	
End Gap	
Standard	.011-.021 (.28-.53)
Wear Limit	.039 (.99)
Side Clearance	
Standard	.0015-.0037 (.038-.094)
Wear Limit	.004 (.10)
No. 3 (Oil)	
End Gap	
Standard	.015-.055 (.38-1.40)
Wear Limit	.074 (1.88)

CYLINDER BLOCK

Application	In. (mm)
Cylinder Bore	
Standard Diameter	3.44 (87.4)
Maximum Taper	.005 (.13)
Maximum Out-Of-Round	.002 (.05)

VALVES & VALVE SPRINGS

Application	Specification
Intake Valves	
Face Angle	45°
Head Diameter	1.60" (40.6 mm)
Minimum Margin	.031" (.79 mm)
Stem Diameter	.3124" (7.935 mm)
Exhaust Valves	
Face Angle	45°
Head Diameter	1.39" (35.3 mm)
Minimum Margin	.047" (1.19 mm)
Stem Diameter	.3103" (7.882 mm)
Valve Springs	
Free Length	
Caravan & Voyager	2.39" (60.7 mm)
Dakota	2.16" (54.9 mm)
Installed Height	1.62-1.68" (41.1-42.7 mm)
Out-Of-Square	.079" (2.01 mm)

	Lbs. @ In. (kg @ mm)
Pressure	
Valve Closed	108-120 @ 1.65 (49-54 @ 42)
Valve Open	
Caravan & Voyager	195-215 @ 1.22 (89-97 @ 31)
Dakota	221-235 @ 1.22 (100-107 @ 31)

CYLINDER HEAD

Application	Specification
Maximum Warpage	.004" (.10 mm)
Valve Seats	
Intake Valve	
Seat Angle	45°
Seat Width	.069-.088" (1.75-2.24 mm)
Maximum Seat Runout	.002" (.05 mm)
Seat Bore Diameter	1.593" (40.46 mm)
Exhaust Valve	
Seat Angle	45°
Seat Width	.059-.078" (1.50-1.98 mm)
Maximum Seat Runout	.002" (.05 mm)
Seat Bore Diameter	1.371" (34.82 mm)
Valve Guides	
Valve Stem-To-Guide Oil Clearance	
Intake	.0009-.0026" (.023-.066 mm)
Exhaust	.0030-.0047" (.076-.119 mm)

CAMSHAFT

Application	In. (mm)
Cam Lobe Wear	.010 (.25)
End Play	
Standard	.005-.013 (.13-.33)
Wear Limit	.020 (.51)
Journal Diameter	
Standard	1.375-1.376 (34.93-34.95)
Oversized	1.395-1.396 (35.43-35.46)

Caravan, Voyager

NOTE: For engine repair procedures not covered in this article, see ENGINE OVERHAUL PROCEDURES in GENERAL INFORMATION.

ENGINE IDENTIFICATION

Engine may be identified by eighth character of Vehicle Identification Number (VIN). The VIN is stamped on a plate on top of instrument panel at lower left of windshield.

ENGINE IDENTIFICATION CODE

Application	Code
3.0L PFI	3

ADJUSTMENTS

VALVE CLEARANCE ADJUSTMENT

Hydraulic lash adjusters are used. No valve adjustment is required.

REMOVAL & INSTALLATION

NOTE: For reassembly reference, label all electrical connectors, vacuum hoses and fuel lines before removal. Also place mating marks on engine hood and other major assemblies before removal.

WARNING: When battery is disconnected, vehicle computer and memory systems may lose memory data. Driveability problems may exist until computer systems have completed a relearn cycle. See COMPUTER RELEARN PROCEDURES article in GENERAL INFORMATION before disconnecting battery.

FUEL PRESSURE RELEASE

CAUTION: Fuel system is under pressure. Pressure must be released before servicing any fuel system components.

1) Loosen fuel tank cap to release pressure. Disconnect injector wiring harness from engine wiring harness. Connect jumper wire from terminal No. 1 of injector harness to ground. See Fig. 1.
2) Connect a second jumper wire to terminal No. 2 of injector harness. Touch jumper wire to positive battery terminal for no more than 5 seconds to release fuel pressure. Remove jumper wires and reconnect wiring harness.

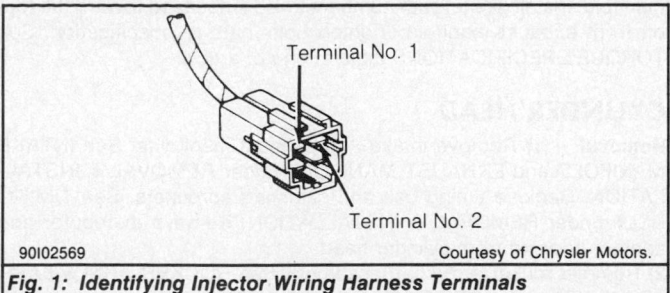

90I02569   Courtesy of Chrysler Motors.

Fig. 1: Identifying Injector Wiring Harness Terminals

ENGINE

NOTE: Remove engine with transaxle remaining in the vehicle.

Removal – 1) Release fuel pressure. See FUEL PRESSURE RELEASE under REMOVAL & INSTALLATION. Disconnect battery. Scribe hood hinge location on hood for reassembly. Remove hood. Drain cooling system and engine oil. Disconnect necessary coolant hoses, control cables, fuel lines, electrical connections and vacuum hoses.
2) Remove air cleaner and radiator/fan assembly. Raise and support vehicle. Remove A/C compressor and power steering pump with hoses attached and set aside (if equipped).

3) Remove starter. Disconnect exhaust pipe at exhaust manifold. Remove torque converter cover. Reference mark flexplate to torque converter for reassembly reference.
4) Remove torque converter-to-flexplate bolts. Attach "C" clamp to bottom front edge of torque converter housing to secure torque converter.
5) Remove lower transaxle-to-cylinder block bolts. Lower vehicle. Support transaxle with floor jack. Attach lifting hoist to engine. Remove remaining transaxle-to-cylinder block bolts.
6) Place reference mark on side rail to indicate right insulator (timing belt side) position for reassembly reference. Remove right insulator-to-side rail bolts.

CAUTION: To ensure proper positioning of the engine, right insulator position on side rail must be marked before removal for reassembly reference. Insulator must be installed in original position.

7) Remove through bolt from left engine mount from inside fenderwell. Insulator bracket-to-transaxle bolts may be removed instead of through bolt. Remove front engine mount bolts. Lift engine from vehicle.

Installation – 1) To install, reverse removal procedure. DO NOT tighten engine mount bolts until all bolts are installed. If vertical bolts on right or left mount were loosened, axle shaft length must be checked.
2) To determine axle shaft length, measure distance between inner edge of outboard boot and inner edge of inboard boot at 6 o'clock position. See Fig. 2.

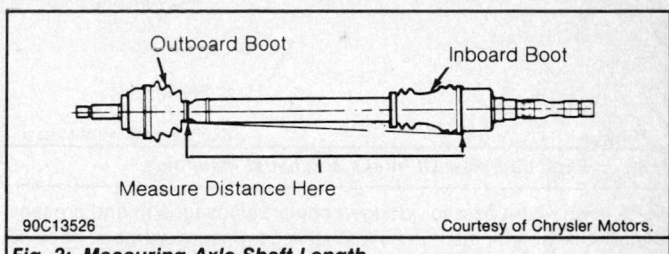

Outboard Boot   Inboard Boot

Measure Distance Here

90C13526   Courtesy of Chrysler Motors.

Fig. 2: Measuring Axle Shaft Length

3) Axle shaft length must be within specification. See AXLE SHAFT LENGTH SPECIFICATIONS table.

AXLE SHAFT LENGTH SPECIFICATIONS

Application	In. (mm)
Right Axle Shaft	20.5-20.9 (521-531)
Left Axle Shaft	9.0-9.4 (229-239)

4) Adjust axle shaft length to specification by sliding engine in slots on engine mounts. Tighten all engine mount bolts once correct axle shaft length is obtained.

CAUTION: Tighten vertical bolt in right mount bracket (timing belt side) before tightening through bolt.

5) Ensure reference mark is aligned on torque converter and flexplate. Tighten bolts to specification. See TORQUE SPECIFICATIONS table at end of article.

INTAKE MANIFOLD

CAUTION: Fuel system is under pressure. Fuel pressure must be released before disconnecting fuel lines.

Removal – 1) Release fuel pressure. See FUEL PRESSURE RELEASE under REMOVAL & INSTALLATION. Disconnect negative battery cable. Drain cooling system. Remove air cleaner hose from throttle body. Remove throttle cable and transaxle kickdown linkage. Disconnect necessary electrical connections and vacuum hoses at throttle body and intake manifold.
2) Remove ignition coil from upper intake manifold. Wrap fuel lines with shop towel and disconnect from fuel rail. Remove retaining bolts,

upper air intake and gaskets. *See Fig. 3*. Cover intake manifold openings with shop towel.

3) Disconnect vacuum hoses from fuel rail and pressure regulator. Disconnect fuel injector wiring harness from engine wiring harness. Remove retaining bolts and pressure regulator from fuel rail.

4) Remove retaining bolts and fuel rail assembly from intake manifold. Disconnect radiator and heater hoses. Remove retaining bolts, intake manifold and gaskets. *See Fig. 3*.

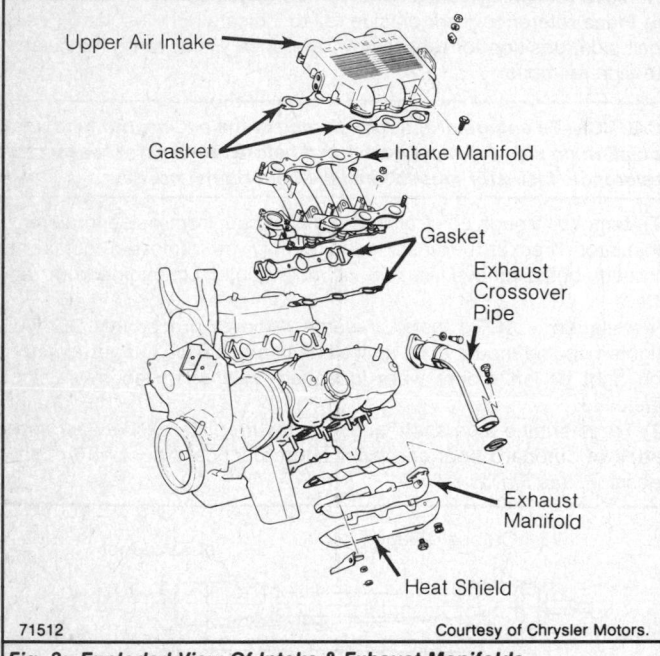

Fig. 3: Exploded View Of Intake & Exhaust Manifolds

Inspection – Inspect for clogged coolant passages in end crossovers. Check mounting surfaces for warpage. Ensure warpage does not exceed specification. See INTAKE MANIFOLD WARPAGE table.

INTAKE MANIFOLD WARPAGE

Application	In. (mm)
Cylinder Head Mounting Surface	
Standard	.003 (.08)
Maximum	.005 (.13)
Upper Air Intake Mounting Surface	
Standard	.004 (.10)
Maximum	.008 (.20)

Installation – **1)** Install gaskets and intake manifold. Tighten intake manifold nuts to specification in sequence. *See Fig. 4*. See TORQUE SPECIFICATIONS table at end of article.

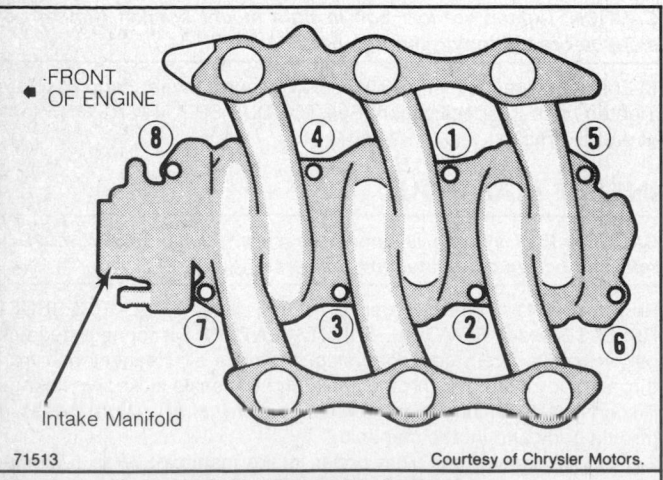

Fig. 4: Intake Manifold Nut Tightening Sequence

2) Ensure injector holes are clean. Lubricate injector "O" rings with engine oil before installing. Install fuel rail and injectors until injectors are firmly seated in port. Install fuel rail retaining bolts. Install pressure regulator. Tighten bolts/nuts to specification. See TORQUE SPECIFICATIONS table at end of article.

3) Install upper air intake gaskets on intake manifold with beaded sealant side upward, away from intake manifold. Install upper air intake. Tighten upper air bolts in sequence to specification. *See Fig. 5*. See TORQUE SPECIFICATIONS table at end of article.

4) To install remaining components, reverse removal procedure. Fill cooling system.

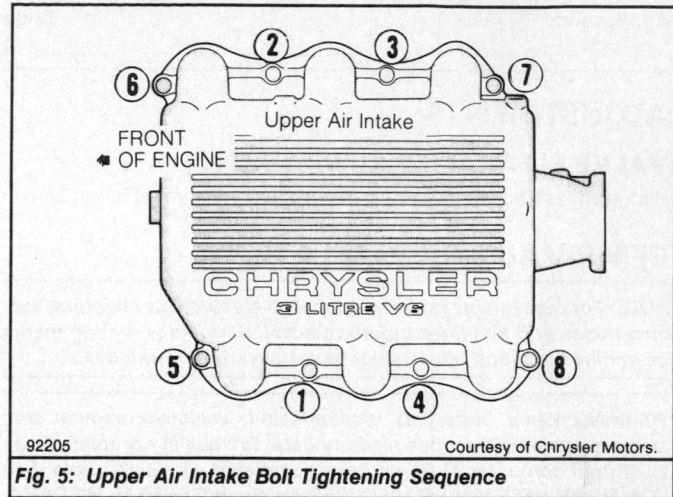

Fig. 5: Upper Air Intake Bolt Tightening Sequence

EXHAUST MANIFOLD

Removal – **1)** Raise and support vehicle. Disconnect exhaust pipe from rear exhaust manifold flange. Disconnect O_2 sensor wiring. Remove exhaust crossover pipe mounting bolts. *See Fig. 3*. Remove rear exhaust manifold retaining nuts, and remove exhaust manifold.

2) Lower vehicle. Remove heat shield-to-front exhaust manifold bolts. Disconnect exhaust crossover pipe at front exhaust manifold. Remove retaining nuts and front exhaust manifold.

Inspection – Check manifolds for cracks, damage and mounting surfaces for warpage. Repair or replace manifold if warpage exceeds **.008" (.20 mm)**.

Installation – To install, reverse removal procedure. Install gasket with numbers 1-3-5 embossed toward the top, on rear exhaust manifold. Install gasket with numbers 2-4-6 embossed toward the top, on front exhaust manifold. Tighten bolts/nuts to specification. See TORQUE SPECIFICATIONS table at end of article.

CYLINDER HEAD

Removal – **1)** Remove intake and exhaust manifolds. See INTAKE MANIFOLD and EXHAUST MANIFOLD under REMOVAL & INSTALLATION. Remove timing belt and camshaft sprockets. See TIMING BELT under REMOVAL & INSTALLATION. Remove distributor and adapter housing from cylinder head.

2) Remove rocker arm shaft assembly. See ROCKER ARM & LASH ADJUSTER under REMOVAL & INSTALLATION. Remove camshaft. Remove cylinder head bolts in sequence. *See Fig. 6*. Remove cylinder head and gasket.

CAUTION: Note location of 10-mm Allen hex cylinder head bolt and washer for reassembly reference. See Fig. 6.

Inspection – Check cylinder head for warpage. Resurface head if warpage exceeds specification. See CYLINDER HEAD table under ENGINE SPECIFICATIONS at end of article.

CAUTION: DO NOT grind more than .008" (.20 mm) combined total from surface of cylinder head and deck surface of cylinder block.

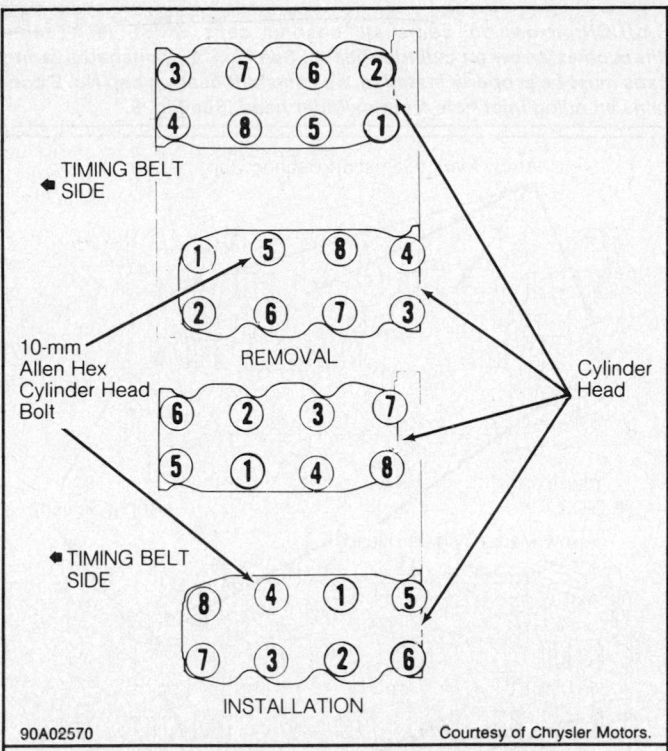

Fig. 6: Cylinder Head Bolt Removal & Installation Sequence

Installation – 1) To install, reverse removal procedure. Ensure 10-mm Allen hex cylinder head bolts and washers are installed in correct location. *See Fig. 6.* Tighten cylinder head bolts to specification in sequence, using 2-3 steps. See TORQUE SPECIFICATIONS table at end of article.

2) Lubricate camshaft with engine oil before installing. To install remaining components, reverse removal procedure. Tighten bolts to specification. See TORQUE SPECIFICATIONS table at end of article.

CRANKSHAFT FRONT SEAL

Removal & Installation – 1) Crankshaft front seal is located in oil pump housing. Timing belt and crankshaft sprocket must be removed for access to crankshaft front seal. Manufacturer does not indicate procedure for seal removal.

2) To install, apply light coat of engine oil on circumference of crankshaft front seal. Use Seal Installer (MB998306) to install crankshaft front seal.

TIMING BELT

Removal – 1) Disconnect negative battery cable. Remove accessory drive belts. Remove A/C compressor with hoses attached, and secure aside. Remove A/C compressor mounting bracket and drive belt tensioner. Remove power steering/alternator belt tensioner. Remove power steering pump with hoses attached and secure aside.

2) Raise and support vehicle. Remove right inner fender shield. Remove crankshaft pulley and vibration damper. Lower vehicle and support engine with floor jack. Separate engine mount from engine mount bracket located in front of timing belt cover. Raise engine slightly. Remove engine mount bracket.

3) Remove timing belt covers, noting bolt length for reassembly reference. Rotate engine and align timing marks on front and rear camshaft sprockets and crankshaft sprocket. *See Fig. 7.* Mark direction of timing belt rotation for reassembly reference.

4) Loosen timing belt tensioner. Remove timing belt. Note direction of flange installation on front of crankshaft and remove (if necessary). If camshaft sprocket removal is required, use Camshaft Sprocket Holder (MB990775) to hold sprocket. Remove retaining bolt and camshaft sprocket.

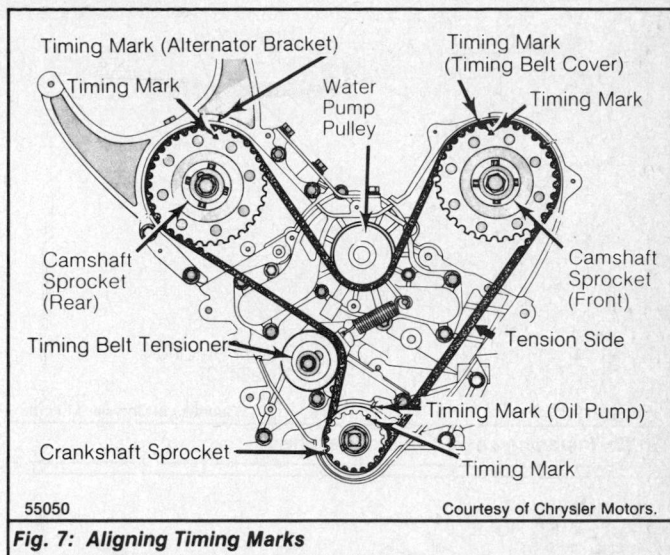

Fig. 7: Aligning Timing Marks

Installation – 1) Install camshaft sprockets (if removed). Using camshaft sprocket holder, tighten camshaft sprocket retaining bolt to specification. See TORQUE SPECIFICATIONS table at end of article. **2)** Ensure all timing marks are aligned. *See Fig. 7.* Rotate timing belt tensioner fully counterclockwise, and temporarily tighten retaining bolt. Install timing belt on crankshaft sprocket while holding belt tight on tension side. *See Fig. 7.*

CAUTION: When installing timing belt, ensure it will turn in original direction.

3) Install timing belt on front (radiator side) camshaft sprocket. Install timing belt on water pump pulley, rear camshaft sprocket and then on timing belt tensioner.

4) Apply rotating force on front (radiator side) camshaft sprocket in opposite direction to apply pressure on tension side of timing belt. Ensure all timing marks align. *See Fig. 7.*

5) Install flange on front of crankshaft sprocket (if removed) with flat side against timing belt and offset side toward front of crankshaft. Loosen timing belt tensioner bolt, allowing spring tension to be applied on timing belt. Rotate crankshaft clockwise 2 full revolutions.

CAUTION: Rotate crankshaft in a clockwise direction. DO NOT rotate crankshaft counterclockwise.

6) Realign all timing marks and tighten timing belt tensioner to specification. See TORQUE SPECIFICATIONS table at end of article. To install remaining components, reverse removal procedure. Ensure timing belt cover bolts are installed in original location. Tighten to specification. See TORQUE SPECIFICATIONS table at end of article.

ROCKER ARM & LASH ADJUSTER

NOTE: Lash adjuster operation should be checked before removing rocker arm.

Removal – 1) Remove air cleaner assembly. Disconnect spark plug wires. Remove valve covers.

2) To check lash adjuster operation, insert a small wire through air bleed hole at top of rocker arm, directly above lash adjuster. Lightly push check ball downward in lash adjuster and check rocker arm for free play. If free play does not exist, replace lash adjuster.

3) Install Lash Adjuster Retainers (MD998443) on rocker arms. *See Fig. 8.* Loosen, but DO NOT remove, camshaft bearing cap bolts. Mark location of rocker arms for reassembly reference. Camshaft bearing caps are numbered for location. *See Fig. 10.* Remove rocker arms, shafts and camshaft bearing caps as an assembly.

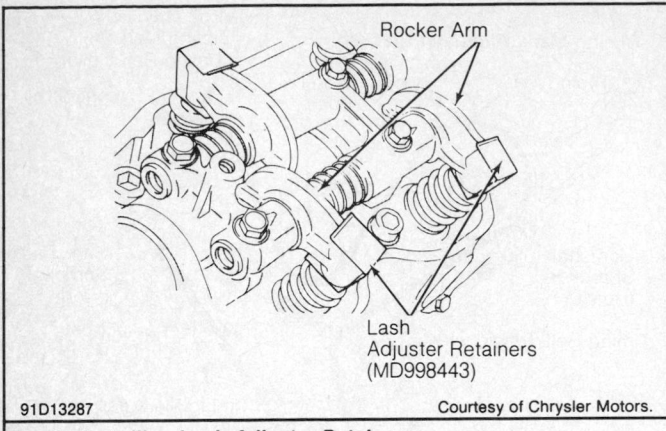

91D13287   Courtesy of Chrysler Motors.

Fig. 8: Installing Lash Adjuster Retainers

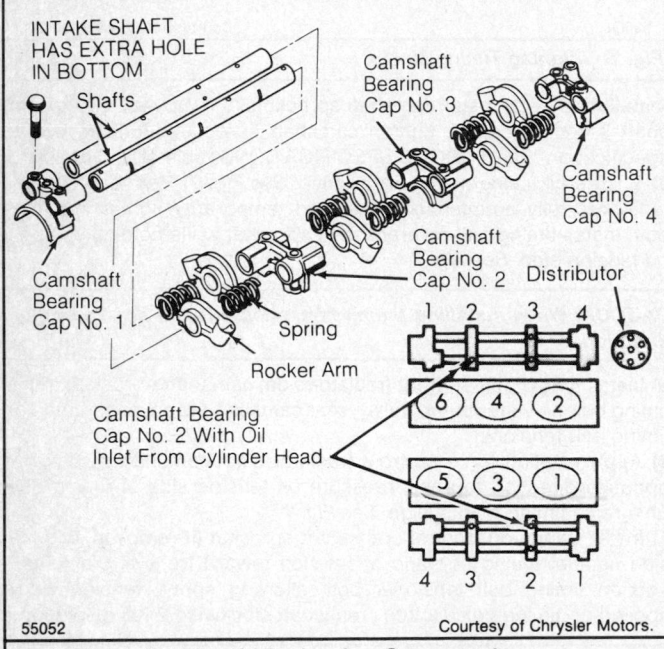

55052   Courtesy of Chrysler Motors.

Fig. 9: Exploded View Of Rocker Arm Components

Installation – 1) Ensure rocker arm shaft for intake valves contains an additional oil feed hole in bottom of shaft. *See Fig. 9.*

2) Ensure No. 1 bearing cap is installed with machined portion of rocker arm shaft facing downward, toward cylinder head. This positions notch areas of rocker arm shafts upward, pointing toward outside of camshaft bearing cap. *See Fig. 10.*

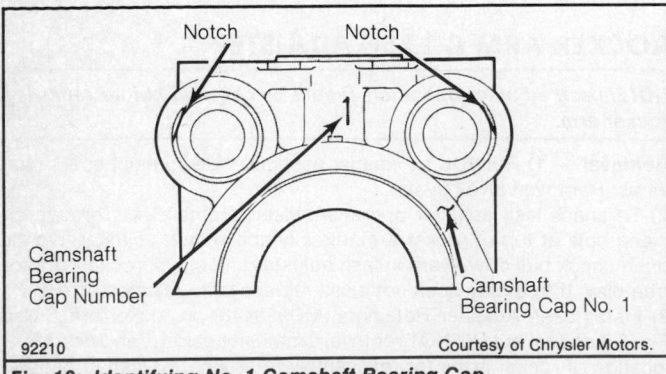

92210   Courtesy of Chrysler Motors.

Fig. 10: Identifying No. 1 Camshaft Bearing Cap

3) Apply sealant on camshaft bearing cap-to-cylinder head mating surfaces at both ends of cylinder head. *See Fig. 11.* Install rocker arm shaft assembly.

CAUTION: *Arrow on camshaft bearing caps MUST face same direction as arrow on cylinder heads. See Fig. 11. Camshaft bearing caps must be properly installed, as camshaft bearing cap No. 2 contains an oiling inlet hole from cylinder head. See Fig. 9.*

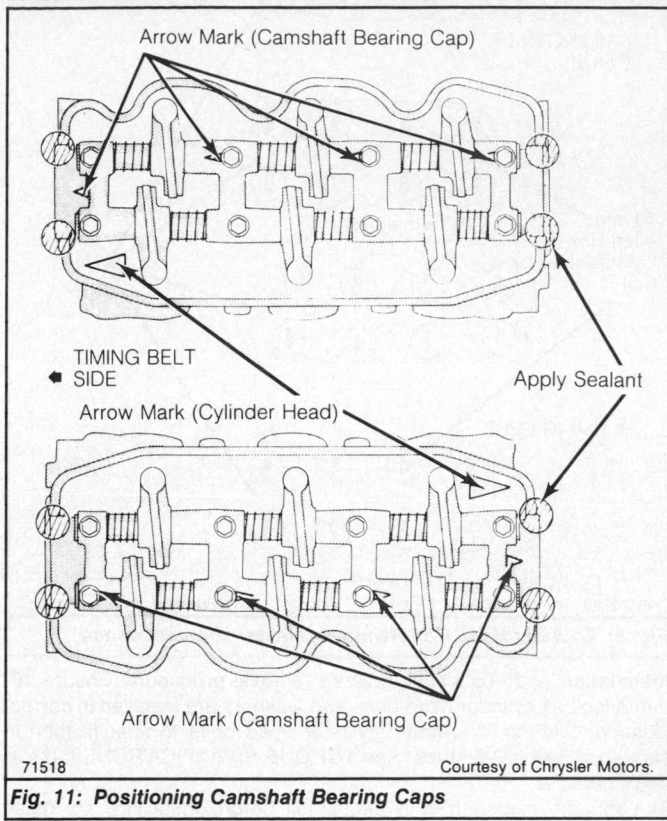

71518   Courtesy of Chrysler Motors.

Fig. 11: Positioning Camshaft Bearing Caps

4) Tighten camshaft bearing cap bolts to specification in 2 steps in the following order: No. 3, No. 2, No. 1 and then No. 4 camshaft bearing cap. See TORQUE SPECIFICATIONS table at end of article.

5) Install distributor adapter (if removed). Tighten bolts to specification. See TORQUE SPECIFICATIONS table at end of article. Coat camshaft oil seal lip with grease.

6) Thread Seal Installer (MD998713) into camshaft and install camshaft oil seal. Using Plug Installer (MD998306), install camshaft plug. Before installing valve cover, apply RTV sealant at front and rear camshaft bearing cap-to-valve cover gasket contact areas.

7) To install remaining components, reverse removal procedure. Tighten bolts to specification. See TORQUE SPECIFICATIONS table at end of article.

CAMSHAFT

Removal – 1) Remove distributor and distributor adapter (if necessary). Remove timing belt. See TIMING BELT under REMOVAL & INSTALLATION.

2) Remove rocker arm and lash adjuster. See ROCKER ARM & LASH ADJUSTER under REMOVAL & INSTALLATION. Remove camshaft and oil seals.

Inspection – Inspect components for damage. Replace if damaged. Ensure all oil holes are not restricted. Inspect camshaft and cylinder head journal areas for damage. Inspect distributor drive gear for damage. Measure lobe height. Replace camshaft if not within specification. See CAMSHAFT table under ENGINE SPECIFICATIONS at end of article.

Installation – To install, reverse removal procedure. Lubricate camshaft with engine oil before installing.

CAUTION: *Ensure proper procedure is used when installing rocker arms, as camshaft bearing caps must be properly installed. See ROCKER ARM & LASH ADJUSTER under REMOVAL & INSTALLATION.*

REAR CRANKSHAFT OIL SEAL

NOTE: Rear crankshaft oil seal is a one-piece oil seal mounted in seal retainer. Manufacturer lists procedure with seal retainer removed from cylinder block.

Removal & Installation – 1) Remove flywheel for access to seal retainer. Remove seal retainer. It may be necessary to remove oil pan, as oil pan seals against seal retainer. Remove oil seal from seal retainer.
2) Using Seal Installer (MD998718), install rear crankshaft oil seal into seal retainer. Before installing seal retainer, apply RTV sealant on seal retainer-to-cylinder block surface. Install seal retainer. To install remaining components, reverse removal procedure. Tighten bolts to specification. See TORQUE SPECIFICATIONS table at end of article.

WATER PUMP

Removal & Installation – 1) Remove timing belt. See TIMING BELT under REMOVAL & INSTALLATION. Drain cooling system. Remove retaining bolts, water pump, gasket and "O" ring on coolant inlet pipe.
2) To install, reverse removal procedure. Install NEW "O" ring on coolant inlet pipe. Apply water to "O" ring before installing water pump. DO NOT apply grease to "O" ring. Tighten bolts to specification. See TORQUE SPECIFICATIONS table at end of article. To install remaining components, reverse removal procedure. Fill cooling system.

OIL PAN

Removal & Installation – 1) Removal procedure is not available from manufacturer. To install, apply a .12" (3.0 mm) diameter bead of RTV sealant around edge of oil pan before installing.
2) Ensure sealant is applied in sealing surface groove and on outside of bolt holes. DO NOT allow sealant to be forced from flange area toward flywheel.
3) Install oil pan. Tighten bolts to specification in sequence. *See Fig. 12.* See TORQUE SPECIFICATIONS table at end of article.

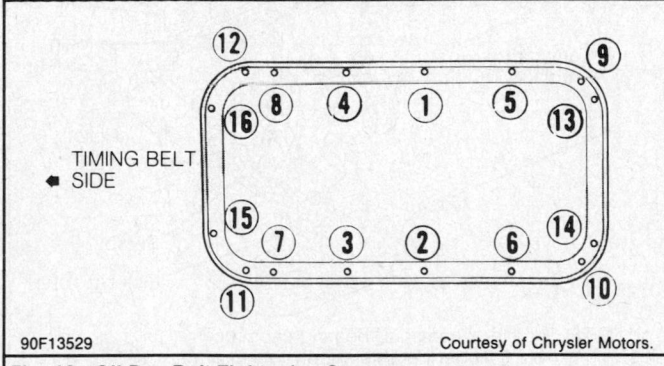

90F13529   Courtesy of Chrysler Motors.

Fig. 12: Oil Pan Bolt Tightening Sequence

OVERHAUL

CYLINDER HEAD

Cylinder Head – Check cylinder head warpage. Resurface cylinder head if warpage exceeds specification. See CYLINDER HEAD table under ENGINE SPECIFICATIONS at end of article.

CAUTION: DO NOT grind more than .008" (.20 mm) combined total from surface of cylinder head and deck surface of cylinder block.

Valve Springs – Check valve spring free length, out-of-square and pressure. Replace valve spring if not within specifications. See VALVES & VALVE SPRINGS table under ENGINE SPECIFICATIONS at end of article.

CAUTION: Valve spring must be installed with enamel-coated end toward spring retainer.

Valve Stem Oil Seals – Umbrella-type oil seals are used on all valves. Seals must be replaced if removed for any reason. When reinstalling valves, DO NOT overcompress valve springs, or valve stem oil seal may be damaged.
Valve Guides – Check valve guide I.D. and valve stem-to-valve guide oil clearance. Clearance must be within specification. See CYLINDER HEAD table under ENGINE SPECIFICATIONS at end of article. No service procedure is available from manufacturer.
Valve Seat – Check valve seat width. Grind valve seat if width is not within specification. See CYLINDER HEAD table under ENGINE SPECIFICATIONS at end of article.
Valves – Check margin and stem diameter. Replace valve if not within specifications. See VALVES & VALVE SPRINGS table under ENGINE SPECIFICATIONS at end of article.
Valve Seat Correction Angles – Use a 15-degree stone to lower valve seat or a 65-degree stone to raise valve seat.

VALVE TRAIN

Rocker Arm Shaft Assembly – 1) Note location and direction of rocker arm components and camshaft bearing caps. Remove camshaft bearing cap bolts. Disassemble rocker arm shaft assembly. *See Fig. 9.*
2) Ensure intake valve rocker arm shaft has a .12" (3 mm) oil hole in bottom of shaft. *See Fig. 9.* Exhaust valve rocker shaft does not have oil hole. Oil hole supplies oil to exhaust valve rocker arm shaft through camshaft bearing cap.
3) Inspect components for damage. Replace if damaged. Ensure all oil holes are not clogged. Reassemble rocker arm shaft assembly.

CAUTION: The No. 1 camshaft bearing cap must be installed with machined portion of rocker arm shaft facing downward, toward cylinder head. This positions notch areas of rocker arm shafts upward, pointing toward outside of camshaft bearing cap. See Fig. 10. Ensure No. 2 camshaft bearing cap contains oil inlet from cylinder head. See Fig. 9.

Lash Adjuster – Lash adjuster is located in rocker arm. Lash adjuster must not be disassembled.

CYLINDER BLOCK ASSEMBLY

Piston & Rod Assembly – For cylinders No. 1, 3 and 5, install pistons with "R" front mark on top of piston toward timing belt side of engine. For cylinders No. 2, 4 and 6, install piston with "L" front mark toward timing belt side of engine. Ensure front mark "72" on connecting rod is facing toward timing belt side of engine. *See Fig. 13.*

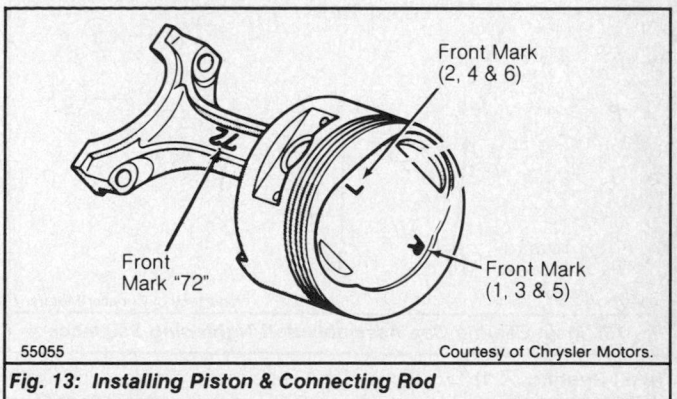

Front Mark (2, 4 & 6)

Front Mark "72"

Front Mark (1, 3 & 5)

55055   Courtesy of Chrysler Motors.

Fig. 13: Installing Piston & Connecting Rod

CAUTION: Pistons are not interchangeable from side-to-side.

Fitting Pistons – Measure cylinder bore diameter and taper at .50" (12.7 mm) below top surface of cylinder bore, middle of bore and .38" (9.6 mm) from bottom of cylinder bore. Measure piston diameter at .08" (2.0 mm) from bottom of piston skirt at right angle to piston pin. Piston diameter and clearance must be within specification. See PISTONS, PINS & RINGS table under ENGINE SPECIFICATIONS at end of article.

1992 ENGINES
3.0L V6 (Cont.)

Piston Rings – Ensure ring end gap and side clearances are within specification. See PISTONS, PINS & RINGS table under ENGINE SPECIFICATIONS at end of article. Ensure piston ring end gaps are properly positioned. *See Fig. 14.*

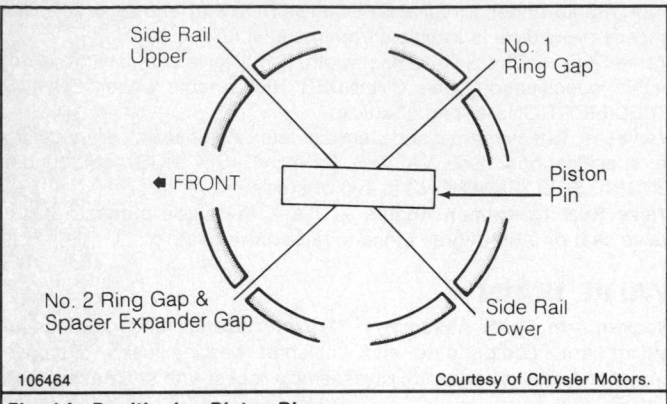

Fig. 14: Positioning Piston Rings

Rod Bearings – **1)** When replacing rod bearings, ensure front mark "72" on connecting rod faces toward timing belt side of engine. *See Fig. 13.*

2) Tighten connecting rod nuts to specification. See TORQUE SPECIFICATIONS table at end of article. Ensure bearing oil clearance and side play are within specifications. See CRANKSHAFT, MAIN & CONNECTING ROD BEARINGS and CONNECTING RODS tables under ENGINE SPECIFICATIONS at end of article.

Crankshaft & Main Bearings – **1)** Upper main bearings contain oil grooves, while lower bearings installed in main bearing cap assembly do not.

2) Main bearing cap assembly must be installed with arrow toward front (timing belt end) of engine. Coat bolts with oil before installing. Tighten bolts to specification in sequence. *See Fig. 15.* See TORQUE SPECIFICATIONS table at end of article.

3) Ensure main bearing oil clearance and crankshaft end play are within specifications. See CRANKSHAFT, MAIN & CONNECTING ROD BEARINGS table under ENGINE SPECIFICATIONS at end of article. Replace thrust bearing if end play is not within specification.

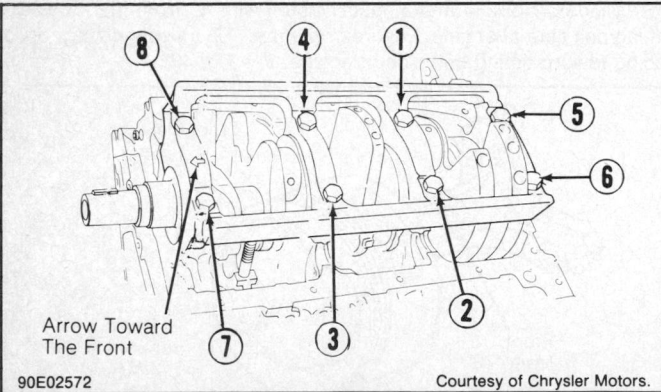

Fig. 15: Main Bearing Cap Assembly Bolt Tightening Sequence

Thrust Bearing – **1)** Two types of thrust bearings are used, one with positioning tabs and another without. One set of thrust bearings (one with positioning tab and one without tab) fit in cylinder block, and another set in main bearing cap assembly at No. 3 main bearing.

2) Thrust bearing without positioning tab fits on front (timing belt side) of cylinder block and rear (flywheel side) of main bearing cap assembly. Thrust bearing with positioning tab fits on rear (flywheel side) of cylinder block and on front (timing belt side) of main bearing cap assembly. Groove side on thrust bearing goes toward crankshaft.

3) Replace thrust bearing if crankshaft end play is not within specification. See CRANKSHAFT, MAIN & CONNECTING ROD BEARINGS table under ENGINE SPECIFICATIONS at end of article.

Cylinder Block – **1)** Using a feeler gauge and straightedge, check cylinder block deck surface for warpage. Surface cylinder block if warpage exceeds specification. See CYLINDER BLOCK table under ENGINE SPECIFICATIONS at end of article.

CAUTION: DO NOT grind more than .008" (.20 mm) combined total from surface of cylinder head and deck surface of cylinder block.

---

2) Check cylinder bore, taper and out-of-round. Measurements should be taken at .50" (12.7 mm) below top surface of cylinder bore, middle of bore and .38" (9.6 mm) from bottom of cylinder bore. Bore cylinder block if not within specification. See CYLINDER BLOCK table under ENGINE SPECIFICATIONS.

ENGINE OILING

ENGINE LUBRICATION SYSTEM

A crankshaft-driven oil pump provides pressurized lubrication to main oil gallery. *See Fig. 16.*

Crankcase Capacity – Oil capacity with oil filter is **4.5 qts. (4.2L)**.

Oil Pressure – Oil pressure is **30-100 psi (2.1-7.0 kg/cm²)** at 3000 RPM with engine at normal operating temperature.

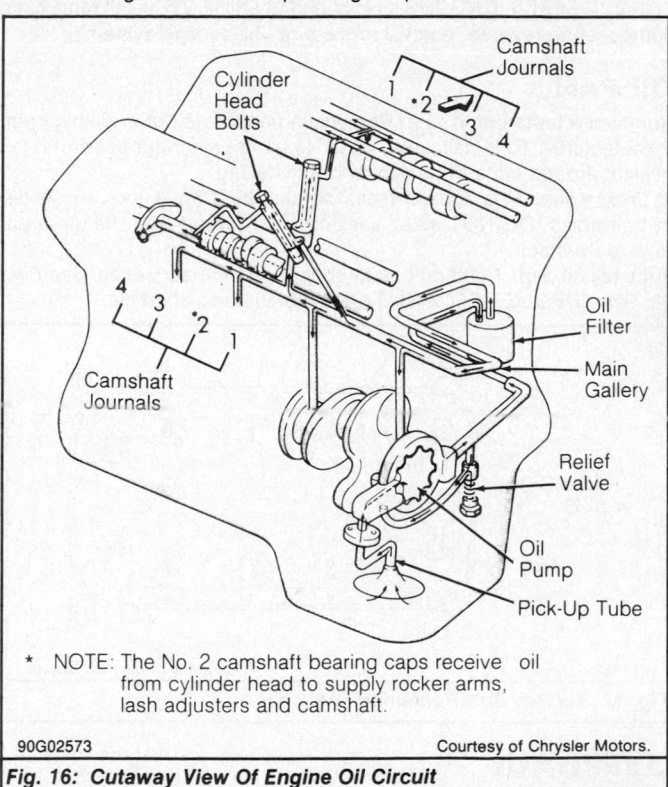

* NOTE: The No. 2 camshaft bearing caps receive oil from cylinder head to supply rocker arms, lash adjusters and camshaft.

Fig. 16: Cutaway View Of Engine Oil Circuit

OIL PUMP

Removal & Disassembly – **1)** Remove timing belt and crankshaft sprocket. See TIMING BELT under REMOVAL & INSTALLATION. Remove oil pan and pick-up tube.

2) Remove oil pump-to-cylinder block bolts. Note bolt location and length for reassembly. Remove oil pump. Disassemble oil pump. *See Fig. 17.* Remove oil seal from oil pump case.

Inspection – **1)** Inspect components for damage. Measure clearance between small area of inner rotor and oil pump case. Measure clearance between outer rotor and oil pump case.

2) With inner and outer rotors installed in oil pump case, place straightedge across oil pump case and both rotors. Using feeler gauge, check rotor end clearance between rotors and straightedge. Ensure relief plunger slides freely in bore. Replace oil pump assembly if clearance exceeds specification. See OIL PUMP SPECIFICATIONS table.

OIL PUMP SPECIFICATIONS

Application	In. (mm)
Inner Rotor Small Diameter-To-Pump Case Clearance	.006 (.15)
Outer Rotor-To-Pump Case Clearance	.004-.007 (.10-.18)
Rotor End Clearance	.0015-.0035 (.038-.089)

Reassembly & Installation – 1) To reassemble, reverse disassembly procedure. Ensure components are installed in original location. If oil seal was removed from oil pump case, use Seal Installer (MB998306) to install NEW seal. Lubricate seal lip with oil before installing.
2) To install, reverse removal procedure. Ensure bolts are installed in original location. *See Fig. 17.* Tighten bolts to specification. See TORQUE SPECIFICATIONS table at end of article.

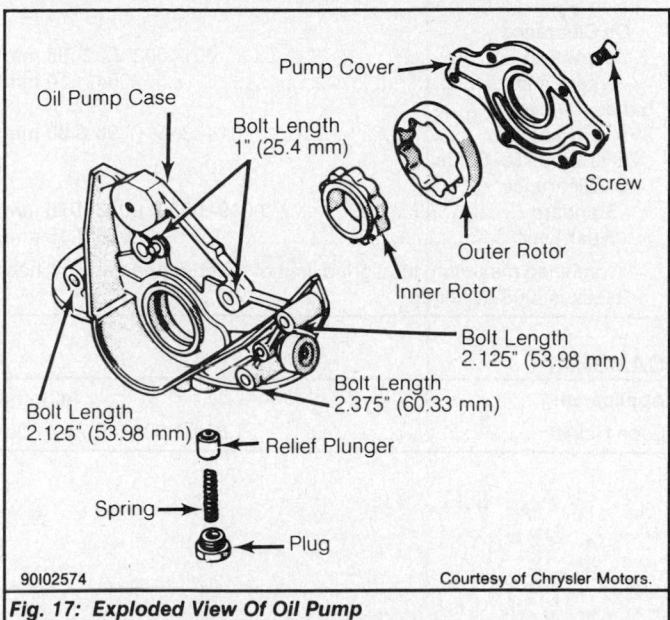

90I02574   Courtesy of Chrysler Motors.

Fig. 17: Exploded View Of Oil Pump

TORQUE SPECIFICATIONS

TORQUE SPECIFICATIONS

Application	Ft. Lbs. (N.m)
A/C Compressor Mount Bolt	40 (54)
Camshaft Bearing Cap Bolt	[1]
Camshaft Sprocket Bolt	70 (95)
Connecting Rod Nut	38 (52)
Crankshaft Belt Pulley Bolt	21 (29)
Cylinder Head Bolt	[2] 70 (95)
Distributor Adapter Bolt	10 (14)
Engine Bracket-To-Cylinder Block Bolt	35 (47)
Exhaust Crossover Pipe Bolt	51 (69)
Exhaust Manifold Heat Shield Bolt	11 (15)
Exhaust Manifold Nut	15 (20)
Flexplate Bolt	70 (95)
Front Mount-To-Cylinder Block Bolt/Nut	
Lower Nut	75 (102)
Upper Bolt	125 (170)
Front Mount-To-Frame Rail Bolt/Nut	40 (54)
Fuel Rail Bolt	10 (14)
Intake Manifold Nut	[3] 14 (19)
Left Mount Through Bolt	50 (68)
Left Mount-To-Frame Rail Bolt	50 (68)

[1] – Tighten camshaft bearing cap bolts to 85 INCH lbs. (10 N.m) in the following sequence: No. 3, No. 2, No. 1, No. 4. Repeat procedure and tighten bolts to 15 ft. lbs. (20 N.m).
[2] – Tighten bolts in sequence. *See Fig. 6.*
[3] – Tighten nuts in sequence. *See Fig. 4.*

TORQUE SPECIFICATIONS (Cont.)

Application	Ft. Lbs. (N.m)
Main Bearing Cap Bolt	[4] 60 (81)
Oil Pick-Up Tube Bolt	16 (22)
Oil Pump Bolt	11 (15)
Oil Pump Relief Plunger Plug	36 (49)
Right Mount (Timing Belt Side)	
Through Bolt	100 (136)
Mount-To-Frame Bolt	50 (68)
Vertical Bolt/Nut	75 (102)
Timing Belt Tensioner Bolt	21 (29)
Torque Converter-To-Flexplate Bolt	55 (75)
Transaxle-To-Cylinder Block Bolt	75 (102)
Upper Air Intake Bolt	[5] 10 (14)
Vibration Damper Bolt	112 (152)
Water Pump Bolt	20 (27)

Application	INCH Lbs. (N.m)
Fuel Pressure Regulator Bolt	95 (11)
Oil Pan Bolt	51 (6)
Oil Pump Cover Screw	104 (12)
Rear Crankshaft Seal Retainer Bolt	104 (12)
Timing Belt Cover Bolt	115 (13)
Valve Cover Bolt	88 (10)

[4] – Coat bolts with oil before installing. Tighten bolts in sequence. *See Fig. 15.*
[5] – Tighten bolts in sequence. *See Fig. 5.*

ENGINE SPECIFICATIONS

GENERAL SPECIFICATIONS

Application	Specification
Displacement	181 Cu. In. (3.0L)
Bore	3.59" (91.1 mm)
Stroke	2.99" (75.9 mm)
Compression Ratio	8.9:1
Fuel System	PFI
Horsepower @ RPM	142 @ 5000
Torque Ft. Lbs. @ RPM	173 @ 2800

CRANKSHAFT, MAIN & CONNECTING ROD BEARINGS

Application	In. (mm)
Crankshaft End Play	
Standard	.002-.010 (.05-.25)
Wear Limit	.012 (.30)
Main Bearings	
Journal Diameter	2.361-2.362 (59.97-59.99)
Journal Out-Of-Round	.001 (.02)
Journal Taper	.0002 (.005)
Oil Clearance	.0006-.0020 (.015-.051)
Connecting Rod Bearings	
Journal Diameter	1.968-1.969 (49.99-50.01)
Journal Out-Of-Round	.001 (.02)
Journal Taper	.0002 (.005)
Oil Clearance	.0008-.0026 (.020-.066)

CONNECTING RODS

Application	In. (mm)
Center-To-Center Length	5.547-5.551 (140.89-140.99)
Maximum Bend & Twist	.0019 (.048)
Side Play	
Standard	.004-.010 (.10-.25)
Wear Limit	.016 (.41)

PISTONS, PINS & RINGS

Application	In. (mm)
Pistons	
Clearance	.0012-.0020 (.030-.051)
Diameter	3.585-3.586 (91.06-91.08)
Rings	
No. 1	
End Gap	
Standard	.012-.018 (.30-.46)
Wear Limit	.031 (.79)
Side Clearance	
Standard	.0020-.0035 (.051-.089)
Wear Limit	.0039 (.099)
No. 2	
End Gap	
Standard	.010-.016 (.25-.41)
Wear Limit	.031 (.79)
Side Clearance	
Standard	.0008-.0020 (.020-.051)
Wear Limit	.0039 (.099)
No. 3 (Oil)	
End Gap	
Standard	.012-.035 (.30-.89)
Wear Limit	.039 (.99)

CYLINDER BLOCK

Application	In. (mm)
Cylinder Bore	
Standard Diameter	3.586-3.587 (91.08-91.10)
Maximum Taper & Out-Of-Round	.0008 (.020)
Maximum Deck Warpage	[1] .0020 (.051)

[1] – Service limit is .0039" (.099 mm). Combined maximum total grind limit of cylinder head and cylinder block is .008" (.20 mm).

VALVES & VALVE SPRINGS

Application	Specification
Intake Valves	
Face Angle	45°
Minimum Margin	.027" (.69 mm)
Stem Diameter	.313-.314" (7.95-7.98 mm)
Exhaust Valves	
Face Angle	45°
Minimum Margin	.059" (1.50 mm)
Stem Diameter	.3120-.3125" (7.92-7.94 mm)
Valve Springs	
Free Length	1.921-1.960" (48.79-49.48 mm)
Out-Of-Square	4°
Pressure	Lbs. @ In. (kg @ mm)
Valve Closed	73 @ 1.59 (33 @ 40.4)

CYLINDER HEAD

Application	Specifications
Maximum Warpage	[1] .002" (.05 mm)
Valve Seats	
Intake Valve	
Seat Angle	44°
Seat Width	.035-.051" (.89-1.30 mm)
Exhaust Valve	
Seat Angle	44°
Seat Width	.035-.051" (.89-1.30 mm)
Valve Guides	
Intake Valve	
Valve Guide I.D.	.314-.315" (7.98-8.00 mm)
Valve Stem-To-Guide	
Oil Clearance	
Standard	.001-.002" (.02-.05 mm)
Wear Limit	.004" (.10 mm)
Exhaust Valve	
Valve Guide I.D.	.314-.315" (7.98-8.00 mm)
Valve Stem-To-Guide	
Oil Clearance	
Standard	.0019-.0030" (.048-.076 mm)
Wear Limit	.006" (.15 mm)

[1] – Combined maximum total grind limit of cylinder head and cylinder block is .008" (.20 mm).

CAMSHAFT

Application	In. (mm)
Lobe Height	1.604-1.624 (40.74-41.25)

Caravan, Town & Country, Voyager

NOTE: For repair procedures not covered in this article, see ENGINE OVERHAUL PROCEDURES article in GENERAL INFORMATION.

ENGINE IDENTIFICATION

Engine may be identified by eighth character of Vehicle Identification Number (VIN). The VIN is stamped on a plate on top of instrument panel, at lower left of windshield.

ENGINE IDENTIFICATION CODE

Engine	Code
3.3L PFI	R

ADJUSTMENTS

VALVE CLEARANCE ADJUSTMENT

Hydraulic valve lifters are used. No valve adjustment is required.

REMOVAL & INSTALLATION

NOTE: For reassembly reference, label all electrical connectors, vacuum hoses and fuel lines before removal. Also place mating marks on engine hood and other major assemblies before removal.

WARNING: When battery is disconnected, vehicle computer and memory systems may lose memory data. Driveability problems may exist until computer systems have completed a relearn cycle. See COMPUTER RELEARN PROCEDURES article in GENERAL INFORMATION before disconnecting battery.

FUEL PRESSURE RELEASE

CAUTION: Fuel system is under pressure. Pressure must be released before servicing any fuel system component.

1) Loosen fuel tank cap to release pressure. Disconnect injector wiring harness from engine wiring harness. Connect jumper wire from terminal No. 1 of injector harness to ground. See Fig. 1.
2) Connect another jumper wire to terminal No. 2 of injector harness. See Fig. 1. Touch jumper wire to positive battery terminal for no more than 5 seconds to release fuel pressure. Remove jumper wires, and reconnect wiring harness.

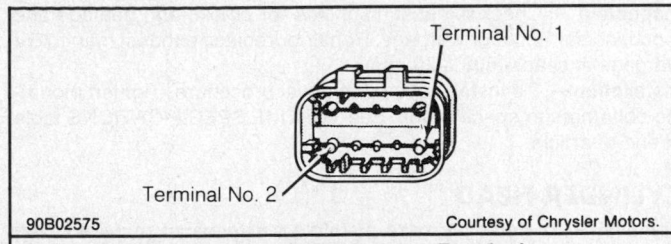

Terminal No. 1

Terminal No. 2

90B02575   Courtesy of Chrysler Motors.

Fig. 1: Identifying Injector Wiring Harness Terminals

COOLING SYSTEM BLEEDING

1) To bleed cooling system, remove engine temperature sending unit. Sending unit is located in front of cylinder head, near thermostat housing, just below spark plug wire holder.
2) Fill cooling system until coolant reaches sending unit level. Install sending unit, and tighten to 60 INCH lbs. (7 N.m). Finish filling cooling system.

ENGINE

NOTE: Remove engine with transaxle remaining in vehicle.

Removal – 1) Release fuel pressure. See FUEL PRESSURE RELEASE under REMOVAL & INSTALLATION. Disconnect negative battery cable. Scribe hood hinge location on hood for reassembly. Remove hood. Drain cooling system. Drain engine oil. Disconnect necessary coolant hoses, control cables, electrical connections and vacuum hoses.
2) Remove air cleaner and radiator/fan assembly. Wrap shop towel around fuel lines. Remove fuel lines from fuel rail by pushing inward on plastic ring, located at end of fuel line fitting, and pulling fuel line from fitting.
3) Raise and support vehicle. Remove A/C compressor and power steering pump with hoses attached, and secure aside.
4) Remove starter. Disconnect exhaust pipe at exhaust manifold. Remove torque converter cover. Mark flexplate to torque converter for reassembly reference.
5) Remove torque converter-to-flexplate bolts. Attach "C" clamp at bottom front edge of torque converter housing to secure converter.
6) Remove lower transaxle-to-cylinder block bolts. Lower vehicle. Support transaxle using floor jack. Attach lifting hoist to engine. Remove remaining transaxle-to-cylinder block bolts.
7) Place reference mark on side rail to indicate right insulator (timing chain side) position for reassembly reference. Remove right insulator-to-side rail bolts.

CAUTION: Right insulator position on side rail must be marked for reassembly reference before removal to ensure proper positioning of engine. Insulator must be installed in original position.

8) Remove through bolt from left engine mount from inside fenderwell. Insulator bracket-to-transaxle bolts may be removed instead of through bolt. Remove front engine mount bolts, and lift engine from vehicle.
Installation – 1) To install, reverse removal procedure. DO NOT tighten engine mount bolts until all bolts are installed. If vertical bolts on right or left mount were loosened, axle shaft length must be checked.
2) To determine axle shaft length, measure distance between inner edge of outboard boot and inner edge of inboard boot at 6 o'clock position. See Fig. 2.

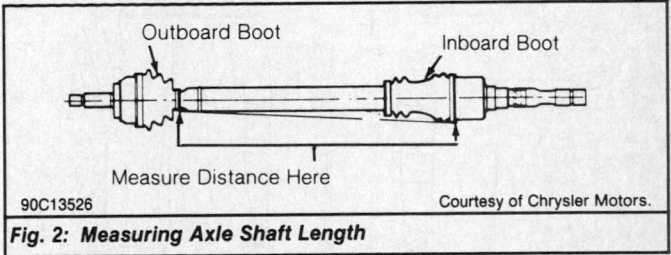

Outboard Boot

Inboard Boot

Measure Distance Here

90C13526   Courtesy of Chrysler Motors.

Fig. 2: Measuring Axle Shaft Length

3) Axle shaft length must be within specification. See AXLE SHAFT LENGTH SPECIFICATIONS table.

AXLE SHAFT LENGTH SPECIFICATIONS

Application	In. (mm)
AWD Models	
Right Axle Shaft	11.5-11.9 (292-302)
Left Axle Shaft	9.0-9.4 (229-239)
2WD Models	
Right Axle Shaft	20.5-20.9 (521-531)
Left Axle Shaft	9.0-9.4 (229-239)

4) Adjust axle shaft length to specification by sliding engine in slots on engine mounts. Tighten all engine mount bolts once correct axle shaft length is obtained.

CAUTION: Tighten vertical bolt in right (timing chain side) mount bracket before tightening through bolt.

5) Ensure reference mark is aligned on torque converter and flexplate. Tighten bolts/nuts to specification. See TORQUE SPECIFICATIONS table at end of article.

6) Lubricate fuel lines with 30W engine oil before reconnecting. Ensure fuel lines are installed by listening for a "click" sound.

NOTE: Fuel supply line is a 5/16" diameter fitting and fuel return line is a 1/4" diameter fitting.

7) Fill and bleed cooling system. See COOLING SYSTEM BLEEDING under REMOVAL & INSTALLATION.

INTAKE MANIFOLD

Removal – 1) Release fuel pressure. See FUEL PRESSURE RELEASE under REMOVAL & INSTALLATION. Disconnect negative battery cable. Drain cooling system. Remove air cleaner-to-throttle body hose.
2) Disconnect control cables and linkages at throttle body. Disconnect Automatic Idle Speed (AIS) motor and Throttle Position Sensor (TPS) wiring harness connectors at throttle body. Remove vacuum hoses from throttle body and intake manifold.
3) Disconnect vacuum hoses and EGR tube flange from air intake plenum (upper intake manifold). Disconnect wiring connectors at charge temperature sensor, MAP sensor and O_2 sensor heater. Remove cylinder head-to-air intake plenum support brace.
4) Wrap shop towel around fuel lines. Remove fuel lines from fuel rail by pushing inward on plastic ring, located at end of fuel line fitting, and pulling fuel line from fitting.
5) Remove ignition coils and alternator bracket from air intake plenum. Remove air intake plenum bolts in sequence. *See Fig. 3.* Rotate air intake plenum back over valve cover. Cover intake manifold ports using shop towels.
6) Disconnect vacuum hose at pressure regulator. Disconnect fuel injector wiring harness from engine wiring harness. Disconnect necessary sensor wiring connectors, near fuel rail and intake manifold.
7) Remove fuel rail retaining bolts and fuel rail. Disconnect coolant hoses at intake manifold. Remove intake manifold retaining bolts in sequence, and remove intake manifold. *See Fig. 4.* Remove intake manifold gasket end seal retaining screws, and remove gasket.

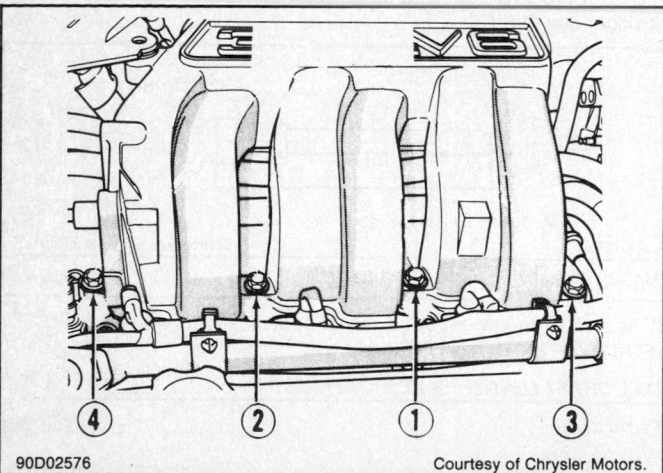
90D02576   Courtesy of Chrysler Motors.

Fig. 3: Air Intake Plenum Bolt Removal & Installation Sequence

CAUTION: Handle intake manifold gasket seal carefully as seal has sharp edges.

Installation – 1) Ensure sealing surfaces are clean. Apply 1/4" (6.4 mm) diameter drop of silicone sealant in 4 corners where intake manifold contacts cylinder head.
2) Install intake manifold gasket. Tighten intake manifold gasket end seal retaining screws to **105 INCH lbs. (12 N.m)**. Install intake manifold. Tighten intake manifold bolts to specification in sequence. *See Fig. 4.* See TORQUE SPECIFICATIONS table at end of article.
3) To install remaining components, reverse removal procedure. Ensure injector holes are clean. Lubricate injector "O" rings with engine oil before installing. Install injector until firmly seated in port.

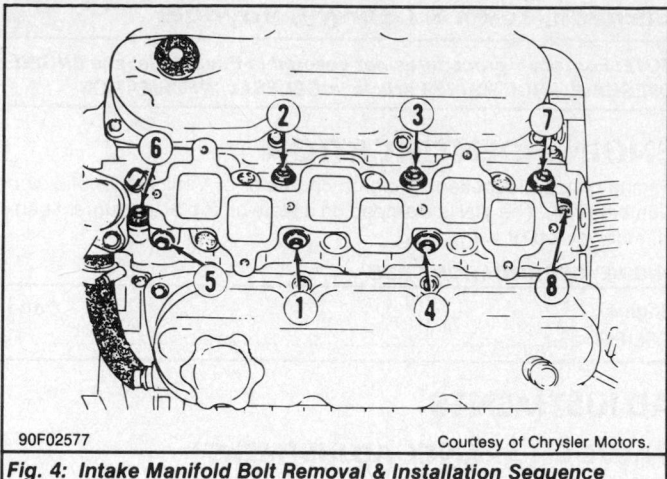
90F02577   Courtesy of Chrysler Motors.

Fig. 4: Intake Manifold Bolt Removal & Installation Sequence

4) Install air intake plenum with bolts finger tight. Loosely install alternator bracket-to-intake manifold bolt and cylinder head-to-intake manifold brace bolts.
5) Tighten air intake plenum bolts to specification in sequence. *See Fig. 3.* See TORQUE SPECIFICATIONS table. Tighten alternator bracket and intake manifold brace bolts.
6) Lubricate fuel lines with 30W engine oil before reconnecting. Ensure fuel lines are installed by listening for a "click" sound.

NOTE: Fuel supply line is a 5/16" diameter fitting and fuel return line is a 1/4" diameter fitting.

7) Fill and bleed cooling system. See COOLING SYSTEM BLEEDING under REMOVAL & INSTALLATION.

EXHAUST MANIFOLD

Removal – 1) Raise and support vehicle. Disconnect exhaust pipe from rear exhaust manifold flange. Disconnect EGR tube from rear exhaust manifold. Disconnect O_2 sensor wiring.
2) Remove alternator assembly support brace at front of exhaust manifold. Remove crossover pipe mounting bolts. Remove retaining bolts and rear exhaust manifold.
3) Lower vehicle. Remove heat shield-to-front exhaust manifold bolts. Disconnect crossover pipe at front exhaust manifold. Remove retaining bolts and front exhaust manifold.
Inspection – Check exhaust manifolds for cracks and damage and mounting surfaces for warpage. Repair or replace exhaust manifold if warpage exceeds .008" (.20 mm).
Installation – To install, reverse removal procedure. Tighten mounting bolts/nuts to specification. See TORQUE SPECIFICATIONS table at end of article.

CYLINDER HEAD

Removal – 1) Remove intake manifold and exhaust manifold. See INTAKE MANIFOLD and EXHAUST MANIFOLD under REMOVAL & INSTALLATION. Disconnect necessary wiring and coolant hoses.
2) Remove rocker arm assembly. See ROCKER ARMS & PUSH RODS under REMOVAL & INSTALLATION. Mark push rod location for reassembly reference. Remove push rods. Remove cylinder head bolts in sequence. *See Fig. 5.* Remove cylinder head.
Inspection – 1) Check cylinder head warpage. Resurface head if warpage exceeds specification. See CYLINDER HEAD table under ENGINE SPECIFICATIONS at end of article.

CAUTION: DO NOT grind more than .008" (.20 mm) total from cylinder head surface and cylinder block deck surface.

2) Hold a straightedge across cylinder head bolt threads. If threads fail to contact straightedge in all areas, cylinder head bolts are stretched and must be replaced.

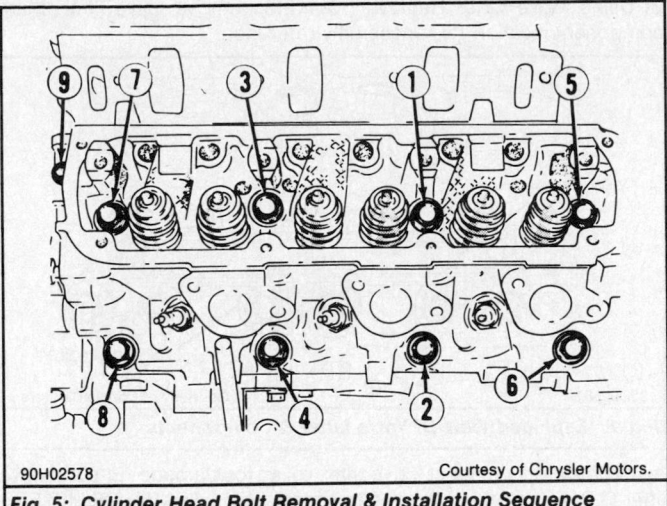

90H02578   Courtesy of Chrysler Motors.

Fig. 5: Cylinder Head Bolt Removal & Installation Sequence

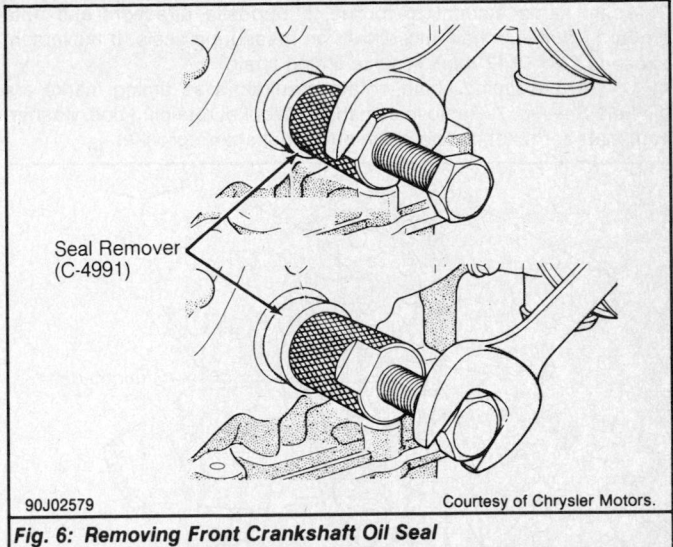

Seal Remover
(C-4991)

90J02579   Courtesy of Chrysler Motors.

Fig. 6: Removing Front Crankshaft Oil Seal

Installation – 1) To install, reverse removal procedure. Ensure cylinder head gasket is installed with identification number facing away from cylinder block. Tighten cylinder head bolts to specification in sequence using 4 steps. *See Fig. 5.* See TORQUE SPECIFICATIONS table at end of article.

CAUTION: No. 9 cylinder head bolt is an 8-mm bolt and must be tightened to specification after 11-mm bolts are tightened in sequence to specification.

2) When tightening cylinder head bolts required additional 1/4 turn, torque should exceed **90 ft. lbs. (122 N.m)**. Replace cylinder head bolt if torque does not exceed specification.
3) To install remaining components, reverse removal procedure. Ensure proper procedure is followed when installing rocker arm assembly and push rods. See ROCKER ARMS & PUSH RODS under REMOVAL & INSTALLATION.
4) Fill and bleed cooling system. See COOLING SYSTEM BLEEDING under REMOVAL & INSTALLATION.

FRONT CRANKSHAFT OIL SEAL

Removal – Raise and support vehicle. Remove right wheel inner splash shield. Remove drive belt. Remove retaining bolt and vibration damper. Using Seal Remover (C-4991), remove seal from timing chain cover. *See Fig. 6.*
Installation – Using Seal Installer (C-4992), install seal until seal is even with timing chain cover surface. Using Plate (L-4524), thrust bearing/washer and bolt, install vibration damper. Tighten bolt to specification. See TORQUE SPECIFICATIONS table at end of article. To install remaining components, reverse removal procedure.

TIMING CHAIN COVER

Removal – 1) Disconnect battery cables. Drain cooling system. Disconnect coolant hoses from timing chain cover. Support engine, and remove right engine mount at timing chain cover. Remove oil pan. See OIL PAN under REMOVAL & INSTALLATION.
2) Remove oil pump pick-up tube. Remove transaxle inspection cover (if necessary). Raise and support vehicle. Remove right wheel and inner splash shield. Remove drive belt.
3) Remove A/C compressor with hoses attached, and secure it aside. Remove A/C compressor mounting bracket. Remove retaining bolt and vibration damper. Remove idler pulley from front engine bracket on front of cylinder block. Remove engine bracket from cylinder block.
4) Note location of cam sensor, located in top of timing chain cover. Disconnect electrical connector at cam sensor. Loosen cam sensor retaining bolt enough for slot in cam sensor to slide past bolt. Pull cam sensor from timing chain cover. Remove timing chain cover retaining bolts, cover, gasket and "O" rings.

NOTE: Tap lightly on top of cam sensor to loosen it (if necessary). DO NOT pull on wiring harness during cam sensor removal.

NOTE: Install front crankshaft oil seal after installing timing chain cover to ensure oil pump engages properly.

Installation – 1) Install new gasket and "O" rings on cylinder block. Rotate crankshaft so oil pump drive areas (flat areas) of crankshaft are positioned vertically.
2) Align flat areas of oil pump in timing chain cover with flat areas on crankshaft. Install timing chain cover. Ensure oil pump engages with crankshaft. Install timing chain cover retaining bolts, and tighten to specification. See TORQUE SPECIFICATIONS table at end of article.
3) Using Seal Installer (C-4992), install front crankshaft oil seal until seal is even with timing chain cover surface. Using Plate (L-4524), thrust bearing/washer and bolt, install vibration damper. Tighten retaining bolt to specification. See TORQUE SPECIFICATIONS table.
4) When installing cam sensor, ensure cam sensor and mounting surface is clean. If original cam sensor is installed, use NEW spacer and "O" ring. If replacement cam sensor is installed, ensure paper spacer and "O" ring are installed on cam sensor.
5) Apply engine oil to cam sensor "O" ring, and install cam sensor in timing chain cover. Hold cam sensor downward until cam sensor contacts camshaft timing gear. Tighten retaining bolt to specification while cam sensor is held downward. See TORQUE SPECIFICATIONS table. Reconnect electrical connector at cam sensor.
6) To install remaining components, reverse removal procedure. Tighten bolts to specification. See TORQUE SPECIFICATIONS table.
7) Fill and bleed cooling system. See COOLING SYSTEM BLEEDING under REMOVAL & INSTALLATION.

TIMING CHAIN

Removal – 1) Remove timing chain cover. See TIMING CHAIN COVER under REMOVAL & INSTALLATION. Check timing chain stretch to determine if chain requires replacement.
2) Position measuring scale near link on timing chain at camshaft sprocket so movement can be measured. Place torque wrench on camshaft sprocket bolt. Apply 30 ft. lbs. (41 N.m) torque with cylinder heads installed or 15 ft. lbs. (20 N.m) with cylinder heads removed on camshaft sprocket bolt in direction of engine rotation. Note reading on measuring scale.

NOTE: When applying torque to camshaft sprocket bolt, DO NOT allow crankshaft to move. If necessary, hold crankshaft.

3) Apply same amount of torque in opposite direction, and note amount of timing chain movement on measuring scale. If movement exceeds **1/8"** (3.17 mm), replace timing chain.

4) To remove timing chain, rotate crankshaft so timing marks are aligned. *See Fig. 7.* Remove camshaft sprocket retaining bolt, washer, camshaft sprocket, timing chain and crankshaft sprocket.

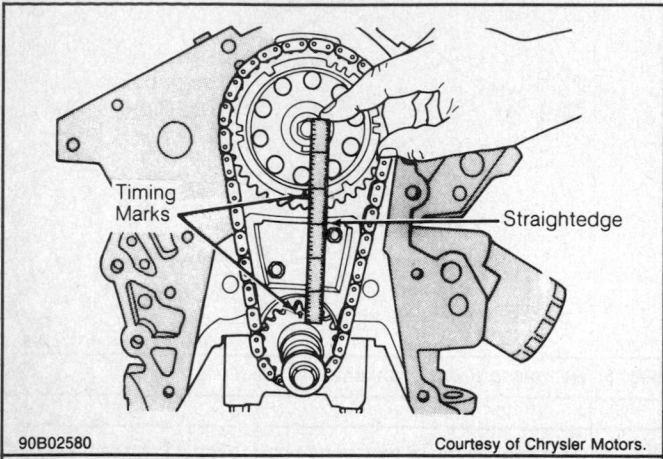

Fig. 7: Aligning Timing Marks

Installation – 1) Install crankshaft sprocket on crankshaft. Rotate crankshaft so timing mark on crankshaft sprocket is at 12 o'clock position.

2) Install timing chain on camshaft sprocket. Position camshaft sprocket so timing mark is at 6 o'clock position. Install timing chain on crankshaft sprocket.

3) Install camshaft sprocket on camshaft. Ensure timing marks are aligned. *See Fig. 7.* Install washer and camshaft sprocket bolt. Tighten camshaft sprocket bolt to specification. See TORQUE SPECIFICA-TIONS table at end of article.

4) Ensure camshaft end play is within specification. See CAMSHAFT table under ENGINE SPECIFICATIONS at end of article. If camshaft end play is not within specification, replace thrust plate, located between camshaft sprocket and camshaft. To install remaining components, reverse removal procedure.

ROCKER ARMS & PUSH RODS

Removal – 1) Remove air intake plenum (upper intake manifold). See INTAKE MANIFOLD under REMOVAL & INSTALLATION. Disconnect spark plug wires. Disconnect closed ventilation system and evaporation control system components from valve cover (if necessary).

2) Remove valve cover. Remove rocker arm and shaft assembly retaining bolts. Remove rocker arm assembly. If removing push rods, mark component location for reassembly reference.

NOTE: If disassembling rocker arm assemblies, mark component location for reassembly reference. Components must be installed in original locations.

CAUTION: DO NOT operate engine until 20 minutes after rocker arm installation and until valve lifters have bled down.

Installation – 1) Ensure push rods are seated in valve lifters. Install rocker arm assembly in original location. Ensure steel retainers are located on retaining bolt area of rocker arm shafts.

2) Slowly tighten rocker arm shaft bolts to specification, starting at center and working out. See TORQUE SPECIFICATIONS table at end of article. To complete installation, reverse removal procedure.

VALVE LIFTERS

Removal – 1) Remove cylinder head. See CYLINDER HEAD under REMOVAL & INSTALLATION. Remove retaining bolts, yoke retainer and aligning yoke. *See Fig. 8.*

2) Using Valve Lifter Remover (C-4129), remove valve lifter. Mark component location for reassembly reference.

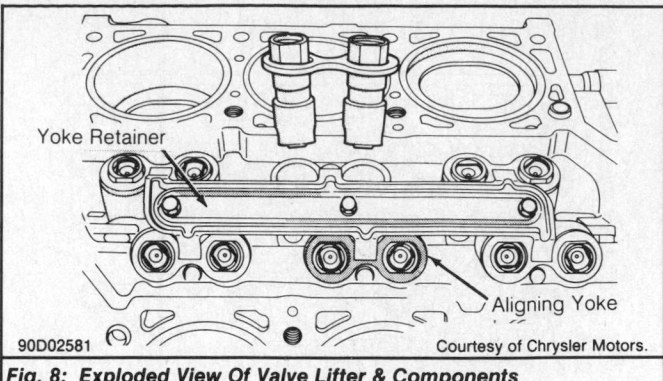

Fig. 8: Exploded View Of Valve Lifter & Components

Inspection – 1) Inspect valve lifter roller for damage. Ensure valve lifter O.D. and oil clearance are to specification. See VALVE LIFTERS table under ENGINE SPECIFICATIONS at end of article. Inspect valve lifter bore in cylinder block and outside surface of lifter for scoring.

2) If scoring exists, ream cylinder block bore for next oversize valve lifter. Oversize valve lifters are available in .001" (.02 mm), .008" (.20 mm) and .030" (.76 mm) sizes.

CAUTION: If camshaft is replaced, valve lifters must also be replaced. Whenever camshaft or valve lifters are replaced, add one pint of Chrysler crankcase conditioner to engine oil for at least 500 miles to aid break-in.

CAUTION: DO NOT allow engine RPM to exceed fast idle until valve lifters have filled with oil and become quiet.

Installation – To install, reverse removal procedure. Ensure components are installed in original locations. Lubricate valve lifters with engine oil before installing. Tighten bolts to specification. See TORQUE SPECIFICATIONS table at end of article.

CAMSHAFT

NOTE: Manufacturer lists camshaft service procedure with engine removed only.

Removal – Remove engine. See ENGINE under REMOVAL & INSTALLATION. Remove valve lifters and timing chain. See VALVE LIFTERS and TIMING CHAIN under REMOVAL & INSTALLATION. Remove camshaft thrust plate retaining bolts. Remove camshaft.

Inspection – Inspect camshaft for wear. Measure camshaft journal diameter. Replace camshaft if it is not within specification. See CAMSHAFT table under ENGINE SPECIFICATIONS at end of article.

CAUTION: If camshaft is replaced, valve lifters must also be replaced. Whenever camshaft or valve lifters are replaced, add one pint of Chrysler crankcase conditioner to engine oil for at least 500 miles to aid in break-in.

CAUTION: DO NOT allow engine RPM to exceed fast idle until valve lifters have filled with oil and become quiet.

Installation – 1) Lubricate camshaft with camshaft lubricant. Install camshaft. Tighten thrust plate bolts to specification. See TORQUE SPECIFICATIONS table at end of article. Ensure camshaft end play is within specification. If camshaft end play is not within specification, replace thrust plate. See CAMSHAFT table under ENGINE SPECIFICATIONS at end of article.

2) To install remaining components, reverse removal procedure. Ensure components are installed in original locations.

CAMSHAFT BEARINGS

Removal & Installation – 1) Inspect camshaft bearing for damage. Replace camshaft bearing if damaged or if I.D. is not within specification. See CAMSHAFT table under ENGINE SPECIFICATIONS at end of article.

CAUTION: Ensure No. 2 camshaft bearing aligns with oil passage to left cylinder head and No. 3 camshaft bearing aligns with oil passage to right cylinder head.

2) Use Camshaft Bearing Remover/Installer (C-3132-A) for camshaft bearing replacement. Ensure all oil holes are aligned.

REAR CRANKSHAFT OIL SEAL

Removal & Installation – 1) Remove transaxle and flexplate. Using screwdriver, pry oil seal from seal retainer.
2) To install, place Oil Seal Installer (C-4681) on crankshaft. Coat oil seal O.D. with Loctite. Install oil seal over oil seal installer. Tap oil seal into seal retainer. Install flexplate and transaxle. Tighten bolts to specification. See TORQUE SPECIFICATIONS table at end of article.

WATER PUMP

Removal & Installation – 1) Drain cooling system. Remove drive belt. Remove right front lower fender shield. Remove water pump pulley. Remove retaining bolts, water pump and "O" ring.
2) To install, reverse removal procedure using new "O" ring. Tighten bolts to specification. See TORQUE SPECIFICATIONS table at end of article.
3) Fill and bleed cooling system. See COOLING SYSTEM BLEEDING under REMOVAL & INSTALLATION.

OIL PAN

Removal & Installation – 1) Disconnect negative battery cable. Remove engine oil dipstick. Raise and support vehicle. Drain engine oil. Remove retaining bolts, oil pan and gasket.
2) To install, reverse removal procedure. Apply silicone sealant at timing chain cover and rear crankshaft seal retainer-to-cylinder block junction areas before installing gasket. Tighten bolts to specification. See TORQUE SPECIFICATIONS table at end of article.

OVERHAUL

CYLINDER HEAD

Cylinder Head – Inspect cylinder head for cracks and warpage. Repair or replace cylinder head if warpage exceeds specification. See CYLINDER HEAD table under ENGINE SPECIFICATIONS at end of article.

CAUTION: DO NOT grind more than .008" (.20 mm) total from cylinder head surface and cylinder block deck surface.

Valve Springs – 1) Check valve spring free length and pressure. Replace valve spring if it is not within specification. See VALVES & VALVE SPRINGS table under ENGINE SPECIFICATIONS at end of article.
2) Measure valve spring installed height from spring seat to bottom of spring retainer. If spacers are installed, measure from top of spacer. If height exceeds 1.594" (40.50 mm), install a .031" (.80 mm) thick spacer in cylinder head counterbore to obtain correct installed height. See VALVES & VALVE SPRINGS table.
Valve Stem Oil Seals – Ensure oversize valve stem seals are used when oversize valves are installed.
Valve Guides – 1) Check valve stem oil clearance. Ensure valve stem diameter is within specification. Valve guide must be reamed for valve with oversize valve stem if oil clearance exceeds specification. See CYLINDER HEAD table under ENGINE SPECIFICATIONS at end of article.

NOTE: DO NOT ream valve guides from standard to maximum oversize in one step. Ream valve guides to oversize in gradual steps so guides are reamed true in relation to valve seat. After reaming valve guides, valve seat runout must be checked.

2) Valves are available with oversize valve stems of .006" (.15 mm), .016" (.40 mm) and .031" (.80 mm). Cylinder head must be replaced if guide cannot be cleaned using a .031" (.80 mm) reamer.
Valve Seat – Check valve seat width and runout. Grind valve seat if it is not within specification. See CYLINDER HEAD table under ENGINE SPECIFICATIONS at end of article. Cylinder head must be replaced if valve seat cannot be corrected.
Valves – Ensure valve margin, head diameter, refinish length and stem diameter are within specification. See VALVES & VALVE SPRINGS table under ENGINE SPECIFICATIONS at end of article. Valves are available with oversize valve stems of .006" (.15 mm), .016" (.40 mm) and .031" (.80 mm).
Seat Correction Angles – Use a 15-degree stone to lower valve seat and a 65-degree stone to raise valve seat.

CYLINDER BLOCK ASSEMBLY

Piston & Rod Assembly – Install piston with notch or groove on top of piston toward front (timing chain end) of engine. Note direction of connecting rod installation on piston before removal. Connecting rod must be installed in original direction. No other information for connecting rod-to-piston installation is available.
Fitting Pistons – 1) Measure piston diameter at 1.65" (41.9 mm) from top of piston at 90-degree angle to piston pin. Measure cylinder bore diameter at .50" (12.7 mm) below top surface of cylinder bore, middle of bore and .50" (12.7 mm) from bottom of cylinder bore.

NOTE: Piston diameter and cylinder bore should be measured at room temperature of approximately 70°F (21°C).

2) Ensure piston diameter and clearance are within specification. See PISTONS, PINS & RINGS table under ENGINE SPECIFICATIONS at end of article.
Piston Rings – Ensure ring end gap and side clearances are within specification. See PISTONS, PINS & RINGS table under ENGINE SPECIFICATIONS at end of article. Ensure piston ring end gaps are properly positioned. *See Fig. 9.*

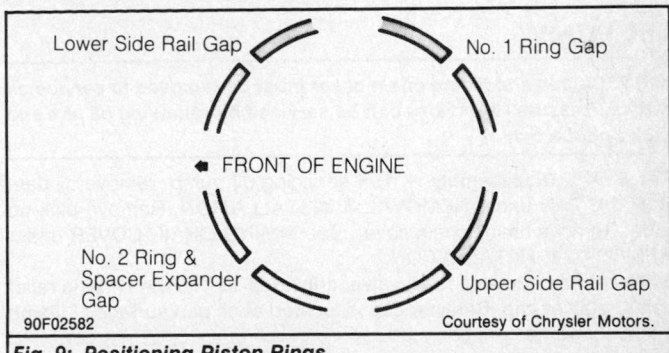

Fig. 9: Positioning Piston Rings

Rod Bearings – 1) Before installing rod bearings, hold a straightedge across threads of connecting rod bolts. If threads fail to contact straightedge in all areas, bolts are stretched and must be replaced.
2) Apply light coat of engine oil to connecting rod bolt threads before tightening nut to specification. See TORQUE SPECIFICATIONS table at end of article. Ensure oil clearance and side play are within specification. See CRANKSHAFT, MAIN & CONNECTING ROD BEARINGS and CONNECTING RODS tables under ENGINE SPECIFICATIONS at end of article.
Crankshaft & Main Bearings – 1) Before installing main bearings, hold a straightedge across threads of main bearing cap bolts. If threads fail to contact straightedge in all areas, bolts are stretched and must be replaced.

CAUTION: *Crankshaft journal grinding should not exceed .012" (.30 mm) undersize. DO NOT grind thrust surfaces of No. 2 main bearing. With cast iron crankshafts, final paper or cloth polishing after regrind must be done in same direction as engine rotation.*

2) Apply light coat of engine oil to threads before tightening bolt to specification. See TORQUE SPECIFICATIONS table at end of article. Ensure oil clearance and end play are within specification. See CRANKSHAFT, MAIN & CONNECTING ROD BEARINGS table under ENGINE SPECIFICATIONS at end of article.
Thrust Bearing – Thrust bearing is located on No. 2 main bearing. Replace thrust bearing if crankshaft end play is not within specification. See CRANKSHAFT, MAIN & CONNECTING ROD BEARINGS table under ENGINE SPECIFICATIONS at end of article.
Cylinder Block – **1)** Check cylinder bore, out-of-round and taper. Measurements should be taken at .50" (12.7 mm) below top surface of cylinder bore, middle of bore and .50" (12.7 mm) from bottom of cylinder bore.

NOTE: *Cylinder bore should be measured at room temperature of approximately 70°F (21°C).*

2) Bore cylinder block if it is not within specification. See CYLINDER BLOCK table under ENGINE SPECIFICATIONS at end of article. Cylinder block warpage information is not available from manufacturer.
3) Check valve lifter bore diameter and for signs of scoring. If scoring exists or lifter bore diameter is not within specification, ream cylinder block bore for next oversize valve lifter. See VALVE LIFTERS table under ENGINE SPECIFICATIONS at end of article.
4) Oversize valve lifters are available in .001" (.02 mm), .008" (.20 mm) and .030" (.76 mm) sizes.

ENGINE OILING

ENGINE LUBRICATION SYSTEM

Crankshaft-driven oil pump provides lubrication to main gallery. *See Fig. 10.*
Crankcase Capacity – Crankcase capacity with oil filter is 4.5 qts. (4.3L).
Oil Pressure – Oil pressure should be **5 psi (.35 kg/cm²)** at curb idle and **30-80 psi (2.1-5.6 kg/cm²)** at 3000 RPM.

OIL PUMP

NOTE: *Oil pan and timing chain cover must be removed to service oil pump. Pressure relief valve can be serviced by removing oil pan and pick-up tube only.*

Removal & Disassembly – **1)** If servicing oil pump, remove oil pan. See OIL PAN under REMOVAL & INSTALLATION. Remove pick-up tube. Remove timing chain cover. See TIMING CHAIN COVER under REMOVAL & INSTALLATION.
2) To service pressure relief valve, drill a 1/8" (3.175 mm) hole in relief valve retainer cap. Retainer cap is located at oil pan surface of timing chain cover, near oil pan stud.
3) Install a self-tapping screw into hole. If timing chain cover is installed, pull self-tapping screw to remove retainer cap.
4) If timing chain cover is removed, clamp self-tapping screw in a vise. Support timing chain cover while lightly tapping on timing chain cover using soft-faced hammer until retainer cap is removed.
5) Remove spring and pressure relief valve. Remove retaining bolts and pump cover. Note direction of rotor installation for reassembly reference. Remove inner and outer rotors. *See Fig. 11.*
Inspection – **1)** Inspect components for damage. Using straightedge and feeler gauge, check pump cover warpage. Replace pump cover if clearance equals or exceeds specification. See OIL PUMP SPECIFICATIONS table.

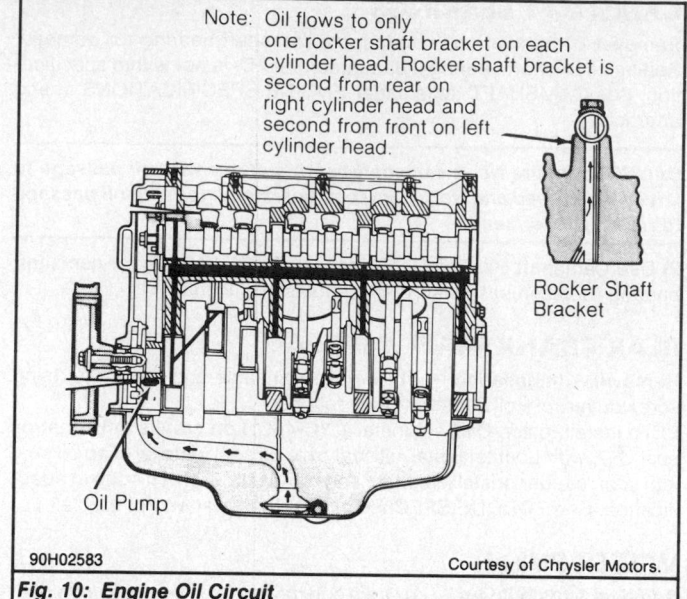

Note: Oil flows to only one rocker shaft bracket on each cylinder head. Rocker shaft bracket is second from rear on right cylinder head and second from front on left cylinder head.

Rocker Shaft Bracket

Oil Pump

90H02583   Courtesy of Chrysler Motors.
Fig. 10: Engine Oil Circuit

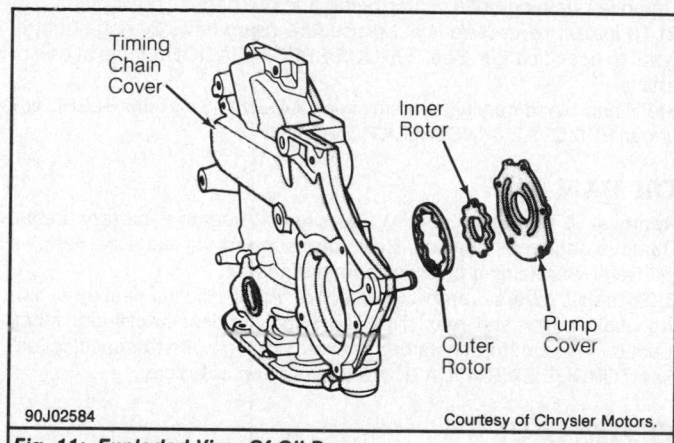

Timing Chain Cover

Inner Rotor

Pump Cover

Outer Rotor

90J02584   Courtesy of Chrysler Motors.
Fig. 11: Exploded View Of Oil Pump

2) Measure thickness of both rotors and outer rotor O.D. Replace rotors if not within specification.
3) Install outer rotor in timing chain cover. Measure clearance between outer rotor and timing chain cover. If clearance equals or exceeds specification but outer rotor O.D. is within specification, replace timing chain cover.
4) Install inner rotor, and measure clearance between inner and outer rotors. Replace pump assembly if clearance is equal to or exceeds specification.
5) Place straightedge across timing chain cover surface. Using feeler gauge, check rotor end clearance between rotors and straightedge. Replace pump if clearance is equal to or exceeds specification.
6) Ensure pressure relief valve slides freely in bore. Check pressure relief valve spring free length and pressure. Replace spring if not within specification.

Reassembly & Installation – To reassemble, reverse disassembly procedure. Install new retainer cap. Tighten pump cover bolts to specification. See TORQUE SPECIFICATIONS table at end of article. Fill rotor cavity with engine oil before installing. To install, reverse removal procedure.

OIL PUMP SPECIFICATIONS

Application	Specification
Inner Rotor-To-Outer Rotor Clearance	.008" (.20 mm)
Outer Rotor O.D.	3.141" (79.78 mm)
Outer Rotor-To-Timing Chain	
Cover Clearance	.002" (.05 mm)
Pressure Relief Valve Spring	
Free Length	1.95" (49.5 mm)
Pressure	19.5-20.5 lbs. @ 1.031"
	(8.8-9.3 kg @ 26.19 mm)
Pump Cover Warpage	.003" (.08 mm)
Rotor End Clearance	.004" (.10 mm)
Rotor Thickness	
Inner Rotor	.301" (7.65 mm)
Outer Rotor	.3005" (7.633 mm)

TORQUE SPECIFICATIONS

TORQUE SPECIFICATIONS

Application	Ft. Lbs. (N.m)
Air Compressor Bolt	50 (68)
Air Intake Plenum Bolt	[1] 21 (29)
Alternator Bracket-To-Manifold Bolt	34 (41)
Camshaft Sprocket Bolt	40 (54)
Connecting Rod Nut	
Step 1	40 (54)
Step 2	Additional 1/4 Turn
Cylinder Head Bolt [2]	
Step 1	45 (61)
Step 2	65 (88)
Step 3	65 (88)
Step 4	[3] Additional 1/4 Turn
EGR Tube Bolt	17 (23)
Engine Bracket Bolt	40 (54)
Exhaust Crossover Pipe Bolt	25 (34)
Exhaust Manifold Bolt	17 (23)
Flexplate Bolt	70 (95)
Front Mount Through Bolt	50 (68)
Front Mount-To-Cylinder Block Bolt	
Lower Bolt	40 (54)
Upper Bolt	75 (102)
Front Mount-To-Frame Rail Bolt/Nut	40 (54)
Fuel Rail Bolt	17 (23)
Intake Manifold Bolt [4]	
Step 1	[5]
Step 2	17 (23)
Step 3	17 (23)
Intake Manifold Brace-To-Cylinder Head Bolt	40 (54)
Left Mount Through Bolt	50 (68)
Left Mount-To-Frame Rail Bolt	50 (68)
Main Bearing Cap Bolt	
Step 1	30 (41)
Step 2	Additional 1/4 Turn
Oil Pump Pick-Up Bolt	21 (29)
Right Mount (Timing Chain Side) Through Bolt	100 (136)
Right Mount (Timing Chain Side)-To-Frame Bolt	50 (68)
Right Mount (Timing Chain Side) Vertical Bolt/Nut	75 (102)
Rocker Arm Shaft Bolt	21 (29)

[1] – Tighten bolts in sequence. *See Fig. 3.*

[2] – All bolts except No. 9 (8 mm) bolt must be tightened to specification in sequence. *See Fig. 5.* No. 9 bolt should be tightened to 25 ft. lbs. (34 N.m) after all other bolts are tightened to specification.

[3] – After additional 1/4 turn, bolt torque should exceed 90 ft. lbs. (122 N.m). If torque is not exceeded, replace cylinder head bolt.

[4] – Tighten bolts in sequence. *See Fig. 4.*

[5] – Tighten bolts in sequence to 10 INCH lbs. (1 N.m).

TORQUE SPECIFICATIONS (Cont.)

Application	Ft. Lbs. (N.m)
Timing Chain Cover	
8-mm Bolt	20 (27)
10-mm Bolt	40 (54)
Torque Converter-To-Flexplate Bolt	55 (75)
Transaxle-To-Cylinder Block Bolt	75 (102)
Vibration Damper Bolt	40 (54)
Water Pump Pulley Bolt	21 (29)
Wheel Lug Nut	95 (129)

Application	INCH Lbs. (N.m)
Cam Sensor Retaining Bolt	105 (12)
Camshaft Thrust Plate Bolt	105 (12)
Ignition Coil Mounting Bolt	105 (12)
Intake Manifold Gasket End Seal Bolt	105 (12)
Oil Pan Bolt	105 (12)
Oil Pump Cover Bolt	105 (12)
Rear Crankshaft Seal Retainer Bolt	105 (12)
Timing Chain Snubber Bolt	105 (12)
Valve Cover Bolt	105 (12)
Valve Lifter Yoke Retainer Bolt	105 (12)
Water Pump Bolt	105 (12)

ENGINE SPECIFICATIONS

GENERAL SPECIFICATIONS

Application	Specification
Displacement	201 Cu. In.
Bore	3.66" (92.9 mm)
Stroke	3.19" (81.0 mm)
Compression Ratio	8.9:1
Fuel System	PFI
Horsepower @ RPM	147 @ 4800
Torque Ft. Lbs. @ RPM	185 @ 3600

CRANKSHAFT, MAIN & CONNECTING ROD BEARINGS

Application	In. (mm)
Crankshaft End Play	
Standard	.003-.009 (.08-.23)
Wear Limit	.015 (.38)
Main Bearings	
Journal Diameter	2.519 (63.98)
Journal Out-Of-Round	.001 (.03)
Journal Taper	.002 (.05)
Oil Clearance	.0007-.0022 (.018-.056)
Connecting Rod Bearings	
Journal Diameter	2.2830 (57.998)
Journal Out-Of-Round	.001 (.03)
Journal Taper	.001 (.03)
Oil Clearance	.0007-.0022 (.018-.056)

CONNECTING RODS

Application	In. (mm)
Side Play	.005-.015 (.13-.38)

PISTONS, PINS & RINGS

Application	In. (mm)
Pistons	
Clearance	.0010-.0022 (.025-.056)
Diameter	3.6594-3.6602 (92.949-92.969)
Pins	
Diameter	.9007-.9009 (22.878-22.883)
Piston Fit	.0002-.0007 (.005-.018)
Rod Fit	[1]
Rings	
No. 1 & 2	
End Gap	
Standard	.012-.022 (.30-.56)
Wear Limit	.039 (.99)
Side Clearance	
Standard	.001-.003 (.03-.08)
Wear Limit	.004 (.10)
No. 3 (Oil)	
End Gap	
Standard	.010-.039 (.25-.99)
Wear Limit	.074 (1.88)
Side Clearance	.0006-.0089 (.015-.226)

[1] – Interference fit.

CYLINDER BLOCK

Application	In. (mm)
Cylinder Bore	
Standard Diameter	3.6610-3.6617 (92.989-93.007)
Maximum Taper	.002 (.05)
Maximum Out-Of-Round	.003 (.08)

VALVES & VALVE SPRINGS

Application	Specification
Intake Valves	
Face Angle	44 1/2°
Head Diameter	1.79" (45.5 mm)
Minimum Margin	.031" (.79 mm)
Minimum Refinish Length	4.916" (124.87 mm)
Stem Diameter	.312-.313" (7.92-7.95 mm)
Exhaust Valves	
Face Angle	44 1/2°
Head Diameter	1.476" (37.49 mm)
Minimum Margin	.047" (1.19 mm)
Minimum Refinish Length	4.941" (125.50 mm)
Stem Diameter	.3112-.3119" (7.905-7.922 mm)
Valve Springs	
Free Length	1.909" (48.49 mm)
Installed Height	1.531-1.594" (38.89-40.49 mm)

	Lbs. @ In. (kg @ mm)
Pressure	
Valve Closed	58-63 @ 1.57 (26-29 @ 39.8)
Valve Open	136-145 @ 1.14 (62-66 @ 28.9)

CYLINDER HEAD

Application	Specification
Maximum Warpage	[1] .00075" Per 1" (.0191 mm Per 25 mm)
Valve Seats	
Intake Valve	
Seat Angle	45°
Seat Width	.069-.088" (1.75-2.24 mm)
Maximum Seat Runout	.002" (.05 mm)
Exhaust Valve	
Seat Angle	45°
Seat Width	.059-.078" (1.49-1.98 mm)
Maximum Seat Runout	.002" (.05 mm)
Valve Guides	
Intake Valve	
Valve Guide I.D.	.3130-.3149" (7.950-7.998 mm)
Valve Stem-To-Guide Oil Clearance	
Standard	.001-.003" (.03-.08 mm)
Wear Limit	[2] .010" (.25 mm)
Exhaust Valve	
Valve Guide I.D.	.3130-.3149" (7.950-7.998 mm)
Valve Stem-To-Guide Oil Clearance	
Standard	.002-.006" (.05-.15 mm)
Wear Limit	[2] .016" (.41 mm)

[1] – Combined maximum total grind limit of cylinder head and cylinder block is .008" (.20 mm).

[2] – Specification applies to measurement obtained by rocking valve stem in valve guide.

CAMSHAFT

Application	In. (mm)
Camshaft Bearing I.D. [1]	
No. 1	2.000-2.001 (50.80-50.83)
No. 2	1.984-1.985 (50.39-50.42)
No. 3	1.969-1.970 (50.01-50.04)
No. 4	1.953-1.954 (49.61-49.63)
End Play	.005-.012 (.13-.30)
Journal Diameter	
No. 1	1.997-1.999 (50.72-50.77)
No. 2	1.980-1.982 (50.29-50.34)
No. 3	1.965-1.967 (49.91-49.96)
No. 4	1.949-1.952 (49.50-49.58)
Oil Clearance	
Standard	.001-.004 (.03-.10)
Wear Limit	.005 (.13)

[1] – Bearings are numbered from front of camshaft.

VALVE LIFTERS

Application	In. (mm)
Bore Diameter	.9051-.9059 (22.990-23.010)
Lifter Diameter	[1] .9035-.9040 (22.949-22.962)
Oil Clearance	.0011-.0024 (.028-.061)

[1] – Standard diameter valve lifter is listed. Oversize valve lifters are available in .001" (.03 mm), .008" (.20 mm) and .030" (.76 mm) sizes.

Dakota, Pickup, Ramcharger, RWD Van

NOTE: For repair procedures not covered in this article, see ENGINE OVERHAUL PROCEDURES article in GENERAL INFORMATION.

ENGINE IDENTIFICATION

Engine may be identified by eighth character of Vehicle Identification Number (VIN) stamped on metal tab, located near lower left corner of windshield.

Engine serial number may be required when ordering replacement parts. On the 3.9L, engine serial number is located on pad on right side of cylinder block. On 5.2L and 5.9L, engine serial number is located on left front corner of cylinder block just below cylinder head.

ENGINE IDENTIFICATION CODES

Engine	Code
3.9L PFI	X
5.2L PFI	Y
5.9L TBI	
Light-Duty Emissions	Z
Heavy-Duty Emissions	5

SPECIAL ENGINE MARKS

Information identifying undersize and oversize components is found at various engine locations and decoded as follows:

Crankshaft & Rod Journals

- "M" or "R" followed by number indicates which main or rod bearing journal is .001" (.02 mm) undersize. Mark is stamped on No. 6 crankshaft counterweight on 3.9L, No. 8 crankshaft counterweight on 5.2L and No. 3 crankshaft counterweight on 5.9L engines.
- "MX" or "RX" indicates all main or rod bearing journals are .010" (.25 mm) undersize. Mark is stamped on No. 6 crankshaft counterweight on 3.9L, No. 8 crankshaft counterweight on 5.2L and No. 3 crankshaft counterweight on 5.9L engines.

Cylinder Block

- Letter "A" following engine serial number indicates .020" (.51 mm) oversize cylinder bores.
- A diamond-shaped stamp, located on top pad at front of engine and stamped on flat area of each oversize lifter bore, indicates .008" (.20 mm) oversize lifters.
- A stamp "X" indicates .005" (.13 mm) oversize valve stems. Stamp is found on machined pad, near two 3/8" tapped holes on each end of cylinder head.

ADJUSTMENTS

VALVE CLEARANCE ADJUSTMENT

Hydraulic valve lifters are used. No valve adjustment is required.

REMOVAL & INSTALLATION

WARNING: When battery is disconnected, vehicle computer and memory systems may lose memory data. Driveability problems may exist until computer systems have completed a relearn cycle. See COMPUTER RELEARN PROCEDURES article in GENERAL INFORMATION before disconnecting battery.

NOTE: For reassembly reference, label all electrical connectors, vacuum hoses and fuel lines before removal. Also place mating marks on engine hood and other major assemblies before removal.

FUEL PRESSURE RELEASE

CAUTION: Fuel system is under pressure. Pressure must be released before servicing fuel system components.

Gasoline (3.9L & 5.2L) – 1) Disconnect negative battery cable. Loosen fuel tank cap to release pressure. Using Fuel Pressure Gauge Tool Set (5069), remove gauge from hose assembly. Place gauge end of hose into an approved container.

2) Remove fuel rail test port protective cap and place a shop towel under test port. To release fuel pressure, screw other end of hose assembly onto test port. Once all fuel pressure is released, replace protective cap on test port.

Compressed Natural Gas Fuel Tube Purging (5.2L) – 1) Close control valve (clockwise) on side mounted fuel cylinder. Close control valves (clockwise) on both of rear mounted fuel cylinders. Open manual shutoff valve.

2) Start and operate engine until it runs out of fuel. Attempt 3 more engine starts. If check valve or fuel fill receptacle is to be serviced, slowly loosen inlet side of fuel fill tube fitting at check valve. It is normal for approximately 25 psi of natural gas pressure to flow from loosened fitting.

At this point, all fuel tubes are purged of natural gas between fuel cylinders and engine. It is now OK to open fuel system.

Compressed Natural Gas Fuel Cylinder Purging (5.2L) – 1) Open manual shutoff valve. Open only the fuel control valve(s) (counterclockwise) on the fuel cylinder(s) to be serviced. Close all other control valve(s) (clockwise) on fuel cylinder(s) not being serviced.

2) Start and operate engine until it runs out of fuel. Attempt 3 more engine starts. At this point, all fuel tubes and opened cylinders are purged of natural gas between fuel cylinders and engine. It is now OK to open fuel system.

Gasoline (5.9L) – 1) Loosen fuel tank cap to release pressure. Disconnect injector wiring harness from engine wiring harness. Connect jumper wire between terminal No. 1 of injector harness and ground. *See Fig. 1.*

2) Connect another jumper wire to terminal No. 2 of injector harness. Touch jumper wire to positive battery terminal for no more than 5 seconds to release fuel pressure. Remove jumper wires and reconnect wiring harness.

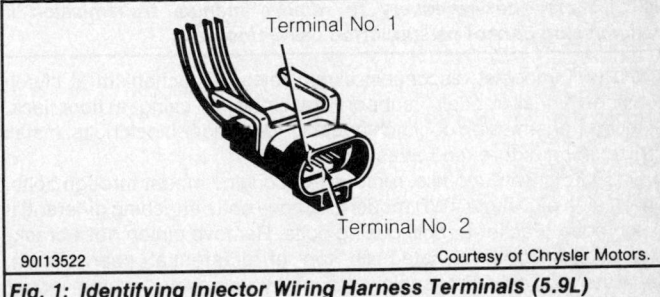

90I13522   Courtesy of Chrysler Motors.

Fig. 1: Identifying Injector Wiring Harness Terminals (5.9L)

ENGINE

CAUTION: DO NOT use lifting tool that bolts to intake manifold in place of throttle body when removing 3.9 and 5.2L engines.

Removal (RWD Van) – 1) Release fuel pressure. See FUEL PRESSURE RELEASE under REMOVAL & INSTALLATION. Disconnect negative battery cable. Scribe hood hinges and remove hood. Drain cooling system and engine oil.

2) Remove engine cover and oil dipstick. On A/C equipped models, discharge A/C system using approved refrigerant recovery equipment. Disconnect A/C lines at condenser. Plug all A/C line openings to prevent contamination. Remove A/C compressor.

3) On all models, remove front bumper, grille and support brace. Disconnect coolant hoses. Remove radiator, condenser and support as an assembly.

4) Remove power steering pump with hoses attached, and secure aside. Remove air pump, spark plug wires and distributor cap. Disconnect necessary electrical connections, fuel lines, coolant hoses and vacuum hoses. Remove air cleaner, throttle body, drive belts, alternator, fan and fan pulley.

5) Raise and support vehicle. Disconnect exhaust crossover pipe. Remove left exhaust manifold and heat shield. Remove starter, oil pan, oil pump and pick-up tube.

6) On A/T models, remove transmission inspection cover. Mark torque converter-to-flexplate position for reassembly reference. Remove torque converter-to-flexplate bolts. On M/T models, disconnect clutch release mechanism at clutch housing.

7) On all models, support transmission using a floor jack. Remove transmission or clutch housing-to-cylinder block bolts. Remove engine mount bolts. Remove engine out front of vehicle.

Installation – 1) To install, reverse removal procedure. Install engine with oil pan removed. Before installing oil pan, place a small amount of RTV sealant at corners where side and front oil pan gaskets meet.

2) Tighten bolts/nuts to specification. See TORQUE SPECIFICATIONS table at end of article. On A/T models, ensure reference marks on torque converter and flexplate are aligned. Evacuate and recharge A/C system.

Removal (All Others) – 1) Release fuel pressure. See FUEL PRESSURE RELEASE under REMOVAL & INSTALLATION. Disconnect and remove battery. Scribe hood hinges and remove hood. Drain cooling system.

2) Disconnect coolant hoses. Remove radiator, fan and shroud. On A/C equipped models, discharge A/C system using approved refrigerant recovery equipment, and disconnect A/C lines. Plug A/C lines to prevent contamination. On all models, remove air cleaner, vacuum lines, distributor cap and wiring.

3) Disconnect necessary electrical connections and fuel lines. Remove throttle body and linkage. Remove starter, alternator, charcoal canister and horns. Disconnect power steering hoses (if equipped). Raise and support vehicle. Disconnect exhaust pipe at exhaust manifold.

4) On A/T models, remove transmission housing inspection plate. Attach "C" clamp to front of housing to secure torque converter. Mark torque converter-to-flexplate position for reassembly reference. Remove torque converter-to-flexplate bolts.

NOTE: It may be necessary to remove manual transmission if transmission cannot be supported using floor jack.

5) On M/T models, disconnect clutch release mechanism at clutch housing. On all models, support transmission using a floor jack. Remove transmission or clutch housing-to-cylinder block bolts. Install engine lifting fixture, and attach chain.

6) On Dakota 2WD models, remove front engine mount through bolts. On left side of Dakota 4WD models, remove bolts attaching differential pinion nose bracket-to-bellhousing bolts. Remove pinion nose bracket-to-adapter bolts (located on top of differential near pinion). Separate engine from engine mount by removing engine mount through bolt and nut located on top of engine mount.

7) On right side of Dakota 4WD models, remove 2 axle-to-bracket bolts and bracket-to-bellhousing bolt. Separate engine from engine mount by removing engine mount through bolt and nut located on top of engine mount.

8) On Pickup and Ramcharger, remove front engine mount bolts. On all models, remove engine.

Installation – To install, reverse removal procedure. Tighten bolts/nuts to specification. See TORQUE SPECIFICATIONS table at end of article. On A/T models, ensure reference marks on torque converter and flexplate are aligned. Evacuate and recharge A/C system.

INTAKE MANIFOLD

Removal – 1) Release fuel pressure. See FUEL PRESSURE RELEASE under REMOVAL & INSTALLATION. Disconnect negative battery cable. Drain cooling system. Disconnect accelerator cable, control cables and fuel lines at throttle body. Remove air cleaner and alternator.

2) Disconnect necessary electrical connections, coolant hoses and vacuum hoses. Remove distributor cap and spark plug wires. Remove valve covers (if necessary).

3) Remove intake manifold bolts, intake manifold and gaskets. Separate throttle body from intake manifold (if necessary).

CAUTION: Intake manifold side gaskets are identified by a cutout "RT" (right side) or "LT" (left side). Ensure gaskets are installed in proper location.

Installation – 1) Install side gaskets on cylinder head. Place a 1/4" (6.4 mm) bead of RTV sealant at all cylinder block-to-cylinder head corners. Coat front and rear intake manifold end gaskets and cylinder block with a quick-dry cement. Allow to dry 4-5 minutes.

2) Install front and rear gaskets. Ensure center hole in front and rear gaskets engage with dowel in cylinder block, and ends of gaskets engage with cylinder head gasket.

3) Install intake manifold and install all bolts finger tight. Tighten bolts to specification in sequence. *See Figs. 2-4.* See TORQUE SPECIFICATIONS table at end of article. To install remaining components, reverse removal procedure.

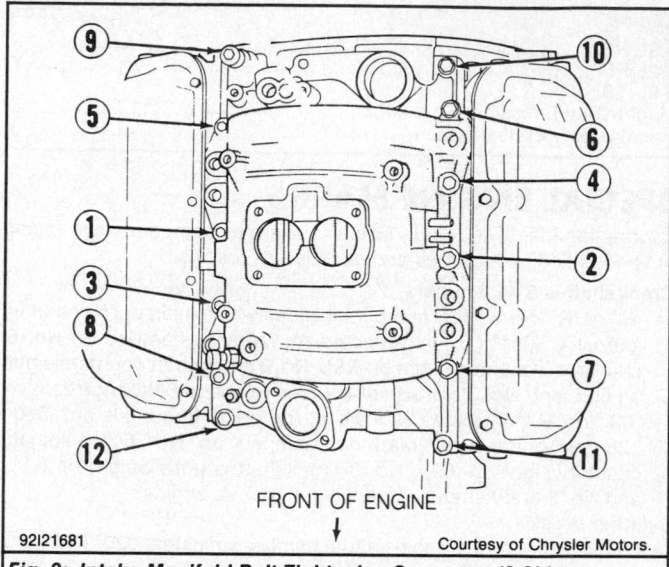

FRONT OF ENGINE

92I21681   Courtesy of Chrysler Motors.

Fig. 2: Intake Manifold Bolt Tightening Sequence (3.9L)

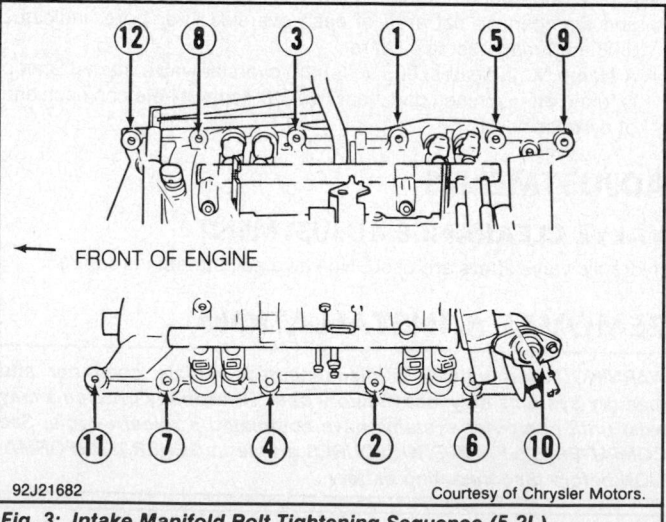

FRONT OF ENGINE

92J21682   Courtesy of Chrysler Motors.

Fig. 3: Intake Manifold Bolt Tightening Sequence (5.2L)

EXHAUST MANIFOLD

Removal – Disconnect negative battery cable. Raise and support vehicle. Disconnect exhaust pipe from exhaust manifold. Remove retaining bolts, nuts, washers and exhaust manifold. Note location of conical washer on bolts. Remove manifold.

Inspection – Check exhaust manifold mating surface warpage. Repair or replace exhaust manifold if warpage exceeds .008" (.20 mm) per 12" (305 mm).

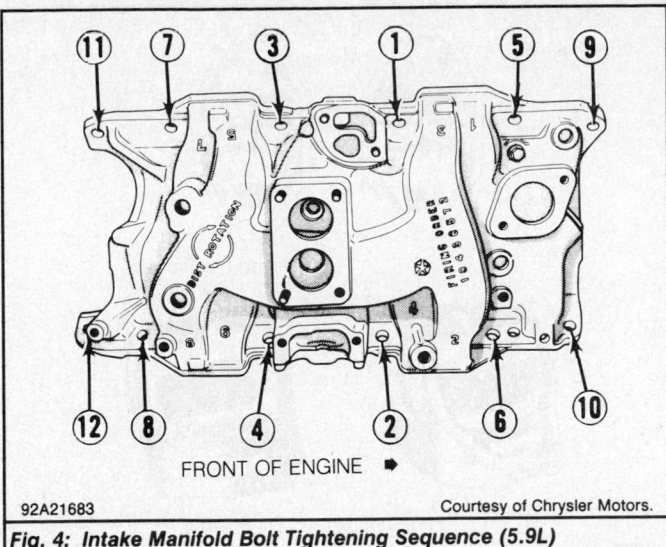

92A21683   Courtesy of Chrysler Motors.
Fig. 4: Intake Manifold Bolt Tightening Sequence (5.9L)

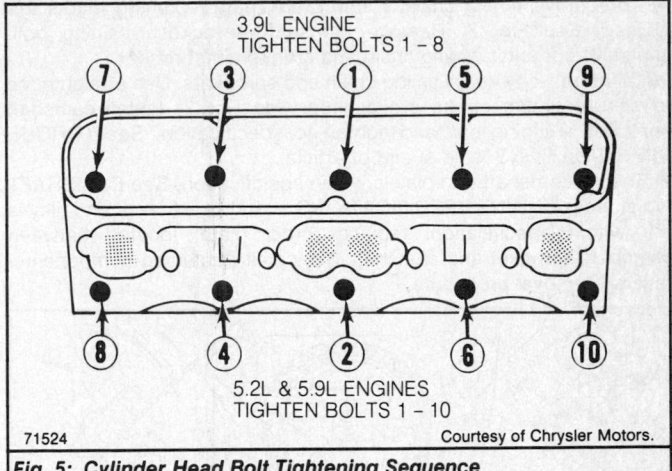

71524   Courtesy of Chrysler Motors.
Fig. 5: Cylinder Head Bolt Tightening Sequence

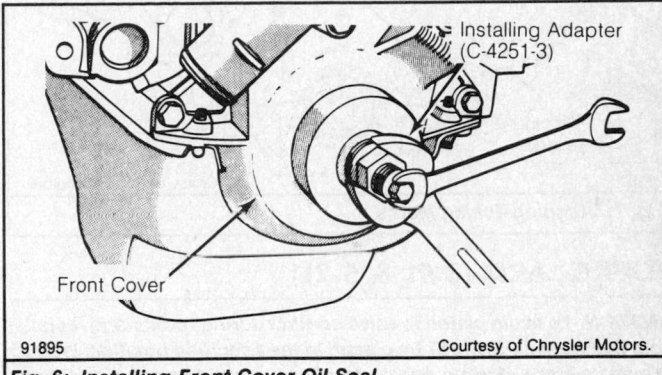

91895   Courtesy of Chrysler Motors.
Fig. 6: Installing Front Cover Oil Seal

CAUTION: Install new studs in cylinder head if studs came out when removing exhaust manifold. Apply sealant to coarse threads of studs before installing.

Installation – **1)** To install, reverse removal procedure. Tighten bolts/nuts to specification, starting at center and working outward. See TORQUE SPECIFICATIONS table at end of article.

2) Ensure conical washers are installed on end studs on 3.9L, and on bolt and stud for front and rear cylinders on 5.2L. DO NOT use conical washers on center bolts.

NOTE: Information is not available from manufacturer on conical washers for 5.9L.

CYLINDER HEAD

Removal (3.9L & 5.2L) – Remove intake and exhaust manifold. See INTAKE MANIFOLD and EXHAUST MANIFOLD under REMOVAL & INSTALLATION. Remove rocker arm shaft assembly. See ROCKER ARM (3.9L & 5.2L) under REMOVAL & INSTALLATION. Remove cylinder head bolts, cylinder head and gasket.

Removal (5.9L) – Remove intake and exhaust manifold. See INTAKE MANIFOLD and EXHAUST MANIFOLD under REMOVAL & INSTALLATION. Remove rocker arm shaft assembly. See ROCKER ARM SHAFT ASSEMBLY (5.9L) under REMOVAL & INSTALLATION. Remove cylinder head bolts, cylinder head and gasket.

Inspection (All Models) – Check cylinder head warpage. Repair or replace cylinder head if warpage exceeds specification. See CYLINDER HEAD table under ENGINE SPECIFICATIONS at end of article.

Installation (All Models) – To install, reverse removal procedure. Tighten cylinder head bolts to specification in sequence using 3 steps. *See Fig. 5.* See TORQUE SPECIFICATIONS table at end of article.

FRONT COVER OIL SEAL

Removal – Disconnect negative battery cable. Remove drive belts from crankshaft pulley. Remove fan and shroud. Remove crankshaft pulley and vibration damper. Pry oil seal from front cover.

Installation – **1)** Use Seal Installer (C-4251) for seal installation. Install threaded shaft of seal installer into crankshaft threads. Install oil seal in front cover with spring facing rear of engine.

2) Position Installing Adapter (C-4251-3) with thrust bearing and nut on shaft. *See Fig. 6.* Tighten nut until installing adapter is even with front cover. Remove installing adapter. To install remaining components, reverse removal procedure. Tighten bolts to specification. See TORQUE SPECIFICATIONS table at end of article.

FRONT COVER

Removal – **1)** Remove water pump. See WATER PUMP under REMOVAL & INSTALLATION. Remove power steering pump (if equipped). Remove remaining drive belts. Remove crankshaft pulley and vibration damper.

2) Loosen oil pan bolts. Remove oil pan-to-front cover bolts on each side of oil pan. Remove retaining bolts, front cover and gasket. Use care not to damage oil pan gasket.

Installation – **1)** Ensure sealing surfaces are clean. Apply a 1/8" (3.2 mm) bead of RTV sealant to oil pan gasket. Lubricate front cover oil seal lip with Lubriplate. Install gasket, front cover and retaining bolts, but DO NOT tighten.

2) Install vibration damper onto crankshaft to align front cover oil seal. Tighten front cover, oil pan and then vibration damper bolts to specification. See TORQUE SPECIFICATIONS table at end of article. To install remaining components, reverse removal procedure.

TIMING CHAIN

Removal – **1)** Remove front cover. See FRONT COVER under REMOVAL & INSTALLATION. Check timing chain stretch to determine if it requires replacement.

2) Position measuring scale near link on timing chain at camshaft sprocket so movement can be measured. Place torque wrench on camshaft sprocket bolt. Apply 30 ft. lbs. (41 N.m) torque with cylinder heads installed or 15 ft. lbs. (20 N.m) with cylinder heads removed on camshaft sprocket bolt in direction of engine rotation. Note reading on measuring scale.

NOTE: When applying torque to camshaft sprocket bolt, DO NOT allow crankshaft to move. It may be necessary to hold crankshaft.

3) Apply same amount of torque in opposite direction and note amount of timing chain movement on measuring scale. If movement exceeds 1/8" (3.17 mm), replace timing chain.

4) To remove timing chain, rotate crankshaft so timing marks are aligned. See Fig. 7. Remove camshaft sprocket retaining bolt, camshaft sprocket, timing chain and crankshaft sprocket.
Installation – 1) Install timing chain and sprockets. Use straightedge to ensure timing marks are aligned. See Fig. 7. Install camshaft sprocket retaining bolt and tighten to specification. See TORQUE SPECIFICATIONS table at end of article.
2) Ensure camshaft end play is within specification. See CAMSHAFT table under ENGINE SPECIFICATIONS at end of article. If end play is not within specification, replace thrust plate, located between camshaft sprocket and camshaft. To install remaining components, reverse removal procedure.

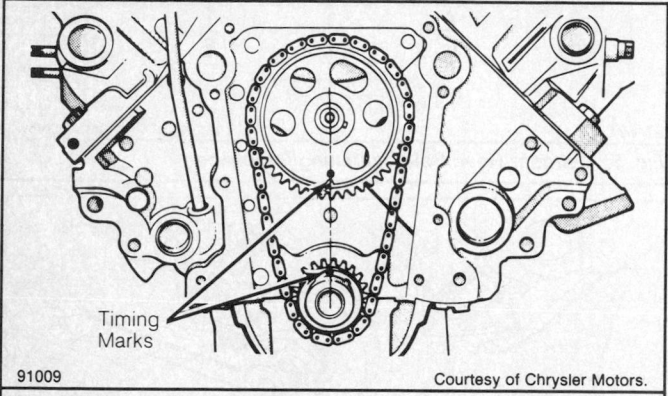

91009   Courtesy of Chrysler Motors.
Fig. 7: Aligning Timing Marks

ROCKER ARM (3.9L & 5.2L)

CAUTION: To avoid piston to valve contact during rocker arm installation, the crankshaft MUST be placed in the specified position. Wait 20 minutes before starting engine to allow valve lifters to bleed down after rocker arm installation.

Removal – Disconnect spark plug wires, PCV and fuel evaporation hoses. Remove valve covers. Remove bolt attaching rocker arm and pivot assembly to cylinder head. Remove rocker arm and pivot. Wire components together for reassembly reference. Mark push rod location and remove (if necessary).
Installation – On 3.9L models, locate "V6" mark stamped on vibration damper at 147° ATDC. On 5.2L models, locate "V8" mark stamped on vibration damper at 17.5° ATDC. On all models, align specified mark with TDC marker. Install rocker arm and pivot assemblies and tighten bolt to **21 ft. lbs. (28 N.m).**

ROCKER ARM SHAFT ASSEMBLY (5.9L)

Removal – 1) Disconnect spark plug wires, PCV and fuel evaporation hoses. Remove valve covers. Remove bolts and retainers attaching rocker arm shaft assembly to cylinder head.
2) Remove rocker arms and shaft as an assembly. Mark push rod location, and remove (if necessary). If rocker arm components are to be separated, note rocker arm identification. See Figs. 8 and 9.

CAUTION: Wait 20 minutes before starting engine to allow valve lifters to bleed down after rocker arm installation.

CAUTION: On engines with exhaust valve rotators, ensure rocker arm for exhaust valve contains relieved area for valve rotator clearance. See Fig. 8.

Installation – 1) Install push rods in original locations. Install rocker arm and shaft assembly with notch on end of rocker arm shaft on bottom and toward front (left bank) or rear (right bank) of engine.
2) Ensure long, stamped-steel retainers are installed on No. 2 and 4 rocker arm shaft retaining bolts. See Fig. 9. Slowly tighten rocker arm shaft bolts to specification, starting at center and working outward. See TORQUE SPECIFICATIONS table at end of article. To install remaining components, reverse removal procedure.

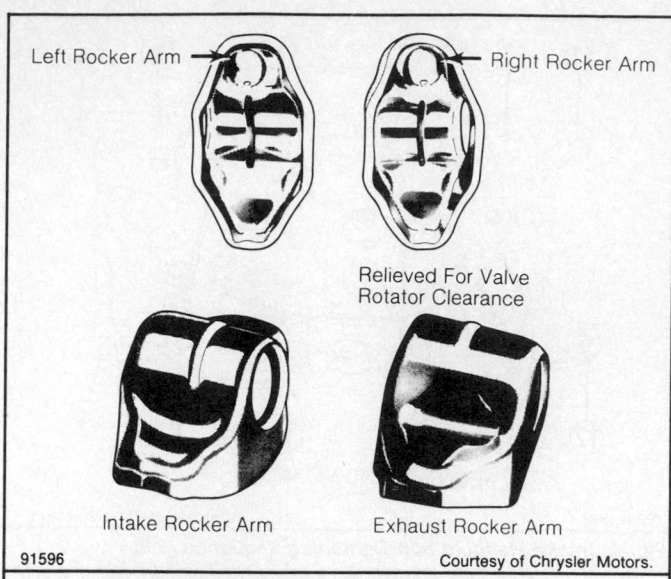

Left Rocker Arm   Right Rocker Arm

Relieved For Valve Rotator Clearance

Intake Rocker Arm   Exhaust Rocker Arm

91596   Courtesy of Chrysler Motors.
Fig. 8: Identifying Rocker Arms (5.9L)

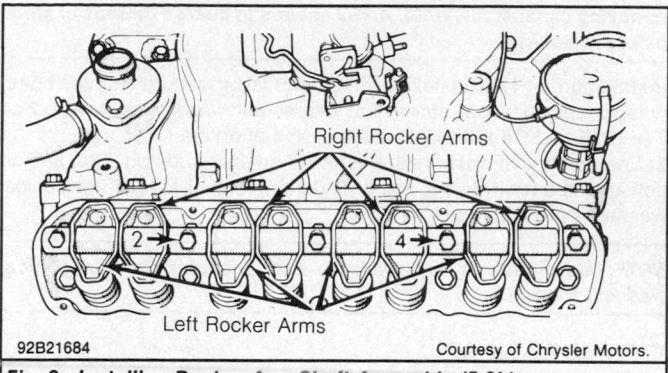

Right Rocker Arms

Left Rocker Arms

92B21684   Courtesy of Chrysler Motors.
Fig. 9: Installing Rocker Arm Shaft Assembly (5.9L)

VALVE LIFTERS

Removal (3.9L & 5.2L) – 1) Remove air cleaner. Remove rocker arms. See ROCKER ARM (3.9L & 5.2L) under REMOVAL & INSTALLATION. Label and remove push rods.
2) Remove intake manifold. See INTAKE MANIFOLD under REMOVAL & INSTALLATION. Remove yoke retainer and aligning yoke. Note if aligning yoke contains an arrow which points toward camshaft. Using Valve Lifter Remover/Installer (C-4129-A), remove valve lifter.
Removal (5.9L) – 1) Remove air cleaner. Remove rocker arm shaft assembly (if equipped). See ROCKER ARM SHAFT ASSEMBLY (5.9L) under REMOVAL & INSTALLATION. Label and remove push rods.
2) Remove intake manifold. See INTAKE MANIFOLD under REMOVAL & INSTALLATION. Remove yoke retainer and aligning yoke. Note if aligning yoke contains an arrow which points toward camshaft. Using Valve Lifter Remover/Installer (C-4129-A), remove valve lifter.
Inspection – Inspect components for damage. Measure lifter O.D. and bore diameter in cylinder block. Determine oil clearance. Clearance must be within specification. See VALVE LIFTERS table under ENGINE SPECIFICATIONS at end of article. Cylinder block can be bored for oversize lifters.

NOTE: Cylinder block must be marked to indicate oversize valve lifters. See SPECIAL ENGINE MARKS.

CAUTION: *If camshaft is replaced, valve lifters must also be replaced. Whenever new camshaft or valve lifters are installed, add one pint of Chrysler crankcase conditioner to engine oil for at least 500 miles to aid break-in.*

Installation – To install, reverse removal procedure. Lubricate valve lifter before installing. Ensure components are installed in original location. Tighten bolts to specification. See TORQUE SPECIFICATIONS table at end of article.

CAUTION: *Ensure valve lifter is installed so oil feed hole in side of valve lifter is facing upward, away from crankshaft. If aligning yoke contains an arrow, ensure aligning yoke is installed with arrow pointing toward camshaft.*

CAUTION: *DO NOT allow engine RPM to exceed fast idle until valve lifters have filled with oil and become quiet.*

CAMSHAFT

NOTE: *Manufacturer lists camshaft service procedure with engine removed.*

Removal – **1)** Remove engine. See ENGINE under REMOVAL & INSTALLATION. Remove front cover and timing chain. See FRONT COVER and TIMING CHAIN under REMOVAL & INSTALLATION. Remove valve lifters. See VALVE LIFTERS under REMOVAL & INSTALLATION.
2) Remove distributor and distributor drive shaft. Remove camshaft thrust plate retaining screws. Note direction of oil tab installation on camshaft thrust plate. See Fig. 10. Remove camshaft.

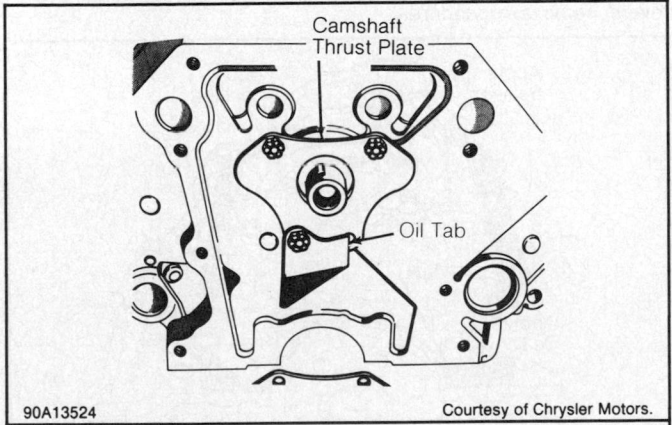

90A13524   Courtesy of Chrysler Motors.
Fig. 10: Positioning Oil Tab

Inspection – Inspect camshaft and camshaft bearings for wear. Measure camshaft journal diameter and camshaft bearing I.D. Replace camshaft or camshaft bearings if not within specification. See CAMSHAFT table under ENGINE SPECIFICATIONS at end of article.

CAUTION: *If camshaft is replaced, valve lifters must also be replaced. Whenever new camshaft or valve lifters are installed, add one pint of Chrysler crankcase conditioner to engine oil for at least 500 miles to aid break-in.*

Installation – **1)** Ensure cup plugs are installed in oil passages behind thrust plate. Lubricate camshaft with camshaft lubricant, and install within approximately 2" (50.8 mm) of final installation location.
2) Install Camshaft Installer (C-3509) with long area behind distributor drive gear. See Fig. 11. This prevents camshaft from contacting plug, located in rear of cylinder block. Install distributor lock bolt to retain camshaft installer.

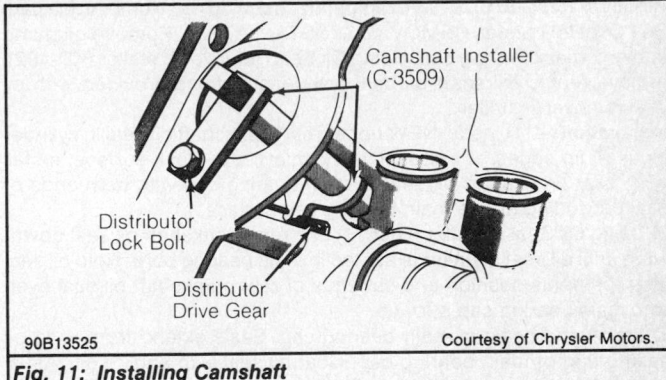

90B13525   Courtesy of Chrysler Motors.
Fig. 11: Installing Camshaft

3) Install camshaft thrust plate. Ensure tang engages with lower right hole of camshaft thrust plate. Tighten camshaft thrust plate bolts to specification. See TORQUE SPECIFICATIONS table at end of article. Top edge of oil tab should be flat against camshaft thrust plate for timing chain lubrication.
4) To install remaining components, reverse removal procedure. Check camshaft end play. If end play exceeds specification, replace thrust plate. See CAMSHAFT table under ENGINE SPECIFICATIONS at end of article. Ensure components are installed in original location.

CAUTION: *DO NOT allow engine RPM to exceed fast idle until valve lifters have filled with oil and become quiet.*

CAMSHAFT BEARINGS

Removal & Installation – **1)** Inspect camshaft bearing for damage. Replace camshaft bearing if damaged or if I.D. is not within specification. See CAMSHAFT table under ENGINE SPECIFICATIONS at end of article.
2) Use Camshaft Bearing Remover/Installer (C-3132-A) for camshaft bearing replacement. Ensure all oil holes are aligned. Install NEW camshaft plug at rear of cylinder block.

CAUTION: *Ensure oil hole in No. 2 bearing aligns with oil hole to left cylinder head, and oil hole in No. 3 bearing (3.9L) or No. 4 bearing (5.2L and 5.9L) aligns with oil hole to right cylinder head.*

DISTRIBUTOR DRIVE SHAFT BUSHING

Removal – **1)** Rotate crankshaft so No. 1 cylinder is at TDC on compression stroke. Remove distributor and distributor drive shaft. Insert Bushing Puller (C-3502) into bushing, and thread down until tight.
2) Hold bushing puller bolt, and rotate bushing puller nut until distributor drive shaft bushing is removed.
Installation – **1)** Install NEW distributor drive shaft bushing over burnishing end of Bushing Installer (C-3503). Insert bushing installer and distributor drive shaft bushing into cylinder block.
2) Using hammer, drive bushing installer and distributor drive shaft bushing into cylinder block. Tighten nut to pull bushing installer through distributor drive shaft bushing. Tightening nut expands bushing tight in cylinder block and burnishes it to correct size.

NOTE: *DO NOT ream distributor drive shaft bushing.*

3) Ensure No. 1 cylinder is at TDC on compression stroke. Install distributor drive shaft so slot is aligned toward left front intake manifold bolt as viewed from rear of engine on 3.9L or is aligned from front to rear of engine on 5.2L and 5.9L. Install distributor with rotor positioned to No. 1 cylinder in distributor cap.

REAR CRANKSHAFT OIL SEAL

NOTE: *The 3.9L and 5.2L use a rope-type rear crankshaft oil seal; 5.9L uses a rubber-type oil seal. Rear crankshaft oil seal can be changed with crankshaft installed.*

Removal (3.9L & 5.2L W/Crankshaft Installed) – Remove oil pan. See OIL PAN under REMOVAL & INSTALLATION. Remove oil pump and rear main bearing cap. Using Oil Seal Remover/Installer (KD-492), remove rear crankshaft oil seal using instructions provided with oil seal remover/installer.

Installation – **1)** Install NEW upper rear crankshaft oil seal in cylinder block. Trim edges of oil seal even with cylinder block surface. Install NEW rear crankshaft oil seal in main bearing cap with both ends of seal protruding above main bearing cap surface.

2) Using Oil Seal Installer (C-3511), tap rear crankshaft oil seal downward until oil seal installer is seated in main bearing bore. Hold oil seal installer in this position and cut ends of rear crankshaft oil seal even with main bearing cap surface.

3) Install end seals in main bearing cap. Seals extend from rope oil seal to end of main bearing cap. Coat oil seal with engine oil. Install main bearing cap and tighten bolts to specification. See TORQUE SPECIFICATIONS table at end of article. To install remaining components, reverse removal procedure.

Removal & Installation (3.9L & 5.2L W/Crankshaft Removed) – **1)** Remove rear crankshaft oil seals from cylinder block and main bearing cap. Install NEW rear crankshaft oil seal in cylinder block and main bearing cap.

2) Using Oil Seal Installer (C-3511), tap oil seal downward until oil seal installer is seated in main bearing bore in cylinder block and main bearing cap. Hold oil seal installer in this position and cut ends of oil seal even with main bearing cap or cylinder block surface.

3) Install end seals in main bearing cap. Seals extend from rope oil seal to end of main bearing cap. Coat oil seal with engine oil.

Removal & Installation (5.9L W/Crankshaft Installed) – **1)** Remove oil pan. See OIL PAN under REMOVAL & INSTALLATION. Remove oil pump and rear main bearing cap. Using small screwdriver, press on rear crankshaft oil seals to remove from cylinder block and main bearing cap.

CAUTION: Clean crankshaft, and lightly oil crankshaft surface and oil seal lips before installing. Rear crankshaft oil seal must be installed with paint stripe toward rear of engine. RTV sealant MUST be applied next to oil seal on main bearing cap surface to prevent oil leakage.

---

2) Rotate rear crankshaft oil seal in cylinder block with paint stripe toward rear of engine. Install rear crankshaft oil seal in main bearing cap with paint stripe toward rear of engine.

3) To prevent oil leakage, apply RTV sealant next to oil seal on main bearing cap surface before installing. Install main bearing cap, and tighten bolts to specification. See TORQUE SPECIFICATIONS table at end of article. To install remaining components, reverse removal procedure.

Removal & Installation (5.9L W/Crankshaft Removed) – Remove rear crankshaft oil seals from cylinder block and main bearing cap. Install rear crankshaft oil seals with paint stripe toward rear of engine. To prevent oil leakage, apply RTV sealant next to oil seal on main bearing cap surface before installing.

WATER PUMP

CAUTION: After removing fan clutch assembly, DO NOT place fan clutch with rear of shaft pointing downward. Silicone fluid from fan clutch may drain into fan drive bearing, causing lubricant failure.

Removal (Dakota) – **1)** Drain cooling system. Note direction of drive belt installation for reassembly reference.

CAUTION: Note direction of accessory drive belt routing. Belt must be installed in correct direction, or engine will overheat due to water pump rotating in wrong direction.

---

2) Remove fan clutch assembly bolts. Remove fan shroud bolts. Remove fan clutch assembly, fan shroud and water pump pulley. Disconnect necessary coolant hoses. Remove retaining bolts, water pump and gasket.

Installation – To install, reverse removal procedure using NEW gasket. Tighten bolts to specification. See TORQUE SPECIFICATIONS table at end of article. Fill system with coolant. Ensure accessory drive belt is installed in original direction to ensure proper rotation of water pump.

Removal (Pickup, Ramcharger & RWD Van) – **1)** Drain cooling system. On models equipped with A/C, remove radiator. On all models, remove drive belts, fan and spacer or fan clutch assembly (if equipped), pulley and bolts.

2) Remove front bracket supporting alternator and A/C compressor or idler pulley (if equipped). Position alternator aside. Remove air pump.

3) Remove power steering pump with hoses attached, and secure aside. Disconnect necessary coolant hoses. Remove retaining bolts, water pump and gasket.

Installation – To install, reverse removal procedure using NEW gasket. Tighten bolts to specification. See TORQUE SPECIFICATIONS table at end of article. Fill system with coolant.

OIL PAN

Removal (Dakota – 2WD) – **1)** Disconnect negative battery cable. Remove oil dipstick and distributor cap. Raise and support vehicle. Drain engine oil.

2) Remove exhaust pipe crossover. Remove side engine mount bolts. Slightly raise engine. When engine is at adequate height, install bolts in side engine mount-to-frame bracket holes to support engine.

3) Lower engine, and allow it to rest on bolts installed in side engine mounts. Remove retaining bolts, oil pan and gaskets.

Installation – To install, reverse removal procedure. Before installing oil pan, apply RTV sealant where front cover contacts cylinder block, oil pan side gaskets meet end seals and end seals contact cylinder block. *See Fig. 12.* Tighten bolts to specification. See TORQUE SPECIFICATIONS table at end of article. To install remaining components, reverse removal procedure.

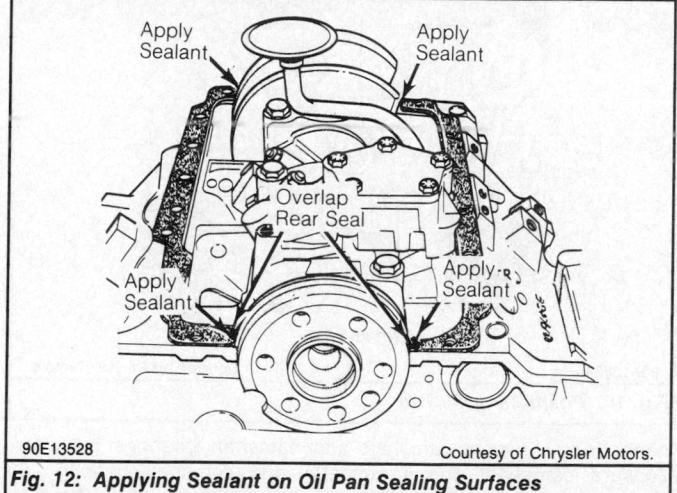

90E13528   Courtesy of Chrysler Motors.

Fig. 12: Applying Sealant on Oil Pan Sealing Surfaces

Removal (Dakota – 4WD) – **1)** Disconnect negative battery cable. Remove oil dipstick. Drain engine oil. Remove exhaust pipe crossover and lower transmission cover.

NOTE: Remove front drive axle for access to oil pan (if necessary). Axle shaft is splined into wheel hub and is retained by a nut.

---

2) For front drive axle removal, loosen wheel lug nuts. Remove cotter pin, lock nut and spring washer. Loosen axle shaft nut with vehicle on floor and brakes applied. Raise and support vehicle.

3) Remove wheels and skid plate. Remove axle shaft nut. Remove axle shaft-to-differential flange bolts at front drive axle. Support axle shaft, and separate axle splines from wheel hub by pulling inward at outer CV joint.

CAUTION: DO NOT pull on rubber boot during axle shaft removal. Pull on outer CV joint only.

4) Remove remaining axle shaft. Mark front drive shaft and transfer case yoke for reassembly reference. Remove front drive shaft from transfer case. Disconnect vacuum hoses from shift motor and electrical connections at shift indicator switch.

5) Support front drive axle using a floor jack. Remove front drive axle and shift motor retaining bolts. Lower floor jack, and remove front drive axle with drive shaft. Remove retaining bolts, oil pan and gaskets.

Installation – 1) To install, reverse removal procedure. Before installing oil pan, apply RTV sealant where front cover contacts cylinder block, oil pan side gaskets meet end seals and end seals contact cylinder block. *See Fig. 12.*

2) When installing front drive axle, loosely install all retaining bolts before tightening to specification. Tighten axle shaft nut to specification with vehicle on ground. See TORQUE SPECIFICATIONS table at end of article. Ensure reference marks on transfer case yoke and front drive shaft are aligned.

Removal (Pickup, Ramcharger & RWD Van – 3.9L) – 1) Disconnect negative battery cable. Remove oil dipstick, engine cover (RWD Van) and air cleaner assembly. Remove engine controller. Raise and support vehicle. Drain engine oil.

2) Remove transmission-to-engine braces. Loosen exhaust pipe support bracket. Remove starter, transmission dust shield, O₂ sensor and air injection tube.

3) Disconnect exhaust pipe. Remove right engine mount nut. Loosen, but DO NOT remove, left engine mount nut. Support right side of engine using jackstand. Remove transmission mount through bolt and support transmission using jackstand.

4) Raise engine and transmission enough for oil pan removal. Remove retaining bolts, oil pan and gaskets.

Installation – To install, reverse removal procedure. Before installing oil pan, apply RTV sealant where front cover contacts cylinder block, oil pan side gaskets meet end seals and end seals contact cylinder block. *See Fig. 12.* Tighten bolts to specification. See TORQUE SPECIFICATIONS table at end of article. To install remaining components, reverse removal procedure.

Removal (Pickup, Ramcharger & RWD Van – 5.2L & 5.9L) – Disconnect negative battery cable. Remove oil dipstick. Raise and support vehicle. Drain engine oil. Remove exhaust crossover pipe. Remove left engine-to-transmission brace. Remove retaining bolts, oil pan and gaskets.

Installation – To install, reverse removal procedure. Before installing oil pan, apply RTV sealant where front cover contacts cylinder block, oil pan side gaskets meet end seals and end seals contact cylinder block. *See Fig. 12.* Tighten bolts to specification. See TORQUE SPECIFICATIONS table at end of article. To install remaining components, reverse removal procedure.

OVERHAUL

CYLINDER HEAD

Cylinder Head – Check cylinder head warpage. Repair or replace cylinder head if warpage exceeds specification. See CYLINDER HEAD table under ENGINE SPECIFICATIONS at end of article.

Valve Springs – 1) Check valve spring free length, out-of-square and pressure. Replace valve spring if not within specification. See VALVES & VALVE SPRINGS table under ENGINE SPECIFICATIONS at end of article.

CAUTION: Installation of wrong spring on exhaust valves with valve rotators can cause severe engine damage. See VALVE SPRING IDENTIFICATION table.

VALVE SPRING IDENTIFICATION

Application	Number Of Coils
Exhaust Valve	
3.9L & 5.2L	5.8
5.9L	5.6
Intake Valve	6.4

2) Measure valve spring installed height from bottom of spring seat (cylinder head surface) to bottom of spring retainer. If spacers are installed, measure from top of spacer.

3) If height exceeds 1.688" (42.86 mm), install a .063" (1.58 mm) thick spacer in cylinder head counterbore to obtain correct installed spring height. See VALVES & VALVE SPRINGS table.

Valve Stem Oil Seals – Cup-type oil seals are used on all valves. Ensure oversize valve stem oil seals are used when oversize valves are installed. When installing valves, DO NOT overcompress valve springs, or damage to valve stem oil seal may result.

Valve Guides – 1) Check valve stem oil clearance. Ensure valve stem diameter is within specification. Valve guide must be reamed for valve with oversize valve stem if oil clearance exceeds specification. See CYLINDER HEAD table under ENGINE SPECIFICATIONS at end of article.

2) Valves are available with oversize valve stems of .005" (.13 mm), .015" (.38 mm) and .030" (.76 mm).

NOTE: DO NOT ream valve guides from standard to maximum oversize in one step. Ream valve guides to oversize in gradual steps so guides are reamed true in relation to valve seat. After reaming valve guides, valve seat runout must be checked.

Valve Seat – Check valve seat width and runout. Grind valve seat if not within specification. See CYLINDER HEAD table under ENGINE SPECIFICATIONS at end of article.

CAUTION: If valve seat is ground, valve stem installed height must be checked. See VALVE STEM INSTALLED HEIGHT.

Valve Stem Installed Height – Valve stem installed height should be checked if valves or valve seats are serviced. Measure valve stem installed height using Valve Stem Installed Height Gauge (C-3968). *See Fig. 13.* Grind off tip of valve stem if too long.

CAUTION: DO NOT grind tip of valve stem on models equipped with exhaust valve rotators.

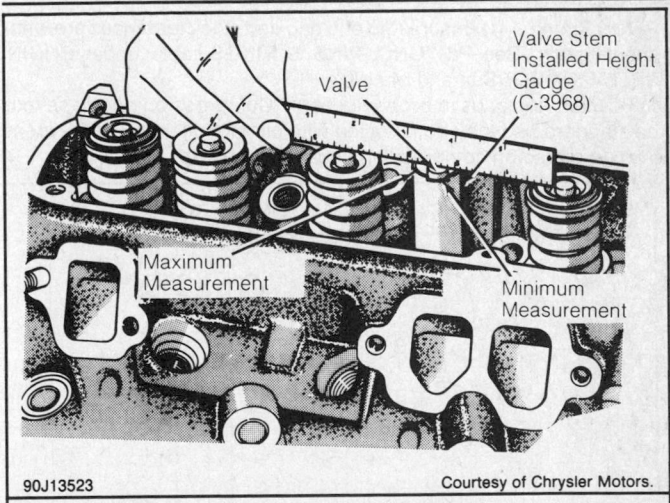

90J13523   Courtesy of Chrysler Motors.

Fig. 13: Measuring Valve Stem Installed Height

Valves – Ensure valve margin, head diameter and stem diameter are within specification. See VALVES & VALVE SPRINGS table under ENGINE SPECIFICATIONS at end of article. Valves are available with oversize valve stems of .005" (.13 mm), .015" (.38 mm) and .030" (.76 mm).

CAUTION: If valves are serviced, valve stem installed height must be checked. See VALVE STEM INSTALLED HEIGHT.

Valve Seat Correction Angles – Use a 15-degree stone to lower valve seat and a 65-degree stone to raise valve seat.

1992 ENGINES
3.9L V6, 5.2L V8 & 5.9L V8 (Cont.)

VALVE TRAIN

Rocker Arm & Pivot (3.9L & 5.2L) – Remove rocker arm and pivot. Inspect for wear. Replace as necessary.

Rocker Arm Shaft Assembly (5.9L) – **1)** If rocker arm components are to be separated, note rocker arm identification. *See Figs. 8 and 9.*

CAUTION: On engines with exhaust valve rotators, ensure rocker arm for exhaust valve contains relieved area for valve rotator clearance. See Fig. 8.

---

2) Install rocker arm and shaft assembly with notch on end of rocker arm shaft on bottom and toward front of engine (left bank) or rear of engine (right bank). Ensure long, stamped-steel retainers are installed on No. 2 and No. 4 rocker arm shaft retaining bolts. *See Fig. 9.*

Valve Lifters – Measure valve lifter diameter and bore diameter in cylinder block. Determine oil clearance. Clearance must be within specification. See VALVE LIFTERS table under ENGINE SPECIFICATIONS at end of article. Cylinder block can be bored for oversize lifters.

NOTE: Cylinder block must be marked to indicate oversize valve lifters. See SPECIAL ENGINE MARKS.

CYLINDER BLOCK ASSEMBLY

Piston & Rod Assembly – Install piston with notch on top of piston toward front of engine (timing chain end) with larger chamfer of connecting rod bore toward crankshaft journal fillet.

Fitting Pistons – **1)** Measure piston diameter at top of piston skirt at 90-degree angle to piston pin. Measure cylinder bore diameter below top surface of cylinder bore, middle of bore and bottom of cylinder bore.

2) Ensure piston diameter and clearance are within specification. See PISTONS, PINS & RINGS table under ENGINE SPECIFICATIONS at end of article.

NOTE: Piston diameter and cylinder bore should be measured at room temperature of approximately 70°F (21°C).

Piston Rings – **1)** Ensure ring end gap and side clearances are within specification. See PISTONS, PINS & RINGS table under ENGINE SPECIFICATIONS at end of article.

2) Position ring gaps in proper location. Compression ring gaps must be staggered so they do not align with oil ring rail gap. Ensure identification marks on compression rings face upward.

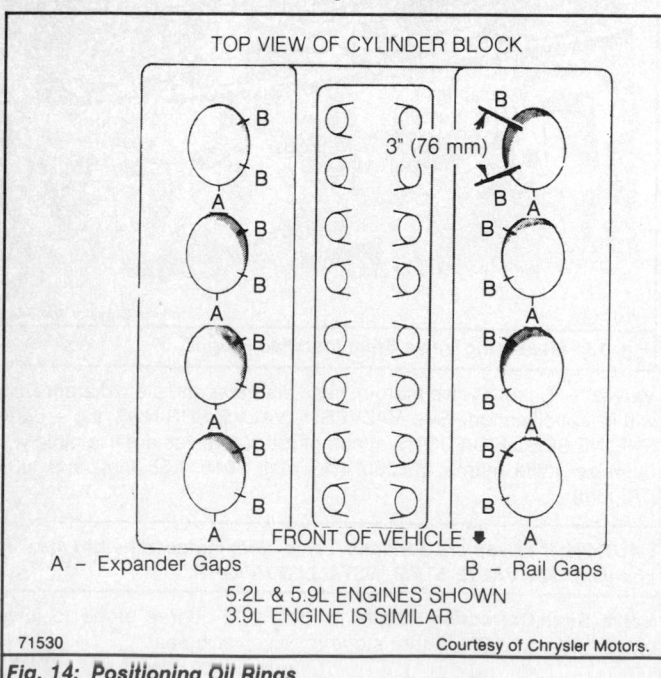

A – Expander Gaps   B – Rail Gaps
5.2L & 5.9L ENGINES SHOWN
3.9L ENGINE IS SIMILAR
71530   Courtesy of Chrysler Motors.

Fig. 14: Positioning Oil Rings

3) Oil ring expander ends should be butted under notch on front of piston. Oil ring rail gaps should be facing middle of engine when installed, and spread 3" (76 mm) apart. *See Fig. 14.*

Rod Bearings – **1)** Crankshaft is marked to indicate undersize rod bearings. See SPECIAL ENGINE MARKS. When replacing connecting rod bearings, ensure connecting rod is installed with larger chamfer of connecting rod bore toward crankshaft journal fillet.

2) Apply light coat of engine oil to connecting rod bolt threads before tightening nut to specification. See TORQUE SPECIFICATIONS table at end of article. Ensure oil clearance and side play are within specification. See CRANKSHAFT, MAIN & CONNECTING ROD BEARINGS table under ENGINE SPECIFICATIONS at end of article.

Crankshaft & Main Bearings – **1)** Crankshaft is marked to indicate undersize main bearings. See SPECIAL ENGINE MARKS. Main bearing cap location and direction of installation should be marked before removal.

2) Ensure journal diameter, taper and out-of-round are within specification. See CRANKSHAFT, MAIN & CONNECTING ROD BEARINGS table under ENGINE SPECIFICATIONS at end of article. Upper main bearings contain oil holes while lower bearings installed in main bearing cap do not.

3) Apply light coat of engine oil to threads before tightening bolt to specification. See TORQUE SPECIFICATIONS table at end of article.

4) Ensure oil clearance and end play are within specification. See CRANKSHAFT, MAIN & CONNECTING ROD BEARINGS table.

CAUTION: Crankshaft journal grinding should not exceed .012" (.30 mm) under standard size. DO NOT grind thrust surfaces of No. 2 main bearing (3.9L) or No. 3 main bearing (5.2L and 5.9L). With cast iron crankshafts, final paper or cloth polishing after regrind must be done in same direction as engine rotation.

Thrust Bearing – Thrust bearing is located on No. 2 main bearing on 3.9L or No. 3 main bearing on 5.2L and 5.9L. Replace thrust bearing if crankshaft end play is not within specification. See CRANKSHAFT, MAIN & CONNECTING ROD BEARINGS table under ENGINE SPECIFICATIONS at end of article.

Cylinder Block – **1)** Check cylinder bore, out-of-round and taper. Measure cylinder bore diameter below top surface of cylinder bore, middle of bore and bottom of cylinder bore.

NOTE: Cylinder bore should be measured at room temperature of approximately 70°F (21°C).

---

2) Bore cylinder block if bore diameter is not within specification. See CYLINDER BLOCK table under ENGINE SPECIFICATIONS at end of article. Cylinder block warpage information is not available from manufacturer.

3) Check valve lifter bore diameter. Check for scoring. If scoring exists or lifter bore diameter is not within specification, ream cylinder block bore for next oversize valve lifter. See VALVE LIFTERS table under ENGINE SPECIFICATIONS at end of article.

NOTE: Cylinder block must be marked to indicate oversize valve lifters. See SPECIAL ENGINE MARKS.

ENGINE OILING

ENGINE LUBRICATION SYSTEM

System has a rotor-type oil pump and full-flow oil filter. Oil is forced by pump through a series of oil passages in engine to provide lubrication to engine components.

On 3.9L and 5.2L oil is supplied to rocker assembly through hollow pushrods. Pushrods are fed oil from lifters.

On 5.9L, oil is supplied to hollow rocker arm shaft (left side) from No. 2 camshaft bearing and hollow rocker arm shaft (right side) No. 4 bearing through indexed holes in camshaft. Oil flows to one support pedestal on each head and into a rocker shaft to lubricate upper valve components.

Crankcase Capacity – Oil capacity with oil filter is **4.5 qts. (4.3L)**.
Oil Pressure – Oil pressure is **6 psi (.4 kg/cm²)** at idle or **30-80 psi (2.1-5.6 kg/cm²)** at 3000 RPM with engine at normal operating temperature.

OIL PUMP

Removal & Disassembly – **1)** Remove oil pan. See OIL PAN under REMOVAL & INSTALLATION. Remove retaining bolts and oil pump from rear main bearing cap.
2) Remove cotter pin, drill a 1/8" (3.2 mm) hole into relief valve retainer cap and insert a self-tapping sheet metal screw into cap. Clamp screw into vise. While supporting pump, remove retainer cap by tapping pump body using soft-faced hammer.
3) Discard retainer cap, and remove spring and relief valve. Remove pump cover and discard oil seal ring. Remove inner rotor and shaft and outer rotor. *See Fig. 15.*

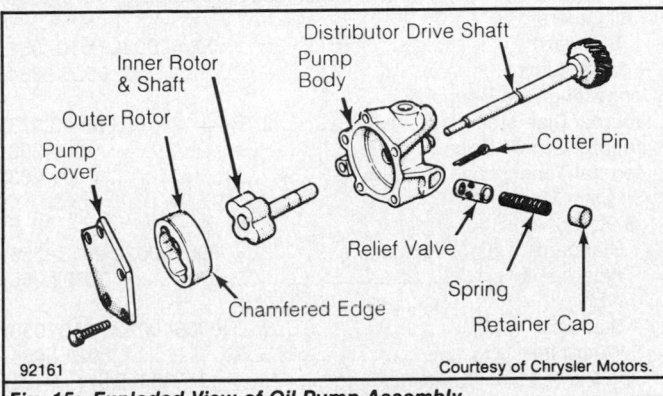

92161	Courtesy of Chrysler Motors.

Fig. 15: Exploded View of Oil Pump Assembly

Inspection – **1)** Inspect components for damage. Using feeler gauge and straightedge, check pump cover flatness. Measure thickness of inner and outer rotors. Measure outer rotor outside diameter. Replace rotors if not to specification. See OIL PUMP SPECIFICATIONS table.
2) Install outer rotor into pump body. Press outer rotor to one side, and measure clearance between outer rotor and pump body. Replace oil pump assembly if clearance exceeds specification. See OIL PUMP SPECIFICATIONS table.
3) With outer rotor installed in pump body, install inner rotor and shaft into pump body. Measure rotor tip clearance between inner and outer rotors. Replace rotors if clearance exceeds specification. See OIL PUMP SPECIFICATIONS table.
4) With rotors installed in pump body, place a straightedge (between bolt holes) across face of pump body. Measure rotor end clearance between rotors and straightedge. Replace oil pump assembly if clearance exceeds specification. See OIL PUMP SPECIFICATIONS table.
5) Ensure relief valve slides freely in bore. Check free length and tension of relief valve spring. Replace spring if not within specification. See OIL PUMP SPECIFICATIONS table.

OIL PUMP SPECIFICATIONS

Application	Specification
Inner & Outer Rotor Thickness	.825" (20.96 mm) Min.
Outer Rotor Diameter	2.47" (62.7 mm) Min.
Outer Rotor-To-Pump Body Clearance	.014" (.36 mm) Max.
Pump Cover Flatness	.0015" (.038 mm) Max.
Rotor End Clearance	.004" (.10 mm)
Rotor Tip Clearance	.008" (.20 mm) Max.
Spring Free Length	1.95" (49.5 mm)
Spring Tension	19.5-20.5 lbs. @ 1.34" (8.8-9.3 kg @ 34.0 mm)

CAUTION: Ensure oil pump fully engages with distributor drive shaft before tightening retaining bolt. It may be necessary to slightly rotate oil pump during installation to align with distributor drive shaft.

Reassembly & Installation – To reassemble, reverse disassembly procedure. Install NEW relief valve retainer cap and oil seal ring. Tighten pump cover bolts. Fill rotor cavity with engine oil before installing. To install, reverse removal procedure.

TORQUE SPECIFICATIONS

TORQUE SPECIFICATIONS

Application	Ft. Lbs. (N.m)
Axle Bracket-To-Bellhousing Bolt	
Dakota 4WD	65 (88)
Axle Shaft Nut	
Dakota 4WD	190 (258)
Axle Shaft-To-Differential Flange Bolt	
Dakota 4WD	65 (88)
Axle-To-Insulator Bolt	
Dakota 4WD	75 (102)
Camshaft Sprocket Bolt	50 (68)
Camshaft Thrust Plate Bolt	18 (24)
Clutch Housing-To-Cylinder Block Bolt	
Dakota & RWD Van	
[1]	30 (41)
[2]	50 (68)
All Others	40 (54)
Connecting Rod Nut	45 (61)
Crankshaft Pulley Bolt	17 (23)
Cylinder Head Bolt [3]	
Step 1	50 (68)
Step 2	105 (142)
Step 3	Recheck At 105 (142)
Differential Pinion Nose Bracket-To-Adapter Bolt	
Dakota 4WD	65 (88)
Differential Pinion Nose Bracket-To-Bellhousing Bolt	
Dakota 4WD	65 (88)
Engine Mount Bracket-To-Frame Rail Bolt	
Dakota 2WD	30 (41)
Engine Mount Through Bolt	
Dakota 2WD	50 (68)
Dakota 4WD	75 (102)
Engine Mount-To-Cylinder Block Bolt	
Dakota	30 (41)
Engine Mount-To-Frame Bracket Bolt/Nut	
Pickup & Ramcharger	75 (102)
RWD Van	68 (92)
Exhaust Manifold	
3.9L & 5.2L	
Bolt & Nut	25 (34)
5.9L	
Bolt	20 (27)
Nut	15 (20)
Flywheel/Flexplate-To-Crankshaft Bolt	55 (75)
Front Cover Bolt	30 (41)
Intake Manifold Bolt [4]	
3.9L & 5.2L	See INCH LBS.
5.9L	
Step 1	All Bolts Finger Tight
Step 2	25 (34)
Step 3	40 (54)
Step 4	Recheck At 40 (54)
Main Bearing Cap Bolt	85 (115)
Oil Filter Adapter Stud	50 (68)
Oil Pan Bolt	17 (23)
Oil Pump Bolt	30 (41)
Rocker Arm Bolt (3.9L & 5.2L)	21 (28)
Rocker Arm Shaft Bolt (5.9L)	17 (23)

[1] – Bolts through clutch housing into cylinder block.
[2] – Bolts through cylinder block into clutch housing.
[3] – Tighten bolts in sequence. *See Fig. 5.*
[4] – Tighten bolts in sequence. *See Figs. 2-4.*

TORQUE SPECIFICATIONS (Cont.)

Application	Ft. Lbs. (N.m)
Shift Motor Bolt	
Dakota 4WD	65 (88)
Spark Plug	30 (41)
Transfer Case Yolk Bolt	
Dakota 4WD	20 (27)
Transmission-To-Cylinder Block Bolt	30 (41)
Vibration Damper Bolt	135 (183)
Water Pump Bolt	30 (41)
Wheel Lug Nut	
1/2"	95 (129)
5/8"	200 (271)

Application	INCH Lbs. (N.m)
Intake Manifold Bolt [4]	
3.9L	
Step 1	[5]
Step 2	Remaining Bolts 72 (8)
Step 3	Recheck At 72 (8)
Step 4	144 (16)
Step 5	Recheck At 144 (16)
5.2L	
Step 1	[6]
Step 2	Remaining Bolts 72 (8)
Step 3	Recheck At 72 (8)
Step 4	144 (16)
Step 5	Recheck At 144 (16)
Oil Pump Cover Bolt	95 (11)
Valve Cover Bolts	80 (9)

[5] – Tighten bolts 1 and 2 in sequence to 72 INCH lbs. (8 N.m) alternating in steps of 12 INCH lbs. (1.4 N.m). *See Fig. 2.*

[6] – Tighten bolts 1 through 4 in sequence to 72 INCH lbs. (8 N.m) alternating in steps of 12 INCH lbs. (1.4 N.m). *See Fig. 3.*

ENGINE SPECIFICATIONS

GENERAL SPECIFICATIONS

Application	Specification
3.9L	
Displacement	239 Cu. In. (3.9L)
Bore	3.91" (99.3 mm)
Stroke	3.31" (84.1 mm)
Compression Ratio	9.0:1
Fuel System	PFI
Horsepower @ RPM	180 @ 4800
Torque Ft. Lbs. @ RPM	225 @ 3200
5.2L	
Displacement	318 Cu. In. (5.2L)
Bore	3.91" (99.3 mm)
Stroke	3.31" (84.1 mm)
Compression Ratio	9.0:1
Fuel System	PFI
Horsepower @ RPM	230 @ 4800
Torque Ft. Lbs. @ RPM	280 @ 3200
5.9L	
Displacement	360 Cu. In. (5.9L)
Bore	4.00" (101.6 mm)
Stroke	3.58" (90.9 mm)
Compression Ratio	8.1:1
Fuel System	TBI
Horsepower @ RPM	190 @ 4000
Torque Ft. Lbs. @ RPM	292 @ 2400

CRANKSHAFT, MAIN & CONNECTING ROD BEARINGS

Application	In. (mm)
3.9L, 5.2L & 5.9L	
Crankshaft End Play	
Standard	.002-.007 (.05-.18)
Wear Limit	.010 (.25)
Main Bearings	
Journal Diameter	
3.9L & 5.2L	2.4995-2.5005 (63.487-63.513)
5.9L	2.8095-2.8105 (71.361-71.387)
Journal Out-Of-Round	.001 (.03)
Journal Taper	.001 (.03)
Oil Clearance	
Journal No. 1	
Standard	.0005-.0015 (.013-.038)
Wear Limit	.0015 (.038)
All Others	
Standard	.0005-.0020 (.013-.051)
Wear Limit	.0025 (.064)
Connecting Rod Bearings	
Journal Diameter	2.124-2.125 (53.950-53.975)
Journal Out-Of-Round	.001 (.03)
Journal Taper	.001 (.03)
Oil Clearance	
3.9L & 5.2L	
Standard	.0005-.0022 (.013-.056)
Wear Limit	.0022 (.056)
5.9L	
Standard	.0005-.0022 (.013-.056)
Wear Limit	.0025 (.064)
Side Play	.006-.014 (.15-.36)

PISTONS, PINS & RINGS

Application	In. (mm)
3.9L, 5.2L & 5.9L	
Pistons	
Clearance	.0005-.0015 (.013-.038)
Pins	
Piston Fit	.00025-.00075 (.0064-.0191)
Rod Fit	Press Fit
Rings	
No. 1 & No. 2	
End Gap	.010-.020 (.25-.51)
Side Clearance	.0015-.0030 (.038-.076)
No. 3 (Oil)	
End Gap	.015-.055 (.38-1.40)
Side Clearance	
3.9L & 5.2L	.0002-.0080 (.005-.203)
5.9L	.0002-.0050 (.005-.127)

CYLINDER BLOCK

Application	In. (mm)
3.9L, 5.2L & 5.9L	
Cylinder Bore	
Standard Diameter	
3.9L & 5.2L	3.910-3.912 (99.31-99.36)
5.9L	4.000-4.002 (101.60-101.61)
Maximum Taper	.010 (.25)
Maximum Out-Of-Round	.005 (.13)

1992 ENGINES
3.9L V6, 5.2L V8 & 5.9L V8 (Cont.)

VALVES & VALVE SPRINGS

Application	Specification
3.9L, 5.2L & 5.9L	
Intake Valves	
Face Angle	
3.9L & 5.2L	43.25-43.75°
5.9L	45°
Head Diameter	1.880" (47.75 mm)
Minimum Margin	.047" (1.19 mm)
Stem Diameter	
3.9L & 5.2L	.313 (7.94)
5.9L	.372-.373" (9.45-9.47 mm)
Exhaust Valves	
Face Angle	
3.9L & 5.2L	43.5°
5.9L	45°
Head Diameter	
3.9L & 5.2L	1.60" (40.64 mm)
5.9L	1.617" (41.07 mm)
Minimum Margin	.047" (1.19 mm)
Stem Diameter	
3.9L & 5.2L	.313 (7.94)
5.9L	.371-.372" (9.42-9.45 mm)
Valve Springs	
Free Length	
Intake	2.00" (50.8 mm)
Exhaust	1.81" (45.9 mm)
Installed Height	
Intake	1.625-1.687" (41.27-42.86 mm)
Exhaust	1.453-1.516" (36.91-38.51 mm)
Out-Of-Square	.078" (1.98 mm)

	Lbs. @ In. (kg @ mm)
Pressure	
Valve Closed	
Intake	78-88 @ 1.687 (35-40 @ 42.85)
Exhaust	80-90 @ 1.484 (36-41 @ 37.70)
Valve Open	
Intake	170-184 @ 1.313 (77-83 @ 33.35)
Exhaust	
3.9L & 5.2L	180-194 @ 1.063 (81-88 @ 27.00)
5.9L	181-197 @ 1.063 (82-89 @ 27.00)

CYLINDER HEAD

Application	Specification
3.9L, 5.2L & 5.9L	
Maximum Warpage	.00075" Per 1" (.0191 mm Per 25 mm)
Valve Seats	
Intake Valve	
Seat Angle	
3.9L & 5.2L	44.5°
5.9L	45°
Seat Width	
3.9L & 5.2L	.040-.060" (1.0-1.5 mm)
5.9L	.065-.085" (1.65-2.16 mm)
Maximum Seat Runout	.003" (.08 mm)
Exhaust Valve	
Seat Angle	
3.9L & 5.2L	44.5°
5.9L	45°
Seat Width	
3.9L & 5.2L	.060-.080" (1.5-2.0 mm)
5.9L	.080-.100" (2.0-2.5 mm)
Maximum Seat Runout	.003" (.08 mm)
Valve Guides	
Intake Valve	
Valve Guide I.D.	
3.9L & 5.2L	.313-.314" (7.94-7.98 mm)
5.9L	.374-.375" (9.50-9.53 mm)

CYLINDER HEAD (Cont.)

Application	Specification
Valve Stem-To-Guide	
Oil Clearance	
Standard	.001-.003" (.02-.08 mm)
Wear Limit	[1] .017" (.43 mm)
Exhaust Valve	
Valve Guide I.D.	
3.9L & 5.2L	.313-.314" (7.94-7.98 mm)
5.9L	.374-.375" (9.50-9.53 mm)
Valve Stem-To-Guide	
Oil Clearance	
Standard	.002-.004" (.05-.10 mm)
Wear Limit	[1] .017" (.43 mm)

[1] – Specification applies to method obtained by rocking valve stem in valve guide.

CAMSHAFT [1]

Application	In. (mm)
3.9L, 5.2L & 5.9L	
End Play	.002-.010 (.05-.25)
Camshaft Bearing I.D.	
3.9L	
No. 1	2.000-2.001 (50.80-50.82)
No. 2	1.984-1.985 (50.39-50.42)
No. 3	1.953-1.954 (49.61-49.63)
No. 4	1.5625-1.5635 (39.688-39.713)
5.2L & 5.9L	
No. 1	2.000-2.001 (50.80-50.82)
No. 2	1.984-1.985 (50.39-50.42)
No. 3	1.969-1.970 (50.01-50.03)
No. 4	1.953-1.954 (49.61-49.63)
No. 5	1.5625-1.5635 (39.688-39.713)
Journal Diameter	
3.9L	
No. 1	1.998-1.999 (50.75-50.77)
No. 2	1.982-1.983 (50.34-50.37)
No. 3	1.951-1.952 (49.56-49.58)
No. 4	1.5605-1.5615 (39.637-39.662)
5.2L & 5.9L	
No. 1	1.998-1.999 (50.75-50.77)
No. 2	1.982-1.983 (50.34-50.37)
No. 3	1.967-1.968 (49.97-49.99)
No. 4	1.951-1.952 (49.56-49.58)
No. 5	1.5605-1.5615 (39.637-39.662)
Oil Clearance	
Standard	.001-.003 (.02-.08)
Wear Limit	.005 (.13)

[1] – Bearings are numbered from front of camshaft.

VALVE LIFTERS

Application	In. (mm)
3.9L, 5.2L & 5.9L	
Bore Diameter	.9051-.9059 (22.990-23.010)
Lifter Diameter	[1] .9035-.9040 (22.949-22.962)
Oil Clearance	.0011-.0024 (.028-.061)

[1] – Standard diameter valve lifter is listed. Oversize valve lifters are available in .001" (.02 mm), .008" (.20 mm) and .030" (.76 mm).

1992 ENGINES
Cummins Diesel "B" Series 5.9L 6-Cylinder

D250/350 Pickup, W250/350 Pickup

NOTE: For repair procedures not covered in this article, see ENGINE OVERHAUL PROCEDURES article in GENERAL INFORMATION.

ENGINE IDENTIFICATION

Engine may be identified by eighth character of Vehicle Identification Number (VIN). VIN is stamped on a metal tab located near lower left corner of windshield.

Engine model code, serial number and Control Parts List (CPL) number are listed on engine data plate. Engine data plate is mounted on fuel injection pump side of timing gear cover. *See Fig. 1.* Serial number and CPL may be required when ordering replacement engine components.

ENGINE IDENTIFICATION CODES

Application	Code
5.9L 6-Cylinder Turbo Diesel	
VIN Engine Code	8
Data Plate Model Code	6BT

ADJUSTMENTS

VALVE CLEARANCE ADJUSTMENT

NOTE: Valve clearance must be adjusted with engine temperature less than 140°F (60°C).

1) Engine can be rotated by removing dust cover from transmission adapter plate and installing Engine Barring Tool (3377462) in adapter plate. *See Fig. 1.* Rotate engine clockwise until No. 1 cylinder is at TDC. Engage timing pin.

CAUTION: Use care when engaging timing pin to avoid breaking tip of timing pin. Ensure timing pin is disengaged before rotating engine.

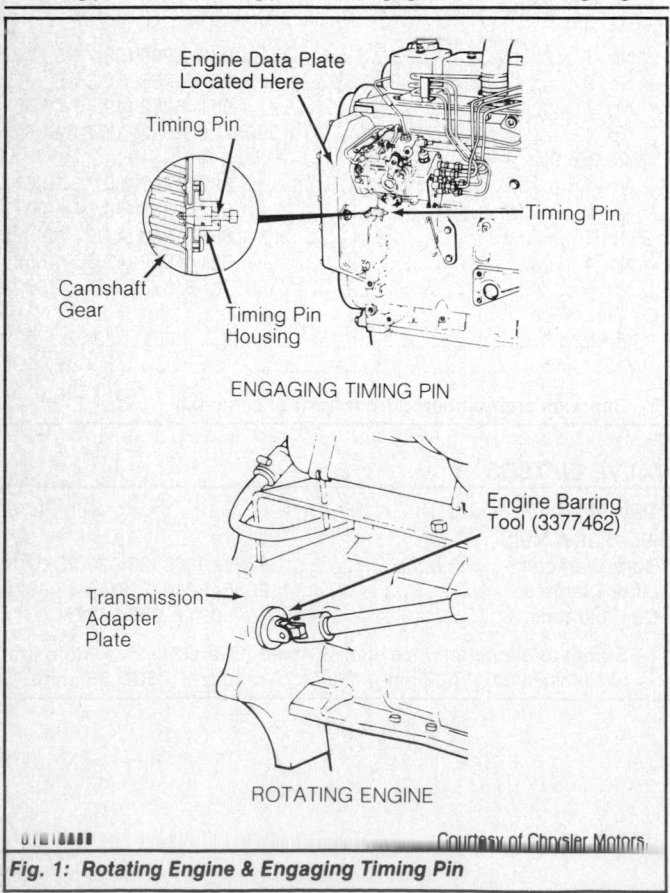

Fig. 1: Rotating Engine & Engaging Timing Pin

2) Remove rocker lever covers, and ensure No. 1 cylinder push rods are loose and valves are closed. If cylinder push rods are not loose or valves are not closed, disengage timing pin and rotate engine 360 degrees. With No. 1 cylinder at TDC, check clearance on proper valves. See VALVE ADJUSTING SEQUENCE table. If clearance is not as specified, adjust using rocker lever adjusting screw. See VALVE CLEARANCE SPECIFICATIONS table.

3) Once valves are checked and adjusted, place reference marks on vibration damper and front timing gear cover. Disengage timing pin, rotate engine 360 degrees, and realign reference marks.

4) Check clearance on proper valves. See VALVE ADJUSTING SEQUENCE table. Adjust clearance if not to specification. See VALVE CLEARANCE SPECIFICATIONS table.

VALVE ADJUSTING SEQUENCE

Procedure	Cylinder Number
Step 1 [1]	
Exhaust Valves	1, 3 & 5
Intake Valves	1, 2 & 4
Step 2 [2]	
Exhaust Valves	2, 4 & 6
Intake Valves	3, 5 & 6

[1] – Adjust clearance with engine cold, timing pin engaged and No. 1 cylinder at TDC.

[2] – Rotate engine 360 degrees from TDC of No. 1 cylinder, and align reference marks.

VALVE CLEARANCE SPECIFICATIONS

Application	[1] In. (mm)
Exhaust Valves	.020 (.51)
Intake Valves	.010 (.25)

[1] – Adjust clearance with engine temperature less than 140°F (60°C).

FUEL INJECTION PUMP TIMING

CAUTION: Special washer must be placed under lock bolt before rotating engine to allow fuel injection pump to rotate. If special washer is not in place, loosen lock bolt and install special washer. Tighten lock bolt to 10 ft. lbs. (14 N.m). See Fig. 17.

1) Ensure special washer is placed under lock bolt. *See Fig. 17.* Rotate engine clockwise until No. 1 cylinder is at TDC. Engage timing pin. *See Fig. 1.* Engine can be rotated by removing dust cover from transmission adapter plate and installing Engine Barring Tool (3377462) in adapter plate.

2) Remove plug from end of fuel injection pump. Install timing indicator in end of fuel injection pump. *See Fig. 2.* It may be necessary to remove some high-pressure fuel lines for timing indicator installation.

NOTE: Note timing indicator range and amount of travel in one revolution. This reading may vary with type of timing indicator used.

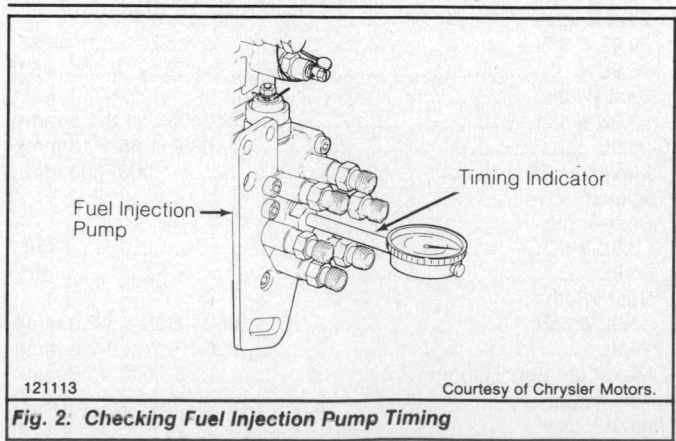

121113   Courtesy of Chrysler Motors.

Fig. 2. Checking Fuel Injection Pump Timing

3) Ensure timing indicator has at least .079" (2.00 mm) of travel. Disengage timing pin. Rotate engine in opposite direction of rotation until dial indicator stops moving. Adjust dial indicator to zero.

1992 ENGINES
Cummins Diesel "B" Series 5.9L 6-Cylinder (Cont.)

CHRY
5-41

4) Rotate engine in direction of rotation to TDC of No. 1 cylinder while counting number of revolutions of dial indicator. Ensure timing pin engages. Reading is plunger lift.

5) Plunger lift should be **0.05" (1.25 mm)**. If plunger lift is not as specified, loosen mounting nuts, and rotate fuel injection pump on mounting studs to obtain correct plunger lift. Tighten mounting nuts to **18 ft. lbs. (24 N.m)**.

6) If new or replacement fuel injection pump is installed, place timing mark on fuel injection pump flange to align with timing mark on gear housing. *See Fig. 17.*

7) Remove timing indicator, and install plug. Tighten plug to **84 INCH lbs. (10 N.m)**. Ensure timing pin is disengaged. Bleed high-pressure fuel lines if fuel lines were disconnected. See FUEL LINE BLEEDING.

THROTTLE POSITION SENSOR (TPS)

NOTE: *Throttle Position Sensor (TPS) is used only on A/T models.*

CAUTION: *Before adjusting TPS, ensure cable rod is adjusted so control lever contacts low-speed screw when in idle position. Ensure control lever moves over center position and rests against break-over spring when in full throttle position. See Fig. 3.*

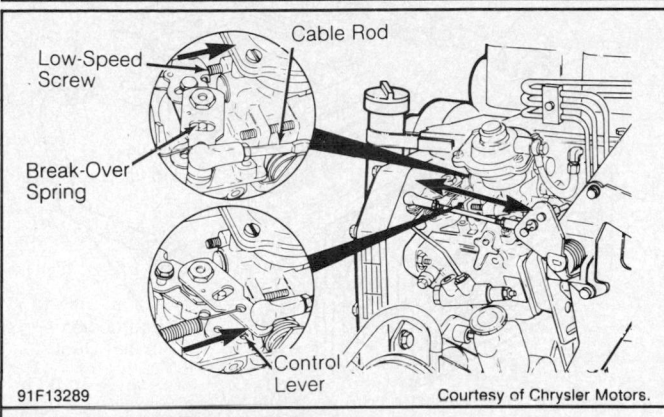

Fig. 3: *Adjusting Throttle Linkage*

1) Connect negative probe of voltmeter to ground. Turn ignition on. Backprobe center wire terminal of TPS electrical connector. With control lever contacting low-speed screw (idle position), voltage should be at least one volt. If voltage is not at least one volt, adjust TPS to obtain correct voltage using 10-mm wrench. *See Fig. 4.*

2) Open throttle to full throttle position. Ensure control lever moves over center position and rests against break-over spring when in full throttle position. *See Fig. 3.* Backprobe center wire terminal at TPS electrical connector.

3) Voltage should be at least 2.25 volts higher than voltage obtained with throttle in idle position. If voltage is not at least 2.25 volts higher than idle position voltage, adjust TPS to obtain correct voltage. *See Fig. 4.*

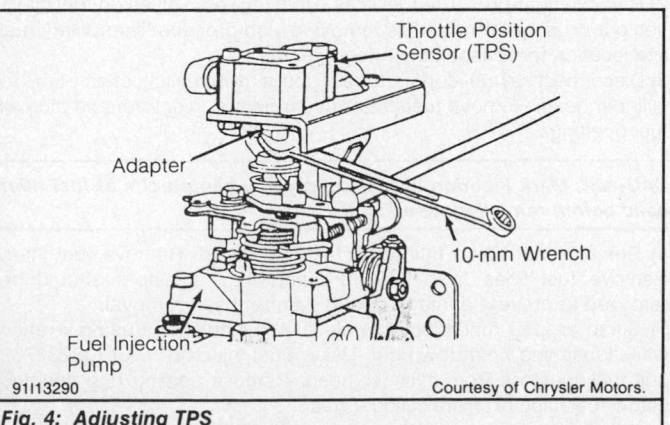

Fig. 4: *Adjusting TPS*

FUEL LINE BLEEDING

WARNING: *DO NOT bleed fuel lines on hot engine, as high exhaust temperatures could cause fire. Use care when bleeding fuel lines, as fuel is under extreme pressure and could penetrate skin, causing personal injury.*

1) To bleed low-pressure fuel lines and fuel filter, open fuel bleed screw on banjo bolt. *See Fig. 5.*

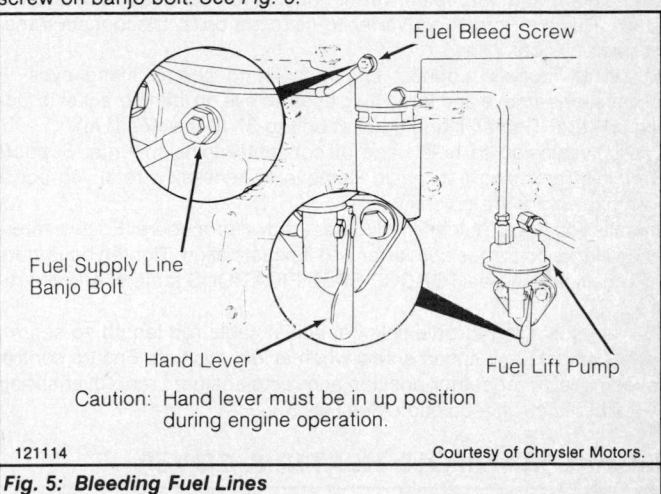

Fig. 5: *Bleeding Fuel Lines*

2) Operate hand lever on fuel lift pump until steady fuel stream flows from fuel bleed screw. Tighten fuel bleed screw to **72 INCH lbs. (8 N.m)**. If hand lever feels like fuel lift pump is not operating, rotate engine 90 degrees, and repeat procedure. Position hand lever in upward position once fuel line is bled.

CAUTION: *Fuel lift pump hand lever must be in upward position once fuel lines are bled.*

3) To bleed high-pressure fuel lines, carefully loosen fuel line nut at fuel injector. Operate starter until steady fuel flow exists, and then tighten fuel line nut to specification. See TORQUE SPECIFICATIONS table at end of article.

CAUTION: *DO NOT operate starter for more than 30 seconds. Allow 2-minute intervals between starter operations.*

4) Start engine, and repeat procedure on each fuel line until engine operates smoothly.

REMOVAL & INSTALLATION

NOTE: *For installation reference, label all electrical connectors, vacuum hoses and fuel lines before removal. Also place mating marks on engine hood and other major assemblies before removal.*

WARNING: *When battery is disconnected, vehicle computer and memory systems may lose memory data. Driveability problems may exist until computer systems have completed a relearn cycle. See COMPUTER RELEARN PROCEDURES article in GENERAL INFORMATION before disconnecting battery.*

ENGINE

Removal – 1) Remove battery. Scribe hood hinges, and remove hood. Drain cooling system and engine oil. Remove fan and fan clutch as an assembly. Remove fan shroud and radiator.

2) Disconnect necessary electrical connections and coolant hoses. Disconnect and remove intercooler outlet duct from intercooler and intake manifold. *See Fig. 7.* Disconnect and remove intercooler inlet duct from turbo and intercooler.

CHRY
5-42

1992 ENGINES
Cummins Diesel "B" Series 5.9L 6-Cylinder (Cont.)

3) Disconnect air inlet tube from turbo. Disconnect control linkages from control lever on fuel injection pump. DO NOT remove control lever from fuel injection pump. *See Fig. 3.*

4) Disconnect exhaust pipe at turbo. On A/C-equipped models, remove A/C compressor with lines attached and secure aside. Disconnect power steering lines, vacuum pump lines and fuel lines.

5) On A/T models, remove torque converter cover. Mark torque converter-to-flexplate position for reassembly reference. Attach "C" clamp on front of torque converter housing to hold torque converter in place. Remove torque converter-to-flexplate bolts. Disconnect transmission oil cooler lines.

6) On all models, connect engine hoist to engine lifting eyes. If necessary, remove and turn lifting eyes so eye on lifting bracket is facing upward. Tighten lifting bracket bolt to **57 ft. lbs. (77 N.m).**

7) Apply tension to hoist, and disconnect engine mounts. Support transmission using floor jack. Remove transmission retaining bolts. Remove engine from vehicle.

Installation – 1) To install, reverse removal procedure. Ensure reference marks on torque converter and flexplate align. Tighten bolts/nuts to specification. See TORQUE SPECIFICATIONS table at end of article.

2) When installing throttle linkage, adjust cable rod length so control lever contacts low-speed screw when in idle position. Ensure control lever moves over center position and rests against break-over spring when in full throttle position. *See Fig. 3.*

INTAKE MANIFOLD HEATER & COVER

NOTE: Intake manifold heater is installed between air inlet housing and intake manifold covers.

Removal – 1) Disconnect intercooler outlet duct from air inlet housing. *See Fig. 7.* Remove high-pressure fuel lines. Hold delivery valves on fuel injection pump using wrench while removing high-pressure lines. Mark fuel line location for reassembly reference.

2) Disconnect intake manifold heater electrical connector. Disconnect fuel heater ground wire (located above fuel filter) from intake manifold cover. Remove retaining bolts, air inlet housing and gasket.

3) Remove intake manifold heater and gasket. Disconnect electrical connectors from charge air temperature sensor and air temperature switch on intake manifold cover. Remove retaining bolts, intake manifold cover and gasket.

Installation – To install, reverse removal procedure using new gaskets. Apply thread sealant to intake manifold cover bolts before installing. Tighten bolts to specification. See TORQUE SPECIFICATIONS table at end of article. Install and bleed high-pressure fuel lines. See FUEL LINE BLEEDING.

EXHAUST MANIFOLD & TURBO

Removal – 1) Disconnect air inlet tube and exhaust pipe from turbo. Remove and plug turbo oil lines. Remove intercooler inlet duct from turbo and intercooler. *See Fig. 7.*

2) Remove retaining nuts, turbo and gasket. Remove coolant line bracket-to-exhaust manifold bolts. Remove retaining bolts, exhaust manifold and gasket.

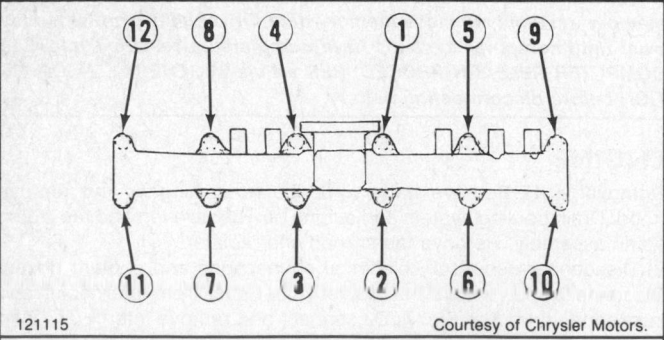

121115   Courtesy of Chrysler Motors.
Fig. 6: Exhaust Manifold Bolt Tightening Sequence

Installation – 1) To install, reverse removal procedure using new gaskets. Tighten exhaust manifold bolts to specification in sequence. *See Fig. 6.* See TORQUE SPECIFICATIONS table at end of article.

2) Install oil drain tube on turbo. Before installing oil supply line, pour **3 ozs. (60 cc)** of clean oil in oil inlet while spinning turbo. To install remaining components, reverse removal procedure. Tighten bolts/nuts to specification. See TORQUE SPECIFICATIONS table.

INTERCOOLER

Removal – 1) Remove grille. Remove front support bracket, located above center of intercooler. On A/C-equipped models, discharge A/C system using approved refrigerant recovery/recycling equipment.

2) Remove bolt from center of sealing plate on A/C lines at condenser. Remove condenser-to-intercooler retaining nuts. Lift condenser and sealing plate from intercooler. Plug all A/C lines to prevent contamination.

3) Remove intercooler inlet and outlet ducts. *See Fig. 7.* Remove intercooler retaining bolts. Pivot intercooler forward and upward to remove.

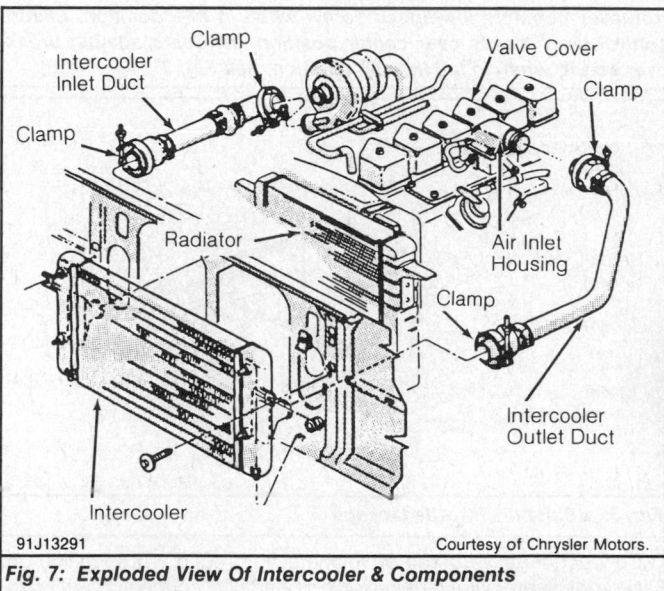

91J13291   Courtesy of Chrysler Motors.
Fig. 7: Exploded View Of Intercooler & Components

Installation – To install, reverse removal procedure. Tighten bolts/nuts to specification. See TORQUE SPECIFICATIONS table at end of article. Evacuate and recharge A/C system (if equipped).

CYLINDER HEAD

Removal – 1) Drain cooling system and engine oil. Disconnect necessary coolant hoses and electrical connections. Remove exhaust manifold and turbo. See EXHAUST MANIFOLD & TURBO under REMOVAL & INSTALLATION. Remove throttle linkage and bracket (if necessary).

2) Remove high-pressure fuel lines. Hold delivery valves on fuel injection pump using wrench while removing high-pressure lines. Mark fuel line location for reassembly reference.

3) Disconnect air/fuel control tube. Tube is from fuel injection pump to cylinder head. Remove fuel drain lines from fuel injectors, and plug all fuel openings.

CAUTION: Mark location of fuel supply line banjo bolts at fuel filter head before removing. See Fig. 5.

4) Remove fuel banjo fittings at fuel filter head. Remove fuel filter. Remove fuel lines from fuel lift pump. Fuel injectors should be removed to prevent damage during cylinder head removal.

5) Clean around fuel injector. Hold fuel injector body using wrench while loosening hold-down nut. Using Fuel Injector Puller (3823276), pull fuel injectors from cylinder head. Remove sealing ring (located below fuel injector) from cylinder head.

1992 ENGINES
Cummins Diesel "B" Series 5.9L 6-Cylinder (Cont.)

CHRY
5-43

6) Remove rocker lever assembly and push rods. See ROCKER LEVER ASSEMBLY & PUSH RODS under REMOVAL & INSTALLATION. Remove cylinder head bolts in sequence. See Fig. 8. Remove cylinder head and gasket.

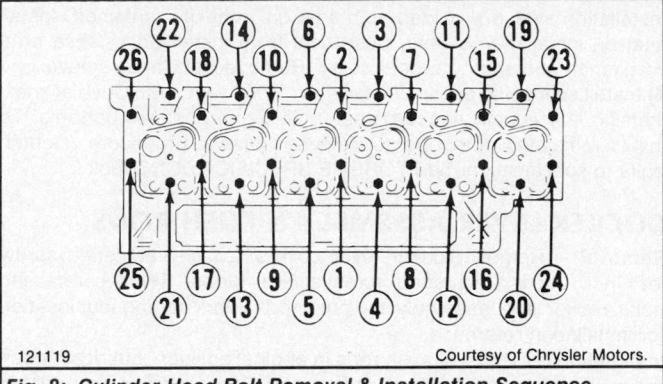

121119   Courtesy of Chrysler Motors.

Fig. 8: Cylinder Head Bolt Removal & Installation Sequence

Inspection – 1) Inspect cylinder head for warpage at deck surface. Resurface cylinder head if warpage exceeds specification. See CYLINDER HEAD table under ENGINE SPECIFICATIONS at end of article. Replace cylinder head if total metal removed exceeds .0393" (.998 mm).

NOTE: Amount of material removed from cylinder head should be stamped on lower right rear corner of cylinder head, above deck surface.

2) Inspect cylinder block warpage. Warpage should not exceed specification. See CYLINDER BLOCK table under ENGINE SPECIFICATIONS at end of article.

CAUTION: Proper head gasket must be installed in accordance with cylinder block height. Different thickness gaskets are used if deck surface is resurfaced.

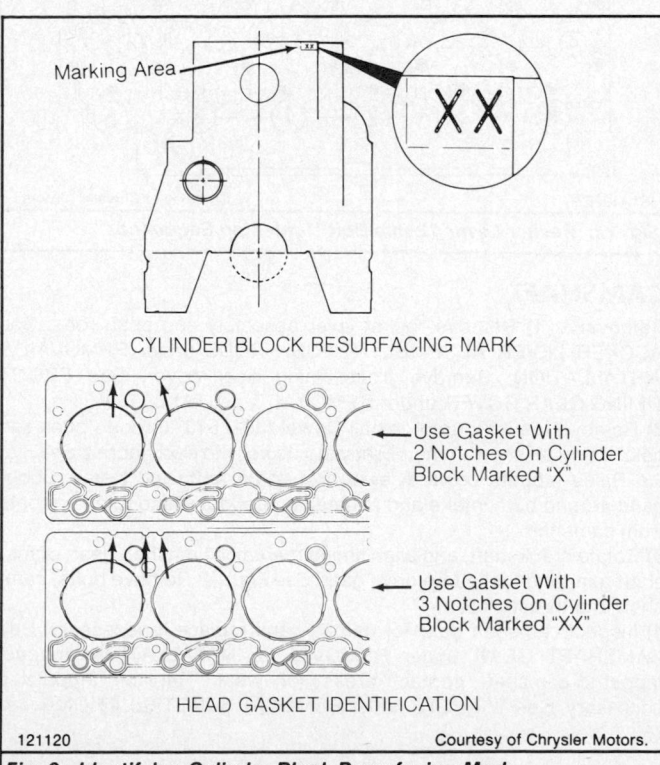

121120   Courtesy of Chrysler Motors.

Fig. 9: Identifying Cylinder Block Resurfacing Mark

Installation – 1) Check upper right corner of cylinder block for marking. See Fig. 9. If no marking exists, cylinder block has not been resurfaced. Cylinder block can only be resurfaced twice: once for .0059" (.149 mm), and then an additional .0138" (.350 mm) for total limit of .0197" (.500 mm).

2) An "X" mark indicates cylinder block was resurfaced .0059" (.149 mm), while "XX" mark indicates block was resurfaced to total of .0197" (.500 mm).

3) Head gasket with 2 notches is used on cylinder block marked "X"; head gasket with 3 notches is used on cylinder block with "XX" mark. See Fig. 9.

NOTE: Consult parts department for proper gasket application to provide proper piston-to-valve clearance.

4) Ensure sealing surfaces, cylinder head bolts and holes are clean and dry. Install dowels in cylinder block (if removed). Install new head gasket. Ensure all holes are aligned.

5) Install cylinder head. Ensure cylinder head properly seats on dowels in cylinder block. Lubricate cylinder head bolts with oil. Install all bolts EXCEPT those for rocker lever pedestals. DO NOT tighten bolts yet. Rocker levers must be installed before tightening cylinder head bolts.

6) Install push rods in original position. Lubricate push rod sockets and valve stems with clean oil. Ensure rocker lever adjusting screw is completely loosened. Install rocker lever pedestals in original position; ensure pedestals align with dowels.

NOTE: If rocker lever pedestal is lifted upward from cylinder head, rotate engine until rocker lever pedestal contacts cylinder head. Ensure adjusting screw is completely loosened.

7) Lubricate remaining bolts with oil, and install. Tighten cylinder head bolts to specification using proper sequence. See Fig. 8. See TORQUE SPECIFICATIONS table at end of article. Tighten remaining rocker lever pedestal bolts to specification.

8) Adjust valve clearance. See VALVE CLEARANCE ADJUSTMENT under ADJUSTMENTS. Replace seal rings on rocker lever cover bolts. Install rocker lever cover, gasket and bolts.

9) Ensure fuel injector sleeve is clean. Install new sealing ring on fuel injector. Coat fuel injector retaining nut and top of fuel injector body with anti-seize compound. Install fuel injector in original position.

10) Ensure protruding side of fuel injector aligns with notch area of cylinder head. Tighten fuel injector retaining nut to specification. See TORQUE SPECIFICATIONS table. Once fuel injector retaining nut is tightened, push "O" ring on top of fuel injector into groove.

CAUTION: Ensure protruding side of fuel injector aligns with notch area of cylinder head.

11) To install remaining components, reverse removal procedure using new sealing washers, gaskets or "O" rings. Ensure banjo bolts for fuel supply line are installed in original location. Install and bleed fuel lines. See FUEL LINE BLEEDING. Fill crankcase and cooling system.

VIBRATION DAMPER

Removal – Remove drive belt. Remove retaining bolts and vibration damper. Inspect mounting hub for cracks. Check for deterioration or missing pieces of rubber. Check alignment of reference marks on inner and outer members. See Fig. 10. Replace vibration damper if reference marks are more than 1/16" out of alignment.

Installation – To install, reverse removal procedure. Tighten vibration damper bolts to specification. See TORQUE SPECIFICATIONS table at end of article. Install drive belt.

CHRY
5-44

1992 ENGINES
Cummins Diesel "B" Series 5.9L 6-Cylinder (Cont.)

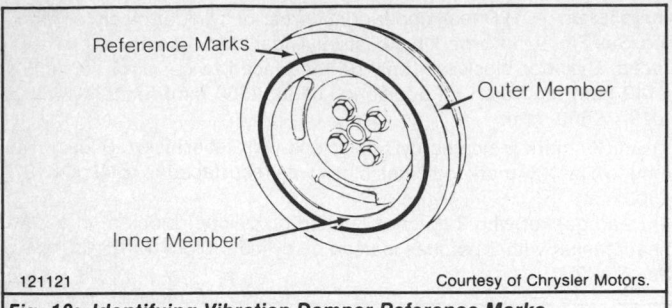

Fig. 10: Identifying Vibration Damper Reference Marks

121121   Courtesy of Chrysler Motors.

CRANKSHAFT FRONT SEAL

Removal – Remove vibration damper. See VIBRATION DAMPER under REMOVAL & INSTALLATION. Drill two 1/8" holes in face of seal, 180 degrees apart. Install sheet metal screws in holes. Using slide hammer, remove crankshaft front seal.

Installation – 1) Ensure seal seating surfaces of crankshaft and front timing gear cover are clean. If front timing gear cover has been recently removed, install aligner/installer provided with crankshaft front seal on front of crankshaft; ensure front timing gear cover and crankshaft align.

CAUTION: Crankshaft and seal must be free of oil during installation to prevent seal leakage.

2) Apply Loctite (277) to outside diameter of seal. Place seal installation sleeve provided with seal on front of crankshaft. Install seal on installation sleeve; push seal from installation sleeve onto crankshaft and start into gear cover. Remove installation sleeve.
3) Install seal using aligner/installer provided with seal. Drive aligner/installer in 4 equally spaced areas until aligner/installer bottoms. To install remaining components, reverse removal procedure. Tighten bolts to specification. See TORQUE SPECIFICATIONS table at end of article.

FRONT TIMING GEAR COVER

Removal – 1) Remove vibration damper. See VIBRATION DAMPER under REMOVAL & INSTALLATION. Remove oil fill tube from front timing gear cover. Remove fan hub and belt tensioner.
2) Remove retaining bolts, front timing gear cover and gasket. *See Fig. 11.* Remove crankshaft front seal from front timing gear cover.

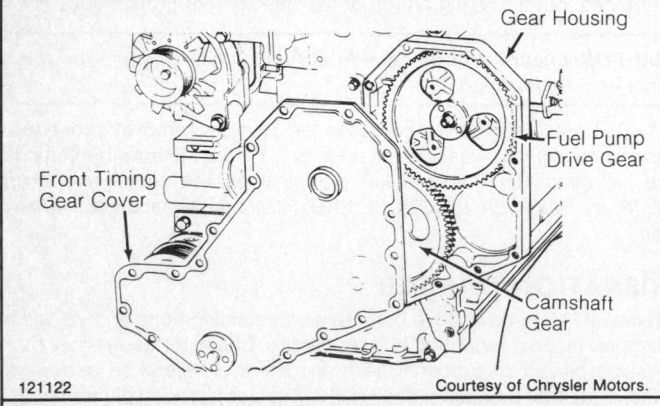

Fig. 11: Identifying Front Timing Gear Cover & Gear Housing

121122   Courtesy of Chrysler Motors.

Installation – 1) Lubricate gear train with oil. Ensure gasket and crankshaft seal surfaces are clean and dry. Install gasket, front timing gear cover and retaining bolts. DO NOT tighten bolts yet.

CAUTION: Crankshaft and seal must be free of oil during installation to prevent seal leakage.

2) Install aligner/installer provided with crankshaft front seal on front of crankshaft. Tighten front timing gear cover retaining bolts to specification, and remove aligner/installer. See TORQUE SPECIFICATIONS table at end of article.
3) Apply Loctite (277) to outside diameter of seal. Place seal installation sleeve provided with seal on front of crankshaft. Install seal on installation sleeve, push seal from installation sleeve onto crankshaft and start into gear cover. Remove installation sleeve.
4) Install seal using aligner/installer provided with seal. Drive aligner/installer in 4 equally spaced areas until aligner/installer bottoms. To install remaining components, reverse removal procedure. Tighten bolts to specification. See TORQUE SPECIFICATIONS table.

ROCKER LEVER ASSEMBLY & PUSH RODS

Removal – Remove rocker lever covers. Loosen adjusting screw lock nut. Loosen adjusting screw until it stops. Remove retaining bolts, rocker lever assembly and push rods. Mark component location for installation reference.
Installation – 1) Install push rods in original position. Lubricate push rod sockets and valve stems with clean oil. Ensure rocker lever adjusting screw is completely loosened. Install rocker lever pedestals in original position; ensure pedestals align with dowels.

NOTE: If rocker lever pedestal is lifted upward from cylinder head, rotate engine until rocker lever pedestal contacts cylinder head. Ensure adjusting screw is completely loosened.

2) Lubricate retaining bolts with oil and install. Tighten rocker lever assembly 12-mm bolts to specification in sequence. *See Fig. 12.* See TORQUE SPECIFICATIONS table at end of article.
3) Tighten 8-mm bolts to specification. See TORQUE SPECIFICATIONS table. Adjust valve clearance. See VALVE CLEARANCE ADJUSTMENT under ADJUSTMENTS. Replace seal rings on rocker cover bolts. Install rocker lever cover, gasket and bolts.

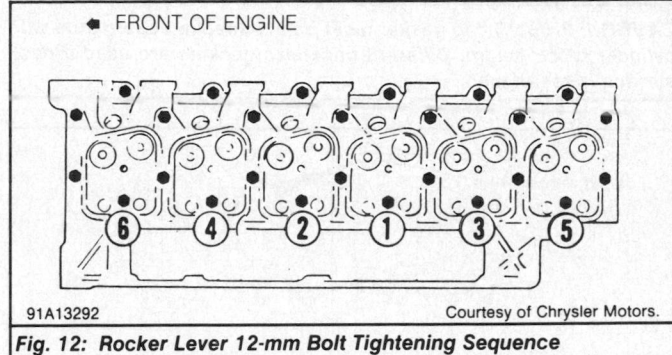

Fig. 12: Rocker Lever 12-mm Bolt Tightening Sequence

91A13292   Courtesy of Chrysler Motors.

CAMSHAFT

Removal – 1) Remove rocker lever assembly and push rods. See ROCKER LEVER ASSEMBLY & PUSH RODS under REMOVAL & INSTALLATION. Remove front timing gear cover. See FRONT TIMING GEAR COVER under REMOVAL & INSTALLATION.
2) Remove fuel lift pump. Install Dowel (3822513) through push rod hole. Using plastic hammer, lightly tap dowel into each tappet. *See Fig. 13.* Raise tappets upward, away from camshaft, and install rubber band around both intake and exhaust tappet dowels to retain tappets from camshaft.
3) Rotate crankshaft, and align timing marks on camshaft gear, crankshaft gear and fuel pump drive gear. *See Fig. 14.* Remove bolts, camshaft and thrust plate.
4) Inspect camshaft gear for damage and replace if necessary. See CAMSHAFT GEAR under REMOVAL & INSTALLATION. Inspect tappet-to-camshaft contact areas for wear. Replace tappets if necessary. See TAPPETS under REMOVAL & INSTALLATION.

1992 ENGINES
Cummins Diesel "B" Series 5.9L 6-Cylinder (Cont.)

CHRY
5-45

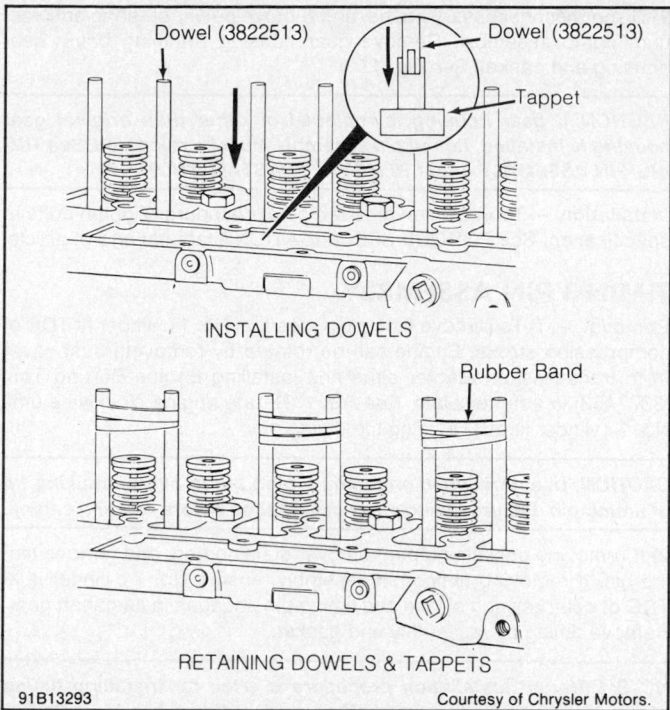

INSTALLING DOWELS

RETAINING DOWELS & TAPPETS

91B13293   Courtesy of Chrysler Motors.

Fig. 13: Retaining Tappet In Cylinder Block

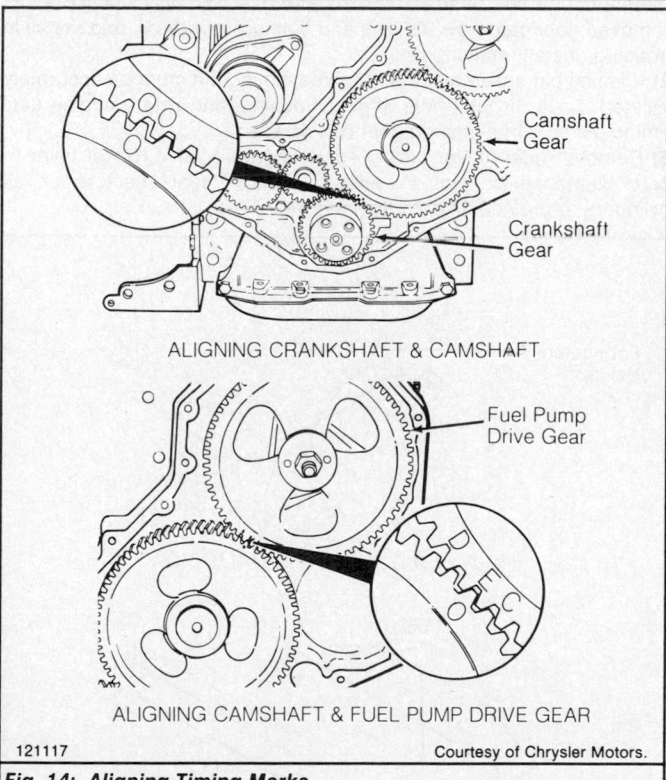

ALIGNING CRANKSHAFT & CAMSHAFT

ALIGNING CAMSHAFT & FUEL PUMP DRIVE GEAR

121117   Courtesy of Chrysler Motors.

Fig. 14: Aligning Timing Marks

Inspection – Inspect camshaft bearings. See CAMSHAFT BEARINGS under REMOVAL & INSTALLATION. Measure camshaft journals and camshaft lobes. Replace camshaft if damaged or not within specification. See CAMSHAFT table under ENGINE SPECIFICATIONS at end of article.
Installation – 1) Coat camshaft bearings, camshaft journals and thrust plate with Lubriplate (105). Install camshaft with all timing marks aligned. See Fig. 14.

CAUTION: DO NOT push camshaft inward beyond area for thrust plate. Excessive inward movement of camshaft will dislodge plug in rear of cylinder block, causing oil leak.

2) Install thrust plate, and tighten retaining bolts to specification. See TORQUE SPECIFICATIONS table at end of article. Using a dial indicator, check gear backlash between camshaft gear, crankshaft gear and fuel pump drive gear. Check camshaft end play.
3) Gear backlash and camshaft end play should be within specification. See CAMSHAFT table under ENGINE SPECIFICATIONS at end of article.
4) To install remaining components, reverse removal procedure. Adjust valve clearance. See VALVE CLEARANCE ADJUSTMENT under ADJUSTMENTS.

CAMSHAFT BEARINGS

NOTE: Camshaft bearing is used only on front camshaft journal and is replaceable. All other camshaft journal bores should have same I.D. as front camshaft bearing. If remaining bores exceed specification, camshaft bores must be machined to accommodate service bearings.

Inspection – Inspect camshaft bearing for scratches or damage. Measure I.D. of camshaft bearing and journal bores. If bore I.D. exceeds specification, replace camshaft bearing, or machine bores for service bearing. See CAMSHAFT table under ENGINE SPECIFICATIONS at end of article.
Removal & Installation – 1) Using camshaft bearing remover/installer, drive camshaft bearing from cylinder block. Mark camshaft bearing and cylinder block for oil hole alignment.
2) Using camshaft bearing remover/installer, install camshaft bearing until camshaft bearing is even with front of cylinder block. Use a .128" (3.25 mm) diameter rod to check alignment between oil hole and cylinder block.

CAMSHAFT GEAR

Removal & Installation – 1) Remove camshaft. See CAMSHAFT under REMOVAL & INSTALLATION. Using press and support blocks, press camshaft from camshaft gear. Ensure camshaft gear keyway and key are free of burrs. Heat camshaft gear to 250°F (121°C) for 45 minutes.
2) Coat camshaft surface with Lubriplate (105). Press camshaft gear on camshaft with timing marks facing away from camshaft. Ensure camshaft gear is seated against camshaft shoulder.

CRANKSHAFT GEAR

NOTE: Manufacturer lists procedure with crankshaft removed.

Removal & Installation – 1) Using gear puller, remove crankshaft gear from crankshaft. To install, install NEW alignment pin (if removed) in crankshaft so pin protrudes .063-.094" (1.60-2.38 mm) above crankshaft.
2) Ensure alignment pin and pin slot in crankshaft gear are free of burrs, and end of crankshaft is smooth. Heat crankshaft gear at 250°F (121°C) for 45 minutes. DO NOT heat for longer than 45 minutes.
3) Install heated crankshaft gear on crankshaft, with timing mark facing outward. Ensure alignment pin and slot in crankshaft gear align. Ensure crankshaft gear is bottomed on crankshaft.

TAPPETS

Removal – 1) Remove camshaft. See CAMSHAFT under REMOVAL & INSTALLATION. Install plastic trough from Tappet Changing Set (3822513) the full length of camshaft bore area of cylinder block. See Fig. 15. Ensure plastic trough is positioned under tappet to retain tappet when dowel is removed.
2) Remove rubber band and dowel (installed during camshaft removal) from tappet. Allow tappet to fall into plastic trough. Ensure tappet in plastic trough falls over. Remove trough and tappet. Mark tappet for location.

CHRY
5-46

1992 ENGINES
Cummins Diesel "B" Series 5.9L 6-Cylinder (Cont.)

CAUTION: DO NOT remove more than one tappet at a time. Ensure tappet in plastic trough falls over before removing. Use care when removing tappets from No. 6 cylinder to prevent shaking tappets over top of plastic trough.

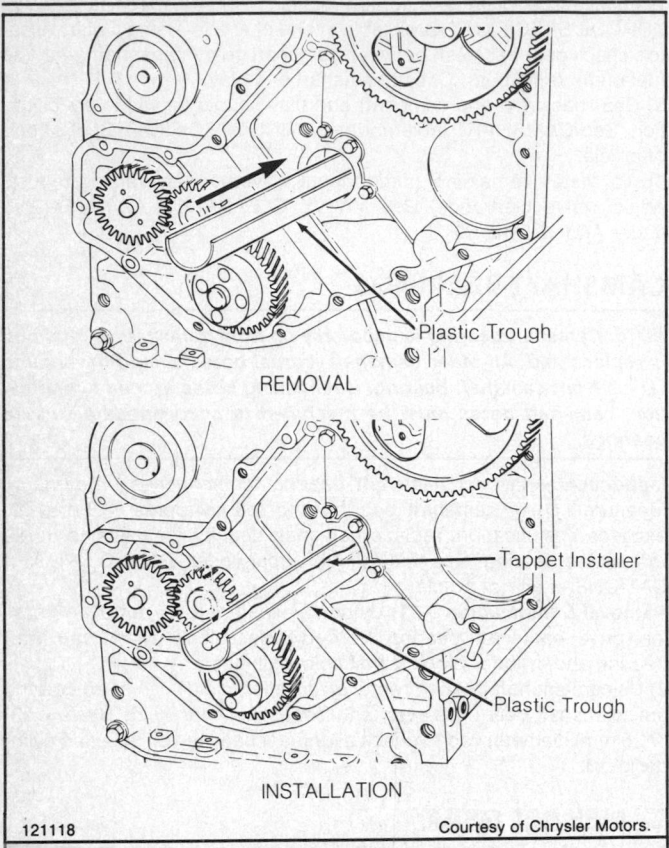

Fig. 15: Removing & Installing Tappets

121118   Courtesy of Chrysler Motors.

Inspection – Inspect tappets for wear in camshaft contact area. Measure tappet stem O.D. at top and bottom of stem. Replace tappet if O.D. is not within specification. Ensure cylinder block tappet bore is within specification. See TAPPETS table under ENGINE SPECIFICATIONS at end of article.

Installation – 1) Install plastic trough in camshaft area of cylinder block. Position tappet installer through push rod hole of cylinder head, and guide out front of plastic trough. *See Fig. 15.* Lubricate tappet with Lubriplate (105).

NOTE: Tappet should be installed on tappet installer several times before installing in cylinder block to aid in removal of tappet installer from tappet once installed in cylinder block.

2) Install tappet on tappet installer. Pull tappet up plastic trough, and align with original installation location. If necessary, pull plastic trough toward front of cylinder block to allow tappet to drop down and align with tappet bore.
3) Once tappet is installed in cylinder block bore, rotate plastic trough so rounded side of trough is against bottom of tappet. This will hold tappet in place. Install dowel and rubber band to retain tappet. Install camshaft and remaining components.

GEAR HOUSING

NOTE: Manufacturer lists procedure with engine removed.

Removal – 1) Remove engine. See ENGINE under REMOVAL & INSTALLATION. Remove camshaft. See CAMSHAFT under REMOVAL & INSTALLATION. Remove fuel injection pump. See FUEL INJECTION PUMP under REMOVAL & INSTALLATION.

2) Disconnect necessary hoses, and remove power steering and vacuum pump assembly. Remove gear housing retaining bolts, gear housing and gasket. *See Fig. 11.*

CAUTION: If gear housing is replaced or other than original gear housing is installed, timing pin assembly must be relocated. See TIMING PIN ASSEMBLY under REMOVAL & INSTALLATION.

Installation – To install, reverse removal procedure. Tighten bolts to specification. See TORQUE SPECIFICATIONS table at end of article.

TIMING PIN ASSEMBLY

Removal – 1) To remove timing pin, position No. 1 cylinder at TDC of compression stroke. Engine can be rotated by removing dust cover from transmission adapter plate and installing Engine Barring Tool (3377462) in adapter plate. *See Fig. 1.* Rotate engine clockwise until No. 1 cylinder is at TDC. Engage timing pin.

CAUTION: Use care when engaging timing pin to avoid breaking tip of timing pin. Ensure timing pin is disengaged before rotating engine.

2) If removing only timing pin, remove retaining ring, and remove timing pin. If removing timing pin assembly, ensure No. 1 cylinder is at TDC of compression stroke and timing pin engages in camshaft gear. Remove timing pin assembly and gasket.

NOTE: Different installation procedure is used for installing timing pin assembly depending on whether or not cylinder head is installed.

Installation (With Cylinder Head Installed) – 1) If only timing pin was removed, lubricate new "O" ring and timing pin with oil, and install in housing. Install retaining ring.
2) If timing pin assembly was removed, timing pin must be accurately located. Look through hole of gear housing, and rotate engine until timing pin hole in camshaft gear can be seen.
3) Remove rocker lever cover. Adjust exhaust valve rocker lever to zero clearance on No. 1 cylinder. Remove fuel injectors on all cylinders to provide smooth engine rotation.

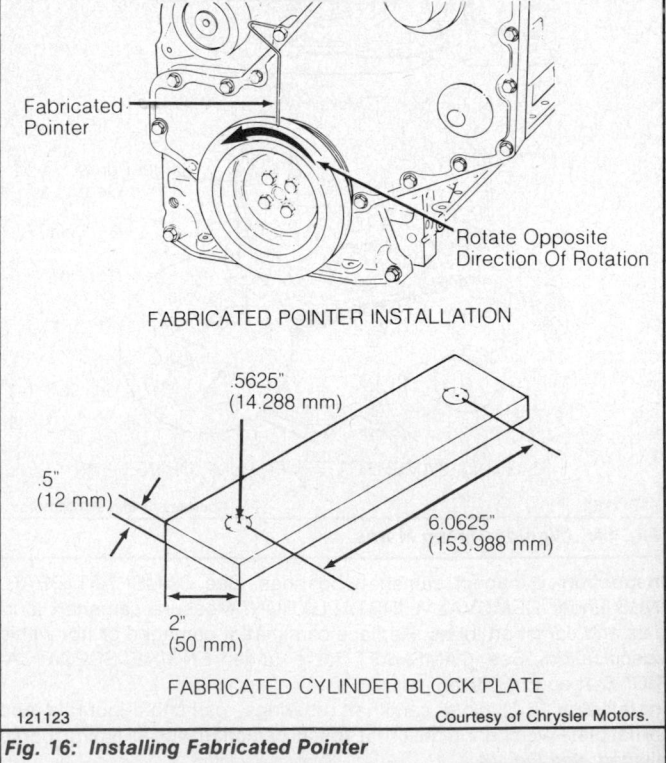

Fig. 16: Installing Fabricated Pointer

121123   Courtesy of Chrysler Motors.

1992 ENGINES
Cummins Diesel "B" Series 5.9L 6-Cylinder (Cont.)

CHRY
5-47

4) Clean around fuel injectors. Disconnect fuel lines from fuel injectors. Hold fuel injector body using wrench while loosening hold-down nut. Remove fuel injector, and mark cylinder location for reassembly reference.

5) Temporarily install vibration damper (if removed). Fabricate and install pointer to align with vibration damper. Rotate crankshaft 1/4 turn counterclockwise, in opposite direction of rotation. See Fig. 16. Tighten adjusting screw for exhaust valve 2 complete turns, and tighten lock nut.

CAUTION: Use care when rotating engine so piston does not contact exhaust valve.

---

6) Slowly rotate crankshaft clockwise until piston slightly contacts exhaust valve. Place reference mark on vibration damper at fabricated pointer.

7) Slowly rotate crankshaft counterclockwise, in opposite direction of rotation, until piston contacts valve with same amount of force. Place reference mark on vibration damper at fabricated pointer.

8) Measure distance between reference marks. Place reference mark on vibration damper at a point halfway between reference marks. This is TDC mark. Completely loosen exhaust valve adjusting screw on No. 1 cylinder.

9) Rotate crankshaft clockwise, in direction of rotation, approximately 180 degrees until fabricated pointer is aligned with TDC mark. Look through back side of gear housing, and note timing pin hole in camshaft gear. If timing pin hole is not visible, rotate crankshaft one revolution.

10) Install timing pin assembly and gasket. Hold timing pin in camshaft gear hole, and align housing with bolt holes. Coat bolts with thread sealant and install. Tighten bolts to specification. See TORQUE SPECIFICATIONS table at end of article. Remove fabricated pointer.

CAUTION: Ensure timing pin is disengaged before rotating engine.

---

11) Adjust valve clearance on No. 1 cylinder. See VALVE CLEARANCE ADJUSTMENT under ADJUSTMENTS. Replace seal rings on rocker cover bolts. Install gasket, rocker lever cover and retaining bolts.

12) Ensure injector sleeve is clean. Install new sealing ring on fuel injector. Coat fuel injector retaining nut and top of fuel injector body with anti-seize compound. Install fuel injectors in original position.

13) Ensure protruding side of fuel injector aligns with notch area of cylinder head. Tighten fuel injector retaining nuts to specification. See TORQUE SPECIFICATIONS table. Once fuel injector retaining nut is tightened, push "O" ring on top of fuel injector into groove. To install remaining components, reverse removal procedure. Install and bleed high-pressure fuel lines. See FUEL LINE BLEEDING.

CAUTION: Ensure protruding side of fuel injector nozzle aligns with notch area of cylinder head.

Installation (With Cylinder Head Removed) – **1)** If only timing pin was removed, coat new "O" ring and timing pin with oil and install in housing. Install retaining ring.

2) If timing pin assembly was removed, timing pin must be accurately located. Temporarily install vibration damper (if removed). Fabricate and install pointer to align with vibration damper. See Fig. 16. If front timing gear cover is removed, install flat washer between gear housing and fabricated pointer to prevent damage to gear housing.

3) Fabricate cylinder block plate. See Fig. 16. Install cylinder block plate over No. 1 cylinder. Rotate crankshaft clockwise, in direction of rotation, until piston contacts cylinder block plate. Place reference mark on vibration damper at fabricated pointer.

4) Slowly rotate crankshaft counterclockwise, in opposite direction of rotation, until piston contacts cylinder block plate. Place reference mark on vibration damper at fabricated pointer.

5) Measure distance between reference marks. Place reference mark on vibration damper at a point halfway between reference marks. This is TDC mark.

6) Remove cylinder block plate. Rotate crankshaft clockwise until fabricated pointer aligns with TDC mark. Look through back side of gear

housing, and note timing pin hole in camshaft gear. If pin hole is not visible, rotate crankshaft one revolution.

7) Install timing pin assembly and gasket. Hold timing pin in camshaft gear hole, and align housing with bolt holes. Coat bolts with thread sealant and install. Tighten bolts to specification. See TORQUE SPECIFICATIONS table at end of article. Remove fabricated pointer.

CAUTION: Ensure timing pin is disengaged before rotating engine.

REAR CRANKSHAFT OIL SEAL

NOTE: Crankshaft and oil seal must be free of oil during installation to prevent seal leakage.

Removal & Installation – **1)** Remove transmission, clutch pressure plate and disc (if equipped), and flywheel. Drill two 1/8" holes in seal face, 180 degrees apart. Install sheet metal screws in holes. Using slide hammer, remove oil seal.

2) To install, ensure all sealing surfaces are clean and dry. Install oil seal pilot provided with rear crankshaft oil seal on rear of crankshaft. Install oil seal on pilot, and push oil seal from oil seal pilot onto crankshaft. Remove oil seal pilot.

3) On oil seals with rubber coating on outer diameter, coat rubber area with soapy water. On oil seals without rubber coating, apply Loctite (277) sealant to outside diameter of oil seal.

4) Install oil seal using oil seal aligner/installer provided with oil seal. Drive oil seal aligner/installer in 4 equally spaced areas until oil seal aligner/installer bottoms. Remove oil seal aligner/installer.

5) To install remaining components, reverse removal procedure. Tighten flywheel bolts in a crisscross pattern to specification. See TORQUE SPECIFICATIONS table at end of article.

REAR CRANKSHAFT OIL SEAL HOUSING

NOTE: Manufacturer lists procedure with transmission, flywheel and oil pan removed.

Removal – Remove retaining bolts, oil seal housing and gasket from rear of cylinder block. Support oil seal housing, and drive oil seal from oil seal housing.

NOTE: Crankshaft and oil seal must be free of oil during installation to prevent seal leakage. Ensure oil seal housing is even with bottom of cylinder block surface to prevent oil leakage.

Installation – **1)** Ensure all sealing surfaces are clean and dry. Install gasket and oil seal housing on cylinder block. DO NOT tighten bolts yet.

2) Install oil seal aligner/installer provided with rear crankshaft oil seal on rear of crankshaft. Ensure oil seal housing is even with bottom of cylinder block surface. Tighten retaining bolts to specification. See TORQUE SPECIFICATIONS table at end of article.

3) Trim oil seal housing gasket even with cylinder block surface. Remove oil seal aligner/installer. Install oil seal pilot provided with rear crankshaft oil seal on rear of crankshaft. Install oil seal on pilot, and push oil seal from oil seal pilot onto crankshaft. Remove oil seal pilot.

4) On oil seals with rubber coating on outer diameter, coat rubber area with soapy water. On oil seals without rubber coating, apply Loctite (277) sealant to outside diameter of oil seal.

5) Install oil seal using oil seal aligner/installer provided with oil seal. Drive on oil seal aligner/installer in 4 equally spaced areas until oil seal aligner/installer bottoms. Remove oil seal aligner/installer.

FLYWHEEL RING GEAR

Removal & Installation – **1)** Remove transmission, clutch pressure plate and disc (if equipped), and flywheel. Note direction of flywheel ring gear installation. Using brass drift and hammer, drive ring gear from flywheel.

CAUTION: Ring gear must be installed with chamfered edge on teeth toward crankshaft side of flywheel.

CHRY
5-48

1992 ENGINES
Cummins Diesel "B" Series 5.9L 6-Cylinder (Cont.)

2) To install, heat ring gear in oven at 250°F (121°C) for 20 minutes. Install flywheel ring gear with chamfered edge on teeth toward crankshaft side of flywheel.

FUEL INJECTION PUMP

Removal – **1)** Disconnect negative battery cable. Disconnect necessary electrical connections at fuel injection pump. Disconnect control linkages from control lever on fuel injection pump. DO NOT remove control lever from fuel injection pump. See Fig. 3.

2) Disconnect control linkage bracket. Remove and cap high-pressure fuel lines. Hold delivery valves on fuel injection pump using wrench while removing high-pressure lines. Mark fuel line location for reassembly reference.

3) Disconnect air fuel control tube. Tube is from fuel injection pump to cylinder head. Disconnect drain tube from fuel injection pump. Disconnect fuel supply line from fuel injection pump.

4) Remove bolt from rear support bracket on fuel injection pump. Remove rear support bracket-to-cylinder block bolts. Loosen center bolt on rear support bracket. Pivot rear support bracket toward rear of engine.

5) Remove oil fill tube from front timing gear cover. Place shop towel in front of fuel pump drive gear to prevent retaining nut and washer from falling during removal. Remove fuel pump drive gear retaining nut and washer.

CAUTION: DO NOT allow fuel pump drive gear retaining nut or washer to fall into front timing gear cover.

6) Rotate engine clockwise so No. 1 cylinder is at TDC of compression stroke. Engine can be rotated by removing dust cover from transmission adapter plate and installing Engine Barring Tool (3377462) in adapter plate. See Fig. 1.

7) When No. 1 cylinder is at TDC, key of fuel injection pump shaft should be pointing toward bottom of engine. Ensure timing pin will engage.

CAUTION: Use care when engaging timing pin to avoid breaking tip of timing pin. DO NOT rotate engine with timing pin engaged.

8) If original fuel injection pump is installed, ensure timing marks on fuel injection pump flange and gear housing are aligned for reassembly reference. See Fig. 17. These factory timing marks apply specifically to original engine and fuel injection pump. Factory timing marks cannot be used if original fuel injection pump is being replaced.

Gear Housing
Timing Marks
Lock Bolt
Fuel Injection Pump Flange
Special Washer

121124   Courtesy of Chrysler Motors.

Fig. 17: Identifying Fuel Injection Pump Timing Marks

9) Loosen lock bolt on fuel injection pump, and remove special washer. See Fig. 17. Tighten lock bolt to **22 ft. lbs. (30 N.m)**, locking fuel injection pump shaft from rotating. Retain special washer for reassembly.

10) Using gear puller and two M8 X 1.25 bolts, pull fuel pump drive gear free from fuel injection pump shaft. Remove retaining nuts, fuel injection pump and gasket.

CAUTION: DO NOT allow key to fall from fuel injection pump shaft during removal.

NOTE: Different installation procedure is used depending on whether original, new or rebuilt component is being installed.

Installation (Original Fuel Injection Pump) – **1)** Ensure gasket surfaces are clean. Ensure No. 1 cylinder is at TDC and timing pin is engaged. Install new gasket on cylinder block. Install key in fuel injection pump shaft, and install fuel injection pump. DO NOT allow key to drop from fuel injection pump shaft.

CAUTION: Use care when installing fuel injection pump to prevent key from dropping from fuel injection pump shaft.

2) Install mounting nuts. DO NOT tighten nuts yet. Fuel injection pump must be free to rotate in slots. Install fuel pump drive gear retaining nut and washer. Tighten fuel pump drive gear retaining nut to **11-15 ft. lbs. (15-20 N.m)**.

3) If fuel injection pump timing marks on fuel injection flange and gear housing were aligned at removal, fuel injection pump timing does not require adjustment. If marks were not aligned, fuel injection pump timing must be checked. See FUEL INJECTION PUMP TIMING under ADJUSTMENTS.

4) If timing marks were aligned at removal, rotate fuel injection pump to align timing marks. Tighten mounting nuts to **18 ft. lbs. (24 N.m)**. On all applications, loosen lock bolt, and install special washer under lock bolt. Tighten lock bolt to **10 ft. lbs. (14 N.m)**. Tighten fuel pump drive gear nut to specification. See TORQUE SPECIFICATIONS table at end of article.

5) Disengage timing pin if not previously done. To install remaining components, reverse removal procedure. Loosely install all bolts in rear support bracket.

6) Tighten rear support bracket bolts to vacuum pump, cylinder block and then to fuel injection pump. Tighten bolts to specification. See TORQUE SPECIFICATIONS table.

7) Install and bleed fuel lines. See FUEL LINE BLEEDING. Adjust cable rod so control lever contacts low-speed screw when in idle position. Ensure control lever moves over center position and rests against break-over spring when in full throttle position. See Fig. 3.

Installation (New Or Rebuilt Fuel Injection Pump) – **1)** Ensure gasket surfaces are clean. Ensure No. 1 cylinder is at TDC and timing pin is engaged. Install new gasket on cylinder block. Install key in fuel injection pump shaft, and install fuel injection pump.

CAUTION: Use care when installing fuel injection pump to prevent key from dropping from fuel injection pump shaft.

2) Install mounting nuts. DO NOT tighten nuts yet. Fuel injection pump must be free to rotate in slots. Install fuel pump drive gear retaining nut and washer. Tighten nut to **11-15 ft. lbs. (15-20 N.m)**.

3) Rotate fuel injection pump toward cylinder head to take up gear lash. Check fuel injection pump timing. See FUEL INJECTION PUMP TIMING under ADJUSTMENTS.

CAUTION: Ensure lock bolt is loosened and special washer is installed under lock bolt. Lock bolt must be tightened to 10 ft. lbs. (14 N.m).

4) Once correct timing is obtained and mounting nuts are tightened, place timing mark on fuel injection pump flange to align with mark on gear housing. See Fig. 17.

5) Disengage timing pin if not previously done. To install remaining components, reverse removal procedure. Install all bolts in rear support.

6) Tighten rear support bracket bolts to vacuum pump, cylinder block and then to fuel injection pump. Tighten bolts to specification. See TORQUE SPECIFICATIONS table at end of article.

7) Install and bleed fuel lines. See FUEL LINE BLEEDING. Adjust cable rod so control lever contacts low-speed screw when in idle position. Ensure control lever moves over center position and rests against break-over spring in full throttle position. See Fig. 3.

1992 ENGINES
Cummins Diesel "B" Series 5.9L 6-Cylinder (Cont.)

CHRY
5-49

THROTTLE POSITION SENSOR (TPS)

Removal – Disconnect electrical connector at TPS. Remove TPS retaining screws. Lift TPS straight up from fuel injection pump.
Installation – 1) Install TPS in bracket on fuel injection pump. Ensure adapter on TPS aligns with opening in fuel injection pump shaft. *See Fig. 4.*
2) If adapter does not align with fuel injection pump shaft, remove TPS bracket retaining screws. Place adapter on fuel injection pump shaft so TPS bracket must be rotated clockwise to align retaining screw holes.
3) Ensure adapter is even or slightly above top of fuel injection pump shaft. To adjust adapter position, hold nylon shaft in place, and rotate adapter. Tighten bracket retaining screws. Adjust TPS. See THROTTLE POSITION SENSOR (TPS) under ADJUSTMENTS.

WATER PUMP

Removal & Installation – Drain cooling system. Remove drive belt. Remove water pump retaining bolts, water pump and "O" ring. To install, reverse removal procedure using new "O" ring. Tighten bolts to specification. See TORQUE SPECIFICATIONS table at end of article. Fill cooling system.

THERMOSTAT

CAUTION: Engine MUST NOT be operated without a thermostat. With no thermostat, coolant passes through by-pass to water pump inlet and causes engine overheating. Thermostat and rubber seal must be installed in correct direction. See Fig. 18.

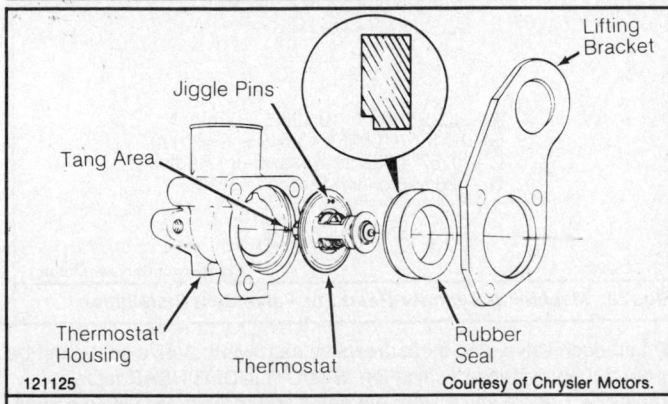

Fig. 18: Removing & Installing Thermostat

Removal – Disconnect negative battery cable. Drain cooling system. Remove drive belt and upper radiator hose. Remove alternator bolt, and rotate alternator aside. Remove retaining bolts, thermostat housing, lifting bracket and thermostat. *See Fig. 18.*
Installation – To install, reverse removal procedure. Thermostat must be installed in housing so tang on thermostat aligns with notch of housing. *See Fig. 18.* Rubber seal must be installed in proper direction. Tighten bolts to specification. See TORQUE SPECIFICATIONS table at end of article. Fill cooling system.

OIL PAN

Removal & Installation – 1) Remove engine. See ENGINE under REMOVAL & INSTALLATION. Remove retaining bolts, oil pan and gasket.
2) To install, reverse removal procedure. Apply sealant at crankshaft rear seal housing and front timing gear cover-to-cylinder block junction areas before installing gasket. Tighten bolts to specification. See TORQUE SPECIFICATIONS table at end of article.

OVERHAUL

CYLINDER HEAD

Cylinder Head – Inspect cylinder head warpage at deck surface. Resurface cylinder head if warpage exceeds specification. See CYL-INDER HEAD table under ENGINE SPECIFICATIONS at end of article. Replace cylinder head if total metal removed exceeds .0393" (.998 mm).

NOTE: Amount of material removed from cylinder head should be stamped on lower right rear corner of cylinder head, above deck surface.

Valve Springs – Check valve spring free length, out-of-square and pressure. Replace valve spring if not to specification. See VALVES & VALVE SPRINGS table under ENGINE SPECIFICATIONS at end of article.
Valve Stem Oil Seals – Intake and exhaust valve stem oil seals are same. Ensure valve stem oil seals are seated on cylinder head.

NOTE: Valve guides may be either thick wall or thin wall. Note wall thickness before servicing valve guides.

Valve Guides – 1) Cylinder head valve guide bore must be reamed if service valve guide I.D. exceeds specification. See CYLINDER HEAD table under ENGINE SPECIFICATIONS at end of article. Ream cylinder head to proper dimension. See VALVE GUIDE INSTALLATION SPECIFICATIONS table.
2) Service valve guides must be centered with valve seats within .01378" (.3500 mm) and squared with deck surface with .004" (.10 mm) within a 1.9685" (49.999 mm) radius. If thin valve guide is used, go to next step. If thick valve guide is used, go to step 5).
3) On thin wall valve guides, lubricate valve guide and install until bottom of valve guide is even with cylinder head boss. *See Fig. 19.*

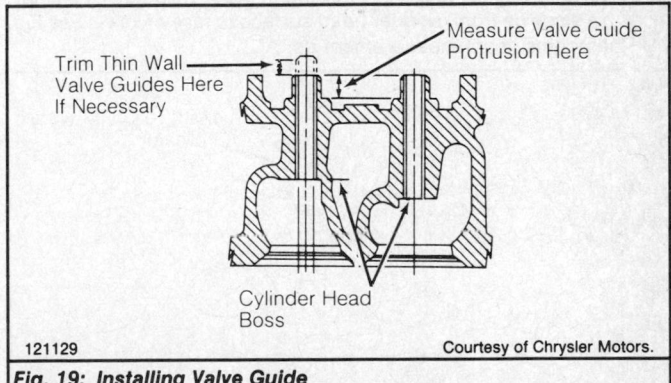

Fig. 19: Installing Valve Guide

4) Valve guide may require trimming so top of valve guide is even with cylinder head boss. Ream valve guide to specification. See VALVE GUIDE INSTALLATION SPECIFICATIONS table.
5) On thick wall valve guides, lubricate valve guide and install until valve guide protrusion above cylinder head is correct. *See Fig. 19.* Valve guide protrusion must be within specification. Ream valve guide to specification. See VALVE GUIDE INSTALLATION SPECIFICATIONS table.

VALVE GUIDE INSTALLATION SPECIFICATIONS

Application	In. (mm)
Cylinder Head Bore Reaming Dimension	
Thick Wall Valve Guide	.5507-.5517 (13.988-14.013)
Thin Wall Valve Guide	.4375-.4385 (11.113-11.138)
Valve Guide Protrusion	
Thick Wall Valve Guide	.4623-.5023 (11.742-12.758)
Valve Guide Reaming Dimension	.3157-.3165 (8.019-8.039)

Valve Seats – 1) On cylinder heads containing integral valve seats, valve seats can be reground only once. Integral valve seats that have been reground must be replaced with service valve seats. Reground valve seats should be identified by an "X" stamped on cylinder head. *See Fig. 20.* Cylinder head should be stamped twice if service valve seats have been installed. *See Fig. 20.*

CHRY
5-50

1992 ENGINES
Cummins Diesel "B" Series 5.9L 6-Cylinder (Cont.)

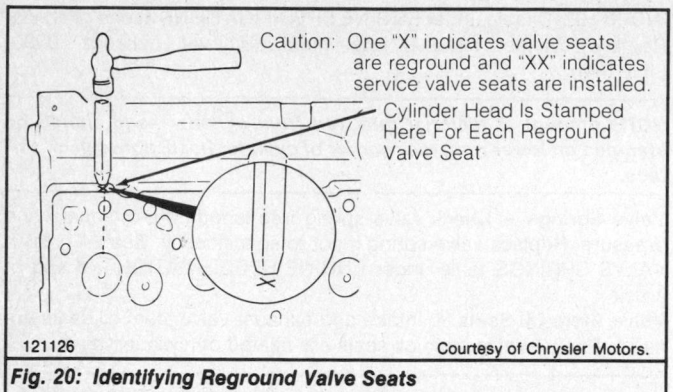

121126

Caution: One "X" indicates valve seats are reground and "XX" indicates service valve seats are installed.

Cylinder Head Is Stamped Here For Each Reground Valve Seat

Courtesy of Chrysler Motors.

Fig. 20: Identifying Reground Valve Seats

CAUTION: On integral valve seats, if material removed from cylinder head is .010" (.25 mm) or more, service valve seats must be installed.

2) To determine if cylinder head has been resurfaced before determining valve grind depth, inspect lower right rear corner of cylinder head, above deck surface, for marking indicating amount of material removed.

3) If no marking exists, measure cylinder head height from deck surface to rocker cover surface. If cylinder head height is 3.730" (94.75 mm) or greater, valve seats can be reground if not previously done.

4) On integral valve seats only, check valve grind depth. Install resurfaced valve in original location of cylinder head. Using dial indicator, measure distance from cylinder head surface to face of valve. *See Fig. 21.* Record this depth measurement as "A".

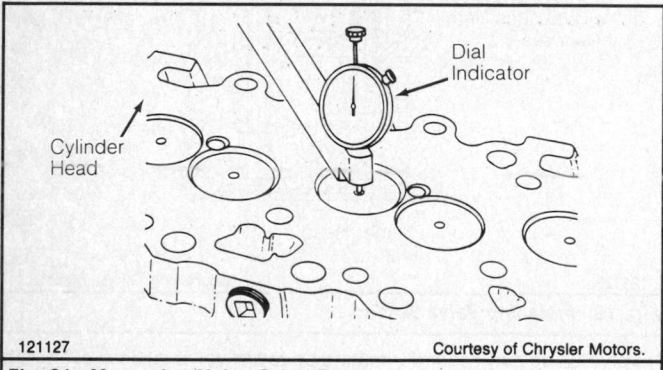

Dial Indicator

Cylinder Head

121127

Courtesy of Chrysler Motors.

Fig. 21: Measuring Valve Grind Depth

5) Grind valve seats at proper angle to remove scores and scratches. See CYLINDER HEAD table under ENGINE SPECIFICATIONS at end of article. Install valve in proper location after grinding valve seat.

6) Measure valve depth again, and record it as measurement "B". To determine valve grind depth, subtract measurement "A" from "B". Service valve seats should be installed if valve grind depth exceeds .010" (.25 mm).

7) Mark cylinder head for reground valve seats. *See Fig. 20.* On integral valve seats and service valve seats, install valves in original location. Measure valve depth again. Replace valve if valve depth is not .039-.060" (.99-1.52 mm).

8) Lap each valve, and measure valve seat width. Valve seat must be ground if not within specification. See CYLINDER HEAD table.

Valve Seat Replacement – **1)** Ensure valve guide I.D. is within specification. See CYLINDER HEAD table under ENGINE SPECIFICATIONS at end of article. Defective valve guides must be replaced before replacing valve seats. Valve seat must be machined to specification for service valve seat installation. *See Fig. 22.*

2) Press service valve seats into cylinder head, and stake valve seats in position. Grind valve seats at proper angle. See CYLINDER HEAD table. Install valve in proper location.

3) Using dial indicator, measure distance from cylinder head surface to face of valve to determine valve depth. Replace valve if valve depth is not .039-.060" (.99-1.52 mm).

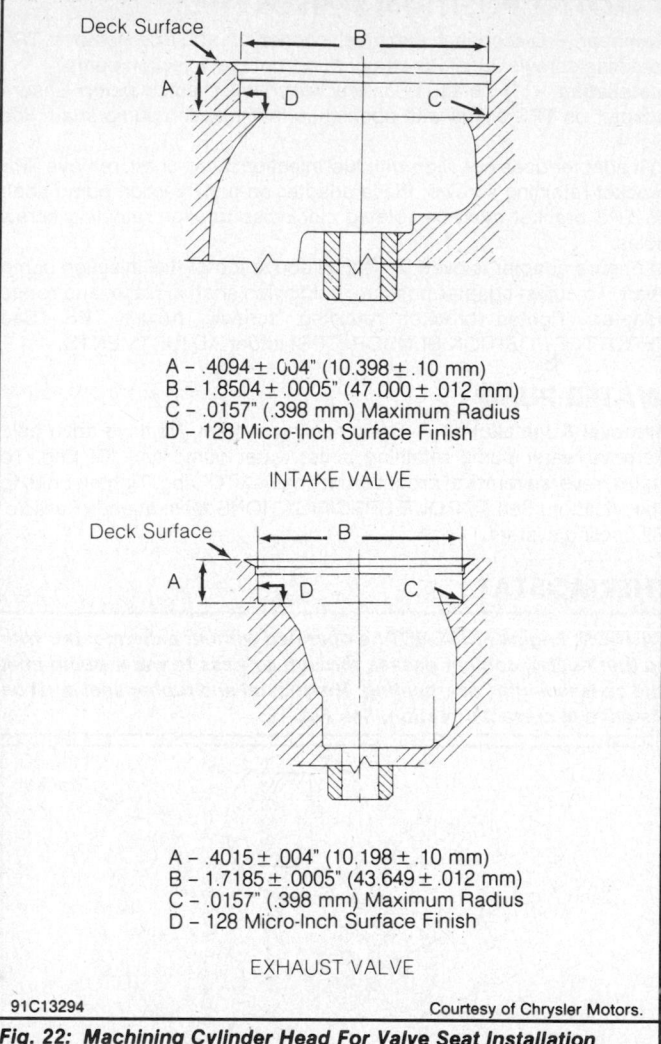

Deck Surface

INTAKE VALVE

A – .4094 ± .004" (10.398 ± .10 mm)
B – 1.8504 ± .0005" (47.000 ± .012 mm)
C – .0157" (.398 mm) Maximum Radius
D – 128 Micro-Inch Surface Finish

Deck Surface

A – .4015 ± .004" (10.198 ± .10 mm)
B – 1.7185 ± .0005" (43.649 ± .012 mm)
C – .0157" (.398 mm) Maximum Radius
D – 128 Micro-Inch Surface Finish

EXHAUST VALVE

91C13294

Courtesy of Chrysler Motors.

Fig. 22: Machining Cylinder Head For Valve Seat Installation

4) Lap each valve, and measure valve seat width. Valve seat must be ground if not within specification. See CYLINDER HEAD table.

Valves – Ensure valve stem diameter and margin are within specification. See VALVES & VALVE SPRINGS table under ENGINE SPECIFICATIONS at end of article. When installing valves, valve spring collets must always be replaced. DO NOT reuse valve spring collets.

Seat Correction Angles – To lower valve seat, use a 15-degree stone; to raise it, use a 65-degree stone.

VALVE TRAIN

Rocker Levers – **1)** To disassemble, remove retaining rings from ends of rocker lever assembly. Remove thrust washers. Mark component location for reassembly reference.

2) Remove rocker levers. DO NOT remove rocker lever shaft from pedestal. Rocker lever shaft and pedestal are serviced as an assembly. Remove adjusting screw and lock nut from rocker lever.

3) Inspect components for damage or wear. Ensure adjusting screw rotates freely in rocker lever. Measure rocker lever bore I.D. and rocker lever shaft O.D. Replace components if not within specification. See ROCKER LEVER SPECIFICATIONS table.

4) To reassemble, coat components with oil, and reverse disassembly procedure. Ensure components are installed in original location. *See Fig. 23.*

ROCKER LEVER SPECIFICATIONS

Application	In. (mm)
Maximum Rocker Lever Bore I.D.	.750 (19.05)
Minimum Rocker Lever Shaft O.D.	.746 (18.94)

1992 ENGINES
Cummins Diesel "B" Series 5.9L 6-Cylinder (Cont.)

CHRY
5-51

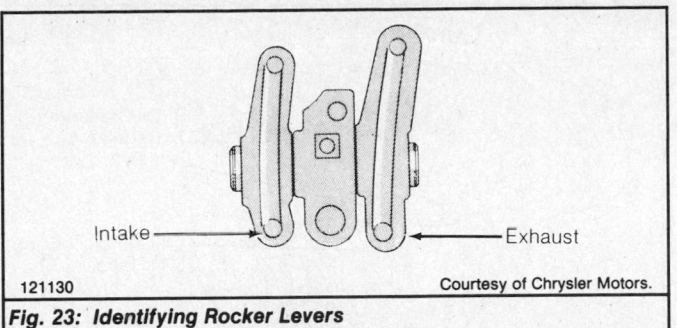

Intake — Exhaust

121130   Courtesy of Chrysler Motors.

Fig. 23: Identifying Rocker Levers

CYLINDER BLOCK ASSEMBLY

Piston & Rod Assembly – Piston must be installed on connecting rod with arrow and connecting rod number properly located. *See Fig. 24.* Piston and connecting rod assembly must be installed with arrow on top of piston toward front of engine.

CAUTION: Four digit number on connecting rod cap and connecting rod must match and be installed toward oil cooler side of engine. See Fig. 24.

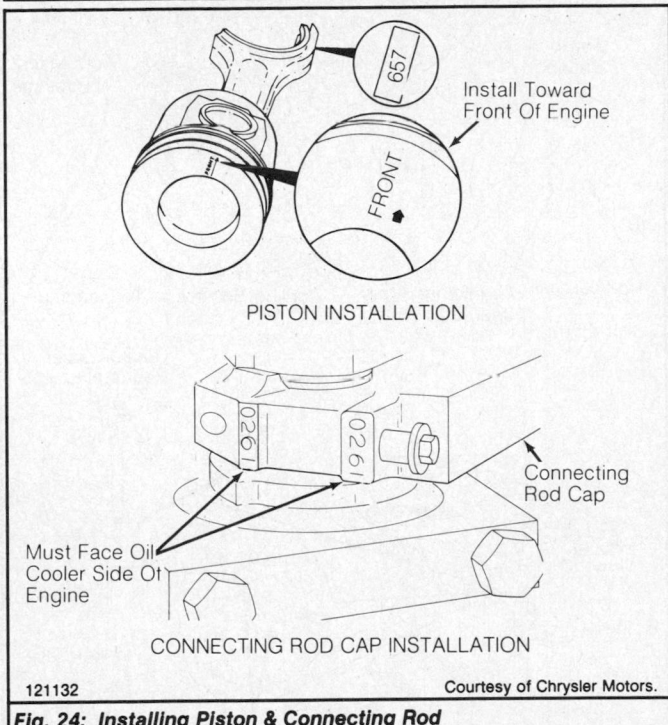

657

Install Toward Front Of Engine

FRONT

PISTON INSTALLATION

026 1   026 1

Connecting Rod Cap

Must Face Oil Cooler Side Of Engine

CONNECTING ROD CAP INSTALLATION

121132   Courtesy of Chrysler Motors.

Fig. 24: Installing Piston & Connecting Rod

Fitting Pistons – Piston diameter should be measured .50" (12.7 mm) from bottom of piston skirt, at 90-degree angle to piston pin. Replace piston if diameter is not within specification. See PISTONS, PINS & RINGS table under ENGINE SPECIFICATIONS at end of article.

CAUTION: Pistons for intercooled and non-intercooled models are different and cannot be interchanged.

Piston Rings – **1)** Ensure piston ring end gap and side clearance are within specification. See PISTONS, PINS & RINGS table under ENGINE SPECIFICATIONS at end of article.
2) Piston rings must be installed with identification mark toward top of piston and rings properly positioned. *See Fig. 25.* Ensure expander in oil control ring is installed with ends of expander ring opposite ends of oil control ring.

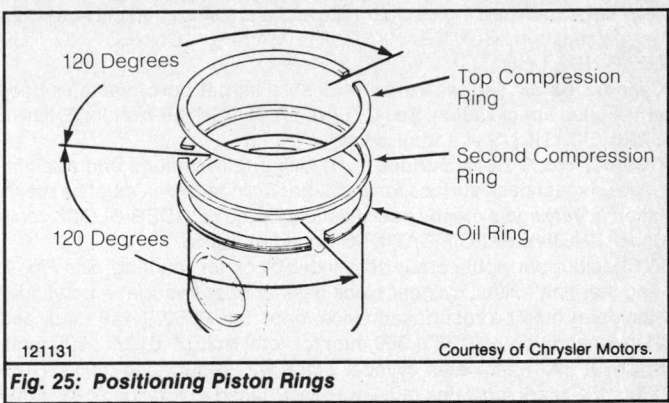

120 Degrees   Top Compression Ring

Second Compression Ring

120 Degrees   Oil Ring

121131   Courtesy of Chrysler Motors.

Fig. 25: Positioning Piston Rings

Rod Bearings – **1)** Before installing rod bearings, lubricate connecting rod bolt threads and head of bolts with engine oil. Install connecting rod so arrow on top of piston is toward front of engine.

CAUTION: Four-digit number on connecting rod cap and connecting rod must match and be installed toward oil cooler side of engine. See Fig. 24.

2) Tighten connecting rod bolts to specification. See TORQUE SPECIFICATIONS table at end of article.
3) Ensure connecting rod bearing oil clearance and side play are within specification. See CRANKSHAFT, MAIN & CONNECTING ROD BEARINGS and CONNECTING RODS tables under ENGINE SPECIFICATIONS at end of article.
Crankshaft & Main Bearings – **1)** Ensure main and connecting rod journal diameters are within specification. See CRANKSHAFT, MAIN & CONNECTING ROD BEARINGS table under ENGINE SPECIFICATIONS at end of article.

CAUTION: Before installing upper main bearings in cylinder block, ensure piston cooling nozzle is installed in bore of cylinder block, next to upper main bearing oil supply passage. The No. 1 main bearing DOES NOT contain a piston cooling nozzle.

2) Ensure dowel rings are installed in main bearing caps before installing. Number on main bearing cap must face oil cooler side of engine. Ensure No. 1 main bearing cap is at front of crankshaft and No. 7 is at flywheel end.
3) Lubricate main bearing cap bolt threads and underside of bolt head with oil before installing. Main bearing cap bolts must be tightened to specification in sequence using 3 steps. *See Fig. 26.* See TORQUE SPECIFICATIONS table at end of article.

CAUTION: Ensure main bearing caps are installed with number on main bearing cap facing oil cooler side of engine. The No. 1 main bearing cap should be at front of crankshaft and No. 7 at flywheel end.

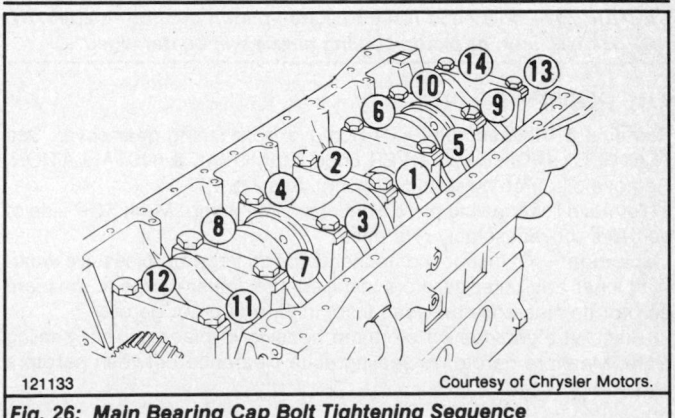

121133   Courtesy of Chrysler Motors.

Fig. 26: Main Bearing Cap Bolt Tightening Sequence

4) Ensure main bearing oil clearance and crankshaft end play are within specification. See CRANKSHAFT, MAIN & CONNECTING ROD BEARINGS table.

Cylinder Block Tappet Bores – Ensure tappet bore diameter does not exceed specification. See CYLINDER BLOCK table under ENGINE SPECIFICATIONS at end of article.

Cylinder Block Deck Surface – **1)** Using feeler gauge and straightedge, inspect deck surface for warpage. Cylinder block must be resurfaced if warpage exceeds specification. See CYLINDER BLOCK table under ENGINE SPECIFICATIONS at end of article.

2) Check upper right corner of cylinder block for marking. *See Fig. 9.* If no marking exists, cylinder block has not been resurfaced. Cylinder block can only be resurfaced twice: once for .0059" (.149 mm), and then an additional .0138" (.350 mm) for total limit of .0197" (.500 mm).

3) An "X" mark indicates cylinder block was resurfaced .0059" (.149 mm); "XX" mark indicates block was resurfaced to total of .0197" (.500 mm). Mark cylinder block if surface is machined.

Cylinder Block Bore – **1)** Measure cylinder bore diameter at 1" (25 mm) and 4.5" (114 mm) below top of cylinder block. Bore cylinder block if diameter, out-of-round or taper exceeds specification. See CYLINDER BLOCK table under ENGINE SPECIFICATIONS at end of article.

2) Cylinder block can be bored twice for oversized pistons and rings. Oversized pistons and rings are available in .0197" (.500 mm) and .0393" (.998 mm) sizes. Cylinder block can also be bored for a repair sleeve, which will restore bore to standard dimensions.

ENGINE OILING

ENGINE LUBRICATION SYSTEM

Gerotor pump provides pressurized lubrication through a cross passage to main passage, and then to overhead, camshaft and crankshaft. Oil passes around cylinder head bolts, into passages of rocker lever pedestals and out to rocker levers. Piston cooling nozzles are located in cylinder block main bearing saddles, except for No. 1 main bearing. *See Fig. 27.*

No piston cooling nozzle is used on No. 1 main bearing saddle. Oil for cylinder No. 1 piston is received from No. 2 main bearing saddle, and oil for No. 2 piston is supplied from No. 3 bearing saddle, etc. Oil cooler housing contains an oil pressure regulator valve.

Crankcase Capacity – Oil capacity is approximately 12 qts. (11.4L) with oil filter.

Oil Pressure – Minimum oil pressure is 10 psi (.7 kg/cm²) at idle and 30 psi (2.1 kg/cm²) at governor rated speed.

PISTON COOLING NOZZLES

Removal & Installation – **1)** Remove crankshaft and upper main bearings. Using a 3/16" pin punch, remove piston cooling nozzle from cylinder block.

2) Inspect piston cooling nozzles for damaged spray tip or cracks. Use pin punch to install piston cooling nozzle until it is even or slightly below main bearing saddle surface.

CAUTION: Use only hand force to install piston cooling nozzles. DO NOT use hammer, or piston cooling nozzle will be damaged.

OIL PUMP

Removal & Disassembly – **1)** Remove front timing gear cover. See FRONT TIMING GEAR COVER under REMOVAL & INSTALLATION. Remove oil pump bolts and oil pump. *See Fig. 27.*

2) Remove rear sealing plate from rear of oil pump. Mark TOP side of gerotors for reassembly reference.

Inspection – **1)** Inspect components for damage or excessive wear. With inner and outer gerotors installed, use feeler gauge to measure gerotor tip clearance between tip of inner and outer gerotor.

2) Place straightedge on oil pump housing in place of rear sealing plate. Measure gerotor-to-sealing plate clearance between gerotors and straightedge.

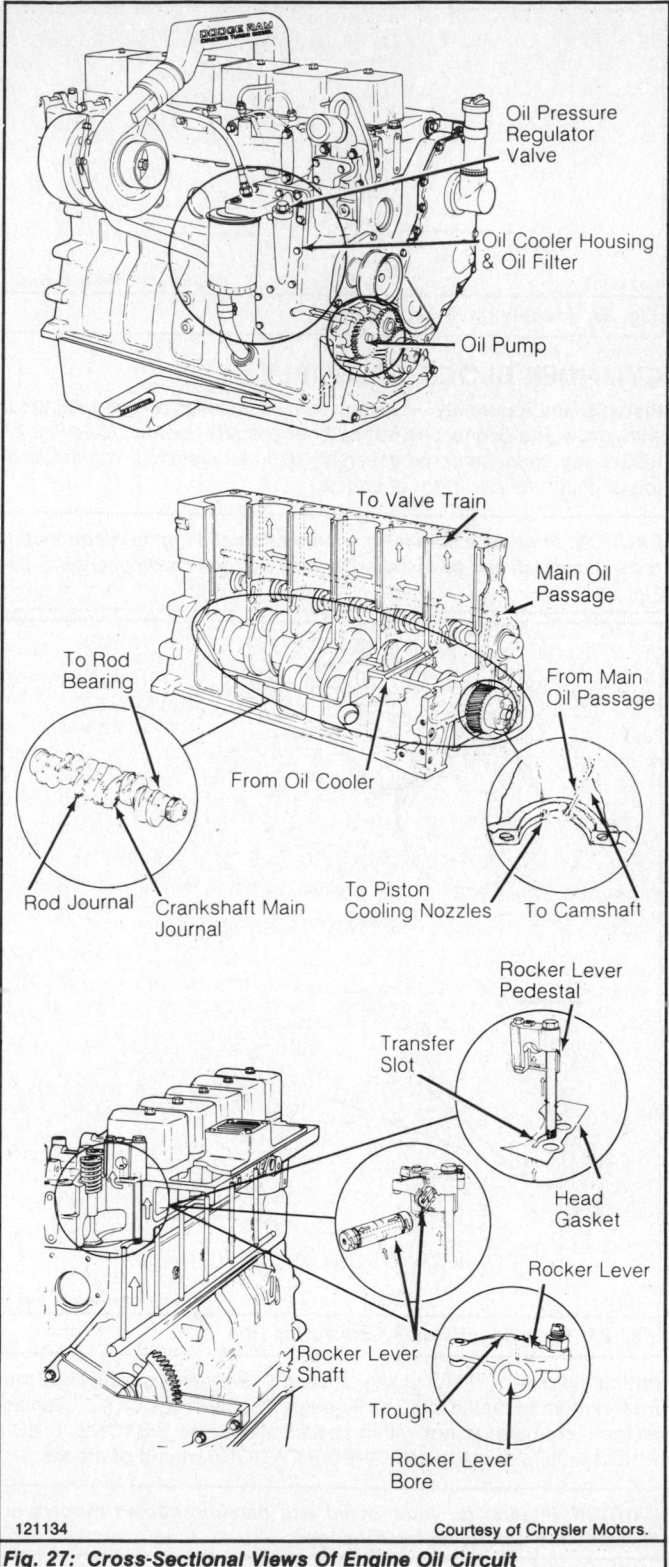

121134   Courtesy of Chrysler Motors.

Fig. 27: Cross-Sectional Views Of Engine Oil Circuit

3) Measure distance between outer gerotor and oil pump housing. Measure backlash between gears on oil pump drive. *See Fig. 28.* Replace oil pump if measurements are not within specification. See OIL PUMP SPECIFICATIONS table.

1992 ENGINES
Cummins Diesel "B" Series 5.9L 6-Cylinder (Cont.)

CHRY
5-53

OIL PUMP SPECIFICATIONS

Application	In. (mm)
Drive Gear Backlash	.003-.015 (.08-.38)
Gerotor Tip Clearance	.007 (.17)
Gerotor-To-Pump Housing Clearance	.015 (.38)
Gerotor-To-Sealing Plate Clearance	.005 (.13)

Reassembly & Installation – 1) To reassemble, reverse disassembly procedure. Ensure gerotors are installed in original location. Lubricate oil pump with engine oil.

2) Install oil pump. Tighten oil pump bolts to specification in sequence. See Fig. 28. See TORQUE SPECIFICATIONS table at end of article.

CAUTION: Ensure idler gear locating pin is aligned with cylinder block during installation. When oil pump is correctly installed, flange on oil pump will not contact cylinder block, as rear sealing plate contacts bottom of bore in cylinder block.

3) Using dial indicator, check oil pump gear backlash on both oil pump gears. Ensure adjoining gear does not rotate while measuring gear backlash. Backlash must be within specification. See Fig. 28. Install remaining components.

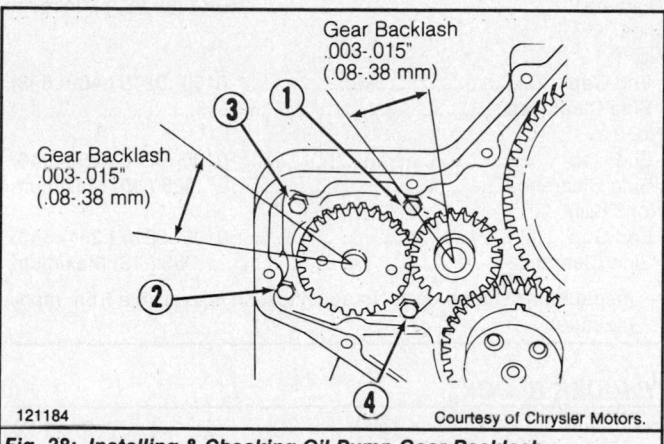

Fig. 28: Installing & Checking Oil Pump Gear Backlash

OIL COOLER

Removal – Drain cooling system. Remove oil filter. Disconnect turbo oil supply line. Remove oil cooler bolts, oil cooler housing, gaskets and cooler element. See Fig. 27.

Testing — 1) Plug outlet fitting of oil cooler element. Install air hose fitting in inlet fitting. Install pressure regulator and air hose. Apply air pressure to oil cooler element. Place oil cooler element in container of water. Element must be covered by water level.

2) Adjust air pressure to **70 psi (4.9 kg/cm²)**. Check for air bubbles, indicating leak exists. Turn off air pressure, and remove test equipment. Replace oil cooler element if leaks exist.

CAUTION: On replacement oil coolers, ensure plastic caps are removed from inlet and outlet ports before installing.

Installation – To install, reverse removal procedure. Fill oil filter with oil before installing.

OIL PRESSURE REGULATOR VALVE

Removal – Remove plug and sealing washer from lower edge of oil cooler housing. See Fig. 27. Remove valve and spring.

Inspection – Inspect plunger for scoring or wear. Ensure plunger moves freely in bore. Using spring tension tester, check spring tension. Replace spring if not to specification. See OIL PRESSURE REGULATOR VALVE SPRING SPECIFICATIONS table.

OIL PRESSURE REGULATOR VALVE SPRING SPECIFICATIONS

Application	Pressure Lbs. @ In. (kg @ mm)
Valve Closed	13.5 @ 1.77 (6.12 @ 44.9)
Valve Open	20.5 @ 1.574 (9.30 @ 39.98)

Installation – To install, reverse removal procedure using new sealing washer on plug. Tighten plug to specification. See TORQUE SPECIFICATIONS table.

TORQUE SPECIFICATIONS

TORQUE SPECIFICATIONS

Application	Ft. Lbs. (N.m)
A/C Compressor Bolt	35 (47)
Air Inlet Housing Bolt	18 (24)
Air Intake Heater Power Supply Nut	10 (14)
Air Crossover Tube Bolt	18 (24)
A/T-To-Cylinder Block Bolt	30 (41)
Belt Tensioner Bolt	32 (43)
Camshaft Thrust Plate Bolt	18 (24)
Clutch Housing-To-Cylinder Block Bolt	30 (41)
Connecting Rod Bolt	
Step 1	26 (35)
Step 2	51 (69)
Step 3	73 (99)
Cylinder Head Bolt [1]	
Step 1 (All Bolts)	66 (90)
Step 2 (Long Bolts) [2]	89 (121)
Step 3 (All Bolts)	Additional 90 Degrees
Engine Mount Through Bolt	30 (41)
Exhaust Manifold Bolt [3]	32 (43)
Fan Assembly [4]	42 (57)
Fan Hub Bearing Retaining Bolt	57 (77)
Fan Hub Mounting Bolt	18 (24)
Flywheel/Flexplate Bolt	101 (137)
Front Timing Gear Cover Bolt	18 (24)
Fuel Heater Mounting Bolt	24 (33)
Fuel High-Pressure Line Nut	18 (24)
Fuel Injection Pump Mounting Nut	18 (24)
Fuel Injection Pump Rear Support Bolt	18 (24)
Fuel Injector Retaining Nut	44 (60)
Fuel Lift Pump Bolt	18 (24)
Fuel Line Banjo Bolt	
At Cylinder Head	18 (24)
At Fuel Injection Pump	24 (33)
Fuel Pump Drive Gear Nut	48 (65)
Gear Housing-To-Cylinder Block Bolt	18 (24)
Intake Manifold Cover Bolt	18 (24)
Lifting Bracket Bolt	57 (77)
Main Bearing Cap Bolt [5]	
Step 1	45 (61)
Step 2	88 (119)
Step 3	129 (175)
Oil Cooler Cover Bolt	18 (24)
Oil Pan Bolt	18 (24)
Oil Pressure Regulator Valve Plug	60 (81)

[1] – Tighten bolts to specification in sequence. See Fig. 8.
[2] – Bolts No. 4, 5, 12, 13, 20 and 21. See Fig. 8.
[3] – Tighten bolts to specification in sequence. See Fig. 6.
[4] – Fan assembly is left-hand thread.
[5] – Tighten bolts to specification in sequence. See Fig. 26.
[6] – Tighten 12-mm bolts to specification in sequence, and then tighten 8-mm bolts to specification. See Fig. 12.

CHRY
5-54

1992 ENGINES
Cummins Diesel "B" Series 5.9L 6-Cylinder (Cont.)

TORQUE SPECIFICATIONS (Cont.)

Application	Ft. Lbs. (N.m)
Oil Pump Bolt	18 (24)
Oil Suction Tube Bolt	18 (24)
Power Steering Pump-To-Vacuum Pump Bolt	18 (24)
Rocker Lever Adjusting Screw Nut	18 (24)
Rocker Lever Cover Bolt	18 (24)
Rocker Lever Pedestal Bolt 6	
8-mm Bolt	18 (24)
12-mm Bolt	
Step 1	66 (90)
Step 2	89 (121)
Step 3	Additional 90 Degrees
Tappet Cover Bolt	18 (24)
Thermostat Housing Bolt	18 (24)
Transmission Adapter Plate Bolt	44 (60)
Turbo Mounting Nut	24 (33)
Turbo Oil Line	
Drain Line	18 (24)
Supply Line	11 (15)
Vacuum Pump-To-Gear Housing Bolt	57 (77)
Vibration Damper Bolt	92 (125)
Water Pump Bolt	18 (24)

Application	INCH Lbs. (N.m)
Air Crossover Tube Clamp	44 (5)
Air Inlet Tube-To-Turbo Clamp	72 (8)
Crankshaft Belt Pulley Bolt	84 (9)
Crankshaft Rear Seal Housing Bolt	84 (9)
Exhaust Pipe-To-Turbo Clamp	72 (8)
Fan Pulley-To-Fan Hub Bolt	84 (9)
Fuel Bleed Screw	72 (8)
Fuel Injector Fuel Line Banjo Bolt	72 (8)
Intercooler Bolt	17 (2)
Intercooler Inlet & Outlet Duct Clamp	72 (8)
Timing Pin Housing Bolt	44 (5)

[1] – Tighten bolts to specification in sequence. See Fig. 8.
[2] – Bolts No. 4, 5, 12, 13, 20 and 21. See Fig. 8.
[3] – Tighten bolts to specification in sequence. See Fig. 6.
[4] – Fan assembly is left-hand thread.
[5] – Tighten bolts to specification in sequence. See Fig. 26.
[6] – Tighten 12-mm bolts to specification in sequence, and then tighten 8-mm bolts to specification. See Fig. 12.

ENGINE SPECIFICATIONS

GENERAL SPECIFICATIONS

Application	Specification
Displacement	360 Cu. In. (5.9L)
Bore	4.02" (102.1 mm)
Stroke	4.72" (119.8 mm)
Compression Ratio	17.5:1
Fuel System	Mechanical Fuel Injection
Horsepower @ RPM	160 @ 2500
Torque Ft. Lbs. @ RPM	400 @ 1750

CONNECTING RODS

Application	In. (mm)
Bore Diameter	
Pin Bore	1.5769 (40.053) Maximum
Side Play	.004-.012 (.10-.30)

CRANKSHAFT, MAIN & CONNECTING ROD BEARINGS

Application	In. (mm)
Crankshaft End Play	.005-.012 (.13-.30)
Main Bearings	
Journal Diameter	3.2662-3.2682 (82.961-83.012)
Journal Out-Of-Round	.002 (.05)
Journal Taper	.0005 (.013)
Oil Clearance	.0047 (.119) Maximum
Connecting Rod Bearings	
Journal Diameter	2.7150-2.7170 (68.961-69.012)
Journal Out-Of-Round	.002 (.05)
Journal Taper	.0005 (.013)
Oil Clearance	.0035 (.089) Maximum

PISTONS, PINS & RINGS

Application	In. (mm)
Pistons	
Diameter	4.009-4.011 (101.83-101.88)
Pin Bore	1.5758 (40.025) Maximum
Pins	
Diameter	1.5744 (39.989) Minimum
Rings	
No. 1	
End Gap	.0160-.0275 (.409-.698)
Side Clearance	[1]
No. 2	
End Gap	.0100-.0215 (.254-.546)
Side Clearance	.006 (.15) Maximum
No. 3 (Oil)	
End Gap	.0100-.0215 (.254-.546)
Side Clearance	.005 (.13) Maximum

[1] – Inspect for damage only. No specification is available from manufacturer.

CYLINDER BLOCK

Application	In. (mm)
Cylinder Bore	
Maximum Diameter	4.0203 (102.116)
Maximum Taper	.003 (.08)
Maximum Out-Of-Round	.0015 (.038)
Maximum Deck Warpage	[1]
Maximum Tappet Bore Diameter	.632 (16.05)

[1] – Warpage should not exceed .0004" (.010 mm) per 2" (51 mm) area; overall or side-to-side warpage should not exceed .012" (.30 mm). See CYLINDER BLOCK DECK SURFACE under CYLINDER BLOCK ASSEMBLY under OVERHAUL for cylinder block marking areas.

VALVES & VALVE SPRINGS

Application	Specification
Intake Valves	
Face Angle	30°
Minimum Margin	.031" (.79 mm)
Stem Diameter	.3126-.3134" (7.940-7.960 mm)
Installed Valve Depth	.039-.060" (.99-1.52 mm)
Exhaust Valves	
Face Angle	45°
Minimum Margin	.031" (.79 mm)
Stem Diameter	.3126-.3134" (7.940-7.960 mm)
Installed Valve Depth	.039-.060" (.99-1.52 mm)
Valve Springs	
Free Length	2.19" (55.6 mm)
Out-Of-Square	.039" (.99 mm)
Pressure	
Valve Closed	65 Lbs. @ 1.94" (29 kg @ 49.3 mm)

1992 ENGINES
Cummins Diesel "B" Series 5.9L 6-Cylinder (Cont.)

CHRY
5-55

CYLINDER HEAD

Application	Specification
Cylinder Head Height	3.730" (94.75 mm)
Maximum Warpage	[1]
Valve Seats	
Intake Valve	
Seat Angle	30°
Seat Width	.060-.080" (1.52-2.03 mm)
Exhaust Valve	
Seat Angle	45°
Seat Width	.060-.080" (1.52-2.03 mm)
Valve Guides	
Valve Guide I.D.	.3157-.3185" (8.019-8.089 mm)
Valve Guide Installed Height	[2]
Valve Stem-To-Guide	
Oil Clearance	.002-.006" (.05-.15 mm)

[1] – Warpage should not exceed .0004" (.010 mm) per 2" (51 mm) area; overall or side-to-side warpage should not exceed .012" (.30 mm).

[2] – See VALVE GUIDES under CYLINDER HEAD under OVERHAUL.

CAMSHAFT

Application	In. (mm)
Maximum Camshaft Bearing & Bore I.D.	
No. 1 Bearing	2.1312 (54.132)
No. 1 Bearing Bore	2.2543 (57.259)
All Other Bores	2.1312 (54.132)
End Play	.006-.010 (.15-.25)
Gear Backlash	.003-.013 (.08-.33)
Minimum Journal Diameter	2.1245 (53.962)
Minimum Lobe Height	
Exhaust	1.841 (46.76)
Intake	1.852 (47.04)
Lift Pump	1.398 (35.51)

TAPPETS

Application	In. (mm)
Bore Diameter	.632 (16.05) Maximum
Tappet Diameter	.627 (15.93) Minimum

1992 ENGINE COOLING
Specifications & Electric Cooling Fans

Caravan, Dakota, Pickup, Ramcharger, RWD Van, Town & Country, Voyager

SPECIFICATIONS

BELT ADJUSTMENT

Belts should be adjusted to proper tension using belt tension gauge. See appropriate BELT ADJUSTMENT SPECIFICATIONS table. Some models may be equipped with automatic belt tensioner to maintain belt tension. Ensure serpentine drive belts are routed properly. *See Figs. 1-6.*

NOTE: *Cracking across belt rib surfaces is considered normal wear. Belt must be replaced if cracks run parallel to rib area.*

4-CYLINDER & V6 BELT ADJUSTMENT SPECIFICATIONS

Application	New Belt Lbs. (kg)	[1] Used Belt Lbs. (kg)
2.5L		
Dakota		
A/C Compressor	160 (72.6)	80 (36.3)
Alternator/Water Pump Poly "V"	160 (72.6)	80 (36.3)
Power Steering Pump	120 (54.4)	80 (36.3)
Caravan & Voyager		
A/C Compressor	125 (56.7)	80 (36.3)
Alternator/Water Pump Poly "V"	130 (60.0)	80 (36.3)
Power Steering Pump	105 (47.6)	80 (36.3)
3.0L		
A/C Compressor	125 (56.7)	80 (36.3)
Serpentine	[2]	[2]
3.3L		
A/C Compressor	[2]	[2]
Serpentine	[2]	[2]
3.9L		
Serpentine	[2]	[2]

[1] – Belt is considered used after 15 minutes of service.
[2] – Equipped with dynamic tensioner; no adjustment is required.

V8 BELT ADJUSTMENT SPECIFICATIONS

Application	Tension Lbs. (kg)
5.2L	
Serpentine	[1]
5.9L	
All Belts [2]	
New Belt	100-140 (45.4-63.5)
Used Belt [3]	60-90 (27.2-40.9)

[1] – Equipped with dynamic tensioner; no adjustment is required.
[2] – Diesel engines have automatic belt tensioner.
[3] – Belt is considered used after 15 minutes of service.

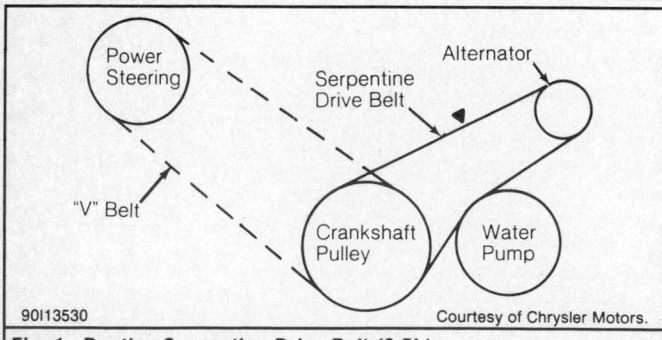

Fig. 1: Routing Serpentine Drive Belt (2.5L)

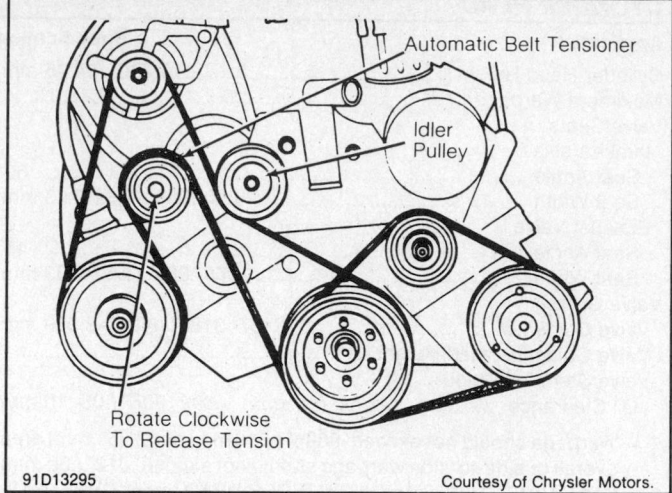

Fig. 2: Routing Serpentine Drive Belt (3.0L)

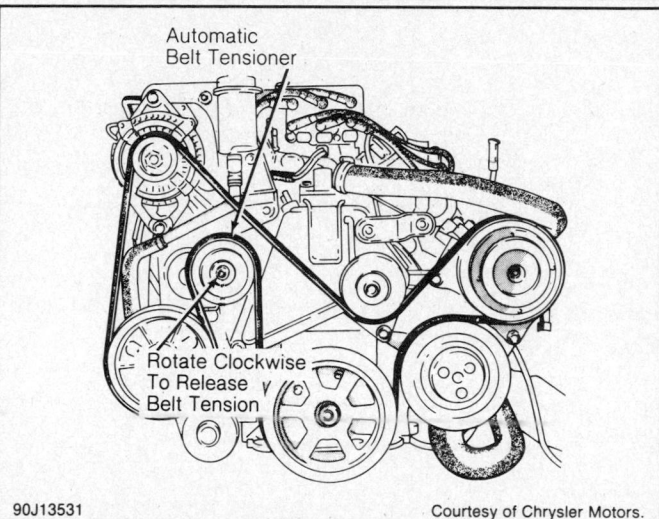

Fig. 3: Routing Serpentine Drive Belt (3.3L)

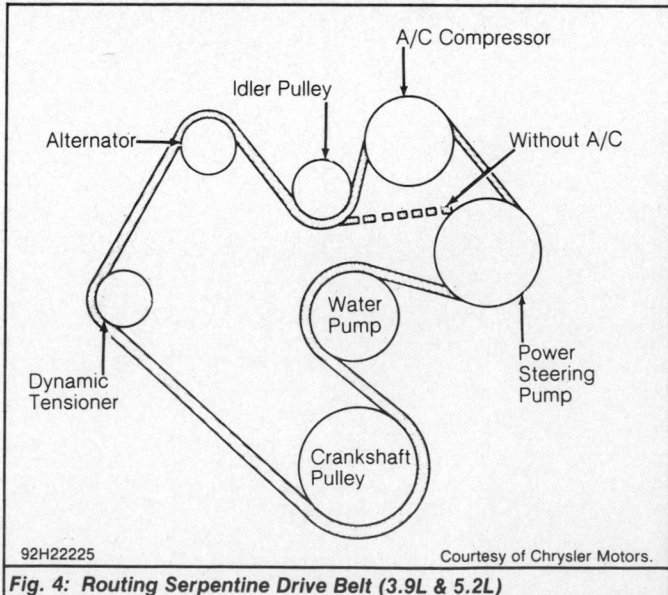

Fig. 4: Routing Serpentine Drive Belt (3.9L & 5.2L)

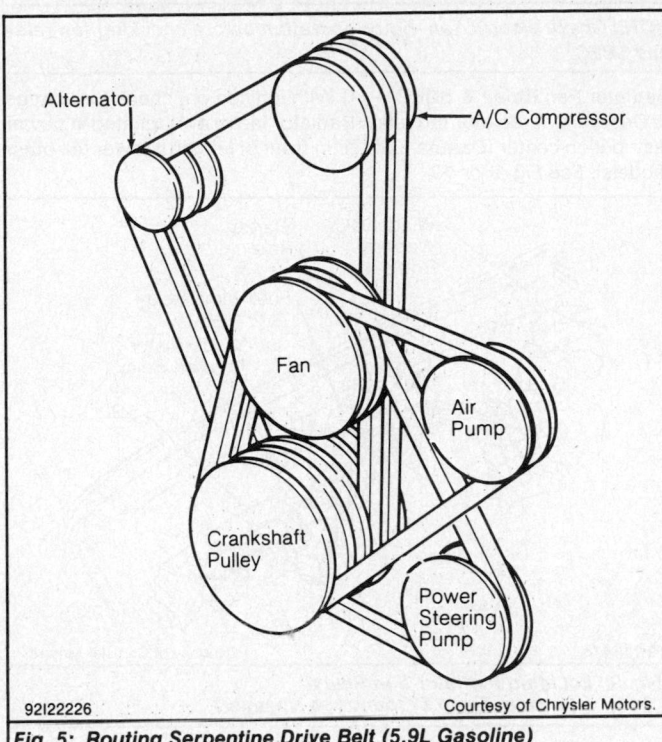

Fig. 5: Routing Serpentine Drive Belt (5.9L Gasoline)

92I22226   Courtesy of Chrysler Motors.

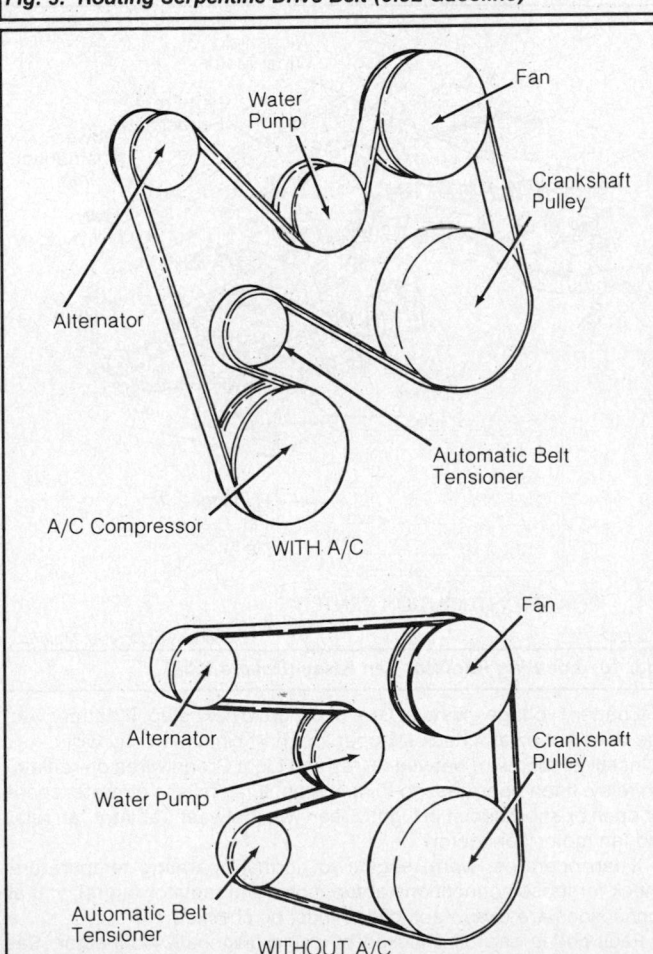

91F13297   Courtesy of Chrysler Motors.

Fig. 6: Routing Serpentine Drive Belt (5.9L Diesel)

COOLING SYSTEM SPECIFICATIONS

COOLING SYSTEM SPECIFICATIONS

Model	Specification
Coolant Replacement Interval	
Except 5.9L Diesel .... [1]	
5.9L Diesel .... 24 Months Or 24,000 miles	
Coolant Capacity [2]	
Caravan, Town & Country, & Voyager	
2.5L .... [3] 9.5 Qts. (9.0L)	
3.0L & 3.3L .... [3] 10.0 Qts. (9.5L)	
Dakota	
2.5L .... 9.8 Qts. (9.3L)	
3.9L .... 14.0 Qts (13.2L)	
5.2L .... 14.3 Qts. (13.5L)	
Pickup & Ramcharger	
3.9L .... 15.1 Qts. (14.3L)	
5.2L	
2WD .... 17.0 Qts. (16.1L)	
4WD .... 16.5 Qts. (15.6L)	
5.9L	
Gasoline Engines	
2WD .... 15.5 Qts. (14.7L)	
4WD .... 15.0 Qts. (14.2L)	
Diesel Engines	
A/T Models .... [4] 16.5 Qts. (15.6L)	
M/T Models .... [4] 15.5 Qts. (14.7L)	
RWD Van	
3.9L .... 14.6 Qts. (13.8L)	
5.2L .... 16.5 Qts. (15.6L)	
5.9L	
With Rear Heater .... 16.0 Qts. (15.1L)	
Without Rear Heater .... 15.0 Qts. (14.2L)	
Pressure Cap .... 16 psi	
Thermostat Temperature Rating	
Caravan, Dakota, Town & Country, & Voyager .... 195°F (90°C)	
Pickup, Ramcharger & RWD Van	
Gasoline Engines .... 192°F (88°C)	
Diesel Engines .... [5]	

[1] – Drain and flush cooling system after 36 months or 52,500 miles and then every 24 months or 30,000 miles thereafter.
[2] – Capacities listed are approximate.
[3] – Capacity includes one pt. (.4L) for coolant recovery tank. Add one qt. (.9L) for models with rear heater.
[4] – Add one qt. (.9L) for coolant recovery bottle.
[5] – Thermostat starts to open at 181°F (83°C) and fully opens at 203°F (95°C).

COOLING SYSTEM BLEEDING

2.5L – Remove vent plug from top of thermostat housing. Fill cooling system, and allow air to bleed from cooling system. Install vent plug once coolant reaches thermostat housing level. Tighten vent plug to **15 ft. lbs. (20 N.m).**

3.3L – 1) Remove engine temperature sending unit. Engine temperature sending unit is located in front of cylinder head, near thermostat housing, just below spark plug wire holder.

2) Fill cooling system until coolant reaches engine temperature sending unit. Install engine temperature sending unit, and tighten to **60 INCH lbs. (7 N.m).** Finish filling cooling system.

ELECTRIC COOLING FAN

OPERATION

Caravan, Dakota 2.5L, Town & Country, & Voyager – Electric cooling fan should not operate during engine cranking. Fan should operate whenever A/C compressor clutch is engaged. If vehicle is not equipped with A/C or if A/C is off, fan should turn on or off as coolant temperature sensor senses following changes in coolant temperatures. See COOLING FAN OPERATING TEMPERATURES table.

COOLING FAN OPERATING TEMPERATURES

Vehicle Speed	Coolant Temp. °F (°C)	Cooling Fan Status
40 MPH Or More	230 (110) Or More	.... Turns On
40 MPH Or More	220 (104) Or Less	.... Shuts Off
40 MPH Or Less	210 (99) Or More	.... Turns On
40 MPH Or Less	200 (93) Or Less	.... Shuts Off

Coolant temperature sensor sends a signal to Single Board Engine Controller (SBEC), which controls cooling fan operation through a radiator fan relay.

On Caravan, Town & Country and Voyager, fan will operate to prevent steaming water vapor from outside of radiator. Fan will operate for 3 minutes when vehicle is stopped with engine idling, coolant temperature is 100-195°F (38-97°C) and ambient temperature is less than 60°F (16°C).

TROUBLE SHOOTING & COMPONENT TESTING

NOTE: If fan motor is noticeably overheated, system voltage may be excessive. Check charging system.

Electric Fan Motor – To check electric fan motor, disconnect fan motor electrical connector. Ensure correct polarity, and connect a 12-volt battery source and ground to fan motor electrical connector. See Fig. 7 or 8. Replace fan motor if it fails to operate.

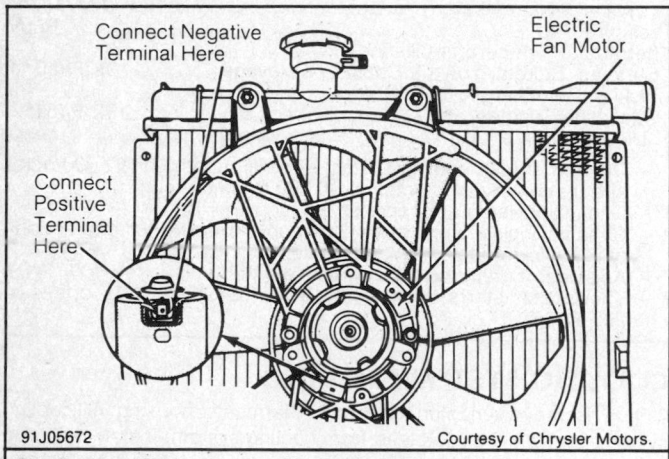

Fig. 7: Identifying Electric Fan Motor Terminals (Caravan, Town & Country, & Voyager)

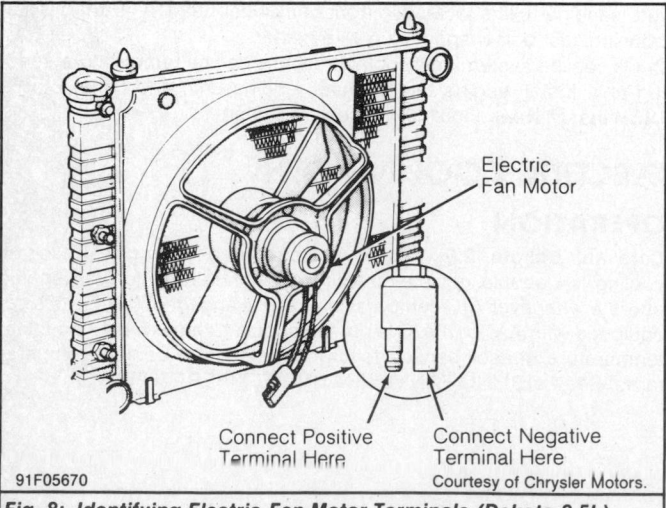

Fig. 8: Identifying Electric Fan Motor Terminals (Dakota 2.5L)

NOTE: Check electric fan motor operation before checking fan relay and SBEC.

Radiator Fan Relay & SBEC – 1) With ignition on, check for voltage at Gray wire of radiator fan relay. Radiator fan relay is located in power distribution center (Dakota 2.5L) or in front of left strut tower (all other models). See Fig. 9 or 10.

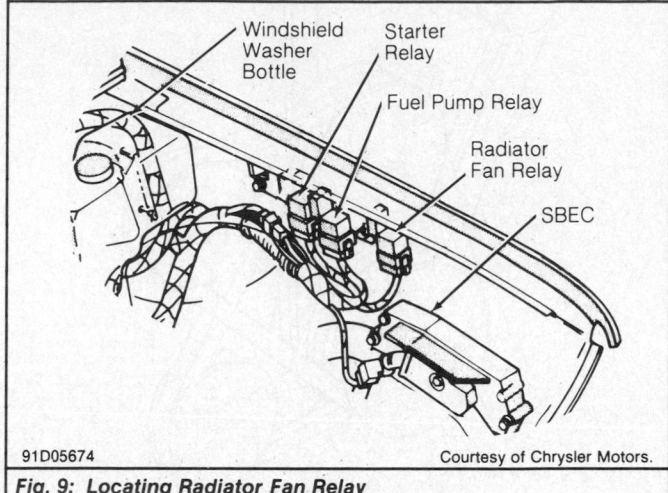

Fig. 9: Locating Radiator Fan Relay (Caravan, Town & Country, & Voyager)

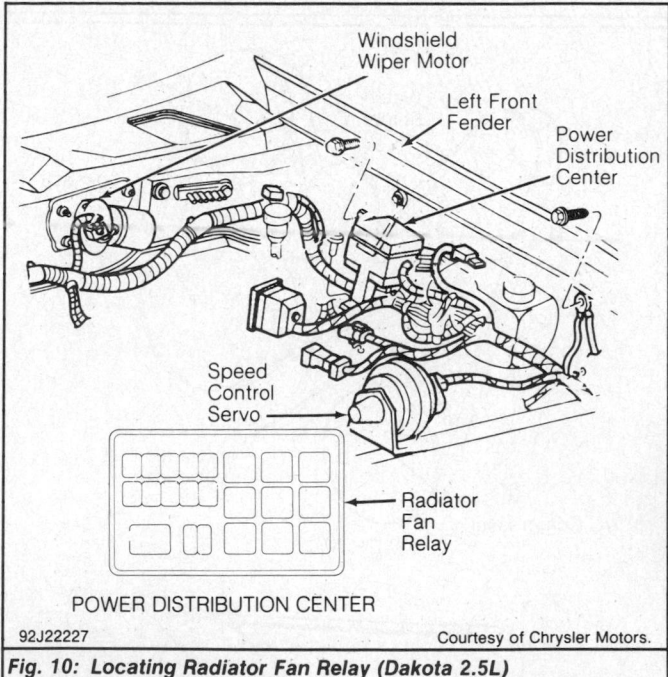

Fig. 10: Locating Radiator Fan Relay (Dakota 2.5L)

2) If battery voltage exists at Gray wire, go to next step. If battery voltage does not exist, check for open or short circuit in Gray wire.
3) Install jumper wire between Gray and Light Green wires on radiator fan relay. If fan operates, go to next step. If fan fails to operate, check for open or short circuit in Light Green wire between radiator fan relay and fan motor connector.
4) If fan operates, warm engine to normal operating temperature. Check for loose connections at fan motor and radiator fan relay. If all connections are okay, fault codes must be checked.
5) Fault codes can be checked by using diagnostic connector. See appropriate SELF-DIAGNOSTICS article in ENGINE PERFORMANCE for complete instructions on connecting diagnostic tester and checking fault codes.

6) If fault code indicates 88-12-35-55 (RADIATOR FAN RELAY), turn ignition on and check for battery voltage at Dark Blue wire of radiator fan relay. If battery voltage exists, go to next step. If voltage is 0-1 volt, go to step **9)**.

7) With ignition off, disconnect 60-pin connector from SBEC, located on right wheelwell of engine compartment (Dakota 2.5L) or left front corner of engine compartment (all other models).

8) Turn ignition on. Check for battery voltage at terminal No. 31 (Dark Blue/Pink) wire of connector. *See Fig. 11.* If battery voltage exists and female terminal is not damaged, replace SBEC. If no voltage exists, repair open or short in Dark Blue/Pink wire from radiator fan relay to SBEC.

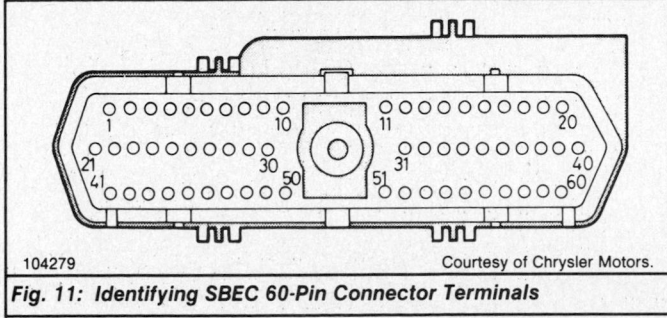

104279   Courtesy of Chrysler Motors.

Fig. 11: *Identifying SBEC 60-Pin Connector Terminals*

9) If voltage is 0-1 volt in step **6)**, turn ignition off. Disconnect 60-pin connector from SBEC. Turn ignition on. Check for battery voltage at Dark Blue wire of radiator fan relay. If battery voltage exists, replace SBEC. If voltage is 0-1 volt, go to next step.

10) With ignition on, test for battery voltage at Dark Blue/Pink wire at radiator fan relay. If battery voltage exists, replace radiator fan relay. If no voltage exists, repair open or short circuit in Dark Blue/Pink wire between radiator fan relay and SBEC. Turn ignition off, reconnect 60-pin connector to SBEC and test system.

WIRING DIAGRAMS

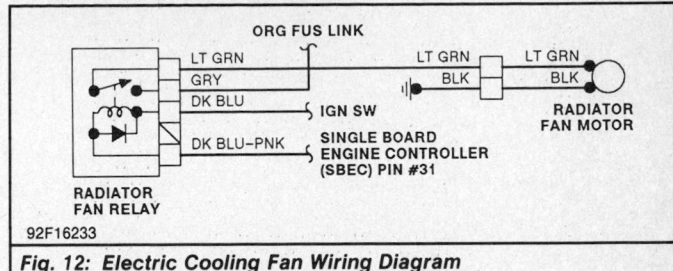

92F16233

Fig. 12: *Electric Cooling Fan Wiring Diagram (Caravan, Town & Country, & Voyager)*

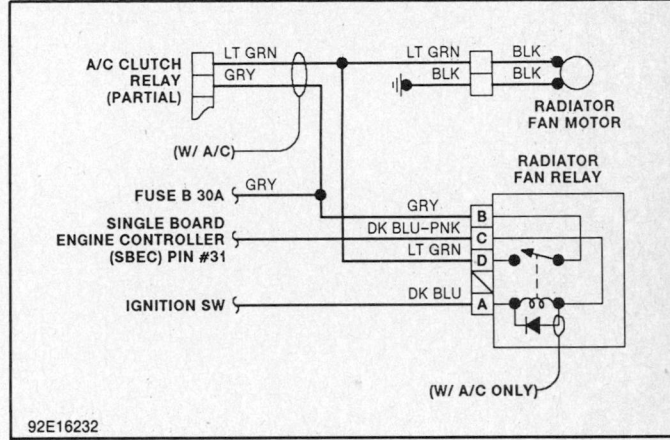

92E16232

Fig. 13: *Electric Cooling Fan Wiring Diagram (Dakota 2.5L)*

Caravan, Voyager

DESCRIPTION

Clutches are a single plate, dry disc-type with a self-adjusting cable release mechanism. *See Fig. 1.* Clutch pedal is connected to a torque shaft which actuates a cable and lever. Upper end of clutch pedal pivots on a pedal bracket using 2 nylon bushings, which do not require periodic lubrication. All models use a constant-running clutch release bearing.

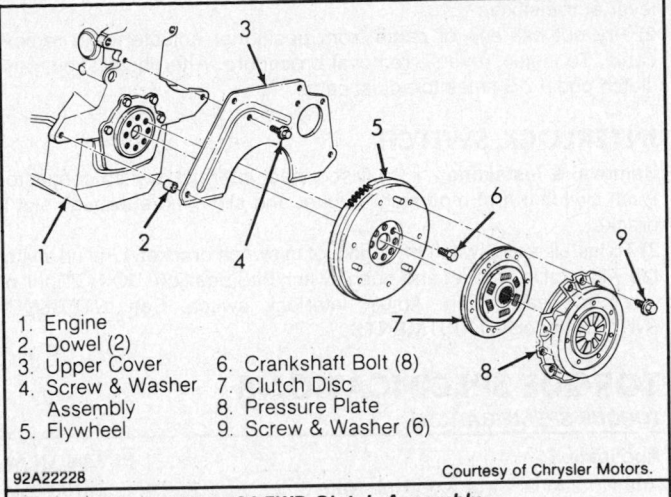

1. Engine
2. Dowel (2)
3. Upper Cover
4. Screw & Washer Assembly
5. Flywheel
6. Crankshaft Bolt (8)
7. Clutch Disc
8. Pressure Plate
9. Screw & Washer (6)

92A22228   Courtesy of Chrysler Motors.

Fig. 1: Exploded View Of FWD Clutch Assembly

ADJUSTMENTS

AXLE SHAFT POSITIONING

1) Engine mount bolt holes are slotted for side-to-side positioning of engine/transaxle assembly. With vehicle completely assembled, ensure front wheels are in straight ahead position. Vehicle should be on platform hoist or alignment rack.

2) Using a tape measure, measure distance from inner edge of outer boot to inner edge of inner boot (dimension "A") on both axle shafts. *See Fig. 2.* This measurement must be taken at bottom of axle shaft only.

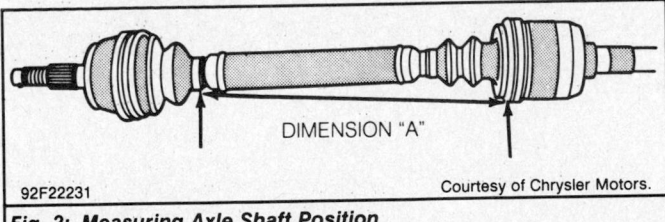

DIMENSION "A"

92F22231   Courtesy of Chrysler Motors.

Fig. 2: Measuring Axle Shaft Position

3) Ensure right dimension "A" measures **18.7-19.1" (475-485 mm)** and left dimension "A" measures **8.4-8.8" (213-224 mm)**. If both axle shafts are within specification, no further service is necessary. If either left or right axle shaft is not within specification, support engine/transaxle assembly using a floor jack.

4) Loosen right engine mount fasteners, front engine mount bracket and front crossmember fasteners. Pry engine right or left as required to obtain correct axle shaft length.

5) Tighten mounting bolts/nuts to specification. Recheck axle shaft length. Install damper weight (if equipped), and tighten to specification. See TORQUE SPECIFICATIONS table at end of article.

CABLE OPERATION

Clutch release cable is self-adjusting. When cable is properly installed, spring on clutch pedal will hold release cable in proper position, regardless of clutch disc wear. *See Fig. 3.*

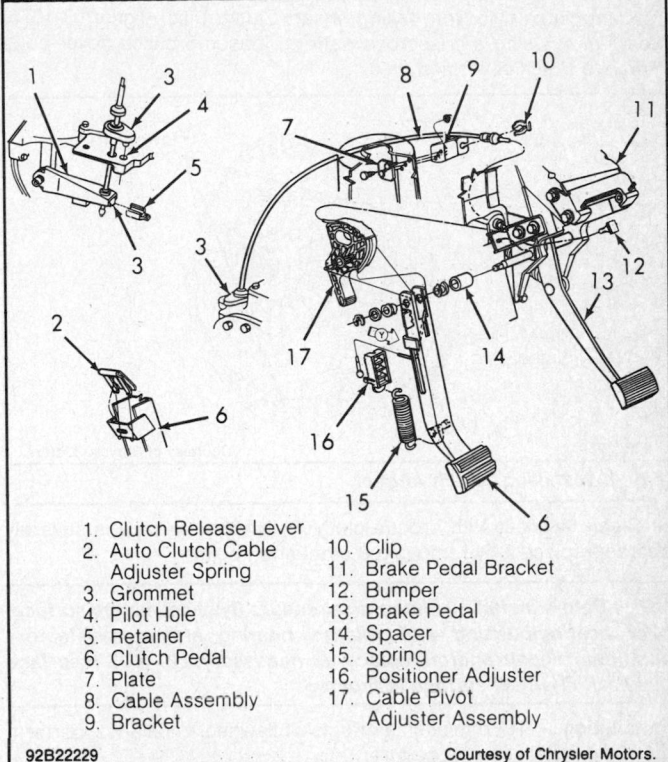

1. Clutch Release Lever
2. Auto Clutch Cable Adjuster Spring
3. Grommet
4. Pilot Hole
5. Retainer
6. Clutch Pedal
7. Plate
8. Cable Assembly
9. Bracket
10. Clip
11. Brake Pedal Bracket
12. Bumper
13. Brake Pedal
14. Spacer
15. Spring
16. Positioner Adjuster
17. Cable Pivot Adjuster Assembly

92B22229   Courtesy of Chrysler Motors.

Fig. 3: Exploded View Of Self-Adjusting Clutch Release Mechanism

INTERLOCK SWITCH

1) Remove floor mat. Set parking brake. Disconnect clutch cable at transaxle. Press clutch pedal and loosen striker adjusting nut, located on left side of clutch pedal.

2) Slide striker plate forward to fully compress interlock switch plunger. Tighten adjusting nut to **105 INCH lbs. (12 N.m)**. Reconnect clutch cable.

REMOVAL & INSTALLATION

WARNING: When battery is disconnected, vehicle computer and memory systems may lose memory data. Driveability problems may exist until computer systems have completed a relearn cycle. See COMPUTER RELEARN PROCEDURES article in GENERAL INFORMATION before disconnecting battery.

CLUTCH ASSEMBLY

CAUTION: When servicing clutch assembly or components, DO NOT create dust by sanding or cleaning clutch parts using dry brush or compressed air.

Removal – 1) Disconnect negative battery cable. Disconnect speedometer cable and clutch cable. Disconnect back-up light harness and starter motor wiring. Remove starter motor.

2) Disconnect gearshift operating lever from selector shaft. Install lifting eye on battery ground strap bolt (on left side of engine). Using an engine support fixture, support engine. Remove operating lever-to-transaxle retaining screw.

3) Raise and support vehicle. Remove front wheels and left front splash shield. Drain transaxle oil. Remove left engine mount from transaxle. Remove anti-rotational link from crossmember bracket, but DO NOT remove bracket from transaxle.

4) Remove left and right axle shafts, and support aside. Secure transaxle jack under transaxle, and remove transaxle-to-engine bolts. Ensure all cables, mounts and wires have been disconnected and do not interfere when lowering transaxle.

5) Scribe reassembly reference mark on clutch cover and flywheel. To prevent clutch disc from falling, insert Clutch Disc Aligner (C-4676). *See Fig. 4.* Using a crisscross pattern, loosen 6 clutch cover bolts. Remove clutch cover and disc.

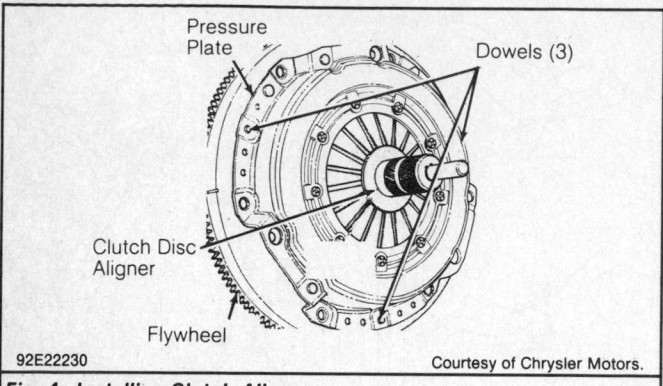

92E22230   Courtesy of Chrysler Motors.

Fig. 4: Installing Clutch Aligner

6) Clean flywheel with crocus cloth. If flywheel surface is severely scored, replace it by removing 8 crankshaft bolts.

NOTE: Before installing clutch disc, ensure flywheel mating surface, pilot bearing/bushing and release bearing are in satisfactory condition. Repair and/or replace as necessary. DO NOT resurface flywheel. Flywheel surface is tapered.

Installation – 1) To minimize effects of flywheel unbalance, perform following installation procedure:
- Using NEW flywheel attaching bolts, loosely assemble flywheel to crankshaft.
- Rotate flywheel until daub of white paint, indicating heavy side, is at 12 o'clock position.
- Using a crisscross pattern, torque flywheel attaching bolts to **70 ft. lbs. (95 N.m).**

2) Align reference marks, and position pressure plate and clutch disc on flywheel. Using clutch aligner, center clutch disc and apply pressure to sliding cone.

3) Install pressure plate-to-flywheel bolts to hold disc in position. Using a crisscross pattern, tighten pressure plate-to-flywheel bolts 1-2 turns at a time to specification. See TORQUE SPECIFICATIONS table at end of article.

4) Remove clutch aligner. To complete installation, reverse removal procedure. Check axle shaft positioning. See AXLE SHAFT POSITIONING under ADJUSTMENTS. Install a NEW gearshift operating lever attaching bolt. Refill transaxle with fluid to proper lever. See appropriate article in TRANSMISSION SERVICING. Push clutch pedal 2-3 times to adjust cable.

CLUTCH CABLE

Removal & Installation – 1) Remove clip from shock tower mount, and remove cable from bracket. Remove retainer from clutch release lever at transaxle.

2) Pry out ball end of cable from positioner adjuster, and remove cable. To install, reverse removal procedure. After installation, push clutch pedal 2-3 times to adjust cable.

INTERLOCK SWITCH

Removal & Installation – 1) Disconnect interlock switch connector. Push switch out of mounting bracket and slide wires through slot in bracket.

2) To install, slide switch through slot in switch bracket. Line up switch tab with slot in bracket and push switch into position. DO NOT pull on wires to seat switch. Adjust interlock switch. See INTERLOCK SWITCH under ADJUSTMENTS.

TORQUE SPECIFICATIONS
TORQUE SPECIFICATIONS

Application	Ft. Lbs. (N.m.)
Anti-Rotational Strut Axle Hub Nut	180 (244)
Ball Joint Clamp Bolt	70 (95)
Bracket-To-Stud Nut	17 (23)
Damper Weight Bolt	21 (28)
Flywheel-To-Crankshaft Bolt	70 (95)
Front Motor Mount Bolt	40 (54)
Left Motor Mount Bolt	40 (54)
Mount-To-Engine Block & Transaxle Case Bolt	70 (95)
Pressure Plate-To-Flywheel Bolt	21 (28)
Transaxle Case-To-Engine Block Bolt	70 (95)
Wheel Lug Nut	95 (129)

	INCH Lbs. (N.m)
Interlock Switch Bracket Nut	105 (12)
Transaxle Cover-To-Case Bolt	105 (12)

Dakota, Pickup, Ramcharger, RWD Van

DESCRIPTION

Clutches on all models are dry, single disc design. Adjustment for wear is not possible. Clutch pedal is connected to release fork through a hydraulic master cylinder and slave cylinder and is not adjustable. Pre-lubricated clutch bearing is constant running type. External adjustments cannot be made.

TRANSMISSION/TRANSFER CASE APPLICATION

Application	Transmission
Dakota	AX 15 & NP 2500
Pickup	¹ G360 & NV 4500
Ramcharger	NV 4500
RWD Van	AX 15
	Transfer Case
Dakota	NP 231
Pickup	
W150	NP 241
W250/350	NP 205
Ramcharger	NP 241

¹ – Diesel only.

ADJUSTMENTS

CLUTCH PEDAL FREE PLAY

NOTE: Clutches are a single, dry disc type. Adjustment for wear is not possible. Clutch is actuated through hydraulic master cylinder and slave cylinder and is self-adjusting.

REMOVAL & INSTALLATION

WARNING: Before removing engine/transmission assembly on compressed natural gas powered vehicles, see COMPRESSED NATURAL GAS SAFETY PRECAUTIONS article in GENERAL INFORMATION.

COMPRESSED NATURAL GAS FUEL SYSTEM PURGING

Fuel Tube Purging – 1) Close control valve (clockwise) on side mounted fuel cylinder. Close control valves (clockwise) on both of rear mounted fuel cylinders. Open manual shutoff valve.

2) Start engine, and operate it until it runs out of fuel. Attempt 3 more engine starts. If check valve or fuel fill receptacle is to be serviced, slowly loosen inlet side of fuel fill tube fitting at check valve. Approximately 25 psi of natural gas pressure may flow from loosened fitting. All fuel tubes are now purged of natural gas between fuel cylinders and engine; fuel system may be opened.

Fuel Cylinder Purging – 1) Open manual shutoff valve. Open only fuel control valves (counterclockwise) on fuel cylinders to be serviced. Close all control valves (clockwise) on fuel cylinders not being serviced.

2) Start engine, and operate it until it runs out of fuel. Attempt 3 more engine starts. All fuel tubes and opened cylinders are now purged of natural gas between fuel cylinders and engine; fuel system may be opened.

TRANSFER CASE

CAUTION: When removing transfer case, DO NOT allow propeller shafts to hang free as damage to universal joints may result.

Removal (NP 205) – 1) Raise and support vehicle. Drain transfer case. Disconnect vehicle speed sensor harness connector. Mark front and rear propeller shaft yokes for installation reference. Disconnect propeller shafts at transfer case, and support to one side.

2) Disconnect shift lever rod from shift lever on transfer case. Secure transfer case to transmission jack using a safety chain. Remove transfer case-to-transmission adapter bolts. Move transfer case to rear until input shaft clears adapter. Lower transfer case from vehicle.

Installation – To install transfer case, reverse removal procedure. Tighten all nuts and bolts to specification. See TORQUE SPECIFICATIONS table at end of article. Fill transfer case with lubricant. Use API Service SG or SG/CD SAE 30 viscosity grade oil.

Removal (NP 231 & NP 241) – 1) Raise and support vehicle, remove drain plug and drain transfer case. Mark front and rear output shaft yokes and propeller shafts for installation reference. Disconnect vehicle speed sensor harness, speedometer cable (if equipped) and vacuum switch hoses. Disconnect shift lever link from operating lever.

2) Support transfer case using suitable transmission jack. On NP 241, remove skid plate and skid plate crossmember. On all models, remove rear crossmember. Disconnect front and rear propeller shafts at yokes, and support to one side. Remove nuts attaching transfer case to transmission adapter.

3) Move transfer case assembly to rear until it is clear of transmission adapter. Remove transfer case from vehicle. Remove all gasket material from rear of transmission adapter housing.

Installation – 1) Install new transmission-to-transfer case gasket with sealer on both sides. Align transfer case with transmission. Rotate transfer case output shaft until transmission output shaft engages transfer case input shaft.

2) Move transfer case until case seats flush against transmission. Install transfer case attaching nuts. To complete installation, reverse removal procedure. Fill transfer case with lubricant. Use Mopar ATF Plus Type 7176 or Dexron-II. Tighten all nuts and bolts to specification. See TORQUE SPECIFICATIONS table at end of article.

TRANSMISSION

Removal (AX 15 & NP 2500) – 1) Shift transmission lever to NEUTRAL position. On NP 2500, remove upper shift lever. On all models, raise and support vehicle. On AX 15, support transmission using jackstand, remove rear crossmember and lower transmission slightly. Press shift lever retainer downward and turn it counterclockwise to release shifter. Allow shift lever to hang from shift boot.

2) On all models, drain transmission fluid. Mark propeller shaft and rear axle yokes for reassembly reference. Disconnect and remove propeller shaft. Disconnect wires from distance sensor. Loosen sensor coupling, and remove sensor from speedometer adapter. Remove speedometer adapter and pinion gear. Disconnect back-up light switch wires.

3) Install Engine Support (C-3487-A) over frame rails. Ensure ends of engine support are positioned against underside of oil pan flange. Raise engine slightly. On AX 15, remove clutch slave cylinder, and secure it aside. Remove engine timing sensor and starter motor. On all models, disconnect insulator from extension housing.

4) On AX 15, remove clutch housing-to-engine bolts. On NP 2500, support transmission using suitable transmission jack and remove center crossmember. Remove transmission-to-clutch housing bolts. Slide transmission rearward until input shaft clears clutch disc. On all models, lower transmission from vehicle.

Installation – To install, reverse removal procedure. Apply high-temperature grease to pilot bushing located in end of crankshaft. Fill transmission with appropriate fluid.

Removal (G360) – 1) Disconnect negative battery cable. Remove upper shift boot attaching screws and upper shift boot. Remove shift lever extension by unthreading it from shift lever stub shaft. Remove lower boot attaching screws and lower boot. Remove shift tower boot. Remove 2 shifter alignment bolts from side of shift tower. Remove snap ring securing stub shaft in tower. Remove stub shaft.

2) Raise and support vehicle. Mark propeller shaft and axle yokes for installation reference, and remove propeller shaft(s). Disconnect speed sensor connector. Support transmission using suitable jackstand. On 4WD models, remove skid plates (if equipped) and transfer case crossmember. Disconnect shift rods at transfer case. Support transfer case using jack. Remove transfer case bolts. Move transfer case rearward, and disengage front input spline.

3) Lower transfer case from vehicle. On all models, remove bolts attaching transmission rear mount to crossmember. Support transmission using suitable transmission jack, and move jackstand underneath engine. Remove crossmember-to-frame braces and crossmember. Remove clutch slave cylinder shield. Remove slave cylinder, and secure it aside. Disconnect back-up light switch connector.

4) Remove transmission-to-clutch housing bolts. Using safety chains, secure transmission to transmission jack. Slide transmission rearward until input shaft clears clutch disc, and lower transmission from vehicle.

Installation – To install, reverse removal procedure. Apply high-temperature grease to pilot bushing located in end of crankshaft.

Removal (NV 4500) – **1)** Disconnect negative battery cable. Shift transmission to Neutral. Disconnect shift boot, and remove shifter lever from transmission stub lever. Raise and support vehicle. Remove skid plate (if equipped). Drain transmission if it is being repaired.

2) Index mark propeller shaft(s) for reassembly reference, and remove shaft(s). Remove front exhaust pipe. Support engine using adjustable jackstand. Disconnect speed sensor harness connector, back-up light harness connector and speedometer cable (if equipped).

3) On 4WD models, remove transfer case. On all models, support transmission using suitable transmission jack and remove rear crossmember. Disconnect transmission harness connectors. Remove clutch slave cylinder, and secure it aside. Remove transmission-to-clutch housing bolts. Slide transmission rearward until input shaft clears clutch assembly. Lower transmission from vehicle.

Installation – To install, reverse removal procedure. Apply high-temperature grease to pilot bushing located in end of crankshaft. Align reference marks made on propeller shaft(s) during removal.

CLUTCH ASSEMBLY

CAUTION: Clutch disc may contain asbestos fibers which can cause serious health risk. DO NOT sand clutch components. DO NOT clean components using compressed air. To clean components, use a water-dampened cloth.

Removal – With transmission and clutch housing removed, mark pressure plate and flywheel for reassembly reference. Install clutch aligner in clutch disc to prevent disc from falling. Loosen pressure plate bolts evenly to avoid warping pressure plate. Remove pressure plate and disc from flywheel. *See Fig. 1.*

Installation – To install, reverse removal procedure using clutch aligner. Ensure reference marks are aligned. Tighten pressure plate bolts evenly to prevent warpage. See TORQUE SPECIFICATIONS table at end of article.

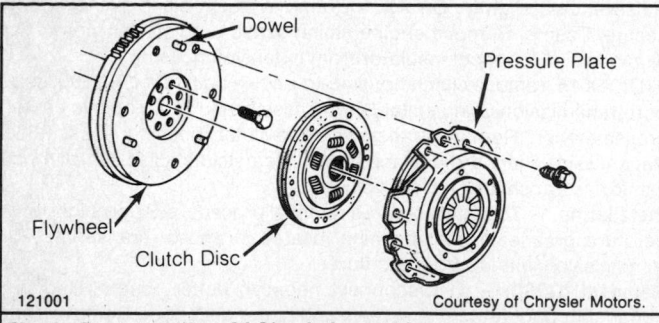

121001   Courtesy of Chrysler Motors.
Fig. 1: Exploded View Of Clutch Assembly

CLUTCH RELEASE BEARING & FORK

Removal – **1)** Remove transmission and clutch housing as an assembly. Disconnect release bearing from fork, and remove bearing. *See Fig. 2.* Remove release fork.

2) Inspect bearing. Bearing should turn smoothly under a light thrust load. Bearing is pre-lubricated, sealed and should not be immersed in solvent. Inspect release fork and fork ball pivot for distortion and wear.

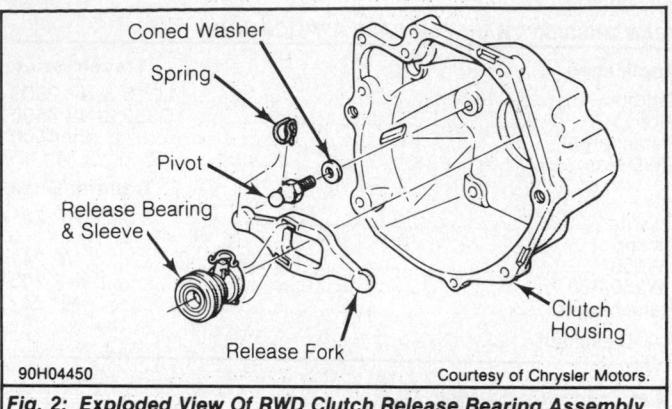

90H04450   Courtesy of Chrysler Motors.
Fig. 2: Exploded View Of RWD Clutch Release Bearing Assembly

Installation – **1)** Lubricate crankshaft pilot bushing, input shaft splines, bearing retainer slide surface, fork pivot and release fork pivot surface with high-temperature wheel bearing grease.

2) Install release fork and release bearing. Ensure fork and bearing are properly secured. Install transmission and clutch housing.

TORQUE SPECIFICATIONS
TORQUE SPECIFICATIONS

Application	Ft. Lbs. (N.m)
Clutch Fork Pivot Bolt	17 (23)
Clutch Housing-To-Engine Bolt [1]	
AX 15 & NP 2500	50 (68)
NV 4500	80 (108)
Clutch Slave Cylinder Nuts	17 (23)
Crossmember-To-Frame Bolts	35 (47)
Engine-To-Clutch Housing [2]	
AX 15 & NP 2500	50 (68)
Pressure Plate Bolt	
5/16"	17 (23)
3/8"	30 (41)
Propeller Shaft Clamp Bolts (AX 15)	14 (19)
Transfer Case-To-Transmission Bolts	35 (47)
Transmission Case-To-Clutch Housing Bolts	50 (68)
Transmission-To-Insulator Bolts	33 (45)

	INCH Lbs. (N.m)
Flywheel Cover Bolt	45 (5)

[1] – Bolts thread into engine from clutch housing side.
[2] – Bolts thread into clutch housing from engine side.

1992 DRIVE AXLES
Dana Full-Floating Axles

Pickup, Ramcharger, RWD Van

DESCRIPTION & OPERATION

Axle assembly is an integral carrier type with hypoid gear ring and pinion. Stamped steel cover is removable for inspection and repair of differential. Vehicle loads are carried by axle housings. Axle shafts of full-floating rear assemblies may be removed without disturbing wheel bearings.

Limited-Slip differential is optional on Model 60 and 70 rear axles. Model 60 uses Trac-Lok differential and Model 70 uses Power-Lock differential. Trac-Lok differential uses a one-piece case. Power-Lock differential uses a 2-piece case. Both differentials use same internal components as a standard differential, plus 2 clutch disc pads.

Vehicles equipped with Rear Wheel Anti-Lock (RWAL) brakes have an exciter ring mounted next to ring gear and a RWAL sensor mounted in drive axle housing.

See appropriate 4WD STEERING KNUCKLES article for removal and installation procedures for front drive axle components.

TROUBLE SHOOTING

NOTE: See TROUBLE SHOOTING article in GENERAL INFORMATION.

AXLE RATIO & IDENTIFICATION

A metal tag on axle is stamped with gear ratio, part numbers and limited slip identification. Use following tables to determine drive axle ratio.

MODEL IDENTIFICATION BY RING GEAR SIZE

Application	Ring Gear Diameter In. (mm)
Model 44 Axle	8.50 (216)
Model 60 Axle	9.75 (248)
Model 70 Axle	10.50 (267)

FRONT AXLE RATIO IDENTIFICATION

Application	Ratio
Model 44 (8.50" Ring Gear)	3.54:1, 3.92:1, 4.09:1
Model 60 (9.75" Ring Gear)	3.54:1, 4.10:1, 4.56:1

REAR AXLE RATIO IDENTIFICATION

Application	Ratio
Model 60 (9.75" Ring Gear)	4.10:1, 4.56:1
Model 70 (10.50" Ring Gear)	3.54:1, 4.10:1, 4.56:1

LUBRICATION

CAUTION: If rear axle is submerged in water, axle lubricant MUST be replaced immediately to avoid premature failure due to contamination.

Use Multipurpose Gear Lubricant (MIL-L-2105-B/API GL-5). Four ounces of Mopar Hypoid Gear Oil Additive Friction Modifier (4318060) MUST be used with every fluid change if equipped with Trac-Lok.

REMOVAL, DISASSEMBLY, REASSEMBLY & INSTALLATION

FRONT HUB, BEARING, SPINDLE & AXLE SHAFT

Removal (Model 44 Axle) – 1) Raise and support vehicle. Remove wheel. Remove caliper and support aside. DO NOT allow caliper to hang by brake hose. Remove grease cap and driving hub snap ring. Remove driving hub and spacer.
2) Remove outer lock nut. Remove tabbed lock washer and inner lock nut. Remove hub and rotor from spindle. Outer bearing will slide off spindle as rotor is removed. Pry inner seal from hub and remove inner bearing.

3) Remove caliper adapter from steering knuckle. Remove nuts and washers from spindle-to-knuckle attaching bolts. Remove brake splash shield. Using soft-faced mallet, strike spindle lightly to loosen from knuckle.
4) Place spindle in soft-jawed vise. DO NOT clamp bearing surfaces. Remove seal. Using Puller (D-131), remove needle bearings from spindle.
5) To remove right axle shaft, carefully pull axle shaft, with spacer, seal and stone shield, from axle housing. Remove seal and stone shield from shaft.
6) To remove left axle, disconnect vacuum lines and electrical connector from switch on disconnect housing assembly. *See Fig. 1.* Remove cover assembly, gasket and shield. Remove intermediate axle shaft from axle without damaging axle shaft seal.

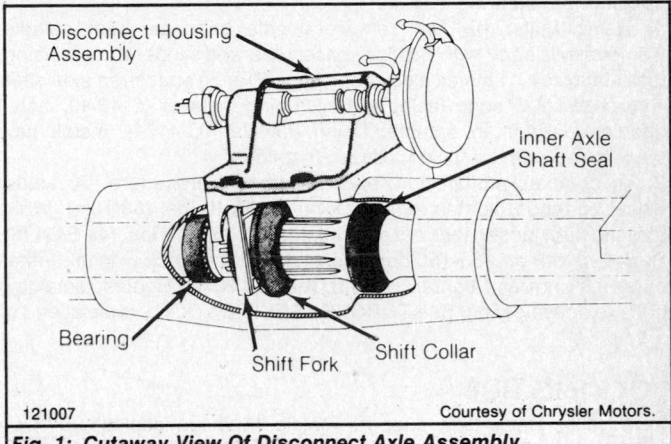

Fig. 1: Cutaway View Of Disconnect Axle Assembly

121007 — Courtesy of Chrysler Motors.

7) Using Bearing Extractor (D-330), remove bearing from inside axle. Remove shift collar from axle. Remove differential cover. Drain gear oil into container.
8) Push inner axle shaft toward center of vehicle. Remove "C" lock from recessed groove on shaft. Using Bar (D 354-4) and Adapter (D-354-3), drive out inner shaft. Using Bar (D-354-4), Remover (D-354-1) and Puller (C-637), remove inner axle shaft bearing. Using Puller (C-637), remove outer axle bearing and seal.
Installation (Left Side) – 1) Using Bar (D-354-4), Installer (D-354-2) and Puller (C-637), install inner axle shaft bearing. Using bar and Adapter (D-354-3), install and seat inner axle shaft. Insert "C" lock in recessed groove in shaft. Position shift collar on splined end of inner axle shaft.
2) Using Installer (D-360) and Handle (C-4171), install outer axle shaft bearing and seal. Using handle and Installer (D-328), install bearing into intermediate axle shaft. Install intermediate axle shaft through seal into housing without damaging shaft seal.
3) Install disconnect housing assembly and gasket while guiding shift fork into groove of shift collar. Install and tighten disconnect housing assembly bolts. See TORQUE SPECIFICATIONS table at end of article.
4) Apply 1/16-3/32" (1.59-2.38 mm) bead of silicone rubber sealant along bolt circle of differential housing cover before installing. Install inner brake pad anti-rattle spring on top of retainer spring plate.
5) To complete installation, reverse removal procedure. To adjust wheel bearings, tighten inner lock nut to **50 ft. lbs. (68 N.m)**. While rotating hub, loosen lock nut and retighten to **30-40 ft. lbs. (41-54 N.m)**. Back lock nut off 135-150 degrees. Install tabbed lock washer. Install outer lock nut and tighten to **50 ft. lbs. (68 N.m)**. Apply silicone rubber sealant to edge of grease cap. Tighten bolts to specification. See TORQUE SPECIFICATIONS table at end of article.
Installation (Right Side) – 1) Position seal on stone shield with seal lip facing toward shaft spline. Install axle shaft into housing without damaging differential seal at side gear. Install inner brake pad anti-rattle spring on top of retainer spring plate.
2) To complete installation, reverse removal procedure. To adjust wheel bearings, tighten inner lock nut to **50 ft. lbs. (68 N.m)**. While rotating hub, loosen lock nut and retighten to **30-40 ft. lbs. (41-54**

N.m). Back lock nut off 135-150 degrees. Install tabbed lock washer. Install outer lock nut and tighten to **50 ft. lbs. (68 N.m)**. Apply silicone rubber sealant to edge of grease cap. Tighten bolts to specification. See TORQUE SPECIFICATIONS table at end of article.

Removal & Installation (Model 60 Axle) – **1)** Block brake pedal in up position. Raise and support vehicle. Remove wheel. Remove caliper-to-adapter Allen head screw. Remove caliper and support aside.

2) Remove locking hub (if equipped). See LOCKING HUB under REMOVAL, DISASSEMBLY, REASSEMBLY & INSTALLATION. Remove outer lock nut, tabbed lock washer, inner lock nut and outer bearing.

3) Remove hub and rotor assembly from spindle. Pry inner seal from hub and remove inner bearing. Remove brake splash shield, brake adapter and spindle-to-steering knuckle nuts and washers. Remove spindle from steering knuckle.

4) Using Puller (D-131), remove needle bearings from spindle. Remove axle shaft with Bronze spacer, seal and slinger from housing.

Installation – **1)** Install axle shaft. Place Bronze spacer on axle shaft with chamfered edge facing inward. Using Installer (C-4370), install needle bearings in spindle. Using Installer (C-4171), install new spindle seal with lip facing axle shaft splines.

2) To complete installation, reverse removal procedure. To adjust wheel bearings, tighten inner lock nut to **50 ft. lbs. (68 N.m)**. While rotating hub, loosen lock nut and retighten to **30-40 ft lbs. (41-54 N.m)**. Back lock nut off 135-150 degrees. Install tabbed lock washer. Install outer lock nut and tighten to **65 ft. lbs. (88 N.m)**. Tighten remaining bolts to specification. See TORQUE SPECIFICATIONS table at end of article.

LOCKING HUB

Removal – Raise and support vehicle. Remove cap-to-hub Allen head screws. Remove cap. Remove axle shaft retaining ring. Remove lock ring from groove in hub. To assist in removal, reinstall 2 Allen head screws in locking hub body. Remove locking hub assembly from hub.

Inspection – Wash parts in mineral spirits, and blow dry with compressed air. Examine components for damage and replace as necessary.

Installation – To install components, reverse removal procedure. Tighten Allen head screws to **35-45 INCH lbs. (4-5 N.m)**.

INTERMEDIATE AXLE SHAFT

Removal (Disconnect Axle Models) – **1)** Remove outer axle. See FRONT HUB, BEARING, SPINDLE & AXLE SHAFT in this article.

2) Remove axle assembly inspection cover and drain fluid. Remove vacuum and electrical connections at shift motor housing. Remove bolts. Pull disconnect housing from axle tube. See Fig. 1.

3) Remove intermediate shaft retaining clip on inner end of axle shaft. Carefully slide intermediate axle shaft through seal and out end of axle tube. Remove shift collar.

4) Inspect intermediate shaft bearings and seals for wear. If replacement of bearings or seal is necessary, use recommended tools.

5) Using Adapter Shaft (D-354-4) and Adapter (D-354-1) with Puller (C-637), remove axle shaft bearing. Use Adapter Shaft (D-354-4) and Adapter (D-354-2) with Puller (C-637) to install new bearing.

6) To install new seal, use Installer (5041-1), Adapter Handle (5041-2) and Adapter (5041-3) to press new axle seal into housing. Use Adapter (D-328) and Driver Handle (C-4171) to install needle bearing on axle shaft.

Installation – **1)** Coat intermediate shaft with lubricant and carefully slide through seal and engage in drive axle splines. Install retaining clip.

2) Install shift collar on axle shaft. Install outer axle shaft and check for smooth operation of shift collar.

3) Apply a bead of silicone sealer to inspection cover and install cover. Fill axle housing with **2.5 pts. (1.2L)** of 75W-90 gear oil. Pour a small amount of gear oil on shift collar and install disconnect housing. Ensure shifting fork is properly positioned in shift collar.

4) To complete installation, reverse removal procedure. Tighten all bolts and nuts to specification. See TORQUE SPECIFICATIONS table at end of article.

PINION FLANGE & SEAL

Removal – **1)** Raise and support vehicle. Disconnect drive shaft and support aside. Using Flange Holder (C-3281), remove pinion nut.

2) Remove flange using Flange Puller (C-542). Remove oil seal from housing using pinion seal puller. See SEAL REMOVAL TOOL APPLICATION table. Use care to avoid damage to housing seal surface.

SEAL REMOVAL TOOL APPLICATION

Application	Seal Removal Tool
Model 44 Axle	D-158
Model 60 Axle	D-162
Model 70 Axle	D-159

NOTE: DO NOT drive flange on with hammer. Hammering could result in damage to ring and pinion gear.

Installation – **1)** Lubricate seal lip with grease. Place seal in axle housing and drive seal in using appropriate seal installer. See SEAL INSTALLATION TOOL APPLICATION table.

SEAL INSTALLATION TOOL APPLICATION

Application	Seal Installation Tool
Model 44 Axle	W-147-E
Model 60 Axle	C-3719-A
Model 70 Axle	C-359

2) Install flange on pinion shaft. Install flange holder and install pinion washer and nut. Tighten pinion nut to specification. See TORQUE SPECIFICATIONS table at end of article.

FRONT AXLE ASSEMBLY

Removal – **1)** Raise and support vehicle. Remove tire and wheel assembly. Support axle housing with transmission jack. Remove hubs, spindles and axles. See FRONT HUB, BEARING, SPINDLE & AXLE SHAFT. Disconnect vacuum hoses and harness connector from shift motor housing.

2) Remove left and right tie rod ends. Remove stabilizer bar links, lower shock mounts and track bar bolt. Disconnect drag link at left steering knuckle arm. Mark drive shaft and front pinion yoke for installation reference. Disconnect front drive shaft at front pinion yoke and support aside. Disconnect axle housing vent tube and plug opening.

3) Remove spring "U" bolt nuts and remove spring. Carefully lower axle assembly from vehicle and remove.

Installation – **1)** Place axle assembly on transmission jack. Position assembly under vehicle and raise until assembly contacts springs. Ensure leaf spring center pin is engaged with hole in axle housing spring plate.

2) Check all bushings and mounting hardware for wear or damage. To complete installation, reverse removal procedure. Tighten all bolts and nuts to specification. See TORQUE SPECIFICATIONS table at end of article. Fill axle assembly with gear oil. Check wheel alignment. See SPECIFICATIONS & PROCEDURES article in WHEEL ALIGNMENT.

REAR HUB, BEARINGS & AXLE SHAFTS

Removal & Installation (Model 60 Axle) – **1)** Raise and support vehicle. Remove wheel. Remove axle shaft nuts, washers and cones. Using dead blow hammer, sharply strike center of axle flange to free cones. Pull axle shaft out of axle tube and remove gasket.

2) Straighten and remove nut lock. Remove adjustment nut and outer bearing. Carefully remove drum assembly. Remove seal and inner bearing from drum assembly.

3) Pack and install inner bearing and seal in drum. Carefully install drum assembly, outer bearing and adjustment nut. Tighten adjustment nut to **120-140 ft. lbs. (163-190 N.m)** while rotating drum.

4) Back off adjustment nut approximately 1/3 turn (120 degrees) to obtain **.001-.008" (0.03-0.20 mm)** end play. Bend nut lock into spindle keyway. Install gasket and axle shaft. Install wheel and lower vehicle. See TORQUE SPECIFICATIONS table at end of article.

REAR HUB BEARING ADJUSTMENT SPECIFICATIONS

Application	[1] Ft. Lbs. (N.m)
Adjusting Nut	
Step 1	120-140 (163-190)
Step 2	Back Off 120 Degrees

[1] – While rotating hub.

Removal (Model 70 Axle) – 1) Raise and support vehicle. Remove wheel and brake drum. Loosen axle housing cover bolts and drain fluid. Remove housing cover. Rotate axle until pinion lock screw is accessible. Remove lock screw and pinion shaft.

2) Push axle toward center of vehicle and remove "C" lock from inner end of shaft. Pull axle out of axle tube, using care not to damage axle shaft bearing in axle tube. Inspect bearing.

3) Using small pry bar, remove seal. Using a bearing and seal remover, remove bearing. Inspect axle tube bore for burrs. Remove burrs if necessary.

Installation – 1) Wipe axle tube bore clean. Lubricate bearing with gear oil. Using a bearing installer, insert bearing into tube. Ensure bearing is not cocked and is seated firmly against tube shoulder. Bearing is properly seated when installer bottoms against bore.

2) Lubricate NEW seal with gear oil and using a seal installer, install seal. Drive seal until flush with axle tube. To complete installation, reverse removal procedure. Pull axle shaft outward after installing "C" lock to seat lock in counterbore of axle side gear. Install pinion shaft and lock screw. To complete installation, reverse removal procedure. Tighten bolts and nuts to specification. See TORQUE SPECIFICATIONS table at end of article.

REAR AXLE ASSEMBLY

Removal – 1) Raise and support vehicle. Remove wheels, hubs and axles. See REAR HUB, BEARINGS & AXLE SHAFTS.

2) Remove lower shock mounts and stabilizer bar mount. Disconnect drive shaft and support aside. Remove hydraulic brake line at junction block and plug to prevent fluid loss. Disconnect RWAL electrical connector (if equipped).

3) Disconnect park brake cables and hydraulic brake lines to wheel cylinders. Remove brake backing plates. Support axle housing with floor jack and remove leaf spring "U" bolts. Carefully lower axle housing and remove from vehicle.

Installation – Place axle housing on floor jack. Raise axle and install "U" bolts and nuts. To complete installation, reverse removal procedure. Tighten all bolts and nuts to specification. See TORQUE SPECIFICATIONS table at end of article and REAR HUB BEARING ADJUSTMENT SPECIFICATIONS table.

OVERHAUL

AXLE SHAFT

NOTE: All front axle shafts use Cardan "U" joints and should be overhauled in same manner as drive shaft "U" joints.

AXLE ASSEMBLY

NOTE: Use extreme care when removing differential case from vehicle to avoid damage to RWAL exciter ring.

Disassembly – 1) Drain lubricant. Remove RWAL sensor (if equipped). Remove axle shafts and housing cover. Using a screwdriver or small pry bar, measure differential side play. Side play resulting from bearing race looseness requires replacement of differential case. Use threaded adjuster to remove side play before measuring ring gear runout. Eliminate any side play. If no side play is found in dif-

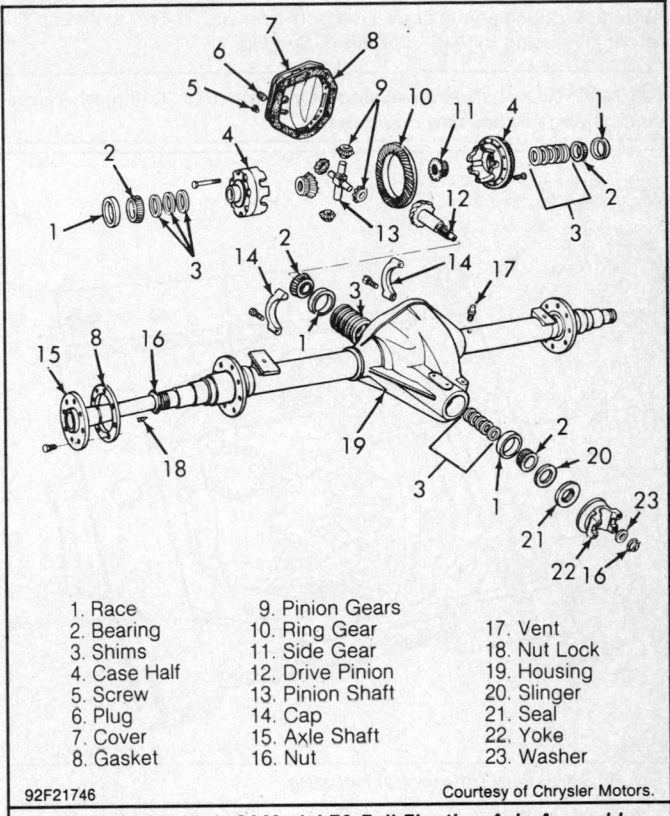

1. Race	9. Pinion Gears
2. Bearing	10. Ring Gear
3. Shims	11. Side Gear
4. Case Half	12. Drive Pinion
5. Screw	13. Pinion Shaft
6. Plug	14. Cap
7. Cover	15. Axle Shaft
8. Gasket	16. Nut

17. Vent	
18. Nut Lock	
19. Housing	
20. Slinger	
21. Seal	
22. Yoke	
23. Washer	

92F21746   Courtesy of Chrysler Motors.

Fig. 2: Exploded View Of Model 70 Full-Floating Axle Assembly

ferential case assembly, mount dial indicator on pilot stud with tip against back of ring gear. *See Fig. 3.* Measure runout of ring gear, marking ring gear and case at point of maximum runout.

2) If total runout exceeds **.005" (.13 mm)**, ring gear could be loose or case could be damaged. Using **.003" (.08 mm)** feeler gauge, try to force feeler gauge between cap and race. If gauge fits, bearing race may have been turning in carrier.

3) If race has been turning, carrier could be damaged. Observe identifying marks stamped into bearing caps and face of carrier sealing surface. Use these matched marks for reassembly reference.

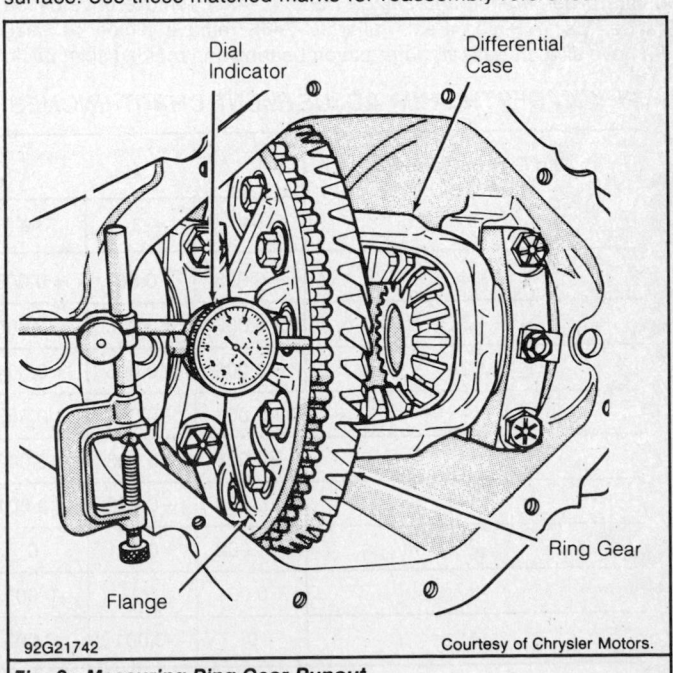

92G21742   Courtesy of Chrysler Motors.

Fig. 3: Measuring Ring Gear Runout

4) Remove side bearing caps. Use Spreader Bar (D-167) to spread differential housing to **.015" (.38 mm)**. *See Fig. 4.*

CAUTION: Do not spread housing more than .015" (.38 mm). Permanent damage to housing could result.

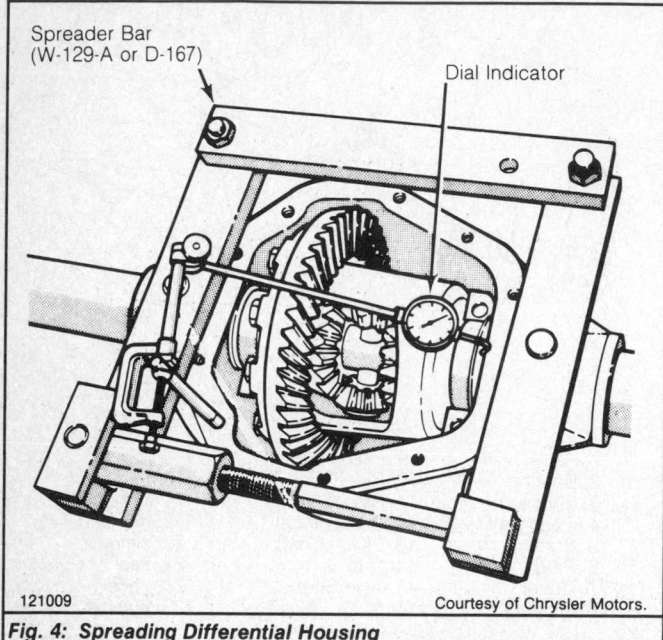

Spreader Bar
(W-129-A or D-167)

Dial Indicator

121009

Courtesy of Chrysler Motors.

Fig. 4: Spreading Differential Housing

5) Remove spreader. Pry differential case out of housing. On models with side bearing shims between carrier and side bearing outer race, record sizes and positions of shims. Be careful not to damage machined surfaces of housing.

6) Put case in soft-jawed vise and remove and discard ring gear bolts. Tap ring gear loose with soft mallet. If earlier ring gear runout measurement exceeded **.005" (.13 mm)**, check differential case flange runout measurement. Total runout of case flange should not exceed **.003" (.08 mm)**. Remove RWAL exciter ring if necessary. Discard ring after removal; DO NOT reuse.

7) Using Flange Holder (C-3281), remove drive pinion nut and washer. Using holder wrench and Flange Puller (C-452), remove drive pinion flange. Using Pinion Seal Puller (C-748), remove pinion oil seal. Remove slinger, gasket, outer pinion bearing and preload shim pack.

8) Remove drive pinion with inner bearing. Remove inner and outer pinion bearing races. Remove and note thickness of shim pack behind inner bearing race. Remove inner pinion bearing from pinion shaft using Puller Press (DD-914-P) with Adapter Ring (DD-914-9) and appropriate pinion bearing puller. See BEARING PULLER TOOL APPLICATION table.

BEARING PULLER TOOL APPLICATION

Application	Bearing Puller
Model 44 Axle	C-748
Model 60 Axle	C-293-37
Model 70 Axle	DD-914-95

NOTE: Pinion bearing adjusting shims may remain on pinion shaft, stick to bearing or fall loose. Collect and save them for reassembly.

9) Remove side bearings with Bearing Puller (DD-914-P), Adapter Ring (DD-914-8), Plate (DD-914-62), Screw Extension (DD-914-7) and Button (DD-914-42). Record shim thickness and location for reassembly reference.

10) Drive out lock pin holding differential pinion shaft to case. Remove differential pinion shaft, gears and thrust washers (one for each gear).

Inspection – 1) Use cleaning solvent to rinse gears and bearings. Check large end of bearing rollers for wear. Check pinion and flange splines for excessive wear. Ensure ring gear teeth are undamaged.

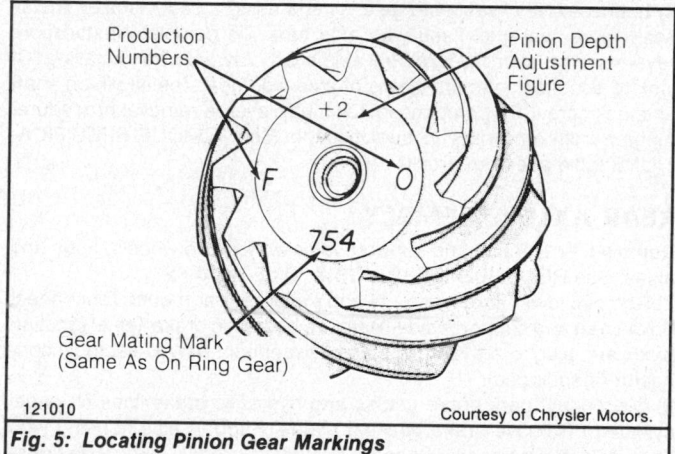

Production
Numbers

Pinion Depth
Adjustment
Figure

+2

F

754

Gear Mating Mark
(Same As On Ring Gear)

121010

Courtesy of Chrysler Motors.

Fig. 5: Locating Pinion Gear Markings

PINION DEPTH SHIM ADJUSTMENT CHART (INCHES)

Old Pinion Marking	New Pinion Marking								
	-4	-3	-2	-1	0	+1	+2	+3	+4
+4	+0.008	+0.007	+0.006	+0.005	+0.004	+0.003	+0.002	+0.001	0
+3	+0.007	+0.006	+0.005	+0.004	+0.003	+0.002	+0.001	0	-0.001
+2	+0.006	+0.005	+0.004	+0.003	+0.002	+0.001	0	-0.001	-0.002
+1	+0.005	+0.004	+0.003	+0.002	+0.001	0	-0.001	-0.002	-0.003
0	+0.004	+0.003	+0.002	+0.001	0	-0.001	-0.002	-0.003	-0.004
-1	+0.003	+0.002	+0.001	0	-0.001	-0.002	-0.003	-0.004	-0.005
-2	+0.002	+0.001	0	-0.001	-0.002	-0.003	-0.004	-0.005	-0.006
-0	+0.001	0	-0.001	-0.002	-0.003	-0.004	-0.005	-0.006	-0.007
-4	0	-0.001	-0.002	-0.003	-0.004	-0.005	-0.006	-0.007	-0.008

2) Check differential case for cracks, scoring of side gears, thrust washers and pinion thrust faces. Check fit of side gears to case and to axle shaft splines. Examine pinion shaft and spacer for scoring or excessive wear.

Reassembly & Adjustments – **1)** When reassembling ring and pinion assembly, pinion depth, pinion bearing preload, side bearing preload and backlash between ring and pinion must be adjusted.

2) If only pinion shaft and ring gear are to be replaced and carrier housing can be reused, compare pinion depth adjustment numbers etched in faces of old and new pinion heads. *See Fig. 5.* Using PINION DEPTH SHIM ADJUSTMENT CHART, correct shims can be selected for new pinion shaft depth adjustment.

NOTE: In order to use PINION DEPTH SHIM ADJUSTMENT CHART procedure, old pinion shaft shim pack dimensions MUST be determined accurately. If original pinion shaft shim pack dimension cannot be determined accurately, Pinion Depth Gauge Set (D-271) must be used to properly determine pinion depth setting. Depth gauge set must also be used if new carrier housing is to be used.

3) Pinion depth adjustment number is determined by manufacturer at time of assembly. Number indicates best running position of pinion shaft. This dimension is controlled by shimming behind the inner pinion bearing cup. *See Fig. 6.*

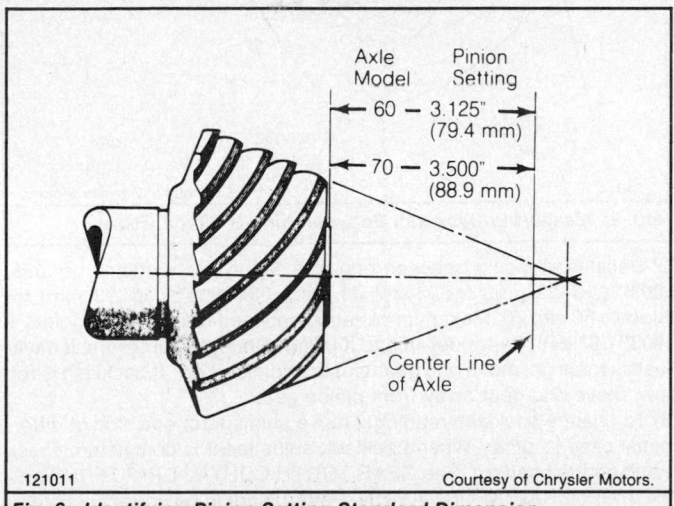

Axle Model	Pinion Setting
60 –	3.125" (79.4 mm)
70 –	3.500" (88.9 mm)

Center Line of Axle

121011   Courtesy of Chrysler Motors.

Fig. 6: Identifying Pinion Setting Standard Dimension

NOTE: Depth shims are available in 0.001" increments from 0.020" to 0.038".

4) Pinion Depth Gauge Set (D-271) allows shim pack adjustments to be made without having to remove and replace differential bearings.

5) Place differential case in holding fixture or vise. Lubricate all parts with gear oil. Place side gears and new thrust washers in case. Place differential pinions and new thrust washers in case. Rotate side gears until holes in pinion gears and washers align with holes in case. Install differential pinion shaft. Install lock pin after aligning hole in shaft with hole in case. Peen edge of hole to keep pin in place.

6) Inspect ring gear and case for any burrs or nicks. If replacing RWAL exciter ring, align exciter ring tab with slot on differential case. Install 2 NEW ring gear bolts to maintain bolt hole alignment. Mount assembly onto hydraulic press and press exciter ring onto case using ring gear as a pilot. Install remaining ring gear bolts and tighten evenly in alternating pattern to specification. See TORQUE SPECIFICATIONS table at end of article.

7) Install Master Bearings into case. Use (D-343) for Model 44 or (D-117) for Models 60 and 70. Install differential case in carrier. Install and tighten side bearing caps finger tight over master bearings. Caps must be in same location as marked during disassembly. Mount dial indicator on carrier with indicator tip against back of ring gear.

8) Pry case assembly aside of carrier. Zero dial indicator and pry case in opposite direction. *See Fig. 7.* Record reading. This indicates thickness of shim pack necessary to eliminate clearance between case and side bearing races.

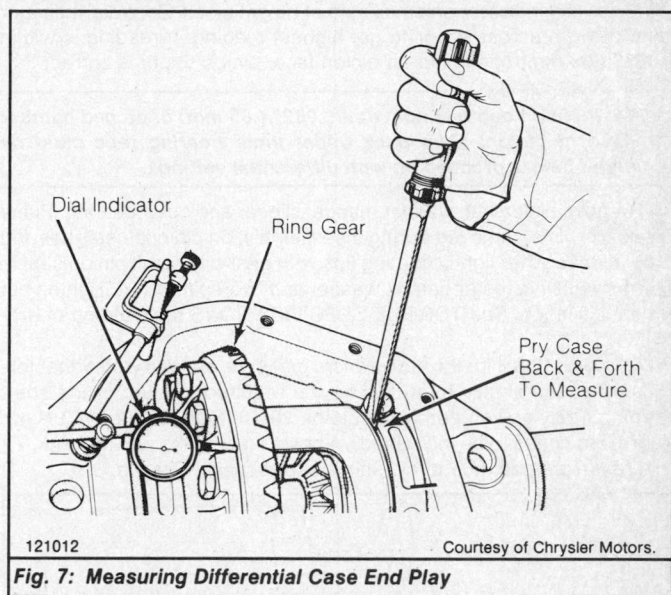

Dial Indicator   Ring Gear

Pry Case Back & Forth To Measure

121012   Courtesy of Chrysler Motors.

Fig. 7: Measuring Differential Case End Play

9) Actual placement of shim pack and necessary preload will be calculated after drive pinion is installed and pinion depth has been determined. Remove dial indicator. Remove bearing caps and differential case from carrier.

NOTE: If new differential side and pinion gears are used with new washers, gear backlash should be correct due to close machine tolerances. If old gears and/or washers are used, gear backlash must be checked.

NOTE: If original ring and pinion are to be used, measure old shim packs and make up packs of same dimensions with new shims. Baffles are considered part of shim pack.

Pinion Depth – **1)** Depth Gauge Set (D-271) is used to determine pinion depth. Place Master Pinion Block (D-139 for Model 44, D-120 for Models 60, or D-137 for Model 70) in pinion bore of carrier. Put Arbor Discs (D-115-4-44 for Model 44, or D-116-2 for Models 60 and 70) on Arbor (D-115-3). Install arbor in carrier with discs riding in bearing bore.

2) Put Pinion Height Block (D-116-1) on top of master pinion block with side against arbor. Place Scooter Block (D-115-2) with Dial Indicator (D-106-5) on lowest step of pinion height block. Zero dial indicator with scooter block flat on pinion height block.

3) Move scooter block so dial indicator tip touches arbor. Move block back and forth (perpendicular to arbor) to get highest reading. This reading, plus or minus value etched on pinion head, is thickness of shim pack necessary for pinion bearing.

4) Measure shims separately with micrometer. If baffle is used, its thickness must be included in shim pack. This is also true if slinger is used between inner bearing and head of pinion shaft. Place pinion height shim pack in carrier bore for inner bearing race. Drive bearing race into carrier, making sure cup is fully seated.

Pinion Bearing Preload – **1)** Drive outer pinion bearing into carrier housing. Press inner pinion bearing onto pinion shaft using Press Tube (C-3095-A). Ensure bearings seat fully. Insert pinion shaft into carrier. Install outer bearing, slinger (if equipped), flange, washer and nut.

NOTE: Pinion preload shims and oil seal should NOT be installed at this time.

2) Using an INCH lb. torque wrench, tighten pinion nut until **10 INCH lbs. (1.13 N.m)** rotational torque is obtained. Recheck pinion depth with arbor and discs at this time. Place pinion height block on face of pinion shaft.

3) Place dial indicator on small step of height block. Zero dial indicator and move it across arbor to get highest reading. If reading is within **.002" (.05 mm)** of etching on pinion face, pinion depth is correct.

NOTE: If pinion depth is not within .002" (.05 mm) of etched number on face of pinion, shim pack under inner bearing race must be changed before proceeding with differential settings.

4) Remove pinion nut, washer, flange, slinger and outer bearing. Place preload shims (removed during disassembly) on pinion. Install bearing and slinger. After lightly coating lips with gear oil, install pinion seal in carrier housing. Install flange, washer and NEW pinion nut. Tighten nut to specification. See TORQUE SPECIFICATIONS table at end of article.

5) Using an INCH lb. torque wrench, measure preload (rotational torque) of pinion shaft. Rotational torque required to keep pinion shaft turning freely and smoothly should be **20-40 INCH lbs. (2.3-4.5 N.m)**. If preload needs to be increased, remove a few shims and recheck. To decrease preload, add a few shims and recheck. *See Fig. 8.*

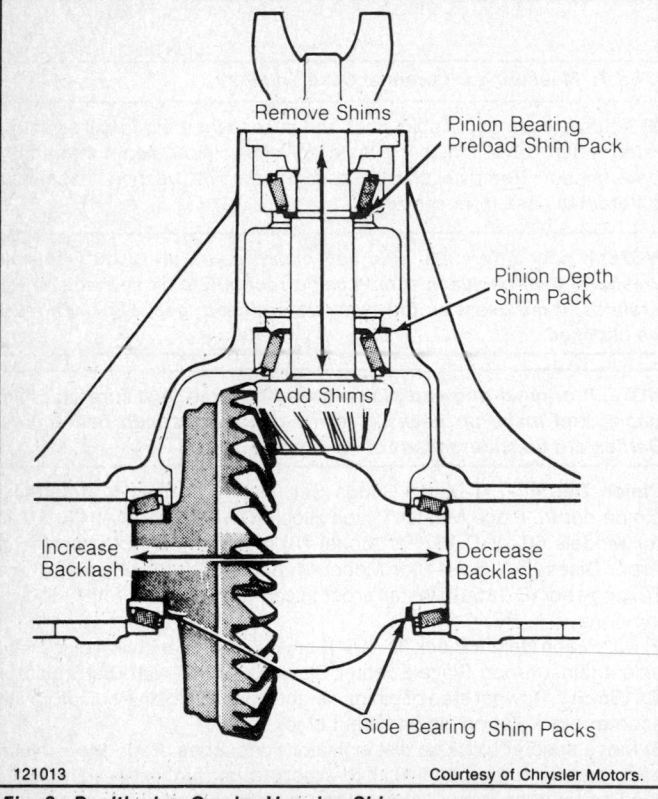

121013   Courtesy of Chrysler Motors.

Fig. 8: Positioning Carrier Housing Shim

Differential Bearing Preload – **1)** Install differential case in housing with master bearings on case. Set up dial indicator in same position as when case end play was checked. *See Fig. 7.* Press ring gear toward pinion head while rocking ring gear so teeth mesh fully. Zero dial indicator while holding ring gear in pinion gear.

2) Press differential case (ring gear) away from pinion gear. Repeat until dial indicator gives same reading each time. This figure is shim pack thickness necessary between case and side bearing on ring gear side. Remove dial indicator and differential case from carrier. Remove master bearings from case.

3) Put calculated shim pack on hub of case at ring gear side. Place side bearing on hub. Use Bearing Installer (C-4025A) and Handle (C-4171) to drive bearing onto case until it is seated. Take remaining shim pack as determined from case end play measurement and install pack on opposite side of case from ring gear.

4) Add **.015" (.38 mm)** thickness to shim pack opposite ring gear to provide side bearing preload. Drive side bearing onto case with installer and handle. Install spreader and dial indicator on carrier housing. Spread housing **.015" (.38 mm)**. Put side bearing races onto side bearings. Install differential case into carrier.

Ring & Pinion Backlash – **1)** Install side bearing caps, making sure reference marks made on caps and carrier match. Tighten cap bolts to **80 ft. lbs. (108 N.m)**. Check backlash between ring and pinion gears at 3 equally spaced points on ring gear. *See Fig. 9.*

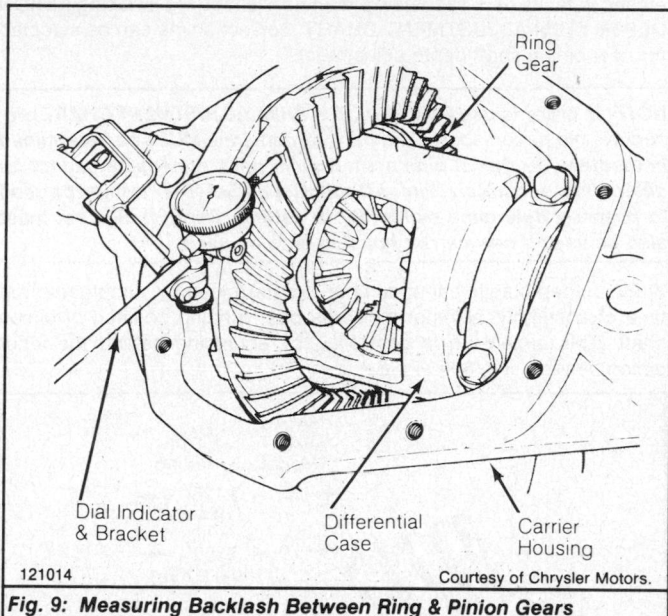

121014   Courtesy of Chrysler Motors.

Fig. 9: Measuring Backlash Between Ring & Pinion Gears

2) Backlash reading between ring and pinion gears should be **.005-.009" (.13-.23 mm)** for Model 44, and **.004-.009" (.10-.23 mm)** for Models 60 and 70. Maximum variation between readings at 3 points is **.003" (.08 mm)** for Model 44 and **.002" (.05 mm)** for all others. If backlash is too high, move ring gear closer to pinion gear. If backlash is too low, move ring gear away from pinion gear.

3) To change backlash readings, move shims from one side of differential case to other. When backlash adjustment is completed, check tooth contact pattern. See GEAR TOOTH CONTACT PATTERNS article in GENERAL INFORMATION. Pattern should be correct if assembly and adjustments have been done properly.

4) When differential is complete and correctly adjusted, install new cover gasket and cover. Tighten cover bolts to **35 ft. lbs. (47 N.m)**. Fill assembly with hypoid lubricant.

AXLE ASSEMBLY SPECIFICATIONS
AXLE ASSEMBLY SPECIFICATIONS

Application	Specifications
Pinion Gear Depth (Nominal Dimension)	
Model 44	2.625" (66.68 mm)
Model 60	3.125" (79.38 mm)
Model 70	3.500" (88.90 mm)
Ring Gear Backlash	.004-.009" (.10-.23 mm)
Side Bearing Preload	.015" (.38 mm)
Pinion Bearing Preload	
New Bearings	20-40 INCH lbs. (2.3-4.5 N.m)
Used Bearings	10-20 INCH lbs. (1.1-2.3 N.m)

TORQUE SPECIFICATIONS

TORQUE SPECIFICATIONS

Applications	Ft. Lbs. (N.m)
Front Axle	
Differential Cap Bearing Bolt	80 (108)
Disconnect Housing Bolt	10 (14)
Drag Link Nut	60 (81)
Drive Shaft Nut	25 (34)
Housing Cover Bolts	35 (47)
Leaf Spring "U" Bolt Nut	110 (149)
Lower Shock Mount Bolt	55 (75)
Pinion Shaft Flange Nut	
Model 44	210 (285)
Model 60	260 (352)
Ring Gear-To-Case Bolt	
Model 44	45-60 (61-81)
Spindle-To-Knuckle Nut	50-70 (68-95)
Stabilizer Bar Link	10 (14)
Tie Rod Nut	60 (81)
Wheel Lug Nut	110 (149)
Rear Axle	
Axle Flange-To-Hub Bolt	
Models 60 & 70	72 (98)
Drive Shaft Bolt	16 (22)
Housing Cover Bolts	35 (47)
Pinion Shaft Flange Nut	
Models 60 & 70	260 (352)
Ring Gear-To-Case Bolt	
Models 60	113 (153)
Model 70	105 (142)
Leaf Spring "U" Bolt Nut	180 (244)
Lower Shock Mount Nut	50 (68)
Side Bearing Cap Bolt	
Model 60	85 (115)
Model 70	88 (119)
Wheel Lug Nut	
Coned	200 (271)
Flanged 5/8 x 18	325 (441)
Flanged 1 1/8 x 16	475 (644)

1992 DRIVE AXLES
Dana Trac-Lok

Pickup, RWD Van

DESCRIPTION

Trac-Lok (limited slip) differential has same internal components as a standard differential, plus 2 clutch disc packs to provide limited slip action. Multiple disc clutches permit differential action when required for turning corners and transmit equal torque to both wheels when driving straight ahead.

When one wheel tries to spin, due to reduced traction, clutch packs automatically provide more torque to wheel with greater traction. Trac-Lok has a one-piece differential case and 2 differential pinion gears.

Vehicles equipped with Rear Wheel Anti-Lock (RWAL) brakes have an exciter ring mounted next to ring gear and a RWAL sensor mounted in drive axle housing.

AXLE RATIO & IDENTIFICATION
REAR AXLE RATIO IDENTIFICATION

Application	Ratio
Model 60 (9.75" Ring Gear)	4.10:1
Model 70 (10.50" Ring Gear)	4.56:1

LUBRICATION

CAUTION: If rear axle is submerged in water, replace axle lubricant immediately to avoid premature failure due to contamination.

Use Multipurpose Gear Lubricant (MIL-L-2105C/API GL-5). Use 4 ozs. of Mopar Hypoid Gear Oil Additive Friction Modifier (4318060) with every fluid change.

TROUBLE SHOOTING
DIFFERENTIAL NOISE

1) Operate vehicle for at least 10 minutes to bring differential lubricant to operating temperature. If noise is still evident, raise vehicle on hoist and drain differential lubricant.
2) Fill differential with MOPAR Hypoid Lubricant (4318058). With rear wheels off ground, start vehicle and operate rear wheels at approximately 40 MPH for at least 10 minutes.
3) Stop vehicle. Remove differential filler plug. Using a suction gun, remove as much lubricant as possible. Add 4 ounces of MOPAR Hypoid Friction Modifier (4318060). Refill differential housing to correct fluid level with MOPAR hypoid gear lubricant. Install filler plug, and tighten to **25 ft. lbs. (35 N.m).**
4) Manufacturer recommends driving vehicle at least 100 miles before re-evaluating differential noise. If noise still exists, replace entire differential case assembly. Ring gear, differential side gears and RWAL exciter ring are only serviceable parts. Differential case and internal parts are serviced as a unit.

TESTING

1) Drive vehicle at least 10 minutes. Place a piece of Kraft paper over a smooth Formica board. Place Formica board with paper under a rear wheel. Block front tires with a 2" wood block.
2) Start vehicle. With gradual throttle pressure, attempt to slowly drive vehicle over wood block. If paper slips out from under wheel before vehicle drives over wood block, move Formica and paper under other rear wheel.
3) Attempt to drive over wood block again. If vehicle drives over wood block with Formica and paper under either wheel, drive axle is considered normal.

REMOVAL & INSTALLATION

Removal and installation procedures are same as Dana 60 rear drive axles. See DANA FULL-FLOATING AXLES article.

OVERHAUL

NOTE: Ring gear, differential side gears and RWAL exciter ring are only replaceable parts. See Fig. 1. Differential case and internal parts are serviced as a unit.

For overhaul procedures, see DANA FULL-FLOATING AXLES article.

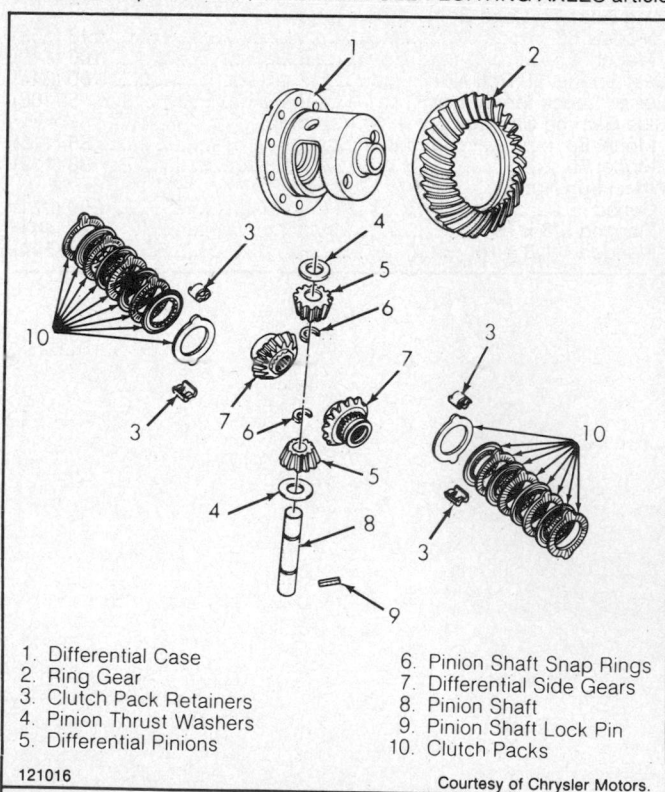

1. Differential Case	6. Pinion Shaft Snap Rings
2. Ring Gear	7. Differential Side Gears
3. Clutch Pack Retainers	8. Pinion Shaft
4. Pinion Thrust Washers	9. Pinion Shaft Lock Pin
5. Differential Pinions	10. Clutch Packs

121016   Courtesy of Chrysler Motors.

Fig. 1: Exploded View Of Dana Trac-Lok Differential

Dakota

DESCRIPTION

On 4WD models, front axle assembly is hypoid gear type. *See Fig. 1.* Assembly has a vacuum-operated shift motor for engaging and disengaging front driving axles. A small metal tag attached to axle housing cover identifies axle ratio.

On 2WD and 4WD models, rear axle assembly is hypoid gear type. Models equipped with Rear Wheel Anti-Lock (RWAL) brakes use a sensor mounted on differential housing and an exciter ring pressed onto differential case for speed sensing. *See Fig. 2.*

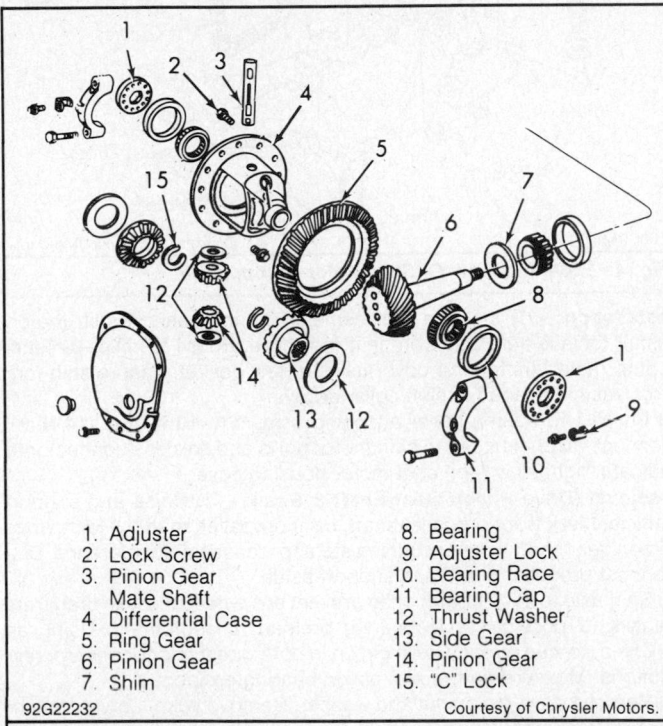

1. Adjuster
2. Lock Screw
3. Pinion Gear Mate Shaft
4. Differential Case
5. Ring Gear
6. Pinion Gear
7. Shim
8. Bearing
9. Adjuster Lock
10. Bearing Race
11. Bearing Cap
12. Thrust Washer
13. Side Gear
14. Pinion Gear
15. "C" Lock

92G22232   Courtesy of Chrysler Motors.

Fig. 1: Exploded View Of 7 1/4" Drive Axle Assembly (Front)

FRONT & REAR AXLE RATIO IDENTIFICATION

Application	Ratio
7 1/4" Ring Gear	2.76:1, 2.94:1, 3.23:1, 3.55:1

LUBRICATION

CAUTION: If front or rear axle is submerged in water, axle lubricant MUST be replaced immediately to avoid premature failure due to contamination.

Use Multipurpose Gear Lubricant (MIL-L-2105-C/API GL-5). Lubricant level should be between 1/4" (6.4 mm) and 1/2" (12.8 mm) below level of filler plug hole.

REMOVAL & INSTALLATION

FRONT AXLE ASSEMBLY

Removal (Left Axle Shaft) – **1)** Raise and support vehicle. Loosen wheel lug nuts, and remove cotter pin, nut lock and spring washer from stub shaft. Remove hub nut and washer. Remove wheel. Disconnect left axle shaft inner tripod joint housing from axle shaft flange. Support axle shaft, and separate stub shaft splines from hub bearing splines. DO NOT pull on boot. Remove axle shaft.

2) Clean area where differential housing cover mates with differential housing. Loosen housing cover bolts, and drain lubricant from housing. Remove housing cover. Rotate differential case so differential pinion gear mate shaft lock screw is accessible.

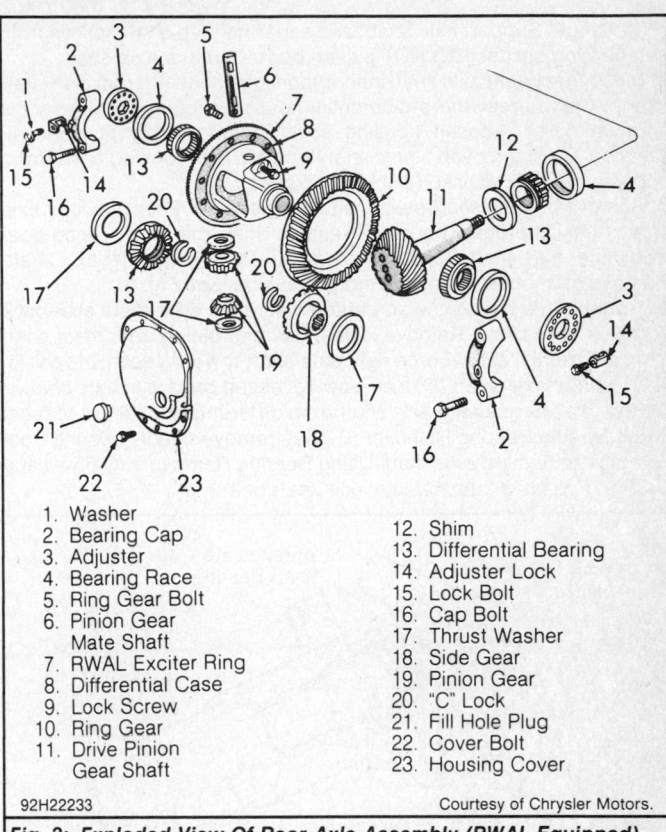

1. Washer
2. Bearing Cap
3. Adjuster
4. Bearing Race
5. Ring Gear Bolt
6. Pinion Gear Mate Shaft
7. RWAL Exciter Ring
8. Differential Case
9. Lock Screw
10. Ring Gear
11. Drive Pinion Gear Shaft
12. Shim
13. Differential Bearing
14. Adjuster Lock
15. Lock Bolt
16. Cap Bolt
17. Thrust Washer
18. Side Gear
19. Pinion Gear
20. "C" Lock
21. Fill Hole Plug
22. Cover Bolt
23. Housing Cover

92H22233   Courtesy of Chrysler Motors.

Fig. 2: Exploded View Of Rear Axle Assembly (RWAL Equipped)

3) Remove lock screw and pinion gear mate shaft from differential case. *See Fig. 1.* Force left axle shaft toward center of vehicle, and remove axle shaft "C" lock from recessed groove in axle shaft. Remove axle shaft from differential housing. DO NOT damage axle shaft bearing, which remains in housing.

4) Inspect axle shaft bearing contact surfaces for brinelling, excessive wear and damage. If any of these conditions exist, replace axle shaft and bearing. Remove axle shaft seal from end of housing bore. Remove axle shaft bearing if it appears damaged or excessively worn. Using Bearing Remover (C-4167) and slide hammer, remove axle shaft bearing.

Installation – 1) Using Bearing Installer (C-4203), install new seal and bearing in housing. When installer contacts housing flange face, seal is positioned at correct depth in bore. Lubricate bearing bore and seal lip.

2) Insert axle shaft into housing bore, and engage splines with differential side gear splines. DO NOT damage axle shaft seal lip. With axle shaft in place, insert "C" lock in recessed groove of axle shaft.

3) Force axle shaft outward to seat "C" lock in differential side gear counterbore. Insert differential pinion gear mate shaft into case and through thrust washers and pinion gears. Align hole in shaft with lock screw hole in differential case, and using Loctite, install lock screw. Tighten lock screw to **96 INCH lbs. (11 N.m).**

4) Remove residual sealant material from differential housing and cover. Thoroughly clean contact surfaces with mineral spirits, and dry surfaces completely. Apply a 1/16" to 3/32" thick bead of silicone rubber sealant around bolt circle on housing.

5) Install housing cover. Install axle gear ratio identification tag with one cover bolt. Tighten cover bolts to **35 ft. lbs. (47 N.m).**

6) Install axle shaft by reversing removal procedure. Remove supports, and lower vehicle until level. Fill differential housing with lubricant, and install fill plug. Lower vehicle, and test axle for correct operation.

Removal (Right & Intermediate Axle Shafts) – **1)** Raise and support vehicle. Loosen wheel lug nuts, and remove cotter pin, nut lock and spring washer from stub shaft. Remove hub nut and washer. Remove wheel. Disconnect right axle shaft inner tripod joint housing from axle shaft flange. Support axle shaft, and separate stub shaft splines from hub bearing splines. DO NOT pull on boot. Remove axle shaft.

2) Disconnect right axle shaft inner tripod joint housing from axle shaft flange. Clean area where differential housing mates with differential housing cover. Loosen housing cover bolts, and drain lubricant. Remove housing cover. Remove shift motor and housing cover from housing. See REMOVAL (SHIFT MOTOR).

3) Remove bearing seal/retainer attaching screws. Remove outer axle shaft from differential housing. Remove snap ring and splined gear from outer axle shaft. Separate bearing and seal from outer axle shaft. Remove shift collar from shift motor housing. See Fig. 3.

4) Rotate differential case so differential pinion gear mate shaft lock screw is accessible. Remove lock screw and pinion gear mate shaft from differential case. Force right axle shaft toward center of vehicle, and remove axle shaft "C" lock from recessed groove in axle shaft.

5) Remove intermediate axle shaft from differential housing and tube. Using Needle Bearing Remover (D-330), remove needle bearing from end of intermediate axle shaft. Using Bearing Removers (D-354-4 and D-354-1), remove intermediate axle shaft bearing.

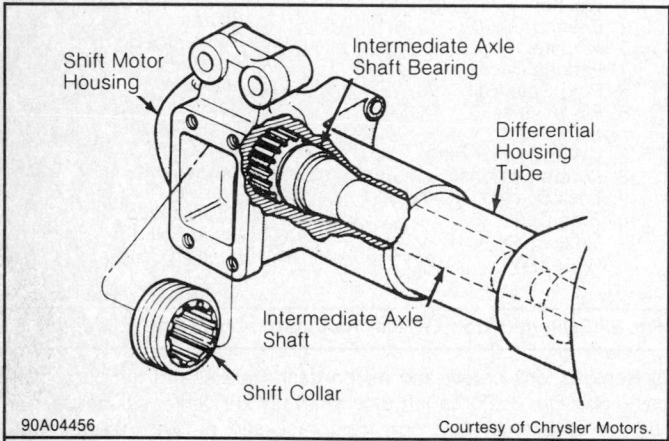

Shift Motor Housing

Intermediate Axle Shaft Bearing

Differential Housing Tube

Intermediate Axle Shaft

Shift Collar

90A04456   Courtesy of Chrysler Motors.

Fig. 3: Identifying Intermediate Axle Shaft, Bearing & Shift Collar

Installation – 1) Using Bearing Installer (D-354-2) and Driver Handle (C-4171), install intermediate axle shaft bearing. Using Bearing Installer (D-328) and Driver Handle (C-4171), install needle bearing in end of intermediate axle shaft. Lubricate bearing. Insert axle shaft into tube and housing bore, and engage splines with differential side gear splines.

2) With axle shaft in place, insert "C" lock in recessed groove of axle shaft. Force axle shaft outward to seat "C" lock in differential side gear counterbore. Insert differential pinion gear mate shaft into case and through thrust washers and pinion gears. Align hole in shaft with lock screw hole in differential case, and using Loctite, install lock screw. Tighten lock screw to **96 INCH lbs. (11 N.m).**

3) Install shift collar on splined end of intermediate axle shaft. Install seal/retainer onto outer axle shaft. Press on replacement bearing. Install splined gear and retaining snap ring. Insert outer axle shaft into shift motor housing. Tighten attaching screws to **17 ft. lbs. (23 N.m).** Install shift motor. See REMOVAL (SHIFT MOTOR). Ensure shift fork is correctly engaged in shift collar groove.

4) Remove residual sealant material from differential housing and cover. Thoroughly clean contact surfaces with mineral spirits, and dry surfaces completely. Apply a 1/16" to 3/32" thick bead of silicone rubber sealant around bolt circle on housing cover.

5) Install housing cover. Install axle gear ratio identification tag with one cover bolt. Tighten cover bolts to **35 ft. lbs. (47 N.m).** Install axle shaft by reversing removal procedure. Remove supports, and lower vehicle until level. Fill differential housing with lubricant, and install fill plug. Lower vehicle, and test axle for correct operation.

Removal (Shift Motor) – 1) Disconnect vacuum hoses to shift motor. Disconnect indicator light harness connector. Remove shift motor housing cover and gasket. See Fig. 4. Remove "E" clips from shift motor armature.

2) Remove shift motor and shift fork from cover. Remove "O" ring seal from shift motor. Remove pads from shift fork. Clean and inspect all components. Replace any worn or damaged component.

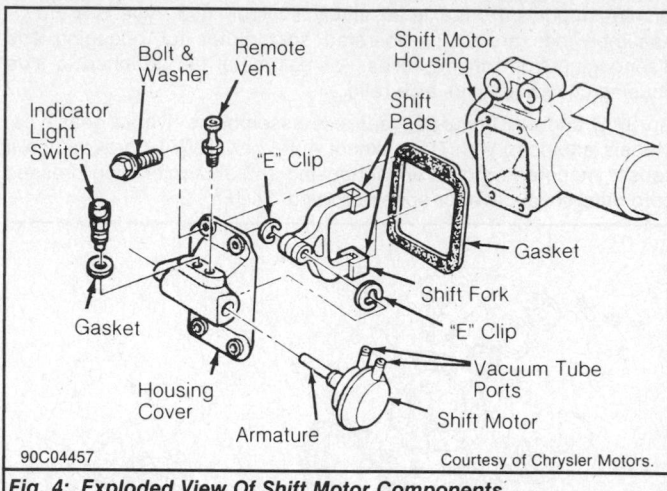

Bolt & Washer

Remote Vent

Shift Motor Housing

Indicator Light Switch

Shift Pads

"E" Clip

Gasket

Gasket

Shift Fork

"E" Clip

Housing Cover

Vacuum Tube Ports

Armature

Shift Motor

90C04457   Courtesy of Chrysler Motors.

Fig. 4: Exploded View Of Shift Motor Components

Installation – 1) Install a replacement "O" ring seal on shift motor. Install replacement pads on shift fork bore. Install "E" clips on shift motor. Install shift motor cover using a new gasket. Ensure shift fork is correctly engaged in shift collar groove.

2) Install and tighten cover attaching screws to **10 ft. lbs. (14 N.m).** Connect vacuum hoses to shift motor ports and harness connector to indicator light switch on shift motor housing cover.

Removal (Drive Pinion Gear Shaft & Seal) – 1) Raise and support vehicle. Mark front propeller shaft, front propeller shaft "U" joint, drive pinion gear shaft yoke and pinion stem for reassembly reference. Disconnect propeller shaft, and support aside.

2) Shift axle to 2WD operation to prevent any wheel or brake drag from causing a possible false bearing preload measurement. Using an INCH-lb. torque wrench, turn pinion in both directions for several revolutions. Measure and record pinion bearing preload.

3) Remove drive pinion nut and washer. Remove yoke. Lower front of vehicle to prevent lubrication leakage from differential housing. Carefully pry out oil seal; DO NOT damage machined surface.

Installation – 1) Install new pinion oil seal squarely into bore in housing until seated. Align marks, and install pinion flange. Install pinion washer (convex side out) and nut. Tighten shaft nut to **210 ft. lbs. (285 N.m),** and rotate pinion to properly seat bearing rollers.

2) Measure pinion bearing preload. Continue tightening pinion nut until preload is same as before disassembly. Preload should NEVER be more than 10 INCH lbs. (1.1 N.m) greater than original setting.

NOTE: *Under NO circumstances should pinion nut be backed off to lessen preload. If desired preload is exceeded, install new collapsible spacer and retighten nut until proper preload is obtained.*

---

3) Install front propeller shaft with reference marks aligned. Tighten "U" joint yoke clamp screws to **14 ft. lbs. (19 N.m).** Check differential housing lubricant level. Add lubricant if needed. Road test vehicle.

Removal (CV Boots) – Remove axle shafts from vehicle. Remove clamps holding boot to CV joint and shaft. Remove CV joint from axle shaft. See INNER CV JOINT and OUTER CV JOINT under OVERHAUL. Remove boot from axle shaft.

Installation – 1) CV joint boot uses 2 sizes of ladder-type clamps. Using Clamp Installer (C-4124), tighten and cut strap clamps.

2) Slide small clamp onto axle shaft. Slide small end of boot onto axle shaft. Position small end of boot at same position on axle as old boot. Position clamp evenly in groove on axle boot. Crimp using installer.

3) Fill boot with lubricant included in boot kit. Install CV joint onto end of axle shaft. Slide boot over edge of CV joint, and clean off excess lubricant. Position clamp into groove on boot. Crimp using installer.

Removal (Differential Housing) – 1) Raise and support vehicle. Remove skid plate. Disconnect axle shafts from axle shaft flanges. Remove front drive shaft from transfer case output shaft flange.

2) Disconnect vacuum hoses and harness connector from shift motor. Using a jack, support differential housing. Lower differential housing with front drive shaft. Remove differential housing from vehicle.

Installation – Support differential housing on jack, and raise into position. Loosely install all bolts and nuts. To complete installation, reverse removal procedure. Tighten all bolts and nuts to specification. See TORQUE SPECIFICATIONS table at end of article.

REAR AXLE ASSEMBLY

Removal (Axle Shaft) – 1) Raise and support vehicle. Remove wheel. Clean area where differential housing cover mates with differential housing. Loosen housing cover bolts, and drain lubricant from housing. Remove housing cover. Rotate differential case so differential pinion gear mate shaft lock screw is accessible. *See Fig. 2.*

2) Remove lock screw and pinion gear mate shaft from differential case. Force axle shaft toward center of vehicle, and remove axle shaft "C" lock from recessed groove in axle shaft. Remove axle shaft from differential housing. DO NOT damage axle shaft bearing, which remains in housing.

3) Inspect axle shaft bearing contact surfaces for brinelling, excessive wear and damage. If any of these conditions exist, replace axle shaft and bearing. Remove axle shaft seal from end of housing bore. Remove axle shaft bearing if it appears damaged or excessively worn. Using Bearing Remover (C-4167) and a slide hammer, remove axle shaft bearing.

Installation – 1) Using Bearing Installer (C-4203), install new seal and bearing in housing. When installer contacts housing flange face, seal will be positioned at correct depth in bore. Lubricate bearing bore and seal lip.

2) Insert axle shaft into housing bore, and engage splines with differential side gear splines. DO NOT damage axle shaft seal lip. With axle shaft in place, insert "C" lock in recessed groove of axle shaft.

3) Force axle shaft outward to seat "C" lock in differential side gear counterbore. Insert differential pinion gear mate shaft into case and through thrust washers and pinion gears. Align hole in shaft with lock screw hole in differential case, and using Loctite, install lock screw. Tighten lock screw to **96 INCH lbs. (11 N.m).**

4) Remove residual sealant material from differential housing and cover. Thoroughly clean contact surfaces with mineral spirits, and dry surfaces completely. Apply a 1/16" to 3/32" thick bead of silicone rubber sealant around bolt circle on housing.

5) Install housing cover. Install axle gear ratio identification tag with one cover bolt. Tighten cover bolts to **35 ft. lbs. (47 N.m).** Remove supports, and lower vehicle until level. Fill differential housing with lubricant, and install fill plug. Lower vehicle, and test axle for correct operation.

Removal (Drive Pinion Gear Shaft & Seal) – 1) Raise and support vehicle. Mark propeller shaft, drive pinion gear shaft yoke and pinion stem for reassembly reference. Disconnect propeller shaft, and support aside.

2) Using an INCH-lb. torque wrench, turn pinion several revolutions in both directions. Measure and record pinion bearing preload.

3) Remove drive pinion nut and washer. Remove yoke. Lower rear of vehicle to prevent lubrication leakage from differential housing. Carefully pry out oil seal; DO NOT damage machined surface.

Installation – 1) Install new pinion oil seal squarely into bore in housing until seated. Align marks, and install pinion flange. Install pinion washer (convex side out) and nut. Tighten shaft nut to **210 ft. lbs. (285 N.m),** and rotate pinion to properly seat bearing rollers.

2) Measure pinion bearing preload. Continue tightening pinion nut until preload is same as before disassembly. Preload should NEVER be more than 10 INCH lbs. (1.1 N.m) greater than original setting.

NOTE: Under NO circumstances should pinion nut be backed off to lessen preload. If desired preload is exceeded, install new collapsible spacer and retighten nut until proper preload is obtained.

---

3) Install drive shaft with reference marks aligned. Tighten "U" joint yoke clamp screws to **14 ft. lbs. (19 N.m).** Check differential housing lubricant level; add lubricant if necessary. Road test vehicle.

Removal & Installation (Differential Housing) – 1) Raise and support vehicle. Block brake pedal in up position. Remove rear wheels. DO NOT remove brake drums. Disconnect brake lines at wheel cylinders and cap lines to prevent fluid loss. Remove differential vent hose from brake tee fitting.

2) Remove brake tee fitting bolt, and disengage brake lines from axle housing clips. Disconnect parking brake cables. Disconnect propeller shaft, and support aside. Remove shock absorber attaching bolts.

3) Remove rear spring "U" bolt nuts. Remove "U" bolts and spring brackets. Carefully lower axle assembly from vehicle.

4) To install axle, reverse removal procedure. On 2WD vehicles, tighten "U" bolt nuts to **65 ft. lbs. (88 N.m).** On 4WD vehicles, tighten "U" bolt nuts to **110 ft. lbs. (149 N.m).** Bleed and adjust brakes. Check differential fluid level; add fluid if necessary.

OVERHAUL

INNER CV JOINT

Disassembly – 1) Remove CV axle shaft. Clamp axle shaft in vise. Remove and discard boot clamps. Pull boot back to reach tripod retainer assembly. Move axle shaft toward end of CV housing. Using a hammer, tap axle to remove end cap.

2) Remove outer snap ring from axle shaft groove. Remove tripod by hand. If necessary, use brass punch to tap tripod body. Remove housing and boot.

Reassembly – 1) Install new boot on axle shaft. Install CV housing. Slide tripod onto axle shaft, chamfered side first. Flat side of tripod should be next to retaining ring groove. Using grease in boot kit, put 2 of 3 packets into boot. Third packet will go into CV housing.

2) Install retaining ring. Place boot over retaining groove in housing, using Clamp Installer (C-4653), clamp boot in position. Install end cap.

OUTER CV JOINT

Disassembly – 1) Remove CV axle shaft from vehicle. Remove and discard boot clamps. Wipe away grease so CV joint body edge is visible. Hold axle shaft in soft jaws of vise. Using soft hammer, give top of CV joint body a sharp blow to break body loose from internal circlip in groove at end of shaft.

2) Wear sleeve on outer CV housing is a wiping surface for hub bearing seal. If wear sleeve is bent or damaged, pry sleeve away from machined ledge of CV joint. Remove and discard circlip from shaft groove.

3) If shaft is damaged, remove heavy spacer ring from inner groove. If joint was operating properly, replace boots only. If joint was noisy or badly worn, replace complete joint. Replace boot whenever joint is replaced.

4) Wipe grease off outer CV joint, and mark inner race (cross), cage and housing with paint. Position joint vertically in vise, using soft jaws to clamp on splined shaft. Press down on one side of inner race to tilt cage, and remove ball from opposite side. Remove all balls.

CAUTION: DO NOT hit cage when using hammer and drift to loosen CV joint.

---

5) If joint is tight, use brass drift and hammer to tap inner race and remove balls. Tilt cage and inner race assembly to vertical position.

6) Remove inner race and cage assembly by pulling up and away from housing. Turn inner race 90 degrees to cage. Align elongated cage window with one spherical land on race. Raise land to cage window, and remove inner race by swinging it out of cage.

Inspection – Check grease for contamination. Wash all parts in solvent, and dry with compressed air. Inspect races, splined shaft and nut threads for damage. Inspect balls and cage for damage.

Reassembly – **1)** Position new wear sleeve on joint housing machined ledge. Lightly oil all components before reassembly. Align parts according to paint markings.

2) Insert one inner race (cross) into cage window, and feed race into cage. Pivot inner race to fully assemble cage and race. Align opposing elongated cage windows with housing land. Feed cage assembly into housing. Pivot cage 90 degrees to complete installation.

3) Counterbore of inner race should face outward from joint. Apply lubricant to ball races from packet in boot kit.

4) Distribute grease equally between all sides of ball grooves. Insert balls into raceways by tilting cage and inner race assembly. Fasten boot to shaft. Insert new circlip from shaft groove kit.

5) Position outer joint on splined end of axle shaft. Put hub nut on stub axle. Engage splines, and use mallet to tap sharply on hub nut. Ensure circlip is properly seated by trying to pull joint off shaft.

6) Install large end of boot over joint housing, ensuring boot is not twisted. Using Clamp Installer (C-4653), clamp boot to housing.

DIFFERENTIAL

NOTE: Differential overhaul procedures for front and rear axle are identical. It is not necessary to remove complete front axle assembly to overhaul differential.

Disassembly – **1)** Mark propeller shaft and "U" joint for reassembly. Remove propeller shaft, and support aside. Drain lubricant, and remove housing cover.

2) Remove differential pinion lock bolt and pinion. On rear axle, push left axle shaft inward, and remove "C" lock. Pull left axle shaft out of differential housing. Remove right axle in same manner.

3) On front axle, remove shift motor and housing cover. Remove bearing seal retainer attaching screws. Remove right axle shaft from differential. Remove snap ring and splined gear from right axle shaft. Separate bearing and seal from right axle shaft. Remove shift collar from shift motor housing.

4) Force intermediate shaft toward center of vehicle, and remove axle shaft "C" lock. Install pinion gear mate shaft and lock screw. Remove intermediate axle shaft.

5) On front and rear axles, measure and record differential side play, ring gear runout and pinion gear shaft preload. Mark differential gear and case at point of maximum runout. Side play should not exist and ring gear runout should not exceed **.005" (.13 mm)**. If ring gear runout exceeds **.005" (.13 mm)**, check differential case flange runout.

6) To check case flange runout, use Hex Adjuster (C-4164). Tighten adjusters until all case side play is eliminated. Remove and discard ring gear bolts (left-hand threads). Using a hammer and brass drift, force ring gear from differential case flange, and remove ring gear.

7) Mount dial indicator to housing, and place dial indicator pointer on ring gear flange of differential case. *See Fig. 5.* Rotate case several times, checking reading on dial indicator. If reading varies more than .003" (.08 mm), replace differential case.

8) Using Flange Holder (C-3281), remove drive pinion flange and pry out seal. Mark side bearing caps and axle housing for reassembly reference. Remove adjuster locks. Loosen, but DO NOT remove, bearing caps. Insert hex adjuster through axle tube, and loosen hex adjuster on each side.

9) Remove bearing caps, adjusters and differential case assembly. Keep all bearing races and adjusters with their respective bearings. Using soft drift punch and hammer, drive pinion shaft out of housing.

NOTE: Bearings, races, collapsible spacer and shim(s) must be replaced after driving out pinion.

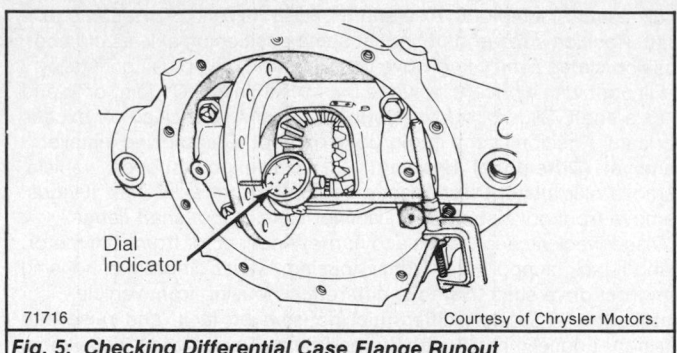

Dial
Indicator

71716   Courtesy of Chrysler Motors.

Fig. 5: Checking Differential Case Flange Runout

10) Using Bearing Remover (C-4306) and Driver Handle (C-4171), drive bearing races out of housing. Using Puller (C-293-PA) and Adapter (C-293-42), remove bearings from pinion shaft. Remove shim(s) from behind rear bearing, and record thickness.

11) Mount differential case assembly in soft-jawed vise. Remove and discard ring gear bolts (left-hand thread). Using soft-faced hammer, drive ring gear off differential case.

NOTE: DO NOT remove ring gear from differential case unless case or gear set is replaced.

Cleaning & Inspection – Clean all components, and inspect for wear. Inspect all bearings and races for wear and pitting, and replace as set. Inspect all gear teeth for wear and chipping, and replace as matched set.

Reassembly & Adjustment – **1)** Install thrust washers on differential side gears, and position gears in differential case. Place thrust washers on differential pinion gears, and position gears in case so gears are 180 degrees apart when meshed with side gears.

2) Rotate side gears until holes in pinion gears are in alignment with pinion shaft holes in case. Install differential pinion shaft. Ensure hole in pinion shaft is aligned with lock bolt hole in case. Using Loctite, install lock bolt, and tighten to **90 INCH lbs. (10 N.m)**.

3) Ensure contact surface of ring gear and case flange is clean and free of all nicks and burrs. Using an Arkansas stone, remove any sharp areas from chamfer on inside diameter of ring gear.

4) Using heat lamp, hot oil or water, heat ring gear. Temperature of ring gear must not exceed 300°F (149°C). DO NOT use torch to heat ring gear. Install 3 equally spaced pilot studs on ring gear. Place heated ring gear on jaws of vise, and install case using new left-hand threaded bolts.

5) Tighten ring gear-to-case bolts alternately and evenly to specifications. Using Bearing Installer (C-3716-A) and Driver Handle (C-4171), install side bearings on case. See TORQUE SPECIFICATIONS table at end of article.

Drive Pinion Depth – **1)** Install both drive pinion bearing races into axle housing bores. Assemble Pinion Locating Spacer (SP-3244) over body of Main Stem (SP-5385) followed by rear pinion bearing cone. Insert assembly into axle carrier from rear.

2) Position bearing and tools in housing. Install Locating Sleeve (SP-3245) and drive pinion gear shaft front bearing. Install Compression Sleeve (SP-3194-B), Centralizing Washer (SP-534) and Compression Nut (SP-3193).

3) Install Gauge Block (SP-3250) on end of main body (SP-5385). Install Cap Screw (SP-536), and tighten securely using Wrench (SP-531). Position Cross Bar Arbor (SP-3243) in axle housing bearing seats. *See Fig. 6.*

4) Using feeler gauge, determine proper thickness of shims so they will fit snugly between arbor and gauge block. Fit must be snug, but not excessively tight.

5) To select correct shim pack, read markings on end of pinion head. When marking is minus, add that amount to feeler gauge thickness to obtain thickness of correct shim pack. When marking is plus, subtract that amount of thickness. Remove all tools.

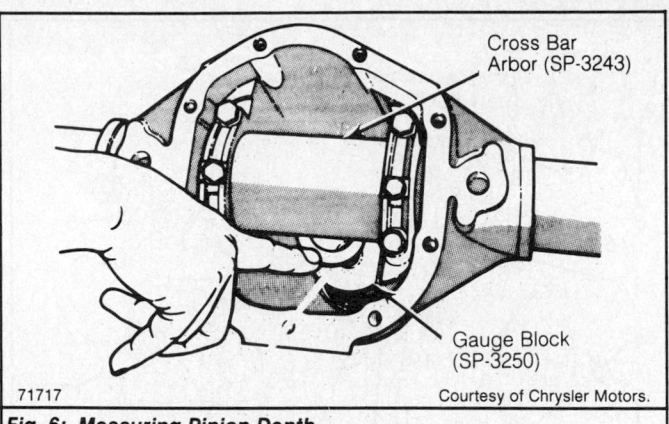

Cross Bar
Arbor (SP-3243)

Gauge Block
(SP-3250)

71717   Courtesy of Chrysler Motors.

Fig. 6: Measuring Pinion Depth

Pinion Bearing Preload – 1) Place selected shim on pinion shaft. Using Press Sleeve (C-3717) and an arbor press, press bearing on pinion shaft. Lubricate pinion and bearing with gear oil.
2) Insert drive pinion assembly through axle housing. Install new collapsible spacer and front pinion bearing onto stem of gear. Using Installer (C-3718) and Holder (C-3281), install pinion flange.

NOTE: DO NOT collapse spacer. If spacer is collapsed, new spacer must be installed.

---

3) Remove pinion flange. Using Seal Installer (C-4076), install new pinion oil seal. Align marks, and install pinion flange, washer (convex side out) and nut. While rotating pinion assembly to ensure proper bearing seating, tighten pinion flange nut until all end play is removed.
4) Tighten drive pinion nut to specification. See TORQUE SPECIFICATIONS at end of article. Using INCH-lb. torque wrench, measure pinion bearing preload by rotating pinion through several revolutions. Continue tightening pinion flange nut in small increments until correct bearing preload is obtained. DO NOT back off nut to lessen bearing preload. If desired preload is exceeded, install new collapsible spacer, and retighten nut until proper preload is obtained.
Backlash & Side Bearing Preload – 1) Observe 2 precautions when checking and adjusting ring gear backlash and differential bearing preload:

- Index gears so same teeth are meshed during all backlash measurements. Permissible backlash variation is **.003" (.08 mm)**. For example, if backlash at minimum point is .006" (.15 mm) and backlash at maximum point is .009" (.23 mm), variation is correct.
- Maintain specified adjuster torque to obtain accurate differential bearing preload.

2) Using Hex Adjuster (C-4164), turn each adjuster until bearing free play is eliminated with approximately .01" (.25 mm) backlash. Seat differential roller bearings, as bearings do not always move with adjusters. To ensure accurate adjustment, bearings must be seated by oscillating drive pinion 1/2 turn in each direction 5-10 times each time adjusters are moved.
3) Install dial indicator on cover flange . Position indicator stem against drive side of ring gear. Check backlash every 90 degrees to find point of minimum backlash. Mark each position so backlash readings will be taken with same teeth meshed. Rotate ring gear to point of minimum backlash.

4) Loosen right adjuster and tighten left adjuster until backlash is .003-.004" (.08-.10 mm) with each adjuster tightened to **10 ft. lbs. (14 N.m)**. Seat bearings as before. Tighten bearing cap bolts to **45 ft. lbs. (61 N.m)**. Using hex adjuster, tighten right adjuster to **70 ft. lbs. (95 N.m)**. Seat bearings, and continue to tighten right adjuster until torque remains constant at **70 ft. lbs. (95 N.m)**.
5) Using indicator, recheck backlash. If backlash is not between .003-.006" (.08-.15 mm), increase torque on right adjuster, and seat bearings. Continue operation until backlash is **.003-.006" (.08-.15 mm)**. Tighten left adjuster to **70 ft. lbs. (95 N.m)**, and seat bearings. With adjustments completed, install adjuster locks. Ensure lock teeth are engaged in adjuster threads. Tighten lock bolts to **90 INCH lbs. (10 N.m)**.
Final Inspection & Assembly – With pinion bearing preload and ring gear backlash properly adjusted, check tooth pattern contact. When pattern is satisfactory, install axle shafts, wheels and axle housing cover. Refill with hypoid gear lubricant.

AXLE ASSEMBLY SPECIFICATIONS

AXLE ASSEMBLY SPECIFICATIONS

Application	Specification
Maximum Ring Gear Runout	.005" (.13 mm)
Maximum Differential Case Flange Runout	.003" (.08 mm)
Pinion Bearing Preload	
New Bearings	10-20 INCH lbs. (1.1-2.3 N.m)
Used Rear & New Front Bearings	[1] 10 INCH lbs. (1.1 N.m)
Ring Gear Backlash	.003-.006" (.08-.15 mm)

[1] – Maximum increase over original preload before disassembly.

TORQUE SPECIFICATIONS

TORQUE SPECIFICATIONS

Application	Ft. Lbs. (N.m)
Axle Housing Cover Bolt	35 (47)
Axle Shaft Nut	190 (258)
Axle "U" Bolt Nut	
2WD	65 (88)
4WD	110 (149)
Drive Pinion Nut (Minimum)	210 (285)
Inner Axle Flange Bolt	65 (88)
Insulator-To-Differential Housing Nut	75 (102)
Insulator-To-Shift Motor Housing Nut	75 (102)
Propeller Shaft Nut	65 (88)
Ring Gear-To-Differential Case Bolt [1]	70 (95)
Side Bearing Cap Bolt	45 (61)
Skid Plate Bolts	17 (23)
Support Bracket-To-Adapter Bolt	65 (88)
Support Bracket-To-Shift Motor Housing Bolt	65 (88)
"U" Joint Yoke Clamp Screws	14 (19)
Wheel Lug Nut	85 (115)
	INCH Lbs. (N.m)
Adjuster Lock Bolt	90 (10)
Differential Case Lock Screw	96 (11)

[1] – Left-hand threaded bolt.

Dakota, Pickup, Ramcharger, RWD Van

DESCRIPTION

Axle assembly is hypoid gear type with an integral carrier housing. It is used on light-duty vehicles with semi-floating axles. Pinion bearing preload adjustment is made with collapsible spacer. Differential bearing preload adjustment is made with adjusting nuts seated on bearing races. Removable housing cover permits inspection and minor servicing of differential without removal from vehicle.

NOTE: If vehicle is equipped with Dana axle assembly, see DANA FULL-FLOATING AXLES article.

Vehicles equipped with Rear Wheel Anti-Lock (RWAL) brakes have an exciter ring pressed onto differential case, next to ring gear, and a RWAL sensor mounted in differential housing. *See Fig. 1.* A small metal tag attached to rear axle housing cover bolt identifies axle ratio.

REAR AXLE RATIO IDENTIFICATION

Application	Ratio
8 1/4" Ring Gear	2.94:1, 3.21:1, 3.55:1, 3.90:1, 4.10:1
8 3/8" Ring Gear	3.21:1, 3.55:1, 3.90:1
9 1/4" Ring Gear	3.55:1, 3.90:1

LUBRICATION

CAUTION: If axle has been submerged in water, axle lubricant MUST be replaced immediately to avoid premature failure due to contamination.

Use Multipurpose Gear Lubricant (MIL-L-2105-C/API GL-5). Lubricant level should be 1/4-1/2" (6.4-12.7 mm) below level of filler hole.

REMOVAL & INSTALLATION

AXLE SHAFTS & BEARINGS

NOTE: During repairs, DO NOT heat (with torch) or hammer bearing cones, races, bores or journals.

Removal – 1) Raise vehicle and remove wheel and brake drum. Clean dirt and foreign material from area of housing cover. *See Fig. 1.* Loosen housing cover attaching bolts and drain lubricant. Remove housing cover. Remove pinion gear mate shaft lock bolt and differential pinion gear mate shaft.

2) Force axle shaft toward center of vehicle. Remove "C" lock from groove in axle shaft. Using care not to damage roller bearing, pull axle shaft out of housing. Remove oil seal from housing bore.

3) To remove axle shaft bearing on 8 1/4" and 8 3/8" ring gears, use Bearing Puller (C-4167). On 9 1/4" ring gear, use Bearing Puller (C-4828). On 8 1/4" and 8 3/8" ring gears, attach slide hammer to puller and remove axle shaft bearing. On 9 1/4" ring gear, use a wrench to turn threaded shaft through puller bar and remove axle shaft bearing. On all models, if either axle or bearing shows any signs of brinnelling, spalling or pitting, replace component.

Installation – 1) Clean all parts thoroughly. Install axle shaft bearing using Bearing Installer (C-4198) for 8 1/4" and 8 3/8" ring gears. Use Bearing Installer (C-4826) with Handle (C-4171) for 9 1/4" ring gear. Ensure bearing is bottomed against shoulder in bore. Lubricate and install new oil seal in housing bore.

2) Slide axle shaft into place. Install "C" lock into groove in axle shaft. Pull outward on axle shaft to seat "C" lock in counterbore of differential side gear.

3) Install differential pinion gear mate shaft. Align hole in shaft with lock bolt hole in case. Using Loctite, install pinion gear mate shaft lock bolt and tighten to **100 INCH lbs. (11 N.m).** Apply 1/16" bead of Silicone Rubber Sealant (4318025) to housing cover sealing surface. Install housing cover and identification tag. Tighten bolts to specification. See TORQUE SPECIFICATIONS table at end of article.

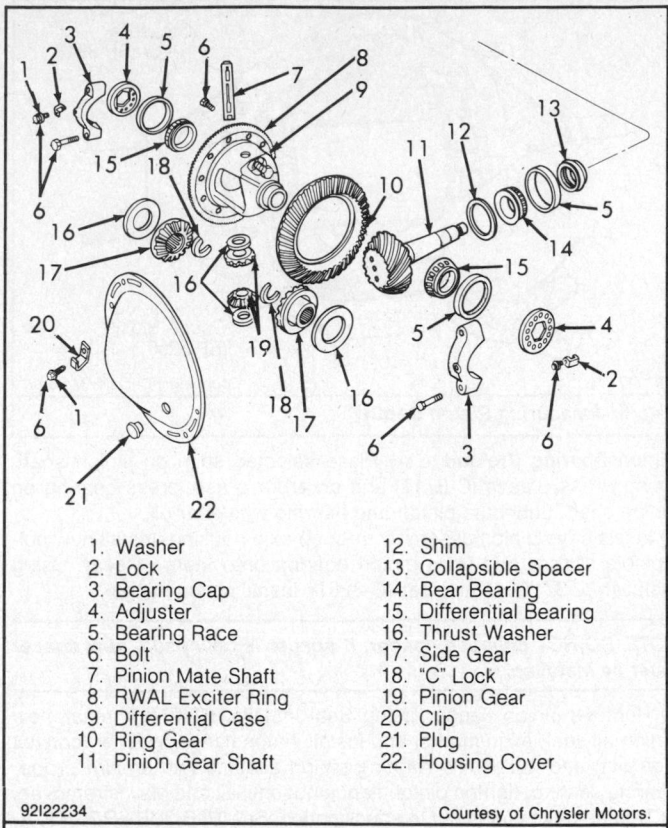

1. Washer	12. Shim
2. Lock	13. Collapsible Spacer
3. Bearing Cap	14. Rear Bearing
4. Adjuster	15. Differential Bearing
5. Bearing Race	16. Thrust Washer
6. Bolt	17. Side Gear
7. Pinion Mate Shaft	18. "C" Lock
8. RWAL Exciter Ring	19. Pinion Gear
9. Differential Case	20. Clip
10. Ring Gear	21. Plug
11. Pinion Gear Shaft	22. Housing Cover

92I22234   Courtesy of Chrysler Motors.

Fig. 1: Exploded View Of Drive Axle Assembly (RWAL Equipped)

PINION FLANGE & SEAL

Removal – 1) Raise vehicle, mark propeller shaft universal joint, drive pinion flange and pinion stem for reassembly. Disconnect propeller shaft and support aside. Remove rear wheels and brake drums to prevent false preload reading.

2) Using INCH-pound torque wrench, rotate pinion nut to measure pinion bearing preload. Record preload reading. Using Pinion Flange Holder (C-3281), remove drive pinion nut and washer. Using 2-jaw puller, pull off flange. Taking care not to damage machined surface, pry out oil seal.

Installation – 1) Examine drive pinion for any burrs or excessive wear. Remove burrs with crocus cloth and replace drive pinion gear if excessively worn. Install new pinion oil seal using Seal Installer (C-4076) for 8 1/4" and 8 3/8" ring gears. Use Seal Installer (C-3980 or C-4109) for 9 1/4" ring gear.

2) Align marks and install pinion flange. Install pinion washer (convex side out) and nut. Using pinion flange holder, tighten nut to specification. See TORQUE SPECIFICATIONS table at end of article. Rotate pinion to properly seat bearing rollers.

3) Measure pinion bearing preload. Continue tightening pinion nut until preload is same as noted before disassembly. Preload should NEVER be greater than original setting by more than 10 INCH lbs. (1.1 N.m).

CAUTION: Under NO circumstances should pinion nut be backed off to lessen preload. If desired preload is exceeded, install new collapsible spacer, and retighten nut until proper preload is obtained.

AXLE ASSEMBLY

Removal & Installation – 1) Raise vehicle and remove wheels and brake drums. Disconnect and cap brake lines at wheel cylinders. Disconnect differential vent hose. Disconnect parking brake cables. Disconnect RWAL sensor electrical connection (if equipped).

2) Mark propeller shaft universal joint, drive pinion flange and pinion stem for reassembly reference. Disconnect propeller shaft and support aside. Remove shock absorbers and rear spring "U" bolts.

1992 DRIVE AXLES
8 1/4", 8 3/8" & 9 1/4" Ring Gears (Cont.)

CHRY
7-15

Remove rear axle assembly. To install, reverse removal procedure. Bleed brakes.

OVERHAUL

DISASSEMBLY

NOTE: It is not necessary to remove complete rear axle assembly to overhaul differential.

Differential – 1) Remove wheels and brake drums. Mark propeller shaft and universal joint for reassembly. Remove propeller shaft and support aside. Drain lubricant and remove housing cover. Remove pinion gear mate shaft lock screw. Remove pinion gear mate shaft.
2) Force both axle shafts toward center of vehicle and remove "C" locks. Remove axles. Measure and record differential side play, ring gear runout and pinion gear shaft preload. Mark differential gear and case at point of maximum runout. No side play should exist and ring gear runout should not exceed .005" (.13 mm). If ring gear runout exceeds .005" (.13 mm), differential case flange runout must be checked.
3) Tighten adjusters until all case side play is eliminated. Remove ring gear bolts from differential case flange and discard bolts (left-hand thread). Mount dial indicator to housing, and place dial indicator pointer on ring gear flange of differential case. *See Fig. 2.*

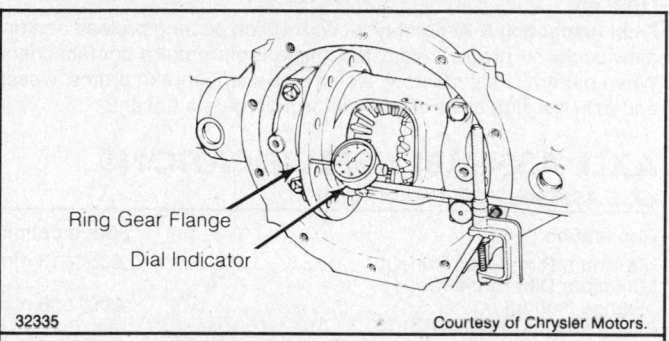

32335   Courtesy of Chrysler Motors.

Fig. 2: Checking Differential Case Flange Runout

Ring Gear Flange
Dial Indicator

4) Rotate case several times, checking reading on dial indicator. If reading varies more than .003" (.08 mm), replace differential case. Remove drive pinion flange and seal as previously described. Mark side bearing caps and axle housing for reassembly. Remove adjuster locks. Loosen, but do not remove, bearing caps. Insert hex adjuster through axle tube and loosen hex adjuster on each side.

CAUTION: Use extreme care when removing differential case from vehicle to avoid damage to RWAL exciter ring.

5) Remove bearing caps, adjusters and differential case assembly. Be sure to keep all bearing races and adjusters with their respective bearings. Using soft drift punch and hammer, drive pinion shaft out of housing.
6) Using hammer and soft drift punch, drive bearing races out of housing. Remove shim(s) from behind rear race and record thickness. Remove bearing cones from pinion shaft using Puller (C-293-PA) and Adapter (C-293-42).

NOTE: DO NOT remove ring gear from differential case unless case, gear set or RWAL exciter ring is being replaced.

7) Mount differential case assembly in soft-jawed vise. Remove and discard ring gear bolts (left-hand thread), if not removed previously. Using soft-faced hammer, drive ring gear off differential case.
8) If RWAL exciter ring is being replaced, use a hammer and punch to drive exciter ring from differential case.

CLEANING & INSPECTION

Differential – Clean all components and inspect for wear. Inspect all bearings and races for wear or pitting and replace as set. Inspect all gear teeth for wear or chipping and replace as matched set only.

REASSEMBLY & ADJUSTMENT

Differential Case Assembly – 1) Install thrust washers on differential side gears, and position gears in differential case. Place thrust washers on differential pinion gears and position gears in case so they are 180 degrees apart when meshed with side gears.
2) Rotate side gears until holes in pinion gears are in alignment with pinion gear mate shaft holes in case. Install differential pinion gear mate shaft. Ensure hole in shaft is aligned with lock bolt hole in case.
3) Ensure contact surface of ring gear and case flange is clean and free of all nicks and burrs. Using an Arkansas stone, remove any sharp areas from chamfer on inside diameter of ring gear.

NOTE: RWAL exciter ring is installed using same heating procedures as ring gear.

4) Using heat lamp, hot oil or water, heat ring gear. Temperature of ring gear must not exceed 300°F (149°C). DO NOT use torch to heat ring gear. Install 3 equally spaced pilot studs on ring gear. Place heated ring gear on jaws of vise and install case using new left-hand threaded bolts.
5) Tighten ring gear-to-case bolts alternately and evenly to specification. See TORQUE SPECIFICATIONS table at end of article. Install side bearings on case using Bearing Installer (C-4340 for 8 1/4" and 8 3/8" ring gears, or C-4213 for 9 1/4" ring gear) and Driver (C-4171). Use these tools in conjunction with an arbor press. Lubricate assembly with hypoid gear lubricant.
Drive Pinion Depth – 1) Install both drive pinion bearing races into axle housing bores. Assemble Pinion Locating Spacer (SP-6030) over body of Main Stem (SP-5385), followed by rear pinion bearing. Insert assembly into axle housing from rear.

NOTE: All tool numbers indicated in procedure apply to 8 1/4" and 8 3/8" ring gear axles. For equivalent tool numbers for 9 1/4" ring gear axles, see EQUIVALENT TOOL NUMBERS table.

EQUIVALENT TOOL NUMBERS

Application	8 1/4" & 8 3/8" Tool No.	9 1/4" Tool No.
Bearing Installer	C-4340	C-4213
Centralizing Washer	SP-534	SP-534
Compression Sleeve	SP-3194-B	SP-535A
Cross Bore Arbor	SP-6029	SP-6018
Gauge Block	SP-5383	SP-6020
Holding Tool	C-3281	C-3281
Main Stem	SP-5385	SP-526
Nut	SP-3193	SP-533
Spacer	SP-5382	SP-1730
Spacer	SP-6030	SP-6017
Washer	SP-6022	SP-6022

2) On 8 1/4" and 8 3/8" ring gear assemblies, hold spacer and main stem assembly in position. Install front pinion bearing over Spacer (SP-5382) and position over main stem of tool. On 9 1/4" and 9 1/4" HD ring gear assemblies, position spacer and main stem assembly in housing. Install front pinion bearing and Washer (SP-6022).
3) Procedure from this point is same for both assemblies, except for tool numbers. See EQUIVALENT TOOL NUMBERS table. Position compression sleeve, centralizing washer and main screw nut on main stem. Hold compression sleeve with companion flange wrench, and tighten nut. *See Fig. 3.* Allow tool to rotate as nut is being tightened to prevent damaging bearings and races.
4) Loosen tool nut then retighten to obtain appropriate pinion bearing preload. See AXLE ASSEMBLY SPECIFICATIONS table. Rotate tool after tightening to properly seat pinion bearings. Install Gauge Block (SP-5383 or SP-6020) on main tool and tighten screw.

CHRY
7-16

1992 DRIVE AXLES
8 1/4", 8 3/8" & 9 1/4" Ring Gears (Cont.)

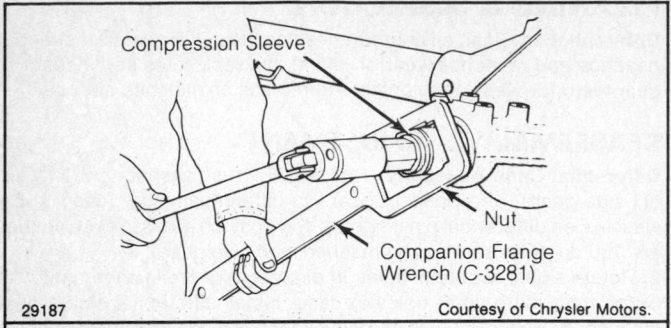

Fig. 3: Seating Pinion Bearing Races

Compression Sleeve

Nut

Companion Flange Wrench (C-3281)

29187   Courtesy of Chrysler Motors.

5) Position Cross Bore Arbor (SP-6029 or SP-6018) in housing side bearing seats, and center arbor in bore. *See Fig. 4.* Position bearing caps on carrier pedestals and insert .002" (.051 mm) spacer between arbor and each cap. Install cap bolts and tighten to **10 ft. lbs. (14 N.m)**.
6) Using feeler gauge, determine proper thickness of shims to fit snugly between arbor and gauge block. Fit must be snug, NOT excessively tight.
7) To select correct shim pack, read markings on end of pinion head. When marking is minus, add that amount of thickness to feeler gauge thickness to obtain thickness of correct shim pack. When marking is plus, subtract that amount of thickness. Remove all tools and rear pinion bearing race from housing.

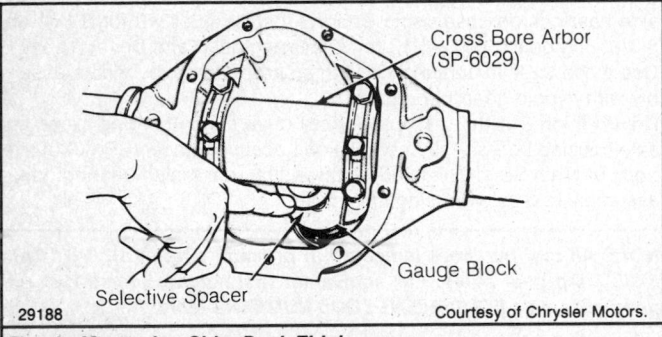

Fig. 4: Measuring Shim Pack Thickness

Cross Bore Arbor (SP-6029)

Gauge Block

Selective Spacer

29188   Courtesy of Chrysler Motors.

Pinion Bearing Preload – **1)** Place selected shim in pinion shaft bore and install rear pinion bearing race. Lubricate rear pinion bearing and press into position on drive pinion stem.
2) Insert drive pinion assembly through axle housing. Install collapsible spacer and front pinion bearing onto stem of gear. Install pinion flange and tighten nut until front bearing is seated.

NOTE: Use care not to collapse spacer. If spacer is collapsed, new spacer must be installed.

---

3) With front bearing fully seated, remove pinion flange. Install new pinion oil seal. Align marks and install pinion flange, washer (convex side out) and nut. While rotating pinion assembly (to ensure proper bearing seating), tighten pinion flange nut until all end play is removed.
4) Tighten pinion nut to specified torque and measure pinion bearing preload, by rotating pinion through several revolutions, with INCH-pound torque wrench. Continue tightening pinion flange nut in small increments until correct bearing preload is obtained.

CAUTION: DO NOT back off nut to decrease bearing preload. If desired preload is exceeded, new collapsible spacer must be installed and nut retightened until proper preload is obtained.

Backlash & Side Bearing Preload – **1)** Observe following 2 precautions when checking and adjusting ring gear backlash and differential bearing preload.
- Index gears so same teeth are meshed during all backlash measurements. Permissible backlash variation is .003" (.08 mm).
- Maintain specified adjuster torque to obtain accurate differential bearing preload.

2) Using hex adjuster, turn each adjuster until bearing free play is eliminated with approximately .010" (.25 mm) backlash. Seat differential roller bearings, as bearings do not always move with adjusters. To ensure accurate adjustment, bearings must be seated by oscillating drive pinion 1/2 turn in each direction 5-10 times each time adjusters are moved.
3) Install dial indicator on cover flange. Position indicator stem against drive side of ring gear. Check backlash every 90 degrees to find point of minimum backlash. Mark each position so backlash readings will be taken with same teeth meshed. Rotate ring gear to point of minimum backlash.
4) Loosen right adjuster, and tighten left adjuster until backlash is .003"-.004" (.08-.10 mm). Tighten each adjuster to **10 ft. lbs. (14 N.m)**. Seat bearings as previously described. Tighten bearing cap bolts to **70 ft. lbs. (95 N.m)** for 8 3/8" ring gear and **100 ft. lbs. (136 N.m)** for 8 1/4" and 9 1/4" ring gears. Using hex adjuster, tighten right adjuster to **75 ft. lbs. (102 N.m)**. Seat bearings, and continue to tighten right adjuster until torque remains constant at 75 ft. lbs. (102 N.m).
5) Check backlash again with indicator. If backlash is not .006-.008" (.15-.20 mm), increase torque on right adjuster and seat bearings. Repeat procedure until backlash is **.006-.008" (.15-.20 mm)**. Tighten left adjuster to **75 ft. lbs. (102 N.m)**, and seat bearings. With adjustments completed, install adjuster locks. Ensure lock teeth are engaged in adjuster threads. Tighten both lock bolts to **90 INCH lbs. (10 N.m)**.

Final Inspection & Assembly – With pinion bearing preload and ring gear backlash properly adjusted, make tooth pattern contact check. When pattern is satisfactory, install axle shafts, brake drums, wheels and axle housing cover. Refill with hypoid gear lubricant.

AXLE ASSEMBLY SPECIFICATIONS

AXLE ASSEMBLY SPECIFICATIONS

Application	Specifications
Maximum Ring Gear Runout	.005" (.13 mm)
Maximum Differential Case	
Flange Runout	.003" (.08 mm)
Pinion Bearing Preload	
New Bearings	
Except 8 1/4" Ring Gear	20-35 INCH Lbs. (2.3-4 N.m)
8 1/4" Ring Gear	10-20 INCH Lbs. (1.1-2.3 N.m)
Used Rear & New Front Bearing	[1] 10 INCH lbs. (1.1 N.m)
Ring Gear Backlash	.006-.008" (.15-.20 mm)

[1] – Maximum increase over original preload reading recorded before disassembly.

TORQUE SPECIFICATIONS

TORQUE SPECIFICATIONS

Application	Ft. Lbs. (N.m)
Differential Bearing Cap Bolts	
8 3/8" Ring Gear	70 (95)
8 1/4" & 9 1/4" Ring Gears	100 (136)
Drive Pinion Nut (Minimum)	210 (285)
Housing Cover Bolts	35 (47)
Propeller Shaft Bolts	14-17 (19-23)
Ring Gear-To-Differential Case Bolts [1]	70 (95)
RWAL Brake Sensor Cover Screw	18 (24)
Shock Absorber Nuts	
8 1/4" Ring Gear	60 (81)
8 3/8" & 9 1/4" Ring Gears	50 (68)
Spring "U" Bolt Nuts	
Except Dakota 4WD	
8 3/8" Ring Gear	45 (61)
8 1/4" & 9 1/4" Ring Gears	65 (88)
Dakota 4WD	110 (149)
Wheel Lug Nuts	
8 1/4" Ring Gear	85 (115)
8 3/8" & 9 1/4" Ring Gears	105 (142)

	INCH Lbs. (N.m)
Bearing Adjuster Lock Screws	90 (10)
Pinion Gear Mate Shaft Lock Bolt	100 (11)

[1] – Left-hand threaded bolts.

1992 DRIVE AXLES
Sure-Grip Differential

Dakota, Pickup, Ramcharger, RWD Van

DESCRIPTION

Sure-Grip differential assembly is an option available only for 8 3/8 and 9 1/4 ring gear rear axle assemblies. The Sure-Grip differential assembly is a positive-traction, limited-slip type differential. It is similar in operation to conventional type differentials, except for helical-grooved clutch cones that grip side gears and inside of differential case simultaneously. See Fig. 1. The helical-grooves assure maximum lubrication of clutch surfaces during differential operation.

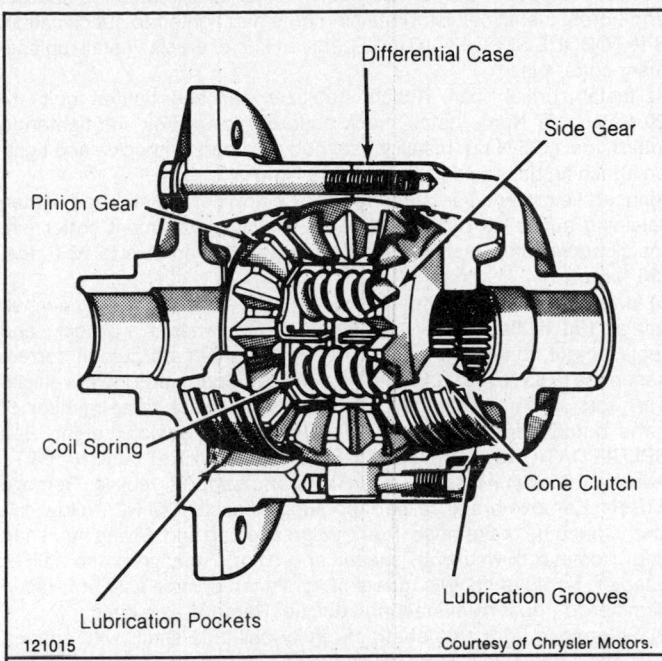

Fig. 1: Cross-Sectional View Of Sure-Grip Differential Assembly

Differential Case

Side Gear

Pinion Gear

Coil Spring

Lubrication Pockets

Cone Clutch

Lubrication Grooves

121015

Courtesy of Chrysler Motors.

AXLE RATIO & IDENTIFICATION

AXLE RATIO SPECIFICATIONS

Application	Ratio
8 3/8" & 9 1/4" Ring Gears	3.21:1, 3.55:1, 3.90:1

Identification – Raise both rear wheels off surface. Place transmission in Neutral. Rotate wheels by hand or by engine power. If both rear wheels rotate in same direction, vehicle is equipped with Sure-Grip differential assembly.

LUBRICATION

CAUTION: If rear axle is submerged in water, rear axle lubricant MUST be replaced immediately to avoid premature differential failure due to oil contamination.

Use Mopar Hypoid Lubricant (4318058) or Multipurpose Gear Lubricant 80W or 80W-90 GL-5 as defined by MIL-L-2105-B (API GL-5). Add 4 ozs. of Mopar Hypoid Gear Oil Additive Friction Modifier (4318060) with every fluid change.

TROUBLE SHOOTING

WARNING: Whenever axle assembly is to be rotated using engine, both rear wheels must be raised off ground to avoid vehicle jumping, which could result in personal injury.

NOTE: If road test produces noise in turns but not during straight-ahead driving, probable cause is incorrect or dissipated rear axle lubricant or additive. Perform following procedure before tear-down.

1) With lubricant of rear axle assembly at operating temperature, raise vehicle so rear wheels are free to turn. Remove axle cover and drain lubricant. Rotate differential so hole in case is facing down. Wipe out all accessible areas of carrier.
2) Scrape gasket material from housing and cover. Thoroughly clean surface with mineral spirits and dry completely to remove any oil residue. Apply a 1/16-3/32" bead of Mopar Silicone Rubber Sealant (4318025) along bolt circle of cover. Install cover to housing with attaching bolts. Install axle gear ratio identification tag under one bolt. Tighten bolts to 35 ft. lbs. (47 N.m).
3) Remove cover filler plug. Add 4 ounces of Mopar Hypoid Gear Oil Additive Friction Modifier (4318060). Refill axle to proper level with Mopar Hypoid Lubricant (4318058). Install filler plug and lower vehicle.
4) After changing lubricant, drive vehicle to a close location and perform 10-12 slow figure-8 turns. This maneuver will pump lubricant through clutches. Road test vehicle and listen for noise condition. If noise persists, replace carrier assembly. See 8 1/4", 8 3/8" & 9 1/4" RING GEAR article.

TESTING

1) Raise rear wheels off ground. Ensure engine is off. On A/T models, place shift lever in PARK position. On M/T models, place shift lever in 1st gear. Grip tread of tire, and attempt to rotate wheel.
2) If rotation is extremely difficult or impossible, differential is performing correctly. If either wheel turns relatively easily or continuously, differential is not performing correctly and should be replaced.

REMOVAL & INSTALLATION

Procedure is same as used to remove and install standard differential case. See 8 1/4", 8 3/8" & 9 1/4" RING GEAR article.

NOTE: During removal and installation of axle shafts, DO NOT rotate one axle shaft unless both axles are installed into differential. Rotation of one axle shaft without other in place may result in misalignment of 2 spline segments with which axle shaft splines engage. This would require difficult realignment procedures when axle shaft is reinstalled.

OVERHAUL

Sure-Grip differential is serviced as an assembly. Under NO circumstances should Sure-Grip differential case be disassembled.

1992 DRIVE AXLES
4WD Steering Knuckles

Dakota, Pickup, Ramcharger

DESCRIPTION

Open type steering knuckles are used on all models. Open type knuckles provide sharper turning angle, decreasing turning radius. Axle shafts are free floating. Depending upon vehicle model, steering knuckles can be attached to axle housing by either ball joints or roller bearings and king (pivot) pins.

NOTE: References to Model 44 and Model 60 refer to axle models used on Pickup and Ramcharger models.

REMOVAL & INSTALLATION

BALL JOINT TYPE

Removal (Dakota) – 1) Remove cotter pin, nut lock, and spring washer from end of stub shaft. Raise and support vehicle. Remove wheel hub nut and washer from end of stub shaft. Remove wheel.

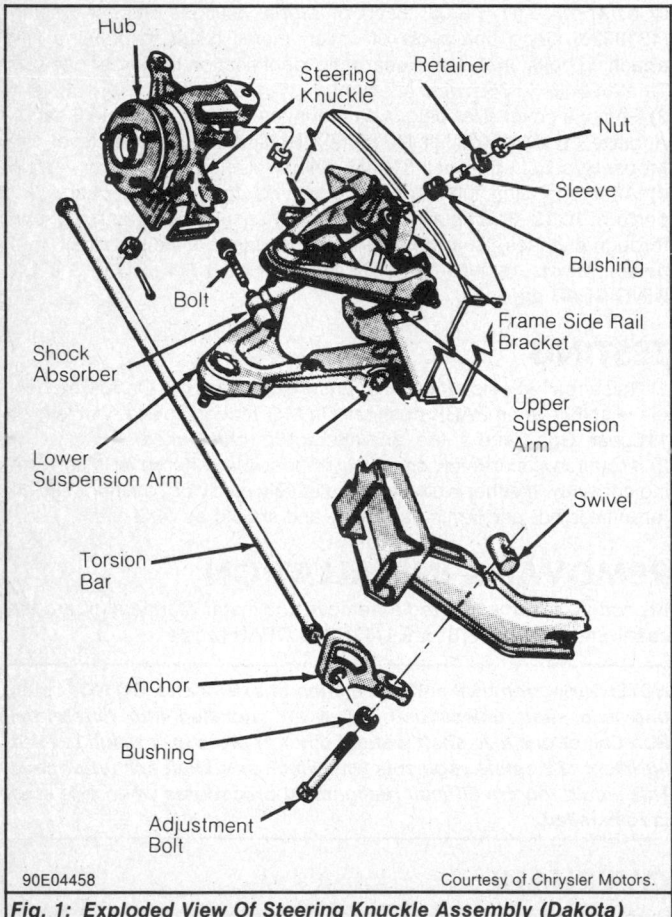

90E04458   Courtesy of Chrysler Motors.

Fig. 1: Exploded View Of Steering Knuckle Assembly (Dakota)

CAUTION: Turn torsion bar adjustment bolt counterclockwise to completely relieve tension from torsion bar.

---

2) While counting number of turns for installation reference, relieve torsion bar tension. Remove brake caliper and support aside. Remove brake rotor. Remove shock absorber lower bolt. Disconnect stabilizer bar from steering knuckle arm. Remove wheel hub-to-steering knuckle attaching bolts and remove wheel hub. See Fig. 1. Remove cotter pin and nut from tie rod end at steering knuckle arm. Using Puller (C-3894-A), remove tie rod end stud from steering knuckle. Remove torsion bar.

0) Remove cotter pin and nut from lower and upper ball joints. Separate lower ball joint from steering knuckle arm bore. Using Ball Joint Remover (C-3564-A) between steering knuckle arms, apply force on

upper ball joint. DO NOT use ball joint remover to force ball joint out of knuckle; strike steering knuckle with hammer to loosen ball joint. Separate upper ball joint from steering knuckle arm bore. Remove steering knuckle. Remove bearing seal from steering knuckle.

Installation – 1) Using multi-purpose lubricant, fill cavity between replacement seal lip and steering knuckle and lubricate lip. Position replacement seal in bore at inner side of steering knuckle and install with Installer (C-4698).

2) Lubricate outer surface area around perimeter of CV drive shaft wear sleeve with multi-purpose lubricant. Position steering knuckle adjacent to suspension arms. Insert ball joints into steering knuckle arm bores. Install ball joint retaining nuts and tighten to specification. See TORQUE SPECIFICATIONS table at end of article. Install replacement cotter pins.

3) Install torsion bar. Attach stabilizer bar and tighten bolts to **20 ft. lbs. (27 N.m)**. Install shock absorber lower bolt and tighten to **100 ft. lbs. (136 N.m)**. Install wheel hub on steering knuckle and tighten attaching bolts to **110 ft. lbs. (149 N.m)**.

4) Insert tie rod end into steering knuckle arm bore. Install and tighten retaining nut to **40 ft. lbs. (54 N.m)**. Install replacement cotter pin. Install brake rotor. Install brake caliper and tighten pins to **22 ft. lbs. (30 N.m)**.

5) Install wheel hub washer and nut on stub shaft. Tighten wheel hub nut to **190 ft. lbs. (258 N.m)**. Install spring washer, nut lock, and replacement cotter pin. Install wheel and tighten lug nuts in correct sequence to **85 ft. lbs. (115 N.m)**. Remove supports and lower vehicle. Turn torsion bar adjustment bolt clockwise, exact same number of turns noted during removal. Adjust front suspension height. See SPECIFICATIONS & PROCEDURES article in WHEEL ALIGNMENT.

Removal (Model 44 Axle) – 1) Raise and support vehicle. Remove wheels. Remove brake caliper and support aside. DO NOT allow caliper to hang by brake hose. Remove grease cap and driving hub snap ring. Remove driving hub, spacer and rotor. Remove brake caliper adapter. Remove spindle nuts and lightly tap spindle with soft-faced hammer to free it from steering knuckle. Remove axle shaft.

2) To remove right axle shaft, carefully pull axle shaft, with spacer, seal and stone shield, from axle housing. To remove left axle, disconnect vacuum lines and electrical connector from switch on disconnect housing assembly. See Fig. 2. Remove cover assembly, gasket and shield. Remove intermediate axle shaft from axle without damaging axle shaft seal. Remove shift collar from axle. Remove differential cover and drain gear oil. Push inner axle shaft toward center of vehicle and remove "C" lock from recessed groove on shaft. Using pry bar, drive out inner shaft.

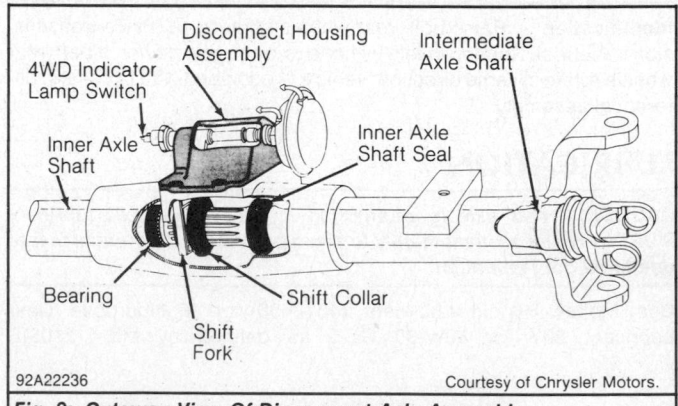

92A22236   Courtesy of Chrysler Motors.

Fig. 2: Cutaway View Of Disconnect Axle Assembly

3) Disconnect tie rod end and drag link studs. Remove nuts and washers from steering knuckle arm. Tap steering knuckle with soft-faced hammer and remove arm. Remove ball joint cotter keys and nuts, discard lower nut. Using a soft-faced hammer, tap steering knuckle to free it from axle tube. Using Yoke Sleeve Removal Wrench (C-4169), remove and discard sleeve from axle shaft tube upper arm bore. Using snap ring pliers, remove lower ball joint retaining snap ring. Press upper and lower ball joints from knuckle.

4) Clean all components with solvent and dry with compressed air. Inspect all parts for burrs, chips, wear, flat spots or cracks. Replace all damaged or worn parts.

NOTE: When aligning upper ball joint nut to install cotter pin, always tighten nut to align holes. Never loosen nut to align holes.

Installation – 1) Press upper and lower ball joints into steering knuckle. Install snap ring on lower ball joint. Install NEW rubber boots over both ball joints. Thread NEW sleeve into axle shaft tube upper arm bore. Leave 2 threads exposed at top of arm.

2) Position steering knuckle on axle shaft arms and install NEW lower ball joint nut. Tighten nut to **80 ft. lbs. (108 N.m)**. Tighten sleeve in yoke arm bore to **40 ft. lbs. (54 N.m)**. Install upper ball joint nut and tighten to **100 ft. lbs. (136 N.m)**. Tighten, DO NOT loosen, nut to install new cotter pin.

3) Position steering knuckle arm on steering knuckle. Install washers and nuts and tighten to **90 ft. lbs. (122 N.m)**. Connect drag link stud to steering knuckle arm. Install retaining nut and tighten to **60 ft. lbs. (81 N.m)**. Install new cotter pin.

4) Connect tie rod end stud to steering knuckle arm. Install retaining nut and tighten to **45 ft. lbs. (61 N.m)**. Install new cotter pin. Install seal on axle shaft shield. Lubricate seal.

5) On left side, install inner axle shaft and insert "C" lock in recessed groove in shaft. Position shift collar on splined end of inner axle shaft. Install intermediate axle shaft. Install disconnect housing assembly and gasket while guiding shift fork into groove of shift collar. Install and tighten disconnect housing assembly bolts. See TORQUE SPEC-IFICATIONS table at end of article. On right side, slide axle shaft into axle shaft tube.

6) To complete installation, reverse removal procedure. To adjust wheel bearings, tighten inner lock nut to **50 ft. lbs. (68 N.m)**. While rotating hub, loosen inner lock nut and retighten to **30-40 ft. lbs. (41-54 N.m)**. Back lock nut off 135-150 degrees. Install tabbed lock washer. Install outer lock nut and tighten to **50 ft. lbs. (68 N.m)**. Apply silicone rubber sealant to edge of grease cap and install cap. Tighten bolts to specification. See TORQUE SPECIFICATIONS table. Remove supports and lower vehicle.

ROLLER BEARING & KING PIN TYPE

Removal (Model 60 Axle) – 1) Block brake pedal in up position. Raise and support vehicle. Remove wheel. Remove caliper-to-adapter Allen head screw. Remove caliper and support aside.

2) To remove locking hub (if equipped), remove cap-to-hub Allen head screws. Remove cap. Remove axle shaft retaining ring. Remove lock ring from groove in hub. To assist in removal, reinstall 2 Allen head screws in locking hub body. Remove locking hub assembly from hub.

3) Remove outer lock nut, tabbed lock washer, inner lock nut and outer bearing. Remove hub and rotor assembly from spindle. Remove brake splash shield, brake adapter and spindle-to-steering knuckle nuts and washers. Remove spindle from steering knuckle.

4) Remove axle shaft with Bronze spacer, seal and slinger from housing. Remove steering knuckle upper cap. Remove spring, retainer and gasket. Discard gasket. Remove steering knuckle lower cap. Remove cap from steering knuckle and yoke. Remove steering knuckle from

axle shaft tube. Remove tapered bushing from top of kingpin in knuckle. Using Remover/Installer (D-192), remove upper kingpin and discard seal.

5) Press out lower ball socket from lower arm bore. Discard grease seal, retainer and lower bearing cup.

Inspection – Wash parts in mineral spirits, and blow dry with compressed air. Examine components for damage and replace as necessary.

Installation – 1) Apply sealant to grease retainer mating surface. Lubricate lower ball socket with Mopar Multi-Mileage lubricant. Install grease retainer in yoke bore with concave side facing upper kingpin. Press grease seal and lower bearing cup into yoke lower bore. Grease retainer area and install bearing cone. Press lower bearing cup and seal into yoke lower arm bore.

2) Using Remover/Installer (D-192), install upper kingpin. Tighten kingpin to **500-600 ft. lbs. (678-813 N.m)**. Install seal over kingpin. Install knuckle on axle yoke. Insert tapered bushing over upper king-pin. Fill socket lower cavity with Mopar Multi-Mileage lubricant. Install lower kingpin and retainer cap on steering knuckle. Install cap screws and tighten to **70-90 ft. lbs. (95-122 N.m)**. Install retainer and compression spring on tapered bushing. Install NEW gasket over steering knuckle upper studs.

3) To complete installation, reverse removal procedure. To adjust wheel bearings, tighten inner lock nut to **50 ft. lbs. (68 N.m)**. While rotating hub, loosen lock nut and retighten to **30-40 ft. lbs. (41-54 N.m)**. Back lock nut off 135-150 degrees. Install tabbed lock washer. Install outer lock nut and tighten to **65 ft. lbs. (88 N.m)**. Tighten locking hub Allen head screws to **35-45 INCH lbs. (4-5 N.m)**. Tighten remaining bolts to specification. See TORQUE SPECIFICATIONS table. Remove supports and lower vehicle.

TORQUE SPECIFICATIONS
TORQUE SPECIFICATIONS

Application	Ft. Lbs. (N.m)
Disconnect Housing Bolt	10 (14)
Drag Link Ball Joint Nut (Model 44 & 60)	60 (81)
Hub-To-Steering Knuckle Bolts (Dakota)	110 (149)
Lower Ball Joint Nut	
Dakota	120 (163)
Model 44	80 (108)
Shift Motor Housing Cover Bolts (Model 44)	10 (14)
Spindle Retaining Nuts	
Model 44	25-35 (34-47)
Model 60	50-70 (68-95)
Steering Knuckle Arm Nuts (Model 44)	90 (122)
Tie Rod-To-Steering Knuckle Nut	
Dakota	40 (54)
Models 44 & 60	45 (61)
Upper Ball Joint Nut	
Dakota	105 (142)
Model 44	100 (136)
Upper Ball Joint Split Retaining Seat (Model 44)	40 (54)
Wheel Hub Nut (Dakota)	190 (258)
Wheel Lug Nuts	
Dakota	85 (115)
Model 44	110 (149)
Model 60	75 (102)

1992 DRIVE AXLES
FWD Axle Shafts

Caravan, Town & Country, Voyager

DESCRIPTION

Front Wheel Drive (FWD) vans use only the unequal length axle shaft system. Unequal length system has a long axle shaft on right side and short axle shaft on left side. *See Fig. 1.*

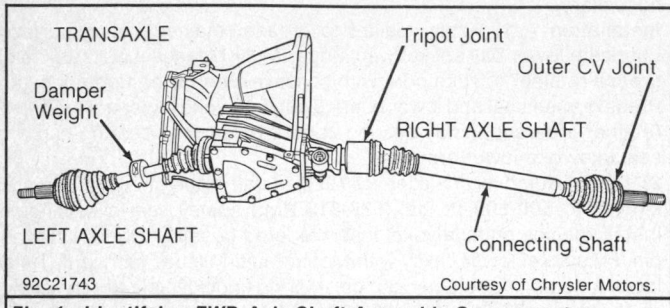

Fig. 1: Identifying FWD Axle Shaft Assembly Components

The short shaft on left side is the same for all transmission and engine applications. The long shaft on right side varies depending on transmission used. Manual transmissions use a tubular shaft, while automatic transmissions use a solid shaft.

Drive shaft assemblies are 3 piece units consisting of outer Constant Velocity (CV) joint, connecting shaft and inner tripot joint. Vehicles are equipped with any one of 3 types of axle shaft assemblies. *See Fig. 2.*

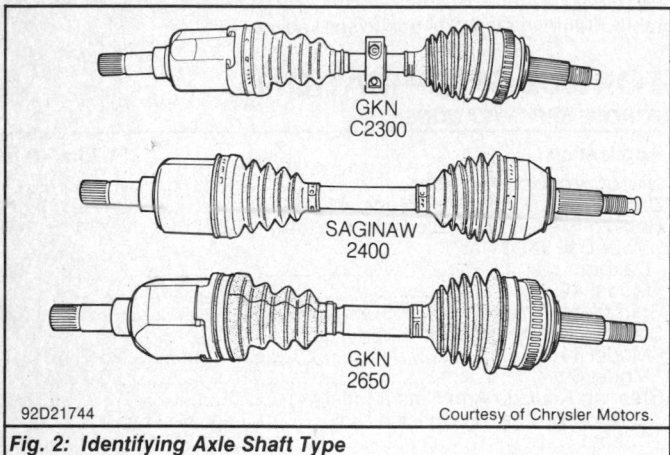

Fig. 2: Identifying Axle Shaft Type

LUBRICATION

CV joints require special lubrication. Joints are enclosed in a boot to contain lubricant and prevent contamination. Periodic lubrication of CV joints is not required, but boots should be inspected at regular intervals.

When adding fluid to transaxle, use Mopar ATF Plus (7176). If Mopar ATF is not available, Dexron-II may be used.

ADJUSTMENTS

AXLE SHAFT POSITIONING

NOTE: Check axle shaft positioning if engine/transaxle is loosened or moved or if front structural damage has occurred. Incorrect axle shaft positioning may result in premature failure of components.

1) Engine mount bolt holes are slotted for side-to-side positioning of engine. With vehicle completely assembled, ensure front wheels are in straight-ahead position. Vehicle should be on platform hoist or alignment rack.

2) Using a tape measure, measure distance from inner edge of outer boot to inner edge of inner boot on both axle shafts. *See Fig. 3.* This measurement must be taken at bottom of axle shaft only.

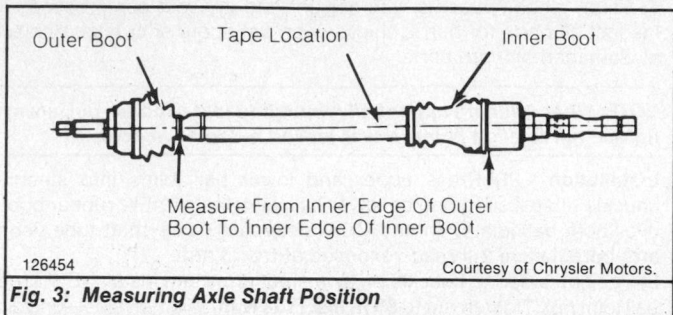

Fig. 3: Measuring Axle Shaft Position

3) If both axle shafts are within specifications, no further service is necessary. If either left or right axle shaft is not within specification, support engine/transaxle assembly using a floor jack. See AXLE SHAFT POSITIONING SPECIFICATIONS table.

4) Loosen right engine mount fasteners, front engine mount bracket and front crossmember fasteners. *See Fig. 4.* Pry engine right or left as required to obtain correct axle shaft length. See AXLE SHAFT POSITIONING SPECIFICATIONS table.

5) Tighten mounting bolts/nuts to specifications. Recheck axle shaft length. Install damper weight (if equipped), and tighten to specification. See TORQUE SPECIFICATIONS table at end of article.

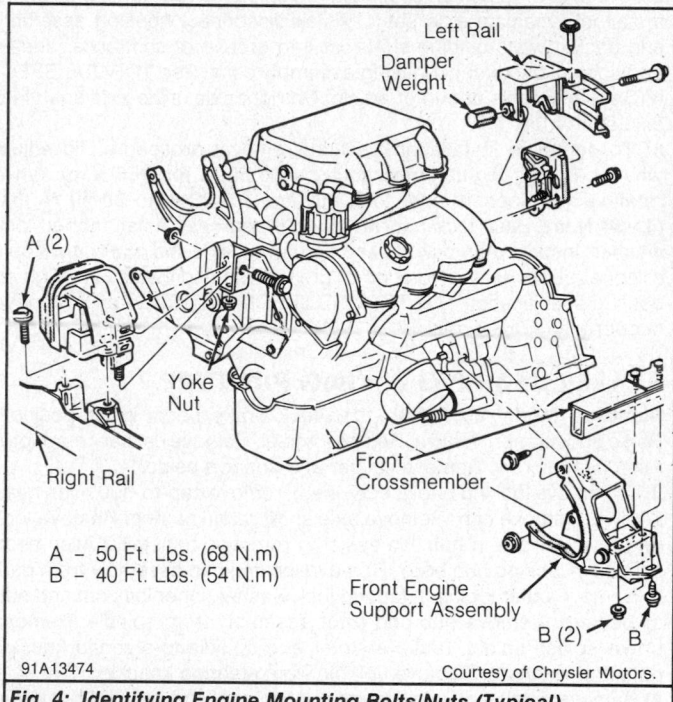

Fig. 4: Identifying Engine Mounting Bolts/Nuts (Typical)

AXLE SHAFT POSITIONING SPECIFICATIONS

Application	Right Side Length In. (mm)	Left Side Length In. (mm)
2WD Automatic		
2.5L	18.9-19.3 (480-490)	7.3-7.7 (185-196)
3.0L & 3.3L	18.7-19.1 (475-485)	7.2-7.6 (183-193)
2WD Manual		
2.5L	18.7-19.1 (475-485)	8.4-8.8 (213-224)
4WD Automatic		
3.3L	11.5-11.9 (292-302)	7.2-7.6 (183-193)

REMOVAL & INSTALLATION

AXLE SHAFTS

Removal – 1) Remove axle nut. Raise and support vehicle. If removing right axle shaft, remove speedometer pinion assembly from transaxle. Using brass hammer, lightly tap axle shaft end to free axle shaft from hub splines. Remove lower ball joint clamp bolt. Separate lower ball joint from steering knuckle.

NOTE: Remove speedometer drive pinion before removing right axle shaft. See SPEEDOMETER PINION GEAR under REMOVAL & INSTALLATION.

2) Pull out on hub/steering knuckle assembly, and separate axle shaft from hub. Grasp both CV joints at outer housings to prevent separation, and pull axle shaft out of transaxle or intermediate shaft. Remove axle shaft from vehicle.

Installation – Grasp both CV joints at outer housings, and insert inner CV joint into transaxle or intermediate shaft. To complete installation, reverse removal procedure. Using multipurpose lubricant, lubricate seal and wear sleeve. Tighten all bolts/nuts to specification. See TORQUE SPECIFICATIONS table at end of article.

CV JOINT BOOTS

Removal – Cut boot clamps. Disassemble CV joint. See appropriate CV JOINT under OVERHAUL. Remove boot from axle shaft.

Installation (Inner Boot) – **1)** Use only strap and buckle type clamp and Strap Installer (C-4653). *See Fig. 5.* Slide small end of boot over shaft. Position boot to edge of locating mark or groove. Slide large diameter of boot into position. Wrap strap around boot twice. Add 2.5" (63.5 mm), and cut strap.

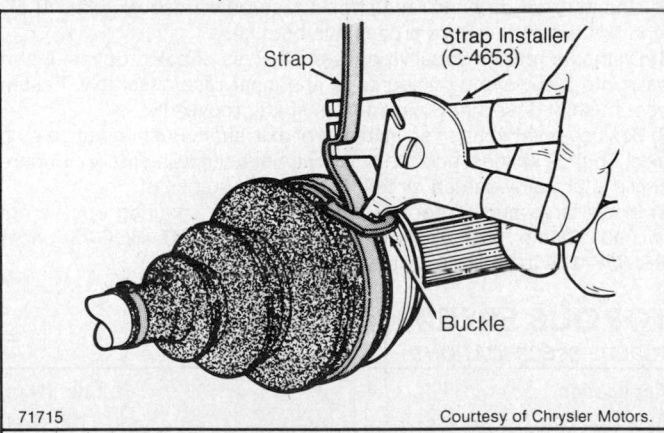

Fig. 5: *Installing Strap On Rubber Inner CV Joint Boot*

2) Remove strap from CV joint. Install buckle on strap, and fold strap back about 1.125" (28.58 mm) on inside of buckle. Wrap strap around CV joint twice, passing strap through buckle on each wrap. Using Strap Installer (C-4653), tighten strap.

3) DO NOT pull installer downward to tighten strap, as strap can break. If necessary, disconnect and reinstall installer to retighten strap. With strap tightened sufficiently, remove installer to side and cut strap .125" (3.18 mm) beyond buckle. Complete by folding strap under buckle.

Installation (Outer Boot) – Slide small diameter boot clamp onto axle shaft. Slide boot onto axle shaft until small end of boot is seated in boot groove on shaft. Position boot clamp evenly in clamp groove on boot. Position tabs on boot clamp in jaws of Clamp Installer (C-4975). *See Fig. 6.* Tighten bolt on clamp installer until tabs on boot clamp interlock.

SPEEDOMETER PINION GEAR

NOTE: Speedometer pinion gear is located on speed sensor in extension housing on right side of transaxle. Pinion must be removed before removing right axle shaft assembly.

Removal – Disconnect speed sensor connector. Remove sensor assembly retaining bolt. Gently remove sensor and pinion gear from housing.

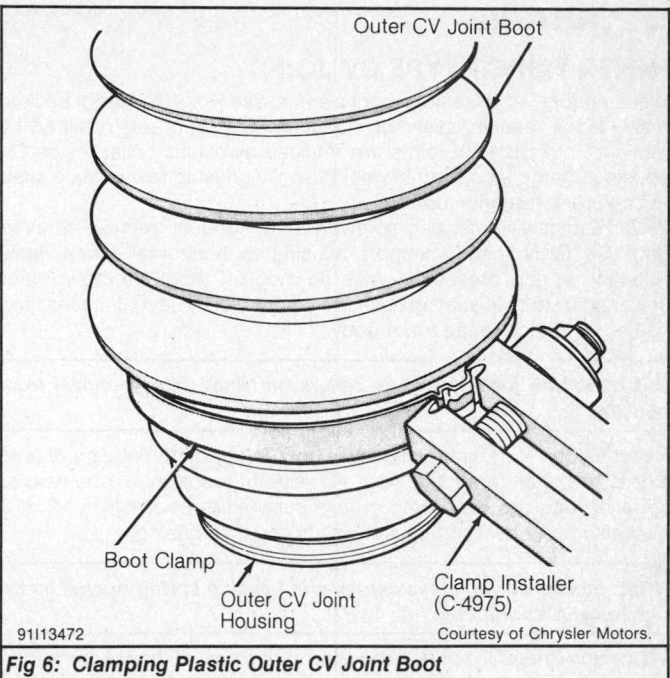

Fig 6: *Clamping Plastic Outer CV Joint Boot*

Installation – To install, reverse removal procedure. Ensure adapter and transaxle housing area are clean. Install and tighten retaining bolt.

AXLE SHAFT DAMPER WEIGHTS

Removal & Installation – Damper weights are split in 2 pieces and are attached by 2 bolts to left axle shaft between inner and outer CV joints. *See Fig. 7.* Damper weights should be removed from axle shaft during axle shaft positioning procedure. Ensure damper weight bolts are tightened to specification. See TORQUE SPECIFICATIONS table at end of article.

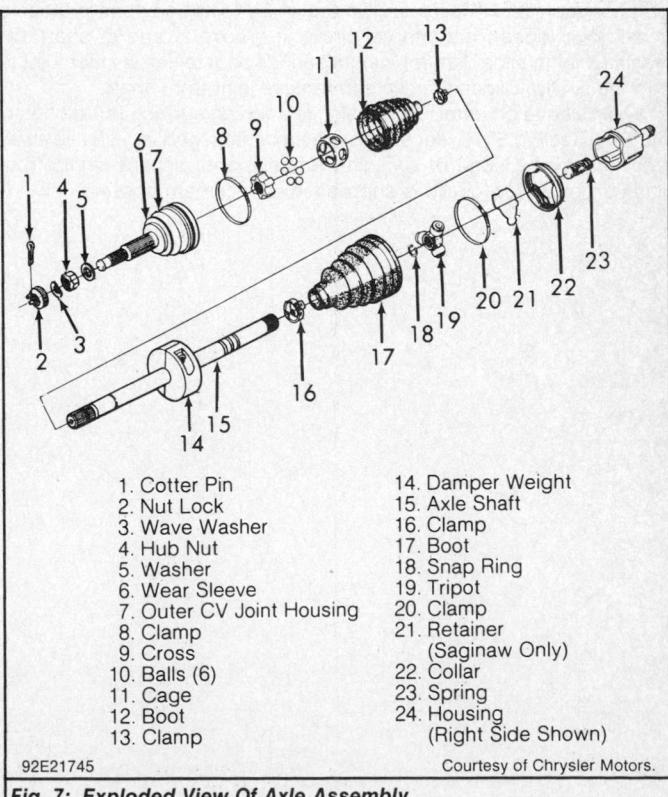

1. Cotter Pin	14. Damper Weight
2. Nut Lock	15. Axle Shaft
3. Wave Washer	16. Clamp
4. Hub Nut	17. Boot
5. Washer	18. Snap Ring
6. Wear Sleeve	19. Tripot
7. Outer CV Joint Housing	20. Clamp
8. Clamp	21. Retainer (Saginaw Only)
9. Cross	22. Collar
10. Balls (6)	23. Spring
11. Cage	24. Housing (Right Side Shown)
12. Boot	
13. Clamp	

Fig. 7: *Exploded View Of Axle Assembly*

OVERHAUL

INNER TRIPOT TYPE CV JOINT

Disassembly – 1) Remove boot clamps. *See Fig. 7.* Pull boot back to reach tripot retainer assembly. Saginaw CV joints are retained by retainer ring. GKN CV joints are retained by plastic collar inside CV housing. Clamp axle shaft in vise. Push CV housing toward axle shaft to compress retention spring.

2) On Saginaw joints, use screwdriver to carefully remove retainer ring. On GKN joints, support housing in horizontal plane while retention spring pressure forces housing off tripot. Remove outer snap ring from axle shaft groove. Remove tripot by hand. If necessary, use brass punch to tap tripot body.

CAUTION: Use tape to secure rollers on tripot, after removal from housing.

Reassembly – 1) Install new axle boot on axle shaft. Slide tripot onto axle shaft, chamfered side first. Flat side of tripot should be next to retaining ring groove. Using grease supplied in boot kit, put 2 of 3 packets into boot. Third packet will go into CV housing.

NOTE: Ensure spring stays centered in housing spring pocket as tripot seats in spring cup.

2) Position retention spring in housing spring pocket. Install spring cup onto exposed end of spring. Lubricate concave surface of spring cup with grease. Install housing over tripot, and place boot over retaining groove in housing. Clamp boot in position. To complete installation, reverse removal procedure.

OUTER CV JOINT

CAUTION: DO NOT strike cage when using hammer and drift to loosen CV joint.

Disassembly – 1) Remove and discard boot clamps. Wipe away grease to expose CV joint. Hold axle shaft in soft jaws of vise. Using soft hammer, on GKN joints give top of CV joint body sharp blow to break joint loose from internal circlip in groove at end of shaft. On Saginaw joint, slide damper weight and CV boot towards inner joint to expose circlip. Expand circlip and remove joint from shaft.

2) Wear sleeve on outer CV housing is a wiping surface for hub bearing seal. *See Fig. 7.* If wear sleeve is bent or damaged, pry sleeve away from machined ledge of CV joint. Remove and discard circlip from shaft groove. New circlip is supplied in replacement boot kit.

3) If shaft is damaged, remove heavy spacer ring from inner groove. If joint was operating properly, replace boots only. If joint was noisy or badly worn, replace complete joint. Replace boot whenever joint is replaced.

4) Wipe grease off outer CV joint, and mark inner race (cross), cage and housing with paint. Position joint vertically in vise, using soft jaws to clamp on splined shaft. Press down on one side of inner race to tilt cage, and remove ball from opposite side. Remove all balls.

5) If joint is very tight, use brass drift and hammer to tap inner race and remove balls. Tilt cage and inner race assembly to vertical.

6) Remove inner race and cage assembly by pulling upward away from housing. Turn inner race 90 degrees to cage. Align elongated cage window with one of spherical lands on race. Raise land to cage window, and remove inner race by swinging it out of cage.

Inspection – Check grease for contamination. Wash all parts, except boots, in solvent, and dry with compressed air. Inspect races, splined shaft and nut threads for damage. Inspect balls and cage for excessive wear or damage. If excessive wear or damage is found, replace CV joint.

Reassembly – 1) Position new wear sleeve on joint housing machined ledge. Lightly oil all components before reassembly. Align parts according to paint markings.

2) Insert one inner race (cross) into cage window, and feed race into cage. Pivot inner race to fully assemble cage and race. Align opposing elongated cage windows with housing land. Feed cage assembly into housing. Pivot cage 90 degrees to complete installation.

3) Counterbore of inner race should face outward from joint. Apply lubricant to ball races from packet in boot kit.

4) Distribute grease equally between all sides of ball grooves. Insert balls into raceways by tilting cage and inner race assembly. Fasten boot to shaft. Insert new circlip from shaft groove kit.

5) Position outer joint on splined end of axle shaft. Put hub nut on stub axle. Engage splines, and tap sharply on hub nut using mallet. Ensure circlip is properly seated by trying to pull joint off shaft.

6) Install large end of boot over joint housing, ensuring boot is not twisted. Clamp boot to housing. See CV JOINT BOOTS under REMOVAL & INSTALLATION

TORQUE SPECIFICATIONS
TORQUE SPECIFICATIONS

Application	Ft. Lbs. (N.m)
Axle Hub Nut	180 (244)
Ball Joint Clamp Nut	70 (95)
Damper Weight Bolts	21 (28)
Wheel Lug Nut	95 (129)

Caravan, Town & Country, Voyager

DESCRIPTION

All-Wheel Drive (AWD) is available on all models equipped with 3.3L engine and A604 transaxle. AWD system consists of rear carrier, torque tube, overrunning clutch assembly, a vacuum operated dog clutch and a viscous coupling in one unit called the Rear Driveline Module (RDLM). Power is supplied by a Power Transfer Unit (PTU) that sits in place of the extension housing on the transmission.

Rear carrier contains conventional open differential with hypoid ring and pinion gear set. *See Fig. 1*. Hypoid gears are lubricated by SAE 85W-90 gear oil.

Torque tube assembly attaches to overrunning clutch case. *See Fig. 2*. A propeller shaft and a sealed front bearing assembly are located inside torque tube housing. A vacuum reservoir and solenoid assembly are bolted to top of torque tube.

Overrunning clutch allows rear wheels to overrun front wheels during rapid front wheel braking. Overrunning clutch prevents feedback of front wheel braking torque to rear wheels and allows braking behavior similar to FWD models. Overrunning clutch has separate oil sump and is filled independently from differential. See LUBRICATION.

Dog clutch provides AWD action in reverse by bridging and locking out overrunning clutch. Dog clutch is operated by double-acting servo using manifold vacuum. Two vacuum solenoids, controlled by back-up light switch, engage and disengage dog clutch. Spring in servo disengages dog clutch if vacuum supply is lost.

Viscous coupling controls and distributes torque to rear wheels. Coupling is similar to a multi-plate clutch. Alternating plates are indexed to front and rear drive units and operate in a silicone fluid. Unit is sealed and requires no maintenance or adjustment.

Rear axle shafts are similar to FWD axle and are serviced using FWD procedures. See. FWD AXLE SHAFTS article in DRIVE AXLES.

AWD AXLE RATIO IDENTIFICATION

Application	Ratio
Power Transfer Unit	3.45:1
Rear Carrier Assembly	3.42:1

LUBRICATION

When adding fluid to overrunning clutch, use Mopar ATF Plus (7176). If Mopar ATF is not available, Dexron-II may be used.

FLUID CAPACITIES

Application	Pts. (L)
Carrier Assembly	4.0 (1.90)
Overrunning Clutch	.8 (.37)
PTU	2.4 (1.15)

TROUBLE SHOOTING

FLUID LEAK DIAGNOSIS

Two weep holes are provided on bottom of rear drive assembly to assist in fluid leakage diagnosis. *See Fig. 3*. If leak is detected from either hole, seal replacement is necessary. Red fluid leaking from weep hole "A" indicates front overrunning clutch seal failure. Red fluid leaking from weep hole "B" indicates rear overrunning clutch seal failure. Brown fluid leaking from weep hole "B" indicates input pinion seal failure.

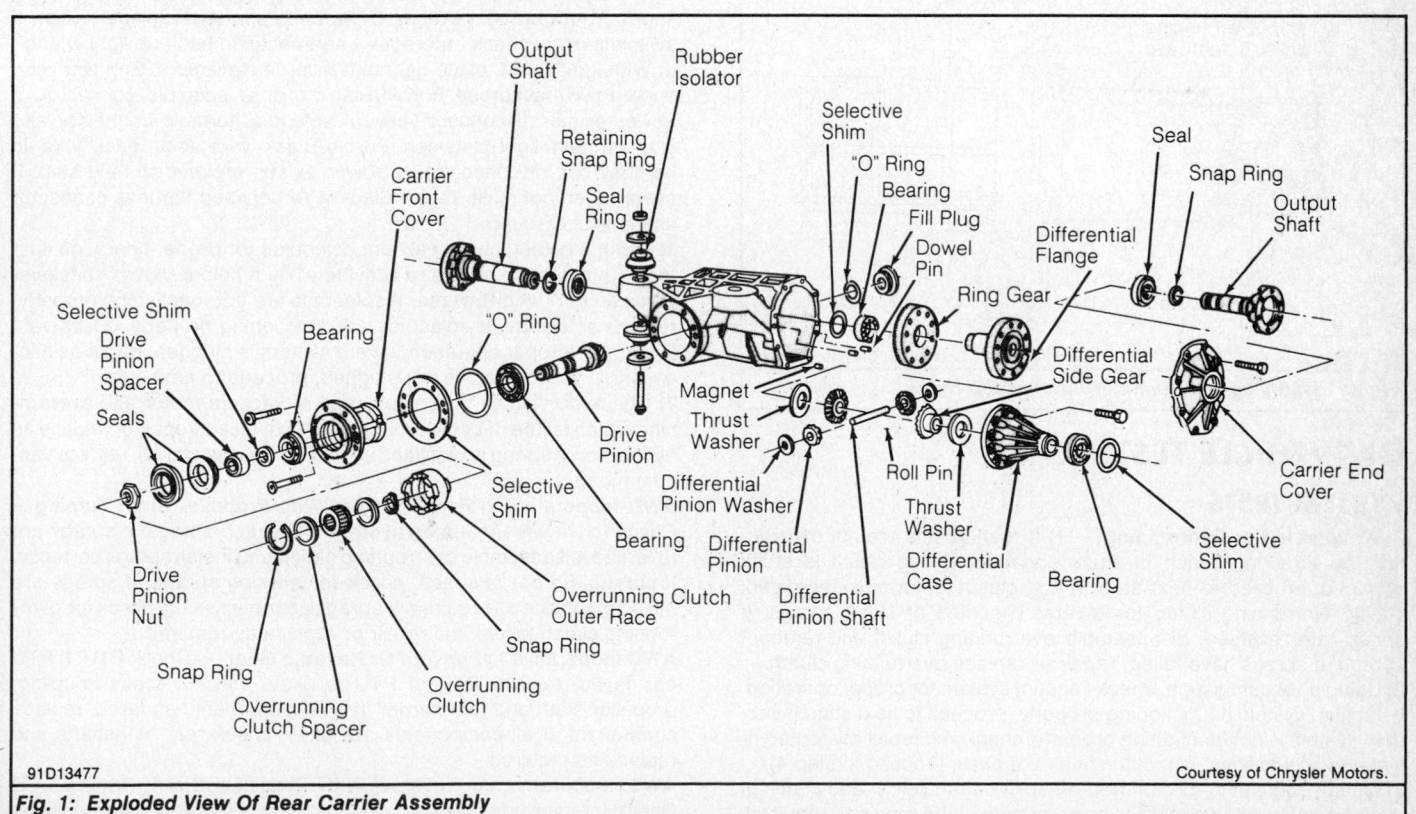

91D13477

Courtesy of Chrysler Motors.

Fig. 1: Exploded View Of Rear Carrier Assembly

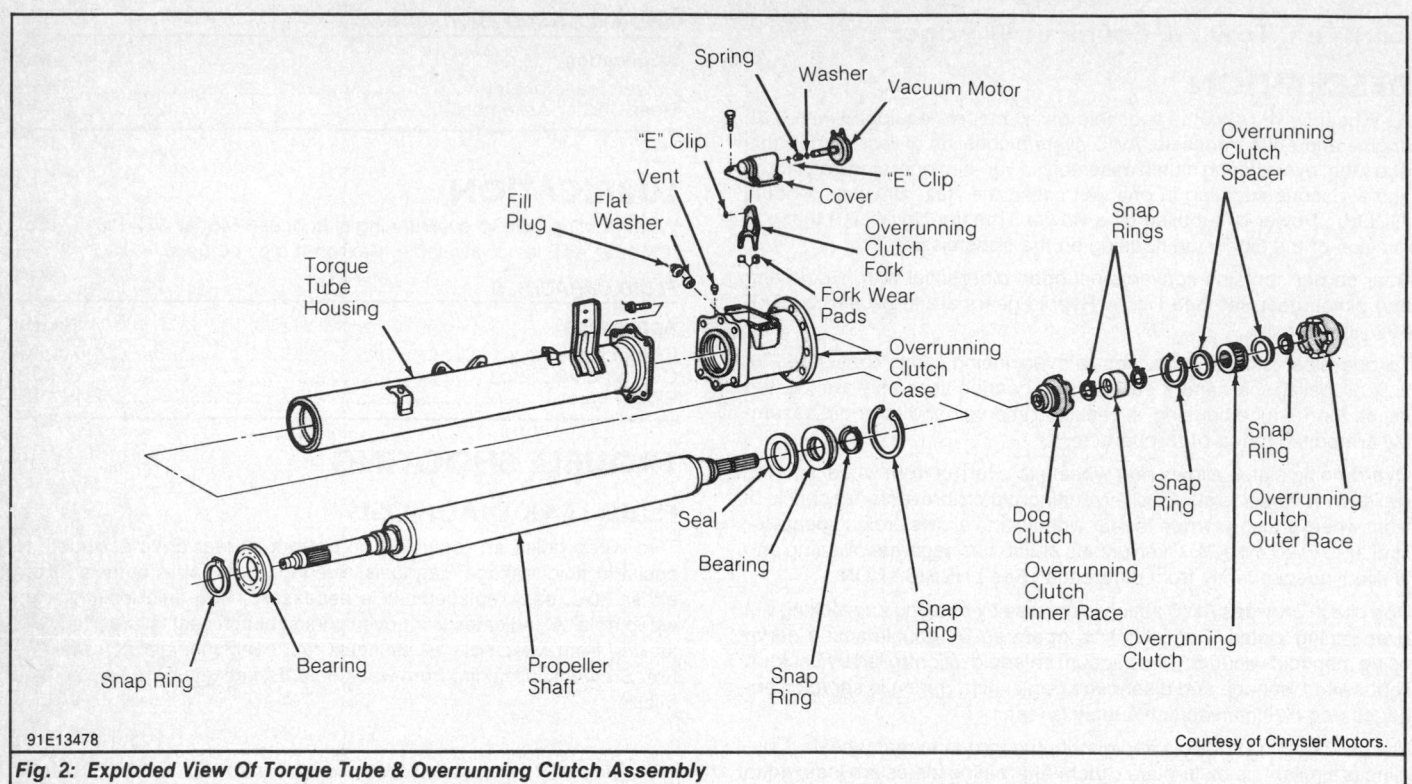

91E13478   Courtesy of Chrysler Motors.

Fig. 2: Exploded View Of Torque Tube & Overrunning Clutch Assembly

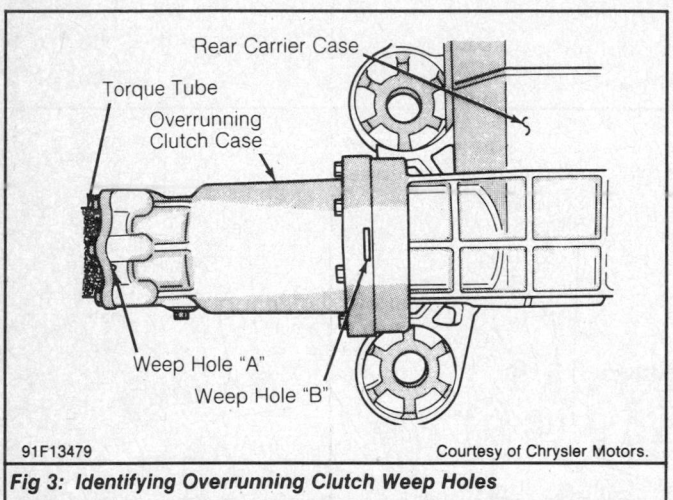

91F13479   Courtesy of Chrysler Motors.

Fig 3: Identifying Overrunning Clutch Weep Holes

ON-VEHICLE TESTING

SYSTEM TESTS

Rear Wheels Not Overrunning – 1) If rear wheels are not overrunning, ensure dog clutch is stuck engaged. If dog clutch is stuck engaged, proceed to next step. If dog clutch is not stuck engaged, check overrunning clutch for reverse mounted or failed sprags. If sprags are reversed, disassemble overrunning clutch and remount sprags. If sprags have failed, repair or replace overrunning clutch.

2) Using a vacuum gauge, check vacuum system for proper operation. If vacuum system if functioning properly, proceed to next step. If vacuum system is not functioning properly, check and repair misrouted or kinked vacuum lines. If vacuum lines are okay, proceed to step **4)**.

3) Check dog clutch for jammed on spline condition. If dog clutch is jammed on spline, inspect for burrs or nicks, and repair as required. If dog clutch is not jammed on spline, check for torsional bind-up condition. If dog clutch is bound up, repair binding condition. If dog clutch is not bound up, check for shift fork interference. If shift fork is interfering, repair or replace as required.

4) Turn ignition on. Place gearshift lever in Park. Using a test light, backprobe Purple/Black wire at vacuum solenoids. If power does not exist, proceed to next step. If power exists, check for failed back-up light relay. If relay has failed, replace relay. If relay is okay, check for shorted back-up light switch. If switch is shorted, replace switch. If switch is okay, check and repair short circuit in back-up light wiring.

5) With ignition on, place gearshift lever in Reverse. Using test light, once again backprobe Purple/Black wire at solenoid connector. If power exists, disconnect vacuum solenoid harness connector and connect test light between Purple/Black wire and Black wire in harness half of connector. If power exists, proceed to next step. If power does not exist, repair Black wire between harness connector and chassis ground.

6) Using a helper, check vacuum solenoids for proper operation. Listen and feel for solenoids to activate while a helper moves shift lever between Park and Reverse. If solenoids are not functioning properly, replace solenoids. If solenoids are functioning properly, check vent system for proper operation. If vent system is plugged, repair as necessary. If vent system is not plugged, proceed to next step.

7) Check dog clutch for combination of vacuum motor and overrunning clutch failure. If both components have failed, repair or replace as necessary. If spring is okay and vacuum motor has failed, replace vacuum motor.

AWD Inoperative In Forward Gear With Propeller Shaft Turning – Check for reverse-mounted overrunning clutch sprags. If sprags are reversed, disassemble overrunning clutch and install sprags correctly. If sprags are not reversed, check for missing sprags. If sprags are missing, replace as required. If sprags are not missing, check for overrunning clutch failure and repair or replace as required.

AWD Inoperative In Forward Or Reverse Gear – Check PTU. If PTU has failed, replace PTU. If PTU is okay, check viscous coupling, propeller shaft and rear carrier. If any component has failed, replace component. If all components are okay, check rear half-shafts and replace as required.

AWD Inoperative In Reverse With Propeller Shaft Turning – 1) Check for missing dog clutch. If dog clutch is missing, install missing parts. If dog clutch is present and inoperative, check vacuum actuation system. If vacuum actuation system is not functioning properly, proceed to step **3)**.

2) If vacuum actuation system is functioning properly, check for dog clutch jammed disengaged, shift fork "E" clip(s) missing, broken shift fork, shift fork interference, or overrunning clutch spring jammed or too strong. If any condition exists, repair or replace as required.

3) Using a test light, backprobe Purple/Black wire at solenoid connector. If power does not exist, proceed to next step. If power exists, check vacuum system to solenoids and solenoid switching. To test solenoid switching, listen and feel for solenoid clicking while a helper moves shift lever between Park and Reverse. If solenoids operate correctly, proceed to step **5)**. If solenoids fail to operate correctly, replace solenoids.

4) Check harness and connector for damage or pushed out terminals. If harness is damaged, or terminals are damaged or pushed out, repair as required. If harness and connectors are okay, check back-up light relay and back-up light switch. If either component is faulty, replace component. If components are okay, check harness between switch, relay and solenoids. If harness is okay check solenoids as described in step **2)**. Repair or replace as necessary.

5) Ensure vacuum valve is installed correctly. If valve is incorrectly installed, replace vacuum reservoir. If vacuum valve is installed correctly, check for leaking vacuum reservoir. If reservoir is leaking, replace reservoir. If vacuum reservoir is okay, check front and rear vacuum harnesses. If vacuum harnesses are okay, proceed to next step. If vacuum harnesses are faulty, repair or replace as required.

6) Check for plugged vacuum filter. If filter is plugged, replace filter. If filter is okay, check vacuum motor for leaks. If vacuum motor is leaking, replace motor. If vacuum motor is not leaking, check for motor shaft jammed condition. If vacuum motor shaft is jammed, replace vacuum motor.

REMOVAL & INSTALLATION

REAR DRIVELINE MODULE (RDLM)

Removal & Installation – 1) Raise and support vehicle. Remove left and right inner half-shaft joint mounting bolts and support half-shafts to one side. Remove propeller shaft-to-viscous coupling bolts and support propeller shaft to one side. Remove viscous coupling retaining nut and slide coupling off RDLM assembly.

2) Disconnect RDLM main vacuum harness. Support RDLM with suitable transmission jack and chain RDLM to jack to prevent assembly falling. Remove RDLM rear mounting bolts. Remove RDLM front mounting bolts. Partially lower RDLM and disconnect remote solenoid vent and remote carrier vent. Carefully lower RDLM from vehicle.

3) To install RDLM, reverse removal procedure. Tighten mounting bolts to specification. See TORQUE SPECIFICATIONS at end of article.

REAR CARRIER UNIT

Removal & Installation – 1) Remove RDLM. See REAR DRIVELINE MODULE (RDLM). Drain oil from overrunning clutch assembly. Remove overrunning clutch-to-rear carrier case bolts. Separate rear carrier case from overrunning clutch case.

2) To install rear carrier, reverse removal procedure. Tighten mounting bolts to specification. See TORQUE SPECIFICATIONS table at end of article.

TORQUE TUBE

Removal & Installation – 1) Remove RDLM. See REAR DRIVELINE MODULE (RDLM). Remove viscous coupling. Remove snap ring and torque tube bearing shield. Remove torque tube-to-overrunning clutch bolts. Slide torque tube off of propeller shaft.

2) To install torque tube, reverse removal procedure. Tighten bolts to specifications. See TORQUE SPECIFICATIONS table at end of article.

PROPELLER SHAFT & REAR HALF-SHAFTS

NOTE: Propeller shaft and rear half-shafts may be removed without removing RDLM from vehicle.

Removal & Installation (Propeller Shaft) – Raise and support vehicle. Remove propeller shaft rear mounting bolts and support shaft. Remove propeller shaft front mounting bolts and remove propeller shaft. To install propeller shaft, reverse removal procedure. Tighten bolts to specification. See TORQUE SPECIFICATIONS at end of article.

Removal & Installation (Rear Half-Shaft) – Raise and support vehicle so that rear wheels hang freely. Remove rear wheel assembly. Remove cotter pin, nut lock and spring washer. Remove hub nut and washer. Remove inner half-shaft mounting bolts. Compress inner half-shaft joint slightly, pull downward to clear differential and remove half-shaft. To install half-shaft, reverse removal procedure. Tighten retaining bolts and axle nut to specifications. See TORQUE SPECIFICATIONS at end of article.

OVERHAUL

NOTE: All overhaul procedures except REAR CARRIER OUTPUT SHAFT SEALS and DIFFERENTIAL SIDE GEARS require removal of RDLM.

REAR CARRIER OUTPUT SHAFT SEALS

Removal & Installation – 1) Remove appropriate inner half-shaft retaining bolts and support shaft to one side. Using 2 pry bars and 2 wooden support blocks, pop out output shaft. *See Fig. 4.* Carefully pry oil seal from rear carrier case so as not to damage bearing race.

2) Clean and inspect shaft and seal area. Install seal using Seal Installer (MD998334). Install output shaft. Using a soft-face mallet, tap output shaft into rear carrier assembly until retainer ring seats. Check and top off differential fluid.

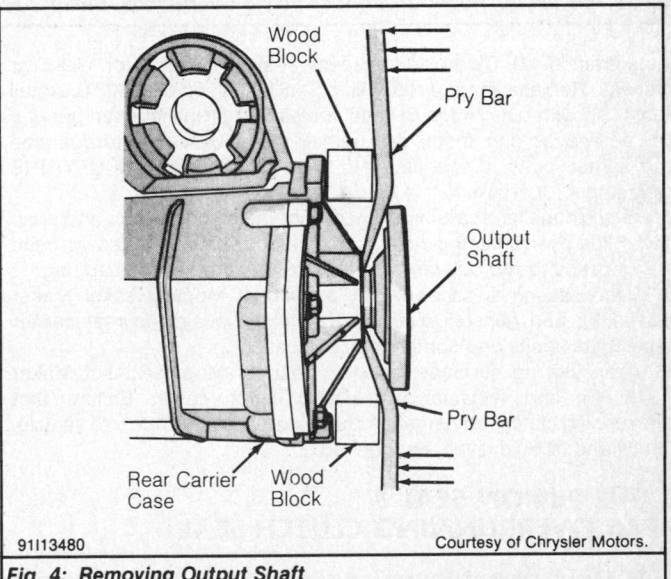

91I13480   Courtesy of Chrysler Motors.

Fig. 4: Removing Output Shaft

FRONT OVERRUNNING CLUTCH SEAL

Removal – 1) Remove RDLM and viscous coupling unit. See REAR DRIVELINE MODULE (RDLM) under REMOVAL & INSTALLATION. Remove overrunning clutch cover assembly. *See Fig. 5.* Drain fluid from overrunning clutch. Remove overrunning clutch case-to-rear carrier bolts. Separate overrunning clutch case from rear carrier case.

2) Remove overrunning clutch inner race snap ring. Slide overrunning clutch inner race off of shaft. Remove shaft snap ring and slide dog clutch off shaft. Remove propeller shaft snap ring and torque tube bearing shield.

3) Remove torque tube retaining bolts. Remove inner propeller shaft bearing snap ring. Separate overrunning clutch case from torque tube. Remove rear propeller shaft bearing retaining outer snap ring in overrunning clutch case. Remove rear propeller shaft bearing. Remove seal using Seal Driver (C-4967).

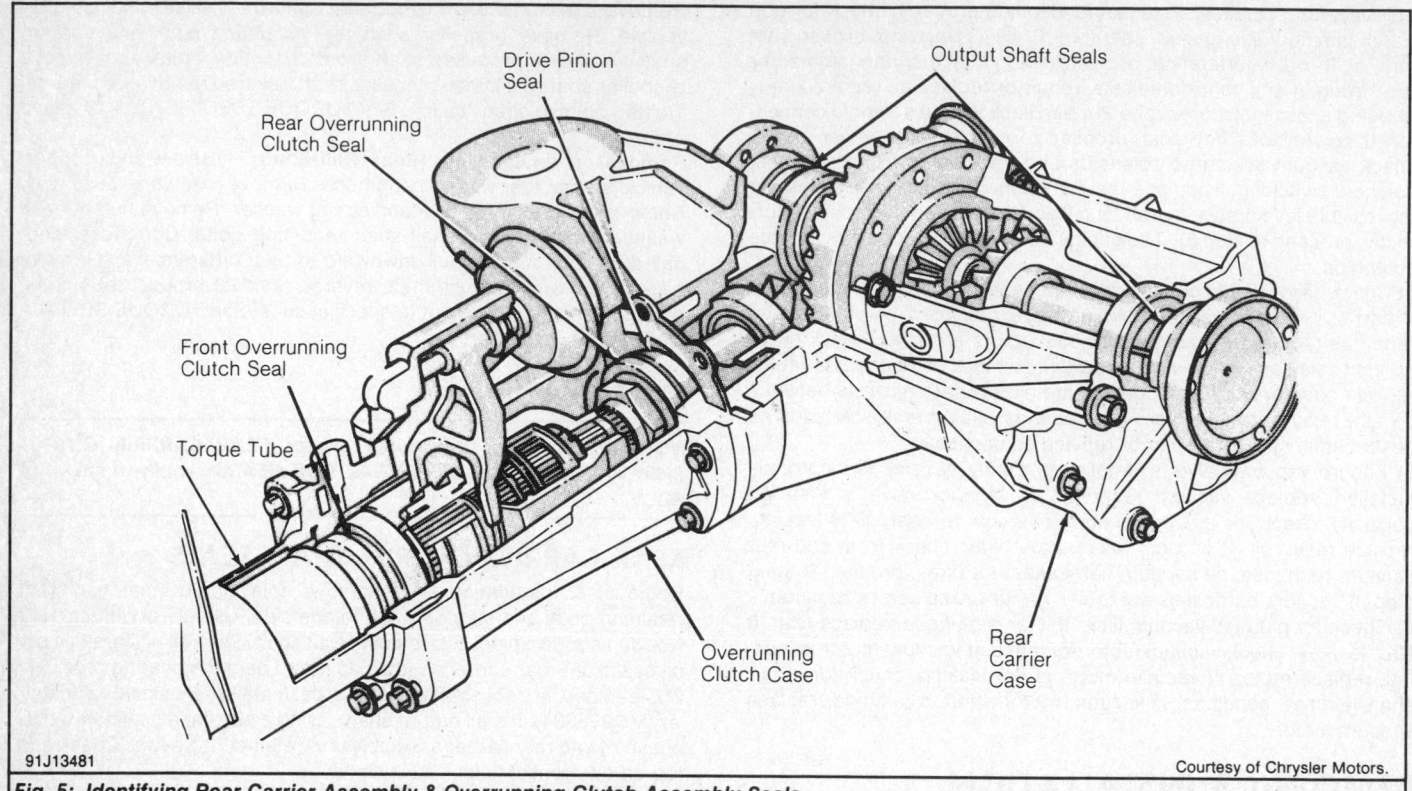

Drive Pinion
Seal

Output Shaft Seals

Rear Overrunning
Clutch Seal

Front Overrunning
Clutch Seal

Torque Tube

Overrunning
Clutch Case

Rear
Carrier
Case

91J13481

Courtesy of Chrysler Motors.

Fig. 5: Identifying Rear Carrier Assembly & Overrunning Clutch Assembly Seals

Installation – 1) Clean and inspect sealing surface for nicks or grooves. Replace as required. Using Seal Installer (MD998334), install seal flush with outer edge of case. Install rear propeller shaft bearing and outer snap ring. Install overrunning clutch case onto torque tube and tighten bolts to specification. See TORQUE SPECIFICATIONS table at end of article.

2) Install propeller shaft inner snap ring. Install dog clutch and snap ring. Slide overrunning clutch inner race onto shaft with tapered end of inner race facing outward. Install inner race retaining snap ring.

3) Clean sealing surfaces, apply a bead of Mopar Gasket Maker (4318083), and reinstall overrunning clutch housing to rear carrier case. Install bolts and tighten to specification.

4) Clean sealing surfaces, apply a bead of Mopar Gasket Maker (4318083), and reinstall overrunning clutch cover. Ensure that overrunning clutch fork engages clutch dog. Install RDLM into vehicle. Check and fill fluid levels as required.

DRIVE PINION SEAL & REAR OVERRUNNING CLUTCH SEAL

NOTE: *Overrunning clutch seal must be removed to gain access to input pinion seal. DO NOT reuse overrunning clutch seal.*

Removal – 1) Remove RDLM. Remove overrunning clutch case-to-rear carrier bolts. Separate overrunning clutch case from differential carrier case. Remove overrunning clutch outer race snap ring. Slide overrunning clutch off of shaft.

2) Using Spline Tool (6534) and a wrench, remove drive pinion nut. Remove front carrier cover retaining screws and remove cover. Remove pinion spacer and bearing shim from pinion shaft by inverting carrier cover and tapping pinion shaft on a block of wood. *See Fig. 6.* Reinstall front carrier cover into carrier case and tighten retaining bolts to **105 INCH lbs. (12 N.m)**.

3) Using Seal Puller (7794-A), remove overrunning clutch seal. If drive pinion seal must be removed, it may now be removed using same puller. *See Fig. 7.*

CAUTION: *Install bearing shim along with cover to avoid possibility of cutting "O" ring.*

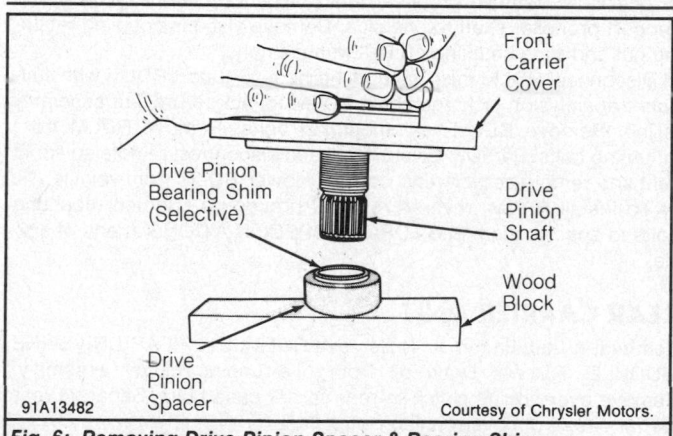

Front
Carrier
Cover

Drive Pinion
Bearing Shim
(Selective)

Drive
Pinion
Shaft

Wood
Block

Drive
Pinion
Spacer

91A13482

Courtesy of Chrysler Motors.

Fig. 6: Removing Drive Pinion Spacer & Bearing Shim

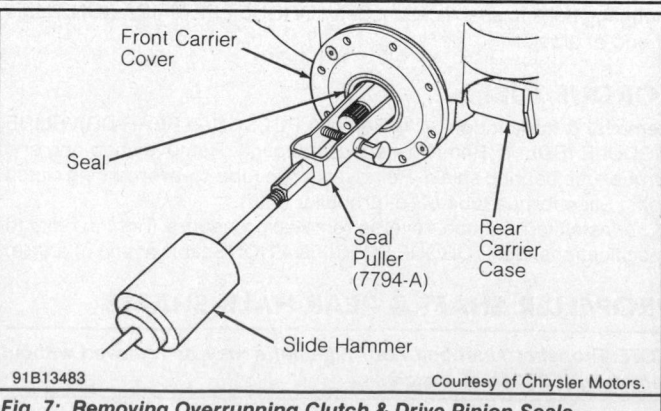

Front Carrier
Cover

Seal

Seal
Puller
(7794-A)

Rear
Carrier
Case

Slide Hammer

91B13483

Courtesy of Chrysler Motors.

Fig. 7: Removing Overrunning Clutch & Drive Pinion Seals

Installation – 1) Apply a light coat of oil to drive pinion seal. Using Seal Installer (6507), install seal with spring side facing toward rear carrier case. Apply a light coat of oil onto drive pinion spacer. Install spacer with tapered side facing outward.

CAUTION: If drive pinion spacer is grooved or damaged, it must be replaced. Replacement spacer may require different size bearing shim. See DRIVE PINION BEARING SHIM SELECTION.

---

2) Apply a light coat of oil onto overrunning clutch seal. Using Seal Installer (6508), install seal with spring side facing AWAY from rear carrier case. Install drive pinion nut and tighten to specification. See TORQUE SPECIFICATIONS at end of article. Install overrunning clutch outer race and snap ring.

3) Apply sealer to overrunning clutch sealing surface and reinstall overrunning clutch case to rear carrier case. Install RDLM into vehicle. Check and fill all fluids as required.

DRIVE PINION BEARING SHIM SELECTION

NOTE: This procedure MUST be performed whenever drive pinion spacer requires replacement.

1) Using a one-inch micrometer, measure thickness of ORIGINAL spacer. *See Fig. 8.* Measure NEW spacer in same manner. If new spacer is same thickness as old spacer, reuse original shim. If new pinion spacer measurement is less than original pinion spacer measurement, a thicker shim is required. If new pinion spacer measurement is greater than original pinion spacer measurement, a thinner shim is required.

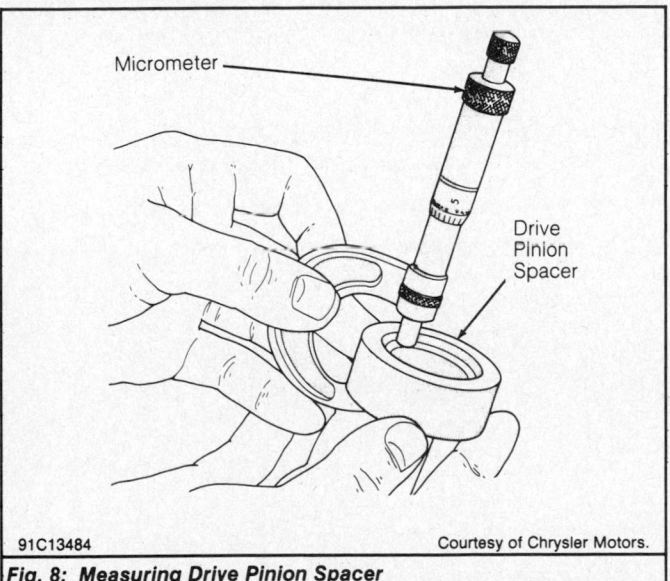

Micrometer

Drive Pinion Spacer

91C13484   Courtesy of Chrysler Motors.

Fig. 8: Measuring Drive Pinion Spacer

2) Record difference in measurements between new spacer and original spacer. Measure and record thickness of original shim. Add or subtract difference in spacer measurements to shim measurement to determine correct shim size.

DIFFERENTIAL SIDE GEARS

Removal – Disconnect both half-shafts from RDLM and support to one side. Using 2 pry bars, pop out output shafts. *See Fig. 4.* Remove differential end cover bolts and remove cover. Remove differential assembly from case.

Disassembly & Inspection – Remove ring gear bolts and separate differential case from differential body. Using a hammer and punch, remove differential pinion shaft roll pin. Remove differential pinion shaft from differential case. Inspect and replace pinion gears, pinion shaft and pinion washers as required.

Installation – To reassemble differential carrier assembly, reverse disassembly procedure. To complete overhaul, install differential assembly into case. Clean sealer surfaces, apply a bead of Mopar Gasket Maker (4318083) and install end cover. Tighten bolts, in sequence, to specification. *See Fig. 9.* See TORQUE SPECIFICATIONS at end of article.

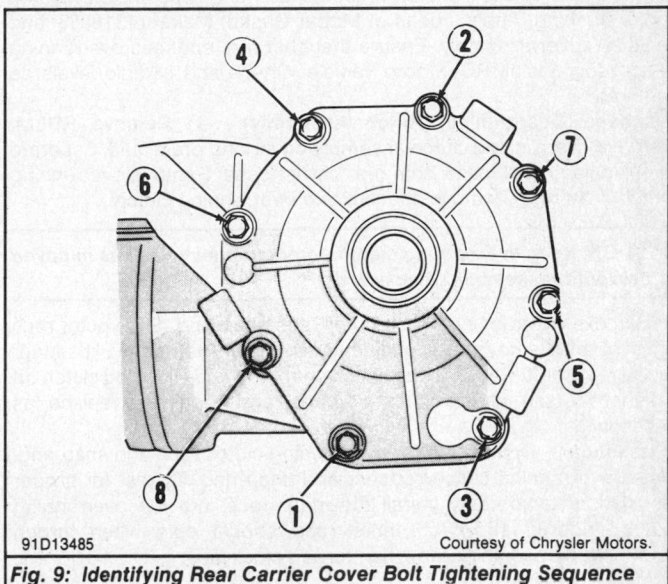

91D13485   Courtesy of Chrysler Motors.

Fig. 9: Identifying Rear Carrier Cover Bolt Tightening Sequence

TORQUE TUBE BEARINGS

Removal & Installation (Front Bearing) – 1) Remove RDLM. Remove viscous coupling. Remove overrunning clutch cover assembly and drain fluid. Remove overrunning clutch case-to-rear carrier case bolts and separate overrunning clutch case from carrier case.

2) Remove overrunning clutch inner race snap ring. Slide overrunning clutch inner race off of shaft. Remove shaft snap ring and slide dog clutch off of shaft. Remove propeller shaft rear bearing snap ring.

3) Remove overrunning clutch case-to-torque tube bolts. Separate torque tube from overrunning clutch case. Remove front snap ring and torque tube bearing shield. Slide propeller shaft out of torque tube. Drive bearing out of housing.

4) To install torque tube front bearing, reverse removal procedure. Tighten bolts to specifications.

Removal & Installation (Rear Bearing) – 1) Remove RDLM. Remove viscous coupling. Remove overrunning clutch cover assembly and drain fluid. Remove overrunning clutch case-to-rear carrier case bolts and separate overrunning clutch case from carrier case.

2) Remove overrunning clutch inner race snap ring. Slide overrunning clutch inner race off of shaft. Remove shaft snap ring and slide dog clutch off of shaft. Remove propeller shaft rear bearing snap ring.

3) Remove overrunning clutch case-to-torque tube bolts. Separate torque tube from overrunning clutch case. Remove rear bearing retaining snap ring in overrunning clutch case. Remove rear torque tube bearing.

4) To install torque tube rear bearing, reverse removal procedure. Tighten bolts to specifications.

OVERRUNNING CLUTCH

Removal (Vacuum Motor) – 1) Remove RDLM. Disconnect hoses to vacuum motor. Remove overrunning clutch cover assembly mounting bolts. Lift overrunning clutch cover assembly off of overrunning clutch case.

2) Clamp assembly in soft-jawed vise. Remove 2 "E" clips from vacuum motor shaft. While holding overrunning clutch shift fork, slide vacuum motor out of housing. Clean and inspect all parts and sealing surfaces. Replace worn or damaged parts.

1992 DRIVE AXLES
All-Wheel Drive Axle (Cont.)

CAUTION: Note position of shift fork before removing vacuum motor as it is possible to install fork backwards. Offset on fork must angle AWAY from vacuum motor.

Installation – Slide vacuum motor into housing and through shift fork. Install 2 "E" clips: one on vacuum motor shaft and one on vacuum motor bushing. Apply a bead of Mopar Gasket Maker (4318083) and reinstall cover assembly. Ensure that shift fork engages overrunning clutch dog. Install RDLM into vehicle. Check and fill fluid levels as required.

Removal (Overrunning Clutch Assembly) – 1) Remove RDLM. Remove overrunning clutch assembly cover and drain fluid. Separate overrunning clutch case from rear carrier case. Remove overrunning clutch snap ring. Remove spacers and overrunning clutch.

CAUTION: Keep overrunning clutch components in order as removed to prevent reassembling backward.

2) Remove overrunning clutch outer race snap ring. Slide outer race off of shaft. Remove overrunning clutch inner snap ring. Slide inner race off of shaft. Remove dog clutch snap ring and slide dog clutch off of shaft. Clean and inspect all parts and repair or replace as necessary.

Installation – 1) Install outer overrunning clutch race and snap ring. Install overrunning clutch spacers and snap ring. To test for proper installation, temporarily install the inner race into the overrunning clutch, tapered end first. Inner race should spin when turned counterclockwise and grab when turned clockwise.

2) Install dog clutch onto shaft and reinstall snap ring. Install overrunning onto the shaft with the tapered end facing outward and install snap ring. Apply Mopar Gasket Maker (4318083) sealer and reinstall overrunning clutch case to rear carrier case. Apply sealer and reinstall overrunning clutch cover making sure that shift fork engages clutch dog. Install RDLM into vehicle. Check and fill fluid levels as required.

TORQUE SPECIFICATIONS
TORQUE SPECIFICATIONS

Application	Ft. Lbs. (N.m)
Axle Nut	180 (244)
Differential End Cover	21 (28)
Drive Pinion Nut	250 (339)
Inner Half Shaft Mounting Bolts	45 (61)
Overrunning Clutch Bolts	
Case-To-Rear Carrier	21 (28)
Case-To-Torque Tube	21 (28)
Cover Assembly	21 (28)
Propeller Shaft Mounting Bolts	
Front & Rear	21 (28)
RDLM Rear Mounting Bolts	40 (54)
Ring Gear Bolts	70 (95)
Torque Tube Mounting Bolts	40 (54)
Viscous Coupling Retaining Nut	180 (244)

	INCH Lbs. (N.m)
Front Carrier Cover	105 (12)

Pickup, Ramcharger

DESCRIPTION

Locking hubs provide a means of engaging and disengaging front wheels from the front transfer case. When locking hubs and transfer case are engaged, power is transmitted to front wheels. When hubs are disengaged and transfer case is not in 4WD, front wheels are free wheeling and axle shafts and differential remain idle.

Engagement is accomplished through gears within the hub. With hub engaged, the inner clutch gear locks with the outer clutch and engages the axle shaft with wheel hub.

REMOVAL & INSTALLATION

Removal – Raise and support vehicle. Remove wheel. Remove caliper, and support it aside. Remove cap-to-hub Allen screws. Remove cap. *See Fig. 1.* Remove axle shaft retaining ring. Remove lock ring from groove in hub. To assist in removal, reinstall 2 Allen screws in locking hub body. Remove locking hub assembly from hub.

Inspection – Wash parts in mineral spirits, and blow dry using compressed air. Examine components for damage, and replace as necessary.

Installation – Lubricate parts lightly with multipurpose lubricant. To install components, reverse removal procedure. Tighten Allen screws to **35-45 INCH lbs. (4-5 N.m).**

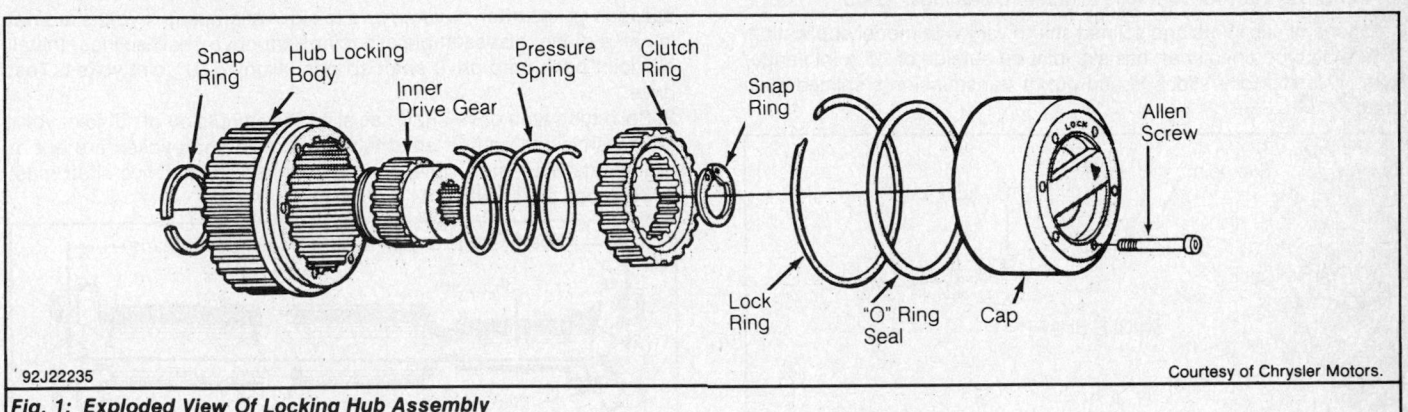

92J22235

Courtesy of Chrysler Motors.

Fig. 1: Exploded View Of Locking Hub Assembly

1992 DRIVE AXLES
Drive Shafts

Dakota, Pickup, Ramcharger, RWD Van

DESCRIPTION

Drive shafts are balanced, tubular shafts with "U" joints attached at each end. Flanges or yokes are used to connect drive shaft "U" joints to rear differential pinion flange or to transmission output shaft. "U" joint bearing caps are bolted to shaft flanges, or are pressed into shaft yokes. Drive shafts can be steel or aluminum.

Number of drive shafts used by vehicle depends on vehicle length and 4WD capability. Long wheel base vehicles use 2 rear drive shafts with a center bearing support assembly. See Fig. 1. The 4WD applications use a double cardan constant velocity joint on front axle drive shaft for correct drive shaft-to-front axle alignment. See Figs. 12-15.

Locations of slip joints and splined shafts vary with model application. Solid tube type drive shaft has slip joint on outside of "U" joint flange/yoke. This slip joint slides in and out of transmission's splined main shaft.

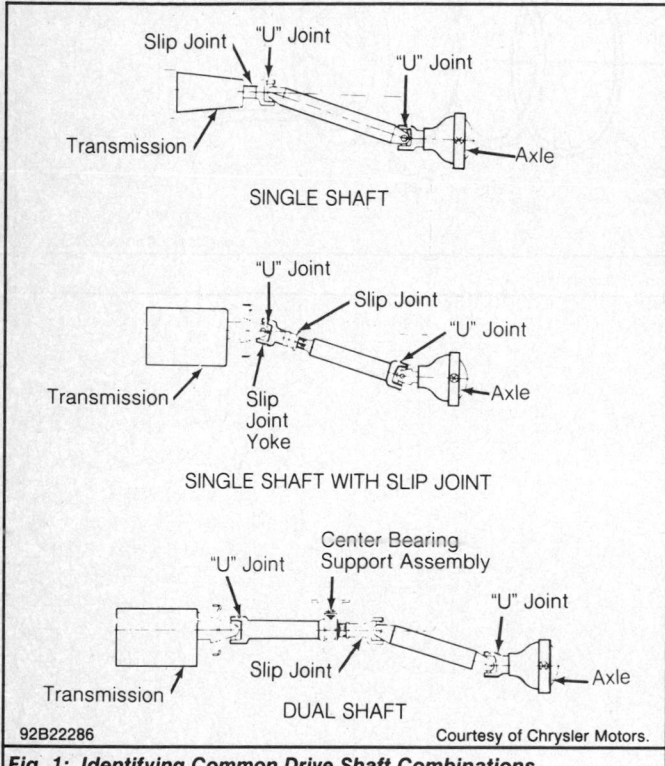

Fig. 1: Identifying Common Drive Shaft Combinations

LUBRICATION

Apply multipurpose lubricant (NLGI grade 2 EP) to "U" joints and slip joint fittings.

INSPECTION

Abnormal vibration and noise can come from many driveline sources. Drive shaft vibration/noise increases with vehicle speed (MPH). A vibration that occurs within a specific speed is not caused by drive shaft imbalance. Before overhauling driveline, check for other causes/sources of possible vibration/noise.

Tires & Wheels – Check tire inflation and wheel balance. Check for foreign objects in tread, damaged tread, mismatched tread patterns or incorrect tire sizes. Check for bent wheels.

Center Bearing – Tighten drive shaft center bearing mounting bolts. If bearing insulator is deteriorated or oil-soaked, or drive shaft can be moved up/down in support, replace center bearing support assembly.

Engine & Transmission Mounts – Tighten mounting bolts. If rubber mounts are deteriorated or broken, replace as needed.

Drive Shaft(s) – Check drive shaft(s) for missing weights, broken welds, or for dents affecting balance. Check for undercoating, mud, snow/ice on drive shaft(s). Clean shafts thoroughly and retest drive.

"U" Joints – Check for foreign material lodged in joints and flange/yokes. Check for loose "U" joint-to-flange mounting bolts. Check for worn "U" joint needle bearings. Check for Reddish-Brown rust-dust around "U" joint caps. Replace "U" joints if necessary.

ADJUSTMENTS

CHECKING DRIVE SHAFT PHASING

1-Piece Shafts – **1)** Ensure "U" joint flanges on either end of drive shaft are in same plane. See Fig. 2. Drive shafts with slip joints between yokes often have arrows to aid in alignment. If yokes are not in same plane, disassemble slip joint from drive shaft splines. Install slip joint back onto drive shaft splines, aligning "U" joint yokes. Test drive.

2) Solid tube type drive shaft has slip joint on outside of "U" joint yoke (at transmission end). If solid tube type drive shaft yokes are out of alignment, this means drive shaft is torque-twisted. Drive shaft must be replaced or rebuilt.

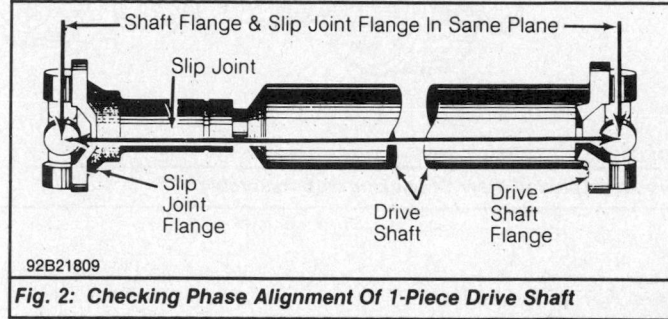

Fig. 2: Checking Phase Alignment Of 1-Piece Drive Shaft

2-Piece Shafts – **1)** On most models with 2-piece shafts, proper yoke phasing is accomplished by "keys" on drive shaft spline and "keyway" in slip joint splines. Most drive shafts of this type will fit together only one way. Other non-key type drive shafts will spline together in any order.

2) Rotate transmission flange/yoke until flange/yoke ears (trunnion axis) are in horizontal plane. Install front drive shaft to transmission flange/yoke keeping flange/yoke in horizontal plane. This means both flange/yoke ears of front drive shaft are in vertical plane. See Fig. 3.

3) Connect center bearing support assembly to crossmember bracket. Ensure front face of center bearing support assembly is perpendicular (90 degrees) to center line of drive shaft. If center bearing support assembly is installed crooked or off center, drive shaft vibration and/or noise will result. See Fig. 8.

4) Align and install rear drive shaft splines into slip yoke splines while keeping rear drive shaft flange/yoke in horizontal plane. Drive shaft rear "U" joint mounting caps will be in vertical plane. Set differential pinion flange in vertical plane. Connect rear drive shaft to pinion flange. If 2-piece shaft is correctly installed, center line of flange/yokes trunnion axis for each individual shaft will be parallel. See Fig. 3.

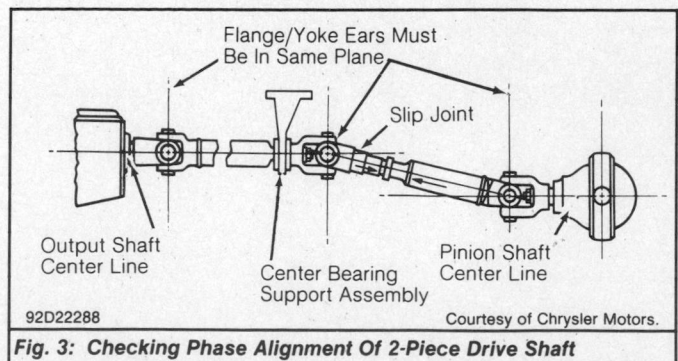

Fig. 3: Checking Phase Alignment Of 2-Piece Drive Shaft

CHECKING RUNOUT

Using dial indicator, measure runout of transmission flange/yoke, center bearing yoke and pinion flange. Replace flange/yoke if runout exceeds .003-.005" (.08-.13 mm).

BALANCING DRIVE SHAFT

1) Perform following procedure only after inspecting all other possible causes of vibration. See INSPECTION. Drive shaft imbalance may often be cured by disconnecting shaft, rotating it 180 degrees and reconnect shaft to flange. Test drive to obtain results.

NOTE: DO NOT run engine for prolonged periods without forced air-low across radiator, as engine or transmission may overheat.

2) To balance drive shaft(s), begin by raising rear wheels off ground and turning drive shaft with engine. Balance testing may be done by marking drive shaft in 4 positions, 90 degrees apart around shaft. Place marks about 6" forward of rear flange/yoke weld. Number the marks 1-4.

3) Install large diameter screw-type hose clamp around drive shaft so clamp's head is in No. 1 position. Rotate drive shaft with engine and note vibrations. If there is little or no change in vibration intensity, move clamp head to No. 2 position, and repeat test.

4) Continue procedure until vibration is at lowest level. If no difference is noted with clamp head moved to all 4 positions, vibrations may not be drive shaft imbalance.

5) If vibration decreases but is not completely eliminated, place a second clamp at same position, and repeat test. Combined weight of both clamps in one position may increase vibration. If so, rotate clamps 1/2" apart, above and below lowest vibration level position, and repeat test.

6) Continue to rotate clamps, as necessary, until vibration is at lowest point. If vibration can be eliminated or reduced to acceptable level, bend back slack end of clamp so screw cannot loosen. If vibration level is still unacceptable, leave rear clamp(s) in place, and repeat procedure at front end of drive shaft. Road test vehicle. On 4WD models, perform procedure on each shaft.

CHECKING VERTICAL ANGLE

1-Piece Shafts – **1)** Raise and support vehicle so rear wheels can be rotated. Rotate drive shaft so a pinion flange bearing cap faces downward. Attach Inclinometer (C-4224) magnet to bearing cap, and measure drive shaft vertical angle. *See Fig. 4.* Remove inclinometer.

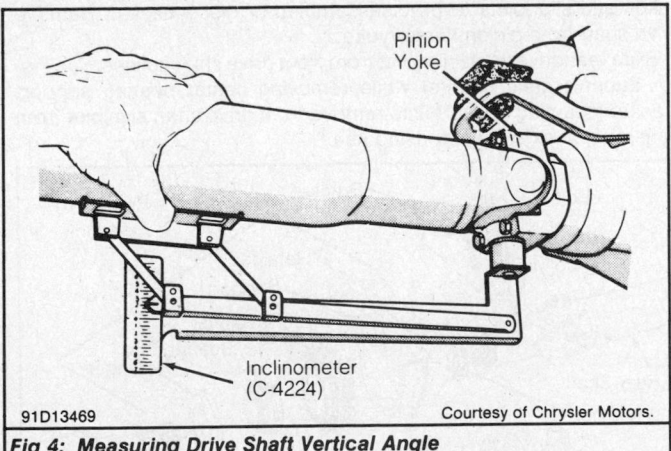
91D13469   Courtesy of Chrysler Motors.
Fig 4: Measuring Drive Shaft Vertical Angle

2) Rotate drive shaft (90°) until drive shaft rear yoke bearing cap faces downward. Attach inclinometer magnet to bearing cap, and measure drive shaft vertical angle. Difference between 2 measured angles is drive shaft rear angle. *See Fig. 5.* Remove inclinometer.

3) Rotate drive shaft until a slip joint yoke bearing cap faces downward. Attach inclinometer magnet to bearing cap, and note angle. Remove inclinometer. Rotate drive shaft (90°) until drive shaft

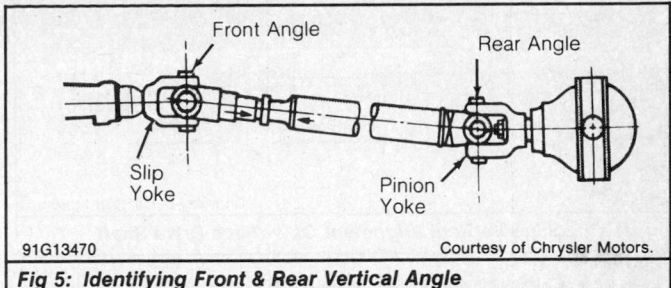
91G13470   Courtesy of Chrysler Motors.
Fig 5: Identifying Front & Rear Vertical Angle

front yoke bearing cap faces downward. Attach inclinometer magnet to bearing cap, and note angle. Remove inclinometer.

4) Difference between 2 measured angles is drive shaft front angle. *See Fig. 5.* Compare front and rear angles. Allowable difference between angles is plus or minus one degree. If difference of angles is greater than specified, adjustment is necessary. See ADJUSTING VERTICAL ANGLE.

2-Piece Non-Parallel Shafts ("Broken Back" Type) – **1)** A "broken back" type driveline is where yokes are not perpendicular to each other in vertical plane. *See Fig. 6.* With non-parallel or "broken back" type installation, working angles of "U" joints of given drive shaft must be equal (angle "A" = angle "B").

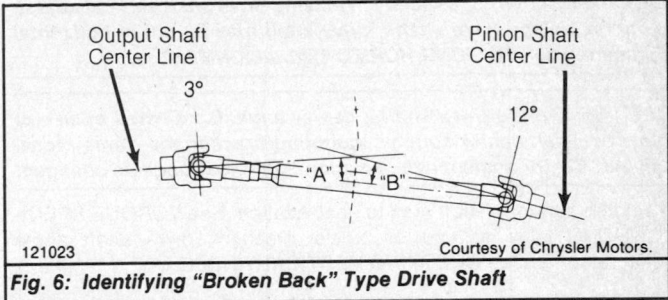
121023   Courtesy of Chrysler Motors.
Fig. 6: Identifying "Broken Back" Type Drive Shaft

2) Calculate by subtracting angle of output shaft center line from angle of drive shaft. Difference should equal front shaft angle subtracted from rear shaft angle.

2-Piece Shafts – **1)** All yokes must be perpendicular in both vertical and horizontal planes to engine crankshaft. Using Inclinometer (C-4224), measure drive shaft vertical angles.

2) Raise and support vehicle so rear wheels can be rotated. Rotate drive shaft so a pinion flange bearing cap faces downward. Attach inclinometer magnet to bearing cap, and note angle. *See Fig. 4.* Remove inclinometer.

3) Rotate drive shaft (90°) until drive shaft rear yoke bearing cap faces downward. Attach inclinometer magnet to bearing cap, and note angle. Difference between 2 measured angles is drive shaft rear angle. *See Fig. 5.* Remove inclinometer.

4) Rotate drive shaft until a slip joint yoke bearing cap faces downward. Attach inclinometer magnet to bearing cap, and note angle. Remove inclinometer. Rotate drive shaft (90°) until drive shaft front yoke bearing cap faces downward. Attach inclinometer magnet to bearing cap, and note angle. Difference between 2 measured angles is drive shaft front angle. *See Fig. 5.* Remove inclinometer.

5) Rotate drive shaft until front yoke of rear shaft faces downward. Attach inclinometer magnet to bearing cap, and note angle. Rotate drive shaft until REAR yoke of front drive shaft faces downward. Attach inclinometer magnet to bearing cap, and note angle. Remove inclinometer.

6) Difference between 2 measured angles is drive shaft center angle. Compare front, center and rear angles. Vertical alignment of 2-piece drive shafts at yokes should be greater than 1/2 degree and must be retained as close to one degree as possible. *See Fig. 7.* If difference of angles is greater than specified, adjustment is necessary. See ADJUSTING VERTICAL ANGLE.

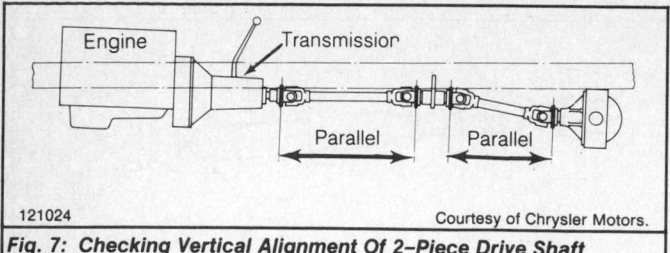

Fig. 7: Checking Vertical Alignment Of 2-Piece Drive Shaft

ADJUSTING VERTICAL ANGLE

1) If front angle minus rear angle is greater than one degree positive (+1 degree), rear angle is too small and must be increased. If front angle minus rear angle is greater than one degree negative (-1 degree), rear angle is too large and must be decreased. To adjust angle, proceed to next step.

2) Raise and support rear of vehicle using jackstands under frame. Position a hydraulic jack under differential housing. Remove rear wheel assemblies. Loosen rear spring "U" bolt nuts. Insert tapered shim between spring and axle spring pad. If increasing angle, insert shim with taper facing front of vehicle. If decreasing angle, insert shim with taper facing rear of vehicle.

NOTE: If encountering difficulty in making drive shaft vertical adjustments on 1-piece drive shafts, drive shaft may be out of horizontal alignment. See CHECKING HORIZONTAL ALIGNMENT.

NOTE: On 2-piece drive shafts, center angle is adjusted by use of shims between center support mounting bracket and frame crossmember. Center angle may need adjusting if rear angle is changed.

3) Tighten spring "U" bolt nuts to specification. See TORQUE SPECIFICATIONS table at end of article. Recheck drive shaft angle measurements. See CHECKING VERTICAL ANGLE.

CHECKING HORIZONTAL ALIGNMENT

1) Drive shaft horizontal alignment should be checked if frame damage is suspected or when major components have been replaced. *See Fig. 8.*

2) Clamp a long straightedge (12" longer than width of rear wheel track) at 90 degrees to frame side rails. *See Fig. 9.* Use large framing squares to align straightedge with side rails.

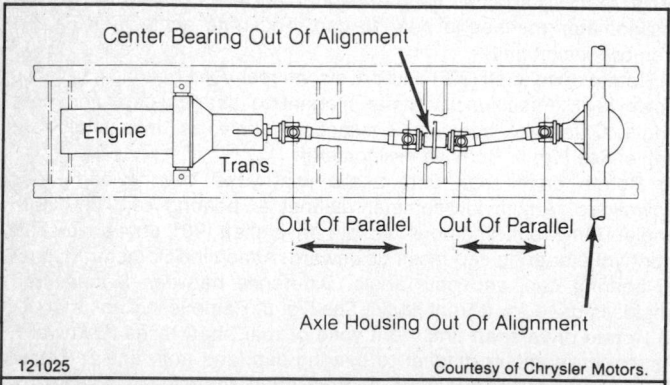

Fig. 8: Identifying Horizontal Misalignment Of Drive Shaft

3) To make horizontal alignment checks, set up straightedges as shown. *See Fig. 9.* Set transmission output flange/yoke horizontally, and clamp straightedge to ·yoke in a horizontal plane. Repeat procedure with drive pinion flange. Ensure flange/yokes are horizontal by checking angle of straightedge using a machinist spirit level.

4) Measure distance "X" at each side. *See Fig. 9.* If measurements are not within 1/16" (1.6 mm) of each other, transmission flange is horizontally misaligned.

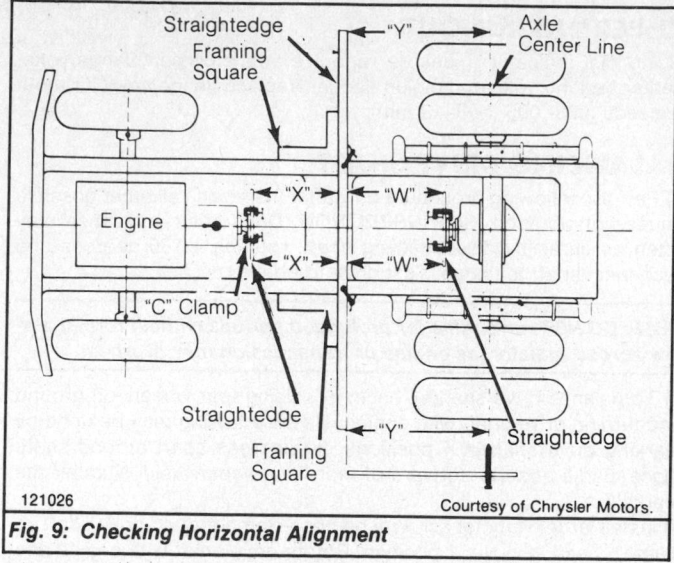

Fig. 9: Checking Horizontal Alignment

5) Measure distance "Y" (edge of straightedge to axle shaft center line) at each side. If measurements are not within 1/8" (3.2 mm) of each other, axle housing is misaligned.

6) Measure distance "W" at each side. If measurements are not within 1/16" (1.6 mm) of each other, pinion flange is horizontally misaligned.

ADJUSTING HORIZONTAL ALIGNMENT

NOTE: Excessive difference in measurements may indicate frame damage. DO NOT attempt to use following correction procedure if more than slight horizontal misalignment exists.

Minor adjustment of drive shaft horizontal alignment may be made by loosening axle housing "U" bolts and moving either side of axle housing forward or backward. If frame is not bent, slight axle movement should make "W" measurements equal. *See Fig. 9.*

REMOVAL & INSTALLATION

CENTER BEARING SUPPORT ASSEMBLY

Removal – 1) Set parking brake or block wheels. Loosen slip yoke-spline protective boot clamps. Scribe alignment marks on all flange/yokes and slip joints to be disassembled or disconnected. Remove drive shaft from pinion flange/yoke.

2) Slide rear drive shaft slip joint from front drive shaft splines. *See Fig. 10.* Support drive shaft(s) while removing center bearing support bracket mounting bolts. Pull to remove front drive shaft slip joint from transmission extension housing shaft.

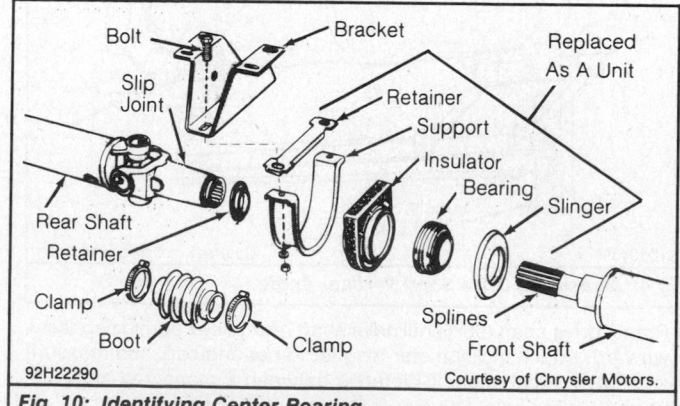

Fig. 10: Identifying Center Bearing Support Assembly Components

CAUTION: DO NOT clamp drive shaft tube or slip joint tube in a vise. Clamp only forged portion of each yoke in vise. To avoid distorting yoke, DO NOT overtighten vise jaws.

Disassembly – 1) Carefully clamp front drive shaft in a soft-jaw vise. If required, disassemble "U" joint from yoke to access yoke-to-drive shaft retaining bolt. Scribe mark yoke or slip joint to drive shaft for reassembly reference. Slide yoke or slip joint off shaft splines.
2) Remove and retain center bearing support bracket and retainer. (Service replacement assembly may not come with these items.) Remove rubber insulator from bearing housing. *See Fig. 10.*
3) Bend slinger away from center bearing to provide clearance for bearing puller. Using bearing puller, remove center bearing from drive shaft. On some applications, outer bearing cover/cage and balls must be removed to attach puller to bearing race.
Reassembly & Installation – Install new slinger to shaft. Install/press bearing onto shaft using appropriate tool or pipe until bearing is seated to shaft shoulder. To complete installation, reverse disassembly and removal procedures. Ensure support bracket angle adjustment shims are reinstalled (if removed).

OVERHAUL

NOTE: Manufacturer recommends replacing "U" joint(s) whenever "U" joint is disassembled from yoke. ALWAYS replace complete "U" joint whenever extreme external lubrication leakage or bearing cap damage exists.

Before disassembly, mark flange/yoke to drive shaft for reassembly reference, and remove "U" joint lube fitting(s). If joints are rusted or corroded, apply penetrating oil before pressing bearing caps out of yoke or off "U" joint trunnion pin.

SINGLE CARDAN "U" JOINTS

Other than adding grease, "U" joint assembly items are not individually serviceable or repairable. If needle bearings, seals, spider, or bearing caps are found to be defective, damaged or excessively worn; complete "U" joint must be replaced.

NOTE: Saturate bearing caps and yokes with penetrating oil before removal.

Removal – Remove drive shaft. *See Fig. 11.* Remove inner or outer type bearing cap retainer clips. Press bearing caps from yokes. Remove bearings, seals and spider from yoke bore and discard.
Cleaning – Clean yoke bores using an appropriate cleaning solvent and wire brush or crocus cloth. Remove all rust, corrosion and foreign matter from yoke bores.
Installation – 1) Apply multipurpose lubricant (NLGI grade 2 EP) to yoke bores and into needle bearings of each bearing cap. Position spider in yoke bores.
2) Install seals onto spider trunnions or onto bearing caps. Lightly tap bearing caps into yoke bore far enough to retain spider in place.

CAUTION: DO NOT clamp drive shaft tube or slip joint tube in a vise. Clamp only forged portion of each yoke in vise. To avoid distorting yoke, DO NOT overtighten vise jaws.

3) Using vise or vertical press, carefully press bearing caps into yoke bores, keeping spider aligned in center of bearing caps. Using socket with diameter slightly smaller than bearing cap, continue pressing caps inward until retainer clips can be installed. Install inner or outer type bearing cap retainer clips.
4) Install lube fitting and lube "U" joint. Install drive shaft. Tighten "U" joint clamp bolts to **14 ft. lbs. (19 N.m)**. Remove supports, and lower vehicle.

DOUBLE CARDAN CONSTANT VELOCITY (CV) JOINT (4WD)

CAUTION: DO NOT allow pinion flange end of front drive shaft to hang free or bend at sharp angle from CV joint. After removal, drive shaft and CV joint assembly may be carried vertically without damage.

NOTE: Other than adding grease, "U" joint assembly items are not individually serviceable or repairable. If needle bearings, seals, spider, or bearing caps are found to be defective, damaged or excessively worn; complete "U" joint assembly must be replaced.

Removal & Disassembly (Dakota) – 1) Mark drive shaft yoke-to-front pinion flange position and transfer case flange-to-CV joint flange position for installation reference. Remove CV joint flange-to-transfer case flange bolts first, then remove pinion flange bolts. Remove front drive shaft from vehicle using care not to bend shaft at sharp angle from CV joint.
2) Mark CV joint components for reassembly reference. Remove all inner or outer type bearing cap retaining clips. *See Fig. 12.* Disassemble components in the following order.
- Bearing Caps Retaining Front Spider In Link Yoke
- Separate Link Yoke From Drive Shaft Yoke
- Bearing Caps Retaining Rear Spider In Link Yoke
- Separate Link Yoke From Socket Yoke
- Bearing Caps And Spider From Socket Yoke
- Bearing Caps And Front Spider From Drive Shaft Yoke

Reassembly & Installation – 1) Clean dirt and rust from all contact areas. Apply multipurpose lubricant (NLGI grade 2 EP) to yoke bores and into needle bearings of each bearing cap. Lube center socket yoke and needle bearings. *See Fig. 12.*

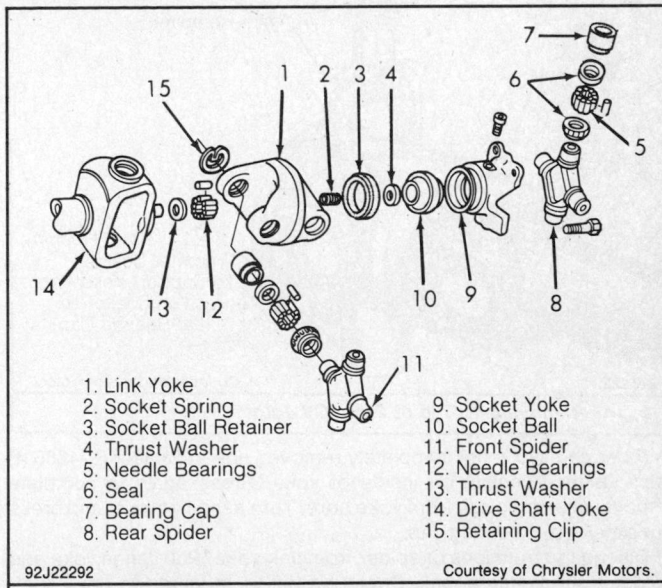

1. Link Yoke
2. Socket Spring
3. Socket Ball Retainer
4. Thrust Washer
5. Needle Bearings
6. Seal
7. Bearing Cap
8. Rear Spider
9. Socket Yoke
10. Socket Ball
11. Front Spider
12. Needle Bearings
13. Thrust Washer
14. Drive Shaft Yoke
15. Retaining Clip

92J22292
Courtesy of Chrysler Motors.

Fig. 12: Exploded View Of Double Cardan Constant Velocity (CV) "U" Joint (Dakota 4WD)

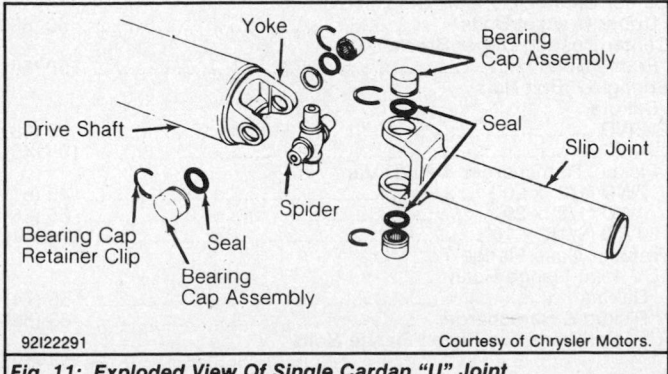

Yoke
Bearing Cap Assembly
Drive Shaft
Seal
Slip Joint
Spider
Bearing Cap Retainer Clip
Seal
Bearing Cap Assembly

92122291
Courtesy of Chrysler Motors.

Fig. 11: Exploded View Of Single Cardan "U" Joint

2) Position spider in drive shaft yoke bore. Reassemble components in reverse order of disassembly, ensuring reference marks align. Install drive shaft in vehicle, and tighten flange bolts to specification. See TORQUE SPECIFICATIONS table at end of article.

Removal & Disassembly (Pickup 4WD & Ramcharger 4WD) – 1) Mark front drive shaft-to-pinion flange position and transfer case flange-to-CV joint flange position for installation reference. Remove front drive shaft from vehicle using care not to bend shaft at sharp angle to CV joint.

2) Mark CV joint components for reassembly reference and to maintain drive shaft balance. *See Figs. 13 and 14.* Remove all inner or outer type bearing cap retaining clips. If retaining clips are not present, original production "U" joints are retained into yokes using injected plastic. Plastic must be removed using high heat (such as acetylene torch). New retaining clips are provided with replacement "U" joints.

WARNING: When heating "U" joint cap and yoke ear to remove plastic, point "U" joint cap away from body, preferably toward ground. When plastic and grease are heated simultaneously, joint cap will loosen quickly without notice.

3) To disassemble CV joint in least amount of time, remove bearing caps in order. *See Fig. 13.* Support drive shaft horizontally while placing CV joint onto base plate of press. Place No. 1 rear ear of link yoke over a 1 1/8" (30 mm) socket. Place Yoke Remover (C-4365-1) onto both outside No. 2 bearing caps in yoke. Press No. 1 bearing cap out of link yoke ear. *See Fig. 14.*

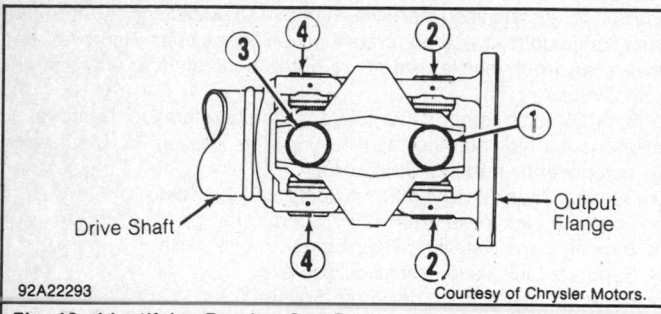

Fig. 13: Identifying Bearing Cap Removal Sequence (Pickup & Ramcharger)

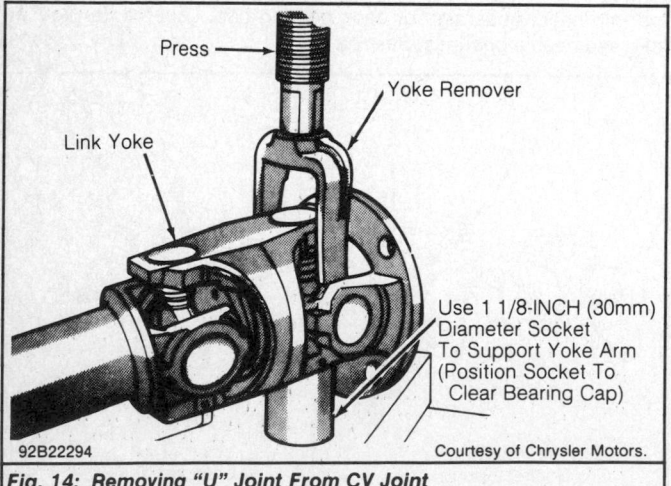

Fig. 14: Removing "U" Joint From CV Joint

4) If bearing cap is not completely removed, insert Spacer (C-4365-4) onto spider trunnion, on inside of yoke. Press again to complete removal of bearing cap from yoke bore. Turn assembly over and press out other No. 1 bearing cap.

5) Disengage trunnions of spider from link yoke. Pull flange yoke and spider from centering ball. Centering ball is mounted to drive shaft yoke ball support. Ball socket is part of flange yoke. Pry seal from ball socket. Remove washers, 3 ball seats and spring. *See Fig. 15.* To remove centering ball, go to next step.

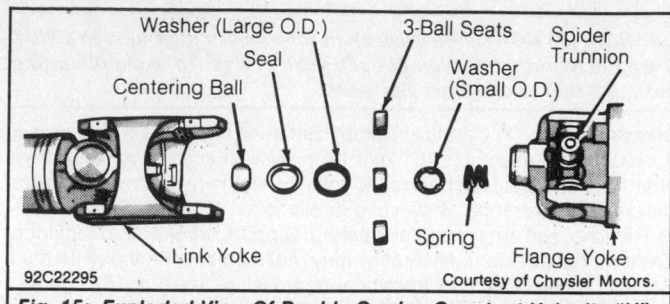

Fig. 15: Exploded View Of Double Cardan Constant Velocity "U" Joint Center Ball Components (Pickup & Ramcharger)

6) Clean and inspect flange yoke ball socket bushing and ball seats for abnormal wear. If abnormal wear is present, replace flange yoke, "U" joint, ball seats, spring and seal. Remove centering ball from drive shaft yoke stud using Remover Kit (components No. C-4365-5 through C-4365-8) and Nut (SP-84).

Reassembly – 1) Using Ball Installer (C-4365-3), drive centering ball onto stud. Ensure ball seats firmly against shoulder at stud base.

2) To install spider, install one bearing cap part way into one side of yoke, and turn this yoke to bottom. Insert spider into yoke so spider trunnion seats into bearing cap.

3) Install opposite bearing cap part way. Press bearing caps inward while working spider to ensure free movement of trunnions in bearing cap needle bearings. When one bearing cap retaining clip groove clears inside of yoke, stop pressing and snap retaining clip into position.

4) Position socket on opposite side bearing cap and continue to press until retaining clip can be snapped into position. If encountering difficulty, strike yoke ear firmly using a hammer to seat retaining clips.

5) Lubricate all ball socket parts with grease provided with ball seat kit. Insert parts into clean ball socket in this order: spring, small O.D. washer, 3 ball seats with large opening outward, and large washer.

6) Lubricate seal lip, and press in seal until flush. Sealing lip should tip inward slightly. Fill cavity with grease provided in service kit. Ensure centering ball and socket are well lubricated with grease. Assemble other half of flange yoke "U" joint into link yoke using same method as steps 2) - 4).

Installation – 1) Before installing drive shaft, clean mating flange, and inspect machined surface for scratches, nicks and burrs.

2) Support drive shaft during installation to prevent bending shaft at sharp angle to CV joint and causing damage to "U" joints. Aligning reference marks, install CV joint flange to transfer case flange first, then install shaft to pinion flange.

3) Attach 2 clamps to pinion flange, and tighten attaching bolts to specification. Install and tighten 4 bolts to CV joint at transfer case flange. See TORQUE SPECIFICATIONS table.

TORQUE SPECIFICATIONS
TORQUE SPECIFICATIONS

Application	Ft. Lbs. (N.m)
Center Bearing Support Bracket-To- Upper Bracket Bolts	50 (68)
Center Bearing Upper Bracket-To- Frame Bolts	50 (68)
Spring "U" Bolt Nuts	
Dakota	
2WD	65 (88)
4WD	110 (149)
Pickup, Ramcharger & RWD Van	
2WD (1/2" x 20")	45 (61)
4WD (1/2" x 20")	65 (88)
4WD (9/16" x 18")	180 (244)
Transfer Case Flange-To- CV Joint Flange Bolts	
Dakota	55 (74)
Pickup & Ramcharger	65 (88)
"U" Joint Clamp-To-Pinion Flange Bolts	
1/4"	14 (19)
5/16"	25 (34)
Wheel Lug Nuts	95 (129)

Caravan, Town & Country, Voyager

MODEL IDENTIFICATION

Vehicle body codes are used throughout self-diagnostic tests. See BODY CODE DESIGNATION table for model identification.

BODY CODE DESIGNATION

Model Name	Body Designation
Caravan, Voyager, Town & Country	AS

DESCRIPTION

Bendix-10 Anti-Lock Brake System (ABS) is designed to prevent wheel lock-up during heavy braking. This allows operator to maintain steering control, while stopping vehicle in shortest distance possible. Major components consist of the following: hydraulic assembly, 4 wheel speed sensors, Controller Anti-Lock Brake (CAB), 2 warning lights (Red BRAKE and Amber ANTI-LOCK) and pump/motor assembly. *See Fig. 1.* ABS has a self-diagnostic system, which detects and trouble shoots system malfunction.

NOTE: For more information on brake system, see appropriate DISC & DRUM article.

OPERATION

Each wheel sensor sends an AC electrical signal to the CAB, which translates this information into wheel speed. If wheel speed in any wheel decelerates excessively in comparison to other wheels, the CAB cycles hydraulic brake pressure to each wheel to equalize decelerating speed of all wheels. ABS does not function at speeds less than 5 MPH. Minor wheel lock-up may occur at speeds less than 5 MPH.

Red BRAKE warning light will come on when ignition switch is in START position. Warning light should go off when ignition switch is released to RUN position. If light does not go off, the following conditions may be the cause: parking brake not fully released, low brake fluid, low accumulator pressure or low hydraulic pressure. See DIAGNOSIS & TESTING.

Amber ANTI-LOCK warning light will come on for 1-30 seconds when ignition switch is turned to ON position, and ABS will perform a self-diagnostic test during this period. If light does not go off after 30 seconds, ABS has found a fault. ABS is deactivated until fault is repaired. Normal braking functions are unaffected. Proceed to DIAGNOSIS & TESTING to locate and correct fault.

PEDAL FEEL CHARACTERISTICS

During ABS stopping, solenoid valve clicking and pump motor operation may be heard, and brake pedal vibration/pulsation may be felt. The ABS prevents complete wheel lock-up, but some tire chirping may occur, depending on road surface. The chirping sound should not be interpreted as total wheel lock-up (although wheel lock-up may occur at speeds less than 5 MPH).

During an ABS stop, the master cylinder is isolated from wheel brakes, producing a hard pedal feel. The ABS is shut off toward end of ABS stop, when speed is less than 5 MPH. A slight brake pedal drop may be felt when ABS is shut off.

The system may detect wheel lock-up and activates ABS under the following conditions: braking on bumpy surface or when sand, gravel or other loose debris is on the road. Under such conditions, hard pedal feel and loss of deceleration may be experienced.

Hard pedal feel WILL NOT illuminate warning lights or set fault code. When investigating a hard pedal feel or excessive system noise, inspect sensor and tone wheel teeth for chips, damaged sensor pole tips, excessive tone wheel runout or gap.

SYSTEM PRECAUTIONS

CAUTION: See ANTI-LOCK BRAKE SAFETY PRECAUTIONS article in GENERAL INFORMATION.

1) DO NOT unplug or plug CAB connector with ignition switch in ON position. Before bleeding brake system or disconnecting any hydraulic brake component (including brake lines), depressurize ABS hydraulic system by turning ignition switch to OFF position, and depressing brake pedal at least 40 times.
2) Unplug CAB and sensor block connectors before using an arc welder on vehicle. When painting vehicle, CAB and sensor block should be insulated or removed before placing vehicle in paint oven.
3) Visually inspect ABS before performing any test. Ensure hydraulic system, normal brake system, charging system and battery are okay. Low battery voltage can cause faulty reading. If necessary, connect a battery charger, and apply slow charge. DO NOT fast charge battery.
4) Ensure parking brake switch, all related electrical wiring, electrical connections and electrical grounds are okay.

BLEEDING BRAKE SYSTEM

WARNING: Depressurize hydraulic accumulator before performing brake bleeding procedure to prevent injury and/or damage to painted surfaces.

Air enters system whenever lines, hoses, calipers or hydraulic assembly are disconnected for service. ABS must be bled if air has entered system. Air inside brake system may set a primary pressure/delta pressure fault in the Controller Anti-Lock Brake (CAB). Refer to DIAGNOSIS & TESTING.

NOTE: During brake bleeding procedure, ensure reservoir fluid level remains full. Check fluid level periodically during procedure, and add DOT 3 brake fluid if necessary.

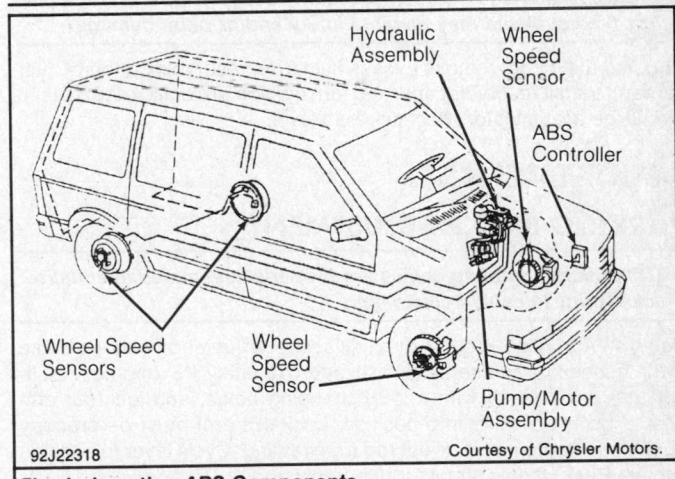

92J22318   Courtesy of Chrysler Motors.

Fig. 1: Locating ABS Components

MANUAL BLEEDING

NOTE: Manual bleeding procedure may require a second technician.

1) Ensure ignition remains in OFF position during brake bleeding procedure. Depressurize accumulator by pumping brake pedal at least 40 times. When a definite increase in pedal effort is felt, pump pedal a few more times to ensure pressure is released.
2) Connect transparent hose to LR caliper/wheel cylinder bleed screw. Submerge free end of hose in clear jar partially filled with clean brake fluid. Slowly pump brake pedal full strokes several times; allow about 5 seconds between pedal strokes. After 2 or 3 strokes, hold pedal at bottom of travel.
3) With pressure on pedal, open caliper/wheel cylinder bleed screw 1/2 - 3/4 turn. Leave bleed screw open until fluid no longer flows from

hose, or fluid level stops rising in bottle. Tighten bleed screw, and release pedal. Repeat procedure until clear, bubble-free fluid flows from hose. Bleed calipers/wheel cylinders in the following order: LR, RR, LF and RF.

PRESSURE BLEEDING

NOTE: Use only diaphragm-type pressure bleeding equipment to prevent air, moisture and other contaminants from entering system.

1) Ensure ignition remains in OFF position during brake bleeding procedure. Depressurize accumulator by pumping brake pedal at least 40 times. When a definite increase in pedal effort is felt, pump pedal a few more times to ensure pressure is released.
2) Remove both reservoir caps. Install pressure bleeder adapter on one reservoir port and dummy cap on the other. Attach bleeding equipment to bleeder adapter per equipment instructions. Charge pressure bleeder to approximately 20 psi (1.4 kg/cm²).
3) Connect transparent hose to LR caliper/wheel cylinder bleed screw. Submerge free end of hose in clear jar partially filled with clean brake fluid. With pressure bleeder turned on, open caliper/wheel cylinder bleed screw 1/2 - 3/4 turn, and allow fluid to flow into container. Leave bleed screw open until clear, bubble-free fluid flows from hose.
4) When installing NEW components or, if master cylinder reservoir was drained or hydraulic assembly removed before bleeding, slowly pump brake pedal 2 times while bleed screw is open and fluid is flowing. This will help purge air from master cylinder and/or hydraulic assembly. Tighten caliper/wheel cylinder bleed screw to **80-170 INCH lbs. (9-19 N.m)**.
5) Bleed calipers/wheel cylinders in the following order: LR, RR, LF and RF. After all calipers/wheel cylinders have been bled, release pressure bleeding equipment air pressure. Close pressure bleeder valve, and slowly unscrew bleeder adapter from hydraulic assembly reservoir. Remove bleeder adapter and bleeder equipment.

WARNING: Failure to release pressure slowly from reservoir will cause fluid spill and may result in injury and/or paint damage.

6) Using a syringe, remove excess fluid from reservoir (to top of filter screen). Install reservoir caps, and turn ignition on to allow ABS pump to charge accumulator. Recheck fluid level.

ADJUSTMENTS

PARKING BRAKE ADJUSTMENT

NOTE: Ensure operating cables are properly assembled to equalizer bracket prior to cable adjustment.

Using a 7/32" Allen wrench, turn hex socket adjuster on parking brake lever assembly counterclockwise approximately 15 degrees. Self-adjuster will release with a loud snapping noise, and lock-out arm should be felt clicking into position. Lock-out arm must be properly positioned to prevent lock-out rod from rattling. Cycle lever to position cables. Rear wheels should rotate freely.

STOPLIGHT SWITCH ADJUSTMENT

Install switch in retaining bracket, and push switch forward as far as possible. The brake pedal will move forward slightly. Gently pull back on pedal, bringing striker back toward switch until pedal will go no further. This ratchets the switch to its correct position. No other adjustment is necessary.

REMOVAL & INSTALLATION

WARNING: When battery is disconnected, vehicle computer and memory systems may lose memory data. Driveability problems may exist until computer systems have completed a relearn cycle. See COMPUTER RELEARN PROCEDURES article in GENERAL INFORMATION before disconnecting battery.

WARNING: To prevent personal injury and vehicle damage, before removing any component, depressurize hydraulic system by turning ignition off and depressing brake pedal at least 40 times. When a definite increase in pedal effort is felt, pump pedal a few more times before disconnecting any hydraulic line or component.

PUMP/MOTOR ASSEMBLY

Removal & Installation – 1) Disconnect negative battery cable, or ensure ignition switch is off and key is removed. Depressurize hydraulic accumulator by pumping brake pedal at least 40 times. Remove fresh air intake ducts from engine induction system.
2) Unclip and disconnect pump/motor harness and connectors from engine compartment harness. Disconnect high and low pressure hoses from hydraulic assembly, and cap reservoir outlet. *See Fig. 2.* Disconnect pump/motor electrical connector from left side engine mount.
3) Remove pump heat shield bolt from front of pump bracket. Remove heat shield. Lift pump/motor assembly from bracket and remove from vehicle. To install, reverse removal procedure.

PRESSURE & RETURN HOSES

Removal & Installation – 1) Disconnect negative battery cable, or ensure ignition switch is off and key is removed. Depressurize hydraulic accumulator by pumping brake pedal at least 40 times. Remove fresh air intake ducts from engine induction system.
2) Remove pump/motor assembly. See PUMP/MOTOR ASSEMBLY. Cut 2 tie straps securing hoses and wiring harness. Remove banjo bolt from pump/motor. Remove pressure and return hoses.
3) To install, reverse removal procedure. Install NEW rubber "O" rings on high and low pressure hoses. Position hose assemblies on pump/motor, and install banjo bolt. Carefully route wiring harness along side of hoses. Install tie straps around hoses and wiring harness. Install pump/motor assembly in vehicle.

HYDRAULIC ASSEMBLY

Removal & Installation – 1) Disconnect negative battery cable, or ensure ignition switch is off and key is removed. Depress brake pedal at least 40 times to depressurize brake system. Remove fresh air intake ducts from engine induction system. Unplug all electrical connectors from hydraulic assembly.
2) With a syringe, remove as much brake fluid as possible from reservoir. Remove high pressure hose fitting from hydraulic assembly. Disconnect pump return hose from filter nipple, and cap fitting on filter. Disconnect all brake lines from hydraulic assembly.
3) From under instrument panel, remove brake pedal clip and pin. Discard clip. Remove 4 hydraulic assembly mounting nuts from firewall. Remove hydraulic assembly, noting position of brake push rod. To install, reverse removal procedure. Install new clip. Bleed brake system. See BLEEDING BRAKE SYSTEM.

RESERVOIR

Removal – 1) Disconnect negative battery cable, or ensure ignition switch is off and key is removed. Depress brake pedal at least 40 times to depressurize brake system. With a syringe, remove as much brake fluid as possible from reservoir.
2) Unscrew and remove accumulator from hydraulic assembly using oil filter wrench. *See Fig. 2.* Remove high pressure hose banjo fitting from hydraulic assembly near accumulator. Using needle-nose pliers, remove 3 locking pins from hydraulic assembly. Carefully pry between reservoir and hydraulic assembly with blunt tool while rocking reservoir to unseat it from grommets. DO NOT damage or puncture reservoir during removal.
3) Remove brake fluid level sensor from bottom of reservoir by squeezing switch retaining barbs and sliding switch out. Remove rubber grommets from assembly and discard.
Installation – To install, reverse removal procedure. Lubricate new reservoir grommets with clean brake fluid and install. Press reservoir into hydraulic assembly. Bleed brake system. See BLEEDING BRAKE SYSTEM.

CAUTION: Press reservoir in by hand using a rocking motion to fully seat hydraulic assembly into 3 grommets. DO NOT pound reservoir into hydraulic assembly using a hammer.

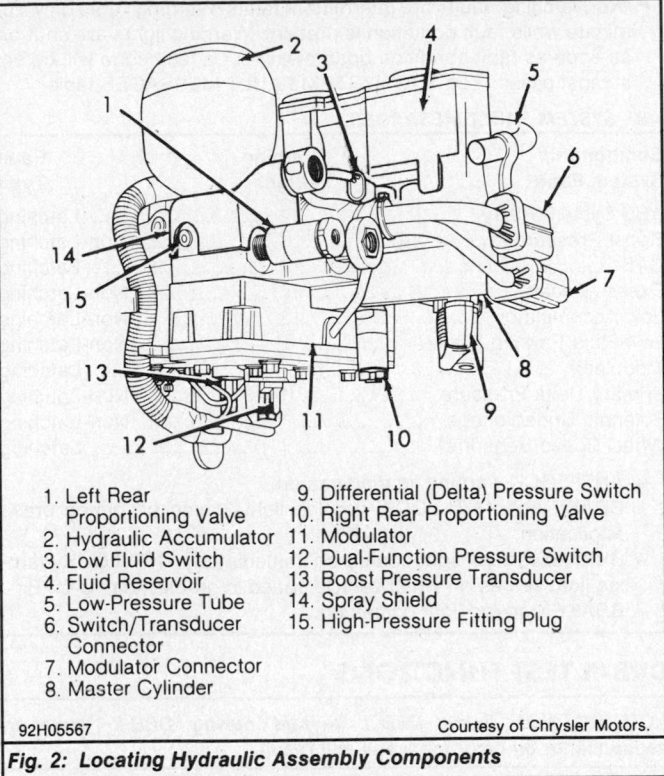

1. Left Rear Proportioning Valve
2. Hydraulic Accumulator
3. Low Fluid Switch
4. Fluid Reservoir
5. Low-Pressure Tube
6. Switch/Transducer Connector
7. Modulator Connector
8. Master Cylinder
9. Differential (Delta) Pressure Switch
10. Right Rear Proportioning Valve
11. Modulator
12. Dual-Function Pressure Switch
13. Boost Pressure Transducer
14. Spray Shield
15. High-Pressure Fitting Plug

92H05567   Courtesy of Chrysler Motors.

Fig. 2: Locating Hydraulic Assembly Components

ACCUMULATOR

Removal – Disconnect negative battery cable, or ensure ignition switch is off and key is removed. Depress brake pedal at least 40 times to depressurize brake system. Unscrew and remove accumulator from hydraulic assembly using oil filter wrench. See Fig. 2.

Installation – Install accumulator onto hydraulic assembly, ensuring "O" ring is fully seated into hydraulic assembly. Tighten accumulator to **35 ft. lbs. (48 N.m)**. Turn ignition on to allow hydraulic system to pressurize. Check for leaks at hydraulic assembly-to-accumulator fitting. Depress brake pedal at least 40 times to depressurize brake system. Open reservoir, and top off brake fluid.

PROPORTIONING VALVES

CAUTION: NEVER disassemble proportioning valves. Valves are NOT repairable and MUST be replaced if faulty.

Removal – **1)** Disconnect negative battery cable, or ensure ignition switch is off and key is removed. Depress brake pedal at least 40 times to depressurize brake system. Proportioning valves are located on bottom and sides of hydraulic assembly. See Fig. 2.

2) Remove air intake ducts and air cleaner assembly. Remove brake tube and fitting from proportioning valve to be replaced. If necessary, remove pressure and return lines from hydraulic assembly to remove proportioning valve.

Installation – Install proportioning valve on hydraulic assembly and tighten to **30 ft. lbs. (40 N.m)**. Install brake tube on proportioning valve and tighten to **11 ft. lbs. (15 N.m)**. Install pressure and return lines to hydraulic assembly. Tighten pressure line to hydraulic assembly to **12 ft. lbs. (16 N.m)**. Tighten return line to metal tube clamp to **10 INCH lbs. (1 N.m)**. Bleed affected brake line. See BLEEDING BRAKE SYSTEM.

CONTROLLER ANTI-LOCK BRAKE (CAB)

Removal & Installation – Disconnect negative battery cable, or ensure ignition switch is off and key is removed. Raise vehicle on

hoist. CAB is located on left front, inner frame rail, under battery tray. Remove transaxle oil cooler line routing retaining clip from CAB. Disconnect vehicle wiring harness 60-way connector from CAB. Remove 3 mounting bolts securing CAB to left frame rail, and remove CAB. To install, reverse removal procedure.

ANTI-LOCK WARNING LIGHT RELAY & ABS SYSTEM RELAY

Removal & Installation – ABS and ANTI-LOCK warning light relays are located in engine compartment, between battery and left inner fender panel. See Fig. 3. Remove relay mounting bracket bolt from fender panel. Remove relay harness connectors by disengaging connector locking tab and pulling each connector straight off relay. To install, reverse removal procedure.

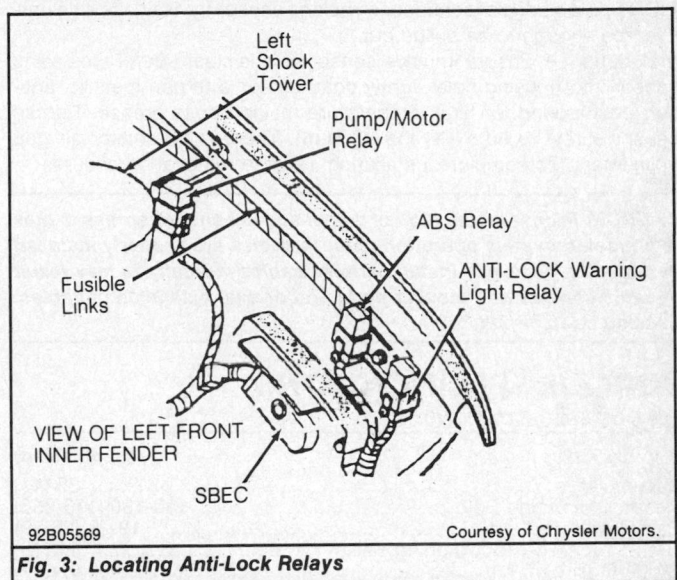

92B05569   Courtesy of Chrysler Motors.

Fig. 3: Locating Anti-Lock Relays

PUMP/MOTOR RELAY

Removal & Installation – Relay is located in engine compartment, on left inner fender panel, in front of strut tower. Remove pump/motor relay by pulling upward from connector. See Fig. 3. To install, push relay firmly into position in connector.

FRONT WHEEL SPEED SENSOR

Removal – **1)** Raise and securely support vehicle. Remove wheel and tire assembly. Remove screw and clip securing sensor harness cable to fender shield. Carefully pull sensor harness grommet from fender shield. DO NOT pull on sensor harness cable. Unplug sensor connector from engine compartment harness. Remove retainer clip from bracket slot on strut. Remove harness cable and grommets from retainer bracket slot.

2) On steering knuckle, remove sensor retaining screw. Carefully remove sensor by pulling straight out from steering knuckle. If sensor is stuck or frozen/corroded in place, DO NOT use pliers to remove. Use hammer and punch to LIGHTLY tap edge of sensor ear, rocking sensor from side to side until it is free enough to be pulled out.

Installation – Ensure knuckle sensor hole is clean. Before installing sensor into housing hole, lightly coat sensor with non-metallic, anti-seize compound, or high-temperature multipurpose grease. Tighten sensor screw to **60 INCH lbs. (7 N.m)**. There is no sensor air gap adjustment. To complete installation, reverse removal procedure.

CAUTION: Proper installation of wheel speed sensor harness cables is critical to system operation. Ensure cables are properly installed in retainers. Failure to install harness cables in retainers may result in cable contact with moving parts and/or over-extension of cables, causing an open circuit.

REAR WHEEL SPEED SENSOR

Removal – 1) Raise and support vehicle. Remove wheel and tire assembly. Remove sensor assembly grommet from underbody, and carefully pull harness cable through hole in underbody until connector is visible. Unplug connector from harness. Remove sensor cable grommet retaining screw from brake hose bracket, located just forward of trailing arm bushing.

2) Remove sensor cable retaining clip located on inboard side of trailing arm. Remove sensor cable wire fastener from rear brake hose bracket. Remove sensor assembly retainer nut from outboard axle housing.

3) Remove sensor head screw. Carefully remove sensor by pulling straight out from housing. If sensor is stuck or frozen/corroded in place, DO NOT use pliers to remove. Use hammer and punch to LIGHTLY tap edge of sensor ear, rocking sensor from side to side until it is free enough to be pulled out.

Installation – Ensure knuckle sensor hole is clean. Before installing sensor into housing hole, lightly coat sensor with non-metallic, anti-seize compound, or high-temperature multipurpose grease. Tighten sensor screw to **60 INCH lbs. (7 N.m)**. There is no sensor air gap adjustment. To complete installation, reverse removal procedure.

CAUTION: Proper installation of wheel speed sensor harness cables is critical to system operation. Ensure cables are properly installed in retainers. Failure to install harness cables in retainers may result in cable contact with moving parts and/or over-extension of cables, causing open circuit.

TORQUE SPECIFICATIONS

TORQUE SPECIFICATIONS

Application	Ft. Lbs. (N.m)
Accumulator	35 (47)
Adapter Mounting Bolt	130-190 (176-258)
Banjo Bolt	19-29 (26-39)
Brake Tube-To-Proportioning Valve	11 (15)
Guide Pins	25-35 (34-47)
Proportioning Valve	30 (40)

	INCH Lbs. (N.m)
Caliper Bleed Screw	80-170 (9-19)
Tubes-To-Fittings	115-175 (13-20)
Wheel Speed Sensor Screw	60 (7)

DIAGNOSIS & TESTING

SELF-DIAGNOSTIC SYSTEM

The Bendix-10 Anti-Lock Brake System (ABS) is controlled and monitored by the Controller Anti-Lock Brake (CAB). In addition to controlling ABS system, CAB has 3 useful diagnostic capabilities.

- Fault codes are stored in memory until they are erased by technician using Chrysler's Diagnostic Readout Box-II (DRB-II) or erased automatically by CAB after 50 ignition cycles.
- More than one fault code can be stored at a time. The number of fault codes stored is displayed by DRB-II. The number of ignition cycles since most recent fault was stored is also displayed.
- Using DRB-II, most functions of CAB and ABS can be accessed by technician for testing and diagnostic purposes.

Start-Up Cycle – The start-up cycle is an electrical check of ABS and ANTI-LOCK warning light relays, which takes place immediately after ignition switch is turned to ON position. During this check, the instrument cluster ANTI-LOCK warning light comes on and then goes out at completion of start-up cycle test. Test cycle lasts 1-2 seconds.

Drive-Off Cycle – The drive-off cycle takes place when vehicle reaches approximately 3 MPH for the first time after start-up cycle. When vehicle is first driven off after engine start-up, a series of rapid clicks from hydraulic assembly will be heard, confirming drive-off cycle operation.

Latching & Non-Latching Faults – Faults detected by CAB are identified as "latching" or "non-latching".

- "Latching" fault is stored in CAB memory and ABS is disabled until ignition switch is cycled again (reset). ANTI-LOCK warning light will remain lit, and ABS will remain disabled even if original fault has disappeared while driving.
- "Non-latching" faults are intermittent faults. Warning lights only illuminate while fault condition is present. Warning lights are shut off as soon as fault condition goes away, but a fault code will be set in most cases. See ABS SYSTEM FAULT MESSAGES table.

ABS SYSTEM FAULT MESSAGES

Component/ System Fault	Warning Light	Fault Type
ABS System Relay	1	Latching
Boost Pressure	2	Non-Latching
CAB	1	Latching
Excess Decay	1	Non-Latching
Low Accumulator	2	Non-Latching
Low Fluid/Parking Brake	3	Non-Latching
Modulator	1	Latching
Primary/Delta Pressure	4	Non-Latching
Solenoid Undervoltage	1	Non-Latching
Wheel Speed Sensor(s)	1	Latching

1 – ANTI-LOCK warning light comes on.
2 – BRAKE and ANTI-LOCK warning lights come on during brake application.
3 – BRAKE warning light comes on immediately; ANTI-LOCK warning light comes on when vehicle speed is greater than 3 MPH.
4 – BRAKE warning light comes on.

DRB-II TEST FUNCTIONS

NOTE: DO NOT touch DRB-II keypad during DRB-II power-up sequence, or an error message will result.

Entering DRB-II Main Menu – **1)** Ensure ignition is off. Attach DRB-II to Chrysler Collision Detection (CCD) BUS diagnostic connector. Diagnostic connector is located under instrument cluster, left of steering column. See Fig. 4. Turn ignition switch to RUN position.

2) All DRB-II character positions will illuminate and copyright information will appear on screen for a few seconds. DRB-II main menu will appear after a few seconds. If DRB-II screen is blank or any error messages appear, refer to DRB-II PROBLEMS & ERROR MESSAGES.

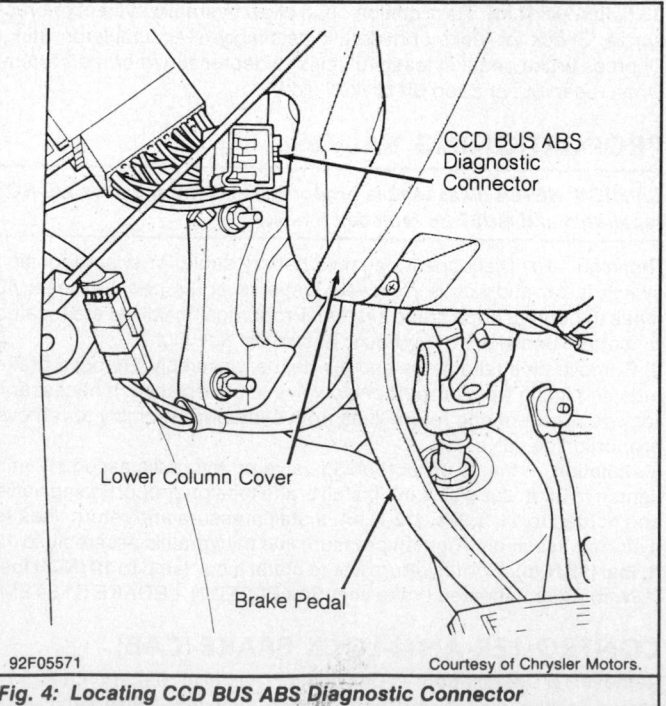

CCD BUS ABS Diagnostic Connector

Lower Column Cover

Brake Pedal

92F05571   Courtesy of Chrysler Motors.

Fig. 4: Locating CCD BUS ABS Diagnostic Connector

ABS Mode – **1)** To perform ABS self-diagnostic tests, DRB-II must be in ABS mode. Access DRB-II main menu. See ENTERING DRB-II MAIN MENU.

2) At DRB-II main menu, press "4" (SELECT SYSTEM) key to enter diagnostic test program. Press Down Arrow 3 times to change menu display.

3) Select "5" (ABS) key to enter ABS mode of DRB-II program. ABS menu will appear after a few seconds. Select ABS type. Screen will display a partial menu of DRB-II test categories for ABS. Press Down Arrow 3 times to view rest of menu.

4) The following test functions can be accessed from the ABS menu: SYSTEM TESTS, READ FAULTS, STATE DISPLAY, ACTUATOR TESTS and ADJUSTMENTS.

- **SYSTEM TESTS** – This function is not available in the ABS diagnostic program.
- **READ FAULTS** – This function allows user to read fault codes.
- **STATE DISPLAY** – This function allows user to read states or values of a variety of sensors, inputs/outputs and components.
- **ACTUATOR TESTS** – This function allows user to activate various outputs, valves and hydraulics to verify proper operation.
- **ADJUSTMENTS** – This function allows user to erase fault codes.

VEHICLES TESTED Mode – **1)** This mode displays vehicle models covered by DRB-II cartridge. To enter this mode, access DRB-II main menu. See ENTERING DRB-II MAIN MENU.

2) At DRB-II menu, press "1" (VEHICLES TESTED) key. Press ENTER key. Screen will display vehicle models covered by cartridge for 5 seconds and then return to DRB-II main menu.

HOW TO USE Mode – Enter DRB-II main menu. See ENTERING DRB-II MAIN MENU. At DRB-II menu, press "2" (HOW TO USE) key. Press ENTER key. A series of screens will be displayed explaining function of DRB-II keys used to move through diagnostic program.

CONFIGURE Mode – **1)** This mode allows user to customize DRB-II display. For example, if metric system is more useful, simply select METRIC from the appropriate menu. All selections made under CONFIGURE mode will remain active until user changes selection.

2) Enter DRB-II main menu in order to access CONFIGURE mode. See ENTERING DRB-II MAIN MENU. At DRB-II main menu, press "3" (CONFIGURE) key. Press ENTER key. DRB-II will display CONFIGURE menu.

DRB-II Volt/Ohmmeter Mode – **1)** To access volt/ohmmeter mode of DRB-II, connect Red volt/ohmmeter test lead to Red port, located on top right of DRB-II.

NOTE: Because DRB-II is grounded through diagnostic connector, only one volt/ohmmeter test lead is required when using volt/ohmmeter mode. DRB-II volt/ohmmeter should only be used when required by self-diagnostic tests.

---

2) To access voltmeter, press VOLT/OHM key once. DRB-II is now in voltmeter mode. Touch test probe to connector or wire to be measured. Voltage reading will be displayed on DRB-II screen. When voltage testing is complete, press VOLT/OHM key 3 times to exit voltmeter mode.

3) To access ohmmeter, press VOLT/OHM key twice. DRB-II is now in ohmmeter mode. Touch test probe to connector or wire to be measured. Resistance reading will be displayed on DRB-II screen. When resistance testing is complete, press VOLT/OHM key twice to exit ohmmeter mode.

DRB-II Continuity Meter Mode – Press VOLT/OHM key 3 times to enter mode. Screen will display NO CONTINUITY message. Touch test probe to connector or wire to be measured. Reading will be displayed on DRB-II screen. When continuity testing is complete, press VOLT/OHM key once to exit continuity meter mode.

DRB-II PROBLEMS & ERROR MESSAGES

Blank Message Screen – **1)** Turn ignition off. Disconnect DRB-II, adapter cable and cartridge. Connect DRB-II to a different vehicle with equipment identical to vehicle being tested.

2) Access DRB-II main menu. If message screen is still blank, adapter cable or DRB-II is faulty. Substitute adapter cable with a known good cable to locate faulty component.

3) If message screen is not blank, DRB-II is functioning properly. If message screen is still blank, inspect diagnostic connector for proper wire placement, corrosion, damaged terminals or pushed-out pins. Repair if necessary.

4) If diagnostic connector is okay, use external voltmeter to measure voltage at Red wire of CCD BUS ABS diagnostic connector. CCD BUS ABS diagnostic connector is located under driver's side of instrument cluster. *See Fig. 4.*

5) If voltmeter reading at Red wire is at least 9 volts, repair open in CCD BUS ABS diagnostic connector Black/Light Green (ground) wire. If voltage is not at least 9 volts, repair open in Red wire to battery.

NO RESPONSE Message – **1)** Disconnect Controller Anti-Lock Brake (CAB) 60-pin connector. Inspect connector for proper wire placement, corrosion, damaged terminals or pushed out pins. Repair if necessary.

2) Select DRB-II in voltmeter mode. See DRB-II VOLT/OHMMETER MODE under DRB-II TEST FUNCTIONS. Probe cavity No. 60 of CAB 60-pin connector. *See Fig. 6.* If voltage is at least 9 volts, go to next step. If voltage is not at least 9 volts, repair open in Dark Blue or Dark Blue/White wire.

3) Place DRB-II in ohmmeter mode. See DRB-II VOLT/OHMMETER MODE under DRB-II TEST FUNCTIONS. Probe cavity No. 5 of CAB 60-pin connector. *See Fig. 6.* If resistance is less than 10 ohms, go to next step. If resistance is 10 ohms or more, repair open Black (ground) wire.

4) Disconnect DRB-II from CCD BUS ABS diagnostic connector. Inspect connector for proper wire placement, corrosion, damaged terminals or pushed out pins. Repair if necessary.

5) If diagnostic connector is okay, use an external ohmmeter to check resistance at White/Violet wire terminal of CCD BUS ABS diagnostic connector. *See Fig. 7.* If resistance is greater than 10 ohms, go to next step. If resistance is 10 ohms or less, repair short circuit to ground in White/Violet wire.

6) Using an external ohmmeter, check resistance at Orange wire terminal of CCD BUS ABS diagnostic connector. If resistance is greater than 10 ohms, go to next step. If resistance is 10 ohms or less, repair short circuit to ground in Orange wire.

7) Connect a jumper wire between ground and cavities No. 11 and 12 of CAB 60-pin connector. *See Fig. 6.* Use an external ohmmeter to check resistance at White/Violet wire terminal of CCD BUS ABS diagnostic connector. If resistance is less than 10 ohms, go to next step. If resistance is 10 ohms or more, repair open White/Violet wire.

8) With jumper wire still connected, use an external ohmmeter to check resistance at Orange wire terminal of CCD BUS ABS diagnostic connector. If resistance is less than 10 ohms, replace CAB. If resistance is 10 ohms or more, repair open Orange wire.

RAM TEST FAILURE Message – Replace DRB-II.

CARTRIDGE ERROR Message – Replace DRB-II diagnostic cartridge.

KEY PAD TEST FAILURE Message – Ensure fingers are off the keypad, and power-up DRB-II again. If error message returns, replace DRB-II.

HIGH BATTERY Or LOW BATTERY Message – Correct condition of vehicle battery, and reconnect DRB-II.

CONNECTOR IDENTIFICATION

CONNECTOR IDENTIFICATION DIRECTORY

Connector	Figure
ABS Boost Pressure Transducer	10
ABS Bulkhead Body Connector	15
ABS Dual-Function Pressure Switch	8
ABS Modulator	9
ABS Primary Pressure Transducer	10
ABS Pump/Motor	11
ABS Pump/Motor Relay	12
ABS Switch/Transducer	13
ABS Relay	5
ABS Wheel Speed Sensor	14
ANTI-LOCK Warning Light Relay	5
CCD BUS ABS Diagnostic Connector	7
Controller Anti-Lock Brake (CAB)	6

1992 BRAKES
Anti-Lock – Bendix-10 (Cont.)

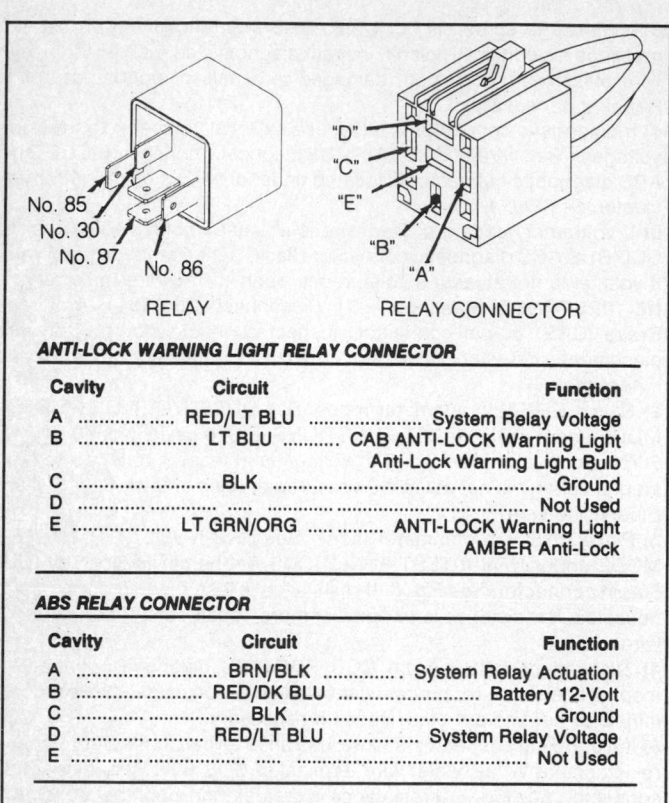

ANTI-LOCK WARNING LIGHT RELAY CONNECTOR

Cavity	Circuit	Function
A	RED/LT BLU	System Relay Voltage
B	LT BLU	CAB ANTI-LOCK Warning Light Anti-Lock Warning Light Bulb
C	BLK	Ground
D		Not Used
E	LT GRN/ORG	ANTI-LOCK Warning Light AMBER Anti-Lock

ABS RELAY CONNECTOR

Cavity	Circuit	Function
A	BRN/BLK	System Relay Actuation
B	RED/DK BLU	Battery 12-Volt
C	BLK	Ground
D	RED/LT BLU	System Relay Voltage
E		Not Used

92H05572   Courtesy of Chrysler Motors.

*Fig. 5: Identifying ANTI-LOCK Warning Light Relay &
ABS Relay Connector Terminals*

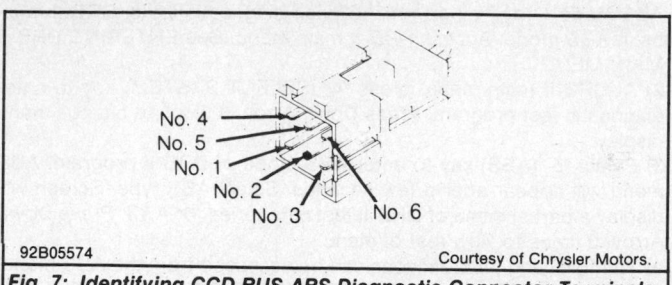

92B05574   Courtesy of Chrysler Motors.

Fig. 7: Identifying CCD BUS ABS Diagnostic Connector Terminals

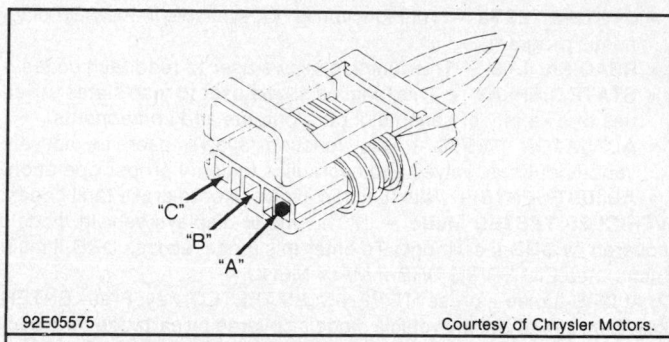

92E05575   Courtesy of Chrysler Motors.

*Fig. 8: Identifying ABS Dual-Function Pressure Switch
Connector Terminals*

CAB 60-PIN CONNECTOR

CAB 60-PIN CONNECTOR

Cavity	Circuit	Function
1	YEL/DK BLU	RR Wheel Sensor –
2	YEL	RR Wheel Sensor +
3	LT GRN/DK BLU	LR Wheel Sensor –
4	LT GRN	LR Wheel Sensor +
5	BLK	Ground
6	WHT/DK BLU	RF Wheel Sensor –
7	WHT	RF Wheel Sensor +
8	RED/DK BLU	LF Wheel Sensor –
9	RED	LF Wheel Sensor +
10	RED/BLK	Transducer Return (–)
11	WHT/VIO	Diagnostic (Data Input)
12	ORG	Diagnostic (Data Output)
13	WHT/TAN	Stop Light Signal
14	GRY/BLK	Brake Fluid Level/Park Brake
15	LT GRN/ORG	ANTI-LOCK Warning Light
16	GRY/RED	Low Fluid Output Sensor
17	RED	Low Accumulator

CAB 60-PIN CONNECTOR (Cont.)

Cavity	Circuit	Function
18	WHT/ORG	Primary Pressure/ Delta Pressure Signal
19	DK BLU	Boost Pressure
20 - 41		Not Used
42	BRN/WHT	LF Build Valve
43	DK GRN/BLK	LF Decay Valve
44		Not Used
45	WHT/LT GRN	LF Isolation Valve
46	BRN/RED	RF Build Valve
47	RED/LT BLU	Solenoid 12-Volt Feed
48	DK GRN/WHT	RF Decay Valve
49	WHT/TAN	RF Isolation Valve
50	RED/LT BLU	ABS Solenoid Feed
51	WHT/BLK	LR Isolation Valve
52	BRN/TAN	RR/LR Build Valve
53		Not Used
54	DK GRN/ORG	RR/LR Decay Valve
55	WHT/PNK	RR Isolation Valve
56		Not Used
57	BRN/BLK	ABS System Relay
58	GRY/LT BLU	Transducer Feed (5-Volt)
59		Not Used
60	DK BLU	Ignition Start/Run

92J05573   Courtesy of Chrysler Motors.

Fig. 6: Identifying CAB Connector Terminals

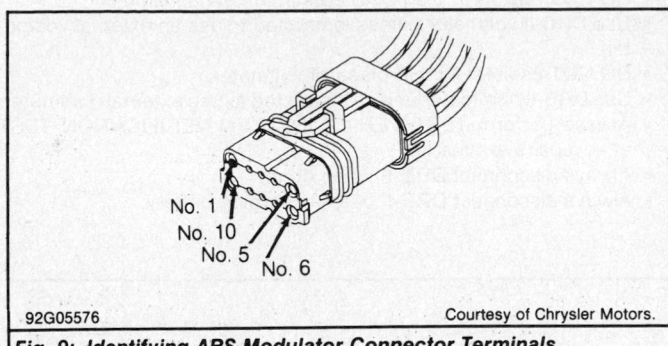

92G05576   Courtesy of Chrysler Motors.

Fig. 9: Identifying ABS Modulator Connector Terminals

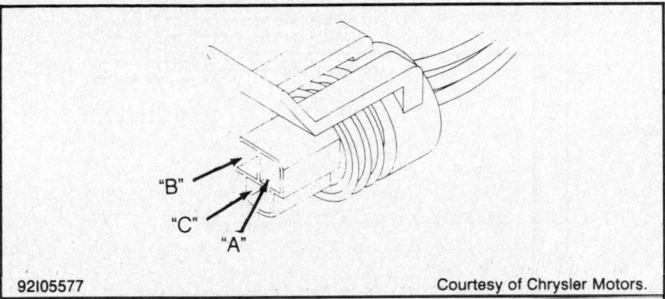

92I05577   Courtesy of Chrysler Motors.

Fig. 10: Identifying ABS Primary Pressure Transducer & Boost Pressure Transducer Connector Terminals

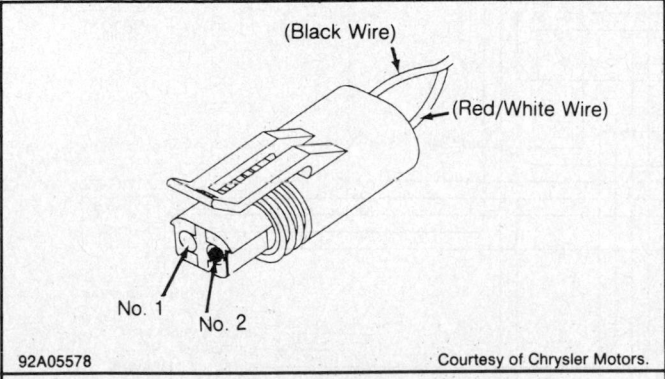

92A05578   Courtesy of Chrysler Motors.

Fig. 11: Identifying ABS Pump/Motor Connector Terminals

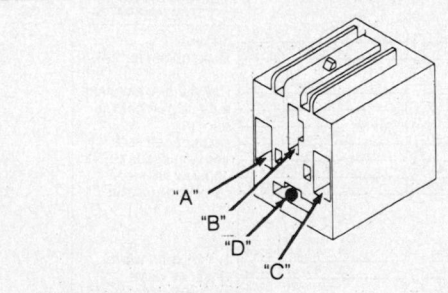

ABS PUMP/MOTOR RELAY

Cavity	Circuit	Function
A	DK BLU	System Relay Voltage
B	RED/DK GRN	Battery 12-Volt
C	GRY	Pump/Motor Ground CAB Controlled
D	BRN/WHT	Pump/Motor & CAB Motor Monitor

92C05579   Courtesy of Chrysler Motors.

Fig. 12: Identifying ABS Pump/Motor Relay Connector Terminals

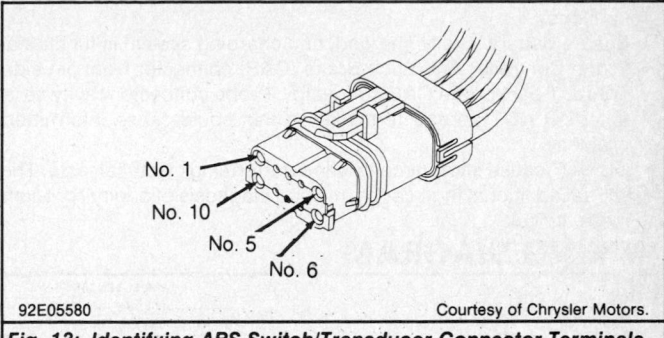

92E05580   Courtesy of Chrysler Motors.

Fig. 13: Identifying ABS Switch/Transducer Connector Terminals

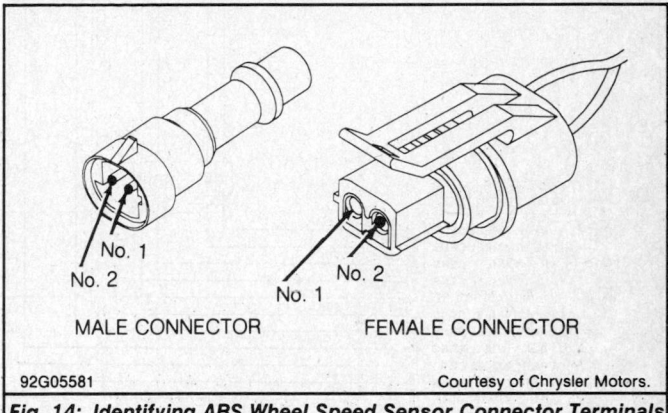

MALE CONNECTOR   FEMALE CONNECTOR

92G05581   Courtesy of Chrysler Motors.

Fig. 14: Identifying ABS Wheel Speed Sensor Connector Terminals

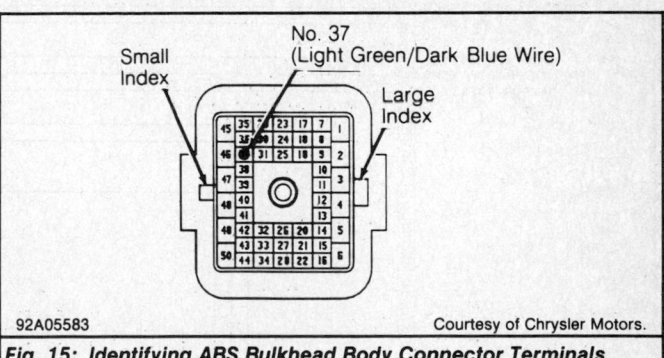

92A05583   Courtesy of Chrysler Motors.

Fig. 15: Identifying ABS Bulkhead Body Connector Terminals

DIAGNOSTIC PROCEDURE

Test Equipment Required – The following equipment is needed to perform self-diagnostic tests:

- Diagnostic Readout Box-II (DRB-II)
- 1992 Diagnostic Program Cartridge
- Body Diagnostic Cable
- High-Impedance VOM
- Jumper Wires

Diagnostic Procedure – Perform VISUAL INSPECTION test before proceeding with any self-diagnostic tests. ALWAYS start diagnosis with TEST 1A: READING FAULT MESSAGES. Starting with any other test may result in incorrect diagnosis.

NOTE: When diagnosing ABS system, DO NOT skip any steps in tests unless directed to do so, or incorrect diagnosis may result.

1992 BRAKES
Anti-Lock – Bendix-10 (Cont.)

Before proceeding with diagnosis, read and observe following precautions:

- Ensure battery is fully charged, and charging system is functional.
- Probe Controller Anti-Lock Brake (CAB) connector from pin side. DO NOT backprobe CAB connector. Probe connector cavity carefully. DO NOT spread terminal, as this could cause intermittent problem.
- DO NOT cause short circuits when performing electrical tests. This will set additional fault codes, making diagnosis of original problem more difficult.

- DO NOT unplug or plug CAB connector with ignition on.
- Use DRB-II voltmeter unless instructed to use an external voltmeter.
- DO NOT use test light in place of voltmeter.
- Use DRB-II ohmmeter unless instructed to use external ohmmeter.
- Always perform TEST VER-1A: SYSTEM VERIFICATION TEST after repairs are made.
- Always disconnect DRB-II when done.
- Always disconnect DRB-II before charging battery.

WIRING DIAGRAM

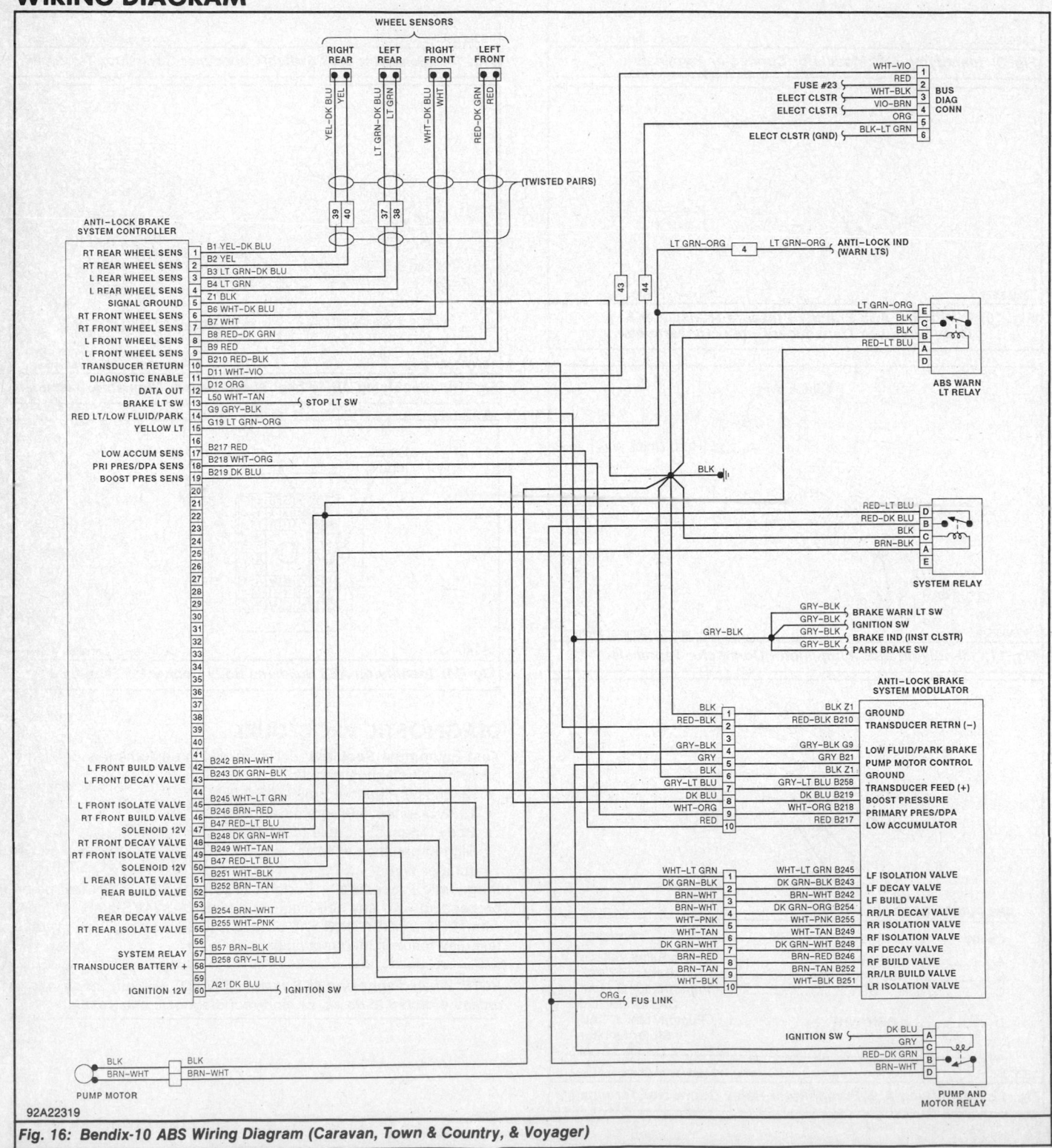

Fig. 16: Bendix-10 ABS Wiring Diagram (Caravan, Town & Country, & Voyager)

92A22319

SELF-DIAGNOSTIC TESTS

NOTE: In the following self-diagnostic tests, illustrations are courtesy of Chrysler Motors.

Perform VISUAL INSPECTION before proceeding with any self-diagnostic tests. ALWAYS begin diagnosis with TEST 1A. DO NOT proceed to any other self-diagnostic test without first performing TEST 1A.

VISUAL INSPECTION

Brake Fluid Level – Check reservoir fluid level AFTER depressing brake pedal 40 times to release brake pressure.
Hydraulic Assembly – Check hydraulic assembly for damaged or disconnected harness connectors and fluid leaks.
Power Distribution Center (PDC) & Relays – Ensure all ABS relays, located near SBEC, battery and power distribution center, are properly installed and secure.
Wheel Speed Sensors & Connectors – Check all 4 wheel speed sensors, connectors and harnesses for damage.
Brake Fluid Lines and Fittings – Check for leaks and damages.
Controller Anti-Lock Brake (CAB) – Check CAB for secure mounting to frame rail. Check CAB connector and harness for damage. Ensure CAB connector and harness are not corroded by battery leaks and acid corrosion.

TEST 1A
READING FAULT MESSAGES

Using DRB-II, read fault messages and perform appropriate test listed in FAULT MESSAGES. If DRB-II displays a blank message screen, perform TEST 2A. If DRB-II displays NO RESPONSE message, perform TEST 3A. If no fault message is displayed, go to TEST 24A. Also check SYMPTOM DIAGNOSIS table for problems described by customers, and perform appropriate test.

FAULT MESSAGES

Fault Message	Perform Test
ANTI-LOCK LIGHT	4A
ANTI-LOCK LIGHT RELAY	5A
CAB	7A
BOOST PRESSURE	6A
EXCESS DECAY	8A
LOW ACCUMULATOR	15A
LOW FLUID/PARKING BRAKE	16A
MODULATOR	17A
SOLENOID UNDERVOLTAGE	23A
SYSTEM RELAY	25A
PRIMARY PRESSURE/DELTA PRESSURE	18A
RR WHEEL SPEED SENSOR CONTINUITY	21A
LR WHEEL SPEED SENSOR CONTINUITY	13A
RF WHEEL SPEED SENSOR CONTINUITY	19A
LF WHEEL SPEED SENSOR CONTINUITY	11A
RR WHEEL SPEED SENSOR	22A
LR WHEEL SPEED SENSOR	14A
RF WHEEL SPEED SENSOR	20A
LF WHEEL SPEED SENSOR	12A

SYMPTOM DIAGNOSIS

Complaint	Perform Test
Hard Pedal/Clicking Noises	26A
Noisy Pump/Motor	27A
Scraping/Whirring Noise At Wheels	28A

TEST 2A
TESTING BLANK DRB-II MESSAGE SCREEN

NOTE: For connector terminal identification, see CONNECTOR IDENTIFICATION. For wiring diagram, see WIRING DIAGRAM.

1) Turn ignition off. Disconnect DRB-II. Turn ignition on. Using DVOM, measure voltage at terminal No. 2 (Red wire) of CCD BUS ABS diagnostic connector. *See Fig. 7.* If voltage is more than 10 volts, go to next step. If voltage is 10 volts or less, go to step 4).
2) Turn ignition off. Using DVOM, measure resistance at terminal No. 6 (Black/Light Green wire) of CCD BUS ABS diagnostic connector. If resistance is 5 ohms or less, go to next step. If resistance is more than 5 ohms, repair open in Black/Light Green wire. After repairs are complete, perform TEST VER-1A.
3) Test DRB-II on another vehicle. If DRB-II functions properly, replace DRB-II cable, and perform TEST VER-1A. If DRB-II still does not function properly, replace DRB-II.
4) Remove fuse No. 23 from Power Distribution Center (PDC). Inspect fuse. If fuse is open (blown), go to step 6). If fuse is good, using DVOM, measure voltage at power-feed side of fuse.
5) If voltage is greater than 10 volts, repair open in Red wire between fuse block and CCD BUS ABS diagnostic connector. If voltage is 10 volts or less, repair open in Red/White wire to fuse block. After repairs are complete, perform TEST VER-1A.
6) Ensure ignition is off. Using DVOM, measure resistance to ground at output side of fuse No. 23. If resistance is less than 5 ohms, repair short to ground in Red wire to fuse block. If resistance is 5 ohms or more, replace fuse. After repairs are complete, perform TEST VER-1A.

TEST 3A
TESTING DRB-II NO RESPONSE MESSAGE

NOTE: For connector terminal identification, see CONNECTOR IDENTIFICATION. For wiring diagram, see WIRING DIAGRAM.

1) Turn ignition off. Disconnect CAB 60-pin connector. *See Fig. 6.* Select DRB-II voltmeter mode. See DRB-II VOLT/OHMMETER MODE under DRB-II TEST FUNCTIONS. Turn ignition on. Measure voltage at CAB 60-pin connector terminal No. 60 (Dark Blue wire). If voltage is more than 9 volts, go to next step. If voltage is 9 volts or less, repair open in Dark Blue wire. After repairs are complete, perform TEST VER-1A.
2) Turn ignition off. Select DRB-II ohmmeter mode. See DRB-II VOLT/OHMMETER MODE under DRB-II TEST FUNCTIONS. Measure resistance at CAB 60-pin connector terminal No. 5 (Black wire). If resistance is less than 5 ohms, go to next step. If resistance is 5 ohms or more, repair open in Black wire to ground. After repairs are complete, perform TEST VER-1A.
3) Ensure ignition is off. Disconnect DRB-II. Using DVOM, measure resistance to ground at CCD BUS ABS diagnostic connector terminal No. 1 (White/Violet wire). *See Fig. 7.* If resistance is more than 5 ohms, go to next step. If resistance is 5 ohms or less, repair short to ground in White/Violet wire. After repairs are complete, perform TEST VER-1A.
4) Using DVOM, measure resistance to ground at CCD BUS ABS diagnostic connector terminal No. 5 (Orange wire). If resistance is less than 5 ohms, repair short to ground in Orange wire. After repairs are complete, perform TEST VER-1A. If resistance is 5 ohms or more, using 2 jumper wires, connect CAB 60-pin connector terminals No. 11 (White/Violet wire) and No. 12 (Orange wire) to ground.
5) Using DVOM, measure resistance to ground at CCD BUS ABS diagnostic connector terminal No. 1 (White/Violet wire). If resistance is 5 ohms or less, go to next step. If resistance is more than 5 ohms, repair open in White/Violet wire. After repairs are complete, perform TEST VER-1A.
6) Measure resistance to ground at CCD BUS ABS diagnostic connector terminal No. 5 (Orange wire). If resistance is more than 5 ohms, repair open in Orange wire. After repairs are complete, perform TEST VER-1A. If resistance is 5 ohms or less, disconnect jumper wires from CAB 60-pin connector terminals No. 11 and No. 12 to ground.
7) Using DVOM, check continuity at CCD BUS ABS diagnostic connector between terminal No. 1 (White/Violet wire) and terminal No. 5 (Orange wire). If resistance is 5 ohms or more, go to next step. If resistance is less than 5 ohms, White/Violet and Orange wires are shorted together. Locate and repair both wires as required. After repairs are complete, perform TEST VER-1A.
8) Turn ignition on. Using DVOM, measure voltage at CCD BUS ABS diagnostic connector terminal No. 1 (White/Violet wire). If there is no voltage, go to next step. If voltage exists, repair short to battery voltage in White/Violet wire. After repairs are complete, perform TEST VER-1A.
9) Measure voltage at terminal No. 5 (Orange wire) of same connector. If voltage is present, repair short to battery voltage in Orange wire. If there is no voltage, replace CAB. After repairs are complete, perform TEST VER-1A.

TEST 4A
ANTI-LOCK LIGHT FAULT

NOTE: For connector terminal identification, see CONNECTOR IDENTIFICATION. For wiring diagram, see WIRING DIAGRAM.

1) Turn ignition on. If ANTI-LOCK warning light is on, go to step **4)**. If ANTI-LOCK warning light is off, depress parking brake pedal. If PARK BRAKE light is on, go to next step. If PARK BRAKE light is off, repair open in ignition voltage circuit to ANTI-LOCK and PARK BRAKE light indicator bulbs.

2) Remove ANTI-LOCK warning light relay. *See Fig. 3.* Check connector terminals and repair if required. Connect jumper wire between ANTI-LOCK warning light relay connector terminal "E" and ground. *See Fig. 5.* If ANTI-LOCK warning light illuminates, system is operating properly at this time. After repairs are complete, perform TEST VER-1A.

3) If ANTI-LOCK warning light does not illuminate, remove ANTI-LOCK warning light bulb from instrument cluster. If bulb is faulty, replace it. If bulb is good, repair open in Light Green/Orange wire between ANTI-LOCK warning light relay and bulb.

4) Remove ANTI-LOCK warning light relay. *See Fig. 3.* Check connector terminals and repair if required. If ANTI-LOCK warning light remains on, repair short to ground in Light Green/White wire. After repairs are complete, perform TEST VER-1A. If ANTI-LOCK warning light goes out, reinstall ANTI-LOCK warning light relay and perform TEST 5A.

TEST 5A
ANTI-LOCK LIGHT RELAY FAULT

NOTE: For connector terminal identification, see CONNECTOR IDENTIFICATION. For wiring diagram, see WIRING DIAGRAM.

1) Using DRB-II, actuate ABS relay output test. While performing ABS relay output test, select DRB-II voltmeter mode. See DRB-II VOLT/OHMMETER MODE under DRB-II TEST FUNCTIONS. DO NOT stop output test. Using DRB-II probe, backprobe terminal "A" (Red/Light Blue wire) at warning light relay connector. *See Fig. 7.*

2) If voltage does not toggle between zero and 12 volts, go to TEST 25A. If voltage toggles between zero and 12 volts, and ANTI-LOCK warning light blinks, go to step **8)**. If voltage toggles between zero and 12 volts, but ANTI-LOCK warning light does not blink, go to next step.

3) Swap ANTI-LOCK warning light relay with ABS relay. Using DRB-II, actuate ABS relay output test again. While performing ABS relay output test, select DRB-II voltmeter mode. DO NOT stop output test. Using DRB-II probe, backprobe ABS warning light relay connector terminal "A" (Red/Light Blue wire).

4) If voltage does not toggle between zero and 12 volts, replace ANTI-LOCK warning light relay, which is now in ABS relay connector. After repairs are complete, perform TEST VER-1A. If voltage toggles between zero and 12 volts, go to next step.

5) Remove relay from ANTI-LOCK warning light relay connector. Using DRB-II voltmeter probe, probe ANTI-LOCK warning light relay connector terminal "A" (Red/Light Blue wire). If voltage is more than 9.5 volts, but does not toggle, repair open in Red/Light Blue wire between the 2 relays. If voltage is more than 9.5 volts and toggles, select DRB-II ohmmeter mode. See DRB-II VOLT/OHMMETER MODE under DRB-II TEST FUNCTIONS.

6) Using DRB-II ohmmeter probe, probe ANTI-LOCK warning light relay connector terminal "B" (Black wire). *See Fig. 5.* If resistance is 5 ohms or more, repair open in Black wire between relay connector and ground. Perform TEST VER-1A. If resistance is less than 5 ohms, go to next step.

7) Probe ANTI-LOCK warning light relay connector terminal "C" (Black wire). If resistance is 5 ohms or more, repair open in Black wire between relay connector and ground. If resistance is less than 5 ohms, go to next step.

8) Turn ignition off. Disconnect CAB 60-pin connector. Check connector terminals. Clean and repair connector if necessary. Remove ANTI-LOCK warning light relay. *See Fig. 3.* Using DRB-II ohmmeter mode, probe ANTI-LOCK warning light relay connector terminal "E" (Light Green/Orange wire). *See Fig. 5.* If resistance is less than 5 ohms, repair short to ground in Light Green/Orange wire. Perform TEST VER-1A. If resistance is 5 ohms or more, go to next step.

9) Using jumper wire, connect terminals "B" and "E" of ANTI-LOCK warning light relay connector. Using DRB-II, probe terminal No. 15 (Light Green/Orange wire) of CAB 60-pin connector. *See Fig. 6.* If resistance is 5 ohms or more, repair open in Light Green/Orange wire. If resistance is less than 5 ohms, replace CAB. Perform TEST VER-1A.

TEST 6A
BOOST PRESSURE FAULT

NOTE: For connector terminal identification, see CONNECTOR IDENTIFICATION. For wiring diagram, see WIRING DIAGRAM.

1) Turn ignition on. Using DRB-II, read boost pressure sensor voltage. If voltage is more than 4 volts, perform TEST 6E. If voltage is zero volt, go to step **4)**. If voltage is 0-4 volts, depress brake pedal to floor and hold.

2) Using DRB-II, read boost pressure sensor voltage. If voltage is less than 1.95 volts, perform TEST 9A. If voltage is 1.95 volts or more, monitor primary and boost pressures on DRB-II while varying brake pedal pressure. Compare boost and primary pressure voltage readings.

3) If boost pressure voltage is less than primary pressure voltage by more than .6 volt, perform TEST 6B. If boost pressure voltage is not less than primary pressure voltage by more than .6 volt, ABS is operating properly. Perform TEST VER-1A.

4) Disconnect switch/transducer connector. *See Fig. 2.* Check connector terminals, and clean and repair as necessary. Connect jumper wire between terminals No. 7 (Gray/Light Blue wire) and No. 8 (Dark Blue wire) of switch/transducer female connector. *See Fig. 13.* If primary pressure voltage is 4.5 volts or less, perform TEST 6C. If primary pressure voltage is more than 4.5 volts, disconnect jumper wire.

5) Select DRB-II ohmmeter mode. See DRB-II VOLT/OHMMETER MODE under DRB-II TEST FUNCTIONS. Probe terminal No. 8 (Dark Blue wire) in switch/transducer female connector. If resistance is 5 ohms or more, perform TEST 6D. If resistance is 5 ohms or less, disconnect boost pressure transducer connector. *See Fig. 2.*

6) Using DRB-II, probe terminal No. 8 (Dark Blue wire) in switch/transducer female connector. If resistance is less than 5 ohms, repair short to ground in Dark Blue wire. If resistance is 5 ohms or more, replace boost pressure transducer. After repairs are complete, perform TEST VER-1A.

TEST 6B
BOOST PRESSURE FAULT

NOTE: For connector terminal identification, see CONNECTOR IDENTIFICATION. For wiring diagram, see WIRING DIAGRAM.

1) Using DRB-II, read boost pressure voltage with brake pedal released. If voltage is not .15-.45 volt, replace boost pressure transducer. Perform TEST VER-1A. If voltage is .15-.45 volt, read primary pressure voltage with brake pedal released.

2) If voltage is not .15-.45 volt, replace primary pressure transducer. Perform TEST VER-1A. If voltage is .15-.45 volt, inspect hydraulic assembly for leaks and repair if necessary. After repairs are complete, perform TEST VER-1A. If no leaks are found, turn off ignition.

3) Release accumulator pressure by pumping brake pedal at least 40 times. Connect Pressure Gauge (MST-6163), Adapter (MST-6505) and Fitting (MST-6491A) to hydraulic assembly. *See Fig. 2 or 6B.* Turn ignition on. Allow pump/motor to re-pressurize fluid system and then shut itself off.

92D22320

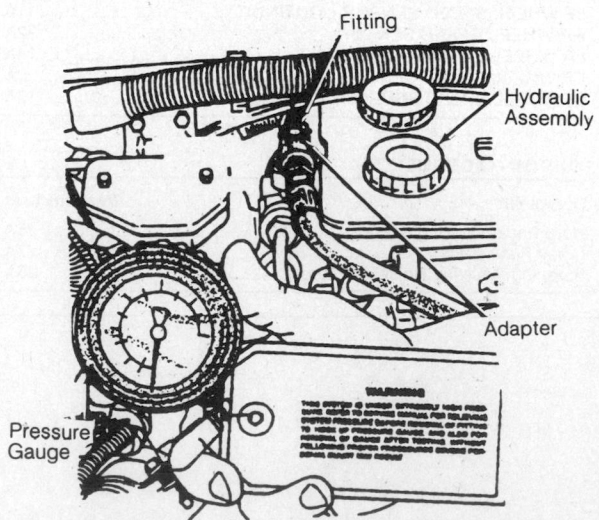

Fig. 6B: Installing Brake Fluid Pressure Gauge & Adapters

TEST 6B (Cont.)

4) Depress brake pedal until gauge pressure indicates 1000 psi and hold pedal at that pressure. Using DRB-II, read boost pressure sensor voltage. If voltage is not 2.03-2.33 volts, replace boost pressure transducer. After repairs are complete, perform TEST VER-1A. If voltage is 2.03-2.33 volts, go to next step.

5) Using DRB-II, read primary pressure sensor voltage. If voltage is not 2.03-2.33 volts, replace primary pressure transducer. If voltage is 2.03-2.33 volts, ABS is operating properly at this time. After repairs are complete, perform TEST VER-1A.

TEST 6C
BOOST PRESSURE FAULT

NOTE: For connector terminal identification, see CONNECTOR IDEN-TIFICATION. For wiring diagram, see WIRING DIAGRAM.

1) Disconnect jumper wire from switch/transducer connector. Disconnect CAB 60-pin connector. Using DRB-II ohmmeter mode, probe terminal No. 8 (Dark Blue wire) of switch/transducer female connector. See Fig. 13. If resistance is less than 5 ohms, repair short to ground in Dark Blue wire. If resistance is 5 ohms or more, connect jumper wire between terminal No. 19 of CAB 60-pin connector and ground. See Fig. 6.

2) Using DRB-II ohmmeter, probe terminal No. 8 (Dark Blue wire) of switch/transducer female connector. If resistance is 5 ohms or more, repair open in Dark Blue wire. After repairs are complete, perform TEST VER-1A. If resistance is less than 5 ohms, go to next step.

3) Probe terminal No. 7 (Gray/Light Blue wire) of switch/transducer female connector. If resistance is less than 5 ohms, repair short to ground in Gray/Light Blue wire. After repairs are complete, perform TEST VER-1A. If resistance is 5 ohms or more, connect jumper wire between terminal No. 58 of CAB 60-pin connector and ground.

4) Using DRB-II ohmmeter, probe terminal No. 7 (Gray/Light Blue wire) of switch/transducer female connector. If resistance is 5 ohms or more, repair open in Gray/Light Blue wire. If resistance is less than 5 ohms, replace CAB. After repairs are complete, perform TEST VER-1A.

TEST 6D
BOOST PRESSURE FAULT

NOTE: For connector terminal identification, see CONNECTOR IDEN-TIFICATION. For wiring diagram, see WIRING DIAGRAM.

1) Disconnect boost pressure transducer connector. See Fig. 2. Connect jumper wires from ground to terminal "B" (Gray/Light Blue wire) and terminal "C" (Dark Blue wire) of boost pressure transducer connector. See Fig. 10.

2) Using DRB-II ohmmeter mode, probe terminal No. 8 (Dark Blue wire) of switch/transducer male connector. If resistance is 5 ohms or more, repair open in Dark Blue wire. After repairs are complete, perform TEST VER-1A. If resistance is less than 5 ohms, using DRB-II, probe terminal No. 7 (Gray/Light Blue wire) of switch/transducer male connector.

3) If resistance is 5 ohms or more, repair open in Gray/Light Blue wire. If resistance is less than 5 ohms, replace boost pressure transducer. After repairs are complete, perform TEST VER-1A.

TEST 6E
BOOST PRESSURE FAULT

NOTE: For connector terminal identification, see CONNECTOR IDEN-TIFICATION. For wiring diagram, see WIRING DIAGRAM.

1) Disconnect CAB 60-pin and boost pressure transducer connectors. Check and clean connector terminals, and repair as necessary. Connect jumper wire between ground and terminal "A" (Red/Black wire) of boost pressure transducer connector. See Fig. 10.

2) Using DRB-II ohmmeter mode, probe terminal No. 10 (Red/Black wire) of CAB connector. See Fig. 6. If resistance is less than 5 ohms, go to step 4). If resistance is 5 ohms or more, disconnect switch/transducer connector. Check and clean connector terminals, and repair as necessary. Using DRB-II ohmmeter, probe terminal No. 2 (Red/Black wire) of male switch/transducer connector.

3) If resistance is less than 5 ohms, repair open in Red/Black wire between CAB and switch/transducer male connector. If resistance is 5 ohms or more, repair open in Red/Black wire between switch/transducer male connector and boost pressure transducer connector. After repairs are complete, perform TEST VER-1A.

TEST 6E (Cont.)

4) Using DVOM, check resistance between terminals "B" and "C" of boost pressure transducer on bottom of hydraulic assembly. See Fig. 10. If resistance is less than 5 ohms, replace boost pressure transducer. If resistance is 5 ohms or more, replace CAB. After repairs are complete, perform TEST VER-1A.

TEST 7A
CAB FAULT

1) Using DRB-II, erase faults. Turn ignition off and then on. Using DRB-II, read fault messages. If DRB-II displays CAB FAULT, replace CAB. After repairs are complete, perform TEST VER-1A. If DRB-II displays any other fault messages, perform TEST 1A. If DRB-II does not display any other fault messages, go to next step.

2) Road test vehicle for a minimum of 5 minutes at speeds greater than 3 MPH. Using DRB-II, read fault messages. If DRB-II displays CAB FAULT, replace CAB. After repairs are complete, perform TEST VER-1A. If DRB-II displays any other fault messages, perform TEST 1A. If DRB-II does not display any other fault messages, ABS is operating properly at this time. Perform TEST VER-1A.

TEST 8A
EXCESS DECAY VALVE FAULT

1) Using DRB-II, erase faults. Inspect vehicle tires for excessive wear or wrong size. Replace if necessary. After repairs are complete, perform TEST VER-1A. If vehicle tires are okay, go to next step.

2) Ensure vehicle brakes are not dragging. If brakes are dragging, repair brakes as necessary, and perform TEST VER-1A. If brakes are not dragging, perform several ABS stops on clean, dry pavement.

3) Using DRB-II, read fault messages. If DRB-II displays EXCESS DECAY message, go to next step. If EXCESS DECAY message is not displayed, go to step 5).

4) Inspect tone wheels for damage (chipping or cracking). If tone wheels are okay, perform TEST 17A. Replace tone wheels if damaged. After repairs are complete, perform TEST VER-1A.

5) Check DRB-II for other fault messages. If other fault messages are displayed, perform TEST 1A. If there are no fault messages, ABS is operating properly at this time. Perform TEST VER-1A.

TEST 9A
HYDRAULIC PRESSURE PERFORMANCE TEST

NOTE: For connector terminal identification, see CONNECTOR IDEN-TIFICATION. For wiring diagram, see WIRING DIAGRAM.

1) Turn off ignition. Reconnect all connectors. Brake system is under extreme pressure. Relieve ABS pressure by depressing brake pedal at least 40 times. Remove high-pressure fitting near bottom of accumulator. See Fig. 2.

2) Connect Pressure Gauge (MST-6163), Adapter (MST-6505) and Fitting (MST-6491A) to accumulator assembly. See Fig. 6B. Turn ignition on. Observe pressure gauge for pressure build rate, and note length of time to transition points.

3) If pressure exceeds 400 psi in 2 minutes, go to next step. If pressure does not exceed 400 psi in 2 minutes, go to TEST 9C.

4) If pressure rises very quickly to 460 psi, go to next step. If pressure does not rise quickly to 460 psi, go to TEST 9B.

5) If pressure build rate slows down after reaching 460 psi, go to next step. If pressure build rate does not slow down after reaching 460 psi, replace pump/motor assembly. After repairs are complete, perform TEST VER-1A.

6) If pressure rises very slowly after reaching 1000 psi, go to next step. If pressure does not rise slowly after reaching 1000 psi, replace accumulator. After repairs are complete, perform TEST VER-1A.

7) If pump/motor stopped running before pressure reaches 1800 psi, replace dual-function pressure switch. If pressure does not reach 1800 psi, go to TEST 9D. If pressure reaches 1800 psi, check pump/motor operation at pressure greater than 2200 psi. If pump/motor keeps running at pressures greater than 2200 psi, replace dual-function pressure switch.

8) If pump/motor stops running before pressure reaches 2200 psi, pump brake pedal while observing pressure gauge. If pump/motor does not start up at about 1600 psi, replace dual-function switch. If pump/motor starts up at about 1600 psi, ABS is operating properly at this time. After repairs are complete, perform TEST VER-1A.

TEST 9B
HYDRAULIC PRESSURE PERFORMANCE TEST

1) Observe pressure gauge. If pressure build rate does not change noticeably at 460 psi, stop test and replace pump/motor assembly. If pressure build rate changes noticeably at 460 psi, but not at 1000 psi, stop test and replace accumulator. After repairs are complete, perform TEST VER-1A.

2) If pressure build rate changes noticeably at 460 psi and 1000 psi, turn ignition off when pressure is at least 1200 psi. Observe pressure gauge for pressure drop. If pressure drops more than 50 psi in one minute, go to TEST 9D. If pressure does not drop more than 50 psi in one minute, ABS is operating properly at this time. After repairs are complete, perform TEST VER-1A.

TEST 9C
HYDRAULIC PRESSURE PERFORMANCE TEST

Turn ignition off. Release accumulator pressure by pumping brake pedal at least 40 times. Depress brake pedal and hold it down. Observe pressure gauge, and turn ignition on. If pressure exceeds 400 psi in 2 minutes, replace hydraulic assembly. If pressure does not exceed 400 psi in 2 minutes, check for hydraulic leaks and repair if necessary. If there are no leaks, perform TEST 9D. After repairs are complete, perform TEST VER-1A.

TEST 9D
HYDRAULIC PRESSURE PERFORMANCE TEST

1) Turn ignition off. Release accumulator pressure by pumping brake pedal at least 40 times. Connect internal leak tester to high-pressure hose and actuator assembly per tester instructions. Open shutoff valve on tester.

2) Turn ignition on. Allow pump/motor to build to its highest steady pressure or until pump/motor turns off. If pressure rises until pump/motor shuts off, go to step **5)**. If pressure does not rise until pump shuts off, close shutoff valve on tester. Observe pressure gauges at actuator assembly and high-pressure line.

3) If pressure of high-pressure hose quickly exceeds highest steady pressure and continues rising, open shutoff valve. Replace complete hydraulic assembly. After repairs are complete, perform TEST VER-1A.

4) If pressure of high-pressure hose does not quickly exceed highest steady pressure, replace pump/motor assembly. After repairs are complete, perform TEST VER-1A.

5) Close shutoff valve. Turn ignition off. Observe pressure gauges at actuator assembly and high-pressure line. If pressure of high pressure hose drops 10 seconds after shutting off valve, replace pump/motor assembly. If pressure of high-pressure hose does not drop, but actuator pressure drops, replace complete hydraulic assembly. After repairs are complete, perform TEST VER-1A.

6) If high-pressure hose and actuator pressures do not drop after valve has been shut off for 10 seconds, open shutoff valve on tester. Turn ignition on. Pump brake pedal 10 times. Allow pump to build pressure and then shut off.

7) Close shutoff valve on tester. Turn ignition off. Observe pressure gauges at actuator assembly and high-pressure line. If after 10 seconds of shutting off valve, pressure at high-pressure hose drops, replace pump/motor assembly. If pressure at high pressure hose does not drop, but actuator pressure drops, replace complete hydraulic assembly. After repairs are complete, perform TEST VER-1A.

8) If after 10 seconds of shutting off valve, high-pressure hose and actuator pressures do not drop, ABS is operating properly at this time. After repairs are complete, perform TEST VER-1A.

TEST 10A
HYDRAULIC PUMP/MOTOR CIRCUIT TEST

NOTE: For connector terminal identification, see CONNECTOR IDENTIFICATION. For wiring diagram, see WIRING DIAGRAM.

NOTE: Perform TEST 15A before proceeding.

1) Perform visual inspection of pump/motor wiring harness and connectors. See Fig. 10A. Repair damaged harness. If there is no visual damage, remove pump/motor relay. See Fig. 3.

TEST 10A (Cont.)

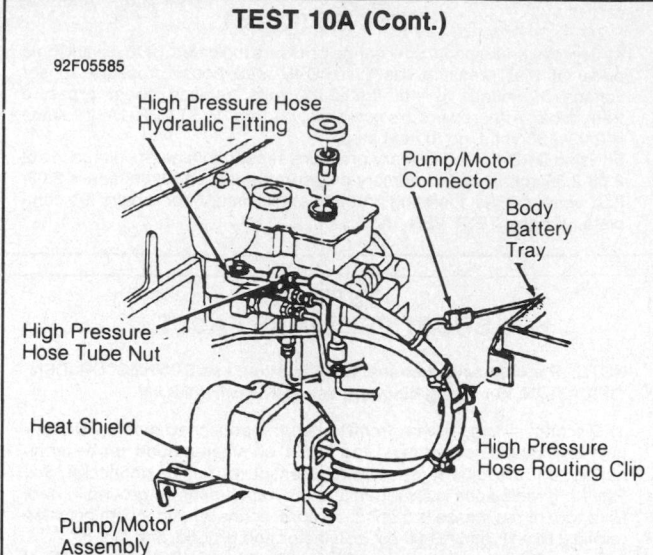

92F05585

Fig. 10A: Identifying Pump/Motor Assembly, Harness & Connectors

2) Using DRB-II ohmmeter mode, probe terminal "B" of pump/motor relay connector. See Figs. 3 and 12. If resistance is less than 5 ohms, repair short to ground in Red/Dark Green wire. Replace fuse cartridge/fuse link. After repairs are complete, perform TEST VER-1A. If resistance is 5 ohms or more, go to next step.

3) Disconnect pump/motor 2-pin connector. See Fig. 10A. Pump/motor 2-pin connector is tied to high-pressure line about 6-10 inches from hydraulic assembly. Check and clean connector terminals; repair if necessary.

4) Using DRB-II, probe terminal "D" (Brown/White wire) of pump/motor relay connector. See Figs. 3 and 12. If resistance is less than 5 ohms, repair short to ground in Brown/White wire, and replace fuse cartridge/fusible link. After repairs are complete, perform TEST VER-1A. If resistance is 5 ohms or more, go to next step.

5) Inspect Red wire from ABS pump/motor. If Red wire is shorted to ground, repair wire and replace fuse cartridge/fusible link. After repairs are complete, perform TEST VER-1A. If Red wire is not shorted to ground, turn ignition off. Replace fuse cartridge/fusible link. See Fig. 3. Reconnect pump/motor 2-pin connector. Reinstall pump/motor relay.

6) Release accumulator pressure by pumping brake pedal at least 40 times. Turn ignition on. Check fuse cartridge/fusible link. If fuse cartridge/fusible link is blown, replace pump/motor assembly. If fuse cartridge/fusible link is not blown, ABS is operating properly at this time. After repairs are complete, perform TEST VER-1A.

TEST 10B
HYDRAULIC PUMP/MOTOR CIRCUIT TEST

NOTE: For connector terminal identification, see CONNECTOR IDENTIFICATION. For wiring diagram, see WIRING DIAGRAM.

1) Turn ignition off. Disconnect switch/transducer connector. See Fig. 2. Check and clean connector terminals; repair as necessary. Release accumulator pressure by pumping brake pedal at least 40 times.

2) Turn ignition on. Connect jumper wire between switch/transducer female connector terminal No. 1 (Gray wire) and ground. See Fig. 13. DO NOT leave jumper wire connected for more than 10 seconds. If pump/motor runs when jumper wire is connected, immediately remove jumper wire and repair intermittent condition. Perform TEST 10C.

3) If pump/motor does not run when jumper wire is connected, disconnect pump/motor 2-pin connector. See Fig. 10A. Pump/motor 2-pin connector is tied to high-pressure hose about 6-10 inches from hydraulic assembly. Select DRB-II voltmeter mode. See DRB-II VOLT/OHMMETER MODE under DRB-II TEST FUNCTIONS. Probe pump/motor 2-pin connector terminal No. 2 (Brown/White wire). See Fig. 11.

4) If voltage is more than 9 volts, perform TEST 10D. If voltage is 9 volts or less, raise ABS pump/motor relay slightly, ensuring there is still contacts between relay terminals and connector terminals. Using DRB-II voltmeter mode, probe terminal "A" (Dark Blue wire) of relay. If voltage

TEST 10B (Cont.)

is 9 volts or less, repair open in Dark Blue wire between relay and ignition switch. If voltage is more than 9 volts, go to next step.

5) Probe terminal "B" of pump/motor relay. If voltage is 9 volts or less, go to step 8). If voltage is more than 9 volts, remove pump/motor relay from connector. See Fig. 3. Using DRB-II ohmmeter mode, probe terminal "C" (Gray wire) of pump/motor relay connector. If resistance is 5 ohms or more, repair open in Gray wire. If resistance is less than 5 ohms, go to next step.

6) Connect jumper wire between terminal No. 2 of pump/motor connector and ground. See Fig. 11. Using DRB-II ohmmeter mode, probe terminal "D" (Brown/White wire) of pump/motor relay connector. See Figs. 3 and 12. If resistance is 5 ohms or more, repair open in Brown/White wire. After repairs are complete, perform TEST VER-1A. If resistance is less than 5 ohms, reconnect switch/transducer connector and install pump/motor relay.

7) Using DRB-II, actuate pump/motor relay. Using DRB-II voltmeter mode, probe terminal No. 2 (Brown/White wire) of pump/motor 2-pin connector. If voltage does not toggle between zero and 9 volts, replace pump/motor relay. If voltage toggles between zero and 9 volts, ABS is operating properly at this time. After repairs are complete, perform TEST VER-1A. Repair open in Red/Dark Green wire. After repairs are complete, perform TEST VER-1A.

TEST 10C
HYDRAULIC PUMP/MOTOR CIRCUIT TEST

NOTE: For connector terminal identification, see CONNECTOR IDENTIFICATION. For wiring diagram, see WIRING DIAGRAM.

1) Disconnect jumper wire in switch/transducer connector. Reconnect switch/transducer connector. Disconnect dual-function pressure switch connector. Check and clean connector terminals; repair if necessary.

2) Connect jumper wire between terminal "B" (Gray wire) and terminal "A" (Black wire) of dual-function pressure switch connector. See Fig. 8. DO NOT leave jumper wire connected for more than 10 seconds. If pump/motor does not run with jumper wire connected, go to next step. If pump/motor runs with jumper wire connected, replace dual-function pressure switch. After repairs are complete, perform TEST VER-1A.

3) Using DRB-II ohmmeter mode, probe terminal "A" (Black wire) of dual-function pressure switch connector. If resistance is 5 ohms or more, repair open in Black wire. If resistance is less than 5 ohms, repair open in Gray wire between dual-function pressure switch and switch/transducer connectors. After repairs are complete, perform TEST VER-1A.

TEST 10D
HYDRAULIC PUMP/MOTOR CIRCUIT TEST

NOTE: For connector terminal identification, see CONNECTOR IDENTIFICATION. For wiring diagram, see WIRING DIAGRAM.

Select DRB-II ohmmeter mode. See DRB-II VOLT/OHMMETER MODE under DRB-II TEST FUNCTIONS. Probe terminal No. 1 (Black wire) of pump/motor connector. See Fig. 11. If resistance is less than 5 ohms, replace pump/motor assembly. If resistance is 5 ohms or more, repair open in Black wire. After repairs are complete, perform TEST VER-1A.

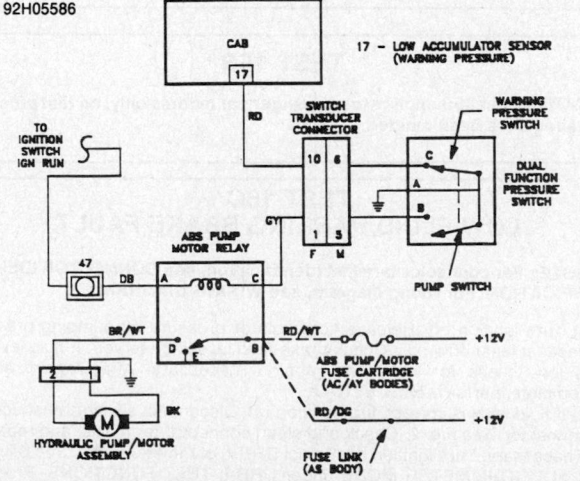

92H05586

Fig. 10D: Hydraulic Pump/Motor Circuit

TEST 11A
LEFT FRONT WHEEL SPEED SENSOR CONTINUITY FAULT

NOTE: For connector terminal identification, see CONNECTOR IDENTIFICATION. For wiring diagram, see WIRING DIAGRAM.

1) Inspect left front Wheel Speed Sensor (WSS). Replace left front WSS if damaged, and perform TEST VER-1A. If left front WSS is okay, go to next step.

2) Disconnect left front WSS 2-pin connector located near brake master cylinder. Using DVOM ohmmeter scale, measure resistance across left front WSS connector terminals. See Fig. 14. If resistance is 1000-4000 ohms, go to next step. If resistance is not 1000-4000 ohms, replace left front WSS. After repairs are complete, perform TEST VER-1A.

3) Turn ignition off. Disconnect CAB 60-pin connector. Select DRB-II ohmmeter mode. See DRB-II VOLT/OHMMETER MODE under DRB-II TEST FUNCTIONS. Measure resistance at CAB 60-pin connector terminal No. 8 (Red/Dark Blue wire). See Fig. 6. If resistance is 5 ohms or more, go to next step. If resistance is less than 5 ohms, repair short to ground in Red/Dark Blue wire. After repairs are complete, perform TEST VER-1A.

4) Measure resistance on CAB 60-pin connector terminal No. 9 (Red wire). If resistance is 5 ohms or more, go to next step. If resistance is less than 5 ohms, repair short to ground in Red wire. After repairs are complete, perform TEST VER-1A.

5) Connect jumper wire between ground and CAB 60-pin connector terminal No. 8 (Red/Dark Blue wire). Using DRB-II, measure resistance at left front WSS harness connector terminal No. 1 (Red/Dark Blue wire). See Fig. 14. If resistance is less than 5 ohms, go to next step. If resistance is 5 ohms or more, repair open in Red/Dark Blue wire. After repairs are complete, perform TEST VER-1A.

6) Disconnect jumper wire from CAB 60-pin connector terminal No. 8 (Red/Dark Blue wire). Connect jumper wire between ground and CAB 60-pin connector terminal No. 9 (Red wire). Measure resistance on left front WSS harness connector terminal No. 2 (Red wire). If resistance is less than 5 ohms, disconnect jumper wire and replace CAB. If resistance is 5 ohms or more, repair open in Red wire. After repairs are complete, perform TEST VER-1A.

TEST 12A
LEFT FRONT WHEEL SPEED SENSOR FAULT

NOTE: For connector terminal identification, see CONNECTOR IDENTIFICATION. For wiring diagram, see WIRING DIAGRAM.

1) Using DRB-II, read fault messages. If DRB-II displays LF WSS CONTINUITY FAULT message, perform TEST 11A. If DRB-II does not display LF WSS CONTINUITY FAULT message, go to next step.

2) Remove and inspect left front Wheel Speed Sensor (WSS). Replace left front WSS if damaged. After repairs are complete, perform TEST VER-1A. If left front WSS is okay, inspect left front tone wheel for damage (chipping, cracking or missing teeth). Replace tone wheel if damaged. After repairs are complete, perform TEST VER-1A. If tone wheel is okay, go to next step.

3) Disconnect left front WSS 2-pin connector located near fender panel, under brake master cylinder. Using DVOM ohmmeter scale, measure resistance across left front WSS connector terminals. See Fig. 14. If resistance is 1000-4000 ohms, inspect and repair ABS wiring harness between CAB and WSS if necessary. If harness is okay, replace CAB. If resistance is not 1000-4000 ohms, replace left front WSS. After repairs are complete, perform TEST VER-1A.

TEST 13A
LEFT REAR WHEEL SPEED SENSOR CONTINUITY FAULT

NOTE: For connector terminal identification, see CONNECTOR IDENTIFICATION. For wiring diagram, see WIRING DIAGRAM.

1) Inspect left rear Wheel Speed Sensor (WSS), harness, connector and tone wheel. Remove rear brake drum to inspect components. Repair or replace any damaged components. After repairs are complete, perform TEST VER-1A. If components are okay, go to next step.

2) Disconnect left rear WSS harness connector. Open rear hatch and remove left rear side panel to locate left rear WSS connector. Using DVOM ohmmeter scale, measure resistance across left rear WSS connector terminals. See Fig. 14. If resistance is not 1000-4000 ohms,

TEST 13A (Cont.)

replace left rear wheel speed sensor. After repairs are complete, perform TEST VER-1A. If resistance is 1000-4000 ohms, go to next step.

3) Disconnect CAB 60-pin connector. Check and clean connector terminals, and repair as necessary. Select DRB-II ohmmeter mode. See DRB-II VOLT/OHMMETER MODE under DRB-II TEST FUNCTIONS. Probe terminal No. 2 (Light Green wire) of left rear WSS harness connector. *See Fig. 14.* If resistance is less than 5 ohms, go to step **6)**. If resistance is 5 ohms or more, go to next step.

4) Probe left rear WSS connector terminal No. 1 (Light Green/Dark Blue wire). If resistance is less than 5 ohms, go to step **8)**. If resistance is 5 ohms or more, connect a jumper wire between each left rear WSS connector terminal and ground. Using DRB-II ohmmeter, probe CAB connector terminal No. 3. *See Fig. 6.* If resistance is 5 ohms or more, go to step **10)**. If resistance is less than 5 ohms, go to next step.

5) Probe CAB connector terminal No. 4. If resistance is 5 ohms or more, go to step **12)**. If resistance is less than 5 ohms, replace CAB. After repairs are complete, perform TEST VER-1A.

6) Disconnect bulkhead body connector located at driver's inner firewall. Select DRB-II ohmmeter mode. Probe terminal No. 2 (Light Green wire) of left rear WSS harness connector. *See Fig. 14.*

7) If resistance is less than 5 ohms, repair short to ground in Light Green wire between WSS and body connector. If resistance is 5 ohms or more, repair short to ground in Light Green wire between CAB and body connector. After repairs are complete, perform TEST VER-1A.

8) Disconnect bulkhead body connector located at driver's inner firewall. Select DRB-II ohmmeter mode. Probe terminal No. 2 (Light Green/Dark Blue wire) of left rear WSS harness connector. *See Fig. 14.*

9) If resistance is less than 5 ohms, repair short to ground in Light Green/Dark Blue wire between WSS and body connector. If resistance is 5 ohms or more, repair short to ground in Light Green/Dark Blue wire between CAB and body connector. After repairs are complete, perform TEST VER-1A.

10) Disconnect bulkhead body connector located at driver's inner firewall. Select DRB-II ohmmeter mode. Probe terminal No. 37 (Light Green/Dark Blue wire) of bulkhead body connector. *See Fig. 15.*

11) If resistance is 5 ohms or more, repair open in Light Green/Dark Blue wire between WSS connector and body wiring harness connector. If resistance is less than 5 ohms, repair open in Light Green/Dark Blue wire between CAB 60-pin connector and body wiring harness connector. After repairs are complete, perform TEST VER-1A.

12) Disconnect bulkhead body connector located at driver's inner firewall. Select DRB-II ohmmeter mode. Probe terminal No. 38 (Light Green wire) of bulkhead body connector. *See Fig. 15.*

13) If resistance is 5 ohms or more, repair open in Light Green wire between WSS connector and body wiring harness connector. If resistance is less than 5 ohms, repair open in Light Green wire between CAB 60-pin connector and body wiring harness connector. After repairs are complete, perform TEST VER-1A.

TEST 14A
LEFT REAR WHEEL SPEED SENSOR FAULT

NOTE: For connector terminal identification, see CONNECTOR IDENTIFICATION. For wiring diagram, see WIRING DIAGRAM.

1) Using DRB-II, read fault messages. If DRB-II displays LR WHEEL SPEED SENSOR CONTINUITY FAULT message, perform TEST 13A. If LR WHEEL SPEED SENSOR CONTINUITY FAULT is not displayed, inspect left rear Wheel Speed Sensor (WSS) harness, connector and tone wheel for damage. Remove rear brake drum to inspect these components.

2) Inspect left rear tone wheel for damage (chipping, cracking, or missing teeth). Repair or replace any components as necessary. After repairs are complete, perform TEST VER-1A. If components are okay, go to next step.

3) Disconnect left rear WSS 2-pin connector. Open rear hatch and remove left rear side panel to locate left rear WSS connector. Using DVOM, measure resistance across left rear WSS connector terminals. *See Fig. 14.* If resistance is not 1000-4000 ohms, replace LR WSS. After repairs are complete, perform TEST VER-1A.

4) If resistance is 1000-4000 ohms, inspect and repair, ABS wiring harness between CAB and left rear WSS. If ABS wiring harness is good, replace CAB. After repairs are complete, perform TEST VER-1A.

TEST 15A
LOW ACCUMULATOR FAULT

NOTE: For connector terminal identification, see CONNECTOR IDENTIFICATION. For wiring diagram, see WIRING DIAGRAM.

1) If the LOW FLUID/PARKING BRAKE FAULT message was set during TEST 1A, perform TEST 16A. If the LOW FLUID/PARKING BRAKE FAULT message was not set, turn ignition off. Release accumulator pressure by pumping brake pedal at least 40 times.

2) Turn ignition on. If pump/motor runs, go to step **4)**. If pump/motor does not run, inspect ABS fuse cartridge/fusible link. *See Fig. 3.* If ABS fuse cartridge/fusible link is blown, perform TEST 10A. If ABS fuse cartridge/fusible link is not blown, disconnect dual-function pressure switch connector and pump/motor connector. *See Figs. 2 and 10A.*

3) Disconnect switch/transducer connector. Check and clean all connectors and terminals, and repair as necessary. After repairs are complete, perform TEST VER-1A. If connector terminals are good, reconnect all connectors and perform TEST 10B.

4) If pump/motor does not stop running within 2 minutes, perform TEST 9A. If pump/motor stops running within 2 minutes, turn ignition off. Disconnect switch/transducer connector. Check and clean connector terminals, and repair if necessary. Turn ignition on.

5) Select DRB-II ohmmeter mode. See DRB-II VOLT/OHMMETER MODE under DRB-II TEST FUNCTIONS. Probe switch/transducer female harness connector terminal No. 10 (Red wire). *See Fig. 13.* If voltage is more than 9 volts, go to step **7)**. If voltage is 9 volts or less, turn ignition off. Disconnect CAB 60-pin connector. Check and clean connector terminals, and repair if necessary.

6) Connect jumper wire between CAB connector terminal No. 17 (Red wire) and ground. *See Fig. 6.* Using DRB-II ohmmeter, probe switch/transducer female connector terminal No. 10 (Red wire). *See Fig. 13.* If resistance is less than 5 ohms, replace CAB. If resistance is 5 ohms or more, repair open in Red wire. After repairs are complete, perform TEST VER-1A.

7) Using DRB-II ohmmeter mode, probe pump/motor connector terminal No. 1 (Black wire). *See Fig. 11.* If resistance is 5 ohms or more, repair open in Black wire to ground. If resistance is less than 5 ohms, using DVOM ohmmeter mode, connect DVOM positive lead to dual-function pressure switch connector terminal "C" (Red wire). *See Fig. 8.* Connect DVOM negative lead to switch/transducer female connector terminal No. 6 (Red wire). *See Fig. 13.*

8) If resistance is 5 ohms or more, repair open in Red wire between dual-function pressure switch connector and switch/transducer connector. If resistance is less than 5 ohms, replace dual-function pressure switch. After repairs are complete, perform TEST VER-1A.

TEST 16A
LOW FLUID/PARKING BRAKE FAULT

NOTE: For connector terminal identification, see CONNECTOR IDENTIFICATION. For wiring diagram, see WIRING DIAGRAM.

Ensure parking brake is fully released. If parking brake is not fully released, release parking brake or repair as necessary. After repairs are complete, perform TEST VER-1A. If parking brake is fully released, perform TEST 16C.

TEST 16B

NOTE: Test 16B applies to passenger car models only, no test procedures have been omitted.

TEST 16C
LOW FLUID/PARKING BRAKE FAULT

NOTE: For connector terminal identification, see CONNECTOR IDENTIFICATION. For wiring diagram, see WIRING DIAGRAM.

1) Turn ignition off. Release accumulator pressure by pumping brake pedal at least 40 times. Check brake fluid level in reservoir. If fluid level is low, check for leaks and repair if necessary. After repairs are complete, perform TEST VER-1A.

2) If fluid level is correct, turn ignition off. Disconnect switch/transducer connector. *See Fig. 2.* Check and clean connector terminals, and repair if necessary. Turn ignition on. Select DRB-II ohmmeter mode. See DRB-II VOLT/OHMMETER MODE under DRB-II TEST FUNCTIONS. Probe switch/transducer male connector terminal No. 4 (Gray/Black wire). *See Fig. 10.*

TEST 16C (Cont.)

3) If resistance is less than 5 ohms, perform TEST 16D. If resistance is 5 ohms or more, probe switch/transducer female connector terminal No. 2 (Gray/Black wire). *See Fig. 13.* If resistance is less than 5 ohms, perform TEST 16E. If resistance is 5 ohms or more, inspect BRAKE warning light circuit (Gray/Black wire) for intermittent short to ground; repair circuit if necessary. If circuit is okay, system is operating properly at this time. Perform TEST VER-1A.

TEST 16D
LOW FLUID/PARKING BRAKE FAULT

NOTE: For connector terminal identification, see CONNECTOR IDEN-TIFICATION. For wiring diagram, see WIRING DIAGRAM.

1) Turn ignition off. Remove brake fluid level switch from bottom of reservoir. Using DVOM ohmmeter scale, check resistance between switch/transducer male connector terminal No. 1 (Black wire) and terminal No. 4 (Gray/Black wire).
2) If resistance is 5 ohms or more, replace brake fluid reservoir. If resistance is less than 5 ohms, replace brake fluid level switch. After repairs are complete, perform TEST VER-1A.

TEST 16E
LOW FLUID/PARKING BRAKE FAULT

NOTE: For connector terminal identification, see CONNECTOR IDEN-TIFICATION. For wiring diagram, see WIRING DIAGRAM.

Disconnect CAB 60-pin connector. Check and clean connector terminals, and repair if necessary. Select DRB-II ohmmeter mode. See DRB-II VOLT/OHMMETER MODE under DRB-II TEST FUNCTIONS. Probe switch/transducer male connector terminal No. 4 (Gray/Black wire). If resistance is less than 5 ohms, repair short to ground in Gray/Black wire. If resistance is 5 ohms or more, replace CAB. After repairs are complete, perform TEST VER-1A.

TEST 17A
MODULATOR FAULT

NOTE: For connector terminal identification, see CONNECTOR IDEN-TIFICATION. For wiring diagram, see WIRING DIAGRAM.

1) Turn ignition on. Disconnect modulator connector. *See Fig. 2.* Check and clean connector terminals, and repair if necessary. Using DRB-II, actuate left front build valve.
2) Hydraulic valve tests will cycle on and off for about 7 minutes. It may be necessary to reactivate test if too much time elapses. If DRB-II shows left front build valve actuating, go to next step. If DRB-II does not show left front build valve actuating, replace CAB. After repairs are complete, perform TEST VER-1A.
3) Select DRB-II voltmeter mode. See DRB-II VOLT/OHMMETER MODE under DRB-II TEST FUNCTIONS. Ensure DRB-II is still actuating left front build valve. Probe modulator female connector terminal No. 3 (Brown/White wire). *See Fig. 9.* If voltage is switching between zero to more than 12 volts, go to next step. If voltage is not switching between zero to more than 12 volts, perform TEST 17B.
4) Using DRB-II, stop actuation test. Using DRB-II, actuate right front build valve. If DRB-II shows right front build valve actuating, go to next step. If DRB-II does not show right front build valve actuating, replace CAB. After repairs are complete, perform TEST VER-1A.
5) Select DRB-II voltmeter mode. See DRB-II VOLT/OHMMETER MODE under DRB-II TEST FUNCTIONS. Ensure DRB-II is still actuating right front build valve. Probe modulator female connector terminal No. 8 (Brown/Red wire). If voltage is switching between zero to more than 12 volts, go to next step. If voltage is not switching between zero to more than 12 volts, perform TEST 17C.
6) Using DRB-II, stop actuation test. Using DRB-II, actuate rear build valve. If DRB-II shows rear build valve actuating, go to next step. If DRB-II does not show rear build valve actuating, replace CAB. After repairs are complete, perform TEST VER-1A.
7) Select DRB-II voltmeter mode. Ensure DRB-II is still actuating rear build valve. Probe modulator female connector terminal No. 9 (Brown/Tan wire). If voltage is switching between zero to more than 12 volts, go to next step. If voltage is not switching between zero to more than 12 volts, perform TEST 17D.
8) Stop actuation test. Using DRB-II, actuate left front decay valve. If DRB-II shows left front decay valve actuating, go to next step. If DRB-II does not show left front decay valve actuating, replace CAB. After repairs are complete, perform TEST VER-1A.

TEST 17A (Cont.)

9) Select DRB-II voltmeter mode. Ensure DRB-II is still actuating left front decay valve. Probe modulator female connector terminal No. 4 (Dark Green/Black wire). If voltage is switching between zero to more than 12 volts, go to next step. If voltage is not switching between zero to more than 12 volts, perform TEST 17E.
10) Stop actuation test. Using DRB-II, actuate right front decay valve. If DRB-II shows right front decay valve actuating, go to next step. If DRB-II does not show right front decay valve actuating, replace CAB. After repairs are complete, perform TEST VER-1A.
11) Select DRB-II voltmeter mode. Ensure DRB-II is still actuating right front decay valve. Probe modulator female connector terminal No. 7 (Dark Green/White wire). If voltage is switching between zero to more than 12 volts, go to next step. If voltage is not switching between zero to more than 12 volts, perform TEST 17F.
12) Stop actuation test. Using DRB-II, actuate rear decay valve. If DRB-II shows rear decay valve actuating, go to next step. If DRB-II does not show rear decay valve actuating, replace CAB. After repairs are complete, perform TEST VER-1A.
13) Select DRB-II voltmeter mode. Ensure DRB-II is still actuating rear decay valve. Probe modulator female connector terminal No. 2 (Dark Green/Orange wire). If voltage is switching between zero to more than 12 volts, go to next step. If voltage is not switching between zero to more than 12 volts, perform TEST 17G.
14) Stop actuation test. Using DRB-II, actuate left front isolation valve. If DRB-II shows left front isolation valve actuating, go to next step. If DRB-II does not show left front isolation valve actuating, replace CAB. After repairs are complete, perform TEST VER-1A.
15) Select DRB-II voltmeter mode. Ensure DRB-II is still actuating left front isolation valve. Probe modulator female connector terminal No. 5 (White/Light Green wire). *See Fig. 9.* If voltage is switching between zero to more than 12 volts, go to next step. If voltage is not switching between zero to more than 12 volts, perform TEST 17H.
16) Stop actuation test. Using DRB-II, actuate right front isolation valve. If DRB-II shows right front isolation valve actuating, go to next step. If DRB-II does not show right front isolation valve actuating, replace CAB. After repairs are complete, perform TEST VER-1A.
17) Select DRB-II voltmeter mode. Ensure DRB-II is still actuating right front isolation valve. Probe modulator female connector terminal No. 6 (White/Tan wire). If voltage is switching between zero to more than 12 volts, go to next step. If voltage is not switching between zero to more than 12 volts, perform TEST 17J.
18) Stop actuation test. Using DRB-II, actuate left rear isolation valve. If DRB-II shows left rear isolation valve actuating, go to next step. If DRB-II does not show left rear isolation valve actuating, replace CAB. After repairs are complete, perform TEST VER-1A.
19) Select DRB-II voltmeter mode. Ensure DRB-II is still actuating left rear isolation valve. Probe modulator female connector terminal No. 10 (White/Black wire). If voltage is switching between zero to more than 12 volts, go to next step. If voltage is not switching between zero to more than 12 volts, perform TEST 17K.
20) Stop actuation test. Using DRB-II, actuate right rear isolation valve. If DRB-II shows right rear isolation valve actuating, go to next step. If DRB-II does not show right rear isolation valve actuating, replace CAB. After repairs are complete, perform TEST VER-1A.
21) Put DRB-II in voltmeter mode. Ensure DRB-II is still actuating right rear isolation valve. Probe modulator female connector terminal No. 1 (White/Pink wire). If voltage is switching between zero to more than 12 volts, go to next step. If voltage is not switching between zero to more than 12 volts, perform TEST 17L. Stop actuation test. Replace complete hydraulic assembly. After repairs are complete, perform TEST VER-1A.

TEST 17B
MODULATOR FAULT

NOTE: For connector terminal identification, see CONNECTOR IDEN-TIFICATION. For wiring diagram, see WIRING DIAGRAM.

1) Turn ignition off. Disconnect CAB 60-pin connector. Check and clean connector terminals, and repair if necessary. Select DRB-II ohmmeter mode. See DRB-II VOLT/OHMMETER MODE under DRB-II TEST FUNCTIONS. Probe modulator female connector terminal No. 3 (Brown/White wire). *See Fig. 9.* If resistance is less than 5 ohms, repair short to ground in Brown/White wire. After repairs are complete, perform TEST VER-1A.
2) If resistance is 5 ohms or more, connect jumper wire between ground and CAB connector terminal No. 42 (Brown/White wire). *See Fig. 6.* Using DRB-II ohmmeter mode, probe modulator female connector terminal No. 3 (Brown/White wire). If resistance is less than 5 ohms, replace CAB. If resistance is 5 ohms or more, repair open in Brown/White wire. After repairs are complete, perform TEST VER-1A.

TEST 17C
MODULATOR FAULT

NOTE: For connector terminal identification, see CONNECTOR IDEN-TIFICATION. For wiring diagram, see WIRING DIAGRAM.

1) Turn ignition off. Disconnect CAB 60-pin connector. Check and clean connector terminals, and repair if necessary. Select DRB-II ohmmeter mode. See DRB-II VOLT/OHMMETER MODE under DRB-II TEST FUNCTIONS. Probe modulator female connector terminal No. 8 (Brown/Red wire). See Fig. 9. If resistance is less than 5 ohms, repair short to ground in Brown/Red wire. After repairs are complete, perform TEST VER-1A.
2) If resistance is 5 ohms or more, connect jumper wire between ground and CAB connector terminal No. 46 (Brown/Red wire). See Fig. 6. Using DRB-II ohmmeter mode, probe modulator female connector terminal No. 8 (Brown/Red wire). If resistance is less than 5 ohms, replace CAB. If resistance is 5 ohms or more, repair open in Brown/Red wire. After repairs are complete, perform TEST VER-1A.

TEST 17D
MODULATOR FAULT

NOTE: For connector terminal identification, see CONNECTOR IDEN-TIFICATION. For wiring diagram, see WIRING DIAGRAM.

1) Turn ignition off. Disconnect CAB 60-pin connector. Check and clean connector terminals, and repair if necessary. Select DRB-II ohmmeter mode. See DRB-II VOLT/OHMMETER MODE under DRB-II TEST FUNCTIONS. Probe modulator female connector terminal No. 9 (Brown/Tan wire). See Fig. 9. If resistance is less than 5 ohms, repair short to ground in Brown/Tan wire. After repairs are complete, perform TEST VER-1A.
2) If resistance is 5 ohms or more, connect jumper wire between ground and CAB connector terminal No. 52 (Brown/Tan wire). See Fig. 6. Using DRB-II ohmmeter mode, probe modulator female connector terminal No. 9 (Brown/Tan wire). If resistance is less than 5 ohms, replace CAB. If resistance is 5 ohms or more, repair open in Brown/Tan wire. After repairs are complete, perform TEST VER-1A.

TEST 17E
MODULATOR FAULT

NOTE: For connector terminal identification, see CONNECTOR IDEN-TIFICATION. For wiring diagram, see WIRING DIAGRAM.

1) Turn ignition off. Disconnect CAB 60-pin connector. Check and clean connector terminals, and repair if necessary. Select DRB-II ohmmeter mode. See DRB-II VOLT/OHMMETER MODE under DRB-II TEST FUNCTIONS. Probe modulator female connector terminal No. 4 (Dark Green/Black wire). See Fig. 9.
2) If resistance is less than 5 ohms, repair short to ground in Dark Green/Black wire. After repairs are complete, perform TEST VER-1A. If resistance is 5 ohms or more, connect jumper wire between ground and CAB connector terminal No. 43 (Dark Green/Black wire). See Fig. 6.
3) Using DRB-II ohmmeter mode, probe modulator female connector terminal No. 4 (Dark Green/Black wire). If resistance is less than 5 ohms, replace CAB. If resistance is 5 ohms or more, repair open in Dark Green/Black wire. After repairs are complete, perform TEST VER-1A.

TEST 17F
MODULATOR FAULT

NOTE: For connector terminal identification, see CONNECTOR IDEN-TIFICATION. For wiring diagram, see WIRING DIAGRAM.

1) Turn ignition off. Disconnect CAB 60-pin connector. Check and clean connector terminals, and repair if necessary. Select DRB-II ohmmeter mode. See DRB-II VOLT/OHMMETER MODE under DRB-II TEST FUNCTIONS. Probe modulator female connector terminal No. 7 (Dark Green/White wire). See Fig. 9.
2) If resistance is less than 5 ohms, repair short to ground in Dark Green/White wire. After repairs are complete, perform TEST VER-1A. If resistance is 5 ohms or more, connect jumper wire between ground and CAB connector terminal No. 48 (Dark Green/White wire). See Fig. 6.
3) Using DRB-II ohmmeter mode, probe modulator female connector terminal No. 7 (Dark Green/White wire). If resistance is less than 5 ohms, replace CAB. If resistance is 5 ohms or more, repair open in Dark Green/White wire. After repairs are complete, perform TEST VER-1A.

TEST 17G
MODULATOR FAULT

NOTE: For connector terminal identification, see CONNECTOR IDEN-TIFICATION. For wiring diagram, see WIRING DIAGRAM.

1) Turn ignition off. Disconnect CAB 60-pin connector. Check and clean connector terminals, and repair if necessary. Select DRB-II ohmmeter mode. See DRB-II VOLT/OHMMETER MODE under DRB-II TEST FUNCTIONS. Probe modulator female connector terminal No. 2 (Dark Green/Orange wire). See Fig. 9.
2) If resistance is less than 5 ohms, repair short to ground in Dark Green/Orange wire. After repairs are complete, perform TEST VER-1A. If resistance is 5 ohms or more, connect jumper wire between ground and CAB connector terminal No. 54 (Dark Green/Orange wire). See Fig. 6.
3) Using DRB-II ohmmeter mode, probe modulator female connector terminal No. 2 (Dark Green/Orange wire). If resistance is less than 5 ohms, replace CAB. If resistance is 5 ohms or more, repair open in Dark Green/Orange wire. After repairs are complete, perform TEST VER-1A.

TEST 17H
MODULATOR FAULT

NOTE: For connector terminal identification, see CONNECTOR IDEN-TIFICATION. For wiring diagram, see WIRING DIAGRAM.

1) Turn ignition off. Disconnect CAB 60-pin connector. Check and clean connector terminals, and repair if necessary. Select DRB-II ohmmeter mode. See DRB-II VOLT/OHMMETER MODE under DRB-II TEST FUNCTIONS. Probe modulator female connector terminal No. 5 (White/Light Green wire). See Fig. 9.
2) If resistance is less than 5 ohms, repair short to ground in White/Light Green wire. After repairs are complete, perform TEST VER-1A. If resistance is 5 ohms or more, connect jumper wire between ground and CAB connector terminal No. 45 (White/Light Green wire). See Fig. 6.
3) Using DRB-II ohmmeter mode, probe modulator female connector terminal No. 5 (White/Light Green wire). If resistance is less than 5 ohms, replace CAB. If resistance is 5 ohms or more, repair open in White/Light Green wire. After repairs are complete, perform TEST VER-1A.

TEST 17J
MODULATOR FAULT

NOTE: For connector terminal identification, see CONNECTOR IDEN-TIFICATION. For wiring diagram, see WIRING DIAGRAM.

1) Turn ignition off. Disconnect CAB 60-pin connector. Check and clean connector terminals, and repair if necessary. Select DRB-II ohmmeter mode. See DRB-II VOLT/OHMMETER MODE under DRB-II TEST FUNCTIONS. Probe modulator female connector terminal No. 6 (White/Tan wire). See Fig. 9.
2) If resistance is less than 5 ohms, repair short to ground in White/Tan wire. After repairs are complete, perform TEST VER-1A. If resistance is 5 ohms or more, connect jumper wire between ground and CAB connector terminal No. 49 (White/Tan wire). See Fig. 6.
3) Using DRB-II ohmmeter mode, probe modulator female connector terminal No. 6 (White/Tan wire). If resistance is less than 5 ohms, replace CAB. If resistance is 5 ohms or more, repair open in White/Tan wire. After repairs are complete, perform TEST VER-1A.

TEST 17K
MODULATOR FAULT

NOTE: For connector terminal identification, see CONNECTOR IDEN-TIFICATION. For wiring diagram, see WIRING DIAGRAM.

1) Turn ignition off. Disconnect CAB 60-pin connector. Check and clean connector terminals, and repair if necessary. Select DRB-II ohmmeter mode. See DRB-II VOLT/OHMMETER MODE under DRB-II TEST FUNCTIONS. Probe modulator female connector terminal No. 10 (White/Black wire). See Fig. 9.
2) If resistance is less than 5 ohms, repair short to ground in White/Black wire. After repairs are complete, perform TEST VER-1A. If resistance is 5 ohms or more, connect jumper wire between ground and CAB connector terminal No. 51 (White/Black wire). See Fig. 6.
3) Using DRB-II ohmmeter mode, probe modulator female connector terminal No. 10 (White/Black wire). If resistance is less than 5 ohms, replace CAB. If resistance is 5 ohms or more, repair open in White/Black wire. After repairs are complete, perform TEST VER-1A.

TEST 17L
MODULATOR FAULT

NOTE: For connector terminal identification, see CONNECTOR IDENTIFICATION. For wiring diagram, see WIRING DIAGRAM.

1) Turn ignition off. Disconnect CAB 60-pin connector. Check and clean connector terminals, and repair if necessary. Select DRB-II ohmmeter mode. See DRB-II VOLT/OHMMETER MODE under DRB-II TEST FUNCTIONS. Probe modulator female connector terminal No. 1 (White/Pink wire). See Fig. 9.
2) If resistance is less than 5 ohms, repair short to ground in White/Pink wire. After repairs are complete, perform TEST VER-1A. If resistance is 5 ohms or more, connect jumper wire between ground and CAB connector terminal No. 55 (White/Pink wire). See Fig. 6.
3) Using DRB-II ohmmeter mode, probe modulator female connector terminal No. 1 (White/Pink wire). If resistance is less than 5 ohms, replace CAB. If resistance is 5 ohms or more, repair open in White/Pink wire. After repairs are complete, perform TEST VER-1A.

TEST 18A
PRIMARY PRESSURE OR
DELTA PRESSURE FAULT

NOTE: For connector terminal identification, see CONNECTOR IDENTIFICATION. For wiring diagram, see WIRING DIAGRAM.

1) Turn ignition on. Using DRB-II, read primary pressure sensor voltage. If voltage is more than 4 volts, perform TEST 18E. If voltage is less than 4 volts, press and hold brake pedal down. Using DRB-II, read primary pressure sensor voltage. If voltage is zero volt, go to step 3). If voltage is greater than zero volt, read boost pressure sensor voltage using DRB-II.
2) Vary brake pedal pressure, and monitor primary pressure sensor voltage and boost pressure sensor voltage. If voltage readings are not equal, perform TEST 18B. If voltage readings are equal, system is operating properly at this time. Ensure condition of ABS wiring harness is good. Repair wiring harness if damaged. After repairs are complete, perform TEST VER-1A.
3) Release brake pedal. Using DRB-II, read primary pressure sensor voltage. If voltage is zero volt, go to step 6). If voltage is greater than zero volt, bleed brake system. See BLEEDING BRAKE SYSTEM.
4) Depress and hold brake pedal down. Using DRB-II, read primary pressure sensor voltage. If voltage is zero volt, go to next step. If voltage is greater than zero volt, ABS is operating properly at this time. Perform TEST VER-1A.
5) Check system for fluid leaks. If leak does not exist, check brake disc pads for excessive or uneven wear. Replace disc pads if necessary. If disc pads are good, ABS is operating properly at this time. If leak exists, repair as necessary and bleed system. After repairs are complete, perform TEST VER-1A.
6) Disconnect switch/transducer connector. See Fig. 2. Check and clean connector terminals, and repair if necessary. Connect jumper wire between switch/transducer female connector terminals No. 9 (White/Orange wire) and No. 7 (Gray/Light Blue wire). See Fig. 13.
7) If primary pressure voltage is 4.5 volts or less, perform TEST 18C. If primary pressure voltage is more than 4.5 volts, disconnect jumper wire. Select DRB-II ohmmeter mode. See DRB-II VOLT/OHMMETER MODE under DRB-II TEST FUNCTIONS. Probe switch/transducer male connector terminal No. 7 (White wire). If resistance is 5 ohms or more, perform TEST 18D. If resistance is less than 5 ohms, disconnect differential (delta) pressure switch connector. See Fig. 2.
8) Using DRB-II ohmmeter mode, probe switch/transducer male connector terminal No. 7 (White wire). If resistance is less than 5 ohms, repair short to ground in White wire. After repairs are complete, perform TEST VER-1A. If resistance is 5 ohms or more, probe terminal No. 1 (Light Green wire) of differential (delta) pressure switch harness connector.
9) If resistance is 5 ohms or more, replace differential (delta) pressure switch. After repairs are complete, perform TEST VER-1A. If resistance is less than 5 ohms, disconnect primary pressure transducer connector. See Fig. 18A. Primary pressure transducer is located on left side of fluid reservoir, near low-pressure tube. Check and clean connector terminals, and repair if necessary.

TEST 18A (Cont.)

92J05587

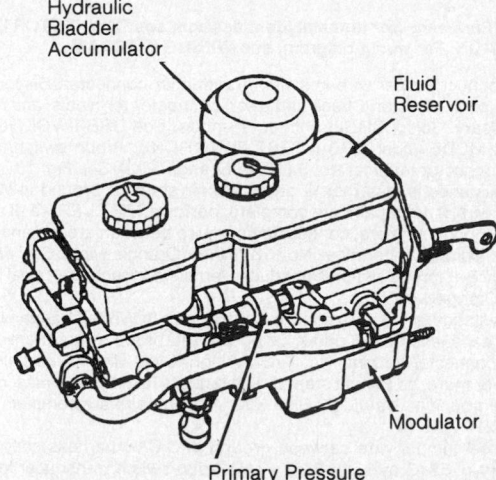

Fig. 18A: Locating Primary Pressure Transducer

10) Using DRB-II ohmmeter mode, probe terminal No. 1 (Light Green wire) of differential (delta) pressure switch harness connector. If resistance is less than 5 ohms, repair short to ground in Light Green wire. After repairs are complete, perform TEST VER-1A. If resistance is 5 ohms or more, probe primary pressure transducer harness connector terminal "B" (Gray/Light Blue wire). See Fig. 10.
11) If resistance is 5 ohms or more, replace primary pressure transducer. After repairs are complete, perform TEST VER-1A. If resistance is less than 5 ohms, disconnect boost pressure transducer connector. See Fig. 2. Using DRB-II ohmmeter mode, probe primary pressure transducer harness connector terminal "B" (Gray/Light Blue wire).
12) If resistance is less than 5 ohms, repair short to ground in Gray/Light Blue wire. If resistance is 5 ohms or more, replace boost pressure transducer. After repairs are complete, perform TEST VER-1A.

TEST 18B
PRIMARY PRESSURE OR
DELTA PRESSURE FAULT

NOTE: For connector terminal identification, see CONNECTOR IDENTIFICATION. For wiring diagram, see WIRING DIAGRAM.

1) Using DRB-II, read boost pressure voltage with brake pedal released. If voltage is not .15-.45 volt, replace boost pressure transducer. Perform TEST VER-1A. If voltage is .15-.45 volt, using DRB-II, read primary pressure voltage with brake pedal released.
2) If voltage is not .15-.45 volt, replace primary pressure transducer. If voltage is .15-.45 volt, check for primary brake system fluid leaks and repair if necessary. After repairs are complete, perform TEST VER-1A. If leak does not exist, go to next step.
3) Bleed brake system. See BLEEDING BRAKE SYSTEM. Perform TEST VER-1A. Using DRB-II, vary brake pedal pressure, and monitor primary and boost pressure voltages. If primary and boost pressure voltages are approximately equal, ABS is operating properly at this time. Perform TEST VER-1A. If primary and boost pressure voltages are not approximately equal, turn ignition off.
4) Release accumulator pressure by pumping brake pedal at least 40 times until a definite increase in pedal effort is felt. Remove high-pressure fitting plug near bottom of accumulator. See Fig. 2. Connect Brake Fluid Pressure Gauge (MST-6163), Adapter (MST-6505) and Fitting (MST-6491A) to fitting hole. Turn ignition on. Allow pump/motor to re-pressurize hydraulic system and then shut itself off.
5) Depress brake pedal until gauge pressure is 1000 psi, and hold pedal at that pressure. Using DRB-II, read boost pressure sensor voltage. If voltage is not 2.03-2.33 volts, replace boost pressure transducer. After repairs are complete, perform TEST VER-1A. If voltage is 2.03-2.33 volts, go to next step.
6) Using DRB-II, read primary pressure sensor voltage. If voltage is not 2.03-2.33 volts, replace primary pressure transducer. If voltage is 2.03-2.33 volts, ABS is operating properly at this time. After repairs are complete, perform TEST VER-1A.

TEST 18C
PRIMARY PRESSURE OR
DELTA PRESSURE FAULT

NOTE: For connector terminal identification, see CONNECTOR IDEN-TIFICATION. For wiring diagram, see WIRING DIAGRAM.

1) Disconnect jumper wire in switch/transducer connector. Disconnect CAB 60-pin connector. Check and clean connector terminals, and repair if necessary. Select DRB-II ohmmeter mode. See DRB-II VOLT/OHM-METER MODE under DRB-II TEST FUNCTIONS. Probe switch/transducer connector terminal No. 9 (White/Orange wire). *See Fig. 13.*
2) If resistance is less than 5 ohms, repair short to ground in White/Orange wire. After repairs are complete, perform TEST VER-1A. If resistance is 5 ohms or more, connect jumper wire between ground and CAB harness connector terminal No. 18 (White/Orange wire). *See Fig. 6.* Using DRB-II, probe switch/transducer female connector terminal No. 9 (White/Orange wire).
3) If resistance is 5 ohms or more, repair open in White/Orange wire. If resistance is less than 5 ohms, using DRB-II, probe switch/transducer female connector terminal No. 7 (Gray/Light Blue wire). If resistance is 5 ohms or more, go to next step. If resistance is less than 5 ohms, repair short to ground in Gray/Light Blue wire. After repairs are complete, perform TEST VER-1A.
4) Connect jumper wire between ground and CAB harness connector terminal No. 58 (Gray/Light Blue wire). Probe switch/transducer female connector terminal No. 7 (Gray/Light Blue wire). If resistance is 5 ohms or more, repair open in Gray/Light Blue wire. If resistance is less than 5 ohms, replace CAB. After repairs are complete, perform TEST VER-1A.

TEST 18D
PRIMARY PRESSURE OR
DELTA PRESSURE FAULT

NOTE: For connector terminal identification, see CONNECTOR IDEN-TIFICATION. For wiring diagram, see WIRING DIAGRAM.

1) Disconnect primary pressure transducer connector. *See Fig. 18A.* Check and clean connector terminals, and repair if necessary.
2) Using 2 jumper wires, connect primary pressure transducer connector terminal "B" (Gray/Light Blue wire) and terminal "C" (Light Green wire) to ground. Select DRB-II ohmmeter mode. See DRB-II VOLT/OHMMETER MODE under DRB-II TEST FUNCTIONS. Probe switch/transducer male connector terminal No. 7 (White wire).
3) If resistance is 5 ohms or more, go to step **4)**. If resistance is less than 5 ohms, probe switch/transducer male connector terminal No. 9 (Gray/Light Blue wire). If resistance is 5 ohms or more, repair open in Gray/Light Blue wire. If resistance is less than 5 ohms, replace primary pressure transducer. After repairs are complete, perform TEST VER-1A.
4) Disconnect differential (delta) pressure switch connector. *See Fig. 2.* Check and clean connector terminals, and repair if necessary. Probe differential (delta) pressure switch harness connector terminal No. 1 (Light Green wire). If resistance is less than 5 ohms, repair open in White wire. If resistance is 5 ohms or more, repair open in Light Green wire. After repairs are complete, perform TEST VER-1A.

TEST 18E
PRIMARY PRESSURE OR
DELTA PRESSURE FAULT

NOTE: For connector terminal identification, see CONNECTOR IDEN-TIFICATION. For wiring diagram, see WIRING DIAGRAM.

1) Disconnect CAB 60-pin harness connector. Disconnect primary pressure transducer connector. *See Fig. 18A.* Check and clean terminals of connectors, and repair if necessary.
2) Connect jumper wire between ground and boost pressure transducer connector terminal "A" (Red/Black wire). *See Fig. 10.* Select DRB-II ohmmeter mode. See DRB-II VOLT/OHMMETER MODE under DRB-II TEST FUNCTIONS. Probe CAB harness connector terminal No. 10 (Red/Black wire). *See Fig. 6.* If resistance is 5 ohms or more, go to step **4)**. If resistance is less than 5 ohms, using DVOM ohmmeter scale, measure resistance between terminals "B" and "C" of primary pressure transducer, located on hydraulic assembly. Refer to harness connector terminals for transducer terminal reference. *See Fig. 10.*
3) If resistance is less than 5 ohms, replace primary pressure transducer. If resistance is 5 ohms or more, replace CAB. After repairs are complete, perform TEST VER-1A.

TEST 18E (Cont.)

4) Disconnect switch/transducer connector. *See Fig. 2.* Check and clean connector terminals, and repair if necessary. Probe switch/transducer male connector terminal No. 2 (Red/Black wire).
5) If resistance is less than 5 ohms, repair open in Red/Black wire between CAB and switch/transducer connector. If resistance is 5 ohms or more, repair open in Red/Black wire between switch/transducer connector and primary pressure transducer. Perform TEST VER-1A.

TEST 19A
RIGHT FRONT WHEEL SPEED SENSOR
CONTINUITY FAULT

NOTE: For connector terminal identification, see CONNECTOR IDEN-TIFICATION. For wiring diagram, see WIRING DIAGRAM.

1) Inspect right front Wheel Speed Sensor (WSS), harness, connectors and tone wheel. Replace damaged component. After repairs are complete, perform TEST VER-1A. If components are okay, disconnect right front WSS connector.
2) Using DVOM ohmmeter scale, measure resistance across right front WSS male connector terminals. If resistance is not 1000-4000 ohms, replace right front WSS. After repairs are complete, perform TEST VER-1A. If resistance is 1000-4000 ohms, turn ignition off.
3) Disconnect CAB 60-pin connector. Check and clean connector terminals, and repair if necessary. Select DRB-II ohmmeter mode. See DRB-II VOLT/OHMMETER MODE under DRB-II TEST FUNCTIONS. Probe CAB connector terminal No. 6 (White/Dark Blue wire). *See Fig. 6.* If resistance is less than 5 ohms, repair short to ground in White/Dark Blue wire. Perform TEST VER-1A. If resistance is 5 ohms or more, go to next step.
4) Probe CAB harness connector terminal No. 7 (White wire). If resistance is less than 5 ohms, repair short to ground in White wire. Perform TEST VER-1A. If resistance is 5 ohms or more, connect jumper wire between ground and CAB harness connector terminal No. 6 (White/Dark Blue wire). Using DRB-II, probe right front WSS harness connector terminal No. 2 (White/Dark Blue wire). *See Fig. 14.*
5) If resistance is more than 5 ohms, repair open in White/Dark Blue wire. Perform TEST VER-1A. If resistance is less than 5 ohms, disconnect jumper wire between ground and CAB harness connector terminal No. 6 (White/Dark Blue wire). Connect jumper wire between ground and CAB harness connector terminal No. 7 (White wire).
6) Using DRB-II, probe right front WSS harness connector terminal No. 1 (White wire). If resistance is 5 ohms or more, repair open in White wire between right front WSS and CAB. If resistance is less than 5 ohms, disconnect jumper wire and replace CAB. After repairs are complete, perform TEST VER-1A.

TEST 20A
RIGHT FRONT WHEEL SPEED SENSOR FAULT

NOTE: For connector terminal identification, see CONNECTOR IDEN-TIFICATION. For wiring diagram, see WIRING DIAGRAM.

1) Using DRB-II, read faults. If DRB-II displays RF WHEEL SPEED SENSOR CONTINUITY FAULT message, perform TEST 19A. If RF WHEEL SPEED SENSOR CONTINUITY FAULT message is not displayed, inspect right front Wheel Speed Sensor (WSS), harness, connectors and tone wheel. Replace damaged component. After repairs are complete, perform TEST VER-1A.
2) If components are okay, remove right front WSS from knuckle. Closely inspect sensor pick-up end and tone wheel for damage or corrosion, and repair or replace as necessary. If no damage exists, disconnect right front WSS harness connector located behind right front strut tower.
3) Using DVOM ohmmeter scale, measure resistance across right front WSS male connector terminals. *See Fig. 14.* If resistance is 1000-4000 ohms, inspect condition of ABS harness between CAB and right front WSS. If harness and/or connectors are damaged, repair or replace as necessary. If no damage exists, replace CAB. If resistance is not 1000-4000 ohms, replace right front WSS. After repairs are complete, perform TEST VER-1A.

TEST 21A
RIGHT REAR WHEEL SPEED SENSOR CONTINUITY FAULT

NOTE: For connector terminal identification, see CONNECTOR IDENTIFICATION. For wiring diagram, see WIRING DIAGRAM.

1) Inspect right rear Wheel Speed Sensor (WSS), harness, connector and tone wheel. Remove rear brake drum to inspect components. If any components are damaged, repair or replace as necessary. After repairs are complete, perform TEST VER-1A.
2) If all components are good, disconnect right rear WSS harness connector. Open rear hatch and remove right rear side panel to locate right rear WSS connector.
3) Using DVOM ohmmeter scale, measure resistance across right rear WSS male connector terminals. See Fig. 14. If resistance is not 1000-4000 ohms, replace right rear WSS. After repairs are complete, perform TEST VER-1A. If resistance is 1000-4000 ohms, disconnect CAB 60-pin connector. Check and clean connector terminals, and repair if necessary.
4) Select DRB-II ohmmeter mode. See DRB-II VOLT/OHMMETER MODE under DRB-II TEST FUNCTIONS. Probe right rear WSS harness connector terminal No. 2 (Yellow wire). If resistance is less than 5 ohms, perform TEST 21B. If resistance is 5 ohms or more, probe right rear WSS harness connector terminal No.1 (Yellow/Dark Blue wire). If resistance is less than 5 ohms, perform TEST 21C. If resistance is 5 ohms or more, connect both terminals of right rear WSS harness connector to ground using 2 jumper wires.
5) Using DRB-II ohmmeter mode, probe CAB connector terminal No. 1 (Yellow/Dark Blue wire). See Fig. 6. If resistance is 5 ohms or more, perform TEST 21D. If resistance is less than 5 ohms, probe CAB connector terminal No. 2 (Yellow wire). If resistance is 5 ohms or more, perform TEST 21E. If resistance is less than 5 ohms, replace CAB. After repairs are complete, perform TEST VER-1A.

TEST 21B
RIGHT REAR WHEEL SPEED SENSOR CONTINUITY FAULT

NOTE: For connector terminal identification, see CONNECTOR IDENTIFICATION. For wiring diagram, see WIRING DIAGRAM.

1) Disconnect bulkhead body connector located at driver's inner firewall. Select DRB-II ohmmeter mode. See DRB-II VOLT/OHMMETER MODE under DRB-II TEST FUNCTIONS. Probe right rear WSS harness connector terminal No. 2 (Yellow wire). See Fig. 14.
2) If resistance is less than 5 ohms, repair short to ground in Yellow wire between right rear WSS and body connector. If resistance is 5 ohms or more, repair short to ground in Yellow wire between CAB and body connector. After repairs are complete, perform TEST VER-1A.

TEST 21C
RIGHT REAR WHEEL SPEED SENSOR CONTINUITY FAULT

NOTE: For connector terminal identification, see CONNECTOR IDENTIFICATION. For wiring diagram, see WIRING DIAGRAM.

1) Disconnect bulkhead body connector located at driver's inner firewall. Select DRB-II ohmmeter mode. See DRB-II VOLT/OHMMETER MODE under DRB-II TEST FUNCTIONS. Probe right rear WSS harness connector terminal No. 1 (Yellow/Dark Blue wire). See Fig. 14.
2) If resistance is less than 5 ohms, repair short to ground in Yellow/Dark Blue wire between right rear WSS and body connector. If resistance is 5 ohms or more, repair short to ground in Yellow/Dark Blue wire between CAB and body connector. After repairs are complete, perform TEST VER-1A.

TEST 21D
RIGHT REAR WHEEL SPEED SENSOR CONTINUITY FAULT

NOTE: For connector terminal identification, see CONNECTOR IDENTIFICATION. For wiring diagram, see WIRING DIAGRAM.

1) Disconnect bulkhead body connector located at driver's inner firewall. Select DRB-II ohmmeter mode. See DRB-II VOLT/OHMMETER MODE under DRB-II TEST FUNCTIONS. Probe bulkhead body connector terminal No. 39 (Yellow/Dark Blue wire). See Fig. 15.
2) If resistance is 5 ohms or more, repair open in Yellow/Dark Blue wire between right rear WSS and body connector. If resistance is less than 5 ohms, repair open in Yellow/Dark Blue wire between CAB and body connector. After repairs are complete, perform TEST VER-1A.

TEST 21E
RIGHT REAR WHEEL SPEED SENSOR CONTINUITY FAULT

NOTE: For connector terminal identification, see CONNECTOR IDENTIFICATION. For wiring diagram, see WIRING DIAGRAM.

1) Disconnect bulkhead body connector located at driver's inner firewall. Select DRB-II ohmmeter mode. See DRB-II VOLT/OHMMETER MODE under DRB-II TEST FUNCTIONS. Probe bulkhead body connector terminal No. 40 (Yellow wire). See Fig. 15.
2) If resistance is 5 ohms or more, repair short to ground in Yellow wire between right rear WSS and body connector. If resistance is less than 5 ohms, repair short to ground in Yellow wire between CAB and body connector. After repairs are complete, perform TEST VER-1A.

TEST 22A
RIGHT REAR WHEEL SPEED SENSOR FAULT

NOTE: For connector terminal identification, see CONNECTOR IDENTIFICATION. For wiring diagram, see WIRING DIAGRAM.

1) Using DRB-II, read faults. If DRB-II displays RR WHEEL SPEED SENSOR CONTINUITY FAULT message, perform TEST 21A. If RR WHEEL SPEED SENSOR CONTINUITY FAULT message is not displayed, inspect right rear Wheel Speed Sensor (WSS), harness, connectors and tone wheel for damages. Remove rear brake drum to inspect components. If any components are damaged, repair or replace as necessary. After repairs are complete, perform TEST VER-1A.
2) If no obvious component damage exists, remove right rear WSS. Closely inspect sensor pick-up end and tone wheel for damage or corrosion, and repair or replace as necessary. If all components are good, disconnect right rear WSS harness connector. Open rear hatch, and remove right rear side panel to locate right rear WSS connector.
3) Using DVOM ohmmeter scale, measure resistance across right rear WSS male connector terminals. See Fig. 14. If resistance is 1000-4000 ohms, inspect condition of ABS harness between CAB and right rear WSS. If harness and/or connectors are damaged, repair or replace as necessary. If no damage exists, replace CAB. If resistance is not 1000-4000 ohms, replace right rear WSS. After repairs are complete, perform TEST VER-1A.

TEST 23A
SOLENOID UNDERVOLTAGE FAULT

NOTE: For connector terminal identification, see CONNECTOR IDENTIFICATION. For wiring diagram, see WIRING DIAGRAM.

1) Inspect for blown fusible links. See Fig. 3. If fusible links are not blown, perform TEST 23B. If fusible links are blown, turn ignition off. Disconnect CAB 60-pin connector. Check and clean connector terminals, and repair as necessary.
2) Disconnect ANTI-LOCK warning light relay and ABS relay. See Fig. 3. Select DRB-II ohmmeter mode. See DRB-II VOLT/OHMMETER MODE under DRB-II TEST FUNCTIONS. Probe ANTI-LOCK relay connector terminal "B" (Red/Dark Blue wire). See Fig. 5.
3) If resistance is less than 5 ohms, repair short to ground in Red/Dark Blue wire between relay connector and fusible link. Replace fusible link. After repairs are complete, perform TEST VER-1A. If resistance is 5 ohms or more, go to next step.

TEST 23A (Cont.)

4) Probe ABS relay connector terminal "D" (Red/Light Blue wire). If resistance is less than 5 ohms, repair short to ground in Red/Light Blue wire. Replace fusible link. If resistance is 5 ohms or more, go to next step.
5) Measure resistance between ANTI-LOCK relay terminals No. 85 and 86 using DVOM. If resistance is less than 5 ohms, replace relay and fusible link. If resistance is 5 ohms or more, go to next step.
6) Replace ABS system fusible link. Road test vehicle, and perform several ABS stops. Check for blown ABS system fusible link. If fusible link is blown, replace CAB and fusible link. If fusible link is not blown, ABS is operating properly at this time. After repairs are complete, perform TEST VER-1A.

TEST 23B
SOLENOID UNDERVOLTAGE FAULT

NOTE: For connector terminal identification, see CONNECTOR IDEN-TIFICATION. For wiring diagram, see WIRING DIAGRAM.

1) Turn ignition on. Using DRB-II, read ABS relay voltage. If voltage is 9 volts or less, go to step 5). If voltage is more than 9 volts, turn ignition off. Disconnect CAB 60-pin connector. Check and clean connector terminals, and repair as necessary.
2) Using DVOM, measure resistance between CAB harness connector terminals No. 47 and 50 (Red/Light Blue wires). See Fig. 6. If resistance is 5 ohms or more, repair open in Red/Light Blue wire between CAB harness connector terminals No. 47 and 50. Perform TEST VER-1A. If resistance is less than 5 ohms, reconnect CAB 60-pin harness connector.
3) Turn ignition on. Using DRB-II, monitor ABS relay voltage while wiggle testing CAB connector and wires. If ABS relay voltage drops to less than 9 volts, repair CAB connector and/or wire terminals as necessary. If ABS system relay voltage does not drop to less than 9 volts, monitor ABS relay voltage while wiggle testing relay connector and wires.
4) If ABS relay voltage drops to less than 9 volts, repair relay connector and/or wire terminals as necessary. If ABS relay voltage does not drop to less than 9 volts, system is operating properly at this time. After repairs are complete, perform TEST VER-1A.
5) Disconnect ABS warning light relay. See Fig. 3. Select DRB-II voltmeter mode. See DRB-II VOLT/OHMMETER MODE under DRB-II TEST FUNCTIONS. Probe ABS warning light relay connector terminal "A". See Fig. 5. If voltage is 9 volts or less, go to next step. If voltage is more than 9 volts, backprobe CAB connector terminals No. 47 and 50. If voltage is more than 9 volts at both terminals, replace CAB. If voltage is 9 volts or less, repair open in Red/Light Blue wire between CAB and relay. Perform TEST VER-1A.
6) Remove ABS relay. Using DRB-II voltmeter mode, probe ABS relay connector terminal "A". See Fig. 5. If voltage is more than 9 volts, go to step 8). If voltage is 9 volts or less, turn ignition off. Disconnect CAB 60-pin connector. Using DRB-II ohmmeter mode, probe ABS system relay connector terminal "A".
7) If resistance is less than 5 ohms, repair short to ground in Brown/Black wire. If resistance is 5 ohms or more, connect jumper wire between CAB connector terminal No. 57 (Brown/Black wire) and ground. See Fig. 6. Probe ABS relay connector terminal "A". If resistance is less than 5 ohms, replace CAB. If resistance is more than 5 ohms, repair open in Brown/Black wire. After repairs are complete, perform TEST VER-1A.
8) Using DVOM ohmmeter scale, measure resistance from ANTI-LOCK warning light relay connector terminal "A" (Red/Light Blue wire) to ABS relay connector terminal "D" (Red/Light Blue wire). See Fig. 5. If resistance is 5 ohms or more, repair open in Red/Light Blue wire. Perform TEST VER-1A. If resistance is less than 5 ohms, using DRB-II voltmeter mode, probe ABS relay connector terminal "B" (Red/Dark Green wire).
9) If voltage is 9 volts or less, repair open in Red/Dark Blue wire. Perform TEST VER-1A. If voltage is more than 9 volts, probe ABS relay connector terminal "C" (Black wire). If resistance is less than 5 ohms, replace ABS relay. If resistance is 5 ohms or more, repair open in Black wire between relay and ground. After repairs are complete, perform TEST VER-1A.

TEST 24A
STOPLIGHT SWITCH INPUT TEST

NOTE: For connector terminal identification, see CONNECTOR IDEN-TIFICATION. For wiring diagram, see WIRING DIAGRAM.

1) Turn ignition on. Press and release brake pedal while observing brakelights. If brakelights do not function properly, repair as necessary. If brakelights function properly, read stoplight switch I/O state using DRB-II. If DRB-II indicates stoplights are on, replace CAB. Perform TEST VER-1A. If DRB-II indicates stoplights are off, go to next step.
2) Depress brake pedal. If DRB-II indicates stoplights are on, ABS is operating properly at this time. Perform TEST VER-1A. If DRB-II indicates stoplights are off, go to next step.
3) Turn ignition off. Disconnect CAB 60-pin connector. Depress brake pedal. Select DRB-II voltmeter mode. See DRB-II VOLT/OHMMETER MODE under DRB-II TEST FUNCTIONS. Probe CAB connector terminal No. 13 (White/Tan wire). See Fig. 6. If voltage is 9 volts or less, repair open in White/Tan wire. If voltage is more than 9 volts, replace CAB. After repairs are complete, perform TEST VER-1A.

TEST 25A
SYSTEM RELAY FAULT

NOTE: For connector terminal identification, see CONNECTOR IDEN-TIFICATION. For wiring diagram, see WIRING DIAGRAM.

1) Using DRB-II, actuate ABS relay test. If ANTI-LOCK warning light blinks, go to step 3). If ANTI-LOCK warning light does not blink, disconnect ABS relay. See Fig. 3. Check and clean connector terminals, and repair if necessary.
2) Using DVOM ohmmeter scale, measure resistance of ABS relay connector between terminals No. 30 and 87. See Fig. 5. If resistance is less than 5 ohms, replace ABS relay. If resistance is 5 ohms or more, select DRB-II voltmeter mode. See DRB-II VOLT/OHMMETER MODE under DRB-II TEST FUNCTIONS. Probe ABS relay connector terminal "D". If voltage is zero volt, go to next step. If voltage is greater than zero, perform TEST 25B.
3) Reinstall ABS relay. Using DRB-II, erase faults. Turn ignition off and then on. Using DRB-II, read faults. If ABS relay fault is not set, ABS is operating properly at this time. If ABS relay fault is set, exchange ABS relay with ANTI-LOCK warning light relay.
4) Using DRB-II, erase faults. Turn ignition off and then on. Using DRB-II, read faults. If DRB-II displays SYSTEM RELAY FAULT message, replace CAB. If SYSTEM RELAY FAULT message is not displayed, replace relay that is now in ANTI-LOCK warning light relay connector. After repairs are complete, perform TEST VER-1A.

TEST 25B
SYSTEM RELAY FAULT

NOTE: For connector terminal identification, see CONNECTOR IDEN-TIFICATION. For wiring diagram, see WIRING DIAGRAM.

Disconnect CAB 60-pin connector. Select DRB-II voltmeter mode. See DRB-II VOLT/OHMMETER MODE under DRB-II TEST FUNCTIONS. Probe ABS relay connector terminal "D" (Red/Light Blue wire). See Fig. 5. If voltage is zero volt, replace CAB. If voltage is greater than zero, repair short to battery voltage in Red/Light Blue wire. After repairs are complete, perform TEST VER-1A.

TEST 26A
COMPLAINT OF "HARD" BRAKE PEDAL, OR "CLICKING" NOISES.
NO BRAKE WARNING LIGHT IS ON & NO FAULTS ARE STORED

1) Check for obstruction of brake pedal travel and repair as necessary. If there are no obstructions, select DRB-II ABS mode. See ABS MODE under DRB-II TEST FUNCTIONS. Monitor isolation valve activity. Road test vehicle under complaint conditions. If isolation valves were not on (ABS inactive mode), go to step **5)**. If isolation valves were on (ABS active) and ABS stop was activated, review pedal feel characteristics. See PEDAL FEEL CHARACTERISTICS at beginning of article.

2) If isolation valves come on (ABS active), but ABS stop was not activated, identify which isolation valve(s) came on. If rear isolation valve came on, go to next step. If rear isolation valve did not come on, inspect tone wheel and WSS to identify suspect valve circuit, and repair or replace as necessary. After repairs are complete, perform TEST VER-1A.

3) Inspect tone wheel and WSS to identify suspect valve circuit, and repair or replace as necessary. Road test vehicle. If isolation valves do not come on, perform TEST VER-1A. If isolation valves continue to come on, verify proper valve operation, and perform TEST 17A.

4) After performing TEST 17A, if isolation valves are not operating properly, repair or replace as necessary. If isolation valves are operating properly, verify proper proportioning valve operation. Perform TEST VER-1A.

5) Inspect pedal feel. If pedal feel is typical of other ABS-equipped vehicles, review pedal feel characteristics. See PEDAL FEEL CHARACTERISTICS at beginning of article. Road test vehicle, and perform ABS stop to verify ABS is operational. If ABS is NOT operating properly, repair as necessary. If ABS is operating properly, read faults using DRB-II. If any fault messages exist, perform TEST VER-1A. If there are no fault messages, system is operating properly at this time.

TEST 27A
COMPLAINT OF NOISY PUMP/MOTOR

Verify noise comes from ABS pump/motor on transaxle. See Fig. 10A. Inspect pump hoses for contact against sheet metal, and repair as necessary. Inspect pump/motor for contact against pump/motor heat shield, and repair as necessary. Inspect pump/motor mounts, and repair or replace as necessary. If noise still exists, perform TEST 9A.

TEST 28A
COMPLAINT OF SCRAPING/WHIRRING NOISE

Verify brake linings and pads are not worn out. Replace if necessary. Inspect Wheel Speed Sensor (WSS) and tone wheel for contact with each other. Repair or replace as necessary. After repairs are complete, perform TEST VER-1A.

TEST VER-1A
SYSTEM VERIFICATION TEST

1) Disconnect all previously connected jumper wires. Reconnect all previously disconnected connectors. Reinstall all previously removed relays. Using DRB-II, erase fault messages. Turn ignition off and then on. Using DRB-II, read fault messages. If any fault messages are displayed, perform TEST 1A. If no fault messages are displayed, go to next step.

2) Road test vehicle for a minimum of 5 minutes at speed of customer complaint (minimum 25-30 MPH). Perform several ABS stops during road test. After completing road test, use DRB-II to read fault messages. If any fault messages are displayed, perform TEST 1A. If no fault messages are displayed, but ABS valves can be heard clicking during normal (non-ABS) stops, go to TEST 26A. If no fault messages are displayed and no ABS valve clicking is heard during normal (non-ABS) stops, ABS is operating properly at this time.

Dakota, Pickup, Ramcharger, RWD Van

DESCRIPTION

The Kelsey-Hayes Rear Wheel Anti-Lock (RWAL) brake system is designed to prevent rear wheel lock-up during heavy braking conditions, no matter what type of road surface vehicle is on. Preventing rear wheel lock-up allows driver to maintain vehicle directional stability during braking. System components include an Electronic Control Module (ECM), speed sensor, 2 warning lights and a dual-solenoid control valve. System has the capability to self-diagnose and store trouble codes to detect problems within the system. Benefit of the RWAL system is limited when vehicle is operating in 4WD mode.

OPERATION

When ignition is turned on, the Electronic Control Module (ECM) performs a self-diagnosis on the system. ECM is located on lower right side cowl panel on Dakota or behind glove box on all others. *See Figs. 1-3.* If ECM detects a problem, the Amber ANTI-LOCK warning light, located on instrument panel, will stay on after engine is started. If ECM stores a trouble code, the Red BRAKES warning light will also come on. If system is okay, both lights will go out in approximately 2 seconds.

As vehicle is moving, speed sensor, located on top of rear differential housing, sends an AC voltage signal to the ECM. ECM translates this signal into wheel speed. Using this signal, ECM detects deceleration from a reduction in wheel speed and electronic signal from stoplight switch. ECM then signals the dual-solenoid hydraulic valve to increase, decrease or maintain rear wheel brake hydraulic pressure to prevent rear wheel lock-up. Dual-solenoid hydraulic valve is located on frame rail.

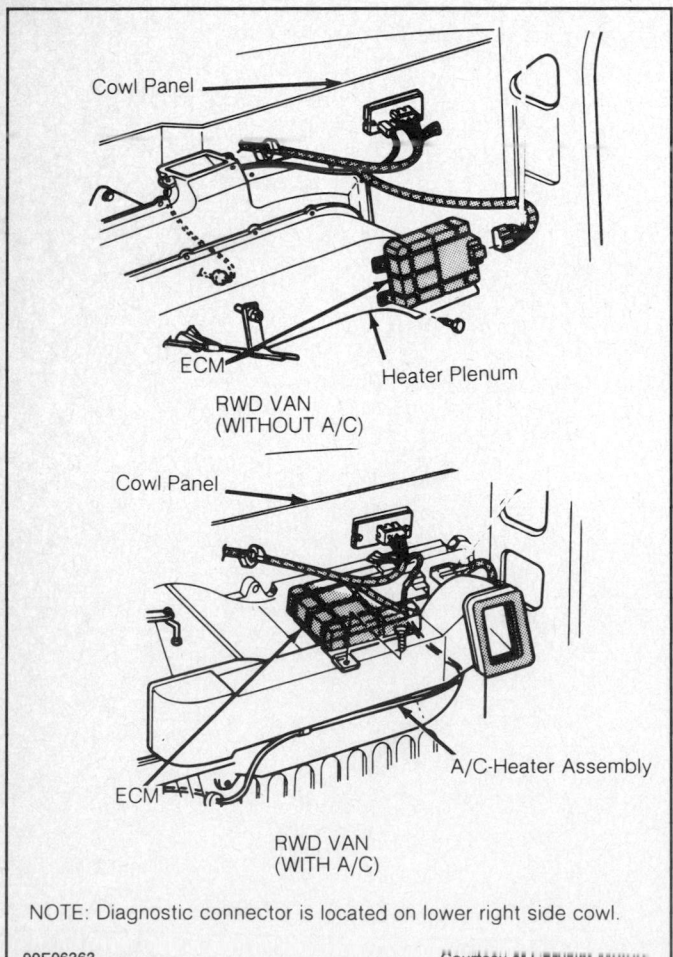

NOTE: Diagnostic connector is located on lower right side cowl.

90E06363   Courtesy of Chrysler Motors.

Fig. 1: Locating Electronic Control Module (RWD Van)

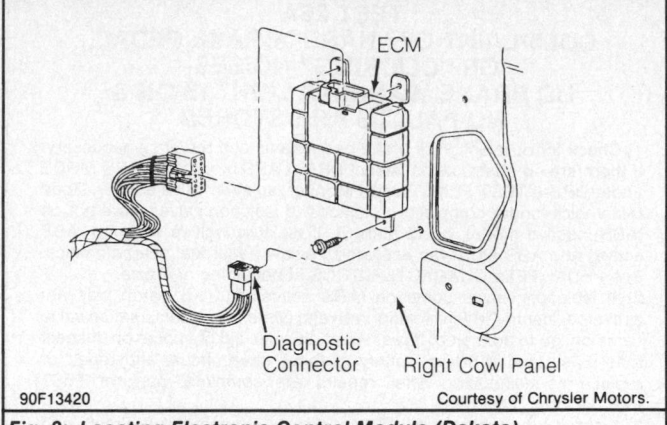

90F13420   Courtesy of Chrysler Motors.

Fig. 2: Locating Electronic Control Module (Dakota)

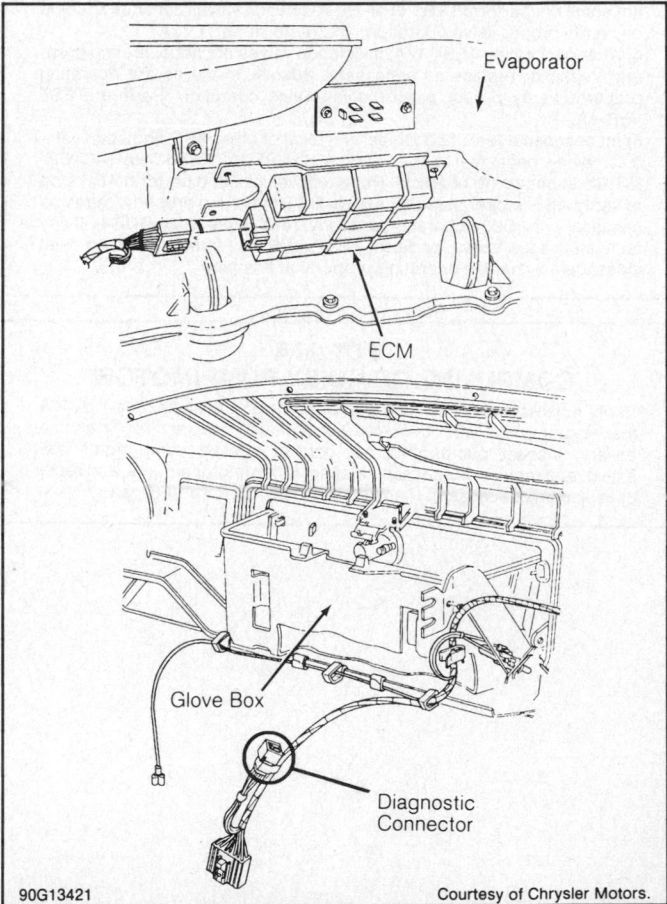

90G13421   Courtesy of Chrysler Motors.

Fig. 3: Locating Electronic Control Module (Pickup & Ramcharger)

BLEEDING BRAKE SYSTEM

Bleed brake system, using pressure bleeder or depressing brake pedal, in the following sequence: dual-solenoid hydraulic valve, right rear, left rear, right front and left front. Use DOT 3 brake fluid.

TESTING

WARNING: When battery is disconnected, vehicle computer and memory systems may lose memory data. Driveability problems may exist until computer systems have completed a relearn cycle. See COMPUTER RELEARN PROCEDURES article in GENERAL INFORMATION before disconnecting battery.

NOTE: *For ECM 14-pin connector terminal identification, see Fig. 5.*

TEST 1 – VISUAL INSPECTION

Check all electrical connectors and terminals, and instrument panel ground before continuing test. Faulty terminals or connectors can lead to misdiagnosis. Loose or faulty instrument panel ground can also lead to misdiagnosis.

TEST 2 – SELF-CHECK

1) Turn ignition on. On diesel engine models, engine must be started. If system is okay, Red BRAKES and Amber ANTI-LOCK warning lights will go off after approximately 2 seconds. If both lights go off, go to TEST 3. If Red BRAKES and Amber ANTI-LOCK warning lights stay on constantly, turn ignition off. Disconnect ECM connector for 5 seconds. Reconnect ECM connector and turn ignition on, or start engine on diesel models. If both lights go off after 2 seconds, intermittent problem has occurred. Road test vehicle and self-check again.

2) If both lights still do not go off, go to TEST 5. If Amber ANTI-LOCK and Red BRAKES lights stay on but flash, go to TEST 8. If Amber ANTI-LOCK light does not come on for 2 seconds and will not self-check, but Red BRAKES light operates properly, go to TEST 6. If Amber ANTI-LOCK light comes on for 2 seconds then goes off, and Red BRAKES light stays on constantly, go to TEST 6. If Red BRAKES light does not come on, but Amber ANTI-LOCK light operates properly, go to TEST 7.

TEST 3 – CHECKING SPEED SENSOR

1) Ensure stoplight switch and stoplights are operating. If not, check stoplight circuit and switch. Ensure stoplight switch is properly adjusted. If stoplight switch and circuit are okay, raise and support rear of vehicle. Remove speed sensor. Ensure sensor and exciter ring are not damaged. Reinstall speed sensor. Ensure air gap between speed sensor pole and exciter ring is **.005-.050" (.13-1.27 mm)**.

2) Block front wheels. On 4WD models, ensure transfer case is in 2WD position. Start engine. Place transmission in gear, and drive rear wheels at 5 MPH.

CAUTION: *Use care when working around rotating wheels.*

3) Set voltmeter on 2-volt AC scale. Check voltage between Red/Violet and White/Violet wires at speed sensor. If voltage is 650 mV or more, go to TEST 4. If voltage is less than 650 mV, check if speed sensor has been previously replaced. If sensor has not been replaced, replace sensor and retest. If sensor has been replaced, go to next step.

4) Turn ignition off. Unplug 14-pin ECM connector and speed sensor connector. Check continuity between Red/Violet wire (pin No. 14) at 14-pin ECM connector and Red/Violet wire at sensor harness connector. If there is continuity, go to next step. If there is no continuity, repair open circuit and retest.

5) Check for continuity between Red/Violet wire (pin No. 14) at 14-pin ECM connector and ground. If there is continuity, repair short to ground. If there is no continuity, check for continuity between White/

Violet wire (pin No. 13) at 14-pin ECM connector and White/Violet wire at sensor harness connector.

6) If there is no continuity, repair open circuit and retest. If there is continuity, check for continuity between White/Violet wire (pin No. 13) at 14-pin ECM connector and ground. If continuity exists, repair short to ground. If continuity does not exist, go to next step.

7) Remove speed sensor from differential. Measure distance between sensor mounting face and pole piece. Measurement should be **1.07-1.08" (27.2-27.4 mm)**. *See Fig. 4.* Measure between sensor mounting face on differential and exciter ring. Measurement should be **1.085-1.120" (27.56-28.45 mm)**.

8) Subtract sensor measurement from differential-to-exciter ring measurement. Difference should be **.005-.050" (.13-1.27 mm)**. If difference is not as specified, recheck measurements. If component measurement is not as specified, replace sensor or disassemble differential and replace exciter ring. If speed sensor gap is correct, go to TEST 4.

TEST 4 – MECHANICAL PROBLEMS CHECK

Drive vehicle and check rear brake operation. If rear brakes are grabbing, locking or pulling, remove brake drum. Check components for wear or damage. If rear brake components are okay, recheck rear brake operation. If mechanical components of rear brakes are operating okay, replace ECM and retest system.

TEST 5 – DIAGNOSTIC CONNECTOR CHECK

1) With all connectors plugged in, turn ignition on. Ground diagnostic connector to ground. *See Figs. 1-3.* Amber ANTI-LOCK warning light should flash a code starting with one long flash, and followed by short flashes. If a code is flashed, count flashes after first long flash, and go to TROUBLE CODES.

2) If no code is flashed, turn ignition off. Unplug 14-pin connector from ECM. Using an ohmmeter, check for continuity between Black/White wire (pin No. 12) at 14-pin ECM connector and Black wire at diagnostic connector. If there is no continuity, repair open circuit and retest.

3) If there is continuity, ensure master cylinder reservoir fluid level is correct. If reservoir fluid level is not correct, check for hydraulic leak. Repair leak and retest system. If reservoir fluid level is correct, reconnect 14-pin ECM connector. Unplug proportioning valve switch connector. Turn ignition on. Check if Amber ANTI-LOCK and Red BRAKES warning lights are on. If lights are not on, check for air in brake system, or damage to brake system.

4) If lights are on, turn ignition off. On gasoline engines, go to step **5)**. On diesel engines, unplug vacuum warning switch connector located on power booster. If both lights go off, repair vacuum system, or replace vacuum warning switch. If both lights are still on, go to next step.

5) Unplug 14-pin ECM connector. Turn ignition on. Check Red BRAKES and Amber ANTI-LOCK warning lights. If both warning lights are off, go to next step. If Amber ANTI-LOCK warning light is on, but Red BRAKES warning light is off, repair short in Orange wire (pin No. 2) between 14-pin ECM connector and Amber ANTI-LOCK light on instrument panel. If Amber ANTI-LOCK warning light is off, but Red BRAKES warning light is on, repair short in speed sensor wiring or vacuum warning switch circuit (diesel engines).

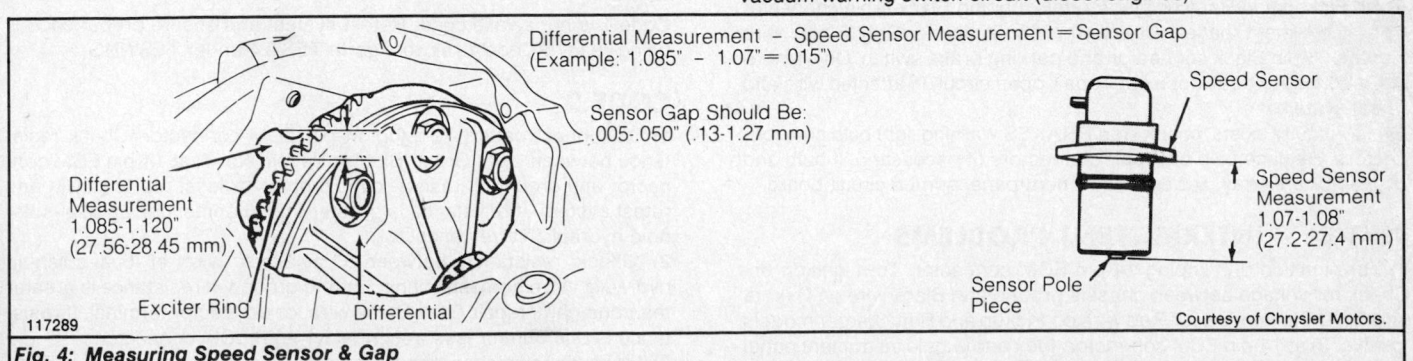

Differential Measurement – Speed Sensor Measurement = Sensor Gap
(Example: 1.085" – 1.07" = .015")

Sensor Gap Should Be:
.005-.050" (.13-1.27 mm)

Differential Measurement 1.085-1.120" (27.56-28.45 mm)

Exciter Ring   Differential

Speed Sensor

Speed Sensor Measurement 1.07-1.08" (27.2-27.4 mm)

Sensor Pole Piece

Courtesy of Chrysler Motors.

117289

Fig. 4: *Measuring Speed Sensor & Gap*

6) Turn ignition off. Reconnect all connectors. Turn ignition on. Check ABS fuse. If fuse is bad, replace fuse and recheck. If fuse is okay, connect a voltmeter between ground and Black wire on Dakota and RWD Van, or Red wire on Pickup and Ramcharger (pin No. 3) at 14-pin ECM connector.

7) If voltage is 9 volts or less, repair open circuit. If voltage is greater than 9 volts, check stoplight fuse. If fuse is bad, replace fuse and retest. If fuse is okay, check voltage between Pink/Dark Blue wire (pin No. 9) at 14-pin ECM connector and ground. If voltage is greater than 9 volts, replace ECM. If voltage is 9 volts or less, repair open in Pink/Dark Blue wire.

TEST 6 – ECM POWER & GROUND

1) Ensure 14-pin ECM connector is connected fully. Improper connection can cause faulty or intermittent ABS failure. If improper connection is found, retest system. If connection is okay, disconnect battery. Unplug 14-pin ECM connector. Check resistance between Black/Light Green wire (pin No. 10) at ECM connector and ground.

2) If resistance is one ohm or more, repair open in Black/Light Green wire. Ensure connector terminals are mating properly. If resistance is less than one ohm, check Amber ANTI-LOCK light fuse. If fuse is bad, replace fuse and retest system. If fuse is okay, reconnect battery. Turn ignition on.

3) Check voltage between Orange wire (pin No. 2) at 14-pin ECM connector and ground. If voltage is 9 volts or more, replace ECM and retest system. If voltage is less than 9 volts, check Amber ANTI-LOCK warning light bulb. If bulb is bad, replace bulb and retest system. If bulb is okay, repair open in Orange wire between pin No. 2 at 14-pin ECM connector and Amber ANTI-LOCK warning light. Retest system.

TEST 7 – PARKING BRAKE CIRCUIT

1) To check parking brake circuit for short, turn ignition off. Ensure all connectors are plugged in. Turn ignition on. Block wheels. Release parking brake and check Red BRAKES warning light operation. If Red BRAKES warning light goes off after releasing parking brake, turn ignition off.

2) Turn ignition on to perform self-diagnosis. If Red BRAKES warning light does not go off, pull parking brake release lever and pull up on parking brake pedal. If Red BRAKES warning light goes off, repair parking brake switch or mechanism. If Red BRAKES warning light does not go off, unplug parking brake switch connector.

3) If Red BRAKES warning light goes off, adjust or replace parking brake switch and retest system. If Red BRAKES warning light does not go off, unplug 14-pin ECM connector. If Red BRAKES warning light is off, replace ECM and retest system. If Red BRAKES warning light does not go off, check for short in White/Black wire on Dakota or Gray/Black on all others to ECM pin No. 5. If no short is found, check for air in hydraulic system or mechanical problem.

4) To check parking brake circuit for open, ensure all connectors are plugged in. If Red BRAKES warning light does not operate, unplug parking brake switch connector. On Dakota and RWD Van models, unplug 11-pin connector (Red on Dakota Black on RWD Van) from instrument panel. Check for continuity in White/Black wire between 11-pin connector and parking brake switch.

5) On Pickup and Ramcharger models, unplug Black 6-pin connector from instrument panel. Check for continuity in Gray/Black wire between 6-pin Black connector and parking brake switch. On all models, if continuity does not exist, repair open circuit in affected wire and retest system.

6) If continuity exists, check Red BRAKES warning light bulb and connectors. Replace bulb or repair connectors (if necessary). If bulb and connector are okay, replace instrument panel printed circuit board.

TEST 8 – INTERMITTENT PROBLEMS

1) Turn ignition off. Unplug 14-pin ECM connector. Turn ignition on. Check for voltage between chassis ground and Black wire on Dakota and RWD Van models, or Red wire on Pickup and Ramcharger models (pin No. 3) at 14-pin ECM connector. Flex and wiggle instrument panel

harness while measuring voltage. If voltage is not a steady 9 volts, repair open circuit in affected wire.

2) If voltage is a steady 9 volts, turn ignition off. Disconnect battery. Check resistance between Black/White wire (pin No. 12) at 14-pin ECM connector and ground. Flex and wiggle instrument panel harness while measuring resistance. If resistance is not 100,000 ohms or more, and steady, repair short to ground in Black/White wire.

3) If resistance is 100,000 ohms or more and steady, check resistance between Black/Light Green wire (pin No. 10) at 14-pin ECM connector and ground. Flex and wiggle instrument panel harness while measuring resistance. If resistance is steady at less than one ohm, replace ECM and retest system. If resistance is not steady at less than one ohm, repair open in Black/Light Green wire.

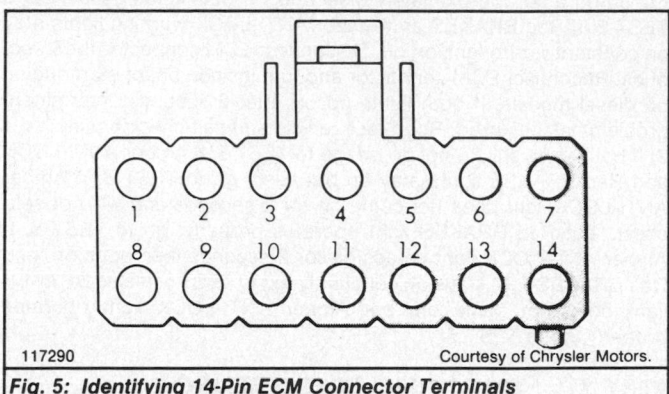

117290   Courtesy of Chrysler Motors.

Fig. 5: Identifying 14-Pin ECM Connector Terminals

TROUBLE CODES

WARNING: When battery is disconnected, vehicle computer and memory systems may lose memory data. Driveability problems may exist until computer systems have completed a relearn cycle. See COMPUTER RELEARN PROCEDURES article in GENERAL INFORMATION before disconnecting battery.

RETRIEVING TROUBLE CODES

To retrieve trouble codes, momentarily ground RWAL diagnostic connector located at ECM. See Figs. 1-3. Count flashes of Amber ANTI-LOCK warning light. The first flash will be a long flash, followed by a number of short flashes. To accurately diagnose system, count all flashes after long flash. Long flash indicates starting of code sequence. Proceed to appropriate test after flashes have been counted.

CLEARING TROUBLE CODES

To clear trouble codes, turn ignition off. Unplug 14-pin ECM connector, or remove battery voltage for 5 seconds. Reconnect battery or connector. During system retest, wait approximately 30 seconds before reading codes.

CODE 1

Code 1 is not a valid code. Retest system and ensure proper code is being read. If Code 1 returns, go to TEST 4 under TESTING.

CODE 2

1) Disconnect battery. Unplug 14-pin ECM connector. Check resistance between Light Green/Black wire (pin No. 1) at 14-pin ECM connector and ground. If resistance is 6 ohms or less, replace ECM and retest system. If resistance is greater than 6 ohms, unplug dual-solenoid hydraulic valve connector.

2) Check resistance between Gray/Black wire at dual-solenoid hydraulic valve harness connector and ground. If resistance is greater than one ohm, repair Gray/Black wire, or connector terminal. If resistance is one ohm or less, reconnect 14-pin ECM connector.

3) Measure resistance between Green wire and Black wire at dual-solenoid hydraulic valve connector. If resistance is more than 6 ohms, replace dual-solenoid hydraulic valve and retest system. If resistance is 6 ohms or less, repair Light Green wire between valve and 14-pin ECM connector (pin No. 1). Retest system.

CODE 3

1) Disconnect battery. Unplug 14-pin ECM connector. Measure resistance between White/Brown wire (pin No. 8) at 14-pin ECM connector and ground. If resistance is 3 ohms or less, replace ECM and retest system. If resistance is greater than 3 ohms, unplug dual-solenoid hydraulic valve connector.
2) Measure resistance between White wire and Black wire at valve connector. If resistance is more than 3 ohms, replace dual-solenoid hydraulic valve. If resistance is 3 ohms or less, repair White/Brown wire between valve and 14-pin ECM connector (pin No. 8).

CODE 4

1) Unplug dual-solenoid hydraulic valve connector. Measure resistance between Light Blue wire on valve connector and ground. If resistance is 10,000 ohms or less, replace dual-solenoid hydraulic valve. Clear trouble code and retest system.
2) If resistance is more than 10,000 ohms, measure resistance between Light Blue wire and Black wire at valve connector. If resistance is 10,000 ohms or less, replace dual-solenoid hydraulic valve. Clear trouble code and retest system. If resistance is more than 10,000 ohms, disconnect battery. Unplug 14-pin ECM connector.
3) Measure resistance between Light Blue wire (pin No. 11) at 14-pin ECM connector and ground. If resistance is more than 100,000 ohms, replace ECM and retest system. If resistance is 100,000 ohms or less, repair short in Light Blue wire between 14-pin ECM connector and valve. Clear trouble code and retest system.

CODE 5

1) If failure occurred with vehicle in 4WD mode, go to step 3). If failure occurred on 2WD models, or on 4WD models with vehicle in 2WD mode, unplug 14-pin ECM connector. Drive vehicle in 2WD with ECM disconnected.
2) Drive vehicle under normal driving conditions to determine rear brake operation. If brakes are operating normally, replace dual valve hydraulic solenoid and retest system. If brakes do not operate properly, repair brake as necessary.
3) Unplug 14-pin ECM connector. Start engine. Place transfer case in 4WD mode. Move vehicle a short distance. Measure voltage between ground and Light Green/Brown wire on Dakota or Dark Green/Gray wire on Pickup and Ramcharger (pin No. 4) at 14-pin ECM connector.
4) If voltage is greater than one volt, repair open circuit in affected wire, or 4WD indicator switch located on transfer case. Retest system. If voltage is one volt or less, replace dual-solenoid hydraulic valve. Clear trouble code and retest system.

CODE 6

1) Recheck code after driving vehicle. If Code 6 does not appear after driving vehicle, clear codes and retest. If Code 6 is reset, disconnect battery. Unplug 14-pin ECM connector. Measure resistance between White/Violet wire (pin No. 13) and Red/Violet wire (pin No. 14) at 14-pin connector.
2) Flex and wiggle ABS wiring harness from ECM to speed sensor while measuring resistance. If resistance is not a constant 1000-2000 ohms, repair wiring or connector and retest system. If resistance is a constant 1000-2000 ohms, remove speed sensor from differential. Check for metal chips on sensor pole.
3) If chips are found, disassemble differential. Check exciter ring for damage. Replace exciter ring if damaged. If exciter ring and sensor are okay, reinstall speed sensor. Locate speed sensor test connector on right of steering column (RWD Van), or on left side cowl panel (all others). Connect a voltmeter between Red/Violet wire and White/Violet wire at test connector.

CAUTION: Use care when working around rotating wheels.

4) Raise and support rear of vehicle. Block front wheels. Ensure vehicle is in 2WD mode. Start engine and place transmission in gear. With vehicle operating at 5 MPH, measure voltage. If voltage is more than 650 mV and steady, replace ECM and retest system. If voltage is 650 mV or lower, and/or is not steady, replace speed sensor and retest system.

CODE 7

1) Unplug dual-solenoid hydraulic valve connector. Measure resistance between Green wire and Black wire at valve connector. If resistance is less than 3 ohms, replace valve. Clear trouble code and retest system. If resistance is 3 ohms or more, disconnect battery.
2) Unplug 14-pin ECM connector. Measure resistance between ground and Light Green/Black wire (pin No. 1) at 14-pin ECM connector. If resistance is 20,000 ohms or less, repair short to ground in Light Green/Black wire. Clear trouble code and retest system. If resistance is greater than 20,000 ohms, replace ECM. Clear trouble code and retest system.

CODE 8

1) Unplug dual-solenoid hydraulic valve connector. Measure resistance between White wire and Black wire at valve connector. If resistance is less than one ohm, replace dual-solenoid hydraulic valve. Clear trouble code and retest system. If resistance is one ohm or more, disconnect battery.
2) Unplug 14-pin ECM connector. Measure resistance between White/Brown wire (pin No. 8) and ground at 14-pin ECM connector. If resistance is more than 20,000 ohms, replace ECM. If resistance is 20,000 ohms or less, repair short to ground in White/Brown wire. Clear trouble code and retest system.

CODE 9

NOTE: Ensure seal is placed between sensor and connector whenever separated.

1) Unplug RWAL speed sensor connector at differential. Measure resistance between sensor terminals. If resistance is 2500 ohms or more, replace speed sensor. Clear trouble code and retest system.
2) If resistance is less than 2500 ohms but not zero, reconnect speed sensor connector. Disconnect battery. Unplug 14-pin ECM connector. Measure resistance between White/Violet wire (pin No. 13) and Red/Violet wire (pin No. 14) at 14-pin ECM connector.
3) If resistance is 2500 ohms or less but not zero, replace ECM. Clear trouble code and retest system. If resistance is more than 2500 ohms, repair open in White/Violet wire or Red/Violet wire. Also ensure connector terminals are mating properly and are not damaged. Clear trouble code and retest system.

CODE 10

NOTE: Ensure seal is placed between sensor and connector whenever separated.

1) Unplug RWAL speed sensor connector at differential. Measure resistance between Pink wire and Light Green/Orange wire at sensor connector. If resistance is less than 1000 ohms, replace sensor. Clear trouble code and retest system.
2) If resistance is 1000 ohms or more but not infinity, disconnect battery. Unplug 14-pin ECM connector. Measure resistance between Red/Violet wire (pin No. 14) and ground at 14-pin ECM connector. If resistance is 20,000 ohms or less, repair short to ground in Red/Violet wire between ECM and sensor. Clear trouble code and retest system.
3) If resistance is more than 20,000 ohms, measure resistance between White/Violet wire (pin No. 13) and Red/Violet wire (pin No. 14) at 14-pin ECM connector. If resistance is more than 20,000 ohms, replace ECM and retest system. If resistance is 20,000 ohms or less, repair short between White/Violet wire and Red/Violet wire. Clear trouble code and retest system.

CODE 11

1) Recheck for Code 11 after driving vehicle at 35 MPH or more. If trouble code reappears after driving 35 MPH or more, apply brake pedal and check stoplight operation.

2) If stoplights do not work, repair stoplight circuit. Clear trouble code and retest system. If stoplights work, turn ignition off. Unplug 14-pin ECM connector. Measure voltage between White/Tan wire (pin No. 7) at 14-pin ECM connector and ground while depressing brake pedal.

3) If voltage is less than 9 volts, repair open circuit in White/Pink or White/Tan wire between stoplight switch and ECM. Clear trouble code and retest system. If voltage is 9 volts or more, ensure 4-way flasher, turn signals, cruise control (if equipped) and stoplight circuits are okay. If circuits are okay, ensure Amber ANTI-LOCK and Red BRAKES warning lights operate properly. Clear trouble code and retest system.

CODE 12 OR HIGHER

Ensure codes are read correctly. Clear trouble code and retest system. If Codes 12, 13, 14, etc. are still recorded, replace ECM and retest system.

REMOVAL & INSTALLATION

SPEED SENSOR

Removal & Installation – Raise and support rear of vehicle. Remove speed sensor mounting bolt. Unplug speed sensor connector. Remove speed sensor. To install, reverse removal procedure. Ensure seal between sensor and connector is in place.

ELECTRONIC CONTROL MODULE (ECM)

Removal & Installation (Dakota) – Remove right side sill plate and cowl cover. Ensure ignition is off. Unplug 14-pin ECM connector. Remove ECM. To install, reverse removal procedure.

Removal & Installation (All Others) – Remove glove box. Ensure ignition is off. Unplug 14-pin ECM connector. Remove ECM. To install, reverse removal procedure.

DUAL SOLENOID HYDRAULIC VALVE

Removal & Installation – Raise and support vehicle. Disconnect and plug hydraulic lines from valve. Unplug valve connector. Remove valve from vehicle. To install, reverse removal procedure. Bleed brake system. See BLEEDING BRAKE SYSTEM.

WIRING DIAGRAMS

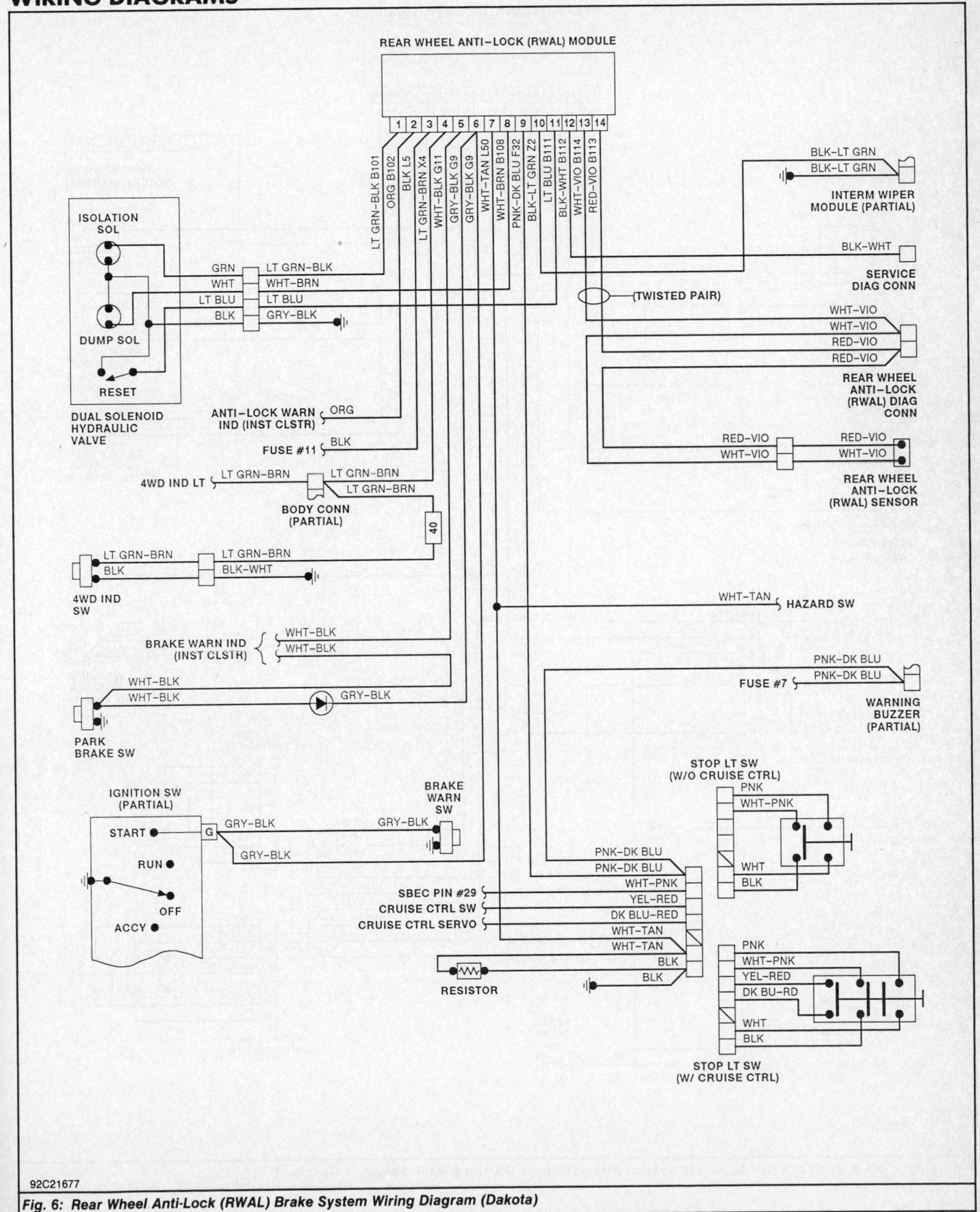

92C21677

Fig. 6: Rear Wheel Anti-Lock (RWAL) Brake System Wiring Diagram (Dakota)

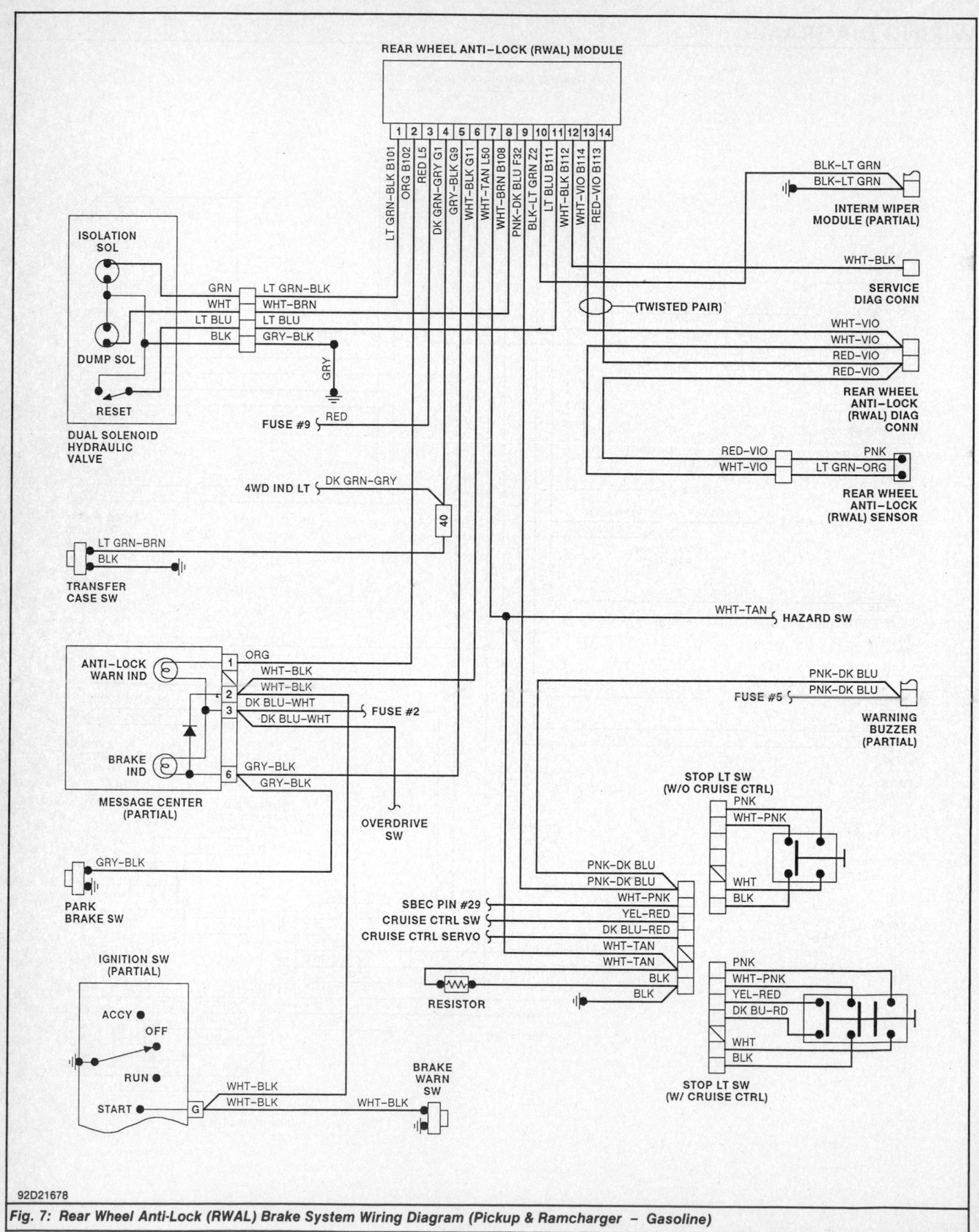

Fig. 7: Rear Wheel Anti-Lock (RWAL) Brake System Wiring Diagram (Pickup & Ramcharger – Gasoline)

92D21678

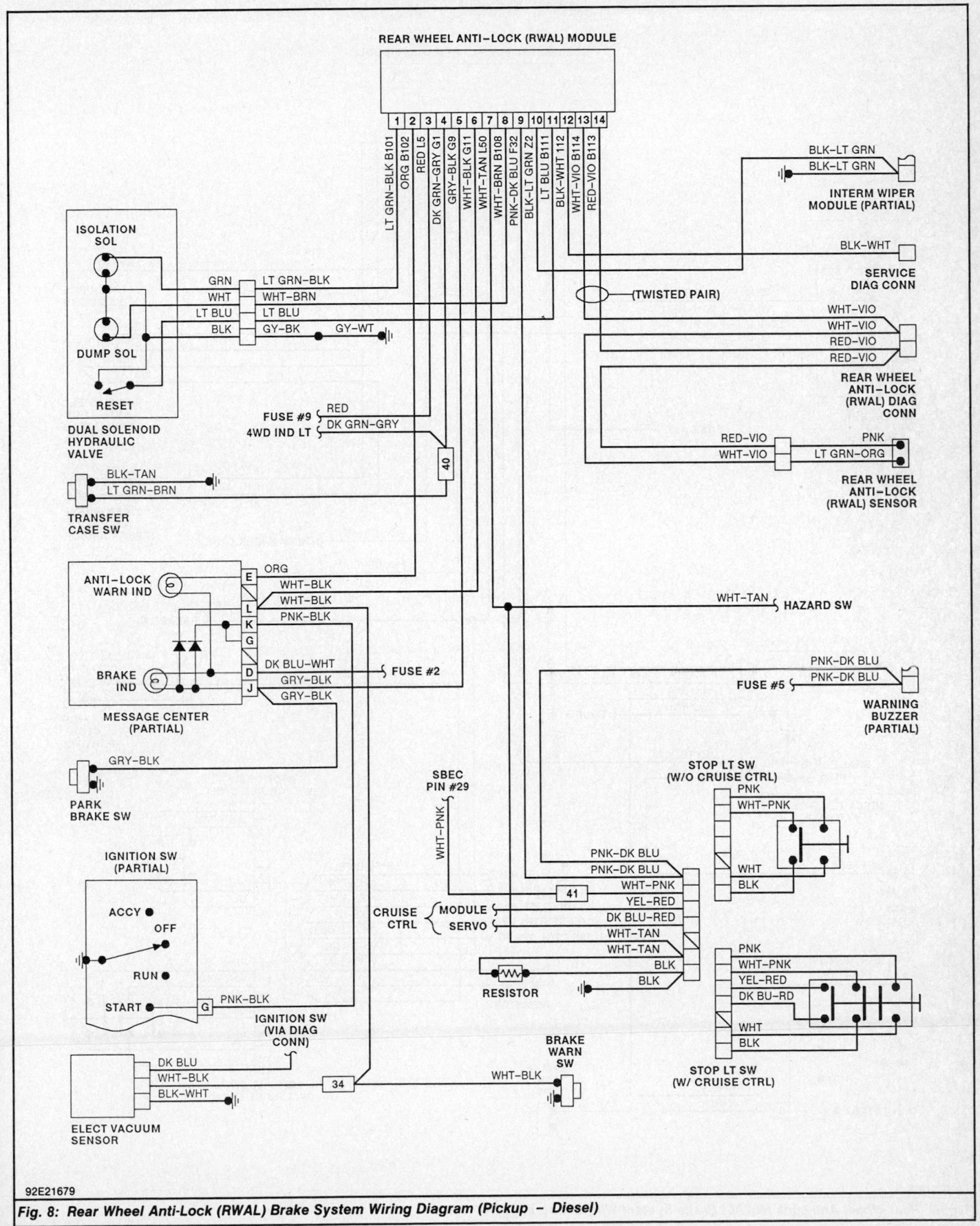

Fig. 8: Rear Wheel Anti-Lock (RWAL) Brake System Wiring Diagram (Pickup – Diesel)

92E21679

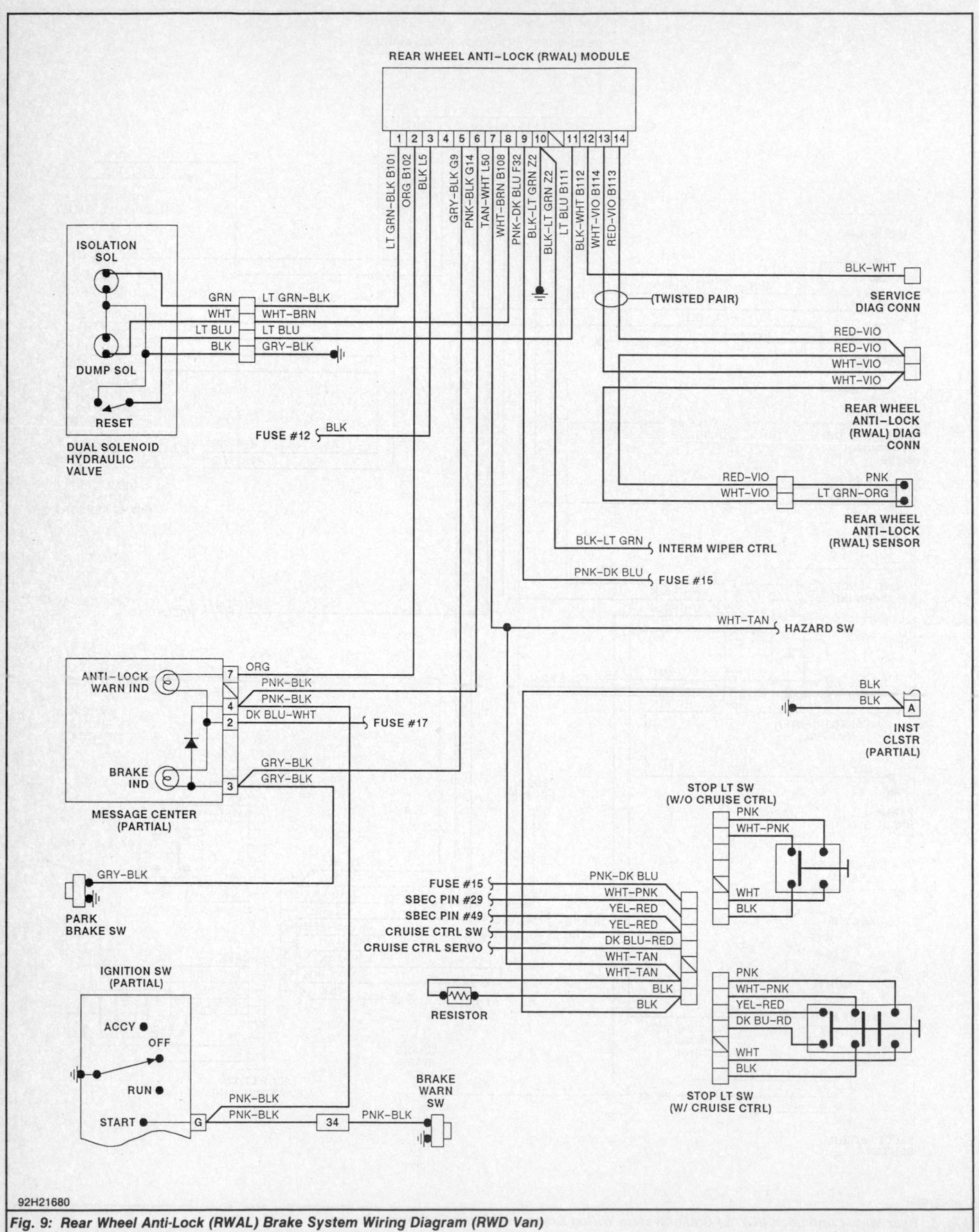

Fig. 9: Rear Wheel Anti-Lock (RWAL) Brake System Wiring Diagram (RWD Van)

1992 BRAKES
Disc & Drum

Caravan, Dakota, Pickup, Ramcharger, RWD Van, Town & Country, Voyager

DESCRIPTION & OPERATION

All models are equipped with single piston, sliding caliper front disc brakes with ventilated cast iron rotors. Rear brakes are equipped with anti-lock drum brakes. System also includes power brake booster, dual reservoir master cylinder, wheel cylinders, brake lines, hoses and combination valve. Combination valve consists of metering valve and pressure differential switch. Caravan, Town & Country and Voyager are also equipped with a height sensing proportioning valve.

Disc brake caliper is free to move laterally on adapter slide surfaces. On brake application, fluid pressure is exerted equally against caliper piston and all surfaces of caliper piston bore. Piston pressure is transmitted directly to inboard disc pad, which presses against disc rotor. Pressure applied to inboard pad makes caliper slide inward. Inward movement presses outboard pad against opposite side of disc rotor to complete braking action. On brake release, piston and caliper return to normal, non-applied position.

Models without full floating rear axle use 9", 10" or 11" single anchor rear brakes. All 3 sizes are of same design. See Fig. 9.

Models with full floating rear axle use 12" single anchor rear brakes of slightly different design than 9", 10" and 11" brakes. See Fig. 10.

NOTE: For information on Anti-Lock Brake Systems (ABS), see appropriate ANTI-LOCK article.

BLEEDING BRAKE SYSTEM

BLEEDING PROCEDURES

Before bleeding system, exhaust all vacuum from power unit by depressing brake pedal several times. Bleed master cylinder with bleeder screws (if equipped). Bleed slave cylinder on vehicles equipped with remote mount power assist units. Bleed wheel cylinders and calipers in sequence. See BLEEDING SEQUENCE table.

BLEEDING SEQUENCE

Application	Sequence
RWD	RR, LR, RF & LF
FWD & 4WD	LR, RF, RR & LF

Master Cylinder (Bench Bleeding) – 1) To prevent excessive amount of air from entering brake system and creating poor brake operation, bleed master cylinder before installation.
2) Place master cylinder in soft-jawed vise. DO NOT tighten vise enough to damage master cylinder. Install bleeder tubes in both outlets of master cylinder. See Fig. 1.

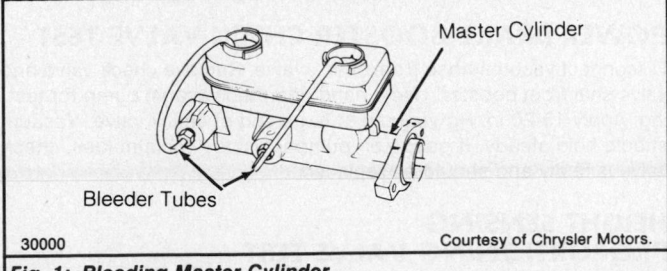

30000   Courtesy of Chrysler Motors.
Fig. 1: Bleeding Master Cylinder

3) Fill master cylinder with clean brake fluid that meets DOT 3 specifications. Ensure ends of bleeder tubes are submerged in brake fluid.
4) Using proper sized rod, apply and release master cylinder until no air bubbles exist in brake fluid flow. Once all air bubbles are gone from master cylinder, secure caps and install on vehicle.
5) Leave bleeder tubes installed on master cylinder until master cylinder is installed. Bleed brake system after installation.

Master Cylinder (On-Vehicle Bleeding) – 1) After bench bleeding, install master cylinder on vehicle. Remove bleeder lines and install brake lines. DO NOT fully tighten brake lines at this time.
2) Slowly force brake pedal to floor, and hold pedal down. Tighten brake lines and release brake pedal. Repeat procedure until no air bubbles exist at brake lines. Wheel cylinders and calipers may also require bleeding.

POSITIONING METERING VALVE BEFORE BLEEDING SYSTEM

Dakota, Pickup, Ramcharger & RWD Van – 1) Before using pressure tank bleeding procedure, correctly position metering valve (incorporated in combination valve) to allow brake fluid to flow through valve to entire brake system.
2) Valve stem may be retained in metering valve during bleeding procedure, using Valve Retainer (C-4121). See Fig. 2. Remove valve retainer once brake bleeding procedure is complete.

CAUTION: DO NOT use rigid clamp to position valve stem. Damage to valve assembly may result, causing brake failure.

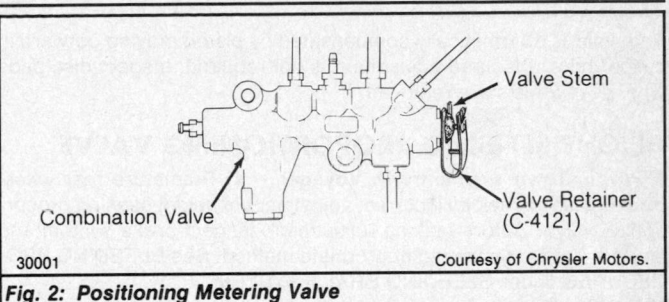

Combination Valve
Valve Stem
Valve Retainer (C-4121)
30001   Courtesy of Chrysler Motors.
Fig. 2: Positioning Metering Valve

VACUUM BLEEDING

Fill master cylinder. Install vacuum bleed equipment to first bleeder valve to be serviced. Open bleeder valve 3/4-1 turn. Depress vacuum pump, and pull fluid into reservoir jar. Bleed each bleeder valve in sequence. See BLEEDING SEQUENCE table.

PRESSURE BLEEDING

CAUTION: When using pressure bleeding method on Dakota, Pickup, Ramcharger and RWD Van, valve stem on combination valve must be pressed in and held in to properly bleed brake system. See POSITIONING METERING VALVE BEFORE BLEEDING SYSTEM.

1) Clean master cylinder cap and surrounding area. Remove cap. With pressure tank at least 1/2 full, connect to master cylinder with appropriate adapters. Attach bleeder hose to first bleeder valve to be serviced. See BLEEDING SEQUENCE table.
2) Submerge other end of hose in clean glass jar partially filled with clean brake fluid. Metering valve must be positioned properly before pressure bleeding. See POSITIONING METERING VALVE BEFORE BLEEDING SYSTEM.
3) Open release valve on pressure bleeder. Follow equipment manufacturer's pressure bleeding instructions or see PRESSURE BLEEDER SETTINGS table. Open bleeder screw 3/4-1 turn, and note fluid flow.
4) Close bleeder screw when fluid flow is free of air bubbles. Repeat procedure on remaining wheels in proper sequence. Check brake pedal operation after bleeding has been completed.
5) Remove pressure bleeding equipment and valve retainer from metering valve. Ensure that master cylinder is full of fluid.

PRESSURE BLEEDER SETTINGS

Application
All Models

MANUAL BLEEDING

NOTE: When bleeding disc brakes, air may tend to cling to caliper walls. Lightly tap caliper, while bleeding, to aid in removal of air.

1) Fill master cylinder. Install bleeder hose on first bleeder valve to be serviced. See BLEEDING SEQUENCE table. Submerge other end of hose in clean glass jar partially filled with clean brake fluid.
2) Open bleeder valve 3/4-1 turn. Depress brake pedal slowly through full travel. Close bleeder valve and release pedal. Repeat procedure until fluid flow is free of air bubbles.

NOTE: When bleeding brake system manually, ensure bleeder valve is closed when brake pedal is released.

ADJUSTMENTS

DISC PAD

NOTE: When replacing pads, ALWAYS replace inner and outer pads on both front wheels.

Pad wear is automatically compensated by piston moving outward in caliper bore. Disc pad adjustment is not required. Inspect disc pads whenever wheels are removed.

HEIGHT SENSING PROPORTIONING VALVE

Caravan, Town & Country, & Voyager – 1) Premature rear wheel skid may be caused by incorrect adjustment of height sensing proportioning valve. Before making adjustment, inspect brake system and bleed entire system using appropriate method. See BLEEDING PROCEDURES under BLEEDING BRAKE SYSTEM.
2) Raise vehicle on hoist and allow rear suspension to hang free with rear wheels removed. Ensure hoist does not contact rear springs. Disconnect shock absorbers. Loosen adjustment nut on actuator assembly. *See Fig. 3.* Ensure actuator assembly hook is correctly seated on proportioning valve lever.
3) Pull actuator assembly toward spring hanger until proportioning valve lever bottoms. Hold proportioning valve lever in this position. and tighten adjustment nut to **25 INCH lbs. (2.8 N.m)**. Install shock absorbers and rear wheels.

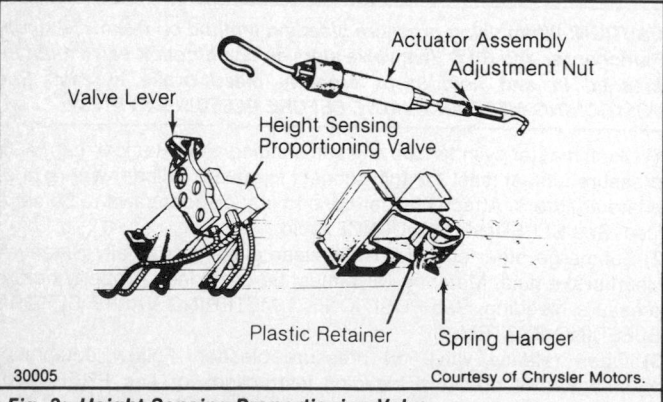

30005   Courtesy of Chrysler Motors.

Fig. 3: Height Sensing Proportioning Valve (Caravan, Town & Country, & Voyager)

PARKING BRAKE

1) Release parking brake, and loosen cable adjusting nut to allow slack in cable. Adjust rear brakes. Tighten cable adjusting nut until a slight drag is felt while rotating rear wheels.
2) Loosen cable adjusting nut until both rear wheels can be rotated freely. Back off adjusting nut an additional 2 turns. Apply and release parking brake several times, checking for free rotation at rear wheels.

REAR BRAKE SHOES

1) Raise and support vehicle. Ensure parking brake lever is fully released. Back off parking brake cable adjustment to ensure cable has slack. Remove adjusting hole cover.
2) Using a brake adjuster, expand brake shoes until slight drag is felt when wheel assembly is rotated. Using thin screwdriver, hold automatic adjusting lever away from adjustment star wheel.
3) Back off adjustment star wheel until wheel assembly rotates freely and brake shoe drag is eliminated. Repeat adjustment for remaining wheels. Adjustment must be equal at all wheels. Replace adjusting hole covers, and adjust parking brake. See PARKING BRAKE under ADJUSTMENTS.

STOPLIGHT SWITCH

Stoplight switch is attached to brake pedal support. Push stoplight switch through clip in mounting bracket until switch seats in bracket. Pull brake pedal backward as far as pedal will travel. Brake pedal will ratchet stoplight switch to correct position. Verify full brake pedal return and that stoplights glow when brake pedal is applied.

TESTING

POWER BRAKE BOOSTER FUNCTIONAL TEST

1) Start engine, and check booster vacuum hose connections. A hissing noise indicates a vacuum leak. Repair any vacuum leaks before proceeding. Stop engine and shift transmission into Neutral. Pump brake pedal until all vacuum reserve in booster is depleted.
2) Hold brake pedal under light foot pressure. If pedal does not hold firm and falls away, master cylinder may be faulty. Bleed system using appropriate method, and repeat step 1). See BLEEDING PROCEDURES under BLEEDING BRAKE SYSTEM. If pedal still does not hold firm, master cylinder is faulty. If pedal holds firm, start engine and observe pedal action. If no pedal action is observed, power booster or vacuum check valve is faulty. Install good check valve, and repeat steps 1) and 2). If pedal falls away slightly under light foot pressure and then holds firm, go to next step .
3) With engine running, rebuild booster vacuum reserve. Release brake pedal. Increase engine speed to 1500 RPM. Close throttle and immediately turn off ignition. Wait at least 90 seconds, and try brake action again. Booster should provide 2 or more vacuum assisted pedal applications. If vacuum assist is not provided, perform booster and check valve vacuum tests.

POWER BRAKE BOOSTER VACUUM TEST

Connect vacuum gauge to booster check valve using "T" fitting. Start engine, and run it at idle speed for one minute. Clamp hose shut between vacuum source and check valve. Stop engine and observe vacuum gauge. If vacuum drops more than one in. Hg within 15 seconds, booster diaphragm or check valve is faulty.

POWER BRAKE BOOSTER CHECK VALVE TEST

Disconnect vacuum hose from check valve. Remove check valve and valve seal from booster. Use a hand operated vacuum pump for testing. Apply 15-20 in. Hg vacuum at large end of check valve. Vacuum should hold steady. If gauge on pump indicates vacuum loss, check valve is faulty and should be replaced.

HEIGHT SENSING PROPORTIONING VALVE TEST

Caravan, Town & Country, & Voyager – 1) Remove actuator assembly adjustment nut. *See Fig. 3.* Disconnect actuator assembly hook from height sensing proportioning valve. Install one gauge and "T" of Height Sensing Proportioning Valve Test Set (C-4007-A) in either line of master cylinder outlet port between master cylinder and brake warning switch.
2) Install other gauge and "T" of test set in either line of proportioning valve outlet port between proportioning valve and rear wheel cylinder. Bleed brake system and gauges.

3) Using an assistant, press and hold brake pedal. Note reading on both gauges. Pressure on inlet gauge (at master cylinder) should be **500 psi (35 kg/cm²)**. Pressure on outlet gauge (at proportioning valve) should be **100-200 psi (7-14 kg/cm²)**.

4) If pressures are not to specification, replace height sensing proportioning valve. If pressures are okay, remove test equipment. Install actuator and adjust. See HEIGHT SENSING PROPORTIONING VALVE under ADJUSTMENTS. Bleed brake system. See appropriate bleeding procedure under BLEEDING BRAKE SYSTEM.

COMBINATION VALVE METERING VALVE TEST

Metering valve operation can be checked visually with aid of an assistant. While an assistant applies and releases brake pedal, observe metering valve stem. If valve is operating correctly, stem will extend slightly when brakes are applied and contract when brakes are released. If valve is faulty, replace combination valve assembly.

COMBINATION VALVE
PRESSURE DIFFERENTIAL SWITCH TEST

1) Using an assistant, observe brake warning light and apply brake pedal. Raise and support vehicle and connect a bleed hose to one rear wheel cylinder. Submerge other end of hose into container partially filled with brake fluid. Have assistant press and hold brake pedal down while observing brake warning light. If warning light glows, switch is operating properly.

2) If warning light fails to glow, check circuit fuse, bulb and wiring. Repair as necessary. Repeat step **1)**. If warning light fails to glow, check brake light, parking brake switches and related wiring. Repair as necessary. Repeat step **1)**. If warning light fails to glow, pressure differential switch is faulty. Replace combination valve assembly, bleed brake system and verify proper valve operation.

REMOVAL & INSTALLATION

CALIPER

CAUTION: DO NOT allow caliper to hang by brake hose. Damage to brake hose could result.

Removal (Bendix) – 1) Raise and support vehicle. Remove wheels. Remove support key retaining screw. *See Fig. 4.* Using drift punch, drive out support key and spring. Remove caliper from adapter, and pry outer pad from caliper.

2) Support caliper aside. Remove inner pad and anti-rattle spring from adapter. Note position of anti-rattle spring on inner pad for installation. If reusing pads, mark pads for installation reference.

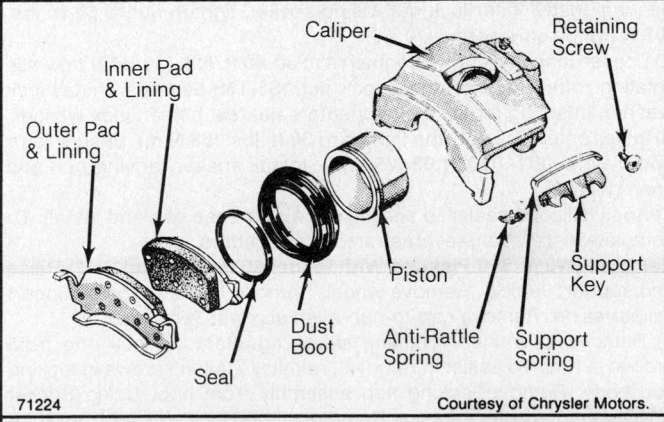

71224　　　　　　　　　　　　　　Courtesy of Chrysler Motors.

Fig. 4: Exploded View Of Single-Piston Sliding Caliper (Bendix)

Inspection – Replace pads if lining is worn to within 1/16" (1.6 mm) of rivet heads. Inspect rotor. See inspection procedure for ROTOR under REMOVAL & INSTALLATION. Check piston seal for leaks and piston boot for cuts. If piston seal leaks or if boot is damaged, overhaul caliper assembly. Disconnect and plug hydraulic brake hose at caliper if caliper overhaul is necessary.

Installation – 1) Clean caliper and adapter slide surfaces using wire brush. Lubricate with multipurpose grease. Install anti-rattle spring on inner pad, ensuring loop portion of spring is away from rotor. Install inner pad in adapter, ensuring spring remains in position.

2) Install outer pad in caliper. Free play should not exist between pad flange (tab) and caliper flange. If free play exists, bend pad flange (tab) until interference fit with caliper is obtained. If disc pad cannot be installed by hand, press into place using a block of wood and "C" clamp. Place caliper into position over rotor. Seat caliper in adapter.

3) Place support spring over support key. Install assembly between adapter and lower caliper machined surfaces. Tap assembly into place using drift punch. Install support key retaining screw, ensuring boss on screw fits into cut-out on support key.

4) If caliper overhaul was necessary, install brake hose. Bleed brake system. See BLEEDING PROCEDURES under BLEEDING BRAKE SYSTEM. Install wheels. Fill reservoir to proper level. Slowly pump brake pedal until firm. Check reservoir fluid level. Road test vehicle.

Removal (Chrysler Motors) – Raise and support vehicle. Remove wheels. Remove caliper retainer bolts, anti-rattle springs and clips. *See Fig. 5.* Carefully lift caliper assembly away from rotor. Pry between outer pad and caliper to remove outer pad. Support caliper aside. Remove inner pad from adapter.

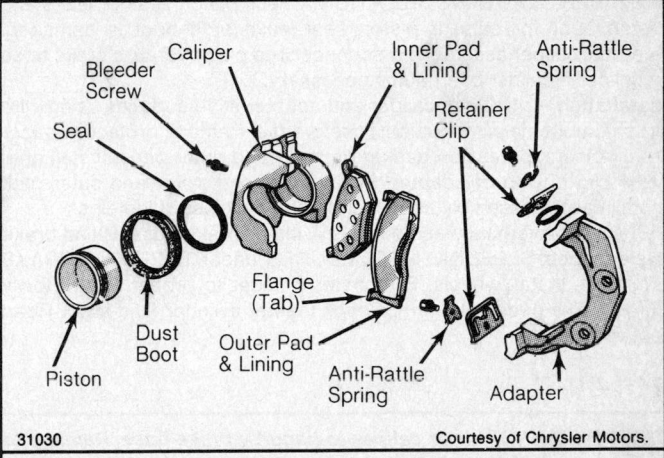

31030　　　　　　　　　　　　　　Courtesy of Chrysler Motors.

Fig. 5: Exploded View Of Single-Piston Sliding Caliper (Chrysler Motors)

Inspection – Measure pad lining thickness. If pad lining is worn to a thickness of 1/8" (3.2 mm) or less, replace pads. Inspect rotor. See inspection procedure for ROTOR under REMOVAL & INSTALLATION. Check piston seal for leaks and piston boot for cuts. If piston seal leaks or if boot is damaged, overhaul caliper assembly. Disconnect and plug hydraulic brake hose at caliper if caliper overhaul is necessary.

Installation – 1) Clean caliper and adapter slide surfaces using wire brush. Install inner pad into adapter. Lubricate slide surfaces of adapter and caliper with multipurpose grease. Remove protective paper from noise suppression gasket on outer pad. Install outer pad in caliper. Free play should not exist between pad flange (tab) and caliper flange. If free play exists, bend pad flange (tab) until interference fit with caliper is obtained.

2) Carefully install caliper over rotor. Align caliper in adapter. Install retainer clips and anti-rattle springs. Install brake hose, if caliper overhaul was necessary. Bleed brake system. See BLEEDING PROCEDURES under BLEEDING BRAKE SYSTEM. Install wheels. Fill master cylinder to proper level. Slowly pump brake pedal to obtain firm pedal. Check master cylinder fluid level. Road test vehicle.

Removal (Kelsey-Hayes Double Pin) – Raise and support vehicle. Remove front wheels. Remove caliper guide pins. Pry caliper away from adapter and pads. *See Fig. 6.* Remove caliper. Support caliper aside. Remove outer pad, rotor and inner pad.

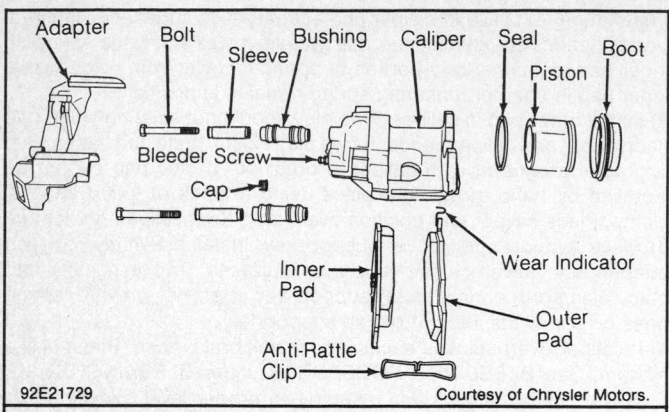

Fig. 6: Exploded View Of Single-Piston Sliding Caliper (Kelsey-Hayes Double Pin)

Inspection – Measure combined thickness of pad and backing at thinnest part of pad. If combined thickness is 1/4" (6.35 mm) or less, replace pads. Inspect rotor. See inspection procedure for ROTOR under REMOVAL & INSTALLATION. Check piston seal for leaks and piston boot for cuts. If piston seal leaks or if boot is damaged, overhaul caliper assembly. Disconnect and plug hydraulic brake hose at caliper if caliper overhaul is necessary.

Installation – **1)** Clean caliper and adapter slide surfaces using wire brush. Lubricate with multipurpose grease. Remove protective paper from noise suppression gasket on inner and outer pads. Install anti-rattle clip on top of adapter. Install inner pad, rotor and outer pad. Install caliper assembly. Install and tighten caliper guide pins.

2) If caliper overhaul was necessary, install brake hose. Bleed brake system. See BLEEDING PROCEDURES under BLEEDING BRAKE SYSTEM. Install wheels. Fill master cylinder to proper level. Slowly pump brake pedal until firm. Check master cylinder fluid level. Road test vehicle.

ROTOR

CAUTION: DO NOT allow caliper to hang by brake hose. Damage to brake hose could result.

Inspection – **1)** Raise and support vehicle. Remove wheels. On Caravan, Dakota 4WD, Town & Country and Voyager, reinstall and tighten lug nuts to secure rotor. On Dakota 2WD, Pickup, Ramcharger and RWD Van, remove dust cap and temporarily adjust wheel bearings to zero end play.

2) On all models, mount dial indicator on steering arm, with plunger contacting rotor approximately 1" (25 mm) from edge of rotor. Slowly rotate rotor and note lateral runout. Lateral runout on either side of rotor should not exceed specification. See DISC BRAKE SPECIFICA-TIONS table.

3) On Caravan, Dakota, Town & Country and Voyager, check runout of hub face if runout exceeds specification. Before removing rotor, make a chalk mark across rotor and one wheel stud. Make mark on high side of runout.

4) Remove rotor from hub. Install dial indicator on steering arm, with stem contacting hub face near outer diameter. Place dial indicator stem outside stud circle but inside chamfer on hub rim. If runout is not within specification, hub must be replaced.

5) If hub runout is within specification, install rotor on hub with chalk marks 180 degrees apart. Install wheel lug nuts and recheck rotor runout. If runout is not within specification, resurface or replace rotor.

6) On all models, measure rotor parallelism. To measure parallelism, measure rotor thickness with micrometer at 12 equal points around rotor radius approximately 1" (25 mm) from edge of rotor. If thickness varies more than parallelism specification, resurface or replace rotor. See DISC BRAKE SPECIFICATIONS table.

Removal (Dakota 2WD, Pickup 2WD, Ramcharger 2WD & RWD Van) – Raise and support vehicle. Remove wheels. Remove brake caliper from adapter. Support caliper aside. Remove grease cap, cot-

ter pin, nut lock, nut, thrust washer and outer wheel bearing. Pull rotor assembly off spindle.

Installation – **1)** Slide rotor assembly into position on spindle. Pack and install outer wheel bearing, thrust washer and nut. While rotating rotor and hub assembly, tighten wheel bearing nut to **20-25 ft. lbs. (27-34 N.m)** on RWD Van and **90 INCH lbs. (10 N.m)** on all other 2WD models.

2) Back off nut to release preload. Retighten nut finger tight. Install nut lock and cotter pin. Coat inside of cap with grease, and install cap. To complete installation, reverse removal procedure.

Removal & Installation (Caravan, Dakota 4WD, Town & Country, & Voyager) – Raise and support vehicle. Remove wheels. Remove brake caliper. Support caliper aside. Remove rotor from drive flange. To install, reverse removal procedure.

Removal (Ramcharger 4WD & W150/250 Pickup With Model 44 Front Axle) – **1)** Raise and support vehicle. Remove wheel. Remove brake caliper and adapter. Support caliper aside. Remove grease cap and driving hub snap ring. Remove drive hub and spacer. *See Fig. 7.*

2) Using Socket (C-4170), remove outer lock nut. Remove lock washer and inner lock nut. Remove rotor. Outer wheel bearing will slide off of spindle as rotor is removed.

1. Cap	10. Wheel Nut
2. Snap Ring	11. Wheel Stud
3. Drive Hub	12. Hub & Rotor
4. Spacer	13. Inner Bearing Cup
5. Outer Lock Nut	14. Inner Bearing
6. Lock Washer	15. Inner Grease Seal
7. Inner Lock Nut	16. Adapter
8. Outer Bearing	17. Adapter-To-Knuckle Bolt
9. Outer Bearing Cup	

Fig. 7: Exploded View Of 4WD Hub/Bearing Assembly (Model 44 Front Axle)

Installation – **1)** Mount rotor on spindle. Pack and install outer wheel bearing. Install inner lock nut. Using socket, tighten nut to **50 ft. lbs. (68 N.m)** to seat bearings.

2) Loosen inner lock nut. Retighten it to **30-40 ft. lbs. (41-54 N.m)** while rotating rotor. Back off inner lock nut 135-150 degrees. Install lock washer, ensuring pin on lock nut enters nearest hole in lock washer.

3) Install outer lock nut, and tighten to **50 ft. lbs. (68 N.m)**. Ensure rotor end play is **.001-.010" (.03-.25 mm)**. Install spacer, driving hub and snap ring.

4) Apply silicone sealer to sealing edge of grease cap and install. To complete installation, reverse removal procedure.

Removal (W250/350 Pickups With Model 60 Front Axle) – **1)** Raise and support vehicle. Remove wheel. Remove brake caliper. Support caliper aside. Remove cap-to-hub Allen screws. *See Fig. 8.*

2) Remove axle shaft retaining snap ring. Remove lock ring from groove in hub. To assist in removal, reinstall 2 Allen screws in locking hub body. Remove locking hub assembly from hub. Using Socket (7158), remove outer lock nut. Remove tabbed lock washer from spindle. Using Socket (7158), remove inner lock nut. Remove hub and rotor assembly from spindle.

Installation – **1)** Mount hub and rotor assembly on spindle. Pack and install outer wheel bearing. Install inner lock nut. Using Socket (7158), tighten nut to **50 ft. lbs. (68 N.m)** to seat bearings.

2) Loosen inner lock nut. Retighten it to **30-40 ft. lbs. (41-54 N.m)** while rotating rotor. Back off inner lock nut 135-150 degrees. Install tabbed

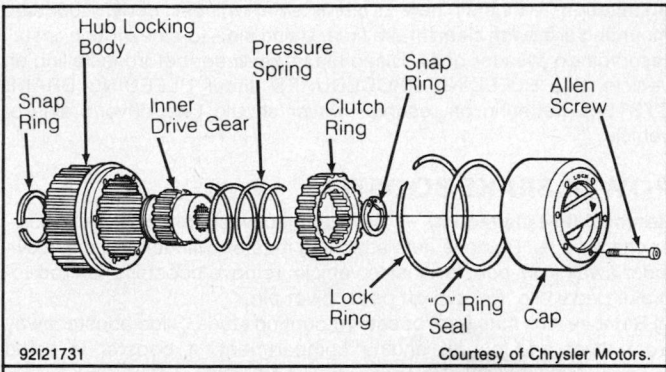

Fig. 8: Exploded View Of Locking Hub Assembly (Model 60 Front Axle)

92I21731

Courtesy of Chrysler Motors.

lock washer. Install outer lock nut, and tighten it to **160-205 ft. lbs. (217-278 N.m)**. Ensure rotor end play is **.001-.010" (.03-.25 mm)**.

3) Install locking hub assembly on hub. Install lock ring in hub groove. Install snap ring on end of axle. Ensure snap ring is seated. Install cap on hub. Ensure "O" ring seal is in place and not distorted. Install and tighten Allen screws to **35-45 INCH lbs. (4-5 N.m.)**. To complete installation, reverse removal procedure.

REAR BRAKE SHOES

WARNING: Use water or brake cleaner to clean brake parts. DO NOT use compressed air to remove dirt and dust.

Removal (9", 10" & 11" Drum) – 1) Remove wheel and drum. Note how secondary spring overlaps primary spring. Using spring remover, remove brake shoe return springs. Slide automatic adjuster cable off anchor. Disconnect cable from adjusting lever.

2) Remove cable, cable guide and anchor plate. See Fig. 9. Disconnect adjusting lever return spring from lever. Remove lever and return spring from pivot pin. Remove shoe-to-shoe spring. Spread shoes and remove adjustment star wheel.

3) Remove shoe retainers, springs and nails. Remove parking brake lever from secondary shoe. Remove shoes and parking brake strut with spring.

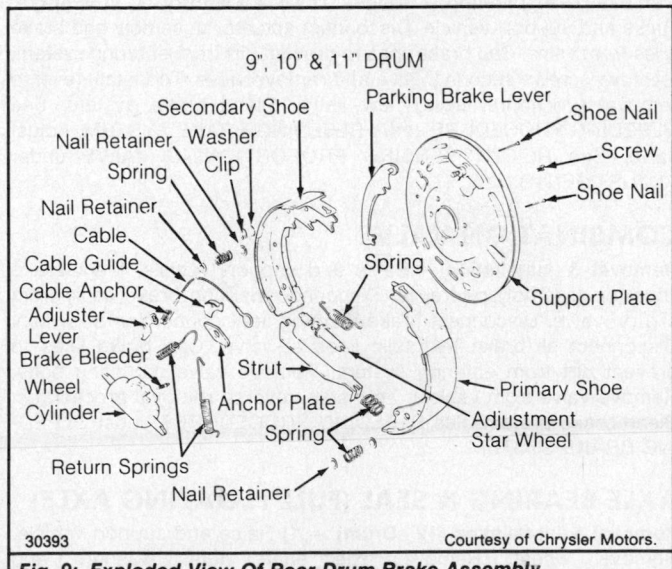

Fig. 9: Exploded View Of Rear Drum Brake Assembly (9", 10" & 11")

30393

Courtesy of Chrysler Motors.

Inspection – Replace brake shoes if worn to within 1/16" (1.6 mm) of rivet heads or if bonded lining is less than 3/16" (4 mm) thick. Discard brake springs and retainer components if worn, distorted or collapsed. Replace support plate if rusted through, bent or distorted.

Installation – 1) Apply thin coat of multipurpose grease to 6 shoe contact pads on support plate. Connect parking brake lever to secondary shoe. Install primary shoe on support plate with shoe nail, spring and retainer.

2) Install spring on parking brake strut and engage strut into primary shoe. Install secondary shoe on support plate with shoe nail, spring and retainer. Insert strut into slot in parking brake lever.

3) Install anchor plate and eye of adjusting cable over anchor. Install primary return spring. Position cable guide over hole in secondary shoe and install secondary return spring.

NOTE: To identify left and right adjustment star wheels, unscrew threaded rod from star wheel. Note stamped "L" or "R" on end of threaded rod.

4) Install adjustment star wheel with wheel closest to secondary shoe. Install shoe-to-shoe spring, engaging in primary shoe first with coil on opposite side of adjusting lever. Install lever spring and adjusting lever over pivot pin.

5) Slide lever rearward to lock in position. Thread adjuster cable over guide and hook end of cable in lever. Verify adjuster operation. Pull adjuster cable upward. Cable should lift lever and rotate star wheel. Ensure adjuster lever properly engages star wheel teeth. Adjust brakes. See REAR BRAKE SHOES under ADJUSTMENTS.

Removal (12" Drum) – 1) Remove drum. See AXLE BEARING & SEAL (FULL FLOATING AXLE) under REMOVAL & INSTALLATION. Disconnect adjusting lever from cable. Disconnect adjusting lever return spring from lever. Remove lever and return spring from pivot pin. Remove upper shoe-to-shoe spring.

2) Disconnect and remove shoe retainers, springs and nails. Disconnect parking brake cable from lever. Remove both brake shoes, lower shoe-to-shoe spring and adjustment star wheel as an assembly. See Fig. 10. Remove lower shoe-to-shoe spring.

NOTE: Adjustment star wheel on left brake assembly has left-hand threads. Right side assembly has right-hand threads.

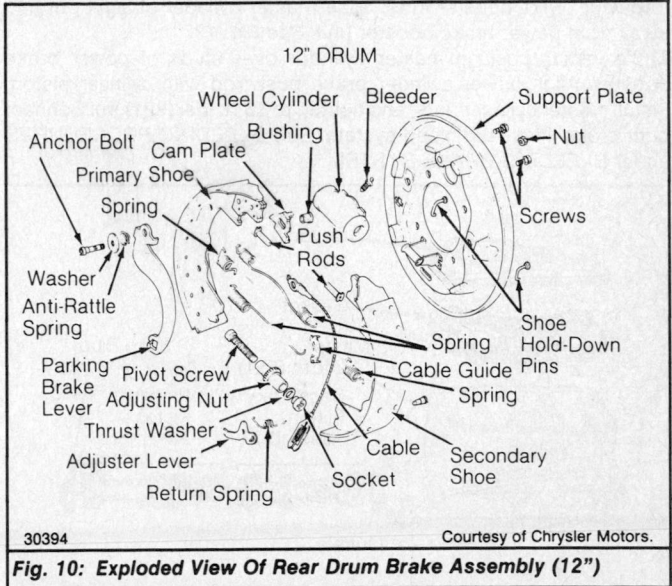

Fig. 10: Exploded View Of Rear Drum Brake Assembly (12")

30394

Courtesy of Chrysler Motors.

Inspection – Replace brake shoes if worn to within 1/16" (1.6 mm) of rivet heads or if bonded lining is less than 3/16" (4 mm) thick. Discard brake springs and retainer components if worn, distorted or collapsed. Replace support plate if rusted through, bent or distorted.

Installation – 1) Lubricate and assemble adjustment star wheel. Apply thin film of multipurpose grease to shoe contact pads on support plate. Assemble lower shoe-to-shoe spring, adjustment star wheel and both shoes. Position shoe assembly on support plate.

2) Attach parking brake cable to lever. Install shoe nails, springs and retainers. Install upper shoe-to-shoe spring. Position adjusting lever return spring on pivot. Install adjusting lever. Route cable, and connect it to adjuster. Install drum assembly and wheel. Adjust brakes. See REAR BRAKE SHOES under ADJUSTMENTS.

WHEEL CYLINDERS

Removal & Installation – **1)** Remove wheel, drum, and brake shoes. Inspect boots for damage and signs of leakage. Disconnect and plug hydraulic brake line from wheel cylinder. Remove attaching bolts, and remove cylinder. See Fig. 11.

2) Apply silicone sealant to cylinder mounting surface, and position cylinder on support plate. Start brake line fitting in wheel cylinder. Install and tighten mounting bolts. Tighten brake line fitting. To complete installation, reverse removal procedure. Fill brake fluid reservoir, and bleed hydraulic system. See BLEEDING PROCEDURES under BLEEDING BRAKE SYSTEM.

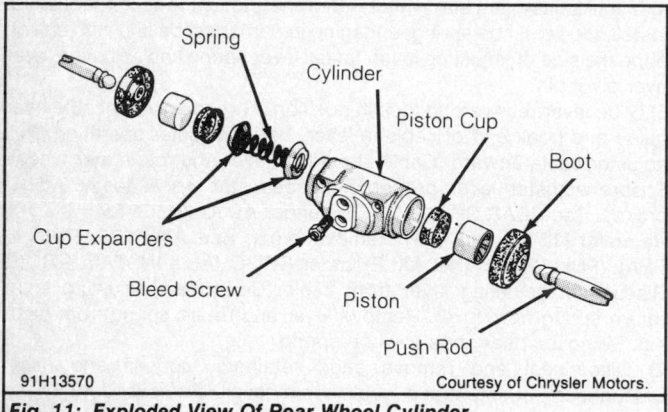

91H13570   Courtesy of Chrysler Motors.

Fig. 11: Exploded View Of Rear Wheel Cylinder

MASTER CYLINDER

Removal & Installation – **1)** Disconnect and plug primary and secondary brake lines from master cylinder. Remove master cylinder-to-power brake booster nuts. Slide master cylinder straight out and away from power brake booster unit. See Fig. 12.

2) To install, position master cylinder over studs of power brake booster. Align power cylinder brake push rod with cylinder piston. Install master cylinder nuts, and tighten to **16 ft. lbs. (22 N.m)**. Connect both brake lines, and bleed system. See BLEEDING PROCEDURES under BLEEDING BRAKE SYSTEM.

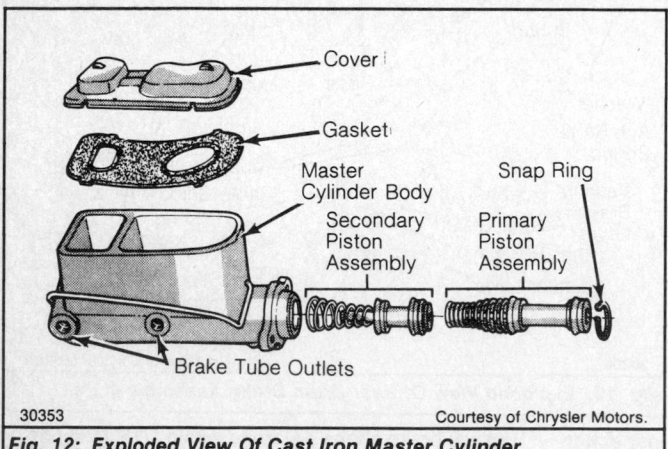

30353   Courtesy of Chrysler Motors.

Fig. 12: Exploded View Of Cast Iron Master Cylinder

RESERVOIR REPLACEMENT (ALUMINUM MASTER CYLINDER)

Removal – Empty brake fluid from reservoir. Position cylinder body in vise. Clean reservoir exterior and master cylinder body. Using side-to-side motion, remove reservoir from cylinder body. Remove grommets from cylinder body.

Installation – Install new grommets in cylinder body. Lubricate mounting area with clean brake fluid. Using side-to-side motion, install reservoir on cylinder body. Bleed master cylinder before installing on vehicle. See BLEEDING PROCEDURES under BLEEDING BRAKE SYSTEM. Lettering on reservoir cover should face driver's side of vehicle.

POWER BRAKE BOOSTER

Removal (In-Line Mount) – **1)** Disconnect vacuum hose from booster check valve. Remove nuts attaching master cylinder and move cylinder away from booster. Inside vehicle, remove booster push rod-to-brake pedal clip. Pry clip off pedal pivot pin.

2) Remove lock nuts from booster mounting studs. Slide booster away from dash and out of engine compartment. If booster is being replaced, remove booster check valve and seal.

Installation – **1)** If new booster is being installed, install check valve and seal. Position booster on dash and install lock nuts on booster mounting studs finger tight. Install booster push rod on brake pedal pin and secure rod with new retaining clip.

2) Tighten booster lock nuts to **18 ft. lbs. (24 N.m)**. Install master cylinder on booster, and tighten mounting nuts to **16 ft. lbs. (22 N.m)**. Connect vacuum hose to booster check valve. Start vehicle, and ensure proper booster operation.

Removal (Transverse Mount) – Disconnect vacuum hose from booster check valve. Remove nuts attaching master cylinder to booster studs. Move master cylinder away from booster. Remove pivot bolt, "O" ring and nut attaching booster rod to bellcrank. Remove lock nuts attaching booster to mounting bracket. Slide booster off mounting bracket and out of engine compartment. If booster is being replaced, remove booster check valve and seal.

Installation – **1)** Install check valve and seal if new booster is being installed. Position booster on mounting bracket and install lock nuts on booster mounting studs finger tight. Align booster rod with bellcrank arm, and install pivot pin, "O" ring and nut.

2) Tighten booster lock nuts and pivot pin nut to **30 ft. lbs. (41 N.m)**. Install master cylinder on booster, and tighten mounting nuts to **16 ft. lbs. (22 N.m)**. Connect vacuum hose to booster check valve. Start vehicle, and ensure proper booster operation.

HEIGHT SENSING PROPORTIONING VALVE

Removal & Installation (Caravan, Town & Country, & Voyager) – Raise and support vehicle. Disconnect actuator assembly and brake lines from valve. Cap brake lines to prevent dirt from entering system. Remove screws securing valve and remove valve. To install, reverse removal procedure, using new valve. Bleed brake system. See BLEEDING PROCEDURE under BLEEDING BRAKE SYSTEM. Adjust valve. See HEIGHT SENSING PROPORTIONING VALVE under ADJUSTMENTS.

COMBINATION VALVE

Removal & Installation – Raise and support vehicle. Mark brake lines for assembly reference. Disconnect parking brake cable from clip on valve. Disconnect brake warning light connection at switch. Disconnect all brake hydraulic lines at valve. Cap brake lines to prevent dirt from entering system. Remove valve mounting bolts. Remove valve from vehicle. To install, reverse removal procedures. Bleed brake system. See BLEEDING PROCEDURES under BLEEDING BRAKE SYSTEM.

AXLE BEARING & SEAL (FULL FLOATING AXLE)

Removal & Installation (12" Drum) – **1)** Raise and support vehicle. Remove wheel. Remove axle shaft nuts, washers and cones. Using dead blow hammer, sharply strike center of axle flange to free cones. Remove axle shaft and gasket.

2) Straighten and remove nut lock. Remove adjustment nut and outer bearing. Carefully remove drum assembly. Remove seal and inner bearing from drum assembly.

3) Pack and install inner bearing and seal in drum. Install drum assembly, outer bearing and adjustment nut. While rotating drum, tighten adjustment nut to **120-140 ft. lbs. (163-190 N.m)**.

4) Back off adjustment nut approximately 1/3 turn (120 degrees) to obtain .001-.008" (0.03-0.20 mm) end play. Bend nut lock into spindle keyway. Install gasket and axle shaft. Install wheel, and lower vehicle. See TORQUE SPECIFICATIONS table.

OVERHAUL

NOTE: When overhauling components, refer to Figs. 4-12.

TORQUE SPECIFICATIONS

TORQUE SPECIFICATIONS

Application	Ft. Lbs. (N.m)
Axle Shaft Flange Or	
Support Plate Mounting Nuts	
3/8"	25-60 (34-81)
7/16"	40-70 (54-95)
1/2"	65-105 (88-142)
Caliper	
Guide Pin(s) (Kelsey-Hayes)	25-35 (34-47)
Retaining Bolt (Chrysler Motors)	17 (23)
Retaining Screw (Bendix)	15 (20)
Caliper Adapter Bolts	
1/2" Bolts	95-125 (129-169)
5/8" Bolts	140-180 (190-244)
Drive Flange Lock Nuts (4WD)	30-40 (41-54)
Master Cylinder Nuts	16 (22)
Pivot Pin	30 (41)
Power Booster Lock Nuts	
In-Line Mount	18 (24)
Transverse Mount	30 (41)
Wheel Bearing Outer Lock Nut (4WD)	65 (88)
Wheel Lug Nuts	
Caravan, Town & Country, & Voyager	95 (129)
Dakota	85 (115)
Pickup, Ramcharger & RWD Van	
Cone 1/2" x 20	105 (142)
Cone 5/8" x 18	200 (271)
Flanged 5/8" x 18	325 (441)
	INCH Lbs. (N.m)
Locking Hub Allen Screws	35-45 (4.0-5.0)
Proportioning Valve Adjusting Nut	25 (2.8)

DISC BRAKE SPECIFICATIONS

DISC BRAKE SPECIFICATIONS

Application	In. (mm)
Disc Diameter	
Caravan, Town & Country, & Voyager	
Standard	10.24 (260)
Heavy Duty	11.14 (283)
Dakota	
Standard	10.70 (272)
Heavy Duty	11.40 (290)
Pickup 2WD	
D150	11.75 (298)
D250/350	12.88 (327)
Pickup 4WD	
W150	11.63 (295)
W250	12.82 (326)
W250/350 With Model 60 Front Axle	12.88 (327)
Ramcharger	
AD100/150	11.75 (298)
AW100/150	11.63 (295)
RWD Van	
B150/250	11.75 (298)
B350	12.82 (326)

DISC BRAKE SPECIFICATIONS (Cont.)

Application	In. (mm)
Lateral Runout	
Caravan, Town & Country, & Voyager	.005 (.13)
Dakota, Pickup [1], Ramcharger & RWD Van	.004 (.10)
Parallelism	
Except W250/350	.0005 (.013)
W250/350	.001 (.025)
Original Thickness	
Caravan, Town & Country, & Voyager	.870 (22.10)
Dakota	.871 (22.12)
Pickup [2] & Ramcharger	1.25 (31.75)
RWD Van	[3]
Minimum Refinish Thickness	
Caravan, Town & Country, & Voyager	.833 (21.16)
Dakota	.811 (20.6)
Pickup & Ramcharger	[4]
RWD Van	
B150/250	1.18 (29.97)
B350	1.25 (31.75)
Discard Thickness	
Caravan, Town & Country, & Voyager	.803 (20.4)
Dakota	.811 (20.6)
Pickup & Ramcharger	[5]
RWD Van	
B150/250	1.18 (29.97)
B350	1.125 (28.58)

[1] – On W250/350, lateral runout is .005" (.127 mm).

[2] – On W250/350 with model 60 front axle, original thickness is 1.19" (30.23).

[3] – Information is not available from manufacturer.

[4] – Discard thickness plus .030" (76 mm) equals minimum refinish thickness.

[5] – Discard thickness is marked on rotor hub.

DRUM BRAKE SPECIFICATIONS

DRUM BRAKE SPECIFICATIONS

Application	In. (mm)
9" Drum	
Drum Width	2.50 (63.5)
Maximum Allowable Diameter	9.060 (230.12)
Wheel Cylinder Diameter	.750 (19.05)
10" Drum	
Drum Width	2.50 (63.5)
Maximum Allowable Diameter	10.060 (255.52)
Wheel Cylinder Diameter	.810 (20.57)
11" Drum	
Drum Width	2.50 (63.5)
Maximum Allowable Diameter	11.060 (280.92)
Wheel Cylinder Diameter	.940 (23.88)
12" Drum	
Drum Width	[1] 2.50 (63.5)
Maximum Allowable Diameter	12.060 (306.32)
Wheel Cylinder Diameter	[2]

[1] – On Pickup and RWD Van B350 with Model 60 front axle, drum width is 3.00" (76.2 mm).

[2] – Wheel cylinder diameter is 1.00" (25.40 mm) on Pickup W250/350, 1.25" (28.58 mm) on Pickup W350 with Model 60 front axle and .940" (23.88 mm) on RWD Van.

Caravan, Dakota, Pickup, Ramcharger RWD Van, Town & Country, Voyager

NOTE: Prior to performing wheel alignment, perform visual and mechanical inspection of wheels, tires and suspension components. See PRE-ALIGNMENT INSTRUCTIONS in WHEEL ALIGNMENT THEORY & OPERATION article in GENERAL INFORMATION.

RIDING HEIGHT ADJUSTMENT

Dakota (4WD) – 1) Vehicle's side-to-side height difference should not be more than .25" (6.4 mm). Measure inner height from floor surface to underside surface of lower control arm rear pivot bores. Outer measurement is from floor surface to underside surface of lower control arm rear edge, at area immediately inboard of steering stop. **2)** Check inner and outer measurements, and adjust height differential to specifications. See ALIGNMENT SPECIFICATIONS at end of article. Adjust each front suspension arm by rotating torsion bar anchor adjustment bolt. After each adjustment, jounce vehicle before measuring height to determine effects of adjustment.

JACKING & HOISTING

FLOOR JACK

Dakota, Pickup & Ramcharger – 1) On Dakota, 2WD Pickup and 2WD Ramcharger, center floor jack under inner edge of lower control arm pivot bolt mounting bracket to raise front end. To raise rear end, position jack under rear axle, next to leaf spring mount. *See Fig. 1.*

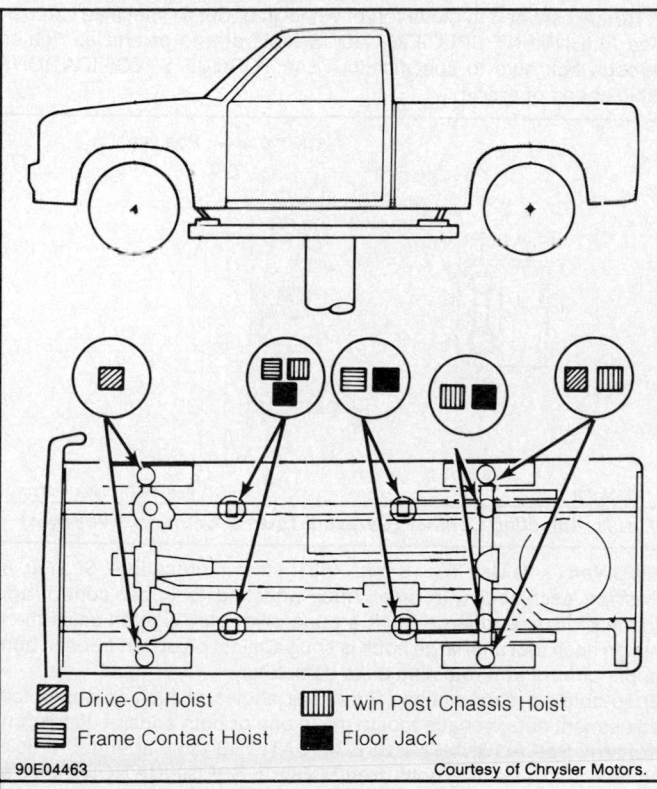

▨ Drive-On Hoist	⊞ Twin Post Chassis Hoist
▤ Frame Contact Hoist	■ Floor Jack

90E04463
Courtesy of Chrysler Motors.

Fig. 1: Identifying Hoisting & Jacking Locations (Dakota, Pickup & Ramcharger)

2) On 4WD Pickup and 4WD Ramcharger, raise front end by placing floor jack under outside of front leaf spring mount, and center it under front axle. To raise rear end, place floor jack under rear axle, next to leaf spring mount. *See Fig. 1.*

CAUTION: DO NOT place jack under any part of vehicle underbody. DO NOT attempt to raise one entire side of vehicle by placing a jack midway between front and rear wheels, as permanent body damage could occur.

Caravan, Town & Country, & Voyager – To raise front end, place floor jack under front crossmember forward flange, inboard of lower control arm pivot. To raise rear end, place floor jack under rear axle, next to leaf spring mount. *See Fig. 2.*

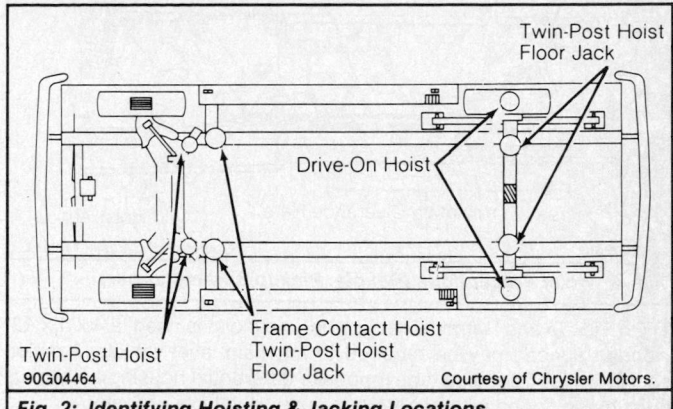

90G04464
Courtesy of Chrysler Motors.

Fig. 2: Identifying Hoisting & Jacking Locations (Caravan, Town & Country, & Voyager)

CAUTION: Never place jack under any part of vehicle underbody. DO NOT attempt to raise one entire side of vehicle by placing a jack midway between front and rear wheels, as permanent body damage could occur.

RWD Van – To raise front end, place floor jack under center of front crossmember, inboard of lower control arm pivot. *See Fig. 3.* To raise rear end, place floor jack under rear axle, next to leaf spring "U" bolt mount.

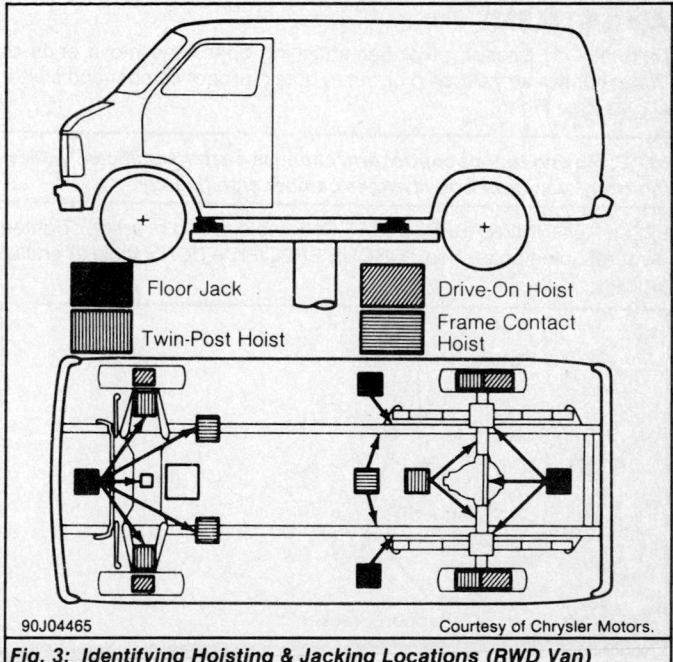

90J04465
Courtesy of Chrysler Motors.

Fig. 3: Identifying Hoisting & Jacking Locations (RWD Van)

HOIST

CAUTION: DO NOT raise vehicle by hoisting or jacking against front lower control arms. If rear axle, fuel tank, spare tire and liftgate will be removed for service, place additional weight on rear end of vehicle. This will prevent tipping as center of gravity changes.

Dakota, Pickup & Ramcharger – 1) Vehicle may be raised on single- or twin-post swiveling arm, or ramp-type drive hoists. If using swiveling arm hoist, ensure lifting arms, pads or ramps are positioned evenly on frame rails, and adequate clearance is maintained for transfer case (4WD models) or skid plate. *See Figs. 1 and 4.*

1992 WHEEL ALIGNMENT
Specifications & Procedures (Cont.)

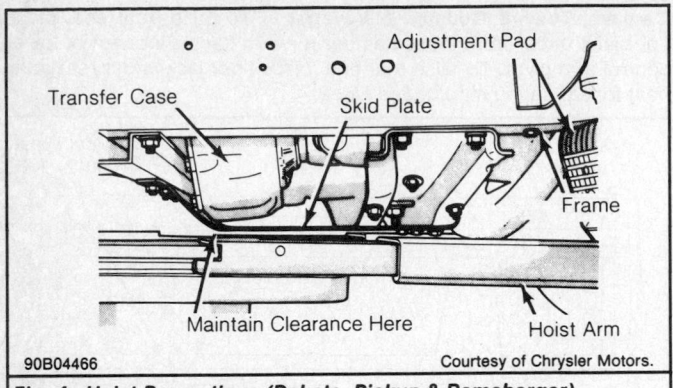

Fig. 4: Hoist Precautions (Dakota, Pickup & Ramcharger)

2) On Pickup and Ramcharger, if twin-post hoist is used, a 4 x 4 x 12" wooden spacer may be required to maintain level vehicle. Position spacer under front axle tube (opposite differential housing). All hoists must be equipped with adapters to support vehicle properly.

CAUTION: On RWD vans, ensure there is adequate drive shaft clearance while raising vehicle.

Caravan, RWD Van, Town & Country, & Voyager – To raise vehicle on single- and twin-post type hoists, ensure hoist pads contact vehicle frame behind front control arm pivots and inside rear wheels on rear axle housing. Always use appropriate hoist adapters. *See Fig. 2 or 3.*

WHEEL ALIGNMENT PROCEDURES

FRONT WHEEL CAMBER & CASTER ADJUSTMENT

Dakota – **1)** Loosen pivot bar attaching bolts, and move ends of upper control arm either in or out to obtain proper camber and caster angles. *See Fig. 5.*

NOTE: Moving rear of control arm changes caster significantly. Moving front of control arm changes camber significantly.

2) See ALIGNMENT SPECIFICATIONS table at end of article. Tighten pivot retaining bolts. See TORQUE SPECIFICATIONS table at end of article.

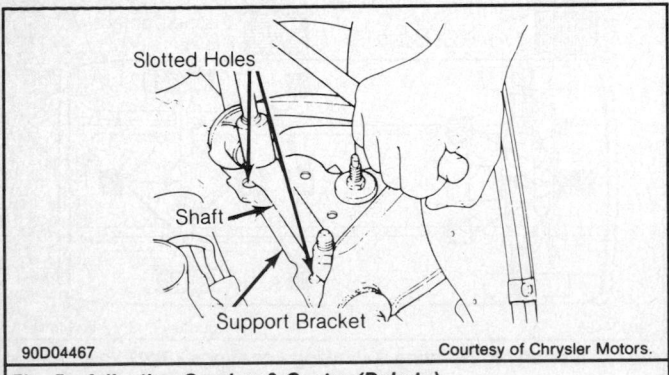

Fig. 5: Adjusting Camber & Caster (Dakota)

Pickup (2WD) & Ramcharger (2WD) – Clean eccentric cam bolt threads. Record camber and caster measurements. Loosen cam bolt retaining nuts. *See Fig. 6.* Adjust camber and caster to specification. See ALIGNMENT SPECIFICATIONS table at end of article. Tighten cam bolt retaining nuts to specification. See TORQUE SPECIFICATIONS table at end of article.

CAUTION: DO NOT adjust camber by heating or bending suspension components. If camber angle is incorrect, replace component(s) causing incorrect angle.

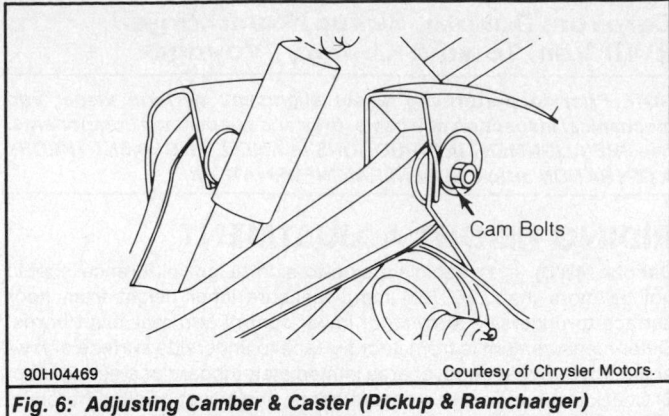

Fig. 6: Adjusting Camber & Caster (Pickup & Ramcharger)

Pickup (4WD) & Ramcharger (4WD) – Camber is not adjustable on 4WD models. Caster angle may be adjusted using shims. Record caster measurements. Remove original caster shims from spring pads, and add or delete shims to meet specifications. See ALIGNMENT SPECIFICATIONS table at end of article.

CAUTION: DO NOT adjust caster by heating or bending suspension components. If caster angle is incorrect, replace component(s) causing incorrect angle.

Caravan, Town & Country, & Voyager – Caster is not adjustable on FWD vehicles. Loosen cam and through bolts on each side. *See Fig. 7.* Rotate cam bolt to move top of wheel in or out to specified camber. See ALIGNMENT SPECIFICATIONS table at end of article. Tighten through bolt nuts to specification. See TORQUE SPECIFICATIONS table at end of article.

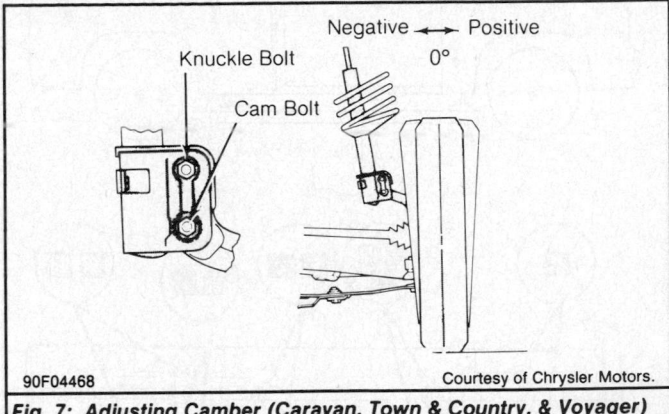

Fig. 7: Adjusting Camber (Caravan, Town & Country, & Voyager)

RWD Van – **1)** Use Tool Set (C-4581) for this procedure. *See Fig. 8.* Position each tool with small hook attached to upper control arm frame bracket and large hook around pivot bar. Tighten adjustment nut on each tool until large hook is snug against pivot bar. Loosen both upper control arm retaining bolts completely.
2) To obtain proper camber and caster angles, tighten or loosen tool adjustment nuts on each tool to move one or both ends of upper control arm. See ALIGNMENT SPECIFICATIONS table at end of article. Tighten pivot retaining bolts. See TORQUE SPECIFICATIONS table at end of article.

FRONT WHEEL TOE ADJUSTMENT

NOTE: Set each front wheel at 1/2 of total toe specification. On vehicles equipped with power steering, set wheel toe position with engine running.

Except RWD Van & 4WD Models – Center steering wheel and hold with steering wheel clamp. Loosen tie rod lock nuts. Rotate rods to set toe to specifications. See ALIGNMENT SPECIFICATIONS table.

1992 WHEEL ALIGNMENT
Specifications & Procedures (Cont.)

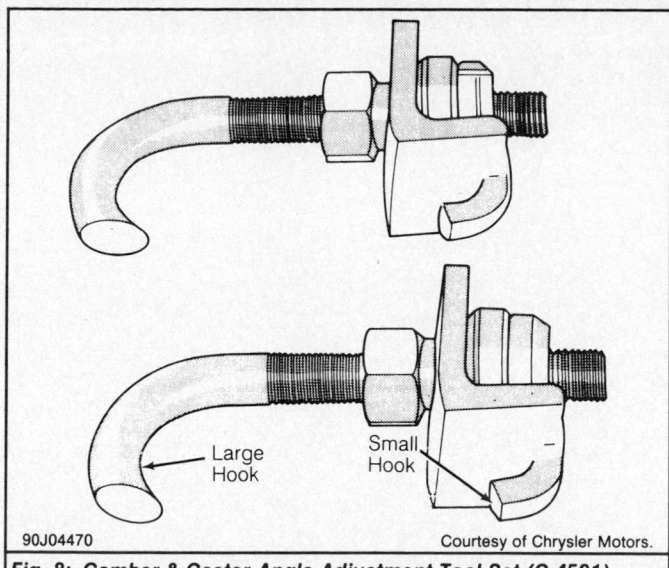

Fig. 8: Camber & Caster Angle Adjustment Tool Set (C-4581)

Tighten tie rod lock nuts to specification. See TORQUE SPECIFICATIONS table. Adjust steering gear to tie rod boots at tie rod. Remove steering wheel clamp.

RWD Van & 4WD Models – Center steering wheel and hold with steering wheel clamp. Loosen tie rod adjustment sleeve clamp bolts. Rotate adjustment sleeve to align toe to specifications. See ALIGNMENT SPECIFICATIONS table. Position sleeve clamps on underside of sleeve so clamp ends are not over sleeve slot, and tighten adjustment sleeve clamp bolts to specification. See TORQUE SPECIFICATIONS table. Remove steering wheel clamp.

REAR WHEEL CAMBER & TOE ADJUSTMENT

NOTE: Rear wheel alignment adjustments, if required, are made by adding 0.01" (.25 mm) shims between spindle mounting surface and axle casting.

Caravan, Town & Country, & Voyager – 1) Block front wheels, and release parking brake. With suspension supported, remove wheel, grease cap, cotter pin, castle lock, adjusting nut and brake drum.
2) Loosen, but DO NOT remove 4 backing plate mounting bolts. Adjust alignment by adding shims. *See Fig. 9.*

NOTE: Each shim changes alignment reading by 19/64° (.3°). DO NOT use more than 2 shims to make adjustments.

3) Tighten 4 backing plate mounting bolts to **80 ft. lbs. (108 N.m).** Install brake drum, and adjusting nut. Tighten adjusting nut to **20-25 ft. lbs. (27-34 N.m)** while rotating wheel. Back off adjusting nut to completely remove preload, and retighten nut finger tight.

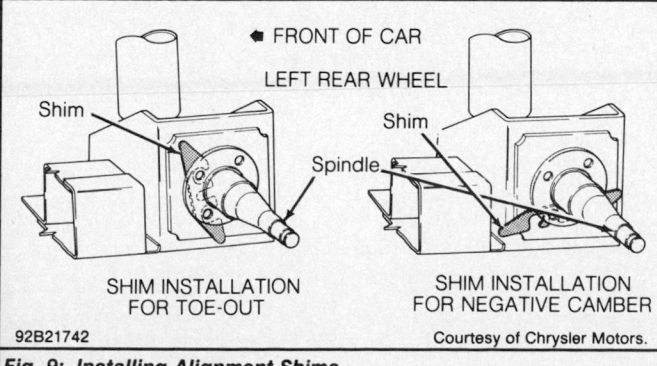

Fig. 9: Installing Alignment Shims

4) Install castle lock, cotter pin, grease cap and wheel. Lower vehicle, and recheck rear wheel alignment.

TORQUE SPECIFICATIONS
TORQUE SPECIFICATIONS

Application	Ft. Lbs. (N.m)
Eccentric Cam Bolt Nuts	
Caravan, Town & Country, & Voyager	[1] 75 (100)
Pickup (2WD) & Ramcharger (2WD)	70 (95)
Pivot Bar Retaining Bolts	
Dakota	155 (210)
RWD Van	195 (264)
Strut Nut	
Dakota, Pickup, Ramcharger & RWD Van	50 (68)
Tie Rod Adjustment Sleeve Bolts	
Except 4WD Models & D350 Pickup	13-17 (18-23)
4WD Models & D350 Pickup	25-26 (34-35)
Tie Rod Lock Nut(s)	
Caravan, Town & Country, & Voyager	55 (75)
All Other Models	13 (18)
Wheel Lug Nuts	
Caravan, Town & Country, & Voyager	95 (129)
Dakota	85 (115)
All Other Models	
1/2 x 20"	105 (142)
5/8 x 18"	200 (271)
Flanged Type Nut	325 (441)

[1] – Tighten 1/4 turn beyond specified torque.

ALIGNMENT SPECIFICATIONS
WHEEL ALIGNMENT SPECIFICATIONS

Application	Fraction	Decimal
Caravan, Town & Country, & Voyager		
Camber (Degrees)		
Front	-13/64 To 13/16	(-0.2 To 0.8)
Rear	-13/16 To 13/32	(-0.8 To 0.4)
Caster (Degrees) [1]	5/64 To 1 13/16	(.08 To 1.8)
Toe-In (Inches)		
Front	0 To 3/32	(0 To 0.1)
Rear	-19/64 To 19/64	(-0.3 To 0.3)
Toe-In (Degrees)		
Front	0 To 13/64	(0 To 0.2)
Rear	-19/32 To 19/32	(-0.6 To 0.6)
Dakota		
Camber (Degrees)	0 To 1.0	(0 To 1.0)
Caster (Degrees) [2][3]	1/2 To 2 1/2	(0.5 To 2.5)
Riding Height (Inches)	1 1/4 ± 1/4	(1.25 ± .25)
Toe-In (Inches)	5/64 To 3/16	(.08 To .18)
Toe-In (Degrees)	5/32 To 11/32	(.15 To .35)
Pickup & Ramcharger		
Camber (Degrees)		
2WD	0 To 1.0	(0 To 1.0)
4WD	-1.0 To 1.0	(-1.0 To 1.0)
Caster (Degrees)		
2WD	-1.0 To 2.0	(-1.0 To 2.0)
4WD	1/2 To 3 1/2	(0.5 To 3.5)
Toe-In (Degrees)		
2WD	0 To 1/2	(0 To 0.5)
4WD	-1/2 To 29/64	(-.05 To .45)
RWD Van		
Camber (Degrees)	-19/32 To 19/32	(-0.6 To 0.6)
Caster (Degrees) [2]	1 1/2 To 3 1/2	(1.5 To 3.5)
Toe-In (Inches)	-1/8 To 1/8	(-.12 To .12)
Toe-In (Degrees)	-1/4 To 1/4	(-.25 To .25)

[1] – Left-to-right caster differential must not exceed 1 1/2° (1.5°).
[2] – Left-to-right caster differential must not exceed 1 1/4° (1.25°).
[3] – If vehicle sways, caster should be increased.

Caravan, Town & Country, Voyager

DESCRIPTION

The front suspension is an independent MacPherson strut type. Struts are attached to upper fender reinforcements and steering knuckles. Lower control arms are attached to crossmember through bushings and to steering knuckles through ball joints. Working through a pivot bearing in upper retainer, upper strut and steering knuckle turn as an assembly during steering maneuvers. *See Fig. 1.*

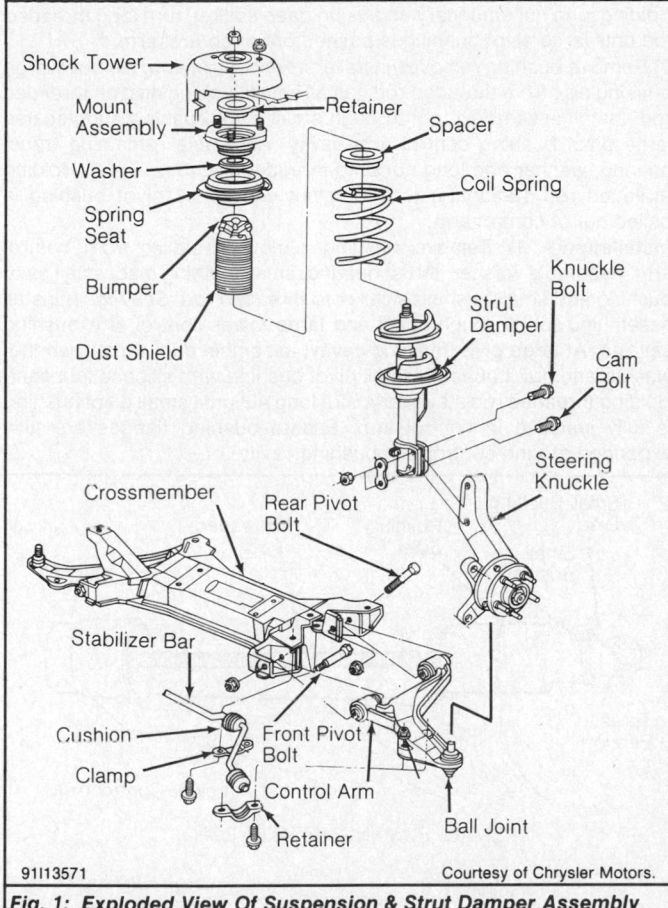

Fig. 1: Exploded View Of Suspension & Strut Damper Assembly

ADJUSTMENTS & INSPECTION

WHEEL ALIGNMENT SPECIFICATIONS & PROCEDURES

NOTE: See SPECIFICATIONS & PROCEDURES article in WHEEL ALIGNMENT.

WHEEL BEARING

Front wheel bearings are permanently sealed; lubrication and adjustment are not required. Hub and bearing unit is replaced as a complete assembly. Tighten hub nut to **180 ft. lbs. (244 N.m)** with brakes applied.

BALL JOINT CHECKING

NOTE: On some models, ball joint is welded to lower control arm and is not a serviceable component. Replace lower control arm assembly if ball joint needs to be replaced.

Lower Ball Joint – With weight of vehicle resting on wheels in normal driving position, grasp ball joint grease fitting and attempt to move it. Replace ball joint if fitting moves freely.

REMOVAL & INSTALLATION

HUB & BEARING ASSEMBLY

NOTE: If service procedures require front hub removal, replace grease seal.

Removal – 1) Remove cotter pin, nut lock and spring washer. *See Fig. 2.* Loosen hub nut with vehicle on ground and brakes applied. Raise and support vehicle. Remove wheel.

2) Remove hub nut. Ensure drive shaft is free to separate from spline in hub. Remove brake hose retainer from strut, and remove brake caliper from steering knuckle. Support caliper aside. Remove rotor from hub studs.

3) Remove cotter pin and nut from tie rod. Using Puller (C-3894-A), disconnect tie rod end from steering arm. Remove clamp bolt securing ball joint stud in steering knuckle. *See Fig. 2.* Separate ball joint stud from steering knuckle assembly.

4) Pull steering knuckle out and away from drive shaft. Remove 4 hub bolts attaching hub and bearing assembly to steering knuckle. Remove hub and bearing assembly.

NOTE: Knuckle and bearing mounting surfaces must be smooth and completely free of foreign material and nicks.

Installation – 1) Install new hub and bearing assembly, and tighten bolts to **45 ft. lbs. (61 N.m)**. Position new seal in recess. Using Seal Installer (C-4698), install seal.

2) Lubricate full circumference of seal and wear sleeve with multipurpose grease. Install drive shaft through hub. Install steering knuckle to suspension. To install remaining components, reverse removal procedure. Tighten all remaining components to specifications. See TORQUE SPECIFICATIONS table at end of article.

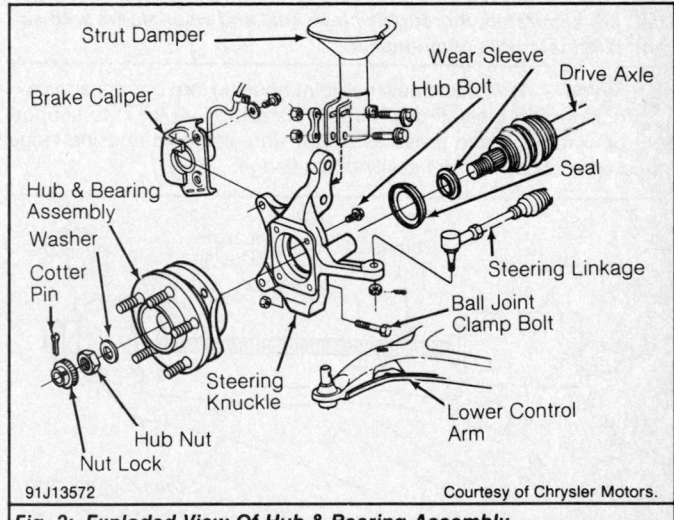

Fig. 2: Exploded View Of Hub & Bearing Assembly

STEERING KNUCKLE

Removal – 1) Remove cotter pin, nut lock and spring washer. Loosen hub nut with vehicle on ground and brakes applied. Raise and support vehicle. Remove wheel. Remove hub nut. Ensure splined drive shaft is free from hub. If necessary, drive shaft may be tapped lightly using soft brass punch.

2) Remove cotter pin and nut from tie rod. Using Puller (C-3894-A), separate tie rod from steering knuckle. Remove brake hose retaining clamp. Remove ball joint clamp stud bolt. Remove caliper adapter bolts with washers attached. Remove caliper, and support it aside. Remove rotor.

3) Mark camber position on upper cam bolt and then remove both bolts. Remove steering knuckle from strut damper and from ball joint stud. *See Fig. 2.* Ensure drive shaft is supported during removal of steering knuckle to prevent damage to constant velocity joints.

Installation – To install, reverse removal procedure. Tighten components to specifications. See TORQUE SPECIFICATIONS table at end of article.

LOWER CONTROL ARM & BALL JOINT

NOTE: On lower control arm with welded lower ball joint and pivot bushing, replace complete assembly if component replacement is necessary.

Removal (Control Arm) – **1)** Raise and support vehicle. Remove front inner pivot bolt. *See Fig. 1.* Remove rear stub strut nut, retainer and bushings. Remove ball joint-to-steering knuckle clamp bolt. Separate ball joint from steering knuckle.

CAUTION: DO NOT pull steering knuckle from vehicle after releasing ball joint or inner constant velocity joint will separate.

2) Remove stabilizer bar-to-control arm end bushing retainer nuts, and rotate control arm over stabilizer bar. Remove stub strut retainer. Check control arm for distortion and bushings for deterioration. Replace component as necessary.

Installation – To install, reverse removal procedure. Ensure control arm mount bolts are tightened with vehicle at normal operating height. Tighten pivot bolts to **125 ft. lbs. (169 N.m).**

Removal (Ball Joint) – **1)** Remove steering knuckle. See STEERING KNUCKLE under REMOVAL & INSTALLATION. Pry off dust seal. Position Receiving Cup (C-4699-2) to support lower control arm while receiving ball joint.

2) Install a 1 1/16" deep socket over stud and against joint upper housing. Use press to remove ball joint assembly from control arm.

NOTE: During any service procedures in which knuckle and drive shaft are separated, thoroughly clean seal and wear sleeve with solvent. Lubricate both components.

Installation – **1)** Position new ball joint housing into control arm cavity. Position assembly in press using Installer (C-4699-1) to support control arm. Align and press assembly until ball joint housing ledge stops against control arm cavity down flange.

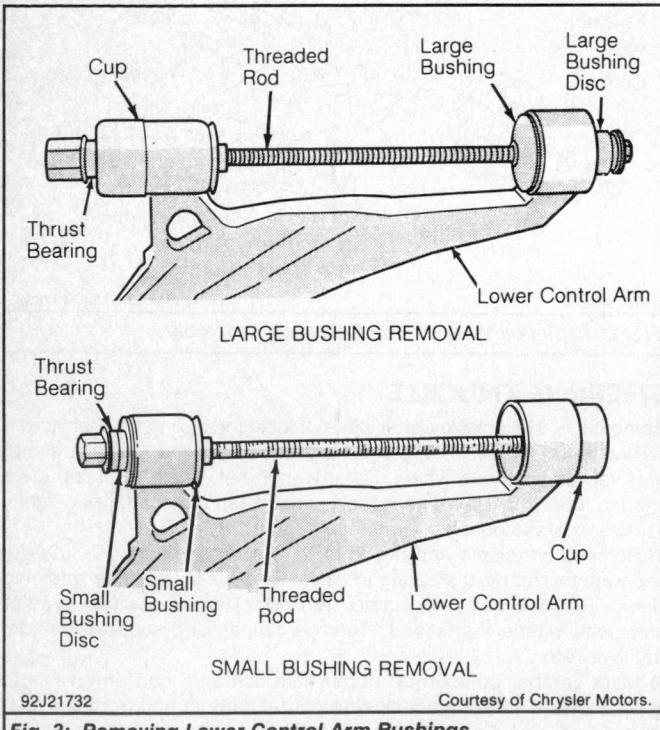

LARGE BUSHING REMOVAL

SMALL BUSHING REMOVAL

92J21732   Courtesy of Chrysler Motors.

Fig. 3: Removing Lower Control Arm Bushings

2) Support ball joint housing using receiving cup. Position new seal over stud and housing. Using a 1 1/2" socket, press seal onto joint housing until seal seats against control arm. To complete installation, reverse removal procedure. Tighten bolts to specification. See TORQUE SPECIFICATIONS table at end of article.

Removal (Pivot Bushing) – **1)** With control arm removed, place control arm in vise. Using Bushing Remover/Installer (6602), assemble washer, thrust bearing and large bushing disc onto threaded rod. *See Fig. 3.* Install assembled tool into large pivot bushing. Assemble remaining cup, thrust bearing, washer and nut onto threaded rod. Holding long nut stationary and using deep socket, turn long threaded rod until large pivot bushing is pushed out of control arm.

2) Remove bushing remover/installer from control arm. Remove large bushing disc from threaded rod. Install small bushing disc on threaded rod. Install assembled tool through small pivot bushing and vacated large pivot bushing control arm cavity. Assemble remaining thrust bearing, washer and long nut onto threaded rod. *See Fig. 3.* Holding threaded rod stationary, turn long nut until small pivot bushing is pulled out of control arm.

Installation – **1)** Remove bushing remover/installer from control arm. Assemble washer, thrust bearing, small bushing disc, small pivot bushing and small bushing sizer onto threaded rod. *See Fig. 4.* Install assembled tool through small and large lower control arm bushing cavities. At large pivot bushing cavity, assemble cup, thrust bearing, washer and nut. Lubricate small pivot bushing with silicone lubricant. Holding threaded rod stationary, turn long nut until small pivot bushing is fully installed in control arm. Ensure bushing flanges are fully expanded around control arm bushing cavity.

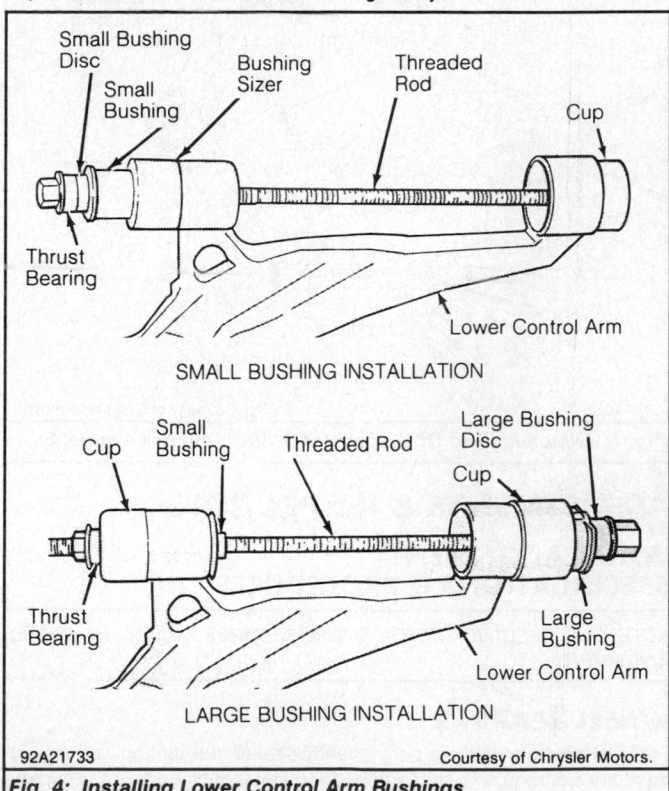

SMALL BUSHING INSTALLATION

LARGE BUSHING INSTALLATION

92A21733   Courtesy of Chrysler Motors.

Fig. 4: Installing Lower Control Arm Bushings

2) Remove bushing remover/installer. Assemble washer, thrust bearing and large pivot bushing cup onto threaded rod. Install assembled tool through small pivot bushing hole and large pivot bushing control arm cavity. At large pivot bushing control arm cavity, assemble large bushing sizer, large bushing cup, large pivot bushing, large bushing disc, thrust bearing, washer and nut onto threaded rod. *See Fig. 4.* Lubricate large pivot bushing with silicone lubricant. Point arrow on large pivot bushing away from lower ball joint. Holding threaded rod stationary, turn long nut until bushing is fully installed into control arm. Ensure bushing flanges are fully expanded around control arm bushing cavity.

3) Ensure arrow on large pivot bushing is pointing away from lower ball joint. If arrow moved during installation, install nut and bolt through bushing and sleeve. Tighten nut and bolt. Using wrench, rotate bolt until arrow is in correct position. To complete installation, reverse removal procedure. Tighten components to specifications. See TORQUE SPECIFICATIONS table at end of article.

STABILIZER BAR

Removal – Raise and support vehicle. Remove nuts, bolts and retainers from control arms. Remove bolts at crossmember clamps. Remove clamps, and remove stabilizer bar. Inspect components for cracks, damage and rubber deterioration.

Bushing Replacement – Inner bushing can be removed by opening split and removing bushing. Outer bushing must be cut or hammered off. Install new outer bushing until 1/2" of stabilizer bar protrudes.

NOTE: Control arm retainers will bend slightly upon installation.

Installation – To install, reverse removal procedure. Install crossmember bushings with curved surface upward and split area to front. Tighten bolts with vehicle at normal operating height. See TORQUE SPECIFICATIONS table at end of article.

STRUT ASSEMBLY

NOTE: When servicing original strut damper and steering knuckle, mark cam adjusting bolt position for reassembly reference.

Removal – **1)** Raise and support vehicle. Remove wheel. Remove cam adjusting bolt and steering knuckle bolt from strut damper assembly. See Fig. 1. Remove brake hose-to-damper bracket retaining bolt.

2) Remove strut damper-to-fender shield mounting nuts. Remove strut damper assembly from vehicle.

Disassembly – **1)** Compress coil spring in Spring Compressor (C-4838), with at least 5 coils of spring between compressor's jaws. See Fig. 5.

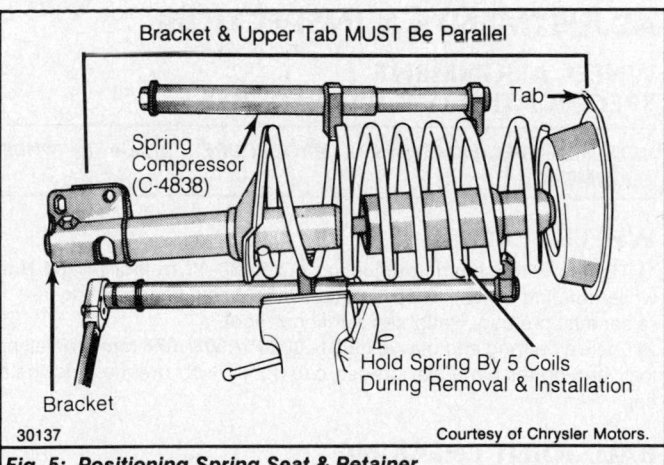

Bracket & Upper Tab MUST Be Parallel

Tab →

Spring Compressor (C-4838)

Hold Spring By 5 Coils During Removal & Installation

Bracket

30137   Courtesy of Chrysler Motors.

Fig. 5: Positioning Spring Seat & Retainer

NOTE: Coil springs are rated separately for each side of vehicle, depending on optional equipment and type of service. If removing springs, ensure to mark springs for installation in original positions.

2) Hold strut rod while loosening strut rod nut. Remove nut. Remove mount assembly. Remove coil spring, and mark it for installation to same side of vehicle. Remove remaining components. See Fig. 1.

Inspection – Inspect all components, and replace any showing signs of leakage, damage or excessive wear. If leakage is found, replace strut damper as an assembly.

Reassembly – **1)** Install dust shield, bumper, spacer and spring seat on top of spring. Install mount to strut rod, ensuring lower washer is in position.

2) Position upper tab parallel to strut damper lower attaching bracket. See Fig. 5. Install rebound retainer and strut rod nut. Using Nut Holder (L-4558), tighten strut rod nut to **60 ft. lbs. (81 N.m)** before releasing spring compressor. Remove spring compressor.

Installation – **1)** Install unit in fender shield. Install retaining nuts and washers. Tighten nuts to **20 ft. lbs. (27 N.m)**. Position steering knuckle into strut damper. Position washer plate, and install cam and steering knuckle bolts.

2) Attach brake hose retainer to strut damper, and tighten retaining bolt to **10 ft. lbs. (14 N.m)**. Index cam bolt to original mark. Place a 4" (102 mm) "C" clamp on strut damper and steering knuckle.

3) Tighten clamp to eliminate any looseness between steering knuckle and strut damper. Tighten bolts to **75 ft. lbs. (102 N.m)** plus 1/4 turn. Remove "C" clamp. Install wheel. Adjust front end alignment.

TORQUE SPECIFICATIONS
TORQUE SPECIFICATIONS

Application	Ft. Lbs. (N.m)
Ball Joint Clamp Bolt	70 (95)
Brake Caliper Adapter Bolt	160 (217)
Brake Caliper Guide Pins	18-26 (24-35)
Brake Hose-To-Strut Retaining Bolt	10 (14)
Control Arm Pivot Bolt	125 (169)
Hub & Bearing Assembly Bolts	45 (61)
Stabilizer Bar-To-Control Arm Bolt	50 (68)
Stabilizer Bar-To-Crossmember Bolt	50 (68)
Strut Damper Rod Nut	60 (81)
Strut Damper-To-Fender Shield Nut	20 (27)
Strut Damper-To-Steering Knuckle Cam & Knuckle Bolt	[1] 75 (102)
Tie Rod End Nut	35 (47)
Wheel Hub Mount Nut	180 (244)
Wheel Nut	95 (129)

[1] – Tighten an additional 1/4 turn.

1992 SUSPENSION
Front – 2WD Coil Spring

Dakota, Pickup, Ramcharger, RWD Van

DESCRIPTION

All models are equipped with independent front suspension, consisting of upper and lower control arms, steering knuckles, coil springs and shock absorbers. *See Figs. 1-3.* Upper control arms are mounted to frame side rails. Lower control arms are mounted to crossmember. Steering knuckles are mounted between upper and lower control arms by conventional ball joints. Coil springs are mounted between seat in frame and lower control arm.

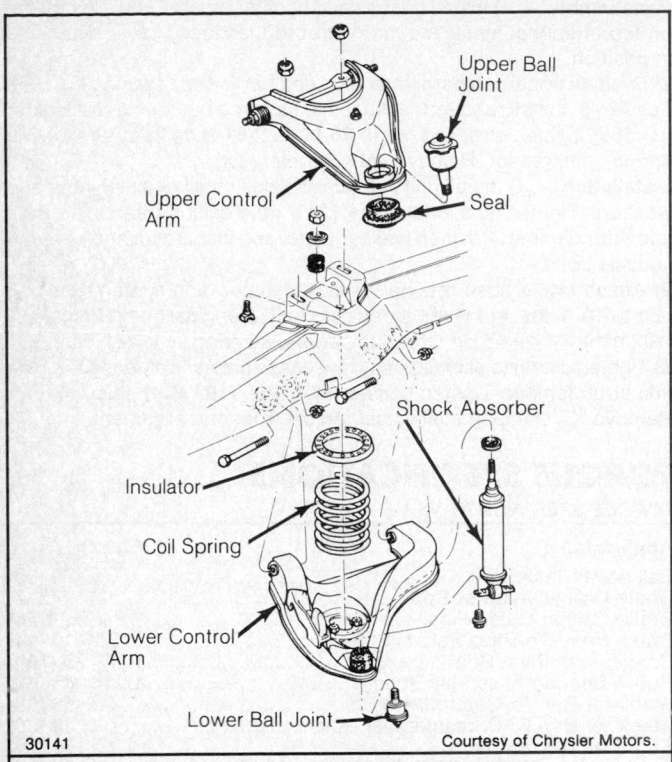

Fig. 1: Exploded View Of Front Suspension (Dakota)

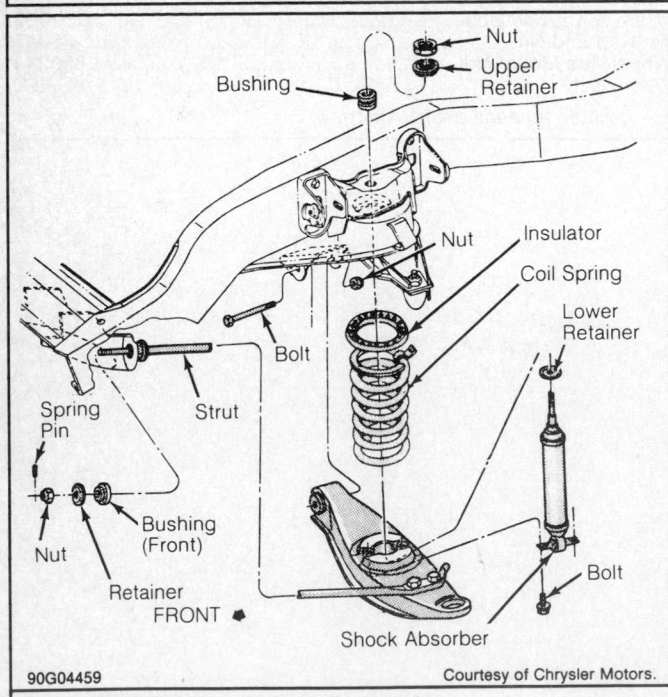

Fig. 2: Exploded View Of Front Suspension (Pickup & Ramcharger)

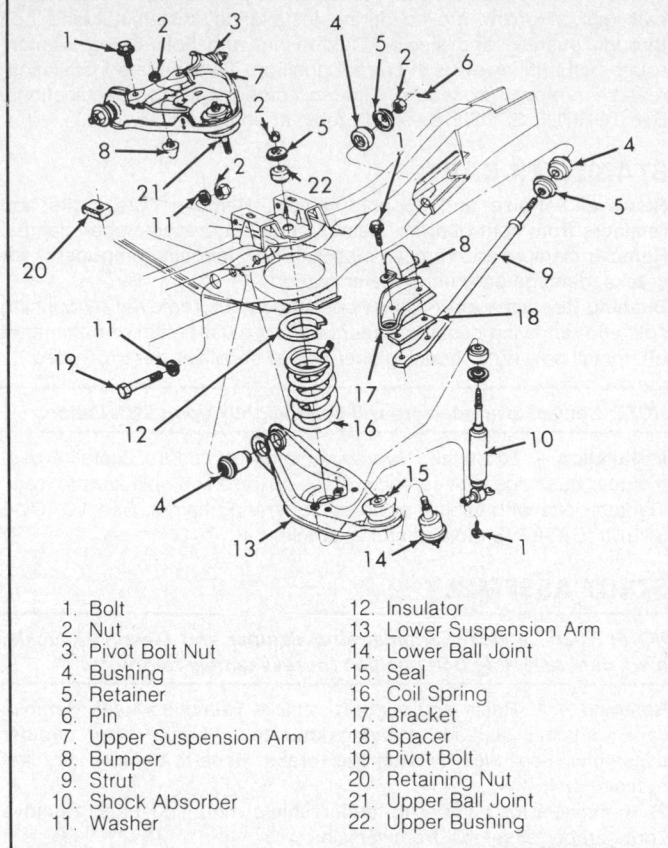

1. Bolt	12. Insulator
2. Nut	13. Lower Suspension Arm
3. Pivot Bolt Nut	14. Lower Ball Joint
4. Bushing	15. Seal
5. Retainer	16. Coil Spring
6. Pin	17. Bracket
7. Upper Suspension Arm	18. Spacer
8. Bumper	19. Pivot Bolt
9. Strut	20. Retaining Nut
10. Shock Absorber	21. Upper Ball Joint
11. Washer	22. Upper Bushing

90I04460   Courtesy of Chrysler Motors.

Fig. 3: Exploded View Of Front Suspension (RWD Van)

ADJUSTMENTS & INSPECTION

WHEEL ALIGNMENT SPECIFICATIONS & PROCEDURES

NOTE: See SPECIFICATIONS & PROCEDURES article in WHEEL ALIGNMENT.

WHEEL BEARING

1) Tighten wheel bearing adjusting nut to **30-40 ft. lbs. (41-54 N.m)** while rotating wheel. Stop rotation, and back off adjusting nut to release all preload. Retighten nut finger tight.
2) Ensure bearing end play is **.0001-.0030" (.003-.076 mm)**. Install nut lock and cotter pin. Coat grease cap lightly with grease, and install cap.

BALL JOINT CHECKING

Ball joints are preloaded. Replace lower ball joint if vertical movement exceeds **.02" (.5 mm)**. Replace upper ball joint if any perceptible lateral movement exists.

REMOVAL & INSTALLATION

COIL SPRING

Removal – **1)** Raise vehicle, position safety stands under frame and remove wheels. Remove brake caliper retainer and brake caliper (if necessary). Support caliper aside. On Pickup and Ramcharger, remove hub.
2) Remove shock absorber. *See Figs. 1-3.* Remove lower control strut rod. Disconnect sway bar (if equipped). Install Spring Compressor (DD-1278), tighten compressor finger tight and then back off 1/2 turn.

3) On all models except Dakota, remove cotter pins and ball joint nuts. Install Ball Joint Breaker (C-3564-A). Turn threaded portion of ball joint breaker to lock against lower stud. Tighten ball joint breaker to place pressure on lower stud.

CAUTION: DO NOT attempt to force ball joint stud from steering knuckle using ball joint breaker only.

4) Using hammer, strike steering knuckle to loosen ball joint stud. Remove ball joint breaker.

5) Slowly loosen spring compressor to relieve tension from coil spring. Remove spring compressor, coil spring and insulator (if equipped).

6) On Dakota, place 2 jacks under lower control arm (straddling bushings). Remove control arm-to-frame bolts. Slowly lower jacks until coil spring tension is released. Remove spring compressor, coil spring and insulator.

Installation – To install, reverse removal procedure. Tighten all nuts and bolts to specifications. See TORQUE SPECIFICATIONS table at end of article.

STEERING KNUCKLE

Removal & Installation – 1) Raise and support vehicle. Remove wheel. Remove caliper retainer and brake caliper. Support caliper aside. Remove inboard brake pad.

2) Remove grease cap, cotter pin, nut, washer and outer wheel bearing. Carefully slide rotor from steering knuckle. Remove splash shield. Remove and discard dust seal.

3) Place jack under outer end of lower control arm. Remove cotter pin and nut from tie rod end. Install Puller (C-3894-A), and apply enough pressure to free tie rod end.

4) Remove cotter pins and nuts from ball joints. Install Ball Joint Breaker (C-3564-A). Turn threaded portion of ball joint breaker to lock against lower stud. Tighten ball joint breaker to place pressure on lower stud.

CAUTION: DO NOT attempt to force ball joint stud from steering knuckle using ball joint breaker only.

5) Using hammer, strike steering knuckle to loosen ball joint stud. Separate ball joint studs from steering knuckle. Remove steering knuckle from vehicle, and separate components.

6) To install, reverse removal procedure. Tighten all nuts and bolts to specifications. See TORQUE SPECIFICATIONS table at end of article.

LOWER CONTROL ARM & BALL JOINT

Removal – 1) Raise and support vehicle. Remove wheel. Remove shock absorber and coil spring. See COIL SPRING under REMOVAL & INSTALLATION.

2) Remove brake caliper retainer and brake caliper. Support caliper aside. Remove cotter pin and lower ball joint nut. Install Ball Joint Breaker (C-3564-A). Turn threaded portion of ball joint breaker to lock against lower stud. Tighten ball joint breaker to place pressure on lower stud.

CAUTION: DO NOT attempt to force ball joint stud from steering knuckle using ball joint breaker only.

3) Using hammer, strike steering knuckle to loosen ball joint stud. Remove pivot bolts and lower control arm. Support lower control arm in vise. Remove ball joint seal. Using Ball Joint Press (C-4212), remove ball joint from lower control arm.

Installation – To install ball joint, use Ball Joint Press (C-4212) to press new ball joint into lower control arm. Using appropriately sized socket, seat ball joint seal until firmly locked. To install remaining components, reverse removal procedure. With vehicle at normal operating height, tighten all nuts and bolts to specifications. See TORQUE SPECIFICATIONS table at end of article.

LOWER CONTROL ARM BUSHINGS

Removal & Installation – Remove lower control arm. See LOWER CONTROL ARM & BALL JOINT under REMOVAL & INSTALLATION. Using a sleeve and press, remove and replace bushings.

STABILIZER BAR

Removal & Installation – Raise and support vehicle. Remove link rod retaining nut at each end of stabilizer bar. Remove outer retainers and rubber bushings from link rods. Remove bolts from "U"-shaped support brackets. Remove stabilizer bar from vehicle. To install, reverse removal procedure. Tighten all nuts and bolts to specifications. See TORQUE SPECIFICATIONS table at end of article.

STRUT ASSEMBLY

Removal & Installation – Raise and support vehicle. Remove stabilizer bar from strut bracket. Using a hammer and punch, remove spring pin from rear end of strut rod. Remove strut rod front retaining nuts and bolts from lower control arm. Remove strut assembly. Replace bushings (if necessary). To install, reverse removal procedure. Tighten all nuts and bolts to specifications. See TORQUE SPECIFICATIONS table at end of article.

UPPER CONTROL ARM & BALL JOINT

Removal – 1) Raise vehicle, and position safety stands under frame. Remove wheel. Remove shock absorber and coil spring. See COIL SPRING under REMOVAL & INSTALLATION.

2) On all models except Ramcharger, remove brake caliper retainer and brake caliper. Support caliper aside. Disconnect ball joint. See steps **2)** and **3)** in LOWER CONTROL ARM & BALL JOINT under REMOVAL & INSTALLATION.

3) On all models, remove pivot bolts and control arm. Support control arm in vise. Using Ball Joint Wrench (C-3561), unscrew ball joint from control arm.

Installation – To install, reverse removal procedure. Ensure ball joint is fully seated against control arm. With vehicle at normal operating height, tighten all nuts and bolts to specifications. See TORQUE SPECIFICATIONS table at end of article.

Bushing Replacement – If bushings are worn, remove upper control arm. Using a sleeve and press, remove and replace bushings.

WHEEL BEARINGS

Removal – 1) Raise and support vehicle. Remove wheel. Remove caliper retainer and anti-rattle springs (if equipped). Remove brake caliper, and support it aside. Remove inboard brake pad (if necessary). Remove grease cap, cotter pin, nut, washer and outer wheel bearing.

CAUTION: DO NOT allow inner bearing and seal to contact spindle threads during removal. Damage to threads, bearing and seal could result.

2) Carefully slide rotor from steering knuckle. Remove oil seal and inner bearing.

Installation – Clean and inspect bearings. Pack or replace bearings as required. Install inner bearing and oil seal. Carefully install rotor and outer bearing, washer and nut. Adjust wheel bearings. See WHEEL BEARING under ADJUSTMENTS & INSPECTION. To install remaining components, reverse removal procedure.

1992 SUSPENSION
Front – 2WD Coil Spring (Cont.)

TORQUE SPECIFICATIONS

TORQUE SPECIFICATIONS

Application	Ft. Lbs. (N.m)
Ball Joint Nuts	
Upper	
Dakota	105 (142)
Pickup, Ramcharger & RWD Van	135 (183)
Lower	
Dakota	135 (183)
Pickup, Ramcharger & RWD Van	
11/16"	135 (183)
3/4"	175 (237)
Brake Caliper Anti-Rattle Spring Retainer Clips	
Pickup, Ramcharger & RWD Van	18 (24)
Lower Control Arm Strut	
Pickup & Ramcharger	
Mounting Bolt	95 (129)
Mounting Nut	50 (68)
RWD Van	
Mounting Bolt	100 (136)
Mounting Nut	52 (71)
Lower Control Arm-To-Crossmember Bolt	
Pickup & Ramcharger	210 (285)
RWD Van	175 (237)
Lower Control Arm-To-Frame Nut (Dakota)	
Front	130 (176)
Rear	80 (108)
Lower Shock Absorber Mounting Bolt	17 (23)
Stabilizer Bar Bolts/Nuts	
Frame End	
Dakota	40 (54)
Pickup, Ramcharger & RWD Van	23 (31)
Link End	
Dakota	17 (23)
Pickup, Ramcharger & RWD Van	[1]

[1] – Tighten to 100 INCH lbs. (11 N.m).

TORQUE SPECIFICATIONS (Cont.)

Application	Ft. Lbs. (N.m)
Tie Rod End Nut	
Dakota, Pickup & Ramcharger	40 (54)
RWD Van	
9/16"-18	55 (75)
9/16"-20	75 (102)
Upper Ball Joint-To-Control Arm Nut	125 (169)
Upper Control Arm Eccentric Cam Bolt	
Pickup & Ramcharger	70 (95)
Upper Control Arm Pivot Bar Bolt	
Dakota	155 (210)
RWD Van	195 (264)
Upper Shock Absorber Mounting Bolt	25 (34)
Wheel Lug Nuts	
Dakota	85 (115)
Pickup & Ramcharger	
Tapered (Coned)	
1/2"-20	105 (142)
5/8"-18	200 (271)
Flat (Flanged)	
5/8"-18	325 (441)
RWD Van	
Except 350 H/D Axle	85-110 (115-149)
350 H/D Axle	
Tapered (Coned)	175-225 (237-305)
Flat (Flanged)	300-350 (407-475)

Pickup 4WD, Ramcharger

DESCRIPTION

Front suspension uses leaf springs which are mounted to frame rail brackets and shackles to provide support for axle housing. Shock absorbers are attached to brackets on frame rails and axle assembly. *See Fig. 1.* Sway bar is mounted to frame rail by brackets and to axle assembly by link assembly. Steering knuckles are mounted at each end of axle assembly.

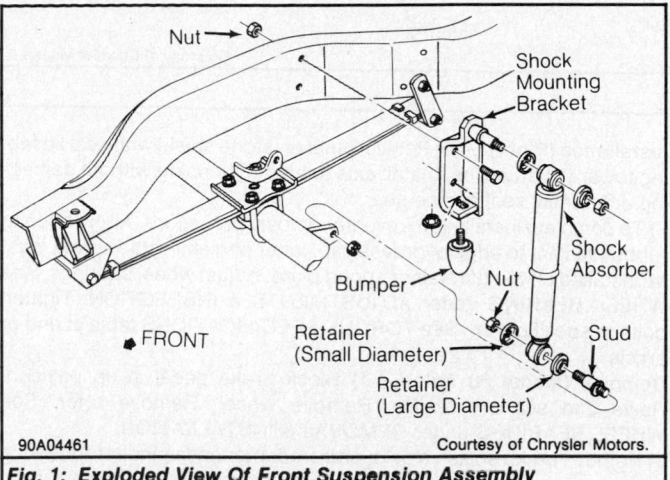

90A04461   Courtesy of Chrysler Motors.

Fig. 1: Exploded View Of Front Suspension Assembly

ADJUSTMENTS & INSPECTION

WHEEL ALIGNMENT
SPECIFICATIONS & PROCEDURES

NOTE: See SPECIFICATIONS & PROCEDURES article in WHEEL ALIGNMENT.

WHEEL BEARING

1) Raise and support vehicle. Remove wheel. On Model 44 axle, remove grease cap and drive hub snap ring. Remove drive hub and spacer. *See Fig. 2.*

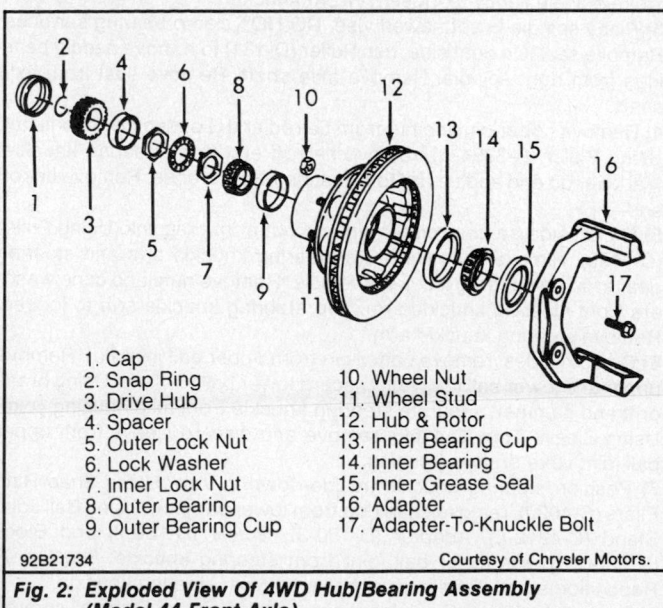

1. Cap
2. Snap Ring
3. Drive Hub
4. Spacer
5. Outer Lock Nut
6. Lock Washer
7. Inner Lock Nut
8. Outer Bearing
9. Outer Bearing Cup
10. Wheel Nut
11. Wheel Stud
12. Hub & Rotor
13. Inner Bearing Cup
14. Inner Bearing
15. Inner Grease Seal
16. Adapter
17. Adapter-To-Knuckle Bolt

92B21734   Courtesy of Chrysler Motors.

Fig. 2: Exploded View Of 4WD Hub/Bearing Assembly (Model 44 Front Axle)

2) On Model 60 axle, remove cap-to-hub Allen screws. *See Fig. 3.* Remove cap. Remove axle shaft retaining ring. Remove lock ring from groove in hub. To assist in removal, reinstall 2 Allen screws in locking hub body. Remove locking hub assembly from hub.

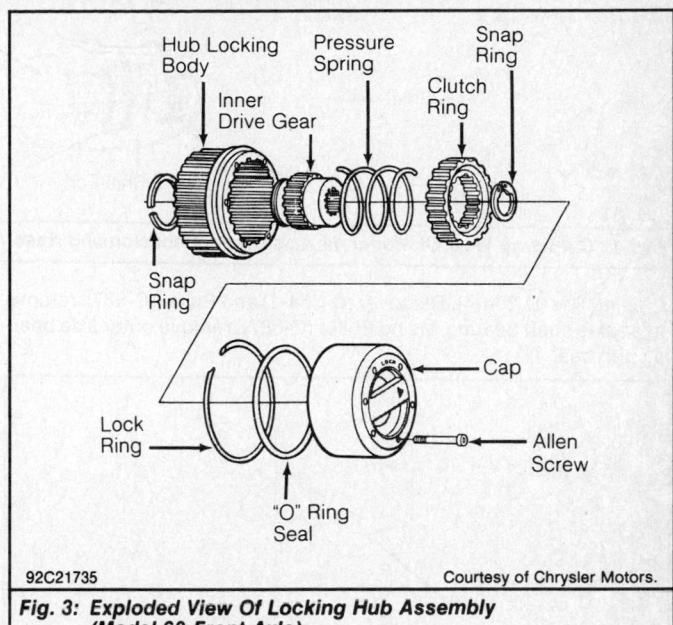

92C21735   Courtesy of Chrysler Motors.

Fig. 3: Exploded View Of Locking Hub Assembly (Model 60 Front Axle)

3) On all models, remove outer lock nut. Remove tabbed lock washer. Loosen and retighten inner lock nut to **50 ft. lbs. (68 N.m)**. While rotating hub, loosen lock nut and retighten to **30-40 ft. lbs. (41-54 N.m)**. Back lock nut off 135-150 degrees.

4) Install tabbed lock washer. Install outer lock nut, and tighten nut to **50 ft. lbs. (68 N.m)** for Model 44 axle or **65 ft. lbs. (88 N.m)** for Model 60 axle. On all models, end play should be **.001-.010" (.03-.25 mm)** after adjustment. To install remaining components, reverse removal procedure. On Model 44 axle, apply silicone sealant to grease cap sealing edge and install cap. On Model 60 axle, tighten Allen screws to **35-45 INCH lbs. (4-5 N.m)**.

BALL JOINT CHECKING

NOTE: Information is not available from manufacturer.

REMOVAL & INSTALLATION

AXLE SHAFTS

Removal (Model 44 Axle) – 1) Raise and support vehicle. Remove wheel. Remove rotor. See WHEEL BEARINGS under REMOVAL & INSTALLATION. Remove caliper adapter from steering knuckle.

2) Remove retaining nuts and washers from spindle-to-steering knuckle bolts. Remove spindle from knuckle. Remove brake splash shield (if equipped). Using soft-faced mallet, strike spindle lightly to loosen it from steering knuckle.

3) To remove right axle shaft, carefully pull axle shaft, with spacer, seal and stone shield, from axle housing. Remove seal and stone shield from shaft.

4) To remove left axle, disconnect vacuum lines and electrical connector from switch on disconnect housing assembly. *See Fig. 4.* Remove cover assembly, gasket and shield. Remove intermediate axle shaft from axle without damaging axle shaft seal.

5) Using Bearing Extractor (D-330), remove bearing from inside axle. Remove shift collar from axle. Remove differential cover. Drain gear oil into container.

6) Push inner axle shaft toward center of vehicle. Remove "C" lock from recessed groove on shaft. Using Bar (D-354-4) and Adapter (D-354-3), drive out inner shaft. *See Figs. 5 and 6.*

1992 SUSPENSION
Front – 4WD Leaf Spring (Cont.)

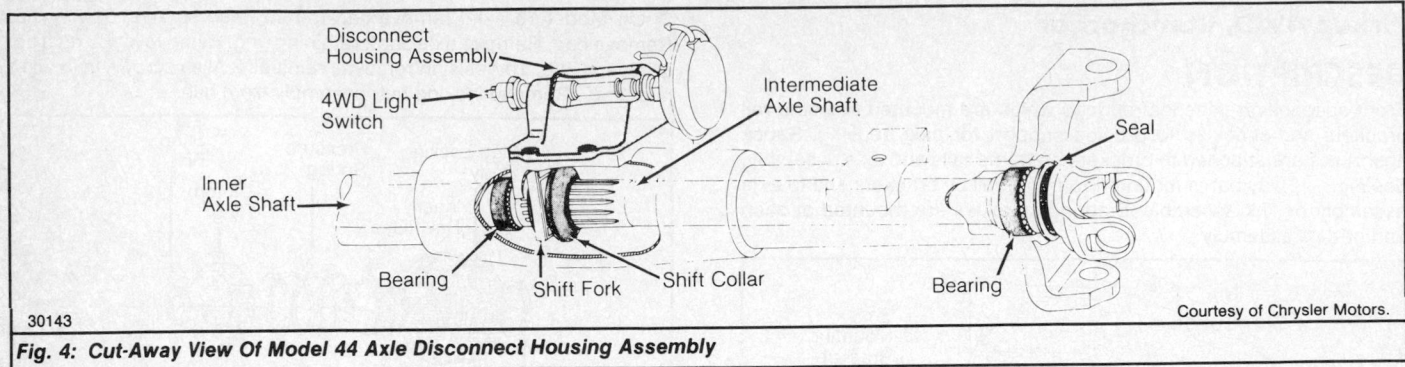

30143   Courtesy of Chrysler Motors.

Fig. 4: Cut-Away View Of Model 44 Axle Disconnect Housing Assembly

7) Using Bar (D-354-4), Remover (D-354-1) and Puller (C-637), remove inner axle shaft bearing. Using Puller (C-637), remove outer axle bearing and seal.

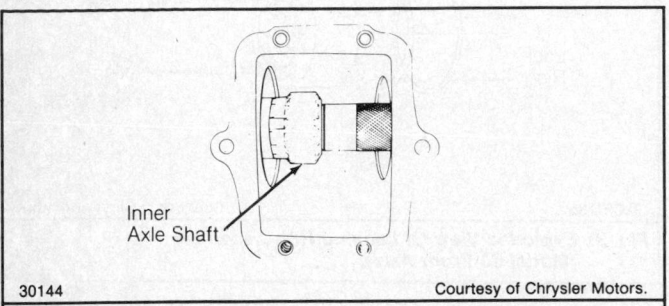

30144   Courtesy of Chrysler Motors.

Fig. 5: Removing Inner Axle Shaft From Model 44 Axle

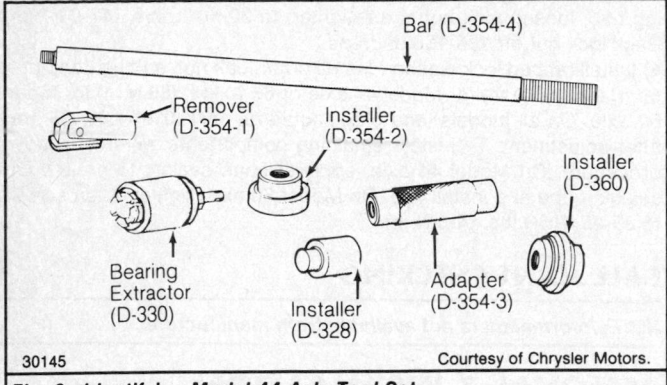

30145   Courtesy of Chrysler Motors.

Fig. 6: Identifying Model 44 Axle Tool Set

Installation (Left) – 1) Using Bar (D-354-4), Installer (D-354-2) and Puller (C-637), install inner axle shaft bearing. *See Fig. 6.* Using bar and Adapter (D-354-3), install and seat inner axle shaft. Insert "C" lock in recessed groove in shaft. Position shift collar on splined end of inner axle shaft.

2) Using Installer (D-360) and Handle (C-4171), install outer axle shaft bearing and seal. Using handle and Installer (D-328), install bearing into intermediate axle shaft. Install intermediate axle shaft through seal into housing without damaging shaft seal.

3) Install disconnect housing assembly and gasket while guiding shift fork into groove of shift collar. Install and tighten disconnect housing assembly bolts.

4) To complete installation, reverse removal procedure. Apply silicone rubber sealant to edge of grease cap. Apply 1/16-3/32" (1.6-2.4 mm) bead of silicone rubber sealant along bolt circle of differential housing cover before installing.

5) Install inner pad anti-rattle spring on top of retainer spring plate. Adjust wheel bearings. See WHEEL BEARING under ADJUSTMENTS & INSPECTION. Tighten bolts to specification. See TORQUE SPECIFICATIONS table at end of article.

Installation (Right) – 1) Position seal on stone shield with seal lip facing toward shaft spline. Install axle shaft into housing without damaging differential seal at side gear.

2) To complete installation, reverse removal procedure. Apply silicone rubber sealant to edge of grease cap. Inner pad anti-rattle spring must be installed on top of retainer spring plate. Adjust wheel bearings. See WHEEL BEARING under ADJUSTMENTS & INSPECTION. Tighten bolts to specification. See TORQUE SPECIFICATIONS table at end of article.

Removal (Model 60 Axle) – 1) Block brake pedal in up position. Raise and support vehicle. Remove wheel. Remove rotor. See WHEEL BEARINGS under REMOVAL & INSTALLATION.

2) Remove brake splash shield, brake adapter and spindle-to-steering knuckle nuts and washers. Remove spindle from steering knuckle. Remove axle shaft, Bronze spacer, seal and slinger from housing.

Installation – Install axle shaft. Place Bronze spacer on axle shaft with chamfered edge facing inward. To complete installation, reverse removal procedure. Adjust wheel bearings. See WHEEL BEARING under ADJUSTMENTS & INSPECTION. Tighten bolts to specification. See TORQUE SPECIFICATIONS table at end of article.

STEERING KNUCKLE, SPINDLE & BALL JOINT

Removal (Model 44 Axle) – 1) Raise and support vehicle. Remove wheel. Remove rotor. See WHEEL BEARINGS under REMOVAL & INSTALLATION. Remove caliper adapter from steering knuckle.

2) Remove and discard nuts and washers from spindle-to-knuckle attaching bolts. Remove brake splash shield. Using soft-faced mallet, strike spindle lightly to loosen it from knuckle.

3) Place spindle in soft-jawed vise. DO NOT clamp bearing surfaces. Remove seal. On right side, use Puller (D-131) to remove needle bearings from right spindle. Remove axle shaft. Remove seal from axle shaft.

4) Remove cotter pin and nut from tie rod end. Loosen clamp bolt nut. Using Puller (C-3894-A), remove tie rod end from steering knuckle. Mark tie rod end and tie rod for reassembly reference. Remove tie rod end.

5) On left side, remove cotter pin and nut from drag link. Using Puller (C-4150), remove drag link from steering knuckle arm and steering gear arm. Lower drag link from vehicle. Remove nuts and cone washers from steering knuckle arm. Tap steering knuckle arm to loosen. Remove steering knuckle arm.

6) On both sides, remove cotter pin from upper ball joint nut. Remove upper and lower ball joint nut. Discard lower ball joint nut. Using brass drift and hammer, separate steering knuckle from axle housing yoke. Using Sleeve Tool (C-4169), remove and discard sleeve from upper ball joint yoke on axle housing.

7) Position steering knuckle upside-down in vise. Using Snap Ring Pliers (C-4020), remove snap ring from lower ball joint. Using Ball Joint Stand (C-4212-L), Adapter (D-150-3), Screw (D-150-2) and Block (D-150-1), press lower ball joint from steering knuckle. *See Fig. 7.* Reposition stand. Press upper ball joint from steering knuckle.

8) Replace ball joints if any looseness or play exists. Clean all components with solvent, and dry using compressed air. Inspect all parts for burrs, chips, wear and cracks. Replace as required.

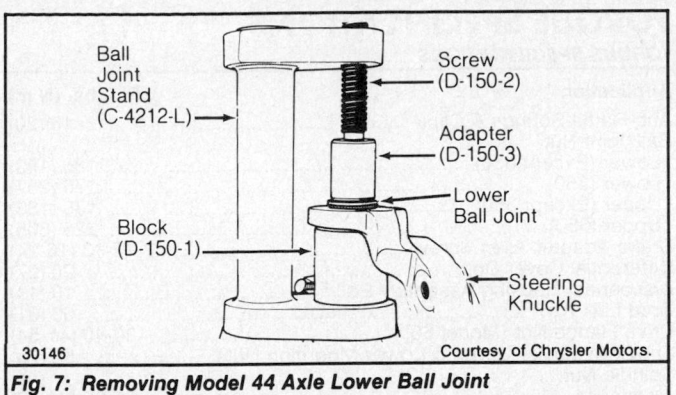

Fig. 7: Removing Model 44 Axle Lower Ball Joint

Installation – 1) Place steering knuckle in vise. Press ball joints into position with stand and components. *See Fig. 8.* Install new boots on ball joints. Remove steering knuckle from vise. Insert new sleeve into upper ball joint yoke of axle housing, allowing 2 threads to be exposed at top of housing.

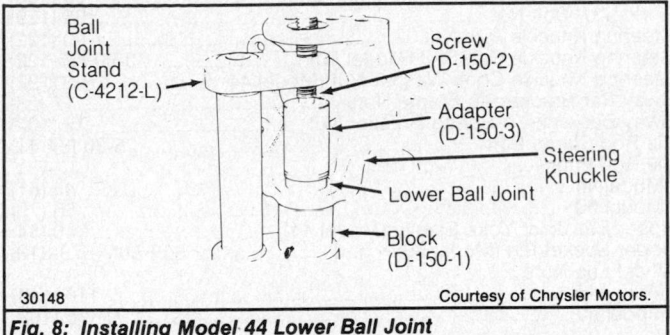

Fig. 8: Installing Model 44 Lower Ball Joint

2) Place steering knuckle on axle housing yoke. Install and tighten NEW lower ball joint nut. Using Sleeve Tool (C-4169) and torque wrench, tighten upper ball joint yoke sleeve to **40 ft. lbs. (54 N.m)**. Install upper ball joint nut, and tighten to **100 ft. lbs. (136 N.m)**.

3) Align cotter pin hole in stud with slot in castellated nut. Tighten nut to align hole and slot. DO NOT loosen nut. Insert cotter pin. Install steering knuckle arm, cone washer and drag link on left side of vehicle.

4) Install tie rod ends. Apply multipurpose grease to seal lip. Install seal on stone shield with seal lip facing axle shaft spline. Install right axle shaft into housing without damaging seal.

5) On left axle shaft, remove disconnect housing assembly. Install shaft. Install disconnect housing assembly. Using Installer (D-360) and Handle (C-4171), install new needle bearings in RIGHT spindle.

6) Using Installer (D-155) and handle, install new brake hub seals. Grease full circumference of seal and spindle thrust surface. Install new spacer on axle shaft. Install spindle and brake splash shield.

7) To complete installation, reverse removal procedure. Ensure inboard brake pad anti-rattle spring is on top of retainer spring plate. Adjust wheel bearings. See WHEEL BEARING under ADJUSTMENTS & INSPECTION. Tighten bolts to specification. See TORQUE SPECIFICATIONS table at end of article.

Removal (Model 60 Axle) – 1) Remove axle shafts. See AXLE SHAFTS under REMOVAL & INSTALLATION. Remove cotter pin and nut from tie rod end. Loosen clamp bolt nut. Using Puller (C-3894-A), remove tie rod end.

2) On left side, remove cotter pin and nut from drag link. Using Puller (C-4150), remove tie rod end from steering knuckle arm. Disconnect drag link from steering knuckle. Remove steering knuckle arm bolts and arm.

3) On both sides, remove upper steering knuckle cap, and discard gasket. Remove spring and upper socket sleeve. Remove lower steering knuckle cap bolts and cap. To separate steering knuckle from axle housing, swing steering knuckle outward at bottom while lifting up and off upper socket pin.

4) Using Socket (D-192), loosen and remove upper socket pin. Remove seal. Using Ball Joint Stand (C-4212-L) and Adapters (C-4366-1 and C-4366-2), press lower ball socket assembly from axle housing. *See Fig. 9.*

5) Clean all components with solvent, and dry using compressed air. Inspect components for burrs, chips, wear, flat spots and cracks. Replace as necessary.

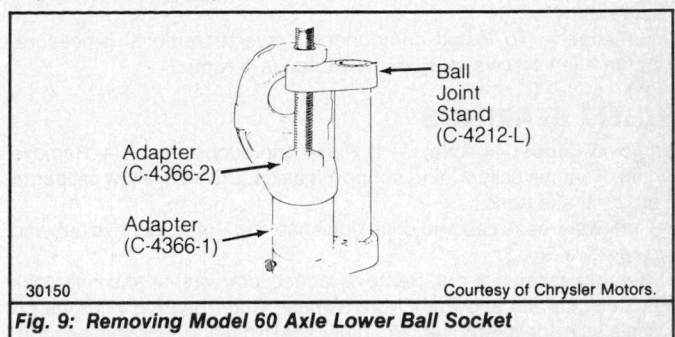

Fig. 9: Removing Model 60 Axle Lower Ball Socket

Installation – 1) Apply multipurpose lubricant to lower ball socket. Using Ball Joint Stand (C-4212-L) and Adapters (C-4366-3, C-4366-4 and C-4366-5), press seal and lower bearing race into axle housing. *See Fig. 10.* Replace adapters. Install lower bearing and seal into housing.

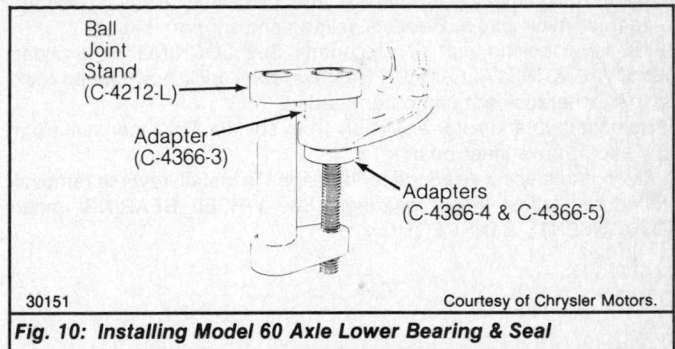

Fig. 10: Installing Model 60 Axle Lower Bearing & Seal

2) Using Socket (D-192) and torque wrench, install and tighten upper socket pin. Install seal over pin. Position steering knuckle over socket pin. Fill lower socket cavity with multipurpose lubricant. Install lower steering knuckle cap.

3) Apply generous amount of multipurpose lubricant to upper socket pin. Align upper socket sleeve in keyway of steering knuckle, and slide into position. *See Fig. 11.* Install new gasket over upper steering knuckle studs. Position upper socket spring over sleeve. Install steering knuckle cap.

4) On left side, connect drag link to steering knuckle. Install nut, and tighten to specification. See TORQUE SPECIFICATIONS table at end of article. Install cotter pin. To complete installation, reverse removal procedure. Adjust wheel bearings. See WHEEL BEARING under ADJUSTMENTS & INSPECTION.

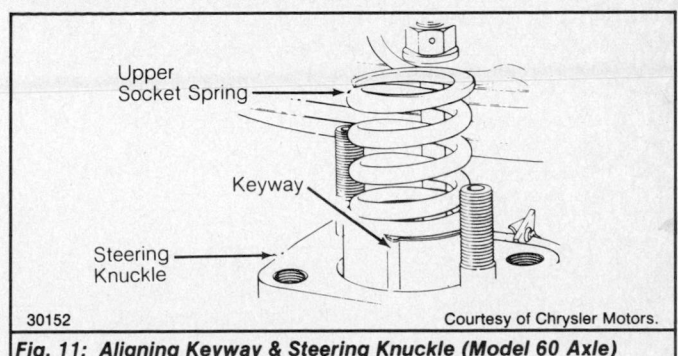

Fig. 11: Aligning Keyway & Steering Knuckle (Model 60 Axle)

1992 SUSPENSION
Front – 4WD Leaf Spring (Cont.)

LOCKING HUB

Removal – Raise and support vehicle. Remove cap-to-hub Allen screws. Remove cap. Remove axle shaft retaining ring. Remove lock ring from groove in hub. To assist removal, reinstall 2 Allen screws in locking hub body. Remove locking hub assembly from hub. *See Fig. 3.*

Inspection – Wash parts in mineral spirits, and blow dry using compressed air. Examine components for damage, and replace as necessary.

Installation – To install components, reverse removal procedure. Tighten Allen screws to **35-45 INCH lbs. (4-5 N.m)**.

WHEEL BEARINGS

Removal (Model 44 Axle) – **1)** Raise and support vehicle. Remove wheel. Remove caliper, and support it aside. DO NOT allow caliper to hang by brake hose.

2) Remove grease cap and drive hub snap ring. Remove drive hub and spacer. *See Fig. 2.*

3) Remove outer lock nut. Remove tabbed lock washer and inner lock nut. Remove hub and rotor from spindle. Outer bearing will slide off spindle as rotor is removed. Pry inner seal from hub. Remove bearing.

Installation – Lubricate and install inner bearing. Using Seal Installer (D-359) and Handle (C-4171), install inner seal. Install rotor on spindle. To complete installation, reverse removal procedure. Adjust bearings. See WHEEL BEARING under ADJUSTMENTS & INSPECTION.

Removal & Installation (Model 60 Axle) – **1)** Block brake pedal in up position. Raise and support vehicle. Remove wheel. Remove caliper-to-adapter Allen screw. Remove caliper, and support it aside.

2) Remove locking hub (if equipped). See LOCKING HUB under REMOVAL & INSTALLATION. Remove outer lock nut, tabbed lock washer, inner lock nut and outer bearing.

3) Remove hub and rotor assembly from spindle. Pry inner seal from hub, and remove inner bearing.

4) Clean and inspect bearings for damage. To install, reverse removal procedure. Adjust wheel bearings. See WHEEL BEARING under ADJUSTMENTS & INSPECTION.

TORQUE SPECIFICATIONS

TORQUE SPECIFICATIONS

Application	Ft. Lbs. (N.m)
Anti-Rattle Springs & Clips	15 (20)
Ball Joint Nut	
Lower (Except 350)	135 (183)
Lower (350)	175 (237)
Upper (Except 350)	135 (183)
Upper (350)	225 (305)
Brake Adapter Allen Screw	12-18 (16-24)
Differential Cover Bolt	20 (27)
Disconnect Housing Assembly Bolt	10 (14)
Drag Link Nut	60 (81)
Drive Flange Nut (Model 60)	30-40 (41-54)
Shock Absorber Upper & Lower Mounting Nuts	55 (75)
Spindle Nut	
Model 44	25-35 (34-47)
Model 60	50-70 (68-95)
Spring Eye Pivot Bolt Nut	80 (108)
Spring Plate Stud Nut	
9/16"-18 Stud	95 (129)
Model 44 Axle	105 (142)
Model 60 Axle	115 (156)
Spring Shackle Bolt	80 (108)
Spring "U" Bolt Nut	95 (129)
Steering Knuckle Arm Nut	90 (122)
Steering Knuckle Cap Bolt (Model 60)	70-90 (95-122)
Steering Knuckle Cone Washer Nut (Model 44)	90 (122)
Sway Bar Bracket-To-Frame Nuts	17 (23)
Sway Bar Link-To-Spring Bracket Nut	75 (102)
Tie Rod Clamp Bolt	25-30 (34-41)
Tie Rod End Nut	
Model 44	45 (61)
Model 60	55 (75)
Upper Ball Joint Yoke Sleeve (Model 44)	40 (54)
Upper Socket Pin (Model 60)	500-600 (678-813)
Wheel Lug Nuts	
Model 44	110 (149)
Model 60	75 (102)

	INCH Lbs. (N.m)
Locking Hub Allen Screws	35-45 (4-5)
Sway Bar Link Rod Nut	100 (11)

Dakota 4WD

DESCRIPTION

Front suspension consists of upper and lower control arms, sway bar, shock absorbers and left and right torsion bars. *See Fig. 1.* Front end of torsion bar is connected to lower control arm. Rear end of torsion bar is mounted to an adjustable arm at crossmember.

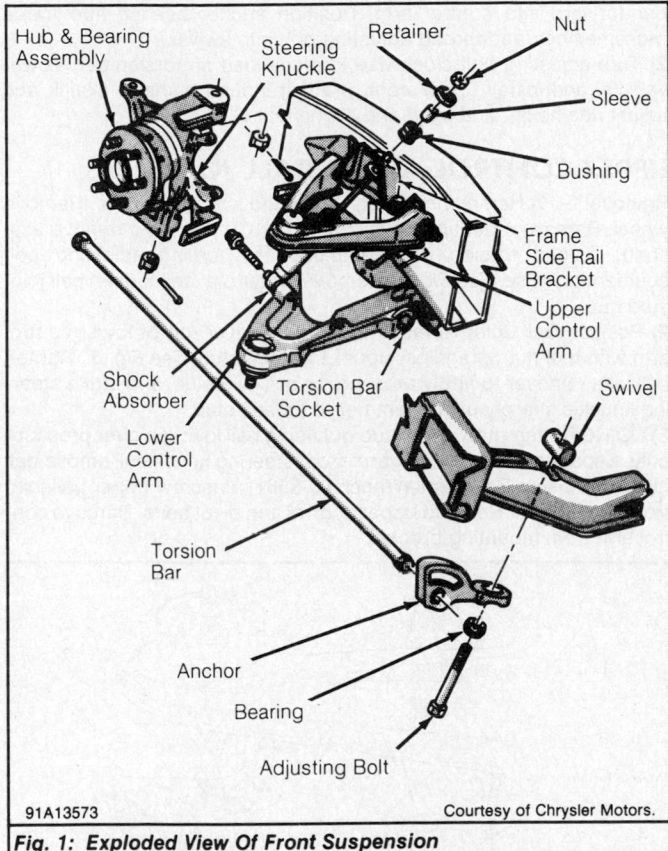

91A13573   Courtesy of Chrysler Motors.

Fig. 1: Exploded View Of Front Suspension

ADJUSTMENTS & INSPECTION

WHEEL ALIGNMENT
SPECIFICATIONS & PROCEDURES

NOTE: See SPECIFICATIONS & PROCEDURES article in WHEEL ALIGNMENT.

WHEEL BEARING

Front wheel bearings are permanently sealed and do not require lubrication or adjustment. Hub and bearing unit is replaced as an assembly. Tighten hub nut to **190 ft. lbs. (258 N.m)** with brakes applied.

RIDING HEIGHT

Vehicle height is adjusted by rotating torsion bar anchor adjusting bolt. Turning adjusting bolt clockwise increases vehicle height. Turning adjusting bolt counterclockwise decreases vehicle height. Adjust riding height with vehicle on a level surface and its tires properly inflated. Measure inner height from floor surface to underside surface of lower control arm rear pivot bores.

Measure outer height from floor surface to underside surface of lower control arm rear edge, at area immediately inboard of steering stop. Check inner and outer measurements, and adjust height differential to specification. Height differential from side to side of vehicle should not be more than .25" (6.4 mm). See SPECIFICATIONS & PROCEDURES

article in WHEEL ALIGNMENT. After each adjustment, jounce vehicle before measuring to determine effects of adjustment.

BALL JOINT CHECKING

Ball joints are preloaded. Replace ball joint if vertical movement exceeds .02" (.5 mm).

REMOVAL & INSTALLATION

AXLE SHAFT

Removal – 1) Remove hub nut. Raise and support vehicle. Remove wheel. Remove inner CV joint mounting bolts, and remove drive axle. Loosen axle housing cover bolts, and drain fluid. Remove axle housing cover.

2) Rotate differential case until pinion shaft lock screw is accessible. Remove lock screw and pinion shaft. Push axle shaft toward center of vehicle. Remove axle shaft "C" lock, and remove axle shaft.

Installation – To install, reverse removal procedure. Install lock screw using Loctite, and tighten screw to **8 ft. lbs. (11 N.m)**. Using silicone sealant, install cover. Tighten remaining bolts and nuts to specification. See TORQUE SPECIFICATIONS table at end of article.

HUB & BEARING ASSEMBLY

Removal – 1) Remove cotter pin, nut lock and spring washer. Loosen hub nut, and then raise and support vehicle. Remove wheel, hub nut and hub washer. Remove brake caliper guide pins, and remove caliper. Support caliper aside. Mark brake rotor and hub, and remove brake rotor.

2) Remove hub and bearing assembly mounting bolts from rear of steering knuckle. *See Fig. 1.* Slide hub and bearing assembly off front axle shaft splines. Inspect steering knuckle grease seal and hub and bearing assembly for excessive wear and damage. Replace components as necessary.

Installation – 1) Install hub and bearing assembly onto steering knuckle, guiding axle shaft through spline in hub. Tighten mounting bolts to **110 ft. lbs. (149 N.m)**.

2) Align marks, and install brake rotor and caliper. Install caliper pins, and tighten to **22 ft. lbs. (30 N.m)**. With brakes applied, tighten hub retainer nut to **190 ft. lbs. (258 N.m)**. Install spring washer, nut lock and new cotter pin. DO NOT back off nut to install cotter pin. To complete installation, reverse removal procedure. See TORQUE SPECIFICATIONS table at end of article.

KNUCKLE ASSEMBLY

Removal – 1) Remove wheel hub. See HUB & BEARING ASSEMBLY under REMOVAL & INSTALLATION. Remove tie rod end nut. Using Tie Rod Puller (C-3894-A), disconnect tie rod end from steering knuckle.

2) Unload torsion bar completely by turning adjusting bolt counterclockwise. *See Fig. 2.* Remove lower shock absorber mounting bolt. Disconnect sway bar from lower control arm.

3) Place Ball Joint Remover (C-3564-A) over top of lower control arm with tool nut up against upper ball joint stud. *See Fig. 3.* Loosen ball joint stud nut. Tighten ball joint remover to apply pressure to ball joint stud, and strike steering knuckle sharply using hammer to loosen stud. Detach opposite ball joint in same manner. DO NOT attempt to force stud out using ball joint remover pressure only.

4) Separate lower ball joint stud from steering knuckle. Remove steering knuckle from vehicle. Inspect steering knuckle grease seal for cuts, distortion and wear. Check steering knuckle and hub and bearing assembly for damage. Replace components as necessary.

Installation – 1) Install new steering knuckle grease seal. Position new grease seal in recess of steering knuckle, and install using Seal Installer (C-4698). Lubricate seal lip with multipurpose grease. Install steering knuckle onto ball joint studs.

2) Install hub and bearing assembly onto steering knuckle, guiding axle shaft through spline in hub. Install tie rod end. Install brake rotor and caliper. Tighten caliper guide pins to **22 ft. lbs. (30 N.m)**.

3) Tighten hub retainer nut to **190 ft. lbs. (258 N.m)** with brakes applied. Install spring washer, nut lock and new cotter pin. DO NOT back off nut to install cotter pin. To complete installation, reverse removal procedure. See TORQUE SPECIFICATIONS table at end of article. Check and adjust ride height.

LOWER CONTROL ARM & BALL JOINT

Removal – 1) Loosen hub nut. Raise and support vehicle. Remove wheel. Remove mounting bolts from inner CV joint, and remove axle shaft. Unload torsion bar completely by turning adjusting bolt counterclockwise. *See Fig. 2.* Remove torsion bar. See TORSION BARS under REMOVAL & INSTALLATION.

2) Remove lower shock absorber mounting bolt. Disconnect sway bar from lower control arm. Disconnect lower ball joint. Separate lower control arm from steering knuckle. Remove lower control arm pivot bolts, and remove lower control arm. Pry retainer off ball joint. Remove ball joint from lower control arm.

Installation – 1) Install new ball joint in lower control arm. Install new ball joint grease seal. Position control arm on vehicle, and install nuts on pivot bolts finger tight.

2) To complete installation, reverse removal procedure. Lubricate ball joint. With vehicle on floor, tighten lower control arm pivot bolts to specification. See TORQUE SPECIFICATIONS table at end of article. Check and adjust ride height and front end alignment.

Bushing Replacement – If bushings are worn, remove lower control arm. Use a sleeve and press to remove and replace bushings.

STABILIZER SHAFT

Removal – Raise and support vehicle. Remove rear support bracket-to-frame crossmember bracket bolts. Remove stabilizer shaft-to-lower control arm "C"-shaped retainer attaching bolts. Remove retainer and stabilizer shaft from vehicle. Remove rear support brackets and stabilizer shaft bushings, if required.

Installation – Install stabilizer shaft bushings and rear support brackets on stabilizer shaft, if removed. Position rear support brackets next to frame crossmember brackets, and install attaching bolts finger tight. Using "C"-shaped retainer and attaching bolts, attach stabilizer shaft to lower control arm. Ensure no interference exists between stabilizer shaft and other components, and ensure spacing is equal on both sides. Tighten all attaching bolts to **20 ft. lbs. (27 N.m).**

TORSION BARS

NOTE: Left and right torsion bars are NOT interchangeable. Torsion bars may be installed with either end facing forward.

Removal – 1) Remove upper control arm rebound bumper, and then raise and support vehicle. Unload torsion bar completely by turning adjusting bolt counterclockwise. *See Fig. 2.*

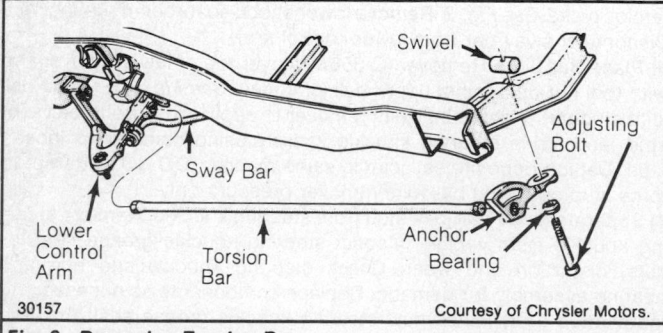

30157   Courtesy of Chrysler Motors.
Fig. 2: Removing Torsion Bar

2) Remove adjusting bolt from anchor, and remove torsion bar and anchor as an assembly from control arm. Separate torsion bar from anchor and bearing.

3) Inspect torsion bars, anchors, swivels, bearings and crossmember support for bend, cracks, deterioration and damage. Check adjusting bolt and nut for damage and stripped threads. Replace components as necessary.

Installation – 1) Install torsion bar through anchor, and slide torsion bar forward into control arm. Position anchor bearing into frame crossmember, and thread adjusting bolt into swivel.

2) Turn adjusting bolt clockwise to place load on torsion bar. Lower vehicle, and install upper control arm rebound bumper. Check and adjust ride height and front end alignment.

UPPER CONTROL ARM & BALL JOINT

Removal – 1) Remove hub nut. Raise and support vehicle. Remove wheel. Remove mounting bolts from inner CV joint, and remove axle shaft. Unload torsion bar completely by turning adjusting bolt counterclockwise. *See Fig. 2.* Remove cotter pin, and loosen ball joint stud nut.

2) Position Ball Joint Remover (C-3564-A) over top of lower control arm with tool nut up against upper ball joint stud. *See Fig. 3.* Tighten ball joint remover to apply pressure to ball joint stud, and strike steering knuckle sharply using hammer to loosen stud.

3) DO NOT attempt to force stud out using ball joint remover pressure only. Separate upper control arm from steering knuckle. Remove ball joint seal. Using Ball Joint Wrench (C-3561), unscrew upper ball joint from control arm. Remove upper control arm pivot bolts. Remove control arm from mounting bracket.

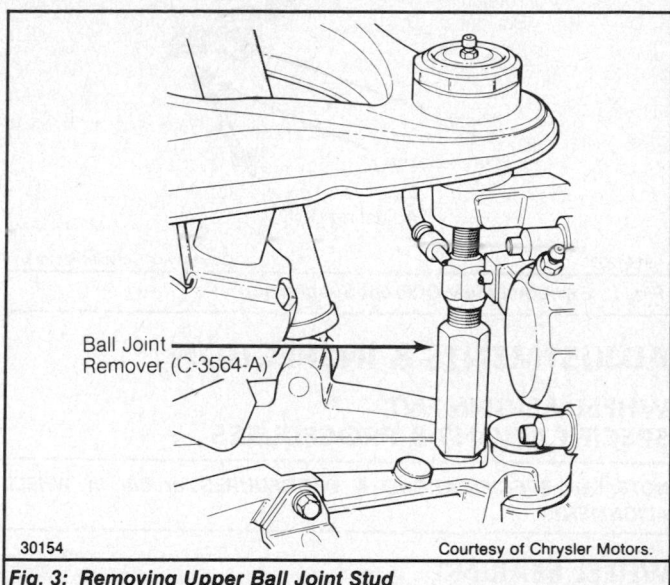

30154   Courtesy of Chrysler Motors.
Fig. 3: Removing Upper Ball Joint Stud

Installation – 1) Position upper control arm onto mounting bracket. Install upper control arm pivot bolts. Tighten bolts finger tight. Using Ball Joint Wrench (C-3561), screw upper ball joint into control arm. Tighten ball joint to **125 ft. lbs. (169 N.m).** Install new ball joint grease seal. Connect steering knuckle to ball joint.

2) To complete installation, reverse removal procedure. With vehicle on floor, tighten upper control arm pivot bolts to specification. See TORQUE SPECIFICATIONS table at end of article. Lubricate ball joint. Check and adjust ride height and front end alignment.

Bushing Replacement – If bushings are worn, remove upper control arm. Use a sleeve and press to remove and replace bushings.

TORQUE SPECIFICATIONS

TORQUE SPECIFICATIONS

Application	Ft. Lbs. (N.m)
Axle Housing Cover Bolts	35 (47)
Ball Joint Stud Nut	
Lower	120 (163)
Upper	105 (142)
Brake Caliper Guide Pins	22 (30)
CV Joint Flange-To-Axle Flange Bolt	65 (88)
Hub & Bearing Assembly-To-Drive Axle	
Retainer Nut	[1] 190 (258)
Hub & Bearing Assembly-To-Steering Knuckle	
Mounting Bolt	110 (149)
Lower Control Arm-To-Frame Pivot Bolt	
Front	80 (108)
Rear	130 (176)
Pinion Shaft Lock Screw	8 (11)
Shock Absorber Bolt	
Lower	100 (136)
Upper	25 (34)
Sway Bar Mounting Bolt	20 (27)
Tie Rod End Nut	50 (68)
Upper Ball Joint-To-Control Arm	125 (169)
Upper Control Arm-To-Frame Pivot Bolt	155 (210)
Wheel Lug Nut	85 (115)

[1] – DO NOT back off retainer nut to install new cotter pin. After reaching specification, tighten nut only enough to align slot.

Caravan, Dakota, Pickup, Ramcharger, RWD Van, Town & Country, Voyager

CAUTION: Caravan, Town & Country and Voyager are equipped with Air Bag Restraint System (ABRS). See AIR BAG PRECAUTIONS before working with air bag system.

WARNING: When battery is disconnected, vehicle computer and memory systems may lose memory data. Driveability problems may exist until computer systems have completed a relearn cycle. See COMPUTER RELEARN PROCEDURES article in GENERAL INFORMATION before disconnecting battery.

DESCRIPTION & OPERATION

All models use collapsible steering columns with an integral ignition switch and locking device. *See Fig. 1.* Optional tilt wheel is available.

WARNING: On models with Air Bag Restraint System (ABRS), observe precautions before any repairs are performed. See AIR BAG PRECAUTIONS. Use caution when working around steering column (air bag could deploy).

AIR BAG PRECAUTIONS

Follow precautions when working with air bag systems:
- When performing air bag repairs, disable ABRS. See COMPLETE SYSTEM DEACTIVATION under AIR BAG DISABLING.
- Use caution when handling a sensor. Never strike or jar a sensor. All sensors or mounting bracket bolts must be carefully torqued to ensure proper sensor operation.
- Never apply power to ABRS if a sensor is not rigidly attached to vehicle.

- To avoid accidental air bag deployment while trouble shooting ABRS, DO NOT use electrical test equipment, such as AC-powered or battery-powered voltmeter, ohmmeter, etc.
- Always carry air bag module with trim cover away from body. Always place inflatable module on workbench with trim cover up, away from loose objects.
- DO NOT install used air bag parts from another vehicle. Use NEW parts only. DO NOT disassemble or tamper with air bag assembly.
- Wait at least 2 minutes after disconnecting battery before proceeding with repairs or trouble shooting system. Some manufacturers recommend waiting up to 20 minutes before making ABRS repairs. For a short time after battery is disconnected, ABRS retains enough voltage to deploy air bag.

NOTE: For additional information on ABRS, see AIR BAG RESTRAINT SYSTEM article in SAFETY EQUIPMENT.

AIR BAG DISABLING

NOTE: Complete system deactivation should be performed only when Air Bag Restraint System (ABRS) is not functioning properly and vehicle needs to be driven.

Complete System Deactivation – Disconnect and isolate negative battery cable. Disconnect 2-way Yellow clockspring harness connector, located on top of fuse block between clockspring and instrument panel wiring harness. Clockspring connector may also be disconnected at Air Bag System Diagnostic Module (ASDM).

WARNING: Wait about 2 minutes after disconnecting negative battery cable before servicing air bag system. System reserve capacitor maintains air bag system voltage for about 2 minutes after battery is disconnected. Servicing air bag system before 2 minutes may cause accidental air bag deployment and possible personal injury.

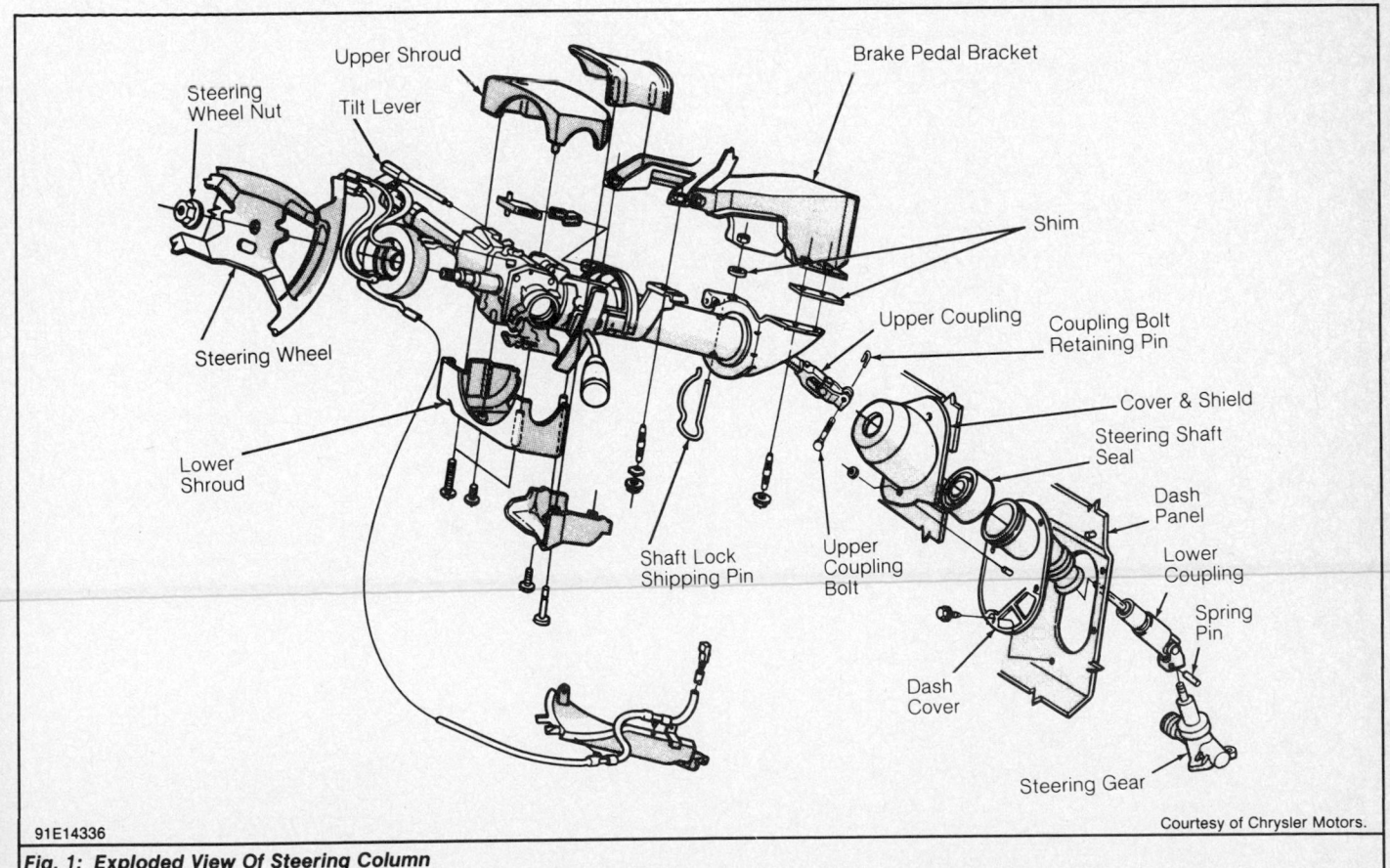

Courtesy of Chrysler Motors.

91E14336

Fig. 1: Exploded View Of Steering Column

ADJUSTMENTS

NOTE: On column shift models, whenever steering column is removed or loosened, shift rod adjustment must be checked.

SHIFT ROD ADJUSTMENT

1) Place shift selector in PARK position. Loosen cable adjusting bracket lock screw on transaxle.

2) Ensure preload adjusting spring engages fork on transaxle bracket. Move shift lever on transaxle all the way to rear detent (Park) position and hold. Tighten lock screw to **100-105 INCH lbs. (11-12 N.m)**.

3) To check adjustment, gearshift lever should be within limits of gate stops when shifted through gear positions. Vehicle must only start in Park or Neutral.

REMOVAL & INSTALLATION

WARNING: When battery is disconnected, vehicle computer and memory systems may lose memory data. Driveability problems may exist until computer systems have completed a relearn cycle. See COMPUTER RELEARN PROCEDURES article in GENERAL INFORMATION before disconnecting battery.

STEERING COLUMN

Removal & Installation – 1) Position front wheels straight ahead. Disconnect and isolate negative battery cable. On column shift models, remove link rod from grommet in shift lever. On all models, remove steering wheel using Puller (C-3428-B).

2) Remove steering column shaft-to-coupler roll pin. Push upper coupler shaft down into lower steering coupler. Remove dash panel column cover. On column shift models, disconnect shift indicator cable.

3) On all models, remove tilt lever (if equipped). Remove upper and lower shroud. Remove lower fixed shroud. Disconnect multifunction switch harness connector. Disconnect harness connectors from ignition switch, key-in light, horn and speed control (if equipped).

4) Loosen upper support bracket nuts and allow column to drop slightly. Remove upper fixed shroud. Disconnect wiring harness retainers from column, and move harness to one side. Remove lower dash panel. Remove lower steering column retaining nuts. Remove column.

5) To install column, reverse removal procedure. Connect clockspring connector. Connect negative battery cable.

CAUTION: DO NOT reuse bushing in shift rod lever once shift rod is removed. Always install a NEW bushing.

6) On column shift models, whenever steering column is removed or loosened, shift rod adjustment must be checked. See SHIFT ROD ADJUSTMENT under ADJUSTMENTS.

OVERHAUL

NOTE: Steering column is not serviceable, except for trim, switches and steering wheel. If service is required, replace column.

TORQUE SPECIFICATIONS
TORQUE SPECIFICATIONS

Application	Ft. Lbs. (N.m)
Steering Wheel Retaining Nut	45 (61)

	INCH Lbs. (N.m)
Steering Column-To-Instrument Panel Bracket Bolt/Nut	
Caravan, Town & Country, & Voyager	105 (12)
All Others	110 (12)

Dakota (2WD)

DESCRIPTION & OPERATION

Manual steering gear rack and pinion assembly converts rotational movement to lateral movement of rack. Steering wheel movement is transmitted by shaft to pinion through steering shaft coupler. Steering gear assembly service is limited to replacement of boot seals, outer tie rod ends or steering gear.

LUBRICATION

Manual rack and pinion gears are permanently lubricated during assembly. Periodic lubrication of the rack is not necessary.

REMOVAL & INSTALLATION

BOOT SEAL

NOTE: Boot seal replacement procedure is with steering gear removed from vehicle.

Removal & Installation – 1) Remove steering gear. See STEERING GEAR under REMOVAL & INSTALLATION. Remove outer tie rod end. See OUTER TIE ROD END under REMOVAL & INSTALLATION.
2) Expand outer boot seal clamp and remove. Cut inner boot seal clamp and remove. *See Fig. 1.* Place reference mark for breather tube location on steering gear housing before removing boot seal. Using a small screwdriver, remove boot seal from groove in steering gear housing and remove boot seal.
3) To install, ensure all surfaces are clean. Lubricate tie rod boot seal groove with silicone lubricant before installing outer clamp. Install boot seal, aligning reference mark with breather tube. Install NEW boot seal clamps and tighten. Ensure boot seal is not twisted. To complete installation, reverse removal procedure.

OUTER TIE ROD END

NOTE: If part replacement is necessary, check part number carefully. 1991-92 models use a larger diameter ball stud on outer tie rod end. Parts are NOT interchangeable with previous model years.

Removal – 1) Place reference mark on outer tie rod end and inner tie rod end for reassembly reference. Loosen lock nut at inner tie rod end. Remove cotter pin and nut from tie rod end at steering knuckle.
2) Using tie rod end Puller Tool (C-3894-A), separate tie rod end from steering knuckle. Unscrew tie rod end from inner tie rod end. It may be necessary to expand or remove outer boot seal clamp.
Installation – 1) To install, reverse removal procedure. Expand or remove outer clamp on boot seal while installing tie rod end. Lubricate groove of boot seal with silicone lubricant.
2) Install tie rod to reference mark made during removal. Adjust toe-in. See SPECIFICATIONS & PROCEDURES article in WHEEL ALIGNMENT. Install and tighten outer clamp on boot seal. Ensure boot seal is not twisted. Tighten lock nut and tie rod end-to-steering knuckle nut to specification. See TORQUE SPECIFICATIONS table at end of article.

STEERING GEAR

Removal – 1) Raise and support vehicle. Remove front wheels. Separate tie rod ends from steering knuckles. See OUTER TIE ROD END under REMOVAL & INSTALLATION.
2) Remove pin from steering shaft coupling at steering gear shaft. Remove steering gear-to-crossmember bolts. Remove steering gear.
Installation – To install, reverse removal procedure. Ensure master serrations align. Adjust toe-in. See SPECIFICATIONS & PROCEDURES article in WHEEL ALIGNMENT.

TORQUE SPECIFICATIONS

TORQUE SPECIFICATIONS

Application	Ft. Lbs. (N.m)
Steering Gear-To-Crossmember Bolt	150 (203)
Tie Rod End-To-Steering Knuckle Nut	40 (54)
Tie Rod Lock Nut	55 (75)
Wheel Lug Nut	85 (115)

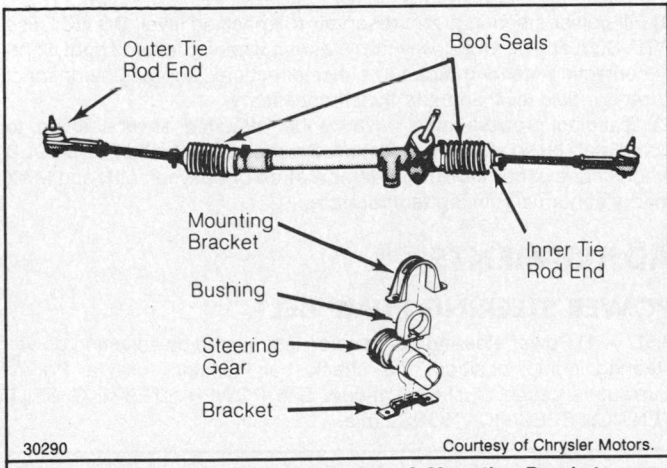

30290   Courtesy of Chrysler Motors.

Fig. 1: Exploded View Of Steering Gear & Mounting Bracket

1992 STEERING
Power Rack & Pinion

Caravan, Dakota (2WD), Town & Country, Voyager

DESCRIPTION & OPERATION

Power rack and pinion steering system uses rotary control valve to direct hydraulic fluid to either side of integral rack piston. Tie rods connect steering gear (rack and pinion) to steering knuckles. See Fig. 1. Loosely fitted pinion drive-tangs will provide manual steering control in case of system malfunction.

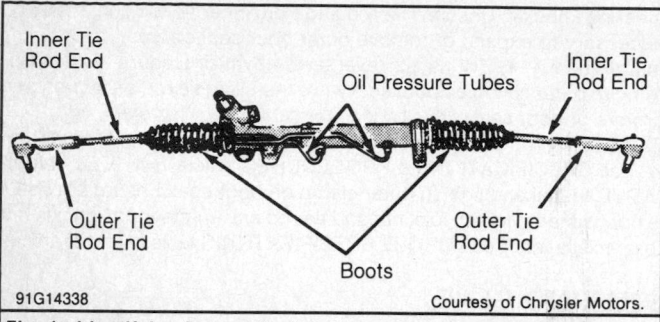

Fig. 1: Identifying Power Rack & Pinion Steering Gear (Typical)

Steering wheel movement is transmitted by steering shaft to pinion through 2 universal joint couplings. Steering gear rack and pinion assembly converts rotational movement of pinion to transverse movement of rack.

Several styles of Saginaw vane submerged power steering pumps are used depending on engine size and type. See POWER STEERING PUMP APPLICATION table. See Figs. 2 and 3. Only fluid reservoirs, caps and pulleys are replaceable on Saginaw pumps. On Ham Can type pumps, reservoir, seals and "O" rings are serviceable. On T/C type pumps, flow control valve "O" ring is also replaceable. See Fig. 5. Internal components are non-serviceable. If pump, reservoir or cap fails or leaks, defective part should be replaced.

POWER STEERING PUMP APPLICATION

Engine Size	Pump Type
Caravan, Town & Country, & Voyager	
2.5L & 3.0L	Saginaw Ham Can
3.3L	Saginaw T/C
Dakota	Saginaw Ham Can

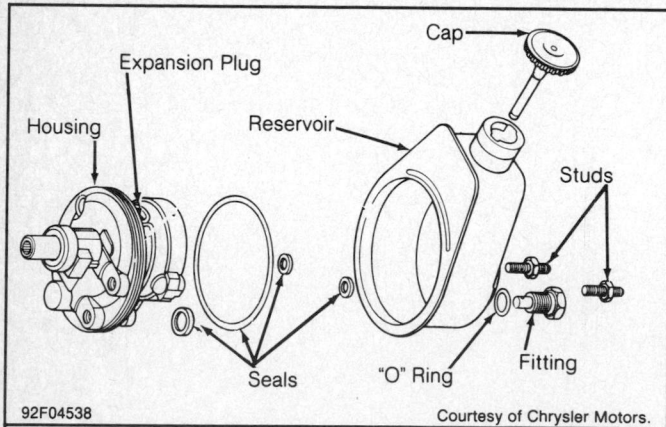

Fig. 2: Identifying Saginaw Ham Can Type Pump Components

LUBRICATION

CAPACITY

Fluid capacity is approximately 1.7 pts. (.81L) for all models.

FLUID TYPE

Use Mopar Power Steering Fluid (4318055).

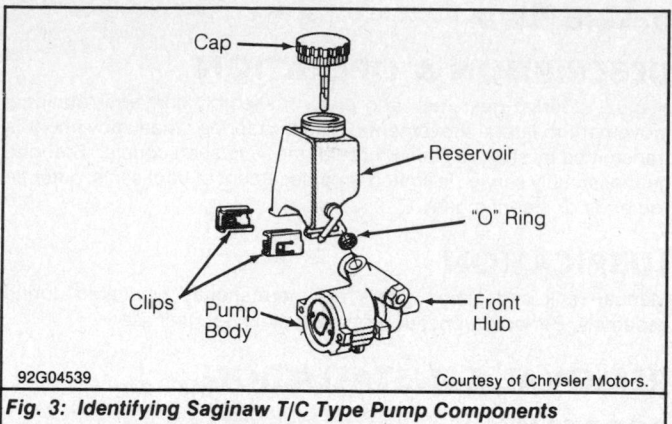

Fig. 3: Identifying Saginaw T/C Type Pump Components

CAUTION: DO NOT use Automatic Transmission Fluid (ATF). Power steering system failure could result.

FLUID LEVEL CHECK

WARNING: Engine must be shut off before checking power steering fluid level or personal injury could result.

Check fluid level with vehicle on level surface, engine shut off and at normal running temperature. Remove fluid level dipstick on reservoir. Dipstick should read FULL COLD when fluid is at normal outside temperature or between MIN and MAX marks at normal running temperature. If needed, add fluid through dipstick opening, and recheck. DO NOT overfill. DO NOT use ATF.

HYDRAULIC SYSTEM BLEEDING

1) Fill power steering pump reservoir to specified level. DO NOT use ATF. Start engine and slowly turn steering wheel to left and right, lightly contacting steering stops in either direction. Stop engine. Inspect reservoir fluid level and add fluid if necessary.

2) Bleeding process may have to be repeated several times to completely bleed all air from system. Dipstick should read FULL COLD when fluid is at normal outside temperature or between MIN and MAX marks at normal running temperature.

ADJUSTMENTS

POWER STEERING PUMP BELT

2.5L – 1) Power steering belt tension is adjusted by adjusting power steering pump position. To check belt tension, use a Poly-V Burroughs gauge or similar gauge. See POWER STEERING BELT TENSION SPECIFICATIONS table.

NOTE: Belt is considered used after 15 minutes of service.

POWER STEERING BELT TENSION SPECIFICATIONS

Application	New Belt Lbs. (kg)	Used Belt Lbs. (kg)
2.5L		
Caravan & Voyager	105 (48)	80 (36)
Dakota	120 (54)	80 (36)
3.0L, 3.3L, 3.9L & 5.2L	[1]	[1]

[1] – Equipped with dynamic tensioner; no adjustment is required.

2) On Caravan and Voyager, belt tension can also be checked using deflection method. Place straightedge across 2 adjacent pulleys, and use a 10 lb. (4.5 kg) push or pull force at midpoint. For new belt, deflection should be **1/4" (6 mm)**. For used belt, deflection should be **7/16" (11 mm)**.

3.0L, 3.3L, 3.9L & 5.2L – Serpentine belt tension is kept in proper adjustment by dynamic tensioner. No tension specifications are provided for belts using dynamic tensioner.

STEERING GEAR

NOTE: *DO NOT attempt to service or adjust power steering gear. If a malfunction or oil leak occurs, replace steering gear as a complete assembly.*

TESTING

NOTE: *Before testing, check fluid level, belt tension, pump pulley, tire pressure and engine idle speed.*

HYDRAULIC SYSTEM PRESSURE TEST

Idle Pressure Test – **1)** Check and adjust power steering pump belt tension as necessary. See POWER STEERING PUMP BELT under ADJUSTMENTS. Remove high pressure hose at steering pump, and connect a spare hose to pump fitting. Connect opposite end of spare hose to Pressure Test Gauge (C-3309E). Connect pressure hose from valve side of steering gear to valve side of gauge. Valve must be installed on outlet side of gauge. *See Fig. 4.*

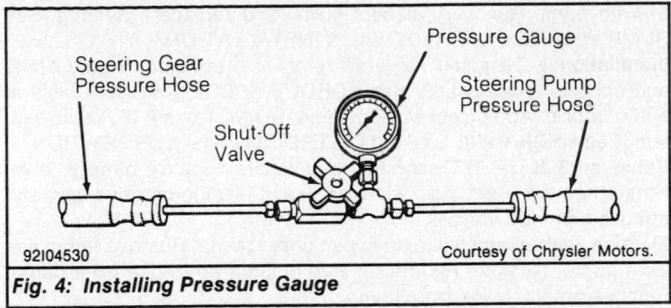

92I04530   Courtesy of Chrysler Motors.

Fig. 4: Installing Pressure Gauge

NOTE: *Replacement fittings are required on Pressure Test Gauge (C-3309E) for adapting to "O" ring type hose tube ends.*

2) Fully open shutoff valve on test gauge. With engine at idle speed and gauge valve open, check initial pressure. If pressure is greater than 125 psi (8.8 kg/cm²) on Dakota or greater than 100 psi (7.0 kg/cm²) on all other models, check for restricted hoses and crimped lines. See POWER STEERING PUMP PRESSURE TEST SPECIFICATIONS table.

POWER STEERING PUMP PRESSURE TEST SPECIFICATIONS

Application	Pressure psi (kg/cm²)
Idle Pressure	
Caravan, Town & Country & Voyager	30-50 (2.1-3.5)
Dakota	50-80 (3.5-5.7)
Relief Pressure	
Caravan, Town & Country & Voyager	1175-1225 (83.0-86.0)
Dakota	
2.5L	1200-1300 (84.5-91.5)
3.9L & 5.2L	1400-1500 (98.5-105.5)

CAUTION: *DO NOT leave shutoff valve closed more than 5 seconds or pump damage could result.*

Relief Pressure Test – **1)** Close gauge shutoff valve completely 3 times. Record highest pressure attained each time. All 3 readings must be above specifications and within 50 psi (3.5 kg/cm²) of each other. See POWER STEERING PUMP PRESSURE TEST SPECIFICATIONS table.
2) If recorded pressures are within specification and range of readings is within 50 psi (3.5 kg/cm²), pump is working properly. If recorded pressures are above specifications but not within 50 psi (3.5 kg/cm²) of each other, replace pump. See POWER STEERING PUMP under REMOVAL & INSTALLATION.

3) If pressures are within 50 psi (3.5 kg/cm²) of each other but below specifications, replace pump. See POWER STEERING PUMP under REMOVAL & INSTALLATION.

CAUTION: *DO NOT hold steering wheel against stops more than 4 seconds or pump damage can result.*

4) Open test valve, and turn steering wheel to left and right stops. Record highest pressure attained at each stop. If output pressures are not same against each stop, gear is leaking internally and must be replaced. See STEERING GEAR under REMOVAL & INSTALLATION.

REMOVAL & INSTALLATION

WARNING: *When battery is disconnected, vehicle computer and memory systems may lose memory data. Driveability problems may exist until computer systems have completed a relearn cycle. See COMPUTER RELEARN PROCEDURES article in GENERAL INFORMATION before disconnecting battery.*

BOOT SEAL

NOTE: *Boot seal replacement procedure is with steering gear removed from vehicle.*

Removal & Installation – **1)** Remove outer tie rod end. See OUTER TIE ROD END under REMOVAL & INSTALLATION. Expand and remove outer boot seal clamp. Cut and remove inner boot seal clamp. **2)** Place reference mark for breather tube location on steering gear housing before removing boot seal. Using a small screwdriver, remove boot seal from groove in steering gear housing and remove boot seal.
3) To install, ensure all surfaces are clean. Lubricate tie rod end boot seal groove with silicone lubricant before installing outer clamp. Install boot seal, aligning reference mark with breather tube. Install and tighten new boot seal clamps. Ensure boot seal is not twisted. To complete installation, reverse removal procedure.

FLOW VALVE "O" RING (T/C TYPE PUMP)

Removal – Remove pressure hose from pump fitting. Remove pump and pulley if necessary. See POWER STEERING PUMP and PUMP PULLEY under REMOVAL & INSTALLATION. Remove fitting from pump housing. Prevent control valve and spring from sliding out of bore. Remove and discard "O" ring. *See Fig. 5.*
Installation – To install, reverse removal procedure. Use NEW "O" ring. Tighten nuts and bolts to specification. See TORQUE SPECIFICATIONS table at end of article. Add power steering fluid. DO NOT use ATF. Bleed system. See HYDRAULIC SYSTEM BLEEDING under LUBRICATION.

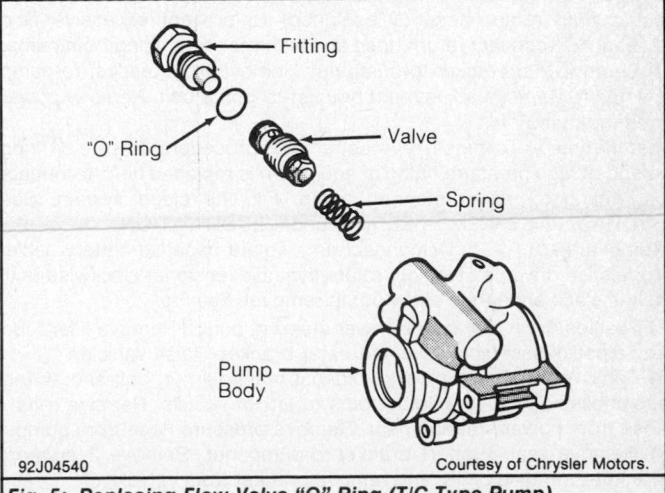

92J04540   Courtesy of Chrysler Motors.

Fig. 5: Replacing Flow Valve "O" Ring (T/C Type Pump)

1992 STEERING
Power Rack & Pinion (Cont.)

OUTER TIE ROD END

Removal – **1)** Place mark on outer tie rod end and inner tie rod end for reassembly reference. Loosen lock nut at inner tie rod end. Remove cotter pin and nut from tie rod end at steering knuckle.

2) Separate tie rod end from steering knuckle. Unscrew tie rod end from inner tie rod end. If necessary, expand or remove outer boot seal clamp.

Installation – **1)** To install, reverse removal procedure. Expand or remove outer clamp on boot seal while installing tie rod end. Lubricate groove of boot seal with silicone lubricant.

2) Install tie rod to mark made during removal. Adjust toe-in. See SPECIFICATIONS & PROCEDURES article in WHEEL ALIGNMENT. Install and tighten outer clamp on boot seal. Ensure boot seal is not twisted. Tighten lock nut and tie rod end-to-steering knuckle nut to specification. See TORQUE SPECIFICATIONS table at end of article.

POWER STEERING PUMP

CAUTION: Excessive belt tension can cause pump shaft bushing to fail. DO NOT pry on reservoir. When filling pump reservoir, DO NOT use ATF.

Removal (2.5L) – **1)** Disconnect and isolate negative battery cable. To release drive belt tension, loosen power steering pump adjustment slot nut and pivot bolt. Loosen rear bracket-to-pump bolts. Turn power steering pump adjustment bolt counterclockwise until belt is slack enough to allow pump removal. *See Fig. 6.*

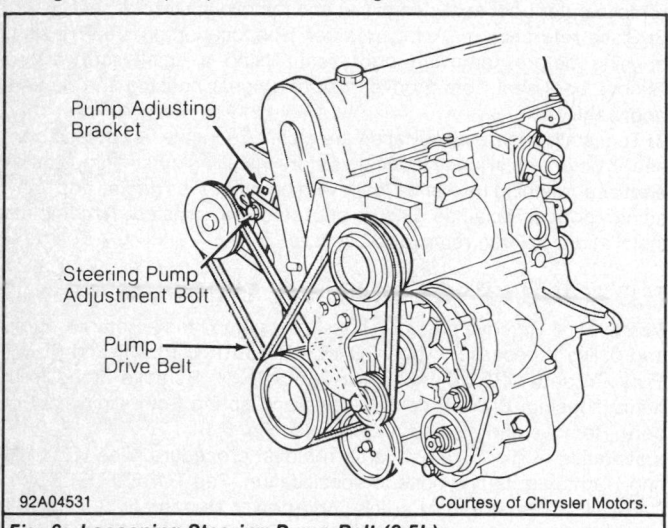

Fig. 6: *Loosening Steering Pump Belt (2.5L)*

2) Position a drain pan under power steering pump. Install a clamp on pump fluid return hose (if equipped) to prevent excessive fluid leakage. Disconnect return hose and high pressure fitting from pump.

3) Remove rear bracket-to-pump nut. Remove front bracket-to-pump pivot bolt. Remove adjustment bracket-to-pump bolt. Remove power steering pump.

Installation – To install, reverse removal procedure. Ensure "O" ring at end of high pressure fitting (if equipped) is replaced before connecting fitting to power steering pump. Fill and bleed system. See HYDRAULIC SYSTEM BLEEDING under LUBRICATION.

Removal (3.0L) – **1)** Disconnect and isolate negative battery cable. To release drive belt tension, rotate dynamic tensioner clockwise until belt is slack enough to allow pump removal. *See Fig. 7.*

2) Position drain pan under power steering pump. Remove filler tube and dipstick assembly from alternator bracket. Raise vehicle.

3) Remove 2 exhaust pipe-to-exhaust manifold nut, bolt and spring assemblies. Remove exhaust pipe to left of vehicle. Remove return hose from power steering gear. Remove pressure hose from pump.

4) Remove rear support bracket-to-pump nut. Remove 2 support bracket-to-engine bolts, and remove bracket from vehicle.

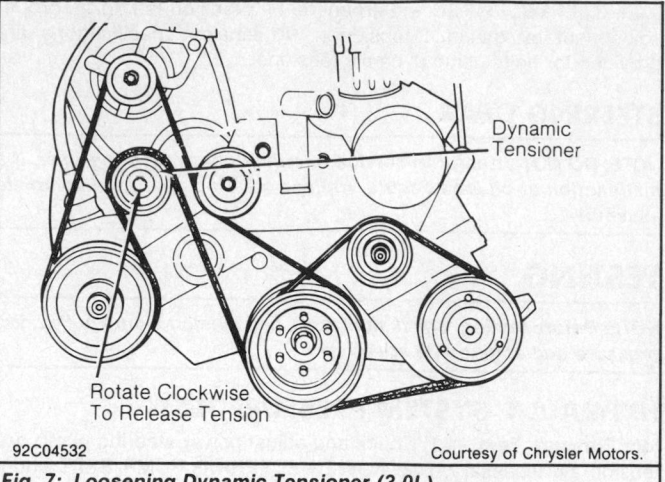

Fig. 7: *Loosening Dynamic Tensioner (3.0L)*

5) Using a deep-well socket to gain access through slots in pump pulley, remove 2 front pump-to-mounting plate bolts. Remove pump assembly through area between floor pan and crossmember at exhaust pipe tunnel.

6) With pump removed, inspect pulley and replace if needed. See PUMP PULLEY under REMOVAL & INSTALLATION.

Installation – To install, reverse removal procedure. Tighten nuts and bolts to specification. See TORQUE SPECIFICATIONS table at end of article. Add power steering fluid. DO NOT use ATF. Bleed system. See HYDRAULIC SYSTEM BLEEDING under LUBRICATION.

Removal (3.3L) – **1)** Disconnect and isolate negative battery cable. Rotate belt tensioner clockwise to release tension on drive belt, and remove belt from vehicle.

2) Raise vehicle, and place drain pan under pump. Remove return line from pump. Remove remote reservoir clamp and hose from pump. Remove pressure line from pump.

3) Remove right front wheel. Remove 3 pump-to-alternator-to-tensioner bracket bolts. *See Fig. 8.*

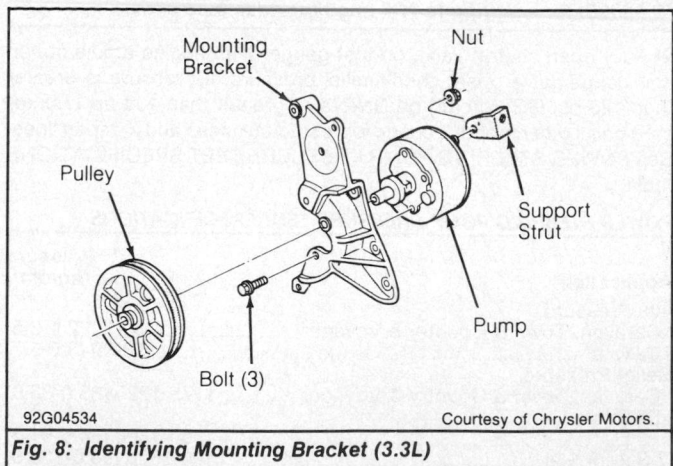

Fig. 8: *Identifying Mounting Bracket (3.3L)*

4) Remove support strut-to-engine nut and bolt. *See Fig. 8.* Lay pump assembly on top of steering gear.

5) Remove tensioner-to-mounting bracket nut. Remove tensioner from bracket.

6) Remove alternator-to-pump support strut nut and bolt. *See Fig. 9.* Lower vehicle.

7) Remove 2 reservoir-to-alternator bracket bolts. Remove tube/hose-to-pump bracket mounting bolt. Remove tube/hose and reservoir as assembly. Remove engine wiring harness clip from alternator bracket. Loosen, but DO NOT remove, engine bracket assembly-to-engine support assembly bolt. *See Fig. 10.*

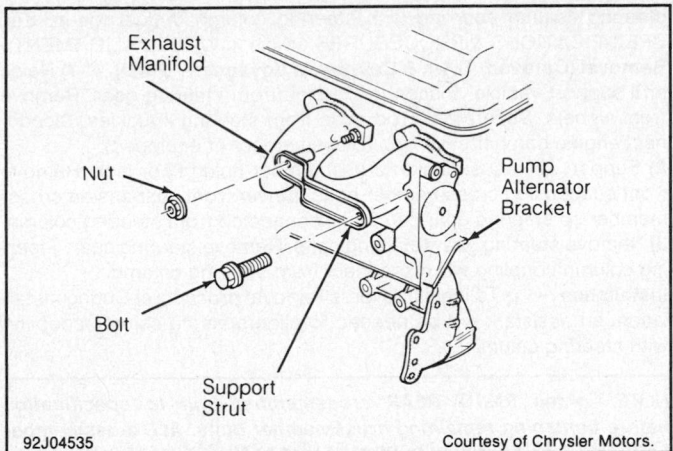

Fig. 9: Identifying Support Strut Bracket (3.3L)

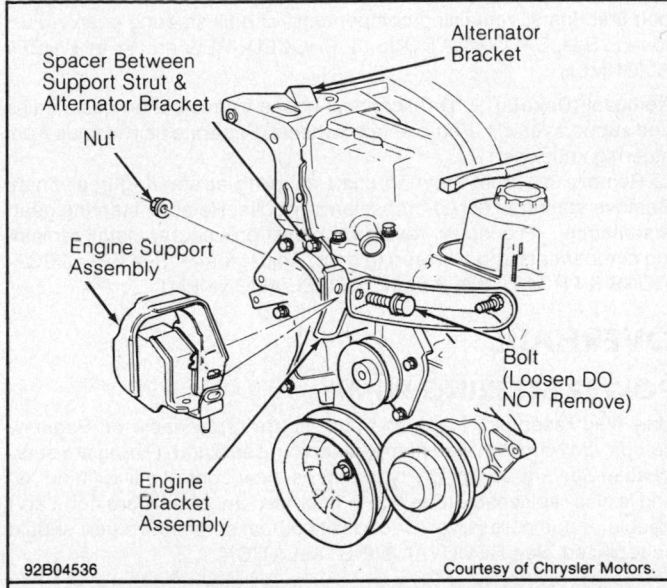

Fig. 10: Identifying Engine Bracket Assembly-To-Engine Support Assembly (3.3L)

8) Remove upper alternator-to-alternator bracket bolt. Rotate alternator back toward dash. Remove 4 alternator bracket-to-intake manifold bolts, and remove bracket.

9) Remove alternator-to-lower bracket bolt. Without removing wiring harness from alternator, remove alternator from bracket and lay alternator on intake manifold.

10) Remove pump through area vacated by alternator. With pump removed, inspect pulley and replace if needed. See PUMP PULLEY under REMOVAL & INSTALLATION.

Installation – To install, reverse removal procedure. Ensure spacer is installed between support strut and alternator bracket. See Fig. 10. Tighten nuts and bolts to specification. See TORQUE SPECIFICATIONS table at end of article. Add power steering fluid. DO NOT use ATF. Bleed system. See HYDRAULIC SYSTEM BLEEDING under LUBRICATION.

Removal (3.9L & 5.2L) – **1)** Disconnect and isolate negative battery cable. Rotate belt tensioner clockwise to release tension on drive belt, and remove belt from vehicle.

2) Clamp fluid return hose, and remove hoses from pump. Cap fittings. Remove pump bracket-to-engine block bolts. Remove pump with pulley and bracket as an assembly.

3) With pump removed, remove pulley. See PUMP PULLEY under REMOVAL & INSTALLATION. Remove bracket-to-pump attaching screws. See Fig. 11.

Installation – To install, reverse removal procedure. Tighten nuts and bolts to specification. See TORQUE SPECIFICATIONS table at end of article. Add power steering fluid. DO NOT use ATF. Bleed system. See HYDRAULIC SYSTEM BLEEDING under LUBRICATION.

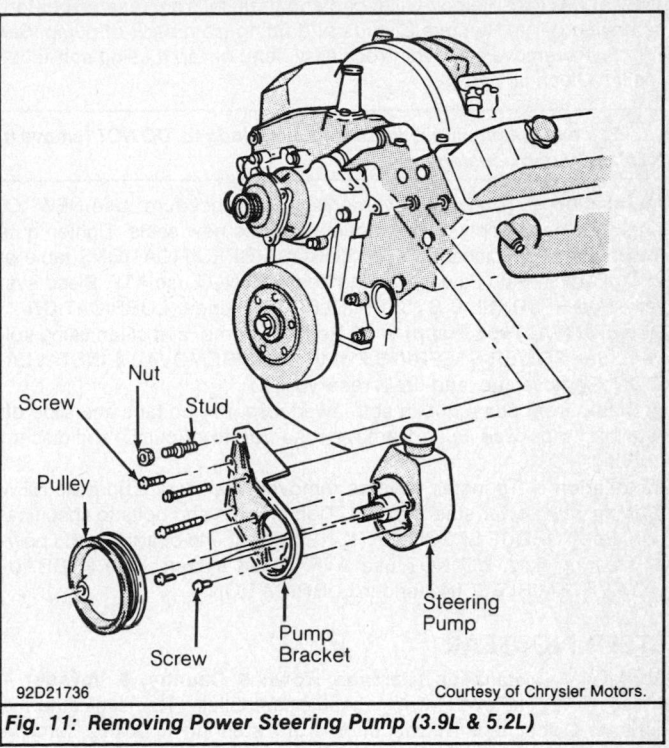

Fig. 11: Removing Power Steering Pump (3.9L & 5.2L)

PUMP PULLEY

CAUTION: Examine exposed end of rotor drive shaft before removal. If it is corroded, clean surface using crocus cloth to prevent damage to shaft bushing during removal.

Removal & Installation – Remove pulley on Ham Can type pump using Puller (C-4068) and Puller Adapter (C-4068-1). Remove pulley from T/C type pump using Remover/Installer (C-4063). See Fig. 12. Replace pulley if bent, cracked or loose. Install Ham Can type and T/C type pump pulleys using Remover/Installer (C-4063). Press pulley until it is flush with shaft end.

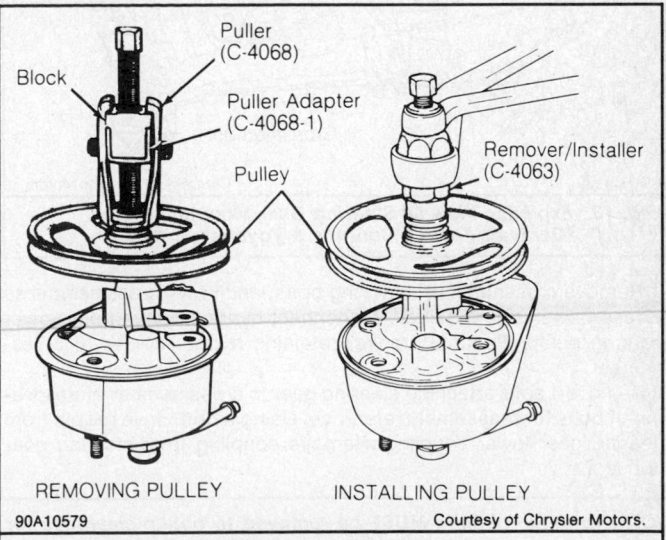

Fig. 12: Removing & Installing Pump Pulley
(Ham Can Type Shown; T/C Type Is Similar)

1992 STEERING
Power Rack & Pinion (Cont.)

RESERVOIR

Removal (Ham Can Type Pump) – Remove pump from vehicle if necessary. See POWER STEERING PUMP under REMOVAL & INSTALLATION. Remove filler cap and drain oil from reservoir before removing parts. Remove 2 studs and fitting from back of pump. *See Fig. 2.* To remove reservoir, rock it by hand or tap it using soft-faced mallet. Clean all parts.

NOTE: If expansion plug is deformed or dislodged, DO NOT remove it. Replace pump housing.

Installation – To install, reverse removal procedure. Use NEW "O" ring and seals. Apply power steering fluid to new seals. Tighten nuts and bolts to specification. See TORQUE SPECIFICATIONS table at end of article. Add power steering fluid. DO NOT use ATF. Bleed system. See HYDRAULIC SYSTEM BLEEDING under LUBRICATION.

Removal (T/C Type Pump) – **1)** Remove pump, and clean using solvent. See POWER STEERING PUMP under REMOVAL & INSTALLATION. Remove cap, and drain reservoir.

2) Clamp front pump hub in soft-jawed vise. Pry up tabs and slide off retaining clips. *See Fig 3.* Remove reservoir from pump, and discard "O" ring.

Installation – To install, reverse removal procedure. Lubricate NEW "O" ring with power steering fluid. Tighten nuts and bolts to specification. See TORQUE SPECIFICATIONS table at end of article. Add power steering fluid. DO NOT use ATF. Bleed system. See HYDRAULIC SYSTEM BLEEDING under LUBRICATION.

STEERING GEAR

Removal & Installation (Caravan, Town & Country, & Voyager – AWD) – **1)** Remove front wheel assemblies. Remove steering column. Disconnect tie rod ends from steering knuckle. Remove bridge assembly attaching nuts and bolts. *See Fig. 13.* Support crossmember using a transmission jack.

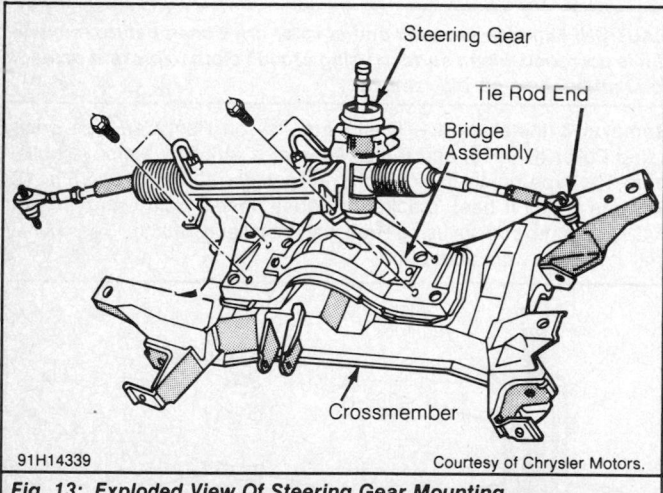

91H14339   Courtesy of Chrysler Motors.

Fig. 13: Exploded View Of Steering Gear Mounting (Caravan, Town & Country, & Voyager – AWD)

2) Remove crossmember attaching bolts, and lower crossmember to access power steering lines. Disconnect hydraulic lines from power steering pump. Remove bracket retaining hydraulic lines to crossmember.

3) Remove 4 bolts attaching steering gear to crossmember. Note location of bolts for reassembly reference. Using a drift, drive roll pin from steering gear lower coupling. Remove coupling from steering gear stub shaft.

NOTE: Pin and coupling MUST be removed to obtain clearance for steering gear removal.

4) Slide gear toward left side of vehicle. Rotate gear housing to clear frame rail, and remove gear assembly. To install gear, reverse removal procedure. During installation, an assistant will be needed to align

steering column coupling with steering column. Adjust toe-in. See SPECIFICATIONS & PROCEDURES article in WHEEL ALIGNMENT.
Removal (Caravan, Town & Country, & Voyager – FWD) – **1)** Raise and support vehicle. Disconnect hoses from steering gear. Remove front wheels. Separate tie rod ends from steering knuckles. Disconnect engine damper strut from crossmember (if equipped).

2) Support front suspension crossmember using floor jack. Remove front suspension crossmember bolts. Lower front suspension crossmember so steering gear can be disconnected from steering column.

3) Remove steering gear retaining bolts. Remove steering gear. Steering column coupling will disconnect from steering column.

Installation – **1)** To install, reverse removal procedure. During installation, an assistant will be needed to align steering column coupling with steering column.

NOTE: Tighten RIGHT REAR crossmember bolt to specification before tightening remaining crossmember bolts. ALL crossmember bolts MUST be tightened to 90 ft. lbs. (122 N.m.)

2) Install all crossmember bolts. Tighten RIGHT REAR crossmember bolt first. Install remaining components, and fill steering gear. Adjust toe-in. See SPECIFICATIONS & PROCEDURES article in WHEEL ALIGNMENT.

Removal (Dakota) – **1)** Disconnect hoses from steering gear. Raise and support vehicle. Remove front wheels. Separate tie rod ends from steering knuckles.

2) Remove pin from steering shaft coupling at steering gear shaft. Remove steering gear-to-crossmember bolts. Remove steering gear.

Installation – To install, reverse removal procedure. Install remaining components and fill steering gear. Adjust toe-in. See SPECIFICATIONS & PROCEDURES under WHEEL ALIGNMENT.

OVERHAUL

POWER STEERING PUMP

Only fluid reservoirs, caps and pulleys are replaceable on Saginaw pumps. On Ham Can type pump, reservoir, seals and "O" ring are serviceable. *See Fig. 2.* On T/C type pumps, flow control valve fitting "O" ring is also replaceable. *See Fig. 5.* Internal components are non-serviceable. If pump, reservoir or cap fails or leaks, defective part should be replaced. See REMOVAL & INSTALLATION.

STEERING GEAR

NOTE: DO NOT attempt to service or adjust power steering gear. If malfunction or oil leak occurs, replace steering gear as complete assembly. See STEERING GEAR under REMOVAL & INSTALLATION.

TORQUE SPECIFICATIONS
TORQUE SPECIFICATIONS

Application	Ft. Lbs. (N.m)
Bridge Assembly Nuts and Bolts	
Caravan, Town & Country, & Voyager	50 (68)
Crossmember Bolt [1]	
Caravan, Town & Country, & Voyager	90 (122)
Flow Control Valve	55 (75)
Pump Bracket Nut	30 (41)
Pressure Hose Fitting	25 (34)
Reservoir-To-Pump Body	35 (47)
Return Hose Fitting	25 (34)
Steering Gear-To-Crossmember Bolt	
Caravan, Town & Country, & Voyager	50 (68)
Dakota	150 (203)
Tie Rod End-To-Steering Knuckle Nut	
Caravan, Town & Country, & Voyager	35 (47)
Dakota	40 (54)
Tie Rod Lock Nut	55 (75)
Wheel Lug Nut	
Caravan, Town & Country, & Voyager	95 (129)
Dakota	85 (115)

[1] – Tighten right rear bolt to specification before tightening other bolts.

RWD Van

DESCRIPTION & OPERATION

The constant control power steering system consists of steering gear, steering linkage, pressure and return fluid hoses and fittings, and a belt-driven hydraulic steering pump with fluid reservoir.

The steering gear is a power assisted recirculating-ball type that acts as a rolling thread between worm shaft and rack piston. When worm shaft is turned, the rack piston moves and piston teeth mesh with sector shaft teeth, turning pitman arm which turns steering linkage.

The steering linkage consists of pitman arm, idler arm(s), tie rods, center link and drag link (if equipped).

The power steering pump is a constant flow rate and displacement, vane-type pump. Pump is connected to steering gear by pressure and return hoses. Pump shaft has pressed on, belt-driven pulley.

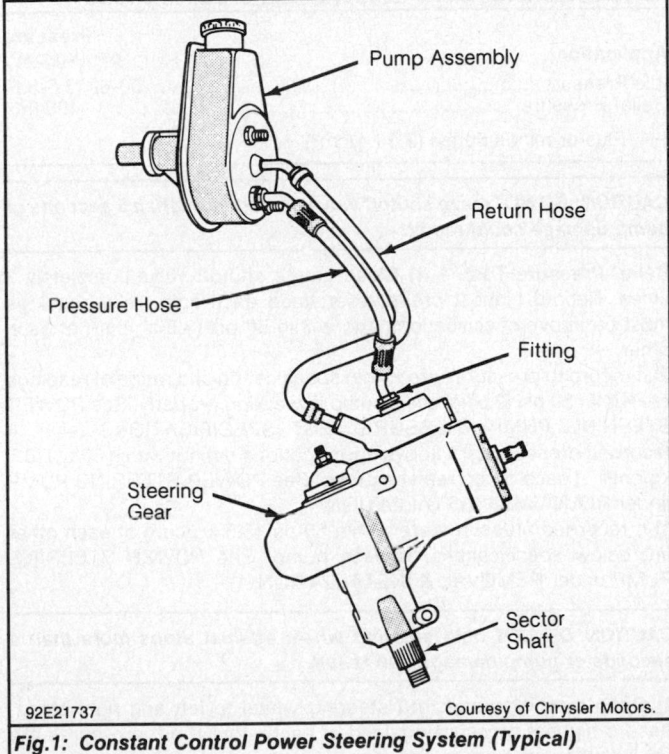

92E21737   Courtesy of Chrysler Motors.

Fig.1: Constant Control Power Steering System (Typical)

LUBRICATION

CAPACITY

Application	Pts. (L)
RWD Van	2.7 (1.3)

FLUID TYPE

Use Mopar Power Steering Fluid (4318055).

CAUTION: DO NOT use Automatic Transmission Fluid (ATF).

FLUID LEVEL CHECK

Check fluid level with engine cold and not running. Remove fluid level cap/dipstick on pump reservoir. Dipstick should indicate FULL COLD with fluid temperature of 70-80°F (21-27°C). If needed, add fluid through dipstick opening, and recheck. DO NOT overfill.

HYDRAULIC SYSTEM BLEEDING

Fill power steering pump reservoir to specified level. Start engine and slowly turn steering wheel to left and right but DO NOT contact steering stops in either direction. Stop engine. Inspect reservoir fluid level and add fluid if necessary. Bleeding process may have to be repeated several times to completely purge all air from system.

ADJUSTMENTS

POWER STEERING PUMP BELT

3.9L & 5.2L – Serpentine belt tension is kept in proper adjustment by dynamic tensioner. No tension specifications are provided for belts using dynamic tensioner.

5.9L – Power steering belt tension is adjusted by adjusting power steering pump position. To check belt tension, use a Poly-V Burroughs type gauge. See POWER STEERING BELT TENSION SPECIFICATIONS table.

POWER STEERING BELT TENSION SPECIFICATIONS

Application	New Belt Lbs. (kg)	Used Belt Lbs. (kg)
3.9L & 5.2L	[1]	[1]
5.9L	100-140 (44-62)	[2] 60-90 (27-40)

[1] – Dynamic tensioner equipped, no adjustment required.
[2] – Belt is considered used after 15 minutes of use.

POWER STEERING PUMP PULLEY

On vehicles equipped with serpentine belts, after pulley installation, run engine until warm. See PUMP PULLEY under REMOVAL & INSTALLATION. If belt chirp exists, move pulley outward approximately .020" (0.5 mm). If noise increases, press pulley inward .040" (1.0 mm). Ensure pulley does not contact mounting bolts.

SECTOR SHAFT PRELOAD

1) Ensure that valve body is centered before adjusting sector shaft preload. See VALVE BODY CENTERING under ADJUSTMENTS. Disconnect drag link from pitman arm. Start engine and run at idle. Turn steering wheel from stop-to-stop and note number of turns. Turn wheel back 1/2 number of turns to center gear.
2) Loosen sector shaft adjuster screw until backlash exists. *See Fig. 2.* Tighten adjuster screw until no backlash exists. Tighten adjuster screw an additional 3/8 to 1/2 turn. Tighten lock nut to **23 ft. lbs. (38 N.m)**.

VALVE BODY CENTERING

NOTE: Valve body centering should only be performed if steering wheel movement is noticed when engine starts or if valve body is removed from steering gear.

1) Start engine and check for steering wheel movement. If movement exists, loosen valve body mounting bolts. Tighten bolts to **84 INCH lbs. (10 N.m)** to allow for valve body centering.
2) Tap control valve up or down until steering wheel movement upon engine start-up stops. To move valve downward, tap on end plug of valve body. To move valve upward, tap on valve body retaining bolt. Turn steering wheel from stop-to-stop several times to bleed air from system.

CAUTION: DO NOT turn steering wheel tightly against stops with valve body mounting bolts loose, or excessive pressure may blow out valve body "O" rings.

3) Check power steering fluid level and fill as necessary. With front wheels in straight-ahead position, start and stop engine several times. If steering wheel moves, repeat steps **1)** and **2)**. If steering wheel does not move, tighten valve body bolts to **17 ft. lbs. (23 N.m)**.

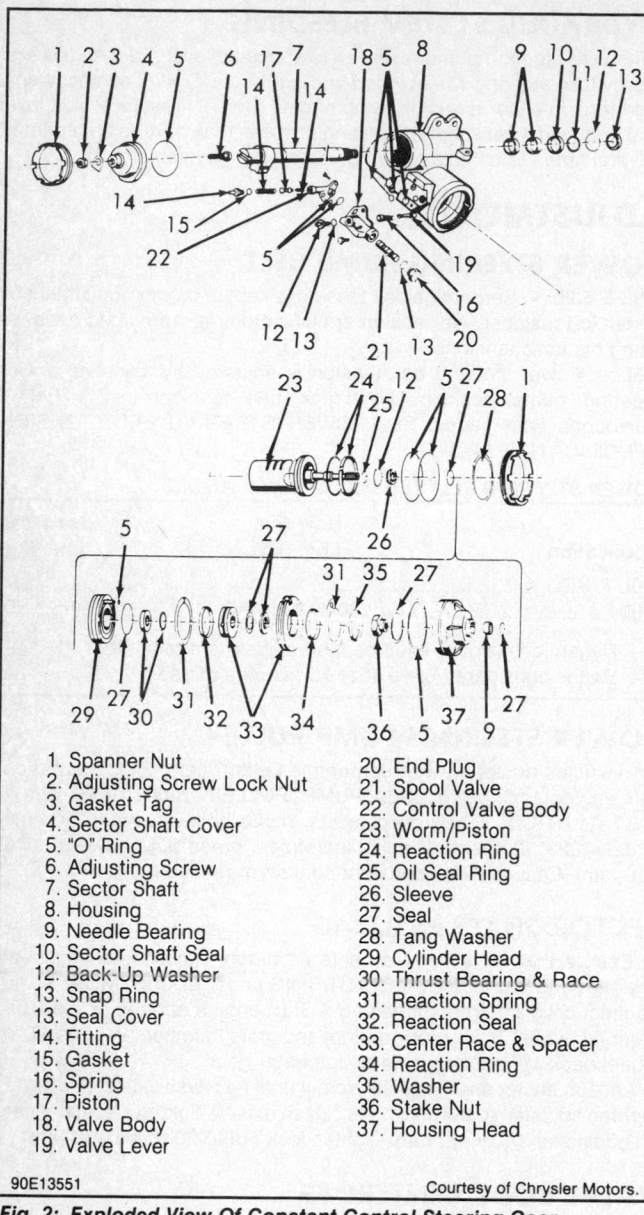

1. Spanner Nut
2. Adjusting Screw Lock Nut
3. Gasket Tag
4. Sector Shaft Cover
5. "O" Ring
6. Adjusting Screw
7. Sector Shaft
8. Housing
9. Needle Bearing
10. Sector Shaft Seal
12. Back-Up Washer
13. Snap Ring
13. Seal Cover
14. Fitting
15. Gasket
16. Spring
17. Piston
18. Valve Body
19. Valve Lever

20. End Plug
21. Spool Valve
22. Control Valve Body
23. Worm/Piston
24. Reaction Ring
25. Oil Seal Ring
26. Sleeve
27. Seal
28. Tang Washer
29. Cylinder Head
30. Thrust Bearing & Race
31. Reaction Spring
32. Reaction Seal
33. Center Race & Spacer
34. Reaction Ring
35. Washer
36. Stake Nut
37. Housing Head

90E13551   Courtesy of Chrysler Motors.

Fig. 2: Exploded View Of Constant Control Steering Gear

TESTING

NOTE: *Before testing, check fluid level, belt tension, pump pulley, tire pressure and engine idle speed.*

HYDRAULIC SYSTEM PRESSURE TEST

Idle Pressure Test – 1) Check and adjust power steering pump belt tension as necessary. See POWER STEERING PUMP BELT under ADJUSTMENTS. Remove high pressure hose at steering pump and connect a spare hose to pump fitting. Connect opposite end of spare hose to Pressure Test Gauge (C-3309E). Connect pressure hose from valve side of steering gear to valve side of gauge. Valve must be installed on outlet side of gauge. *See Fig. 3.*

NOTE: *Replacement fittings are required on Pressure Test Gauge (C-3309E) for adapting to "O" ring type hose tube ends.*

2) Fully open shutoff valve on test gauge. With a thermometer in fluid reservoir, start engine and warm fluid to 150-170°F (66-77°C). Turning wheels from stop-to-stop will aid in warming fluid. DO NOT hold wheels against stop.

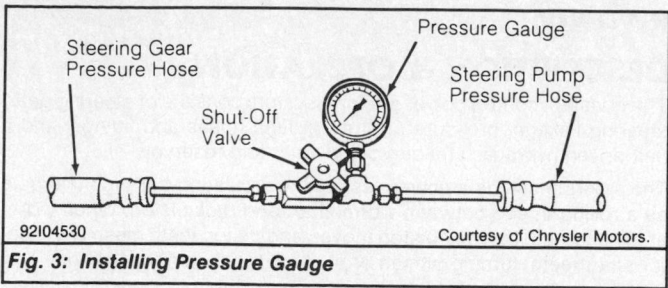

92I04530   Courtesy of Chrysler Motors.

Fig. 3: Installing Pressure Gauge

3) With engine at idle and gauge valve open, check initial pressure. See POWER STEERING PUMP PRESSURE TEST SPECIFICATIONS table. If pressure is greater than 125 psi (8.8 kg/cm²), check for restricted hoses or crimped lines.

POWER STEERING PUMP PRESSURE TEST SPECIFICATIONS

Application	Pressure psi (kg/cm²)
Idle Pressure	50-80 (3.5-5.6)
Relief Pressure	¹ 1400 (98)

¹ – Plus or minus 50 psi (3.5 kg/cm²).

CAUTION: *DO NOT leave shutoff valve closed more than 5 seconds or pump damage could result.*

Relief Pressure Test – 1) Close gauge shutoff valve completely 3 times. Record highest pressure attained each time. All 3 readings must be above specifications and within 50 psi (3.5 kg/cm²) of each other.

2) If recorded pressures are within specification and range of readings are within 50 psi (3.5 kg/cm²), pump is working properly. See POWER STEERING PUMP PRESSURE TEST SPECIFICATIONS table. If recorded pressures are above specifications but not within 50 psi (3.5 kg/cm²) of each other, replace pump. See POWER STEERING PUMP under REMOVAL & INSTALLATION.

3) If recorded pressures are within 50 psi (3.5 kg/cm²) of each other but below specifications, replace pump. See POWER STEERING PUMP under REMOVAL & INSTALLATION.

CAUTION: *DO NOT hold steering wheel against stops more than 4 seconds or pump damage can result.*

4) Open test valve and turn steering wheel to left and right stops. Record highest pressure attained at each stop. If out pressures are not equal against each stop, gear is leaking internally and must be repaired or replaced. See STEERING GEAR under REMOVAL & INSTALLATION or under OVERHAUL. Shut off engine, remove test gauge and connect pressure hose.

REMOVAL & INSTALLATION

WARNING: *When battery is disconnected, vehicle computer and memory systems may lose memory data. Driveability problems may exist until computer systems have completed a relearn cycle. See COMPUTER RELEARN PROCEDURES article in GENERAL INFORMATION before disconnecting battery.*

WARNING: *Safety goggles should be worn whenever servicing power steering pump or steering gear.*

PUMP PULLEY

CAUTION: *Examine exposed end of rotor drive shaft before removal. If it is corroded, clean surface with crocus cloth to prevent damage to shaft bushing during removal.*

Removal & Installation – Remove pump from vehicle if necessary. See POWER STEERING PUMP under REMOVAL & INSTALLATION. Using Puller (C-4068) and Puller Adapter (C-4068-1), remove pump pulley. *See Fig. 4.* Replace pulley if bent, cracked or loose. Using Installer (C-4063), press pulley until flush with shaft end. If belt chirp exists after starting engine, see POWER STEERING PUMP PULLEY under ADJUSTMENTS.

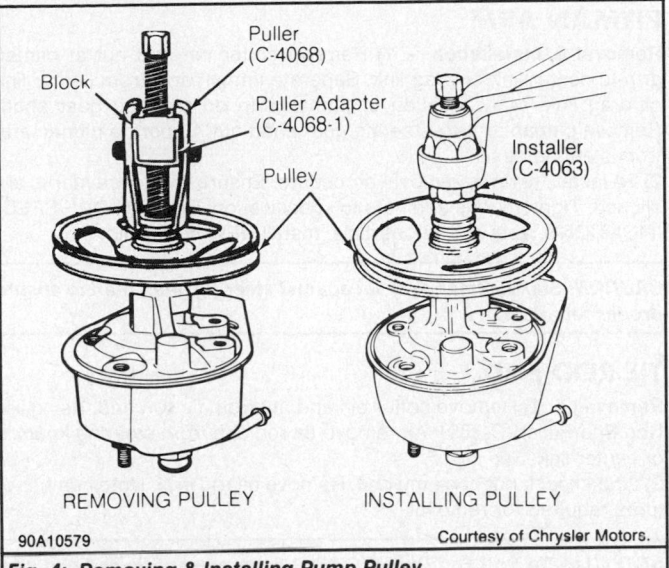

REMOVING PULLEY   INSTALLING PULLEY

90A10579   Courtesy of Chrysler Motors.

Fig. 4: Removing & Installing Pump Pulley

PUMP RESERVOIR

Removal – **1)** Remove pump from vehicle if necessary. See POWER STEERING PUMP under REMOVAL AND INSTALLATION. Remove filler cap and drain oil from reservoir before removing parts. Remove 2 studs and fitting from back of pump. *See Fig. 5.*

2) Rock reservoir by hand or tap with soft-faced mallet to remove it. Remove "O" ring seals from housing and reservoir. Remove flow control valve and spring from rear of pump housing. *See Fig. 6.* Clean all parts.

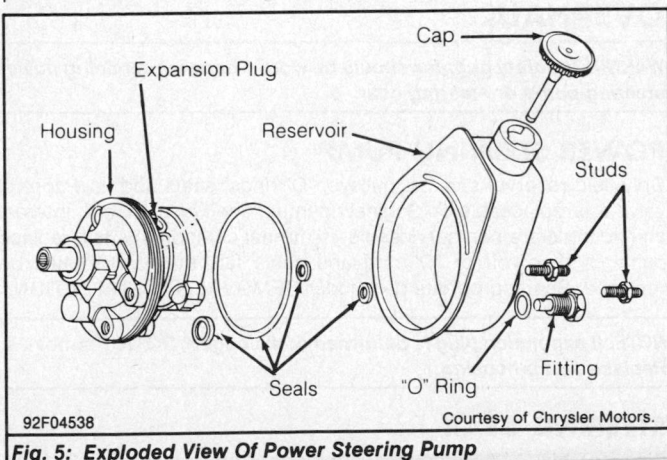

92F04538   Courtesy of Chrysler Motors.

Fig. 5: Exploded View Of Power Steering Pump

NOTE: *If expansion plug is deformed or dislodged, DO NOT remove it. Replace pump housing.*

Installation – To install, reverse removal procedure. Use NEW "O" ring, seals and flow control valve. Tighten flow control valve fitting to **55 ft. lbs. (75 N.m).** Apply power steering fluid to new seals. Tighten nuts and bolts to specification. See TORQUE SPECIFICATIONS table at end of article. Add power steering fluid. DO NOT use ATF. Bleed system. See HYDRAULIC SYSTEM BLEEDING under LUBRICATION.

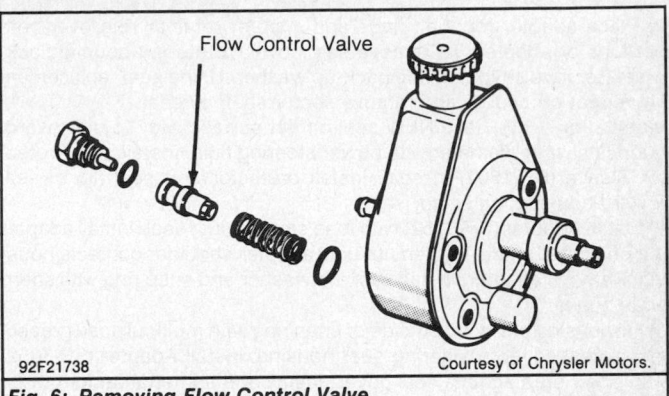

92F21738   Courtesy of Chrysler Motors.

Fig. 6: Removing Flow Control Valve

POWER STEERING PUMP

WARNING: *DO NOT attempt to remove power steering pump without removing power steering pump belt. Personal injury or pulley damage could result.*

Removal (3.9L & 5.2L) – **1)** Disconnect and isolate negative battery cable. To remove serpentine belt, rotate tensioner clockwise and hold in place, then slide belt from tensioner pulley. Place drain pan under pump. Disconnect and cap hoses.

2) Remove bracket-to-engine block attaching bolts. Remove pump, pulley and mounting bracket as an assembly. To allow access to pump attaching screws, remove pump pulley. See PUMP PULLEY under REMOVAL & INSTALLATION. Remove bracket-to-pump attaching screws.

Installation – To install pump, reverse removal procedure. Fill and bleed system. See HYDRAULIC SYSTEM BLEEDING under LUBRICATION.

Removal & Installation (5.9L) – Disconnect and isolate negative battery cable. Remove belt from pump pulley. Place drain pan under pump. Disconnect and cap hoses. Remove front bracket bolts. Remove rear pump-to-rear bracket nuts/bolts. Remove pump. Remove front bracket from pump if needed. To install, reverse removal procedure. Fill and bleed system. See HYDRAULIC SYSTEM BLEEDING under LUBRICATION.

STEERING GEAR

NOTE: *To avoid damaging collapsible steering column, disconnect steering column from floor panel and instrument panel. See STEERING COLUMNS article.*

Removal – **1)** Disconnect and isolate negative battery cable. Detach steering column from floor panel and instrument panel. Disconnect and cap pressure and return hoses at steering gear.

2) Remove nut and pitman arm from sector shaft. Remove steering gear-to-frame bolts and remove steering gear.

Installation – To install, reverse removal procedure. Rotate worm shaft by hand, and position sector shaft at midpoint of travel. Install pitman arm and remaining components. Tighten bolts to specification. See TORQUE SPECIFICATIONS table at end of article. Fill pump with fluid and start engine. Turn steering wheel from stop-to-stop several times to bleed system. Stop engine and refill pump (if necessary).

SECTOR SHAFT OIL SEAL

NOTE: *Removing steering gear is not necessary for seal replacement.*

Removal – **1)** Remove nut and pitman arm from sector shaft. Using Seal Replacement Kit (C-3350-A), slide threaded adapter over sector shaft and thread nut on sector shaft. *See Fig. 2.* Maintain pressure on threaded adapter with adapter nut, while screwing adapter inward enough to engage metal portion of seal cover.

2) Place adapter tool half rings and adapter retainer ring over both portions of adapter. To remove seal cover, rotate nut counterclockwise. Remove snap ring and back-up washer. Using seal replacement kit, repeat procedure and remove sector shaft oil seal.

Installation – 1) Place NEW seal on flat surface with lip downward. Lubricate inner diameter with power steering fluid. Install Seal Protector Sleeve (SP-1601) in seal. Install protector and seal (lip of seal toward housing) on sector shaft.

2) Install Adapter (SP-3052) with long step against seal. Install adapter nut on sector shaft. Tighten nut until adapter shoulder contacts housing. Remove adapter. Install back-up washer and snap ring with sharp edge outward.

3) Fill housing cavity on outside of snap ring with multipurpose grease. Install seal cover in steering gear housing. Install Adapter (SP-3052) with short step against seal cover. Install and tighten adapter nut on sector shaft until shoulder contacts steering gear housing. Remove adapter.

4) Place steering gear and steering wheel in straight-ahead position. Install pitman arm and tighten nut to specification. See TORQUE SPECIFICATIONS table at end of article. Fill power steering pump with power steering fluid (if necessary).

WORM SHAFT SEAL

NOTE: Removing steering gear is not necessary for seal replacement.

Removal & Installation – 1) Remove steering column. See STEERING COLUMNS article. Using Seal Remover (C-3638), remove seal from steering gear.

2) To install, use Seal Installer (C-3650). Install seal with seal lip toward steering gear housing. Force seal inward until seal installer contacts housing. To install remaining components, reverse removal procedure.

CENTER LINK

Removal & Installation – Separate tie rods, idler arm, steering and drag link (if equipped) from center link. *See Fig. 7.* Remove center link. To install, reverse removal procedure. Tighten retaining nuts to specification. See TORQUE SPECIFICATIONS table at end of article.

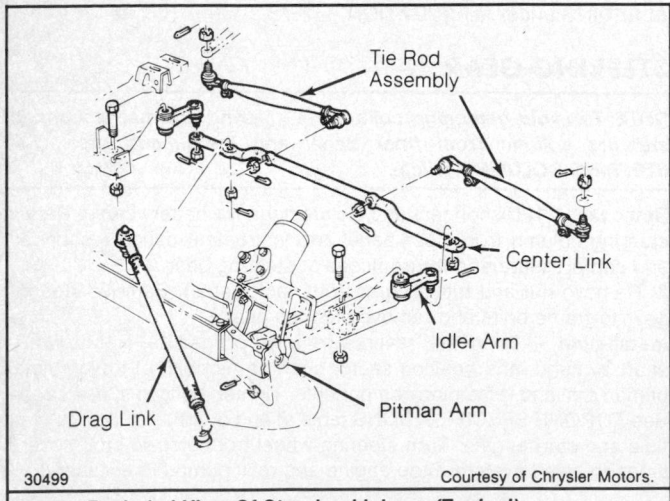

Fig. 7: *Exploded View Of Steering Linkage (Typical)*

30499   Courtesy of Chrysler Motors.

DRAG LINK

Removal & Installation – Remove cotter pin and drag link nut. Using Separator (C-4150), separate drag link from center link and pitman arm. Remove drag link. To install drag link, reverse removal procedure. Install drag link retaining nut and NEW cotter pin.

IDLER ARM

Removal & Installation – Remove cotter pin and nut from idler arm. Separate idler arm from center link. Remove idler arm retaining bolt(s). Remove idler arm. To install, reverse removal procedure. Tighten bolts to specification. See TORQUE SPECIFICATIONS table at end of article. Install NEW cotter pin.

PITMAN ARM

Removal & Installation – 1) Remove cotter pin and nut at pitman arm-to-center link or drag link. Separate pitman arm from center link or drag link. Mark location of pitman arm on steering gear shaft. Remove pitman arm-to-steering gear shaft nut. Separate pitman arm from steering gear.

2) To install, reverse removal procedure. Ensure reference marks are aligned. Tighten bolts and nuts to specification. See TORQUE SPECIFICATIONS table at end of article. Install NEW cotter pin.

CAUTION: Stake pitman arm nut against steering gear shaft to ensure proper retention.

TIE ROD END

Removal – 1) Remove cotter pin and nut from tie rod end. Using Tie Rod End Puller (C-3894-A), remove tie rod end from steering knuckle or center link. *See Fig. 7.*

2) Loosen lock nut or clamp bolt. Remove tie rod end. Note number of turns required for removal.

NOTE: Use Tie Rod End Puller (C-3894-A) to prevent tie rod end seal damage.

Installation – 1) To install, reverse removal procedure. Ensure tie rod end is installed at same location. Position clamp sleeve with bolt located on bottom. Clamp opening should be aligned with slot in sleeve.

2) Tighten tie rod end nut to specification. See TORQUE SPECIFICATIONS table at end of article. Install NEW cotter pin. Check and adjust toe-in. See SPECIFICATIONS & PROCEDURES article in WHEEL ALIGNMENT. Tighten clamp bolt to specification.

OVERHAUL

WARNING: Safety goggles should be worn whenever servicing power steering pump or steering gear.

POWER STEERING PUMP

Only fluid reservoirs, caps, pulleys, "O" rings, seals and flow control valve are replaceable on Saginaw pumps. *See Figs. 5 and 6.* Internal components are non-serviceable. If internal components fail, replace pump. If reservoir or "O" ring and seals fail, that part should be replaced. See appropriate part under REMOVAL & INSTALLATION.

NOTE: If expansion plug is deformed or dislodged, DO NOT remove it. Replace pump housing.

STEERING GEAR

Disassembly – 1) Remove steering gear from vehicle. See STEERING GEAR under REMOVAL & INSTALLATION. Clean exterior of steering gear and clamp it in a soft-jawed vise. Rotate worm and piston assembly shaft from stop-to-stop several times to drain fluid. Remove valve body and "O" rings from valve body housing. *See Fig. 2.* Remove spring. Using a screwdriver, pry valve lever up and then outward.

CAUTION: DO NOT collapse slotted valve lever end. This will destroy bearing tolerances of spherical head.

2) Loosen sector shaft adjusting screw lock nut. Using Spanner Wrench (C-3988), remove spanner nut from sector shaft cover. Position sector shaft teeth at center of travel. Using Spanner Wrench (C-3989), loosen worm and piston spanner nut. Install Arbor (C-3786) on threaded end of sector shaft. *See Fig. 8.* Slide arbor into housing until both arbor and shaft engage with bearings.

CAUTION: Keep worm and piston firmly compressed to keep retaining rings from dislodging.

---

3) Compress housing head components by rotating worm shaft to full left turn position. Using spanner wrench, remove spanner nut and tang washer. Remove worm and piston assembly cover nut and tang washer. Using a screwdriver and sector shaft as fulcrum, pry on worm and piston teeth and remove assembly. *See Fig. 8.*

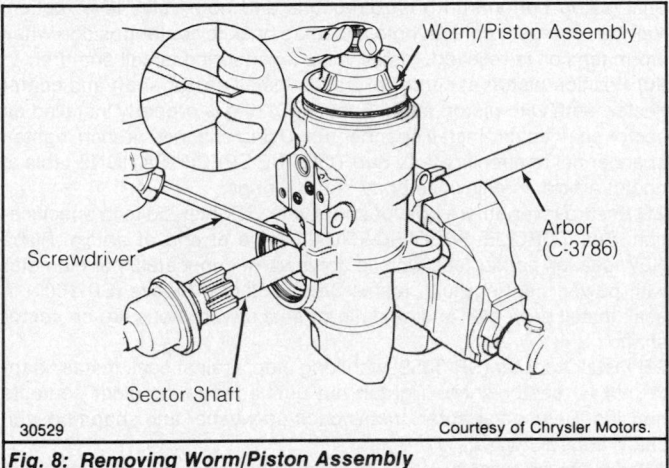

30529   Courtesy of Chrysler Motors.

Fig. 8: Removing Worm/Piston Assembly

---

4) Place worm and piston assembly vertically in a soft-jawed vise. Raise housing head until worm shaft oil seal clears worm shaft. Position Arbor (C-3929) on top of worm shaft and extend into oil seal. Arbor retains needle bearings in place.

CAUTION: Arbor must be inserted into housing head during removal to hold needle bearings in place. If replacing worm shaft oil seal, remove seal with housing head assembled in steering gear housing.

---

5) With arbor installed, pull upward on housing head until arbor is fully engaged in bearing. Remove housing head and arbor as a unit. If needle bearings dislodge, use wheel bearing grease to hold in position during installation.
6) Remove large "O" ring from housing head. Apply air to housing head chamber to remove reaction seal from groove. *See Fig. 9.* Remove reaction spring, reaction ring, balancing ring and spacer. Hold worm shaft and remove staked nut.

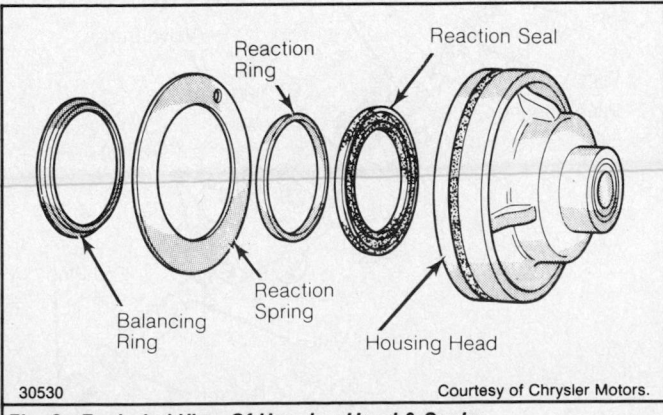

30530   Courtesy of Chrysler Motors.

Fig. 9: Exploded View Of Housing Head & Seals

---

7) Remove upper thrust bearing race and bearing from worm shaft. Remove center race from worm shaft. Remove lower thrust bearing and race from worm shaft. Remove reaction ring and reaction spring.
8) Remove cylinder head assembly. Remove "O" rings from outside of cylinder head. Apply air to oil hole between "O" ring grooves of cylinder head to remove reaction ring "O" ring from cylinder head.

NOTE: Worm and piston are serviced as an assembly only. DO NOT disassemble.

---

9) Remove snap ring, sleeve and rectangular oil seal from cylinder head counterbore. Using INCH-pound torque wrench, check torque required to rotate worm shaft through its travel. Torque should not exceed **1.50 INCH lbs. (.17 N.m)**.
Inspection – 1) Place worm and piston in a soft-jawed vise with rack teeth facing upward and worm centered. Attach a dial indicator and position pointer on worm shaft at 2.313" (58.75 mm) from piston flange.
2) Vertical side play should not exceed **.008" (.20 mm)** with a lifting force of 1 lb. (4.4 N) at end of worm shaft. Inspect Teflon piston ring for wear and cuts. Replace with cast iron piston ring and sealing ring (if necessary).

NOTE: Lubricate all seals and "O" rings with power steering fluid before installing.

Reassembly – 1) If replacing piston ring, replace rubber seal ring and cast iron ring in piston groove. Place piston and ring assembly into Piston Ring Installer (C-3676), with lower part of piston ring on piston ring installer. *See Fig. 10.*

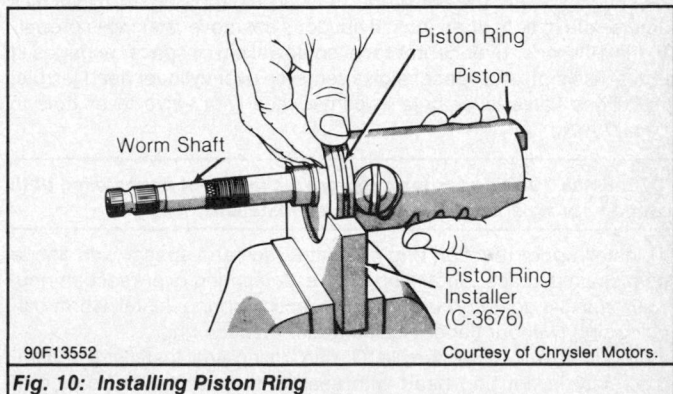

90F13552   Courtesy of Chrysler Motors.

Fig. 10: Installing Piston Ring

---

2) Press downward on piston and rotate to seat ring in groove, forcing ends of ring out for ease of locking. Place worm/piston assembly in a soft-jawed vise with worm shaft upward.
3) Ensure cylinder head oil passage is not restricted. Lubricate large "O" rings and install in cylinder head grooves.
4) Install rectangular oil seal, sleeve and snap ring in cylinder head. Install reaction ring "O" ring in cylinder head.

CAUTION: Ensure piston ring end gap is closed before installing cylinder head to avoid damaging "O" ring.

---

5) Slide cylinder head assembly on worm shaft with ferrule end upward. *See Fig. 11.* Lubricate components with power steering fluid and install in following order:
- Inner thrust bearing (thick) race
- Inner thrust bearing
- Inner reaction spring (small hole over ferrule rod)
- Reaction ring (flange side up through reaction spring to contact "O" ring in cylinder head)
- Thrust bearing center race
- Outer thrust bearing
- Outer thrust bearing (thin) race
- NEW staked nut (finger tight only)

NOTE: DO NOT tighten staked nut.

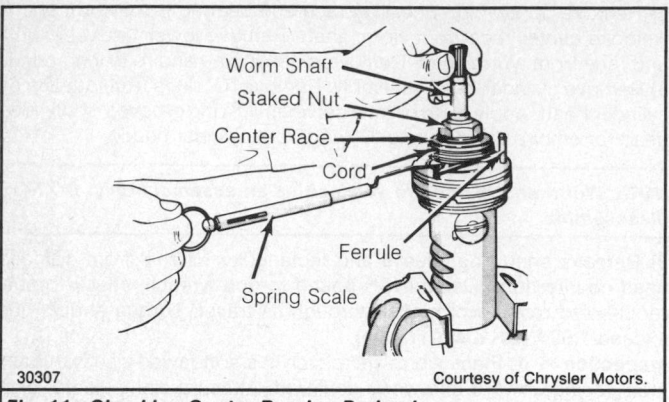

30307   Courtesy of Chrysler Motors.

Fig. 11: Checking Center Bearing Preload

6) Rotate worm shaft clockwise 1/2 turn. Hold worm shaft in this position with Splined Nut (C-3637) and socket wrench. Tighten staked nut to **50 ft. lbs. (68 N.m)**, to pre-stretch threads, then loosen.

7) Place several rounds of cord around center race. Attach a spring scale. Pull on cord to rotate bearing. *See Fig. 11.* Tighten nut while pulling cord. Adjustment is correct when reading on spring scale is **16-24 oz. (4.4-6.7 N)** with race rotating.

8) Using a 1/4" punch, stake upper portion of stake nut into knurled area of worm shaft. If nut moves while staking, tap in opposite direction to regain proper adjustment. Recheck center bearing preload adjustment.

9) If adjustment is correct, stake nut in 3 areas and recheck adjustment. Check nut for proper staking by applying **20 ft. lbs. (27 N.m)** torque in both directions. If nut does not move, staking is proper.

10) Install spacer over center race, so dowel pin of spacer engages in center race slot, and spacer slot is centered over cylinder head ferrule. This aligns valve lever hole in center race with valve lever hole in spacer.

NOTE: Small "O" ring for ferrule groove should not be installed until reaction spring and spacer have been installed.

11) Install upper reaction ring on center race and spacer with flange down against spacer. Install upper reaction spring over reaction ring. Ensure ferrule goes through hole in reaction spring. Install worm balancing ring (without flange) inside upper reaction ring.

12) Lubricate and install ferrule "O" ring. Using Seal Installer (C-3650), install seal in housing head with seal lip toward needle bearing (if removed) until seal installer bottoms.

13) Lubricate and install reaction seal in inner face of housing head with seal flat side out. *See Fig. 9.* Install "O" ring on housing head.

14) Slide housing head over worm shaft, engaging cylinder head ferrule and "O" ring. Ensure reaction rings enter groove in housing head. Lubricate worm/piston bore of housing. Rotate worm shaft fully counterclockwise to retain reaction rings in place. Install worm/piston assembly.

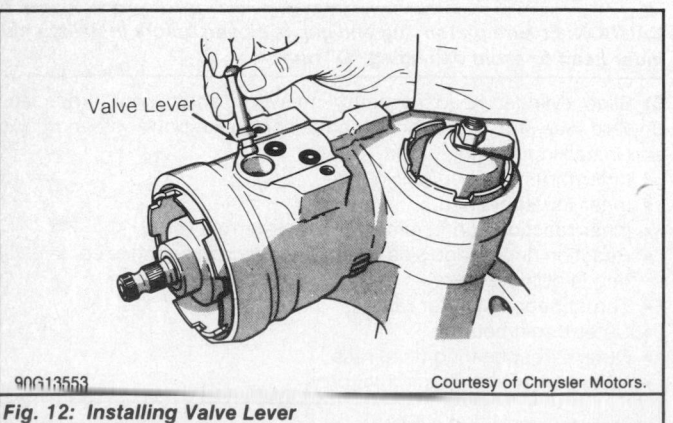

90G13553   Courtesy of Chrysler Motors.

Fig. 12: Installing Valve Lever

CAUTION: Ensure cylinder head is bottomed on housing shoulder.

15) Ensure piston teeth face right and valve lever hole in spacer faces upward. Align valve lever hole in center race and spacer with valve lever hole in gear housing.

16) Install valve lever with double bearing end first, through hole in housing. *See Fig. 12.* Ensure slots in lever are parallel to worm shaft.

17) Lightly tap end of valve lever to seat lower pivot point in center race. Center valve lever in steering gear by tapping on reinforcing to slightly rotate housing head.

18) Align tang washer with groove in housing and install. Install spanner nut. Using spanner wrench, tighten spanner nut to specification. See TORQUE SPECIFICATIONS table at end of article.

19) Ensure valve lever remains centered in hole. Rotate worm shaft until piston bottoms in both directions and note valve lever action. Valve lever must center in hole and snap back to center position when worm tension is relieved. Install valve lever spring, small end first.

20) Position piston at center of travel. Install sector shaft and center sector teeth with piston teeth. Ensure "O" ring is properly installed on sector shaft cover. Install spanner nut. Using spanner wrench, tighten spanner nut to specification. See TORQUE SPECIFICATIONS table at end of article. Install valve body and "O" rings.

21) Ensure lever enters hole of spool valve. Tighten bolts to specification. See TORQUE SPECIFICATIONS table at end of article. Place NEW seal on flat surface with lip downward. Lubricate inner diameter with power steering fluid. Install Seal Protector Sleeve (SP-1601) in seal. Install protector and seal (lip of seal toward housing) on sector shaft.

22) Install Adapter (SP-3052) with long step against seal. Install adapter nut on sector shaft. Tighten nut until adapter shoulder contacts housing. Remove adapter. Install back-up washer and snap ring with sharp edge outward.

23) Fill housing cavity on outside of snap ring with multipurpose grease. Install seal cover in steering gear housing. Install Adapter (SP-3052) with short step against seal cover. Install and tighten adapter nut on sector shaft until shoulder contacts steering gear housing. Remove adapter.

24) Adjust sector shaft preload. See SECTOR SHAFT PRELOAD under ADJUSTMENTS.

VALVE BODY

Disassembly – 1) Disconnect and cap pressure and return hoses from valve body. Tie hoses above power steering pump fluid level to prevent drainage. Remove mounting bolts and lift valve body assembly from steering gear. Remove control valve body-to-valve body bolts.

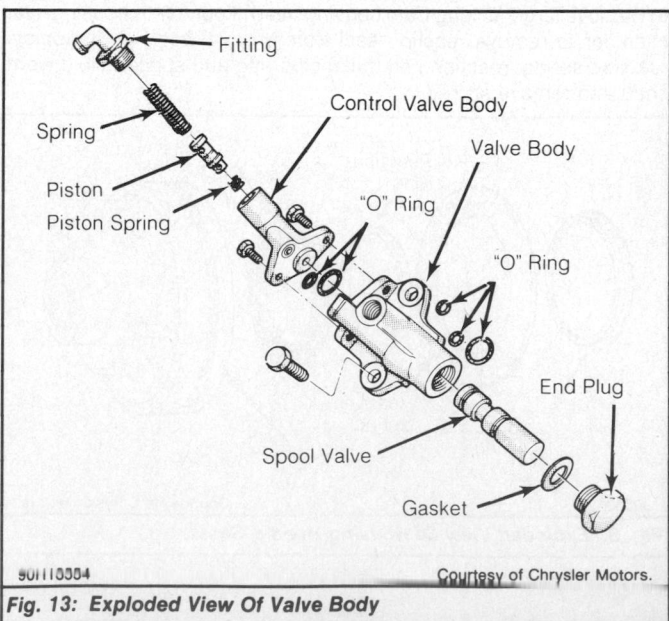

90I110354   Courtesy of Chrysler Motors.

Fig. 13: Exploded View Of Valve Body

NOTE: DO NOT remove end plug from valve unless gasket is leaking.

2) Separate both valve bodies. *See Fig. 13.* Remove pump inlet fitting, washer, spring, piston and piston spring. Remove spool valve from steering body and inspect for nicks, burrs and scores. Replace complete assembly if damage exists.

Reassembly – 1) Install spool valve in valve body so valve lever hole is aligned with lever opening of valve body. Ensure valve slides freely in valve body. Install a NEW gasket on end plug (if removed). Install and tighten end plug to **25 ft. lbs. (34 N.m)**.

2) Install piston spring in control valve body. Ensure spring seats in counterbore at bottom of housing. Lubricate piston and properly install piston in control valve body. *See Fig. 13.* Ensure piston slides freely in bore. Install other spring on top of piston.

3) Install NEW washer and pump inlet fitting. Tighten fitting to **40 ft. lbs. (55 N.m)**. Install NEW "O" rings between control valve body and valve body. Install and tighten attaching bolts to **95 INCH lbs. (11 N.m)**. Align lever hole in spool valve with lever opening in valve body. Install valve body on steering gear.

4) Install valve body-to-steering gear bolts. Tighten bolts to **84 INCH lbs. (10 N.m)**. Valve body must be centered. See VALVE BODY CENTERING under ADJUSTMENTS. With valve body centered, tighten mounting bolts to final specification. See TORQUE SPECIFICATIONS table.

TORQUE SPECIFICATIONS
TORQUE SPECIFICATIONS

Application	Ft. Lbs. (N.m)
Drag Link-To-Center Link Nut	55 (75)
Housing Head Spanner Nut	162 (220)
Idler Arm-To-Center Link Nut	47 (64)
Idler Arm-To-Frame Bolt	70 (95)
Pitman Arm Nut	175 (237)
Pitman Arm-To-Steering Gear Nut	175 (237)
Pump Inlet Fitting	40 (54)
Sector Shaft Adjuster Screw Lock Nut	28 (38)
Sector Shaft Spanner Nut	155 (210)
Steering Gear Assembly-To-Frame Bolt	100 (136)
Tie Rod Clamp Bolt	
B150/250	17 (23)
B350	26 (35)
Tie Rod Nut	
9/16"	55 (75)
5/8"	75 (102)
Valve Body End Plug	25 (34)
Valve Body-To-Steering Gear Housing Bolt	17 (23)
	INCH Lbs. (N.m)
Control Valve Body-To-Valve Body Bolt	95 (11)

1992 STEERING
Power Recirculating Ball

Dakota (4WD), Pickup, Ramcharger

DESCRIPTION & OPERATION

The recirculating ball power steering system consists of steering gear, steering linkage, pressure and return fluid hoses and fittings, and a hydraulic steering pump with fluid reservoir. *See Fig. 1.*

The steering gear is a power assisted recirculating-ball type that acts as a rolling thread between worm shaft and rack piston. When worm shaft is turned, the rack piston moves and piston teeth mesh with sector shaft teeth, turning pitman arm, which turns steering linkage.

The steering linkage consists of pitman arm, idler arm(s), tie rods, center link and drag link (if equipped).

The power steering pump is a constant flow rate and displacement, vane-type pump. Pump is connected to steering gear by pressure and return hoses. On gasoline models, pump shaft has pressed on belt-driven pulley

On diesel models, power steering pump is bolted onto rear of vacuum pump and is driven by a common shaft

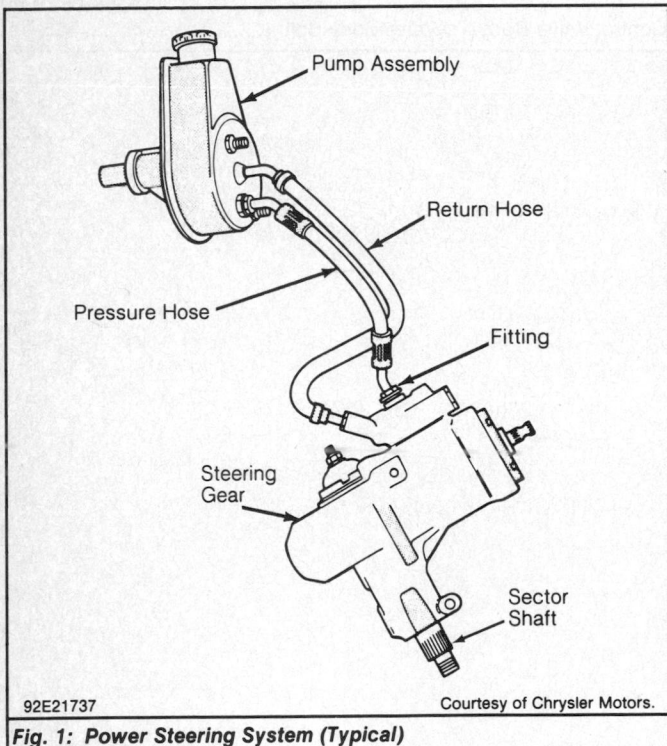

Fig. 1: Power Steering System (Typical)

LUBRICATION

CAPACITY

CAPACITY

Models	Pts. (L)
Dakota (4WD)	2.5 (1.2)
Pickup & Ramcharger	2.7 (1.3)

FLUID TYPE

Use Mopar Power Steering Fluid (4318055).

CAUTION: DO NOT use Automatic Transmission Fluid (ATF).

FLUID LEVEL CHECK

Check fluid level with engine cold and not running. Remove fluid level dipstick on pump reservoir. Dipstick should indicate FULL COLD with fluid temperature of 70-80°F (21-27°C). If needed, add fluid through dipstick opening, and recheck. DO NOT overfill.

HYDRAULIC SYSTEM BLEEDING

Fill power steering pump reservoir to specified level. Start engine and slowly turn steering wheel to left and right but DO NOT contact steering stops in either direction. Stop engine. Inspect reservoir fluid level and add fluid if necessary. Bleeding process may have to be repeated several times to completely purge all air from system.

ADJUSTMENTS

POWER STEERING PUMP BELT

2.5L, 3.9L, 5.2L & 5.9L (Gasoline) – Power steering belt tension is adjusted by adjusting power steering pump position. To check belt tension, use a Poly-V Burroughs gauge or similar gauge. See POWER STEERING BELT TENSION SPECIFICATIONS table.

POWER STEERING BELT TENSION SPECIFICATIONS

Application	New Belt Lbs. (kg)	[1] Used Belt Lbs. (kg)
2.5L	120 (53)	80 (36)
3.9L & 5.2L	[2]	[2]
5.9L (Gasoline)	100-140 (44-62)	60-90 (27-40)
5.9L (Diesel)	[2]	[2]

[1] – Belt is considered used after 15 minutes of operation.
[2] – Equipped with dynamic tensioner; no adjustment is required.

POWER STEERING PUMP PULLEY

On vehicles equipped with serpentine belts, after pulley installation, run engine until warm. See PUMP PULLEY under REMOVAL & INSTALLATION. If belt chirp exists, move pulley outward approximately .020" (0.5 mm). If noise increases, press pulley inward .040" (1.0 mm). Ensure pulley does not contact mounting bolts.

THRUST BEARING PRELOAD

NOTE: Manufacturer recommends removing steering gear from vehicle before performing any adjustments.

1) Remove steering gear from vehicle. See STEERING GEAR under REMOVAL & INSTALLATION. Ensure steering gear is empty of hydraulic fluid. Rotate steering from stop-to-stop several times to drain fluid. Loosen lock nut on adjuster plug. *See Fig. 3.* Using spanner wrench, rotate adjuster plug clockwise until plug is seated in housing. Torque will be approximately 20 ft. lbs. (27 N.m).

2) Place reference mark on steering gear housing adjacent to one hole in adjuster plug. Measure counterclockwise about 1/2" (13 mm) from reference mark and place a second reference mark on steering gear housing. Rotate adjuster plug counterclockwise until hole in adjuster plug aligns with second mark on steering gear housing.

3) Tighten lock nut on adjuster plug to 80 ft. lbs. (108 N.m). Ensure adjuster plug DOES NOT move while tightening lock nut.

OVER-CENTER PRELOAD

CAUTION: Thrust bearing preload MUST be adjusted before adjusting over-center preload.

1) Loosen lock nut on sector shaft adjuster screw. *See Fig. 4.* Rotate stub shaft and count turns required to go from stop-to-stop. Turn stub shaft back 1/2 number of turns to center steering gear.

2) Rotate sector shaft adjuster screw counterclockwise until fully extended, then turn clockwise one full turn.

3) Attach INCH-pound torque wrench to end of stub shaft. Position torque wrench handle in a vertical position. Rotate stub shaft 45 degrees from vertical position in each direction, and record highest reading. *See Fig. 4.*

4) Turn adjuster in until torque required to turn stub shaft is 6-10 INCH lbs. (0.7-1.1 N.m) more than reading in step 3). Hold adjuster screw, and tighten lock nut to 20 ft. lbs. (27 N.m).

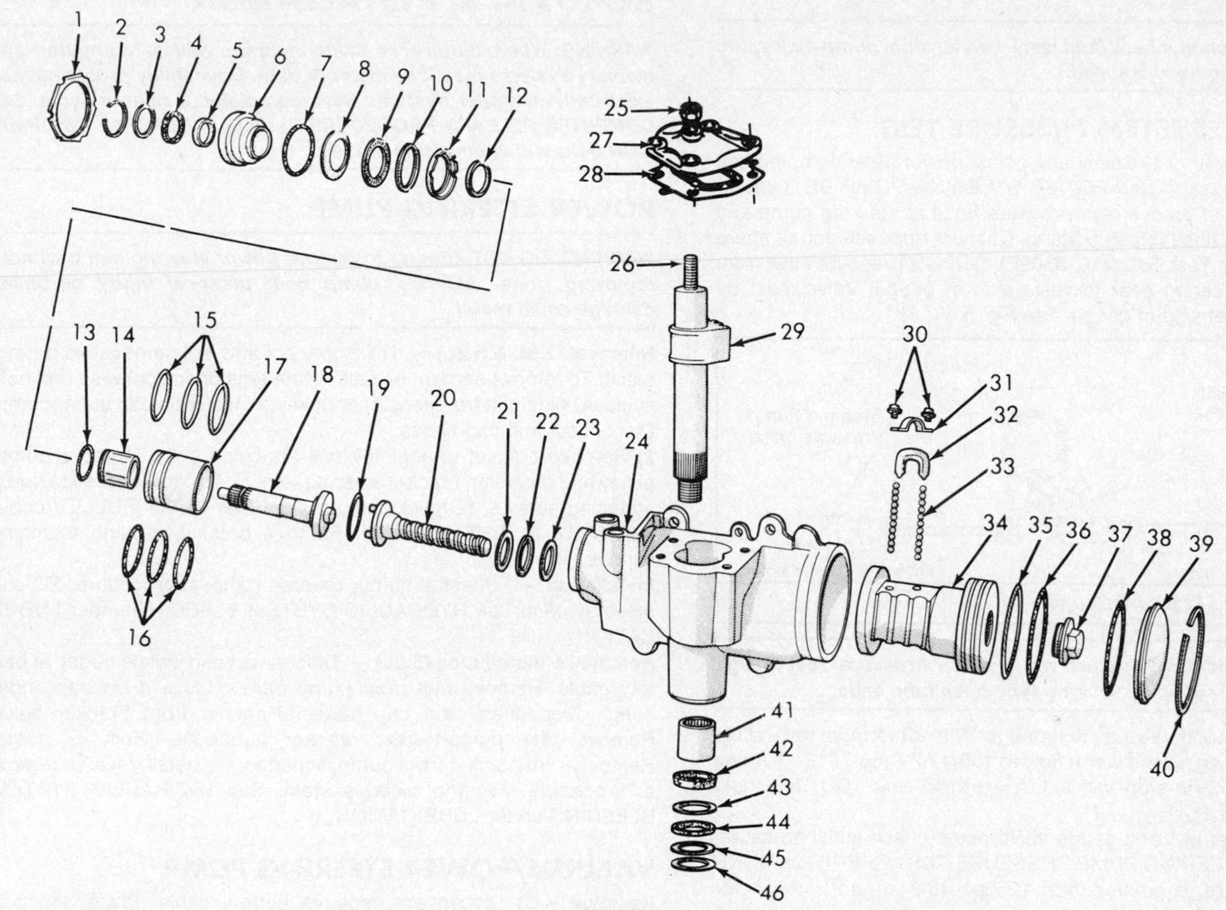

1. Lock Nut	12. Retainer	23. Bearing Race	34. Rack Piston	45. Steel Washer
2. Retaining Ring	13. "O" Ring	24. Steering Gear Housing	35. "O" Ring	46. Retaining Ring
3. Dust Seal	14. Spool Valve	25. Lock Nut	36. Teflon Ring	
4. Oil Seal	15. Teflon Rings	26. Sector Shaft Adjuster Screw	37. End Plug	
5. Needle Bearing	16. "O" Rings	27. Side Cover	38. "O" Ring	
6. Adjuster Plug	17. Valve Body	28. Gasket	39. Housing End Cover	
7. "O" Ring	18. Stub Shaft	29. Sector Shaft	40. Retainer Ring	
8. Large Bearing Race	19. "O" Ring	30. Retainer Screws	41. Sector Shaft Bearing	
9. Thrust Bearing	20. Worm Shaft	31. Guide Clamp	42. Upper Oil Seal (Single Lip)	
10. Small Bearing Race	21. Bearing Race	32. Ball Guide	43. Steel Washer	
11. Spacer	22. Lower Thrust Bearing	33. Recirculating Balls	44. Lower Oil Seal (Double Lip)	

90113555

Courtesy of General Motors Corp.

Fig. 2: Exploded View Of Saginaw Rotary Valve Power Steering Gear

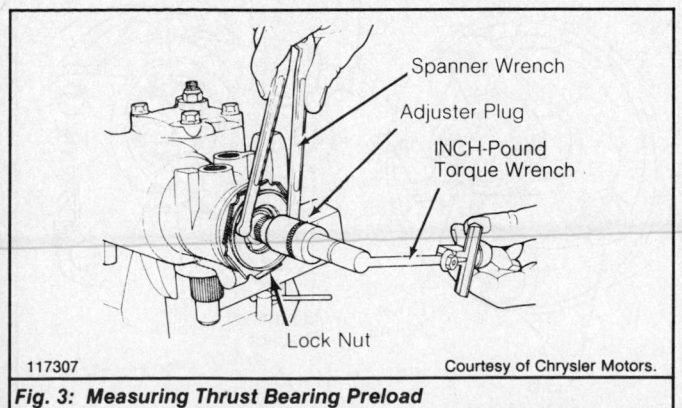

117307

Courtesy of Chrysler Motors.

Fig. 3: Measuring Thrust Bearing Preload

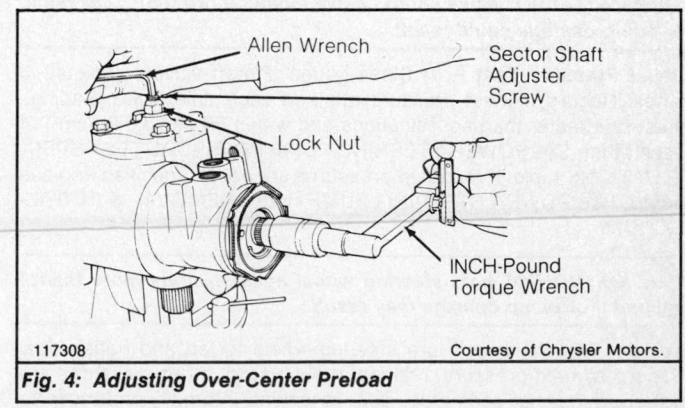

117308

Courtesy of Chrysler Motors.

Fig. 4: Adjusting Over-Center Preload

TESTING

NOTE: Before testing, check fluid level, belt tension, pump pulley, tire pressure and engine idle speed.

HYDRAULIC SYSTEM PRESSURE TEST

Idle Pressure Test – 1) Check and adjust power steering pump belt tension as necessary. See POWER STEERING PUMP BELT under ADJUSTMENTS. Remove high pressure hose at steering pump and connect a spare hose to pump fitting. Connect opposite end of spare hose to Pressure Test Gauge (C-3309E). Connect pressure hose from valve side of steering gear to valve side of gauge. Valve must be installed on outlet side of gauge. *See Fig. 5.*

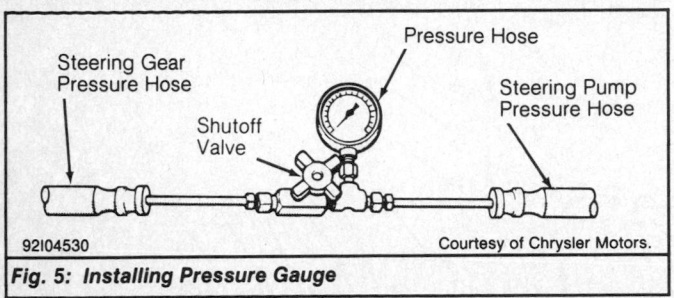

Fig. 5: Installing Pressure Gauge

92I04530   Courtesy of Chrysler Motors.

NOTE: Replacement fittings are required on Pressure Test Gauge (C-3309E) for adapting to "O" ring type hose tube ends.

2) Fully open shutoff valve on test gauge. With a thermometer in fluid reservoir, start engine and warm fluid to 150-170°F (66-77°C). Turning wheels from stop-to-stop will aid in warming fluid. DO NOT hold wheels against stop.
3) With engine at idle and gauge valve open, check initial pressure. See POWER STEERING PUMP PRESSURE TEST SPECIFICATIONS table. If pressure is greater than 125 psi (8.8 kg/cm²), check for restricted hoses or crimped lines.

POWER STEERING PUMP PRESSURE TEST SPECIFICATIONS

Application	Pressure psi (kg/cm²)
Idle Pressure	50-80 (3.5-5.6)
Relief Pressure [1]	
Dakota	
2.5L	1250 (88)
3.9L & 5.2L	1450 (102)
Pickup & Ramcharger	1400 (98)

[1] – Specification may vary by 50 psi (3.5 kg/cm²).

CAUTION: DO NOT leave shutoff valve closed more than 5 seconds, or pump damage could result.

Relief Pressure Test – 1) Close gauge shutoff valve completely 3 times. Record highest pressure attained each time. All 3 readings must be greater than specifications and within 50 psi (3.5 kg/cm²) of each other. See POWER STEERING PUMP PRESSURE TEST SPECIFICATIONS table. If recorded pressures are not as specified, replace pump. See POWER STEERING PUMP under REMOVAL & INSTALLATION.

CAUTION: DO NOT hold steering wheel against stops more than 4 seconds, or pump damage may result.

2) Open test valve and turn steering wheel to left and right stops. Record highest pressure attained at each stop. If out pressures are not equal against each stop, gear is leaking internally and must be repaired or replaced; see applicable STEERING GEAR procedure under OVERHAUL or REMOVAL & INSTALLATION. Shut off engine, remove test gauge, and connect pressure hose.

REMOVAL & INSTALLATION

WARNING: When battery is disconnected, vehicle computer and memory systems may lose memory data. Driveability problems may exist until computer systems have completed a relearn cycle. See COMPUTER RELEARN PROCEDURES article in GENERAL INFORMATION before disconnecting battery.

POWER STEERING PUMP

WARNING: DO NOT attempt to remove power steering pump without removing power steering pump belt; personal injury or pulley damage could result.

Removal (3.9L & 5.2L) – 1) Disconnect and isolate negative battery cable. To remove serpentine belt, rotate tensioner clockwise and hold in place, slide belt from tensioner pulley. Place drain pan under pump. Disconnect and cap hoses.
2) Remove bracket-to-engine block attaching bolts. Remove pump, pulley and mounting bracket as an assembly. To allow access to pump attaching screws, remove pump pulley. See PUMP PULLEY under REMOVAL & INSTALLATION. Remove bracket-to-pump attaching screws.
Installation – To install pump, reverse removal procedure. Fill and bleed system. See HYDRAULIC SYSTEM BLEEDING under LUBRICATION.
Removal & Installation (5.9L) – Disconnect and isolate negative battery cable. Remove belt from pump pulley. Place drain pan under pump. Disconnect and cap hoses. Remove front bracket bolts. Remove rear pump-to-rear bracket nuts/bolts. Remove pump. Remove front bracket from pump if needed. To install, reverse removal procedure. Fill and bleed system. See HYDRAULIC SYSTEM BLEEDING under LUBRICATION.

VACUUM/POWER STEERING PUMP

Removal – 1) Disconnect negative battery cable. Place drip pan under vacuum/power pump. Disconnect and cap power brake booster hose at upper vacuum pump and hydraulic lines at power steering pump. Disconnect oil pressure sending unit electrical connector. Remove sending unit from engine block and plug hole in block. Disconnect and cap oil feed line from bottom of vacuum pump.

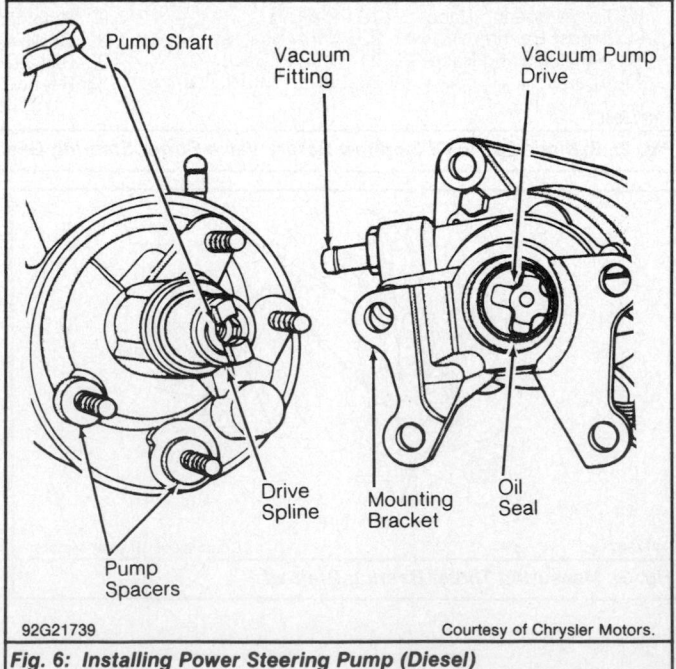

92G21739   Courtesy of Chrysler Motors.

Fig. 6: Installing Power Steering Pump (Diesel)

2) Remove nuts and bolts attaching vacuum/power steering pump to engine block and attaching bracket, remove upper pump bolt last, and remove pump. Drain fluid from steering pump reservoir. Remove gaskets from mounting surfaces.

CAUTION: DO NOT damage internal vacuum pump oil seal when separating steering pump from vacuum pump. See Fig. 6.

---

3) Remove steering pump-to-vacuum pump bracket bolts. Carefully slide steering pump from bracket. Remove 2 pump body spacers. *See Fig. 6.*

Installation – 1) Install 2 pump body spacers and rotate drive gear until steering pump and vacuum pump drive splines align. *See Fig. 6.* Carefully install steering pump on vacuum pump bracket to prevent damaging oil seal.

NOTE: Steering pump housing and spacers must mate completely with vacuum pump bracket.

---

2) Install 3 vacuum pump bracket-to-steering pump nuts and tighten to **18 ft. lbs. (24 N.m).** Using silicone sealer if needed, position new gaskets on mounting surfaces.

3) Ensuring steering pump stud is inserted into block bracket, align and install pump assembly. Tighten pump assembly-to-engine block bolts to **57 ft. lbs. (77 N.m).** Install steering pump-to-bracket nut, tighten to **18 ft. lbs. (24 N.m).**

4) Remove cap from engine block and install oil sending unit. Tighten sending unit to **60 INCH lbs. (7 N.m)** and install electrical connector. Install oil feed line to vacuum pump and tighten to **60 INCH lbs. (7 N.m).** To complete installation, reverse removal procedure. Fill and bleed system. See HYDRAULIC SYSTEM BLEEDING under LUBRICATION. Start engine. Ensure brakes are operating properly.

PUMP PULLEY

CAUTION: Examine exposed end of rotor drive shaft before removal. If it is corroded, clean surface with crocus cloth to prevent damage to shaft bushing during removal.

Removal & Installation (Gasoline) – Remove pump from vehicle if necessary. See POWER STEERING PUMP under REMOVAL & INSTALLATION. Using Puller (C-4068) and Puller Adapter (C-4068-1), remove pump pulley. *See Fig. 7.* Replace pulley if bent, cracked or loose. Using Installer (C-4063), Press pulley until flush with shaft end. If belt chirp exists after starting engine, See POWER STEERING PUMP PULLEY under ADJUSTMENTS.

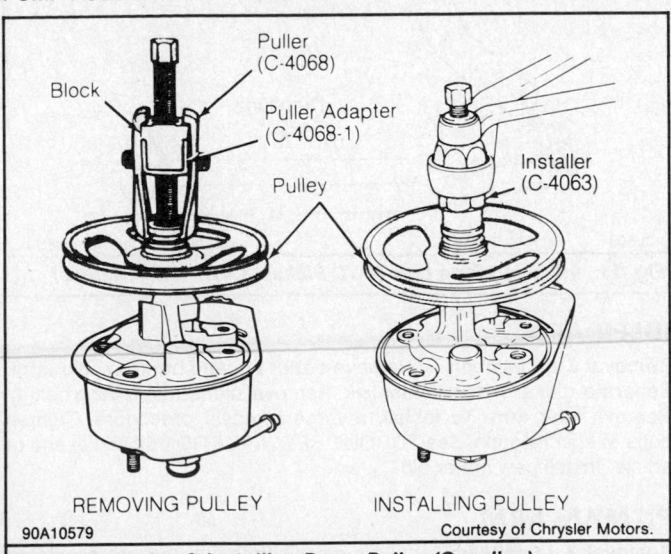

REMOVING PULLEY   INSTALLING PULLEY

90A10579   Courtesy of Chrysler Motors.

Fig. 7: Removing & Installing Pump Pulley (Gasoline)

PUMP RESERVOIR

Removal – 1) Remove pump from vehicle if necessary. See POWER STEERING PUMP under REMOVAL & INSTALLATION. Remove filler cap and drain oil from reservoir before removing parts. Remove 2 studs and fitting from back of pump. *See Fig. 8.*

2) Rock reservoir by hand or tap with soft-faced mallet to remove it. Remove "O" ring seals from housing and reservoir. Remove flow control valve and spring from rear of pump housing. *See Fig. 9.* Clean all parts.

NOTE: If expansion plug is deformed or dislodged, DO NOT remove it. Replace pump housing.

Installation – To install, reverse removal procedure. Use NEW "O" ring, seals and flow control valve. Tighten flow control valve fitting to **55 ft. lbs. (75 N.m).** Apply power steering fluid to new seals. Tighten nuts and bolts to specification. See TORQUE SPECIFICATIONS table at end of article. Add power steering fluid. DO NOT use ATF. Bleed system. See HYDRAULIC SYSTEM BLEEDING under LUBRICATION.

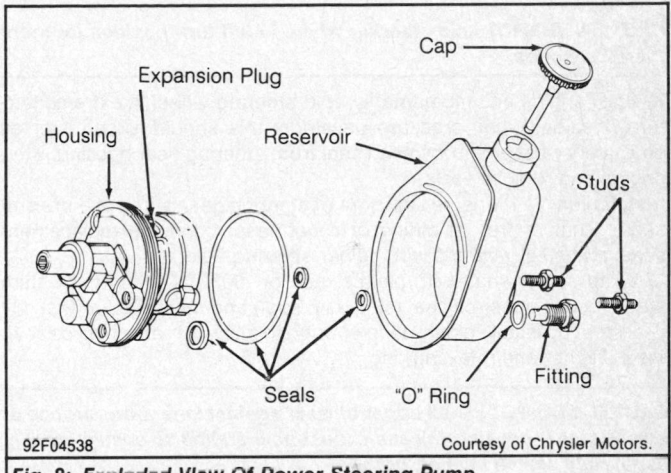

92F04538   Courtesy of Chrysler Motors.

Fig. 8: Exploded View Of Power Steering Pump

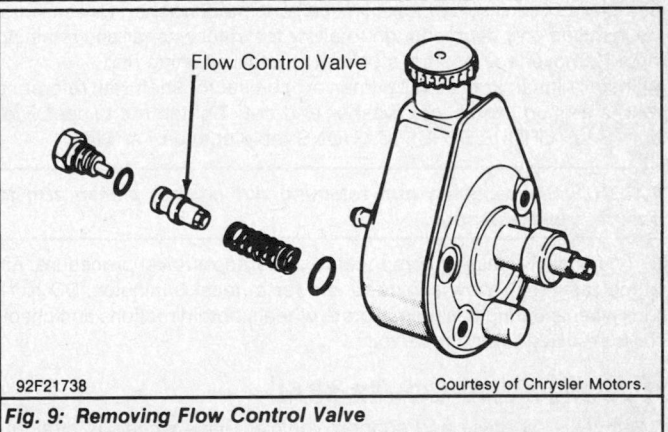

92F21738   Courtesy of Chrysler Motors.

Fig. 9: Removing Flow Control Valve

STEERING GEAR

Removal – 1) Place wheels in straight-ahead position. Place drain pan under steering gear assembly. Disconnect and cap pressure and return hoses from steering gear. Disconnect steering column shaft coupling from steering gear stub shaft.

2) Raise and support vehicle. Disconnect steering linkage (center link) from pitman arm. *See Fig. 10.* Disconnect stabilizer bar (if necessary). Place reference mark on pitman arm and sector shaft. Remove nut and pitman arm from sector shaft. Remove steering gear-to-frame bolts. Remove steering gear.

Installation – 1) Install steering gear with retaining bolts finger tight. Center steering gear and align stub shaft with steering column. Install steering column shaft coupling bolt and tighten to specification. See TORQUE SPECIFICATIONS table at end of article.

2) Reposition steering gear to eliminate binding and tighten retaining bolts to specification. Install pitman arm on sector shaft with reference marks aligned. Install lock washer and nut. Tighten nut to specification.

CAUTION: Stake pitman arm retaining nut against pitman arm to ensure proper retention.

3) To install, remaining components, reverse removal procedure. Fill pump reservoir. Bleed air from system. See HYDRAULIC SYSTEM BLEEDING under LUBRICATION.

SECTOR SHAFT OIL SEAL

Removal – 1) Raise and support vehicle. Place wheels in straight-ahead position. Disconnect steering linkage (center link) from pitman arm. Disconnect stabilizer bar (if necessary).
2) Place reference mark on pitman arm and sector shaft. Remove nut and pitman arm from sector shaft. Place drain pan under steering gear. Remove retaining ring and steel washer. *See Fig. 2.*

CAUTION: DO NOT hold steering wheel in left-turn position for more than 2 seconds.

3) Start engine and momentarily hold steering wheel in extreme left-turn position. When pressure develops, this should force upper oil seal, steel washer and lower oil seal from steering gear housing. Stop engine and remove seals.
Installation – 1) Ensure seal bore of steering gear is free of burrs and sector shaft is free of pitting or roughness. Lubricate replacement seals and steel washers with power steering fluid.
2) Wrap sector shaft with plastic tape or .005" (.13 mm) thick shim stock. Install upper oil seal (single lip seal) and steel washer first. Oil seal must be installed only deep enough to allow for remaining oil seal, steel washer and retaining ring.

CAUTION: DO NOT install upper oil seal against inner bore surface of steering gear housing. Oil seals must be installed so each oil seal is separately seated in shaft bore.

3) Install lower oil seal (double lip seal) and steel washer. Oil seal must be installed only deep enough to allow for steel washer and retaining ring. Remove tape or shim stock and install retaining ring.
4) Install pitman arm. Install pitman arm on sector shaft with reference marks aligned. Install lock washer and nut. Tighten nut to specification. See TORQUE SPECIFICATIONS table at end of article.

CAUTION: Stake pitman arm retaining nut against pitman arm to ensure proper retention.

5) To install, remaining components, reverse removal procedure. Fill pump reservoir. Allow engine to idle for at least 3 minutes. DO NOT turn wheels during this time. Rotate wheels both directions and check for leaks. Refill pump reservoir.

HOUSING END COVER SEAL

Removal – 1) Raise and support vehicle. Place wheels in straight-ahead position. Place drain pan under steering gear.
2) Rotate housing end cover retainer ring until one end of ring is under small hole in steering gear housing. *See Fig. 2.* Insert punch through small hole and depress retainer ring. Remove retainer ring.
3) Rotate steering wheel to left until rack piston forces housing end cover from steering gear housing. Turn steering wheel back to center position. Remove housing end cover and "O" ring.

CAUTION: DO NOT rotate steering wheel any more than necessary, as recirculating balls may fall from rack piston.

Installation – Lubricate "O" ring with power steering fluid and install on housing end cover. Install housing end cover and retainer ring. Fill pump reservoir. Allow engine to idle for at least 3 minutes. DO NOT

turn wheels during this time. Rotate wheels both directions and check for leaks. Refill pump reservoir.

CENTER LINK

Removal & Installation – Separate tie rods, idler arm, steering and drag link (if equipped) from center link. Remove center link. To install, reverse removal procedure. Tighten retaining nuts to specification.

CAUTION: Ensure center link is installed so link ends turn upward when viewed from front of vehicle.

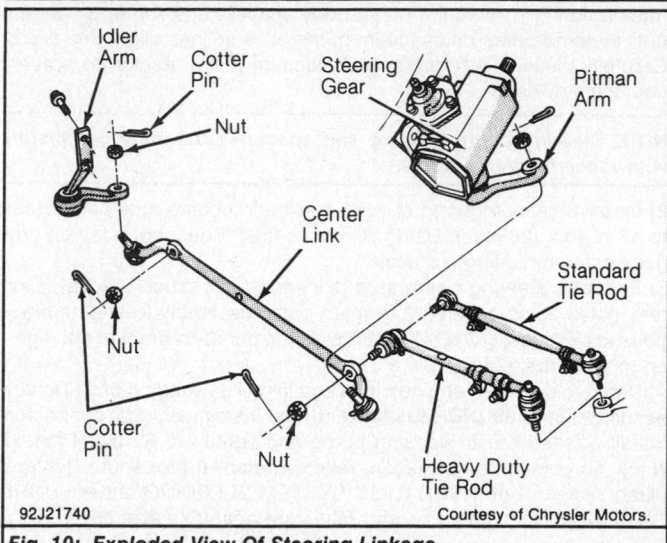

92J21740   Courtesy of Chrysler Motors.
Fig. 10: Exploded View Of Steering Linkage

DRAG LINK

Removal – Remove cotter pins and drag link nuts. Using Separator (C-4150), separate drag link from steering knuckle or center link and pitman arm.
Installation – On 4WD Pickup and 4WD Ramcharger, drag link must be installed to steering knuckle with short distance ("A") attached to steering knuckle. *See Fig. 11.* On all models, install drag link and retaining nuts. Tighten nuts to specification. See TORQUE SPECIFICATIONS table at end of article. Install cotter pins.

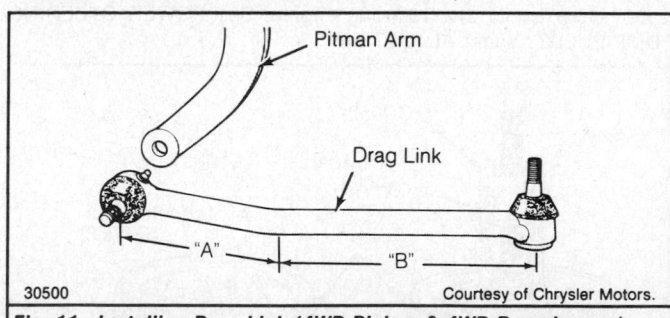

30500   Courtesy of Chrysler Motors.
Fig. 11: Installing Drag Link (4WD Pickup & 4WD Ramcharger)

IDLER ARM

Removal & Installation – Remove cotter pin and nut from idler arm. Separate idler arm from center link. Remove idler arm retaining bolt(s). Remove idler arm. To install, reverse removal procedure. Tighten bolts to specification. See TORQUE SPECIFICATIONS table at end of article. Install new cotter pin.

PITMAN ARM

Removal & Installation – 1) Remove cotter pin and nut at pitman arm-to-center link or drag link. Separate pitman arm from center link or drag link. Mark location of pitman arm on steering gear shaft. Remove pitman arm-to-steering gear shaft nut. Separate pitman arm from steering gear.

2) To install, reverse removal procedure. Ensure reference marks are aligned. Tighten bolts and nuts to specification. Install new cotter pin.

CAUTION: Stake pitman arm nut against steering gear shaft to ensure proper retention.

TIE ROD END

Removal – 1) Remove cotter pin and nut from tie rod end. Using Tie Rod End Puller (C-3894-A), remove tie rod end from steering knuckle or center link.
2) Loosen lock nut or clamp bolt. Remove tie rod end. Note number of turns required for removal.

NOTE: Use Tie Rod End Puller (C-3894-A) to prevent tie rod end seal damage.

Installation – 1) To install, reverse removal procedure. Ensure tie rod end is installed at same location. Position clamp sleeve with bolt located on bottom. Clamp opening should be aligned with slot in sleeve.
2) Tighten tie rod end nut to specification. Install cotter pin. Check and adjust toe-in. See SPECIFICATIONS & PROCEDURES article in WHEEL ALIGNMENT. Tighten clamp bolt to specification. See TORQUE SPECIFICATIONS table at end of article.

OVERHAUL

POWER STEERING PUMP

Only fluid reservoirs, caps, pulleys, "O" rings, seals and flow control valve are replaceable on Saginaw pumps. *See Figs. 8 and 9.* Internal components are non-serviceable. If internal components fail, replace pump. Replace reservoir, or "O" ring and seals if damaged. See appropriate component under REMOVAL & INSTALLATION.

NOTE: If expansion plug is deformed or dislodged, DO NOT remove it. Replace pump housing.

STEERING GEAR

Disassembly – 1) Remove steering gear from vehicle. See STEERING GEAR under REMOVAL & INSTALLATION. Clean exterior of steering gear, and clamp it in a soft-jawed vise so sector shaft is pointing downward. Rotate housing end cover retainer ring until one end of plug is over hole in steering gear housing. *See Fig. 2.*
2) Force end of retainer ring from groove in steering gear housing and remove ring. Rotate stub shaft counterclockwise to force housing end cover from steering gear housing. Rotate stub shaft clockwise 1/2 turn to move rack piston inward.

CAUTION: DO NOT rotate stub shaft more than necessary, or recirculating balls may fall from rack piston.

---

3) Using soft-faced hammer, tap on end plug. Hit end plug with a soft-faced hammer to unseat it. Remove end plug. Remove lock nut from sector shaft adjuster screw. Remove side cover bolts.
4) Rotate sector shaft adjuster screw while holding side cover until side cover and gasket can be removed. *See Fig. 2.* Rotate stub shaft until sector shaft teeth are centered in steering gear housing.
5) Using a soft-faced hammer, tap end of sector shaft to free it from steering gear housing. Remove sector shaft. Remove retainer adjuster plug lock nut. Using a spanner wrench, remove adjuster plug.
6) Insert Rack Piston Arbor (C-4175) into end of rack piston assembly until arbor just contacts worm shaft. Rack piston arbor will retain recirculating balls in rack piston. Rotate stub shaft counterclockwise to force rack piston onto rack piston arbor. Remove rack piston and arbor as an assembly.
7) Remove stub shaft and valve body from steering gear housing by pulling outward on stub shaft splined end. Remove worm shaft, lower thrust bearing and bearing races from steering gear housing.

Cleaning – 1) Clean all internal parts in solvent and dry with compressed air. Avoid wiping valve parts with cloth. Lint may cause binding of mechanism.
2) DO NOT steam clean hydraulic parts. If further disassembly is required, see appropriate sub-assembly heading under OVERHAUL.
Reassembly – 1) Lubricate all parts with power steering fluid before reassembly. Mount steering gear in vise so sector shaft points downward. Install lower thrust bearing and bearing races on worm shaft. *See Fig. 12.*

NOTE: Install bearing races so cone (raised area) faces toward steering gear housing. See Fig. 12.

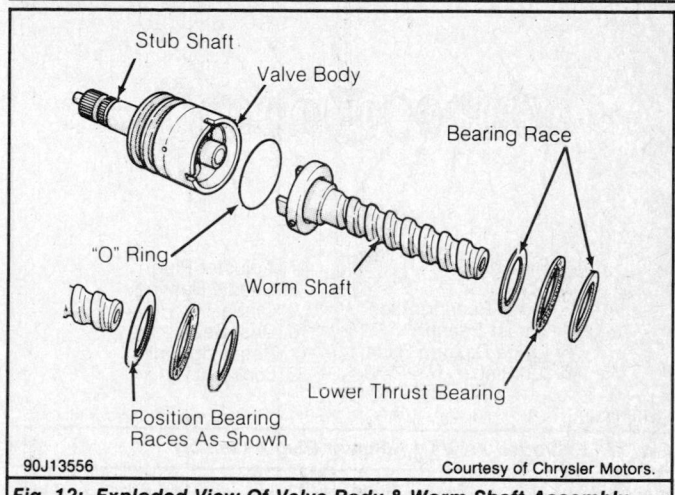

90J13556   Courtesy of Chrysler Motors.

Fig. 12: Exploded View Of Valve Body & Worm Shaft Assembly

2) Place worm shaft in valve body. Install "O" ring in valve body. Ensure "O" ring is seated against inner edge of stub shaft. Align notch in valve body with drive pin in worm shaft.
3) Install valve body and worm shaft assembly into steering gear housing. Seat valve body in steering gear housing by pressing on outer diameter surface of valve body with fingertips.
4) Ensure Teflon rings do not bind in steering gear housing. Valve body is seated when all or most of fluid return port in steering gear housing is fully visible.

CAUTION: DO NOT press against stub shaft while seating valve body in steering gear housing. This may cause stub shaft to separate from valve body and allow spool valve "O" ring to fall into fluid passages.

---

5) Place Seal Protector (C-4182) over stub shaft. Using new "O" ring, install adjuster plug on stub shaft. Using spanner wrench, tighten adjuster plug until it seats against valve body. Approximately 20 ft. lbs. (27 N.m) is required to seat adjuster plug.
6) Remove seal protector. Loosely install adjuster plug lock nut. Install rack piston (with rack piston arbor to retain recirculating balls) into steering gear housing until worm shaft engages with valve body and stub shaft. Rotate stub shaft clockwise to force rack piston into steering gear housing. Maintain pressure on rack piston arbor until worm shaft is fully engaged.
7) Rotate stub shaft clockwise to align center groove of rack piston with center of sector shaft bearing bore. Remove arbor. Lubricate rubber portion of sector shaft cover gasket with petroleum jelly.
8) Install gasket on sector shaft cover. Ensure rubber portion is seated in groove of sector shaft cover. Install sector shaft cover on sector shaft adjuster screw.
9) Thread sector shaft cover onto adjuster screw until cover contacts sector shaft. Install sector shaft so center gear tooth meshes with center groove in rack piston. Install sector shaft cover bolts and tighten to specification.
10) Install NEW lock nut half-way on sector shaft adjuster screw. Install end plug in rack piston and tighten to specification. Install housing end plug, end plug and retainer ring.

11) Ensure end of retainer ring is not aligned with hole in steering gear housing. Lightly tap on housing end cover to ensure retainer ring is fully seated. Adjust worm bearing preload and over-center preload. See THRUST BEARING PRELOAD and OVER-CENTER PRELOAD under ADJUSTMENTS.

ADJUSTER PLUG

Disassembly – **1)** Using a screwdriver, carefully remove and discard retainer. See Fig. 13. Remove spacer, thrust bearing and bearing races. Note direction of bearing race installation for reassembly. Remove and discard "O" ring.

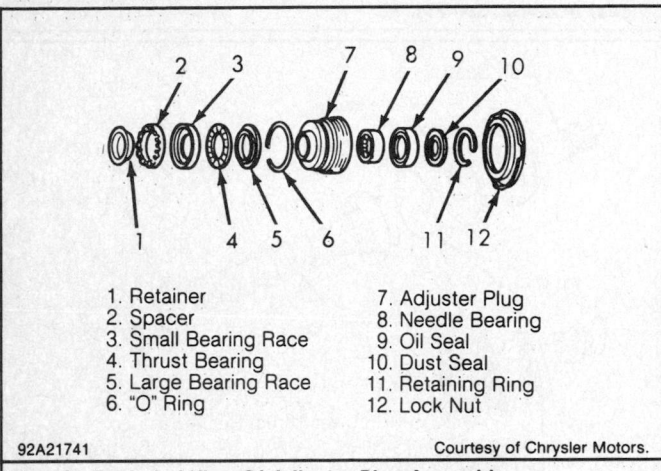

1. Retainer
2. Spacer
3. Small Bearing Race
4. Thrust Bearing
5. Large Bearing Race
6. "O" Ring
7. Adjuster Plug
8. Needle Bearing
9. Oil Seal
10. Dust Seal
11. Retaining Ring
12. Lock Nut

92A21741   Courtesy of Chrysler Motors.

Fig. 13: Exploded View Of Adjuster Plug Assembly

2) Remove lock nut and retaining ring. Remove dust seal. Pry oil seal from adjuster plug. Inspect needle bearing. Remove needle bearing by pressing bearing out of adjuster plug from spacer end of adjuster plug (if necessary). See Fig. 13.

Inspection – Inspect thrust bearing for cracks. Check rollers for pitting, scoring, or cracking. Check bearing races and spacer for damage. Replace components as necessary.

Reassembly – **1)** Lubricate components with power steering fluid. Press needle bearing into adjuster plug with identification number away from adjuster plug until bearing bottoms in bore. Install oil seal with seal lip toward adjuster plug.

2) Lubricate dust seal with petroleum jelly. Install dust seal with rubber side away from adjuster plug. Install retaining ring. Ensure retaining ring is fully seated.

3) Lubricate "O" ring with petroleum jelly and install on adjuster plug. Assemble thrust bearing, bearing races, and spacer on adjuster plug. Ensure bearing races are installed in correct location. See Fig. 13. Using a punch, tap NEW retainer into adjuster plug.

RACK PISTON & WORM SHAFT

Disassembly – **1)** Remove ball guide clamp. Place assembly over container to catch recirculating balls. Remove ball guides, worm shaft with arbor and recirculating balls. Ensure 24 recirculating balls are removed.

2) Remove rack piston arbor (if installed). Remove Teflon and "O" rings from rack piston.

Inspection – **1)** Clean and dry all parts. Inspect worm shaft and rack piston grooves for scoring. Inspect ball bearings for damage. If any ball bearings are damaged, replace entire set. Check ball guides for pinching of ends.

2) Inspect lower thrust bearing and races for cracking, scoring, or pitting. Inspect rack piston teeth for chips, cracks, dents or scoring. Replace components as necessary.

Reassembly – **1)** Lubricate all components with power steering fluid. Install new "O" ring onto rack piston. Ensure "O" ring is not twisted. Install new Teflon seal over "O" Ring. Insert worm shaft completely into rack piston.

2) Install recirculating balls in rack piston by alternately installing one Black ball and then one Silver ball. See Fig. 14. Press each ball downward to allow installation of next ball.

NOTE: Ensure a Black ball is installed first, and then a Silver ball is alternately installed in rack piston.

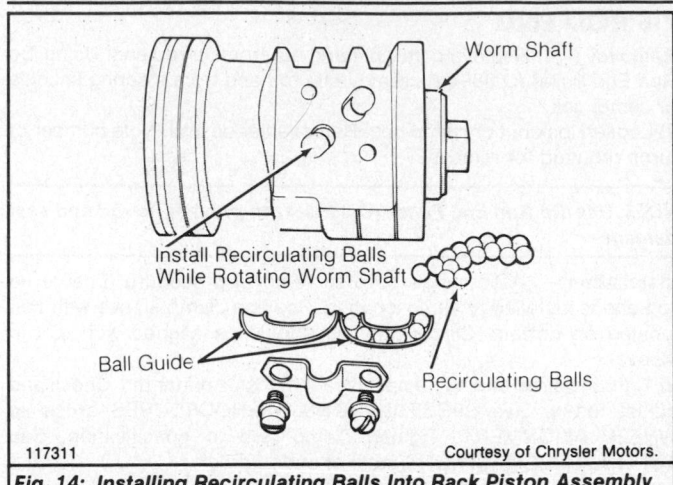

Worm Shaft

Install Recirculating Balls While Rotating Worm Shaft

Ball Guide

Recirculating Balls

117311   Courtesy of Chrysler Motors.

Fig. 14: Installing Recirculating Balls Into Rack Piston Assembly

3) A total of 18 balls should be installed in rack piston. Rotate worm shaft counterclockwise as viewed from steering shaft end to install recirculating balls in rack piston.

4) Apply petroleum jelly to one ball guide and install 6 recirculating balls. Ensure a Black ball is followed by a Silver ball and is in sequence with those installed in rack piston.

5) Install remaining ball guide and install both ball guides in rack piston. Install clamp, and tighten bolts to **48 INCH lbs. (5 N.m).** Insert Rack Piston Arbor (C-4175) into rack piston until it contacts worm shaft.

CAUTION: DO NOT allow rack piston arbor to separate from worm shaft until rack piston is fully installed on worm shaft.

VALVE BODY & STUB SHAFT

NOTE: Valve body and stub shaft should not be disassembled unless necessary. If components are defective, valve body and stub shaft must be replaced as a unit. If "O" ring seal requires replacement, remove spool valve only.

Disassembly – **1)** Lightly tap end of stub shaft against wooden block until cap (large end) of stub shaft is free of valve body. Remove stub shaft cap-to-wormshaft "O" ring. Pull stub shaft outward from valve body until drive pin hole is visible. See Fig. 15.

CAUTION: DO NOT pull stub shaft outward more than 1/4" (6 mm) or spool valve may become cocked in valve body.

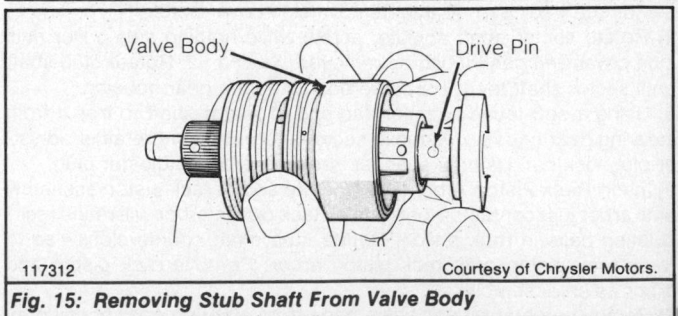

Valve Body

Drive Pin

117312   Courtesy of Chrysler Motors.

Fig. 15: Removing Stub Shaft From Valve Body

2) Disengage drive pin. See Fig. 15. Rotate and remove stub shaft from valve body. Remove spool valve from valve body. If spool valve becomes cocked, realign spool valve and remove. Carefully cut, remove and discard all "O" rings and Teflon rings. *See Fig. 16.*

CAUTION: DO NOT force stub shaft or spool valve out of valve body.

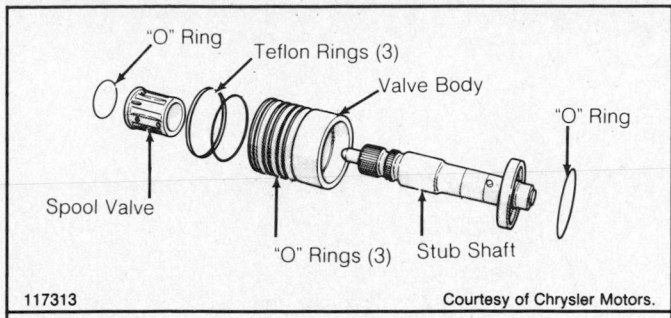

117313   Courtesy of Chrysler Motors.

Fig. 16: Exploded View Of Valve Body Assembly

Inspection – 1) Wash all parts in solvent and blow dry. Check for leaks between stub shaft and torsion bar. Check for nicks and scores on stub shaft. Sand down with Crocus cloth, if possible. Check drive pin notch in valve body skirt for wear. Check stub shaft drive pin for damage.

2) Lubricate spool valve with power steering fluid. Check spool valve fit in valve body, with "O" ring removed, by rotating spool valve in valve body. If valve does not rotate freely, replace complete valve.

3) Valve assembly is balanced during assembly. If replacing any parts other than "O" rings or Teflon seals, replace complete assembly.

Reassembly – 1) Lubricate valve body components with power steering fluid. Install new "O" rings in seal grooves. Install new Teflon rings over "O" rings. DO NOT damage seal rings during installation.

NOTE: Teflon seal rings may appear to be distorted after installation, but heat during operation will straighten them.

---

2) Lubricate replacement spool valve "O" ring with power steering fluid and install on spool valve. *See Fig. 16.* Carefully install spool valve in valve body.

3) Push spool valve through valve body until stub shaft drive pin hole is visible on valve body and spool valve is even with notched end of valve body. Install stub shaft into spool valve and valve body.

4) Align notch at top of stub shaft with pin in valve body. *See Fig. 17.* Press stub shaft and spool valve into valve body. Install "O" ring in groove on stub shaft.

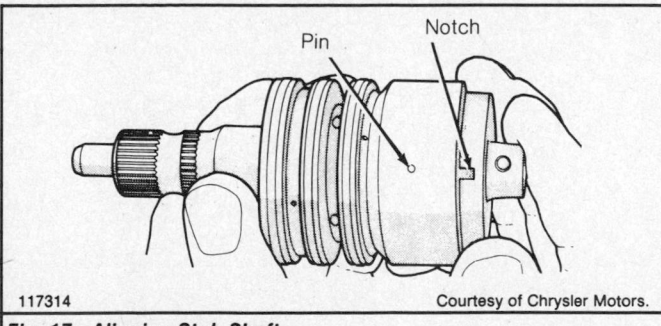

117314   Courtesy of Chrysler Motors.

Fig. 17: Aligning Stub Shaft

STEERING GEAR HOUSING

NOTE: Sector shaft threads and splines should be covered with vinyl tape during installation to protect replacement seal lips.

Disassembly – Remove sector shaft seal retaining ring. *See Fig. 2.* Remove steel washer, lower oil seal, steel washer and upper oil seal from housing. Press sector shaft bearing from steering gear housing.

Reassembly – 1) Lubricate steering housing bore, steel washers and oil seals with power steering fluid. *See Fig. 2.* Install sector shaft bearing in steering gear housing using Handle (C-4171) and Adapter (C-4178). Bearing should be installed until bearing is .030" (.76 mm) below shoulder of inner bore.

2) Install upper oil seal (single lip seal) and steel washer. Oil seal lip should face toward steering gear housing, and must be installed only deep enough to allow for remaining oil seal, steel washer and retaining ring to be installed.

CAUTION: DO NOT install upper oil seal against inner bore surface of steering gear housing. Oil seals must be installed so each oil seal is separately seated in shaft bore.

---

3) Install lower oil seal (double lip seal) and steel washer. Oil seal must be installed only deep enough to allow for steel washer and retaining ring to be installed. Lips of both seals should face toward steering gear housing bore. Install retaining ring.

TORQUE SPECIFICATIONS
TORQUE SPECIFICATIONS

Application	Ft. Lbs. (N.m)
Adjuster Plug Lock Nut	85 (115)
Ball Guide Clamp Bolt	10 (14)
Center Link-To-Pitman Arm Nut	
Dakota (4WD)	38 (52)
Pickup & Ramcharger	40 (54)
Drag Link Nut	60 (81)
Flow Control Valve Fitting	40 (54)
Idler Arm-To-Center Link Nut	38 (52)
Idler Arm-To-Frame Bolt	
Dakota (4WD)	65 (88)
Pickup & Ramcharger	40 (54)
Mounting Studs	35 (47)
Pitman Arm Nut [1]	185 (251)
Rack Piston End Plug	50 (68)
Sector Shaft Adjuster Screw Lock Nut	20 (27)
Side Cover Bolt	28 (38)
Steering Gear Housing-To-Frame Bolt	
2WD Models	100 (136)
4WD Models	165 (223)
Tie Rod Clamp Bolt	
Dakota (4WD)	17 (23)
Pickup & Ramcharger	15 (20)
Tie Rod Nut	
2WD Models	40 (54)
4WD Models	60 (81)
Vacuum/Power Steering Pump	
Assembly-To-Engine Bolts	57 (77)
Vacuum Pump-To-Power Steering Pump	
Attaching Nuts	18 (24)

[1] – Retaining nut must be staked against pitman arm threads.

Caravan, Town & Country, Voyager

IDENTIFICATION

TRANSAXLE APPLICATION

Application	Model
2.5L	A-413/30TH 3-Speed
3.0L	A-670/31TH 3-Speed & A-604/41TE 4-Speed
3.3L	[1] A-604/141TE 4-Speed

[1] – AWD is equipped with A-604/141TE 4-speed transaxle & Power Transfer Unit (PTU).

LUBRICATION

SERVICE INTERVALS

Light duty service requires no transaxle servicing. Vehicles subjected to severe heavy-duty conditions should have transaxle serviced (fluid drained and refilled, bands adjusted) every 15,000 miles.

CHECKING FLUID LEVEL

1) Check fluid level with vehicle parked on level surface, engine idling at normal operating temperature for a minimum of 60 seconds and parking brake applied. Move selector lever through all gear ranges, ending in "P".

2) Fluid level should be in WARM crosshatched area of dipstick with transaxle fluid temperature about 100°F (38°C) and in HOT cross-hatched area of dipstick with transaxle temperature about 180°F (82°C). Check condition of fluid for contamination or burnt smell.

RECOMMENDED FLUID

It is important that proper lubricant be used in transaxle. Mopar ATF Plus automatic transaxle fluid Type 7176 should be used to aid in assuring optimum transaxle performance. Fluids of the type labeled Dexron-II should be used only if recommended fluid is not available.

FLUID CAPACITIES

NOTE: Transaxle total refill capacities listed in table should only be used as a guide. Correct fluid level should always be determined by marks on dipstick. See DRAINING & REFILLING when performing regular servicing.

TRANSMISSION REFILL CAPACITIES

Application	Qts. (L)
A-413/30TH & A-670/31TH	
Overhaul [1]	
Except Fleet	8.5 (8.0)
Fleet	9.2 (8.7)
Service	4.0 (3.8)
A-604/41TE	
Overhaul [1]	9.1 (8.6)
Service	4.0 (3.8)
Power Transfer Unit (PTU)	1.22 (1.15)

[1] – Fill capacity with converter empty.

DRAINING & REFILLING

NOTE: Torque converter is not equipped with a drain.

1) Loosen oil pan bolts. Break pan loose by tapping lightly on one corner of pan and allow fluid to drain. Remove pan. Install new filter on bottom of valve body and tighten retaining screws to 40 INCH lbs. (5 N.m). Clean oil pan. Clean magnet (if equipped), and place over boss in right rear corner of pan. Install pan with new gasket. *See Figs. 1 and 2.* Tighten pan bolts to **165 INCH lbs. (19 N.m)**.

2) Add 4 qts. (3.8L) ATF to transaxle. Start engine and run at idle for at least one minute. Apply parking brake and move shift selector lever through all ranges, ending in "P". Add fluid to 1/8" below middle hole on dipstick. DO NOT overfill. Recheck fluid level when transaxle reaches normal operating temperature.

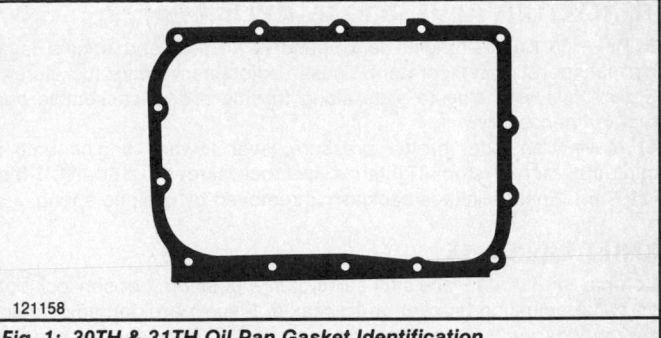

Fig. 1: 30TH & 31TH Oil Pan Gasket Identification

121158

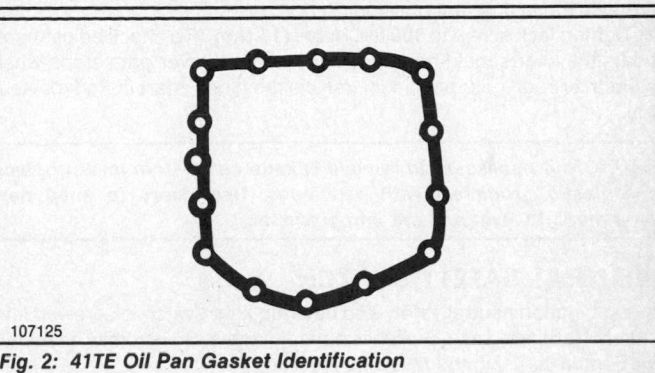

Fig. 2: 41TE Oil Pan Gasket Identification

107125

ADJUSTMENTS

NOTE: 41TE transaxle does not have any bands. Kickdown band adjusting screw is located on left side (top front) of transaxle case.

KICKDOWN (FRONT) BAND

30TH & 31TH Transaxle – 1) Locate kickdown band adjusting screw on left side (top front) of transaxle case. Loosen adjusting screw lock nut and back off screw 5 turns. Ensure adjusting screw turns freely in case.

2) Using Wrench (C-3380-A) with Adapter (C-3705), tighten adjusting screw to 48 INCH lbs. (5 N.m). If adapter is not used, tighten adjusting screw to 72 INCH lbs. (8 N.m).

3) Back off front adjusting screw 2 1/2 turns. Hold adjusting screw and tighten lock nut to 35 ft. lbs. (47 N.m).

LOW-REVERSE (REAR) BAND

30TH & 31TH Transaxle – 1) Drain transaxle fluid and remove oil pan. Apply 30 psi (2.1 kg/cm²) air pressure to low-reverse servo and measure gap between band ends. If gap is less than .080" (2.0 mm), band is excessively worn and should be replaced.

2) To adjust band, loosen lock nut approximately 5 turns and tighten adjusting screw to 44 INCH lbs. (5 N.m). Back off adjusting screw 3 1/2 turns. Hold screw in position and tighten lock nut to 120 INCH lbs. (14 N.m).

THROTTLE VALVE CABLE

30TH – 1) Ensure engine idle speed is correct and engine is at normal operating temperature. Loosen adjustment bracket lock screw. Bracket must have both bracket alignment tabs touching transaxle cast surface. Tighten lock screw to 105 INCH lbs. (12 N.m).

2) Release cross-lock on cable assembly by pulling upward. Ensure adjustment is correct. Cable must be free to slide toward engine, against its stop, after cross-lock is released.

3) Move transaxle throttle control lever fully clockwise against its internal stop. Press cross-lock downward into locked position. Move transaxle throttle lever counterclockwise. Slowly release it to ensure it will return to full clockwise position.

1992 TRANSMISSION SERVICING
Automatic Transaxle – FWD (Cont.)

THROTTLE VALVE ROD (6-CYLINDER)

31TH – 1) Ensure engine idle speed is correct and engine is at normal operating temperature. Loosen adjustment swivel lock screw. Ensure swivel is free to slide along throttle rod. Disassemble and repair if necessary.

2) Move transaxle throttle pressure lever toward engine until it contacts internal stop. Tighten swivel lock screw to **100 INCH lbs. (11 N.m)**. Ensure linkage backlash is removed by preload spring.

SHIFT LINKAGE

Column Shift – 1) Place shift selector in P position. Loosen lock bolt on cable adjusting bracket on transaxle. Ensure preload adjustment spring engages fork on transaxle bracket. Pull shift lever by hand all the way to front detent position (Park).

2) Tighten lock screw to **100 INCH lbs. (11 N.m)**. To check adjustment, gearshift lever should be within limits of hand lever gate stops when shifted through gear positions. Vehicle must only start in Park or Neutral.

CAUTION: If necessary to remove linkage cable from lever, replace old plastic grommets with new ones. Use pliers to snap new grommet into lever and rod into grommet.

NEUTRAL SAFETY SWITCH

A combination neutral safety and back-up light switch is screwed into side of transaxle case. Switch is nonadjustable. Switch may be tested for continuity using the following method.

NOTE: Before replacing a switch that fails test, ensure gearshift linkage is properly adjusted.

Testing – 1) With transaxle linkage properly adjusted, switch should allow starter operation in "P" and "N" only. To test switch, remove wire connector and test for continuity between switch center pin and transaxle case. Continuity should exist only when transaxle is in "P" or "N".

2) Check for continuity between 2 outer pins. Continuity should exist with transaxle in "R" position only. There should be no continuity between either outside pin and the transaxle case.

3) To replace neutral safety switch, remove switch from case and allow fluid to drain. Move selector lever to "P" and "N" positions and ensure switch operating fingers are centered in switch opening. Install new switch and seal. Tighten to **25 ft. lbs. (34 N.m)**. Retest switch for continuity and add transaxle fluid as required.

TORQUE SPECIFICATIONS
TORQUE SPECIFICATIONS

Application	Ft. Lbs. (N.m)
Kickdown (Front) Band Adjustment Lock Nut	35 (47)
Neutral Safety Switch	25 (34)

	INCH Lbs. (N.m)
Band Adjusting Screws [1]	
Kickdown (Front)	
With Adapter	48 (5)
Without Adapter	72 (8)
Rear [2]	44 (5)
Filter Retaining Screws	40 (5)
Gearshift Linkage Lock Screw	
30TH & 31TH	105 (12)
41TE	100 (11)
Pan Bolts	165 (19)
Rear Band Adjustment Lock Nut	120 (14)
Throttle Pressure Cable-To-Transaxle Lock Screw	105 (12)
Throttle Pressure Linkage Rod Swivel Screw	100 (11)

[1] – Tighten to specification, then back off 2 1/2 turns.
[2] – Tighten to specification, then back off 3 1/2 turns.

Dakota, Pickup, Ramcharger, RWD Van

IDENTIFICATION

TRANSMISSION/TRANSFER CASE APPLICATION

Application	Transmission
Dakota	
3.9L	42RH 4-Speed
5.2L	46RH 4-Speed
Pickup, Ramcharger & RWD Van	
3.9L & 5.2L [1]	32RH 3-Speed & 42RH 4-Speed
5.9L Gas	36RH 3-Speed & 46RH 4-Speed
Diesel	37RH 3-Speed & [2] 46RH 4-Speed

	Transfer Case
Dakota	NP-231
Pickup	
W150	NP-241
W250/350	NP-205
Ramcharger	NP-241

[1] – Some 5.2L models are equipped with either 36RH 3-Speed or 46RH 4-Speed.

[2] – Heavy duty version.

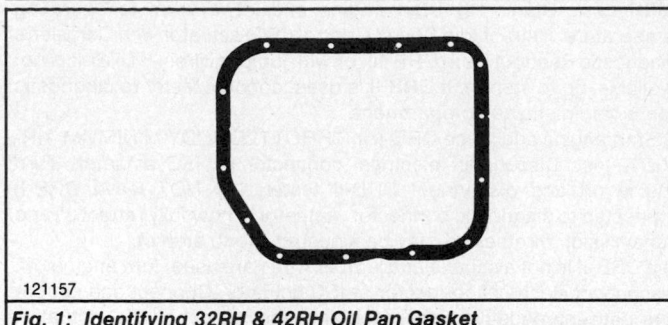

121157

Fig. 1: Identifying 32RH & 42RH Oil Pan Gasket

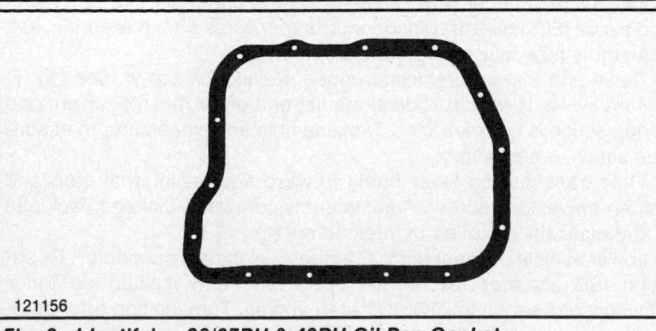

121156

Fig. 2: Identifying 36/37RH & 46RH Oil Pan Gasket

LUBRICATION

SERVICE INTERVALS

Transmission – Light-duty service requires transmission servicing (fluid drained and refilled, bands adjusted) every 37,500 miles. Under normal heavy-duty conditions, service transmission every 24,000 miles. Vehicles subjected to severe heavy-duty conditions should have transmission serviced every 12,000 miles.

Transfer Case – Light-duty service requires transfer case servicing (fluid drained and refilled) every 37,500 miles. Under normal heavy-duty conditions, service transmission every 36,000 miles.

CHECKING FLUID LEVEL

Transmission – 1) Check fluid level with vehicle parked on level surface, engine idling at normal operating temperature and parking brake applied. Move selector lever through all gear ranges, ending in "N".
2) Fluid level when warm, 85-125°F (29-52°C), should be between 2 dimples on dipstick. Fluid level when hot, 180°F (82°C), should be in the "OK" crosshatched area of dipstick. Check condition of fluid for contamination or burnt smell.

Transfer Case – With vehicle in level position, remove filler plug and check fluid level. Add lubricant If level is below bottom of filler plug hole.

RECOMMENDED FLUID

Transmission – It is important that proper lubricant be used in transmission. Mopar ATF Plus automatic transmission fluid Type 7176 should be used. Fluids labeled Dexron-II should be used only if recommended fluid is not available.
Transfer Case (NP-205) – Engine oils labeled for API Service SG or SG/CD with a SAE 30 viscosity grade should be used.
Transfer Case (NP-241 & NP-231) – Fluids labeled Mopar ATF Plus type 7176, or Dexron-II are recommended.

FLUID CAPACITIES

NOTE: Use capacities listed in TOTAL REFILL CAPACITIES table only as a guide. Correct fluid level should always be determined by marks on dipstick. Capacities listed are total system capacity including torque converter. See DRAINING & REFILLING when performing regular servicing.

TOTAL REFILL CAPACITIES

Application	Qts. (L)
Transmission [1]	
32RH	8.6 (8.1)
36RH	8.4 (7.9)
37RH	8.6 (8.1)
42RH/46RH	10.2 (9.6)

	Pts. (L)
Transfer Case	
NP-205	4.5 (2.4)
NP-231	2.5 (1.2)
NP-241	6.0 (2.8)

[1] – Includes torque converter.

DRAINING & REFILLING

NOTE: Converter is not equipped with a drain. No attempt should be made to drain torque converter.

Transmission – 1) Raise and support vehicle. Loosen oil pan bolts. Tap lightly on one corner of pan to break loose, and allow fluid to drain. Remove pan. Install new filter on bottom of valve body. Torque filter retaining screws to **35 INCH lbs. (4 N.m)**.
2) Clean oil pan. Ensure magnet (if equipped) is over boss in right front corner of pan. Install pan with new gasket. Torque oil pan bolts to **150 INCH lbs. (17 N.m)**.
3) Refill transmission with 4 qts. (3.8L) of recommended fluid. See RECOMMENDED FLUID. Start engine and allow to run at idle for at least 2 minutes. With engine at curb idle and parking brake applied, move shift selector lever through all ranges, ending in "N".
4) Add fluid up to 2 dimples on dipstick. DO NOT overfill. Recheck fluid level when transmission reaches normal operating temperature. See CHECKING FLUID LEVEL.
Transfer Case – Raise and support vehicle. Position drain pan under transfer case. Remove drain and fill plugs. Drain lubricant. Install drain plug. Tighten drain plug to **40 ft. lbs. (54 N.m)**. Remove drain pan. Using recommended lubricant, fill transfer case to bottom edge of fill plug opening. See RECOMMENDED FLUID. Lower vehicle.

ADJUSTMENTS

KICKDOWN (FRONT) BAND

1) Locate kickdown band adjusting screw on left side of transmission case, near throttle lever shaft. *See Fig. 3.* Loosen adjusting screw lock nut and back off screw 5 turns. Ensure adjusting screw turns freely in case.

2) Using Wrench (C-3380-A) with Adapter (C-3705), tighten adjusting screw to **48 INCH lbs. (5 N.m)**. If adapter is not used, tighten adjusting screw to **72 INCH lbs. (8 N.m)**.

3) Back off front adjusting screw 2 1/2 turns. Hold adjusting screw in position and tighten lock nut to **35 ft. lbs. (47 N.m)**.

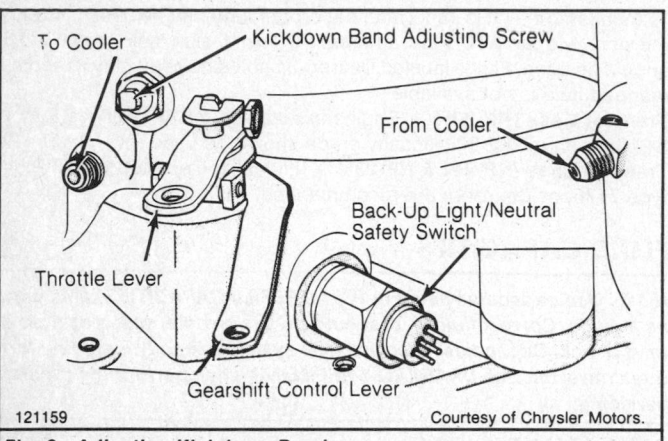

Fig. 3: Adjusting Kickdown Band

LOW-REVERSE (REAR) BAND

1) Drain transmission and remove oil pan. Locate low-reverse band adjusting screw on rear servo lever. *See Fig. 4*. Loosen adjusting screw lock nut and back off screw about 5 turns. Ensure screw turns freely in lever. Using Wrench (C-3380-A), tighten adjusting screw to **72 INCH lbs. (8 N.m)**.

2) Back off rear adjusting screw specified number of turns. See LOW-REVERSE (REAR) BAND ADJUSTMENT table. Hold adjusting screw in position and tighten lock nut to **35 ft. lbs. (47 N.m)**. Clean oil pan, install new gasket with pan and fill transmission with fluid. See DRAINING & REFILLING under LUBRICATION.

LOW-REVERSE (REAR) BAND ADJUSTMENT

Application	Back Off Screw
32RH	4 Turns
36/37RH	2 Turns

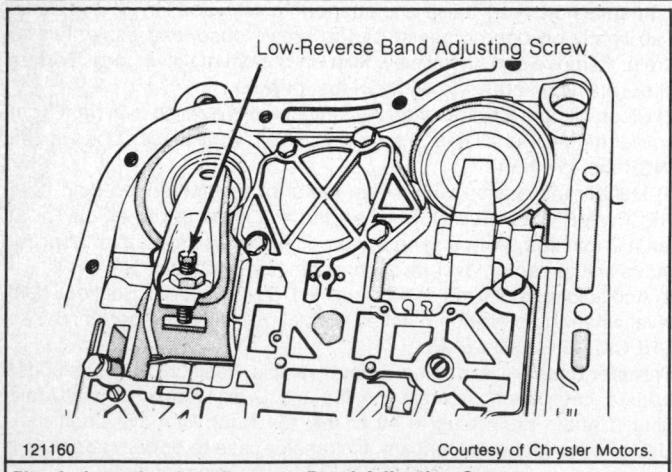

Fig. 4: Locating Low-Reverse Band Adjusting Screw

THROTTLE PRESSURE CABLE

NOTE: A .180" (4.57 mm) diameter gauge is required to check and adjust throttle pressure cable on diesel models. Use a drill of correct diameter or fabricate gauge from metal stock.

37RH (5.9L Diesel) – 1) Start engine and let it warm to operating temperature. Adjust idle speed if necessary. Using gauge, check clearance between rear of cable actuating pin and end of slot in throttle pressure cable.

2) Clearance should be .180" (4.57 mm). If clearance is okay, cable adjustment is correct. If clearance is not as specified, proceed to next step.

3) Release cable lock pawl. Insert gauge between cable actuating pin and end of slot in cable. Slide cable forward or rearward to obtain specified clearance. Press cable lock pawl down until it snaps into locked position. Recheck clearance.

All Others – 1) Start engine and let it warm to operating temperature. Adjust idle speed if necessary. Push and hold cable lock button to release cable. Pull cable housing toward rear of vehicle until fully retracted. Release cable lock button.

2) Raise and support vehicle. Rotate throttle valve lever toward front of vehicle. Cable housing should ratchet back through lock mechanism. Continue rotating throttle valve lever until ratcheting stops.

3) To check adjustment, observe throttle valve lever while a helper opens throttle lever on throttle body. Throttle valve lever should begin to move just as throttle lever comes off curb idle position. Readjust as necessary.

THROTTLE PRESSURE LINKAGE ROD

36RH (5.9L Gas) – 1) Start engine and let it warm to operating temperature. Retract Idle Speed Control (ISC) actuator with Chrysler's Diagnostic Readout Box (DRB-II), or with jumper wires. If DRB-II is not available, go to step 3). If DRB-II is used, connect tester to diagnostic connector in engine compartment.

2) Start engine and place DRB-II in THROTTLE BODY MINIMUM AIRFLOW test. Disconnect electrical connector on ISC actuator. Turn engine off and disconnect DRB-II tester. DO NOT leave DRB-II connected to diagnostic connector. Actuator is now fully retracted and transmission throttle rod may be adjusted. Go to step 4).

3) If DRB-II is not available and jumper wires are used, turn engine off. Disconnect electrical connector at ISC actuator. Connect one jumper wire between negative battery terminal and top pin on ISC actuator. Connect other jumper wire between positive battery terminal and second pin on ISC actuator. Disconnect jumper wires after 5 seconds. ISC actuator is now fully retracted. Go to next step.

4) Raise and support vehicle. Loosen swivel lock screw. *See Fig. 5*. Ensure swivel is free to slide along flat end of throttle rod so preload spring action is not restricted. Disassemble and clean parts to assure free action, if necessary.

5) Hold transmission lever firmly forward against internal stop and tighten swivel lock screw. Adjustment is complete. Linkage backlash is automatically removed by preload spring.

6) Lower vehicle. Reconnect ISC actuator electrical connector. Reposition ISC actuator for normal operation. Turn ignition on for a minimum of 5 seconds. DO NOT start engine. Turn ignition off. Actuator is now positioned for normal operation.

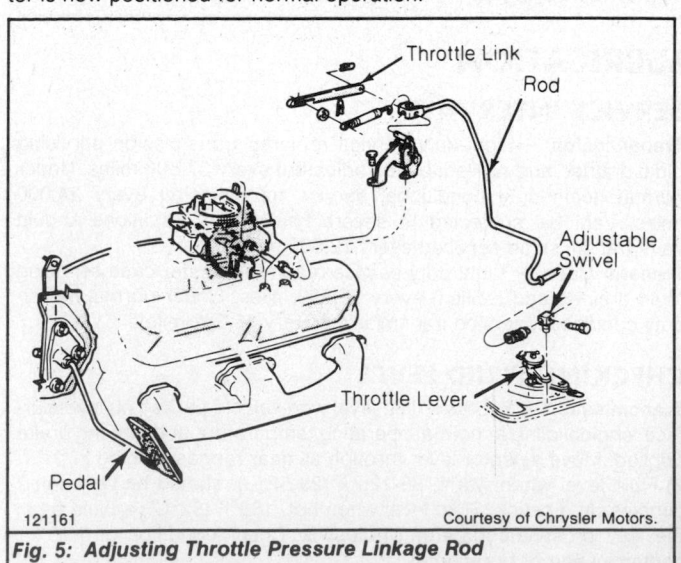

Fig. 5: Adjusting Throttle Pressure Linkage Rod

GEARSHIFT LINKAGE

1) With column shift lever in "P" position, loosen adjustable swivel lock screw. *See Fig. 6.* Ensure swivel is free to move on shift rod. Disassemble and clean components if required.

2) Move shift lever on transmission to full rear detent ("P") position and tighten swivel lock screw. When linkage is properly adjusted, detent positions for "N" and "D" will be within limits of shift lever gate stops and engine will start only in "P" or "N".

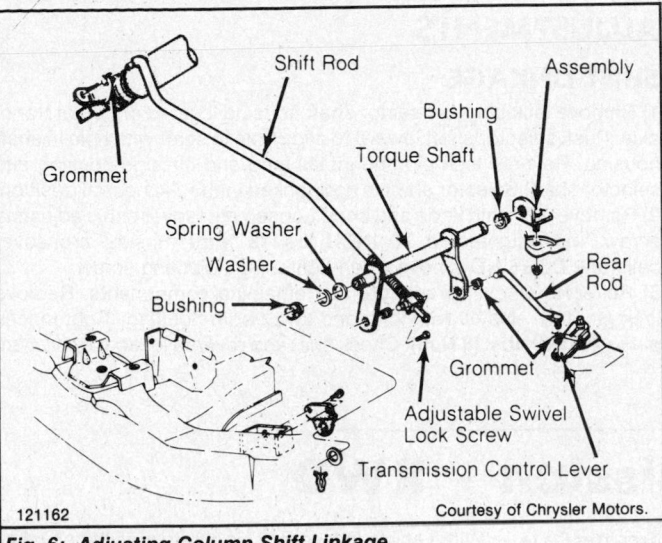

121162   Courtesy of Chrysler Motors.

Fig. 6: Adjusting Column Shift Linkage

NEUTRAL SAFETY SWITCH

A combination neutral safety and back-up light switch is screwed into side of transmission case. Switch is not adjustable. Switch may be tested for continuity using the following method.

NOTE: Before replacing a switch that fails tests, ensure gearshift linkage is properly adjusted.

Testing – 1) With transmission linkage properly adjusted, switch should allow starter operation in "P" and "N" only. To test switch, remove wire connector. Using an ohmmeter, test for continuity between center pin of switch and case. Continuity should exist only with transmission in "P" or "N".

2) Check for continuity between 2 outer pins. Continuity should exist with transmission in Reverse only. There should be no continuity between either outside pin or transmission case.

3) To replace neutral safety switch, remove switch from case and allow fluid to drain. Move selector lever to "P" and "N" positions and ensure switch operating fingers are centered in switch opening. Install new switch and seal. Tighten to **25 ft. lbs. (34 N.m)**. Retest switch for continuity and add transmission fluid.

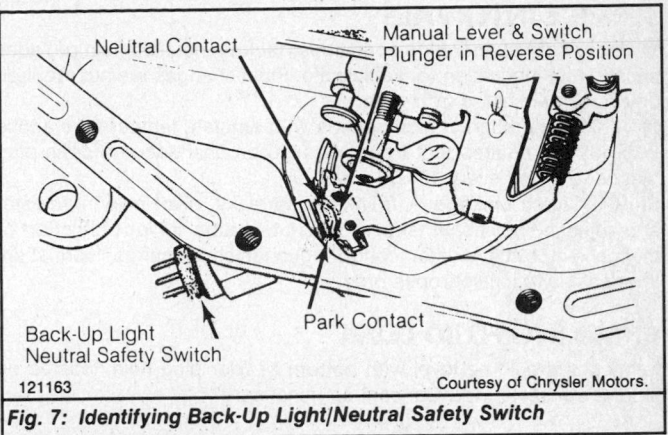

121163   Courtesy of Chrysler Motors.

Fig. 7: Identifying Back-Up Light/Neutral Safety Switch

TORQUE SPECIFICATIONS
TORQUE SPECIFICATIONS

Application	Ft. Lbs. (N.m)
Kickdown (Front) Band Adjustment Lock Nut	30 (41)
Neutral Safety Switch	25 (34)
Rear Band Adjustment Lock Nut	25 (34)

	INCH Lbs. (N.m)
Band Adjusting Screws [1]	
Kickdown (Front)	
With Adapter	48 (5)
Without Adapter	72 (8)
Low-Reverse (Rear) [2]	44 (5)
Filter Retaining Screws	35 (4)
Gearshift Linkage Lock Screw	90 (10)
Pan Bolts	150 (17)
Throttle Pressure Linkage Rod Swivel Screw	90 (10)

[1] – Tighten to specification, then back off 2 1/2 turns.

[2] – Tighten to specification, then back off 4 turns on 32RH or 2 turns on 36/37RH.

1992 TRANSMISSION SERVICING
Manual Transaxle – FWD

Caravan, Voyager
IDENTIFICATION

NOTE: All models use A-523 5-Speed manual transaxle.

LUBRICATION

SERVICE INTERVALS

1) Under normal operating conditions, factory installed fluid provides satisfactory lubrication for vehicle life. Fluid changes are not required unless contaminated with water.
2) Vehicle operation at high speeds with ambient temperature above 90°F (32°C) requires that transaxle fluid be changed and drain plug magnet cleaned every 15,000 miles.
Shift & Clutch Linkage – If linkage squeaks, pivot hole in adjuster and adjusting positioner teeth require lubrication. If high shift effort or mechanism rattle exists, control mechanism requires lubrication. Lubricate with multipurpose grease.

CHECKING FLUID LEVEL

Lubricant should be level with bottom of filler plug hole, located on side of transaxle. Add lubricant as necessary.

RECOMMENDED FLUID

SAE 5W-30 (Grade SG or SG-CC) engine oil.

TRANSMISSION REFILL CAPACITIES

Application	Qts (L)
All Models [1]	2.3 (2.2)

[1] – Measure given is approximate; level with bottom of fill hole.

ADJUSTMENTS

SHIFT LINKAGE

1) Remove lock pin from sector shaft housing located on top of transaxle. Push selector shaft inward to align hole in shaft with hole in shaft housing. Reverse lock pin and install long end through housing into selector shaft. Selector shaft is now locked in the 3-4 neutral position.
2) Remove gearshift knob and boot. Loosen crossover cable adjusting screw and retighten to **70 INCH lbs. (8 N.m)**. Ensure crossover bellcrank DOES NOT move when tightening adjusting screw.
3) Reverse removal procedure for remaining components. Remove lock pin and reinstall with long end away from housing. Tighten lock pin to **70 INCH lbs. (8 N.m)**. Check shift and reverse lockout operation.

Manual Transmission – RWD

Dakota, Pickup, Ramcharger, RWD Van
IDENTIFICATION
TRANSMISSION/TRANSFER CASE APPLICATION

Application	Transmission
Dakota	AX 15 & NP 2500
Pickup	[1] G360 & NV 4500
Ramcharger	NV 4500
RWD Van	AX 15

	Transfer Case
Dakota	NP 231
Pickup	
W150	NP 241
W250/350	NP 205
Ramcharger	NP 241

[1] – Diesel only.

LUBRICATION

SERVICE INTERVALS

Transmission – Light-duty service requires transmission servicing (fluid drained and refilled) every 37,500 miles. Under normal heavy-duty conditions, service transmission every 36,000 miles. Vehicles subjected to severe heavy-duty conditions should have transmission serviced every 18,000 miles.
Shift Linkage – Gearshift control mechanism should be lubricated every 2 years or 22,500 miles with multipurpose grease. Lubricate if shift effort or noise is apparent.
Transfer Case – Light-duty service requires transfer case servicing (fluid drained and refilled) every 37,500 miles. Under normal heavy-duty conditions, service transmission every 36,000 miles.

CHECKING FLUID LEVEL

Transmission – With vehicle in level position, check lubricant level at filler plug hole on side of transmission. Lubricant should be level with bottom of filler plug hole. Add lubricant as needed to bring to correct level.

Transfer Case – With vehicle in level position, remove filler plug and check fluid level. If level is below bottom of filler plug hole, add lubricant to bottom of filler hole.

RECOMMENDED FLUID

Transmission (G360 5-Speed) – Use API SG or SG-CD SAE 5W-30 engine oil.
Transmission (NP 2500 5-Speed) – Use API SG or SG/CD SAE 10W-30 engine oil. Dexron-II ATF may be used if high shift effort is experienced during warm-up in cold weather. Drain 10W-30 engine oil from transmission and refill with Dexron-II ATF.
Transmission (NV 4500 5-Speed) – Use Castrol Syntorq SAE 75W-90 synthetic gear lubricant. Manufacturer specifies Syntorq as the only lubricant to use in NV 4500.
Transfer Case (NP 205) – Engine oils labeled for API Service SG or SG/CD with a SAE 30 viscosity grade should be used.
Transfer Case (NP 241 & NP 231) – Fluids labeled Mopar ATF Plus type 7176, or Dexron-II are recommended.

FLUID CAPACITIES

TRANSMISSION REFILL CAPACITIES

Application	Pts. (L)
Transmission	
AX 15 5-Speed	6.55 (3.1)
G360 5-Speed	7.0 (3.3)
NP 2500 & NV 4500 5-Speed	8.0 (3.8)

	Qts. (L)
Transfer Case	
NP 205	4.5 (2.1)
NP 231	2.5 (1.2)
NP 241	6.0 (2.8)

Caravan, Town & Country, Voyager

WARNING: When battery is disconnected, vehicle computer and memory systems may lose memory data. Driveability problems may exist until computer systems have completed a relearn cycle. See COMPUTER RELEARN PROCEDURES article in GENERAL INFORMATION before disconnecting battery.

MANUAL TRANSAXLE

NOTE: For manual transmission replacement procedures, see appropriate CLUTCHES article.

POWER TRANSFER UNIT (PTU)

Removal & Installation − **1)** Raise and support vehicle. Remove front wheel assemblies. Remove drive shaft. Remove crossmember bridge attaching bolts. Remove power steering hose bracket attaching bolt. Using tie wraps, secure steering gear assembly to frame rails.

2) Disconnect ball joints from steering knuckles. Remove lower transaxle-to-crossmember strut bolt. Support crossmember with suitable transmission jack. Remove crossmember attaching bolts and remove crossmember from vehicle.

3) Remove right front drive axle. Remove PTU support bracket and strut assembly. Remove rear PTU brace attaching bolts. Remove speed sensor. Remove PTU remote vent from left engine mount. Remove 4 PTU mounting bolts and remove PTU. To install PTU, reverse removal procedure.

AUTOMATIC TRANSAXLE

NOTE: Transaxle removal does not require engine removal.

CAUTION: Transaxle and torque converter must be removed as an assembly to avoid damage to torque converter drive plate, pump bushing or oil seal. Transaxle weight should NOT be allowed to rest on drive plate during removal.

Removal & Installation − **1)** Disconnect negative battery cable. Disconnect throttle linkage and shift linkage from transaxle. Remove upper and lower oil cooler hoses. Support engine using engine support fixture. Remove bellhousing upper bolts.

2) Remove wheel hub cotter pin, nut lock and spring washer. Loosen hub nut and wheel nuts with vehicle on ground. Raise and support vehicle. Remove hub nut, washer and tire.

3) Remove speedometer adapter and pinion as an assembly. Remove ball joint-to-steering knuckle clamp bolt.

4) Separate ball joint stud from steering knuckle by prying against knuckle leg and control arm. Separate outer Constant Velocity (CV) joint splined shaft from hub by holding CV housing while moving knuckle (hub) assembly away.

CAUTION: DO NOT pull on shaft when removing drive shaft assembly.

5) Support axle shaft at CV joint housings. Remove axle shaft by pulling outward on inner CV joint housing. DO NOT pull on shaft. Remove left splash shield.

6) Remove torque converter dust cover. Mark torque converter and flexplate for installation reference. Remove flexplate-to-torque converter bolts. Remove access plug in right splash shield to rotate engine crankshaft.

7) Disconnect neutral safety switch. Remove engine mount bracket from front crossmember. Remove front mount insulator through-bolt and bellhousing bolts. Position transmission jack under transaxle. Remove left engine mount. Remove starter. Remove lower bellhousing bolts.

8) Attach a small "C" clamp to edge of bellhousing to hold torque converter in place during transaxle removal. Slowly lower transaxle.

9) To install, reverse removal procedure. Adjust gearshift and throttle cables. Torque all nuts and bolts to specification. Refill transaxle with Mopar ATF Plus Type 7176 or if not available, use Dexron-II automatic transmission fluid.

TORQUE SPECIFICATIONS
TORQUE SPECIFICATIONS

Application	Ft. Lbs. (N.m)
Ball Joint-To-Steering Knuckle Clamp Bolt	100 (136)
Crossmember-To-Frame Bolts & Nuts	90 (122)
Flexplate-To-Crankshaft Bolts	70 (95)
Flexplate-To-Torque Converter Bolts	55 (75)
Front Motor Mount Bolts	40 (54)
Hub Nut	180 (244)
Left Motor Mount Bolts	40 (54)
Manual Cable-To-Transaxle Case Bolts	21 (28)
PTU-To-Transaxle Attaching Bolts	21 (28)
Starter-To-Transaxle Bellhousing Bolts	40 (54)
Transaxle-To-Cylinder Block Bolts	70 (95)
Wheel Lug Nuts	95 (129)

	INCH Lbs. (N.m)
Bellhousing Cover Bolts	108 (12)
Lower Bellhousing Cover Bolts	108 (12)
Manual Control Lever Bolts	108 (12)
Power Steering Line Bracket Bolt	70 (8)
Speedometer-To-Extension Bolts	60 (7)
Throttle Cable-To-Transaxle Case Bolts	108 (12)
Throttle Lever-To-Transaxle Shaft Bolts	108 (12)

1992 TRANSMISSION SERVICING
Transmission Removal & Installation – RWD

Dakota, Pickup, Ramcharger, RWD Van

WARNING: Before removing engine/transmission assembly on compressed natural gas powered vehicles, see COMPRESSED NATURAL GAS SAFETY PRECAUTIONS article in GENERAL INFORMATION.

WARNING: When battery is disconnected, vehicle computer and memory systems may lose memory data. Driveability problems may exist until computer systems have completed a relearn cycle. See COMPUTER RELEARN PROCEDURES article in GENERAL INFORMATION before disconnecting battery.

COMPRESSED NATURAL GAS FUEL SYSTEM PURGING

Fuel Tube Purging – 1) Close control valve (clockwise) on side mounted fuel cylinder. Close control valves (clockwise) on both rear mounted fuel cylinders. Open manual shutoff valve.

2) Start and operate engine until it runs out of fuel. Attempt 3 more engine starts. If check valve or fuel fill receptacle is to be serviced, slowly loosen inlet side of fuel fill tube fitting at check valve. It is normal for approximately 25 psi of natural gas pressure to flow from loosened fitting.

At this point, all fuel tubes are purged of natural gas between fuel cylinders and engine. It is now OK to open fuel system.

Fuel Cylinder Purging – 1) Open manual shutoff valve. Open only the fuel control valve(s) (counterclockwise) on the fuel cylinder(s) to be serviced. Close all other control valve(s) (clockwise) on fuel cylinder(s) not being serviced.

2) Start and operate engine until it runs out of fuel. Attempt 3 more engine starts. At this point, all fuel tubes and opened cylinders are purged of natural gas between fuel cylinders and engine. It is now OK to open fuel system.

MANUAL TRANSMISSION

NOTE: For manual transmission replacement procedures, see appropriate CLUTCHES article.

TRANSFER CASE (A/T)

MODEL NP-205

Removal – 1) Raise and support vehicle. Drain transfer case. Mark front and rear drive shaft yokes for installation reference. Disconnect drive shaft at transfer case and support to one side. Disconnect shift lever rod from shift rail link.

CAUTION: DO NOT allow drive shaft to hang free, as damage to universal joints may result.

2) Secure transfer case to transmission jack using a safety chain. Remove transfer case-to-transmission adapter bolts and nuts. Move transfer case to rear until input shaft clears adapter. Lower transfer case from vehicle.

Installation – To install transfer case, reverse removal procedure. Torque all nuts and bolts to specification. See TORQUE SPECIFICATIONS table. With vehicle in level position, remove filler plug and add lubricant until fluid level reaches bottom of filler hole. Use engine oil labeled API Service SG or SG/CD SAE 30 viscosity grade.

MODELS NP-231 & NP-241

Removal – 1) Raise and support vehicle. Drain transfer case. Mark front and rear output shaft yokes and drive shaft for installation reference. Disconnect speedometer cable (if equipped) and vacuum switch hoses.

2) Disconnect shift lever link from operating lever. Support transfer case with transmission jack. Remove crossmember. Disconnect front and rear drive shaft yokes and support to one side.

3) Remove transfer case-to-transmission nuts. Move transfer case assembly to rear until clear of transmission output shaft. Lower transfer case from vehicle. Remove all gasket material from rear of transmission adapter housing.

Installation – 1) Install new transmission-to-transfer case gasket with sealer on both sides. Align transfer case with transmission. Rotate transfer case output shaft until transmission output shaft engages transfer case input shaft.

2) Move transfer case until case seats flush against transmission. Install transfer case attaching bolts. To complete installation, reverse removal procedure. With vehicle in level position, remove filler plug and add lubricant until fluid level reaches bottom of filler hole.

3) Use Mopar ATF Plus type 7176, or Dexron-II transmission fluid. Torque all nuts and bolts to specification. See TORQUE SPECIFICATIONS table.

OVERDRIVE UNIT

Removal & Installation – 1) Shift transmission to Park. Raise and support vehicle. Remove transmission pan. Drain fluid. Reinstall pan.

NOTE: If overdrive unit has failed or fluid is contaminated, remove entire transmission. If clutch or governor problems exist, remove only overdrive unit.

2) Mark drive shaft(s) for installation reference. Remove drive shaft(s). Remove transfer case (if equipped). See TRANSFER CASE (A/T). Remove overdrive unit attaching bolts.

3) Carefully pull overdrive unit off intermediate shaft. Remove and retain overdrive piston thrust bearing. Bearing may be located on piston or in clutch hub. To install overdrive unit, reverse removal procedure.

AUTOMATIC TRANSMISSION

CAUTION: Transmission and converter must be removed and installed as an assembly to prevent damage to converter drive plate, front pump bushing, and oil seal. DO NOT allow weight of transmission to rest on drive plate during removal or installation.

Removal – 1) Remove transfer case from 4WD vehicles. See TRANSFER CASE (A/T). Disconnect negative battery cable. Disconnect and lower exhaust system as needed for removal clearance. Remove engine-to-transmission struts (if equipped). Disconnect cooler lines at transmission. Remove starter, cooler line bracket and converter access cover.

NOTE: Crankshaft flange bolt circle, inner and outer circle of holes in drive plate and tapped holes in converter all have one hole offset so parts can only be installed in original position.

2) Loosen oil pan bolts. Tap pan to break loose and allow fluid to drain. Reinstall pan. Mark torque converter and flexplate for installation reference. Rotate crankshaft CLOCKWISE with socket on vibration damper bolt to access torque converter-to-flexplate bolts. Remove bolts. Mark drive shaft for installation reference. Remove from vehicle.

3) Disconnect wiring connector from back-up light/neutral safety switch. Remove crankshaft position sensor. Disconnect gearshift rod and torque shaft assembly from transmission. Disconnect transmission throttle rod from lever. Remove linkage bellcrank assembly (if equipped). Remove oil filler tube. Disconnect speedometer cable (if equipped).

4) Install engine support fixture under rear of engine. Raise transmission with service jack to relieve load on rear mount. Remove rear mount bolt and bolts securing crossmember to frame. Remove crossmember. Remove all converter housing-to-engine attaching bolts.

5) Carefully work transmission and converter assembly rearward off engine block dowel pins, disengaging converter hub from end of crankshaft. Attach a small "C" clamp on edge of converter housing to hold converter in place while transmission is being removed. Lower transmission. Remove from vehicle.

Inspection – 1) Before installing converter, rotate front pump rotors with Aligner (C-3756) until 2 holes in tool handle are vertical. Slide torque converter over input and reaction shafts. Ensure converter hub slots are vertical and fully engage pump inner rotor lugs.

2) Test for full engagement by placing a straightedge across face of transmission case. Surface of converter front cover lug should be at least 1/2" to rear of straightedge when converter is fully engaged. Attach small "C" clamp to edge of converter housing to hold converter in place while installing transmission.

3) Inspect converter drive plate for distortion or cracks and replace if necessary. Install drive plate and tighten bolts to specification.

Installation – 1) Coat converter hub hole in crankshaft with multipurpose grease. Place transmission assembly on jack and position under vehicle. Ensure marks on converter and drive plate (made during removal) are aligned.

2) Carefully work transmission assembly into position over dowels. Install all converter housing-to-engine bolts. Tighten to specification.

3) To complete installation, reverse removal procedure. Install crankshaft position sensor. Adjust shift and throttle linkages and fill transmission with fluid. Use Mopar ATF Plus Type 7176 or Dexron-II automatic transmission fluid. On 4WD models, install transfer case.

TORQUE SPECIFICATIONS

TORQUE SPECIFICATIONS

Application	Ft. Lbs. (N.m)
Converter Housing-To-Engine Bolts	30 (41)
Cooler Line Fitting	13 (18)
Drain & Fill Plugs	40 (54)
Oil Pan Bolts	12 (16)
Overdrive Unit-To-Transmission Bolts	25 (34)
Propeller Shaft Clamp Bolts (1/4")	14 (19)
Propeller Shaft Clamp Bolts (5/16")	25 (34)
Rear Mount Bolt	50 (68)
Torque Converter-To-Flexplate Bolts	
9 1/2" 3-Bolt	40 (54)
9 1/2" & 10" 4-Bolt	55 (75)
10 3/4"	23 (31)
12 1/4" [1]	35 (47)
Transfer Case-To-Transmission Nuts	35 (47)

[1] – Diesel models.

FORD MOTOR CO.

NOTE: Includes 1991-92 Cruise Control Systems.

GENERAL INFORMATION [1]

[1] – For GENERAL INFORMATION, see front of this manual.

ENGINE PERFORMANCE

ENGINE PERFORMANCE (Cont.)

1992 FORD MOTOR CO. CONTENTS (Cont.)

STEERING (Cont.)

TRANSMISSION SERVICING

1992 MODEL COVERAGE

MODEL	ENGINE	ENGINE ID	FUEL SYSTEM	IGNITION SYSTEM
Aerostar	3.0L	U	PFI	TFI-IV
	4.0L	X	PFI-MA	EDIS
Bronco	4.9L	Y	PFI	TFI-IV
	5.0L	N	PFI	TFI-IV
	5.8L	H	PFI	TFI-IV
"E" Series Van (E150/350)	4.9L	Y	PFI	TFI-IV
	5.0L	N	PFI	TFI-IV
	5.8L	H	PFI	TFI-IV
	¹ 7.3L	M	Diesel	
	7.5L	G	PFI	TFI-IV
Explorer	4.0L	X	PFI-MA	EDIS
"F" Series Pickup (F150/350)	4.9L	Y	PFI	TFI-IV
	5.0L	N	PFI	TFI-IV
	5.8L	H	PFI	TFI-IV
	¹ 7.3L	M	Diesel	
	7.5L	G	PFI	TFI-IV
Ranger	2.3L	A	PFI-MA	DIS
	2.9L	T	PFI	TFI-IV
	3.0L	U	PFI-MA	TFI-IV
	4.0L	X	PFI-MA	EDIS

¹ – Available only with F250 Heavy Duty, F350 and E350.

VIN DEFINITION

1FTBF25X5NLA00001
① ② ③ ④ ⑤ ⑥ ⑦ ⑧ ⑨ ⑩ ⑪ ⑫ ⑬ ⑭ ⑮ ⑯ ⑰

①②③ Indicates Manufacturer, Make and Type.
④ Indicates Brake System/GVWR Class.
⑤⑥⑦ Indicates Model or Line.
⑧ **Indicates Engine Code.**
⑨ Indicates Check Digit.
⑩ **Indicates Model Year.**
⑪ Indicates Assembly Plant.
⑫ Constant A.
⑬⑭⑮⑯⑰ Indicates Plant Sequential Number.

MODEL YEAR VIN CODE APPLICATION

VIN Code	Model Year
L	1990
M	1991
N	1992

ENGINE CODE LOCATION

NOTE: Emission calibration number label is located on driver's door or door post pillar as well as engine. It also identifies engine code number and revision number. Engine code and calibration number may be needed when ordering parts.

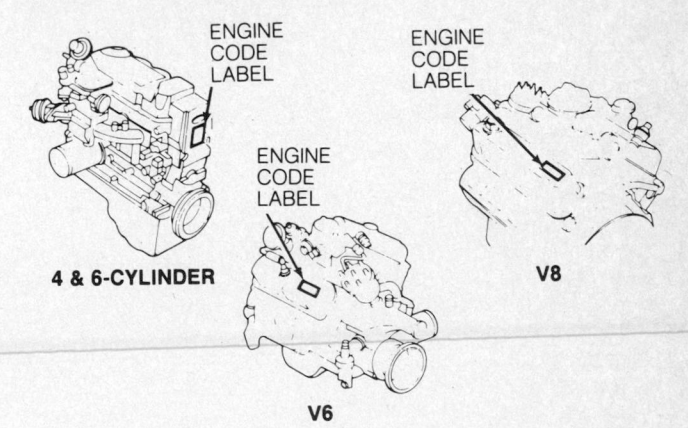

ENGINE CODE LABEL

4 & 6-CYLINDER

ENGINE CODE LABEL

V6

ENGINE CODE LABEL

V8

90J14448 90E10037 90F10038

Courtesy of Ford Motor Co.

1992 ENGINE PERFORMANCE
Emission Applications

1992 FORD MOTOR CO.

Engine & Fuel System Light Duty Emissions (8500 GVW Or Less)	Emission Control Systems & Devices
2.3L (140") 4-Cyl. PFI-MA	PCV, EVAP, TWC, FR, [1] EGR, SPK, AP, O₂, CEC, CE, AP-BPV, EGR-EVRV
2.9L (177") V6 PFI	PCV, EVAP, TWC, FR, SPK, AP, O₂, CEC, CE, AP-BPV
3.0L (183") V6 PFI	PCV, EVAP, TWC, FR, SPK, AP, O₂, CEC, CE, AP-BPV
3.0L (183") V6 PFI-MA	PCV, EVAP, TWC, FR, SPK, AP, O₂, CEC, CE, AP-BPV
4.0L (246") V6 PFI-MA	PCV, EVAP, TWC, FR, SPK, AP, O₂, CEC, CE, AP-BPV
4.9L (300") 6-Cyl. PFI	PCV, EVAP, TWC/OC, FR, EGR, SPK, AP, O₂, CEC, CE, AP-BPV, EGR-EVRV
5.0L (302") V8 PFI	PCV, EVAP, TWC/OC, FR, EGR, SPK, AP, O₂, CEC, CE, AP-BPV, EGR-EVRV
5.8L (351") V8 PFI	PCV, EVAP, TWC, FR, EGR, SPK, AP, O₂, CEC, CE, AP-BPV, EGR-EVRV
Heavy Duty Emissions (8501 GVW Or More)	
4.9L (300") 6-Cyl. PFI	PCV, EVAP, TWC/OC, FR, EGR, SPK, AP, O₂, CEC, CE, AP-BPV, EGR-EVRV
5.8L (351") V8 PFI	PCV, EVAP, TWC, FR, EGR, SPK, AP, O₂, CEC, CE, AP-BPV, EGR-EVRV
7.3L (446") V8 Diesel	PCV
7.5L (460") V8 PFI	PCV, EVAP, OC, FR, EGR, SPK, AP, O₂, CEC, CE, AP-BPV, EGR-EVRV

[1] – Some models.

NOTE: For quick reference, major emission control systems and devices are listed in bold type; components and other related devices are listed in light type.

AP – Air Pump Injection System	**GVW** – Gross Vehicle Weight
AP-BPV – Air By-Pass Valve	**O₂** – Oxygen Sensor
CE – Check Engine Light	**OC** – Oxidation Catalyst
CEC – Computerized Engine Controls	**PCV** – Positive Crankcase Ventilation
EGR – Exhaust Gas Recirculation	**PFI** – Port Fuel Injection
EGR-EVRV – EGR Electronic Vacuum Regulator Valve	**PFI-MA** – PFI Mass Airflow Sensor
EVAP – Fuel Evaporative System	**SPK** – Spark Controls
FR – Fill Pipe Restrictor	**TWC** – Three-Way Catalyst
	TWC/OC – Three-Way Catalyst/Oxidation Catalyst

Aerostar, Bronco, Explorer, Pickup, Ranger, Van

NOTE: Unless otherwise specified, references to Pickup include the F350 Super Duty commercial chassis.

MODEL IDENTIFICATION

Series [1]	Model
"A"	Aerostar
"E"	RWD Van
"F"	Pickup
"R"	Ranger
"U"	Bronco & Explorer

[1] – Vehicle series is fifth character of VIN.

INTRODUCTION

Use this article to find specifications related to servicing and on-vehicle adjustments. This article may be used as a quick reference when you are familiar with proper adjustment procedures but need a specification.

CAPACITIES

BATTERY SPECIFICATIONS

Application & Group	Amp Hour Rating
Aerostar, Bronco, Explorer & "F" Series	
Standard BXT-65	650
Optional BXT-65	850
Ranger	
Regular Cab 2.3, 2.9L & 3.0L BX-58C	N/A
Optional BXT-65	650
Regular Cab 4.0L BXT-65	650
Optional BXT-65	850
Super Cab All Engines BXT-65	650
Optional BXT-65	850
"E" Series	
Standard BXT-64A	N/A
Auxiliary BH-27A	N/A

COOLING SYSTEM CAPACITIES

Application	Qts. (L)
Aerostar, Explorer & Ranger	
2.3L	
Automatic or Manual Transmission	7.2 (6.8)
2.9L	
Automatic or Manual Transmission [1]	7.2 (6.8)
Automatic or Manual Transmission [2]	7.8 (7.4)
3.0L	
Automatic or Manual Transmission	11.8 (11.2)
4.0L	
Automatic Transmission [2][3]	8.3 (7.9)
Automatic or Manual Transmission [1]	7.8 (7.4)
Bronco & "F" Series	
4.9L	
Automatic or Manual Transmission [1]	13 (12)
Automatic Transmission [2][5]	15 (14)
Automatic Transmission [5]	14 (13)
Manual Transmission [4]	14 (13)
Manual Transmission [2][3]	15 (14)
5.0L	
Automatic Transmission [1]	14 (13)
Automatic or Manual Transmission [2]	14 (13)
Automatic or Manual Transmission [3]	15 (14)
Manual Transmission [1]	13 (12)
5.8L	
Automatic Transmission [1]	16 (15)
Automatic or Manual Transmission [2]	16 (15)
Automatic or Manual Transmission [3]	17 (16)
Manual Transmission [1]	15 (14)
7.3L	[6] 29 (27)
7.5L	18 (17)

COOLING SYSTEM CAPACITIES (Cont.)

Application	Qts. (L)
"E" Series	
4.9L	
Automatic or Manual Transmission [1]	15 (14)
Automatic or Manual Transmission [4]	18 (17)
5.0L	
Automatic or Manual Transmission [1][2]	17.5 (16.6)
Automatic or Manual Transmission [3]	18.5 (17.5)
5.8L	
Automatic or Manual Transmission [1]	20 (19)
Automatic or Manual Transmission [4]	21 (20)
7.3L	[6] 31 (29)
7.5L	28 (26)

[1] – With Standard Cooling.
[2] – With A/C.
[3] – With Super Cooling.
[4] – With A/C or Super Cooling.
[5] – With Standard or Super Cooling.
[6] – Include 5 quarts (4.7L) in reservoir bottle.

CRANKCASE CAPACITIES

Application	[1] Qts. (L)
All Engines Except 3.0L & 7.3L	[2] 5.0 (4.7)
3.0L	4.5 (4.25)
7.3L	10.0 (9.5)

[1] – Add 1/2 qt. if equipped with oil cooler.
[2] – "F" Series, 6 quarts (5.6L).

TRANSMISSION & TRANSFER CASE CAPACITIES

Application	Specification	Quantity
Aerostar		
A4LD Auto.	Mercon	9.7 Qts. (9.2L)
E4WD Auto.	Mercon	10.0 Qts. (9.5L)
5-Speed Overdrive (Mazda R-1)	Mercon	5.6 Pts. (2.65L)
Transfer Case (TC-28 Dana)	Mercon	4.5 Qts. (4.3L)
Bronco		
AOD Auto.	Mercon	12.3 Qts. (11.6L)
C-6 Auto. (4X4)	Mercon	13.5 Qts. (12.7L)
E4OD Auto. (4X2)	Mercon	16.2 Qts. (15.3L)
4-Speed (Warner T-18)	SAE 80W-90	3.5 Qts. (3.3L)
5-Speed Overdrive (Mazda R-2)	Mercon	3.8 Qts. (3.6L)
Transfer Case (1356 Warner)	Mercon	2.0 Qts. (1.9L)
Explorer		
A4LD Auto. (4X2)	Mercon	9.7 Qts. (9.2L)
A4LD Auto. (4X4)	Mercon	10.0 Qts. (9.5L)
5-Speed Overdrive (Mazda R-1)	Mercon	5.6 Pts. (2.65L)
Transfer Case 13-54 Warner	Mercon	2.5 Pts. (1.2L)
Ranger		
A4LD Auto. (4X2)	Mercon	9.7 Qts. (9.2L)
A4LD Auto. (4X4)	Mercon	10.0 Qts. (9.5L)
5-Speed Overdrive (Mazda R-1)	Mercon	5.6 Pts. (2.65L)
5-Speed Overdrive (Mitsubishi)	SAE 80W-85	4.8 Pts. (2.3L)
Transfer Case 13-54 Warner	Mercon	2.5 Pts. (1.2L)
"E" Series		
AOD Auto.	Mercon	12.3 Qts. (11.6L)
C-6 Auto.	Mercon	12.0 Qts. (11.4L)
E4OD Auto.	Mercon	15.7 Qts. (14.8L)
5-Speed Overdrive (ZF HD)	Mercon	3.4 Qts. (3.2L)

TRANSMISSION & TRANSFER CASE CAPACITIES (Cont.)

Application	Specification	Quantity
"F" Series		
AOD Auto. (4X2)	Mercon	12.3 Qts. (11.6L)
C-6 Auto. (4X2)	Mercon	12.0 Qts. (11.4L)
C-6 Auto. (4X4)	Mercon	13.5 Qts. (12.7L)
E4OD Auto. (4X2)	Mercon	15.7 Qts. (14.8L)
E4OD Auto. (4X4)	Mercon	16.2 Qts. (15.3L)
4-Speed (Warner T-18)	SAE 80W-90	3.5 Qts. (3.3L)
5-Speed Overdrive (Mazda R-2)	Mercon	3.8 Qts. (3.6L)
5-Speed Overdrive (ZF S5-42)	Mercon	3.4 Qts. (3.2L)
Transfer Case (1356 Warner)	Mercon	2.0 Qts. (1.9L)

AXLE CAPACITIES

Application	Pts. (L)
Aerostar	
Front	2.2 (1.0)
Rear	
7.5" Ford [1]	[2] 3.5 (1.65)
8.8" Ford [1]	[2] 5.0 (2.4)
Bronco	
Front	3.8 (1.8)
Rear (8.8" Ford [1])	[2] 5.5 (2.6)
Explorer	
Front (Dana 35)	3.5 (1.65)
Rear (8.8" Ford [1])	[2] 5.5 (2.6)
Ranger	
Front (Dana 35)	3.5 (1.65)
Rear (7.5" & 8.8" Ford) [1]	[2] 5.0 (2.4)
"E" Series	
Rear	
8.8" Ford [1]	[2] 5.5 (2.6)
9.75" Dana M60-1U	6.3 (3.0)
10.5" Dana M70-2U	6.6 (3.1)
"F" Series	
Front	
Dana 44-IFS L.D.	3.6 (1.7)
Dana 50-IFS H.D.	3.8 (1.8)
Dana 60 Monobeam	5.8 (2.8)
Rear	
8.8" Ford	5.5 (2.6)
10.25" Ford [3]	7.5 (3.5)
11.25" Dana 80	8.3 (3.9)

[1] – Conventional and Traction-Lok.
[2] – Add 4 oz. Friction Modifier for Traction-Lok Axles.
[3] – Conventional and Traction-Lok, Semi and Full Float.

QUICK-SERVICE

SERVICE INTERVALS & SPECIFICATIONS
REPLACEMENT INTERVALS

Component	Interval (Miles)
Gasoline Engines	
Air Filter	30,000
Cam Timing Belt	60,000
Coolant	30,000
Crankcase Ventilation Filter	30,000
Fuel Filter	30,000
Oil & Filter	7500
PCV Valve	60,000
Spark Plugs (Standard)	30,000
Spark Plugs (Platinum)	60,000
Spark Plug Wires	60,000
Transfer Case Oil	60,000
Transmission Oil	
Automatic Transmission	30,000
Manual Transmission	60,000

REPLACEMENT INTERVALS (Cont.)

Component	Interval (Miles)
Diesel Engines	
Air Filter	30,000
Coolant	30,000
Fuel Filter	[1] 60,000
Oil & Filter	5000
Transfer Case Oil	60,000
Transmission Oil	
Automatic Transmission	30,000
Manual Transmission	60,000

[1] – Drain water from fuel filter bowl every 5000 miles.

BELT ADJUSTMENT

Application	New Belt Lbs. (kg)	[1] Used Belt Lbs. (kg)
2.3L		
Fixed	150-190 (68-86)	140-160 (64-73)
With Tensioner [2]	150-190 (68-86)	140-160 (64-73)
2.9L	120-160 (54-73)	110-130 (50-59)
3.0L		
Fixed	100-140 (45-64)	80-100 (36-45)
With Tensioner [2]	150-190 (68-86)	140-160 (64-73)
4.0L With Tensioner [2]	108-132 (49-60)	108-132 (49-60)
4.9L With Tensioner [2]	[3]	[3]
5.0L With Tensioner [2]	[4]	[4]
5.8L With Tensioner [2]	[4]	[4]
7.3L Except Ambulance		
Vac. Pump W/ 3/8" Belt	90-130 (41-59)	65-85 (30-39)
Vac. Pump W/ 1/2" Belt	110-150 (50-68)	75-95 (34-43)
All Others W/ 1/2" Belt	140-180 (64-82)	95-115 (43-52)
7.3L Ambulance		
Alternator	140-160 (64-73)	140-160 (64-73)
Vac. Pump	90-130 (41-59)	65-85 (30-39)
A/C & P/S	140-180 (64-82)	95-115 (43-52)
7.5L		
With Tensioner [2]	[5]	[5]
Alt. & Air Pump	160-200 (73-91)	110-130 (50-59)

[1] – Any belt operated for 10 minutes.
[2] – Tension is correct if tensioner is within indicator marks.
[3] – 90 lbs. (41 kg) minimum for vehicles with 60 & 75 amp alternators. 117 lbs. (53 kg) minimum for vehicles with 100 amp alternators.
[4] – 77 lbs. (35 kg) minimum for vehicles with 60 & 75 amp alternators. 111 lbs. (50 kg) minimum for vehicles with 100 amp alternators.
[5] – 94 lbs. (43 kg) minimum tension.

NOTE: To check belt tension and routing, refer to Figs. 1-8.

MECHANICAL CHECKS

ENGINE COMPRESSION

Check engine compression at specified cranking speed with engine at normal operating temperature, all spark plugs removed (on dual plugs, remove exhaust side only) and throttle wide open. Ensure crankcase is full and oil is of correct viscosity. With compression gauge installed, use remote starter to crank engine.

Crank engine at least 5 revolutions, and record highest reading. Repeat procedure for all cylinders using approximately same number of revolutions. Lowest compression reading should not be less than 75 percent of highest compression reading. No cylinder compression reading should be less than 100 psi (7 kg/cm^2).

4-CYLINDER COMPRESSION RATIO SPECIFICATIONS

Application	Compression Ratio
2.3L	9.5:1

6-CYLINDER COMPRESSION RATIO SPECIFICATIONS

Application	Compression Ratio
4.9L	8.8:1

V6 COMPRESSION RATIO SPECIFICATIONS

Application	Compression Ratio
2.9L & 4.0L	9.0:1
3.0L	9.3:1

V8 COMPRESSION RATIO SPECIFICATIONS

Application	Compression Ratio
5.0L	9.0:1
5.8L	8.8:1
7.3L (Diesel)	21.5:1
7.5L	8.0:1

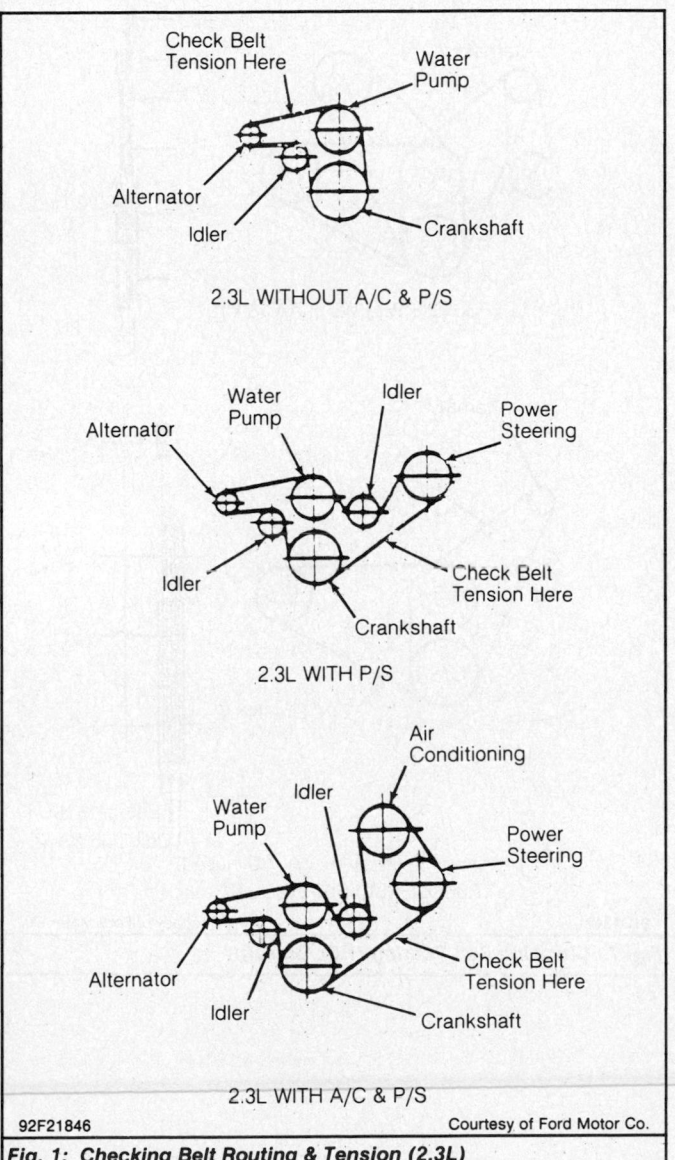

92F21846 Courtesy of Ford Motor Co.

Fig. 1: Checking Belt Routing & Tension (2.3L)

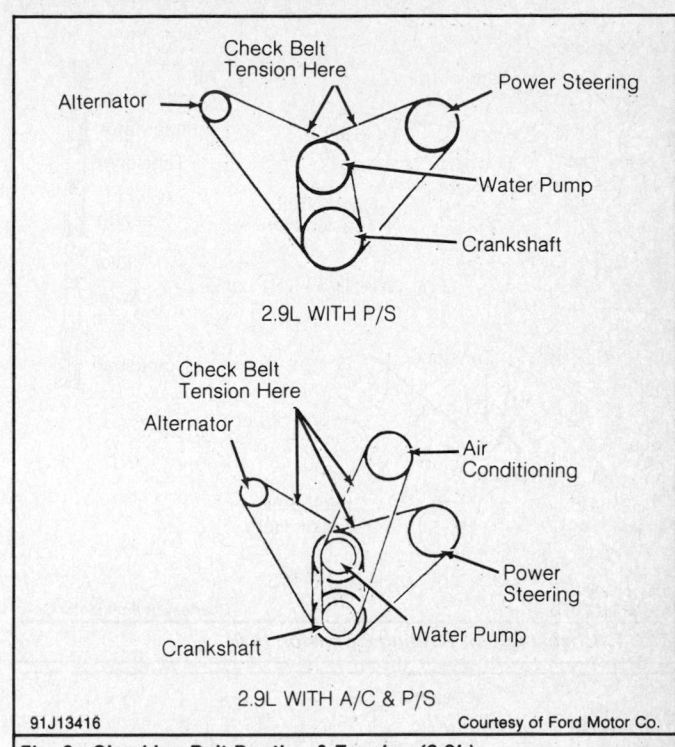

91J13416 Courtesy of Ford Motor Co.

Fig. 2: Checking Belt Routing & Tension (2.9L)

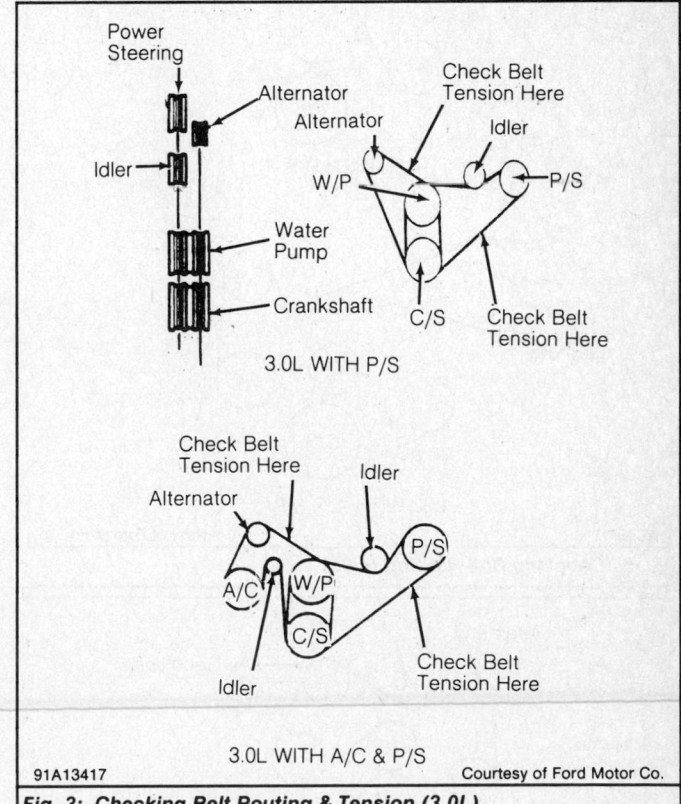

91A13417 Courtesy of Ford Motor Co.

Fig. 3: Checking Belt Routing & Tension (3.0L)

1992 ENGINE PERFORMANCE
Service & Adjustment Specifications (Cont.)

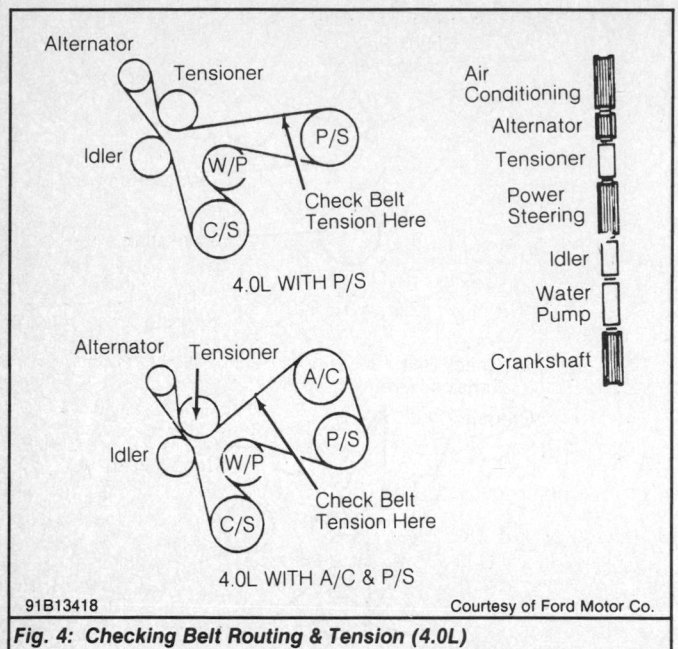

4.0L WITH P/S

4.0L WITH A/C & P/S

Check Belt Tension Here

Air Conditioning
Alternator
Tensioner
Power Steering
Idler
Water Pump
Crankshaft

91B13418   Courtesy of Ford Motor Co.

Fig. 4: Checking Belt Routing & Tension (4.0L)

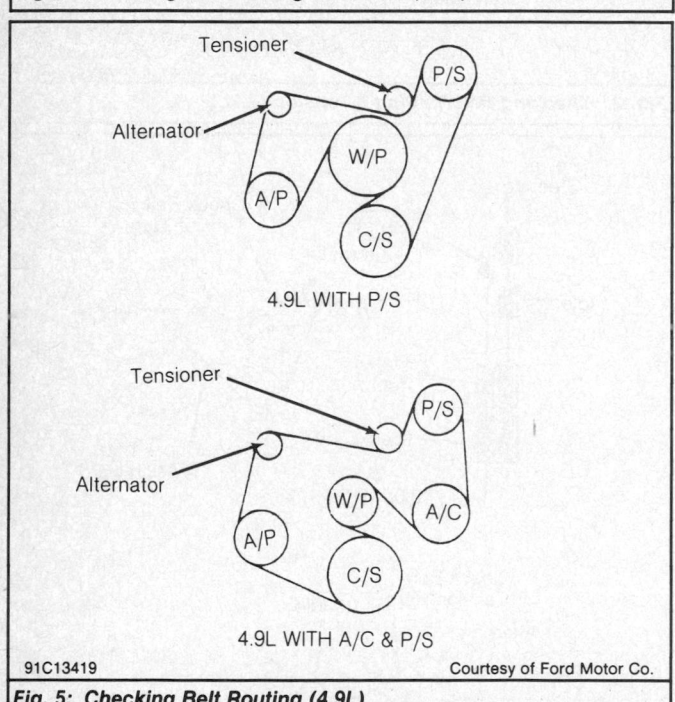

4.9L WITH P/S

4.9L WITH A/C & P/S

91C13419   Courtesy of Ford Motor Co.

Fig. 5: Checking Belt Routing (4.9L)

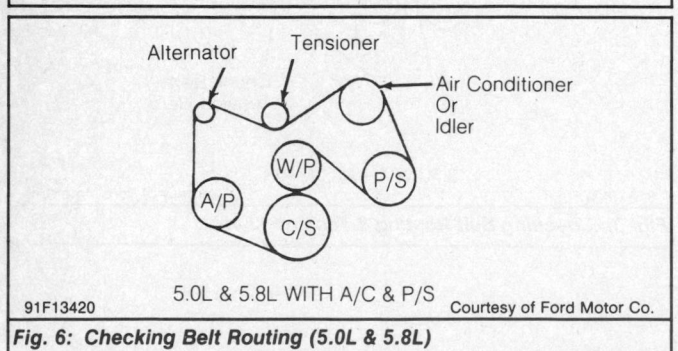

5.0L & 5.8L WITH A/C & P/S

91F13420   Courtesy of Ford Motor Co.

Fig. 6: Checking Belt Routing (5.0L & 5.8L)

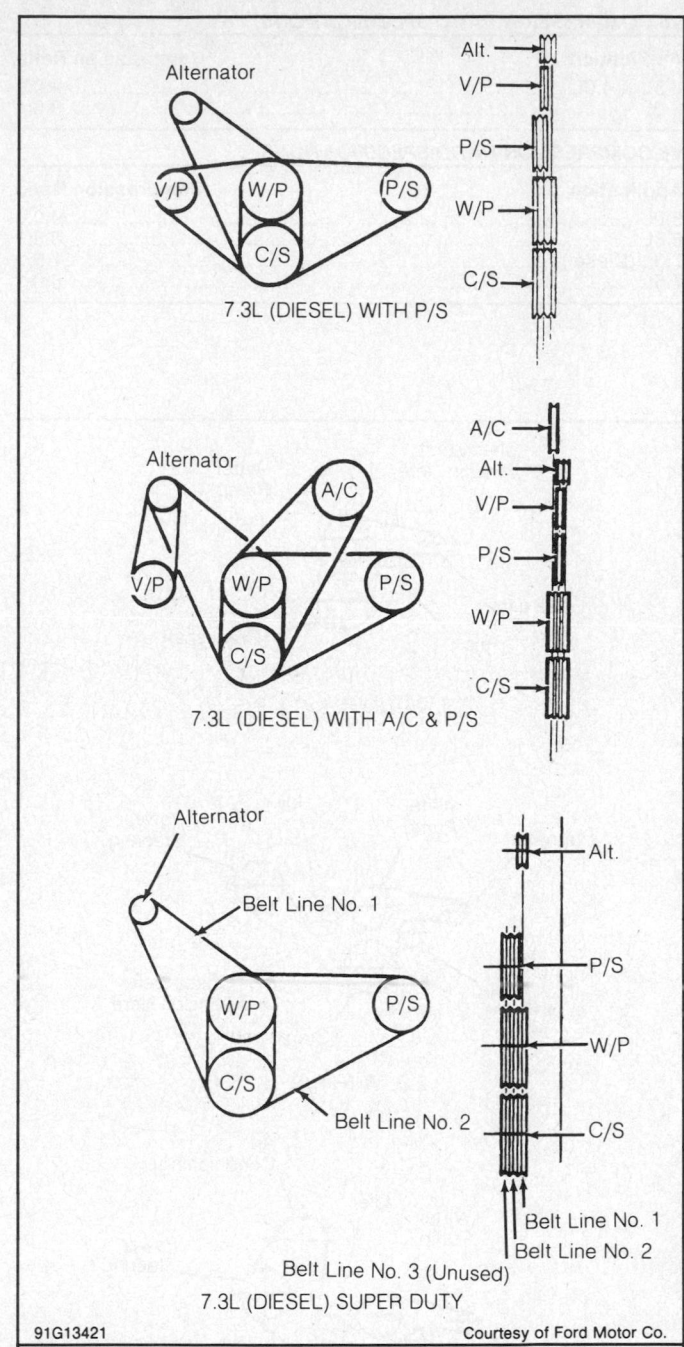

7.3L (DIESEL) WITH P/S

7.3L (DIESEL) WITH A/C & P/S

Belt Line No. 1
Belt Line No. 2
Belt Line No. 1
Belt Line No. 2
Belt Line No. 3 (Unused)
7.3L (DIESEL) SUPER DUTY

91G13421   Courtesy of Ford Motor Co.

Fig. 7: Checking Belt Routing (7.3L Diesel)

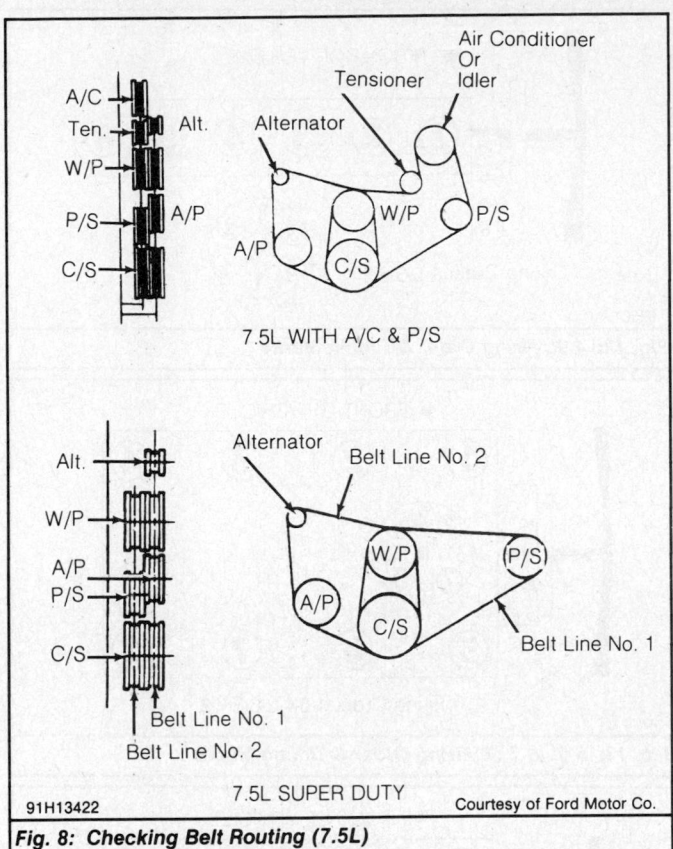

91H13422   Courtesy of Ford Motor Co.

Fig. 8: Checking Belt Routing (7.5L)

VALVE CLEARANCE

NOTE: On 2.9L models, valve clearance is set by turning adjusting screw an additional 1 1/2 turns past zero lash. On all other models, no valve adjustment is required as hydraulic valve lifters are used. If incorrect valve clearance is suspected, collapse lifter before checking clearance.

4-CYLINDER COLLAPSED VALVE LIFTER CLEARANCE

Application	In. (mm)
2.3L OHC	.035-.055 (.89-1.39)

6-CYLINDER COLLAPSED VALVE LIFTER CLEARANCE

Application	In. (mm)
4.9L	
Allowable	.100-.200 (2.54-5.10)
Desired	.125-.175 (3.18-4.45)

V6 COLLAPSED VALVE LIFTER CLEARANCE

Application	In. (mm)
2.9L	[1]
3.0L	.088-.189 (2.23-4.77)
4.0L	[2]

[1] – Valve clearance is set by turning adjusting screw an additional 1 1/2 turns past zero lash.
[2] – Information not available from manufacturer.

V8 COLLAPSED VALVE LIFTER CLEARANCE

Application	In. (mm)
5.0L	
Allowable	.071-.193 (1.80-4.90)
Desired	.096-.165 (2.44-4.19)
5.8L	
Allowable	.098-.198 (2.48-5.03)
Desired	.123-.173 (3.12-4.39)
7.3L (Diesel)	[1] .185 (4.70)
7.5L	
Allowable	.075-.175 (1.91-4.45)
Desired	.100-.150 (2.54-4.81)

[1] – Maximum clearance value.

IGNITION SYSTEM

IGNITION COIL

4-CYLINDER IGNITION COIL RESISTANCE

Application	Primary Ohms	Secondary Ohms
2.3L DIS	.5	[1]

[1] – Information not available from manufacturer.

6-CYLINDER IGNITION COIL RESISTANCE

Application	Primary Ohms	Secondary Ohms
4.9L TFI-IV	.8-1.6	8000-11,500

V6 IGNITION COIL RESISTANCE

Application	Primary Ohms	Secondary Ohms
2.9L & 3.0L TFI-IV	.8-1.6	8000-11,500
4.0L EDIS	.5	[1]

[1] – Information not available from manufacturer.

V8 IGNITION COIL RESISTANCE

Application	Primary Ohms	Secondary Ohms
5.0L & 5.8L TFI-IV	.8-1.6	8700-11,500
7.5L TFI-IV/(CBD)	.8-1.6	8700-11,500

HIGH TENSION WIRE RESISTANCE

HIGH TENSION WIRE RESISTANCE

Application	Ohms
DIS, EDIS & TFI-IV	7000 Per Foot

SPARK PLUGS

NOTE: See Vehicle Emissions Information decal for spark plug gap specification.

1992 ENGINE PERFORMANCE
Service & Adjustment Specifications (Cont.)

SPARK PLUG TYPE

Application	Motorcraft No.
2.3L	AWSF-32C
2.9L	AWSF-42C
3.0L	AWSF-32P
4.0L	
Aerostar & Ranger	AWSF-42P
Explorer	AWSF-42C
4.9L	BSF-44C
5.0L	ASF-42C
5.8L	ASF-32C
7.5L	ASF-44P

FIRING ORDER & TIMING MARKS

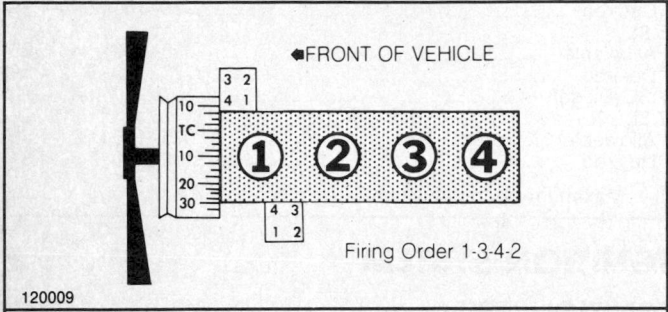

Firing Order 1-3-4-2

Fig. 9: 2.3L Firing Order & Timing Marks

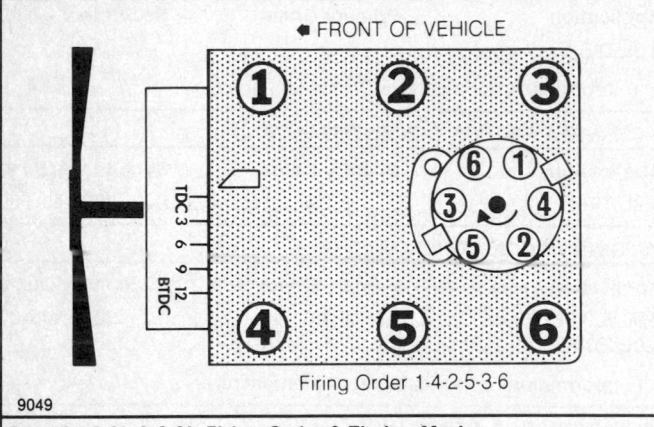

Firing Order 1-4-2-5-3-6

Fig. 10: 2.9L & 3.0L Firing Order & Timing Marks

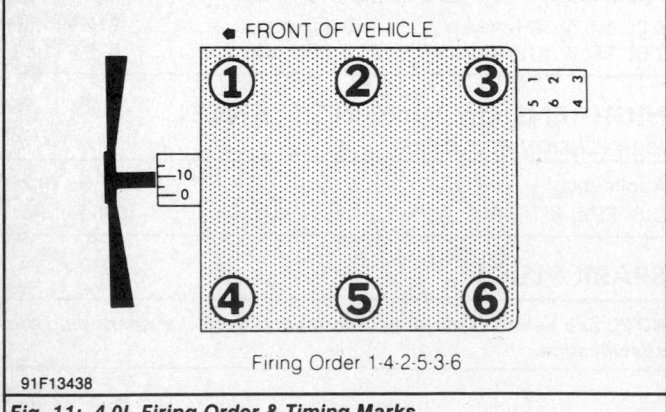

Firing Order 1-4-2-5-3-6

Fig. 11: 4.0L Firing Order & Timing Marks

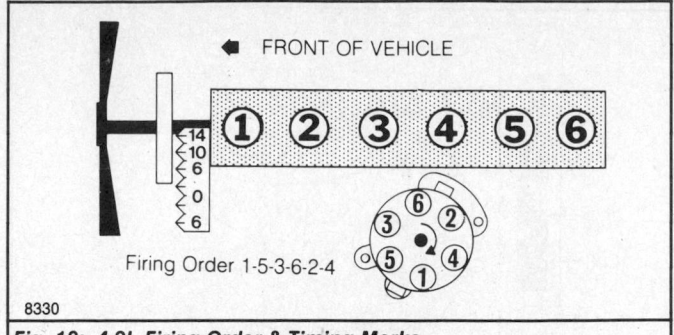

Firing Order 1-5-3-6-2-4

Fig. 12: 4.9L Firing Order & Timing Marks

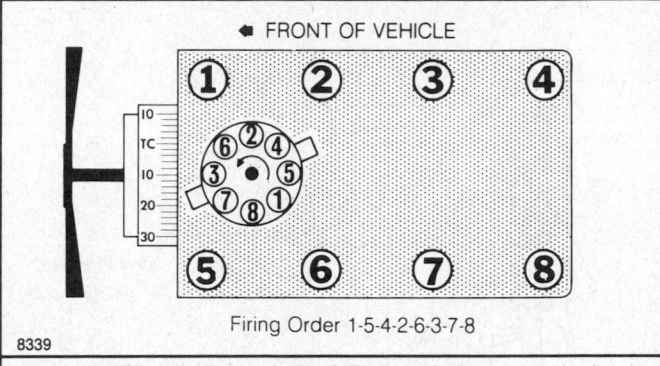

Firing Order 1-5-4-2-6-3-7-8

Fig. 13: 5.0L & 7.5L Firing Order & Timing Marks

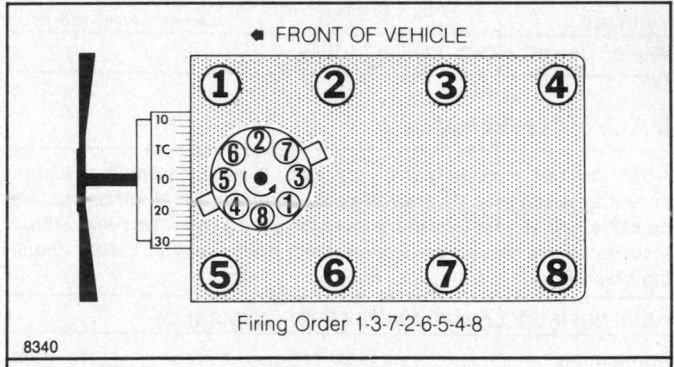

Firing Order 1-3-7-2-6-5-4-8

Fig. 14: 5.8L Firing Order & Timing Marks

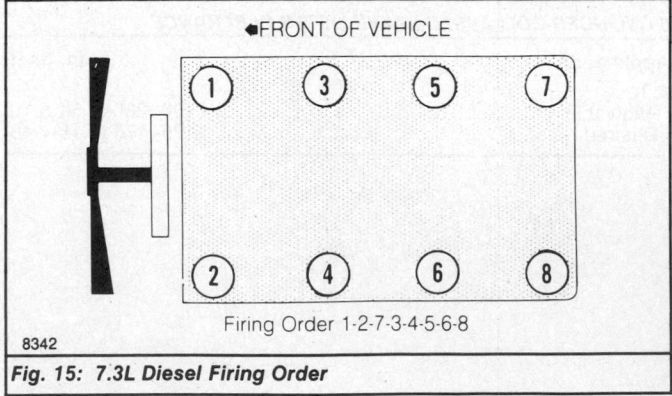

Firing Order 1-2-7-3-4-5-6-8

Fig. 15: 7.3L Diesel Firing Order

IGNITION TIMING
4-CYLINDER BASE IGNITION TIMING

Application	Degrees BTDC @ RPM
2.3L	Timing Not Adjustable.

6-CYLINDER BASE IGNITION TIMING

Application	Degrees BTDC @ RPM
4.9L	10 @ [1]

[1] – Information not available from manufacturer.

V6 BASE IGNITION TIMING

Application [1]	Degrees BTDC @ RPM
2.9L	
Automatic Transmission	10 @ 800
Manual Transmission	10 @ 850
3.0L	10 @ [2]
4.0L	Timing Not Adjustable.

[1] – With SPOUT in-line connector disconnected.
[2] – Information not available from manufacturer.

V8 BASE IGNITION TIMING

Application	[1] Degrees BTDC @ RPM
5.0L	
Automatic Transmission	10 @ 525-825
Manual Transmission	10 @ 550-850
5.8L	
C6 Automatic Transmission	10 @ 630-930
E4OD Automatic Transmission	10 @ 580-880
Manual Transmission	10 @ 580-880
7.5L	10 @ 500-800

[1] – With SPOUT in-line connector disconnected.

NOTE: For 7.3L injection pump timing procedures, see ON-VEHICLE ADJUSTMENTS article.

DISTRIBUTOR SPECIFICATIONS

NOTE: All models use computed timing advance. No adjustment is possible.

FUEL SYSTEM

FUEL PUMP

NOTE: Fuel pump performance is a measurement of fuel pressure and volume availability, not regulated fuel pressure.

FUEL PUMP PERFORMANCE

Application	Specification
Gasoline Engines	
Fuel Line Pressure	
4.9L [1]	[2] 50-60 psi (3.5-4.2 kg/cm²)
All Others [1]	[2] 35-45 psi (2.5-3.2 kg/cm²)
Volume	1.5 Pts. (.72L) In 30 Seconds.
Diesel Engines	
Fuel Line Pressure	[3] 6-8 psi (.42-.56 kg/cm²)
Volume	1 Pt. (.5L) In 30 Seconds.

[1] – Key on, engine off.
[2] – Engine running pressure may be 5 psi (.4 kg/cm²) less.
[3] – At idle.

IDLE SPEED & MIXTURE

NOTE: No idle mixture adjustments are possible. If engine performance is unsatisfactory, see appropriate SELF-DIAGNOSTICS article.

FAST IDLE SPEED

NOTE: Refer to underhood engine decal for engine fast idle RPM specification.

THROTTLE POSITION SENSOR/SWITCH
TPS VOLTAGE SPECIFICATIONS [1]

Application	Idle	Wide Open Throttle
2.3L, 2.9L [2], 3.0L & 4.0L	0.20	4.84
2.9L [3], 4.9L, 5.0L, 5.8L & 7.5L	0.34	4.84

[1] – Minimum and maximum specifications are given.
[2] – Vehicles equipped with mass airflow sensor only.
[3] – Except vehicles equipped with mass airflow sensor.

1992 ENGINE PERFORMANCE
On-Vehicle Adjustments

Aerostar, Bronco, Explorer, Pickup, Ranger, Van

NOTE: Unless otherwise specified, references to Pickup include the F350 Super Duty commercial chassis.

MODEL IDENTIFICATION

Series [1]	Model
"A"	Aerostar
"E"	RWD Van
"F"	Pickup
"R"	Ranger
"U"	Bronco & Explorer

[1] – Vehicle series is fifth character of VIN.

ENGINE MECHANICAL

Before performing any on-vehicle adjustments to fuel or ignition systems, ensure engine mechanical condition is okay.

VALVE CLEARANCE

NOTE: Valve cover(s) must be removed before performing valve adjustment. See appropriate article in ENGINES for removal and installation procedures.

2.3L VALVE CLEARANCE ADJUSTMENT

NOTE: Valve clearance is nonadjustable, but clearance can be checked to determine if worn components exist.

1) Rotate camshaft so base circle of camshaft lobe is positioned on valve to be checked. Using Valve Spring Compressor (T88T-6565-BH), apply pressure on cam follower until lash adjuster is fully collapsed.
2) While holding lash adjuster in fully collapsed position, use feeler gauge to measure clearance between base circle of camshaft and camshaft follower. See 2.3L COLLAPSED LIFTER VALVE CLEARANCE table.
3) If clearance is not within specification, inspect camshaft follower for damage. If camshaft follower is not damaged, check for sticking valve, worn valve spring or camshaft lobe(s). If components are okay, check for defective lash adjuster. Replace components as necessary.

2.3L COLLAPSED VALVE LIFTER CLEARANCE

Application	In. (mm)
2.3L	
Allowable	.100-.200 (2.50-5.08)
Desired	.035-.055 (.89-1.40)

2.9L VALVE CLEARANCE ADJUSTMENT

1) Position camshaft lobe on cylinder to be adjusted so that rocker arm is on the base circle area. Loosen adjusting screw on rocker arm until a distinct lash between rocker arm pad and valve tip can be noticed. Plunger of lash adjuster should be fully extended.
2) Carefully screw in the adjusting screw until rocker arm slightly touches valve stem. To achieve nominal working position of the plunger, screw in adjusting screw an additional **1 1/2 turns**, which is equivalent to **.07" (2 mm)**.

3.0L VALVE CLEARANCE ADJUSTMENT

NOTE: Hydraulic valve lifters are used; no valve adjustment is required. If incorrect valve clearance is suspected, lifter must be collapsed before clearance can be checked.

1) Position No. 1 piston at TDC of compression stroke. Slowly apply pressure until valve lifter is completely collapsed on No. 1 intake.
2) Holding lifter in collapsed position, measure clearance between rocker arm and tip of valve stem. If clearance is not within

specification, repair or replace components as necessary. See 3.0L COLLAPSED VALVE LIFTER SPECIFICATIONS table.
3) Repeat procedure for exhaust valves No. 1, No. 2 and No. 4, and intake valves No. 3 and No. 6. Rotate crankshaft 360 degrees (one revolution). Repeat procedure for exhaust valves No. 3, No. 5 and No. 6, and intake valves No. 2, No. 4 and No. 5.

3.0L COLLAPSED VALVE LIFTER SPECIFICATIONS

Application	In. (mm)
All Valves	.088-.189 (2.23-4.77)

4.0L VALVE CLEARANCE ADJUSTMENT

NOTE: Hydraulic roller valve lifters and nonadjustable rocker arms are used; valve adjustment is not possible. Manufacturer supplies no procedure for checking valve clearance. If valve lifters are found to be excessively worn or noisy, test and repair or replace as necessary.

4.9L VALVE CLEARANCE ADJUSTMENT

NOTE: Hydraulic valve lifters are used; no valve adjustment is required. If valve clearance is incorrect, use oversize or undersize push rods to correct clearance.

1) Position crankshaft so No. 1 piston is at TDC on compression stroke. Using chalk, make 2 marks on vibration damper. The first mark must be 120 degrees from timing mark. Make the second mark 120 degrees from first mark. This will divide the damper into three equal parts to facilitate checking valve clearance on all cylinders.
2) Ensure rocker arm bolts on cylinder No. 1 are tightened to **17-23 ft. lbs. (23-31 N.m)**. Using Lifter Bleed Down Wrench (T70P-6513-A), slowly apply pressure to bleed down lifter until plunger is completely bottomed.
3) Measure clearance between rocker arm and valve stem. See 4.9L COLLAPSED VALVE LIFTER CLEARANCE table. If clearance is not within specification, install longer or shorter push rod to obtain correct clearance.
4) Rotate engine to next mark on vibration damper. Repeat procedure on each succeeding cylinder in firing order (1-5-3-6-2-4), rotating engine to next mark on damper before checking clearance.

4.9L COLLAPSED VALVE LIFTER CLEARANCE

Application	In. (mm)
4.9L	
Allowable	.100-.200 (2.50-5.08)
Desired	.125-.175 (3.18-4.45)

5.0L VALVE CLEARANCE ADJUSTMENT

NOTE: Hydraulic valve lifters are used; no valve adjustment is required. If valve clearance is incorrect, use oversize or undersize push rods to correct clearance.

1) Rotate crankshaft in normal operation direction until No. 1 cylinder is at TDC of compression stroke. Using Lifter Bleed Down Wrench (T71P-6513-B), apply pressure to No. 1 intake valve lifter tappet until lifter is completely bottomed.
2) Hold valve lifter in this position while measuring clearance between valve lifter and valve stem. Record measurement. Repeat this procedure for intake valves No. 7 and No. 8, and exhaust valves No. 1, No. 5 and No. 4.
3) Rotate crankshaft 180 degrees (1/2 turn). Bleed lifter and check intake valves No. 5 and No. 4, and exhaust valves No. 2 and No. 6. Rotate crankshaft 270 degrees (3/4 turn). Bleed lifter down and check intake valves No. 2, No. 3 and No. 6, and exhaust valves No. 3, No. 7 and No. 8. Record measurement and compare it to specification. See 5.0L COLLAPSED VALVE LIFTER CLEARANCE table. If clearance is not within specification, use shorter or longer push rod to obtain correct clearance.

5.0L COLLAPSED VALVE LIFTER CLEARANCE

Application	In. (mm)
5.0L	
Allowable	.071-.193 (1.80-4.90)
Desired	.096-.165 (2.44-4.19)

5.8L VALVE CLEARANCE ADJUSTMENT

NOTE: Hydraulic valve lifters are used; no valve adjustment is required. If valve clearance is incorrect, use oversize or undersize push rod to obtain correct clearance.

1) Rotate crankshaft in normal operation direction until No. 1 cylinder is at TDC of compression stroke. Using Lifter Bleed Down Wrench (T71P-6513-B), apply pressure to No. 1 intake valve lifter until lifter is completely bottomed.
2) Hold valve lifter in this position while measuring clearance between valve lifter and valve stem. Record measurement. Repeat this procedure for intake valves No. 4 and No. 8, and exhaust valves No. 1, No. 3 and No. 7.
3) Rotate crankshaft 180 degrees (1/2 turn). Bleed lifter and check intake valves No. 3 and No. 7, and exhaust valves No. 2 and No. 6. Rotate crankshaft 270 degrees (3/4 turn). Bleed lifter down and check intake valves No. 2, No. 5 and No. 6, and exhaust valves No. 4, No. 5 and No. 8. Record measurement and compare it to specification. See 5.8L COLLAPSED VALVE LIFTER CLEARANCE table. If clearance is not within specification, use shorter or longer push rod to obtain correct clearance.

5.8L COLLAPSED VALVE LIFTER CLEARANCE

Application	In. (mm)
5.8L	
Allowable	.098-.198 (2.48-5.03)
Desired	.123-.173 (3.12-4.39)

7.3L (DIESEL) VALVE CLEARANCE ADJUSTMENT

NOTE: Hydraulic valve lifters are used; no valve adjustment is required. If incorrect valve clearance is suspected, lifter must be collapsed before clearance can be checked.

Position each piston at TDC of compression stroke so both valves are closed. Using Lifter Bleed Down Wrench (T83T-6500-A), bleed down lifters until lifter plunger bottoms. Check valve clearance. See 7.3L (DIESEL) COLLAPSED VALVE LIFTER SPECIFICATIONS table. If clearances are not correct, check valve train components for wear and damage. Replace as necessary.

7.3L (DIESEL) COLLAPSED VALVE LIFTER SPECIFICATIONS

Application	In. (mm)
All Valves	.185 (4.70)

7.5L VALVE CLEARANCE ADJUSTMENT

NOTE: Hydraulic valve lifters are used and no valve adjustment is required. If valve clearance is incorrect, use oversize or undersize push rod to obtain correct clearance.

1) Rotate crankshaft in normal operation direction until No. 1 cylinder is at TDC of compression stroke. Using Lifter Bleed Down Wrench (T71P-6513-B), apply pressure to No. 1 intake valve lifter until lifter is completely bottomed.
2) Hold valve lifter in this position while measuring clearance between lifter and valve stem. Record measurement. Repeat this procedure for intake valves No. 3, No. 7 and No. 8, and exhaust valves No. 1, No. 4, No. 5 and No. 8.
3) Rotate crankshaft 360 degrees (one turn). Bleed lifter and check intake valves No. 2, No. 4, No. 5 and No. 6, and exhaust valves No. 2, No. 3, No. 6 and No. 7. Record measurement and compare it to spec-

ification. See 7.5L COLLAPSED VALVE LIFTER CLEARANCE table. If clearance is not within specification, use shorter or longer push rod to obtain correct clearance.

7.5L COLLAPSED VALVE LIFTER CLEARANCE

Application	In. (mm)
7.5L	
Allowable	.075-.175 (1.91-4.45)
Desired	.100-.150 (2.54-4.81)

IGNITION TIMING

GASOLINE ENGINES

NOTE: Ignition timing on 2.3L with DIS and 4.0L with EDIS is not adjustable.

Initial Timing (TFI-IV) – 1) Place transmission in Park or Neutral. Ensure A/C and heater are off. Connect inductive timing light and tachometer to engine. With engine off, disconnect the single-wire in-line SPOUT (Yellow/Light Green wire near distributor) connector or remove shorting bar from the double-wire SPOUT connector. Start and warm engine to normal operating temperature.
2) With engine at idle speed, check/adjust initial timing to **10 degrees BTDC**. Turn engine off and reconnect the single-wire in-line SPOUT connector or reinstall shorting bar on double-wire SPOUT connector. Start engine and check timing advance to verify distributor is advancing beyond initial setting. Remove test equipment and reconnect all disconnected components.

7.3L DIESEL INJECTION TIMING

STATIC TIMING

1) Remove fast idle bracket and solenoid from injection pump. Using Pump Mounting Wrench (T83T-9000-B), loosen nuts holding injection pump to pump mounting adapter. Install Rotating Wrench (T83T-9000-C) on front of pump, and rotate to align timing mark on pump mounting flange with timing mark on pump mounting adapter. *See Fig. 1.*
2) Align timing marks to within .030". Remove rotating wrench and tighten nuts to **84 INCH lbs. (9.5 N.m)**. Ensure timing marks are aligned. Install fast idle bracket and solenoid.

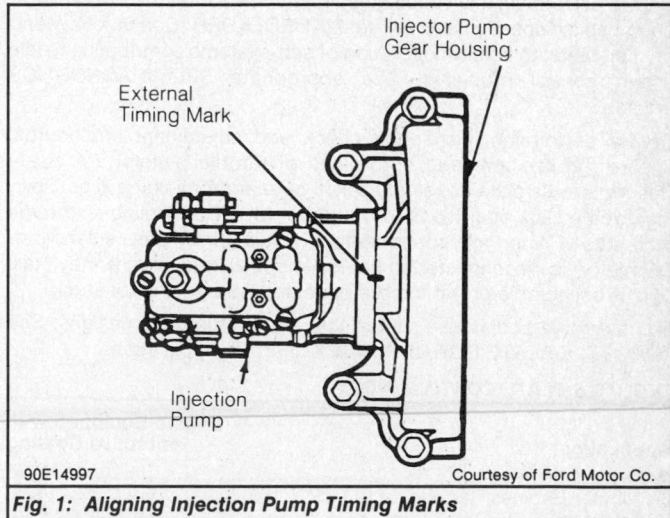

90E14997   Courtesy of Ford Motor Co.

Fig. 1: Aligning Injection Pump Timing Marks

DYNAMIC TIMING

NOTE: Engine must be at normal operating temperature of 192-212°F (89-100°C) when checking/setting dynamic timing.

1) Bring engine to normal operating temperature. Stop engine and install Dynamic Timing Meter (078-00200) into timing probe hole until it almost touches vibration damper. *See Fig. 2.*

2) Attach clamp from Timing Meter Adapter (078-00201) to line pressure sensor on No. 1 injector nozzle ("F" Series) or No. 4 injector nozzle ("E" Series), and connect to dynamic timing meter. Connect dynamic timing meter to battery and dial in minus 20 degrees offset on meter.

3) Disconnect cold start advance terminal connector from solenoid terminal. *See Fig. 3.* With transmission in Neutral and rear wheels raised, start engine. Using Throttle Control Tool (D83T-9000-E), set engine speed to 2000 RPM with no accessory load.

4) Observe injection timing on dynamic timing meter. Injection timing should be **8.5 degrees BTDC at 2000 RPM.** Apply battery voltage to cold start advance solenoid. Activating cold start advance solenoid terminal can increase engine speed. Adjust throttle if necessary.

5) Timing at 2000 RPM should be at least one degree before the timing obtained in first timing check. If advance is less than one degree, replace fuel injection pump top cover assembly. If dynamic timing is not within ±2 degrees of specification, adjust pump timing.

IDLE SPEED & MIXTURE

COLD (FAST) IDLE

Gasoline Engines – Fast idle speed is computer controlled. Adjustment procedures are not supplied by manufacturer.

7.3L Diesel – **1)** Connect tachometer. Place transmission in Neutral or Park. Start engine and bring to normal operating temperature. Disconnect fast idle solenoid from harness and apply battery voltage to activate solenoid.

2) Rev engine momentarily to set solenoid. Fast idle should be 800-850 RPM. Adjust by turning solenoid plunger. *See Fig. 3.* Recheck fast idle and adjust if necessary. Reconnect solenoid connector.

IDLE ADJUSTMENT PROCEDURES
(GASOLINE ENGINES)

Idle Adjustment Precautions – Idle speed, on all engines, is controlled by ECA and idle speed control air by-pass valve. If control system is operating properly, engine idle RPM is fixed and cannot be changed by standard adjustments. Many engines do not provide an RPM specification. A scan tester must be used on these systems because control strategy and idle speed specification is controlled by ECA.

Before performing idle speed adjustment procedure, complete a thorough basic inspection and self-test (KOEO, KOER, Continuous Memory self-tests) to confirm operation of sub-systems contributing to idle speed control problems. See appropriate SELF-DIAGNOSTICS article.

Before performing idle speed check and adjustment procedures, ensure throttle bore and both sides of throttle plate(s) are clean. Ensure throttle plate does not stick in bore and/or linkage is not limiting throttle plate operation. Throttle lever MUST be resting on throttle stop screw. When idle speed control device (air by-pass solenoid or DC motor) is disconnected to set minimum air rate, engine may stall. This is acceptable only if throttle plate and linkage are not stuck.

Some throttle bodies use sludge tolerant throttle plate designs. See THROTTLE PLATE COATING INDEX chart for application.

THROTTLE PLATE COATING INDEX [1]

Application	Engine Equipped with Protective Coating
4-Cylinder Engines	2.3L
6-Cylinder Engines	4.9L
V6 Engines	3.0L & [1] 4.0L
V8 Engines	5.0L, 5.8L & [1] 7.5L

[1] – Sludge tolerant throttle body introduced 1991 1/2.

These units must not be cleaned because a protective coating is applied to the lip of throttle plate(s). *See Fig. 4* for location of identification label.

Turn off all accessories before checking and adjusting idle speed. Ensure cooling system is filled to correct level. Ensure there are no vacuum leaks or unmetered air entering the throttle chamber on mass airflow design systems. If vehicle is equipped with electric cooling fan, check and adjust idle speed when fan is off.

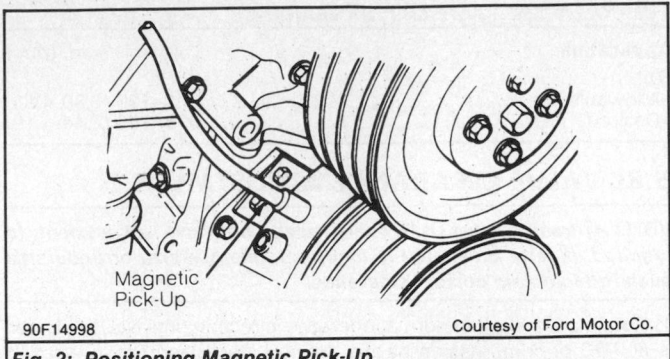

Magnetic Pick-Up

90F14998   Courtesy of Ford Motor Co.

Fig. 2: Positioning Magnetic Pick-Up

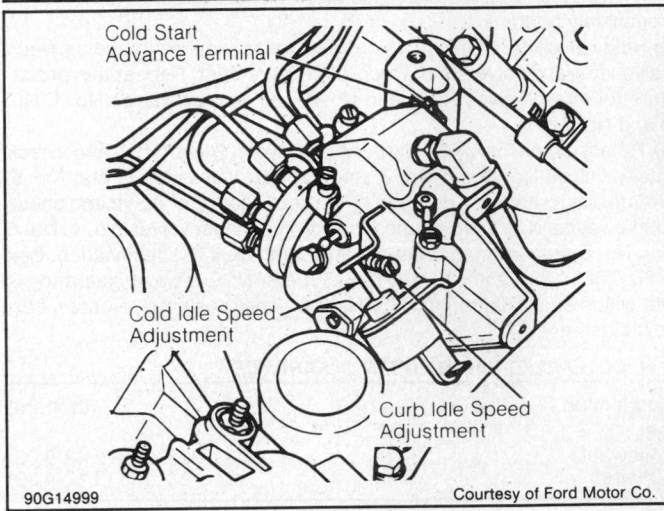

Cold Start Advance Terminal

Cold Idle Speed Adjustment

Curb Idle Speed Adjustment

90G14999   Courtesy of Ford Motor Co.

Fig. 3: Locating Idle Speed Adjusting Screw

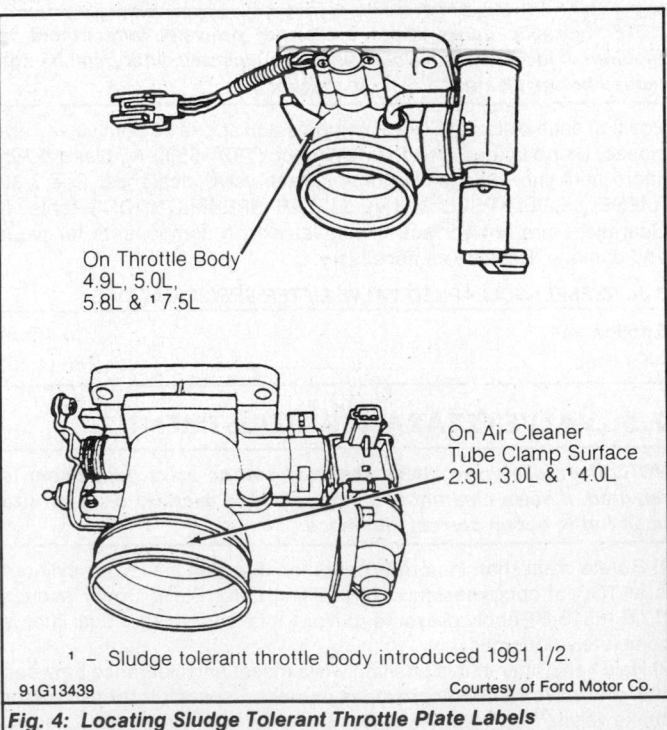

On Throttle Body
4.9L, 5.0L,
5.8L & [1] 7.5L

On Air Cleaner
Tube Clamp Surface
2.3L, 3.0L & [1] 4.0L

[1] – Sludge tolerant throttle body introduced 1991 1/2.

91G13439   Courtesy of Ford Motor Co.

Fig. 4: Locating Sludge Tolerant Throttle Plate Labels

2.3L OHC, 3.0L, 4.0L & 7.5L With Sludge Tolerant Throttle Body – 1) With engine off, disconnect negative battery cable for at least 5 minutes then reconnect it. Start engine and allow idle speed to stabilize for 2 minutes. Snap throttle open and return to idle. Lightly depress and release accelerator and allow engine to idle. If engine idles properly, idle speed adjustment is not required.

2) If engine does not idle properly, disconnect the SPOUT in-line connector and verify base ignition timing is correct (2.3L only). With ignition off, disconnect idle speed control air by-pass solenoid. Start engine and run at 2500 RPM for 30 seconds. Place A/T in Park (Neutral on M/T) and apply parking brake. Check idle speed. If idle speed is less than 475-575 RPM (2.3L), 550-675 RPM (3.0L), 555-725 RPM (4.0L) or 500-800 RPM (7.5L), go to next step. If idle speed is greater than specified, go to step **5)**.

3) If idle speed is too low, check throttle body for presence of throttle plate orifice plug. See Fig. 5. If there is no plug, turn idle adjusting screw CLOCKWISE only to adjust idle speed. If there is a plug from previous service, remove it and turn screw to obtain correct idle speed. After adjustment, idle adjusting screw MUST be in contact with throttle lever pad.

4) Turn engine off and disconnect battery for 5 minutes. Reconnect SPOUT in-line connector and ISC by-pass solenoid power lead. Move throttle plate to ensure it is not stuck in bore. Start engine and stabilize for 2 minutes. Snap throttle open and let it return to idle. With engine idling, lightly depress and release accelerator to exercise the ISC solenoid.

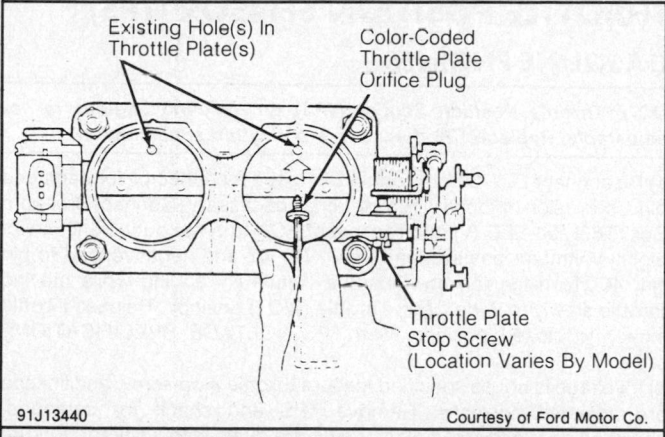

91J13440   Courtesy of Ford Motor Co.

Fig. 5: Locating Throttle Plate Orifices & Installing Plug

5) If idle speed is too high, turn ignition off. Disconnect air cleaner hose. Using tape, block off orifice in throttle plate. See Fig. 5. If orifice is already plugged, go to next step. On mass airflow engines, reconnect air cleaner hose. On all models, restart engine and check idle speed. If engine stalls, crack throttle plate open using throttle plate stop screw. See Fig. 6. If idle speed is still too high, go next step. If idle speed drops to specification, drops lower than specification, or engine stalls, go to step **7)**.

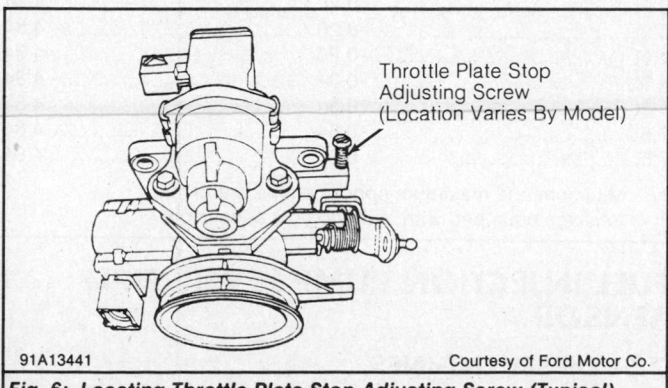

91A13441   Courtesy of Ford Motor Co.

Fig. 6: Locating Throttle Plate Stop Adjusting Screw (Typical)

6) Perform a KOEO self-test. Check for fault codes, especially TPS fault code. If fault codes are present, repair as necessary. See appropriate SELF-DIAGNOSTICS article. If TPS fault code is present, check for proper TPS output. See THROTTLE POSITION SENSOR (TPS). If no fault codes are present, remove tape. Exit this procedure and refer to TROUBLE SHOOTING – NO CODES article.

7) Turn ignition off. Remove air cleaner hose. Remove tape covering the throttle plate orifice. See Fig. 5. Select correct plug for the orifice. Plugs are available in Throttle Plate Plug Kit (FOPE-9F652-AA).

8) Reconnect air cleaner hose and start engine. Recheck idle speed. If idle speed is not within specification, turn adjusting screw CLOCKWISE to obtain correct idle speed. Turn ignition off. Connect SPOUT in-line connector (2.3L only) and ISC by-pass solenoid power lead.

9) Move throttle plate to ensure it is not stuck in bore and linkage is not keeping throttle from closing. Start engine and stabilize for 2 minutes. Snap throttle open and return to idle. With engine idling, lightly depress and release accelerator to exercise ISC solenoid. If idle problem is still present, refer to TROUBLE SHOOTING – NO CODES article to locate other possible causes of high idle.

2.9L, 4.0L & 7.5L Without Sludge Tolerant Throttle Body – 1) With engine off, disconnect negative battery cable for at least 5 minutes then reconnect it. Start engine and allow idle speed to stabilize for 2 minutes. Snap throttle open and return to idle. Lightly depress and release accelerator.

2) Allow engine to idle. Ensure electric cooling fan is off. If engine idle is okay, idle speed adjustment is not required. If engine does not idle properly, turn ignition off. Disconnect idle speed control air by-pass solenoid.

3) Place A/T in Park (Neutral on M/T). Start engine and run at 2500 RPM for 30 seconds. Apply parking brake. Check idle speed. If idle speed is not 600-725 RPM (2.9L), 550-725 RPM (4.0L) or 500-800 RPM (7.5L), turn throttle plate stop screw to obtain specification. See Fig. 6. Turn ignition off. Reconnect idle speed control air by-pass solenoid and recheck idle speed.

4) If idle speed is still not correct, perform a KOEO self-test. Check for fault codes, especially TPS fault code. If fault codes are present, repair as necessary. See appropriate SELF-DIAGNOSTICS article. If TPS fault code is present, check for proper TPS output. See THROTTLE POSITION SENSOR (TPS). If fault codes are not present, exit this procedure and refer to TROUBLE SHOOTING – NO CODES article.

5) Move throttle plate to ensure it is not stuck in bore and linkage is not keeping throttle from closing. Start engine and stabilize for 2 minutes. Snap throttle open and return to idle. With engine idling, lightly depress and release accelerator. If idle problem is still present, refer to TROUBLE SHOOTING – NO CODES article to locate other possible causes of high idle.

5.0L (Except E4OD) – 1) With engine off, disconnect negative battery cable for at least 5 minutes then reconnect it. Start engine and allow idle speed to stabilize for 2 minutes. Snap throttle open and return to idle. Lightly depress and release accelerator, and allow engine to idle. If engine idles properly, idle speed adjustment is not required.

2) If engine does not idle properly, turn engine off. Install a .050" (1.27 mm) feeler gauge (A/T) or .030" (.76 mm) feeler gauge (M/T) between throttle plate stop screw and throttle lever. Disconnect SPOUT in-line connector and verify base ignition timing is correct. With ignition off, disconnect idle speed control air by-pass solenoid. Start engine and allow to idle for 120 seconds. Place A/T in Park (Neutral on M/T) and apply parking brake. Check idle speed. If idle speed is less than 525-825 RPM (A/T) or 550-850 RPM (M/T), go to next step. If idle speed is greater than specified, go to step **5)**.

3) If idle speed is too low, check throttle body for presence of throttle plate orifice plug. See Fig. 5. If there is no plug, turn idle adjusting screw CLOCKWISE only to adjust idle speed. If there is a plug from previous service, remove it and turn screw to obtain correct idle speed. After adjustment, idle adjusting screw MUST be in contact with lever pad.

4) Turn engine off and disconnect battery for 5 minutes. Reconnect SPOUT in-line connector and ISC by-pass solenoid power lead. Move throttle plate to ensure it is not stuck in bore. Start engine and stabilize for 2 minutes. Snap throttle open and let it return to idle. With engine idling, lightly depress and release accelerator to activate the ISC solenoid.

5) If idle speed is too high, turn ignition off. Disconnect air cleaner hose. Using tape, block off orifice in throttle plate. *See Fig. 5.* If orifice is already plugged, go to next step. On mass airflow engines, reconnect air cleaner hose. On all models, restart engine and check idle speed. If engine stalls, crack throttle plate open using throttle plate stop screw. *See Fig. 6.* If idle speed is still too high, go to next step. If idle speed drops to specification, drops lower than specification, or engine stalls, go to step **7)**.

6) Perform a KOEO self-test. Check for fault codes, especially TPS fault code. If fault codes are present, repair as necessary. See appropriate SELF-DIAGNOSTICS article. If TPS fault code is present, check for proper TPS output. See THROTTLE POSITION SENSOR (TPS). If fault codes are not present, remove tape. Exit this procedure and refer to TROUBLE SHOOTING – NO CODES article.

7) Turn ignition off. Remove air cleaner hose. Remove tape covering throttle plate orifice. *See Fig. 5.* Select correct plug for orifice. Plugs are available in Throttle Plate Plug Kit (FOPE-9F652-AA).

8) Reconnect air cleaner hose, remove feeler gauge and start engine. Recheck idle speed. If idle speed is not within specification, turn adjusting screw CLOCKWISE to obtain correct idle speed. Turn ignition off. Connect SPOUT in-line connector and ISC by-pass solenoid power lead.

9) Move throttle plate to ensure it is not stuck in bore and linkage is not keeping throttle from closing. Start engine and stabilize for 2 minutes. Snap throttle open and return to idle. With engine idling, lightly depress and release accelerator to activate ISC solenoid. If idle problem is still present, refer to TROUBLE SHOOTING – NO CODES article to locate other possible causes of high idle.

10) On vehicles equipped with AOD transmission, check throttle valve pressure adjustment.

NOTE: Engine RPM oscillations may occur if throttle plate is open far enough to expose canister purge port. To verify, disconnect and plug purge port on throttle body. If problem no longer exists, close throttle plate just enough to eliminate oscillations.

4.9L, 5.0L (With E4OD) & 5.8L – **1)** Connect scan tester to diagnostic connector. Enter KOER self-test. A single-pulse tone indicates entry mode has been successfully entered. Observe scan tester read-out.

2) If a constant tone, solid light or STO LO is displayed, base idle speed is within range and adjustment is not necessary. Exit self-test.

3) If a beeping tone, flashing light or STO LO at 8 Hz is displayed, TPS is out of range and adjustment may be required. Perform adjustment and repeat test.

4) If a beeping tone, flashing light or STO LO at 4 Hz is displayed, base idle speed is too high. Go to step **8)**.

5) If a beeping tone, flashing light or STO LO at one Hz is displayed, base idle speed is too low. Go to next step.

6) DO NOT clean throttle bore. Check throttle plate for presence of throttle plate orifice plug. *See Fig. 5.* If there is no plug, turn idle adjusting screw CLOCKWISE only to adjust idle speed until conditions in step **2)** are obtained. If there is a plug from previous service, remove plug and turn screw to obtain conditions in step **2)**. After adjustment, screw MUST be in contact with throttle lever pad.

7) Perform a KOEO Self-Test to ensure TPS fault code is not present. Move throttle plate to ensure it is not stuck in bore and linkage is not keeping throttle from closing. On models with automatic overdrive transmissions, check throttle valve adjustment.

8) If idle speed is too high, turn engine off. Using tape, block off orifice in throttle plate. *See Fig. 5.*

9) If orifice is already plugged, go to next step. On mass airflow engines, reconnect air cleaner hose. On all models, restart engine and check idle speed. If engine stalls, crack throttle plate open using throttle plate stop screw. If idle speed is still too high, go to next step. If idle speed drops to specification or drops lower than specification, go to step **11)**

10) Perform KOEO self-test. If fault codes are present, repair as necessary. See appropriate SELF-DIAGNOSTICS article. If TPS fault

code is present, check for proper TPS output. See THROTTLE POSITION SENSOR (TPS). Ensure adjustment screw is in contact with lever pad. If fault codes are not present, see TROUBLE SHOOTING – NO CODES article.

11) Turn ignition off. Remove air cleaner hose and remove tape covering throttle plate orifice. Select correct color plug for orifice. Plugs are available in Throttle Plate Plug Kit (FOPE-9F652-AA).

12) Reconnect air cleaner hose and start engine. Recheck idle speed. If idle speed is not within specification, turn adjusting screw CLOCKWISE to obtain correct idle speed. After adjustment, screw MUST be in contact with throttle lever pad.

13) On all models, perform a KOEO self-test to ensure TPS fault code is not present. Move throttle plate to ensure it is not stuck in bore and linkage is not keeping throttle from closing. On models with automatic overdrive transmissions, check throttle valve pressure adjustment.

IDLE ADJUSTMENT PROCEDURES (DIESEL ENGINES)

1) Place transmission in Neutral or Park and bring engine up to normal operating temperature. Check idle speed with transmission in Neutral (M/T) or Drive (A/T). Ensure curb idle adjustment screw is against the stop. If adjustment screw is not against the stop, correct linkage.

2) Connect tachometer and check curb idle speed. Idle speed should be 600-700 RPM. Adjust idle speed using curb idle speed adjustment screw. *See Fig. 3.* Repeat check, and adjust again if necessary.

THROTTLE POSITION SENSOR (TPS)

GASOLINE ENGINES

NOTE: Throttle Position Sensor (TPS) on gasoline engines is not adjustable. Replace TPS if sensor is not within specification.

1) Disconnect ECA 60-pin connector. Inspect connector for damaged pins, corrosion or loose wires; repair as necessary. Connect Breakout Box (T83L-50-EEC-IV) and reconnect ECA to breakout box. Connect digital voltmeter positive lead to pin No. 47 and negative lead to pin No. 46. Turn ignition on. Observe voltmeter reading while moving throttle slowly to Wide Open Throttle (WOT) position. Release throttle slowly to closed position. See TPS VOLTAGE SPECIFICATIONS table.

2) If voltage is not as specified, ensure throttle stop screw and linkage are adjusted correctly. Remove TPS and check for damaged, corroded or misadjusted pins. If pins are okay, install sensor. Ensure sensor is seated correctly. Repeat step **1)**. If voltage is not as specified, perform KOEO self-test. See appropriate SELF-DIAGNOSTICS article.

TPS VOLTAGE SPECIFICATIONS [1]

Application	Idle	Wide Open Throttle
2.3L	0.20	4.84
2.9L	0.34	4.84
2.9L [2]	0.20	4.84
3.0L	0.20	4.84
4.0L	0.20	4.84
4.9L	0.34	4.84
5.0L	0.34	4.84
5.8L	0.34	4.84
7.5L	0.34	4.84

[1] – Minimum and maximum specifications are given.
[2] – Vehicles equipped with mass airflow sensor only.

FUEL INJECTION PUMP LEVER (FIPL) SENSOR

7.3L DIESEL ENGINES

1) Install scan tester and enter Key On Engine Off (KOEO) self-test while holding throttle in Wide Open Throttle (WOT) position. After last

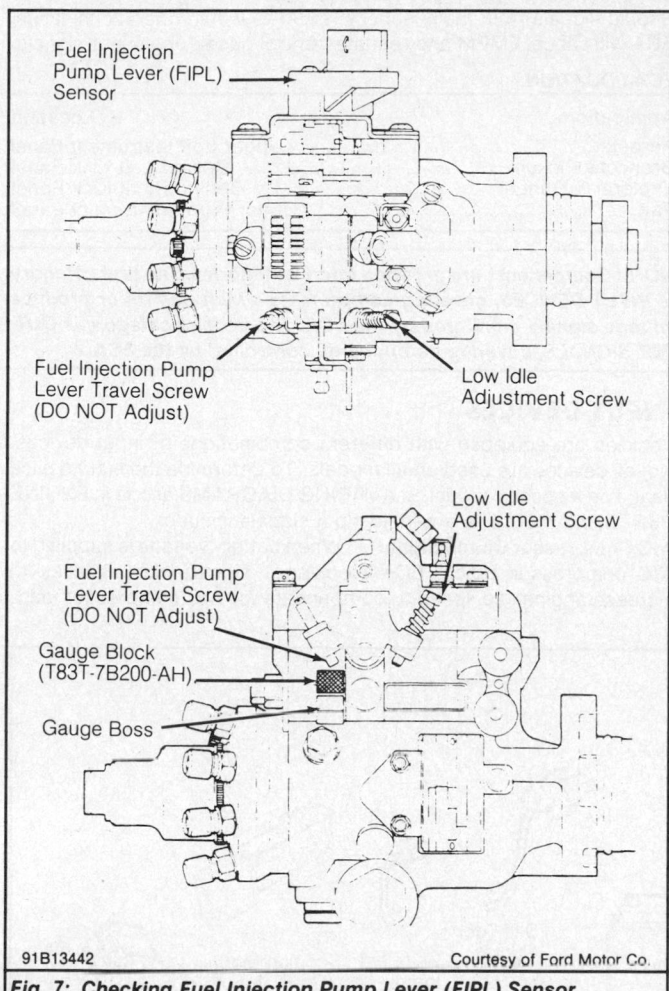

Fuel Injection
Pump Lever (FIPL)
Sensor

Fuel Injection Pump
Lever Travel Screw
(DO NOT Adjust)

Low Idle
Adjustment Screw

Low Idle
Adjustment Screw

Fuel Injection Pump
Lever Travel Screw
(DO NOT Adjust)

Gauge Block
(T83T-7B200-AH)

Gauge Boss

91B13442   Courtesy of Ford Motor Co.

Fig. 7: Checking Fuel Injection Pump Lever (FIPL) Sensor

service code has been displayed, remain in self-test. Place a **0.515"** **(13.08 mm)** Gauge Block (T83T-7B200-AH) between fuel pump lever travel screw and gauge boss. *See Fig. 7.*

2) Cycle Overdrive Cancel Switch (OCS) once. Observe Self-Test Output (STO) on scan tester for the following conditions:

- Constant tone, solid light, or STO LO readout indicates throttle position sensor is within range. Cycle OCS to exit test.
- Fast beeping tone, flashing light, or STO LO erratic readout (4 per second) indicates throttle position sensor requires adjustment.
- Slow beeping tone, flashing light, or STO LO erratic readout (one per second) indicates throttle position sensor requires adjustment.
- No tone, solid light, or STO LO readout indicates throttle position sensor may have worn internal components. Check by trying to move sensor.

3) If FIPL sensor and bracket screws are tight and there are no signs of wear between mounted parts, loosen FIPL sensor attachment screws. *See Fig. 8.* Rotate sensor one way or the other until a constant tone, solid light, or STO LO readout is obtained. Tighten FIPL sensor attachment screws. Remove gauge block. Cycle throttle lever to WOT 5 times. Reinsert gauge block to verify setting.

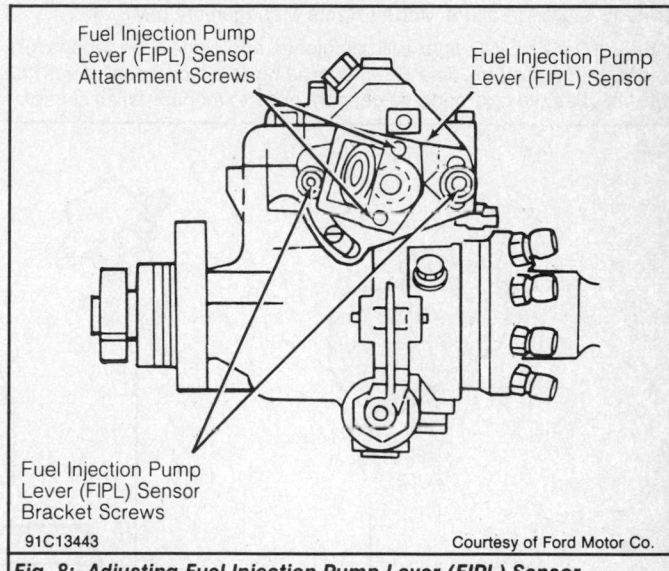

Fuel Injection Pump
Lever (FIPL) Sensor
Attachment Screws

Fuel Injection Pump
Lever (FIPL) Sensor

Fuel Injection Pump
Lever (FIPL) Sensor
Bracket Screws

91C13443   Courtesy of Ford Motor Co.

Fig. 8: Adjusting Fuel Injection Pump Lever (FIPL) Sensor

1992 ENGINE PERFORMANCE
Theory & Operation

Aerostar, Bronco, Explorer, Pickup, Ranger, Van

NOTE: *Unless otherwise specified, references to Pickup include the F350 Super Duty commercial chassis.*

INTRODUCTION

This article covers basic description and operation of engine performance-related systems and components. Read this article before diagnosing vehicles or systems with which you are not completely familiar.

COMPUTERIZED ENGINE CONTROLS

ELECTRONIC CONTROL ASSEMBLY (ECA)

During system operation, ECA transmits electrical reference signals to engine sensors and analyzes return signals to determine engine operating conditions. *See Fig. 1.* If a sensor or actuator fails, ECA initiates an alternative strategy, allowing vehicle to maintain driveability. This strategy is called Failure Mode Effects Management (FMEM).

The CHECK ENGINE light will illuminate and remain on whenever FMEM is in operation. The ECA, overriding failed component with a FMEM substitute operation value, continues to monitor failed sensor.

Should signals from faulty sensor return to within operational limits, ECA will cancel FMEM and resume control based on sensor signals.

ECA LOCATION

Application	Location
Aerostar	Under Left Instrument Panel
Bronco & Pickup	Behind Left Kick Panel
Explorer & Ranger	Behind Right Kick Panel
Van	Under Right Instrument Panel

NOTE: *Components are grouped into 2 categories. The first category is INPUT DEVICES, covering components which control or produce voltage signals monitored by the ECA. The second category is OUTPUT SIGNALS, covering components controlled by the ECA.*

INPUT DEVICES

Vehicles are equipped with different combinations of input devices. Not all devices are used on all models. To determine the input device usage on a specific model, see WIRING DIAGRAMS article in ENGINE PERFORMANCE. The available input signals include:

A/C Compressor Clutch Signal – When battery voltage is supplied to A/C compressor clutch, ECA receives a signal, which it uses to increase engine idle speed to compensate for A/C compressor load.

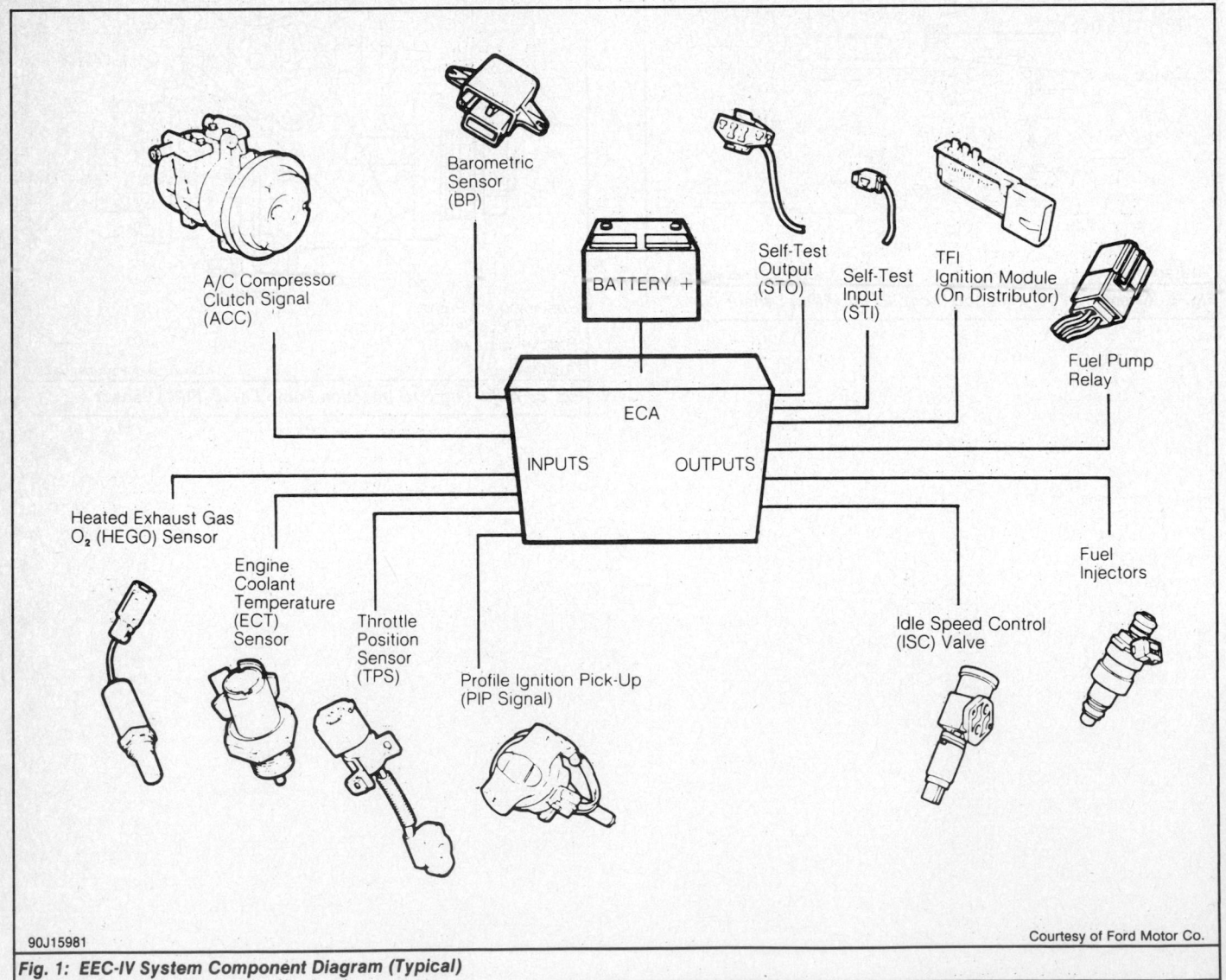

A/C Compressor Clutch Signal (ACC)

Barometric Sensor (BP)

BATTERY +

Self-Test Output (STO)

Self-Test Input (STI)

TFI Ignition Module (On Distributor)

Fuel Pump Relay

ECA

INPUTS   OUTPUTS

Heated Exhaust Gas O₂ (HEGO) Sensor

Engine Coolant Temperature (ECT) Sensor

Throttle Position Sensor (TPS)

Profile Ignition Pick-Up (PIP Signal)

Idle Speed Control (ISC) Valve

Fuel Injectors

90J15981

Courtesy of Ford Motor Co.

Fig. 1: EEC-IV System Component Diagram (Typical)

Air Charge Temperature (ACT) Sensor – Threaded into a cylinder runner of intake manifold, the ACT sensor provides electronic fuel injection system with mixture temperature information. The ACT sensor is used both as a density corrector for airflow calculation and to proportion cold enrichment fuel flow.

Barometric Pressure (BP) Sensor – BP sensor measures barometric pressure of atmosphere. Variations in atmospheric pressure (changes in altitude) modify an electrical signal monitored by ECA. The BP sensor input affects spark advance, EGR flow and air/fuel mixture adjustments by ECA. Sensor input is updated during key-on and wide open throttle applications. The sensor looks identical to Manifold Absolute Pressure (MAP) sensor, except tubing nipple on BP sensor is open to atmosphere, while tubing nipple on MAP sensor is connected to intake manifold.

Brake On-Off (BOO) Switch – The BOO switch is mounted on brake pedal. It signals deceleration for air/fuel ratio adjustment.

Clutch Engage Switch – This switch is mounted at clutch pedal and signals ECA when transmission is in gear. Clutch engage switch signal to ECA affects air/fuel ratio and idle speed.

Coolant Temperature Sensor – See ENGINE COOLANT TEMPERATURE (ECT) SENSOR.

Crankshaft Sensor – A dual Hall Effect crankshaft sensor, mounted at crankshaft pulley, is used on 2.3L dual-plug Distributorless Ignition System (DIS). Sensor signals are generated when 2 trigger wheels, mounted on pulley assembly, pass through air gap of 2 Hall Effect switches. One switch produces a Profile Ignition Pick-up (PIP) signal, monitored by DIS ignition module to provide RPM signal to ECA. The second switch produces Cylinder Identification (CID) signal, used by DIS ignition module to identify which coil pack to trigger. If CID signal is not present, vehicle will be hard to start.

EGR Valve Position (EVP) Sensor – Mounted on EGR valve, EVP sensor detects EGR valve position and transmits this information to ECA. The EVP signal affects EGR flow and ignition timing.

Engine Coolant Temperature (ECT) Sensor – Threaded into an engine coolant passage near thermostat housing, ECT sensor inputs coolant temperature to ECA. The signal from ECT affects air/fuel ratio, idle speed, EGR flow, purge flow, fuel pressure, boost pressure (turbo engine) and ignition timing output signal from ECA.

Fuel Injection Pump Lever (FIPL) Sensor – The FIPL sensor is used on 7.3L vehicles with E40D automatic transmission. FIPL is mounted to fuel injection pump and actuated by throttle lever. FIPL transmits a signal, proportional to level of fuel delivery, to the Transmission Electronic Control Assembly (TECA) for assisting in transmission shift and torque capacity.

If FIPL circuit malfunctions, TECA will recognize erroneous signals and provide high capacity operating mode to protect transmission from damage. High capacity operating mode includes singular shift schedule at maximum throttle valve pressure, resulting in harsh shifting.

Heated Exhaust Gas Oxygen (HEGO) Sensor – The O₂ sensor is mounted in exhaust manifold. When at operating temperature, the O₂ sensor monitors oxygen content of exhaust gases. A heating circuit is used to warm O₂ sensor to operating temperature, enabling faster conversion of feedback system to closed loop operation.

The O₂ sensor produces low voltage (less than .4 volt) to indicate a lean mixture (high amount of oxygen) and a high voltage (more than .6 volt) to indicate a rich mixture (low amount of oxygen). This voltage signal is transmitted to ECA.

Manifold Absolute Pressure (MAP) Sensor – Manifold pressure and temperature are used by the ECA to calculate the airflow rate. The MAP sensor responds to manifold vacuum changes due to engine load and speed changes.

The MAP sensor uses frequency to measure manifold vacuum. The MAP sensor is used as a barometric sensor for altitude compensation, updating the ECA during Key On, Engine Off (KOEO) and at Wide Open Throttle (WOT). By monitoring MAP sensor output voltage, the ECA can determine correct rate of spark advance, EGR flow and air/fuel ratio. If MAP sensor fails, the ECA will supply a fixed MAP value and use the Throttle Position Sensor (TPS) to control fuel distribution.

Mass Airflow (MAF) Sensor – MAF sensor measures flow of air entering the engine. This measurement of airflow is a reflection of engine load (throttle opening). The sensing element (hot wire) is a thin platinum wire wound on a ceramic bobbin and coated with glass. The hot wire is maintained at **392°F (200°C)** above cold wire (ambient) temperature. Cold wire is located downstream of hot wire. As air passes through the airflow sensor, the air temperature is measured as air passes over the cold wire sensor. The ECA uses this information to control fuel delivery.

Neutral Gear Switch (NGS) – The NGS monitors in-gear conditions and signals ECA. This signal affects air/fuel ratio, idle speed and ignition timing.

Neutral Safety Switch (NSS) – Mounted on side of transmission, this switch monitors gear position on automatic transmission vehicles. The signal affects air/fuel ratio, idle speed and EGR flow.

Power Steering (P/S) Pressure Switch – The P/S pressure switch monitors power steering pressure, signaling ECA to adjust engine idle speed under load conditions. The switch is located in high pressure line from P/S pump to steering rack assembly.

Profile Ignition Pick-Up (PIP) – On 2.3L DIS ignition systems, modulated PIP and CID signals are produced by dual Hall Effect crankshaft sensor and monitored by DIS ignition module. See CRANKSHAFT SENSOR under INPUT DEVICES. Ignition module relays the PIP signal to ECA, which uses it as an RPM reference to determine timing adjustments.

ECA timing control returns to ignition module in form of a Spark Output (SPOUT) signal. The leading edge of SPOUT signal fires coil, and trailing edge controls dwell on-time.

On 4.0L EDIS ignition systems, PIP signal is generated by Variable Reluctance Sensor (VRS), located near crankshaft pulley. The VRS is a Permanent Magnet (PM) generator, which produces an AC voltage signal which increases with RPM. The EDIS ignition module monitors this signal, passes this information on to ECA and modifies coil triggering signal based upon a Spark Angle Word (SAW) signal sent from ECA.

On distributor-type ignition systems, PIP signal is provided by a 12-volt reference from ignition module to Hall Effect switch, inside distributor. This reference voltage is modulated by window/shutter Hall Effect switch. Monitored reference is pulled low when shutter blade is out of Hall Effect switch window.

When shutter blade enters window, 12-volt reference returns, and TFI ignition module sends PIP signal to ECA. ECA uses the PIP signal as an RPM reference to calculate timing adjustments. ECA timing control returns to ignition module in form of a Spark Output (SPOUT) signal.

Self-Test Output/Self-Test Input (STO/STI) Connectors – The STO connector is a 6-pin connector used to perform self-test diagnostic procedure. The STI is a single-pin connector, located next to STO. When STI is grounded, it activates fault code output function. Codes are retrieved through STO connector.

Throttle Position Sensor (TPS) – Mounted on throttle body at throttle plate rod, TPS monitors throttle plate opening. The TPS signal to ECA is proportional to throttle opening angle. The TPS signal affects air/fuel ratio, injector timing, idle speed, EGR flow and fuel pressure. If TPS system malfunctions, Code 12 will be set in ECA memory.

Variable Reluctance Sensor (VRS) – The VRS is used on 4.0L Electronic Distributorless Ignition System (EDIS). The VRS transmits crankshaft position and RPM information. It is a passive electromagnetic device, which senses movement of a 35-tooth wheel (with a gap at 60 degrees BTDC, where the 36th tooth would have been, for triggering). The VRS is located behind crankshaft pulley.

An AC voltage signal, generated by VRS, increases with engine RPM and provides basic spark timing information to EDIS ignition module. Ignition module uses this input to produce a PIP signal to ECA. The ECA responds with a Spark Angle Word (SAW) signal, which, along with VRS signal, is used by ignition module to compute basic spark timing and to determine which coil pack to trigger.

Vehicle Speed Sensor (VSS) – The transmission-mounted VSS sends a pulsing signal to ECA when vehicle is moving. The VSS generates pulses with axle shaft revolution. The ECA interprets speed sensor input along with TPS closed throttle input.

This input enables ECA to differentiate between closed throttle deceleration and closed throttle idle (vehicle stopped) conditions. During deceleration, ECA controls Idle Speed Control (ISC) Valve to maintain a desired manifold pressure. During idle, ECA controls ISC motor to maintain a desired idle speed.

OUTPUT SIGNALS

NOTE: Vehicles are equipped with different combinations of computer-controlled components. Not all components listed below are used on every vehicle. For theory and operation on components, refer to indicated system.

A/C Clutch Cycling Switch – See MISCELLANEOUS CONTROLS.
Canister Purge Solenoid Valve – See EMISSION SYSTEMS.
CHECK ENGINE Light – See SELF-DIAGNOSTIC SYSTEM.
Cooling Fan – See MISCELLANEOUS CONTROLS.
EGR System – See EMISSION SYSTEMS.
Fuel Injectors – See FUEL SYSTEMS.
Fuel Pump – See FUEL SYSTEMS.
Fuel Pressure Regulator – See FUEL SYSTEMS.
Idle Speed Control (ISC) Valve – See FUEL SYSTEMS.
Self-Diagnostic – See SELF-DIAGNOSTIC SYSTEM.
Self-Test Output/Self-Test Input Connectors – See SELF-DIAGNOSTIC SYSTEM.
Wide Open Throttle Cutoff – See MISCELLANEOUS CONTROLS.

FUEL SYSTEMS

FUEL DELIVERY

System Types – Fuel delivery systems differ in design depending upon model. System designs use one of the following configurations:
- Single tank with single pump.
- Single tank with dual pump.
- Dual tank with mechanical selector valve/reservoir.

Low Pressure Fuel Pump – All vehicles are equipped with a high pressure pump, but some vehicles use multiple pump systems. These systems have a primary, low pressure in-tank pump for supplying fuel to reservoir. The low pressure pump rests in a sump (depression) in fuel tank. A nylon screen protects low pressure pump inlet from contaminating particles, but allows passage of small amounts of water which may accumulate in fuel tank sump.

When dual tanks are used, each tank is equipped with a low pressure pump. Such a system has a total of 3 pumps: 2 low pressure and one high pressure.

High Pressure Fuel Pump – The high pressure fuel pump is positioned inside fuel tank. A reservoir is built onto pump and sender assembly, instead of as part of tank.

In a 2-tank system, sender assembly handles switching of high pressure fuel through internal valves. Should one tank overfill during use (return line returns fuel to wrong tank), pump and sender unit in overfilling tank need replacement.

The high pressure fuel pump is capable of pumping over 33 gallons (125 liters) of fuel per hour at a working pressure of **39.2 psi (2.75 kg/cm²)**. This pump also has internal pressure relief and discharge check valves.

Mechanical Fuel Pump – The 7.3L diesel engine uses a mechanical fuel pump to pump fuel from fuel tank to a combination fuel filter/fuel heater/water separator.

Mechanical Selector Valve – A driver-operated selector switch controls selector valve for switching fuel supply from one tank to other. The mechanical selector valve is contained within 6-port reservoir assembly. This valve switches fuel supply and return lines from one tank to other in response to fuel pressure from in-tank pumps acting on its actuating diaphragm.

The diaphragm switches tank connection when less than 2 psi of fuel pressure is acting on upper side of front tank and lower side of rear

tank. Valve functioning depends upon proper operation of in-tank low pressure pumps. In all dual tank vehicles, excess fuel not used by engine is returned to same tank from which it was pumped.

Reservoirs & Filters – Fuel reservoirs are used to prevent fuel flow interruptions during extreme vehicle maneuvers with low tank fill levels. Models using multiple pumps use in-line reservoirs, frame mounted between low and high pressure pumps. On models using one pump, reservoir is either molded or welded into either tank or fuel pump and sender plastic housing.

There are 2 types of in-line reservoirs: single function and dual function. Both contain a fine mesh in-filter; the dual function contains a mechanical selector valve.

Fuel Supply Manifold Assembly – Fuel supply manifold assembly (fuel rail) delivers high pressure fuel from fuel pump supply line to fuel injectors. Fuel rail consists of tubular rail or stamping with injector connectors. Fuel pressure regulator is mounted on flange attached to rail. Rail also has mounting attachments which secure fuel injectors in intake manifold.

Fuel Pressure Regulator – The fuel pressure regulator is attached to fuel supply manifold assembly, downstream of fuel injectors. It regulates fuel pressure supplied to injectors. Regulator is a diaphragm-operated valve with one side responding to fuel pressure and the other side to intake manifold vacuum.

When intake manifold vacuum is low, an internal spring increases pressure on diaphragm, blocking off fuel return passage and increasing fuel pressure. When manifold pressure is high, spring pressure is overcome by vacuum, opening fuel return passage and lowering fuel pressure. Excess fuel is by-passed through regulator and returned to fuel tank.

The regulator also controls fuel line vapor formation, allowing for rapid restarts, assistance in engine idle stabilization and maintenance of fuel pressure when engine is turned off. Pressure is adjusted at factory to compensate for fuel flow differences between injectors.

Fuel Pump Actuation – When ignition switch is turned to START position, ECA operates fuel pump relay to provide fuel for starting engine. ECA senses engine speed and shuts off fuel pump by opening ground circuit to fuel pump relay when engine stops or speed drops to less than 120 RPM. When ignition switch is in ON position, EEC power relay is energized (contacts closed). Power is provided to fuel pump relay and timer in ECA. Fuel pump receives power through fuel pump relay contacts.

Fuel Pump Shutoff (Inertia) Switch – All models use an electrical interrupt switch in fuel system. During a collision or vehicle roll-over, electrical contacts within inertia switch open, shutting off fuel supply to electric fuel pump. Fuel supply is interrupted even when engine is running.

A reset button is located on switch assembly. If electrical circuit trips, vehicle will not re-start until switch is reset. Fuel system should be inspected before resetting switch.

On Aerostar, inertia switch is located in right kick panel. On Van, inertia switch is located on right cowl panel, near front of door. On Bronco and Pickup, inertia switch is located on left toe board, near parking brake assembly. On Ranger and Explorer, inertia switch is located on toe board, near right side of transmission hump.

NOTE: DO NOT reset fuel pump shutoff (inertia) switch after an accident until inspecting entire fuel system for leaks.

FUEL CONTROL (GASOLINE ENGINES)

Precise fuel metering is accomplished with EEC-IV system. The ECA continually monitors engine operating conditions based on information received from various sensors and switches. In response to information received, ECA calculates optimum air/fuel mixture in relation to present engine operating conditions and affects required metering adjustments through output actuators control.

Fuel Injection – The ECA controls fuel injectors to meter pulse width or time each injector is energized. Each injector receives battery voltage through ignition switch circuit. The ECA-controlled ground circuit completes circuit to energize injector. The ECA receives inputs from engine sensors to compute fuel flow necessary to maintain air/fuel mixture ratio throughout entire engine operational range.

Each cylinder has a solenoid-operated injector which sprays fuel toward back of each intake valve. Injector bodies consist of solenoid-actuated pintle and needle valve assembly. Injector flow orifice is fixed, and fuel pressure at injector tip is constant. Atomizing spray is obtained by shape of pintle.

Throttle Body Assembly – The throttle body assembly controls airflow to engine through a butterfly valve. Throttle position is controlled by either linkage or cable/cam mechanism. Body is one-piece aluminum casting with single bore and air by-pass channel.

FUEL CONTROL (7.3L DIESEL)

The fuel pump delivers fuel from fuel tank to the fuel filter. After being filtered, fuel enters the injection pump and is delivered under high pressure through injection nozzles into cylinders. Injectors are equipped with a fuel return outlet. Excess fuel collected at the injectors and injector pump are recirculated back to the fuel tank.

IDLE SPEED (GASOLINE ENGINES)

Idle Speed Control (ISC) Valve – The ISC valve, mounted on the throttle body, controls idle smoothness by regulating throttle plate by-pass air. ISC valve consists of an air by-pass valve, which functions during cold engine conditions below **122°F (50°C)**, and the idle speed control solenoid valve, which works throughout the entire temperature range. The air by-pass valve is affected by the engine coolant temperature. The idle speed control solenoid is controlled by ECA.

Idle is controlled by idle speed control air by-pass valve. The throttle air by-pass valve is a solenoid-operated valve controlled by ECA. The valve allows air to by-pass throttle plates to control cold engine fast idle, no-touch start, dashpot, overtemperature idle boost and engine load idle correction.

Air by-pass channel carries idle airflow regulated by air by-pass valve. Air by-pass valve is controlled by ECA to adjust both cold and warm idle speeds. Air by-pass valve uses solenoid valve to vary idle airflow volume allowed to enter engine.

IDLE SPEED (7.3L DIESEL)

Idle is controlled by curb idle speed adjustment screw, located on injection pump. Fast (cold) idle is controlled by cold idle solenoid, located by curb idle speed adjustment screw. For additional information, see ON-VEHICLE ADJUSTMENTS article.

IGNITION SYSTEMS

Distributorless Ignition System (DIS) – The DIS system, used on 4-cylinder engines, is a dual plug system consisting of a crankshaft-mounted dual Hall Effect sensor, two 4-tower DIS coil packs and a DIS ignition module.

The DIS eliminates distributor by using multiple coils, each of which simultaneously fires 2 paired spark plugs. The first time a pair of spark plugs is fired, one fires during compression stroke and other during exhaust stroke. The next time same pair of spark plugs is fired, the roles are reversed. Although spark in exhaust stroke is wasted, little of coil's energy is lost.

Two ignition coils are mounted together in a coil pack. Since there are 2 plugs per cylinder, 2 coil packs are required. The right coil pack operates continuously, whereas left coil pack may be switched on or off by ECA.

The ECA computes spark angle and dwell for ignition system. The crankshaft-mounted dual Hall Effect sensor is a dual digital output device, which responds to 2 rotating metallic shutters mounted on crankshaft. One output from hall effect sensor, Profile Ignition Pick-Up (PIP), is a 50 percent duty cycle signal, providing base spark timing information. The other output signal, Cylinder Identification (CID) signal, is required for DIS module to know which coil to fire. CID is high (battery voltage) for half of crankshaft revolution (180 degrees) and low (zero volts) for other half of revolution.

The ECA determines Spark Output (SPOUT) by using PIP signal to establish base timing. The SPOUT signal is produced and sent by ECA to DIS module and serves 2 purposes: the leading edge of signal fires coil, and trailing edge of signal controls dwell on-time. This feature is called Computer Controlled Dwell (CCD).

Another feature of system is Ignition Diagnostic Monitor (IDM). This is an output from DIS module to ECA which provides diagnostic information about ignition system for self-test.

Dual Plug Inhibit (DPI), another system feature, allows ECA processor to switch ignition system from single-to-dual plug operation. During cranking, vehicle is in single plug mode: only plugs on right side of engine fire. When engine starts, ECA sends a command to DIS module to switch to dual plug operation.

If CID circuit fails, DIS module will randomly select one of 2 coils to fire. If hard starting results, turning key off and then cranking again will result in another random selection. Several attempts may be needed before DIS module selects proper coil, which will allow vehicle to start and be driven until repairs can be made.

The Failure Mode Effects Management (FMEM) system will keep vehicle drivable in event of an EEC-IV system or ignition failure, which would otherwise prevent spark angle or dwell commands. During FMEM, ECA opens SPOUT line and DIS module fires coils directly from PIP output. This results in a fixed spark angle of 10 degrees and a fixed dwell.

Electronic Distributorless Ignition System (EDIS) – System is used on 4.0L engines and consists of a Variable Reluctance Sensor (VRS), an EDIS ignition module, an ECA and one 6-tower coil pack.

During system operation, EDIS ignition module receives crankshaft position information from VRS. In turn, EDIS ignition module generates a Profile Ignition Pick-Up (PIP) signal and sends it to ECA. The ECA responds with a Spark Angle Word (SAW) signal containing advance or retard timing information, which it sends to EDIS module. The EDIS ignition module then processes VRS and SAW signals to decide which coils to fire. In addition, EDIS ignition module generates an Ignition Diagnostic Monitor (IDM) signal and sends it to ECA, which uses it during failure mode to provide a tach output signal.

The EDIS ignition module is a microprocessor and makes decisions about spark timing and coil firing. The EDIS ignition module turns coils on and off at correct times and in proper sequence, based on VRS and SAW signals. The EDIS ignition module, upon receiving VRS and SAW signals, produces PIP and IDM output signals and sends these signals to ECA.

The ECA receives IGN GND and PIP signals from EDIS ignition module, and then generates a SAW output signal, based upon fuel, air and other sensor information. ECA also receives an IDM signal from EDIS ignition module to determine if a failure mode should be recorded.

The coil pack receives active low signals from EDIS ignition module and fires 2 spark plugs at a time. One plug is for cylinder which is to be fired (on compression stroke) and other goes to mating cylinder (on exhaust stroke). The next time coil is fired, situation is reversed. Coils are fired according to engine firing order.

Thick Film Ignition (TFI) – All engines, except those with distributorless ignition systems, use TFI ignition systems. The TFI distributor is a gear-driven, die-cast unit. A Hall Effect stator assembly is used to trigger ignition coil. This distributor does not use conventional centrifugal/vacuum advance mechanisms. The TFI ignition module may be mounted in base of distributor bowl or on cowl behind engine. Vehicles which have a remotely mounted module are often referred to as Closed Bowl Distributor (CBD) TFI systems.

The TFI distributor uses a Hall Effect switch mechanism to switch primary voltage and send a Profile Ignition Pick-Up (PIP) signal to ECA. The ECA uses PIP input signal to produce a Spark Output signal (SPOUT), which is sent to TFI ignition module to trigger coil secondary voltage discharge.

On manual transaxle vehicles, the TFI ignition module features a push start mode, which allows vehicle to be push started if necessary. An "E" core ignition coil is used.

EMISSION SYSTEMS

Several systems and components are used to control emissions. Operation and actuation method is provided for most devices. For testing procedures, refer to specific system in SYSTEM & COMPONENT TESTING article.

Temperature Vacuum Switch (TVS) – The TVS incorporates a bimetallic disc which opens and closes vacuum ports. TVS may be used in conjunction with distributor, canister purge or EGR systems.

Vacuum Control Valve – This temperature-operated vacuum switch has 2 or more ports. Valve uses a wax pellet or bimetallic material to open or close vacuum ports at normal engine operating temperatures. Vacuum control valve is usually mounted in some part of cooling system with its base immersed in coolant. Valve may be either normally open or closed.

Vacuum Delay Valve – Vacuum delay valve is inserted in vacuum lines to provide gradual application or vacuum release to engine or emission control devices. One-way or two-way valve may be used, depending on function and system.

Vacuum Reservoir – The vacuum reservoir stores vacuum and provides an amplified vacuum signal, preventing rapid fluctuations or sudden drops in a vacuum signal during such conditions as acceleration.

Vacuum Restrictor – This orifice-type flow restrictor is used as an emission calibration to control flow rate and/or actuation timing of components and systems.

Vacuum Vent Valve – Vacuum vent valve controls induction of fresh air into system, preventing accumulation of fuel vapors which could cause decay of vacuum diaphragms. Valve may be vent only or combined vent and delay valve. Valve should always be mounted with ports pointing downward.

AIR INJECTION SYSTEM

The air injection system reduces carbon monoxide (CO) and hydrocarbon (HC) content of exhaust gases. It injects fresh air into exhaust gas stream, which continues combustion of unburned gases. Air can be by-passed to atmosphere by a thermactor air by-pass valve and/or directed near exhaust manifold or catalytic converter.

Depending upon engine size and application, individual systems may vary in number and type of components. All systems use same basic components: air supply pump, air by-pass valve, filter, check valve(s), air control valve, air manifold and air hoses. Some models may use a combined air by-pass/air control valve.

Air By-Pass Valve – Valve directs airflow from thermactor air pump to exhaust system or atmosphere as required. Valve may be mounted on air pump or in-line (remote). Air by-pass valve is vacuum operated and may be either normally open or closed.

Normally closed valve supplies air to exhaust system with medium and high applied vacuum signals during normal modes, short idles and some acceleration. With low or no vacuum applied, pump air is dumped through silencer valve ports.

Normally open valve with a vacuum vent provides a timed air dump during deceleration. Valve also dumps when a vacuum pressure difference is maintained between signal and vent ports.

Air Pump – The air pump is a belt-driven, positive displacement, vane-type pump which provides air for air injection system. Air is received from a remote silencer/filter, attached to air inlet nipple of pump, or through a centrifugal fan on front of pump. The by-pass valve performs pressure relief.

The air pump supplies air under pressure to exhaust port near exhaust valve by either an external air manifold or through an internal drilled passage in cylinder head or exhaust manifold. This pressurized air, combined with hot exhaust gases, creates a secondary combustion stage, which produces carbon dioxide and water.

Air Supply Control Valve – Operated by vacuum, this valve directs air pump output upstream to exhaust manifold or downstream to catalytic converter.

Check Valves – Check valves are used on all thermactor systems in various locations. These valves allow airflow in one direction only.

Combination Air By-Pass & Air Control Valve – By-pass valve routes thermactor air to either the exhaust system or atmosphere. When air is routed to exhaust system, control valve routes air either upstream to exhaust manifolds or downstream to catalytic converter.

Both valves are normally closed and come in either a bleed or non-bleed type. Bleed-type valves will have bleed percentage molded into plastic case.

Dual Thermactor Air Control Solenoid Valve – The dual thermactor air control solenoid valve assembly consists of 2 normally closed solenoid valves with vents. One valve controls thermactor air by-pass valve and other controls thermactor air diverter valve. Both valves pass air when deactivated and do not pass air when activated.

Thermactor Idle Vacuum (TIV) Valve – The TIV valve vents vacuum signal to atmosphere when preset manifold vacuum or pressure is exceeded. During periods of extended idle, this valve is used to divert thermactor airflow to limit exhaust temperature. This prevents excessive underbody temperature. TIV valve also cuts EGR in a heavy boost mode for turbocharged applications.

EGR SYSTEM

NOTE: Not all vehicles use EGR systems. EGR system usage depends on engine application.

The Exhaust Gas Recirculation (EGR) system distributes exhaust gas into intake mixture. This lowers combustion temperatures due to lower concentrations of oxygen. Lowering combustion temperatures reduces NOx emissions.

Electronic EGR Valve – The Electronic EGR valve is required in EEC systems where EGR flow is controlled according to computer demands of EGR Valve Position (EVP) sensor. The EGR valve is operated by a vacuum signal from EGR Vacuum Regulator (EVR).

EGR valve is mounted on top of an intake and exhaust gas port. The EGR pintle blocks exhaust gas from entering intake system. When vacuum is applied to EGR valve, the diaphragm is actuated. This lifts EGR pintle (attached to diaphragm) and allows exhaust gas to recirculate into intake system.

EGR Vacuum Regulator (EVR) – The vacuum regulator is an electro-magnetic device controlling vacuum to EGR valve. Regulator operation is measured as a duty cycle: increased duty means increased vacuum to EGR.

EGR Valve Position (EVP) Sensor – This sensor is attached to EGR valve assembly and indicates EGR valve position to ECA.

EVAPORATIVE EMISSION CONTROL

NOTE: Not all listed components are used on every vehicle system. Component usage depends on calibration of vehicle.

The function of evaporative emission control system is to store gasoline fumes from fuel system in a carbon canister when engine is not running. During engine operation, fumes are drawn into engine for burning during combustion process, purging canister.

Three basic components are used in evaporative emission system:
- Activated carbon canister.
- Computer-controlled solenoid.
- Tank pressure control cap.

For specific component application and vacuum hose routing, see VACUUM DIAGRAMS article.

Carbon Canister – Carbon canister storage is used for evaporative fuel control on all vehicles.

Canister Purge Solenoid Valve – This normally closed solenoid valve controls fuel vapor flow from canister to intake manifold. It is opened or closed by a signal from ECA during various engine operating modes.

Fill Control/Vent System – Fill limiting is accomplished through configuration of fill neck and/or internal vent lines. Vent system is designed to permit air space in 10-12 percent of tank to allow for thermal expansion.

Vapor generated in fuel supply line is continuously vented back to fuel tank. Venting prevents engine surging from fuel enrichment and assists in hydrocarbon (HC) emission control.

Pressure/Vacuum Relief Fuel Cap – This system consists of a sealed filler cap with an integral pressure/vacuum relief valve. Fuel system vacuum relief is provided after 1.0 in. Hg of vacuum. Pressure relief is provided after 1.8 psi (.13 kg/cm²). Under normal conditions, fill cap allows air to enter fuel tank as fuel is used, without allowing fuel vapors to escape.

Vapor Vent System – System provides a vapor space above gasoline surface in fuel tank. This area is sufficient to permit adequate breathing room for tank vapor valve assembly.

All vapor valves are mounted on fuel tank and use a small orifice which allows vapor (but not liquid) fuel to pass into line running to canister. Fuel vapors in fuel tank are vented though vapor valve assembly on top of fuel tank. Vapors are routed through a vapor line to carbon canister in engine compartment.

POSITIVE CRANKCASE VENTILATION (PCV)

The PCV system uses intake manifold vacuum to eliminate blow-by gases from crankcase. Manifold vacuum draws gases from crankcase, through PCV hose, into combustion chamber. The PCV valve is positioned in hose through which blow-by gases flow on their way to combustion chamber.

By opening and closing in direct relation to engine vacuum, the PCV valve meters blow-by gas flow to combustion chamber. During periods of high manifold vacuum, such as at idle and deceleration, valve is almost completely closed, limiting flow of gases. During cruise speeds, valve permits greatest flow of gases.

Under conditions in which excessively high amounts of blow-by gases are produced (such as worn cylinders or rings), system allows excess gases to flow back through crankcase vent hose and into intake manifold.

SELF-DIAGNOSTIC SYSTEM

NOTE: All systems have self-diagnostic capabilities. For information on procedures for entering self-test modes and reading service codes, see appropriate SELF-DIAGNOSTICS article.

CHECK ENGINE LIGHT

The CHECK ENGINE light (if equipped) will illuminate whenever ignition is turned to ON position (bulb check) or systems related to the EEC-IV system malfunction during normal engine operation. For additional information, see appropriate SELF-DIAGNOSTICS article.

SELF-TEST OUTPUT/SELF-TEST INPUT (STO/STI) CONNECTORS

The STO connector is a 6-pin connector used to perform self-test diagnostic procedure. The STI is a single-pin connector, located next to STO. When STI is grounded, it activates fault code output function. Codes are retrieved through STO connector.

MISCELLANEOUS CONTROLS

A/C CLUTCH CYCLING PRESSURE SWITCH (CCPS)

On models with manual A/C system, the CCPS is mounted on top of the receiver-drier. Based on refrigerant system pressure, a signal is sent to the ECA. The ECA uses this signal to maintain system pressure within the programmed range.

COOLING FAN

The ECA regulates operation of the electric cooling fan through an ECA-controlled relay, which controls the ground or power circuit of the cooling fan. This allows the ECA to operate the cooling fan based on engine temperature. A malfunction of the cooling fan will cause engine overheating and possible detonation.

WIDE OPEN THROTTLE A/C (WAC) CUTOFF

During wide open throttle, WAC circuit interrupts power to A/C compressor clutch. The A/C remains off for about 3 seconds after returning from WOT.

WAIT TO START INDICATOR LIGHT

On 7.3L models, this light comes on when engine is cold and ignition is in the RUN position. The light will remain on for 5-10 seconds, depending on time required for glow plugs to warm.

WATER IN FUEL INDICATOR LIGHT

On 7.3L models, this light comes on when engine is in the START position. The light will remain on if fuel filter water separator has a water level that exceeds predetermined level.

1992 ENGINE PERFORMANCE
Basic Diagnostic Procedures

Aerostar, Bronco, Explorer, Pickup, Ranger, Van

NOTE: Unless otherwise specified, references to Pickup include the F350 Super Duty commercial chassis.

MODEL IDENTIFICATION

Series [1]	Model
"A"	Aerostar
"E"	RWD Van
"F"	Pickup
"R"	Ranger
"U"	Bronco & Explorer

[1] – Vehicle series is fifth character of VIN.

INTRODUCTION

The following diagnostic steps will help prevent overlooking a simple problem. This is also where to begin diagnosis for a no-start condition.

The first step in diagnosing any driveability problem is verifying the customer's complaint with a test drive under the conditions the problem reportedly occurred.

Before entering self-diagnostics, perform a careful and complete visual inspection. Most engine control problems result from mechanical breakdowns, poor electrical connections or damaged/misrouted vacuum hoses. Before condemning the computerized system, perform each test listed in this article.

NOTE: Perform all voltage tests with a Digital Volt-Ohmmeter (DVOM) with a minimum 10-megohm input impedance, unless stated otherwise in test procedure.

PRELIMINARY INSPECTION & ADJUSTMENTS

VISUAL INSPECTION

Visually inspect all electrical wiring, looking for chafed, stretched, cut or pinched wiring. Ensure electrical connectors fit tightly and are not corroded. Ensure vacuum hoses are properly routed and are not pinched or cut. See VACUUM DIAGRAMS article to verify routing and connections (if necessary). Inspect air induction system for possible vacuum leaks.

MECHANICAL INSPECTION

Compression – Check engine mechanical condition using a compression gauge, vacuum gauge or engine analyzer. If using engine analyzer, see engine analyzer manual for specific instructions. Compression pressures are considered within specifications if lowest reading cylinder is within 75 percent of highest reading cylinder.

WARNING: Because fuel injectors on many models are triggered by the ignition switch, DO NOT use ignition switch during compression tests on fuel injected vehicles. Use a remote starter to crank engine to prevent fire hazard or engine oiling system contamination.

Exhaust System Backpressure – Using a vacuum or pressure gauge, check exhaust system. Remove O_2 sensor or air injection check valve (if equipped). Connect a 0-5 psi pressure gauge, and run engine at 2500 RPM. If exhaust system backpressure is greater than 2 psi, exhaust system or catalytic converter is plugged.

If using a vacuum gauge, connect vacuum gauge hose to intake manifold vacuum port, and start engine. Observe vacuum gauge. Open throttle part way and hold steady. If vacuum gauge reading slowly drops after stabilizing, check exhaust system for restrictions.

NO-START DIAGNOSIS

NOTE: For diesel information, see TROUBLE SHOOTING – NO CODES article.

Definition – No-start is defined as engine cranks okay, but does not start. Engine may fire a few times.

PRELIMINARY CHECKS

Before diagnosing problems in ignition system, ensure following systems and components are in good condition and operating properly.
- Battery
- State of tune
- Fuel delivery and injection system
- All wiring and vacuum connections
- Air cleaner and ducts
- Cooling system

DISTRIBUTORLESS IGNITION SYSTEM (DIS)

Spark Output Check – **1)** Check EEC-IV system for fault codes and repair if necessary. See QUICK TEST in SELF-DIAGNOSTICS – EEC-IV article. If no fault codes are retrieved, check ignition system wiring harness connectors for corrosion and tight fit. *See Fig. 1.*
2) If wiring and connectors are okay, use Neon Bulb Spark Tester (D89P-6666-A) to check for spark at each spark plug wire while cranking engine. If spark is consistent and equal at each spark plug (one spark per crankshaft revolution), ignition system is okay. If spark is not present, go to IGNITION SYSTEMS in SYSTEM & COMPONENT TESTING article.

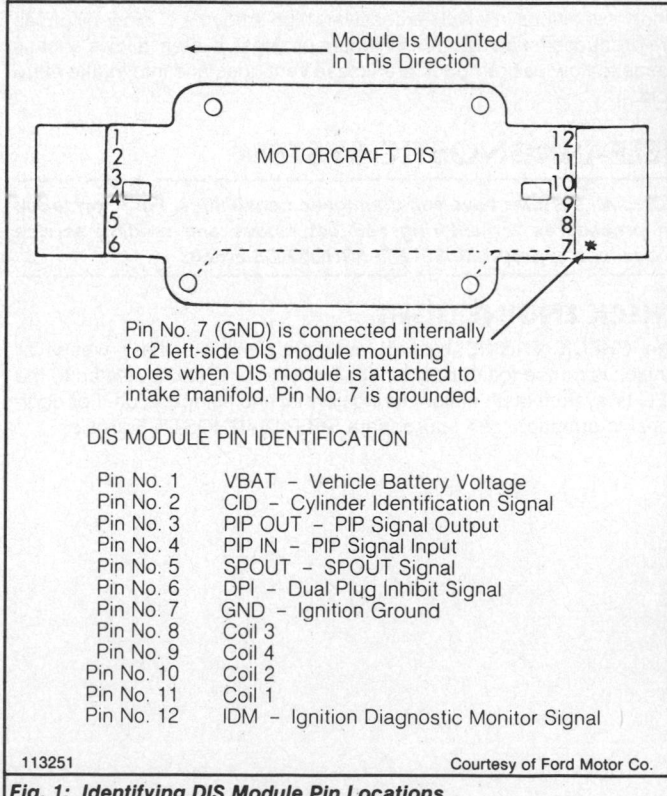

Pin No. 7 (GND) is connected internally to 2 left-side DIS module mounting holes when DIS module is attached to intake manifold. Pin No. 7 is grounded.

DIS MODULE PIN IDENTIFICATION

Pin No. 1	VBAT – Vehicle Battery Voltage
Pin No. 2	CID – Cylinder Identification Signal
Pin No. 3	PIP OUT – PIP Signal Output
Pin No. 4	PIP IN – PIP Signal Input
Pin No. 5	SPOUT – SPOUT Signal
Pin No. 6	DPI – Dual Plug Inhibit Signal
Pin No. 7	GND – Ignition Ground
Pin No. 8	Coil 3
Pin No. 9	Coil 4
Pin No. 10	Coil 2
Pin No. 11	Coil 1
Pin No. 12	IDM – Ignition Diagnostic Monitor Signal

113251   Courtesy of Ford Motor Co.

Fig. 1: Identifying DIS Module Pin Locations

ELECTRONIC DISTRIBUTORLESS IGNITION SYSTEM (EDIS)

Spark Output Check – **1)** Check EEC-IV system for fault codes and repair if necessary. See QUICK TEST in SELF-DIAGNOSTICS – EEC-IV article. If no fault codes are retrieved, check ignition system wiring harness connectors for corrosion and tight fit. Repair or replace as necessary.

2) If wiring and connectors are okay, use Neon Bulb Spark Tester (D89P-6666-A) to check for spark at each spark plug wire while cranking engine. If spark is consistent and equal at each spark plug (one spark per crankshaft revolution), ignition system is okay. If spark is not present, go to IGNITION SYSTEMS in SYSTEM & COMPONENT TESTING article.

THICK FILM IGNITION (TFI) IV

Spark Check – **1)** Using a high output spark tester, check for spark at coil wire while cranking engine. If spark is present, go to step **2)**. If spark is not present, remove distributor cap, and crank engine to check for distributor rotation. If distributor rotation is okay, check coil secondary wire resistance. Resistance should not be greater than 7000 ohms per foot.

2) Place transmission in Neutral. Disconnect TFI wiring harness connector. Attach TFI Ignition Tester (105-000003). Connect Red lead of tester to 12 volts. Attach remote starter to "S" terminal of starter relay. While observing 2 LED lights on tester, use remote starter to crank engine. If PIP light blinks, go to step **4)**. If PIP light does not blink, remove distributor.

3) Remove TFI module from distributor. Using an ohmmeter, ensure all circuit resistance values are correct. See TFI MODULE CIRCUIT RESISTANCE SPECIFICATIONS table. *See Fig. 2.* If readings are incorrect, replace TFI module. If readings are correct, check stator for open winding or short to ground. See SYSTEM & COMPONENT TESTING article.

TFI MODULE CIRCUIT RESISTANCE SPECIFICATIONS

TFI Terminals [1]	Ohms
Ground Pin – PIP	More Than 500
Power Pin – PIP Input Pin	Less Than 2000
Power Pin – TFI Power	Less Than 200
Ground Pin – Ignition Ground	Less Than 2
PIP Input Pin – PIP	Less Than 200

[1] – See Fig. 2 for terminal identification.

4) If PIP light did not blink in step **2)**, replace TFI module, and repeat step **1)**. If spark is still not present, replace ignition coil and module connector. If PIP light did blink in step **2)**, substitute ignition coil with a known working unit, and repeat step **1)**. If spark is now present, ensure coil secondary wire resistance is not greater than 7000 ohms per foot, and replace ignition coil.

5) If spark was not present in step **4)**, connect original vehicle coil and spark tester. Remove pin-in-line connector located near distributor. Crank engine while checking for spark. If spark is present, inspect PIP and ignition ground circuits to verify continuity, and repair as necessary.

6) If spark was not present in step **5)**, measure battery voltage with negative lead from voltmeter attached to base of distributor. Measure voltage at ignition coil positive (+) terminal. Ignition coil positive (+) terminal voltage should be at least 90 percent of battery voltage. If not, check circuitry between ignition coil and ignition switch for wear or damage. Repair as necessary.

7) If ignition coil positive (+) terminal voltage was at least 90 percent of battery voltage in step **6)**, remove connector from ignition module. Disconnect starter relay "S" terminal. Turn ignition on. Measure voltage at ignition module connector power terminals No. 3 and 4. *See Fig. 2.* See TFI MODULE VOLTAGE TEST TERMINALS table. Voltage should be at least 90 percent of battery voltage.

TFI MODULE VOLTAGE TEST TERMINALS

TFI Terminal	Ignition Switch Position
With CCD [1]	
No. 3	Run & Start
Without CCD [1]	
No. 3	Run & Start
No. 4	Start

[1] – Computer Controlled Dwell.

8) If voltage is not at least 90 percent of battery voltage, check circuitry between ignition coil and ignition switch for wear or damage. Repair as necessary. If voltage was at least 90 percent of battery voltage in step **7)**, inspect wiring between ignition module terminal No. 2 and coil. If okay, check all related circuitry. Replace or repair as necessary.

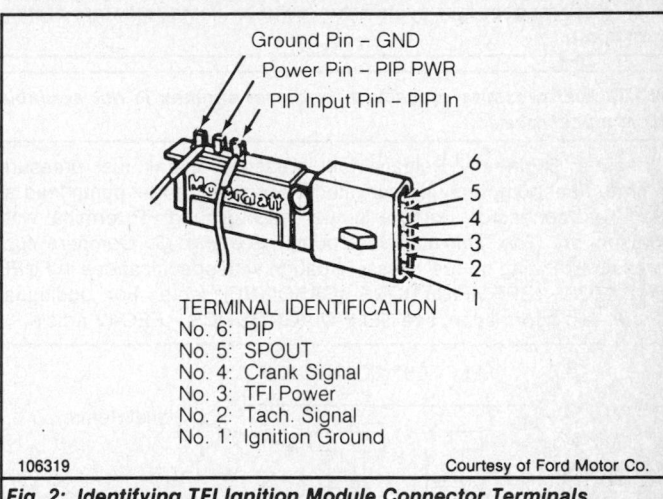

Ground Pin – GND
Power Pin – PIP PWR
PIP Input Pin – PIP In

TERMINAL IDENTIFICATION
No. 6: PIP
No. 5: SPOUT
No. 4: Crank Signal
No. 3: TFI Power
No. 2: Tach. Signal
No. 1: Ignition Ground

106319   Courtesy of Ford Motor Co.

Fig. 2: Identifying TFI Ignition Module Connector Terminals

IGNITION COIL RESISTANCE

IGNITION COIL RESISTANCE – OHMS @ 75°F (24°C)

Application	Primary	Secondary
DIS, EDIS	.5	[1]
TFI-IV	0.8-1.6	8000-11,500

[1] – Resistance values are not provided by manufacturer.

FUEL SYSTEM

PRELIMINARY CHECKS

Ensure following systems and components are in good condition and operating properly before diagnosing problems in fuel injection system.

- Battery
- State of tune
- Fuel delivery system
- All wiring and vacuum connections
- Air cleaner and ducts
- Cooling system

Engine Does Not Crank – Check for hydrostatic lock (liquid in cylinder). Repair as needed. Check for starting and charging system problems.

Engine Cranks But Will Not Start – **1)** Check fuel tank contents and fuel gauge accuracy. Check for dirt, water or other contamination in fuel.

2) Check ignition system for strong secondary current at spark plugs. If no spark exists or if spark is weak, repair ignition system problem.

3) Check fuel lines and fittings for leaks. If no leaks are found, check fuel delivery system for proper pressure and volumes. Reset inertia switch (if necessary).

4) Check for a defective fuel injector or coolant temperature sensor. Ensure TPS does not stick.

WARNING: Always relieve fuel pressure before disconnecting any fuel injection-related component. DO NOT allow fuel to contact engine or electrical components.

FUEL PRESSURE RELEASE

Gasoline Engines – Disconnect negative battery cable. Remove fuel cap to release fuel tank pressure. Using EFI Pressure Gauge (T80L-

9974-B), release fuel pressure from relief valve. Relief valve is located on fuel supply manifold.

FUEL PRESSURE

WARNING: Inspect fuel system for leaks or damage before testing fuel pump.

NOTE: Fuel pressure procedure for diesel engines is not available from manufacturer.

Gasoline Engines – Release fuel pressure. Install fuel pressure gauge. Fuel pump may be activated by grounding fuel pump lead at Self-Test connector. Using a jumper lead, ground FP terminal with ignition on. This activates fuel pump. *See Fig. 3.* Compare fuel pressure reading on fuel pressure gauge with specifications in FUEL PRESSURE SPECIFICATIONS (GASOLINE) table. For additional circuit test information, see SELF-DIAGNOSTICS – EEC-IV article.

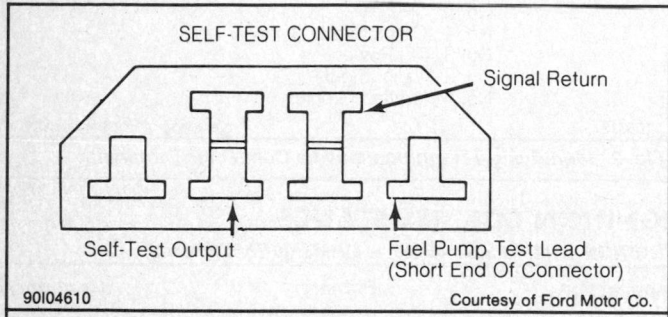

SELF-TEST CONNECTOR

Signal Return

Self-Test Output

Fuel Pump Test Lead
(Short End Of Connector)

90I04610   Courtesy of Ford Motor Co.

Fig. 3: Identifying Fuel Pump Self-Test Connector

FUEL PRESSURE SPECIFICATIONS (GASOLINE)

Engine	Pressure KOER psi (kg/cm²)	Pressure KOEO psi (kg/cm²)
4.9L	45-60 (3.2-4.2)	[1] 50-60 (3.5-4.2)
All Others	30-45 (2.1-4.2)	[1] 35-45 (2.5-4.2)

[1] – Fuel pump outlet pressure (maximum output).

FUEL PRESSURE SPECIFICATIONS (DIESEL)

Application	psi (kg/cm²)
Filter Inlet	[1] 2 (.14)
Filter Outlet	[2] 1 (.07)
Return Line	[2] 2 (.14)

[1] – At idle.
[2] – At 3300 RPM.

FUEL INJECTORS

Fuel Injector Check – **1)** Connect tachometer to engine. Run engine at idle. Disconnect and reconnect injectors individually. If each injector causes a momentary drop in engine speed of at least 100 RPM, injectors are providing proper fuel delivery. RPM drop should only be momentary, as ISC will attempt to re-establish correct idle RPM.
2) Replace any injectors not causing sufficient drop in engine speed. When test is complete, turn engine off. To check curb idle, refer to emission control specifications on decal in engine compartment or IDLE SPEED & MIXTURE in ON-VEHICLE ADJUSTMENTS article.
Fuel Injector Circuit – Disconnect all injector harness connectors. Using digital ohmmeter, check resistance across terminals of each injector. See INDIVIDUAL INJECTOR RESISTANCE table. Disconnect injector bank harness connector, and check resistance of injector bank. See INJECTOR BANK RESISTANCE table. Repair injector bank or any injector not within specifications.

NOTE: For further component testing and information, see SELF-DIAGNOSTICS – EEC-IV article.

INDIVIDUAL INJECTOR RESISTANCE [1]

Engine	Ohms
2.3L & 3.0L	15-18
All Others	13-16

[1] – Resistance values are for a single injector.

INJECTOR BANK RESISTANCE

Engine	Ohms
2.3L	7.0-9.5
2.9L, 3.0L & 4.9L	5.0-6.5
4.0L	4.0-5.5
5.0L, 5.8L & 7.5L	3.0-4.0

INERTIA SWITCH

WARNING: DO NOT reset inertia switch until fuel system has been inspected for leaks.

1) In event of a collision, electrical contacts in inertia switch open, automatically shutting off fuel pump. Fuel pump shuts off even if engine does not stop running. Engine eventually stops due to lack of fuel.
2) Engine cannot be restarted until inertia switch is manually reset. To reset inertia switch, depress button on switch. Inertia switches may be found in following locations:
- Aerostar & Van – On right kick panel, just forward of door opening.
- Bronco & Pickup – On floorboard, left of and above steering column.
- Explorer & Ranger – Under instrument panel, right of transmission hump.

IDLE SPEED & IGNITION TIMING
BASE IGNITION TIMING

NOTE: Ignition timing is not adjustable on models with DIS or EDIS.

Ensure idle speed and ignition timing are set to specification. For adjustment procedures, see ON-VEHICLE ADJUSTMENTS article. Ensure all accessories are off and transmission is in Park or Neutral. Set parking brake. Disconnect automatic parking brake release (if equipped). Ensure vehicle front wheels are in straight-ahead position and curb idle speed set to specification.

4-CYLINDER BASE IGNITION TIMING

Application	Degrees BTDC @ RPM
2.3L	[1]

[1] – Timing is not adjustable.

6-CYLINDER BASE IGNITION TIMING

Application	Degrees BTDC @ RPM
4.9L	10 @ Idle

V6 BASE IGNITION TIMING

Application [1]	Degrees BTDC @ RPM
2.9L	
Automatic Transmission	10 @ 800
Manual Transmission	10 @ 850
3.0L	10 @ Idle
4.0L	[2]

[1] – With SPOUT in-line connector disconnected.
[2] – Timing is not adjustable.

V8 BASE IGNITION TIMING

Application	[1] Degrees BTDC @ RPM
5.0L	
Automatic Transmission	10 @ 525-825
Manual Transmission	10 @ 550-850
5.8L	
C6 Automatic Transmission	10 @ 630-930
E4OD Automatic Transmission	10 @ 580-880
Manual Transmission	10 @ 580-880
7.5L	10 @ 500-800

[1] – With SPOUT in-line connector disconnected.

IDLE SPEED

Idle speed is controlled by ECA and idle speed control air by-pass valve on all engines. If control system is operating properly, engine idle RPM is fixed and cannot be changed by standard adjustments. Manufacturer does not provide RPM specifications for many engines. A scan tester must be used on these systems because control strategy and idle speed specification are controlled by ECA. See ON-VEHICLE ADJUSTMENTS article.

Before performing idle speed adjustment procedure, complete a thorough basic inspection and self-test (KOEO, KOER, Continuous Memory self-tests) to confirm operation of sub-systems contributing to idle speed control. See SELF-DIAGNOSTICS – EEC-IV article.

IDLE MIXTURE ADJUSTMENT

NOTE: No idle mixture adjustments are possible on any models. See SELF-DIAGNOSTICS – EEC-IV article for diagnosis of incorrect idle mixture.

THROTTLE POSITION SENSOR (TPS) ADJUSTMENT

NOTE: Throttle Position Sensor (TPS) on gasoline engines is not adjustable. Replace TPS if sensor is not within specifications.

TPS VOLTAGE SPECIFICATIONS [1]

Application	Idle	Wide Open Throttle
2.3L, 2.9L [2], 3.0L & 4.0L	0.20	4.84
2.9L [3], 4.9L, 5.0L, 5.8L & 7.5L	0.34	4.84

[1] – Minimum and maximum specifications are given.
[2] – Vehicles equipped with mass airflow sensor only.
[3] – Except vehicles equipped with mass airflow sensor.

FUEL INJECTION PUMP LEVER (FIPL) SENSOR ADJUSTMENT

For Fuel Injection Pump Lever (FIPL) sensor adjustment, see ON-VEHICLE ADJUSTMENTS article.

SUMMARY

If no faults were found while performing BASIC DIAGNOSTIC PROCEDURES, proceed to SELF-DIAGNOSTICS – EEC-IV article. If no hard codes are found in self-diagnostics or if vehicle does not have a self-diagnostic system, proceed to TROUBLE SHOOTING – NO CODES article for diagnosis by symptom (i.e., ROUGH IDLE, NO START, etc.) or intermittent diagnostic procedures.

1992 ENGINE PERFORMANCE
Self-Diagnostics – EEC-IV

Aerostar, Bronco, Explorer, Pickup, Ranger, Van

NOTE: Unless otherwise specified, references to Pickup include the F350 Super Duty commercial chassis.

INTRODUCTION

Perform all steps in BASIC DIAGNOSTIC PROCEDURES article in ENGINE PERFORMANCE. If no fault is found while performing BASIC DIAGNOSTIC PROCEDURES, proceed with self-diagnostics. If no service code or only pass codes are found during self-diagnostics, proceed to TROUBLE SHOOTING – NO CODES article in ENGINE PERFORMANCE for diagnosis by symptoms.

SELF-DIAGNOSTIC SYSTEM

WARNING: When battery is disconnected, vehicle computer and memory systems may lose memory data. Driveability problems may exist until computer systems have completed a relearn cycle. See COMPUTER RELEARN PROCEDURES article in GENERAL INFORMATION before disconnecting battery.

DIAGNOSTIC FORMATS

QUICK TEST and CIRCUIT TESTS are diagnostic formats used to test and service EEC-IV system. QUICK TEST allows technician to identify problems and retrieve service codes. CIRCUIT TESTS check circuits, sensors and actuators.

Before starting any CIRCUIT TEST, follow all steps under QUICK TEST to find correct CIRCUIT TEST. If vehicle passes QUICK TEST and no driveability symptoms or intermittent faults exist, EEC-IV system is okay.

SERVICE CODES

During QUICK TEST, 3 types of service codes are retrieved: KOEO, KOER and Continuous Memory codes. See QUICK TEST for self-test procedures. Codes may be cleared from ECA memory after they have been recorded or repaired. See CLEARING CODES.

KOEO & KOER Codes (Hard Faults) – These codes indicate faults are present at time of testing. A hard fault may cause CHECK ENGINE or Malfunction Indicator Light (MIL) to glow and remain on until fault is repaired. If KOEO or KOER codes are retrieved during KOEO SELF-TEST or KOER SELF-TEST, use SERVICE CODE REFERENCE CHARTS to find correct testing and repair procedures.

Continuous Memory Codes (Soft Faults) – These codes indicate a fault that may or may not be present at time of testing. These codes are used to diagnose intermittent problems. Continuous Memory Codes are retrieved during KOEO SELF-TEST. Some codes may turn on MIL or CHECK ENGINE light. Corresponding soft trouble code will be retained in ECA memory. If fault does not reoccur within 40 warm-up cycles (80 cycles on some models), ECA will automatically clear code.

Technician may clear service codes from memory. See CLEARING CODES. Intermittent faults may be caused by a sensor, connector or wiring-related problems. See INTERMITTENTS in TROUBLE SHOOTING – NO CODES article.

CAUTION: Continuous Memory Codes should be recorded when retrieved during KOEO SELF-TEST. These codes may be used to identify intermittent problems that exist after all KOEO and KOER codes have been repaired and a Code 11 or 111 (pass code) has been obtained. Failure to follow this procedure may result in unnecessary testing. Some Continuous Memory Codes faults may not be valid after KOEO and KOER codes are repaired.

RETRIEVING CODES

Service codes are retrieved from EEC-IV system through self-test connector. Various methods and test equipment may be used to access these codes:

- Analog Volt-Ohmmeter (VOM)
- Scan Tester
- In-Dash Malfunction Indicator Light (MIL) Or CHECK ENGINE Light

SELF-TEST CONNECTOR LOCATIONS

Application	Location
Aerostar	Left front inner fender panel
Bronco & Pickup	Left front inner fender panel
Explorer & Ranger	Right front inner fender panel
Van	Right front inner fender panel

READING CODES

KOEO & KOER SELF-TEST Codes – All service codes are 2- or 3-digit numbers. ECA outputs codes one digit at a time. These codes indicate current faults in system and should be serviced in order of appearance. Use SERVICE CODE REFERENCE CHARTS to find correct CIRCUIT TEST.

Codes are shown as voltage pulses. If using CHECK ENGINE light, service codes are displayed as light pulses. If using Volt-Ohmmeter (VOM), service codes are displayed as needle sweeps. See Fig. 1.

Pay careful attention to length of pauses in order to read codes correctly. A 1/2-second pause occurs between number of sweeps in a digit and a 2-second pause occurs between digits in a code. A 4-second pause occurs between each code. KOEO codes are separated from Continuous Memory Codes by a 6-second delay, a single 1/2-second sweep (Separator) and another 6-second delay. Record codes in order received.

Scan tester, if used, will count pulses and display them as a digital code. STAR Series Tester will add a zero (0) to single-digit Separator Code (10) and Dynamic Response Code (10). Dynamic Response Code is displayed in KOER SELF-TEST. See Fig. 1.

Separator Code – Single 1/2-second separator pulse is issued 6-9 seconds after last KOEO code. Continuous Memory Codes (soft faults) are then displayed 6-9 seconds after 1/2-second separator code. Some digital test equipment may display separator code as "10" instead of "1".

Pass Codes – Code 11 or 111 indicates system passes that portion of test. If Code 11 or 111 is not retrieved in KOEO SELF-TEST, codes retrieved during KOER SELF-TEST may not be valid. Code 11-1-11 or 111-1-111, output during KOEO SELF-TEST, indicates no KOEO code or Continuous Memory Code was recorded.

Continuous Memory Codes – Continuous Memory Codes are displayed after separator pulse code in KOEO SELF-TEST. These codes result from information stored by ECA during continuous self-test monitoring. These codes indicate faults recorded within last 40 engine starts (80 engine starts on some models). Fault may or may not be currently present. See SERVICE CODE REFERENCE CHARTS. Use these codes for diagnosis only when KOEO SELF-TEST and KOER SELF-TEST result in Code 11 or 111.

Fast Codes – At start of KOEO SELF-TEST and after Wide Open Throttle (WOT) request in KOER SELF-TEST, ECA outputs short bursts of information, known as FAST CODES, which were used by manufacturer during assembly. With most equipment, these code bursts are not visible; an entire code sequence lasts less than 1/2 second. If this fluctuation is visible on test equipment, ignore it.

CLEARING CODES

CAUTION: DO NOT disconnect vehicle battery to clear codes, as this will erase stored operating information from Keep-Alive Memory (KAM).

To clear codes from ECA memory, start KOEO SELF-TEST. When service codes appear on test equipment or CHECK ENGINE light, disconnect jumper wire from Self-Test Input (STI) connector. If using STAR Series Tester, unlatch center button. This procedure erases Continuous Memory Codes from ECA memory. If problem has not been corrected or fault is still present, hard code will immediately be reset in ECA memory.

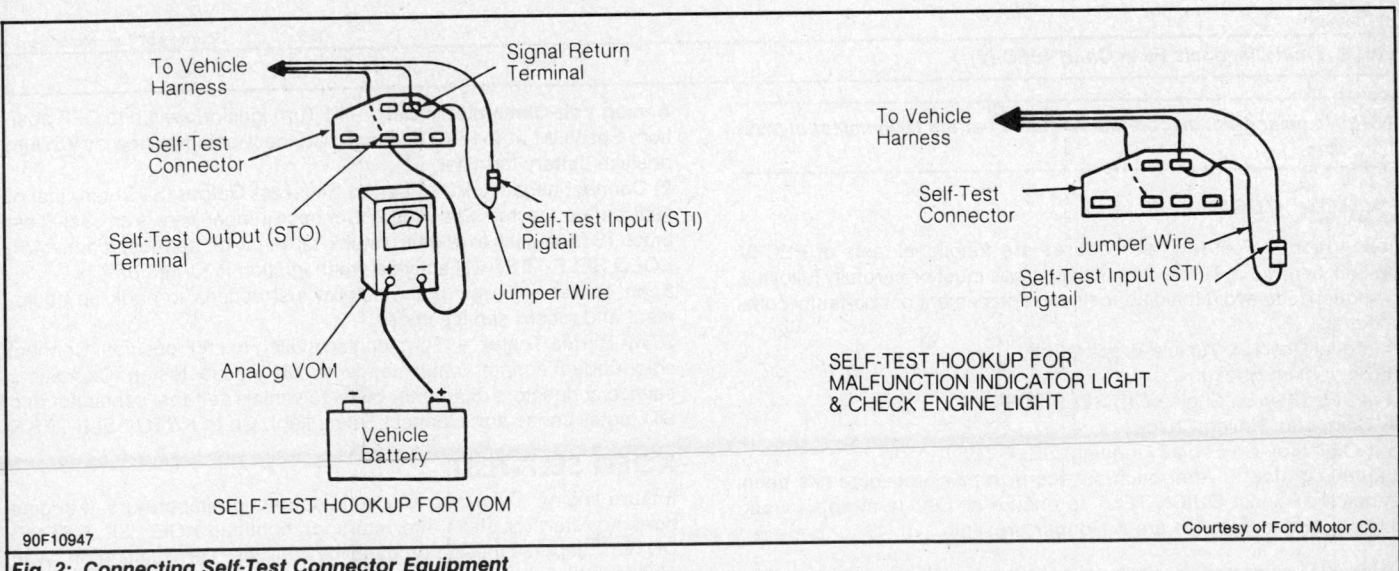

KOEO & CONTINUOUS MEMORY CODE FORMAT
Example Code 11-10-11 (Pass Code)

FAST CODES

4 Seconds

KOEO CODES

6-9 Seconds

SEPARATOR CODES

6-9 Seconds

4 Seconds

CONTINUOUS MEMORY CODES
(Outputted During KOEO Only)

KOER SELF-TEST CODE FORMAT

Engine ID Pulse

6-20 Seconds

DYNAMIC RESPONSE (GOOSE) REQUEST CODE

4-15 Seconds

FAST CODES

4 Seconds

KOER CODES

1st DIGIT = 2

2nd DIGIT = 3

Dash Light — "CHECK ENGINE" OR "SERVICE ENGINE SOON" — 1 Light Flash

2-SECOND PAUSE BETWEEN DIGITS

Analog VOM

1/2 SECOND PAUSE

1 NEEDLE PULSE (SWEEP) + 1 NEEDLE PULSE (SWEEP)

1 NEEDLE PULSE (SWEEP) FOR 1/2 SECOND + 1 NEEDLE PULSE (SWEEP) FOR 1/2 SECOND + 1 NEEDLE PULSE (SWEEP) FOR 1/2 SECOND

23
SERVICE CODE

4-SECOND PAUSE BETWEEN SERVICE CODES, WHEN MORE THAN ONE CODE IS INDICATED

90E10946

Courtesy of Ford Motor Co.

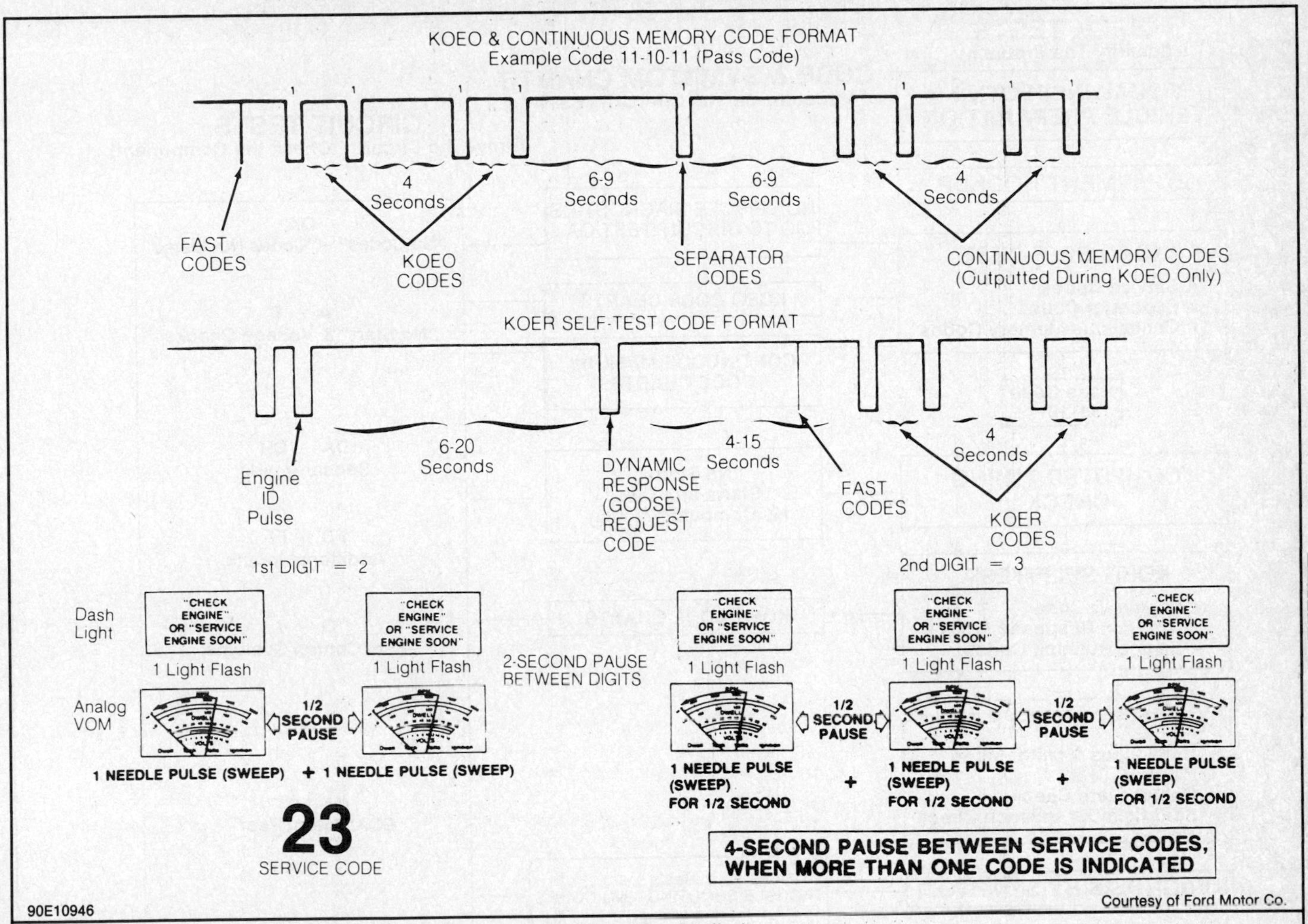

Fig. 1: Reading Service Codes (2-Digit Codes Shown; 3-Digit Codes Are Similar)

To Vehicle Harness

Signal Return Terminal

Self-Test Connector

Self-Test Output (STO) Terminal

Self-Test Input (STI) Pigtail

Jumper Wire

Analog VOM

Vehicle Battery

SELF-TEST HOOKUP FOR VOM

To Vehicle Harness

Self-Test Connector

Jumper Wire

Self-Test Input (STI) Pigtail

SELF-TEST HOOKUP FOR MALFUNCTION INDICATOR LIGHT & CHECK ENGINE LIGHT

90F10947

Courtesy of Ford Motor Co.

Fig. 2: Connecting Self-Test Connector Equipment

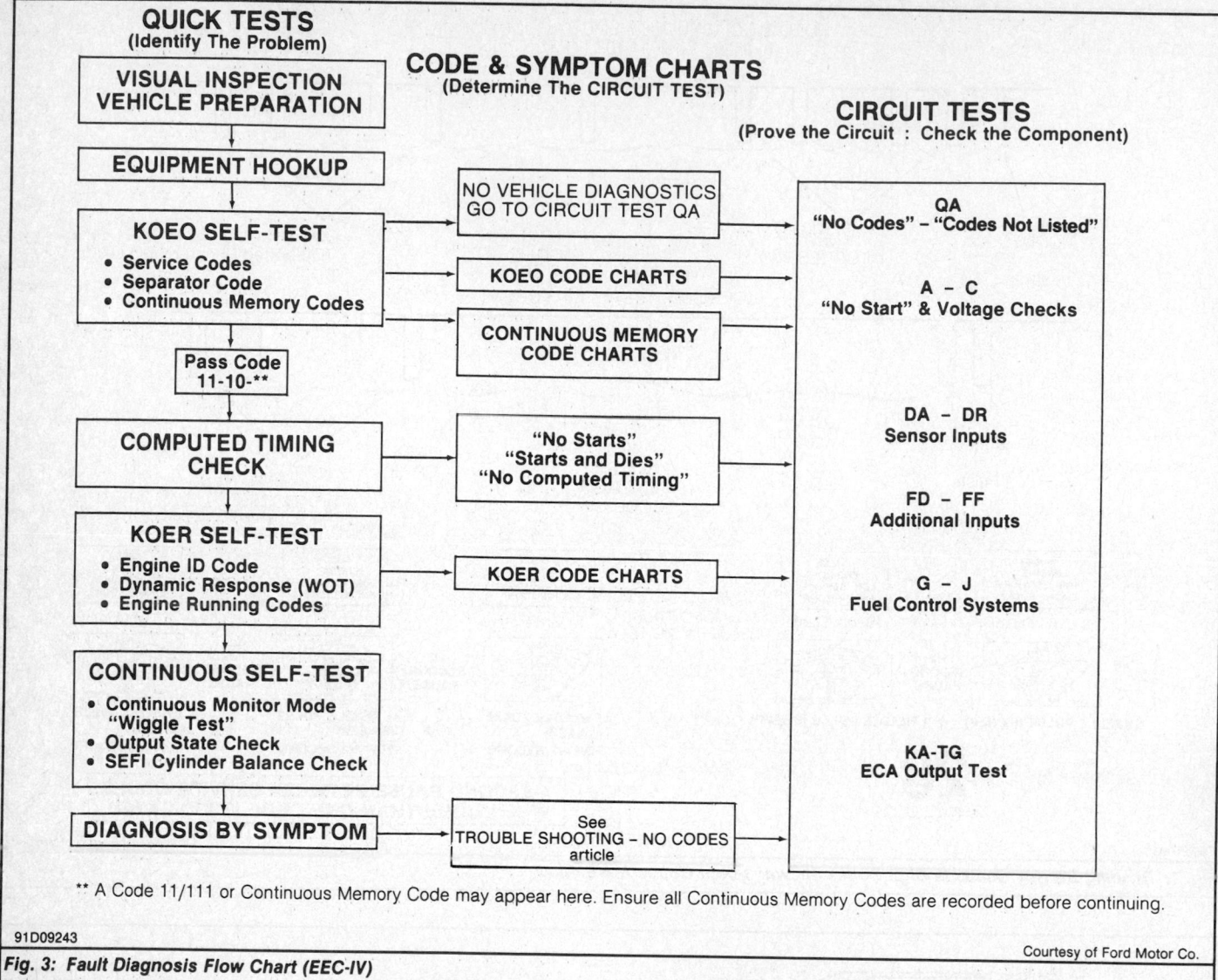

QUICK TESTS
(Identify The Problem)

VISUAL INSPECTION VEHICLE PREPARATION

CODE & SYMPTOM CHARTS
(Determine The CIRCUIT TEST)

CIRCUIT TESTS
(Prove the Circuit : Check the Component)

EQUIPMENT HOOKUP

NO VEHICLE DIAGNOSTICS GO TO CIRCUIT TEST QA

QA
"No Codes" – "Codes Not Listed"

KOEO SELF-TEST
• Service Codes
• Separator Code
• Continuous Memory Codes

KOEO CODE CHARTS

A – C
"No Start" & Voltage Checks

CONTINUOUS MEMORY CODE CHARTS

Pass Code 11-10-**

DA – DR
Sensor Inputs

COMPUTED TIMING CHECK

"No Starts"
"Starts and Dies"
"No Computed Timing"

FD – FF
Additional Inputs

KOER SELF-TEST
• Engine ID Code
• Dynamic Response (WOT)
• Engine Running Codes

KOER CODE CHARTS

G – J
Fuel Control Systems

CONTINUOUS SELF-TEST
• Continuous Monitor Mode "Wiggle Test"
• Output State Check
• SEFI Cylinder Balance Check

KA-TG
ECA Output Test

DIAGNOSIS BY SYMPTOM

See TROUBLE SHOOTING – NO CODES article

** A Code 11/111 or Continuous Memory Code may appear here. Ensure all Continuous Memory Codes are recorded before continuing.

91D09243

Courtesy of Ford Motor Co.

Fig. 3: Fault Diagnosis Flow Chart (EEC-IV)

NOTE: To clear KAM, disconnect negative battery terminal for at least 5 minutes.

QUICK TEST

Description – Following procedures are functional tests of EEC-IV system. See Fig. 3. These 5 basic test steps must be carefully followed in sequence to avoid misdiagnosis or replacement of non-faulty components.
• Visual Check & Vehicle Preparation
• Equipment Hookup
• KOEO (Key On Engine Off) SELF-TEST
• Computed Timing Check
• KOER (Key On Engine Running) SELF-TEST

Diagnostic Aids – After each service or repair procedure has been completed, repeat QUICK TEST to ensure all EEC-IV systems work properly and fault codes are no longer present.

VISUAL CHECK & EQUIPMENT HOOKUP

Complete all steps in BASIC DIAGNOSTIC PROCEDURES article before proceeding to self-diagnostic tests. Ensure vacuum hoses and EEC-IV wiring harnesses are properly connected.

Apply parking brake, and place shift lever in PARK (A/T) or NEUTRAL (M/T) position. Block drive wheels. Turn off all electrical loads. Connect appropriate test equipment to vehicle as follows:

Analog Volt-Ohmmeter (VOM) – 1) Turn ignition switch to OFF position. Set VOM at 0-15V DC range. Connect positive lead of VOM to positive battery terminal.

2) Connect negative VOM lead to Self-Test Output (STO) terminal of self-test connector. See Fig. 2. Connect jumper wire from Self-Test Input (STI) pigtail to signal return terminal of self-test connector. KOEO SELF-TEST will activate when ignition is turned on.

Scan Tester – Follow manufacturer instructions to hook up equipment and record service codes.

STAR Series Tester – Turn ignition switch to OFF position. Connect color-coded adapter cable leads to diagnostic tester. Connect 2 service connectors of adapter cable to vehicle self-test connector and STI pigtail connector. Connect timing light. Go to KOEO SELF-TEST.

KOEO SELF-TEST

Ensure engine is warmed to normal operating temperature. If engine does not start (or stalls after starting), continue KOEO SELF-TEST. DO NOT depress throttle on gasoline vehicles. Turn ignition off. Wait 10 seconds. Ensure test equipment is properly attached. Turn ignition on (engine off). Record all KOEO and Continuous Memory Codes.

If a Code 11 or 111 (pass code) is not retrieved in KOEO portion of test, service KOEO codes. See SERVICE CODE REFERENCE CHARTS. If ECA will not output codes, go to CIRCUIT TEST QA. If service codes are retrieved:

- Service codes in order retrieved. See SERVICE CODE REFERENCE CHARTS.
- On DIS and EDIS models, see IGNITION SYSTEM in SYSTEM & COMPONENT TESTING – EEC-IV article if Continuous Memory Code 45, 46, 48, 215, 216, 217, 232 or 238 is retrieved during KOEO SELF-TEST.
- If vehicle has a no-start condition, go to CIRCUIT TEST AA (TFI), CIRCUIT TEST AB (DIS) or CIRCUIT TEST AC (EDIS).
- If vehicle displays a Code 11 or 111 (pass code) and does not have any of symptoms described in previous steps, go to COMPUTED TIMING CHECK.

COMPUTED TIMING CHECK

Turn ignition off. Connect timing light. Using jumper wire or test equipment, activate KOER SELF-TEST. If engine starts and stalls (or stalls during self-test), go to CIRCUIT TEST S. Start engine, and check for following:

- If Code 98 or 998 is displayed, EEC-IV system is operating in Failure Mode Effects Management (FMEM). Vehicle cannot be diagnosed in KOER SELF-TEST; rerun KOEO SELF-TEST.
- Check computed timing after last service code has been displayed. Timing will remain fixed for 2 minutes after last code has been retrieved unless self-test is deactivated.
- Computed timing, at crankshaft, should equal base timing (see vehicle emission decal) plus 20 degrees BTDC. This timing may vary 3 degrees (+/−). If computed timing is within specification, perform KOER SELF-TEST. If timing is not within specification, go to step 2) of CIRCUIT TEST PA (TFI), of CIRCUIT TEST PB (DIS) or of CIRCUIT TEST PC (EDIS).

KOER SELF-TEST

Diagnostic Aids – DO NOT enter this test sequence until a Code 11 or 111 (pass code) has been retrieved in KOEO SELF-TEST. If system has not passed KOEO SELF-TEST, codes recorded in KOER SELF-TEST may not be valid.

Deactivate self-test by removing and reconnecting jumper wire or by procedure specified by test equipment in use. Start engine, and run it for 2 minutes at 2000 RPM to warm Heated Exhaust Gas Oxygen (HEGO) sensor. Turn engine off, and wait 10 seconds. Activate KOER SELF-TEST using a jumper wire or appropriate procedure for test equipment used. Start engine. Record all service codes displayed. Check following items:

- If engine starts and stalls (or stalls during self-test), go to CIRCUIT TEST S.
- If Code 98 or 998 is displayed, EEC-IV system is operating in Failure Management Effects Mode (FMEM) and vehicle has not passed KOEO SELF-TEST. Vehicle cannot be diagnosed while in FMEM mode. See Code 98 or 998 in SERVICE CODE REFERENCE CHARTS.
- If vehicle is equipped with a Brake On-Off (BOO) switch, brake pedal must be depressed and released after ID code portion of test.
- On vehicles with Power Steering Pressure Switch (PSPS), turn steering wheel at least 1/2 turn and release within 1-2 seconds after ID code portion of test.
- On vehicles with E4OD transmissions, Overdrive Cancel Switch (OCS) must be cycled after ID code portion of test.
- If Dynamic Response Code appears, perform a brief Wide Open Throttle (WOT). DO NOT perform WOT unless requested.
- If a Code 11 or 111 (pass code) is retrieved during KOER SELF-TEST, service Continuous Memory Codes retrieved in KOEO SELF-TEST. See SERVICE CODE REFERENCE CHARTS.
- If a Code 11 or 111 (pass code) is retrieved during Continuous Memory Code portion of KOEO SELF-TEST (Code 11-1-11 or Code 111-1-111) and no driveability problem exists, EEC-IV testing is complete. If driveability problems are still present, go to TROUBLE SHOOTING – NO CODES article.

- If KOER codes are present, see SERVICE CODE REFERENCE CHARTS. If system will not output codes, go to CIRCUIT TEST QA.

CONTINUOUS MONITOR MODE (WIGGLE TEST)

Continuous Monitor Mode allows technician to attempt to recreate an intermittent fault while monitoring system. This mode, also called wiggle test, may be used in both KOEO SELF-TEST and KOER SELF-TEST. CIRCUIT TESTS specify use of this procedure to identify intermittent faults in specific circuits or components.

KOEO Wiggle Test – Connect test equipment. Turn ignition on, and activate self-test using jumper lead or diagnostic tester. Wait 10 seconds, and then deactivate and reactivate self-test. Wiggle test mode is now activated. Tap, move and wiggle suspect sensor and/or harness area. If a fault is detected, a service code may be stored in memory and indicated at diagnostic tester or scan tester. Retrieve code, and perform appropriate test. See SERVICE CODE REFERENCE CHARTS.

KOER Wiggle Test – Connect test equipment. Turn ignition off, and wait 10 seconds. Start engine. Activate self-test using jumper lead or diagnostic tester. Wait 10 seconds, and then deactivate and reactivate self-test. DO NOT turn engine off. KOER wiggle test mode is now activated. Tap, move and wiggle suspect sensor and/or harness area. If a fault is detected, a service code may be stored in memory and indicated at diagnostic tester or scan tester. Retrieve code, and perform appropriate test. See SERVICE CODE REFERENCE CHARTS.

ADDITIONAL SYSTEM FUNCTIONS

Additional diagnostic system features are available to help diagnose driveability problems and service EEC-IV systems.

CHECK ENGINE Light & Malfunction Indicator Light (MIL) – CHECK ENGINE light and MIL are intended to alert driver of certain malfunctions in EEC-IV system.

Light may also be used to retrieve service codes stored in ECA. When hooked up for KOEO SELF-TEST or KOER SELF-TEST, light will display all codes which turn on light during vehicle operation, not just Continuous Memory Codes.

If light comes on during vehicle operation, vehicle should be inspected as soon as possible. Immediately turning off engine is not necessary; vehicle can be driven with light on.

If light comes on and then goes off during vehicle operation, code causing light to glow will be stored in ECA memory as a Continuous Memory Code.

Light should come on when ignition is turned on and go out when engine is started. If light does not come on, see SYMPTOMS in TROUBLE SHOOTING – NO CODES article. If hard fault codes are not present, ECA turns out light when it receives a Profile Ignition Pick-Up (PIP) signal.

Output State Check – Output state check is used as an aid for servicing EEC-IV system output actuators. It allows technicians to operate most output actuators on command. This mode is entered from KOEO SELF-TEST after all codes have been retrieved. Leave SELF-TEST activated, and depress throttle to initiate test sequence. Each time throttle is depressed and released, output actuators will change from on to off or off to on.

Failure Mode Effects Management (FMEM), Code 98 Or 998 – FMEM mode allows system operation when sensors fail or transmit signals that are out of normal operating range. During FMEM mode, ECA substitutes a mid-range signal for defective sensor while continuing to monitor sensor. If faulty sensor's signals return to normal operating range, ECA will use those signals. A Code 98 or 998 will be displayed when FMEM mode is in effect.

Hardware Limited Operational Strategy (HLOS) – If a number of system or sensor failures are present and ECA is not receiving enough information to operate, ECA will switch to HLOS mode. ECA will output fixed values to allow operation of vehicle. Driveability performance will be reduced.

1992 ENGINE PERFORMANCE
Self-Diagnostics – EEC-IV (Cont.)

Cylinder Balance Test – This test helps identify a weak or non-contributing cylinder in engines with sequential PFI fuel systems. ECA shuts off fuel supply to each injector and measures RPM drop. It computes variation between cylinders and identifies weak ones. This test mode is entered from KOER SELF-TEST after all codes have been displayed. Within 2 minutes after codes have been displayed, lightly depress throttle (a 2-3 degree throttle angle is required, not a wide open throttle). After a brief stabilizing period, ECA will activate test procedure. Test will be repeated if throttle is depressed within 2 minutes of final code output. During second and third test sequences, percentage of allowable variation between cylinders is reduced. Service codes displayed during this test identify weak or non-contributing cylinder. See CYLINDER BALANCE TEST SERVICE CODES table. If Code 90 is displayed during this test, system has passed test. If Code 77 is displayed, repeat cylinder balance test. If throttle is moved during this test, Code 77 will appear, indicating test is not completed. Total test time is about 3 minutes.

CYLINDER BALANCE TEST SERVICE CODES

Service Code	Application
90	Pass
10	Cylinder No. 1
20	Cylinder No. 2
30	Cylinder No. 3
40	Cylinder No. 4
50	Cylinder No. 5
60	Cylinder No. 6
70	Cylinder No. 7
80	Cylinder No. 8
77	Retest

SUMMARY

If no service code or Code 11-1-11 or 111-1-111 (pass code) is present, but driveability problem still exists, proceed to EEC-IV DIAGNOSIS BY SYMPTOM table. If driveability problem still cannot be located, go to TROUBLE SHOOTING – NO CODES article for diagnosis by symptoms or intermittent diagnostic procedures.

EEC-IV DIAGNOSIS BY SYMPTOM

Symptom	Application	Circuit Test
A/C Compressor Runs Continuously	2.3L & 4.9L	KM – Step 35)
A/C Does Not Cut Off During WOT	All Models	KM – Step 15)
A/C Not Functioning	All Models	KM – Step 1)
Black Exhaust Smoke	Except 7.3L	H – Step 1)
CHECK ENGINE Light Always On	[1] Except 7.3L	ML – Step 1)
CHECK ENGINE Light Flashing With Erratic Idle	[1] Except 7.3L	ML – Step 15)
CHECK ENGINE Light Never On	[1] Except 7.3L	ML – Step 4)
CHECK ENGINE Light On Intermittently	[1] Except 7.3L	ML – Step 10)
Difficult Start	Ranger 2.3L	NB – Step 25)
Engine Detonates	2.3L & 4.0L	KP – Step 5)
Engine Hesitates After Hot Restart	[1] Except 7.3L	H – Step 21)
Engine Hesitation	[1] Except 7.3L	S – Step 2)
Engine Lacks Power Or Loses Power	[1] Except 7.3L	S – Step 2)
Engine Miss At Idle, Acceleration Or Cruise	[1] Except 7.3L	S – Step 2)
Engine Runs Rough At All Times	[1] Except 7.3L	S – Step 2)
Engine Stalls	Except 7.3L	S – Step 2)
Engine Stalls During Trans. Downshift	Models With E4OD	TC – Step 1)
Engine Stalls During Trans. Engagement	Models With E4OD	TC – Step 1)
Engine Stalls When Parking	Models With PSPS	FF – Step 3)
Engine Surge At Acceleration Or Cruise	[1] Except 7.3L	S – Step 2)
Engine Surge At Idle With A/C On	[1] 2.3L	KM – Step 30)
Erratic RPM	[1] Except 7.3L	S – Step 2)
Gasoline Fumes	Models With CANP	KD – Step 1)
Late Shift Into 4x4 High	Models With E4OD	TB – Step 5)
Low Idle With A/C on	Except 7.3L	KM – Step 43)
Overdrive Cancel Indicator Off	Models With E4OD	TB – Step 4)
4x4 Low Light Always Off & Harsh Shift	Models With E4OD	TB – Step 2)
4x4 Low Light Always On & Shift Slipping	Models With E4OD	TB – Step 2)

[1] – On models equipped with mass airflow system, ensure air induction and electrical connections are clean and tight.

1992 ENGINE PERFORMANCE
Self-Diagnostics – EEC-IV (Cont.)

SERVICE CODE REFERENCE CHARTS

2-DIGIT SERVICE CODE REFERENCE CHART

Code	Application	KOEO	KOER	CONT.
No Codes	All Models	QA1	QA1	QA1
11	All Models	Pass	Pass	Pass
12	All Models			KE1
13	All Models			KE15
14	7.3L Diesel All Other Models			DJ1 NA1
15	All Models	Replace ECA		QB1
16	All Models			KE1
18	All Models		PA1	NA3
19	All Models		Replace ECA	
21	All Models	DA1	DA1	
	All Other Models	DF1	DF7	DF90
23	7.3L Diesel All Other Models	DQ1 DH2	DQ1 DH1	
24	All Models	DA1	DA1	
25	All Models		DG1	
26	Bronco, E & F Series All Other Models	TE1 DC2	TE1 DC1	
29	Bronco, E & F Series All Other Models			DS1 DP1
31	All Models	DN1	DN1	DN90
32	All Models	DN25	DN25	DN90
33	All Models		DN40	DN110
34	All Models	DN20	DN20	DN115
35	All Models	DN5	DN5	DN90
41	All Models		H1	H1
42	All Models		H1	
44	All Models		KC1	
45	All Models		KC1	
46	All Models		KC1	
47	All Models	TB1		
49	All Models			TG90
51	All Models	DA10		DA90
52	All Models	FF1	FF5	
53	7.3L Diesel All Other Models	DQ2 DH3		DQ90 DH90
54	All Models	DA10		DA90
56	Bronco, E & F Series All Other Models	TE10 DC20		TG90 DC20

Code	Application	KOEO	KOER	CONT.
57	All Models	KP1		
59	All Models			TG90
61	All Models	DA20		DA90
62	All Models			TG90
63	7.3L Diesel All Other Models	DQ10 DH10		DQ94 DH94
64	All Models	DA20		DA90
65	All Models		TB1	
66	Bronco, E & F Series All Other Models	TE20		TG90 DC10
67	Bronco (Exc. 4.9L M/T) E & F Series (Exc. 4.9L M/T) All Other Models	KM40 TA1		TG90 TA1
69	All Models			TG90
72	All Models		DF10	
73	All Models		DH20	
74	All Models		FD1	
75	All Models		FD10	
77	All Models		M1	
79	All Models	KM40		
81	All Models	KC8		DF11
82	All Models	KC8		
84	All Models	DN10		
85	All Models	KD6		
86	All Models	TC10		
87	All Models	J7		J95
89	All Models	TC10		
91	All Models	TC1	H1	H1
92	All Models	TC1	H1	
93	All Models	TC1		
94	All Models	TC1	KC1	
95	All Models	J20		J90
96	All Models	J30		J93
97	All Models	TB1		
98	7.3L Diesel All Other Models	TC10 FMEM	FMEM	FMEM
99	All Models	TC10	TG90	TG90
Code Not Listed	All Models	QA1	QA1	QA1

1992 ENGINE PERFORMANCE
Self-Diagnostics – EEC-IV (Cont.)

3-DIGIT SERVICE CODE REFERENCE CHART (1 OF 2)

3-DIGIT SERVICE CODE DEFINITIONS		Go To Circuit Test:		
Code	Application	KOEO	KOER	CONT.
No Codes	All Models	QA1	QA1	QA1
111	All Models	Pass	Pass	Pass
112	All Models	DA20		DA90
113	All Models	DA10		DA90
114	All Models	DA1	DA1	
116	All Models	DA1	DA1	
117	All Models	DA20		DA90
118	All Models	DA10		DA90
121	All Models	DH2	DH1	G1
122	All Models	DH10		DH94
123	All Models	DH3		DH90
124	All Models			G1
125	All Models			G1
126	All Models	DF1	DF1	DF90
128	All Models			DF11
129	Aerostar, Explorer & Ranger		DC10	
	All Other Models		DF10	
136	All Models		H1	
137	All Models		H1	
139	All Models			H1
144	All Models			H1
157	All Models			DC10
158	All Models	DC20		DC20
159	All Models	DC1	DC1	
167	All Models		DH20	
171	All Models			H1
172	All Models		H1	H1
173	All Models		H1	H1
174	All Models			H1
175	All Models			H1
176	All Models			H1
177	All Models			H1
178	All Models			H1
179	All Models			HA15
181	All Models			HA1
182	All Models			HA15
183	All Models			HA1
184	All Models			G5
185	All Models			G5

3-DIGIT SERVICE CODE DEFINITIONS		Go To Circuit Test:		
Code	Application	KOEO	KOER	CONT.
186	All Models			G7
187	All Models			G7
188	All Models			HA15
189	All Models			HA1
191	All Models			HA15
192	All Models			HA1
194	All Models			H5
195	All Models			H5
211	All W/ TFI Ignition			NA1
	All W/ DIS Ignition			NB1
	All W/ EDIS Ignition			NC1
212	W/ TFI Ignition			
	3.0L PFI Truck			NA2
	All Other TFI Trucks			NA3
	All W/ DIS Ignition			NB2
	All W/ EDIS Ignition			NC3
213	All W/ TFI Ignition		PA1	
	All W/ DIS Ignition		PB1	
	All W/ EDIS Ignition		PC1	
215	All Models			(1)
216	All Models			(1)
217	All Models			(1)
218	All Models			(1)
219	All Models			PB10
222	All Models			(1)
223	All Models			(1)
224	All Models			(1)
225	All Models		DG1	
226	All Models	NC2		
232	All Models			(1)
238	All Models			(1)
311	All Models		KC1	
312	All Models		KC1	
313	All Models		KC1	
314	All Models		KC1	
327	All Models	DN1	DN1	DN90
328	All Models	DN25	DN25	DN90
332	All Models		DN40	DN110
334	All Models	DN20	DN20	DN115
337	All Models	DN5	DN5	DN90
338	All Models			DA100
339	All Models			DA101

(1) - Refer to the SYSTEM & COMPONENT TESTING article.

3-DIGIT SERVICE CODE REFERENCE CHART (2 OF 2)

Code	Application	KOEO	KOER	CONT.
341	All Models	KP1		
411	All Models		KE15	
412	All Models		KE1	
452	Aerostar, Bronco, E & F Series			DS1
	All Other Models			DP1
511	All Models	Replace ECA		
512	All Models			QB1
513	All Models	Replace ECA		
519	All Models	FF1		
521	All Models		FF5	
522	All Models	TA1		
525	All Models	TA1		TA1
528				TA1
529				ML25
533				ML25
536			FD1	FD90
538			M1	
539		KM40		
542	All Models	J20		J90
543	All Models	J30		J93
552	All Models	KC8		
553	All Models	KC8		
556	All Models	J7		J95
558	All Models	DN10		
565	All Models	KD6		
566	All Models	TC10		
569	All Models	KD6		
617	All Models			TG90
618	All Models			TG90
619	All Models			TG90

Code	Application	KOEO	KOER	CONT.
621	All Models	TC1		
622	All Models	TC1		
624	All Models	TC10		TG90
625	All Models	TC10		TG90
626	All Models	TC1		
627	All Models	TC1		
628	All Models			TG90
629	Aerostar, Explorer & Ranger	TC10		
	All Other Models	TC1		TC90
631	All Models	TB1		
632	All Models		TB1	
633	All Models	TB1		
634	Bronco, E & F Series	TD1		TD1
	All Other Models	TD1		TG90
636	All Models	TE1	TE1	
637	All Models	TE10		TG91
638	All Models	TE20		TG91
641	All Models	TC1		
643	All Models	TC20		TC30
645	All Models			TG90
646	All Models			TG90
647	All Models			TG90
648	All Models			TG90
649	All Models			TG90
651	All Models			TG90
652	All Models	TC1		
654	All Models	TD1		
656	All Models			
998	All Models	FMEM	FMEM	FMEM
Code Not Listed	All Models	QA1	QA1	QA1

1992 ENGINE PERFORMANCE
Self-Diagnostics – EEC-IV (Cont.)

SERVICE CODE DEFINITION CHARTS

SERVICE CODE DEFINITION (RANGER 2.3L – 1 OF 2)	
SERVICE CODE	**SERVICE CODE DEFINITION**
111 orc	▶ System PASS
112 oc	▶ ACT indicated 123°C (254°F) / circuit grounded
113 oc	▶ ACT indicated -40°C (-40°F) / circuit open
114 or	▶ Air Charge Temp (ACT) out of Self-Test range
116 or	▶ Engine Coolant Temp (ECT) out of Self-Test range
117 oc	▶ ECT indicated 123° C (254°F) / circuit grounded
118 oc	▶ ECT indicated -40°C (-40°F) / circuit open
121 orc	▶ Throttle Position (TP) out of Self-Test range
122 oc	▶ TP circuit below minimum voltage
123 oc	▶ TP circuit above maximum voltage
124 c	▶ Throttle Position (TP) Sensor voltage higher than expected
125 c	▶ Throttle Position (TP) Sensor voltage lower than expected
129 r	▶ Insufficient MAP change during Dynamic Response Test
157 c	▶ MAF circuit below minimum voltage
158 oc	▶ MAF circuit above maximum voltage
159 or	▶ Mass Air Flow (MAF) out of Self-Test range
167 r	▶ Insufficient TP change during Dynamic Response Test
171 c	▶ Fuel system at adaptive limits, Oxygen Sensor (HEGO) unable to switch
172 rc	▶ Lack of Oxygen Sensor (HEGO) switches, indicates lean
173 rc	▶ Lack of Oxygen Sensor (HEGO) switches, indicates rich
179 c	▶ Fuel system at lean adaptive limit at part throttle, system rich
181 c	▶ Fuel system at rich adaptive limit at part throttle, system lean
184 c	▶ Mass Air Flow (MAF) higher than expected
185 c	▶ Mass Air Flow (MAF) lower than expected
186 c	▶ Injector pulse width higher than expected
187 c	▶ Injector pulse width lower than expected
211 c	▶ PIP circuit failure
213 r	▶ SPOUT circuit open
218 c	▶ Loss of IDM (left side)
222 c	▶ Loss of IDM (right side)
223 c	▶ Loss of Dual Plug Input control
224 c	▶ Erratic IDM input to processor
327 orc	▶ EVP circuit below minimum voltage
328 orc	▶ EVP voltage below closed limit
332 rc	▶ EGR valve opening not detected
334 orc	▶ EVP voltage above closed limit
337 orc	▶ EVP circuit above maximum voltage
341	▶ Octane Adjust circuit open
411 r	▶ Cannot control rpm during Self-Test low rpm check
412 r	▶ Cannot control rpm during Self-Test high rpm check
452 c	▶ Insufficient input from Vehicle Speed Sensor (VSS)
511 o	▶ EEC processor Read Only Memory (ROM) test failed
512 c	▶ EEC processor Keep Alive Memory (KAM) test failed
513 o	▶ Failure in EEC processor internal voltage
519 o	▶ Power Steering Pressure Switch (PSPS) circuit open
521 r	▶ PSPS circuit did not change states
522 o	▶ Vehicle not in PARK or NEUTRAL during KOEO
536 r	▶ Brake On / Off (BOO) circuit failure / not actuated during Self-Test

SERVICE CODE DEFINITION (RANGER 2.3L – 2 OF 2)

SERVICE CODE		SERVICE CODE DEFINITION
538 r	▶	Operator error (Dynamic Response / Cylinder Balance Tests)
539 o	▶	A / C ON / Defrost ON during Self-Test
542 oc	▶	Fuel Pump circuit open - EEC processor to motor ground
543 oc	▶	Fuel Pump circuit open - battery to EEC processor
556 oc	▶	Primary Fuel Pump circuit failure
558 o	▶	EGR Vacuum Regulator (EVR) circuit failure
566 o	▶	Shift Solenoid (SS) circuit failure
629 o	▶	Clutch Converter Override (CCO) circuit failure
998 r	▶	Hard fault present
NO CODES		Unable to initiate Self-Test or unable to output Self-Test codes
CODES NOT LISTED		Service codes displayed are not applicable to the vehicle being tested

KEY: o = Key On Engine Off (KOEO); r = Key On Engine Running (KOER); c = Continuous Memory

SERVICE CODE DEFINITION (RANGER 2.9L)

SERVICE CODE		SERVICE CODE DEFINITION
11 orc	▶	System PASS
12 r	▶	Cannot control rpm during Self-Test high rpm check
13 r	▶	Cannot control rpm during Self-Test low rpm check
14 c	▶	PIP circuit failure
15 o	▶	EEC processor Read Only Memory (ROM) test failed
15 c	▶	EEC processor Keep Alive Memory (KAM) test failed
18 r	▶	SPOUT circuit open
18 c	▶	Loss of IDM input to processor / SPOUT circuit grounded
19 o	▶	Failure in EEC processor internal voltage
21 or	▶	Engine Coolant Temp (ECT) out of Self-Test range
22 orc	▶	Manifold Absolute Pressure (MAP) out of Self-Test range
23 or	▶	Throttle Position (TP) out of Self-Test range
24 or	▶	Air Charge Temp (ACT) out of Self-Test range
29 c	▶	Insufficient input from Vehicle Speed Sensor (VSS)
41 r	▶	HEGO sensor circuit indicates system lean
41 c	▶	No HEGO switch detected
42 r	▶	HEGO sensor circuit indicates system rich
51 oc	▶	ECT indicated -40°C (-40°F) / circuit open
53 oc	▶	TP circuit above maximum voltage
54 oc	▶	ACT indicated -40°C (-40°F) / circuit open
61 oc	▶	ECT indicated 123°C (254°F) / circuit grounded
63 oc	▶	TP circuit below minimum voltage
64 oc	▶	ACT indicated 123°C (254°F) / circuit grounded
67 o	▶	Neutral Drive Switch (NDS) circuit open / A / C ON
67 c	▶	Clutch Switch circuit failure
72 r	▶	Insufficient MAP change during Dynamic Response Test
73 r	▶	Insufficient TP change during Dynamic Response Test
74 r	▶	Brake On / Off (BOO) circuit failure / not actuated during Self-Test
77 r	▶	Operator error (Dynamic Response / Cylinder Balance Tests)
86 o	▶	Shift Solenoid (SS) circuit failure
87 oc	▶	Primary Fuel Pump circuit failure
89 o	▶	Clutch Converter Override (CCO) circuit failure
95 oc	▶	Fuel Pump circuit open - EEC processor to motor ground
96 oc	▶	Fuel Pump circuit open - battery to EEC processor
98 r	▶	Hard fault present
NO CODES	▶	Unable to initiate Self-Test or unable to output Self-Test codes
CODES NOT LISTED		Service codes displayed are not applicable to the vehicle being tested

KEY: o = Key On Engine Off (KOEO); r = Key On Engine Running (KOER); c = Continuous Memory

SERVICE CODE DEFINITION (BRONCO 4.9L, PICKUP 4.9L & VAN 4.9L – 1 OF 2)

SERVICE CODE		SERVICE CODE DEFINITION
111	▶	System PASS
112	▶	ACT indicated 123°C (254°F) / circuit grounded
113	▶	ACT indicated -40°C (-40°F) / circuit open
114	▶	Air Charge Temperature (ACT) sensor out of Self-Test range
116	▶	Engine Cooling Temperature (ECT) sensor out of Self-Test range
117	▶	ECT indicated 123°C (254°F) / circuit grounded
118	▶	ECT indicated -40°C (-40°F) / circuit open
121	▶	Throttle Position (TP) sensor out of Self-Test range
122	▶	TP circuit below minimum voltage
123	▶	TP sensor above maximum voltage
126	▶	Manifold Absolute Pressure (MAP) sensor out of Self-Test range
129	▶	Insufficient MAP change during Dynamic Response Test
144	▶	No HEGO switch detected
172	▶	HEGO sensor circuit indicates system lean
173	▶	HEGO sensor circuit indicates system rich
176	▶	Insufficient TP change during Dynamic Response Test
179	▶	Adaptive fuel limit lean
181	▶	Adaptive fuel limit rich
182	▶	Adaptive fuel limit lean @ idle
183	▶	Adaptive fuel limit rich @ idle
211	▶	PIP circuit failure
213	▶	SPOUT circuit open
224	▶	Loss of IDM input to processor / SPOUT circuit grounded
311	▶	Thermactor air system inoperative
312	▶	Thermactor air upstream during Self-Test
313	▶	Thermactor air not bypassed during Self-Test
327	▶	EVP circuit below minimum voltage
328	▶	EVP voltage below closed limit
332	▶	EGR valve opening not detected
334	▶	EVP voltage above closed limit
337	▶	EVP circuit above maximum voltage
411	▶	Cannot control rpm during Self-Test low rpm check
412	▶	Cannot control rpm during Self-Test high rpm check
452	▶	Insufficient input from the Vehicle Speed Sensor (VSS)
511	▶	EEC processor Read Only Memory (ROM) test failed
512	▶	EEC processor Keep Alive Memory (KAM) test failed
513	▶	Failure in EEC processor internal voltage
527	▶	Neutral Drive Switch (NDS) circuit open / A/C on
536	▶	Brake On / Off (BOO) circuit open / not actuated during Self-Test
538	▶	Operator error (Dynamic Response / Cylinder Balance Tests)
542	▶	Fuel pump circuit open -EEC processor to motor ground
543	▶	Fuel pump circuit open - battery to EEC processor
552	▶	Air Management 1 (AM1) circuit failure
553	▶	Air Management 2 (AM2) circuit failure
556	▶	Primary Fuel Pump circuit failure
558	▶	EGR Vacuum Regulator (EVR) circuit failure
565	▶	Canister Purge (CANP) circuit failure
617	▶	1-2 shift error (E4OD)

SERVICE CODE DEFINITION (BRONCO 4.9L, PICKUP 4.9L & VAN 4.9L – 2 OF 2)

SERVICE CODE	SERVICE CODE DEFINITION
618	▶ 2-3 shift error (E4OD)
619	▶ 3-4 shift error (E4OD)
621	▶ Shift Solenoid 1 (SS1) circuit failure (E4OD)
622	▶ Shift Solenoid 2 (SS2) circuit failure (E4OD)
624	▶ Electronic Pressure Control (EPC) circuit
625	▶ Electronic Pressure Control (EPC) driver open in EEC processor (E4OD)
626	▶ Coast Clutch Solenoid (CCS) circuit failure (E4OD)
627	▶ Converter Clutch Control (CCC) solenoid circuit failure (E4OD)
628	▶ Converter clutch error (E4OD)
631	▶ Overdrive Cancel Indicator Light (OCIL) circuit failure (E4OD)
632	▶ Overdrive Cancel Switch (OCS) not changing state (E4OD)
633	▶ 4 x 4 switch is closed (E4OD)
634	▶ Manual Lever Position (MLP) sensor out of range / A/C ON (E4OD)
636	▶ Transmission Oil Temperature (TOT) sensor out of Self-Test range (E4OD)
637	▶ TOT indicated -40°C (-40°F) / circuit open (E4OD)
638	▶ TOT indicated 143°C (290°F) / circuit grounded (E4OD)
654	▶ (MLP) sensor not in Park position
998	▶ Hard fault present
NO CODES	Unable to initiate Self-Test or unable to output Self-Test codes
CODES NOT LISTED	Services codes displayed are not applicable to the vehicle being tested

KEY: o = Key On Engine Off (KOEO); r = Key On Engine Running (KOER); c = Continuous Memory

1992 ENGINE PERFORMANCE
Self-Diagnostics − EEC-IV (Cont.)

SERVICE CODE DEFINITION (VAN 5.0L)

SERVICE CODE		SERVICE CODE DEFINITION
111 orc	▶	System PASS
112 oc	▶	ACT indicated 123°C (254°F) / circuit grounded
113 oc	▶	ACT indicated -40°C (-40°F) / circuit open
114 or	▶	Air Charge Temperature (ACT) Sensor out of Self-Test range
116 or	▶	Engine Cooling Temperature (ECT) Sensor out of Self-Test range
117 oc	▶	ECT indicated 123°C (254°F) / circuit grounded
118 oc	▶	ECT indicated -40°C (-40°F) / circuit open
121 orc	▶	Throttle Position (TP) Sensor out of Self-Test range
122 oc	▶	TP circuit below minimum voltage
123 oc	▶	TP above maximum voltage
126 orc	▶	Manifold Absolute Pressure (MAP) Sensor out of Self-Test range
128 c	▶	MAP vacuum circuit failure
129 r	▶	Insufficient MAP change during Dynamic Response Test
167 r	▶	Insufficient TP change during Dynamic Response Test
171 c	▶	Fuel system at adaptive limits, Oxygen Sensor (HEGO) unable to switch
172 rc	▶	Lack of Oxygen Sensor (HEGO) switches, indicates lean
173 rc	▶	Lack of Oxygen Sensor (HEGO) switches, indicates rich
179 c	▶	Fuel system at lean adaptive limit at part throttle, system rich
181 c	▶	Fuel system at rich adaptive limit at part throttle, system lean
211 c	▶	PIP circuit failure
212 c	▶	Loss of IDM input to processor / SPOUT circuit grounded
213 r	▶	SPOUT circuit open
225 r	▶	Knock not sensed during Dynamic Response Test
311 r	▶	Thermactor air system inoperative
312 r	▶	Thermactor air upstream during Self-Test
313 r	▶	Thermactor air not bypassed during Self-Test
327 orc	▶	EVP circuit below minimum voltage
328 orc	▶	EVP voltage below closed limit
332 rc	▶	EGR valve opening not detected
334 orc	▶	EVP voltage above closed limit
337 orc	▶	EVP circuit above maximum voltage
411 r	▶	Cannot control rpm during Self-Test low rpm check
412 r	▶	Cannot control rpm during Self-Test high rpm check
452 c	▶	Insufficient input from Progammable Speedometer / Odometer Module (PSOM)
511 o	▶	EEC processor Read Only Memory (ROM) test failed
512 c	▶	EEC processor Keep Alive Memory (KAM) test failed
513 o	▶	Failure in EEC processor internal voltage
522 o	▶	Vehicle not in PARK or NEUTRAL during KOEO
528 c	▶	Clutch switch circuit failure
538 r	▶	Operator error Dynamic Response Test
542 oc	▶	Fuel Pump circuit open - EEC processor to motor ground
543 oc	▶	Fuel Pump circuit open - battery to EEC processor
552 o	▶	Air Management 1 (AM1) circuit failure
553 o	▶	Air Management 2 (AM2) circuit failure
556 oc	▶	Primary fuel pump circuit failure
558 o	▶	EGR Vacuum Regulator (EVR) circuit failure
565 o	▶	Canister Purge (CANP) circuit failure
998 r	▶	Hard fault present
NO CODES		Unable to initiate Self-Test or unable to output Self-Test codes
CODES NOT LISTED		Services codes displayed are not applicable to the vehicle being tested

KEY: o = Key On Engine Off (KOEO); r = Key On Engine Running (KOER); c = Continuous Memory

SERVICE CODE DEFINITION (BRONCO 5.0L & PICKUP 5.0L WITH E4OD – 1 OF 2)

SERVICE CODE	SERVICE CODE DEFINITION
111 orc	▶ System PASS
112 oc	▶ ACT indicated 123°C (254°F) / circuit grounded
113 oc	▶ ACT indicated -40°C (-40°F) / circuit open
114 or	▶ Air Charge Temperature (ACT) Sensor out of Self-Test range
116 or	▶ Engine Cooling Temperature (ECT) Sensor out of Self-Test range
117 oc	▶ ECT indicated 123°C (254°F) / circuit grounded
118 oc	▶ ECT indicated -40°C (-40°F) / circuit open
121 orc	▶ Throttle Position (TP) Sensor out of Self-Test range
122 oc	▶ TP circuit below minimum voltage
123 oc	▶ TP above maximum voltage
126 orc	▶ Manifold Absolute Pressure (MAP) Sensor out of Self-Test range
128 c	▶ MAP vacuum circuit failure
129 r	▶ Insufficient MAP change during Dynamic Response Test
167 r	▶ Insufficient TP change during Dynamic Response Test
171 c	▶ Fuel system at adaptive limits, Oxygen Sensor (HEGO) unable to switch
172 rc	▶ Lack of Oxygen Sensor (HEGO) switches, indicates lean
173 rc	▶ Lack of Oxygen Sensor (HEGO) switches, indicates rich
179 c	▶ Fuel system at lean adaptive limit at part throttle, system rich
181 c	▶ Fuel system at rich adaptive limit at part throttle, system lean
211 c	▶ PIP circuit failure
212 c	▶ Loss of IDM input to processor / SPOUT circuit grounded
213 r	▶ SPOUT circuit open
225 r	▶ Knock not sensed during Dynamic Response Test
311 r	▶ Thermactor air system inoperative
312 r	▶ Thermactor air upstream during Self-Test
313 r	▶ Thermactor air not bypassed during Self-Test
327 orc	▶ EVP circuit below minimum voltage
328 orc	▶ EVP voltage below closed limit
332 rc	▶ EGR valve opening not detected
334 orc	▶ EVP voltage above closed limit
337 orc	▶ EVP circuit above maximum voltage
411 r	▶ Cannot control rpm during Self-Test low rpm check
412 r	▶ Cannot control rpm during Self-Test high rpm check
452 c	▶ Insufficient input from Progammable Speedometer / Odometer Module (PSOM)
511 o	▶ EEC processor Read Only Memory (ROM) test failed
512 c	▶ EEC processor Keep Alive Memory (KAM) test failed
513 o	▶ Failure in EEC processor internal voltage
536 rc	▶ Brake On / Off (BOO) circuit open—not actuated during Self-Test
538 r	▶ Operator error Dynamic Response Test
539 o	▶ A / C on / Defrost on during Self-Test
542 oc	▶ Fuel Pump circuit open - EEC processor to motor ground
543 oc	▶ Fuel Pump circuit open - battery to EEC processor
552 o	▶ Air Management 1 (AM1) circuit failure
553 o	▶ Air Management 2 (AM2) circuit failure
556 oc	▶ Primary fuel pump circuit failure
558 o	▶ EGR Vacuum Regulator (EVR) circuit failure

SERVICE CODE DEFINITION (BRONCO 5.0L & PICKUP 5.0L WITH E4OD – 2 OF 2)

SERVICE CODE		SERVICE CODE DEFINITION
565 o	▶	Canister Purge (CANP) circuit failure
617 c	▶	1-2 shift error
618 c	▶	2-3 shift error
619 c	▶	3-4 shift error
621 o	▶	Shift Solenoid 1 (SS1) circuit failure
622 o	▶	Shift Solenoid 2 (SS2) circuit failure
624 oc	▶	Electronic Pressure Control (EPC) circuit failure
625 o	▶	Electronic Pressure Control (EPC) driver failure in processor
626 o	▶	Coast Clutch Solenoid (CCS) circuit failure
628 o	▶	Converter clutch error
629 o	▶	Converter Clutch Control (CCC) solenoid circuit failure
631 o	▶	Overdrive Cancel Indicator Light (OCIL) circuit failure
632 r	▶	Overdrive Cancel Switch (OCS) not changing state
633 o	▶	4 x 4 switch is closed
634 c	▶	MLP sensor out of range
636 or	▶	Transmission Oil Temperature (TOT) sensor out of Self-Test range
637 oc	▶	TOT indicated -40°C (-40°F) / circuit OPEN
638 oc	▶	TOT indicated 290°C (143°F) / circuit grounded
654 o	▶	Manual Lever Position (MLP) Sensor not in Park position
998 r	▶	Hard fault present
NO CODES		Unable to initiate Self-Test or unable to output Self-Test codes
CODES NOT LISTED		Services codes displayed are not applicable to the vehicle being tested

KEY: o = Key On Engine Off (KOEO); r = Key On Engine Running (KOER); c = Continuous Memory

SERVICE CODE DEFINITION (BRONCO 5.0L & PICKUP 5.0L WITHOUT E4OD)

SERVICE CODE	SERVICE CODE DEFINITION
11 orc	System PASS
12 r	Cannot control rpm during Self-Test high rpm check
13 r	Cannot control rpm during Self-Test low rpm check
14 c	PIP circuit failure
15 o	EEC processor Read Only Memory (ROM) test failed
15 c	EEC processor Keep Alive Memory (KAM) test failed
18 r	SPOUT circuit open
18 c	Loss of IDM input to processor / SPOUT circuit grounded
19 o	Failure in EEC processor internal voltage
21 or	Engine Cooling Temperature (ECT) sensor out of Self-Test range
22 orc	Manifold Absolute Pressure (MAP) sensor out of Self-Test range
23 orc	Throttle Position (TP) sensor out of Self-Test range
24 or	Air Charge Temperature (ACT) sensor out of Self-Test range
25 r	Knock not sensed during Dynamic Response Test
29 c	Insufficient input from Progammable Speedometer / Odometer Module (PSOM)
31 orc	EVP circuit below minimum voltage
32 orc	EVP voltage below closed limit
33 rc	EGR valve opening not detected
34 orc	EVP voltage above closed limit
35 orc	EVP circuit above maximum voltage
41 r	HEGO sensor circuit indicates system lean
41 c	No HEGO switching detected
42 r	HEGO sensor circuit indicates system rich
44 r	Thermactor air system inoperative
45 r	Thermactor air upstream during Self-Test
46 r	Thermactor air not bypassed during Self-Test
51 oc	ECT indicated -40°C (-40°F) / circuit open
52 o	Power Steering Pressirue Switch (PSPS) circuit open
52 r	PSPS circuit did not change states
53 oc	TP above maximum voltage
54 oc	ACT indicated -40°C (-40°F) / circuit open
61 oc	ECT indicated 123°C (254°F) / circuit grounded
63 oc	TP circuit below minimum voltage
64 oc	ACT indicated 123°C (254°F) / circuit grounded
67 o	Neutral Drive Switch (NDS) circuit open; A/C ON (Manual)
72 r	Insufficient MAP change during Dynamic Response Test
73 r	Insufficient TP change during Dynamic Response Test
74 rc	Brake On / Off (BOO) circuit open—not actuated during Self-Test
77 r	Operator error Dynamic Response Test
81 o	Air Management 2 (AM2) circuit failure
82 o	Air Management 1 (AM1) circuit failure
84 o	EGR Vacuum Regulator (EVR) circuit failure
85 o	Canister Purge (CANP) circuit failure
87 oc	Primary fuel pump circuit failure
95 oc	Fuel Pump circuit open - EEC processor to motor ground
96 oc	Fuel Pump circuit open - battery to EEC processor
98 r	Hard fault present
NO CODES	Unable to initiate Self-Test or unable to output Self-Test codes
CODES NOT LISTED	Services codes displayed are not applicable to the vehicle being tested

KEY: o = Key On Engine Off (KOEO); r = Key On Engine Running (KOER); c = Continuous Memory

SERVICE CODE DEFINITION (BRONCO 5.8L, PICKUP 5.8L & VAN 5.8L – 1 OF 2)

SERVICE CODE	SERVICE CODE DEFINITION
111	▶ System PASS
112	▶ ACT indicated 123°C (254°F) / circuit grounded
113	▶ ACT indicated -40°C (-40°F) / circuit open
114	▶ Air Charge Temperature (ACT) sensor out of Self-Test range
116	▶ Engine Cooling Temperature (ECT) sensor out of Self-Test range
117	▶ ECT indicated 123°C (254°F) / circuit grounded
118	▶ ECT indicated -40°C (-40°F) / circuit open
121	▶ Throttle Position (TP) sensor out of Self-Test range
122	▶ TP circuit below minimum voltage
123	▶ TP above maximum voltage
126	▶ Manifold Absolute Pressure (MAP) sensor out of Self-Test range
128	▶ MAP Vacuum circuit failure
129	▶ Insufficient MAP change during Dynamic Response Test
144	▶ No HEGO switching detected
167	▶ Insufficient TP change during Dynamic Response Test
172	▶ HEGO sensor circuit indicates system lean
173	▶ HEGO sensor circuit indicates system rich
179	▶ Adaptive Fuel limit lean
181	▶ Adaptive Fuel limit rich
182	▶ Adaptive Fuel limit lean @ idle
183	▶ Adaptive Fuel limit rich @ idle
211	▶ PIP circuit failure
212	▶ Loss of IDM input to processor / SPOUT circuit grounded
213	▶ SPOUT circuit open
311	▶ Thermactor air system inoperative
312	▶ Thermactor air upstream during Self-Test
313	▶ Thermactor air not bypassed during Self-Test
327	▶ EVP circuit below minimum voltage
328	▶ EVP voltage below closed limit
332	▶ EGR valve opening not detected
334	▶ EVP voltage above closed limit
337	▶ EVP circuit above maximum voltage
411	▶ Cannot control rpm during Self-Test low rpm check
412	▶ Cannot control rpm during Self-Test high rpm check
452	▶ Insufficient input from Vehicle Speed Sensor (VSS)
511	▶ EEC processor Read Only Memory (ROM) test failed
512	▶ EEC processor Keep Alive Memory (KAM) test failed
513	▶ Failure in EEC processor internal voltage
527	▶ Neutral Drive Switch (NDS) circuit open; A/C ON (Manual)
536	▶ Brake On/Off (BOO) circuit open—not actuated during Self-Test
538	▶ Operator error Dynamic Response Test
542	▶ Fuel Pump circuit open - EEC processor to motor ground
543	▶ Fuel Pump circuit open - battery to EEC processor
552	▶ Air Management 1 (AM1) circuit failure
553	▶ Air Management 2 (AM2) circuit failure
556	▶ Primary fuel pump circuit failure
558	▶ EGR Vacuum Regulator (EVR) circuit failure
565	▶ Canister Purge (CANP) circuit failure

SERVICE CODE DEFINITION (BRONCO 5.8L, PICKUP 5.8L & VAN 5.8L — 2 OF 2)

SERVICE CODE	SERVICE CODE DEFINITION
617	▶ 1-2 shift error (E4OD)
618	▶ 2-3 shift error (E4OD)
619	▶ 3-4 shift error (E4OD)
621	▶ Shift Solenoid 1 (SS1) circuit failure (E4OD)
622	▶ Shift Solenoid 2 (SS2) circuit failure (E4OD)
624	▶ Electronic Pressure Control (EPC) circuit failure (E4OD)
625	▶ Electronic Pressure Control (EPC) driver failure in processor (E4OD)
626	▶ Coast Clutch Solenoid (CCS) circuit failure (E4OD)
627	▶ Converter Clutch Control (CCC) solenoid circuit failure (E4OD)
628	▶ Converter clutch error (E4OD)
631	▶ Overdrive Cancel Indicator Light (OCIL) circuit failure (E4OD)
632	▶ Overdrive Cancel Switch (OCS) not changing state (E4OD)
633	▶ 4 x 4 switch is closed (E4OD)
634	▶ MLP sensor out of range; A/C ON (E4OD)
636	▶ Transmission Oil Temperature (TOT) sensor out of Self-Test range (E4OD)
637	▶ TOT indicated -40°C (-40°F) / circuit open (E4OD)
638	▶ TOT indicated 143°C (290°F) / circuit grounded (E4OD)
654	▶ MLP sensor not in Park position
998	▶ Hard fault present
NO CODES	Unable to initiate Self-Test or unable to output Self-Test codes
CODES NOT LISTED	Services codes displayed are not applicable to the vehicle being tested

SERVICE CODE DEFINITION (PICKUP 7.3L & VAN 7.3L)

SERVICE CODE	SERVICE CODE DEFINITION
11 orc	▶ System PASS
14 c	▶ Engine rpm sensor (rpms) circuit fault
15 o	▶ EEC processor Read Only Memory (ROM) test failed
15 c	▶ EEC processor Keep Alive Memory (KAM) test failed
19 o	▶ Failure in EEC processor internal voltage
22 orc	▶ Barometric Pressure (BP) out of Self-Test range
23 or	▶ Throttle Position Sensor (TPS) out of Self-Test range
26 or	▶ Transmission Oil Temp (TOT) out of Self-Test range
29 c	▶ Insufficient input from the Programmable Speedometer / Odometer Module PSOM)
47 o	▶ 4 x 4 switch is closed
49 c	▶ 1-2 Shift error
53 oc	▶ Throttle Position Sensor (TPS) circuit above maximum voltage
56 oc	▶ Transmission Oil Temp (TOT) indicated -40°C (-40°F) / circuit open
59 c	▶ 2-3 Shift error
62 c	▶ Converter Clutch error
63 oc	▶ Throttle Position Sensor (TPS) circuit below minimum voltage
65 r	▶ Overdrive Cancel Switch (OCS) circuit did not change states
66 oc	▶ Transmission Oil Temp (TOT) indicated 143°C (290°F) / circuit grounded
67 oc	▶ Manual Lever Position (MLP) sensor out of range / A/C ON
69 c	▶ 3-4 Shift error
74 r	▶ Brake On/Off (BOO) circuit open / not actuated during Self-Test
91 o	▶ Shift Solenoid 1 (SS1) circuit failure
92 o	▶ Shift Solenoid 2 (SS2) circuit failure
93 o	▶ Coast Clutch Solenoid (CCS) circuit failure
94 o	▶ Converter Clutch Control (CCC) Solenoid circuit failure
97 o	▶ Overdrive Cancel Indicator Light (OCIL) circuit failure
98 o	▶ Electronic Pressure Control (EPC) driver open in EEC processor
99 oc	▶ Electronic Pressure Control (EPC) circuit failure
NO CODES	Unable to initiate Self-Test or unable to output Self-Test codes
CODES NOT LISTED	Service codes displayed are not applicable to the vehicle being tested

KEY: o = Key On Engine Off (KOEO); r = Key On Engine Running (KOER); c = Continuous Memory

SERVICE CODE DEFINITION (PICKUP 7.5L & VAN 7.5L – 1 OF 2)

SERVICE CODE	SERVICE CODE DEFINITION
111	▶ System PASS
112	▶ ACT indicated 123°C (254°F) / circuit grounded
113	▶ ACT indicated -40°C (-40°F) / circuit open
114	▶ Air Charge Temperature (ACT) sensor input is out of Self-Test range
116	▶ Engine Cooling Temperature (ECT) sensor input is out of Self-Test range
117	▶ ECT indicated 123°C (254°F) / circuit grounded
118	▶ ECT indicated -40°C (40°F) / circuit open
121	▶ Throttle Position (TP) sensor input is out of Self-Test range
122	▶ TP circuit below minimum voltage
123	▶ TP above maximum voltage
126	▶ Manifold Absolute Pressure (MAP) sensor input is out of Self-Test range
129	▶ Insufficient MAP change during Dynamic Response Test
144	▶ No HEGO switching detected
167	▶ Insufficient TP change during Dynamic Response Test
172	▶ HEGO sensor circuit indicates system lean
173	▶ HEGO sensor circuit indicates system rich
179	▶ Adaptive Fuel limit lean
181	▶ Adaptive Fuel limit rich
182	▶ Adaptive Fuel limit lean @ idle
183	▶ Adaptive Fuel limit rich @ idle
211	▶ PIP circuit failure
212	▶ SPOUT circuit grounded
213	▶ SPOUT circuit open
311	▶ Thermactor air system inoperative
327	▶ EVP circuit below minimum voltage
328	▶ EVP voltage below closed limit
332	▶ EGR valve opening not detected
334	▶ EVP voltage above closed limit
337	▶ EVP circuit above maximum voltage
411	▶ Cannot control rpm during Self-Test low rpm check
412	▶ Cannot control rpm during Self-Test high rpm check
452	▶ Insufficient input from the Vehicle Speed Sensor (VSS)
511	▶ EEC processor Read Only Memory (ROM) test failed
512	▶ EEC processor Keep Alive Memory (KAM) test failed
513	▶ Failure in EEC processor internal voltage
527	▶ Neutral Drive Switch (NDS) circuit open; A/C ON (Manual/C6)
536	▶ Brake On/Off (BOO) circuit open - not actuated during Self-Test
538	▶ Operator error Dynamic Response Test
542	▶ Fuel pump circuit open EEC processor to motor ground
543	▶ Fuel pump circuit open battery to EEC processor
552	▶ Air Management 1 (AM1) circuit failure
556	▶ Primary fuel pump circuit failure
558	▶ EGR Vacuum Regulator (EVR) circuit failure
565	▶ Canister Purge (CANP) circuit failure
617	▶ 1-2 shift error (E4OD)

SERVICE CODE DEFINITION (PICKUP 7.5L & VAN 7.5L – 2 OF 2)

SERVICE CODE	SERVICE CODE DEFINITION
618	▶ 2-3 shift error (E4OD)
619	▶ 3-4 shift error (E4OD)
621	▶ Shift Solenoid 1 (SS1) circuit failure (E4OD)
622	▶ Shift Solenoid 2 (SS2) circuit failure (E4OD)
624	▶ Electronic Pressure Control (EPC) circuit failure (E4OD)
625	▶ Electronic Pressure Control (EPC) driver failure in processor (E4OD)
626	▶ Coast Clutch Solenoid (CCS) circuit failure (E4OD)
627	▶ Converter Clutch Control (CCC) solenoid circuit failure (E4OD)
628	▶ Converter clutch error (E4OD)
631	▶ Overdrive Cancel Indicator Light (OCIL) circuit failure (E4OD)
632	▶ Overdrive Cancel Switch (OCS) not changing state (E4OD)
633	▶ 4 x 4 switch is closed (E4OD)
634	▶ Manual Lever Position (MLP) sensor out of range; A/C on (E4OD)
636	▶ Transmission Oil Temperature (TOT) sensor input is out of Self-Test range (E4OD)
637	▶ TOT indicated -40°C (-40°F) / circuit open (E4OD)
638	▶ TOT indicated 143°C (290°F) / circuit grounded (E4OD)
654	▶ MLP Sensor not in Park position
998	▶ Hard fault is present
NO CODES	Unable to initiate Self-Test or unable to output Self-Test codes
CODES NOT LISTED	Service codes displayed are not applicable to the vehicle being tested

KEY: o = Key On Engine Off (KOEO); r = Key On Engine Running (KOER); c = Continuous Memory

CIRCUIT TESTS

NOTE: A breakout box, connected to vehicle harness at ECA, is necessary to perform most circuit tests. References to Test Pin No. found in CIRCUIT TEST steps refer to test terminals on manufacturer breakout box overlay. Circuit diagrams at beginning of each test identify circuit and wire colors.

HOW TO USE CIRCUIT TESTS

1) Ensure all non-EEC-IV related faults found while performing steps in BASIC DIAGNOSTIC PROCEDURES article have been corrected. DO NOT perform any CIRCUIT TEST unless instructed by a QUICK TEST procedure. Follow each test step in order until fault is found. When more than one code is retrieved, start with first code displayed.
2) CIRCUIT TESTS ensure electrical circuits are okay before sensors or other components are replaced. Always test circuits for continuity between sensor and ECA. Test all circuits for short to power, opens or short to ground. Voltage Reference (VREF) and Voltage Power (VPWR) circuits should be tested with ignition on unless otherwise specified in CIRCUIT TESTS.
3) DO NOT measure voltage or resistance at ECA. DO NOT connect any test light unless specified in testing procedure. All measurements are made by probing rear of connector. Isolate both ends of a circuit and turn ignition off when checking continuity, unless instructed otherwise.
4) Disconnect solenoids and switches from harness before measuring continuity and resistance or applying voltage. After each repair, check all component connections and repeat QUICK TEST.
5) An open circuit is defined as a resistance reading of greater than 5 ohms. This specification tolerance may be too high for some items in EEC-IV system. If resistance approaches 5 ohms, always clean suspect connector and coat it with protective dielectric silicone grease. A short is defined as a resistance reading of less than 10,000 ohms to ground, unless stated otherwise in CIRCUIT TEST.

Diagnostic Aids – Fuel-contaminated engine oil may affect some codes. If oil is suspect, remove PCV valve from valve cover and repeat QUICK TEST. If problem is corrected, change engine oil.

On CIRCUIT TEST H and CIRCUIT TEST J, vacuum leaks in non-EEC related areas may cause Code 41 or 91 to be displayed. Check vacuum motors, engine seals, EGR system, PCV system, Canister Purge (CANP), HEGO sensor and between airflow meter and throttle body for unmetered air leaks. Code 42 or 92 may be caused by fuel-contaminated engine oil, ignition misfire, or EGR system or CANP problems.

NOTE: In following tests, circuit diagrams and illustrations are courtesy of Ford Motor Co.

CIRCUIT TESTS are grouped as follows.
- A-C – No Start & Voltage Tests
- DA-DS – Input Sensor Tests
- FD-FF – Additional Input Component Tests
- G-J – Fuel Control System Tests
- KC-TG – ECA (Processor) Output Tests

CIRCUIT TEST INDEX

CIRCUIT TEST AA

NO START
(TFI IGNITION SYSTEMS)

CAUTION: Stop this test at first sign of a fuel leak. DO NOT allow smoking or an open flame in vicinity of vehicle during these tests.

Diagnostic Aids – Enter this CIRCUIT TEST only when steps in QUICK TEST have been successfully completed but engine still does not start or if directed here from another test or chart.

This test is only intended to diagnose following EEC-IV ignition systems and circuits:
- Thick Film Ignition (TFI) Systems
- Electronic Control Assembly (ECA)
- Spark (ECA-controlled)
- Wiring Harness Circuits (PIP, SPOUT, IGN GND And VPWR)

NOTE: Vehicles are equipped with either a Closed Bowl Distributor (CBD) TFI module (remote mounted) or a standard TFI module (distributor mounted).

90J18829

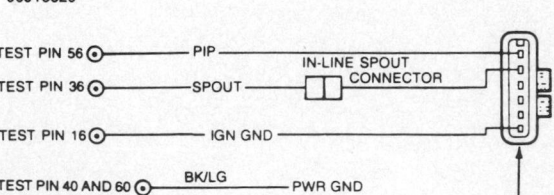

Fig. AA1: Distributor Mounted TFI Module Circuits

CIRCUIT TEST AA (Cont.)

91I06925

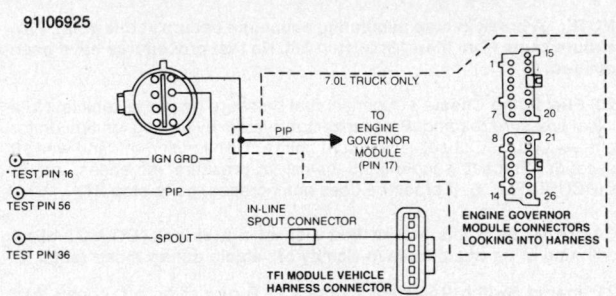

Fig. AA2: Remote Mounted TFI Module Circuits (Except Aerostar 3.0L & Ranger 3.0L)

91A06926

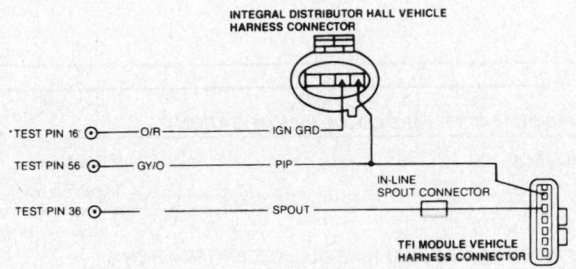

Fig. AA3: Remote Mounted TFI Module Circuits (Aerostar 3.0L & Ranger 3.0L)

TEST PIN NO. 16 (IGN GND) WIRE COLOR IDENTIFICATION

Application	Wire Color
All Models	Orange/Red

TEST PIN NO. 36 (SPOUT) WIRE COLOR IDENTIFICATION

Application	Wire Color
Ranger (2.9L & 3.0L) & 7.5L	Pink
Except Ranger (2.9L & 3.0L) & 7.5L	Yellow/Light Green

TEST PIN NO. 56 (PIP) WIRE COLOR IDENTIFICATION

Application	Wire Color
Ranger (2.9L & 3.0L), Aerostar (3.0L) & 7.5L	Gray/Orange
All Others	Dark Blue

To prevent replacement of good components, be aware following non-EEC related areas and components may be cause of problem:
- Fuel quality and quantity.
- Ignition (general system condition).
- Engine mechanical components.
- Starter and battery circuits.
- Dual Hall sensor.
- Distributor.
- Camshaft (CID) sensor.
- Crankshaft (PIP) Hall sensor.
- Ignition coil.

1) Starting System – Try to start engine. If engine does not crank, check vehicle starting and charging systems. If engine cranks, verify inertia switch button is pushed in. If inertia switch button is pushed in, go to step **2)**.

CIRCUIT TEST AA (Cont.)

2) Check VREF Signal At TPS – Turn ignition off, and wait 10 seconds. Set DVOM on 20-volt scale. Disconnect Throttle Position Sensor (TPS). Turn ignition on (engine off). Measure voltage at TPS harness connector between VREF and SIG RTN. See Fig. AA4. If voltage is 4-6 volts, reconnect TPS and go to step **3)**. If voltage is not 4-6 volts, go to CIRCUIT TEST C.

90B10950

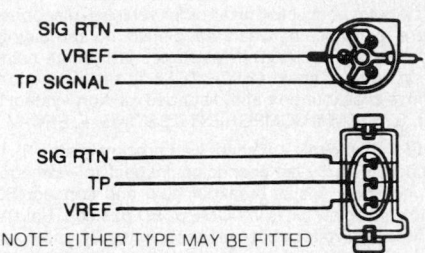

NOTE: EITHER TYPE MAY BE FITTED

Fig. AA4: Identifying TPS Harness Connector Terminals

3) Check For Spark At Plugs – Disconnect any spark plug wire. Connect spark tester between spark plug wire and ground. Crank engine and check for spark. If spark is present and consistent, connect spark plug wire and go to step **13)**. If spark does not exist, connect spark plug wire and go to step **4)**.

4) Check For Spark At Coil – Remove high-tension coil wire from distributor. Install spark tester. Check for spark while cranking engine. If spark exists, connect coil wire, and service ignition secondary system. If no spark exists, connect coil wire and go to step **5)**.

5) Check Ignition Circuit Ground Continuity – Turn ignition off. Wait 10 seconds. Disconnect and inspect ECA 60-pin connector. Install Breakout Box (T83L-50-EEC-IV), leaving ECA disconnected. Disconnect TFI module. Disconnect Hall sensor or Crank Angle Sensor (CAS) if equipped. Measure resistance between test pin No. 16 at breakout box and IGN GND circuit of TFI, Hall sensor or CAS harness connector. If reading is more than 5 ohms, repair open in IGN GND circuit and repeat QUICK TEST. If reading is 5 ohms or less, go to step **6)**.

6) Isolate SPOUT Circuit Fault – Connect TFI module, CAS or distributor hall connector as applicable. Connect ECA to breakout box. Set breakout box timing switch to DIST position. Try to start vehicle. If vehicle starts, go to step **11)**. If vehicle does not start, go to step **7)**.

7) Check SPOUT Signal – Turn ignition off. Move breakout box timing switch to DIST position. Set DVOM on 20-volt scale. Turn ignition on. Measure voltage between test pin No. 36 at breakout box and negative battery terminal while cranking engine. If voltage is 3-6 volts, EEC-IV system is not at fault. Diagnose ignition system. See TFI-IV SYSTEM in SYSTEM & COMPONENT TESTING – EEC-IV article. If voltage is not 3-6 volts, go to step **8)**.

8) Check SPOUT & PIP Circuits For Short Circuit – Turn ignition off. With breakout box installed, move timing switch to COMPUTED position. On models with remote mounted TFI-IV module, disconnect distributor connector; on all other models, disconnect TFI module. Disconnect ECA. Turn ignition on. Measure voltage between test pin No. 36 (SPOUT) and negative battery terminal. Measure resistance between test pin No. 56 (PIP) and negative battery terminal. If voltage is more than 10.5 volts, repair circuit for a short to power and repeat QUICK TEST. If engine still does not start or if all voltages are 10.5 volts or less, go to step **9)**.

9) Turn ignition off. On models with remote mounted TFI-IV module, disconnect distributor connector; on all other models, disconnect TFI module. Measure resistance between test pin No. 36 (SPOUT) and test pins No. 16, 20, 40, 46 and 60 for short to ground. Measure resistance between test pin No. 36 and test pin No. 56 for short to PIP. Measure resistance between test pin No. 56 (PIP) and test pins No. 16, 20, 40, 46 and 60. If all readings are 10,000 ohms or more, go to step **10)**. If any reading is less than 10,000 ohms, repair short in harness and repeat QUICK TEST. If engine still does not start, go to step **10)**.

10) Isolate Shorts In ECA – Turn ignition off. With breakout box installed, reconnect ECA. Measure resistance between test pin No. 36 (SPOUT) and test pins No. 37, 40, 57 and 60. Measure resistance between test pin No. 56 (PIP) and test pins No. 37, 40, 57 and 60. If any reading is less than 500 ohms, replace ECA and repeat QUICK TEST. If all readings are 500 ohms or more, connect TFI and go to step **11)**.

CIRCUIT TEST AA (Cont.)

11) Check PIP Signal – Turn ignition off. Set DVOM on 20-volt scale. With breakout box installed, move timing switch to COMPUTED position. While cranking engine, measure voltage between test pin No. 56 (PIP) and test pins No. 40 and 60. If voltage is 3-7 volts, replace ECA. Repeat QUICK TEST. If voltage is not 3-7 volts, go to step **12)**.

12) Check Continuity Of PIP Circuit – Turn ignition off. Disconnect ECA from breakout box. On models with remote mounted TFI-IV module, disconnect distributor connector; on all other vehicles, disconnect TFI module. Measure resistance between test pin No. 56 and distributor or TFI module connector PIP circuit. If resistance is 5 ohms or more, repair open PIP circuit and repeat QUICK TEST. If resistance is less than 5 ohms, remove breakout box and diagnose ignition system. See TFI-IV SYSTEM in SYSTEM & COMPONENT TESTING – EEC-IV article.

13) Verify SPOUT Signal – If spark was present in step **3)**, turn ignition off. Disconnect ECA 60-pin connector. Inspect for damaged pins and repair as necessary. Install breakout box, and connect ECA. Ensure breakout box timing switch is in COMPUTED position. Set DVOM on 20-volt scale. Measure voltage between test pin No. 36 and pins No. 40 and 60 while cranking engine. If voltage is 3-6 volts, go to step **20)**. If voltage is not 3-6 volts, return to step **8)**.

→

CIRCUIT TEST AA (Cont.)

NOTE: A break in step numbering sequence occurs at this point. Procedure skips from step 13) to step 20). No test procedures have been omitted.

20) Fuel Pump Check – Connect fuel pressure gauge to vehicle. Note initial pressure reading. Pressurize fuel system by turning ignition on for one second, and observe pressure gauge. Turn ignition off, and wait 10 seconds. Repeat sequence 5 times. If pressure increases, go to CIRCUIT TEST S. If pressure does not increase, go to step **21)**.

CAUTION: Stop this test at first sign of a fuel leak. DO NOT allow smoking or an open flame in vicinity of vehicle during these tests.

21) Inertia Switch Resistance Check – Turn ignition off. Locate fuel pump inertia switch. Ensure button on switch is pushed down to ON position. Measure resistance of switch. If resistance is 5 ohms or more, replace switch. If resistance is less than 5 ohms, inertia switch is okay. For additional fuel system test procedures, see FUEL SYSTEM in SYSTEM & COMPONENT TESTING – EEC-IV article.

CIRCUIT TEST AB

NO START
(DIS IGNITION SYSTEMS)

CAUTION: Stop this test at first sign of a fuel leak. DO NOT allow smoking or an open flame in vicinity of vehicle during these tests.

Diagnostic Aids – Enter this CIRCUIT TEST only when steps in QUICK TEST has been successfully completed but engine still does not start or if directed here from another test or chart. This test is only intended to diagnose following EEC-IV ignition systems and circuits:
- Distributorless Ignition Systems (DIS).
- Spark (ECA-controlled).
- Wiring harness circuits (PIP, SPOUT, IGN GND and VPWR).
- ECA.

To prevent replacement of good components, be aware following non-EEC related areas and components may be cause of problem:
- Fuel quality and quantity.
- Ignition (general system condition).
- Engine mechanical components.
- Starter and battery circuits.
- Dual Hall sensor.
- DIS module.
- Camshaft (CID) sensor.
- Crankshaft Hall (PIP) sensor.
- DIS coil.

TEST PIN NO. 4 (IDM) WIRE COLOR IDENTIFICATION

Application	Wire Color
2.3L	Tan/Yellow

TEST PIN NO. 16 (IGN GND) WIRE COLOR IDENTIFICATION

Application	Wire Color
2.3L	Orange/Red

1) Starting System – Try to start engine. If engine does not crank, check vehicle starting and charging systems. If engine cranks, go to next step.

2) Check VREF Signal At TPS – Ensure fuel pump inertia switch is set (button pushed in). Turn ignition off. Set DVOM on 20-volt scale. Disconnect Throttle Position Sensor (TPS). Turn ignition on (engine off). Measure voltage at TPS harness connector between VREF and SIG RTN. *See Fig. AB2.* If voltage is not 4-6 volts, go to CIRCUIT TEST C. If voltage is 4-6 volts, reconnect TPS and go to step **3)**.

91E06828

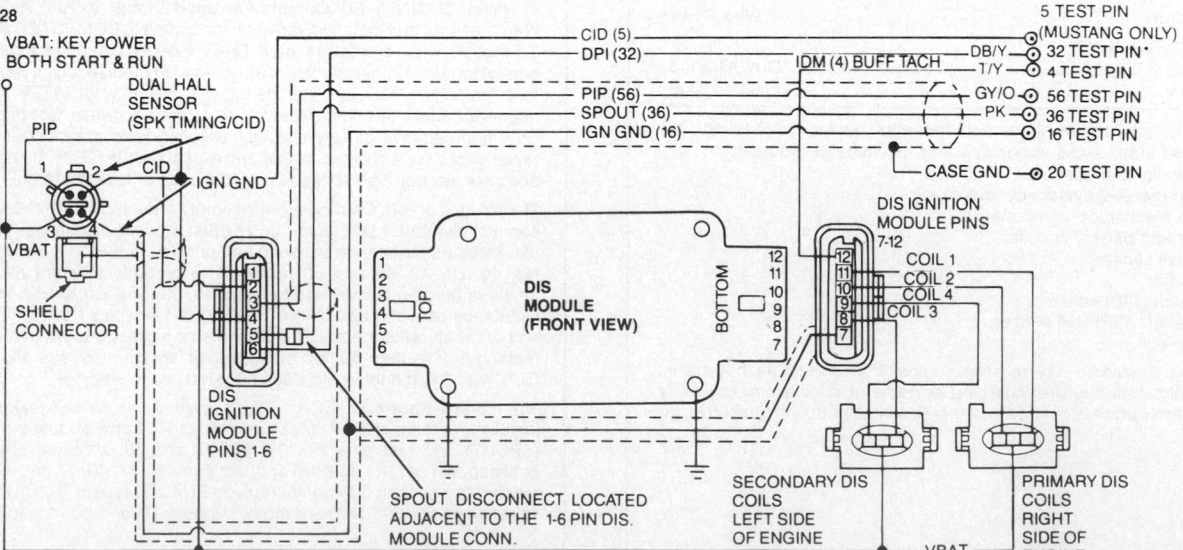

Fig. AB1: Distributorless Ignition System (DIS) Wiring Diagram

CIRCUIT TEST AB (Cont.)

90B10950

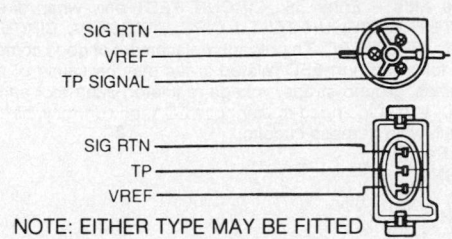

NOTE: EITHER TYPE MAY BE FITTED

Fig. AB2: Identifying TPS Harness Connector Terminals

3) Check For Spark At Plugs – Disconnect any spark plug wire from exhaust-side spark plug. Connect spark tester between spark plug wire and ground. Crank engine and check for spark. If spark is present and consistent, connect spark plug wire and go to step **7)**. If no spark exists, connect spark plug wire and go to step **4)**.

4) Check PIP Circuit – Turn ignition off, and wait 10 seconds. Install Breakout Box (T83L-50-EEC-IV), leaving ECA disconnected. Disconnect DIS module pins No. 1-6. Measure resistance between test pin No. 56 (PIP) and test pins No. 16, 20, 40, 46, and 60 for short to ground. Measure resistance between test pin No. 56 and test pins No. 26, 37 and 57 for short to power. If resistance is less than 10,000 ohms, repair short circuit and repeat QUICK TEST. If resistance is 10,000 ohms or more, go to step **5)**.

5) Isolate Short At ECA – Ensure ignition is off. Connect ECA to breakout box. Disconnect DIS pins No. 1-6. Measure resistance between test pin No. 56 (PIP) and test pins No. 40 and 60 for short to ground. Measure resistance between test pin No. 56 and test pins No. 37 and 57 for short to power. If resistance is less than 10,000 ohms, replace ECA and repeat QUICK TEST. If resistance is 10,000 ohms or more, go to step **6)**.

6) Check IGN GND Circuit Continuity (ECA Disconnected) – Ensure ignition is off. Disconnect from ECA breakout box. Disconnect DIS module pins No. 7-12. Measure resistance between test pin No. 16 and DIS module wiring harness connector IGN GND terminal. If resistance is 5 ohms or more, repair open IGN GND circuit. If resistance is less than 5 ohms, go to DIS SYSTEM in SYSTEM & COMPONENT TESTING – EEC-IV article.

7) Check PIP Signal – Turn ignition off. Connect ECA to breakout box. Set DVOM on 20-volt scale. Turn timing switch to DIST position on breakout box. Measure voltage between test pins No. 56 and 16 while cranking engine. If voltage is 3-7 volts, go to step **8)**. If voltage is not 3-7 volts, go to step **9)**.

8) Check IGN GND Circuit Continuity (ECA Connected) – Turn ignition off. Wait 10 seconds. Disconnect ECA 60-pin connector. Inspect it for damaged pins and repair if necessary. Install breakout box, leaving ECA connected. Disconnect DIS module pins No. 7-12. Measure resistance between test pin No. 16 and DIS module wiring harness connector IGN GND terminal. If resistance is 5 ohms or more, repair open IGN GND circuit. If resistance is less than 5 ohms, go to step **10)**.

9) Check Continuity Of PIP Circuit – Turn ignition off. Disconnect ECA 60-pin connector. Disconnect DIS module pins No. 1-6. Measure resistance between test pin No. 56 and DIS module wiring harness connector PIP terminal. If resistance is 5 ohms or more, repair open PIP circuit and repeat QUICK TEST. If resistance is less than 5 ohms, go to DIS SYSTEM in SYSTEM & COMPONENT TESTING – EEC-IV article.

10) Fuel Pump Check – Connect fuel pressure gauge to vehicle. Note initial pressure reading. Pressurize fuel system by turning ignition on for one second, and observe pressure gauge. Turn ignition off, and wait 10 seconds. Repeat sequence 5 times. If pressure does not increase, go to step **11)**. If pressure increases, go to CIRCUIT TEST S.

11) Check ECA Output To Fuel Pump – Turn ignition off. Measure voltage between test pins No. 22 and 37 or 57 while cranking engine. If voltage is less than 10.5 volts, replace ECA and repeat QUICK TEST. If voltage is 10.5 volts or more, go to FUEL SYSTEM in SYSTEM & COMPONENT TESTING – EEC-IV article.

CIRCUIT TEST AC

NO START
(EDIS IGNITION SYSTEMS)

CAUTION: Stop this test at first sign of a fuel leak. DO NOT allow smoking or an open flame in vicinity of vehicle during these tests.

Diagnostic Aids – Enter this CIRCUIT TEST only when all steps under QUICK TEST have been successfully completed and engine still does not start or if directed here from another test or chart. This test is only intended to diagnose:
- Spark (ECA-controlled).
- Wiring harness circuits (PIP, IGN GND and VPWR).
- ECA.

To prevent replacement of good components, be aware following non-EEC related areas and components may be cause of problem:
- Fuel Quality And Quantity
- Ignition (General Condition)
- Engine Mechanical Components
- Starter And Battery Circuits
- Variable Reluctance Sensor (VRS)
- EDIS Module
- Coil Packs

91G06929

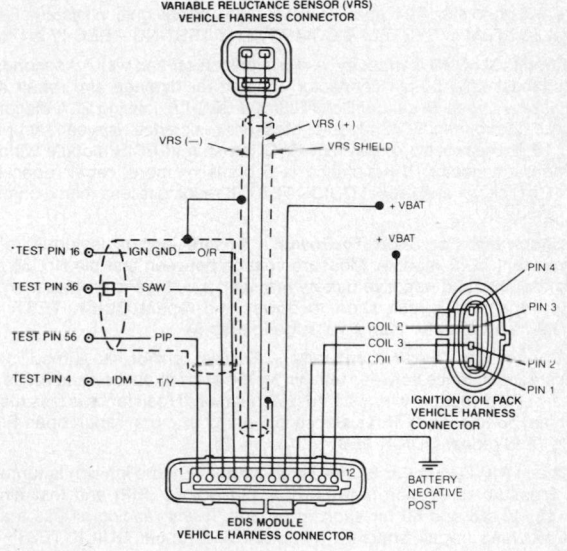

Fig. AC1: EDIS Module Circuits (4.0L)

TEST PIN NO. 4 (IDM) WIRE COLOR IDENTIFICATION

Application	Wire Color
4.0L	Tan/Yellow

TEST PIN NO. 36 (SAW) WIRE COLOR IDENTIFICATION

Application	Wire Color
4.0L	
Aerostar	Yellow/Light Green
Explorer & Ranger	Pink

TEST PIN NO. 56 (PIP) WIRE COLOR IDENTIFICATION

Application	Wire Color
4.0L	Gray/Orange

1) Starting System – Ensure fuel pump inertia switch is closed (button pushed in). Try to start engine. If engine does not crank, check vehicle starting and charging systems. If engine cranks, go to step **2)**.

CIRCUIT TEST AC (Cont.)

2) Check VREF Signal At TPS – Turn ignition off. Disconnect Throttle Position Sensor (TPS). Turn ignition on (engine off). Measure voltage between VREF and SIG RTN at TPS harness connector. *See Fig. AC2*. If voltage is not 4-6 volts, go to CIRCUIT TEST C. If voltage is 4-6 volts, reconnect TPS and go to step **3)**.

90B10950

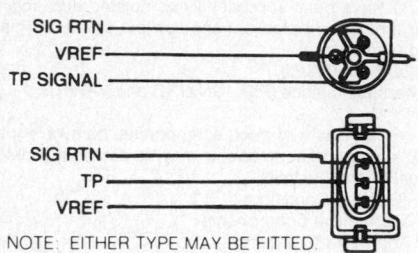

NOTE: EITHER TYPE MAY BE FITTED.

Fig. AC2: Identifying TPS Harness Connector Terminals

3) Check For Spark At Plugs – Disconnect any spark plug wire. Connect spark tester between plug wire and engine ground. Crank engine and check for spark. If spark is present, reconnect spark plug wire and go to step **4)**. If spark is not present, check ignition system. See EDIS SYSTEM in SYSTEM & COMPONENT TESTING – EEC-IV article.

4) Check IGN GND Continuity – Turn ignition off and wait 10 seconds. Disconnect ECA 60-pin connector. Inspect for damage and repair as necessary. Install Breakout Box (T83L-50-EEC-IV), leaving ECA disconnected. Disconnect EDIS module. Measure resistance between test pin No. 16 at breakout box and IGN GND terminal at EDIS module wiring harness connector. If resistance is 5 ohms or more, repair open in IGN GND circuit and repeat QUICK TEST. If reading is less than 5 ohms, go to step **5)**.

5) Check PIP For Short To Power – Ensure ignition is turned off. Disconnect EDIS module. Measure voltage between test pin No. 56 at breakout box and negative battery terminal. If voltage is greater than 7 volts, repair PIP circuit short to power and repeat QUICK TEST. If voltage is not greater than 7 volts, go to step **6)**.

6) Check PIP Circuit Continuity – Ensure ignition is turned off. Measure resistance between test pin No. 56 at breakout box and PIP terminal at EDIS module wiring harness connector. If resistance is less than 5 ohms, go to step **7)**. If resistance is 5 ohms or more, repair open PIP circuit and repeat QUICK TEST.

7) Check PIP Circuit For Shorts To Ground – Ensure ignition is turned off. Measure resistance between test pin No. 56 (PIP) and test pins No. 16, 40, 46 and 60 for short to ground. If any reading is less than 10,000 ohms, repair short in PIP circuit and repeat QUICK TEST. If engine still does not start, go to step **8)**. If all readings are 10,000 ohms or more, go to step **8)**.

8) Isolate Shorts In ECA – Ensure ignition is turned off. With breakout box installed, connect ECA to breakout box. Disconnect EDIS module. Measure resistance between test pin No. 56 (PIP) and test pins No. 37 and 57 for short to power. Measure resistance between test pin No. 56 and test pins No. 40 and 60 for short to ground. If any resistance is not 20,000-150,000 ohms, replace ECA and repeat QUICK TEST. If all resistances are 20,000-150,000 ohms, go to step **9)**.

9) Check PIP Signal – Turn ignition off. Wait 10 seconds. With breakout box installed, disconnect ECA. Reconnect EDIS module. Measure voltage between test pin No. 56 and test pin No. 16 at breakout box while cranking engine. Record voltage. If voltage is 3-7 volts, go to step **10)**. If voltage is not 3-7 volts, replace EDIS module and repeat QUICK TEST.

10) Fuel Pump Check – Connect fuel pressure gauge to vehicle. Note initial pressure reading. Pressurize fuel system by turning ignition on for one second. Record system pressure. Turn ignition off, and wait 10 seconds. Repeat sequence 5 times. If pressure increases, go to CIRCUIT TEST S. If pressure does not increase, go to FUEL SYSTEM in SYSTEM & COMPONENT TESTING – EEC-IV.

CIRCUIT TEST B

CHECKING VEHICLE BATTERY

Diagnostic Aids – Enter this CIRCUIT TEST only when directed by CIRCUIT TEST C, CIRCUIT TEST J, CIRCUIT TEST PA, CIRCUIT TEST PB or CIRCUIT TEST PC. To prevent replacement of good components, be aware following non-EEC related areas may be cause of problem: battery cables, ground straps, voltage regulator, alternator and ignition switch. This test is intended to diagnose ECA, power relay, battery voltage and following harness circuits.

- Signal Return
- PWR GND
- VPWR
- KAPWR
- VREF
- Ignition Switch

92G03817

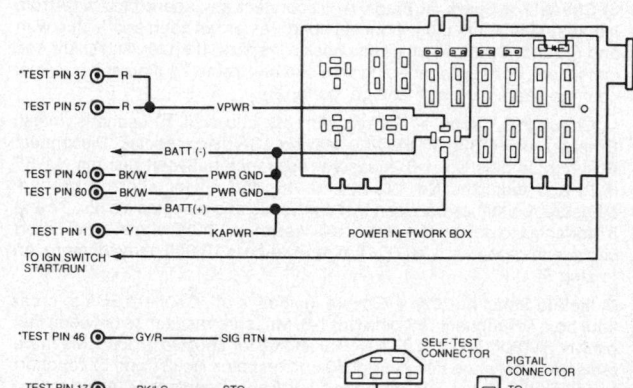

*TEST PINS LOCATED ON BREAKOUT BOX.
ALL HARNESS CONNECTORS VIEWED INTO MATING SURFACE.*

Fig. B1: Identifying Power Relay Circuits (Van)

92I03818

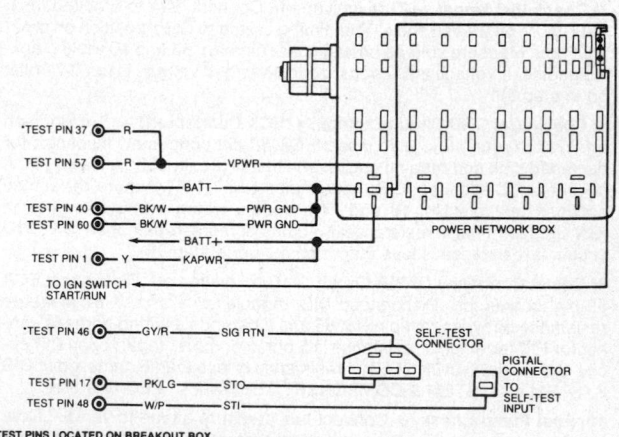

*TEST PINS LOCATED ON BREAKOUT BOX.
ALL HARNESS CONNECTORS VIEWED INTO MATING SURFACE.*

Fig. B2: Identifying Power Relay Circuits (Bronco & Pickup)

CIRCUIT TEST B (Cont.)

92A03819

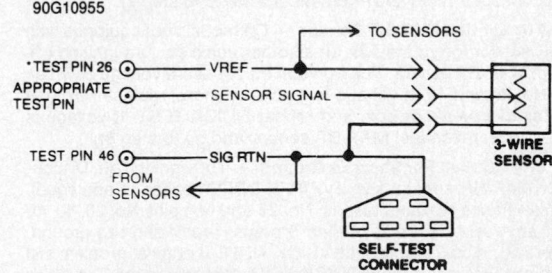

Fig. B3: Identifying Power Relay Circuits Terminals (Except Bronco, Pickup & Van)

TEST PIN NO. 1 (KAPWR) WIRE COLOR IDENTIFICATION

Application	Wire Color
All Models	Yellow

TEST PIN NO. 17 (STO) WIRE COLOR IDENTIFICATION

Application	Wire Color
Aerostar	Tan/Red
Bronco, Pickup & Van	Pink/Light Green
Except Aerostar, Bronco, Pickup & Van	Yellow/Black

TEST PIN NO. 48 (STI) WIRE COLOR IDENTIFICATION

Application	Wire Color
Aerostar (3.0L)	White/Red
Except Aerostar (3.0L)	White/Pink

WARNING: When battery is disconnected, vehicle computer and memory systems may lose memory data. Driveability problems may exist until computer systems have completed a relearn cycle. See COMPUTER RELEARN PROCEDURES article in GENERAL INFORMATION before disconnecting battery.

1) **Battery Voltage Check** – Turn ignition on (engine off). Measure battery voltage. If voltage is less than 10.5 volts, recharge or replace battery. If voltage is 10.5 volts or more, go to step **2)**.

2) **Check Continuity Of PWR GND Circuit** – Turn ignition off. Wait 10 seconds. Disconnect ECA. Inspect connector pins for damage and repair as necessary. Install Breakout Box (T83L-50-EEC-IV). Connect ECA to breakout box. Measure resistance between test pins No. 40 and 60 at breakout box and negative battery terminal. If resistance is 5 ohms or more, repair open in PWR GND circuit. Remove breakout box, and repeat QUICK TEST. If both resistances are less than 5 ohms, go to next step.

3) **Check For Open Between SIG RTN & PWR GND Circuits At ECA** – Ensure ignition is turned off. With breakout box installed and ECA connected, set DVOM on 200-ohm scale. Measure resistance between test pin No. 46 and test pins No. 40 and 60 at breakout box. If readings are 5 ohms or more, disconnect ECA connector. Inspect connector pins for damage and repair as necessary. If fault is still present, replace ECA and repeat QUICK TEST. If readings are less than 5 ohms, go to step **4)**.

4) **Check Continuity Of SIG RTN Circuit** – Ensure ignition is turned off. Measure resistance between test pin No. 46 at breakout box and SIG RTN terminal at self-test connector. If resistance is 5 ohms or more, repair open in SIG RTN circuit. Remove breakout box, and repeat QUICK TEST. If reading is less than 5 ohms, go to step **5)**.

CIRCUIT TEST B (Cont.)

5) **Check KAPWR Circuit Voltage At EEC Power Relay** – Turn ignition off. Locate relay block in engine compartment. Disconnect EEC power relay from relay block. Turn ignition on. Measure voltage between negative battery terminal and KAPWR terminal at EEC power relay connector. If voltage is 10.5 volts or less, check KAPWR circuit between EEC power relay and battery power for open circuit. If voltage is 10.5 volts or more, go to step **6)**.

6) **Check Ignition Circuit Voltage At EEC Power Relay** – Ensure EEC power relay is disconnected. Turn ignition on. Measure voltage between negative battery terminal and IGNITION terminal at EEC power relay connector. If voltage is less than 10.5 volts, check for open in ignition switch circuits. Repair wiring, and repeat QUICK TEST. If voltage is 10.5 volts or more, go to step **7)**.

7) **Check PWR GND Circuit Continuity** – Turn ignition off, and wait 10 seconds. With ECA connected to breakout box, measure resistance between negative battery terminal and PWR GND terminal at EEC power relay connector. If resistance is 10 ohms or more, repair open circuit in ground circuit. Repeat QUICK TEST. If reading is less than 10 ohms, go to step **8)**.

8) **Check VPWR Circuit Continuity** – Turn ignition off. Measure resistance between test pins No. 37 and 57 (VPWR) at breakout box and VPWR terminal of EEC power relay connector. If resistance is 5 ohms or more, repair VPWR open circuit between EEC power relay and ECA. Repeat QUICK TEST. If reading is less than 5 ohms, go to step **9)**.

9) **Check VPWR Circuit Voltage** – Turn ignition off. Install EEC power relay. Turn ignition on. With ECA connected, measure voltage between test pins No. 37 and 57 (VPWR) and test pins No. 40 and 60 (PWR GND) and 46 (SIG RTN) at breakout box. If voltage is 10.5 volts or more, repair circuit between ECA and EEC power relay. Repeat QUICK TEST. If voltage is less than 10.5 volts, replace EEC power relay. Repeat QUICK TEST.

CIRCUIT TEST C

REFERENCE VOLTAGE

Diagnostic Aids – Perform this test when a check for VREF signal has failed in sensor input CIRCUIT TEST DA and CIRCUIT TEST DS, or if directed by CIRCUIT TEST A or CIRCUIT TEST QA. SIG RTN is a dedicated ground used by most EEC-IV system sensors. VREF is a 5-volt reference voltage that is continuously output by ECA. This consistent voltage signal is used on all 3-wire sensors. This circuit test is only intended to diagnose SIG RTN, VREF, TP, EVP, PFE, DPFE, MAP and BP circuits.

90G10955

*TEST PINS LOCATED ON BREAKOUT BOX.
ALL HARNESS CONNECTORS VIEWED INTO MATING SURFACE.

Fig. C1: Identifying Reference Voltage Circuits & Connector Terminals

TEST PIN NO. 26 (VREF) WIRE COLOR IDENTIFICATION

Application	Wire Color
All Models	Brown/White

CIRCUIT TEST C (Cont.)

TEST PIN NO. 46 (SIG RTN) WIRE COLOR IDENTIFICATION

Application	Wire Color
All Models	Gray/Red

1) Check Battery Power Circuit – Turn ignition off, and wait 10 seconds. Disconnect ECA 60-pin connector. Inspect for damage and repair as necessary. Install Breakout Box (T83L-50-EEC-IV), leaving ECA connected. Turn ignition on. Measure and record voltage between breakout box test pin No. 37 and SIG RTN terminal of self-test connector. Measure and record voltage across battery terminals. If both readings are less than 10.5 volts, or if they differ by more than 1.0 volt, reconnect sensor (if applicable) and go to CIRCUIT TEST B. If voltages are 10.5 volts or more and do not differ from one another by more than one volt, go to step **2)**.

2) Check VREF Voltage – With breakout box installed and ECA connected, set DVOM on 20-volt scale. Turn ignition on. Measure voltage between test pins No. 26 and 46 at breakout box. If voltage is 4-6 volts, go to step **3)**. If voltage is more than 6 volts, go to step **4)**. If voltage is less than 4 volts, go to step **5)**.

3) Check VREF & SIG RTN Circuit Continuity – Turn ignition off. If directed here by a sensor test, ensure sensor is disconnected. Measure resistance between test pin No. 26 and VREF terminal at wiring harness connector of applicable sensor. Measure resistance between test pin No. 46 and SIG RTN circuit terminal at wiring harness connector of applicable sensor. If both readings are less than 5 ohms, VREF circuit is okay. If either reading is 5 ohms or more, repair open in VREF or SIG RTN circuit and repeat QUICK TEST.

4) Check For Excess VREF Circuit Voltage – Turn ignition off. With breakout box installed, disconnect ECA and scan tester or STAR tester (if applicable). Turn ignition on. Measure voltage between test pin No. 26 and battery ground. If voltage is less than 0.5 volt, replace ECA and repeat QUICK TEST. If voltage is 0.5 volt or more, repair short to battery power in wiring harness. Remove breakout box and repeat QUICK TEST. Replace ECA if fault still occurs.

5) Check For Shorted TPS – Turn ignition off. Connect ECA to breakout box. Disconnect Throttle Position Sensor (TPS) from wiring harness. Turn ignition on. Measure voltage between test pins No. 26 and 46 at breakout box. If voltage is 4 volts or more, replace TPS and repeat QUICK TEST. If voltage is less than 4 volts on models with EVP, PFE or DPFE sensor, go to step **6)**; if voltage is less than 4 volts on all other models, go to step **7)**.

6) Check For Shorted EVP/PFE/DPFE Sensor – Turn ignition off. Disconnect EVP/PFE/DPFE sensor. Turn ignition on. Measure voltage between test pins No. 26 and 46. If voltage is 4 volts or more, replace EVP/PFE/DPFE sensor and repeat QUICK TEST. If voltage is less than 4 volts, reconnect EVP/PFE/DPFE sensor and go to step **7)**.

7) Check For Shorted MAP/BP Sensor – On models not equipped with a MAP/BP sensor, go to step **8)**; on all other vehicles, turn ignition off. Disconnect MAP/BP sensor. Turn ignition on. Measure voltage between test pins No. 26 and 46. If voltage is 4 volts or more, replace MAP/BP sensor. Remove breakout box, and repeat QUICK TEST. If voltage is less than 4 volts, reconnect MAP/BP sensor and go to step **8)**.

8) Check VREF Circuit For Short To Ground – Turn ignition off. Disconnect TPS, MAP/BP sensor and EVP/PFE/DPFE sensor (if equipped). Measure resistance between test pin No. 26 and test pins No. 20, 40, 46 and 60. If any resistance is less than 5 ohms, repair short to ground. Remove breakout box, and repeat QUICK TEST. If original problem still exists, replace ECA and repeat QUICK TEST. If readings are 5 ohms or more, replace ECA and repeat QUICK TEST.

CIRCUIT TEST DA

TEMPERATURE SENSOR TEST (ACT & ECT)

Diagnostic Aids – Perform this test only when directed by QUICK TEST. Ambient air temperature must be at least 50°F (10°C) to receive valid input from ACT and VAT sensors. Engine coolant temperature must be greater than 50°F (10°C) to pass KOEO SELF-TEST and greater than 180°F (82°C) to pass KOER SELF-TEST. Voltage values in this test are based on a 5-volt VREF signal. Values may vary up to 15% due to sensor and VREF variations.

CIRCUIT TEST DA (Cont.)

This circuit test is intended to diagnose following components and circuits:
- Air Charge Temperature (ACT) sensor.
- Engine Charge Temperature (ECT) sensor.
- Wiring harness circuits (ACT, ECT and SIG RTN).
- Electronic Control Assembly (ECA).

To prevent replacing good components, ensure following non-EEC areas or components are not cause of problem:
- Coolant Level Low
- Cooling System, Water Pump Or Fan
- Electro Drive Cooling Fan
- Engine Operating Temperature Low
- Engine Oil Level Low
- Thermostat
- Air Cleaner Duct
- Ambient Temperature Too Low

90I10957

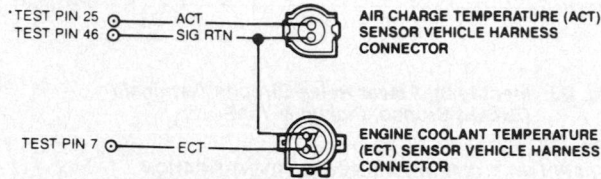

*TEST PINS LOCATED ON BREAKOUT BOX.
ALL HARNESS CONNECTORS VIEWED INTO MATING SURFACE.

Fig. DA1: Identifying Temperature Sensor Circuits & Connector Terminals

TEST PIN NO. 7 (ECT) WIRE COLOR IDENTIFICATION

Application	Wire Color
All Models	Light Green/Red

TEST PIN NO. 25 (ACT) WIRE COLOR IDENTIFICATION

Application	Wire Color
All Models	Gray

TEST PIN NO. 46 (SIG RTN) WIRE COLOR IDENTIFICATION

Application	Wire Color
All Models	Gray/Red

1) Code 21/116 Or 24/114 – Code 21/116 (ECT) or 24/114 (ACT) indicates corresponding sensor is out of self-test range. Correct range for measurement is .3-3.7 volts. Check for following possible causes:
- Low ambient temperature (less than 50°F).
- Low coolant level.
- Faulty harness connector.
- Faulty sensor.
- ACT sensor improperly mounted in air cleaner.

If vehicle cannot be started, go to step **3)**. If vehicle stalls, go to CIRCUIT TEST S. Ensure upper radiator hose is hot and pressurized. Repeat QUICK TEST. If Code 21, 24, 114 or 116 is present, go to step **2)**. If none of these codes are present, service other codes as necessary.

2) Check VREF Circuit Voltage At TPS – Turn ignition off. Disconnect Throttle Position Sensor (TPS). Turn ignition on. Measure voltage at TPS wiring harness connector between VREF and SIG RTN. *See Fig. DA2*. If voltage is 4-6 volts, reconnect TPS and go to step **3)**. If voltage is not 4-6 volts, go to CIRCUIT TEST C.

3) Check Temperature Sensor Resistance – Turn ignition off. Disconnect suspect sensor. Measure resistance between sensor signal circuit and SIG RTN circuit at sensor. If resistance is not within specification, replace suspected sensor. See ACT & ECT SENSOR SPECIFICATIONS table. Reconnect wiring harness, and repeat QUICK TEST. If resistance is within specification, perform following step as applicable.
- For diagnosing vehicles with ECT sensor and a no-start condition, DO NOT service Code 21/116 at this time. Go to CIRCUIT TEST AA for TFI, CIRCUIT TEST AB for DIS and CIRCUIT TEST AC for EDIS.
- For other vehicles, go to step **4)**.

CIRCUIT TEST DA (Cont.)

ACT & ECT SENSOR SPECIFICATIONS

Temperature °F (°C)	Voltage	Ohms
50 (10)	3.5	58,750
68 (20)	3.1	37,300
86 (30)	2.6	24,270
104 (40)	2.1	16,150
122 (50)	1.7	10,970
140 (60)	1.3	7700
158 (70)	1.0	5370
176 (80)	.8	384
194 (90)	.6	280
212 (100)	.5	207
230 (110)	.4	155

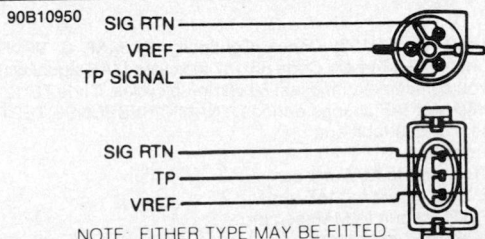

90B10950 SIG RTN
VREF
TP SIGNAL

SIG RTN
TP
VREF

NOTE: EITHER TYPE MAY BE FITTED

Fig. DA2: Identifying TPS Harness Connector Terminals

4) Warm engine to normal operating temperature. Turn ignition off. Disconnect suspect sensor. Run engine at 2000 RPM for 2 minutes. Measure resistance between sensor signal circuit and SIG RTN circuit at temperature sensor. See ACT & ECT SENSOR SPECIFICATIONS table. If resistance is within specification, replace ECA and repeat QUICK TEST. If sensor is not within specification, replace sensor and repeat QUICK TEST.

NOTE: A break in step numbering sequence occurs at this point. Procedure skips from step 4) to step 10). No test procedures have been omitted.

10) Code 51/118 Or 54/113: Induce Opposite Code (Code 61/117 Or 64/112) – Code 51/118 (ECT) or 54/113 (ACT) indicate corresponding sensor signal is greater than self-test maximum. Maximum signal voltage for ECT and ACT sensor is 4.6 volts. Possible causes for excess voltage signals are:

- Open circuit in wiring harness (ACT or ECT).
- Faulty connection.
- Faulty sensor.
- Faulty ECA.

Turn ignition off. Disconnect suspect temperature sensor. Connect a jumper wire between sensor SIG RTN terminal and SIG RTN terminal at temperature sensor wiring harness connector. Repeat QUICK TEST. If Code 61, 64, 112 or 117 is displayed, replace suspect sensor and repeat QUICK TEST. If Code 61, 64, 112 or 117 is not displayed, remove jumper wire and go to next step.

11) Check Continuity Of Sensor Signal & SIG RTN Circuits – Turn ignition off. Ensure suspect temperature sensor is disconnected. Disconnect ECA 60-pin connector. Check for damaged wiring, and repair as necessary. Install Breakout Box (T83L-50-EEC-IV), leaving ECA disconnected. Measure resistance between test pin No. 7 (ECT sensor) or test pin No. 25 (ACT sensor) at breakout box and SIG RTN terminal at sensor wiring harness connector. Also measure resistance between test pin No. 46 and SIG RTN circuit at sensor wiring harness connector. If both readings are less than 5 ohms, replace ECA and repeat QUICK TEST. If either reading is 5 ohms or more, repair open circuit. Remove breakout box and repeat QUICK TEST.

NOTE: A break in step numbering sequence occurs at this point. Procedure skips from step 11) to step 20). No test procedures have been omitted.

20) Code 61/117 or 64/112: Induce Opposite Code (51/118 or 54/113) – Code 61/117 (ECT) or 64/112 (ACT) indicates sensor signal is less than self-test minimum. Minimum signal for ACT and ECT sensor is 0.2 volt. Possible causes for this fault are:

- Circuit grounded in wiring harness (ACT or ECT).
- Faulty sensor.
- Faulty ECA.
- Faulty connection.

Turn ignition off. Disconnect wiring harness connector from suspect sensor. Check for damaged wiring, and repair as necessary. Repeat KOEO SELF-TEST. If Code 51, 54, 113 or 118 is displayed, replace sensor repeat QUICK TEST. If Codes 51, 54, 113 and 118 is not displayed, go to step 21).

CIRCUIT TEST DA (Cont.)

21) Check VREF Circuit Voltage At TPS – Turn ignition off. Disconnect wiring harness connector from suspect sensor. Disconnect TPS. Turn ignition on. Measure voltage between VREF and SIG RTN at TPS wiring harness connector.
If voltage is not 4-6 volts, go to CIRCUIT TEST C. If voltage is 4-6 volts, connect TPS and go to step 22).

22) Check Temperature Sensor Signal For Shorts To Ground – Turn ignition off. Disconnect suspect sensor. Disconnect ECA 60-pin connector. Inspect for damage and repair as necessary. Install Breakout Box (T83L-50-EEC-IV), leaving ECA disconnected. Measure resistance between test pin No. 7 (ECT) or 25 (ACT) and pins No. 40, 46 and 60. If any reading is less than 10,000 ohms, repair short circuit and repeat QUICK TEST. If all readings are 10,000 ohms or more, replace ECA and repeat QUICK TEST.

NOTE: A break in step numbering sequence occurs at this point. Procedure skips from step 22) to step 90). No test procedures have been omitted.

90) Continuous Memory Code 51/118, 54/113, 61/117 Or 64/112 – A Continuous Memory Code 51/118 or 54/113 indicates sensor signal is greater than self-test maximum of 4.6 volts. Code is set during normal driving conditions. Continuous Memory Code 61/117 or 64/112 indicates sensor signal is less than self-test minimum of 0.2 volt. Code is set during normal driving conditions. Possible causes for these faults are:

- Faulty sensor.
- Open or grounded circuit in harness.
- Faulty ECA.

SENSOR CODES

Sensor	Continuous Memory Code
ACT	54/113, 64/112
ECT	51/118, 61/117

Enter KOEO wiggle test mode. See CONTINUOUS MONITOR MODE (WIGGLE TEST) under QUICK TEST. Observe analog voltmeter or scan tester for indication of fault while tapping sensor lightly and wiggling sensor connector. If fault is indicated, disconnect and inspect connector and terminals. If connector and terminals are okay, replace sensor, clear continuous memory and repeat QUICK TEST. If fault is not indicated, go to step 91).

91) Check EEC-IV Wiring Harness – While in CONTINUOUS MONITOR MODE (WIGGLE TEST), observe analog voltmeter or scan tester while wiggling and bending wiring harness, a small section at a time, from sensor to cowl. Also check harness from cowl to ECA. If fault is indicated, isolate fault and repair as necessary. Clear continuous memory, and repeat QUICK TEST. If no fault is found, go to step 92).

92) Inspect ECA & Wiring Harness Connectors – Turn ignition off. Disconnect ECA 60-pin connector. Inspect both connector and connector terminals for damage. If connectors and terminals are damaged, repair as necessary and repeat QUICK TEST. If connectors and terminals are okay and fault cannot be duplicated at this time, see INTERMITTENTS in TROUBLE SHOOTING – NO CODES article.

NOTE: A break in step numbering sequence occurs at this point. Procedure skips from step 92) to step 100). No test procedures have been omitted.

100) Continuous Memory Code 338 – A Continuous Memory Code 338 indicates cooling system has not reached normal operating temperature. Possible causes for this fault are:

- Thermostat stuck open.
- Coolant outlet gasket leak.
- Water pump gasket leak.

Repair cooling system as necessary. Clear continuous memory, and repeat QUICK TEST.

101) Continuous Memory Code 339 – A Continuous Memory Code 339 indicates cooling system has overheated. Possible causes for this fault are:

- Coolant level low.
- Thermostat stuck closed.
- Coolant system clogged.
- Radiator fins clogged.
- Water pump damaged or worn.
- Radiator cap damaged or worn.
- Cooling fan damaged or worn.

Repair cooling system as necessary. Clear continuous memory, and repeat QUICK TEST.

CIRCUIT TEST DC

MASS AIRFLOW (MAF) SENSOR

Diagnostic Aids – Perform this test when directed by QUICK TEST. This test procedure is only intended to diagnose MAF sensor, ECA and wiring harness circuits (VPWR, PWR GND, MAF and MAF RTN).

To prevent replacement of good components, be aware following non-EEC related areas may be cause of problem:

- Air Cleaner Element
- Inlet Air Duct
- Throttle Body

Code 26/159, retrieved during KOEO SELF-TEST, indicates voltage exceeded .7-volt test range. Code 26/159, retrieved during KOER SELF-TEST, indicates voltage is not within .2-1.5 volts operating range. Possible causes are faulty MAF sensor or ECA.

92E03821

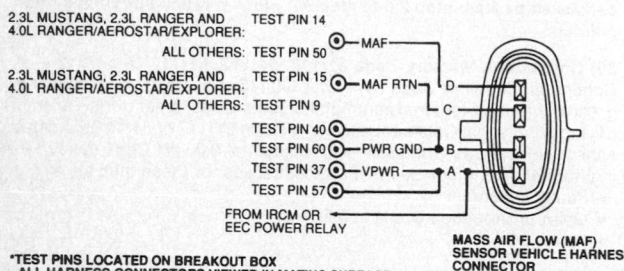

*TEST PINS LOCATED ON BREAKOUT BOX
ALL HARNESS CONNECTORS VIEWED IN MATING SURFACE

Fig. DC1: Identifying Mass Airflow (MAF) Sensor Circuits & Connector Terminals

TEST PIN NO. 14 OR 50 (MAF) WIRE COLOR IDENTIFICATION

Application	Wire Color
2.3L, 3.0L & 4.0L	Light Blue/Red

TEST PIN NO. 9 OR 15 (MAF RTN) WIRE COLOR IDENTIFICATION

Application	Wire Color
2.3L, 3.0L & 4.0L	Tan/Light Blue

TEST PINS NO. 37 & 57 (VPWR) WIRE COLOR IDENTIFICATION

Application	Wire Color
All Models	Red

TEST PINS NO. 40 & 60 (PWR GND) WIRE COLOR IDENTIFICATION

Application	Wire Color
Aerostar	Black/Light Green
Except Aerostar	Black/White

MAF SIGNAL VOLTAGE [1]

Application	Volts
Idle	.6
20 MPH	1.1
40 MPH	1.7
60 MPH	2.1

[1] – MAF signal voltage is typical for normal operating temperature. Voltage signal may vary due to engine load and temperature.

NOTE: Code 26/159 may be caused by use of a garage exhaust ventilation system. Ensure vehicle is vented to outside atmosphere before repeating QUICK TEST.

CIRCUIT TEST DC (Cont.)

1) Code 26/159: Check VPWR Circuit Voltage – Turn ignition off. Disconnect MAF sensor connector. Set DVOM on 20-volt scale. Turn ignition on. Measure voltage between VPWR terminal at MAF sensor wiring harness connector and negative battery terminal. If voltage is less than 10.5 volts, repair open in VPWR circuit and repeat QUICK TEST. If voltage is 10.5 volts or more, go to step **2)**.

2) Check MAF Sensor Ground – Turn ignition on. Disconnect MAF sensor. Measure voltage between VPWR terminal and PWR GND terminal at MAF sensor connector. If voltage is less than 10.5 volts, repair open PWR GND circuit. Connect MAF sensor, and repeat QUICK TEST. If voltage is 10.5 volts or more, go to step **10)**.

NOTE: A break in step numbering sequence occurs at this point. Procedure skips from step 2) to step 10). No test procedures have been omitted.

10) Code 66/157 Or 72/129: Check Continuity Of MAF & VPWR Circuits – Continuous Memory Code 66/157 indicates MAF signal was less than 0.4 volt sometime during last 80 warm-up cycles. Code 72/129 indicates insufficient MAF change during DYNAMIC RESPONSE TEST. Possible causes for this fault are:

- Open MAF circuit.
- Open VPWR circuit to MAF sensor.
- Open PWR GND circuit to MAF sensor.
- Open MAF RTN circuit to MAF sensor.
- MAF circuit shorted to ground.
- Faulty ECA or MAF sensor.
- Air leak before or after MAF sensor.
- MAF sensor disconnected.

Turn ignition off. Disconnect MAF sensor. Disconnect ECA 60-pin connector. Inspect for damage and repair as necessary. Install EEC-IV Breakout Box (T83L-50-EEC-IV), leaving ECA disconnected. Measure resistance between VPWR terminal at MAF sensor wiring harness connector and test pins No. 37 and 57 at breakout box. On all models except 2.3L and 4.0L, measure resistance between MAF terminal at MAF sensor wiring harness connector and test pin No. 14 at breakout box. On 2.3L and 4.0L models, measure resistance between MAF terminal at MAF sensor wiring harness connector and test pin No. 50 at breakout box. If all resistances are less than 5 ohms, go to step **11)**. If any resistance is 5 ohms or more, repair open MAF circuit and repeat QUICK TEST.

11) Check MAF & MAF RTN Circuit – On all models except 2.3L and 4.0L, measure resistance between test pin No. 14 and test pins No. 15, 40 and 60 at breakout box. On 2.3L and 4.0L models, measure resistance between test pin No. 50 and test pins No. 9, 40 and 60 at breakout box. If resistance in any circuit is less than 10,000 ohms, repair short circuit and repeat QUICK TEST. If all circuit resistances are 10,000 ohms or more, go to step **12)**.

12) Check Continuity Of PWR GND Circuit – Turn ignition off. Set DVOM on 200-ohm scale. Measure resistance between PWR GND terminal at MAF sensor wiring harness connector and negative battery terminal. If resistance is 10 ohms or more, repair open PWR GND circuit and repeat QUICK TEST. If resistance is less than 10 ohms, go to next step.

13) Check Continuity Of MAF RTN Circuit – On all models except 2.3L and 4.0L, measure resistance between MAF RTN terminal at MAF sensor wiring harness connector and test pin No. 15 at breakout box. On 2.3L and 4.0L models, measure resistance between MAF RTN terminal at MAF sensor wiring harness connector and test pin No. 9 at breakout box. If resistance is less than 5 ohms, go to step **14)**. If resistance is 5 ohms or more, repair open MAF RTN circuit and repeat QUICK TEST.

14) Check MAF Signal For Short To Ground – Turn ignition off. Disconnect MAF sensor. Connect ECA to breakout box. On all models except 2.3L and 4.0L, measure resistance between test pin No. 14 and test pins No. 15, 40 and 60 at breakout box. On 2.3L and 4.0L models, measure resistance between test pin No. 50 and pins No. 9, 40 and 60 at breakout box. If any circuit resistance is less than 10,000 ohms, replace ECA and repeat QUICK TEST. If each circuit resistance is 10,000 ohms or more, go to step **15)**.

15) Check MAF Circuit Output – Turn ignition off. Connect MAF sensor wiring harness connector. Set DVOM on 20-volt scale. Start engine. On all models except 2.3L and 4.0L, measure voltage between test pin No. 14 at breakout box and negative battery terminal. On 2.3L and 4.0L models, measure voltage between test pin No. 50 at breakout box and negative battery terminal. If voltage is 0.4-1.5 volts, go to step **16)**. If voltage is not 0.4-1.5 volts, replace MAF sensor. Repeat QUICK TEST.

CIRCUIT TEST DC (Cont.)

16) Start engine. On all models except 2.3L and 4.0L, measure voltage between test pin No. 14 and test pin No. 15 at breakout box. On 2.3L and 4.0L models, measure voltage between test pins No. 9 and 50 at breakout box. If voltage is 0.4-1.5 volts, replace ECA and repeat QUICK TEST. If voltage is not 0.4-1.5 volts, replace MAF sensor and repeat QUICK TEST.

NOTE: A break in step numbering sequence occurs at this point. Procedure skips from step 16) to step 20). No test procedures have been omitted.

20) Code 56/158 – Turn ignition off. Disconnect MAF sensor wiring harness connector. Start engine, and allow it to idle for one minute. Turn ignition off. Repeat KOEO SELF-TEST. If Code 66 or 157 is present, replace MAF sensor and repeat QUICK TEST. If Code 66 or 157 is not present, go to step 21).

21) Check MAF Circuit For Short To VPWR – Turn ignition off. Disconnect ECA 60-pin connector, and inspect it for damaged or corroded terminals. Service if necessary. Measure resistance between MAF and VPWR terminals at MAF sensor wiring harness connector. If resistance is 10,000 ohms or more, replace ECA and repeat QUICK TEST. If resistance is less than 10,000 ohms, repair short circuit and repeat QUICK TEST.

CIRCUIT TEST DF

MANIFOLD ABSOLUTE PRESSURE (MAP)/ BAROMETRIC PRESSURE (BP) SENSOR

Diagnostic Aids – Perform this test when directed by QUICK TEST or CIRCUIT TEST S. Barometric pressure sensor output is digital and must be measured using an oscilloscope or MAP/BP tester. To prevent replacement of good components, be aware following non-EEC related areas may be cause of problem:

- Unusually high or low atmospheric barometric pressure.
- Kinked or blocked vacuum lines.
- Engine mechanical condition (valves, vacuum leaks, valve timing, EGR valve, etc.).

This test is intended to diagnose following:

- MAP/BP sensor.
- Wiring harness circuits (VREF, MAP/BP SIG and SIG RTN).
- MAP vacuum line.
- ECA.

90B10968

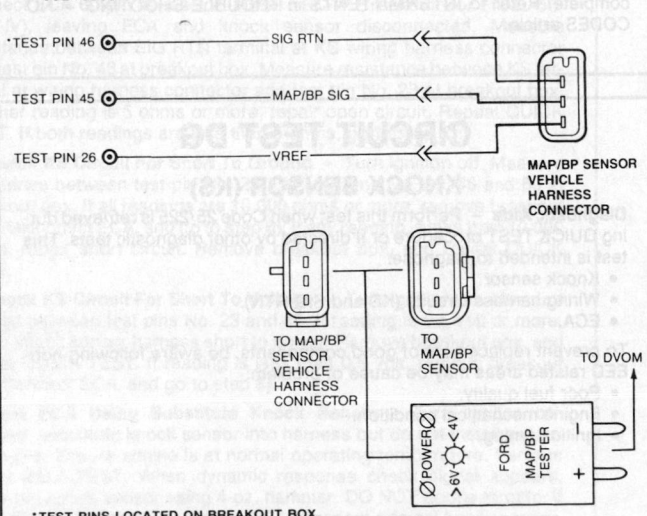

*TEST PINS LOCATED ON BREAKOUT BOX.
ALL HARNESS CONNECTORS VIEWED INTO MATING SURFACE.

Fig. DF1: Identifying MAP/BP Sensor Circuits, Connector Terminals & Tester Hookup

CIRCUIT TEST DF (Cont.)

TEST PIN NO. 26 (VREF) WIRE COLOR IDENTIFICATION

Application	Wire Color
All Models	Brown/White

TEST PIN NO. 45 (MAP/BP SIG) WIRE COLOR IDENTIFICATION

Application	Wire Color
All Models	Light Green/Black

TEST PIN NO. 46 (SIG RTN) WIRE COLOR IDENTIFICATION

Application	Wire Color
All Models	Gray/Red

MAP SENSOR SPECIFICATIONS

Manifold Vacuum In. Hg	Frequency Hz
0	159
3	150
6	141
9	133
12	125
15	117
18	109
21	102
24	95
27	88
30	80

MAP/BP SENSOR SPECIFICATIONS

Barometric Pressure In. Hg	Frequency Hz
17.1	122.4
18.3	125.5
19.5	128.7
20.7	131.9
21.8	135.1
23.0	138.3
24.2	141.8
25.4	145.4
26.6	148.9
27.7	152.5
28.9	156.1
30.1	159.6
31.0	162.4

1) Code 22/126: Check Power To MAP/BP Sensor – Code 22/126 indicates MAP/BP sensor is out of self-test voltage range (1.4-1.6 volts). Following are possible causes of this code:

- Vacuum trapped at MAP/BP sensor.
- High atmospheric pressure.
- MAP/BP signal circuit open between sensor and ECA.
- MAP/BP signal circuit shorted to VREF, SIG RTN or ground.
- VREF circuit open at sensor.
- SIG RTN circuit open at sensor.
- Faulty MAP/BP sensor.
- Faulty ECA.

Turn ignition off. Disconnect MAP/BP sensor from wiring harness. Connect MAP/BP tester between wiring harness and MAP/BP sensor. Connect banana plugs of tester into DVOM. Set DVOM on 20-volt scale. Turn ignition on. If Red light or no light is on, VREF is out of range. Go to step 2). If Green light is on, VREF is okay. Go to step 3).

2) Check Power At Sensor Wiring Harness Connector – Disconnect MAP/BP sensor. Turn ignition on. If Green light on tester is lit, replace MAP/BP sensor and repeat QUICK TEST. If Green light is not on, remove MAP/BP tester. Connect MAP/BP sensor, and go to CIRCUIT TEST C.

CIRCUIT TEST DH (Cont.)

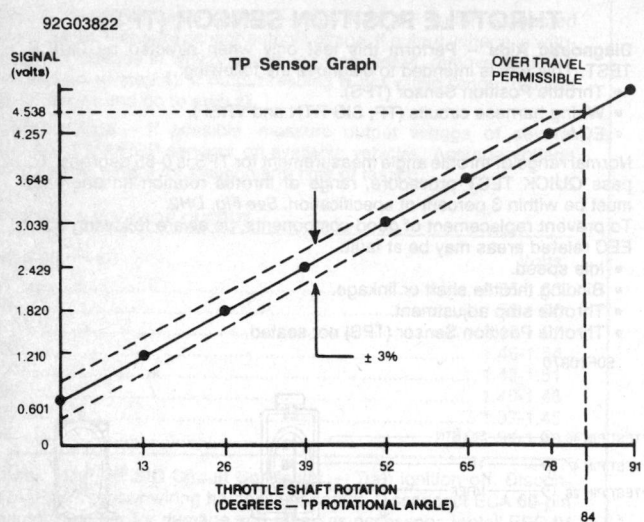

Fig. DH2: TPS Specification Chart

1) Code 23/121: Check For Other Codes – Code 23/121 indicates TPS rotational setting may be out of self-test range. Possible causes for this fault are:

- Binding throttle linkage.
- TPS not seated correctly.
- Faulty TPS.
- Faulty ECA.

Perform KOER SELF-TEST. Check for Code 31/327. If either of these codes are present with Code 23/121, service Code 31/327 and repeat QUICK TEST. If these codes are not present, go to step **2)**.

2) Code 23/121: Check For Binding Throttle Plate – Inspect throttle body and linkage for binding. If throttle plate is binding, check for binding throttle or cruise control linkage, vacuum line or harness interference, etc. Repair as necessary, and repeat QUICK TEST. If no mechanical problem is found, go to step **3)**.

3) Code 53/123: Attempt To Generate Code 63/122 – Code 53/123 indicates TPS signal is greater than self-test maximum value. Possible causes for this fault are:

- TPS not seated properly.
- Faulty TPS.
- VREF circuit shorted in wiring harness.
- Faulty ECA.

Turn ignition off. Disconnect TPS wiring harness connector. Inspect and repair connector pins if damaged. Repeat KOEO SELF-TEST. Ignore all other codes at this time. If Code 63/122 is not displayed, go to step **5)**. If Code 63/122 is displayed, go to step **4)**.

4) Check VREF Circuit Voltage – Turn ignition on. Measure voltage between VREF and SIG RTN terminals at TPS wiring harness connector. If reading is 4-6 volts, replace TPS and repeat QUICK TEST. If reading is not 4-6 volts, reconnect sensor and go to CIRCUIT TEST C.

5) Check TP Circuit For Short To Power – Turn ignition off. Disconnect TPS from wiring harness. Disconnect ECA 60-pin connector. Inspect for damage and repair as necessary. Install EEC-IV Breakout Box (T83L-50-EEC-IV), leaving ECA disconnected. Measure resistance between test pin No. 47 and test pins No. 26 and 57. If either resistance is less than 10,000 ohms, repair short circuit in wiring harness and repeat QUICK TEST. If both resistances are 10,000 ohms or more, replace ECA and repeat QUICK TEST.

NOTE: A break in step numbering sequence occurs at this point. Procedure skips from step 5) to step 10). No test procedures have been omitted.

CIRCUIT TEST DH (Cont.)

10) Code 63/122: Attempt To Generate Code 53/123 Or 23/121 – Code 63/122 indicates TP signal is less than minimum self-test value. Possible causes for this fault are:

- TPS not seated correctly.
- Faulty TPS.
- Open circuit in wiring harness.
- Grounded circuit in wiring harness.
- Faulty ECA.

Turn ignition off, and wait 10 seconds. Disconnect TPS from harness. Install a jumper wire between VREF and TP terminals at TPS wiring harness connector. Perform KOEO SELF-TEST. If either Code 53/123 or 23/121 is present, replace TPS and repeat QUICK TEST. If Codes 53/123 and 23/121 are not present, remove jumper wire and go to step **11)**. If any other codes are present, ignore at this time. If no codes are present, remove jumper wire and go to step **13)**.

11) Check VREF Circuit Voltage – Turn ignition on. Measure voltage between VREF and SIG RTN terminals at TPS wiring harness connector. If voltage is not 4-6 volts, reconnect all components and go to CIRCUIT TEST C. If voltage is 4-6 volts, go to step **12)**.

12) Check TPS Circuit Continuity – Turn ignition off. Leave TPS disconnected. Disconnect ECA 60-pin connector. Inspect for damage and repair as necessary. Install EEC-IV Breakout Box (T83L-50-EEC-IV), leaving ECA disconnected. Measure resistance between TP terminal at TPS wiring harness connector and test pin No. 47. If resistance is 5 ohms or more, repair open circuit and repeat QUICK TEST. If resistance is less than 5 ohms, go to step **13)**.

13) Check TP Circuit For Shorts To Ground – Turn ignition off. Leave TPS disconnected. Disconnect ECA 60-pin connector. Inspect for damage and repair as necessary. Measure resistance between test pin No. 47 and test pins No. 40, 46 and 60. If any reading is less than 10,000 ohms, repair short circuit and repeat QUICK TEST. If all readings are 10,000 ohms or more, replace ECA and repeat QUICK TEST.

NOTE: A break in step numbering sequence occurs at this point. Procedure skips from step 13) to step 20). No test procedures have been omitted.

20) KOER Code 73/167: Repeat Dynamic Response Test – KOER Code 73/167 indicates TPS did not exceed 25% rotation during dynamic response portion of KOER SELF-TEST. A complete Wide Open Throttle (WOT) must be performed during dynamic response portion of test. Perform KOER SELF-TEST. Ensure WOT is obtained during dynamic response portion of test. If Code 73/167 is still present, go to step **21)**. If code is not present, system is unable to duplicate Code 73/167 at this time. Service any other KOER codes. If no other service codes are present, testing is complete.

21) Check TPS Movement During Dynamic Response Test – Turn ignition off. Disconnect ECA 60-pin connector. Inspect for damage and repair as necessary. Install EEC-IV Breakout Box (T83L-50-EEC-IV), leaving ECA connected. Connect DVOM between test pins No. 46 and 47 at breakout box. Perform KOER SELF-TEST. Ensure a WOT is obtained during dynamic response portion of test. If DVOM reading exceeds 3.5 volts, replace ECA and repeat QUICK TEST. If reading does not exceed 3.5 volts, ensure TPS is correctly installed and adjusted. If TPS is correctly installed and adjusted, replace TPS. Repeat QUICK TEST.

NOTE: A break in step numbering sequence occurs at this point. Procedure skips from step 21) to step 90). No test procedures have been omitted.

90) Continuous Memory Code 53/123 – This test monitors TPS under simulated road conditions. Enter wiggle test. See CONTINUOUS MONITOR MODE (WIGGLE TEST) under QUICK TEST. Fully open throttle while observing DVOM or diagnostic tester for indication of fault. Slowly bring throttle to closed position. Lightly tap TPS and wiggle harness connector. If no fault is indicated, go to step **92)**. If fault is indicated, go to step **91)**.

91) Measure TP Circuit Voltage While Exercising TPS – Turn ignition off, and wait 10 seconds. Disconnect ECA 60-pin connector. Inspect it for damaged wiring, and repair if necessary. Install EEC-IV Breakout Box (T83L-50-EEC-IV), leaving ECA connected. Stay in wiggle test (as in previous step). Connect DVOM between test pins No. 47 and 46. Set DVOM on 20-volt scale. Turn ignition on. Observe DVOM and repeat step **90)**. If fault occurs at less than 4.25 volts, inspect TPS connectors and terminals. If connectors and terminals are okay, replace TPS and repeat QUICK TEST. If fault does not occur at less than 4.25 volts, TPS over-travel may have caused Continuous Memory Code 53/123. TPS is okay. Go to step **92)** to check wiring harness.

CIRCUIT TEST DH (Cont.)

92) Check EEC-IV Wiring Harness – While in wiggle test, bend and shake small sections of EEC-IV harness from TPS connector to firewall and from firewall to ECA while observing analog voltmeter or scan tester. If fault is indicated, isolate fault in wiring and repair as necessary. Clear codes, and repeat QUICK TEST. If no fault is indicated, go to next step.

93) Check ECA & Harness Connectors – Turn ignition off, and wait 10 seconds. Disconnect ECA 60-pin connector from breakout box and inspect for damage. If connectors and terminals are okay, fault cannot be duplicated at this time. Continuous Memory Code 53/123 testing is complete. If connector or terminals are damaged, repair as necessary. Clear codes from ECA memory, and repeat QUICK TEST.

94) Continuous Memory Code 63/122 – This test checks for open or short circuit in TPS and wiring harness under simulated road conditions. Enter wiggle test. See CONTINUOUS MONITOR MODE (WIGGLE TEST) under QUICK TEST. Observe VOM or diagnostic tester for indication of fault while performing following:
- Fully open throttle to WOT.
- Slowly bring throttle to closed position.
- Lightly tap TPS and wiggle connector.

If fault is indicated, disconnect TPS. Inspect connectors and terminals. If connectors and terminals are okay, replace TPS. Clear codes from ECA memory, and repeat QUICK TEST. If no fault is indicated, go to next step.

95) Check EEC-IV Wiring Harness – Stay in wiggle test (as in previous step). Bend, wiggle and shake small sections of EEC-IV harness from TPS wiring harness connector to firewall and from firewall to ECA while observing analog voltmeter or scan tester. If fault is indicated, isolate fault in wiring and repair as necessary and repeat QUICK TEST. If no fault is indicated, go to step **96)**.

96) Check ECA & Harness Connectors – Turn ignition off, and wait 10 seconds. Disconnect ECA 60-pin connector. Inspect connectors and terminals for damage. If connectors and terminals are damaged, repair as necessary and repeat QUICK TEST. If connectors and terminals are okay, fault cannot be duplicated at this time. Continuous Memory Code 63/122 testing is complete.

CIRCUIT TEST DJ

ENGINE RPM SENSOR (7.3L DIESEL)

NOTE: Perform this test when Code 14 is displayed during QUICK TEST or when directed here by other test procedures. This test is intended to diagnose only the following components:
- Engine RPM Sensor (RPMS)
- ECA
- RPMS (+) And RPMS (−) Vehicle Harness Circuits

To prevent replacement of good components, verify RPM sensor is correctly installed and circuits/connectors are in good condition:

91F14253

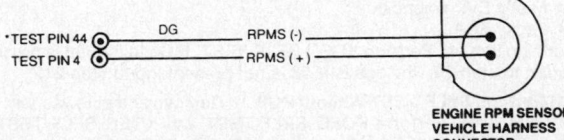

*TEST PINS LOCATED ON BREAKOUT BOX.
ALL HARNESS CONNECTORS VIEWED INTO MATING SURFACE.

Fig. DJ1: RPM Sensor Circuit

TEST PIN 4 (RPMS +) WIRE COLOR IDENTIFICATION

Application	Wire Color
Pickup & Van	Tan/Yellow

1) Code 14: Erratic RPM Signal – Code 14 indicates RPM signal output was missing pulses while engine was running. Check EEC-IV sys-

CIRCUIT TEST DJ (Cont.)

tem for loose wires or connectors. If vehicle is equipped with 2-way radio or telephone, check for correct installation. Enter KOER CONTINUOUS MONITOR MODE (WIGGLE TEST). See QUICK TEST. Observe VOM or diagnostic tester while lightly tapping engine RPM sensor and wiggling RPM sensor connector. If fault is detected, repair as necessary. Clear memory and repeat QUICK TEST to verify repair. If fault is not detected, go to step **2)**.

2) Remain in KOER CONTINUOUS MONITOR MODE. Observe VOM or diagnostic tester for indication of fault while bending or wiggling small sections of harness from sensor connector to dash panel and from dash panel to ECA. If fault is detected, repair as necessary. Clear memory and repeat QUICK TEST to verify repair. If fault is not detected, go to step **3)**.

3) Turn ignition off. Disconnect ECA 60-pin connector. Inspect connector for damage and repair as necessary. Install EEC-IV Breakout Box (T83L-50-EEC-IV), leaving ECA disconnected. Disconnect engine RPM sensor connector. Use ohmmeter to measure resistance between test pin No. 4 and RPMS (+) terminal at sensor. Measure resistance between test pin No. 44 and RPMS (−) terminal at sensor. If either circuit resistance is 5 ohms or more, repair open circuit and repeat QUICK TEST. If resistance is less than 5 ohms, go to step **4)**.

4) Ensure ignition is off and RPM sensor is disconnected. Measure resistance between test pin No. 4 and test pin Nos. 37/57, 40 and 44 at breakout box. Measure resistance between test pin No. 44 and test pin Nos. 37/57 at breakout box. If each resistance is less than 10,000 ohms, repair short circuit. Remove breakout box, connect all components and repeat QUICK TEST. If resistance is 10,000 ohms or more, go to step **5)**.

5) Ensure ignition is off and RPM sensor is disconnected. Measure resistance between engine RPM sensor terminals. If resistance is 2400-2800 ohms, replace ECA and repeat QUICK TEST. If resistance is not 2400-2800 ohms, sensor and circuit are okay. Test is complete.

CIRCUIT TEST DN

EGR VALVE POSITION (EVP) SENSOR & EGR VALVE REGULATOR (EVR) SOLENOID

Diagnostic Aids – Perform this test when instructed by QUICK TEST or if directed by other test procedures. To prevent replacement of good components, be aware a damaged EGR valve may be cause of problem. This CIRCUIT TEST is intended to diagnose the following:
- EVP Sensor
- EVR Solenoid
- EGR Valve Assembly
- ECA
- EGR And EVR Vacuum Lines
- VREF, EVP, SIG RTN, EVR And VPWR Harness Circuits

EVR solenoid receives variable input from ECA, which allows it to control vacuum level to EGR valve. Vacuum not used by EGR is routed to EVR solenoid and vented to atmosphere.

90H12382

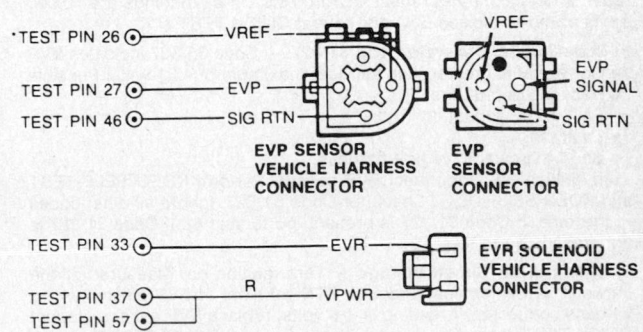

*TEST PINS LOCATED ON BREAKOUT BOX.
ALL HARNESS CONNECTORS VIEWED INTO MATING SURFACE.

Fig. DN1: Identifying EVP Sensor & EVR Solenoid Circuits & Connectors

CIRCUIT TEST DN (Cont.)

TEST PIN NO. 26 (VREF) WIRE COLOR IDENTIFICATION

Application	Wire Color
All Models	Brown/White

TEST PIN NO. 27 (EVP) WIRE COLOR IDENTIFICATION

Application	Wire Color
2.3L, 4.9L & 5.0L	Brown/Light Green

TEST PIN NO. 33 (EVR) WIRE COLOR IDENTIFICATION

Application	Wire Color
2.3L, 4.9L & 5.0L	Brown/Pink

TEST PIN NO. 46 (SIG RTN) WIRE COLOR IDENTIFICATION

Application	Wire Color
All Models	Gray/Red

NOTE: EVR sensor is preloaded when attached to EGR valve. Valve failure causing EVR sensor to lose preload may set Code 31/327.

1) Code 31/327: Generate Code 35/337 – Code 31/327 indicates EVP sensor signal is less than self-test minimum of 0.2 volt. Possible causes for this fault are:
- Faulty EVP sensor.
- Open or grounded harness.
- Faulty ECA.

Turn ignition off. Disconnect EVP wiring harness connector at sensor. Install a jumper wire between VREF terminal and EVP terminal at EVP sensor wiring harness connector. Repeat KOEO SELF-TEST and KOER SELF-TEST. Check for Code 337. Ignore all other codes at this time. If Code 35/337 is present, replace EVP sensor and repeat QUICK TEST. If Code 35/337 is not present, remove jumper wire and go to step 2).

2) Check VREF Circuit Voltage – Disconnect EVP sensor. Turn ignition on. Measure voltage between VREF terminal and SIG RTN terminal at EVP sensor wiring harness connector. If voltage is 4-6 volts, go to step 3). If voltage is not 4-6 volts, go to CIRCUIT TEST C.

3) Check EVP Circuit Resistance – Turn ignition off, and wait 10 seconds. Disconnect ECA 60-pin connector. Inspect terminals, and repair if damaged. Install EEC-IV Breakout Box (T83L-50-EEC-IV) leaving ECA disconnected. Measure resistance between EVP terminal at EVP sensor wiring harness connector and test pin No. 27. If resistance is 5 ohms or more, repair open circuit and repeat QUICK TEST. If resistance is less than 5 ohms, go to step 4).

4) Check EVP Circuit For Shorts To Ground – With ignition off and EVP sensor disconnected, measure resistance between test pin No. 27 and test pins No. 40, 46 and 60. If any resistance is less than 10,000 ohms, repair short circuit and repeat QUICK TEST. If all readings are 10,000 ohms or more, replace ECA and repeat QUICK TEST.

5) Code 35/337: Generate Code 31/327 – Code 35/337 indicates EVP sensor signal is greater than self-test maximum of 4.81 volts. Possible causes for this fault are:
- Faulty EVP sensor.
- Faulty ECA.
- Short to power in vehicle harness.

Turn ignition off. Disconnect EVP sensor. Perform KOEO SELF-TEST and KOER SELF-TEST. Check for Code 31/327. Ignore all other codes at this time. If Code 31/327 is present, go to step 6). If Code 31/327 is not present, go to step 7).

6) Check VREF Circuit Voltage – Turn ignition on. Measure voltage between VREF terminal and SIG RTN terminal at EVP sensor wiring harness connector. If reading is 4-6 volts, replace EVP sensor. Repeat QUICK TEST. If reading is not 4-6 volts, go to CIRCUIT TEST C.

7) Check EVP Circuit For Short To Power – Turn ignition off. Inspect ECA 60-pin connector terminals, and repair if damaged. Install EEC-IV Breakout Box (T83L-50-EEC-IV), leaving ECA disconnected. Measure resistance between test pin No. 27 and test pins No. 26 and 57 at breakout box. If either reading is less than 10,000 ohms, repair short circuit and repeat QUICK TEST. If both readings are 10,000 ohms or more, replace ECA and repeat QUICK TEST.

CIRCUIT TEST DN (Cont.)

NOTE: A break in step numbering sequence occurs at this point. Procedure skips from step 7) to step 10). No test procedures have been omitted.

10) Code 84/558: Check EVR Solenoid Resistance – Code 84/558 indicates fault in EVR solenoid circuit. Possible causes for this fault are:
- Faulty EVR solenoid.
- Faulty ECA.
- Shorted or open harness.

Turn ignition off. Disconnect EVR solenoid connector. Measure resistance across EVR solenoid terminals. If reading is not within specification, replace EVR solenoid assembly and repeat QUICK TEST. See EVR SOLENOID RESISTANCE table. If reading is within specification, go to step 11).

EVR SOLENOID RESISTANCE

Application	Ohms
7.5L	100-135
Except 7.5L	20-70

11) Check VPWR Circuit Voltage – Turn ignition on. Measure voltage between negative battery terminal and VPWR terminal at EVR solenoid wiring harness connector. If reading is less than 10.5 volts, repair open in VPWR circuit and repeat QUICK TEST. If reading is 10.5 volts or more, go to step 12).

12) Check EVR Circuit Continuity – Turn ignition off. Disconnect EVR solenoid. Disconnect ECA 60-pin connector. Inspect terminals, and repair if damaged. Install EEC-IV Breakout Box (T83L-50-EEC-IV), leaving ECA disconnected. Set DVOM on 200-ohm scale. Measure resistance between EVR terminal at EVR solenoid wiring harness connector and test pin No. 33. If reading is less than 5 ohms, go to next step. If reading is 5 ohms or more, repair open circuit and repeat QUICK TEST.

13) Check EVR Circuit For Shorts To Power Or Ground – Turn ignition off. Measure resistance between test pin No. 33 and pins No. 37, 40, 46, 57 and 60 at breakout box. If any reading is less than 10,000 ohms, repair short circuit and repeat QUICK TEST. If code is repeated, replace ECA. If all readings are 10,000 ohms or more, replace ECA. Remove breakout box, and repeat QUICK TEST.

NOTE: A break in step numbering sequence occurs at this point. Procedure skips from step 13) to step 20). No test procedures have been omitted.

20) Code 34/334: Check For Code 84/558 – Code 34/334 indicates EGR valve and/or EVP is not fully seated in closed position. EVP voltage signal, in closed position, is greater than self-test maximum of 0.67 volt. Because of EVP sensor preload, determining whether EGR valve is seated or EVP sensor contacts EGR valve stem is difficult. Possible causes for this fault are:
- Poor contact in EVP sensor circuit.
- EGR valve not seated.
- Faulty EGR valve.
- Faulty EVP sensor.
- Faulty EVP solenoid.
- Faulty ECA.

Turn ignition off. Perform KOEO SELF-TEST. If Code 84/558 is present, return to step 10). If Code 84/558 is not present, go to step 21).

21) Perform SELF-TEST Without EGR – Remove and plug vacuum line to EGR valve. Perform KOEO SELF-TEST and KOER SELF-TEST. If Code 34/334 is still present, go to step 22). If Code 34/334 is not present, check EVR solenoid for obstructions. Replace EVR solenoid if no obstructions are present.

22) Check EGR Valve & EVP Sensor Operation – Turn ignition off. Disconnect EVP sensor. Inspect harness and connector. Service if necessary. Remove and plug vacuum hose to EGR valve. Install vacuum gauge at EGR valve vacuum hose. Operate EGR valve by applying and releasing vacuum. Install vacuum hose to EGR valve. Repeat KOEO SELF-TEST and KOER SELF-TEST. If Code 34/334 is present, go to step 23). If Code 34/334 is not present, original fault was caused by poor continuity at EVP sensor connector or binding **of EGR valve stem.

23) Check EVP Signal Voltage – Turn ignition off. Disconnect ECA 60-pin connector. Inspect terminals, and repair if damaged. Install EEC-IV Breakout Box (T83L-50-EEC-IV). Connect ECA to breakout box. Turn

CIRCUIT TEST DN (Cont.)

ignition on. Measure voltage between test pin No. 27 and test pin No. 46 at breakout box. If voltage is less than 0.67 volt, replace ECA and repeat QUICK TEST. If voltage is greater than 0.67 volt, go to step 24).

24) **EGR Valve/EVP Sensor Fault Isolation** – Remove EGR valve and EVP sensor. Inspect valve and sensor for binding, carbon deposits, excessive wear and damage. Repair or replace as necessary. Install EGR valve and EVP sensor. Perform KOEO SELF-TEST and KOER SELF-TEST. If Code 34/334 is still present, replace EGR valve. If Code 34/334 is not present, testing is complete.

25) **Service Code 32/328** – Service Code 32/328 indicates EVP sensor is lower than normal (0.24 volt) in closed position. Possible causes for this fault are:
- Faulty EGR valve.
- Faulty EVP sensor.
- Faulty ECA.
- Open or shorted EVP sensor.

Turn ignition off. Disconnect EVP sensor. Inspect harness and connector, and service as necessary. Remove and plug vacuum hose to EGR valve. Install vacuum gauge at EGR valve vacuum hose. Operate EGR valve by applying and releasing vacuum. Install vacuum hose to EGR valve. Repeat KOEO SELF-TEST and KOER SELF-TEST. If Code 32/328 is not present, original fault was caused by poor continuity at EVP sensor connector or binding/sticking of EGR valve stem. If Code 32/328 is present, go to step 26).

26) **Check EVP Signal Voltage** – Turn ignition off. Disconnect ECA 60-pin connector. Inspect terminals, and repair if damaged. Install EEC-IV Breakout Box (T83L-50-EEC-IV). Connect ECA to breakout box. Remove and plug vacuum hose to EGR valve. Install vacuum gauge at EGR valve vacuum hose. Turn ignition on. Measure voltage between test pin No. 27 and test pin No. 46 at breakout box while performing following: apply 6 in. Hg to EGR valve and slowly bleed vacuum completely off. If voltage drops to less than 0.24 volt, replace ECA and repeat QUICK TEST. If voltage remains more than 0.24 volt, go to step 27).

27) **Substitute EVP Sensor On Original EGR Valve** – Turn ignition off. Install a known good EVP sensor on original EGR valve. Ensure all hoses and electrical connectors are attached. Perform KOEO SELF-TEST and KOER SELF-TEST. If Code 32/328 is present, check EGR valve for mechanical malfunction. If Code 32/328 is not present, replace original EVP sensor. Repeat QUICK TEST.

NOTE: A break in step numbering sequence occurs at this point. Procedure skips from step 27) to step 40). No test procedures have been omitted.

40) **KOER Code 33/332: Check Vacuum At EGR** – KOER Code 33/332 indicates EVP sensor input did not change after ECA signaled operation of EGR. Because Code 84/558 was not retrieved in KOEO SELF-TEST, EVR solenoid electrical function is okay. Lack of Code 32/328 or 34/334 indicates EVP sensor is within closed position specifications. Possible causes for this fault are:
- Leaking vacuum hose.
- Restricted vacuum hose.
- Restricted EVR solenoid.
- Faulty EGR valve.

Turn ignition off. Disconnect vacuum line from EGR valve. Connect a vacuum gauge at open end of line. Perform KOER SELF-TEST while observing vacuum gauge. If vacuum reading is more than 1.0 in. Hg, remove vacuum gauge and go to step 43). If reading is 1.0 in. Hg or less, go to step 41).

41) **Verify Vacuum Supply To EVR Solenoid** – Turn ignition off. Disconnect vacuum hose to EVR solenoid at source. Install vacuum gauge at source. Start engine and check vacuum. If reading is 10 in. Hg or more, go to step 42). If reading is less than 10 in. Hg, check vacuum line to EVR solenoid. Repair if necessary. Repeat QUICK TEST.

42) **Check Vacuum Between EVR Solenoid & EGR Valve** – Carefully check vacuum hose for cracks, loose connections, blockage and kinks. Repair or replace vacuum hose if necessary, and repeat QUICK TEST. If vacuum hose is okay, check EVR solenoid filter for obstructions. Replace if necessary. If filter is okay, replace EVR solenoid. After repairs are made, repeat QUICK TEST.

43) **Check EVP Sensor & EGR Valve Operation** – Turn ignition off. Disconnect vacuum hose at EGR valve. Inspect connector and harness for damage, and service as necessary. Remove and plug vacuum hose from EGR valve. Connect vacuum pump to EGR valve. Test EGR valve operation by applying and releasing vacuum. Connect vacuum line to EGR valve. Connect wiring harness connector to EVP sensor. Repeat KOER SELF-

CIRCUIT TEST DN (Cont.)

TEST. If Code 33/332 is still present, go to step 44). If Code 33/332 is not present, original code was set either by poor continuity at EVP sensor connector or sticking EGR valve. Test is complete.

44) **Verify EGR Valve Vacuum Control** – Turn ignition off. Install tachometer. Remove idle air by-pass wiring harness connector. Remove and plug vacuum hose from EGR valve. Start engine, and allow it to idle with transmission in Neutral. Ensure idle speed is adjusted correctly. Connect vacuum pump to EGR valve. Slowly apply 5-10 in. Hg. If vacuum drops more than 100 RPM with vacuum applied and returns to correct idle with vacuum released, replace EVP sensor. If vacuum does not drop more than 100 RPM with vacuum applied, repair or replace EGR valve.

NOTE: A break in step numbering sequence occurs at this point. Procedure skips from step 44) to step 90). No test procedures have been omitted.

90) **Continuous Memory Code 31/327, 32/328 Or 35/337** – Continuous Memory Code 31/327 or 32/328 indicates EGR valve closed further than normal or EVP circuit failed with intermittent low voltage sometime during engine operation. Code 35/337 indicates EVP signal to ECA was above maximum self-test limit sometime during engine operation. Possible causes for these faults are:
- Obstructed vacuum valve.
- Faulty EVP sensor.
- EGR valve.

Turn ignition off, and wait 10 seconds. Disconnect ECA 60-pin connector. Inspect terminals, and repair if damaged. Install EEC-IV Breakout Box (T83L-50-EEC-IV). Connect ECA to breakout box. Turn ignition on. Connect DVOM between test pins No. 27 and 46 at breakout box. Wiggle wiring harness and lightly tap on EVP sensor. If voltage remains steady at .24-.67 volt, go to step 91). If voltage is erratic or not within .24-.67 volt range, remove and inspect EVP sensor wiring harness connector. Repair or replace if necessary. If sensor connector is okay, replace EVP sensor.

91) **Check Wiring Harness** – Connect DVOM between test pins No. 27 and 46 at breakout box. Turn ignition on. Observe DVOM for fault indication while wiggling and bending small sections of wiring harness near sensor, working from sensor toward firewall. Wiggle and bend wiring harness from firewall to ECA. If fault is indicated, isolate fault and repair wiring harness. Clear codes, and repeat QUICK TEST. If fault is not found, go to step 92).

92) **Measure EVP Signal Voltage While Exercising EVP Sensor** – Remove and plug vacuum hose to EGR valve. Install vacuum gauge at EGR valve vacuum hose. Turn ignition on. Measure voltage between test pin No. 27 and test pin No. 46 at breakout box while performing following: apply 5-10 in. Hg to EGR valve and slowly bleed vacuum completely off. If voltage steadily fluctuates between 0.24-4.81 volts, problem is intermittent and cannot be duplicated at this time. If voltage does not fluctuate between 0.24-4.81 volts, replace EVP sensor and repeat QUICK TEST.

NOTE: A break in step numbering sequence occurs at this point. Procedure skips from step 92) to step 110). No test procedures have been omitted.

110) **Continuous Memory Code 33/332** – Code 33/332 indicates EGR valve did not open with engine at normal operating temperature and with EVR solenoid signal present sometime during engine operation. Possible causes of this fault are:
- Fault in vacuum line.
- Faulty EGR valve.
- Open or shorted EVR circuit.

Turn ignition off. Disconnect vacuum hose at EGR valve. Connect vacuum pump to valve. Apply 10-20 in. Hg to EGR valve. If EGR valve opens and holds vacuum, go to step 111). If EGR valve does not open and hold vacuum, service or replace EGR valve as necessary and repeat QUICK TEST.

111) **EVR Solenoid & Wiring Harness Check** – Turn ignition off. Disconnect vacuum hose from EGR valve. Connect EGR valve hose to vacuum gauge. Disconnect ECA 60-pin connector. Inspect for damaged terminals and repair as necessary. Install EEC-IV Breakout Box (T83L-50-EEC-IV). Connect ECA to breakout box. Start engine, and allow it to idle. Connect jumper wire between test pins No. 33 and 40. Tap on EVR sensor and wiggle wiring harness while observing vacuum gauge. If vacuum gauge shows a sudden drop in vacuum, isolate cause and repair as necessary. If vacuum gauge does not show a drop in vacuum, problem is intermittent and cannot be duplicated at this time.

CIRCUIT TEST DN (Cont.)

NOTE: A break in step numbering sequence occurs at this point. Procedure skips from step 111) to step 115). No test procedures have been omitted.

115) Continuous Memory Code 34/334: – Code 34/334 indicates EGR valve was open with engine idling at normal operating temperature. Possible causes for this fault are:
- Faulty EVR sensor.
- Faulty EVR solenoid.
- Faulty EGR valve.

Turn ignition off. Disconnect vacuum hose from EGR valve. Connect EGR valve hose to vacuum gauge. Start engine, and allow it to idle. Tap on EVR sensor and wiggle wiring harness while observing vacuum gauge. If vacuum gauge reading does not remain below 1.0 in. Hg and/or has sudden vacuum increase, service or replace EVR solenoid. If vacuum gauge reading remains below 1.0 in. Hg with no sudden increase, go to step **116)**.

116) EVR Solenoid Check – Leave engine idling and vacuum gauge connected to EGR valve hose. Observe vacuum gauge while wiggling and bending small sections of wiring harness near EVR sensor, working from sensor toward firewall. Wiggle and bend wiring harness from firewall to ECA. If vacuum gauge shows an increase in vacuum, isolate cause and repair as necessary. If vacuum gauge does not show an increase in vacuum, go to step **117)**.

117) Check EVR Signal At ECA – Turn ignition off, and wait 10 seconds. Disconnect ECA 60-pin connector. Inspect terminals, and repair if damaged. Install EEC-IV Breakout Box (T83L-50-EEC-IV). Connect ECA to breakout box. Start engine, and allow it to idle. Connect DVOM between test pins No. 27 and 46 at breakout box. Wiggle wiring harness and lightly tap on EVP sensor. If voltage increases to more than 0.67 volt, remove and service EGR valve. If voltage is still more than 0.67 volt, replace EVP sensor. If voltage is 0.67 volt or less, problem is intermittent and cannot be duplicated at this time.

CIRCUIT TEST DP

VEHICLE SPEED SENSOR (VSS)

Diagnostic Aids – Perform this test when directed by QUICK TEST. This CIRCUIT TEST is intended to diagnose:
- Vehicle Speed Sensor (VSS)
- VSS Wiring Harness Circuits
- ECA

91J14257

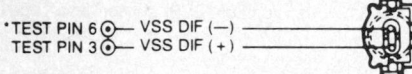

*TEST PIN 6 — VSS DIF (−)
TEST PIN 3 — VSS DIF (+)

VEHICLE SPEED SENSOR (VSS) VEHICLE HARNESS CONNECTOR

*TEST PINS LOCATED ON BREAKOUT BOX. ALL HARNESS CONNECTORS VIEWED INTO MATING SURFACE.

Fig. DP1: Vehicle Speed Sensor Circuit

TEST PIN NO. 3 (VSS +) WIRE COLOR IDENTIFICATION

Application	Wire Color
Ranger & Explorer	Gray/Black

TEST PIN NO. 6 (VSS −) WIRE COLOR IDENTIFICATION

Application	Wire Color
Ranger & Explorer	Pink/Orange

Preliminary Instructions (A/T) – Record and clear continuous memory codes. Warm engine to normal operating temperature. In Low gear, accelerate hard to 35 MPH and coast down to a stop. Shut off engine. Perform KOEO SELF-TEST. Go to step **1)**.

Preliminary Instructions (M/T) – Record and clear continuous memory codes. Warm engine to normal operating temperature. Accelerate moderately to 40 MPH. Start engine in first gear, shifting no higher than second gear. Coast down to idle, and stop. Shut engine off. Perform KOEO SELF-TEST and record continuous memory codes. Go to step **1)**.

CIRCUIT TEST DP (Cont.)

1) Continuous Memory Code 29/452 – Code 29/452 indicates ECA detected incorrect output from VSS sometime during vehicle operation. Possible causes for this code are:
- Faulty VSS
- Open Or Shorted Circuit
- Faulty ECA

Perform appropriate drive cycle procedure. See PRELIMINARY INSTRUCTIONS (A/T) or PRELIMINARY INSTRUCTIONS (M/T). Ensure driveability complaint can be verified. If Code 29/452 is still present or driveability complaint can be verified, go to step **2)**. If code is not present or complaint cannot be verified, fault cannot be duplicated at this time. Clear codes, and see SYMPTOMS in TROUBLE SHOOTING – NO CODES article.

2) Check VSS Circuit Continuity – Turn ignition off. Disconnect VSS sensor. Remove ECA 60-pin connector. Inspect terminals, and repair if damaged. Install EEC-IV Breakout Box (T83L-50-EEC-IV) leaving ECA disconnected. Measure resistance between VSS DIF (+) terminal at VSS wiring harness connector and test pin No. 3 at breakout box. Measure resistance between VSS DIF (−) terminal at VSS wiring harness connector and test pin No. 6 at breakout box. If any resistance reading is more than 5 ohms, service open circuit in VSS wiring harness and repeat step **1)**. If both resistance readings are 5 ohms or less, go to next step.

3) Check VSS Circuits For Shorts To Power Or Ground – Turn ignition off. Ensure ECA and VSS are disconnected. Measure resistance between test pin No. 3 and test pins No. 6, 37 and 40 at breakout box. If any reading is less than 500 ohms, repair shorts in VSS wiring harness and repeat step **1)**. If all readings are greater than 500 ohms, go to next step.

4) Check VSS Resistance – Turn ignition off, and wait 10 seconds. Disconnect VSS wiring harness connector. Measure resistance across VSS terminals. If reading is 190-250 ohms, replace ECA and repeat step **1)**. If reading is not 190-250 ohms, replace VSS and repeat step **1)**.

CIRCUIT TEST DQ

FUEL INJECTION PUMP LEVER (FIPL)

91G14254

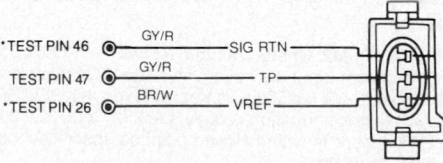

*TEST PIN 46 — GY/R — SIG RTN
*TEST PIN 47 — GY/R — TP
*TEST PIN 26 — BR/W — VREF

Fig. DQ1: FIPL Connector & Circuits

Diagnostic Aids – Enter this CIRCUIT TEST only when instructed during QUICK TEST. If you were directed here from KOEO Code 23 but an engine ID code of 5.0 was not received, go to CIRCUIT TEST DJ.

1) Service Code 23: Throttle Linkage Check – Inspect throttle linkage for binding, sticking or interference. If throttle linkage does not operate smoothly, service as necessary and repeat QUICK TEST. If throttle does operate smoothly, go to next step.

2) Service Code 53: Attempt to Generate Code 63 – With ignition off, and FIPL disconnected, inspect and repair any corroded or damaged pins. Perform KOEO self test. If Code 63 is present, go to next step. If code 63 is not present, go to step **4)**.

3) VREF Circuit Voltage Check – With ignition off and FIPL disconnected, measure voltage at SIG RTN and VREF circuit at connector. If voltage is not 4.0-6.0 volts, connect all components and go to CIRCUIT TEST C, step **1)**. If voltage is 4.0-6.0 volts, connect all components and go to step **14)**.

4) Check for Shorts to Power – With ignition off and FIPL disconnected, install breakout box leaving ECA disconnected. Set DVOM on 200-k/ohm scale. Measure resistance between test pin No. 47 and test pins No. 26 and 57. If resistance is 10,000 ohms or more, replace ECA; remove breakout box and reconnect components. Repeat QUICK TEST. If resistance is less than 10,000 ohms, repair short circuit; remove breakout box and reconnect all components. Repeat QUICK TEST.

CIRCUIT TEST DQ (Cont.)

NOTE: A break in step numbering sequence occurs at this point. Procedure skips from step 4) to step 10). No test procedures have been omitted.

10) Service Code 63: Attempt to Generate Code 53/23 – With ignition off, disconnect FIPL wiring harness connector. Inspect connector and harness for damage, and service as necessary. Connect jumper wire between VREF and TP circuit at FIPL wiring harness connector. Perform KOEO SELF TEST. If no codes are present, go to step **13)**. If Codes 23 or 53 are present, remove jumper wire and go to step **14)**. If Codes 23 or 53 are not present, go to next step.

11) VREF Circuit Voltage Check – With ignition off and FIPL disconnected, measure voltage at SIG RTN and VREF circuit at connector. If voltage is not 4.0-6.0 volts, connect all components and go to CIRCUIT TEST C, step **1)**. If voltage is 4.0-6.0 volts, connect all components and go to step **12)**.

12) FIPL Circuit Continuity Check – With ignition off and FIPL disconnected, install breakout box leaving ECA connected. Inspect connector and harness for damage, and service as necessary. Measure resistance between test pin No. 47 and TP circuit at FIPL wiring harness connector. If resistance is 5 ohms or more, repair open circuit; remove breakout box and reconnect components. Repeat QUICK TEST. If resistance is less than 5 ohms, go to next step.

13) Check for Shorts to Ground – With ignition off and FIPL disconnected, install breakout box leaving ECA disconnected. Inspect connector and harness for damage, and service as necessary. Set DVOM on 200-k/ohm scale. Measure resistance between test pin No. 47 and test pins No. 40, 46 and 60 at breakout box. If resistance is 10,000 ohms or more, replace ECA; remove breakout box and reconnect components. Repeat QUICK TEST. If resistance is less than 10,000 ohms, repair short circuit; remove breakout box and reconnect all components. Repeat QUICK TEST.

NOTE: Super STAR II scan tester is required for FIPL adjustment.

14) FIPL Sensor Adjustment – Perform KOEO SELF-TEST while holding throttle fully open. After last service code has been received, remain in self-test. Place 0.515" gauge between FIPL travel screw and gauge boss. Cycle overdrive cancel switch. Observe Super STAR II tester for one of the following modes:
- Constant tone, solid light or consistent STO LO readout indicates FIPL sensor is within range. Cycle overdrive cancel switch to exit test.
- Beeping tone, flashing light or erratic STO readout indicates adjustment is required.
- If tone is undetectable, FIPL sensor may be worn.
- If adjustment is required, loosen adjusting screws and rotate sensor until a constant tone, solid light or consistent STO LO readout appears. Tighten adjusting screws, and remove gauge block. Repeat QUICK TEST. If service codes are still present or constant tone cannot be obtained, replace FIPL sensor.

91H14255

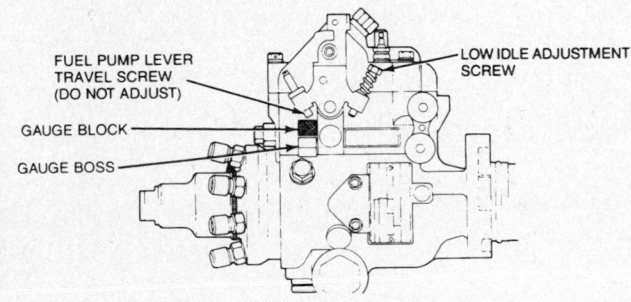

FUEL PUMP LEVER TRAVEL SCREW (DO NOT ADJUST)

LOW IDLE ADJUSTMENT SCREW

GAUGE BLOCK

GAUGE BOSS

Fig. DQ2: Adjusting FIPL Sensor

CIRCUIT TEST DQ (Cont.)

NOTE: A break in step numbering sequence occurs at this point. Procedure skips from step 14) to step 90). No test procedures have been omitted.

90) Continuous Memory Code 53: Monitor FIPL Circuit Under Simulated Road Conditions – Enter KOEO wiggle test. See CONTINUOUS MONITOR MODE (WIGGLE TEST) under QUICK TEST. Observe DVOM or diagnostic tester for indication of fault while slowly opening throttle to WOT. Slowly bring throttle to closed position, and lightly tap FIPL and wiggle harness connector. This test checks for open or short in FIPL, connectors and wiring harness. If no fault is indicated, go to step **92)**. If fault is indicated, go to step **91)**.

91) Measure TP Circuit Voltage While Exercising FIPL – Turn ignition off and wait 10 seconds. Disconnect ECA 60-pin connector. Install EEC-IV Breakout Box (T83L-50-EEC-IV) leaving ECA connected. Stay in KOEO wiggle test (as in previous step). Connect DVOM between test pins No. 46 and 47. Turn ignition on. Observe DVOM and repeat step **90)**. If fault occurs at less than 4.25 volts, inspect FIPL connectors and terminals. If connectors and terminals are okay, go to step **14)**. If fault does not occur at less than 4.25 volts, go to step **92)**.

92) Check EEC-IV Vehicle Harness – While in KOEO wiggle test, shake, bend and wiggle small sections of EEC-IV harness from FIPL vehicle harness connector to firewall, and from firewall to ECA. If fault is indicated, isolate fault in wiring and repair as necessary. Clear codes and repeat QUICK TEST. If no fault is indicated, go to step **93)**.

93) Check ECA & Harness Connectors – Turn ignition off. Inspect ECA 60-pin connector and terminal for damage. Repair as necessary. Clear Continuous Memory Codes and repeat QUICK TEST. If connectors and terminals are okay, fault cannot be duplicated at this time. Testing is complete.

94) Continuous Memory Code 63: Monitor TP Circuit Under Simulated Road Conditions – Enter KOEO wiggle test. See CONTINUOUS MONITOR MODE (WIGGLE TEST) under QUICK TEST. Check VOM or diagnostic tester for fault while performing the following:
- Slowly open throttle to WOT.
- Slowly bring throttle to closed position.
- Lightly tap FIPL and wiggle connector.

This test checks for open or short in FIPL, connectors and vehicle harness. If fault is indicated, disconnect FIPL. Inspect connector and terminal. If connector and terminals are okay, go to step **14)**. If no fault is indicated, go to step **95)**.

95) Check EEC-IV Vehicle Harness – While in KOEO wiggle test (CONTINUOUS MONITOR MODE), shake, bend and wiggle small sections of EEC-IV harness from FIPL vehicle harness connector to firewall, and from firewall to ECA. If fault is indicated, isolate fault in wiring and repair as necessary. Clear Continuous Memory Codes and repeat QUICK TEST. If no fault is indicated, go to step **96)**.

96) Check ECA and Harness Connectors – Turn ignition off and wait 10 seconds. Disconnect ECA 60-pin connector. Inspect connector and terminal for damage. Repair as necessary. Clear Continuous Memory Codes and repeat QUICK TEST. If connectors and terminals are okay, fault cannot be duplicated at this time. Continuous Memory Code 63/122 testing is complete.

CIRCUIT TEST DS

PROGRAMMABLE SPEEDOMETER/ODOMETER MODULE (PSOM)

Diagnostic Aids – Perform this test when directed by QUICK TEST. This CIRCUIT TEST is intended to diagnose:
- PSOM output to ECA.
- PSOM (+) and PSOM (–) wiring harness circuits.
- ECA.

To prevent replacement of good components, be aware following non-EEC related areas and components may be cause of problem:
- Cruise control system.
- Rear anti-lock brake system.
- Instrumentation system.

92A03824

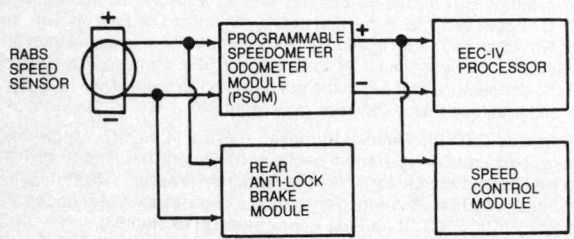

Fig. DS1: Programmable Speedometer/Odometer Module (PSOM) Circuit

92D03825

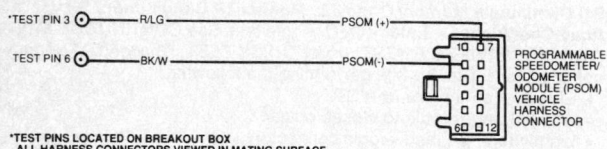

*TEST PINS LOCATED ON BREAKOUT BOX
ALL HARNESS CONNECTORS VIEWED IN MATING SURFACE

Fig. DS2: Identifying Programmable Speedometer/Odometer Module (PSOM) Connector Terminals

CIRCUIT TEST DS (Cont.)

TEST PIN NO. 3 (PSOM +) WIRE COLOR IDENTIFICATION

Application	Wire Color
Aerostar	Dark Green/White
Van	Red/Light Green
Except Aerostar & Van	Gray/Black

TEST PIN NO. 6 (PSOM –) WIRE COLOR IDENTIFICATION

Application	Wire Color
Aerostar	Black/Yellow
Except Aerostar	Pink/Orange

1) Continuous Memory Code 29/452 – Code 29/452 indicates ECA detected incorrect output from VSS sometime during vehicle operation. Following are possible causes of code.
- PSOM Output To ECA
- PSOM (+) And PSOM (–) Wiring Harness Circuits
- ECA

Turn ignition off. Remove ECA 60-pin connector. Inspect terminals, and repair if damaged. Install EEC-IV Breakout Box (T83L-50-EEC-IV), leaving ECA disconnected. Measure resistance between test pins No. 3 and 6 at breakout box. If reading is 21,000–55,000 ohms, go to step **4)**. If resistance is not 21,000–55,000 ohms, go to step **2)**.

2) Check PSOM Circuit Continuity – Ensure ignition is off. Disconnect PSOM wiring harness connector. Measure resistance between test pin No. 3 at breakout box and PSOM + circuit at PSOM wiring harness connector. If resistance is less than 5 ohms, repair open circuit and repeat QUICK TEST. If resistance is more than 5 ohms, go to step **3)**.

3) Check PSOM Circuit For Open – Ensure ignition is off. Measure resistance between test pin No. 3 and test pins No. 6, 37 and 40 at breakout box. If resistance is 10,000 ohms or less, repair open circuit and repeat QUICK TEST. If resistance is more than 10,000 ohms, go to step **4)**.

4) Turn ignition off. Connect ECA to breakout box. Connect wiring harness connector to PSOM. Set DVOM on 20-volt AC scale. Start engine, and warm it to normal operating temperature. Measure voltage between test pins No. 3 and 6 while gradually increasing vehicle speed to 50 MPH. If maximum voltage is less than 4.5 volts, fault is in instrument cluster. If maximum voltage received is more than 4.5 volts, replace ECA.

CIRCUIT TEST FD

BRAKE ON-OFF (BOO) SWITCH

Diagnostic Aids – Perform this test when directed by QUICK TEST. This test is intended to diagnose a faulty BOO switch circuit or ECA. To prevent replacement of good components, be aware following non-EEC related areas may be at fault:

- Brakelight bulb.
- Brakelight switch or brakelight fuse.

92F22769

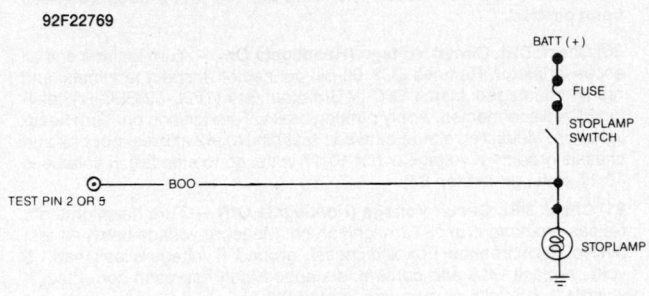

* TEST PINS LOCATED ON BREAKOUT BOX.
ALL HARNESS CONNECTORS VIEWED INTO MATING SURFACES.

Fig. FD1: BOO Switch Circuit

TEST PIN 2 (BOO) WIRE COLOR IDENTIFICATION

Application	Wire Color
Aerostar	Red/Light Green
Except Aerostar	Light Green

1) Code 74/536: Verify Brake Pedal Was Depressed – Code 74/536 indicates that when brake pedal is depressed during KOER SELF-TEST, BOO signal did not cycle high and low. Possible causes for this fault are:

- Brake pedal not depressed during self-test.
- Brake pedal pressed during entire self-test.
- Open brakelight circuit.
- Short to ground or power.
- Faulty ECA.

If brake was not depressed during KOER SELF-TEST, repeat test. Depress and release brake pedal only once during test. If pedal was depressed, go to step 2).

2) Check Operation Of Brakelights – With ignition on, check operation of brakelights. If brakelights operate normally, go to step 3). If brakelights do not operate, go to step 4). If brakelights are always on, go to step 5).

3) Check For BOO Switch Circuit Cycling – Turn ignition off. Wait 10 seconds. Disconnect ECA 60-pin connector. Inspect terminals, and repair if damaged. Install EEC-IV Breakout Box (T83L-50-EEC-IV), leaving ECA disconnected. Set DVOM on 20-volt scale. Measure voltage between test pins No. 2 and 40 while applying and releasing brake. If voltage cycles, replace ECA and repeat QUICK TEST. If voltage does not cycle, repair open circuit in BOO switch circuit between ECA and BOO switch connection to brakelight circuit. Repeat QUICK TEST.

4) Check For Power To Brake Switch – Ensure related fuses and brakelight bulbs are in good condition. Turn ignition off. Disconnect brakelight switch (located on brake pedal). Measure voltage between BATT (+) input to brakelight switch and ground. If voltage is greater than 10 volts, check condition of brakelight switch. If brakelight switch is okay, repair open circuit between brakelight switch and brakelight ground. Repeat QUICK TEST. If voltage is less than 10 volts, repair open BATT (+) circuit to brakelight switch and repeat QUICK TEST.

5) Verify Brake Switch Is Not Always Closed – Turn ignition off. Disconnect brakelight switch (located on brake pedal). Turn ignition on. If brakelights are still on, go to step 6). If brakelights are not on, verify correct installation of brakelight switch. If installation is okay, replace brakelight switch and repeat QUICK TEST.

6) Check For Short To Power In ECA – Turn ignition off. Disconnect ECA. Turn ignition on, and check brakelights. If brakelights are on, repair short to power between ECA and harness connector and repeat QUICK TEST. If brakelights are not on, replace ECA and repeat QUICK TEST.

CIRCUIT TEST FD (Cont.)

NOTE: A break in step numbering sequence occurs at this point. Procedure skips from step 6) to step 10). No test procedures have been omitted.

10) Code 75/531 – Code 75/531 indicates that while brake pedal was released during KOER SELF-TEST, BOO switch signal was high. Possible causes for this fault are:

- Brake pedal depressed during entire self-test.
- Open BOO switch/brakelight circuit (between ECA and brakelight ground).
- Short to POWER.
- Faulty brakelight switch.
- Faulty ECA.

Turn ignition on. Check brakelight operation. If brakelights operate normally, go to step 11). If brakelights are always on, go to step 5). If brakelights are off, inspect brakelight bulbs. If bulb is okay, repair open circuit between BOO switch connection to brakelight circuit and brakelight ground.

11) Check Continuity Of BOO Switch Circuit – Turn ignition off. Disconnect brakelight switch (located on brake pedal). Install EEC-IV Breakout Box (T83L-50-EEC-IV), leaving ECA disconnected. Measure resistance between test pin No. 2 at breakout box and BOO switch terminal at switch wiring harness connector. If resistance is less than 5 ohms, replace ECA and repeat QUICK TEST. If resistance is 5 ohms or more, repair open circuit between ECA and BOO switch connection to brakelight circuit and repeat KOER SELF-TEST.

NOTE: A break in step numbering sequence occurs at this point. Procedure skips from step 11) to step 90). No test procedures have been omitted.

90) Continuous Memory Code 536 – Code 536 indicates a BOO switch circuit failure. If BOO switch input does not cycle after a predetermined number of transitions from zero MPH to a specific speed, BOO switch input failure is presumed and Code 536 is set. Possible causes for this code are:

- Brakelight switch improperly installed.
- Open brakelight/BOO switch circuit.
- Damaged brakelight switch.
- Poor brakelight ground connection.

Inspect brakelight switch for incorrect installation, poor alignment with pedal and damaged wiring. Repair if necessary, and repeat QUICK TEST. If all components are in good condition, go to step 91).

91) Check Brakelight For Ground – Check brakelight connector and wires for corrosion and damage. If connector or wires are corroded or damaged, repair as necessary, and repeat QUICK TEST. If brakelight connector and wires are okay, go to step 92).

92) Check BOO Switch Circuits For Short To Power – DO NOT depress brake pedal during this test. Turn ignition on. While watching brakelights, wiggle brakelight/BOO switch circuit wires and connectors. If brakelights flash, isolate and repair short to power. Repeat QUICK TEST. If brakelights do not flash, go to step 93).

93) Check Brakelight Circuit Continuity – Turn ignition off. Depress and hold brake pedal. Observe brakelights. Tap brakelight switch to simulate road shock. Wiggle brakelight circuit wires and connectors. If brakelights blink or go off, isolate and repair open in brakelight circuit. Clear codes, and repeat QUICK TEST. If brakelights are on constantly and do not blink or go off, go to step 94).

94) Check Continuity Of BOO Switch Circuit – Turn ignition off. Disconnect ECA 60-pin connector. Inspect and repair any damaged terminals. Install EEC-IV Breakout Box (T83L-50-EEC-IV), leaving ECA disconnected. Set DVOM on 200-ohm scale. Measure resistance between test pin No. 2 at breakout box and brakelight circuit at brakelight switch connector. While observing DVOM, wiggle BOO switch circuit wires and connectors. If resistance is 5 ohms or more, isolate and repair open circuit in BOO switch circuit. Repeat QUICK TEST. If resistance is less than 5 ohms, fault cannot be duplicated at this time. See SYMPTOMS in TROUBLE SHOOTING – NO CODES article.

CIRCUIT TEST FE

ELECTRICAL LOAD INPUTS

Diagnostic Aids – Perform this test when directed by QUICK TEST or CIRCUIT TEST S. This CIRCUIT TEST is intended to diagnose:

- Blower motor input circuit.
- Daytime Running Lights (DRL) input circuit.
- Headlight input circuit.
- Rear window defrost input circuit.
- ECA.

Electrical load inputs are used for idle speed control strategy so correct idle can be maintained regardless of electrical demands on engine. ECA uses 4 accessories to determine electrical load status: blower motor, headlights, rear window defroster, and daytime running lights (if equipped).

Fig. FE1: Electrical Load Input Circuit

1) Isolate Faulty System – If idle speed fault occurs when blower motor is on, go to step 10). If idle speed fault occurs when daytime running lights are on, go to step 20). If idle speed fault occurs when headlights are on, go to step 30). If idle speed fault occurs when rear window defroster is on, go to step 40).

NOTE: A break in step numbering sequence occurs at this point. Procedure skips from step 1) to step 10). No test procedures have been omitted.

10) Check Blower Motor Switch (Low Speed) – Turn ignition and all accessories off. Remove ECA 60-pin connector. Inspect terminals, and repair if damaged. Install EEC-IV Breakout Box (T83L-50-EEC-IV), leaving ECA disconnected. Turn ignition on. Turn climate control motor switch to low-speed position "1" or "2". Measure voltage between test pin No. 14 at breakout box and chassis ground. If voltage is not 10-17 volts, go to step 13). If voltage is 10-17 volts, go to step 11).

11) Check Blower Motor Switch (High Speed) – Turn ignition and all accessories off. Turn climate control motor switch to high-speed position "3" or "4". Turn ignition on. Measure voltage between test pin No. 14 at breakout box and chassis ground. If voltage is less than 1.5 volts, replace ECA and confirm idle speed fault has been corrected. If voltage is 1.5 volts or more, go to step 12).

12) Check Blower Circuit For Short To Power – Turn ignition off. Disconnect blower motor relay. Measure resistance between test pin No. 14 and pins No. 37 and 57 at breakout box. If resistance is more than 10,000 ohms, check for damaged blower motor or relay. If resistance is 10,000 ohms or less, repair short circuit.

13) Check Blower Circuit Continuity – Turn ignition off. Disconnect blower motor relay. Measure resistance between BLR terminal at power distributor box and test pin No. 14 at breakout box. If resistance is 5 ohms or more, repair open circuit. If resistance is less than 5 ohms, go to step 14).

CIRCUIT TEST FE (Cont.)

14) Check Blower Circuit For Short To Power – Turn ignition off. Disconnect blower motor relay. Measure resistance between test pin No. 14 and test pins No. 40, 46 and 60 at breakout box. If resistance is more than 10,000 ohms, check for damaged blower motor or relay. If resistance is 10,000 ohms or less, repair short circuit.

NOTE: A break in step numbering sequence occurs at this point. Procedure skips from step 14) to step 20). No test procedures have been omitted.

20) Check DRL Circuit Voltage (Headlights On) – Turn ignition and all accessories off. Remove ECA 60-pin connector. Inspect terminals, and repair if damaged. Install EEC-IV Breakout Box (T83L-50-EEC-IV), leaving ECA disconnected. Apply parking brake. Turn ignition on. Turn headlights on. Measure voltage between test pin No. 42 at breakout box and chassis ground. If voltage is not 10-17 volts, go to step 23). If voltage is 10-17 volts, go to step 21).

21) Check DRL Circuit Voltage (Headlights Off) – Turn headlights off. Release parking brake. Turn ignition on. Measure voltage between test pin No. 42 at breakout box and chassis ground. If voltage is less than 1.5 volts, replace ECA and confirm idle speed fault has been corrected. If voltage is 1.5 volts or more, go to step 22).

22) Check DRL Circuit For Short To Power – Turn ignition off. Disconnect DRL relay. Measure resistance between test pin No. 42 and pins No. 37 and 57 at breakout box. If resistance is more than 10,000 ohms, check daytime running lights module for malfunction. If resistance is 10,000 ohms or less, repair short circuit and confirm idle speed fault has been corrected.

23) Check DRL Circuit Continuity – Turn ignition off. Disconnect daytime running lights relay. Measure resistance between DRL relay connector and test pin No. 42 at breakout box. If resistance is 5 ohms or more, repair open circuit and confirm idle speed fault has been corrected. If resistance is less than 5 ohms, go to step 24).

24) Check DRL Circuit For Short To Power – Turn ignition off. Disconnect daytime running lights relay. Measure resistance between test pin No. 42 and test pins No. 40, 46 and 60 at breakout box. If resistance is more than 10,000 ohms, check daytime running lights module for malfunction. If resistance is 10,000 ohms or less, repair short circuit and confirm idle speed fault has been corrected.

NOTE: A break in step numbering sequence occurs at this point. Procedure skips from step 24) to step 30). No test procedures have been omitted.

30) Check Headlight Circuit Voltage (Headlights Off) – Turn ignition and all accessories off. Remove ECA 60-pin connector. Inspect terminals, and repair if damaged. Install EEC-IV Breakout Box (T83L-50-EEC-IV), leaving ECA disconnected. Turn ignition on. Measure voltage between test pin No. 45 at breakout box and chassis ground. If voltage is 1.5 volts or more, go to step 34). If voltage is less than 1.5 volts, go to step 31).

31) Check Headlight Circuit Voltage (Headlights On) – Turn all accessories off. Turn ignition on. Turn headlights on. Measure voltage between test pin No. 45 at breakout box and chassis ground. If voltage is 10-17 volts, replace ECA and confirm idle speed fault has been corrected. If voltage is not 10-17 volts, go to step 32).

32) Check HDL Circuit Continuity – Turn ignition off. Disconnect headlight relay. Measure resistance between HDL terminal at power distribution box and test pin No. 45 at breakout box. If resistance is 5 ohms or more, repair open circuit and confirm idle speed fault has been corrected. If resistance is less than 5 ohms, go to step 33).

33) Check HDL Circuit For Short To Ground – Turn ignition off. Disconnect headlight relay. Measure resistance between test pin No. 45 and test pins No. 40, 46 and 60 at breakout box. If each resistance is more than 10,000 ohms, check headlight switch for malfunction. If any circuit resistance is 10,000 ohms or less, repair short circuit and confirm idle speed fault has been corrected.

34) Check HDL Circuit For Short To Power – Turn ignition off. Disconnect headlight relay. Measure resistance between test pin No. 45 and pins No. 37 and 57 at breakout box. If resistance is more than 10,000 ohms, check headlight switch for malfunction. If resistance is 10,000 ohms or less, repair short circuit and confirm idle speed fault has been corrected.

NOTE: A break in step numbering sequence occurs at this point. Procedure skips from step 34) to step 40). No test procedures have been omitted.

CIRCUIT TEST FE (Cont.)

40) Check DEF Circuit Voltage (Defrost Off) – Turn ignition off. Turn all accessories off. Remove ECA 60-pin connector. Inspect terminals, and repair if damaged. Install EEC-IV Breakout Box (T83L-50-EEC-IV), leaving ECA disconnected. Turn ignition on. Measure voltage between test pin No. 15 at breakout box and chassis ground. If voltage is 10-17 volts, go to step **41)**. If voltage is not 10-17 volts, go to step **43)**.

41) Check DEF Circuit Voltage (Defrost On) – Turn ignition on. Turn rear window defroster on. Measure voltage between test pin No. 15 at breakout box and chassis ground. If voltage is less than 3 volts, replace ECA and confirm idle speed fault has been corrected. If voltage is 3 volts or more, go to step **42)**.

42) Check DEF Circuit For Short To Power – Turn ignition off. Disconnect rear window defroster relay. Measure resistance between test pin No. 15 and test pins No. 37 and 57 at breakout box. If resistance is more than 10,000 ohms, check DEF switch or relay for malfunction. If resistance is 10,000 ohms or less, repair short circuit and confirm idle speed fault has been corrected.

43) Check DEF Circuit Continuity – Turn ignition off. Disconnect rear window defroster switch. Measure resistance between DEF terminal at power distribution box and test pin No. 15 at breakout box. If resistance is less than 5 ohms, go to step **44)**. If resistance is 5 ohms or more, repair open circuit and confirm idle speed fault has been corrected.

44) Check DEF Circuit For Short To Ground – Turn ignition off. Disconnect rear window defroster relay. Measure resistance between test pin No. 15 and test pins No. 40, 46 and 60 at breakout box. If each circuit resistance is more than 10,000 ohms, check DEF switch and relay circuit for malfunction. If any circuit resistance is 10,000 ohms or less, repair short circuit and confirm idle speed fault has been corrected.

CIRCUIT TEST FF

POWER STEERING PRESSURE SWITCH (PSPS)

Diagnostic Aids – Perform this test when instructed during QUICK TEST or if directed by other test procedures. Some vehicles may not have power steering, but ECA may be equipped with PSPS software strategy. Disregard KOEO Code 52/519 if vehicle is not equipped with power steering. This test is only intended to diagnose:
- Power Steering Pressure Switch (PSPS).
- PSPS and SIG RTN wiring harness circuits.
- ECA.

To prevent replacement of good components, be aware following non-EEC related areas may be at fault:
- Idle speed/throttle stop adjustment.
- Binding throttle shaft/linkage.
- Cruise control linkage.
- Power steering hydraulic system.

91J06940

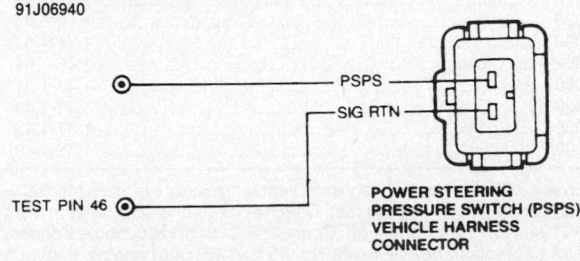

```
                                      ── PSPS
                                      ── SIG RTN

TEST PIN 46  ●─────────────          POWER STEERING
                                     PRESSURE SWITCH (PSPS)
                                     VEHICLE HARNESS
                                     CONNECTOR
```

*TEST PINS LOCATED ON BREAKOUT BOX.
ALL HARNESS CONNECTORS VIEWED INTO MATING SURFACE.

Fig. FF1: Power Steering Pressure Switch (PSPS) Circuit

TEST PIN NO. 24 (PSPS) WIRE COLOR IDENTIFICATION

Application	Wire Color
Bronco 5.0L, Pickup 5.0L & Ranger 2.3L	Yellow/Light Green

CIRCUIT TEST FF (Cont.)

TEST PIN NO. 46 (SIG RTN) WIRE COLOR IDENTIFICATION

Application	Wire Color
All Models	Gray/Red

1) Code 52/519: Attempt To Eliminate Code – Code 52/519 indicates PSPS circuit is open. Turn ignition off. Disconnect PSPS switch. Install jumper wire between PSPS terminal and SIG RTN terminal at wiring harness connector. Repeat KOEO SELF-TEST. If Code 52/519 is not displayed, replace PSPS and repeat QUICK TEST. If Code 52/519 is displayed, remove jumper wire and go to step **2)**.

2) Check Continuity Of PSPS Circuits – Turn ignition off, and wait 10 seconds. Disconnect ECA 60-pin connector. Inspect terminals and repair if damaged. Install EEC-IV Breakout Box (T83L-50-EEC-IV), leaving ECA disconnected. Set DVOM on 200-ohm scale. Measure resistance between test pin No. 46 and SIG RTN terminal at PSPS wiring harness connector. Also measure resistance between test pin No. 24 at breakout box and PSPS terminal at switch wiring harness connector. If both readings are less than 5 ohms, replace ECA and repeat QUICK TEST. If readings are 5 ohms or more, repair open circuit and repeat QUICK TEST.

3) Check PSPS Operation – Turn ignition off. Connect tachometer, and start engine. Allow engine to idle in Park or Neutral. Disconnect PSPS switch connector. If RPM increases, replace PSPS switch and recheck system. If RPM does not increase, go to step **4)**.

4) Check PSPS Circuits For Shorts – Turn ignition off. Disconnect PSPS switch. Disconnect ECA 60-pin connector. Inspect terminals, and repair if damaged. Install EEC-IV Breakout Box (T83L-50-EEC-IV), leaving ECA disconnected. Set DVOM on 200-k/ohm scale. Measure resistance between test pin No. 24 and test pin No. 46 at breakout box. If resistance is 10,000 ohms or less, repair short in harness and recheck symptom. If reading is more than 10,000 ohms, replace ECA and recheck symptom.

5) KOER SELF-TEST Code 52/521 – Disregard this code if vehicle does not have power steering. Code 52/521 indicates PSPS did not change states due to open or closed switch. If steering wheel was turned 1/2 turn within 2 seconds after engine ID code and front wheels were centered in a no-load condition, go to step **6)**. If steering wheel was not turned, repeat QUICK TEST.

6) Check ECA Open Circuit Identifying Capabilities – Turn ignition off. Disconnect PSPS. Perform KOEO SELF-TEST. If Code 52/519 is present, go to step **8)**. If Code 52/519 is not present, go to step **7)**.

7) Check PSPS Circuits For Shorts – Turn ignition off. Disconnect PSPS switch. Disconnect ECA 60-pin connector. Inspect terminals, and repair if damaged. Install EEC-IV Breakout Box (T83L-50-EEC-IV), leaving ECA disconnected. Set DVOM on 200-k/ohm scale. Measure resistance between test pin No. 24 and test pin No. 46 at breakout box. If reading is 10,000 ohms or less, repair short circuit and repeat QUICK TEST. If reading is more than 10,000 ohms, replace ECA and repeat QUICK TEST.

8) Check PSPS Position Comparison – Turn ignition off. Install EEC-IV Breakout Box (T83L-50-EEC-IV), leaving ECA connected. With PSPS connected, set DVOM on 200-ohm scale. Turn ignition on. Measure resistance between test pin No. 24 and test pin No. 46 at breakout box. Start engine. Measure resistance between test pin No. 24 and test pin No. 46 at breakout box. If reading shows less than 10 ohms difference between key on engine off and key on engine running, go to step **9)**. If reading is not as described, replace PSPS switch and repeat QUICK TEST.

9) Check PSPS With Engine Running (Load & No Load) – Connect PSPS, and set DVOM on 200-ohm scale. Start engine, and allow it to idle. Measure resistance between test pin No. 24 and test pin No. 46 at breakout box. Turn steering wheel 1/2 turn and return to center position. If resistance changes from less than 10 ohms to infinity and then returns to 10 ohms or less (when steering wheel is centered), PSPS system is okay. Testing is complete. If reading does not change as indicated, replace PSPS switch.

10) Code 519: Attempt To Eliminate Code 519 – Disregard this code if vehicle does not have power steering. Code 519 indicates PSPS circuit is closed. Turn ignition off. Disconnect PSPS switch connector. Repeat KOEO SELF-TEST. Measure resistance between test pin No. 24 and test pin No. 46 at breakout box. If Code 519 is not present, replace PSPS switch. If Code 519 is present, go to step **11)**.

CIRCUIT TEST FF (Cont.)

11) Check PSPS Circuit For Short – Turn ignition off. Disconnect ECA 60-pin connector. Inspect terminals, and repair if damaged. Install EEC-IV Breakout Box (T83L-50-EEC-IV), leaving ECA disconnected. Measure resistance between test pin No. 24 and test pin No. 46 at breakout box. If reading is 10,000 ohms or less, repair short circuit and repeat QUICK TEST. If reading is more than 10,000 ohms, replace ECA and repeat QUICK TEST.

NOTE: A break in step numbering sequence occurs at this point. Procedure skips from step 11) to step 15). No test procedures have been omitted.

15) Check PSPS Operation – Connect tachometer, and start engine. Allow engine to idle in Park or Neutral. Disconnect PSPS switch connector. If RPM increases, replace PSPS switch and recheck system. If RPM does not increase, go to step **16)**.

16) Check Continuity Of PSPS Circuits – Turn ignition off, and wait 10 seconds. Disconnect ECA 60-pin connector. Inspect terminals, and repair if damaged. Install EEC-IV Breakout Box (T83L-50-EEC-IV), leaving ECA disconnected. Set DVOM on 200-ohm scale. Measure resistance between test pin No. 46 and SIG RTN terminal at PSPS wiring harness connector. Also measure resistance between test pin No. 24 at breakout box and PSPS terminal at PSPS wiring harness connector. If both readings are less than 5 ohms, replace ECA and repeat QUICK TEST. If any reading is 5 ohms or more, repair open circuit and repeat QUICK TEST.

NOTE: A break in step numbering sequence occurs at this point. Procedure skips from step 16) to step 20). No test procedures have been omitted.

20) KOER SELF-TEST Code 521 – Disregard this code if vehicle does not have power steering. Code 521 indicates PSPS did not change states due to open or closed switch. If steering wheel was turned 1/2 turn within 2 seconds after engine ID code and front wheels were centered in a no-load condition, go to step **21)**. If steering wheel was not turned, repeat QUICK TEST.

21) Check ECA Closed Circuit Identifying Capabilities – Turn ignition off. Disconnect PSPS switch. Connect jumper wire between PSPS terminal and SIG RTN terminal at PSPS switch wiring harness connector. Perform KOEO SELF-TEST. If Code 519 is present, remove jumper wire and go to step **23)**. If Code 519 is not present, go to step **22)**.

22) Check Continuity Of PSPS Circuits – Turn ignition off, and wait 10 seconds. Disconnect ECA 60-pin connector. Inspect terminals, and repair if damaged. Install EEC-IV Breakout Box (T83L-50-EEC-IV), leaving ECA disconnected. Set DVOM on 200-ohm scale. Measure resistance between test pin No. 24 at breakout box and PSPS terminal at PSPS wiring harness connector. Also measure resistance between test pin No. 46 at breakout box and SIG RTN terminal at PSPS wiring harness connector. If both readings are less than 5 ohms, replace ECA and repeat QUICK TEST. If either reading is 5 ohms or more, repair open circuit and repeat QUICK TEST.

23) Check PSPS Position Comparison – Turn ignition off. Install EEC-IV Breakout Box (T83L-50-EEC-IV), leaving ECA connected. With PSPS connected, set DVOM on 200-ohm scale. Turn ignition on. Measure resistance between test pin No. 24 and test pin No. 46 at breakout box. Start engine. If reading shows less than 10 ohms difference between key on engine off and key on engine running, go to step **24)**. If reading is not as described, replace PSPS switch and repeat QUICK TEST.

24) Check PSPS With Engine Running (Load & No Load) – Start engine, and allow it to idle. Measure resistance between test pin No. 24 and test pin No. 46 at breakout box. Turn steering wheel 1/2 turn and return to center position. If resistance changes from less than 10 ohms to infinity and then returns to 30 ohms or less (when steering wheel is centered), PSPS system is okay. Testing is complete. If reading does not change as indicated, replace PSPS switch.

CIRCUIT TEST G

MAF/TPS FUEL INJECTOR PULSE WIDTH TEST

Diagnostic Aids – To prevent replacement of good components, be aware following non-EEC related areas may be at fault:
- PCV malfunction.
- Excessive blow-by.
- PCV malfunction.
- Vacuum leaks.
- Incorrect fuel pressure.
- Throttle binding.

Perform this test when instructed during QUICK TEST or if directed by other test procedures. This test is only intended to diagnose:
- MAP/BP sensor.
- Throttle Position Sensor (TPS).
- Mass Airflow (MAF) sensor.
- Air Charge Temperature (ACT) sensor.
- Fuel injectors.

1) Throttle Position Sensor (TPS) Integrity – Code 121 indicates TPS is inconsistent with MAF value. Code 124 indicates TPS value is higher than expected. Code 125 indicates TPS value is lower than expected. Turn ignition off. Disconnect ECA 60-pin connector. Inspect terminals, and repair if damaged. Install EEC-IV Breakout Box (T83L-50-EEC-IV). Connect ECA to breakout box. Set DVOM on 20-volt scale. Connect DVOM to test pins No. 46 and 47. Slowly apply throttle to wide open position and release to closed position. See CIRCUIT TEST DH for schematic and specific TPS values. If voltage varies suddenly, ensure TPS is properly installed on throttle body. If TPS is properly installed, replace TPS and repeat QUICK TEST. If voltage does not vary suddenly, go to step **6)** for Continuous Memory Code 121 or step **2)** for all other codes.

2) Check Throttle Body – Check throttle and/or cruise control linkage for binding or rough operation. Inspect throttle body for sludge build-up. Check engine vacuum hoses. Refer to Vehicle Emission Control Information (VECI) decal for proper vacuum hose routing. Check for air leak between ISC solenoid and MAF sensor. Repair as necessary and repeat QUICK TEST. If no problems are found, go to step **3)**.

3) Check MAP/BP Sensor Output – Refer to CIRCUIT TEST DF for MAP/BP sensor output check. *See Fig. DF1* for connector terminal identification and MAP/BP tester hookup. With tester connected and ignition on, measure sensor output voltage. If output voltage is within range for specified altitude, remove MAP/BP tester and go to step **4)**. See MAP SENSOR VOLTAGE OUTPUT table for specification. If output voltage is not within range, replace MAP/BP sensor and repeat QUICK TEST.

Diagnostic Aids – If possible, measure several known good MAP/BP sensors. Average voltage reading will be typical for location and day of testing.

MAP SENSOR VOLTAGE OUTPUT

Elevation (Feet)	Volts
0	1.55-1.63
1000	1.52-1.60
2000	1.49-1.57
3000	1.46-1.54
4000	1.43-1.51
5000	1.40-1.48
6000	1.37-1.45
7000	1.35-1.43

4) Check ACT Sensor – Ensure ambient temperature is more than 50°F (10°C) before performing this test. Check and repair any air leaks in front of ACT sensor. Turn ignition off. Connect ECA to breakout box. Connect DVOM to breakout box test pins No. 25 and 46. Start engine, and let it idle. Monitor voltage as engine warms up. See CIRCUIT TEST DA for voltage specifications. If voltage does not decrease smoothly and stabilize after engine reaches operating temperature, replace ACT sensor and repeat QUICK TEST. If voltage decreases smoothly and stabilizes when engine reaches operating conditions, system is operating properly at this time. Reconnect all components, and repeat QUICK TEST.

5) Code 184 Or 185: Visually Inspect MAF Sensor – Code 184 indicates MAF sensor signal is higher than expected. Code 185 indicates MAF sensor signal is lower than expected. Turn ignition off. Check for air leaks between ISC solenoid and MAF sensor. Inspect MAF sensor for oil contamination caused by excessive blow-by or malfunctioning PCV. If problems are found, repair as necessary. Clear codes, and repeat QUICK TEST. If all checks are okay, go to step **8)**.

CIRCUIT TEST G (Cont.)

6) Check MAF Sensor – Turn ignition off. Disconnect ECA 60-pin connector. Inspect and repair any damaged terminals. Connect ECA to breakout box. Set DVOM on 20-volt scale. Start engine, and warm it to normal operating temperature. Measure voltage between test pins No. 40 and 60 and MAF test pin at breakout box. See MAF TEST PIN NO. IDENTIFICATION table. If voltage is not within specification, replace MAF sensor and repeat QUICK TEST, See MAF SENSOR DATA table. *See Fig. G1*. If voltage is within acceptable range, system is operating normally at this time. See SYMPTOMS in TROUBLE SHOOTING – NO CODES article.

MAF TEST PIN NO. IDENTIFICATION

Application	Test Pin No.
Aerostar, Explorer, Ranger (except 3.0L)	14
Ranger 3.0L	50

MAF SENSOR DATA

Engine Condition	[1] Voltage
Idle	0.8
20 MPH	1.0
40 MPH	1.7
60 MPH	2.1

[1] – With engine at normal operating temperature.

91B06941

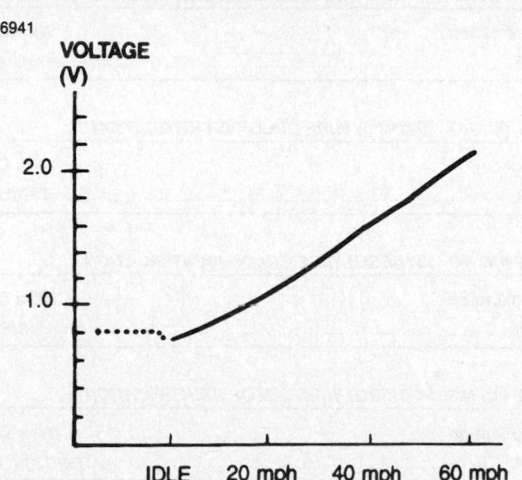

Fig. G1: MAF Sensor Graph

7) Visual Vacuum Checks – Code 186 indicates fuel injector pulse width is longer than expected (rich). Code 187 indicates fuel injector pulse width is shorter than expected (lean). Inspect air cleaner and air inlet duct. Replace or repair an necessary. Check for unmetered air leaks between MAF sensor and ISC by-pass solenoid. Check all engine vacuum hoses for damage, blockage and improper routing. Make necessary repairs, and repeat QUICK TEST. If all checks are okay, go to step **8)**.

8) Check Fuel Pressure – Turn ignition off. Install fuel pressure gauge. Ensure fuel pressure regulator vacuum hose is connected (if applicable). Start engine, and allow it to idle. If fuel pressure is within specifications, go to step **9)**. See FUEL PRESSURE SPECIFICATIONS table. If fuel pressure is not within specifications, repair as necessary. See FUEL SYSTEM in SYSTEM & COMPONENT TESTING article.

FUEL PRESSURE SPECIFICATIONS

Engine	KOER PRESSURE psi (kg/cm²)	KOEO PRESSURE psi (kg/cm²)
4.9L PFI	45-60 (3.2-4.2)	50-60 (3.5-4.2)
Except 4.9L PFI	30-45 (2.1-3.2)	35-45 (2.5-3.2)

CIRCUIT TEST G (Cont.)

9) Verify Fuel Pressure Retention Ability – Turn ignition on. If fuel pressure remains at specification for 60 seconds, go to next step (SEFI) or go to CIRCUIT TEST H, step **7)** (except SEFI). If fuel pressure does not remain at specification, repair fuel delivery system as necessary. See FUEL SYSTEM in SYSTEM & COMPONENT TESTING article.

10) Cylinder Balance Test – Perform KOER SELF-TEST. After last code, wait 5-10 seconds, and then goose throttle lightly (not wide open throttle). This will activate cylinder balance test. If Code 90 is present after test, go back to step **5)**. If Code 90 is not present after test, go to CIRCUIT TEST H, step **4)**.

CIRCUIT TEST H

FUEL CONTROL

Diagnostic Aids – Perform this test when instructed during QUICK TEST or if directed by other test procedures. Fuel-contaminated engine oil may affect Codes 41/172, 91/136, 42/173 and 92/137. If fuel-contaminated engine oil is suspected, remove PCV valve from valve cover and repeat QUICK TEST. If problem is corrected, change engine oil and filter. Only use this test to diagnose:
* HEGO sensor.
* HEGO signal, ground circuit and sensor connection.
* Vacuum systems.
* Fuel injector and/or fuel injector circuitry.
* ECA.
* Electrical circuits (HEGO GND, HEGO, INJ 1-8, VPWR and SIG RTN).

To prevent replacement of good components, be aware following non-EEC areas may be cause of driveability concerns:
* Ignition system.
* Faulty evaporative emission system.
* EGR system.
* Air intake system.
* Engine oil contamination.
* Fuel system.
* Intake or exhaust system leaks.
* Engine cooling system.

INDIVIDUAL INJECTOR RESISTANCE [1]

Engine	Ohms
All Models	13-16

[1] – Resistance values are for a single injector.

INJECTOR BANK RESISTANCE

Engine	Ohms
2.3L	6.0-8.5
2.9L, 3.0L, 4.0L & 4.9L	4.0-5.5
5.0L, 5.8L & 7.5L	0.5-3.0

FUEL PRESSURE SPECIFICATIONS

Engine	KOER PRESSURE psi (kg/cm²)	KOEO PRESSURE psi (kg/cm²)
4.9L	45-60 (3.2-4.2)	50-60 (3.5-4.2)
Except 4.9L	30-45 (2.1-3.2)	35-45 (2.5-3.2)

1992 ENGINE PERFORMANCE
Self-Diagnostics – EEC-IV (Cont.)

CIRCUIT TEST H (Cont.)

92B03829

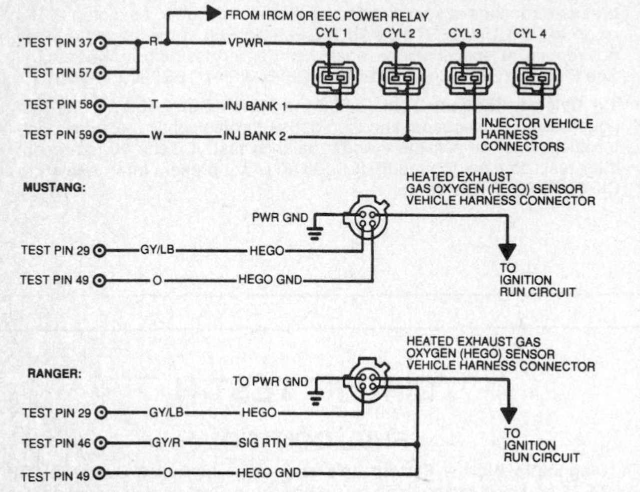

Fig. H1: Test Schematic (2.3L)

92D03830

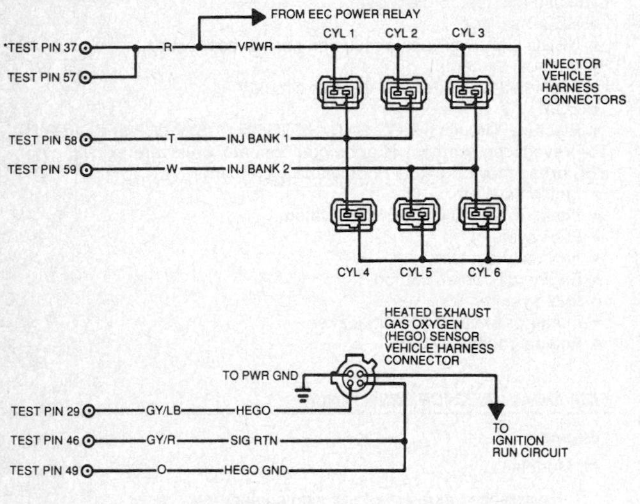

*TEST PINS LOCATED ON BREAKOUT BOX
ALL HARNESS CONNECTORS VIEWED IN MATING SURFACE

Fig. H2: Test Schematic (2.9L & 4.0L)

92J03833

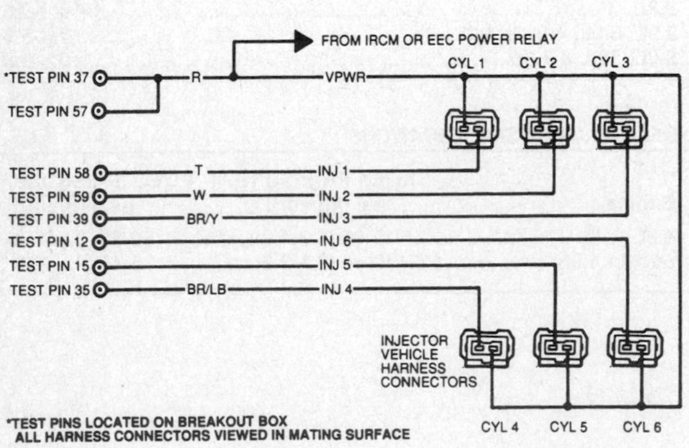

*TEST PINS LOCATED ON BREAKOUT BOX
ALL HARNESS CONNECTORS VIEWED IN MATING SURFACE

Fig. H3: Test Schematic (3.0L)

CIRCUIT TEST H (Cont.)

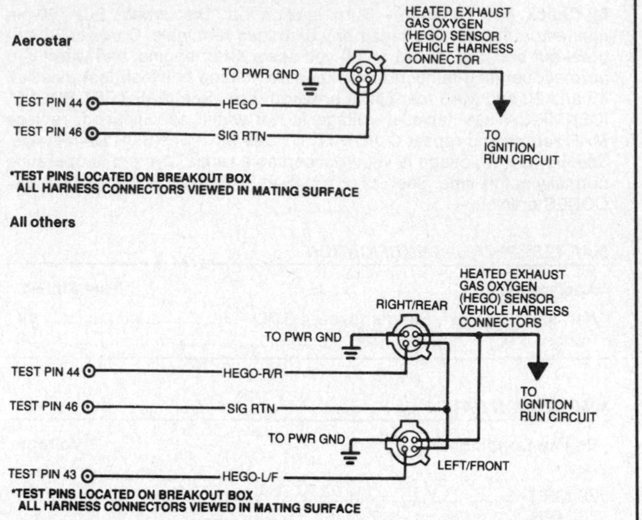

Fig. H3: Test Schematic (3.0L – Cont.)

TEST PIN NO. 12 (INJ 6) WIRE COLOR IDENTIFICATION

Application	Wire Color
3.0L	Light Green/Orange

TEST PIN NO. 15 (INJ 5) WIRE COLOR IDENTIFICATION

Application	Wire Color
3.0L	Tan/Black

TEST PIN NO. 43 (HEGO) WIRE COLOR IDENTIFICATION

Application	Wire Color
3.0L	Red/Black

TEST PIN NO. 44 (HEGO) WIRE COLOR IDENTIFICATION

Application	Wire Color
3.0L	Gray/Light Blue

TEST PIN NO. 46 WIRE COLOR IDENTIFICATION

Application	Wire Color
All Models	Green/Red

92E03835

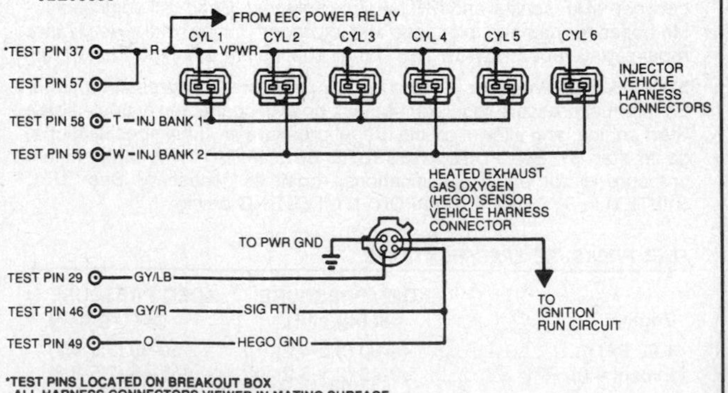

*TEST PINS LOCATED ON BREAKOUT BOX
ALL HARNESS CONNECTORS VIEWED IN MATING SURFACE

Fig. H4: Test Schematic (4.9L)

CIRCUIT TEST H (Cont.)

92I03837

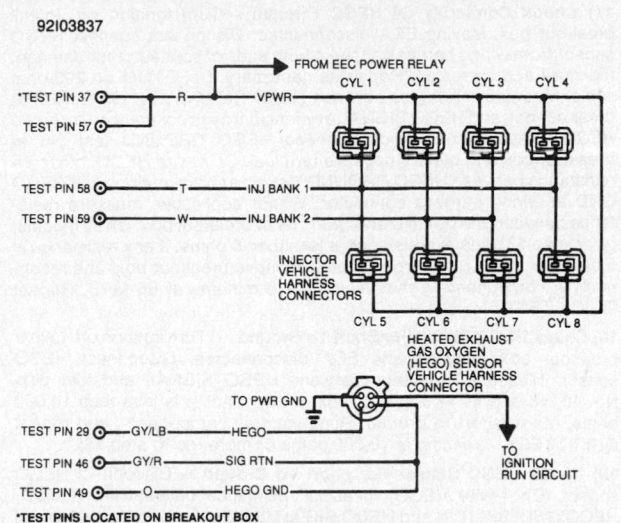

Fig. H5: Test Schematic (5.0L, 5.8L & 7.5L)

CIRCUIT TEST H ACRONYMS

Acronym	Definition
HEGO	Heated Exhaust Gas Oxygen Sensor
SEFI	Sequential Electronic Fuel Injection

1) Check For Contaminated Engine Oil – Turn ignition off. Remove PCV valve from valve cover. Inspect PCV system for damage. Inspect valve for blockage and movement of valve plunger. Repair as necessary. Perform KOER SELF-TEST. If vehicle is a no-start, go to step **2)**. If KOER Code 41/172, 42/173, 91/136 or 92/137 or Continuous Memory Code 171, 174, 175, 176, 177, 178, 41/441 or 91/139 is set, install PCV valve and go to step **2)**. If no codes are set, change engine oil and filter. Install PCV valve, and drive vehicle for 5 miles at 55 MPH. Repeat QUICK TEST.

2) Check Fuel Pressure – Turn ignition off. Install fuel pressure gauge. Ensure manifold vacuum supply is connected to fuel pressure regulator (if equipped). Run engine at idle and check fuel pressure. If vehicle will not start, cycle ignition on and off several times. Check fuel pressure. See FUEL PRESSURE SPECIFICATIONS table. If fuel pressure is within specification, go to step **3)**. If pressure is not within specification, go to FUEL SYSTEM in SYSTEM & COMPONENT TESTING – EEC-IV article.

3) Check System Ability To Hold Fuel Pressure – Turn ignition on. If fuel pressure remains at specification for 60 seconds, go to step **4)** (no-starts), step **5)** (non-SEFI) or step **6)** (SEFI). If fuel pressure is not as described, repair fuel delivery system as necessary.

4) Fuel Delivery Test – Release fuel system pressure. Install fuel pressure gauge, and pressurize fuel system as in step **1)**. Disconnect inertia switch. Crank engine 5 seconds. If fuel pressure drop is greater than 5 psi after 5 seconds of cranking, EEC-IV system is not causing no-start condition. Check additional no-start tests in TROUBLE SHOOTING – NO CODES article. If fuel pressure drop is less than 5 psi, remove fuel pressure gauge. Connect inertia switch. Go to step **7)** for non-SEFI or step **8)** for SEFI.

5) Cylinder Balance Test (Non-SEFI) – Connect a tachometer to engine. Start engine, and run it at idle. Disconnect and reconnect injectors individually, noting RPM drop as each injector is disconnected. ISC motor will attempt to re-establish RPM. If each injector does not produce a momentary drop in RPM, go to step **7)**. If each injector produces a momentary drop in RPM, go to step **13)** for Codes 41/172, 91/136 or 176. For Codes 42/173, 92/137 or 177, go to step **24)**. Go to step **14)** for all other codes.

6) Cylinder Balance Test (SEFI) – Perform KOER SELF-TEST. After last code is displayed, wait 5-10 seconds. Enter CYLINDER BALANCE TEST by lightly goosing throttle (not WOT). Test time is about 2-3

CIRCUIT TEST H (Cont.)

minutes. To interpret codes retrieved from test, refer to CYLINDER BALANCE TEST SERVICE CODES table. If cylinder balance fault code is present, go to step **8)**. If a cylinder balance fault code is not present, fuel delivery is okay; fault is in area common to all cylinders. Code 77/538 indicates throttle was touched when test was ran and test is not completed. Code 538 could also be output if Continuous Memory Code 214 (CID) is present. If Continuous Memory Code 214 Is present, see appropriate chart under SERVICE CODE REFERENCE CHARTS for instruction. For symptoms or Code 41/172, 91/136 or 176, go to step **13)**. For Code 42/173, 92/137 or 177, go to step **24)**. For all other codes, go to step **14)**.

CYLINDER BALANCE TEST SERVICE CODES

Service Code	Application
90	Pass
10	Cylinder No. 1
20	Cylinder No. 2
30	Cylinder No. 3
40	Cylinder No. 4
50	Cylinder No. 5
60	Cylinder No. 6
70	Cylinder No. 7
80	Cylinder No. 8
77/538	Retest

7) Check Injector & Harness Resistance (Non-SEFI) – Turn ignition off. Wait 10 seconds. Disconnect ECA 60-pin connector. Inspect pins for damage and repair if necessary. Install breakout box, leaving ECA disconnected. Set DVOM on 200-ohm scale. Measure resistance of injector banks between test pins No. 37 and 58 at breakout box. Measure resistance of injector banks between test pins No. 37 and 59 at breakout box. Record resistances. Refer to INJECTOR BANK RESISTANCE table in this circuit test. If each resistance is within specifications, go to step **12)**. If resistance is not as specified, repair open circuit on VPWR circuit (for no-start) or go to step **9)** (for all other conditions).

8) Check Injector & Harness Resistance (SEFI) – Turn ignition off and wait 10 seconds. Disconnect ECA 60-pin connector. Install EEC-IV Breakout Box (T83L-50-EEC-IV), leaving ECA disconnected. Set DVOM on 200-ohm scale. Measure and record resistance between suspected injector circuit test pin and test pin No. 37. For no starts, measure and record resistance between any injector circuit test pin and test pin No. 37. Refer to INJECTOR BANK RESISTANCE table in this circuit test. If each resistance is within specification, go to step **12)**. If resistance is not as specified, repair open circuit on VPWR circuit (for no-start) or go to step **9)** (for all other conditions).

9) Check Continuity Of Fuel Injector Harness – Turn ignition off. Disconnect injector wiring harness connector at injectors. Set DVOM to 200-ohm scale. Measure resistance between test pins No. 37 and 57 at breakout box and each injector VPWR terminal at wiring harness connector. Measure resistance between injector test pin(s) at breakout box and same injector circuit terminal at each injector wiring harness connector. If each resistance is less than 5 ohms, go to step **10)**. If each resistance is 5 ohms or more, repair open circuit. Remove breakout box, reconnect all components and drive vehicle for 5 miles at 55 MPH. Repeat QUICK TEST.

10) Check Injector Harness Circuit For Short To Power Or Ground – Turn ignition off, and wait for 10 seconds. With breakout box installed and ECA disconnected, disconnect fuel injector wiring harness. Set DVOM to 200-k/ohm scale. Measure resistance between injector test pin(s) and test pins No. 37, 40, 46, 57 and 60. Measure resistance between injector test pin(s) at breakout box and chassis ground. If each resistance is 10,000 ohms or more, replace injector per cylinder balance test service code and repeat QUICK TEST (SEFI) or go to next step (non-SEFI). If each resistance is less than 10,000 ohms, repair short. Remove breakout box, reconnect all components and drive vehicle for 5 miles at 55 MPH. Repeat QUICK TEST.

11) Isolate Faulty Injector Circuit – Turn ignition off. Install breakout box, and disconnect ECA. Disconnect all injectors on suspect bank. With DVOM set on 200-ohm scale, connect one injector and measure resistance between test pins No. 37 and 58 (injector bank No. 1) or 59 (injector bank No. 2). Disconnect injector, and repeat process for all other injectors. See INDIVIDUAL INJECTOR RESISTANCE table. If all injectors are within specification, go to step **12)**. If injectors are not as specified, replace injector. Remove breakout box, and reconnect components. Drive vehicle for 5 miles at 55 MPH. Repeat QUICK TEST.

CIRCUIT TEST H (Cont.)

12) Check Injector Drive Signal – With ignition off and breakout box installed, connect ECA to breakout box. Use a non-powered 12-volt test light, and connect as follows:

- **Non-SEFI** – Connect test light between test pins No. 37 and 58 at breakout box. Connect light between test pins No. 37 and 59 at breakout box.
- **SEFI** – Connect test light between test pin No. 37 and suspect injector test pin at breakout box.

Crank or start engine. If test light glows dimly, system is operating correctly. Clean injectors, and drive vehicle for 5 miles at 55 MPH. Repeat QUICK TEST and CYLINDER BALANCE TEST. If test light does not glow dimly (no light/bright light), replace ECA. Reconnect all components, and drive vehicle for 5 miles at 55 MPH. Repeat QUICK TEST.

13) Check Thermactor Operation – If vehicle is equipped with pulse-air or does not have thermactor system, go to step **14)**. A HEGO which is always lean could be caused by thermactor air being diverted upstream from HEGO sensor. With dual HEGO, Code 41/172 applies to right or rear HEGO and Code 91/136 or 176 applies to left or front HEGO. Turn ignition off. Disconnect thermactor air hose(s) from thermactor pump. Run KOER SELF-TEST. If Code 41/172, 91/136 or 176 is present, reconnect thermactor air hoses and go to step **14)**. If codes are not present, repair thermactor system as necessary.

14) Check HEGO Integrity – A HEGO sensor which is always lean, slow to switch or does not switch could be caused by:

- Moisture inside HEGO sensor or connector causing a short to ground.
- HEGO sensor coated with contaminants.
- HEGO circuit open.
- HEGO circuit shorted to ground.

Turn ignition off. Inspect HEGO wiring harness for damage. Inspect HEGO sensor and connector for signs of fluid entry. Repair or replace as necessary. Start engine, and run it at 2000 RPM for 2 minutes. Turn ignition off. Run KOER SELF-TEST. If fault codes are present, go to step **15)** (MAP sensor-equipped models) or step **16)** (MAF sensor-equipped models). If no code is present, go to step **21)**.

15) Check HEGO Sensor (Engines With MAP Sensors) – Vacuum or air leaks in non-EEC-IV areas could cause Code 41, 91, 136, 172 or 176. Check following possibilities before continuing:

- Leaking vacuum actuated motor.
- Leaking intake gasket.
- EGR system.
- PCV system.
- Lead-contaminated HEGO sensor.

Turn ignition off. Ensure MAP sensor output voltage is correct. See CIRCUIT TEST DF, step **3)**. Disconnect appropriate HEGO sensor from wiring harness. Connect DVOM to HEGO SIGNAL lead at sensor from wiring harness. On 3-wire HEGO, connect DVOM to HEGO SIGNAL lead at sensor connector and battery negative terminal. On 4-wire HEGO, connect DVOM to HEGO SIGNAL and HEGO GND leads at sensor connector. On all models, disconnect and plug vacuum line at MAP sensor. Start engine, and apply 10-14 in. Hg to MAP sensor. Run engine at 2000 RPM for 2 minutes. If reading is 0.5 volt or more, go to step **17)**. If reading is less than 0.5 volt, replace HEGO sensor and repeat QUICK TEST.

16) Check HEGO Sensor (Engines With MAF Sensor) – Purpose of this test is to verify HEGO sensor can generate a voltage signal of greater than 0.5 volt during KOER SELF-TEST. With ignition off and DVOM set on 20-volt scale, disconnect appropriate HEGO sensor from harness. On 4-wire HEGO, connect DVOM between HEGO SIGNAL and HEGO GND at HEGO sensor connector. On 3-wire HEGO, connect DVOM to HEGO SIGNAL at sensor and battery negative terminal. On all models, run engine at 2000 RPM for 2 minutes. Repeat KOER SELF-TEST and monitor HEGO sensor voltage. If voltage is 0.5 volt or more at end of self-test, go to step **17)**. If voltage is less than 0.5 volt, replace HEGO sensor and repeat QUICK TEST.

CIRCUIT TEST H (Cont.)

17) Check Continuity Of HEGO Circuits – Turn ignition off. Install breakout box, leaving ECA disconnected. Disconnect suspect HEGO sensor from wiring harness. Inspect both ends of connector for damage, moisture and corrosion. Repair as necessary. Set DVOM on 200-ohm scale. Measure resistance between HEGO SIGNAL (test pin No. 29) at breakout box and HEGO SIGNAL at wiring harness connector. On 3-wire HEGO, measure resistance between HEGO GROUND test pin at breakout box and battery negative terminal. On 4-wire HEGO, measure resistance between HEGO GROUND test pin at breakout box and HEGO GND at wiring harness connector. Where applicable, measure resistance between HEGO GND and SIG RTN at breakout box. On all models, go to step **18)** if each resistance is less than 5 ohms. If any resistance is 5 ohms or more, repair open circuit. Remove breakout box, and reconnect all components. Drive vehicle for 5 minutes at 55 MPH. Repeat QUICK TEST.

18) Check HEGO Circuit For Short To Ground – Turn ignition off. Leave breakout box installed and ECA disconnected. Disconnect HEGO sensor. Measure resistance between HEGO SIGNAL and test pins No. 40, 46 and 49 at breakout box. If any reading is less than 10,000 ohms, repair short to ground. Reconnect all components, and repeat QUICK TEST. If reading is 10,000 ohms or more, go to step **19)**.

19) Check HEGO Sensor For Short To Ground – Disconnect HEGO sensor. On 4-wire HEGO, measure resistance between PWR GND, HEGO GND, SIG RTN and HEGO SIG at HEGO sensor connector. On all HEGO sensors, measure resistance between PWR GND and HEGO SIGNAL at HEGO sensor connector. If resistance is less than 10,000 ohms, replace HEGO sensor. Connect all components, and drive vehicle for 5 miles at 55 MPH. Repeat QUICK TEST. If resistance is 10,000 ohms or more, perform following procedure as applicable.

- For Codes 144/41, 139/91, 171, 174, 175 and 178, go to step **90)**.
- For all other codes, go to step **20)** if engine is equipped with MAP sensor. If engine is equipped with MAF sensor, replace ECA. Drive vehicle for 5 miles at 55 MPH, and repeat QUICK TEST.

20) Attempt To Eliminate Code 41/172, 91/136 Or 176 (Engines With MAP Sensor) – Turn ignition off. Connect ECA to breakout box. Connect HEGO sensor. Disconnect and plug MAP sensor vacuum hose. Apply 10-14 in. Hg to MAP sensor. Start and run engine at 2000 RPM for 2 minutes. Allow engine to return to idle. Perform KOER SELF-TEST. If diagnosing continuous memory codes, drive vehicle 5 miles at 55 MPH. If Code 41/172, 91/136 or 176 is still present, remove breakout box. Connect all components. If engine runs rough, go to step **2)** of CIRCUIT TEST S. If engine does not run rough, replace ECA, drive vehicle 5 miles at 55 MPH and repeat QUICK TEST. If code is not present, remove breakout box and connect all components. HEGO input circuit and fuel delivery are okay; fault is in area common to all systems. See TROUBLE SHOOTING – NO CODES article.

21) Check Resistance Of HEGO Heating Element – Turn ignition off. Disconnect suspect HEGO sensor. Inspect both ends of connector for damage, moisture and corrosion. Repair if necessary. Set DVOM on 200-ohm scale. Measure resistance between IGNITION RUN circuit and PWR GND circuit at HEGO sensor connector. Hot to warm engine resistance should be 5-30 ohms. Cold engine resistance is 2-5 ohms. If resistance is within specification, go to step **22)**. If resistance is not as specified, replace HEGO sensor and repeat QUICK TEST.

22) Check For Power At HEGO Harness Connector – Disconnect HEGO sensor. Turn ignition on. Measure voltage between IGNITION RUN and PWR GND circuits at HEGO wiring harness connector. If voltage is 10.5 volts or more, HEGO system and fuel delivery are okay. HEGO sensor may have cooled before KOER SELF-TEST. If driveability symptom continues, fault is in area common to all cylinders. See TROUBLE SHOOTING – NO CODES article. If voltage is less than 10.5 volts, go to step **23)**.

CIRCUIT TEST H (Cont.)

23) Check Continuity Of Power Ground Circuit – Turn ignition off. Measure resistance between PWR GND circuit at HEGO wiring harness connector and negative battery terminal. If resistance is less than 5 ohms, repair open in IGNITION RUN circuit and repeat QUICK TEST. If resistance is 5 ohms or more, repair open in PWR GND circuit and repeat QUICK TEST.

24) Check HEGO SIGNAL For Short To Power – On dual HEGO systems, Code 42/173 applies to right or rear HEGO. Codes 92/137 and 177 applies to left or front HEGO. Turn ignition off. Disconnect appropriate HEGO sensor. Turn ignition on. Measure voltage between HEGO SIG and PWR GND at HEGO wiring harness connector. If reading is less than 0.5 volt, go to step **26)**. If reading is 0.5 volt or more, go to step **25)**.

25) Check For Short To Power – Turn ignition off. Disconnect HEGO sensor. Inspect both ends of connector for damage, moisture and corrosion. Repair if necessary. Drive vehicle 5 miles at 55 MPH and repeat QUICK TEST. If connector is okay, go to step **26)**.

26) Check HEGO Sensor For Short To IGNITION RUN Circuit – Turn ignition off, and wait 10 seconds. Disconnect HEGO. Set DVOM to 200-k/ohm scale. Measure resistance between IGNITION RUN circuit and HEGO SIG circuit at HEGO sensor connector. If resistance is 10,000 ohms or more, go to step **27)** for Codes 42/173, 92/137 and 177; for codes 171, 174, 175 and 178, go to step **28)** (MAP sensor) or **30)** (MAF sensor). If resistance is less than 10,000 ohms, replace HEGO sensor. Drive vehicle for 5 miles at 55 MPH, and repeat QUICK TEST.

27) Attempt To Generate Code 41/172, 91/136 Or 176 – Turn ignition off. Disconnect appropriate HEGO sensor. Using jumper wire, connect HEGO SIG circuit at HEGO wiring harness connector to negative battery terminal. Repeat KOER SELF-TEST. If Code 41/172, 91/136 or 176 is present, remove jumper wire and go to step **28)** for engines with MAP sensor or step **30)** for engines with MAF sensor. If Codes 41/172, 91/136 and 176 are not present, remove jumper wire. Disconnect ECA connector, and inspect it for damage. If connector is okay, replace ECA. Drive vehicle for 5 miles at 55 MPH. Repeat QUICK TEST.

Diagnostic Aids – Because MAP sensor greatly influences fuel control, MAP sensor may malfunction without setting Code 22/126. Next 2 steps test MAP vacuum circuit.

28) Check MAP Sensor For Vacuum Leaks – Turn ignition off. Disconnect vacuum hose from MAP sensor. Connect vacuum pump to sensor. Apply 18 in. Hg to MAP sensor. If sensor does not hold vacuum, replace MAP sensor. Drive vehicle for 5 miles at 55 MPH. Repeat QUICK TEST. If sensor holds vacuum, release vacuum and go to step **29)**.

29) Check For Loss Of Vacuum To MAP Sensor – Using vacuum "T", connect vacuum gauge in MAP sensor vacuum hose. Start engine. Note vacuum reading at idle stabilizes. Turn ignition off. Remove "T" and vacuum gauge. Reconnect hose to MAP sensor. Connect vacuum gauge at a different manifold vacuum location. Start engine, and note vacuum reading. If readings do not differ by more than 1 in. Hg, go to next step. If readings differ by more than 1 in. Hg, inspect vacuum hoses for leaks, kinks and blockage. Repair as necessary. Connect all components, and drive vehicle for 5 miles at 55 MPH. Repeat QUICK TEST.

30) HEGO Sensor Check – Turn ignition off. Disconnect HEGO sensor. For 4-wire HEGO sensor, connect DVOM to HEGO and HEGO GND or SIG RTN at HEGO sensor connector. For 3-wire HEGO sensor, connect DVOM to HEGO SIGNAL at HEGO sensor connector and negative battery terminal. On all models, remove PCV valve from hose. Start engine, and run it at about 2000 RPM. DVOM should indicate less than 0.4 volt within 30 seconds. If voltage is not as specified, replace HEGO sensor. Reconnect vacuum hoses, and drive vehicle for 5 miles at 55 MPH. Repeat QUICK TEST. If voltage is as specified, go to step **90)**.

NOTE: A break in step numbering sequence occurs at this point. Procedure skips from step 30) to step 90). No test procedures have been omitted.

CIRCUIT TEST H (Cont.)

90) Check Continuous Monitor Mode – Start engine, and warm it to normal operating temperature. Raise engine speed to 2000 RPM for 2 minutes and then return to idle. Enter KOER wiggle test. See CONTINUOUS MONITOR MODE (WIGGLE TEST) under QUICK TEST. While observing DVOM or scan tester, shake or bend small sections of wiring harness from HEGO sensor to ECA. Wiggle, shake or bend small sections of wiring harness from HEGO GND to ECA. If no fault is indicated, remain in CONTINUOUS MONITOR MODE and go to step **91)**. If fault is indicated, isolate and repair fault as necessary. Clear codes. Repeat QUICK TEST.

91) Continuous Monitor Test Drive Check – While still in KOER wiggle test, drive vehicle for 5 miles at 55 MPH over smooth roads. Drive an additional 5 miles at 55 MPH over rough roads. If possible, drive vehicle through a pool of water to wet HEGO sensor and connector. If fault is indicated, isolate fault and repair as necessary. Clear codes, and remove breakout box. Repeat QUICK TEST. If no codes are indicated, exit KOER wiggle test and go to next step.

92) Check HEGO Switching – Turn ignition off. Inspect wire harness for proper routing. Check for burnt, chaffed or open wires. Repair if necessary. Disconnect ECA 60-pin connector. Inspect it for damaged or pushed-out pins and repair as necessary. Install breakout box. Connect ECA to breakout box. Connect analog voltmeter to suspect HEGO sensor test pin and HEGO GND at breakout box. Test drive vehicle for 5 miles at 55 MPH while observing voltmeter. HEGO should switch fluctuate between .3 and .9 volt in 3 second cycles. If HEGO does not switch as described, replace HEGO sensor. Connect all components, and repeat QUICK TEST. If HEGO switches as described, fault cannot be identified at this time. See INTERMITTENTS in TROUBLE SHOOTING (EEC-IV) – NO CODES article.

CIRCUIT TEST HA

ADAPTIVE FUEL

Diagnostic Aids – Perform this test when directed by QUICK TEST. ECA uses adaptive fuel logic to compensate for normal variances in fuel system components. If fuel system appears to be too rich or too lean, adaptive fuel will make appropriate shift in fuel delivery calculations to compensate.

FUEL PRESSURE SPECIFICATIONS

Engine	KOER PRESSURE psi (kg/cm²)	KOEO PRESSURE psi (kg/cm²)
4.9L	45-60 (3.2-4.2)	50-60 (3.5-4.2)
Except 4.9L	30-45 (2.1-3.2)	35-45 (2.5-3.2)

If possible, measure several known good MAP/BP sensors. Average voltage reading will be typical for location and day of testing.

MAP SENSOR VOLTAGE OUTPUT

Elevation (Feet)	Volts
0	1.55-1.63
1000	1.52-1.60
2000	1.49-1.57
3000	1.46-1.54
4000	1.43-1.51
5000	1.40-1.48
6000	1.37-1.45
7000	1.35-1.43

CIRCUIT TEST HA (Cont.)

CIRCUIT TEST HA ACRONYMS

Acronym	Definition
HEGO	Heated Exhaust Gas Oxygen Sensor
KAM	Keep-Alive Memory
SEFI	Sequential Electronic Fuel Injection

1) Continuous Memory Codes 181, 183, 189 & 192 – This test identifies areas which could cause HEGO sensor to detect excessive oxygen, resulting in adaptive fuel enriching system to compensate. Excessive oxygen will be detected with lean conditions and certain rich conditions. For models with dual HEGO sensors, a related fuel code from both HEGO sensors could indicate a problem common to all cylinders. If a code is present from only one HEGO, this may help isolate a problem or be an early indication of a common problem.

- **Code 183** – Indicates single right or rear HEGO detected a problem and adaptive fuel rich limit has been reached at idle.
- **Code 192** – Indicates left or front HEGO detected a problem and adaptive fuel rich limit has been reached at idle.
- **Code 181** – Indicates single right or rear HEGO detected a problem and adaptive fuel rich limit has been reached.
- **Code 189** – Indicates left or front HEGO detected a problem and adaptive fuel rich limit has been reached.

Ensure a pass Code (111) is retrieved during both KOEO SELF-TEST and KOER SELF-TEST. Whenever a repair is made, clear KAM. If driveability symptoms are not present, be aware of other temporary conditions which may have set this code, such as fuel contamination or vehicle is out of fuel. For SEFI models, go to step **2)**. For non-SEFI models, go to step **3)**.

2) Run Cylinder Balance Test – Run KOER SELF-TEST. After last repeated code, wait 5-10 seconds then goose throttle lightly (not WOT). Cylinder balance test will be activated. If Code 90 is present, go to next step. If Code 90 is not present, go to step **35)**.

3) Check For Vacuum/Air Induction Leaks – Check vacuum hoses, air induction system and EGR tube for leaks and damage. Repair if necessary. Clear KAM, and repeat QUICK TEST. If leak or damage is not found, go to step **4)**.

4) Check For Low Fuel Pressure – Turn ignition off. Release fuel system pressure. Install fuel pressure gauge. Cycle ignition from OFF to RUN position twice. Observe KOEO fuel pressure. Start engine. Observe and record KOER fuel pressure. Compare fuel pressure readings with FUEL PRESSURE SPECIFICATIONS table. If fuel pressure is within specification, go to step **5)**. If fuel pressure is not within specification, repair fuel system. Clear KAM, and repeat QUICK TEST.

5) Check System Ability To Hold Fuel Pressure – With fuel pressure gauge installed, cycle ignition from OFF to ON position twice to pressurize fuel system (DO NOT start engine). If fuel pressure remains at specification for 60 seconds, go to step **6)** (MAP/BP equipped vehicles) or step **7)** (all other vehicles). If fuel pressure does not remain at specification for 60 seconds, repair fuel system as necessary. Clear KAM, and repeat QUICK TEST.

6) Check MAP/BP Frequency – Turn ignition off. Connect MAP/BP tester to MAP/BP sensor. *See Fig. DF1* in CIRCUIT TEST DF. Turn ignition on. If MAP/BP voltage is within specification, go to step **7)**. See MAP SENSOR VOLTAGE OUTPUT table. If voltage is not within specification, check wiring to MAP/BP sensor for corrosion and other damage. Repair as necessary. Clear KAM, and repeat QUICK TEST. If wiring is okay, replace MAP/BP sensor. Clear KAM, and repeat QUICK TEST.

7) Check For Proper Battery Voltage To Fuel Injectors – Turn ignition on. Measure and record voltage across battery terminals. Disconnect any fuel injector harness connector. Measure and record voltage between VPWR circuit at fuel injector wiring harness connector and battery negative terminal. If both voltage readings are within one volt of each other, go to step **8)**. If voltage readings differ by more than one volt, fuel injectors are not getting correct voltage. Repair as necessary. Clear KAM, and repeat QUICK TEST.

8) Verify CANP Solenoid Is Not Stuck Closed – Enter OUTPUT STATE CHECK. See ADDITIONAL SYSTEM FUNCTIONS. Disconnect hose to manifold vacuum at CANP solenoid. Check for blockage. Repair or replace hose as necessary. With outputs off, apply 16 in. Hg vacuum to manifold vacuum side of CANP. Apply throttle to cycle outputs on. If vac-

CIRCUIT TEST HA (Cont.)

uum releases, reconnect vacuum hose to CANP and go to step **9)** (thermactor-equipped vehicles) or step **25)** (all other vehicles). If vacuum does not release, repeat this step to verify results. If vacuum now releases, go to step **9)** (thermactor-equipped vehicles) or step **25)** (all other vehicles). If vacuum will not release, replace CANP solenoid. Clear KAM, and repeat QUICK TEST.

9) Check Thermactor System For Upstream Air Leak – Check thermactor air control and vacuum control valves. See SYSTEM & COMPONENT TESTING – EEC-IV article. If air control valve is operating properly, go to step **25)**. If air control valve is not operating properly, repair or replace valve as necessary. Clear KAM, and repeat QUICK TEST.

NOTE: A break in step numbering sequence occurs at this point. Procedure skips from step 9) to step 15). No test procedures have been omitted.

15) Continuous Memory Codes 179, 182, 188 & 191 – This test identifies areas which could cause engine to run rich, resulting in adaptive fuel reducing system to compensate. For vehicles with dual HEGO sensors, a related fuel code from both HEGO sensors could indicate a problem common to all cylinders. If a code is present from only one HEGO, this may help isolate a problem or it may be an early indication of a common problem.

- **Code 179** – Indicates single right or rear HEGO detected a problem and adaptive fuel lean limit has been reached.
- **Code 182** – Indicates single right or rear HEGO detected a problem and adaptive fuel lean limit has been reached at idle.
- **Code 188** – Indicates left or front HEGO detected a problem and adaptive fuel lean limit has been reached.
- **Code 191** – Indicates left or front HEGO detected a problem and adaptive fuel lean limit has been reached at idle.

Ensure a pass Code (111) is received during both KOEO SELF-TEST and KOER SELF-TEST. Whenever a repair is made, clear KAM. For SEFI vehicles, go to step **16)**. For non-SEFI vehicles, go to step **17)**.

16) Run Cylinder Balance Test – Run KOER SELF-TEST. After last repeated code, wait 5-10 seconds and then goose throttle lightly (not WOT). Cylinder balance test will be activated. If Code 90 is present, go to next step. If Code 90 is not present, go to step **35)**.

17) Check For Low Fuel Pressure – Turn ignition off. Release fuel system pressure. Install fuel pressure gauge. Cycle ignition from OFF to RUN position twice. Observe KOEO fuel pressure. Start engine. Observe and record KOER fuel pressure. Compare fuel pressure readings with FUEL PRESSURE SPECIFICATIONS table. If fuel pressure is within specification, go to step **18)**. If fuel pressure is not within specification, repair fuel system as necessary. Clear KAM, and repeat QUICK TEST.

18) Check System Ability To Hold Fuel Pressure – With fuel pressure gauge installed, cycle ignition from OFF to ON position twice to pressurize fuel system (do not start engine). If fuel pressure remains at specification for 60 seconds, go to step **19)** (MAP/BP-equipped vehicles) or step **20)** (all other vehicles). If fuel pressure does not remain at specification for 60 seconds, repair fuel system as necessary. Clear KAM, and repeat QUICK TEST.

19) Check MAP/BP Frequency – Turn ignition off. Connect MAP/BP tester to MAP/BP sensor. Turn ignition on. Refer to MAP SENSOR VOLTAGE OUTPUT table. If voltage is not within specification, check wiring to MAP/BP sensor for corrosion or other damage. Repair if necessary. Clear KAM, and repeat QUICK TEST. If wiring is okay, replace MAP/BP sensor. Clear KAM, and repeat QUICK TEST. If MAP/BP voltage is within specification, go to step **20)**.

20) Check Throttle Body & Air Induction System – Check throttle body and air induction system for contamination and obstruction. Repair if necessary. Clear KAM, and repeat QUICK TEST. If throttle body and air induction system are okay, go to step **21)**.

21) Check PCV Valve – Turn ignition off. Remove and shake PCV valve. If PCV valve rattles freely when shaken, go to step **26)**. Replace PCV valve if it does not rattle. Clear KAM, and repeat QUICK TEST.

NOTE: A break in step numbering sequence occurs at this point. Procedure skips from step 21) to step 26). No test procedures have been omitted.

CIRCUIT TEST HA (Cont.)

26) Check HEGO Heater Circuit – Turn ignition off. Disconnect HEGO sensor(s). Measure resistance between IGNITION RUN circuit and PWR GND circuit at HEGO sensor connectors. Resistance should be 2 ohms (cold) or 35 ohms (hot). Set DVOM to 20-volt scale. Turn ignition on. Measure voltage between IGNITION RUN circuit and PWR GND circuit at HEGO sensor connectors. Voltage should be 10.5 volts. If HEGO circuit checks are within specification, go to step **27)**. If HEGO circuit check are not within specification, isolate problem and repair as necessary. Clear KAM, and repeat QUICK TEST.

27) Inspect HEGO Sensor For Contamination – Remove HEGO sensor(s) from exhaust manifold. Visually inspect for contamination and other damage. If HEGO sensors appear okay, go to step **28)** (models with EGR) or step **30)** (models without EGR). If HEGO sensors are contaminated or damaged, replace HEGO sensor. Clear KAM, and repeat QUICK TEST.

28) Check EGR Vacuum Supply At Idle – Disconnect vacuum line at EGR valve. Connect vacuum gauge to EGR vacuum line. Start engine, and let it idle. If vacuum reading is less than 2.5 in. Hg, go to step **29)**. If vacuum reading is 2.5 in. Hg or more, check EVR solenoid filter for obstructions. Repair as necessary. If EVR filter is okay, replace EVR solenoid. Connect all components, clear KAM, and repeat QUICK TEST.

29) Verify EGR Valve Is Fully Seated – Inspect EGR valve to ensure proper seating. If EGR valve is fully seated, reconnect vacuum line to EGR valve and go to step **30)**. If EGR valve is not fully seated, service or replace EGR valve as necessary. Clear KAM, and repeat QUICK TEST.

30) Check Cooling System – Ensure cooling system is in good condition and all components are operating properly. If cooling system is okay, go to step **35)**. If cooling system requires service, repair or replace as necessary. Clear KAM, and repeat QUICK TEST.

NOTE: A break in step numbering sequence occurs at this point. Procedure skips from step 30) to step 35). No test procedures have been omitted.

35) Check Ignition System – Ensure ignition system is operating properly. Scope check engine to verify no abnormal primary or secondary ignition firing lines exist. If ignition system is operating properly, go to step **36)**. If system is not operating properly, make necessary repairs. See IGNITION SYSTEMS in SYSTEM & COMPONENT TESTING – EEC-IV article. Clear KAM, and repeat QUICK TEST.

36) Injector Flow Check – Check fuel injector flow using Fuel Injector Tester (Rotunda 113-00001). If injector flow is okay, go to step **37)**. If injectors are restricted, clean or replace injectors as necessary. Clear KAM, and repeat QUICK TEST.

CIRCUIT TEST HA (Cont.)

37) Check Cylinder Compression – Check cylinder compression. See MECHANICAL INSPECTION in BASIC DIAGNOSTIC PROCEDURES article. If cylinder compression is not within specifications, repair or replace engine as necessary. Clear KAM, and repeat QUICK TEST. If cylinder compression is within specification, go to step **40)**.

NOTE: A break in step numbering sequence occurs at this point. Procedure skips from step 37) to step 40). No test procedures have been omitted.

WARNING: Following road test is an optional procedure. Follow all applicable safety procedures and traffic laws. This road test requires a driver and an assistant. Assistant should make measurements, observe changes and record notes. If this test is not performed, go to TROUBLE SHOOTING – NO CODES article for other possible causes.

40) Road Test Vehicle – Purpose of this test is to identify faults by monitoring certain controlled parameters while trying to recreate a driveability fault or symptom. To prepare for road test:

- Install fuel pressure gauge.
- Install MAP/BP tester.
- Disconnect ECA 60-pin connector, install breakout box and reconnect ECA to breakout box.
- Connect "T" vacuum gauge into manifold vacuum line.
- Have DVOM, writing materials, appropriate schematics and pin voltage charts available.

With ignition on and negative lead of DVOM connected to battery negative terminal, ensure following signals are correct:

- POWERS: KAPWR (pin No. 1) is more than 10.5 volts, VPWR (pins No. 37 and 57) is more than 10.5 volts and VREF (pin No. 26) is 4-6 volts.
- GROUNDS: PWR GND (pins No. 40 and 60), SIG RTN (pin No. 46) and IGN GND (pin No. 16) are 0-.5 volt.
- OPTIONAL GROUNDS: HEGO GND (pin No. 49), CSE GND (pin No. 20) and MAF RTN (pin No. 9 or 15) are 0-.5 volt.

Drive vehicle and attempt to induce symptom. Information provided by vehicle operator may help when trying to recreate symptom. When symptom occurs, assistant should observe and record changes in voltage signals. Information about symptom, operating condition value of voltage signal and any other information available should be recorded for analysis. If unable to duplicate symptom during road test, verify EEC-IV values are within acceptable range. After road test is completed, analyze results to locate and repair fault causing symptom. If problem cannot be identified, go to TROUBLE SHOOTING – NO CODES article for other possible causes of symptom.

CIRCUIT TEST J

FUEL PUMP CIRCUIT
(RELAY & INERTIA SWITCH)

Diagnostic Aids – Perform this test when instructed by QUICK TEST or CIRCUIT TEST AA. This test is only intended to diagnose:
- Fuel pump relay.
- Inertia switch.
- Wiring harness circuits (BATT +, VPWR, FUEL PUMP, GND and POWER-TO-PUMP).
- ECA.

92J22771

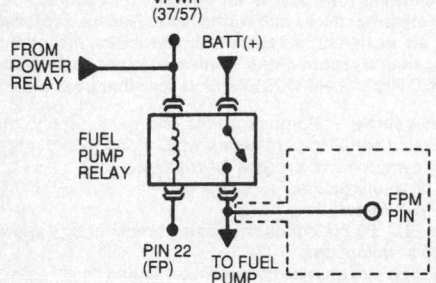

Fig. J1: **Fuel Pump Monitor Circuit Diagram (Typical)**

92A22772

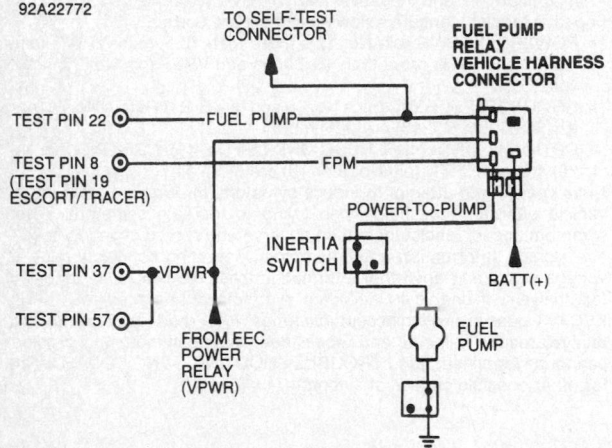

Fig. J2: **Fuel Pump Monitor Circuit Diagram (Aerostar, Explorer & Ranger)**

TEST PIN NO. 8 (FPM) WIRE COLOR IDENTIFICATION

Application	Wire Color
Aerostar	Pink/Black
Except Aerostar	Dark Green/Yellow

TEST PIN NO. 22 (FP) WIRE COLOR IDENTIFICATION

Application	Wire Color
All Models	Light Blue/Orange

TEST PIN NO. 37 & 57 (VPWR) WIRE COLOR IDENTIFICATION

Application	Wire Color
All Models	Red

CIRCUIT TEST J (Cont.)

92E03848

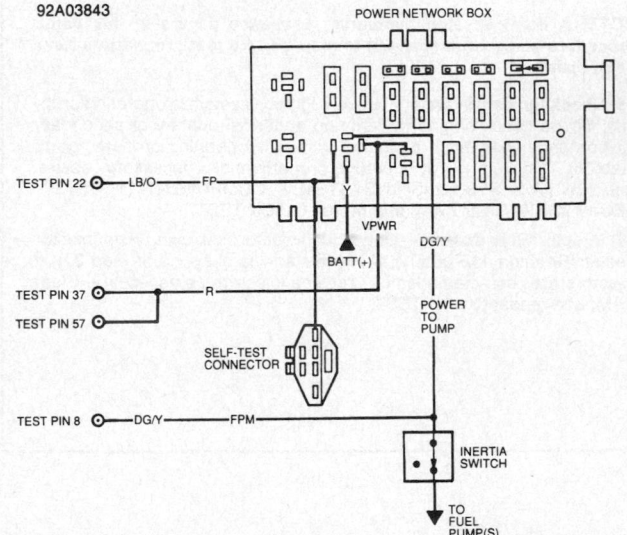

Fig. J3: **Fuel Pump Monitor Circuit Diagram (Bronco & Pickup)**

92A03843

Fig. J4: **Fuel Pump Monitor Circuit Diagram (Van)**

1) No Fuel System Pressure: Check Fuel Pump Operation – Turn ignition switch from OFF to RUN position several times (DO NOT turn to START position). If fuel pump runs briefly each time ignition is turned to RUN position, fuel pump circuit is okay. If fuel pump does not run, go to step **2)**.

2) Check For VPWR To ECA – Turn ignition off. Install EEC-IV Breakout Box (T83L-50-EEC-IV). Connect ECA to breakout box. Turn ignition on. Measure voltage between test pins No. 37 and 40 at breakout box. Measure voltage between test pins No. 57 and 60 at breakout box. If both voltage readings are more than 10.5 volts, go to step **3)**. If voltage is 10.5 volts or less, go to CIRCUIT TEST B, step **1)**.

3) Check Voltage To POWER-TO-PUMP Circuit – With ignition on, measure voltage between chassis ground and POWER-TO-PUMP circuit at fuel pump relay while cranking engine. If reading is less than 8 volts, go to step **4)**. If reading is 8 volts or more, check fuse to fuel pump relay. If fuse is okay, repair open in BATT+ circuit between fuel pump relay and battery positive terminal. Remove breakout box, and repeat QUICK TEST.

CIRCUIT TEST J (Cont.)

4) Checking BATT (+) Circuit To Fuel Pump Relay – Turn ignition on. Leave breakout box installed and ECA connected. Locate fuel pump relay. Measure voltage between chassis ground and BATT (+) circuit at fuel pump relay. If voltage is less than 10.5 volts, repair open in BATT (+) circuit between fuel pump relay and positive battery terminal. Repeat QUICK TEST. If reading is 10.5 volts or more, go to step **5)**.

5) Check Voltage At POWER-TO-PUMP Circuit – Turn ignition off. Connect jumper wire from test pin No. 22 to test pin No. 40 or 60 at breakout box. Turn ignition on. Measure voltage between chassis ground and POWER-TO-PUMP circuit at fuel pump relay. If voltage is 10.5 volts or more, replace ECA and repeat QUICK TEST. If voltage is less than 10.5 volts, replace fuel pump relay, and repeat QUICK TEST.

NOTE: A break in step numbering sequence occurs at this point. Procedure skips from step 5) to step 7). No test procedures have been omitted.

7) Code 87/556: Check VPWR To Fuel Pump Relay – Code 87/556 indicates a fuel pump primary circuit failure. Possible causes for this fault are:
- Inertia switch not reset or circuit open.
- Open or shorted circuit.
- Faulty fuel pump relay.
- Faulty ECA.

Disconnect fuel pump relay. Turn ignition on. Measure voltage between chassis ground and VPWR circuit at fuel pump relay wiring harness connector. If reading is 10.5 volts or more, go to step **8)**. If reading is less than 10.5 volts, verify inertia switch is in ON position. If switch is okay, repair open in VPWR circuit between EEC power relay and fuel pump relay. Connect fuel pump relay and repeat QUICK TEST.

8) Check Fuel Pump Relay – Turn ignition off. Disconnect fuel pump relay. *See Fig. J5.* Set DVOM on 200-ohm scale. On Bronco, Pickup and Van relays, measure resistance between terminals No. 85 and 86. On all other relays, measure resistance between VPWR pin and FUEL PUMP circuit pin at fuel pump relay. Both resistances should be 40-85 ohms. Set DVOM to 20-k/ohm scale. On Bronco, Pickup and Van relays, measure resistance between terminal No. 85 and terminals No. 30 and 87. On all other relays, measure resistance between FUEL PUMP circuit pin and both POWER-TO-PUMP and BATT (+) pins at fuel pump relay. All resistances should be greater than 10,000 ohms. If resistances are as specified, go to step **9)**. If resistances are not as specified, replace fuel pump relay and repeat QUICK TEST.

92B22773

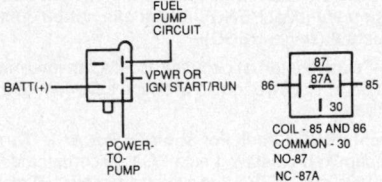

EXCEPT BRONCO, PICKUP & VAN — **BRONCO, PICKUP & VAN**

Fig. J5: Identifying Fuel Pump Relay Connector Terminals

9) Check For Short To Power – Turn ignition off. Disconnect fuel pump relay. Disconnect 60-pin ECA connector. Inspect terminals, and repair if damaged. Install EEC-IV Breakout Box (T83L-50-EEC-IV), leaving ECA disconnected. Turn ignition on. Measure voltage between test pin No. 22 and negative battery terminal. If voltage is less than 1.0 volt, go to step **10)**. If voltage is 1.0 volt or more, repair short circuit. Reconnect ECA, and attempt to start vehicle. If vehicle fails to start, replace ECA. Repeat QUICK TEST.

10) Check For Shorts To Ground – Turn ignition off. Leave fuel pump relay disconnected. Measure resistance between test pin No. 22 and test pins No. 40 and 60. If resistance is less than 10,000 ohms, repair short in FUEL PUMP circuit. Remove breakout box, and repeat QUICK TEST. If resistance is 10,000 ohms or more, go to step **11)**.

11) Check Fuel Pump Circuit Continuity – Turn ignition off. Leave fuel pump relay disconnected. Measure resistance between FUEL PUMP circuit at fuel pump relay wiring harness connector and test pin No. 22 at breakout box. If resistance is less than 5 ohms, replace ECA and repeat QUICK TEST. If resistance is 5 ohms or more, repair open circuit. Reconnect all components, and repeat QUICK TEST.

CIRCUIT TEST J (Cont.)

NOTE: A break in step numbering sequence occurs at this point. Procedure skips from step 11) to step 20). No test procedures have been omitted.

20) Code 95/542 – A KOEO Code 95/542 indicates one of following conditions:
Engine Starts:
- Fuel pump secondary circuit shorted to power.
- Fuel pump relay contacts always closed.
- Open in Fuel Pump Monitor (FPM) circuit between ECA and connection to POWER-TO-PUMP circuit.
- HEGO short to power (dual HEGO applications).
- Faulty ECA.

No Start:
- Inertia switch not reset or electrically open.
- Open circuit in or between ECA and fuel pump.
- Faulty ground connection at fuel pump.

If engine starts, go to step **21)**. If engine does not start, go to step **24)**.

21) Check Fuel Pump Operation – Turn ignition on. Wait 5 seconds. Listen for fuel pump operation. If fuel pump is off, go to step **23)**. If fuel pump is on, go to step **22)**.

22) Check For Fuel Pump Relay Always Closed – Turn ignition off. Disconnect fuel pump relay. Turn ignition on. If fuel pump is off with relay disconnected, replace fuel pump relay and repeat QUICK TEST. If fuel pump is on with relay disconnected, repair short to power in POWER-TO-PUMP/FPM circuit. (For models with relay block, also check fuel pump prime plug circuit). Repeat QUICK TEST.

23) Check Continuity Of Fuel Pump Monitor (FPM) Circuit – Turn ignition off. Disconnect ECA 60-pin connector. Inspect and repair any damaged terminals. Install EEC-IV Breakout Box (T83L-50-EEC-IV), leaving ECA disconnected. Disconnect fuel pump relay. Measure resistance between test pin No. 8 at breakout box and POWER-TO-PUMP circuit at fuel pump relay wiring harness connector. If resistance is less than 5 ohms, go to step **35)** (dual HEGO) or replace ECA and repeat QUICK TEST (single HEGO). If resistance is 5 ohms or more, repair open circuit and repeat QUICK TEST.

24) Check Inertia Switch – Turn ignition off. Disconnect fuel pump inertia switch. Ensure switch is reset. Measure resistance of inertia switch. If resistance is less than 5 ohms, reconnect switch and check for open in POWER-TO-PUMP circuit, poor fuel pump ground or open in fuel pump. If resistance is 5 ohms or more, reset or replace inertia switch. Repeat QUICK TEST.

NOTE: A break in step numbering sequence occurs at this point. Procedure skips from step 24) to step 30). No test procedures have been omitted.

30) Code 96/543 – Code 96/543 indicates fuel pump secondary circuit failure between BATT (+) supply and FPM connection to POWER-TO-PUMP circuit. Following are possible causes:
No Start:
- Open circuit between BATT (+) supply and FPM connection to POWER-TO-PUMP circuit.
- Fuel pump relay contacts are always open.

Engine Starts:
- HEGO short to power (dual HEGO models).
- Faulty ECA.

If engine starts, go to step **35)** (dual HEGO) or replace ECA and repeat QUICK TEST (single HEGO). If engine does not start, go to step **31)**.

31) Check For BATT (+) To Fuel Pump Relay – Turn ignition off. Disconnect fuel pump relay. Connect DVOM between BATT (+) terminal at fuel pump relay wiring harness connector and negative battery terminal. If voltage is 10.5 volts or more, go to step **32)**. If voltage is less than 10.5 volts, check fuse/fusible link for BATT (+) supply to fuel pump relay. If fuse/fusible link is okay, repair open circuit in BATT (+) circuit. Repeat QUICK TEST.

32) Check POWER-TO-PUMP Circuit Continuity – Turn ignition off. With fuel pump relay disconnected, measure resistance between POWER-TO-PUMP terminal at fuel pump relay wiring harness connector and negative battery terminal. If resistance is less than 10 ohms, replace fuel pump relay. Reconnect relay and repeat QUICK TEST. If resistance is 10 ohms or more, repair open circuit in POWER-TO-PUMP circuit between FPM splice and fuel pump relay. Repeat QUICK TEST.

NOTE: A break in step numbering sequence occurs at this point. Procedure skips from step 32) to step 35). No test procedures have been omitted.

CIRCUIT TEST J (Cont.)

Diagnostic Aids – Due to internal circuitry of ECA, a left/front HEGO signal short to power could produce a Code 95/542 or 96/543.

35) Check Left/Front HEGO Sensor For Short To Power – Turn ignition off. Disconnect left or front HEGO sensor. *See Fig. J6.* Measure resistance between HEGO SIGNAL terminal and KEY POWER terminal at HEGO sensor wiring harness connector. *See Fig. J7.* If resistance is 10,000 ohms or more, go to step **36)**. If resistance is less than 10,000 ohms, replace HEGO sensor. Clear KAM, and repeat QUICK TEST.

91D06956

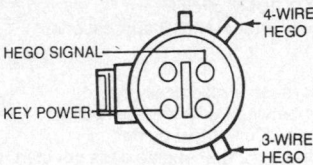

Fig. J6: HEGO Sensor Connector

91F06957

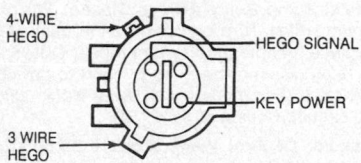

Fig. J7: HEGO Sensor Vehicle Harness Connector

36) Check HEGO Circuit For Short To Power – Turn ignition off. Disconnect ECA. Inspect and repair any damaged terminals. Turn ignition on. With left or front HEGO sensor disconnected, measure voltage between HEGO SIGNAL at HEGO wiring harness connector and chassis ground. If voltage is less than 2 volts, replace ECA and repeat QUICK TEST. If voltage is 2 volts or more, repair short circuit. Reconnect ECA and HEGO sensor. Clear KAM, and repeat QUICK TEST.

NOTE: A break in step numbering sequence occurs at this point. Procedure skips from step 36) to step 90). No test procedures have been omitted.

90) Continuous Memory Code 95/542 – Code 95/542 indicates one of following conditions:
- Faulty ground circuit at fuel pump.
- FPM or POWER-TO-PUMP circuit short to power.
- Fuel pump relay contacts stuck closed.
- Open circuit in or between fuel pump and FPM circuit at ECA.
- Left or front HEGO circuit short to power (dual HEGO system).
- FUEL PUMP circuit is activated at a time that is not programmed into ECA strategy.

Start engine, and enter wiggle test. See CONTINUOUS MONITOR MODE (WIGGLE TEST) under QUICK TEST. Check for engine miss or intermittent fuel pump deactivation while performing following:
- Shake and bend POWER-TO-PUMP circuit wiring harness connector between fuel pump relay and fuel pump.
- Shake and bend fuel pump ground circuit between fuel pump and ground.
- Lightly tap fuel pump to simulate road shock.
- Lightly tap inertia switch to simulate road shock.

With ignition off, check harness connectors for corrosion and damage. Isolate and repair any faults. Clear continuous memory, and repeat QUICK TEST. If no faults are found, go to step **91)**.

91) Check FPM Circuit – Turn ignition off. Disconnect ECA 60-pin connector. Inspect terminals, and repair if damaged. Install EEC-IV Breakout Box (T83L-50-EEC-IV), leaving ECA disconnected. Connect test light between test pin No. 8 and test pin No. 37 at breakout box. With test light on, perform wiggle test on FPM circuit between fuel pump and ECA. Light will go out if fault is found, indicating an open circuit. If a fault is found, repair as necessary and repeat QUICK TEST. If no fault is found, go to step **92)**.

92) Check For Shorts To Power – Connect a test light between breakout box test pin No. 8 and test pin No. 40. Test light should be off. Observe test light while bending and shaking FPM circuit and POWER-TO-PUMP circuit. Lightly tap fuel pump relay to simulate road shock.

CIRCUIT TEST J (Cont.)

Fault is indicated if test light comes on. Isolate and repair fault as necessary, and repeat QUICK TEST. If no fault is found, go to step **96)** (dual HEGO) or step **99)** (single HEGO).

93) Continuous Memory Code 96/543: Check For Continuous Memory Code 87/556 – If Code 87 or 556 is present, go to step **95)**. If Codes 87 and 556 are not displayed, go to step **94)**.

94) Check EEC-IV Harness – A Continuous Memory Code 96/543, without an accompanying Continuous Memory Code 87/556, indicates one of following conditions has occurred during vehicle operation:
- An open in BATT (+) circuit between BATT (+) and fuel pump relay.
- Fuel pump relay contacts open.
- Open in POWER-TO-PUMP circuit between fuel pump relay to FPM splice (if applicable).
- Left/front HEGO circuit short to power (dual HEGO).

Start engine. Check for engine miss or intermittent fuel pump deactivation while performing following:
- Shake and bend BATT (+) circuit wiring harness between power source and fuel pump relay.
- Shake and bend POWER-TO-PUMP circuit wiring harness connector between fuel pump relay and FPM splice (if applicable).
- Lightly tap fuel pump relay to simulate road shock.

Turn ignition off. Inspect all fuel pump relay and BATT (+) connectors for damage and corrosion. If fault is found, repair as necessary. Clear and repeat QUICK TEST. If no fault is found, a Continuous Memory Code 95/543 may have been set without a Continuous Memory Code 87/556 under certain conditions, even though a fault has occurred in fuel pump primary circuit. Go to step **95)** for fuel pump primary circuit check.

95) Continuous Memory Code 87/556: Check EEC-IV Harness – A Continuous Memory Code 87 or 556 indicates primary fuel pump circuit has failed during vehicle operation. Possible causes for this fault are:
- Open in VPWR circuit between EEC power relay and fuel pump relay.
- Open coil in fuel pump relay.
- Open in fuel pump circuit (pin No. 22).
- Faulty inertia switch.

Start engine. Check for engine miss or intermittent fuel pump deactivation while performing following:
- Shake and bend VPWR circuit wiring harness between EEC and fuel pump relay.
- Shake and bend FP circuit wiring harness connector between fuel pump relay and ECA.
- Lightly tap fuel pump relay to simulate road shock.
- Lightly tap inertia switch to simulate road shock (if equipped).

Turn ignition off. Disconnect ECA 60-pin connector. Inspect terminals, and repair if damaged. Install EEC-IV Breakout Box (T83L-50-EEC-IV), leaving ECA disconnected. If fault is found, isolate and repair as necessary. Repeat QUICK TEST. If no faults are found but Code 96/543 is present, go to step **96)** (dual HEGO). If fault can not be duplicated at this time, go to step **99)** (single HEGO).

Diagnostic Aids – Due to internal circuitry of ECA, an intermittent left/front HEGO signal short to power could produce a Continuous Memory Code 95/542 or 96/543.

96) Check Left/Front HEGO Circuit For Short To Power – Turn ignition off. Breakout box should be installed with ECA disconnected. Connect test light between left/front HEGO test pin and pin No. 40 at breakout box. Test light should be off. Observe test light while shaking left/front HEGO circuit from HEGO sensor to ECA. Lightly tap HEGO SENSOR to simulate road shock. Fault is indicated if test light comes on. Isolate and repair as necessary. Clear Keep-Alive Memory (KAM), and repeat QUICK TEST. If no fault is indicated, go to step **99)**.

NOTE: A break in step numbering sequence occurs at this point. Procedure skips from step 96) to step 99). No test procedures have been omitted.

WARNING: Following road test is an optional procedure. Follow all applicable safety procedures and traffic laws. This road test requires a driver and an assistant. Assistant should make measurements, observe changes and record notes. If this test is not performed, go to TROUBLE SHOOTING – NO CODES article for other possible causes.

99) Road Test Vehicle – Purpose of this test is to identify faults by monitoring certain controlled parameters while trying to recreate a driveability or MIL light symptom. To prepare for road test:
- Install fuel pressure gauge.
- Install MAP/BP tester.
- Disconnect ECA 60-pin connector, install breakout box and reconnect ECA to breakout box.

CIRCUIT TEST J (Cont.)

- Connect "T" vacuum gauge into manifold vacuum line.
- Have DVOM, writing materials and appropriate schematics and pin voltage charts available.

With ignition on and negative lead of DVOM connected to negative battery terminal, ensure following signals are correct:

- POWERS: KAPWR (pin No. 1) is greater than 10.5 volts, VPWR (pins No. 37 and 57) is greater than 10.5 volts and VREF (pin No. 26) is 4-6 volts.
- GROUNDS: PWR GND (pins No. 40 and 60), SIG RTN (pin No. 46) and IGN GND (pin No. 16) are 0.0-0.5 volt.
- OPTIONAL GROUNDS: HEGO GND (pin No. 49), CSE GND (pin No. 20) and MAF RTN (pin No. 9 or 15) are 0.0-0.5 volt.

Diagnostic Aids – Test lights and DVOM are useful during diagnosis. For example: with Continuous Memory Code 87/556 (fuel pump primary circuit failure) and a surge or stall symptom, connect a test light to fuel pump relay between VPWR and ground. Connect DVOM between FP circuit at fuel pump relay and breakout box test pin No. 1. Under normal driving conditions, test light will be on and DVOM will read battery voltage. If vehicle stalls, ECA will open FP circuit and DVOM voltage will be low. If fault is in fuel pump circuit, test light and DVOM status will change as fault occurs. If test light at VPWR circuit goes out, fault is in VPWR circuit to fuel pump relay. If test light and DVOM status do not change and Continuous Memory Code 87/556 is set again, replace fuel pump relay. If only FP voltage goes low, fault is in FP circuit or ECA. To diagnose FP circuit and ECA, connect DVOM between breakout box test pin No. 1 and 22. If voltage goes low as symptom occurs, replace ECA. If voltage stays high as symptom occurs, fault is in FP circuit. For fuel pump secondary circuit Codes 95/542 and 96/543, circuits BATT (+), POWER-TO-PUMP and FPM can be diagnosed using same procedure. Drive vehicle and attempt to induce symptom. Information provided by vehicle operator may help when trying to recreate symptom. When symptom occurs, assistant should observe and record changes in voltage signals. Information about symptom and operating condition value of voltage signal and any other information available should be recorded for analysis. If unable to duplicate symptom during road test, verify EEC-IV values are within acceptable range. After test is completed, analyze results to locate and repair fault causing symptom. If problem cannot be identified, go to TROUBLE SHOOTING – NO CODES article for other possible causes of symptom.

CIRCUIT TEST KA

EGR VACUUM REGULATOR (EVR) SOLENOID

Diagnostic Aids – Perform this test when instructed by QUICK TEST. To prevent replacement of good components, be aware following non-EEC related areas may be at fault:

- Damaged vacuum hoses.
- Damaged Backpressure Transducer (BPT).
- EGR valve.
- EVP sensor.

This test is only intended to diagnose:

- EVR solenoid.
- ECA.
- EVR and VPWR harness circuits.

EVR solenoid regulate vacuum to EGR valve by way of Backpressure Transducer (BPT). When energized, EVR opens a port between manifold vacuum and EGR valve. When not energized, EVR closes port to EGR and vacuum is vented to atmosphere.

92J03847

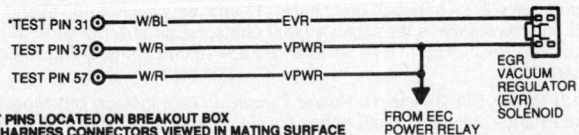

```
*TEST PIN 31 ⊘—W/BL————EVR——————⌐
*TEST PIN 37 ⊘—W/R—————VPWR—————|  EGR
*TEST PIN 57 ⊘—W/R—————VPWR—————⌐  VACUUM
                                    REGULATOR
*TEST PINS LOCATED ON BREAKOUT BOX    (EVR)
ALL HARNESS CONNECTORS VIEWED IN MATING SURFACE   SOLENOID
                              FROM EEC
                              POWER RELAY
```

Fig. KA1: Identifying EGR Valve Regulator (EVR) Solenoid Circuits & Connector Terminals

CIRCUIT TEST KA (Cont.)

1) Code 558 – Code 558 indicates failure in EVR solenoid circuit. Possible causes for this fault are:

- Faulty EVR solenoid.
- Faulty vacuum hoses.
- Open or ground circuit in wiring harness.
- Faulty ECA.

Turn ignition off. Remove scan tester (if applicable). Disconnect cruise control servo wiring harness connector. Connect DVOM negative lead to STO terminal at Self-Test connector. Connect positive lead to positive battery terminal. Install a jumper wire between STI terminal and SIG RTN terminal at Self-Test connector. *See Figs. B1-B3 in CIRCUIT TEST B.* Perform KOEO SELF-TEST until continuous memory test is complete. DVOM will read less than 1.0 volt when test is complete to indicate ECA has entered OUTPUT STATE CHECK. Depress and release throttle. If voltage does not increase, fully apply throttle and release. If STO voltage remains low, go to CIRCUIT TEST QC. If voltage increases, remain in OUTPUT STATE CHECK and go to step **2)**.

2) Check EVR Solenoid Electrical – Turn ignition off. Disconnect EVR solenoid wiring harness connector. Connect DVOM positive lead to VPWR terminal and negative test lead to EVR terminal at EVR solenoid wiring harness connector. Depress and release throttle 3-5 times to cycle solenoid output. If EVR solenoid voltage output change is 0.5 volt or more, go to step **3)**. If EVR solenoid voltage output change is less than 0.5 volt, go to step **5)**.

3) Check EVR Solenoid Vacuum – Turn ignition on. Disconnect EVR solenoid vacuum hoses. Install vacuum pump on EVR solenoid vacuum source port. Install vacuum gauge on solenoid output port. Apply 6 in. Hg, and hold. Depress and release throttle 3-5 times to cycle solenoid output. Turn ignition off. If vacuum gauge shows vacuum cycling at output port, go to step **4)**. If vacuum gauge does not show vacuum cycling at output port, replace EVR solenoid and repeat QUICK TEST.

4) Check EVR Vacuum Hoses – Remove jumper wire, vacuum pump and gauge. Remove vacuum hoses individually. Plug one end of hose. Connect vacuum pump at opposite end. Apply vacuum and observe gauge. If vacuum is not held, replace hose and repeat QUICK TEST. If vacuum is held, ensure vacuum port between BPT and EGR is not restricted. If vacuum port is clear, go to step **5)**.

5) Check EVR Solenoid VPWR – Turn ignition off. Disconnect EVR solenoid wiring harness connector. Turn ignition on. Measure voltage between VPWR at EVR solenoid wiring harness connector and negative battery terminal. If voltage is 10.5 volts or more, go to step **6)**. If voltage is less than 10.5 volts, repair open VPWR circuit and repeat QUICK TEST.

6) Check EVR Solenoid Circuit Continuity – Turn ignition off. Disconnect ECA 60-pin connector. Inspect terminals, and repair if damaged. Install EEC-IV Breakout Box (T83L-50-EEC-IV), leaving ECA disconnected. Measure resistance between EVR terminal at EVR solenoid wiring harness connector and test pin No. 31. If reading is less than 5 ohms, go to step **7)**. If resistance is 5 ohms or more, repair open circuit and repeat QUICK TEST.

7) Check EVR Solenoid Circuit For Short – Turn ignition off. Measure resistance between test pin No. 31 and test pins No. 37 and 57 at breakout box. If each resistance is 10,000 ohms or more, replace ECA and repeat QUICK TEST. If reading is less than 10,000 ohms, repair short circuit and repeat QUICK TEST.

CIRCUIT TEST KC

AIR MANAGEMENT SYSTEM (AM1/AM2)

Diagnostic Aids – Perform this test when instructed by QUICK TEST or if directed by other test procedures. This test is only intended to diagnose:

- AM1 or AM2 solenoid valve assembly.
- Wiring harness circuits (AM1, AM2 and VPWR).
- Vacuum supply.
- ECA.

To prevent replacement of good components, be aware following non-EEC related areas may be at fault:

- Thermactor air system drive belt, air pump and valve.
- Blocked or restricted thermactor air passages in engine.

92B03848

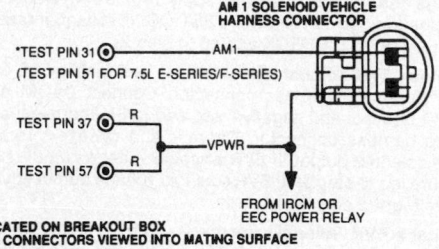

Fig. KC1: Air Management Circuits (Pickup & Van 7.5L)

TEST PIN NO. 11 (AM2) WIRE COLOR IDENTIFICATION

Application	Wire Color
4.9L, 5.0L & 5.8L	White/Brown

TEST PIN NO. 51 (AM1) WIRE COLOR IDENTIFICATION

Application	Wire Color
4.9L, 5.0L, 5.8L & 7.5L	White/Orange

92C22774

Fig. KC2: Air Management Circuits (Except Pickup & Van 7.5L)

1) Codes 44/311, 45/312, 46/313 & 94/314 – Code 44/311 or 94/314 indicates thermactor system is inoperative. Code 45/312 indicates thermactor air is incorrectly routed. Code 46/313 indicates thermactor air is not by-passed when directed. Possible causes for these faults are:

- Vacuum hoses leaking, blocked or kinked.
- Air pump or diverter valve inoperative.
- Air Management (AM) solenoid defective or blocked.

Check for correct vacuum hose routing to AM1/AM2 solenoids and by-pass diverter valve. See Vehicle Emission Control Information (VECI) label. Check for kinked disconnected, or blocked vacuum hoses. Check for kinked or blocked air hoses. If faults are detected, repair as necessary and repeat QUICK TEST. If no faults are detected and Code 44/311 or 94/314 is present, go to step **4)**. If Code 46/313 is present, go to step **3)**. If Code 45/312 is present, go to step **2)**.

2) Attempt To Eliminate Code 45/312 – Disconnect and plug vacuum hose at diverter valve. Turn ignition off. Repeat KOER SELF-TEST, and record codes. If Code 45/312 is present, EEC-IV system is okay. Inspect diverter valve and check valve for faults. If Code 45/312 is not present, go to step **4)**.

3) Attempt To Eliminate Code 46/313 – Disconnect and plug vacuum hose at by-pass valve. Turn ignition off. Repeat KOER SELF-TEST, and record codes. If Code 46/313 is present, EEC-IV system is okay. Check by-pass valve for problem. If Code 46/313 is not present, go to step **4)**.

CIRCUIT TEST KC (Cont.)

4) Output Check – Enter OUTPUT STATE CHECK. See ADDITIONAL SYSTEM FUNCTIONS. Use only a VOM or DVOM for this step. DO NOT use scan tester. Turn ignition off. Disconnect cruise control servo (if equipped). With DVOM on 20-volt scale, connect DVOM negative lead to STO terminal at self-test connector. Connect positive lead to positive battery terminal. Using jumper wire, connect STI to SIG RTN at self-test connector. *See Figs. B1-B3* in CIRCUIT TEST B. Perform KOEO SELF-TEST until continuous memory test is complete. DVOM will read less than 1.0 volt when test is complete. Depress and release throttle. If voltage increases, remain in OUTPUT STATE CHECK and go to step **5)**. If voltage does not increase, depress throttle to WOT and release. If STO voltage does not go high, go to CIRCUIT TEST QC.

5) Check Solenoid Electrical Operation – Set DVOM on 20-volt scale. Disconnect AM solenoids. Connect DVOM positive lead to VPWR terminal and negative lead to AM1 terminal at AM1 solenoid wiring harness connector. While observing DVOM, depress and release throttle several times to cycle output on and off. Repeat test for AM2 solenoid. Connect DVOM positive lead to VPWR terminal and negative test lead to AM2 terminal on AM2 solenoid wiring harness connector. Cycle AM2 solenoid on and off. If either solenoid does not cycle more than 0.5 volt, remove jumper and go to step **9)**. If both solenoids cycle more than 0.5 volt, stay in OUTPUT STATE CHECK, reconnect solenoids and go to step **6)**.

6) Check Solenoids For Vacuum Cycling – Connect vacuum pump to AM1 solenoid vacuum supply port. Connect vacuum gauge to output port. Maintain vacuum at source while depressing and releasing throttle to cycle output on and off. Observe vacuum gauge. Repeat for AM2 solenoid. If either output does not cycle on and off, replace solenoid assembly and repeat QUICK TEST. If both outputs cycle on and off, exit OUTPUT STATE CHECK and go to step **7)**.

7) Check Solenoids For Internal Vacuum Leaks – Connect a vacuum pump to AM1 solenoid supply port. Connect a vacuum gauge to AM1 solenoid output port. Apply 15 in. Hg vacuum and observe gauge. Repeat test for AM2 solenoid. If vacuum gauge reading holds vacuum for each solenoid, check vacuum source for blockage and leakage from manifold to solenoids and control valves. If vacuum source is okay, inspect thermactor air tube and air passages in cylinder head for carbon blockage. Repeat QUICK TEST. If vacuum gauge does not hold vacuum, replace solenoid assembly and repeat QUICK TEST.

8) Codes 81/553 & 82/552: Check VPWR Circuit Voltage – Codes 81/553 and 82/552 indicate voltage output for thermactor air solenoid did not change when activated. Possible causes for this fault are:

- Shorted or open circuits.
- Solenoid resistance out of range.
- Faulty ECA.

Disconnect both solenoid connectors. Turn ignition on. Measure voltage between VPWR terminal of wiring harness connector and battery ground for both solenoids. If either voltage reading is less than 10.5 volts, repair wiring harness open circuit. Connect solenoid connectors, and repeat QUICK TEST. If both readings are 10.5 volts or more, go to step **9)**.

9) Measure Solenoid Resistance – Turn ignition off. Set DVOM on 200-ohm scale. Disconnect AM1 and AM2 solenoid connectors. Measure resistance of both solenoids. If either resistance is not 50-100 ohms, replace solenoid assembly and repeat QUICK TEST. If both resistances are 50-100 ohms, go to step **10)**.

10) Check Circuit Continuity – Turn ignition off. Disconnect ECA 60-pin connector. Inspect terminals, and repair if damaged. Install EEC-IV Breakout Box (T83L-50-EEC-IV), leaving ECA disconnected. Set DVOM on 200-ohm scale. Measure resistance between test pin No. 51 and AM1 terminal at wiring harness connector. Measure resistance between test pin No. 11 and AM2 terminal at wiring harness connector. If either resistance is 5 ohms or more, repair open circuit and repeat QUICK TEST. If both resistances are less than 5 ohms, go to step **11)**.

11) Check For Short To Ground – Turn ignition off. Measure resistance between breakout box test pin No. 51 and pins No. 40, 46 and 60. Measure resistance between test pin No. 11 and test pins No. 40, 46 and 60. If any resistance is less than 10,000 ohms, repair short to ground and repeat QUICK TEST. If all resistances are 10,000 ohms or more, go to step **12)**.

12) Check For Shorts To Power Circuit – Turn ignition off. Measure resistance between breakout box pin No. 51 and test pins No. 37 and 57. Also measure resistance between test pin No. 11 and test pins No. 37 and 57. If any resistance is less than 10,000 ohms, repair short to power and repeat QUICK TEST. If code is repeated, replace ECA. If all resistances are 10,000 ohms or more, replace ECA, and repeat QUICK TEST.

CIRCUIT TEST KD

CANISTER PURGE (CANP)

Diagnostic Aids – Perform this test when instructed by QUICK TEST or if directed by other test procedures. This test is only intended to diagnose:

- CANP solenoid.
- Harness circuits (CANP and VPWR).
- ECA.

92F03850

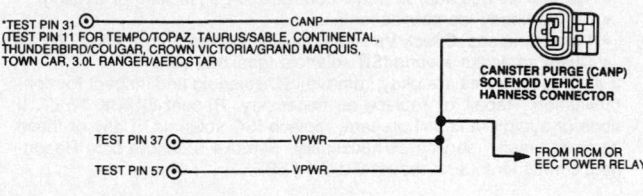

*TEST PIN 31 — CANP
(TEST PIN 11 FOR TEMPO/TOPAZ, TAURUS/SABLE, CONTINENTAL, THUNDERBIRD/COUGAR, CROWN VICTORIA/GRAND MARQUIS, TOWN CAR, 3.0L RANGER/AEROSTAR)

CANISTER PURGE (CANP) SOLENOID VEHICLE HARNESS CONNECTOR

TEST PIN 37 — VPWR
TEST PIN 57 — VPWR

FROM IRCM OR EEC POWER RELAY

*TEST PINS LOCATED ON BREAKOUT BOX
ALL HARNESS CONNECTORS VIEWED INTO MATING SURFACE

Fig. KD1: Canister Purge (CANP) Circuit

TEST PIN NO. 11 Or 31 (CANP) WIRE COLOR IDENTIFICATION

Application	Wire Color
3.0L, 4.0L, 4.9L, 5.0L, 5.8L & 7.5L	Gray/Yellow

TEST PINS NO. 37 & 57 (VPWR) WIRE COLOR IDENTIFICATION

Application	Wire Color
All Models	Red

1) Check System Function – Use only VOM or DVOM for this step. DO NOT use scan tester. Turn ignition off. Disconnect cruise control servo wiring harness connector. Connect DVOM negative lead to STO terminal at self-test connector. Connect positive lead to positive battery terminal. Install a jumper wire between STI terminal and SIG RTN terminal at self-test connector. See Figs. B1-B3 in CIRCUIT TEST B. Perform KOEO SELF-TEST until continuous memory test is complete. DVOM will read less than one volt when test is complete to indicate ECA has entered OUTPUT STATE CHECK. Depress and release throttle. If voltage increases, remain in OUTPUT STATE CHECK and go to step **2)**. If voltage does not increase, apply full throttle and release. If STO voltage does not increase, leave test equipment hooked up and go to CIRCUIT TEST QC.

2) Check CANP Solenoid Electrical Function – Turn ignition on. Disconnect CANP solenoid. Connect DVOM positive test lead to VPWR terminal and negative test lead to CANP terminal at solenoid wiring harness connector. While observing DVOM, depress and release throttle several times to cycle output on and off. If CANP circuit voltage does not cycle 0.5 volt or more, remove jumper wire and go to step **6)**. If CANP circuit voltage cycles, remain in OUTPUT STATE CHECK and go to step **3)**.

3) Check Solenoid For Vacuum Leaks – Turn ignition on. Leave CANP solenoid disconnected. Disconnect vacuum hose at CANP solenoid from manifold vacuum side of solenoid. Apply 16 in. Hg vacuum to manifold vacuum side of CANP solenoid. If CANP solenoid does not hold vacuum for 20 seconds, replace solenoid and repeat QUICK TEST. If fault is still present, service fuel evaporation canister or hoses. If CANP holds vacuum for 20 seconds, remain in OUTPUT STATE CHECK, leave vacuum pump attached and go to step **4)**.

4) Check Solenoid Mechanical Operation – Connect CANP solenoid connector. Apply 16 in. Hg vacuum to manifold vacuum side of CANP solenoid. Depress and release throttle. If vacuum is released, check hose from CANP solenoid to canister for leaks and cracks. If hose is okay, remove jumper wire from STI to SIG RTN and go to step **5)**. If vacuum is not released, check hose from CANP solenoid to canister for leaks and cracks. If hose is okay, replace CANP solenoid and repeat QUICK TEST.

5) Check Vacuum Supply To CANP Solenoid – Disconnect vacuum hose from CANP solenoid on manifold vacuum (PCV) side. Start engine. If vacuum is present at vacuum hose, EEC system is okay. Check evaporative canister. If vacuum is not present at hose, check vacuum hose for improper routing, kinks and blockage. If hose is okay, check engine for cause of low vacuum.

6) Code 85/565 Or 569: Check CANP Solenoid Resistance – Code 85/565 or 569 indicates fault in CANP solenoid circuit. For vehicles with

CIRCUIT TEST KD (Cont.)

dual CANP systems, Code 565 refers to CANP 1; Code 569 refers to CANP 2. Possible causes for this fault are:

- Faulty CANP solenoid.
- Open in wiring harness circuit.
- Shorted wiring harness circuit.
- Faulty ECA.

Turn ignition off. Set DVOM on 200 ohm scale. Disconnect CANP solenoid connector. Measure CANP solenoid resistance. If resistance is 40-90 ohms, go to step **7)**. If resistance is not 40-90 ohms, replace CANP solenoid and repeat QUICK TEST.

7) Check Voltage Of VPWR Circuit – With CANP solenoid disconnected, turn ignition on. Measure voltage between VPWR terminal at CANP solenoid harness connector and negative battery terminal. If resistance is 10.5 volts or more, go to step **8)**. If resistance is less than 10.5 volts, repair open circuit and repeat QUICK TEST.

8) Check Continuity Of CANP Circuit – Turn ignition off. Disconnect CANP solenoid. Disconnect 60-pin ECA connector. Inspect terminals, and repair if damaged. Install EEC-IV Breakout Box (T83L-50-EEC-IV), leaving ECA disconnected. Measure resistance between test pin No. 31 and CANP terminal at solenoid wiring harness connector. If resistance is less than 5 ohms, go to step **9)**. If resistance is 5 ohms or more, repair open circuit and repeat QUICK TEST.

9) Check CANP Circuit For Short To Ground – Turn ignition off. With CANP solenoid disconnected, measure resistance between test pin No. 31 and pins No. 40, 46 and 60 at breakout box. If all resistances are 10,000 ohms or more, go to step **10)**. If any resistance is less than 10,000 ohms, repair short to ground and repeat QUICK TEST.

10) Check CANP Circuit For Short To Power – Turn ignition off. With CANP solenoid disconnected, measure resistance between test pin No. 31 and test pins No. 37 and 57 at breakout box. If all resistances are 10,000 ohms or more, replace ECA and repeat QUICK TEST. If any resistance is less than 10,000 ohms, repair circuit short to power and repeat QUICK TEST. If code is repeated, replace ECA and repeat QUICK TEST.

CIRCUIT TEST KE

IDLE SPEED CONTROL (AIR BY-PASS)

Diagnostic Aids – Perform this test when instructed by QUICK TEST or if directed by other test procedures. If engine is running rough or has rough idle, correct these conditions before performing test. Causes may be in ignition system, fuel system or EGR system. This test is terminals intended to diagnose:

- RPM during SELF-TEST mode.
- ISC solenoid.
- Wiring harness circuits (ISC and VPWR).
- ECA.

To prevent replacement of good components, be aware following non-EEC related areas may be at fault:

- Engine temperature under or over correct operating range.
- A/C input (electrical problem).
- Incorrect idle speed or throttle stop adjustment.
- Faulty cruise control linkage.

92H03851

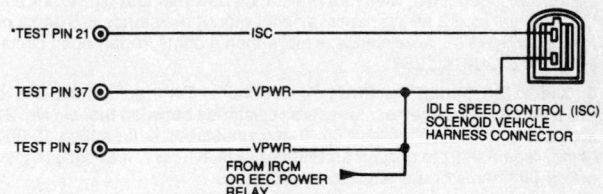

*TEST PIN 21 — ISC

TEST PIN 37 — VPWR
TEST PIN 57 — VPWR

IDLE SPEED CONTROL (ISC) SOLENOID VEHICLE HARNESS CONNECTOR

FROM IRCM OR EEC POWER RELAY

Fig. KE1: Idle Speed Control (Air By-Pass) Circuit

TEST PIN NO. 21 (ISC) WIRE COLOR IDENTIFICATION

Application	Wire Color
All Models	White/Light Blue

CIRCUIT TEST KE (Cont.)

TEST PINS NO. 37 & 57 (VPWR) WIRE COLOR IDENTIFICATION

Application	Wire Color
All Models	Red

1) Code 12/412 Or 16 – Code 12/412 indicates engine RPM could not be controlled within upper RPM limit during KOER SELF-TEST. Code 16 indicates engine RPM was too low to perform HEGO test during KOER SELF-TEST. Possible causes for this fault are:
- Open or shorted circuit.
- Sticking or binding throttle linkage.
- Incorrect idle airflow setting.
- Throttle body or ISC solenoid contaminated.
- Faulty ISC solenoid.
- Faulty ECA.
- Mechanical faults unrelated to EEC-IV which could affect RPM.

Turn ignition off. Connect tachometer to engine. Start engine. Disconnect Idle Speed Control (ISC) harness. If RPM drops or engine stalls, go to step **2)**. If RPM does not drop or engine does not stall, go to step **3)**.

2) Check For EGR Codes – If EGR service Code 31/327, 32/326/328, 33/332, 34/336/334 or 213 is displayed, reconnect ISC solenoid. Go to appropriate KOER SELF-TEST. See SERVICE CODE REFERENCE CHARTS. If these codes are not displayed, go to step **3)**.

3) Check For Other EEC-IV Codes – If Code 22/126, 41/172, 42/173, 91/136 or 92/137 is displayed, reconnect ISC solenoid. Go to appropriate KOER SELF-TEST. See SERVICE CODE REFERENCE CHARTS. If these codes are not displayed, go to step **4)**.

4) Measure ISC Solenoid Resistance – Turn ignition off. Disconnect ISC solenoid. Connect DVOM positive lead to VPWR terminal and negative lead to ISC terminal. See Fig. KE2. Measure resistance of ISC solenoid. If resistance is not 6-13 ohms, replace ISC solenoid and repeat QUICK TEST. If resistance is 6-13 ohms, go to step **5)**.

90H13141

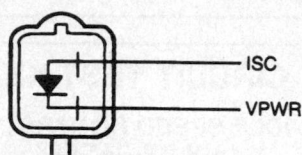

Fig. KE2: ISC Solenoid Connector

5) Check For Internal Short To ISC Solenoid Case – Turn ignition off. With ISC solenoid disconnected, measure resistance from either ISC terminal pin to ISC solenoid housing. If resistance is more than 10,000 ohms, go to step **6)**. If resistance is 10,000 ohms or less, replace ISC solenoid. Repeat QUICK TEST.

6) Check VPWR Circuit Voltage – Leave ISC harness disconnected. Turn ignition on. Measure voltage between VPWR terminal at ISC harness connector and battery ground terminal. If voltage is 10.5 volts or more, go to step **7)**. If voltage is less than 10.5 volts, repair open in circuit and repeat QUICK TEST.

7) Check ISC Circuit Continuity – Turn ignition off. Leave ISC solenoid disconnected. Disconnect 60-pin ECA connector. Inspect terminals, and repair if damaged. Install EEC-IV Breakout Box (T83L-50-EEC-IV), leaving ECA disconnected. Measure resistance between test pin No. 21 and ISC terminal at ISC wiring harness connector. If resistance is 5 ohms or less, go to step **8)**. If resistance is more than 5 ohms, repair open circuit and repeat QUICK TEST.

8) Check ISC Circuit For Short To Ground – Turn ignition off. Leave ISC solenoid disconnected. Measure resistance between test pin No. 21 and test pins No. 40, 46 and 60. If any resistance is less than 10,000 ohms, repair short to ground and repeat QUICK TEST. If all resistances are 10,000 ohms or more, go to step **9)**.

9) Check ISC Circuit For Short To Power – Turn ignition on. Measure voltage between breakout box test pin No. 21 and chassis ground. If voltage is more than 1.0 volt, repair short circuit. Reconnect all components, and repeat QUICK TEST. If code or symptom is still present, replace ECA. If voltage is 1.0 volt or less, go to step **10)**.

10) Check ISC Signal From ECA – Turn ignition off. Reconnect ISC solenoid. Connect ECA to breakout box. Set DVOM on 20-volt scale. Connect DVOM between test pins No. 21 and 40 at breakout box. Start engine. Observe DVOM while slowly increasing engine speed to 3000 RPM. If DVOM voltage reading is 3.0-11.5 volts, go to step **11)**. If DVOM voltage reading is not 3.0-11.5 volts, remove ISC solenoid to confirm that it is not open. If ISC is okay, replace ECA and repeat QUICK TEST.

CIRCUIT TEST KE (Cont.)

11) Check Base Idle – Verify base idle speed is correct. See ON-VEHICLE ADJUSTMENTS article. If base idle speed is within specification, remove ISC solenoid and inspect for contamination. Repair or replace as necessary. Repeat QUICK TEST. If code or symptom is still present, replace ISC solenoid. If base idle speed is not correct, reset idle speed to specification. Repeat QUICK TEST. If unable to set idle to specification, go to step **12)**.

12) Check For Faults Affecting Idle Speed – Check following mechanical items for faults:
- Throttle linkage and/or cruise control linkage (sticking or binding).
- Throttle body (contamination).
- Vacuum hoses. Check Vehicle Emission Control Information (VECI).
- Check for leaks around ISC solenoid (gaskets, etc.).

If all of these items are okay, remove ISC solenoid and inspect for contamination. Repair or replace as necessary. Repeat QUICK TEST. If code or symptom is still present, replace ISC solenoid. If any of these items are faulty, service as necessary. Remove breakout box. Reconnect components, and repeat QUICK TEST.

NOTE: A break in step numbering sequence occurs at this point. Procedure skips from step 12) to step 15). No test procedures have been omitted.

15) Code 13/411 – Code 13/411 indicates engine RPM could not be controlled within lower RPM limit during KOER SELF-TEST. Possible causes for this fault are:
- Incorrect idle airflow setting.
- Vacuum leaks.
- Sticking or binding throttle linkage.
- Throttle plates open.
- Incorrect ignition timing (TFI ignition only).
- Throttle body or ISC solenoid contamination.
- ISC circuit shorted to ground.
- Faulty ISC solenoid.

If above items are okay and idle is set to specification, remove ISC solenoid and inspect for contamination. Repair or replace as necessary. Repeat QUICK TEST. If code or symptom is present, replace ISC solenoid. If idle speed is not set to specification, reset and repeat QUICK TEST. If idle speed cannot be set to specification, go to next step.

16) Check For Conditions Affecting Idle Speed – Check following mechanical components:
- Vacuum hoses. Check Vehicle Emission Control Information (VECI).
- Throttle linkage and/or cruise control linkage (sticking or binding).
- Induction system (vacuum leaks).
- Throttle body (contamination).
- Ensure throttle plates are fully closed.
- Ensure CANP solenoid is not stuck open.
- Ensure base ignition timing is to specification on emission decal (TFI vehicles only).

If above items are okay, go to step **17)**. If fault is found, service as necessary and repeat QUICK TEST.

17) Check For Internal Short To ISC Solenoid Case – With ignition off and ISC solenoid disconnected, set DVOM on 200-k/ohm scale. Measure resistance from either ISC terminal pin to ISC solenoid housing. If resistance is more than 10,000 ohms, go to step **18)**. If resistance is 10,000 ohms or less, replace ISC solenoid. Repeat QUICK TEST.

18) Check ISC Circuit For Short To Ground – Turn ignition off. Leave ISC solenoid disconnected. Disconnect 60-pin ECA connector. Inspect terminals, and repair if damaged. Install EEC-IV Breakout Box (T83L-50-EEC-IV), leaving ECA disconnected. Measure resistance between test pin No. 21 and test pins No. 40, 46 and 60. If any resistance is less than 10,000 ohms, repair short to ground. Reconnect components, and repeat QUICK TEST. If all resistances are 10,000 ohms or more, go to step **19)**.

19) Check ISC Signal From ECA – Turn ignition off. Connect ECA to breakout box. Reconnect ISC solenoid. Set DVOM on 20-volt scale. Connect DVOM between test pins No. 21 and 40. Start engine. Observe DVOM while slowly increasing and decreasing engine RPM. If voltage is 3.0-11.5 volts, remove ISC solenoid and inspect for contamination. Repair or replace as necessary, and repeat QUICK TEST. If code or symptom is still present, replace ISC solenoid. If voltage is not 3.0-11.5 volts, replace ECA and repeat QUICK TEST.

CIRCUIT TEST KM

WIDE OPEN THROTTLE A/C CUT-OUT (WAC) & A/C DEMAND SWITCH

Diagnostic Aids – Perform this test when diagnosing a symptom. To prevent replacing good components, check following non-EEC components and systems:

- Refrigerant charge.
- Low ambient temperature (less than 45°F).

This test is only intended to diagnose:

- Wiring harness circuits (WAC, VPWR, GND, POWER-TO-CLUTCH and ACD).
- WAC relay.
- A/C fan controller.
- ECA.

92E03864

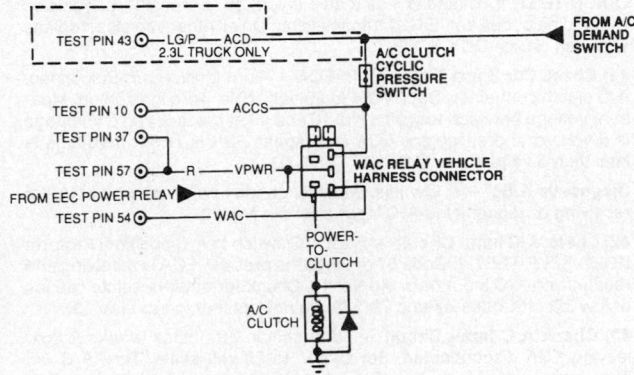

Fig. KM1: WOT A/C Cut-Out Circuit (Aerostar, Explorer & Ranger)

91E09205

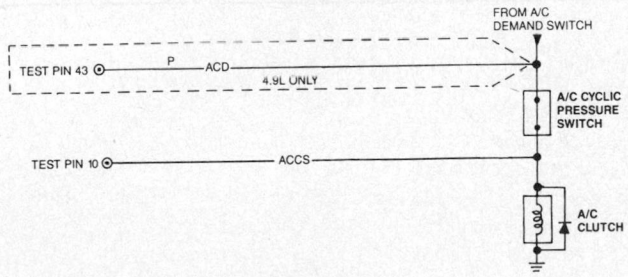

Fig. KM2: WOT A/C Cut-Out Circuit (Bronco, Pickup & Van)

TEST PIN NO. 10 (ACCS) WIRE COLOR IDENTIFICATION

Application	Wire Color
Aerostar, Bronco, Pickup & Van	Black/Yellow
Explorer & Ranger	Dark Green/Orange

TEST PIN NO. 54 (WAC) WIRE COLOR IDENTIFICATION

Application	Wire Color
Aerostar	Gray/White
Explorer & Ranger	Pink/Yellow

1) No A/C: Check For Voltage At A/C Clutch – Check all A/C-related fuses in fuse panel before proceeding with this test. Turn ignition off. Disconnect A/C clutch wiring harness connector. Turn A/C switch to A/C position. Start engine, and wait 10 seconds. Measure voltage between power side of A/C clutch wiring harness connector and negative battery terminal. If voltage is 10.5 volts or more, EEC-IV system is okay. Check A/C system. If voltage is less than 10.5 volts, go to next step.

2) Check Continuity Of POWER-TO-CLUTCH Circuit – Turn ignition off. Disconnect A/C clutch and WAC relay wiring harness connectors.

CIRCUIT TEST KM (Cont.)

Measure resistance between power side of A/C clutch wiring harness connector and POWER-TO-CLUTCH terminal at WAC relay wiring harness connector. If resistance is 5 ohms or less, reconnect A/C clutch and go to step 3). If resistance is more than 5 ohms, repair open circuit and retest system.

3) Check For Power On A/C Demand Circuit – Turn ignition on. Turn A/C switch on. Set DVOM to 20-volt scale. Measure voltage between A/C demand input terminal at WAC relay wiring harness connector and chassis ground.

If voltage is 10.5 volts or more, go to step 5). If voltage is less than 10.5 volts, verify operation of A/C clutch cycling pressure switch and A/C demand switch. If components are okay, repair open circuit and reconnect all components. Recheck system.

4) Check Continuity Between WAC Relay & A/C Relay – Turn ignition off. Disconnect WAC and A/C relays. Set DVOM on 200-ohm scale. Measure resistance between A/C relay output to WAC relay circuit at A/C relay wiring harness connector and A/C relay input at WAC relay wiring harness connector. If resistance is less than 5 ohms, reconnect WAC relay and check A/C system. If resistance is 5 ohms or more, repair open circuit. Connect relays, and check system operation.

5) Check WAC Circuit For Short To Ground – Turn ignition off. Disconnect 60-pin ECA connector. Disconnect WAC relay. Inspect wiring, and repair if damaged. Measure resistance between WAC terminal at WAC relay and chassis ground. If resistance is less than 10,000 ohms, repair short and recheck system operation. If resistance is 10,000 ohms or more, go to step 6).

6) Check For Voltage At ACCS Input To ECA – Turn ignition off. Install EEC-IV Breakout Box (T83L-50-EEC-IV), leaving ECA disconnected. Set A/C switch to A/C position. Turn ignition on. Measure voltage between test pins No. 10 and 40 at breakout box. If voltage is 10.5 volts or less, repair open circuit. Connect all components, and check system operation. If voltage is more than 10.5 volts, go to step 7).

7) Check WAC Relay – Turn ignition off. Connect WAC relay, leaving A/C clutch disconnected. Turn ignition on. Set A/C switch to A/C position. Measure voltage between power side of A/C clutch wiring harness connector and negative battery terminal. If voltage is 10.5 volts or more, replace ECA. If voltage is less than 10.5 volts, replace WAC relay.

NOTE: A break in step numbering sequence occurs at this point. Procedure skips from step 7) to step 15). No test procedures have been omitted.

15) No A/C Output At WOT: Enter Output State Check – Use only VOM or DVOM for this step. DO NOT use scan tester. Turn ignition off. Disconnect cruise control servo wiring harness connector. Connect DVOM negative lead to STO terminal at self-test connector. Connect positive lead to positive battery terminal. Install a jumper wire between STI terminal and SIG RTN terminal at self-test connector. *See Fig. QA1* in CIRCUIT TEST QA. Perform KOEO SELF-TEST until continuous memory test is complete. DVOM will read less than 1.0 volt when test is complete to indicate ECA has entered OUTPUT STATE CHECK. Depress and release throttle. If voltage increases to 10.5 volts or more, remain in OUTPUT STATE CHECK and go to step 16). If voltage does not increase to 10.5 volts, depress throttle to WOT and release. If STO voltage does not go high, leave test equipment connected and go to CIRCUIT TEST QC, step 2).

16) Check For VPWR To Relay – With vehicle in OUTPUT STATE CHECK, disconnect wiring harness from WAC relay. Measure voltage between VPWR circuit at WAC relay wiring harness connector and chassis ground. If voltage is less than 10.5 volts, repair open in VPWR circuit between EEC power relay and WAC relay. Remove test equipment, and retest system. If voltage is 10.5 volts or more, go to step 17).

17) Check WAC System For Cycling – Leave vehicle in OUTPUT STATE CHECK. Disconnect WAC relay wiring harness connector. Connect DVOM positive test lead to VPWR circuit and connect negative test lead to WAC circuit at WAC relay wiring harness connector. Check DVOM while depressing and releasing throttle several times to cycle output on and off. If voltage cycles from high to low, replace WAC relay. If voltage does not cycle, remove test leads. Reconnect speed control servo, and go to step 18).

18) Check Continuity Of WAC Circuit – Turn ignition off. Disconnect 60-pin ECA connector. Inspect terminals, and repair if damaged. Install EEC-IV Breakout Box (T83L-50-EEC-IV), leaving ECA disconnected. Measure resistance between test pin No. 54 and WAC terminal at WAC relay wiring harness connector. If resistance is 5 ohms or more, repair open circuit. Reconnect all components, and retest system. If resistance is less than 5 ohms, go to step 19).

CIRCUIT TEST KM (Cont.)

19) Check WAC Circuit For Short To Power – Turn ignition off. Leave ECA and WAC relay disconnected. Turn ignition on. Measure voltage between test pin No. 54 and chassis ground. If voltage is 1.0 volt or less, replace ECA and retest system. If voltage is more than 1.0 volt, repair short circuit. If symptom is still present, replace ECA.

NOTE: A break in step numbering sequence occurs at this point. Procedure skips from step 19) to step 30). No test procedures have been omitted.

30) Cycle A/C Demand Switch – Turn ignition off. Disconnect 60-pin ECA connector. Inspect terminals, and repair if damaged. Install EEC-IV Breakout Box (T83L-50-EEC-IV), leaving ECA disconnected. Connect DVOM negative test lead to test pin No. 40 and positive test lead to test pin No. 43. Turn ignition on. Cycle A/C switch. If voltage goes high and low as switch is cycled, go to step **43)**. If voltage does not cycle, go to step **31)**.

31) Check Continuity Of A/C Demand (ACD) Circuit – Turn ignition off. Measure resistance between test pin No. 43 at breakout box and A/C Demand switch. If resistance is more than 5 ohms, repair open in ACD circuit and repeat QUICK TEST. If resistance is 5 ohms or less, EEC-IV system is okay. Remove breakout box, and reconnect components. Fault is in A/C system.

NOTE: A break in step numbering sequence occurs at this point. Procedure skips from step 31) to step 35). No test procedures have been omitted.

35) Check A/C Demand Circuit For Short To Power – Turn ignition off. Disconnect WAC relay (except 4.9L). Disconnect 60-pin ECA connector. Inspect terminals, and repair if damaged. Install EEC-IV Breakout Box (T83L-50-EEC-IV), leaving ECA disconnected. With A/C Demand switch in OFF position, turn ignition on. Measure voltage between chassis ground and test pin No. 43 at breakout box. If voltage is 1.0 volt or less, EEC-IV system is okay. Fault is in A/C system. If voltage is more than 1.0 volt, check operation of A/C Demand switch. If switch operation is okay, repair short circuit and retest system.

CIRCUIT TEST KM (Cont.)

NOTE: A break in step numbering sequence occurs at this point. Procedure skips from step 35) to step 40). No test procedures have been omitted.

Diagnostic Aids – Before entering this test, ensure A/C selector is in OFF position and shift selector is in PARK position (AXOD-E and E4OD vehicles). If A/C was on, repeat QUICK TEST. If Code 67 or 79/539 is present, continue with this test.

40) Check A/C Input – Code 79/539 indicates ACCS input to ECA was high during SELF-TEST. Code 67 indicates Neutral Drive Switch (NDS) or ACCS circuit voltage was high during SELF-TEST. Turn ignition off. Disconnect 60-pin ECA connector. Inspect terminals, and repair if damaged. Install EEC-IV Breakout Box (T83L-50-EEC-IV), leaving ECA disconnected. Set DVOM to 20-volt scale. Turn ignition on. Measure voltage between test pin No. 10 at breakout box and chassis ground. If voltage is 1.0 volt or more, repair short to power in A/C circuit and repeat QUICK TEST. If voltage is less than 1.0 volt, go to step **41)** for vehicles with 2-digit codes and E4OD transmission. On all other vehicles, replace ECA and repeat QUICK TEST.

41) Check For Short To Power In ECA – Turn ignition off. Disconnect A/C clutch connector. Set DVOM to 20-volt scale. Turn ignition on. Measure voltage between test pins No. 10 and 40 at breakout box. If voltage is 5 volts or more, replace ECA and repeat QUICK TEST. If voltage is less than 5 volts, go to CIRCUIT TEST TD.

Diagnostic Aids – A low idle with A/C on may be caused by ECA not receiving or recognizing A/C input from pin No. 10

42) Check A/C Input Circuit – Turn A/C switch to A/C position. Perform KOEO SELF-TEST. If Code 67 or 79/539 is present, ECA is receiving and recognizing A/C input from pin No. 10. Check for other possible causes of low idle. If Codes 67 and 79/539 are not present, go to step **43)**.

43) Check A/C Input Circuit – Turn ignition off. Install breakout box, leaving ECA disconnected. Set DVOM to 20-volt scale. Turn A/C on. Turn ignition on. Measure voltage between test pins No. 10 and 40. If voltage is 10.5 volts or more, replace ECA and repeat QUICK TEST. If voltage is less than 10.5 volts, repair open A/C circuit. Remove breakout box, reconnect all components and repeat QUICK TEST.

CIRCUIT TEST KP

OCTANE ADJUST

Diagnostic Aids – Enter this test when directed by QUICK TEST. This test is only intended to diagnose:

- Harness circuits (SIG RTN and OCT ADJ).
- Octane shorting bar connector.

Purpose of Octane Adjust Shorting Bar is to provide optimum spark advance for fuel used. If engine detonates (spark knock), remove Octane Shorting Bar. This retards spark advance about 3-4 degrees. If engine continues to detonate, use fuel with a higher octane rating.

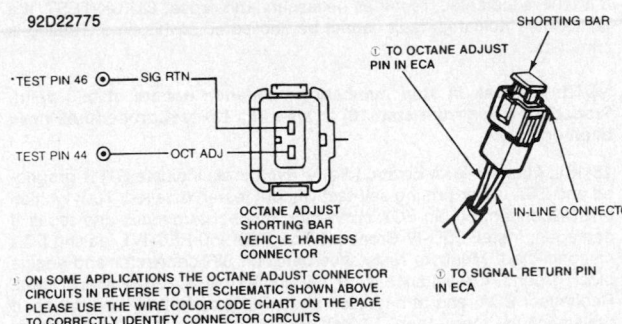

92D22775

① ON SOME APPLICATIONS THE OCTANE ADJUST CONNECTOR CIRCUITS IN REVERSE TO THE SCHEMATIC SHOWN ABOVE. PLEASE USE THE WIRE COLOR CODE CHART ON THE PAGE TO CORRECTLY IDENTIFY CONNECTOR CIRCUITS

*TEST PINS LOCATED ON BREAKOUT BOX.
ALL HARNESS CONNECTORS VIEWED INTO MATING SURFACE.

Fig. KP1: Octane Adjust Circuit

TEST PINS NO. 44 (OCT ADJ) WIRE COLOR IDENTIFICATION

Application	Wire Color
Aerostar 4.0L	Orange
Explorer & Ranger (2.3L & 4.0L)	Dark Green

TEST PIN NO. 46 (SIG RTN) WIRE COLOR IDENTIFICATION

Application	Wire Color
All Models	Gray/Red

1) Code 57/341 – Code 57/431 indicates Octane Adjust Shorting Bar is not in place or OCT ADJ circuit is open. Turn ignition off. Inspect Octane Adjust in-line connector. If shorting bar has been removed, go to step **2)**. If shorting bar is in place, go to step **4)**.

2) Check For Modification Decal – If vehicle has modification decal indicating OCT ADJ shorting bar was removed as a factory authorized procedure, testing is complete. If engine is detonating, go to TROUBLE SHOOTING – NO CODES article. If vehicle does not have modification decal, go to step **3)**.

3) Check For Code 57/341 – Replace OCT ADJ shorting bar. Perform KOEO SELF-TEST. If Code 57/341 is present, go to step **4)**. If code is not present, testing is complete. If driveability faults are present, go to TROUBLE SHOOTING – NO CODES article.

4) Check Octane Adjust Circuit Continuity – Continuity should exist from OCT ADJ circuit, through in-line connector and shorting bar, to SIG RTN circuit. Turn ignition off. Disconnect 60-pin ECA connector. Inspect terminals, and repair if damaged. Install EEC-IV Breakout Box (T83L-50-EEC-IV), leaving ECA disconnected. Measure resistance between test pin No. 46 and OCT ADJ test pin at breakout box. If resistance is more than 5 ohms, repair open OCT ADJ circuit, shorting bar or SIG RTN circuit. Repeat QUICK TEST. If resistance is 5 ohms or less, replace ECA and repeat QUICK TEST.

5) Check For Code 11 – Start engine. Warm it to normal operating temperature. Turn ignition off. Perform KOEO SELF-TEST. If Code 11 or 111 is present, go to step **6)**. If Code 11 or 111 is not present, use higher octane fuel or check for other possible causes for Code 57/341. For all other codes, return to QUICK TEST.

6) Verify In-Line Shorting Bar Is Installed – Turn ignition off. Inspect Octane Adjust in-line connector. If shorting bar is installed, go to step **8)**. If shorting bar is not installed, go to step **7)**.

7) Check For Modification Decal – If vehicle has modification decal indicating OCT ADJ shorting bar was removed as a factory authorized procedure, testing is complete. If engine is detonating, go to TROUBLE SHOOTING – NO CODES article. If vehicle does not have modification decal, go to step **10)**.

CIRCUIT TEST KP (Cont.)

8) Check For Technical Service Bulletin (TSB) – If a TSB authorizing removal of OCT ADJ shorting bar exists, go to step **9)**. If a TSB authorizing removal of OCT ADJ shorting bar does not exist, testing is complete. If driveability faults are present, go to TROUBLE SHOOTING – NO CODES article.

9) Verify Drive Concern – Turn ignition off. Locate and remove shorting bar. Test drive vehicle to verify complaint. If detonation is present, go to step **10)**. If detonation is not present, EEC-IV is okay, testing is complete.

10) Check Octane Adjust Circuit For Short To Ground – Turn ignition off. Disconnect 60-pin ECA connector. Inspect terminals, and repair if damaged. Install EEC-IV Breakout Box (T83L-50-EEC-IV), leaving ECA disconnected. Measure resistance between OCT ADJ circuit at in-line connector and test pins No. 40 and 60 at breakout box. If resistance is 10,000 ohms or less, repair short circuit and repeat QUICK TEST. If each resistance is more than 10,000 ohms, go to step **11)**.

11) Check ECA – Turn ignition off. Disconnect OCT ADJ shorting bar. Turn ignition on. Measure voltage between breakout box OCT ADJ test pin terminal and test pins No. 40 and 60. If voltage is less than 4 volts, replace ECA. If engine still detonates, go to TROUBLE SHOOTING – NO CODES article. If voltage is 4 volts or more, remove breakout box and go to TROUBLE SHOOTING – NO CODES article.

CIRCUIT TEST M

DYNAMIC RESPONSE TEST

Diagnostic Aids – Perform this test only when directed by QUICK TEST. To prevent replacing good components, be aware following non-EEC related areas may be cause of problem:

- Technician did not perform brief Wide Open Throttle (WOT) after Dynamic Response Code.
- Faulty mechanical engine components.
- Engine did not go over 2000 RPM during WOT.

This test is only intended to diagnose:

- Throttle movement (minimum 3/4 throttle).
- RPM increase is more than 2000 RPM.

If throttle is snapped open briefly, it may not pass WOT test. Ensure throttle is depressed fully to WOT and engine speed exceeds 2000 RPM.

1) Code 77/538 Displayed: System Failed To Recognize WOT Test – Repeat KOER SELF-TEST as follows:

- Activate SELF-TEST.
- Start engine.
- Observe ID Code start of test.
- Observe Dynamic Response Code 1 (Code 0 with STAR tester).
- Perform brief WOT.
- Testing is complete; service code output begins.

Ensure vehicle speed reached 2000 RPM during WOT. If Code 77/538 is present, replace ECA. If Code 77/538 is not present, vehicle has passed dynamic response test. Service other codes if necessary.

CIRCUIT TEST ML

SELF-TEST OUTPUT (STO) OR MALFUNCTION INDICATOR LIGHT (MIL)

Diagnostic Aids – Perform this test only when instructed by QUICK TEST or if directed by CIRCUIT TEST QA. This circuit test does not apply to vehicles with electronic instrument cluster. To prevent replacing good components, be aware that fuse, bulb or bulb socket may be cause of problem. This test is only intended to diagnose:

- STO/MIL circuit.
- ECA.

92E22776

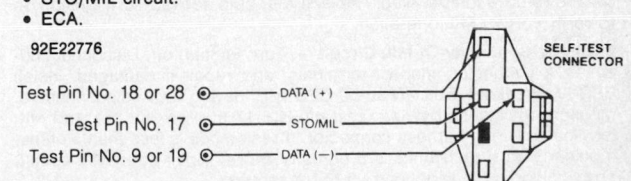

Test Pin No. 18 or 28 — DATA (+)
Test Pin No. 17 — STO/MIL
Test Pin No. 9 or 19 — DATA (–)

SELF-TEST CONNECTOR

*TEST PINS LOCATED ON BREAKOUT BOX
HARNESS CONNECTOR VIEWED INTO MATING SURFACE

Fig. ML1: Identifying Data Communication Link (DCL) Circuit

CIRCUIT TEST ML (Cont.)

TEST PIN NO. 17 (STO/MIL) WIRE COLOR IDENTIFICATION

Application	Wire Color
Aerostar	Tan/Red
Except Aerostar	Pink/Light Green

TEST PIN NO. 18 OR 28 (DATA +) WIRE COLOR IDENTIFICATION

Application	Test Pin No.	Wire Color
Aerostar 3.0L	18	Orange/Black
Aerostar 4.0L	28	Orange/Black
Ranger 3.0L	18	Tan/Orange
All Other Models	28	Tan/Orange

TEST PIN NO. 9 OR 19 (DATA –) WIRE COLOR IDENTIFICATION [1]

Application	Test Pin No.	Wire Color
Aerostar 3.0L	19	Black/Orange
Aerostar 4.0L	9	Black/Orange
Except Aerostar [2]	9	Pink/Light Blue

[1] – Test Pin is not available on 7.3L or 7.5L.

[2] – Test Pin is not available on Bronco 5.0L or Pickup 5.0L, except models equipped with E4OD A/T.

1) Malfunction Indicator Light (MIL) Always On – If vehicle will not start, go to appropriate circuit test:
- For TFI, CIRCUIT TEST AA.
- For DIS, CIRCUIT TEST AB.
- For EDIS, CIRCUIT TEST AC.

Service all KOEO and Continuous Memory Codes before proceeding with this test. Turn ignition off. Disconnect 60-pin ECA connector. Inspect terminals, and repair if damaged. Install EEC-IV Breakout Box (T83L-50-EEC-IV), leaving ECA disconnected. Measure resistance between test pins No. 17 and 40 at breakout box. If resistance is more than 5 ohms, replace ECA and repeat QUICK TEST. If resistance is 5 ohms or less, repair short between test pin No. 17 and self-test connector or between test pin No. 17 and MIL light. Reconnect all components, and repeat QUICK TEST.

NOTE: A break in step numbering sequence occurs at this point. Procedure skips from step 1) to step 4). No test procedures have been omitted.

4) Malfunction Indicator Light (MIL) Does Not Light – If vehicle will not start, go to step 1). Turn ignition on. Measure voltage between negative battery terminal to ground side of MIL fuse. If voltage is more than 10.5 volts, go to step 6). If voltage is 10.5 volts or less, go to step 5).

5) Check For Voltage At Fuse – Turn ignition on. Measure voltage from negative battery terminal to power side of MIL fuse. If voltage is more than 10.5 volts, replace fuse. Verify repair by turning ignition switch to RUN position. If voltage is 10.5 volts or less, repair open MIL/VBAT circuit. Verify repair by turning ignition switch to RUN position.

6) Check Voltage At VBAT Circuit – Turn ignition on. Measure voltage between VBAT side of MIL bulb and negative battery terminal. If voltage is 10.5 volts or less, repair open in MIL circuit between fuse and bulb. Verify repair by turning ignition switch to RUN position. If voltage is more than 10.5 volts, go to step 7).

7) Check MIL Bulb Response To Grounding – Turn ignition off. Attach jumper wire between ground side of MIL bulb socket and chassis ground. Turn ignition on. If MIL light comes on, turn ignition off. Remove jumper wire, and go to step 8). If MIL light does not come on, turn ignition off and remove jumper wire. Replace MIL bulb socket. Turn ignition on to verify correct MIL operation.

8) Check Continuity Of MIL Circuit – Turn ignition off. Disconnect 60-pin ECA connector. Inspect terminals, and repair if damaged. Install EEC-IV Breakout Box (T83L-50-EEC-IV), leaving ECA disconnected. Measure resistance between test pin No. 17 at breakout box and MIL terminal at wiring harness connector. If resistance is less than 5 ohms, replace ECA. If resistance is 5 ohms or more, repair open MIL circuit. Turn ignition on to verify correct MIL operation.

NOTE: A break in step numbering sequence occurs at this point. Procedure skips from step 8) to step 10). No test procedures have been omitted.

CIRCUIT TEST ML (Cont.)

10) MIL On Intermittently, Check For Intermittent Short From STO To Ground – If vehicle does not start, go to step 1). Light comes on when a fault code is present. Service all fault codes before proceeding. If no codes are output, proceed with this test. Enter KOEO wiggle test. See CONTINUOUS MONITOR MODE (WIGGLE TEST) under QUICK TEST. Check DVOM for indication of fault while performing wiggle test on harness in following areas:
- From self-test connector to dash panel.
- Dash panel to ECA.
- Dash panel to Malfunction Indicator Light (MIL).

If a fault is indicated, repair as necessary and repeat QUICK TEST. If a fault is not indicated, fault cannot be duplicated at this time. Testing is complete.

NOTE: A break in step numbering sequence occurs at this point. Procedure skips from step 10) to step 15). No test procedures have been omitted.

15) MIL Flashes With Erratic Idle – Symptoms indicate STI is grounded and ECA is performing self-test without tester installed. Turn ignition off. Disconnect 60-pin ECA connector. Inspect terminals, and repair if damaged. Install EEC-IV Breakout Box (T83L-50-EEC-IV), leaving ECA disconnected. Measure resistance between STI connector and engine block ground. If resistance is 10,000 ohms or less, repair short circuit. Reconnect ECA, and turn ignition on to verify correct MIL operation. If resistance is more than 10,000 ohms, MIL circuit is okay. Verify symptom, and test for other rough idle symptoms.

NOTE: A break in step numbering sequence occurs at this point. Procedure skips from step 15) to step 20). No test procedures have been omitted.

20) CHECK ENGINE Message Displayed – If vehicle will not start, go to step 1). Perform KOEO SELF-TEST. If result is Code 11-10-11 or Code 111-10-111 (pass code), fault is in instrument cluster. If pass code is not displayed, service codes as necessary.

NOTE: A break in step numbering sequence occurs at this point. Procedure skips from step 20) to step 25). No test procedures have been omitted.

25) Continuous Memory Code 529 Or 533: CHECK ENGINE Or CHECK DCL Message Displayed – Codes 529 and 533 indicate circuit fault has occurred on Data Communications Link (DCL). These codes can occur alone or with another code. Fault will occur under following conditions:
- Code 529 indicates ECA or Data Communicator Link (DCL) circuit failure.
- Code 533 indicates Data Communication Link to Electronic Instrument Cluster circuit failure.

If vehicle does not start, go to step 1). If vehicle starts, clear continuous memory codes. Wait 5 minutes, and repeat KOEO SELF-TEST. If result is pass code (Code 11-10-11 or 111-10-111), fault is in instrument cluster. If pass code is not displayed, service codes as necessary.

CIRCUIT TEST NA

TFI
IGNITION DIAGNOSTIC MONITOR (IDM)

Diagnostic Aids – Perform this test when directed by QUICK TEST. This test is only intended to diagnose EEC-IV portion of ignition system. For additional information on ignition system and component testing, see SYSTEM & COMPONENT TESTING – EEC-IV article. To prevent replacing good components, be aware following non-EEC related areas may be cause of problem:
- TFI module.
- Ignition coil.
- Spark plugs and/or wires.
- Distributor.
- Secondary ignition short to ground.

This test is intended to diagnose:
- IDM circuit.
- ECA assembly.

CIRCUIT TEST NA (Cont.)

91E09210

Fig. NA1: IDM Circuit Schematic (2.9L, 4.9L, 5.0L, 5.8L & 7.5L)

91G09211

Fig. NA2: IDM Circuit Schematic (3.0L)

TEST PIN NO. 4 (IDM) WIRE COLOR IDENTIFICATION

Application	Wire Color
3.0L	White/Pink
Except 3.0L	Tan/Yellow

TEST PIN NO. 36 (SPOUT) WIRE COLOR IDENTIFICATION

Application	Wire Color
Aerostar	Yellow/Light Green
Except Aerostar	Pink

1) Continuous Memory Code 14/211 – Code 14/211 indicates 2 successive erratic Profile Ignition Pick-Up (PIP) pulses occurred, resulting in a possible engine miss or stall. Check for following possible causes of fault:
- Loose wires or connectors.
- Secondary ignition short to ground.
- On-board transmitter equipment (2-way radio).

Repair any problems found as necessary. Clear code, and repeat QUICK TEST. If problem is not found, go to step **2)** for vehicles with Computer-Controlled Dwell (CCD) or step **3)** for all others. For ignition system application, see FORD MOTOR CO. INTRODUCTION article.

2) Code 18/212: Check IDM Circuit Continuity (CCD) – Continuous Memory Code 18/212 indicates loss of IDM input to ECA. Possible causes for this fault are:
- Open or shorted circuit in wiring harness.
- Faulty TFI module.
- Faulty ECA.

Turn ignition off. Disconnect 60-pin ECA connector. Inspect terminals, and repair if damaged. Install EEC-IV Breakout Box (T83L-50-EEC-IV), leaving ECA disconnected. Disconnect TFI module. Measure resistance between test pin No. 4 at breakout box and IDM terminal at TFI wiring harness connector. If resistance is 5 ohms or less, go to step **4)**. If any resistance is more than 5 ohms, repair open circuit. Clear codes, and repeat QUICK TEST.

CIRCUIT TEST NA (Cont.)

3) Code 18/212: Check IDM Circuit Continuity (Non-CCD) – Continuous Memory Code 18/212 indicates loss of IDM input to ECA. Possible causes for this fault are:
- Open or shorted circuit in wiring harness.
- Faulty TFI module.
- Faulty ECA.

Turn ignition off. Disconnect 60-pin ECA connector. Inspect terminals, and repair if damaged. Install EEC-IV Breakout Box (T83L-50-EEC-IV), leaving ECA disconnected. Disconnect ignition coil and TFI module. Measure resistance between test pin No. 4 at breakout box and IDM terminal at TFI wiring harness connector. If resistance is not 20,000-24,000 ohms, repair open circuit. Clear codes, and repeat QUICK TEST. If resistance is 20,000-24,000 ohms, go to step **4)**.

4) Check IDM Circuit For Short To Power (Except VREF) – Turn ignition off. Leave TFI module disconnected. Measure voltage between breakout box test pin No. 4 and negative battery terminal. Measure voltage between test pin No. 4 and test pins No. 40 and 60 at breakout box. If voltage is more than 10.5 volts, repair short circuit. Clear codes, and repeat QUICK TEST. If voltage is 10.5 volts or less, go to step **5)**.

5) Check IDM Circuit For Short To PIP & VREF – Turn ignition off. Leave ECA and TFI module disconnected. For shorts to PIP, measure resistance between test pins No. 4 and 56 at breakout box. For shorts to VREF, measure resistance between test pins No. 4 and 26 at breakout box. If either resistance is 10,000 ohms or less, repair short circuit and repeat QUICK TEST. If each resistance is more than 10,000 ohms, go to step **6)**.

6) Check IDM Circuit For Short To Ground – Turn ignition off. Disconnect ignition coil on vehicles without CCD. On all models, set DVOM to 200-k/ohm scale. Measure resistance between test pin No. 4 and test pins No. 40, 46 and 60 at breakout box. If each resistance is more than 10,000 ohms, go to step **7)**. If any resistance is 10,000 ohms or less, repair short to ground in IDM circuit. Clear codes, and repeat QUICK TEST.

7) Check TFI Module – Turn ignition off. Connect ECA to breakout box. Connect TFI wiring harness connector. Set DVOM to 20-volt scale. Connect DVOM between test pins No. 4 and 16 at breakout box. Start engine. Observe DVOM for voltage surge while lightly tapping on TFI module to simulate road shock. Wiggle all TFI wiring and harness connectors. If fault (voltage surge) is indicated, disconnect and inspect TFI harness connectors and terminals for damage. If connector and terminals are okay, check ignition system. See SYSTEM & COMPONENT TESTING – EEC-IV article. If fault (voltage surge) is indicated, go to step **8)**.

8) Check ECA & Harness Connectors – Turn ignition off. Disconnect ECA 60-pin connector. Inspect connector for damaged pins, corrosion and loose wires. If connector is damaged, repair as necessary. Clear codes, and repeat QUICK TEST. If connector is okay, go to step **9)**.

9) Check ECA For Short To Power – Turn ignition off. Connect ECA to breakout box. Disconnect TFI module. Measure voltage between test pin No. 4 at breakout box and chassis ground. Turn ignition on. Measure voltage between test pin No. 4 and test pins No. 40, 46 and 60 at breakout box. If either voltage reading is more than 10.5 volts, replace ECA and repeat QUICK TEST. If both voltage readings are 10.5 volts or less, go to step **10)**.

10) Check ECA For Short To Ground – Turn ignition off. Connect ECA to breakout box. On models without CCD, disconnect ignition coil. On all models, disconnect TFI module. Measure resistance between test pin No. 4 and test pins No. 40, 46 and 60 at breakout box. If resistance is more than 10,000 ohms, check ignition system. See SYSTEM & COMPONENT TESTING – EEC-IV article. If resistance is 10,000 ohms or less, replace ECA and repeat QUICK TEST.

CIRCUIT TEST NB

DIS
IGNITION DIAGNOSTIC MONITOR (IDM)

Diagnostic Aids – Perform this test when directed by QUICK TEST. This test is only intended to diagnose EEC-IV portion of ignition system. For additional information on ignition system and component testing, see SYSTEM & COMPONENT TESTING – EEC-IV article. To prevent replacing good components, be aware following non-EEC related areas may be cause of problem:
- DIS ignition module.
- DIS coil packs.
- Spark plugs and/or wires.
- Crankshaft sensor.
- Camshaft sensor (if equipped).
- Secondary ignition short to ground.

This test is intended to diagnose:
- IDM, DPI and SAW wiring harness circuits.
- ECA assembly.

91I09212

Fig. NB1: IDM Circuit Schematic (Ranger 2.3L)

TEST PIN NO. 4 (IDM) WIRE COLOR IDENTIFICATION

Application	Wire Color
Ranger 2.3L	Tan/Yellow

DIS MODULE LOCATION TABLE

Application	Location
Ranger 2.3L	Near Right Fuel Rail

1) Continuous Memory Code 211: Erratic Ignition – Code 211 indicates 2 successive erratic Profile Ignition Pick-Up (PIP) pulses occurred. Possible causes for this fault are:
- Loose wires or connectors.
- Secondary ignition short to ground.
- On-board transmitter equipment (2-way radio).

Repair any problems found as necessary. Clear code, and repeat QUICK TEST. If problem is not found, go to step **4)**.

2) Continuous Memory Code 212: Check For Other Codes – Continuous Memory Code 212 indicates loss of IDM input signal to ECA. Possible causes for this fault are:
- Open or shorted harness.
- Faulty DIS module.
- Faulty ECA.

If Continuous Memory Code 215, 216 or 217 is present, go to IGNITION SYSTEMS in SYSTEM & COMPONENT TESTING – EEC-IV article. If Code 215, 216 or 217 is not present, go to step **3)**.

3) Continuous Memory Code 212, 218 Or 222 – Code 212 indicates loss of IDM input signal. Possible causes are:
- Open or shorted wiring harness circuit.
- Faulty ignition module.
- Faulty ECA.

Code 222 indicates IDM input signal is always low. Possible causes are:
- Open or shorted wiring harness circuit.
- Faulty CID sensor.
- VBAT (battery voltage) low at DIS.
- Faulty DIS module.
- Faulty ECA.

CIRCUIT TEST NB (Cont.)

Code 218 indicates IDM input signal is always high. Possible causes are:
- Open signal in wiring harness.
- VBAT open at secondary coil.
- VBAT low at secondary coil.

Turn ignition off. Disconnect 60-pin ECA connector. Inspect terminals, and repair if damaged. Install EEC-IV Breakout Box (T83L-50-EEC-IV), leaving ECA disconnected. Disconnect DIS module connector (pins No. 7-12). Measure resistance between test pin No. 4 at breakout box and DIS module wiring harness connector pin No. 12. If resistance is 5 ohms or less, go to step **4)**. If resistance is more than 5 ohms, repair open circuit. Clear codes, and repeat QUICK TEST.

4) Check IDM Circuit For Short To Power – Turn ignition off. Disconnect DIS module connector (pins No. 1-6). Leave ECA disconnected from breakout box. Turn ignition on. Measure voltage between test pin No. 4 and test pins No. 40 and 60 at breakout box. If voltage is less than 10.5 volts, go to step **5)**. If voltage is 10.5 volts or more, repair short circuit.

5) Check IDM Circuit For Short To VREF & PIP – Turn ignition off. Ensure DIS module (pins No. 1-6) is disconnected. Check VREF circuit by measuring resistance between test pins No. 4 and 26. Check PIP circuit by measuring resistance between test pins No. 4 and 56. If either resistance is less than 10,000 ohms, repair short circuit and repeat QUICK TEST. If each resistance is 10,000 ohms or more, go to step **6)**.

6) Check IDM Circuit For Short To Ground – Turn ignition off. Disconnect DIS module connector (pins No. 7-12). Leave ECA disconnected from breakout box. Measure resistance between test pin No. 4 and test pins No. 16, 20, 40, 46 and 60 at breakout box. If any resistance is less than 10,000 ohms, repair short to ground and repeat QUICK TEST. If each resistance is 10,000 ohms or more, go to step **7)**.

7) Check DIS Module – Turn ignition off. Connect DIS module and ECA to breakout box. Start engine, and allow it to idle. Connect positive lead of DVOM to test pin No. 4 and negative lead to test pin No. 16 and test pin No. 32. Observe DVOM for voltage surge (fault) while lightly tapping on ignition components to simulate road shock. Wiggle all DIS harness connectors. If fault is not indicated, disconnect and inspect DIS wiring harness connectors and terminals for damage. If connectors and terminals are okay, check ignition system. See SYSTEM & COMPONENT TESTING – EEC-IV article. If fault is indicated, leave DVOM connected to breakout box and go to step **8)**.

8) Check EEC-IV Harness – Ensure engine is idling at correct RPM. Wiggle, shake or bend small sections of harness, working from DIS connectors to firewall. Observe DVOM for indication of fault. Repeat process from firewall to ECA. If fault is indicated, isolate fault and repair wiring harness. Repeat QUICK TEST. If no fault is indicated, go to step **9)**.

9) Check ECA & Harness Connectors – Turn ignition off. Disconnect ECA 60-pin connector. Inspect connector for damaged pins, corrosion and loose wires. If connector is damaged, repair as necessary. Clear codes, and repeat QUICK TEST. If connector is okay, go to step **10)**.

10) Check ECA For Short To Ground – Turn ignition off. Disconnect DIS module connector (pins No. 7-12). Connect ECA to breakout box. Measure resistance between test pin No. 4 and pins No. 40, 46 and 60. If each resistance is more than 10,000 ohms, check ignition system. See SYSTEM & COMPONENT TESTING – EEC-IV article. If any resistance is 10,000 ohms or less, replace ECA and repeat QUICK TEST.

NOTE: A break in step numbering sequence occurs at this point. Procedure skips from step 10) to step 20). No test procedures have been omitted.

20) Continuous Memory Code 223 (Ranger 2.3L) – Code 223 indicates open in Dual Plug Inhibit (DPI) circuit or open or short to ground in coil No. 4. Possible causes for this fault are:
- Open or short circuit in wiring harness.
- Faulty ECA.
- Faulty DIS module.
- Faulty coil No. 4.

Turn ignition off. Disconnect DIS connector (pins No. 1-6). Disconnect 60-pin ECA connector. Inspect terminals, and repair if damaged. Install EEC-IV Breakout Box (T83L-50-EEC-IV), leaving ECA disconnected. Measure resistance between pin No. 6 at DIS vehicle harness connector and test pin No. 32 at breakout box. If resistance is 5 ohms or more, repair open circuit and repeat QUICK TEST. If resistance is less than 5 ohms, check ignition system. See SYSTEM & COMPONENT TESTING – EEC-IV article. If ignition system is okay, replace ECA.

CIRCUIT TEST NB (Cont.)

NOTE: A break in step numbering sequence occurs at this point. Procedure skips from step 20) to step 25). No test procedures have been omitted.

25) Hard To Start: Check For Spark During Crank – Use spark tester to check for spark at all spark plug wires while cranking engine. If spark is present and consistent, go to step **26).** If spark is not present or if spark is inconsistent, replace spark plug or spark plug wire and repeat QUICK TEST.

26) Hard To Start: Check DPI Circuit – Turn ignition off. Disconnect DIS module (pins No. 1-6). Disconnect 60-pin ECA connector. Inspect terminals and repair if damaged. Install EEC-IV Breakout Box (T83L-50-EEC-IV), leaving ECA disconnected. Measure resistance between test pin No. 32 and test pins No. 40 and 60 at breakout box. If resistance is 100,000 ohms or less, repair short circuit and repeat QUICK TEST. If resistance is more than 100,000 ohms, go to step **27).**

27) Check ECA For Short To Ground – Turn ignition off. Connect ECA to breakout box. Measure resistance between test pin No. 32 and test pins No. 40 and 60 at breakout box. If resistance is 500 ohms or less, replace ECA and repeat QUICK TEST. If resistance is more than 500 ohms, check ignition system. See SYSTEM & COMPONENT TESTING – EEC-IV article.

CIRCUIT TEST NC

EDIS
IGNITION DIAGNOSTIC MONITOR (IDM)

Diagnostic Aids – Perform this test when directed by QUICK TEST. This test is only intended to diagnose EEC-IV portion of ignition system. For additional information on ignition system and component testing, see SYSTEM & COMPONENT TESTING – EEC-IV article. To prevent replacing good components, be aware following non-EEC related areas may be at fault:
- EDIS ignition module.
- EDIS coil packs.
- Spark plugs and/or wires.
- Variable reluctance sensor.
- Secondary ignition short to ground.

This test is intended to diagnose:
- IDM and SAW harness circuits.
- ECA assembly.

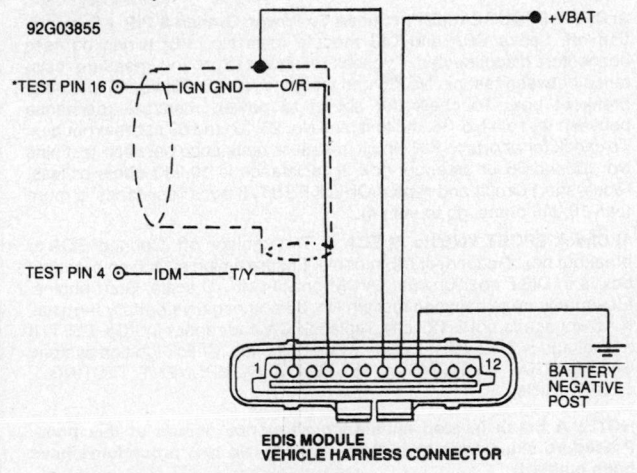

**EDIS MODULE
VEHICLE HARNESS CONNECTOR**

***TEST PINS LOCATED ON BREAKOUT BOX
ALL HARNESS CONNECTORS VIEWED INTO MATING SURFACE**

Fig. NC1: IDM Circuit Schematic (4.0L)

CIRCUIT TEST NC (Cont.)

1) Continuous Memory Code 211: Erratic Ignition – Code 211 indicates 2 successive erratic Profile Ignition Pick-Up (PIP) pulses occurred. Possible causes for this fault are:
- Loose wires or connectors.
- Secondary ignition short to ground.
- On-board transmitter equipment (2-way radio).

Repair any problems found as necessary. Clear codes, and repeat QUICK TEST. If problem is not found, go to step **4).**

2) Code 226: IDM Circuit Failure – Code 226 indicates ECA did not receive IDM signal from EDIS module in KOEO SELF-TEST. Possible causes for this problem are:
- Open or short in IDM or IGN GND circuit wiring harness.
- Faulty EDIS module.

If engine does not start, go to IGNITION SYSTEMS in SYSTEM & COMPONENT TESTING – EEC-IV article. If engine starts, go to step **4).**

3) Continuous Memory Code 212: Check For Other Codes – Code 212 indicates loss of IDM input signal to ECA. Possible causes for this fault are:
- Open or short circuit in wiring harness.
- Faulty EDIS module.
- Faulty ECA.

If Continuous Memory Code 215, 216 or 217 is also present, go to IGNITION SYSTEMS in SYSTEM & COMPONENT TESTING – EEC-IV article. If Code 215, 216 or 217 is not also present, go to step **4).**

4) Continuous Memory Code 212: Check IDM Circuit Continuity – Turn ignition off. Disconnect EDIS module. Disconnect 60-pin ECA connector. Inspect terminals, and repair if damaged. Install EEC-IV Breakout Box (T83L-50-EEC-IV), leaving ECA disconnected. Measure resistance between test pin No. 4 at breakout box and pin No. 2 at EDIS module wiring harness connector. If resistance is 5 ohms or more, repair open circuit. Clear codes, and repeat QUICK TEST. If resistance is less than 5 ohms, go to step **5).**

5) Check IDM Circuit For Short To Power (Except VREF) – Turn ignition off. Ensure ECA and EDIS module are disconnected. Monitor circuit voltage by connecting DVOM between test pin No. 4 and test pins No. 40 and 60. To check VBAT circuit, turn ignition off. To check VPWR circuit, turn ignition on. If either voltage reading is more than 10.5 volts, repair short circuit and repeat QUICK TEST. If voltage is 10.5 volts or less, go to step **6).**

6) Check IDM Circuit For Short To VREF & PIP – Turn ignition off. Ensure ECA and EDIS module are disconnected. To check for shorts to VREF, use DVOM to measure resistance between test pins No. 4 and 26 at breakout box. To test for shorts to PIP, measure resistance between test pins No. 4 and 56 at breakout box. If either resistance is 10,000 ohms or less, repair short circuit and repeat QUICK TEST. If each resistance is more than 10,000 ohms, go to step **7).**

Diagnostic Aids – When 4-wire HEGO is connected to vehicle harness, a short to SIG RTN (pin No. 46) may be indicated along with an actual short to PWR GND.

7) Check IDM Circuit For Short To Ground – Turn ignition off. Ensure ECA and EDIS module are disconnected. Measure resistance between test pin No. 4 and test pins No. 40, 46 and 60 at breakout box. If any resistance is less than 10,000 ohms, repair short to ground in IDM circuit and repeat QUICK TEST. If all resistances are 10,000 ohms or more, go to step **8).**

8) Check EDIS Module – Turn ignition off. Connect EDIS module to wiring harness connector. Connect ECA to breakout box. Start engine, and allow it to idle. Connect positive lead of DVOM to test pin No. 4 and negative lead to test pin No. 16. Observe DVOM for voltage surge (fault) while lightly tapping on ignition components to simulate road shock. Wiggle all EDIS harness connectors. If fault is not indicated, disconnect and inspect EDIS wiring harness connectors and terminals for damage. If connectors and terminals are okay, check ignition system. See SYSTEM & COMPONENT TESTING – EEC-IV article. If fault is indicated, leave DVOM connected to breakout box and go to step **9).**

9) Check EEC-IV Harness – Ensure engine is idling at correct RPM. Wiggle, shake or bend small sections of harness, working from DIS connectors to firewall. Observe DVOM for indication of fault. Repeat process from firewall to ECA. If fault is indicated, isolate fault and repair wiring harness. Repeat QUICK TEST. If no fault is indicated, go to step **10).**

10) Check ECA & Harness Connectors – Turn ignition off. Disconnect ECA 60-pin connector. Inspect connector for damaged pins, corrosion and loose wires. If connector is damaged, repair as necessary ford repeat QUICK TEST. If connector is okay, go to step **11).**

CIRCUIT TEST NC (Cont.)

11) Check ECA For Short To Ground – Turn ignition off. Disconnect EDIS module connector. Connect ECA to breakout box. Measure resistance between test pin No. 4 and test pins No. 16, 20, 40, 46 and 60. If each resistance is more than 10,000 ohms, check ignition system. See SYSTEM & COMPONENT TESTING – EEC-IV article. If any resistance is 10,000 ohms or less, replace ECA and repeat QUICK TEST.

CIRCUIT TEST PA

SPARK TIMING CHECK
(TFI VEHICLES)

Diagnostic Aids – Perform this test when checking computed timing or if directed by QUICK TEST. This test is intended to diagnose:
- SPOUT wiring harness circuit.
- Base timing.
- Faulty ECA.

To prevent replacing good components, be aware following non-EEC related areas may be at fault:
- Basic engine condition (valves, vacuum leaks, valve timing, etc.).
- Distributor.
- TFI module.

91J09217

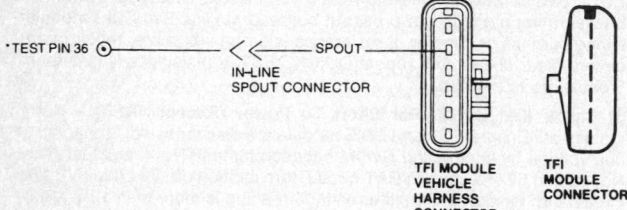

Fig. PA1: TFI Spark Timing Check Circuit

TEST PIN NO. 36 (SPOUT) WIRE COLOR IDENTIFICATION

Application	Wire Color
Aerostar	Yellow/Light Green
All Others	Pink

1) Check For Power To ECA – Turn ignition off. Disconnect 60-pin ECA connector. Inspect terminals, and repair if damaged. Install EEC-IV Breakout Box (T83L-50-EEC-IV), leaving ECA disconnected. Turn ignition on. Measure voltage between test pins No. 37 and 40 and between test pins No. 57 and 60 at breakout box. If either voltage reading is less than 10.5 volts, go to CIRCUIT TEST B. If both voltage readings are 10.5 volts or more, go to step 2).

2) Check SPOUT Circuit For Continuity – Turn ignition off. Disconnect TFI module. Measure resistance between test pin No. 36 at breakout box and SPOUT terminal at TFI module wiring harness connector. If resistance is more than 5 ohms, repair open circuit. Reconnect all components, and verify ignition timing is correct. If resistance is 5 ohms or less, go to step 3).

3) Check SPOUT Voltage At ECA – Turn ignition off. Connect ECA to breakout box. Reconnect TFI module. Ensure timing switch on breakout box is in DIST position. Set DVOM on 20-volt AC scale. Start engine. Measure voltage between test pin No. 36 and negative battery terminal. If voltage is 3-10 volts AC, EEC-IV system is okay. Check ignition system. See IGNITION SYSTEMS in SYSTEM & COMPONENT TESTING – EEC-IV article. If voltage is not 3-10 volts, replace ECA and repeat QUICK TEST.

CIRCUIT TEST PB

SPARK TIMING CHECK
(DIS VEHICLES)

Diagnostic Aids – Perform this test when checking computed timing or if directed by QUICK TEST. This test is intended to diagnose:
- SPOUT wiring harness circuit.
- Base timing.
- Faulty ECA.

To prevent replacing good components, be aware following non-EEC related areas may be at fault:
- Basic engine condition (valves, vacuum leaks, valve timing, etc.).
- DIS module.
- Camshaft sensor.
- Crankshaft sensor.

92A03857

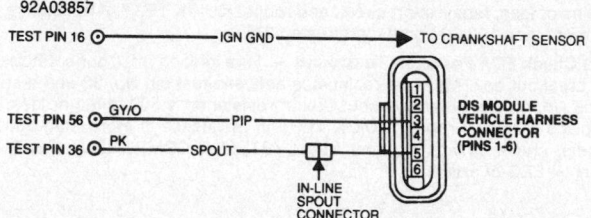

Fig. PB1: Identifying DIS Module Wiring Harness Connector Terminals (Ranger 2.3L)

TEST PIN NO. 16 (IGN GND) WIRE COLOR IDENTIFICATION

Application	Wire Color
Ranger 2.3L	Orange/Red

1) Check For Power To ECA – Turn ignition off. Disconnect 60-pin ECA connector. Inspect terminals, and repair if damaged. Install EEC-IV Breakout Box (T83L-50-EEC-IV), leaving ECA disconnected. Turn ignition on. Measure voltage between test pins No. 37 and 40 and between test pins No. 57 and 60 at breakout box. If either reading is less than 10.5 volts, go to CIRCUIT TEST B. If both readings are 10.5 volts or more, go to step 2).

2) Check SPOUT Circuit For Continuity – Turn ignition off. Disconnect DIS module wiring harness connector (pins No. 1-6). Measure resistance between test pin No. 36 at breakout box and SPOUT terminal at DIS module wiring harness connector. If resistance is more than 5 ohms, repair open circuit and check ignition timing. If resistance is 5 ohms or less, go to step 3).

3) Check SPOUT Circuit For Shorts To Power, Ground & PIP – Turn ignition off. Leave ECA and DIS module (pins No. 1-6) wiring harness connectors disconnected. To check for shorts to ground, measure resistance between test pins No. 16, 20, 40, 46 and 60 at breakout box. To check for shorts to power, measure resistance between test pin No. 36 and test pins No. 26, 37 and 57 at breakout box. To check for shorts to PIP circuit, measure resistance between test pins No. 36 and 56 at breakout box. If resistance is 10,000 ohms or less, repair short circuit and repeat QUICK TEST. If each resistance is more than 10,000 ohms, go to step 4).

4) Check SPOUT Voltage At ECA – Turn ignition off. Connect ECA to breakout box. Reconnect DIS module. Ensure timing switch on breakout box is in DIST position. Set DVOM on 20-volt AC scale. Start engine. Measure voltage between test pin No. 36 and negative battery terminal. If AC voltage is not 3-12 volts, replace ECA and repeat QUICK TEST. If AC voltage is 3-12 volts, EEC-IV system is okay. Check ignition system. See IGNITION SYSTEMS in SYSTEM & COMPONENT TESTING – EEC-IV article.

NOTE: A break in step numbering sequence occurs at this point. Procedure skips from step 4) to step 10). No test procedures have been omitted.

10) Continuous Memory Code 219: Check SPOUT Circuit Continuity – Code 219 indicates ignition timing has defaulted to 10 degrees BTDC. SPOUT signal has a variable duty cycle, with voltage varying from 0.4 volt to battery voltage. In event of a SPOUT failure, DIS module will generate a fixed dwell and constant spark angle, based on CID and PIP signals (FMEM mode). Possible causes for this fault are:
- Faulty DIS module.
- Faulty SPOUT circuit.

CIRCUIT TEST PB (Cont.)

Turn ignition off. Disconnect 60-pin ECA connector. Inspect terminals, and repair if damaged. Install EEC-IV Breakout Box (T83L-50-EEC-IV), leaving ECA disconnected. Disconnect DIS module (pins No. 1-6). Measure resistance between test pin No. 36 at breakout box and SPOUT terminal at DIS module harness connector. If resistance is 5 ohms or less, go to step **11)**. If resistance is more than 5 ohms, check SPOUT in-line connector. If connector is okay, repair open circuit and repeat QUICK TEST.

11) Check SPOUT For Short To Power & Ground – Turn ignition off. Leave ECA and DIS module disconnected. Measure resistance between test pin No. 36 and test pins No. 16 and 40 at breakout box. Measure resistance between test pin No. 36 and negative battery terminal. If any resistance is 10,000 ohms or less, repair short circuit and repeat QUICK TEST. If each resistance is more than 10,000 ohms, EEC system is okay. Check ignition system. See IGNITION SYSTEMS in SYSTEM & COMPONENT TESTING – EEC-IV article.

CIRCUIT TEST PC

SPARK TIMING CHECK (EDIS VEHICLES)

Diagnostic Aids – Perform this test when checking computed timing or if directed by QUICK TEST. This test is intended to diagnose:
- SAW wiring harness circuit.
- Base timing.
- Faulty ECA.

To prevent replacing good components, be aware following non-EEC related areas may be at fault:
- Basic engine condition (valves, vacuum leaks, valve timing, etc.).
- EDIS module.

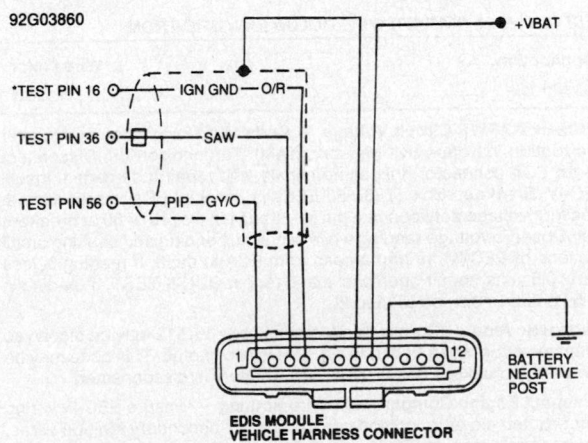

92G03860

Fig. PC1: Identifying EDIS Connector Terminals (4.0L)

TEST PIN NO. 36 (SAW) WIRE COLOR IDENTIFICATION (4.0L)

Application	Wire Color
Aerostar	Yellow/Light Green
Explorer & Ranger	Pink

1) Check For Power To ECA – Turn ignition off. Disconnect 60-pin ECA connector. Inspect terminals, and repair if damaged. Install EEC-IV Breakout Box (T83L-50-EEC-IV), leaving ECA disconnected. Turn ignition on. Measure voltage between test pins No. 37 and 40 at breakout box. Measure voltage between test pins No. 57 and 60 at breakout box. If both readings are 10.5 volts or more, go to step **2)**. If either reading is less than 10.5 volts, go to CIRCUIT TEST B.

CIRCUIT TEST PC (Cont.)

2) Check SAW Circuit For Continuity – Turn ignition off. Disconnect EDIS module. Measure resistance between test pin No. 36 at breakout box and SAW terminal at EDIS module wiring harness connector. See Fig. PC2. If resistance is 5 ohms or less, go to step **3)**. If resistance is more than 5 ohms, repair open circuit. Reconnect all components, and check ignition timing.

91B09223

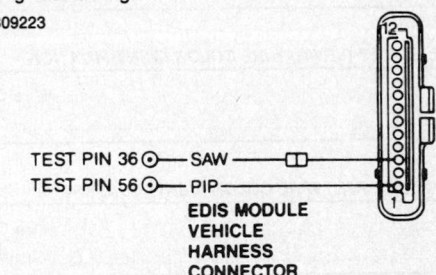

Fig. PC2: Identifying Module Connector Terminals

3) Check SAW Circuit For Shorts To Power (Except VREF) – Turn ignition off. Leave ECA and EDIS module disconnected. Measure voltage between test pin No. 36 and test pin No. 40 or 60 at breakout box. To check for short to VBAT, turn ignition off. To check for short to VPWR, turn ignition on. If any reading is more than 10.5 volts, repair short circuit and repeat QUICK TEST. If voltage is 10.5 volts or less, go to step **4)**.

4) Check SAW Circuit For Shorts To VREF, Ground & PIP – Turn ignition off. Leave ECA and EDIS module disconnected. To check for shorts to ground, measure resistance between test pin No. 36 and test pins No. 16, 20, 40, 46 and 60. To check for shorts to VREF, measure resistance between test pins No. 26 and 36. To check for shorts to PIP circuit, measure resistance between test pins No. 36 and 56. If each resistance is more than 10,000 ohms, go to step **5)**. If resistance is 10,000 ohms or less, repair short circuit and repeat QUICK TEST.

Diagnostic Aids – During this test, a short to SIG RTN (pin No. 46) may be indicated along with an actual short to PWR GND when 4-wire HEGO is connected to vehicle wiring harness.

5) Check SAW Voltage At ECA – Turn ignition off. Connect ECA to breakout box. Reconnect EDIS module. Place timing switch on breakout box in DIST position. Set DVOM on 20-volt AC scale. Start engine. Measure voltage between test pin No. 36 and negative battery terminal. If AC voltage is not 0.1-1.9 volts, replace ECA and repeat QUICK TEST. If AC voltage within specification, EEC-IV system is okay. Remove breakout box, reconnect ECA and check ignition system. See SYSTEM & COMPONENT TESTING – EEC-IV article.

CIRCUIT TEST QA

NO CODES/CODES NOT LISTED

Diagnostic Aids – Perform this test when directed by QUICK TEST or other test procedures. This test is intended to diagnose:
- ECA.
- EEC power relay.
- Harness circuits (SIG RTN, STO, STI, VPWR and VREF).

Aftermarket devices, such as alarm system, may cause SELF-TEST to abort if wiring is connected to certain EEC components. If a device is installed, disconnect it completely from EEC system. Before continuing with this circuit test, restore EEC circuits to original state and repeat QUICK TEST.

92A03862

*TEST PIN 46 ⊙ — SIG RTN
MALFUNCTION INDICATOR LIGHT (MIL)
VBAT — MIL
TEST PIN 17 ⊙ — STO
TEST PIN 48 ⊙ — STI
TEST PIN 37 ⊙ — VPWR
TEST PIN 57 ⊙ — VPWR
SELF-TEST CONNECTOR
PIGTAIL CONNECTOR TO SELF-TEST INPUT
FROM EEC POWER RELAY OR IRCM

*TEST PIN LOCATED ON BREAKOUT BOX
ALL HARNESS CONNECTORS VIEWED INTO MATING SURFACES

Fig. QA1: No Codes/Codes Not Listed Circuits

CIRCUIT TEST QA (Cont.)

TEST PIN NO. 17 (STO & MIL) WIRE COLOR IDENTIFICATION

Application	Wire Color
Aerostar	Tan/Red
Except Aerostar	Pink/Light Green

TEST PINS NO. 37 & 57 (VPWR) WIRE COLOR IDENTIFICATION

Application	Wire Color
All Models	Red

TEST PIN NO. 46 (SIG RTN) WIRE COLOR IDENTIFICATION

Application	Wire Color
All Models	Gray/Red

TEST PIN NO. 48 (STI) WIRE COLOR IDENTIFICATION

Application	Wire Color
Aerostar	White/Red
Except Aerostar	White/Pink

1) Check VREF Voltage At Self-Test Connector – Turn ignition off. Disconnect 60-pin ECA connector. Inspect terminals, and repair if damaged. Install EEC-IV Breakout Box (T83L-50-EEC-IV). Connect ECA to breakout box. Set DVOM on 20-volt scale. Turn ignition on. Measure voltage between test pin No. 26 at breakout box and SIG RTN terminal at self-test connector. If reading is 4-6 volts, go to step **3)**. If reading is not 4-6 volts, go to step **2)**.

2) Check STI Circuit Continuity – Turn ignition off. Disconnect ECA from breakout box. Measure resistance between test pin No. 48 at breakout box and SIG RTN terminal at self-test connector. If resistance is less than 5 ohms, go to CIRCUIT TEST C. If resistance is 5 ohms or more, repair open circuit and repeat QUICK TEST.

3) Check STI Circuit Continuity – Turn ignition off. Disconnect ECA from breakout box. Measure resistance between test pin No. 48 at breakout box and Self-Test Input (STI) terminal at pigtail connector. If resistance is 5 ohms or more, repair open circuit and repeat QUICK TEST. If resistance is less than 5 ohms, go to step **4)**.

4) Check STO Circuit Continuity – Turn ignition off. Leave ECA disconnected from breakout box. Measure resistance between test pin No. 17 at breakout box and STO terminal at self-test connector. If resistance is less than 5 ohms, go to step **5)**. If resistance is 5 ohms or more, repair open circuit and repeat QUICK TEST.

5) Check EGO Signal For Short To Power – Turn ignition off. Leave ECA disconnected from breakout box. Measure voltage between test pin No. 40 or 60 and HEGO SIGNAL test pin No. 29 or 44 at breakout box. For HEGO circuit schematics, see Figs. H1-H5 in CIRCUIT TEST H. If voltage is more than 2 volts, go to step **6)**. If voltage is 2 volts or less, go to step **7)**.

6) Isolate Short To Harness Or HEGO Sensor – Turn ignition off. Leave ECA disconnected from breakout box. Disconnect right/rear HEGO sensor connector. Turn ignition on. Measure voltage between HEGO SIGNAL test pin No. 29 or 44 and test pin No. 40 or 60 at breakout box. If voltage is 2 volts or more, repair short to power in HEGO SIGNAL circuit. Reconnect all components, and repeat QUICK TEST. If voltage is less than 2 volts, replace right/rear HEGO sensor. Reconnect all components, and repeat QUICK TEST.

7) Check STO Circuit For Short To Ground – Turn ignition off. Leave ECA disconnected from breakout box. Measure resistance between STO terminal at self-test connector and engine ground. If resistance is more than 5 ohms, go to step **8)**. If resistance is 5 ohms or less, repair STO or MIL circuit for short to ground and repeat QUICK TEST.

8) Check If Power Relay Is Always On – Turn ignition off. Leave ECA disconnected from breakout box. Connect DVOM between test pin No. 37 or 57 and pin No. 40 or 60 at breakout box. Turn ignition on and then off. Wait 10 seconds. If voltage does not change from 10.5 volts (or more) to less than 1.0 volt, go to step **9)**. If voltage changes from 10.5 volts (or more) to less than 1.0 volt, go to step **10)**.

CIRCUIT TEST QA (Cont.)

9) Check VPWR Circuit For Short To Power – Turn ignition off. Leave ECA disconnected from breakout box. Disconnect EEC power relay. Connect DVOM to test pin No. 37 or 57 and test pin No. 40 or 46 at breakout box. If voltage is more than 1.0 volt, repair VPWR circuit short to power. Reconnect ECA, and repeat QUICK TEST. If voltage is 1.0 volt or less, replace EEC-IV power relay. Reconnect ECA, and repeat QUICK TEST.

10) Check Malfunction Indicator Light (MIL) Function – If MIL is always on, go to CIRCUIT TEST ML, step **1)**. If MIL is always off, go to CIRCUIT TEST ML, step **4)**. If MIL is working normally, replace ECA and repeat QUICK TEST.

CIRCUIT TEST QB

CONTINUOUS MEMORY CODE 15 OR 512

Diagnostic Aids – Perform this test when directed by QUICK TEST. This test is intended to diagnose:

- ECA.
- KAPWR wiring harness circuits.

92C03863

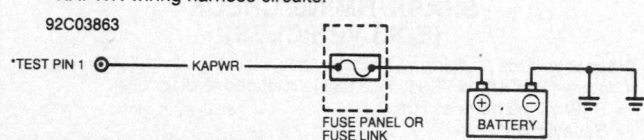

* TEST PINS LOCATED ON BREAKOUT BOX. ALL HARNESS CONNECTORS VIEWED INTO MATING SURFACES.

Fig. QB1: KAPWR Circuit

TEST PIN NO. 1 (KAPWR) WIRE COLOR IDENTIFICATION

Application	Wire Color
All Models	Yellow

1) Check KAPWR Circuit Voltage – Code 15/512 indicates ECA power interruption in Keep-Alive Memory (KAM). Turn ignition off. Disconnect 60-pin ECA connector. Inspect terminals, and repair if damaged. Install EEC-IV Breakout Box (T83L-50-EEC-IV), leaving ECA disconnected. Measure voltage between test pin No. 1 and pin No. 40 or 60 at breakout box. Observe voltage reading while wiggling, bending and shaking small sections of EEC-IV wiring harness from ECA to dash. If reading is less than 10.5 volts, repair open circuit and repeat QUICK TEST. If reading is 10.5 volts or more, go to step **2)**.

Diagnostic Aids – Continuous Memory Code 15/512 may be displayed when power between ECA and KAPWR is interrupted. This code may be set when a breakout box is installed or battery is disconnected.

2) Inspect Engine Compartment Wire Routing – Ensure EEC-IV wiring is not routed close to ignition components or secondary ignition wires. If necessary, reroute EEC wiring. Clear codes, and wait 5 minutes. Repeat KOEO SELF-TEST. If Continuous Memory Code 15/512 is no longer displayed, Continuous Memory Code 15/512 testing is complete. If Continuous Memory Code 15/512 is still present, replace ECA and repeat QUICK TEST.

CIRCUIT TEST QC

OUTPUT STATE CHECK NOT FUNCTIONING

Diagnostic Aids – Perform this circuit test when directed by other CIRCUIT TESTS. This test is only intended to diagnose:
- ECA.
- Throttle plate linkage.

1) Check For Codes 23, 53, 63, 121, 122 & 123 – Disconnect cruise control servo wiring harness connector. Perform KOEO SELF-TEST. If Code 23, 53, 63, 121, 122 or 123 is present, go to appropriate CIRCUIT TEST. See SERVICE CODE REFERENCE CHARTS. Service code(s) as necessary. If pass code (11/111) is displayed, go to step **2**). If no code is displayed, go to CIRCUIT TEST QA.

2) Check Throttle Linkage – Check throttle and linkage for sticking and binding. If throttle and linkage are okay, replace Throttle Position Sensor (TPS) and repeat QUICK TEST. If throttle and linkage are binding, repair as necessary and repeat QUICK TEST.

CIRCUIT TEST S

SYSTEM CHECK

Diagnostic Aids – Perform this test only when directed by CIRCUIT TEST AA, CIRCUIT TEST AB or CIRCUIT TEST AC. This test is intended to diagnose:
- ISC by-pass air system.
- MAP system.
- EGR system.
- MAF system.

To prevent replacing good components, be aware following non-EEC-IV areas may be at fault:
- Faulty power or ground connections.
- Ignition system (distributor cap, rotor, wires, coil and plugs).
- Engine mechanical components (cam timing, valves, etc.).

1) ISC-BPA Check – Try to start engine at part throttle. If engine starts and runs smoothly at part throttle, go to CIRCUIT TEST KE, step **4**). If engine does not run as described, go to step **2**).

2) Check For RPM Drop – Turn ignition off. Connect a tachometer to engine. Start engine. Disconnect ISC solenoid. If RPM drops or engine stalls, reconnect ISC solenoid and go to step **3**). If RPM does not drop, go to step **4**).

3) Power To MAP/BP Sensor – If vehicle is not equipped with a MAP/BP sensor, go to step **8**). Test MAP/BP using Ford Motor Co. MAP/BP tester. Disconnect MAP/BP sensor. Turn ignition off. Connect MAP/BP tester between wiring harness and MAP/BP sensor. See Fig. S1. Connect banana plugs of tester into DVOM. Set DVOM on 20-volt scale. With tester connected, turn ignition on. If Green light is on, go to step **4**). If light is not on, repair open in VREF circuit and remove MAP/BP tester. Reconnect components, and retest symptom.

90H14511

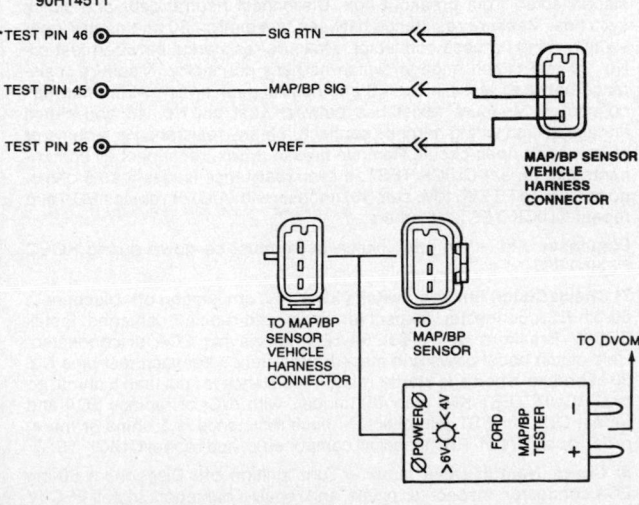

Fig. S1: MAP/BP Tester & Circuit

CIRCUIT TEST S (Cont.)

4) MAP/BP Tester Output Reading – Measure several known good MAP/BP sensors to obtain average voltage for location and date of testing. With MAP/BP tester and DVOM connected, turn ignition on. Measure MAP/BP voltage at MAP sensor. If voltage is in within specification for specific altitude, go to step **5**). See MAP VOLTAGE OUTPUT table. If voltage is not within specification for specific altitude, replace MAP/BP sensor.

MAP VOLTAGE OUTPUT

Approximate Elevation (Ft.)	Voltage Output (Volts)
0	1.59
1000	1.56
2000	1.53
3000	1.50
4000	1.47
5000	1.44
6000	1.41
7000	1.39

5) Check Vacuum Lines – Check vacuum lines for correct routing. Refer to VECI decal. Check MAP sensor vacuum line for leaks and blockage. If vacuum lines are okay, go to step **6**). If vacuum lines are not okay, repair as necessary. Repeat QUICK TEST.

6) Check MAP Sensor – Turn ignition off. Disconnect vacuum hose from manifold vacuum source. Install vacuum pump to MAP sensor hose. Apply 18 in. Hg vacuum to MAP sensor. If MAP sensor holds vacuum, release vacuum and remove vacuum pump. Reconnect vacuum hose to MAP sensor, and go to step **7**). If MAP sensor does not hold vacuum, replace MAP sensor or hose and repeat QUICK TEST.

7) Check Vacuum Manifold Source – Turn ignition off. Disconnect MAP sensor vacuum hose from manifold vacuum source. Install vacuum gauge at manifold vacuum source. Start engine and observe vacuum gauge. If manifold vacuum is present, remove vacuum gauge. Reconnect MAP sensor vacuum hose, and go to step **8**). If vacuum is not present, remove obstruction. Reconnect all components, and repeat QUICK TEST.

8) Check EGR Vacuum – If vehicle is not equipped with EGR system, go to CIRCUIT TEST H, step **2**). Disconnect and plug vacuum line at EGR valve. Attempt to start engine. If vehicle did not start previously but starts now or if driveability symptoms are eliminated, go to CIRCUIT TEST DN, step **42**). If vehicle could not start previously and still does not start or if vehicle driveability fault is still present, go to step **9**).

9) Check EGR Valve – Inspect EGR valve for leaks. If valve is fully closed, go to CIRCUIT TEST H, step **2**). If EGR valve is leaking or is not fully seated, repair or replace valve as necessary.

CIRCUIT TEST TA

NEUTRAL DRIVE INPUT

Diagnostic Aids – Perform this test only when directed by QUICK TEST. This test is intended to diagnose:

- Clutch Engage/Interlock Switch.
- Neutral Drive/Gear Switch.
- ECA.
- Wiring harness circuits CES, CIS, NDS, NGS and SIG RTN.

92F03874

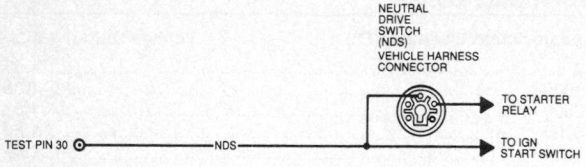

Fig. TA1: Neutral Drive Input Circuit (A/T)

92J03871

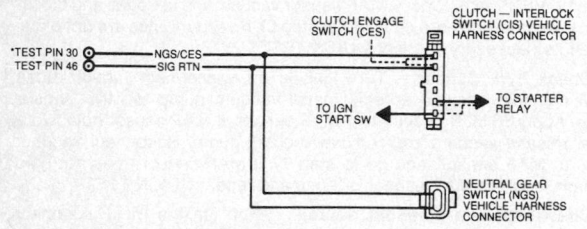

*TEST PINS LOCATED ON BREAKOUT BOX.
ALL HARNESS CONNECTORS VIEWED INTO MATING SURFACE.

Fig. TA2: Neutral Drive Input Circuit (M/T – Aerostar, Explorer, Ranger 2.9L & Ranger 4.0L)

92I03875

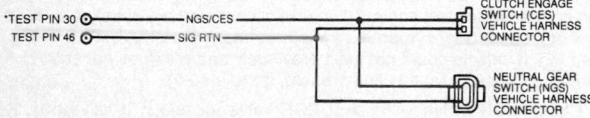

*TEST PIN LOCATED ON BREAKOUT BOX
ALL HARNESS CONNECTORS VIEWED INTO MATING SURFACES

Fig. TA3: Neutral Drive Input Circuit (M/T – Ranger 2.3L)

92B03872

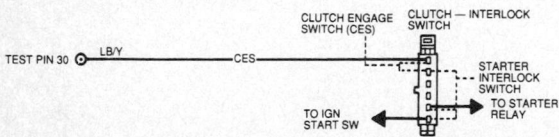

Fig. TA4: Neutral Drive Input Circuit (M/T – 4.9L)

TEST PIN NO. 30 (NDS/NGS) WIRE COLOR IDENTIFICATION

Application	Wire Color
All Models	Light Blue/Yellow

TEST PIN NO. 46 (SIG RTN) WIRE COLOR IDENTIFICATION

Application	Wire Color
All Models	Gray/Red

1) Code 67/522, 525, 527, 528 Or 634 System Identification – Code 67/522, 525, 527 or 528 is a result of voltage being high at either pin No. 10 (A/C input) or 30 (neutral drive) while cranking engine or during KOEO SELF-TEST. Possible causes for these faults are:

CIRCUIT TEST TA (Cont.)

- A/C circuit shorted to power.
- Clutch engage/interlock circuits open.
- Neutral drive/gear switch open.
- Faulty ECA.
- Starter relay disconnected during self-test.

On all A/T models, go to step **8**). For 4.9L M/T, go to step **7**). On all other M/T models, go to step **2**).

2) Check Neutral Gear/Clutch Input – Turn ignition off. Turn A/C off (if equipped). Disconnect 60-pin ECA connector. Inspect terminals, and repair if damaged. Install EEC-IV Breakout Box (T83L-50-EEC-IV), leaving ECA disconnected. Measure resistance between test pins No. 30 and 46 with transmission in Neutral and clutch pedal up. Measure resistance between test pins No. 30 and 46 with transmission in gear and clutch pedal down. If each resistance is less than 5 ohms, go to step **3**). If resistance is 5 ohms or more, go to step **5**).

3) Check Neutral Gear/Clutch Input Integrity – Turn ignition off. Leave ECA disconnected from breakout box. Measure resistance between test pins No. 30 and 46 with transmission in any gear and clutch pedal up. *See Fig. TA5.* If resistance is less than 5 ohms, go to CIRCUIT TEST KM, step **40**) (models with A/C) or replace ECA and repeat QUICK TEST (all others). If resistance is 5 ohms or more, go to step **4**).

91G09230

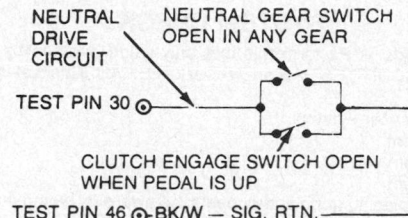

Fig. TA5: Neutral Gear/Clutch Input Circuit

4) Check For Short To Ground – Turn ignition off. Leave ECA disconnected from breakout box. Disconnect clutch engage switch. Measure resistance between test pins No. 30 and 46. If resistance is 10,000 ohms or more, go to CIRCUIT TEST KM, step **40**) (models with A/C) or replace ECA and repeat QUICK TEST (all others). If resistance is less than 10,000 ohms, repair short circuit. Reconnect all components, and repeat QUICK TEST.

5) Check Neutral Gear/Clutch Engage Switch – Turn ignition off. Leave ECA disconnected from breakout box. Locate neutral gear switch (on transmission) and clutch engage switch (at clutch pedal linkage). Disconnect wiring harness at both switches, and inspect connectors for pushed-back pins. Measure resistance across neutral gear switch terminals with transmission in Neutral. Measure resistance across clutch engage switch with clutch pedal down. If each resistance is 5 ohms or less, go to step **6**). If resistance is more than 5 ohms, replace open switch. Reconnect all components, and repeat QUICK TEST.

6) Check Neutral Gear/Clutch Harness – Turn ignition off. Leave ECA disconnected from breakout box. Disconnect neutral gear and clutch switches. Measure resistance between test pin No. 30 and neutral gear switch wiring harness connector. Measure resistance between test pin No. 30 and clutch engage switch harness connector. Measure resistance between test pin No. 46 and neutral gear switch wiring harness connector. Measure resistance between test pin No. 46 and clutch engage switch wiring harness connector. If any resistance is 5 ohms or more, repair open circuit. Remove breakout box, reconnect all components and repeat QUICK TEST. If each resistance is less than 5 ohms, go to CIRCUIT TEST KM, step **40**) (models with A/C) or replace ECA and repeat QUICK TEST (all others).

Diagnostic Aid – On 4.9L, clutch pedal must be down during KOEO SELF-TEST.

7) Check Clutch Engage Switch (4.9L) – Turn ignition off. Disconnect 60-pin ECA connector. Inspect terminals, and repair if damaged. Install EEC-IV Breakout Box (T83L-50-EEC-IV), leaving ECA disconnected. Hold clutch pedal down and measure resistance between test pin No. 30 at breakout box and starter relay. If resistance is less than 5 ohms, go to CIRCUIT TEST KM, step **40**) (models with A/C) or replace ECA and repeat QUICK TEST (all others). If each resistance is 5 ohms or more, repair open circuit. Reconnect all components, and repeat QUICK TEST.

8) Check Neutral Drive Input – Turn ignition off. Disconnect 60-pin ECA connector. Inspect terminals, and repair if damaged. Install EEC-IV Breakout Box (T83L-50-EEC-IV), leaving ECA disconnected. Ensure

CIRCUIT TEST TA (Cont.)

A/C is off (if equipped). Ensure transmission is in Neutral or Park. Turn ignition on. Measure voltage between test pin No. 30 and chassis ground. If voltage is less than 1.0 volt, go to CIRCUIT TEST KM, step **40**) (models with A/C) or replace ECA and repeat QUICK TEST (all others). If voltage is 1.0 volt or more, go to step **9**).

9) Check Neutral Drive Switch Resistance – Turn ignition off. Leave ECA disconnected from breakout box. Disconnect wiring harness from neutral drive switch. Measure resistance across switch terminals. If resistance is less than 5 ohms, repair open in NDS circuit. Reconnect all components, and repeat QUICK TEST. If resistance is 5 ohms or more, replace neutral drive switch. Reconnect all components, and repeat QUICK TEST.

NOTE: A break in step numbering sequence occurs at this point. Procedure skips from step 9) to step 12). No test procedures have been omitted.

12) Check NDS Circuit For Short To Ground Or Closed Neutral Drive Switch – Turn ignition off. Leave ECA disconnected from breakout box. Place transmission in Drive. Measure resistance between test pin No. 30 and test pins No. 40 and 60 at breakout box. If resistance is 10,000 ohms or more, NDS circuit is okay. Diagnose other possible causes. If resistance is less than 10,000 ohms, repair closed neutral drive switch or short circuit. Reconnect all components, and repeat QUICK TEST.

CIRCUIT TEST TB

4X4 LOW & OVERDRIVE CANCEL SWITCH (OCS)

Diagnostic Aids – Perform this test only when directed by QUICK TEST. To prevent replacing good components, be aware following non-EEC areas may be at fault:
- Engine base condition (cam timing, valves, rings, etc.).
- Brakes.
- Transmission fluid, friction elements and cooling.
- Transfer case linkage or internal condition.
This test is only intended to diagnose:
- Harness circuits 4x4 LOW/ OCIL and OCS.
- Faulty ECA.

92C03877

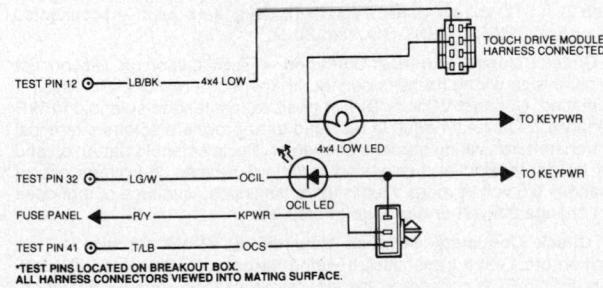

TEST PINS LOCATED ON BREAKOUT BOX. ALL HARNESS CONNECTORS VIEWED INTO MATING SURFACE.

Fig. TB1: 4x4 Low & Overdrive Cancel Circuits (Touch Drive Option)

92E03878

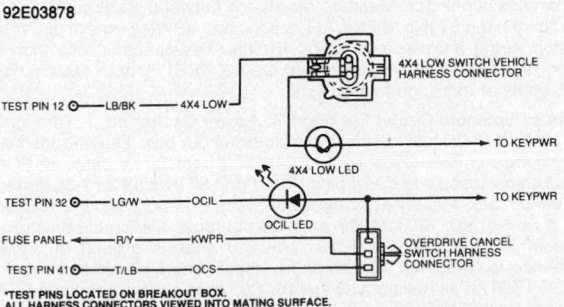

TEST PINS LOCATED ON BREAKOUT BOX. ALL HARNESS CONNECTORS VIEWED INTO MATING SURFACE.

Fig. TB2: 4x4 Low & Overdrive Cancel Circuits (Without Touch Drive Option)

1) Code 47/633, 65/632 Or 97/631 – Code 47/633 indicates 4x4 Low selector lever is not in 4x2 or 4x4 HIGH position during KOEO SELF-

CIRCUIT TEST TB (Cont.)

TEST. Code 65/632 indicates Overdrive Cancel Switch (OCS) is not cycled between engine ID code and WOT check during KOER SELF-TEST. Code 97/631 indicates OCS circuit fault during KOEO SELF-TEST. Possible causes for these faults are:
- Faulty 4x4 Low switch or 4x4 selector lever position.
- Faulty OCS switch or switch not cycled.
- OCS bulb burned out.
- OCS circuit open or grounded.
- Faulty ECA.

Perform QUICK TEST. If no codes are present, fault is intermittent and cannot be duplicated at this time. If Code 47/633 or 65/632 is present, go to step **2**). If Code 97/631 is present, go to step **3**).

2) Cycle 4x4 Or Overdrive Cancel Switch – Turn ignition off. Disconnect 60-pin ECA connector. Inspect terminals, and repair if damaged. Install EEC-IV Breakout Box (T83L-50-EEC-IV), leaving ECA disconnected. Turn ignition on. To check 4x4 LOW circuit, measure voltage between test pin No. 12 and test pins No. 40 and 60 at breakout box. To check OCS circuit, measure voltage between test pin No. 41 and test pins No. 40 and 60 at breakout box while cycling overdrive cancel switch. If voltage cycles, replace ECA and repeat QUICK TEST. If voltage does not cycle, go to step **3**).

3) Check Circuits For Short To Ground – Turn ignition off. Leave ECA disconnected from breakout box. Disconnect switch. To check 4x4 LOW circuit, measure resistance between test pin No. 12 and test pins No. 40 and 60 at breakout box. To check OCS circuit, measure resistance between test pin No. 41 and pins No. 40 and 60 at breakout box. If resistance is more than 10,000 ohms, go to step **4**) (Code 97/631) or step **6**) (Code 47/633 or 65/632). If resistance is 10,000 ohms or less, repair short circuit. Repeat QUICK TEST. If code is still present, go to step **5**).

4) Check Power Through OCIL Circuit – Turn ignition off. Leave ECA disconnected from breakout box. Measure voltage between test pin No. 32 and test pins No. 40 and 60 at breakout box. If voltage is more than 10.5 volts, replace ECA and repeat QUICK TEST. If voltage is 10.5 volts or less, go to step **5**).

5) Check Output Driver Voltage Signal – Turn ignition off. Leave ECA disconnected from breakout box. Disconnect switch. To check 4x4 LOW circuit, connect DVOM positive lead on KEY POWER terminal of fuse panel and negative lead on test pin No. 12 at breakout box. *See Fig. TB3.* To check OCS circuit, connect DVOM positive lead on KEY POWER terminal of fuse panel and negative lead on test pin No. 32 at breakout box. If either voltage reading is less than 2 volts, check bulb and fuse. If bulb and fuse are okay, repair open circuit and repeat QUICK TEST. If both voltage readings are 2 volts or more, go to step **6**).

92G03879

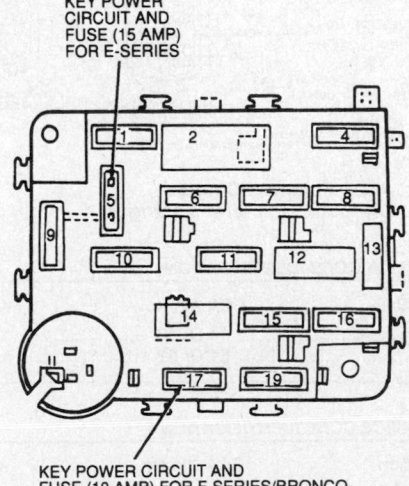

Fig. TB3: Identifying KEY POWER Terminal in Fuse Panel

6) Check Circuit Continuity – Turn ignition off. Leave ECA disconnected from breakout box. Disconnect switch. To check 4x4 LOW circuit, connect DVOM positive lead on KEY POWER terminal of fuse panel and negative lead on test pin No. 12 at breakout box. To check OCS circuit, connect DVOM positive lead on KEY POWER terminal of fuse panel and negative lead on power side of OCS wiring harness connector. Connect

CIRCUIT TEST TB (Cont.)

DVOM positive lead on test pin No. 41 at breakout box and negative lead on power side of OCS wiring harness connector. If either resistance reading is 5 ohms or more, repair open circuit and repeat QUICK TEST. If both resistance readings are less than 5 ohms, go to step 7).

7) Check Circuits For Short To Power – Turn ignition off. Leave ECA disconnected from breakout box. Disconnect switch. To check 4x4 LOW circuit, measure resistance between test pin No. 12 and test pins No. 37 and 57 at breakout box. To check OCS circuit, measure resistance between test pin No. 32 and test pins No. 37 and 57 at breakout box. Measure resistance between test pin No. 41 and test pins No. 37 and 57 at breakout box. If resistances are more than 10,000 ohms, replace switch and repeat QUICK TEST. If any resistance is 10,000 ohms or less, repair short circuit and repeat QUICK TEST.

CIRCUIT TEST TC

TRANSMISSION SOLENOIDS

Diagnostic Aids – Perform this test only when directed by QUICK TEST. To prevent replacing good components, be aware following non-EEC areas may be at fault:
- Engine base condition (cam timing, valves rings, etc.).
- Brakes.
- Transmission fluid, friction elements and cooling.

This test is not intended to diagnose transmission. This test is intended to diagnose:
- Wiring harness circuits M/CCC, CCO, CCS, EPC, SS3/4, SS1, SS2, SS3, SIG RTN, EPC PWR and VPWR.
- Faulty ECA.

CIRCUIT TEST TC ACRONYMS

Acronym	Definition
CCO	Converter Clutch Overdrive
CCS	Coast Clutch Control
CCC	Converter Clutch Control
EPC	Electronic Pressure Control
MCCC	Modulated Converter Clutch Control
SS	Shift Solenoid

92I03880

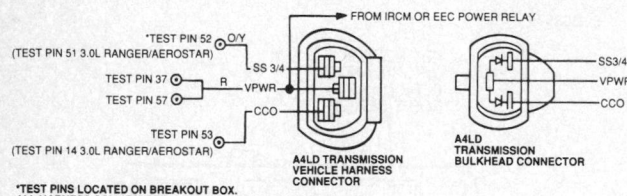

Fig. TC1: A4LD Solenoid Circuits
(Aerostar, Explorer & Ranger)

A4LD SERVICE CODE IDENTIFICATION

Application	ECA Pin No.	KOEO Code
CCO	14 Or 53	89/629
SS3/4	51 Or 52	86/566

E4OD SERVICE CODE IDENTIFICATION

Application	ECA Pin No.	KOEO Code
CCC	53	94/627
CCS	55	93/626
EPC	38	99/624, 998
SS1	52	91/621
SS2	19	92/622

CIRCUIT TEST TC (Cont.)

92A03881

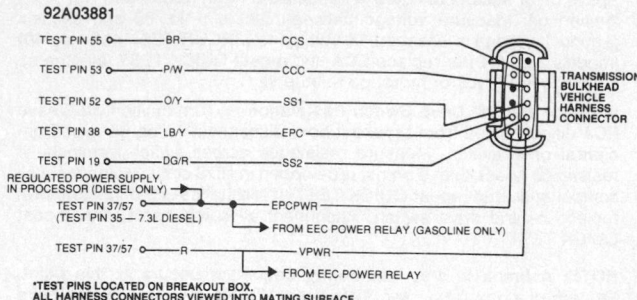

Fig. TC2: E4OD Solenoid Circuits
(Bronco, Pickup & Van)

TEST PINS NO. 37 & 57 (EPC PWR) WIRE COLOR [1] IDENTIFICATION

Application	Wire Color
Bronco, Pickup & Van	Red Or Red/White

[1] – On 7.3L, use test pin No. 35 (Red/White) for EPC PWR circuit.

1) OUTPUT STATE CHECK – Code 91/621, 92/622, 93/626, 94/627, 629, 641 or 652 indicates shift solenoid did not respond to ECA command. Possible causes for these faults are:
- Faulty Manual Lever Position (MLP) sensor.
- Circuit open or grounded.
- Faulty ECA.

To enter OUTPUT STATE CHECK, use only VOM or DVOM. DO NOT use scan tester. Turn ignition off. Disconnect cruise control servo wiring harness connector. Connect DVOM negative lead to STO terminal at self-test connector. Connect positive lead to positive battery terminal. Install a jumper wire between SIG RTN terminal at self-test connector and STI terminal. See Fig. QA1 in CIRCUIT TEST QA. Perform KOEO SELF-TEST until continuous memory test is complete. DVOM will read less than 1.0 volt when test is complete to indicate ECA has entered OUTPUT STATE CHECK. Depress and release throttle. If voltage increases, remain in OUTPUT STATE CHECK and go to step 2). If voltage does not increase, depress throttle to WOT and release. If STO voltage goes high, go to step 2). If STO voltage does not go high, leave test equipment connected and go to CIRCUIT TEST QC, step 2).

2) Check Solenoid Electrical Condition – Turn ignition off. Disconnect transmission wiring harness connector. Inspect terminals, and repair if damaged. Connect VOM or DVOM positive test lead to solenoid VPWR connector. Connect negative test lead to appropriate solenoid terminal at transmission wiring harness connector. Cycle solenoid output on and off by depressing and releasing throttle 3-5 times. If voltage output changes 0.5 volt or more, fault is in transmission. If voltage does not change 0.5 volt or more, go to step 3).

3) Check Continuity Between Solenoid & VPWR Circuits – Turn ignition off. Leave transmission wiring harness disconnected. Disconnect 60-pin ECA connector. Inspect terminals, and repair if damaged. Install EEC-IV Breakout Box (T83L-50-EEC-IV), leaving ECA disconnected. Measure resistance between ECA output signal terminal at ECA wiring harness connector and output signal terminal at transmission wiring harness connector. Measure resistance between breakout box test pins No. 37 and 57 (No. 35 for 7.3L diesel) and VPWR terminal at transmission wiring harness connector. If either resistance is less than 5 ohms, repair open circuit and repeat QUICK TEST. If both resistances are 5 ohms or more, go to step 4).

4) Check Solenoid Circuit For Short To Power Or Ground – Turn ignition off. Leave ECA disconnected from breakout box. Leave transmission wiring harness disconnected. Measure resistance between ECA output signal test pin and test pins No. 37 and 57 (No. 35 for 7.3L diesel) at breakout box. Measure resistance between ECA output signal test pin and pins No. 40, 46 and 60 at breakout box. Measure resistance between ECA output signal test pin and chassis ground. If either resistance is less than 10,000 ohms, repair short circuit and repeat QUICK TEST. If all resistances are 10,000 ohms or more, replace ECA and repeat QUICK TEST.

NOTE: A break in step numbering sequence occurs at this point. Procedure skips from step 4) to step 10). No test procedures have been omitted.

CIRCUIT TEST TC (Cont.)

10) Check VPWR To Solenoid – Code 86/566 or 89/629 indicates shift solenoid did not respond to ECA command. Code 99/624 indicates failure of EPC circuit. Code 98/625 indicates EPC driver failure. Possible causes for these faults are:
- Faulty solenoid.
- Circuit open or grounded.
- Faulty ECA.

Turn ignition off. Disconnect transmission wiring harness connector. Turn ignition on. Measure resistance between VPWR and EPC PWR terminal at transmission wiring harness connector and chassis ground. If voltage is less than 10.5 volts, repair open circuit and repeat QUICK TEST. If voltage is 10.5 volts or more, go to step 11).

11) Check Solenoid Resistance – Turn ignition off. Leave transmission wiring harness connector disconnected. Measure resistance between VPWR and EPC PWR terminal and suspect component terminal at transmission wiring harness connector. If resistance is not 26-40 ohms (A4LD) or 3-7 ohms (except A4LD), fault is in transmission. If resistance is 26-40 ohms (A4LD) or 3-7 ohms (except A4LD), go to step 12).

12) Check Solenoid Signal & VPWR Circuit Continuity – Turn ignition off. Disconnect 60-pin ECA connector. Inspect terminals, and repair if damaged. Install EEC-IV Breakout Box (T83L-50-EEC-IV), leaving ECA disconnected. Measure resistance between breakout box test pins No. 37 and 57 (No. 35 for 7.3L diesel) and VPWR/EPC PWR terminal at transmission wiring harness connector. On A4LD models, measure resistance between CCO or SS3/4 test pin at breakout box and solenoid terminal at transmission wiring harness connector; on all models except A4LD, measure resistance between test pin No. 32 at breakout box and EPC solenoid terminal at transmission wiring harness connector. If resistance is 5 ohms or more, repair open circuit and repeat QUICK TEST. If resistance is more than 5 ohms, go to step 13).

13) Check Circuit For Short To Power Or Ground – Turn ignition off. Leave ECA disconnected from breakout box. Leave transmission wiring harness connector disconnected. On A4LD models, measure resistance between test pin No. 52 or 53 and pins No. 37 and 57 (No. 35 for 7.3L diesel) at breakout box. Measure resistance between test pin No. 52 or 53 and pins No. 40, 46 and 60 at breakout box. On all models except A4LD, measure resistance between test pin No. 38 and test pins No. 37 and 57 (No. 35 for 7.3L diesel) at breakout box. Measure resistance between test pin No. 38 and test pins No. 40, 46 and 60 at breakout box. If either resistance is less than 10,000 ohms, repair short circuit and repeat QUICK TEST. If all resistances are 10,000 ohms or more, replace ECA and repeat QUICK TEST.

NOTE: A break in step numbering sequence occurs at this point. Procedure skips from step 13) to step 20). No test procedures have been omitted.

20) Check Solenoid Resistance – KOEO Code 621 (SS1), 622 (SS2), 641 (SS3) or 643 (CCC) indicates failure in shift solenoid circuit. Possible causes for these faults are:
- Faulty shift solenoid.
- Circuit open or grounded.
- Faulty ECA.

Turn ignition off. Disconnect transmission wiring harness connector. Measure resistance between suspect shift solenoid at transmission wiring harness connector and chassis ground. If resistance is 13-17 ohms, go to step 21). If resistance is not 13-17 ohms, go to step 22).

21) Check Shift Solenoid For Short To Power – Turn ignition off. Disconnect transmission wiring harness connector. Disconnect 60-pin ECA connector. Inspect terminals, and repair if damaged. Turn ignition on. Measure voltage between suspect shift solenoid at transmission wiring harness connector and chassis ground. If voltage is more than 0.5 volt, repair short to power and repeat QUICK TEST. If voltage is 0.5 volt or less, go to step 22).

22) Check Shift Solenoid For Short To Ground – Turn ignition off. Leave transmission wiring harness connector disconnected. Measure resistance between suspect shift solenoid at transmission wiring harness connector and chassis ground. Measure resistance between suspect shift solenoid and other circuits at transmission wiring harness connector. If either resistance is less than 10,000 ohms, repair short circuit and repeat QUICK TEST. If all resistances are 10,000 ohms or more, go to step 23).

23) Check Shift Solenoid Circuit Continuity – Turn ignition off. Leave transmission wiring harness connector disconnected. Install EEC-IV Breakout Box (T83L-50-EEC-IV) or 4EAT tester, leaving ECA disconnected. Measure resistance between suspect shift solenoid at breakout box and suspect shift solenoid terminal at transmission wiring harness

CIRCUIT TEST TC (Cont.)

connector. If resistance is 5 ohms or more, repair open circuit and repeat QUICK TEST. If resistance is less than 5 ohms, go to step 24).

24) Check Shift Solenoid For Short To Power In Transmission – Turn ignition off. Leave ECA disconnected from breakout box. Reconnect transmission wiring harness connector. Measure voltage between test pin No. 60 and suspect shift solenoid terminal at breakout box. If voltage is 0.5 volt or more, replace or repair solenoid short to power. If voltage is less than 0.5 volt, replace ECA and repeat QUICK TEST.

NOTE: A break in step numbering sequence occurs at this point. Procedure skips from step 24) to step 30). No test procedures have been omitted.

30) Continuous Memory Codes 621, 622, 641 & 643 – Continuous Memory Code 621 (SS1), 622 (SS2), 641 (SS3) or 643 (CCC) indicates a failure was detected in shift solenoid circuit during last 80 warm-up cycles. Possible causes for these faults are:
- Faulty shift solenoid.
- Circuit open or grounded.

Turn ignition off. Check shift solenoid circuit between ECA and transmission. Repair or replace as necessary. If circuits are okay, go to step 31).

31) Check For Intermittent Short Or Open – Turn ignition off. Disconnect 60-pin ECA connector. Inspect terminals, and repair if damaged. Install EEC-IV Breakout Box (T83L-50-EEC-IV), leaving ECA disconnected. Turn ignition on. Connect test light between test pin No. 37 and suspect shift solenoid terminal at breakout box. Test light should be at partial brightness. Observe test light while wiggling and bending shift solenoid circuit between transmission and ECA. An open or short to power will be indicated by light going off. A short to ground will be indicated by light getting bright. Repeat procedure for all solenoids. If fault is indicated, isolate and repair as necessary. If no fault is indicated, go to step 32).

IDENTIFYING SHIFT SOLENOID TEST CIRCUITS

Shift Solenoid	Test Pin No.
SS1	11
SS2	51
SS3	52
CCC	55

32) Check For Intermittent Short To Ground – Turn ignition off. Leave ECA disconnected from breakout box. Disconnect transmission wiring harness connector. Turn ignition on. Connect test light between test pin No. 37 (No. 35 for 7.3L diesel) and suspect shift solenoid terminal at breakout box. Test light should be off. Observe test light while wiggling and bending shift solenoid circuit between transmission and ECA. A short to ground will be indicated by light turning on. Repeat procedure for all solenoids. If fault is indicated, isolate and repair as necessary. If no fault is indicated, problem is intermittent and cannot be duplicated at this time.

CIRCUIT TEST TD

MANUAL LEVER POSITION (MLP) SENSOR

Diagnostic Aids – Perform this test only when directed by QUICK TEST. To prevent replacing good components, be aware following non-EEC areas may be at fault:
- Engine base condition (cam timing, valves rings, etc.).
- Electrical (alternator, battery, add-on devices, etc.).
- Transmission shift linkage.

This test is not intended to diagnose transmission. This test is intended to diagnose:
- Wiring harness circuits MLP, TSR, TSL, TSD, TSOD and SIG RTN.
- ECA.

92B03886

*TEST PINS LOCATED ON BREAKOUT BOX.
ALL HARNESS CONNECTORS VIEWED INTO MATING SURFACE.

Fig. TD1: Manual Lever Position (MLP) Sensor Circuit

CIRCUIT TEST TD Cont.)

TEST PIN NO. 30 (MLP) WIRE COLOR IDENTIFICATION

Application	Wire Color
Bronco, Pickup & Van	Light Blue/Yellow

TEST PIN NO. 46 (SIG RTN) WIRE COLOR IDENTIFICATION

Application	Wire Color
Bronco, Pickup & Van	Gray/Red

1) KOEO Codes 67/634, 522 & 654 – KOEO Codes 67/634 522 and 654 indicate MLP sensor is out of self-test range (3770-4607 ohms) when gear selector is in PARK position. Possible causes for these faults are:
- Linkage not adjusted correctly.
- Faulty Manual Lever Position (MLP) sensor.
- Circuit open or grounded.
- Faulty ECA.

Turn ignition off. Apply parking brake. Place transmission gear selector in NEUTRAL position. Place Manual Lever Position Sensor Gauge (T89T-70010-J) in sensor slot. If gauge does not fit, loosen MLP mounting bolts and adjust sensor as necessary. If gauge fits, go to step **2)**.

2) Check MLP Sensor Circuit Continuity – Turn ignition off. Disconnect MLP sensor wiring harness connector. Disconnect 60-pin ECA connector. Inspect terminals, and repair if damaged. Install EEC-IV Breakout Box (T83L-50-EEC-IV), leaving ECA disconnected. Measure resistance between MLP terminal at MLP sensor wiring harness connector and test pin No. 30 at breakout box. Measure resistance between SIG RTN terminal at MLP sensor wiring harness connector and test pin No. 46 at breakout box. If either resistance is more than 5 ohms, repair open circuit and repeat QUICK TEST. If both resistances are 5 ohms or less, go to step **3)**.

3) Check MLP Sensor For Short To Power & Ground – Turn ignition off. Leave ECA and MLP sensor disconnected. Measure resistance between test pin No. 30 and test pins No. 40, 46 and 60 at breakout box. Measure resistance between test pin No. 30 and chassis ground. If resistance is less than 10,000 ohms, repair short circuit and repeat QUICK TEST. If resistance is 10,000 ohms or more, go to step **4)**.

4) Check MLP Sensor Resistance – Turn ignition off. Connect MLP sensor. Leave ECA disconnected from breakout box. Measure resistance between test pins No. 30 and 46 at breakout box while cycling gear selector. See MLP SENSOR RESISTANCE table. If resistance is within specification, replace ECA and repeat QUICK TEST. If resistance is not within specification, replace MLP sensor and repeat QUICK TEST.

MLP SENSOR RESISTANCE

Gear Selected	Ohms
Park	3770-4607
Reverse	1304-1593
Neutral	660-807
Overdrive	361-442
Drive	190-232
First	190-232

NOTE: A break in step numbering sequence occurs at this point. Procedure skips from step 4) to step 7). No test procedures have been omitted.

7) Incorrect Shift/No Shift – Turn ignition off. Check transmission fluid. Add or replace if necessary. Test drive vehicle to determine transmission shift patterns. If transmission always remains in 3rd gear when vehicle is operated with shift lever in Drive or Overdrive position, go to next step. If transmission does not operate as described, go to step **9)**.

8) Visual Inspection – Visually check select switch and solenoid wiring harness between ECA and transmission. Repair or replace wiring harness if necessary and repeat QUICK TEST. If wiring harness is okay, go to step **9)**.

9) Diagnose Transmission Shift Patterns – If transmission upshifts and downshifts correctly, EEC-IV system is okay. Fault is in transmission. If transmission does not shift correctly, turn ignition off. Inspect transmission switches and harness connectors for corrosion and damaged pins. Inspect wiring harness for incorrect routing. If any faults are found, repair or replace as necessary. If no faults are found, problem is intermittent and cannot be found at this time.

CIRCUIT TEST TE

TRANSMISSION OIL TEMPERATURE (TOT) SENSOR

Diagnostic Aids – Perform this test only when directed by QUICK TEST. To prevent replacing good components, be aware following non-EEC areas may be at fault:
- Transmission fluid level.
- Transmission fluid temperature.
- Ambient temperature.

This test is intended to diagnose:
- TOT sensor.
- Wiring harness circuits TOT and SIG RTN.
- Faulty ECA.

92J03890

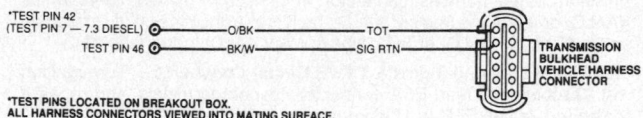

*TEST PIN 42
(TEST PIN 7 — 7.3 DIESEL) — O/BK — TOT
TEST PIN 46 — BK/W — SIG RTN
TRANSMISSION BULKHEAD VEHICLE HARNESS CONNECTOR

*TEST PINS LOCATED ON BREAKOUT BOX.
ALL HARNESS CONNECTORS VIEWED INTO MATING SURFACE.

Fig. TE1: Transmission Oil Temperature (TOT) Sensor Circuit (Bronco, Pickup & Van)

TOT SENSOR (AXOD-E) SPECIFICATIONS

Temperature °F (°C)	¹ Volts	¹ Ohms
32 (0)	3.88	96,255
41 (5)	3.71	75,201
50 (10)	3.53	59,175
59 (15)	3.32	46,883
68 (20)	3.10	37,387
77 (25)	2.86	30,000
86 (30)	2.62	24,215
95 (35)	2.38	19,657
104 (40)	2.15	16,043
113 (45)	1.92	13,161
122 (50)	1.71	10,050
131 (55)	1.51	8990
140 (60)	1.33	7487
149 (65)	1.17	6265
158 (70)	1.03	5260
167 (75)	0.90	4450
176 (80)	0.78	3775
185 (85)	0.69	3215
194 (90)	0.60	2750
200 (95)	0.52	2361

¹ – Value may vary by 15 percent.

1) KOEO Code 26/636 – KOEO Code 26/636 indicate TOT sensor is out of self-test range. Possible causes for these faults are:
- Transmission fluid incorrect temperature.
- Incorrect sensor resistance.
- Faulty ECA.

Ensure transmission fluid temperature is more than 50°F (10°C). Repeat QUICK TEST. If Code 26/636 is present, go to step **2)**. If Code 26/636 is not present, test is complete.

2) Check VREF At Throttle Position Sensor (TPS) – Turn ignition off. Disconnect TPS sensor wiring harness connector. Disconnect 60-pin ECA connector. Inspect terminals, and repair if damaged. Install EEC-IV Breakout Box (T83L-50-EEC-IV). Connect ECA to breakout box. Turn ignition on. Measure voltage between VREF and SIG RTN terminals at TPS wiring harness connector. If voltage is 4-6 volts, go to step **3)**. If voltage is not 4-6 volts, go to CIRCUIT TEST C.

3) Check TOT Sensor Resistance – Turn ignition off. Disconnect ECA from breakout box. Allow transmission to cool. Turn ignition on. Measure and record voltage between test pin No. 46 and TOT test pin at breakout box. Start engine, and warm transmission to normal operating temperature. Disconnect ECA from breakout box. Measure voltage between test pin No. 46 and TOT test pin at breakout box. If voltage is within specification, replace ECA and repeat QUICK TEST. If voltage is not within specification, replace TOT sensor and repeat QUICK TEST.

CIRCUIT TEST TE (Cont.)

NOTE: A break in step numbering sequence occurs at this point. Procedure skips from step 3) to step 10). No test procedures have been omitted.

10) KOEO Code 56 Or 637 – KOEO Code 56 and 637 indicate TOT sensor output exceeds self-test maximum voltage. Possible causes for these faults are:
- Transmission fluid temperature incorrect.
- Open wiring harness circuit.
- Faulty ECA.

Turn ignition off. Disconnect TOT wiring harness connector. Inspect terminals, and repair if damaged. Connect jumper wire between TOT and SIG RTN terminals. Perform KOER SELF-TEST. If Code 66/638 is present, replace TOT sensor and repeat QUICK TEST. If Code 66/638 is not present, go to step **11)**.

11) Check TOT & SIG RTN Circuit Continuity – Turn ignition off. Leave TOT sensor disconnected. Disconnect 60-pin ECA connector. Inspect terminals, and repair if damaged. Install EEC-IV Breakout Box (T83L-50-EEC-IV), leaving ECA disconnected. Measure resistance between TOT circuit at TOT wiring harness connector and TOT test pin at breakout box. Measure resistance between SIG RTN circuit at TOT wiring harness connector and TOT test pin at breakout box. If either resistance is more than 5 ohms, repair open circuit and repeat QUICK TEST. If each resistance is 5 ohms or less, go to step **12)**.

12) Check TOT Sensor For Short To VPWR – Turn ignition off. Leave ECA and TOT sensor disconnected. Measure resistance between TOT test pin and test pins No. 37 and 57 at breakout box. If resistance is more than 10,000 ohms, replace ECA and repeat QUICK TEST. If resistance is 10,000 ohms or less, repair short circuit and repeat QUICK TEST.

NOTE: A break in step numbering sequence occurs at this point. Procedure skips from step 12) to step 20). No test procedures have been omitted.

20) KOEO Code 66 Or 638 – KOEO Code 66 and 638 indicate TOT sensor output is lower than self-test minimum voltage. Possible causes for these faults are:
- Damaged TOT sensor.
- Shorted wiring harness circuit.
- Faulty ECA.

Turn ignition off. Disconnect transmission wiring harness connector. Inspect terminals, and repair if damaged. Perform KOEO SELF-TEST. If Code 56 or 637 is present, replace TOT sensor and repeat QUICK TEST. If Code 66/638 is not present, go to step **21)**.

21) Check VREF At Throttle Position Sensor (TPS) – Turn ignition off. Disconnect TPS sensor wiring harness connector. Disconnect 60-pin ECA connector. Inspect terminals, and repair if damaged. Install EEC-IV Breakout Box (T83L-50-EEC-IV). Connect ECA to breakout box. Turn ignition on. Measure voltage between VREF and SIG RTN terminals at TPS wiring harness connector. *See Fig. TE2.* If voltage is 4-6 volts, go to step **22)**. If voltage is not 4-6 volts, go to CIRCUIT TEST C.

90B10950

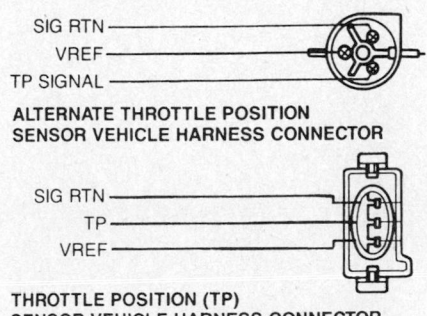

SIG RTN
VREF
TP SIGNAL

ALTERNATE THROTTLE POSITION SENSOR VEHICLE HARNESS CONNECTOR

SIG RTN
TP
VREF

THROTTLE POSITION (TP) SENSOR VEHICLE HARNESS CONNECTOR

NOTE: EITHER TYPE MAY BE FITTED

Fig. TE2: Identifying Throttle Position Sensor (TPS) Connector Terminals

22) Check TOT Sensor Resistance – Turn ignition off. Disconnect ECA from breakout box. Measure resistance between TOT test pin at

CIRCUIT TEST TE (Cont.)

breakout box and test pins No. 40, 46 and 60. If resistance is more than 10,000 ohms, replace ECA and repeat QUICK TEST. If resistance is 10,000 ohms or less, repair short circuit and repeat QUICK TEST.

NOTE: A break in step numbering sequence occurs at this point. Procedure skips from step 22) to step 25). No test procedures have been omitted.

25) Check Transmission Wiring Harness – Turn ignition off. Check transmission internal and external wiring and connectors for damage and corrosion. Repair or replace if necessary. If wiring is okay, replace TOT sensor and repeat QUICK TEST.

NOTE: A break in step numbering sequence occurs at this point. Procedure skips from step 25) to step 90). No test procedures have been omitted.

90) Continuous Memory Code 637/638 – Continuous Memory Code 637/638 indicates that a fault has been detected in TOT circuit at one or more times during previous 80 warm-up cycles. Possible causes for these faults are:
- Intermittent fault in TOT sensor.
- Intermittent short or open in wiring harness.

Turn ignition off. Disconnect 60-pin ECA connector. Inspect terminals, and repair if damaged. Install EEC-IV Breakout Box (T83L-50-EEC-IV). Connect ECA to breakout box. Connect DVOM between test pins No. 2 and 46 at breakout box. Turn ignition on. Shake and bend TOT and SIG RTN wires between transmission and ECA. Voltage should remain stable or change gradually. If voltage drops or surges abruptly, fault in circuit is indicated. If fault is indicated, isolate and repair as necessary. If no faults are found, problem cannot be located at this time.

CIRCUIT TEST TG

ELECTRONIC TRANSMISSION CONTINUOUS MEMORY SERVICE CODES

Diagnostic Aids – Perform this test only when directed by QUICK TEST. This test is intended to diagnose:
- Wiring harness circuits CLS, SS1, SS3, EPC, MCCC, TOT, MLP and VPWR.
- ECA.

92I03899

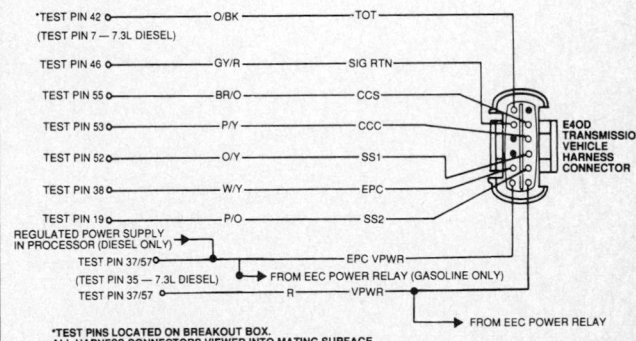

Fig. TG1: E4OD Electronic Transmission Circuit (Bronco, Pickup & Van)

TEST PINS NO. 37 & 57 (EPC PWR) WIRE COLOR [1] IDENTIFICATION

Application	Wire Color
Bronco, Pickup & Van	Red

[1] – On 7.3L, use test pin No. 35 (Red/White) for EPC PWR circuit.

NOTE: Procedure begins with step 90). No test procedures have been omitted.

90) Vehicle Preparation – Ensure all components are properly connected. Ensure transmission fluid is correct level. Warm engine to normal operating temperature. Perform KOEO and CONTINUOUS MEMORY CODE SELF-TEST. If Code 49/617, 56/637, 59/618, 66/638,

CIRCUIT TEST TG (Cont.)

69/619, 62/628, 645, 646, 647, 648 or 656 is present, go to step **93)**. If none of these codes are present, go to step **91)**.

91) Drive Cycle Test (E4OD) – With transmission gear selector in DRIVE position, press Overdrive Cancel Switch (LED should light). Moderately accelerate vehicle to 40 MPH for at least 15 seconds (30 seconds above 4000' elevation). Transmission should be in 3rd gear. While holding speed steady, press Overdrive Cancel Switch (LED should go off) and accelerate from 40 MPH to 50 MPH. Transmission should shift from 3rd gear to 4th gear. Hold speed steady for 15 seconds. While holding speed steady, lightly apply and release brakes to turn brakelights on. Maintain 50 MPH for about 5 seconds. Stop and park vehicle for a minimum of 20 seconds with transmission gear selector in DRIVE position. Repeat procedure 5 times.

After completing DRIVE CYCLE TEST, perform KOEO and CONTINUOUS MEMORY CODE SELF-TEST. If Code 99/624, 67/634 or 651 is present, go to step **92)**. If none of these codes are present but Code 29/452 is present, go to CIRCUIT TEST DS. If Code 11/111 (pass code) is present, fault cannot be duplicated at this time.

92) Code 99/624, 67/634 Or 651 – Code 99/624 and 651 indicate Electronic Pressure Control (EPC) failure. Code 67/634 indicates that Manual Lever Position (MLP) sensor is out of calibration. Possible causes for these faults are:
- Faulty EPC solenoid.
- Faulty MLP sensor.
- Circuit open or grounded.
- Damaged ECA connector pins.

Turn ignition off. Disconnect 60-pin ECA connector. Inspect terminals, and repair if damaged. Install EEC-IV Breakout Box (T83L-50-EEC-IV). Connect ECA to breakout box. To test EPC solenoid, connect DVOM to EPC test pin and EPC VPWR test pin at breakout box. To test MLP sen-

CIRCUIT TEST TG (Cont.)

sor, connect DVOM to MLP test pin and test pin No. 46 at breakout box. For EPC solenoid and MLP sensor, turn ignition on. Voltage for EPC should be less than 10 volts. Voltage for MLP should be less than 5 volts. Shake and bend EPC/MLP wiring harness. Lightly tap on components to simulate road shock. Voltage should remain stable. If voltage changes or exceeds specification, fault in circuit is indicated. If fault is indicated, isolate and repair as necessary. Clear continuous memory codes, and repeat QUICK TEST. If no faults are found, problem cannot be located at this time.

93) Check Circuit Harness & Connectors – Shake and bend EEC-IV wiring harness. Lightly tap on components to simulate road shock. Perform KOEO Continuous Monitor Mode. See CIRCUIT TEST KOEO CONTINUOUS MEMORY CODES table. If fault is indicated, isolate and repair as necessary. Clear continuous memory codes, and repeat QUICK TEST. If no faults are found, problem cannot be located at this time.

CIRCUIT TEST KOEO CONTINUOUS MEMORY CODES

Code	Fault
49/617	1 - 2 Shift Incorrect
56/637	Excessive TOT Circuit Voltage
59/618	2 - 3 Shift Incorrect
66/638	Inadequate TOT Circuit Voltage
69/628	2 - 3 Shift Incorrect
619	3 - 4 Shift Incorrect
645	Inadequate 1st Gear Command Response
646	Inadequate 2nd Gear Command Response
647	Inadequate 3rd Gear Command Response
648	Inadequate 4th Gear Command Response
656	Continuous Slippage Detected

Aerostar, Bronco, Explorer, Pickup, Ranger, Van

NOTE: Unless otherwise specified, references to Pickup include the F350 Super Duty commercial chassis.

MODEL IDENTIFICATION

Series [1]	Model
"A"	Aerostar
"E"	RWD Van
"F"	Pickup
"R"	Ranger
"U"	Bronco & Explorer

[1] – Vehicle series is fifth character of VIN.

INTRODUCTION

Use this article to diagnose driveability problems or for reference to correct component repair procedure. Follow diagnostic or test procedures listed in the articles referenced by these charts. Intermittent faults may also be diagnosed using the procedures in this article.

NOTE: Some driveability problems may have been corrected by manufacturer with a revised computer calibration chip or computer control unit. Check with manufacturer for latest chip or computer application.

Symptom checks can direct the technician to malfunctioning component(s) for further diagnosis. A symptom should lead to a specific component or system test and/or adjustment.

Use intermittent test procedures to locate driveability problems that DO NOT occur when the vehicle is being tested. These test procedures should also be used if a soft (intermittent) trouble code was present, but no problem was found during self-diagnostic testing.

NOTE: For specific testing procedures, see SYSTEM & COMPONENT TESTING – EEC-IV article. For specifications, see ON-VEHICLE ADJUSTMENTS or SERVICE & ADJUSTMENT SPECIFICATIONS article.

SYMPTOMS

SYMPTOM DIAGNOSIS

Symptom checks cannot be used properly unless problem occurs while vehicle is being tested. To reduce diagnostic time, ensure steps in BASIC DIAGNOSTIC PROCEDURES and SELF-DIAGNOSTICS – EEC-IV articles were performed before diagnosing a symptom.

Use diagnostic charts to identify systems and components that should be checked for fault. See DIAGNOSTIC CHART INDEX table. Perform check or adjustment procedure indicated in appropriate diagnostic chart.

DIAGNOSTIC CHART INDEX

Driveability Symptom	See Fig.
Starting	
No Crank	1
Hard Start/Long Crank	2
Stall After Start	3
No Start/Normal Crank	4
Idle	
Slow To Return To Idle	5
Rough Idle	6
High Idle	7
Low/Slow Idle	8
Stalls/Quits	
At Idle	3
On Acceleration	9
At Cruising Speed	9
On Deceleration	8
Runs Rough	
At Idle	6
On Acceleration	10
At Cruising Speed	10

DIAGNOSTIC CHART INDEX (Cont.)

Driveability Symptom	See Fig.
Misses	
At Idle	6
On Acceleration	10
At Cruising Speed	10
Buck/Jerk	9
Hesitation	
On Acceleration	9
Surge	
On Acceleration	9
At Cruising Speed	11
Backfires	12
Lack/Loss Of Power	13
Spark Knock (Pings)	14
Diesels/Runs On	7
Poor Fuel Economy	15
Improper Shift	18
Emissions Compliance	16
Engine	
High Oil Consumption	19
Noise	24
Runs Cold	21
Runs Hot	20
Exhaust Smoke	22
Fuel Odor	23
Vibration	25

INTERMITTENTS

INTERMITTENT PROBLEM DIAGNOSIS

Intermittent fault testing requires duplicating circuit or component failure to identify the problem. These procedures may lead to the computer setting a fault code (on some systems), which may help in diagnosis.

If vehicle does not produce fault codes, monitor voltage or resistance using a DVOM while attempting to reproduce conditions causing intermittent fault. A status change on DVOM indicates a fault has been located.

Use a DVOM to pinpoint faults. When monitoring voltage, ensure ignition switch is in ON position or engine is running. Ensure ignition switch is in OFF position or negative battery cable is disconnected when monitoring circuit resistance. Status changes on DVOM during test procedures indicate area of fault.

TEST PROCEDURES

Intermittent Simulation – To reproduce the conditions creating an intermittent fault, use the following methods:
- Lightly vibrate component.
- Heat component.
- Wiggle or bend wiring harness.
- Spray component with water.
- Remove/apply vacuum source.

Monitor circuit/component voltage or resistance while simulating intermittent. If engine is running, monitor for self-diagnostic codes. See SELF-DIAGNOSTICS – EEC-IV article. Use test results to identify a faulty component or circuit.

NOTE: For test equipment connection and CONTINUOUS MONITOR MODE test operation, see SELF-DIAGNOSTICS – EEC-IV article.

Continuous Monitor Mode (WIGGLE TEST) – In this mode, the technician can attempt to re-create an intermittent fault while monitoring the system. This mode, also called the WIGGLE TEST, may be used in Key On Engine Off (KOEO) and Key On Engine Running (KOER) self-test modes. See SELF-DIAGNOSTICS – EEC-IV article for instructions on the use of this procedure to identify intermittent faults in specific circuits or components.

KOEO WIGGLE TEST Procedure – Connect test equipment. See SELF-DIAGNOSTICS – EEC-IV article. Turn ignition on. Activate self-test using jumper lead or diagnostic tester. Wait 10 seconds, and then

1992 ENGINE PERFORMANCE
Trouble Shooting – No Codes (Cont.)

deactivate and reactivate self-test to enter WIGGLE TEST. Tap, move and wiggle the suspected sensor and/or harness area. If a fault is detected, a code may be stored in memory and indicated at the diagnostic tester or Scan tool. Record or retrieve code, and perform CIRCUIT TEST indicated in SELF-DIAGNOSTICS – EEC-IV article.

KOER WIGGLE TEST Procedure – Connect test equipment. See SELF-DIAGNOSTICS – EEC-IV article. Turn ignition off, and wait 10 seconds. Start engine. Activate self-test using jumper lead or diagnostic tester. Wait 10 seconds, and then deactivate and reactivate self-test to enter WIGGLE TEST. DO NOT turn engine off. Tap, move and wiggle the suspected sensor and/or harness area. If a fault is detected, a code may be stored in memory and indicated at the diagnostic or scan tester. Record or retrieve code, and perform CIRCUIT TEST indicated in SELF-DIAGNOSTICS – EEC-IV article.

DIAGNOSTIC CHARTS

NOTE: For SYSTEM & COMPONENT TESTING references, see SYSTEM & COMPONENT TESTING – EEC-IV article.

NO CRANK		
System	**Component**	**Reference**
Starting	Battery Starter Relay Starter Neutral Drive Switch / Clutch Switch Brake Interlock Switch Ignition Switch Transmission Linkage Adjustment	Charge Or Replace Battery Check Charging And Starting Systems
EEC	Neutral Drive Switch / Clutch Switch	See SELF-DIAGNOSTICS – EEC-IV article.
Base Engine	Flywheel Engine Seized	Check Engine Mechanical Condition
Fuel / Throttle Body	Injectors (hydro-lock)	See FUEL SYSTEM in SYSTEM & COMPONENT TESTING Article
Ignition	Harness (START wire short to GND)	See SYSTEM & COMPONENT TESTING Article

92J04168

Courtesy of Ford Motor Co.

Fig. 1: No Crank

1992 ENGINE PERFORMANCE
Trouble Shooting – No Codes (Cont.)

CRANKS NORMALLY BUT SLOW TO START

System	Component	Reference
Ignition	Scope engine for: Spark Plugs Coil Secondary Ignition Wires Spark Plugs Fouled **TFI IV:** Distributor Cap, Adapter and Rotor **DIS/EDIS:** Single or Dual Hall Crankshaft Sensors Hall Camshaft Sensor DIS/EDIS Ignition Module Coil Pack(s)	**TFI IV:** See IGNITION SYSTEMS in SYSTEM & COMPONENT TESTING Article **DIS/EDIS:** See IGNITION SYSTEMS in SYSTEM & COMPONENT TESTING Article
EEC	EEC-IV Quick Test	See SELF-DIAGNOSTICS – EEC-IV article.
Fuel/Throttle Body	Filter Pump Water/Dirt/Rust Contamination in Fuel Fuel Lines Fuel Pressure Regulator Sender Filter Injectors Improper Fuel Idle Airflow	Perform a Visual Inspection See FUEL SYSTEM in SYSTEM & COMPONENT TESTING Article
Exhaust	Component (restricted)	Inspect Exhaust System
Air Intake and Vacuum Distribution	Vacuum Leaks Air Cleaner Element Restricted	Perform a Visual & Audible Inspection
Cooling	Electric Fan (Hot Start Only)	Check Cooling System
EGR	Valve	See SYSTEM & COMPONENT TESTING Article
PCV	Valve	
EVAP	Components	

92B04169

Courtesy Of Ford Motor Co.

Fig. 2: Cranks Normally But Slow To Start

1992 ENGINE PERFORMANCE
Trouble Shooting – No Codes (Cont.)

CRANKS NORMALLY BUT WON'T RUN (STALLS)

System	Component	Reference
EEC	EEC-IV Quick Test	See SELF-DIAGNOSTICS – EEC-IV article.
Fuel / Throttle Body	Idle Airflow Electrical and Vacuum Connections Fuel Filter Fuel Pump Water / Dirt / Rust Contamination in Fuel Fuel Lines Tank (Fuel Supply) Sender Filter Fuel Pressure Regulator Injectors Improper Fuel	Perform a Visual Inspection See FUEL SYSTEM in SYSTEM & COMPONENT TESTING Article
Vacuum Distribution	Vacuum Leaks	Perform a Visual & Audible Inspection
Ignition	Electrical Connections Secondary Ignition Wires Ignition Switch **TFI IV:** Ignition Coil Ignition Module Rotor Alignment Distributor Cap, Adapter, Rotor and Stator Ballast Resistor **DIS (Thunderbird SC only):** Hall Camshaft Sensor (CID)	**TFI IV:** See IGNITION SYSTEMS in SYSTEM & COMPONENT TESTING Article **DIS (Thunderbird SC only):** See IGNITION SYSTEMS in SYSTEM & COMPONENT TESTING Article
Exhaust	Component (restricted)	Inspect Exhaust System
EGR	Valve	See SYSTEM & COMPONENT TESTING Article
Air Intake System	Air Tube Intercooler Tube (Thunderbird SC)	Check Connections
Base Engine	Camshaft and Valve Train	Check Engine Mechanical Condition

92D04170

Courtesy Of Ford Motor Co.

Fig. 3: Cranks Normally But Won't Run (Stalls)

1992 ENGINE PERFORMANCE
Trouble Shooting – No Codes (Cont.)

CRANKS NORMALLY BUT WON'T START

NOTE: Extended cranking, due to no-start condition, can load the exhaust system with raw fuel, which can ruin the catalytic converter after the engine is started. After servicing no-start condition, disconnect the thermactor air supply, operate engine until surplus fuel is used up, and then reconnect the thermactor air supply.

System	Component	Reference
EEC	EEC-IV Quick Test	See SELF-DIAGNOSTICS – EEC-IV article.
Ignition	Electrical Connections Secondary Ignition Wires Spark Plugs Fouled Ignition Switch **TFI IV:** Ignition Coil Ignition Module Rotor Alignment Distributor Cap, Adapter, Rotor and Stator **DIS/EDIS:** Single and Dual Hall Crankshaft Sensors Hall Camshaft Sensor DIS/EDIS Ignition Module Coil Pack(s)	**TFI IV:** Perform a Visual Inspection See IGNITION SYSTEMS in SYSTEM & COMPONENT TESTING Article **DIS/EDIS:** Perform a Visual Inspection See IGNITION SYSTEMS in SYSTEM & COMPONENT TESTING Article
Fuel/Throttle Body	Fuel Filter Fuel Pump Water/Dirt/Rust Contamination in Fuel Fuel Lines Tank (Fuel Supply) Fuel Sender Filter Fuel Pressure Regulator Injectors Inertia Switch	Perform a Visual Inspection See FUEL SYSTEM in SYSTEM & COMPONENT TESTING Article
Base Engine	Compression Camshaft Timing	Check Engine Mechanical Condition
EGR	Valve	See SYSTEM & COMPONENT TESTING Article
Exhaust	Component (Restricted)	Inspect Exhaust System
Air Intake	Air Tube	Check Connections

92F04171 Courtesy Of Ford Motor Co.

Fig. 4: Cranks Normally But Won't Start

SLOW RETURN TO IDLE

System	Component	Reference
EEC	EEC-IV Quick Test	See SELF-DIAGNOSTICS – EEC-IV article.
Fuel/Throttle Body	Contamination Throttle Linkage	Perform a Visual Inspection
Vacuum Distribution	Vacuum Leaks	Perform a Visual & Audible Inspection
Air Intake	Air Leak	

92H04172 Courtesy Of Ford Motor Co.

Fig. 5: Slow Return To Idle

1992 ENGINE PERFORMANCE
Trouble Shooting – No Codes (Cont.)

ROUGH IDLE

System	Component	Reference
Ignition	Scope Engine For: Spark Plug, Coil, Secondary Ignition Wires, Distributor Cap, Adapter and Rotor, Ignition Timing	See BASIC DIAGNOSTIC PROCEDURES Article
EEC	EEC-IV Quick Test	See SELF-DIAGNOSTICS – EEC-IV article.
Fuel / Throttle Body	Idle Airflow Electrical and Vacuum Connections Fuel Pressure Regulator Injectors Fuel Rail Fuel Lines	Perform a Visual Inspection See FUEL SYSTEM in SYSTEM & COMPONENT TESTING Article
Vacuum Distribution	Vacuum Leaks	Perform a Visual & Audible Inspection
Cooling	Thermostat Fan (loose or cracked)	Check Cooling System
EGR	Valve	See SYSTEM & COMPONENT TESTING Article
Base Engine	Compression Valve Train Camshaft Intake Manifold Gaskets	Check Engine Mechanical Condition
PCV	Valve	See SYSTEM & COMPONENT TESTING Article
EVAP	Components	
Air Intake System	Air Tube Intercooler Tube (Thunderbird SC)	Check Connections
Charging System	Components	Check Charging System
Exhaust	Components	Inspect Exhaust System
Thermactor	Thermactor System Components	See SYSTEM & COMPONENT TESTING Article

92J04173

Courtesy Of Ford Motor Co.

Fig. 6: Rough idle

HIGH IDLE (ENGINE "DIESELS")

System	Component	Reference
Fuel / Throttle Body	Idle Airflow Throttle Plate and Linkage Speed Control Chain	Perform a Visual Inspection See FUEL SYSTEM in SYSTEM & COMPONENT TESTING Article
Vacuum Distribution	Vacuum Leaks	Perform a Visual & Audible Inspection
EEC	EEC-IV Quick Test	See SELF-DIAGNOSTICS – EEC-IV article.
Air Intake System	Air Tube Intake Manifold Gasket	Perform a Visual & Audible Inspection
Cooling	Overheating	Check Cooling System
Air Conditioning	A / C Clutch A / C Demand A / C Cyclic Pressure Switch A / C Refrigerant Charge	Check Air Conditioning System

92B04174

Courtesy Of Ford Motor Co.

Fig. 7: High Idle (Engine "Diesels")

1992 ENGINE PERFORMANCE
Trouble Shooting – No Codes (Cont.)

LOW IDLE (STALLS ON DECELERATION OR QUICK STOP)

System	Component	Reference
Fuel / Throttle Body	Idle Airflow Electrical and Vacuum Connections	Perform a Visual Inspection
EEC	EEC-IV Quick Test	See SELF-DIAGNOSTICS – EEC-IV article.
EGR	Valve	See SYSTEM & COMPONENT TESTING Article
Base Transmission (A / T with overdrive)	Transmission Oil Level Converter Clutch Control Solenoid Modulated Converter Clutch Control Solenoid	See SELF-DIAGNOSTICS – EEC-IV article.

92E04175

Courtesy Of Ford Motor Co.

Fig. 8: Low Idle (Stalls On Deceleration Or Quick Stop)

HESITATES OR STALLS

System	Component	Reference
EEC	EEC-IV Quick Test	See SELF-DIAGNOSTICS – EEC-IV article.
Ignition	Scope engine for: Spark Plug, Coil, Secondary Wires, Distributor Cap and Rotor, Crossed Wires Ignition Timing	See BASIC DIAGNOSTIC PROCEDURES Article
Fuel / Throttle Body	Idle Airflow Fuel Filter Fuel Pump Water / Dirt / Rust Contamination in Fuel Fuel Lines Fuel Pressure Regulator Sender Filter Injectors	Perform a Visual Inspection See FUEL SYSTEM in SYSTEM & COMPONENT TESTING Article
Vacuum Distribution	Vacuum Leaks	Perform a Visual & Audible Inspection
Air Intake Systems	Air Cleaner, Air Duct Intercooler Tube (Thunderbird SC)	Check Connections
EGR	Valve	See SYSTEM & COMPONENT TESTING Article
PCV	Valve	
Exhaust	Restriction (with Backpressure EGR system (PFE))	See SYSTEM & COMPONENT TESTING Article
Base Transmission (A / T with Overdrive)	Converter Clutch Control Solenoid Converter Clutch Override Converter Clutch Modulated Converter Clutch Control Solenoid	
Base Engine	Components	Check Engine Mechanical Condition

92G04176

Courtesy Of Ford Motor Co.

Fig. 9: Hesitates Or Stalls

1992 ENGINE PERFORMANCE
Trouble Shooting – No Codes (Cont.)

MISSES UNDER LOAD

System	Component	Reference
Ignition	Scope engine for: Spark Plug, Coil, Secondary Wires, Distributor Cap, Adapter and Rotor Ignition Timing	See BASIC DIAGNOSTIC PROCEDURES Article
EEC	EEC-IV Quick Test	See SELF-DIAGNOSTICS – EEC-IV article.
Fuel / Throttle Body	Fuel Filter Fuel Pump Fuel Lines Fuel Pressure Regulator Sender Filter Injectors	Perform a Visual Inspection See FUEL SYSTEM in SYSTEM & COMPONENT TESTING Article
EGR	Valve	See SYSTEM & COMPONENT TESTING Article
Vacuum Distribution	Vacuum Leaks	Perform a Visual & Audible Inspection
Base Engine	Components	Check Engine Mechanical Condition

92I04177

Courtesy of Ford Motor Co.

Fig. 10: Misses Under Load

SURGES AT STEADY SPEED

System	Component	Reference
EEC	EEC-IV Quick Test	See SELF-DIAGNOSTICS – EEC-IV article.
Fuel / Throttle Body	Filter Pump Lines Fuel Pressure Regulator Sender Filter Octane Idle Airflow	Perform a Visual Inspection See FUEL SYSTEM in SYSTEM & COMPONENT TESTING Article
Ignition	Scope engine for: Spark Plugs, Wires, Coil, etc Secondary Ignition Wires Timing	See BASIC DIAGNOSTIC PROCEDURES Article
Vacuum Distribution	Vacuum Leaks	Perform a Visual & Audible Inspection
EGR	Valve	See SYSTEM & COMPONENT TESTING Article
Air Intake System	Air Intake Components	Perform a Visual Inspection
EVAP	Components	See SYSTEM & COMPONENT TESTING Article
Base Engine	Valve Train and Camshaft Intake Manifold and Gaskets	Check Engine Mechanical Condition
Thermactor	Thermactor System Components	See SYSTEM & COMPONENT TESTING Article
Supercharger	Assembly	
Base Transmission (A / T with Overdrive)	Converter Clutch Control Components	See SELF-DIAGNOSTICS – EEC-IV article.

92A04178

Courtesy Of Ford Motor Co.

Fig. 11: Surges At Steady Speed

1992 ENGINE PERFORMANCE
Trouble Shooting – No Codes (Cont.)

BACKFIRE (INTAKE OR EXHAUST)

System	Component	Reference
Ignition	Scope engine for: Spark Plugs, Wires, Coil, etc. Crossed Wires, Ignition Timing	See BASIC DIAGNOSTIC PROCEDURES Article
Vacuum Distribution	Vacuum Hoses, Connections	Perform a Visual & Audible Inspection
EEC	EEC-IV Quick Test	See SELF-DIAGNOSTICS – EEC-IV article.
Thermactor	Thermactor System Components	See SYSTEM & COMPONENT TESTING Article
Base Engine	Intake Manifold Gaskets Compression Checks Camshaft Valves	Check Engine Mechanical Condition
Exhaust	Components (restricted)	Inspect Exhaust System
Fuel / Throttle Body	Filter Pump Water / Dirt / Rust / Contamination in Fuel Lines Fuel Pressure Regulator Injectors Sender Filter Octane	Perform a Visual Inspection See FUEL SYSTEM in SYSTEM & COMPONENT TESTING Article

92C04179 Courtesy of Ford Motor Co.

Fig. 12: Backfire (Intake Or Exhaust)

LACK OF POWER

System	Component	Reference
Ignition	Scope engine for: Spark Plugs, Wires, Coil, etc. Timing	See BASIC DIAGNOSTIC PROCEDURES Article
EEC	EEC-IV Quick Test	See SELF-DIAGNOSTICS – EEC-IV article.
Fuel / Throttle Body	Filter Pump Lines Fuel Pressure Regulator Fuel Sender Filter Injectors Idle Airflow	Perform a Visual Inspection See FUEL SYSTEM in SYSTEM & COMPONENT TESTING Article
Exhaust	Component (restricted)	Inspect Exhaust System
Cooling	Thermostat	Check Cooling System
Vacuum Distribution	Vacuum Leaks	Perform a Visual Inspection
Air Intake Systems	Air Cleaner Duct and Element	See SYSTEM & COMPONENT TESTING Article
EGR	Valve	
Base Engine	Compression Check Camshaft Valves	Check Engine Mechanical Condition
Drivetrain	Clutch, Automatic Transmission, Brakes	Check Transmission & Drive Train Components
Supercharger	Assembly	See SYSTEM & COMPONENT TESTING Article

92E04180 Courtesy Of Ford Motor Co.

Fig. 13: Lack Of Power

SPARK KNOCK (PINGS)

System	Component	Reference
Ignition	Timing	See ON-VEHICLE ADJUSTMENTS Article
EEC	EEC-IV Quick Test	See SELF-DIAGNOSTICS – EEC-IV article.
Cooling	Overheating	Check Cooling System
Base Engine	Oil Level Compression Check Intake Manifold Gasket	Check Engine Mechanical Condition
Fuel / Throttle Body	Filter Pump Lines Fuel Pressure Regulator Sender Filter Injectors	Perform a Visual Inspection. See FUEL SYSTEMS in SYSTEM & COMPONENT TESTING article.
PCV	Valve	See SYSTEM & COMPONENT TESTING Article
EGR	Verify Correct Application, then Diagnose	
Air Intake System	Air Cleaner Duct and Element	
Thermactor	Thermactor System Components	
Base Transmission (E4OD, AODE, AXOD-E)	Transmission Controls	See SELF-DIAGNOSTICS – EEC-IV Article

92G04181   Courtesy of Ford Motor Co.

Fig. 14: Spark Knock (Pings)

POOR FUEL ECONOMY

NOTE: Fuel consumption increases drastically in city driving, short-run operation, stop-and-go driving, trailer towing, extended winter warm-up periods, etc. Determine if these factors are the cause of poor fuel mileage before proceeding with diagnostic procedure.

System	Component	Reference
Fuel / Throttle Body	Fuel Pressure Regulator Fuel Return Line Blocked	See SYSTEM & COMPONENT TESTING Article
Air Intake System	Air Cleaner Duct and Element	Perform a Visual Inspection
Ignition	Scope engine for: Spark Plugs, Wires, Coil, Secondary Wires, Distributor Cap, etc. Timing	See IGNITION SYSTEMS in SYSTEM & COMPONENT TESTING Article
EEC	EEC-IV Quick Test	See SELF-DIAGNOSTICS – EEC-IV article.
Cooling	Thermostat	Check Cooling System
Factors External to the Engine	Tire Pressure Clutch Operation Converter Clutch Override Automatic Transmission Shift Pattern and Fluid Level Brake Drag Exhaust System Speedometer / Odometer Gear Ratio Axle Ratio Vehicle Load Road and Weather Conditions Aftermarket Add Ons	Perform a Manual & Visual Inspection
Base Transmission (A / T with Overdrive)	Converter Clutch Control Components Modulated Converter Clutch Control Solenoid	See SELF-DIAGNOSTICS – EEC-IV article.
EGR	Valve Operation	See SYSTEM & COMPONENT TESTING Article

92I04102   Courtesy Of Ford Motor Co.

Fig. 15: Poor Fuel Economy

STATE EMISSION TEST FAILURE

NOTE: Canada and some states or metropolitan areas in the United States require periodic idle emission tests. All Ford products have been designed to pass these tests. If a Ford product fails an idle Emission test, it is probable that 1), the engine temperature was not warm and stabilized prior to the test, or 2), the vehicle had idled excessively long prior to the test.

Before starting any services, verify complaints of idle emission test failure by using test procedure of area that failed vehicle. The following encompasses most of the emissions measurement modes of current state idle test procedures:

- Ensure engine is at normal operating temperature and all accessories are turned off.
- Read emissions at idle.
- Operate engine at 2200-2800 RPM.
- Read emissions within 30 seconds.
- Return engine speed to idle.
- Read emissions within 30 seconds.

If any emission component is changed, Keep-Alive Memory (KAM) should be cleared before repeating state emission test procedure. See SELF-DIAGNOSTICS – EEC-IV article.

System	Component	Reference
EEC	EEC-IV Quick Test	See SELF-DIAGNOSTICS – EEC-IV article.
Ignition	Scope engine for: Spark Plugs, Wires, Coil, Timing, etc.	See BASIC DIAGNOSTIC PROCEDURES Article
Vacuum Distribution	Vacuum Leaks/Blockage	Perform a Visual & Audible Inspection
Fuel/Throttle Body	Idle Airflow Injectors Fuel Rail Fuel Pressure	Perform a Visual Inspection See FUEL SYSTEM in SYSTEM & COMPONENT TESTING Article
EGR	Valve Vacuum Regulator	See SYSTEM & COMPONENT TESTING Article
PCV	Valve	
EVAP	Valve	
Thermactor	Thermactor System Components	
Exhaust	Pipes, Muffler, Catalysts, Resonator, etc.	Inspect Exhaust System
Cooling	Unstabilized Engine Temperature	Check Cooling System
Base Engine	Scheduled Maintenance Compression Valve Train Camshaft Intake Manifold Leaks	Check Engine Mechanical Condition

92A04183

Courtesy of Ford Motor Co.

Fig. 16: State Emission Test Failure

NOTE: This chart DOES NOT apply to Light Trucks

SHIFT INDICATOR LIGHT & AUDIBLE CHIMES ON

NOTE: Verify that the customer has read the Owner Guide on the Thunderbird SC overheat protection feature.

The Thunderbird SC is equipped with a Shift Indicator Light and Audible Chime that warns the customer when the engine oil or coolant overheats while the vehicle is operated at high speeds (above 100 MPH) for extended periods of time. The Shift Indicator Light and Chime will also warn the customer when the engine has reached too high an RPM for that gear. The EEC-IV processor will reduce vehicle speed by limiting fuel to the engine when one of these overheat conditions has been reached. The customer may then notice a loss of power and/or a slight vibration. The Shift Indicator Light will "light" and the Audible Chime will produce a "steady tone" to alert the customer to upshift at the time. Full power will be restored and the Shift Indicator Light and Chimes will turn off when the vehicle returns to normal operating termperatures.

System	Component	Reference
EEC	EEC-IV Quick Test SIL Circuit Top Gear Switch	See SELF-DIAGNOSTICS – EEC-IV article.
Thunderbird SC	Audible Chime System	See CIRCUIT TEST KL in SELF-DIAGNOSTICS – EEC-IV article.

92C04184

Courtesy of Ford Motor Co.

Fig. 17: Shift Indicator Light & Audible Chimes On

IMPROPER SHIFT

System	Component	Reference
Base Transmission (4EAT, A4LD, AOD-E, AXOD-E, E4OD)	Converter Clutch Control Solenoid Converter Clutch Electronic Pressure Control Solenoid Shift Solenoids Modulated Converter Clutch Control Solenoid 4x4 Low Switch	See SELF-DIAGNOSTICS – EEC-IV article.
EEC (EEC Controlled Electronic Transmission)	EEC-IV Quick Test	See SELF-DIAGNOSTICS – EEC-IV article.

92F04185

Courtesy of Ford Motor Co.

Fig. 18: Improper Shift

1992 ENGINE PERFORMANCE
Trouble Shooting – No Codes (Cont.)

HIGH OIL CONSUMPTION

System	Component	Reference
External Leaks	Rocker Cover Gasket, Crankshaft Seals, etc.	Perform a Visual Inspection
Proper Dipstick	Over / Under Filling of Crankcase	Perform a Visual Inspection
PCV	Valve	
Internal Leaks (Blue smoke from the tailpipe)	Valve Guides Valve Stem Seals Intake Manifold Gaskets Cylinder Head Drain Passages Piston Rings	Check Engine Mechanical Condition

92H04186

Courtesy of Ford Motor Co.

Fig. 19: High Oil Consumption

ENGINE RUNS HOT

System	Component	Reference
Cooling	Thermostat Coolant Level Radiator or A / C Condenser Pressure Cap and / or Overflow System External Leaks Belts and Tension Fan and Fan Clutch Electric Fan (if equipped)	Perform a Visual Inspection Check Cooling System
Gauges	Sending Unit	1
EEC	EEC-IV Quick Test	See SELF-DIAGNOSTICS – EEC-IV article.
Ignition	Timing	See ON-VEHICLE ADJUSTMENTS Article
Base Engine	Water Pump Core Sand in Block / Heads Internal Leaks	Check Engine Mechanical Condition
Brakes	Brakes Dragging	Check Brake System

1 – See Appropriate INSTRUMENT PANELS Article in SAFETY EQUIPMENT

92J04187

Courtesy of Ford Motor Co.

Fig. 20: Engine Runs Hot

ENGINE RUNS COLD

System	Component	Reference
Gauge System	Gauge Sender	See appropriate SAFETY EQUIPMENT article.
Cooling	Thermostat	Check Cooling System

92B04188

Courtesy of Ford Motor Co.

Fig. 21: Engine Runs Cold

1992 ENGINE PERFORMANCE
Trouble Shooting – No Codes (Cont.)

EXHAUST SMOKE

System	Component	Reference
Black Smoke (Rich Mixture)	Air Cleaner Element Restricted Fuel Pressure Regulator Injectors Return Fuel Line Restricted	Perform a Visual Inspection See FUEL SYSTEM in SYSTEM & COMPONENT TESTING Article
	EEC Components	See SELF-DIAGNOSTICS – EEC-IV article.
Blue Smoke (Burning Oil)	PCV Valve Guides / Stems / Seals Oil Drain Passages in Heads Piston Rings (not seated, seized, etc) Cylinder Bores (scuffed)	Check Engine Mechanical Condition
White Smoke (Coolant in Combustion)	Intake Manifold Gasket Leaks, Cracked, Porous Cylinder Head Gasket Leaks, Cracked, Porous Engine Block Cracked, Porous	Perform a Visual Inspection Check Cooling System

92D04189

Courtesy of Ford Motor Co.

Fig. 22: Exhaust Smoke

GAS SMELL

System	Component	Reference
Fuel / Throttle Body	Fuel Filter Leaks Injectors Leak Fuel Pump Leaks Fuel Lines Leak Fuel Tank Leaks Fuel Tank Filler Neck Leaks Fuel Tank Sender Leaks Fuel Return Line Blocked Fuel Pressure Regulator Leaks	Perform a Visual Inspection See FUEL SYSTEM in SYSTEM & COMPONENT TESTING Article
CANP	Carbon Canister, Solenoid, Hoses Leak	See SYSTEM & COMPONENT TESTING Article
EEC	EEC-IV Quick Test	See SELF-DIAGNOSTICS – EEC-IV article.

92F04190

Courtesy of Ford Motor Co.

Fig. 23: Gas Smell

1992 ENGINE PERFORMANCE
Trouble Shooting – No Codes (Cont.)

ENGINE NOISE

System	Component	Reference
Squeal, Click, Chirp	Oil Level Low Valve Train Drive Belts (loose, worn) Drive Belt Components EEC Solenoids	Perform a Visual & Audible Inspection Check Engine Mechanical Condition
Rumble, Grind	Belt Driven Components	Perform a Visual & Audible Inspection
Rattle	Loose Components	
Hiss	Thermactor System Leaks Vacuum Distribution System Leaks Air Induction System Leaks Spark Plugs Loose Cooling System Leaks EVAP System Leaks	Perform a Visual & Audible Inspection
Snap	Secondary Ignition	
Rap, Roar	Exhaust System Leaks Thermactor System	Perform a Visual & Audible Inspection Inspect Exhaust System
Knock	Connecting Rod Bearings Worn Main Bearings Worn Piston Pins Loose Piston to Bore clearance Detonation (Spark Knock)	Check Engine Mechanical Condition *See Fig. 14.*

92H04191 Courtesy of Ford Motor Co.

Fig. 24: Engine Noise

ENGINE VIBRATES AT NORMAL SPEEDS

System	Component	Reference
Engine Accessories	Fan Belt Drive Components Engine Mounts Engine Vibration Damper	Perform a Manual & Visual Inspection
Non-Engine	Driveline Tires, Wheels Tire Balance	Perform a Manual & Visual Inspection
3.8L SC	Shift Indicator Light and Audible Chime "ON"	*See Fig. 17.*

92J04192 Courtesy of Ford Motor Co.

Fig. 25: Engine Vibrates At Normal Speeds

1992 ENGINE PERFORMANCE
System & Component Testing – EEC-IV

Aerostar, Bronco, Explorer, Pickup, Ranger, Van

NOTE: Unless otherwise specified, references to Pickup include the F350 Super Duty commercial chassis.

MODEL IDENTIFICATION

Series [1]	Model
"A"	Aerostar
"E"	Van
"F"	Pickup
"R"	Ranger
"U"	Bronco & Explorer

[1] – Vehicle series is fifth character of VIN.

INTRODUCTION

Prior to testing separate components or systems, it is recommended that all procedures listed in BASIC DIAGNOSTIC PROCEDURES article be performed. Since many computer controlled and monitored components will set a service code if they malfunction, check EEC-IV system and retrieve service codes. See Quick Test procedure in SELF-DIAGNOSTICS – EEC-IV article. If service codes are present see appropriate CIRCUIT TEST in SELF-DIAGNOSTICS – EEC-IV article.

NOTE: Testing individual components does not isolate wiring circuit shorts or opens. Perform all voltage tests with a Digital Volt-Ohmmeter (DVOM) that has a minimum 10-megohm input impedance, unless stated otherwise in test procedure. Use ohmmeter to isolate wiring harness shorts or opens.

NOTE: For wiring diagrams not shown in testing procedures, see WIRING DIAGRAMS article in ENGINE PERFORMANCE.

COMPUTERIZED ENGINE CONTROLS

ELECTRONIC CONTROL ASSEMBLY (ECA)

Ground Circuits – 1) Using a DVOM, check for continuity to ground on ECA terminals No. 20, 40 and 60. *See Fig. 1.* Resistance should be zero ohms. If resistance is not zero ohms, repair open to ground.
2) Using a voltmeter, touch negative lead of voltmeter to a good ground. Touch positive lead of voltmeter to each ground terminal. With vehicle running, voltmeter should indicate less than one volt. If voltmeter reading is greater than one volt, check for open, corrosion or loose connection on ground lead.
Power Circuits – Using a voltmeter, check for battery voltage between ECA terminal No. 1 (KAPWR) and ground. Check for battery voltage at terminals No. 37 and 57 (VPWR). If battery voltage is not present, power is not being supplied from EEC power relay. See CIRCUIT TEST B in SELF-DIAGNOSTICS – EEC-IV article.

ECA LOCATION

Application	Location
Aerostar	Left Of Master Cylinder.
Bronco & Pickup	Below Brake Fluid Reservoir.
Explorer & Ranger	Behind Right Kick Panel.
Van	Right Fender Apron, Under Blower Motor.

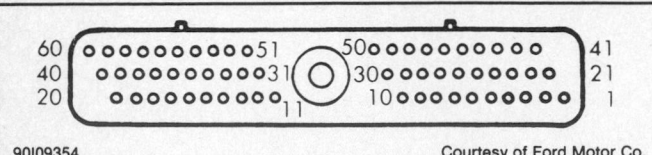

90I09354   Courtesy of Ford Motor Co.

Fig. 1: Identifying ECA 60-Pin Connector Terminals

ENGINE SENSORS & SWITCHES (ECA INPUTS)

NOTE: For additional sensor testing specifications, see SENSOR OPERATING RANGE CHARTS article.

Air Charge Temperature (ACT) Sensor – 1) Sensor is located in intake runner. Sensor requires a 5-volt reference signal during engine operation. With sensor disconnected, sensor may be checked by measuring resistance between sensor terminals.

NOTE: Engine Coolant Temperature (ECT) sensor and ACT sensor terminal connectors are identical. Ensure testing is done on proper component.

2) For specifications, see SENSOR OPERATING RANGE CHARTS article. For additional testing information and circuit testing of sensor, see CIRCUIT TEST DA in SELF-DIAGNOSTICS – EEC-IV article.
Barometric Pressure Sensor (BP) – Faults in barometric pressure sensor or circuit should set a service code. See Quick Test procedure in SELF-DIAGNOSTICS – EEC-IV article. If no service code has been set, see CIRCUIT TEST DF in SELF-DIAGNOSTICS – EEC-IV article for sensor specifications.
Clutch Switch – See NEUTRAL DRIVE SWITCH (NDS) A/C INPUT.
Cylinder Identification Sensor (CID) & Crankshaft Sensor – CID sensor is mounted at crankshaft. Disconnect sensor connector and measure resistance across sensor terminals. Resistance should be 300-750 ohms. If resistance is not as specified, replace sensor.
Engine Coolant Temperature (ECT) Sensor – Sensor is located in intake manifold coolant passage at front of most engines. On 2.3L, sensor is mounted on left side of engine, above oil filter. Sensor requires a 5-volt reference signal during engine operation. With sensor disconnected, sensor may be checked by measuring resistance between sensor terminals. For specifications, see SENSOR OPERATING RANGE CHARTS article. For additional testing information and circuit testing of sensor, see CIRCUIT TEST DA in SELF-DIAGNOSTICS – EEC-IV article.
EGR Valve Position (EVP) Sensor/EGR Vacuum Regulator (EVR) Solenoid – Faults in sensor or circuit should set a service code. See Quick Test procedure in SELF-DIAGNOSTICS – EEC-IV article. If no service code has been set, see CIRCUIT TEST DN in SELF-DIAGNOSTICS – EEC-IV article for sensor specifications and circuit testing procedure.
Engine RPM Sensor (RPMS) – This sensor is used only on diesel engines. Disconnect RPMS electrical connector. Using DVOM, measure resistance across sensor terminals. Resistance should be 2400-2800 ohms. Replace sensor if not as specified. Faults in RPMS or circuit should set a service code. See Quick Test procedure in SELF-DIAGNOSTICS – EEC-IV article. If no service code has been set, see CIRCUIT TEST DJ in SELF-DIAGNOSTICS – EEC-IV article for additional sensor testing and specifications.
Fuel Injection Pump Lever (FIPL) Sensor (7.3L Diesel) – This sensor may also be referred to as Throttle Position Sensor (TP or TPS). Faults in FIPL sensor or circuit should set a service code. See Quick Test procedure in SELF-DIAGNOSTICS – EEC-IV article. If no service code has been set, see CIRCUIT TEST DQ in SELF-DIAGNOSTICS – EEC-IV article for additional sensor testing and specifications. Ensure none of the following conditions exist.
• Binding throttle or speed control linkage
• Idle speed and throttle stop improperly adjusted
• Choke/high cam system sticking
Heated Exhaust Gas Oxygen (HEGO) Sensor – Vehicle may be equipped with one or 2 HEGO sensors. They are located in the exhaust pipe upstream of the catalytic converters. Faults in sensor or circuit should set a service code. See Quick Test procedure in SELF-DIAGNOSTICS – EEC-IV article. If no service code has been set, see CIRCUIT TEST H in SELF-DIAGNOSTICS – EEC-IV article for additional sensor specifications and circuit testing procedures. Ensure that none of the following conditions exist.

- Moisture inside sensor/harness connector
- HEGO sensor coated with contaminants
- Sensor circuit open or shorted to ground

Inertia Switch – Ensure key is off. Inertia switches may be found in the following locations:

- On Aerostar & Van, on right kick panel, just forward of door opening.
- On Bronco & Pickup, on floorboard to left and above steering column.
- On Explorer, under instrument panel, to right of transmission hump.

Push down on reset button to ensure switch is closed. Measure resistance between terminals on switch. If resistance is 5 ohms or less, switch is okay. For additional circuit testing information refer to CIRCUIT TEST J in SELF-DIAGNOSTICS – EEC-IV article. If resistance is greater than 5 ohms, replace switch.

NOTE: In closed position, reset button can be depressed an additional 1/16" against spring. This is normal and does not affect switch operation.

Knock Sensor (KS) – KS is located on cylinder block. Faults in sensor or circuit should set a service code. See Quick Test procedure in SELF-DIAGNOSTICS – EEC-IV article. If no service code has been set, see CIRCUIT TEST DG in SELF-DIAGNOSTICS – EEC-IV article for additional sensor specifications and circuit testing procedures. Sensor is tested by substitution or by manually generating a knock to ensure sensor will set a service code.

Manifold Absolute Pressure (MAP) Sensor – Sensor is located on engine or firewall and is connected to intake manifold by a vacuum supply hose. Remove vacuum supply hose to sensor. Install vacuum pump to sensor and apply 18 in. Hg vacuum. Sensor should hold vacuum. If sensor does not hold vacuum, replace sensor. Faults in MAP sensor or circuit should set a service code. See Quick Test procedure in SELF-DIAGNOSTICS – EEC-IV article. If no service code has been set, see CIRCUIT TEST DF in SELF-DIAGNOSTICS – EEC-IV article for additional sensor testing and specifications.

Mass Airflow (MAF) Sensor – Faults in MAF sensor or circuit should set a service code. See Quick Test procedure in SELF-DIAGNOSTICS – EEC-IV article. If no service code has been set, see CIRCUIT TEST DC in SELF-DIAGNOSTICS – EEC-IV article for sensor and circuit testing and specifications.

Neutral Drive Switch (NDS) A/C Input – With ignition switch in OFF position, set DVOM to 200-ohm scale. Locate NDS switch (on transmission) and clutch switch (on clutch pedal linkage). Disconnect harness at both switches. Measure resistance across NDS terminals with transmission in Neutral and across clutch switch terminals with clutch pedal fully depressed. If any resistance is greater than 5 ohms, switch is open. Replace switch as necessary. Faults in switches or switch circuits should set a service code. See Quick Test procedure in SELF-DIAGNOSTICS – EEC-IV article. If no service code has been set, see CIRCUIT TEST TA in SELF-DIAGNOSTICS – EEC-IV article for additional switch testing and specifications.

Power Steering Pressure Switch (PSPS) – **1)** Disconnect PSPS connector at steering gearbox or line. Set DVOM to 200-ohm scale and connect test leads to switch. With steering wheel centered, resistance should be less than 10 ohms. Start engine and turn steering wheel one-half turn and then return it to centered position.

2) Resistance should change from less than 10 ohms to infinity and return to less than 10 ohms when steering wheel is returned to centered position. Faulty PSPS or circuit should set a service code. See Quick Test procedure in SELF-DIAGNOSTICS – EEC-IV article. If no service code has been set, see CIRCUIT TEST FF in SELF-DIAGNOSTICS – EEC-IV article for additional switch testing and specifications.

Throttle Position Sensor (TP Or TPS – Gasoline) – For diesel TPS, see FUEL INJECTION PUMP LEVER (FIPL) SENSOR. Faults in TP sensor or circuit should set a service code. See Quick Test procedure in SELF-DIAGNOSTICS – EEC-IV article. If no service code has been set, see CIRCUIT TEST DH in SELF-DIAGNOSTICS – EEC-IV article

for additional sensor testing and specifications. Ensure none of the following conditions exist:

- Binding throttle linkage
- TP sensor loose or not seated properly
- Throttle plate not fully closed

Vehicle Speed Sensor (VSS) – Disconnect VSS electrical connector. Using DVOM measure resistance across sensor terminals. Resistance should be 190-250 ohms. Replace sensor if not within specification. Faults in VSS sensor or circuit should set a service code. See Quick Test procedure in SELF-DIAGNOSTICS – EEC-IV article. If no service code has been set, see CIRCUIT TEST DP in SELF-DIAGNOSTICS – EEC-IV article for additional sensor testing and specifications.

MODULES, MOTORS, RELAYS & SOLENOIDS

RELAYS

Fuel Pump Relay – Remove relay from vehicle. Connect battery voltage to terminal "C". Ground terminal "D". *See Fig. 2.* Measure resistance between terminals "A" and "B". Resistance should be less than one ohm with power applied and greater than 10 k/ohms with power removed.

NOTE: For more fuel delivery system testing, see CIRCUIT TEST J in SELF-DIAGNOSTICS article.

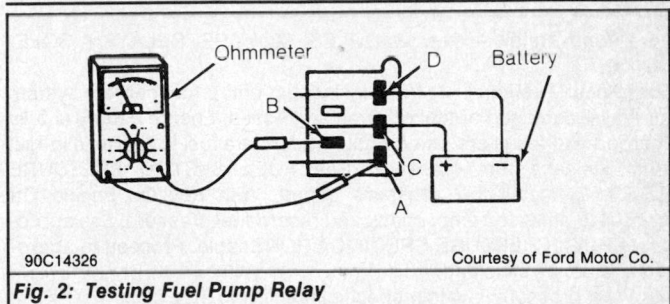

90C14326   Courtesy of Ford Motor Co.

Fig. 2: Testing Fuel Pump Relay

SOLENOIDS

Air Management Solenoids (AM1 & AM2) – Disconnect solenoid harness connectors, and measure resistance across terminals. Resistance should be 50-100 ohms. If resistance is not as specified, replace solenoid. Faults in AM1 or AM2 solenoids or circuits should set a service code. See Quick Test procedure in SELF-DIAGNOSTICS – EEC-IV article. If no service code has been set, see CIRCUIT TEST KC in SELF-DIAGNOSTICS – EEC-IV article for additional solenoid and circuit testing.

Canister Purge (CANP) Solenoid – See FUEL EVAPORATION under EMISSION SYSTEMS & SUB-SYSTEMS.

EGR Solenoid – See EXHAUST GAS RECIRCULATION (EGR) under EMISSION SYSTEMS & SUB-SYSTEMS.

Idle Speed Control (ISC) Solenoid – **1)** Solenoid is by-pass air type. Ensure ignition is off. Disconnect ISC solenoid harness connector. Set DVOM to 200-ohm scale. Measure resistance between ISC solenoid

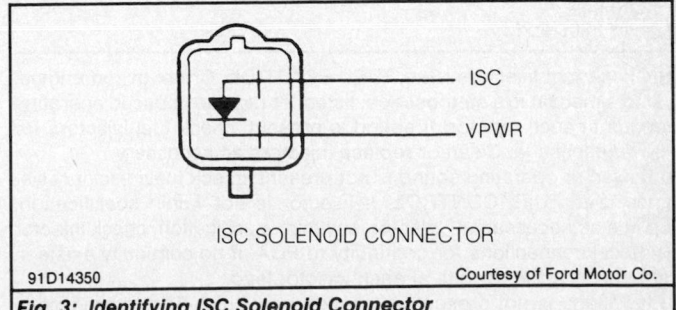

ISC SOLENOID CONNECTOR

91D14350   Courtesy of Ford Motor Co.

Fig. 3: Identifying ISC Solenoid Connector

terminals. *See Fig. 3.* There is a diode in solenoid, connect DVOM (+) test lead to VPWR terminal and DVOM (–) lead to ISC terminal.

2) Resistance should be 7-13 ohms. If resistance is not as specified, replace solenoid. Faults in ISC solenoid or circuit should set a service code. See Quick Test procedure in SELF-DIAGNOSTICS – EEC-IV article. If no service code has been set, see CIRCUIT TEST KE in SELF-DIAGNOSTICS – EEC-IV article for additional solenoid testing and specifications.

FUEL SYSTEM

NOTE: In testing procedures, references to KOEO refer to Key On Engine Off. References to KOER refer to Key On Engine Running.

FUEL SYSTEM PRESSURE RELEASE

1) Remove fuel tank cap. Using Fuel Pressure Gauge (T80L-9974-B), release pressure from system at pressure relief valve (Schrader valve), located on fuel injection manifold rail.

2) If fuel pressure gauge is not available, disconnect electrical connector to inertia switch located on left side of luggage compartment. Remove fuel cap to release fuel tank pressure. Crank engine for 15 seconds to release system pressure.

FUEL DELIVERY

NOTE: For fuel system pressure testing and fuel pressure specifications, see BASIC DIAGNOSTIC PROCEDURES article.

Fuel Pump Relay – See MODULES, MOTORS, RELAYS & SOLENOIDS.

Fuel Pump Testing – 1) Visually inspect entire fuel delivery system for leaks, damaged or kinked lines and hoses. Ensure battery is fully charged and fuses are okay. Ensure adequate fuel is available in fuel tank. Release fuel pressure. See FUEL SYSTEM PRESSURE RELEASE. Install fuel pressure gauge. With Key On Engine Off (KOEO) to activate pump, check and record fuel pressure. See appropriate FUEL PRESSURE SPECIFICATIONS table. Proceed to appropriate step, as indicated:

- If fuel pressure is within specification, go to step **2)**.
- If fuel pressure is zero, go to step **5)**.
- If fuel pressure is low, go to step **11)**.
- If fuel pressure is high, go to step **12)**.

FUEL PRESSURE SPECIFICATIONS (GASOLINE)

Engine	psi (kg/cm²) KOER	psi (kg/cm²) KOEO
4.9L	45-60 (3.16-4.22)	40-60 (3.52-4.22)
All Others	30-45 (2.11-3.16)	35-40 (2.46-2.81)

FUEL PRESSURE SPECIFICATIONS (DIESEL)

Application	psi (kg/cm²)
Filter Inlet	[1] 2 (.14)
Filter Outlet	[2] 1 (.07)
Return Line	[2] 2 (.14)

[1] – At idle.
[2] – At 3300 RPM.

2) Check fuel injectors. See FUEL CONTROL. Crank or run engine. Using a mechanic's stethoscope, listen for regularly spaced operating sounds at each injector. If sound is present, check fuel injectors for flow and leakage. Clean or replace injectors as necessary.

3) If injector operating sound is not present, check fuel injector resistance. See FUEL CONTROL. If injector is not within specification, replace as necessary. If injector is within specification, check injector electrical connections for continuity to ECA. If no continuity exists in circuit, check for 12 volts at each injector lead.

4) If voltage is not present at injector, see Quick Test procedure in SELF-DIAGNOSTICS – EEC-IV article. Faults in injector circuit

should set a service code. If no service code has been set, see CIRCUIT TEST H in SELF-DIAGNOSTICS – EEC-IV article.

5) If fuel pressure is zero, ensure battery is fully charged and key is off. Ground fuel pump lead. Using a jumper lead, ground FP terminal at SELF-TEST connector. *See Fig. 4.* Ensure connection is okay at pump/sender unit. Turn ignition on, engine off. Listen for sound of fuel pump running. If pump is running, proceed to next step. If fuel pump is not running, proceed to step **7)**.

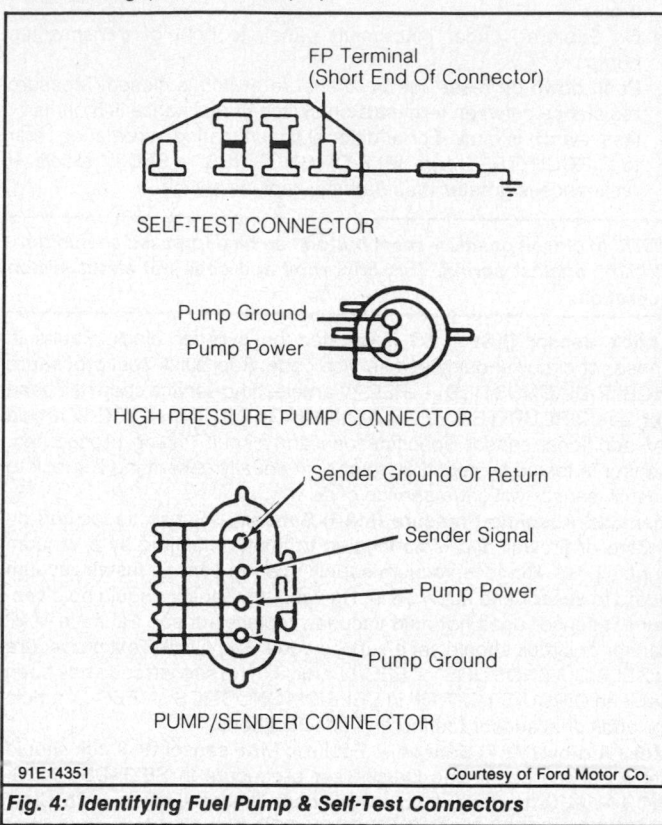

91E14351   Courtesy of Ford Motor Co.

Fig. 4: Identifying Fuel Pump & Self-Test Connectors

6) Check condition of high-pressure fuel filter. If filter is free of contamination check fuel pressure regulator, go to step **12)**. If filter is contaminated, replace filter and recheck system pressure as outlined in step **1)**.

7) Turn ignition off and disconnect fuel pump/sender or high pressure pump connector. Set DVOM on 200-ohm scale. Measure resistance between pump ground at connector and chassis ground. If resistance is one ohm or more, repair open circuit to ground. If resistance is less than one ohm, go to next step.

8) Ensure ignition is off and battery is fully charged. Disconnect harness connector from pump/sender unit. Ground FP terminal at SELF-TEST connector. With KOEO and DVOM on 20-volt scale, measure voltage at Pump Power terminal of pump/sender or high pressure pump connector. If voltage is 10.5 volts or more, replace pump/sender assembly. If voltage is not as specified, go to next step.

9) With KOEO, check voltage at fuel pump inertia switch. If voltage is 10.5 volts or more at both inertia switch terminals, repair wire between inertia switch and pump. If voltage is not as specified, reset or replace inertia switch as necessary and go to next step.

10) Ensure ignition is off and battery is fully charged. Ground FP terminal at SELF-TEST connector. With KOEO and DVOM on 20-volt scale, measure voltage at fuel pump relay (Brown wire). If voltage is 10.5 volts or more at relay, repair Brown wire between fuel pump relay and inertia switch. If voltage is not as specified, check voltage supply to fuel pump relay and to terminal No. 1 at ECA. For additional circuit testing information see CIRCUIT TEST J in SELF-DIAGNOSTICS EEC-IV article.

11) Ground FP terminal at SELF-TEST connector. Using a DVOM, check voltage at fuel pump terminal (Pink/Black wire). If voltage at fuel pump is within .5 volt of battery voltage, go to step **6)**. If voltage is not as specified, go to step **5)**.

12) Check engine compartment vacuum hose for leaks and ensure engine produces normal engine vacuum. See FUEL PRESSURE REGULATOR test procedure.

CAUTION: Inspect fuel system for leaks or damage before testing fuel pump.

Fuel Pressure Regulator (Gasoline) – 1) Ensure key is off. Connect fuel pressure gauge to Schrader valve on fuel rail. Ensure manifold vacuum supply tube is connected to fuel pressure regulator. Start and run engine for 10 seconds. Stop engine and wait 10 seconds. Start and operate engine for 10 seconds. Stop engine and remove pressure regulator vacuum hose. *See Fig. 5.* Check vacuum port for fuel.

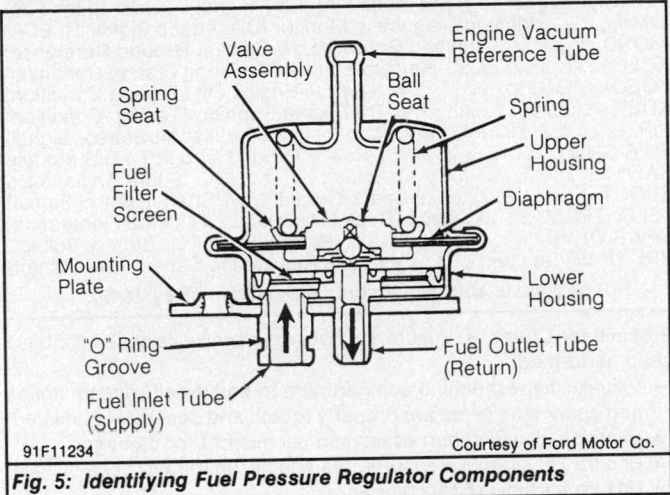

91F11234   Courtesy of Ford Motor Co.

Fig. 5: Identifying Fuel Pressure Regulator Components

2) If fuel is present, replace fuel pressure regulator and repeat test. If fuel is not present, start and run engine for 30 seconds. Stop engine and check fuel pressure gauge. If fuel pressure does not drop, go to

step **4**). If fuel pressure drops more than 5 psi (.4 kg/cm²) in 60 seconds, disconnect and plug fuel return line at engine. Cycle ignition key on and off until normal fuel pressure is obtained.

3) Turn key off and check fuel pressure gauge. If gauge drops more than 5 psi (.4 kg/cm²) in 30 seconds, replace high pressure fuel pump (dual pump system) or fuel sender/pump assembly (single pump type). If gauge does not drop more than 5 psi (.4 kg/cm²) in 30 seconds, replace fuel pressure regulator.

4) Ensure key is off. Relieve fuel pressure. Remove fuel pressure regulator. Check "O" ring, gasket and mounting surfaces for cracks, cuts or other damage. Connect vacuum pump to fuel return tube and apply 20 in. Hg. If maximum vacuum loss exceeds 10 in. Hg in 10 seconds, replace regulator. If maximum vacuum loss does not exceed 10 in. Hg in 10 seconds, recheck entire fuel delivery system for cause of fuel pressure loss.

Fuel Selector Valve (Diesel) – 1) Disconnect electrical connector from tank selector valve. Turn ignition to RUN position. Move selector switch to FRONT position and check for voltage at selector valve terminals No. 1 and 2. *See Fig. 6.* If voltage is present, go to step **2**). If voltage is not present, check fuse No. 15 (10A) or related circuit.

2) Check voltage between selector valve motor terminal No. 2 and ground. If voltage is present, go to step **3**). If voltage is not present, check fuse No. 15 (10A) or related circuit. Replace fuse or repair circuit as necessary. Test system. If system is still inoperative, go to next step.

3) Jumper selector valve terminal No. 2 to battery positive and terminal No. 1 to frame ground. *See Fig. 6.* Valve motor should operate. Reverse jumper leads to motor. Motor should operate in opposite direction. If motor does not operate in one or both directions, replace fuel selector valve assembly.

Fuel Selector Valve (Gasoline) – Fuel selector valve is mechanically operated and uses in-tank pump pressure to control fuel supply and return. Front or rear tank indication is controlled by the selector switch.

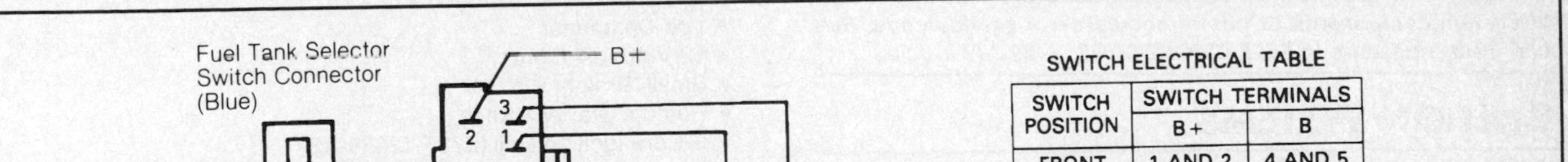

SWITCH ELECTRICAL TABLE

| SWITCH | SWITCH TERMINALS | |
POSITION	B+	B
FRONT	1 AND 2	4 AND 5
REAR	2 AND 3	5 AND 6

VALVE ELECTRICAL TABLE

| VALVE | VALVE TERMINALS | | | | |
POSITION	1	2	3	4	5
FRONT	–	+	SHORTED	OPEN	
REAR	+	–	OPEN	SHORTED	

Courtesy of Ford Motor Co.

92B22195

Fig. 6: Diesel Fuel Selector Valve Wiring Schematic (F250/350)

FUEL CONTROL

Fuel Injectors – 1) Connect tachometer to engine. Run engine at idle. Disconnect and reconnect injectors individually. If each injector causes a momentary drop in engine speed of at least 100 RPM, injectors are giving proper fuel delivery. RPM drop should only be momentary as ISC will attempt to re-establish correct idle RPM.

2) Replace any injectors that do not cause sufficient drop in engine speed. When test is complete and all injectors cause equal drop in speed, shut off engine. In order to check curb idle, refer to emission control specifications on decal in engine compartment.

Injector Circuit – 1) Disconnect all injector harness connectors. Using a DVOM, check resistance across terminals of each injector. See INDIVIDUAL INJECTOR RESISTANCE table.

2) Disconnect injector bank harness connector, and check resistance of injector bank. See INJECTOR BANK RESISTANCE table. Repair wiring or replace any injector circuit not within specification.

INDIVIDUAL INJECTOR RESISTANCE

Engine	Ohms
2.3L & 3.0L	15.0-18.0
All Others	13.0-16.0

INJECTOR BANK RESISTANCE

Engine	Ohms
2.3L	7.0-9.5
2.9L, 3.0L & 4.9L	5.0-6.5
5.0L, 5.8L & 7.5L	3.0-4.0

IDLE CONTROL SYSTEM

NOTE: See IDLE SPEED CONTROL (ISC) SOLENOID test procedures under SOLENOIDS. Curb idle and fast idle speed is controlled by ECA and is not adjustable. Some throttle bodies have a sludge-tolerant design with a special coated throttle bore. A Yellow/Black warning decal on these units warns against backing off throttle plate adjustment screw to avoid throttle plate sticking in bore. Faults in idle control system components or circuit should set a service code. See Quick Test procedure in SELF-DIAGNOSTICS – EEC-IV article.

IGNITION SYSTEMS

NOTE: For additional information and descriptions see IGNITION SYSTEMS in THEORY & OPERATION article. Perform spark output check in BASIC DIAGNOSTIC PROCEDURES article before entering these tests. Some ignition systems require that Quick Test procedure be performed prior to testing. This will retrieve trouble codes from the EEC-IV system. See SELF-DIAGNOSTICS – EEC-IV article.

IGNITION SYSTEM IDENTIFICATION

Application	System
2.3L Ranger	DIS
2.9L Ranger	TFI-IV
3.0L Aerostar & Ranger	TFI-IV
4.0L Aerostar, Explorer & Ranger	EDIS
4.9L Bronco, Pickup & Van	TFI-IV
5.0L Bronco, Pickup & Van	TFI-IV
5.8L Bronco, Pickup & Van	TFI-IV
7.5L Pickup & Van	[1] TFI-IV

[1] – Closed Bowl Distributor (CBD)

TFI-IV SYSTEM (2.9L & 3.0L RANGER, 3.0L AEROSTAR & 4.9L, 5.0L, 5.8L & 7.5L BRONCO, PICKUP & VAN)

NOTE: Before testing components and circuits of this system, ensure system is identified as to location of TFI module (distributor mounted or CBD type) and if dwell is controlled by TFI module or ECA (Non-CCD or CCD type). Additional system and circuit testing for this system is located in appropriate CIRCUIT TESTS in SELF-DIAGNOSTICS – EEC-IV article.

IGNITION SYSTEM ACRONYMS [1]

Acronym	Definition
BAT+ Or BAT (+)	Battery Positive
BAT– Or BAT (–)	Battery Negative
BOB	Breakout Box
CBD	Closed Bowl Distributor (TFI-IV)
CCD	Computer Controlled Dwell (TFI-IV)
CID	Cylinder Identification
C1, C2, C3	Coil Drive (Coils 1, 2 & 3)
DIS	Distributorless Ignition System
ECA	Electronic Control Assembly (EEC-Processor, Computer, Processor)
EDIS	Electronic Distributorless Ignition System
DPI	Dual Plug Inhibit (High Signal – Right Plugs Fire, Low Signal – Both Sides Fire)
IDM	Ignition Diagnostic Monitor (Diagnostic Signal To ECA)
IGGND	Ignition Ground (Low Current Ground Reference)
KOEC	Key On Engine Cranking (Testing Condition)
KOEO	Key On Engine Off (Testing Condition)
KOER	Key On Engine Running (Testing Condition)
PIP	Profile Ignition Pickup (Crankshaft Sensor Signal)
PWR GND	Power Ground Circuit To DIS Module
SAW	Spark Angle Word
SPOUT	Spark Output (ECA Spark Control Signal)
TFI Or TFI-IV	Thick Film Ignition (IV Is 4th Generation)
VPWR Or VBAT	Battery Power Or Battery Voltage
VRS Or VR Sensor	Variable Reluctance Sensor (Crankshaft)

[1] – Not all circuits and components are used in all systems.

Preliminary Check – Ensure the following preliminary checks have been performed:
- Visually inspect engine compartment to ensure all vacuum hoses and spark plug wires are properly routed and securely connected.
- Examine all wiring harnesses and connectors for damage.
- Ensure TFI module is securely fastened to distributor base or cowl.
- Ensure battery is fully charged.
- Turn all accessories off during diagnosis.

Test Equipment – The following test equipment or equivalent should be used in TFI-IV ignition system tests.
- Spark Tester (D81P-6666-A)
- Volt-Ohmmeter
- 12-Volt Test Light
- Small Straight Pin
- Remote Starter Switch
- E-Core Ignition Coil (E73F-12029-AB)
- Ignition Coil Secondary Wire

Diagnostic Aids – Following information should be noted during testing:
- A spark plug with a broken side electrode is NOT sufficient to check for spark and may lead to incorrect results.
- When instructed to inspect a wiring harness, both a visual inspection and a continuity test should be performed.
- When making measurements on a wiring harness or connector, perform a WIGGLE test while measuring.
- References to SPOUT in-line connector apply to both in-line and shorting-bar type connectors.
- Test procedures are intended to identify faulty components or wiring while fault is present. If complaint is an intermittent condition, refer to TROUBLE SHOOTING – NO CODES article.

Primary Circuit Test (Except Closed Bowl Distributor) – 1) Disconnect terminal "S" at starter relay to allow testing of ignition primary circuit without cranking motor. Ensure ignition is off. Push down on connector tab and disconnect harness connector from TFI module. Ensure TFI module connector is not corroded or swollen. Repair or replace connector as necessary.

NOTE: If connector is damaged or has broken tabs due to misuse, replace connector. A loose or damaged connector may cause ignition signal faults during KOER operation.

2) Use a straight pin or terminal spade from an old TFI module to probe connector. Attach negative DVOM lead to distributor base. Avoid ground contact with straight pin or positive terminal lead during testing. Turn ignition on and measure voltage at following TFI module harness connector terminals: *See Fig. 7.*

Key On Engine Cranking (KOEC)
- No. 3 (Power/Run Circuit)
- No. 4 (Start Circuit)

Key On Engine Off (KOEO)
- No. 3 (Power/Run Circuit)

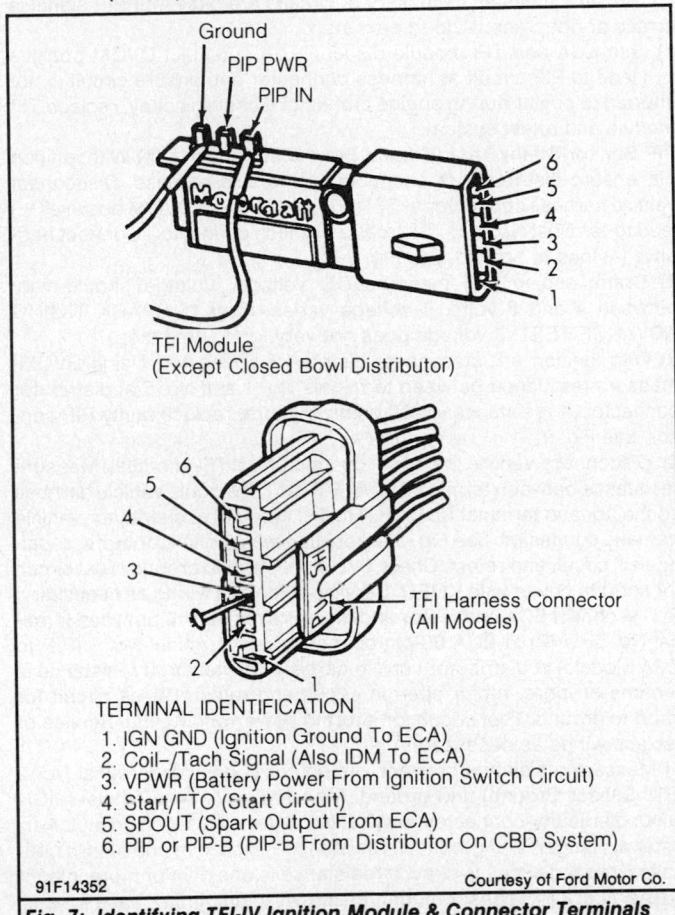

Ground
PIP PWR
PIP IN

TFI Module
(Except Closed Bowl Distributor)

TFI Harness Connector
(All Models)

TERMINAL IDENTIFICATION

1. IGN GND (Ignition Ground To ECA)
2. Coil−/Tach Signal (Also IDM To ECA)
3. VPWR (Battery Power From Ignition Switch Circuit)
4. Start/ГТО (Start Circuit)
5. SPOUT (Spark Output From ECA)
6. PIP or PIP-B (PIP-B From Distributor On CBD System)

91F14352   Courtesy of Ford Motor Co.

Fig. 7: Identifying TFI-IV Ignition Module & Connector Terminals

3) Turn ignition off and remove test pin. Reconnect wire to "S" terminal on relay. If approximately 90% of Battery Voltage (VBAT) is not present at these terminals, repair open circuits in wiring harness as necessary. Check ignition switch for faults. See appropriate wiring diagram. If voltage was as specified, reconnect module and go to next step.

4) Attach a 12-volt test light between ground and coil negative (−)/tach terminal No. 2 at TFI module. Turn ignition on, and crank engine. If test light flashes brightly during cranking, go to appropriate PIP SENSOR/STATOR TEST. If test light stays on during cranking, check for open in coil negative circuit between coil and TFI module connector. Repair circuit as necessary. If no open circuits are found, ignition module is shorted internally. Replace TFI module and retest.

5) If test light is always dim or off during cranking, check voltage to coil positive (+) terminal. If voltage is not present with key on or during cranking, repair open in primary circuit between battery and coil positive (+). If light flashes intermittently, check ignition module resistance. If voltage is available at coil, go to COIL TEST and check ignition coil.

Primary Circuit Test (Closed Bowl Distributor) – 1) Disconnect terminal "S" at starter relay to allow testing of ignition primary circuit without cranking motor. Ensure ignition is off. Push down on connector tab and disconnect harness connector from TFI module. Ensure TFI module connector is not corroded or swollen. Repair or replace connector as necessary.

NOTE: If connector is damaged or has broken tabs due to misuse, replace connector. A loose or damaged connector may cause ignition signal faults during KOER operation.

2) Use a straight pin or terminal spade from an old TFI module to probe connector. Avoid ground contact, between straight pin and ground, during testing. Using a DVOM, turn ignition on and measure voltage at following vehicle harness connector terminals of cowl mounted TFI module: *See Fig. 7.*

Key On Engine Cranking (KOEC)
- No. 3 (Power/Run Circuit)
- No. 4 (Start Circuit)

Key On Engine Off (KOEO)
- No. 3 (Power/Run Circuit)

If approximate Battery Voltage (VBAT) is not present at these terminals, repair open circuits in wiring harness as necessary. See appropriate wiring diagram in WIRING DIAGRAMS article in ENGINE PERFORMANCE.

3) If battery voltage is as specified, check module ground circuit. With TFI module disconnected and KOEO, measure voltage at terminal No. 6. If voltage is greater than .5 volt, ground circuit has high resistance or is open. Repair as necessary.

4) Ensure ignition is off. Disconnect distributor connector. Turn ignition on. With DVOM set on DC voltage scale, connect positive (+) lead to terminal No. 8 (terminal No. 4 on 3.0L Aerostar and Ranger). Connect negative (−) lead to distributor or engine ground. *See Fig. 8.*

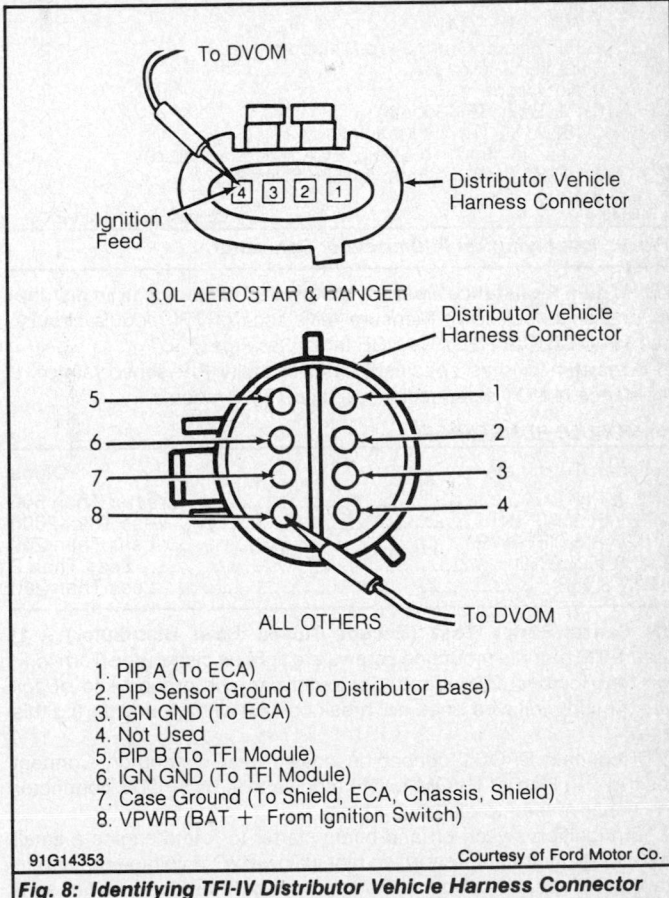

To DVOM

Distributor Vehicle Harness Connector

Ignition Feed

3.0L AEROSTAR & RANGER

Distributor Vehicle Harness Connector

To DVOM

ALL OTHERS

1. PIP A (To ECA)
2. PIP Sensor Ground (To Distributor Base)
3. IGN GND (To ECA)
4. Not Used
5. PIP B (To TFI Module)
6. IGN GND (To TFI Module)
7. Case Ground (To Shield, ECA, Chassis, Shield)
8. VPWR (BAT + From Ignition Switch)

91G14353   Courtesy of Ford Motor Co.

Fig. 8: Identifying TFI-IV Distributor Vehicle Harness Connector

5) Cycle ignition switch between ON and START positions. Battery voltage should be present in both positions. If not, service or repair circuit as necessary. If okay, go to next step.

6) Using a DVOM, check ignition ground circuits continuity. Measure resistance between distributor base and terminals No. 2 and No. 6 at distributor connector (terminal No. 3 on 3.0L Aerostar and Ranger). If resistance at each terminal is less than 3 ohms, circuit is okay. If resistance is 3 ohms or greater, repair ground circuit as necessary. *See Fig. 9.*

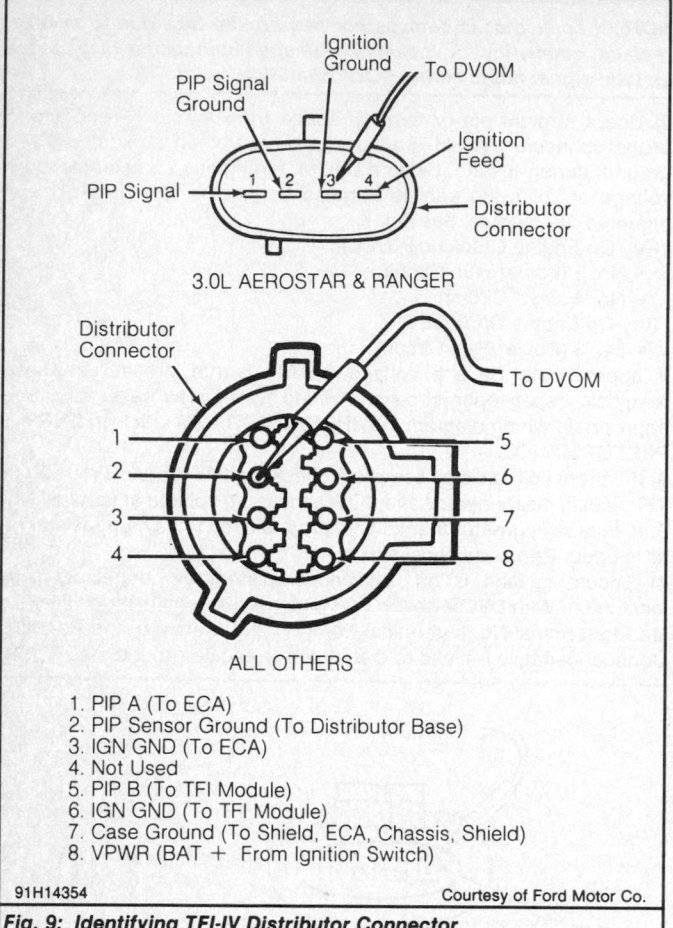

1. PIP A (To ECA)
2. PIP Sensor Ground (To Distributor Base)
3. IGN GND (To ECA)
4. Not Used
5. PIP B (To TFI Module)
6. IGN GND (To TFI Module)
7. Case Ground (To Shield, ECA, Chassis, Shield)
8. VPWR (BAT + From Ignition Switch)

91H14354   Courtesy of Ford Motor Co.

Fig. 9: Identifying TFI-IV Distributor Connector

TFI Module Resistance Test – 1) Remove TFI module from distributor or disconnect cowl. Measure resistance of TFI module circuits. See TFI MODULE RESISTANCE table. See Figs. 7-9.
2) If resistance is as specified, suspect faulty PIP sensor/stator. If resistance is NOT as specified, replace TFI-IV module.

TFI MODULE RESISTANCE

Between Terminals	Ohms
GND & PIP IN	Greater Than 500
PIP PWR & PIP IN	Less Than 2000
PIP PWR & TFI PWR	Less Than 200
GND & IGN GND	Less Than 2
PIP IN & PIP	Less Than 200

PIP Sensor/Stator Test (Except Closed Bowl Distributor) – 1) Ensure TFI module mounting screws are tight on distributor. Turn ignition off. Remove coil wire at distributor cap and ground end of coil wire. Ensure coil wire does not break contact with ground during this test.
2) Disconnect SPOUT connector located near distributor. Connect positive (+) lead of DVOM to TFI module side of SPOUT connector and negative lead to distributor base.
3) Turn ignition switch on and bump starter to rotate engine a small amount. Measure and record voltage (allow DVOM voltage reading to stabilize). Repeat procedure 10 times. Voltage should vary as hall sensor vanes and windows rotate through PIP sensor.
4) Voltage reading should vary between .5 volt and 11.5 volts (90% of battery voltage). If the higher voltage readings are only about 70% of battery voltage, go to TFI MODULE RESISTANCE TEST. If TFI module resistance is greater than specified, replace TFI module. If resistance is less than specified, replace PIP sensor.
5) If the lower voltage readings are greater than .5 volt and ignition module resistance is within specification, replace PIP sensor. If PIP

sensor and module test okay, go to next step to check for PIP signal at ECA during cranking.
6) Turn ignition off and install Break Out Box (BOB) at ECA connector. Connect a DVOM between test terminals No. 56 (PIP) and No. 16 (IGN GND). Measure PIP signal voltage while cranking engine. Voltage should vary between 4 and 6 volts. If not, check for an open or grounded PIP circuit or an open IGN GND circuit at test terminal No. 16. Repair circuits as necessary. If circuits are okay, but PIP signal is erratic or not present, go to next step.
7) With ECA and TFI module disconnected, connect DVOM positive (+) lead to PIP circuit at harness connector and ensure circuit is not shorted to power during engine cranking. If circuit is okay, replace TFI module and retest system.

PIP Sensor/Stator Test (Closed Bowl Distributor) – 1) With ignition off, ensure distributor is connected to vehicle harness. Disconnect vehicle harness connector at TFI module. Connect DVOM positive (+) lead to terminal No. 6 at TFI vehicle harness connector. Connect negative (–) lead to ground. See Fig. 8.
2) Crank engine and measure DC voltage. Voltage should vary between 4 and 6 volts. If voltage varies, refer to SPARK TIMING ADVANCE TEST. If voltage does not vary, go to next step.
3) With ignition off, disconnect distributor connector. Using DVOM, measure resistance between terminals No. 1 and No. 5 at distributor connector. If resistance is 200 ohms or more, replace faulty PIP sensor. See Fig. 9.
4) Disconnect vehicle harness connector at TFI module. Measure resistance between terminal No. 6 (PIP) at TFI module vehicle harness connector and terminal No. 5 (PIP to TFI Module) at distributor vehicle harness connector. See Fig. 8. If resistance is 5 ohms or more, repair open in circuit and retest. Check circuit for short to ground. Test circuit for short to power with KOEO. Service or replace wiring as necessary.
5) Disconnect ECA connector and measure resistance between terminal No. 56 (PIP) at ECA 60-pin connector and terminal No. 1 (PIP to ECA Module) at distributor vehicle harness connector. If resistance is 5 ohms or more, repair open in circuit and retest. Check circuit for short to ground. Test circuit for short to power with KOEO. Service or replace wiring as necessary.
6) Measure resistance between distributor connector terminal No. 2 (PIP Sensor Ground) and ground. Measure resistance between IGN GND, distributor connector terminal No. 6 (terminal No. 3 on 3.0L Aerostar or Ranger) and ground. If resistance is less than one ohm in both cases, ground circuit is okay. If resistance is one ohm or more in both cases, check PIP sensor mounting screws in distributor base for corrosion and tightness.

Coil Test – 1) Connect negative (–) DVOM lead to distributor base and measure battery voltage. Turn ignition switch to RUN position. Measure voltage at coil positive (+) terminal and turn ignition off. Voltage should be 10.5-12 volts. If voltage is as specified, go to next step. If voltage is not as specified, repair or replace ignition switch or wiring circuit to coil. See appropriate wiring diagram in WIRING DIAGRAMS article in ENGINE PERFORMANCE.
2) Ensure ignition is off. Disconnect coil primary connector and inspect both contacts for corrosion or damage. Service or replace as necessary. Using a DVOM, measure primary circuit resistance. If resistance is not .3-1.0 ohm at 70°F, replace coil and retest system.
3) Remove secondary coil wire from coil tower and inspect contact for signs of arcing or corrosion. Using a DVOM, measure resistance between coil tower connector and coil negative (–) terminal. If resistance is not 8000-11,500 ohms, replace coil.

Spark Timing Advance Test – 1) This procedure is applicable to all TFI-IV equipped vehicles. Spark advance is controlled by ECA. This procedure checks capability of ignition module to receive spark timing commands from ECA on the SPOUT circuit. A varying voltage signal is necessary on SPOUT circuit for ECA to transmit data. A KOER Code 18 or Code 213 may be set when SPOUT circuit is open or shorted. For additional information on TFI ignition systems, see THEORY & OPERATION article.
2) Check SPOUT circuit voltage at TFI module. Ensure ignition switch is in OFF position. Disconnect SPOUT in-line connector near TFI module. If connector is SHORTING BAR type, remove SHORTING BAR.

3) Attach negative (–) voltmeter lead to distributor base and positive (+) lead to TFI module side of the SPOUT connector. Start engine and measure voltage at idle. Measure voltage at ECA side of SPOUT connector.

4) Voltage readings should be 4-8 volts. If voltage on TFI module side is okay, TFI module is okay. This voltage signal is necessary for TFI module to receive ECA SPOUT signal. If voltage signal from ECA to SPOUT connector is as specified, circuit from ECA to SPOUT connector is okay. If either voltage signal is not as specified, go to next test. If both voltage signals are as specified, check ignition timing advance.

5) Check SPOUT circuit continuity. Push TFI module connector tab to release connector. Separate wiring harness connector from ignition module. Inspect for dirt, corrosion and damage.

6) Using a small straight pin inserted into harness connector terminal No. 5, measure resistance between terminal and TFI module side of SPOUT connector. Resistance should be less than 5 ohms. If resistance is 5 ohms or more, repair wiring as necessary.

7) Measure resistance between ECA side of SPOUT connector and pin No. 36 at ECA connector. If resistance is less than 5 ohms, go to next step. If resistance is 5 ohms or more, repair wiring between SPOUT connector and ECA.

8) Check Ignition Timing Advance. With SPOUT connector disconnected, run engine at idle and ensure timing is at base timing adjustment. See ON-VEHICLE ADJUSTMENTS article. Stop engine.

9) Connect SPOUT connector and start engine. Timing should advance from base timing specification. Increase engine RPM and ensure timing advances. If time does not advance, check TFI module. If module is okay, replace ECA.

DIS SYSTEM (2.3L RANGER)

NOTE: Start all diagnostics with EEC-IV Quick Test. See SELF-DIAGNOSTICS – EEC-IV article. These tests are dependent on results and service codes received during Quick Test procedures.

CAUTION: DO NOT connect ECA to DIS diagnostic cable. The 60-pin connector on this harness may be connected to an additional Breakout Box (BOB) only. If ECA is connected to DIS diagnostic cable, it may be damaged.

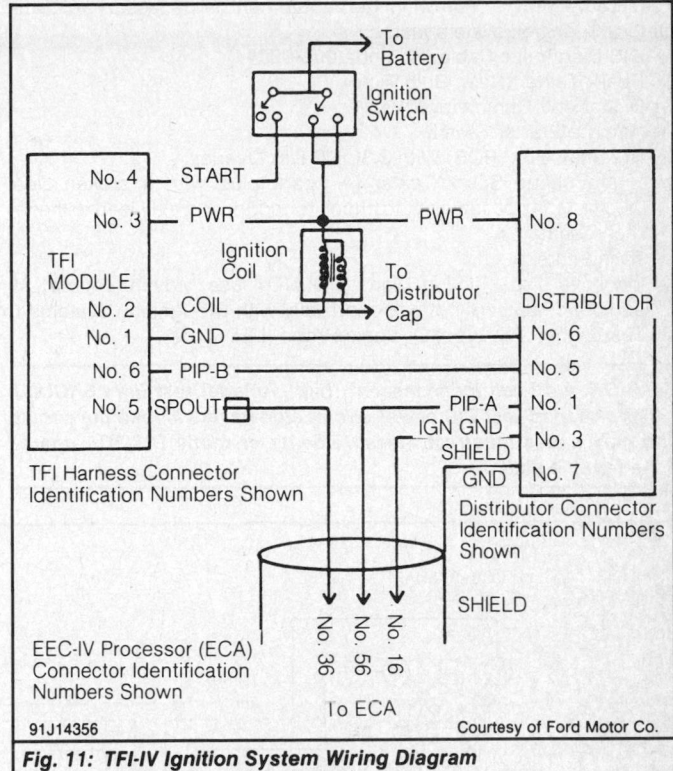

Fig. 11: TFI-IV Ignition System Wiring Diagram (Closed Bowl Distributor)

Preliminary Check – Ensure following preliminary checks have been performed:

- Visually inspect engine compartment to ensure all vacuum hoses and spark plug wires are properly and securely connected.
- Check all wiring harnesses and connectors for damaged insulation, burned, overheating, damaged pins, loose or broken conditions. Check sensor shield connector. Ensure DIS module mounting screws are tight.
- Ensure battery is fully charged.
- Turn all accessories off during diagnosis.

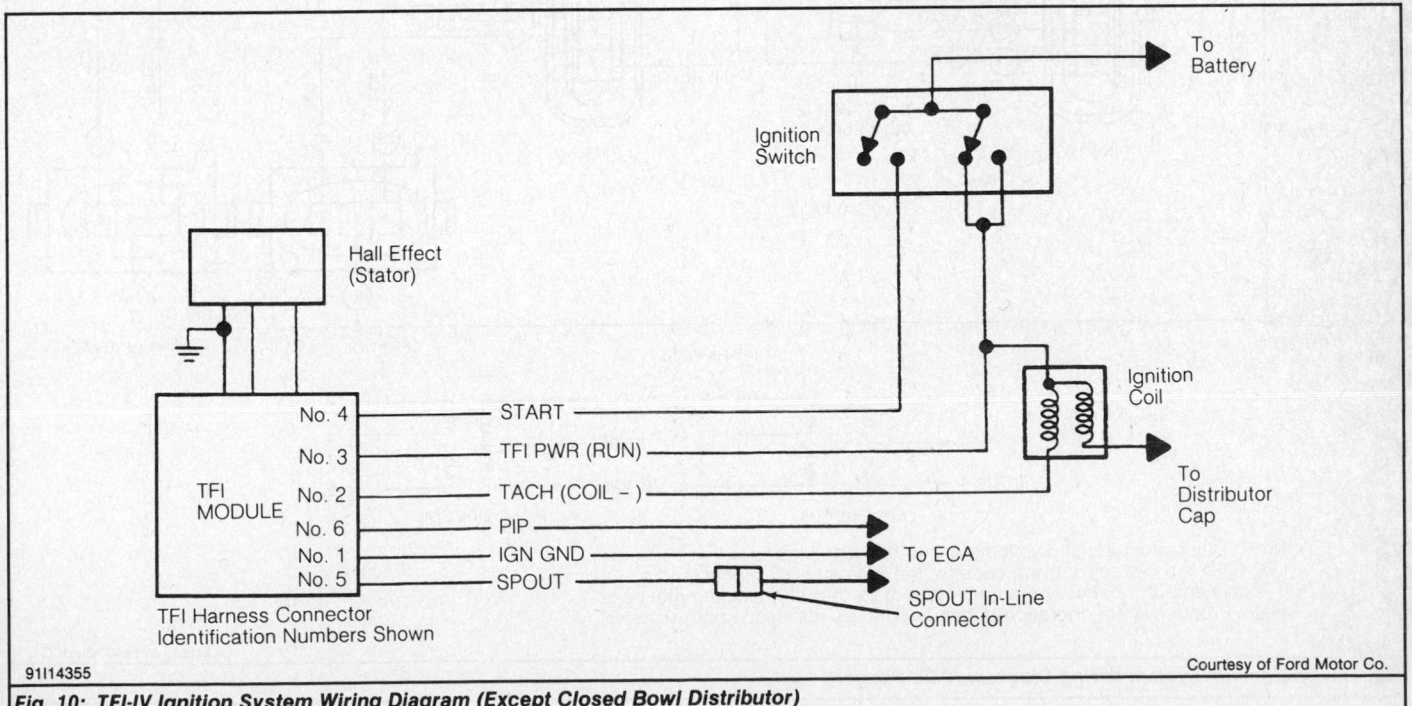

Fig. 10: TFI-IV Ignition System Wiring Diagram (Except Closed Bowl Distributor)

1992 ENGINE PERFORMANCE
System & Component Testing – EEC-IV (Cont.)

Test Equipment – Following test equipment is necessary to complete DIS ignition system tests.

- DIS Diagnostic Cable (Rotunda 007-00044)
- Spark Tester (Neon Bulb Type)
- Digital Volt-Ohmmeter (DVOM)
- Remote Starter Switch
- Breakout Box (BOB) With 2.3L DP DIS Overlay
- High Voltage Spark Tester (A spark plug with a broken side electrode is not sufficient to check for spark and may lead to incorrect results.)
- Tachometer
- Inductive Type Timing Light (DO NOT use "advance knob", if equipped, as it will not work correctly with DIS Ignition Systems.)
- Test Light (LED Type) Or Logic Probe (LED Type)

CAUTION: A 12-volt incandescent (high voltage) test light SHOULD NOT be used to test CID or PIP circuit signals. It will load the circuit and may cause incorrect measurements or faulty DIS/ECA operations (engine stall).

Diagnostic Aids – PINPOINT TESTS A through F are intended to diagnose hard faults. Intermittent failures may be difficult to diagnose using these procedures.

A Breakout Box (BOB) connected to DIS diagnostic cable is referred to as DIS BOB. If a second BOB is connected to the ECA vehicle harness connector it is referred to as ECA BOB. This test setup allows testing of DIS components and vehicle harness circuits.

Circuits are identified in all capitals, example: IGND = Ignition Ground. Manufacturers BOB overlay identification is in brackets, example: (J2) = IGND (J2). This indicates test terminal number or circuit identification number.

NOTE: Unless specified otherwise in a specific test step, all voltage and resistance tests of DIS ignition system are performed at the BOB connected to the DIS diagnostic cable.

NOTE: When performing PINPOINT TEST procedures for the 2.3L DIS (Ranger) system, refer to Figs. 12 and 13.

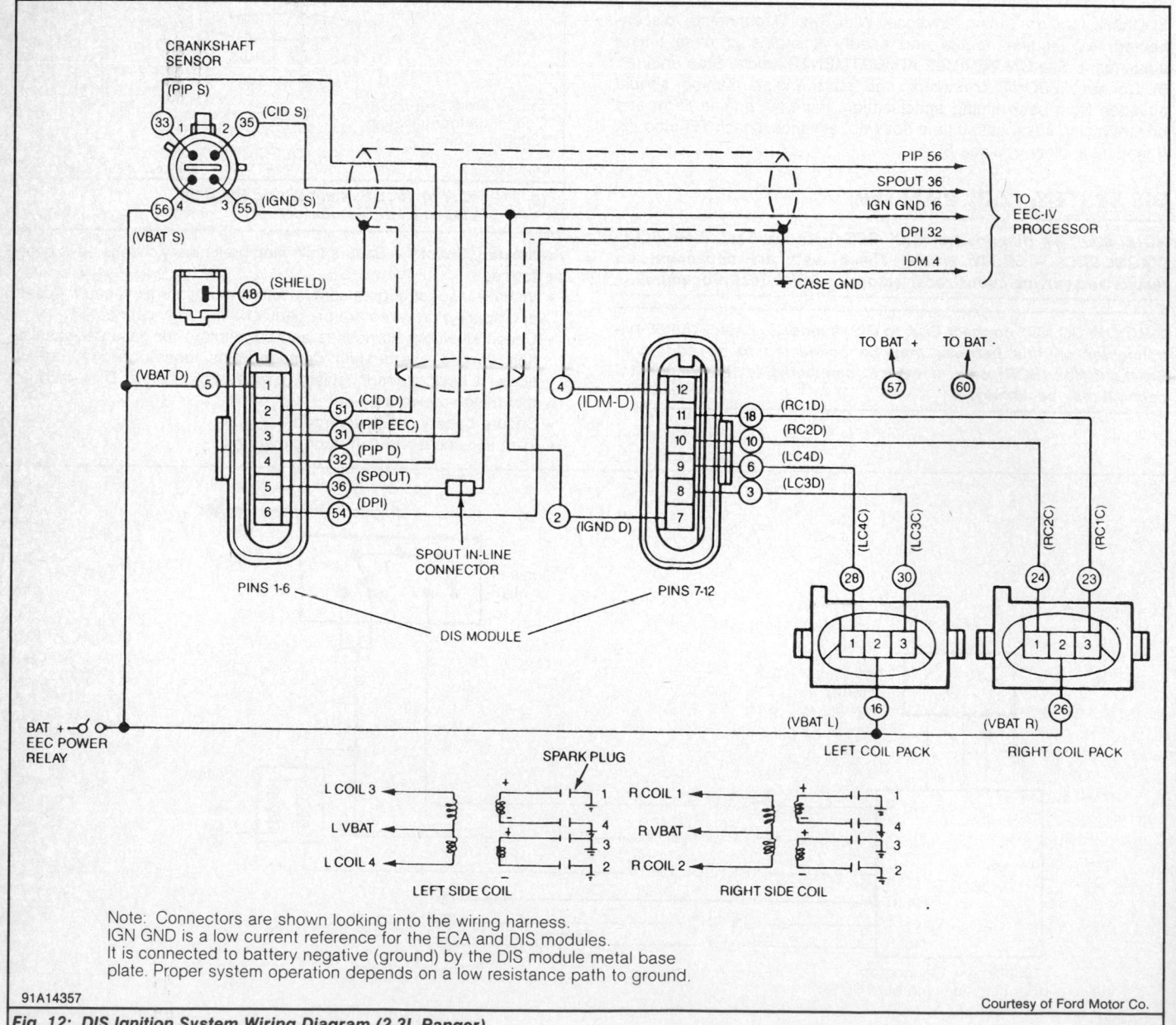

Note: Connectors are shown looking into the wiring harness.
IGN GND is a low current reference for the ECA and DIS modules.
It is connected to battery negative (ground) by the DIS module metal base plate. Proper system operation depends on a low resistance path to ground.

91A14357

Courtesy of Ford Motor Co.

Fig. 12: DIS Ignition System Wiring Diagram (2.3L Ranger)

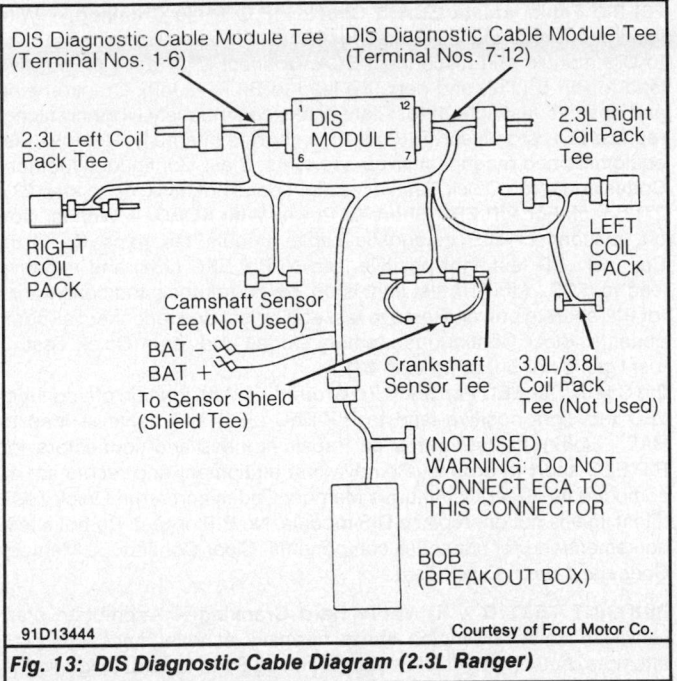

DIS Diagnostic Cable Module Tee (Terminal Nos. 1-6)
DIS Diagnostic Cable Module Tee (Terminal Nos. 7-12)
2.3L Left Coil Pack Tee
2.3L Right Coil Pack Tee
RIGHT COIL PACK
LEFT COIL PACK
Camshaft Sensor Tee (Not Used)
BAT –
BAT +
To Sensor Shield (Shield Tee)
Crankshaft Sensor Tee
3.0L/3.8L Coil Pack Tee (Not Used)
(NOT USED) WARNING: DO NOT CONNECT ECA TO THIS CONNECTOR
BOB (BREAKOUT BOX)

91D13444   Courtesy of Ford Motor Co.

Fig. 13: DIS Diagnostic Cable Diagram (2.3L Ranger)

2.3L RANGER DIS PINPOINT TEST INDEX

PINPOINT TEST A – 1) Perform EEC-IV Quick Test – See SELF-DIAGNOSTICS – EEC-IV article. If service codes are not present, go to step 2). If service codes (KOEO, KOER or Continuous Memory Codes) are present, service the codes first. If vehicle still will not start, go to step 2).

2) Check For Spark During Cranking – Using a Neon Bulb Spark Tester (D89P6666-A), check for spark at each right side spark plug wire while cranking. If spark is consistent on all right side plug wires (one spark per crank revolution), go to step 3). If spark is not consistent, go to step 8).

3) Check PIP Circuit At DIS Module When Cranking – Connect DIS diagnostic cable to BOB (DIS BOB). Use 2.3L DP DIS overlay. Connect LED test light positive lead to BOB PIP EEC (J31) and negative lead to BOB BAT – (J60). Crank engine. If LED test light blinks continuously during cranking, go to step 4). If LED test light does not blink continuously during cranking, replace DIS module, there is no PIP output. Remove all test equipment. Reconnect all components. Clear Continuous Memory Codes and rerun Quick Test.

4) Check PIP Circuit To ECA Continuity With Key Off – Ensure ignition is off. Disconnect vehicle harness from ECA. Set DVOM on 200-ohm scale. Measure resistance between PIP EEC (J31) at DIS BOB and vehicle harness connector pin PIP (No. 56). If resistance is less than 5 ohms, go to CIRCUIT TEST AB in SELF-DIAGNOSTICS article. If resistance is 5 ohms or more, PIP circuit is open, repair harness or connectors as necessary. Remove all test equipment. Reconnect all components. Clear Continuous Memory Codes and rerun Quick Test.

5) Spark Fault, Determine Missing Spark Combination – As a result of an inconsistent spark test in step No. 2), determine if spark is missing from cylinders No. 1 and 4 or from cylinders No. 2 and 3. If spark is missing from either pair of cylinders, go to step 7). If spark is not missing from a pair of cylinders, go to step 6).

6) Spark Fault, Check Plugs & Wires – Ensure ignition is off. Check plug wires for insulation damage, looseness, shorting or other damage. Remove plugs and check for damage, wear, carbon deposits and proper plug gap. If plugs and wires are okay, reinstall and proceed to step 7). If plugs and wires are not okay, service or replace defective plugs or wires as necessary. Remove all test equipment. Reconnect all components. Clear Continuous Memory Codes and rerun Quick Test.

7) Spark Fault, Check VBAT At DIS BOB – Ensure DIS diagnostic cable is connected to BOB. Select 2.3L DP DIS overlay. Connect LED test light negative lead to IGN D (J2) and positive LED test light lead to VBAT D (J5). Turn ignition on. If LED test light is on, go to step 8). If LED test light is not on, service harness and connectors. Remove all test equipment and reconnect all components. Clear Continuous Memory Codes and rerun Quick Test.

8) Check Ignition Ground Circuit (IGND) At DIS Module – Ensure ignition is off. Set DVOM on 200-ohm scale. Measure resistance between IGND D (J2) at DIS BOB and ground (J60 or VBAT–). If resistance is less than 5 ohms, go to step 10). If resistance is 5 ohms or more, go to step 9).

9) IGND Circuit Fault, Check DIS Mounting Screws – Ensure ignition is off. If mounting surface and screws are clean and tight, fault is an open in ignition ground circuit, replace DIS module. If they are not, clean, tighten or replace mounting screws. Clean mounting surface area of DIS module. Ensure mounting surface is coated with heat sink compound. Remove all test equipment and reconnect all components. Clear Continuous Memory Codes and rerun Quick Test.

10) Spark Fault, Check Voltage At RC1D & RC2D During Engine Cranking – With ignition off, install right side ignition coil (C1 and C2) diagnostic cable tee. Turn ignition on. Connect LED test light positive lead to RC1D (J18) and connect negative lead to BAT – (J60). Then connect LED test light positive lead to RC2D (J10) and connect negative lead to BAT – (J60). If test light was on in both test positions, go to step 14). If test light was not on in both test positions, go to next step.

11) Right Coil Fault, Isolate DIS Module – With ignition off, disconnect DIS diagnostic cable module tee (pins No. 7-12) from DIS module. Repeat procedure in step 10). If LED test light was on in both test positions, replace DIS module. Coil packs may be damaged as module was shorting C1 and C2 driver circuit to ground. Remove all test equipment and reconnect all components. Clear Continuous Memory Codes and rerun Quick Test. If LED test light was not on in both test positions, go to step 12).

12) Check VBAT, Right Coil Pack – Connect LED test light positive lead to VBAT R (J26) and negative lead to BAT – (J60). Turn ignition on. If LED test light is on, go to step 13). If LED test light is not on, locate and repair open circuit in right side coil VBAT. Remove all test equipment and reconnect all components. Clear Continuous Memory Codes and rerun Quick Test.

13) Check Right Coil Circuit – Connect LED test light positive lead to RC1C (J23) and connect negative lead to BAT – (J60). Then connect LED test light positive lead to RC2C (J24) and connect negative lead to BAT – (J60). Turn ignition on in each test position and observe test light. If test light was on in both test positions, one or both coil wires are shorted to VBAT. Repair or replace harness or connectors. Remove all test equipment and reconnect all components. Clear Continuous Memory Codes and rerun Quick Test. If test light was not on in both test positions, replace right coil pack. Remove all test equipment and reconnect all components. Clear Continuous Memory Codes and rerun Quick Test.

14) Check PIP D At DIS Module – Connect LED test light positive lead to PIP D (J32) and negative lead to BAT – (J60). Crank engine and observe test light. If test light blinks continuously during cranking, go to step 15). If test light does not blink continuously during cranking, go to step 19).

15) Check DIS Module Coil Drivers – Connect LED test light positive lead to RC1D (J18) and negative lead to BAT – (J60). Then connect LED test light positive lead to RC2D (J10) and negative lead to BAT – (J60). Crank engine and observe test light. If test light blinks continuously during cranking in both test positions, go to step 16). If test light does not blink continuously during cranking, replace DIS module. Remove all test equipment and reconnect all components. Clear Continuous Memory Codes and rerun Quick Test.

16) Check VBAT, Right Coil Pack – Connect LED test light positive lead to VBAT R (J26) and negative lead to BAT – (J60). Turn ignition on. If LED test light is on, go to step **17)**. If LED test light is not on, locate and repair open circuit in right side coil VBAT. Remove all test equipment and reconnect all components. Clear Continuous Memory Codes and rerun Quick Test.

17) Check Right Coil Circuit – Connect LED test light positive lead to RC1C (J23) and connect negative lead to BAT – (J60). Then connect LED test light positive lead to RC2C (J24) and connect negative lead to BAT – (J60). Turn ignition on in each test position and observe test light. If test light was on in both test positions, go to step **18)**. If test light was not on in both test positions, one or both coil wires may be shorted to ground. Repair or replace harness or connectors. Remove all test equipment and reconnect all components. Clear Continuous Memory Codes and rerun Quick Test.

18) Check Right Coil Circuit – Repeat test procedure in step **17)** and crank engine at each test position. If test light blinks continuously during cranking, replace right coil pack. Remove all test equipment and reconnect all components. Clear Continuous Memory Codes and rerun Quick Test. If test light does not blink continuously, one or both coil wires may be open. Check connections, repair or replace harness as necessary. Remove all test equipment and reconnect all components. Clear Continuous Memory Codes and rerun Quick Test.

19) Isolate DIS Module From PIP D During Cranking – With ignition off, disconnect DIS diagnostic cable module tee (pins No. 1-6) from DIS module. Connect LED test light positive lead to PIP D (J32) and negative lead to IGND S (J55). Crank engine and observe test light. If test light blinks continuously during cranking, go to step **26)**. If test light does not blink during cranking, go to step **20)**.

20) Check Crankshaft Sensor VBAT – With ignition on, connect LED test light positive lead to VBAT (J56) and negative lead to IGND D (J2). If test light is on, go to step **21)**. If test light is not on, locate and repair open in VBAT circuit to sensor. Remove all test equipment and reconnect all components. Clear Continuous Memory Codes and rerun Quick Test.

21) Check Crankshaft Sensor Ignition Ground – Turn ignition off and disconnect ECA. Disconnect diagnostic cable from crankshaft sensor. Set DVOM to 200-ohm scale. Measure resistance between IGND S (J55) and BAT – (J60). If resistance is less than 5 ohms, go to step **22)**. If resistance is 5 ohms or greater, locate and repair open or high resistance in circuit. Remove all test equipment and reconnect all components. Clear Continuous Memory Codes and rerun Quick Test.

22) Check Crankshaft Sensor PIP S Circuit – Turn ignition off and reconnect ECA to harness. Connect diagnostic cable to crankshaft sensor. Connect LED test light positive lead to PIP S (J33) and negative lead to IGND D (J2). Crank engine and observe test light. If test light blinks continuously, locate and repair open circuit between sensor and DIS module. Remove all test equipment and reconnect all components. Clear Continuous Memory Codes and rerun Quick Test. If test light does not blink, go to step **23)**.

23) Check PIP Circuit For Short To Ground – Turn ignition off and disconnect diagnostic cable from DIS module (pins No. 1-6). Connect LED test light positive lead to PIP S (J33) and negative lead to BAT + (J57). Turn ignition on and observe test light. If test light is on, locate and repair short to ground in PIP circuit. Remove all test equipment and reconnect all components. Clear Continuous Memory Codes and rerun Quick Test. If test light is not on, go to step **24)**.

24) Check PIP S Circuit For Short To VBAT – With ignition on, connect LED test light positive lead to PIP S (J33) and negative lead to BAT – (J60). If test light is on, locate and repair short to VBAT in sensor harness. Remove all test equipment and reconnect all components. Clear Continuous Memory Codes and rerun Quick Test. If test light is not on, go to step **25)**.

25) PIP Fault, Check Crankshaft Vane – If crankshaft vane moves through sensor air gap when engine is cranked, replace crankshaft sensor. Remove test equipment and reconnect all components. Clear Continuous Memory Codes and rerun Quick Test. If vane does not move through air gap, repair damaged crankshaft vane.

26) PIP Fault, Isolate ECA & Check PIP D While Cranking – With ignition off, reconnect DIS diagnostic cable module tee (pins No. 1-6) to DIS module and disconnect ECA. Connect LED test light positive lead to PIP D (J32) and negative lead to BAT – (J60). Crank engine and observe test light. If test light blinks continuously while cranking, replace ECA processor. PIP circuit is shorted internally. Remove test equipment and reconnect all components. Clear Continuous Memory Codes and rerun Quick Test. If test light does not blink, go to step **27)**.

27) Check For PIP EEC Short To Power With KOEO – With ignition off, disconnect DIS diagnostic cable module tee (pins No. 1-6). Connect LED test light positive lead to PIP EEC (J31) and negative lead to BAT – (J60). If test light is on, repair harness and connectors for PIP short to power. Remove test equipment and reconnect all components. Clear Continuous Memory Codes and rerun Quick Test. If test light is not on, go to step **28)**.

28) Check PIP EEC For Short To Ground – With ignition off, connect LED test light positive lead to PIP EEC (J31) and negative lead to BAT + (J57). If test light is on, repair harness and connectors for PIP EEC short to ground. Remove test equipment and reconnect all components. Clear Continuous Memory Codes and rerun Quick Test. If test light is not on, replace DIS module. No PIP output. Remove test equipment and reconnect all components. Clear Continuous Memory Codes and rerun Quick Test.

PINPOINT TEST B – 1) Verify Hard Cranking – Attempt to start vehicle 5 times. If engine starts normally at least once out of 5 attempts, but when it fails to start cranking RPM is erratic, ignition is firing out of time due to CID signal fault. If engine fails to start at least once, go to step **2)**. If engine starts at least once, go to step **8)**.

2) CID Fault, Check CID D Circuit During KOER – With ignition off, install DIS diagnostic cable module tee (pins No. 1-6) to DIS module. Connect diagnostic cable negative lead to battery. Connect diagnostic cable to DIS BOB. Use 2.3L DP DIS overlay. Connect LED test light positive lead to CID D (J51) and negative lead to IGND D (J2). Start engine and observe test light. If test light blinks continuously, replace DIS module. Module does not respond to CID input. Remove test equipment and reconnect all components. Clear Continuous Memory Codes and rerun Quick Test. If test light does not blink, go to step **3)**.

3) Isolate DIS Module From CID Circuit – Turn ignition off and disconnect diagnostic cable from DIS module (pins No. 1-6). Crank engine and observe test light. If test light blinks continuously, replace DIS module. Remove all test equipment and reconnect all components. Clear Continuous Memory Codes and rerun Quick Test. If test light does not blink, go to step **4)**.

4) Check Crankshaft Sensor CID Signal Output – Turn ignition off and reconnect diagnostic cable connector to DIS module (pins No. 1-6). Connect LED test light positive lead to CID S (J35) and negative lead to BAT – (J60). Start engine and observe test light. If test light blinks continuously, locate and repair open in CID circuit. Remove all test equipment and reconnect all components. Clear Continuous Memory Codes and rerun Quick Test. If test light does not blink, go to step **5)**.

5) Check CID For Short To Ground – With ignition off, disconnect diagnostic cable CID sensor tee from CID sensor. Disconnect diagnostic cable from DIS module (pins No. 1-6). Connect LED test light positive lead to BAT + (J57) and negative lead to CID D (J51). Turn ignition on and observe test light. If test light is on, service or repair connectors or harness. CID is shorted to ground. Remove test equipment and reconnect all components. Clear Continuous Memory Codes and rerun Quick Test. If test light is not on, go to step **6)**.

6) Check For CID Short To Power – With ignition still on, connect LED test light positive lead to CID D (J51) and negative lead to BAT – (J60). If test light is on, check and repair connectors and harness as necessary. CID is shorted to power. Remove test equipment and reconnect all components. Clear Continuous Memory Codes and rerun Quick Test. If test light is not on, go to step **7)**.

7) Check CID Vane – If crankshaft vane moves through sensor air gap when engine is cranked, replace crankshaft sensor. Remove test equipment and reconnect all components. Clear Continuous Memory Codes and rerun Quick Test. If vane does not move through air gap, repair damaged crankshaft vane.

8) Check DPI Signal At DIS Module – With ignition off, install DIS diagnostic cable module tee (pins No. 1-6) to DIS module. Connect DIS diagnostic cable to ECA BOB. Use 2.3L DP DIS overlay. Turn ignition on and connect LED test light positive lead to DPI (J54) and negative lead to BAT – (J60). If test light is on, go to step **11)**. If test light is not on, go to step **9)**.

9) Isolate DIS Module From DPI Circuit – With ignition off, disconnect DIS diagnostic cable module tee (pins No. 1-6) from DIS module and turn ignition on. If test light is off, replace DIS module. Remove test equipment and reconnect all components. Clear Continuous Memory Codes and rerun Quick Test. If test light is on, go to step **10)**.

10) Isolate ECA From DPI Circuit – With ignition off, disconnect ECA from vehicle harness. Connect LED test light positive lead to DPI (J54) and negative lead to BAT – (J60). Turn ignition on and observe test light. If test light is on, locate and repair short to VBAT in harness. Remove all test equipment and reconnect all components. Clear Continuous Memory Codes and rerun Quick Test. If test light is not on, replace ECA. Remove test equipment and reconnect all components. Clear Continuous Memory Codes and rerun Quick Test.

11) Check IDM Signal At DIS Module – Connect LED test light positive lead to IDM (J4) and negative lead to BAT – (J60). Start engine and observe test light. If test light blinks continuously, replace ECA. IDM is okay at DIS module. If test light does not blink, go to step **12)**.

12) Isolate ECA From IDM Circuit – Turn ignition off and disconnect ECA. Crank engine and observe test light. If test light blinks continuously, replace ECA as it is holding the IDM signal low. If test light does not blink, go to step **13)**.

13) Check IDM For Short To Ground – Turn ignition off and disconnect HEGO sensor. Disconnect diagnostic cable from DIS module (pins No. 7-12). Set DVOM to 20 k/ohm scale. Measure resistance between IDM (J4) and BAT – (J60). If resistance is less than 10 k/ohms, locate and repair short to ground in harness between DIS module and ECA. Remove all test equipment and reconnect all components. Clear Continuous Memory Codes and rerun Quick Test. If resistance is 10 k/ohms or more, replace DIS module. Remove all test equipment and reconnect all components. Clear Continuous Memory Codes and rerun Quick Test.

PINPOINT TEST C – 1) Check For Left Side Spark With KOER – Start engine and using spark tester, check for spark at each left spark plug wire. If spark is present at any left spark plug wire, go to step **2)**. If spark is not present, go to PINPOINT TEST D, Step **1)**.

2) Check IDM With KOER – With ignition off, install DIS diagnostic cable module tee (pins No. 7-12) to DIS module. Connect DIS diagnostic cable to BOB. Use 2.3L DP DIS overlay. Connect LED test light positive lead to IDM (J4) and negative lead to BAT – (J60). Start engine and observe test light. If test light blinks continuously, go to step **3)**. If test light does not blink, go to step **4)**.

3) Check IDM To ECA Continuity To ECA – With ignition off, disconnect ECA. Crank engine and observe test light. If test light blinks continuously, replace ECA. ECA does not respond to IDM input. Remove test equipment and reconnect all components. Clear Continuous Memory Codes and rerun Quick Test. If test light does not blink, go to step **4)**.

4) Isolate ECA & Check IDM Circuit During Cranking – With ignition off, disconnect ECA. Crank engine and observe test light. If test light blinks continuously, replace ECA, the ECA is shorting IDM circuit. If test light does not blink, go to step **5)**.

5) Check IDM For Short To Power – With ignition off, and disconnect HEGO sensor. Disconnect DIS diagnostic cable module tee (pins No. 7-12) from DIS module. Set DVOM on 20 k/ohm scale. Measure resistance between IDM (J4) and VBAT D (J5). If resistance is less than 10 k/ohms, check connectors and service or replace harness. IDM is shorted to VBAT. Remove test equipment and reconnect all components. Clear Continuous Memory Codes and rerun Quick Test. If resistance is 10 k/ohms or more, go to step **6)**.

6) Check IDM For Short To Ground – With ignition off, disconnect diagnostic cable connector from DIS module (pins No. 7-12). Set DVOM on 20 k/ohm scale. Measure resistance between IDM (J4) and BAT – (J60). If resistance is 10 k/ohm or less, check connectors and service or replace harness. IDM is shorted to ground. Remove test

equipment and reconnect all components. Clear Continuous Memory Codes and rerun Quick Test. If resistance is 10 k/ohm or more, replace DIS module. IDM is shorted in DIS module. Remove test equipment and reconnect all components. Clear Continuous Memory Codes and rerun Quick Test.

PINPOINT TEST D – 1) Check For Spark During Cranking – Using a spark tester, check for spark at all spark plug wires with engine running. If spark is consistent on all spark plug wires, go to PINPOINT TEST E, step **1)**. If spark us not consistent, go to step **2)**.

2) Check For Spark At Right Plug Wires During Cranking – If spark is present on all right side spark plug wires, go to step **3)**. If spark is not present on all right side spark plug wires, go to step **10)**.

3) Left Spark Fault, Isolate Plugs & Wires – If spark was missing from both cylinders No. 1 and 4 or both cylinders No. 2 and 3, go top step **5)**. If not go to step **4)**.

4) Check Left Side Spark Plugs & Wires – Check left spark plug wires for insulation damage, looseness, shorting or damage. Remove and check left spark plugs for damage, wear, carbon deposits and proper plug gap. If spark plugs and wires are okay, reinstall plugs and wires and go to step **5)**. If spark plugs or wires are defective, service or replace damaged component. Remove test equipment and reconnect all components. Clear Continuous Memory Codes and rerun Quick Test.

5) Left Spark Fault, Check Module Output – With ignition off, install diagnostic cable. Connect diagnostic cable to breakout box. Use 2.3L overlay. Disconnect diagnostic cable connector from DIS module vehicle harness connector (pins No. 7-12). Connect a jumper wire between IGND S (J55) and BAT – (J60). Connect a jumper wire between DPI (J54) and IGND S (J55). If spark was missing from cylinders No. 1 and 4, connect LED test light positive lead to VBAT D (J5) and negative lead to LC3D (J3). If spark was missing from cylinders No. 2 and 3, connect LED test light positive lead to VBAT D (J5) and negative lead to LC4D (J6). Crank engine and observe test light. If test light blinks continuously, go to step **6)**. If test light does not blink, replace DIS module. Remove all test equipment and reconnect all components. Clear Continuous Memory Codes and rerun Quick Test.

6) Left Spark Fault, Check Left Coil Pack VBAT – Turn ignition off and remove jumper wires. Reconnect diagnostic cable connector to DIS module harness (pins No. 7-12). Connect LED test light positive lead to BAT L (J15) and negative lead to BAT – (J60). Turn ignition on and observe test light. If test light is on, go to step **7)**. If test light is not on, locate and repair open circuit in left coil pack. Remove all test equipment and reconnect all components. Clear Continuous Memory Codes and rerun Quick Test.

7) Left Spark Fault, Isolate Left Coil Pack – Turn ignition off and disconnect HEGO sensor. Disconnect diagnostic cable from left coil pack. If spark was missing from cylinders No. 1 and 4 in step **3)**, connect LED test light positive lead to BAT + (J57) and negative lead to LC3C (J30). If spark was missing from cylinders No. 2 and 3 in step **3)**, connect LED test light positive lead to BAT + (J57) and negative lead to LC4C (J28). Crank engine and observe test light. If test light blink continuously. replace left coil pack. Remove all test equipment and reconnect all components. Clear Continuous Memory Codes and rerun Quick Test. If test light does not blink, go to step **8)**.

8) Check For Open Circuit – Turn ignition off and disconnect diagnostic cable connector from DIS module (pins No. 7-12). Set DVOM to 20-ohm scale. If spark was missing from cylinders No. 1 and 4, measure resistance between LC3D (J3) and LC3C (J30). If spark was missing from cylinders No. 2 and 3, measure resistance between LC4D (J6) and LC4C (J28). If resistance is less than 5 ohms, go to next step. If resistance is 5 ohms or more, locate and repair open circuit between left coil pack and DIS module. Remove all test equipment and reconnect all components. Clear Continuous Memory Codes and rerun Quick Test.

9) Check For Shorts – If spark was missing from cylinders No. 1 and 4, measure resistance between LC3D (J3) and BAT – (J57). If spark was missing from cylinders No. 2 and 3, measure resistance between LC4D (J6) and BAT – (J57). If resistance is less than 10 k/ohms, locate and repair short VBAT between DIS module and coil pack. Remove all test equipment and reconnect all components. Clear Continuous

Memory Codes and rerun Quick Test. If resistance is 10 k/ohms or more, locate and repair short to ground. Remove all test equipment and reconnect all components. Clear Continuous Memory Codes and rerun Quick Test.

10) Check Module Output – Turn ignition off and disconnect HEGO sensor. Install diagnostic cable and disconnect diagnostic cable from DIS module harness (pins No. 7-12). Connect diagnostic cable to breakout box and select 2.3L DIS overlay. Connect jumper wire between IGNDS (J55) and BAT – (J60) at breakout box. If spark was missing from cylinders No. 1 and 4, connect LED test light positive lead to RC1D (J18) and negative lead to BAT + (J57). If spark was missing from cylinders No. 2 and 3, connect LED test light positive lead to RC2D (J10) and negative lead to BAT + (J57). Crank engine and observe test light. If test light blinks continuously, go to step **11)**. If test light does not blink, replace DIS module. Remove all test equipment and reconnect all components. Clear Continuous Memory Codes and rerun Quick Test.

11) Isolate Right Coil Pack – Turn ignition off and disconnect diagnostic cable from right coil pack. If spark was missing from cylinders No. 1 and 4, connect LED test light positive lead to RC1C (J23) and negative lead to BAT + (J57). If spark was missing from cylinders No. 2 and 3, connect LED test light positive lead to RC2C (J24) and negative lead to BAT + (J57). Crank engine and observe test light. If test light blinks continuously, replace right coil pack. Remove all test equipment and reconnect all components. Clear Continuous Memory Codes and rerun Quick Test. If test light did not blink, go to step **12)**.

12) Check For Open Circuit – Turn ignition off and disconnect diagnostic cable connector from DIS module (pins No. 7-12). Set DVOM to 20-ohm scale. If spark was missing from cylinders No. 1 and 4, measure resistance between RC1D (J18) and RC1C (J23). If spark was missing from cylinders No. 2 and 3, measure resistance between RC2D (J10) and RC1C (J23). If resistance is less than 5 ohms, go to step **13)**. If resistance is 5 ohms or more, locate and repair open circuit between right coil pack and DIS module. Remove all test equipment and reconnect all components. Clear Continuous Memory Codes and rerun Quick Test.

13) Check For Shorts – Disconnect HEGO sensor. If spark was missing from cylinders No. 1 and 4, measure resistance between RC1D (J18) and BAT – (J60). If spark was missing from cylinders No. 2 and 3, measure resistance between RC2D (J10) and BAT – (J60). If resistance is less than 10 k/ohms, locate and repair short to ground between DIS module and coil pack. Remove all test equipment and reconnect all components. Clear Continuous Memory Codes and rerun Quick Test. If resistance is 10 k/ohms or more, locate and repair short to VBAT. Remove all test equipment and reconnect all components. Clear Continuous Memory Codes and rerun Quick Test.

PINPOINT TEST E – 1) Isolate SPOUT High Circuit – With ignition off, disconnect HEGO sensor. Install DIS diagnostic cable to DIS BOB and DIS module. Use 2.3L DP DIS overlay. Connect LED test light positive lead to SPOUT (J36) and negative lead to BAT – (J60). Start engine and observe test light. If test light blinks continuously, go to step **2)**. If test light does not blink, go step **3)** and check SPOUT.

2) Check Dual Plug Operation – Using a Neon Spark Tester, check for spark at each left side plug wire with engine running. If spark is present at one or more wires, go to step **6)**. If spark was not present at one or more wires, go to step **11)**.

3) Isolate SPOUT To ECA – Turn ignition off. Remove SPOUT harness plug from SPOUT in-line vehicle harness connector. Connect LED test light positive lead to ECA side of SPOUT vehicle harness connector and negative lead to main ground. See Fig. 14. If test light blinks continuously after engine is started, go to step **5)**. If test light does not blink continuously after engine is started, go to step **4)**.

4) Check For Short To VBAT – Turn ignition off and disconnect ECA. Disconnect positive battery cable. Set DVOM to 20 k/ohm scale. Measure resistance between VBAT + (J57) and ECA side of SPOUT vehicle harness connector. See Fig. 14. If resistance is 10 k/ohms or more, locate and repair short to VBAT in harness between SPOUT connector and ECA. Remove all test equipment and reconnect all components. Clear Continuous Memory Codes and rerun Quick Test. If

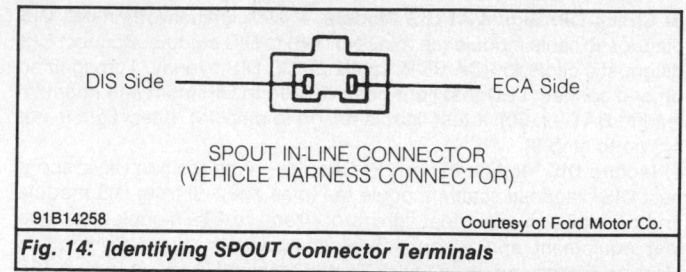

SPOUT IN-LINE CONNECTOR
(VEHICLE HARNESS CONNECTOR)

91B14258   Courtesy of Ford Motor Co.

Fig. 14: Identifying SPOUT Connector Terminals

resistance is 10 k/ohms or more, replace ECA. Remove all test equipment and reconnect all components. Clear Continuous Memory Codes and rerun Quick Test.

5) Check For Short To VBAT – Turn ignition off. Disconnect diagnostic cable connector from DIS module (pins No. 1-6). Set DVOM to 20 k/ohm scale. Measure resistance between VBAT + (J57) and DIS side of SPOUT vehicle harness connector. See Fig. 14. If resistance is less than 10 k/ohms, locate and repair short to VBAT + in harness between SPOUT connector and DIS module. Remove all test equipment and reconnect all components. Clear Continuous Memory Codes and rerun Quick Test. If resistance is 10 k/ohms or more, replace DIS module. Remove all test equipment and reconnect all components. Clear Continuous Memory Codes and rerun Quick Test.

6) Check DIS Module IDM Output – Connect LED test light positive lead to IDM D (J4) and negative lead to BAT – (J60). Crank or start engine and observe test light. If test light blinks continuously, go to step **7)**. If test light does not blink, go to step **8)**.

7) Check IDM Circuit Continuity – Turn ignition off and set DVOM to 20-ohm scale. Measure resistance between test pin No. 4 (IDM) at ECA vehicle harness connector and IDM (J4) at DIS connector. If resistance is less than 5 ohms, replace ECA. Remove all test equipment and reconnect all components. Clear Continuous Memory Codes and rerun Quick Test. If resistance is 5 ohms or more, locate and repair open in IDM circuit between DIS module and ECA. Remove all test equipment and reconnect all components. Clear Continuous Memory Codes and rerun Quick Test.

8) Isolate ECA – Turn ignition off and disconnect ECA. Crank engine and observe test light. If test light blinks continuously, replace ECA. Remove all test equipment and reconnect all components. Clear Continuous Memory Codes and rerun Quick Test. If test light does not blink, go to step **9)**.

9) Check For Short To Ground – Turn ignition off. Disconnect diagnostic cable connector from DIS module (pins No. 7-12). Remove LED test light. Set DVOM to 20-ohm scale. Measure resistance between IDM (J4) and BAT – (J60). If resistance is less than 5 ohms, locate and repair short to ground in IDM circuit. Remove all test equipment and reconnect all components. Clear Continuous Memory Codes and rerun Quick Test. If resistance is 5 ohms or more, go to step **10)**.

10) Check For Short To VBAT – Measure resistance between IDM (J4) and BAT + (J57). If resistance is less than 5 ohms, locate and repair short to VBAT between DIS module and ECA. Remove all test equipment and reconnect all components. Clear Continuous Memory Codes and rerun Quick Test. If resistance is 5 ohms or more, replace DIS module. Remove all test equipment and reconnect all components. Clear Continuous Memory Codes and rerun Quick Test.

11) Check Continuity – Turn ignition off and install diagnostic cable. Disconnect diagnostic cable connector from DIS module (pins No. 1-6). Connect diagnostic cable to breakout box. Select 2.3L overlay. Disconnect ECA. Set DVOM to 20-ohm scale. Measure resistance between DPI (pin No. 32) of ECA harness connector and DPI (J54) of breakout box. If resistance is less than 5 ohms, go to step **12)**. If resistance is 5 ohms or more, locate and repair open DPI circuit between DIS module and ECA. Remove all test equipment and reconnect all components. Clear Continuous Memory Codes and rerun Quick Test.

12) Check For Short To VBAT – Measure resistance between DPI (J54) and BAT + (J57). If resistance is 5 ohms or more, go to step **13)**. If resistance is less than 5 ohms, locate and repair to VBAT in harness between DIS module and ECA. Remove all test equipment and reconnect all components. Clear Continuous Memory Codes and rerun Quick Test.

CAUTION: In the next step, be careful not to jumper the DPI (J54) circuit to VBAT + or BAT + as high voltage will damage the ECA on this circuit.

13) Isolate ECA – Turn ignition off. Reconnect ECA and connect a jumper wire between DPI (J54) and BAT – (J60). Start engine and check for spark at any left side spark plug or wire. If spark is present, replace ECA. Remove all test equipment and reconnect all components. Clear Continuous Memory Codes and rerun Quick Test. If spark is not present, replace DIS module. Remove all test equipment and reconnect all components. Clear Continuous Memory Codes and rerun Quick Test.

PINPOINT TEST F – 1) Check Timing At Idle – With ignition off, install timing light. Ensure transmission is in Park or Neutral. Check timing with engine running at normal operating temperature. If timing advance is greater than 19 degrees BTDC, timing advance is okay, check engine mechanical condition, see BASIC DIAGNOSTIC PROCEDURES article. If timing is not as specified, go to step **2)**.

2) Check SPOUT Function – Turn ignition off and disconnect HEGO sensor. Install diagnostic cable and connect diagnostic cable to breakout box. Use 2.3L overlay. Disconnect diagnostic cable from DIS module (pins No. 1-6). Connect LED test light positive lead to SPOUT (J36) and negative lead to BAT – (J60). Crank or start engine and observe test light. If test light blinks continuously, replace DIS module. Remove all test equipment and reconnect all components. Clear Continuous Memory Codes and rerun Quick Test. If problem still exists, replace ECA. Remove all test equipment and reconnect all components. Clear Continuous Memory Codes and rerun Quick Test. If test light does not blink, go to step **3)**.

3) Isolate SPOUT Fault – Turn ignition off. Remove SPOUT harness jumper plug from SPOUT vehicle harness connector. Connect diagnostic cable to DIS module (pins. No. 1-6). Connect LED test light positive lead to EEC side of SPOUT vehicle harness connector and negative lead to BAT – (J60). Start engine and observe test light. If test light blinks continuously, reconnect diagnostic cable connector to DIS module (pins No. 1-6) and go to step **6)**. If test light does not blink continuously, reconnect diagnostic cable connector to DIS module (pins No. 1-6) and go to step **4)**.

4) Check Continuity – Turn ignition off and disconnect ECA. Set DVOM to 20-ohm scale. Measure resistance between SPOUT (pin No. 36) of ECA vehicle harness connector and ECA side of SPOUT vehicle harness connector. If resistance is less than 5 ohms, go to step **5)**. If resistance is 5 ohms or more, locate and repair open circuit between SPOUT connector and ECA. Remove all test equipment and reconnect all components. Clear Continuous Memory Codes and rerun Quick Test.

5) Check SPOUT For Short To Ground – Turn ignition off and disconnect ECA. Set DVOM to 20 k/ohm scale. Measure resistance between BAT – (J60) and ECA side of SPOUT vehicle harness connector. If resistance is less than 10 k/ohms, locate and repair short to ground between ECA and SPOUT connector. Remove all test equipment and reconnect all components. Clear Continuous Memory Codes and rerun Quick Test. If resistance is 10 k/ohms or more, replace ECA. Remove all test equipment and reconnect all components. Clear Continuous Memory Codes and rerun Quick Test.

6) Check SPOUT Circuit Continuity – Turn ignition off. Measure resistance between SPOUT (J36) and DIS side of SPOUT vehicle harness connector. If resistance is less than 5 ohms, go to step **7)**. If resistance is 5 ohms or more, locate and repair open circuit between DIS module and SPOUT vehicle harness connector. Remove all test equipment and reconnect all components. Clear Continuous Memory Codes and rerun Quick Test.

7) Check SPOUT For Short To Ground – Turn ignition off. Disconnect diagnostic cable connector from DIS module (pins No. 1-6). Measure resistance between BAT – (J60) and SPOUT (J36). If resistance

is less than 10 k/ohms, locate and repair short to ground in harness between DIS module and SPOUT vehicle harness connector. Remove all test equipment and reconnect all components. Clear Continuous Memory Codes and rerun Quick Test. If resistance is 10 k/ohms or more, replace DIS module. Remove all test equipment and reconnect all components. Clear Continuous Memory Codes and rerun Quick Test.

EDIS SYSTEM
(4.0L – AEROSTAR, EXPLORER & RANGER)

NOTE: Start all diagnostics with charts in TROUBLE SHOOTING – NO CODES article. Perform Quick Test procedure in SELF-DIAGNOSTICS – EEC-IV article before entering this test. These tests are dependent on results of Quick Test procedure.

NOTE: The EDIS Diagnostic Cable (Rotunda 007-00059) should be used to diagnose this system. This cable is equipped with additional resistors, circuits and components used to enhance and modify signals for testing purposes. If an aftermarket test cable is used, or diagnosis is being performed using only a DVOM, ensure technician is familiar with system wiring diagram and system operation.

Preliminary Checkout – Visually inspect engine compartment to ensure all vacuum hoses and spark plug wires are properly and securely connected. Examine all wiring harnesses and connectors for damaged insulation, burned, overheated, damaged pins, loose or broken conditions. Check sensor shield connector. Ensure EDIS module mounting screw is tight. Ensure battery is fully charged and all accessories are off during diagnosis.

Test Equipment – Following test equipment or equivalent should be used in these test procedures.
• EDIS Diagnostic Cable (Rotunda 007-00059)
• Spark Tester (Neon Bulb Type)
• Volt-Ohmmeter (Rotunda 007-00001)
• Remote Starter Switch
• 2 Breakout Boxes (BOB), For DIS (DIS BOB) And ECA (ECA BOB)
• Spark Tester (D81P-6666-A Or equivalent)
• Inductive Timing Light
• Test Light (LED Type) Or Logic Probe (LED Type)

Diagnostic Aids – When making measurements on a wiring harness, both a visual inspection and a continuity test should be performed. Inspect terminal connector pins for damage and corrosion, when directed to remove a connector.
• Spark timing adjustments are not possible. Timing is controlled by the EDIS module with input from the ECA.
• When checking voltage drop to GROUND, circuit must have a voltage drop of less than one volt.
• Battery voltage (VBAT) is any voltage reading within 2 volts of actual battery voltage.
• Spark timing will vary at idle due to feedback spark strategy used to control idle speed.
• DO NOT connect positive lead of EDIS diagnostic cable to battery or connect cable to VR sensor until directed to.
• SAW and IDM signal detectors in EDIS diagnostic cable will not work unless diagnostic cable battery leads are connected to battery.
• When using DVOM to measure DC voltage always connect positive lead to BOB terminal A (+) and negative lead to A (–).

CAUTION: DO NOT use a 12-volt incandescent (high voltage) test light to test circuit signals, as it will load the circuit and may cause incorrect measurements or faulty EDIS/ECA operations (engine stall).

NOTE: When using PINPOINT TEST procedures for the 4.0L EDIS (Aerostar, Explorer & Ranger) system, refer to Figs. 15 & 16.

1992 ENGINE PERFORMANCE
System & Component Testing – EEC-IV (Cont.)

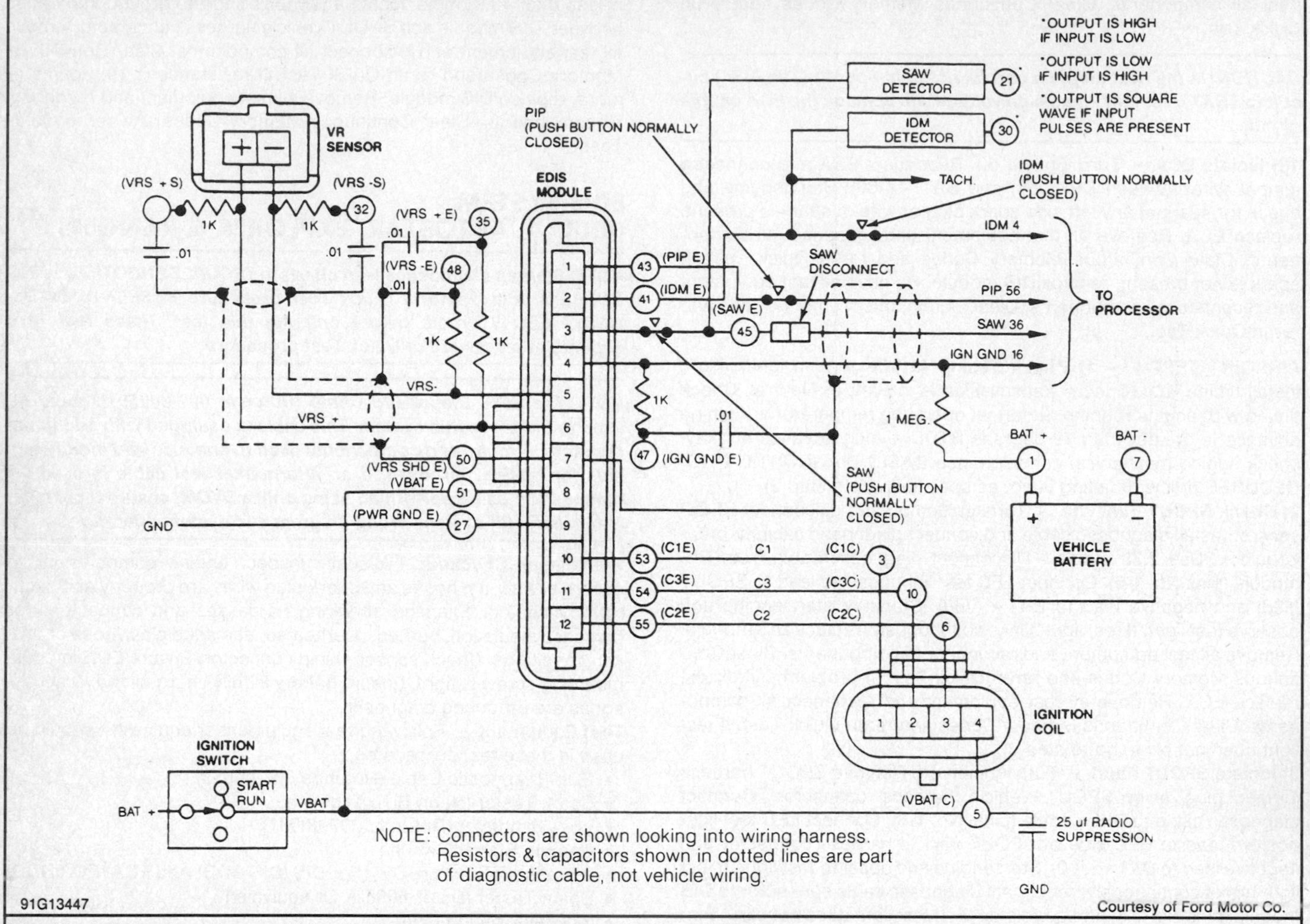

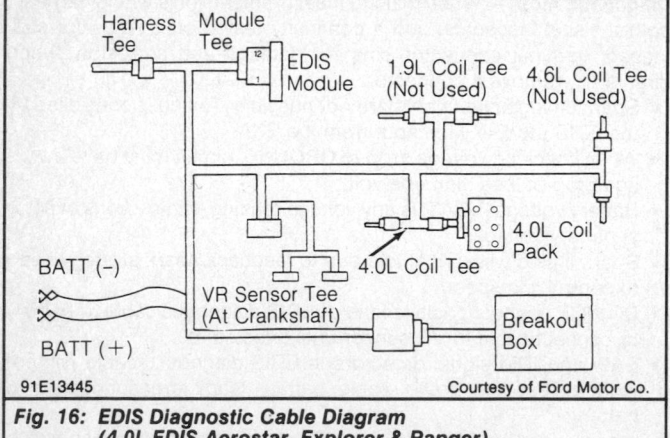

Fig. 15: EDIS Ignition System Wiring Diagram (4.0L EDIS Aerostar, Explorer & Ranger)

Fig. 16: EDIS Diagnostic Cable Diagram (4.0L EDIS Aerostar, Explorer & Ranger)

4.0L EDIS PINPOINT TEST INDEX

Result	Pinpoint Test & Step
No Start	
No Codes	A1
Continuous Memory Code 14 (PIP Signal At ECA fault)	A1
KOEO Code 16 (IDM, GND and IGN GND at EAC fault)	A1
KOER Code 18 (EAC/EDIS fault)	A1
"CHECK ENGINE" Light Stays On During Engine Cranking	A1
Engine Runs	
Continuous Memory Code 18 (IDM To ECA Circuit Fault)	B1
Continuous Memory Code 45 (Coil Fault)	D1
Lack Of Power Or Poor Fuel Economy	C1

WARNING: DO NOT connect ECA to EDIS diagnostic cable. The 60-pin connector on this harness may be connected to a Breakout Box (BOB) only. If ECA is connected to EDIS diagnostic cable it may be damaged. Some tests may require a second BOB (ECA BOB) to be connected to ECA 60-pin connector. When a second BOB is used, ECA should be disconnected at all times. Never connect ECA to BOB when performing EDIS diagnostics

WARNING: DO NOT bring a fluorescent trouble light (drop light) close to vehicle ignition system wiring. If ignition is on and VR sensor is disconnected, fluorescent light may cause EDIS module to fire ignition coil.

PINPOINT TEST A – 1) Perform EEC-IV Quick Test – If Quick Test was performed according to procedures in SELF-DIAGNOSTICS – EEC-IV article, go to step **2)**. If Quick Test was not tested as specified, go to article and perform Quick Test procedure.

2) Check For Spark During Cranking – Using a spark tester, check for spark at all spark plug wires while cranking. If spark was present and consistent on ALL spark plug wires (one spark per crankshaft revolution), go to next step. If spark was not available, go to step **7)**.

3) Check PIP Signal At EDIS Module – With ignition off, connect EDIS diagnostic cable to BOB, EDIS module and coil pack. DO NOT connect VR sensor tee. Use EDIS diagnostic "6" overlay on BOB (if available). Connect EDIS diagnostic cable negative lead to battery, leaving positive lead disconnected. Set EDIS diagnostic cable box switch to "4/6 Cylinder" position. Set DVOM on 20-volt AC scale. Crank engine, and measure voltage between PIP E (43) and BAT– (7) at BOB. If stabilized AC voltage reading is 4.5 volts or greater, go to next step. If reading was less than 4.5 volts, go to step **8)**.

4) Check For PIP Open To ECA – With ignition off, disconnect ECA. Connect ECA BOB to ECA harness connector. Set DVOM on 200-ohm scale. Measure resistance between PIP E (43) at BOB and PIP (56) at ECA BOB. If resistance is less than 5 ohms, go to next step. If resistance is 5 ohms or greater, repair open circuit. Remove test equipment and reconnect all components. Clear Continuous Memory Codes and rerun Quick Test.

5) Check IGN GND At EDIS Module – With ignition off and ECA disconnected, set DVOM on 2 k/ohm scale. Measure resistance between IGN GND E (47) and BAT– (7) at BOB. If resistance is less than 1025 ohms, go to next step. If resistance is 1025 ohms or greater, go to step **11)**.

6) Check IGN GND Open Circuit To ECA – With ignition off, and ECA disconnected, set DVOM on 2 k/ohm scale, measure resistance between IGN GND E (47) at BOB and terminal No. 16 (IGN GND) of ECA BOB. If resistance is less than 1025 ohms, remove test equipment. Reconnect all components. Clear Continuous Memory Codes and rerun Quick Test. If Continuous Memory Code 16 and/or 18 is still present, go to PINPOINT TEST B, Step **1)**. If no codes are present, go to TROUBLE SHOOTING – NO CODES article for no start problems. If resistance is 1025 ohms or greater, repair ignition ground to ECA open circuit. Remove test equipment and reconnect all components. Clear Continuous Memory Codes and rerun Quick Test.

7) Check Spark Plugs & Wires – Check spark plug wires for insulation damage, looseness or shorts. Remove and check spark plugs for damage, wear, carbon deposits and correct plug gap. If spark plugs and wires are okay, reinstall plugs and wires and go to step **12)**. If spark plugs and wires are defective, repair or replace damaged components as necessary. Remove test equipment and reconnect all components. Clear Continuous Memory Codes and rerun Quick Test.

8) Isolate EDIS Module – PIP Fault – With ignition off, connect EDIS diagnostic cable positive lead to battery. Set DVOM to 20-volt AC scale. Hold the EDIS diagnostic cable PIP Push Button down. Crank engine and measure voltage between PIP E (43) and BAT– (7) at BOB. If settled AC voltage reading is 4 volts or greater, go to next step. If voltage is less than 4 volts, repair or replace damaged component. Remove test equipment, and reconnect all components. Clear Continuous Memory Codes, and Rerun Quick Test.

9) Check For PIP Short To Ground – Isolate EDIS Module & ECA – With ignition off, disconnect ECA. Disconnect EDIS module from EDIS module tee. Leave EDIS diagnostic cable connected to EDIS module side of vehicle harness connector. Disconnect EDIS diagnostic cable positive lead at battery. Set DVOM on 200-ohm scale. Measure resistance between PIP E (43) and BAT– (7) at BOB. If resistance is less than 10 ohms, repair PIP short circuit to ground. Remove test equipment and reconnect all components. Clear Continuous Memory and Rerun Quick Test. If resistance is 10 ohms or greater, go to next step.

10) Check For PIP Short To VBAT – Isolate EDIS Module & ECA – With ignition off and ECA disconnected, set DVOM on 20-volt DC scale. With KOEO, measure voltage between PIP E (43) and BAT– (7) at BOB. If DC voltage is .5 volt or greater, repair short circuit. PIP is shorted to power. Remove test equipment and reconnect all components. Clear Continuous Memory Codes and rerun Quick Test. If voltage less than .5 volt, replace ECA. PIP circuit is shorted internally in ECA. Remove test equipment and reconnect all components. Clear Continuous Memory and Rerun Quick Test.

11) Check PWR GND To EDIS Module – IGN GND Fault – With ignition off, set DVOM on 2 k/ohm scale. Measure resistance between PWR GND E (27) and BAT– (7) at BOB. If resistance is less than 1050 ohms, replace EDIS module. Ground circuit is open in EDIS module. Remove test equipment and reconnect all components. Clear Continuous Memory Codes and rerun Quick Test. If resistance is 1050 ohms or greater, repair open circuit. PWR GND circuit to EDIS module is open. Remove test equipment and reconnect all components. Clear Continuous Memory and Rerun Quick Test.

12) Check Vehicle Performance – If the original problem was vehicle cranks but does not start, go to next step. If not, go to PINPOINT TEST D step **1)**.

13) Check PWR GND to EDIS Module – With ignition off and ECA disconnected, connect EDIS diagnostic cable to BOB, EDIS module, and coil pack. Do not connect VR sensor tee. Use EDIS "6" overlay (if available). Connect EDIS diagnostic cable negative lead to battery, leave positive lead disconnected. Set EDIS diagnostic cable box switch to "4/6 cylinder" position. Set DVOM on 2 k/ohm scale. measure resistance between PWR GND (27) and BAT– (7) at BOB. If resistance is less than 5 ohms, go to next step. If resistance is 5 ohms or greater, repair open circuit. Remove all test equipment and reconnect all components. Clear Continuous Memory Codes and rerun Quick Test.

14) Check For VBAT Open To EDIS Module – With ignition off and ECA disconnected, set DVOM on 20-volt DC scale. With KOEO, measure voltage between VBAT E (51) and BAT– (7) at BOB. If DC voltage is 10.5 volts or greater, go to next step. If voltage is less than 10.5 volts, repair open VBAT to EDIS module circuit. Remove all test equipment and reconnect all components. Clear Continuous Memory and Rerun Quick Test.

15) Check VRS (+) Bias At EDIS Module – With ignition off and ECA disconnected, set DVOM on 20-volt DC scale. With KOEO, measure voltage between VRS+ E (35) and BAT– (7) at BOB. If the DC voltage is .8-2.2 volts, proceed to next step. If voltage is not as specified, proceed to step **17)**.

16) Check VRS Amplitude At EDIS Module – With ignition off, reconnect ECA. Disconnect EDIS diagnostic cable negative lead from battery. Set DVOM on 20-volt AC scale. Crank engine, and measure voltage between VRS+ E (35) and VRS– E (48) at BOB. If stabilized AC voltage reading is .4 volt or greater, go to PINPOINT TEST D, step **1)**. If voltage is less than .4 volt, go to step **25)**.

17) Check VRS (+) Bias – Isolate VR Sensor – With ignition off and ECA disconnected, disconnect VR sensor from vehicle harness connector. Set DVOM on 20-volt DC scale. With KOEO, measure voltage between VRS+ E (35) and BAT– (7) at BOB. If DC voltage is .8-2.2 volts, go to step **21)**. If voltage is not .8-2.2 volts, go to next step.

18) Check VRS (+) High Or Low – If bias voltage reading in step **17)** was less than .8 volt, go to next step. If bias voltage reading in step **17)** was .8 volt or greater, go to step **20)**.

19) Check VRS (+) For Short To Ground – Isolate EDIS Module – With ignition off and ECA disconnected, disconnect EDIS module from EDIS diagnostic cable module tee, leave diagnostic cable connected to vehicle harness connector. Set DVOM on 2 k/ohm scale. Measure resistance between VRS+ E (35) and BAT– (7) at BOB. If resistance is less than 1025 ohms, repair short circuit. VRS (+) is shorted to ground. Remove test equipment and reconnect all components. Clear Continuous Memory Codes and rerun Quick Test. If resistance is 1025 ohms or greater, replace EDIS module. VRS (+) is shorted to ground. Remove test equipment and reconnect all components. Clear Continuous Memory Codes and rerun Quick Test.

20) Check VRS (+) For Short To Power – Isolate EDIS Module – With ignition off and ECA disconnected, disconnect EDIS module from EDIS diagnostic cable module tee, leave EDIS diagnostic cable connected to vehicle harness connector. Set DVOM on 20-volt DC scale. With KOEO, measure voltage between VRS+ E (35) and BAT– (7) at BOB. If DC voltage is .5 volt or greater, repair short circuit. VRS (+) circuit is shorted to power. Remove test equipment and reconnect all components. Clear Continuous Memory Codes and rerun Quick Test. If voltage is less than .5 volt, replace EDIS module. VRS (+) circuit is shorted to power. Remove test equipment and reconnect all components. Clear Continuous Memory Codes and rerun Quick Test.

21) Check VRS (–) Bias – With ignition off and ECA disconnected, set DVOM on 20-volt DC scale. With KOEO, measure voltage between VRS– E (48) and BAT– (7) at BOB. If DC voltage is .8-2.2 volts, replace VR sensor. Short to ground in VR sensor. Remove test equipment and reconnect all components. Clear Continuous Memory Codes and rerun Quick Test. If voltage is not .8-2.2 volts, proceed to next step.

22) Check VRS (–) Signal High Or Low – If DC bias voltage reading in step **21)** is less than .8 volt, go to next step. If voltage is .8 volt or greater, go to step **24)**.

23) Check VRS (–) For Short To Ground – Isolate EDIS Module – With ignition off and ECA disconnected, disconnect EDIS module from EDIS diagnostic cable module tee, leave diagnostic cable connected to vehicle harness connector. Set DVOM on 2 k/ohm scale. Measure resistance between VRS– E (48) and BAT– (7) at BOB. If resistance is less than 1025 ohms, repair short circuit. VRS circuit is shorted to ground. Remove test equipment and reconnect all components. Clear Continuous Memory Codes and rerun Quick Test. If resistance is 1025 ohms or greater, replace EDIS module. VRS circuit is shorted to ground. Remove test equipment and reconnect all components. Clear Continuous Memory Codes and rerun Quick Test.

24) Check VRS (–) For Short To VBAT – Isolate EDIS Module – With ignition off and ECA disconnected, disconnect EDIS module from EDIS diagnostic cable module tee, leaving EDIS diagnostic cable connected to vehicle harness connector. Set DVOM on 20-volt DC scale. With KOEO, measure voltage between VRS– E (48) and BAT– (7) at BOB. If DC voltage is .5 volt or greater, repair short circuit. VRS (–) circuit is shorted to VBAT. Remove test equipment, and reconnect all components. Clear Continuous Memory Codes, and rerun Quick Test. If voltage is less than .5 volt, replace EDIS module. VRS (–) circuit is shorted to VBAT. Remove test equipment, and reconnect all components. Clear Continuous Memory Codes, and rerun Quick Test.

25) Check VRS Amplitude At EDIS Module – Isolate EDIS Module – With ignition off and ECA disconnected, disconnect EDIS module from EDIS diagnostic cable module tee, leave diagnostic cable connected to vehicle harness connector. Set DVOM on 20-volt AC scale. Crank engine and measure voltage between VRS+ E (35) and VRS– E (48) at BOB. If stabilized AC voltage reading is .4 volt or greater, replace EDIS module. VRS (+) circuit is shorted to VRS (–). Remove test equipment and reconnect all components. Clear Continuous Memory Codes and rerun Quick Test. If stabilized AC voltage reading is less than .4 volt, go to next step.

26) Check VRS Resistance – With ignition off and ECA disconnected, disconnect EDIS diagnostic cable negative lead from battery. Set DVOM on 20 k/ohm scale. Measure resistance between VRS– E (48) and VRS+ E (35) at BOB. If resistance is 2580-2700 ohms, go to next step. If resistance is not 2580-2700 ohms, go to step **28)**.

27) Check VRS Air Gap – With ignition off, check VRS air gap. Ensure there is an air gap between sensor and trigger wheel. Air gap is not adjustable. If air gap is okay, replace VR sensor. Remove all test equipment and reconnect all components. Clear Continuous Memory Codes and rerun Quick Test. If air gap is not okay, repair or replace components as required. Remove test equipment and reconnect all components. Clear Continuous Memory Codes and rerun Quick Test.

28) Check VRS High Or Low Resistance – With ignition off and ECA disconnected, disconnect EDIS diagnostic cable negative lead from battery. Set DVOM on 20 k/ohm scale. Measure resistance between VRS– E (48) and VRS+ E (35) at BOB. If resistance is less than 2550 ohms, go to next step. If resistance is 2550 ohms or greater, go to step **30)**.

29) Check VRS (+) For Short To VRS (–) (Isolate VRS) – With ignition off and ECA disconnected, disconnect VR sensor from vehicle harness connector. Set DVOM on 200 k/ohm scale. Measure resistance between VRS+ E (35) and VRS– E (48) at BOB. If resistance is 3000 ohms or greater, replace VR sensor. Sensor windings are shorted. Remove test equipment and reconnect all components. Clear Continuous Memory Codes and rerun Quick Test. If resistance is less than 3000 ohms, repair short circuit. VRS (+) shorted to VRS (–). Remove test equipment and reconnect all components. Clear Continuous Memory Codes and rerun Quick Test.

30) Check For VRS (+) Open Circuit (Resistance High Fault) – With ignition off and ECA disconnected, connect EDIS diagnostic cable VR sensor tee to VR sensor and vehicle harness connector. Set DVOM on 20 k/ohm scale. Measure resistance between VRS+ S (31) and VRS+ E (35) at BOB. If resistance is 2025 ohms or greater, repair open circuit. VRS (+) circuit is open. Remove test equipment and reconnect all components. Clear Continuous Memory Codes and rerun Quick Test. If resistance is less than 2025 ohms, go to next step.

31) Check For VRS (–) Open Circuit (Resistance High Fault) – With ignition off and ECA disconnected, set DVOM on 20 k/ohm scale. Measure resistance between VRS– S (32) and VRS– E (48) at BOB. If resistance is less than 2025 ohms, replace VR sensor. Resistance is high. Remove test equipment and reconnect all components. Clear Continuous Memory Codes and rerun Quick Test. If resistance is 2025

ohms or greater, repair open circuit. VRS (–) circuit is open. Remove test equipment and reconnect all components. Clear Continuous Memory Codes and rerun Quick Test.

CAUTION: Never connect ECA to ECA BOB when performing EDIS diagnostics unless directed to do so.

PINPOINT TEST B – 1) Check For IDM Short High – With ignition off, connect EDIS diagnostic cable to BOB, EDIS module, and coil pack. Do not connect VR sensor tee. Use EDIS "6" overlay. Connect EDIS diagnostic cable negative and positive leads to battery. Set EDIS diagnostic cable box switch to "4/6 cylinder" position. Set DVOM on 20-volt DC scale. Start engine and measure voltage between diagnostic cable IDM DETECTOR (30) and BAT– (7) at BOB. If pulses are present, the IDM detector output will be 5-7 volts DC. If DC voltage is 5-7 volts, go to next step. If DC voltage is not 5-7 volts, go to step **3)**.

2) Check For IDM Open – With ignition off, disconnect ECA. Disconnect EDIS module from EDIS module tee, leave EDIS diagnostic cable connected to vehicle harness connector. Connect ECA BOB to ECA harness connector. Set DVOM on 200-ohm scale. Measure resistance between IDM E (41) at BOB, and terminal No. 4 at ECA BOB. If resistance is less than 5 ohms, replace ECA. IDM signal at ECA is okay. Remove test equipment and reconnect all components. Clear Continuous Memory Codes and rerun Quick Test. If resistance is 5 ohms or greater, repair open circuit. Remove test equipment and reconnect all components. Clear Continuous Memory Codes and rerun Quick Test.

3) Check IDM Output From EDIS Module – Isolate Harness – With ignition off, ensure ECA is connected. Set DVOM on 20-volt DC scale. Start engine and push EDIS IDM button at the EDIS diagnostic cable connector to BOB. Measure voltage between diagnostic cable IDM DETECTOR (30) and BAT– (7) at BOB. If DC voltage is 5-7 volts, go to next step. If voltage is not 5-7 volts, replace EDIS module. No IDM output from module. Remove test equipment and reconnect all components. Clear Continuous Memory Codes and rerun Quick Test.

4) Check For IDM Short In ECA – Isolate ECA – With ignition off, disconnect ECA. Set DVOM on 20-volt DC scale. Crank engine and measure voltage between diagnostic cable IDM DETECTOR (30) and BAT– (7) at BOB. If DC voltage is 4.4-6.0 volts, replace ECA. IDM circuit is shorted in ECA. Remove test equipment and reconnect all components. Clear Continuous Memory Codes and rerun Quick Test. If voltage is not as specified, go to next step.

5) Check For IDM Short To Ground In Harness – With ignition off, disconnect ECA. Disconnect EDIS module from diagnostic cable module tee, leave EDIS diagnostic cable connected to vehicle harness connector. Set DVOM on 20 k/ohm scale. Measure resistance between IDM E (41) and BAT– (7) at BOB. If resistance is less than 5 ohms, repair short circuit. IDM is shorted to VBAT. Remove test equipment and reconnect all components. Clear Continuous Memory Codes and rerun Quick Test. If resistance is 5 ohms or greater, go to next step.

6) Check For IDM Short To VBAT In Harness – With ignition off, disconnect ECA. Set DVOM on 20-volt DC scale. With KOEO, measure voltage between IDM E (41) and BAT– (7) at BOB. If DC voltage is .5 volt or greater, repair short circuit. IDM is shorted to VBAT between EDIS module and ECA. Remove test equipment and reconnect all components. Clear Continuous Memory Codes and rerun Quick Test. If voltage is not as specified, repair short circuit or replace harness IDM is shorted to another wire between EDIS module and ECA. Remove test equipment and reconnect all components. Clear Continuous Memory Codes and rerun Quick Test.

CAUTION: Never connect ECA to ECA BOB when performing EDIS diagnostics unless directed to do so.

PINPOINT TEST C – 1) Check Base Ignition Timing – With ignition off, install EDIS diagnostic cable to BOB, EDIS module, and coil pack. Do not connect VR sensor tee. Use EDIS "6" overlay (if available). Connect EDIS diagnostic cable negative and positive leads to battery. Set EDIS diagnostic cable box switch to "4/6 cylinder" position. Connect timing light (must be EDIS/DIS compatible). Start engine and allow it to warm up. If timing is 10±2 degrees BTDC when EDIS diagnostic cable SAW button is pushed, go to step **2)**. If timing is not as specified, proceed to step **8)**.

2) Check For Advance Spark Angle – If engine timing is greater than 15 degrees BTDC when diagnostic cable SAW button is released, EDIS Ignition System is okay. Go to TROUBLE SHOOTING – NO-CODES article for further driveability symptom diagnosis. If timing is not as specified, go to next step.

3) Check SAW At EDIS Module – With ignition off, set DVOM on 20-volt DC scale. Start engine and measure voltage between EDIS diagnostic cable SAW DETECTOR (21) and BAT– (7) at BOB. If DC voltage reading is 5-7 volts, replace EDIS module. SAW input to EDIS module is okay but no spark advance is present. Remove test equipment and reconnect all components. Clear Continuous Memory Codes and rerun Quick Test. If DC voltage is not 5-7 volts, proceed to next step.

4) Check For SAW Short In EDIS Module – Isolate EDIS Module – With ignition off and ECA connected, set DVOM on 20-volt DC scale. Push EDIS diagnostic cable SAW button at EDIS diagnostic cable connector to BOB. Start engine and measure voltage between SAW DETECTOR (21) and BAT– (7) at BOB. If DC voltage reading is 5-7 volts, replace EDIS module. SAW circuit is shorted in EDIS module. Remove test equipment and reconnect all components. Clear Continuous Memory Codes and rerun Quick Test. If DC voltage is not 5-7 volts, proceed to next step.

5) Check For SAW Short To Ground In Harness – With ignition off, disconnect ECA. Disconnect EDIS module from EDIS diagnostic cable module tee. Leave EDIS diagnostic cable connected to vehicle harness connector. Disconnect HEGO connector. Set DVOM on 200-ohm scale. Measure resistance between SAW E (45) and BAT– (7) at BOB. If resistance is less or greater than 100 ohms, repair short circuit. Remove test equipment and reconnect all components. Clear Continuous Memory Codes and rerun Quick Test. If resistance is 100 ohms or greater, reconnect HEGO sensor and go to next step.

6) Check For SAW Short To VBAT In Harness – With ignition off, and ECA disconnected, set DVOM on 20-volt DC scale. With KOEO, measure voltage between SAW E (45) and BAT– (7) at BOB. If DC voltage reading is less than .5 volt, repair short circuit. SAW is shorted to VBAT. Remove test equipment and reconnect all components. Clear Continuous Memory Codes and rerun Quick Test. If voltage is .5 volt or greater, go to next step.

7) Check For SAW Open – With ignition off and ECA disconnected, connect ECA BOB to ECA harness connector. Set DVOM on 200-ohm scale. Measure resistance between SAW E (45) at BOB and terminal No. 36 at ECA BOB. If resistance is less than 5 ohms, replace ECA. SAW is not being transmitted by ECA. Remove test equipment and reconnect all components. Clear Continuous Memory Codes and rerun Quick Test. If resistance is not as specified, repair open circuit. Remove test equipment and reconnect all components. Clear Continuous Memory Codes and rerun Quick Test.

8) Inspect VR Sensor/Trigger Wheel – If VR sensor or trigger wheel is damaged, loose or misaligned, replace or repair components as required. Remove test equipment and reconnect all components. Clear Continuous Memory Codes and rerun Quick Test. If trigger wheel and VR sensor are not damaged or loose, replace EDIS module. Module cannot control timing. Remove test equipment and reconnect all components. Clear Continuous Memory Codes and rerun Quick Test.

CAUTION: Never connect ECA to ECA BOB when performing EDIS diagnostics unless directed to do so.

PINPOINT TEST D – 1) Check For VBAT Open To Coil – With ignition off and ECA connected, install EDIS diagnostic cable to BOB, EDIS module, and coil pack. Do not connect VR sensor tee. Use EDIS "6" overlay (if available). Connect EDIS diagnostic cable negative lead to battery. Set EDIS diagnostic cable box switch to "4/6 cylinder" position. Set DVOM on 20-volt DC scale. With KOEO, measure voltage between VBAT C (5) and BAT– (7) at BOB. If DC voltage is 10.5 volts or greater, go to next step. If voltage is less than 10.5, repair open VBAT to EDIS module circuit. Remove test equipment and reconnect

all components. Clear Continuous Memory Codes and rerun Quick Test.

2) Verify Vehicle Operating Mode – If vehicle will crank and start, go to step **4)**. If vehicle will not crank and start, go to next step.

3) Check C1, C2, C3 In Sequence At Coil Pack During Cranking – With ignition off and ECA connected, set DVOM on 20-volt AC scale, crank engine and measure voltage between BAT– (7) and each coil C1C (3), C2C (6), C3C (10) at BOB. If stabilized AC voltage reading is less than .2 volt, replace coil pack. Remove all test equipment and reconnect all components. Clear Continuous Memory Codes and rerun Quick Test. If voltage is .2 volt or greater, go to step **5)**.

4) Check C1, C2, C3 In Sequence At Coil Pack With Engine Running – With ignition off and ECA connected, set DVOM on 20-volt AC scale, crank engine and measure voltage between BAT– (7) and each coil C1C (3), C2C (6), C3C (10) at BOB. If stabilized AC voltage reading is less than 1.0 volt, replace coil pack. Remove all test equipment, and reconnect all components. Clear Continuous Memory Codes, and rerun Quick Test. If voltage is 1.0 volt or greater, go to next step.

5) Check C1, C2, C3 In Sequence At Coil Pack – KOEO Coil Fault – With ignition off and ECA disconnected, set DVOM on 20-volt DC scale. With KOEO, measure voltage between BAT– (7) and each coil C1C (3), C2C (6), C3C (10) at BOB. If each DC voltage reading is 10.5 volts or greater, go to next step. If voltage is less than 10.5 volts, go to step **10)**.

6) Check C1, C2, C3 In Sequence At EDIS Module – KOEO Coil Fault – With ignition off and ECA disconnected, set DVOM on 20-volt DC scale. With KOEO, measure voltage between BAT– (7) and each coil C1E (53), C2E (55), C3E (54) at BOB. If each DC voltage reading is 10.5 volts or greater, go to step **7)**. If voltage is less than 10.5 volts, repair open circuit. Remove all test equipment and reconnect all components. Clear Continuous Memory Codes and rerun Quick Test.

7) Check C1, C2, C3 In Sequence At Coil Pack – Isolate Coil – With ignition off and ECA disconnected, disconnect coil pack from coil tee. Leave EDIS diagnostic cable connected to vehicle harness connector. Set DVOM on 20-volt DC scale. With KOEO, measure voltage between BAT– (7) and each coil C1C (3), C2C (6), C3C (10) at BOB. If each DC voltage reading is less than .5 volt, go to step **9)**. If voltage is .5 volt or greater, go to next step.

8) Check C1, C2, C3 In Sequence At Coil Pack – Isolate EDIS Module – With ignition off and ECA disconnected, disconnect EDIS module from EDIS module tee. Leave EDIS diagnostic cable connected to vehicle harness connector. Set DVOM on 20-volt DC scale. With KOEO, measure voltage between BAT– (7) and each coil C1C (3), C2C (6), C3C (10) at BOB. If each DC voltage reading is less than .5 volt, replace EDIS module. Remove all test equipment and reconnect all components. Clear Continuous Memory Codes and rerun Quick Test. If voltage is .5 volt or greater, repair short circuit. Remove all test equipment and reconnect all components. Clear Continuous Memory Codes and rerun Quick Test.

9) Check C1, C2, C3 Coil Primary – With ignition off and ECA disconnected, reconnect coil pack to coil tee. Set DVOM on 20-ohm scale. Measure resistance between VBAT C (5) and each coil C1C (3), C2C (6), C3C (10) at BOB. If each resistance reading is .8 ohms or greater, replace EDIS module. Remove all test equipment and reconnect all components. Clear Continuous Memory Codes and rerun Quick Test. If resistance reading is less than .8 ohm, replace coil pack. Remove all test equipment and reconnect all components. Clear Continuous Memory Codes and rerun Quick Test.

10) Check C1, C2, C3 Short To Ground In Coil Pack – With ignition off and ECA disconnected, set DVOM on 2 k/ohm scale. Measure resistance between BAT– (7) and each coil C1C (3), C2C (6), C3C (10) at BOB. If each resistance reading is less than 1200 ohms, go to next step. If resistance reading is 1200 ohms or greater, replace coil pack. Remove all test equipment, and reconnect all components. Clear Continuous Memory Codes, and rerun Quick Test.

11) Check C1, C2, C3 Short To Ground In Harness – With ignition off and ECA disconnected, disconnect EDIS coil tee from coil pack and vehicle harness connector. Disconnect EDIS module from EDIS module tee, leaving EDIS cable connected to vehicle harness connector.

Set DVOM on 2 k/ohm scale. Measure resistance between BAT– (7) and each coil C1C (3), C2C (6), C3C (10) at BOB. If any resistance reading is less than 5 ohms, repair short. Remove all test equipment, and reconnect all components. Clear Continuous Memory Codes, and rerun Quick Test. If any resistance reading is 5 ohms or greater, replace EDIS module. Remove all test equipment, and reconnect all components. Clear Continuous Memory Codes, and rerun Quick Test.

EMISSION SYSTEMS & SUB-SYSTEMS

AIR INJECTION

Air Supply Pump – Check belt tension and adjust to proper tension, if necessary. Disconnect air supply hose from by-pass control valve. Start engine. Pump is operating satisfactorily if airflow is felt at pump outlet and airflow increases as engine speed is increased. If pump does not operate as specified, replace pump.

CAUTION: DO NOT pry on the air supply pump to adjust belt tension. Aluminum housing of pump may collapse.

Air Silencer/Filter (Air Pump & Pulse Air Inlet) – Inspect hoses and air silencer for leaks. Disconnect hose from air silencer outlet. Remove silencer from vehicle, and visually inspect for plugging. If no plugging or leaks are found, silencer is okay. If any plugging or leaks are found, repair or replace as required.

Air By-Pass Valve (Normally Closed) – **1)** Disconnect air supply hose at valve outlet. *See Fig. 17.* Remove vacuum line from vacuum nipple and check for presence of vacuum at nipple. There must be vacuum present at nipple before proceeding.

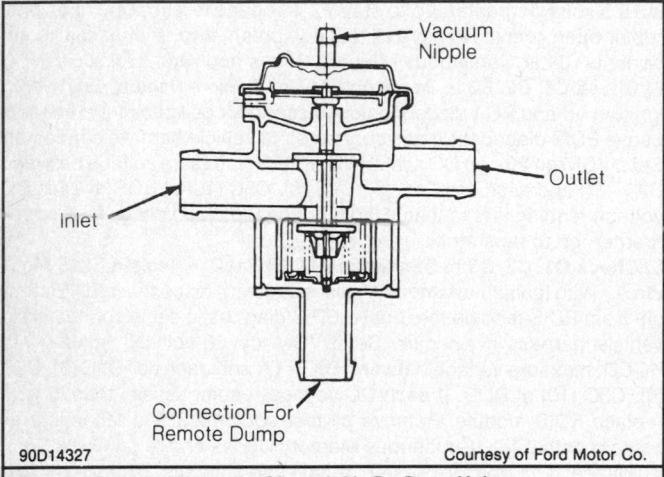

90D14327   Courtesy of Ford Motor Co.

Fig. 17: Testing Normally Closed Air By-Pass Valve

2) Reconnect vacuum line to vacuum nipple. With engine at 1500 RPM, air pump supply air should be heard and felt at air by-pass valve outlet.
3) With engine still at 1500 RPM, disconnect vacuum line. Air at outlet should decrease significantly or shut off. Air pump supply air should now be heard or felt at silencer ports or at dump port.
4) If the normally closed air by-pass valve does not perform as described in steps **2)** and **3)**, check the air pump for faults. If air pump is operating satisfactorily, replace air by-pass valve.
Air Check Valve – **1)** Visually inspect thermactor hoses, tubes, control valve(s) and check valve(s) for leaks that may be due to backflow of exhaust gases. If holes are found and/or traces of exhaust gas products are evident, check valve may be suspect.
2) Valve should allow free flow of air in direction of arrow only. *See Fig. 18.* The valve(s) should check (or block) the free flow of exhaust gas air in the opposite direction.
3) If air does not flow as indicated or if exhaust gas backflows opposite of direction of arrow in illustration, replace check valve.
Air Supply Control Valve – **1)** Disconnect air supply hose at inlet. Accelerate engine to 1500 RPM and verify presence of airflow in hose. Reconnect air supply hose to valve inlet.

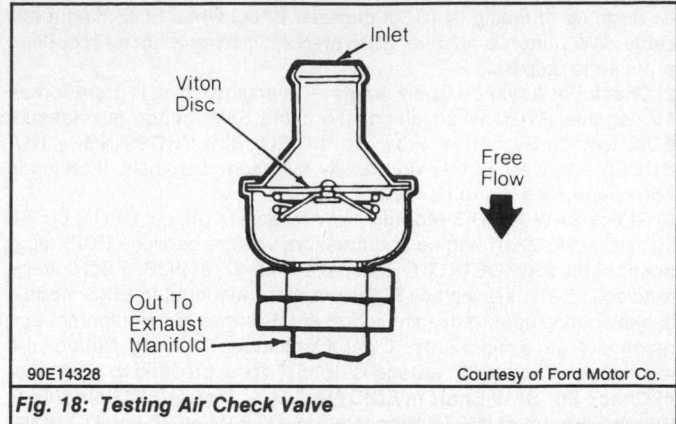

90E14328   Courtesy of Ford Motor Co.

Fig. 18: Testing Air Check Valve

2) Disconnect air supply hoses at outlets "A" and "B". *See Fig. 19.* Remove vacuum line at vacuum nipple. Accelerate engine to 1500 RPM. Airflow should be heard and felt at outlet "B" with little or no airflow at outlet "A".

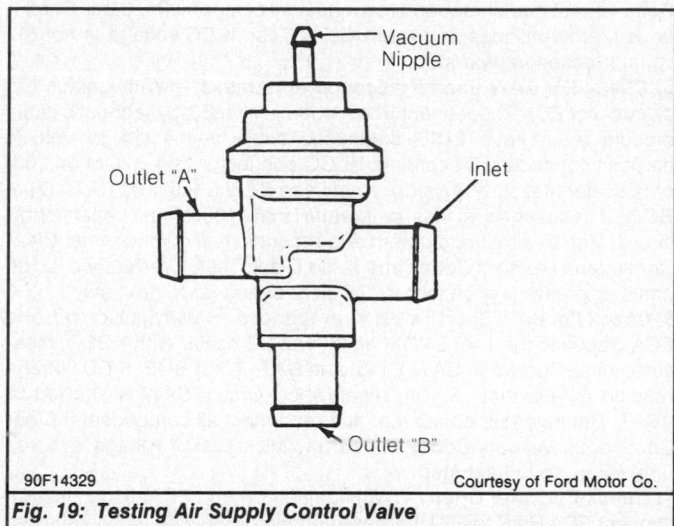

90F14329   Courtesy of Ford Motor Co.

Fig. 19: Testing Air Supply Control Valve

3) Connect a vacuum line from manifold vacuum fitting to air supply control valve vacuum nipple. Accelerate engine to 1500 RPM. Airflow should be heard and felt at outlet "A" with little or no airflow at outlet "B".
4) If valve does not operate as specified, replace valve. If airflow operates as described in steps **1)**, **2)** and **3)**, valve is okay. Reinstall hoses and clamps.

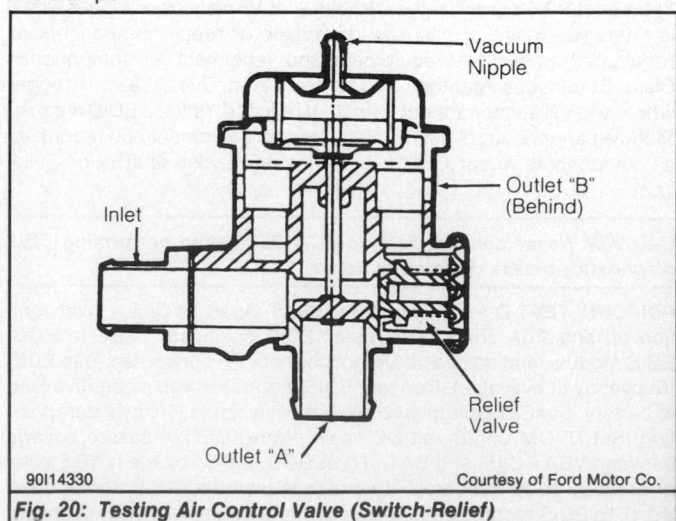

90I14330   Courtesy of Ford Motor Co.

Fig. 20: Testing Air Control Valve (Switch-Relief)

Air Control Valve (Switch-Relief) – **1)** Disconnect air supply hose at inlet. Accelerate engine to 1500 RPM and verify presence of airflow in hose. Reconnect air supply hose to valve inlet.

2) Carefully disconnect the air supply hoses at outlets "A" and "B". *See Fig. 20.* Carefully remove vacuum line at vacuum nipple. Accelerate engine to 1500 RPM. Airflow should be heard and felt at outlet "B" with little or no airflow at outlet "A".

3) Connect a vacuum line from manifold vacuum fitting to air control valve vacuum nipple. Accelerate engine to 1500 RPM. Airflow should be heard and felt at outlet "A" with little or no airflow at outlet "B".

4) If conditions in steps **2)** and **3)** are not as specified, replace air control valve. If the valve operates satisfactorily, restore all hose and vacuum connections.

Air Pump Resonator – Visually inspect for holes. Remove hoses and check for restricted ports. Replace resonator if holes or ports are restricted. Reconnect hoses and install clamps.

Combination Air By-Pass/Air Control Valve – **1)** Disconnect hoses from outlets "A" and "B". *See Fig. 21.* Disconnect and plug vacuum line to port "D". With engine operating at 1500 RPM, airflow should be flowing from by-pass vents.

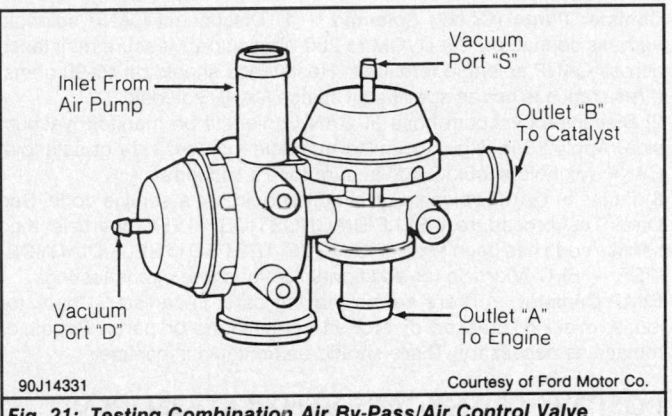

90J14331

Courtesy of Ford Motor Co.

Fig. 21: Testing Combination Air By-Pass/Air Control Valve

2) Reconnect vacuum line to port "D". Disconnect and plug vacuum line to port "S". Ensure vacuum is present in line to vacuum port "D". Accelerate engine to 1500 RPM. Airflow should be noted coming out of outlet "B". No airflow should be detected at outlet "A".

3) Apply 8-10 in. Hg vacuum to port "S". With engine operating at 1500 RPM, airflow should be noted coming out of outlet "A". If valve is bleed type, less air will flow from outlet "A" or "B", and the main discharge will change when vacuum is applied to port "S".

4) If the conditions in the above steps are not met, replace valve. If above conditions are met, valve is okay. Reconnect hoses and vacuum lines.

Dual Thermactor Air Control Solenoid Valve – Function of each valve can be determined by externally energizing valve with vacuum lines attached. Check resistance of each solenoid. Resistance should be 51-108 ohms when checked at coil terminals. If resistance is not 51-108 ohms, solenoid should be replaced.

Thermactor Idle Vacuum (TIV) Valve – **1)** With engine at idle and transmission in Neutral, apply vacuum to small nipple and place fingers over the TIV valve atmospheric vent holes. *See Fig. 22.* If no vacuum is sensed, the TIV is damaged and must be replaced. If vacuum is sensed, go to next step.

2) With engine still at idle, apply vacuum to TIV valve large nipple using a vacuum pump. See TIV VALVE (LARGE NIPPLE) VACUUM SPECIFICATIONS table. If vacuum is not held, the TIV is damaged and must be replaced. If no vacuum is sensed, replace valve.

TIV VALVE (LARGE NIPPLE) VACUUM SPECIFICATIONS

TIV Decal Color Code	In. Hg
Ash	5.1-10
Red	11.8-15.2

Vacuum Control Valve (VCV) – **1)** A 2-port valve may be in open or closed position when engine is cold, but should reverse when engine is warmed to operating temperature.

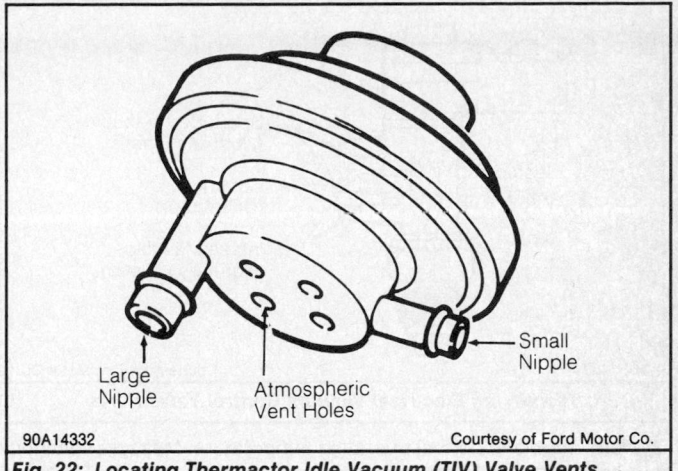

90A14332

Courtesy of Ford Motor Co.

Fig. 22: Locating Thermactor Idle Vacuum (TIV) Valve Vents

2) For 3-port valves, with a cold engine, passage "A" to "B" should be closed and passage "A" to "C" should be open. *See Fig. 23.* With engine at normal operating temperature, the VCV should be open between "A" and "B" and closed between "A" and "C".

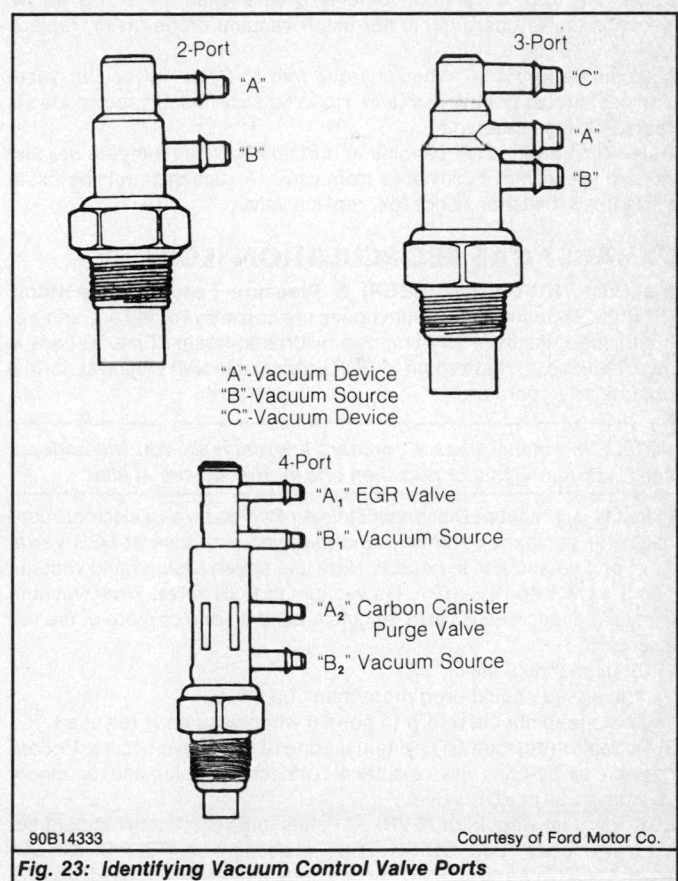

90B14333

Courtesy of Ford Motor Co.

Fig. 23: Identifying Vacuum Control Valve Ports

3) For the 4-port valve, check "A₁" to "B₁" and "A₂" to "B₂" separately. *See Fig. 23.* A 4-port valve may be in open or closed position when engine is cold, but should reverse when engine is warmed to operating temperature. If valve does not operate as specified, replace the valve.

Electrical Vacuum Control Valve – **1)** Electrical vacuum control valve may be either open or closed at room temperature, but should reverse the position when engine is at full operating temperature. While engine is cold, measure continuity across switch terminals. *See Fig. 24.* Note if switch is open or closed.

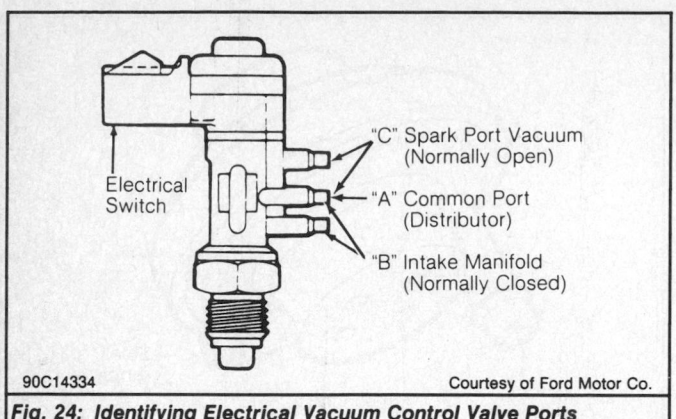

"C" Spark Port Vacuum (Normally Open)

Electrical Switch

"A" Common Port (Distributor)

"B" Intake Manifold (Normally Closed)

90C14334   Courtesy of Ford Motor Co.

Fig. 24: Identifying Electrical Vacuum Control Valve Ports

2) Warm engine to normal operating temperature. Measure continuity across switch terminals again. Continuity should be opposite of cold condition. If switch continuity does not switch, replace valve. Check vacuum function of valve as described in VACUUM CONTROL VALVE.

Vacuum Check Valve – Apply 16 in. Hg vacuum to check side of valve and trap. If vacuum remains greater than 15 in. Hg for 10 seconds, valve operation is normal. If vacuum drops faster, replace valve.

Vacuum Reservoir – When charged with 15-20 in. Hg vacuum, vacuum loss should not exceed .5 in. Hg in 60 seconds. If vacuum loss is faster, replace reservoir.

Pulse Air Valve – With engine at normal operating temperature and at curb idle, remove inlet hose from valve. A suction should be felt at valve inlet. If suction is not felt, replace valve.

EXHAUST GAS RECIRCULATION (EGR)

Electronic EGR Valve (EEGR) & Pressure Feedback Electronic (PFE) – 1) Ensure all vacuum hoses are correctly routed and securely attached. Replace any crimped or broken hoses. Ensure there is less than one in. Hg vacuum to EGR valve at idle with engine at normal operating temperature.

NOTE: EVR solenoid has a constant internal leak. You will notice a small vacuum signal of less than one in. Hg vacuum at idle.

---

2) Install tachometer. Disconnect Idle Air By-Pass Valve electrical connector (if equipped). Remove and plug vacuum hose at EGR valve. Start engine and idle in neutral. Note idle speed. Using hand vacuum pump, slowly apply 5-10 in. Hg vacuum to EGR valve. When vacuum is fully applied to EGR valve, engine should do one or more of the following:
- Engine should stall.
- Idle speed should drop more than 100 RPM.
- Idle speed should return to normal when vacuum is released.

3) Repair or replace EGR system if none of the above occurs. Reconnect idle air by-pass valve electrical connector. Unplug and reconnect vacuum hose at EGR valve.

EGR Vacuum Regulator (EVR) – Faults in EVR or circuit should set a service code. See QUICK TEST procedure in SELF-DIAGNOSTICS – EEC-IV article. If no service code has been set, see CIRCUIT TEST DN in SELF-DIAGNOSTICS – EEC-IV article for diagnostic procedures.

On 2.3L Ranger (1989-92), intermittent operation or failure of EVR may be caused by water in EVR or vacuum hoses connected to it. If water or moisture is found in EVR or hoses connected to it, install new service part, available from manufacturer, in an inverted position. Use shop air to clear water and moisture from vacuum hoses. Clear Continuous Memory Codes if set and run Quick Test to verify repair.

EGR Solenoid – Remove EGR solenoid harness connector. Measure resistance across solenoid terminals. Resistance should be 65-110 ohms. Set DVOM to 200 k/ohm scale. Measure resistance between each solenoid terminal and ground or side of solenoid. Resistance should be 10 k/ohms or more. If resistance is not as specified in either test, replace solenoid.

Vacuum Check Valve – Apply 16 in. Hg vacuum to check side of valve and trap. If vacuum remains greater than 15 in. Hg for 10 seconds, valve operation is normal. If vacuum does not remain greater than 15 in. Hg for 10 seconds, replace valve.

Vacuum Reservoir – When charged with 15-20 in. Hg vacuum, vacuum loss should not exceed .5 in. Hg in 60 seconds. If vacuum loss is greater than specified, replace reservoir.

FUEL EVAPORATION

Canister Purge Regulator (CPR) Valve – With CPR valve de-energized, apply 5 in. Hg vacuum to source port. Valve should not pass air. Apply 9-14 volts to one electrical terminal and ground the other. Valve should open and pass air. If valve does not operate as described, replace valve.

Canister Purge (CANP) Solenoid – 1) Disconnect CANP solenoid harness connector. Set DVOM to 200-ohm scale. Measure resistance across CANP solenoid terminals. Resistance should be 40-90 ohms. If resistance is not as specified, replace CANP solenoid.

2) Disconnect vacuum hose at CANP solenoid on manifold vacuum side. Apply 16 in. Hg vacuum to manifold vacuum side of solenoid. CANP solenoid should hold vacuum for 20 seconds.

3) Faults in CANP solenoid or circuit should set a service code. See Quick Test procedure in SELF-DIAGNOSTICS – EEC-IV article. If no service code has been set, see CIRCUIT TEST KD in SELF-DIAGNOSTICS – EEC-IV article for additional solenoid and circuit testing.

EVAP Canister – There are no moving parts in canister. Check for loose, missing, cracked or broken connections or parts. Repair or replace as necessary. There should be no liquid in canister.

POSITIVE CRANKCASE VENTILATION (PCV)

PCV Valve – 1) Remove PCV valve from rocker cover grommet. Shake valve. Valve should rattle when shaken. If valve does not rattle, replace valve.

2) Start engine and warm to normal operating temperature. On 2.3L, 2.9L and 4.9L engines, remove corrugated hose from oil separator nipple. Place stiff piece of paper over nipple end and wait 60 seconds.

3) On all other engines, disconnect hose from remote air cleaner or outlet tube. Place stiff piece of paper over hose end and wait 60 seconds. Vacuum should hold paper in place. If vacuum does not hold paper in place, replace valve.

THERMOSTATIC AIR CLEANER (TAC)

Air Cleaner Temperature Sensor – Bring temperature of sensor to less than 75°F (24°C), and apply 8 in. Hg vacuum to source port. Duct door should close. If door does not close, replace sensor. Sensor will bleed off vacuum to allow duct door to open and let in fresh air at specific temperatures. See AIR CLEANER TEMPERATURE SENSOR OPENING table.

AIR CLEANER TEMPERATURE SENSOR OPENING

Color	Temperature
Brown	70°F (21°C)
Pink, Black Or Red	90°F (32°C)
Blue, Yellow Or Green	105°F (41°C)

Air Control Door – When a vacuum of 8 in. Hg or more is applied to vacuum motor, door should stay in proper position for as long as vacuum is applied. If vacuum bleeds off and door returns to rest position, replace vacuum motor.

Aerostar, Bronco, Explorer, Pickup, Ranger, Van

NOTE: Unless otherwise specified, references to Pickup include the F350 Super Duty commercial chassis.

MODEL IDENTIFICATION

Series [1]	Model
"A"	Aerostar
"E"	RWD Van
"F"	Pickup
"R"	Ranger
"U"	Bronco & Explorer

[1] – Vehicle series is fifth character of VIN.

INTRODUCTION

Pin voltage charts are supplied to reduce diagnostic time. Checking pin voltages at the Electronic Control Assembly (ECA), determines whether it's receiving and transmitting proper voltage signals. Charts may also help determine if ECA harness is shorted or opened.

Diagnostic values are based on engine at normal operating temperature. Key On Engine Off (KOEO) and Hot Idle tests are recorded with transmission selector lever in Park (A/T) or Neutral (M/T) position. Vehicles with manual transmission use 3rd gear for 30 MPH values and 4th gear for 55 MPH values.

Reference values may differ due to component tolerances, driving conditions and weather. The ACT and ECT values may vary greatly with temperature. The values given were recorded at approximately 600 feet above sea level at 50-70°F (15°C).

NOTE: Unless stated otherwise in testing procedures, perform all voltage tests using a Digital Volt-Ohmmeter (DVOM) with a minimum 10-megohm input impedance. Voltage readings may vary slightly due to battery condition or charging rate.

ECA LOCATION

ECA LOCATION

Application	Location
Aerostar	On Left Side Of Firewall.
Bronco & Pickup	Near Brake Fluid Reservoir.
Explorer	Above Right Kick Panel.
Ranger	Behind Right Kick Panel.
Van	On Right Side Of Firewall, Under Blower Motor.

ECA CONNECTOR

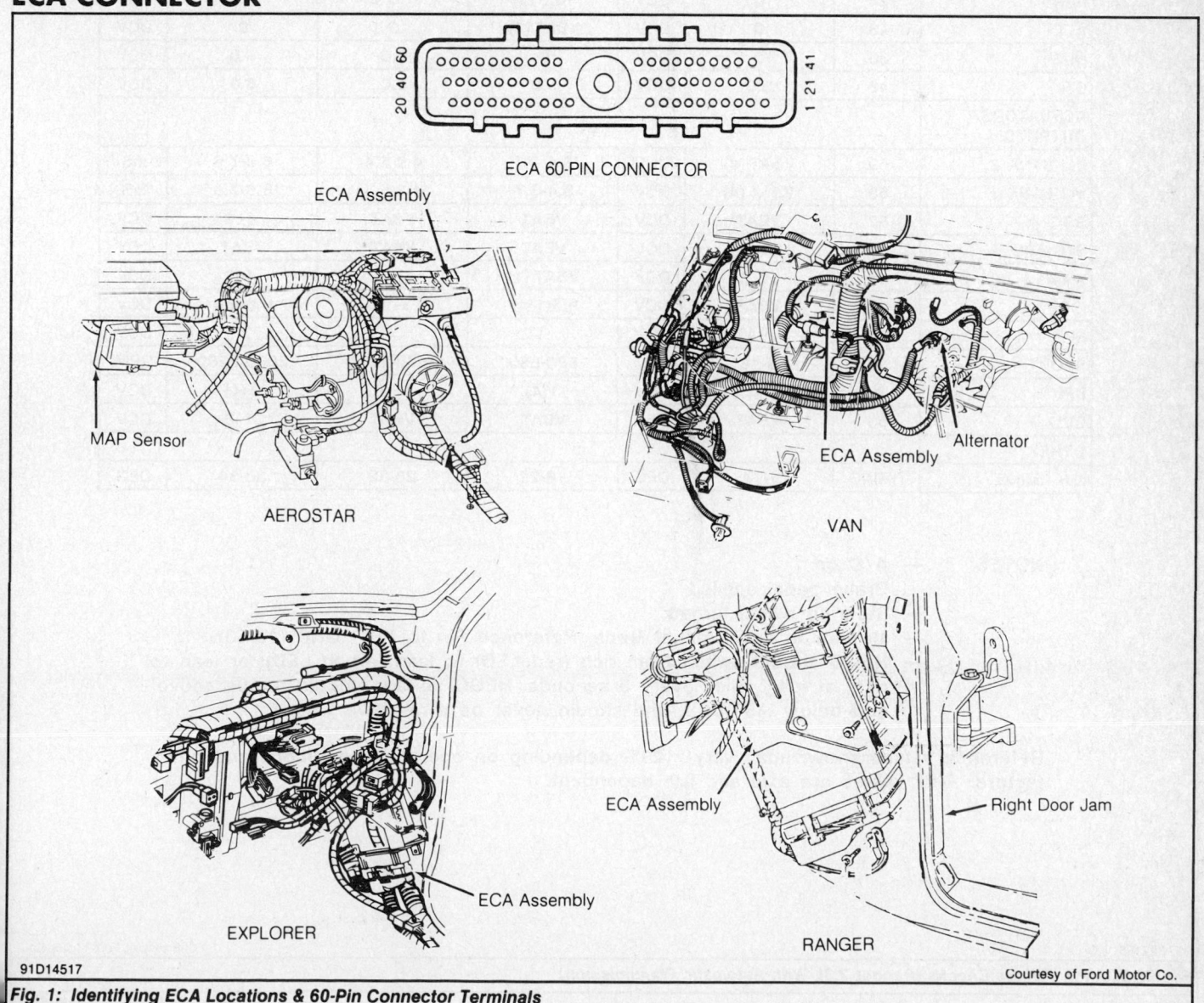

ECA 60-PIN CONNECTOR

AEROSTAR

VAN

EXPLORER

RANGER

91D14517

Courtesy of Ford Motor Co.

Fig. 1: Identifying ECA Locations & 60-Pin Connector Terminals

1992 ENGINE PERFORMANCE
Pin Voltage Charts (Cont.)

ECA CHECKS

2.3L RANGER
AUTOMATIC TRANSMISSION

SENSORS/ INPUTS	Signal Pin #	KOEO	Units	HOT IDLE	30 MPH	55 MPH	Units
OCT ADJ	44	0	DCV	0	0	0	DCV
MAF - red	14	0 (4)	DCV	.5-.7 (4)	1.1-1.6 (4)	1.6-2.3 (4)	DCV
TP	47	.9-1.0	DCV	.9-1.0	1.0-1.2	1.2-1.6	DCV
ECT	7	.8-.9	DCV	.8-.9	.7-.8	.7-.8	DCV
ACT	25	.7-1.9	DCV	.7-1.9	.7-1.9	.7-1.9	DCV
IDM	4	8-16	RPM	680-880	1670-1770	2090-2250	RPM
PIP	56	8-16	RPM	680-880	1670-1770	2090-2250	RPM
HEGO	29	0	DCV	switching (5)	switching (5)	switching (5)	DCV
BOO	2	0	DCV	VBAT (2)	0	0	DCV
FPM - red	8	0	DCV	VBAT	VBAT	VBAT	DCV
ACCS	10	0	DCV	VBAT (1)	0	0	DCV
VSS+	3	1	MPH	1	30	55	MPH
PSPS	24	0	DCV	10.0 (3)	0	0	DCV
ACD	43	0	DCV	VBAT (1)	0	0	DCV
NDS	30	0	DCV	0	5.0	5.0	DCV
STI	48	5.0	DCV	5.0	5.0	5.0	DCV
ACTUATORS/ OUTPUTS							
INJ BANK 2	59	VBAT (4)	DCV	3.4-3.7	4.9-5.4	6.6-7.6	mS
INJ BANK 1	58	VBAT (4)	DCV	3.4-3.7	4.9-5.4	6.6-7.6	mS
SS 3/4	52	VBAT	DCV	VBAT	VBAT	.1-.3	DCV
STO/MIL	17	.1-.2	DCV	VBAT	VBAT	VBAT	DCV
WAC	54	.1-.2	DCV	VBAT (1)	.1-.2	.1-.2	DCV
ISC	21	VBAT	DCV	9.5-11.5	8.3-10.3	6.6-9.4	DCV
FP	22	VBAT	DCV	.1	.1	.1	DCV
SPOUT	36	8-16	RPM	680-880	1670-1770	2090-2250	RPM
DPI	32	11.0-12.0 (4)	DCV	0 (4)	0 (4)	0 (4)	DCV
CCO	53	VBAT	DCV	VBAT	VBAT	.1-.3	DCV
OTHER							
IGN TIMING	TIMING	N/A	DEG	18-22	28-32	30-34	DEG

NOTES: ① — A/C on.
② — Brake pedal applied.
③ — Steering wheel turned.
④ — Monitor in DCV Manual Mode, Reference Pin to PWR GND (40/60).
⑤ — HEGO should switch from rich (red LED) to lean (green LED), or lean to rich, at least once every 3 seconds. HEGO voltage should toggle above and below .450 DCV, and should never be a negative value.

Reference values shown may vary ± 20% depending on operating conditions and other factors. RPM values are axle and tire dependent.

92C22196

Courtesy of Ford Motor Co.

Fig. 2: ECA Pin Voltage Checks (Ranger 2.3L With Automatic Transmission)

1992 ENGINE PERFORMANCE
Pin Voltage Charts (Cont.)

2.3L RANGER
MANUAL TRANSMISSION

SENSORS/ INPUTS	Signal Pin #	KOEO	Units	HOT IDLE	30 MPH	55 MPH	Units
OCT ADJ	44	0	DCV	0	0	0	DCV
MAF - red	14	0 (4)	DCV	.5-.7 (4)	1.1-1.6 (4)	1.6-2.3 (4)	DCV
TP	47	.9-1.0	DCV	.9-1.0	1.0-1.2	1.2-1.6	DCV
EVP	27	.3-.4	DCV	.3-.4	.3-1.1	.8-2.0	DCV
ECT	7	.8-.9	DCV	.8-.9	.7-.8	.7-.8	DCV
ACT	25	.7-1.9	DCV	.7-1.9	.7-1.9	.7-1.9	DCV
IDM	4	8-16	RPM	750-900	1420-1480	2090-2190	RPM
PIP	56	8-16	RPM	750-900	1420-1480	2090-2190	RPM
HEGO	29	0	DCV	switching (5)	switching (5)	switching (5)	DCV
BOO	2	0	DCV	VBAT (2)	0	0	DCV
FPM - red	8	0	DCV	VBAT	VBAT	VBAT	DCV
ACCS	10	0	DCV	VBAT (1)	0	0	DCV
VSS+	3	1	MPH	1	30	55	MPH
PSPS	24	0	DCV	10.0 (3)	0	0	DCV
ACD	43	0	DCV	VBAT (1)	0	0	DCV
STI	48	5.0	DCV	5.0	5.0	5.0	DCV
ACTUATORS/ OUTPUTS							
INJ BANK 2	59	VBAT (4)	DCV	3.1-3.5	3.6-4.8	5.4-7.2	mS
INJ BANK 1	58	VBAT (4)	DCV	3.1-3.5	3.6-4.8	5.4-7.2	mS
EVR	33	VBAT (4)	DCV	0	0-40	25-50	%
STO/MIL	17	.1-.2	DCV	VBAT	VBAT	VBAT	DCV
WAC	54	.1-.2	DCV	VBAT (1)	.1-.2	.1-.2	DCV
ISC	21	VBAT	DCV	9.5-11.5	8.3-10.3	6.6-9.4	DCV
FP	22	VBAT	DCV	.1	.1	.1	DCV
SPOUT	36	8-16	RPM	750-900	1420-1480	2090-2190	RPM
DPI	32	11.0-12.0 (4)	DCV	0 (4)	0 (4)	0 (4)	DCV
OTHER							
IGN TIMING	TIMING	N/A	DEG	18-22	28-32	30-34	DEG

NOTES:
① — A/C on.
② — Brake pedal applied.
③ — Steering wheel turned.
④ — Monitor in DCV Manual Mode, Reference Pin to PWR GND (40/60).
⑤ — HEGO should switch from rich (red LED) to lean (green LED), or lean to rich, at least once every 3 seconds. HEGO voltage should toggle above and below .450 DCV, and should never be a negative value.

Reference values shown may vary ± 20% depending on operating conditions and other factors. RPM values are axle and tire dependent.

92D22197

Courtesy of Ford Motor Co.

Fig. 3: ECA Pin Voltage Checks (Ranger 2.3L With Manual Transmission)

1992 ENGINE PERFORMANCE
Pin Voltage Charts (Cont.)

2.9L RANGER
AUTOMATIC TRANSMISSION

SENSORS/ INPUTS	Signal Pin #	KOEO	Units	HOT IDLE	30 MPH	55 MPH	Units
TP	47	.9-1.0	DCV	.9-1.0	1.0-1.2	1.2-1.5	DCV
ECT	7	.5-.7	DCV	.5-.7	.5-.7	.5-.7	DCV
ACT	25	.7-2.8	DCV	.7-2.8	.7-2.8	.7-2.8	DCV
MAP	45	158	Hz	104-108	106-118	118-132	Hz
IDM	4	2-12	RPM	810-890	1450-1600	1940-2080	RPM
PIP	56	2-12	RPM	810-890	1450-1600	1940-2080	RPM
HEGO	29	0	DCV	switching (3)	switching (3)	switching (3)	DCV
FPM - red	8	0	DCV	VBAT	VBAT	VBAT	DCV
ACCS	10	.1-.2	DCV	VBAT (1)	.1-.2	.1-.2	DCV
VSS+	3	1	MPH	1	30	55	MPH
NDS	30	0	DCV	0	5.0	5.0	DCV
STI	48	5.0	DCV	5.0	5.0	5.0	DCV
ACTUATORS/ OUTPUTS							
INJ BANK 2	59	VBAT (2)	DCV	3.2-3.5	4.0-5.8	5.5-7.0	mS
INJ BANK 1	58	VBAT (2)	DCV	3.2-3.5	4.0-5.8	5.5-7.0	mS
SS 3/4	52	VBAT	DCV	VBAT	VBAT	.1-.3	DCV
STO/MIL	17	.1-.2	DCV	VBAT	VBAT	VBAT	DCV
WAC	54	.1-.2	DCV	VBAT (1)	.1-.2	.1-.2	DCV
ISC	21	VBAT	DCV	10.1-11.1	8.5-11.0	4.6-10.0	DCV
FP	22	VBAT	DCV	.1-.9	.1-.9	.1-.9	DCV
SPOUT	36	2-12	RPM	810-890	1450-1600	1940-2080	RPM
CCO	53	VBAT	DCV	VBAT	VBAT	.1-.3	DCV
OTHER							
IGN TIMING	TIMING	N/A	DEG	24-28	30-36	32-36	DEG

NOTES: ① — A/C on.
② — Monitor in DCV Manual Mode, Reference Pin to PWR GND (40/60).
③ — HEGO should switch from rich (red LED) to lean (green LED), or lean to rich, at least once every 3 seconds. HEGO voltage should toggle above and below .450 DCV, and should never be a negative value.

Reference values shown may vary ± 20% depending on operating conditions and other factors. RPM values are axle and tire dependent.

92E22198

Fig. 4: ECA Pin Voltage Checks (Ranger 2.9L With Automatic Transmission)

1992 ENGINE PERFORMANCE
Pin Voltage Charts (Cont.)

2.9L RANGER
MANUAL TRANSMISSION

SENSORS/ INPUTS	Signal Pin #	KOEO	Units	HOT IDLE	30 MPH	55 MPH	Units
TP	47	.9-1.0	DCV	.9-1.0	1.0-1.2	1.2-1.5	DCV
ECT	7	.5-.7	DCV	.5-.7	.5-.7	.5-.7	DCV
ACT	25	.7-2.8	DCV	.7-2.8	.7-2.8	.7-2.8	DCV
MAP	45	158	Hz	104-108	106-118	118-132	Hz
IDM	4	2-12	RPM	810-890	1340-1500	2040-2140	RPM
PIP	56	2-12	RPM	810-890	1340-1500	2040-2140	RPM
HEGO	29	0	DCV	switching (3)	switching (3)	switching (3)	DCV
FPM - red	8	0	DCV	VBAT	VBAT	VBAT	DCV
ACCS	10	.1-.2	DCV	VBAT (1)	.1-.2	.1-.2	DCV
VSS+	3	1	MPH	1	30	55	MPH
NGS/CES	30	0	DCV	0	VBAT	VBAT	DCV
STI	48	5.0	DCV	5.0	5.0	5.0	DCV
ACTUATORS/ OUTPUTS							
INJ BANK 2	59	VBAT (2)	DCV	3.2-3.5	4.0-5.8	5.5-7.0	mS
INJ BANK 1	58	VBAT (2)	DCV	3.2-3.5	4.0-5.8	5.5-7.0	mS
STO/MIL	17	.6	DCV	VBAT	VBAT	VBAT	DCV
WAC	54	.1-.2	DCV	VBAT (1)	.1-.2	.1-.2	DCV
ISC	21	VBAT	DCV	10.1-11.1	8.5-11.0	4.6-10.0	DCV
FP	22	VBAT	DCV	.1-.9	.1-.9	.1-.9	DCV
SPOUT	36	2-12	RPM	810-890	1340-1500	2040-2140	RPM
OTHER							
IGN TIMING	TIMING	N/A	DEG	24-28	28-34	30-36	DEG

NOTES: ① — A/C on.
② — Monitor in DCV Manual Mode, Reference Pin to PWR GND (40/60).
③ — HEGO should switch from rich (red LED) to lean (green LED), or lean to rich, at least once every 3 seconds. HEGO voltage should toggle above and below .450 DCV, and should never be a negative value.

Reference values shown may vary ± 20% depending on operating conditions and other factors. RPM values are axle and tire dependent.

92F22199

Courtesy of Ford Motor Co.

Fig. 5: ECA Pin Voltage Checks (Ranger 2.9L With Manual Transmission)

1992 ENGINE PERFORMANCE
Pin Voltage Charts (Cont.)

3.0L AEROSTAR
AUTOMATIC TRANSMISSION

SENSORS/ INPUTS	Signal Pin #	KOEO	Units	HOT IDLE	30 MPH	55 MPH	Units
TP	47	.6-.7	DCV	.6-.7	.8-1.0	1.1-1.5	DCV
MAF	50	0	DCV	.9-1.0	1.4-2.0	2.3-2.7	DCV
ECT	7	.5-.7	DCV	.5-.7	.5-.7	.5-.7	DCV
ACT	25	.7-2.8	DCV	.7-2.8	.7-2.8	.7-2.8	DCV
IDM	4	0-12	RPM	710-810	1620-1720	1870-1980	RPM
PIP	56	0-12	RPM	710-810	1620-1720	1870-1980	RPM
HEGO	44	0	DCV	switching (4)	switching (4)	switching (4)	DCV
BOO	2	0	DCV	VBAT (2)	0	0	DCV
ACCS	10	0-.1	DCV	VBAT (1)	0-.1	0-.1	DCV
PSOM +	3	1	MPH	1	30	55	MPH
NDS	30	0	DCV	0	5.0	5.0	DCV
FPM - red	8	0	DCV	VBAT	VBAT	VBAT	DCV
STI	48	3.3-4.9	DCV	3.3-4.9	3.3-4.9	3.3-4.9	DCV
ACTUATORS/ OUTPUTS							
INJ 3	39	VBAT (3)	DCV	5.0-5.5	5.5-7.5	9.6-12.4	mS
INJ 5	15	VBAT (3)	DCV	5.0-5.5	5.5-7.5	9.6-12.4	mS
INJ 4	35	VBAT (3)	DCV	5.0-5.5	5.5-7.5	9.6-12.4	mS
INJ 2	59	VBAT (3)	DCV	5.0-5.5	5.5-7.5	9.6-12.4	mS
INJ 1	58	VBAT (3)	DCV	5.0-5.5	5.5-7.5	9.6-12.4	mS
STO-MIL	17	0-.2	DCV	VBAT	VBAT	VBAT	DCV
WAC	54	.1-.2	DCV	VBAT (1)	.1-.2	.1-.2	DCV
ISC	21	VBAT	DCV	11.8-12.6	11.1-12.1	11.1-12.1	DCV
FP	22	VBAT	DCV	.1-.2	.1-.2	.1-.2	DCV
INJ 6	12	VBAT (3)	DCV	5.0-5.5	5.5-7.5	9.6-12.4	mS
SPOUT	36	0-12	RPM	710-810	1620-1720	1870-1980	RPM
CCO	14	VBAT	DCV	VBAT	VBAT	.2-.4	DCV
SS 3/4	51	VBAT	DCV	VBAT	VBAT	.2-.4	DCV
CANP	11	VBAT	DCV	VBAT	11.4-VBAT	.2-12.0	DCV
OTHER							
IGN TIMING	TIMING	N/A	DEG	24-28	28-35	28-34	DEG

NOTES: ① — A/C on.
② — Monitor in DCV Manual Mode, Reference Pin to PWR GND (40/60).
③ — HEGO should switch from rich (red LED) to lean (green LED), or lean to rich, at least once every 3 seconds. HEGO voltage should toggle above and below .450 DCV, and should never be a negative value.

Reference values shown may vary ± 20% depending on operating conditions and other factors. RPM values are axle and tire dependent.

92I22200

Courtesy of Ford Motor Co.

Fig. 6: ECA Pin Voltage Checks (Aerostar 3.0L With Automatic Transmission)

1992 ENGINE PERFORMANCE
Pin Voltage Charts (Cont.)

3.0L AEROSTAR
MANUAL TRANSMISSION

SENSORS/ INPUTS	Signal Pin #	KOEO	Units	HOT IDLE	30 MPH	55 MPH	Units
TP	47	.6-.7	DCV	.6-.7	.8-1.0	1.0-1.2	DCV
MAF	50	0	DCV	.9-1.0	1.4-2.0	2.1-2.7	DCV
ECT	7	.5-.7	DCV	.5-.7	.5-.7	.5-.7	DCV
ACT	25	.7-2.8	DCV	.7-2.8	.7-2.8	.7-2.8	DCV
IDM	4	0-12	RPM	780-880	1360-1500	1990-2150	RPM
PIP	56	0-12	RPM	780-880	1360-1500	1990-2150	RPM
HEGO	44	0	DCV	switching (3)	switching (3)	switching (3)	DCV
ACCS	10	0-.1	DCV	VBAT (1)	0-.1	0-.1	DCV
PSOM +	3	1	MPH	1	30	55	MPH
FPM - red	8	0	DCV	VBAT	VBAT	VBAT	DCV
STI	48	3.3-4.9	DCV	3.3-4.9	3.3-4.9	3.3-4.9	DCV
ACTUATORS/ OUTPUTS							
INJ BANK 3	39	VBAT (2	DCV	5.0-5.5	5.5-7.5	8.0-11.2	mS
INJ BANK 5	15	VBAT (2)	DCV	5.0-5.5	5.5-7.5	8.0-11.2	mS
INJ BANK 4	35	VBAT (2)	DCV	5.0-5.5	5.5-7.5	8.0-11.2	mS
INJ BANK 2	59	VBAT (2)	DCV	5.0-5.5	5.5-7.5	8.0-11.2	mS
INJ BANK 1	58	VBAT (2)	DCV	5.0-5.5	5.5-7.5	8.0-11.2	mS
STO/MIL	17	0-.2	DCV	VBAT	VBAT	VBAT	DCV
WAC	54	.1-.2	DCV	VBAT (1)	.1-.2	.1-.2	DCV
ISC	21	VBAT	DCV	10.8-11.8	9.7-10.7	8.4-9.2	DCV
FP	22	VBAT	DCV	.1-.2	.1-.2	.1-.2	DCV
INJ 6	12	VBAT (2)	DCV	5.0-5.5	5.5-7.5	8.0-11.2	mS
SPOUT	36	0-12	RPM	780-880	1360-1500	1990-2150	RPM
CANP	11	VBAT	DCV	VBAT	.2-VBAT	.2-12.0	DCV
OTHER							
IGN TIMING	TIMING	N/A	DEG	24-28	33-37	34-38	DEG

NOTES: ① — A/C on.
② — Monitor in DCV Manual Mode, Reference Pin to PWR GND (40/60).
③ — HEGO should switch from rich (red LED) to lean (green LED), or lean to rich, at least once every 3 seconds. HEGO voltage should toggle above and below .450 DCV, and should never be a negative value.

Reference values shown may vary ± 20% depending on operating conditions and other factors. RPM values are axle and tire dependent.

92J22201

Courtesy of Ford Motor Co.

Fig. 7: ECA Pin Voltage Checks (Aerostar 3.0L With Manual Transmission)

1992 ENGINE PERFORMANCE
Pin Voltage Charts (Cont.)

3.0L RANGER
AUTOMATIC TRANSMISSION

SENSORS/ INPUTS	Signal Pin #	KOEO	Units	HOT IDLE	30 MPH	55 MPH	Units
TP	47	.6-.7	DCV	.6-.7	.8-1.0	1.1-1.5	DCV
MAF	50	0	DCV	.9-1.0	1.4-2.0	2.3-2.7	DCV
ECT	7	.5-.7	DCV	.5-.7	.5-.7	.5-.7	DCV
ACT	25	.7-2.8	DCV	.7-2.8	.7-2.8	.7-2.8	DCV
IDM	4	0-12	RPM	710-810	1620-1720	1870-1980	RPM
PIP	56	0-12	RPM	710-810	1620-1720	1870-1980	RPM
HEGO-R	44	0	DCV	switching (4)	switching (4)	switching (4)	DCV
BOO	2	0	DCV	VBAT (2)	0	0	DCV
ACCS	10	0-.1	DCV	VBAT (1)	0-.1	0-.1	DCV
VSS+	3	1	MPH	1	30	55	MPH
HEGO-L	43	0	DCV	switching (4)	switching (4)	switching (4)	DCV
NDS	30	0	DCV	0	5.0	5.0	DCV
FPM - red	8	0	DCV	VBAT	VBAT	VBAT	DCV
STI	48	3.3-4.9	DCV	3.3-4.9	3.3-4.9	3.3-4.9	DCV
ACTUATORS/ OUTPUTS							
INJ 3	39	VBAT (3)	DCV	5.0-5.5	5.5-7.5	9.6-12.4	mS
INJ 5	15	VBAT (3)	DCV	5.0-5.5	5.5-7.5	9.6-12.4	mS
INJ 4	35	VBAT (3)	DCV	5.0-5.5	5.5-7.5	9.6-12.4	mS
INJ 2	59	VBAT (3)	DCV	5.0-5.5	5.5-7.5	9.6-12.4	mS
INJ 1	58	VBAT (3)	DCV	5.0-5.5	5.5-7.5	9.6-12.4	mS
STO-MIL	17	0-.2	DCV	VBAT	VBAT	VBAT	DCV
WAC	54	.1-.2	DCV	VBAT (1)	.1-.2	.1-.2	DCV
ISC	21	VBAT	DCV	11.8-12.6	11.1-12.1	11.1-12.1	DCV
FP	22	VBAT	DCV	.1-.2	.1-.2	.1-.2	DCV
INJ 6	12	VBAT (3)	DCV	5.0-5.5	5.5-7.5	9.6-12.4	mS
SPOUT	36	0-12	RPM	710-810	1620-1720	1870-1980	RPM
CCO	14	VBAT	DCV	VBAT	VBAT	.2-.4	DCV
SS 3/4	51	VBAT	DCV	VBAT	VBAT	.2-.4	DCV
CANP	11	VBAT	DCV	VBAT	11.4-VBAT	.2-12.0	DCV
OTHER							
IGN TIMING	TIMING	N/A	DEG	24-28	28-35	28-34	DEG

NOTES: ① — A/C on.
    ② — Brake pedal applied.
    ③ — Monitor in DCV Manual Mode, Reference Pin to PWR GND (40/60).
    ④ — HEGO should switch from rich (red LED) to lean (green LED), or lean to rich, at least once every 3 seconds. HEGO voltage should toggle above and below .450 DCV, and should never be a negative value.

Reference values shown may vary ± 20% depending on operating conditions and other factors. RPM values are axle and tire dependent.

92A22202

Fig. 8: ECA Pin Voltage Checks (Ranger 3.0L With Automatic Transmission)

1992 ENGINE PERFORMANCE
Pin Voltage Charts (Cont.)

3.0L RANGER
MANUAL TRANSMISSION

SENSORS/ INPUTS	Signal Pin #	KOEO	Units	HOT IDLE	30 MPH	55 MPH	Units
TP	47	.6-.7	DCV	.6-.7	.8-1.0	1.0-1.2	DCV
MAF	50	0	DCV	.9-1.0	1.4-2.0	2.1-2.7	DCV
ECT	7	.5-.7	DCV	.5-.7	.5-.7	.5-.7	DCV
ACT	25	.7-2.8	DCV	.7-2.8	.7-2.8	.7-2.8	DCV
IDM	4	0-12	RPM	780-880	1360-1500	1990-2150	RPM
PIP	56	0-12	RPM	780-880	1360-1500	1990-2150	RPM
HEGO-R	44	0	DCV	switching (3)	switching (3)	switching (3)	DCV
ACCS	10	0-.1	DCV	VBAT (1)	0-.1	0-.1	DCV
VSS+	3	1	MPH	1	30	55	MPH
HEGO-L	43	0	DCV	switching (3)	switching (3)	switching (3)	DCV
FPM - red	8	0	DCV	VBAT	VBAT	VBAT	DCV
STI	48	3.3-4.9	DCV	3.3-4.9	3.3-4.9	3.3-4.9	DCV
ACTUATORS/ OUTPUTS							
INJ BANK 3	39	VBAT (2)	DCV	5.0-5.5	5.5-7.5	8.0-11.2	mS
INJ BANK 5	15	VBAT (2)	DCV	5.0-5.5	5.5-7.5	8.0-11.2	mS
INJ BANK 4	35	VBAT (2)	DCV	5.0-5.5	5.5-7.5	8.0-11.2	mS
INJ BANK 2	59	VBAT (2)	DCV	5.0-5.5	5.5-7.5	8.0-11.2	mS
INJ BANK 1	58	VBAT (2)	DCV	5.0-5.5	5.5-7.5	8.0-11.2	mS
STO/MIL	17	0-.2	DCV	VBAT	VBAT	VBAT	DCV
WAC	54	.1-.2	DCV	VBAT (1)	.1-.2	.1-.2	DCV
ISC-BPA	21	VBAT	DCV	10.8-11.8	9.7-10.7	8.4-9.2	DCV
FP	22	VBAT	DCV	.1-.2	.1-.2	.1-.2	DCV
INJ 6	12	VBAT (2)	DCV	5.0-5.5	5.5-7.5	8.0-11.2	mS
SPOUT	36	0-12	RPM	780-880	1360-1500	1990-2150	RPM
CANP	11	VBAT	DCV	VBAT	.2-VBAT	.2-12.0	DCV
OTHER							
IGN TIMING	TIMING	N/A	DEG	24-28	33-37	34-38	DEG

NOTES: ① — A/C on.
② — Monitor in DCV Manual Mode, Reference Pin to PWR GND (40/60).
③ — HEGO should switch from rich (red LED) to lean (green LED), or lean to rich, at least once every 3 seconds. HEGO voltage should toggle above and below .450 DCV, and should never be a negative value.

Reference values shown may vary ± 20% depending on operating conditions and other factors. RPM values are axle and tire dependent.

92B22203

Courtesy of Ford Motor Co.

Fig. 9: ECA Pin Voltage Checks (Ranger 3.0L With Manual Transmission)

1992 ENGINE PERFORMANCE
Pin Voltage Charts (Cont.)

4.0L AEROSTAR
AUTOMATIC TRANSMISSION

SENSORS/ INPUTS	Signal Pin #	KOEO	Units	HOT IDLE	30 MPH	55 MPH	Units
OCT ADJ	44	0	DCV	0	0	0	DCV
MAF - red	14	0 (3)	DCV	.6-.7 (3)	1.0-1.4 (3)	1.5-2.0 (3)	DCV
TP	47	.8-.9	DCV	.8-.9	1.0-1.2	1.2-1.5	DCV
ECT	7	.5-.7	DCV	.5-.7	.5-.7	.5-.7	DCV
ACT	25	.7-2.8	DCV	.7-2.8	.7-2.8	.7-2.8	DCV
IDM	4	70-100	RPM	730-830	1360-1460	1580-1780	RPM
PIP	56	0-12	RPM	730-830	1360-1460	1580-1780	RPM
HEGO	29	0	DCV	switching (4)	switching (4)	switching (4)	DCV
BOO	2	0	DCV	VBAT (2)	0	0	DCV
FPM - red	8	0	DCV	VBAT	VBAT	VBAT	DCV
ACCS	10	0	DCV	VBAT (1)	0	0	DCV
PSOM +	3	1	MPH	1	30	55	MPH
NDS	30	0	DCV	0	5.0	5.0	DCV
STI	48	5.0	DCV	5.0	5.0	5.0	DCV
ACTUATORS/ OUTPUTS							
INJ BANK 2	59	VBAT (3)	DCV	3.3-3.6	3.6-4.4	4.8-5.6	mS
INJ BANK 1	58	VBAT (3)	DCV	3.3-3.6	3.6-4.4	4.8-5.6	mS
SS 3/4	52	VBAT	DCV	VBAT	VBAT	.2-.4	DCV
STO/MIL	17	.1-.2	DCV	VBAT	VBAT	VBAT	DCV
CANP	31	VBAT	DCV	VBAT	7.0-VBAT	.1-9.2	DCV
WAC	54	.1	DCV	VBAT (1)	.1	.1	DCV
ISC	21	VBAT	DCV	10.0-11.8	9.5-10.3	8.3-9.8	DCV
FP	22	VBAT	DCV	.1	.1	.1	DCV
SAW	36	0-12	RPM	730-830	1360-1460	1580-1780	RPM
CCO	53	VBAT	DCV	VBAT	VBAT	.2-.4	DCV
OTHER							
IGN TIMING	TIMING	N/A	DEG	N/A	N/A	N/A	DEG

NOTES: ① — A/C on.
② — Brake pedal applied.
③ — Monitor in DCV Manual Mode, Reference Pin to PWR GND (40/60).
④ — HEGO should switch from rich (red LED) to lean (green LED), or lean to rich, at least once every 3 seconds. HEGO voltage should toggle above and below .450 DCV, and should never be a negative value.

Reference values shown may vary ± 20% depending on operating conditions and other factors. RPM values are axle and tire dependent.

92C22204

Courtesy of Ford Motor Co.

Fig. 10: ECA Pin Voltage Checks (Aerostar 4.0L With Automatic Transmission)

1992 ENGINE PERFORMANCE
Pin Voltage Charts (Cont.)

4.0L EXPLORER
AUTOMATIC TRANSMISSION

SENSORS/ INPUTS	Signal Pin #	KOEO	Units	HOT IDLE	30 MPH	55 MPH	Units
OCT ADJ	44	0	DCV	0	0	0	DCV
MAF - red	14	0 (3)	DCV	.6-.7 (3)	1.0-1.4 (3)	1.5-2.0 (3)	DCV
TP	47	.8-.9	DCV	.8-.9	1.0-1.2	1.2-1.5	DCV
ECT	7	.5-.7	DCV	.5-.7	.5-.7	.5-.7	DCV
ACT	25	.7-2.8	DCV	.7-2.8	.7-2.8	.7-2.8	DCV
IDM	4	70-100	RPM	730-830	1360-1460	1580-1780	RPM
PIP	56	0-12	RPM	730-830	1360-1460	1580-1780	RPM
HEGO	29	0	DCV	switching (4)	switching (4)	switching (4)	DCV
BOO	2	0	DCV	VBAT (2)	0	0	DCV
FPM - red	8	0	DCV	VBAT	VBAT	VBAT	DCV
ACCS	10	0	DCV	VBAT (1)	0	0	DCV
VSS+	3	1	MPH	1	30	55	MPH
NDS	30	0	DCV	0	5.0	5.0	DCV
STI	48	5.0	DCV	5.0	5.0	5.0	DCV
ACTUATORS/ OUTPUTS							
INJ BANK 2	59	VBAT (3)	DCV	3.3-3.6	3.6-4.4	4.8-5.6	mS
INJ BANK 1	58	VBAT (3)	DCV	3.3-3.6	3.6-4.4	4.8-5.6	mS
SS 3/4	52	VBAT	DCV	VBAT	VBAT	.2-.4	DCV
STO/MIL	17	.1-.2	DCV	VBAT	VBAT	VBAT	DCV
CANP	31	VBAT	DCV	VBAT	7.0-VBAT	.1-9.2	DCV
WAC	54	.1	DCV	VBAT (1)	.1	.1	DCV
ISC	21	VBAT	DCV	8.0-VBAT	9.5-10.3	8.3-9.8	DCV
FP	22	VBAT	DCV	10.0-11.8	.1	.1	DCV
SAW	36	0-12	RPM	730-830	1360-1460	1580-1780	RPM
CCO	53	VBAT	DCV	VBAT	VBAT	.2-.4	DCV
OTHER							
IGN TIMING	TIMING	N/A	DEG	N/A	N/A	N/A	DEG

NOTES: ① — A/C on.
② — Brake pedal applied.
③ — Monitor in DCV Manual Mode, Reference Pin to PWR GND (40/60).
④ — HEGO should switch from rich (red LED) to lean (green LED), or lean to rich, at least once every 3 seconds. HEGO voltage should toggle above and below .450 DCV, and should never be a negative value.

Reference values shown may vary ± 20% depending on operating conditions and other factors. RPM values are axle and tire dependent.

92D22205

Courtesy of Ford Motor Co.

Fig. 11: ECA Pin Voltage Checks (Explorer 4.0L With Automatic Transmission)

1992 ENGINE PERFORMANCE
Pin Voltage Charts (Cont.)

4.0L EXPLORER
MANUAL TRANSMISSION

SENSORS/ INPUTS	Signal Pin #	KOEO	Units	HOT IDLE	30 MPH	55 MPH	Units
OCT ADJ	44	0	DCV	0	0	0	DCV
MAF - red	14	0 (3)	DCV	.6-.7 (3)	1.0-1.4 (3)	1.5-2.0 (3)	DCV
TP	47	.8-.9	DCV	.8-.9	1.0-1.2	1.2-1.5	DCV
ECT	7	.5-.7	DCV	.5-.7	.5-.7	.5-.7	DCV
ACT	25	.7-2.8	DCV	.7-2.8	.7-2.8	.7-2.8	DCV
IDM	4	70-100	RPM	730-830	1140-1300	1680-1820	RPM
PIP	56	0-12	RPM	730-830	1140-1300	1680-1820	RPM
HEGO	29	0	DCV	switching (4)	switching (4)	switching (4)	DCV
BOO	2	0	DCV	VBAT (2)	0	0	DCV
FPM - red	8	0	DCV	VBAT	VBAT	VBAT	DCV
ACCS	10	0	DCV	VBAT (1)	0	0	DCV
VSS+	3	1	MPH	1	30	55	MPH
NGS/CES	30	0	DCV	0	5.0	5.0	DCV
STI	48	5.0	DCV	5.0	5.0	5.0	DCV
ACTUATORS/ OUTPUTS							
INJ BANK 2	59	VBAT (3)	DCV	3.3-3.6	3.6-4.4	4.8-5.6	mS
INJ BANK 1	58	VBAT (3)	DCV	3.3-3.6	3.6-4.4	4.8-5.6	mS
STO/MIL	17	.1-.2	DCV	VBAT	VBAT	VBAT	DCV
CANP	31	VBAT	DCV	VBAT	7.0-VBAT	.1-9.2	DCV
WAC	54	.1	DCV	VBAT (1)	.1	.1	DCV
ISC	21	VBAT	DCV	10.0-11.8	9.5-10.3	8.3-9.8	DCV
FP	22	VBAT	DCV	.1	.1	.1	DCV
SAW	36	0-12	RPM	730-830	1140-1300	1680-1820	RPM
OTHER							
IGN TIMING	TIMING	N/A	DEG	N/A	N/A	N/A	DEG

NOTES: ① — A/C on.
② — Brake pedal applied.
③ — Monitor in DCV Manual Mode, Reference Pin to PWR GND (40/60).
④ — HEGO should switch from rich (red LED) to lean (green LED), or lean to rich, at least once every 3 seconds. HEGO voltage should toggle above and below .450 DCV, and should never be a negative value.

Reference values shown may vary ± 20% depending on operating conditions and other factors. RPM values are axle and tire dependent.

92E22206

Courtesy of Ford Motor Co.

Fig. 12: ECA Pin Voltage Checks (Explorer 4.0L With Manual Transmission)

1992 ENGINE PERFORMANCE
Pin Voltage Charts (Cont.)

4.0L RANGER
AUTOMATIC TRANSMISSION

SENSORS/ INPUTS	Signal Pin #	KOEO	Units	HOT IDLE	30 MPH	55 MPH	Units
OCT ADJ	44	0	DCV	0	0	0	DCV
MAF - red	14	0 (3)	DCV	.6-.7 (3)	1.0-1.4 (3)	1.5-2.0 (3)	DCV
TP	47	.8-.9	DCV	.8-.9	1.0-1.2	1.2-1.5	DCV
ECT	7	.5-.7	DCV	.5-.7	.5-.7	.5-.7	DCV
ACT	25	.7-2.8	DCV	.7-2.8	.7-2.8	.7-2.8	DCV
IDM	4	70-100	RPM	730-830	1360-1460	1580-1780	RPM
PIP	56	0-12	RPM	730-830	1360-1460	1580-1780	RPM
HEGO	29	0	DCV	switching (4)	switching (4)	switching (4)	DCV
BOO	2	0	DCV	VBAT (2)	0	0	DCV
FPM - red	8	0	DCV	VBAT	VBAT	VBAT	DCV
ACCS	10	0	DCV	VBAT (1)	0	0	DCV
VSS+	3	1	MPH	1	30	55	MPH
NDS	30	0	DCV	0	5.0	5.0	DCV
STI	48	5.0	DCV	5.0	5.0	5.0	DCV
ACTUATORS/ OUTPUTS							
INJ BANK 2	59	VBAT (3)	DCV	3.3-3.6	3.6-4.4	4.8-5.6	mS
INJ BANK 1	58	VBAT (3)	DCV	3.3-3.6	3.6-4.4	4.8-5.6	mS
SS 3/4	52	VBAT	DCV	VBAT	VBAT	.2-.4	DCV
STO/MIL	17	.1-.2	DCV	VBAT	VBAT	VBAT	DCV
CANP	31	VBAT	DCV	VBAT	7.0-VBAT	.1-9.2	DCV
WAC	54	.1	DCV	VBAT (1)	.1	.1	DCV
ISC	21	VBAT	DCV	10.0-11.8	9.5-10.3	8.3-9.8	DCV
FP	22	VBAT	DCV	.1	.1	.1	DCV
SAW	36	0-12	RPM	730-830	1360-1460	1580-1780	RPM
CCO	53	VBAT	DCV	VBAT	VBAT	.2-.4	DCV
OTHER							
IGN TIMING	TIMING	N/A	DEG	N/A	N/A	N/A	DEG

NOTES: ① — A/C on.
② — Brake pedal applied.
③ — Monitor in DCV Manual Mode, Reference Pin to PWR GND (40/60).
④ — HEGO should switch from rich (red LED) to lean (green LED), or lean to rich, at least once every 3 seconds. HEGO voltage should toggle above and below .450 DCV, and should never be a negative value.

Reference values shown may vary ± 20% depending on operating conditions and other factors. RPM values are axle and tire dependent.

92F22207

Courtesy of Ford Motor Co.

Fig. 13: ECA Pin Voltage Checks (Ranger 4.0L With Automatic Transmission)

1992 ENGINE PERFORMANCE
Pin Voltage Charts (Cont.)

4.0L RANGER
MANUAL TRANSMISSION

SENSORS/ INPUTS	Signal Pin #	KOEO	Units	HOT IDLE	30 MPH	55 MPH	Units
OCT ADJ	44	0	DCV	0	0	0	DCV
MAF - red	14	0 (3)	DCV	.6-.7 (3)	1.0-1.4 (3)	1.5-2.0 (3)	DCV
TP	47	.8-.9	DCV	.8-.9	1.0-1.2	1.2-1.5	DCV
ECT	7	.5-.7	DCV	.5-.7	.5-.7	.5-.7	DCV
ACT	25	.7-2.8	DCV	.7-2.8	.7-2.8	.7-2.8	DCV
IDM	4	70-100	RPM	730-830	1140-1300	1680-1820	RPM
PIP	56	0-12	RPM	730-830	1140-1300	1680-1820	RPM
HEGO	29	0	DCV	switching (4)	switching (4)	switching (4)	DCV
BOO	2	0	DCV	VBAT (2)	0	0	DCV
FPM - red	8	0	DCV	VBAT	VBAT	VBAT	DCV
ACCS	10	0	DCV	VBAT (1)	0	0	DCV
VSS+	3	1	MPH	1	30	55	MPH
NGS/CES	30	0	DCV	0	5.0	5.0	DCV
STI	48	5.0	DCV	5.0	5.0	5.0	DCV
ACTUATORS/ OUTPUTS							
INJ BANK 2	59	VBAT (3)	DCV	3.3-3.6	3.6-4.4	4.8-5.6	mS
INJ BANK 1	58	VBAT (3)	DCV	3.3-3.6	3.6-4.4	4.8-5.6	mS
STO/MIL	17	.1-.2	DCV	VBAT	VBAT	VBAT	DCV
CANP	31	VBAT	DCV	VBAT	7.0-VBAT	.1-9.2	DCV
WAC	54	.1	DCV	VBAT (1)	.1	.1	DCV
ISC	21	VBAT	DCV	10.0-11.8	9.5-10.3	8.3-9.8	DCV
FP	22	VBAT	DCV	.1	.1	.1	DCV
SAW	36	0-12	RPM	730-830	1140-1300	1680-1820	RPM
OTHER							
IGN TIMING	TIMING	N/A	DEG	N/A	N/A	N/A	DEG

NOTES: ① — A/C on.
② — Brake pedal applied.
③ — Monitor in DCV Manual Mode, Reference Pin to PWR GND (40/60).
④ — HEGO should switch from rich (red LED) to lean (green LED), or lean to rich, at least once every 3 seconds. HEGO voltage should toggle above and below .450 DCV, and should never be a negative value.

Reference values shown may vary ± 20% depending on operating conditions and other factors. RPM values are axle and tire dependent.

92G22208

Courtesy of Ford Motor Co.

Fig. 14: ECA Pin Voltage Checks (Ranger 4.0L With Manual Transmission)

1992 ENGINE PERFORMANCE
Pin Voltage Charts (Cont.)

4.9L BRONCO, PICKUP & VAN
AUTOMATIC TRANSMISSION (EXCEPT E4OD)

SENSORS/ INPUTS	Signal Pin #	KOEO	Units	HOT IDLE	30 MPH	55 MPH	Units
TP	47	.9-1.0	DCV	.9-1.0	1.1-1.3	1.4-1.8	DCV
EVP	27	.3-.4	DCV	.3-.4	1.2-2.6	2.5-3.5	DCV
ECT	7	.5-.7	DCV	.5-.7	.5-.7	.5-.7	DCV
ACT	25	.7-2.8	DCV	.7-2.8	.7-2.8	.7-2.8	DCV
MAP	45	158	Hz	102-106	112-120	118-136	Hz
IDM	4	0-12	RPM	670-770	1230-1360	1500-1680	RPM
OCS -red	41	.1-.2	DCV	.1-.2	.1-.2	.1-.2	DCV
PIP	56	0-12	RPM	670-770	1230-1360	1500-1680	RPM
TOT - red	42	.8-2.0 (3)	DCV	.8-2.0 (3)	1.3-1.7 (3)	1.0-1.2 (3)	DCV
KS	23	2.5	DCV	2.5	2.5	2.5	DCV
HEGO	29	0	DCV	switching (4)	switching (4)	switching (4)	DCV
4x4L - red	12	VBAT (3)	DCV	VBAT (3)	VBAT (3)	VBAT (3)	DCV
BOO	2	0	DCV	VBAT (2)	0	0	DCV
FPM - red	8	0	DCV	VBAT	VBAT	VBAT	DCV
ACCS	10	0	DCV	VBAT (1)	0	0	DCV
PSOM+	3	1	MPH	1	30	55	MPH
ACD	43	0	DCV	VBAT (1)	0	0	DCV
MLPS	30	4.4	DCV	4.4	2.1	2.1	DCV
STI	48	5.0	DCV	5.0	5.0	5.0	DCV
ACTUATORS/ OUTPUTS							
INJ BANK 2	59	VBAT (3)	DCV	6.2-7.4	8.4-11.6	13.0-17.6	mS
INJ BANK 1	58	VBAT (3)	DCV	6.2-7.4	8.4-11.6	13.0-17.6	mS
SS1	52	.3-.4	DCV	.3-.4	VBAT	VBAT	DCV
EVR	33	VBAT (3)	DCV	VBAT (3)	9.8-11.3 (3)	6.3-9.8 (3)	DCV
EPC	38	6.8-7.3	DCV	7.7-8.7	7.7-9.4	8.2-9.4	DCV
STO/MIL	17	.1-.2	DCV	VBAT	VBAT	VBAT	DCV
ISC	21	VBAT	DCV	8.5-10.5	8.0-9.0	5.5-7.5	DCV
FP	22	VBAT	DCV	.1	.1	.1	DCV
SS2 - blue	19	VBAT	DCV	VBAT	.3-.4	VBAT	DCV
SPOUT	36	0-12	RPM	670-770	1230-1360	1500-1680	RPM
OCIL	32	VBAT (3)	DCV	VBAT (3)	VBAT (3)	VBAT (3)	DCV
AM1	51	VBAT	DCV	VBAT	.1	.1	DCV
CCC	53	VBAT	DCV	VBAT	.2-.8	.2-.8	DCV
CCS	55	VBAT	DCV	VBAT	VBAT	VBAT	DCV
OTHER							
IGN TIMING	TIMING	N/A	DEG	20-24	28-32	24-30	DEG

NOTES: ① — A/C on.
② — Brake pedal applied.
③ — Monitor in DCV Manual Mode, Reference Pin to PWR GND (40/60).
④ — HEGO should switch from rich (red LED) to lean (green LED), or lean to rich, at least once every 3 seconds. HEGO voltage should toggle above and below .450 DCV, and should never be a negative value.

Reference values shown may vary ± 20% depending on operating conditions and other factors. RPM values are axle and tire dependent.

92H22209

Courtesy of Ford Motor Co.

Fig. 15: ECA Pin Voltage Checks (Bronco, Pickup & Van 4.9L With Automatic Transmission; Except E4OD)

1992 ENGINE PERFORMANCE
Pin Voltage Charts (Cont.)

4.9L BRONCO & PICKUP
MANUAL TRANSMISSION

SENSORS/ INPUTS	Signal Pin #	KOEO	Units	HOT IDLE	30 MPH	55 MPH	Units
TP	47	.9-1.0	DCV	.9-1.0	1.1-1.3	1.3-1.6	DCV
EVP	27	.3-.4	DCV	.3-.4	1.2-2.6	2.5-3.5	DCV
ECT	7	.5-.7	DCV	.5-.7	.5-.7	.5-.7	DCV
ACT	25	.7-2.8	DCV	.7-2.8	.7-2.8	.7-2.8	DCV
MAP	45	158	Hz	104-106	112-120	118-136	Hz
IDM	4	0-12	RPM	700-800	1100-1200	1630-1730	RPM
PIP	56	0-12	RPM	700-800	1100-1200	1630-1730	RPM
KS	23	2.5	DCV	2.5	2.5	2.5	DCV
HEGO	29	0	DCV	switching (4)	switching (4)	switching (4)	DCV
FPM - red	8	0	DCV	VBAT	VBAT	VBAT	DCV
ACCS	10	0	DCV	VBAT (1)	0	0	DCV
PSOM +	3	1	MPH	1	30	55	MPH
ACD	43	0	DCV	VBAT (1)	0	0	DCV
CES	30	5.0-VBAT	DCV	0 (2)	5.0/VBAT	5.0/VBAT	DCV
STI	48	5.0	DCV	5.0	5.0	5.0	DCV
ACTUATORS/ OUTPUTS							
INJ BANK 2	59	VBAT (3)	DCV	6.2-6.4	8.5-9.5	12.5-13.5	mS
INJ BANK 1	58	VBAT (3)	DCV	6.2-6.4	8.5-9.5	12.5-13.5	mS
EVR	33	VBAT (3)	DCV	VBAT (3)	9.8-11.3 (3)	6.3-9.8 (3)	DCV
STO/MIL	17	.1-.2	DCV	VBAT	VBAT	VBAT	DCV
CANP	31	VBAT	DCV	VBAT	.2-5.0	.2	DCV
ISC	21	VBAT	DCV	8.0-11.0	6.5-9.0	5.0-6.5	DCV
FP	22	VBAT	DCV	.1	.1	.1	DCV
SPOUT	36	0-12	RPM	700-800	1100-1200	1630-1730	RPM
AM1	51	VBAT	DCV	VBAT	.1	.1	DCV
AM2	11	VBAT	DCV	VBAT	VBAT	VBAT	DCV
OTHER							
IGN TIMING	TIMING	N/A	DEG	17-20	24-28	24-30	DEG

NOTES: ① — A/C on.
       ② — Brake pedal applied.
       ③ — Monitor in DCV Manual Mode, Reference Pin to PWR GND (40/60).
       ④ — HEGO should switch from rich (red LED) to lean (green LED), or lean to rich, at least once every 3 seconds. HEGO voltage should toggle above and below .450 DCV, and should never be a negative value.

Reference values shown may vary ± 20% depending on operating conditions and other factors. RPM values are axle and tire dependent.

92A22210

Courtesy of Ford Motor Co.

Fig. 16: ECA Pin Voltage Checks (Bronco & Pickup 4.9L With Manual Transmission)

1992 ENGINE PERFORMANCE
Pin Voltage Charts (Cont.)

4.9L PICKUP & VAN
AUTOMATIC TRANSMISSION (E4OD)

SENSORS/ INPUTS	Signal Pin #	KOEO	Units	HOT IDLE	30 MPH	55 MPH	Units
TP	47	.9-1.0	DCV	.9-1.0	1.1-1.3	1.3-1.6	DCV
EVP	27	.3-.4	DCV	.3-.4	1.2-2.6	2.5-3.5	DCV
ECT	7	.5-.7	DCV	.5-.7	.5-.7	.5-.7	DCV
ACT	25	.7-2.8	DCV	.7-2.8	.7-2.8	.7-2.8	DCV
MAP	45	158	Hz	104-106	112-120	118-136	Hz
IDM	4	0-12	RPM	600-700	1050-1150	1840-1940	RPM
PIP	56	0-12	RPM	600-700	1050-1150	1840-1940	RPM
KS	23	2.5	DCV	2.5	2.5	2.5	DCV
HEGO	29	0	DCV	switching (4)	switching (4)	switching (4)	DCV
FPM - red	8	0	DCV	VBAT	VBAT	VBAT	DCV
ACCS	10	0	DCV	VBAT (1)	0	0	DCV
PSOM+	3	1	MPH	1	30	55	MPH
ACD	43	0	DCV	VBAT (1)	0	0	DCV
NDS	30	0	DCV	0	5.0/VBAT	5.0/VBAT	DCV
STI	48	5.0	DCV	5.0	5.0	5.0	DCV
ACTUATORS/ OUTPUTS							
INJ BANK 2	59	VBAT (3)	DCV	6.8-7.0	9.5-10.5	12.0-13.0	mS
INJ BANK 1	58	VBAT (3)	DCV	6.8-7.0	9.5-10.5	12.0-13.0	mS
EVR	33	VBAT (3)	DCV	VBAT (3)	9.8-11 (3)	6.3-9.8 (3)	DCV
STO/MIL	17	.1-.2	DCV	VBAT	VBAT	VBAT	DCV
CANP	31	VBAT	DCV	VBAT	.2-5.0	.2	DCV
ISC	21	VBAT	DCV	8.0-11.0	6.5-9.0	5.0-6.5	DCV
FP	22	VBAT	DCV	.1	.1	.1	DCV
SPOUT	36	0-12	RPM	600-700	1050-1150	1840-1940	RPM
AM1	51	VBAT	DCV	VBAT	.1	.1	DCV
AM2 (2)	11	VBAT	DCV	VBAT	VBAT	VBAT	DCV
OTHER							
IGN TIMING	TIMING	N/A	DEG	17-20	24-28	24-30	DEG

NOTES: ① — A/C on.
② — Brake pedal applied.
③ — Monitor in DCV Manual Mode, Reference Pin to PWR GND (40/60).
④ — HEGO should switch from rich (red LED) to lean (green LED), or lean to rich, at least once every 3 seconds. HEGO voltage should toggle above and below .450 DCV, and should never be a negative value.

Reference values shown may vary ± 20% depending on operating conditions and other factors. RPM values are axle and tire dependent.

92B22211

Courtesy of Ford Motor Co.

Fig. 17: ECA Pin Voltage Checks (Pickup & Van 4.9L With Automatic Transmission; E4OD)

1992 ENGINE PERFORMANCE
Pin Voltage Charts (Cont.)

5.0L BRONCO & PICKUP
AUTOMATIC TRANSMISSION (EXCEPT E4OD)

SENSORS/ INPUTS	Signal Pin #	KOEO	Units	HOT IDLE	30 MPH	55 MPH	Units
TP	47	.8-.9	DCV	.8-.9	.9-1.1	1.1-1.3	DCV
EVP	27	.3-.4	DCV	.3-.4	.3-2.5	2.1-3.8	DCV
ECT	7	.5-.7	DCV	.5-.7	.5-.7	.5-.7	DCV
ACT	25	.7-2.8	DCV	.7-2.8	.7-2.8	.7-2.8	DCV
MAP	45	157	Hz	103-105	104-114	112-124	Hz
IDM	4	0-12	RPM	660-800	1160-1400	1760-2300	RPM
PIP	56	0-12	RPM	660-800	1160-1400	1760-2300	RPM
KS	23	2.5	DCV	2.5	2.5	2.5	DCV
HEGO	29	0	DCV	switching (4)	switching (4)	switching (4)	DCV
FPM - red	8	0 (3)	DCV	VBAT (3)	VBAT (3)	VBAT (3)	DCV
ACCS	10	0	DCV	VBAT (1)	0	0	DCV
PSOM+	3	1	MPH	1	30	55	MPH
PSPS	24	0	DCV	10.0-11.0 (2)	0	0	DCV
NDS	30	0	DCV	0	5.0/VBAT	5.0/VBAT	DCV
STI	48	5.0	DCV	5.0	5.0	5.0	DCV
ACTUATORS/ OUTPUTS							
INJ BANK 2	59	VBAT (3)	DCV	4.4-5.6	5.6-7.6	7.2-11.4	mS
INJ BANK 1	58	VBAT (3)	DCV	4.4-5.6	5.6-7.6	7.2-11.4	mS
EVR	33	VBAT (3)	DCV	0	30-60	65-90	%
STO/MIL	17	.6	DCV	VBAT	VBAT	VBAT	DCV
ISC	21	VBAT	DCV	7.5-10.5	6.0-9.6	4.5-8.8	DCV
FP	22	VBAT	DCV	.8-.9	.8-.9	.8-.9	DCV
SPOUT	36	0-12	RPM	660-800	1160-1400	1760-2300	RPM
AM1	51	VBAT	DCV	VBAT	.1-.2	.1-.2	DCV
AM2	11	VBAT	DCV	VBAT	VBAT	VBAT	DCV
OTHER							
IGN TIMING	TIMING	N/A	DEG	14-20	28-36	30-40	DEG

NOTES: ① — A/C on.
② — Brake pedal applied.
③ — Monitor in DCV Manual Mode, Reference Pin to PWR GND (40/60).
④ — HEGO should switch from rich (red LED) to lean (green LED), or lean to rich, at least once every 3 seconds. HEGO voltage should toggle above and below .450 DCV, and should never be a negative value.

Reference values shown may vary ± 20% depending on operating conditions and other factors. RPM values are axle and tire dependent.

92C22212

Courtesy of Ford Motor Co.

Fig. 18: ECA Pin Voltage Checks (Bronco & Pickup 5.0L With Automatic Transmission – Except E4OD)

5.0L VAN
AUTOMATIC TRANSMISSION

SENSORS/ INPUTS	Signal Pin #	KOEO	Units	HOT IDLE	30 MPH	55 MPH	Units
TP	47	.8-.9	DCV	.8-.9	.9-1.1	1.1-1.3	DCV
EVP	27	.3-.4	DCV	.3-.4	.3-2.5	2.1-3.8	DCV
ECT	7	.5-.7	DCV	.5-.7	.5-.7	.5-.7	DCV
ACT	25	.7-2.8	DCV	.7-2.8	.7-2.8	.7-2.8	DCV
MAP	45	157	Hz	103-105	104-114	112-124	Hz
IDM	4	0-12	RPM	660-800	1160-1400	1760-2300	RPM
PIP	56	0-12	RPM	660-800	1160-1400	1760-2300	RPM
KS	23	2.5	DCV	2.5	2.5	2.5	DCV
HEGO	29	0	DCV	switching (3)	switching (3)	switching (3)	DCV
FPM - red	8	0 (2)	DCV	VBAT (2)	VBAT (2)	VBAT (2)	DCV
ACCS	10	0	DCV	VBAT (1)	0	0	DCV
PSOM+	3	1	MPH	1	30	55	MPH
NDS	30	0	DCV	0	5.0/VBAT	5.0/VBAT	DCV
STI	48	5.0	DCV	5.0	5.0	5.0	DCV
ACTUATORS/ OUTPUTS							
INJ BANK 2	59	VBAT (2)	DCV	4.4-5.6	5.6-7.6	7.2-11.4	mS
INJ BANK 1	58	VBAT (2)	DCV	4.4-5.6	5.6-7.6	7.2-11.4	mS
EVR	33	VBAT (2)	DCV	VBAT (2)	9.8-11.3 (2)	6.3-9.8 (2)	DCV
STO/MIL	17	.6	DCV	VBAT	VBAT	VBAT	DCV
ISC	21	VBAT	DCV	7.5-10.5	6.0-9.6	4.5-8.8	DCV
FP	22	VBAT	DCV	.8-.9	.8-.9	.8-.9	DCV
SPOUT	36	0-12	RPM	660-800	1160-1400	1760-2300	RPM
AM1	51	VBAT	DCV	VBAT	.1-.2	.1-.2	DCV
AM2	11	VBAT	DCV	VBAT	VBAT	VBAT	DCV
OTHER							
IGN TIMING	TIMING	N/A	DEG	14-20	28-36	30-40	DEG

NOTES:
① — A/C on.
② — Monitor in DCV Manual Mode, Reference Pin to PWR GND (40/60).
③ — HEGO should switch from rich (red LED) to lean (green LED), or lean to rich, at least once every 3 seconds. HEGO voltage should toggle above and below .450 DCV, and should never be a negative value.

Reference values shown may vary ± 20% depending on operating conditions and other factors. RPM values are axle and tire dependent.

Courtesy of Ford Motor Co.

92D22213

Fig. 19: ECA Pin Voltage Checks (Van 5.0L With Automatic Transmission)

1992 ENGINE PERFORMANCE
Pin Voltage Charts (Cont.)

5.0L BRONCO & PICKUP
AUTOMATIC TRANSMISSION (E4OD)

SENSORS/ INPUTS	Signal Pin #	KOEO	Units	HOT IDLE	30 MPH	55 MPH	Units
TP	47	.8-.9	DCV	.8-.9	1.1-1.3	1.2-1.4	DCV
EVP	27	.3-.4	DCV	.3-.4	.3-2.5	2.1-3.5	DCV
ECT	7	.5-.7	DCV	.5-.7	.5-.7	.5-.7	DCV
ACT	25	.7-2.8	DCV	.7-2.8	.7-2.8	.7-2.8	DCV
MAP	45	157	Hz	103-107	104-120	118-140	Hz
IDM	4	0-12	RPM	640-740	1230-1380	1600-1750	RPM
OCS - red	41	.1	DCV	.1	.1	.1	DCV
PIP	56	0-12	RPM	640-740	1230-1380	1600-1750	RPM
TOT - red	42	.6-2.0 (3)	DCV	.6-2.0 (3)	1.3-1.7 (3)	.8-1.2 (3)	DCV
KS	23	2.5	DCV	2.5	2.5	2.5	DCV
HEGO	29	0	DCV	switching (4)	switching (4)	.1 (4)	DCV
4x4L - red	12	VBAT (3)	DCV	VBAT (3)	VBAT (3)	VBAT (3)	DCV
BOO	2	0	DCV	VBAT (2)	0	0	DCV
FPM - red	8	0 (3)	DCV	VBAT (3)	VBAT (3)	VBAT (3)	DCV
ACCS	10	0	DCV	VBAT (1)	0	0	DCV
PSOM+	3	1	MPH	1	30	55	MPH
MLPS	30	4.4	DCV	4.4	2.1	2.1	DCV
STI	48	5.0	DCV	5.0	5.0	5.0	DCV
ACTUATORS/ OUTPUTS							
INJ BANK 2	59	VBAT (3)	DCV	4.7-5.1	5.6-7.8	8.3-12.0	mS
INJ BANK 1	58	VBAT (3)	DCV	4.7-5.1	5.6-7.8	8.3-12.0	mS
SS1	52	.2-.8 (3)	DCV	.2-.8 (3)	VBAT (3)	VBAT (3)	DCV
EVR	33	VBAT (3)	DCV	VBAT (3)	7.6-12.1 (3)	5.6-10.6 (3)	DCV
EPC	38	6.6-10.4	DCV	8.6-12.0	8.6-9.6	8.6-9.4	DCV
STO/MIL	17	.1-.6	DCV	VBAT	VBAT	VBAT	DCV
CANP	31	VBAT	DCV	VBAT	.1-8.8	.1-.2	DCV
ISC	21	VBAT	DCV	8.3-9.9	8.5-9.6	3.2-8.8	DCV
FP	22	VBAT	DCV	.1-.9	.1-.9	.1-.9	DCV
SS2 - blue	19	VBAT	DCV	VBAT	.2-.8	VBAT	DCV
SPOUT	36	0-12	RPM	640-740	1230-1380	1600-1750	RPM
OCIL	32	VBAT	DCV	VBAT	VBAT	VBAT	DCV
AM1	51	VBAT	DCV	.1-.2	VBAT	VBAT	DCV
AM2	11	VBAT	DCV	VBAT	VBAT	VBAT	DCV
CCC	53	VBAT	DCV	VBAT	.2-.8	.2-.8	DCV
CCS	55	VBAT	DCV	VBAT	VBAT	VBAT	DCV
OTHER							
IGN TIMING	TIMING	N/A	DEG	18-22	36-40	36-42	DEG

NOTES: ① — A/C on.
② — Brake pedal applied.
③ — Monitor in DCV Manual Mode, Reference Pin to PWR GND (40/60).
④ — HEGO should switch from rich (red LED) to lean (green LED), or lean to rich, at least once every 3 seconds. HEGO voltage should toggle above and below .450 DCV, and should never be a negative value.

Reference values shown may vary ± 20% depending on operating conditions and other factors. RPM values are axle and tire dependent.

92E22214

Courtesy of Ford Motor Co.

Fig. 20: ECA Pin Voltage Checks (Bronco & Pickup 5.0L With Automatic Transmission; E4OD)

1992 ENGINE PERFORMANCE
Pin Voltage Charts (Cont.)

5.0L BRONCO & PICKUP
MANUAL TRANSMISSION

SENSORS/ INPUTS	Signal Pin #	KOEO	Units	HOT IDLE	30 MPH	55 MPH	Units
TP	47	.7-.8	DCV	.7-.8	.9-1.0	1.1-1.3	DCV
EVP	27	.3-.4	DCV	.3-.4	.3-2.5	2.1-3.8	DCV
ECT	7	.5-.7	DCV	.5-.7	.5-.7	.5-.7	DCV
ACT	25	.7-2.8	DCV	.7-2.8	.7-2.8	.7-2.8	DCV
MAP	45	157	Hz	103-105	104-114	112-124	Hz
IDM	4	0-12	RPM	660-760	1160-1260	1760-2300	RPM
PIP	56	0-12	RPM	660-760	1160-1260	1760-2300	RPM
KS	23	2.5	DCV	2.5	2.5	2.5	DCV
HEGO	29	0	DCV	switching (5)	switching (5)	switching (5)	DCV
FPM - red	8	0 (4)	DCV	VBAT (4)	VBAT (4)	VBAT (4)	DCV
ACCS	10	0	DCV	VBAT (1)	0	0	DCV
PSOM+	3	1	MPH	1	30	55	MPH
PSPS	24	0	DCV	10.0-11.0 (3)	0	0	DCV
CES	30	5.0/VBAT	DCV	0 (2)	5.0/VBAT	5.0/VBAT	DCV
STI	48	5.0	DCV	5.0	5.0	5.0	DCV
ACTUATORS/ OUTPUTS							
INJ BANK 2	59	VBAT (4)	DCV	4.4-5.4	5.6-7.6	7.2-9.2	mS
INJ BANK 1	58	VBAT (4)	DCV	4.4-5.4	5.6-7.6	7.2-9.2	mS
EVR	33	VBAT (4)	DCV	0	30-60	65-90	%
STO/MIL	17	.6	DCV	VBAT	VBAT	VBAT	DCV
ISC	21	VBAT	DCV	9.5-10.5	8.4-9.6	4.5-8.8	DCV
FP	22	VBAT	DCV	.8-.9	.8-.9	.8-.9	DCV
SPOUT	36	0-12	RPM	660-760	1160-1260	1760-2300	RPM
AM1	51	VBAT	DCV	VBAT	.1-.2	VBAT	DCV
AM2	11	VBAT	DCV	VBAT	VBAT	VBAT	DCV
OTHER							
IGN TIMING	TIMING	N/A	DEG	12-14	26-30	38-42	DEG

NOTES: ① — A/C on.
② — Brake pedal applied.
③ — Steering wheel turned.
④ — Monitor in DCV Manual Mode, Reference Pin to PWR GND (40/60).
⑤ — HEGO should switch from rich (red LED) to lean (green LED), or lean to rich, at least once every 3 seconds. HEGO voltage should toggle above and below .450 DCV, and should never be a negative value.

Reference values shown may vary ± 20% depending on operating conditions and other factors. RPM values are axle and tire dependent.

92F22215

Courtesy of Ford Motor Co.

Fig. 21: ECA Pin Voltage Checks (Bronco & Pickup 5.0L With Manual Transmission)

1992 ENGINE PERFORMANCE
Pin Voltage Charts (Cont.)

5.8L BRONCO, PICKUP & VAN
AUTOMATIC TRANSMISSION (E4OD)

SENSORS/ INPUTS	Signal Pin #	KOEO	Units	HOT IDLE	30 MPH	55 MPH	Units
TP	47	.8-1.0	DCV	.8-1.0	1.1-1.2	1.2-1.4	DCV
EVP	27	.3-.4	DCV	.3-.4	.6-1.3	.9-2.8	DCV
ECT	7	.5-.7	DCV	.5-.7	.5-.7	.5-.7	DCV
ACT	25	.7-2.8	DCV	.7-2.8	.7-2.8	.7-2.8	DCV
MAP	45	157	Hz	106-110	110-122	118-138	Hz
IDM	4	0-12	RPM	750-850	1200-1380	1450-1750	RPM
OCS - red	41	.1	DCV	.1	.1	.1	DCV
PIP	56	0-12	RPM	750-850	1200-1380	1450-1750	RPM
TOT - red	42	.6-2.0	DCV	.6-2.0	.6-1.7	.6-1.2	DCV
HEGO	29	0	DCV	switching (4)	switching (4)	switching (4)	DCV
4x4L - red	12	VBAT	DCV	VBAT	VBAT	VBAT	DCV
BOO	2	0	DCV	VBAT (2)	0	0	DCV
FPM - red	8	0	DCV	VBAT	VBAT	VBAT	DCV
ACCS	10	0	DCV	VBAT (1)	0	0	DCV
PSOM+	3	1	MPH	1	30	55	MPH
MLPS	30	4.4	DCV	4.4	2.1	2.1	DCV
STI	48	5.0	DCV	5.0	5.0	5.0	DCV
ACTUATORS/ OUTPUTS							
INJ BANK 2	59	VBAT (3)	DCV	3.5-4.0	4.0-6.0	5.4-7.0	mS
INJ BANK 1	58	VBAT (3)	DCV	3.5-4.0	4.0-6.0	5.4-7.0	mS
SS1	52	.2-.8	DCV	.2-.8	VBAT	VBAT	DCV
EVR	33	VBAT (3)	DCV	VBAT (3)	0 (3)	0 (3)	DCV
EPC	38	6.6-10.4	DCV	8.3-12.0	8.3-9.6	8.3-9.4	DCV
STO/MIL	17	.1-.6	DCV	VBAT	VBAT	VBAT	DCV
CANP	31	VBAT	DCV	VBAT	.1-9.5	.1-.2	DCV
ISC	21	VBAT	DCV	7.0-10.1	5.6-8.5	2.0-6.0	DCV
FP	22	VBAT	DCV	.1-.9	.1-.9	.1-.9	DCV
SS2 - blue	19	VBAT	DCV	VBAT	.2-.8	VBAT	DCV
SPOUT	36	0-12	RPM	750-850	1200-1380	1450-1750	RPM
OCIL	32	VBAT	DCV	VBAT	VBAT	VBAT	DCV
AM1	51	VBAT	DCV	.1-.2	VBAT	VBAT	DCV
AM2	11	VBAT	DCV	VBAT	VBAT	VBAT	DCV
CCC	53	VBAT	DCV	VBAT	.2-.8	.2-.8	DCV
CCS	55	VBAT	DCV	VBAT	VBAT	VBAT	DCV
OTHER							
IGN TIMING	TIMING	N/A	DEG	16-22	32-38	36-42	DEG

NOTES: ① — A/C on.
② — Brake pedal applied.
③ — Monitor in DCV Manual Mode, Reference Pin to PWR GND (40/60).
④ — HEGO should switch from rich (red LED) to lean (green LED), or lean to rich, at least once every 3 seconds. HEGO voltage should toggle above and below .450 DCV, and should never be a negative value.

Reference values shown may vary ± 20% depending on operating conditions and other factors. RPM values are axle and tire dependent.

92G22216

Courtesy of Ford Motor Co.

Fig. 22: ECA Pin Voltage Checks (Bronco, Pickup & Van 5.8L With Automatic Transmission; E4OD)

1992 ENGINE PERFORMANCE
Pin Voltage Charts (Cont.)

5.8L PICKUP
AUTOMATIC TRANSMISSION (EXCEPT E4OD)

SENSORS/ INPUTS	Signal Pin #	KOEO	Units	HOT IDLE	30 MPH	55 MPH	Units
TP	47	.9	DCV	.9	1.0-1.2	1.2-1.4	DCV
EVP	27	.3-.4	DCV	.3-.4	.3-.4	.6-2.8	DCV
ECT	7	.5-.7	DCV	.5-.7	.5-.7	.5-.7	DCV
ACT	25	.7-2.8	DCV	.7-2.8	.7-2.8	.7-2.8	DCV
MAP	45	157	Hz	106-110	110-122	118-138	Hz
IDM	4	0-12	RPM	750-850	1250-1458	1700-2230	RPM
PIP	56	0-12	RPM	750-850	1250-1458	1700-2230	RPM
HEGO	29	0	DCV	switching (3)	switching (3)	switching (3)	DCV
FPM - red	8	0	DCV	VBAT	VBAT	VBAT	DCV
ACCS	10	0	DCV	VBAT (1)	0	0	DCV
PSOM +	3	1	MPH	1	30	55	MPH
NDS	30	0	DCV	0	5.0/VBAT	5.0/VBAT	DCV
STI	48	5.0	DCV	5.0	5.0	5.0	DCV
ACTUATORS/ OUTPUTS							
INJ BANK 2	59	VBAT (2)	DCV	3.5-5.0	4.0-6.0	5.6-7.0	mS
INJ BANK 1	58	VBAT (2)	DCV	3.5-5.0	4.0-6.0	5.6-7.0	mS
EVR	33	VBAT (2)	DCV	VBAT (2)	11.4-VBAT (2)	9.5-11.6 (2)	DCV
STO/MIL	17	.1-.6	DCV	VBAT	VBAT	VBAT	DCV
CANP	31	VBAT	DCV	VBAT	.1-9.5	.1-.2	DCV
ISC	21	VBAT	DCV	7.0-9.2	5.6-8.5	2.0-5.0	DCV
FP	22	VBAT	DCV	.1-.9	.1-.9	.1-.9	DCV
SPOUT	36	0-12	RPM	750-850	1250-1350	1700-2230	RPM
AM1	51	VBAT	DCV	.1-.2	.1-.2	.1-.2	DCV
AM2	11	VBAT	DCV	VBAT	VBAT	VBAT	DCV
OTHER							
IGN TIMING	TIMING	N/A	DEG	16-20	32-36	36-42	DEG

NOTES: ① — A/C on.
② — Monitor in DCV Manual Mode, Reference Pin to PWR GND (40/60).
③ — HEGO should switch from rich (red LED) to lean (green LED), or lean to rich, at least once every 3 seconds. HEGO voltage should toggle above and below .450 DCV, and should never be a negative value.

Reference values shown may vary ± 20% depending on operating conditions and other factors. RPM values are axle and tire dependent.

92H22217

Courtesy of Ford Motor Co.

Fig. 23: ECA Pin Voltage Checks (Pickup 5.8L With Automatic Transmission – Except E4OD)

1992 ENGINE PERFORMANCE
Pin Voltage Charts (Cont.)

5.8L PICKUP
MANUAL TRANSMISSION

SENSORS/ INPUTS	Signal Pin #	KOEO	Units	HOT IDLE	30 MPH	55 MPH	Units
TP	47	.9	DCV	.9	1.0-1.2	1.2-1.4	DCV
EVP	27	.3-.4	DCV	.3-.4	.3-.4	.6-2.8	DCV
ECT	7	.5-.7	DCV	.5-.7	.5-.7	.5-.7	DCV
ACT	25	.7-2.8	DCV	.7-2.8	.7-2.8	.7-2.8	DCV
MAP	45	157	Hz	106-110	112-122	118-138	Hz
IDM	4	0-12	RPM	750-850	1250-1480	1600-1950	RPM
PIP	56	0-12	RPM	750-850	1250-1480	1600-1950	RPM
HEGO	29	0	DCV	switching (4)	switching (4)	switching (4)	DCV
FPM - red	8	0	DCV	VBAT	VBAT	VBAT	DCV
ACCS	10	0	DCV	VBAT (1)	0	0	DCV
PSOM+	3	1	MPH	1	30	55	MPH
CES	30	5.0/VBAT	DCV	0 (2)	5.0/VBAT	5.0/VBAT	DCV
STI	48	5.0	DCV	5.0	5.0	5.0	DCV
ACTUATORS/ OUTPUTS							
INJ BANK 2	59	VBAT (3)	DCV	3.5-4.0	4.0-6.0	5.6-7.0	mS
INJ BANK 1	58	VBAT (3)	DCV	3.5-4.0	4.0-6.0	5.6-7.0	mS
EVR	33	VBAT (3)	DCV	VBAT (3)	11.4-VBAT (3)	9.5-11.6 (3)	DCV
STO/MIL	17	.1-.6	DCV	VBAT	VBAT	VBAT	DCV
CANP	31	VBAT	DCV	VBAT	.1-9.5	.1-.2	DCV
ISC	21	VBAT	DCV	7.0-9.2	5.6-8.5	2.0-5.0	DCV
FP	22	VBAT	DCV	.1-.9	.1-.9	.1-.9	DCV
SPOUT	36	0-12	RPM	750-850	1250-1480	1600-1950	RPM
AM1	51	VBAT	DCV	.1-.2	.1-.2	.1-.2	DCV
AM2	11	VBAT	DCV	VBAT	VBAT	VBAT	DCV
OTHER							
IGN TIMING	TIMING	N/A	DEG	16-20	32-36	36-42	DEG

NOTES: ① — A/C on.
② — Brake pedal applied.
③ — Monitor in DCV Manual Mode, Reference Pin to PWR GND (40/60).
④ — HEGO should switch from rich (red LED) to lean (green LED), or lean to rich, at least once every 3 seconds. HEGO voltage should toggle above and below .450 DCV, and should never be a negative value.

Reference values shown may vary ± 20% depending on operating conditions and other factors. RPM values are axle and tire dependent.

92I22218

Courtesy of Ford Motor Co.

Fig. 24: ECA Pin Voltage Checks (Pickup 5.8L With Manual Transmission)

1992 ENGINE PERFORMANCE
Pin Voltage Charts (Cont.)

7.3L DIESEL PICKUP & VAN
AUTOMATIC TRANSMISSION (E4OD)

SENSORS/ INPUTS	Signal Pin #	KOEO	Units	HOT IDLE	30 MPH	55 MPH	Units
TP	47	1.0-1.1	DCV	1.0-1.1	1.6-1.9	2.0-2.4	DCV
TOT	7	.6-2.3	DCV	.6-2.3	.6-2.3	.6-2.3	DCV
BP	45	157	Hz	157	157	157	Hz
RPMS(+)	4	0-12	RPM	3510-5010	2700-3370	2130-2890	RPM
OCS - red	41	.1	DCV	.1	.1	.1	DCV
4x4L - red	12	VBAT	DCV	VBAT	VBAT	VBAT	DCV
BOO	2	0	DCV	VBAT (2)	0	0	DCV
ACCS	10	0	DCV	VBAT (1)	0	0	DCV
PSOM +	3	1	MPH	1	30	55	MPH
MLPS	30	4.4	DCV	4.4	2.1	2.1	DCV
STI	48	5.0	DCV	5.0	5.0	5.0	DCV
ACTUATORS/ OUTPUTS							
SS1	52	.2-.8	DCV	.2-.8	VBAT	VBAT	DCV
EPC	38	6.2-10.4	DCV	7.0-8.2	7.1-8.5	7.3-9.1	DCV
STO	17	VBAT	DCV	VBAT	VBAT	VBAT	DCV
SS2 - blue	19	VBAT	DCV	VBAT	.2-.8	VBAT	DCV
TAC	36	0-12	RPM	0-12	0-12	0-12	RPM
OCIL/TMIL	32	VBAT	DCV	VBAT	VBAT	VBAT	DCV
CCC	53	VBAT	DCV	VBAT	.2-.8	.2-.8	DCV
CCS	55	VBAT	DCV	VBAT	VBAT	VBAT	DCV
OTHER							
IGN TIMING	TIMING	N/A	DEG	N/A	N/A	N/A	DEG

NOTES: ① — A/C on.
② — Brake pedal applies.

Reference values shown may vary ± 20% depending on operating conditions and other factors. RPM values are axle and tire dependent.

92D22221

Courtesy of Ford Motor Co.

Fig. 25: ECA Pin Voltage Checks (Pickup & Van 7.3L Diesel Automatic Transmission; E4OD)

7.5L PICKUP & VAN
AUTOMATIC TRANSMISSION (EXCEPT E4OD)

SENSORS/ INPUTS	Signal Pin #	KOEO	Units	HOT IDLE	30 MPH	55 MPH	Units
TP	47	.9-1.0	DCV	.9-1.0	1.2-1.4	1.4-1.7	DCV
EVP	27	.3-.4	DCV	.3-.4	.3-.4	1.8-4.4	DCV
ECT	7	.5-.7	DCV	.5-.7	.5-.7	.5-.7	DCV
ACT	25	.7-2.8	DCV	.7-2.8	.7-2.8	.7-2.8	DCV
MAP	45	157	Hz	103-106	106-118	118-136	Hz
IDM	4	0-12	RPM	650-750	1520-1710	2080-2380	RPM
PIP	56	0-12	RPM	650-750	1520-1710	2080-2380	RPM
HEGO	29	0	DCV	switching (3)	switching (3)	switching (3)	DCV
FPM - red	8	0	DCV	VBAT	VBAT	VBAT	DCV
ACCS	10	0	DCV	VBAT (1)	0	0	DCV
NDS	30	0	DCV	0	5.0/VBAT	5.0/VBAT	DCV
STI	48	5.0	DCV	5.0	5.0	5.0	DCV
ACTUATORS/ OUTPUTS							
INJ BANK 2	59	VBAT (2)	DCV	5.0-5.8	6.6-8.2	8.2-10.6	mS
INJ BANK 1	58	VBAT (2)	DCV	5.0-5.8	6.6-8.2	8.2-10.6	mS
EVR	33	VBAT (2)	DCV	0	0	50-75	%
STO/MIL	17	.1-.9	DCV	VBAT	VBAT	VBAT	DCV
CANP	31	VBAT	DCV	VBAT	.1-.2	.1-.2	DCV
ISC	21	VBAT	DCV	8.0-10.0	8.0-9.5	6.0-8.2	DCV
FP	22	VBAT	DCV	.1-.9	.1-.9	.1-.9	DCV
SPOUT	36	0-12	RPM	650-750	1520-1710	2080-2380	RPM
AM1	51	VBAT	DCV	.1-.2	.1-.2	.1-.2	DCV
OTHER							
IGN TIMING	TIMING	N/A	DEG	20-24	38-42	42-48	DEG

NOTES: (1) — A/C on.

(2) — Monitor in DCV Manual Mode, Reference Pin to PWR GND (40/60).

(3) — HEGO should switch from rich (red LED) to lean (green LED), or lean to rich, at least once every 3 seconds. HEGO voltage should toggle above and below .450 DCV, and should never be a negative value.

Reference values shown may vary ± 20% depending on operating conditions and other factors. RPM values are axle and tire dependent.

1992 ENGINE PERFORMANCE
Pin Voltage Charts (Cont.)

7.5L PICKUP & VAN
AUTOMATIC TRANSMISSION (E4OD)

SENSORS/ INPUTS	Signal Pin #	KOEO	Units	HOT IDLE	30 MPH	55 MPH	Units
TP	47	.8-.9	DCV	.8-.9	1.0-1.2	1.1-1.4	DCV
EVP	27	.3-.4	DCV	.3-.4	.3-.4	.3-2.5	DCV
ECT	7	.5-.7	DCV	.5-.7	.5-.7	.5-.7	DCV
ACT	25	.7-2.8	DCV	.7-2.8	.7-2.8	.7-2.8	DCV
MAP	45	157	Hz	103-106	106-118	112-130	Hz
IDM	4	0-12	RPM	650-750	1260-1360	1550-1830	RPM
OCS - red	41	.1	DCV	.1	.1	.1	DCV
PIP	56	0-12	RPM	650-750	1260-1360	1550-1830	RPM
TOT - red	42	.6-2.3	DCV	.6-2.3	.6-2.3	.6-2.3	DCV
HEGO	29	0	DCV	switching (4)	switching (4)	switching (4)	DCV
4x4L - red	12	VBAT	DCV	VBAT	VBAT	VBAT	DCV
BOO	2	0	DCV	VBAT (2)	0	0	DCV
FPM - red	8	0	DCV	VBAT	VBAT	VBAT	DCV
ACCS	10	0	DCV	VBAT (1)	0	0	DCV
PSOM+	3	1	MPH	1	30	55	MPH
MLPS	30	4.4	DCV	4.4	2.1	2.1	DCV
STI	48	5.0	DCV	5.0	5.0	5.0	DCV
ACTUATORS/ OUTPUTS							
INJ BANK 2	59	VBAT (3)	DCV	6.0-6.8	6.8-9.6	8.2-11.4	mS
INJ BANK 1	58	VBAT (3)	DCV	6.0-6.8	6.8-9.6	8.2-11.4	mS
SS1	52	.2-.8	DCV	.2-.8	VBAT	VBAT	DCV
EVR	33	VBAT (3)	DCV	0	0	0-40	%
EPC	38	5.9-8.0	DCV	7.5-9.0	8.3-9.6	8.2-9.4	DCV
STO/MIL	17	.1-.9	DCV	VBAT	VBAT	VBAT	DCV
CANP	31	VBAT	DCV	VBAT	VBAT	.1-.2	DCV
ISC	21	VBAT	DCV	8.0-10.0	7.0-8.8	4.0-6.5	DCV
FP	22	VBAT	DCV	.1-.9	.1-.9	.1-.9	DCV
SS2 - blue	19	VBAT	DCV	VBAT	.2-.8	VBAT	DCV
SPOUT	36	0-12	RPM	650-750	1260-1360	1550-1830	RPM
OCIL	32	VBAT	DCV	VBAT	VBAT	VBAT	DCV
AM1	51	VBAT	DCV	.1-.2	.1-.2	.1-.2	DCV
CCC	53	VBAT	DCV	VBAT	.2-.8	.2-.8	DCV
CCS	55	VBAT	DCV	VBAT	VBAT	VBAT	DCV
OTHER							
IGN TIMING	TIMING	N/A	DEG	22-28	36-40	36-40	DEG

NOTES: ① — A/C on.
② — Brake pedal applied.
③ — Monitor in DCV Manual Mode, Reference Pin to PWR GND (40/60).
④ — HEGO should switch from rich (red LED) to lean (green LED), or lean to rich, at least once every 3 seconds. HEGO voltage should toggle above and below .450 DCV, and should never be a negative value.

Reference values shown may vary ± 20% depending on operating conditions and other factors. RPM values are axle and tire dependent.

92H21813

Courtesy of Ford Motor Co.

Fig. 27: ECA Pin Voltage Checks (Pickup & Van 7.5L With Automatic Transmission; E4OD)

1992 ENGINE PERFORMANCE
Pin Voltage Charts (Cont.)

7.5L PICKUP & VAN
MANUAL TRANSMISSION

SENSORS/ INPUTS	Signal Pin #	KOEO	Units	HOT IDLE	30 MPH	55 MPH	Units
TP	47	.9-1.0	DCV	.9-1.0	1.2-1.4	1.4-1.7	DCV
EVP	27	.3-.4	DCV	.3-.4	.3-.4	1.8-4.4	DCV
ECT	7	.5-.7	DCV	.5-.7	.5-.7	.5-.7	DCV
ACT	25	.7-2.8	DCV	.7-2.8	.7-2.8	.7-2.8	DCV
MAP	45	157	Hz	103-106	106-118	118-136	Hz
IDM	4	0-12	RPM	650-750	1520-1710	2080-2380	RPM
PIP	56	0-12	RPM	650-750	1520-1710	2080-2380	RPM
HEGO	29	0	DCV	switching (4)	switching (4)	switching (4)	DCV
FPM - red	8	0	DCV	VBAT	VBAT	VBAT	DCV
ACCS	10	0	DCV	VBAT (1)	0	0	DCV
NGS/CES	30	5.0/VBAT	DCV	0 (2)	5.0/VBAT	5.0/VBAT	DCV
STI	48	5.0	DCV	5.0	5.0	5.0	DCV
ACTUATORS/ OUTPUTS							
INJ BANK 2	59	VBAT (3)	DCV	5.0-5.8	6.6-8.2	8.2-10.6	mS
INJ BANK 1	58	VBAT (3)	DCV	5.0-5.8	6.6-8.2	8.2-10.6	mS
EVR	33	VBAT (3)	DCV	0	0	50-75	%
STO/MIL	17	.1-.9	DCV	VBAT	VBAT	VBAT	DCV
CANP	31	VBAT	DCV	VBAT	.1-.2	.1-.2	DCV
ISC	21	VBAT	DCV	9.4-10.0	8.0-9.5	6.0-8.2	DCV
FP	22	VBAT	DCV	.1-.9	.1-.9	.1-.9	DCV
SPOUT	36	0-12	RPM	650-750	1520-1710	2080-2380	RPM
AM1	51	VBAT	DCV	.1-.2	.1-.2	.1-.2	DCV
OTHER							
IGN TIMING	TIMING	N/A	DEG	20-24	38-42	42-48	DEG

NOTES: ① — A/C on.
② — Brake pedal applied.
③ — Monitor in DCV Manual Mode, Reference Pin to PWR GND (40/60).
④ — HEGO should switch from rich (red LED) to lean (green LED), or lean to rich, at least once every 3 seconds. HEGO voltage should toggle above and below .450 DCV, and should never be a negative value.

Reference values shown may vary ± 20% depending on operating conditions and other factors. RPM values are axle and tire dependent.

92I21814

Courtesy of Ford Motor Co.

Fig. 28: ECA Pin Voltage Checks (Pickup & Van 7.5L With Manual Transmission)

Aerostar, Bronco, Explorer, Pickup, Ranger, Van

NOTE: Unless otherwise specified, references to Pickup include the F350 Super Duty commercial chassis.

INTRODUCTION

Sensor operating range information can help determine if a sensor is out of calibration. An out-of-calibration sensor may not set a trouble code, but it will cause driveability problems.

NOTE: Unless specified otherwise, perform all voltage tests using a Digital Volt-Ohmmeter (DVOM) with a minimum 10-megohm input impedance.

AIR CHARGE TEMPERATURE (ACT) & ENGINE COOLANT TEMPERATURE (ECT) SENSORS
ACT & ECT SENSORS SPECIFICATIONS

Temperature °F (°C)	[1] Volts	Ohms
50 (10)	3.51	58,700
68 (20)	3.07	37,300
86 (30)	2.60	24,200
104 (40)	2.13	16,150
122 (50)	1.70	10,970
140 (60)	1.33	7700
158 (70)	1.04	5370
176 (80)	0.78	3840
194 (90)	0.60	2800
212 (100)	0.46	2007

[1] – Voltage calculations are based on a Voltage Reference (VREF) of 5 volts. Actual values may vary by as much as 15 percent due to sensor and VREF variations.

EGR VALVE POSITION (EVP) SENSOR
EVP SENSOR VOLTAGE

EGR Valve Opening (%)	[1] Volts
0	0.40
10	0.75
20	1.10
30	1.45
40	1.80
50	2.15
60	2.50
70	2.85
80	3.20
90	3.55
100	3.90

[1] – Voltage calculations are based on a Voltage Reference (VREF) of 5 volts. Actual values may vary by as much as 15 percent due to sensor and VREF variations.

EXHAUST GAS OXYGEN (EGO) SENSOR
EGO SENSOR VOLTAGE

Condition	[1] Voltage
Rich	Increases
Lean	Decreases

[1] – Measure between oxygen sensor connector and ground. Range should be 0.2-0.8 volt.

MASS AIRFLOW (MAF) SENSOR
MAF SENSOR VOLTAGE

Engine Condition [1]	[2] Volts
Idle	0.8
20 MPH	1.0
40 MPH	1.7
60 MPH	2.1

[1] – Engine at normal operating temperature.
[2] – Voltage may vary depending on engine load and temperature.

MANIFOLD ABSOLUTE PRESSURE/BAROMETRIC PRESSURE (MAP/BP) SENSOR
MAP/BP FREQUENCY (BAROMETRIC PRESSURE)

Barometric Pressure (In. Hg)	[1] Frequency (Hz)
17.1	122.4
18.3	125.5
19.5	128.7
20.7	131.9
21.8	135.1
23.0	138.3
24.2	141.8
25.4	145.4
26.6	148.9
27.7	152.5
28.9	156.1
30.1	159.6
31.0	162.4

[1] – Values may vary by as much as 6 Hz.

MAP/BP FREQUENCY (MANIFOLD VACUUM) [1]

Manifold Vacuum (In. Hg)	[2] Frequency (Hz)
0	159
3	150
6	141
9	133
12	125
15	117
18	109
21	102
24	95
27	88
30	80

[1] – Based on barometric pressure of 30.0 in. Hg.
[2] – Values may vary by as much as 6 Hz.

MAP/BP VOLTAGE (ELEVATION)

Elevation (Feet)	Volts
0	1.55-1.63
1000	1.52-1.60
2000	1.49-1.57
3000	1.46-1.54
4000	1.43-1.51
5000	1.40-1.48
6000	1.37-1.45
7000	1.35-1.43

MANUAL LEVER POSITION (MLP) SENSOR
MLP SENSOR SPECIFICATIONS

Position	[1] Volts	[1] Ohms
P	4.41	4160
R	3.60	1440
N	2.83	733
D	2.09	401
2	1.37	211
1	0.68	81

[1] – Values may vary by as much as 15 percent.

PRESSURE FEEDBACK EGR (PFE) SENSOR
PFE SENSOR VOLTAGE

psi [1]	Volts
0.46	3.63
0.91	4.00
1.36	4.38
1.82 psi	4.75

In. Hg [2]	
0	3.25
5.0	1.22
7.4	0.25

[1] – To avoid sensor damage, DO NOT exceed 1.82 psi. Hg during testing.

[2] – To avoid sensor damage, DO NOT exceed 7.4 in. Hg during testing.

THROTTLE POSITION SENSOR (TPS)
TPS VOLTAGE

Throttle Angle	[1] Volts
0°	0.50
10°	0.97
20°	1.44
30°	1.90
40°	2.37
50°	2.84
60°	3.31
70°	3.78
80°	4.24

[1] – Voltage may vary by as much as 15 percent.

TRANSMISSION OIL TEMPERATURE (TOT) SENSOR
TOT SENSOR SPECIFICATIONS

Temperature °F (°C)	[1] Volts	[1] Ohms
50 (10)	3.52	58,750
68 (20)	3.06	37,300
86 (30)	2.62	24,270
104 (40)	2.16	16,150
122 (50)	1.72	10,970
140 (60)	1.35	7600
158 (70)	1.04	5370
176 (80)	0.80	3840
194 (90)	0.61	2800
212 (100)	0.47	2070
230 (110)	0.36	1550
248 (120)	0.28	1180

[1] – Values may vary by as much as 15 percent.

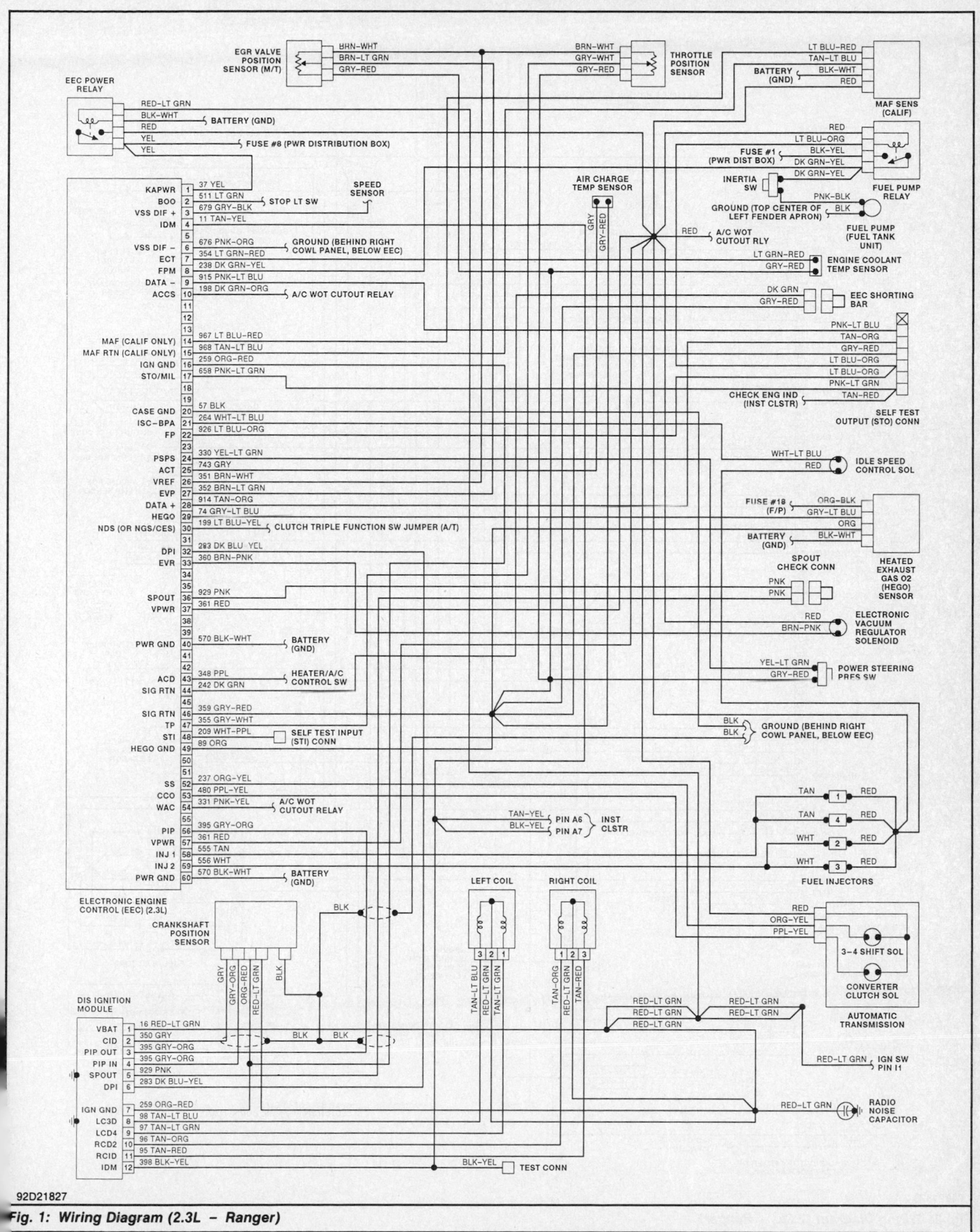

92D21827

Fig. 1: Wiring Diagram (2.3L - Ranger)

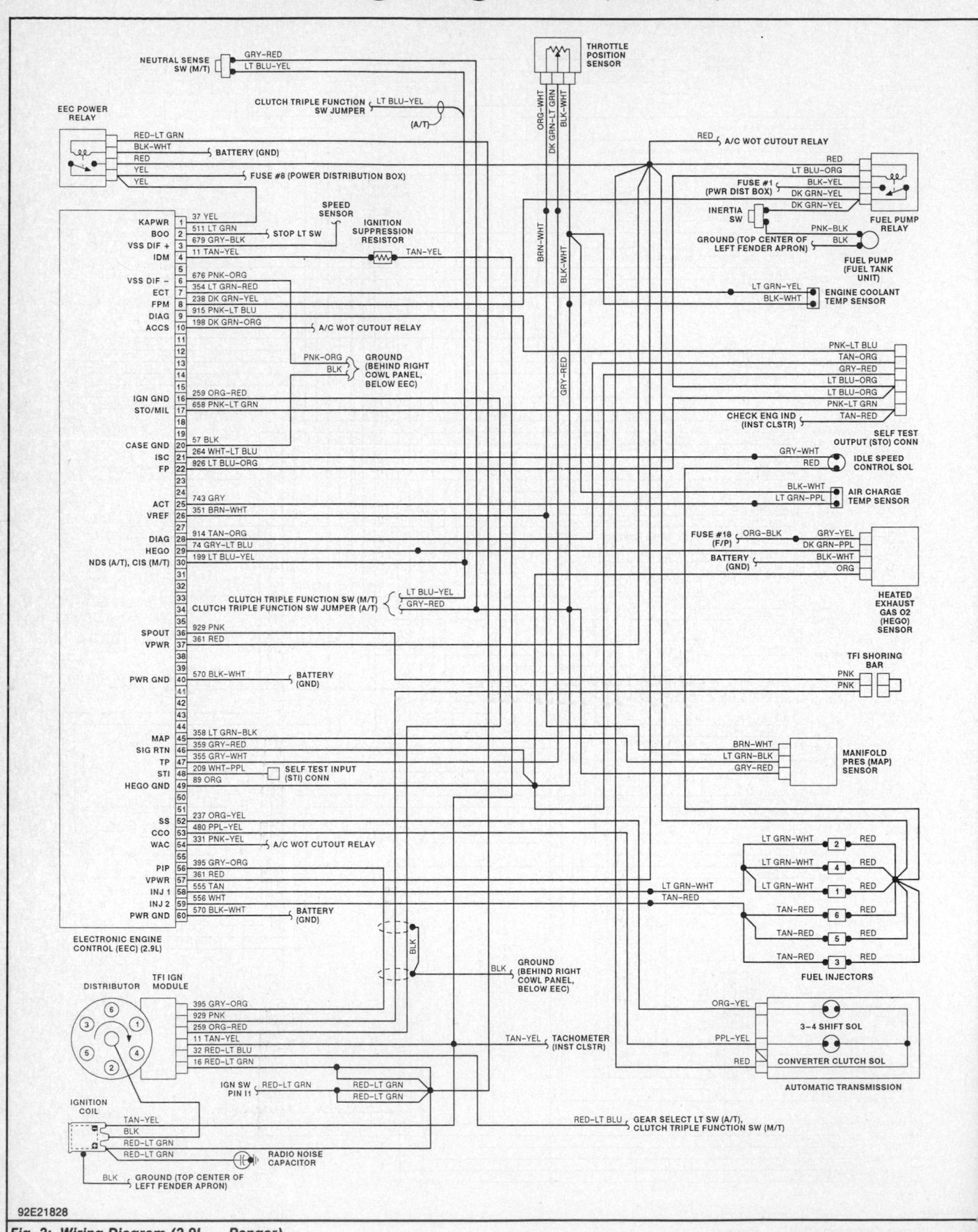

92E21828

Fig. 2: Wiring Diagram (2.9L – Ranger)

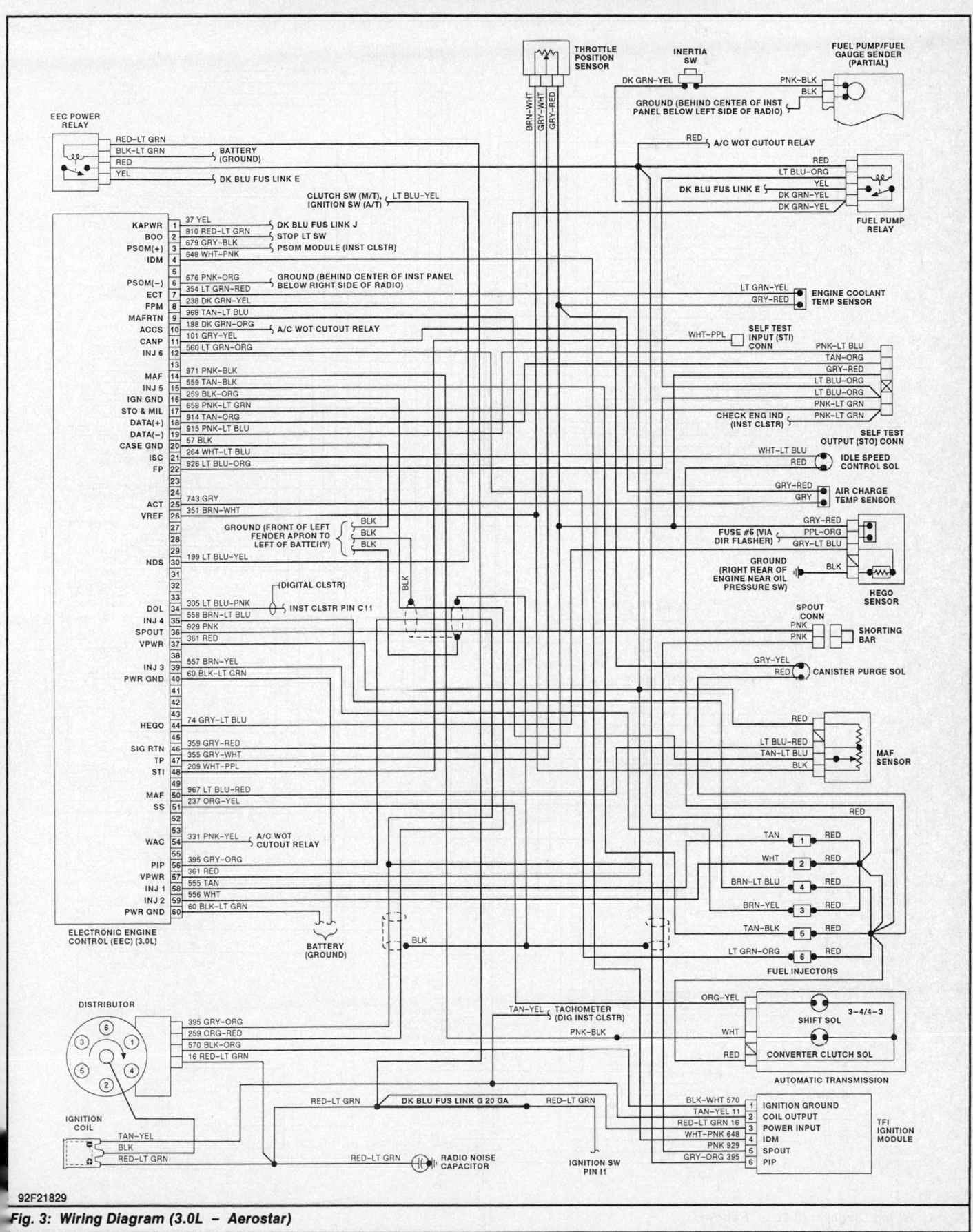

Fig. 3: Wiring Diagram (3.0L – Aerostar)

92F21829

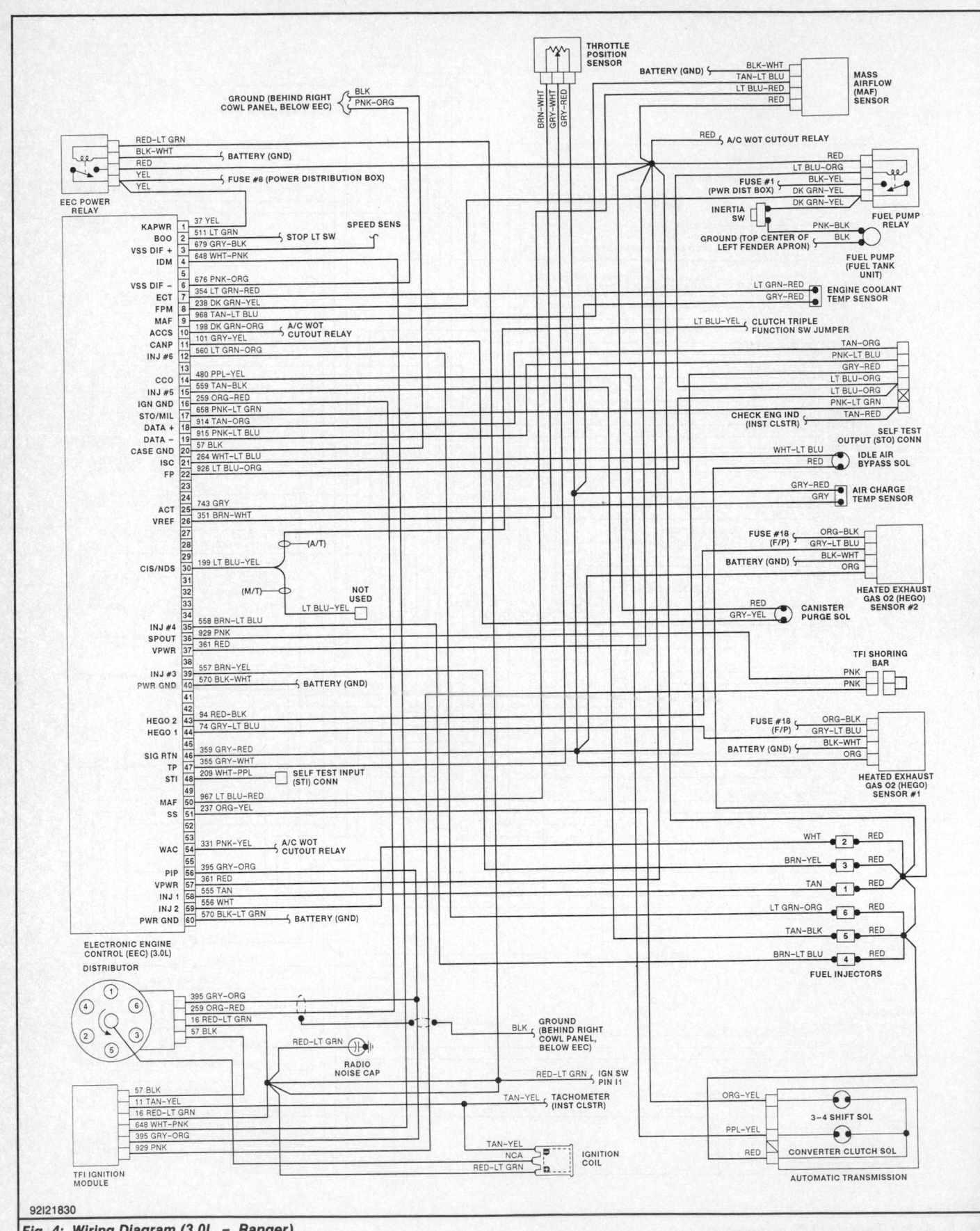

92121830

Fig. 4: Wiring Diagram (3.0L – Ranger)

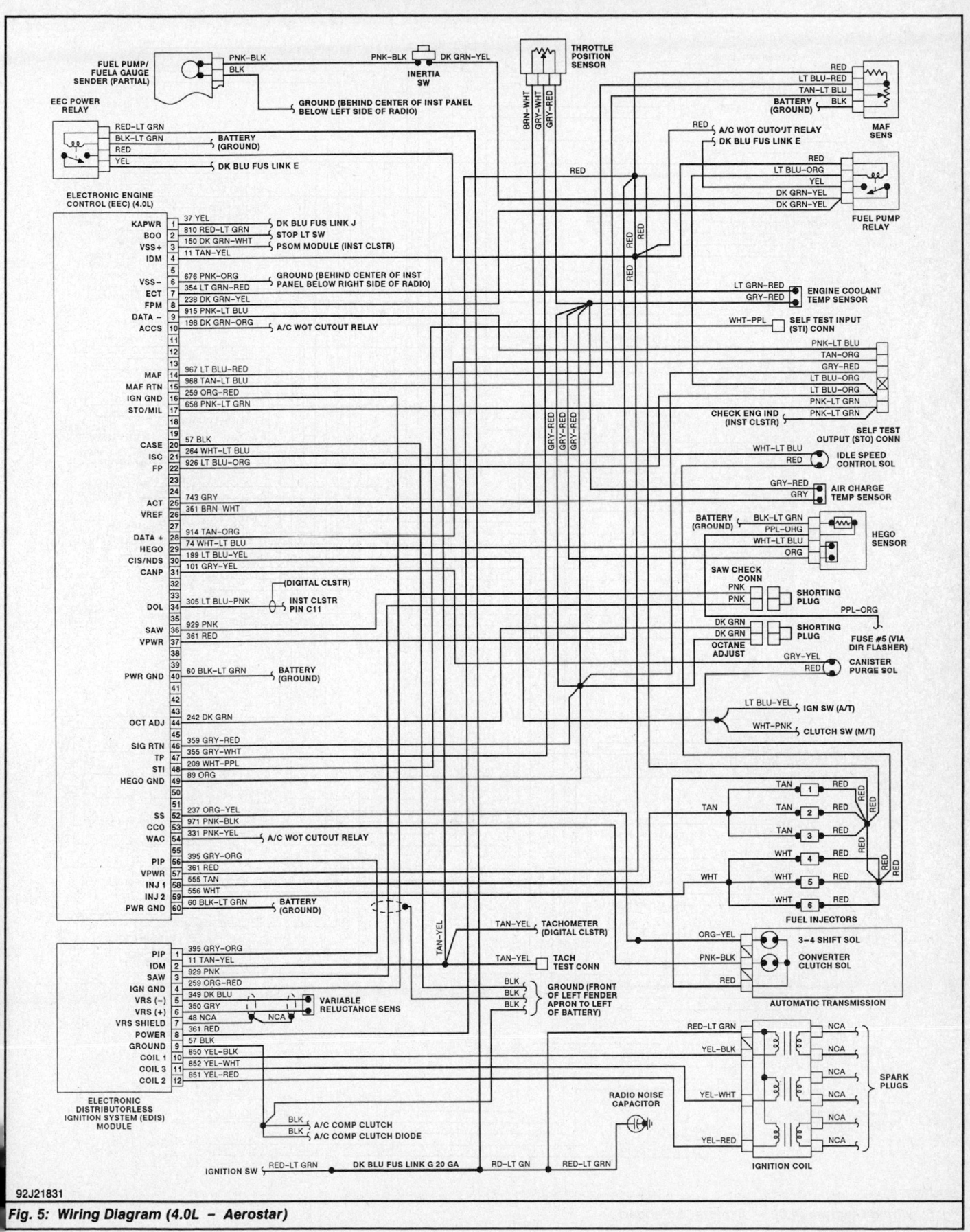

Fig. 5: Wiring Diagram (4.0L – Aerostar)

92J21831

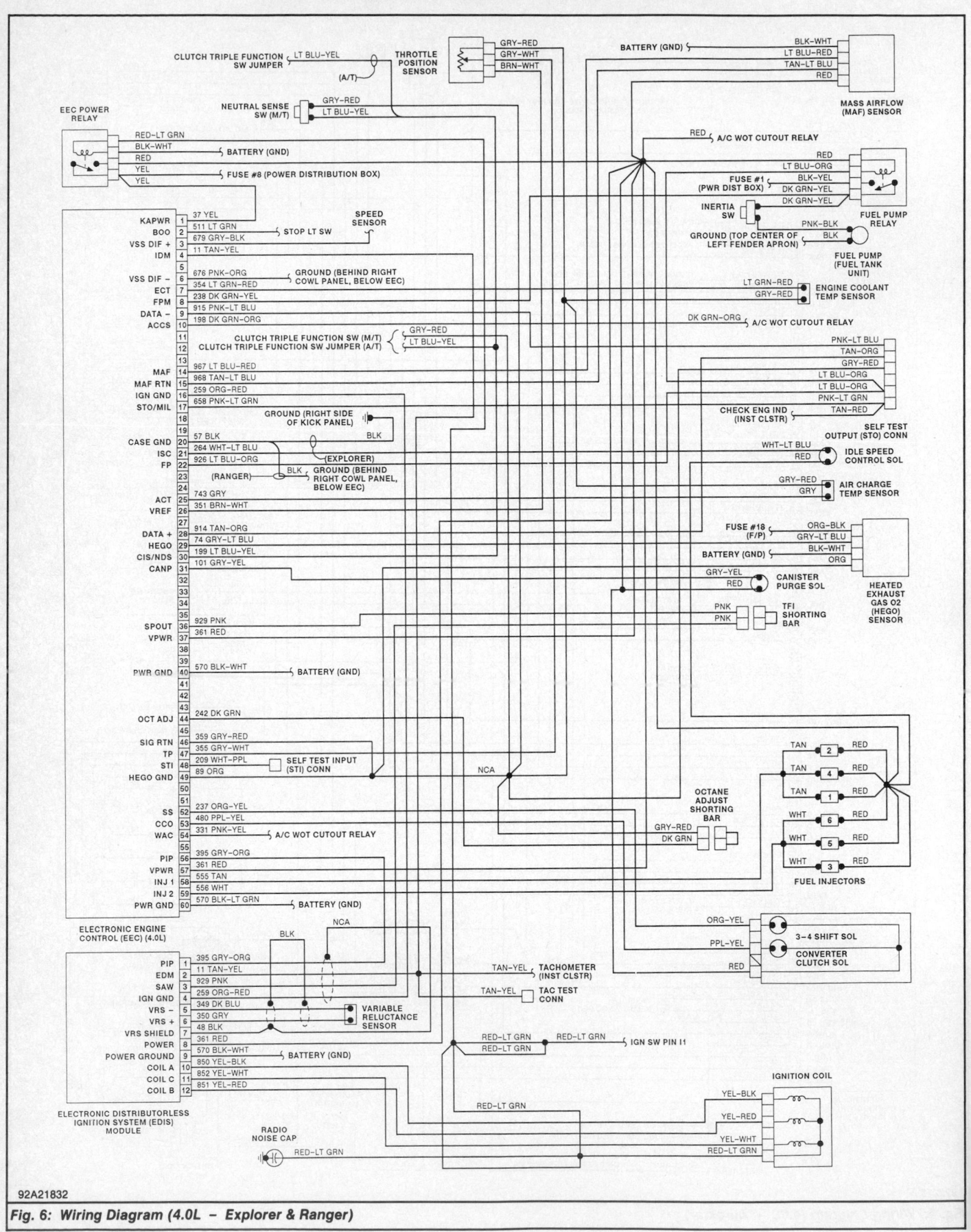

92A21832

Fig. 6: Wiring Diagram (4.0L - Explorer & Ranger)

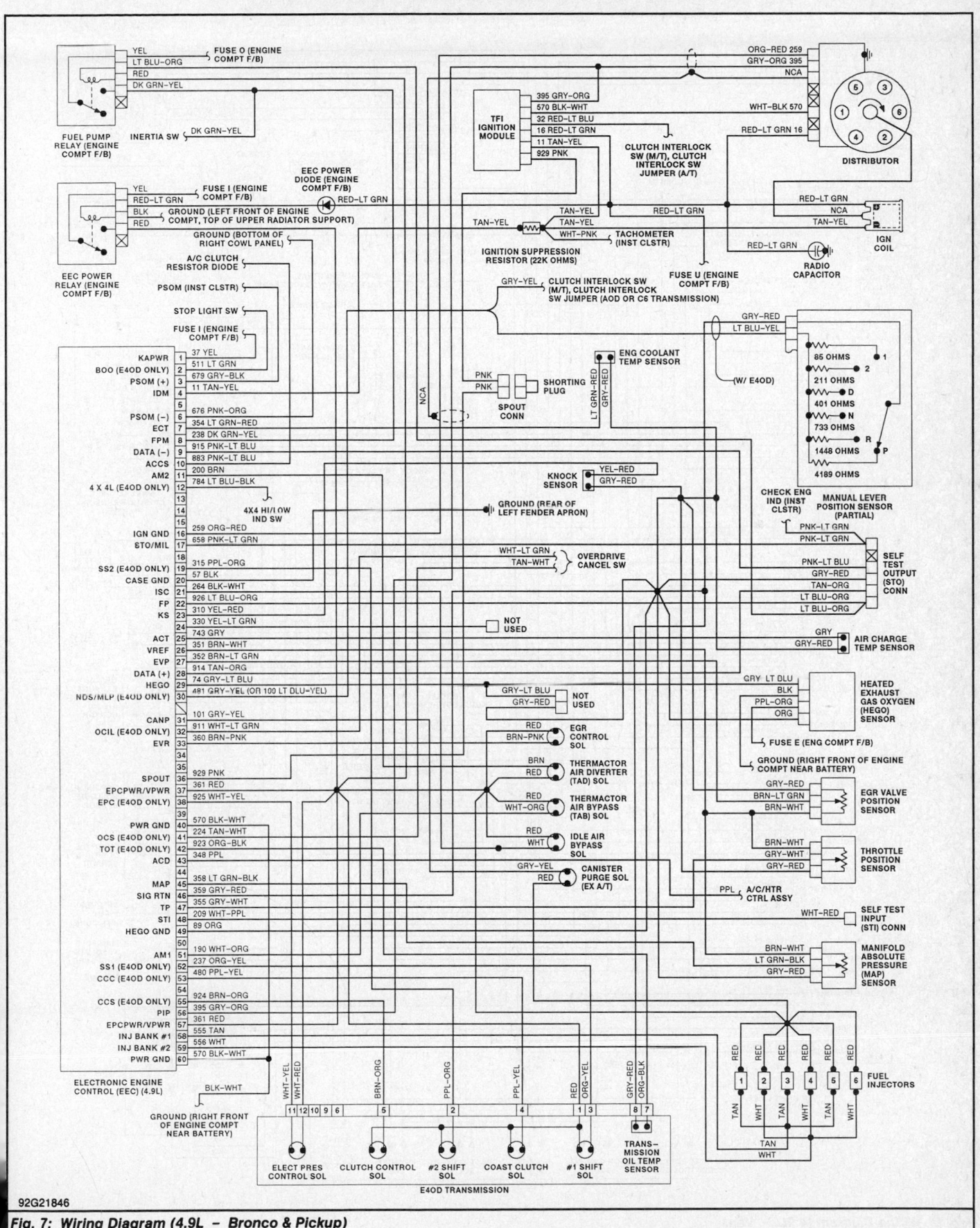

Fig. 7: Wiring Diagram (4.9L – Bronco & Pickup)

92G21846

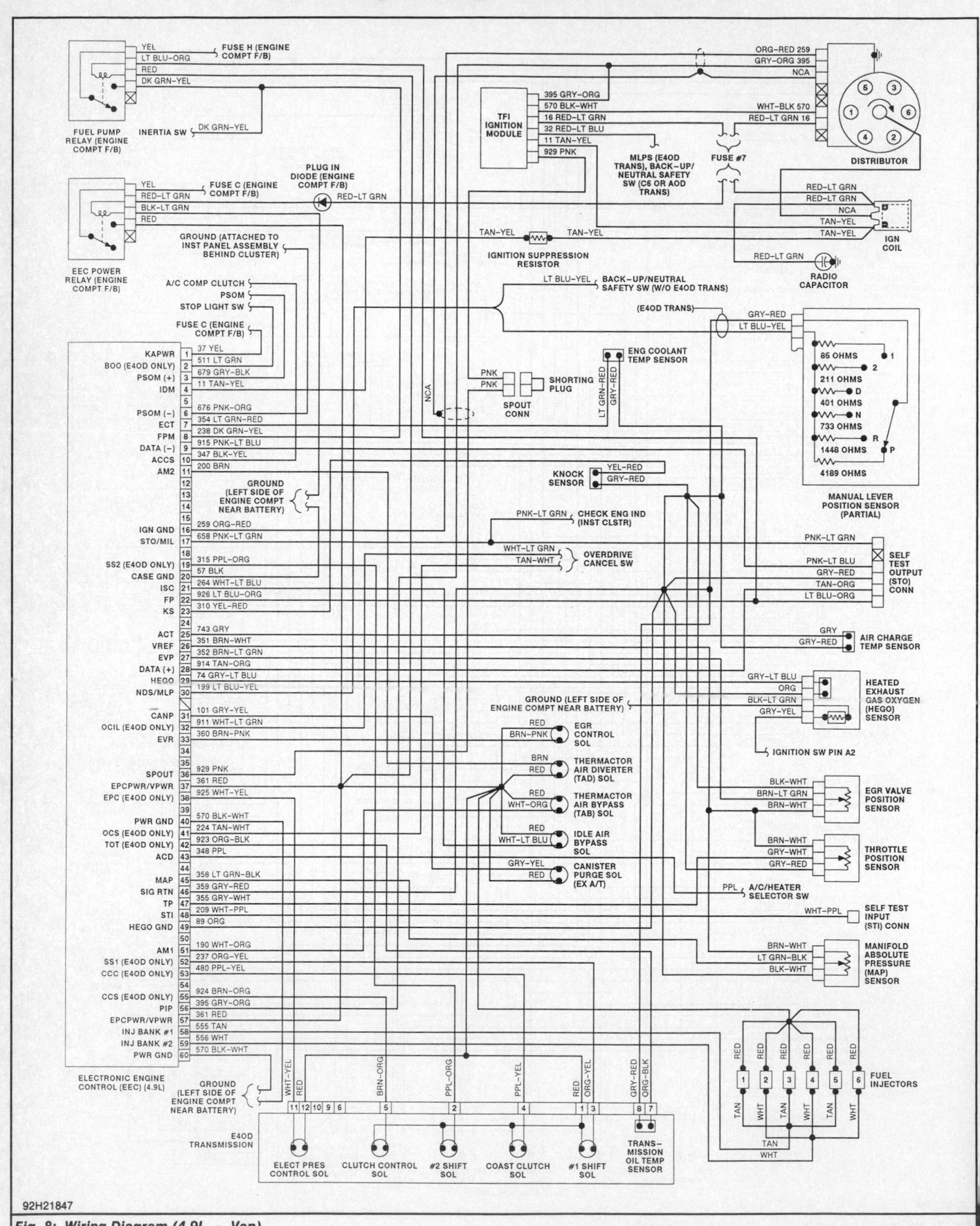

92H21847

Fig. 8: *Wiring Diagram (4.9L – Van)*

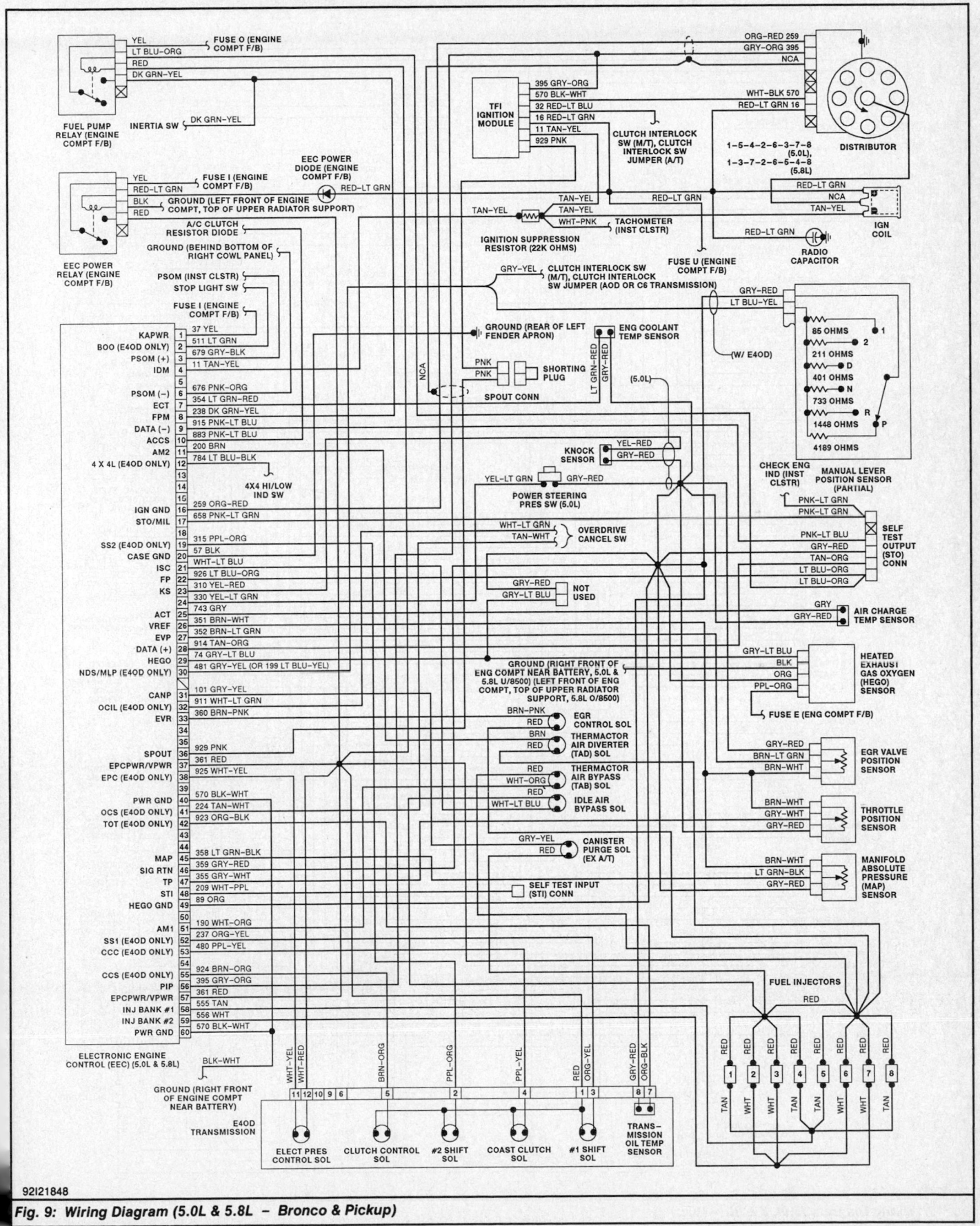

Fig. 9: Wiring Diagram (5.0L & 5.8L – Bronco & Pickup)

92121848

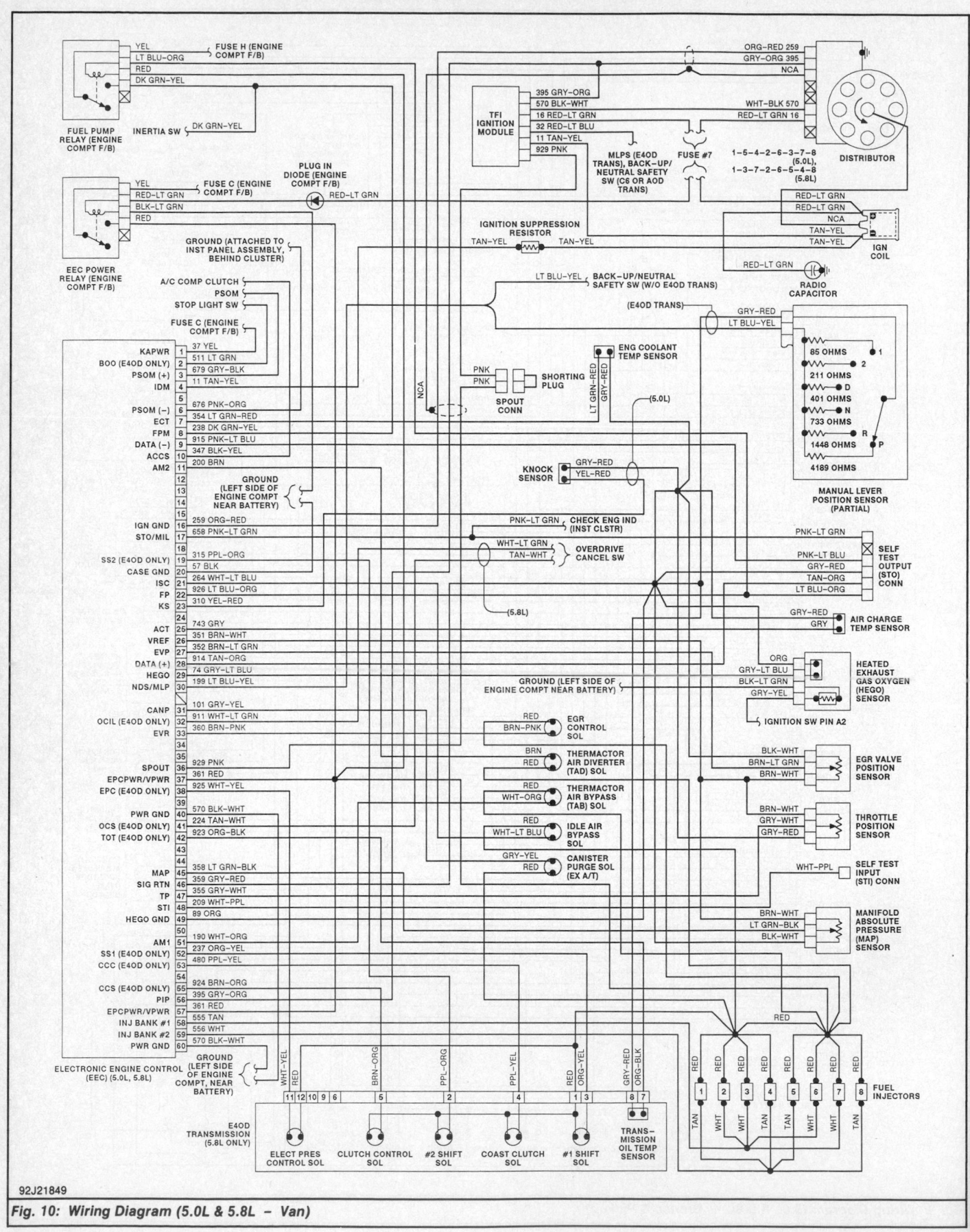

92J21849

Fig. 10: Wiring Diagram (5.0L & 5.8L – Van)

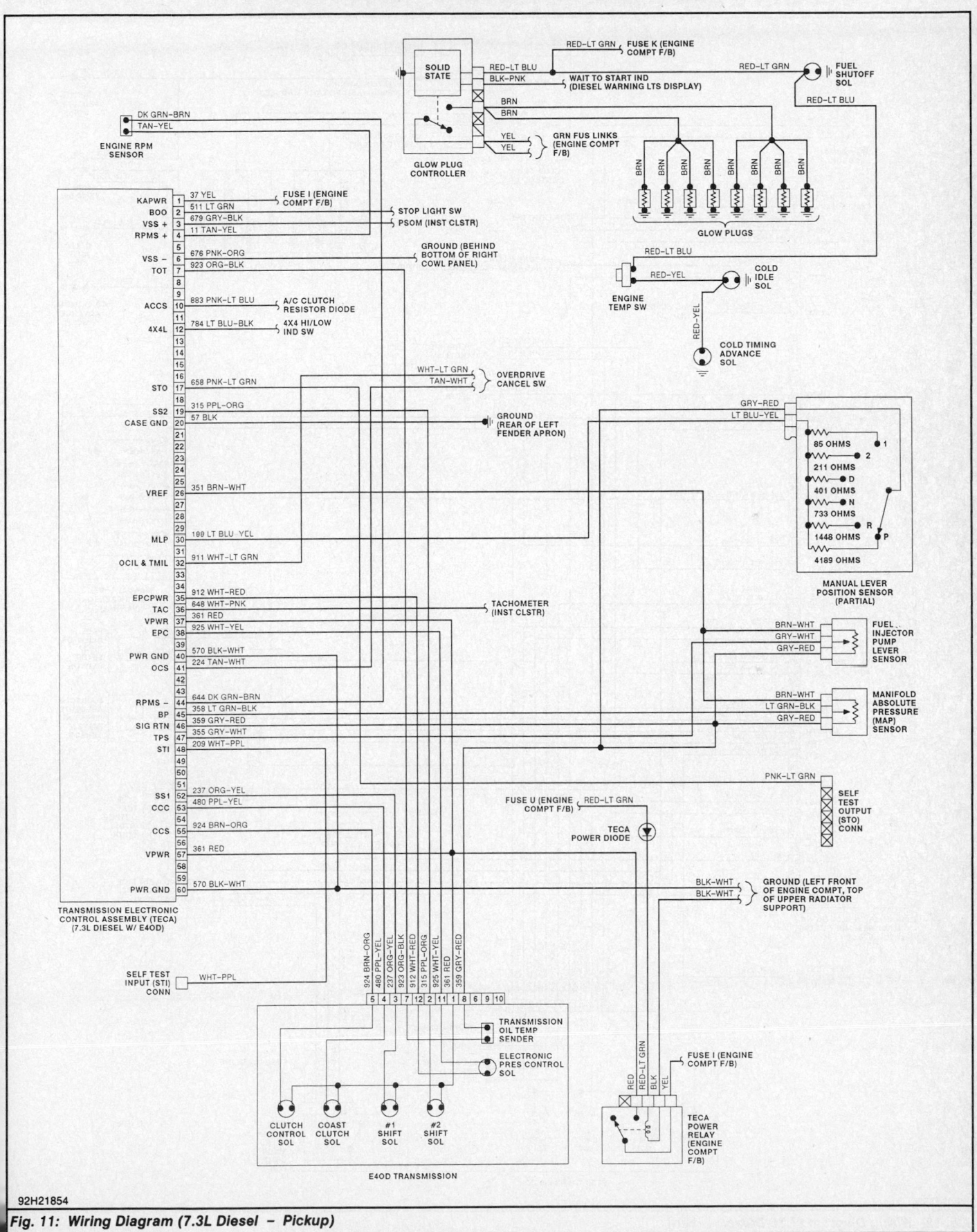

Fig. 11: *Wiring Diagram (7.3L Diesel – Pickup)*

92H21854

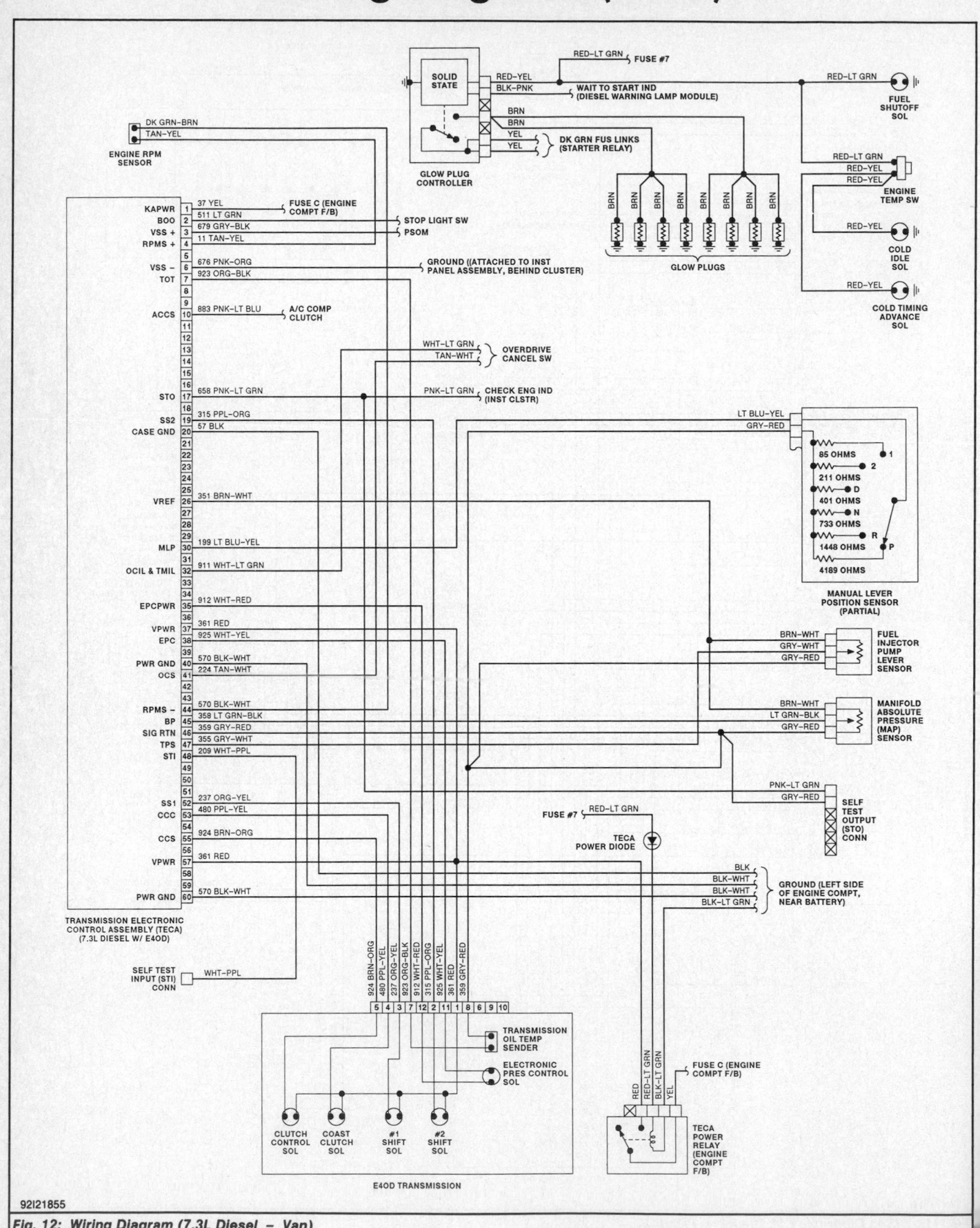

92121855
Fig. 12: Wiring Diagram (7.3L Diesel – Van)

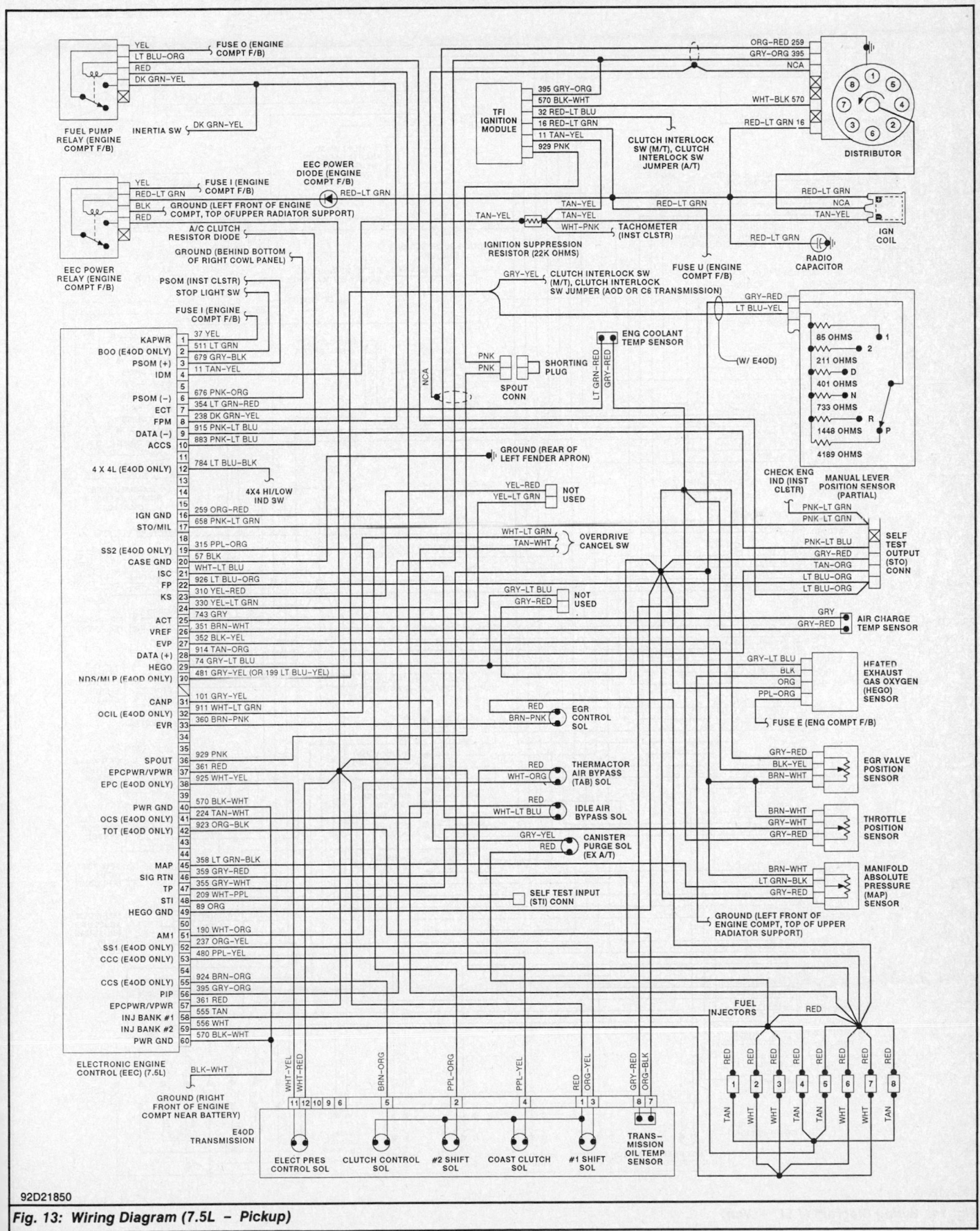

92D21850

Fig. 13: Wiring Diagram (7.5L - Pickup)

1992 ENGINE PERFORMANCE
Wiring Diagrams (Cont.)

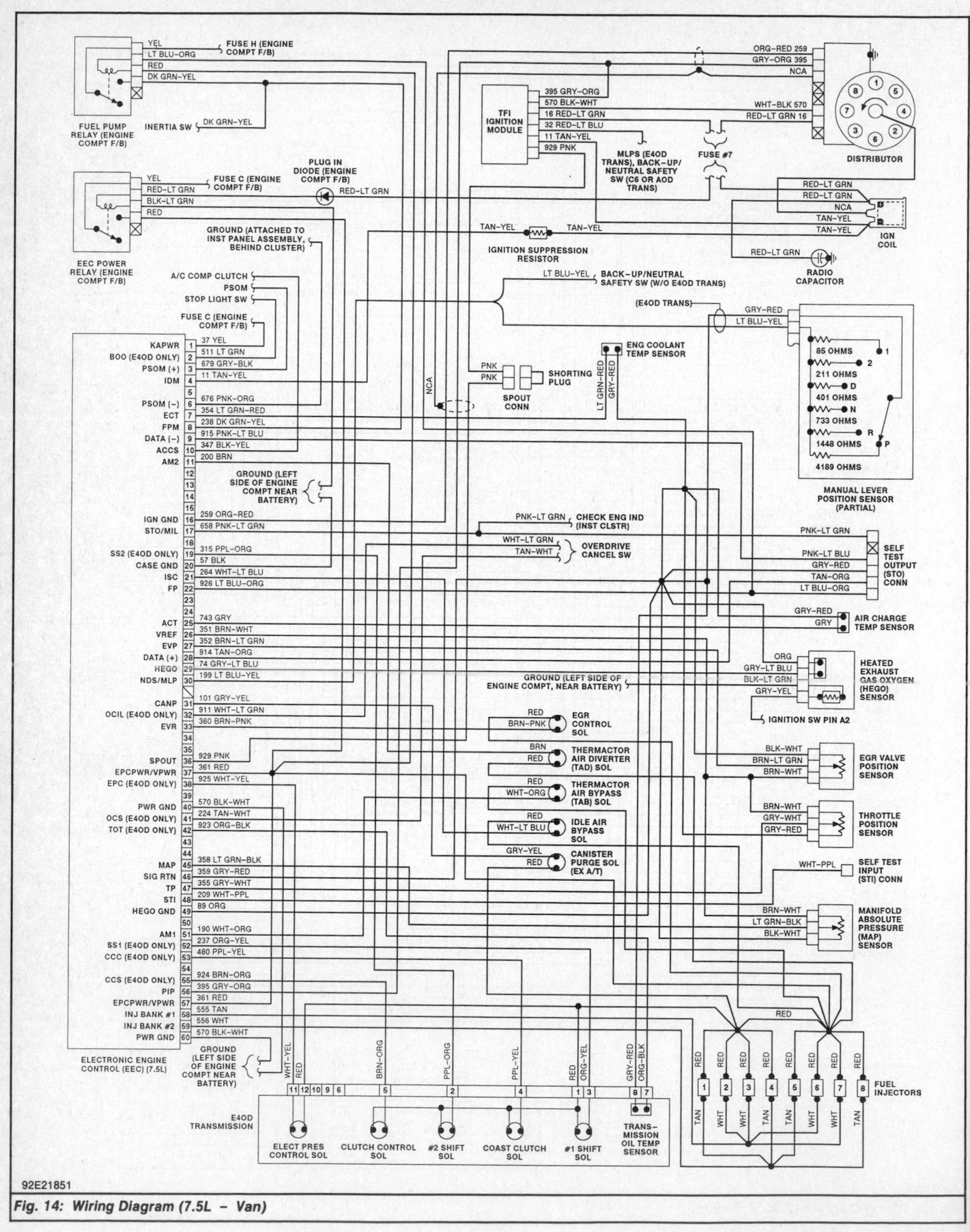

Fig. 14: Wiring Diagram (7.5L - Van)

92E21851

1992 ENGINE PERFORMANCE
Vacuum Diagrams

Aerostar, Bronco, Explorer, Pickup, Ranger, Van

NOTE: Unless otherwise specified, references to Pickup include the F350 Super Duty commercial chassis.

INSTRUCTIONS

Engine calibration number can be found on Emission Calibration Label located on driver's door or "B" pillar post. *See Fig. 1*. Using calibration number and VACUUM DIAGRAM INDEX, determine which vacuum diagram is used for vehicle being serviced.

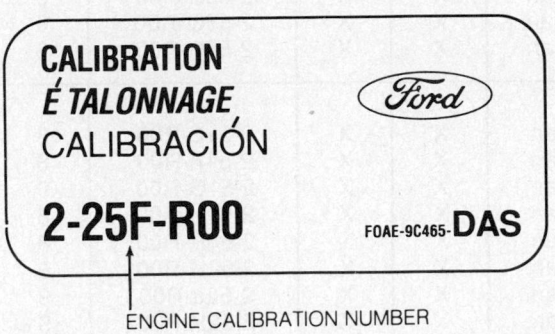

CALIBRATION
ÉTALONNAGE
CALIBRACIÓN

2-25F-R00   FOAE-9C465-**DAS**

ENGINE CALIBRATION NUMBER

92J21922

Fig. 1: Emission Calibration Label Example

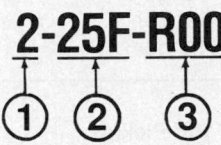

CALIBRATION CODE

1. **MODEL YEAR** – Represents model year that calibration was introduced. In this case 2 represents the last digit of the year 1992.
2. **CALIBRATION DESIGN LEVEL** – Indicates design level assigned to engine. In this case 25F.
3. **CALIBRATION REVISION LEVEL** – Represents revision level of calibration. In this case R00. Numbers will advance as revisions occur.

Courtesy of Ford Motor Co.

VACUUM DIAGRAM INDEX

Engine & Model	Application	Transmission	A/C	Non A/C	Calibration	Fig. No.
2.3L 4-Cylinder						
Ranger [1]	Fed.	Auto./Man.	X	X	2-49S-R00	2
Ranger [1]	Calif./Fed	Auto./Man.	X	X	2-49T-R00	2
Ranger [1]	Calif./Fed	Auto./Man.	X	X	2-50S-R00	2
2.9L V6						
Ranger [1]	Calif./Fed.	Auto./Man.	X	X	9-65H-R00	3
Ranger [1]	Calif./Fed.	Auto./Man.	X	X	0-66H-R10	3
3.0L V6						
Aerostar [1]	Calif./Fed.	Auto./Man.	X	X	2-55F-R00	4
Aerostar	Calif./Fed.	Auto./Man.	X	X	2-55J-R00	4
Aerostar	Calif./Fed.	Auto./Man.	X	X	2-55T-R00	4
Aerostar	Calif./Fed	Auto./Man.	X	X	2-56F-R00	4
Aerostar	Calif./Fed	Auto./Man.	X	X	2-56J-R00	5
Aerostar	Calif./Fed	Auto./Man.	X	X	2-56T-R00	5
4.0L V6						
Aerostar, Explorer, Ranger [1,2]	Fed.	Auto./Man.	X	X	2-57B-R00	6
Aerostar, Explorer, Ranger [1,2]	Calif./Fed.	Auto./Man.	X	X	2-57F-R00	6
Aerostar, Explorer, Ranger [1,2]	Calif.Fed.	Auto./Man.	X	X	2-57H-R00	6
Aerostar, Explorer, Ranger [1,2]	Calif, Fed.	Auto./Man.	X	X	2-57R-R00	6
Aerostar, Explorer, Ranger [1]	Fed.	Auto./Man	X	X	2-58A-R00	6
Aerostar, Explorer, Ranger [1]	Fed.	Auto./Man	X	X	2-58B-R00	6
Aerostar, Explorer, Ranger [1]	Calif., Fed.	Auto./Man	X	X	2-58F-R00	6
Aerostar, Explorer, Ranger [1,2]	Calif., Fed.	Auto./Man	X	X	2-58H-R00	6
Aerostar, Explorer, Ranger [2]	Fed.	Auto./Man	X	X	2-58J-R00	6
Aerostar, Explorer, Ranger [2]	Fed.	Auto./Man	X	X	2-58K-R00	7

[1] – Equipped with A/CL-DV.
[2] – Over 3450 lbs. Curb Weight.

VACUUM DIAGRAM INDEX (Cont.)

Engine & Model	Application	Transmission	A/C	Non A/C	Calibration	Fig. No.
4.0L V6 (Cont.)						
Aerostar, Explorer, Ranger [2]	Calif.	Auto./Man	X	X	2-58L-R00	7
Aerostar, Explorer, Ranger [1]	Calif.	Auto./Man	X	X	2-58P-R00	6
Aerostar, Explorer, Ranger [1]	Calif.	Auto./Man	X	X	2-58Q-R00	6
Aerostar, Explorer, Ranger	Calif.	Auto./Man	X	X	2-58R-R00	6
4.9L 6-Cylinder						
Bronco/E150 Van/F150 Pickup	Fed.	Auto./Man.	X	X	2-51E-R00	8
Bronco/E150 Van/F150 Pickup	Fed.	Auto./Man.	X	X	2-51F-R00	8
Bronco/E150 Van/F150 Pickup	Fed.	Auto./Man.	X	X	2-51G-R00	8
Bronco/E150 Van/F150 Pickup	Fed.	Auto./Man.	X	X	2-51H-R00	8
Bronco/E150 Van/F150 Pickup	Fed.	Auto./Man.	X	X	2-51R-R00	8
Bronco/E150 Van/F150 Pickup	Fed.	Auto./Man.	X	X	2-52H-R00	9
Bronco/E150 Van/F150 Pickup	Fed.	Auto./Man.	X	X	2-52J-R00	9
Bronco/E150 Van/F150 Pickup	Fed.	Auto./Man.	X	X	2-52K-R00	9
Bronco/E150 Van/F150 Pickup	Fed.	Auto./Man.	X	X	2-52L-R00	9
Bronco/E150 Van/F150 Pickup	Fed.	Auto./Man.	X	X	2-52Q-R00	9
Bronco/E150 Van/F150 Pickup	Fed.	Auto./Man.	X	X	2-52R-R00	9
Bronco/E150 Van/F150 Pickup	Fed.	Auto./Man.	X	X	2-52S-R00	9
4.9L 6-Cylinder, Heavy Duty						
Bronco, Pickup, Van [3]	Fed.	Man.	X	X	1-71J-R10	4
Bronco, Pickup, Van [3]	Fed.	Auto.	X	X	1-72J-R10	4
Bronco, Pickup, Van [3]	Fed.	Auto.,/Man.	X	X	2-52K-R00	4
Bronco, Pickup, Van [3]	Fed.	Auto./Man.	X	X	2-52L-R00	4
Bronco, Pickup, Van [3]	Fed.	Auto./Man.	X	X	2-72M-R00	4
5.0L V8						
Bronco, Pickup, Van [3]	[4]	Auto./Man.	X	X	2-53E-R10	4
Bronco, Pickup, Van [3]	[4]	Auto./Man.	X	X	2-53F-R10	4
Bronco, Pickup, Van [3]	[4]	Auto./Man.	X	X	2-54E-R10	4
Bronco, Pickup, Van [3]	[4]	Auto./Man.	X	X	2-54J-R10	4
Bronco, Pickup, Van [3]	[4]	Auto./Man.	X	X	2-54K-R10	4
Bronco, Pickup, Van [3]	[4]	Auto./Man.	X	X	2-54L-R10	4
Bronco, Pickup, Van [3]	[4]	Auto./Man.	X	X	2-54P-R10	4
Bronco, Pickup, Van [3]	[4]	Auto./Man.	X	X	2-54T-R10	4
Bronco, Pickup, Van [3]	[4]	Auto./Man.	X	X	2-54V-R10	4
Bronco, Pickup, Van [3]	[4]	Auto./Man.	X	X	2-54W-R10	4
Bronco, Pickup, Van [3]	[4]	Auto./Man.	X	X	2-54X-R10	4
Bronco, Pickup, Van [3]	[4]	Auto./Man.	X	X	2-54Z-R10	4
5.8L V8						
Bronco, Pickup, Van	Fed.	Auto./Man. [5]	X	X	1-64E-R10	10
Bronco, Pickup, Van	Calif./Fed.	Auto./Man. [5]	X	X	1-64H-R10	11
Bronco, Pickup, Van [3]	Fed.	Auto./Man. [5]	[4]	[4]	1-64J-R10	11
Bronco, Pickup, Van [3]	Fed.	Auto./Man. [5]	[4]	[4]	1-64M-R10	11
Bronco, Pickup, Van [3]	[4]	Auto./Man. [5]	[4]	[4]	1-64P-R10	11
Bronco, Pickup, Van [3]	[4]	Auto./Man. [5]	[4]	[4]	1-64R-R10	4
Bronco, Pickup, Van [3]	Fed.	Auto./Man. [5]	[4]	[4]	2-64E-R10	11
Bronco, Pickup, Van [3]	Fed.	Auto./Man. [5]	[4]	[4]	2-64H-R10	11
Bronco, Pickup, Van [3]	Fed.	Auto./Man. [5]	[4]	[4]	2-64J-R10	11
Bronco, Pickup, Van [3]	Fed.	Auto./Man. [5]	[4]	[4]	2-64K-R10	11
Bronco, Pickup, Van [3]	Fed.	Auto./Man. [5]	[4]	[4]	2-64M-R10	11
Bronco, Pickup, Van [3]	[4]	Auto./Man. [5]	[4]	[4]	2-64P-R10	11
Bronco, Pickup, Van [3]	Calif.	Auto./Man. [5]	[4]	[4]	2-64R-R10	11
Bronco, Pickup, Van [3]	[4]	Auto./Man. [5]	[4]	[4]	2-64S-R10	4

[1] – Equipped with A/CL-DV.
[2] – Over 3450 lbs. Curb Weight.
[3] – Over 6000 lbs. GVWR.
[4] – Information not available.
[5] – M/T in F250 HD and F350.

VACUUM DIAGRAM INDEX (Cont.)

Engine & Model	Application	Transmission	A/C	Non A/C	Calibration	Fig. No.
5.8L V8, Heavy Duty						
Bronco, Pickup, Van [3]	Calif.	Auto./Man.[5]	4	4	1-75A-R00	12
Bronco, Pickup, Van [3]	Calif.	Auto./Man.[5]	4	4	1-76A-R00	12
Bronco, Pickup, Van [3]	Calif.	Auto./Man.[5]	4	4	1-76C-R00	12
Bronco, Pickup, Van [3]	Calif./Fed.	Auto./Man.[5]	4	4	2-64K-R00	11
7.5L V8						
F250/350 Pickup, E250/350 Van	Calif., Fed.	Auto./Man.	4	4	1-98F-R00	13
7.5L V8, Heavy Duty						
F250/350 Pickup, E250/350 Van	Calif./Fed.	Auto./Man[6]	4	4	1-97A-R00	13
F250/350 Pickup, E250/350 Van	Calif./Fed.	Auto./Man[6]	4	4	1-98A-R00	13
F250/350 Pickup, E250/350 Van	Calif./Fed.	Auto./Man[6]	4	4	1-98B-R00	13
F250/350 Pickup, E250/350 Van	Calif./Fed.	Auto./Man[6]	4	4	2-98A-R00	13
F250/350 Pickup, E250/350 Van	Calif.	Auto./Man[6]	4	4	2-98B-R00	13
F250/350 Pickup, E250/350 Van	Calif./Fed.	Auto./Man[6]	4	4	2-98E-R00	13
F250/350 Pickup, E250/350 Van	Calif./Fed.	Auto./Man[6]	4	4	2-98E-R10	13

[1] – Equipped with A/CL-DV.
[2] – Over 3450 lbs. Curb Weight.
[3] – Over 6000 lbs. GVWR.
[4] – Information not available.
[5] – M/T in F250 HD and F350.
[6] – E/F Series M/T and A/T. E350 A/T. Calif. "F" Series HD M/T.

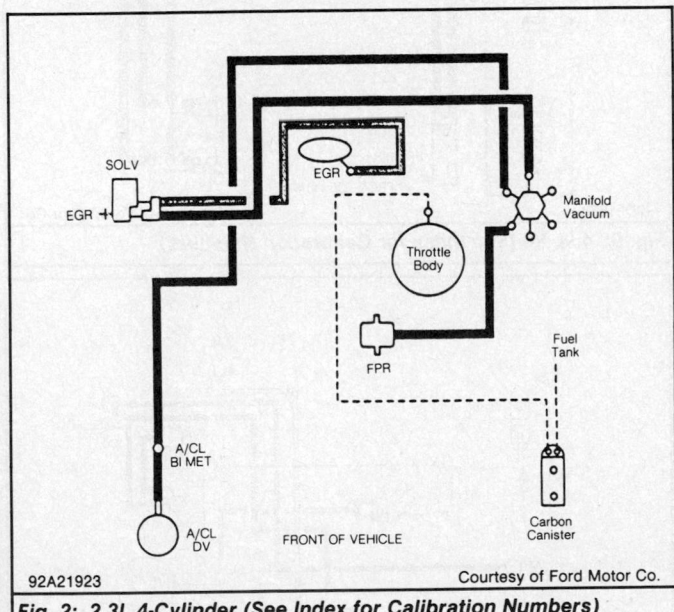

Fig. 2: 2.3L 4-Cylinder (See Index for Calibration Numbers)

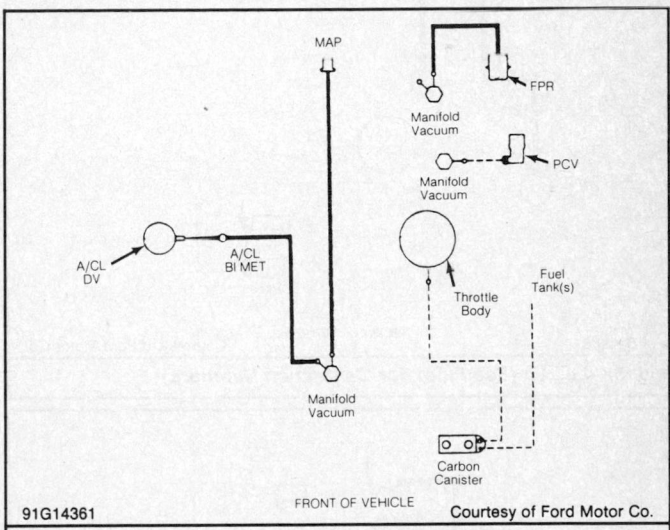

Fig. 3: 2.9L V6 (See Index for Calibration Numbers)

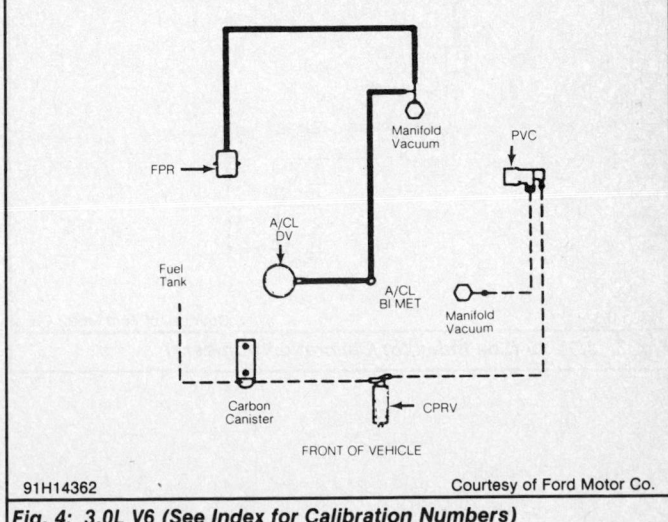

Fig. 4: 3.0L V6 (See Index for Calibration Numbers)

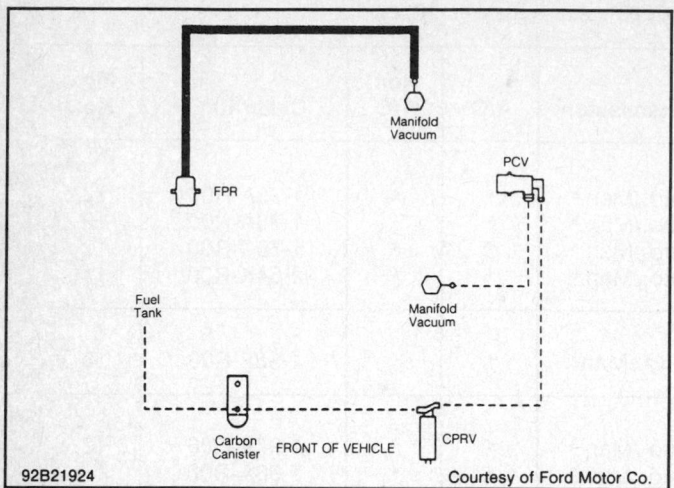

Fig. 5: 3.0L V6 (See Index for Calibration Numbers)

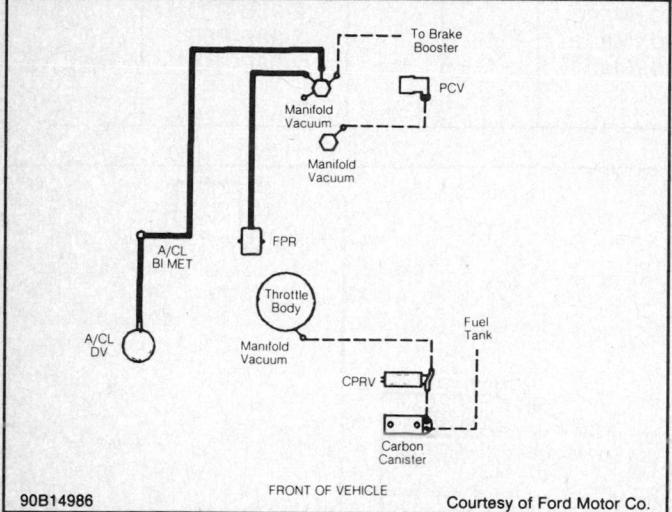

Fig. 6: 4.0L V6 (See Index for Calibration Numbers)

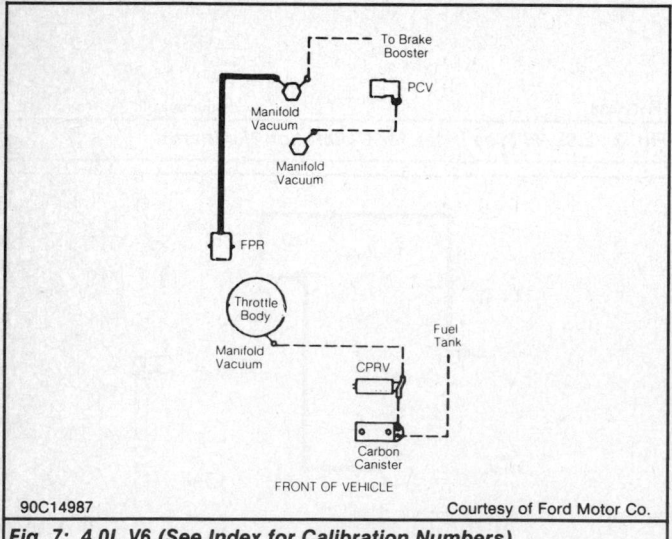

Fig. 7: 4.0L V6 (See Index for Calibration Numbers)

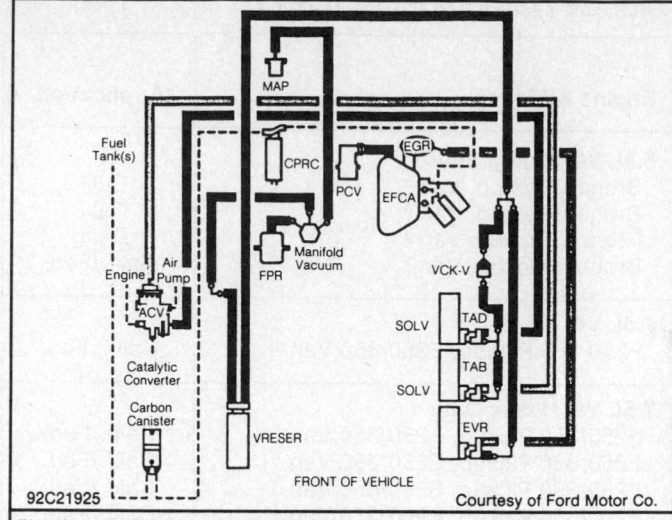

Fig. 8: 4.9L V6 (See Index for Calibration Numbers)

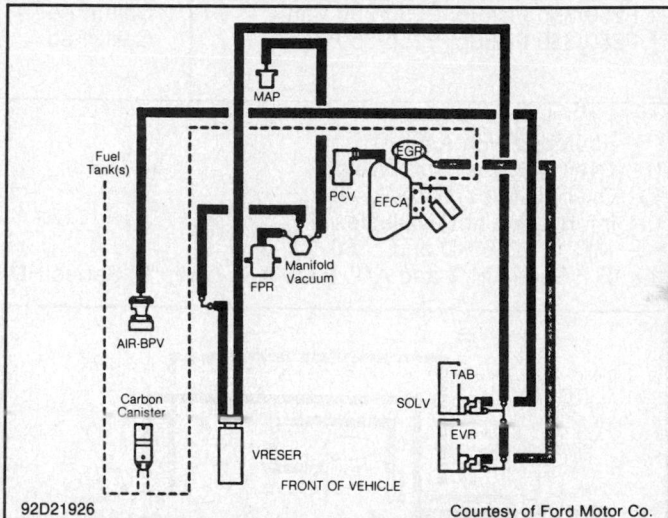

Fig. 9: 4.9L V6 (See Index for Calibration Numbers)

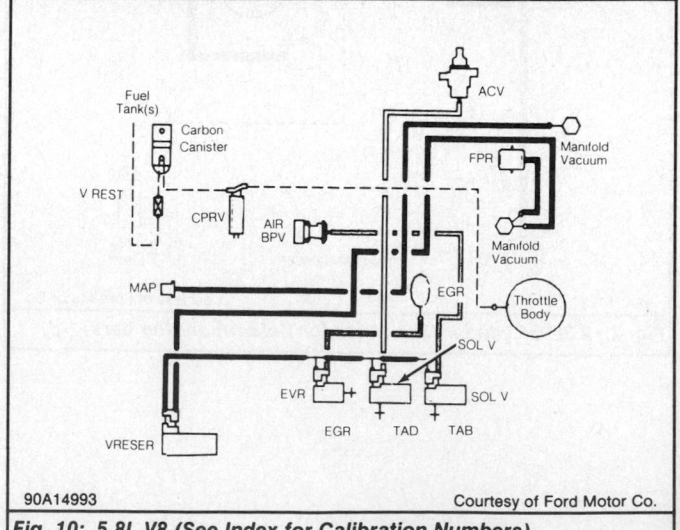

Fig. 10: 5.8L V8 (See Index for Calibration Numbers)

1992 ENGINE PERFORMANCE
Vacuum Diagrams (Cont.)

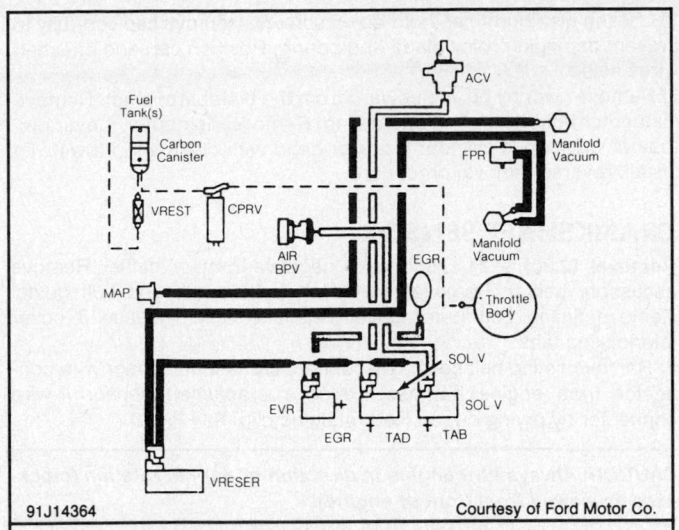

91J14364 Courtesy of Ford Motor Co.

Fig. 11: 5.8L V8 (See Index for Calibration Numbers)

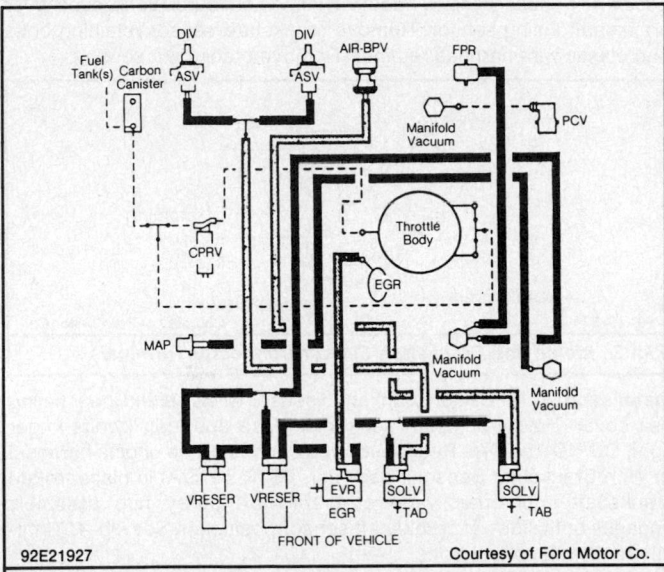

92E21927 Courtesy of Ford Motor Co.

Fig. 12: 5.8L V8 (See Index for Calibration Numbers)

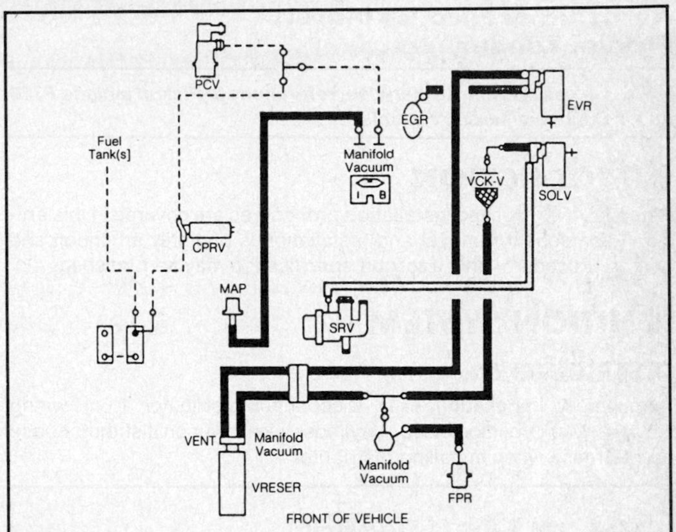

92G21929 Courtesy of Ford Motor Co.

Fig. 13: 7.5L V8 (See Index for Calibration Numbers)

EMISSION CONTROL DEVICE ABBREVIATIONS

A/CL-BI MET – Air Cleaner Bimetallic Sensor
A/CL-DV – Air Cleaner Duct Valve
ACV – Air Control Valve
AIR-BPV – Air By-Pass Valve
AIS – Air Injection System
AM1 – Thermactor Air Management 1 (TAB)
AM2 – Thermactor Air Management 2 (TAB or TAD)
ASV – Air Switching Valve
CAT – Catalytic Converter
CPRV – Canister Purge Regulator Valve
DIV – Diverter
EFCA – Electronic Fuel Control Assembly
EGR – Exhaust Gas Recirculation
EVR – Emission Vacuum Regulator
FPR – Fuel Pressure Regulator
MAP – Manifold Absolute Pressure
PCV – Positive Crankcase Ventilation
SOLV – Vacuum Solenoid Valve
SRV – AIS Solenoid Valve
TAB – Thermactor By-pass
TAD – Thermactor Diverter
TB – Throttle Body
VCK-V – Vacuum Check Valve
VRESER – Vacuum Reservoir
V-REST – Vacuum Restrictor

1992 ENGINE PERFORMANCE
Removal, Overhaul & Installation

Aerostar, Bronco, Explorer, Pickup, Ranger, Van

NOTE: Unless specified otherwise, references to Pickup include F350 Super Duty commercial chassis.

INTRODUCTION

Removal, overhaul and installation procedures are covered in this article. If component removal and installation is primarily an unbolt and bolt-on procedure, only a torque specification may be furnished.

IGNITION SYSTEM

DISTRIBUTOR

Removal & Installation – 1) Disconnect distributor from wiring harness. Mark position of No. 1 cylinder wire tower on distributor base for reference when installing distributor.

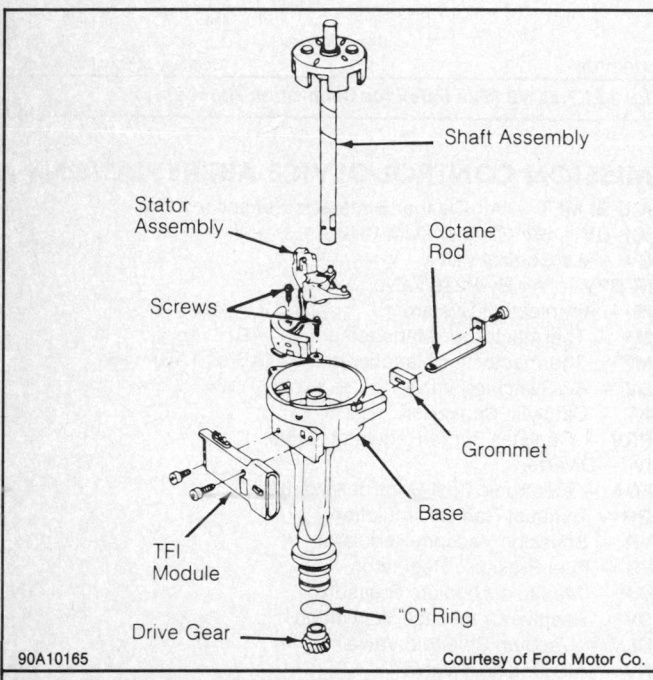

Fig. 1: Exploded View Of TFI-IV Open Bowl Distributor (2.9L, 4.9L, 5.0L & 5.8L)

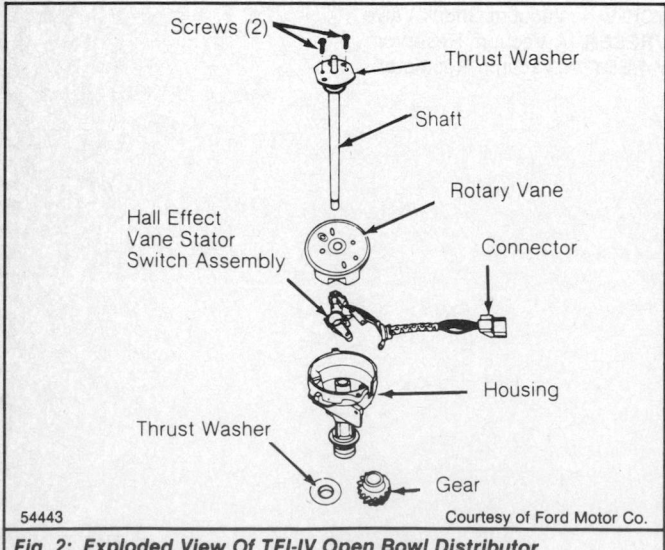

Fig. 2: Exploded View Of TFI-IV Open Bowl Distributor (3.0L & 7.5L)

2) Loosen distributor cap hold-down screws. Remove cap carefully to prevent damaging rotor blade and spring. Position cap and attached wires aside.

3) Remove rotor by pulling upward from the distributor shaft. Remove distributor hold-down bolt and clamp. Remove distributor. Cover distributor opening in cylinder block or head with clean shop towel. To install, reverse removal procedure.

CRANKSHAFT SENSOR

Removal (2.3L) – 1) Disconnect negative battery cable. Remove accessory belt(s). Remove crankshaft pulley, hub and belt guide. Remove timing belt outer cover retaining bolt. Release 8 cover interlocking tabs.

2) Remove timing belt cover. Disconnect crankshaft sensor wire connector from engine harness. Remove crankshaft sensor 4-wire connector by prying out on Red retaining clip. *See Fig. 3.*

CAUTION: Always turn engine in direction of normal rotation (clockwise as viewed from front of engine).

3) Rotate crankshaft and position crankshaft keyway at 10 o'clock position to place vane window of inner and outer vane cups over crankshaft timing sensor. Remove crankshaft sensor retaining bolts and plastic wire harness retainer. Remove crankshaft sensor.

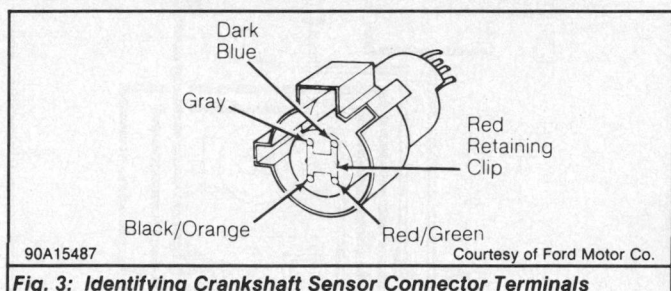

Fig. 3: Identifying Crankshaft Sensor Connector Terminals

Installation – 1) Position crankshaft sensor wires behind inner timing belt cover. Hold crankshaft sensor in place and install bolts finger tight. DO NOT tighten. Reconnect wire connectors to engine harness.

2) With Crankshaft Sensor Positioner (T89P-6316-A) in place, rotate crankshaft until outer vane of crankshaft pulley hub assembly engages both sides of crankshaft sensor positioner. *See Fig. 4.* Tighten crankshaft sensor bolts.

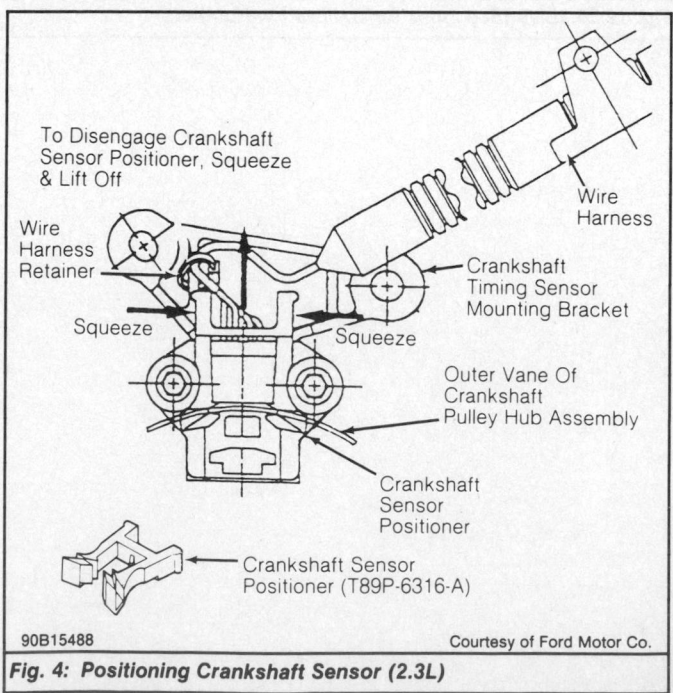

Fig. 4: Positioning Crankshaft Sensor (2.3L)

CAUTION: Always turn engine in direction of normal rotation (clockwise as viewed from front of engine).

3) Rotate crankshaft until vane on crankshaft pulley hub assembly is no longer engaged in crankshaft sensor positioner. Remove crankshaft sensor positioner. Install NEW plastic wire harness retainer and trim off excess.

4) Rotate crankshaft 90 degrees (1/4 turn) clockwise and measure outer vane-to-sensor air gap. Air gap must be .018-.039" (.46-1.0 mm). To complete installation, reverse removal procedure.

Removal (4.0L) – Disconnect negative battery cable. Disconnect crankshaft (variable reluctance) sensor wire connector from engine harness. Remove crankshaft sensor mounting screws. Remove crankshaft sensor. See Fig. 5.

Installation – Place crankshaft sensor in correct position. Install mounting screws and tighten. Reconnect crankshaft sensor wire connector.

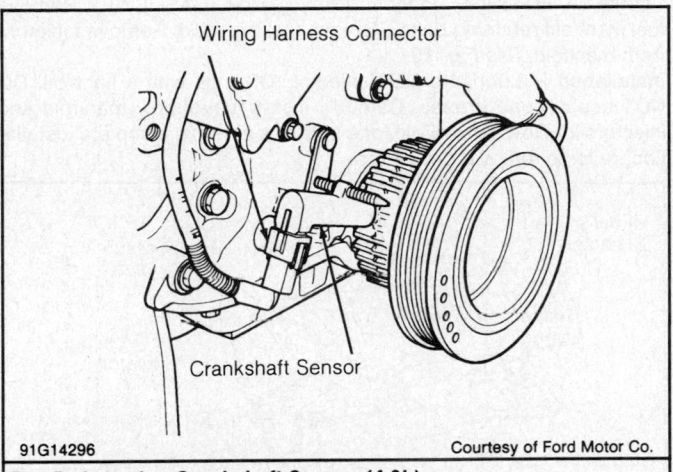

Fig. 5: Locating Crankshaft Sensor (4.0L)

FUEL SYSTEM (GASOLINE)

FUEL PRESSURE RELEASE

WARNING: ALWAYS relieve fuel pressure before disconnecting any fuel injection-related component. DO NOT allow fuel to contact engine or electrical components.

Disconnect negative battery cable. Remove fuel cap to release fuel tank pressure. Using EFI Pressure Gauge (T80L-9974-B), release fuel pressure from relief valve. Relief valve is located on fuel supply manifold.

FUEL PUMP

Removal (Except Van) – Release fuel pressure. See FUEL PRESSURE RELEASE under FUEL SYSTEM (GASOLINE). Remove fuel tank. Using hammer and brass drift punch, carefully tap lock ring counterclockwise to release pump. Remove fuel pump from tank.

Installation – Wipe seal area of tank clean. Position a new "O" ring seal on pump. Position fuel pump in tank so fuel return hose is not kinked. Install lock ring. Using hammer and brass drift punch, drive ring around clockwise to lock pump in place. DO NOT overtighten pump lock ring, as it may leak. Install fuel tank.

Removal & Installation (Van – High Pressure Fuel Pump) – Release fuel pressure. See FUEL PRESSURE RELEASE under FUEL SYSTEM (GASOLINE). Locate fuel pump on left rail. Remove fuel pump bracket attaching screws. Remove fuel pump hoses. Remove fuel pump from bracket. See Fig. 6. To install, reverse removal procedure.

Removal & Installation (Van – Low Pressure Fuel Pump) – Van low pressure (boost) fuel pump is located inside the fuel tank. Removal and installation procedures are the same as removal and installation procedures for Aerostar, Bronco, Explorer, Pickup and Ranger.

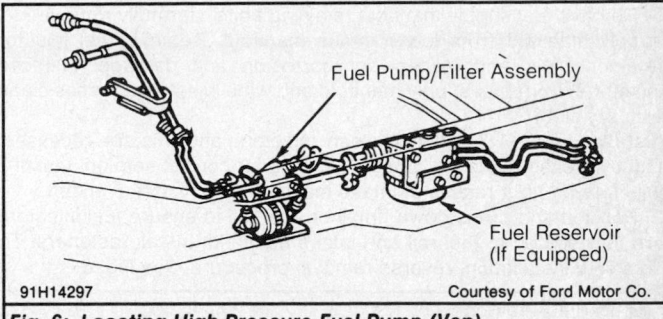

Fig. 6: Locating High Pressure Fuel Pump (Van)

FUEL SUPPLY MANIFOLD ASSEMBLY

Removal (2.3L) – **1)** Release fuel pressure. See FUEL PRESSURE RELEASE under FUEL SYSTEM (GASOLINE). Disconnect fuel supply and return lines. See PUSH-CONNECT FITTINGS under FUEL SYSTEM (GASOLINE).

2) Remove upper intake manifold and throttle body assembly. See UPPER INTAKE MANIFOLD & THROTTLE BODY under FUEL SYSTEM (GASOLINE). Disconnect wiring harness from injectors. Remove fuel supply manifold retaining bolts. Carefully disengage manifold and fuel injectors from engine. Remove manifold and injectors. See Fig. 7.

Installation – **1)** To install, reverse removal procedure. Lubricate NEW "O" rings with a light oil. Install 2 "O" rings on each injector (one per injector if injectors were not removed from fuel supply manifold). DO NOT use silicone grease.

2) Install fuel injector supply manifold and injectors in intake manifold; ensure injectors are seated. Secure fuel manifold assembly with retaining bolts. Connect injector wiring harness.

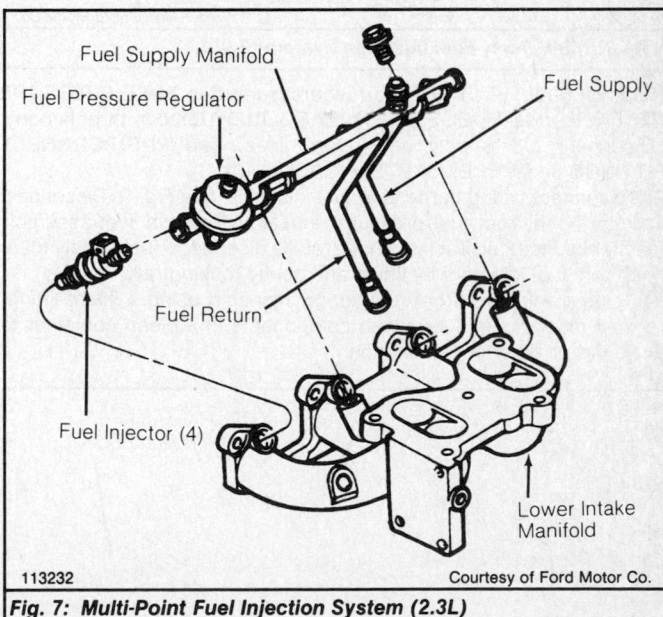

Fig. 7: Multi-Point Fuel Injection System (2.3L)

Removal (2.9L) – **1)** Disconnect negative battery cable. Remove air inlet tube from air cleaner to throttle body. Release fuel pressure. See FUEL PRESSURE RELEASE under FUEL SYSTEM (GASOLINE).

NOTE: Ensure engine is clean before removing fuel supply manifold assembly.

2) Remove upper intake manifold and throttle body assembly. See UPPER INTAKE MANIFOLD & THROTTLE BODY under FUEL SYSTEM (GASOLINE). Disconnect crossover fuel hose, fuel supply, and fuel return line from fuel supply manifold. See PUSH-CONNECT FITTINGS under FUEL SYSTEM (GASOLINE).

3) Remove fuel supply manifold retaining bolts. Carefully remove fuel supply manifold from lower intake manifold. Remove fuel injector retainer clips, and inspect for corrosion and damage. Remove injector(s) from fuel supply manifold and wipe injector recesses clean with dry cloth.

Installation – 1) To install, clean injectors and injector recesses. Lightly grease recesses. Check "O" rings for correct seating. Install 3 injectors on right recess of intake manifold, then install 3 on left.

2) Position and press down firmly on fuel rail to ensure fuel injectors are fully seated in fuel rail and intake manifold. Install fasteners. To complete installation, reverse removal procedure. *See Fig. 8.*

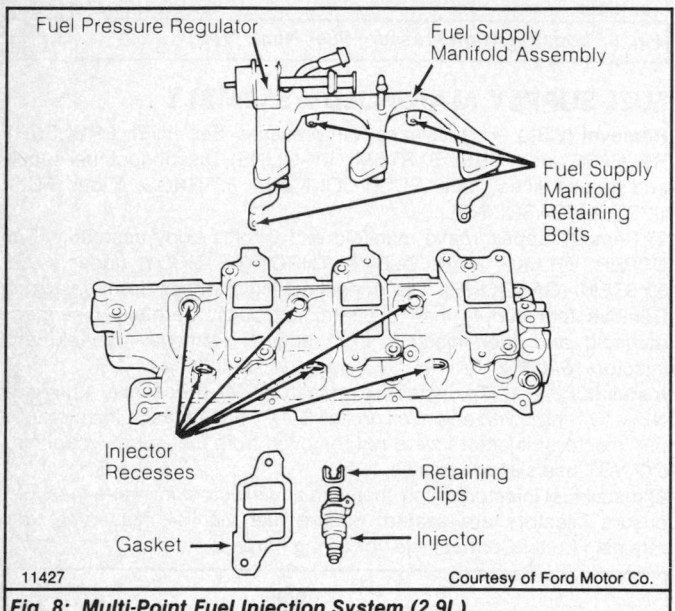

Fig. 8: Multi-Point Fuel Injection System (2.9L)

Removal (3.0L) – 1) Release fuel pressure. See FUEL PRESSURE RELEASE under FUEL SYSTEM (GASOLINE). Remove throttle body. Disconnect fuel supply and return lines. See PUSH-CONNECT FITTINGS under FUEL SYSTEM (GASOLINE).

2) Disconnect wiring harness at fuel injectors. *See Fig. 9.* Disconnect vacuum hose from fuel pressure regulator. Remove fuel assembly manifold bolts (2 on each side). Carefully disengage fuel supply manifold from fuel injectors by lifting and gently rocking rail.

3) Remove injectors from fuel supply manifold using a slight lifting/rocking motion. Place removed components in a clean container to avoid dirt or other contamination.

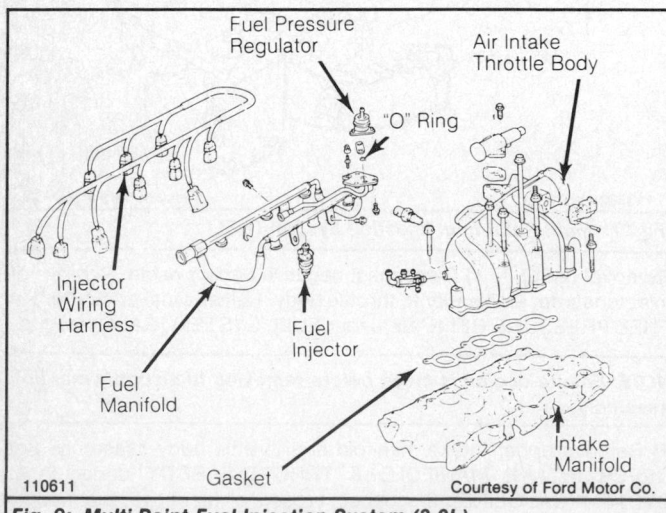

Fig. 9: Multi-Point Fuel Injection System (3.0L)

Installation – Lubricate NEW injector "O" rings with a light oil. DO NOT use silicone grease. Carefully install fuel supply manifold and injectors into lower manifold, one side at a time. To complete installation, reverse removal procedure.

Removal (4.0L) – 1) Disconnect negative battery cable. Remove snow/ice shield. Remove air inlet tube from air cleaner to throttle body. Release fuel pressure. See FUEL PRESSURE RELEASE under FUEL SYSTEM (GASOLINE).

NOTE: Ensure engine is clean before removing fuel supply manifold assembly.

---

2) Remove upper intake manifold and throttle body assembly. See UPPER INTAKE MANIFOLD & THROTTLE BODY under FUEL SYSTEM (GASOLINE). Disconnect fuel supply line fitting at fuel manifold.

3) Disconnect fuel return line from fuel pressure regulator. See PUSH-CONNECT FITTINGS under FUEL SYSTEM (GASOLINE). Remove fuel manifold retaining bolts. Remove fuel manifold. Remove injectors from manifold. *See Fig. 10.*

Installation – Lubricate NEW injector "O" rings with a light oil. DO NOT use silicone grease. Carefully install fuel supply manifold and injectors into lower manifold, one side at a time. To complete installation, reverse removal procedure.

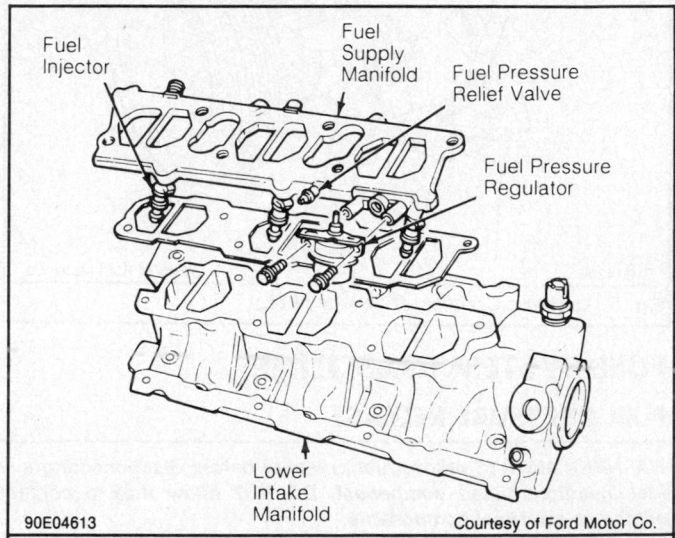

Fig. 10: Multi-Point Fuel Injection System (4.0L)

Removal & Installation (4.9L) – 1) Disconnect negative battery cable. Release fuel pressure. See FUEL PRESSURE RELEASE under FUEL SYSTEM (GASOLINE). Remove upper intake manifold assembly. See UPPER INTAKE MANIFOLD & THROTTLE BODY under FUEL SYSTEM (GASOLINE). Disconnect fuel supply and fuel return lines. See PUSH-CONNECT FITTINGS under FUEL SYSTEM (GASOLINE).

2) Disconnect vacuum hose from fuel pressure regulator. Remove strap surrounding fuel supply manifold, injector electrical harness, and main vacuum harness.

3) Remove fuel supply manifold retaining studs. Carefully disengage fuel supply manifold from fuel injectors, and remove manifold. To install, reverse removal procedure. Ensure injectors are well seated in manifold assembly.

Removal & Installation (5.0L, 5.8L & 7.5L) – 1) Disconnect negative battery cable. Release fuel pressure. See FUEL PRESSURE RELEASE under FUEL SYSTEM (GASOLINE). Remove upper intake manifold and throttle body assembly. See UPPER INTAKE MANIFOLD & THROTTLE BODY under FUEL SYSTEM (GASOLINE).

2) Disconnect fuel supply and return line connections at fuel supply manifold. See PUSH-CONNECT FITTINGS under FUEL SYSTEM (GASOLINE). Remove fuel supply manifold retaining bolts. Carefully disengage fuel supply manifold from fuel injectors. To install, reverse removal procedure. *See Figs. 11 and 12.*

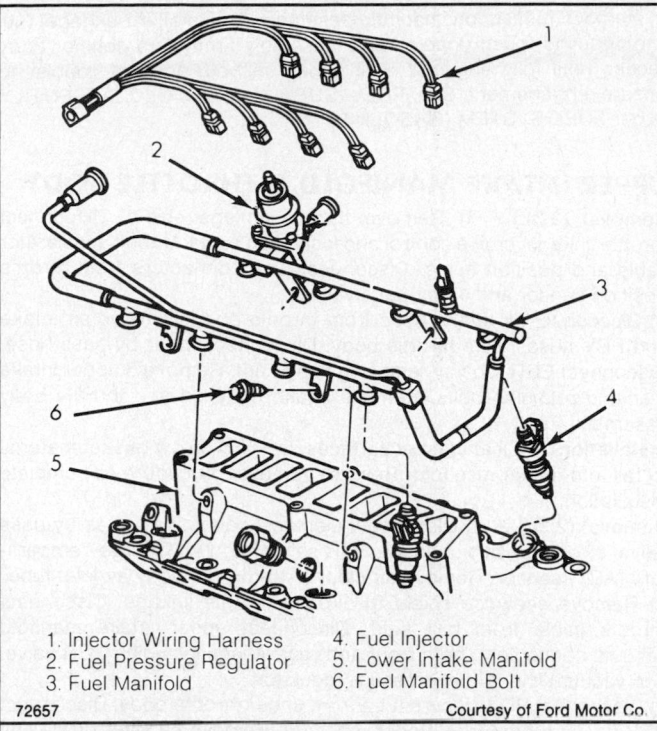

1. Injector Wiring Harness
2. Fuel Pressure Regulator
3. Fuel Manifold
4. Fuel Injector
5. Lower Intake Manifold
6. Fuel Manifold Bolt

72657   Courtesy of Ford Motor Co.

Fig. 11: Multi-Point Fuel Injection System (5.0L & 5.8L)

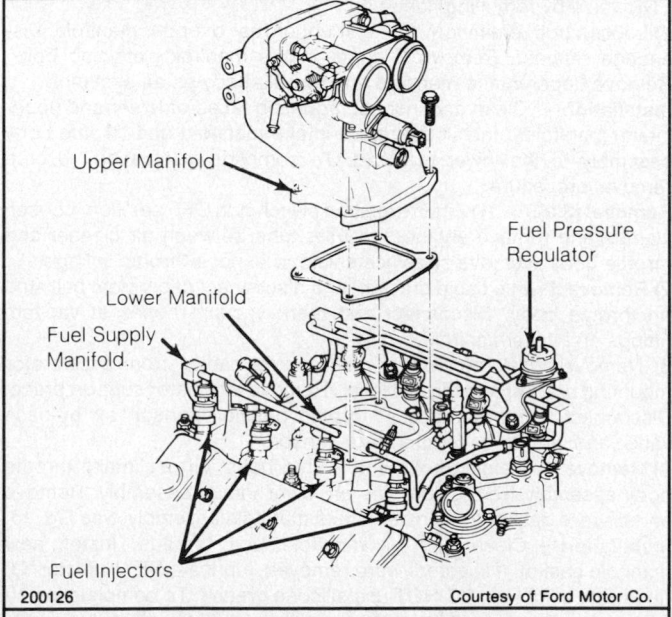

Upper Manifold

Lower Manifold

Fuel Supply Manifold.

Fuel Pressure Regulator

Fuel Injectors

200126   Courtesy of Ford Motor Co.

Fig. 12: Multi-Point Fuel Injection System (7.5L)

FUEL INJECTORS

Removal (2.3L & 3.0L) – 1) Release fuel pressure. See FUEL PRESSURE RELEASE under FUEL SYSTEM (GASOLINE). Disconnect wiring harness from each injector.

2) Remove fuel supply manifold. See FUEL SUPPLY MANIFOLD ASSEMBLY under FUEL SYSTEM (GASOLINE). Remove injectors from fuel supply manifold using a rocking/pulling motion.

Installation – Lubricate NEW injector "O" rings with a light oil. DO NOT use silicone grease. To complete installation, reverse removal procedure.

Removal (2.9L & 4.0L) – 1) Release fuel pressure. See FUEL PRESSURE RELEASE under FUEL SYSTEM (GASOLINE). Remove upper intake manifold and throttle body assembly. See UPPER INTAKE MANIFOLD & THROTTLE BODY under FUEL SYSTEM (GASOLINE).

2) Remove fuel supply manifold. See FUEL SUPPLY MANIFOLD ASSEMBLY under FUEL SYSTEM (GASOLINE). Remove wiring harness from injector(s). Remove injector retaining clips(s). Remove injectors from fuel supply manifold using a rocking/pulling motion.

Installation – Lubricate NEW injector "O" rings with a light oil. DO NOT use silicone grease. To complete installation, reverse removal procedure.

Removal (4.9L, 5.0L, 5.8L & 7.5L) – 1) Disconnect negative battery cable. Release fuel pressure. See FUEL PRESSURE RELEASE under FUEL SYSTEM (GASOLINE). Remove upper intake manifold assembly. See UPPER INTAKE MANIFOLD & THROTTLE BODY under FUEL SYSTEM (GASOLINE).

2) Carefully disconnect electrical lead(s) from injector(s). Remove injector(s) from fuel supply manifold using a slight rocking/pulling motion.

Installation – Lubricate NEW injector "O" rings with a light oil. DO NOT use silicone grease. To complete installation, reverse removal procedure.

FUEL PRESSURE REGULATOR

Removal (2.3L, 2.9L 3.0L & 4.0L) – 1) Disconnect negative battery cable. Release fuel pressure. See FUEL PRESSURE RELEASE under FUEL SYSTEM (GASOLINE). Remove vacuum hose at fuel pressure regulator. Remove fuel line.

2) On 3.0L models, loosen or remove fuel rail-to-intake manifold bolts for access to regulator housing screws. On all models, remove screws from regulator housing. Remove pressure regulator, gasket, and "O" ring.

Installation – Lubricate "O" ring with a light oil. DO NOT use silicone grease. Ensure regulator and manifold gasket surfaces are clean and dry. To complete installation, reverse removal procedure.

Removal (4.9L, 5.0L, 5.8L & 7.5L) – 1) Disconnect negative battery cable. Release fuel pressure. See FUEL PRESSURE RELEASE under FUEL SYSTEM (GASOLINE).

2) Remove vacuum hose from fuel pressure regulator. Remove Allen head screws from fuel pressure regulator housing. Remove fuel pressure regulator, gasket, and "O" ring.

Installation – Lubricate "O" ring with a light oil. DO NOT use silicone grease. Ensure regulator and manifold gasket surfaces are clean and dry. To complete installation, reverse removal procedure.

HEATED EXHAUST GAS OXYGEN (HEGO) SENSOR

Removal – 1) Disconnect negative battery cable. locate O_2 sensor mounted in the exhaust pipe below exhaust manifold or "Y" pipe junction, near catalytic converter inlet. Ensure sensor is free of contaminants. DO NOT use cleaning solvents of any type.

2) Disconnect electrical connector from O_2 sensor. Sensor may be difficult to remove when engine temperature is less than 120°F (48°C). Carefully remove O_2 sensor from exhaust pipe.

Installation – Whenever replacing O_2 sensor, coat threads with anti-seize compound before installation. New O_2 sensors should already have this compound applied to threads. Install O_2 sensor. Reconnect electrical connector to O_2 sensor. Tighten sensor to **30 ft. lbs. (41 N.m)**. Reconnect negative battery terminal.

PUSH-CONNECT FITTINGS

Removal & Installation (3/8", 1/2" & 5/8" Spring Lock Coupling) – 1) Release fuel pressure. See FUEL PRESSURE RELEASE under FUEL SYSTEM (GASOLINE). Place indicated spring lock coupler over coupling. See SPRING LOCK COUPLER IDENTIFICATION table. To release female fitting from garter spring, push coupler along tube into coupling. See Fig. 13.

2) Pull spring lock coupling apart. Remove coupler from disconnected spring lock coupling. Check for damaged garter spring and "O" rings. Wipe end of lines with clean cloth.

3) To install, place NEW "O" rings onto tube. Lubricate ends of lines with clean refrigerant oil. Locate White indicator ring (if equipped) which may have slipped down length of tube. Insert White indicator ring into cage of male fitting.

4) Push fitting together with a slight twisting motion. The White indicator ring should pop free of cage to indicate that male fitting is properly seated over flared end of female fitting.

SPRING LOCK COUPLER IDENTIFICATION

Application	Tool Number
3/8" Line	D87L-9280-A
1/2" Line	D87L-9280-B
5/8" Line	T83P-19623-C

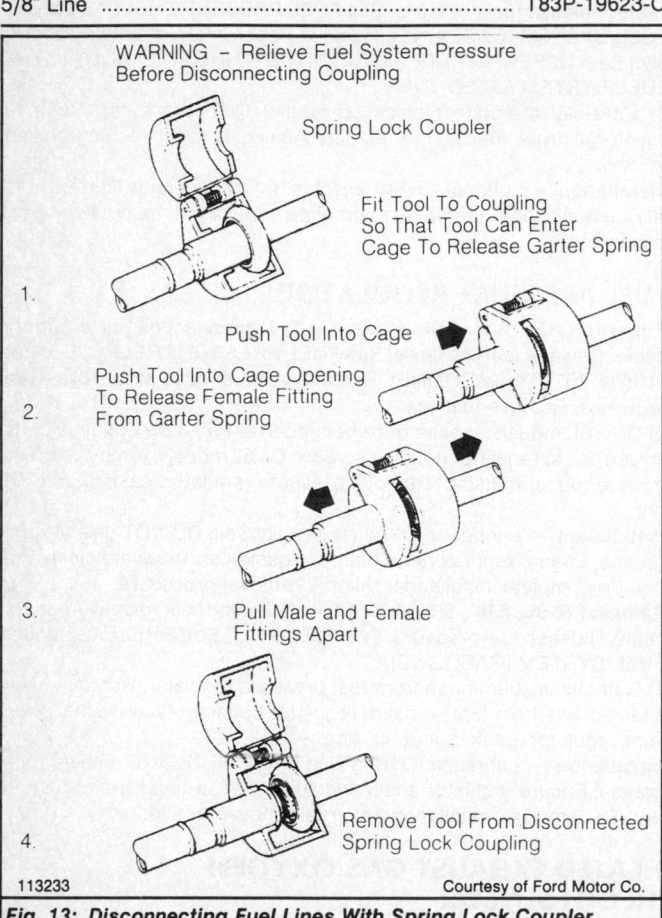

WARNING – Relieve Fuel System Pressure Before Disconnecting Coupling

Spring Lock Coupler

Fit Tool To Coupling So That Tool Can Enter Cage To Release Garter Spring

1.

Push Tool Into Cage

Push Tool Into Cage Opening To Release Female Fitting From Garter Spring

2.

3. Pull Male and Female Fittings Apart

4. Remove Tool From Disconnected Spring Lock Coupling

113233   Courtesy of Ford Motor Co.

Fig. 13: Disconnecting Fuel Lines With Spring Lock Coupler

Removal & Installation (Fuel Line Coupler) – **1)** Disengage locking tabs on connector retainer and separate retainer halves. Disengage fitting from regulator by pushing fitting toward regulator and inserting Fuel Line Coupling Key (T90P-9550-A). See Fig. 14.

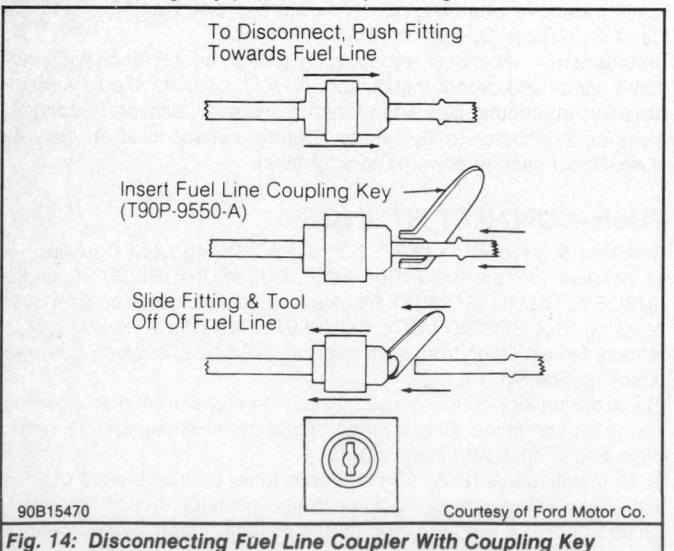

To Disconnect, Push Fitting Towards Fuel Line

Insert Fuel Line Coupling Key (T90P-9550-A)

Slide Fitting & Tool Off Of Fuel Line

90B15470   Courtesy of Ford Motor Co.

Fig. 14: Disconnecting Fuel Line Coupler With Coupling Key

2) Remove fuel supply manifold assembly. To install (re-engage) fuel line coupling, push coupler tube assembly firmly into coupler body recess until fully engaged. Pull gently on both ends of coupler to ensure engagement See FUEL SUPPLY MANIFOLD ASSEMBLY under FUEL SYSTEM (GASOLINE).

UPPER INTAKE MANIFOLD & THROTTLE BODY

Removal (2.3L) – **1)** Remove throttle linkage shield. Disconnect throttle linkage, cruise control and kickdown cable. Unbolt accelerator cable and position aside. Disconnect wire connectors from throttle position sensor and air by-pass valve.

2) Disconnect air intake hose from throttle body. Remove air intake and PCV hoses from throttle body. Disconnect water by-pass hose. Disconnect EGR tube by removing flange nut. Remove 5 upper intake manifold retaining bolts. Remove intake manifold and throttle body assembly.

Installation – Clean gasket surfaces. DO NOT allow gasket material to fall into intake manifold. Reverse removal procedure to complete installation.

Removal (2.9L) – **1)** Disconnect electrical connectors at air by-pass valve, throttle position sensor, EGR sensor and Air Charge Temperature (ACT) sensor. Remove air cleaner-to-throttle body air inlet tube.

2) Remove snow/ice shield to expose throttle linkage. Disconnect throttle cable from ball stud. Disconnect upper intake manifold vacuum connectors, both front and rear fittings including EGR valve, and vacuum line to fuel pressure regulator.

3) Disconnect PCV closure tube from under throttle body. Disconnect PCV vacuum tube from under manifold. Remove canister purge line from fitting near power steering pump. Disconnect EGR tube from EGR valve by removing flange nut.

4) Loosen bolt retaining A/C line at upper rear of upper manifold. Disengage retainer. Remove 6 upper intake manifold retaining bolts. Remove upper intake manifold and throttle body as an assembly.

Installation – Clean and inspect mounting faces of lower and upper intake manifolds. Install the upper intake manifold and throttle body assembly to the lower manifold. To complete installation, reverse removal procedure.

Removal (3.0L) – **1)** Ensure ignition switch is in OFF position. Loosen clamps and remove engine air outlet tube between air cleaner and throttle body. Remove snow/ice shield to expose throttle linkage.

2) Remove throttle cable bracket, and disconnect cable from ball stud on throttle body. Disconnect and mark vacuum hoses at vacuum fittings on intake manifold.

3) Remove accelerator and cruise control cables from accelerator mounting bracket and throttle lever. Remove alternator support brace. Disconnect wiring harness at throttle position sensor, air by-pass valve, and air charge temperature sensor.

4) Remove 4 retaining bolts and 2 stud bolts. Lift air intake throttle body assembly from guide pins on lower intake assembly. Remove and discard gasket from lower intake manifold assembly. See Fig. 15.

Installation – Clean and oil manifold bolt threads. Install new manifold gasket. If injectors were removed, lubricate NEW injector "O" rings with a light oil. DO NOT use silicone grease. To complete installation, reverse removal procedure.

Removal (4.0L) – **1)** Disconnect electrical connectors at air by-pass valve, throttle position sensor and air charge temperature sensor. Remove snow/ice shield to expose throttle linkage. Remove throttle cable bracket.

2) Disconnect cable from ball stud on throttle body. Remove air cleaner-to-throttle body air inlet tube. Disconnect upper intake manifold vacuum connectors. Disconnect PCV valve from rocker cover.

3) Disconnect spark plug wires at rear of manifold. Remove canister purge line from fitting in throttle housing. On Aerostar, remove bolt retaining engine oil dipstick tube.

4) On all models, remove A/C line-to-upper upper manifold bolt. Remove 6 upper manifold retaining bolts. Remove upper intake and throttle body, as an assembly, from lower intake and fuel supply manifolds. See Fig. 16.

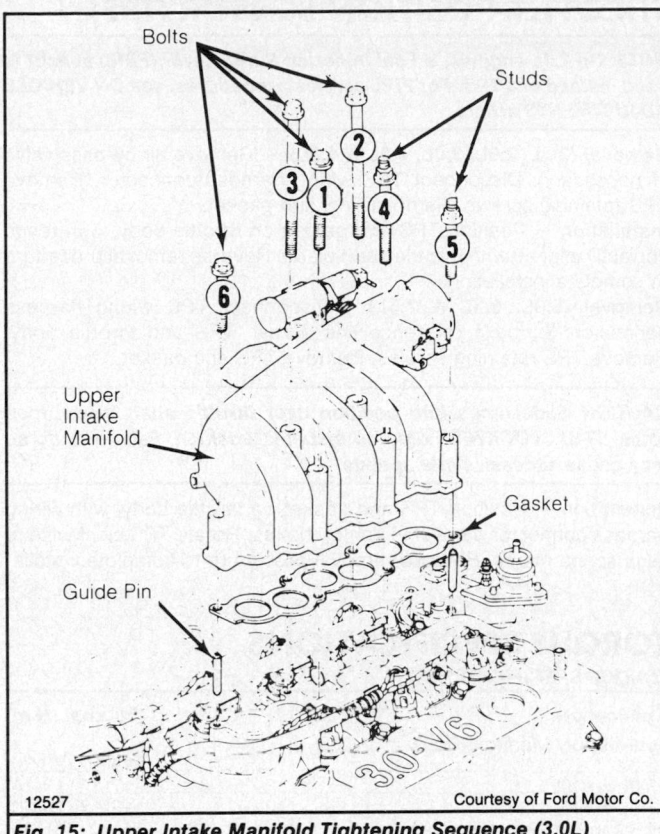

Fig. 15: Upper Intake Manifold Tightening Sequence (3.0L)

Installation – Clean and oil manifold bolt threads. Install NEW manifold gasket. If injectors were removed, lubricate NEW injector "O" rings with a light oil. DO NOT use silicone grease. To complete installation, reverse removal procedure.

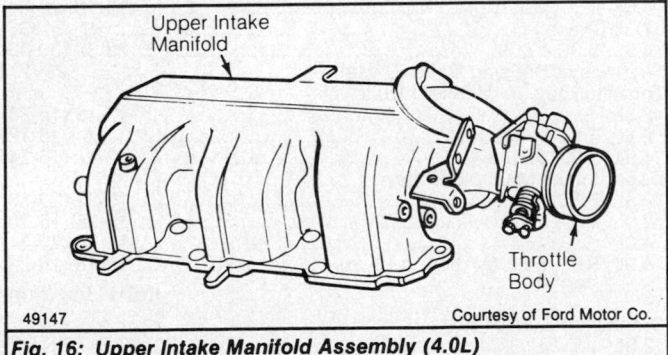

Fig. 16: Upper Intake Manifold Assembly (4.0L)

Removal (4.9L) – **1)** Disconnect electrical connectors at EGR Valve Positioner (EVP) sensor located on EGR valve. Disconnect throttle position sensor and air by-pass valve. Label and disconnect all vacuum hoses connected to upper intake manifold and throttle body assembly.
2) Disconnect PCV hose from fitting located on side of intake manifold. See Fig. 17. Remove throttle linkage shield. Disconnect throttle linkage and cruise control cables. Disconnect accelerator cable from bracket and position cable aside.
3) Disconnect air inlet hoses from throttle body. Disconnect EGR tube from EGR valve and exhaust manifold. Remove thermactor (air injection) tube assembly from lower intake manifold.
4) Remove nut attaching thermactor by-pass valve bracket to lower intake manifold. On van, remove nut attaching transmission filler tube. Remove tube bracket from intake manifold stud.
5) On all models, remove 7 studs retaining upper intake manifold. Remove screw and washer attaching upper intake manifold support

bracket to intake manifold. Remove upper intake manifold and throttle body as an assembly.
Installation – To install, reverse removal procedure. Use NEW gasket between upper and lower intake manifolds.

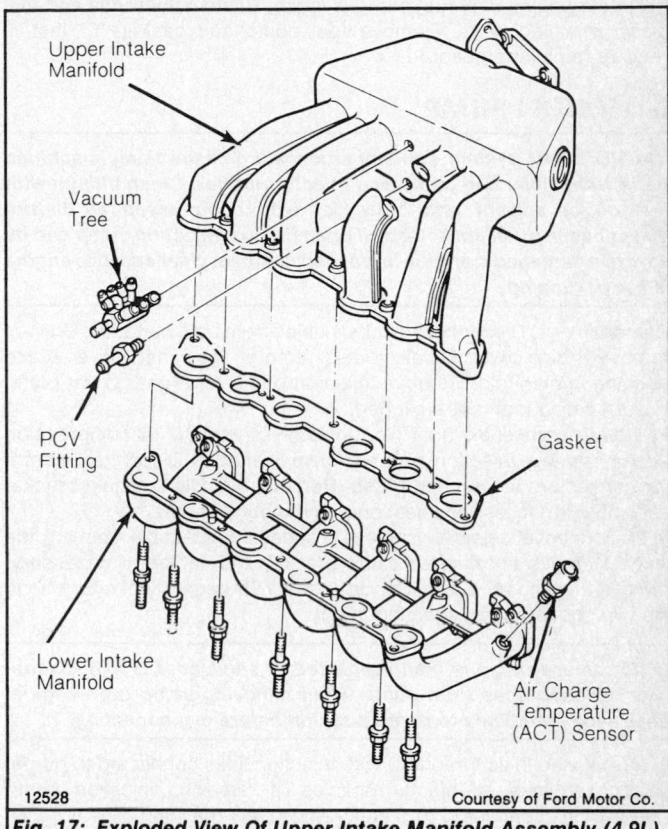

Fig. 17: Exploded View Of Upper Intake Manifold Assembly (4.9L)

Removal (5.0L, 5.8L & 7.5L) – **1)** Disconnect electrical leads at air by-pass valve, throttle position sensor, and EGR position sensor. Disconnect throttle linkage at pivot ball. On 5.0L A/T models, remove transmission linkage from throttle body.
2) On all models, remove bracket-to-intake manifold bolts. Position bracket and cables out of way. Remove vacuum hoses at upper intake manifold vacuum tee, EGR valve, and fuel pressure regulator.
3) Disconnect PCV system by removing hose from fitting on rear of upper intake manifold. Remove 2 canister purge lines from fitting on throttle body. Disconnect heater hoses from throttle body.
4) Disconnect EGR tube from EGR valve. Remove upper intake manifold support bracket. Remove manifold retaining bolts. Remove upper intake manifold and throttle body as an assembly.
Installation – To install, reverse removal procedure. Use NEW gasket between upper and lower intake manifolds.

FUEL SYSTEM (DIESEL)

FUEL INJECTION LINES

Removal – **1)** Clean nozzle and surrounding area. Disconnect negative battery terminal. On van, remove engine cover. On all models, disconnect air cleaner.
2) Disconnect accelerator cable and bracket from intake manifold. Disconnect fuel filter-to-injection pump fuel line. Remove fuel filter-to-injection pump fuel line. Remove fuel line caps. Remove fuel line clamps from fuel lines to be removed.
3) Remove injection pump inlet elbow and inlet fitting adaptor. Remove injection nozzle lines from injection pump using Fuel Line Nut Wrench (T83T-9396-A). Tag lines for reassembly reference. Cap all openings.
Installation – Remove caps and install injection lines. Ensure lines are properly positioned. Reverse removal procedure to complete installation. Start engine and check for leaks.

FUEL PUMP

Removal & Installation – 1) Loosen but DO NOT remove fuel lines and fuel pump retaining bolts. Fuel pump should be loose. If fuel pump is not loose, apply hand pressure to break gasket seal.
2) Rotate engine until fuel pump is loose. Remove fuel lines and fuel pump retaining bolts. Remove fuel pump and gasket. To install, reverse removal procedure.

INJECTION PUMP

CAUTION: Fuel system contamination will damage finely machined parts within injection pump and injector nozzles. Clean fittings with fuel oil or solvent and blow dry with compressed air before disconnecting fuel lines. Cap all open fittings. Injection pump can be severely damaged if engine is washed or steam cleaned while engine is hot or running.

Removal – 1) Disconnect ground cables from both batteries. On van, remove engine cover. On all models, remove air cleaner. Cover intake opening in manifold. Remove injection pump drive gear cover plate. Ensure timing marks are aligned.
2) Rotate crankshaft until No. 1 piston is at TDC of compression stroke. Remove injection pump-to-drive gear bolts. Disconnect electrical connectors at injection pump. Remove fast idle solenoid bracket assembly for access to injection pump mounting nuts.
3) Disconnect accelerator cable and speed control cable from throttle lever. Remove accelerator cable bracket and cables. If necessary, remove fuel filter and bracket. Disconnect 90-degree fuel return hose elbow at governor on injection pump.

NOTE: Unless pump is being replaced or serviced, DO NOT disconnect injection lines from pump when removing pump from engine. Reference mark lines-to-pump position before disconnecting.

4) If removing injection pump with injection lines connected to pump, disconnect lines at injector nozzles. If removing injection pump without lines connected to pump, remove line retaining clips.
5) Disconnect lines from pump using Fuel Line Nut Wrench (T83T-9396-A). Remove injection lines in the following sequence: 5-6-4-8-3-1-7-2. Odd number cylinders are on right bank, with No. 1 cylinder closest to front of engine.

CAUTION: Ensure No. 1 piston is at TDC of compression stroke before removing injector pump. Pulley "Y" marks should be aligned.

6) On all applications, remove 3 injection pump-to-injection pump drive gear cover nuts using Injection Pump Mounting Wrench (T86T-9000-C). On Pickup, lift injection pump (or pump with lines connected) out of engine compartment. On Van, remove injection pump (or pump with lines attached) through passenger compartment.
Installation – 1) Install NEW "O" ring on injection pump drive gear end. Install pump into position, aligning dowel on pump drive shaft with hole in drive gear. If necessary, rotate pump drive shaft to align dowel with hole.
2) Install and hand tighten 3 injection pump-to-drive gear cover nuts. Align timing mark on top radius of injection pump with mark on injection pump drive gear cover. To complete installation, reverse removal procedure.

THROTTLE POSITION SENSOR (TPS)

NOTE: On 7.3L engines, a Fuel Injection Pump Lever (FIPL) sensor is used instead of a TPS. For FIPL service procedures, see ON-VEHICLE ADJUSTMENTS article.

Removal (2.3L, 2.9L, 3.0L, 4.0L & 4.9L) – Remove air by-pass valve (if necessary). Disconnect TPS wiring harness connector. Remove TPS retaining screws. Remove TPS and gasket.
Installation – Position TPS and gasket on throttle body, with tangs correctly aligned with throttle shaft blade. Reverse removal procedure to complete installation.
Removal (5.0L, 5.8L & 7.5L) – Disconnect TPS wiring harness connector. Scribe a reference line across TPS and throttle body. Remove TPS retaining screws. Remove TPS and gasket.

CAUTION: Slide tangs into position over throttle shaft blade, then rotate TPS, CLOCKWISE only, to installed position. Failure to do so may cause excessive idle speeds.

Installation – Position TPS and gasket on throttle body, with wiring harness connector parallel to venturi boxes. Rotate TPS clockwise to align scribe marks. Reverse removal procedure to complete installation.

TORQUE SPECIFICATIONS
TORQUE SPECIFICATIONS

Application	Ft. Lbs. (N.m)
Fuel Supply Manifold Bolts	
2.3L	15-22 (20-30)
3.0L & 4.0L	7-10 (10-14)
4.9L & 5.0L	12-15 (16-20)
Injection Line Fittings (Diesel)	22 (30)
Injection Pump Gear Cover Bolts (Diesel)	14 (19)
Injection Pump Gear Mounting Bolts (Diesel)	25 (34)
Lower Intake Manifold Bolts	
2.3L & 7.5L	15-22 (20-30)
2.9L	11-15 (15-20)
3.0L	24 (32)
4.0L	15-18 (20-24)
7.3L (Diesel)	24 (33)
4.9L, 5.0L & 5.8L	22-32 (30-43)
Thermostat Housing Bolts (Diesel)	120 (27)
Throttle Body-To-Manifold Bolts	
2.3L	12-18 (16-24)
2.9L, 3.0L & 4.0L	6-9 (8-12)
4.9L, 5.0L, 5.8L & 7.5L	12-18 (16-24)
Upper Intake Manifold Bolts	
2.3L & 3.0L	15-22 (20-30)
2.9L	11-15 (15-20)
4.0L	15-18 (20-24)
4.9L, 5.0L, 5.8L & 7.5	12-18 (16-24)

	INCH Lbs. (N.m)
Crankshaft Sensor Bolts	
2.3L	22-31 (2.5-3.5)
4.0L	75-106 (9-12)
Fuel Pressure Regulator Bolts	
Except 2.9L & 4.0L	26-40 (3-4.5)
2.9L & 4.0L	72-96 (8-11)
Fuel Supply Manifold Bolts	
2.9L & 3.0L	72-84 (8-11)
Pressure Relief Valve Cap	4-6 (.5-.7)
Thermostat Housing Bolts (Except Diesel)	72-96 (8-11)
Throttle Position Sensor Screws	
2.3L & 2.9L	25-33 (2.8-3.8)
3.0L	15 (1.5)
4.0L	11-16 (1.2-2.8)
4.9L, 5.0L & 5.8L	18-27 (2.0-3.0)

Alternators – With Integral Regulator

Aerostar, Bronco, Explorer
Ranger, Pickup, Van

NOTE: Unless otherwise specified, references to Pickup include the F350 Super Duty commercial chassis.

DESCRIPTION

Major components of the Motorcraft Integral Alternator-Regulator (IAR) system with external fan are end frames, rotor, stator, rectifier assembly and electronic voltage regulator mounted on the rear of the alternator. *See Fig. 1.*

ADJUSTMENTS

BELT TENSION

Check condition and tension of alternator drive belt prior to performing any on-vehicle charging system tests. Replace belt and/or repair tensioner mechanism if necessary. On vehicles with automatic belt tensioner, belt tension is okay if belt length indicator is within limit marks on tensioner. On vehicles without automatic belt tensioner, adjust alternator drive belt to specification. See ALTERNATOR BELT ADJUSTMENT SPECIFICATIONS table.

ALTERNATOR BELT ADJUSTMENT SPECIFICATIONS

Application	New Belt Lbs. (kg)	[1] Used Belt Lbs. (kg)
2.9L	120-160 (54-73)	110-130 (50-59)
3.0L	120-160 (54-73)	110-130 (50-59)
7.3L With 1/2" Belt	140-180 (64-82)	95-115 (43-52)
7.3L Ambulance	140-160 (64-73)	140-160 (64-73)
7.5L	160-200 (73-91)	110-130 (50-59)

[1] – Any belt operated for 10 minutes.

TROUBLE SHOOTING

NOTE: See TROUBLE SHOOTING article in GENERAL INFORMATION.

ON-VEHICLE TESTING

SYSTEM TEST

1) Check condition of fuse link, battery terminals, battery cables, connections and belt tension. Make any required corrections. Ensure battery is in good condition and is fully charged. Go to next step.
2) Connect voltmeter to battery posts. Record voltmeter indication as base voltage. Start and run engine at 1500 RPM with no electrical load. Read voltmeter when voltage stabilizes. If there is no voltage increase, or if voltage increases to less than .5 volt greater than base voltage, go to step 4). If voltage increase is no greater than 2.0 volts, go to step 3). If voltage increase is greater than 2.0 volts, go to step 10).

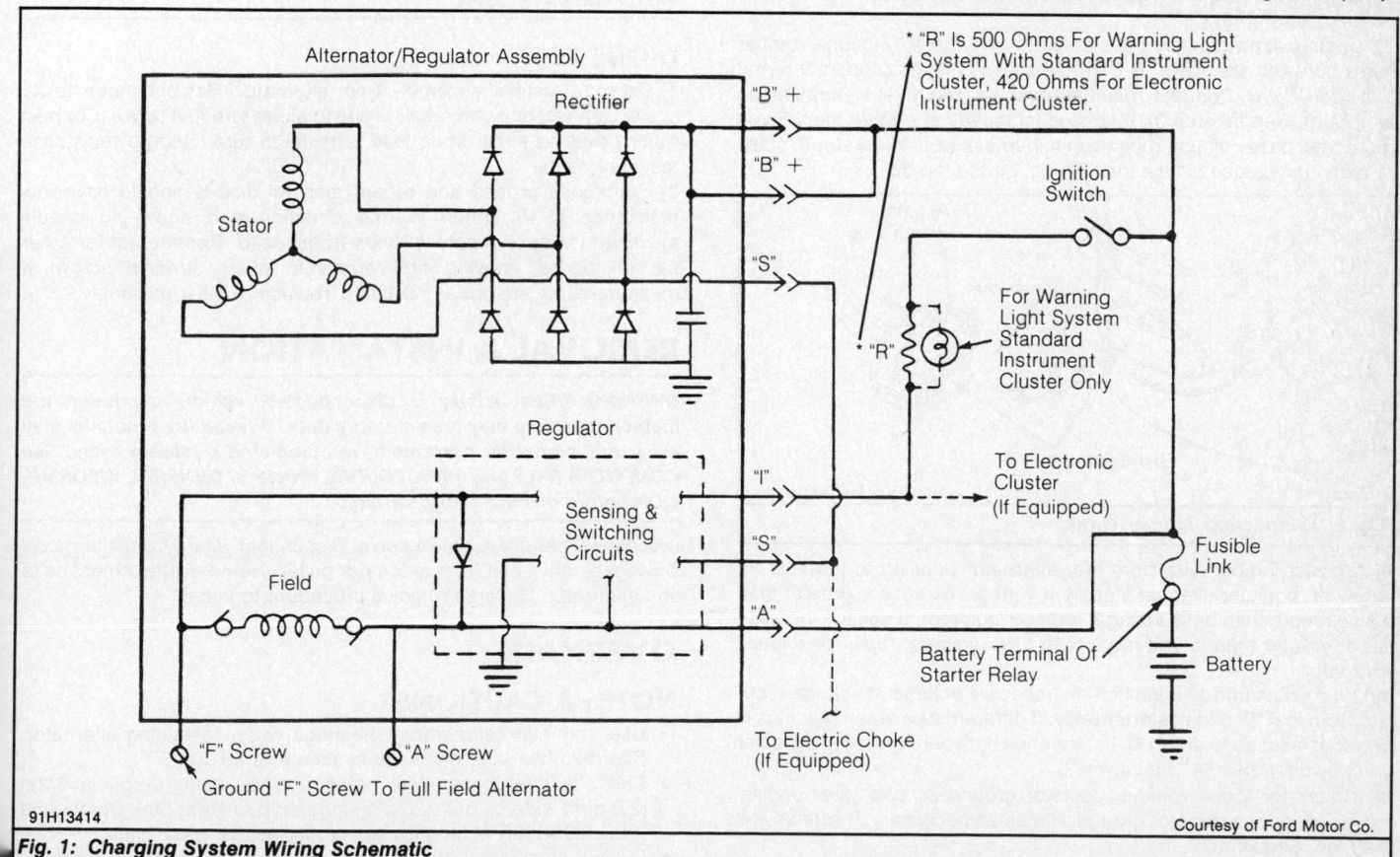

Fig. 1: Charging System Wiring Schematic

91H13414

Courtesy of Ford Motor Co.

3) Load alternator by switching heater/air conditioner blower motor to high speed and headlights to high beam. Increase engine speed to 2000 RPM. Voltmeter should indicate at least .5 volt higher than base voltage. If voltage increase is within specification, alternator operation is normal. If voltage increases to less than .5 volt higher than base voltage, go to step **4)**.

4) Unplug connector from voltage regulator. Measure resistance between regulator "A" and "F" terminals. If resistance is greater than 2.4 ohms, go to step **5)**. If resistance is not greater than 2.4 ohms, replace voltage regulator.

5) Connect wiring to regulator. Connect voltmeter negative lead to rear alternator housing. Connect voltmeter positive lead to terminal "A" screw of regulator. *See Fig. 2*. Meter should indicate battery voltage. If battery voltage is not present, service "A" circuit wiring.

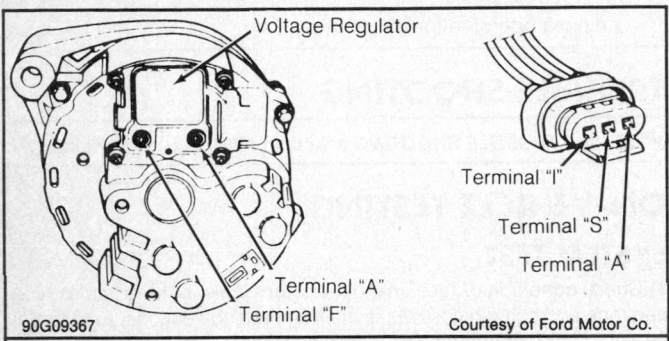

Fig. 2: Identifying Alternator And Regulator Terminals

6) With ignition off, connect voltmeter positive lead to terminal "F" screw of regulator. If battery voltage is present, go to step **7)**. If battery voltage is not present, repair or replace alternator.

7) Set ignition switch to ON position (engine not running). If meter indicates more than 1.5 volts, go to step **8)**. If meter indicates less than 1.5 volts, go to step **9)**.

8) Unplug alternator wiring connector. Connect 12-gauge jumper wires between alternator "B+" terminals and mating connector terminals. *See Fig. 3*. Connect voltmeter positive lead to "B+" terminal on alternator. Repeat step **3)**. If voltage increases to greater than .5 volt more than base voltage, repair wiring harness from alternator to starter relay. If increase is less than .5 volt, go to step **9)**.

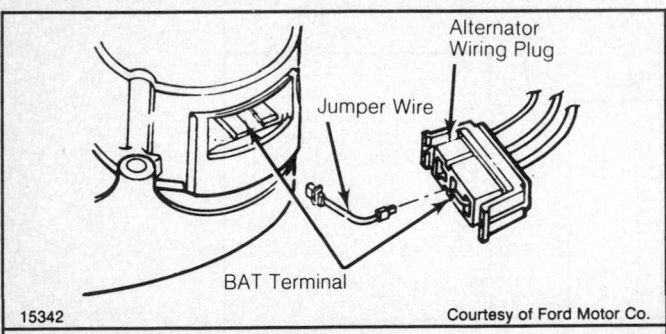

Fig. 3: Connecting Jumper Wires

9) Connect jumper wire from rear alternator housing to terminal "F" screw of regulator. Repeat step **3)**. If voltage increase is greater than 0.5 volt more than base voltage, replace regulator. If voltage increase is not greater than .5 volt more than base voltage, repair or replace alternator.

10) With engine off and ignition on, measure voltage at voltage regulator terminal "F" and at starter relay. If difference between readings is .5 volt or less, go to step **11)**. If difference between readings is greater than .5 volt, repair "A" circuit wiring.

11) Check for loose voltage regulator ground screws, poor engine ground, or poor alternator ground. Repair as necessary. If screws are okay, go to next step.

12) With ignition off, measure voltage at voltage regulator "A" and "F" terminals. If battery voltage does not exist at each terminal, repair or

replace alternator. If battery voltage exists at each terminal, replace voltage regulator.

BENCH TESTING

STATOR GROUND TEST

1) Remove stator from alternator. Set ohmmeter to X1000 scale. Connect one ohmmeter probe to any stator lead. Connect other probe to stator core. Ohmmeter indication should be infinity.

2) If meter needle moves, stator winding is shorted to core and must be replaced. Repeat test for each stator lead. DO NOT touch probes or stator leads, as an incorrect reading will result.

STATOR CONTINUITY TEST

Disconnect stator from rectifier assembly. Set ohmmeter to X1 range. Connect one ohmmeter probe to any stator lead. Connect other ohmmeter probe to another stator lead. If continuity does not exist, stator is open, and should be replaced. Repeat test for each pair of stator leads.

ROTOR TEST

1) Remove rotor from alternator. Set ohmmeter to X1 scale. Measure resistance between rotor slip ring. Resistance should be **2.0-3.9 ohms**. Replace rotor if resistance is not within specification.

2) Set ohmmeter to X1000 scale. Connect one ohmmeter probe to either slip ring. Connect other probe to rotor shaft. Resistance other than infinity indicates rotor is shorted to shaft and must be replaced. Damaged slip ring terminals or solder touching rotor shaft can cause shorted condition.

NOTE: Digital ohmmeter CANNOT be used for following test. Resistance measurements may differ slightly from specification, depending on ohmmeter used.

DIODE TEST

1) Remove rectifier assembly from alternator. Set ohmmeter to X1 scale. Connect one ohmmeter probe to either terminal screw. Connect other probe to each diode lead terminal in turn. Record resistance measurements.

2) Transpose probes and repeat test. All diodes should have low resistance (6-10 ohms) in one direction and show no needle movement with ohmmeter probes transposed. Repeat test for other set of diodes, moving first probe to other terminal screw. If measurements are not as specified, replace rectifier assembly.

REMOVAL & INSTALLATION

WARNING: When battery is disconnected, vehicle computer and memory systems may lose memory data. Driveability problems may exist until computer systems have completed a relearn cycle. See COMPUTER RELEARN PROCEDURES article in GENERAL INFORMATION before disconnecting battery.

Disconnect battery negative cable. Disconnect wiring from alternator. Disengage drive belt from alternator pulley. Remove attachment bolts and alternator. Reverse removal procedure to install.

OVERHAUL

NOTES & CAUTIONS

- Use only high-temperature bearings when rebuilding alternator. Standard bearings will result in alternator failure.
- Clean rectifier base plate using a clean cloth. Apply a 3/32" (2.0 mm) wide by 3/4" (20 mm) long strip of Heat Sink Compound (ESF-M99G138-A) lengthwise across rectifier base plate.
- Place a small amount of waterproof sealant over brush pin hole. DO NOT use silicone sealant. Rotate pulley to check for freedom of movement.
- For exploded view of alternator, *see Fig. 4*.

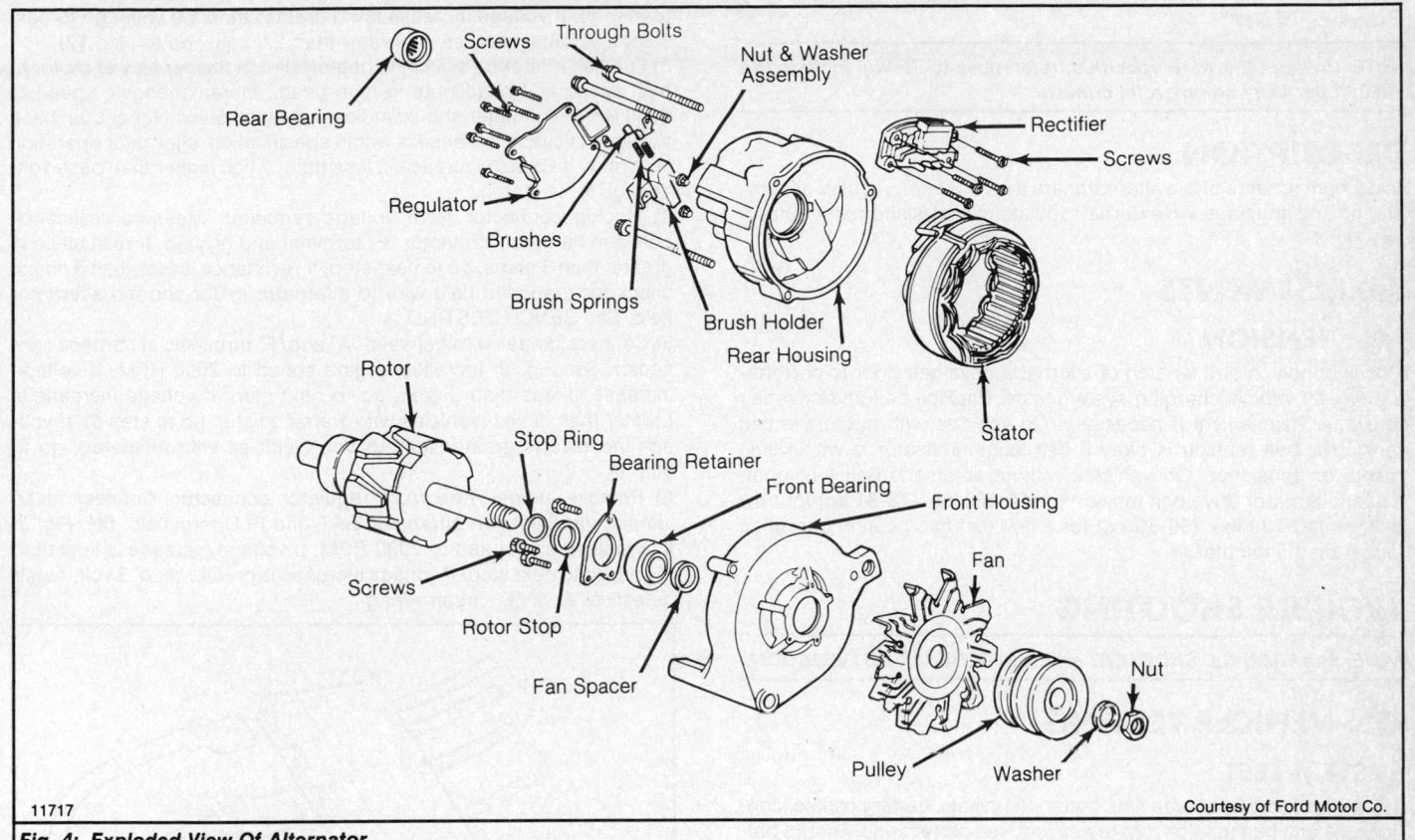

11717   Courtesy of Ford Motor Co.

Fig. 4: Exploded View Of Alternator

Pickup, Van

NOTE: Unless otherwise specified, references to Pickup include the F350 Super Duty commercial chassis.

DESCRIPTION

Major components of the alternator are a rotor, stator, rectifier assembly and end housings. An external regulator controls alternator output. *See Fig. 1.*

ADJUSTMENTS

BELT TENSION

Check condition and tension of alternator drive belt prior to performing any on-vehicle charging system tests. Replace belt and/or repair tensioner mechanism if necessary. On vehicles with automatic belt tensioner, belt tension is okay if belt length indicator is within limit marks on tensioner. On vehicles without automatic belt tensioner, adjust alternator drive belt tension to **160-200 lbs. (73-91 kg)** for new belt, or **110-130 lbs. (50-59 kg)** for a belt that has been in operation longer than 5 minutes.

TROUBLE SHOOTING

NOTE: See TROUBLE SHOOTING article in GENERAL INFORMATION.

ON-VEHICLE TESTING

SYSTEM TEST

1) Check condition of fuse link, battery terminals, battery cables, connections and belt tension. Make any required corrections. Ensure battery is in good condition and is fully charged.

2) Connect voltmeter to battery posts. Record voltmeter indication as base voltage. Start engine and operate at 1500 RPM with no electrical load. Read voltmeter when voltage stabilizes. If there is no voltage increase, or voltage increase is less than .5 volt over base voltage, go

to step **4)**. If voltage increase is no greater than 2.0 volts, go to next step. If voltage increase is greater than 2.0 volts, go to step **12)**.

3) Load alternator by switching heater/air conditioner blower motor to high speed and headlights to high beam. Increase engine speed to 2000 RPM. Voltmeter should indicate at least .5 volt higher than base voltage. If voltage increase is within specification, alternator operation is normal. If voltage increase is less than .5 volt higher than base voltage, go to next step.

4) Unplug connector from voltage regulator. Measure resistance between harness connector "F" terminal and ground. If resistance is greater than 3 ohms, go to next step. If resistance is less than 3 ohms, check for grounded field wire to alternator or for shorted alternator field. See BENCH TESTING.

5) Connect jumper wire between "A" and "F" terminals at harness connector. *See Fig. 2.* Increase engine speed to 2000 RPM. If voltage increase is less than .5 volt, go to next step. If voltage increase is greater than .5 volt (vehicles with warning light), go to step **8)**. If voltage increase is greater than .5 volt (vehicles with ammeter), go to step **9)**.

6) Remove jumper wire from regulator connector. Connect fused jumper wire between alternator BAT and FLD terminals. *See Fig. 3.* Increase engine speed to 2000 RPM. If voltage increase is less than .5 volt, go to next step. If voltage increase is greater than .5 volt, repair defective "A" or "F" circuit wiring.

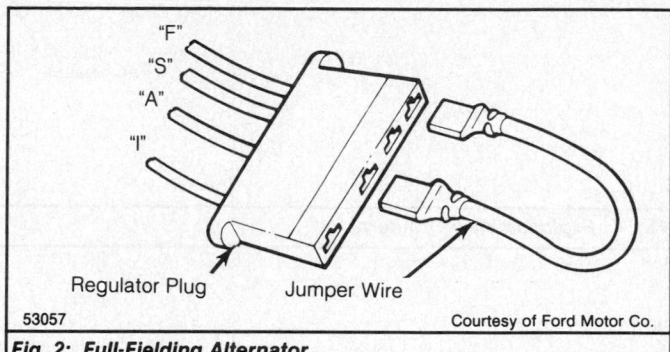

"F"
"S"
"A"
"I"

Regulator Plug   Jumper Wire

53057   Courtesy of Ford Motor Co.

Fig. 2: Full-Fielding Alternator

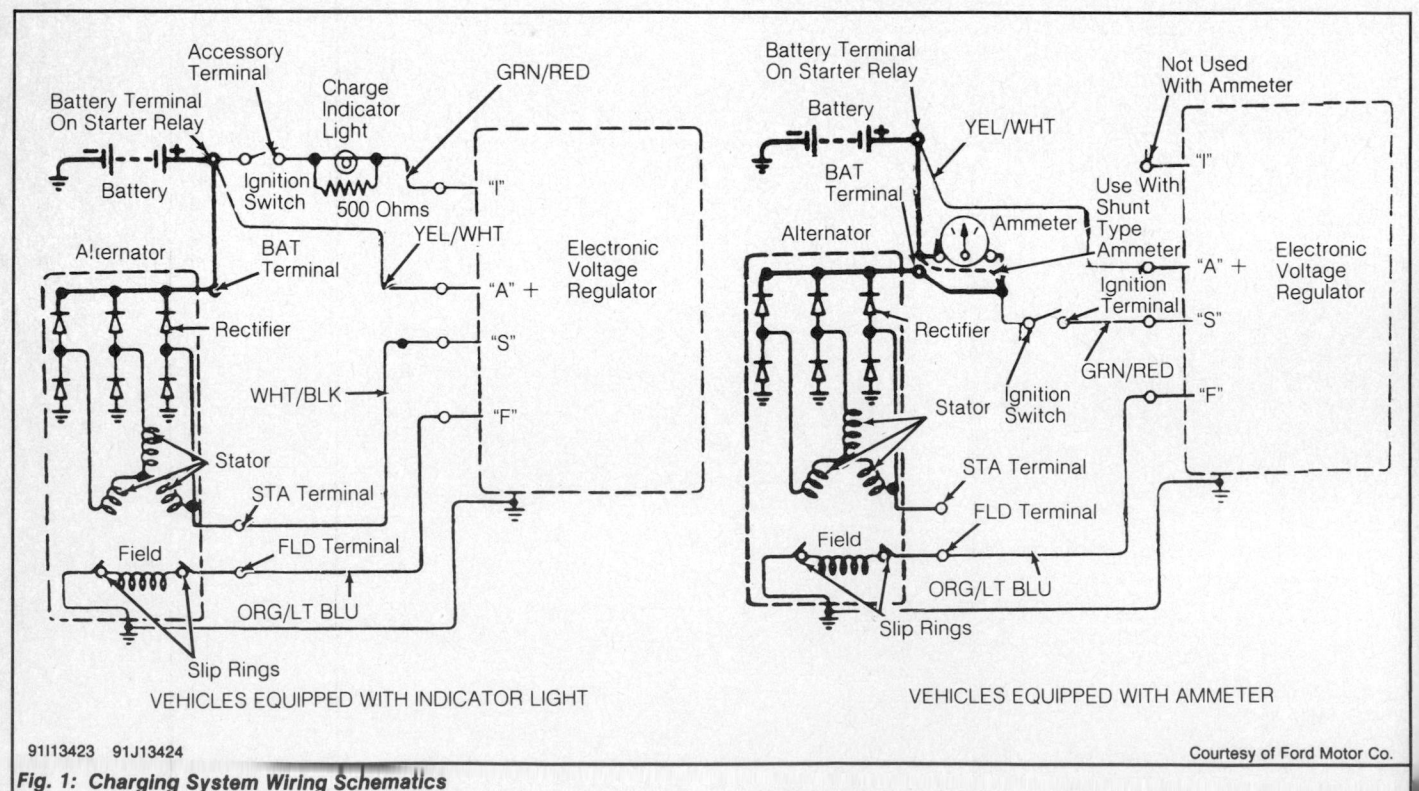

VEHICLES EQUIPPED WITH INDICATOR LIGHT   VEHICLES EQUIPPED WITH AMMETER

91I13423   91J13424   Courtesy of Ford Motor Co.

Fig. 1: Charging System Wiring Schematics

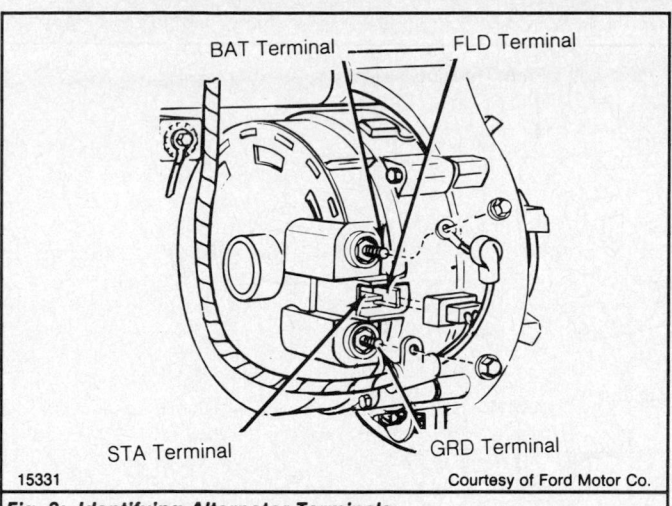

BAT Terminal ————— FLD Terminal

STA Terminal ————— GRD Terminal

15331   Courtesy of Ford Motor Co.

Fig. 3: Identifying Alternator Terminals

7) Stop engine. Measure voltage at alternator BAT terminal. If voltage is equal to base voltage, service alternator. If voltage is not equal to base voltage, repair circuit between alternator and battery.

8) Turn off all loads. Turn ignition off. Connect jumper between "A" and "F" terminals at voltage regulator harness. Start and idle engine. If voltage at regulator harness connector "S" terminal is not approximately 1/2 base voltage, go to step **10)**. If voltage is approximately 1/2 base voltage, replace voltage regulator. If voltage at "I" terminal is not approximately battery voltage, repair defective "I" circuit between indicator light and alternator.

9) Turn off all loads. With ignition on, but engine not running, measure voltage at "I" terminal at regulator harness connector. If voltage is approximately battery voltage, replace voltage regulator. If voltage is not approximately battery voltage, repair defective "I" circuitry.

10) With engine idling, measure voltage at voltage regulator harness connector "S" terminal. If voltage is approximately 1/2 base voltage, replace voltage regulator. If voltage is approximately zero, go to next step.

11) With engine idling, measure voltage at alternator "S" terminal. If voltage is approximately 1/2 base voltage, repair wire between alternator "S" terminal and voltage regulator harness connector. If voltage is not approximately 1/2 base voltage, service alternator.

12) Connect jumper wire between regulator base and alternator frame. If overvoltage condition still exists, go to next step. If overvoltage condition is eliminated, repair voltage regulator ground.

13) Unplug regulator harness connector. If condition is corrected, replace regulator. If overvoltage condition is still present with regulator disconnected, repair short in wiring harness between alternator and regulator ("A" and "F" circuits).

BENCH TESTING

STATOR GROUND TEST

1) Remove stator from alternator. Set ohmmeter to X1000 scale. Connect one ohmmeter probe to any stator lead. Connect other probe to stator core. Ohmmeter indication should be infinity.

2) If meter indicates continuity, stator winding is shorted to core, and must be replaced. Repeat test for each stator lead. DO NOT touch probes or stator leads, as an incorrect reading will result.

STATOR CONTINUITY TEST

NOTE: On alternators with delta stators, a single open phase CANNOT be detected by testing with ohmmeter. Delta stators have 2 wires at each terminal.

Disconnect stator from rectifier assembly. Set ohmmeter to X1 range. Connect one ohmmeter probe to any stator lead. Connect other ohmmeter probe to another stator lead. If no continuity exists, stator is open, and must be replaced. Repeat test for each pair of stator leads.

ROTOR TEST

1) Remove rotor from alternator. Set ohmmeter to X1 scale. Measure resistance between rotor slip ring. Resistance should be **2.0-3.5 ohms**. Replace rotor if resistance is not within specification.

2) Set ohmmeter to X1000 scale. Connect one ohmmeter probe to either slip ring. Connect other probe to rotor shaft. Resistance other than infinity indicates rotor is shorted to shaft and must be replaced. Damaged slip ring terminals or solder touching rotor shaft can cause shorted condition.

NOTE: Following test requires use of analog ohmmeter.

DIODE TEST

1) Remove rectifier assembly from alternator. Set ohmmeter to X1 scale. Connect one ohmmeter probe to either terminal screw. Connect other probe to each diode lead terminal in turn. Record resistance measurements.

2) Transpose probes and repeat test. All diodes should have resistance of approximately 6-10 ohms in one direction and no needle movement with probes transposed. Repeat test for other set of diodes, moving first probe to other terminal screw. If measurements are not as specified, replace rectifier assembly.

REMOVAL & INSTALLATION

WARNING: When battery is disconnected, vehicle computer and memory systems may lose memory data. Driveability problems may exist until computer systems have completed a relearn cycle. See COMPUTER RELEARN PROCEDURES article in GENERAL INFORMATION before disconnecting battery.

Disconnect battery negative cable. Disconnect wiring from alternator. Disengage drive belt from alternator pulley. Remove attachment bolts and alternator. Reverse removal procedure to install.

OVERHAUL

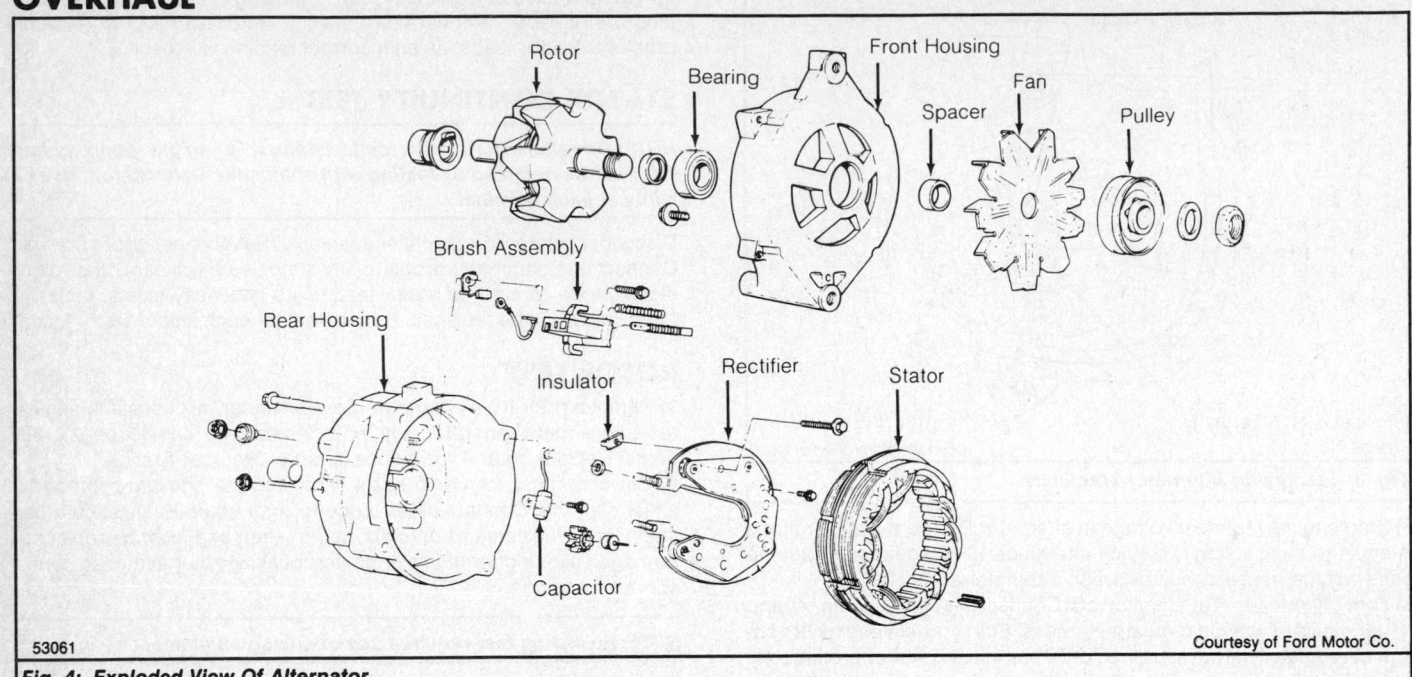

53061   Courtesy of Ford Motor Co.

Fig. 4: Exploded View Of Alternator

Aerostar, Explorer, Ranger

DESCRIPTION

Major components of the Motorcraft Integral Alternator-Regulator (IAR) system with internal fan are end frames, rotor, stator, rectifier assembly and electronic voltage regulator mounted on the rear of the alternator. *See Fig. 1.*

ADJUSTMENTS

BELT TENSION

Check condition and tension of alternator drive belt prior to performing any on-vehicle charging system tests. Replace belt and/or repair tensioner mechanism if necessary. Belt tension is okay if belt length indicator is within limit marks on tensioner.

TROUBLE SHOOTING

NOTE: See TROUBLE SHOOTING article in GENERAL INFORMATION.

ON-VEHICLE TESTING

BASE VOLTAGE TEST

NOTE: Prior to performing BASE VOLTAGE TEST, turn on headlights for 10-15 seconds to remove any surface charge from battery.

Ensure battery is in good condition and fully charged. Connect negative voltmeter lead to negative battery post, and positive voltmeter lead to positive battery post. Record battery voltage. This reading is base voltage.

NO-LOAD TEST

1) Connect tachometer to engine. Start engine and operate at 1500 RPM with no electrical load (foot off brake and doors closed).

2) Measure voltage when needle stops moving. This may require waiting a few minutes. Voltmeter reading should increase, but not more than 3 volts greater than base voltage. See BASE VOLTAGE TEST.
3) If the voltage increases at least .5 volt over base voltage, go to LOAD TEST. If voltage increase is more than 3 volts, proceed to HIGH VOLTAGE TEST. If there is no voltage increase, or voltage increase is less than .5 volt, proceed to LOW VOLTAGE TEST.

LOAD TEST

1) Connect tachometer to engine. Start engine. Load alternator by switching heater/air conditioner blower motor to high position and headlights to high beam. Increase engine speed to 2000 RPM.
2) Voltmeter should indicate at least .5 volt more than base voltage. If voltage is within specification, alternator operation is normal. If voltmeter indicates high voltage (3 volts greater than base voltage), go to HIGH VOLTAGE TEST. If voltmeter does not indicate at least .5 volt greater than base voltage, go to LOW VOLTAGE TEST.

HIGH VOLTAGE TEST

1) Set ignition switch to RUN position (engine off). Measure voltage at alternator output connection, at starter relay and at regulator terminal "A" screw head. *See Fig. 2.*
2) A voltage difference between 2 locations of greater than .5 volt, indicates high resistance in circuit "A" wiring. Repair circuit "A" and rerun NO-LOAD TEST and LOAD TEST.
3) If high voltage condition still exists, inspect alternator and regulator ground screws for looseness. Tighten grounding screws and repeat NO-LOAD TEST and LOAD TEST. *See Fig. 3.*
4) If high voltage condition still exists, connect voltmeter negative lead to ground. Ensure ignition is off. Measure voltage at regulator terminal "A" screw head and then at regulator terminal "F" screw head. Different voltages at 2 screw heads indicates a malfunctioning regulator grounded brush lead or a grounded rotor coil. Replace alternator/regulator assembly.
5) If same voltage (battery voltage) exists at both regulator terminal "A" and "F" screw heads, there is no short to ground through alternator

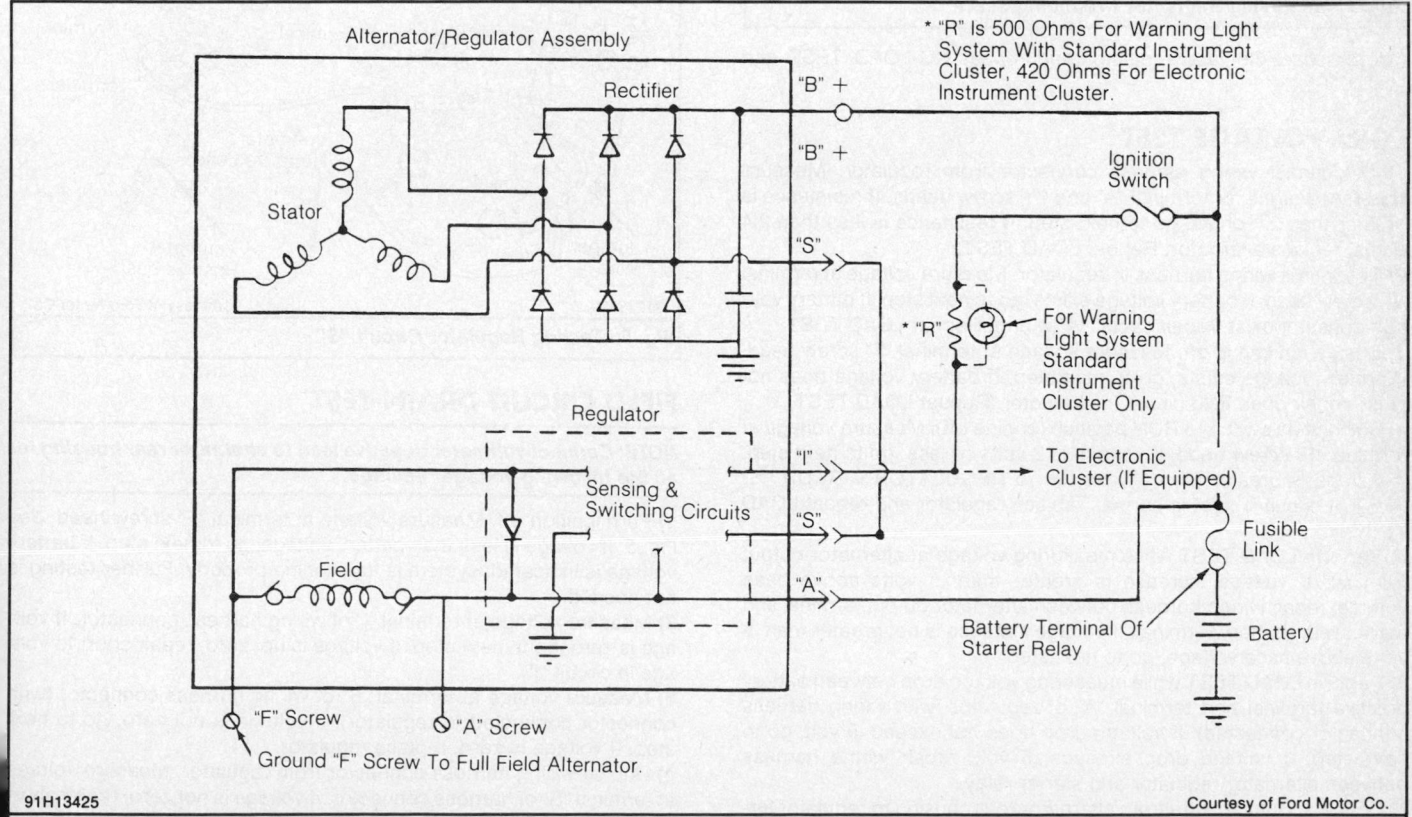

91H13425

Courtesy of Ford Motor Co.

Fig. 1: Charging System Wiring Schematic

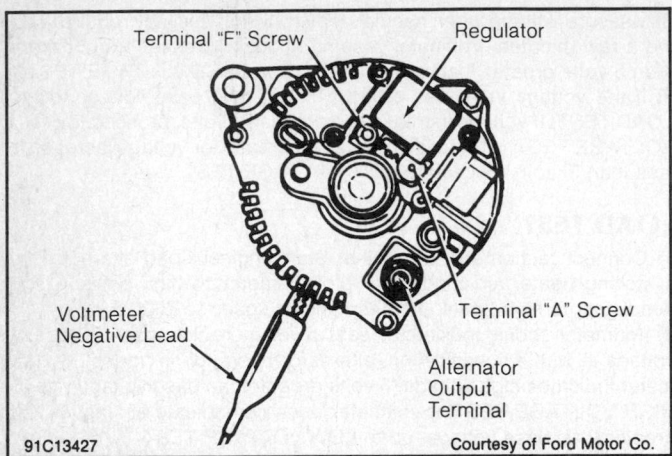

Fig. 2: Identifying Regulator Terminal "A" & "F" Screw Heads

91C13427   Courtesy of Ford Motor Co.

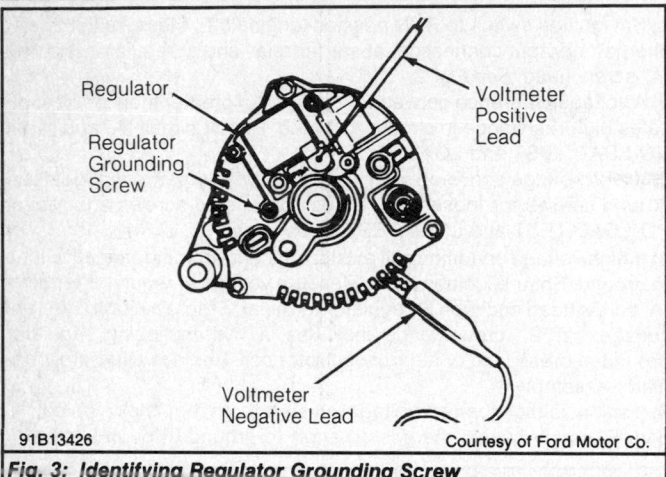

Fig. 3: Identifying Regulator Grounding Screw

91B13426   Courtesy of Ford Motor Co.

field/brushes. Replace regulator and repeat NO-LOAD TEST and LOAD TEST.

LOW VOLTAGE TEST

1) Disconnect wiring harness connector from regulator. Measure resistance regulator terminal "A" and "F" screw heads. If resistance is greater than 2.4 ohms, go to next step. If resistance is less than 2.4 ohms, replace alternator. Repeat LOAD TEST.

2) Reconnect wiring harness to regulator. Measure voltage at terminal "A" screw head. If battery voltage exists, go to next step. If battery voltage does not exist, repair circuit "A" wiring. Repeat LOAD TEST.

3) Ensure ignition is off. Measure voltage at terminal "F" screw head. If battery voltage exists, go to next step. If battery voltage does not exist, repair open field circuit in alternator. Repeat LOAD TEST.

4) Set ignition switch to RUN position (engine off). Measure voltage at terminal "F" screw head. If voltage is 2 volts or less, go to next step. If voltage is greater than 2 volts, go to REGULATOR CIRCUIT "S" TEST. If circuit "I" test is normal, replace regulator and repeat LOAD TEST.

5) Perform LOAD TEST while measuring voltage at alternator output terminal. If voltage increase is greater than .5 volts above base voltage, repair wiring harness between alternator output terminal and starter relay battery terminal. If voltage increase is not greater than .5 volts above base voltage, go to next step.

6) Perform LOAD TEST while measuring voltage drop between battery positive terminal and terminal "A" of regulator (with wiring harness connector connected). If voltage drop does not exceed .5 volt, go to next step. If voltage drop exceeds .5 volt, repair wiring harness between alternator regulator and starter relay.

7) Connect a jumper wire from alternator rear housing to regulator terminal "F" screw. See Fig. 4. Perform LOAD TEST while measuring volt-

age at alternator output terminal. If voltage increases .5 volt or more greater than base voltage, replace regulator. If voltage increase is not at least .5 volt greater than base voltage, replace alternator.

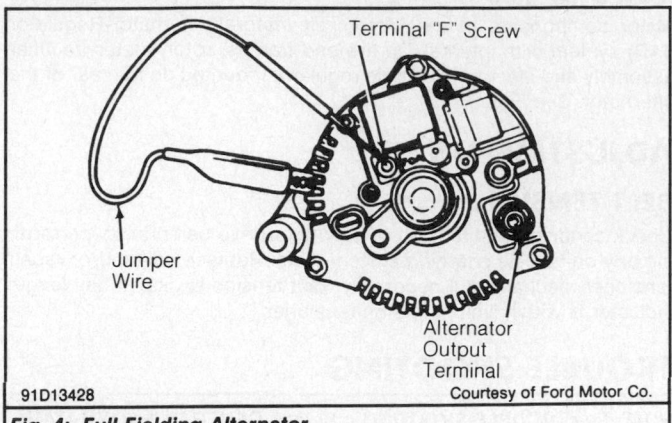

Fig. 4: Full-Fielding Alternator

91D13428   Courtesy of Ford Motor Co.

REGULATOR CIRCUIT "S" TEST

1) Unplug wiring harness connector from regulator. Connect jumper wire between regulator terminal "A" and terminal "A" of harness connector. Connect a jumper wire between regulator terminal "F" screw head and ground on alternator rear housing. See Fig. 5.

2) Start and idle engine. Measure voltage at terminal "S" and at terminal "I" of wiring harness connector. Voltage at terminal "S" should be approximately half that at terminal "I". If voltages are normal, remove jumper wires. Replace regulator. Repeat LOAD TEST.

3) If voltage at terminal "S" is not approximately half that at terminal "I", repair faulty wiring circuit or replace alternator. Reconnect regulator harness. Repeat LOAD TEST to confirm repair.

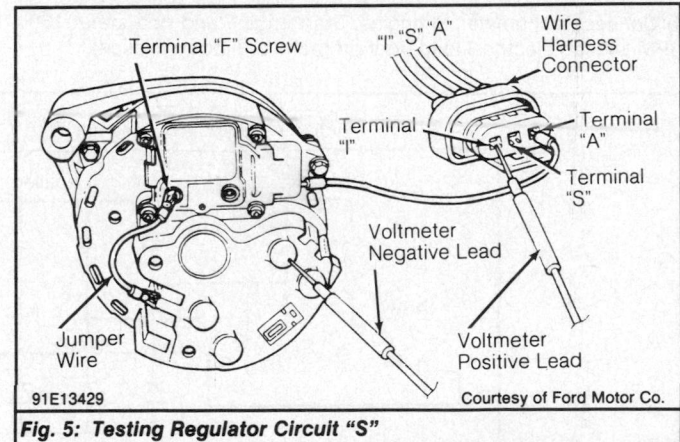

Fig. 5: Testing Regulator Circuit "S"

91E13429   Courtesy of Ford Motor Co.

FIELD CIRCUIT DRAIN TEST

NOTE: Connect voltmeter negative lead to alternator rear housing for all the following voltage readings.

1) Turn ignition off. Measure voltage at terminal "F" screw head. See Fig. 5. If voltage is less than battery voltage, go to next step. If battery voltage is indicated, system is functioning properly. Further testing is not needed.

2) Measure voltage at terminal "I" of wiring harness connector. If voltage is zero, go to next step. If voltage is not zero, repair short to voltage in circuit "I".

3) Measure voltage at terminal "S" of wiring harness connector (with connector connected to regulator). If voltage is not zero, go to next step. If voltage is zero, replace regulator.

4) Unplug wiring harness connector from regulator. Measure voltage at terminal "S" of harness connector. If voltage is not zero, repair short to voltage in wiring harness. If voltage is zero, replace alternator.

REMOVAL & INSTALLATION

WARNING: When battery is disconnected, vehicle computer and memory systems may lose memory data. Driveability problems may exist until computer systems have completed a relearn cycle. See COMPUTER RELEARN PROCEDURES article in GENERAL INFORMATION before disconnecting battery.

Disconnect battery negative cable. Remove snow/ice shield. Remove fresh air inlet duct. Disconnect wiring from alternator. Remove connector bracket. Disengage drive belt. Remove attachment bolts and alternator. Reverse removal procedure to install.

BENCH TESTING & OVERHAUL

Manufacturer states that alternator is serviced only as an assembly.

1992 ELECTRICAL
Alternators – Leece-Neville 165-Amp

Pickup, Van

NOTE: Unless otherwise specified, references to Pickup include the F350 Super Duty commercial chassis.

DESCRIPTION

Major components of the Leece-Neville 165-amp alternator are end frames, rotor, stator, fan, rectifier assembly and electronic voltage regulator mounted on the rear of the alternator. *See Fig. 1.*

Brushes and voltage regulator are located in a waterproof housing that may be removed for service or inspection without disassembling alternator.

ADJUSTMENTS

BELT TENSION

Inspect belt for fraying and proper routing. If fraying has occurred, ensure belt and pulleys are properly aligned. Adjust alternator drive belt tension to **160-200 lbs. (73-91 kg)** for new belt, or **110-130 lbs. (50-59 kg)** for a belt that has been in operation longer than 10 minutes.

TROUBLE SHOOTING

NOTE: See TROUBLE SHOOTING article in GENERAL INFORMATION.

ON-VEHICLE TESTING

OUTPUT TEST

NOTE: Before performing test, ensure drive belt is properly adjusted and all electrical accessories are off. Ensure battery is in good condition and is fully charged.

1) With engine off, connect digital volt-ohmmeter (DVOM) across battery terminals. Record voltage. Start engine. Read DVOM when

voltage stabilizes. If voltage increase is excessive, charging system may be defective or may require adjustment.

2) Remove nylon screw from voltage regulator. Run engine at approximately 1000 RPM. Carefully turn adjusting screw clockwise to increase or counterclockwise to decrease voltage to **14.2-14.3 volts**. *See Fig. 2.* DO NOT turn adjuster screw beyond stop, as damage will occur. Reinstall nylon screw to prevent entry of foreign material.

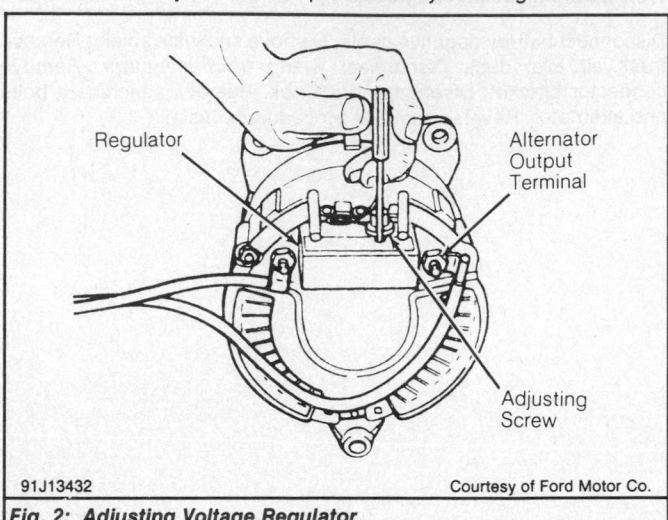

91J13432   Courtesy of Ford Motor Co.

Fig. 2: Adjusting Voltage Regulator

3) If output voltage is excessive and cannot be lowered by adjustment, regulator is at fault and must be replaced. If output voltage is low and cannot be increased by adjustment, either alternator or regulator may be at fault. To determine if fault is with alternator or regulator, go to next step.

4) Connect one end of short jumper wire to negative rectifier terminal. Connect other end to a stiff piece of wire at least 1 1/2" long. Insert wire with jumper wire attached into small hole in end of brush holder

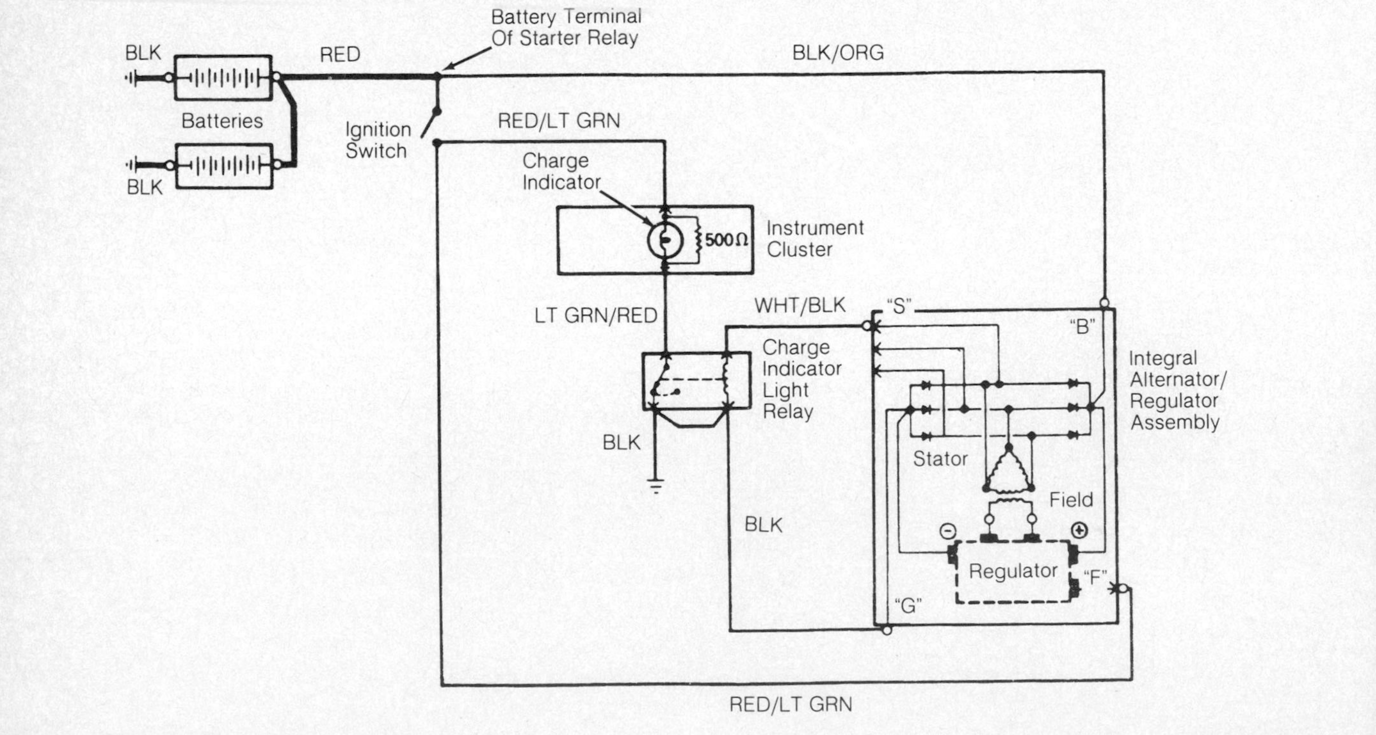

91I13431   Courtesy of Ford Motor Co.

Fig. 1: Charging System Wiring Diagram

so it firmly contacts terminal of outer brush. *See Fig. 3*. With engine at fast idle, read DVOM. If output voltage increases, alternator is okay. Replace regulator. If output voltage does not increase, alternator is defective.

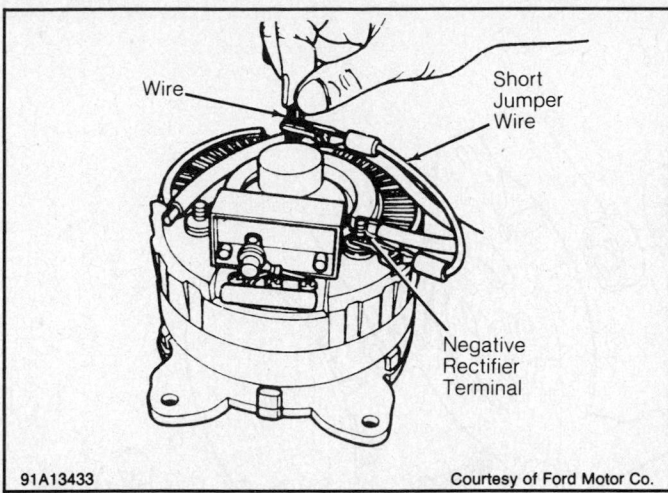

Fig. 3: Full-Fielding Alternator

BENCH TESTING

DIODE TEST

NOTE: These tests may be performed on heat sink assemblies without removing them from brush end housing. Stator and capacitor must be disconnected from heat sinks. Diodes should be tested with a diode tester, but an ohmmeter or a battery powered test light may be substituted.

Positive Heat Sink Test – 1) Connect diode tester positive lead to positive heat sink. Touch negative lead to each diode terminal in turn. *See Fig. 4*. If any diode exhibits low resistance, replace heat sink.

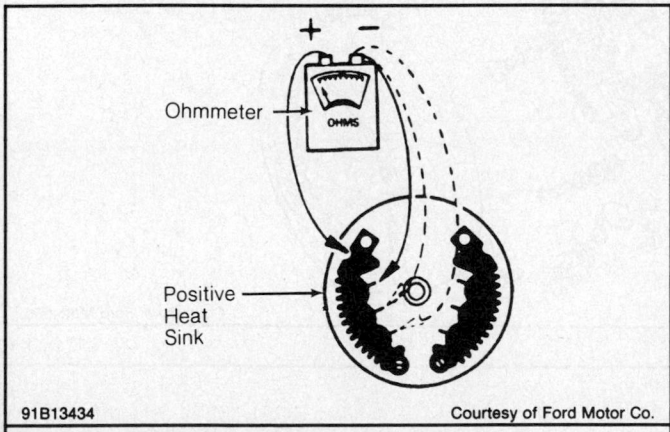

Fig. 4: Testing Positive Heat Sink

2) Transpose test leads so that negative test lead is connected to positive heat sink. Touch negative lead to each diode terminal in turn. If any diode exhibits high resistance, replace heat sink.
Negative Heat Sink Test – 1) Connect diode tester negative lead to negative heat sink. Touch positive lead to each diode terminal in turn. If any diode exhibits low resistance, replace heat sink.

2) Transpose test leads so that positive test lead is connected to negative heat sink. Touch negative lead to each diode terminal in turn. If any diode exhibits high resistance, replace heat sink.

CAPACITOR TEST

1) The capacitor connected across the heat sinks may be tested with a capacitor tester. Capacitance should be **.158 microfarad**.
2) If a capacitor tester is not available, an ohmmeter may be used to test capacitor for shorts. Connect ohmmeter across capacitor terminals. Resistance less than 20 m/ohms indicates a shorted or leaking capacitor, which must be replaced.

ROTOR TEST

1) Connect one ohmmeter test lead to rotor shaft. Touch other test lead to each slip ring. If continuity exists, rotor assembly is grounded and must be replaced.
2) Measure resistance between slip rings. If resistance is not 2.6-2.9 ohms, connect ohmmeter test leads to rotor coil soldered connections. If resistance is now 2.6-2.9 ohms, resolder connections. If resistance is not 2.6-2.9 ohms, replace rotor.

STATOR TEST

1) Visually inspect stator. If windings appear charred, burned, or if insulation is missing and bare copper is exposed, replace stator.
2) Using a DVOM, check for grounds between stator lamination and each stator terminal. If continuity exists, stator must be replaced.
3) Using a DVOM set to lowest scale, check stator phase resistance across stator terminals. *See Fig. 5*. If resistance is about the same for each of the 3 phases, stator is okay.

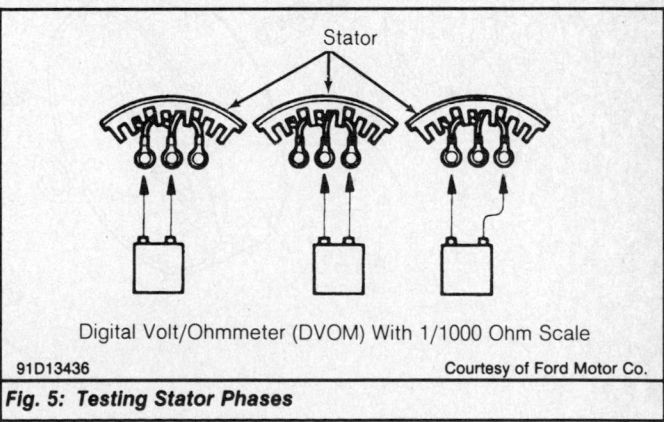

Fig. 5: Testing Stator Phases

REMOVAL & INSTALLATION

WARNING: When battery is disconnected, vehicle computer and memory systems may lose memory data. Driveability problems may exist until computer systems have completed a relearn cycle See COMPUTER RELEARN PROCEDURES article in GENERAL INFORMATION before disconnecting battery.

Disconnect battery negative cable. Disconnect wiring from alternator. Loosen pivot bolt. Remove adjuster bolt. Disengage drive belt. Remove pivot bolt and alternator as an assembly. Reverse removal procedure to install.

OVERHAUL

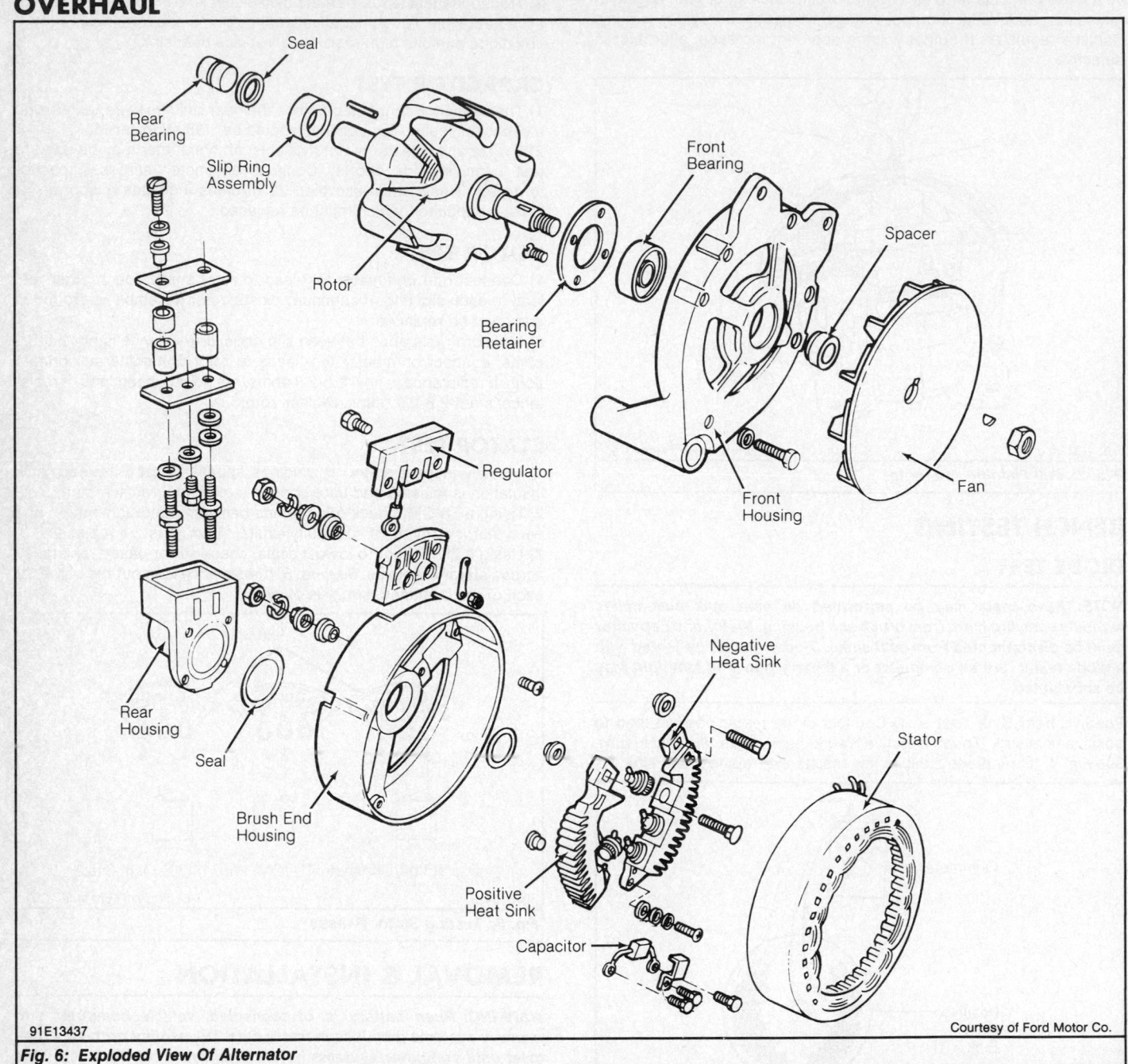

Seal

Rear
Bearing

Slip Ring
Assembly

Rotor

Bearing
Retainer

Front
Bearing

Spacer

Fan

Regulator

Front
Housing

Rear
Housing

Seal

Brush End
Housing

Negative
Heat Sink

Stator

Positive
Heat Sink

Capacitor

91E13437

Courtesy of Ford Motor Co.

Fig. 6: Exploded View Of Alternator

Pickup, Van

NOTE: Unless otherwise specified, references to Pickup include the F350 Super Duty commercial chassis.

DESCRIPTION

The starter used on the 7.3L diesel engine uses permanent magnet fields, internal gear reduction and an externally mounted solenoid. System consists of a starter (ignition) switch, starter relay, batteries and wiring. *See Fig. 1.*

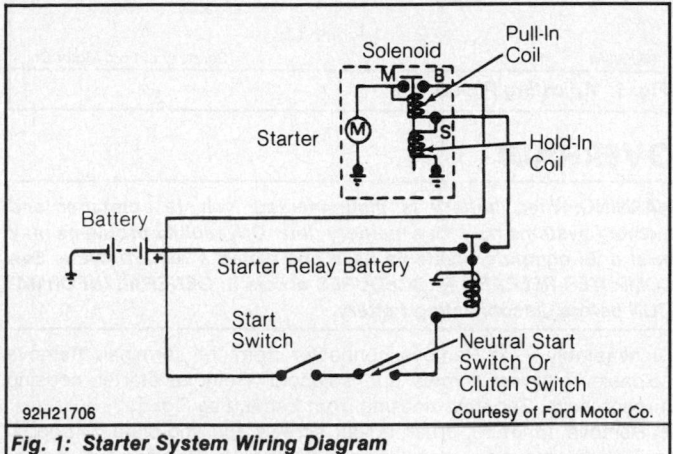

92H21706   Courtesy of Ford Motor Co.

Fig. 1: Starter System Wiring Diagram

TROUBLE SHOOTING

NOTE: See TROUBLE SHOOTING article in GENERAL INFORMATION.

ON-VEHICLE TESTING

CAUTION: Before testing starter, ensure transmission is in Park on A/T models or in Neutral on M/T models.

STARTER MOTOR TEST

1) Ensure batteries are fully charged and in good condition. Ensure battery cables and connections are in good condition. Measure voltage at starter solenoid battery cable terminal. If voltage is battery voltage, go to step 2). If voltage is less than 12 volts, recheck battery cables and connections. Service as necessary.

2) Connect one lead of remote starter switch to starter solenoid battery cable terminal. Connect other lead to "S" terminal on starter solenoid. Operate remote starter switch. If engine does not crank, repair or replace starter. If engine cranks normally, starter is okay; go to STARTER RELAY TEST. If engine cranks sluggishly, recheck batteries, cables, and connections. Repair or replace starter if batteries, cables, and connections are good.

STARTER RELAY TEST

1) Disconnect wire from terminal "S" of starter relay. Connect remote starter switch between terminal "S" and positive battery terminal. Ensure transmission is in Park on A/T models or in Neutral on M/T models.

2) Attempt to crank engine with remote starter switch. If engine cranks, relay is okay. Check ignition switch, neutral or clutch switch, and circuitry for open or loose connections. If engine does not crank, replace relay.

SOLENOID TEST

With all solenoid wiring disconnected, check for continuity between terminals. See SOLENOID SPECIFICATIONS table. Check contact plate for excessive pitting. Repair or replace as necessary.

SOLENOID SPECIFICATIONS

Terminals	Ohmmeter Reading
"S" & "M"	Continuity
"S" & Ground	Continuity
"B" & "M"	No Continuity

BENCH TESTING

WARNING: When battery is disconnected, vehicle computer and memory systems may lose memory data. Driveability problems may exist until computer systems have completed a relearn cycle. See COMPUTER RELEARN PROCEDURES article in GENERAL INFORMATION before disconnecting battery.

NO-LOAD TEST

1) Secure starter in vise. Ensure pinion gap is correct. See ADJUSTMENTS. Connect jumper lead between battery positive post and solenoid terminal "B". Connect remote start switch between battery positive post and solenoid terminal "S". *See Fig. 2.*

2) Starter should rotate at a smooth, consistent speed. If not, ensure shim adjustment for armature-to-starter housing clearance is correct. If shim adjustment is okay, replace starter.

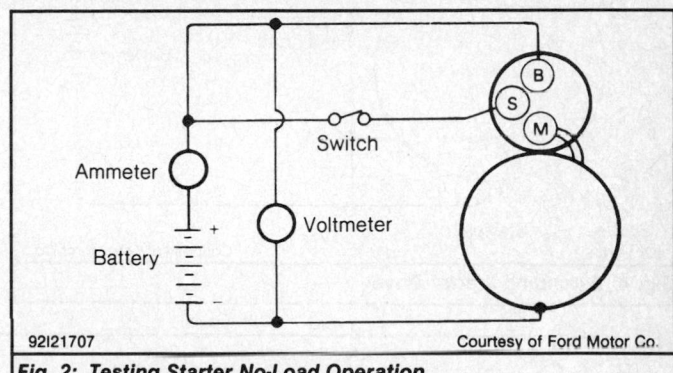

92I21707   Courtesy of Ford Motor Co.

Fig. 2: Testing Starter No-Load Operation

ARMATURE OPEN CIRCUIT TEST

An open armature circuit can be often detected by inspecting the commutator for evidence of burning. If burning is present, replace armature. Check for damage to other related components.

ARMATURE GROUNDED CIRCUIT TEST

Connect voltmeter leads to negative battery terminal and starter commutator. Connect jumper cable to positive battery terminals and armature. *See Fig. 3.* If meter indicates any voltage, windings are grounded.

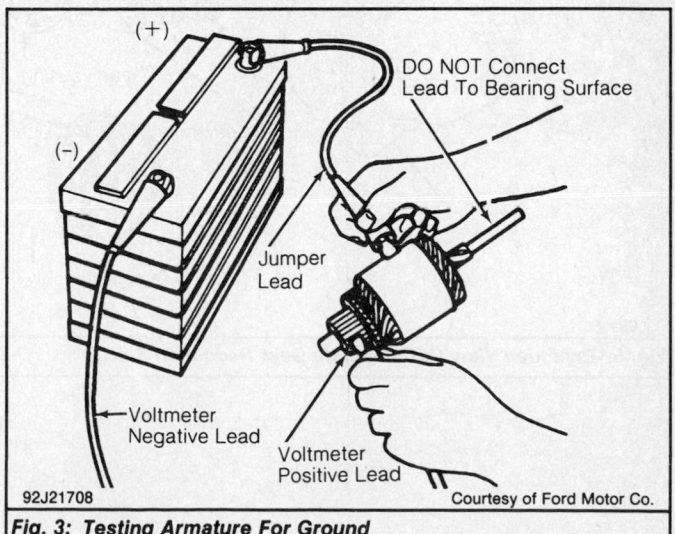

92J21708   Courtesy of Ford Motor Co.

Fig. 3: Testing Armature For Ground

ADJUSTMENTS

PINION GAP

1) Secure starter in vise. Connect a switch in series with starter solenoid and battery. Connect second switch in series with starter field wire. *See Fig. 4.*

2) Turn both switches on. Starter drive should extend and motor should run. Turn switch No. 2 off. Starter should stop running, but drive pinion should remain extended. With the drive pinion extended, measure gap between pinion and stop ring.

3) Pinion gap should be .004-.079" (.10-2.0 mm). If adjustment is required, insert or remove shims between solenoid and drive end housing. Add shims to decrease gap and remove shims to increase gap. *See Fig. 6.*

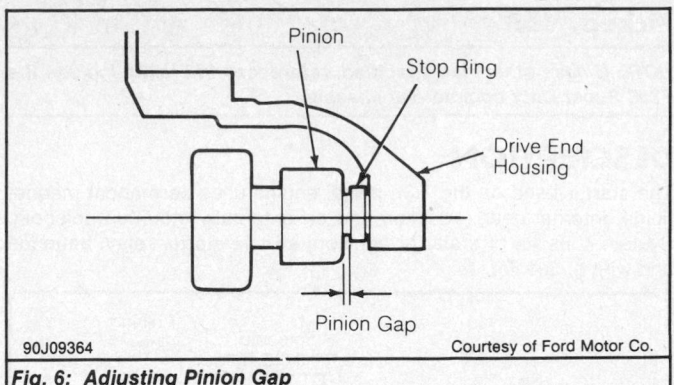

Fig. 6: **Adjusting Pinion Gap**

OVERHAUL

WARNING: When battery is disconnected, vehicle computer and memory systems may lose memory data. Driveability problems may exist until computer systems have completed a relearn cycle. See COMPUTER RELEARN PROCEDURES article in GENERAL INFORMATION before disconnecting battery.

Disassembly – 1) Remove connector from "M" terminal. Remove solenoid retaining screws and solenoid. Remove starter housing through bolts. Separate housing from frame. *See Fig. 5.*

2) Remove armature, brush holder screws and end plate. Lift brush springs to remove brushes. Remove brush plate. Remove seal, holder and spacer. Remove inner gear housing and gear/shaft assembly.

3) Remove drive assembly by placing a pipe over end of shaft and tapping pipe to loosen retaining ring to expose retaining clip. Remove retaining clip, ring and drive assembly.

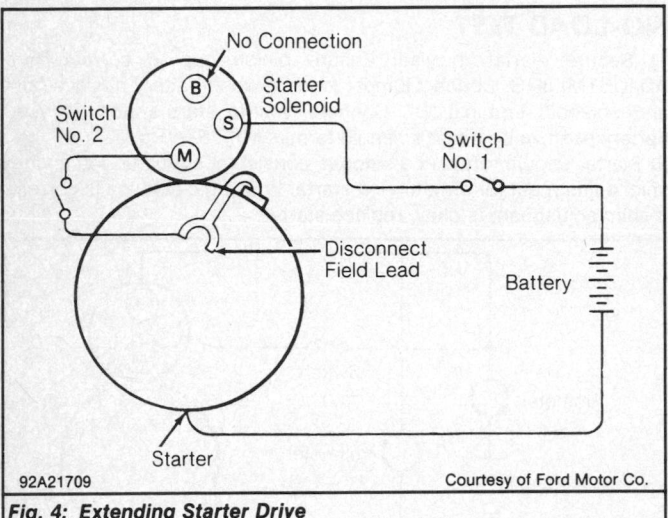

Fig. 4: **Extending Starter Drive**

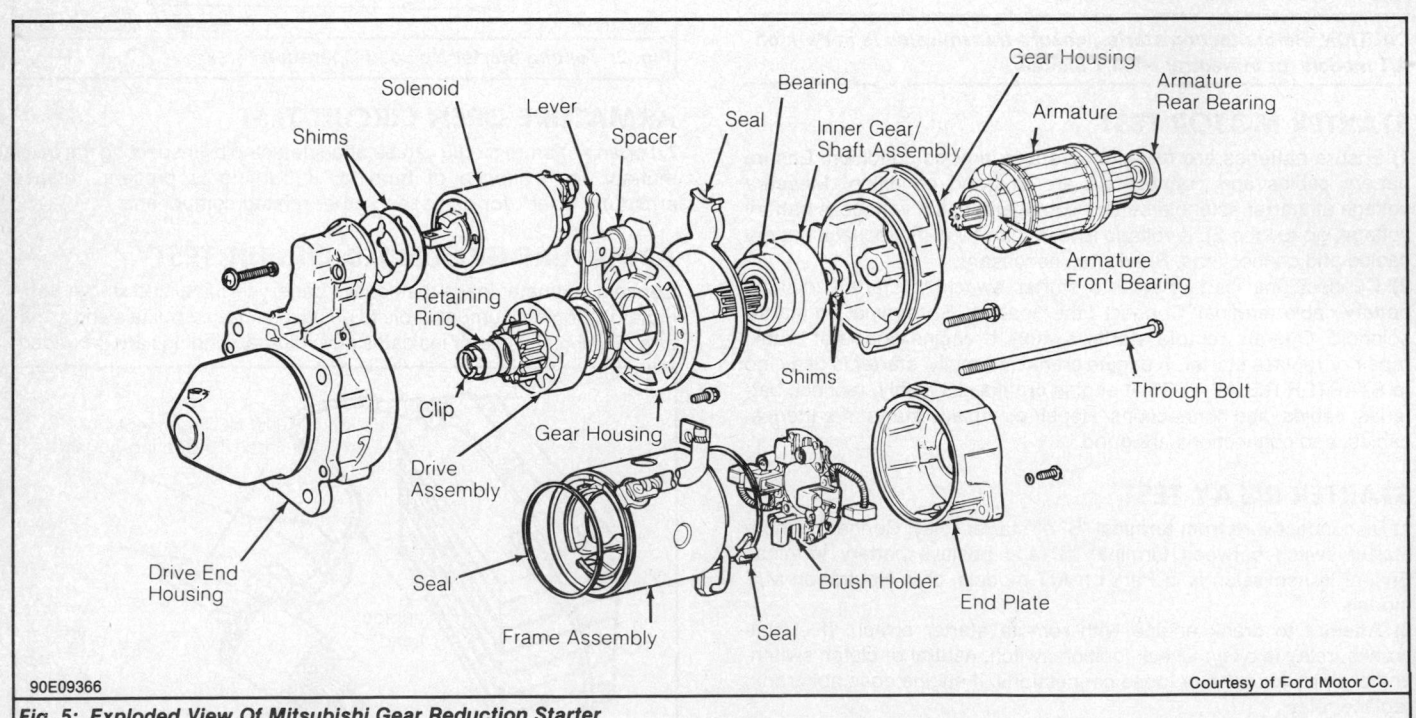

Fig. 5: ***Exploded View Of Mitsubishi Gear Reduction Starter***

Starters – Mitsubishi Gear Reduction (Cont.)

Inspection – Check armature winding for separated or burned insulation. Check for open or shorted circuits. *See Fig. 3.* Check armature shaft and bearings for scoring or excessive wear. Check commutator for excessive runout. Machine commutator if runout exceeds .005" (.12 mm).

Reassembly – To reassemble, reverse disassembly procedure. Lubricate all sliding/pivot points with Multemp MS #2. Adjust shaft end play to **.001-.020" (.02-.05 mm)** gap between inner gear housing and outer gear housing. Add or remove shim(s) as necessary. Ensure pinion gap is okay. See PINION GAP under ADJUSTMENTS.

TORQUE SPECIFICATIONS
TORQUE SPECIFICATIONS

Application	Ft. Lbs. (N.m)
Starter Mounting Bolts	15-20 (20-27)
	INCH Lbs. (N.m)
Battery Cable Retaining Nut	70-130 (7.9-14.7)

Aerostar, Bronco, Explorer, Pickup, Ranger, Van

NOTE: Unless otherwise specified, references to Pickup include the F350 Super Duty commercial chassis.

DESCRIPTION

The permanent magnet, gear reduction type starter is used on all gasoline engines. An internal planetary gear reduction unit provides increased cranking torque. The starting system consists of a starter, ignition/starter switch, relay, neutral start switch (A/T) or clutch switch (M/T), battery and wiring.

ON-VEHICLE TESTING

CAUTION: Before testing starter, ensure transmission is in Park on A/T models or Neutral on M/T models.

STARTER MOTOR TEST

1) Ensure battery is fully charged and in good condition. Ensure battery cables and connections are in good condition. Measure voltage at starter solenoid battery cable terminal. If voltage is battery voltage, go to step 2). If voltage is less than 12 volts, recheck battery cables and connections. Service as necessary.

2) Connect one lead of remote starter switch to starter solenoid battery cable terminal. Connect other lead to "S" terminal on starter solenoid. Operate remote starter switch. If engine does not crank, repair or replace starter. If engine cranks vigorously, starter is okay; go to STARTER RELAY TEST. If cranking is sluggish, go to LOAD TEST.

STARTER RELAY TEST

1) Disconnect terminal "S" of starter relay. *See Fig. 1.* Connect remote starter switch between terminal "S" and positive battery terminal. Ensure transmission is in Park on A/T models or Neutral on M/T models.

2) Crank engine with remote starter. If engine cranks, relay is okay. Check ignition switch, neutral or clutch switch and circuitry for open or loose connections. If engine does not crank, replace relay.

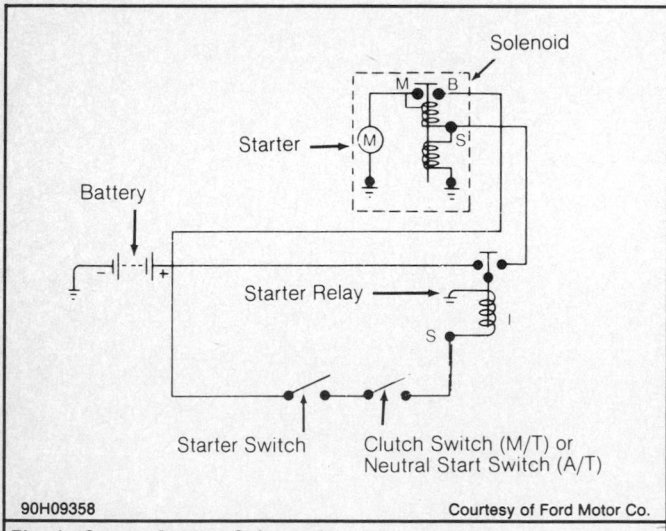

Fig. 1: Starter System Schematic

LOAD TEST

1) Connect starter load tester and voltmeter to battery terminals. Ensure no current is flowing through the ammeter and carbon pile of tester. Disconnect terminal "S" of starter relay.

2) Connect remote starter switch between terminal "S" and positive battery terminal. Ensure transmission is in Park on A/T models, or Neutral on M/T models.

3) Crank engine with ignition off and note voltmeter reading. Stop cranking engine. Turn tester carbon pile rheostat knob to match voltage obtained while cranking. Note ammeter reading. Replace or repair starter if current exceeds specification. See STARTER SPECIFICATIONS table at end of article.

BENCH TESTING

NO-LOAD TEST

1) Mount starter securely in vise. Connect voltmeter to battery terminals. Connect battery, jumper cables and starter load tester to starter. *See Fig. 2.* Ensure no current is flowing through the ammeter and carbon pile of tester.

2) Note voltmeter reading. Disconnect battery from starter. Turn carbon pile to achieve voltage obtained while starter was operating. Note ammeter reading. Replace or repair starter if current exceeds specification. See STARTER SPECIFICATIONS table at end of article.

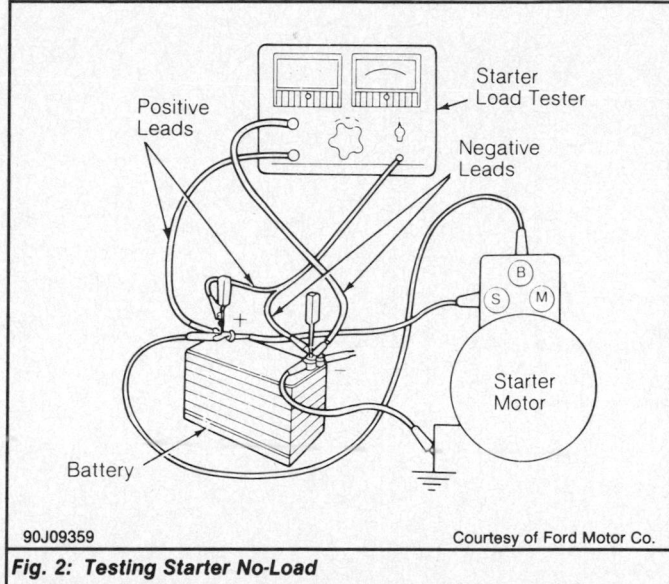

Fig. 2: Testing Starter No-Load

ARMATURE OPEN CIRCUIT TEST

An open armature circuit can sometimes be detected by inspecting the commutator for evidence of burning. If burning is present, replace armature. Check for damage to other related components.

ARMATURE GROUNDED CIRCUIT TEST

Connect ohmmeter leads to the armature and commutator. *See Fig. 3.* Ohmmeter should indicate no continuity. If continuity exists, replace armature.

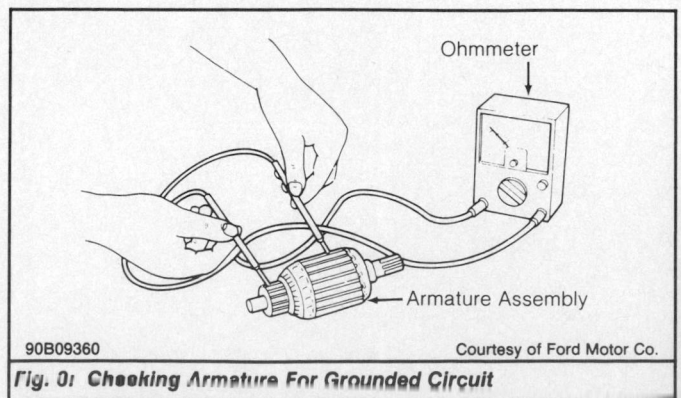

Fig. 3: Checking Armature For Grounded Circuit

REMOVAL & INSTALLATION

WARNING: When battery is disconnected, vehicle computer and memory systems may lose memory data. Driveability problems may exist until computer systems have completed a relearn cycle. See COMPUTER RELEARN PROCEDURES article in GENERAL INFORMATION before disconnecting battery.

Removal – Disconnect negative battery cable. Raise vehicle. Disconnect battery cable from starter. Disconnect starter solenoid wiring. Remove starter mounting bolts or nuts. Remove starter from vehicle.

Installation – 1) Position starter assembly onto flywheel housing. Start bolts. Hold starter against mounting surface, fully inserted into pilot hole. Tighten bolts or nuts to specification.

2) Connect battery cable and solenoid wiring to starter. Tighten to specification. Lower vehicle. Connect negative battery cable. Check starter operation.

OVERHAUL

NOTE: For exploded view of starter, see Fig. 4.

STARTER SPECIFICATIONS

STARTER SPECIFICATIONS

Application	Specifications
Brush Length Wear Limit	.66" (16.8 mm)
Current Draw	
No-Load	60-80 Amps
Under Load	140-200 Amps
Normal Cranking RPM	170-220

TORQUE SPECIFICATIONS

TORQUE SPECIFICATIONS

Application	Ft. Lbs. (N.m)
Mounting Bolts	15-20 (20-27)

	INCH Lbs. (N.m)
"B" & "M" Terminal Nut	80-120 (9.0-13.6)
Brush Plate Screws	20-30 (2.3-3.4)
Cable Terminal Nut	70-130 (7.9-14.7)
Solenoid Bolts	45-54 (5.1-6.1)
Through Bolts	55-75 (6.2-8.5)

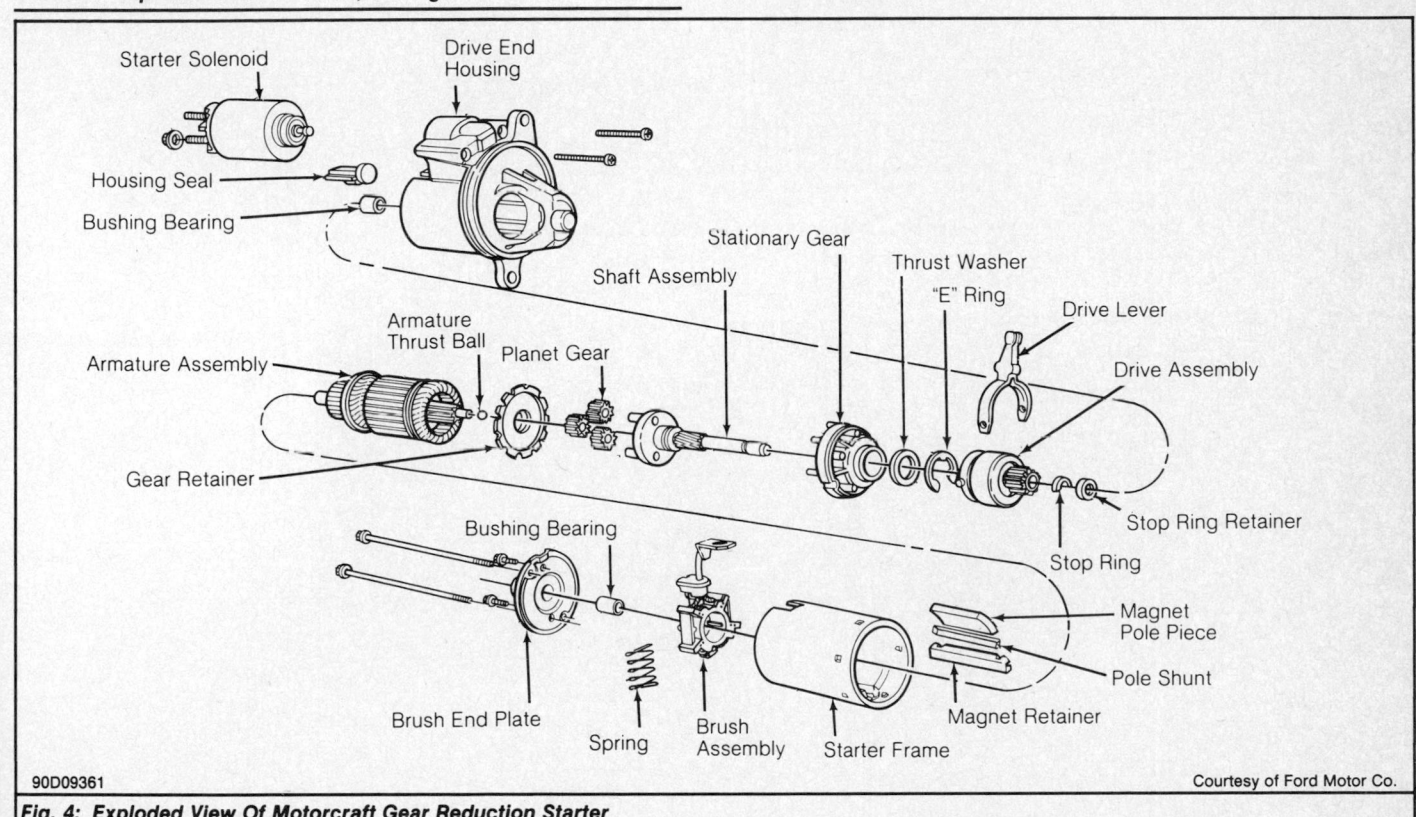

90D09361

Courtesy of Ford Motor Co.

Fig. 4: Exploded View Of Motorcraft Gear Reduction Starter

COMPONENT LOCATOR:

A/C WOT CUTOUT RELAY .... B 16
A/C/HEATER SW .... A 16
ABS SYSTEM .... A–B 28–29
AIRBAG SYSTEM .... C–E 32–34
ANALOG INST CLSTR .... C–E 28
AUTOLAMP DUAL COIL RELAY .... D 24
AUXILIARY BLOWER SWS .... B–C 19
AUXILIARY POWER RELAY .... A 18
BACK-UP LT SW (M/T) .... D 35
BACK-UP/NEUTRAL
  SAFETY SW (A/T) .... D–E 35
BATTERY .... A 2
BLOWER MOTOR SW .... A 17
BRAKE FLUID LEVEL SW .... C 31
BRAKE WARNING RESISTOR/DIODE
  ASSEMBLY .... C 28
BUTTON CONN. .... B 27/E 31
CIG LTRS. .... D–E 22
CLOCKSPRING ASSEMBLY ...... E 17, E 32
CLUTCH SW (M/T) .... B 14, D 17
COURTESY LAMP RELAY .... E 20
CRUISE CONTROL AMP .... D 16
CTSY LTS. .... B–C 20–22
DIFFERENTIAL SPEED SENSOR ...... B 30
DIGITAL INST CLSTR .... A–D 24
DIR FLASHER .... D 13
DOOR AJAR SWS .... A 27/D 31
EDIS MODULE (4.0L) .... E 8
EEC POWER RELAY .... A 4
EEC POWER RELAY (4.0L) .... A 8
ELECTRONIC ENGINE CONTROL
  (EEC) (3.0L) .... A–D 4
ELECTRONIC ENGINE CONTROL
  (EEC) (4.0L) .... A–D 8
ENG COMPT LT SW .... B 1
FUEL PUMP RELAY (3.0L) .... A 7
FUEL PUMP RELAY (4.0L) .... A 11
FUEL PUMP/FUEL GAUGE SENDER .. C–D 27
FUS LINKS .... B 2–3
FUSE BLOCK .... C–D 13–14
GROUND A .... A 1
GROUND B .... A 2
GROUND C .... A 2
GROUND D .... D 1
GROUND E (3.0L) .... C 7
GROUND F .... D 32
GROUND G .... B 32
GROUND H .... A 39
GROUND I .... B 37
GROUND J .... E 38
HAZARD FLASHER .... C 12
HEATER SW (W/O A/C) .... A 19
HEGO SENSOR (3.0L) .... C 7
HEGO SENSOR (4.0L) .... C 11
HORN RELAY .... C 3
IGN COIL (3.0L) .... E 4
IGN COIL (4.0L) .... E 11
IGN SW. .... A 12–15
ILLUM LTS .... D–E 12–15
ILLUMINATED ENTRY TIMER ...... D–E 23
INERTIA SW (3.0L) .... A 6
INTEGRAL ALTERNATOR
  REGULATOR (IAR) .... C 3
INTERIOR LTS .... D–E 20–23
INTERVAL GOVERNOR .... E 19
LCD DIMMING RELAY .... D 27
LIFTGATE WIPER MOTOR .... C 37–38
LIFTGATE WIPER/WASHER SW ..... B 37
LOW OIL LEVEL RELAY
  (ANALOG CLSTR) .... C 31
LT SENSOR AMPLIFIER .... E 24
LUMBAR SEATS .... D 36
MAF SENSOR (4.0L) .....
MAIN LT SW (W/ AUTOLAMPS) .. E 24–27
MAIN LT SW (W/O AUTOLAMPS) .. A 20–22
MULTI-FUNCTION SW .... A–C 23
POWER DOOR LOCKS .... A–C 36–38
POWER MIRRORS .... B–C 34–35
POWER WINDOWS .... A 34–35
RABS MODULE .... A 28
REAR DEFOG SW .... A–B 38
REAR DOOR SWS .... D 22
SEAT BELT SW .... D 22
SHIFT LOCK ACTUATOR .... C 19
SLIDING DOOR AJAR RELAY .... B 27/D 31
STARTER RELAY .... B 3
STO CONN (3.0L) .... B 7
STO CONN (4.0L) .... B 11
STOP LT SW .... C 16
TFI IGNITION MODULE (3.0L) ... E 7
TRAILER TOW RELAY MODULE ... E 36–38
WARNING MODULE .... C–D 23
WIPER MOTOR .... E 3
WIPER/WASHER SW .... D 18
4WD MODULE .... A 31

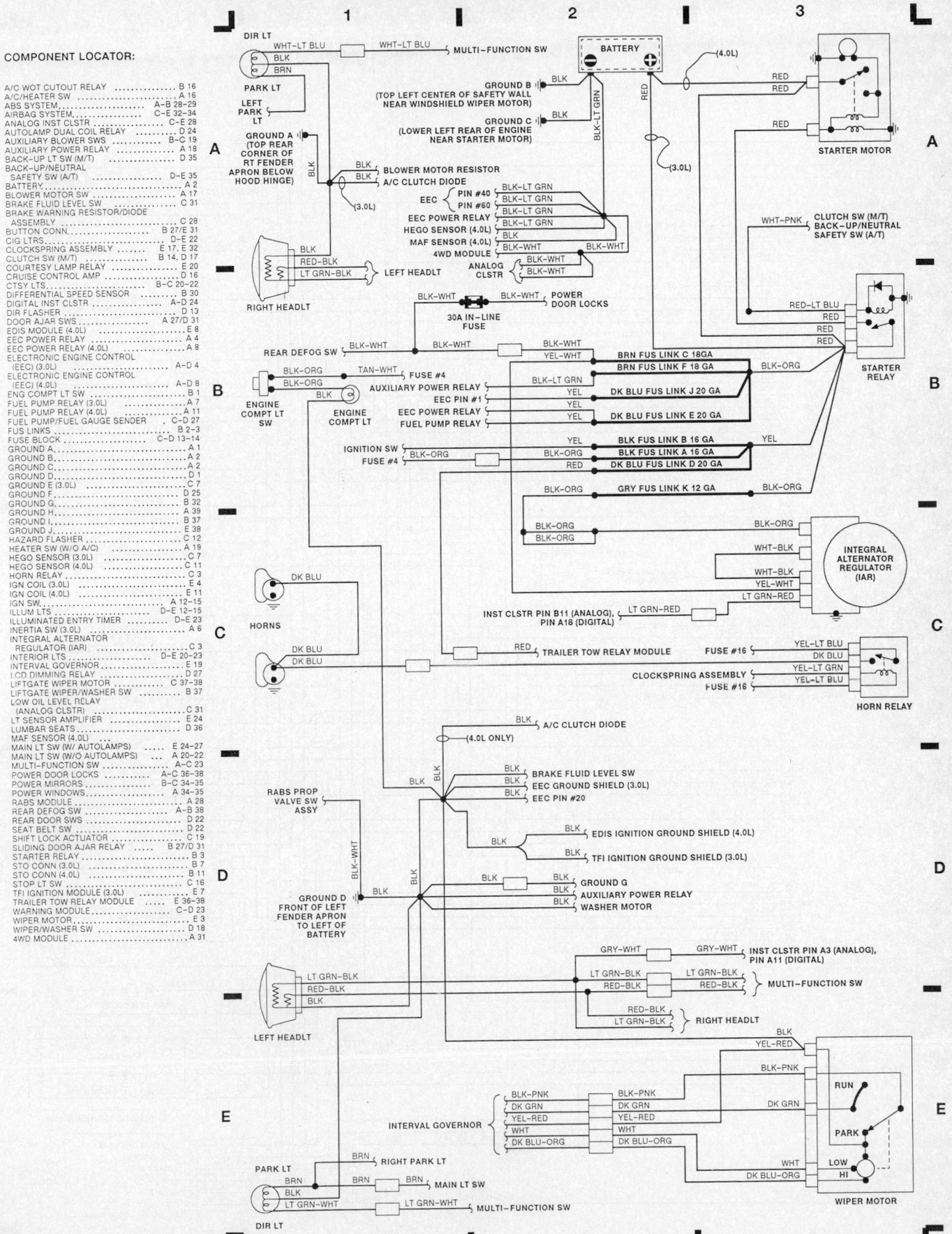

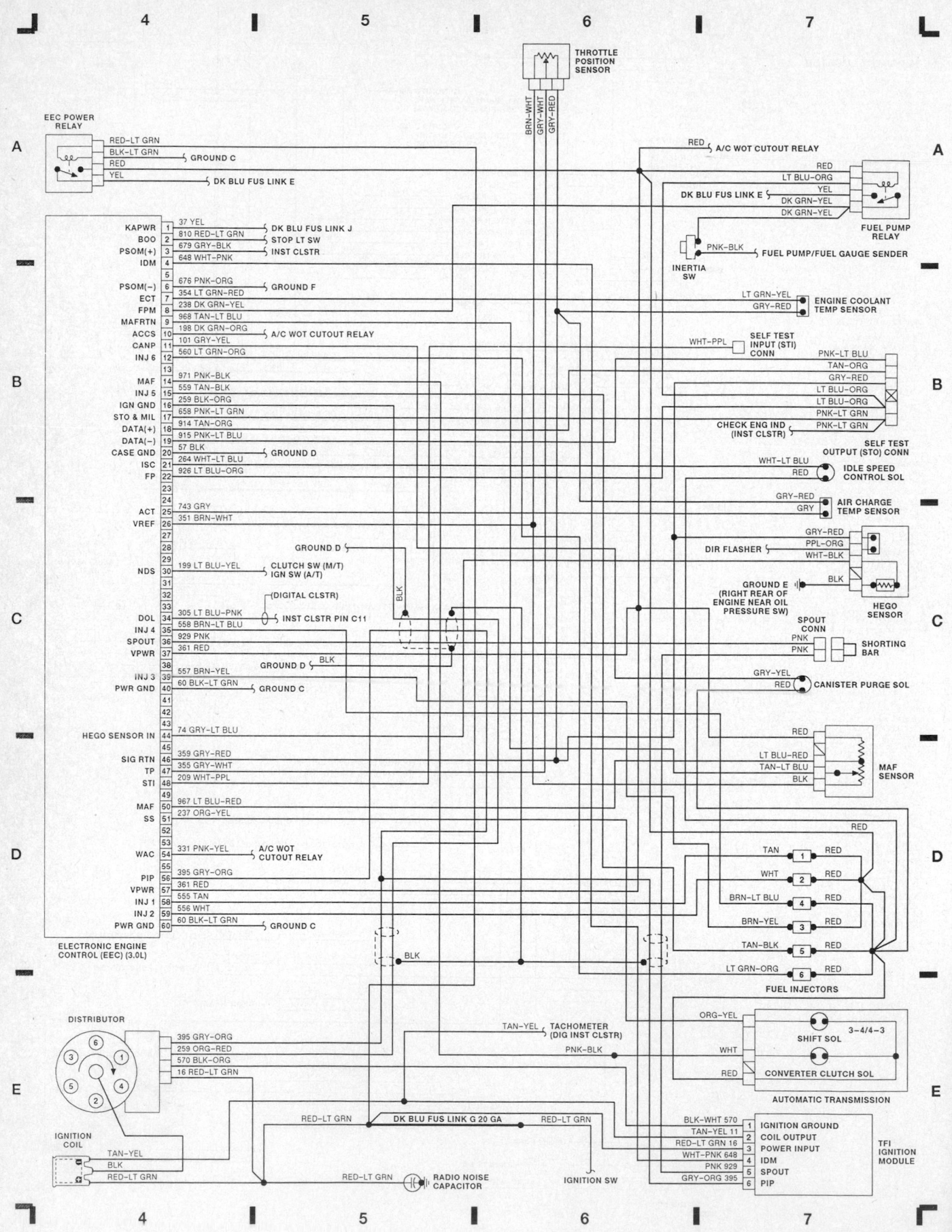

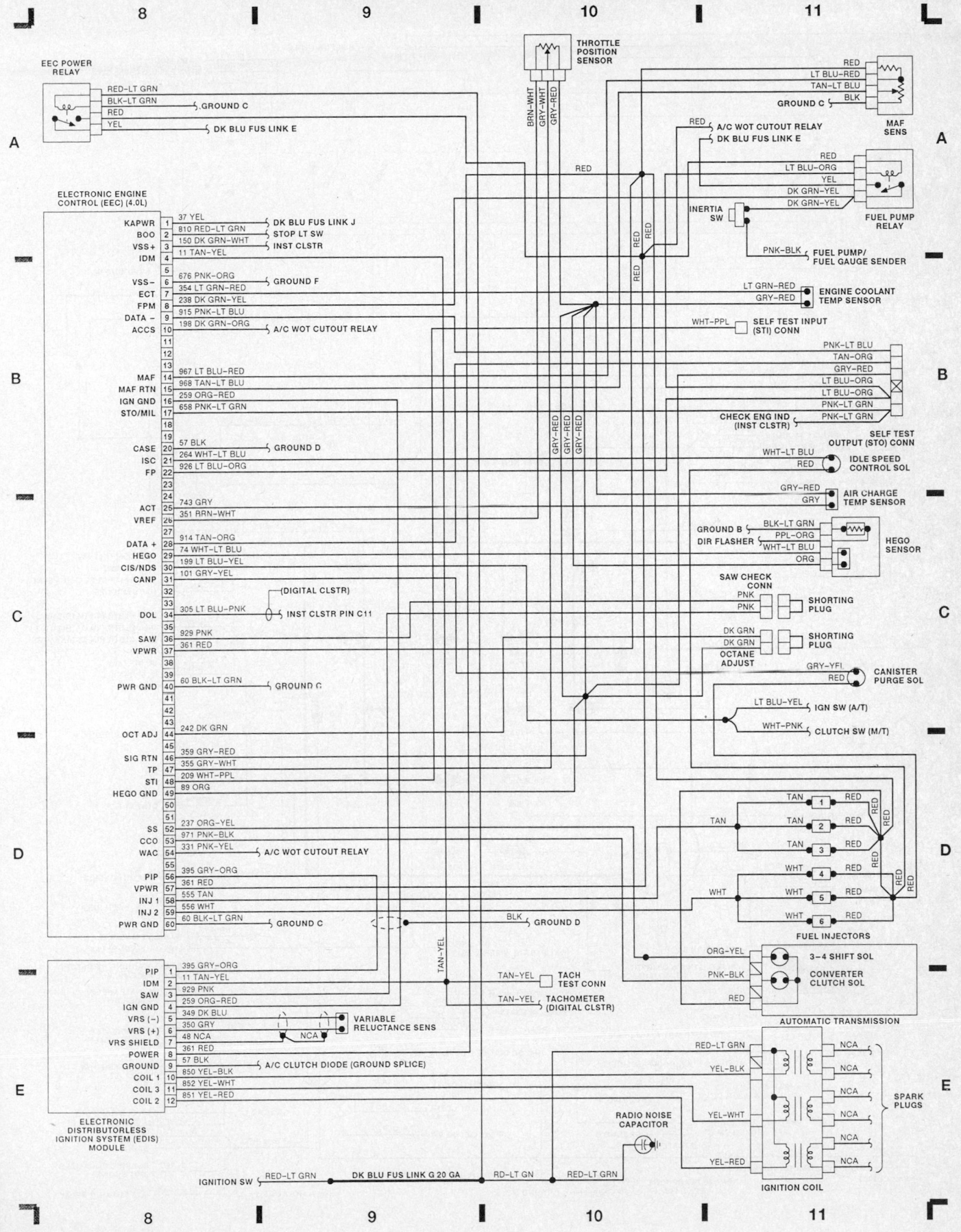

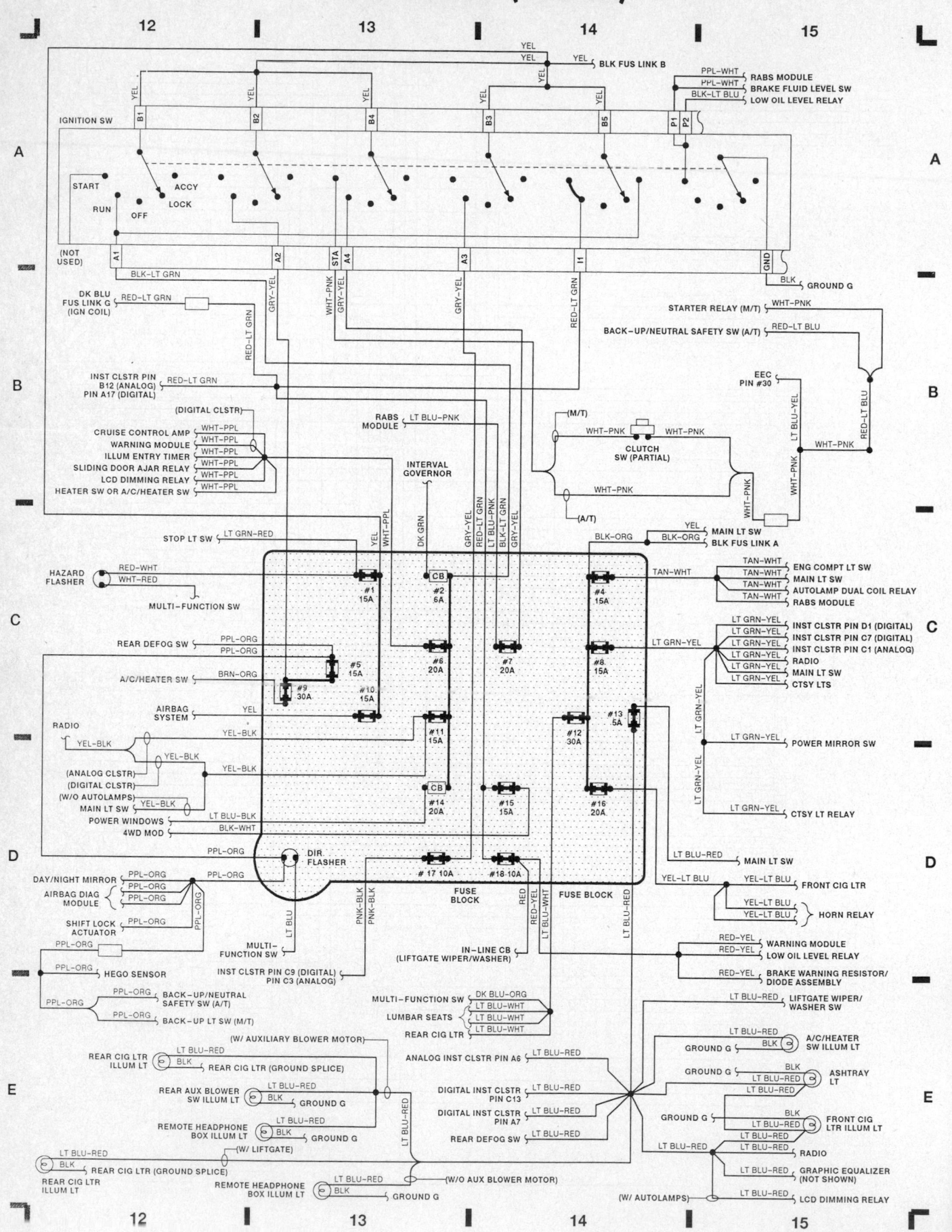

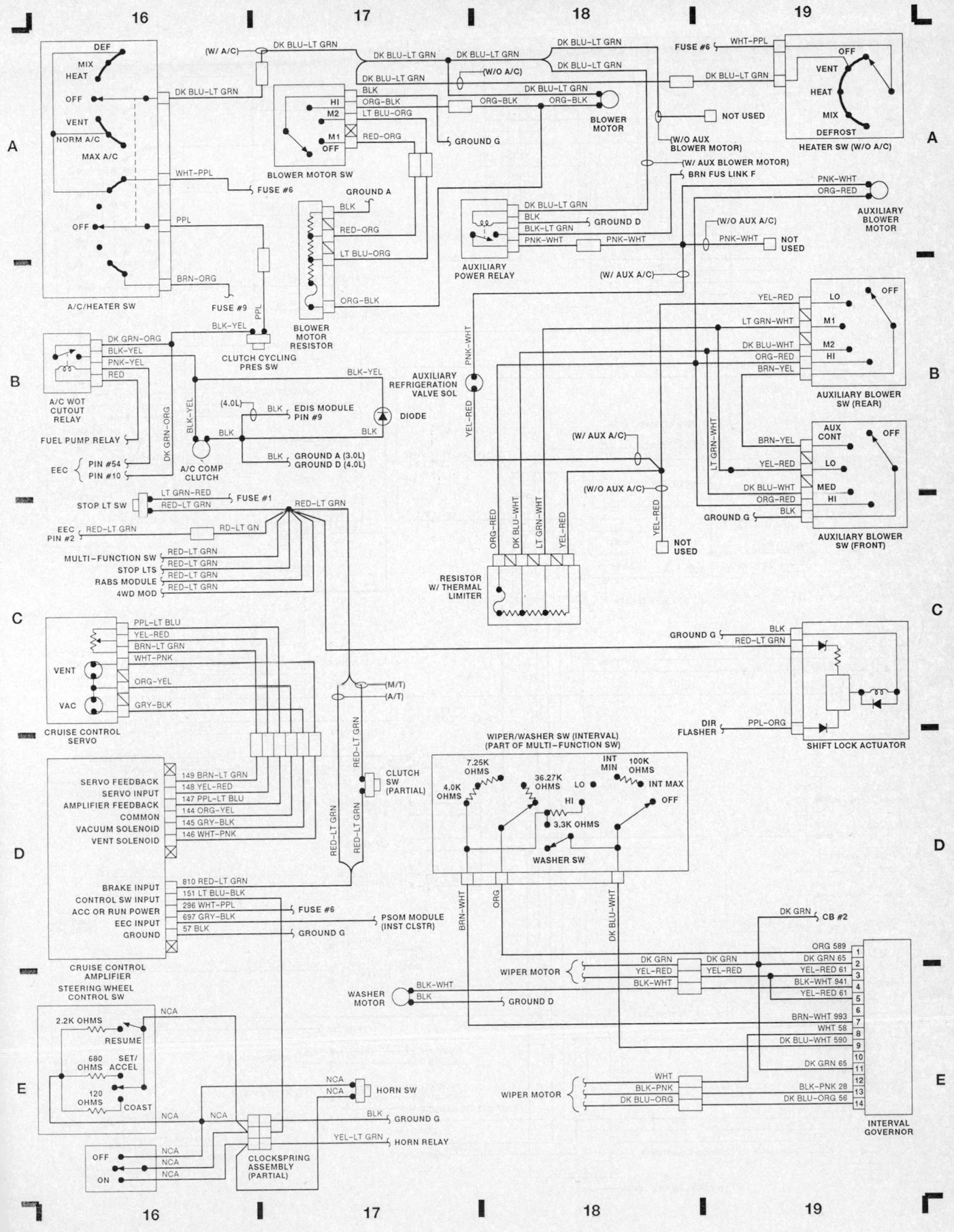

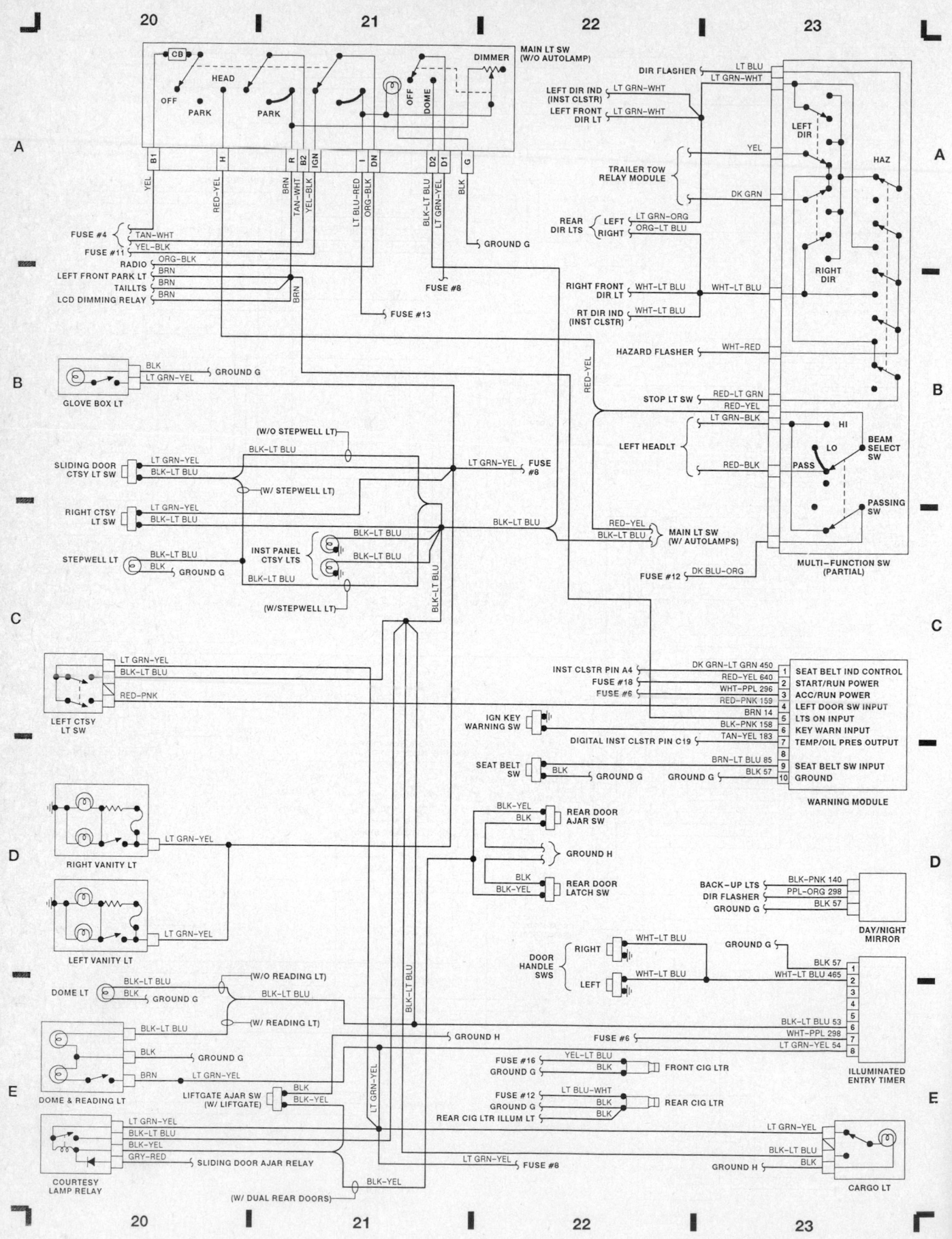

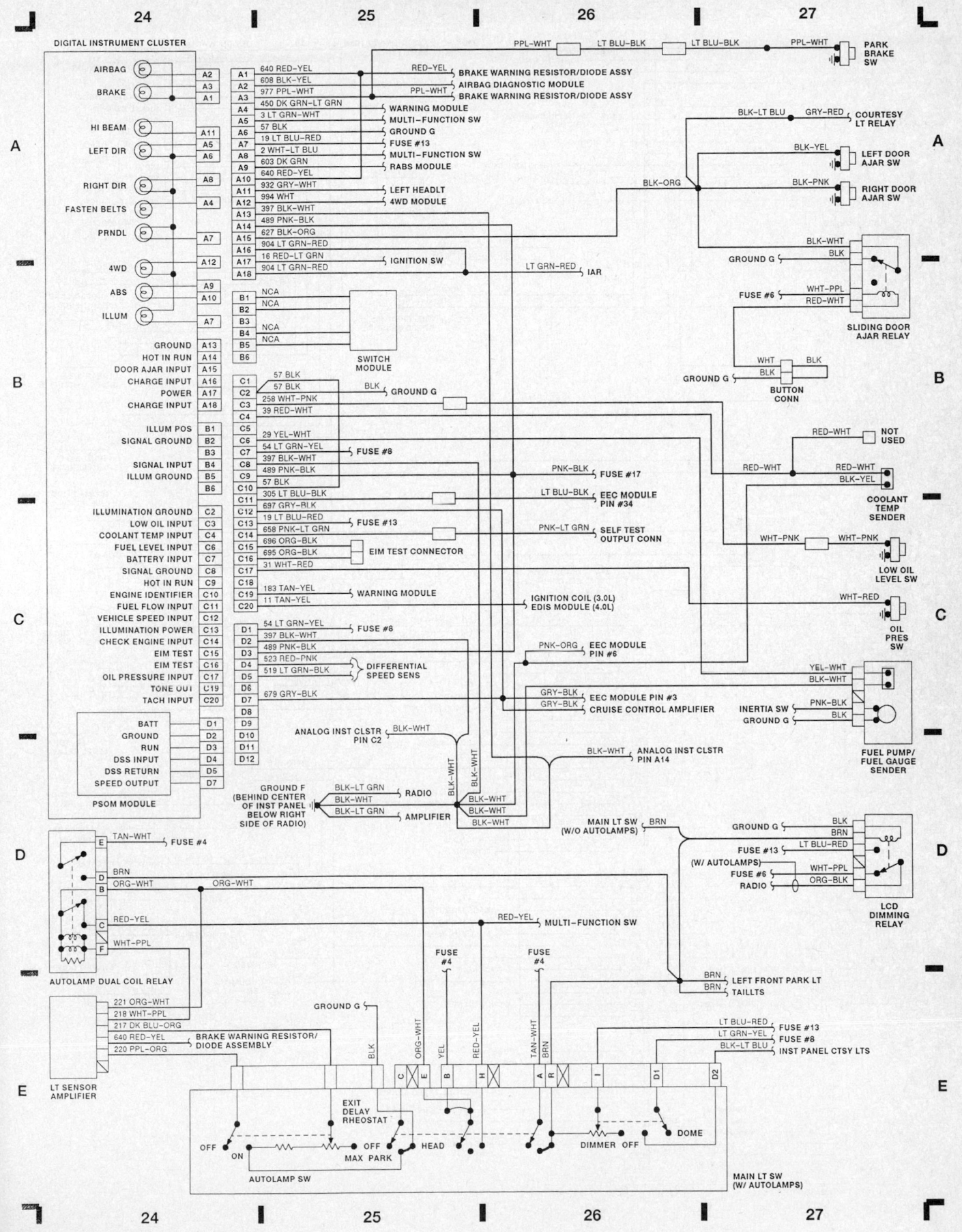

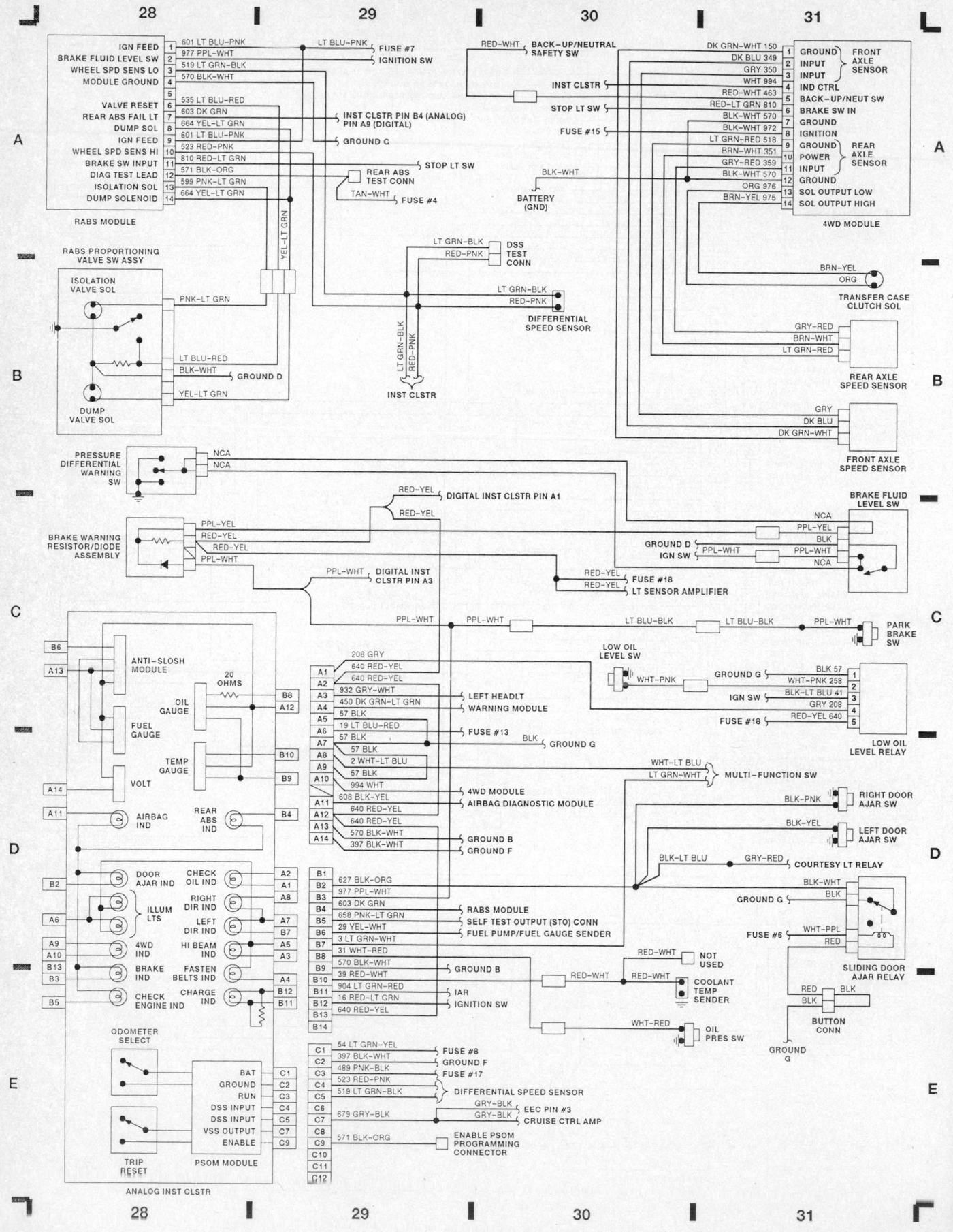

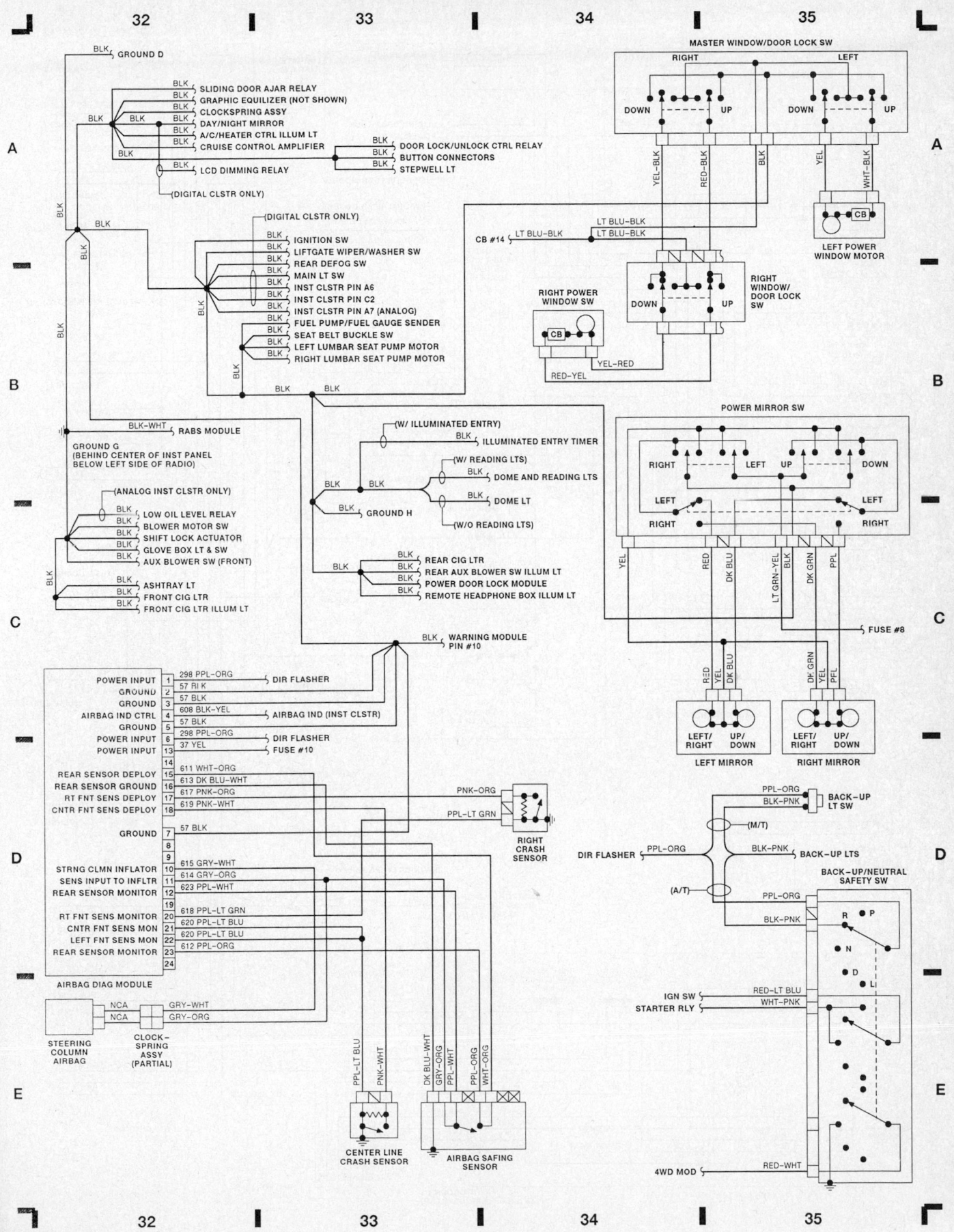

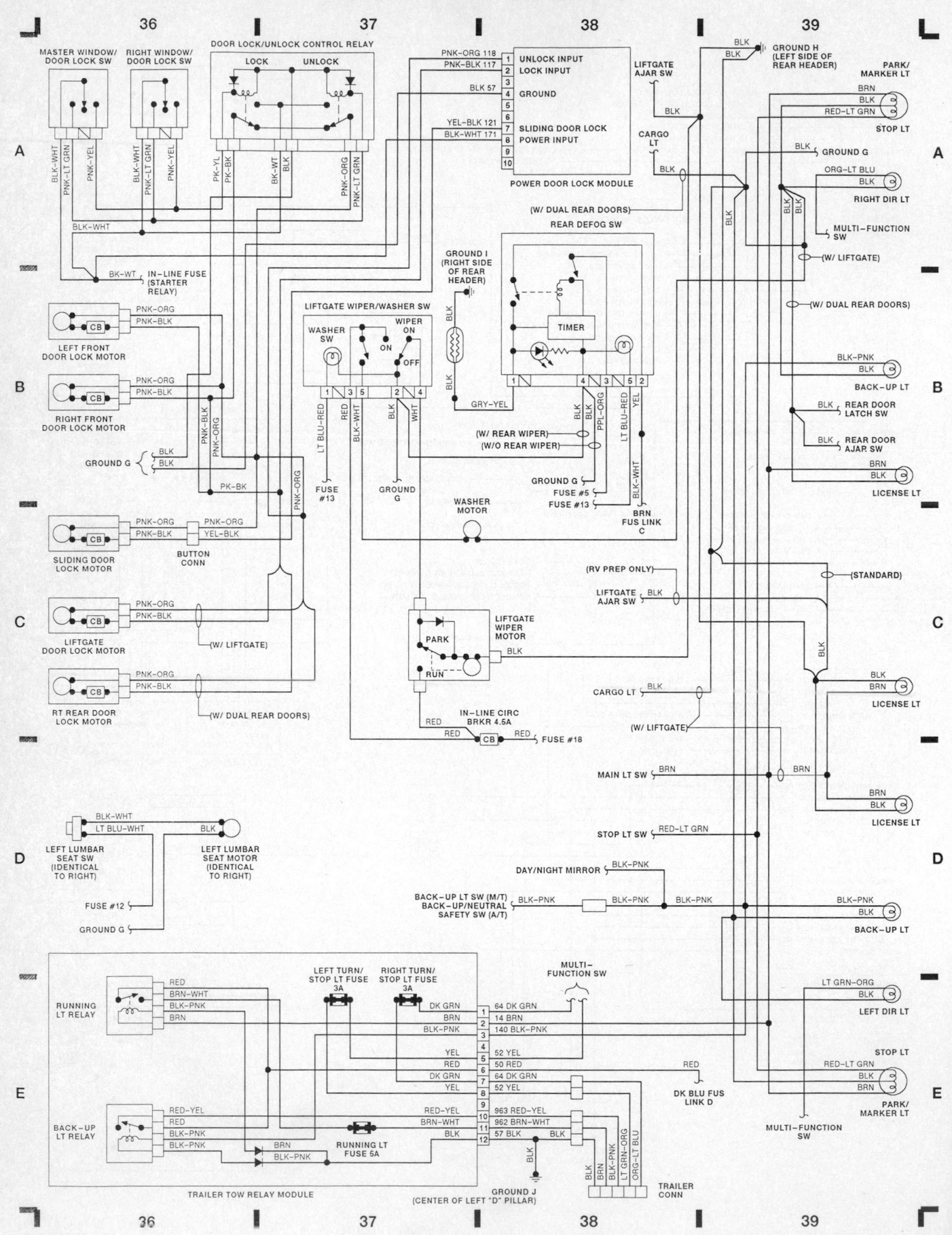

COMPONENT LOCATOR:

A/C CLUTCH RESISTOR DIODE .... E 34
A/C COMP CLUTCH .... E 33
A/C/HEATER CONTROL ASSEMBLY . D-E 32
ALTERNATOR .... B 3, C 3, D 3
ASHTRAY LT .... C 27
AUXILIARY POWER SOCKET .... C 27
BACK-UP LT SW .... D 46
BACK-UP/NEUTRAL SAFETY SW ... A 30-31
BATTERY .... A 2
BATTERY (DIESEL) .... A 2
BEAM SELECT SW .... D 24
BLOWER RESISTOR .... D 33, E 35
BLOWER SW .... E 35, D 33
BRAKE FLUID LEVEL SW .... C 35
BRAKE WARNING RESISTOR/DIODE
  ASSEMBLY .... C 34
CAB MARKER LTS .... A 44-45
CHARGE INDICATOR RELAY .... E 3
CHASSIS CAB ACCESSORY
  MARKER LAMP CONN .... A 46
CIG LTR .... C 24
CLUTCH CYCLING PRES SW .... D 33
CLUTCH INTERLOCK SW .... A 28
CLUTCH INTERLOCK SW JUMPER ... B 31
COLD IDLE SOL (DIESEL) .... B 23
COLD TIMING ADVANCE
  SOL (DIESEL) .... B 23
CRUISE CONTROL MODULE .... E 31
DIESEL WARNING LAMPS DISPLAY ... E 36
DIR FLASHER .... C 26
DIR/HAZ SW .... C 29
DISTRIBUTOR .... A 11, A 15, A 19
E40D TRANSMISSION ...... E 9, E 17, E 21
EEC (4.9L) .... B-E 8
EEC (5.0L & 5.8L) .... B-E 14
EEC (7.5L) .... B-E 16
EEC POWER RELAY .... A 8, A 12, A 16
ELECTRO-HYDRAULIC VALVE ... A-B 36
ELECTRONIC SHIFT
  CONTROL MODULE .... A 39
ELECTRONIC SHIFT CONTROL SW ... A 37
ENGINE COMPT FUSE BOX ...... B-C 6-7
ENGINE COMPT LT .... C 2
ENGINE TEMP SW (DIESEL) .... B 22
FRONT DOOR COURTESY LTS .... D 37
FUEL LINE HEATER (DIESEL) .... A 5
FUEL PUMP RELAY .... A 8, A 12, A 16
FUEL SHUTOFF SOL (DIESEL) .... A 23
FUEL TANK SELECT SW .... B 43
FUEL TANK SELECTOR SW .... C 41
FUEL TANK SENDERS .... C 42
FUEL TANK UNIT .... A 42, A 43
FUEL WATER SW .... D 36
FUSE BLOCK .... C 25-26
GLOVE BOX LT .... E 39
GLOW PLUG CONTROLLER .... A 21
GROUND A .... A 2
GROUND B .... B 1
GROUND C .... A 1
GROUND D .... A 2
GROUND E .... E 4
GROUND F .... A 4
GROUND G ...... C 10, B 14, B 18, B 22
GROUND H .... C 36
GROUND I .... A 41
GROUND J .... A 45
HAZARD FLASHER .... D 28
HEATER CONTROL ASSEMBLY ...... E 34
HEATER CONTROL ILLUM LT .... D 34
HEGO SENSOR ...... C 11, C 15, C 19
HORN RELAY .... D 28
HORN SW .... E 28, E 29
IGN SUPPRESSION RESISTOR .. A 10, A 14, A 18
IGNITION COIL ...... A 11, A 15, A 19
IGNITION SW .... A 24-27
INERTIA SW .... B 43, A 42
INSIDE CARGO LT .... E 39
INSTRUMENT CLUSTER .... A-D 32
INTERVAL GOVERNOR .... B 28
LEFT DOOR SW .... E 37
LEFT SIDE BODY MARKER LTS ...... E 47
LOW VACUUM WARNING SW .... C 35
LUMBAR SEATS .... B 41-42
MAIN LIGHT SW .... D-E 27
MAP/DOME LTS .... D 39
MLPS ...... B 11, B 15, B 19, B 23, A 29
MULTI-FUNCTION SW ... D 24, C 29-31
OUTSIDE CARGO/HIGH
  MOUNT STOP LTS .... E 44
OVERDRIVE CANCEL SW .... C 36
POWER DOOR LOCKS .... C-D 40-41
POWER MIRRORS .... D-E 41-42
POWER WINDOWS .... B-C 40-41
PSOM .... C 32
RABS MODULE .... A 37
REAR DEFOGGER .... A 40
REAR DOOR COURTESY LTS .... D 37
SEAT BELT SW .... D 35
STARTER .... B 3
STARTER RELAY .... A 3
STO CONN ...... C 11, C 15, C 19, D 23
STOP LT SW .... D 30
TAILGATE WINDOW .... D-E 43
TECA .... E 22
TECA POWER RELAY .... E 22
TFI IGNITION MODULE ... A 10, A 14, A 18
TRAILER BACK-UP LAMPS RELAY ... B 44, D 44
TRAILER BATTERY CHARGE RELAY . C 44, D 44
TRAILER CONN .... C 46, D 46
TRAILER MARKER LAMPS RELAY ... A-B 44
W/SHIELD WIPER MOTOR .... C 28
WARNING CHIME MODULE .... D 35
WASHER MOTOR .... B 29
4X4 HI/LOW IND SW .... B 35

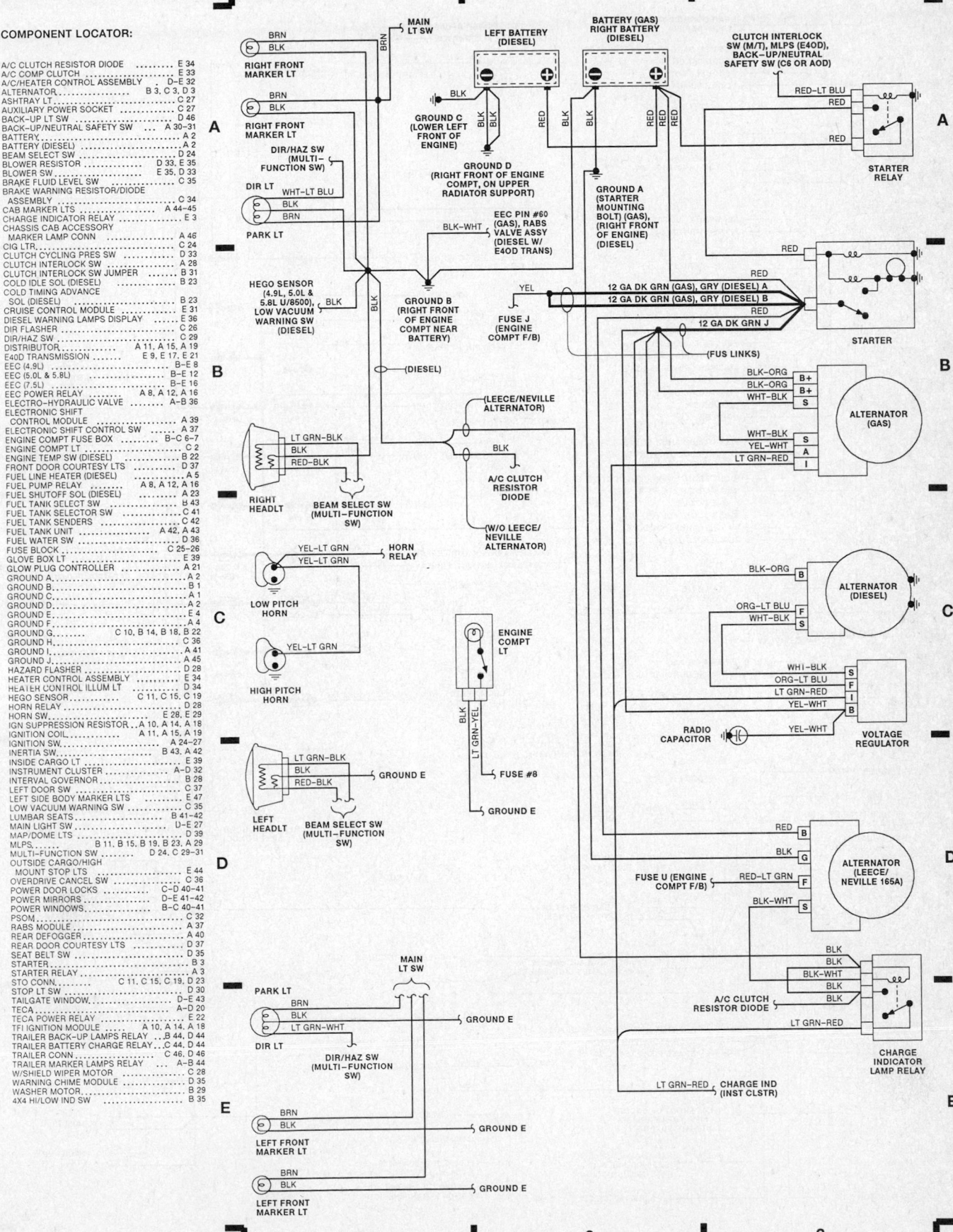

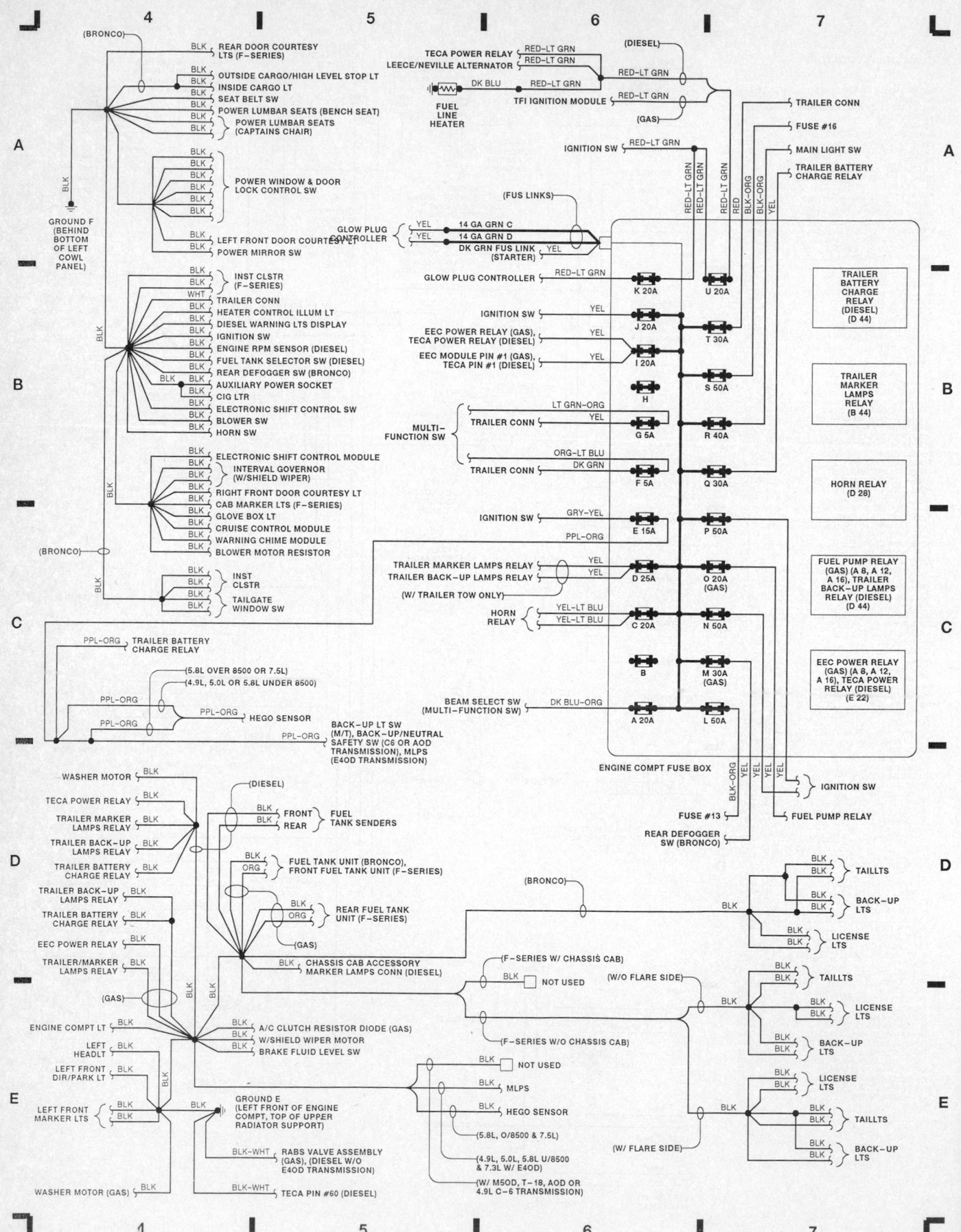

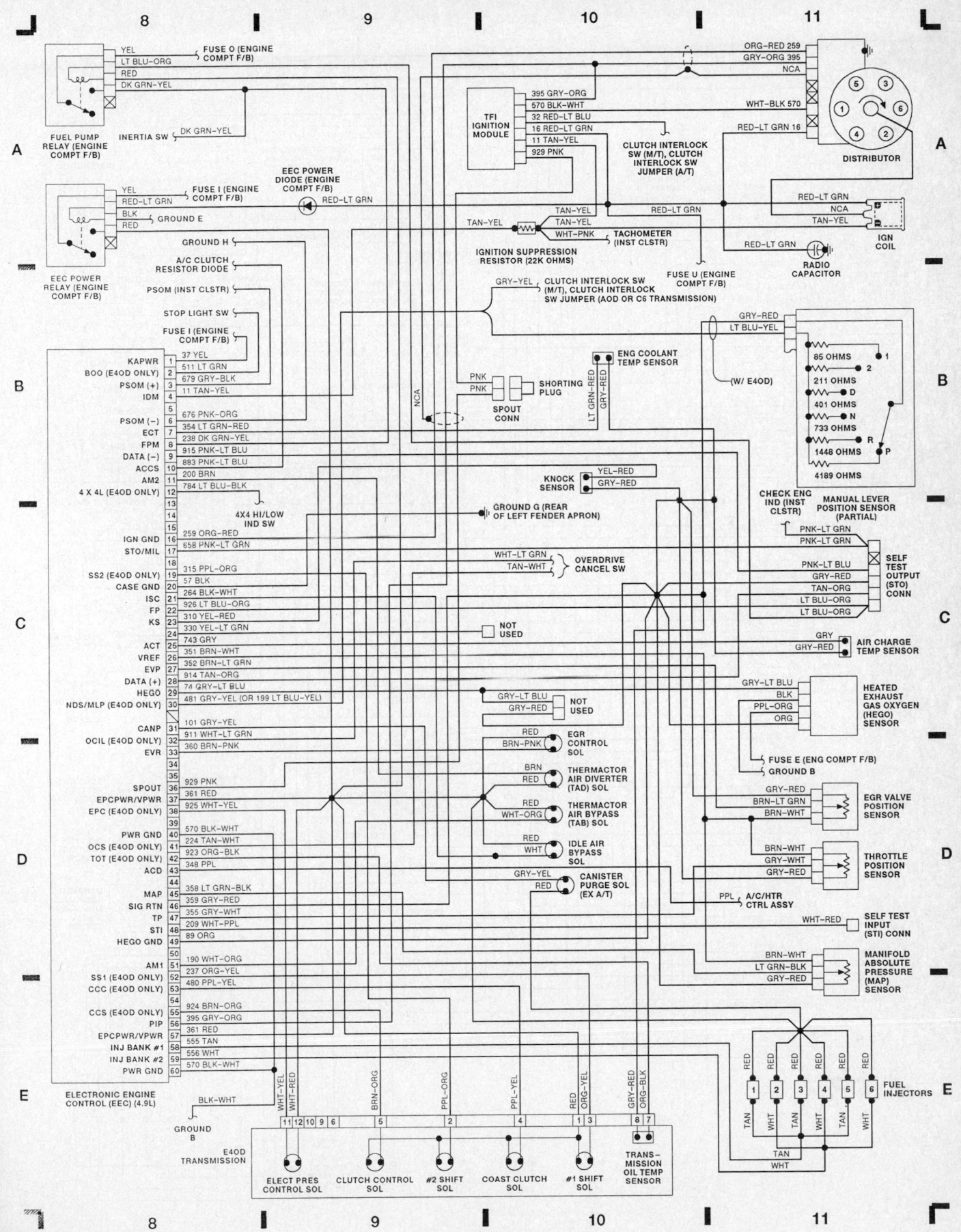

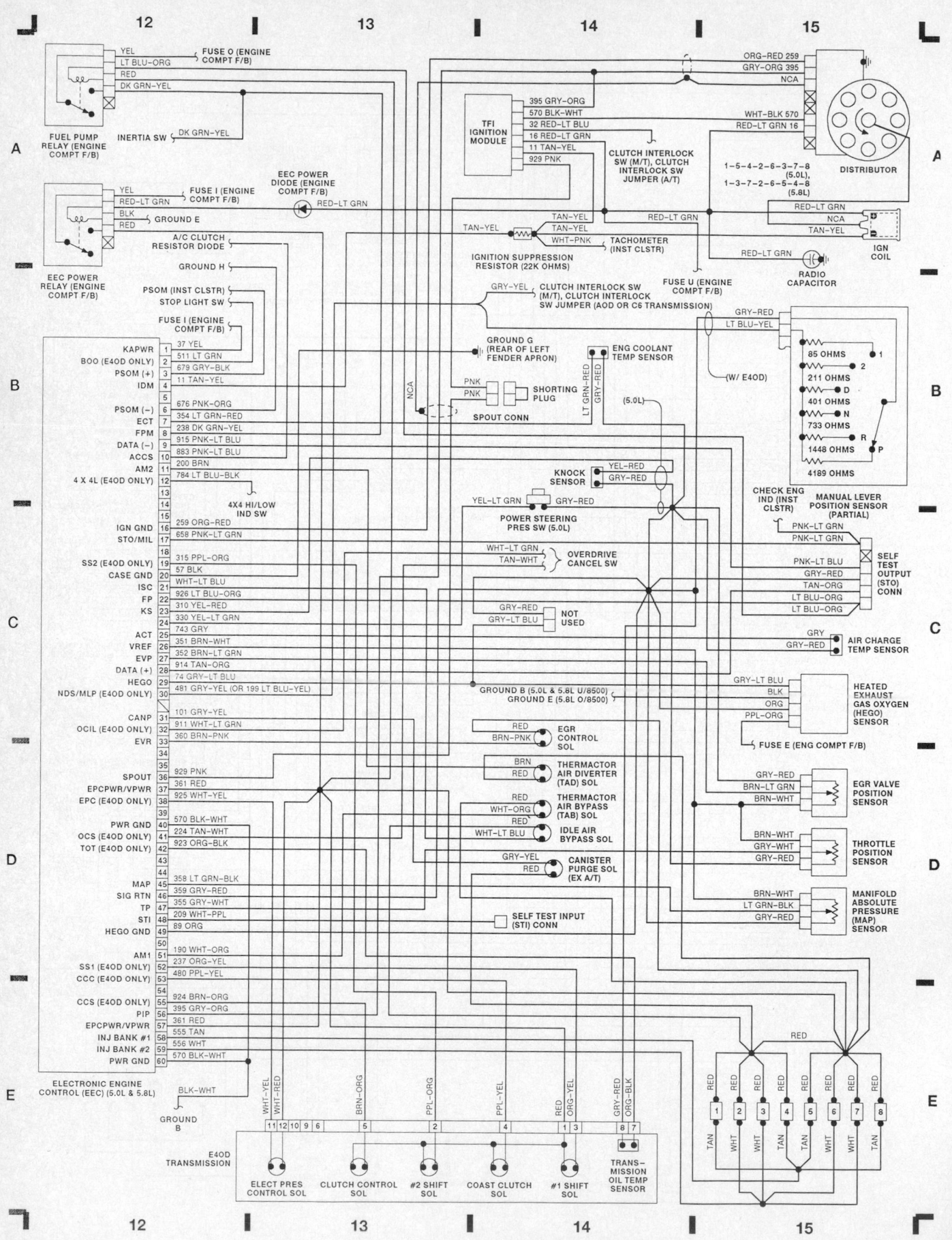

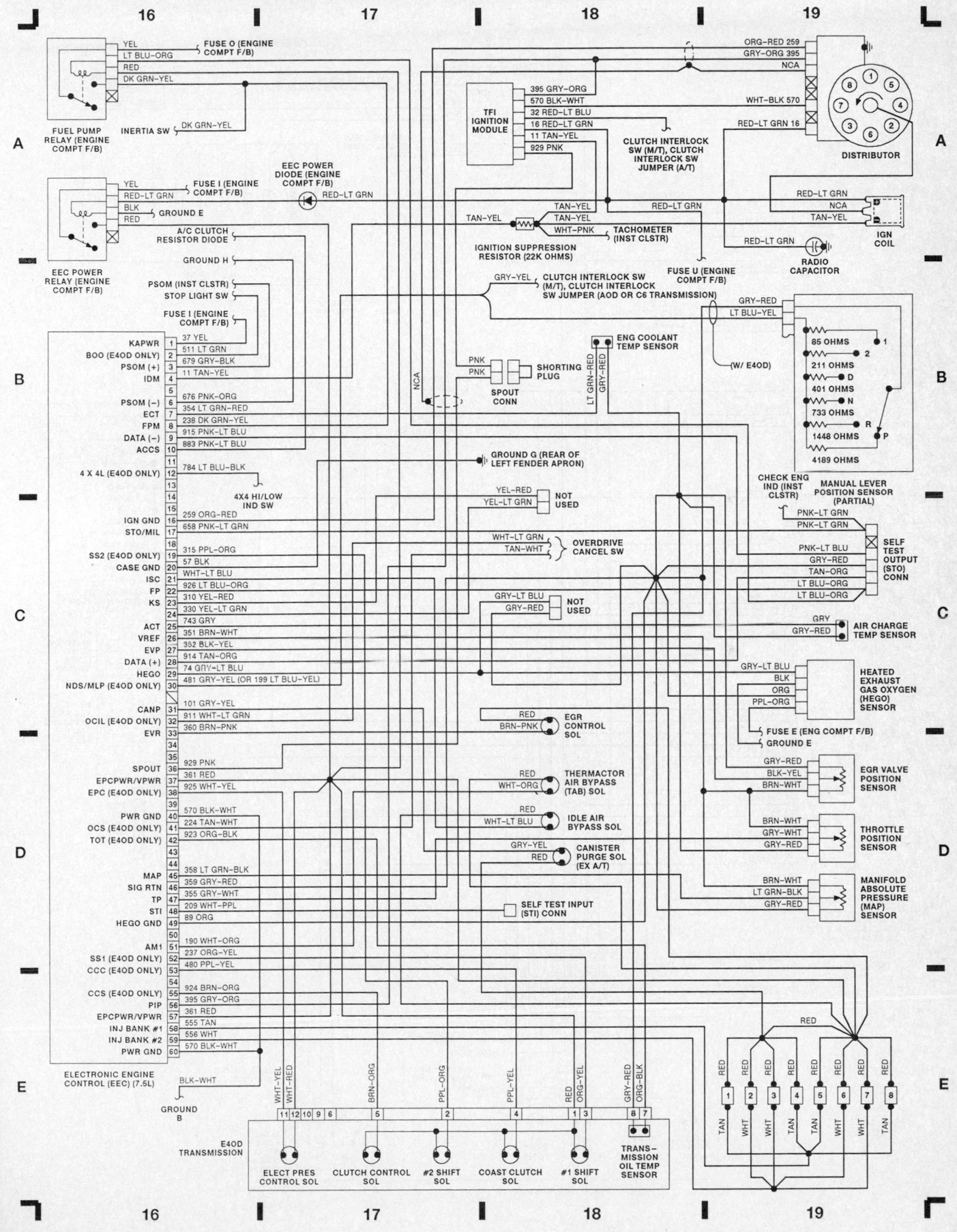

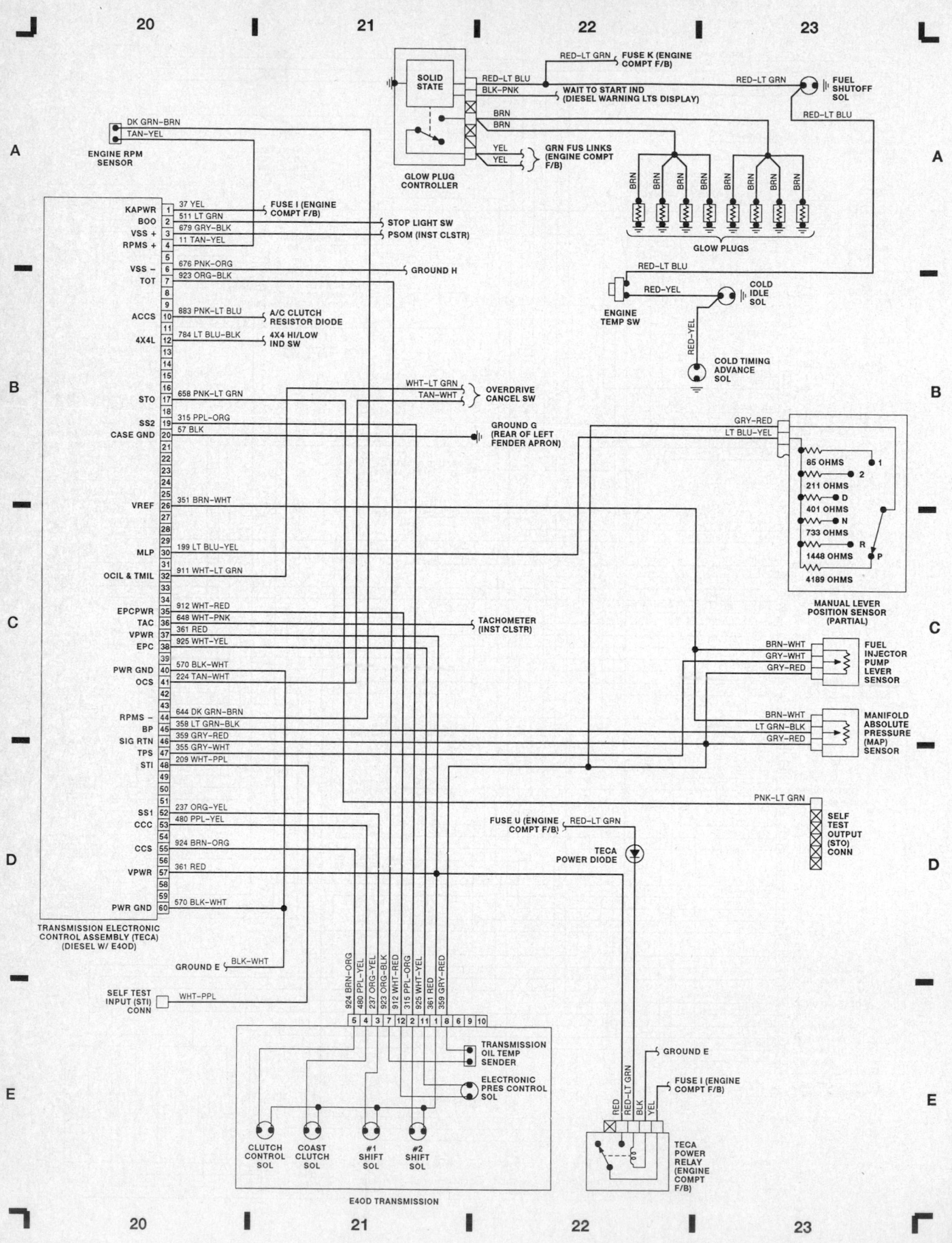

E40D TRANSMISSION

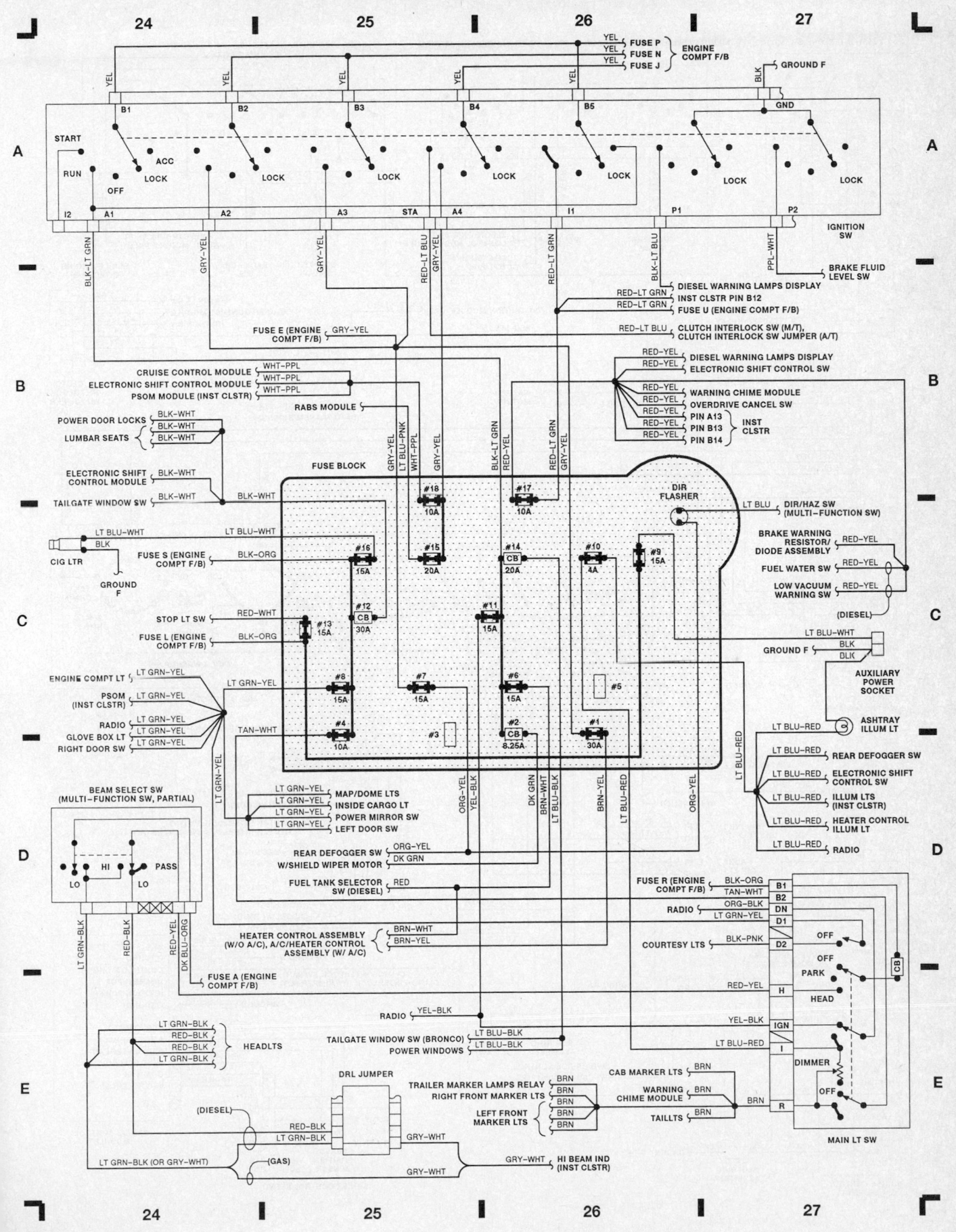

1992 WIRING DIAGRAMS
Bronco & Pickup (Cont.)

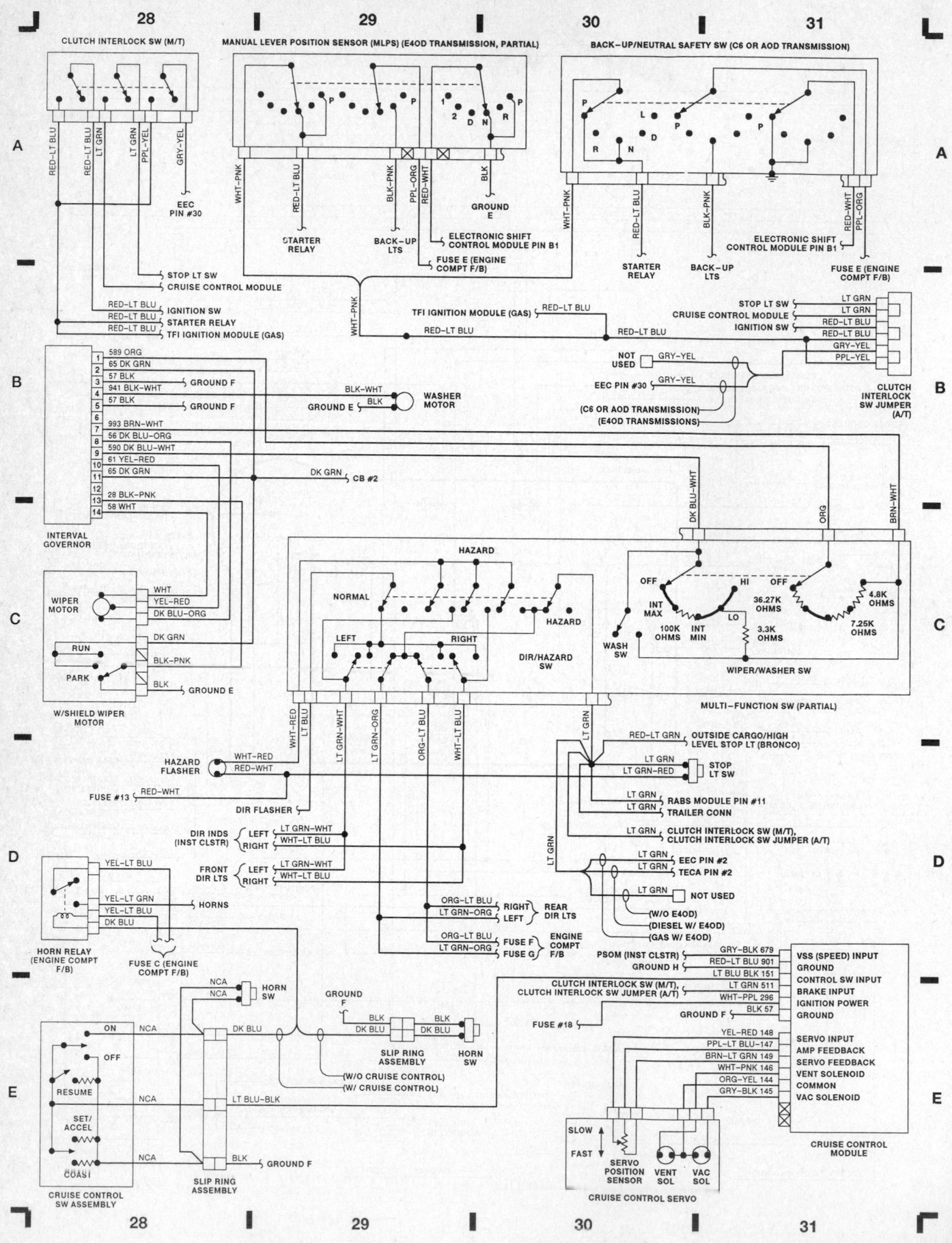

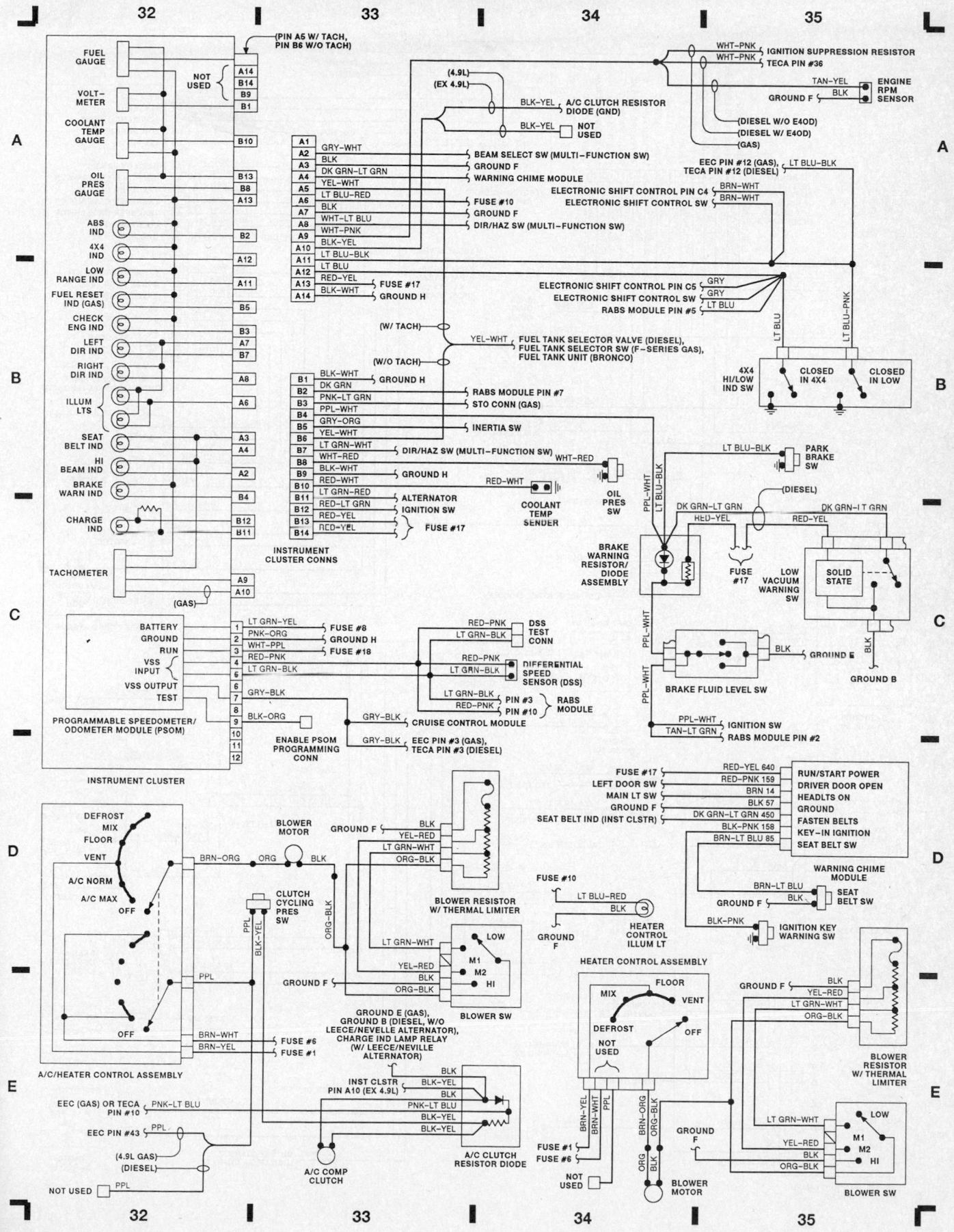

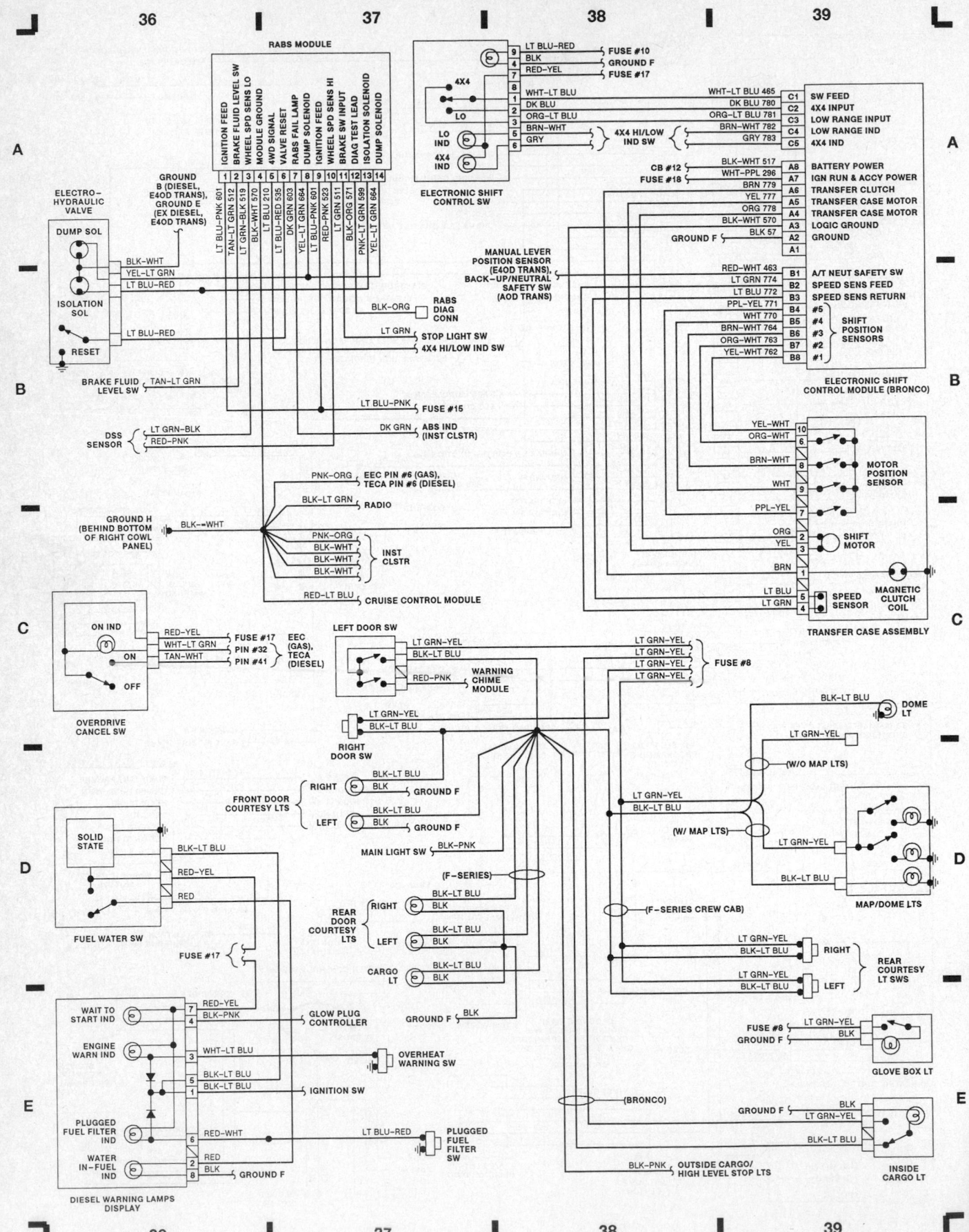

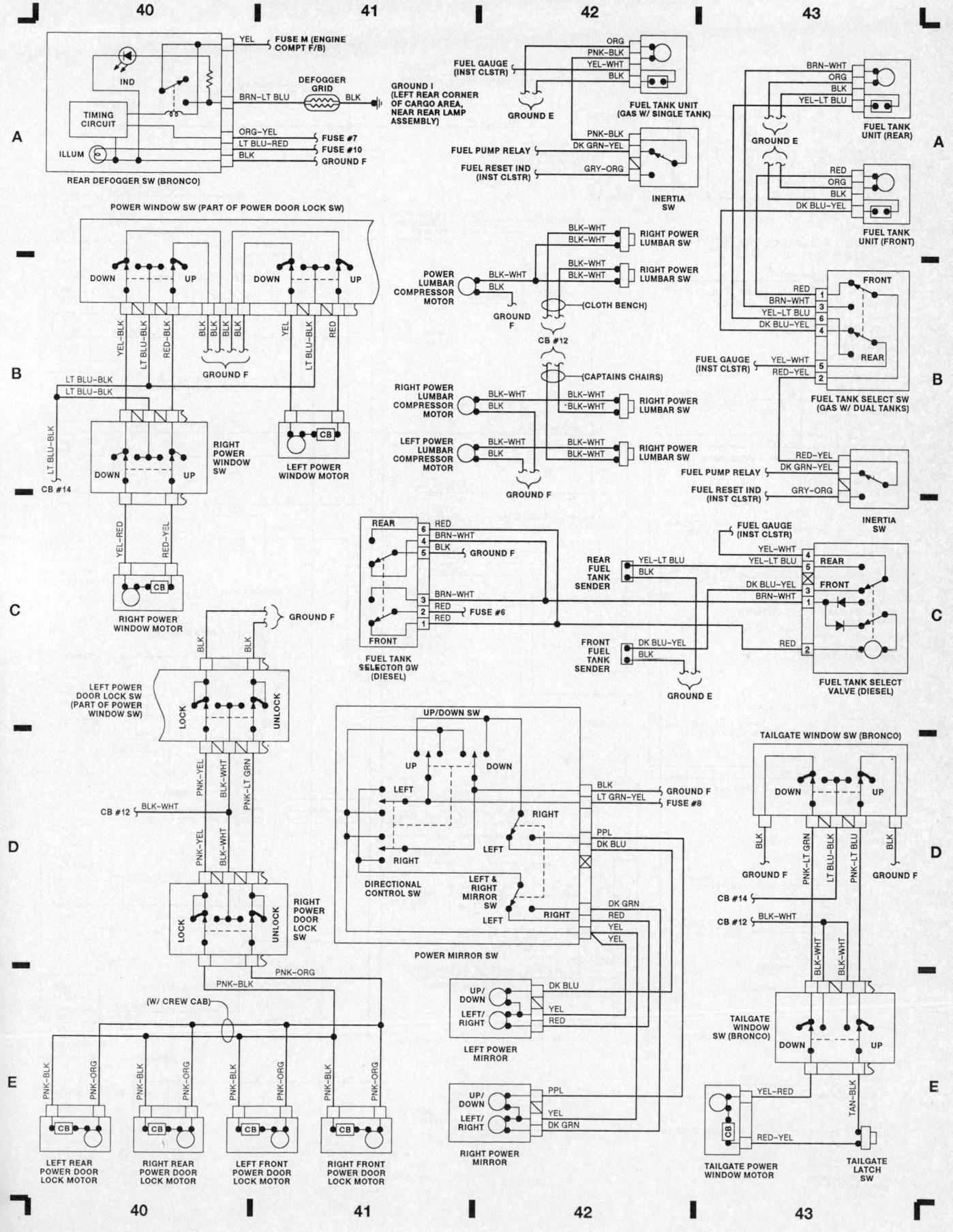

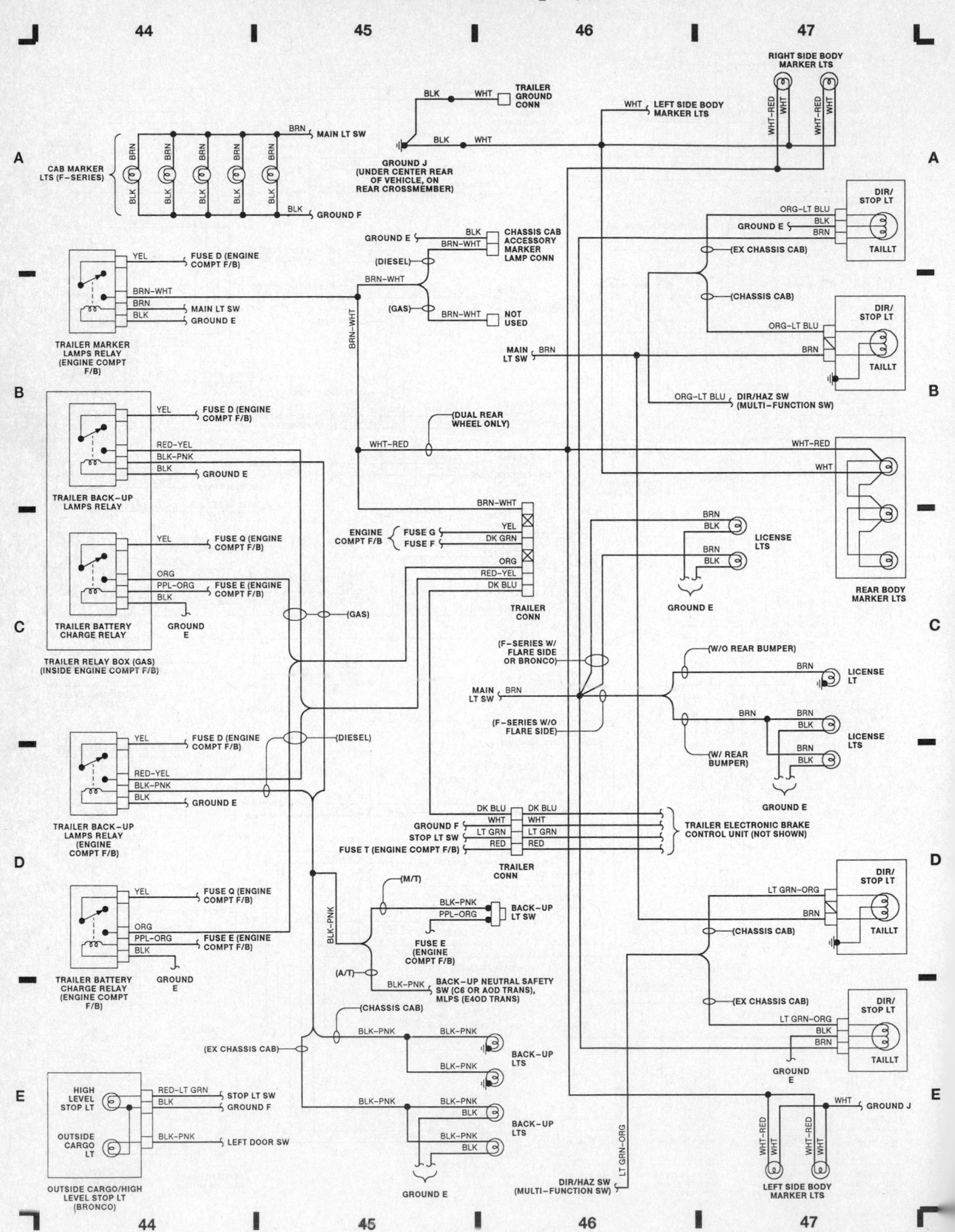

COMPONENT LOCATOR:

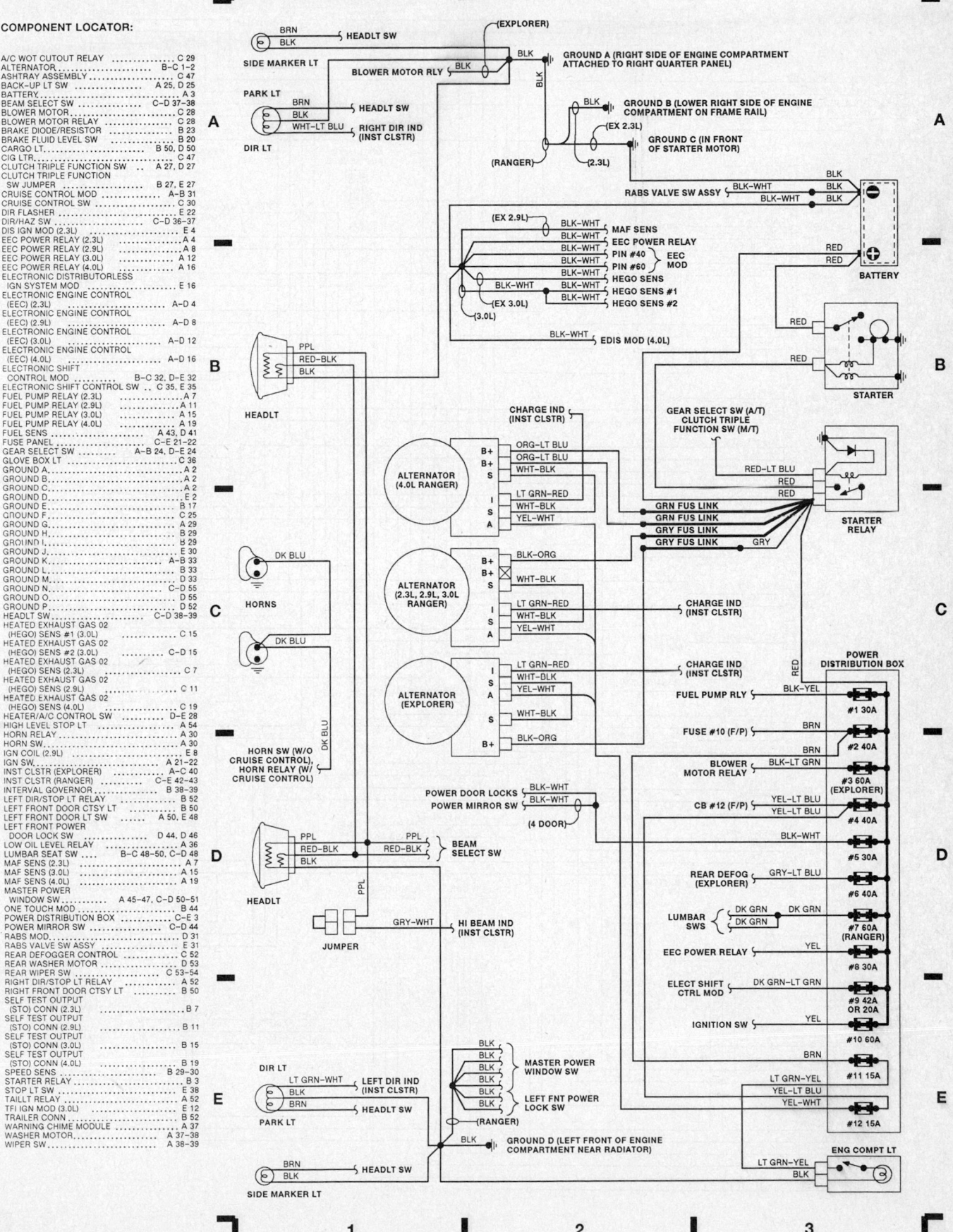

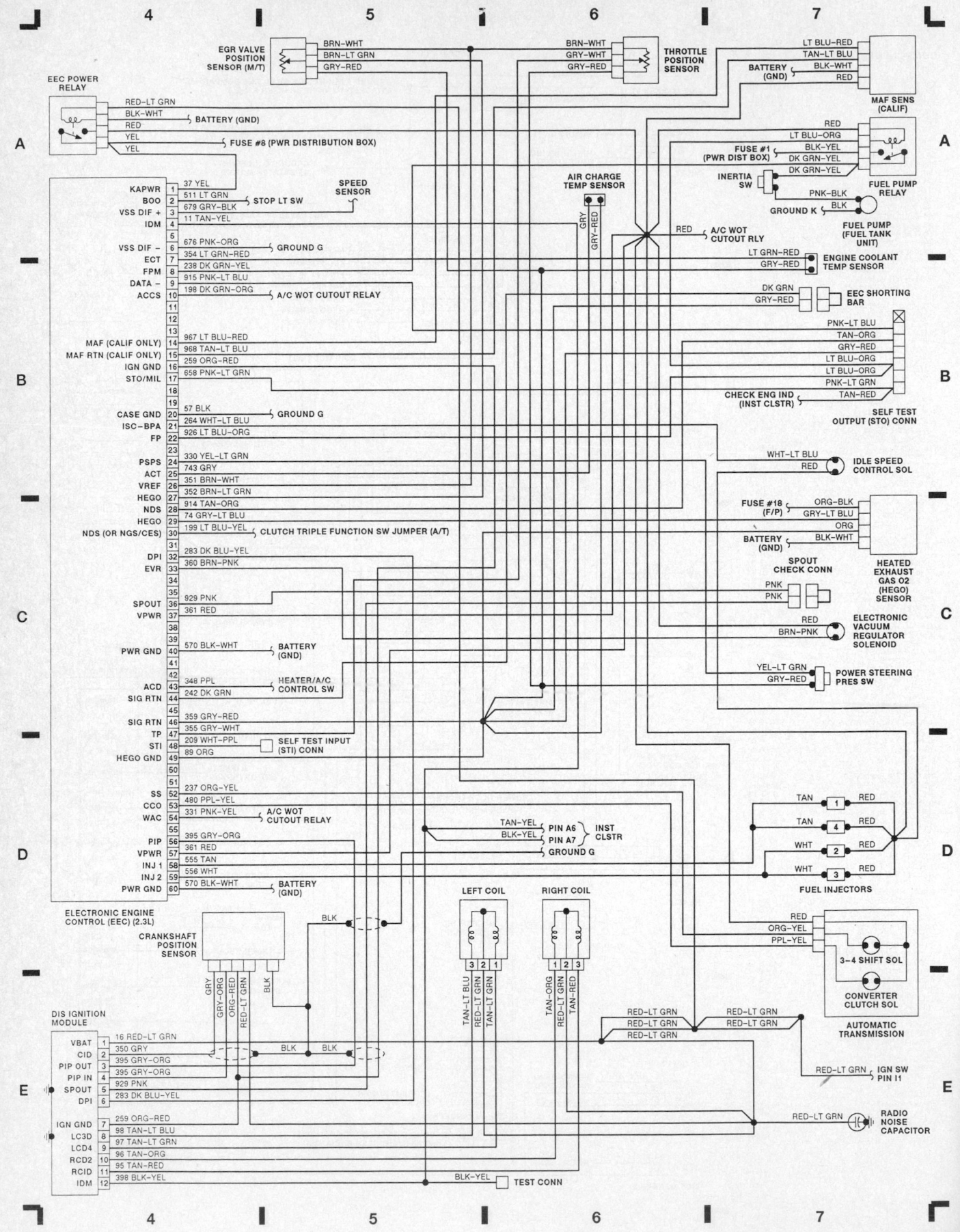

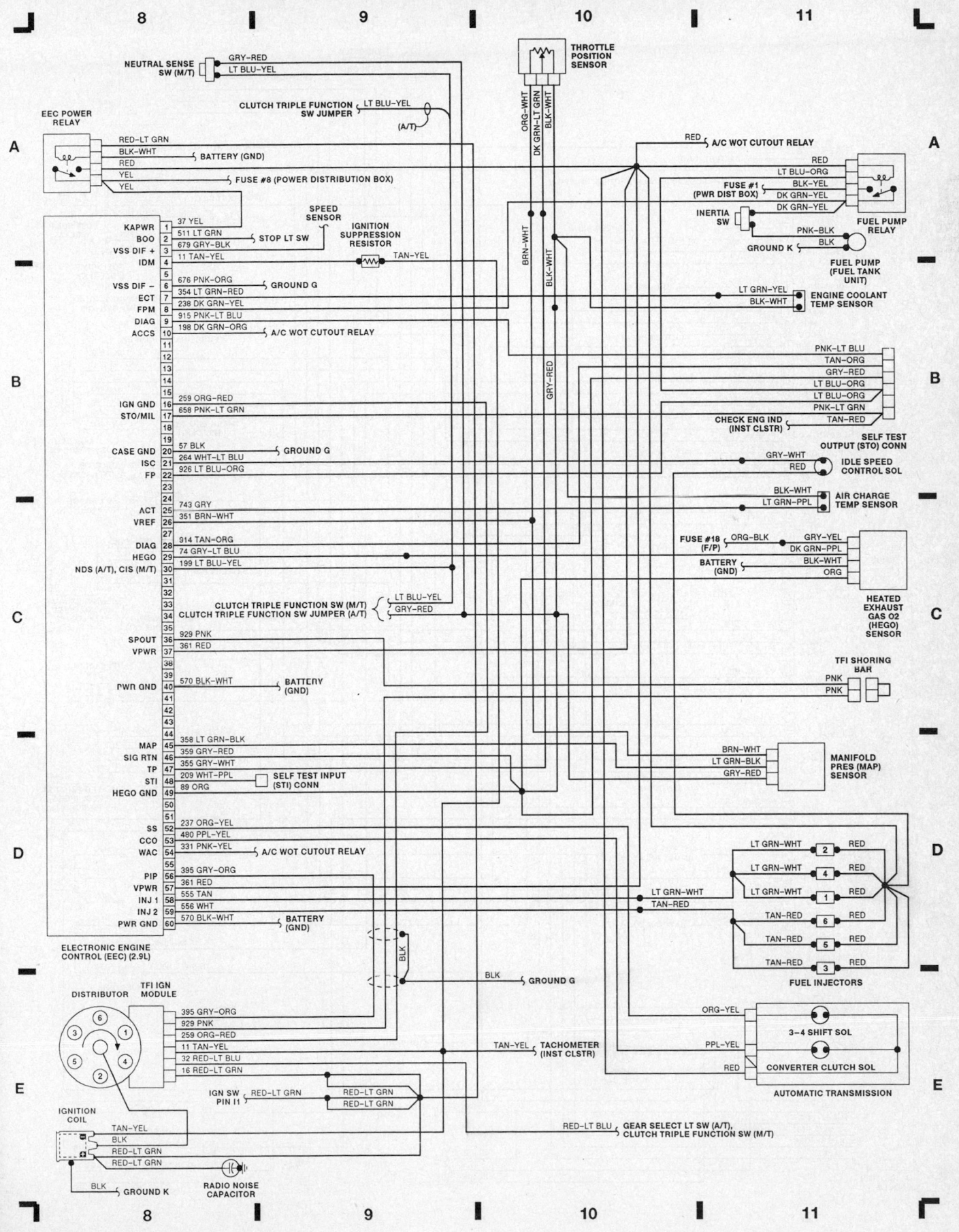

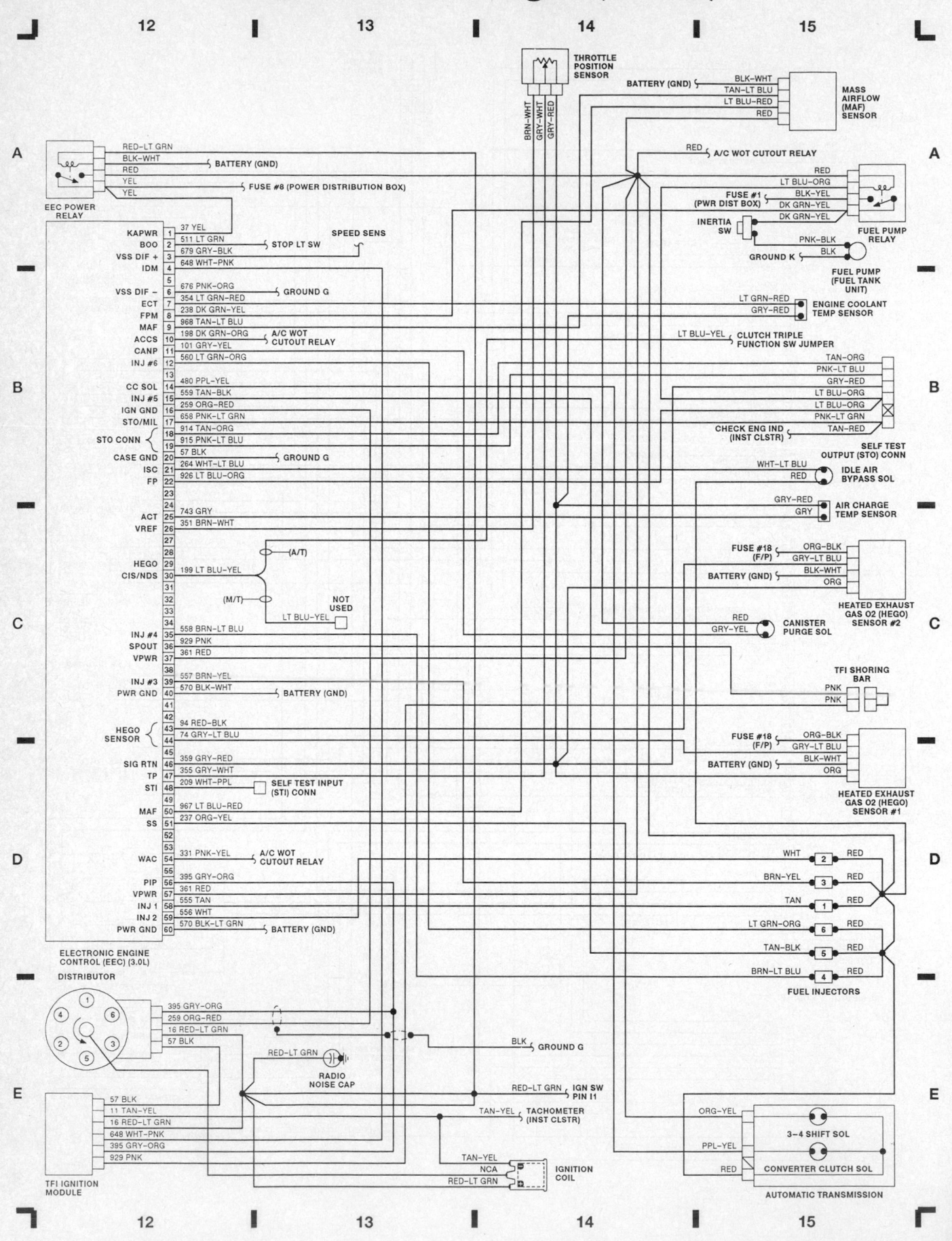

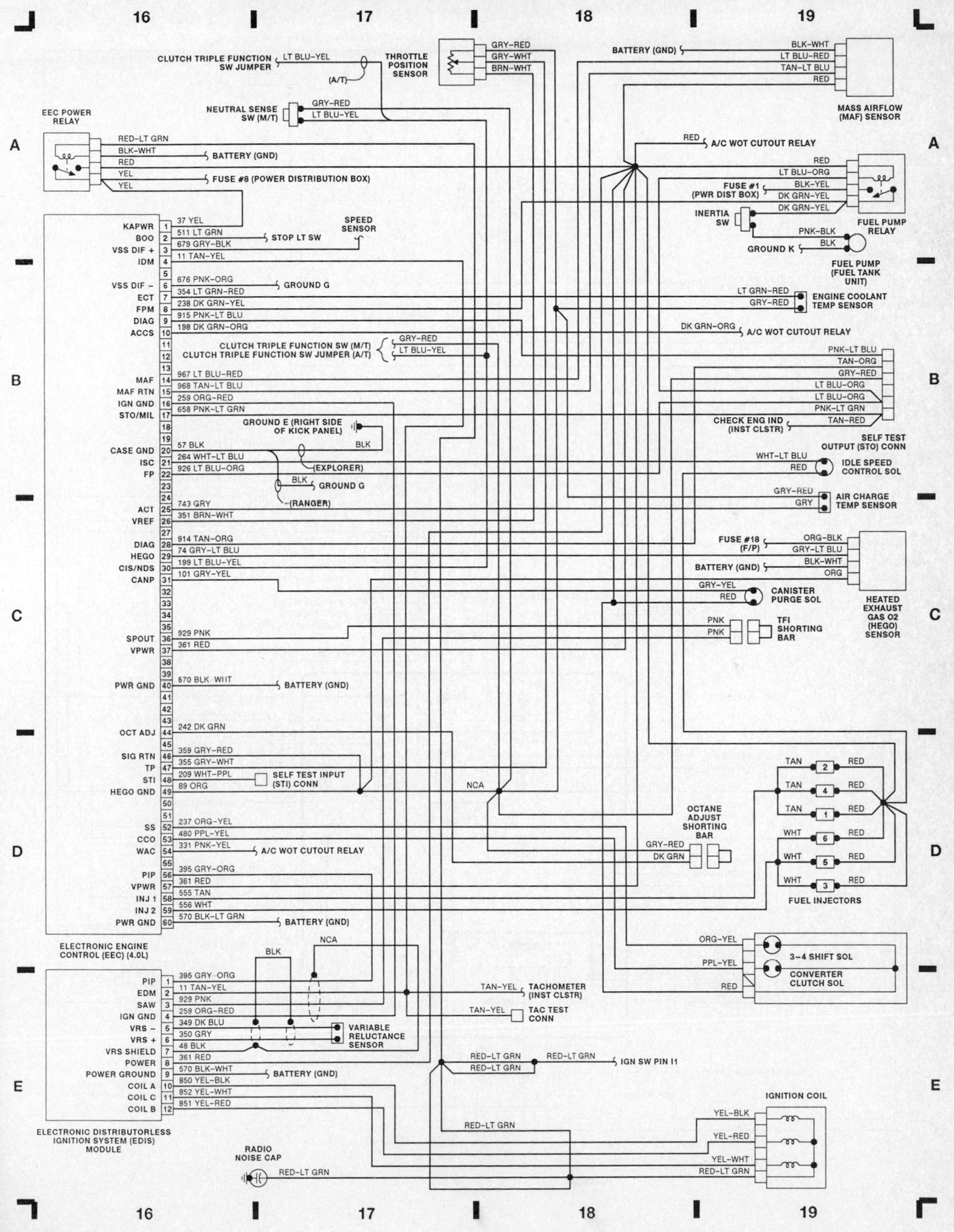

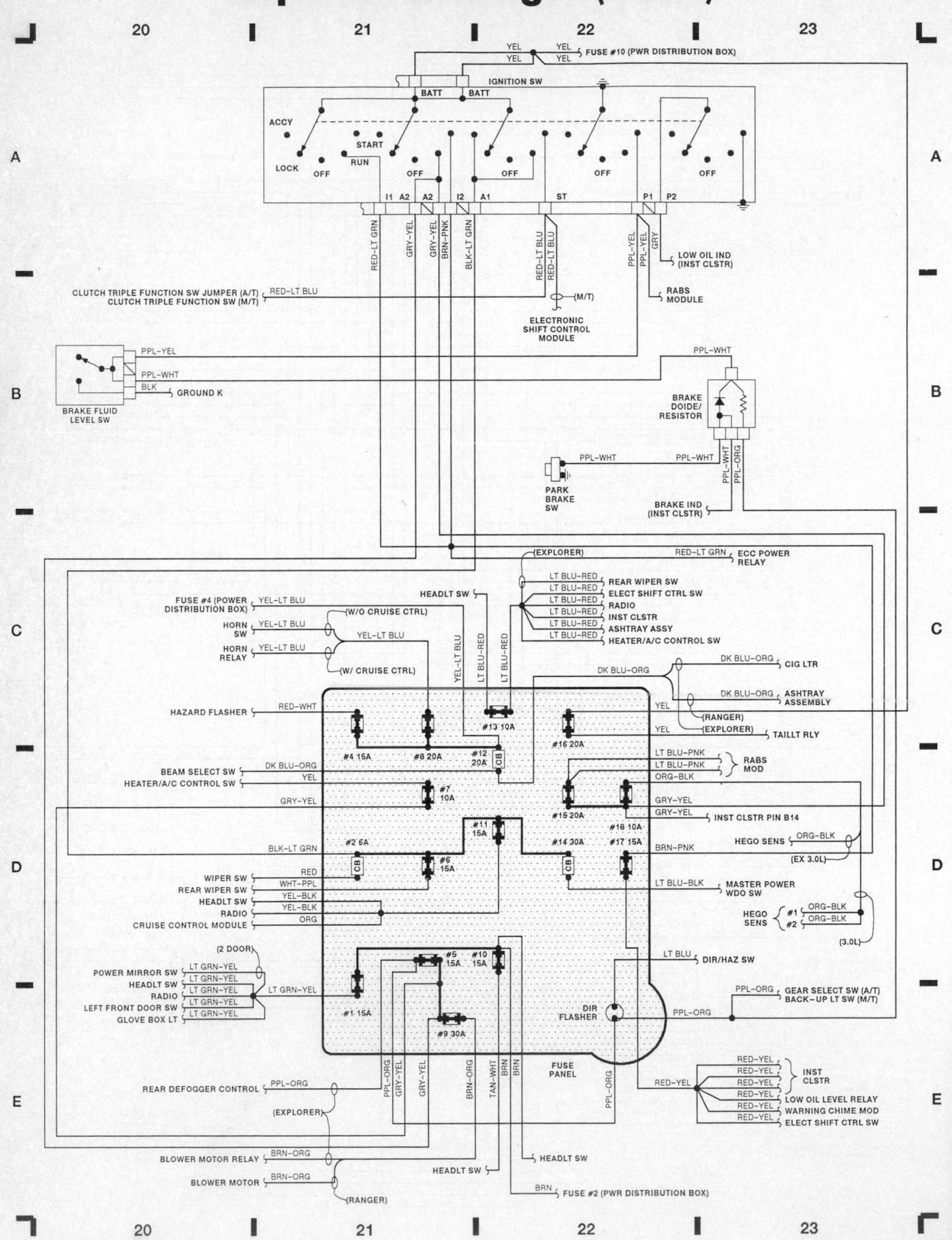

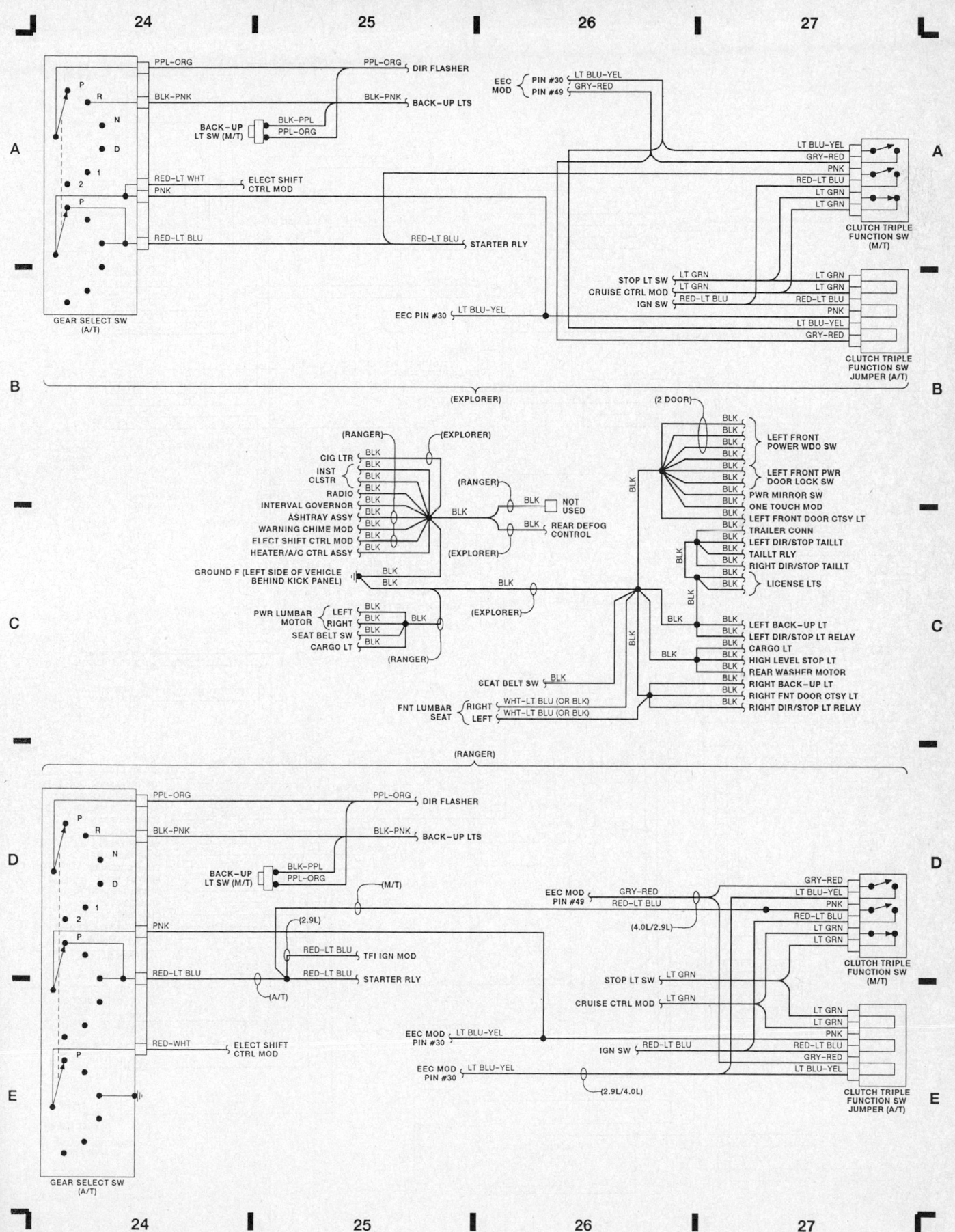

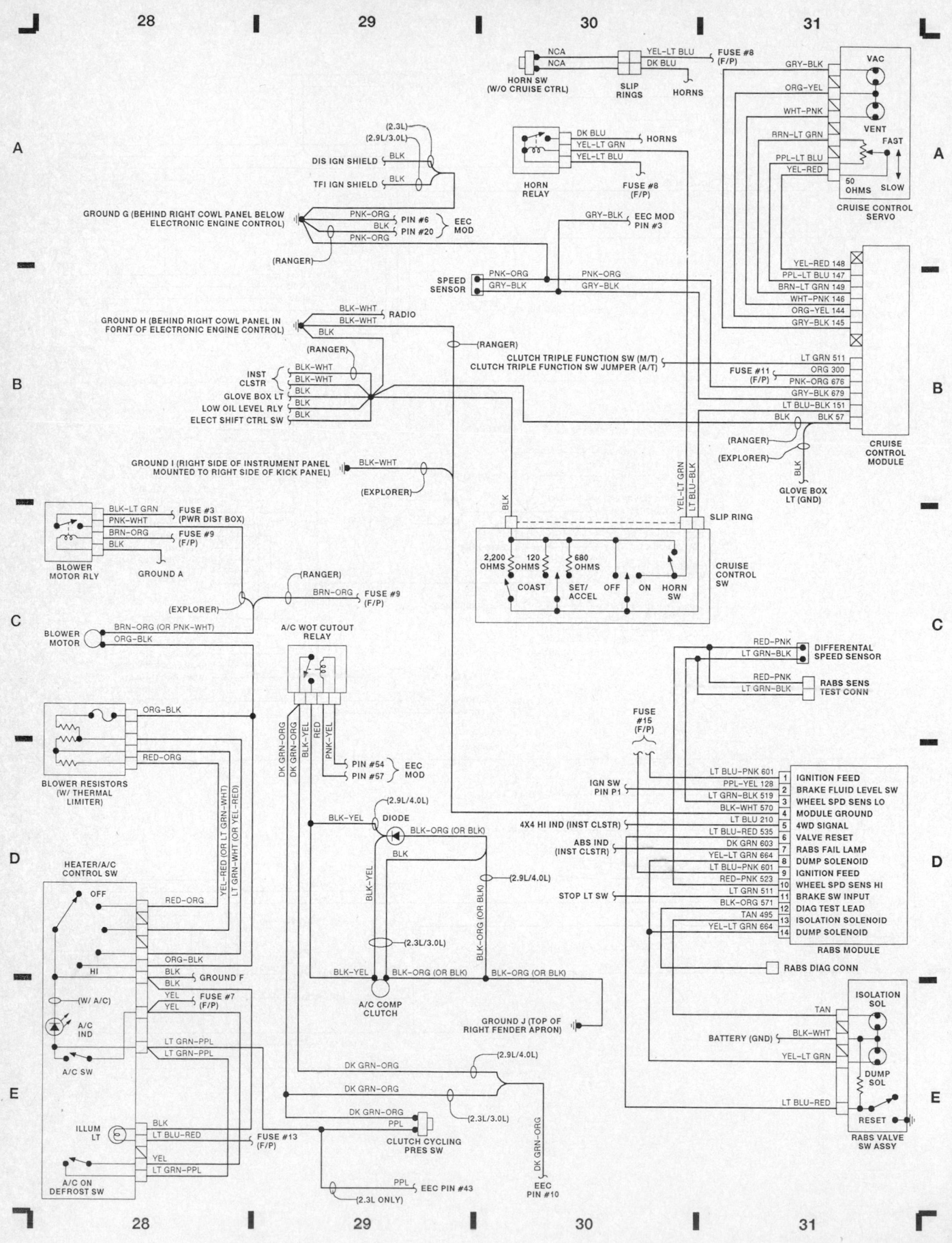

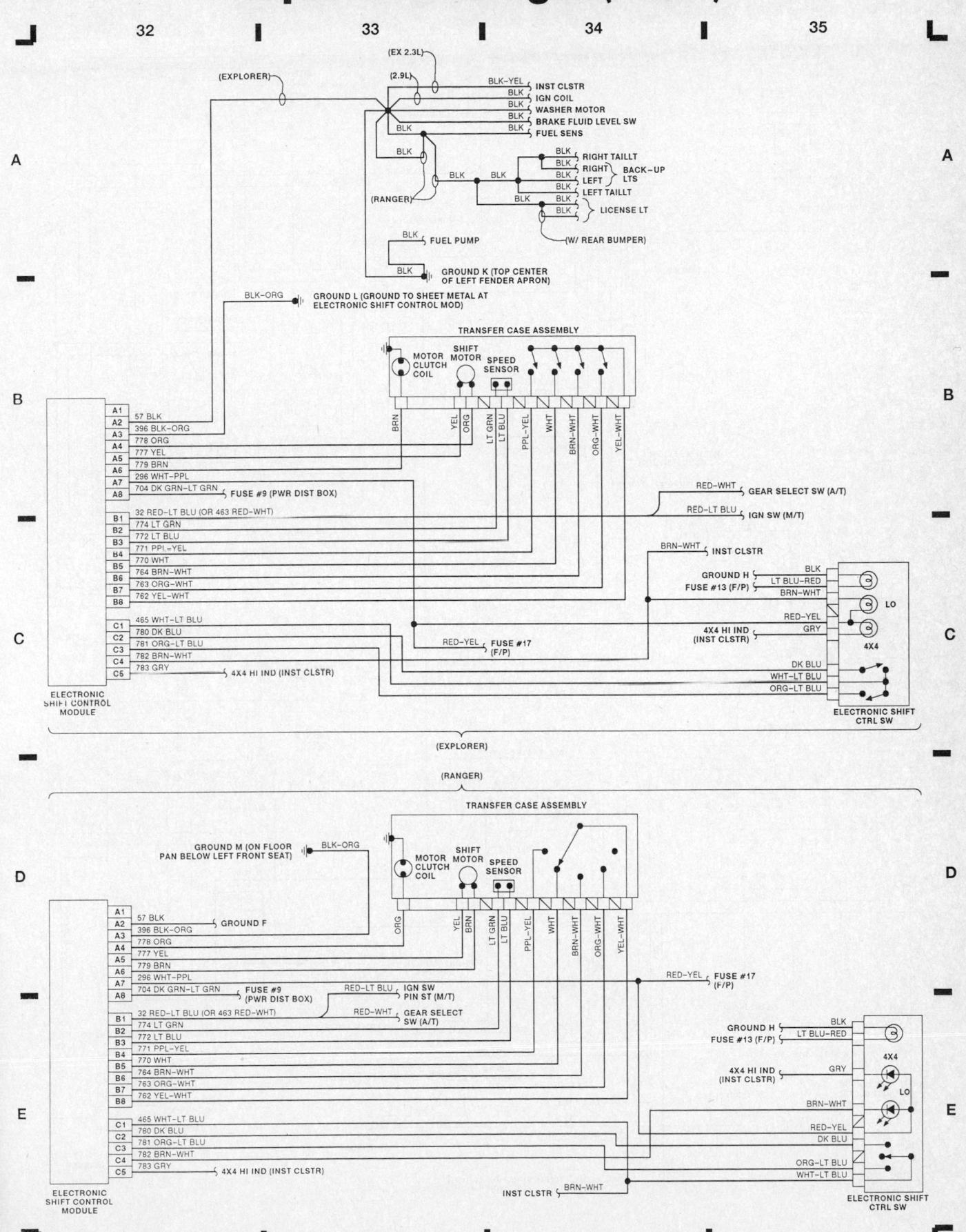

1992 WIRING DIAGRAMS
Explorer & Ranger (Cont.)

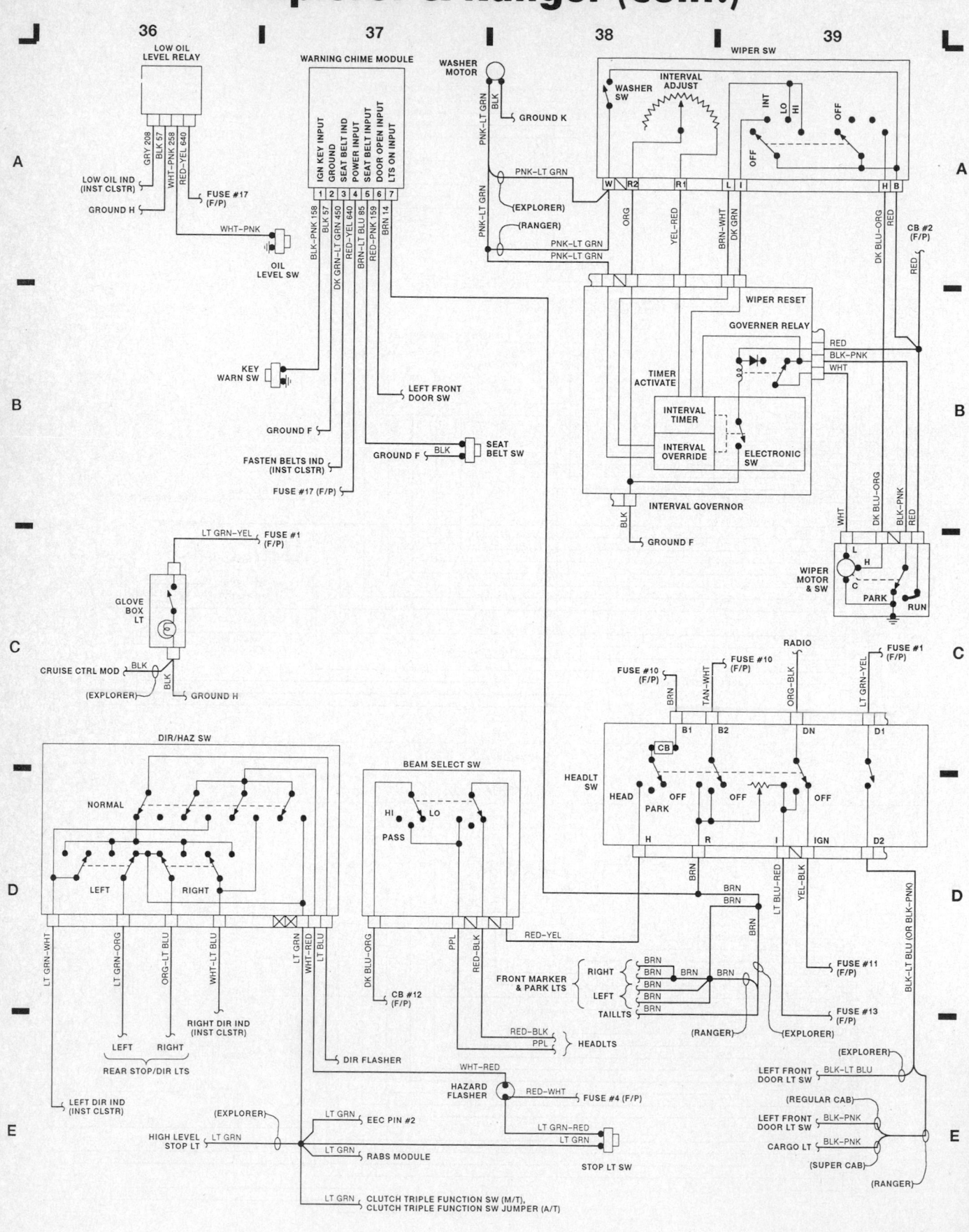

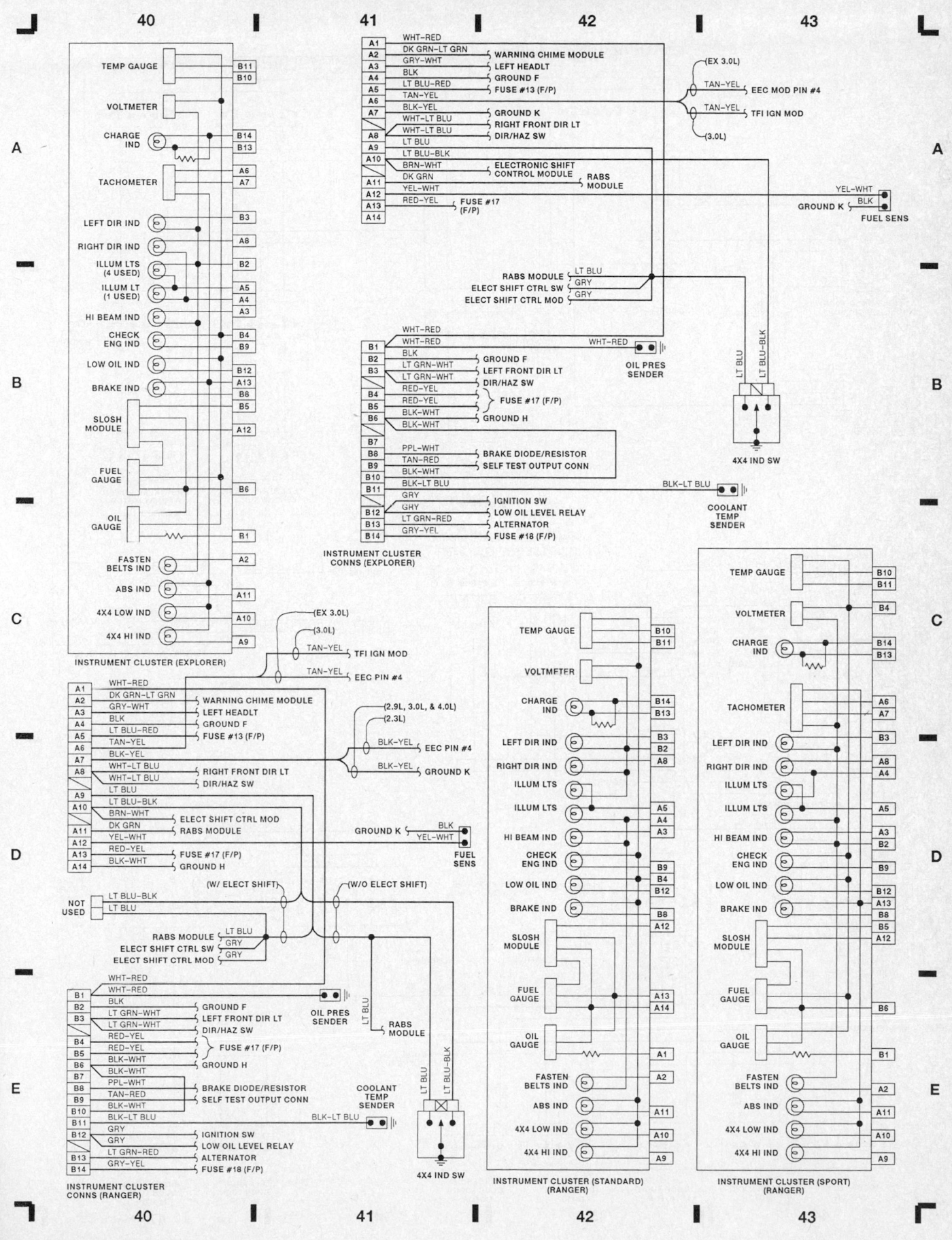

INSTRUMENT CLUSTER (EXPLORER)

INSTRUMENT CLUSTER CONNS (EXPLORER)

INSTRUMENT CLUSTER CONNS (RANGER)

INSTRUMENT CLUSTER (STANDARD) (RANGER)

INSTRUMENT CLUSTER (SPORT) (RANGER)

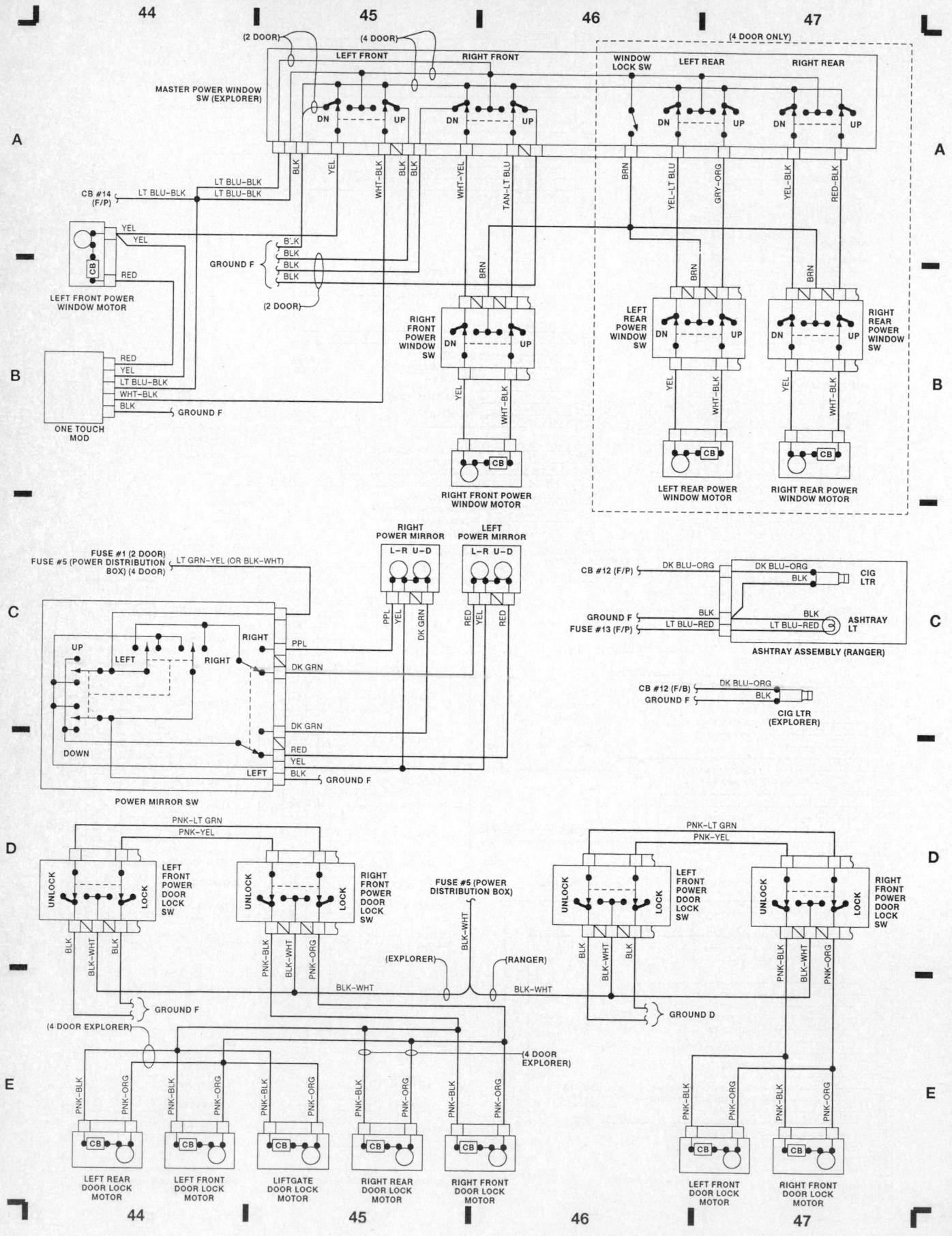

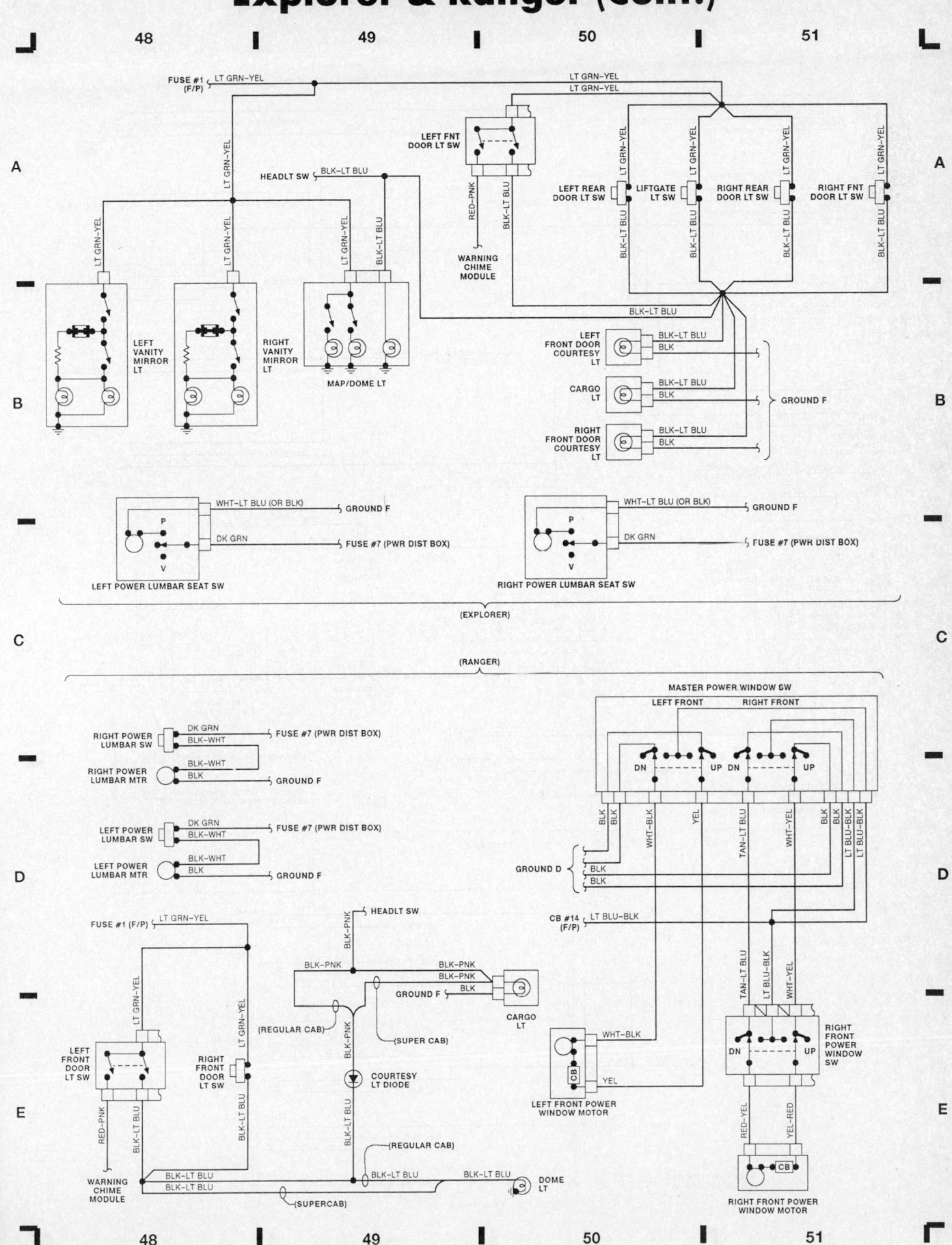

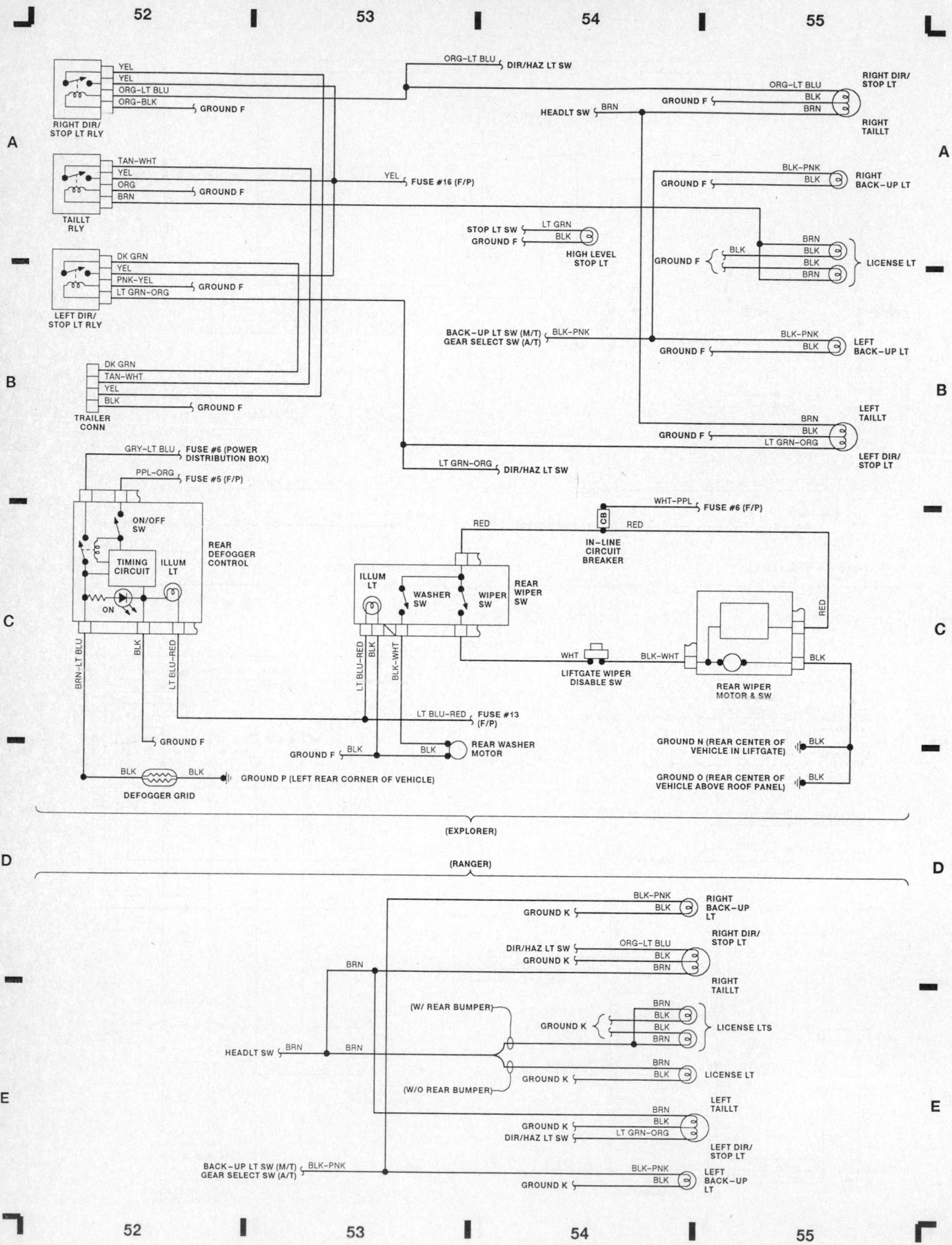

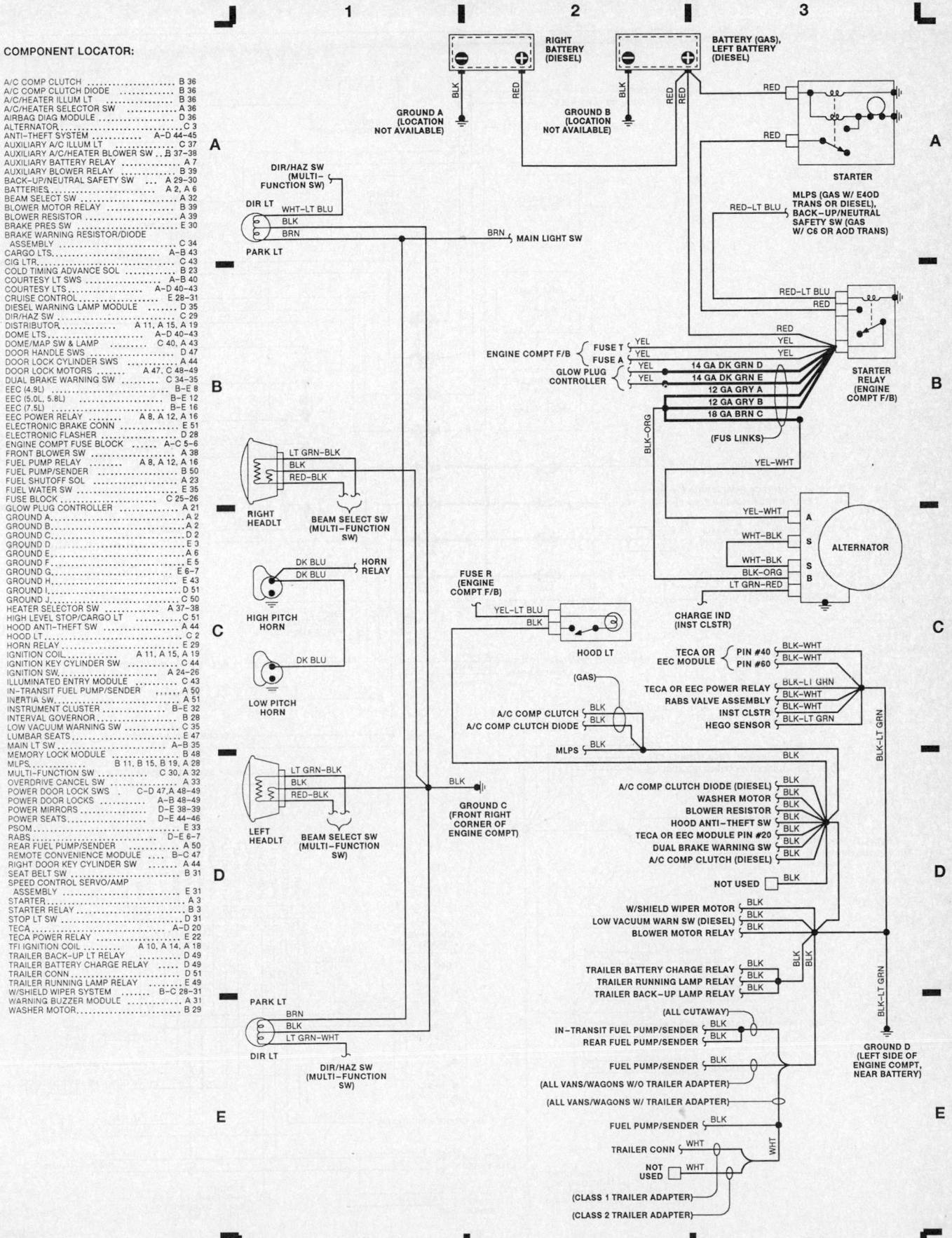

COMPONENT LOCATOR:

A/C COMP CLUTCH .... B 36
A/C COMP CLUTCH DIODE .... B 36
A/C/HEATER ILLUM LT .... B 36
A/C/HEATER SELECTOR SW .... A 36
AIRBAG DIAG MODULE .... D 36
ALTERNATOR .... C 3
ANTI-THEFT SYSTEM .... A–D 44–45
AUXILIARY A/C ILLUM LT .... C 37
AUXILIARY A/C/HEATER BLOWER SW . B 37–38
AUXILIARY BATTERY RELAY .... A 7
AUXILIARY BLOWER RELAY .... B 39
BACK-UP/NEUTRAL SAFETY SW ... A 29–30
BATTERIES .... A 2, A 6
BEAM SELECT SW .... A 32
BLOWER MOTOR RELAY .... B 39
BLOWER RESISTOR .... A 39
BRAKE PRES SW .... E 30
BRAKE WARNING RESISTOR/DIODE
  ASSEMBLY .... C 34
CARGO LTS. .... A–B 43
CIG LTR. .... C 43
COLD TIMING ADVANCE SOL ...... B 23
COURTESY LT SWS .... A–B 42
COURTESY LTS .... A–D 40–43
CRUISE CONTROL .... E 28–31
DIESEL WARNING LAMP MODULE .. D 35
DIR/HAZ SW .... C 29
DISTRIBUTOR .... A 11, A 15, A 19
DOME LTS .... A–D 40–43
DOME/MAP SW & LAMP .... C 40, A 43
DOOR HANDLE SWS .... D 47
DOOR LOCK CYLINDER SWS ..... A 44
DOOR LOCK MOTORS .... A 47, C 48–49
DUAL BRAKE WARNING SW ..... C 34–35
EEC (4.9L) .... B–E 8
EEC (5.0L, 5.8L) .... B–E 12
EEC (7.5L) .... B–E 16
EEC POWER RELAY ..... A 8, A 12, A 16
ELECTRONIC BRAKE CONN .... E 51
ELECTRONIC FLASHER .... D 28
ENGINE COMPT FUSE BLOCK ... A–C 5–6
FRONT BLOWER SW .... A 38
FUEL PUMP RELAY ...... A 8, A 12, A 16
FUEL PUMP/SENDER .... B 50
FUEL SHUTOFF SOL .... A 23
FUEL WATER SW .... A 35
FUSE BLOCK .... C 25–26
GLOW PLUG CONTROLLER .... A 21
GROUND A .... A 2
GROUND B .... A 2
GROUND C .... D 2
GROUND D .... E 3
GROUND E .... A 6
GROUND F .... E 5
GROUND G .... E 6–7
GROUND H .... E 43
GROUND I .... D 51
GROUND J .... C 50
HEATER SELECTOR SW .... A 37–38
HIGH LEVEL STOP/CARGO LT ..... C 51
HOOD ANTI-THEFT SW .... A 44
HOOD LT .... C 2
HORN RELAY .... E 29
IGNITION COIL .... A 11, A 15, A 19
IGNITION KEY CYLINDER SW ..... C 44
IGNITION SW .... A 24–26
ILLUMINATED ENTRY MODULE ... C 43
IN-TRANSIT FUEL PUMP/SENDER ... A 50
INERTIA SW. .... A 51
INSTRUMENT CLUSTER .... B–E 32
INTERVAL GOVERNOR .... B 28
LOW VACUUM WARNING SW ..... C 35
LUMBAR SEATS .... E 47
MAIN LT SW .... A–B 35
MEMORY LOCK MODULE .... B 48
MLPS .... B 11, B 15, B 19, A 28
MULTI-FUNCTION SW .... C 30, A 32
OVERDRIVE CANCEL SW .... A 33
POWER DOOR LOCK SWS . C–D 47, A 48–49
POWER DOOR LOCKS .... A–B 48–49
POWER MIRRORS .... D–E 38–39
POWER SEATS .... D–E 44–46
PSOM .... E 33
RABS .... D–E 6–7
REAR FUEL PUMP/SENDER ...... A 50
REMOTE CONVENIENCE MODULE .... B–C 47
RIGHT DOOR KEY CYLINDER SW ... A 44
SEAT BELT SW .... B 31
SPEED CONTROL SERVO/AMP
  ASSEMBLY .... E 31
STARTER .... A 3
STARTER RELAY .... B 3
STOP LT SW .... D 31
TECA .... A–D 20
TECA POWER RELAY .... E 22
TFI IGNITION COIL ... A 10, A 14, A 18
TRAILER BACK-UP LT RELAY ..... D 49
TRAILER BATTERY CHARGE RELAY . D 49
TRAILER CONN .... D 51
TRAILER RUNNING LAMP RELAY .. E 49
W/SHIELD WIPER SYSTEM .... B–C 28–31
WARNING BUZZER MODULE ..... A 31
WASHER MOTOR. .... B 29

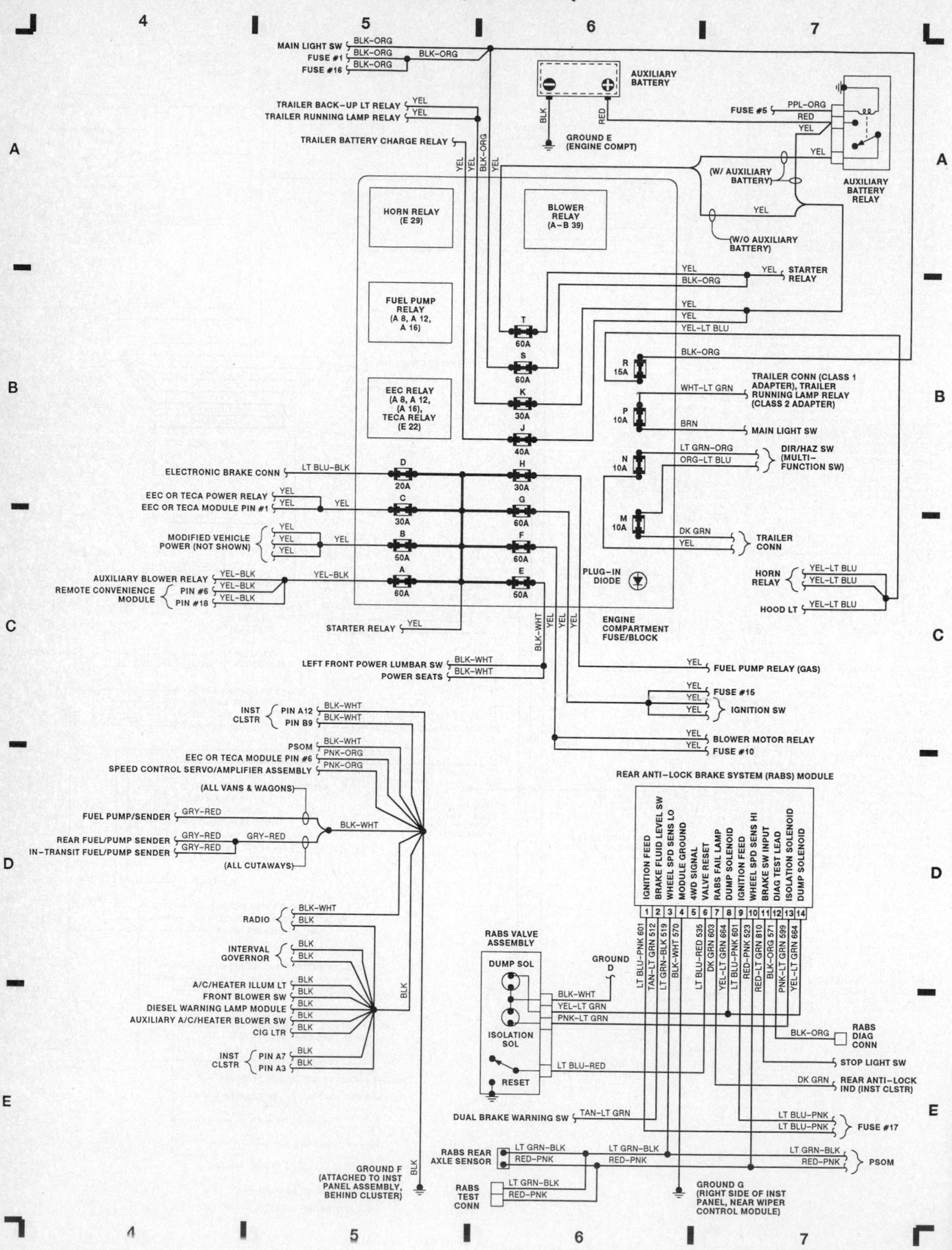

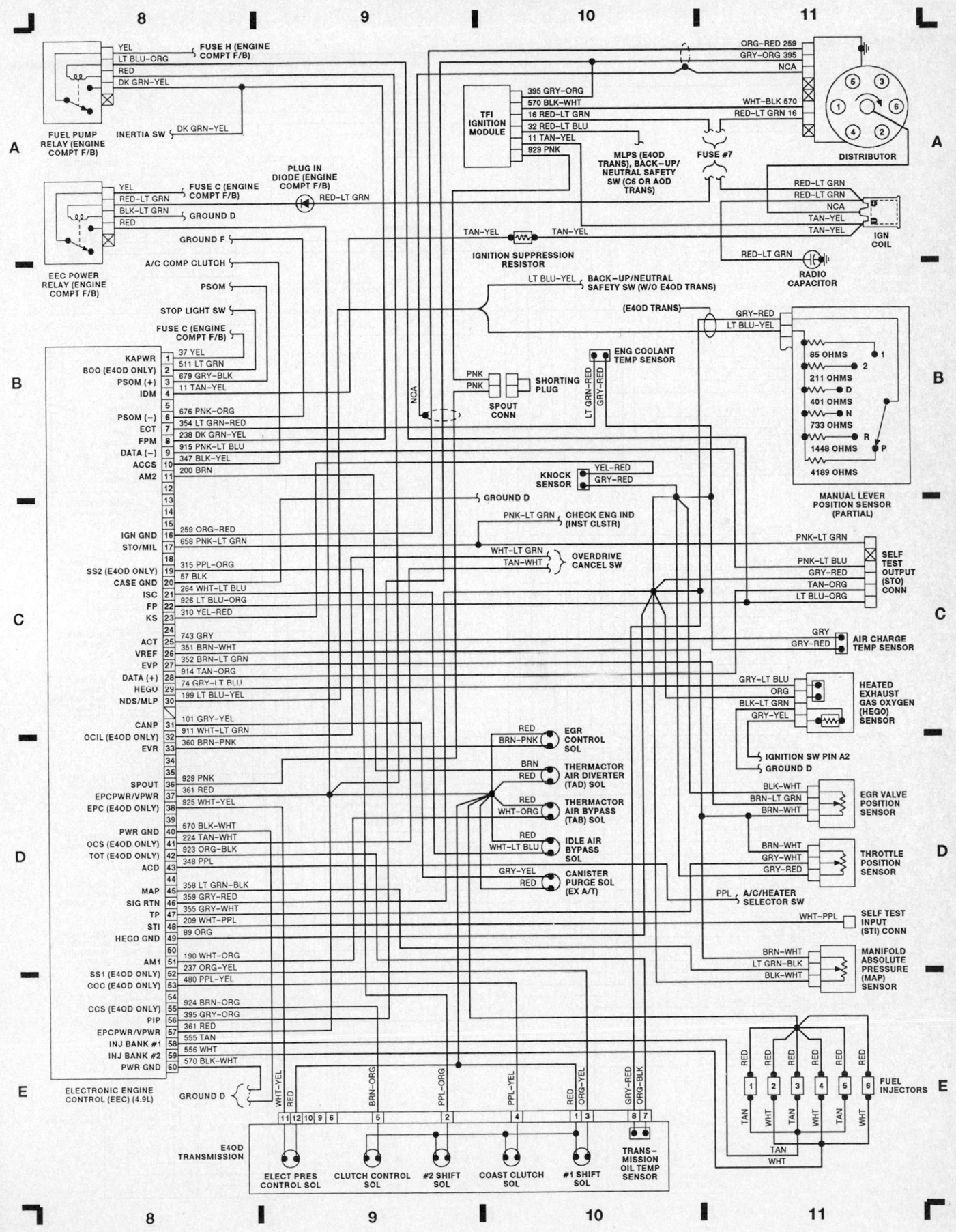

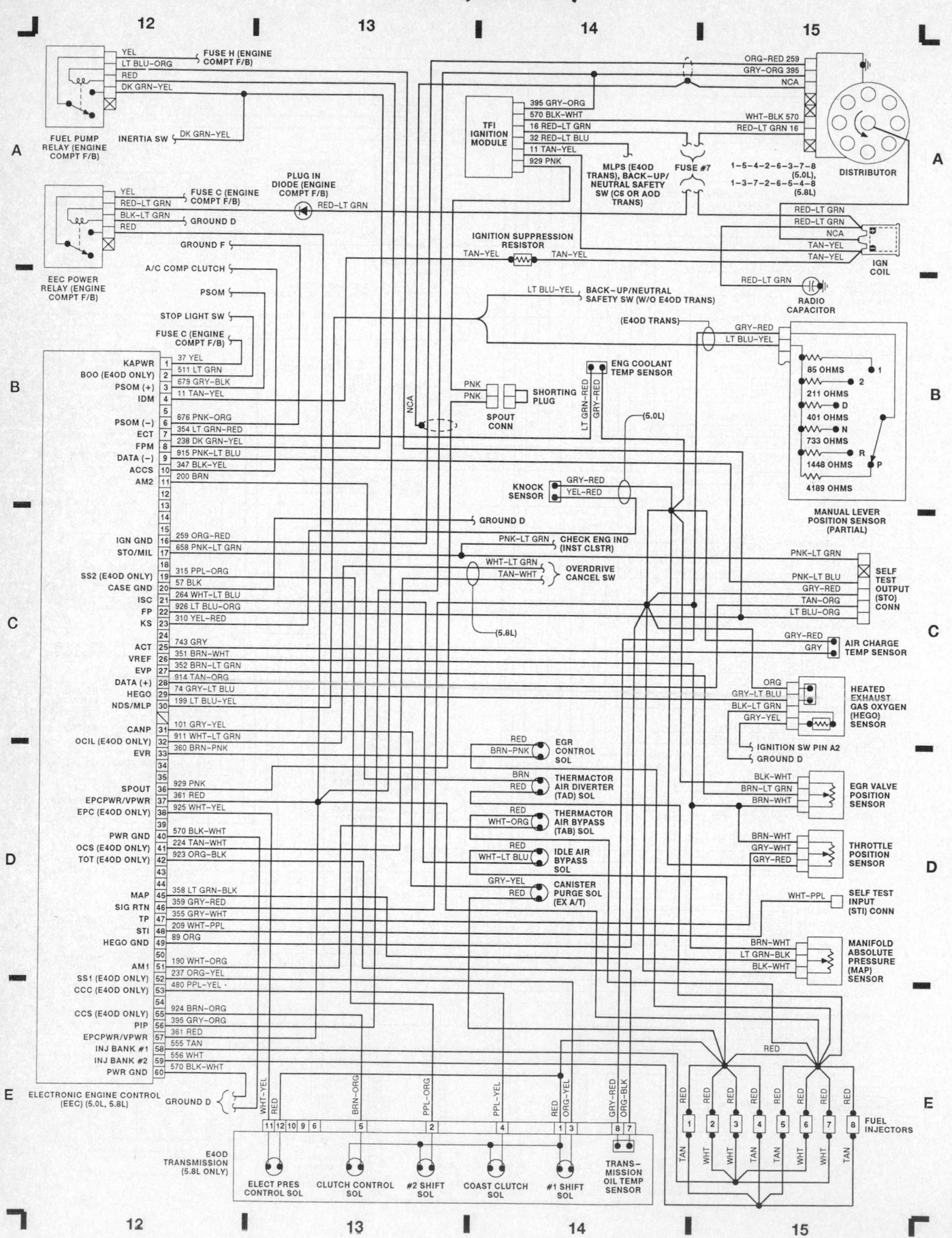

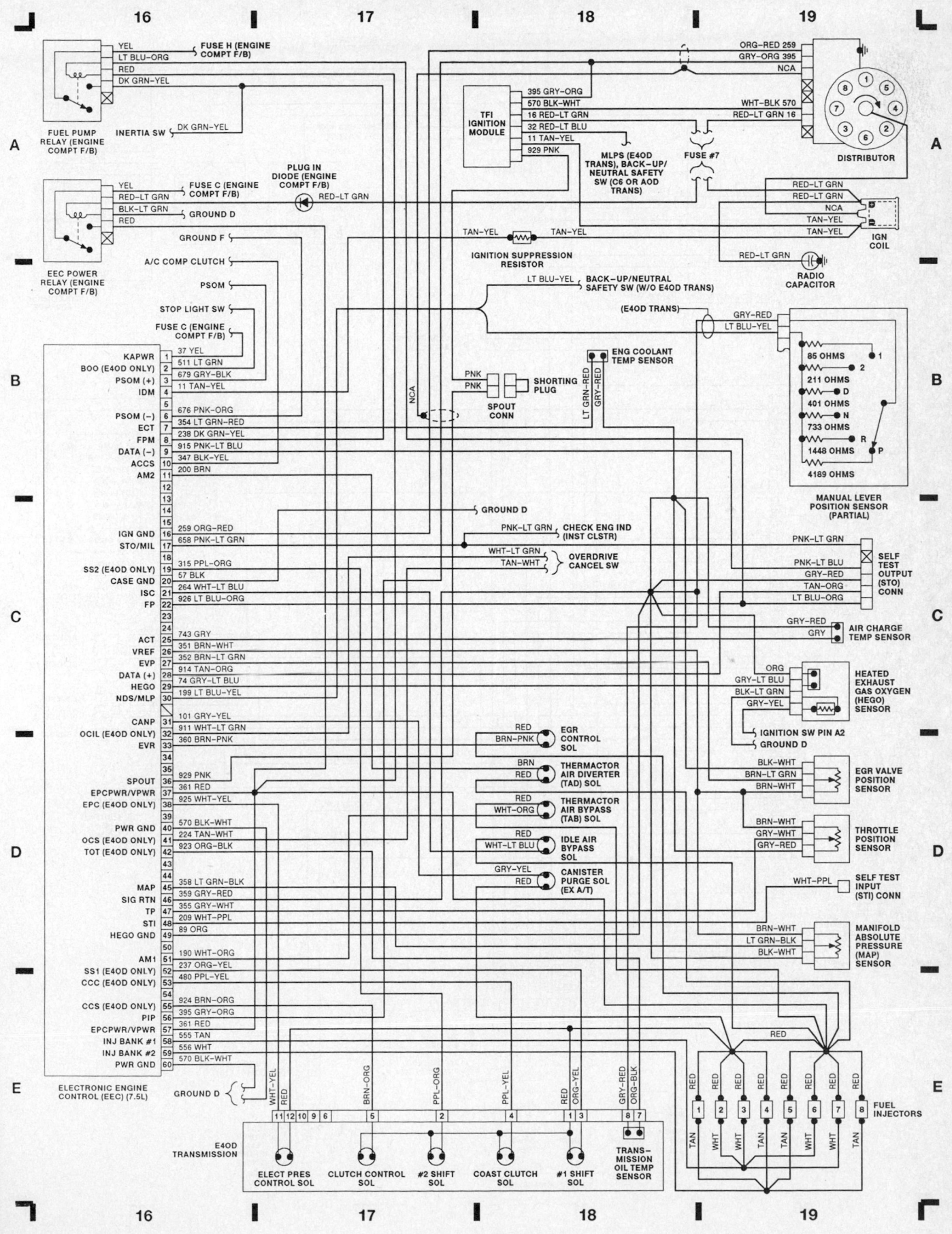

1992 WIRING DIAGRAMS
Van (Cont.)

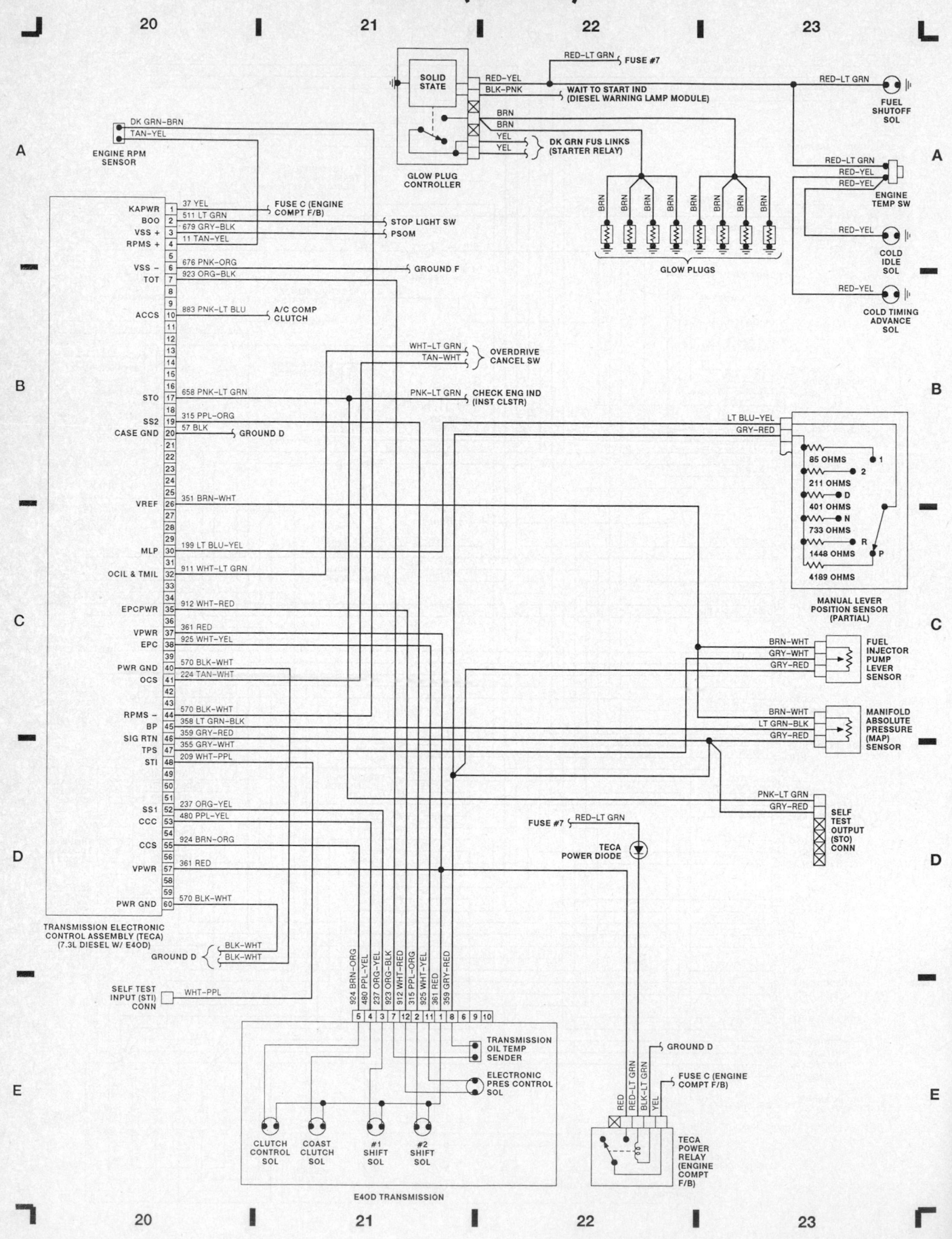

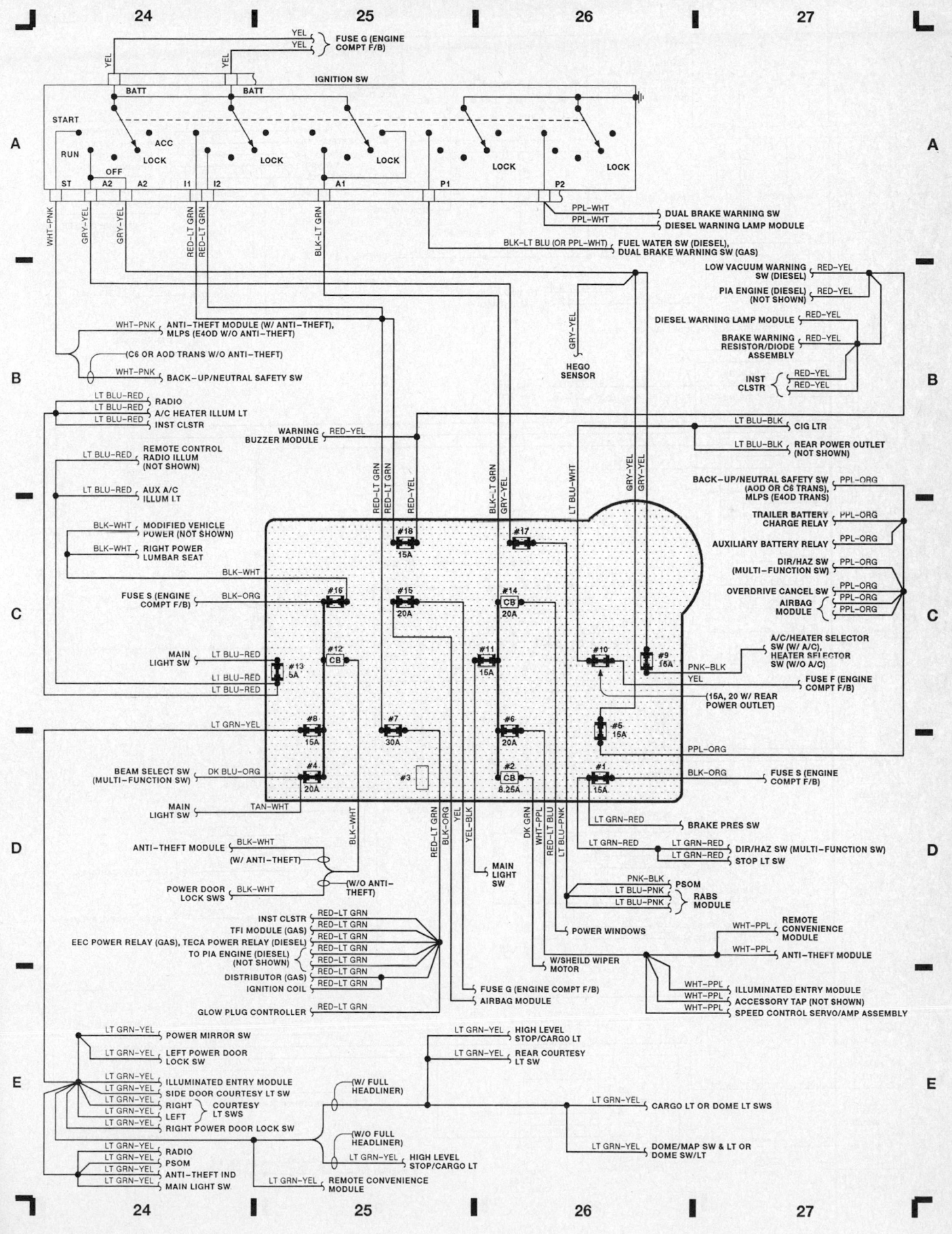

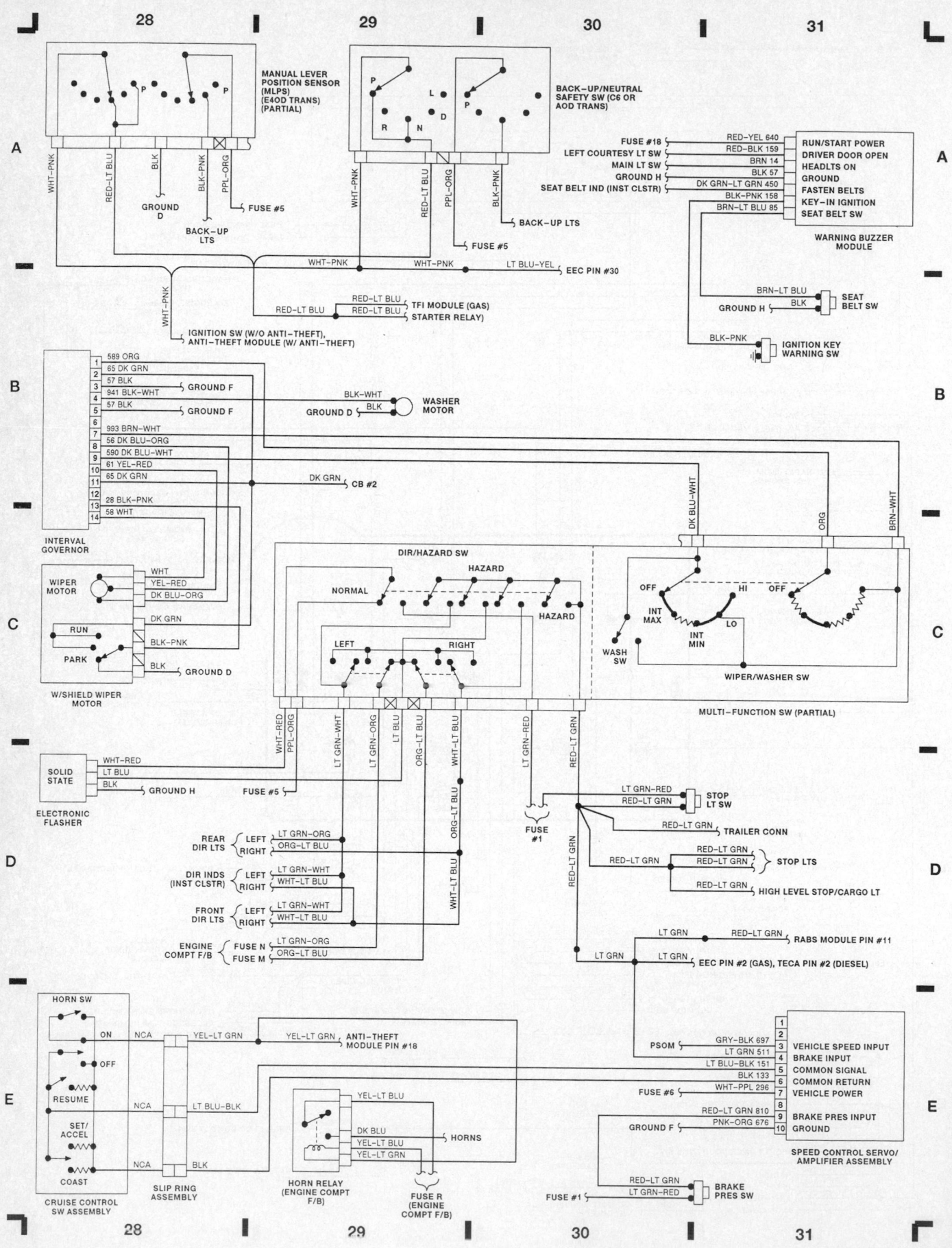

28   29   30   31

MANUAL LEVER
POSITION SENSOR
(MLPS)
(E4OD TRANS)
(PARTIAL)

BACK-UP/NEUTRAL
SAFETY SW (C6 OR
AOD TRANS)

WHT-PNK
RED-LT BLU
BLK
BLK-PNK
PPL-ORG

GROUND
D

FUSE #5

BACK-UP
LTS

WHT-PNK
RED-LT BLU
PPL-ORG
BLK-PNK

BACK-UP LTS

FUSE #5

		RUN/START POWER
FUSE #18	RED-YEL 640	
LEFT COURTESY LT SW	RED-BLK 159	DRIVER DOOR OPEN
MAIN LT SW	BRN 14	HEADLTS ON
GROUND H	BLK 57	GROUND
SEAT BELT IND (INST CLSTR)	DK GRN-LT GRN 450	FASTEN BELTS
	BLK-PNK 158	KEY-IN IGNITION
	BRN-LT BLU 85	SEAT BELT SW

WARNING BUZZER
MODULE

WHT-PNK   WHT-PNK

LT BLU-YEL   EEC PIN #30

BRN-LT BLU   SEAT
GROUND H   BLK   BELT SW

RED-LT BLU   TFI MODULE (GAS)
RED-LT BLU   RED-LT BLU
RED-LT BLU   STARTER RELAY)

WHT-PNK

IGNITION SW (W/O ANTI-THEFT)
ANTI-THEFT MODULE (W/ ANTI-THEFT)

BLK-PNK   IGNITION KEY
WARNING SW

1	589 ORG
2	65 DK GRN
3	57 BLK
4	941 BLK-WHT
5	57 BLK
6	
7	993 BRN-WHT
8	56 DK BLU-ORG
9	590 DK BLU-WHT
10	61 YEL-RED
11	65 DK GRN
12	28 BLK-PNK
13	
14	58 WHT

GROUND F
GROUND F

BLK-WHT   WASHER
GROUND D   BLK   MOTOR

DK GRN   CB #2

INTERVAL
GOVERNOR

DK BLU-WHT
ORG
BRN-WHT

WIPER
MOTOR
WHT
YEL-RED
DK BLU-ORG

RUN
BLK-PNK
PARK
BLK   GROUND D

W/SHIELD WIPER
MOTOR

DIR/HAZARD SW

HAZARD
NORMAL
HAZARD
LEFT   RIGHT

OFF   HI   OFF
INT MAX
INT MIN
LO
WASH SW

MULTI-FUNCTION SW (PARTIAL)
WIPER/WASHER SW

WHT-RED   PPL-ORG
LT GRN-WHT
LT GRN-ORG
LT BLU
ORG-LT BLU
WHT-LT BLU
LT GRN-RED
RED-LT GRN

SOLID
STATE
WHT-RED
LT BLU
BLK   GROUND H   FUSE #5

ELECTRONIC
FLASHER

REAR DIR LTS	LEFT	LT GRN-ORG
	RIGHT	ORG-LT BLU
DIR INDS (INST CLSTR)	LEFT	LT GRN-WHT
	RIGHT	WHT-LT BLU
FRONT DIR LTS	LEFT	LT GRN-WHT
	RIGHT	WHT-LT BLU
ENGINE COMPT F/B	FUSE N	LT GRN-ORG
	FUSE M	ORG-LT BLU

FUSE #1

LT GRN-RED   STOP
RED-LT GRN   LT SW

RED-LT GRN   TRAILER CONN

RED-LT GRN   RED-LT GRN
RED-LT GRN   RED-LT GRN   STOP LTS

RED-LT GRN   HIGH LEVEL STOP/CARGO LT

LT GRN   RED-LT GRN   RABS MODULE PIN #11

LT GRN   LT GRN   EEC PIN #2 (GAS), TECA PIN #2 (DIESEL)

HORN SW

ON   NCA   YEL-LT GRN   YEL-LT GRN   ANTI-THEFT
OFF   MODULE PIN #18
RESUME   NCA   LT BLU-BLK
SET/ACCEL
COAST   NCA   BLK

CRUISE CONTROL
SW ASSEMBLY

SLIP RING
ASSEMBLY

YEL-LT BLU
DK BLU
YEL-LT BLU   HORNS
YEL-LT GRN

HORN RELAY
(ENGINE COMPT
F/B)

FUSE R
(ENGINE COMPT
F/B)

		VEHICLE SPEED INPUT
1		
2		
PSOM	GRY-BLK 697	3
	LT GRN 511	4 BRAKE INPUT
	LT BLU-BLK 151	5 COMMON SIGNAL
	BLK 133	6 COMMON RETURN
FUSE #6	WHT-PPL 296	7 VEHICLE POWER
		8
	RED-LT GRN 810	9 BRAKE PRES INPUT
GROUND F	PNK-ORG 676	10 GROUND

SPEED CONTROL SERVO/
AMPLIFIER ASSEMBLY

FUSE #1   RED-LT GRN   BRAKE
LT GRN-RED   PRES SW

28   29   30   31

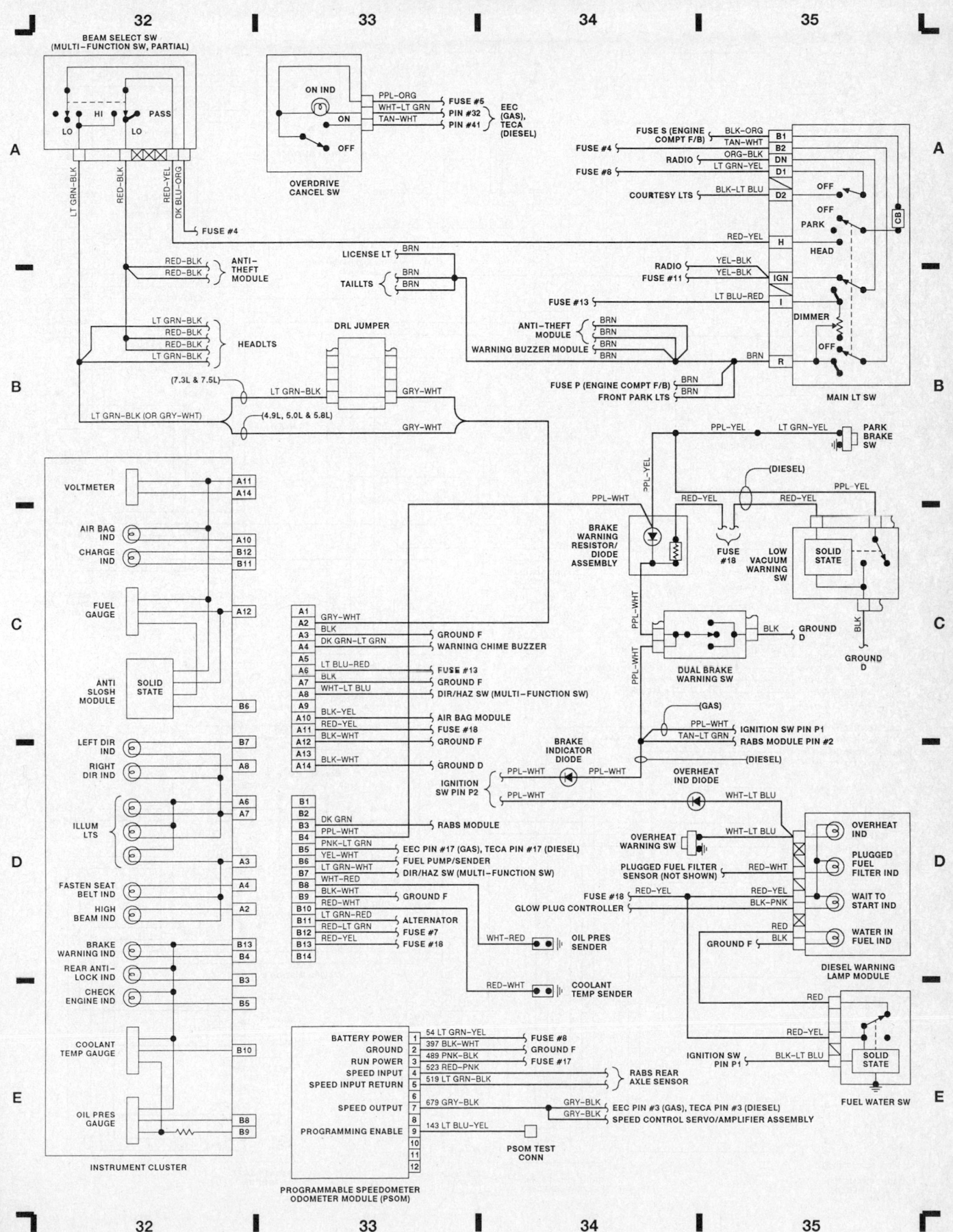

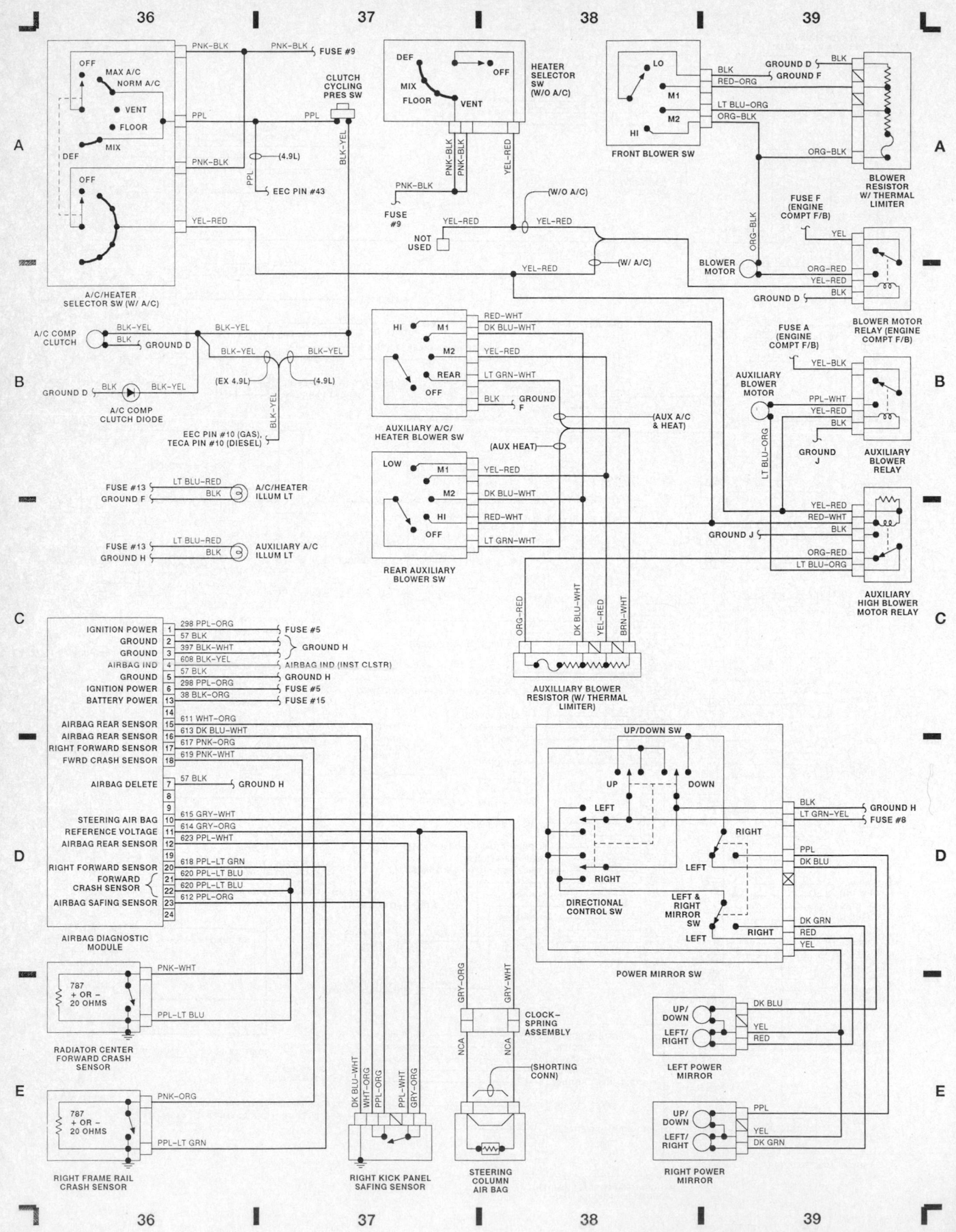

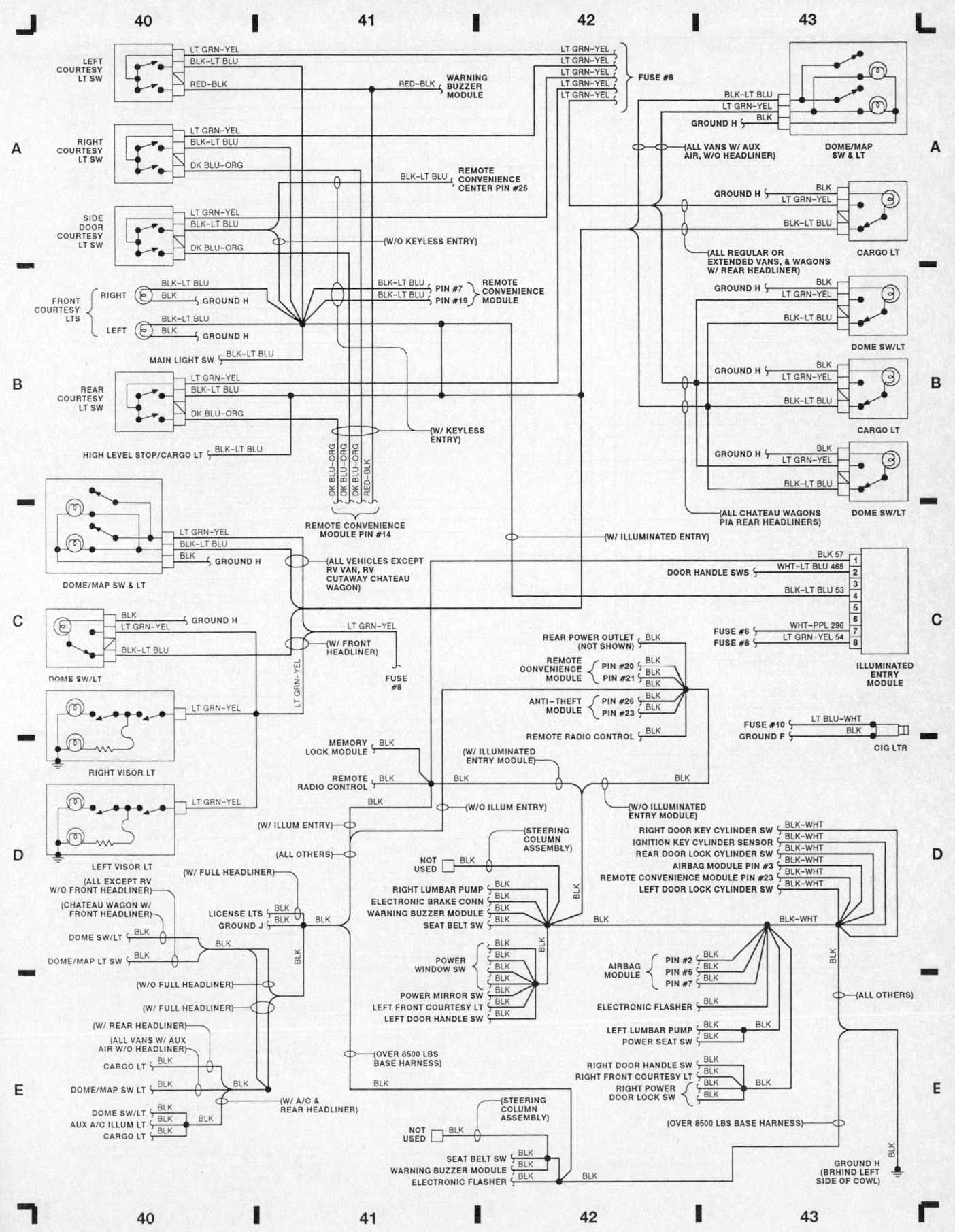

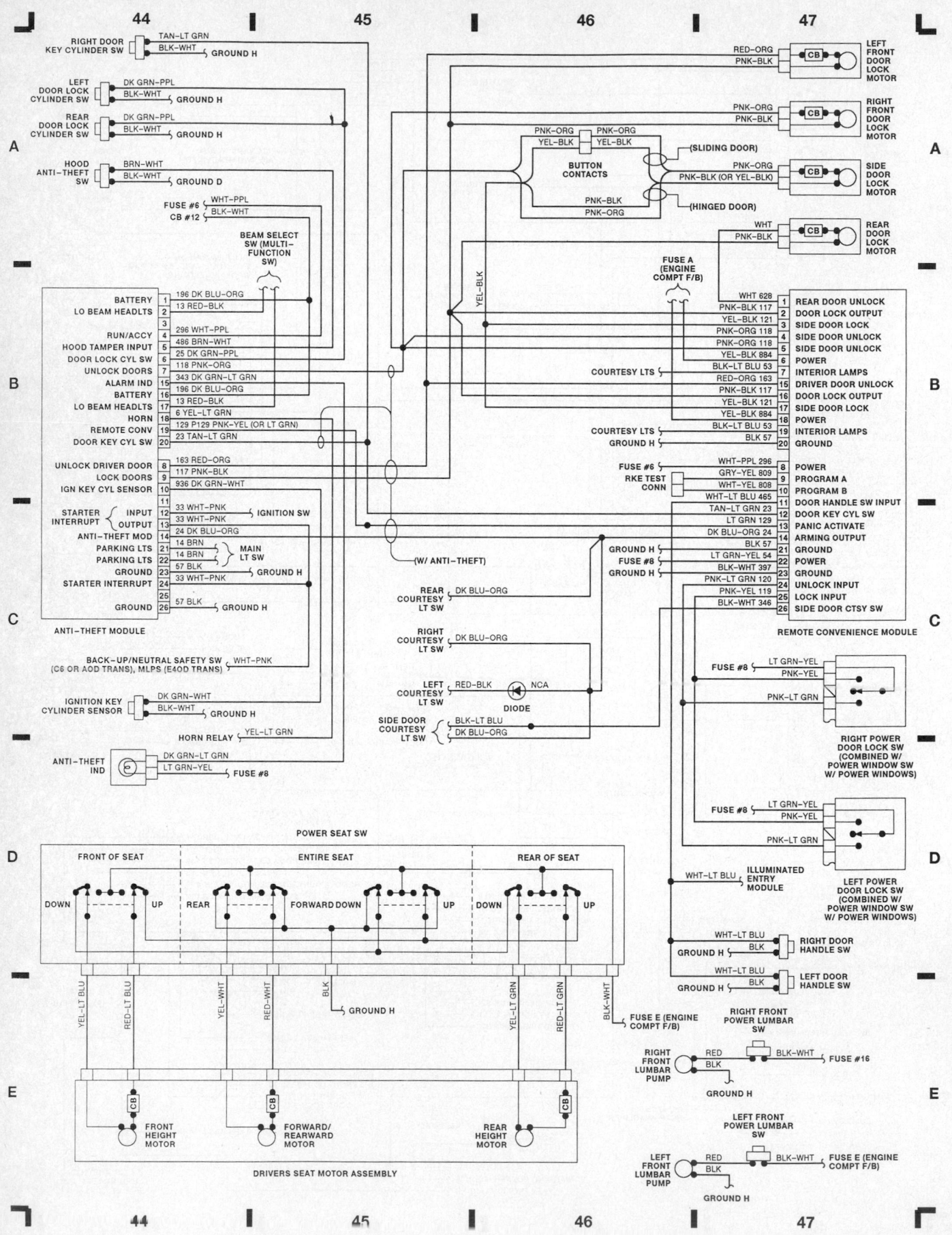

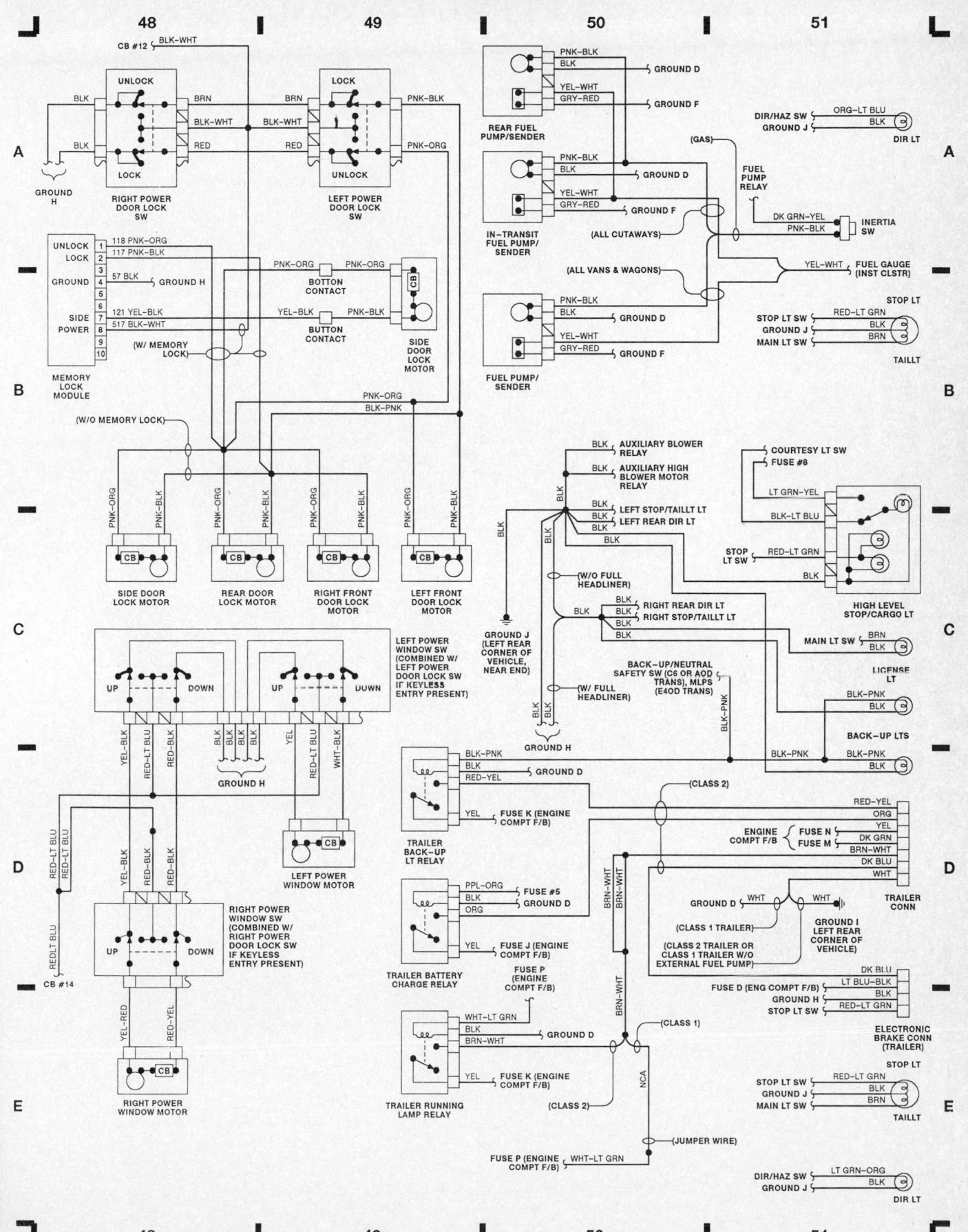

Aerostar, Van

WARNING: To avoid injury from accidental air bag deployment, read and carefully follow all WARNINGS and SERVICE PRECAUTIONS.

NOTE: For information on air bag DIAGNOSIS & TESTING or DISPOSAL PROCEDURES, see the MITCHELL ® AIR BAG SERVICE & REPAIR MANUAL, DOMESTIC & IMPORTED MODELS.

DESCRIPTION & OPERATION

The Supplemental Restraint System (SRS) is designed to provide increased accident protection for the driver by deploying air bag in a front-end collision. During a front-end collision, impact sensors complete an electrical circuit which ignites the inflator to deploy air bag. At least 2 sensors, one safing and one front impact, must activate simultaneously to inflate air bag.

Major components of the SRS are diagnostic monitor, air bag module, system readiness light (AIR BAG warning light), impact and safing sensors, ignitor assembly (in air bag module), clockspring and associated wiring. See Fig. 1 or 2.

An AIR BAG warning light informs the driver of system readiness. It is also used in diagnosing air bag system malfunctions.

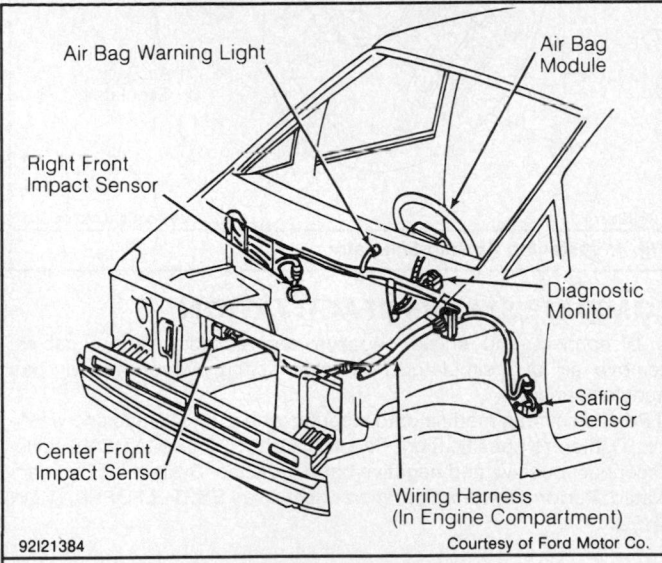

92I21384   Courtesy of Ford Motor Co.

Fig. 1: Locating SRS Components (Aerostar)

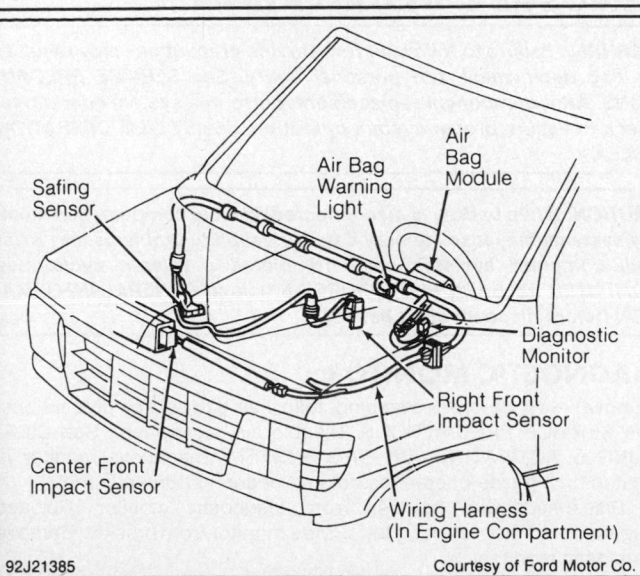

92J21385   Courtesy of Ford Motor Co.

Fig. 2: Locating SRS Components (Van)

AIR BAG MODULE

Air bag module is mounted under steering wheel trim cover. When impact sensors close, an integral ignitor causes a gas generator to produce nitrogen, which inflates the air bag. The air bag module is serviced only as an assembly.

DIAGNOSTIC MONITOR

On all models, diagnostic monitor is located on left side of steering column, beneath instrument panel. Diagnostic monitor performs a system self-check of system's internal circuits every time ignition switch is set to RUN position. Monitor also energizes air bag system readiness indicator light (AIR BAG warning light) during initial system self-check, and whenever a fault is detected.

If a system fault exists and/or AIR BAG warning light malfunctions, a tone will sound, indicating need for service. Diagnostic monitor can also disarm air bag system if certain faults occur.

A back-up power supply within the diagnostic monitor is used on all models. If battery or battery cables are damaged in an accident before impact sensors close the circuit, back-up power supply will deploy air bag. Back-up power supply will hold a charge for approximately one minute after loss of vehicle power.

ELECTRICAL SYSTEM

Air bag system is powered directly from battery, and can function with ignition switch in any position. System can also function when driver and passenger seats are unoccupied. The main functions performed by electrical system are detecting impact, switching electric power to ignitor for air bag, and monitoring air bag system readiness.

SENSORS

Each sensor reacts to impacts according to direction and force. It discriminates between impacts that require air bag inflation and impacts that do not require air bag inflation. When an impact occurs requiring air bag inflation, sensor contacts close, completing electrical circuit necessary for system operation. See Fig. 3. Minimum of 2 sensors, one safing and one impact, must activate simultaneously to inflate air bag. There are 3 sensors: 2 front impact sensors and one safing sensor.

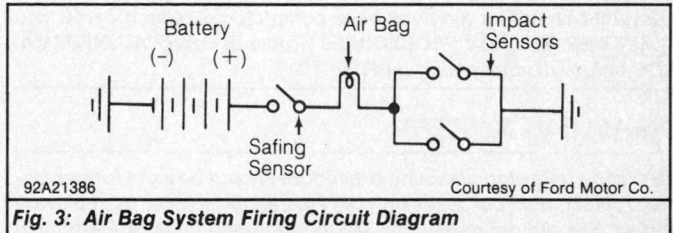

92A21386   Courtesy of Ford Motor Co.

Fig. 3: Air Bag System Firing Circuit Diagram

SYSTEM OPERATION CHECK

1) Whenever checking air bag system operation, and at completion of each circuit test, check for faults in air bag system. To check system, set ignition switch to RUN position. If AIR BAG warning light glows for 4-8 seconds and then goes out, air bag system is functioning properly, and no fault codes exist.

2) If a fault code is detected in air bag system during system operation check, AIR BAG warning light will fail to light, stay on continuously, or flash a code sequence, thus indicating need for service. If a system fault code exists and AIR BAG warning light fails to function, a tone will sound, indicating AIR BAG warning light is out and service is required.

SERVICE PRECAUTIONS

The following precautions must be observed when working with air bag systems.

- Disable air bag system before servicing any air bag system or steering column components. Failure to do so may result in accidental air bag deployment and cause personal injury. See DISABLING & ACTIVATING AIR BAG SYSTEM.

- Back-up power supply will hold a deployment charge for approximately one minute after positive battery cable is disconnected. Servicing SRS before one-minute period may cause accidental air bag deployment and possible personal injury.
- Because of critical system operating requirements, DO NOT service sensors, clockspring, monitor, or air bag module. Corrections are made by replacement only.
- Always wear safety glasses whenever servicing an air bag equipped vehicle or handling an air bag.
- When carrying a live air bag module, ensure air bag module and trim cover are pointed away from your body. This minimizes chance of injury in event of an accidental deployment.
- When placing a live air bag module on a bench or other surface, always face air bag module and trim cover up, away from surface. This will reduce motion of module if it is accidentally deployed.
- After deployment, air bag surface may contain deposits of sodium hydroxide, which may irritate skin. Sodium hydroxide is a product of the gas generant combustion. Always wear gloves and safety glasses when handling a deployed air bag. Wash your hands using mild soap and water. Follow correct disposal procedures.
- If a part is replaced and new part does not correct condition, reinstall original part and perform diagnostic procedure again.
- Never probe connectors on air bag module. Doing so may cause air bag deployment and/or personal injury.
- The instruction to DISCONNECT always refers to a connector. DO NOT remove a component from vehicle when instructed to DISCONNECT.
- After repairs, ensure AIR BAG warning light does not indicate any other faults. See SYSTEM OPERATION CHECK.

DISABLING & ACTIVATING AIR BAG SYSTEM

WARNING: Back-up power supply will hold a deployment charge for approximately one minute after positive battery cable is disconnected. Servicing SRS before one-minute period may cause accidental air bag deployment and possible personal injury.

WARNING: When battery is disconnected, vehicle computer and memory systems may lose memory data. Driveability problems may exist until computer systems have completed a relearn cycle. See COMPUTER RELEARN PROCEDURES article in GENERAL INFORMATION before disconnecting battery.

DISABLING SYSTEM

NOTE: The following disabling procedure should be used for component replacement purposes only. If vehicle was involved in a collision and air bag did not deploy, or SRS is not functioning properly, and vehicle must be driven, complete system deactivation is required. See COMPLETE SYSTEM DEACTIVATION.

Disconnect negative then positive battery cable. Shield both cables. Air bag system contains a back-up power supply built into the diagnostic monitor. Wait a minimum of one minute before servicing any air bag system components. System is now disabled.

ACTIVATING SYSTEM

Connect positive and negative battery cables. System is now activated. From outside of vehicle (driver's side), set ignition switch to RUN position. Perform system operation check. See SYSTEM OPERATION CHECK.

COMPLETE SYSTEM DEACTIVATION

WARNING: Back-up power supply will hold a deployment charge for approximately one minute after positive battery cable is disconnected. Always deactivate air bag module before attempting any service procedures.

NOTE: Complete system deactivation sequence is required for the following situations:

- *Vehicle was involved in a collision, air bag DID NOT deploy, and vehicle must be driven.*
- *Air bag system is not functioning properly and vehicle must be driven.*
- *Diagnosis and testing purposes.*

1) Disconnect and shield negative and positive battery cables. Wait at least one minute to deplete charge in back-up power supply. Remove nuts and washers which retain air bag module to steering wheel. Remove air bag from steering wheel. Unplug air bag module connector.
2) Connect Air Bag Simulator (105-00008) to clockspring connector. *See Fig. 4.* Connect positive and negative battery cables. To reactivate air bag system, see COMPLETE SYSTEM REACTIVATION.

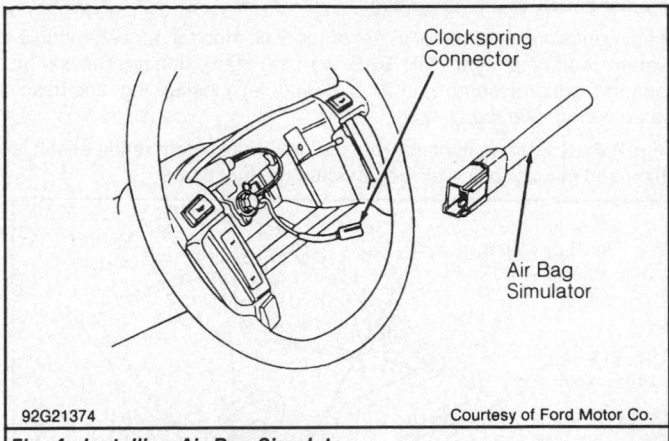

Clockspring Connector

Air Bag Simulator

92G21374   Courtesy of Ford Motor Co.

Fig. 4: Installing Air Bag Simulator

COMPLETE SYSTEM REACTIVATION

1) Disconnect and shield negative and positive battery cables. Remove air bag simulator from clockspring. Reconnect air bag module connector.
2) Position air bag module onto steering wheel. Install nuts and washers. Tighten to specification. See TORQUE SPECIFICATIONS table. Reconnect positive and negative battery cables. System is now reactivated. Perform system operation check. See SYSTEM OPERATION CHECK.

REMOVAL & INSTALLATION

WARNING: Failure to follow air bag service precautions may result in air bag deployment and personal injury. See SERVICE PRECAUTIONS. After component replacement, perform a system operational check to assure proper system operation. See SYSTEM OPERATION CHECK.

CAUTION: When battery is disconnected, vehicle computer and memory systems may lose memory data. Driveability problems may exist until computer systems have completed a relearn cycle. See COMPUTER RELEARN PROCEDURES article in GENERAL INFORMATION before disconnecting battery.

DIAGNOSTIC MONITOR

Removal – 1) Before proceeding, follow air bag service precautions. See SERVICE PRECAUTIONS. Disable air bag system. See DISABLING & ACTIVATING AIR BAG SYSTEM. Diagnostic monitor is located on left side of steering column under instrument panel.
2) Disconnect wire harness from diagnostic monitor. Release diagnostic monitor retaining tabs. Slide monitor from bracket. Remove diagnostic monitor.

Installation – To install diagnostic monitor, reverse removal procedure. Activate air bag system. Check AIR BAG warning light to assure system is functioning properly. See SYSTEM OPERATION CHECK.

CENTER FRONT IMPACT SENSORS

NOTE: Vehicle sensor orientation is critical for proper system operation. If a vehicle equipped with air bag system is involved in a collision, where fenders or grille area have been damaged, inspect sensor mounting brackets for deformation. If damaged, system should be deactivated to ensure air bag does not deploy. Damaged sensor(s) should be replaced regardless of whether or not air bag has been deployed. In addition, ensure body structure in area of sensor mounting is restored to its original condition.

Removal – Before proceeding, follow air bag service precautions. See SERVICE PRECAUTIONS. Disable air bag system. See DISABLING & ACTIVATING AIR BAG SYSTEM. Center sensor is located on upper radiator support. *See Fig. 5.* Disconnect wire harness from sensor. Remove retaining screws and sensor.

Installation – Install sensor and secure with retaining screws. Tighten retaining screws to specification. See TORQUE SPECIFICATIONS table. Reverse removal procedure to complete installation. Activate air bag system. Check AIR BAG warning light to assure system is functioning properly. See SYSTEM OPERATION CHECK.

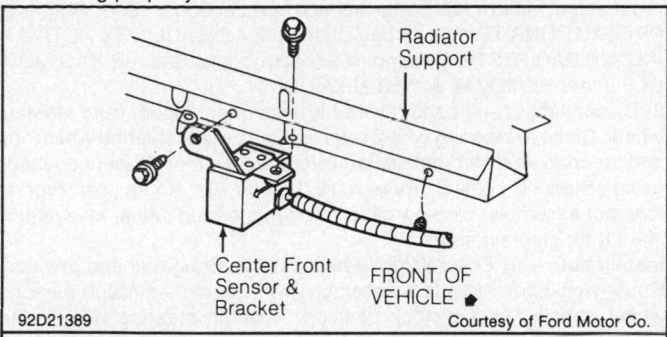

92D21389   Courtesy of Ford Motor Co.

Fig. 5: Locating Center Front Impact Sensor (Aerostar Is Shown; Van Is Similar)

RIGHT FRONT IMPACT SENSORS

NOTE: Vehicle sensor orientation is critical for proper system operation. If a vehicle equipped with air bag system is involved in a collision, where fenders or grille area have been damaged, inspect sensor mounting brackets for deformation. If damaged, system should be deactivated to ensure air bag does not deploy. Damaged sensor(s) should be replaced regardless of whether or not air bag has been deployed. In addition, ensure body structure in area of sensor mounting is restored to its original condition.

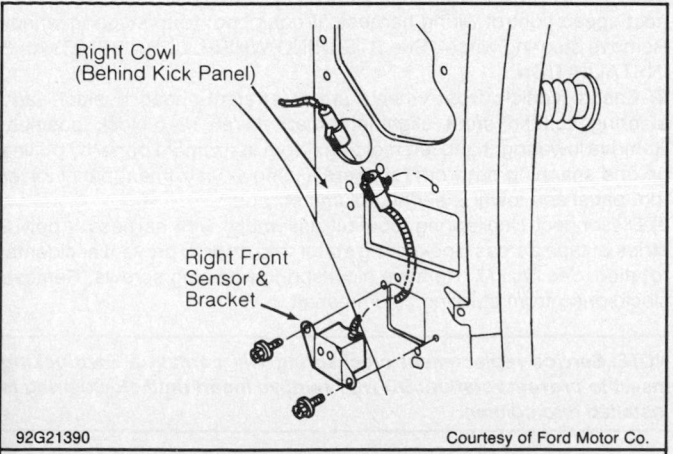

92G21390   Courtesy of Ford Motor Co.

Fig. 6: Locating Right Front Impact Sensor (Aerostar)

Removal (Aerostar) – Before proceeding, follow air bag service precautions. See SERVICE PRECAUTIONS. Disable air bag system. See DISABLING & ACTIVATING AIR BAG SYSTEM. Right front sensor is attached to right cowl, behind kick panel. *See Fig. 6.* Remove right side kick panel. Disconnect wire harness from sensor. Remove retaining screws and sensor.

Installation – Install sensor and secure with retaining screws. Tighten retaining screws to specification. See TORQUE SPECIFICATIONS table. Reverse removal procedure to complete installation. Activate air bag system. Check AIR BAG warning light to assure system is functioning properly. See SYSTEM OPERATION CHECK.

Removal (Van) – Before proceeding, follow air bag service precautions. See SERVICE PRECAUTIONS. Disable air bag system. See DISABLING & ACTIVATING AIR BAG SYSTEM. Right front sensor is located under vehicle, attached to right frame rail *See Fig. 7.* Disconnect wire harness from sensor. Remove retaining screws and sensor.

Installation – Install sensor and secure with retaining screws. Tighten retaining screws to specification. See TORQUE SPECIFICATIONS table. Reverse removal procedure to complete installation. Activate air bag system. Check AIR BAG warning light to assure system is functioning properly. See SYSTEM OPERATION CHECK.

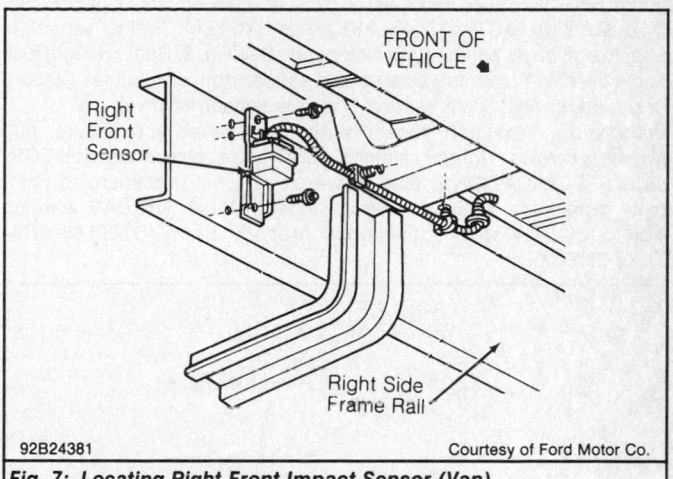

92B24381   Courtesy of Ford Motor Co.

Fig. 7: Locating Right Front Impact Sensor (Van)

SAFING SENSOR

NOTE: Vehicle sensor orientation is critical for proper system operation. If a vehicle equipped with air bag system is involved in a collision, where fenders or grille area have been damaged, inspect sensor mounting brackets for deformation. If damaged, system should be deactivated to ensure air bag does not deploy. Damaged sensor(s) should be replaced regardless of whether or not air bag has been deployed. In addition, ensure body structure in area of sensor mounting is restored to its original condition.

Removal (Aerostar) – Before proceeding, follow air bag service precautions. See SERVICE PRECAUTIONS. Disable air bag system. See DISABLING & ACTIVATING AIR BAG SYSTEM. Safing sensor is attached to cowl, behind left kick panel. *See Fig. 8.* Remove left kick panel. Remove retaining screws and sensor from cowl panel. Disconnect wire harness from sensor. Remove sensor from vehicle.

Installation – Position sensor onto cowl panel, and secure with retaining screws. Reverse removal procedure to complete installation. Tighten screws to specification. See TORQUE SPECIFICATIONS table. Activate air bag system. Check AIR BAG warning light to assure system is functioning properly. See SYSTEM OPERATION CHECK.

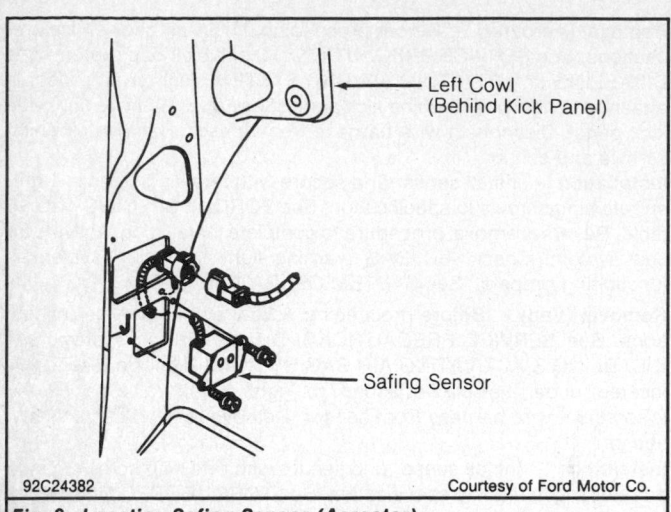

92C24382   Courtesy of Ford Motor Co.

Fig. 8: Locating Safing Sensor (Aerostar)

Removal (Van) – Before proceeding, follow air bag service precautions. See SERVICE PRECAUTIONS. Disable air bag system. See DISABLING & ACTIVATING AIR BAG SYSTEM. Safing sensor is attached to cowl, behind right kick panel. *See Fig. 9.* Remove right kick panel. Remove retaining screws and sensor from cowl panel. Disconnect wire harness from sensor. Remove sensor from vehicle.

Installation – Position sensor onto cowl panel, and secure with retaining screws. Tighten retaining screws to specification. See TORQUE SPECIFICATIONS table. Reverse removal procedure to complete installation. Activate air bag system. Check AIR BAG warning light to assure system is functioning properly. See SYSTEM OPERATION CHECK.

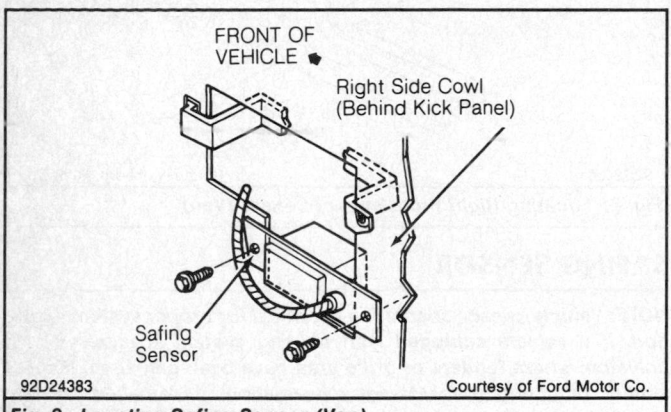

92D24383   Courtesy of Ford Motor Co.

Fig. 9: Locating Safing Sensor (Van)

AIR BAG MODULE

Removal – Before proceeding, follow air bag service precautions. See SERVICE PRECAUTIONS. Disable air bag system. See DISABLING & ACTIVATING AIR BAG SYSTEM. Remove nuts and washers retaining air bag module to steering wheel. *See Fig. 10.* Disconnect air bag wiring from clockspring (contact assembly). Remove air bag module.

WARNING: When placing a live air bag on a bench or other surface, always face air bag and trim cover up, away from surface. This will reduce motion of air bag module if it is accidentally deployed.

Installation – Connect air bag module wiring connector to clockspring (contact assembly) connector. Position air bag module onto steering wheel. Install air bag module nuts and washers. Tighten to specification. See TORQUE SPECIFICATIONS table. Activate air bag system. Check AIR BAG warning light to assure system is functioning properly. See SYSTEM OPERATION CHECK.

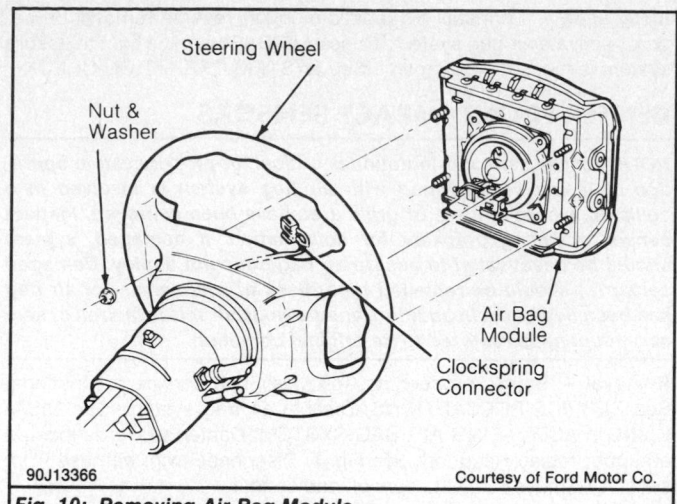

90J13366   Courtesy of Ford Motor Co.

Fig. 10: Removing Air Bag Module

STEERING WHEEL

Removal – 1) Center front wheels to straight-ahead position. Before proceeding, follow air bag service precautions. See SERVICE PRECAUTIONS. Disable air bag system. See DISABLING & ACTIVATING AIR BAG SYSTEM. Remove air bag module. See AIR BAG MODULE under REMOVAL & INSTALLATION.

2) Disconnect speed control wire harness (if equipped) from steering wheel. Remove steering wheel retaining bolt. Mark steering wheel hub and steering shaft for installation reference. Remove steering wheel, using Steering Wheel Puller (T67L-3600-A). Route clockspring (contact assembly) wire harness through steering wheel as wheel is lifted from steering shaft.

Installation – 1) Ensure front wheels are in straight-ahead position. Route clockspring (contact assembly) wire harness through steering wheel opening at 3 o'clock position. Position steering wheel onto steering shaft and align with marks made during removal procedure.

2) Ensure air bag clockspring wire is not pinched when positioning steering wheel. Install NEW steering wheel retaining bolt, and tighten to specification. See TORQUE SPECIFICATIONS table. Connect speed control wire harness (if equipped) to steering wheel, and snap connector assembly into steering wheel clip.

3) Install air bag module. Reconnect positive, then negative battery cable. Activate air bag system. Check AIR BAG warning light to assure system is functioning properly. See SYSTEM OPERATION CHECK.

CLOCKSPRING

Removal – 1) Before proceeding, follow air bag service precautions. See SERVICE PRECAUTIONS. Disable air bag system. See DISABLING & ACTIVATING AIR BAG SYSTEM. Remove air bag module. See AIR BAG MODULE under REMOVAL & INSTALLATION. Disconnect speed control wiring harness (if equipped) from steering wheel. Remove steering wheel. See STEERING WHEEL under REMOVAL & INSTALLATION.

2) Ensure vehicle front wheels are in straight-ahead position, and steering column shaft alignment mark is at 12 o'clock position. Remove lower right and left moldings from instrument panel by pulling up and snapping out from retainers. Remove instrument panel lower trim panel and lower steering column shroud.

3) Disconnect clockspring (contact assembly) wire harness. Apply 2 strips of tape across clockspring stator and rotor to prevent accidental rotation. *See Fig. 11.* Remove clockspring retaining screws. Remove clockspring from steering column shaft.

NOTE: Service replacement clockspring will contain a Red locking insert to prevent rotation. DO NOT remove insert until clockspring is installed into column.

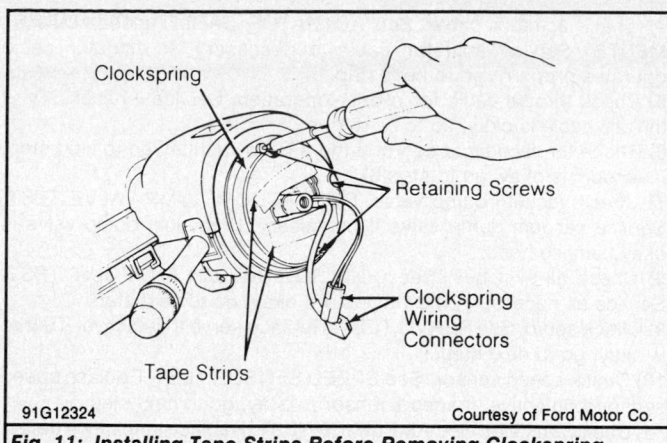

Clockspring

Retaining Screws

Clockspring
Wiring
Connectors

Tape Strips

91G12324

Courtesy of Ford Motor Co.

Fig. 11: Installing Tape Strips Before Removing Clockspring

Installation – 1) Ensure vehicle front wheels are in straight-ahead position and steering column shaft alignment mark is at 12 o'clock position.

2) Align clockspring (contact assembly) with column shaft and mounting bosses. Slide clockspring onto shaft. Install retaining screws and tighten to specification. See TORQUE SPECIFICATIONS table.

NOTE: If a new clockspring (contact assembly) is being installed, remove plastic lock mechanism after clockspring is secured to column before installing lower shroud.

3) Remove tape strips. Route clockspring wiring down column, and connect to wire harness. Install lower shroud and instrument panel cover. Install lower right and left instrument panel moldings. Install air bag module and steering wheel.

4) Reconnect positive then negative battery cable. Activate air bag system. Check AIR BAG warning light to assure system is functioning properly. See SYSTEM OPERATION CHECK.

ADJUSTMENTS
See CLOCKSPRING under REMOVAL & INSTALLATION.

TORQUE SPECIFICATIONS
TORQUE SPECIFICATIONS

Application	Ft. Lbs. (N.m)
Steering Wheel Bolt	23-33 (31-45)

	INCH Lbs. (N.m)
Air Bag Clockspring Retaining Screws	18-26 (2.0-2.9)
Air Bag Module-To-Steering Wheel Nuts	35-50 (4.0-5.6)
Center Front Sensor Screws	91-122 (10.2-13.8)
Right Front Sensor Screws	
Aerostar	91-122 (10.2-13.8)
Van	113-151 (12.8-17.2)
Safing Sensor Screws	
Aerostar	91-122 (10.2-13.8)
Van	68-92 (7.6-10.4)

1991-92 SAFETY EQUIPMENT
Cruise Control Systems

**Aerostar, Bronco, Explorer,
Pickup, Ranger, 1991 Van**

NOTE: Vans have a different cruise control system for 1992. See CRUISE CONTROL SYSTEMS article under 1992 SAFETY EQUIPMENT.

DESCRIPTION

The cruise control system consists of switch buttons (ON, OFF, SET-ACCEL, COAST, and RESUME), servo throttle actuator assembly, speed control sensor, clutch position sensor switch (M/T), amplifier, vacuum dump valve, wiring, and vacuum hoses. Vehicles equipped with overdrive or diesel engines also have a vacuum reservoir.

OPERATION

ENGAGING & DISENGAGING SYSTEM

System is operational at speeds greater than 30 MPH. When ON-OFF switch is set to ON position and SET-ACCEL switch is pressed, vehicle speed will be maintained until new speed is set, brake pedal is pressed, clutch pedal is pressed (M/T), ON-OFF switch is set to OFF position, or hazard lights are activated.

Clutch position sensor switch (M/T) disengages speed control system, preventing engine acceleration when clutch pedal is pressed. If actual vehicle speed drops more than 10 MPH below set speed, because of system malfunction or vehicle limitation, system will automatically disengage.

ADJUSTMENTS

ACTUATOR CABLE

Aerostar, Explorer & Ranger – Remove cable retaining clip. Disengage throttle positioner. Set engine at hot idle. Pull actuator cable to take up slack. While holding cable, insert cable retaining clip.

Bronco, Pickup & 1991 Van – 1) Snap molded actuator cable retainer over accelerator cable end fitting on throttle ball stud. Remove adjuster retainer clip, if installed, from adjuster mounting tab. Insert actuator cable adjuster mounting tab into accelerator cable support bracket slot.

2) Pull cable through adjuster until slight tension is felt without opening throttle plate or increasing idle RPM. Insert adjuster retainer clip slowly until engagement is felt. Push downward until it locks in position.

VACUUM DUMP VALVE

Aerostar, Explorer & Ranger – Firmly pull brake pedal rearward. Push in dump valve until valve collar bottoms against retaining clip.

Bronco, Pickup & 1991 Van – 1) Ensure brake pedal is against stop in released position. Move dump valve in retaining clip until 1/8" or less of valve plunger is exposed.

2) Tip of valve plunger should contact brake pedal adapter. Ensure brake pedal is against stop (released position). Press brake pedal. If vacuum still does not release, replace dump valve.

DIAGNOSIS & TESTING

NOTE: Vehicles with computerized engine controls should be tested for stored computer codes. Codes and related problems must be repaired prior to cruise control diagnosis and repair. For additional information, see appropriate SELF-DIAGNOSTICS article in ENGINE PERFORMANCE.

SPEED CONTROL DOES NOT WORK

1) Inspect all electrical and vacuum connections. Repair as necessary. If all connections are okay, go to net step.
2) Step on brake pedal. Check for proper stoplight operation. Repair stoplight circuit if necessary. If stoplights operate properly, go to next step if vehicle has M/T, or to step **4)** if vehicle has A/T.
3) Check clutch switch. See CLUTCH SWITCH TEST. Service switch if necessary. If clutch switch operates properly, go to next step.

4) Check actuator cable. See ACTUATOR CABLE under ADJUSTMENTS. Service actuator cable if necessary. If actuator cable operates properly, go to next step.
5) Check throttle cable for proper operation. Service if necessary. If throttle cable is okay, go to next step.
6) Check for vacuum at servo. If there is no vacuum, go to next step. If vacuum is okay, go to step **8)**.
7) Check vacuum dump valve. See VACUUM DUMP VALVE TEST. Service vacuum dump valve if necessary. If vacuum dump valve is okay, service hose.
8) Check all switches. See CONTROL SWITCH & CIRCUIT TEST. Service as necessary. If switches are okay, go to next step.
9) Check servo. See SERVO TEST. Replace servo if defective. If servo is okay, go to next step.
10) Check speed sensor. See SPEED SENSOR TEST. Replace speed sensor if defective. If speed sensor is okay, go to next step.
11) Check amplifier. See AMPLIFIER TEST. Replace amplifier if defective. If amplifier is okay, recheck all electrical and vacuum connections.

SPEED CONTROL IS INTERMITTENT

1) Road test vehicle to verify condition. Note when intermittent condition occurs.
2) Inspect all electrical and vacuum connections. Repair as necessary. If condition occurs while cruising, go to next step. If condition occurs while operating switches or while turning steering wheel, go to step **5)**.
3) Check for vacuum at servo. If there is no vacuum, service vacuum supply. If vacuum is okay, go to next step.
4) Check servo. See SERVO TEST. Tap servo body lightly while testing. Replace servo if defective. If servo is okay, substitute known good amplifier, then go to next step.
5) Check all switches. See CONTROL SWITCH & CIRCUIT TEST. Service as necessary.

SPEED CONTROL OPERATES BUT DOES NOT RESUME, ACCELERATE OR COAST DOWN

1) Visually inspect system. Check all electrical and vacuum connections. Repair as necessary. If all connections are okay, go to next step.
2) Check all switches. See CONTROL SWITCH & CIRCUIT TEST. Service as necessary. If switches are okay, go to next step.
3) Check servo. See SERVO TEST. Tap servo body lightly while testing. Replace servo if defective. If servo is okay, substitute known good amplifier, then go to next step.
4) Check amplifier. See AMPLIFIER TEST. Replace amplifier if defective. If amplifier is okay, recheck all electrical and vacuum connections.

SPEED VARIES UP & DOWN

Aerostar, Explorer & Ranger – 1) Check throttle actuator for proper operation and adjustment. See ACTUATOR CABLE under ADJUSTMENTS. Service as necessary. If okay, go to next step.
2) Check servo. See SERVO TEST. Tap servo body lightly while testing. If servo is okay, go to next step. Replace servo if defective.
3) Inspect speedometer cables (if equipped) for proper routing, sharp bends, or binding. Service cables if necessary. Go to next step if cables are okay.
4) Measure speed sensor output voltage. Output voltage at 30 MPH should be **2.5-4.9 volts AC**. Replace speed sensor if output voltage is not within specification. If output voltage is okay, go to next step.
5) Check speed sensor. See SPEED SENSOR TEST. Replace speed sensor if defective. If speed sensor is okay, go to next step.
6) Check vacuum dump valve. See VACUUM DUMP VALVE TEST. Service vacuum dump valve if necessary. If vacuum dump valve is okay, go to next step.
7) Check amplifier. See AMPLIFIER TEST. Replace amplifier if defective. If amplifier is okay, check all connectors and wiring.
Bronco, Pickup & 1991 Van – 1) Check throttle actuator for proper operation and adjustment. See ACTUATOR CABLE under ADJUSTMENTS. Service as necessary. If actuator is okay, go to next step.

2) Check Yellow/Red, Purple/Light Blue, and Brown/Light Green wires for shorts or open circuits between servo and amplifier. Repair as necessary. If wires are okay, go to next step.

3) Check servo. See SERVO TEST. Tap servo body lightly while testing. Replace servo if defective. If servo is okay, go to next step.

4) Measure speed sensor output voltage. Output voltage at 30 MPH should be **2.5-4.9 volts AC**. Replace speed sensor if output voltage is not within specification. If output voltage is okay, go to next step.

5) Check speed sensor. See SPEED SENSOR TEST. Replace speed sensor if defective. If speed sensor is okay, go to next step.

6) Check vacuum dump valve. See VACUUM DUMP VALVE TEST. Service vacuum dump valve if necessary. If vacuum dump valve is okay, go to next step.

7) Check amplifier. See AMPLIFIER TEST. Replace amplifier if defective. If amplifier is okay, check all connectors and wiring.

SPEED CONTROL DOES NOT DISENGAGE WHEN BRAKES ARE APPLIED

1) Step on brake pedal. Check for proper stoplight operation. See BRAKELIGHT SWITCH TEST. Repair stoplight circuit if necessary. If stoplights operate properly, go to next step.

2) Check vacuum dump valve. See VACUUM DUMP VALVE TEST. Service vacuum dump valve if necessary. If vacuum dump valve is okay, go to next step.

3) Check servo. See SERVO TEST. Tap servo body lightly while testing. Replace servo if defective. If servo is okay, go to next step.

4) Check amplifier. See AMPLIFIER TEST. Replace amplifier if defective. If amplifier is okay, check all connectors and wiring.

SPEED WILL NOT SET

1) Inspect throttle actuator for proper operation and adjustment. Service or adjust as necessary. See ACTUATOR CABLE under ADJUSTMENTS. Go to next step if actuator is okay.

2) Inspect all electrical and vacuum connections. Repair as necessary. If all connections are okay, go to next step.

3) Check control switch and circuit. See CONTROL SWITCH & CIRCUIT TEST. Service and retest if necessary. If okay, go to next step.

4) Check vacuum dump valve. See VACUUM DUMP VALVE TEST. Service vacuum dump valve if necessary. If vacuum dump valve is okay, go to next step for vehicles with A/T, or to step 6) for vehicles with M/T.

5) Check clutch switch (if equipped). See CLUTCH SWITCH TEST. Service clutch switch if necessary. If clutch switch is okay, go to next step.

6) Step on brake pedal. Check for proper stoplight operation. Repair stoplight circuit if necessary. If stoplights operate properly, go to next step.

7) Check servo. See SERVO TEST. Tap servo body lightly while testing. Replace servo if defective. If servo is okay, go to next step.

8) Check speed sensor. See SPEED SENSOR TEST. Replace speed sensor if defective. If speed sensor is okay, perform AMPLIFIER TEST.

SPEED CONTROL DOES NOT DISENGAGE WHEN CLUTCH PEDAL IS PRESSED

Verify stoplights and clutch switch operate properly. See CLUTCH SWITCH TEST. If stoplights and clutch switch are okay, service clutch switch wiring.

SPEED GRADUALLY INCREASES OR DECREASES AFTER SPEED IS SET

1) Ensure engine performs normally. Perform SPEED DECREASES ON STEEP GRADES OR UNDER HEAVY LOADS test. Ensure accelerator pedal and linkage open throttle fully. Go to next step.

2) Check vacuum dump valve. See VACUUM DUMP VALVE TEST. Service vacuum dump valve if necessary. If vacuum dump valve is okay, go to next step.

3) Check servo. See SERVO TEST. Tap servo body lightly while testing. Replace servo if defective. If servo is okay, perform AMPLIFIER TEST.

SPEED DECREASES ON STEEP GRADES OR UNDER HEAVY LOADS

Road test vehicle. Set speed to about 55 MPH. Proceed up steep grade. When speed decreases 4-6 MPH, press accelerator pedal. If vehicle can maintain set speed without downshift (downshift is okay with overdrive transmission), problem exists in speed control system. If set speed cannot be maintained without downshift, power train capacity is limiting factor.

CONTROL SWITCH & CIRCUIT TEST

WARNING: On models with air bag, observe the following precautions. Disconnect negative and then positive battery cables. Shield both cables. Air bag system contains a back-up power supply built into the air bag diagnostic monitor. Wait a minimum of one minute before servicing any air bag system components. System is now disabled. See AIR BAG RESTRAINT SYSTEM article.

NOTE: Horn and/or cruise control may operate intermittently if ground brush is missing.

Aerostar, Explorer & Ranger – 1) Press brake pedal. Go to next step if stoplights operate properly. If stoplights do not operate properly, repair as necessary.

2) Attempt to sound horn. Go to next step if horn operates properly. If horn does not operate properly, repair as necessary.

3) Locate 6-pin connector at amplifier. See AMPLIFIER LOCATION table under REMOVAL & INSTALLATION. Using DVOM, check for continuity between circuit No. 57 (Black wire on vehicles with analog cluster) or circuit No. 397 (Black/White wire on Aerostar with electronic cluster) and ground. Repair amplifier ground circuit if necessary. If ground circuit is okay, go to next step.

4) Turn ignition on. Check for battery voltage at circuit No. 296 (White/Purple wire on Aerostar) or circuit No. 302 (Dark Blue wire on Explorer and Ranger). If battery voltage is present, go to next step. If battery voltage is not present, check fuse and wiring back to fuse panel.

5) Press brake pedal. Check for battery voltage at circuit No. 511 (Light Green wire) on Explorer and Ranger or circuit No. 810 (Red/Light Green wire) on Aerostar. If battery voltage exists, go to next step. If battery voltage does not exist, repair wiring between brakelight switch and amplifier and repair as necessary. If continuity exists between brakelight switch and amplifier, check amplifier. See AMPLIFIER TEST.

6) Measure voltage at circuit No. 151 (Light Blue/Black wire). If meter indicates approximately 7.8 volts, go to next step. If meter indicates approximately 12 volts, service sticking speed control ON button or short to ground on circuit No. 151 (Light Blue/Black wire). If voltage is approximately zero, service shorted clockspring on Aerostar. If circuit No. 151 (Light Blue/Black wire) and ON-OFF buttons are both okay, substitute a known good amplifier and repeat test.

7) Measure voltage at circuit No. 151 (Light Blue/Black wire) while turning steering wheel 1/4 turn left and right with specified control switch pressed. See CONTROL SWITCH VOLTAGE table.

CONTROL SWITCH VOLTAGE

Switch Position	Approximate Voltage
No Button Pressed	7.8
ON	12.0
OFF	0
RESUME	6.5
SET-ACCEL	4.5
COAST	1.5

8) If voltages are correct, cruise control switches are operating properly; go to step 15). If voltages are incorrect or fluctuate, go to next step.

9) Turn ignition off. Unplug 6-pin connector at amplifier. Measure resistances between circuit No. 151 (Light Blue/Black wire) and amplifier ground with specified switch pressed. See CONTROL SWITCH RESISTANCE table. If values are correct, replace amplifier and retest. If values are incorrect, go to next step.

CONTROL SWITCH RESISTANCE

Switch	Ohms
OFF	0-1
SET-ACCEL	646-714
COAST	114-126
RESUME	2090-2310

10) Remove horn pad or air bag module (if equipped). Unplug 6-pin horn pad connector from steering wheel. Connect ohmmeter between circuits No. 151 (Yellow/Light Blue wire) and No. 6 (Dark Blue wire) on horn pad connector.

11) Press ON button. If resistance is greater than one ohm, replace cruise control switch assembly. If resistance is okay, connect ohmmeter between circuits No. 151 (Yellow/Light Blue wire) and No. 57 (Black wire) on horn pad connector. Check for resistance values specified in CONTROL SWITCH RESISTANCE table.

12) If values are correct, replace amplifier and retest. If resistance values are incorrect, remove steering wheel. Check circuits No. 151 (Light Blue/Black wire) and No. 57 (Black wire) for continuity between 6-pin connector and brush assembly (Explorer and Ranger) or clockspring (Aerostar).

13) If continuity does not exist, check for continuity between 3-pin brush connector and brush assembly. Also check for continuity of each wire between 3-pin connector and amplifier 6-pin connector. Repair wiring or replace brush assembly as required.

14) If continuity exists on both circuits, clean brush assembly (Explorer and Ranger) or clockspring (Aerostar) with solvent, then lubricate with Speed Control Slip Ring Grease (ESA-M1C122-A). Reinstall steering wheel and horn pad.

15) Measure resistance between circuit No. 150 (Green/White wire) and circuit No. 397 (Black/White wire) on Aerostar, or between circuit No. 563 (Orange/Yellow wire) and circuit No. 397 (Black/White wire) on Explorer and Ranger. If resistance is not 180-250 ohms, check for continuity between 6-pin amplifier connector and 2-pin speed sensor connector at transmission. If wiring is okay, perform SPEED SENSOR TEST.

Bronco, Pickup & 1991 Van – **1)** Unplug 6-pin connector at amplifier. See AMPLIFIER LOCATION table under REMOVAL & INSTALLATION. Check for battery voltage at circuit No. 151 (Light Blue/Black wire) with speed control ON switch pressed. If battery voltage is present, circuit is okay. If battery voltage is not present, go to next step.

2) Check for continuity between Light Blue/Black wire and ground while pressing speed control OFF switch. If resistance is greater than one ohm, wiring to steering columns, slip rings, or switch is at fault, or steering column may not be properly grounded.

3) To check steering column ground, measure resistance between ground and steering column upper flange. Resistance should be less than .5 ohm. Rotate steering wheel to check flexible coupling. If resistance is greater than 3 ohms, clean horn brush contacts and ground brush.

NOTE: Before performing following steps, ensure resistance between steering column and ground is less than one ohm.

4) With ohmmeter connected between circuit No. 151 (Light Blue/Black wire) and ground, press and hold SET-ACCEL switch. If resistance is not approximately 680 ohms, replace switch.

5) Press and hold COAST switch. If resistance is not approximately 120 ohms, replace switch. Press and hold RESUME switch. If resistance is not approximately 2200 ohms, replace switch.

SPEED SENSOR TEST

NOTE: Not all speed sensor problems can be detected with resistance checks. Substitution with a known good speed sensor may be necessary.

Aerostar, Explorer & Ranger – Locate speed sensor at transmission or transfer case. Disconnect speedometer cable from sensor. Unplug electrical connector from speed sensor. Measure resistance between speed sensor terminals. If resistance is approximately 180-250 ohms, and speedometer operates properly, speed sensor is probably good.
Bronco, Pickup & 1991 Van – Unplug 6-pin connector at amplifier. Measure resistance between circuits No. 150 (Dark Green/White wire) and No. 57A (Black wire). If resistance is approximately 200 ohms, and speedometer operates properly, speed sensor is probably good.

SERVO TEST

1) Unplug 8-pin connector at amplifier. See AMPLIFIER LOCATION table under REMOVAL & INSTALLATION. Measure resistance at specified wires on harness connector. See SERVO RESISTANCE table.

SERVO RESISTANCE

Circuit	Ohms
Aerostar, Explorer & Ranger	
144 (Orange/Yellow) - 145 (Gray/Black)	40-70
144 (Orange/Yellow) - 146 (White/Pink)	100-150
147 (Purple/Blue) - 149 (Brown/Green)	35,000-70,000
147 (Purple/Blue) - 148 (Yellow/Red)	15,000-35,000
148 (Yellow/Red) - 149 (Brown/Green)	15,000-35,000
Bronco, Pickup & 1991 Van	
144 (Orange/Yellow) - 145 (Gray/Black)	40-125
144 (Orange/Yellow) - 146 (White/Pink)	60-190

NOTE: Resistance between circuits No. 147 and 148 should be nearly the same as resistance between circuits No. 148 and 149. If the difference is more than 5 k/ohms and vehicle has a surging problem, perform step 2).

2) If resistances are not correct, unplug 6-pin connector at servo. Ensure terminals are clean. Measure resistances at connector. If resistance is correct, check wiring harness and repair as necessary. If resistance is incorrect, replace servo and retest.

CAUTION: If Orange/Yellow wire is shorted to either White/Pink wire or Gray/Black wire, damage to amplifier may occur.

3) Disconnect servo. Start engine. Ensure vacuum to servo is at least 2.5 in. Hg. Connect circuit No. 144 (Orange/Yellow wire) of servo to positive battery terminal. Connect circuit No. 146 (White/Pink wire) of servo to ground. Momentarily connect circuit No. 145 (Gray/Black wire) of servo to ground.

4) Servo throttle actuator arm should pull in and engine speed should increase. The throttle should hold in that position or slowly release. When circuit No. 146 (White/Pink wire) is removed from ground, servo should release. Replace servo if it fails test.

AMPLIFIER TEST

CAUTION: DO NOT use a test light to perform amplifier tests, as excessive current draw will damage the amplifier. Use only a DVOM with minimum 10 megohms input impedance.

NOTE: To test for a malfunctioning amplifier on Aerostar, Explorer, and Ranger, substitute a known good unit. On Bronco, Pickup, and 1991 Van, begin testing with ON CIRCUIT TEST.

ON Circuit Test – **1)** DO NOT substitute a new amplifier until throttle actuator has been tested. See SERVO TEST. Turn ignition on. Connect voltmeter between circuit No. 151 (Light Blue/Black wire) of amplifier connector and ground.

2) Press speed control ON button. Voltmeter should indicate battery voltage. If battery voltage does not exist, check horn relay circuit and control switch test. See HORN RELAY CIRCUIT TEST and CONTROL SWITCH & CIRCUIT TEST.

3) Release ON button. Voltmeter should indicate approximately **7.8 volts**. If meter does not indicate approximately 7.8 volts, check for bad connector on circuit No. 151 (Light Blue/Black wire) of amplifier connector, ground circuit No. 57 (Black wire) to amplifier, or fuse.

OFF Circuit Test – With ignition on, connect DVOM between ground and circuit No. 151 (Light Blue/Black wire) at amplifier 6-pin connector. Press OFF switch. If voltage does not drop to zero volts, perform CONTROL SWITCH & CIRCUIT TEST. If switches are okay, install a known good amplifier and retest.

SET-ACCEL Circuit Test – With ignition on, connect voltmeter between ground and circuit No. 151 (Light Blue/Black wire) of amplifier connector. Press ON button, then press and hold SET-ACCEL button. Voltmeter should indicate approximately **4.5** volts. Rotate steering wheel while observing voltmeter for variation. If voltage varies more than .5 volt, perform CONTROL SWITCH & CIRCUIT TEST.

COAST Circuit Test – With ignition on, connect voltmeter between ground and circuit No. 151 (Light Blue/Black wire) of amplifier connector. Press ON switch, then press and hold COAST button. Voltmeter should indicate approximately **1.5 volts**. If all functions are okay, perform SERVO TEST and SPEED SENSOR TEST, and substitute a known good amplifier.

NOTE: DO NOT substitute a new amplifier until actuator coils in servo have been tested. See SERVO TEST.

RESUME Circuit Test – With ignition on, connect voltmeter between ground and circuit No. 151 (Light Blue/Black wire) of amplifier connector. Press ON switch. Press and hold RESUME switch. Voltmeter should indicate approximately **6.5 volts**. If all functions are okay, perform SERVO TEST and install a known good amplifier.

HORN RELAY CIRCUIT TEST

NOTE: Electrical connectors must remain connected during horn relay testing.

---

1) Locate horn relay. See HORN RELAY LOCATION table. Check for battery voltage at Yellow/Light Blue wire at horn relay. If battery voltage is not present, check fuse and/or wiring back to fuse panel.

HORN RELAY LOCATION

Vehicle	Location
Aerostar	Right Side Of Steering Column, On Relay Bracket
Bronco, Pickup & 1991 Van	Engine Compartment Fuse Panel
Explorer & Ranger	Behind Lower Dash Panel, To Right Of Steering Column

2) If battery voltage is present in step **1)**, check for battery voltage at Dark Blue wire on socket side of connector. If battery voltage is present, press horn button. Voltage should drop to **zero volts** and horn should sound. If horn does not sound and voltage remains at 12 volts, ground Dark Blue wire.

3) If horn still does not sound, check for battery voltage on Dark Blue wire when horn button is pressed. If battery voltage is present, repair open between horn and horn relay. If voltage is not present, replace relay.

CLUTCH SWITCH TEST

NOTE: Test switch only with DVOM. DO NOT use magnetized tools near switch.

Unplug clutch switch connector. Connect ohmmeter to switch terminals No. 3 and 4. *See Fig. 1*. With clutch pedal released, continuity should exist. Press clutch pedal. Switch should open before pedal travels 2" (50 mm). Replace switch if it fails test.

BRAKELIGHT SWITCH TEST

NOTE: Perform this test when brake pedal actuation does not disengage speed control system. On vehicles with M/T, ensure clutch switch operates properly before performing this test.

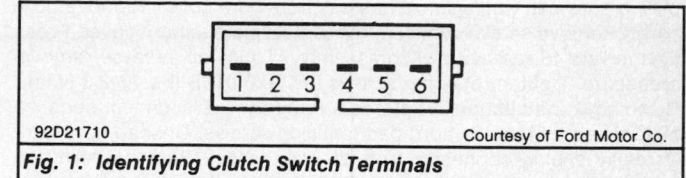

92D21710 · Courtesy of Ford Motor Co.

Fig. 1: Identifying Clutch Switch Terminals

---

1) Check for stoplight operation with maximum brake pedal pressure of 6 lbs. (2.7 kg). If stoplights operate correctly, go to step **2)**. Repair stoplight circuit if necessary.

2) Measure voltage on circuit No. 296 (White/Purple wire) of amplifier 6-pin connector. While stepping on brake pedal, measure voltage on circuit No. 511A (Light Green wire) on Bronco, Pickup and 1991 Van, or circuit No. 511B (Light Green wire) on Aerostar, Explorer and Ranger. If difference between measurements is greater than 1.5 volts, check circuit to find source of high resistance.

VACUUM DUMP VALVE TEST

1) Check vacuum dump valve whenever brake application does not release speed control. Ensure no more than 1/8" of plunger tip is extended when brake pedal is fully released. Disconnect vacuum hose from dump valve to servo, at servo unit. Connect hand-held vacuum pump to hose. Apply vacuum to hose and dump valve.

2) Press brake pedal. Vacuum should be released. If vacuum is not released, adjust or replace dump valve. If vacuum cannot be obtained, hose or dump valve leaks, and should be replaced.

VACUUM RESERVOIR TEST

1) Locate vacuum reservoir on right or left fender apron, depending on model. Disconnect vacuum hose at servo. Connect vacuum gauge to hose. Start engine. Observe vacuum gauge reading.

2) Vacuum should be at least 20 in. Hg. If vacuum is not within specification, check for leaking vacuum hose or faulty vacuum pump.

3) Turn engine off after vacuum has stabilized at more than 20 in. Hg. Vacuum should hold steady. After 24 hours, vacuum should be a minimum of 15 in. Hg. If vacuum fails to hold, replace vacuum reservoir.

REMOVAL & INSTALLATION

WARNING: On models with air bag, observe the following precautions. Disconnect negative and then positive battery cables. Shield both cables. Air bag system contains a back-up power supply built into the air bag diagnostic monitor. Wait a minimum of one minute before servicing any air bag system components. System is now disabled. See AIR BAG RESTRAINT SYSTEM article.

WARNING: When battery is disconnected, vehicle computer and memory systems may lose memory data. Driveability problems may exist until computer systems have completed a relearn cycle. See COMPUTER RELEARN PROCEDURES article in GENERAL INFORMATION before disconnecting battery.

SPEED CONTROL SWITCHES

Removal & Installation (Aerostar) – 1) Disconnect negative battery cable. Remove air bag module retaining nuts and washers. Lift module away from steering wheel. Unplug electrical connector. Remove air bag module.

WARNING: Place air bag module on bench with trim cover facing upward.

---

2) Unplug horn/speed control harness connector from clockspring. Remove retaining screws from switches. Remove tape from connectors. Disconnect switch wires. Remove switches. To install switches, reverse removal procedure. Tighten air bag module nuts to **35-53 INCH lbs. (4-6 N.m)**.

Removal & Installation (Bronco, Pickup & 1991 Van) – Press inward on sides of horn cover. Unsnap horn cover from steering wheel by pulling outward. Unplug wire harness from horn cover. Remove horn cover. Remove screws which retain contact plate to horn cover. Press tabs inward to remove switch assembly. To install, reverse removal procedure. Tighten retaining screws to **18-20 INCH lbs. (2-2.3 N.m).**

Removal & Installation (Explorer & Ranger) – Disconnect negative battery cable. Remove horn pad retaining screws. Unsnap horn pad. Carefully unplug connector from steering wheel. Remove horn pad and switch assembly. Remove speed control switch retaining screws. Unplug connectors from horn pad. Remove switch assembly. To install switch assembly, reverse removal procedure. Tighten retaining screws to **8-11 INCH lbs. (.9-1.2 N.m).**

SPEED SENSOR

Removal & Installation – Speed sensor is located at transmission on Aerostar, Explorer, and Ranger, and at rear axle on Bronco, Pickup, and 1991 van. Disconnect speedometer cable (if equipped). Unplug connector. Remove retaining bolt. Remove speed sensor. To install, reverse removal procedure.

AMPLIFIER

Removal & Installation – Locate amplifier. See AMPLIFIER LOCATION table. Unplug connectors. Remove amplifier and bracket as an assembly. Separate amplifier from bracket. To install, reverse removal procedure. Check system for proper operation.

AMPLIFIER LOCATION

Vehicle	Location
Aerostar	Behind Right Side Of Instrument Panel, Above Cowl Panel, Or Behind Left End Of Instrument Panel
Bronco, Pickup & 1991 Van	Behind Lower Center Of Instrument Panel
Explorer & Ranger	Behind Left Side Of Instrument Panel, Or Above Glove Box

SERVO

Removal & Installation – Unplug connectors from servo. Disconnect adjuster from accelerator cable. Disconnect vacuum hose. Remove retaining nuts and servo assembly. To install, reverse removal procedure.

VACUUM DUMP VALVE

Removal & Installation – Vacuum dump valve is located at brake pedal lever. Disconnect vacuum hose. Remove valve from bracket. To install, reverse removal procedure.

CLUTCH SWITCH

Removal & Installation – Clutch switch is located at clutch pedal lever. Unplug harness connector. Pull clip downward to separate it from tab on switch. Rotate switch to expose retainer. Squeeze tabs to permit retainer to slide to rear. Remove switch. To install, reverse removal procedure.

VACUUM RESERVOIR

Removal & Installation – Vacuum reservoir is located on left or right fender apron. Disconnect vacuum hoses. Remove retaining nuts and vacuum reservoir. To install, reverse removal procedure.

WIRING DIAGRAMS

For 1992 wiring diagrams, see appropriate chassis wiring diagram in WIRING DIAGRAMS.

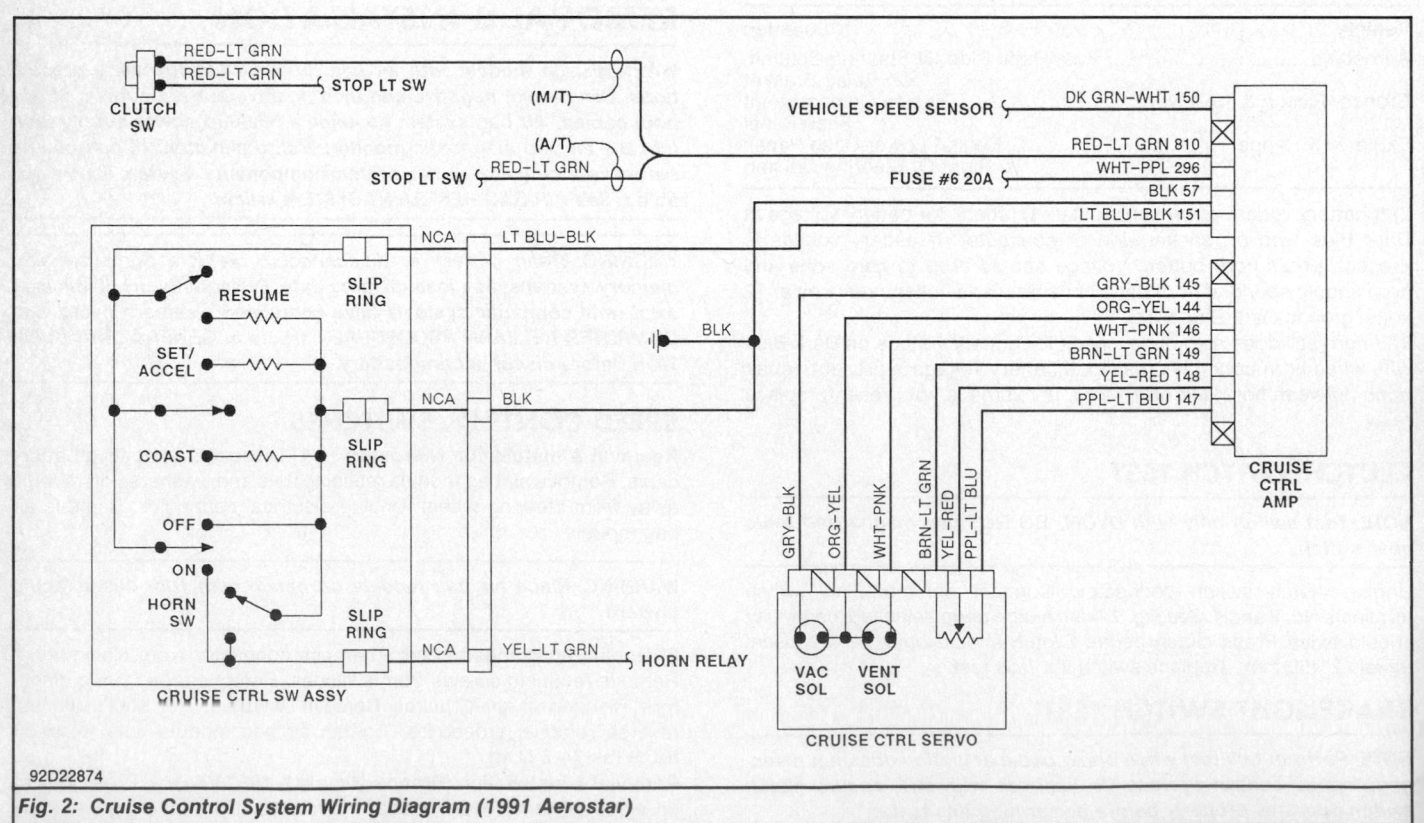

92D22874

Fig. 2: Cruise Control System Wiring Diagram (1991 Aerostar)

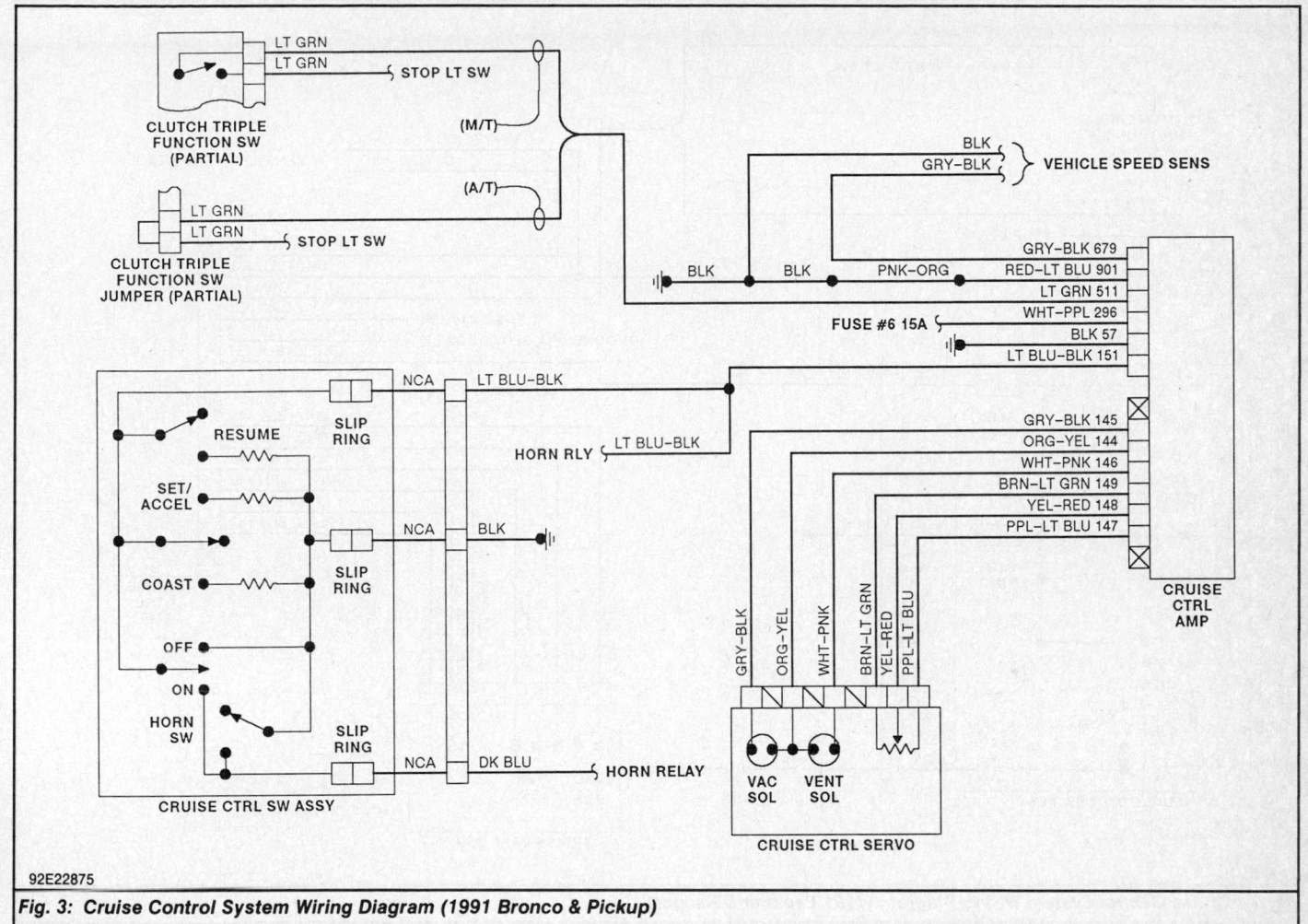

Fig. 3: Cruise Control System Wiring Diagram (1991 Bronco & Pickup)

92E22875

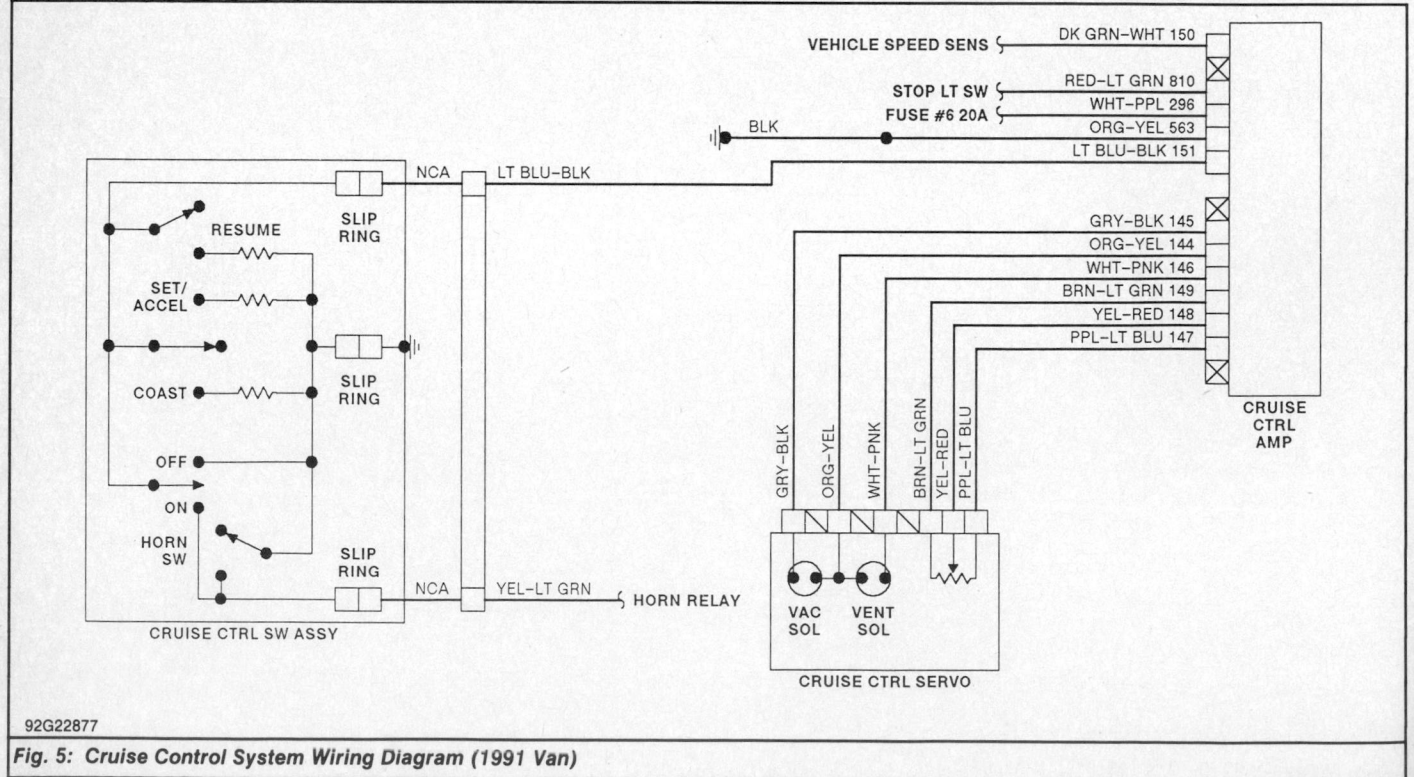

92F22876

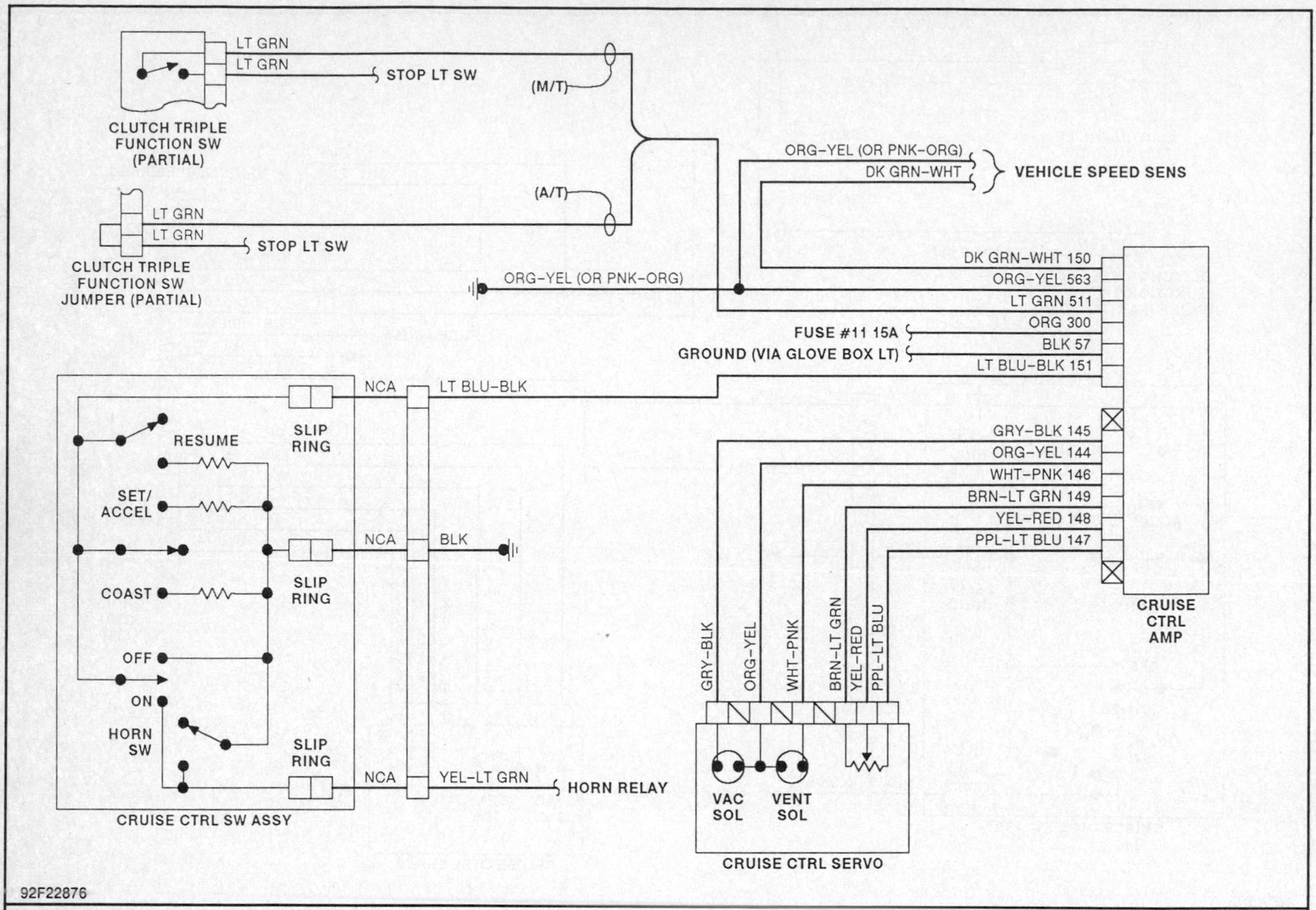

Fig. 4: Cruise Control System Wiring Diagram (1991 Explorer & Ranger)

92G22877

Fig. 5: Cruise Control System Wiring Diagram (1991 Van)

Van

DESCRIPTION

The cruise control system consists of 5 control switches (ON, OFF, SET-ACCEL, COAST, and RESUME), servo throttle actuator/amplifier assembly, speed sensor, deactivator switch, and wiring.

OPERATION

ENGAGING & DISENGAGING SYSTEM

System is operational at speeds greater than 30 MPH. When ON and SET-ACCEL switches have been pressed, vehicle speed will be maintained until new speed is set, brake pedal is pressed, OFF switch has been pressed, or hazard lights are activated.

ADJUSTMENTS

ACTUATOR CABLE

Remove cable retaining clip. Set throttle plate to closed position. Pull actuator cable to take up slack. Back off at least one notch so that there is .04" (one mm) slack in cable. While holding cable, insert cable retaining clip.

DIAGNOSIS & TESTING

NOTE: *Vehicles with computerized engine controls should be tested for stored computer codes. Codes and related problems must be repaired prior to cruise control diagnosis and repair. For additional information, see SELF-DIAGNOSTICS article in ENGINE PERFORMANCE.*

NOTE: *When diagnosing any speed control system malfunction, perform the following tests in the order they are presented. Some of the tests depend on proper results from previous tests.*

SPEED CONTROL INOPERATIVE

1) Perform complete visual inspection of system. Repair as necessary. If all connections and components appear to be okay, go to next step.
2) Unplug harness connector from servo, near master cylinder. Use only DVOM to make measurements specified in steps 3) through 11).
3) Turn ignition on. Check for battery voltage between harness connector pins No. 7 (White/Purple wire) and No. 10 (Black wire) at servo. If battery voltage exists, go to next step. If there is no voltage, go to NO POWER TO SERVO test.
4) With brake pedal in released position, measure voltage between servo harness connector pins No. 4 (Light Green wire) and No. 10 (Black wire). If voltage is zero, stoplight switch is not stuck on; go to next step. If battery voltage exists, replace stoplight switch.
5) Turn ignition off. Measure resistance between servo harness connector pins No. 4 (Light Green wire) and No. 10 (Black wire). If resistance is less than 20 ohms, go to next step. If resistance is greater than 20 ohms, repair stoplight circuit.
6) With ignition off and brake pedal released, measure voltage between servo harness connector pins No. 9 (Red/Light Green wire) and No. 10 (Black wire). If meter indicates battery voltage, go to next step. If meter indicates zero, go to NO POWER ON DEACTIVATOR SWITCH CIRCUIT.
7) With no steering wheel switches pressed, measure voltage between servo harness connector pins No. 5 (Light Blue/Black wire) and No. 10 (Black wire). If voltage is zero, ON switch is not stuck; go to next step. If battery voltage exists, replace ON switch.
8) With ignition off, measure voltage between servo harness connector pins No. 5 (Light Blue/Black wire) and No. 10 (Black wire) while pressing ON switch. If battery voltage exists, ON switch is okay; go to next step. If voltage is zero, go to "ON" SWITCH INOPERATIVE test.
9) With no steering wheel switches pressed, measure resistance between servo harness connector pins No. 5 (Light Blue/Pink wire) and No. 6 (Black wire). If resistance is greater than 3000 ohms, no switches are stuck; go to next step. If resistance is less than 3000 ohms, replace stuck command switch.
10) With SET-ACCEL switch pressed, measure resistance between harness connector pins No. 5 (Light Blue/Pink wire) and No. 6 (Black wire). If resistance is 640-720 ohms, SET-ACCEL switch is okay; go to next step. If resistance is not 640-720 ohms, replace SET-ACCEL switch.
11) Raise and support vehicle with rear wheels free. Run rear wheels at 30 MPH. Measure voltage between harness connector pins No. 3 (Red/Light Green wire) and No. 10 (Black wire). If meter indicates 4-5 volts, speed signal is okay; go to next step. If voltage is zero, service programmable speedometer/odometer module. See appropriate INSTRUMENT PANELS article.
12) Remove cable from servo. Check for broken cable by pulling end of cable and observing throttle movement. Replace cable if necessary. If cable is okay, replace servo.

NO POWER TO SERVO

1) Turn ignition on. Check for battery voltage at servo harness connector pin No. 7 (White/Purple wire) at servo. If battery voltage exists, go to next step. If there is no voltage, replace fuse or repair White/Purple wire.
2) Turn ignition off. Check for continuity between servo harness connector pin No. 10 (Black wire) and ground at servo. If continuity does not exist, repair Black wire to ground.

NO POWER ON DEACTIVATOR SWITCH CIRCUIT

1) Locate deactivator switch, near left frame rail below floor pan. With ignition off and brake pedal released, measure voltage between deactivator switch harness connector pins No. 9 (Red/Light Green wire) and No. 10 (Black wire). If meter indicates battery voltage, power to switch is okay. If meter indicates zero, go to next step.
2) Unplug harness connector from deactivator switch. With ignition off and brake pedal released, measure resistance between switch terminals. If resistance is less than one ohm, go to next step. If resistance is one ohm or greater, replace switch.
3) Measure voltage between deactivator switch harness connector pin No. 1 (Light Green/Red wire) and ground. If meter indicates battery voltage, go to next step. If meter indicates zero, replace fuse or repair Light Green wire from fuse panel.
4) Measure resistance between deactivator switch harness connector pin No. 2 (Red/Light Green wire) and pin No. 9 (Red/Light Green wire) on servo harness connector. If resistance is less than one ohm, circuit is okay. If circuit is open, repair Red/Light Green wire.

"ON" SWITCH INOPERATIVE

1) Unplug harness connector from servo. With ignition off, measure voltage between harness connector pins No. 5 (Light Blue/Black wire) and No. 10 (Black wire) while pressing ON switch. If battery voltage exists, ON switch is okay. If battery voltage does not exist, repeat SPEED CONTROL INOPERATIVE test.
2) While pressing horn button, measure voltage between servo harness connector pin No. 6 (Black wire) and ground. If meter indicates battery voltage, replace ON switch. If meter indicates zero voltage, replace fuse, repair open Yellow/Light Green wire between fuse panel and switch, or open Black ground wire to switch.

SPEED CONTROL SURGES

Check actuator cable and throttle linkage for binding. Repair as necessary. If no binding exists, replace servo.

COAST/TAP-DOWN FUNCTION INOPERATIVE

1) Turn ignition off. Unplug 10-pin connector from servo. While pressing COAST switch, measure resistance between servo harness connector pins No. 5 (Light Blue/Pink wire) and No. 6 (Black wire). Rotate steering wheel through full range while making measurement.

If resistance is 114-126 ohms, switch is okay; go to next step. If resistance is not 114-126 ohms, replace switch.

2) Check for continuity between harness connector pins No. 10 (Pink/Orange wire) and No. 6 (Black wire). If continuity does not exist, switch circuit is okay. If continuity exists, repair switch ground circuit (Black wire).

ACCEL/TAP FUNCTION INOPERATIVE

1) Turn ignition off. Unplug 10-pin connector from servo. While pressing SET-ACCEL switch, measure resistance between servo harness connector pins No. 5 (Light Blue/Pink wire) and No. 6 (Black wire). Rotate steering wheel through full range while making measurement. If resistance is 646-714 ohms, switch is okay; go to next step. If resistance is not 646-714 ohms, replace switch.

2) Check for continuity between harness connector pins No. 10 (Pink/Orange wire) and No. 6 (Black wire). If continuity does not exist, switch circuit is okay. If continuity exists, repair switch ground circuit (Black wire).

RESUME FUNCTION INOPERATIVE

1) Turn ignition off. Unplug 10-pin connector from servo. While pressing RESUME switch, measure resistance between servo harness connector pins No. 5 (Light Blue/Pink wire) and No. 6 (Black wire). Rotate steering wheel through full range while making measurement. If resistance is 2090-2310 ohms, switch is okay; go to next step. If resistance is not 2090-2310 ohms, replace switch.

2) Check for continuity between harness connector pins No. 10 (Pink/Orange wire) and No. 6 (Black wire). If continuity does not exist, switch circuit is okay. If continuity exists, repair switch ground circuit (Black wire).

NO BRAKE SWITCH SHUTOFF

1) Turn ignition off. Unplug 10-pin connector from servo. Check actuator cable and throttle linkage for binding. Repair as necessary. If no binding exists, go to next step.

2) While applying brake, check for battery voltage between harness connector pins No. 4 (Light Green wire) and No. 10 (Pink/Orange wire). If battery voltage exists, replace servo. If battery voltage does not exist, service stoplight switch circuit.

SPEED CONTROL WILL NOT TURN OFF WITH "OFF" SWITCH

Turn ignition off. Unplug 10-pin connector from servo. While pressing OFF switch, measure resistance between harness connector pins No. 5 (Light Blue/Pink wire) and No. 6 (Black wire). Rotate steering wheel through full range while making measurement. If resistance is greater than 4 ohms, replace OFF switch. If resistance is less than 4 ohms, replace servo.

REMOVAL & INSTALLATION

WARNING: When battery is disconnected, vehicle computer and memory systems may lose memory data. Driveability problems may exist until computer systems have completed a relearn cycle. See COMPUTER RELEARN PROCEDURES article in GENERAL INFORMATION before disconnecting battery.

SERVO

Removal – Remove battery and battery tray. Remove speed control bracket mounting screws. Unplug connector from servo. While pressing accelerator pedal, push locking arm on actuator cap. Rotate cap counterclockwise. Remove cable ball from pulley.

Installation – Connect wire harness. While pressing accelerator pedal, lock cable ball into servo pulley. Insert locking tabs into servo. Install actuator and bracket. To complete installation, reverse removal procedure. Adjust cable. See ACTUATOR CABLE under ADJUSTMENTS.

COMMAND SWITCHES (VEHICLES WITH AIR BAG)

WARNING: On vehicles with air bag, observe all service precautions. See SERVICE PRECAUTIONS in AIR BAG RESTRAINT SYSTEM article. Disable air bag system. See SERVICE PRECAUTIONS and DISABLING & ACTIVATING AIR BAG SYSTEM in AIR BAG RESTRAINT SYSTEM article.

Removal – 1) Before proceeding, follow air bag service precautions. See SERVICE PRECAUTIONS in AIR BAG RESTRAINT SYSTEM article. Disable air bag system. See DISABLING & ACTIVATING AIR BAG SYSTEM in AIR BAG RESTRAINT SYSTEM article. Remove nuts and washers retaining air bag module to steering wheel. Disconnect air bag electrical connector from clockspring (contact assembly). Remove air bag module.

WARNING: Place air bag module on bench with trim cover facing upward.

2) Unplug horn/speed control harness connector from clockspring. Remove retaining screws from switches. Remove tape from connectors. Disconnect switch wires. Remove switches.

Installation – Install switches and retaining screws. Connect air bag module wiring connector to clockspring (contact assembly). Position air bag module onto steering wheel. Install air bag module nuts and washers. Tighten nuts to 35-50 INCH lbs. (4.0-5.6 N.m). Activate air bag system. Check AIR BAG warning light to assure system is functioning properly. See SYSTEM OPERATION CHECK in AIR BAG RESTRAINT SYSTEM article.

COMMAND SWITCHES (VEHICLES WITHOUT AIR BAG)

Removal & Installation – Press inward on sides of horn cover. Unsnap horn cover from steering wheel by pulling outward. Unplug wire harness from horn cover. Remove horn cover. Remove screws which retain contact plate to horn cover. Press tabs inward to remove switch assembly. To install, reverse removal procedure.

DEACTIVATOR (BRAKE PRESSURE) SWITCH

Removal & Installation – Deactivator switch is located near left frame rail, below floor pan. Unplug harness connector. Unscrew switch. To install, reverse removal procedure. Bleed brake system. See DISC & DRUM article in BRAKES.

SPEED SENSOR

Removal & Installation – Speed sensor is located at differential housing. Unplug connector. Remove retaining bolt. Remove speed sensor. To install, reverse removal procedure.

WIRING DIAGRAM

See appropriate chassis wiring diagram in WIRING DIAGRAMS.

Aerostar, Bronco, Explorer

DESCRIPTION & OPERATION

Rear defogger system consists of a control assembly, an indicator light, grid lines on inside surface of window and system wiring. Each grid line consists of 2 layers. The first layer is Brown as viewed from the exterior. The second layer is Silver as viewed from interior. A 40-amp, in-line circuit breaker and 15-amp fuse protect defogger circuitry on Aerostar. A fusible link and 15-amp fuse protect Bronco and Explorer defogger circuits.

The 40-amp circuit breaker is in underhood power distribution box. The fusible link is connected near the starter relay. A control switch turns system on or off. A timer-controlled relay turns system off after about 10 minutes of operation. When switch is in ON position, contacts in control assembly are mechanically closed. This provides current to grids, indicator light and control timer.

Contacts will remain closed until control timer turns system off, or ignition switch is turned off. Power to grids and indicator light is supplied directly from battery side of starter relay through a fusible link on Aerostar and Bronco. Power for control timer comes from accessory terminal of ignition switch. Power is available when ignition switch is in RUN or ACC position.

TESTING

NOTE: Rear defogger test procedure for Bronco and control switch test procedure for Aerostar are not available from manufacturer.

REAR DEFOGGER SWITCH TEST

Explorer – 1) Ground pin No. 4, and connect a jumper wire between pins No. 2 and 3. *See Fig. 1.* Connect a 12-volt test light between pin No. 1 and ground. Apply power to pin No. 2. Test light and indicator light should not come on. If test light and/or indicator light come on, replace switch.

2) Momentarily push right side of defogger rocker switch to ON position. Test light and indicator light should come on and stay on after switch is released. Test light and indicator light should go off when defogger switch is pushed to OFF position, 10 minutes have passed, or jumper wire between pins No. 2 and 3 is removed.

WINDOW GRID

1) Using a bright light inside vehicle, visually inspect wire grid from outside. A broken grid wire will appear as a brown spot. Start engine and run at idle. Put control switch in ON position. Indicator light should come on.

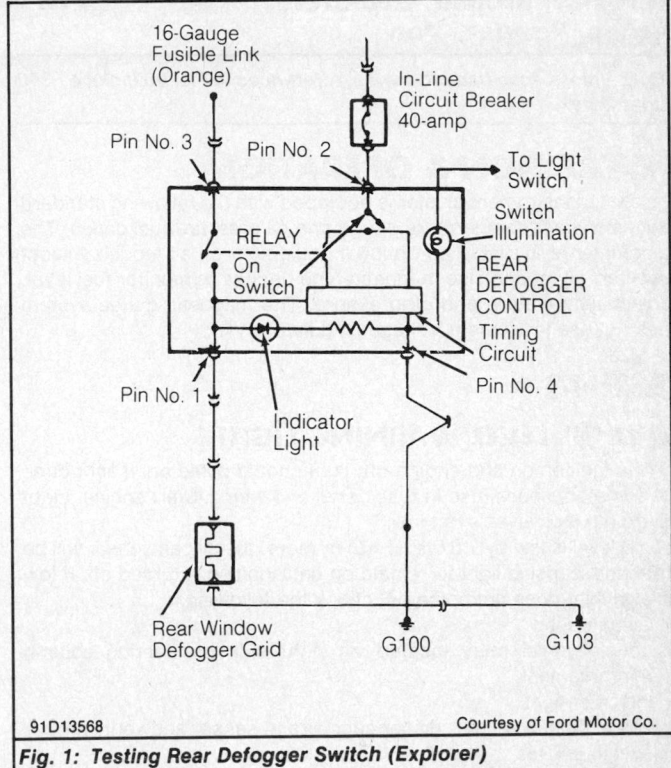

91D13568   Courtesy of Ford Motor Co.

Fig. 1: Testing Rear Defogger Switch (Explorer)

2) Using a voltmeter, check for **10-13 volts** at broad Red/Brown strips on rear window. A low voltage reading indicates a loose ground wire (pigtail) connection at ground screw. With negative voltmeter lead grounded, touch positive lead to each ground line of heated rear window at its midpoint.

3) A reading of approximately **6 volts** indicates proper circuit function. If zero volts are found, circuit is broken between midpoint and hot side of grid line. A reading of 12 volts indicates circuit is broken between midpoint of grid line and ground.

WIRING DIAGRAMS

See appropriate chassis wiring diagram in WIRING DIAGRAMS.

Aerostar, Bronco, Explorer, Pickup, Ranger, Van

NOTE: Unless specified otherwise, references to Pickup include F350 Super Duty.

DESCRIPTION & OPERATION

The analog instrument cluster is equipped with the following standard gauges: voltage/temperature gauge and oil pressure/fuel gauge. The tachometer is available as optional equipment on all models except Aerostar. All models use magnetic-type gauges to monitor fuel level, coolant temperature and oil pressure. The magnetic gauge system does not use Instrument Voltage Regulator (IVR).

TESTING

LOW OIL LEVEL WARNING LIGHT

1) With ignition on and engine off, light should come on. If light does not come on, check fuse in fuse panel and wiring. Start engine. Light will go out if oil level is not low.
2) If oil level is low by 1.5 qts. (1.4L) or more, the oil pan sensor will be grounded, causing light to remain on until ignition is turned off. If low oil level light does not come on, check the following:
  • Circuit fuse
  • Low oil level relay located on right side of steering column reinforcement
  • Indicator light
3) To test oil pan sensor, disconnect wire at sensor and verify proper oil level in engine.
4) Connect a Digital Volt-Ohmmeter (DVOM) to sensor terminal and ground. With oil at proper full level, reading should be greater than **100,000 ohms** (sensor open). Drain 2 qts. of oil from oil pan and recheck. Reading should be less than **1000 ohms**.

NOTE: It may take 5 minutes or more for oil to drain from sensor to get low oil level reading. Sensor must be horizontal when performing this test.

CHARGE INDICATOR LIGHT

1) The Integral Alternator Regulator (IAR) has a circuit that will indicate a high or low battery voltage condition. The charge indicator light will come on if alternator is not charging, or is overcharging. If either of these conditions exists, see appropriate ALTERNATORS article in ELECTRICAL.
2) If charge indicator light does not come on with ignition switch in RUN position (engine off), check ignition switch-to-regulator terminal "I" circuit. Verify circuit is not open or indicator bulb is not blown. Replace bulb if necessary and recheck.
3) If indicator light still does not come on, disconnect wiring connector from regulator. Connect a jumper wire from "I" terminal to negative battery cable. *See Fig. 1.* Turn ignition switch to RUN position (engine off). If indicator light does not come on, check bulb for continuity and replace if necessary. If bulb is good on Aerostar, Explorer and Ranger, perform voltage regulator "I" circuit tests. See appropriate ALTERNATORS article in ELECTRICAL.
4) On Bronco, Pickup and Van, if indicator light does not come on, check 500-ohm resistor across indicator light. Replace as necessary. On Aerostar, Explorer and Ranger, if indicator light comes on when jumper is connected between "I" terminal and negative battery cable, remove jumper wire and reconnect regulator connector.
5) Connect DVOM negative lead to negative battery post. Connect positive lead to voltage regulator terminal "A" screw at alternator. Battery voltage should be indicated.
6) If battery voltage is not indicated, repair circuit "A" wiring. If battery voltage is present, clean and tighten ground connections of alternator and regulator. Turn ignition on (engine off). If indicator light still does not come on, replace regulator.

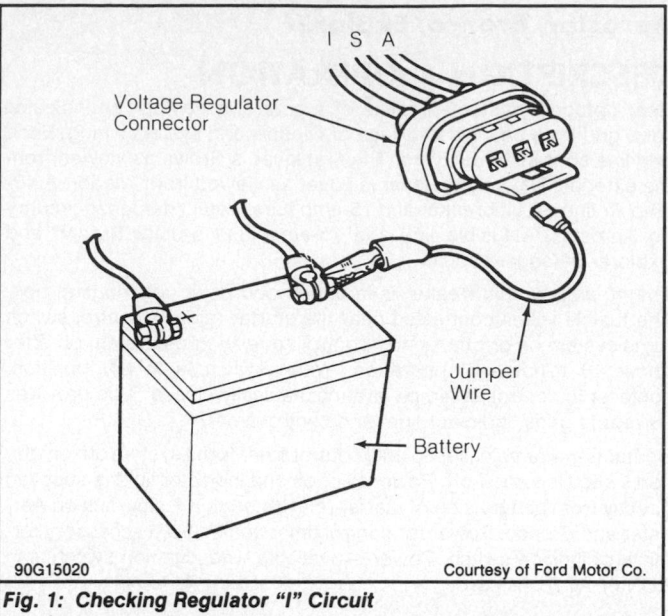

90G15020   Courtesy of Ford Motor Co.
Fig. 1: Checking Regulator "I" Circuit

4WD INDICATOR

If the 4WD or low range indicator lights do not come on when 4WD or low range is engaged, check fuse No. 18. If fuse is okay, check indicator bulbs. If bulbs are okay, check indicator switch continuity. Replace switch as necessary.

ANTI-LOCK BRAKE INDICATOR

See ANTI-LOCK – RABS article in BRAKES.

VOLTMETER

Turn ignition and headlights on with engine off. Voltmeter should read approximately **12-12.5 volts**. If gauge does not move, check battery-to-circuit breaker wire connections. If connections are tight and voltmeter shows no movement, check wire continuity. If continuity is okay, replace voltmeter.

FUEL LEVEL GAUGE

Calibration Test (With Tester) – 1) Use Rotunda Gauge Tester (021-00055) to check fuel gauge. Turn ignition off. Install rotunda gauge tester in circuit. Set tester to 22-ohm position. Turn ignition on. Wait 60 seconds, and then read fuel gauge.
2) If gauge reads "E", go to step 5). If gauge does not read "E", turn ignition switch off, then turn it back on. Tap on instrument panel and wait one minute. If gauge goes to "E", check for intermittent B+ connection at cluster connector, or for damaged printed circuit.
3) Repair as necessary and repeat test. If after repeating test, gauge does not read "E", turn ignition off. Remove instrument cluster and inspect printed circuit for damage. Remove slosh module located on back of cluster. Connect jumper wire from gauge tester to fuel gauge connector terminal "S" (Yellow/White wire).
4) Turn ignition on and observe gauge. If gauge does not read "E", replace gauge. If gauge reads "E", replace slosh module.
5) If gauge reads "E" in step 2), turn ignition off. Set rotunda gauge tester to 145-ohm setting. Turn ignition on, wait 60 seconds, and read fuel gauge. If gauge reads "F", check sender circuit wiring for shorts or opens with ohmmeter. If gauge does not read "F", turn ignition off and remove instrument cluster. See INSTRUMENT CLUSTER under REMOVAL & INSTALLATION.
6) Inspect printed circuit to ensure loop connecting fuel sender input to fuel gauge is cut. If loop is not cut, correctly cut printed circuit at loop. Remove slosh module from rear of cluster, and connect jumper wire from gauge tester to fuel gauge connector terminal "S" (Yellow/White wire). Reconnect cluster connector and recheck gauge.

7) If fuel gauge reads "F", replace slosh module. If gauge does not read "F", replace gauge. Check fuel gauge resistance using ohmmeter. Gauge should read EMPTY at 22.5 ohms and FULL at 145 ohms.
Calibration Test (Without Tester) – 1) Use a DVOM to check gauge calibration. With sending unit float arm in empty stop position, resistance should be **15 ohms**. With sending unit float arm in full stop position, resistance should be **160 ohms**.
2) Fuel gauge should begin to read empty at 22.5 ohms and full at 145 ohms.

OIL PRESSURE GAUGE

Calibration Test (With Tester) – 1) Disconnect connector from oil sender and connect to Rotunda Gauge Tester (021-00055). Connect other tester lead to ground on vehicle. Turn ignition switch to ACC position.
2) Place tester switch in LOW (73 ohms) position. If gauge does not move, go to next step. If gauge reads "L", set gauge tester to HIGH (9.7 ohms) position. If gauge reads approximately midrange on scale, replace sender. If gauge does not read approximately midrange on scale, go to next step.
3) Check sender circuit wiring for shorts and opens with ohmmeter. If wiring is okay, replace gauge. If wiring is shorted or open, repair wiring as necessary. See appropriate chassis wiring diagram in WIRING DIAGRAMS.
Calibration Test (Without Tester) – 1) Test oil pressure gauge with a 10-ohm resistor for high calibration, and a 73-ohm resistor for low calibration. Turn ignition on and connect a 10-ohm resistor between gauge lead and ground. Oil pressure gauge pointer should read at midrange on scale.
2) Remove 10-ohm resistor, and connect 73-ohm resistor. Oil pressure gauge pointer should be around the "L" mark. If gauge readings are not as indicated, replace gauge and retest. If readings are as indicated, replace oil pressure sender.

TEMPERATURE GAUGE

Calibration Test (With Tester) – 1) Disconnect connector from temperature sender and connect to Rotunda Gauge Tester (021-00055). Connect other tester lead to ground on vehicle. Turn ignition switch to ACC position.
2) Place tester switch in LOW (73 ohms) position. If gauge does not move, go to next step. If gauge reads "C", set gauge tester to HIGH (9.7 ohms) position. If gauge reads "H", replace sender. If gauge does not read "H", go to next step.
3) Check sender circuit wiring for shorts and opens with ohmmeter. If wiring is okay, replace gauge. If wiring is shorted or open, repair wiring as necessary. See appropriate chassis wiring diagram in WIRING DIAGRAMS.
Calibration Test (Without Tester) – 1) Test temperature gauge with a 10-ohm resistor for high calibration, and a 73-ohm resistor for low calibration.
2) Turn ignition on and connect a 10-ohm resistor between gauge lead and ground. Temperature gauge pointer should read within band around "H" mark. Connect 73-ohm resistor in place of 10-ohm resistor.
3) Gauge should now read around "C" mark. If gauge readings are not as indicated, replace gauge and retest. If readings are as indicated, replace temperature sender.

TACHOMETER

NOTE: Information is not available on Aerostar, Explorer and Ranger.

WARNING: When battery is disconnected, vehicle computer and memory systems may lose memory data. Driveability problems may exist until computer systems have completed a relearn cycle. See COMPUTER RELEARN PROCEDURES article in GENERAL INFORMATION before disconnecting battery.

Bronco, Pickup & Van Series (Gasoline Engines) – 1) The tachometer on Bronco and Pickup can be used on 6-cylinder or 8-cylinder engines. Tachometer terminals "B" (12 volts), "C" (coil negative) and

"G" (ground) are connected when used on 6-cylinder engines. A fourth terminal, "8" (ground), is grounded through wiring harness for operation on 8-cylinder engines. *See Fig. 2.*

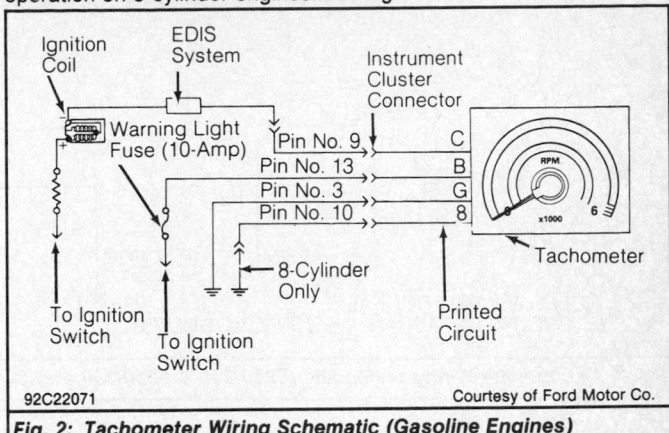

Fig. 2: Tachometer Wiring Schematic (Gasoline Engines)

2) Check fuse and replace if blown. Check for loose wiring connections in engine compartment or at instrument cluster. Secure where necessary. Disconnect negative battery cable. Remove instrument cluster. See INSTRUMENT CLUSTER under REMOVAL & INSTALLATION. Check resistance and voltage using a Volt-Ohmmeter (VOM).
3) Check pin No. 2 of instrument cluster harness connector "B" for resistance to ground. Reading should be **one ohm or less**. *See Fig. 3.* Check pin No. 3 of instrument cluster harness connector "A" for resistance to ground (8-cylinder), or open circuit (6-cylinder). Reading should be **one ohm or less**.

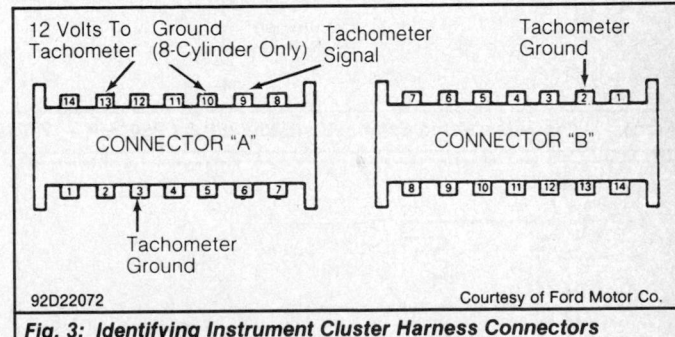

Fig. 3: Identifying Instrument Cluster Harness Connectors "A" & "B" Terminals (Gasoline Engines)

4) Check pin No. 9 of connector "A" for resistance to negative terminal of ignition coil. Reading should be **one ohm or less**. Connect battery and turn ignition on. Check voltage at pin No. 13 of connector "A". Voltage should be **12 volts**. Turn ignition off. Disconnect battery.
5) If readings are not as specified, problem is not in tachometer. Check wiring. If readings are as specified, check for loose or missing cluster connection clips. Check for damaged printed circuit. Reseat or replace missing clips. Replace printed circuit as necessary. If connection clips and printed circuit are okay, replace tachometer.
E250/350 & F250/350 (7.3L Diesel) – 1) The electronically-operated tachometer, mounted in the instrument cluster assembly, indicates engine speed in Revolutions Per Minute (RPM). The tachometer receives its signal from the Variable Reluctance Sensor (VRS) mounted in injection pump timing gear cover.
2) If tachometer is inoperative or erratic, check fuse. If fuse is blown, check for short circuit. Check for loose wire connections in engine compartment or at instrument cluster. If connections are okay, go to next step.
3) Disconnect battery. Remove instrument cluster. See INSTRUMENT CLUSTER under REMOVAL & INSTALLATION. Using DVOM, check resistance and voltage at instrument cluster harness connectors.

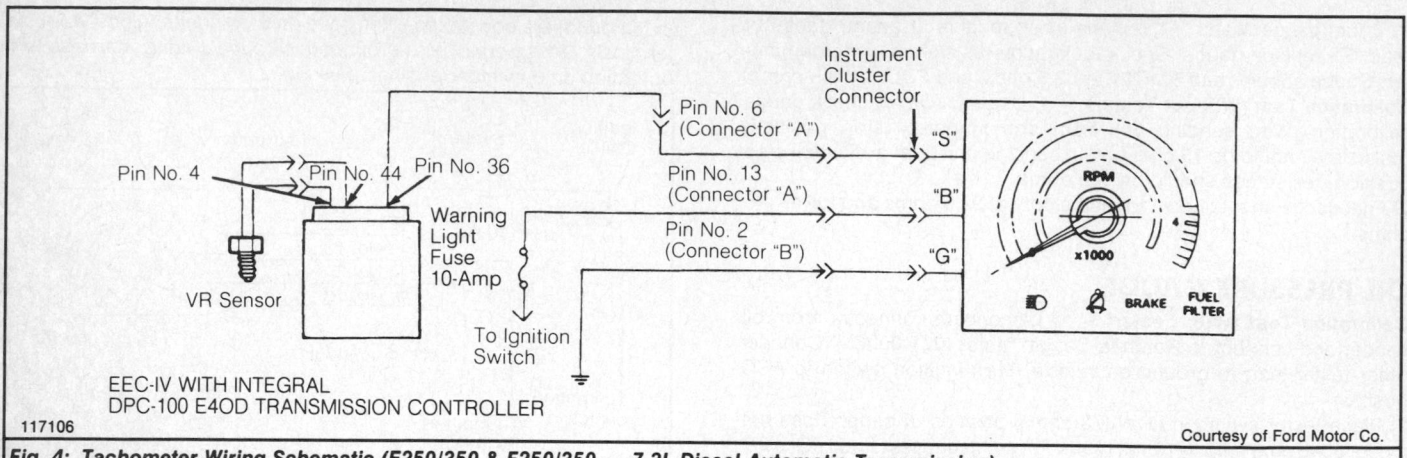

Fig. 4: Tachometer Wiring Schematic (E250/350 & F250/350 – 7.3L Diesel Automatic Transmission)

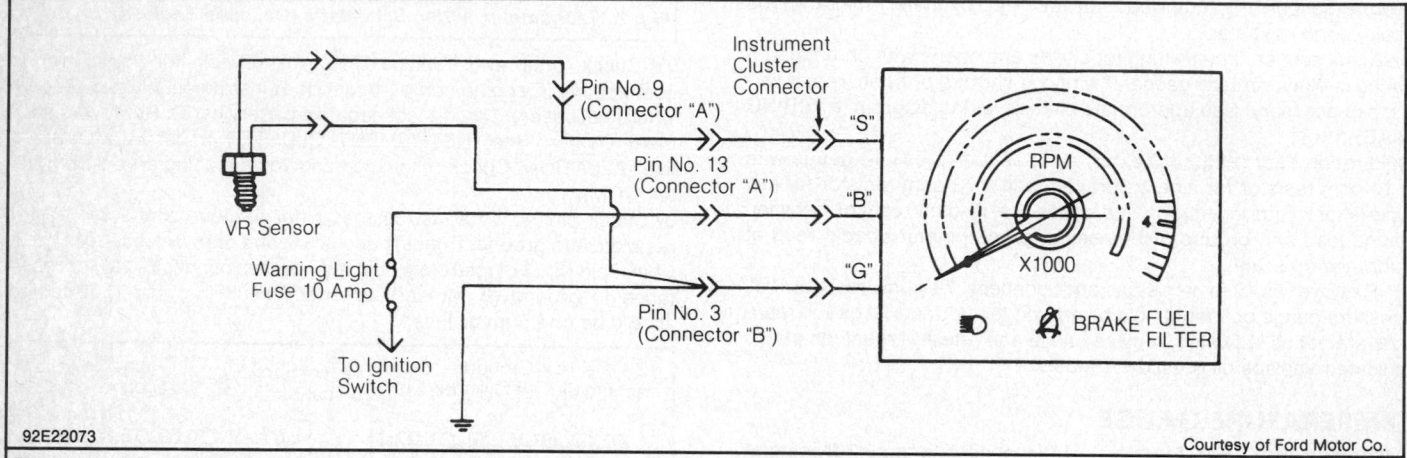

Fig. 5: Tachometer Wiring Schematic (E250/350 & F250/350 – 7.3L Diesel Manual Transmission)

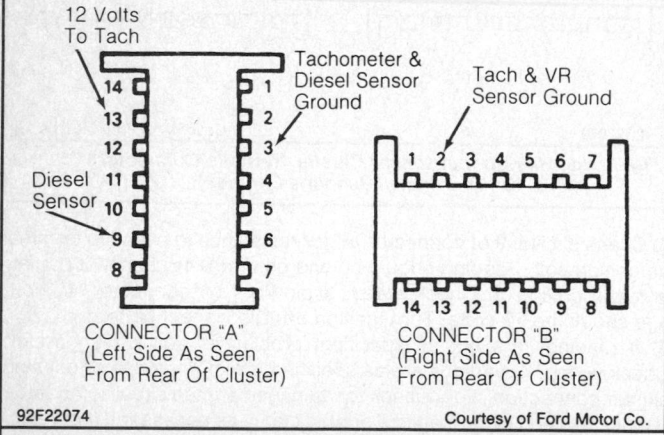

Fig. 6: Identifying Instrument Cluster Harness Connectors "A" & "B" Terminals (7.3L Diesel)

4) Check resistance to ground at pin No. 3 of connector "A". See Figs. 4-6. Check resistance between pin No. 9 of connector "A" and corresponding mating connector pin of diesel sensor. Reading should be **one ohm or less**.

5) On vehicles with E4OD transmissions, check resistance between diesel sensor and Electronic Distributorless Ignition System (EDIS) module. Reading should be one ohm or less.

6) On all models, connect battery. Turn ignition on. Check voltage at pin No. 13 of connector "A". Voltage should be **12 volts**. If readings are not as indicated, problem is not in tachometer. Turn ignition off and disconnect battery. Repair wiring as necessary.

7) If resistance and voltage readings are as indicated, check for loose tachometer retention clips at rear of instrument cluster. Check for damaged printed circuit. Check VRS in injection pump timing gear cover. Repair or replace as necessary.

8) Remove sensor and check resistance across sensor terminals. If reading is not 2000-3000 ohms, replace sensor.

REMOVAL & INSTALLATION

CAUTION: When battery is disconnected, vehicle computer and memory systems may lose memory data. Driveability problems may exist until computer systems have completed a relearn cycle. See COMPUTER RELEARN PROCEDURES article in GENERAL INFORMATION before disconnecting battery.

INSTRUMENT CLUSTER

NOTE: In some cases, it may be necessary to remove speedometer cable at the transmission and pull cable through cowl.

Removal & Installation (Aerostar) – 1) Disconnect negative battery cable. Remove cluster housing-to-cluster screws. Remove cluster housing. Remove transmission shift indicator cable from stud on shift lever. Remove thumb wheel bracket from steering column.

2) Remove 4 cluster-to-instrument panel screws. See Fig. 7. Pull cluster from dash bottom first. Disconnect wiring harness connectors from rear of cluster. Remove instrument cluster.

3) To install, reverse removal procedure. Check operation of all gauges, lights and signals.

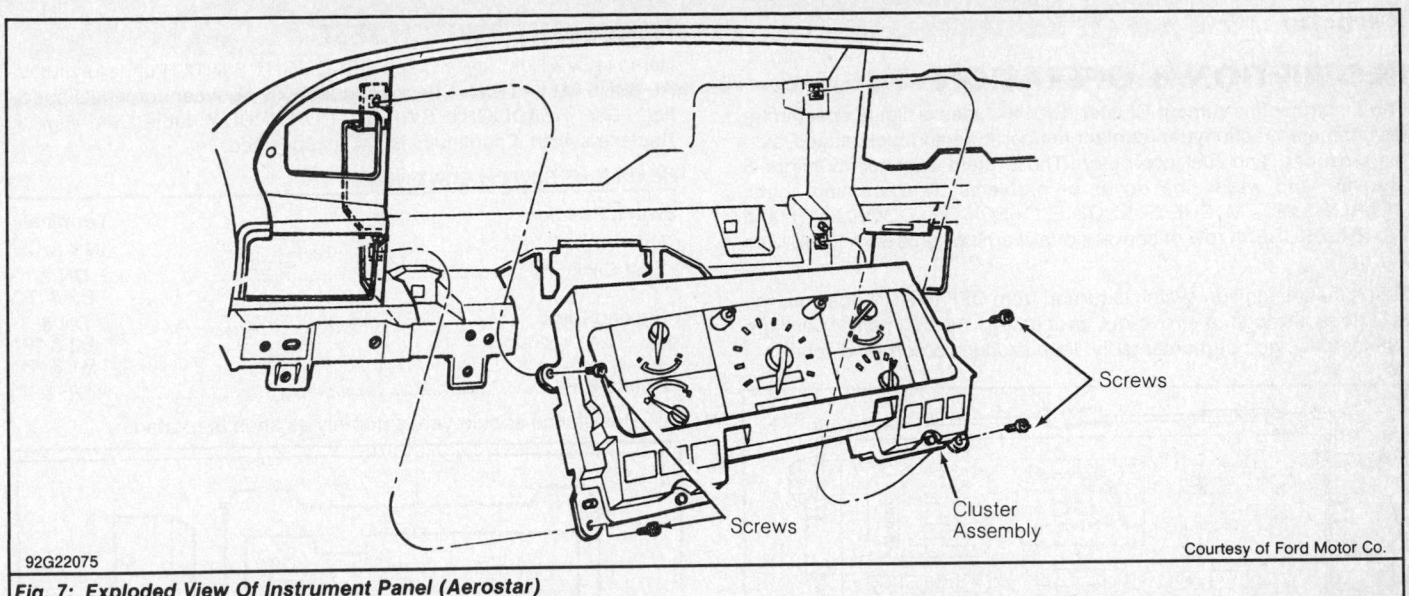

Fig. 7: Exploded View Of Instrument Panel (Aerostar)

92G22075

Courtesy of Ford Motor Co.

Removal & Installation (Explorer & Ranger) – 1) Disconnect negative battery cable. Open ash tray and remove 2 screws attaching ashtray to dash. Remove ashtray. Unsnap cluster trim panel by pulling rearward. Press hazard switch and remove cluster trim panel.

2) Remove 4 cluster-to-panel screws. Pull cluster slightly away from panel. *See Fig. 8*. On A/T models, the PRNDL indicator needs to be removed. Remove 2 PRNDL indicator-to-cluster screws. Slide PRNDL indicator down and out of cluster. On all models, disconnect speedometer cable at speedometer.

3) If there is not enough room, detach cable at transmission. Disconnect wiring harness connector from printed circuit. Before installation, apply a 3/16" ball of silicone lubricant to drive hole of speedometer head.

4) To install, reverse removal procedure. Check operation of all gauges, lights and signals.

Removal & Installation (Bronco, Pickup & Van) – 1) Disconnect negative battery cable. On models with tilt column, position steering wheel in full down position. On models with column shift, set parking brake and move shift lever to lowest position. On all models, unsnap right and left molding.

2) Remove headlight knob. Use a hook tool to release knob lock spring. Remove 2 exposed screws under right and left molding. Unsnap 5 retaining clips by pulling cluster trim panel rearward. On A/T models, remove loop on shift indicator cable from column retainer pin.

3) On all models, remove thumb wheel bracket screw and detach bracket from steering column. Remove cluster finish panel. Remove 4 cluster-to-panel screws. Pull cluster away from panel to disconnect electrical connectors. To install, reverse removal procedure.

WIRING DIAGRAMS

See appropriate chassis wiring diagram in WIRING DIAGRAMS.

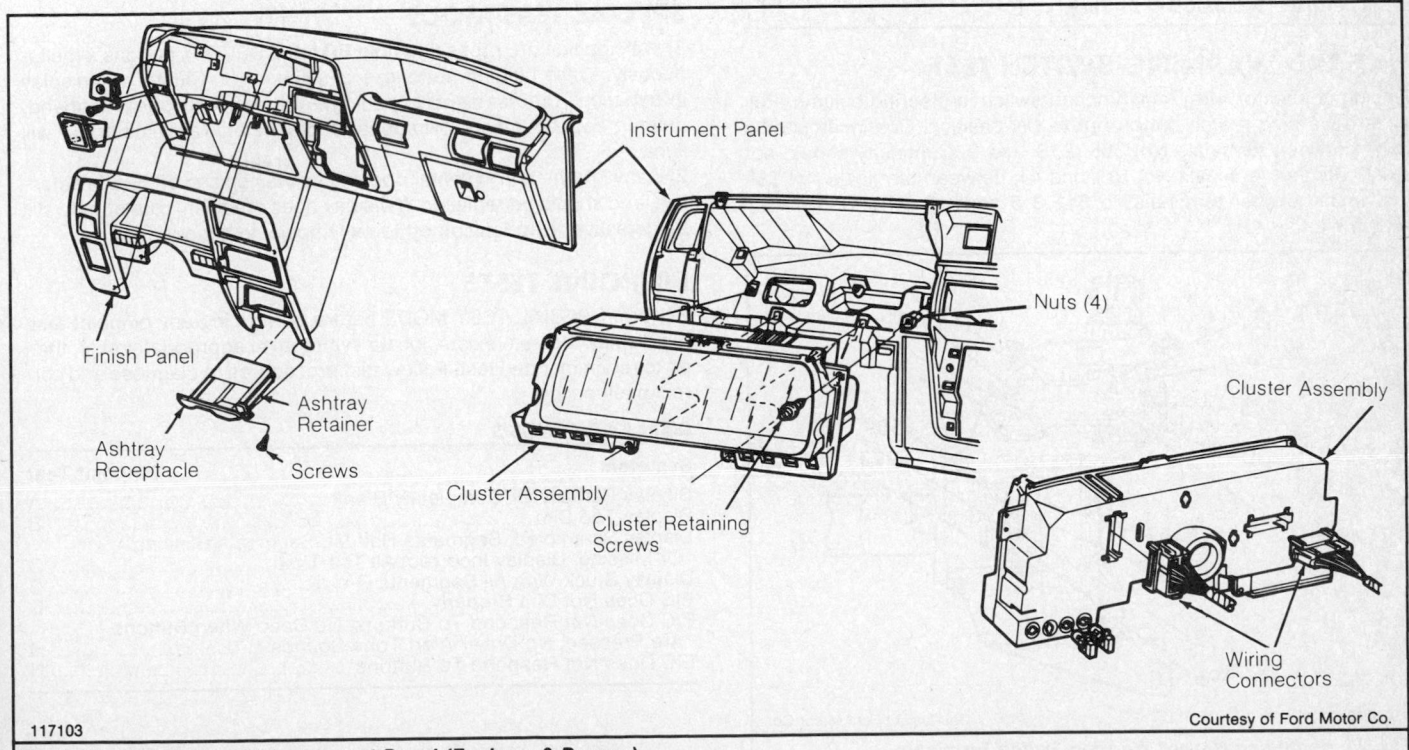

117103

Courtesy of Ford Motor Co.

Fig. 8: Exploded View Of Instrument Panel (Explorer & Ranger)

Aerostar

DESCRIPTION & OPERATION

The Electronic Instrument Cluster (EIC) includes a digital speedometer/odometer, tachometer, coolant temperature and fuel gauges, system scanner, and fuel computer. The system scanner monitors 5 systems, and warns the driver of problems by 5 warning lights: CHARGE SYSTEM, CHECK ENGINE, CHECK OIL, DOOR AJAR, and OIL PRESSURE. A row of conventional warning lights is included. See Fig. 1.

Each time the ignition switch is turned from OFF to RUN position, the EIC goes through a prove-out procedure. All segments will light momentarily, go out momentarily, then produce a normal display.

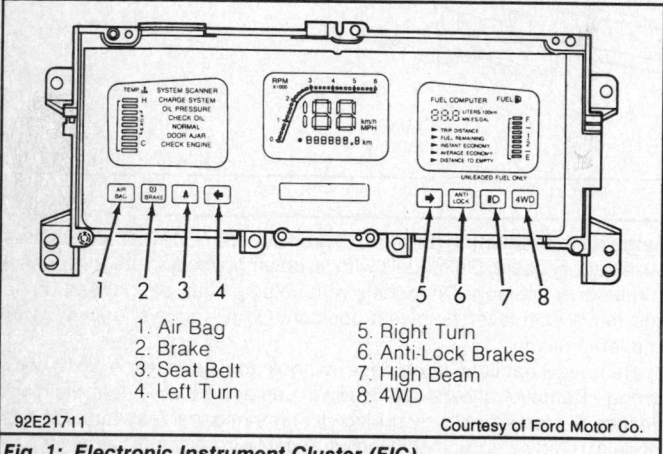

1. Air Bag
2. Brake
3. Seat Belt
4. Left Turn
5. Right Turn
6. Anti-Lock Brakes
7. High Beam
8. 4WD

92E21711   Courtesy of Ford Motor Co.

Fig. 1: Electronic Instrument Cluster (EIC)

TESTING

WARNING: When battery is disconnected, vehicle computer and memory systems may lose memory data. Driveability problems may exist until computer systems have completed a relearn cycle. See COMPUTER RELEARN PROCEDURES article in GENERAL INFORMATION before disconnecting battery.

HAZARD WARNING SWITCH TEST

Unplug connector from multifunction switch in steering column. Pull hazard warning switch button out to ON position. Continuity should exist between terminals No. 385, 2, 3 and 9. Continuity should not exist between terminals No. 511 and 44; between terminals No. 385 and 44; or between terminals No. 511, 3, 5 and 9. See Fig. 2. Replace switch if it fails test.

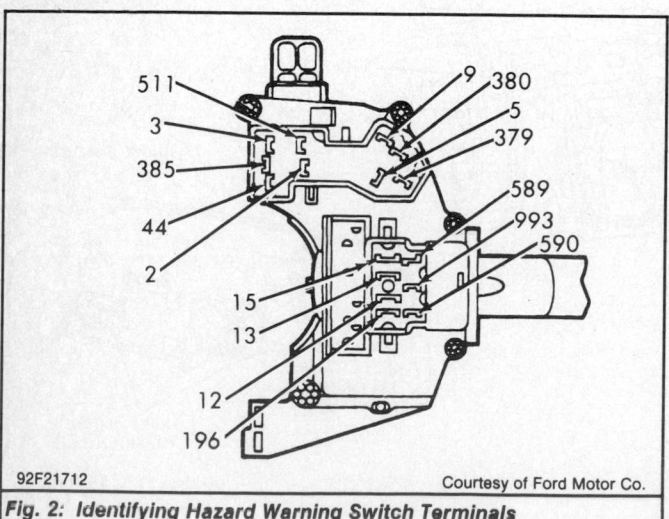

92F21712   Courtesy of Ford Motor Co.

Fig. 2: Identifying Hazard Warning Switch Terminals

HEADLIGHT SWITCH TEST

Remove headlight switch. See HEADLIGHT SWITCH under REMOVAL & INSTALLATION. Check for continuity between terminals specified. See HEADLIGHT SWITCH CONTINUITY table. See Fig. 3. Replace switch if continuity is not as specified.

HEADLIGHT SWITCH CONTINUITY

Switch Position	Terminals
Off	IGN & DN
First Click	DN & "I"
	B2 & "R"
Second Click	DN & "I"
	B2 & "R"
	B1 & "H"
Rotate Knob	[1] "R" & "I"

[1] – Resistance should vary smoothly as knob is rotated.

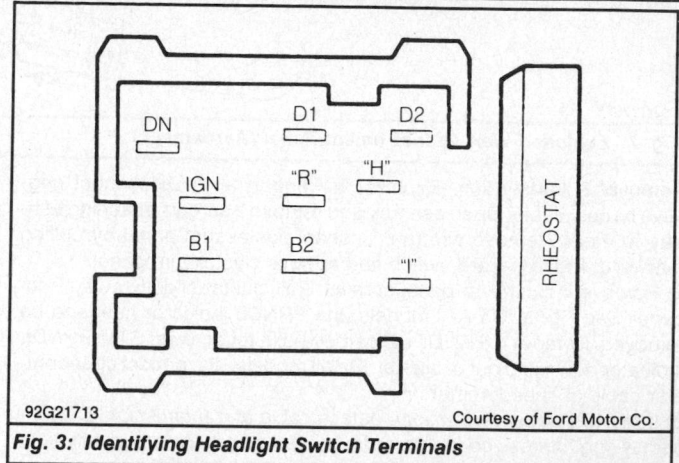

92G21713   Courtesy of Ford Motor Co.

Fig. 3: Identifying Headlight Switch Terminals

WIPER SWITCH

For testing information on wipers, see appropriate WIPER/WASHER SYSTEMS article.

SPECIAL TEST MODE

1) With ignition off, press and hold E/M and SELECT buttons simultaneously. While holding buttons, turn ignition on. Cluster will display information in center display opening. A number will appear in speedometer, and 2 numbers will appear in odometer. Tachometer bar will light.

2) If any information in center opening flashes on and off, EIC is defective, and should be replaced. If display does not flash, cluster may still be defective. Turn ignition off to exit special test mode.

PINPOINT TESTS

Perform SPECIAL TEST MODE before performing any pinpoint test. If a display problem exists, locate symptom in appropriate table, then go to recommended test. Follow test procedures to diagnose and correct malfunction.

DISPLAY DIAGNOSIS

Symptom	Pinpoint Test
Display Partially Or Completely Blank	A
Display Too Dim	B
Display Scrambled, Segments Half Lit, Segments Blinking Or Missing, Display Incorrect All The Time	C
Display Stuck With All Segments On	C
EIC Does Not Dim Properly	D
EIC Does Not Respond To Buttons, No Beep When Buttons Are Pressed, No Driver Alert Tone Sounds	H
EIC Does Not Respond To Buttons	H

TEMPERATURE GAUGE DIAGNOSIS

Symptom	Pinpoint Test
Gauge Blanks Out Thermometer Symbol, Top 2 & Bottom 2 Bars Appear On Gauge	E
No Warning Tone When Thermometer Symbol Blinks	F
Temperature Gauge Always Indicates Cold	G

SPEEDOMETER DIAGNOSIS

Symptom	Pinpoint Test
Indicates Zero When Vehicle Is In Motion	J
Speedometer Inoperative	AA

ODOMETER DIAGNOSIS

Symptom	Pinpoint Test
Odometer Displays Error, Service Symbol On	K
Odometer Displays "S"	L
Odometer Does Not Accumulate, Or Accumulates And Loses Mileage	M
Odometer Indication Incorrect	N

TACHOMETER DIAGNOSIS

Symptom	Pinpoint Test
Tachometer Indication Incorrect, No Tachometer Indication, Tachometer Indication Erratic	Q

FUEL COMPUTER DIAGNOSIS

Symptom	Pinpoint Test
Instantaneous Fuel Economy Always Indicates Zero MPG or 99 L/100 km	R
Trip Distance Does Not Accumulate	S
Distance To Empty Does Not Go Below 200 Miles With Fuel Tank Empty	T

FUEL GAUGE DIAGNOSIS

Symptom	Pinpoint Test
Gauge Displays CO	U
Gauge Displays CS	V
Fuel Quantity Indication Inaccurate	W

SYSTEM SCANNER DIAGNOSIS

Symptom	Pinpoint Test
Door Ajar Warning Light Always On, Or Never Comes On	X
Oil Pressure Warning Light On At All Times, Or Never Comes On	Y
Check Oil Warning Light Operates Improperly	Z

PINPOINT TEST A, DISPLAY PARTIALLY OR COMPLETELY BLANK

1) Turn ignition on. If display is partially lit, go to step **2)**. If display is totally blank, go to step **3)**.

2) Check to see if all choices except the one selected go blank. If all choices except the one selected go blank, system is okay. If EIC remains partially blank, replace EIC.

3) Check fuses No. 8 and 17. If either or both fuses are blown, go to next step. If fuses are okay, go to step **5)**.

4) Turn ignition off. Disconnect negative battery cable. Check for continuity between circuit with blown fuse and ground. If continuity exists, repair shorted circuit. If continuity does not exist, replace fuse.

5) Connect battery if it had been disconnected. Turn ignition on. Measure voltage at fuses No. 8 and No. 17. If meter indicates at least 9 volts at each circuit, go to step **6)**. If meter indicates less than 9 volts, repair fuse holder.

PINPOINT TEST A (Cont.)

6) Remove EIC, but leave it connected to wiring harness. See INSTRUMENT CLUSTER under REMOVAL & INSTALLATION. Connect battery. Turn ignition on. Wiggle connectors at rear of EIC. Service loose connectors as necessary. If connectors are not loose, go to step **7)**.

7) Turn ignition off. Remove EIC. Turn ignition on. Check for battery voltage at Light Green/Yellow and Pink/Black wires at EIC harness connector. Check for continuity between Black/White wire and ground, and between Black wires and ground. If battery voltage does not exist, repair Light Green/Yellow or Pink/Black wire. Repair Black/White or Black wires if continuity does not exist.

8) With EIC removed, inspect flexible circuit traces connected to power and ground circuits. If traces are defective, replace flexible circuit. If traces are okay, replace EIC.

PINPOINT TEST B, DISPLAY TOO DIM

1) Turn ignition on. Examine EIC. If all displays are too dim, go to step **2)**. Replace EIC if parts are okay and other parts are too dim.

2) Ensure headlights are off; display normally dims to almost off when headlights are on. Examine EIC. If all displays are still too dim, go to step **3)**.

3) Remove EIC. See INSTRUMENT CLUSTER under REMOVAL & INSTALLATION. Connect battery. Turn ignition on. Ensure headlights are off. Measure dimmer voltage at Black EIC harness connector pin No.13 (Light Blue/Red wire). If voltage is less than 3 volts, replace EIC. If voltage is not less than 3 volts, repair short to voltage on Light Blue/Red wire.

PINPOINT TEST C, DISPLAY SCRAMBLED, SEGMENTS HALF LIT, SEGMENTS BLINKING OR MISSING, DISPLAY INCORRECT ALL THE TIME

Turn ignition on. Observe display. All segments should light for one second, go out for one second, then exhibit a normal display. If prove-out is as specified, display is okay. If prove-out is not as specified, replace EIC.

PINPOINT TEST D, EIC DOES NOT DIM PROPERLY

1) Turn ignition and headlights on. Rotate panel dimmer control. If EIC does not dim properly, go to step **2)**. If display dims from approximately 65 percent to almost off, system is okay.

2) Remove EIC. See INSTRUMENT CLUSTER under REMOVAL & INSTALLATION. Connect battery. Turn ignition on. Turn headlights on. Measure voltage at Black EIC harness connector "B" pin No. 13 (Light Blue/Red wire) while rotating dimmer control. If voltage varies from 5 volts to battery voltage, system is okay. If voltage is not as specified, replace EIC.

PINPOINT TEST E, TEMPERATURE GAUGE BLANKS OUT THERMOMETER SYMBOL, TOP 2 AND BOTTOM 2 BARS APPEAR ON GAUGE

1) Unplug connector at temperature sending unit, located at front of intake manifold. Turn ignition on. If temperature gauge indicates cold, with only bottom bar displayed, replace temperature sending unit. If display is anything else, go to step **2)**.

2) Disconnect negative battery cable. Unplug harness connector at temperature sending unit. Remove EIC. See INSTRUMENT CLUSTER under REMOVAL & INSTALLATION. Measure resistance between Black EIC harness connector pins No. 4 (Red/White wire) and No. 8 (Black/White wire). If resistance is greater than 15,000 ohms, replace EIC. If resistance is not greater than 15,000 ohms, repair short to ground on Red/White wire.

PINPOINT TEST F,
NO WARNING TONE WHEN
THERMOMETER SYMBOL BLINKS

1) Driver alert tone does not sound unless engine is running. Tone does not sound if module is producing another sound. Tone sounds only for temperature above normal.

2) Turn ignition on. Listen for beep tone while pressing any cluster control button. If beep occurs, system is okay. If beep does not occur, go to PINPOINT TEST H.

PINPOINT TEST G,
TEMPERATURE GAUGE ALWAYS
INDICATES COLD

1) Unplug connector at temperature sending unit. Connect jumper wire from Red/White wire at harness connector to a good engine ground. Turn ignition on. If top 2 and bottom 2 bars of gauge light, remove jumper wire and go to step 3). If top 2 and bottom 2 bars of gauge do not light, leave jumper in place and go to step 2).

2) Remove EIC. See INSTRUMENT CLUSTER under REMOVAL & INSTALLATION. Check for continuity between Black EIC harness connector pins No. 4 (Red/White wire) and No. 8 (Black/White wire). If continuity exists, replace EIC. If continuity does not exist, repair open circuit in Red/White wire, or repair temperature ground circuit.

3) Start and warm engine to normal operating temperature. Measure resistance of temperature sending unit. If resistance is not less than 8000 ohms, go to step 4). If resistance is less than 8000 ohms, replace EIC.

4) Check entire cooling system for proper operation. Repair cooling system as necessary. If cooling system is okay, replace temperature sending unit.

PINPOINT TEST H,
EIC DOES NOT RESPOND TO BUTTONS,
NO BEEP WHEN BUTTONS ARE PRESSED,
NO DRIVER ALERT TONE SOUNDS

1) EIC responds to buttons only when ignition is on. Tone does not sound if module is producing another sound. If display does not respond to buttons, go to step 2). If display responds to buttons, but no beep sounds, go to step 3).

2) Check for seat belt or key warning chime. If either chime sounds, go to step 5). If chime does not sound, service chime warning module.

3) Remove cluster finish panel. Check connections at switch panel. Service connections and recheck if connections are defective. If connections are secure, go to step 4).

4) Unplug 6-pin connector from front of EIC. Measure resistance between connector pins No. 2 (Yellow wire) and No. 4 (Orange wire) while pressing one button at a time. Resistances should be as follows:

- E/M button – 900-5400 ohms
- SELECT button – 2200-2400 ohms
- RESET button – 320-360 ohms
- No button pressed – 17,000-17,800 ohms

If resistance is within specification, go to step 5). If resistance is not within specification, replace switch module.

5) Inspect EIC and switch harness connector for missing or damaged pins. If EIC pins are damaged or missing, replace EIC. If switch module pins are damaged or missing, replace switch module. If all pins are okay, replace EIC.

6) Remove EIC. See INSTRUMENT CLUSTER under REMOVAL & INSTALLATION. Connect battery cable. Turn ignition on. Wait for seat belt warning chime to end. Connect jumper wire between Black harness connector pin No. 19 (Tan/Yellow wire) and ground. If chime sounds, replace EIC. If chime does not sound, repair Tan/Yellow wire to chime module. Check for installation of proper chime module.

PINPOINT TEST J,
SPEEDOMETER INDICATES ZERO AT ALL
TIMES WHEN VEHICLE IS IN MOTION

1) Turn ignition on. Observe display. All segments should light for one second, go out for one second, then exhibit a normal display. If prove-out is as specified, go to step 2). If display is otherwise, replace EIC:

2) Drive vehicle. Determine whether odometer advances. If odometer does not advance, go to step 3). If odometer advances, replace EIC.

3) Drive vehicle. Select TRIP DISTANCE. If distance advances, replace EIC. If distance does not advance, go to PINPOINT TEST AA.

PINPOINT TEST K,
ODOMETER DISPLAYS ERROR,
SERVICE SYMBOL ON

If odometer displays ERROR, and service symbol appears, replace EIC.

PINPOINT TEST L,
ODOMETER DISPLAYS "S"

Verify that "S" appears in odometer. Determine whether speedometer/odometer module has been replaced. If module is original, replace EIC. If module has been replaced, "S" display is normal.

PINPOINT TEST M,
ODOMETER DOES NOT ACCUMULATE,
OR ACCUMULATES AND LOSES MILEAGE

1) If odometer does not accumulate mileage, go to step 2). If odometer accumulates 10 miles, then loses 10 miles, replace EIC.

2) Check whether speedometer operates properly. If speedometer is okay, replace EIC. If speedometer does not operate properly, go to PINPOINT TEST J.

PINPOINT TEST N, ODOMETER
INDICATION INCORRECT

Perform SPECIAL TEST MODE under TESTING. If display does not flash, go to PINPOINT TEST J. If display flashes, replace EIC.

PINPOINT TEST Q,
TACHOMETER INDICATION INCORRECT,
NO TACHOMETER INDICATION,
TACHOMETER INDICATION ERRATIC

1) Check engine performance. Ensure engine does not misfire.

2) Remove EIC. See INSTRUMENT CLUSTER under REMOVAL & INSTALLATION. Measure resistance between Black harness connector pin No. 20 (Tan/Yellow wire) and coil. If resistance is not greater than 100 ohms, replace EIC. If resistance is greater than 100 ohms, repair open circuit in Tan/Yellow wire to coil.

PINPOINT TEST R,
INSTANTANEOUS FUEL ECONOMY ALWAYS
INDICATES ZERO MPG OR 99L/100 KM

1) Drive vehicle. If speedometer operates properly, go to step 2). If speedometer does not operate properly, go to PINPOINT TEST L.

2) Check Light Blue/Pink wire between EIC Black connector pin No. 11 (Light Blue/Pink wire) to EEC module near left side of master cylinder. If Light Blue/Pink wire is okay, go to PINPOINT TEST U. Service wiring as necessary.

3) Verify fuel flow function in EEC. See appropriate SELF-DIAGNOSTICS article in ENGINE PERFORMANCE. If EEC operates properly, replace fuel computer module in EIC. If EEC does not operate properly, replace EEC or fuel flow sensor.

PINPOINT TEST S, TRIP DISTANCE DOES NOT ACCUMULATE

Drive vehicle. If speedometer operates properly, replace EIC. If speedometer does not operate properly, go to PINPOINT TEST L.

PINPOINT TEST T, DISTANCE TO EMPTY DOES NOT GO BELOW 200 MILES WITH FUEL TANK EMPTY

1) Determine whether fuel gauge operates properly. If gauge operates properly, go to step 2). If gauge does not operate properly, go to PINPOINT TEST U or V.

2) Check whether speedometer operates properly. If speedometer operates properly, go to step 3). If speedometer does not operate properly, go to PINPOINT TEST J.

3) Verify fuel flow function in EEC. See appropriate SELF-DIAGNOSTICS article in ENGINE PERFORMANCE. If EEC operates properly, replace fuel computer module in EIC. If EEC does not operate properly, replace EEC or fuel flow sensor.

PINPOINT TEST U, FUEL GAUGE DISPLAYS CO, LIGHTS TOP 2 & BOTTOM 2 BARS, BLANKS OUT FUEL TANK SYMBOL

1) Turn ignition on. If CO appears on fuel gauge, go to step 2).

2) Disconnect negative battery cable. Lower fuel tank. Unplug fuel sending unit connector. Connect jumper wire between Yellow/White and Black/White wires at harness connector. Reconnect battery. Turn ignition on. Wait several minutes. If CO message appears on fuel gauge, go to step 4). If CS appears, remove jumper and go to step 3).

3) Turn ignition off. Measure resistance between fuel sending unit terminals (Yellow/White and Black/White wires on mating connector). If resistance is not 11-168 ohms, replace fuel tank sending unit. If resistance is 112-168 ohms, inspect harness connector for loose terminals or other defects.

4) Disconnect negative battery cable. Remove EIC. See INSTRUMENT CLUSTER under REMOVAL & INSTALLATION. Connect jumper wire between Yellow/White and Black/White wires at sending unit harness connector. Check for continuity between EIC Black harness connector pins No. 6 (Yellow/White wire) and No. 8 (Black/White wire). If continuity exists, replace EIC. If continuity does not exist, repair open circuit in Yellow/White or Black/White wire to fuel sending unit.

PINPOINT TEST V, FUEL GAUGE DISPLAYS CS, LIGHTS TOP 2 & BOTTOM 2 BARS, BLANKS OUT FUEL TANK SYMBOL

1) Turn ignition on. If CS appears on fuel gauge, go to step 2).

2) Disconnect negative battery cable. Remove EIC. See INSTRUMENT CLUSTER under REMOVAL & INSTALLATION. Measure resistance between EIC Black harness connector pins No. 6 (Yellow/White wire) and No. 8 (Black/White wire). If resistance is not 11-168 ohms, go to next step. If resistance is 112-168 ohms, replace EIC.

3) Disconnect negative battery cable. Lower fuel tank. Unplug fuel sending unit connector. Measure resistance between EIC Black harness connector pins No. 6 (Yellow/White wire) and No. 8 (Black/White wire). If resistance is greater than 10,000 ohms, replace fuel tank sending unit. If resistance is not greater than 10,000 ohms, repair short in Yellow/White wire between EIC and fuel tank sending unit.

PINPOINT TEST W, FUEL QUANTITY INDICATION INACCURATE

1) Disconnect negative battery cable. Lower fuel tank. Unplug fuel sending unit connector. Connect 43-ohm resistor between Yellow/White and Black/White wires at harness connector. Reconnect battery. Turn ignition on. Observe fuel gauge. If gauge displays 2 or 3 bars, and 3-4 gals. (13L-15L) fuel remaining, go to step 3). If gauge indicates anything else, go to step 2).

PINPOINT TEST W (Cont.)

2) Disconnect negative battery cable. Remove EIC. See INSTRUMENT CLUSTER under REMOVAL & INSTALLATION. Secure connectors to prevent shorts. Measure resistance between EIC Black harness connector pins No. 6 (Yellow/White wire) and No. 8 (Black/White wire). If resistance is 42-45 ohms, replace EIC. If resistance is not 42-45 ohms, repair short or open circuit in Yellow/White wire between EIC and fuel tank sending unit.

3) Disconnect negative battery cable. Inspect fuel tank sending unit for binding, sticking, misalignment, or other defects. Service sending unit as necessary. If sending unit is okay, go to step 4).

4) Inspect fuel tank for dents, bulges, or other damage. Verify fuel filler tube is installed correctly. If okay, fault is not in fuel level indication circuitry. If fuel tank is damaged, or fill tube is installed incorrectly, service as necessary.

PINPOINT TEST X, DOOR AJAR WARNING LIGHT ALWAYS ON, OR NEVER COMES ON

1) If warning is always on, go to step 2). If warning never comes on, go to step 4).

2) Turn ignition off. Remove connector from driver's door switch. Turn ignition on. Observe warning indicator. Repeat this step for other front door, then rear doors, until no warning appears, or until all switches have been tested. If warning still appears, go to step 3). If no warning appears, service last switch tested.

3) Disconnect negative battery cable. Remove EIC. See INSTRUMENT CLUSTER under REMOVAL & INSTALLATION. Check for continuity between EIC Gray connector pins No. 13 (Black/White wire) and No. 15 (Black/Orange wire). If no continuity exists, replace EIC. If continuity exists, repair shorted Black/Orange wire.

4) Turn ignition off. Remove connector from driver's door switch. Turn ignition on. Connect jumper wire from wire on connector to a good ground. Observe warning indicator. Repeat this step for other front door, then sliding door, until no warning appears, or until all switches have been tested. If warning still does not appear, go to step 5). If warning appears, replace last switch tested.

5) Disconnect negative battery cable. Remove EIC. See INSTRUMENT CLUSTER under REMOVAL & INSTALLATION. Check for continuity between EIC Gray connector pin No. 15 (Black/Orange wire) and wire at each door switch connector. If continuity exists, replace EIC. If continuity does not exist, repair open circuit between EIC Gray connector pin No. 15 (Black/Orange wire) and connector at appropriate door switch.

NOTE: If continuity does not exist to any switch, the most probable problem area is splice S266 (Black/Orange, Black/White, Black/Light Blue, Black/White and Black/Pink wires). Splice S266 is located in main harness, near breakout to brake warning resistor/diode.

PINPOINT TEST Y, OIL PRESSURE WARNING LIGHT ON AT ALL TIMES, OR NEVER COMES ON

1) Observe warning with engine running, and with engine off and ignition on. If warning appears under both conditions, go to step 2). If warning does not come on, go to step 5).

2) Unplug connector from oil pressure switch, located behind right cylinder head. With engine off, check for continuity between switch terminal and ground. If continuity exists, go to step 3). If continuity does not exist, replace oil pressure switch.

3) Reconnect wiring to sensor. Disconnect negative battery cable. Remove EIC. See INSTRUMENT CLUSTER under REMOVAL & INSTALLATION. Check for continuity between EIC Gray connector pins No. 17 (White/Red wire) and No. 8 (Black/White wire). If continuity exists, go to step 4). If continuity does not exist, repair White/Red wire between EIC connector and oil pressure switch, or Black/White wire to ground.

4) Inspect Black EIC harness connector for damaged or dirty terminals. Install EIC. Reconnect battery. Turn ignition on. Wiggle Black connector. If warning appears, repair connector. If warning does not appear, replace EIC.

5) Start engine. Ensure oil pressure is greater than 8 psi. Unplug connector from oil pressure switch. With engine running, check for continuity between switch terminal and a good ground. If continuity does not exist, go to step 6). If continuity exists, replace oil pressure switch.

PINPOINT TEST Y (Cont.)

6) Turn ignition off. Reconnect wiring to sensor. Disconnect negative battery cable. Remove EIC. See INSTRUMENT CLUSTER under REMOVAL & INSTALLATION. Reconnect battery. With engine running, check for continuity between EIC Gray connector pins No. 17 (White/Red wire) and No. 8 (Black/White wire). If continuity does not exist, go to next step. If continuity exists, repair shorted White/Red wire.

7) Turn engine off. Remove EIC. Inspect Black EIC harness connector for damaged or shorted pins. Service connector if necessary. If pins are okay, replace EIC.

PINPOINT TEST Z,
CHECK OIL WARNING LIGHT
OPERATES IMPROPERLY

1) Park vehicle on level surface. Ensure oil level is at FULL mark on dipstick. Turn ignition off. Wait at least 2 minutes. Turn ignition on. If warning appears, go to step **2)**. If warning does not appear, system is okay.

2) Turn ignition off. Unplug connector from sensor, threaded into oil pan. Wait at least 2 minutes. Turn ignition on. If warning appears, go to next step. If warning does not appear, replace sensor.

3) Disconnect negative battery cable. Remove EIC. See INSTRUMENT CLUSTER under REMOVAL & INSTALLATION. Unplug connector from sensor, threaded into oil pan. Check for continuity between Gray EIC connector pins No. 3 (White/Pink wire) and No. 8 (Black/White wire). If continuity exists, repair shorted White/Pink wire between EIC and sensor. If no continuity exists, replace EIC.

PINPOINT TEST AA,
SPEEDOMETER INOPERATIVE

NOTE: Perform this test only if directed to do so from another pinpoint test.

1) Turn ignition on. If ANTI-LOCK light goes out after self-test, go to next step. If ANTI-LOCK light does not go out after self-test, see appropriate ANTI-LOCK article in BRAKES.

2) Backprobe EIC 12-pin connector pins No. 7 (Green Yellow/Black wire) and No. 2 (Black/White wire). If voltage does not increase smoothly from zero to approximately 4.5 volts AC as vehicle speed increases from zero to approximately 30 MPH, service wiring between speedometer and programmable odometer/speedometer module (PSOM), located on back side of EIC. If voltage increase is as specified, go to step **3)**.

3) Backprobe EIC 12-pin connector pins No. 4 (Red/Pink wire) and No. 2 (Black/White wire). If voltage increases smoothly from zero to approximately 3.5 volts AC as vehicle speed increases from zero to approximately 30 MPH, replace EIC. If voltage increase is not as specified, repair wiring between speed sensor and PSOM module. If wiring is okay, see appropriate ANTI-LOCK article in BRAKES.

REMOVAL & INSTALLATION

WARNING: On models with air bag, observe the following precautions. Disconnect negative and then positive battery cables. Shield both cables. Air bag system contains a back-up power supply built into the air bag diagnostic monitor. Wait a minimum of one minute before servicing any air bag system components. System is now disabled. See AIR BAG RESTRAINT SYSTEM article.

WARNING: When battery is disconnected, vehicle computer and memory systems may lose memory data. Driveability problems may exist until computer systems have completed a relearn cycle. See COMPUTER RELEARN PROCEDURES article in GENERAL INFORMATION before disconnecting battery.

HEADLIGHT SWITCH

Removal & Installation – 1) Disconnect negative battery cable. Insert hooked tool into knob slot to release clip. Pull knob from shaft. Remove Autolamp knob (if equipped). Remove steering column cover. Remove 2 center finish panel retaining screws, located in depression below ashtray. Pull left finish panel loose, and allow it to hang down.
2) Remove left finish panel. Remove 5 cluster finish panel retaining screws and finish panel. Remove 2 headlight switch bracket retaining screws. Pull headlight switch out to remove connectors. To install headlight switch, reverse removal procedure.

INSTRUMENT CLUSTER

Removal – 1) Disconnect negative battery cable. Remove cluster opening finish panel. Remove transmission indicator cable loop from ball stud on selector lever. Remove thumbwheel bracket screw. Detach bracket from steering column.
2) Remove EIC mounting screws. Unplug trip computer connector from front of EIC. Pull top of EIC toward steering wheel. Reach behind EIC to unplug 3 connectors. Swing bottom of EIC outward to remove.
Installation – To install, reverse removal procedure. Move transmission range selector fully clockwise. Move transmission range selector 3 detent positions clockwise. Hang 3-lb. weight on end of lever. Rotate thumbwheel to center pointer at middle of "D".

WIRING DIAGRAMS
See appropriate chassis wiring diagram in WIRING DIAGRAMS.

Aerostar, Bronco, Explorer, Pickup, Ranger, Van

NOTE: Unless otherwise specified, references to Pickup include the F350 Super Duty commercial chassis.

DESCRIPTION & OPERATION

Multifunction switch includes headlight dimmer, flash-to-pass and windshield wiper/washer switches. Multifunction switch is mounted on steering column. Ignition switch and lock cylinder are also mounted on steering column, and actuated by ignition key.

TESTING

WARNING: On models with air bag, observe the following precautions. The air bag is powered directly from the battery and back-up power supply. Before performing any repairs, disconnect and shield negative battery cable. Disconnect back-up power supply before servicing ANY air bag system component. Use caution when working around steering column. See AIR BAG RESTRAINT SYSTEM article.

WARNING: When battery is disconnected, vehicle computer and memory systems may lose memory data. Driveability problems may exist until computer systems have completed a relearn cycle. See COMPUTER RELEARN PROCEDURES article in GENERAL INFORMATION before disconnecting battery.

HAZARD SWITCH POWER TEST

Connect test light to ground. Touch test light probe to hazard or multifunction switch harness connector terminal (circuit No. 385, White/Red wire). *See Fig. 1, 2 or 3.* If test light glows, power circuit to hazard switch is okay. If test light does not glow, check for open circuit between hazard switch and fuse block. Repair as necessary. See appropriate MULTIFUNCTION SWITCH CONTINUITY table.

TURN SIGNAL SWITCH POWER TEST

1) Set ignition switch to RUN position. Connect test light to ground. Touch test light probe to turn signal or multifunction switch feed terminal (circuit No. 44, Light Blue wire). *See Fig. 1, 2 or 3.* If test light flashes, power circuit to turn signal switch is okay.
2) If test light does not flash, replace flasher or check for open circuit No. 44 (Light Blue wire) and repair as necessary. See appropriate MULTIFUNCTION SWITCH CONTINUITY table.

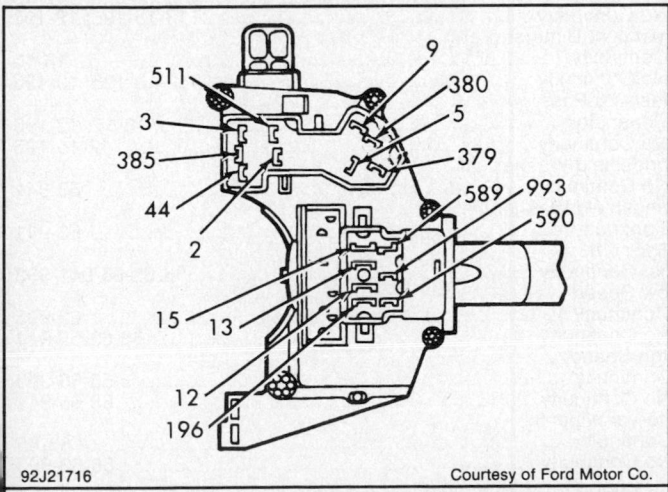

92J21716   Courtesy of Ford Motor Co.

Fig. 1: Testing Multifunction Switch (Aerostar, Bronco & Pickup)

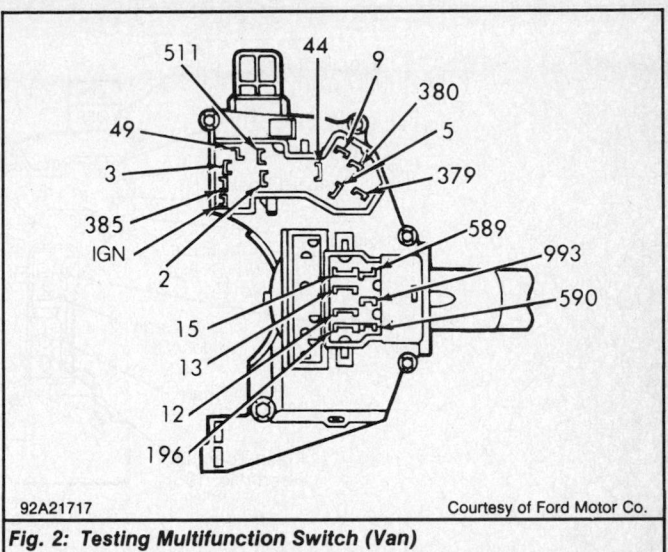

92A21717   Courtesy of Ford Motor Co.

Fig. 2: Testing Multifunction Switch (Van)

MULTIFUNCTION SWITCH CONTINUITY (AEROSTAR)

Switch Position & Condition	Between Circuit No.
Turn Signal Off	
No Continuity	2-3-511; 2-3-5-9-44
Continuity	5-9-511
Left Turn	
No Continuity	2-3-9-511; 2-5-44
Continuity	3-9-44; 5-511; 15-380
Right Turn	
No Continuity	2-3-5-511; 3-9-44
Continuity	2-5-44; 9-511; 15-379
Hazard	
No Continuity	44-385-511; 44-511
Continuity	2-3-9-385
Headlight Dimmer (Low)	
No Continuity	12-15; 12-13-196
Continuity	13-15
Headlight Dimmer (High)	
No Continuity	13-15-196
Continuity	12-15
Flash-To-Pass	
No Continuity	12-15
Continuity	12-196; 13-15
Turn Signal Off/Wash Off	
No Continuity	590-993
Wash On	
Continuity	590-993
Wiper Off	
No Continuity	589-590
Continuity	[1] 589-993; 590-993
Wiper LO	
No Continuity	589-590
Continuity	[2] 589-993; 590-993
Wiper HI	
No Continuity	589-993
Continuity	[3] 590-993
MAX Interval	
No Continuity	589-590
Continuity	[4] 590-993
MIN Interval	
No Continuity	589-590
Continuity	[5] 589-993; 590-993

[1] – Resistance: 589-993, 47.6 k/ohms; 590-993, 103.3 k/ohms
[2] – Resistance: 589-993, 4.1 k/ohms; 590-993, 3.3 k/ohms
[3] – Resistance: 590-993, 3.3 k/ohms
[4] – Resistance: 590-993, 103.3 k/ohms
[5] – Resistance: 589-993, 11.3 k/ohms; 590-993, 3.3 k/ohms

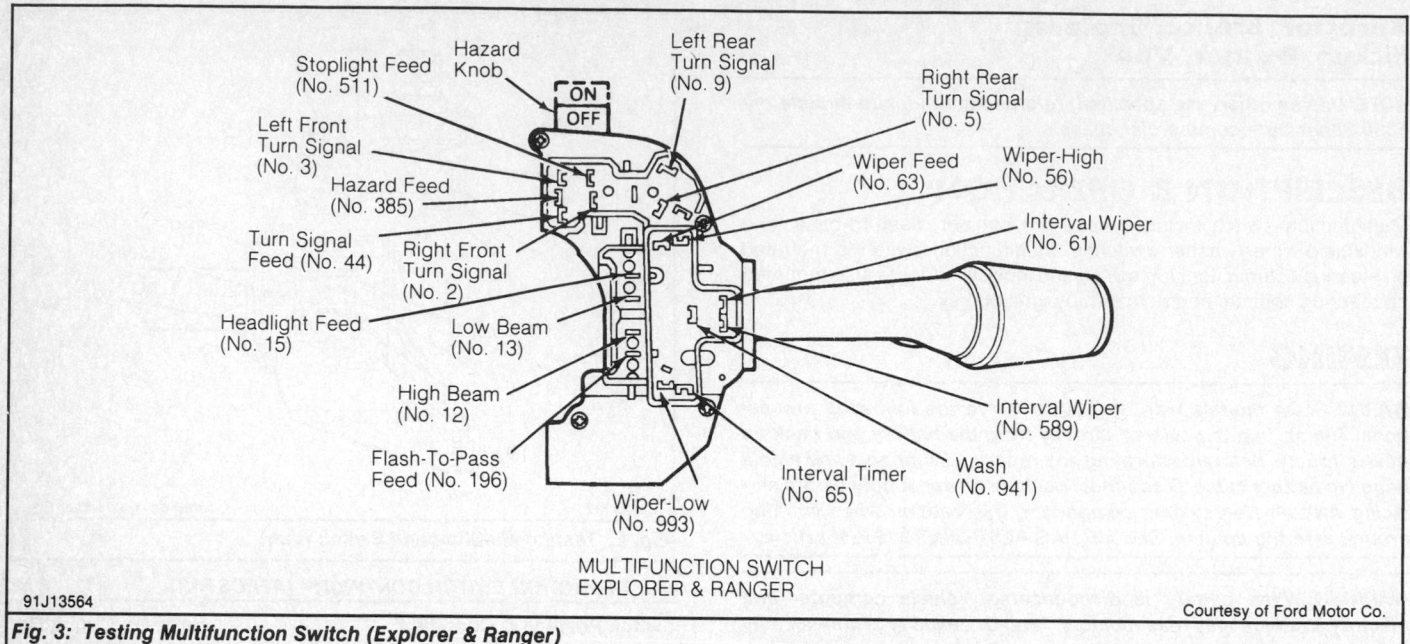

MULTIFUNCTION SWITCH
EXPLORER & RANGER

91J13564

Courtesy of Ford Motor Co.

Fig. 3: Testing Multifunction Switch (Explorer & Ranger)

MULTIFUNCTION SWITCH CONTINUITY (BRONCO, PICKUP & VAN)

Switch Position & Condition	Between Circuit No.
Turn Signal Off	
Continuity	5-9-511
No Continuity	2-3-511; 2-3-5-9-44
Left Turn	
Continuity	5-511; 3-9-44; 15-380
No Continuity	2-3-5-9-511; 2-5-44
Right Turn	
Continuity	9-511; 2-5-44; 15-379
No Continuity	2-3-5-511; 3-9-44
Hazard	
Continuity	2-3-5-9-385
No Continuity	44-511; 44-385-511
Headlight Dimmer (High)	
Continuity	12-15
No Continuity	13-15-196
Headlight Dimmer (Low)	
Continuity	13-15
No Continuity	12-15; 12-13-196
Flash-To-Pass	
Continuity	13-15; 12-196
No Continuity	12-15
Windshield Washer Off	
No Continuity	590-993
Windshield Washer On	
Continuity	590-993
Wiper Off	
No Continuity	589-590
Low Speed	
Continuity	[1] 589-993; 590-993
No Continuity	589-590
High Speed	
Continuity	[2] 589-993; 590-993
No Continuity	589-590
Interval Wiper (MAX)	
Continuity	[3] 589-993; 590-993
No Continuity	589-590
Interval Wiper (MIN)	
Continuity	[4] 589-993; 590-993
No Continuity	589-590

[1] – Resistance: 589-993, 47.6 k/ohms; 590-993, 103.3 k/ohms
[2] – Resistance: 589-993, 4.1 k/ohms; 590-993, 3.3 k/ohms
[3] – Resistance: 589-993, 11.3 k/ohms; 590-993, 103.3 k/ohms
[4] – Resistance: 589-993, 11.3 k/ohms; 590-993, 3.3 k/ohms

MULTIFUNCTION SWITCH CONTINUITY (EXPLORER & RANGER)

Switch Position & Condition	Between Circuit No.
Turn Signal Off	
Continuity	511-5-9
No Continuity	2-3-44-385-511; 2-3-5-9-44-385; 2-3-385
Left Turn	
Continuity	5-511; 3-9-44
No Continuity	3-9-44-385-511; 2-5-44-385; 2-385
Right Turn	
Continuity	9-511; 2-5-44
No Continuity	2-5-511; 44-385; 3-9-44-385; 2-385
Hazard	
Continuity	2-3-5-9-385-511
No Continuity	44-385; 2-3-5-9-44
Headlight Dimmer (High)	
Continuity	12-15
No Continuity	13-15-196; 12-196
Headlight Dimmer (Low)	
Continuity	13-15
No Continuity	12-15-196; 13-196
Flash-To-Pass	
Continuity	13-15; 12-196
No Continuity	12-15-196
Windshield Washer Off	
No Continuity	63-941
Windshield Washer On	
Continuity	63-941
Wiper Off	
No Continuity	56-63-65-941-993
Low Speed	
Continuity	63-993
No Continuity	56-63-65-941
High Speed	
Continuity	56-63-993
No Continuity	63-65-941
Interval Wiper [1]	
Continuity	[2] 63-65
No Continuity	56-63-993

[1] – Knob turned to maximum time interval.
[2] – Resistance between circuits No. 61 and 589 should be 7000-13,000 ohms. When knob is rotated to minimum interval position, resistance should be 420-880 ohms.

IGNITION SWITCH

1) To check steering column ignition system for mechanical operation, rotate lock cylinder through all switch positions. Lock cylinder should not bind, and should return from START to RUN position without assistance.

2) If binding or incorrect modes occur, ignition switch should be adjusted. After adjustment, if binding or incorrect modes are still evident, lock cylinder should either be disassembled and inspected for damage, or ignition switch should be replaced.

3) To check electrical function of ignition switch, lower steering column and unplug ignition switch connector. Test switch continuity using a self-powered test light or ohmmeter. Continuity should not exist between chassis ground and any terminal, except circuits No. 41 and 977 in START position only.

4) See IGNITION SWITCH CONTINUITY table. *See Fig. 4.* If continuity is not as specified, replace ignition switch.

IGNITION SWITCH CONTINUITY

Switch Position	Continuity Between Circuit No.
Accessory	37 & 297
Lock	No Continuity
Off	No Continuity
Run	37-16-687-297
Start	977-41-Ground; 37-32-262-Possibly 16

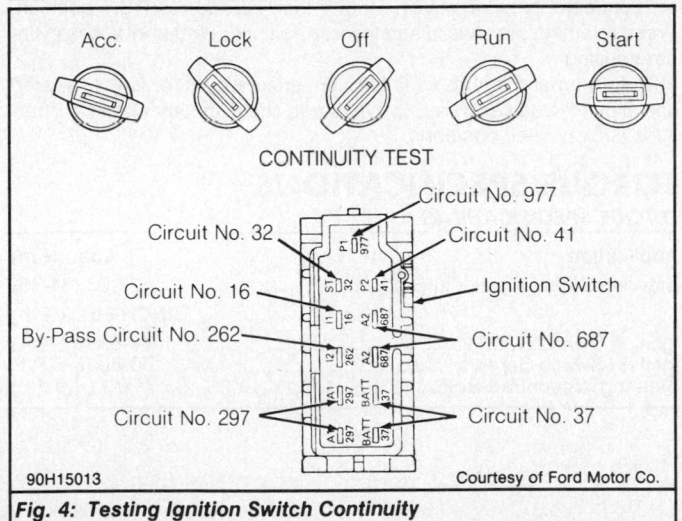

Fig. 4: Testing Ignition Switch Continuity

ADJUSTMENTS

WARNING: When battery is disconnected, vehicle computer and memory systems may lose memory data. Driveability problems may exist until computer systems have completed a relearn cycle. See COMPUTER RELEARN PROCEDURES article in GENERAL INFORMATION before disconnecting battery.

IGNITION SWITCH

Ignition switch is properly adjusted if:

- In ACCESSORY, accessory circuit is operative and steering wheel is locked. Automatic shift lever cannot be moved.
- In LOCK, all ignition switch electrical circuits are inoperative and steering wheel is locked. Automatic shift lever cannot be moved.
- In OFF, all ignition switch electrical circuits are inoperative and steering wheel is unlocked. Automatic shift lever can be moved.
- In ON (RUN), all ignition switch circuits or accessory circuits are operative except starter circuit and warning light check circuit. Steering wheel is unlocked and automatic shift lever can be moved.
- In START, only engine ignition, warning light check, and starter circuits are operative. Steering wheel is unlocked and automatic shift lever can be moved.

Aerostar, Bronco, Pickup & Van – Disconnect negative battery cable. Set ignition switch to ON position. Align switch pin with slot in lock/column assembly. Position slots in column/lock assembly with index mark on casting.

Explorer & Ranger – **1)** Disconnect negative battery cable. Locate ignition switch on top of steering column tube. Remove ignition switch connector. Rotate ignition key back and forth to each side of LOCK position until a 5/64 " (1.98 mm) drill bit can be inserted into ignition switch lock pin hole.

2) Loosen 2 ignition switch mounting nuts, turn switch to LOCK position (feel for detent) and remove ignition key from cylinder. Move switch up or down along column tube. Locate mid-position of rod lash. Tighten 2 mounting nuts to **40-65 INCH lbs. (4.51-7.34 N.m)**.

3) Remove drill bit. Connect wiring. Ensure all accessories are deactivated when switch is in OFF position, and ensure all modes function correctly.

REMOVAL & INSTALLATION

WARNING: On models with air bag, observe the following precautions. The air bag is powered directly from the battery and back-up power supply. Before performing any repairs, disconnect and shield negative battery cable. Disconnect back-up power supply before servicing ANY air bag system component. Use caution when working around steering column. See AIR BAG RESTRAINT SYSTEM article.

WARNING: When battery is disconnected, vehicle computer and memory systems may lose memory data. Driveability problems may exist until computer systems have completed a relearn cycle. See COMPUTER RELEARN PROCEDURES article in GENERAL INFORMATION before disconnecting battery.

STEERING WHEEL

Removal (Models With Air Bag) – **1)** Position front wheels straight ahead. Disconnect negative battery cable and back-up power supply. Remove air bag module retaining nuts. Unplug wire harness from air bag module. Remove air bag module.

2) Disconnect speed control wiring (if equipped). Mark steering wheel and shaft for installation reference. Remove and discard steering wheel bolt. Using Steering Wheel Puller (T67L-3600-A), remove steering wheel. Route contact assembly wiring through steering wheel as it is removed.

Installation – **1)** Ensure front wheels are straight ahead. Route contact assembly wire harness through steering wheel at 3 o'clock position. Position steering wheel onto shaft, ensuring marks are aligned. Ensure air bag wiring is not pinched.

2) Install NEW steering wheel bolt. Tighten bolt to **23-33 ft. lbs. (31-45 N.m)**. Connect speed control wiring (if equipped). Ensure wiring is not trapped between steering wheel and contact assembly. To complete installation, reverse removal procedure.

Removal & Installation (Models Without Air Bag) – **1)** Disconnect negative battery cable. Position front wheels straight ahead. On pickup and van, unsnap horn cover by grasping sides and pulling away from column. On Explorer and Ranger, remove retaining bolts and steering wheel pad. Disconnect wiring. Mark steering wheel and shaft for installation reference. Remove steering wheel bolt.

2) Using Steering Wheel Puller (T67L-3600-A), remove steering wheel. To install, reverse removal procedure. Align reference marks. Install retaining nut. See TORQUE SPECIFICATIONS table.

MULTIFUNCTION SWITCH

Removal & Installation – Disconnect negative battery cable. Remove steering column shroud. Remove retaining screws and multifunction switch. Unplug electrical connector. Remove switch. To install, reverse removal procedure.

IGNITION SWITCH

Removal – Disconnect negative battery cable. Remove steering column shroud and lower column. Unplug switch connector. Remove retaining nuts or screws. Lift switch vertically to disengage actuator. Remove switch.

Installation – **1)** With lock cylinder and switch in LOCK position, position ignition switch onto column and actuator rod. New ignition switches come positioned in LOCK position with shipping pin in side of switch. Position switch on column, and install, but do not tighten, retaining nuts.

2) Move switch up and down along column to locate mid-position of rod lash. Tighten retaining nuts to **40-65 INCH lbs. (4.5-7.3 N.m)**. Remove shipping pin from side of ignition switch. Connect battery cable. Check for proper starter operation in Park and Neutral. Ensure accessories are not on with ignition switch in OFF position and are on with switch in RUN position.

LOCK CYLINDER

Removal (Aerostar, With Key) – Disconnect negative battery cable. Rotate lock cylinder to RUN position. Using a 1/8" drift, through access hole in cylinder, press retaining pin inward and remove lock cylinder.

Installation – Rotate lock cylinder to RUN position. Push retaining pin inward. Insert lock cylinder into housing. Ensure lock cylinder is fully seated and aligned in interlocking washer before turning to OFF position. Rotate lock cylinder with key to check for proper mechanical operation.

Removal (Aerostar, Without Key) – **1)** Disconnect negative battery cable. Remove steering wheel. See STEERING WHEEL. Using vise-type pliers, twist lock cylinder cap until it separates from lock cylinder. Using 3/8" bit, drill center of key slot approximately 1 3/4" (44 mm) deep until lock cylinder breaks away from base.

2) Remove retainer, washer, ignition switch, and actuator. Clean all drill shavings and other foreign material from housing. Inspect housing for damage. If damage exists, replace housing.

Installation – Install actuator, ignition switch, trim, and electrical parts. Rotate lock cylinder to RUN position. Push retaining pin inward. Insert lock cylinder into housing. Ensure lock cylinder is fully seated and aligned in interlocking washer before turning to OFF position. Rotate lock cylinder with key to check for proper mechanical operation. To complete installation, reverse removal procedure.

Removal & Installation (Except Aerostar, With Key) – **1)** Disconnect negative battery cable. Remove steering wheel. See STEERING WHEEL. Remove trim shrouds. Set ignition switch to RUN position. On vehicles with A/T, set selector lever to Park position.

2) Push retaining pin inward and pull out lock cylinder. Unplug wiring from lock cylinder. To install, lubricate lock cylinder. Turn lock cylinder to ON position. Push retaining pin inward and insert lock cylinder into housing. To install remaining components, reverse removal procedure.

Removal (Except Aerostar, Without Key) – **1)** Use this procedure to remove ignition lock cylinder if key is missing or cylinder is frozen. Disconnect negative battery cable. Remove steering wheel. See STEERING WHEEL. Remove steering column trim shrouds and tilt lever (if equipped). Use a 1/8" (3.17 mm) bit to drill out retaining pin. DO NOT drill deeper than 1/2" (12.7 mm).

2) Place a chisel at base of lock cylinder cap. Strike chisel with sharp blows to break cap away from lock cylinder. Using a 3/8" (9.52 mm) bit, drill out center of lock cylinder key slot. Drill approximately 1 3/4" (44 mm) deep until lock cylinder breaks away from base.

3) Remove metal shavings from lock cylinder housing. Remove drive gear, bearing retainer, and actuator. Thoroughly clean all metal shavings and other foreign materials from housing. Carefully inspect housing for damage. If damage is apparent, replace housing.

Installation – **1)** Lubricate and install drive gear, bearing, and retainer. Lubricate cylinder cavity. Rotate lock cylinder to RUN position. Press retaining pin inward and insert new lock cylinder into lock cylinder housing.

2) Before turning key to OFF position, ensure cylinder is fully seated and aligned. Use key to rotate cylinder to check that mechanical operation is okay in all positions.

TORQUE SPECIFICATIONS
TORQUE SPECIFICATIONS

Application	Ft. Lbs. (N.m)
Steering Wheel Retaining Bolt	23-33 (31-45)
	INCH Lbs. (N.m)
Ignition Switch Nuts	40-63 (4.5-7.1)
Ignition Switch Screws	50-63 (5.6-7.1)
Steering Wheel Pad Bolts	8-11 (.9-1.3)

DESCRIPTION & OPERATION

Windshield wipers are operated by a permanent magnet motor. Wiper arms and blades are mounted on pivot shafts at each side of windshield.

Aerostar uses standard and interval wipers. Explorer and Ranger are equipped only with the interval wiper/washer system. The circuit is protected by a circuit breaker located at the fuse block.

Aerostar and Explorer rear window wiper system consists of a motor mounted inside liftgate, arm and blade assembly, control switch, and circuit breaker.

INTERVAL WIPER/WASHER

Low and high speed wiper operation is the same as standard wiper system. When wiper control switch is in interval (INT) position, wipers make single sweeps, separated by a pause. The control wheel above wiper control switch lever sets length of pause, from about one second to about 12 seconds.

ADJUSTMENTS

WIPER ARM ADJUSTMENT

On Aerostar, distance between wiper blade and top of cowl grille should be **2.4-3.5"** (61-89 mm) on windshield and **2.3-3.3"** (56-84 mm) on rear window. On Explorer and Ranger, measurement is **2-3.2"** (51-81 mm) on driver's side and **2.2-3.4"** (56-86 mm) on passenger's side.

TROUBLE SHOOTING

WIPERS INOPERATIVE IN ALL POSITIONS

Battery Voltage Test – **1)** Unplug wiper motor connector. Set control switch to HIGH position. Check for battery voltage on circuits No. 63 (Red wire) and No. 56 (Dark Blue/Orange wire). See appropriate chassis wiring diagram in WIRING DIAGRAMS.
2) If battery voltage is present on both terminals, go to GROUND TEST. If battery voltage does not exist on Dark Blue/Orange wire, check for the following conditions, and service as necessary.
- Malfunctioning interval governor
- Malfunctioning wiper switch
- Open connector
- Open in circuit No. 56 (Dark Blue/Orange)

3) If voltage is not present at either terminal, check for the following conditions, and service or repair as necessary.
- Open circuit breaker in fuse panel
- Open connector
- Open in circuit No. 63 (Red wire)

Ground Test – Ground wiper motor case to good body ground. If wiper motor runs, repair wiper motor ground wire. If wiper motor does not run, perform wiper motor current draw test. See WIPER MOTOR CURRENT DRAW TEST under TESTING.

WIPERS INOPERATIVE OR ERRATIC IN INTERMITTENT OR LOW

1) Run wipers in HIGH position. If wipers do not hesitate, go to step **2)**. If wipers hesitate when they pass through park position, check interval governor ground under mounting screw. If ground is okay, interval governor is defective; service as required. If ground is not secure, tighten interval governor mounting screws.
2) Unplug wiper motor connector. Set wiper switch to LOW position. Check circuit No. 58 (White wire) for battery voltage. If battery voltage exists, check for malfunctioning wiper motor. Perform WIPER MOTOR CURRENT DRAW TEST and service as required.
3) If voltage is not present, check for the following conditions, and service or replace as necessary.
- Open connector
- Malfunctioning wiper switch
- Malfunctioning interval governor
- Open in circuit No. 58 (White wire)

WIPERS RUN IN OFF POSITION

Unplug wiper control switch. Turn ignition on. If wipers park, replace wiper control switch. If wipers continue to run, check for a malfunctioning interval governor or wiper motor.

WIPERS WILL NOT PARK

Turn off ignition to stop wipers so they are not in park position. Unplug wiper motor. Connect jumpers to motor connector. *See Fig. 1 or 2.* If wipers park, check for the following conditions.
- Open connection
- Malfunctioning interval governor
- Open in circuits No. 58 (White wire) or 28 (Black/Pink wire)

Service or repair as required. If wipers do not park, replace wiper motor.

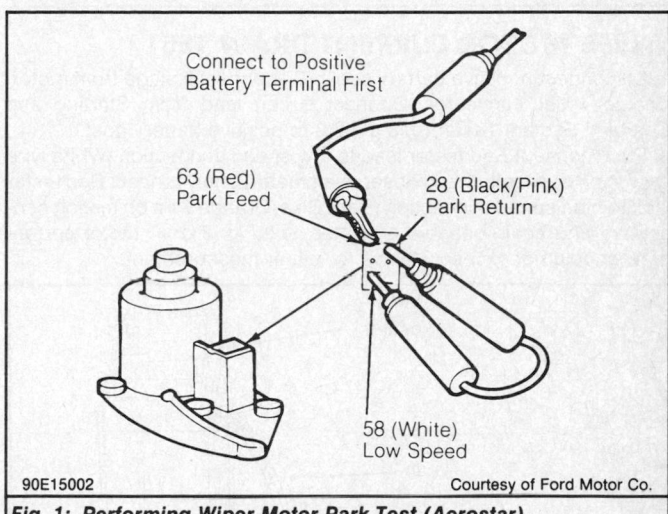

Fig. 1: *Performing Wiper Motor Park Test (Aerostar)*

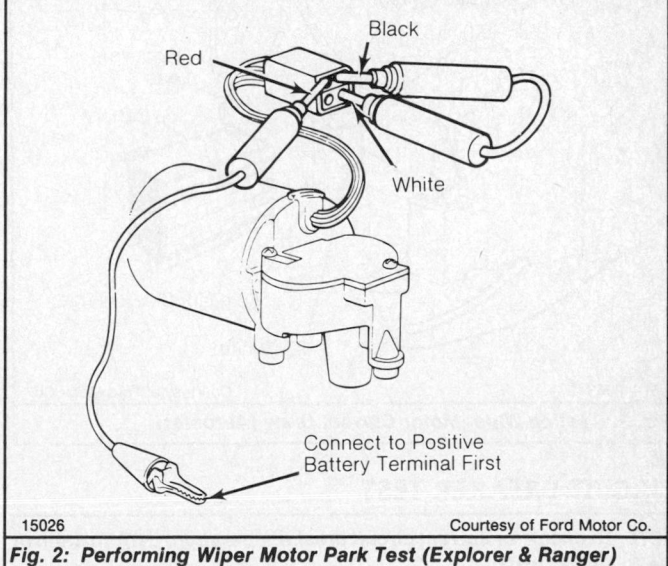

Fig. 2: *Performing Wiper Motor Park Test (Explorer & Ranger)*

WIPERS DO NOT RUN WHEN WASHER IS ACTIVATED

Ensure wipers operate with switch in LOW and HIGH positions. If wipers work, replace interval governor. If wipers do not work, check for malfunctioning wiper switch and interval governor. Service or replace as required.

FORD
4-30

1992 SAFETY EQUIPMENT
Wiper/Washer Systems
Aerostar, Explorer & Ranger (Cont.)

TESTING

WARNING: On models with air bag, observe the following precautions. Disconnect negative and then positive battery cables. Shield both cables. Air bag system contains a back-up power supply built into the air bag diagnostic monitor. Wait a minimum of one minute before servicing any air bag system components. System is now disabled. See appropriate AIR BAG RESTRAINT SYSTEM article.

WARNING: When battery is disconnected, vehicle computer and memory systems may lose memory data. Driveability problems may exist until computer systems have completed a relearn cycle. See COMPUTER RELEARN PROCEDURES article in GENERAL INFORMATION before disconnecting battery.

WIPER MOTOR CURRENT DRAW TEST

1) Disconnect negative battery cable. Disconnect linkage from motor. Unplug wiper connector. Connect Green lead from Starting and Charging System Tester (078-00005) to positive battery post.
2) First, connect Red tester lead to low speed connection (White wire on mating connector), and observe ammeter. Then connect Red tester lead to high speed connection (Dark Blue/Orange wire on mating connector), and again observe ammeter. *See Fig. 3 or 4.* Motor current draw should not exceed 3 amps for either measurement.

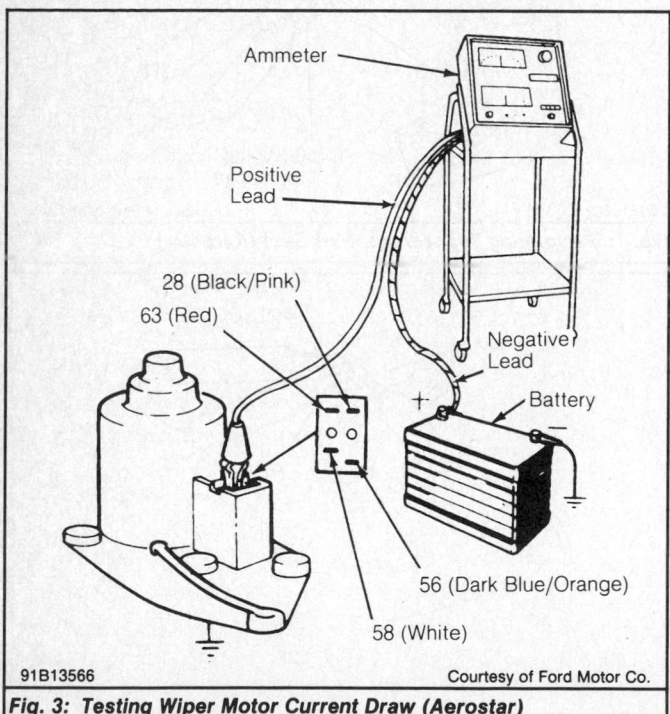

91B13566   Courtesy of Ford Motor Co.

Fig. 3: Testing Wiper Motor Current Draw (Aerostar)

CIRCUIT BREAKER TEST

NOTE: To check for correct circuit breaker operation, perform both of the following tests.

1) Before connecting circuit breaker to tester, short tester leads together, and adjust current draw until it equals circuit breaker rating. Connect breaker to tester. Leave breaker connected to tester for 10 minutes while maintaining rated current. If circuit breaker opens within 10 minutes, replace circuit breaker.

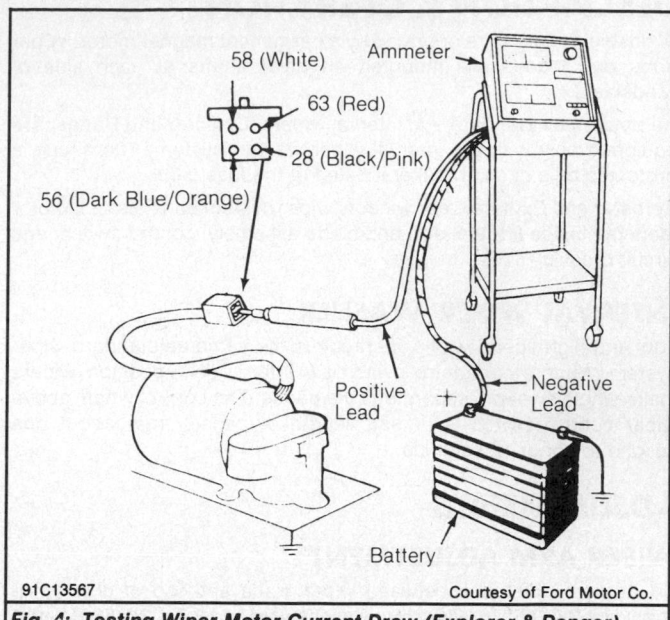

91C13567   Courtesy of Ford Motor Co.

Fig. 4: Testing Wiper Motor Current Draw (Explorer & Ranger)

2) Again short tester leads together. Adjust current draw until it is twice rated current. Connect breaker. Maintain twice rated current. Circuit breaker should open within 30 seconds. If not, replace circuit breaker.

WIPER SWITCH CONTINUITY TEST

1) Check continuity between switch terminals. *See Fig. 5 or 6.* See appropriate WIPER SWITCH CONTINUITY table. Either a self-powered test light or an ohmmeter can be used with standard system. An ohmmeter must be used with interval wiper system.
2) To detect marginal operation of switch, move switch lever while making measurements. If continuity or resistance is not as specified, or if continuity is poor in any position, replace switch.

WIPER SWITCH CONTINUITY (Aerostar)

Position	Terminals	Condition
Wash OFF	590-993	No Continuity
Wash ON	590-993	Continuity
Wiper OFF	589-590	No Continuity
Wash OFF	590-993	103.3 k/ohms
	589-993	47.6 k/ohms
Wiper LO	589-590	No Continuity
Wash OFF	590-993	3.3 k/ohms
	589-993	4.1 k/ohms
Wiper HI	589-993	No Continuity
Wash OFF	590-993	3.3 k/ohms
Interval Wipe	589-590	No Continuity
(Maximum Delay)	590-993	103.3 k/ohms
Interval Wipe	589-590	No Continuity
(Minimum Delay)	590-993	3.3 k/ohms
	589-993	11.3 k/ohms

1992 SAFETY EQUIPMENT
Wiper/Washer Systems
Aerostar, Explorer & Ranger (Cont.)

FORD
4-31

WIPER SWITCH CONTINUITY (Explorer & Ranger)

Position	Terminals	Condition
Wash OFF	63-941	No Continuity
Wash ON	63-941	Continuity
Wiper OFF	56, 63, 65,	No Continuity
Wash OFF	941, 993	
Wiper LO	63-993	Continuity
Wash OFF	63-641, 65-941	No Continuity
Wiper HI	65, 63, 993	Continuity
Wash OFF	63, 65, 941	No Continuity
Interval Wipe	63-65	Continuity
(Maximum Delay)	63-993, 56-941	No Continuity
Wash OFF	61-589	7-13 k/ohms
Interval Wipe	63-65	Continuity
(Minimum Delay)	63-993, 56-941	No Continuity
Wash OFF	61-589	420-880 ohms

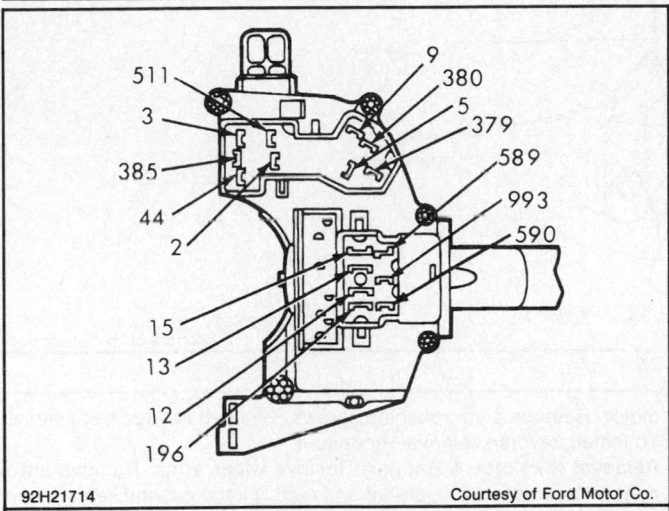

92H21714   Courtesy of Ford Motor Co.

Fig. 5: Identifying Wiper Switch Terminals (Aerostar)

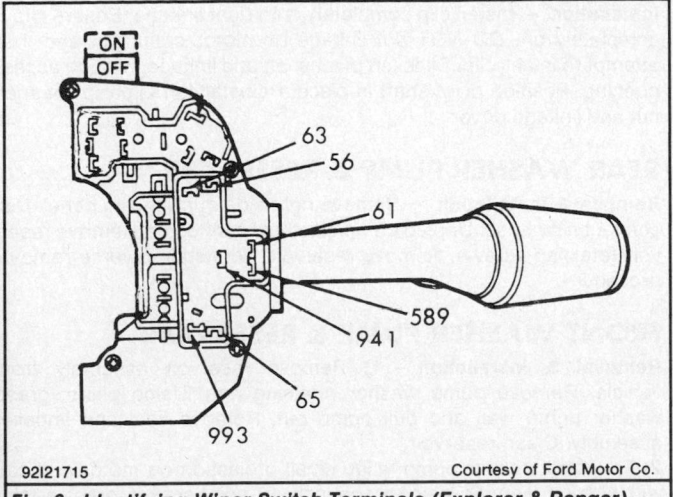

92I21715   Courtesy of Ford Motor Co.

Fig. 6: Identifying Wiper Switch Terminals (Explorer & Ranger)

PARK TEST

1) Turn wipers on. Use ignition switch to stop wiper blades so blades are not in park position. Connect jumper wires as shown. *See Fig. 1 or 2.* Wiper should run one full cycle and then park. If motor does not park or will not run to park position, replace motor.

2) If motor stops, check windshield wiper manual control switch and wiring for continuity. If switch and wiring are okay and wiper does not stop in OFF or INT positions of switch, replace interval governor.

INTERVAL GOVERNOR TEST

If interval operation is not correct, check wiper motor current draw, wiper control switch, and all connecting wires for continuity. If these components and wiring are okay, replace interval governor.

WASHER PUMP CURRENT DRAW TEST

Connect ammeter in series with washer pump. Acceptable current draw is **1.7-4 amps** while washer pump is running. If draw is too high, check for plugged outlet lines or a dirty screen in reservoir.

REMOVAL & INSTALLATION

WARNING: On models with air bag, observe the following precautions. Disconnect negative and then positive battery cables. Shield both cables. Air bag system contains a back-up power supply built into the air bag diagnostic monitor. Wait a minimum of one minute before servicing any air bag system components. System is now disabled. See appropriate AIR BAG RESTRAINT SYSTEM article.

WARNING: When battery is disconnected, vehicle computer and memory systems may lose memory data. Driveability problems may exist until computer systems have completed a relearn cycle. See COMPUTER RELEARN PROCEDURES article in GENERAL INFORMATION before disconnecting battery.

REAR WIPER MOTOR

Removal & Installation (Aerostar & Explorer) – 1) Disconnect negative battery cable. Remove wiper arm and blade assembly. Remove pivot shaft attaching nut, washer and pivot block. Remove liftgate trim panel.

2) On Aerostar, unplug electrical connector and remove motor wiring pins from inner panel. Remove rear wiper motor.

3) On Explorer, remove motor bracket attaching screw and rectangular plate. Unplug the electrical connector. Disengage wiring locator pins. Remove motor assembly. To install, reverse removal procedure.

WINDSHIELD WIPER MOTOR

Removal & Installation (Aerostar) – 1) Turn wipers on. Use ignition switch to stop wipers when blades are vertical. Unplug wiper motor connector. Remove wiper arms and cowl grille.

2) Remove linkage retaining clip and linkage from motor crank arm. Remove wiper motor retaining nuts and motor. To install, reverse removal procedure.

Removal & Installation (Explorer & Ranger) – 1) Turn wipers on. Use ignition switch to stop wipers when blades are vertical. Unplug wiper motor connector. Remove right wiper arm and blade. Disconnect negative battery cable. Remove right pivot nut. Allow linkage to drop into cowl.

2) Remove linkage access cover. Reach through access cover opening and unsnap wiper motor clip. Push clip away from linkage until it clears nib on crank pin. Push clip from linkage. Remove wiper linkage from motor crank pin. Remove wiper motor retaining screws and motor. To install, reverse removal procedure.

REAR WIPER CONTROL SWITCH

Removal & Installation (Aerostar) – Disconnect negative battery cable. Remove trim shrouds. Remove left switch pod. Disconnect electrical connector. Remove 2 cross-recessed screws. Remove switch. To install, reverse removal procedure.

Removal & Installation (Explorer) – Disconnect negative battery cable. Remove 2 ashtray retaining screws and ashtray. Remove

FORD
4-32

1992 SAFETY EQUIPMENT
Wiper/Washer Systems
Aerostar, Explorer & Ranger (Cont.)

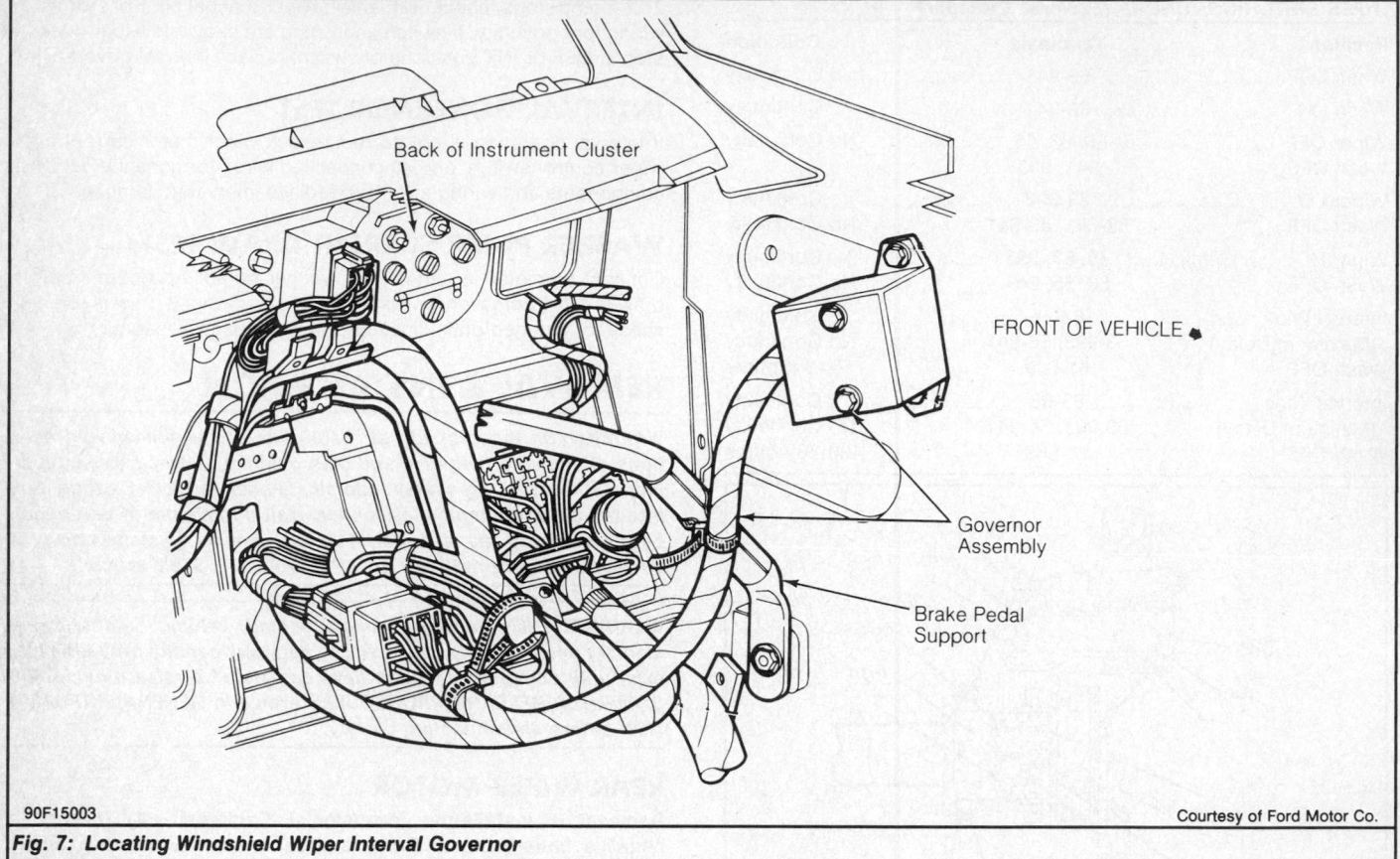

Back of Instrument Cluster

FRONT OF VEHICLE

Governor
Assembly

Brake Pedal
Support

90F15003

Courtesy of Ford Motor Co.

Fig. 7: Locating Windshield Wiper Interval Governor

instrument cluster trim panel. Remove switch mounting bezel. Disconnect electrical connector. Push from connector side mounting bezel until snap-in mounting clips release switch. To install, reverse removal procedure.

WINDSHIELD WIPER CONTROL SWITCH

Removal & Installation – Disconnect negative battery cable. Remove steering column shrouds. Remove switch retaining screws. Unplug electrical connectors. To install, reverse removal procedure. Ensure PRNDL adjustment is correct after installation.

INTERVAL GOVERNOR

Removal & Installation – Interval governor is located under left center of instrument panel. Disconnect negative battery cable. Remove steering column shroud. Unplug interval governor connector from wiper control switch. Unplug interval governor connector from instrument panel wiring harness. Remove mounting screws and interval governor. *See Fig. 7.* To install, reverse removal procedure.

WIPER ARMS

Removal – Raise wiper blade away from windshield. Move slide latch away from pivot shaft to unlock wiper arm from pivot shaft. Pull off wiper arm.
Installation – 1) Ensure pivot shaft is in park position. Push main arm head over pivot shaft. Hold main arm head onto pivot shaft while raising blade end of wiper arm.
2) Push slide latch into lock under pivot shaft head. Lower blade to windshield. If blade does not touch windshield, slide latch is not properly positioned.

PIVOT SHAFT & LINKAGE

Removal & Installation (Aerostar) – Remove wiper arms. Remove cowl top grille. Remove clip retaining linkage to crank arm of wiper

motor. Remove pivot retaining screws. Remove linkage from vehicle. To install, reverse removal procedure.
Removal (Explorer & Ranger) Remove wiper arms. Remove left or right linkage access cover (left and right linkage assemblies are serviced separately). Remove left pivot nut. Lower linkage. Slide linkage out through left access opening.
Installation – Install clip completely onto right linkage. Ensure clip is completely on. DO NOT put linkage on motor crank pin and then attempt to install clip. Slide left pivot shaft and linkage through access opening. Position pivot shaft in place. Reinstall left wiper pivot shaft nut and linkage cover.

REAR WASHER PUMP & RESERVOIR

Removal & Installation – Remove right side quarter trim panel. Disconnect filler hose. Unplug pump electrical connector. Remove reservoir retaining screws. Remove reservoir. To install, reverse removal procedure.

FRONT WASHER PUMP & RESERVOIR

Removal & Installation – 1) Remove reservoir assembly from vehicle. Remove pump washer retaining ring. Using pliers, grasp washer pump wall and pull pump out. Remove seal and impeller assembly. Clean reservoir.
2) To install washer pump, align small projection on motor end cap with slot in reservoir. Using a one-inch, 12-point socket, press retaining ring with hand pressure against motor end plate. Install reservoir.

WIRING DIAGRAMS

See appropriate chassis wiring diagram in WIRING DIAGRAMS.

NOTE: Unless otherwise specified, references to Pickup include the F350 Super Duty commercial chassis.

DESCRIPTION & OPERATION

Windshield wipers are operated by a permanent magnet motor. Wiper arms and blades are mounted on pivot shafts at each side of windshield. Interval wipers are available on all vehicles. The circuit is protected by a circuit breaker.

On interval systems, low and high speed wiper operation is the same as standard wiper system. When wiper control switch is in interval (INT) position, wipers make single sweeps, separated by driver-adjustable pauses.

ADJUSTMENTS

WIPER ARM & BLADE ASSEMBLY

1) Remove wiper arm and blade assemblies from pivot shafts. Turn on wipers to allow motor to operate 3 or 4 cycles, then turn wipers off. Wiper pivot shafts will be in Park position.

2) Install arm and blade assemblies onto pivot shafts. Adjust clearance between wiper blade and cowl top. On Bronco and Pickup, clearance should be **1.4-2.5"** (36-64 mm) for driver side, and **2.0-3.2"** (51-81 mm) for passenger side. On Van, clearance should be **2.1-3.0"** (53-76 mm) for driver side, and **2.2-3.1"** (56-79 mm) for passenger side.

DIAGNOSIS & TESTING

WARNING: On models with air bag, observe the following precautions. Disconnect negative and then positive battery cables. Shield both cables. Air bag system contains a back-up power supply built into the air bag diagnostic monitor. Wait a minimum of one minute before servicing any air bag system components. System is now disabled. See AIR BAG RESTRAINT SYSTEM article.

WARNING: When battery is disconnected, vehicle computer and memory systems may lose memory data. Driveability problems may exist until computer systems have completed a relearn cycle. See COMPUTER RELEARN PROCEDURES article in GENERAL INFORMATION before disconnecting battery.

STANDARD WIPER SYSTEM TESTS

High Speed Test – **1)** When wiper switch is in HI position, current flows from ignition switch, through wiper switch, to wiper motor high speed terminal. *See Fig. 1.* If problem exists in high speed circuit, check for voltage at wiper motor circuit No. 56 (Blue/Orange wire).

2) If voltage is not present, check voltage at circuit No. 297 (Black/Light Green wire) of multifunction switch connector. If voltage is present at circuit No. 297 (Black/Light Green wire) but not at circuit No. 56 (Blue/Orange wire), replace multifunction switch.

3) If voltage is not present at circuit No. 297 (Black/Light Green wire), locate short or open. If voltage is present at circuit No. 56 (Blue/Orange wire) and wiper motor does not run, connect jumper wire between wiper motor ground circuit and chassis ground. If motor runs, repair ground connection. If motor does not run, replace wiper motor.

Low Speed Test – **1)** When wiper switch is in LO position, current flows from ignition switch, through wiper switch, to wiper motor low speed terminal. *See Fig. 1.* If problem exists in low speed circuit, check for voltage at circuit No. 58 (White wire) of wiper motor harness connector.

2) If voltage is not present, check for voltage at circuit No. 297 (Black/Light Green wire) of multifunction switch connector. If voltage is present at circuit No. 297 (Black/Light Green wire) but not at circuit No. 58 (White wire), replace multifunction switch. If voltage is not present at circuit No. 297 (Black/Light Green wire), trace circuit back to source of problem.

3) If voltage is present at circuit No. 58 (White wire), but wiper motor does not run, connect a jumper wire between wiper motor and chassis ground. If wiper motor runs, repair ground connection. If motor does not run, replace wiper motor.

Park Test – **1)** When wipers are turned off, system will complete one cycle through wiper motor park switch. Current flows from ignition switch, through wiper switch, to wiper motor park switch for 9/10th of one cycle. *See Fig. 1.*

2) At last 1/10th of cycle, park switch moves from run position to park position (ground). This stops wiper motor in park position. If a problem exists in park circuit, check for voltage at circuits No. 58 (White wire), No. 28 (Black/Pink wire), and No. 63 (Red wire) of wiper motor connector.

3) If voltage is present on all 3 circuits, but wiper blades are not parked, connect jumper wire between motor and vehicle body. If motor parks, repair ground connection. If motor does not park, replace motor. If voltage is present only at circuit No. 63 (Red wire), replace wiper motor.

4) If voltage is present only at circuits No. 63 (Red wire) and No. 28 (Black/Pink wire), replace multifunction switch. If voltage is still not present at circuit No. 58 (White wire) , check circuits No. 58 and No. 28 (Black/Pink wire) for opens or shorts.

INTERVAL WIPER SYSTEM TESTS

NOTE: If governor relay is inoperative, wipers will operate in high speed and park modes only.

High Speed Test – **1)** With wiper switch in HI position, current flows from ignition switch through wiper switch to governor. From governor, current flows to wiper motor then to ground. *See Fig. 2.*

2) If a problem occurs in system, check for voltage at circuit No. 56 (Blue/Orange wire) of wiper motor connector. If voltage is present and wiper motor does not run, ground wiper motor to vehicle body. If wiper motor runs, repair wiper motor ground connection.

3) If wiper motor does not run, replace motor. If voltage is present on circuit No. 63 (Red wire) but not on circuit No. 56 (Blue/Orange wire), replace multifunction switch. If voltage is not present on circuit No. 63 (Red wire), disconnect multifunction switch connector and check for voltage on circuit No. 297 (Black/Light Green wire). If voltage is present, replace multifunction switch. If voltage is not present, trace circuit to locate short or open.

Low Speed Test – **1)** With wiper switch in LO position, current flows from ignition switch through wiper switch and energized relay contacts of governor to wiper motor. *See Fig. 2.* To locate a low speed problem in system, check for voltage at circuit No. 58 (White wire).

2) If voltage is present but wiper motor does not run, ground wiper motor to vehicle body. If motor runs, repair motor ground connection. If motor does not run, replace motor. If voltage is present on circuit No. 63 (Red wire) but not on No. 58 (White wire), ground control circuits No. 57 (Black wire) and No. 28 (Black/Pink wire) at multifunction switch connector.

3) If voltage is now present on circuit No. 58 (White wire), replace multifunction switch. If no voltage is present, replace governor. If no voltage is present on circuit No. 63 (Red wire), remove multifunction switch connector and check for voltage on circuit No. 297 (Black/Light Green wire). If voltage is present, replace multifunction switch. If voltage is not present, trace circuit to locate short or open.

NOTE: Before trouble shooting interval mode, wiper system must perform properly in low speed and park modes. If wipers run continuously at low speed, or interval delay is excessive, remove multifunction switch and check continuity and resistance values. If switch is okay, replace governor.

Interval Test – **1)** When wiper switch is set to Interval mode, wiper motor park switch contacts are grounded and governor relay is energized. Initially current flows from ignition switch, through wiper switch, through a diode and energized contacts in governor, to wiper motor low speed brush. *See Fig. 2.*

FORD
4-34

1992 SAFETY EQUIPMENT
Wiper/Washer Systems
Bronco, Pickup & Van (Cont.)

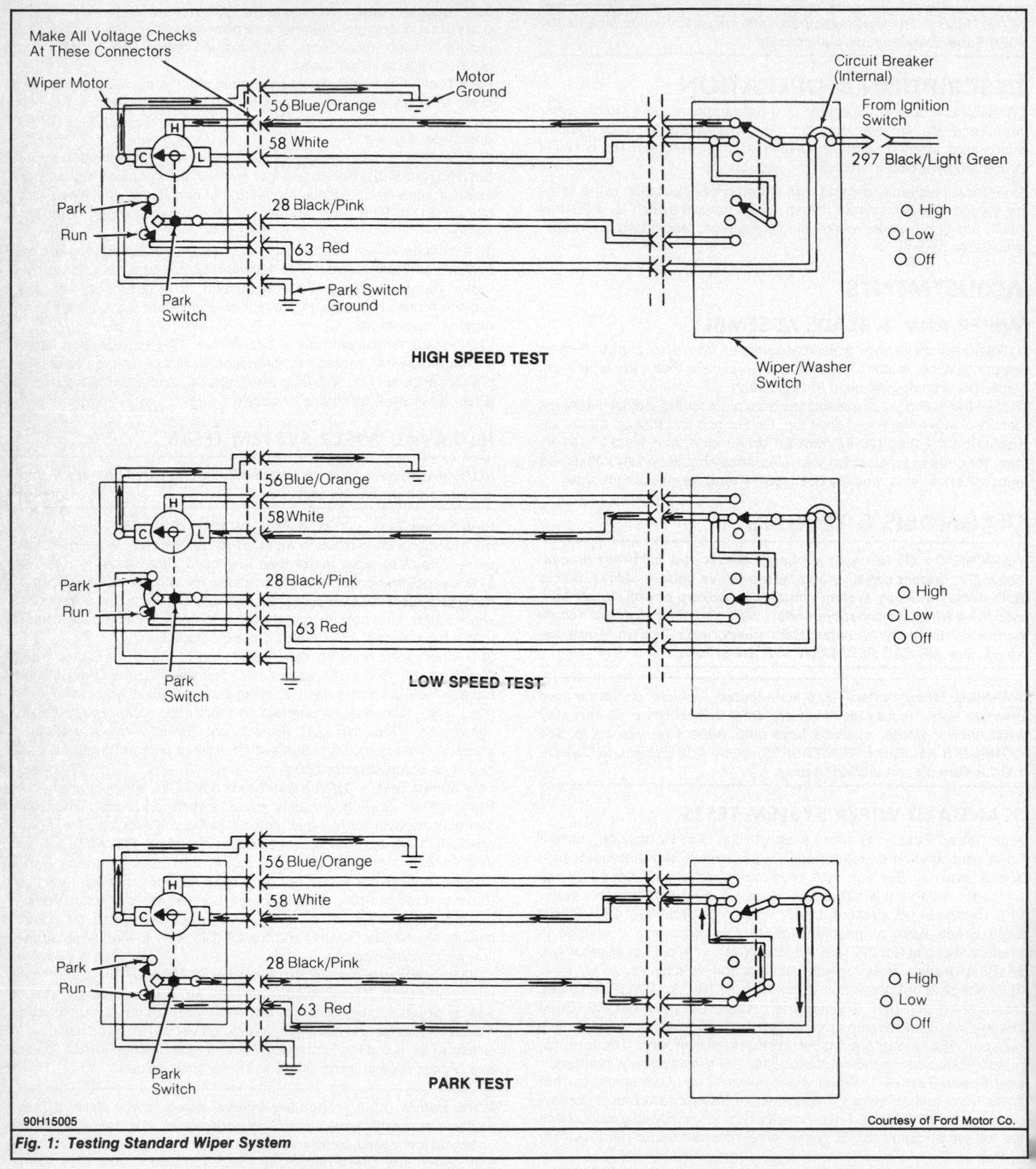

Fig. 1: Testing Standard Wiper System

90H15005

Courtesy of Ford Motor Co.

1992 SAFETY EQUIPMENT
Wiper/Washer Systems
Bronco, Pickup & Van (Cont.)

FORD
4-35

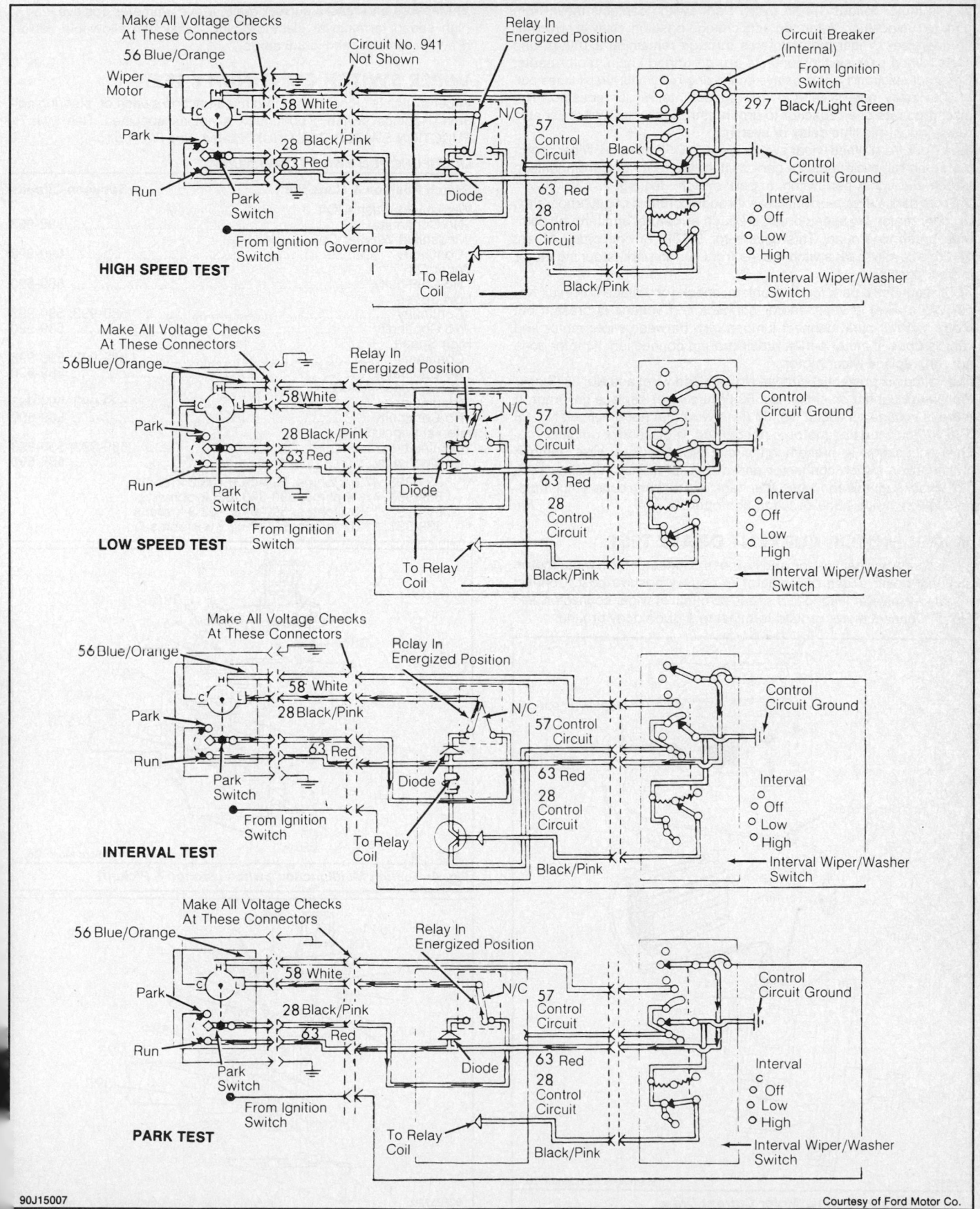

90J15007

Courtesy of Ford Motor Co.

Fig. 2: Testing Interval Wiper System

FORD
4-36

1992 SAFETY EQUIPMENT
Wiper/Washer Systems
Bronco, Pickup & Van (Cont.)

2) The motor rotates 1/10th cycle. Park switch contacts move from park to run position. After contacts change position, relay in governor de-energizes. Wiper motor rotates through remaining 9/10th of one cycle. When park switch contacts are grounded again, motor parks. Governor electronic circuit delays energizing relay until circuit times out.

3) The relay energizes and low speed interval is repeated. The discharge rate of a capacitor to ground through wiper switch variable resistor controls time delay of system.

Park Test – 1) When wiper switch is set to OFF position, wipers complete one full cycle through park switch. Current flows from ignition switch, through wiper switch, to park switch. *See Fig. 2.*

2) From park switch, current flows through contacts of governor relay, to wiper motor low speed brush, through armature, and through common brush to ground. This occurs for 9/10th of one cycle. At last 1/10th of cycle, park switch moves from run to park, stopping motor in park position.

3) To diagnose a park mode problem, check for voltage on circuit No. 58 (White wire) of wiper motor connector. If voltage is present but motor will not park, connect jumper wire between wiper motor and vehicle body. If motor parks, repair ground connection. If motor does not run, replace wiper motor.

4) If voltage is present at circuits No. 63 (Red wire) and No. 28 (Black/Pink wire), but not on circuit No. 58 (White wire), replace governor. If there is voltage on circuit No. 63 (Red wire) but not on circuit No. 28 (Black/Pink wire) and motor is not parked, replace wiper motor.

5) If no voltage is present on circuit No. 63 (Red wire), remove multifunction switch connector and check for voltage on circuit No. 297 (Black/Light Green wire). If voltage is present, replace multifunction switch. If not, trace circuit to find open.

WIPER MOTOR CURRENT DRAW TEST

1) Disconnect wiper linkage and harness connector from wiper motor. Connect positive lead of ammeter to battery positive post. Connect negative ammeter lead to low speed terminal at wiper connector. *See Fig. 3.* Connect motor ground terminal to a good body ground.

2) Measure and record current draw. Move ammeter positive lead to high speed terminal at electrical plug. Maximum allowable current draw for either speed is **3.5 amps**.

WIPER SWITCH CONTINUITY TEST

Wiper switch is incorporated into multifunction switch on steering column. Replace switch if continuity is not as specified. See MULTIFUNCTION SWITCH CONTINUITY table. *See Fig. 4 or 5.*

MULTIFUNCTION SWITCH CONTINUITY

Switch Position & Condition	Between Circuits
Windshield Washer Off	
No Continuity	590-993
Windshield Washer On	
Continuity	590-993
Wiper Off	
No Continuity	589-590
Low Speed	
Continuity	[1] 589-993; 590-993
No Continuity	589-590
High Speed	
Continuity	[2] 589-993; 590-993
No Continuity	589-590
Interval Wiper (MAX)	
Continuity	[3] 589-993; 590-993
No Continuity	589-590
Interval Wiper (MIN)	
Continuity	[4] 589-993; 590-993
No Continuity	589-590

[1] – 589-993, 47.6 k/ohms; 590-993, 103.3 k/ohms.
[2] – 589-993, 4.1 k/ohms; 590-993, 3.3 k/ohms.
[3] – 589-993, 11.3 k/ohms; 590-993, 103.3 k/ohms.
[4] – 589-993, 11.3 k/ohms; 590-993, 3.3 k/ohms.

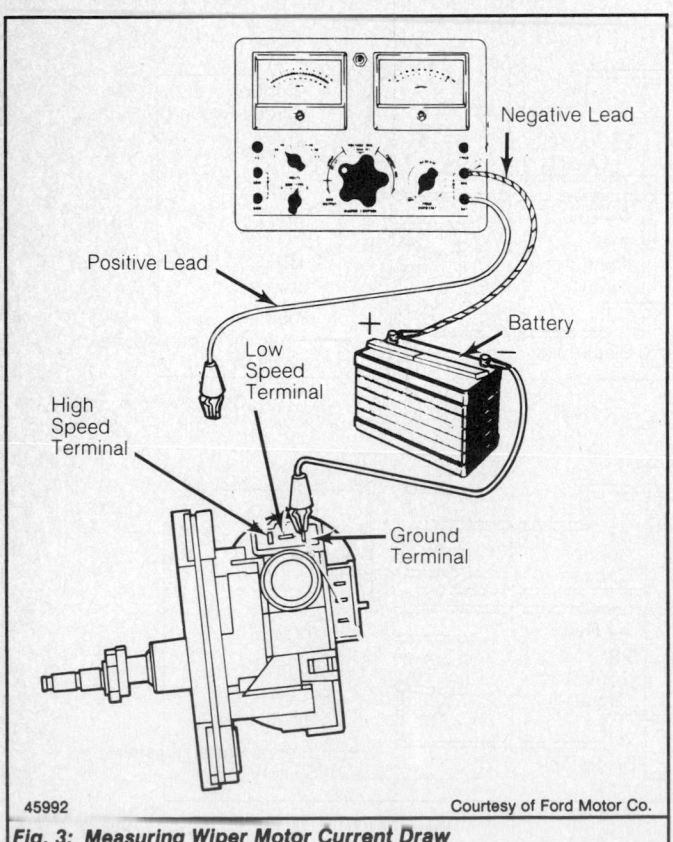

Fig. 3: Measuring Wiper Motor Current Draw

45992
Courtesy of Ford Motor Co.

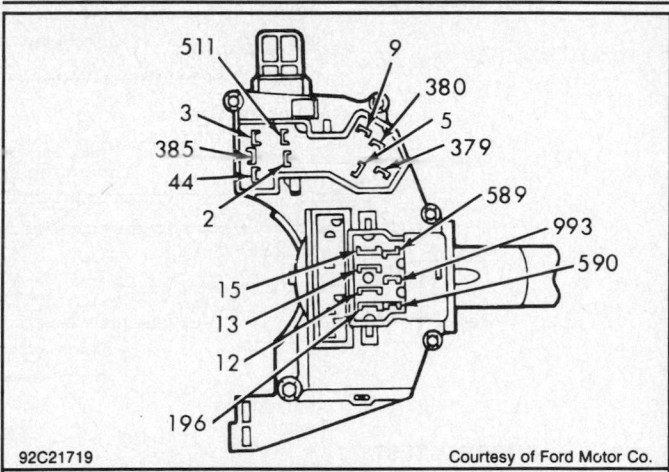

92C21719
Courtesy of Ford Motor Co.

Fig. 4: Testing Multifunction Switch (Bronco & Pickup)

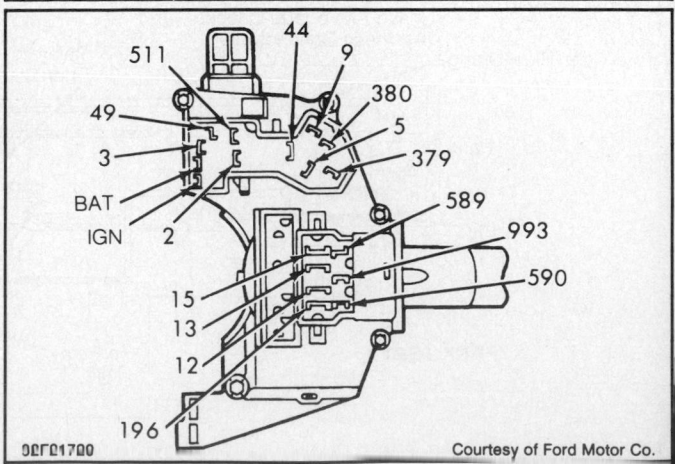

92C21720
Courtesy of Ford Motor Co.

Fig. 5: Testing Multifunction Switch (Van)

1992 SAFETY EQUIPMENT
Wiper/Washer Systems
Bronco, Pickup & Van (Cont.)

FORD
4-37

INTERVAL GOVERNOR TEST

If interval operation is unsatisfactory, check motor current draw, control switch and appropriate wiring. If motor, switch and wiring are okay, replace interval governor assembly.

WASHER PUMP MOTOR CURRENT DRAW TEST

Connect ammeter negative lead to battery positive and positive lead to washer motor terminal. Connect jumper wire from remaining washer motor terminal to negative battery post. Operate washer pump. Acceptable current draw is **1.7-4.0 amps** while washer motor is running. Replace washer motor if current draw is not within specification.

REMOVAL & INSTALLATION

WARNING: On models with air bag, observe the following precautions. Disconnect negative and then positive battery cables. Shield both cables. Air bag system contains a back-up power supply built into the air bag diagnostic monitor. Wait a minimum of one minute before servicing any air bag system components. System is now disabled. See AIR BAG RESTRAINT SYSTEM article.

WARNING: When battery is disconnected, vehicle computer and memory systems may lose memory data. Driveability problems may exist until computer systems have completed a relearn cycle. See COMPUTER RELEARN PROCEDURES article in GENERAL INFORMATION before disconnecting battery.

WIPER MOTOR

Removal & Installation (Bronco & Pickup) – 1) Disconnect negative battery cable. Remove wiper arms and blade assemblies. Remove cowl grille retaining screws. Raise cowl. Disconnect washer hose. Remove cowl grille.

2) Remove wiper linkage clips from motor output arm. Disconnect motor wiring. Remove motor mounting bolts and motor. To install, reverse removal procedure. Tighten mounting bolts to **60-85 INCH lbs. (6.8-9.6 N.m)**.

Removal & Installation (Van) – 1) Disconnect battery negative cable. Remove wiper arms and blade assemblies. Disconnect wiring at motor.

2) Remove outer air inlet cowl. Remove motor drive arm retaining clip. Remove motor mounting bolts and motor. To install, reverse removal procedure. Motor must be in park position during installation. Tighten mounting bolts to **60-85 INCH lbs. (6.8-9.6 N.m)**.

MULTIFUNCTION SWITCH

Removal & Installation – Disconnect negative battery cable. Remove steering column shroud. Remove retaining screws and multifunction switch. Unplug electrical connector. Remove switch. To install, reverse removal procedure.

INTERVAL GOVERNOR

Removal & Installation – Governor is mounted on lower left side of instrument panel. Remove rear window defogger switch assembly (if equipped) to gain access to right governor retaining screw. Unplug harness connector from governor. Remove governor retaining screws. To install, reverse removal procedure.

WASHER PUMP & RESERVOIR

Removal & Installation – Using a small screwdriver, release connector. Remove hose. Drain reservoir. Remove pump retaining screws. Remove reservoir retaining screws. To install, reverse removal procedure. Fill reservoir before making electrical connections.

WIRING DIAGRAMS

See appropriate chassis wiring diagram in WIRING DIAGRAMS.

Ranger

NOTE: For repair procedures not covered in this article, see ENGINE OVERHAUL PROCEDURES article in GENERAL INFORMATION.

ENGINE IDENTIFICATION

Engine is identified by the eighth character of Vehicle Identification Number (VIN). VIN is stamped on a metal tag, and is visible through windshield on driver's side. VIN is also located on the Safety Compliance Certification Label on edge of driver's door.

VIN ENGINE CODE

Engine	Code
2.3L PFI	A

ADJUSTMENTS

VALVE CLEARANCE ADJUSTMENT

NOTE: Valve lifters are set at zero lash. No adjustment is necessary. If valve seat/face has been serviced or worn parts are suspected, check valve clearance.

1) Remove valve cover. Rotate camshaft so base circle of lobe faces the cam follower to be checked. Using Valve Spring Compressor Lever (T88T-6565-BH), apply pressure on cam follower until valve lifter is fully collapsed.

2) While holding valve lifter fully collapsed, use feeler gauge to measure clearance between base circle of camshaft and camshaft follower. Clearance should preferably be .040-.050" (1.01-1.27 mm), but allowable clearance is .035-.055" (.89-1.40 mm). See VALVE LIFTERS table under ENGINE SPECIFICATIONS at end of article.

3) If clearance exceeds specification, inspect camshaft follower for damage. If camshaft follower is not damaged, check for sticking valve. Ensure valve spring height and camshaft lobe lift are within specification. See VALVES & VALVE SPRINGS table and CAMSHAFT & AUXILIARY SHAFT table under ENGINE SPECIFICATIONS at end of article.

4) If components are within specification, inspect valve lifter for faulty operation. See HYDRAULIC VALVE LIFTER under REMOVAL & INSTALLATION. Replace components as necessary. Install valve cover.

REMOVAL & INSTALLATION

WARNING: When battery is disconnected, vehicle computer and memory systems may lose memory data. Driveability problems may exist until computer systems have completed a relearn cycle. See COMPUTER RELEARN PROCEDURES article in GENERAL INFORMATION before disconnecting battery.

NOTE: For reassembly reference, label all electrical connectors, vacuum hoses and fuel lines before removal. Also place mating marks on engine hood and other major assemblies before removal.

NOTE: Discharge A/C system using approved refrigerant recovery/recycling equipment.

FUEL PRESSURE RELEASE

To release fuel pressure, disconnect negative battery cable. Remove fuel cap to release fuel tank pressure. Remove relief valve cap from fuel rail. Connect fuel pressure gauge to relief valve and release fuel into a suitable container.

COOLING SYSTEM BLEEDING

1) Fill cooling system with 50/50 mixture of coolant and water. Pause several minutes for circulation. Fill radiator to filler neck seat. Install radiator cap fully, then back off to first stop.

WARNING: When engine is operating, NEVER remove radiator cap under any conditions. Failure to follow instruction could cause personal injury, or damage cooling system or engine. Always wrap protective material around radiator cap to avoid injury from hot coolant.

2) Place heater controls to maximum heat. Start engine and operate at 2000 RPM for approximately 3-4 minutes. Turn engine off. Using protective rag, carefully remove radiator cap. Add coolant to filler neck seat.

3) Install radiator cap fully, then back off to first stop. Start engine and allow to operate at 2000 RPM until upper radiator hose is warm. Check heater output. Turn engine off. Using protective rag, carefully remove radiator cap. Add coolant to filler neck seat if necessary.

4) Tightly install radiator cap. Remove small cap (large cap is for windshield washer reservoir) on coolant recovery reservoir. Add 1.1 qt. (1L) of 50/50 mixture of coolant and water to reservoir. Install reservoir cap.

ENGINE

Removal – 1) Disconnect battery cables and remove battery. Drain cooling system. Disconnect air cleaner outlet tube at throttle body. Mark location of hood hinges and remove hood.

2) Remove radiator shroud attaching screws. Remove upper radiator supports. Remove cooling fan and shroud. Disconnect radiator hoses at engine and remove radiator with hoses attached. Disconnect engine wiring harness from body wiring harness.

3) Disconnect wiring from alternator and starter. Disconnect accelerator cable and A/T kickdown cable (if equipped) from throttle body. Remove A/C compressor from bracket and set aside with hoses attached (if equipped).

4) Disconnect power brake vacuum hose. Release fuel pressure. See FUEL PRESSURE RELEASE. Using Disconnect Tool (T81P-19623-G1) for 3/8" line or (T81P-19623-G2) for 1/2" line, disconnect fuel supply and return lines. See Fig. 1.

5) Remove heater hoses from engine. Remove engine mount nuts. Raise vehicle and drain crankcase. Remove starter motor. Disconnect exhaust pipe from manifold. Remove dust cover from transmission. On M/T models, remove flywheel housing cover bolts.

6) On A/T models, remove converter-to-flywheel and bellhousing lower bolts. On all applications, support transmission and lower vehicle. Remove upper bellhousing-to-engine bolts. Attach engine hoist and lift engine from vehicle.

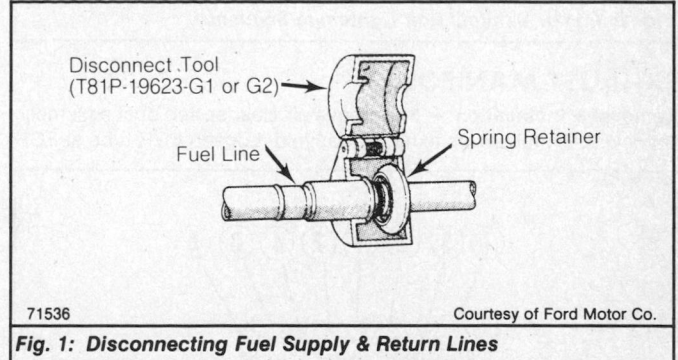

Disconnect Tool
(T81P-19623-G1 or G2)

Fuel Line

Spring Retainer

71536 Courtesy of Ford Motor Co.

Fig. 1: Disconnecting Fuel Supply & Return Lines

Installation – To install, reverse removal procedure. Tighten bolts to specification. See TORQUE SPECIFICATIONS table at end of article. Fill or top off all engine fluids. Fill and bleed air from cooling system. See COOLING SYSTEM BLEEDING.

INTAKE MANIFOLDS

Removal (Upper & Lower) – 1) Disconnect negative battery cable. Drain coolant. Release fuel pressure. See FUEL PRESSURE RELEASE. Mark and disconnect electrical wiring, vacuum lines and vacuum fittings from upper intake manifold. Remove throttle linkage shield. Remove throttle, cruise control and kickdown linkages.

2) Remove air intake hose and crankcase vent hose. Disconnect PCV hose from underside of upper intake manifold. Disconnect coolant by-pass hose at lower intake manifold. Disconnect EGR tube from EGR valve.

3) Using Disconnect Tool (T81P-19623-G1) for 3/8" line or (T81P-19623-G2) for 1/2" line, disconnect fuel supply and return lines. *See Fig. 1.* Remove upper intake manifold bolts. Remove upper intake manifold and throttle body assembly. Remove lower intake manifold bolts. Remove manifold and gasket.

Installation – 1) Clean gasket mating surfaces. Clean and oil bolt threads. Install new gasket. Position lower intake manifold to cylinder head and install bolts finger tight.

2) Tighten bolts in sequence to specification *See Fig. 2.* See TORQUE SPECIFICATIONS table at end of article. To complete installation, reverse removal procedure. Fill and bleed air from cooling system. See COOLING SYSTEM BLEEDING.

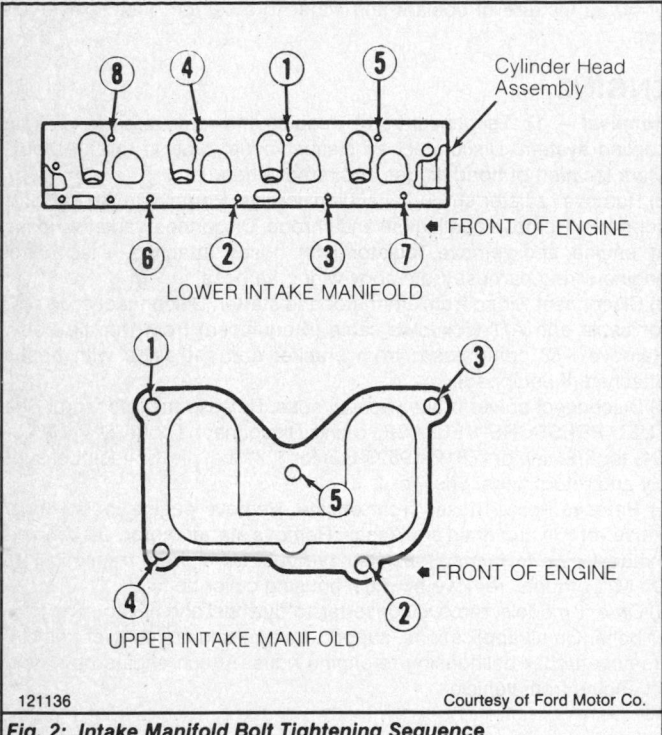

121136   Courtesy of Ford Motor Co.

Fig. 2: Intake Manifold Bolt Tightening Sequence

EXHAUST MANIFOLD

Removal & Installation – 1) Remove air cleaner and duct assembly. Remove EGR tube from exhaust manifold. Loosen EGR tube at EGR

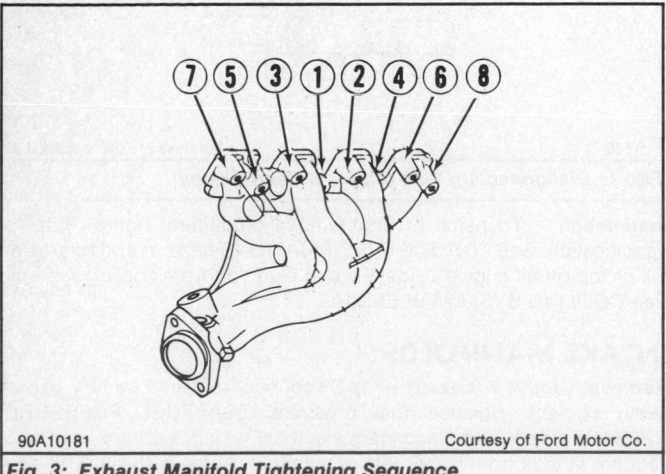

90A10181   Courtesy of Ford Motor Co.

Fig. 3: Exhaust Manifold Tightening Sequence

---

valve. Disconnect oxygen sensor. Remove coil pack from cylinder head and secure it aside. Remove heat shield from exhaust manifold.

2) Remove exhaust manifold mounting bolts and exhaust pipe bolts. Remove manifold. To install, position exhaust manifold on cylinder head; tighten bolts, in sequence, to specification in 2 steps. *See Fig. 3.* See TORQUE SPECIFICATIONS table at end of article. To complete installation, reverse removal procedure.

CYLINDER HEAD

Removal – 1) Drain cooling system. Remove air cleaner assembly and air inlet tube. Remove heater hose attached to valve cover. Remove spark plug wires. Remove spark plugs and oil dipstick. Mark and disconnect vacuum hoses. Remove valve cover.

2) Remove upper and lower intake manifolds. See INTAKE MANIFOLDS. Remove accessory belt(s). Remove alternator and bracket retaining bolts. Remove power steering pump and bracket (if equipped). Remove upper radiator hose. Remove timing belt cover and remove belt. See TIMING BELT & COVER.

3) Remove 4 nuts and/or stud bolts retaining heat stove to exhaust manifold. Remove exhaust manifold. Remove timing belt idler and 2 bracket bolts. Remove timing belt idler spring stop from cylinder head. Remove cylinder head bolts evenly. Lift cylinder head off engine, using care not to bend inner timing belt cover.

Inspection – Inspect cylinder head for warpage. Resurface if warpage exceeds specification. See CYLINDER HEAD table under ENGINE SPECIFICATIONS at end of article. DO NOT machine more than .010" (.25 mm) from original cylinder head thickness. Clean and tap cylinder head bolt holes in cylinder block.

CAUTION: Before installing cylinder head, ensure crankshaft is at TDC. Position camshaft so valves for No. 1 cylinder are closed. Failure to properly position camshaft and crankshaft may result in valves contacting pistons during installation. See Fig. 4.

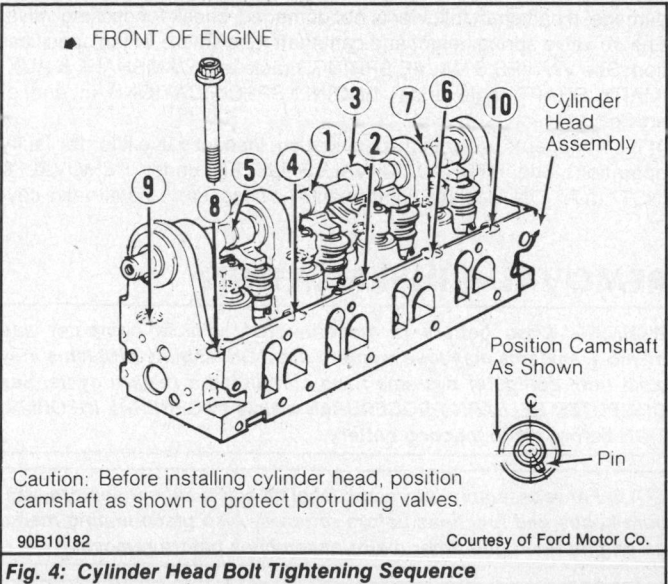

90B10182   Courtesy of Ford Motor Co.

Fig. 4: Cylinder Head Bolt Tightening Sequence

Installation – Clean all gasket mating surfaces and replace all gaskets. Install new head gasket on block. Install cylinder head and tighten bolts to specification in 2 steps, and in sequence. *See Fig. 4.* See TORQUE SPECIFICATIONS table at end of article. To complete installation, reverse removal procedure. Fill and bleed cooling system. See COOLING SYSTEM BLEEDING under REMOVAL & INSTALLATION.

CAUTION: If valves/seats were serviced, check and adjust valve clearance. See VALVE CLEARANCE ADJUSTMENT under ADJUSTMENTS.

CAMSHAFT, FRONT CRANKSHAFT & AUXILIARY SHAFT OIL SEALS

Removal – **1)** Ensure crankshaft is set at TDC and camshaft sprocket timing mark is aligned with cover pointer. *See Fig. 5.* Remove timing belt cover and timing belt. See TIMING BELT & COVER.
2) Using Crankshaft Sprocket Remover (T74P-6306-A), remove crankshaft sprocket. Using Camshaft/Auxiliary Shaft Sprocket Remover (T74P-6256-B), remove camshaft or auxiliary shaft sprocket. Using Seal Remover (T74P-6700-B), remove camshaft, crankshaft or auxiliary shaft oil seals.

CAUTION: Always rotate crankshaft in direction of normal rotation (clockwise as viewed from front of engine).

Installation – **1)** Install new seal using Seal Installer (T74P-6150-A). Install timing belt. Release belt tensioner pulley. Remove one spark plug from each cylinder to ensure timing belt does not jump timing during crankshaft rotation.
2) Rotate crankshaft clockwise 2 complete turns to remove slack from belt. Tighten tensioner adjustment and pivot bolts. To complete installation, reverse removal procedure. Fill and bleed cooling system. See COOLING SYSTEM BLEEDING under REMOVAL & INSTALLATION.

CHECKING VALVE TIMING

CAUTION: Always rotate crankshaft in direction of normal rotation (clockwise as viewed from front of engine). Reverse rotation may cause timing belt to jump time.

---

1) Remove access plug from engine timing belt cover. Rotate crankshaft clockwise and position No. 1 cylinder on TDC of compression stroke. Align crankshaft damper TDC mark with pointer on timing belt cover.
2) Looking through plug hole of outer timing belt cover, ensure camshaft sprocket timing mark is aligned with cover pointer. *See Fig. 5.* If all timing marks are not aligned, timing belt must be removed, sprockets properly positioned and timing belt reinstalled.

TIMING BELT & COVER

Removal – **1)** Ensure crankshaft is set at TDC and camshaft sprocket timing mark is aligned with cover pointer. *See Fig. 5.* Disconnect negative battery cable. Drain cooling system and remove upper radiator hose. Remove accessory belt(s). Remove spark plugs to ensure belt does not jump time during rotation.
2) Remove cooling fan and water pump pulley. Remove crankshaft pulley, hub and belt guide. Remove timing belt outer cover retaining bolt. Release 8 cover interlocking tabs. Remove timing belt cover. Loosen timing belt tensioner pulley bolt. Pry tensioner away from timing belt and tighten bolt to hold tensioner in place. Remove timing belt.

NOTE: If crankshaft timing sensor was removed, see CRANKSHAFT TIMING SENSOR for installation procedure.

CAUTION: Always rotate engine in direction of normal rotation (clockwise as viewed from front of engine).

Installation – **1)** Ensure crankshaft is set at TDC and camshaft sprocket timing mark is aligned with cover pointer. *See Fig. 5.* Install crankshaft sprocket (if removed) with recessed area toward crankshaft. *See Fig. 5.*
2) Install belt guide with flat side toward camshaft sprocket. *See Fig. 5.* Install new timing belt. Loosen tensioner bolt. Allow tensioner to adjust itself, and retighten bolt. Rotate crankshaft clockwise 2 complete turns to remove slack from belt.
3) Loosen tensioner bolt. Allow tensioner to adjust itself and retighten bolt. To complete installation, reverse removal procedure. Fill and bleed cooling system. See COOLING SYSTEM BLEEDING under REMOVAL & INSTALLATION.

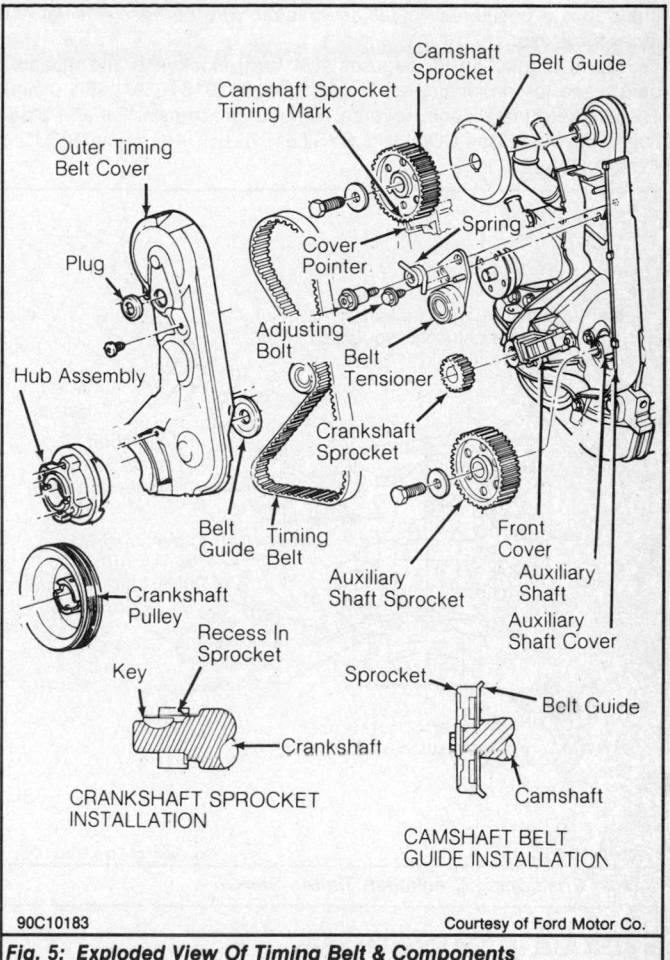

Fig. 5: Exploded View Of Timing Belt & Components

90C10183   Courtesy of Ford Motor Co.

CRANKSHAFT TIMING SENSOR

Removal – **1)** Disconnect negative battery cable. Drain cooling system and remove upper radiator hose. Remove accessory belt(s). Remove cooling fan and water pump pulley. Remove crankshaft pulley, hub and belt guide.
2) Remove thermostat housing and cover. Remove power steering pump mounting bracket and position aside. Remove timing belt outer cover retaining bolt. Release 8 cover interlocking tabs. Remove timing belt cover.

CAUTION: Always rotate engine in direction of normal rotation (clockwise as viewed from front of engine).

---

3) Disconnect crankshaft timing sensor wire connector from engine harness. Remove crankshaft timing sensor 4-wire connector by prying out Red retaining clip. Rotate crankshaft to position crankshaft keyway at 10 o'clock position.
4) This will place vane window of both inner and outer vane cups over the crankshaft timing sensor. Remove crankshaft timing sensor retaining bolts and plastic wire harness retainer. Remove crankshaft timing sensor assembly.
Installation – **1)** Position crankshaft timing sensor wires behind the inner timing belt cover. Hold crankshaft timing sensor in place and install bolts finger tight. DO NOT tighten. Reconnect wire connectors to engine harness.
2) With Crankshaft Sensor Positioner (T89P-6316-A) in place, rotate crankshaft until outer vane on crankshaft pulley hub assembly engages both sides of crankshaft sensor positioner. *See Fig. 6.* Tighten crankshaft timing sensor bolts.
3) Rotate crankshaft until vane on crankshaft pulley hub assembly is no longer engaged in crankshaft sensor positioner. Remove crank-

shaft sensor positioner. Install new plastic wire harness retainer and trim off excess.

4) Rotate crankshaft 90 degrees (1/4 turn) clockwise and measure outer vane-to-sensor air gap. Air gap must be .018-.039" (.46-1.0 mm). To complete installation, reverse removal procedure. Fill and bleed cooling system. See COOLING SYSTEM BLEEDING under REMOVAL & INSTALLATION.

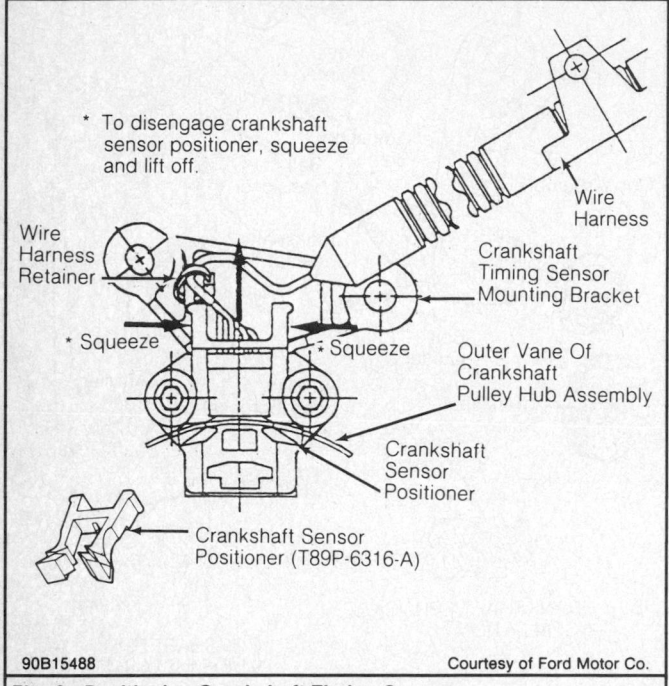

90B15488   Courtesy of Ford Motor Co.

Fig. 6: Positioning Crankshaft Timing Sensor

HYDRAULIC VALVE LIFTER

Removal – Remove valve cover. Rotate camshaft so base circle of cam is facing the lifter to be removed. Using Valve Spring Compressor Lever (T88T-6565-BH), collapse valve spring and rotate cam follower to one side. Remove valve lifter.
Inspection – Replace valve lifters as complete assemblies only. Test lifters with Leak-Down Tester 6500-E. Lifters cannot be checked with engine oil in them. Use hydraulic tester fluid. Fluid can be obtained from tester manufacturer. Time required for the plunger to leak down 1/8" (3.2 mm) travel with 50-lb. load is 2-8 seconds.
Installation – To install, reverse removal procedure.

CAMSHAFT

NOTE: To ensure installation to original location, keep all components in order.

Removal – **1)** Drain cooling system. Remove air cleaner assembly. Mark and disconnect spark plug wires and vacuum hoses. Remove valve cover. Remove upper radiator hose. Remove alternator belt. Remove alternator mounting bracket bolts and position bracket aside. Remove fan shroud.
2) Remove timing belt. See TIMING BELT & COVER under REMOVAL & INSTALLATION. Remove camshaft sprocket using Cam and Auxiliary Shaft Sprocket Remover (T74P-6256-B). Using a Valve Spring Compressor Lever (T88T-6565-BH), depress and remove camshaft followers. Remove camshaft seal using Seal Remover (T74P-6700-B).
3) Check camshaft end play. If end play is not within specification, replace thrust plate. See CAMSHAFT & AUXILIARY SHAFT table under ENGINE SPECIFICATIONS at end of article. Remove camshaft rear thrust plate. Raise vehicle and remove both left and right engine support bolts and nuts.
4) Place a block of wood between engine block and transmission jack. Raise engine as high as it will go. Place block of wood between engine

mount and chassis brackets. Carefully remove camshaft to avoid damaging journals and lobes.

NOTE: When replacing camshaft, ensure threaded plug is in the rear of new camshaft. If plug is missing, remove threaded plug from old camshaft and install.

Inspection – **1)** Clean all components and gasket mating surfaces. Check lobe lift and camshaft-to-bearing clearance. To check camshaft lobe lift, measure distances "A" and "B" of each cam lobe. *See Fig. 7.*
2) Distance "A" minus distance "B" equals cam lobe lift. Check lift of each lobe and note all readings. If readings are not within specification, replace camshaft and all rocker arms. See CAMSHAFT & AUXILIARY SHAFT table under ENGINE SPECIFICATIONS at end of article.

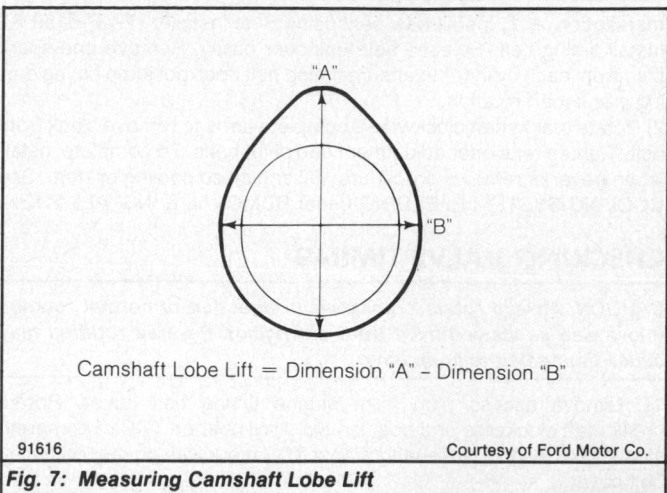

Camshaft Lobe Lift = Dimension "A" – Dimension "B"

91616   Courtesy of Ford Motor Co.

Fig. 7: Measuring Camshaft Lobe Lift

Installation – **1)** Completely dip camshaft in engine oil. Carefully slide camshaft into cylinder head. Lower engine and tighten engine mount bolts or nuts. Install camshaft rear thrust plate. Recheck camshaft end play.
2) If end play is not within specification, replace thrust plate. See CAMSHAFT & AUXILIARY SHAFT table under ENGINE SPECIFICATIONS at end of article. Lubricate camshaft seal and install using Seal Installer (T74P-6150-A). Install camshaft sprocket. To complete installation, reverse removal procedure. Fill and bleed cooling system. See COOLING SYSTEM BLEEDING under REMOVAL & INSTALLATION.

AUXILIARY SHAFT

Removal & Installation – **1)** Remove timing belt. See TIMING BELT & COVER under REMOVAL & INSTALLATION. Remove auxiliary shaft sprocket bolt and remove sprocket. Check auxiliary shaft end play. If end play is not within specification, replace thrust plate. See CAMSHAFT & AUXILIARY SHAFT table under ENGINE SPECIFICATIONS at end of article.
2) Remove thrust plate bolts and remove thrust plate. Carefully pull out auxiliary shaft. If bearings are to be replaced, use a slide hammer with Puller Attachment Tool (T58L-101-B) to remove bearings, and a driver to install bearings. Ensure oil holes in bearings align with oil holes in cylinder block.
3) To install, completely dip auxiliary shaft in engine oil. Carefully slide shaft into bore. Ensure shaft rotates freely. To complete installation, reverse removal procedure.

REAR CRANKSHAFT OIL SEAL

Removal & Installation – Remove transmission. Remove flywheel/flexplate. Remove rear oil seal with slide hammer. Use care not to damage crankshaft sealing surface. Coat seal surfaces with engine oil. Using Rear Main Bearing Seal Installer (T82L-6701-A), install seal until firmly seated. *See Fig. 8.* To complete installation, reverse removal procedure.

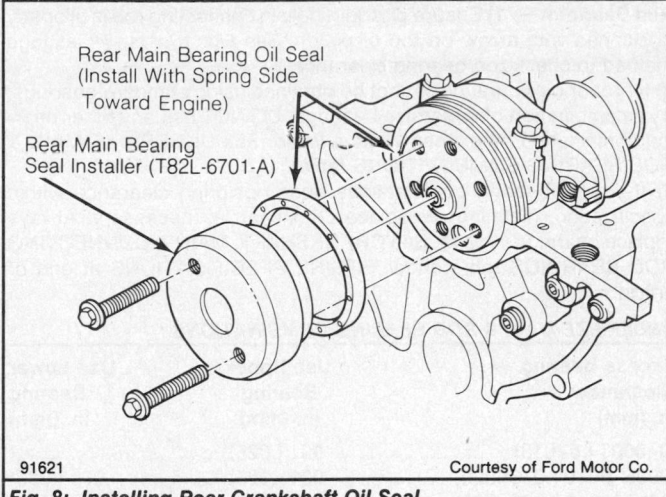

Fig. 8: Installing Rear Crankshaft Oil Seal

91621   Courtesy of Ford Motor Co.

WATER PUMP

Removal – 1) Drain cooling system. Remove accessory belts. Remove fan shroud and position over fan. Remove 4 fan retaining bolts. Remove fan and pulley.
2) Remove vent tube to canister. Remove heater hose from water pump. Remove timing belt cover. See TIMING BELT & COVER under REMOVAL & INSTALLATION. Remove lower radiator hose from water pump. Remove water pump from engine.
Installation – Ensure gasket surfaces are clean. Apply Teflon sealant to water pump bolts before installation. To complete installation, reverse removal procedure. Fill and bleed cooling system. See COOLING SYSTEM BLEEDING under REMOVAL & INSTALLATION.

OIL PAN

Removal & Installation – 1) Remove engine assembly. See ENGINE under REMOVAL & INSTALLATION. Mount engine on engine stand. Remove oil pan retaining bolts and remove pan. To install, use a new oil pan gasket. Install oil pan so the transmission mounting face of oil pan is even with engine block rear face.

NOTE: The transmission bolts to the engine and oil pan. It is necessary to measure the gap between the rear face of oil pan and rear face of engine block.

---

2) Tighten oil pan retaining bolts. *See Fig. 9.* Place a straightedge across engine block and oil pan-to-transmission bolt mounting pads. Use a feeler gauge to measure gap between mounting pad and straightedge. Repeat procedure on opposite mounting pad.
3) If necessary, select spacers and install to mounting pads on oil pan before bolting engine and transmission together. See SPACER SELECTION table. To complete installation, reverse removal procedure.

SPACER SELECTION

Measured Gap In. (mm)	Spacer/Color In. (mm)
0-.010 (0-.254)	None
.011-.020 (.27-.51)	.010 (.254) Yellow
.021-.030 (.52-.76)	.020 (.51) Blue
.031-.040 (.78-1.01)	.030 (.762) Pink

CAUTION: Failure to measure gap and install spacer can result in insufficient or excessive space between oil pan transmission. This can cause oil pan damage or oil leaks.

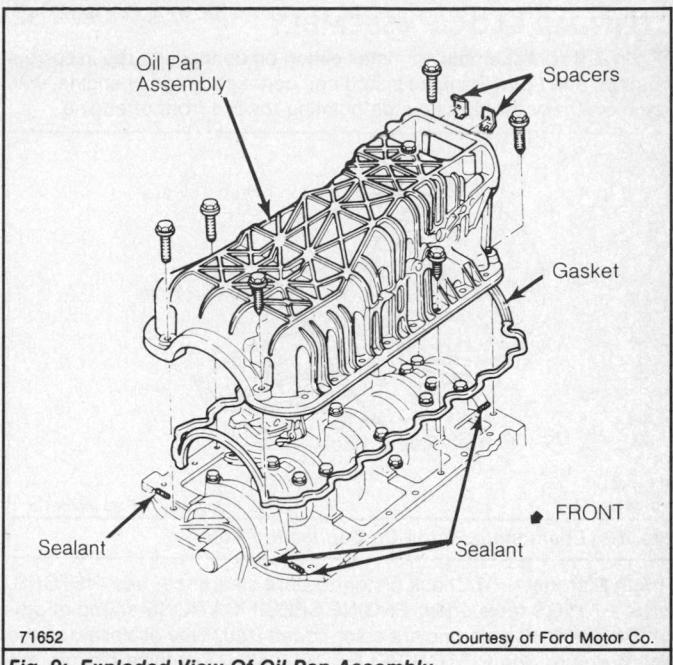

Fig. 9: Exploded View Of Oil Pan Assembly

71652   Courtesy of Ford Motor Co.

OVERHAUL

CYLINDER HEAD

Cylinder Head – Inspect cylinder head for warpage. Resurface cylinder head if warpage exceeds specification. DO NOT machine more than .010" (.25 mm) from original cylinder head thickness. See CYLINDER HEAD table under ENGINE SPECIFICATIONS at end of article.
Valve Springs – 1) Check valve spring installed height from top spring coil to spring seat of cylinder head. If installed height is greater than specification, spacer(s) may be installed between cylinder head and valve spring to obtain correct installed height. See VALVES & VALVE SPRINGS table under ENGINE SPECIFICATIONS at end of article.

CAUTION: DO NOT install spacers unless necessary. Use of excess spacers will cause premature component failure.

---

2) With spring(s) removed, measure spring out-of-square, free length and pressure at specified length. If measurements are not within specification, replace spring(s). See VALVES & VALVE SPRINGS table.
Valve Stem Oil Seals – Use Valve Stem Oil Seal Installer (T87L-6571-AH) to install seal. Install seal until it bottoms on valve guide. Oversize seals must be used on guides that have been reamed for oversize valves.
Valve Guides – Valve guides must be reamed for an oversized valve if valve stem oil clearance is not within specification. See CYLINDER HEAD table under ENGINE SPECIFICATIONS at end of article. Always use reamers in proper sequence (smallest first). If oversized valve or valve stem seal is not available, valve guide may be bored out to use a service bushing.

NOTE: Always grind valve seat after valve guide has been reamed or service bushing has been installed.

Valve Seat – Grind valve seat to a 45-degree angle. If seat width is too wide after grinding, use a 30-degree stone to lower seat or a 60-degree stone to raise seat.
Valves – Check valve stem diameter and stem clearance. During valve grinding, DO NOT remove more than .010" (.25 mm) from end of valve stem. After grinding, ensure margin is within specifications.

CYLINDER BLOCK ASSEMBLY

Piston & Rod Assembly – Install piston on connecting rod in correct location. *See Fig. 10.* Install piston and connecting rod in engine, with notch or arrow on top of piston pointing toward front of engine.

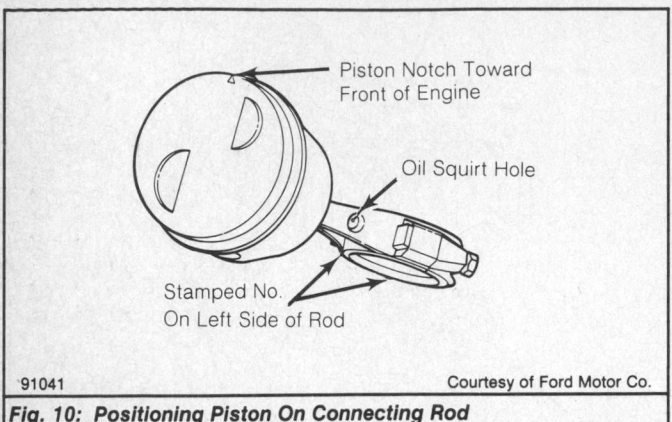

91041   Courtesy of Ford Motor Co.

Fig. 10: Positioning Piston On Connecting Rod

Fitting Pistons – **1)** Check piston-to-bore clearance. See PISTONS, PINS & RINGS table under ENGINE SPECIFICATIONS at end of article. Standard size pistons are color-coded Red, Blue or Yellow on the piston dome. See PISTON SELECTION table. Oversize pistons are also available.

2) If bore diameter is in lower one-third of specification, use a Red-coded piston. If bore diameter is in middle one-third of specification, use a Blue-coded piston. If bore diameter is in upper one-third of specification, use a Yellow-coded piston. Use proper size piston to obtain specified clearance.

PISTON SELECTION

Cylinder Bore Diameter In. (mm)	Piston Color Code
3.7795-3.7810 (95.999-96.037)	Red
3.7810-3.7825 (96.037-96.076)	Blue
3.7825-3.7840 (96.076-96.114)	Yellow

Piston Rings – **1)** Select proper ring set for bore diameter. Place ring in cylinder bore in which it will be installed. Use piston to square ring and place ring below normal ring wear area. Measure ring end gap. If ring gap is not within specification, try another ring set. See PISTONS, PINS & RINGS table under ENGINE SPECIFICATIONS at end of article.

2) Check side clearance of rings after installing on piston. Ensure clearance is within specification around entire circumference. Replace piston and/or rings if clearance is not within specification. See PISTONS, PINS & RINGS table. Ensure rings are properly spaced on piston before installing piston into cylinder. *See Fig. 11.*

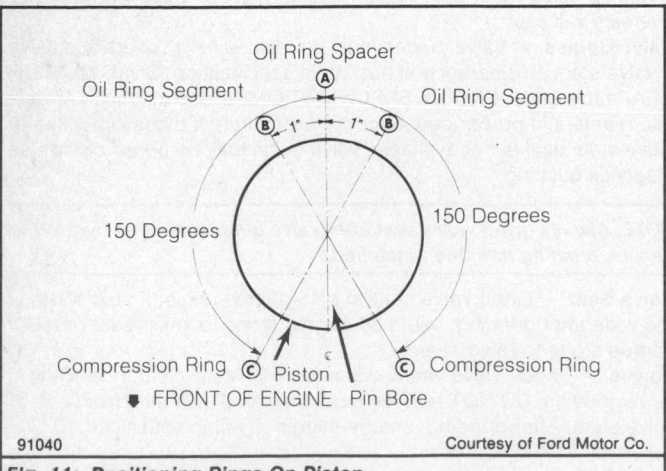

91040   Courtesy of Ford Motor Co.

Fig. 11: Positioning Rings On Piston

Rod Bearings – **1)** Ensure oil squirt hole in connecting rod is properly positioned with arrow on top of piston. *See Fig. 10.* Use Plastigage method to check rod bearing clearance.

2) If proper oil clearance cannot be obtained using standard bearings, try a combination of undersize bearings. DO NOT use any other bearing combination other than what is listed. See UNDERSIZE MAIN & ROD BEARING COMBINATIONS table.

3) If use of bearing combinations does not bring clearance within specification, machine or replace crankshaft as necessary. Always replace bearings in pairs. See CRANKSHAFT, MAIN & CONNECTING ROD BEARINGS table under ENGINE SPECIFICATIONS at end of article.

UNDERSIZE MAIN & ROD BEARING COMBINATIONS [1]

Excess Bearing Clearance In. (mm)	Use Upper Bearing In. (mm)	Use Lower Bearing In. (mm)
.0-.0005 (.0-.013)	.001 (.025)	[2]
.0005-.0010 (.013-.026)	.001 (.025)	.001 (.025)
.0010-.0015 (.026-.039)	.002 (.05)	.001 (.025)
.0015-.0020 (.039-.052)	.002 (.05)	.002 (.05)

[1] – DO NOT use any other bearing combination other than what is listed. If use of bearing combinations does not bring clearance within specification, machine or replace crankshaft as necessary.

[2] – Use standard bearing.

Crankshaft & Main Bearings – **1)** When checking main bearing clearance in vehicle, position a jack under adjoining bearing counterweight being checked. Remove only one main bearing cap at a time.

2) Use Plastigage method to check main bearing clearance. If clearance is not within specification, replace bearings. Machine or replace crankshaft as necessary. See CRANKSHAFT, MAIN & CONNECTING ROD BEARINGS table under ENGINE SPECIFICATIONS at end of article.

3) If proper oil clearance cannot be obtained using standard bearings, try a combination of undersize bearings. DO NOT use any other bearing combination other than what is listed. See UNDERSIZE MAIN & ROD BEARING COMBINATIONS table.

4) If use of bearing combinations does not bring clearance within specification, machine or replace crankshaft as necessary. Always replace bearings in pairs. See CRANKSHAFT, MAIN & CONNECTING ROD BEARINGS table under ENGINE SPECIFICATIONS.

5) Tighten main bearing cap bolts finger tight. Pry crankshaft forward and tighten bearing caps to specification. See TORQUE SPECIFICATIONS table at end of article.

6) Check crankshaft end play. Replace thrust bearing if end play is not within specification. Thrust bearing is No. 3 (from front) main bearing in block. See CRANKSHAFT, MAIN & CONNECTING ROD BEARINGS table under ENGINE SPECIFICATIONS.

Cylinder Block – **1)** Using a feeler gauge and straightedge, check cylinder block head gasket surface for warpage. DO NOT machine more than .010" (.25 mm) from original gasket surface. Check cylinder bore for wear, taper, out-of-round and piston fit. Repair or replace as necessary. See CYLINDER BLOCK table under ENGINE SPECIFICATIONS at end of article.

2) Install all main bearing caps and tighten to specification before honing cylinder bore. See TORQUE SPECIFICATIONS table at end of article. Use ONLY a spring-loaded type cylinder hone. After honing, thoroughly clean bore with detergent and water solution. Rinse solution from bore thoroughly with clean water. Wipe bore clean with lint free cloth. Lubricate cylinder bores with engine oil.

ENGINE OILING

ENGINE LUBRICATION SYSTEM

System is pressure fed from a rotor-type oil pump. Oil flows through oil filter before entering main oil gallery. *See Fig. 12.*

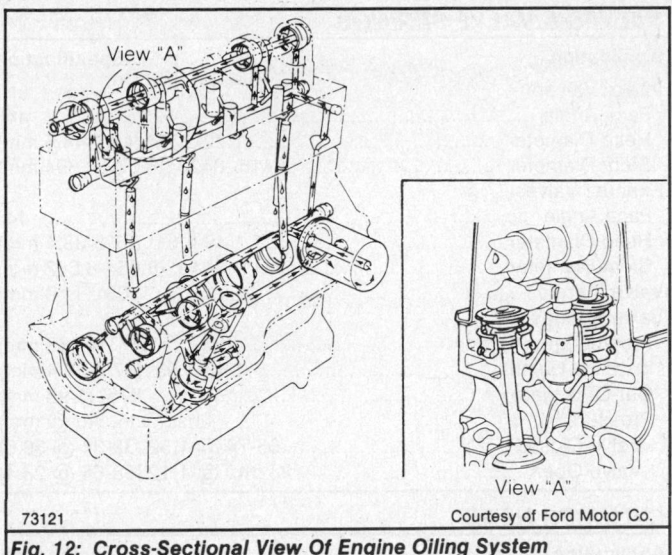

Fig. 12: Cross-Sectional View Of Engine Oiling System

73121 — Courtesy of Ford Motor Co.

Crankcase Capacity – Crankcase capacity is 4 qts. (3.79L) without oil filter and 5 qts. (4.74L) with oil filter.

Oil Pressure – Normal oil pressure at 2000 RPM should be 40-60 psi (2.8-4.2 kg/cm²) with engine at normal operating temperature.

Oil Pressure Relief Valve – Oil pressure relief valve is located in oil pump body. Valve is not adjustable.

OIL PUMP

Removal & Disassembly – 1) Remove oil pan. See OIL PAN under REMOVAL & INSTALLATION. Disconnect pick-up tube from main bearing cap stud. Remove oil pump attaching bolts. Remove oil pump assembly with oil pump drive shaft.
2) Remove pick-up tube from pump. Disassemble oil pump. Note direction of component installation for reassembly reference.

Inspection – Inspect components for damage. Measure rotor end clearance, outer race-to-housing clearance and rotor tip clearance. Check clearance between pressure relief valve and bore. Measure relief valve tension. Replace oil pump assembly if measurements are not within specifications. See OIL PUMP SPECIFICATIONS table.

OIL PUMP SPECIFICATIONS

Application	In. (mm)
Drive Shaft-To-Housing	
Bearing Clearance	.0015-.0030 (.038-.076)
Maximum Assembled	
Rotor End Clearance	.004 (.10)
Maximum Rotor Tip Clearance	.012 (.30)
Outer Race-To-Housing	
Clearance	.001-.013 (.03-.33)
Relief Valve-To-Bore	
Clearance	.0015-.0030 (.038-.076)
Relief Valve Spring Tension	¹

¹ – Spring tension should be 12.6-14.5 lbs. @ 1.20" (5.7-6.8 kg @ 30.5 mm).

Reassembly & Installation – To reassemble, reverse disassembly procedure. Ensure rotors are installed in original location. Ensure oil pump spins freely after reassembly. To install, reverse removal procedure using new gaskets. Prime oil pump assembly before installation.

TORQUE SPECIFICATIONS

TORQUE SPECIFICATIONS

Application	Ft. Lbs. (N.m)
Auxiliary Shaft Sprocket Bolt	28-40 (38-54)
Bellhousing-To-Engine Bolt	28-38 (38-51)
Camshaft Sprocket Bolt	50-71 (68-97)

TORQUE SPECIFICATIONS (Cont.)

Application	Ft. Lbs. (N.m)
Connecting Rod Cap Nut	
Step 1	25-30 (34-41)
Step 2	30-36 (41-49)
Crankshaft Damper Bolt	103-133 (140-180)
Cylinder Head Bolt ¹	
Step 1	50-60 (68-81)
Step 2	80-90 (109-122)
Engine Mount Bracket-To-Engine Bolt	45-60 (62-81)
Engine Mount Nuts	65-85 (88-115)
Engine Mount-To- Bracket Bolt	65-85 (88-115)
Exhaust Manifold Bolt ²	
Step 1	15-17 (20-23)
Step 2	20-30 (27-41)
Flexplate-To-Converter Bolt	20-34 (27-46)
Flywheel-To-Crankshaft Bolt	56-64 (76-87)
Lower Intake Manifold Bolt ³	15-22 (20-30)
Main Bearing Cap Nut	
Step 1	50-60 (68-81)
Step 2	75-85 (102-115)
Oil Pan-To-Transmission Bolt	30-39 (41-53)
Oil Pump Pick-Up Tube Nut	30-41 (41-56)
Oil Pump-To-Block Bolt	15-22 (20-30)
Rear Mount-To-Crossmember Nut	65-80 (88-108)
Rear Mount-To-Transmission Bolt	60-80 (81-108)
Starter Bolt	15-20 (20-27)
Transmission Oil Cooler Lines	16-22 (22-30)
Upper Intake Manifold Bolt ³	15-22 (20-30)
Water Pump Bolt ⁴	15-22 (20-30)

	INCH Lbs. (N.m)
Auxiliary Shaft Thrust Plate Bolt	72-108 (8-12)
Camshaft Thrust Plate Bolt	72-108 (8-12)
Engine Timing Belt Cover Bolt	72-108 (8-12)
Oil Pan-To-Block Bolt	90-120 (10-14)
Spark Plug	60-120 (7-14)
Valve Cover Bolt	60-97 (7-11)

¹ – Tighten in proper sequence. *See Fig. 4.*
² – Tighten in proper sequence. *See Fig. 3.*
³ – Tighten in proper sequence. *See Fig. 2.*
⁴ – Apply sealant to bolt threads.

ENGINE SPECIFICATIONS

GENERAL SPECIFICATIONS

Application	Specification
Displacement	140 Cu. In. (2.3L)
Bore	3.78" (96.0 mm)
Stroke	3.126" (79.40 mm)
Compression Ratio	9.5:1
Fuel System	PFI
Horsepower @ RPM	90 @ 4000
Torque Ft. Lbs.@ RPM	134 @ 2000

CONNECTING RODS

Application	In. (mm)
Bore Diameter	
Pin Bore	.9096-.9112 (23.104-23.144)
Center-To-Center Length	5.2031-5.2063 (132.159-132.240)
Maximum Bend	.012 (.30)
Maximum Twist	.024 (.61)
Side Play	
Standard	.0035-.0105 (.089-.267)
Service Limit	.014 (.36)

CRANKSHAFT, MAIN & CONNECTING ROD BEARINGS

Application	In. (mm)
Crankshaft	
End Play	
Desired	.004-.008 (.10-.20)
Allowable	.012 (.30)
Main Bearings	
Journal Diameter	2.3982-2.3990 (60.914-60.935)
Journal Out-Of-Round	.0006 (.015)
Journal Taper [1]	.0006 (.015)
Oil Clearance	
Desired	.0008-.0015 (.020-.038)
Allowable	.0008-.0026 (.020-.066)
Connecting Rod Bearings	
Journal Diameter	2.0462-2.0472 (51.973-51.998)
Journal Out-Of-Round	.0006 (.015)
Journal Taper [1]	.0006 (.015)
Oil Clearance	
Desired	.0008-.0015 (.020-.038)
Allowable	.0008-.0026 (.020-.066)

[1] – Specification listed is per 1" (25.4 mm)

PISTONS, PINS & RINGS

Application	In. (mm)
Pistons	
Clearance	.0014-.0022 (.036-.056)
Diameter [1]	
Red	3.7768-3.7779 (95.931-95.959)
Pins	
Diameter [2]	.9119-.9124 (23.162-23.175)
Piston Fit	.0002-.0004 (.005-.010)
Rod Fit	Press Fit
Rings	
No. 1 & 2	
End Gap	.010-.020 (.25-.50)
Side Clearance	.002-.004 (.05-.10)
No. 3 (Oil)	
End Gap (Steel Rail)	.015-.049 (.38-1.24)
Side Clearance	Snug Fit

[1] – Diameter of Blue and Yellow pistons are not available from manufacturer. Piston diameter is measured at .57" (14.6 mm) from bottom of skirt, at 90 degrees to piston pin. To select correct pistons, see FITTING PISTONS under CYLINDER BLOCK ASSEMBLY.

[2] – Standard diameter listed. Available in .001" (.02 mm) and .002" (.05 mm) oversize.

CYLINDER BLOCK

Application	In. (mm)
Cylinder Bore	
Standard Diameter	3.7795-3.7825 (95.999-96.076)
Maximum Deck Warpage [1]	.003 (.08)
Maximum Out-Of-Round	.0015 (.038)
Maximum Taper	.010 (.25)

[1] – Specification listed is per 6" (152.4 mm). Maximum of .006" (.15 mm) overall. DO NOT machine more than .010" (.25 mm) from original gasket surface.

VALVES & VALVE SPRINGS

Application	Specification
Intake Valves	
Face Angle	44°
Head Diameter	1.72-1.75" (43.7-44.5 mm)
Stem Diameter	.3416-.3423" (8.677-8.694 mm)
Exhaust Valves	
Face Angle	44°
Head Diameter	1.49-1.51" (37.8-38.4 mm)
Stem Diameter	.3411-.3418" (8.664-8.682 mm)
Valve Margin	.031" (.79 mm)
Valve Springs	
Free Length (Approx.)	1.877" (47.68 mm)
Installed Height	1.49-1.55" (37.8-39.4 mm)
Out-Of-Square	.078" (1.98 mm)
Pressure	Lbs. @ In. (kg @ mm)
Valve Closed	66-74 @ 1.52 (30-34 @ 38.6)
Valve Open	128-142 @ 1.12 (58-64 @ 28.4)

CYLINDER HEAD

Application	Specification
Maximum Warpage [1]	.003" (.08 mm)
Valve Seats	
Intake Valve	
Seat Angle	45°
Seat Width	.060-.080" (1.52-2.03 mm)
Maximum Seat Runout	.0016" (.041 mm)
Exhaust Valve	
Seat Angle	45°
Seat Width	.070-.090" (1.78-2.29 mm)
Maximum Seat Runout	.0016" (.041 mm)
Valve Guides	
Intake Valve	
Valve Stem-To-Guide	
Oil Clearance	
Standard	.0010-.0027" (.025-.069 mm)
Service Limit	.0055" (.140 mm)
Exhaust Valve	
Valve Stem-To-Guide	
Oil Clearance	
Standard	.0015-.0032" (.038-.081 mm)
Service Limit	.0055" (.140 mm)

[1] – Specification listed is taken within a 6" (152 mm) area. Overall warpage is .006" (.15 mm). DO NOT machine more than .010" (.25 mm) from original gasket surface.

VALVE LIFTERS

Application	In. (mm)
Bore Diameter	.8430-.9449 (21.412-24.000)
Collapsed Lifter Clearance	
Desired	.040-.050 (1.02-1.27)
Allowable	.035-.055 (.89-1.40)
Lifter Diameter	.8422-.8427 (21.392-21.405)
Oil Clearance	.0007-.0027 (.018-.069)

CAMSHAFT & AUXILIARY SHAFT

Application	In. (mm)
Auxiliary Shaft	
End Play	.001-.007 (.03-.18)
Camshaft	
End Play	
Standard	.001-.007 (.03-.18)
Service Limit	.006 (.15)
Journal Diameter	1.7713-1.7720 (44.991-45.009)
Lobe Lift	.2381 (6.048)
Oil Clearance	
Standard	.001-.003 (.03-.08)
Service Limit	.006 (.15)

Ranger

NOTE: For repair procedures not covered in this article, see ENGINE OVERHAUL PROCEDURES article in GENERAL INFORMATION.

ENGINE IDENTIFICATION

Engine is identified by the eighth character of Vehicle Identification Number (VIN). The VIN is stamped on a metal plate, and is visible through windshield on left upper side of instrument panel. VIN is also located on Safety Compliance Certification Label attached to left door or left door pillar.

VIN ENGINE CODE

Engine	Code
2.9L PFI	T

ADJUSTMENTS

VALVE CLEARANCE ADJUSTMENT

1) Adjust one cylinder at a time. Rotate crankshaft and position valve being adjusted on lowest portion of camshaft lobe (valve completely closed). Loosen adjusting screw until rocker arm backlash is achieved. Turn in adjusting screw until rocker arm initially contacts valve tip.

2) To achieve nominal working position of valve lifter, turn in adjusting screw 2 turns, or the equivalent of .11" (2.7 mm). Repeat procedure to adjust remaining valves.

REMOVAL & INSTALLATION

WARNING: When battery is disconnected, vehicle computer and memory systems may lose memory data. Driveability problems may exist until computer systems have completed a relearn cycle. See COMPUTER RELEARN PROCEDURES article in GENERAL INFORMATION before disconnecting battery.

NOTE: For installation reference, label all electrical connectors, vacuum hoses and fuel lines before removal. Also place mating marks on engine hood and other major assemblies before removal.

NOTE: Discharge A/C system using approved refrigerant recovery/recycling equipment.

FUEL PRESSURE RELEASE

To release fuel pressure, disconnect negative battery cable. Remove fuel cap to release fuel tank pressure. Remove relief valve cap from fuel rail. Connect fuel pressure gauge to relief valve and release fuel pressure into a suitable container.

COOLING SYSTEM BLEEDING

1) Fill cooling system with 50/50 mixture of coolant and water. Pause several minutes for circulation. Fill radiator to filler neck seat. Install radiator cap fully, then back off to first stop.

WARNING: NEVER remove radiator cap with engine operating under any conditions. Failure to follow instruction may cause damage to cooling system, engine or personal injury. Always wrap protective material around radiator cap to avoid injury from hot coolant.

2) Place heater controls to maximum heat. Start engine and operate at 2000 RPM for approximately 3-4 minutes. Turn engine off. Using a protective rag, carefully remove radiator cap. Add coolant to filler neck seat.

3) Install radiator cap fully and back off to first stop. Start engine and allow to operate at 2000 RPM until upper radiator hose is warm. Check heater output. Turn engine off. Using a rag, carefully remove radiator cap. Add coolant to filler neck seat if necessary.

4) Tightly install radiator cap. Remove small cap (large cap is for windshield washer reservoir) on coolant recovery reservoir. Add 1.1 qt. (1L) of 50/50 water and coolant mixture to reservoir. Install reservoir cap.

ENGINE

Removal – 1) Disconnect negative battery cable and drain cooling system. Remove hood, air cleaner and intake duct assembly. Remove fan shroud and position over fan. Remove radiator with hoses and shroud. Remove alternator and bracket.

2) Remove A/C compressor and power steering pump with hoses attached (if equipped). Disconnect heater hoses from engine. Release fuel pressure. See FUEL PRESSURE RELEASE. Disconnect fuel supply line from fuel injector rail. Using Fuel Line Coupling Key (T90P-9550-A), disconnect fuel return line from fuel pressure regulator. *See Fig. 1.*

3) Disconnect brake booster vacuum hose. Disconnect throttle cable linkage and shield at throttle body and intake manifold. Disconnect all vacuum hoses from rear vacuum fitting in upper intake manifold.

4) Disconnect wiring from coil, oil pressure sending unit and engine coolant temperature sending units. Disconnect injector harness, air charge temperature sensor and throttle position sensor.

5) Raise and support vehicle. Disconnect exhaust pipes from manifolds. Remove starter and front engine mount nuts or through bolts. Remove ground wires from engine block. On A/T vehicles, remove converter inspection cover and disconnect flywheel from converter.

6) Remove kickdown rod and bellhousing mounting bolts. Remove adapter plate-to-converter housing bolt. On M/T vehicles, remove clutch housing bolts and hydraulic clutch hose. On all models, remove engine front support-to-crossmember nuts and bolts.

7) Lower vehicle and attach engine hoist to brackets at exhaust manifolds. Ensure all wires and hoses are disconnected before raising engine. Support transmission. Raise engine slightly and carefully pull engine forward from transmission without damaging rear cover plate. Remove engine from vehicle.

Installation – To install, reverse removal procedure. Tighten bolts to specification. See TORQUE SPECIFICATIONS table at end of article. Fill or top off all engine fluids. Fill and bleed air from cooling system. See COOLING SYSTEM BLEEDING.

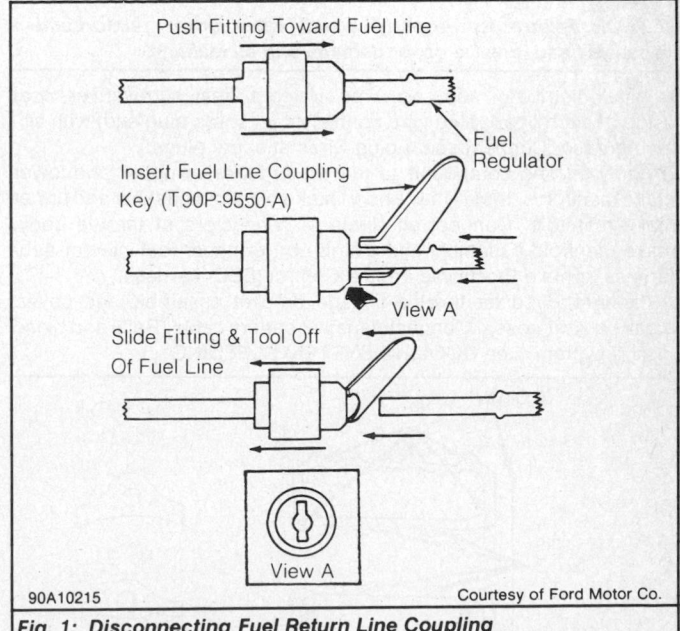

Push Fitting Toward Fuel Line

Insert Fuel Line Coupling Key (T90P-9550-A)

Fuel Regulator

View A

Slide Fitting & Tool Off Of Fuel Line

View A

90A10215

Courtesy of Ford Motor Co.

Fig. 1: Disconnecting Fuel Return Line Coupling

INTAKE MANIFOLDS

Removal (Upper & Lower) – 1) Disconnect negative battery cable. Remove air intake duct. Release fuel system pressure. See FUEL PRESSURE RELEASE.

2) Disconnect fuel supply line from fuel rail. Using Fuel Line Coupling Key (T90P-9550-A), disconnect fuel return line from pressure regulator. *See Fig. 1.* Disconnect throttle cable and bracket assembly.

3) Disconnect vacuum hoses from upper intake manifold. Disconnect electrical connectors at throttle body, upper and lower intake manifolds and distributor. Disconnect fuel injector wiring harness.

4) Remove upper intake manifold. Drain cooling system. Remove coolant hoses as necessary. Remove distributor cap and spark plug wires as an assembly. Rotate engine and position No. 1 cylinder on TDC of compression stroke.

5) Mark location of distributor rotor and housing for installation. Remove distributor hold-down and distributor. Note location of valve cover reinforcement pieces and remove valve covers.

6) Remove lower intake manifold bolts/nuts, noting length of bolts for installation to original position. Remove lower intake manifold. Remove gasket material from lower intake manifold and cylinder block.

Installation – 1) Apply sealing compound to mating surfaces. Place new lower intake manifold gasket into position. Ensure tab on right cylinder head gasket fits into cutout in lower intake manifold gasket.

2) Apply sealing compound to attaching bolt bosses on lower intake manifold and position manifold onto engine. Tighten bolts in sequence to specification. *See Fig. 2.* See TORQUE SPECIFICATIONS table at end of article.

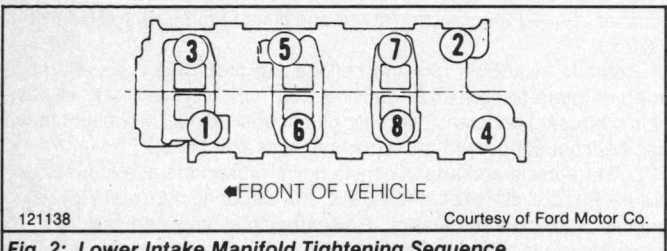

121138   Courtesy of Ford Motor Co.

Fig. 2: Lower Intake Manifold Tightening Sequence

3) Noting reference marks made in removal procedure, install distributor. Install new valve cover gaskets and valve covers. Install valve cover retaining bolts with reinforcement pieces in original position. *See Fig. 3.*

CAUTION: Failure to properly install valve cover reinforcement pieces will cause valve cover damage and oil leakage.

4) Install distributor cap and wires. Using a small screwdriver, coat inside of each spark plug wire connector (at spark plug end) with silicone grease. Connect spark plug wires at spark plugs.

5) Apply sealing compound to mating surfaces of upper and lower intake manifolds. Install new upper intake manifold gaskets and upper intake manifold. Connect all electrical connectors at throttle body, intake manifold assembly and distributor. Connect fuel injector subharness to main Electronic Engine Control (EEC) harness.

6) Install and adjust throttle linkage bracket assembly and cover. Install coolant hoses. Connect negative battery cable. Refill and bleed cooling system. See COOLING SYSTEM BLEEDING.

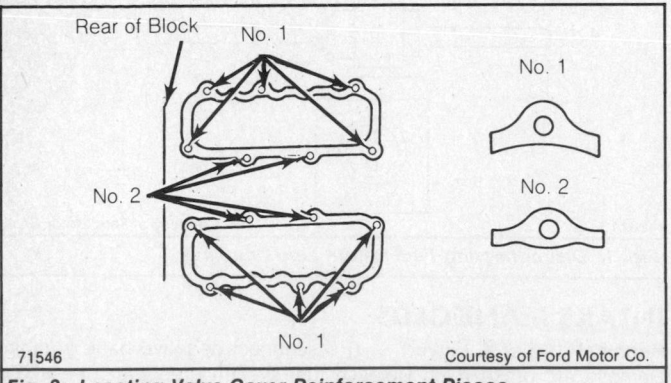

71546   Courtesy of Ford Motor Co.

Fig. 3: Locating Valve Cover Reinforcement Pieces

7) Check ignition timing and reset idle speed to specification as listed on emissions label. Run engine at fast idle and check for coolant and oil leaks.

EXHAUST MANIFOLD

Removal & Installation – Disconnect exhaust pipe from exhaust manifold. Remove exhaust manifold-to-cylinder head bolts. Lift exhaust manifold from cylinder head and out of vehicle. To install, reverse removal procedure. Tighten all bolts to specification. See TORQUE SPECIFICATIONS table at end of article.

CYLINDER HEAD

Removal – 1) Disconnect negative battery cable. Drain coolant and remove upper radiator hose. Remove upper and lower intake manifolds. See INTAKE MANIFOLDS. Remove intake tube from throttle body and disconnect throttle linkage. Remove distributor cap and wires.

2) Mark position of distributor rotor and remove distributor. Remove rocker shaft assembly. See VALVE COVER & ROCKER ARM SHAFT ASSEMBLY under REMOVAL & INSTALLATION. Remove fuel line from fuel rail. Remove push rods and keep in order for installation to original location.

3) Remove exhaust manifold from cylinder head. Loosen and remove cylinder head bolts evenly. Discard cylinder head bolts. Remove cylinder head. Remove and discard cylinder head gasket.

Inspection – Measure cylinder head and cylinder block mating surfaces for warpage. If cylinder head or cylinder block warpage exceeds specification, DO NOT remove more than .010" (.25 mm) material from original surface of cylinder head or block. See CYLINDER HEAD table under ENGINE SPECIFICATIONS at end of article.

CAUTION: Left and right head gaskets are not interchangeable. Each gasket has FRONT and TOP marks. Always use NEW cylinder head bolts.

Installation – 1) Position head gasket on cylinder block with FRONT and TOP marks in proper position. Install fabricated alignment dowels in cylinder block to keep gasket in place and assist in cylinder head alignment. Position cylinder head on block. Install NEW cylinder head bolts.

2) Tighten cylinder head bolts in sequence to specification. *See Fig. 4.* See TORQUE SPECIFICATIONS table at end of article. Apply heavy SF engine oil to both ends of push rods and install.

3) To complete installation, reverse removal procedure. Adjust valve clearance. See VALVE CLEARANCE ADJUSTMENT under ADJUSTMENTS. Fill and bleed cooling system. See COOLING SYSTEM BLEEDING under REMOVAL & INSTALLATION.

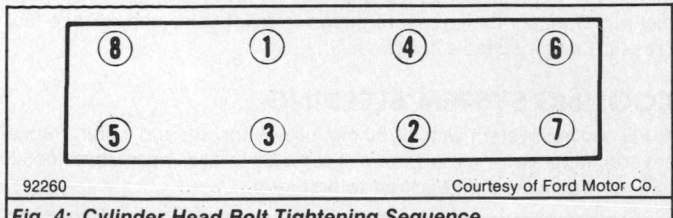

92260   Courtesy of Ford Motor Co.

Fig. 4: Cylinder Head Bolt Tightening Sequence

TIMING CHAIN COVER OIL SEAL

Removal – Drain cooling system and remove radiator. Remove water pump drive belt, crankshaft pulley and vibration damper. Use Seal Remover (1175-AC) and a slide hammer to remove timing chain cover oil seal.

Installation – Coat sealing surface of new seal with heavy SF engine oil. Slide oil seal onto crankshaft. Use Seal Installer (T47P-6700-A) to install oil seal. Install seal into recess of timing chain cover until even with surface of cover. To complete installation, reverse removal procedure. Fill and bleed cooling system. See COOLING SYSTEM BLEEDING under REMOVAL & INSTALLATION.

TIMING CHAIN & SPROCKETS

Removal – 1) Remove oil pan. See OIL PAN under REMOVAL & INSTALLATION. Position No. 1 cylinder on TDC of compression stroke. Ensure damper timing marks align properly. Drain cooling system and remove radiator. Remove heater and radiator hoses.

2) Remove accessory drive belts. Remove A/C compressor and power steering bracket (if equipped). Remove alternator and drive belt(s).

NOTE: Fan clutch nut has a left-hand thread. Remove by turning nut clockwise as viewed from front of engine.

3) Remove fan and clutch assembly using Fan Clutch Holder (T83T-6312-A) and Nut Wrench (T83T-6312-B). *See Fig. 6.* Remove timing chain cover bolts and cover. Remove water pump. Remove crankshaft damper.

CAUTION: Note timing mark alignment of camshaft and crankshaft sprockets for installation reference.

4) Secure timing chain tensioner with clip. Remove camshaft sprocket retaining bolt. Remove camshaft sprocket and timing chain. Remove crankshaft sprocket.

Installation – 1) Ensure crankshaft and camshaft are in TDC position. Slot on camshaft should face slot on crankshaft. Align position dowel on back of crankshaft sprocket with slot on crankshaft face. Install crankshaft sprocket until it seats against crankshaft.

2) Feed timing chain around crankshaft sprocket and camshaft sprocket. Install camshaft sprocket and timing chain as an assembly. Install camshaft sprocket bolt and tighten to specification. See TORQUE SPECIFICATIONS table at end of article.

3) To complete installation, reverse removal procedure. Fill and bleed cooling system. See COOLING SYSTEM BLEEDING under REMOVAL & INSTALLATION. Operate engine at fast idle and check for coolant and oil leaks. Adjust ignition timing.

VALVE COVER & ROCKER ARM SHAFT ASSEMBLY

Removal – 1) Disconnect negative battery cable. Remove intake shield and air intake tube. Release pressure from fuel system. See FUEL PRESSURE RELEASE under REMOVAL & INSTALLATION. Remove spark plug wires. Remove plastic retainer from coupling at fuel pressure regulator. Disconnect fuel line coupling using Fuel Line Coupling Key (T90P-9550-A). *See Fig. 1.* Using 2 wrenches, disconnect fuel supply line.

2) On vehicles with A/C, remove dipstick tube and bracket and left engine lifting hook. On all models, remove PCV valve hose and breather. Remove valve cover bolts and reinforcement pieces, and note location for installation. Lightly tap valve cover with plastic hammer to break valve cover seal and remove valve cover.

3) Remove rocker arm shaft assembly retaining bolts evenly, 2 turns at a time. Remove rocker arm shaft assembly and oil baffle. Remove push rods and keep in order for installation to original location.

Installation – 1) Loosen all valve lash adjusting screws. Apply SF engine oil to rocker arm shaft assembly. Install oil baffle and rocker arm shaft assembly. Install rocker arm shaft bolts. Guide adjusting screws into push rods. Tighten bolts evenly, 2 turns at a time to specification.

2) Adjust valve clearance. See VALVE CLEARANCE ADJUSTMENT under ADJUSTMENTS. Remove old valve cover gasket material. Install new gaskets on valve covers. Install valve covers. Install valve cover retaining bolts with reinforcement pieces in proper position. *See Fig. 3.*

3) Tighten retaining bolts to specification. See TORQUE SPECIFICATIONS table at end of article. To complete installation, reverse removal procedure.

CAUTION: Failure to properly install reinforcement pieces will cause valve cover damage and oil leakage.

CAMSHAFT

Removal – 1) Disconnect negative battery. Remove upper and lower intake manifolds. See INTAKE MANIFOLDS under REMOVAL & INSTALLATION. Remove rocker arm shaft assemblies and push rods. See VALVE COVER & ROCKER ARM SHAFT ASSEMBLY.

2) Remove timing chain and camshaft sprocket. See TIMING CHAIN & SPROCKETS. Remove valve lifters and keep in order for installation to original location. Remove camshaft thrust plate and spacer ring. Carefully remove camshaft out of cylinder block.

Inspection – Measure camshaft bearing journals and lobes for wear. If journals and lobes are not within specification, replace camshaft and valve lifters. See CAMSHAFT and VALVE LIFTERS tables under ENGINE SPECIFICATIONS at end of article.

Installation – 1) Coat camshaft journals and lobes with heavy SF engine oil (50W). Install spacer ring with chamfered side toward camshaft. Install key into camshaft. Carefully install camshaft into cylinder block.

2) Install thrust plate and tighten bolts. Ensure thrust plate covers main oil galley hole. *See Fig. 5.* Check camshaft end play. If end play is not within specification, replace thrust plate. See CAMSHAFT table under ENGINE SPECIFICATIONS at end of article.

3) To complete installation, reverse removal procedure. Adjust valve clearance. See VALVE CLEARANCE ADJUSTMENT under ADJUSTMENTS.

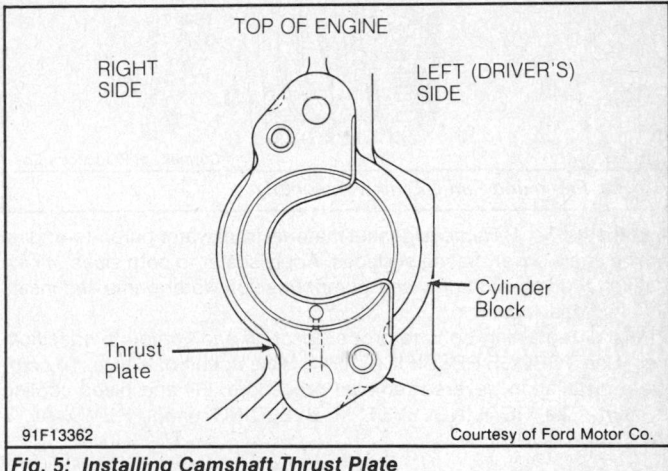

TOP OF ENGINE

RIGHT SIDE

LEFT (DRIVER'S) SIDE

Cylinder Block

Thrust Plate

91F13362

Courtesy of Ford Motor Co.

Fig. 5: Installing Camshaft Thrust Plate

CAMSHAFT BEARINGS

Removal – Remove engine and camshaft. See ENGINE and CAMSHAFT under REMOVAL & INSTALLATION. Remove flywheel/flexplate and rear bearing core plug. Using Cam Bearing Replacer Kit (T71P-6250-A), remove camshaft bearings. To remove front and rear bearings, use Cam Bearing Remover Adapter Tube (T72C-6250).

Installation – 1) Install camshaft bearings using Cam Bearing Replacer Kit. Ensure oil hole in bearing aligns with oil hole in cylinder block.

2) Check oil hole alignment of No. 2 and 3 bearings by inserting a rod of smaller diameter into oil passage. Rod should pass into camshaft bore. Coat sealing edge of new rear bearing core plug with oil resistant sealer.

3) Use a proper size driver ONLY and install core plug. To complete installation, reverse removal procedure.

REAR MAIN BEARING OIL SEAL

Removal – 1) Remove transmission. Remove clutch assembly (if equipped) and flywheel/flexplate. Punch 2 holes in oil seal, one on each side of crankshaft, just above bearing cap-to-block split line.

2) Install a sheet metal screw in each hole. Use pry bars to pry on both screws at the same time to remove oil seal. DO NOT damage crankshaft sealing surface.

Installation – Coat sealing surface of crankshaft and seal with heavy SF engine oil. Using Rear Oil Seal Installer (T72C-6165-R), install seal until firmly seated. To complete installation, reverse removal procedure.

WATER PUMP

NOTE: Fan clutch nut has a left-hand thread. Remove by turning nut clockwise as viewed from front of engine.

Removal – 1) Drain cooling system. Disconnect lower radiator hose and heater return hose from water pump. Remove fan and clutch assembly using Fan Clutch Holder (T83T-6312-A) and Nut Wrench (T83T-6312-B). *See Fig. 6.* Remove by turning nut clockwise, as nut has left-hand thread.
2) Remove alternator belt. Remove alternator and bracket (if A/C equipped). Remove water pump pulley. Remove water pump attaching bolts and note different bolt lengths for installation reference. Remove water pump assembly.

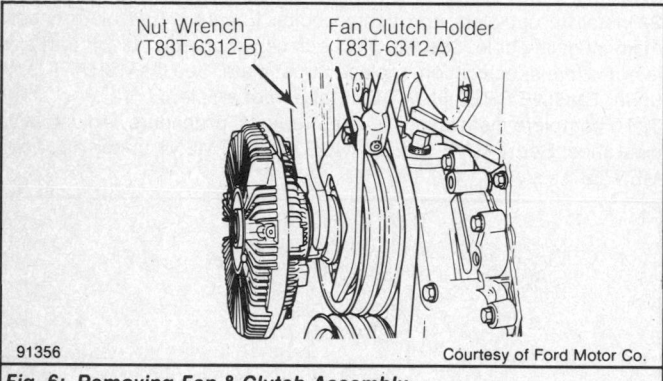

Fig. 6: Removing Fan & Clutch Assembly

Nut Wrench (T83T-6312-B)   Fan Clutch Holder (T83T-6312-A)

91356   Courtesy of Ford Motor Co.

Installation – 1) Remove gasket material from water pump-to-engine timing chain cover mating surfaces. Apply sealer to both sides of new gasket. Place gasket on water pump. Position water pump and install 2 bolts finger tight.
2) Install remaining bolts to proper location and tighten to specification. See TORQUE SPECIFICATIONS table at end of article. To complete installation, reverse removal procedure. Fill and bleed cooling system. See COOLING SYSTEM BLEEDING under REMOVAL & INSTALLATION.

OIL PAN

Removal – 1) Disconnect negative battery cable. Remove air intake tube. Position No. 1 cylinder on TDC of compression stroke. Remove distributor cap. Reference mark distributor rotor and body, and remove distributor. Remove fan shroud, and position back over cooling fan.
2) Remove front engine mount-to-crossmember nuts. Raise and support vehicle. Drain engine oil and remove oil filter. On A/T vehicles, disconnect transmission filler tube and oil cooler lines.
3) On 4WD vehicles, disconnect exhaust pipes from exhaust manifolds. On all models, disconnect front stabilizer bar (if equipped). Disconnect and lower oil cooler bracket (if equipped). Remove starter motor.
4) Raise engine slightly. Place wooden blocks between front engine mounts and crossmember, and lower engine. Remove oil pan bolts. On 4WD vehicles, remove oil pump retaining bolts and lower pump into oil pan. On all models, remove oil pan and gasket.
Installation – 1) To install, reverse removal procedure. Apply silicone sealant at front and rear corners of oil pan surface and cylinder block, and where timing chain cover meets the cylinder block.
2) Install oil pan bolts. Tighten bolts in 2 steps to specification using specified procedure. *See Fig. 7.* See TORQUE SPECIFICATIONS table at end of article. To install remaining components, reverse removal procedure. Tighten bolts to specification.

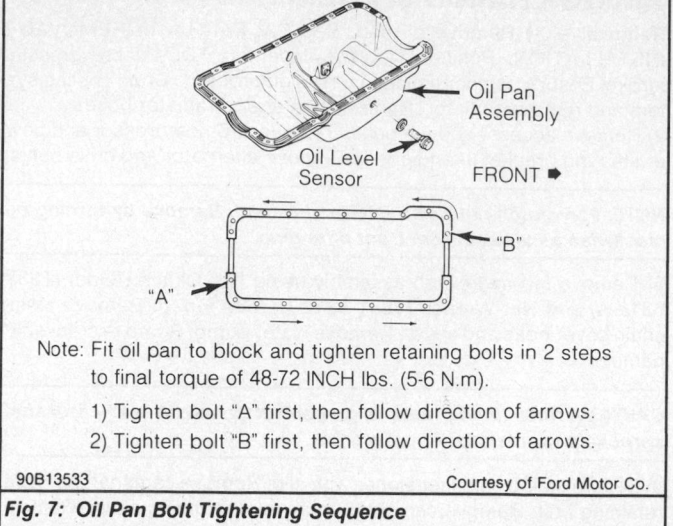

Oil Pan Assembly
Oil Level Sensor
FRONT ➡
"B"
"A"

Note: Fit oil pan to block and tighten retaining bolts in 2 steps to final torque of 48-72 INCH lbs. (5-6 N.m).
   1) Tighten bolt "A" first, then follow direction of arrows.
   2) Tighten bolt "B" first, then follow direction of arrows.

90B13533   Courtesy of Ford Motor Co.

Fig. 7: Oil Pan Bolt Tightening Sequence

OVERHAUL

CYLINDER HEAD

Cylinder Head – 1) Clean head gasket mating surface. Clean carbon from combustion chambers. Use care not to damage surfaces. Check cylinder head for cracks, burrs, nicks and warpage.
2) DO NOT machine more than .010" (.25 mm) from original cylinder head surface to correct warpage. Replace cylinder head as necessary. See CYLINDER HEAD table under ENGINE SPECIFICATIONS at end of article.

CAUTION: DO NOT machine more than .010" (.25 mm) from cylinder head original thickness.

Valve Springs – 1) Inspect valve spring free length and pressure. Replace valve spring if free length and pressure are not within specification. See VALVES & VALVE SPRINGS table under ENGINE SPECIFICATIONS at end of article.
2) Measure valve spring installed height from top of spring seat to underside of spring retainer. Ensure installed height is within specification. See VALVES & VALVE SPRINGS table under ENGINE SPECIFICATIONS at end of article.
3) If installed height is not within specification, a .03" (.8 mm) shim can be installed between cylinder head and valve spring to obtain correct height.

CAUTION: DO NOT install valve spring spacers unless necessary. Using more spacers than required can result in spring breakage or worn camshaft lobes.

Valve Stem Oil Seals – Use Valve Stem Oil Seal Installer (T73P-6571-A) for seal installation. Install seal until it bottoms on valve guide. Oversize seals must be used on guides that have been reamed for oversize valves.

Valve Guides – 1) Valve guides must be reamed for an oversized valve if valve stem oil clearance is not within specification. See CYLINDER HEAD table under ENGINE SPECIFICATIONS at end of article. Valves are available in .008" (.20 mm), .016" (.39 mm) and .030" (.76 mm) oversizes.
2) If oversized valves or oversized valve stem oil seals are not available, valve guide may be bored out to use a service bushing. Always use reamers in proper sequence (smallest first).

NOTE: Always grind valve seat after valve guide has been reamed or service bushing has been installed.

Valve Seat – 1) Grind valve seat to a 45-degree angle. If seat width is too wide after grinding, use a 30-degree stone to lower seat or a 60-

degree stone to raise seat. Ensure valve seat angle, seat width and seat runout are within specification.

2) See CYLINDER HEAD table under ENGINE SPECIFICATIONS at end of article. Valve seats must be ground when valve guide is reamed or replaced. Replacement information is not available from manufacturer.

Valves – Ensure head diameter, valve face runout, stem diameter and valve margin are within specification. See VALVES & VALVE SPRINGS table under ENGINE SPECIFICATIONS at end of article.

CAUTION: DO NOT remove more than .010" (.25 mm) from end of valve stem when resurfacing tip of valve.

CYLINDER BLOCK ASSEMBLY

CAUTION: NEVER cut into ring travel area more than 1/32" when removing ridge ring at top of cylinder bore.

Piston & Rod Assembly – Note installed position of rod in relation to piston for correct assembly. Install piston and connecting rod in engine, with ARROW on top of piston pointing towards front of engine.

Fitting Pistons – 1) Each cylinder bore must be measured for out-of-round, taper and piston-to-cylinder bore clearance. If measurements are not within specification or if cylinder walls are deeply scored, cylinders must be honed or bored. See PISTONS, PINS & RINGS table under ENGINE SPECIFICATIONS at end of article.

2) Measure cylinder diameter in 3 places: 1/2" (12.7 mm) below top surface of cylinder block, at center of piston travel in bore, and 1/2" (12.7 mm) above top of piston with piston at lowest point in cylinder. Pistons are available in .020" (.51 mm) oversize. A Red coded piston is standard size.

3) Measure piston diameter in line with center line of piston pin, and at 90 degrees to piston pin axis.

Piston Rings – 1) Select proper ring set for bore diameter. Place ring in cylinder bore in which it will be installed. Use piston to square ring and place ring below normal ring wear area. Measure ring end gap. If ring gap is not within specification, try another ring set. See PISTONS, PINS & RINGS table under ENGINE SPECIFICATIONS at end of article.

2) Check side clearance of rings after installing on piston. Ensure clearance is within specification around entire circumference. Replace piston and/or rings if clearance is not within specification. See PISTONS, PINS & RINGS table under ENGINE SPECIFICATIONS at end of article. Ensure rings are properly spaced on piston before installing pistons into cylinder. *See Fig. 8.*

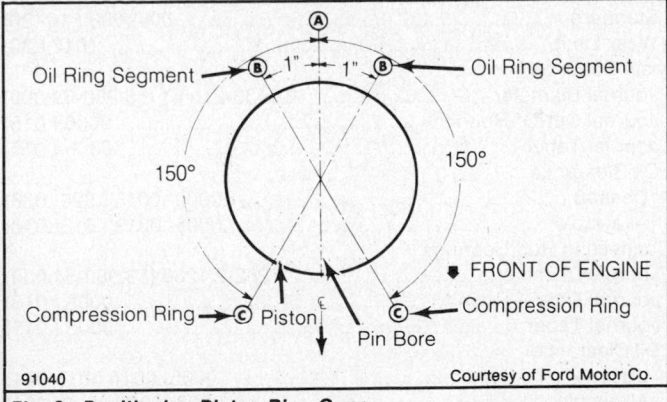

Fig. 8: Positioning Piston Ring Gaps

91040   Courtesy of Ford Motor Co.

Rod Bearings – 1) Clean crankshaft journal and rod bearing bore. Ensure oil hole on rod is not restricted. Check each crankshaft journal for out-of-round. Use Plastigage method to check rod bearing clearance.

2) If proper oil clearance cannot be obtained with standard bearings, try a combination of undersize bearings. DO NOT use any other bearing combination other than what is listed. See UNDERSIZE MAIN & ROD BEARING COMBINATIONS table.

3) If use of bearing combinations does not bring oil clearance within specification, machine or replace crankshaft as necessary. Always replace bearings in pairs. See CRANKSHAFT, MAIN & CONNECTING ROD BEARINGS table under ENGINE SPECIFICATIONS at end of article.

UNDERSIZE MAIN & ROD BEARING COMBINATIONS [1]

Excess Bearing Clearance In. (mm)	Use Upper Bearing In. (mm)	Use Lower Bearing In. (mm)
.0-.0005 (.0-.013)	.001 (.025)	[2]
.0005-.0010 (.013-.026)	.001 (.025)	.001 (.025)
.0010-.0015 (.026-.039)	.002 (.05)	.001 (.025)
.0015-.0020 (.039-.05)	.002 (.05)	.002 (.05)

[1] – DO NOT use any other bearing combination other than what is listed. If use of bearing combinations does not bring clearance within specification, machine or replace crankshaft as necessary.

[2] – Use standard bearing.

Crankshaft & Main Bearings – 1) When checking main bearing clearance in vehicle, position a jack under adjoining bearing counterweight being checked. Remove only one main bearing cap at a time.

2) Use Plastigage method and check main bearing clearance. If clearance is not within specification, replace bearings. Machine or replace crankshaft as necessary. See CRANKSHAFT, MAIN & CONNECTING ROD BEARINGS table under ENGINE SPECIFICATIONS at end of article.

3) If proper oil clearance cannot be obtained with standard bearings, try a combination of undersize bearings. DO NOT use any other bearing combination other than what is listed. See UNDERSIZE MAIN & ROD BEARING COMBINATIONS table.

4) If use of bearing combinations does not bring clearance within specification, machine or replace crankshaft as necessary. Always replace bearings in pairs. See CRANKSHAFT, MAIN & CONNECTING ROD BEARINGS table under ENGINE SPECIFICATIONS at end of article.

5) Install main bearing caps in original location. Ensure arrow on No. 1 and No. 3 main bearing caps face towards front of engine. Tighten main bearing cap bolts finger tight. Pry crankshaft forward and tighten bearing caps to specification.

6) Check crankshaft end play. Replace thrust bearing if end play is not within specification. See CRANKSHAFT, MAIN & CONNECTING ROD BEARINGS table under ENGINE SPECIFICATIONS at end of article. Thrust bearing is No. 3 (from front) main bearing in block.

Cylinder Block – 1) Using a feeler gauge and straightedge, check cylinder block head gasket surface for warpage. Check cylinder bore for wear, taper, out-of-round and piston fit. Repair or replace as necessary. See CYLINDER BLOCK table under ENGINE SPECIFICATIONS at end of article.

2) Install all main bearing caps and tighten to specification before honing cylinder bore. See TORQUE SPECIFICATIONS table at end of article. Use ONLY a spring-loaded type cylinder hone. After honing, thoroughly clean bore with detergent and water solution. Rinse solution from bore thoroughly with clean water. Wipe bore clean with lint-free cloth. Lubricate cylinder bores with engine oil.

ENGINE OILING

ENGINE LUBRICATION SYSTEM

System is pressure fed from a rotor-type oil pump. Oil flows through oil filter before entering main oil gallery.

Crankcase Capacity – Crankcase capacity is 4 qts. (3.8L) without filter and 5 qts. (4.75L) with filter.

Oil Pressure – Normal oil pressure at 2000 RPM should be 40-60 psi (2.8-4.2 kg/cm²) with engine at normal operating temperature.

Oil Pressure Regulator Valve – Oil pressure regulator valve is located in oil pump body. Valve is nonadjustable.

OIL PUMP

Removal & Disassembly – Remove oil pan. See OIL PAN under REMOVAL & INSTALLATION. Remove oil pump attaching bolts. Remove oil pump assembly with oil pump drive shaft attached. On all models, remove pick-up tube from pump. Disassemble oil pump. Note direction of component installation for reassembly reference.

Inspection – Inspect components for damage. Measure rotor end clearance, outer race-to-housing clearance and rotor tip clearance. Check clearance between pressure relief valve and bore. Measure relief valve tension. Replace oil pump assembly if measurements are not within specifications. See OIL PUMP SPECIFICATIONS table.

NOTE: Oil pump is serviced as an assembly only. Replace assembly if measurements are not within specification. See OIL PUMP SPECIFICATIONS table.

OIL PUMP SPECIFICATIONS

Application	Specification In. (mm)
Drive Shaft-To-Housing Bearing Clearance	.0015-.0030 (.038-.076)
Outer Race-To-Housing Clearance	.001-.013 (.03-.33)
Relief Valve Spring Tension	[1]
Relief Valve-To-Bore Clearance	.0015-.0030 (.038-.076)
Rotor Assembly End Play	.004 (.10)

[1] – Relief valve spring tension should be 13.6-14.7 lbs. @ 1.39" (6.2-6.7 kg @ 35.3 mm).

Reassembly & Installation – To reassemble, reverse disassembly procedure. Ensure rotors are installed in original location. Ensure oil pump spins freely after reassembly. To install, reverse removal procedure; use new gaskets. Tighten bolts to specification. See TORQUE SPECIFICATIONS table. Prime oil pump assembly before installation.

TORQUE SPECIFICATIONS

TORQUE SPECIFICATIONS

Application	Ft. Lbs. (N.m)
Bellhousing-To-Engine Bolt	28-38 (38-51)
Camshaft Sprocket Bolt	19-28 (26-38)
Camshaft Thrust Plate Bolt	13-16 (18-22)
Connecting Rod Nut	19-24 (26-33)
Crankshaft Damper Bolt	85-96 (116-131)
Cylinder Head Bolt [1]	
Step 1	22 (30)
Step 2	51-55 (69-75)
Step 3	Additional 90 degrees
Engine Mount-To-Chassis Bolt	71-94 (96-127)
Engine Mount-To-Engine Bracket Bolt	65-85 (88-115)
Exhaust Manifold Bolt	20-30 (27-41)
Fan Clutch-To-Water Pump Nut [2]	30-100 (41-137)
Flexplate-To-Converter Bolt	20-34 (27-46)
Flywheel-To-Crankshaft Bolt	47-52 (64-71)
Front Cover Bolt	13-16 (18-22)
Main Bearing Cap Bolt	65-75 (88-102)
Rear Mount-To-Crossmember Nut	65-85 (88-115)
Rear Mount-To-Transmission Bolt	60-80 (81-108)
Rocker Arm Shaft Bolt	43-50 (58-68)
Starter Bolt	15-20 (20-27)
Water Pump Pulley Bolt	14-22 (19-30)

[1] – Tighten in sequence. See Fig. 4.
[2] – Left-hand thread.
[3] – Tighten in sequence. See Fig. 2.
[4] – Repeat tightening procedure after engine reaches normal operating temperature.
[5] – Tighten in sequence. See Fig. 7.
[6] – Tightening sequence is not available from manufacturer.

TORQUE SPECIFICATIONS (Cont.)

Application	INCH Lbs. (N.m)
Lower Intake Manifold Bolt [3]	
Step 1	Hand Start & Snug
Step 2	36-72 (4-8)
Step 3	72-132 (8-15)
Step 4	132-180 (15-21)
Step 5 [4]	180-216 (21-25)
Oil Pan Bolt [5]	48-72 (5-8)
Oil Pump Case Bolt	80-115 (9-13)
Throttle Body-To-Intake Bolt	80-115 (9-13)
Timing Chain	
Guide Bolt	80-115 (9-13)
Tensioner Bolt	80-115 (9-13)
Upper Intake Manifold Bolt [6]	
Step 1	84 (10)
Step 2	180-216 (21-25)
Valve Cover Bolt	36-60 (4-7)
Water Pump Bolt	84-108 (10-12)

[1] – Tighten in sequence. See Fig. 4.
[2] – Left-hand thread.
[3] – Tighten in sequence. See Fig. 2.
[4] – Repeat tightening procedure after engine reaches normal operating temperature.
[5] – Tighten in sequence. See Fig. 7.
[6] – Tightening sequence is not available from manufacturer.

ENGINE SPECIFICATIONS

GENERAL SPECIFICATIONS

Application	Specification
Displacement	177 Cu. In.
Bore	3.66" (92.9 mm)
Stroke	2.83" (71.9 mm)
Compression Ratio	9.0:1
Fuel System	PFI
Horsepower @ RPM	140 @ 4600
Torque Ft. Lbs. @ RPM	170 @ 2600

CRANKSHAFT, MAIN & CONNECTING ROD BEARINGS

Application	In. (mm)
Crankshaft End Play	
Standard	.004-.008 (.10-.20)
Wear Limit	.012 (.30)
Main Bearings	
Journal Diameter	2.2433-2.2441 (56.980-57.000)
Journal Out-Of-Round	.0006 (.015)
Journal Taper [1]	.0006 (.015)
Oil Clearance	
Desired	.0008-.0015 (.020-.038)
Allowable	.0005-.0019 (.013-.048)
Connecting Rod Bearings	
Journal Diameter	2.1252-2.1260 (53.980-54.000)
Journal Out-Of-Round	.0006 (.015)
Journal Taper [1]	.0006 (.015)
Oil Clearance	
Desired	.0006-.0016 (.015-041)
Allowable	.0005-.0022 (.013-.056)

[1] – Specification is per 1" (25.4 mm).

CONNECTING RODS

Application	In. (mm)
Bore Diameter	
Pin Bore	.9450-.9452 (24.003-24.008)
Crankpin Bore	2.2370-2.2378 (56.820-56.840)
Center-To-Center Length	5.139-5.141 (130.51-130.58)
Maximum Bend [1]	.002 (.05)
Maximum Twist [1]	.006 (.15)
Side Play	
Standard	.004-.011 (.10-.28)
Wear Limit	.014 (.36)

[1] – Specification listed is measured at the ends of an 8" (203 mm) bar, 4" (102 mm) on each side of rod center line.

PISTONS, PINS & RINGS

Application	In. (mm)
Pistons	
Clearance	.0011-.0019 (.028-.048)
Diameter [1]	3.6605-3.6615 (92.976-93.002)
Pins	
Piston Fit	.0003-.0006 (.008-.015)
Rings	
No. 1 & 2	
End Gap	.015-.023 (.038-.058)
Side Clearance	.0020-.0033 (.051-.084)
No. 3 (Oil)	
End Gap	.015-.055 (.38-1.40)
Side Clearance	Snug Fit

[1] – Measured at piston pin bore center line, at 90-degree angle to piston pin.

CYLINDER BLOCK

Application	In. (mm)
Cylinder Bore	
Standard Diameter	3.6614-3.6630 (93.000-93.040)
Maximum Taper	.010 (.25)
Out-Of-Round	
Standard	.0015 (.038)
Wear Limit	.005 (.13)
Maximum Deck Warpage	[1]

[1] – No more than .003" (.08 mm) in any 6" (152.4 mm) section and no more than .006" (.15 mm) overall. DO NOT remove more than .010" (.25 mm) material from original deck if machining is required.

VALVES & VALVE SPRINGS

Application	Specification
Intake Valves	
Face Angle	44°
Head Diameter	1.78-1.81" (45.2-46.0 mm)
Minimum Margin	.031" (.79 mm)
Stem Diameter	.3159-.3167" (8.024-8.044 mm)
Exhaust Valves	
Face Angle	44°
Head Diameter	1.41-1.42" (35.8-36.1 mm)
Minimum Margin	.031" (.79 mm)
Stem Diameter	.3149-.3156" (7.998-8.016 mm)
Valve Springs	
Free Length	1.91" (49.0 mm)
Installed Height	1.58-1.61" (40.1-40.9 mm)
Out-Of-Square	.078" (1.98 mm)

	Lbs. @ In. (kg @ mm)
Pressure	
Valve Closed	60-68 @ 1.59 (27-31 @ 40.4)
Valve Open	138-149 @ 1.22 (63-68 @ 31.0)

CYLINDER HEAD

Application	Specification
Maximum Warpage	[1]
Valve Seats	
Intake Valve	
Seat Angle	45°
Seat Width	.060-.079" (1.52-2.01 mm)
Maximum Seat Runout	.0015" (.038 mm)
Exhaust Valve	
Seat Angle	45°
Seat Width	.060-.079" (1.52-2.01 mm)
Maximum Seat Runout	.0015" (.038 mm)
Valve Guides	
Valve Guide I.D.	.3174-.3184" (8.062-8.087 mm)
Intake Valve	
Valve Stem-To-Guide	
Oil Clearance	.0008-.0025" (.020-.064 mm)
Exhaust Valve	
Valve Stem-To-Guide	
Oil Clearance	.0018-.0035" (.046-.089 mm)

[1] – No more than .003" (.08 mm) in any 6" (152.4 mm) section and no more than .006" (.15 mm) overall. DO NOT remove more than .010" (.25 mm) material from original surface if machining is required.

CAMSHAFT

Application	In. (mm)
Journal Diameter	
Journal No. 1	1.7285-1.7293 (43.904-43.924)
Journal No. 2	1.7135-1.7143 (43.523-43.543)
Journal No. 3	1.6985-1.6992 (43.142-43.160)
Journal No. 4	1.6835-1.6842 (42.761-42.779)
Bearing I.D.	
Journal No. 1	1.7302-1.7310 (43.947-43.967)
Journal No. 2	1.7152-1.7160 (43.566-43.586)
Journal No. 3	1.7002-1.7010 (43.185-43.205)
Journal No. 4	1.6852-1.6860 (42.804-42.824)
End Play	
Standard	.0008-.0040 (.020-.101)
Wear Limit	.009 (.23)
Journal Runout	.005 (.13)
Journal Out-Of-Round	.0003 (.008)
Lobe Lift	
Intake	.3588 (9.113)
Exhaust	.3703 (9.406)
Maximum Lobe Wear	.005 (.13)
Journal-To-Bearing	
Oil Clearance	
Standard	.0010-.0026 (.025-.066)
Wear Limit	.006 (.15)

VALVE LIFTERS

Application	In. (mm)
Lifter Diameter	.8736-.8741 (22.189-22.202)
Oil Clearance	
Standard	.0009-.0024 (.023-.061)
Wear Limit	.005 (.13)

Aerostar, Ranger

NOTE: For repair procedures not covered in this article, see ENGINE OVERHAUL PROCEDURES article in GENERAL INFORMATION.

ENGINE IDENTIFICATION

Engine may be identified by the eighth character of the Vehicle Identification Number (VIN). VIN plate is attached to upper left corner of instrument panel, near windshield. The VIN is also found on the Safety Compliance Certification Label on left door lock pillar.

VIN ENGINE CODE

Engine	Code
3.0L PFI	U

ADJUSTMENTS

VALVE CLEARANCE CHECK

NOTE: Valve lifters are set at zero lash. No adjustment is necessary. If valve train has been disassembled or worn parts are suspected, check valve clearance.

1) Following procedure is done with timing chain cover removed. Rotate crankshaft to position "A". *See Fig. 1.* Using Tappet Collapser (T82L-6500-A), completely collapse No. 1 intake valve lifter. While holding valve lifter fully collapsed, use feeler gauge to measure clearance of No. 1 intake valve between rocker arm and tip of valve stem.
2) Collapsed valve clearance should be .088-.189" (2.23-4.80 mm) on all valves. Repeat procedure for specified valves. See VALVE ADJUSTMENT SEQUENCE table.

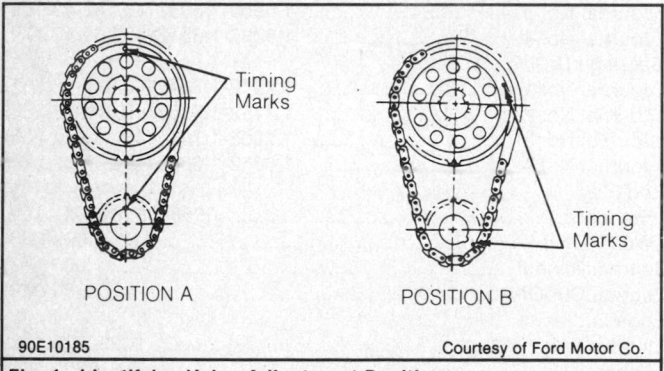

90E10185   Courtesy of Ford Motor Co.

Fig. 1: Identifying Valve Adjustment Positions

3) Rotate crankshaft to position "B". *See Fig. 1.* While holding valve lifter fully collapsed, use feeler gauge to measure clearance of No. 1 exhaust valve between rocker arm and tip of valve stem. Repeat procedure for specified valves. See VALVE ADJUSTMENT SEQUENCE table. See VALVE LIFTERS table under ENGINE SPECIFICATIONS at end of article.
4) If valve clearance on any cylinder is greater than .088-.189" (2.23-4.80 mm), all valve train components for that cylinder must be inspected for excessive wear. Replace as necessary.
5) If valve clearance on any cylinder is less than .088-.189" (2.23-4.80 mm), tappet may not be collapsing or valve stem may be too long as a result of valve seat or valve grinding. Inspect tappet and/or grind valve stem as necessary. See VALVES & VALVE SPRINGS table under ENGINE SPECIFICATIONS at end of article.

NOTE: DO NOT remove more than .010" (.25) from end of valve stem when resurfacing tip of valve.

VALVE ADJUSTMENT SEQUENCE

Crankshaft Position	Adjust Exhaust Valves Of Cylinders	Adjust Intake Valves Of Cylinders
A	.... 2 & 5	.... 1 & 4
B	.... 1, 3, 4 & 6	.... 2, 3, 5 & 6

REMOVAL & INSTALLATION

WARNING: When battery is disconnected, vehicle computer and memory systems may lose memory data. Driveability problems may exist until computer systems have completed a relearn cycle. See COMPUTER RELEARN PROCEDURES article in GENERAL INFORMATION before disconnecting battery.

FUEL PRESSURE RELEASE

To release fuel pressure, disconnect negative battery cable. Remove fuel cap to release fuel tank pressure. Remove relief valve cap from fuel rail. Connect fuel pressure gauge to relief valve and release fuel into a suitable container.

COOLING SYSTEM BLEEDING

1) Fill cooling system with 50/50 mixture of coolant and water. Pause several minutes for circulation. Fill radiator to filler neck seat. Install radiator cap fully, then back off to first stop.

WARNING: When engine is operating, NEVER remove radiator cap under any conditions. Failure to follow instruction could damage cooling system or engine, or cause personal injury. Always wrap protective material around radiator cap to avoid injury from hot coolant.

2) Place heater controls to maximum heat. Start engine and operate at 2000 RPM for approximately 3-4 minutes. Turn engine off. Using a protective rag, carefully remove radiator cap. Add coolant to filler neck seat.
3) Install radiator cap fully then back off to first stop. Start engine and allow to operate at 2000 RPM until upper radiator hose is warm. Check heater output. Turn engine off. Using a protective rag, carefully remove radiator cap. Add coolant to filler neck seat if necessary.
4) Tightly install radiator cap. Remove small cap (large cap is for windshield washer reservoir) on coolant recovery reservoir. Add 1.1 qt. (1L) of 50/50 mixture of coolant and water to reservoir. Install reservoir cap.

ENGINE

Removal (Aerostar) – 1) Disconnect negative battery cable. Drain cooling system. Remove air cleaner and intake duct assembly. Remove radiator hoses and fan shroud. Remove left-handed nut retaining clutch fan to pulley. Remove cooling fan. Disconnect Barometric Manifold Absolute Pressure (BMAP) sensor. Remove throttle linkage shroud.
2) Disconnect throttle linkage at throttle body. Remove accessory drive belts. Disconnect injector harness connector from main Electronic Engine Control (EEC) harness. Disconnect Engine Coolant Temperature (ECT) sensor.
3) Disconnect canister purge solenoid hoses from solenoid. Disconnect power steering pump pressure switch. Remove heater hoses. Remove breather tube from air cleaner and valve cover. Remove transmission oil cooler lines from radiator (if equipped).
4) Remove radiator retaining bolts and radiator. Remove oil fill tube-to-alternator bracket nut. Remove A/C compressor and set aside (if equipped). Remove transmission oil fill tube bolt from top of manifold (if equipped). Disconnect alternator connectors.
5) Remove brake booster vacuum line from brake booster. Remove bolt retaining steering gear at top of shaft. Remove engine cover. Disconnect radio frequency interference suppressor.

6) Disconnect Thick Film Ignition (TFI) connector at distributor. Disconnect oil pressure sender. Release fuel pressure. See FUEL PRESSURE RELEASE. Using Disconnect Tool (D87L-9280-A) for 3/8" line or (D87L-9280-B) for 1/2" line, disconnect fuel supply and return lines. *See Fig. 2.*

7) On M/T models, position shifter in Neutral. Remove shift lever-to-floor retaining bolts. Remove shift lever-to-transmission retaining bolts. Remove shift lever. Raise and support vehicle.

8) Disconnect oil level sensor connector from oil pan. Mark drive shaft-to-flange position and remove drive shaft. Pull speedometer cable from rear of transmission. Remove starter connections and remove starter.

9) On M/T models, remove hydraulic hose-to-slave cylinder lock pin in clutch housing. Remove and plug hose. Disconnect back-up light switch, shift indicator and neutral switch wires. On A/T models, disconnect neutral start switch and 3-4 shift solenoid connectors. Disconnect selector and kickdown cable from transmission lever.

10) Disconnect vacuum modulator hose. Remove converter access cover and adapter plate bolts from lower end of converter housing. Remove flywheel-to-converter retaining nuts. Disconnect oxygen sensor. Disconnect transmission oil cooler lines from transmission (if equipped).

11) Place transmission jack under transmission. Place a safety chain around transmission. Raise transmission slightly. Remove transmission mount-to-crossmember nuts. Remove mount (if necessary). Remove crossmember-to-bracket bolts and nuts. Remove crossmember.

12) Remove bellhousing-to-engine fasteners. Slide transmission rearward. Lower transmission from vehicle. Disconnect exhaust pipes from manifolds. Remove exhaust pipe and converter. Remove front wheels. Remove engine ground straps. Remove stabilizer bar nuts and disconnect stabilizer bar from lower control arms.

13) Disconnect and plug brake lines at bracket on frame behind spindles. Place jack under lower control arm and raise jack until tension is applied to coil spring. Remove upper spindle-to-control arm ball joint bolt and nut. Slowly lower jack to disconnect spindle from ball joint.

14) Position Drive Train Removal Lift (109-00002) under crossmember and engine assembly. Lower vehicle until crossmember rests on lift. Place wood blocks under front crossmember and rear of engine (or transmission if assembled) to keep unit level.

15) Install safety chains around crossmember and lift. With engine and crossmember securely supported on lift, remove 3 engine and crossmember-to-frame retaining bolts from each side of vehicle.

16) Slowly lower engine assembly from vehicle. Ensure A/C compressor and wiring harnesses do not interfere with removal process. Raise body from engine and crossmember assembly. Remove motor mount nuts. Remove engine from crossmember.

Installation – To install, reverse removal procedure. Tighten bolts to specification. See TORQUE SPECIFICATIONS table at end of article. Check and fill all fluid levels. Bleed brakes. Fill and bleed air from cooling system. See COOLING SYSTEM BLEEDING. Start engine and check for leaks. Check front end alignment and adjust as necessary.

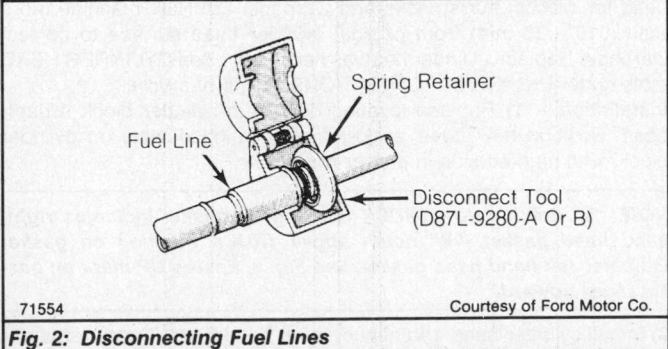

71554   Courtesy of Ford Motor Co.

Fig. 2: Disconnecting Fuel Lines

Removal (Ranger) – **1)** Disconnect negative battery cable and drain cooling system. Remove hood, air cleaner and intake duct assembly. Remove fan shroud and position over fan. Remove radiator with hoses and shroud. Remove alternator and bracket.

2) Remove A/C compressor and power steering pump with hoses attached (if equipped). Disconnect heater hoses from engine. Release fuel pressure. See FUEL PRESSURE RELEASE. Using Disconnect Tool (D87L-9280-A) for 3/8" line or (D87L-9280-B) for 1/2" line, disconnect fuel supply and return lines. *See Fig. 2.*

3) Disconnect brake booster vacuum hose. Disconnect throttle cable linkage and shield at throttle body and intake manifold. Disconnect all vacuum hoses from rear vacuum fitting in upper intake manifold.

4) Disconnect wiring from coil, oil pressure sending unit and engine coolant temperature sending units. Disconnect injector harness, air charge temperature sensor and throttle position sensor.

5) Mark distributor rotor and body position for installation reference. Remove distributor. Raise and support vehicle. Remove 2 lower bolts from A/C compressor. Disconnect oil level sensor connector from oil pan. Disconnect oil pressure sender connector.

6) Remove transmission oil cooler line bracket from right side of engine. Disconnect exhaust pipes from manifolds. Remove starter and front engine mount nuts or through bolts. Remove ground wires from engine block. On A/T models, remove converter inspection cover and disconnect flywheel from converter.

7) Remove kickdown rod and bellhousing mounting bolts. Remove adapter plate-to-converter housing bolt. On M/T models, remove bellhousing bolts and hydraulic clutch hose. On all models, remove engine front support-to-crossmember nuts and bolts.

8) Lower vehicle and attach engine hoist to brackets at exhaust manifolds. Remove remaining A/C compressor bolts and set compressor aside. Ensure all wires and hoses are disconnected before raising engine. Support transmission. Raise engine slightly and carefully pull engine forward from transmission without damaging rear cover plate. Remove engine from vehicle.

Installation – To install, reverse removal procedure. Tighten bolts to specification. See TORQUE SPECIFICATIONS table at end of article. Fill or top off all engine fluids. Fill and bleed air from cooling system. See COOLING SYSTEM BLEEDING. Bleed clutch hydraulic system (if equipped). Adjust ignition timing and idle speed.

INTAKE MANIFOLDS

NOTE: Upper and lower intake manifold service procedures are covered separately.

Removal (Upper) – **1)** Disconnect negative battery cable. Remove air cleaner duct hose. Remove throttle linkage shield and disconnect linkage. Mark and disconnect vacuum hoses from throttle body. Mark and disconnect electrical connectors.

2) Disconnect PCV hose. Remove alternator support brace. Remove 6 upper intake manifold assembly bolts. Remove upper intake manifold assembly and gasket.

Installation – Clean gasket mating surfaces. Install a new gasket. Use guide pins and install upper intake manifold. Tighten bolts in sequence to specification. *See Fig. 3.* See TORQUE SPECIFICATIONS table at end of article. To complete installation, reverse removal procedure.

Removal (Lower) – **1)** Disconnect negative battery cable. Drain cooling system. Remove air cleaner duct hose. Relieve fuel pressure. See FUEL PRESSURE RELEASE under REMOVAL & INSTALLATION. Using Disconnect Tool (D87L-9280-A) for 3/8" line or (D87L-9280-B) for 1/2" line, disconnect fuel supply and return lines. *See Fig. 2.*

2) Remove throttle linkage shield and disconnect linkage. Mark and disconnect vacuum hoses from throttle body. Mark and disconnect electrical connectors. Disconnect upper radiator hose from thermostat housing. Remove ignition coil from throttle body.

3) Remove throttle body. Remove alternator support brace. Disconnect fuel injector harness connectors. Disconnect heater hoses. Mark distributor housing location and note rotor position. Remove distributor. Remove valve covers. See VALVE COVERS.

4) Loosen cylinder No. 3 intake valve rocker arm. Rotate rocker arm off push rod. Remove push rod. Remove intake manifold retaining bolts. Remove alternator if necessary. Remove intake manifold.

Installation – 1) Lightly oil all retaining bolts and stud threads before installation. Apply silicone sealer to 4 intersecting corners of cylinder block and cylinder head. Install front and rear intake manifold seals. Position lower intake manifold gaskets in place with locking tabs over tabs on cylinder head gaskets.

2) Carefully install lower intake manifold. Install manifold retaining bolts and tighten in sequence to specification. *See Fig. 4.* See TORQUE SPECIFICATIONS table at end of article.

3) Install No. 3 cylinder intake valve push rod. Rotate crankshaft until No. 3 intake push rod is at its lowest point on camshaft lobe. Position rocker arm on valve and tighten rocker arm bolt to specification. See TORQUE SPECIFICATIONS table.

4) To complete installation, reverse removal procedure. Fill and bleed cooling system. See COOLING SYSTEM BLEEDING under REMOVAL & INSTALLATION.

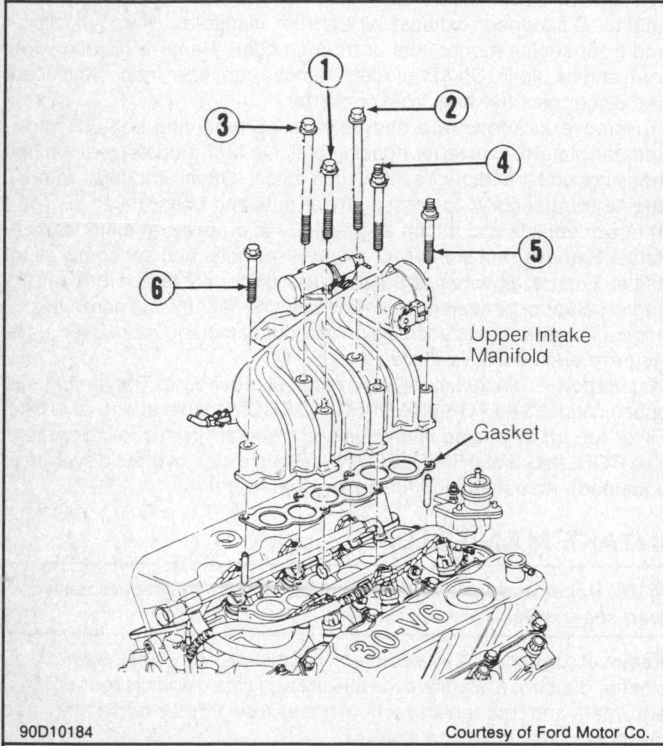

90D10184   Courtesy of Ford Motor Co.

Fig. 3: Upper Intake Manifold Tightening Sequence

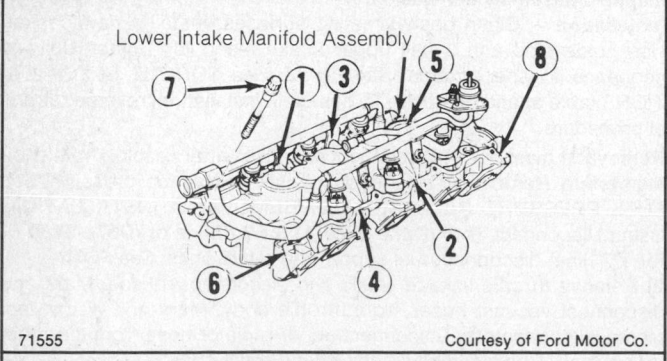

71555   Courtesy of Ford Motor Co.

Fig. 4: Lower Intake Manifold Tightening Sequence

EXHAUST MANIFOLDS

Removal – Disconnect negative battery cable. Remove spark plugs. Remove oil dipstick tube retaining nut from left cylinder head, and rotate tube off of stud. Separate exhaust pipe from exhaust manifold. Remove exhaust manifold bolts. Remove exhaust manifold.

Installation – Clean carbon from mating surfaces. Lightly oil threads of bolts and stud before installation. Install exhaust manifold(s) and

tighten bolts to specification. See TORQUE SPECIFICATIONS table at end of article. To complete installation, reverse removal procedure.

VALVE COVERS

NOTE: Valve covers have integral (built-in) gaskets which are made to last the life of the vehicle. If necessary, replacement gaskets are available.

Removal – 1) Disconnect negative battery cable. On Aerostar, remove fresh air hose from air cleaner. On all models, mark and remove spark plug wires from spark plugs. Remove spark plug wire separators from valve cover studs. For left valve cover, remove upper intake manifold. See INTAKE MANIFOLDS under REMOVAL & INSTALLATION.

2) Remove PCV valve. Disconnect injector wiring harness bracket from left valve cover studs. For right valve cover on Aerostar, remove oil filler tube. On Ranger, disconnect engine wiring harness connectors from right valve cover.

3) On all models, disconnect injector wiring harness bracket from right valve cover studs. Disconnect breather hose. On all applications, remove valve cover retaining bolts and studs.

4) Carefully slide a thin knife between cylinder head and valve cover. Cut silicone sealer; DO NOT cut integral gasket. Remove valve cover(s).

Installation – 1) Replace valve cover gasket if necessary. Ensure gasket lies flat in valve cover channel. Lightly oil threads of bolts and studs. Ensure sealing surfaces are clean.

2) Apply a bead of silicone sealant to intake manifold-to-cylinder head joining area. Install valve cover and tighten bolts to specification. See TORQUE SPECIFICATIONS table at end of article. To complete installation, reverse removal procedure.

CYLINDER HEAD

Removal – 1) Remove upper and lower intake manifolds. See INTAKE MANIFOLDS under REMOVAL & INSTALLATION. Remove accessory drive belts and idler. When removing left cylinder head, remove power steering pump bracket retaining bolts. Remove power steering pump and bracket as an assembly (with hoses attached).

2) On Aerostar, remove ignition coil bracket and coil. On all models, remove dipstick tube retaining nut from exhaust manifold. Rotate or remove dipstick tube. When removing right cylinder head, remove alternator bracket and adjusting arm.

3) Remove spark plugs. Remove exhaust manifolds. See EXHAUST MANIFOLDS. Remove PCV valve and valve covers. See VALVE COVERS.

4) Loosen rocker arm bolts and move rocker arm off push rod. Keep push rods in order for installation reference, and remove push rods. Remove and discard cylinder head retaining bolts. Remove cylinder head and gasket.

Inspection – Clean head gasket mating surfaces. Clean carbon from combustion chambers. DO NOT damage surfaces. Check cylinder head for cracks, burrs, nicks and warpage. DO NOT machine more than .010" (.25 mm) from original cylinder head surface to correct warpage. Replace cylinder head as necessary. See CYLINDER HEAD table under ENGINE SPECIFICATIONS at end of article.

Installation – 1) Replace locating dowels in cylinder block if damaged. Position new head gasket over locating dowels on cylinder block, with marked side in proper position.

NOTE: "V" notch below TRUCK marking on gasket indicates right-hand head gasket. "V" notch above TRUCK marking on gasket indicates left-hand head gasket. See Fig. 5. Ensure UP mark on gasket faces upward.

2) Install cylinder head and new cylinder head bolts. Tighten cylinder head bolts in sequence to specification. *See Fig. 5.* See TORQUE SPECIFICATIONS table at end of article. Dip each push rod end in Oil Conditioner (D9AZ-19579-CA). Install push rods in their original location.

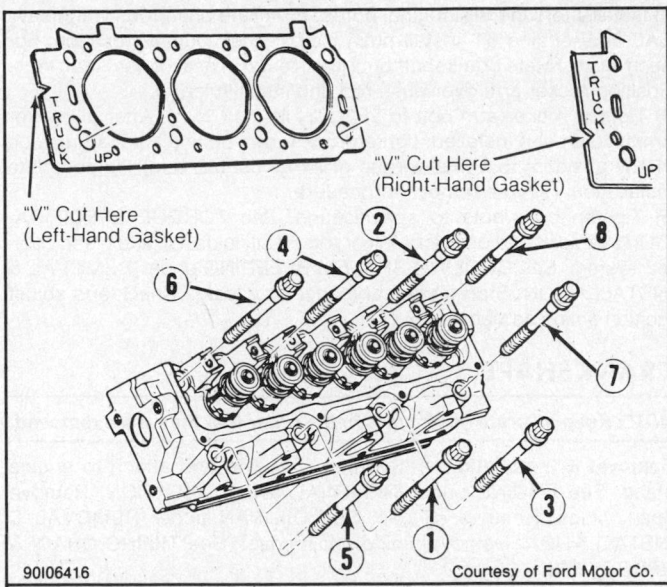

Fig. 5: Cylinder Head Gasket Position & Head Bolt Tightening Sequence

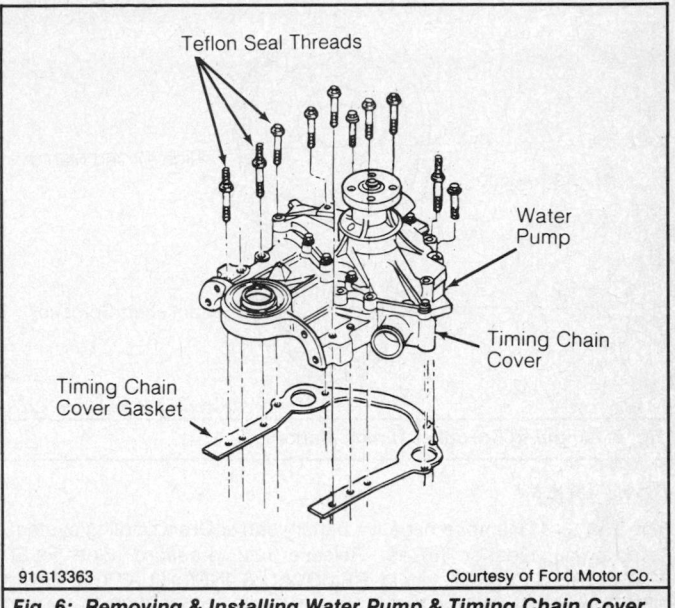

Fig. 6: Removing & Installing Water Pump & Timing Chain Cover Assembly

3) For each valve, rotate crankshaft until lifter rests on heel of camshaft lobe. Position rocker arm over push rod and install fulcrum. Tighten rocker arm bolt to 96 INCH lbs. (11 N.m). After all rocker arms have been installed, tighten rocker arm bolts (camshaft may be in any position) to a final torque of 24 ft. lbs. (33 N.m).

CAUTION: Rocker arms must be fully seated in cylinder head and push rods must be seated in rocker arm sockets before final tightening. If all original components removed are reinstalled, valve clearance check is not required. If valves/seats were serviced, check and adjust valve clearance. See VALVE CLEARANCE CHECK under ADJUSTMENTS.

4) To complete installation, reverse removal procedure. Tighten all bolts/nuts to specification. See TORQUE SPECIFICATIONS table at end of article. Fill and bleed cooling system. See COOLING SYSTEM BLEEDING under REMOVAL & INSTALLATION.

FRONT CRANKSHAFT OIL SEAL

Removal – Disconnect negative battery cable. Remove accessory drive belts. Remove crankshaft belt pulley. Remove crankshaft damper using Crankshaft Damper Remover and Adapter (T58P-6316-D and T82L-6316-B). Pry seal out carefully to avoid damaging sealing surface.

Installation – Lubricate lip of seal with clean engine oil. Using a proper size seal installer, install seal. Lubricate damper seal surface with engine oil. Apply RTV sealer to damper keyway. To complete installation, reverse removal procedure. Tighten bolts to specification. See TORQUE SPECIFICATIONS table at end of article.

TIMING CHAIN COVER

Removal – 1) Remove negative battery cable. Drain cooling system. Remove accessory drive belts. Remove left-handed nut retaining clutch fan to pulley. Remove cooling fan and water pump pulley. Remove A/C bracket, brace and compressor as an assembly (if equipped). Remove alternator adjusting arm and brace, and position alternator aside.

2) On Ranger, remove upper motor mount nuts. Position No. 1 piston on TDC of compression stroke. Remove distributor cap with plug wires. Mark distributor rotor and body position for installation reference. Remove distributor.

3) On all models, remove crankshaft belt pulley. Using Crankshaft Damper Remover and Adapter (T58P-6316-D and T82L-6316-B), remove crankshaft damper. Remove hoses from water pump.

4) Remove oil pan. See OIL PAN under REMOVAL & INSTALLATION. Remove 10 bolts retaining timing chain cover and water pump assembly to engine. *See Fig. 6.* Remove timing chain cover and water pump as an assembly.

Installation – 1) Clean all gasket mating surfaces. Coat both surfaces of new timing chain cover gasket with sealing compound. Install timing chain cover gasket. Install timing chain cover. Lightly oil threads of bolt and stud, except those with Teflon sealant, before installation. *See Fig. 6.*

2) Tighten bolts to specifications. See TORQUE SPECIFICATIONS table at end of article. To complete installation, reverse removal procedure. Fill and bleed cooling system. See COOLING SYSTEM BLEEDING under REMOVAL & INSTALLATION.

TIMING CHAIN & SPROCKETS

NOTE: Check timing chain deflection (stretch) before removal to determine component wear.

Inspection – 1) Remove left-side valve cover. See VALVE COVERS under REMOVAL & INSTALLATION. Loosen No. 5 exhaust rocker arm and rotate to one side. Install a dial indicator on end of push rod. Turn crankshaft clockwise until No. 1 piston is at TDC to take up slack on right side of chain. The damper timing mark should point to TDC.

2) Zero dial indicator. Slowly turn crankshaft counterclockwise until slightest movement is seen on dial indicator. Note the number of degrees of travel from TDC. If reading exceeds 6 degrees, replace timing chain and sprockets.

Removal – Position No. 1 piston on TDC of compression stroke. Remove timing chain cover. See TIMING CHAIN COVER under REMOVAL & INSTALLATION. Check alignment of camshaft and crankshaft sprocket timing marks. Check timing chain deflection. See INSPECTION. Remove camshaft sprocket retaining bolt and washer. Slide sprockets and timing chain forward and remove as an assembly.

CAUTION: DO NOT replace camshaft sprocket retaining bolt with standard bolt. Original camshaft bolt has a drilled oil passage.

Installation – 1) Ensure No. 1 piston is still at TDC of compression stroke. Assemble timing chain and sprockets so sprocket timing marks are aligned. *See Fig. 7.* Install chain and sprockets as an assembly. Lubricate timing chain and sprockets with engine oil.

2) Apply RTV sealer to damper keyway. To complete installation, reverse removal procedure. Tighten bolts and nuts to specifications. See TORQUE SPECIFICATIONS table at end of article.

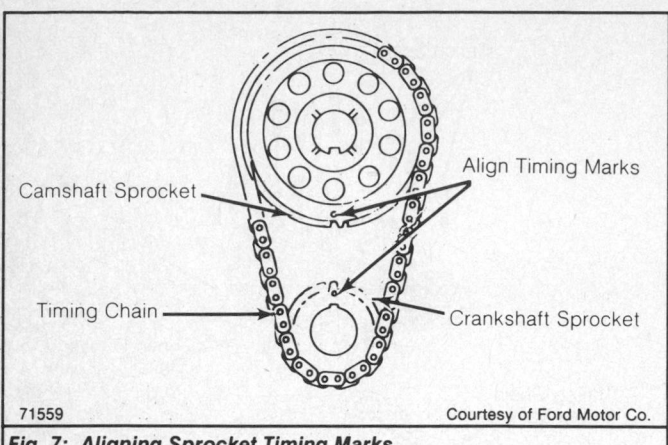

71559   Courtesy of Ford Motor Co.

Fig. 7: Aligning Sprocket Timing Marks

CAMSHAFT

Removal – **1)** Remove negative battery cable. Drain cooling system. Remove air cleaner hoses. Release fuel pressure. See FUEL PRESSURE RELEASE under REMOVAL & INSTALLATION. Using Disconnect Tool (D87L-9280-A) for 3/8" line or (D87L-9280-B) for 1/2" line, disconnect fuel supply and return lines. *See Fig. 2.*

2) Mark and disconnect vacuum hoses and electrical connectors. Remove upper radiator hose and heater hoses. On Ranger, remove ignition coil. On all models, remove throttle body. Disconnect fuel injector harness. Mark distributor rotor and body location for installation reference. Remove distributor.

3) On Aerostar, remove ignition coil from left cylinder head. On all models, remove valve covers. See VALVE COVERS under REMOVAL & INSTALLATION. Remove lower intake manifold. See INTAKE MANIFOLDS under REMOVAL & INSTALLATION.

4) With No. 1 piston on TDC of compression stroke, loosen rocker arm retaining bolts. Remove push rods, keeping them in order. Remove lifter guide plate retainer retaining bolts. Remove guide plate retainer. Remove lifter guide plates from lifters.

5) Remove lifters, keeping them in order. Remove radiator, shroud and A/C condenser (if equipped). Remove left-handed nut retaining clutch fan to pulley and remove cooling fan. Remove accessory drive belts. Remove water pump pulley. Remove A/C compressor (if equipped).

6) Remove crankshaft pulley. Using Crankshaft Damper Remover and Adapter (T58P-6316-D and T82L-6316-B), remove crankshaft damper. Remove lower radiator hose. Remove oil pan. See OIL PAN under REMOVAL & INSTALLATION. Remove timing chain cover. See TIMING CHAIN & SPROCKETS.

7) Align camshaft and crankshaft timing marks. *See Fig.* 7. Check camshaft end play. If end play is not within specification, replace thrust plate. See CAMSHAFT table under ENGINE SPECIFICATIONS at end of article.

8) Check timing chain deflection. See TIMING CHAIN & SPROCKETS. Remove timing chain and camshaft sprocket. Remove camshaft thrust plate. Remove camshaft.

Inspection – Inspect journal diameter, lobe lift, oil clearance and runout. Replace camshaft if these are not within specification. See CAMSHAFT table under ENGINE SPECIFICATIONS at end of article.

Installation – **1)** Lubricate camshaft lobes and journals with heavy SAE 50W engine oil. Carefully slide camshaft through bearings in cylinder block. Install thrust plate and recheck camshaft end play. Install timing chain and sprocket as an assembly.

CAUTION: DO NOT replace camshaft sprocket retaining bolt with standard bolt. Original camshaft bolt has a drilled oil passage.

2) Ensure crankshaft and camshaft sprockets are aligned. *See Fig. 7.* Install camshaft sprocket washer and retaining bolt, and tighten to specification. See TORQUE SPECIFICATIONS table at end of article. Lubricate hydraulic valve lifters and bores with heavy SAE 50W engine oil.

3) Install lifters in their original bores. Lubricate push rods with heavy SAE 50W engine oil. Install push rods in their original location. For each valve, rotate crankshaft until lifter rests on heel of camshaft lobe. Position rocker arm over push rod and install fulcrum.

4) Tighten rocker arm bolt to 96 INCH lbs. (11 N.m). After all rocker arms have been installed, tighten rocker arm bolts (camshaft may be in any position) to a final torque of 24 ft. lbs. (33 N.m). To complete installation, reverse removal procedure.

5) Tighten bolts/nuts to specification. See TORQUE SPECIFICATIONS table at end of article. Fill or top off all fluids. Fill and bleed cooling system. See COOLING SYSTEM BLEEDING under REMOVAL & INSTALLATION. Start engine and check for leaks. Check and adjust ignition timing as necessary.

CRANKSHAFT

NOTE: Keep all crankshaft parts in the order that they were removed.

Removal & Installation – **1)** Remove engine and attach to engine stand. See ENGINE under REMOVAL & INSTALLATION. Remove spark plugs. Remove oil pan. See OIL PAN under REMOVAL & INSTALLATION. Remove timing chain cover. See TIMING CHAIN & SPROCKETS.

2) Check timing chain deflection. See TIMING CHAIN & SPROCKETS. Remove timing chain and sprockets as an assembly. Remove flywheel. Remove oil pump. Rotate crankshaft to position connecting rod caps at bottom of stroke. Tap cap with plastic mallet to separate from rod.

3) Remove connecting rod caps. Cover connecting rod bolts with protective rubber caps. Use wooden hammer handle to tap piston into cylinder bore. Remove crankshaft main bearing caps. Carefully remove crankshaft. To install, reverse removal. Tighten nut/bolts to specifications. See TORQUE SPECIFICATIONS table at end of article.

CAMSHAFT BEARINGS

Removal – Remove engine and attach to engine stand. See ENGINE under REMOVAL & INSTALLATION. Remove camshaft and crankshaft. See CAMSHAFT and CRANKSHAFT. Remove camshaft rear bearing plug. Remove camshaft bearings with Camshaft Bearing Remover/Installer (T65L-6250-A).

NOTE: When installing new camshaft bearings, ensure bearing oil hole is aligned with oil hole in bearing bore.

Installation – **1)** Align oil hole in bearing with oil hole in bearing bore. Using Camshaft Bearing Remover/Installer, install new camshaft bearings. Ensure front bearing is installed .020-.035" (.51-.89 mm) below front face of cylinder block.

2) Coat sealing edge of new rear camshaft bearing bore plug with oil resistant sealer and install bore plug. To complete installation, reverse removal procedure.

REAR CRANKSHAFT OIL SEAL

Removal & Installation – Remove transmission. See TRANSMISSION REMOVAL & INSTALLATION article in TRANSMISSION SERVICING. Remove clutch assembly (if equipped). Remove flywheel/flexplate. Using a slide hammer, remove rear oil seal. Use care not to damage crankshaft sealing surface. Coat seal surfaces with heavy SF engine oil. Use proper size seal installer. Install seal until firmly seated. To complete installation, reverse removal procedure.

WATER PUMP

Removal – **1)** Disconnect negative battery cable. Drain cooling system. Remove left-handed nut retaining clutch fan to pulley. Remove cooling fan. Remove accessory drive belts. Remove water pump pulley.

2) Remove alternator adjusting arm and brace from throttle body. Remove lower radiator and heater hose from water pump. Rotate belt adjuster aside. Remove 11 water pump bolts. Remove water pump. See Fig. 6.

Installation – Clean all gasket surfaces. Lightly oil threads of bolt and stud, except those with Teflon sealant, before installation. *See Fig. 6.* Use sealant on bolts going into water jacket. Apply contact adhesive to new gasket and position on water pump. Install water pump. To complete installation, reverse removal procedure. Fill and bleed system. See COOLING SYSTEM BLEEDING under REMOVAL & INSTALLATION.

OIL PAN

Removal (Aerostar) – Disconnect negative battery cable. Remove dipstick. Raise and support vehicle. Remove retainer clip and electrical connector at oil low level sensor (if equipped). Drain engine oil. Remove starter motor. Remove transmission inspection cover. Remove oil pan bolts, oil pan and gasket.

Installation – To install, reverse removal procedure. Apply silicone sealant at front and rear corners of oil pan surface and cylinder block, and where timing cover meets cylinder block. Tighten bolts to specification. See TORQUE SPECIFICATIONS table at end of article. Start engine and check for oil leaks.

Removal (Ranger) – **1)** Disconnect negative battery cable. Remove dipstick. Disconnect fan shroud and position over fan. Remove motor mount nuts from frame. Position No. 1 piston at TDC of compression stroke.

2) Mark distributor rotor and body location for installation reference. Remove distributor. Raise and support vehicle. Remove retainer clip and electrical connector at oil low level sensor. Drain engine oil.

3) Remove starter motor. Remove transmission inspection cover. On 2WD models, remove right front axle assembly. See AXLE under REMOVAL & INSTALLATION in appropriate SUSPENSION article.

4) Remove oil pan bolts. Using a suitable lifting device, raise engine approximately 2 inches. Be careful not to damage oil pump pick-up tube and carefully remove oil pan. Remove oil pan gasket.

Installation – Clean gasket mating surfaces. To install, reverse removal procedure. Apply silicone sealant at front and rear corners of oil pan surface and cylinder block, and where timing chain cover meets cylinder block. Tighten bolts to specification. See TORQUE SPECIFICATIONS table at end of article. Start engine and check for leaks.

OVERHAUL

CYLINDER HEAD

Cylinder Head – **1)** Clean head gasket mating surface. Clean carbon from combustion chambers. Use care not to damage surfaces. Check cylinder head for cracks, burrs, nicks and warpage.

2) DO NOT machine more than .010" (.25 mm) from original cylinder head surface to correct warpage. Replace cylinder head as necessary. See CYLINDER HEAD table under ENGINE SPECIFICATIONS at end of article.

CAUTION: DO NOT machine more than .010" (.25 mm) from cylinder head original thickness.

Valve Springs – **1)** Inspect valve spring free length and pressure. Replace valve spring if free length and pressure are not within specification. See VALVES & VALVE SPRINGS table under ENGINE SPECIFICATIONS at end of article.

2) Measure valve spring installed height from top of spring seat to underside of spring retainer. Ensure installed height is within specification. See VALVES & VALVE SPRINGS table.

3) If installed height is not within specification, a .03" (.8 mm) shim can be installed between cylinder head and valve spring to obtain correct height.

CAUTION: DO NOT install valve spring spacers unless necessary. Using more spacers than required can result in spring breakage or worn camshaft lobes.

Valve Stem Oil Seals – Use Valve Stem Oil Seal Installer (T73P-6571-A) for seal installation. Install seal until it bottoms on valve guide. Oversize seals must be used on guides that have been reamed for oversize valves.

Valve Guides – **1)** Valve guides must be reamed for an oversized valve if valve stem oil clearance is not within specification. See CYLINDER HEAD table under ENGINE SPECIFICATIONS at end of article. Valves are available in .015" (.38 mm) and .030" (.76 mm) oversize.

2) If oversized valves or oversized valve stem oil seals are not available, valve guide may be bored out to use a service bushing. Always use reamers in proper sequence (smallest first).

NOTE: Always grind valve seat after valve guide has been reamed or service bushing has been installed.

Valve Seat – **1)** Grind valve seat to a 45-degree angle. If seat width is too wide after grinding, use a 30-degree stone to lower seat or a 60-degree stone to raise seat. Ensure valve seat angle, seat width and seat runout are within specification.

2) See CYLINDER HEAD table under ENGINE SPECIFICATIONS at end of article. Valve seats must be ground when valve guide is reamed or replaced. Replacement information is not available from manufacturer.

Valves – Ensure head diameter, valve face runout, stem diameter and valve margin are within specification. See VALVES & VALVE SPRINGS table under ENGINE SPECIFICATIONS at end of article.

CAUTION: DO NOT remove more than .010" (.25 mm) from end of valve stem when resurfacing tip of valve.

CYLINDER BLOCK ASSEMBLY

Piston & Rod Assembly – Install piston on connecting rod, with piston notch on the same side as the button on connecting rod. *See Fig. 8.* Install piston and connecting rod in engine, with notch on top of piston toward front of engine.

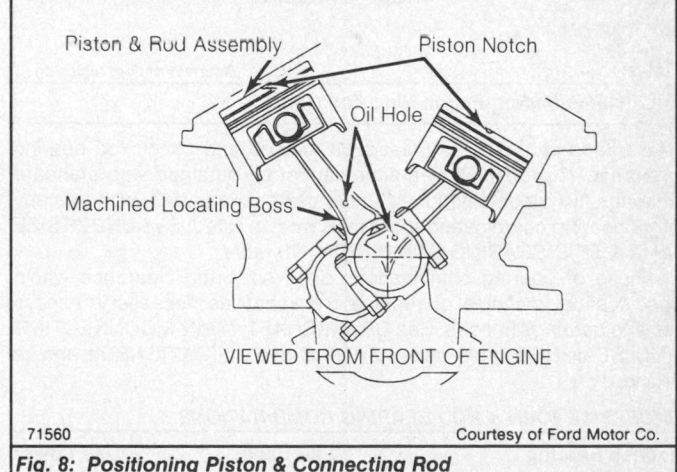

71560   Courtesy of Ford Motor Co.

Fig. 8: Positioning Piston & Connecting Rod

Fitting Pistons – **1)** Check piston-to-bore clearance. See PISTONS, PINS & RINGS table under ENGINE SPECIFICATIONS at end of article. Standard size pistons are color-coded Red, Blue or Yellow on the piston dome. See PISTONS, PINS & RINGS table. Oversize pistons are also available.

2) If bore diameter is in lower one-third of specification, use a Red coded piston. If bore diameter is in middle one-third of specification, use a Blue coded piston. If bore diameter is in upper one-third of specification, use Yellow coded piston. Use proper size piston to obtain specified clearance. See PISTON SELECTION table.

PISTON SELECTION

Cylinder Bore Diameter In. (mm)	Piston Color Code
3.5043-3.5053 (89.009-89.035)	Red
3.5053-3.5063 (89.035-89.060)	Blue
3.5063-3.5073 (89.060-89.085)	Yellow

Piston Rings – 1) Select rings for bore diameter. Place ring in cylinder bore in which it will be installed. Use piston to square ring in bore and place ring below normal ring wear area. Measure ring end gap. If ring gap is not within specification, try another ring set. See PISTONS, PINS & RINGS table under ENGINE SPECIFICATIONS at end of article.

2) Check side clearance of rings after installing on piston. Ensure clearance is within specification around entire circumference. Replace piston and/or rings if clearance is not as specified. See PISTONS, PINS & RINGS table. Ensure rings are properly spaced on piston before installing pistons into cylinder. *See Fig. 9.*

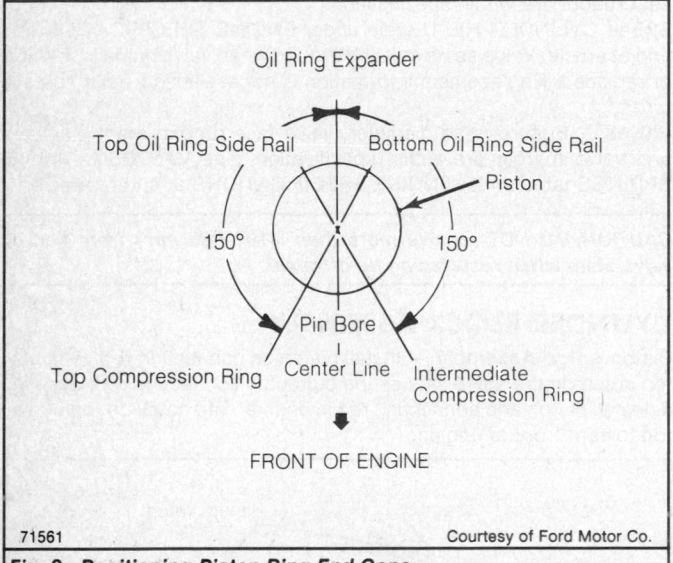

71561   Courtesy of Ford Motor Co.

Fig. 9: Positioning Piston Ring End Gaps

Rod Bearings – 1) Use Plastigage method and check rod bearing clearance. If proper oil clearance cannot be obtained with standard bearings, try a combination of undersize bearings. DO NOT use any other bearing combination other than what is listed. See UNDERSIZE MAIN & ROD BEARING COMBINATIONS table.

2) If use of bearing combinations does not bring clearance within specification, machine or replace crankshaft as necessary. Always replace bearings in pairs. See CRANKSHAFT, MAIN & CONNECTING ROD BEARINGS table under ENGINE SPECIFICATIONS at end of article.

UNDERSIZE MAIN & ROD BEARING COMBINATIONS [1]

Excess Bearing Clearance In. (mm)	Use Upper Bearing In. (mm)	Use Lower Bearing In. (mm)
.0-.0005 (.0-.013)	.001 (.025)	[2]
.0005-.0010 (.013-.025)	.001 (.025)	.001 (.025)
.0010-.0015 (.025-.039)	.002 (.050)	.001 (.025)
.0015-.0020 (.039-.050)	.002 (.050)	.002 (.050)

[1] – DO NOT use any other bearing combination other than what is listed. If use of bearing combinations does not bring clearance within specification, machine or replace crankshaft as necessary.

[2] – Use standard bearing.

Crankshaft & Main Bearings – 1) When checking main bearing clearance in vehicle, position a jack under adjoining bearing counterweight being checked. Remove only one main bearing cap at a time.

2) Use Plastigage method and check main bearing clearance. If proper oil clearance cannot be obtained with standard bearings, try a combination of undersize bearings. DO NOT use any other bearing combination other than what is listed. See UNDERSIZE MAIN & ROD BEARING COMBINATIONS table.

3) If use of bearing combinations does not bring clearance within specification, machine or replace crankshaft as necessary. Always replace bearings in pairs. See CRANKSHAFT, MAIN & CONNECTING ROD BEARINGS table under ENGINE SPECIFICATIONS at end of article.

4) Tighten main bearing cap bolts finger tight. Pry crankshaft forward and tighten bearing caps to specification. See TORQUE SPECIFICATIONS table at end of article.

5) Check crankshaft end play. Replace thrust bearing if end play is not within specification. Thrust bearing is No. 3 (from front) main bearing in block. See CRANKSHAFT, MAIN & CONNECTING ROD BEARINGS table.

Cylinder Block – 1) Using a feeler gauge and straightedge, check cylinder block head gasket surface for warpage. Check cylinder bore for wear, taper, out-of-round and piston fit. See CYLINDER BLOCK table under ENGINE SPECIFICATIONS at end of article.

CAUTION: DO NOT machine more than .010" (.25 mm) of material from original cylinder block head surface.

2) Install all main bearing caps and tighten to specification before honing cylinder bore. Ensure bearing caps are installed in their original location, with arrow on cap pointing toward front of engine.

3) Use ONLY a spring-loaded type cylinder hone. After honing, thoroughly clean bore with detergent and water solution. Rinse solution from bore thoroughly with clean water. Wipe bore clean with lint-free cloth. Lubricate cylinder bores with engine oil.

ENGINE OILING

ENGINE LUBRICATION SYSTEM

Engine lubrication system is a force-feed type. The oil is supplied under full pressure to crankshaft, connecting rods, camshaft bearing and valve lifters. A controlled volume of oil is supplied to rocker arms and push rods. All other moving parts are lubricated by splash or gravity flow. Oil flows through oil filter before entering main oil gallery.

Crankcase Capacity – Crankcase capacity is 4.5 qts. (4.25L) with oil filter.

Oil Pressure – Normal oil pressure at 2500 RPM should be 40-60 psi (2.8-4.2 kg/cm²) with engine at normal operating temperature.

Pressure Relief Valve – Pressure relief valve is located in oil pump and is not adjustable.

OIL PUMP

Removal & Disassembly – Remove oil pan. See OIL PAN under REMOVAL & INSTALLATION. Remove oil pump baffle. Remove oil pump retaining bolts. Remove oil pump and pick-up tube assembly. Remove oil pump drive shaft. Remove and replace gasket. Disassemble oil pump. Note direction of component installation for reassembly reference.

Inspection – Inspect components for damage. Measure rotor end clearance, outer race-to-housing clearance and rotor tip clearance. Check clearance between pressure relief valve and bore. Measure relief valve tension. Replace oil pump assembly if measurements are not within specifications. See OIL PUMP SPECIFICATIONS table.

NOTE: Oil pump is serviced as an assembly only. Replace assembly if measurements are not within specifications. See OIL PUMP SPECIFICATIONS table.

OIL PUMP SPECIFICATIONS

Application	In. (mm)
Drive Shaft-To-Housing Clearance	.0005-.0019 (.013-.048)
Gear Backlash	.008-.012 (.20-.31)
Gear Height Clearance	.0003-.0032 (.008-.081)
Idler Shaft-To-Idler Gear	.0015-.0027 (.038-.069)
Idler-To-Driver Gear	
Radial Clearance	.002-.006 (.05-.15)
Relief Valve Spring Tension	[1]
Relief Valve-To-Bore Clearance	.0017-.0029 (.043-.074)

[1] – Tension should be 9-10 lbs. @ 1.11" (4.08-4.54 kg @ 28.2 mm).

Reassembly & Installation – To reassemble, reverse disassembly procedure. Ensure components are installed in original location. To install, reverse removal procedure. Tighten bolts to specification. See TORQUE SPECIFICATIONS table. Fill crankcase.

TORQUE SPECIFICATIONS

TORQUE SPECIFICATIONS

Application	Ft. Lbs. (N.m)
Bellhousing-To-Engine Bolt	28-38 (38-51)
Camshaft Sprocket Bolt	46 (62)
Connecting Rod Cap Nut	26 (35)
Crankshaft Damper Bolt	107 (145)
Cylinder Head Bolt [1]	
Step 1	59 (80)
Step 2	Loosen One Full Turn
Step 3	37 (51)
Step 4	68 (92)
Engine Front Cover-To-Block	
6-mm Bolt	[2]
8-mm Bolt	19 (25)
Engine Mount-To-Chassis Bolt	71-94 (96-127)
Engine Mount-To-Engine Bracket Bolt	71-94 (96-127)
Exhaust Manifold Bolt	19 (25)
Fan Clutch-To-Water Pump Nut [3]	30-100 (41-137)
Flexplate-To-Converter Bolt	20-34 (27-46)
Flywheel Bolt	59 (80)
Front Crossmember-To-Frame Nut	145-195 (196-264)
Idler Pulley Bolt	30-40 (40-55)
Lower Intake Manifold Bolt [4]	
1st Step	11 (15)
2nd Step	18 (24)
Main Bearing Cap Bolt	66 (90)
Oil Pump Bolt	30-40 (40-55)
Rear Mount-To-Crossmember Nut	71-94 (96-127)
Rear Mount-To-Transmission Bolt	60-80 (81-108)
Rocker Arm Bolt	
Step 1	[5]
Step 2	24 (33)
Spark Plug	11 (15)
Starter Bolt	15-20 (20-27)
Upper Intake Manifold Bolt [6]	15-22 (20-30)

	INCH Lbs. (N.m)
Camshaft Thrust Plate Bolt	84 (10)
Fuel Rail Bolt	84 (10)
Oil Pan Bolt	84 (10)
Valve Cover Bolt	108 (12)
Water Pump Bolt [7]	84 (10)

[1] – Tighten bolts in sequence. See Fig. 5.
[2] – Tighten to 84 INCH lbs. (10 N.m).
[3] – Left-hand thread.
[4] – Tighten bolts in sequence. See Fig. 4.
[5] – Tighten to 96 INCH lbs. (11 N.m).
[6] – Tighten in sequence. See Fig. 3.
[7] – Apply sealant to designated bolts. See Fig. 6.

ENGINE SPECIFICATIONS

GENERAL SPECIFICATIONS

Application	Specification
Displacement	182 Cu. In. (3.0L)
Bore	3.50" (89 mm)
Stroke	3.14" (80 mm)
Compression Ratio	9.3:1
Fuel System	PFI
Horsepower @ RPM	145 @ 4800
Torque Ft. Lbs. @ RPM	165 @ 3000

CRANKSHAFT, MAIN & CONNECTING ROD BEARINGS

Application	In. (mm)
Crankshaft End Play	.004-.008 (.10-.20)
Main Bearings	
Journal Diameter	2.5190-2.5198 (63.973-64.003)
Journal Out-Of-Round	.0003 (.008)
Journal Taper	[1] .0003 (.008)
Journal Runout	.002 (.05)
Oil Clearance	
Desired	.0010-.0014 (.025-.036)
Allowable	.0005-.0023 (.013-.058)
Connecting Rod Bearings	
Journal Diameter	2.1253-2.1261 (53.983-54.003)
Journal Out-Of-Round	.0003 (.008)
Journal Taper	[1] .0003 (.008)
Oil Clearance	
Desired	.0010-.0014 (.025-.036)
Allowable	.0009-.0027 (.023-.069)

[1] – Specification listed is per 1" (25.4 mm).

CONNECTING RODS

Application	In. (mm)
Bore Diameter	
Pin Bore	.9096-.9112 (23.104-23.145)
Crankpin Bore	2.250 (57.15)
Center-To-Center Length	5.53 (140.5)
Maximum Bend	[1] .0016 (.040)
Maximum Twist	[1] .003 (.08)
Side Play	.006-.014 (.15-.36)

[1] – Specification listed is per 1" (25.4 mm)

PISTONS, PINS & RINGS

Application	In. (mm)
Pistons [1]	
Clearance	.0012-.0023 (.030-.058)
Diameter	
Red	3.5024-3.5031 (89.962-89.978)
Blue	3.5035-3.5041 (88.988-89.004)
Yellow	3.5045-3.5051 (89.014-89.030)
Pins	
Diameter	.9119-.9124 (23.162-23.175)
Piston Fit	.0002-.0005 (.005-.013)
Rod Fit	Press Fit
Rings	
No. 1 & 2	
End Gap	.010-.020 (.25-.51)
Side Clearance	.0016-.0037 (.041-.094)
No. 3 (Oil)	
End Gap	.010-.049 (.25-1.24)
Side Clearance	Snug Fit

[1] – Pistons are color-coded on dome of pistons. For correct piston selection, see FITTING PISTONS under CYLINDER BLOCK ASSEMBLY.

CYLINDER HEAD

Application	Specification
Maximum Warpage	[1] .007" (.18 mm)
Valve Seats	
Seat Angle	45°
Seat Width	.06-.08" (1.5-2.0 mm)
Maximum Seat Runout	.001" (.03 mm)
Valve Guides	
Intake Valve	
Valve Guide I.D.	.3433-.3443" (8.720-8.745 mm)
Valve Stem-To-Guide	
Oil Clearance	.0010-.0027 (.025-.069 mm)
Exhaust Valve	
Valve Guide I.D.	.3433-.3443" (8.720-8.745 mm)
Valve Stem-To-Guide	
Oil Clearance	.0015-.0032" (.038-.081 mm)

[1] – Maximum cylinder head wear limit is .010" (2.5 mm). DO NOT machine more than .010" (.25 mm) from original cylinder head thickness.

CAMSHAFT

Application	In. (mm)
Bearing Bore	
1 & 4	2.1531-2.1541 (54.689-54.714)
2 & 3	2.1334-2.1344 (54.188-54.214)
End Play	.001 (.03)
Journal Diameter	2.0074-2.0084 (50.988-51.013)
Journal Runout	.002 (.05)
Lobe Lift	.26 (6.60)
Lobe Wear Limit	.005 (.13)
Oil Clearance	.001-.003 (.03-.08)

VALVE LIFTERS

Application	In. (mm)
Bore Diameter	.8752-.8767 (22.230-22.268)
Collapsed Lifter Clearance	.088-.189 (2.24-4.80)
Lifter Diameter	.874 (22.20)
Oil Clearance	.0007-.0027 (.018-.069)

CYLINDER BLOCK

Application	In. (mm)
Cylinder Bore	
Standard Diameter	3.50 (89.0)
Maximum Taper	.002 (.05)
Maximum Out-Of-Round	.002 (.05)
Maximum Deck Warpage	[1] .003 (.08)

[1] – Specification is within a 6" (152 mm) area. DO NOT machine more than .010" (.25 mm) from original gasket surface.

VALVES & VALVE SPRINGS

Application	Specification
Intake Valves	
Face Angle	44°
Head Diameter	1.57" (39.9 mm)
Minimum Margin	.0313" (.794 mm)
Stem Diameter	.3126-.3134" (7.940-7.960 mm)
Exhaust Valves	
Face Angle	44°
Head Diameter	1.30" (33.0 mm)
Minimum Margin	.0313" (.794 mm)
Stem Diameter	.3121-.3129" (7.927-7.948 mm)
Valve Springs	
Free Length	1.84" (46.7 mm)
Installed Height	1.58" (40.1 mm)
Out-Of-Square	.078" (1.98 mm)

	Lbs. @ In. (kg @ mm)
Pressure	
Valve Closed	65 @ 1.58 (30 @ 40.1)
Valve Open	180 @ 1.16 (82 @ 29.5)

Aerostar, Explorer, Ranger

NOTE: For repair procedures not covered in this article, see ENGINE OVERHAUL PROCEDURES article in GENERAL INFORMATION.

ENGINE IDENTIFICATION

The 4.0L V6 engine may be identified by Vehicle Identification Number (VIN). The VIN is stamped on a metal tab attached to left side of instrument panel, and is visible through the windshield. The VIN is also stamped on the Safety Certification Decals mounted on driver's front door lock panel, and on the Engine Identification Label mounted on valve cover.

The eighth character of VIN identifies the engine, and tenth character, letter "N", indicates 1992 model. All label numbers are necessary for determining correct and unique parts to specific engines. DO NOT remove labels at any time.

VIN ENGINE CODE

Engine	Code
4.0L PFI	X

ADJUSTMENTS

VALVE CLEARANCE

NOTE: Information on valve clearance check is not available from manufacturer.

The 4.0L engine uses hydraulic roller lifters and nonadjustable rocker arms. Lifters are not adjustable; if lifters are found to be excessively worn or noisy, repair or replace as necessary.

REMOVAL & INSTALLATION

WARNING: When battery is disconnected, vehicle computer and memory systems may lose memory data. Driveability problems may exist until computer systems have completed a relearn cycle. See COMPUTER RELEARN PROCEDURES article in GENERAL INFORMATION before disconnecting battery.

NOTE: Discharge A/C system using approved refrigerant recovery/ recycling equipment.

FUEL PRESSURE RELEASE

Disconnect negative battery cable. Remove fuel tank filler cap to release tank pressure. Attach a fuel pressure gauge to pressure relief valve on fuel rail. Release fuel pressure.

COOLING SYSTEM BLEEDING

1) Fill cooling system with 50/50 mixture of coolant and water. Pause several minutes for circulation. Fill radiator to filler neck seat. Install radiator cap fully then back off to first stop.

WARNING: When engine is operating, NEVER remove radiator cap under any conditions. Failure to follow instruction could damage cooling system or engine, or cause personal injury. Always wrap protective material around radiator cap to avoid injury from hot coolant.

2) Place heater controls to maximum heat. Start engine and operate at 2000 RPM for approximately 3-4 minutes. Turn engine off. Use a protective rag, and carefully remove radiator cap. Add coolant to filler neck seat.
3) Install radiator cap fully, then back off to first stop. Start engine and allow to operate at 2000 RPM until upper radiator hose is warm. Check heater output. Turn engine off. Use protective rag, and carefully remove radiator cap. Add coolant to filler neck seat if necessary.

4) Tightly install radiator cap. Remove small cap (large cap is for windshield washer reservoir) on coolant recovery reservoir. Add 1.1 qt. (1L) of 50/50 mixture of coolant and water to reservoir. Install reservoir cap.

ENGINE

NOTE: Aerostar engine assembly can be removed through the front of the engine compartment without transmission attached.

Removal – 1) Disconnect negative battery cable. On Aerostar, remove front grille and bumper cover. On Explorer and Ranger, remove hood. On all models, remove air cleaner tube and assembly. Discharge A/C system (if equipped) and remove A/C condenser. Drain engine oil. Disconnect and remove power steering and transmission coolers.
2) Drain cooling system. Remove upper and lower radiator hoses. Disconnect radiator fan shroud and position over fan. Remove radiator. Remove accessory drive belt. On Aerostar, remove right front air diverter flap. Remove center hood latch support.
3) Remove A/C compressor (if equipped). Remove oil fill tube. Remove engine cover. Remove ice/snow shield. Remove power steering hoses, pump and bracket. Remove transmission dipstick tube. On all models, remove alternator. Disconnect exhaust system from exhaust manifolds. Disconnect wiring and remove starter.
4) On A/T models, remove converter-to-flexplate bolts. Remove bolt securing transmission oil cooler bracket. Remove both engine mount-to-frame bolts. Remove converter housing-to-engine bolts, except 2 upper bolts. Remove left motor mount from engine. Remove 2 upper converter housing bolts.
5) On M/T models, disconnect electrical connectors at transmission and transfer case. On all models, release fuel pressure. See FUEL PRESSURE RELEASE. Using Fuel Line Coupling Key (T90P-9550-A), disconnect fuel supply and return lines at fuel supply manifold. *See Fig. 1.* Disconnect throttle linkage and bracket. Remove heater hoses.
6) Mark and disconnect all engine vacuum hoses. Disconnect throttle position switch connector. Remove throttle body from upper intake manifold. Disconnect engine wiring harness main connectors. Install engine lifting brackets on right-front and left-rear of engine. Remove engine.

Installation – To install, reverse removal procedure. Evacuate and recharge A/C system (if equipped). Check and top off all fluid levels. Fill and bleed air from cooling system. See COOLING SYSTEM BLEEDING.

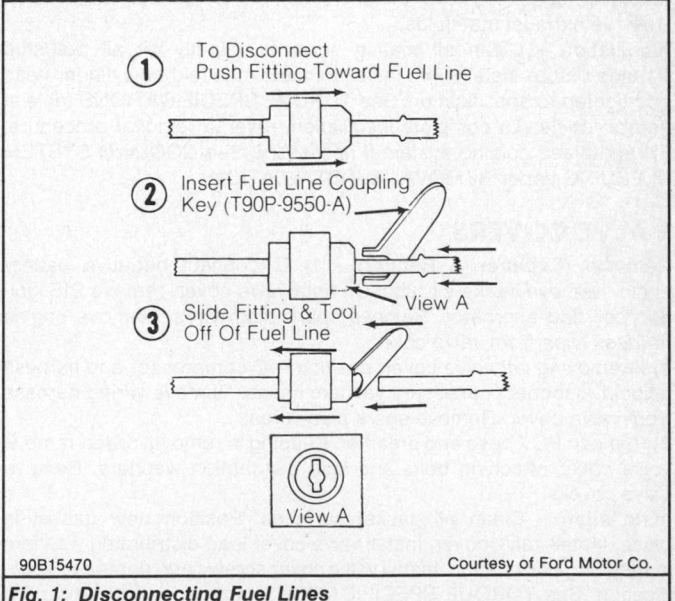

① To Disconnect
Push Fitting Toward Fuel Line

② Insert Fuel Line Coupling Key (T90P-9550-A)

View A

③ Slide Fitting & Tool Off Of Fuel Line

View A

90B15470
Courtesy of Ford Motor Co.

Fig. 1: Disconnecting Fuel Lines

INTAKE MANIFOLDS

Removal (Upper) – 1) Remove negative battery cable. Remove air cleaner intake duct from throttle body. Remove snow/ice shield to expose throttle linkage. Remove throttle cable and bracket from throttle body.

2) Disconnect all vacuum hoses. Disconnect all electrical connectors. Relieve fuel pressure. See FUEL PRESSURE RELEASE under REMOVAL & INSTALLATION. Using Fuel Line Coupling Key (T90P-9550-A), disconnect fuel supply and return lines at fuel supply manifold. *See Fig. 1.* Remove ignition coil. Remove upper intake manifold bolts. Remove upper intake manifold and throttle body as an assembly.

Installation – Clean and inspect mounting surfaces. Position new gasket on mounting studs. Install upper intake manifold and tighten bolts to specifications. See TORQUE SPECIFICATIONS table at end of article. To complete installation, reverse removal procedure.

Removal (Lower) – With upper intake manifold removed, remove valve covers. See VALVE COVERS. Remove manifold attaching bolts. Remove lower intake manifold assembly and gasket.

Installation – Clean gasket mating surfaces. Install intake manifold gaskets. Apply silicone sealer at 4 corners of cylinder block sealing surface. Install lower intake manifold within 15 minutes of silicone sealer application. Tighten bolts in sequence to specification. *See Fig. 2.* See TORQUE SPECIFICATIONS table at end of article.

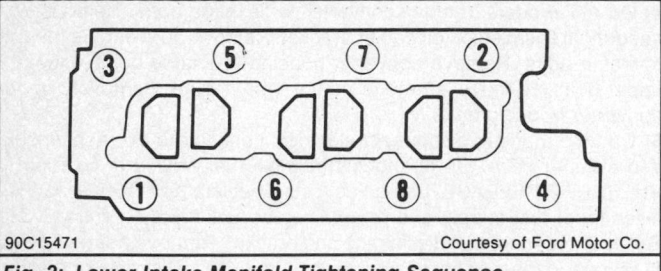

90C15471   Courtesy of Ford Motor Co.

Fig. 2: Lower Intake Manifold Tightening Sequence

EXHAUST MANIFOLDS

Removal – 1) On left exhaust manifold, remove oil dipstick tube support bracket. It may be necessary to remove power steering pressure and return hose. If removing right exhaust manifold, disconnect heater hoses.

2) On both exhaust manifolds, remove exhaust pipe-to-manifold attaching bolts. Remove exhaust manifold-to-cylinder head bolts. Remove exhaust manifolds.

Installation – Clean all mating surfaces. Lightly oil all bolt/stud threads before installation. Install exhaust manifold on cylinder head and tighten to specification. See TORQUE SPECIFICATIONS table at end of article. To complete installation, reverse removal procedure. Fill and bleed cooling system if necessary. See COOLING SYSTEM BLEEDING under REMOVAL & INSTALLATION.

VALVE COVERS

Removal (Explorer & Ranger) – 1) Disconnect negative battery cable. Remove intake air tube. On right valve cover, remove DIS ignition coil and alternator. Remove spark plug wires. Remove engine harness clips from valve cover.

2) If removing left valve cover, position A/C compressor and harness aside. Disconnect necessary vacuum hoses. Remove wiring harness from valve cover. Remove spark plug wires.

3) Remove PCV hose and breather. Keeping in removal order, remove valve cover attaching bolts and load distribution washers. Remove valve covers.

Installation – Clean all gasket surfaces. Position new gasket in place. Install valve cover. Install valve cover load distribution washers in their original location. Install valve cover screws and tighten to specification. See TORQUE SPECIFICATIONS table at end of article. To complete installation, reverse removal procedure.

Removal (Aerostar) – 1) Disconnect negative battery cable. Remove intake air tube. Remove interior engine cover. For right valve cover, remove oil filler tube and dipstick tube.

2) Remove transmission dipstick tube. Remove alternator and ignition coil. Remove spark plug wires. Remove left valve cover attaching bolts. Remove valve cover. For right valve cover, remove intake manifold. See INTAKE MANIFOLDS.

3) Remove A/C compressor from bracket and set aside. Remove right valve cover attaching bolts and remove right valve cover.

Installation – Clean all gasket surfaces. Position new gasket in place. Install valve cover. Install valve cover load distribution washers in their original location. Install valve cover screws and tighten to specification. See TORQUE SPECIFICATIONS table at end of article. To complete installation, reverse removal procedure.

CAUTION: Failure to use new valve cover gaskets and valve cover load distribution washers will result in oil leaks.

CYLINDER HEAD

Removal – 1) Disconnect negative battery cable. Drain cooling system. Release fuel pressure. See FUEL PRESSURE RELEASE under REMOVAL & INSTALLATION. Remove upper and lower intake manifolds. See INTAKE MANIFOLDS under REMOVAL & INSTALLATION. Remove exhaust manifold. See EXHAUST MANIFOLDS under REMOVAL & INSTALLATION.

2) Remove valve covers. See VALVE COVERS. Remove spark plugs. Remove accessory drive belt. If removing left cylinder head, remove A/C compressor (if equipped). Remove power steering pump and bracket, and position aside.

3) If removing right cylinder head, remove alternator and bracket. On all cylinder heads, remove rocker arm shaft bolts evenly by loosening bolts 2 turns at a time. Remove rocker arm shaft assembly.

CAUTION: If rocker arm shafts are not loosened gradually, shafts may become bent or damaged.

4) Mark push rod location for installation reference, and remove push rods. Remove and discard cylinder head bolts. Remove cylinder head(s) and gaskets.

Inspection – Check dowels in cylinder block and replace as necessary. Check cylinder head warpage. Resurface cylinder head if warpage exceeds specification. See CYLINDER HEAD table under ENGINE SPECIFICATIONS at end of article. DO NOT machine more than .010" (.25 mm) from original cylinder head surface.

CAUTION: Always use NEW cylinder head bolts when installing cylinder heads.

Installation – 1) Ensure all bolt holes in cylinder block are clean. Install head gasket and cylinder head. Install new cylinder head bolts. Tighten cylinder head bolts in sequence to specification. *See Fig. 3.* See TORQUE SPECIFICATIONS table at end of article.

2) Coat push rods with Oil Conditioner (D9AZ-19579-CA) and install in original position. Install rocker arm shaft assembly to cylinder head. Guide rocker arms onto push rods.

3) Tighten rocker arm bolts evenly to specification. To complete installation, reverse removal installation. Fill and bleed cooling system. See COOLING SYSTEM BLEEDING under REMOVAL & INSTALLATION.

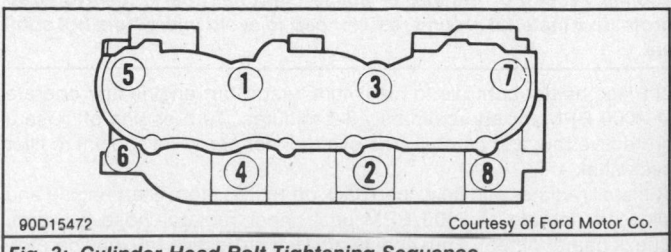

90D15472   Courtesy of Ford Motor Co.

Fig. 3: Cylinder Head Bolt Tightening Sequence

FRONT CRANKSHAFT OIL SEAL

Removal & Installation – **1)** Remove accessory drive belts. Remove crankshaft damper retaining bolt. Using Crankshaft Damper Remover (T74P-6316-A), remove crankshaft damper. Carefully pry seal from timing chain cover; DO NOT damage timing chain cover or crankshaft.
2) To install, lubricate new seal lip with engine oil. Using Timing Chain Cover Aligner (T74P-6019-A) and Crankshaft Front Seal Installer (T90T-6701-A), install front crankshaft seal. Apply silicone sealer to crankshaft keyway.
3) Coat crankshaft damper sealing surface with engine oil. Install crankshaft damper. Tighten to specification. See TORQUE SPECIFI-CATIONS table at end of article. Install accessory drive belts.

TIMING CHAIN COVER

Removal – **1)** Remove oil pan. See OIL PAN under REMOVAL & INSTALLATION. Drain cooling system. Remove upper and lower radiator hoses. Remove radiator. Remove coolant hoses from water pump. Remove A/C compressor and power steering bracket (if equipped).
2) Remove alternator and drive belt(s). Using Fan Clutch Pulley Holder (T84T-6312-C) and Fan Clutch Nut Wrench (T84T-6312-D), remove fan and clutch assembly. *See Fig. 8.*

CAUTION: Fan clutch nut has left-hand threads. Remove nut by turn-ing nut clockwise as viewed from front of engine.

---

3) If equipped with A/C, remove alternator and bracket. Remove water pump pulley. Remove water pump attaching bolts and remove pump. Remove gasket. Using Crankshaft Damper Remover (T74P-6316-A), remove crankshaft damper.
4) Remove crankshaft timing sensor assembly. Note bolt location for installation reference; timing chain cover bolts have different lengths. Remove timing chain cover bolts and remove cover. Remove gasket.
Installation – **1)** Clean timing chain cover mating surfaces. Apply sealing compound to gasket surfaces. Place new timing chain cover gasket into position. Position timing chain cover on engine. Insert bolts into their original location.
2) Tighten bolts to specification. See TORQUE SPECIFICATIONS table at end of article. Apply silicone sealer to crankshaft keyway. To complete installation, reverse removal procedure. Install oil pan. See OIL PAN under REMOVAL & INSTALLATION. Fill or top off all fluids. Fill and bleed air from cooling system. See COOLING SYSTEM BLEEDING under REMOVAL & INSTALLATION.

TIMING CHAIN & SPROCKETS

Removal – **1)** Position No. 1 piston at TDC of compression stroke. Remove timing chain cover. See TIMING CHAIN COVER. Remove oil pan. See OIL PAN under REMOVAL & INSTALLATION.
2) Ensure all timing marks are aligned. *See Fig. 4.* Check camshaft end play. If end play is not within specification, replace camshaft thrust plate. See CAMSHAFT table under ENGINE SPECIFICATIONS at end of article.
3) Remove camshaft sprocket retaining bolt and crankshaft sprocket Woodruff key. Remove tensioner and guide rail; replace as necessary. Remove crankshaft, camshaft sprockets and timing chain as an assembly.
4) If crankshaft sprocket is difficult to remove, carefully pry off with a pair of screwdrivers positioned evenly on sprocket.
Installation – **1)** Install guide rail to cylinder block, with pin inserted into oil hole of block. Install 2 tensioner retaining bolts. Ensure timing marks are aligned. *See Fig. 4.* If camshaft thrust plate was removed, install thrust plate so that it covers main oil gallery. *See Fig. 5.*
2) Install crankshaft, camshaft sprocket and timing chain as an assembly. Install tensioner with clip in place to lock tensioner in retracted position. *See Fig. 4.* Install camshaft sprocket bolt and tighten to spec-ification. See TORQUE SPECIFICATIONS table at end of article.
3) Remove clip from tensioner assembly. To complete installation, reverse removal procedure. Fill and bleed cooling system. See COOL-ING SYSTEM BLEEDING under REMOVAL & INSTALLATION.

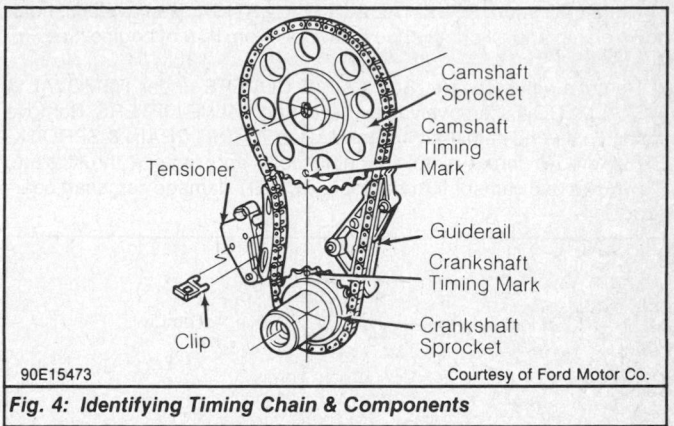

Fig. 4: Identifying Timing Chain & Components

NOTE: Ensure tensioner side of timing chain is held inward, and guide side is straight and tight. Ensure clip is removed from tension-er before installing timing chain cover.

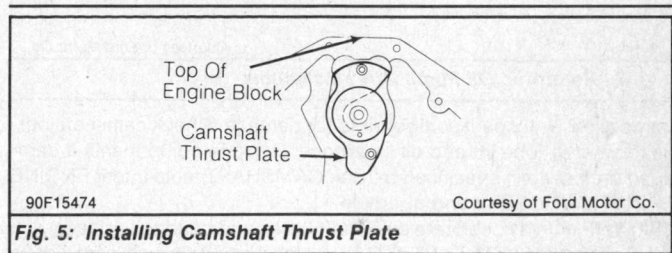

Fig. 5: Installing Camshaft Thrust Plate

VALVE LIFTERS

Removal – Remove cylinder head. See CYLINDER HEAD under REMOVAL & INSTALLATION.

CAUTION: If rocker arm shafts are not loosened gradually, shafts may become bent or damaged.

Inspection – Inspect lifter for damage. Ensure roller rotates smooth-ly. Measure lifter O.D. and cylinder block lifter bore I.D. Replace com-ponents if oil clearance is not within specification. See VALVE LIFTERS table under ENGINE SPECIFICATIONS at end of article.
Installation – **1)** Lubricate lifter and cylinder block bore with Oil Con-ditioner (D9AZ-19579-CA) or heavy engine oil. Install lifter in original location, with alignment tab in locating groove of bore. *See Fig. 6.* Ensure lifters slide freely in bore.
2) To install cylinder head, reverse removal procedure. See CYLIN-DER HEAD under REMOVAL & INSTALLATION. Tighten bolts/nuts to specification. See TORQUE SPECIFICATIONS table at end of article. To install remaining components, reverse removal procedure.

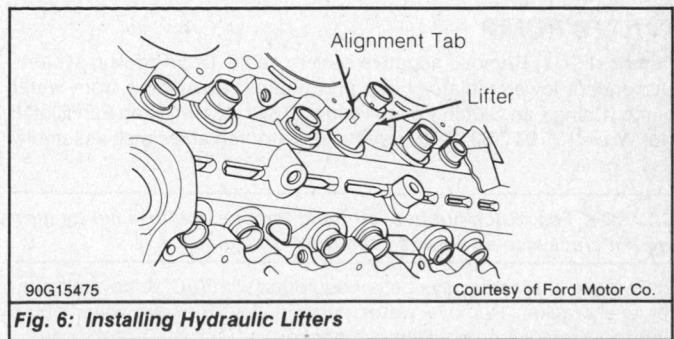

Fig. 6: Installing Hydraulic Lifters

CAMSHAFT

Removal – **1)** Disconnect negative battery cable. Remove timing chain cover. See TIMING CHAIN COVER under REMOVAL & INSTAL-LATION. Remove upper and lower intake manifolds. See INTAKE

MANIFOLDS under REMOVAL & INSTALLATION. Remove bolt, hold-down clamp and oil pump drive assembly from rear of engine. See Fig. 7.

2) Remove valve covers. See VALVE COVERS under REMOVAL & INSTALLATION. Remove valve lifters. See VALVE LIFTERS. Remove timing chain and camshaft sprocket. See TIMING CHAIN & SPROCKETS. Remove thrust plate attaching bolts and remove thrust plate. Slowly remove camshaft from block; DO NOT damage camshaft bearings.

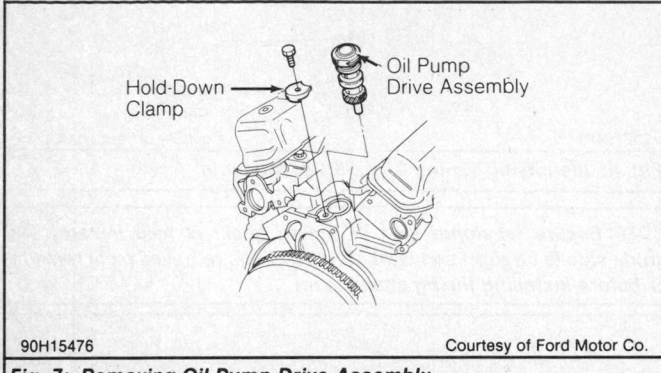

90H15476   Courtesy of Ford Motor Co.

Fig. 7: Removing Oil Pump Drive Assembly

Inspection – Inspect components for damage. Check camshaft journal diameter, lobe lift and oil clearance. Replace components if damaged or not within specification. See CAMSHAFT table under ENGINE SPECIFICATIONS at end of article.

Installation – **1)** Lubricate camshaft lobes and bearing surfaces with Oil Conditioner (D9AZ-19579-CA). Install camshaft; use care not to damage bearings and journal surfaces. If camshaft thrust plate was removed, install thrust plate so it covers main oil gallery. See Fig. 5.

2) Ensure camshaft end play is within specification. See CAMSHAFT table under ENGINE SPECIFICATIONS at end of article. To complete installation, reverse removal procedure. Fill and bleed cooling system. See COOLING SYSTEM BLEEDING under REMOVAL & INSTALLATION.

REAR CRANKSHAFT OIL SEAL

Removal & Installation – **1)** Rear main bearing oil seal is a one-piece seal. Remove transmission. On M/T models, remove clutch assembly. On all models, remove flywheel/flexplate. Punch hole in metal portion of seal with an awl. Remove seal using a slide hammer.

2) To install, lubricate seal and mating surfaces with engine oil. Install seal on crankshaft, with spring side toward crankshaft. Using Crankshaft Rear Oil Seal Replacer (T72C-6165-R), install seal into position until seal is firmly seated. To install remaining components, reverse removal procedure.

WATER PUMP

Removal – **1)** Remove negative battery cable. Drain cooling system. Disconnect lower radiator hose and heater return hose from water pump. Using Fan Clutch Pulley Holder (T84T-6312-C) and Fan Clutch Nut Wrench (T84T-6312-D), remove radiator fan and clutch assembly. See Fig. 8.

CAUTION: Fan clutch nut has left-hand threads. Remove nut by turning nut clockwise as viewed from front of engine.

2) Remove alternator drive belt. If equipped with A/C, remove alternator and bracket. Remove water pump pulley. Remove water pump bolts and remove pump. Remove gasket.

Installation – Clean all gasket surfaces. Apply sealer to both sides of new gasket, and position gasket on water pump. Install water pump. To complete installation, reverse removal procedure. Fill and bleed cooling system. See COOLING SYSTEM BLEEDING under REMOVAL & INSTALLATION.

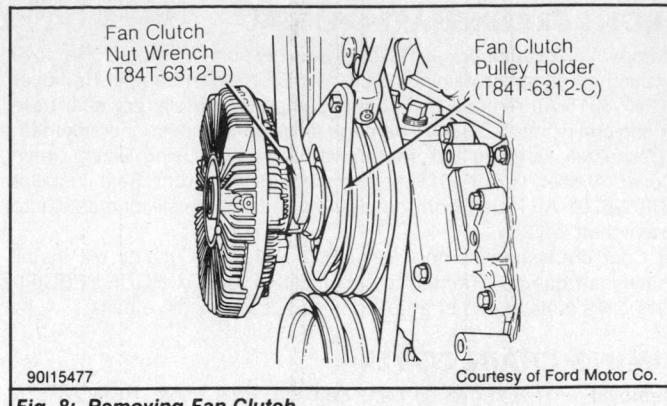

90I15477   Courtesy of Ford Motor Co.

Fig. 8: Removing Fan Clutch

OIL PAN

Removal (Aerostar) – **1)** Disconnect negative battery cable. Raise and support vehicle. Remove starter. On 4WD models, remove front wheels. Remove pivot bolts/nuts from both lower control arms and allow control arms to hang free.

2) Remove lower control arm rear pivot bracket from crossmember. Remove lower nuts from both motor mounts. Remove front drive axle assembly. See AXLE SHAFT under REMOVAL & INSTALLATION in appropriate SUSPENSION article. On all models, drain engine oil and remove oil filter.

3) Disconnect low oil level sensor connector from engine oil pan. Remove 2 engine-to-transmission bolts and spacers. Remove oil pan retaining bolts/nuts. On 4WD, raise engine approximately 1" (25 mm). On all models, remove oil pan. Remove oil pan gasket and crankshaft rear main bearing cap wedge seal. See Fig. 9.

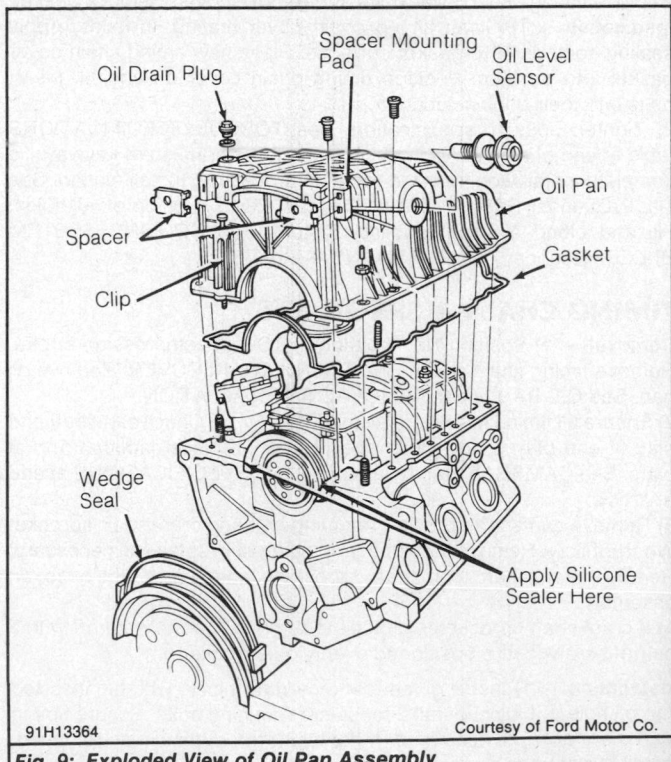

91H13364   Courtesy of Ford Motor Co.

Fig. 9: Exploded View of Oil Pan Assembly

Installation – **1)** Clean gasket mating surfaces. Apply small amount of silicone sealant to engine block where oil pan, rear seal and block mate. See Fig. 9.

2) Install new crankshaft rear main bearing cap wedge seal. Wedge seal should fit snug into sides of rear main bearing cap. Position new oil pan gasket into groove in oil pan. If installing original oil pan, go to step **4)**. If installing new oil pan, go to next step.

CAUTION: If installing original oil pan, existing oil pan spacers may be used. If installing new oil pan, measure oil pan-to-transmission clearance and install correct spacers to prevent oil pan damage and/ or oil leaks.

3) Position oil pan on engine without spacers. Install oil pan retaining nuts on 4 locating studs. Using a feeler gauge, measure gap between locating pads on oil pan and transmission bellhousing. Determine spacer thickness from measured clearance. See SPACER SELECTION table.

SPACER SELECTION

Clearance In. (mm)	Shim Thickness In. (mm)	Shim Color Code
.011-.020 (.28-.51)	.010 (.25)	Yellow
.021-.029 (.53-.74)	.020 (.51)	Blue
.030-.039 (.76-.99)	.030 (.76)	Pink

4) Remove oil pan. Position oil pan spacers on oil pan locating pads. Install oil pan. Tighten retaining bolts/nuts tight enough to compress oil pan gasket so transmission bolts align with holes in oil pan, but loose enough to allow oil pan to move when transmission bolts are installed.
5) Install transmission-to-oil pan bolts and tighten to specification. Install and tighten all oil pan bolts to specification. See TORQUE SPECIFICATIONS table at end of article. To complete installation, reverse removal procedure. Fill or top off fluids. Start engine and check for leaks.

Removal (Explorer) – Remove engine. See ENGINE under REMOVAL & INSTALLATION. Mount engine on engine stand with oil pan facing up. Remove oil pan, gasket and rear main bearing cap wedge seal. Clean gasket mating surfaces.
Installation – **1)** Install new crankshaft rear main bearing cap wedge seal. Wedge seal should fit snugly into sides of rear main bearing cap. Position new oil pan gasket into groove in oil pan. Position oil pan on engine.
2) Install oil pan retaining bolts/nuts and tighten to specification. See TORQUE SPECIFICATIONS table at end of article. Position a straight-edge along rear of engine block so it extends over one of the oil pan spacer mounting pads. *See Fig. 10.*
3) Using a feeler gauge, measure gap between mounting pad and straightedge. Repeat procedure for other mounting pad. Determine spacer thickness from measured clearance. See SPACER SELECTION table. To complete installation, reverse removal procedure. Fill or top off all fluids. Start engine and check for leaks.

NOTE: Oil pan spacers must be installed before bolting engine to transmission.

Removal & Installation (Ranger) – Information is not available from manufacturer.

OVERHAUL

CYLINDER HEAD

Cylinder Head – **1)** Clean head gasket mating surface. Clean carbon from combustion chambers. Use care not to damage surfaces. Check cylinder head for cracks, burrs, nicks and warpage.
2) Check cylinder head warpage. Resurface cylinder head if warpage exceeds specification. See CYLINDER HEAD table under ENGINE SPECIFICATIONS at end of article. DO NOT machine more than .010" (.25 mm) from original cylinder head surface.
Valve Springs – **1)** Measure valve spring installed height from surface of cylinder head spring pad to underside of spring retainer. If installed height is not within specification, a .03" (.8 mm) shim can be installed between cylinder head and valve spring to obtain correct height.

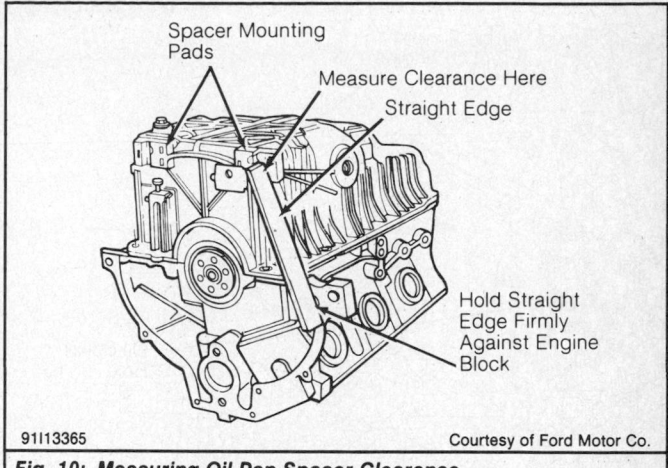

Fig. 10: *Measuring Oil Pan Spacer Clearance (Explorer Shown, Ranger Is Similar)*

91I13365 — Courtesy of Ford Motor Co.

2) Inspect valve spring free length and pressure. Replace valve spring if free length and pressure are not within specification. See VALVES & VALVE SPRINGS table under ENGINE SPECIFICATIONS at end of article.

CAUTION: DO NOT install valve spring spacers unless necessary. Using more spacers than required can result in spring breakage or worn camshaft lobes.

Valve Stem Oil Seals – Different types of valve stem oil seals are used on intake and exhaust valves. Use Valve Stem Installer (T90T-6571-A) to install new valve stem seals. Ensure oil seal bottoms on valve guide. Oversized oil seals must be installed when using oversized valves.
Valve Guides – **1)** Valve guides must be reamed for an oversized valve if valve stem oil clearance exceeds specification. See CYLINDER HEAD table under ENGINE SPECIFICATIONS at end of article. Valves are available in .008" (.20 mm) and .016" (.41 mm) oversize.
2) If oversized valves or oversized valve stem oil seals are not available, valve guide may be bored out to use a service bushing. Always use reamers in proper sequence (smallest first).

NOTE: Always grind valve seat after valve guide has been reamed or service bushing has been installed.

Valve Seat – Ensure valve seat angle, seat width and seat runout are within specification. See CYLINDER HEAD table under ENGINE SPECIFICATIONS at end of article. Valve seats must be ground when valve guide is reamed or replaced. Replacement information is not available from manufacturer.
Valves – **1)** Ensure head diameter, valve face runout, stem diameter and valve margin are within specification. See VALVES & VALVE SPRINGS table under ENGINE SPECIFICATIONS at end of article.
2) Oversize valves are available in .008" (.20 mm) and .016" (.41 mm). When servicing valve stem tip, DO NOT remove more than **.010" (.25)** from end of valve stem.
Seat Correction Angles – Grind valve seat to a true 45-degree angle. If seat width is too wide after grinding, use a 30-degree stone to lower seat or a 60-degree stone to raise seat. See CYLINDER HEAD table under ENGINE SPECIFICATIONS at end of article.

CYLINDER BLOCK ASSEMBLY

Piston & Rod Assembly – Ensure pistons and rods are installed in cylinder from which they were removed. Note direction of connecting rod installation on piston before removal. Ensure arrow on piston dome is facing front of engine, and connecting rod oil squirt hole is as shown. *See Fig. 11.*

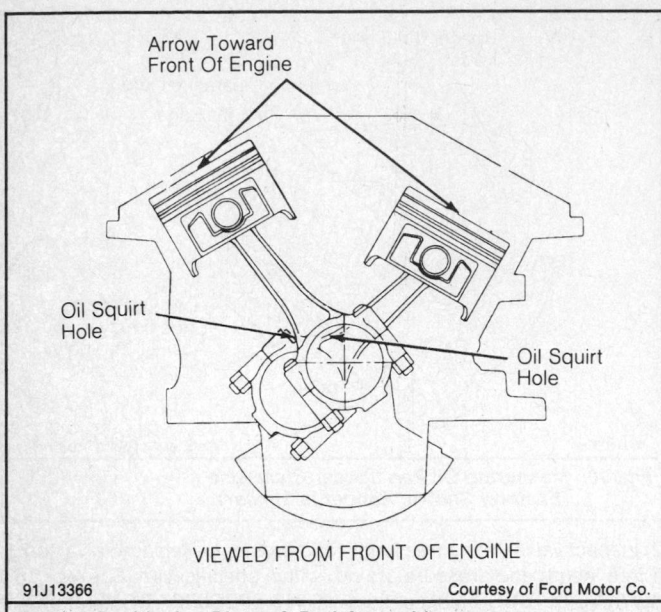

Fig. 11: Positioning Piston & Rod Assembly

Fitting Pistons – Measure cylinder bore for out-of-round, taper and piston-to-cylinder bore clearance. Measure with components at about 70°F (21°C). If measurements are not within specification, hone or bore cylinders. See CYLINDER BLOCK and PISTONS, PINS & RINGS tables under ENGINE SPECIFICATIONS at end of article.

Piston Rings – 1) Select rings for bore diameter. Place ring in cylinder bore in which it will be installed. Use piston to square ring in bore and place ring below normal ring wear area. Measure ring end gap. If ring gap is not within specification, try another ring set. See PISTONS, PINS & RINGS table under ENGINE SPECIFICATIONS at end of article.

2) Check side clearance of rings after installing on piston. Ensure clearance is within specification around entire circumference. Replace piston and/or rings if clearance is not within specification. See PISTONS, PINS & RINGS table. Ensure rings are properly spaced on piston before installing pistons into cylinder. *See Fig. 12.*

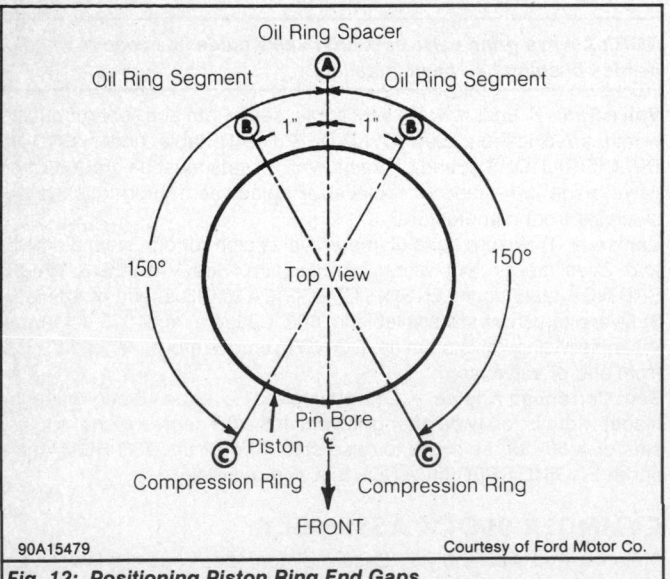

Fig. 12: Positioning Piston Ring End Gaps

Rod Bearings – 1) Use Plastigage to check rod bearing clearance. If proper oil clearance cannot be obtained with standard bearings, try a combination of undersize bearings. DO NOT use any other bearing combination other than what is listed. See UNDERSIZE MAIN & ROD BEARING COMBINATIONS table.

2) If use of bearing combinations does not bring clearance within specification, machine or replace crankshaft as necessary. Always replace bearings in pairs. See CRANKSHAFT, MAIN & CONNECTING ROD BEARINGS table under ENGINE SPECIFICATIONS at end of article.

UNDERSIZE MAIN & ROD BEARING COMBINATIONS [1]

Excess Bearing Clearance In. (mm)	Use Upper Bearing In. (mm)	Use Lower Bearing In. (mm)
.0-.0005 (.0-.013)	.001 (.025)	[2]
.0005-.0010 (.013-.025)	.001 (.025)	.001 (.025)
.0010-.0015 (.025-.039)	.002 (.050)	.001 (.025)
.0015-.0020 (.039-.050)	.002 (.050)	.002 (.050)

[1] – DO NOT use any other bearing combination other than what is listed. If use of bearing combinations does not bring clearance within specification, machine or replace crankshaft as necessary.

[2] – Use standard bearing.

Crankshaft & Main Bearings – 1) When checking main bearing clearance in vehicle, position a jack under adjoining bearing counterweight being checked. Remove only one main bearing cap at a time.

2) Use Plastigage to check main bearing clearance. If proper oil clearance cannot be obtained with standard bearings, try a combination of undersize bearings. DO NOT use any other bearing combination other than what is listed. See UNDERSIZE MAIN & ROD BEARING COMBINATIONS table.

3) If use of bearing combinations does not bring clearance within specification, machine or replace crankshaft as necessary. Always replace bearings in pairs. See CRANKSHAFT, MAIN & CONNECTING ROD BEARINGS table under ENGINE SPECIFICATIONS at end of article.

4) Tighten main bearing cap bolts finger tight. Pry crankshaft forward and tighten bearing caps to specification. See TORQUE SPECIFICATIONS table at end of article.

5) Check crankshaft end play. Replace thrust bearing if end play is not within specification. Thrust bearing is No. 3 (from front) main bearing in block. See CRANKSHAFT, MAIN & CONNECTING ROD BEARINGS table under ENGINE SPECIFICATIONS at end of article.

Cylinder Block – 1) Using a feeler gauge and straightedge, check cylinder block head gasket surface for warpage. Check cylinder bore for wear, taper, out-of-round and piston fit. See CYLINDER BLOCK table under ENGINE SPECIFICATIONS at end of article.

CAUTION: DO NOT machine more than .010" (.25 mm) of material from original cylinder block head surface.

2) Install all main bearing caps and tighten to specification before honing cylinder bore. See TORQUE SPECIFICATIONS table at end of article. Ensure bearing caps are installed in their original location, with arrow on cap pointing towards front of engine.

3) Use ONLY a spring-loaded type cylinder hone. After honing, thoroughly clean bore with detergent and water solution. Rinse solution from bore thoroughly with clean water. Wipe bore clean with lint-free cloth. Lubricate cylinder bores with engine oil.

ENGINE OILING

ENGINE LUBRICATION SYSTEM

Engine lubrication system is a force-feed type. The oil is supplied under full pressure to crankshaft, connecting rods, camshaft bearing and valve lifters. *See Fig. 13.* A controlled volume of oil is supplied to rocker arms and push rods. All other moving parts are lubricated by splash or gravity flow. Oil flows through oil filter before entering main oil gallery.

Crankcase Capacity – Crankcase capacity is **5 qts. (4.75L)** with oil filter.

Oil Pressure – Oil pressure with engine at normal operating temperature is **40-60 psi (2.8-4.2 kg/cm²)** at 2000 RPM.

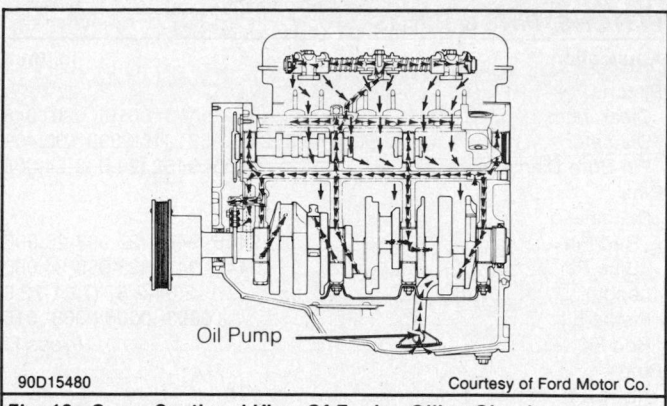

90D15480   Courtesy of Ford Motor Co.

Fig. 13: Cross-Sectional View Of Engine Oiling Circuit

OIL PUMP

Removal & Disassembly – Remove oil pan. See OIL PAN under REMOVAL & INSTALLATION. Remove oil pump attaching bolts. Remove oil pump and oil pump drive shaft. Disassemble oil pump. Note direction of component installation for reassembly reference.

Inspection – Inspect components for damage. Measure rotor end play and outer rotor-to-housing clearance. Measure relief valve-to-housing clearance and relief valve tension. Replace oil pump assembly if measurements are not within specifications. See OIL PUMP SPECIFICATIONS table.

NOTE: Oil pump is serviced as an assembly only. Replace assembly if measurements are not within specifications. See OIL PUMP SPECIFICATIONS table.

OIL PUMP SPECIFICATIONS

Application	Specification In. (mm)
Outer Rotor-To-Housing	
Clearance	.001-.013 (.03-.33)
Rotor End Play	.004 (.10) Max.
Shaft-To-Housing	
Clearance	.0015-.0030 (.038-.076)
Relief Valve Spring Tension	[1]
Relief Valve-To-Housing	
Clearance	.0015-.0030 (.038-.076)

[1] – Spring tension is 13.6-14.7 lbs. @ 1.39" (6.2-6.7 kg @ 35 mm).

Reassembly & Installation – **1)** To reassemble, reverse disassembly procedure. Ensure components are installed in original location. To install, prime oil pump with engine oil. Rotate oil pump drive shaft to distribute oil within pump body.

2) Insert oil pump drive shaft into engine block, with pointed end of oil pump drive shaft inward. Pointed end is closest to the pressed-on retainer ring. *See Fig. 14.*

3) Position new gasket in place and install oil pump. To complete installation, reverse removal procedure. Tighten bolts to specification. See TORQUE SPECIFICATIONS table.

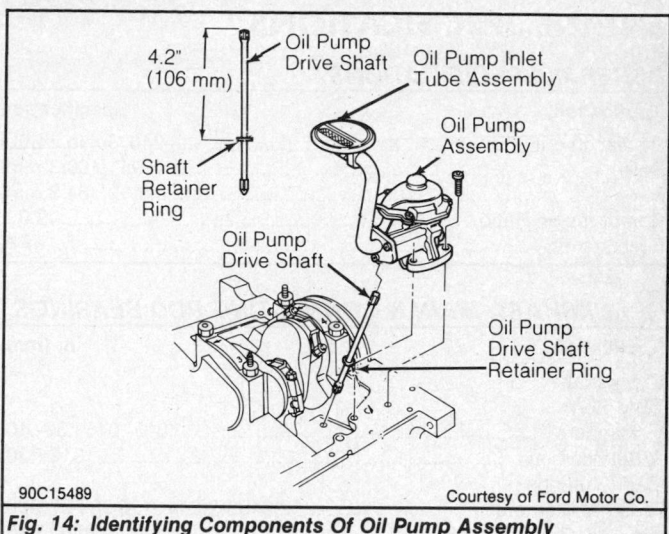

90C15489   Courtesy of Ford Motor Co.

Fig. 14: Identifying Components Of Oil Pump Assembly

TORQUE SPECIFICATIONS

TORQUE SPECIFICATIONS

Application	Ft. Lbs. (N.m)
Bellhousing-To-Engine Bolt	28-38 (38-51)
Camshaft Sprocket Bolt	44-50 (60-68)
Connecting Rod Nut	18-24 (24-33)
Crankshaft Damper-To-Crankshaft Bolt	
Step 1	30-37 (41-51)
Step 2	[1]
Cylinder Head Bolt [2]	59 (80)
Engine Mount-To-Crossmember Nut	71-94 (96-127)
Engine Mount-To-Engine Bolt	45-60 (88-81)
Exhaust Manifold Bolt	19 (26)
Flexplate-To-Converter Bolt	20-34 (27-46)
Flywheel-To-Crankshaft Bolt	59 (80)
Front Cover Bolt	13-15 (18-21)
Lower Intake Manifold Bolts/Nuts [3]	
Step 1	[4]
Step 2	6-11 (8-15)
Step 3	11-15 (15-21)
Step 4	15-18 (21-24)
Main Bearing Cap Bolt	66-77 (90-104)
Oil Level Sensor	13-20 (18-27)
Oil Pump Retaining Bolt	13-15 (18-21)
Rear Mount-To-Crossmember Nut	65-85 (88-115)
Rear Mount-To-Transmission Bolt	60-80 (81-108)
Rocker Arm Assembly Bolt [5]	46-52 (62-71)
Starter Bolt	15-20 (20-27)
Transmission Crossmember Bolt	65-85 (88-115)
Upper Intake Manifold Bolt	15-18 (21-24)
	INCH Lbs. (N.m)
Camshaft Thrust Plate Bolt	84-120 (8-13)
Oil Pan Bolt/Nut	60-84 (7-9)
Valve Cover Bolt	36-60 (4-7)

[1] – Tighten an additional 80-90 degrees.
[2] – Tighten in sequence. *See Fig. 3.*
[3] – Tighten in sequence. *See Fig. 2.*
[4] – Tighten to 36 INCH lbs. (4-8 N.m)
[5] – Tighten bolts evenly, 2 turns at a time.

ENGINE SPECIFICATIONS

GENERAL SPECIFICATIONS

Application	Specification
Displacement	246 Cu. In. (4.0L)
Bore	3.95" (100.3 mm)
Stroke	3.32" (84.3 mm)
Compression Ratio	9.0:1
Fuel System	PFI

CRANKSHAFT, MAIN & CONNECTING ROD BEARINGS

Application	In. (mm)
Crankshaft	
End Play	
Standard	.012-.016 (.30-.40)
Service Limit	.012 (.30)
Main Bearings	
Journal Diameter	2.2433-2.2441 (56.980-57.000)
Journal Out-Of-Round	.0006 (.015)
Journal Taper	[1] .0006 (.015)
Journal Runout	
Standard	.002 (.05)
Service Limit	.005 (.13)
Oil Clearance	
Desired	.0008-.0015 (.020-.038)
Allowable	.0005-.0019 (.013-.048)
Connecting Rod Bearings	
Journal Diameter	2.1252-2.1260 (53.980-54.000)
Journal Out-Of-Round	.0006 (.015)
Journal Taper	[1] .0006 (.015)
Oil Clearance.	
Desired	.0005-.0022 (.013-.056)
Allowable	.0003-.0024 (.008-.061)

[1] – Specification listed is per 1" (25.4 mm).

CONNECTING RODS

Application	In. (mm)
Bore Diameter	
Pin Bore	.9432-.9439 (23.957-23.975)
Crankpin Bore	2.2370-2.2378 (56.820-56.840)
Center-To-Center Length	5.1386-5.1413 (130.520-130.589)
Maximum Bend [1]	.002 (.05)
Maximum Twist [1]	.006 (.15)
Side Play	[2] N/A
Service Limit	.014 (.36)

[1] – Specification listed is measured at the ends of an 8" (203 mm) bar, 4" (102 mm) on each side of rod center line.

[2] – Information not available from manufacturer.

PISTONS, PINS & RINGS

Application	In. (mm)
Pistons	
Clearance	.0008-.0019 (.020-.048)
Diameter	[1] 3.9524-3.9531 (100.390-100.409)
Pin Bore Diameter	.9450-.9452 (24.003-24.008)
Pins	
Diameter	
Red Pin	.9446-.9448 (23.993-23.998)
Blue Pin	.9448-.9449 (23.998-24.000)
Length	2.84-2.87 (72.1-72.9)
Piston Fit	.0003-.0006 (.008-.015)
Rod Fit	Press Fit
Rings	
No. 1 & 2	
End Gap	.015-.023 (.38-.58)
Side Clearance	.0020.0033 (.051-.084)
No. 3 (Oil)	
End Gap (Steel Rail)	.015-.055 (.38-1.40)
Side Clearance	Snug Fit

[1] – Measure at piston pin bore, 90 degrees to pin.

CYLINDER BLOCK

Application	In. (mm)
Cylinder Bore	
Standard Diameter	3.9527-3.9543 (100.398-100.439)
Maximum Taper	.010 (.25)
Maximum Out-Of-Round	
Standard	.0015 (.038)
Service Limit	.005 (.13)
Maximum Deck Warpage [1]	
Standard Service	.003 (.08)
Service Limit	.006 (.15)

[1] – Within a 6" (152 mm) area.

VALVES & VALVE SPRINGS

Application	Specification
Face Angle	44°
Head Diameter	
Intake	1.71" (43.5 mm)
Exhaust	1.36" (34.5 mm)
Stem Diameter	
Intake	.3159-.3167" (8.024-8.044 mm)
Exhaust	.3149-.3156" (8.998-8.016 mm)
Valve Margin	.031" (.79 mm)
Valve Springs	
Free Length	1.91" (48.5 mm)
Installed Height	1.58-1.61" (40.1-40.9 mm)
Out-Of-Square	.078" (1.98 mm)

	Lbs. @ In. (kg @ mm)
Pressure	
Intake & Exhaust	
Closed	60-68 @ 1.59 (27-31 @ 37.8)
Open	138-149 @ 1.22 (63-68 @ 31.0)

CYLINDER HEAD

Application	Specification
Maximum Warpage [1]	.003" (.08 mm)
Valve Seats	
Seat Angle	45°
Seat Width	.060-.079" (1.52-2.00 mm)
Maximum Seat Runout	.0015" (.038 mm)
Valve Guides	
Valve Guide Bore I.D.	.3174-.3184" (8.062-8.087 mm)
Valve Stem-To-Guide	
Oil Clearance	
Intake	.0008-.0025" (.020-.064 mm)
Exhaust	.0018-.0035" (.046-.089 mm)

[1] – Specification listed is within 6" (152 mm). Overall warpage is .006" (.15 mm). DO NOT machine more than .010" (.25 mm) from original gasket surface.

CAMSHAFT

Application	In. (mm)
Camshaft Bearing I.D.	
No. 1	1.954-1.955 (49.64-49.66)
No. 2	1.939-1.940 (49.26-49.28)
No. 3	1.919-1.920 (48.75-48.77)
No. 4	1.924-1.925 (48.88-48.90)
End Play	
Standard	.004-.008 (.10-.20)
Service Limit	.009 (.23)
Journal Runout	.005 (.13)
Lobe Lift	.4024 (10.220)
Lobe Lift Wear Limit	.005 (.13)
Oil Clearance	
Standard	.0010-.0026 (.025-.066)
Service Limit	.006 (.15)

VALVE LIFTERS

Application	In. (mm)
Lifter Diameter	.8742-.8755 (22.205-22.238)
Oil Clearance	
Standard	.0005-.0022 (.013-.056)
Service Limit	.005 (.13)

1992 ENGINES
4.9L 6-Cylinder

Bronco, Pickup, Van

NOTE: Unless otherwise specified, references to Pickup include the F350 Super Duty commercial chassis.
For engine repair procedures not covered in this article, see ENGINE OVERHAUL PROCEDURES article in GENERAL INFORMATION.

ENGINE IDENTIFICATION

Engine is identified by eighth character of Vehicle Identification Number (VIN). VIN is visible through windshield on left side of instrument panel. VIN is also located on Safety Compliance Certification Label attached to left door lock pillar.

VIN ENGINE CODE

Engine	Code
4.9L (300 Cu. In.) PFI	Y

ADJUSTMENTS

VALVE CLEARANCE ADJUSTMENT

In most cases, valve clearance adjustment is not required. Positive-stop rocker arm bolts and hydraulic valve lifters automatically adjust stem-to-rocker arm clearance. However, repeated valve and/or valve seat refacing will change stem-to-rocker arm clearance.

When this occurs, stem-to-rocker arm clearance will be insufficient. If clearance is excessive, it will cause valve train noise; if clearance is insufficient, it will prevent valve from seating. To compensate for excessive changes in stem-to-rocker arm clearance, a longer or shorter push rod must be installed. Push rods are available in .060" (1.52 mm) longer or shorter than original.

1) Install an auxiliary starter switch, so engine can be cranked with ignition off. Make 2 chalk marks on crankshaft damper. Space marks 120 degrees apart. Including the timing mark, damper should be divided into 3 equal parts. Remove valve cover.
2) Rotate crankshaft until No. 1 piston is at TDC of compression stroke. Ensure intake and exhaust rocker arms of No. 1 cylinder are tightened to specifications. See TORQUE SPECIFICATIONS table at end of article. Slowly collapse lifter plunger using Tappet Bleed Down Wrench (T70P-6513-A) until completely bottomed.
3) While maintaining pressure on lifter, use feeler gauge to check clearance between rocker arm and valve stem tip. On all valves, desired clearance is **.125-.175" (3.18-4.45 mm)**, and allowable range is .100-.200" (2.54-5.08 mm).
4) If clearance is less than specification, install shorter push rod. If clearance is greater than specification, install longer push rod. Rotate crankshaft 120 degrees (in direction of normal rotation) to check next set of valves in firing order sequence. Firing order is 1-5-3-6-2-4. Repeat procedure for remaining valves.

REMOVAL & INSTALLATION

WARNING: When battery is disconnected, vehicle computer and memory systems may lose memory data. Driveability problems may exist until computer systems have completed a relearn cycle. See COMPUTER RELEARN PROCEDURES article in GENERAL INFORMATION before disconnecting battery.

NOTE: Discharge A/C system using approved refrigerant recovery/recycling equipment.

FUEL PRESSURE RELEASE

Disconnect negative battery cable. Remove fuel tank filler cap to release tank pressure. Attach a fuel pressure gauge to pressure relief valve on fuel rail. Release fuel pressure.

COOLING SYSTEM BLEEDING

1) To bleed trapped air from cooling system, disconnect heater hose from water pump. Using 50/50 mixture of coolant and water, fill radiator until coolant flows from heater hose fitting at water pump. Reconnect heater hose.
2) Fill radiator until coolant is 1.5" (38 mm) below radiator cap seal. Install radiator cap. Run engine until warm. Turn off engine. CAREFULLY remove radiator cap and check level. Fill as required.

ENGINE

NOTE: Engine removal and installation procedures are for engine without transmission attached.

Removal (Bronco & Pickup) – 1) Disconnect battery cables. Drain cooling system and crankcase. Scribe hood hinge position and remove hood. Remove throttle body inlet tubes. Remove heater hoses and air cleaner assembly. Release fuel pressure. See FUEL PRESSURE RELEASE.

NOTE: Fan clutch/water pump hub has right-hand thread.

2) Using Disconnect Tool (D87L-9280-A) for 3/8" line or (D87L-9280-B) for 1/2" line, disconnect fuel supply and return lines. *See Fig. 1.* Remove radiator shroud and radiator. Using Fan Clutch Pulley Holder (T84T-6312-C) and Fan Clutch Nut Wrench (T84T-6312-D), remove fan and clutch assembly.
3) Remove water pump pulley. Disconnect accelerator cable at throttle body and remove return spring. Remove power brake vacuum hose at intake manifold. Disconnect kickdown cable at throttle body (A/T). Separate exhaust pipe from manifold.
4) Remove wiring harness from coil and all sending units. Disconnect all Electronic Engine Control (EEC) sensor connectors. Remove alternator mounting bolts and set alternator aside with wires attached. Remove power steering pump from mounting brackets and set aside with lines attached.

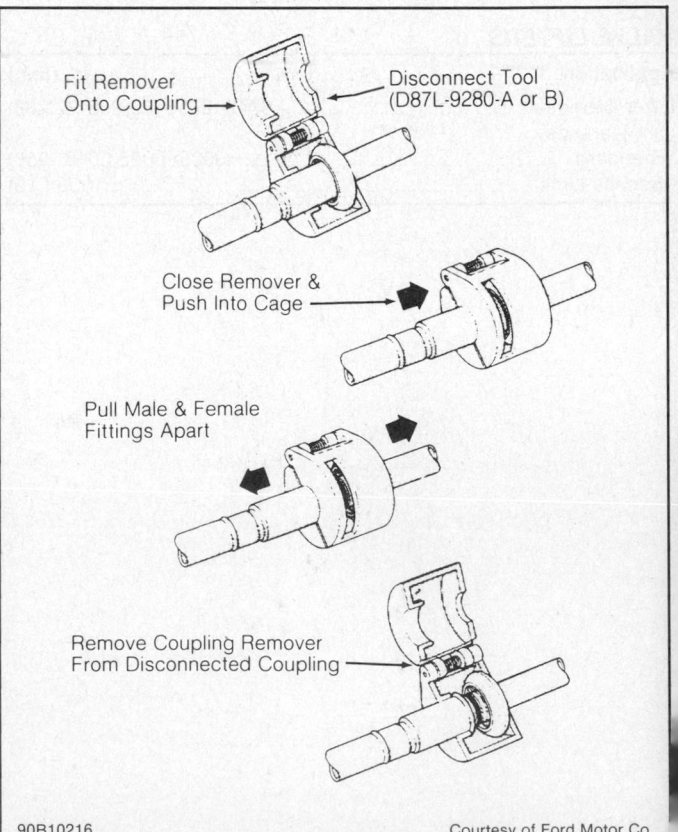

Fit Remover Onto Coupling

Disconnect Tool (D87L-9280-A or B)

Close Remover & Push Into Cage

Pull Male & Female Fittings Apart

Remove Coupling Remover From Disconnected Coupling

90B10216

Courtesy of Ford Motor Co.

Fig. 1: Disconnecting Fuel Lines

5) On A/C-equipped models, discharge system and disconnect pressure lines. On all models, raise and support vehicle. Remove starter and A/T filler tube bracket (if equipped). Remove upper right bolt from engine rear plate.

6) Remove all bellhousing lower retaining bolts and disconnect clutch retracting spring (if equipped). On A/T models, remove converter housing access cover and remove flex plate-to-converter nuts. Secure converter assembly in housing.

7) Remove transmission cooler lines from clip at engine. Remove converter housing lower retaining bolts. On all models, remove insulator support bracket nut from each front engine support. Lower vehicle and support transmission with floor jack.

8) Remove remaining bellhousing-to-engine bolts. Attach engine hoist to engine. Raise engine slightly to separate from transmission. Remove engine from vehicle.

Installation – To install, reverse removal procedure. Tighten bolts to specification. See TORQUE SPECIFICATIONS table at end of article. Fill or top off all fluid levels. Fill and bleed air from cooling system. See COOLING SYSTEM BLEEDING.

Removal (Van) – 1) Remove engine cover and air cleaner assembly. Drain cooling system. Disconnect battery. Remove front bumper, grille and lower gravel deflector. Disconnect coolant hoses and transmission oil lines from radiator (if equipped).

2) Remove radiator and shroud. Disconnect brake booster and heater hoses at intake manifold. Disconnect alternator and set aside. Remove power steering pump drive belt, pump and bracket from engine.

3) Release fuel pressure. See FUEL PRESSURE RELEASE. Using Disconnect Tool (D87L-9280-A) for 3/8" line or (D87L-9280-B) for 1/2" line, disconnect fuel supply and return lines. See Fig. 1.

4) Disconnect distributor, Electronic Engine Control (EEC) sensors and sending unit wires from engine. Disconnect accelerator cable and remove bracket from engine. Disconnect A/T kickdown cable at throttle body. Remove exhaust manifold heat deflector and exhaust pipe-to-manifold nuts.

5) Disconnect A/T vacuum line at intake manifold junction. Remove upper transmission-to-engine bolts. Remove A/T dipstick tube support at intake manifold. Raise vehicle. Drain crankcase and remove oil filter.

6) Disconnect starter wiring and remove starter. On A/T models, remove flywheel inspection cover and flexplate-to-converter nuts. On all applications, remove front engine mount nuts. Remove remaining transmission-to-engine bolts. Lower vehicle from hoist. Attach lifting device to engine. Remove engine from vehicle.

Installation – To install, reverse removal procedure. Tighten bolts to specification. See TORQUE SPECIFICATIONS table at end of article. Fill or top off all fluid levels. Fill and bleed air from cooling system. See COOLING SYSTEM BLEEDING.

INTAKE & EXHAUST MANIFOLDS

Removal – 1) Disconnect negative battery cable. Disconnect electrical connectors as necessary. Disconnect PCV hose from underside of upper intake manifold. Remove throttle linkage shield.

CAUTION: When disconnecting throttle cable from ball stud, use screwdriver or similar tool to pry off. Removing by hand may damage cable.

---

2) Disconnect accelerator cable and speed control cable. Remove throttle body inlet hoses. Disconnect accelerator cable from bracket and set aside. Remove cable retracting spring. Disconnect and remove EGR tube.

3) Release fuel system pressure. See FUEL PRESSURE RELEASE under REMOVAL & INSTALLATION. Using Disconnect Tool (D87L-9280-A) for 3/8" line or (D87L-9280-B) for 1/2" line, disconnect fuel supply and return lines. See Fig. 1.

4) Remove thermactor tube assembly from lower intake manifold. Remove thermactor by-pass valve bracket retaining nut from lower intake manifold. On Van models, remove transmission fill tube retaining nut.

5) On all models, remove upper intake manifold retaining nuts. Remove screw and washer attaching upper intake manifold support bracket to upper intake manifold. Remove upper intake manifold and throttle body as an assembly. Remove injector heat shield.

6) Disconnect exhaust pipes from exhaust manifolds. Mark and disconnect vacuum lines for installation reference. Disconnect power brake vacuum line (if equipped). Remove lower intake manifold and exhaust manifold-to-cylinder head bolts. Remove lower intake manifold and exhaust manifolds.

Installation – 1) Clean mating surfaces of manifolds and cylinder head. Lightly coat mating surfaces with graphite grease. Install new intake/exhaust manifold gasket on cylinder head.

NOTE: If installing original exhaust manifolds, install new exhaust manifold gaskets. If installing new exhaust manifolds, install exhaust manifolds without gaskets.

---

2) Position lower intake/exhaust manifold assembly on cylinder head. Ensure gasket remains in position. Tighten bolts and nuts in sequence to specification. See Fig. 2. See TORQUE SPECIFICATIONS table at end of article. To complete installation, reverse removal procedure.

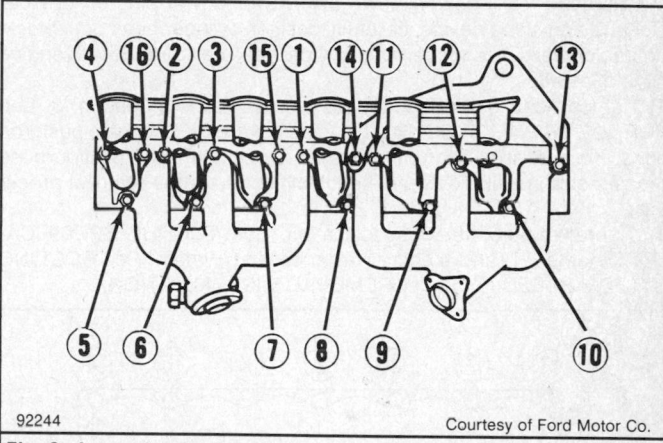

92244   Courtesy of Ford Motor Co.

Fig. 2: Lower Intake & Exhaust Manifold Tightening Sequence

CYLINDER HEAD

NOTE: Cylinder head can be removed with intake and exhaust manifolds connected.

Removal – 1) Scribe hood hinge position and remove hood. Disconnect negative battery cable. Drain cooling system and crankcase. Remove throttle body inlet tubes. Discharge A/C system. Remove the A/C compressor and condenser.

2) Disconnect heater hoses from water pump and thermostat housing. Release pressure from fuel system. See FUEL PRESSURE RELEASE under REMOVAL & INSTALLATION.

NOTE: Fan clutch/water pump hub has right-hand thread.

---

3) Using Disconnect Tool (D87L-9280-A) for 3/8" line or (D87L-9280-B) for 1/2" line, disconnect fuel supply and return lines. See Fig. 1. DO NOT bend fuel rail. Remove radiator and shroud. Using Fan Clutch Pulley Holder (T84T-6312-C) and Fan Clutch Nut Wrench (T84T-6312-D), remove fan and clutch assembly.

4) Remove water pump pulley and fan drive belt. Disconnect accelerator cable and return spring from throttle body. Disconnect power brake vacuum line from intake manifold (if equipped). Disconnect transmission kickdown cable from throttle body (if equipped).

5) Disconnect exhaust pipes from exhaust manifolds. Disconnect body ground strap and negative battery cable from engine. Disconnect Electronic Engine Control (EEC) harness and engine wiring harness from all electrical components on engine.

6) Leaving wiring attached, remove alternator and set aside. Remove air pump and alternator/air pump bracket. Remove power steering pump with hoses attached and set aside. Remove power steering pump and A/C compressor bracket.

7) Remove coil bracket and set aside. Remove rocker arm cover. Loosen rocker arm bolts and rotate rocker arms aside. Mark and remove push rods for installation reference. Disconnect spark plug wires from spark plugs.

8) Remove cylinder head bolts. Lift cylinder head and manifold assemblies from engine using appropriate lifting device. DO NOT pry between cylinder head and block, as machined surfaces may be damaged.

Inspection – 1) Clean gasket mating surfaces. Check cylinder head warpage. Resurface cylinder head if warpage exceeds specification. See CYLINDER HEAD table under ENGINE SPECIFICATIONS at end of article. Check cylinder block deck surface for warpage.

2) Resurface cylinder block if warpage exceeds specification. See CYLINDER BLOCK table under ENGINE SPECIFICATIONS at end of article. If cylinder head or cylinder block warpage exceeds specification, DO NOT remove more than .010" (.25 mm) material from original surface of cylinder head or block.

Installation – 1) Position new gasket over dowel pins on cylinder block. Using lifting device, carefully position cylinder head onto block. Ensure dowel pins engage in head. Coat head bolt threads with engine oil and install.

2) Tighten head bolts in sequence to specification. *See Fig. 3.* See TORQUE SPECIFICATIONS table at end of article. Lubricate push rod ends, rocker arm fulcrum seats and sockets with multipurpose grease, and install. To complete installation, reverse removal procedure.

3) Tighten nuts/bolts to specification. See TORQUE SPECIFICATIONS table. Fill and bleed air from cooling system. See COOLING SYSTEM BLEEDING under REMOVAL & INSTALLATION.

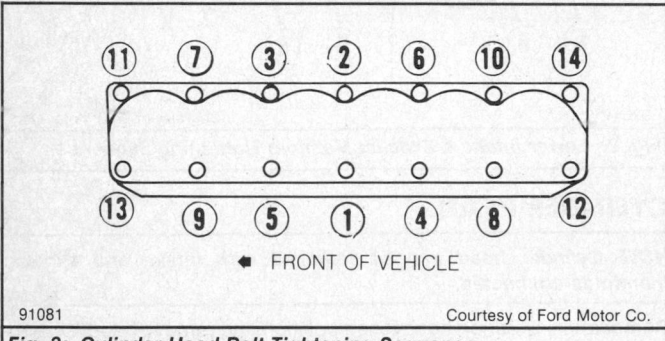

← FRONT OF VEHICLE

91081   Courtesy of Ford Motor Co.

Fig. 3: Cylinder Head Bolt Tightening Sequence

FRONT CRANKSHAFT OIL SEAL

Removal – 1) Remove fan and shroud. Remove drive belt. Remove crankshaft pulley. Using Vibration Damper Remover (T58P-6316-D), remove vibration damper. Position Timing Gear Cover Seal Remover (T70P-6B070-B) onto seal and tighten 2 through bolts to force seal puller under the seal flange.

2) Alternately tighten 4 puller bolts 1/2 turn at a time. Remove oil seal from the timing gear cover. Clean seal recess in timing gear cover.

Installation – 1) Lubricate crankshaft stub, vibration damper hub I.D. and sealing surface of timing gear cover seal with clean engine oil. DO NOT apply grease to seal. Position seal onto Timing Gear Cover Seal Installer (T70P-6B070-A).

2) Position Timing Gear Cover Seal Installer and seal onto the crankshaft end. Force seal into recess by tightening bolt. *See Fig. 4.* Remove timing gear cover seal installer. Apply a 1/4" (6 mm) bead of silicone sealer to keyway inside vibration damper hub.

3) Using Vibration Damper Installer (T52L-6306-AEE), install vibration damper. To complete installation, reverse removal procedure. See TORQUE SPECIFICATIONS table at end of article.

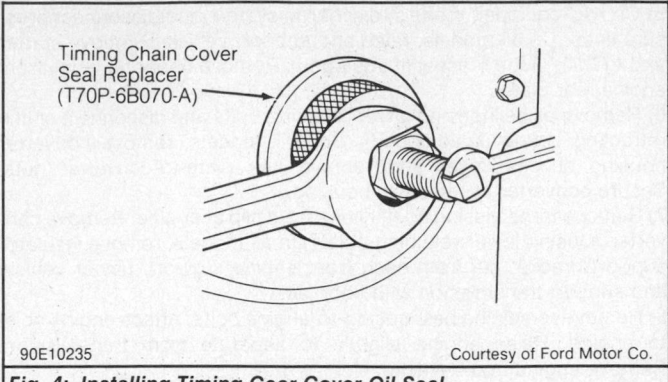

Timing Chain Cover
Seal Replacer
(T70P-6B070-A)

90E10235   Courtesy of Ford Motor Co.

Fig. 4: Installing Timing Gear Cover Oil Seal

TIMING GEAR COVER

Removal – 1) Drain cooling system and crankcase. Remove shroud and radiator. Remove drive belts. Using Fan Clutch Pulley Holder (T84T-6312-C) and Fan Clutch Nut Wrench (T84T-6312-D), remove fan and clutch assembly.

2) Remove water pump pulley. Remove power steering pump and bracket. Remove crankshaft damper retaining bolt and washer. Using Vibration Damper Remover (T58P-6316-D), remove vibration damper.

3) Remove timing gear cover and front oil pan bolts. Loosen first 6 bolts on each side of oil pan. Lightly push down oil pan to relieve pressure on timing gear cover. Remove timing gear cover and gasket.

NOTE: Always replace timing gear cover oil seal whenever timing gear cover is removed.

Installation – 1) Clean timing gear cover and cylinder block mating surfaces. Coat cylinder block and timing gear cover gasket surfaces with oil resistant sealer. Install timing gear cover gasket. Apply silicone sealer to block/pan junction and to oil pan gasket sealing surface.

2) Position timing gear cover on cylinder block. Hand-start timing gear cover and pan bolts. To aid timing gear cover alignment, slide Timing Gear Cover Aligner (T61P-6019-B) over crankshaft and into seal bore.

3) Tighten timing gear cover bolts first to obtain proper alignment, then tighten oil pan bolts. Remove timing gear cover aligner. Install and lubricate timing gear cover oil seal. See FRONT CRANKSHAFT OIL SEAL.

4) Lubricate crankshaft stub, vibration damper hub I.D. and sealing surface of timing gear cover seal with clean engine oil. DO NOT apply grease to seal. Apply a 1/4" (6 mm) bead of silicone sealer to keyway inside vibration damper hub.

5) Using Vibration Damper Replacer (T52L-6306-AEE), install vibration damper. To install remaining components, reverse removal procedure. Tighten bolts to specification. See TORQUE SPECIFICATIONS table at end of article. Fill and bleed air from cooling system. See COOLING SYSTEM BLEEDING under REMOVAL & INSTALLATION.

TIMING GEARS

CAUTION: To avoid valve train damage, NEVER rotate camshaft or crankshaft unless timing gears are installed.

Checking Timing Gear Backlash – 1) Remove timing gear cover. See TIMING GEAR COVER. Attach a dial indicator to engine block, with sensing stylus on camshaft gear tooth.

2) Using a dial indicator, measure gear backlash between camshaft gear and crankshaft gear at 6 equally spaced teeth. To obtain an accurate reading, hold gear firmly against block. Backlash should be .004-.010" (.10-.25 mm). If any of the 6 readings are not within specification, replace timing gears.

Removal – 1) Drain cooling system and crankcase. Remove timing gear cover. See TIMING GEAR COVER. Check camshaft end play. If end play is not within specification, replace camshaft thrust plate. See CAMSHAFT table under ENGINE SPECIFICATIONS at end of article.
2) Rotate engine (in direction of normal rotation) until camshaft and crankshaft gear timing marks are aligned. *See Fig. 5.* Using Camshaft Gear Puller (T82T-6256-A), remove camshaft gear. Using Vibration Damper Remover (T52L-6306-AEE), remove crankshaft gear. Remove Woodruff keys from camshaft and crankshaft.

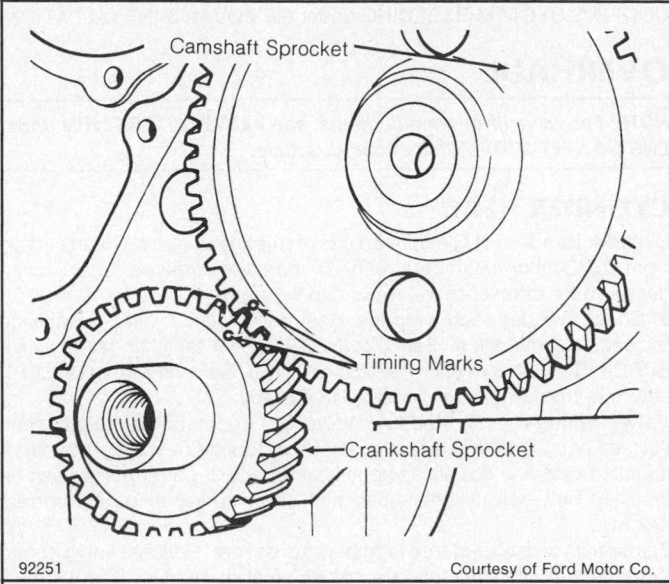

92251   Courtesy of Ford Motor Co.

Fig. 5: Aligning Timing Marks

Installation – 1) Ensure camshaft key spacer and thrust plate are correctly installed. Install Woodruff key into camshaft. Align camshaft gear keyway with camshaft key and install gear using Camshaft Gear Replacing Adapter (T65L-6306-A).
2) Install Woodruff key into crankshaft. Align crankshaft gear keyway with key and install crankshaft gear. Ensure timing marks on camshaft and crankshaft gears are still aligned.
3) To complete installation, reverse removal procedure. Tighten bolts to specification. See TORQUE SPECIFICATIONS table at end of article. Fill or top off all fluids. Fill and bleed air from cooling system. See COOLING SYSTEM BLEEDING under REMOVAL & INSTALLATION.

CAMSHAFT

Removal – 1) Drain cooling system and crankcase. Remove radiator and shroud. Remove rocker arm cover. Rotate engine (in direction of rotation) until No. 1 piston is at TDC. Remove distributor cap.
2) Mark distributor rotor and housing for installation reference. Remove distributor. Loosen rocker arm bolts and turn rocker arms aside. Remove push rods and mark for installation reference.
3) Remove engine side cover to expose valve lifters. Remove lifters and mark for installation reference. Remove engine timing gear cover. See TIMING GEAR COVER under REMOVAL & INSTALLATION. Check and note camshaft end play.
4) Replace camshaft thrust plate if end play is not within specification. See CAMSHAFT table under ENGINE SPECIFICATIONS at end of article. Turn crankshaft to align gear timing marks. *See Fig. 5.*
5) Remove camshaft thrust plate bolts. Remove camshaft gear using Camshaft Gear Puller (T82T-6256-A). Remove Woodruff key, thrust plate and spacer. Carefully remove camshaft to avoid damaging lobes or bearings.
Inspection – Inspect components for damage. Check camshaft journal diameter, lobe lift, and oil clearance. Replace components if damaged or not within specification. See CAMSHAFT table under ENGINE SPECIFICATIONS at end of article.
Installation – 1) Coat camshaft lobes with multipurpose grease. Coat bearing journals with clean engine oil. Install Woodruff key,

spacer and thrust plate on camshaft. Align gear keyway with key and install gear using Camshaft Gear Replacing Adapter (T65L-6306-A).
2) Install camshaft, spacer, thrust plate and gear as an assembly, ensuring timing marks are aligned. *See Fig. 5.* Tighten thrust plate bolts. Ensure camshaft end play is within specification. See CAMSHAFT table under ENGINE SPECIFICATIONS at end of article.
3) To complete installation, reverse removal procedure. Tighten bolts to specification. See TORQUE SPECIFICATIONS table at end of article. Fill and bleed air from cooling system. See COOLING SYSTEM BLEEDING under REMOVAL & INSTALLATION.

CAMSHAFT BEARINGS

NOTE: It may be necessary to remove crankshaft for access to camshaft bearings.

Removal – 1) Remove engine. See ENGINE under REMOVAL & INSTALLATION. Install engine on engine stand. Remove flywheel/flexplate. Remove camshaft rear bearing bore plug.
2) Remove camshaft and crankshaft. See CAMSHAFT and CRANKSHAFT. Push pistons to top of cylinders. Use Camshaft Bearing Remover/Installer (T65L-6250-A) to remove cam bearings. To remove front bearing, place bearing puller in cam bore from rear of cylinder block.
Installation – To install cam bearings, reverse removal procedure. Ensure oil holes in bearings align with oil holes in cylinder block when installing camshaft bearings. Install front bearing so .020-.035" (.51-.89 mm) exists between front edge of bearing and face of cylinder block.

CRANKSHAFT

NOTE: Unless parts are being discarded, keep all crankshaft parts in the order that they were removed.

Removal & Installation – 1) Remove engine and attach to engine stand. See ENGINE under REMOVAL & INSTALLATION. Remove spark plugs. Remove oil pan. See OIL PAN under REMOVAL & INSTALLATION. Remove timing gear cover. See TIMING GEAR COVER under REMOVAL & INSTALLATION.
2) Using Camshaft Gear Puller (T82T-6256-A), remove camshaft gear. Using Vibration Damper Remover (T52L-6306-AEE), remove crankshaft gear. Remove flywheel. Remove oil pump. Rotate crankshaft to position connecting rod caps at bottom of stroke. Remove connecting rod cap nuts. Tap cap with plastic mallet to separate from rod.
3) Remove connecting rod caps. Cover connecting rod bolts with protective rubber caps. Use wooden hammer handle to tap piston into cylinder bore. Ensure main bearing caps are marked. Remove crankshaft main bearing caps.
4) Carefully remove crankshaft. To install, reverse removal. Once bearings are installed apply a coat of heavy engine oil to crankshaft and bearings. Tighten nut/bolts to specifications. See TORQUE SPECIFICATIONS table at end of article.

REAR CRANKSHAFT OIL SEAL

Removal – 1) Remove starter and transmission. See TRANSMISSION REMOVAL & INSTALLATION article in TRANSMISSION SERVICING. Remove clutch assembly (if equipped). Remove flexplate/flywheel. Remove engine rear cover plate. Using an awl, punch hole in oil seal metal surface between lip and block.
2) Carefully pry oil seal from recess without damaging seal surface. Clean oil seal recess in block and main bearing cap.
Installation – 1) Inspect and clean crankshaft surface. Lightly coat crankshaft and sealing surface of new oil seal with engine oil. Place seal in position with lip facing inward, and install seal using seal installer.
2) Keep installer straight in respect to center line of crankshaft. Seal is properly installed when seal installer contacts cylinder block. Coat threads of flywheel bolts with oil resistant sealer. To complete installation, reverse removal procedure. Tighten bolts to specification. See TORQUE SPECIFICATIONS table at end of article.

WATER PUMP

NOTE: Fan clutch/water pump hub has right-hand thread.

Removal – Drain cooling system. Remove accessory drive belt by using a 5/8" (16 mm) open-end wrench. Lift belt tensioner away from belt. Using Fan Clutch Pulley Holder (T84T-6312-C) and Fan Clutch Nut Wrench (T84T-6312-D), remove fan and clutch assembly. Remove water pump pulley. Disconnect coolant hoses from water pump. Remove water pump.

Installation – **1)** Clean all gasket mating surfaces. Coat new gasket on both sides with gasket sealer and position gasket on water pump. Install water pump and tighten attaching bolts.

2) To install remaining components, reverse removal procedure. Fill and bleed air from cooling system. See COOLING SYSTEM BLEEDING under REMOVAL & INSTALLATION.

OIL PAN

Removal (Bronco & Pickup) – **1)** Drain engine oil and cooling system. Remove upper intake manifold and throttle body. See INTAKE & EXHAUST MANIFOLDS under REMOVAL & INSTALLATION. Disconnect negative battery cable. Raise and support vehicle. Remove starter. Remove both front engine mount-to-engine mount bracket nuts.

2) Raise engine and place 1" (25.4 mm) wood blocks between front engine mount insulators and frame brackets. Remove oil pan bolts. Lower pan and remove oil pump bolts and pick-up tube nut. Lower oil pump assembly into pan. Remove pan.

Installation – **1)** To install, reverse removal procedure. Apply silicone sealant at front and rear corners of oil pan surface and cylinder block, and where timing gear cover meets the cylinder block.

2) Install oil pan bolts and tighten using specified procedure. *See Fig. 6.* To install remaining components, reverse removal procedure. Tighten bolts to specification. See TORQUE SPECIFICATIONS table at end of article. Fill or top off fluids. Fill and bleed air from cooling system. See COOLING SYSTEM BLEEDING under REMOVAL & INSTALLATION.

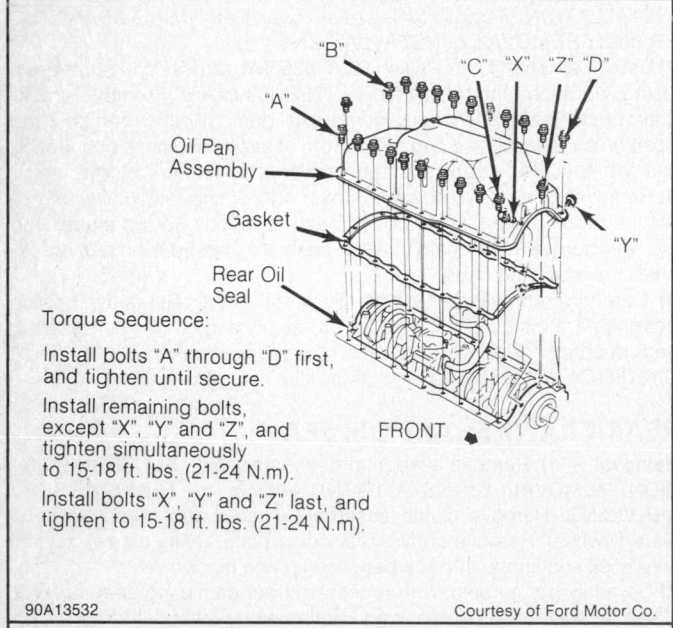

90A13532   Courtesy of Ford Motor Co.

Fig. 6: Oil Pan Bolt Tightening Sequence

Removal (Van) – **1)** Remove engine cover, air cleaner and air inlet tubes from throttle body. Position idle air by-pass valve aside. Unbolt fan shroud and let it rest on fan. Remove oil filler tube bracket. Drain engine oil and cooling system. Remove upper and lower radiator hoses.

2) Put vehicle on jack stands. Remove front engine mount nuts. Raise engine approximately 3" and place wooden block under engine

mounts. Remove oil pan bolts. Remove oil pick-up tube from oil pump. Remove oil pan and gaskets.

Installation – **1)** To install, reverse removal procedure. Apply silicone sealant at front and rear corners of oil pan surface and cylinder block, and where timing gear cover meets the cylinder block.

2) Install oil pan bolts and tighten using specified procedure. *See Fig. 6.* To install remaining components, reverse removal procedure. Tighten bolts to specification. See TORQUE SPECIFICATIONS table at end of article.

3) Fill or top off fluids. Fill and bleed air from cooling system. See COOLING SYSTEM BLEEDING under REMOVAL & INSTALLATION.

OVERHAUL

NOTE: For valve lifter specifications, see VALVE LIFTERS table under ENGINE SPECIFICATIONS at end of article.

CYLINDER HEAD

Cylinder Head – **1)** Clean head gasket mating surface. Clean carbon from combustion chambers. DO NOT damage surfaces. Check cylinder head for cracks, burrs, nicks and warpage.

2) Check cylinder head warpage. Resurface cylinder head if warpage exceeds specification. See CYLINDER HEAD table under ENGINE SPECIFICATIONS at end of article. DO NOT machine more than .010" (.25 mm) from original cylinder head surface.

Valve Springs – **1)** Measure valve spring installed height from surface of cylinder head spring pad to underside of spring retainer. If installed height is not within specification, a .03" (.8 mm) shim can be installed between cylinder head and valve spring to obtain correct height.

2) Inspect valve spring free length and pressure. Replace valve spring if free length and pressure are not within specification. See VALVES & VALVE SPRINGS table under ENGINE SPECIFICATIONS at end of article.

CAUTION: DO NOT install valve spring spacers unless necessary. Using more spacers than required can result in spring breakage or worn camshaft lobes.

Valve Stem Oil Seals – When installing new valve stem seals, ensure oil seal bottoms on valve guide. Oversized valve stem seals must be installed when oversized valves are used.

Valve Guides – **1)** Valve guides must be reamed for an oversized valve if valve stem oil clearance exceeds specification. See CYLINDER HEAD table under ENGINE SPECIFICATIONS at end of article. Valves are available with .015" (.38 mm) and .030" (.76 mm) oversize stems.

2) If oversized valves or oversized valve stem oil seals are not available, valve guide may be bored out to use a service bushing. Always use reamers in proper sequence (smallest first).

NOTE: Always grind valve seat after valve guide has been reamed or service bushing has been installed.

Valve Seat – Ensure valve seat angle, seat width and seat runout are within specification. See CYLINDER HEAD table under ENGINE SPECIFICATIONS at end of article. Valve seats must be ground when valve guide is reamed or replaced. Seat replacement information is not available from manufacturer.

Valves – **1)** Ensure head diameter, valve face runout, stem diameter and valve margin are within specification. See VALVES & VALVE SPRINGS table under ENGINE SPECIFICATIONS at end of article.

2) Oversize valves are available in .015" (.38 mm) and .030" (.76 mm). When servicing valve stem tip, DO NOT remove more than .010" (.25) from end of valve stem.

Seat Correction Angles – Grind valve seat to a true 45-degree angle. If seat width is too wide after grinding, use a 30-degree stone to lower seat or a 60-degree stone to raise seat. See CYLINDER HEAD table under ENGINE SPECIFICATIONS at end of article.

CYLINDER BLOCK ASSEMBLY

CAUTION: NEVER cut into ring travel area more than 1/32" when removing ridge ring at top of bore.

Piston & Rod Assembly – Note direction of connecting rod installation on piston before removal. Ensure pistons and rods are installed in cylinder from which they were removed. When installing piston in bore, ensure arrow on top of piston is facing front of engine and bearing tang on connecting rod is facing camshaft. *See Fig. 7.*

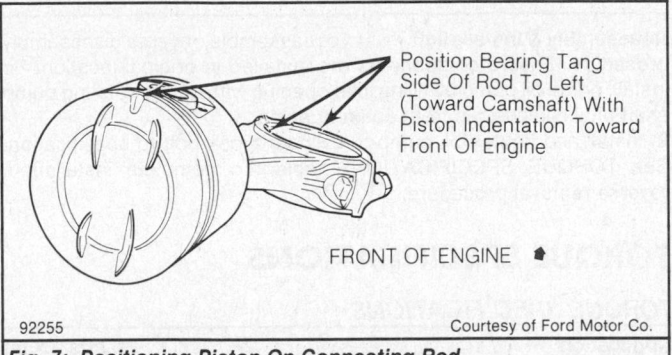

Position Bearing Tang Side Of Rod To Left (Toward Camshaft) With Piston Indentation Toward Front Of Engine

FRONT OF ENGINE

92255   Courtesy of Ford Motor Co.

Fig. 7: Positioning Piston On Connecting Rod

NOTE: Make all measurements with piston and block are at normal room temperature of 70°F (21°C).

Fitting Pistons – **1)** Check piston-to-bore clearance. See PISTONS, PINS & RINGS table under ENGINE SPECIFICATIONS at end of article. Standard size pistons are color-coded Red, Blue or Yellow on the piston dome. See PISTONS, PINS & RINGS table. Oversize pistons are also available.

2) If bore diameter is in lower one-third of specification, use a Red coded piston. If bore diameter is in middle one-third of specification, use a Blue coded piston. If bore diameter is in upper one-third of specification, use Yellow coded piston. Use proper size piston to obtain specified clearance. See PISTONS, PINS & RINGS table.

Piston Rings – **1)** Select rings for bore diameter. Place ring in cylinder bore in which it will be installed. Use piston to square ring in bore and place ring below normal ring wear area. Measure ring end gap. If ring gap is not within specification, try another ring set. See PISTONS, PINS & RINGS table under ENGINE SPECIFICATIONS at end of article.

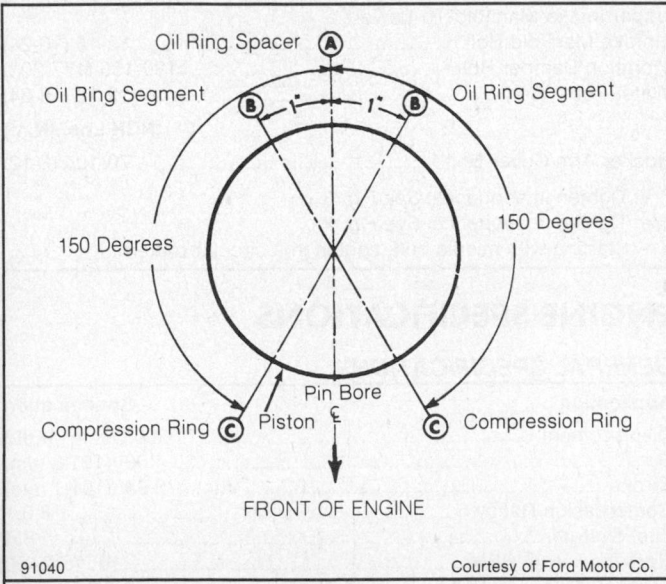

91040   Courtesy of Ford Motor Co.

Fig. 8: Positioning Rings On Piston

2) Check side clearance of rings after installing on piston. Ensure clearance is within specification around entire circumference. Replace piston and/or rings if clearance is not within specification. See PISTONS, PINS & RINGS table. Ensure rings are properly spaced on piston before installing pistons into cylinder. *See Fig. 8.*

Piston Pin Replacement – **1)** Remove bearing inserts from connecting rod and cap. Mark pistons and pins to ensure assembly to original location. Remove piston rings. Using a press and Piston Pin Remover/Replacer (T81P-6135-A), press piston pin from piston and connecting rod.

2) Before assembling piston and rod, ensure connecting rod pin bore diameter and piston diameter are within specification. See PISTONS, PINS & RINGS table under ENGINE SPECIFICATIONS at end of article. Apply light coat of engine oil to parts to be assembled. When installing piston pin, ensure piston and connecting rod are assembled as shown. *See Fig. 7.*

Rod Bearings – **1)** Use Plastigage to check rod bearing clearance. If proper oil clearance cannot be obtained with standard bearings, try a combination of undersize bearings. DO NOT use any other bearing combination other than what is listed. See UNDERSIZE MAIN & ROD BEARING COMBINATIONS table.

2) If bearing combinations cannot bring clearance within specification, machine or replace crankshaft as necessary. Always replace bearings in pairs. See CRANKSHAFT, MAIN & CONNECTING ROD BEARINGS table under ENGINE SPECIFICATIONS at end of article.

UNDERSIZE MAIN & ROD BEARING COMBINATIONS [1]

Excess Bearing Clearance In. (mm)	Use Upper Bearing In. (mm)	Use Lower Bearing In. (mm)
.0-.0005 (.0-.013)	.001 (.025)	[2]
.0005-.0010 (.013-.025)	.001 (.025)	.001 (.025)
.0010-.0015 (.025-.039)	.002 (.050)	.001 (.025)
.0015-.0020 (.039-.050)	.002 (.050)	.002 (.050)

[1] – DO NOT use any other bearing combination other than what is listed. If use of bearing combinations does not bring clearance within specification, machine or replace crankshaft as necessary.
[2] – Use standard bearing.

Crankshaft & Main Bearings – **1)** When checking main bearing clearance in vehicle, position a jack under adjoining bearing counterweight being checked. Remove only one main bearing cap at a time.

2) Use Plastigage to check main bearing clearance. If proper oil clearance cannot be obtained with standard bearings, try a combination of undersize bearings. DO NOT use any other bearing combination other than what is listed. See UNDERSIZE MAIN & ROD BEARING COMBINATIONS table.

3) If use of bearing combinations does not bring clearance within specification, machine or replace crankshaft as necessary. Always replace bearings in pairs. See CRANKSHAFT, MAIN & CONNECTING ROD BEARINGS table under ENGINE SPECIFICATIONS at end of article.

4) Install all bearing caps except thrust bearing cap (No. 5 from front of engine). Tighten main bearing cap bolts to specifications. See TORQUE SPECIFICATIONS table at end of article. Install No. 5 bearing cap and tighten bolts finger tight. Pry crankshaft forward and pry No. 5 bearing cap to rear of engine to align thrust bearing. While retaining forward pressure on crankshaft, tighten bearing cap bolts to specifications. See TORQUE SPECIFICATIONS table.

5) Ensure crankshaft end play is within specification. Replace thrust bearing if end play is not within specification. See CRANKSHAFT, MAIN & CONNECTING ROD BEARINGS table.

Cylinder Block – **1)** Using a feeler gauge and straightedge, check cylinder block head gasket surface for warpage. Check cylinder bore for wear, taper, out-of-round and piston fit. See CYLINDER BLOCK table under ENGINE SPECIFICATIONS at end of article.

CAUTION: DO NOT machine more than .010" (.25 mm) of material from original cylinder block head surface.

2) Install all main bearing caps and tighten to specification before honing cylinder bore. Ensure bearing caps are installed in their original location, with arrow on cap pointing towards front of engine.

3) Use ONLY a spring-loaded type cylinder hone. After honing, thoroughly clean bore with detergent and water solution. Rinse solution from bore thoroughly with clean water. Wipe bore clean with lint-free cloth. Lubricate cylinder bores with engine oil.

ENGINE OILING

ENGINE LUBRICATION SYSTEM

Oil supply from pan is forced through lubrication system by rotor oil pump. Oil flows through full-flow oil filter, which routes oil into main oil gallery. *See Fig. 9.*

Oil gallery supplies oil to all internal engine bearings and lifters. Oil from lifters is forced through push rods to lubricate valve train. Timing gears are lubricated by splash method. Spring-loaded oil pressure relief valve is located in pump body and is nonadjustable.

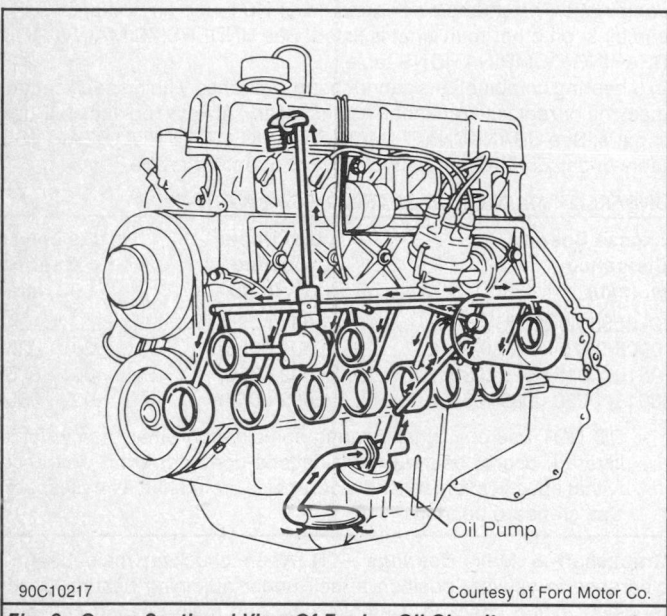

90C10217   Courtesy of Ford Motor Co.

Fig. 9: Cross-Sectional View Of Engine Oil Circuit

Crankcase Capacity – Crankcase capacity is 5 qts. (4.75L). Add 1 qt. (.95L) when replacing oil filter.

Oil Pressure – Normal oil pressure at 2000 RPM should be 40-60 psi (2.8-4.2 kg/cm²) with engine at normal operating temperature.

OIL PUMP

Removal & Disassembly – Remove oil pan. See OIL PAN under REMOVAL & INSTALLATION. Remove oil pump retaining bolts and remove oil pump assembly. Disassemble oil pump. Note location of component installation for reassembly reference.

Inspection – Inspect components for damage. Measure rotor end play, rotor tip clearance and outer rotor-to-housing clearance. Measure relief valve-to-bore clearance and relief valve tension. Replace oil pump assembly if measurements are not within specifications. See OIL PUMP SPECIFICATIONS table.

NOTE: Oil pump is serviced as an assembly only. Replace assembly if measurements are not within specification. See OIL PUMP SPECIFICATIONS table.

OIL PUMP SPECIFICATIONS

Application	Specification In. (mm)
Drive Shaft-To-Housing Clearance	.0015-.0030 (.038-.076)
Outer Rotor-To-Housing Clearance	.001-.013 (.03-.33)
Relief Valve Spring Tension	[1]
Relief Valve-To-Bore Clearance	.0015-.0030 (.038-.076)
Rotor End Play	.004 (.10) Max.
Rotor Tip Clearance	.012 (.31) Max.
Shaft-To-Housing Clearance	.0015-.0030 (.038-.076)

[1] - Spring tension is 20.6-22.6 lbs.@ 2.49" (9.3-10.3 kg @ 63.2 mm).

Reassembly & Installation – **1)** To reassemble, reverse disassembly procedure. Ensure components are installed in original location. To install, prime oil pump by filling inlet opening with oil and rotating pump shaft until oil emerges from outlet opening.

2) Install and tighten oil pump-to-cylinder block bolt to specification. See TORQUE SPECIFICATIONS table. To complete installation, reverse removal procedure.

TORQUE SPECIFICATIONS

TORQUE SPECIFICATIONS

Application	Ft. Lbs. (N.m)
Bellhousing-To-Engine Bolt	40-50 (54-68)
Camshaft Thrust Plate Bolt	12-18 (16-24)
Connecting Rod Cap Nut	40-45 (54-61)
Cylinder Head Bolt [1]	
Step 1	50-55 (68-75)
Step 2	60-65 (82-88)
Step 3	70-85 (95-116)
Engine Mount-To-Bracket Bolt	54-74 (73-100)
Flexplate-To-Converter Bolt	20-30 (27-41)
Flywheel-To-Crankshaft Bolt	75-85 (102-116)
Front Cover Bolt	12-18 (16-24)
Fuel Supply Manifold Bolt	12-15 (16-20)
Lower Intake & Exhaust	
Manifold Assembly Nut [2]	22-32 (30-44)
Main Bearing Cap Bolt	60-70 (82-95)
Oil Filter Adapter Bolt	40-50 (54-68)
Oil Pan Bolt	15-18 (21-24)
Oil Pump Attaching Bolt	10-12 (14-20)
Oil Pump Pick-Up Tube Nut	22-32 (30-43)
Rocker Arm Bolt	17-23 (23-31)
Throttle Body-To-Upper Intake Manifold Bolt	14-20 (19-27)
Upper Intake Manifold-To-Lower	
Intake Manifold Bolt	12-18 (16-24)
Vibration Damper Bolt	130-150 (177-203)
Water Pump Bolt	12-18 (16-24)
	INCH Lbs. (N.m)
Rocker Arm Cover Bolt [3]	70-105 (8-12)

[1] – Tighten in sequence. *See Fig. 3.*
[2] – Tighten in sequence. *See Fig. 2.*
[3] – Starting with middle bolt, tighten in a circular pattern.

ENGINE SPECIFICATIONS

GENERAL SPECIFICATIONS

Application	Specification
Displacement	300 Cu. In. (4.9L)
Bore	4.00" (101.6 mm)
Stroke	3.98" (101.1 mm)
Compression Ratio	8.8:1
Fuel System	PFI
Horsepower @ RPM	145 @ 3400
Torque Ft. Lbs. @ RPM	260 @ 2000

CRANKSHAFT, MAIN & CONNECTING ROD BEARINGS

Application	In. (mm)
Crankshaft	
End Play	
Standard	.004-.008 (.10-.20)
Wear Limit	.012 (.30)
Runout	
Standard	.002 (.05)
Wear Limit	.005 (.13)
Main Bearings	
Journal Diameter	2.3982-2.3990 (60.914-60.935)
Journal Out-Of-Round	.0006 (.015)
Journal Taper	.0005 (.013) per 1" (25.4 mm)
Oil Clearance	
Desired	.0008-.0015 (.020-.038)
Allowable	.0010-.0028 (.025-.071)
Connecting Rod Bearings	
Journal Diameter	2.1228-2.1236 (53.919-53.939)
Journal Out-Of-Round	.0006 (.015)
Journal Taper	.0006 (.015) per 1" (25.4 mm)
Oil Clearance	
Desired	.0008-.0015 (.020-038)
Allowable	.0007-.0024 (.018-.061)

PISTONS, PINS & RINGS

Application	In. (mm)
Pistons	
Clearance	.0010-.0018 (.025-.046)
Diameter [1]	
Red Piston	3.9982-3.9988 (101.554-101.570)
Blue Piston	3.9994-4.0000 (101.585-101.600)
Yellow Piston [2]	4.0008-4.0014 (101.620-101.636)
Pins	
Diameter	
Standard	.9749-.9754 (24.762-24.775)
.001" (.03 mm) Oversize	.9760-.9763 (24.790-24.798)
.002" (.05 mm) Oversize	.9770-.9773 (24.816-24.823)
Piston Fit	[2] .0002-.0004 (.005-.010)
Rings	
No. 1	
End Gap	.010-.020 (.25-.51)
Side Clearance	
Standard	.0019-.0036 (.048-.091)
Wear Limit	.0056 (.142)
No. 2	
End Gap	.010-.020 (.25-.51)
Side Clearance	
Standard	.002-.004 (.05-.10)
Wear Limit	.006 (.15)
No. 3 (Oil)	
End Gap (Steel Rail)	.015-.055 (.38-1.40)
Side Clearance	Snug Fit

[1] – Measured at piston pin bore center line, at 90° angle to piston pin.
[2] – Piston fit is .0003-.0005" (.007-.013 mm) on vehicles under 8500 lbs. GVW.

CYLINDER BLOCK

Application	In. (mm)
Cylinder Bore	
Standard Diameter	4.0000-4.0048 (101.600-101.722)
Maximum Taper	.010 (.25)
Maximum Out-Of-Round	.0015 (.038)
Maximum Deck Warpage	[1]

[1] – No more than .003" (.08 mm) within a 6" (152 mm) area, and no more than .006" (.15 mm) overall. DO NOT remove more than .010" (.25 mm) material from original deck if machining is required.

CONNECTING RODS

Application	In. (mm)
Bore Diameter	
Pin Bore	.9734-.9742 (24.724-24.745)
Crankpin Bore	2.2750-2.2758 (57.785-57.805)
Crankpin Bearing Bore	
Out-Of-Round	.0006 (.015)
Center-To-Center Length	6.2082-6.2112 (157.688-157.764)
Maximum Bend [1]	.012 (.30)
Maximum Twist [1]	.024 (.61)
Side Play	
Standard	.006-.013 (.15-.33)
Wear Limit	.018 (.46)

[1] – Specification listed is measured at the ends of an 8" (203 mm) bar, 4" (102 mm) on each side of rod center line.

VALVES & VALVE SPRINGS

Application	Specification
Face Angle	44°
Head Diameter	
Intake Valve	1.769-1.793" (44.93-45.54 mm)
Exhaust Valve	1.551-1.569" (39.40-39.85 mm)
Minimum Margin	.031" (.79 mm)
Stem Diameter	
Standard	.3416-.3423" (8.677-8.694 mm)
.015 Oversize	.3566-.3573" (9.058-9.075 mm)
.030 Oversize	.3716-.3723" (9.439-9.456 mm)
Valve Springs	
Free Length	
Intake	1.96" (49.78 mm)
Exhaust	1.78" (45.21 mm)
Installed Height	
Intake	1.61-1.67" (40.89-42.42 mm)
Exhaust	1.44-1.50" (36.58-38.10 mm)
Out-Of-Square	.078" (1.98 mm)

	Lbs. @ In. (kg @ mm)
Pressure	
Valve Closed	
Intake	66-74 @ 1.640 (30-34 @ 41.65)
Exhaust	66-74 @ 1.470 (30-34 @ 37.34)
Valve Open	
Intake	166-184 @ 1.240 (75-83 @ 31.50)
Exhaust	166-184 @ 1.070 (75-83 @ 27.18)

CYLINDER HEAD

Application	Specification
Maximum Warpage	[1]
Valve Seats	
Seat Angle	45°
Seat Width	
Intake	.060-.080" (1.52-2.03 mm)
Exhaust	.070-.090" (1.78-2.29 mm)
Maximum Seat Runout	.002" (.05 mm)
Valve Guides	
Intake	
Valve Guide I.D.	.3433-.3443" (8.720-8.745 mm)
Valve Stem-To-Guide	
Oil Clearance	
Standard	.0010-.0027" (.025-.069 mm)
Wear Limit	.0055" (.140 mm)

[1] – No more than .006" (.15 mm) within a 6" (152 mm) area, and no more than .007" (.18 mm) overall. DO NOT remove more than .010" (.25 mm) material from original surface if machining is required.

CAMSHAFT

Application	In. (mm)
Journal Diameter	2.017-2.018 (51.23-51.26)
Bearing I.D.	2.019-2.020 (51.28-51.31)
End Play	
Standard	.001-.007 (.03-.18)
Wear Limit	.009 (.23)
Journal Runout	.005 (.13)
Lobe Lift	[1] .249 (6.32)
Maximum Lobe Wear	.005 (.13)
Journal-To-Bearing	
Oil Clearance	
Standard	.001-.003 (.03-.08)
Wear Limit	.006 (.15)

[1] – Lobe lift is .247" (6.27 mm) on F150 (Federal emissions) with 2.47:1 or 2.75:1 axle ratio and manual transmission.

VALVE LIFTERS

Application	In. (mm)
Lifter Diameter	.8740-.8745 (22.200-22.212)
Oil Clearance	
Standard	.0007-.0027 (.018-.069)
Wear Limit	.005 (.13)

Bronco, Pickup, Van

NOTE: Unless otherwise specified, references to Pickup include the F350 Super Duty commercial chassis.
For engine repair procedures not covered in this article, see ENGINE OVERHAUL PROCEDURES article in GENERAL INFORMATION.

ENGINE IDENTIFICATION

Engine may be identified by the eighth character of the Vehicle Identification Number (VIN). VIN plate is attached to upper left corner of instrument panel, near windshield. The VIN is also found on the Safety Compliance Certification Label on left door or left door pillar.

VIN ENGINE CODES

Engine	Code
5.0L PFI	N
5.8L PFI	H

ADJUSTMENTS

VALVE CLEARANCE ADJUSTMENT

NOTE: The use of positive stop rocker arm bolts eliminates the need to adjust valve clearance. If valve seat/face has been serviced or worn parts are suspected, check valve clearance.

1) Using a remote starter (ignition off), rotate crankshaft until No. 1 piston is at TDC of compression stroke. Reference mark "A" indicates TDC. With No. 1 piston at TDC, mark references "B" and "C", 90 degrees apart. *See Fig. 1.*

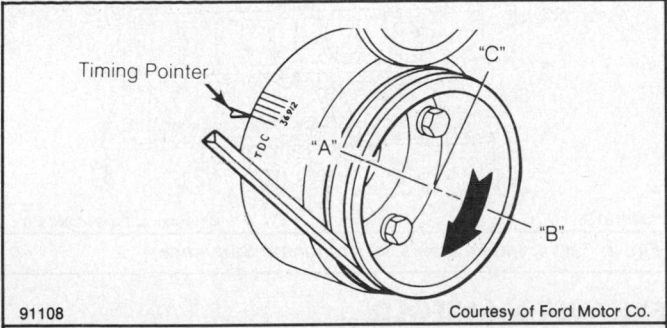

91108 Courtesy of Ford Motor Co.

Fig. 1: Identifying Crankshaft Positions For Valve Adjustment

2) Slowly bleed lifter down (until bottomed) using Tappet Bleed Down Wrench (T71P-6513-B) on appropriate cylinder. See VALVE CLEARANCE ADJUSTMENT table. With lifter plunger bottomed, use a feeler gauge to measure clearance between rocker arm and valve stem tip. See VALVE LIFTERS table under ENGINE SPECIFICATIONS at end of article.
3) If clearance is insufficient, install .060" (1.52 mm) undersize push rod. If clearance is excessive, install .060" (1.52 mm) oversize push rod. Check and/or adjust valve clearance on proper cylinders in relation to crankshaft position. See VALVE CLEARANCE ADJUSTMENT table.

VALVE CLEARANCE ADJUSTMENT

Crankshaft Position	Check Intake Nos.	Check Exhaust Nos.
5.0L		
"A"	1, 7, 8	1, 5, 4
"B"	5, 4	2, 6
"C"	2, 3, 6	7, 3, 8
5.8L		
"A"	1, 4, 8	1, 3, 7
"B"	3, 7	2, 6
"C"	2, 5, 6	4, 5, 8

REMOVAL & INSTALLATION

WARNING: When battery is disconnected, vehicle computer and memory systems may lose memory data. Driveability problems may exist until computer systems have completed a relearn cycle. See COMPUTER RELEARN PROCEDURES article in GENERAL INFORMATION before disconnecting battery.

NOTE: Discharge A/C system using approved refrigerant recovery/recycling equipment.

FUEL PRESSURE RELEASE

Remove fuel cap to release fuel tank pressure. Remove relief valve cap. Relief valve is located on fuel rail. Connect fuel pressure gauge to relief valve. Release fuel into a suitable container.

COOLING SYSTEM BLEEDING

WARNING: When engine is operating, NEVER remove radiator cap under any conditions. Failure to follow instruction could damage cooling system or engine, or cause personal injury. Always wrap protective material around radiator cap to avoid injury from hot steam or hot coolant.

1) Fill cooling system with 50/50 mixture of water and coolant. Pause several minutes for circulation. Fill radiator to filler neck seat. Disconnect heater outlet hose at water pump to bleed off trapped air. Fill radiator until coolant begins to escape.
2) Connect heater outlet hose. Fill radiator until coolant is between the cap seal in the filler neck to 1.5" (38 mm) below cap seal. Install radiator cap. Start engine and allow to warm up. Shut engine off. Allow engine to cool. Remove radiator cap and check coolant level. Top off radiator coolant as necessary.

ENGINE

Removal (Bronco & Pickup) – 1) Drain cooling system and crankcase. Mark hood hinges and remove hood. Disconnect battery and ground cables from cylinder block. Disconnect EGR tube (if equipped). On 5.0L models, remove air intake hoses, PCV tube and carbon canister hose.
2) On 5.8L models, remove air cleaner and intake duct assembly with crankcase ventilation and carbon canister hoses attached. On all models, disconnect radiator hoses. Disconnect transmission cooler lines (if equipped). Disconnect oil cooler lines at oil filter adapter (if equipped).
3) Disconnect power steering hoses and thermactor hoses. On models with A/C, discharge A/C system. Disconnect hoses at compressor and remove A/C condenser. On all models, remove fan shroud, spacer, pulley and radiator. Remove and position alternator aside.
4) Remove brackets for thermactor pump, power steering pump, alternator and A/C compressor. Disconnect oil pressure sending unit wire. Release fuel pressure. See FUEL PRESSURE RELEASE. Using Disconnect Tool (D87L-9280-A) for 3/8" line or (D87L-9280-B) for 1/2" line, disconnect fuel supply and return lines. *See Fig. 2.*
5) If hairpin-type clip is used, remove hairpin by bending tab downward so it will clear body. Using your hands, spread clip legs and push legs into fitting. Pull hairpin clip from fitting. *See Fig. 2.* Disconnect accelerator cable, transmission shift rod and speed control linkages from throttle body.
6) Disconnect throttle bracket from upper intake manifold and set aside with cables attached. Disconnect vacuum lines, carbon canister hose, heater hoses and electrical wiring from engine. Disconnect primary wire at coil and brake booster hose at engine.
7) Remove bellhousing-to-engine upper bolts. Raise front of vehicle. Remove starter. Separate exhaust pipes from manifolds. Disconnect engine mounts from brackets on frame. On A/T models, remove converter inspection plate and flex plate-to-converter bolts.
8) On all models, remove remaining bellhousing-to-engine bolts. Lower vehicle and support transmission. Attach engine hoist and carefully

separate engine from transmission. Carefully lift engine from vehicle without damaging rear cover plate.

Installation – To install, reverse removal procedure. Tighten bolts to specification. See TORQUE SPECIFICATIONS table at end of article. Check and top off all engine fluids. Fill and bleed air from cooling system. See COOLING SYSTEM BLEEDING.

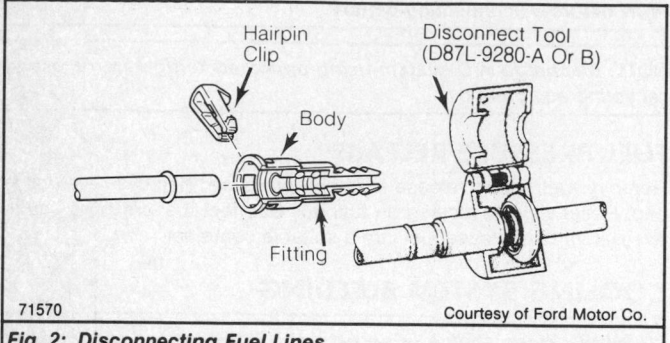

71570   Courtesy of Ford Motor Co.

Fig. 2: Disconnecting Fuel Lines

Removal (Van) – **1)** Remove engine cover. Disconnect battery. Drain cooling system. Remove air cleaner. Remove grille and radiator air deflector. Remove headlight and side marker light assemblies. Remove fan shroud and radiator.

2) Discharge A/C system. Remove A/C condenser. Remove hood lock leaving cable attached. Remove stone deflector and upper radiator support. Disconnect air bag electrical connector. Remove heater hoses. Remove oil filler tube. Disconnect alternator and junction box.

3) Disconnect lines at A/C compressor. Remove upper intake manifold. See INTAKE MANIFOLDS under REMOVAL & INSTALLATION. Disconnect transmission filler tube. Release fuel pressure. See FUEL PRESSURE RELEASE.

4) Disconnect fuel inlet and return lines using Disconnect Tool (D87L-9280-A or B). *See Fig. 2.* Disconnect thermactor lines. Remove distributor cap, rotor and spark plug wires. Remove 3 top engine-to-transmission bolts. Raise vehicle and remove power steering pump hoses.

5) Disconnect starter wiring and remove starter. Disconnect exhaust pipes from manifolds. On A/T vehicles, remove converter inspection cover bolts. Remove flex plate-to-converter nuts. Remove front engine mount attaching bolts and nuts.

6) Support vehicle on jack stands. Support transmission with jack. Remove remaining engine-to-transmission bolts. Connect engine to engine hoist and lift engine out of engine compartment.

Installation – To install, reverse removal procedure. Tighten bolts to specification. See TORQUE SPECIFICATIONS table at end of article. Check and top off all engine fluids. Fill and bleed air from cooling system. See COOLING SYSTEM BLEEDING.

INTAKE MANIFOLDS

Removal (Upper) – **1)** Disconnect negative battery cable. Mark and disconnect electrical connectors at upper intake components. Disconnect throttle linkage by prying with screwdriver. DO NOT pull off by hand. Disconnect kickdown linkage from throttle body. Remove throttle linkage cable bracket.

2) Mark and disconnect vacuum lines at upper intake. Disconnect PCV hose from rear of upper intake. On Van models, remove oil filler tube. On all models, remove 2 canister purge lines from throttle body. Disconnect heater hoses attached to throttle body. Disconnect EGR tube from EGR valve.

3) Remove upper intake support bracket. Remove 6 upper intake manifold mounting bolts. Remove upper intake manifold and throttle body as an assembly. Remove intake manifold gasket.

Installation – **1)** Ensure gasket mating surfaces are clean and flat. Install new gasket on lower intake manifold. If available, install 2 guide pins in opposite corners. Install upper intake manifold and tighten bolts finger tight.

2) Evenly tighten bolts to specification. See TORQUE SPECIFICATIONS table at end of article. To complete installation, reverse removal procedure. Fill and bleed air from cooling system. See COOLING SYSTEM BLEEDING under REMOVAL & INSTALLATION.

Removal (Lower) – **1)** Disconnect negative battery cable. Remove upper intake manifold. See INTAKE MANIFOLDS. Drain cooling system. Remove distributor cap and plug wires as an assembly. Mark and remove distributor assembly.

2) Mark and disconnect electrical connectors and vacuum hoses from lower manifold. Remove fuel injector wiring harness. Release fuel pressure. See FUEL PRESSURE RELEASE under REMOVAL & INSTALLATION.

3) Using Disconnect Tool (D87L-9280-A or B), disconnect fuel supply and return line. *See Fig. 2.* Remove upper radiator hose, by-pass hose and heater outlet hose. Remove lower intake manifold bolts evenly. Remove lower intake manifold and gaskets.

Installation – **1)** Clean gasket mating surfaces. Apply a 1/16" (1.6 mm) bead of silicone rubber sealer on full width of each intake manifold seal (4 places). Install new lower intake manifold gaskets on cylinder block and heads.

2) Ensure gaskets are interlocked with end rubber gaskets. Install 2 guide pins in opposite corners. Install lower intake manifold and tighten bolts finger tight. Tighten bolts evenly in sequence to specification. *See Fig. 3.* See TORQUE SPECIFICATIONS table at end of article. To complete installation, reverse removal procedure. Fill and bleed air from cooling system. See COOLING SYSTEM BLEEDING under REMOVAL & INSTALLATION.

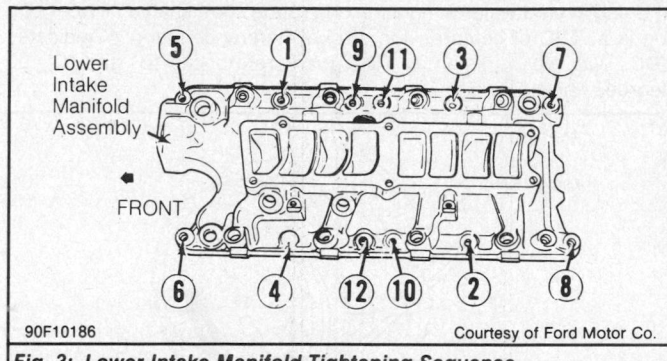

90F10186   Courtesy of Ford Motor Co.

Fig. 3: Lower Intake Manifold Tightening Sequence

EXHAUST MANIFOLD

Removal – **1)** Raise vehicle. Remove exhaust pipe-to-exhaust manifold nuts. Lower vehicle. On Van, remove interior engine cover. On right manifold, remove air cleaner, intake duct assembly and crankcase ventilation hose.

2) On vehicles with C6 transmission, remove thermactor manifold from exhaust manifold. On all models, remove upper intake manifold support bracket and transmission dipstick tube bracket. Remove EGR valve assembly. Remove spark plug shield and right side exhaust manifold. Removal of left side exhaust manifold is similar to right side.

Installation – Ensure gasket mating surfaces are clean and flat. Install exhaust manifold and bolts. Tighten bolts, starting from center and moving outward, to specification. See TORQUE SPECIFICATIONS table at end of article. To complete installation, reverse removal procedure.

CYLINDER HEAD

Removal – **1)** Remove lower intake manifold. See INTAKE MANIFOLDS under REMOVAL & INSTALLATION. Remove valve cover(s). Remove drive belt. On Van, remove ignition coil and air cleaner duct. On all models, if left cylinder head is being removed, remove A/C compressor and power steering bracket.

2) Remove oil dipstick tube and speed control bracket (if equipped). On right cylinder head, remove alternator and air pump mounting bracket complete with accessories. Swing alternator down and position aside.

3) Disconnect exhaust manifold(s) from exhaust pipe(s). Loosen rocker arm bolts and pivot rocker arm off push rods. Mark push rods for installation reference and remove.

4). On Bronco and Pickup, disconnect thermactor air supply hoses at check valves and plug check valve. On Van, remove air supply tube assembly from rear of cylinder head On all models, remove cylinder head bolts in reverse order of tightening sequence. *See Fig. 4.* Remove cylinder head and gasket.

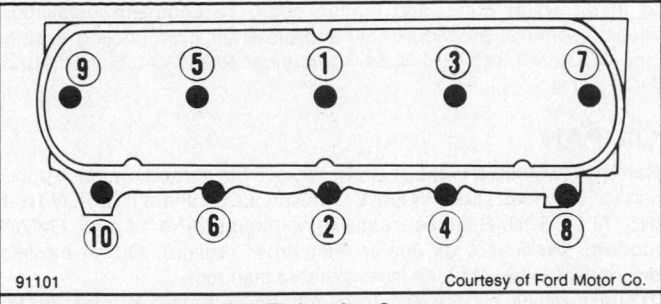

Fig. 4: Cylinder Head Bolt Tightening Sequence

Inspection – Inspect cylinder head for warpage. Resurface if warpage exceeds specification. See CYLINDER HEAD table under ENGINE SPECIFICATIONS at end of article. DO NOT machine more than .010" (.25 mm) from original cylinder head thickness. Clean and tap cylinder head bolt holes in cylinder block.

Installation – **1)** Ensure gasket mating surfaces are clean and flat. Properly install new cylinder head gasket as marked on gasket. DO NOT use sealer on head gasket. Install cylinder head and bolts. Tighten bolts in sequence to specification. *See Fig. 4.* See TORQUE SPECIFICATIONS table at end of article.

2) Lubricate push rod ends, valve stem tips, rocker arms and fulcrum seats with Multipurpose Grease (DOAZ-19584-AA). To complete installation, reverse removal procedure. Fill and bleed air from cooling system. See COOLING SYSTEM BLEEDING under REMOVAL & INSTALLATION.

CAUTION: If valves/seats were serviced, check and adjust valve clearance. See VALVE CLEARANCE ADJUSTMENT under ADJUSTMENTS.

TIMING CHAIN COVER OIL SEAL

NOTE: Front cover seal can be replaced without removing front cover. Use Seal Remover (T70P-6B070-B) and Seal Installer (T70P-6B070-A) to remove and install cover seal.

Removal – **1)** Remove fan shroud attaching bolts. Remove fan, clutch and shroud. Remove serpentine drive belt. Remove crankshaft pulley and damper. Place Seal Remover (T70P-6B070-B) onto timing chain cover plate over front seal.

2) Tighten 2 bolts, forcing seal remover under seal flange. Alternately tighten 2 bolts one-half turn at a time until seal is removed from engine.

Installation – Coat new seal with Lubriplate. Using Seal Installer (T70P-6B070-A), install new timing chain cover seal. Ensure seal is fully seated and spring is properly positioned in seal. To complete installation, reverse removal procedure.

TIMING CHAIN COVER

Removal (Bronco & Pickup) – **1)** Drain cooling system. Loosen fan clutch bolts. Remove fan shroud-to-radiator bolts (if equipped), and position shroud over fan. Remove idler pulley belt. Remove all hoses and brackets attached to water pump.

2) Remove fan, clutch and pulley. Remove fan shroud (if equipped). Remove crankshaft pulley bolt. Remove crankshaft pulley and damper. Remove oil pan-to-cylinder block timing chain cover bolts. Remove timing chain cover and water pump as an assembly.

3) Cut oil pan gasket even with cylinder block. If replacement of timing chain cover seal is necessary, drive out old seal with pin punch. DO NOT damage timing chain cover seal recess.

Installation – **1)** Clean all gasket surfaces. If timing chain cover seal was removed, install new timing chain cover oil seal. Cut and fit new oil pan gasket. Apply sealer to oil pan gasket surface and install new gasket. Coat block and timing chain cover with gasket sealer, and position new gasket on block.

2) Place timing chain cover on cylinder block. Install Timing Chain Cover Aligner (T61P-6019-B). It may be necessary to force cover downward slightly to compress pan gasket. Coat timing chain cover bolts with oil-resistant sealer, and install bolts.

3) Tighten oil pan-to-timing chain cover bolts while pushing in on timing chain cover aligner. Tighten timing chain cover bolts. Remove aligner. To complete installation, reverse removal procedure. Fill and bleed air from cooling system. See COOLING SYSTEM BLEEDING under REMOVAL & INSTALLATION.

Removal (Van) – **1)** Drain cooling system. Remove upper and lower radiator hoses. Remove radiator. Remove cooling fan and shroud. Raise vehicle on hoist. Remove A/C compressor and power steering pump bracket, and accessories. Remove crankshaft pulley.

2) Remove crankshaft damper using Crankshaft Damper Remover (T-79T-6316-A). Remove oil pan-to-timing chain cover bolts. Remove timing chain cover and water pump as an assembly.

3) If replacement of timing chain cover seal is necessary, drive out old seal with pin punch, taking care not to damage timing chain cover seal recess. Cut oil pan gasket even with cylinder block.

Installation – **1)** Clean all gasket surfaces. If timing chain cover seal was removed, install new timing chain cover oil seal. Cut and fit new oil pan gasket. Apply sealer to oil pan gasket surface and install new gasket. Coat block and timing chain cover with gasket sealer and position new gasket on block.

2) Place timing chain cover on cylinder block. It may be necessary to force cover downward slightly to compress pan gasket. Coat timing chain cover bolts with oil-resistant sealer, and install bolts.

3) Tighten oil pan-to-timing chain cover bolts. Tighten timing chain cover bolts to specification. See TORQUE SPECIFICATIONS table at end of article. To complete installation, reverse removal procedure. Fill and bleed air from cooling system. See COOLING SYSTEM BLEEDING under REMOVAL & INSTALLATION.

TIMING CHAIN & SPROCKET

Removal – **1)** Position No. 1 piston on TDC of compression stroke. Remove timing chain cover. See TIMING CHAIN COVER. Check alignment of camshaft and crankshaft sprocket timing marks. *See Fig. 5.* Check timing chain deflection.

2) If chain deflection is not within specification, replace timing chain and sprockets. See CAMSHAFT table under ENGINE SPECIFICATIONS at end of article. Remove camshaft sprocket bolt and washer. Slide sprockets and timing chain forward and remove as an assembly.

Installation – Install crankshaft sprocket, camshaft sprocket and timing chain as an assembly. Ensure timing marks are properly aligned. *See Fig. 5.* Apply oil to timing chain and sprockets. To complete installation, reverse removal procedure. Tighten bolts and nuts to specifications. See TORQUE SPECIFICATIONS table at end of article.

CAMSHAFT

Removal – **1)** On Van, remove front grille. On all models, drain cooling system. Disconnect upper and lower radiator hoses. Disconnect transmission oil cooler lines (if equipped). Remove radiator. Remove engine timing chain cover. See TIMING CHAIN COVER under REMOVAL & INSTALLATION.

2) Remove timing chain. See TIMING CHAIN & SPROCKET. Remove upper intake manifold and throttle body as an assembly. See INTAKE MANIFOLDS under REMOVAL & INSTALLATION. Remove valve covers.

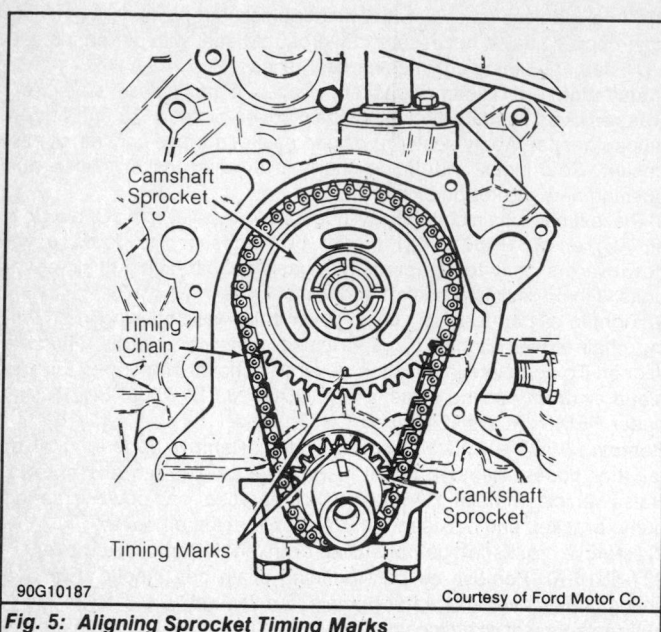

Camshaft
Sprocket

Timing
Chain

Crankshaft
Sprocket

Timing Marks

90G10187   Courtesy of Ford Motor Co.

Fig. 5: Aligning Sprocket Timing Marks

3) Loosen rocker arm fulcrum bolts, and rotate rocker arms to one side. Mark and remove push rods and valve lifters for installation reference. Check camshaft end play. If not within specification, replace camshaft thrust plate. See CAMSHAFT table under ENGINE SPECIFICATIONS.

4) Remove camshaft thrust plate and remove camshaft. Use care to avoid damage to camshaft bearings and journals.

Inspection – Clean all components and gasket mating surfaces. Check lobe lift and camshaft-to-bearing clearance. See CAMSHAFT table under ENGINE SPECIFICATIONS.

Installation – 1) Oil camshaft journals and apply polyethylene grease to lobes. Carefully slide camshaft into position. Coat camshaft thrust plate with engine oil, and install with groove toward cylinder block.

2) Lubricate lifters with engine oil and install in the bores from which they were removed. Lubricate rocker arms, fulcrum seats, valve stem tips and push rod ends with polyethylene grease before installing.

3) To complete installation, reverse removal procedure; use new gaskets. Check and adjust valve clearance as necessary. See VALVE CLEARANCE ADJUSTMENT under ADJUSTMENTS.

REAR CRANKSHAFT OIL SEAL

Removal – 1) Disconnect negative battery cable and remove starter. Remove transmission. Remove flywheel/flexplate and engine rear cover plate. Using a sharp awl, punch a hole into seal metal surface, between lip and block.

2) Using Jet Plug Puller (T77L-9533), screw in threaded end of puller. Remove rear oil seal.

NOTE: Use caution to prevent scratching or damaging crankshaft seal surfaces.

Installation – Coat seal surfaces with light engine oil. DO NOT use grease for seal lubrication. Using Seal Installer (T65P-6701-A), install seal until firmly seated. To install remaining components, reverse removal procedure.

WATER PUMP

Removal (Bronco & Pickup) – Drain cooling system. Loosen bolts on fan clutch. Disconnect fan shroud and position over fan. Remove drive belt. Remove all hoses and brackets attached to water pump. Remove fan, clutch and pulley. Remove A/C compressor and power steering pump bracket. Remove bolts attaching water pump to engine block.

Removal (Van) – Remove air cleaner duct assembly. Drain cooling system. Remove all hoses and brackets attached to water pump. Remove radiator. Remove drive belt, fan clutch and water pump pulley. Remove A/C compressor and power steering pump bracket. Remove bolts attaching water pump to engine block.

Installation – 1) Clean all gasket mating surfaces. Coat both sides of new gasket with gasket sealer, and position on cylinder timing chain cover.

2) Install water pump and tighten bolts. To complete installation, reverse removal procedure. Fill and bleed air from cooling system. See COOLING SYSTEM BLEEDING under REMOVAL & INSTALLATION.

OIL PAN

Removal (Bronco & Pickup) – 1) Remove fan shroud. Remove upper intake manifold. See INTAKE MANIFOLDS under REMOVAL & INSTALLATION. Remove front engine mount-to-frame nuts. On A/T models, disconnect oil cooler lines from radiator. On all models, disconnect exhaust pipes from exhaust manifold.

2) Drain engine oil. Support transmission and remove transmission crossmember. Remove oil pan bolts and lower oil pan. Remove oil pump bolts and pick-up tube nut. Lower oil pump assembly into pan. Remove oil pan.

Installation – To install, reverse removal procedure. Apply silicone sealant at front and rear corners of oil pan surface and cylinder block, and where timing chain cover meets the cylinder block. To install remaining components, reverse removal procedure.

Removal (Van) – 1) Disconnect battery. Remove engine cover and air cleaner. Drain cooling system and engine oil. Remove power steering pump and A/C compressor with hoses attached and set aside (if equipped). Remove fan shroud and oil filler tube. Disconnect radiator hoses. Remove oil dipstick tube bolts and remove dipstick.

2) Raise and support vehicle. Remove splash shield from under alternator. On A/T models, disconnect transmission cooler lines at radiator. Remove transmission dipstick and tube. On all models, release fuel pressure. See FUEL PRESSURE RELEASE under REMOVAL & INSTALLATION. Disconnect fuel line at fuel rail.

3) Disconnect exhaust pipes from manifold. On M/T models, disconnect manual linkage at transmission. On all models, remove center drive shaft support and remove drive shaft from transmission. Remove engine mount nuts.

4) Place a transmission jack, with wooden support, under oil pan. Raise engine and transmission assembly. Engine and transmission assembly will pivot around rear engine mount.

5) Engine and transmission assembly must remain centered in engine compartment in order for it to be raised approximately 4" (120 mm) at front engine mounts. Use wooden blocks to support engine assembly in this position.

6) Remove oil pan bolts and lower oil pan. Lower oil pump assembly into pan. Remove oil pan and oil pump intermediate shaft.

Installation – 1) To install, reverse removal procedure. Apply silicone sealant at front and rear corners of oil pan surface and cylinder block, and where timing chain cover meets the cylinder block. Position new gasket and seals to engine block.

2) Position oil pan with pump to engine, and install oil pump. To complete installation, reverse removal procedure. Fill or top off all fluids. Fill and bleed air from cooling system. See COOLING SYSTEM BLEEDING under REMOVAL & INSTALLATION.

OVERHAUL

CYLINDER HEAD

Cylinder Head – 1) Clean head gasket mating surface. Clean carbon from combustion chambers. Use care not to damage surfaces. Check cylinder head for cracks, burrs, nicks and warpage.

2) DO NOT machine more than .010" (.25 mm) from original cylinder head surface to correct warpage. Replace cylinder head as necessary. See CYLINDER HEAD table under ENGINE SPECIFICATIONS at end of article.

Valve Springs – 1) Measure valve spring installed height from top of spring seat to underside of spring retainer. Ensure installed height is within specification. See VALVES & VALVE SPRINGS table under ENGINE SPECIFICATIONS at end of article.

2) If installed height is not within specification, a .03" (.8 mm) shim can be installed between cylinder head and valve spring to obtain correct height. Inspect valve spring free length and pressure. Replace valve spring if free length and pressure are not within specification. See VALVES & VALVE SPRINGS table.

CAUTION: DO NOT install valve spring spacers unless necessary. Using more spacers than required can result in spring breakage or worn camshaft lobes.

Valve Stem Oil Seals – When installing new valve stem seals, ensure oil seal bottoms on valve guide. Oversized valve stem seals must be installed when oversized valves are used.

Valve Guides – 1) Valve guides must be reamed for an oversized valve if valve stem oil clearance exceeds specification. See CYLINDER HEAD table under ENGINE SPECIFICATIONS at end of article. Valves are available in .015" (.38 mm) and .030" (.76 mm) oversize.

2) If oversized valves or oversized valve stem oil seals are not available, valve guide may be bored out to use a service bushing. Always use reamers in proper sequence (smallest first).

NOTE: Always grind valve seat after valve guide has been reamed or service bushing has been installed.

Valve Seat – 1) Grind valve seat to a true 45-degree angle. If seat width is too wide after grinding, use a 30-degree stone to lower seat or a 60-degree stone to raise seat. See CYLINDER HEAD table under ENGINE SPECIFICATIONS at end of article.

2) Ensure valve seat angle, seat width and seat runout are within specification. See CYLINDER HEAD table under ENGINE SPECIFICATIONS at end of article. Valve seats must be ground when valve guide is reamed or replaced. Replacement information is not available from manufacturer.

Valves – Ensure head diameter, valve face runout, stem diameter and valve margin are within specification. See VALVES & VALVE SPRINGS table under ENGINE SPECIFICATIONS at end of article.

CAUTION: DO NOT remove more than .010" (.25 mm) from end of valve stem when resurfacing tip of valve.

CYLINDER BLOCK ASSEMBLY

Piston & Rod Assembly – 1) Ensure pistons and rods are installed in cylinder from which they were removed. Ensure indentation on piston top is positioned as shown in illustration. *See Fig. 6.*

2) Ensure numbered side of rod faces outward. *See Fig. 6.* When installing replacement rods, ensure large-chamfered side of connection rod bearing bore is toward crankshaft cheek, facing front of engine for right rods and rear of engine for left rods.

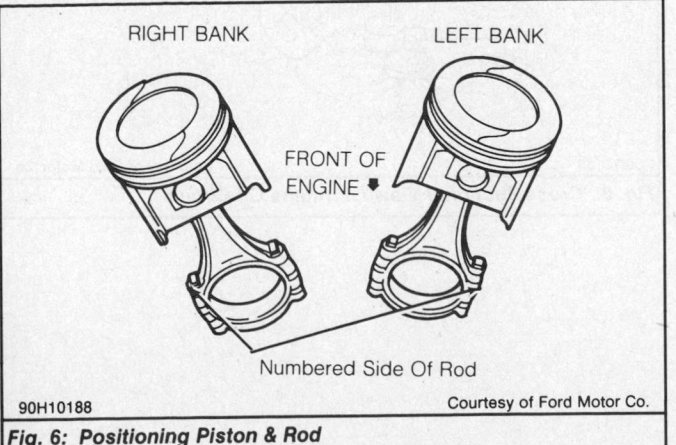

90H10188   Courtesy of Ford Motor Co.

Fig. 6: Positioning Piston & Rod

NOTE: Take measurements with components at about 70°F (21°C).

Fitting Pistons – 1) Check piston-to-bore clearance. See PISTONS, PINS & RINGS table under ENGINE SPECIFICATIONS at end of article. Standard size pistons are color-coded Red, Blue or Yellow on the piston dome. See PISTONS, PINS & RINGS table. Oversize pistons are also available.

2) If bore diameter is in lower one-third of specification, use a Red coded piston. If bore diameter is in middle one-third of specification, use a Blue coded piston. If bore diameter is in upper one-third of specification, use Yellow coded piston. Use proper size piston to obtain specified clearance. See PISTONS, PINS & RINGS table.

Piston Rings – 1) Select rings for bore diameter. Place ring in cylinder bore in which it will be installed. Use piston to square ring in bore and place ring below normal ring wear area. Measure ring end gap. If ring gap is not within specification, try another ring set. See PISTONS, PINS & RINGS table under ENGINE SPECIFICATIONS at end of article.

2) Check side clearance of rings after installing on piston. Ensure clearance is within specification around entire circumference. Replace piston and/or rings if clearance is not within specification. See PISTONS, PINS & RINGS table. Ensure rings are properly spaced on piston before installing pistons into cylinder. *See Fig. 7.*

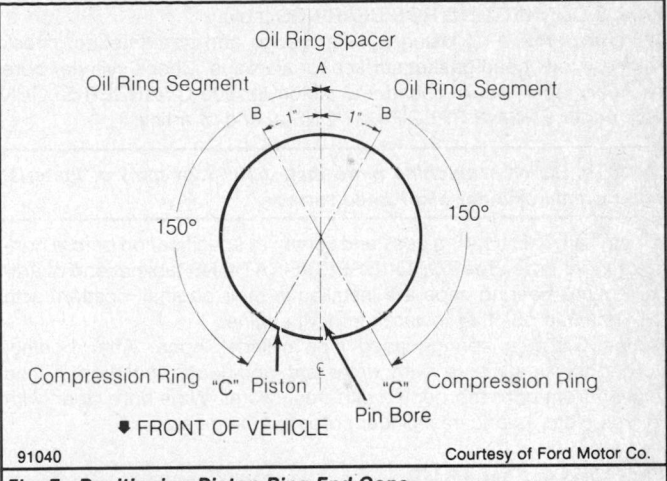

91040   Courtesy of Ford Motor Co.

Fig. 7: Positioning Piston Ring End Gaps

Rod Bearings – 1) Use Plastigage to check rod bearing clearance. If proper oil clearance cannot be obtained with standard bearings, try a combination of undersize bearings. DO NOT use any other bearing combination other than what is listed. See UNDERSIZE MAIN & ROD BEARING COMBINATIONS table.

2) If use of bearing combinations does not bring clearance within specification, machine or replace crankshaft as necessary. Always replace bearings in pairs. See CRANKSHAFT, MAIN & CONNECTING ROD BEARINGS table under ENGINE SPECIFICATIONS at end of article.

UNDERSIZE MAIN & ROD BEARING COMBINATIONS [1]

Excess Bearing Clearance In. (mm)	Use Upper Bearing In. (mm)	Use Lower Bearing In. (mm)
.0-.0005 (.0-.013)	.001 (.025)	[2]
.0005-.0010 (.013-.025)	.001 (.025)	.001 (.025)
.0010-.0015 (.025-.039)	.002 (.050)	.001 (.025)
.0015-.0020 (.039-.050)	.002 (.050)	.002 (.050)

[1] – DO NOT use any other bearing combination other than what is listed. If use of bearing combinations does not bring clearance within specification, machine or replace crankshaft as necessary.

[2] – Use standard bearing.

Crankshaft & Main Bearings – 1) When checking main bearing clearance in vehicle, position a jack under adjoining bearing counterweight being checked. Remove only one main bearing cap at a time.

2) Use Plastigage to check main bearing clearance. If proper oil clearance cannot be obtained with standard bearings, try a combination of undersize bearings. DO NOT use any other bearing combination other than what is listed. See UNDERSIZE MAIN & ROD BEARING COMBINATIONS table.

3) If use of bearing combinations does not bring clearance within specification, machine or replace crankshaft as necessary. Always replace bearings in pairs. See CRANKSHAFT, MAIN & CONNECTING ROD BEARINGS table under ENGINE SPECIFICATIONS at end of article.

4) Install all bearing caps except thrust bearing cap (No. 3 from front of engine). Tighten main bearing cap bolts to specification. See TORQUE SPECIFICATIONS table at end of article. Install No. 3 bearing cap and tighten bolts finger tight.

5) Pry crankshaft forward and pry No. 3 bearing cap to rear of engine to align thrust bearing. While retaining forward pressure on crankshaft, tighten bearing cap to specification. See TORQUE SPECIFICATIONS table.

6) Ensure crankshaft end play is within specification. Replace thrust bearing if end play is not within specification. See CRANKSHAFT, MAIN & CONNECTING ROD BEARINGS table.

Cylinder Block – 1) Using a feeler gauge and straightedge, check cylinder block head gasket surface for warpage. Check cylinder bore for wear, taper, out-of-round and piston fit. See CYLINDER BLOCK table under ENGINE SPECIFICATIONS at end of article.

CAUTION: DO NOT machine more than .010" (.25 mm) of material from original cylinder block head surface.

---

2) Install all main bearing caps and tighten to specification before honing cylinder bore. See TORQUE SPECIFICATIONS table at end of article. Ensure bearing caps are installed in their original location, with arrow on cap pointing towards front of engine.

3) Use ONLY a spring-loaded type cylinder hone. After honing, thoroughly clean bore with detergent and water solution. Rinse solution from bore thoroughly with clean water. Wipe bore clean with lint-free cloth. Lubricate cylinder bores with engine oil.

ENGINE OILING

ENGINE LUBRICATION SYSTEM

Engine lubrication system is a force-feed type. The oil is supplied under full pressure to crankshaft, connecting rods, camshaft bearing and valve lifters. A controlled volume of oil is supplied to rocker arms and push rods. All other moving parts are lubricated by splash or gravity flow. Oil flows through oil filter before entering main oil gallery. *See Fig. 8.*

Crankcase Capacity – Crankcase capacity is 5 qts. (4.75L). Add one additional quart (.95L) when replacing oil filter.

Oil Pressure – Normal oil pressure at 2000 RPM should be 40-60 psi (2.8-4.2 kg/cm²) with engine at normal operating temperature.

Pressure Relief Valve – Pressure relief valve is located in oil pump and is not adjustable.

OIL PUMP

Removal & Disassembly – 1) Remove oil pan. See OIL PAN under REMOVAL & INSTALLATION. Remove oil pump from oil pan. Remove oil pump drive shaft. Disassemble oil pump.

2) Note direction of component installation for reassembly reference. Drill a small hole in oil pressure relief valve cap. Install self-threading screw in drilled hole and pull on screw to remove cap.

Inspection – Inspect components for damage and wear. Measure rotor end play and outer rotor-to-housing clearance. Measure relief valve-to-bore clearance and relief valve tension. Replace oil pump assembly if measurements are not within specifications. See OIL PUMP SPECIFICATIONS table.

OIL PUMP SPECIFICATIONS

Application	Specification
Outer Rotor-To-Housing	
Clearance	.001-.013" (.03-.33 mm)
Relief Valve Spring Tension	
5.0L	10.6-12.2 lbs. @ 1.74" (4.8-5.5 kg @ 44.2 mm)
5.8L	18.2-20.2 lbs. @ 2.49" (8.3-9.2 kg @ 63.2 mm)
Relief Valve-To-Housing	
Clearance	.0015-.0030" (.038-.076 mm)
Rotor End Play	.004" (.10 mm) Max.
Shaft-To-Housing	
Clearance	.0015-.0030" (.038-.076 mm)

NOTE: Oil pump is serviced as an assembly only. Replace assembly if measurements are not to specifications. See OIL PUMP SPECIFICATIONS table.

Reassembly & Installation – 1) To reassemble, reverse disassembly procedure. Ensure components are installed in original location. Install new oil pressure relief valve cap. To install, prime oil pump by filling inlet opening with oil, and rotating pump shaft until oil emerges from outlet opening.

2) Install and tighten oil pump-to-cylinder block bolt to specification. See TORQUE SPECIFICATIONS table. To complete installation, reverse removal procedure.

CAUTION: If pump and drive shaft do not seat readily, DO NOT force into position. Realign drive shaft hex with distributor shaft socket and reinstall.

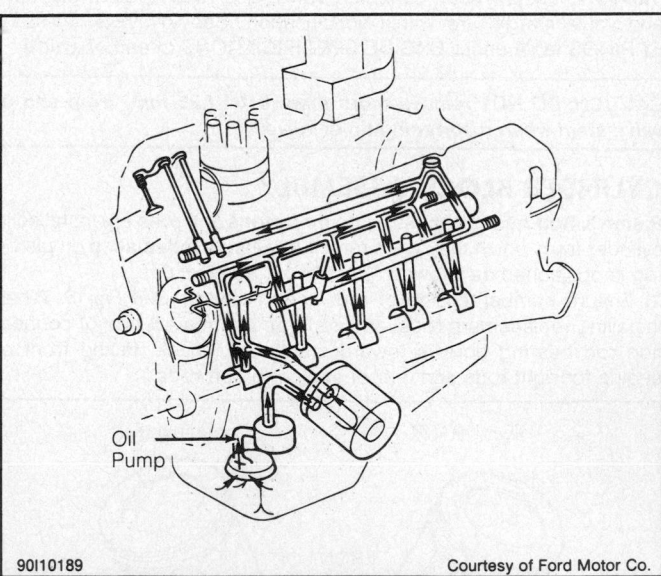

90I10189   Courtesy of Ford Motor Co.

Fig. 8: Cross-Sectional View Of Engine Oil Circuit

TORQUE SPECIFICATIONS

TORQUE SPECIFICATIONS

Application	Ft. Lbs. (N.m)
Bellhousing-To-Engine Bolt	40-50 (54-68)
Camshaft Sprocket Bolt	40-45 (54-61)
Connecting Rod Cap Nut	
5.0L	19-24 (26-33)
5.8L	40-45 (54-61)
Crankshaft Damper Bolt	70-90 (95-122)
Cylinder Head Bolt [1]	
5.0L	
Step 1	55-65 (75-88)
Step 2	65-72 (88-98)
5.8L	
Step 1	85 (116)
Step 2	95 (129)
Step 3	105-112 (143-152)
Exhaust Manifold Bolt	18-24 (24-33)
Flexplate-To-Converter Bolt	20-30 (27-41)
Flywheel-To-Crankshaft Bolt	75-85 (102-116)
Intake Manifold Bolts & Stud	
Lower [2]	23-25 (31-34)
Upper	12-18 (17-24)
Main Bearing Cap Bolt	
5.0L	60-70 (82-95)
5.8L	95-105 (129-143)
Oil Pan-To-Cylinder Block Bolt	11 (14)
Oil Pump Inlet Tube	10-15 (30-20)
Oil Pump-To-Cylinder Block Bolt	22-32 (30-44)
Rear Mount-To-Crossmember Nut	60-80 (81-108)
Rocker Arm Fulcrum Bolt	18-25 (24-34)
Starter Bolt	40-50 (54-68)
Timing Chain Cover Bolt	12-18 (17-24)

	INCH Lbs. (N.m)
Camshaft Thrust Plate Bolt	108-144 (12-16)
Valve Cover Bolt	36-60 (4-6)

[1] – Tighten in sequence. *See Fig. 4.*
[2] – Tighten in sequence. *See Fig. 3.*

ENGINE SPECIFICATIONS

GENERAL SPECIFICATIONS

Application	Specification
5.0L & 5.8L	
Displacement	
5.0L	302 Cu. In.
5.8L	351 Cu. In.
Bore	4.00" (101.6 mm)
Stroke	
5.0L	3.00" (76.2 mm)
5.8L	3.50" (88.9 mm)
Compression Ratio	
5.0L	9.0:1
5.8L	8.8:1
Fuel System	
5.0L	PFI
5.8L	PFI
Horsepower @ RPM	
5.0L	185 @ 3800
5.8L	210 @ 3800
Torque Ft. Lbs.@ RPM	
5.0L	270 @ 2400
5.8L	315 @ 2800

CRANKSHAFT, MAIN & CONNECTING ROD BEARINGS

Application	In. (mm)
5.0L & 5.8L	
Crankshaft	
End Play	.004-.008 (.10-.20)
Main Bearings	
Journal Diameter	
5.0L	2.2482-2.2490 (57.104-57.125)
5.8L	2.9994-3.0002 (76.185-76.205)
Journal Out-Of-Round	.0006 (.015)
Journal Taper [1]	.0005 (.013)
Journal Runout	.002 (.05)
Oil Clearance	
5.0L	
No. 1 Bearing	
Desired	.0001-.0015 (.003-.038)
Allowable	.0001-.0020 (.003-.050)
All Other Bearings	
Desired	.0008-.0015 (.020-.038)
Allowable	.0008-.0024 (.020-.061)
5.8L	
Desired	.0008-.0015 (.020-.038)
Allowable	.0008-.0026 (.020-.066)
Connecting Rod Bearings	
Journal Diameter	
5.0L	2.1228-2.1236 (53.919-53.939)
5.8L	2.3103-2.3111 (58.682-58.702)
Journal Taper [1]	.0006 (.015)
Journal Out-Of-Round	.0006 (.015)
Oil Clearance	
5.0L	
Desired	.0008-.0015 (.020-.038)
Allowable	.0007-.0024 (.018-.061)
5.8L	
Desired	.0008-.0015 (.020-.038)
Allowable	.0008-.0025 (.020-.064)

[1] – Within a 1" (25 mm) area.

CONNECTING RODS

Application	In. (mm)
5.0L & 5.8L	
Bore Diameter	
Pin Bore	.9096-.9112 (23.104-23.144)
Crankpin Bore	
5.0L	2.2390-2.2398 (56.871-56.891)
5.8L	2.4265-2.4273 (61.633-61.653)
Center-To-Center Length	
5.0L	5.0885-5.0915 (129.248-129.324)
5.8L	5.9545-5.9575 (151.244-151.321)
Maximum Bend [1]	.012 (.30)
Maximum Twist [1]	.024 (.61)
Side Play	
Standard	.010-.020 (.25-.51)
Service Limit	.023 (.58)

[1] – Specification listed is measured at the ends of an 8" (203 mm) bar, 4" (102 mm) on each side of rod center line.

PISTONS, PINS & RINGS

Application	In. (mm)
5.0L & 5.8L	
Pistons	
Clearance	
5.0L	.0014-.0022 (.036-.056)
5.8L	.0018-.0026 (.046-.066)
Diameter (5.0L) [1]	
Red	3.9989-3.9995 (101.572-101.587)
Blue	4.0001-4.0007 (101.603-101.618)
Yellow	4.0013-4.0019 (101.633-101.648)
Diameter (5.8L) [1]	
Red	3.9978-3.9984 (101.544-101.559)
Blue	3.9990-3.9996 (101.575-101.590)
Yellow	4.0002-4.0008 (101.605-101.620)
Pins	
Diameter	.9119-.9124 (23.16-23.17)
Length	3.01-3.04 (76.45-77.21)
Piston Fit	
5.0L	.0002-.0004 (.005-.010)
5.8L	.0003-.0005 (.008-.013)
Rod Fit	Press Fit
Rings	
No. 1 & 2	
End Gap	.010-.020 (.25-.51)
Side Clearance	
No. 1	.0013-.0033 (.033-.084)
No. 2	.002-.004 (.05-.10)
No. 3 (Oil)	
End Gap (Steel Rail)	.015-.055 (.38-1.40)
Side Clearance	Snug Fit

[1] – Standard pistons are color-coded Red, Blue and Yellow on piston dome.

CYLINDER BLOCK

Application	In. (mm)
5.0 & 5.8L	
Cylinder Bore	
Standard Diameter	4.000-4.005 (101.60-101.73)
Maximum Taper	.010 (.25)
Maximum Out-Of-Round	
Standard	.0015 (.038)
Service Limit	.005 (.13)
Maximum Deck Warpage [1]	.003 (.08)

[1] – Specification is within a 6" (152 mm) area. Overall warpage is .006" (.15 mm). DO NOT machine more than .010" (.25 mm) from original gasket surface.

VALVES & VALVE SPRINGS

Application	Specification
5.0L & 5.8L	
Face Angle	44°
Head Diameter	
5.0L	
Intake	1.69" (42.9 mm)
Exhaust	1.44-1.46" (36.6-37.1 mm)
5.8L	
Intake	1.77-1.79" (45.0-45.5 mm)
Exhaust	1.45-1.47" (36.8-37.3 mm)
Stem Diameter	
Intake	.3416-.3423" (8.677-8.694 mm)
Exhaust	.3411-.3418" (8.664-8.682 mm)
Valve Margin	.031" (.79 mm)
Valve Springs	
Free Length	
Intake	2.04" (51.8 mm)
Exhaust	1.85" (47.0 mm)
Installed Height	
5.0L	
Intake	1.67-1.70 (42.4-43.2)
Exhaust	1.58-1.61 (40.1-40.9)
5.8L	
Intake	1.77-1.80 (45.0-45.7)
Exhaust	1.58-1.61 (40.1-40.9)
Out-Of-Square	.078" (1.98 mm)

	Lbs. @ In. (kg @ mm)
Pressure	
Intake Valve Closed	
5.0L	74-82 @ 1.50 (34-37 @ 45)
5.8L	74-82 @ 1.50 (34-37 @ 45)
Intake Valve Open	
5.0L	196-212 @ 1.36 (89-96 @ 35)
5.8L	190-210 @ 1.20 (86-95 @ 31)
Exhaust Valve Closed	
5.0L	76-84 @ 1.60 (34-38 @ 41)
5.8L	76-84 @ 1.60 (34-38 @ 41)
Exhaust Valve Open	
5.0L	190-210 @ 1.20 (86-95 @ 31)
5.8L	190-210 @ 1.20 (86-95 @ 31)

CYLINDER HEAD

Application	Specification
5.0L & 5.8L	
Maximum Warpage [1]	.003" (.08 mm)
Valve Seats	
Seat Angle	45°
Seat Width	
5.0L	.06" (1.5 mm)
5.8L	.08" (2.0 mm)
Maximum Seat Runout	.002" (.05 mm)
Valve Guides	
Intake Valve	
Valve Guide Bore I.D.	.3433-.3443" (8.720-8.745 mm)
Valve Stem-To-Guide	
Oil Clearance	.0010-.0027" (.025-.069 mm)
Exhaust Valve	
Valve Guide Bore I.D.	.3433-.3443" (8.720-8.745 mm)
Valve Stem-To-Guide	
Oil Clearance	.0015-.0032" (.038-.081 mm)

[1] – Specification listed is within 6" (152 mm). Overall warpage is .006" (.15 mm). DO NOT machine more than .010" (.25 mm) from original gasket surface.

CAMSHAFT

Application	In. (mm)
5.0L & 5.8L	
Bearing I.D. Diameter	
No. 1	2.0825-2.0835 (52.896-52.921)
No. 2	2.0675-2.0685 (52.515-52.540)
No. 3	2.0525-2.0535 (52.134-52.159)
No. 4	2.0375-2.0385 (51.753-51.778)
No. 5	2.0225-2.0235 (51.372-51.397)
End Play	.001-.007 (.03-.18)
Journal Diameter	
No. 1	2.0805-2.0815 (52.845-52.870)
No. 2	2.0655-2.0665 (52.464-52.489)
No. 3	2.0505-2.0515 (52.083-52.108)
No. 4	2.0355-2.0365 (51.702-51.727)
No. 5	2.0205-2.0215 (51.321-51.346)
Journal Runout	.005 (.13)
Lobe Lift (5.0L)	
Intake	.2375 (6.033)
Exhaust	.2474 (6.284)
Lobe Lift (5.8L)	
Intake	.278 (7.06)
Exhaust	.283 (7.19)
Lobe Wear Limit	.005 (.13)
Oil Clearance	.001-.003 (.03-.08)
Timing Chain Deflection	.500 (12.70)

VALVE LIFTERS

Application	In. (mm)
5.0L & 5.8L	
Lifter Diameter	.8740-.8745 (22.200-22.212)
Oil Clearance	.0007-.0027 (.018-.069)
Collapsed Lifter Clearance	
5.0L	
Desired	.096-.165 (2.44-4.19)
Allowable	.071-.193 (1.80-4.90)
5.8L	
Desired	.123-.173 (3.12-4.39)
Allowable	.098-.198 (2.49-5.03)

1992 ENGINES
7.3L V8 Diesel

Pickup, Van

NOTE: Unless otherwise specified, references to Pickup include the F350 Super Duty commercial chassis.
For engine repair procedures not covered in this article, see ENGINE OVERHAUL PROCEDURES article in GENERAL INFORMATION.

ENGINE IDENTIFICATION

The eighth character of the Vehicle Identification Number (VIN) identifies the engine. The VIN is stamped on a metal tab attached to top left end of instrument panel and is visible through windshield. VIN is also located on Vehicle Safety Compliance Certification Label on left door or left door post pillar.

ENGINE IDENTIFICATION CODE

Application	Code
7.3L Diesel	M

ADJUSTMENTS

VALVE CLEARANCE CHECK

NOTE: Valve lifters are set at zero lash. No adjustment is necessary. If valve train has been disassembled or worn parts are suspected, valve clearance can be checked. Information not available from manufacturer.

REMOVAL & INSTALLATION

COOLING SYSTEM BLEEDING

WARNING: When battery is disconnected, vehicle computer and memory systems may lose memory data. Driveability problems may exist until computer systems have completed a relearn cycle. See COMPUTER RELEARN PROCEDURES article in GENERAL INFORMATION before disconnecting battery.

WARNING: When engine is operating, NEVER remove radiator cap under any conditions. Failure to follow instruction could damage cooling system or engine, or cause personal injury. Always wrap protective material around radiator cap to avoid injury from hot steam or hot coolant.

1) Fill cooling system with 50/50 mixture of water and coolant. Pause several minutes for circulation. Fill radiator to filler neck seat. Disconnect heater outlet hose at water pump to bleed off trapped air. Fill radiator until coolant begins to escape.
2) Connect heater outlet hose. Fill radiator until coolant is between the cap seal in the filler neck to 1.5" (38 mm) below cap seal. Install radiator cap. Start engine and allow to warm up. Shut engine off. Allow engine to cool. Remove radiator cap and check coolant level. Top off radiator coolant as necessary.

ENGINE

Removal (Pickup) – 1) Disconnect negative battery cable from both batteries. Scribe hood hinge location and remove hood. Drain cooling system. Remove air cleaner and intake duct assembly. Cover intake opening.

NOTE: Fan and fan clutch assembly are secured with left-hand threads.

2) Disconnect fan shroud and place shroud over fan. Using Fan Clutch Pulley Holder (T83T-6312-A) and Fan Clutch Nut Wrench (T83T-6312-B), remove fan and clutch assembly. Remove fan shroud. Remove A/T cooler lines from radiator (if equipped).
3) Remove radiator with hoses attached. Remove A/C compressor drive belt and A/C compressor; position on upper radiator support

with lines attached (if equipped). Remove power steering pump drive belt. Remove power steering pump with hoses attached and position aside.
4) Disconnect all sending unit wires and alternator wiring from engine. Disconnect accelerator and cruise control cables from injection pump. Remove accelerator cable bracket from engine and position aside. Remove transmission kickdown rod from injection pump (if equipped).
5) Disconnect main wiring harness connector from right side of engine. Disconnect engine ground strap from rear of engine. Disconnect fuel return hose from left rear of engine. Remove vacuum supply hose from pump. Remove upper transmission-to-engine bolts. Disconnect heater hoses from engine. Raise vehicle.
6) Disconnect both battery ground cables at engine. Disconnect and plug fuel supply line at fuel supply pump. Disconnect starter cables and remove starter. Disconnect exhaust pipes from manifolds. Remove engine mount-to-engine nuts. Remove flywheel inspection plate.
7) Remove flexplate-to-converter bolts (if equipped). Lower vehicle. Support transmission with floor jack. Remove 4 lower transmission-to-engine bolts. Attach lifting device to engine. Lift engine to clear No. 1 crossmember. Pull engine forward, rotate 45 degrees to left and carefully lift engine from vehicle.
Installation – To install, reverse removal procedure. Tighten bolts to specification. See TORQUE SPECIFICATIONS table at end of article. Check and top off all engine fluids. Fill and bleed air from cooling system. See COOLING SYSTEM BLEEDING. Evacuate and recharge A/C system (if equipped).
Removal (Van) – 1) Remove engine cover. Disconnect negative battery cable from both batteries. Drain coolant. Remove air cleaner and air intake hoses. On models equipped with A/C, discharge A/C system. Remove front bumper, grille, air deflector and gravel deflector.
2) Remove headlight and side light assemblies. Remove transmission oil cooler and brackets. Remove lower grille. Remove latch leaving cable attached. Remove fan shroud and radiator. Disconnect hoses from condenser and remove condenser. Disconnect oil cooler lines.

NOTE: Fan and fan clutch assembly are secured with left-hand threads.

3) Using Fan Clutch Pulley Holder (T83T-9424-A) and Fan Clutch Nut Wrench (T83T-6312-B), remove fan and clutch assembly. Remove all belts. Disconnect hoses and electrical connectors from A/C compressor. Remove A/C compressor. Remove power steering pump with pressure hose attached.
4) Remove radiator hoses. Disconnect wiring from alternator. Disconnect wiring from engine sensors and switches as necessary. Disconnect heater hoses from heater core. Remove fuel filter assembly. Remove fuel return hose and transmission dipstick tube.
5) Remove the top 3 transmission-to-engine bolts. Raise vehicle. Disconnect starter and transmission electrical connectors. Remove exhaust manifold-to-exhaust pipe bolts. On vehicles with A/T, remove flywheel housing cover.
6) Remove torque converter nuts. Remove 4 engine mount nuts. Lower vehicle and support transmission. Attach engine hoist to engine. Remove remaining engine-to-transmission bolts. Remove engine and attach to engine stand.
Installation – To install, reverse removal procedure. Tighten bolts to specification. See TORQUE SPECIFICATIONS table at end of article. Check and top off all engine fluids. Fill and bleed air from cooling system. See COOLING SYSTEM BLEEDING. Evacuate and recharge A/C system (if equipped).

INJECTION PUMP

CAUTION: Fuel system contamination will damage finely machined parts within injection pump and injector nozzles. Clean fittings with fuel oil or solvent and blow dry with compressed air before disconnecting fuel lines. Cap all open fittings. Injection pump can be severely damaged if engine is washed or steam cleaned while engine is hot or running.

Removal – 1) Disconnect ground cables from both batteries. On Van, remove engine cover. On all models, remove air cleaner. Cover intake opening in manifold.

2) Remove injection pump drive gear cover plate. Remove injection pump-to-drive gear bolts. Disconnect electrical connectors at injection pump. Remove fast idle solenoid bracket assembly for access to injection pump mounting nuts.

3) Disconnect accelerator cable and speed control cable from throttle lever. Remove accelerator cable bracket and cables. On Van, disconnect fuel inlet and return lines from fuel filter. Remove fuel filter. Disconnect 90-degree fuel return hose elbow at governor on injection pump.

NOTE: DO NOT disconnect injection lines from pump when removing pump from engine unless pump is being replaced or serviced. Reference mark lines-to-pump position before disconnecting.

4) If removing injection pump with injection lines connected to pump, disconnect lines at injector nozzles. If removing injection pump without lines connected to pump, remove line retaining clips.

CAUTION: Ensure No. 1 piston is at TDC of compression stroke before removing injector pump. Pulley "Y" marks should be aligned. See Fig. 1.

5) Disconnect lines from pump using Fuel Line Nut Wrench (T83T-9396-A). On all applications, remove 3 injection pump-to-injection pump drive gear cover nuts using Injection Pump Mounting Wrench (T86T-9000-B).

6) On Pickup, lift injection pump (or pump with lines connected) out of engine compartment. On Van, remove injection pump (or pump with lines attached) through passenger compartment.

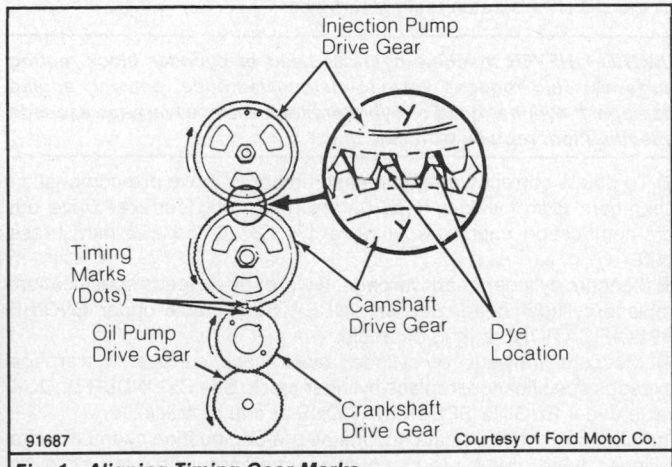

Fig. 1: Aligning Timing Gear Marks

Installation – 1) Install new "O" ring on injection pump drive gear end. Install pump into position, aligning dowel on pump drive shaft with hole in drive gear. If necessary, rotate pump drive shaft to align dowel with hole.

2) Install and hand tighten 3 injection pump-to-drive gear cover nuts. Align timing mark on top radius of injection pump with mark on injection pump drive gear cover. See Fig. 2. To complete installation, reverse removal procedure.

INJECTION PUMP DRIVE GEAR

CAUTION: To maintain injection pump drive gear-to-camshaft gear timing, CAREFULLY follow removal and installation procedures.

Removal – 1) Disconnect negative cable from both batteries. On Van, remove engine cover. On all models, remove air cleaner. Cover opening in intake manifold. Remove injection pump. See INJECTION PUMP. Remove injection pump drive gear cover. DO NOT remove drive gear.

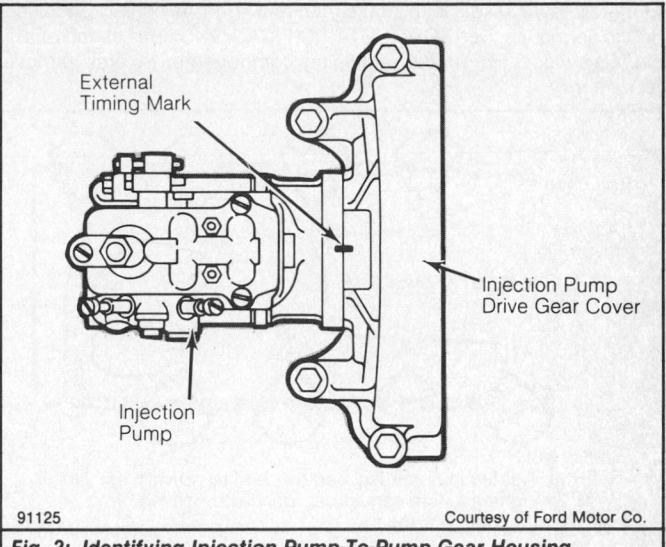

Fig. 2: Identifying Injection Pump-To-Pump Gear Housing Timing Marks

2) Using Glow Plug Socket (D83T-6002-2), remove glow plugs. Rotate crankshaft until No. 1 piston is at TDC of compression stroke. If injection pump drive gear dowel is at 4 o'clock position as viewed from front of engine, No. 1 cylinder is on compression stroke.

3) Ensure timing mark on vibration damper is set at TDC. Ensure "Y" timing mark on injection pump drive gear is aligned with "Y" timing mark on camshaft gear. See Fig. 1.

4) Without removing injection pump drive gear, slide gear back enough to expose top of camshaft gear. Note permanently dyed camshaft gear teeth adjacent to "Y" mark on camshaft gear. Remove injection pump drive gear.

Installation – 1) Clean gasket and sealing surfaces. Ensure No. 1 piston is at TDC of compression stroke. See steps **2)** and **3)** of removal procedure. Install drive gear, ensuring "Y" timing marks are properly aligned.

2) Apply a 1/8" (3.2 mm) bead of silicone sealer along bottom surface of drive gear cover. Apply thread sealing compound to drive gear cover bolt threads. Install drive gear cover and tighten to specification. See TORQUE SPECIFICATIONS table at end of article.

NOTE: With drive gear cover installed, gear remains stationary and cannot jump timing.

3) Install injection pump. Install air cleaner. Reconnect negative cables to both batteries. Run engine and check for oil, fuel and coolant leaks.

INTAKE MANIFOLD

Removal – 1) Disconnect battery ground cable from both batteries. Remove air cleaner. Cover intake opening in manifold. On Van, disconnect fuel inlet and return lines from fuel filter. Remove fuel filter and bracket as an assembly.

2) On all models, remove injection pump. See INJECTION PUMP under REMOVAL & INSTALLATION. On Pickup, disconnect fuel return hoses from No. 7 and No. 8 (rear) injector nozzles. Disconnect return hose to fuel tank. On all models, remove glow plug harness and controller. Remove engine wiring harness from engine.

3) Remove engine harness ground cable from rear of left cylinder head. Remove intake manifold-to-cylinder head bolts. Remove intake manifold. Remove valley cover (if necessary) by removing drain plug and Crankcase Depression Regulator (CDR) valve tube. Remove valley cover.

Installation – 1) Clean gasket mating surfaces. If valley cover was removed, install new valley cover with 1/8 (3.2 mm) bead of silicone sealer at ends of cylinder block.

2) Install new gaskets with intake manifold. Tighten bolts to specification in sequence. See TORQUE SPECIFICATIONS table at end of article. *See Fig. 3.* To install remaining components, reverse removal procedure.

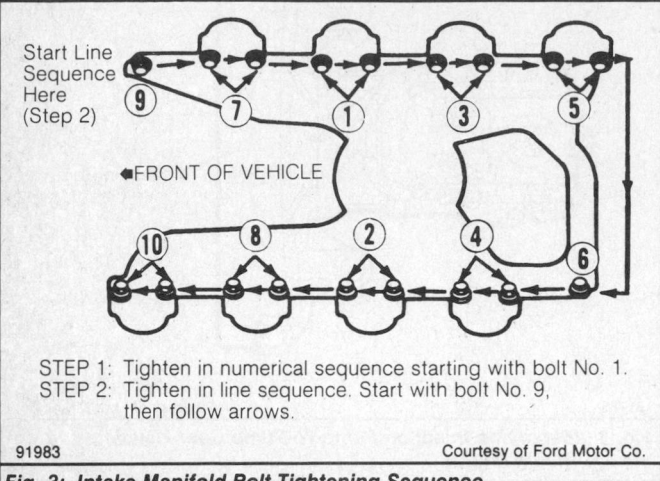

Start Line Sequence Here (Step 2)

◄FRONT OF VEHICLE

STEP 1: Tighten in numerical sequence starting with bolt No. 1.
STEP 2: Tighten in line sequence. Start with bolt No. 9, then follow arrows.

91983   Courtesy of Ford Motor Co.

Fig. 3: Intake Manifold Bolt Tightening Sequence

EXHAUST MANIFOLDS

Removal – Disconnect negative battery cable from both batteries. Raise and support vehicle. Disconnect exhaust pipes from manifolds. If removing right manifold, lower vehicle. If removing left manifold, leave vehicle in raised position. Remove bolts and remove exhaust manifold(s).

Installation – To install, reverse removal procedure. Apply anti-seize to manifold bolts. Install and tighten exhaust manifold bolts to specification in sequence. See TORQUE SPECIFICATIONS table at end of article. *See Fig. 4 .*

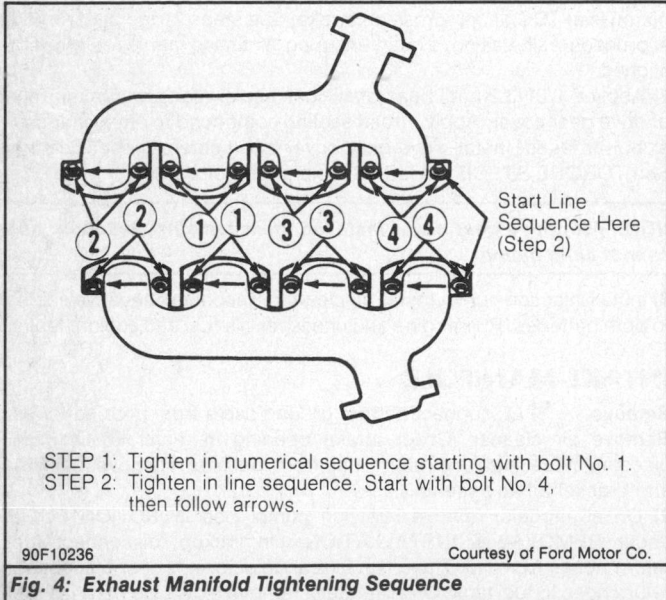

Start Line Sequence Here (Step 2)

STEP 1: Tighten in numerical sequence starting with bolt No. 1.
STEP 2: Tighten in line sequence. Start with bolt No. 4, then follow arrows.

90F10236   Courtesy of Ford Motor Co.

Fig. 4: Exhaust Manifold Tightening Sequence

CYLINDER HEADS

NOTE: The following cylinder head removal and installation procedures are for right cylinder head. Procedures for left cylinder head are similar. New cylinder heads and gaskets are interchangeable. Used cylinder heads should be installed in their original positions.

Removal – **1)** Disconnect battery ground cable from both batteries. Drain cooling system. Disconnect fan shroud and position shroud over fan. Using Fan Clutch Pulley Holder (T83T-6312-A) and Fan Clutch Nut

Wrench (T83T-6312-B), remove fan and clutch assembly. Remove fan shroud.

NOTE: Fan and fan clutch assembly are secured with left-hand threads.

2) Disconnect wiring harness electrical connector from top of fuel filter. Remove alternator. Remove vacuum pump. On Pickup, remove fuel filter inlet, outlet and return lines. Cap lines and fittings to prevent fuel system contamination.

3) Remove fuel filter and bracket. On all models, remove alternator and vacuum pump mounting bracket. Remove heater hose from cylinder head. On all models, remove injection pump. See INJECTION PUMP under REMOVAL & INSTALLATION.

4) Remove intake manifold and valley cover. See INTAKE MANIFOLD under REMOVAL & INSTALLATION. Raise vehicle. Disconnect exhaust pipe from exhaust manifolds. Remove transmission dipstick tube-to-cylinder head bolt (if equipped). Lower vehicle.

CAUTION: Pre-combustion chamber inserts may fall out of cylinder head when cylinder head is removed. Ensure pre-combustion chambers DO NOT fall into combustion chamber when installing cylinder head.

5) Remove engine oil dipstick tube bolts. Remove exhaust manifold. See EXHAUST MANIFOLDS under REMOVAL & INSTALLATION. Remove engine oil dipstick, dipstick tube and "O" ring.

6) Remove valve cover. Keeping in order of removal, remove rocker arms and push rods. Remove injector nozzles and glow plugs. Remove and discard cylinder head bolts. Remove cylinder head.

Inspection – **1)** Clean all carbon from cylinder head combustion chambers. Remove all gasket material from cylinder head and cylinder block. DO NOT scratch mating surfaces.

CAUTION: NEVER machine cylinder head or cylinder block mating surfaces. This reduces valve-to-piston clearance, causing engine damage. If cylinder head or cylinder block surface warpage exceeds specification, replace with new unit.

2) To obtain correct warpage measurement, remove pre-combustion chambers from cylinder head before measuring surface. Drive out pre-combustion chambers using a 1/4 x 8" (6.35 x 203 mm) brass drift.

3) Measure cylinder head warpage. If warpage exceeds specification, replace cylinder head. See CYLINDER HEAD table under ENGINE SPECIFICATIONS at end of article.

4) Measure warpage of cylinder block deck surface. If warpage exceeds specification, replace cylinder block. See CYLINDER BLOCK table under ENGINE SPECIFICATIONS at end of article.

Installation – **1)** Lubricate and install pre-combustion chambers into cylinder head. Seat pre-combustion chamber within its bore by tapping with plastic mallet. Install cylinder head(s). DO NOT use sealer on head gaskets.

2) Install and tighten new head bolts to specification in sequence. See TORQUE SPECIFICATIONS table at end of article. *See Fig. 5.* To complete installation, reverse removal procedure. Fill and bleed air from cooling system. See COOLING SYSTEM BLEEDING under REMOVAL & INSTALLATION.

HYDRAULIC VALVE LIFTERS

Removal – Remove intake manifold and valley cover. See INTAKE MANIFOLD under REMOVAL & INSTALLATION. Remove valve covers, rocker arms and push rods, marking all components for installation to original location. Remove lifter guide retainers. Remove valve lifters, marking each one for installation to original location.

Inspection – **1)** Clean valve lifters in solvent or diesel fuel. Check valve lifter-to-bore oil clearance. If oil clearance is not within specification, replace valve lifter. See VALVE LIFTERS table under ENGINE SPECIFICATIONS at end of article.

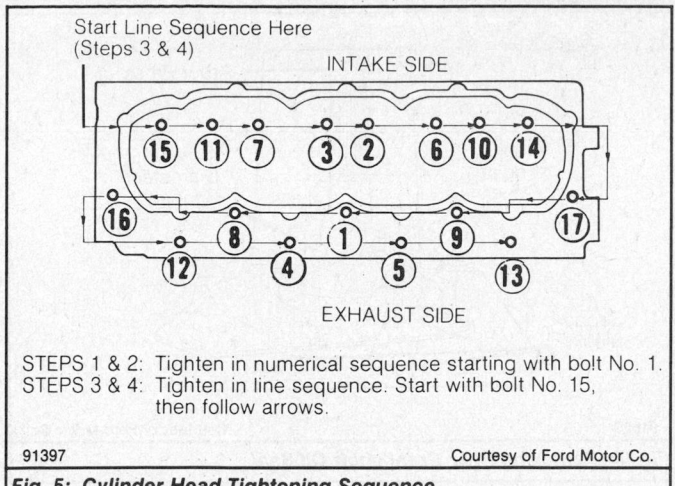

Start Line Sequence Here
(Steps 3 & 4)

INTAKE SIDE

EXHAUST SIDE

STEPS 1 & 2: Tighten in numerical sequence starting with bolt No. 1.
STEPS 3 & 4: Tighten in line sequence. Start with bolt No. 15,
then follow arrows.

91397   Courtesy of Ford Motor Co.

Fig. 5: Cylinder Head Tightening Sequence

2) Replace lifter if any part shows pitting, scoring, galling or evidence of non-rotation. Ensure lifter roller operates smoothly and without excessive play.
Installation – 1) Lubricate valve lifters and bores with clean engine oil. Install valve lifters in original positions in block. Install valve lifter guide retainers.
2) Install push rods with copper-colored end toward rocker arm. To complete installation, reverse removal procedure. Tighten bolts to specification. See TORQUE SPECIFICATIONS table at end of article.

FRONT CRANKSHAFT OIL SEAL

NOTE: Fan and fan clutch assembly are secured with left-hand threads.

Removal – 1) Front crankshaft oil seal can be removed without removing timing gear cover. Disconnect battery cables from both batteries. Disconnect fan shroud and place shroud over fan. Using Fan Clutch Pulley Holder (T83T-6312-A) and Fan Clutch Nut Wrench (T83T-6312-B), remove fan and clutch assembly. Remove fan shroud.
2) Remove accessory drive belts. Raise and support vehicle. Remove crankshaft pulley. Remove vibration damper-to-crankshaft bolt. Install Crank/Cam Gear and Damper Remover (T83T-6316-A), and remove vibration damper. Pry oil seal out with screwdriver.

NOTE: On some timing gear covers, 3 nuts are welded to front surface of cover around the outer circumference of oil seal. Seal Installer (T83T-6700-A) consists of 3 pieces: seal installer, large square washer and bridge assembly. Bridge assembly is used to install seal only if timing gear cover is equipped with welded nuts.

Installation – 1) Coat sealing surface of new seal with multipurpose grease. Install oil seal using Seal Installer (T83T-6700-A). Place seal into seal installer. If necessary, rotate crankshaft to align damper key with seal installer. Install seal and seal installer over end of crankshaft.
2) If timing gear cover is equipped with welded nuts, attach bridge to welded nuts. Draw seal into timing gear cover by rotating center screw clockwise. Seal installer should bottom on timing gear cover.
3) If timing gear cover is not equipped with welded nuts, install Crank/Cam Gear Installer (T83T-6316-B) onto crankshaft end. Draw seal into timing gear cover by rotating center screw clockwise. Seal installer should bottom on timing gear cover.
4) On all engines, apply a 1/8" (3.2 mm) bead of silicone sealer around outside diameter of oil seal where it contacts timing gear cover. Lubricate sealing surface of damper with engine oil. Install vibration damper using Crank/Cam Gear and Damper Installer (T83T-6316-B).
5) To prevent oil leakage past vibration damper keyway, apply silicone sealer to engine side of damper washer in area of keyway. Install and tighten vibration damper bolt and crankshaft pulley to specification.

See TORQUE SPECIFICATIONS table at end of article. To complete installation, reverse removal procedure.

TIMING GEAR COVER

NOTE: Fan and fan clutch assembly are secured with left-hand threads.

Removal – 1) Disconnect negative battery cables from both batteries. Drain cooling system. Remove air cleaner. Cover intake opening in manifold. Disconnect fan shroud and place shroud over fan. Using Fan Clutch Pulley Holder (T83T-9424-A) and Fan Clutch Nut Wrench (T83T-6312-B), remove fan and clutch assembly. Remove fan shroud.
2) Remove injection pump and injection pump drive gear cover. See INJECTION PUMP DRIVE GEAR under REMOVAL & INSTALLATION. Remove water pump. See WATER PUMP under REMOVAL & INSTALLATION.
3) Raise and support vehicle. Remove crankshaft pulley. Using Crank/Cam Gear and Damper Remover (T83T-6316-A), remove vibration damper. Disconnect ground cables from front of engine.
4) Remove timing gear cover-to-oil pan bolts. Lower vehicle. Remove timing gear cover-to-engine block bolts. Remove timing gear cover. Remove oil seal from timing gear cover.
Installation – 1) Coat sealing surface of new oil seal with multipurpose grease and install seal. Clean gasket surfaces of engine block, oil pan, timing gear cover and water pump.
2) Apply silicone sealer to sealing surfaces of cylinder block and timing gear cover. Install timing gear cover gasket to cylinder block. Apply a 1/8" (3.2 mm) bead of silicone sealer to front of oil pan, including oil pan-to-cylinder block junction.
3) Place timing gear cover into position, aligning holes in timing gear cover with fabricated oil pan dowel pins (if necessary) and fabricated cylinder block dowel pins (if necessary). Install 2 bolts at top of timing gear cover and one bolt at bottom left of cover.
4) Remove fabricated dowels (if used). Install remaining timing gear cover bolts and oil pan bolts. Tighten to specification. See TORQUE SPECIFICATIONS table at end of article.
5) When installing water pump, apply silicone sealant to bolts as shown. *See Fig. 8* To prevent oil leakage past keyway, apply silicone sealer to engine side of vibration damper washer (in area of keyway).
6) To complete installation, reverse removal procedure. Tighten bolts to specification. See TORQUE SPECIFICATIONS table at end of article. Fill and bleed air from cooling system. See COOLING SYSTEM BLEEDING under REMOVAL & INSTALLATION.

CAMSHAFT

Removal – 1) Remove engine from vehicle. See ENGINE under REMOVAL & INSTALLATION. Remove injection pump, intake manifold and hydraulic valve lifters. See INJECTION PUMP, INTAKE MANIFOLD and HYDRAULIC VALVE LIFTERS under REMOVAL & INSTALLATION. Remove timing gear cover. See TIMING GEAR COVER.
2) Disconnect fuel lines from fuel pump. Remove fuel pump. Remove camshaft Allen screw and washer. Using Gear Puller (T83T-6316-A), remove camshaft gear. Using Gear Puller (T77F-4220-B1), remove fuel pump cam and thrust flange spacer from camshaft. *See Fig. 6.* Remove thrust plate. Remove camshaft from engine.
Inspection – Measure camshaft bearing journals for wear. If journal diameter is not within specification, replace camshaft and valve lifters. See CAMSHAFT table under ENGINE SPECIFICATIONS at end of article.
Installation – 1) Lubricate camshaft journals with engine oil. Coat camshaft lobes with multipurpose grease. Install camshaft into bore. Install thrust plate. Ensure camshaft end play is within specification. See CAMSHAFT table under ENGINE SPECIFICATIONS at end of article.
2) Install thrust flange spacer and fuel pump cam using Crank/Cam Gear and Damper Installer (T83T-6316-B). Position camshaft to align timing marks on gears. *See Fig. 1.*

3) Install camshaft gear using crank/cam gear and damper installer. Tighten camshaft gear Allen screw to specification. See TORQUE SPECIFICATIONS table at end of article. To complete installation, reverse removal procedure.

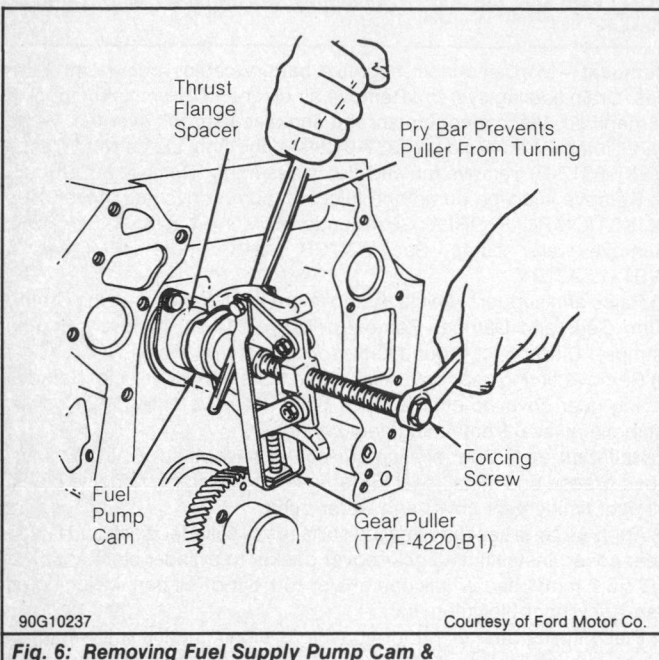

90G10237   Courtesy of Ford Motor Co.

Fig. 6: Removing Fuel Supply Pump Cam & Thrust Flange Spacer

CAMSHAFT BEARINGS

NOTE: All camshaft bearings are interchangeable except front bearing, which is wider than others.

Removal – 1) Remove engine from vehicle. See ENGINE under REMOVAL & INSTALLATION. Remove camshaft. See CAMSHAFT under REMOVAL & INSTALLATION. Remove flywheel, crankshaft and rear cylinder block camshaft core plug.
2) DO NOT damage piston cooling jets at bottom of cylinder wall. Push pistons to top of cylinders. Using Camshaft Bearing Remover/Installer (T65L-6250-A), remove camshaft bearings.
Installation – 1) Install camshaft bearings using Camshaft Bearing Remover/Installer (T65L-6250-A). Ensure bearing oil holes are properly aligned with oil holes in cylinder block.
2) Install front bearing **.020-.050" (.51-1.27 mm)** below front face of cylinder block. Check bearing installation with straightedge and feeler gauge. Install new cylinder block camshaft core plug. To complete installation, reverse removal procedure.

REAR CRANKSHAFT OIL SEAL

Removal – Remove transmission. Remove clutch assembly (if equipped). Remove flywheel/flexplate. Remove rear engine cover-to-engine bolts and remove rear cover. Position rear cover on arbor press as shown. *See Fig. 7.* Using arbor press and 4 1/8" (105 mm) diameter spacer, remove rear oil seal from cover.
Installation – 1) Clean rear cover and engine block gasket surfaces. Remove old silicone sealer from oil pan sealing surface. Clean surface with solvent and dry thoroughly.

CAUTION: Install new oil seal, from engine block side of rear cover, even with seal bore inner surface.

2) Apply thin coat of gasket adhesive to seal bore I.D. in rear cover. Using an arbor press and Rear Crankshaft Seal Installer (T83T-6701-A), install new rear crankshaft oil seal.

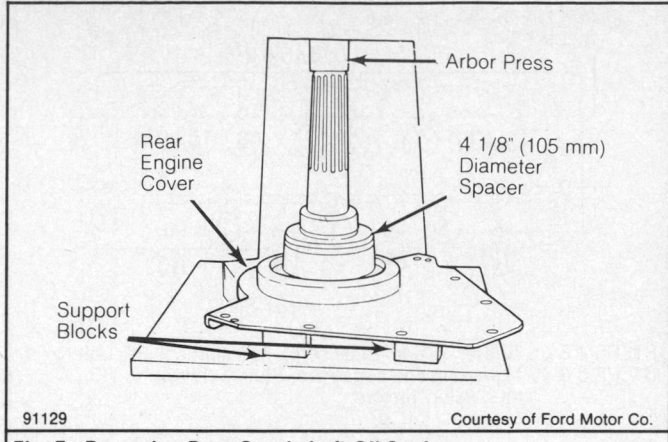

91129   Courtesy of Ford Motor Co.

Fig. 7: Removing Rear Crankshaft Oil Seal

3) Apply a 1/8" (3.2 mm) bead of silicone sealer around O.D. of rear seal and edge of rear cover. Apply gasket adhesive to engine block and rear cover gasket surfaces. Install rear cover gasket to engine block.
4) To aid rear cover alignment, install Rear Seal Pilot (T83T-6701-B) on crankshaft. Immediately before installing rear cover, apply 1/4" (6.35 mm) bead of silicone sealer to oil pan sealing surface, including corner of cylinder block-to-pan junction.
5) Position rear cover on engine block. Install bolts and tighten to specification. See TORQUE SPECIFICATIONS table at end of article. Remove rear seal pilot from crankshaft. To complete installation, reverse removal procedure.

WATER PUMP

NOTE: Fan and fan clutch assembly are secured with left-hand threads.

Removal – 1) Disconnect ground cables from both batteries. Drain cooling system. Disconnect fan shroud and place shroud over fan. Using Fan Clutch Pulley Holder (T83T-6312-A) and Fan Clutch Nut Wrench (T83T-6312-B), remove fan and clutch assembly. Remove fan shroud.
2) Remove accessory drive belts. Disconnect heater hose from water pump. Remove heater hose fitting from water pump. Remove water pump pulley. Remove alternator adjusting arm and adjusting arm bracket.
3) Remove A/C compressor with hoses attached and set aside. Remove A/C brackets. Remove power steering pump with hoses attached and set aside. Remove power steering bracket. Note bolt location and remove water pump bolts. Remove water pump.
Installation – 1) Clean gasket surfaces and bolt threads. Coat 2 top bolts and 2 bottom bolts with silicone sealer. *See Fig. 8.* Install water pump and tighten to specification. See TORQUE SPECIFICATIONS table at end of article.
2) To complete installation, reverse removal procedure. Fill and bleed air from cooling system. See COOLING SYSTEM BLEEDING under REMOVAL & INSTALLATION. Start engine and check for coolant leaks.

OIL PAN

Removal – 1) Disconnect negative cable from both batteries. Remove engine oil dipstick and transmission dipstick and tube (A/T models). Remove air cleaner and install Intake Manifold Cover (T83T-9424-A).

NOTE: Fan and fan clutch assembly are secured with left-hand threads.

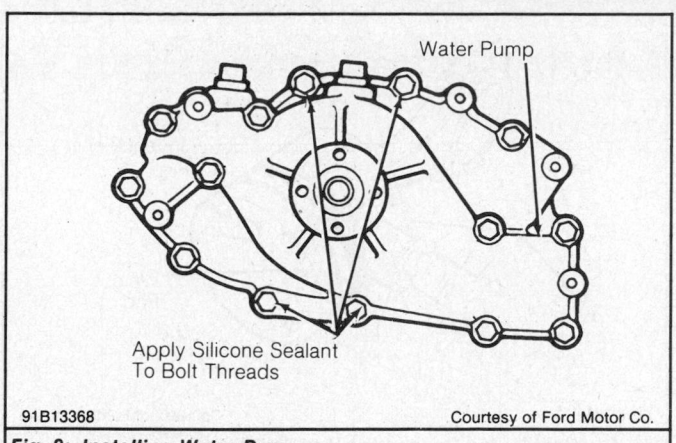

Fig. 8: Installing Water Pump

2) Drain cooling system and remove lower radiator hose. Using Fan Clutch Pulley Holder (T83T-6312-A) and Fan Clutch Nut Wrench (T83T-6312-B), remove fan and clutch assembly.

3) Disconnect power steering return hose from pump and plug openings. Disconnect alternator wiring harness and fuel line heater connector from alternator. Raise and support vehicle. Disconnect and plug transmission cooler lines (if equipped).

4) Disconnect and plug fuel pump inlet line. Drain engine oil and remove oil filter. Disconnect exhaust pipe at manifolds. Remove muffler inlet pipe from muffler flange. Remove upper inlet pipe mounting stud on right-side exhaust manifold.

5) Remove front engine mount nuts from crossmember. On A/T models, remove 2 bolts securing shift linkage bell crank to transmission. Allow linkage to hang freely. On all models, lower vehicle. On Van, install Rotunda Engine Lifting Brackets (014-00312) to front of engine.

6) Connect Rotunda Engine Lifting Brackets (T70P-6000) to lift sling and raise engine until transmission contacts body. On Pickup, install lifting sling to lifting eyes on intake manifold and raise engine until transmission contacts body.

7) Use wooden blocks to support engine; block right side up 2" and left side up 2 3/4". Remove flywheel inspection plate. Move fuel pump inlet line to rear crossmember. Remove oil pan bolts.

8) Remove transmission mount nuts. Using a transmission jack, raise transmission approximately 1". Lower oil pan. It may be necessary to release oil pan from cylinder block by prying on oil pan at front and rear of pan, on left side of cylinder block in dowel holes.

9) On Pickup, remove oil pump bolts and pick-up tube nut. Lower oil pump assembly into oil pan. On all models, remove oil pan. It may be necessary to rotate crankshaft to remove oil pan.

Installation – 1) To install, reverse removal procedure. Apply a 1/8" (3.2 mm) bead of silicone sealant on pan rails and a 1/4" (6.4 mm) bead of sealant on oil pan sealing surfaces of front and rear covers.

2) To install remaining components, reverse removal procedure. Fill or top off all fluids. Fill and bleed air from cooling system. See COOLING SYSTEM BLEEDING under REMOVAL & INSTALLATION.

OIL COOLER ASSEMBLY

Removal & Disassembly – 1) Disconnect negative cable from both batteries. Drain cooling system. Disconnect fan shroud and position shroud over fan. Using Fan Clutch Pulley Holder (T83T-6312-A) and Fan Clutch Nut Wrench (T83T-6312-B), remove fan and clutch assembly. Remove fan shroud.

NOTE: Fan and fan clutch assembly are secured with left-hand threads.

2) Raise vehicle. Drain crankcase and remove oil filter. On Pickup, remove left engine mount insulator-to-frame nut. Raise vehicle slightly.

3) Install a 1" wood block between engine mount insulator and frame. Lower engine on block. On all models, remove oil cooler-to-engine block bolts. Remove oil cooler.

4) To disassemble, use a soft-faced hammer and gently tap front and rear (filter) headers to loosen "O" rings. See Fig. 9. Separate headers from tube assembly. Thoroughly clean tube assembly and headers in solvent. Drain residue and blow dry with compressed air.

CAUTION: To prevent leakage, use new "O" rings when assembling oil cooler assembly.

Reassembly & Installation – 1) Lubricate all "O" rings and "O" ring mating surfaces with clean engine oil. Install large "O" ring and then small "O" ring onto oil cooler tube (bundle). Push assembly together, ensuring locating clips align in slots.

2) To install, position oil cooler assembly on cylinder block with new gaskets and tighten to specification. See TORQUE SPECIFICATIONS table at end of article. On Pickup, raise engine. Remove wood block and lower vehicle. Install engine mount insulator washer and nut.

3) On all models, apply thin coat of oil to oil filter gasket surface and install filter. Lower vehicle. To complete installation, reverse removal procedure.

4) Fill or top off all fluids. Fill and bleed air from cooling system. See COOLING SYSTEM BLEEDING under REMOVAL & INSTALLATION. Start engine and check for oil and coolant leaks.

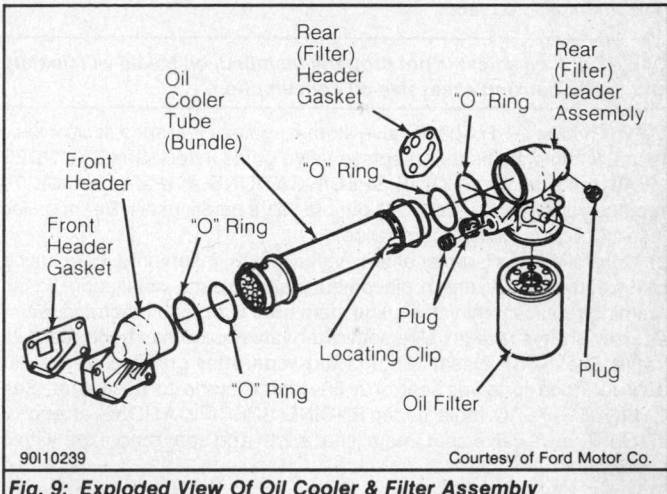

Fig. 9: Exploded View Of Oil Cooler & Filter Assembly

OVERHAUL

CYLINDER HEAD

Cylinder Head – 1) Clean head gasket mating surface. Clean carbon from combustion chambers. DO NOT damage surfaces. Check cylinder head for cracks, burrs, nicks and warpage.

2) If cylinder head warpage exceeds specification, replace cylinder head. DO NOT machine cylinder head to correct warpage. See CYLINDER HEAD table under ENGINE SPECIFICATIONS at end of article.

3) Check pre-combustion chambers for cracks. Pre-combustion chamber cracks are acceptable if cracking is within the fire ring. See Fig. 10. If cracking extends past fire ring, replace pre-combustion chamber insert.

Valve Springs – Inspect valve spring free length and pressure. Replace valve spring if free length and pressure are not within specification. See VALVES & VALVE SPRINGS table under ENGINE SPECIFICATIONS at end of article.

Valve Stem Oil Seals – Valve stem seals are used on intake valves only. Lubricate and install a new valve stem oil seal using Valve Stem Seal Replacer (T83T-6571-A).

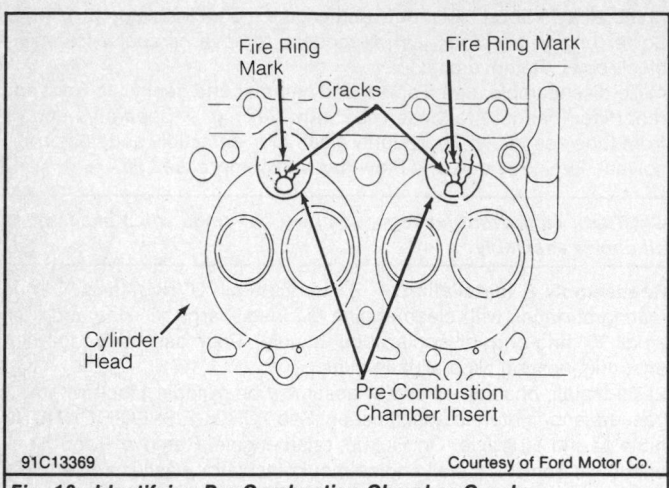

Fig. 10: Identifying Pre-Combustion Chamber Cracks

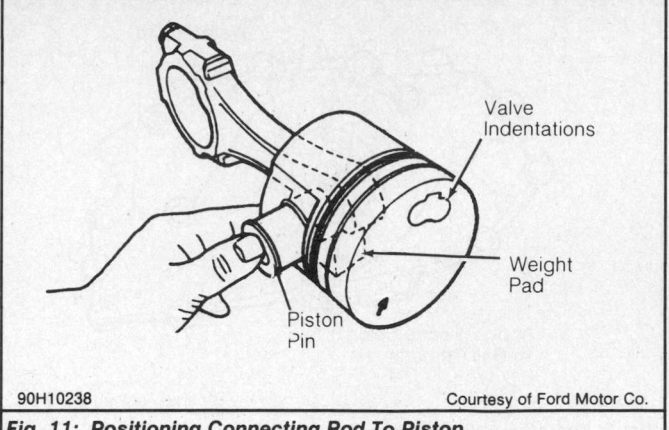

Fig. 11: Positioning Connecting Rod To Piston

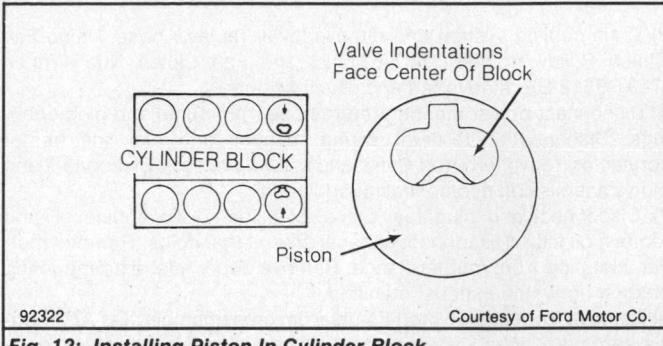

Fig. 12: Installing Piston In Cylinder Block

Valve Stem Oil Shields – Both intake and exhaust valves use valve stem oil shields. Intake and exhaust oil shields are not interchangeable. Intake oil shield is smaller than exhaust oil shield. Using hand pressure, install new oil shield into underside of spring retainer until shield snaps into place.

CAUTION: If oil shield is not properly installed, oil shield will float up and down, causing excessive oil consumption.

Valve Guides – 1) Check valve stem-to-guide clearance. If clearance is not within specification, replace valve guide insert. See CYLINDER HEAD table under ENGINE SPECIFICATIONS at end of article. To replace valve guide insert, drill out old valve guide insert. Ream drilled insert bore for replacement guide.

2) Carefully install replacement valve guide insert into bore using press. If necessary, chill replacement insert to ease installation. Finish reaming replacement valve guide stem bore with recommended reamer size. Always reface valve seat after valve guide has been reamed.

Valve Seat – 1) If seat width is too wide after grinding, use a 15-degree stone to lower seat or a 60-degree stone to raise seat. See CYLINDER HEAD table under ENGINE SPECIFICATIONS at end of article. Ensure valve seat angle, seat width and seat runout are within specification.

2) See CYLINDER HEAD table. Valve seats must be ground when valve guide is reamed or replaced. Use Exhaust Valve Seat Remover/Replacer (D83T-6084-A) to remove and install exhaust valve seats. Intake valve seat replacement information is not available from manufacturer.

Valves – Ensure head diameter, valve face runout, stem diameter and valve margin are within specification. See VALVES & VALVE SPRINGS table under ENGINE SPECIFICATIONS at end of article.

CAUTION: DO NOT remove more than .010" (.25 mm) from end of valve stem when resurfacing tip of valve.

CYLINDER BLOCK ASSEMBLY

Piston & Rod Assembly – Ensure weight pad on connecting rod is facing away from valve indentations on top of piston. *See Fig. 11.* Ensure pistons and rods are installed in same cylinders from which they were removed. Ensure valve indentations on top of piston face center of cylinder block when installed. *See Fig. 12.*

Fitting Pistons – 1) Measure piston diameter 1.23" (31.2 mm) below lower land of oil ring. Measure at piston pin center line, at 90-degree angle to piston pin. Measure cylinder bore for out-of-round, taper and piston-to-cylinder bore clearance.

2) If measurements are not within specification, hone or bore cylinders. See CYLINDER BLOCK and PISTONS, PINS & RINGS

tables under ENGINE SPECIFICATIONS at end of article. If cylinder block needs to be bored, pistons are available in .010" (.25 mm), .020" (.51 mm) and .030" (.76 mm) oversize.

Piston Rings – 1) Select rings for bore diameter. Place ring in cylinder bore in which it will be installed. Use piston to square ring in bore and place ring below normal ring wear area. Measure ring end gap. If ring gap is not within specification, try another ring set. See PISTONS, PINS & RINGS table under ENGINE SPECIFICATIONS at end of article.

2) Check side clearance of rings after installing on piston. Ensure clearance is within specification around entire circumference. Replace piston and/or rings if clearance is not within specification. See PISTONS, PINS & RINGS table.

3) Top and intermediate rings are identified by one dot (top ring) and 2 dots (intermediate ring) stamped on surface of ring, near end gap. Ensure rings are properly spaced on piston before installing pistons into cylinder. *See Fig. 13.*

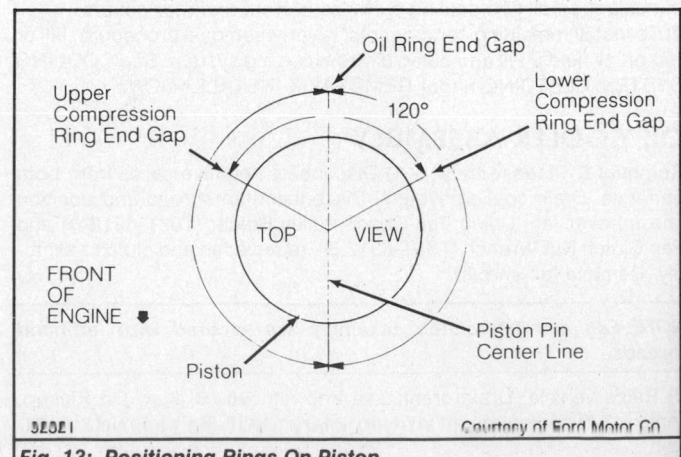

Fig. 13: Positioning Rings On Piston

Rod Bearings — Use Plastigage to check rod bearing clearance. If clearance is not within specification, machine or replace crankshaft as necessary. Always replace bearings in pairs. See CRANKSHAFT, MAIN & CONNECTING ROD BEARINGS table under ENGINE SPECIFICATIONS at end of article.

Crankshaft & Main Bearings — **1)** When checking main bearing clearance in vehicle, position a jack under adjoining bearing counterweight being checked. Remove only one main bearing cap at a time.

2) Use Plastigage to check main bearing clearance. If clearance is not within specification, machine or replace crankshaft as necessary. Always replace bearings in pairs. See CRANKSHAFT, MAIN & CONNECTING ROD BEARINGS table under ENGINE SPECIFICATIONS at end of article.

3) Install all bearing caps except thrust bearing cap (No. 3 from front of engine). Ensure bearing caps are installed in their original location. Tighten main bearing cap bolts to specification. See TORQUE SPECIFICATIONS table at end of article. Install No. 3 bearing cap and tighten bolts finger tight.

4) Pry crankshaft forward and pry No. 3 bearing cap to rear of engine to align thrust bearing. While retaining forward pressure on crankshaft, tighten bearing cap to specification. See TORQUE SPECIFICATIONS table.

5) Ensure crankshaft end play is within specification. Replace thrust bearing if end play is not within specification. See CRANKSHAFT, MAIN & CONNECTING ROD BEARINGS table.

CAUTION: Remove piston cooling jets before machining cylinder bores. Special "patch" bolts, included with new cooling jets, are used to install piston cooling jets. DO NOT use standard bolts.

Cylinder Block — **1)** Check cylinder bore for wear, taper, out-of-round and piston fit. Using a feeler gauge and straightedge, check cylinder block deck surface for warpage. If deck surface warpage exceeds specification, replace cylinder block. DO NOT machine cylinder block to correct warpage. See CYLINDER BLOCK table under ENGINE SPECIFICATIONS at end of article.

2) Install all main bearing caps and tighten to specification before honing cylinder bore. See TORQUE SPECIFICATIONS table. Ensure bearing caps are installed in their original location, with arrow on cap pointing toward front of engine.

3) Use ONLY a spring-loaded type cylinder hone. After honing, thoroughly clean bore with detergent and water solution. Rinse solution from bore thoroughly with clean water. Wipe bore clean with lint-free cloth. Lubricate cylinder bores with engine oil.

ENGINE OILING

ENGINE LUBRICATION SYSTEM

Full pressure lubrication through a full flow oil filter and oil cooler is supplied by a gear-driven oil pump. Main oil gallery feeds oil through passages to camshaft and crankshaft. Valve lifter gallery feeds valve lifters. Rocker arms are fed through hollow push rods.

Oil Cooler Assembly — Oil flows from pump to oil cooler located on left side of engine block. *See Figs. 9 and 14.* Oil flows around the outside of heat exchanger tubes inside oil cooler. Coolant flows through heat exchanger tubes where heat is transferred to coolant.

If oil is found in coolant or coolant is found in oil, check oil cooler for leakage. Areas of possible leakage include "O" rings, heat exchanger tubes inside cooler, front header and rear header.

Crankcase Capacity — Crankcase capacity is 10 qts. (9.5L) including filter change.

Oil Pressure — Normal oil pressure at 3300 RPM should be **40-70 psi (2.81-4.92 kg/cm²)**.

OIL PUMP

Removal & Disassembly — Remove oil pan. See OIL PAN under REMOVAL & INSTALLATION. On Pickup, remove oil pump retaining

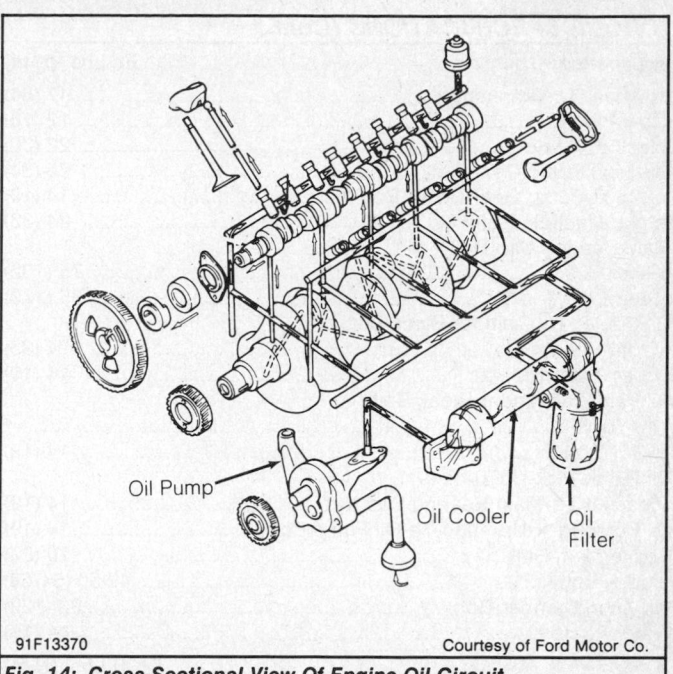

91F13370   Courtesy of Ford Motor Co.

Fig. 14: Cross-Sectional View Of Engine Oil Circuit

bolts. Remove oil pump and pick-up tube assembly. On Van, remove oil pump from oil pan. Disassemble oil pump. Note direction of component installation for reassembly reference.

Inspection — Inspect components for damage and wear. Check oil pump drive gear backlash. If backlash is not **.006-.010" (.15-.25 mm)**, replace oil pump. Oil pump is serviced as an assembly.

Reassembly & Installation — **1)** To reassemble, reverse disassembly procedure. Ensure components are installed in original location. To install, prime oil pump by filling inlet opening with oil and rotating pump shaft until oil emerges from outlet opening.

2) Install and tighten oil pump-to-cylinder block bolt to specification. See TORQUE SPECIFICATIONS table. To complete installation, reverse removal procedure.

TORQUE SPECIFICATIONS

TORQUE SPECIFICATIONS

Application	Ft. Lbs. (N.m)
Bellhousing-To-Engine Bolt	50-65 (68-88)
Camshaft Gear Allen Screw	15 (21)
Connecting Rod Nut	
Step 1	38 (52)
Step 2	51 (69)
Cylinder Head Bolt [1]	
Step 1	65 (88)
Step 2	90 (122)
Step 3	110 (150)
Engine Mount Bracket-To-Engine Bolt	65-85 (88-115)
Exhaust Manifold Bolt [2]	35 (47)
Flexplate-To-Converter Bolt	20-30 (27-41)

[1] – At steps 1 and 2, tighten bolts in numerical sequence beginning with bolt No. 1. At steps 3 and 4, tighten bolts in line sequence beginning with bolt No. 15. *See Fig. 5.*

[2] – Tighten to specification in numerical sequence beginning with bolt No. 1, then tighten again to same specification in line sequence beginning with bolt No. 4. *See Fig. 4.*

TORQUE SPECIFICATIONS (Cont.)

Application	Ft. Lbs. (N.m)
Flywheel-To-Crankshaft [3]	47 (64)
Glow Plug	12 (16)
Injector Nozzle	22 (30)
Injection Pump Gear Bolt	25 (34)
Injection Pump Gear Cover Bolt [3]	14 (19)
Intake Manifold Bolt [4]	24 (33)
Main Bearing Cap Bolt	
Step 1	75 (102)
Step 2	95 (129)
Oil Cooler-To-Cylinder Block Bolt	
Front Header	24 (33)
Rear (Filter) Header	14 (19)
Oil Pan-To-Cylinder Block Bolt	
1/4" Bolt	[5]
5/16" Bolt	14 (19)
Oil Pump Pick-Up Tube	
Bracket-To-Main Bearing Cap Nut	14 (19)
Oil Pump Pick-Up Tube-To-Oil Pump Bolt	14 (19)
Rocker Arm Bolt	20 (27)
Starter Bolt	40-50 (54-68)
Vibration Damper Bolt	90 (122)
Water Pump [6]	14 (19)

Application	INCH Lbs. (N.m)
Rocker Arm Cover Bolt	72 (8)
Rear Engine Cover Bolt	84 (9)

[3] – Coat threads with thread sealing compound.
[4] – Tighten to specification in numerical sequence beginning with bolt No. 1, then tighten again to same specification in line sequence beginning with bolt No. 9. See Fig. 3.
[5] – Tighten to 84 INCH lbs. (9 N.m).
[6] – Apply sealant to specified bolts. See Fig. 8.

ENGINE SPECIFICATIONS

GENERAL SPECIFICATIONS

Application	Specification
Displacement	444 Cu. In. (7.3L)
Bore	4.1095" (104.381 mm)
Stroke	4.1120" (104.445 mm)
Compression Ratio	21.5:1
Fuel System	Mechanical Fuel Injection
Horsepower @ RPM	180 @ 3300
Torque Ft. Lbs. @ RPM	345 @ 1400

CONNECTING RODS

Application	In. (mm)
Bore Diameter	
Pin Bore	1.1105-1.1108 (28.207-28.214)
Crankpin Bore	2.5001-2.5016 (63.503-63.541)
Crankpin Bearing Bore	
Maximum Out-Of-Round	.0005 (.013)
Maximum Taper	.0005 (.013)
Center-To-Center Length	7.128-7.132 (181.05-181.15)
Maximum Bend	[1] .002 (.05)
Maximum Twist	[1] .002 (.05)
Side Play	.012-.024 (.30-.61)

[1] – Specification listed is measured at the ends of an 8" (203 mm) bar, 4" (102 mm) on each side of rod center line.

CRANKSHAFT, MAIN & CONNECTING ROD BEARINGS

Application	In. (mm)
Crankshaft	
End Play	
Standard	.0025-.0085 (.064-.216)
Wear Limit	.012 (.30)
Main Bearings	
Journal Diameter	3.1228-3.1236 (79.319-79.339)
Journal Out-Of-Round	.0002 (.005)
Journal Taper [1]	.0005 (.013)
Runout	
Standard	.002 (.05)
Wear Limit	.005 (.13)
Oil Clearance	
Desired	.0018-.0036 (.046-.091)
Allowable	.0018-.0046 (.046-.117)
Connecting Rod Bearings	
Journal Diameter	2.4980-2.4990 (63.450-63.475)
Journal Out-Of-Round	.0003 (.008)
Journal Taper [1]	.0005 (.013)
Oil Clearance	.0011-.0036 (.028-.091)

[1] – Specification is within a 1" (25 mm) area.

PISTONS, PINS & RINGS

Application	In. (mm)
Pistons	
Diameter	[1] 4.1035-4.1040 (104.229-104.242)
Clearance	
Bores 1-6	.0055-.0085 (.140-.216)
Bores 7 & 8	.0060-.0085 (.152-.216)
Piston Height Above Crankcase	.010-.031 (.25-.79)
Pins	
Diameter	1.1099-1.1101 (28.191-28.197)
Piston Fit	.0003-.0007 (.007-.018)
Rod Fit	.0004-.0009 (.010-.023)
Rings	
No. 1	
End Gap	.013-.045 (.33-1.14)
Side Clearance	
Standard	.002-.004 (.05-.10)
Wear Limit	.006 (.15)
No. 2	
End Gap	.060-.085 (1.52-2.16)
Side Clearance	
Standard	.002-.004 (.05-.10)
Wear Limit	.006 (.15)
No. 3 (Oil)	
Side Clearance	
Standard	.001-.003 (.03-.08)
Wear Limit	.005 (.13)

[1] – Measure 1.23" (31.2 mm) below lower land of oil ring. Measure at piston pin bore center line, at 90-degree angle to piston pin.

CYLINDER BLOCK

Application	In. (mm)
Cylinder Bore	
Standard Diameter	
Bores 1-6	4.1095-4.1115 (104.381-104.432)
Bores 7 & 8	4.1100-4.1120 (104.394-104.445)
Maximum Out-Of-Round	.002 (.05)
Maximum Taper	.002 (.05)
Maximum Deck Warpage [1]	.003 (.08)

[1] – Specification is within a 6" (152.4 mm) area. Overall warpage is .006" (.15 mm). DO NOT machine cylinder block deck surface. If deck warpage exceeds specification, replace cylinder block.

VALVES & VALVE SPRINGS

Application	Specification
Intake Valves	
Face Angle	30°
Minimum Margin	.112" (2.84 mm)
Stem Diameter	.37165-.37235" (9.4399-9.4577 mm)
Exhaust Valves	
Face Angle	37.5°
Minimum Margin	.053" (1.35 mm)
Stem Diameter	.37165-.37235" (9.4399-9.4577 mm)
Valve Springs	
Free Length	
Intake & Exhaust	1.925-2.225" (48.90-56.52 mm)
Installed Height	
Intake	1.767" (44.88 mm)
Exhaust	1.833" (46.56 mm)
Out-Of-Square	.078" (1.98 mm)

	Lbs. @ In. (kg @ mm)
Pressure	
Valve Closed	
Intake & Exhaust	80 @ 1.833 (36 @ 46.56)

CYLINDER HEAD

Application	Specification
Maximum Warpage [1]	.003" (.08 mm)
Prechamber Protrusion	[2]
Valve Seats	
Intake Valve	
Seat Angle	30°
Seat Width	.065-.095" (1.65-2.41 mm)
Maximum Seat Runout	.002" (.05 mm)
Exhaust Valve	
Seat Angle	37.5°
Seat Width	.065-.095" (1.65-2.41 mm)
Maximum Seat Runout	.002" (.05 mm)
Valve Guides	
Intake & Exhaust	
Valve Guide I.D.	.3736-.3746" (9.489-9.515 mm)
Valve Stem-To-Guide	
Maximum Oil Clearance	.0055" (.140 mm)

[1] – Specification is within a 6" (152.4 mm) area. Overall warpage is .006" (.15 mm). DO NOT machine cylinder head surface. If head warpage exceeds specification, replace cylinder head.

[2] – Within .0025" (.064 mm) above or below face of prechamber bore.

CAMSHAFT

Application	In. (mm)
End Play	.002-.009 (.05-.23)
Journal Diameter	2.0990-2.1000 (53.315-53.340)
Bearing I.D.	2.1015-2.1025 (53.378-53.404)
Oil Clearance	.0015-.0035 (.038-.089)
Front Bearing Installed Depth [1]	.020-.050 (.51-1.27)

[1] – Specification listed is distance from face of cylinder block to bearing.

VALVE LIFTERS

Application	In. (mm)
Lifter Diameter	.9209-.9217 (23.391-23.411)
Oil Clearance	.0011-.0034 (.028-.086)
Collapsed Lifter Clearance	.185 (4.70)

1992 ENGINES
7.5L V8

Pickup, Van

NOTE: Unless otherwise specified, references to Pickup include the F350 Super Duty commercial chassis.
For engine repair procedures not covered in this article, see ENGINE OVERHAUL PROCEDURES article in GENERAL INFORMATION.

ENGINE IDENTIFICATION

The eighth character of the Vehicle Identification Number (VIN) identifies engine. VIN is located near windshield on left side of instrument panel. The VIN number is also on the Safety Compliance Certification Label attached to left door lock pillar.

VIN ENGINE CODE

Engine	Code
7.5L PFI	G

ADJUSTMENTS

VALVE CLEARANCE ADJUSTMENT

1) Rotate crankshaft and position No. 1 piston on TDC of compression stroke. Make chalk mark at points "A" and "B" on crankshaft pulley at TDC. *See Fig. 1.* Rotate crankshaft 360 degrees for mark "B".
2) Using Lifter Bleed-Down Wrench (T71B-6513-B), apply pressure to push rod end of rocker arm. Slowly bleed down lifter until lifter plunger is completely bottomed. See VALVE CLEARANCE ADJUSTMENT table.
3) While holding lifter in this position, check clearance between rocker arm and valve stem tip using feeler gauge. If clearance is less than specified, install a .060" (1.52 mm) shorter push rod. If clearance is greater that specified, install a .060" (1.52 mm) longer push rod. See CAMSHAFT table under ENGINE SPECIFICATIONS at end of article.

VALVE CLEARANCE ADJUSTMENT [1]

Crankshaft Position	Check Intake Valve Nos.	Check Exhaust Valve Nos.
"A"	1, 3, 7 & 8	1, 4, 5 & 8
"B"	2, 4, 5 & 6	2, 3, 6 & 7

[1] – See Fig. 1 for crankshaft positions.

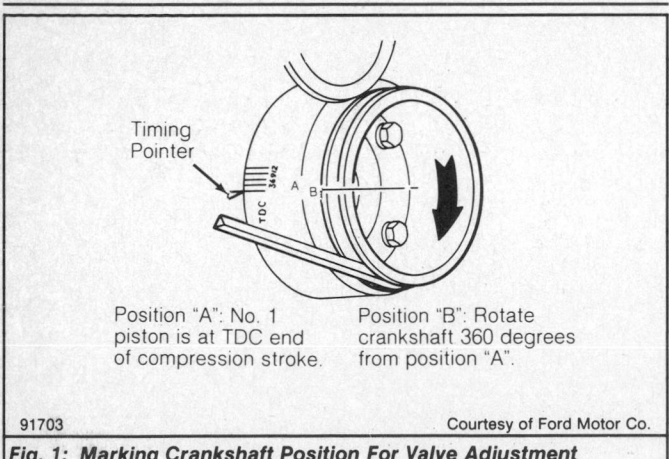

Position "A": No. 1 piston is at TDC end of compression stroke.

Position "B": Rotate crankshaft 360 degrees from position "A".

91703   Courtesy of Ford Motor Co.

Fig. 1: Marking Crankshaft Position For Valve Adjustment

REMOVAL & INSTALLATION

NOTE: For reassembly reference, label all electrical connectors, vacuum hoses and fuel lines before removal. Also place mating marks on engine hood and other major assemblies before removal.

WARNING: When battery is disconnected, vehicle computer and memory systems may lose memory data. Driveability problems may exist until computer systems have completed a relearn cycle. See COMPUTER RELEARN PROCEDURES article in GENERAL INFORMATION before disconnecting battery.

NOTE: Discharge A/C system using approved refrigerant recovery/recycling equipment.

FUEL PRESSURE RELEASE

Remove fuel cap to release fuel tank pressure. Remove relief valve cap. Relief valve is located on fuel rail. Connect fuel pressure gauge to relief valve. Release fuel pressure into a suitable container.

COOLING SYSTEM BLEEDING

WARNING: When engine is operating, NEVER remove radiator cap under any conditions. Failure to follow instruction could damage cooling system or engine, or cause personal injury. Always wrap protective material around radiator cap to avoid injury from hot steam or hot coolant.

1) Fill cooling system with 50/50 mixture of water and coolant. Pause several minutes for circulation. Fill radiator to filler neck seat. Disconnect heater outlet hose at water pump to bleed off trapped air. Fill radiator until coolant begins to escape.
2) Connect heater outlet hose. Fill radiator until coolant is between cap seal in filler neck to 1.5" (38 mm) below cap seal. Install radiator cap. Start engine and allow to warm up. Shut engine off. Allow engine to cool. Remove radiator cap and check coolant level. Top off radiator coolant as necessary.

ENGINE

Removal (Pickup) – 1) Drain cooling system and crankcase. Mark hood hinges and remove hood. Disconnect battery and ground cables from cylinder block. Remove air cleaner and intake duct assembly with crankcase ventilation and carbon canister hoses attached.
2) Disconnect radiator hoses. Disconnect transmission cooler lines (if equipped). Disconnect oil cooler lines at oil filter adapter (if equipped).

CAUTION: DO NOT attempt to disconnect engine oil cooler lines at quick-disconnect fittings behind or at oil cooler, or damage to fittings will occur.

3) Disconnect thermactor hoses. On models with A/C, discharge A/C system. Remove condenser and disconnect hoses at compressor. On all models, remove fan shroud, spacer, pulley and radiator. Remove and position alternator aside.
4) Disconnect oil pressure sending unit wire. Release fuel pressure. See FUEL PRESSURE RELEASE. Disconnect fuel supply and return lines; use Disconnect Tool (D87L-9280-A) for 3/8" line or (D87L-9280-B) for 1/2" line. *See Fig. 2.*
5) If hairpin-type clip is used, remove hairpin by bending tab downward so it will clear body. Using your hands, spread clip legs .125" (3 mm) and push legs into fitting. Pull hairpin clip from fitting. *See Fig. 2.*
6) Disconnect accelerator cable, transmission shift rod and speed control linkages from throttle body. Disconnect throttle bracket from upper intake manifold and set aside with cables attached. Disconnect EGR tube. Disconnect vacuum lines, carbon canister hose, heater hoses and electrical wiring from engine.
7) Disconnect brake booster hose. Remove bellhousing-to-engine upper bolts. Remove oil fill dipstick and tube. Raise and support vehicle. Remove starter. Separate exhaust pipes from manifolds. Disconnect engine mounts from frame brackets. On A/T models, remove converter inspection plate and flex plate-to-converter bolts.

8) On all models, remove remaining bellhousing-to-engine bolts. Lower vehicle and support transmission. Attach engine hoist and carefully separate engine from transmission. Carefully lift engine from vehicle without damaging rear cover plate.

Installation – To install, reverse removal procedure. Tighten bolts to specification. See TORQUE SPECIFICATIONS table at end of article. Check and top off all engine fluids. Fill and bleed air from cooling system. See COOLING SYSTEM BLEEDING. Evacuate and recharge A/C system (if equipped).

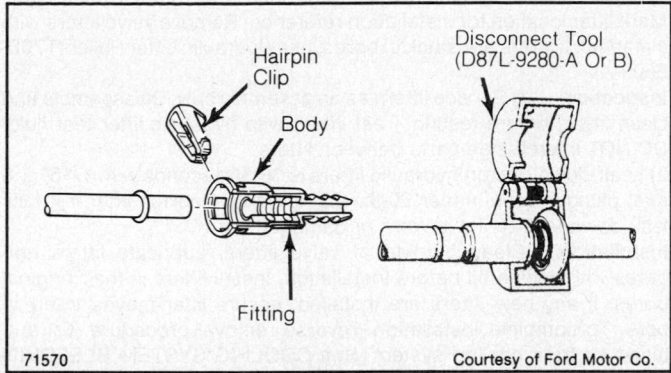

Hairpin Clip
Body
Fitting
Disconnect Tool (D87L-9280-A Or B)

71570   Courtesy of Ford Motor Co.

Fig. 2: Disconnecting Fuel Lines

Removal (Van) – 1) Remove engine cover. Disconnect battery. Drain cooling system. Remove air deflector, grille assembly and gravel deflector. Remove hood latch. Remove headlight and parking light assemblies. Remove air cleaner and air ducts.

2) Remove upper grille support, hood lock support and condenser upper mounting brackets (if equipped). On models with A/C, discharge A/C system. Remove condenser and disconnect lines at A/C compressor. On all models, remove radiator hoses and heater hoses from engine. Disconnect power steering hoses. Remove power steering pump and bracket from front of engine.

3) Disconnect A/T lines at radiator. Remove fan, shroud and radiator. Disconnect EGR tube. Disconnect thermactor air pump hoses. Remove air cleaner assembly. Disconnect accelerator cable, transmission shift rod and speed control linkages from throttle body.

4) Disconnect throttle bracket from upper intake manifold and set aside with cables attached. Release fuel pressure. See FUEL PRESSURE RELEASE. Disconnect fuel inlet and return lines using Disconnect Tool (D87L-9280-A Or B). *See Fig. 2.*

5) Raise and support vehicle. Drain crankcase and remove oil filter. Disconnect exhaust pipes from manifolds. Disconnect transmission filler tube from right cylinder head. Remove engine mount attaching bolts and nuts. Remove starter wiring and remove starter.

NOTE: Right engine mount through bolt is installed from front of vehicle. Left engine mount through bolt is installed from rear.

6) Remove converter inspection cover bolts and remove cover. Remove flex plate-to-converter nuts. Remove bellhousing lower bolts. Remove ground strap from engine block. Lower vehicle and support transmission.

7) Disconnect engine wiring loom and position aside. Attach lifting device to engine. Remove upper bellhousing-to-engine bolts. Carefully remove engine from vehicle.

Installation – To install, reverse removal procedure. Tighten bolts to specification. See TORQUE SPECIFICATIONS table at end of article. Check and top off all engine fluids. Fill and bleed air from cooling system. See COOLING SYSTEM BLEEDING. Evacuate and recharge A/C system (if equipped).

INTAKE MANIFOLDS

NOTE: On Pickup, it is possible to remove upper and lower intake manifolds as an assembly. On Van, upper manifold must be removed first.

Removal (Upper) – 1) Disconnect negative battery cable. Disconnect throttle and A/T linkage (if equipped) from throttle body. Remove 2 bracket-to-intake manifold bolts. Set bracket and cables aside.

2) Disconnect electrical connectors and upper manifold vacuum hose connections as necessary. Disconnect EGR and PCV systems. Disconnect clean air supply hose of idle by-pass valve. Remove 4 upper intake manifold bolts. Remove upper intake manifold and throttle body as an assembly.

Installation – Clean all gasket surfaces. Position new gasket on lower intake manifold. Ensure new gasket is aligned. To complete installation, reverse removal procedure. Tighten bolts to specification. See TORQUE SPECIFICATIONS table at end of article.

Removal (Lower) – 1) Disconnect negative battery cable. Remove upper intake manifold as previously described. Position No. 1 piston on TDC of compression stroke. Remove distributor cap and wires. Mark distributor location for installation reference. Remove distributor.

2) Remove air cleaner and duct assembly. Release fuel system pressure. See FUEL PRESSURE RELEASE under REMOVAL & INSTALLATION. Disconnect fuel inlet and return lines with Disconnect Tool (D87L-9280-A Or B).

3) If hairpin-type retainer is used, remove hairpin by bending tab downward so it clears body. Spread clip legs .125" (3 mm) and push legs into fitting. Gently pull hairpin clip from fitting. *See Fig. 2.*

4) Remove upper radiator hose. Disconnect coolant hoses at intake manifold and water pump. Label and disconnect vacuum hoses as necessary. Remove both thermactor exhaust air supply tubes. Remove ignition coil and mounting bracket.

5) Disconnect wiring harness from main wiring. Remove wiring harness and lower intake manifold as an assembly. Label and disconnect all other electrical wiring from intake manifold. Remove attaching bolts, and lift lower intake manifold and throttle body as an assembly.

Installation – 1) Clean all gasket surfaces. Apply 1/8" (3 mm) bead silicone sealer to 4 corners of cylinder block seal mounting surface. Install manifold gasket, front seal and rear seal. Apply 1/16" (1.5mm) bead silicone sealer along full width of front and rear seal ends.

2) Install intake manifold within 15 minutes of applying sealer. Position intake manifold over 4 studs in cylinder heads. Check gasket and seal alignment before tightening.

3) Install manifold attaching bolts, studs and nuts. Tighten bolts in sequence to specification. *See Fig. 3.* See TORQUE SPECIFICATIONS table at end of article. Install fuel lines, electrical connectors and vacuum hoses. To install remaining components, reverse removal procedure.

4) Fill and bleed air from cooling system. See COOLING SYSTEM BLEEDING under REMOVAL & INSTALLATION. Check and adjust ignition timing as necessary. Start engine and allow it to reach operating temperature. Turn off engine. Retorque bolts and nuts sequentially to **22-35 ft. lbs. (30-47 N.m)** to complete installation.

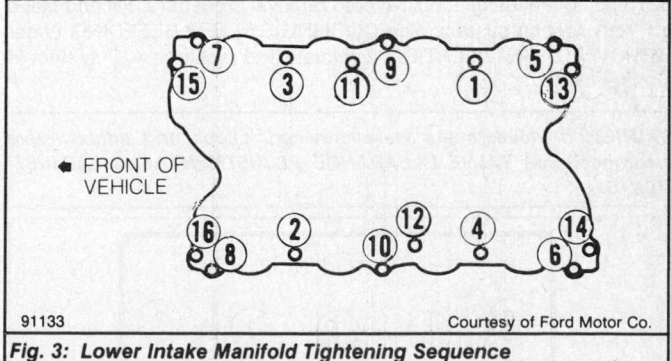

FRONT OF VEHICLE

91133   Courtesy of Ford Motor Co.

Fig. 3: Lower Intake Manifold Tightening Sequence

EXHAUST MANIFOLD

Removal – 1) If removing right exhaust manifold, remove spark plug heat shield. If removing left exhaust manifold, disconnect EGR tube. On Van, remove power steering pump support bracket.

2) On all models, remove oil dipstick tube from left exhaust manifold. Disconnect spark plug wires. Disconnect exhaust pipe(s) from manifold(s). Remove exhaust manifold-to-cylinder head bolts. Remove exhaust manifold(s).
Installation – 1) Inspect manifold(s) for cracks, damaged sealing surfaces, or other wear or damage. Replace manifold(s) as necessary. Clean cylinder head and manifold mating surfaces.
2) Clean mounting flange of manifold and exhaust pipe. Apply light film of graphite grease to manifold-machined surface. Position spark plug wire heat shields and exhaust manifold on cylinder head.
3) Install attaching bolts and washers, starting at fourth bolt hole from front of each manifold. Tighten bolts to specification, starting at center bolts and working outward. See TORQUE SPECIFICATIONS table at end of article.

CYLINDER HEAD

Removal – 1) Drain cooling system. Remove upper and lower intake manifolds. See INTAKE MANIFOLDS under REMOVAL & INSTALLATION. Disconnect exhaust pipes at manifolds. Remove drive belts. Remove thermactor air pump and bracket from right cylinder head. Remove alternator.
2) On models with A/C, discharge A/C system. Remove valves and hoses from compressor. Remove A/C compressor support bracket nuts from water pump. Remove and position compressor aside. Remove compressor mounting bracket from cylinder head.
3) On models without A/C, remove power steering pump bracket-to-left cylinder head bolts. Position pump and bracket aside. On Van, disconnect oil filler tube. On all models, remove valve covers.
4) Mark location for installation reference, and remove rocker arm assemblies and push rods. Remove cylinder head and exhaust manifold assemblies. Discard cylinder head gasket. Remove exhaust manifolds.
Inspection – Measure cylinder head and cylinder block mating surfaces for warpage. If cylinder head or cylinder block warpage exceeds specification, DO NOT remove more than .010" (.25 mm) material from original surface of cylinder head or block to correct warpage. See CYLINDER HEAD table under ENGINE SPECIFICATIONS at end of article.
Installation – 1) Clean gasket mating surfaces. Check flatness of cylinder head and block mating surfaces. If exhaust manifolds were removed, coat cylinder head and manifold port areas with a thin film of graphite grease, and install manifold on cylinder head.
2) Place 2 long head bolts in 2 rear lower bolt holes of left cylinder head. Place one long head bolt in rear lower bolt hole of right cylinder head. Keep bolts in position until heads are installed.
3) Position new head gaskets on block. DO NOT apply sealer to head gasket surfaces. Install cylinder head bolts. Tighten bolts in sequence to specification. *See Fig. 4.* See TORQUE SPECIFICATIONS table at end of article.
4) To complete installation, reverse removal procedure. Fill and bleed air from cooling system. See COOLING SYSTEM BLEEDING under REMOVAL & INSTALLATION. Evacuate and recharge A/C system (if equipped).

CAUTION: If valves/seats were serviced, check and adjust valve clearance. See VALVE CLEARANCE ADJUSTMENT under ADJUSTMENTS.

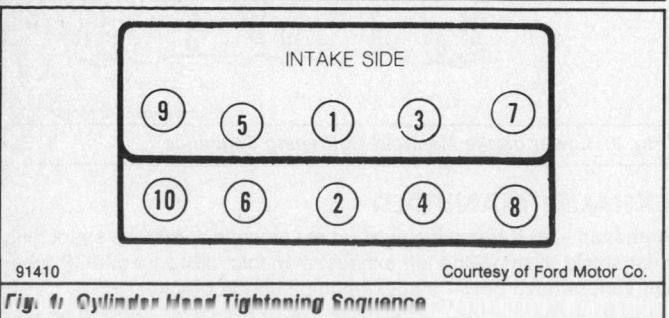

91410   Courtesy of Ford Motor Co.

Fig. 4: Cylinder Head Tightening Sequence

HYDRAULIC VALVE LIFTERS

NOTE: Before replacing a noisy hydraulic valve lifter, ensure valve clearance is correct. See VALVE CLEARANCE ADJUSTMENT under ADJUSTMENTS.

Removal – 1) Remove upper and lower intake manifolds. See INTAKE MANIFOLDS under REMOVAL & INSTALLATION. Remove valve covers. Loosen rocker arm fulcrum bolts and turn to one side.
2) Mark location for installation reference and remove push rods. Mark lifter location for installation reference. Remove valve lifters with a magnet. If lifters are stuck in bores, use Hydraulic Lifter Puller (T70L-6500-A).
Inspection – 1) Service lifters as an assembly only. Disassemble and clean lifters before testing. Test lifters with hydraulic lifter test fluid. DO NOT interchange parts between lifters.
2) Leak-down rate on hydraulic lifters is 10-50 seconds with 1/16" (1.6 mm) plunger travel under 50-lb. (23 kg) load. Replace lifter if it fails leak-down test, or if it is worn or damaged.
Installation – Clean outside of valve lifters. Lubricate lifters and bores with engine oil before installation. Install lifters in their original bores. If any new lifters are installed, ensure lifter moves freely in bore. To complete installation, reverse removal procedure. Fill and bleed air from cooling system. See COOLING SYSTEM BLEEDING under REMOVAL & INSTALLATION.

FRONT CRANKSHAFT OIL SEAL

NOTE: Front crankshaft seal can be replaced without removing timing chain cover.

Removal – Remove radiator fan, spacer and shroud. Remove drive belts. Remove crankshaft pulley and vibration damper. Place Seal Remover (T70P-6B070-B) onto timing chain cover plate over front seal. Tighten 2 bolts, forcing seal remover under seal flange. Alternately tighten 2 bolts, one-half turn at a time, until seal is removed from engine.
Installation – Coat new seal with polyethylene grease and install seal using Seal Installer (T70P-6B070-A). Ensure seal is fully seated. To install remaining components, reverse removal procedure.

TIMING CHAIN COVER

NOTE: Front crankshaft oil seal should be replaced whenever timing chain cover is removed.

Removal – 1) Disconnect negative battery cable. Drain cooling system and crankcase. Remove fan and radiator shroud. Disconnect radiator hoses at engine. Disconnect oil cooler lines (if equipped) at radiator. Remove upper radiator support and remove radiator.
2) Remove all drive belts and water pump pulley. Remove alternator and air pump assemblies with brackets. Remove A/C compressor and support bracket (if equipped). Disconnect heater hose from water pump, and loosen by-pass hose clamp at pump.
3) Remove crankshaft pulley. Using Vibration Damper Remover (T58P-6316-D), remove vibration damper and Woodruff key from crankshaft. Remove timing chain cover-to-cylinder block bolts. Remove timing chain cover and water pump as an assembly.
4) Cut oil pan gasket even with cylinder block face. Discard timing chain cover gasket and pan gasket. Carefully remove old seal using a pin punch; DO NOT damage front crankshaft seal recess.
Installation – 1) Install new timing chain cover oil seal. Coat gasket surface of oil pan with gasket sealer. Cut and position new gasket on oil pan. Apply silicone sealer at block-to-oil pan junction. Apply gasket sealer to timing chain cover and cylinder block gasket surfaces. Position new timing chain cover gasket in place.
2) Position timing chain cover on cylinder block. Install Timing Chain Cover Aligner (T68P-6019-A) on crankshaft. *See Fig. 5.* Coat threads of cover bolts with oil-resistant sealer and install bolts. It may be necessary to push cover downward to compress pan gasket.

3) While pushing in on Timing Chain Cover Aligner (T68P-6019-A), tighten oil pan-to-cover bolts. Remove timing chain cover aligner and tighten timing chain cover-to-cylinder block bolts. To complete installation, reverse removal procedure. Fill engine crankcase with proper grade oil. Fill and bleed air from cooling system. See COOLING SYSTEM BLEEDING under REMOVAL & INSTALLATION.

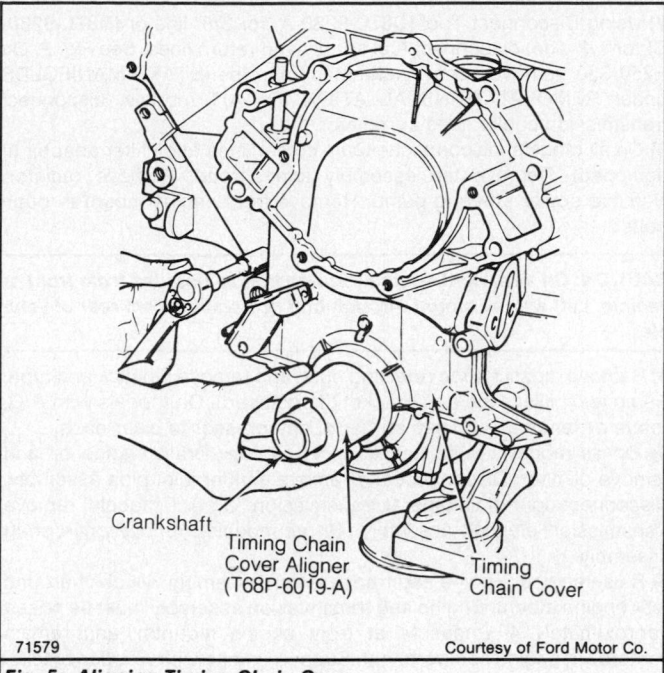

Crankshaft
Timing Chain
Cover Aligner
(T68P-6019-A)
Timing
Chain Cover

71579   Courtesy of Ford Motor Co.

Fig. 5: Aligning Timing Chain Cover

TIMING CHAIN & SPROCKET

Removal – 1) Position No. 1 piston on TDC of compression stroke. Remove timing chain cover. See TIMING CHAIN COVER. Check alignment of camshaft gear and crankshaft gear timing marks. See Fig. 6.
2) Check timing chain deflection (stretch) for excessive wear. See CAMSHAFT table under ENGINE SPECIFICATIONS at end of article. Remove camshaft sprocket bolt and washer. Slide timing chain and sprockets forward and remove as an assembly.
Installation – Assemble and align timing chain and sprockets. See Fig. 6. Install chain and sprockets as an assembly. Lubricate timing chain with engine oil. Tighten bolts to specification. See TORQUE SPECIFICATIONS table at end of article. To complete installation, reverse removal procedure.

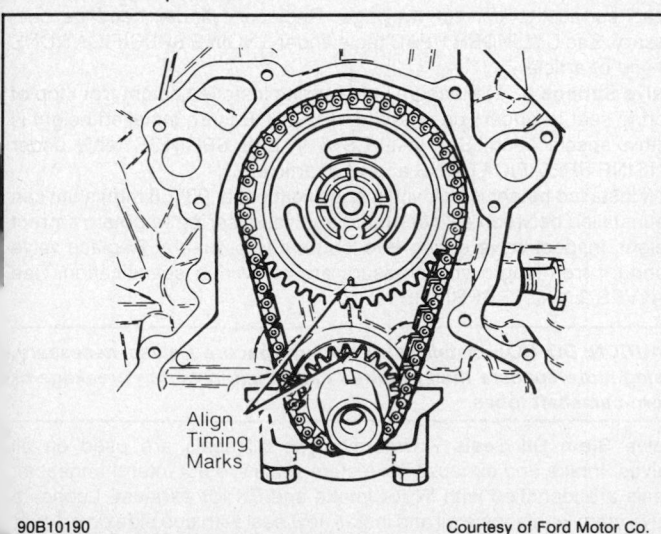

Align
Timing
Marks

90B10190   Courtesy of Ford Motor Co.

Fig. 6: Aligning Timing Marks

CAMSHAFT

Removal – 1) Remove timing chain cover, timing chain and sprockets. See TIMING CHAIN COVER and TIMING CHAIN & SPROCKET. Remove intake manifolds. See INTAKE MANIFOLDS under REMOVAL & INSTALLATION. Remove valve covers.
2) Loosen all rocker arm bolts and rotate rocker arms aside. Remove push rods and valve lifters, keeping them in order for installation in original locations.

NOTE: Use Hydraulic Lifter Puller (T70L-6500-A) to remove stuck lifters.

3) Remove A/C condenser-to-chassis bolts (if equipped) and set condenser aside. Remove front grille. Check camshaft end play. If not within specification, replace thrust plate. See CAMSHAFT table under ENGINE SPECIFICATIONS at end of article. Remove camshaft thrust plate. Carefully remove camshaft without damaging bearings or journals.
Inspection – Measure camshaft bearing journals and lobes for wear. If measurements are not within specification, replace camshaft and valve lifters. See CAMSHAFT table under ENGINE SPECIFICATIONS at end of article.
Installation – 1) Oil camshaft journals and apply polyethylene grease to camshaft lobes. Carefully slide camshaft into position. Install and tighten thrust plate. Recheck camshaft end play. Lubricate lifters with engine oil and install.
2) Lubricate rocker arms, fulcrum seats, valve stem tips and push rods with polyethylene grease before installing. Rotate crankshaft until No. 1 piston is on TDC of compression stroke.
3) Install rocker arm, fulcrum seats, oil deflection and fulcrum bolts to the appropriate valves. See VALVE CLEARANCE ADJUSTMENT table under ADJUSTMENTS. Rotate crankshaft 360 degrees and install rocker arm components on remaining valves.
4) Ensure fulcrum seat base is inserted into slot on cylinder head before tightening fulcrum bolts. To complete installation, reverse removal procedure. Use new gaskets where required.

CAMSHAFT BEARINGS

NOTE: It may be necessary to remove crankshaft for access to camshaft bearings.

Removal – Remove engine from vehicle. See ENGINE under REMOVAL & INSTALLATION. Remove camshaft. See CAMSHAFT. Remove flywheel. Push pistons to top of cylinders. Remove camshaft rear bearing bore plug. Using Camshaft Bearing Remover/Installer Set (T65L-6250-A), remove camshaft bearings.
Installation – Using camshaft bearing remover/installer, install bearings into place. Ensure oil holes in bearings and cylinder block are aligned. Install front bearing .040-.060" (1.02-1.52 mm) behind front face of cylinder block. Coat new rear bore plug with sealer and install. To complete installation, reverse removal procedure.

REAR CRANKSHAFT OIL SEAL

Removal – 1) Remove oil pan. See OIL PAN under REMOVAL & INSTALLATION. Loosen all main bearing cap bolts to slightly lower crankshaft. DO NOT lower more than 1/32" (.79 mm). Remove rear main bearing cap and lower oil seal half. Use seal remover to remove upper seal.
2) If seal remover is not available, install a small metal screw in one end of seal. Carefully pull on screw to remove seal without damaging sealing surface.
Installation – 1) Carefully clean oil seal grooves in bearing cap and block. Coat split-lip seal halves with engine oil. Carefully install upper seal into groove in cylinder block, with undercut side of seal toward front of engine.

NOTE: DO NOT damage outside diameter of seal when installing in groove. DO NOT allow oil to get on area where sealer is applied.

2) Rotate seal on crankshaft journal until about 3/8" (9.5 mm) of seal protrudes below parting face. *See Fig. 7.* Tighten all main bearing cap bolts except the rear main. Install lower seal in rear main bearing cap, with undercut side of seal toward front of engine.

3) Allow seal to protrude about 3/8" (9.5 mm) above parting surface to mate with upper seal when cap is installed. Apply 1/16" (1.5 mm) bead of silicone sealer to both sides of cylinder block-to-cap mating surface and both sides of bearing cap. *See Fig. 8.*

4) Install and tighten rear main bearing cap before sealer sets (about 15 minutes). To complete installation, reverse removal procedure.

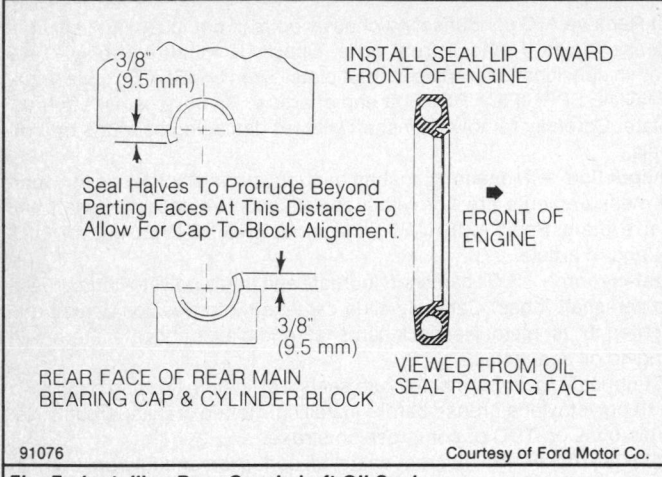

91076   Courtesy of Ford Motor Co.

Fig. 7: Installing Rear Crankshaft Oil Seal

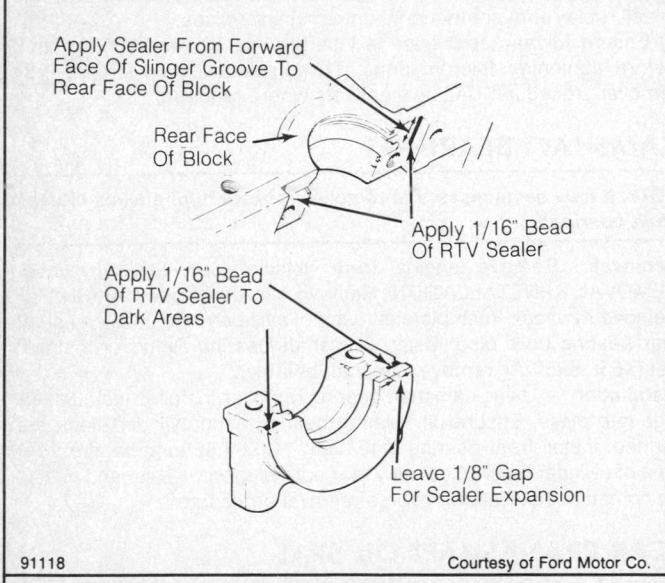

91118   Courtesy of Ford Motor Co.

Fig. 8: Identifying Silicone Sealer Application Points

WATER PUMP

Removal – 1) Remove negative battery cable. Drain cooling system. Remove fan shroud and fan. Loosen power steering pump attaching bolts. Remove A/C compressor (if equipped). Remove A/C compressor and power steering bracket.

2) Remove all drive belts. Remove air pump, alternator and bracket. Disconnect all hoses from water pump and loosen by-pass hose clamp at pump. Remove remaining bolts and remove water pump. Remove separator plate from water pump and discard gaskets.

Installation – Clean all gasket surfaces. To install, reverse removal procedure. Use new gaskets coated on both sides with water-resistant sealer. Fill and bleed air from cooling system. See COOLING SYSTEM BLEEDING under REMOVAL & INSTALLATION.

OIL PAN

Removal – 1) Remove engine cover (if equipped) and disconnect battery. Drain cooling system. Disconnect upper and lower radiator hoses. Disconnect and remove air cleaner assembly. Release fuel pressure. See FUEL PRESSURE RELEASE under REMOVAL & INSTALLATION.

2) Using Disconnect Tool (D87L-9280-A) for 3/8" line or (D87L-9280-B) for 1/2" line, disconnect fuel supply and return lines. *See Fig. 2.* On E250/350, remove upper intake manifold. See INTAKE MANIFOLDS under REMOVAL & INSTALLATION. On A/T models, disconnect transmission cooler lines at radiator.

3) On all models, disconnect engine cooler lines at oil filter adapter (if equipped). Remove fan assembly and shroud. Remove radiator. Remove power steering pump. Remove front engine mount through bolts.

CAUTION: On Van, right engine through bolt is installed from front of vehicle. Left engine mount through bolt is installed from rear of vehicle.

4) Remove dipstick tube retaining nuts, and remove dipstick and tube. Remove oil filler tube and bracket (if equipped). On models with A/C, rotate or remove A/C lines at rear of compressor to clear dash.

5) On all models, raise and support vehicle. Drain engine oil and remove oil filter. Disconnect and remove muffler inlet pipe assembly. Disconnect control linkage at transmission. On A/T models, remove transmission dipstick assembly. On all models, remove drive shaft assembly.

6) Raise engine. Engine and transmission assembly will pivot around rear engine mount. Engine and transmission assembly must be raised approximately 4" (measure at front engine mounts), and remain centered in engine compartment. Support engine with wooden blocks.

7) Remove oil pan bolts and lower oil pan. Remove oil pump bolts and pick-up tube nut. Lower oil pump assembly into pan. Remove oil pan.

Installation – To install, reverse removal procedure. Tighten bolts to specification. See TORQUE SPECIFICATIONS table at end of article. Fill or top off all fluids. Fill and bleed air from cooling system. See COOLING SYSTEM BLEEDING under REMOVAL & INSTALLATION. Start engine and check for leaks.

OVERHAUL

CYLINDER HEAD

Cylinder Head – 1) Clean head gasket mating surface. Clean carbon from combustion chambers. Use care not to damage surfaces. Check cylinder head for cracks, burrs, nicks and warpage.

2) DO NOT machine more than .010" (.25 mm) from original cylinder head surface to correct warpage. Replace cylinder head as necessary. See CYLINDER HEAD table under ENGINE SPECIFICATIONS at end of article.

Valve Springs – 1) Measure valve spring installed height from top of spring seat to underside of spring retainer. Ensure installed height is within specification. See VALVES & VALVE SPRINGS table under ENGINE SPECIFICATIONS at end of article.

2) If installed height is not within specification, a .03" (.8 mm) shim can be installed between cylinder head and valve spring to obtain correct height. Inspect valve spring free length and pressure. Replace valve spring if free length and pressure are not within specification. See VALVES & VALVE SPRINGS table.

CAUTION: DO NOT install valve spring spacers unless necessary. Using more spacers than required can result in spring breakage or worn camshaft lobes.

Valve Stem Oil Seals – Umbrella-type oil seals are used on all valves. Intake and exhaust valve stem seals are not interchangeable. Seals are identified with IN for intake and EX for exhaust. Lubricate valve stem with engine oil and install new seal with cup side down over valve guide.

Valve Guides – 1) Valve guides must be reamed for an oversized valve if valve stem oil clearance exceeds specification. See CYLINDER HEAD table under ENGINE SPECIFICATIONS at end of article. Valves are available with .015" (.38 mm) and .030" (.76 mm) oversize stems.

2) If oversized valves or oversized valve stem oil seals are not available, valve guide may be bored out to use a service bushing. Always use reamers in proper sequence (smallest first).

NOTE: Always grind valve seat after valve guide has been reamed or service bushing has been installed.

Valve Seat – 1) Grind valve seat to a true 45-degree angle. If seat width is too wide after grinding, use a 30-degree stone to lower seat or a 60-degree stone to raise seat. See CYLINDER HEAD table under ENGINE SPECIFICATIONS at end of article.

2) Ensure valve seat angle, seat width and seat runout are within specification. See CYLINDER HEAD table under ENGINE SPECIFICATIONS at end of article. Valve seats must be ground when valve guide is reamed or replaced. Replacement information is not available from manufacturer.

Valves – Ensure head diameter, valve face runout, stem diameter and valve margin are within specification. See VALVES & VALVE SPRINGS table under ENGINE SPECIFICATIONS at end of article.

CAUTION: DO NOT remove more than .010" (.25 mm) from end of valve stem when resurfacing tip of valve.

CYLINDER BLOCK ASSEMBLY

Pistons & Rod Assembly – Ensure pistons and rods are installed in their original cylinder. Ensure notch on piston top faces forward, and numbered side of rod faces outward. *See Fig. 9.* Check side play of connecting rod. See CONNECTING RODS table under ENGINE SPECIFICATIONS at end of article.

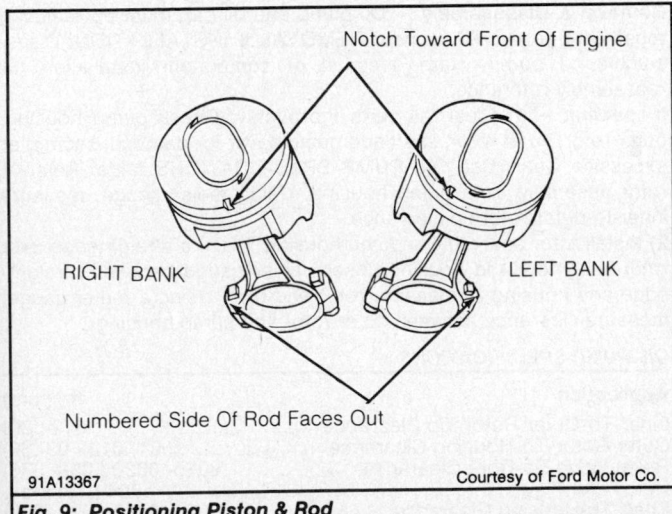

Fig. 9: Positioning Piston & Rod

Fitting Pistons – 1) Check piston-to-bore clearance. See PISTONS, PINS & RINGS table under ENGINE SPECIFICATIONS at end of article. Standard size pistons are color-coded Red, Blue or Yellow on the piston dome. See PISTONS, PINS & RINGS table. Oversize pistons are also available.

2) If bore diameter is in lower one-third of specification, use a Red coded piston. If bore diameter is in middle one-third of specification, use a Blue coded piston. If bore diameter is in upper one-third of specification, use Yellow coded piston. Use proper size piston to obtain specified clearance. See PISTONS, PINS & RINGS table under ENGINE SPECIFICATIONS.

Piston Rings – 1) Select rings for bore diameter. Place ring in cylinder bore in which it will be installed. Use piston to square ring in bore and place ring below normal ring wear area. Measure ring end gap. If ring gap is not within specification, try another ring set. See PISTONS, PINS & RINGS table.

2) Check side clearance of rings after installing on piston. Ensure clearance is within specification around entire circumference. Replace piston and/or rings if clearance is not within specification. See PISTONS, PINS & RINGS table. Ensure rings are properly spaced on piston before installing pistons into cylinder. *See Fig. 10.*

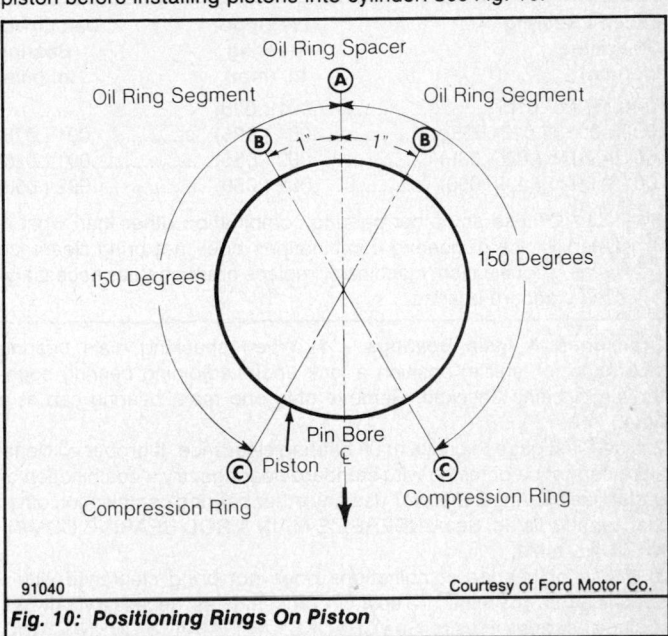

Fig. 10: Positioning Rings On Piston

Piston Pin Replacement – 1) Using an arbor press and Piston Pin Remover/Installer (T68P-6135-A), press piston pin from piston and connecting rod. *See Fig. 11.* Ensure connecting rod piston pin bore and piston pin are within specification. See CONNECTING RODS and PISTONS, PINS & RINGS tables under ENGINE SPECIFICATIONS at end of article.

2) Apply light coat of engine oil to all parts to be assembled. Assemble piston to connecting rod, with numbered side of rod toward outside of engine and notch in piston head toward front of engine. *See Fig. 9.*

3) Position piston pin in piston and connecting rod. Using arbor press and pin remover/installer, press pin into piston and connecting rod until end of pin is 1/16 - 1/8" (1.6-3.2 mm) below chamfer of piston pin bore.

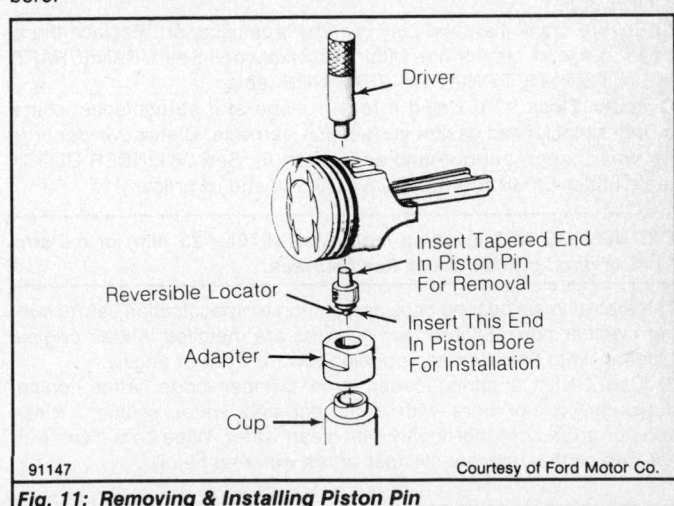

Fig. 11: Removing & Installing Piston Pin

Rod Bearings – 1) Use Plastigage to check rod bearing clearance. If proper oil clearance cannot be obtained with standard bearings, try a combination of undersize bearings. DO NOT use any other bearing combination other than what is listed. See UNDERSIZE MAIN & ROD BEARING COMBINATIONS table.

2) If use of bearing combinations does not bring clearance within specification, machine or replace crankshaft as necessary. Always replace bearings in pairs. See CRANKSHAFT, MAIN & CONNECTING ROD BEARINGS table under ENGINE SPECIFICATIONS at end of article.

UNDERSIZE MAIN & ROD BEARING COMBINATIONS [1]

Excess Bearing Clearance In. (mm)	Use Upper Bearing In. (mm)	Use Lower Bearing In. (mm)
.0-.0005 (.0-.013)	.001 (.025)	[2]
.0005-.0010 (.013-.025)	.001 (.025)	.001 (.025)
.0010-.0015 (.025-.039)	.002 (.050)	.001 (.025)
.0015-.0020 (.039-.050)	.002 (.050)	.002 (.050)

[1] – DO NOT use any other bearing combination other than what is listed. If use of bearing combinations does not bring clearance within specification, machine or replace crankshaft as necessary.

[2] – Use standard bearing.

Crankshaft & Main Bearings – 1) When checking main bearing clearance in vehicle, position a jack under adjoining bearing counterweight being checked. Remove only one main bearing cap at a time.

2) Use Plastigage to check main bearing clearance. If proper oil clearance cannot be obtained with standard bearings, try a combination of undersize bearings. DO NOT use any other bearing combination other than what is listed. See UNDERSIZE MAIN & ROD BEARING COMBINATIONS table.

3) If use of bearing combinations does not bring clearance within specification, machine or replace crankshaft as necessary. Always replace bearings in pairs. See CRANKSHAFT, MAIN & CONNECTING ROD BEARINGS table under ENGINE SPECIFICATIONS at end of article.

NOTE: Ensure main bearing oil holes are aligned with cylinder block oil holes.

4) Install all bearing caps except thrust bearing cap (No. 3 from front of engine). Tighten main bearing cap bolts to specification. See TORQUE SPECIFICATIONS table at end of article. Install No. 3 bearing cap and tighten bolts finger tight.

5) Pry crankshaft forward and pry No. 3 bearing cap to rear of engine to align thrust bearing. While retaining forward pressure on crankshaft, tighten bearing cap to specification. See TORQUE SPECIFICATIONS table.

6) Ensure crankshaft end play is within specification. Replace thrust bearing if end play is not within specification. See CRANKSHAFT, MAIN & CONNECTING ROD BEARINGS table.

Cylinder Block – 1) Using a feeler gauge and straightedge, check cylinder block head gasket surface for warpage. Check cylinder bore for wear, taper, out-of-round and piston fit. See CYLINDER BLOCK table under ENGINE SPECIFICATIONS at end of article.

CAUTION: DO NOT machine more than .010" (.25 mm) of material from original cylinder block head surface.

2) Install all main bearing caps and tighten to specification before honing cylinder bore. Ensure bearing caps are installed in their original location, with arrow on cap pointing toward front of engine.

3) Use ONLY a spring-loaded type cylinder hone. After honing, thoroughly clean bore with detergent and water solution. Rinse solution from bore thoroughly with clean water. Wipe bore clean with lint-free cloth. Lubricate cylinder bores with engine oil.

ENGINE OILING

ENGINE LUBRICATION SYSTEM

Engine lubrication is a force-feed system. The oil is supplied under full pressure to crankshaft, connecting rods, camshaft bearing and valve lifters. A controlled volume of oil is supplied to rocker arms and push

rods. All other moving parts are lubricated by splash or gravity flow. Oil flows through oil filter before entering main oil gallery. *See Fig. 12.*

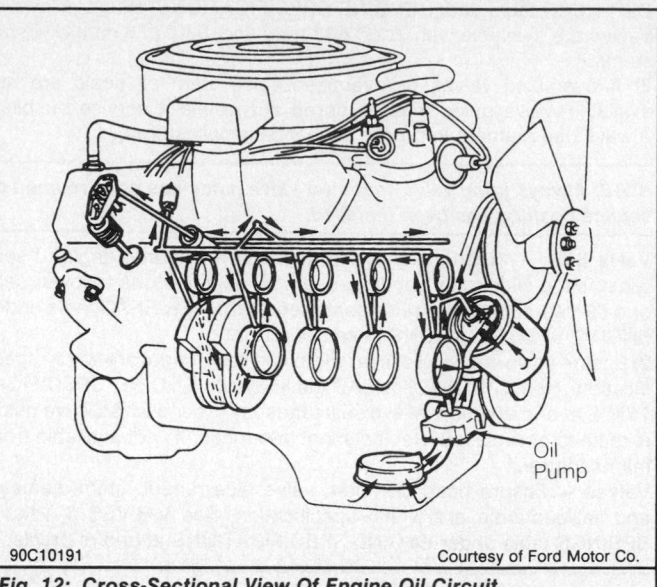

90C10191   Courtesy of Ford Motor Co.

Fig. 12: Cross-Sectional View Of Engine Oil Circuit

Crankcase Capacity – Crankcase capacity is **5 qts. (4.75L)**. Add one additional quart (.95L) when replacing oil filter.

Oil Pressure – Normal oil pressure at 2000 RPM should be **40-65 psi (2.8-4.6 kg/cm²)** with engine at operating temperature.

Oil Pressure Relief Valve – Nonadjustable oil pressure regulator valve is located in pump body.

OIL PUMP

Removal & Disassembly – Oil pump and oil pan must be removed together. See OIL PAN under REMOVAL & INSTALLATION. Disassemble oil pump. Note direction of component installation for reassembly reference.

Inspection – 1) Clean all parts thoroughly. Check pump housing, outer rotor, inner rotor, shaft and pump cover for damage, scoring or excessive wear. See OIL PUMP SPECIFICATIONS table. Remove rotor assembly from pump housing. Using feeler gauge, measure inner-to-outer rotor tip clearance.

2) Install rotor assembly in pump housing. Place a straightedge over rotor assembly and housing. Insert feeler gauge between straightedge and housing to measure rotor end play. Using a feeler gauge, measure clearance between outer rotor and pump housing.

OIL PUMP SPECIFICATIONS

Application	In. (mm)
Inner-To-Outer Rotor Tip Clearance	.012 (.30)
Outer Rotor-To-Housing Clearance	.001-.013 (.03-.33)
Relief Valve-To-Bore Clearance	.0015-.0030 (.038-.076)
Rotor End Play	.004 (.10) Max.
Shaft-To-Housing Clearance	.0015-.0030 (.038-.076)

Reassembly & Installation – 1) To reassemble, reverse disassembly procedure. Ensure components are installed in original location. Ensure oil pump spins freely after reassembly. To install, prime oil pump by filling inlet opening with oil and rotating pump shaft until oil emerges from outlet opening.

2) Install oil pump assembly and pan. To complete installation, reverse removal procedure. Tighten bolts to specification. See TORQUE SPECIFICATIONS table.

TORQUE SPECIFICATIONS

TORQUE SPECIFICATIONS

Application	Ft. Lbs. (N.m)
Bellhousing-To-Engine Bolt	40-50 (54-68)
Camshaft Sprocket Bolt	40-50 (54-68)
Connecting Rod Nut	41-45 (56-61)
Cylinder Head Bolt [1]	
Step 1	70-80 (95-109)
Step 2	100-110 (136-149)
Step 3	130-140 (176-190)
Front Engine Mount Nut	60-85 (81-115)
Front Engine Mount Through Bolt	40-58 (54-79)
Engine Mount-To-Engine Bolt	50-70 (68-95)
Exhaust Manifold Bolt	22-30 (30-41)
Flexplate-To-Converter Bolt	20-30 (27-41)
Flywheel-To-Crankshaft Bolt	75-85 (102-115)
Lower Intake Manifold Bolts/Nuts [2]	
Step 1	10-12 (14-16)
Step 2	12-22 (16-30)
Step 3	22-35 (30-47)
Step 4	[3]
Main Bearing Cap Bolt	95-105 (129-142)
Oil Pan-To-Engine Block Bolt	[4]
Oil Pump Attaching Bolt	22-32 (30-44)
Rear Mount-To-Crossmember Bolt/Nut	60-80 (81-109)
Rocker Arm Fulcrum Bolt	18-25 (24-34)
Starter Bolt	40-50 (54-68)
Timing Chain Cover	12-18 (16-24)
Upper Intake Manifold Bolt	12-18 (16-24)
Vibration Damper-To-Crankshaft Bolt	70-90 (95-122)
Water Pump Bolt	12-18 (16-24)
	INCH Lbs. (N.m)
Camshaft Thrust Plate Bolt	71-108 (8-12)
Valve Cover Bolt [5]	108-132 (12-15)

[1] – Tighten in sequence. *See Fig. 4.*
[2] – Tighten in sequence. *See Fig. 3.*
[3] – Allow engine to reach normal operating temperature. Retorque lower exhaust manifold bolts/nuts to 22-35 ft. lbs. (30-47 N.m)
[4] – Tighten 1/4" bolt to 84-108 INCH lbs. (10-12 N.m). Tighten 5/16" bolt to 96-132 INCH lbs. (11-15 N.m)
[5] – Tighten in sequence, from rear to front on left side of engine and front to rear on right side of engine.

ENGINE SPECIFICATIONS

GENERAL SPECIFICATIONS

Application	Specification
Displacement	460 Cu. In. (7.5L)
Bore	4.36" (110.7 mm)
Stroke	3.85" (97.8 mm)
Compression Ratio	8.5:1
Fuel System	PFI
Horsepower @ RPM	230 @ 3600
Torque Ft. Lbs. @ RPM	390 @ 2200

CRANKSHAFT, MAIN & CONNECTING ROD BEARINGS

Application	In. (mm)
Crankshaft	
End Play	
Standard	.004-.008 (.10-.20)
Service Limit	.012 (.30)
Main Bearings	
Journal Diameter	2.9994-3.0002 (76.185-76.205)
Journal Taper	.0005 (.013)
Journal Runout	
Standard	.002 (.05)
Service Limit	.005 (.13)
Maximum Journal Out-Of-Round	.0006 (.02)
Oil Clearance	
Desired	.0008-.0015 (.020-.038)
Allowable	.0008-.0026 (.020-.066)
Connecting Rod Bearings	
Journal Diameter	2.4992-2.5000 (63.480-63.500)
Journal Taper	.0006 (.015)
Maximum Journal Out-Of-Round	.0006 (.02)
Oil Clearance	
Desired	.0008-.0015 (.020-.038)
Allowable	.0008-.0025 (.020-.064)

CONNECTING RODS

Application	In. (mm)
Bore Diameter	
Pin Bore	1.0386-1.0393 (26.380-26.398)
Crankpin Bore	2.6522-2.6530 (67.366-67.386)
Center-To-Center Length	6.6035-6.6065 (167.729-167.805)
Maximum Bend [1]	.012 (.30)
Maximum Twist [1]	.024 (.61)
Side Play	
Standard	.010-.020 (.25-.51)
Service Limit	.023 (.058)

[1] – Specification listed is measured at the ends of an 8" (203 mm) bar, 4" (102 mm) on each side of rod center line.

PISTONS, PINS & RINGS

Application	In. (mm)
Pistons	
Clearance	.0022-.0030 (.056-.076)
Diameter [1]	
Red Piston	4.3577-4.3583 (110.686-110.701)
Blue Piston	4.3589-4.3595 (110.716-110.731)
Yellow Piston	4.3601-4.3607 (110.747-110.762)
Pins	
Diameter	1.0398-1.0403 (26.411-26.424)
Length	3.29-3.32 (83.6-84.3)
Piston Fit	.0002-.0005 (.005-.013)
Rod Fit	Press Fit
Rings	
No. 1 & 2	
End Gap	.010-.020 (.25-.51)
Side Clearance	.0025-.0045 (.064-.114)
No. 3 (Oil)	
End Gap (Steel Rail)	.010-.035 (.25-.89)
Side Clearance	Snug Fit

[1] – Standard pistons are color-coded Red, Blue and Yellow on piston dome.

CYLINDER BLOCK

Application	In. (mm)
Cylinder Bore	
Standard Diameter	4.3600-4.3636 (110.744-110.835)
Maximum Deck Warpage [1]	.003 (.08)
Maximum Out-Of-Round	
Standard	.0015 (.038)
Service Limit	.005 (.13)
Maximum Taper	.010 (.25)

[1] – Specification is within a 6" (152 mm) area. Overall warpage is .006" (.15 mm). DO NOT machine more than .010" (.25 mm) from original gasket surface.

VALVES & VALVE SPRINGS

Application	Specification
Face Angle	44°
Head Diameter	
Intake	1.97-1.99" (50.0-50.5 mm)
Exhaust	1.65-1.66" (41.9-42.2 mm)
Stem Diameter	.3415-.3423" (8.674-8.694 mm)
Valve Margin	.031" (.79 mm)
Valve Springs	
Free Length	2.06" (52.3 mm)
Installed Height	1.80-1.83" (45.7-46.5 mm)
Out-Of-Square	.078" (1.98 mm)

	Lbs. @ In. (kg @ mm)
Pressure	
Intake & Exhaust	
Closed	74-84 @ 1.81 (35-38 @ 46)
Open	218-240 @ 1.33 (99-109 @ 34)

CYLINDER HEAD

Application	Specification
Maximum Warpage [1]	.003" (.08 mm)
Valve Seats	
Seat Angle	45°
Seat Width	.060-.080" (1.52-2.03 mm)
Maximum Seat Runout	.002" (.05 mm)
Valve Guides	
Valve Guide Bore I.D.	.3433-.3443" (8.720-8.745 mm)
Valve Stem-To-Guide	
Oil Clearance	.0010-.0027" (.025-.069 mm)

[1] – Specification is taken within a 6" (152 mm) area. Overall warpage is .006" (.15 mm). DO NOT machine more than .010" (.25 mm) from original cylinder head thickness.

CAMSHAFT

Application	In. (mm)
Camshaft Bearing I.D.	2.1258-2.1268 (53.995-54.021)
Journal Diameter	2.1238-2.1248 (53.945-53.970)
End Play	
Standard	.001-.006 (.03-.15)
Service Limit	.006 (.15)
Lobe Lift	
Intake	.252 (6.40)
Exhaust	.278 (7.06)
Lobe Wear	.005 (.13)
Maximum Journal Runout	.005 (.13)
Oil Clearance	
Standard	.001-.003 (.03-.08)
Service Limit	.006 (.15)
Timing Chain Deflection	.500 (12.7)

VALVE LIFTERS

Application	In. (mm)
Lifter Diameter	.8740-.8745 (22.200-22.212)
Oil Clearance	.0007-.0027 (.018-.069)
Collapsed Lifter Clearance	
Desired	.100-.150 (2.54-3.81)
Allowable	.075-.175 (1.91-4.45)

Aerostar, Bronco, Explorer, Pickup, Ranger, Van

NOTE: Unless otherwise specified, references to Pickup include the F350 Super Duty commercial chassis.

SPECIFICATIONS

BELT ADJUSTMENT

Inspect belt for fraying. If fraying has occurred, ensure belt and tensioner are aligned properly. *See Fig. 1.* If tensioner has reached its limit of travel, belt is excessively stretched and replacement of belt is required. If excessive noise is noticed from tensioner or idler, check for possible bearing failure. Belt tension adjustment is not required on vehicles with automatic belt tensioners. DO NOT apply belt dressing or any other additive to belt(s). Ensure belts are properly installed. *See Figs. 2-10.* See BELT TENSION ADJUSTMENT SPECIFICATIONS table.

Proper Alignment	
Improper Alignment	

92411 · Courtesy of Ford Motor Co.

Fig. 1: Aligning Serpentine Belt

BELT TENSION ADJUSTMENT SPECIFICATIONS

Application	New Belt Lbs. (kg)	[1] Used Belt Lbs. (kg)
2.3L, 3.0L [2]	110-140 (50-64)	110-130 (50-59)
2.9L	120-160 (54-73)	110-130 (50-59)
3.0L [2]	110-140 (50-64)	110-130 (50-59)
4.0L [2]	108-132 (49-60)	108-132 (49-60)
4.9L [2]	90-117 (41-53) [3]	90-117 (41-53) [3]
5.0L & 5.8L [2]	77-111 (35-50) [4]	77-111 (35-50) [4]
7.3L Except Ambulance		
Vac. Pump W/ 3/8" Belt	90-130 (41-59)	65-85 (30-39)
Vac. Pump W/ 1/2" Belt	110-150 (50-68)	75-95 (34-43)
All Other W/ 1/2" Belt	140-180 (64-82)	95-115 (43-52)
7.3L Ambulance		
Alternator	140-160 (64-73)	140-160 (64-73)
Vac. Pump	90-130 (41-59)	65-85 (30-39)
A/C & P/S	140-180 (64-82)	95-115 (43-52)
7.5L		
With Tensioner [2]	[5]	[5]
Alt. & Air Pump	160-200 (73-91)	110-130 (50-59)

[1] – Any belt that has been in operation for 10 minutes.
[2] – Tension is correct if tensioner is within indicator marks.
[3] – For vehicles with 60, 75 and 100-amp alternators.
[4] – For vehicles with 60, 75 and 100-amp alternators.
[5] – 94 lbs. (43 kg) minimum tension.

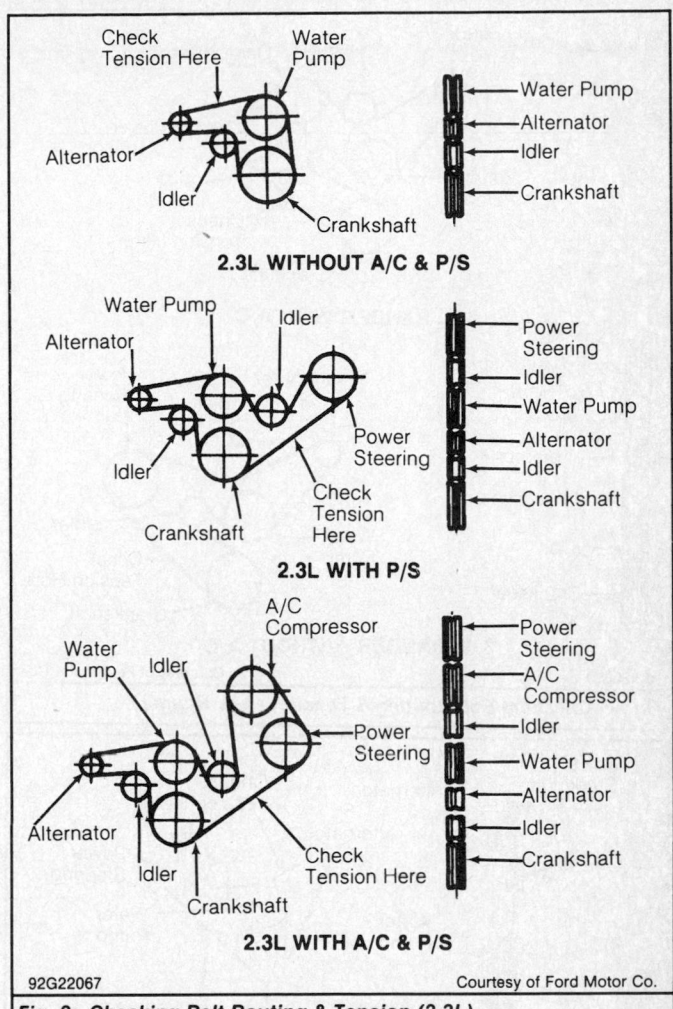

2.3L WITHOUT A/C & P/S

2.3L WITH P/S

2.3L WITH A/C & P/S

92G22067 · Courtesy of Ford Motor Co.

Fig. 2: Checking Belt Routing & Tension (2.3L)

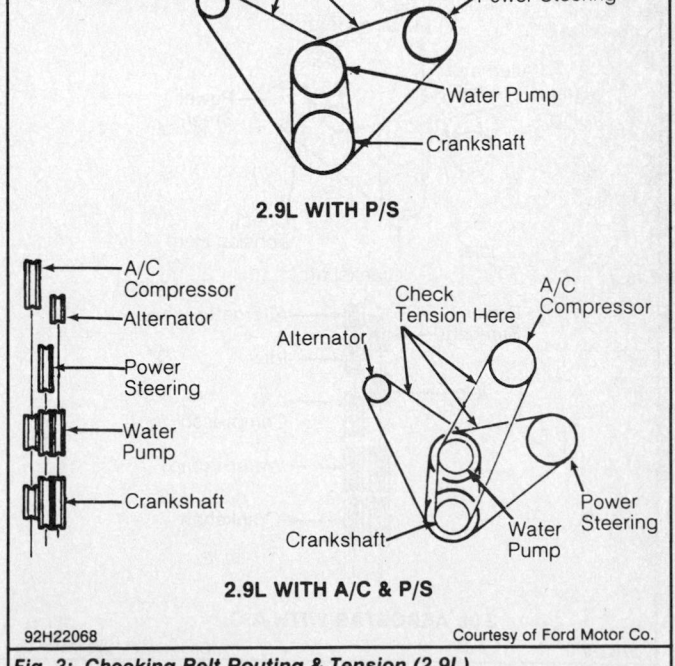

2.9L WITH P/S

2.9L WITH A/C & P/S

92H22068 · Courtesy of Ford Motor Co.

Fig. 3: Checking Belt Routing & Tension (2.9L)

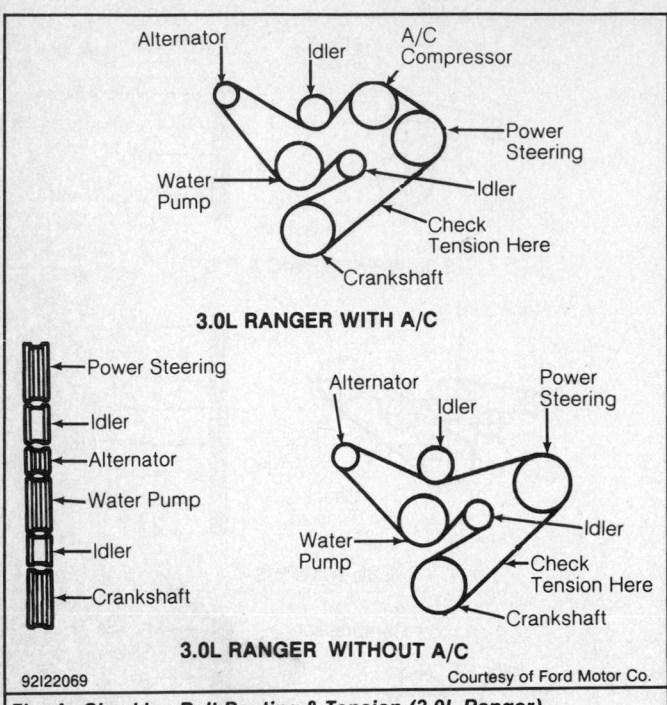

3.0L RANGER WITH A/C

3.0L RANGER WITHOUT A/C

92I22069   Courtesy of Ford Motor Co.

Fig. 4: Checking Belt Routing & Tension (3.0L Ranger)

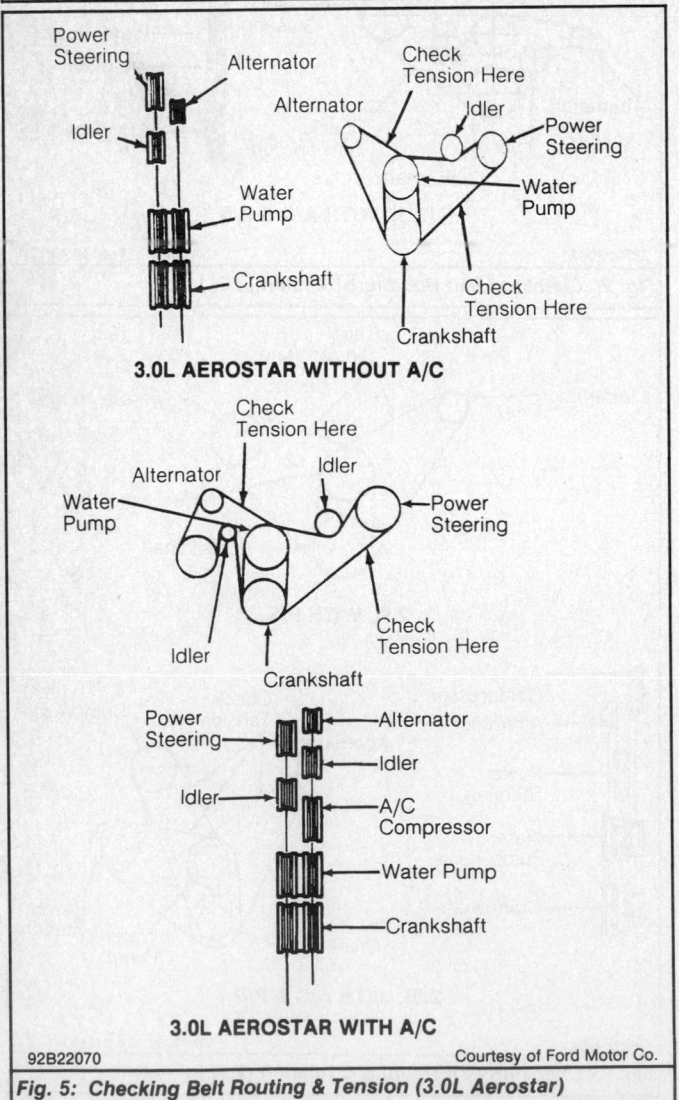

3.0L AEROSTAR WITHOUT A/C

3.0L AEROSTAR WITH A/C

92B22070   Courtesy of Ford Motor Co.

Fig. 5: Checking Belt Routing & Tension (3.0L Aerostar)

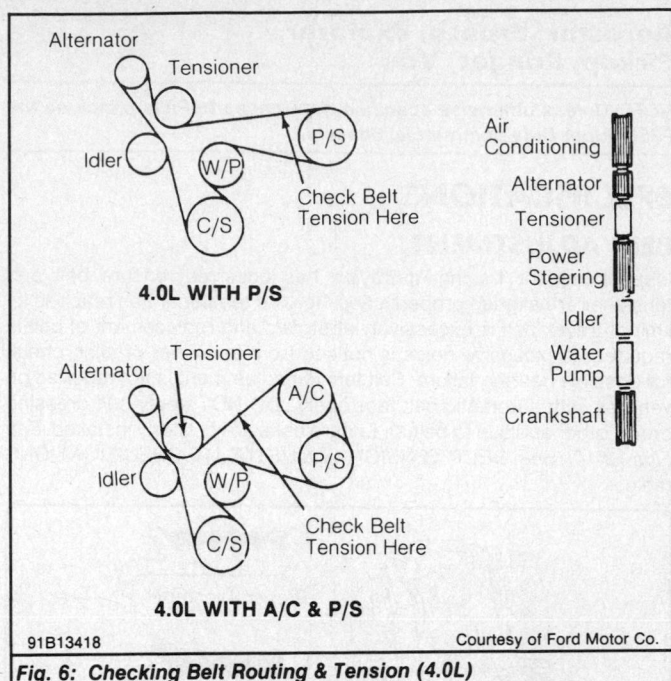

4.0L WITH P/S

4.0L WITH A/C & P/S

91B13418   Courtesy of Ford Motor Co.

Fig. 6: Checking Belt Routing & Tension (4.0L)

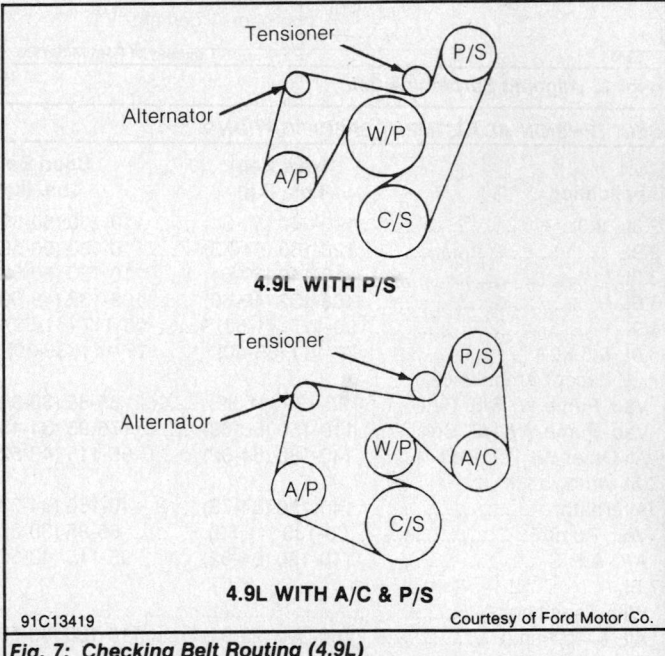

4.9L WITH P/S

4.9L WITH A/C & P/S

91C13419   Courtesy of Ford Motor Co.

Fig. 7: Checking Belt Routing (4.9L)

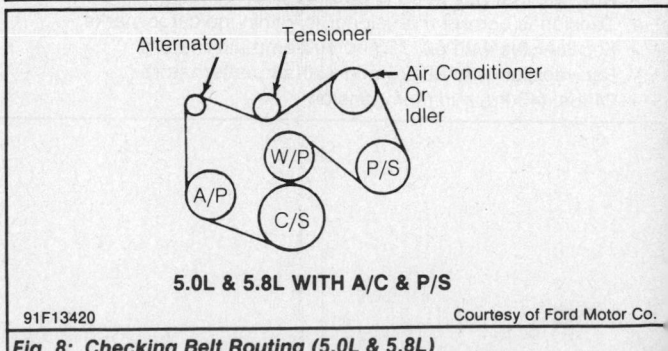

5.0L & 5.8L WITH A/C & P/S

91F13420   Courtesy of Ford Motor Co.

Fig. 8: Checking Belt Routing (5.0L & 5.8L)

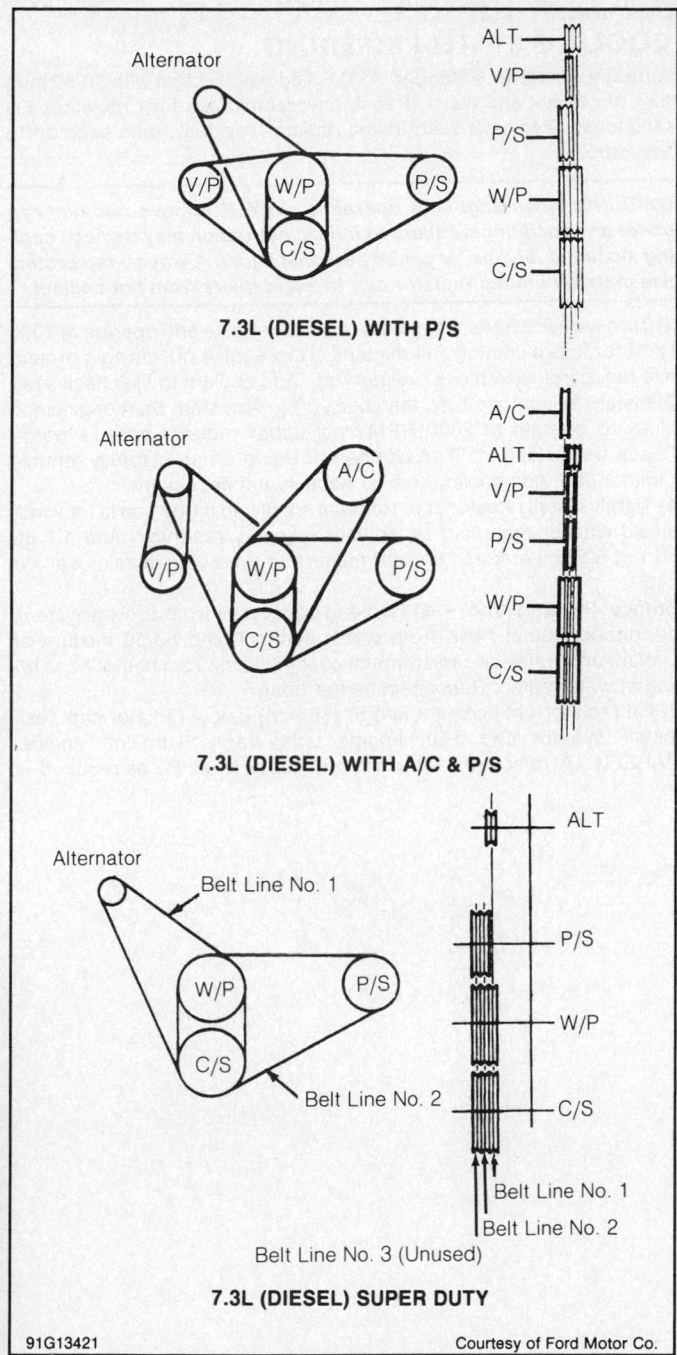

7.3L (DIESEL) WITH P/S

7.3L (DIESEL) WITH A/C & P/S

7.3L (DIESEL) SUPER DUTY

91G13421   Courtesy of Ford Motor Co.

Fig. 9: Checking Belt Routing (7.3L Diesel)

7.5L WITH A/C & P/S

7.5L SUPER DUTY

91H13422   Courtesy of Ford Motor Co.

Fig. 10: Checking Belt Routing (7.5L)

COOLING SYSTEM SPECIFICATIONS
COOLING SYSTEM CAPACITIES

Application	Specification
Coolant Replacement Interval	
All Models	30,000 Miles or 36 Months
Coolant Capacity	
Aerostar	
3.0L	11.8 qts. (11.2L)
4.0L	
Manual or Automatic Transmission [1]	8.1 qts. (7.6L)
Automatic Transmission [2]	8.5 qts. (8.0L)
Bronco & Pickup	
4.9L	
Manual or Automatic Transmission [1]	13 qts. (12L)
Manual Transmission [2]	14 qts. (13L)
Automatic Transmission [3] [4]	15 qts. (14L)
Automatic Transmission [4]	14 qts. (13L)
5.0L	
Manual Transmission [1]	13 qts. (12L)
Automatic Transmission [1]	14 qts. (13L)
Manual or Automatic Transmission [3]	14 qts. (13L)
Manual or Automatic Transmission [5]	15 qts. (14L)
5.8L	
Manual Transmission [1]	15 qts. (14L)
Automatic Transmission [1]	16 qts. (15L)
Manual or Automatic Transmission [3]	16 qts. (15L)
Manual or Automatic Transmission [5]	17 qts. (16L)
7.3L	[6] 29 qts. (27L)
7.5L	18 qts. (17L)
Explorer	
4.0L	
Manual or Automatic Transmission [1]	8.1 qts. (7.6L)
Automatic Transmission [2]	8.5 qts. (8.0L)

[1] – With standard cooling.
[2] – With A/C or super cooling.
[3] – With A/C.
[4] – With standard or super cooling.
[5] – With super cooling.
[6] – Include 5 qts. (4.7L) in reservoir bottle.
[7] – Information is not available from manufacturer.

1992 ENGINE COOLING
Specifications (Cont.)

COOLING SYSTEM CAPACITIES (Cont.)

Application	Specification
Ranger	
2.3L	
Manual or Automatic Transmission	7.2 qts. (6.8L)
2.9L	
Manual or Automatic Transmission [1]	7.2 qts. (6.8L)
Manual or Automatic Transmission [3]	7.8 qts. (7.4L)
3.0L	
Manual or Automatic Transmission	11.8 qts. (11.2L)
4.0L	
Manual or Automatic Transmission [1]	8.1 qts. (7.6L)
Automatic Transmission [2]	8.5 qts. (8.0L)
Van	
4.9L	
Manual or Automatic Transmission [1]	15 qts. (14L)
Manual or Automatic Transmission [2]	18 qts. (17L)
5.0L	
Manual or Automatic Transmission [1][3]	17.5 qts. (16.6L)
Manual or Automatic Transmission [5]	18.5 qts. (17.5L)
5.8L	
Manual or Automatic Transmission [1]	20 qts. (19L)
Manual or Automatic Transmission [2]	21 qts. (20L)
7.3L	[6] 31 qts. (29L)
7.5L	28 qts. (26L)
Pressure Cap	
All Models	13 PSI
Thermostat Opens	
7.3L Diesel	
Starts	180-192°F (82-89°C)
Fully Open	200-212°F (93-100°C)
Gasoline Engines	[7]

[1] – With standard cooling.
[2] – With A/C or super cooling.
[3] – With A/C.
[4] – With standard or super cooling.
[5] – With super cooling.
[6] – Include 5 qts. (4.7L) in reservoir bottle.
[7] – Information is not available from manufacturer.

COOLING SYSTEM BLEEDING

Aerostar, Explorer & Ranger – 1) Fill cooling system with 50/50 mixture of coolant and water. Pause several minutes for circulation. Fill radiator to filler neck seat. Install radiator cap fully, then back off to first stop.

WARNING: When engine is operating, NEVER remove radiator cap under any conditions. Failure to follow instruction may damage cooling system or engine, or cause personal injury. Always wrap protective material around radiator cap to avoid injury from hot coolant.

2) Turn heater controls to maximum. Start engine and operate at 2000 RPM for approximately 3-4 minutes. Turn engine off. Using a protective rag, carefully remove radiator cap. Add coolant to filler neck seat. **3)** Install radiator cap fully, then back off to first stop. Start engine and allow to operate at 2000 RPM until upper radiator hose is warm. Check heater output. Turn engine off. Using a rag, carefully remove radiator cap. Add coolant to filler neck seat if necessary. **4)** Tightly install radiator cap. Remove small cap (large cap is for windshield washer reservoir) on coolant recovery reservoir. Add **1.1 qt. (1L)** of 50/50 water and coolant mixture to reservoir. Install reservoir cap.

Bronco, Pickup & Van – 1) To bleed trapped air from cooling system, disconnect heater hose from water pump. Using 50/50 mixture of coolant and water, fill radiator until coolant flows from heater hose fitting at water pump. Reconnect heater hose.

2) Fill radiator until coolant is 1.5" (38 mm) below radiator cap seal. Install radiator cap. Run engine until warm. Turn off engine. CAREFULLY remove radiator cap and check level. Fill as required.

Aerostar, Bronco, Explorer, Pickup, Ranger, Van

NOTE: Unless otherwise specified, references to Pickup include the F350 Super Duty commercial chassis.

DESCRIPTION

The hydraulic clutch control consists of the hydraulic master cylinder, slave cylinder, reservoir, and connecting hydraulic lines. The clutch disc and pressure plate are single-disc type. The clutch release bearing or bearing arm is activated by hydraulic pressure.

The pilot bearing is mounted inside the bellhousing and requires no lubrication unless the clutch assembly is serviced. The clutch linkage or pedal position requires no adjustments.

TRANSMISSION & TRANSFER CASE APPLICATION

Vehicle Model	Transmission Model
Aerostar & Explorer	Mazda M50D 5-Speed O/D
Bronco	Borg-Warner T-18 4-Speed
	Ford S5-42 ZF 5-Speed
	Mazda M50D 5-Speed O/D
Pickup	Borg-Warner T-18 4-Speed
	Ford S5-42 ZF 5-Speed
	Mazda M50D 5-Speed O/D
Ranger	
2WD	Mazda M50D 5-Speed O/D
4WD	Mitsubishi FM146 5-Speed O/D
Van	
E350	Ford S5-42 ZF 5-Speed

	Transfer Case Model
Aerostar	Spicer TC-28
Bronco	Borg-Warner 1356
Explorer & Ranger	Borg-Warner 1354
Pickup	Borg-Warner 1356
	Borg-Warner 1345

ADJUSTMENTS

CLUTCH MASTER CYLINDER PUSH ROD LENGTH ADJUSTMENT

Bronco & Pickup – **1)** Ensure attaching nut on left side of clutch pedal is tight. Remove clutch master cylinder push rod from cross shaft lever pin. If push rod is in alignment with cross shaft lever pin, adjustment is okay.

2) If push rod is not in alignment with cross shaft lever pin, reinstall push rod to cross shaft lever pin. Pump clutch pedal several times to reset position of shaft to pedal slot.

3) Remove clutch master cylinder push rod from lever pin and evaluate alignment. If push rod is aligned with pin, adjustment is okay. If 2 components are still not in alignment, replace cross shaft lever. *See Fig. 1.*

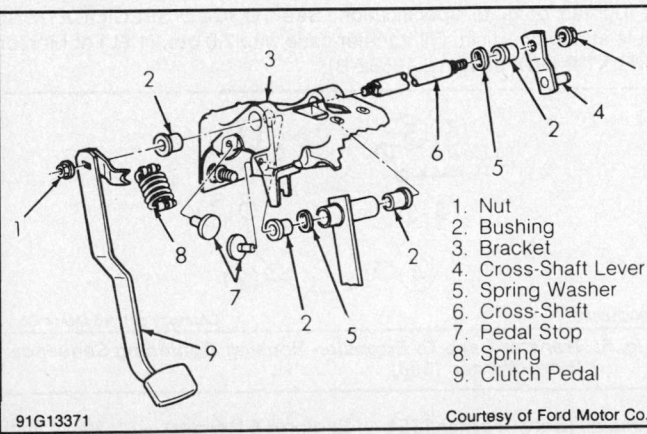

1. Nut
2. Bushing
3. Bracket
4. Cross-Shaft Lever
5. Spring Washer
6. Cross-Shaft
7. Pedal Stop
8. Spring
9. Clutch Pedal

91G13371   Courtesy of Ford Motor Co.

Fig. 1: Exploded View Of Clutch Pedal Assembly (Bronco & Pickup)

CLUTCH RELEASE BEARING TRAVEL MEASUREMENT

Externally Mounted Slave Cylinder – **1)** Remove slave cylinder dust shield. With clutch pedal fully depressed, measure external slave cylinder push rod travel.

2) Push rod should travel a minimum of **0.43" (10.9 mm)**. DO NOT replace clutch hydraulic system if measurement exceeds specification. If slave cylinder travel is less than specification, check hydraulic reservoir fluid level.

Internally Mounted Slave Cylinder – **1)** Remove rubber plug from inspection port in transmission bellhousing. Position Bearing Travel Measurement Tool (D87T-4201A) through opening and against slave cylinder. *See Fig. 2.*

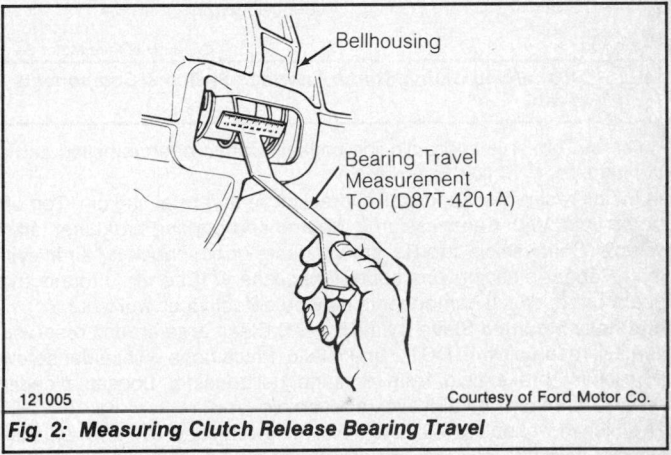

Bellhousing

Bearing Travel Measurement Tool (D87T-4201A)

121005   Courtesy of Ford Motor Co.

Fig. 2: Measuring Clutch Release Bearing Travel

2) Using rear edge of Black plastic bearing retainer as an indicator, take a reading with clutch pedal fully up. With clutch pedal fully depressed, take another measurement.

3) Difference between 2 readings is total bearing travel. If bearing travel is greater than .295" (7.49 mm), replace pressure plate and or clutch disc.

4) If bearing travel is .295" (7.49 mm) or less, inspect hydraulic system for leaks. Repair leak. If no leak is found, bleed system. See HYDRAULIC SYSTEM BLEEDING under IN-VEHICLE SERVICE. Recheck bearing travel after repairs have been completed.

IN-VEHICLE SERVICE

CLUTCH/STARTER INTERLOCK SWITCH

1) Disconnect wiring connector at switch by flexing retaining tab. Test electrical continuity of switch using an ohmmeter. Switch should be open (infinity) when pedal is up and clutch is engaged. Switch should be closed (zero ohms) when clutch pedal is pressed to floor. On all models except Van, if switch does not function as specified, replace switch.

2) On Van, if switch does not operate properly, check position of self-adjusting clip. Adjust switch by removing both halves of clip and positioning clip closer to switch body. Reset switch by depressing clutch pedal to floor. If switch still does not operate properly, replace switch. *See Fig. 3 or 4.*

HYDRAULIC SYSTEM BLEEDING

Externally Mounted Slave Cylinder – **1)** Remove slave cylinder from transmission bellhousing. Using a 3/32" diameter punch, remove pin that holds hydraulic line in slave cylinder. Remove hydraulic line from slave cylinder.

2) Place hydraulic line into container for waste fluid. Hold slave cylinder so hydraulic line port is at highest point. Fill slave cylinder through hydraulic line port with DOT 3 brake fluid. Gently push on slave cylinder push rod to expel all air.

3) When all air has been expelled, install slave cylinder. Remove clutch master cylinder reservoir cap. While maintaining fluid level in

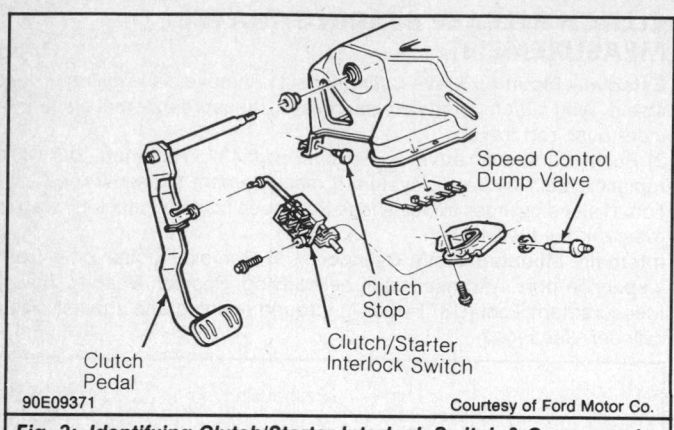

Fig. 3: Identifying Clutch/Starter Interlock Switch & Components (Van)

90E09371   Courtesy of Ford Motor Co.

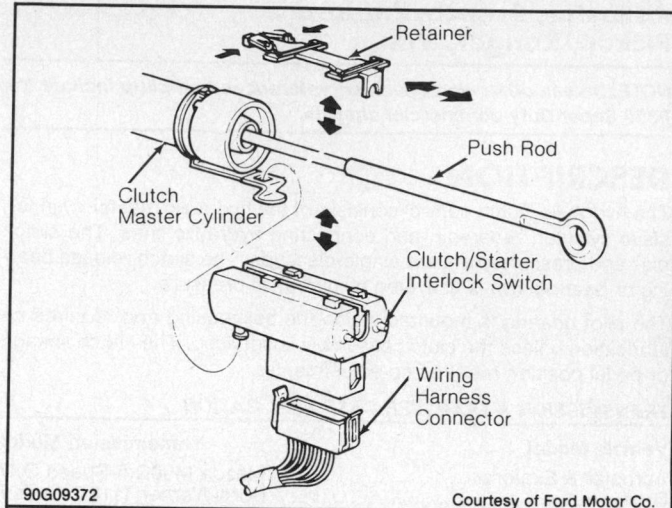

Fig. 4: Identifying Clutch/Starter Interlock Switch & Components (Except Van)

90G09372   Courtesy of Ford Motor Co.

reservoir, observe hydraulic line until all air has been expelled and a steady stream of fluid is flowing.

4) Install reservoir cap. Install hydraulic line and retaining pin. Top off brake fluid. With transmission in Neutral and parking brake set, start vehicle. Shift vehicle into Reverse. If gears grind, check for air in system. Repeat bleeding procedure if necessary. If no air is found and gears grind, clutch components may be defective or worn out.

Internally Mounted Slave Cylinder – 1) Clean area around reservoir cap. Fill reservoir with DOT 3 brake fluid. Place hose on bleeder screw to prevent brake fluid from entering bellhousing. Loosen bleeder screw and maintain fluid level in reservoir.

2) Fluid and bubbles will flow from hose attached to slave cylinder bleeder screw. Close bleeder screw when fluid stream is free of air bubbles. Ensure fluid level is correct and install reservoir cap.

3) Place light pressure on clutch pedal and open bleeder screw. Maintain pressure until pedal contacts floor. Close bleeder screw while pedal is fully depressed. DO NOT allow pedal to return before bleeder screw is fully closed. Recheck fluid level.

4) Test system operation by starting vehicle, depressing clutch and placing gearshift in Reverse. No grinding should be heard or felt with clutch pedal within 1/2" (13 mm) of floor. If noise is heard, check for air in system. Repeat bleeding procedure if necessary.

REMOVAL & INSTALLATION

WARNING: When battery is disconnected, vehicle computer and memory systems may lose memory data. Driveability problems may exist until computer systems have completed a relearn cycle. See COMPUTER RELEARN PROCEDURES article in GENERAL INFORMATION before disconnecting battery.

TRANSFER CASE

Removal (Spicer TC-28 – Aerostar) – 1) Raise vehicle. Remove drain plug and drain fluid from transfer case. Install plug. Disconnect electrical connector from rear of transfer case.

2) Disconnect front and rear drive shafts from transfer case output shaft yokes. Disconnect speedometer drive gear from transfer case rear cover. Remove cylinder block-to-transfer case strut.

3) Support transfer case with jack and remove bolts attaching transfer case to transmission extension housing. Slide transfer case off transmission output shaft. Lower transfer case from vehicle. Remove gasket between transfer case and transmission extension housing.

Installation – 1) Install new transfer case-to-extension housing gasket. To complete installation, reverse removal procedure. Tighten transfer case-to-extension housing bolts in sequence. *See Fig. 5.*

2) Tighten bolts to specification. See TORQUE SPECIFICATIONS table at end of article. Fill transfer case with **2.3 qts. (2.2L)** of Mercon ATF (XT-2-QDX or E4AZ-19582-B).

Removal (Borg-Warner 1356 – Bronco & Pickup) – 1) Raise vehicle. Remove skid plate (if equipped). Remove drain plug and drain fluid

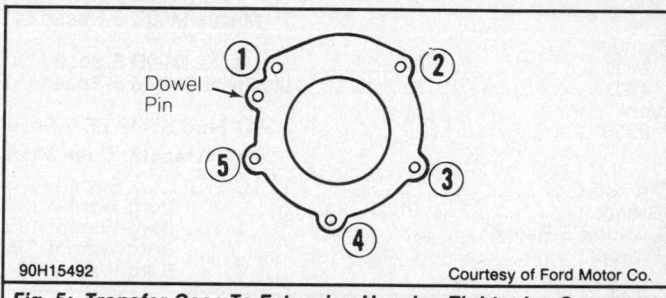

Fig. 5: Transfer Case-To-Extension Housing Tightening Sequence (Spicer TC-28 & Borg-Warner 1354)

90H15492   Courtesy of Ford Motor Co.

from transfer case. Install plug. Disconnect 4WD indicator switch at transfer case.

2) Disconnect front and rear drive shafts from transfer case output shaft yokes. Disconnect speedometer drive gear from transfer case rear cover. Disconnect vent hose from mounting bracket. Disconnect shift rod between transfer case shift lever and control lever assembly.

3) Support transfer case with jack and remove bolts attaching transfer case to transmission extension housing. Slide transfer case off transmission output shaft. Lower transfer case from vehicle. Remove gasket between transfer case and transmission extension housing.

Installation – 1) Install new transfer case-to-extension housing gasket. To complete installation, reverse removal procedure. Tighten transfer case-to-extension housing bolts in sequence. *See Fig. 6.*

2) Tighten bolts to specification. See TORQUE SPECIFICATIONS table at end of article. Fill transfer case with **2.0 qts. (1.9L)** of Mercon ATF (XT-2-QDX or E4AZ-19582-B).

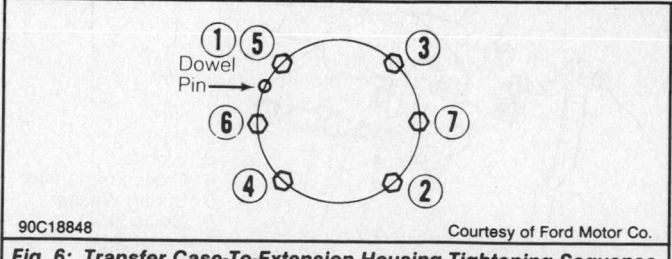

Fig. 6: Transfer Case-To-Extension Housing Tightening Sequence (Borg-Warner 1356)

90C18848   Courtesy of Ford Motor Co.

Removal (Borg-Warner 1354 – Explorer & Ranger) – 1) Raise vehicle. Remove skid plate (if equipped). Remove damper from transfer case (if equipped). Remove drain plug and drain fluid from transfer case. Install plug. Disconnect 4WD indicator switch at transfer case.

2) Disconnect front and rear drive shafts from transfer case output shaft yokes. Disconnect speedometer drive gear from transfer case rear cover. Disconnect vent hose from control lever. Remove shift lever retaining nut and lever.

3) Loosen or remove both large and small bolt retaining shifter to extension housing. Remove lever assembly and bushing. Support transfer case with jack and remove bolts attaching transfer case to transmission extension housing.

4) Slide transfer case rearward off transmission output shaft. Lower transfer case from vehicle. Remove gasket from transfer case and transmission extension housing.

Installation – **1)** Install new transfer case-to-extension housing gasket. To complete installation, reverse removal procedure. Tighten transfer case-to-extension housing bolts in sequence. See Fig. 5.

NOTE: *When installing shift lever assembly, ensure large bolt is tightened first, then small bolt.*

---

2) Tighten bolts to specifications. See TORQUE SPECIFICATIONS table at end of article. Fill transfer case with **1.3 qts. (1.2L)** of Mercon ATF (XT-2-QDX or E4AZ-19582-B).

Removal (Borg-Warner 1345 – F150/250 4WD) – 1) Raise vehicle. Remove drain plug and drain fluid from transfer case. Replace plug. Disconnect 4WD indicator switch connector at transfer case. Remove skid plate (if equipped).

2) Disconnect front and rear drive shafts from transfer case output shaft yokes. Wire drive shaft aside. Disconnect speedometer drive gear from transfer case rear cover.

3) Remove retaining clips and shift rod from transfer case control and transfer case shift levers. Disconnect vent hose from transfer case. Remove heat shield. Support transfer case with transmission jack.

4) Remove transfer case-to-extension housing bolts. Slide transfer case off transmission output shaft. Lower transfer case from vehicle. Remove transfer case-to-extension housing gasket.

Installation – Install new transfer case-to-extension housing gasket. To complete installation, reverse removal procedure. Tighten transfer case-to-extension housing bolts in sequence. See Fig. 7. Tighten bolts to specifications. See TORQUE SPECIFICATIONS table at end of article. Fill transfer case with **3.3 qts. (3.0L)** of Mercon ATF (XT-2-QDX or E4AZ-19582-B).

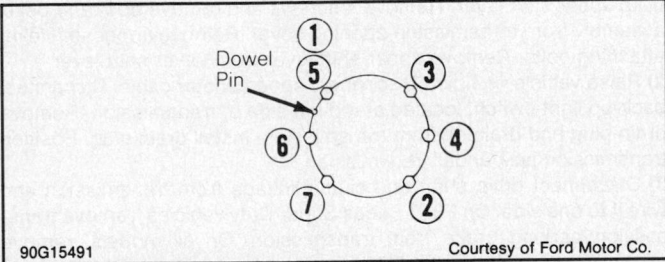

90G15491   Courtesy of Ford Motor Co.

Fig. 7: Transfer Case-To-Extension Housing Tightening Sequence (Borg-Warner 1345)

TRANSMISSION

Removal (Mazda M50D 5-Speed Overdrive – Aerostar, Explorer & Ranger) – 1) Disconnect negative battery cable from battery. Shift transmission into Neutral. Remove boot assembly-to-floor bolts. Remove boot from shift lever assembly.

2) Remove shift lever retaining bolt. Remove shift lever, ball and boot assembly. Raise vehicle on hoist. Scribe a mark on drive shaft and rear axle flange for installation reference.

3) Disconnect drive shaft at rear drive axle flange. Remove drive shaft. Cap transmission extension housing to prevent lubricant spillage. Disconnect starter cable and wires. Remove starter.

4) Disconnect clutch slave cylinder hydraulic line by pressing White retainer bushing with Disconnect Tool (T88T-70522-A) while pulling on line. See Fig. 8. Cap end of line to prevent fluid leakage.

5) Disconnect back-up lamp switch from sender on transmission. Remove speedometer cable from extension housing or transfer case

(if equipped). Position jack under engine, protecting oil pan with wood block.

6) On 4WD models, remove transfer case. See TRANSFER CASE under REMOVAL & INSTALLATION. Remove transmission mount/damper-to-crossmember nuts/bolts.

7) Position transmission jack under transmission. Place jack safety chain around transmission. Slightly raise transmission. Remove nuts and bolts retaining crossmember to frame. Remove crossmember.

8) Remove bellhousing-to-engine bolts. Slide transmission rearward to separate bellhousing from dowel pins on rear of engine block. Lower transmission from vehicle.

Installation – **1)** Ensure mating surfaces and locating dowels are clean and free of burrs. Ensure transmission input shaft splines are clean. Place transmission on transmission jack and position under vehicle.

2) Raise transmission into position and start input shaft into clutch disc. Align splines on input shaft with splines on clutch disc. Move transmission forward until bellhousing seats on locating dowels.

3) Install bellhousing-to-engine block bolts. Tighten bolts to specification. See TORQUE SPECIFICATIONS table at end of article. To complete installation, reverse removal procedure.

4) Bleed hydraulic clutch system. See HYDRAULIC SYSTEM BLEEDING under IN-VEHICLE SERVICE. For recommended fluid and capacity, see AUTOMATIC/MANUAL TRANSMISSION article in TRANSMISSION SERVICING.

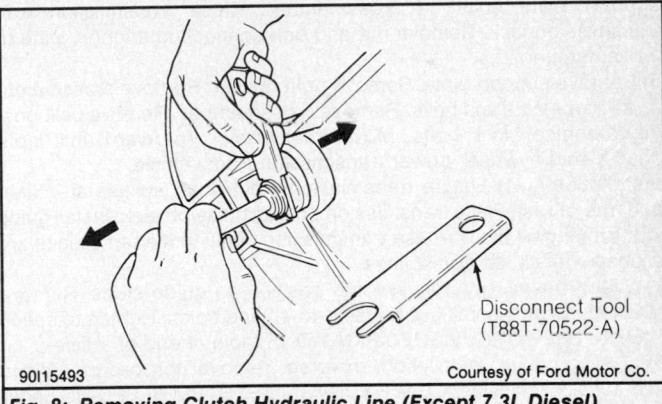

Disconnect Tool (T88T-70522-A)

90I15493   Courtesy of Ford Motor Co.

Fig. 8: Removing Clutch Hydraulic Line (Except 7.3L Diesel)

Removal (Mazda M50D 5-Speed Overdrive – Pickup 2WD) – 1) Shift transmission into Neutral. Remove carpet or floor mat for access. Remove shifter boot retainer screws. Slide boot up shift lever shaft. Remove shift lever retainer bolt and shift lever.

2) Raise vehicle on hoist. Disconnect speedometer cable. Disconnect back-up light switch, located on top left of transmission. Remove drain plug and drain gear oil. Install drain plug. Position transmission jack under transmission.

3) Disconnect drive shaft from extension housing and wire to one side. On models with 7.3L engine, disconnect clutch slave cylinder hydraulic line. On all others, remove clutch slave cylinder hydraulic line by pressing White retainer bushing with Disconnect Tool (T88T-70522-A) while pulling on line. See Fig. 8.

4) Remove transmission rear mount and lower retainer. Remove skid plate (if equipped). Remove catalytic converter heat shield. Remove 2 upper gusset-to-frame nuts from both sides. Remove transmission-to-transmission support plate bolts on crossmember. Raise transmission with transmission jack.

5) Remove nut and bolt connecting support plate to crossmember. Remove support plate. Remove right gusset. Remove nuts and bolts holding crossmember to frame. Remove crossmember.

6) Remove transmission-to-engine block bolts. Move transmission rearward until input shaft clears flywheel. Lower transmission from vehicle.

Installation – **1)** Ensure transmission input shaft splines are clean and free of rust. Place transmission on transmission jack. Install guide studs in engine block. Raise transmission until input shaft splines are aligned with clutch disc splines.

2) Slide transmission forward into position on guide studs. Remove guide studs and install bell housing-to-engine bolts. Tighten to specification. See TORQUE SPECIFICATIONS table at end of article.

3) To complete installation, reverse removal procedure. Bleed hydraulic clutch system. See HYDRAULIC SYSTEM BLEEDING under IN-VEHICLE SERVICE. For recommended fluid and capacity, see AUTOMATIC/MANUAL TRANSMISSION article in TRANSMISSION SERVICING.

Removal (Mazda M50D 5-Speed Overdrive – Bronco & Pickup 4WD) – 1) Shift transmission into Neutral. Remove carpet or floor mat for access. Remove shifter boot retainer screws. Slide boot up shift lever shaft. Remove shift lever retainer bolt and shift lever.

2) Raise vehicle on hoist. Remove drain plugs and drain gear oil from transmission and transfer case. Install drain plugs. Disconnect front and rear drive shafts from transfer case.

3) Remove clutch slave cylinder hydraulic line by pressing White retainer bushing with Disconnect Tool (T88T-70522-A) while pulling on line. *See Fig. 8.* Disconnect back-up light switch. Disconnect speedometer cable from transfer case.

4) Remove skid plate (if equipped). Position transmission jack under transfer case. Remove transfer case-to-transmission bolts. Lower transfer case. Ensure transfer case shift lever clears opening in floor pan. Remove transmission rear mount and lower retainer.

5) Remove catalytic converter heat shield. Remove 2 upper gusset-to-frame nuts from both sides. Remove transmission-to-transmission support plate bolts on crossmember. Raise transmission with transmission jack. Remove nut and bolt connecting support plate to crossmember.

6) Remove support plate. Remove right gusset. Remove crossmember-to-frame nuts and bolts. Remove crossmember. Remove bellhousing-to-engine block bolts. Move transmission rearward until input shaft clears flywheel. Lower transmission from vehicle.

Installation – 1) Ensure transmission input shaft splines are clean and free of rust. Place transmission on transmission jack. Install guide studs in engine block. Raise transmission until input shaft splines are aligned with clutch disc splines.

2) Slide transmission forward into position on guide studs. Remove guide studs and install bell housing-to-engine bolts. Tighten to specification. See TORQUE SPECIFICATIONS table at end of article.

3) To complete installation, reverse removal procedure. Bleed hydraulic clutch system. See HYDRAULIC SYSTEM BLEEDING under IN-VEHICLE SERVICE. For recommended fluid and capacity, see AUTOMATIC/MANUAL TRANSMISSION article in TRANSMISSION SERVICING.

Removal (Borg-Warner T-18 4-Speed – F150/250 2WD) – 1) Remove floor mat and body floor pan cover. Remove gearshift lever shift ball and boot. Remove insulator pad. Raise vehicle on hoist.

2) Remove drain plug and drain transmission. Install drain plug. Remove clutch slave cylinder hydraulic line by pressing White retainer bushing with Disconnect Tool (T88T-70522-A) while pulling on line. *See Fig. 8.*

3) Position transmission jack under transmission. Disconnect speedometer cable. Disconnect back-up light switch connector from rear of gearshift housing cover. Disconnect drive shaft or coupling shaft.

4) Disconnect clutch linkage from transmission and wire it aside. Remove skid plate (if equipped). Remove nuts connecting upper gusset to frame on both sides of frame. Remove nut/bolt connecting gusset to crossmember.

5) Remove left side gusset. Remove transmission mount-to-transmission bolts. Raise transmission with transmission jack. Remove nuts attaching transmission mount-to-crossmember. Remove right side gusset. Remove nuts/bolts connecting crossmember-to-frame.

6) Remove crossmember. Remove transmission-to-bellhousing bolts. Move transmission to rear until input shaft clears bellhousing. Lower and remove transmission.

Installation – 1) Ensure transmission input shaft splines are clean and free of rust. Place transmission on transmission jack. Install guide studs in engine block. Raise transmission until input shaft splines are aligned with clutch disc splines.

2) Slide transmission forward into position on guide studs. Remove guide studs and install bell housing-to-engine bolts. Tighten to specification. See TORQUE SPECIFICATIONS table at end of article.

3) To complete installation, reverse removal procedure. Bleed hydraulic clutch system. See HYDRAULIC SYSTEM BLEEDING under IN-VEHICLE SERVICE. For recommended fluid and capacity, see AUTOMATIC/MANUAL TRANSMISSION article in TRANSMISSION SERVICING.

Removal (Borg-Warner T-18 4-Speed – Bronco & F150/250 4WD) – 1) Remove floor mat and body floor pan cover. Place shift lever in REVERSE position. Remove gearshift cover. Remove insulator and dust cover. Remove transfer case shift lever, shift ball and boot as an assembly.

2) Remove transmission shift lever, shift ball and boot as an assembly. Raise vehicle on hoist. Remove drain plug and drain transmission and transfer case. Install drain plug.

3) Disconnect rear and front drive shafts and wire them aside. Remove shift linkage from transmission. Remove speedometer cable. Position transmission jack under transfer case.

4) Remove transfer case-to-transmission bolts. Remove clutch slave cylinder hydraulic line by pressing White retainer bushing with Disconnect Tool (T88T-70522-A) while pulling on line. *See Fig. 8.*

5) Remove transfer case. Remove rear support bracket-to-transmission bolts. Position transmission jack under transmission. Remove rear support bracket brace. Remove transmission-to-bellhousing bolts. Remove transmission.

Installation – 1) Ensure transmission input shaft splines are clean and free of rust. Place transmission on transmission jack. Install guide studs in engine block. Raise transmission until input shaft splines are aligned with clutch disc splines.

2) Slide transmission forward onto guide studs. Remove guide studs and install bellhousing-to-engine bolts. Tighten to specification. See TORQUE SPECIFICATIONS table at end of article.

3) To complete installation, reverse removal procedure. Bleed hydraulic clutch system. See HYDRAULIC SYSTEM BLEEDING under IN-VEHICLE SERVICE. For recommended fluid and capacity, see AUTOMATIC/MANUAL TRANSMISSION article in TRANSMISSION SERVICING.

Removal (Ford S5-42 ZF 5-Speed – E350 & Pickup 2WD) – 1) Shift transmission into Neutral. Remove carpet or floor mat. Remove ball from upper shift lever. Remove 4 screws and remove boot and bezel assembly from transmission opening cover. Remove upper shift lever attaching bolts. Remove upper shift lever from lower shift lever.

2) Raise vehicle on hoist. Disconnect speedometer cable. Disconnect back-up light switch, located at top left side of transmission. Remove drain plug and drain oil from transmission. Install drain plug. Position transmission jack under transmission.

3) Disconnect drive shaft and clutch linkage from transmission and wire it to one side. On F350 Series Super Duty vehicles, remove transmission parking brake from transmission. On all models, remove transmission rear mount and lower retainer.

4) On models with 7.3L engine, disconnect clutch slave cylinder hydraulic line. On all other models, remove clutch slave cylinder hydraulic line by pressing White retainer bushing with Disconnect Tool (T88T-70522-A) while pulling on line. *See Fig. 8.*

5) Remove skid plate (if equipped). Remove 2 upper gusset-to-frame nuts from both sides. Remove transmission-to-transmission support plate bolts on crossmember. Raise transmission with transmission jack. Remove nut and bolt connecting support plate to crossmember.

6) Remove support plate. Remove right gusset. Remove crossmember-to-frame nuts and bolts. Remove crossmember. Remove bellhousing-to-engine bolts. Move transmission to rear until input shaft clears engine flywheel. Lower transmission from vehicle.

Installation – 1) Ensure transmission input shaft splines are clean and free of rust. Place transmission on transmission jack. Install guide studs in engine block. Raise transmission until input shaft splines are aligned with clutch disc splines.

2) Slide transmission forward onto guide studs. Remove guide studs and install bellhousing-to-engine bolts. Tighten to specification. See TORQUE SPECIFICATIONS table at end of article.

3) To complete installation, reverse removal procedure. Bleed hydraulic clutch system. See HYDRAULIC SYSTEM BLEEDING under IN-VEHICLE SERVICE. For recommended fluid and capacity, see AUTOMATIC/MANUAL TRANSMISSION article in TRANSMISSION SERVICING.

Removal (Ford S5-42 ZF 5-Speed – Bronco & Pickup 4WD) –
1) Shift transmission into Neutral. Remove carpet or floor mat. Remove 4 screws and remove boot and bezel assembly from transmission opening cover. Remove 2 bolts and upper shift lever from lower shift lever.

2) Raise vehicle on hoist. Remove drain plugs and drain transmission and transfer case. Install drain plug. Disconnect rear drive shaft from transfer case and wire it aside. Disconnect front drive shaft from transfer case and wire aside.

3) Disconnect back-up light switch. Remove speedometer cable from transfer case. Remove skid plate (if equipped). Position transmission jack under transfer case.

4) On models with 7.3L engine, disconnect clutch slave cylinder hydraulic line. On all others models, remove clutch slave cylinder hydraulic line by pressing White retainer bushing with Disconnect Tool (T88T-70522-A) while pulling on line. *See Fig. 8.*

5) Remove transfer case-to-transmission bolts. Remove carrier case-to-transmission bolts. Carefully lower transfer case from vehicle, ensuring shift lever clears opening in floor pan. Remove transmission rear mount and lower retainer.

6) Remove 2 upper gusset-to-frame nuts from both sides. Remove transmission-to-transmission support plate bolts on crossmember. Raise transmission with transmission jack. Remove nut and bolt connecting support plate to crossmember.

7) Remove support plate. Remove right gusset. Remove crossmember-to-frame nuts and bolts. Remove crossmember. Remove bellhousing-to-engine bolts. Move transmission to rear until input shaft clears engine flywheel housing. Lower transmission from vehicle.

Installation – 1) Ensure transmission input shaft splines are clean and free of rust. Place transmission on transmission jack. Install guide studs in engine block. Raise transmission until input shaft splines are aligned with clutch disc splines.

2) Slide transmission forward into position on guide studs. Remove guide studs. Install bell housing-to-engine bolts and tighten to specification. See TORQUE SPECIFICATIONS table at end of article.

3) Bleed hydraulic clutch system. See HYDRAULIC SYSTEM BLEEDING under IN-VEHICLE SERVICE. To complete installation, reverse removal procedure. For recommended fluid and capacity, see AUTOMATIC/MANUAL TRANSMISSION article in TRANSMISSION SERVICING.

Removal (Mitsubishi FM146 5-Speed Overdrive – Ranger 4WD) –
1) Disconnect negative battery cable. Place gearshift selector in Neutral. Remove shift boot retainer bolts. Remove bolts attaching retainer cover to gearshift lever retainer.

2) Pull gearshift lever assembly out of control housing. Cover opening in control housing to prevent dirt from falling into transmission. Raise vehicle. Index rear drive shaft axle flange and front transfer case flange.

3) Disconnect drive shaft at both rear axle flange and transfer case. Remove front drive shaft. Install plug in transfer case adapter to prevent lubricant leakage.

4) Pull rear drive shaft rearward and disconnect drive shaft from transmission. Remove bellhousing dust shield. Disconnect clutch slave cylinder hydraulic line by pressing White retainer bushing with Disconnect Tool (T88T-70522-A) while pulling on line. *See Fig. 8.* Plug line to prevent leakage.

5) Disconnect speedometer cable. Disconnect starter motor cable, back-up light switch wire and neutral position switch wire. Place jack under engine block, protecting oil pan with wood block. Remove transfer case. See TRANSFER CASE under REMOVAL & INSTALLATION.

6) Remove starter. Place a transmission jack under transmission. Remove bolts attaching bellhousing-to-engine. Remove nuts/bolts attaching transmission mount and damper to crossmember.

7) Remove nuts attaching crossmember to frame side rails and remove crossmember. Lower engine jack. Work bellhousing off locat-

ing dowels and slide transmission rearward until input shaft clears clutch disc. Remove transmission from vehicle.

Installation – 1) Ensure mating surfaces and locating dowels are free of burrs. Ensure transmission input shaft splines are clean. Place transmission on transmission jack and position under vehicle. Raise transmission into position and start input shaft into clutch disc.

2) Align splines on input shaft with splines on clutch disc. Move transmission forward until bellhousing seats on locating dowels. Install bolts retaining bellhousing-to-engine block.

3) Tighten bolts to specification. See TORQUE SPECIFICATIONS table at end of article. To complete installation, reverse removal procedure. Bleed hydraulic clutch system. See HYDRAULIC SYSTEM BLEEDING under IN-VEHICLE SERVICE. For recommended fluid and capacity, see AUTOMATIC/MANUAL TRANSMISSION article in TRANSMISSION SERVICING.

CLUTCH DISC & PRESSURE PLATE

Removal – 1) Disconnect negative battery cable. Disconnect clutch master cylinder push rod. Raise vehicle and remove starter. Disconnect clutch slave cylinder hydraulic line by pressing White retainer bushing with Disconnect Tool (T88T-70522-A) while pulling on line. *See Fig. 8.*

2) Remove transmission. See TRANSMISSION under REMOVAL & INSTALLATION. Place reference mark on pressure plate and flywheel for reassembly reference. Loosen pressure plate-to-flywheel bolts evenly until springs are expanded. Remove pressure plate and clutch disc.

Installation – 1) Clean pressure plate and flywheel surface with alcohol-based solvent. Place clutch disc on flywheel. Align disc center with pilot bearing using old input shaft or clutch pilot shaft.

2) Place pressure plate on flywheel and align reference mark. Tighten bolts evenly in a crisscross sequence. Remove clutch pilot shaft. To complete installation, reverse removal procedure.

CLUTCH RELEASE BEARING

Removal (Internally Mounted Slave Cylinder) – With transmission removed, twist release bearing and carrier assembly until resistance is felt. Turning assembly further will allow preload spring to push bearing assembly from slave cylinder. *See Fig. 9.*

Installation – Prior to installation, lubricate bearing bore and bearing carrier with multipurpose grease. Install release bearing assembly to clutch slave cylinder by pushing into place.

CLUTCH PILOT BEARING

Removal – Remove transmission. See TRANSMISSION under REMOVAL & INSTALLATION. Remove pressure plate and clutch disc. See CLUTCH DISC & PRESSURE PLATE under REMOVAL & INSTALLATION. Use Impact Slide Hammer Puller (T58L-101-B) to remove pilot bearing.

Installation – Lightly coat crankshaft bore with lithium-based grease. Using Bearing Driver (T71P-7137-H) and Adapter (T74P-7137-A), install pilot bearing with seal toward transmission. Install clutch disc, pressure plate and transmission.

NOTE: Use Adapter (T74P-7137-C) on 3.0L engine.

CLUTCH HYDRAULIC SYSTEM

CAUTION: On all models, disconnect master cylinder push rod if slave cylinder is to be disconnected from release lever or bearing. Permanent damage to master cylinder will occur if master cylinder is activated with slave cylinder disconnected.

Removal – 1) Note position of clutch pedal push rod. Disconnect master cylinder push rod from clutch pedal by prying retainer bushing and push rod off shaft. Disconnect clutch/starter interlock switch connector.

2) Remove 2 nuts and support bracket retaining clutch reservoir and master cylinder assembly to firewall. On models with 7.3L engine, dis-

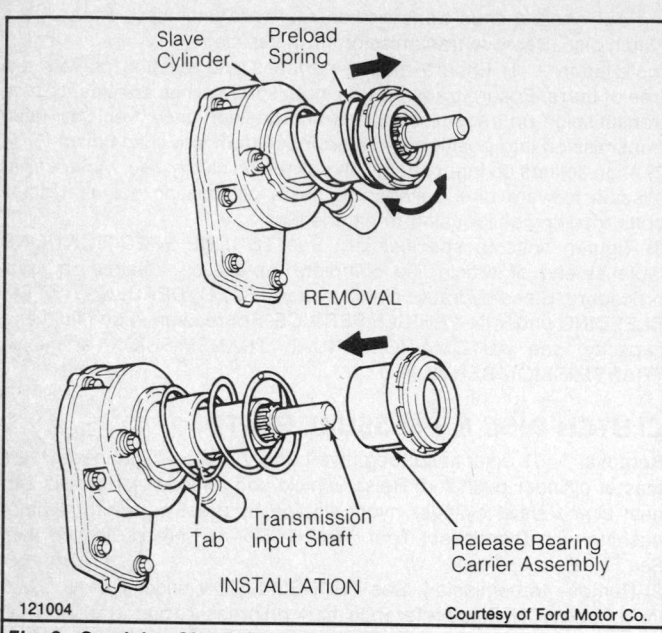

Fig. 9: Servicing Clutch Release Bearing

Courtesy of Ford Motor Co.

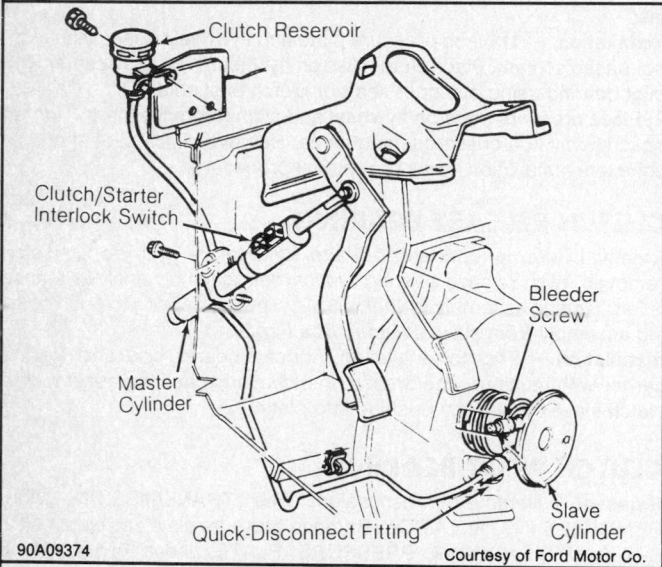

Fig. 10: Schematic Of Internal Slave Cylinder Hydraulic Clutch System (Typical)

Courtesy of Ford Motor Co.

connect clutch slave cylinder hydraulic line. On all other models, disconnect clutch slave cylinder hydraulic line by pressing White retainer bushing with Disconnect Tool (T88T-70522-A) while pulling on line. See Fig. 8. Plug line to prevent leakage.

3) On Bronco and Pickup, when master cylinder studs are free of dash panel, rotate cylinder 105 degrees counterclockwise to permit interlock switch to clear dash panel.

4) On all models, remove master cylinder, reservoir and hydraulic line. See Fig. 10. Plug lines. If removing slave cylinder on vehicles with externally mounted slave cylinder, remove slave cylinder from bellhousing.

5) On vehicles with internally mounted slave cylinder, remove transmission and bellhousing. See TRANSMISSION under REMOVAL & INSTALLATION. Note position of slave cylinder and remove from bellhousing.

Installation – 1) Install slave cylinder (if removed). On models with internally mounted slave cylinders, ensure slave cylinder is properly engaged in notches of bellhousing. Install transmission and bellhousing. On all models, insert master cylinder push rod through opening in firewall.

2) Ensure push rod is located on correct side of clutch pedal. Attach master cylinder to firewall. Insert hydraulic line and fitting in clutch slave cylinder. Install fluid reservoir on access cover.

3) Install push rod on clutch pedal. Bleed hydraulic system. See HYDRAULIC SYSTEM BLEEDING under IN-VEHICLE SERVICE. Depress clutch pedal at least 10 times to check for proper release and smooth operation.

CLUTCH PEDAL

Removal (Aerostar, Explorer & Ranger) – 1) Disconnect push rod from clutch pedal. Disconnect clutch/starter interlock switch from pedal. Remove retainer clip from pedal shaft.

2) On Explorer and Ranger, remove left kick panel. Remove parking brake assembly and secure away from work area. On all models, remove pedal and shaft assembly from bracket.

3) Remove bushings from bracket. Remove retainer clip from end of clutch pedal shaft. Remove clutch pedal and shaft from mounting bracket.

NOTE: When clutch pedal shaft is removed from bracket, brake pedal, bushings and spring washer will fall.

Installation – To install, reverse removal procedure. Inspect and lubricate bushings with a light film of SAE 30 engine oil. Replace bushings if worn.

Removal (Bronco, Pickup & Van) – 1) On Bronco and Pickup models, disconnect clutch pedal retracting spring from clutch pedal and bracket. On Van, disconnect barbed retainer bushing on clutch/starter interlock switch rod from clutch pedal.

2) On all models, remove retainer clip from end of clutch pedal shaft. Remove clutch pedal and shaft from mounting bracket.

Installation – To install, reverse removal procedure. Compress retracting spring in a vise and secure with wire until it is in place. Inspect and lubricate bushings with a light film of SAE 30 engine oil or replace bushings.

TORQUE SPECIFICATIONS
TORQUE SPECIFICATIONS

Application	Ft. Lbs. (N.m)
Aerostar, Explorer & Ranger	
Bellhousing-To-Engine Bolt	28-38 (38-52)
Drive Shaft U-Bolt	10-15 (14-21)
Starter Bolt	15-20 (21-27)
Transfer Case-To-Extension Housing	
Aerostar (Spicer TC-28) [1]	23-35 (31-47)
Explorer & Ranger (Borg-Warner 1354) [1]	25-35 (34-47)
Transmission Mount-To-Crossmember Nut	60-80 (81-109)
Transmission-To-Bellhousing Bolt	30-40 (41-54)
Crossmember-To-Right Frame Nut	110-140 (149-190)
Crossmember-To-Left Frame Nut	
Except Ranger 2.3L 4WD	110-140 (149-190)
Ranger 2.3L 4WD	75-95 (102-129)
Pressure Plate Bolts [2]	15-24 (21-33)
Bronco, Pickup & Van	
Bellhousing-To-Engine Bolt	40-50 (54-68)
Front Drive Shaft-To-Front Output Yoke Nut	10-15 (14-21)
Starter Bolt	15-20 (21-27)
Transfer Case-To-Extension Housing	
Bronco & Pickup (Borg-Warner 1356) [3]	25-43 (34-58)
F150/250 4WD (Borg-Warner 1345) [4]	25-43 (34-58)
Transmission Mount-To-Crossmember Nut	60-80 (81-109)
Pressure Plate-To-Flywheel Bolt [2]	
4.9L, 5.0L & 5.8L	
10" Clutch	15-20 (21-27)
11" Clutch	20-29 (27-39)
7.3L & 7.5L	15-20 (21-27)
All Other Models	20-29 (27-39)

[1] – Tighten in sequence. See Fig. 5.
[2] – Tighten in a crisscross pattern.
[3] – Tighten in sequence. See Fig. 6.
[4] – Tighten in sequence. See Fig. 7.

Aerostar, Bronco, Explorer, Pickup, Ranger, Van

NOTE: Unless otherwise specified, references to Pickup include the F350 Super Duty commercial chassis.

MODEL IDENTIFICATION

Series [1]	Model
"A"	Aerostar
"E"	RWD Van
"F"	Pickup
"R"	Ranger
"U"	Bronco & Explorer

[1] – Vehicle series is fifth character of VIN.

IDENTIFICATION

Front axle identification tag is located under cover-to-carrier bolt. Rear axle identification tag is located under cover-to-carrier bolt or on front side of differential carrier. See appropriate differential article for identification tag interpretation. Vehicle axle application can also be determined through axle code on the Safety Certification Label located on left door pillar.

NOTE: All differential codes listed in AXLE RATIO IDENTIFICATION table are Ford Motor Co. production number codes.

AXLE RATIO IDENTIFICATION

Application	Ratio
Front Axles (4WD)	
Aerostar	
Dana 28-2	
519A-BA	3.27:1
519A-AB	3.73:1
Bronco & F150	
Dana 44 IFS	
F2TA-PA [2], F2TA-RA [2], F2TA-RB [2]	3.07:1
F2TA-SA [2], F2TA-SB [2], F2TA-TA [2], F2TA-UA [4]	3.54:1
F2TA-VA [2]	4.09:1
Explorer & Ranger	
Dana 35 IFS	
E87A-GB [2], E87A-DB [2]	3.45:1
FO7A-GC [2], FO7A-LB [2]	
F17A-JA [2], F27A-LA [2], F27A-MA [2]	3.55:1
FO7A-EB [2], FO7A-EC [2], FO7A-BB [2]	
F17A-HB [2], F27A-LA [2], F27A-NA [2], FO7A-BC [2]	3.73:1
E87A-JB [2], E87A-FB [2]	4.10:1
F250	
Dana 44 IFS-HD	
F1TA-LA [2], F1TA-LA [2]	3.54:1
E8TA-TC [2], E8TA-UC [2], E8TA-ZC [2]	3.55:1
F1TA-MA [2]	4.09:1
F250 Heavy Duty	
Dana 50 IFS	
E8TA-YC [2], F1TA-PA [2]	4.10:1
F350	
Dana 60 Monobeam	
F2TA-AA [4], F2TA-AB [4], F2TA-DA [2], F2TA-DB [2]	3.54:1
F2TA-FA [2], F2TA-FB [2], F2TA-BA [4], F2TA-BB [4]	
F2TA-CA [2], F2TA-CB [2], F2TA-EA [2], F2TA-EB [2]	4.10:1
Rear Axles	
Aerostar	
7 1/2" Ring Gear [1]	
S688-A, S688-B	3.27:1
S692-A, S692-C, S692-W	3.45:1
S696-A, S696-C, S696-W	3.73:1
S668-A [2]	4.10:1
7 1/2" Ring Gear [2]	
S697-A, S697-C, S697-W	3.73:1
S699-A, S699-C, S699-W	4.10:1
8 3/4" Ring Gear [1]	
S672-A, S672-B	3.27:1
S674-A, S674-B, S675-A, S675-B	3.55:1

[1] – Non-limited slip differential.
[2] – Limited slip differential.

AXLE RATIO IDENTIFICATION (Cont.)

Application	Ratio
Bronco, E150 & F150	
8 3/4" Ring Gear [1]	
S812-D, S842-A, S842-B, S736-A, S736-D, S736-G	2.73:1
S806-D, S836-A, S836-B, S738-A, S738-D, S738-G	3.08:1
S740-G	3.31:1
S808-D, S814-P, S838-B, S844-A, S844-B,	
S742-A, S742-D, S742-G, S744-A, S744-D, S744-G	3.55:1
8 3/4" Ring Gear [2]	
S805-D, S805-D, S835-A,	
S835-B, S739-A, S739-D,	
S739-G, S739-A, S739-D, S739-G	3.08:1
S741-G	3.31:1
S807-D, S817-P, S837-A, S837-B,	
S847-A, S847-B, S743-A, S743-D,	
S743-G, S745-A, S745-D, S745-G	3.55:1
S815-D, S845-A, S845-B	4.10:1
Explorer	
8 3/4" Ring Gear [1]	
S624-B, S624-D	3.08:1
S622-B, S622-D	3.27:1
S626-B	3.55:1
S628-A	3.73:1
E250/350	
Dana 60	
9 3/4" Ring Gear [2]	
F2UA-KD, F0UA-YA, F2UA-KC	3.54:1
F0UA-JB, F2UA-BD, F2UA-UA	3.73:1
F0UA-LB, F2UA-PA, F2UA-EC, F2UA-ED	4.10:1
9 3/4" Ring Gear [1]	
F0UA-RB, F2UA-JD, F2UA-CC,	
F2UA-CC, F2UA-CD, F2UA-PB	3.54:1
F0UA-HB, F2UA-AD, F2UA-TA	3.73:1
F0UA-KB, F2UA-DC, F2UA-DD, F2UA-NA, F2UA-DD	4.10:1
9 3/4" Ring Gear [1]	
E350 (Dual Rear Wheel)	
Dana 70	
10 1/2" Ring Gear [2]	
F0UA-NC, F0UA-ND, F2UA-HC,	
F2UA-HD, F2UA-SA, F2US-DB	4.10:1
10 1/2" Ring Gear [1]	
F0UA-SC, F0UA-SD, F0UA-MC,	
F0UA-MD, F0US-AA, F0US-AB,	
F0US-AC, F2UA-GC, F2UA-GC,	
F2UA-GD, F2UA-RA, F2US-AB, F2US-AC	4.10:1
"F" Series Super Duty, Stripped &	
Motorhome Chassis	
Dana 80	
11 1/4" Ring Gear [1]	
F1TA-AA, F2TA-LA	4.63:1
11 1/4" Ring Gear [1]	
F0TA-XA, F0TD-AA, F1TA-BA, F2TA-MA, F2TD-AB	5.13:1
Ranger	
7 1/2" Ring Gear [1]	
S314-C, S314-F, S360-A	3.08:1
S366-A, S302-C,	
S302-F, S304-C, S304-F, S362-A	3.45:1
S308-C, S308-F,	
S310-C, S310-F, S368-A, S370-A	3.73:1
S312-C, S312-F, S322-C, S322-F	4.10:1
7 1/2" Ring Gear [2]	
S307-C, S307-F	
S309-C, S309-F, S363-A, S367-A	3.73:1
S313-C, S313-F	4.10:1
8 3/4" Ring Gear [1]	
S324-A, S324-C,	
S326-A, S326-C, S350-A, S352-A	3.08:1
S328-C, S356-A	3.27:1
S336-A, S336-C, S358-A	3.55:1
S354-A	3.73:1
8 3/4 Ring Gear [2]	
S335-A, S335-C,	
S337-A, S337-C, S355-A, S357-A	3.55:1
S329-A, S329-C, S359-A	3.73:1

[1] – Non-limited slip differential.
[2] – Limited slip differential.

SAFETY CERTIFICATION LABEL AXLE CODE

Code	Type	Ratio
Aerostar		
B2	Limited Slip	4.10:1
B4	Limited Slip	3.73:1
B9	Limited Slip	3.55:1
23	Conventional	3.45:1
24 & 34	Conventional	3.73:1
25	Conventional	3.27:1
29	Conventional	3.55:1
Bronco & Pickup [1]		
B5	Limited Slip	4.10:1
B9	Limited Slip	3.55:1
C5	Limited Slip	4.10:1
C9	Limited Slip	3.55:1
D5	Limited Slip	4.10:1
F5	Limited Slip	4.10:1
H5	Limited Slip	4.10:1
H8	Limited Slip	3.08:1
H9	Limited Slip	3.55:1
W5	Limited Slip	4.00:1
12	Conventional	2.73:1
18	Conventional	3.08:1
19	Conventional	3.55:1
25	Conventional	4.10:1
29	Conventional	3.55:1
35	Conventional	4.10:1
39	Conventional	3.55:1
45	Conventional	4.10:1
49	Conventional	3.55:1
65	Conventional	4.10:1
69	Conventional	3.55:1
72	Conventional	4.63:1
73	Conventional	5.13:1
Explorer (Rear)		
D4	Limited Slip	3.73:1
41	Conventional	3.27:1
43	Conventional	3.08:1
45	Conventional	3.55:1

[1] – On front axles, when "2" is used as the third digit in axle code, front axle is limited slip design.

SAFETY CERTIFICATION LABEL AXLE CODE (Cont.)

Code	Type	Ratio
Ranger (Rear)		
F5	Limited Slip	3.55:1
F6	Limited Slip	3.73:1
F7	Limited Slip	4.10:1
82	Conventional	3.08:1
84	Conventional	3.45:1
85	Conventional	3.55:1
86	Conventional	3.73:1
87	Conventional	4.10:1
92	Conventional	3.08:1
95	Conventional	3.55:1
Van (Rear)		
B4	Limited Slip	3.73:1
C2	Limited Slip	4.10:1
C3	Limited Slip	3.54:1
E2	Limited Slip	4.10:1
F2	Limited Slip	4.10:1
H8	Limited Slip	3.08:1
H9	Limited Slip	3.08:1
12	Conventional	2.73:1
18	Conventional	3.08:1
19	Conventional	3.55:1
23	Conventional	3.54:1
24	Conventional	3.73:1
32	Conventional	4.10:1
33	Conventional	3.54:1
52	Conventional	4.10:1
53	Conventional	3.54:1
62	Conventional	4.10:1

Aerostar, Ranger

NOTE: The 7 1/2" ring gear differential is used in Ford integral rear axles only. For Aerostar front differential, see DANA 28-2 FRONT AXLE – AEROSTAR article. For Ranger front differential, see DANA IFS FRONT AXLE article.

DESCRIPTION & OPERATION

Rear axle is a hypoid design ring and pinion gear encased in an integral cast iron differential housing. The hypoid gear set contains a pinion supported by tapered roller bearings. Pinion bearing preload is maintained by a collapsible spacer on the pinion. Semi-floating axle shafts are retained by "C" locks at splined end of axle shafts.

On models equipped with Rear Anti-Lock Brake System (RABS), a multi-tooth exciter ring is pressed on differential case behind the ring gear. An electronic speed sensor is retained in a bore on top of differential housing.

AXLE RATIO & IDENTIFICATION

Metal identification tag stamped with date of manufacture, ratio, ring gear diameter and assembly plant coding is attached to rear cover on the housing. *See Fig. 1.* Use information to order replacement parts. Vehicle axle application can also be determined through axle code on Safety Certification Label located on driver's door pillar. See AXLE RATIO IDENTIFICATION article.

NOTE: If rear axle is a limited slip version, an "L" will be displayed with the ratio. For example, a limited slip axle ratio would be listed as 3L45.

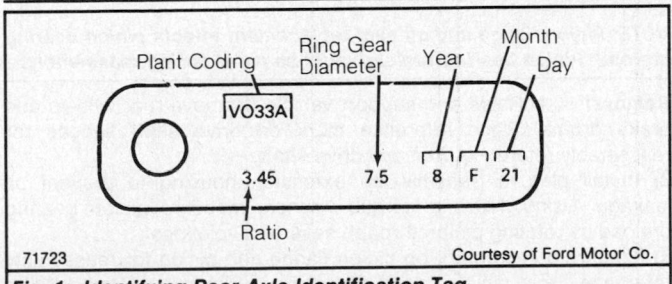

Fig. 1: Identifying Rear Axle Identification Tag

LUBRICATION

CAPACITY

REAR AXLE CAPACITY [1]

Application	Pts. (L)
Aerostar	3.5 (1.7)
Ranger	5.0 (2.4)

[1] – Approximate capacity is listed. Fill differential until fluid level is approximately 1/4" below bottom of filler plug hole.

FLUID TYPE

Use Hypoid Gear Lubricant (EQAZ-19580-AA).

CAUTION: On models with limited slip differential, additional 4 ounces of Friction Modifier (C8AZ-19B546-A) is required. Friction modifier must be added to prevent damage to differential.

TROUBLE SHOOTING

NOTE: See TROUBLE SHOOTING article in GENERAL INFORMATION.

REMOVAL & INSTALLATION

AXLE SHAFT & BEARING

Removal – 1) Raise and support vehicle. Remove wheel and brake drum. Remove housing cover and drain lubricant.
2) For all ratio axles except 3.73:1 and 4.10:1, remove differential pinion shaft lock bolt and pinion shaft. Push axle toward center, and remove "C" locks from splined end of axle shaft.

NOTE: Pinion gears may be left in place. When axle shafts are removed, reinstall pinion shaft and lock bolt to retain components in position.

3) On 3.73:1 and 4.10:1 ratio axles, remove pinion shaft lock bolt. Place hand behind differential case and push pinion shaft outward until step on pinion shaft contacts ring gear. Remove "C" locks from splined end of axle shaft.
4) On all ratio axles, carefully remove axle shaft, using care not to damage oil seal. Using slide hammer and Bearing Remover (T85L-1225-AH), remove wheel bearing and axle shaft seal as a unit from differential housing.
Installation – 1) Lubricate wheel bearing with rear axle lubricant. Using Bearing Installer (T78P-1225-A), install wheel bearing in differential housing. Lubricate lips of axle shaft seal with grease. Using Seal Installer (T78P-1177-A), install axle shaft seal. If seal becomes cocked during installation, remove and replace seal.

NOTE: On 3.73:1 and 4.10:1 ratio axles, ensure pinion shaft step contacts ring gear before installing axle shaft.

2) Install axle shaft, using care not to damage oil seal. Engage axle shaft with splines and push firmly inward.
3) Install "C" locks, and then pull axle shaft outward to seat "C" locks in counterbore of side gear. Install pinion shaft through differential case and pinion gears. Align pinion shaft hole with pinion shaft lock bolt hole.
4) Install and tighten pinion shaft lock bolt to specification. See TORQUE SPECIFICATIONS table at end of article.

NOTE: Aerostar models use a plastic housing cover. Housing cover and retaining bolts must be replaced. DO NOT reuse housing cover or retaining bolts. Ranger models use a metal housing cover and can be reused.

5) Ensure all sealing surfaces are clean. Apply a 3/16" diameter bead of silicone sealant on housing cover sealing surface, on inside area of bolt holes.
6) Install housing cover and retaining cover bolts. Use NEW retaining bolts on Aerostar models. Tighten retaining bolts to specification. See TORQUE SPECIFICATIONS table. Fill axle with lubricant and install filler plug. To install remaining components, reverse removal procedure.

DIFFERENTIAL HOUSING ASSEMBLY

Removal (Aerostar) – 1) Raise and support vehicle. Remove rear wheels. Ensure parking brake is released. From underneath vehicle, pull front cable for parking brake rearward approximately 2".
2) Carefully clamp cable behind crossmember, ensuring cable coating is not damaged. Remove parking brake cables from equalizer. Compress tabs on retainers and pull parking brake cables through rear crossmember.
3) Place jack stands on frame lift points or under rear bumper support brackets. Place reference mark on drive shaft flanges for reassembly reference. Remove drive shaft. Install plug in transmission extension housing to prevent oil leakage.
4) Disconnect brake line from junction on frame rail. Support differential housing assembly with jack. Disconnect shock absorber from low-

er control arm. Lower differential assembly until coil springs are fully extended with no pressure on coil spring.

5) Ensure no pressure exists on coil spring. Remove bolt and nut from upper and lower coil spring retainers. Remove coil spring, noting direction of installation for reassembly reference.

6) Note direction of upper and lower control arm-to-differential housing assembly bolt installation for reassembly reference. Raise differential housing assembly to normal operating height.

7) Remove differential housing assembly-to-lower control arm retaining bolt. Remove retaining bolt and separate upper control arm from differential housing assembly.

8) Place reference mark on bushing and cam adjuster for reassembly reference. *See Fig. 2.* Lower differential housing assembly and remove.

CAUTION: Ensure bushing and cam adjuster are marked for reassembly reference. Components must be installed in original location to obtain correct rear axle pinion angle.

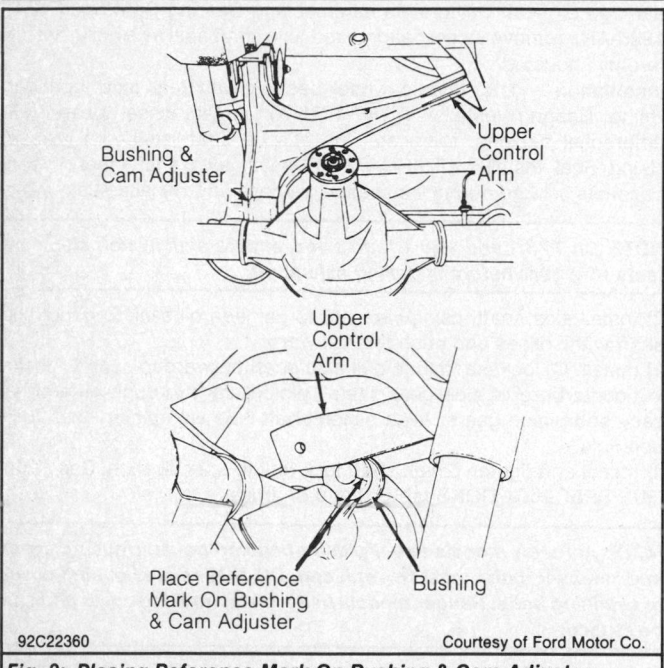

Bushing & Cam Adjuster

Upper Control Arm

Upper Control Arm

Place Reference Mark On Bushing & Cam Adjuster

Bushing

92C22360   Courtesy of Ford Motor Co.

Fig. 2: Placing Reference Mark On Bushing & Cam Adjuster

Installation – 1) Raise differential housing assembly so upper control arm fits over cam adjuster and bushing. Ensure reference mark on bushing and cam adjuster are still aligned. Install bolt, retainer and nut in upper control arm. Tighten bolt and nut until it is snug. DO NOT tighten to specification at this time.

2) Lower differential housing assembly for coil spring installation. Install lower insulator for coil spring on lower control arm. Install upper insulator on tapered coil (White colored end) of coil spring.

CAUTION: Coil spring must be installed with tapered coil (White colored end) toward the body.

---

3) Install coil spring. Install upper and lower coil spring retainers and tighten bolt/nut to specification. See TORQUE SPECIFICATIONS table at end of article.

4) Raise differential housing assembly to normal operating height. Install lower control arm-to-differential housing bolt. Tighten upper and lower control arm-to-differential housing bolts/nuts to specification. See TORQUE SPECIFICATIONS table.

CAUTION: Ensure bushing and cam adjuster mark are still aligned. Components must be in original location to obtain correct rear axle pinion angle. Upper and lower control arm-to-differential housing assembly bolts must be tightened to specification with differential housing assembly at normal operating height.

---

5) To install remaining components, reverse removal procedure. Apply Loctite to drive shaft flange bolt threads before installing. Ensure reference mark on drive shaft flanges are aligned. Tighten all bolts/nuts to specification. See TORQUE SPECIFICATIONS table. Bleed brake system.

Removal (Ranger) – 1) Manufacturer recommends removing brake backing plates so brake lines are not disconnected. Remove axle shaft. See AXLE SHAFT & BEARING under REMOVAL & INSTALLATION. Remove retaining nuts and brake backing plates.

2) Disconnect vent from differential housing assembly. Disengage brake lines from clips on differential housing assembly. Place reference mark on drive shaft flanges for reassembly reference. Remove drive shaft.

3) Install plug in transmission extension housing to prevent oil leakage. Support differential housing assembly with floor jack. Remove retaining nuts and disconnect shock absorbers from brackets on differential housing assembly.

4) Remove nuts, "U" bolts and plates. Lower floor jack and remove differential housing assembly.

Installation – 1) To install, reverse removal procedure. Apply thread sealant to vent before installing. Apply Loctite to drive shaft flange bolt threads before installing. Ensure reference mark on drive shaft flanges are aligned.

2) Before installing housing cover, ensure all sealing surfaces are clean. Apply a 3/16" diameter bead of silicone sealant on housing cover sealing surface on inside area of the bolt holes.

3) Install housing cover and retaining cover bolts. Tighten all bolts/nuts to specification. See TORQUE SPECIFICATIONS table at end of article.

PINION FLANGE & OIL SEAL

NOTE: Pinion flange and oil seal replacement affects pinion bearing preload. Pinion bearing preload must be reset during reassembly.

Removal – 1) Raise and support vehicle. Remove rear wheels and brake drums. Place reference mark on drive shaft flanges for reassembly reference. Remove drive shaft.

2) Install plug in transmission extension housing to prevent oil leakage. Using INCH lb. torque wrench, measure pinion bearing preload by rotating pinion through several revolutions.

3) Place reference mark on pinion flange and pinion for reassembly reference. Hold pinion flange and remove pinion nut. Using Puller (T77F-4220-B1), remove pinion flange.

4) Using screwdriver, pry metal area of oil seal upward. Grip metal area of oil seal and pull from differential housing.

Installation – 1) Ensure pinion splines are free of burrs. If necessary, remove burrs using fine crocus cloth. Lubricate area between lips of oil seal with grease. Using Oil Seal Installer (T79P-4676-A), install oil seal.

NOTE: If oil seal becomes cocked during installation, replace oil seal.

---

2) Lubricate pinion flange splines with oil. Install pinion flange on pinion with reference marks aligned.

CAUTION: DO NOT hammer pinion flange or use power tools to install pinion flange.

---

3) Install NEW pinion nut. DO NOT reuse pinion nut. Hold pinion flange and gradually tighten pinion nut. Rotate pinion while tightening pinion nut to ensure proper seating of the bearing.

4) Using INCH lb. torque wrench, measure pinion bearing preload at different stages when tightening pinion nut. Tighten pinion nut until original pinion bearing preload is obtained.

5) If original pinion bearing preload is less than 8-14 INCH lbs. (.9-1.6 N.m), tighten pinion nut to obtain correct pinion bearing preload. If original pinion bearing preload is greater than specification, tighten pinion nut to obtain the original bearing preload reading.

CAUTION: DO NOT back off pinion nut to reduce pinion rotating torque. If reduced pinion bearing preload is required, install a new collapsible spacer, and retighten pinion nut to obtain correct bearing preload.

6) To install remaining components, reverse removal procedure. Apply Loctite to drive shaft flange bolt threads before installing. Ensure reference mark on drive shaft flanges are aligned.

7) Tighten all bolts/nuts to specification. See TORQUE SPECIFICATIONS table at end of article. Fill axle with lubricant. Install and tighten filler plug.

DAMPER ASSEMBLY

Removal & Installation (Aerostar) – 1) Damper assembly is bolted on right side of differential housing assembly, near the pinion. Remove retaining bolts and damper assembly.

2) To install, reverse removal procedure using NEW retaining bolts. DO NOT reuse retaining bolts. Tighten retaining bolts to specification. See TORQUE SPECIFICATIONS table at end of article.

DIFFERENTIAL ASSEMBLY

Removal & Installation – Removal and installation of differential assembly is covered in overhaul procedure. See DIFFERENTIAL ASSEMBLY under OVERHAUL.

REAR ANTI-LOCK BRAKE SENSOR ASSEMBLY

Removal – Rear anti-lock brake sensor is located on top of differential housing assembly. Clean area around rear anti-lock brake sensor. Disconnect electrical connector. Remove retaining bolt, rear anti-lock brake sensor and "O" ring.

Installation – 1) Replace "O" ring if using original rear anti-lock brake sensor. Lubricate "O" ring with engine oil. Hold rear anti-lock brake sensor on both sides and install. DO NOT push downward on electrical connector area.

2) Install retaining bolt and tighten to specification. See TORQUE SPECIFICATIONS table at end of article. Install electrical connector.

RING GEAR & DIFFERENTIAL CASE RUNOUT CHECKING PROCEDURE

RING GEAR RUNOUT

NOTE: Check ring gear runout before disassembling differential assembly.

1) Assemble dial indicator on differential housing assembly with tip of dial indicator contacting back face of ring gear.

NOTE: A space is provided between exciter ring and ring gear for measuring ring gear runout.

2) Adjust dial indicator to zero. Rotate ring gear and note ring gear runout. Maximum ring gear runout is .004" (.10 mm). If ring gear runout exceeds .004" (.10 mm), check for improper tightening on ring gear bolts or foreign material between ring gear and differential case.

3) If ring gear runout still exceeds .004" (.10 mm), check for warped ring gear, worn differential bearings or warped differential case by checking differential case runout. See DIFFERENTIAL CASE RUNOUT.

DIFFERENTIAL CASE RUNOUT

1) Remove differential case from differential housing assembly. Remove retaining bolts and ring gear. Install differential case with bearing races and preload shims into differential housing assembly.

2) Install bearing caps in original location, Install and tighten bearing cap retaining bolts to specification. See TORQUE SPECIFICATIONS table at end of article. Rotate differential case to ensure bearings are properly seated.

3) Assemble dial indicator on differential housing assembly with tip of dial indicator contacting ring gear surface of differential case. Adjust dial indicator to zero.

4) Rotate differential case and note differential case runout. If differential case runout is within .003" (.08 mm), install a new ring gear and pinion.

5) If differential case runout exceeds .003" (.08 mm), ring gear is okay. The problem area is damaged differential housing assembly or worn bearings on differential case.

6) Visually check for damaged bearings. If bearings are okay, replace both bearings and differential case. Recheck differential case runout using new components.

7) If differential case is now within .003" (.08 mm), use the new bearings and components for reassembly. If differential case runout exceeds .003" (.08 mm), differential housing assembly is damaged and should be replaced.

OVERHAUL

DIFFERENTIAL ASSEMBLY

NOTE: Differential case and pinion may be serviced in the vehicle. Some models may be a limited slip axle. To service differential case and components on limited slip axles, see TRACTION-LOK 7 1/2" & 8 3/4" DIFFERENTIALS article in DRIVE AXLES.

Disassembly – 1) Raise and support vehicle. Remove axle shafts. See AXLE SHAFT & BEARING under REMOVAL & INSTALLATION.

2) Place reference mark on drive shaft flanges for reassembly reference. Remove drive shaft. Install plug in transmission extension housing to prevent oil leakage.

3) Check and record ring gear runout. See RING GEAR RUNOUT under RING GEAR & DIFFERENTIAL CASE RUNOUT CHECKING PROCEDURE. Place reference mark on bearing cap and differential housing assembly for reassembly reference.

CAUTION: Ensure bearing cap location is marked for reassembly reference. Bearing caps must be installed in original location. Arrow or triangle area between bolt holes on bearing cap must point away from ring gear (toward axle shaft end of housing).

4) Loosen bearing cap retaining bolts. Pry differential case, bearing races and preload shims until loose in bearing caps. *See Fig. 3.* Remove retaining bolts, bearing caps and differential case.

CAUTION: Mark bearing races and preload shim location for reassembly reference if components are to be reused. Components must be installed in original location. DO NOT damage rear anti-lock brake sensor when removing differential case.

5) Using puller, remove bearings from differential case (if replacement is required). If removing ring gear, place reference mark on differential case and ring gear for reassembly reference. Remove retaining bolts and tap ring gear from differential case.

NOTE: Exciter ring must be replaced if removed from differential case. DO NOT reuse exciter ring.

6) If removing exciter ring, use soft-faced hammer and tap exciter ring from differential case. Remove pinion shaft, side gears, thrust washer and pinion gears (if necessary). *See Fig. 3.*

7) Place reference mark on pinion flange and pinion for reassembly reference. Hold pinion flange and remove pinion nut. Using Puller (T77F-4220-B1), remove pinion flange.

8) Using soft-faced hammer, tap pinion out of front bearing assembly. Remove pinion from differential housing assembly. Using Oil Seal Remover (1175-AC and T50T-100A), remove pinion oil seal.

9) Remove front bearing assembly and collapsible spacer from differential housing assembly. *See Fig. 3.* If removing rear pinion bearing from pinion, use press and bearing Bearing Replacer (T71P-4621-B) to press bearing from pinion.

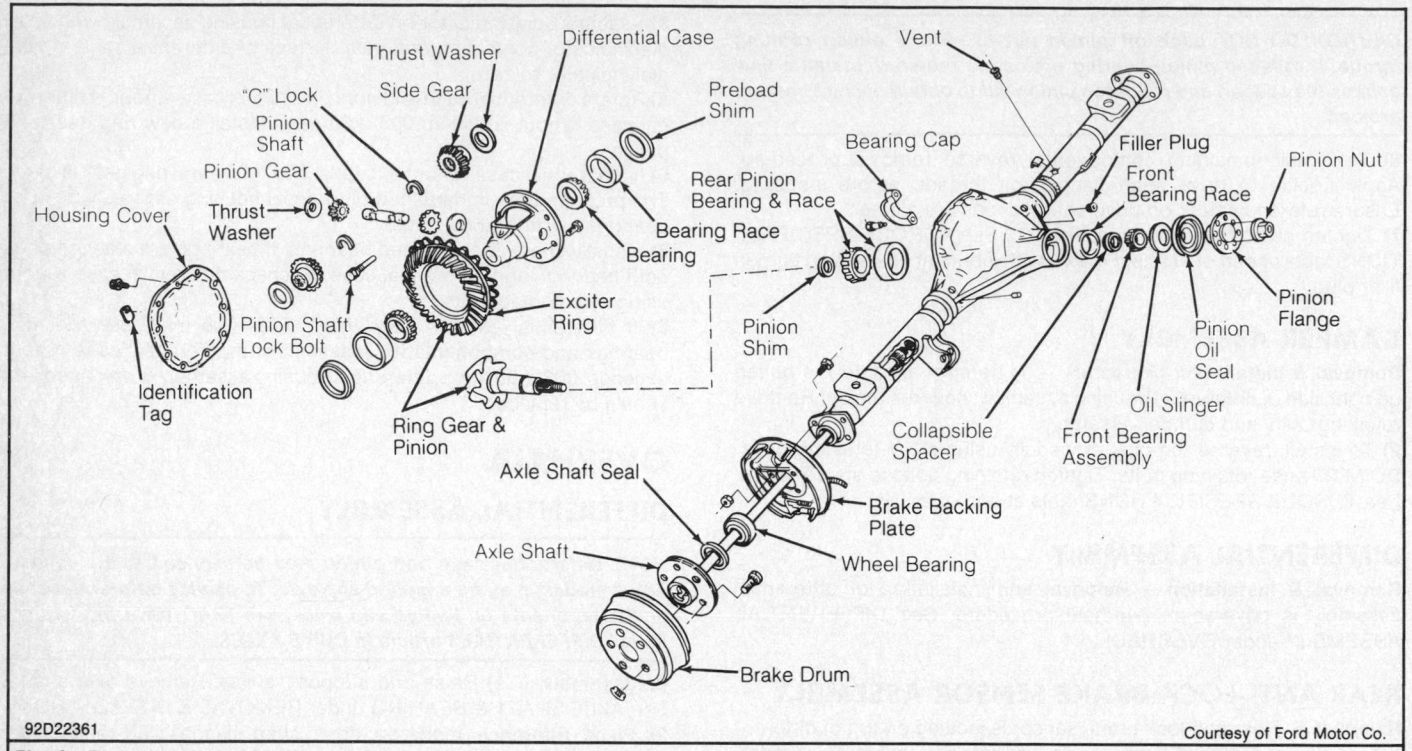

Fig. 3: Exploded View Of Differential Axle Housing & Components (Ranger Shown, Aerostar Is Similar)

10) Measure and record thickness of pinion shim located between pinion and rear pinion bearing for reassembly reference.

NOTE: DO NOT remove pinion bearing races from differential housing assembly unless replacement is required. Pinion bearings must also be replaced if bearing races are replaced.

Cleaning & Inspection – Clean components with solvent and dry with compressed air.thoroughly in cleaning solvent. Examine pinion and ring gear teeth for scoring, excessive wear and chipping. Check bearing races for deep scores or galling. Check all bearings for pitting and scoring. Replace damaged components.

NOTE: Replace ring gear and pinion as a matched sets.

Reassembly & Adjustments – **1)** To reassemble differential case, lubricate all components with rear axle lubricant. Install side gears, pinion gears and thrust washers in differential case.

NOTE: On 3.73:1 and 4.10:1 ratio axles, pinion shaft must be installed in differential case before installing ring gear. On all applications, exciter ring must be replaced if removed from differential case. DO NOT reuse exciter ring.

2) Install ring gear and NEW exciter ring (if removed) on differential case. Ensure reference mark on ring gear aligns with mark on differential case. Tab on exciter ring must align with slot on differential case. *See Fig. 4.* Start 2 ring gear retaining bolts into differential case.

CAUTION: Ensure tab on exciter ring aligns with slot on differential case.

---

3) Place differential case in press with ring gear facing downward. Press ring gear and exciter ring on differential case. Remove the 2 ring gear retaining bolts.
4) Apply Loctite to ring gear retaining bolt threads. Install and tighten ring gear retaining bolts to specification. See TORQUE SPECIFICATIONS table at end of article.
5) If replacing front or rear bearing races, install bearing races in differential housing assembly. To ensure bearing races are fully

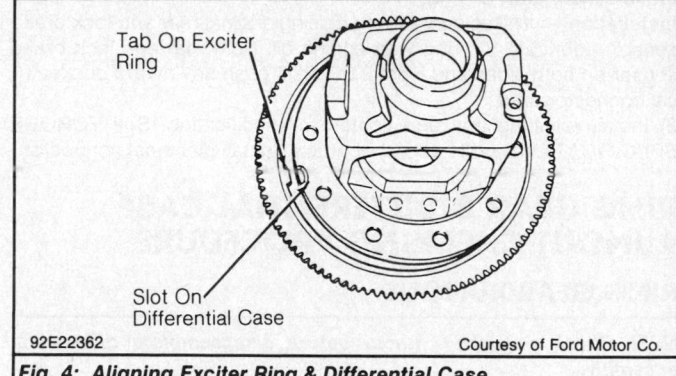

Fig. 4: Aligning Exciter Ring & Differential Case

seated, verify that a .0015" (.038 mm) feeler gauge will not fit between bearing race and bottom of bore.
6) Pinion depth, pinion bearing preload, differential bearing preload and ring gear backlash must be checked.
Pinion Depth – **1)** Pinion Depth Gauge Set (T79P-4020-A) is used for checking pinion depth. Assemble gauge block, gauge disc, aligning adapter and screw. *See Fig. 5.*
2) Place rear pinion bearing over aligning adapter and into bearing race of differential housing assembly. *See Fig. 5.* Install front pinion bearing into front bearing race.
3) Install handle onto screw and tighten to **20 ft. lbs. (27 N.m)**. Apply a light film of oil to pinion bearings. Rotate gauge block several times to seat bearings. Rotational torque on gauge block assembly with new bearings should be **20 INCH lbs. (2.25 N.m)**. Position gauge block at approximately 45-degree angle to axle shaft center line. *See Fig. 6.*
4) Thoroughly clean differential case bearing bores. Install gauge tube so it is centered in differential housing assembly. Install bearing caps in original location.

CAUTION: Ensure bearing caps are installed in original location. Arrow or triangle area between bolt holes on bearing cap must point away from ring gear (toward axle shaft end of housing).

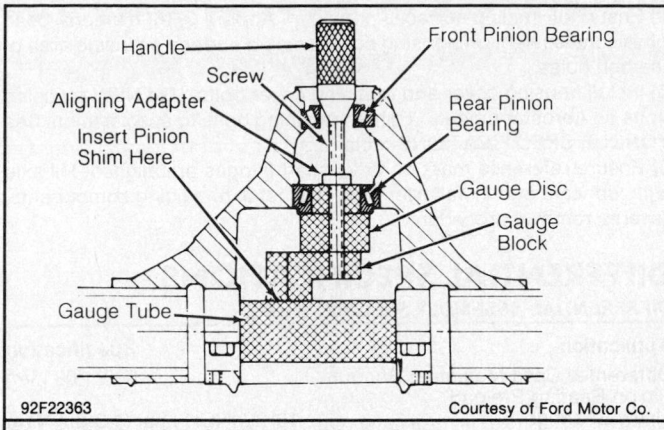

92F22363   Courtesy of Ford Motor Co.

Fig. 5: Assembling & Checking Pinion Depth

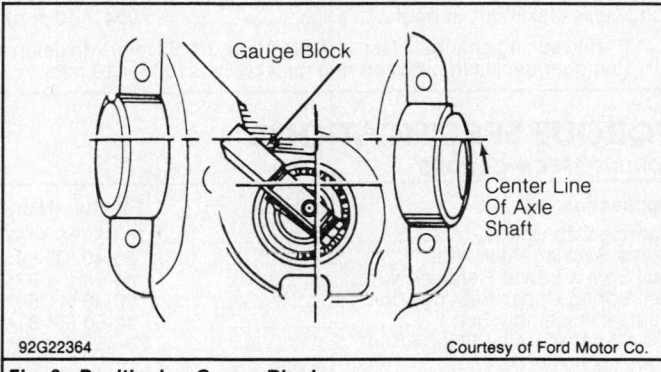

92G22364   Courtesy of Ford Motor Co.

Fig. 6: Positioning Gauge Block

5) Install bearing cap bolts and tighten to specification. See TORQUE SPECIFICATIONS table at end of article. Ensure pinion depth gauge set components are properly installed. *See Fig. 5.*

6) Hold pinion depth gauge and insert a pinion shim as a gauge for shim selection, between gauge block and gauge tube. Ensure pinion shim is clean and flat.

NOTE: DO NOT force pinion shim between gauge block and gauge tube. A slight drag should be felt if correct thickness pinion shim is selected.

7) If pinion has a plus (+) marking on head of pinion, subtract this amount from measured clearance. If pinion has a minus (–) marking, add this amount to measured clearance.

8) Correct pinion shim selection is accomplished when a slight drag is felt as shim is drawn between gauge block and gauge tube. Remove pinion depth gauge set components.

Pinion Bearing Preload – 1) Place pre-selected pinion shim on the pinion. Press rear pinion bearing on pinion. Ensure bearing and pinion shim are firmly seated against shoulder of pinion shaft.

2) Install NEW collapsible spacer on pinion. Lubricate bearings with axle lubricant. Install front pinion bearing and oil slinger (if equipped) in differential housing assembly.

3) Using Oil Seal Installer (T79P-4676-A), install new pinion oil seal. Lubricate lips of pinion oil seal with grease. From rear of differential housing assembly, install pinion into front pinion bearing.

4) Lubricate pinion flange splines with oil. Install pinion flange on pinion with reference marks aligned.

CAUTION: DO NOT hammer pinion flange or use power tools to install pinion flange.

5) Install NEW pinion nut. DO NOT reuse pinion nut. Hold pinion flange and gradually tighten pinion nut. Rotate pinion while tightening pinion nut to ensure proper seating of the bearing.

6) Using INCH lb. torque wrench, measure pinion bearing preload at different stages when tightening pinion nut. Tighten pinion nut to obtain correct bearing preload. See DIFFERENTIAL ASSEMBLY SPECIFICATIONS table under DIFFERENTIAL SPECIFICATIONS at end of article.

7) If bearing preload is exceeded, replace collapsible spacer, install new pinion nut, and repeat procedures. DO NOT exceed pinion nut torque specification. See TORQUE SPECIFICATIONS table at end of article.

CAUTION: DO NOT back off pinion nut to reduce pinion rotating torque. If reduced pinion bearing preload is required, install a new collapsible spacer, and retighten pinion nut to obtain correct bearing preload.

Differential Bearing Preload & Ring Gear Backlash – 1) With pinion depth set and pinion installed, place differential case and ring gear assembly with bearings and races into differential housing assembly.

2) Install a .265" (6.73 mm) preload shim on left (ring gear side) side of differential case. Install left bearing cap, and tighten retaining bolts finger tight.

CAUTION: Ensure bearing caps are installed in original location. Arrow or triangle area between bolt holes on bearing cap must point away from ring gear (toward axle shaft end of housing).

3) Apply pressure on left (ring gear) side of differential case to ensure bearing is fully seated in bearing race. Select largest preload shim which will fit with on the right (pinion) side. Preload shim should fit with a slight drag.

4) Install preload shim on right (pinion) side of differential case. Install right bearing cap. Arrow or triangle area between bolt holes on bearing cap must point away from ring gear (toward axle shaft end of housing). Install and tighten all bearing cap bolts to specification. See TORQUE SPECIFICATIONS table at end of article.

5) Ensure differential case rotates smoothly. Using dial indicator, hold pinion and measure ring gear backlash. *See Fig. 7.* Ring gear backlash may be adjusted if not within .008-.015" (.20-.38 mm).

6) If no ring gear backlash exists, remove .020" (.51 mm) from left (ring gear) side and add to the right (pinion) side. If ring gear backlash is not within specification, note direction that differential case must be moved for backlash adjustment. *See Fig. 8.*

7) Ring gear backlash can be changed by increasing thickness of one preload shim and decreasing thickness on the other preload shim the same amount. Changing preload shim thickness will change ring gear backlash a designated amount. See BACKLASH-TO-SHIM THICKNESS CONVERSION table.

BACKLASH-TO-SHIM THICKNESS CONVERSION

Required Change In Backlash In. (mm)	Change In Shim Thickness In. (mm)
.001 (.03)	.002 (.05)
.002 (.05)	.002 (.05)
.003 (.08)	.004 (.10)
.004 (.10)	.006 (.15)
.005 (.13)	.006 (.15)
.006 (.15)	.008 (.20)
.007 (.18)	.010 (.25)
.008 (.20)	.010 (.25)
.009 (.23)	.012 (.30)
.010 (.25)	.014 (.35)
.011 (.28)	.014 (.35)
.012 (.30)	.016 (.41)
.013 (.33)	.018 (.46)
.014 (.35)	.018 (.46)
.015 (.38)	.020 (.51)

8) Install proper preload shim. Tighten bearing cap bolts to specification. Rotate ring gear assembly several times. Recheck and correct ring gear backlash as necessary.

9) Once correct ring gear backlash is obtained, remove bearing caps and preload shims. Increase both left and right preload shim thickness .006" (.15 mm), and reinstall to obtain correct bearing preload. Install bearing caps and tighten bolts to specification. See TORQUE SPECIFICATIONS table.

10) Using white marking compound, check gear tooth contact pattern. See GEAR TOOTH CONTACT PATTERNS article in GENERAL INFORMATION.

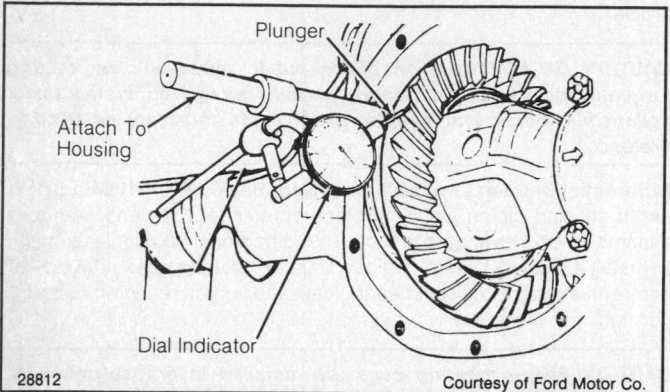

Fig. 7: **Measuring Ring Gear Backlash**

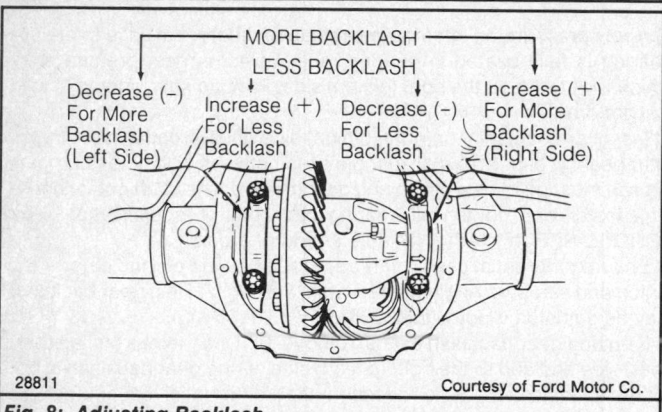

Fig. 8: **Adjusting Backlash**

Final Assembly – 1) Install axle shaft, using care not to damage oil seal. Engage axle shaft with splines and push firmly inward.

2) Install "C" locks, and then pull axle shaft outward to seat "C" locks in counterbore of side gear. Install pinion shaft through differential case and pinion gears. Align pinion shaft hole with pinion shaft lock bolt hole.

3) Install and tighten pinion shaft lock bolt to specification. See TORQUE SPECIFICATIONS table.

NOTE: *Aerostar uses a plastic housing cover. Housing cover and retaining bolts must be replaced. DO NOT reuse housing cover or retaining bolts. Ranger uses a metal housing cover and can be reused.*

4) Ensure all sealing surfaces are clean. Apply a 3/16" diameter bead of silicone sealant on housing cover sealing surface on inside area of the bolt holes.

5) Install housing cover and retaining cover bolts. Use NEW retaining bolts on Aerostar models. Tighten retaining bolts to specification. See TORQUE SPECIFICATIONS table.

6) Ensure reference mark on drive shaft flanges are aligned. Fill axle with lubricant and install filler plug. To install remaining components, reverse removal procedure.

DIFFERENTIAL SPECIFICATIONS
DIFFERENTIAL ASSEMBLY SPECIFICATIONS

Application	Specification
Differential Case Maximum Runout	.003" (.08 mm)
Pinion Bearing Preload	
New Bearings	16-29 INCH Lbs. (1.8-3.2 N.m)
Used Bearings	8-14 INCH Lbs. (.9-1.6 N.m)
Ring Gear Backlash	[1] .008-.015" (.20-.38 mm)
Ring Gear Maximum Runout	.004" (.10 mm)

[1] – Preferred ring gear backlash is .012-.015" (.30-.38 mm). Maximum ring gear backlash between ring gear teeth is .004" (.10 mm).

TORQUE SPECIFICATIONS
TORQUE SPECIFICATIONS

Application	Ft. Lbs. (N.m)
Bearing Cap Bolt	70-85 (95-115)
Brake Backing Plate Nut	20-40 (27-54)
Coil Spring Lower Retainer Nut	41-64 (56-87)
Coil Spring Upper Retainer Bolt	30-40 (41-54)
Damper Assembly Bolt [1]	40-60 (54-81)
Drive Shaft-To-Axle Flange Bolt	70-95 (95-129)
Housing Cover Bolt	
Aerostar [1]	15-20 (20-27)
Ranger	25-35 (34-47)
Lower Control Arm-To-Differential Housing	
Assembly Bolt [2]	95-130 (129-176)
Pinion Nut	170 (230)
Pinion Shaft Lock Bolt	15-30 (20-41)
Rear Anti-Lock Brake Sensor Bolt	25-30 (34-41)
Ring Gear Bolt [3]	70-85 (95-115)
Shock Absorber-To-Lower Control	
Arm Bolt/Nut	40-60 (54-81)
"U" Bolt	55-75 (75-102)
Upper Control Arm-To-Differential Housing	
Assembly Bolt [2]	155-210 (210-286)
Wheel Lug Nut	85-115 (115-156)

[1] – Use NEW bolt. DO NOT reuse bolt.
[2] – Tighten to specification with vehicle at normal ride height.
[3] – Apply Loctite to bolt threads.

Aerostar, Bronco, Explorer, Pickup, Ranger, Van

NOTE: Unless otherwise specified, references to Pickup include the F350 Super Duty commercial chassis.

MODEL IDENTIFICATION

Series [1]	Model
"A"	Aerostar
"E"	RWD Van
"F"	Pickup
"R"	Ranger
"U"	Bronco & Explorer

[1] – Vehicle series is fifth character of VIN.

DESCRIPTION

Rear axle is a hypoid-design ring and pinion gear encased in an integral cast iron axle housing. A one-piece differential case contains a conventional 2-pinion differential assembly.

To signal rear anti-lock brake system operation, rear axles use an exciter ring pressed on the differential case behind the ring gear, and a sensor mounted in axle housing. A space is provided between ring gear and exciter ring for measuring ring gear runout.

Aerostar, Bronco, Explorer, Ranger, E150 and F150 are equipped with 8 3/4 ring gear differential. The F250 Heavy Duty (HD) and F350 with full-floating axles, and the F250 with semi-floating axles are equipped with 10 3/4 ring gear differential. On all models except Aerostar, rear axle housing is equipped with leaf springs. On Aerostar, rear axle housing is equipped with coil springs.

AXLE RATIO & IDENTIFICATION

A metal tag stamped with axle model, date of manufacture, ratio, ring gear diameter and assembly plant is attached to rear cover. Use information on tag to order replacement parts. *See Fig. 1.* Vehicle axle application can also be determined by axle code on the Safety Certification Label located on left door pillar. See AXLE RATIO IDENTIFICATION article.

LUBRICATION

CAPACITY

REAR AXLE CAPACITY [1]

Application	Pts. (L)
Aerostar & Ranger	5.0 (2.4)
Bronco, Explorer, E150 & F150	5.5 (2.6)
All Others	6.5 (3.0)

[1] – Approximate capacity is listed. Fill differential until fluid level is approximately 1/4" below bottom of filler plug hole.

FLUID TYPE

Use Hypoid Gear Lubricant (EQAZ-19580-AA) for differentials.

CAUTION: On models with limited slip differential, add an additional 4 ozs. of Friction Modifier (C8AZ-19B546-A). Friction modifier must be added to prevent damage to differential.

TROUBLE SHOOTING

See TROUBLE SHOOTING article in GENERAL INFORMATION.

REMOVAL & INSTALLATION

AXLE SHAFT & BEARING

Removal (Semi-Floating) – **1)** Raise and support vehicle. Remove wheel assembly and brake drum. Remove housing cover, and drain lubricant.

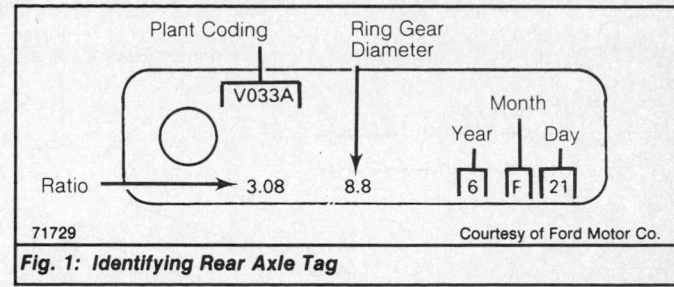

Fig. 1: Identifying Rear Axle Tag

71729   Courtesy of Ford Motor Co.

2) Remove differential pinion shaft lock bolt and remove pinion shaft. *See Fig. 2.* Push axle shaft inward and remove "C" locks.

CAUTION: DO NOT damage "O" ring in axle shaft groove under "C" lock.

3) Remove axle shaft, being careful not to cut axle seal. Using a slide hammer and puller, remove bearing and oil seal as a unit.

NOTE: Aerostar and Explorer models use a plastic housing cover. Housing cover and retaining bolts must be replaced. DO NOT reuse housing cover or retaining bolts. All other models use a metal housing cover and can be reused. No gasket, other than silicone sealant, is used. Housing cover must be installed within 15 minutes of sealant application.

Installation – **1)** Lubricate bearing with rear axle lubricant and install bearing with a driver. Install oil seal. If seal becomes cocked during installation, remove seal and replace with a new one.
2) Carefully insert axle in housing to avoid damaging oil seal. Install "C" locks, and push shafts outward to seat locks in counterbore of differential side gears.
3) Replace pinion gears and thrust washers (if removed). Turn gear assembly to align pinion gear and thrust washer bores with pinion shaft holes on case. Install pinion shaft. Apply Loctite to lock bolt and tighten to specification. See TORQUE SPECIFICATIONS table at end of article.
4) Clean gasket mating surfaces and apply 1/8 - 3/16" wide bead of silicone sealant on axle housing cover. Install housing cover. Tighten cover bolts to specification in a crisscross pattern. See TORQUE SPECIFICATIONS table at end of article. Fill differential until fluid level is approximately 1/4" below bottom of filler plug hole.

Removal (Full-Floating) – **1)** Set parking brake and loosen 8 axle shaft bolts. Raise vehicle, keeping axle parallel to floor. Release parking brake.
2) Remove wheel assembly and brake drum (back off rear brake adjustment if necessary). *See Fig. 3.* Discard push-on drum retainer nuts. Remove axle shaft bolts and remove axle shaft.

NOTE: Left-side hub nut has left-hand threads. Right-side hub nut has right-hand threads. Hub nut is stamped with RH for right side, or LH for left side.

3) Install Hub Wrench (T85T-4252-AH) so drive tangs engage 4 slots in hub nut. Remove hub nut. Hub nut will ratchet during removal.
4) Install Step Plate Adapter (D80L-630-7) onto spindle. Install Hub Puller (D80L-1002-L) onto hub assembly. Loosen hub to point of removal. Remove puller and step plate. Remove hub assembly.
5) Place hub in soft-jawed vise. Remove hub oil seal and inner bearing. Reposition hub in vise and remove inner and outer bearing race with brass drift.

Installation – **1)** While holding Driver Handle (T80T-4000-W) and Bearing Race Replacer (T75T-1225-A) straight, install outer and inner bearing races. Pack inner bearing with lithium-based lubricant and place into inner race.
2) Install oil seal using Hub Oil Seal Installer (T85T-1175-AH), ensuring Ford logo on seal faces up. Strike tool handle until oil seal seats fully. Coat inner diameter of oil seal lip with axle lubricant.

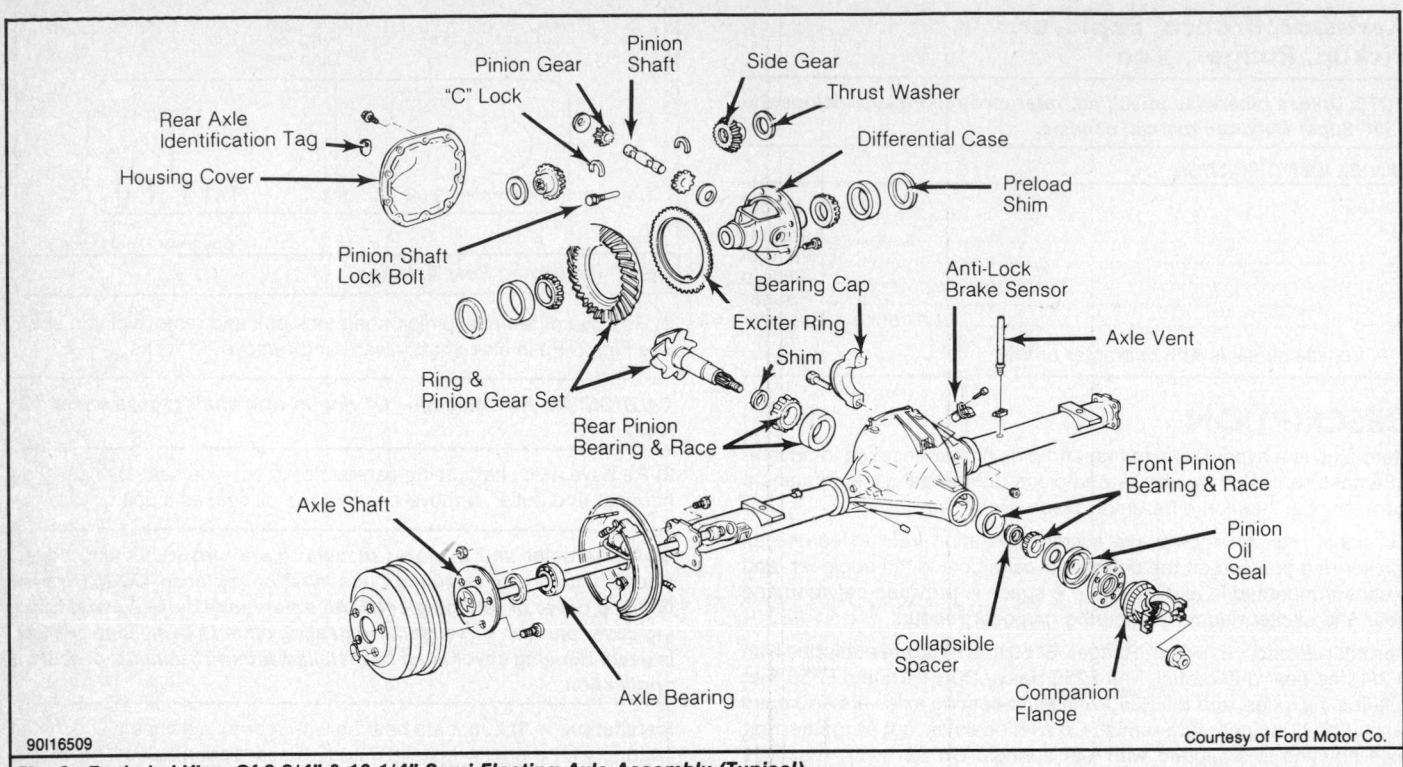

Rear Axle Identification Tag
Housing Cover
"C" Lock
Pinion Gear
Pinion Shaft
Side Gear
Thrust Washer
Differential Case
Preload Shim
Pinion Shaft Lock Bolt
Bearing Cap
Anti-Lock Brake Sensor
Axle Vent
Ring & Pinion Gear Set
Exciter Ring
Shim
Rear Pinion Bearing & Race
Front Pinion Bearing & Race
Pinion Oil Seal
Axle Shaft
Axle Bearing
Collapsible Spacer
Companion Flange

90I16509

Courtesy of Ford Motor Co.

Fig. 2: Exploded View Of 8 3/4" & 10 1/4" Semi-Floating Axle Assembly (Typical)

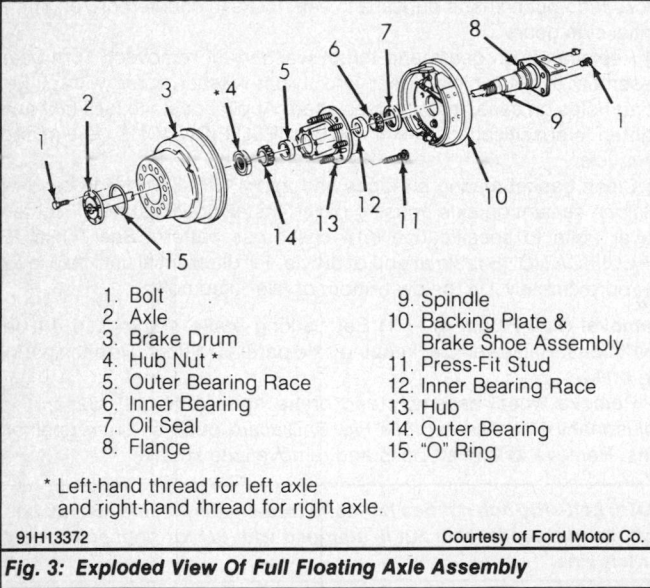

1. Bolt
2. Axle
3. Brake Drum
4. Hub Nut *
5. Outer Bearing Race
6. Inner Bearing
7. Oil Seal
8. Flange
9. Spindle
10. Backing Plate & Brake Shoe Assembly
11. Press-Fit Stud
12. Inner Bearing Race
13. Hub
14. Outer Bearing
15. "O" Ring

* Left-hand thread for left axle and right-hand thread for right axle.

91H13372

Courtesy of Ford Motor Co.

Fig. 3: Exploded View Of Full Floating Axle Assembly

3) Clean spindle and coat with axle lubricant. Pack outer bearing with lithium-based lubricant. Push hub onto spindle. Install outer bearing into hub. Install hub nut on spindle.

CAUTION: Ensure hub nut tab is located in spindle keyway before thread engagement.

4) Install Hub Wrench (T85T-4252-AH) onto hub nut. Tighten hub nut to 55-65 ft. lbs. (75-88 N.m). After tightening to specification, ratchet back 5 clicks on hub nut. Clicking will be heard if procedure is performed correctly.
5) Check axle shaft "O" ring and replace if necessary. Install axle shaft. Coat axle shaft bolt threads with Loctite. Install axle shaft bolts until seated, but DO NOT tighten.

6) Install brake drum and wheel assembly. Check lubricant level and add if necessary. Tighten wheel lug nuts and adjust brakes (if necessary). Lower vehicle and tighten axle shaft bolts to specification. See TORQUE SPECIFICATIONS table at end of article.

AXLE HOUSING ASSEMBLY
Removal (Aerostar) – 1) Raise and support vehicle. Ensure parking brake is released. Remove rear wheels and brake drums. From underneath vehicle, pull front cable for parking brake rearward approximately 2".
2) Carefully clamp cable behind crossmember, ensuring cable coating is not damaged. Remove parking brake cables from equalizer. Compress tabs on retainers; pull cables through rear crossmember.
3) Place jack stands on frame lift points or under rear bumper support brackets. Place reference mark on drive shaft flanges for reassembly reference. Remove drive shaft. Install plug in transmission extension housing to prevent oil leakage.
4) Disconnect hydraulic brake lines. Support axle housing with floor jack. Disconnect shock absorbers from lower control arms. Lower axle housing until coil springs are no longer under compression. Remove lower coil spring retainer first, then remove upper retainer. Remove coil springs and spring insulators.
5) Raise axle housing to normal load position. Note axle housing-to-lower control arm bolt position for installation reference. Remove lower control arms.
6) Remove upper control arm-to-axle housing bolt. Remove upper control arm from axle housing. Mark cam adjuster-to-axle housing bushing position for installation reference. *See Fig. 4.* Lower axle housing and remove from vehicle.

CAUTION: Upper control arm bushing is an eccentric-type bushing which, depending on its position, controls drive pinion angle. When removing upper control arm, ALWAYS mark cam adjuster-to-axle housing bushing position for installation reference. Nominal position (zero degree) of drive pinion angle is with axle housing bushing notch at 6 o'clock position. See Fig. 4.

1992 DRIVE AXLES
8 3/4" & 10 1/4" Ring Gear Differentials (Cont.)

FORD
7-11

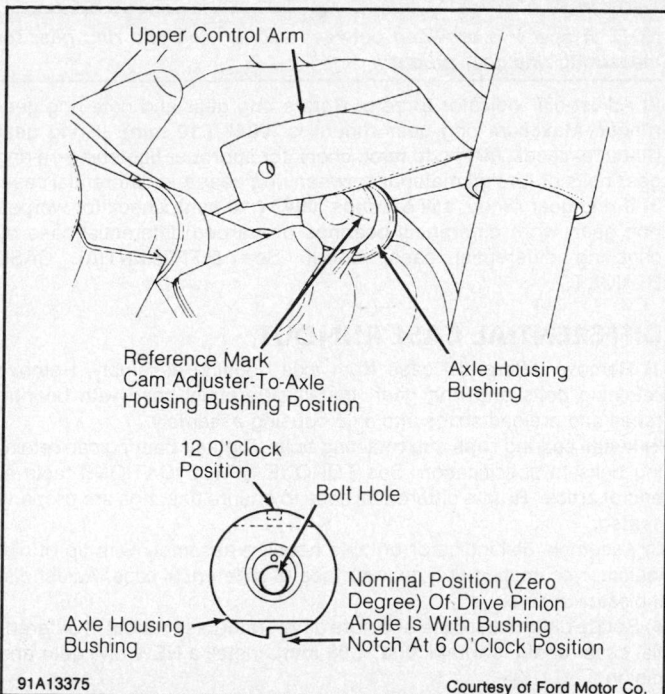

Upper Control Arm

Reference Mark
Cam Adjuster-To-Axle
Housing Bushing Position

Axle Housing
Bushing

12 O'Clock
Position

Bolt Hole

Axle Housing
Bushing

Nominal Position (Zero
Degree) Of Drive Pinion
Angle Is With Bushing
Notch At 6 O'Clock Position

91A13375 · Courtesy of Ford Motor Co.

Fig. 4: Referencing Cam Adjuster To Axle Housing Bushing

Installation – 1) Raise axle housing assembly so upper control arm fits over cam adjuster and bushing. Ensure reference mark on bushing and cam adjuster are still aligned. Install bolt and nut in upper control arm. Tighten bolt and nut until snug. DO NOT tighten to specification at this time.

2) Lower axle housing assembly for coil spring installation. Install lower insulator for coil spring on lower control arm. Install upper insulator on tapered coil (White colored end) of coil spring.

CAUTION: Coil spring must be installed with tapered coil (White colored end) toward vehicle body.

---

3) Install coil spring. Install upper and lower coil spring retainers and tighten nut to specification. See TORQUE SPECIFICATIONS table at end of article.

4) Raise axle housing assembly to normal load position. Install lower control arm-to-axle housing bolt. Tighten upper and lower control arm-to-axle housing bolts to specification. See TORQUE SPECIFICATIONS table at end of article.

CAUTION: Ensure bushing and cam adjuster mark are still aligned. Components must be in original location to obtain correct rear axle pinion angle. Upper and lower control arm-to-axle housing assembly bolts must be tightened to specification with axle housing assembly at normal operating height.

---

5) To install remaining components, reverse removal procedure. Apply Loctite to drive shaft flange bolt threads before installing. Ensure reference mark on drive shaft flanges are aligned. Tighten all bolts/nuts to specification. See TORQUE SPECIFICATIONS table at end of article. Bleed brake system. Fill differential until fluid level is approximately 1/4" below bottom of filler plug hole.

Removal (Explorer) – 1) Raise and support vehicle. Remove wheel assembly and brake drum. Manufacturer recommends removing brake backing plates so brake lines are not disconnected. Remove axle shaft. See AXLE SHAFT & BEARING under REMOVAL & INSTALLATION. Remove retaining nuts and brake backing plates.

2) Disconnect vent hose from axle housing. Disengage brake lines from clips on axle housing. Remove hydraulic brake junction block from axle housing. DO NOT disconnect brake lines from block. Place

reference mark on drive shaft flanges for reassembly reference. Remove drive shaft. Install plug in transmission extension housing to prevent oil leakage.

3) Support axle housing with transmission jack. Remove nuts, "U" bolts and shock absorber mounting plates. Remove stabilizer bar bracket bolts from axle housing. Position stabilizer bar away from axle housing. Raise axle housing off leaf spring toward right side of vehicle. Lower left side of axle housing below leaf spring Remove axle housing from vehicle.

Installation – 1) To install, reverse removal procedure. Apply Loctite to drive shaft flange bolt threads before installing. Ensure reference mark on drive shaft flanges are aligned. Apply thread sealant to brake junction block bolt prior to installation. Tighten all bolts and nuts to specification.

2) Clean gasket mating surfaces and apply 1/8 - 3/16" wide bead of silicone sealant on axle housing cover. Install NEW housing cover. Tighten NEW cover bolts to specification in a crisscross pattern. See TORQUE SPECIFICATIONS table at end of article. Fill differential until fluid level is approximately 1/4" below bottom of filler plug hole.

NOTE: Explorer models use a plastic housing cover. Housing cover and retaining bolts must be replaced. DO NOT reuse housing cover or retaining bolts. No gasket, other than silicone sealant, is used. Housing cover must be installed within 15 minutes of sealant application.

Removal (Bronco, Pickup, Ranger & Van) – 1) Raise and support vehicle. Remove wheel assembly and brake drum. Manufacturer recommends removing brake backing plates so brake lines are not disconnected. Remove axle shaft. See AXLE SHAFT & BEARING under REMOVAL & INSTALLATION. Remove retaining nuts and brake backing plates.

2) Disconnect vent hose from axle housing. Disengage brake lines from clips on axle housing. Remove hydraulic brake junction block from axle housing. DO NOT disconnect brake lines from block. Place reference mark on drive shaft flanges for reassembly reference. Remove drive shaft. Install plug in transmission extension housing to prevent oil leakage.

3) Support axle housing with floor jack. Remove retaining nuts and disconnect shock absorbers from plates on axle housing. Remove nuts, "U" bolts and plates. Lower floor jack and remove axle housing.

Installation – 1) To install, reverse removal procedure. Apply thread sealant to brake junction block bolt prior to installation. Connect vent hose to axle housing. Apply Loctite to drive shaft flange bolt threads before installing. Ensure reference mark on drive shaft flanges are aligned.

2) Before installing housing cover, ensure all sealing surfaces are clean. Apply a 3/16" diameter bead of silicone sealant on housing cover sealing surface on inside area of bolt holes. Install housing cover and retaining cover bolts. Tighten all bolts and nuts to specification. See TORQUE SPECIFICATIONS table at end of article. Fill differential until fluid level is approximately 1/4" below bottom of filler plug hole.

Removal (All Others) – 1) Loosen wheel lug nuts and axle shaft retaining bolts. Disconnect shock absorbers from axle housing. Disconnect stabilizer bar mounts. Raise vehicle until weight is off rear springs.

2) Disconnect hydraulic brake hose. Remove axle housing vent hose and brake junction block. Remove parking brake cable from cable support and brackets. Mark drive shaft for installation reference. Disconnect rear "U" joint and remove drive shaft. Install plug in transmission extension housing to prevent oil leakage.

3) Disconnect anti-lock wiring from axle sensor and height sensing linkage (if equipped). Support axle housing assembly with floor jack. Remove spring "U" bolt nuts and remove "U" bolts. Carefully lower axle housing from vehicle. Roll axle housing out from vehicle. Drain lubricant. Remove wheels and mount axle housing on workbench.

Installation – To install, reverse removal procedure. Apply locking compound to threads holding axle housing brake junction block to axle housing. Adjust parking brake. Bleed brakes. Fill differential until fluid level is approximately 1/4" below bottom of filler plug hole.

FORD
7-12

1992 DRIVE AXLES
8 3/4" & 10 1/4" Ring Gear Differentials (Cont.)

PINION FLANGE & OIL SEAL

NOTE: Pinion flange and oil seal replacement affects bearing preload. Preload must be carefully reset during reassembly.

Removal – 1) Raise and support vehicle. Scribe alignment marks on companion flange and drive shaft end yoke for installation reference. Remove drive shaft.

2) Install plug in transmission extension housing to prevent oil leakage. Using an INCH lb. torque wrench, measure and record torque required to rotate pinion through several revolutions.

3) Mark companion flange or end yoke in relation to pinion shaft for installation reference. Hold companion flange or end yoke and remove pinion nut. Using Puller (T77FP-4220-B1), remove companion flange. Using screwdriver, remove pinion seal.

Installation – 1) Ensure pinion shaft splines are free of burrs. Remove burrs with fine crocus cloth if necessary. Lubricate area between oil seal lip, and install oil seal into axle housing using Pinion Oil Seal Replacer (T83T-4676-A).

NOTE: If oil seal becomes cocked during installation, remove seal and install new oil seal.

2) Align marks on companion flange and pinion. Apply a small amount of lubricant to companion flange splines. Install companion flange and NEW pinion nut. Hold companion flange or end yoke, and gradually tighten nut while rotating pinion.

3) Check pinion bearing preload often, until correct preload is obtained. DO NOT back off pinion nut to reduce preload. See DIFFERENTIAL ASSEMBLY SPECIFICATIONS table under DIFFERENTIAL SPECIFICATIONS at end of article.

NOTE: If desired preload is exceeded, a new collapsible spacer must be installed. Tighten nut to obtain proper preload.

4) Remove plug from transmission extension housing. Install front end of drive shaft on transmission output shaft. Connect rear end of drive shaft to companion flange, aligning scribed marks.

5) Apply locking compound to drive shaft bolt threads and tighten bolts to specification. See TORQUE SPECIFICATIONS table at end of article. Fill differential until fluid level is approximately 1/4" below bottom of filler plug hole.

DIFFERENTIAL ASSEMBLY

Removal & Installation – Removal and installation procedure is included in overhaul procedure. See DIFFERENTIAL ASSEMBLY under OVERHAUL.

REAR ANTI-LOCK BRAKE SENSOR ASSEMBLY

Removal – Rear anti-lock brake sensor is located on top of axle housing assembly. Clean area around rear anti-lock brake sensor. Disconnect electrical connector. Remove retaining bolt, rear anti-lock brake sensor and "O" ring.

Installation – Replace "O" ring if using original rear anti-lock brake sensor. Lubricate "O" ring with engine oil. Hold rear anti-lock brake sensor on both sides and install. DO NOT push downward on electrical connector area. Install retaining bolt and tighten to specification. See TORQUE SPECIFICATIONS table at end of article. Install electrical connector.

RING GEAR & DIFFERENTIAL CASE RUNOUT CHECKING PROCEDURE

RING GEAR RUNOUT

NOTE: Ring gear runout should be checked before disassembling differential assembly.

1) Assemble dial indicator on axle housing assembly with tip of dial indicator contacting back face of ring gear.

NOTE: A space is provided between exciter ring and ring gear for measuring ring gear runout.

2) Adjust dial indicator to zero. Rotate ring gear and note ring gear runout. Maximum ring gear runout is .004" (.10 mm). If ring gear runout exceeds .004" (.10 mm), check for improper tightening on ring gear bolts or foreign material between ring gear and differential case.

3) If ring gear runout still exceeds .004" (.10 mm), check for warped ring gear, worn differential bearings or warped differential case by checking differential case runout. See DIFFERENTIAL CASE RUNOUT.

DIFFERENTIAL CASE RUNOUT

1) Remove differential case from axle housing assembly. Remove retaining bolts and ring gear. Install differential case with bearing races and preload shims into axle housing assembly.

2) Install bearing caps and retaining bolts. Tighten bearing cap retaining bolts to specification. See TORQUE SPECIFICATIONS table at end of article. Rotate differential case to ensure bearings are properly seated.

3) Assemble dial indicator on axle housing assembly with tip of dial indicator contacting ring gear surface of differential case. Adjust dial indicator to zero.

4) Rotate differential case and note differential case runout. If differential case runout is within .003" (.08 mm), install a NEW ring gear and pinion.

5) If differential case runout exceeds .003" (.08 mm), ring gear is okay. The problem area is damaged axle housing assembly or worn bearings on differential case.

6) Visually check for damaged bearings. If bearings are okay, replace both bearings and differential case. Recheck differential case runout using NEW components.

7) If differential case is now within .003" (.08 mm), use components for reassembly. If differential case runout exceeds .003" (.08 mm), axle housing assembly is damaged and should be replaced.

OVERHAUL

DIFFERENTIAL ASSEMBLY

NOTE: Differential case and drive pinion may be serviced in vehicle.

Disassembly – 1) Raise and support vehicle. Drain lubricant and remove housing cover. Mount dial indicator and measure and record ring gear runout. See RING GEAR & DIFFERENTIAL CASE RUNOUT CHECKING PROCEDURE. Measure and record ring gear backlash. See Fig. 7 and DIFFERENTIAL BEARING PRELOAD & RING GEAR BACKLASH procedure.

2) Remove axle shafts. See AXLE SHAFT & BEARING under REMOVAL & INSTALLATION. Place alignment marks on drive shaft, yoke and companion flange for reassembly reference.

3) Remove drive shaft. Install plug in transmission extension housing to prevent oil leakage. Mark differential bearing caps for reassembly reference and note arrow position. Loosen bearing cap bolts. Pry out differential case, bearing races and shims until loose in bearing caps.

NOTE: Bearing races and caps must be installed in original positions.

4) Remove bearing caps and differential. Remove pinion nut and companion flange. Drive pinion out of front bearing using soft-faced hammer. Remove pinion from housing. Remove oil seal using slide hammer.

5) Remove front bearing. Mount bearing puller on pinion shaft, and press shaft out of bearing. Remove, measure, and record thickness of shim located behind bearing. Remove differential side bearings with a puller.

NOTE: DO NOT remove pinion bearing races unless damaged. If races are replaced, bearings must also be replaced.

1992 DRIVE AXLES
8 3/4" & 10 1/4" Ring Gear Differentials (Cont.)

FORD
7-13

6) Mark differential case and ring gear for reassembly reference. Remove and discard ring gear mounting bolts. Press or tap off ring gear. Remove exciter ring from differential case (if necessary). If exciter ring is removed from differential case, a NEW exciter ring must be installed. Remove pinion shaft lock bolt and remove shaft. Remove pinion gears, side gears and thrust washers.

NOTE: Tab on exciter ring must be aligned with slot in differential case.

Cleaning & Inspection – Clean all parts thoroughly in solvent. Examine pinion and ring gear teeth for scoring, excessive wear, nicks and chipping. Check bearing races for deep scores or galling. Check carrier bearings for wear or damage. Replace components as necessary.

Anti-Lock Brake Sensor – Check sensor pole piece for loose metal particles. Clean if necessary.

Exciter Ring – Ensure exciter ring is properly pressed onto differential case. Examine ring for chips or missing teeth.

Bearing Races – Check bearing races for scores or galling. If a .0015" (.038 mm) feeler gauge can be inserted between a race and bottom of its bore at any point around the race, race must be reseated.

Bearing & Roller Assemblies – When operated in races, bearing rollers must turn without roughness. Examine roller ends for step wear. If damaged, both parts should be replaced.

Companion Flange – Ensure flange half-rounds and lugs have not been damaged. End of flange contacting bearing, counterbore and seal surface must be smooth and free of damage.

Gears – Examine pinion and ring gear teeth for scoring, excessive wear, and excessive chipping. Worn or damaged gears CANNOT be rebuilt to correct noisy condition.

Axle Housing – Ensure differential and pinion bearing bores are smooth. Remove any nicks or burrs from mounting surfaces.

Differential Case – Ensure hubs where bearings mount are smooth. Check differential case bearing shoulders for damage. Bearing assemblies will fail if they do not seat firmly against shoulders. Ensure differential side gears rotate freely in counterbores.

NOTE: Ring and pinion gear set must be replaced in matched sets.

Reassembly & Adjustments – 1) Lubricate all parts with axle lubricant. Place side gears and thrust washers into case. Place pinion gears and thrust washers opposite each other in case openings, and in mesh with side gears.

2) Install ring gear with NEW mounting bolts. If bolts are covered with Green coating over 1/2" of threaded area, install and tighten bolts. If new bolts DO NOT have Green coating, apply small amount of Loctite to bolt threads then tighten bolts.

3) If bearing races have been replaced, NEW bearing and roller assemblies should be installed. Races must be seated in bores so a .0015" (.038 mm) feeler gauge will not fit between race and bottom of bore.

Pinion Depth – 1) Assemble Axle Pinion Depth Gauge Set (T79P-4020-A) and install aligning adapter, gauge disc, gauge block screw and gauge block.

2) Place rear pinion bearing over aligning disc and into bearing race of axle housing. Install front pinion bearing into front bearing race. Place tool handle onto screw and finger tighten. *See Fig. 5.*

3) Ensure pinion depth measuring tools are properly installed and tightened. Apply a light film of oil to pinion bearings. Rotate gauge block several times to seat bearings.

4) Tighten tool handle to 20 ft. lbs. (27 N.m). Final position of gauge block should be 45 degrees above axle shaft centerline. Clean differential bearing bores thoroughly and install gauge tube.

5) Tighten bearing cap bolts to specification. See TORQUE SPECIFICATIONS table at end of article. Using flat pinion shims as a gauge for shim selection, hold gauge block in proper position and measure clearance between gauge block and tube.

6) Correct shim selection is accomplished when a slight drag is felt as shim is drawn between gauge block and tube.

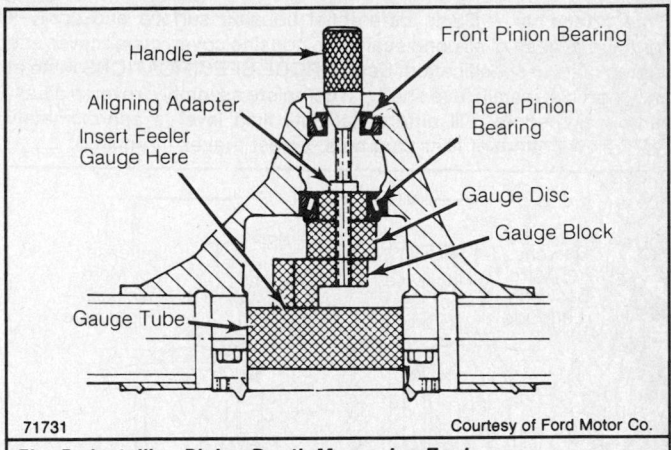

71731   Courtesy of Ford Motor Co.

Fig. 5: Installing Pinion Depth Measuring Tools
(Tools Are Included In Axle Pinion Depth Gauge Set)

Pinion Bearing Preload – 1) Place pre-selected shim on pinion shaft. Press bearing onto shaft until bearing and shim are firmly seated against shoulder of shaft. Install NEW collapsible spacer on pinion shaft.

2) Lubricate bearings with axle lubricant. Install front pinion bearing in housing. Install NEW pinion oil seal. Insert companion flange into oil seal and hold firmly in place.

3) From rear of axle housing, insert pinion shaft into flange. Install a NEW pinion nut on pinion shaft and gradually tighten pinion nut while holding flange.

NOTE: If installing a new companion flange, disregard scribed mark on pinion shaft.

---

4) Check bearing preload often. As soon as preload is measured, turn pinion shaft in both directions several times to seat bearings. Hold companion flange with Companion Flange Holder (T78P-4851-A) while tightening nut.

5) Tighten pinion nut and continue to measure pinion bearing preload until specified pinion torque is obtained. See DIFFERENTIAL ASSEMBLY SPECIFICATIONS table under DIFFERENTIAL SPECIFICATIONS at end of article. If bearing preload is exceeded before torque specification is reached, replace collapsible spacer.

6) Install NEW pinion nut and repeat procedures. DO NOT loosen pinion nut to reduce pinion bearing preload.

Differential Bearing Preload & Ring Gear Backlash – 1) With pinion depth set and pinion installed, place differential case and gear assembly with bearings and races into axle housing.

2) Install a .265" (6.73 mm) shim on left (ring gear side) side of differential. Install left bearing cap and bolts. Tighten bolts finger tight.

3) Select and install largest shim that will fit, with a slight drag, on pinion gear side (right side) of differential. Install right bearing cap and bolts and tighten all cap bolts to specification. See TORQUE SPECIFICATIONS table at end of article.

4) Rotate gear assembly to ensure free operation. Check ring and pinion backlash. *See Fig. 7.* If backlash is .008-.015" (.20-.38 mm), proceed to step 6). If backlash is zero, add .020" (.51 mm) to shim size on right side, and subtract .020" (.51 mm) from shim size on left side.

5) If backlash is less than .008" (.20 mm) or more than .015" (.38 mm), increase or decrease shim size where necessary to correct reading. *See Fig. 6* and BACKLASH-TO-SHIM THICKNESS CONVERSION table.

6) Retighten bearing cap bolts and rotate gear assembly several times. Recheck backlash and correct if necessary. Increase both left and right shim sizes .006" (.15 mm), and reinstall for correct preload.

7) Ensure shims are seated and gear assembly turns freely. Using marking compound, check gear tooth contact pattern. See GEAR TOOTH CONTACT PATTERNS article in GENERAL INFORMATION.

FORD
7-14

1992 DRIVE AXLES
8 3/4" & 10 1/4" Ring Gear Differentials (Cont.)

Final Assembly – Clean differential housing surface and apply a continuous bead of silicone sealant to housing cover. Install cover and tighten bolts to specification. See TORQUE SPECIFICATIONS table at end of article. Install drive shaft. To complete assembly, reverse disassembly procedure. Fill differential until fluid level is approximately 1/4" below bottom of filler plug hole. Adjust brakes if required.

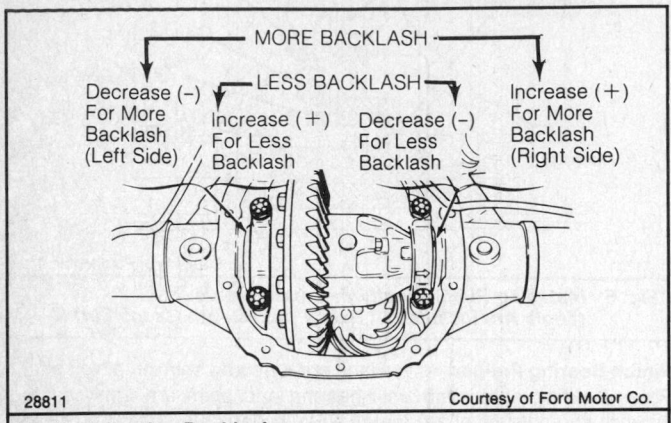

28811   Courtesy of Ford Motor Co.

Fig. 6: Adjusting Backlash

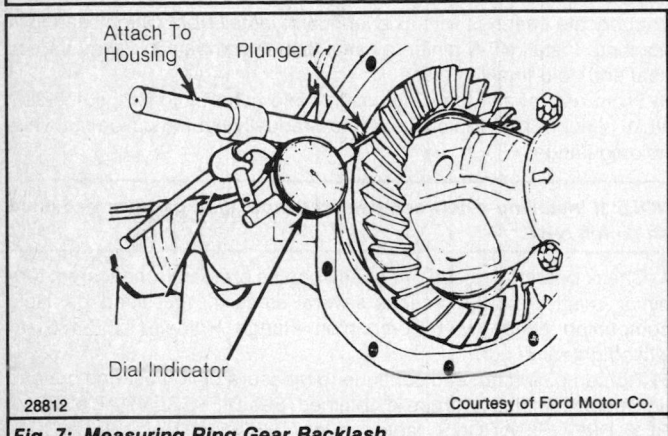

28812   Courtesy of Ford Motor Co.

Fig. 7: Measuring Ring Gear Backlash

BACKLASH-TO-SHIM THICKNESS CONVERSION

Required Change In Backlash In. (mm)	Change In Shim Thickness In. (mm)
.001 (.03)	.002 (.05)
.002 (.05)	.002 (.05)
.003 (.08)	.004 (.10)
.004 (.10)	.006 (.15)
.005 (.13)	.006 (.15)
.006 (.15)	.008 (.20)
.007 (.18)	.010 (.25)
.008 (.20)	.010 (.25)
.009 (.23)	.012 (.30)
.010 (.25)	.014 (.35)
.011 (.28)	.014 (.35)
.012 (.30)	.016 (.41)
.013 (.33)	.018 (.46)
.014 (.35)	.018 (.46)
.015 (.38)	.020 (.51)

DIFFERENTIAL SPECIFICATIONS
DIFFERENTIAL ASSEMBLY SPECIFICATIONS

Application	Specification
Differential Case Flange Runout	.003" (.08 mm)
Maximum Backlash Variation Between Teeth	.004" (.10 mm)
Nominal Pinion Shim Thickness	.030" (.76 mm)
Pinion Gear Thrust Washer Thickness	.030-.032" (.76-.81 mm)
Ring Gear Back Face Runout	.004" (.10 mm)
Ring Gear Backlash [1]	.008-.015" (.20-.38 mm)
Side Gear Thrust Washer Thickness	.030-.032" (.76-.81 mm)
	INCH Lbs. (N.m)
Pinion Bearing Preload New Bearings	16-29 (1.8-3.2)
Original Bearings (With Oil Seal)	8-14 (.9-1.6)

[1] – Preferred setting is .012-.015" (.30-.38 mm).

TORQUE SPECIFICATIONS
TORQUE SPECIFICATIONS

Application	Ft. Lbs. (N.m)
ABS Sensor Bolt	26-30 (35-41)
Axle Shaft Bolt (Full-Floating)	60-80 (81-108)
Backing Plate Retainer Nut	20-40 (27-54)
Bearing Cap Bolt	
8 3/4" Ring Gear	70-85 (95-115)
10 1/4" Ring Gear	80-95 (108-129)
Brake Junction Block Bolt	25-30 (34-41)
Coil Spring Retainer Nut (Aerostar)	
Lower	41-64 (56-87)
Upper	30-40 (41-54)
Driveshaft-To-Circular Companion Flange Bolt	70-95 (95-129)
Driveshaft-To-Half Round Companion Flange Bolt	10-15 (14-21)
Housing Cover Bolt	
8 3/4" Ring Gear	15-20 (21-27)
10 1/4" Ring Gear	25-35 (34-47)
Hub Nut (Full-Floating)	[1] 55-65 (75-88)
Lower Control Arm-To-Axle Housing Bolt (Aerostar)	95-130 (129-176)
Pinion Nut (Minimum)	[2] 160 (217)
Pinion Shaft Lock Bolt	15-30 (21-41)
Ring Gear Bolt	
8 3/4" Ring Gear	70-85 (95-115)
10 1/4" Ring Gear	100-120 (136-163)
Shock Absorber Nut	
Aerostar	
Lower	41-65 (56-88)
Upper	25-35 (34-47)
Bronco & Pickup	
Lower	52-74 (71-100)
Upper	40-60 (54-81)
Explorer	
Lower	27-41 (37-56)
Upper	41-63 (56-85)
Van	
Lower	50-68 (68-92)
Upper	25-34 (34-46)
Ranger	
Lower & Upper	39-53 (53-72)
Stabilizer Bar Nut	30-42 (41-57)
"U" Bolt Nut	
Ranger	66-80 (89-108)
Explorer	88-108 (119-146)
Pickup	75-115 (102-156)
Van	72-98 (98-133)
Wheel Lug Nut	
Aerostar	85-115 (115-156)
Bronco, Explorer & Ranger	100 (136)
All Others	140 (190)

[1] – Ratchet back 5 clicks after initial torque.

[2] – If bearing preload exceeds specification before torque specification is reached, install NEW collapsible spacer.

Front Axle: F350
Rear Axle: E250, E350,
F350 Super Duty

DESCRIPTION & OPERATION

NOTE: Axles designed so axle housing supports the load are called "full floating axles". Axles designed so axle shaft supports the load are called "semi-floating axles".

DANA DRIVE AXLE APPLICATION

Application	Axle Type	Dana Axle
E250 (Rear)	Semi-Floating	Model 60
E350 (Rear)		
Single Wheels	Full-Floating	Model 60
Dual Wheels	Full-Floating	Model 70
F350 4WD (Front)	Full-Floating	[1] Model 60
"F" Series Super Duty		
(Rear)	Full-Floating	Model 80

[1] – Model 60 monobeam is identical to other Model 60 drive axles, except for components unique to front wheel drive.

All Dana axle assemblies are an integral-type housing with hypoid-type ring and pinion gear. Stamped steel cover is removable for inspection and repair of differential. Drive pinion depth, pinion bearing preload and differential side bearing preload are all set by shims.

On Dana axle assemblies with full-floating axle shafts, vehicle loads are supported by axle housings. Axle shafts of full-floating rear assemblies may be removed without disturbing wheel bearings. Full-floating axle shafts are held in place by bolts attached to hub.

On Dana axle assemblies with semi-floating axle shafts, the axle shaft rides on axle bearing, which is pressed into outer end of axle housing tube. Semi-floating axles are retained in the axle by "C" clips positioned in a slot at end of splined axle shaft.

Power is transmitted through driveshaft to the drive pinion located in the differential carrier housing. *See Fig. 2.* Drive pinion shaft is supported by 2 opposed tapered roller bearings. Power is transmitted from pinion gear through ring gear and differential pinion gears to axle shafts and wheels.

NOTE: For removal and installation procedures for F350 4WD front drive axle component parts not covered in this article, see appropriate LOCKING HUBS and 4WD STEERING KNUCKLES articles.

AXLE RATIO & IDENTIFICATION

Axle identification can be determined by the axle code on the Safety Certification Label on left door pillar. In addition, a metal identification tag stamped with gear ratio and diameter is secured to axle housing by 2 bolts. *See Fig. 1.* If axle is equipped with limited-slip differential, the gear ratio will have the letter "L" in the number. See AXLE RATIO IDENTIFICATION article.

LUBRICATION

CAPACITY

DIFFERENTIAL LUBRICATION CAPACITY

Application	Pts. (L)
Model 60 (Front)	5.8 (2.7)
Model 60 (Rear)	6.3 (3.0)
Model 70	6.6 (3.1)
Model 70 HD	7.4 (3.5)
Model 80	8.5 (4.0)

FLUID TYPE

All model use Hypoid Gear Lubricant (C6AZ-19580-E). Limited Slip Differentials (LSD) require an additional 8 ounces of Friction Modifier (C8AZ-19B546-A)

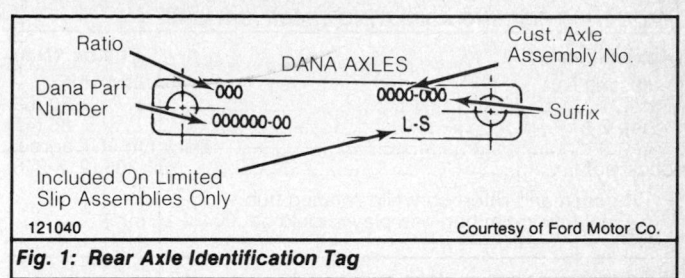

Fig. 1: Rear Axle Identification Tag

121040   Courtesy of Ford Motor Co.

TROUBLE SHOOTING

NOTE: See TROUBLE SHOOTING article in GENERAL INFORMATION.

REMOVAL & INSTALLATION

HUB, BEARING & AXLE SHAFT (FULL-FLOATING)

Removal (F350 – Front) – 1) Raise and support vehicle. Remove tire and wheel assembly. Remove disc brake caliper and support out of way. Remove caliper and secure to frame. Remove locking hub screws and remove hub cover.

2) Remove snap ring from end of axle. Remove outer hub retaining ring from hub housing. Remove locking hub from housing by installing 2 cap screws into locking hub outer ring and pull out of hub.

3) Using Spanner Lock Nut Wrench (D85T-1197-A), remove spindle lock nut, retaining washer, and bearing adjusting nut. Pull hub and rotor assembly off spindle. Remove inner grease seal and bearing.

4) Inspect bearings and bearing races for wear and pitting. If replacement is necessary, drive outer race from bearing hub using a punch and hammer. Install new race; be careful not to chip or dent race. Ensure new race is fully seated in hub.

5) Match mark spindle and knuckle, and remove nuts. Tap spindle with soft-faced hammer, and remove spindle and splash shield. Pull axle shaft through knuckle. Remove spacer from axle shaft, if necessary.

6) Inspect needle bearing and seal in spindle. If replacement is necessary, remove seal. Remove bearing using Bridge Assembly (D80L-100-W), Actuator Pin D80L-100-H, the 1 1/2 - 1 3/4" Collet (D80L-100-T). Inspect axle shaft "U" joint and shaft splines for wear. Replace as necessary.

Installation – 1) If removed, install needle bearing using driver handle and Spindle Bearing Replacer (T80-4000-R). Lettering on spindle needle bearing must face rear of spindle. Install seal into spindle. Seal should spin freely when installed.

2) Install axle shaft through knuckle and engage into axle gear splines. Install spacer (if removed) with chamfered side inboard against axle shaft. Install splash shield. Align match marks and install spindle. Clean bearings and hub. Pack bearings with multipurpose grease and apply grease to hub races.

3) Install inner bearing and new grease seal. Wipe spindle clean, and lightly coat spindle with grease. Install hub onto spindle. Use care not to damage seal. Install outer bearing adjusting nut.

4) Using spanner lock nut wrench, tighten bearing adjusting nut in 3 steps. See FRONT HUB BEARING ADJUSTING SPECIFICATIONS table. Install retaining ring. Ensure adjusting nut lock pin engages hole in ring. Install spindle lock nut and tighten to specification. See FRONT HUB BEARING ADJUSTING SPECIFICATIONS table.

5) Lightly grease locking hub assembly and install into hub. Install outer retaining ring and axle snap ring. Install locking hub cover and tighten retaining screws. See TORQUE SPECIFICATIONS table at end of article. To complete installation, reverse removal procedure. Check hub for proper operation.

FRONT HUB BEARING ADJUSTING SPECIFICATIONS

Application	Ft. Lbs. (N.m)
Adjusting Nut	
Step 1	50 (68)
Step 2 [1]	35 (47)
Step 3 [2]	Back Off 90 Degrees
Lock Nut	160-205 (217-278)

[1] – Loosen and retorque while rotating hub.
[2] – Final maximum hub end play should be .004" (.10 mm).

CAUTION: On E350 & F350 Super Duty, hub nuts have right-hand threads for both spindles. Nuts are marked RH for thread direction. DO NOT use power impact tools on hub nuts.

Removal (E350 & F350 Super Duty) – **1)** Set parking brake. Loosen axle-to-hub bolts. *See Fig. 2*. Release parking brake. Raise and support vehicle. Remove tire and wheel assembly.
2) Remove axle-to-hub bolts and lock washers. Discard bolts and washers. Remove axle shaft, and discard gasket. Remove brake drums. Using Hub Wrench (T85T-4252-AH), remove bearing adjusting nut(s). Remove hub assembly. Remove hub seal and inner bearing. Inspect bearings and races for wear.
Installation – **1)** To replace bearing race, drive race from bearing hub using a brass drift and hammer. Install new bearing race using Bearing Replacer (T75T-1225-A or B). Use care not to chip or dent race. Ensure new race is fully seated in hub.
2) Pack bearings with lithium-base grease. Install new seal. Carefully install hub onto axle spindle to avoid damaging seal lip and spindle threads. Install outer bearing and adjusting nut.

3) Install adjusting nut. Ensure nut tab aligns with keyway in axle. Using Hub Wrench (T85T-4252-AH), tighten bearing adjusting nut in 3 steps. See REAR HUB BEARING ADJUSTING SPECIFICATIONS table. Hub will ratchet as torque is applied.
4) To complete installation, reverse removal procedure. Install new axle-to-hub bolts, lock washers and gasket. Tighten lug nuts to specification. See TORQUE SPECIFICATIONS table.

NOTE: On dual wheel models, use only new-style 2-piece, swiveling lug nuts and wheel components. DO NOT use the old-style (pre-1985) 1-piece, cone-shaped lug nuts or wheel components

REAR HUB BEARING ADJUSTING SPECIFICATIONS

Application	Ft. Lbs. (N.m)
Adjusting Nut	
Step 1	65-75 (88-102)
Step 2	[1] Back Off 90 Degrees
Step 3	[2] 15-20 (20-27)

[1] – Loosen and retorque.
[2] – There should be no end play.

AXLE SHAFTS & BEARINGS (SEMI-FLOATING)

Removal (E250) – **1)** Raise and support vehicle. Remove wheels and brake drums. Remove housing cover to drain lubricant. Remove lock bolt from pinion shaft in differential case. *See Fig. 3*.
2) Remove differential pinion shaft from differential case. Push flanged end of axle shaft toward center of vehicle. Remove "C" clip from inner end of axle shaft. Pull axle shaft out of housing tube.

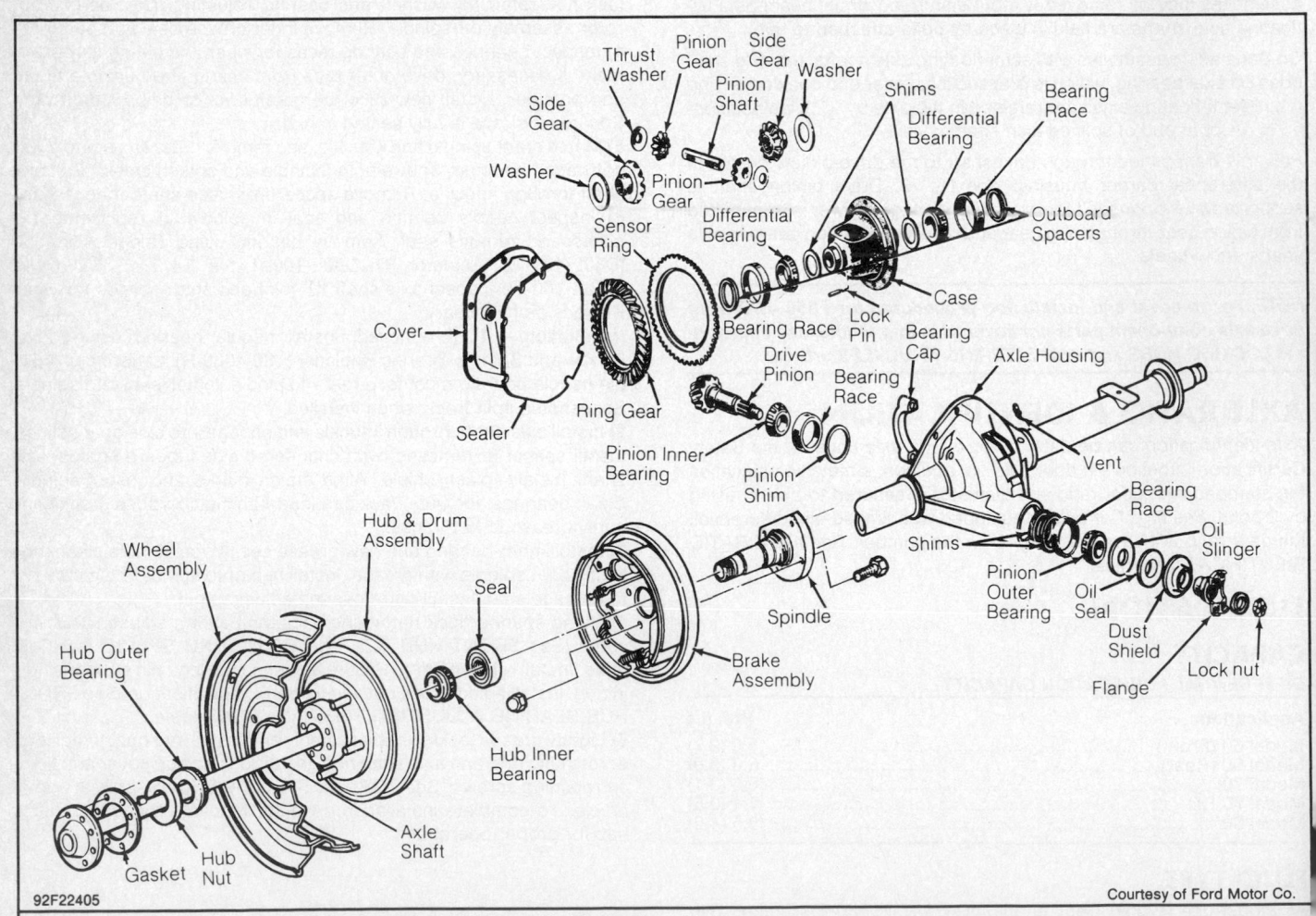

92F22405

Courtesy of Ford Motor Co.

Fig. 2: *Exploded View Of Dana Full-Floating Axle Assembly (Typical)*

NOTE: DO NOT rotate differential side gears when removing axle shafts. Turning gears may cause gear and thrust washers to fall out of opening in differential case.

3) Pry oil seal out of axle tube and discard seal. Using Push-Puller (T81P-1104-C), Adapters (T81P-1104-B) for coarse threads or (D81T-1104-A) for fine threads, and Rear Wheel Bearing Remover (T81T-1225-A), remove bearing from axle housing.

WARNING: Wear safety glasses when removing bearing from housing, as bearing could shatter under pressure.

4) Ensure bearing bore has no burrs or excessive wear. Clean bore with metal cleaning solvent. Contamination in bore could cause premature failure of new bearing.

Installation – **1)** Coat bearing with axle lubricant before installing into axle bore. Using push-puller, adapters, Step Plate (D80L-630-1) and Rear Axle Bearing Installer (T80T-4000-X), install bearing into axle bore. Ensure bearing does not cock in bore while installing.
2) Install NEW oil seal into bore using push-puller, adapters, step plate, and Rear Oil Seal Installer (T80T-4000-Y). Ensure seal does not cock in bore. Fill space between seal and bearing with Premium Long-Life Grease XG-1-C or XG-1-K.
3) Carefully slide axle shaft through seal and bearing. Engage splines on axle shaft with side gear. Push axle shaft inward and install "C" clip. Install differential pinion shaft. Ensure differential pinion gear thrust washers are in place.

CAUTION: One type of pinion shaft lock bolt has a 6-point socket head and locking compound on threads. DO NOT reuse this type. The other type has 12-point drive head and off-set threads. Lock bolts with off-set threads may be reused up to 4 times.

4) Align hole in pinion shaft with hole in differential case. Install lock bolt and tighten to **20-25 ft. lbs. (27-34 N.m)**. Clean any oil film off sealing surfaces. Apply bead of silicone rubber sealer 1/8 - 1/4" high and wide onto cover plate in place of gasket. Bead must go inside bolt holes, not outside or over holes.
5) Install 2 bolts into cover as guides while mounting cover onto axle housing. Install remaining bolts and tighten evenly to **30-40 ft. lbs. (41-**

54 N.m). Allow one-hour drying time before filling axle housing and operating vehicle. To complete installation, reverse removal procedure.

AXLE HOUSING ASSEMBLY

Removal (F350 – Front) – **1)** Raise and support vehicle. Remove tire and wheel assembly. Remove hubs, spindles and axles. See HUB, BEARING & AXLE SHAFT (FULL-FLOATING) under REMOVAL & INSTALLATION.
2) Remove left and right tie rod ends. Remove stabilizer bar links, lower shock mounts and track bar bolt. Mark drive shaft position for installation reference. Disconnect front drive shaft at front pinion yoke, and wire shaft to frame. Disconnect axle housing vent tube, and plug opening.
3) Support axle housing with floor jack. Remove spring "U" bolt nuts, and remove "U" bolt. Carefully lower axle housing assembly from vehicle and remove.
Installation – **1)** Check all bushings and mounting hardware for wear or damage. Place axle housing assembly onto floor jack. Position assembly under vehicle and raise until assembly contacts springs. Ensure bolt head protruding from leaf spring plate is seated in spring mounting plate recess.
2) To complete installation, reverse removal procedure. Tighten all bolts and nuts to specification. See FRONT HUB BEARING ADJUSTING SPECIFICATIONS table under HUB, BEARING & AXLE SHAFT (FULL-FLOATING), and TORQUE SPECIFICATIONS table. Fill axle housing assembly with gear oil. Check wheel alignment.
Removal & Installation (E250, E350 & "F" Super Duty – Rear) – **1)** Loosen wheel lug nuts and axle shaft retaining bolts. Remove shock absorbers and stabilizer bar mounts. Raise vehicle until weight is off the rear springs.
2) Disconnect brake hose from frame and parking brake cable at equalizer. Remove parking brake cable from cable support and brackets. Disconnect rear "U" joint. Disconnect anti-lock wiring from axle sensor and height sensing linkage (if equipped).
3) Support axle assembly with floor jack. Remove spring "U" bolt nuts, and remove "U" bolt. Carefully lower axle housing assembly from vehicle. Roll axle housing assembly out from vehicle. Drain lubricant. Remove wheels and mount assembly onto workbench. To install, reverse removal procedure.

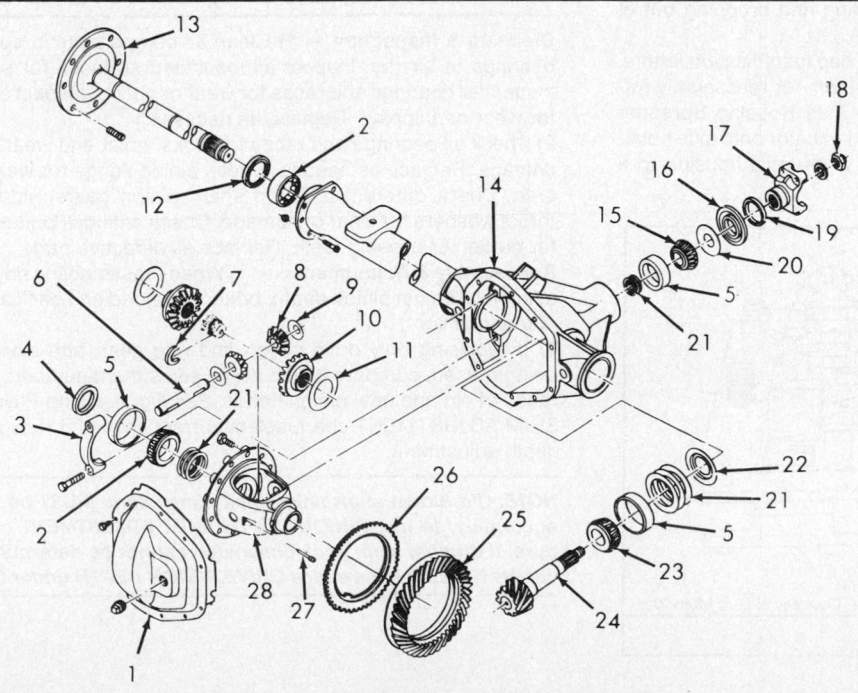

1. Cover
2. Bearing
3. Bearing Cap
4. Outboard Spacer
5. Race
6. Pinion Shaft
7. "C" Clip
8. Pinion Gear
9. Thrust Washer
10. Side Gear
11. Washer
12. Seal
13. Axle
14. Axle Housing
15. Pinion Outer Bearing
16. Pinion Seal
17. Pinion Flange
18. Nut
19. Dust Shield
20. Oil Slinger
21. Shims
22. Baffle
23. Pinion Inner Bearing
24. Drive Pinion
25. Ring Gear
26. Sensor Ring
27. Lock Bolt
28. Differential Case

91I13373

Courtesy of Ford Motor Co.

Fig. 3: Exploded View Of Dana 60 Rear Semi-Floating Axle Assembly (E250)

PINION FLANGE & SEAL

Removal – 1) Raise and support vehicle. Mark drive shaft position for installation reference. Disconnect drive shaft and wire shaft to frame. Using Pinion Flange Holder (T57T-4851-B), remove pinion nut.

CAUTION: Hammering on companion flange could result in damage to ring and pinion gear.

2) Using Puller (T80L-4851-B), remove pinion flange. Carefully remove pinion oil seal so as not to damage housing seal surface.
Installation – 1) Lubricate seal lip with gear lubricant. Using Oil Seal Replacer (T83T-4676-A), install pinion seal into axle housing.
2) Install pinion flange onto pinion shaft. Install pinion washer and nut. Using pinion flange holder, tighten pinion nut to specification. See TORQUE SPECIFICATIONS table. To complete installation, reverse removal procedure.

DIFFERENTIAL ASSEMBLY

Removal & Installation – Removal and installation procedure is included in overhaul procedure. See DIFFERENTIAL ASSEMBLY under OVERHAUL.

OVERHAUL

DIFFERENTIAL ASSEMBLY

NOTE: It is recommended, but not necessary, that axle housing be removed for overhaul. See Fig. 2 or 3 to identify differential components throughout overhaul procedure.

Pre-Disassembly – 1) Before disassembly, visually inspect differential parts for wear and/or damage. Rotate gears and check for any roughness which would indicate damaged bearings or gears.
2) Check ring gear teeth for scoring, nicks, chips or wear. Measure ring gear runout. Mount dial indicator onto axle housing so tip of dial indicator contacts back of ring gear. Runout should not exceed **.004"** **(.10 mm)**.
Disassembly – 1) Remove axle housing cover. Remove axle shafts. See HUB, BEARING & AXLE SHAFT (FULL-FLOATING) or AXLE SHAFTS & BEARINGS (SEMI-FLOATING) under REMOVAL & INSTALLATION. On E250, install pinion shaft and lock bolt to keep pinion gears and thrust washers from rotating and dropping out of case.
2) On all models, note orientation of bearing cap identification letters. If side bearing caps are not identified, mark them for reassembly reference. Remove side bearing caps. Install Axle Housing Spreader (4000-E) onto housing. *See Fig. 4.* Mount dial indicator onto axle housing to measure amount of spread. Spread differential housing to a maximum of **.015" (.38 mm)**.

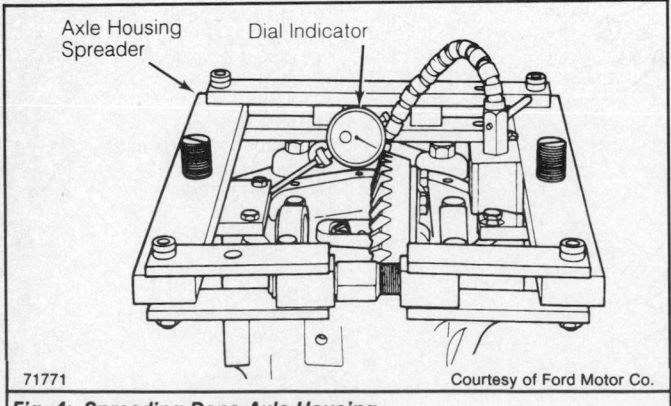

Axle Housing
Spreader

Dial Indicator

71771   Courtesy of Ford Motor Co.
Fig. 4: Spreading Dana Axle Housing

CAUTION: DO NOT spread axle housing more than .015" (.38 mm).

3) Remove dial indicator after housing has been spread. Carefully pry differential assembly out of housing. Remove spreader tool immediately to avoid housing distortion. Mark bearing races to identify which side they were removed from. Record size and position of side bearing shims between axle housing and side bearings outer races.
4) Place Universal Bearing Remover (D81L-4220-A) into vise while removing differential side bearings. Keep bearings, bearing races and shims in sets, marked with bearings' location in axle housing. Place differential case into vise with rags underneath to protect ring gear.

NOTE: If anti-lock brake sensor ring is removed from axle housing, a new sensor ring must be installed.

5) Remove and discard ring gear bolts. Remove ring gear by tapping with soft-faced mallet. On E250, remove pinion shaft lock bolt. On all other models, remove pinion shaft lock pin. On all models, remove pinion shaft. Rotate side gears until pinion gears align with case opening. Remove pinion gears and thrust washers.
6) Remove side gears with thrust washers. Rotate nose of axle housing to horizontal position. Hold pinion flange with Pinion Flange Holder (T57T-4851-B). Remove pinion nut and washer. Using Flange Puller (D80L-1002-L), remove pinion flange. Using soft-faced hammer, tap drive pinion out of housing.

NOTE: Pinion bearing adjusting shims and pre-load spacer (if equipped) may remain on pinion shaft, stick to bearing, or fall loose. Collect and save shims for reassembly.

7) Remove pinion seal with Bearing Race Puller (T77F-1102-A) and slide hammer. Discard seal. Remove drive pinion outer bearing and oil slinger. Turn nose of axle housing downward.
8) Remove pinion outer bearing race and inner bearing race using appropriate Bearing Race Driver (D81T-4628-A/B or D) and Driver Handle (D81L-4000-A).
9) Remove shims and baffle (if used) from bearing race bore in axle housing. Using universal bearing remover, remove pinion inner bearing from drive pinion shaft.

NOTE: Both oil slinger and baffle (if used) are part of shim pack and must be reused or replaced during reassembly procedure.

Cleaning & Inspection – 1) Clean all components in solvent. Allow bearings to air dry. Inspect all machined surfaces for smoothness. Inspect all bearings and races for wear or pitting. Inspect all gear teeth for wear or chipping. Replace as necessary.
2) Check all bearings and races for nicks, roller end wear, grooves or damage. Replace as needed. Check pinion flange for wear in sealing area. Check differential pinion shaft, pinion gears, side gears and thrust washers for wear or damage. Check anti-lock brake sensor ring for broken or missing teeth. Replace all defective parts.
Reassembly & Adjustments – 1) When reassembling ring and pinion assembly, adjust pinion depth, bearing preload and backlash between ring and pinion.
2) If replacing only drive pinion and ring gear, and axle housing is being reused, compare pinion depth adjustment numbers etched into faces of old and new pinion heads. *See Fig. 5.* Using PINION DEPTH SHIM ADJUSTMENT chart, select correct shims for new pinion shaft depth adjustment.

NOTE: Old pinion shaft shim pack dimensions MUST be determined accurately, to use PINION DEPTH SHIM ADJUSTMENT chart procedure. If original shim pack dimension cannot be determined or if the carrier housing is new, see DRIVE PINION DEPTH under OVERHAUL.

PINION DEPTH SHIM ADJUSTMENT CHART (INCHES)

Old Pinion Marking	New Pinion Marking								
	-4	-3	-2	-1	0	+1	+2	+3	+4
+4	+0.008	+0.007	+0.006	+0.005	+0.004	+0.003	+0.002	+0.001	0
+3	+0.007	+0.006	+0.005	+0.004	+0.003	+0.002	+0.001	0	-0.001
+2	+0.006	+0.005	+0.004	+0.003	+0.002	+0.001	0	-0.001	-0.002
+1	+0.005	+0.004	+0.003	+0.002	+0.001	0	-0.001	-0.002	-0.003
0	+0.004	+0.003	+0.002	+0.001	0	-0.001	-0.002	-0.003	-0.004
-1	+0.003	+0.002	+0.001	0	-0.001	-0.002	-0.003	-0.004	-0.005
-2	+0.002	+0.001	0	-0.001	-0.002	-0.003	-0.004	-0.005	-0.006
-3	+0.001	0	-0.001	-0.002	-0.003	-0.004	-0.005	-0.006	-0.007
-4	0	-0.001	-0.002	-0.003	-0.004	-0.005	-0.006	-0.007	-0.008

PINION DEPTH SHIM ADJUSTMENT CHART (MILLIMETERS)

Old Pinion Marking	New Pinion Marking								
	-10	-8	-5	-3	0	+3	+5	+8	+10
+10	+0.20	+0.18	+0.15	+0.13	+0.10	+0.08	+0.05	+0.03	0
+8	+0.18	+0.15	+0.13	+0.10	+0.08	+0.05	+0.03	0	-0.03
+5	+0.15	+0.13	+0.10	+0.08	+0.05	+0.03	0	-0.03	-0.05
+3	+0.13	+0.10	+0.08	+0.05	+0.03	0	-0.03	-0.05	-0.08
0	+0.10	+0.08	+0.05	+0.03	0	-0.03	-0.05	-0.08	-0.10
-3	+0.08	+0.05	+0.03	0	-0.03	-0.05	-0.08	-0.10	-0.13
-5	+0.05	+0.03	0	-0.03	-0.05	-0.08	-0.10	-0.13	-0.15
-8	+0.03	0	-0.03	-0.05	-0.08	-0.10	-0.13	-0.15	-0.18
-10	0	-0.03	-0.05	-0.08	-0.10	-0.13	-0.15	-0.18	-0.20

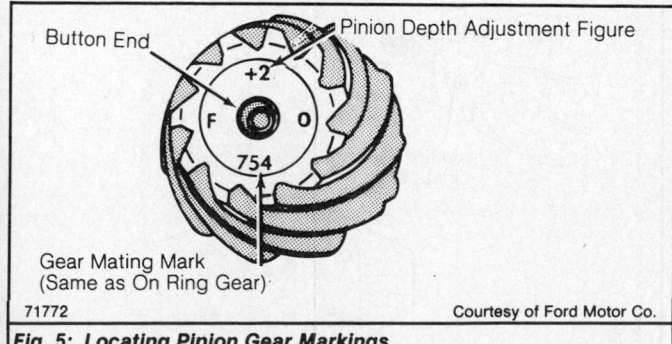

71772   Courtesy of Ford Motor Co.

Fig. 5: Locating Pinion Gear Markings

3) The pinion depth adjustment number is determined by manufacturer at time of assembly. Number represents distance that pinion shaft deviates from distance between back-face of pinion gear to center line of ring gear. *See Fig. 6* for specified distances.
4) Ring gear and pinion gear are supplied in matched sets only. Matching numbers are etched onto ring and pinion gears. If using new gear set, verify matching gear mating marks. *See Fig. 5.*

5) Pinion Depth Gauge Set (T80T-4020-A) allows shim pack adjustments to be made without having to remove and replace differential bearings when setting up shim packs. *See Fig. 7.*
6) Use gear tooth contact pattern as a verification of final pinion position for pinion gears. See GEAR TOOTH CONTACT PATTERNS article in GENERAL INFORMATION.

Differential Case – 1) Place differential case into vise. Use multipurpose grease to lubricate side gears, pinion gears and all thrust washers. Install into case. Rotate side gears until holes in pinion gears and washers line up with holes in case.
2) Install differential pinion shaft. On E250, install new lock bolt, but DO NOT tighten at this time. On all other models, install lock pin. Using a punch and hammer, peen metal of differential case over lock pin at 90 degrees to the left and right of lock pin slot.

NOTE: Tab on anti-lock sensor ring must be aligned with slot in differential case.

3) Align tab in anti-lock sensor ring with slot in differential case. Install 2 ring gear bolts, but DO NOT tighten. Using an arbor press, press sensor ring and ring gear onto differential case.

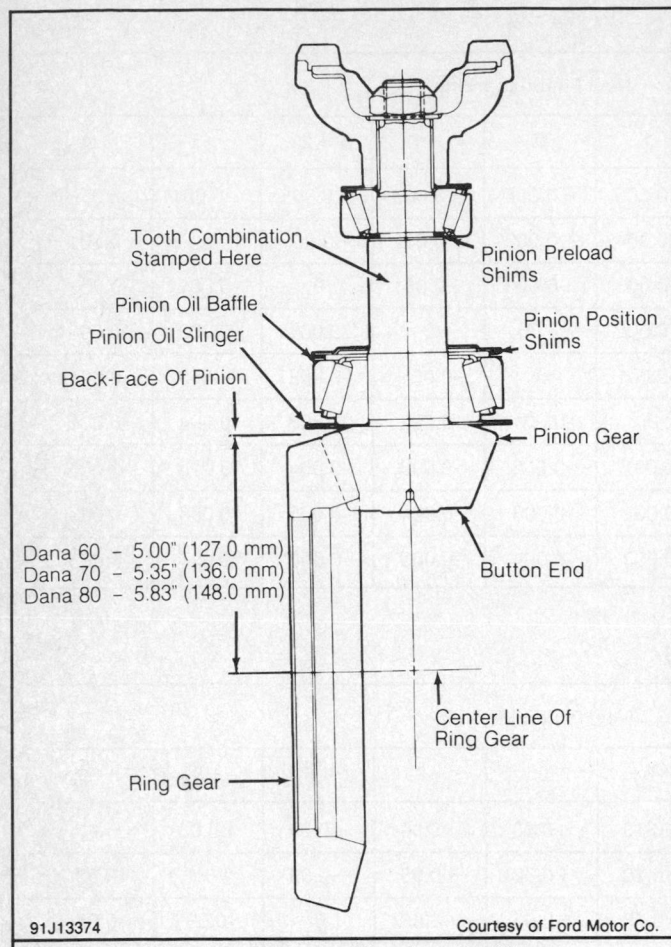

Tooth Combination Stamped Here

Pinion Preload Shims

Pinion Oil Baffle

Pinion Oil Slinger

Pinion Position Shims

Back-Face Of Pinion

Pinion Gear

Dana 60 – 5.00" (127.0 mm)
Dana 70 – 5.35" (136.0 mm)
Dana 80 – 5.83" (148.0 mm)

Button End

Center Line Of Ring Gear

Ring Gear

91J13374   Courtesy of Ford Motor Co.

Fig. 6: Identifying Drive Pinion-To-Ring Gear Position

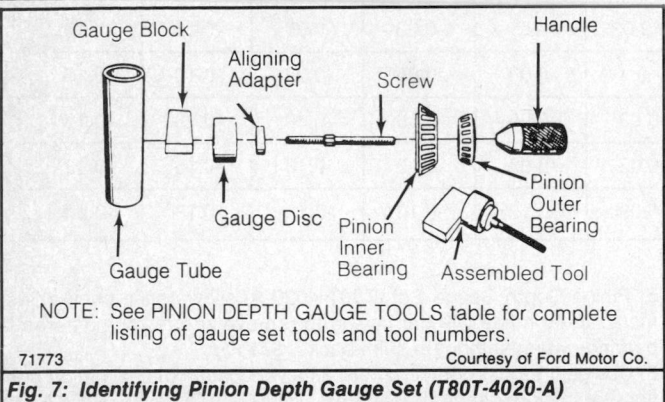

Gauge Block

Aligning Adapter

Screw

Handle

Gauge Disc

Gauge Tube

Pinion Inner Bearing

Pinion Outer Bearing

Assembled Tool

NOTE: See PINION DEPTH GAUGE TOOLS table for complete listing of gauge set tools and tool numbers.

71773   Courtesy of Ford Motor Co.

Fig. 7: Identifying Pinion Depth Gauge Set (T80T-4020-A)

4) Apply Thread Lock Sealer (EOAZ-19554-AA) to new ring gear bolts. Install NEW ring gear bolts and tighten evenly to specification. See TORQUE SPECIFICATIONS table.

5) On Dana 60 and 70 axles, install Master Differential Bearings (D81T-4222-D) onto differential case. On Dana 80 and 70 HD axles, install Master Differential Bearings (D81T-4222-E). On all axles, install outboard spacers (if equipped) into case. Install case into housing (without shims).

6) Mount dial indicator with indicator tip against back of ring gear, at 90 degrees to gear. Measure and record total end play of differential case by moving it back and forth with screwdriver. See Fig. 8.

7) This measurement will be used later to determine proper shim pack dimension. Remove case from housing. Leave master bearings on case at this time.

Drive Pinion Bearing Outer Race Installation – **1)** Place drive pinion inner and outer bearing outer races into bores of axle housing. Place appropriate pinion inner bearing race installer onto inner bearing outer race, and appropriate pinion outer bearing race installer onto pinion outer bearing outer race. See PINION BEARING OUTER RACE INSTALLER table.

2) Install Threaded Drawbar (T75T-1176-A) through both pinion bearings outer races. See Fig. 9. Tighten drawbar until bearing outer races are seated in axle housing bore. Both pinion bearing outer races are installed, into axle housing, at the same time.

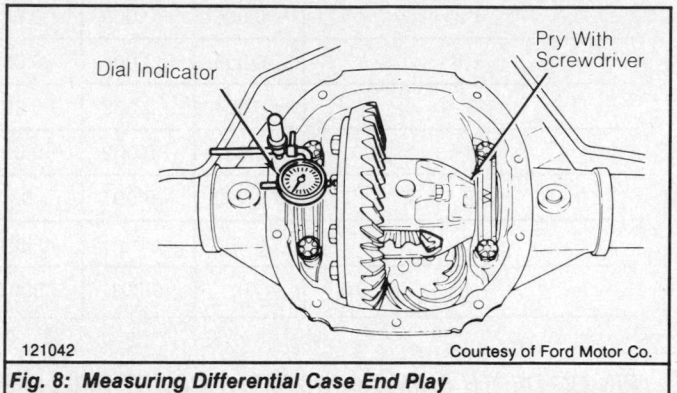

Dial Indicator

Pry With Screwdriver

121042   Courtesy of Ford Motor Co.

Fig. 8: Measuring Differential Case End Play

PINION BEARING OUTER RACE INSTALLER

Application	Tool No.
Inner Bearing Outer Race	
Dana 60 & 70	T56T-4616-B2
Dana 70-HD & 80	D81T-4616-A
Outer Bearing Outer Race	
Dana 60, 70 & 70-HD	T56T-4616-B1
Dana 80	D67P-4616-A

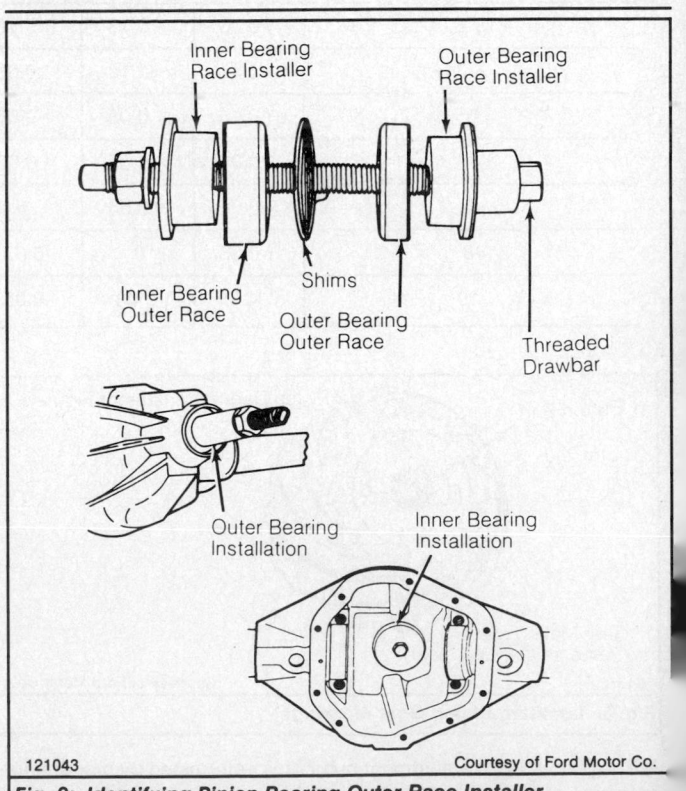

Inner Bearing Race Installer

Outer Bearing Race Installer

Inner Bearing Outer Race

Shims

Outer Bearing Outer Race

Threaded Drawbar

Outer Bearing Installation

Inner Bearing Installation

121043   Courtesy of Ford Motor Co.

Fig. 9: Identifying Pinion Bearing Outer Race Installer

NOTE: Check pinion depth gauge tools before each use. Any nicks o
damage MUST be removed to ensure accurate readings.

Drive Pinion Depth – 1) Install new drive pinion inner bearing onto appropriate aligning adapter and gauge disc. See PINION DEPTH GAUGE TOOLS table. *See Fig. 7.* Install pinion outer bearing (new or good used) into outer race in housing. Place gauge assembly into housing, with Screw (T80T-4020-F43) extending through outer bearing.

PINION DEPTH GAUGE TOOLS [1]

Application	Tool No.
Aligning Adapter	
Dana 60	T76P-4020-A3
Dana 70	T80T-4020-F48
Dana 80	D80T-4020-R60
Gauge Block	T80T-4020-F42
Gauge Disc	
Dana 60	T78P-4020-A15
Dana 70	D80T-4020-F45
Dana 80	T88T-4020-A
Gauge Tube	
Dana 60 & 70	D80T-4020-F48
Dana 80	D81T-4020-F51
Handle	
Dana 60 & 70	T76P-4020-A11
Dana 80	T88T-4020-B
Screw	T80T-4020-F43

[1] – Complete tool set is Pinion Depth Gauge Set (T80T-4020-A).

2) Thread appropriate handle onto screw finger tight. Using 3/8" torque wrench in square drive on handle, tighten handle until preload on bearings is **20-40 INCH lbs. (2.26-4.52 N.m)**. Center appropriate gauge tube in side bearing bore. Install side bearing caps and tighten bolts to **80-90 ft. lbs. (108-122 N.m)**.

3) Place Gauge Block (T80T-4020-F42) on top of the drive pinion face underneath gauge tube. Using feeler gauge, determine clearance between gauge block and gauge tube. Correct feeler gauge will give slight drag feeling as gauge strip passes between tube and block.

4) Thickness of correct feeler gauge is thickness of shim pack to be installed under inner bearing race, when drive pinion has no number marked on face. If drive pinion has a plus (+) number marked on face, subtract that number from thickness dimension. If drive pinion has a minus (−) number marked on face, add that number to thickness dimension.

NOTE: New pinion bearings used during depth measurement procedure MUST be used during final assembly in order for drive pinion depth to be correct. New oil slinger and/or baffle (if used) are measured as part of shim pack.

---

5) Remove drive pinion inner bearing outer race from axle housing bore. Install shim pack with baffle (if used) into housing bearing bore. Reinstall inner bearing outer race into axle housing.

6) Using Axle Bearing/Seal Plate (T75L-1165-B), arbor press and appropriate axle bearing/seal replacer, press drive pinion inner bearing and oil slinger (if used) onto drive pinion. See AXLE BEARING/SEAL REPLACER table.

AXLE BEARING/SEAL REPLACER

Application	Tool No.
Dana 60	T75L-1165-DA
Dana 70	T53T-4621-C
Dana 80	D80T-4200-B

Drive Pinion Bearing Preload – 1) Install preload shims and slinger (if used) onto drive pinion. Install drive pinion into housing. Install drive pinion outer bearing using press, axle bearing/seal plate and axle bearing/seal installer. Install drive pinion flange with washer and NEW nut. Tighten nut to specification. See TORQUE SPECIFICATIONS table.

2) Using INCH lb. torque wrench on pinion flange nut, measure torque required to rotate pinion. Pinion preload torque should be **20-40 INCH lbs. (2.26-4.52 N.m)** for NEW bearings. If preload reading is too low, remove preload shims from drive pinion. If preload reading is too high, add preload shims to drive pinion. *See Fig. 10.*

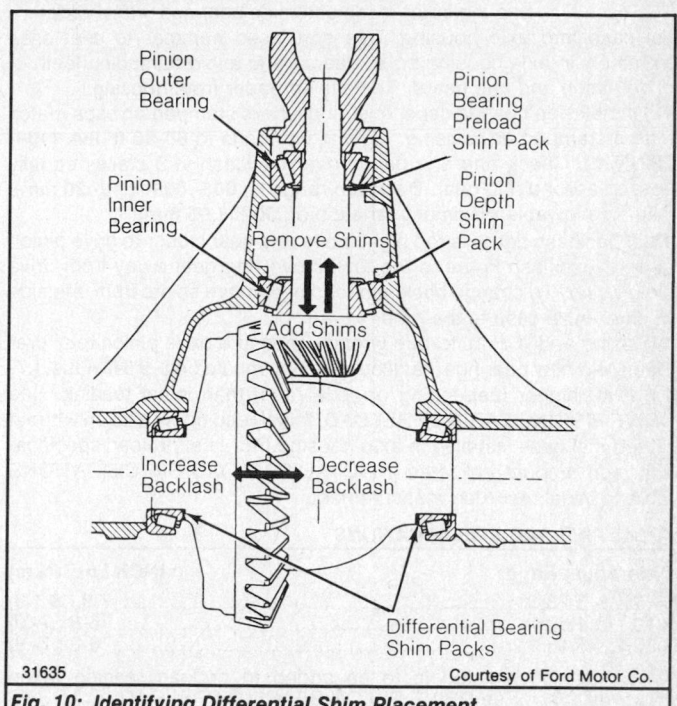

Fig. 10: Identifying Differential Shim Placement

Ring & Pinion Gear Backlash – 1) With drive pinion depth and preload adjustments correct, remove pinion flange using holder and flange remover. Coat pinion oil seal with multipurpose grease. Install pinion oil seal.

2) Ensure spring behind lip of seal remains in place during seal installation. If spring is dislodged, remove and replace seal. Install pinion flange and tighten nut to specification. See TORQUE SPECIFICATIONS table.

3) Install differential case into axle housing. Differential master bearings should still be on case. Install outboard spacers. Set dial indicator so dial indicator tip is against back of ring gear, at 90 degrees to gear.

4) Force ring gear away from drive pinion gear. With force still applied to ring gear, zero the dial indicator. Force ring gear and case toward drive pinion gear to obtain a reading on indicator. Repeat this procedure until same reading is obtained each time.

5) The reading obtained is thickness of shim pack that must go under differential side bearing on ring gear side of case. Remove dial indicator. Remove differential case from housing. Remove master bearings from differential case. Place shim pack of correct thickness onto ring gear hub. *See Fig. 10.*

6) Drive side bearing onto case using Side Bearing Installer (D81T-4221-A). On Dana 60 axle, support case on opposite side with Step Plate (D80L-630-7) while installing side bearing. On Dana 70 and 80 axles, use Step Plate (D80L-630-8).

7) On all applications, to determine the correct amount of shims to placed onto pinion gear side hub, subtract thickness of shim pack installed on ring gear side of case from total differential case end play. Total differential case end play was recorded in step 6) in DIFFERENTIAL CASE procedure under OVERHAUL.

8) On Dana 60 axle, add **.015" (.38 mm)** to figure for remaining end play. On Dana 70 and 80 axles, add **.010" (.25 mm)** to figure. On all applications, result is thickness of shim pack to be installed onto hub of differential case opposite ring gear (drive pinion side of case).

9) Place shim pack on case hub and drive side bearing onto case using side bearing installer. Support case with step plate to protect side bearing already installed onto ring gear side of case.

10) Install housing spreader and dial indicator onto axle housing. Set tip of dial indicator at same point used when case was removed from housing during disassembly procedure. Spread housing to a maximum of **.015" (.38 mm)**. Damage could occur if housing is spread further. Remove dial indicator.

11) Place side bearing outer races onto side bearings. Install differential case into axle housing. Use soft-faced hammer to seat case assembly in axle housing bore. Use care to avoid damaging teeth of drive pinion and ring gears. Remove spreader from housing.

12) Install side bearing caps, ensuring letters stamped on caps match letters stamped on housing. Tighten cap bolts to **80-90 ft. lbs. (108-122 N.m)**. Check ring and pinion gear backlash in 3 places equally spaced around ring gear. Backlash range is **.005-.008" (.13-.20 mm)**, with an allowable maximum variation of **.002" (.05 mm)**.

13) If backlash figure is too high, move ring gear closer to drive pinion gear. If backlash figure is too low, move ring gear away from drive pinion gear. To change backlash readings, move shims from one side of differential case to the other.

14) Using an INCH lb. torque wrench, measure drive pinion total preload. With new bearings installed, reading should be **6-9 INCH lbs. (.7-1.0 N.m)** higher (depending on axle ratio) than initial reading. See DRIVE PINION BEARING PRELOAD. Initial reading was taken without differential case installed in axle housing. For final preload specification, add amount indicated in TOTAL PRELOAD SPECIFICATIONS table to initial recorded measurement.

TOTAL PRELOAD SPECIFICATIONS

Differential Ratio	[1] INCH Lbs. (N.m)
3.45:1 & 3.73:1	7-9 (.8-1.0)
4.10:1 & 4.56:1	6-8 (.7-.9)
4.63:1 & 5.13:1	6-8 (.7-.9)

[1] – Specification listed is to be added to preload reading taken previously. See DRIVE PINION BEARING PRELOAD.

15) If total preload reading is too high, remove an equal amount of shims from each differential case hub. If total preload reading is too low, add an equal amount of shims to each differential case hub.

16) Verify final pinion position using gear tooth contact pattern. See GEAR TOOTH CONTACT PATTERNS article in GENERAL INFORMATION. Pattern should be correct if assembly and adjustments have been done properly.

17) When backlash is correct, install axle shafts. See HUB, BEARING & AXLE SHAFT (FULL-FLOATING) or AXLE SHAFTS & BEARINGS (SEMI-FLOATING) under REMOVAL & INSTALLATION. Install new gasket (if applicable) and housing cover. Tighten cover bolts to **30-40 ft. lbs. (41-54 N.m)**. Fill assembly with hypoid lubricant.

DIFFERENTIAL SPECIFICATIONS
DIFFERENTIAL ASSEMBLY SPECIFICATIONS

Application	In. (mm)
Axle Shaft End Play	Nonadjustable
Ring Gear Backlash	.005-.008 (.13-.20)
Ring Gear Backlash Maximum Variation Between Teeth	.002 (.05)

	INCH Lbs. (N.m)
Pinion Bearing Preload	
New Bearings	20-40 (2-5)
Used Bearings	10-20 (1-2)

TORQUE SPECIFICATIONS
TORQUE SPECIFICATIONS

Application	Ft. Lbs. (N.m)
Axle-To-Hub Bolt	
Except F350 Super Duty	41-55 (56-75)
F350 Super Duty	70-85 (95-115)
Ball Joint Nut (F-350)	
Lower	
Step 1	35 (47)
Step 2	150 (203)
Upper	70 (95)
Housing Cover Bolt	30-40 (41-54)
Pinion Flange Nut	
Dana 60 & 70	250-270 (339-366)
Dana 80	440-500 (597-678)
Pinion Shaft Lock Bolt	20-25 (27-34)
"U" Joint Bolt	15-20 (20-27)
Ring Gear Bolt	
Dana 60 & 70	100-120 (136-163)
Dana 80	200-240 (271-325)
Side Bearing Cap Bolt	80-90 (108-122)
Spindle-To-Steering Knuckle Nut (F-350)	50-60 (68-81)
Stabilizer Bar Link Nut (F-350)	21-33 (28-45)
Stabilizer Bar "U" Bolt (F-350)	48-68 (65-92)
Tie Rod End Nut (F-350)	70-100 (95-136)
Track Bar Bolt (F-350)	163-203 (221-275)
Wheel Lug Nut	140 (190)

	INCH Lbs. (N.m)
Locking Hub Cover Screw (F-350)	35-53 (4-6)

DESCRIPTION

Dana model 28-2 front axle is an integral carrier housing. *See Fig. 1.* Center line of drive pinion is mounted on center line of ring gear. Axle housing is made of aluminum and is mounted to sub-frame assembly. Inner axle shafts are retained in axle housing by "C" clips in differential case. Outer half-shaft drive axles bolt to inner drive axle shaft flanges and are supported on outboard end by rotor and hub assembly.

Drive pinion depth and differential side bearing preload are set by use of shims. Pinion bearing preload is set by use of collapsible pinion spacer.

AXLE RATIO & IDENTIFICATION

Axle application can be determined through the axle code on the Safety Certification Label on left door pillar. Additionally, a metal identification tag stamped with gear ratio and diameter is secured to housing cover. See AXLE RATIO IDENTIFICATION article.

REMOVAL & INSTALLATION

AXLE SHAFT, BEARING & OIL SEAL

Removal – 1) Remove axle housing assembly. See AXLE HOUSING ASSEMBLY under REMOVAL & INSTALLATION. Remove axle housing cover and drain differential fluid. Mount axle housing in Holding Fixture (T57L-500-B) using Adapters (T90T-4000-A) and Spacer (T80T-4000-B2).

2) Rotate shafts until open side of "C" clip on inner end of axle shaft can be reached. Remove "C" clip. Remove axle shaft. Remove axle

housing oil seal and needle bearings using slide hammer, Collet (D80L-100-A) and Actuator Pin (D80L-100-H).

Installation – 1) Ensure bearing bore is clean and has no nicks. Place new caged needle bearing on Needle Bearing Installer (T83T-1244-A). Ensure bearing manufacturer's name and part number is facing toward tool when installed in housing bore.

2) Drive needle bearing in until bearing is fully seated in housing bore. Coat lip of seal with multipurpose grease. Drive seal into carrier using Seal Installer (T90T-3110-A). Install axle shaft so groove on shaft is visible inside differential case.

3) Install "C" clip into groove on axle shaft. DO NOT tap on center of "C" clip, as clip will be damaged. Clean all sealant, oil and dirt from housing-to-cover mating surfaces. Apply continuous bead of RTV sealant, 1/4 - 3/8" wide, on housing.

NOTE: Install housing cover within 5 minutes after applying RTV sealant.

---

4) Sealant bead should not pass over or outside holes. Install housing cover. To complete installation, reverse removal procedure. Wait one hour before filling differential.

AXLE HOUSING ASSEMBLY

Removal – 1) Raise vehicle, and install safety stands under front lifting points. Mark position of drive shaft and axle flanges for installation reference. Disconnect front drive shaft from front axle companion flange.

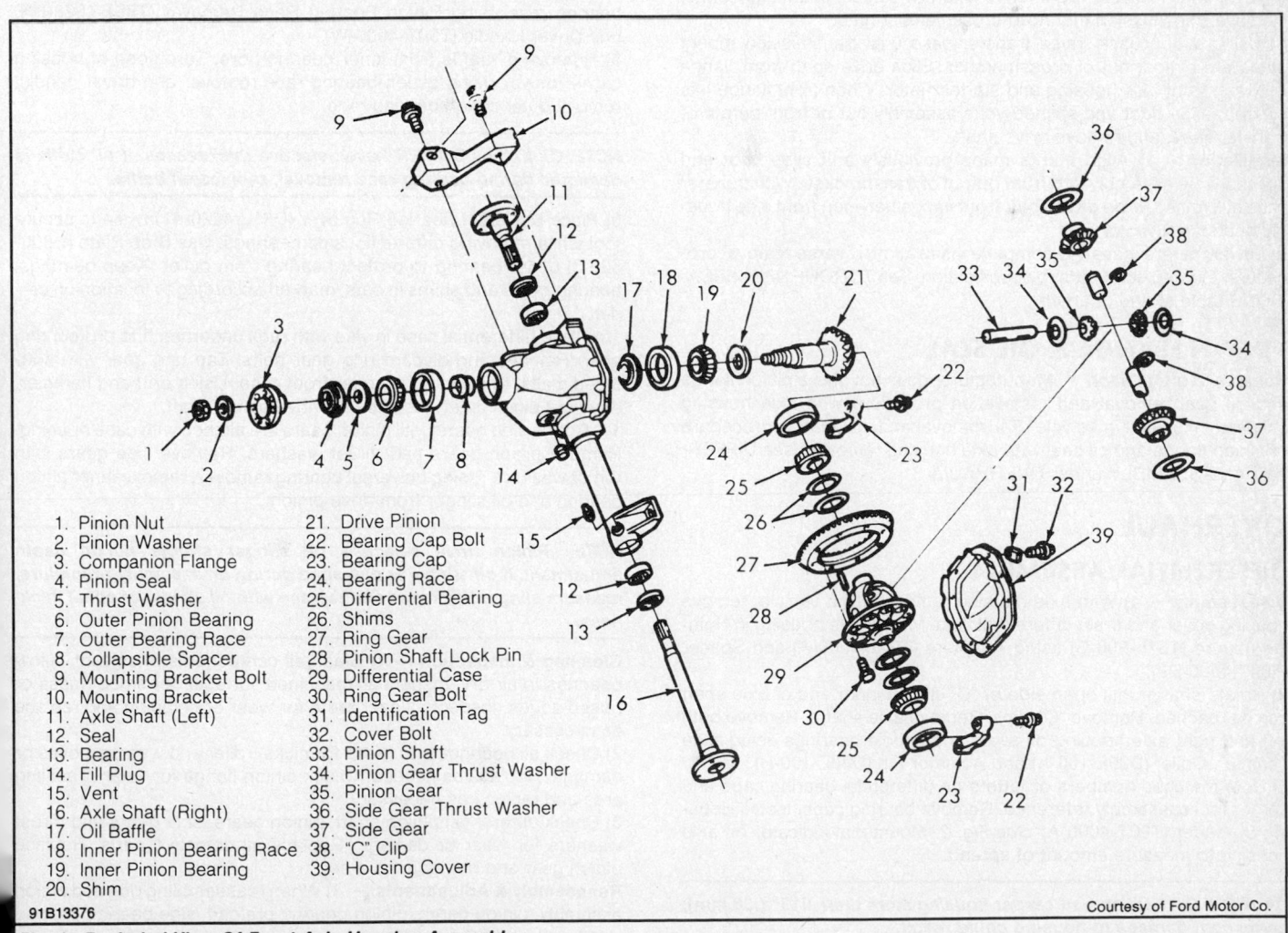

1. Pinion Nut
2. Pinion Washer
3. Companion Flange
4. Pinion Seal
5. Thrust Washer
6. Outer Pinion Bearing
7. Outer Bearing Race
8. Collapsible Spacer
9. Mounting Bracket Bolt
10. Mounting Bracket
11. Axle Shaft (Left)
12. Seal
13. Bearing
14. Fill Plug
15. Vent
16. Axle Shaft (Right)
17. Oil Baffle
18. Inner Pinion Bearing Race
19. Inner Pinion Bearing
20. Shim
21. Drive Pinion
22. Bearing Cap Bolt
23. Bearing Cap
24. Bearing Race
25. Differential Bearing
26. Shims
27. Ring Gear
28. Pinion Shaft Lock Pin
29. Differential Case
30. Ring Gear Bolt
31. Identification Tag
32. Cover Bolt
33. Pinion Shaft
34. Pinion Gear Thrust Washer
35. Pinion Gear
36. Side Gear Thrust Washer
37. Side Gear
38. "C" Clip
39. Housing Cover

91B13376

Courtesy of Ford Motor Co.

Fig. 1: Exploded View Of Front Axle Housing Assembly

FORD
7-24

1992 DRIVE AXLES
Dana 28-2 Front Axle – Aerostar (Cont.)

2) Remove inboard half-shaft flange-to-axle shaft bolts (both sides). Wire half-shafts aside, maintaining level position. Remove vent hose from axle housing and cap vent fitting to prevent fluid leakage.

3) Remove snubber from rear support crossmember, located below drive pinion. Support axle housing assembly with floor jack. Remove axle mounting bracket-to-crossmember lock nuts (4 places). Lower floor jack and remove axle housing assembly. Remove axle mounting bracket from axle housing, if necessary.

Installation – 1) Install axle mounting bracket to axle housing, if removed. Install mounting bracket bolts using Loctite and tighten to specification. See TORQUE SPECIFICATIONS table.

NOTE: If using new axle housing mounting bushings, tighten each lock nut to full torque in one step.

---

2) Insert axle housing bushing studs (4) through axle mounting brackets. Install axle housing mounting bushing stud lock nuts using Loctite, and tighten in sequence to specification.

3) Tightening sequence is as follows: left front, right front, pinion and rear. See TORQUE SPECIFICATIONS table at end of article. To complete installation, reverse removal procedure.

DRIVE SHAFT

Removal – 1) Raise and support vehicle. Mark position of drive shaft, companion flanges and splined yoke assembly-to-transfer case for installation reference. Release clamp on drive shaft dust boot using Clamp Remover (D87P-1090-A), and pull boot from transfer case.

2) Remove snubber from rear support crossmember, located below drive pinion. Remove front drive shaft-to-companion flange bolts. Remove transmission mount-to-crossmember nuts.

3) Using a floor jack, raise transfer case until transmission mount studs are almost out of crossmember. Slide drive shaft front flange between front axle housing and starter motor. When front flange has cleared, slide boot and splined yoke assembly out of front output of transfer case, and remove drive shaft.

Installation – 1) Align marks made previously and slide boot and splined yoke assembly into front output of transfer case. With transfer case still raised, slide drive shaft front flange between front axle housing and starter motor.

2) Lower transfer case. To complete installation, reverse removal procedure. Tighten bolts/nuts to specification. See TORQUE SPECIFICATIONS table at end of article.

PINION FLANGE & OIL SEAL

Removal & Installation – Manufacturer does not give a pinion flange and oil seal removal and installation procedure with axle housing assembly installed in vehicle. For removal and installation procedure of pinion flange and oil seal with axle housing removed, see DIFFERENTIAL ASSEMBLY under OVERHAUL.

OVERHAUL

DIFFERENTIAL ASSEMBLY

Disassembly – 1) With axle housing removed from vehicle, remove housing cover and drain differential fluid. Mount axle housing in Holding Fixture (T57L-500-B) using Adapters (T90T-4000-A) and Spacer (T80T-4000-B2).

2) Rotate shafts until open side of "C" clip on inner end of axle shaft can be reached. Remove "C" clips. Remove axle shafts. Remove both left and right axle housing oil seals and needle bearings using slide hammer, Collet (D80L-100-A) and Actuator Pin (D80L-100-H).

3) Note matched numbers or letters on differential bearing caps and carrier for reassembly reference. Remove bearing caps. Install Housing Spreader (T90T-4000-A). See Fig. 2. Mount dial indicator on axle housing to measure amount of spread.

CAUTION: DO NOT spread carrier housing more than .015" (.38 mm); permanent damage to housing could result.

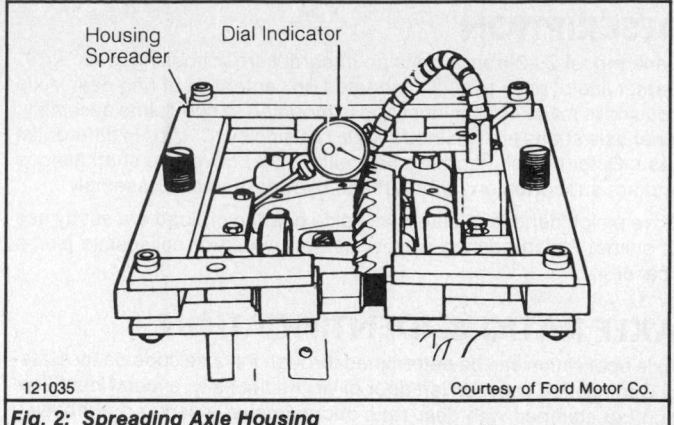

Housing Spreader   Dial Indicator

121035   Courtesy of Ford Motor Co.

Fig. 2: Spreading Axle Housing

4) Spread axle housing to a maximum of .015" (.38 mm). Remove dial indicator. Carefully pry differential assembly out of housing. Remove spreader immediately so housing does not permanently distort.

5) Remove and tag side bearing races to indicate from which side of carrier they were removed. Turn nose of axle housing up. Mark pinion companion flange-to-drive pinion position for installation reference.

6) Using Companion Flange Holder (T78P-4851-A), hold companion flange while removing drive pinion nut and washer. Remove companion flange. If flange shows wear in sealing area, replace flange. Remove drive pinion by tapping with soft-faced mallet.

7) Remove and discard drive pinion oil seal. Remove outer pinion bearing, oil slinger and collapsible spacer. Drive out inner drive pinion bearing race using Pinion Bearing Race Remover (T86T-4628-BH) and Driver Handle (T80T-4000-W).

8) Remove oil baffle from inner bearing bore. Turn nose of housing carrier down. Using pinion bearing race remover and driver handle, remove outer pinion bearing race.

NOTE: Oil baffles DO NOT have selective thicknesses. If oil baffle is damaged during bearing race removal, replace oil baffle.

---

9) Place Universal Bearing Remover (D81L-4220-A) in vise to secure tool while removing differential side bearings. Use Step Plate (D80L-630-3) under bearing to protect bearing from puller. Keep bearings, bearing races and shims in sets, marked according to location on carrier.

10) Place differential case in vise with rags underneath to protect ring gear. Remove and discard ring gear bolts. Tap ring gear with soft-faced mallet to remove ring gear from case. Using drift and hammer, drive out pinion shaft lock pin. Remove pinion shaft.

11) Rotate side gears until pinion gears are aligned with case opening. Remove pinion gears and thrust washers. Remove side gears with thrust washers. Using universal bearing remover, remove inner pinion bearing and oil slinger from drive pinion.

NOTE: Pinion drive selective oil slinger affects pinion depth adjustment. If oil slinger is damaged during disassembly procedure, measure slinger thickness and replace with oil slinger of equal thickness.

Cleaning & Inspection – 1) Clean all components in solvent. Allow bearings to air dry. Inspect all machined surfaces for smoothness or raised edges. Inspect all gear teeth for wear or chipping and replace as necessary.

2) Check all bearings and races for nicks, roller end wear, grooves or damage. Replace as needed. Check pinion flange for wear in sealing area and replace as necessary.

3) Check differential pinion shaft, pinion gears, side gears and thrust washers for wear or damage. Replace all defective parts. Replace pinion gear and ring gear as a set.

Reassembly & Adjustments – 1) When reassembling ring and pinion assembly, pinion depth, pinion bearing preload, side bearing preload and backlash between ring and pinion must be adjusted.

1992 DRIVE AXLES
Dana 28-2 Front Axle – Aerostar (Cont.)

**FORD
7-25**

2) If only replacing pinion shaft and ring gear and carrier housing can be reused, compare pinion depth adjustment numbers etched in faces of old and new pinion heads. *See Fig. 3.*

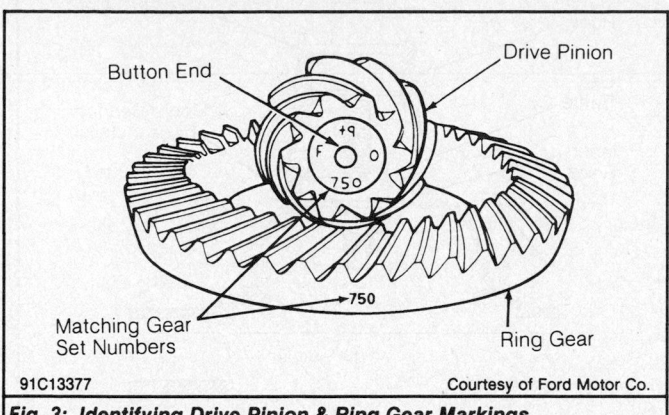

Button End
Drive Pinion
Matching Gear Set Numbers
Ring Gear
→750
91C13377
Courtesy of Ford Motor Co.

Fig. 3: Identifying Drive Pinion & Ring Gear Markings

3) Drive pinion end has a plus figure (+), minus figure (–) or a zero figure (0). Figure is determined by manufacturer at time of assembly.

Number represents nominal distance that pinion shaft deviates from distance between pinion gear face and center line of axle.

4) Nominal distance is measured from center line of ring gear to face of gear on drive pinion shaft. Using PINION DEPTH SHIM ADJUSTMENT CHART, correct shims can be selected for new pinion shaft depth adjustment.

5) For example, if original drive pinion is etched +4" (+10 mm) and new drive pinion is etched zero (0), then new selective oil slinger would be .004" (.10 mm) thicker than original selective oil slinger. See PINION DEPTH SHIM ADJUSTMENT CHART.

6) Ring gear and pinion gear are supplied in matched sets only. Matching numbers are etched on ring and pinion gears. If using new gear set, verify matching gear set numbers. *See Fig. 3.*

7) Pinion depth gauge set allows oil slinger adjustments to be made without having to remove and replace differential bearings when figuring correct pinion depth. *See Fig. 4.*

NOTE: To use PINION DEPTH SHIM ADJUSTMENT CHART procedure, old drive pinion oil slinger dimension MUST be determined accurately. If original drive pinion oil slinger dimension cannot be accurately determined, use pinion depth gauge set to determine correct pinion depth setting. Use depth gauge set if using new carrier housing.

PINION DEPTH SHIM ADJUSTMENT CHART (INCHES)

Old Pinion Marking	New Pinion Marking								
	-4	-3	-2	-1	0	+1	+2	+3	+4
+4	+0.008	+0.007	+0.006	+0.005	+0.004	+0.003	+0.002	+0.001	0
+3	+0.007	+0.006	+0.005	+0.004	+0.003	+0.002	+0.001	0	-0.001
+2	+0.006	+0.005	+0.004	+0.003	+0.002	+0.001	0	-0.001	-0.002
+1	+0.005	+0.004	+0.003	+0.002	+0.001	0	-0.001	-0.002	-0.003
0	+0.004	+0.003	+0.002	+0.001	0	-0.001	-0.002	-0.003	-0.004
-1	+0.003	+0.002	+0.001	0	-0.001	-0.002	-0.003	-0.004	-0.005
-2	+0.002	+0.001	0	-0.001	-0.002	-0.003	-0.004	-0.005	-0.006
-3	+0.001	0	-0.001	-0.002	-0.003	-0.004	-0.005	-0.006	-0.007
-4	0	-0.001	-0.002	-0.003	-0.004	-0.005	-0.006	-0.007	-0.008

PINION DEPTH SHIM ADJUSTMENT CHART (MILLIMETERS)

Old Pinion Marking	New Pinion Marking								
	-10	-8	-5	-3	0	+3	+5	+8	+10
+10	+0.20	+0.18	+0.15	+0.13	+0.10	+0.08	+0.05	+0.03	0
+8	+0.18	+0.15	+0.13	+0.10	+0.08	+0.05	+0.03	0	-0.03
+5	+0.15	+0.13	+0.10	+0.08	+0.05	+0.03	0	-0.03	-0.05
+3	+0.13	+0.10	+0.08	+0.05	+0.03	0	-0.03	-0.05	-0.08
0	+0.10	+0.08	+0.05	+0.03	0	-0.03	-0.05	-0.08	-0.10
-3	+0.08	+0.05	+0.03	0	-0.03	-0.05	-0.08	-0.10	-0.13
-5	+0.05	+0.03	0	-0.03	-0.05	-0.08	-0.10	-0.13	-0.15
-8	+0.03	0	-0.03	-0.05	-0.08	-0.10	-0.13	-0.15	-0.18
-10	0	-0.03	-0.05	-0.08	-0.10	-0.13	-0.15	-0.18	-0.20

FORD
7-26

1992 DRIVE AXLES
Dana 28-2 Front Axle – Aerostar (Cont.)

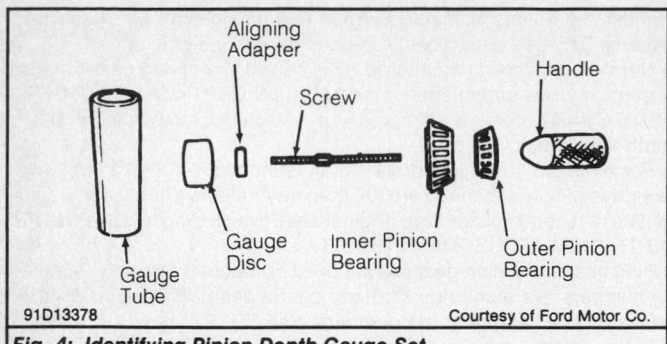

Fig. 4: Identifying Pinion Depth Gauge Set

Differential Case Reassembly – 1) Position ring gear to differential case. Install NEW ring gear bolts and tighten to specification in a circular pattern. Place differential case into position in axle housing. Install Master Differential Bearings (T83T-4222-A) on differential case.

2) Remove all burrs and nicks from hubs so master bearings rotate freely. Install differential case in housing without shims. Mount dial indicator with indicator tip at 90 degrees to flat surface on head of ring gear bolt or flat machined surface of ring gear.

3) Using screwdriver, force differential case toward dial indicator as far as possible. Zero dial indicator with force still applied. Force differential case away from dial indicator as far as possible. Read gauge. Repeat this procedure until same reading is obtained. *See Fig. 5.*

4) This measurement is total differential case end play and will be used later to determine proper shim pack dimension. Use multipurpose grease to lubricate side gears, pinion gears and all thrust washers. Install components in differential case. Rotate side gears until holes in pinion gears and washers line up with holes in case.

5) Install differential pinion shaft. Install lock pin. Using a punch and hammer, peen metal of differential case over lock pin at 2 locations, 90 degrees to the left and right of lock pin slot. Remove differential case from housing. Leave master bearings on case at this time.

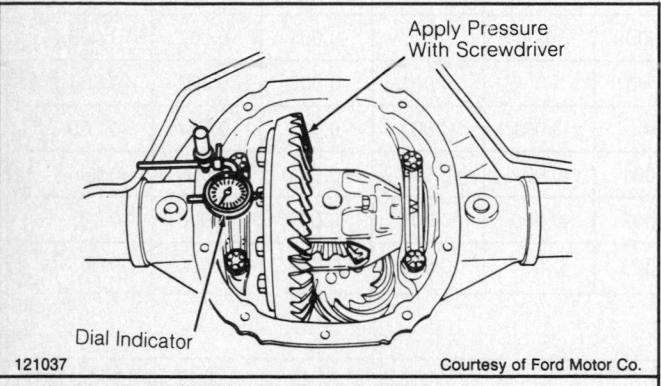

Fig. 5: Measuring Differential Case End Play

Drive Pinion Bearing Race Installation – 1) Install oil baffle in inner bearing race bore of housing. Place inner and outer pinion bearing races in bores of axle housing.

2) Place Inner/Outer Race Installers (T71P-4616-A) on bearing races. *See Fig. 6.* Install Forcing Screw (T75T-1176-A) through bearing races. Tighten forcing screw until both bearing races are seated in axle housing.

NOTE: Check tools in pinion depth gauge set for nicks or damage before each use. Remove any high spots on tools to ensure accurate readings.

Drive Pinion Depth – 1) Put new inner drive pinion bearing on Aligning Adapter (T76P-4020-A1), and assemble using Gauge Disc Block (T90T-4020-A). *See Fig. 4.* Put outer pinion bearing (new or good used) into race. Place depth gauge assembly into housing with Screw (T76P-4020-A9), extending through outer bearing.

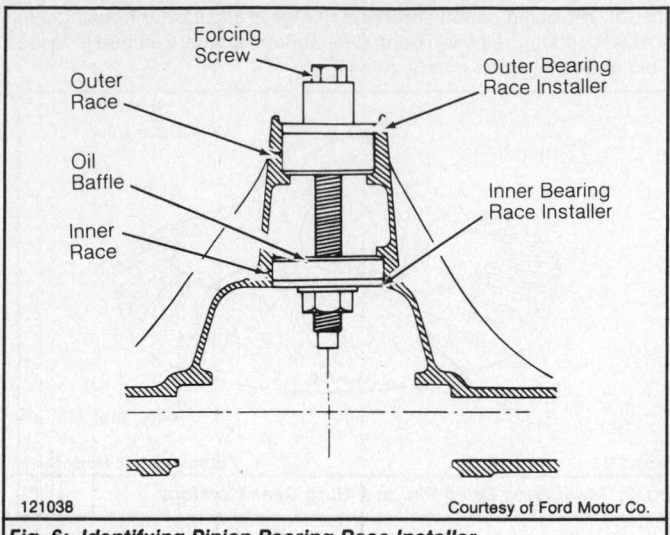

Fig. 6: Identifying Pinion Bearing Race Installer

2) Thread Handle (T76P-4020-A11) onto screw finger tight. Install and center Gauge Tube (T76P-4020-A7) into differential bearing bore. Install bearing caps and tighten to specification. See TORQUE SPECIFICATIONS table at end of article. Using 3/8" drive torque wrench in square drive on handle, tighten handle until preload on bearings is 20-40 INCH lbs. (2.3-4.5 N.m).

3) Determine clearance between gauge block and gauge tube using feeler gauge. Correct feeler gauge will give feeling of slight drag as gauge passes between tube and block. *See Fig. 7.*

4) Thickness of correct feeler gauge is thickness of selective oil slinger to be installed between drive pinion head and inner pinion bearing, if drive pinion has zero marking. If drive pinion has plus (+) marking on face, subtract that number from thickness dimension. If drive pinion has minus (–) marking on face, add that number to thickness dimension.

NOTE: Inner bearing used for depth measurement must be bearing used for final assembly.

5) Using a micrometer, measure oil slinger to verify size. Place oil slinger on drive pinion. Press inner drive pinion bearing and oil slinger on drive pinion, using Axle Bearing/Seal Plate (T75L-1165-B), Pinion Bearing Replacer (T57L-4621-B) and arbor press.

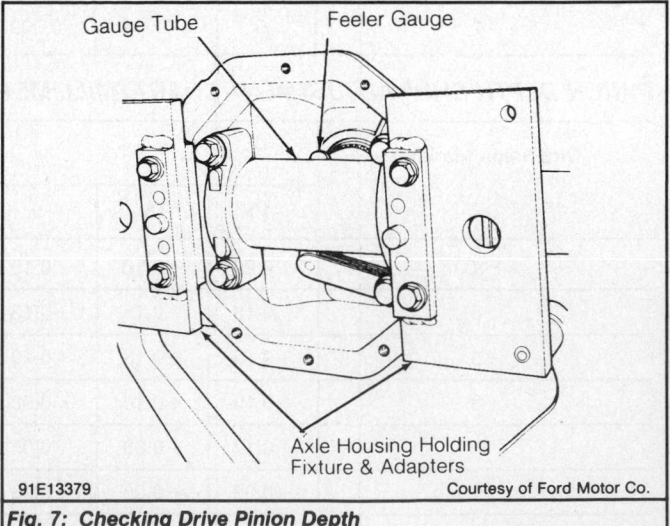

Fig. 7: Checking Drive Pinion Depth

Drive Pinion Bearing Preload – 1) Install drive pinion in axle housing. Install NEW collapsible spacer. Install outer pinion bearing and thrust

1992 DRIVE AXLES
Dana 28-2 Front Axle – Aerostar (Cont.)

**FORD
7-27**

washer. Lubricate and install drive pinion oil seal. Noting alignment marks made previously, install pinion companion flange, washer and NEW nut on pinion shaft. Tighten pinion nut to specification. See TORQUE SPECIFICATIONS table at end of article.

2) Using an INCH-pound torque wrench, check rotational torque necessary to turn pinion. Rotational torque should be **15-35 INCH lbs. (1.7-4.0 N.m)**. If rotational torque is less than specification, tighten pinion nut in small increments until correct rotational torque is reached. If reading exceeds 35 INCH lbs (4.0 N.m), remove pinion and replace collapsible spacer.

CAUTION: Always use NEW collapsible spacer when reassembling drive pinion. NEVER tighten pinion flange nut more than 275 ft. lbs. (373 N.m) as collapsible spacer will be compressed too far.

Ring & Pinion Gear Backlash – 1) With drive pinion depth and preload adjustments properly made, install differential case into housing. Differential master bearings should still be on case. Force differential case away from drive pinion gear so case is fully seated in cross bores of housing.

2) Set dial indicator so tip is against head of ring gear bolt at 90 degrees to bolt. Rock ring gear so teeth of ring gear mesh fully with drive pinion gear teeth. Force ring gear teeth against drive pinion gear teeth and zero dial indicator. Force ring gear and case away from drive pinion gear. Read gauge. Repeat this procedure until same reading is obtained each time.

3) This reading, less .005" (.13 mm), is thickness of shim pack that must go under differential side bearing on ring gear side of case. Remove case from axle housing. Remove master bearings from case. Place correct shim pack on ring gear hub of case. Place side bearing on hub of case. Drive bearing onto case using Step plate (D80L-630-3), Side Bearing Replacer (T83T-4221-A) and Handle (T80T-4000-W).

4) To determine correct amount of shims to place on pinion gear side hub, subtract thickness of shim pack installed on ring gear side of case from total of differential case end play. Total differential case end play was previously determined in steps **1) - 4)** of DIFFERENTIAL CASE REASSEMBLY. Add .010" (.25 mm) to figure determined for shim pack thickness on side opposite ring gear.

5) Place required thickness shim pack on hub of case opposite ring gear. Place step plate on ring gear side bearing to protect bearing. Drive remaining side bearing onto case with side bearing replacer. Install side bearing races on side bearings.

6) Install housing spreader and dial indicator on carrier. Spread housing to maximum of .015" (.37 mm). Install differential case in housing. Use soft-faced hammer to ensure that case seats fully in housing bore. Use care to avoid damaging teeth of ring and pinion gears.

7) Remove housing spreader and dial indicator. Install side bearing caps, ensuring letters stamped on caps match letters stamped on housing. Tighten bearing cap bolts to specification. See TORQUE SPECIFICATIONS table at end of article.

8) Check ring and pinion gear backlash in 3 places equally spaced around ring gear. Backlash range is **.005-.008" (.13-20 mm)** with allowable maximum variation of .003" (.08 mm). If backlash figure is too high, move ring gear closer to drive pinion gear.

9) If backlash figure is too low, move ring gear away from drive pinion gear. To change backlash readings, move shims from one side of differential case to other. DO NOT change total thickness of end play shim packs.

10) When backlash adjustment is completed, check tooth contact pattern. See GEAR TOOTH CONTACT PATTERNS article in GENERAL INFORMATION. Pattern will be correct if assembly and adjustments have been done properly. When backlash is correct, apply continuous bead of RTV sealant, 1/4 - 3/8" wide, on housing.

11) Sealant bead should not pass over or outside holes. Install housing cover. To complete installation, reverse removal procedure. Allow one hour cure time before filling differential.

ASSEMBLY SPECIFICATIONS
AXLE ASSEMBLY SPECIFICATIONS

Application	In. (mm)
Axle Shaft End Play	Non-Adjustable
Ring Gear-To-Pinion Backlash [1]	.005-.008 (.13-.20)

	INCH Lbs. (N.m)
Drive Pinion Bearing Preload New Bearings	15-35 (1.7-4.0)

[1] – Maximum backlash variation between 3 equally spaced check points is .003" (.08 mm).

TORQUE SPECIFICATIONS
TORQUE SPECIFICATIONS

Application	Ft. Lbs. (N.m)
Axle Mounting Bracket-To-Axle Housing Bolt	70-80 (95-108)
Axle Snubber Bolt	17-24 (23-33)
Axle-To-Crossmember Mounting Bushing Nut	65-85 (88-115)
Flange Bolt	22-29 (30-39)
Housing Cover Bolt	20-25 (27-34)
Pinion Flange Nut	[1] 140-275 (190-373)
Ring Gear-To-Case Bolt	45-65 (61-86)
Side Bearing Cap Bolt	30-45 (41-61)
Wheel Lug Nuts	100 (136)

[1] – Collapsible pinion spacer used. Tighten pinion nut until rotational torque of pinion is 15-35 ft. lbs. (1.7-4.0 N.m)

1992 DRIVE AXLES
Dana IFS Front Axle

Bronco, Explorer, Pickup, Ranger

NOTE: References to Pickup include the F150 & F250 but NOT F350 Super Duty commercial chassis.

DESCRIPTION & OPERATION

Independent Front Suspension (IFS) front axle is of integral carrier housing, hypoid gear type. Centerline of drive pinion is mounted above centerline of ring gear. Drive pinion and ring gear bearing adjustments are all accomplished with shims.

Dana 35 IFS axle is used on 4WD Explorer and 4WD Ranger models. Dana 44 IFS axle is used on Bronco and F150 4WD. Dana 44 IFS-HD axle is used on F250 4WD. Dana 50 IFS axle is used on F250 HD 4WD. Dana 35 IFS and 44 IFS axles are equipped with coil springs. Dana 44 IFS-HD and 50 IFS axles are equipped with leaf springs.

Power is transmitted through transfer case driveshaft to the drive pinion located in the differential carrier housing. *See Fig. 1.* Drive pinion shaft is supported by 2 opposed tapered roller bearings. Power is transmitted from pinion gear through ring gear and differential pinion gears to axle shafts and wheels.

AXLE RATIO & IDENTIFICATION

Axle application can be determined through the axle code on the Safety Certification Label on left door pillar. Additionally, a metal identification tag stamped with gear ratio and diameter, is secured to carrier housing. If axle is equipped with limited slip differential, gear ratio will have letter "L" in the number. To further identify differential ring gear size and drive axle ratio, see AXLE RATIO IDENTIFICATION article.

LUBRICATION

CAPACITY
DIFFERENTIAL LUBRICATION CAPACITY

Application	Pts. (L)
Model 35	3.6 (1.7)
Model 44	3.9 (1.8)
Model 50	4.1 (1.9)

FLUID TYPE

All models use Hypoid Gear Lubricant (C6AZ-19580-E). Limited Slip Differentials (LSD) require an additional 4 ozs. of Friction Modifier (C8AZ-19B546-A)

TROUBLE SHOOTING

NOTE: See TROUBLE SHOOTING article in GENERAL INFORMATION.

REMOVAL & INSTALLATION

NOTE: For removal and installation procedures of front drive axle component parts not covered in this article, see appropriate LOCKING HUBS and 4WD STEERING KNUCKLES articles.

HUBS & BEARINGS

Removal (Explorer & Ranger With Dana 35 IFS) – **1)** Raise and support vehicle. Remove wheels and tires. Remove retainer washers from wheel lug nut studs. Remove caliper with brake line attached and secure to frame with wire. DO NOT hang caliper with any tension on brake hose. Remove manual or automatic locking hub assemblies.
2) On models with manual locking hubs, remove snap ring and axle shaft spacer from spindle. Remove outer bearing lock nut with Spanner Lock Nut Wrench (T86T-1197-B). Remove lock nut washer and inner bearing adjusting nut.
3) On models with automatic locking hubs, remove snap ring and axle shaft spacer. Carefully pull plastic cam assembly from bearing adjusting nut. Remove 2 plastic thrust washers from adjusting nut.

CAUTION: Before removing adjusting nut, remove locking key from spindle keyway. Failure to clear keyway will result in thread damage on spindle.

4) Using magnet, remove locking key from spindle keyway. It may be necessary to rotate adjusting nut slightly to relieve pressure for locking key removal. Remove adjusting nut with 2 3/8" Hex Socket (T70T-4252-B).
5) On all models, remove hub and rotor. Remove outer bearing. Using Seal Remover (1175-AC), remove grease seal from rotor. Remove inner bearing. If bearings require replacement, remove races from hub using Internal Puller (D80L-943-A) and attached slide hammer.
Installation & Adjustment (With Manual Locking Hubs) – **1)** If bearings are replaced, drive new races into hub. Lubricate bearings with lithium base multipurpose wheel bearing grease. Install inner bearing and seal into hub. Install hub and rotor assembly on spindle. Install outer bearing and adjusting nut. Tighten adjusting nut to 35 ft. lbs. (47 N.m) while turning hub back and forth to seat bearings.
2) Spin hub and back off adjusting nut 1/4 turn (90 degrees). Install lock washer on spindle. Mount lock washer over pin on adjusting nut, turning nut slightly if necessary to align pin. Install and tighten outer lock nut to 150 ft. lbs. (203 N.m) using spanner lock nut wrench.
3) Install axle shaft spacer. Install snap ring on end of spindle. Install manual hub assembly. Install retaining washers, wheel and tire. Check hub and rotor assembly end play. End play should be 0-.003" (0-.08 mm). To complete installation, reverse removal procedure.
Installation & Adjustment (With Automatic Locking Hubs) – **1)** If bearings are replaced, drive new races into hub. Lubricate bearings with lithium base multipurpose wheel bearing grease. Install inner bearing and seal into hub. Install hub on spindle.
2) Install outer bearing and adjusting nut. Tighten adjusting nut to 35 ft. lbs. (47 N.m) while turning hub back and forth to seat bearings. Spin hub and back off adjusting nut 1/4 turn (90 degrees). Retighten adjusting nut to 16 INCH lbs. (1.8 N.m).
3) Align nearest hole in adjusting nut with center of spindle keyway slot. Advance nut to next lug, if necessary. Install locking key into spindle keyway under adjusting nut. Install 2 thrust washers. Press plastic cam assembly onto adjusting nut while lining up key in fixed cam with spindle keyway.
4) Install axle shaft spacer. Clip snap ring onto end of spindle. Install automatic locking hub assembly with 3 legs of hub assembly inserted into 3 pockets of cam assembly. Install retaining washers, wheel and tire. Check hub and rotor assembly end play. End play should be 0-.003" (0-.08 mm). To complete installation, reverse removal procedure.

WARNING: Use great care in aligning spindle nut lug with center of spindle keyway. Damage to locking key may allow wheel assembly to come off vehicle while in motion.

Removal (Bronco & F150/250 With Manual Locking Hubs) – **1)** Raise and support front of vehicle. Remove front wheels. Remove locking hubs. See LOCKING HUBS article. Remove caliper with brake line attached and secure to frame with wire. Do not hang caliper with any tension on brake hose.
2) Remove hub bearing lock nut, lock ring and adjusting nut. Using Spanner Lock Nut Wrench (T86T-1197-A), remove nuts. Remove hub and rotor. Outer bearing will slide off with hub. Remove grease seal and inner bearing. If bearings require replacement, remove races from hub with Internal Puller (T77F-1102-A) and attached slide hammer.
Installation & Adjustment – **1)** If bearings are replaced, drive new races into hub. Lubricate bearings with lithium base multipurpose wheel bearing grease. Install inner bearing and seal into hub.
2) Install hub and rotor assemble on spindle. Install outer bearing and adjusting nut. Using torque wrench and Spanner Lock Nut Wrench (T86T-1197-A) tighten adjusting nut to 50-60 ft. lbs. (68-81 N.m) while turning wheel back and forth.
3) Applying inward pressure to spanner lock nut wrench to disengage locking splines, back off adjusting nut approximately 1/2 turn (180 degrees). Retighten adjusting nut to 15 ft. lbs. (20 N.m). Check hub

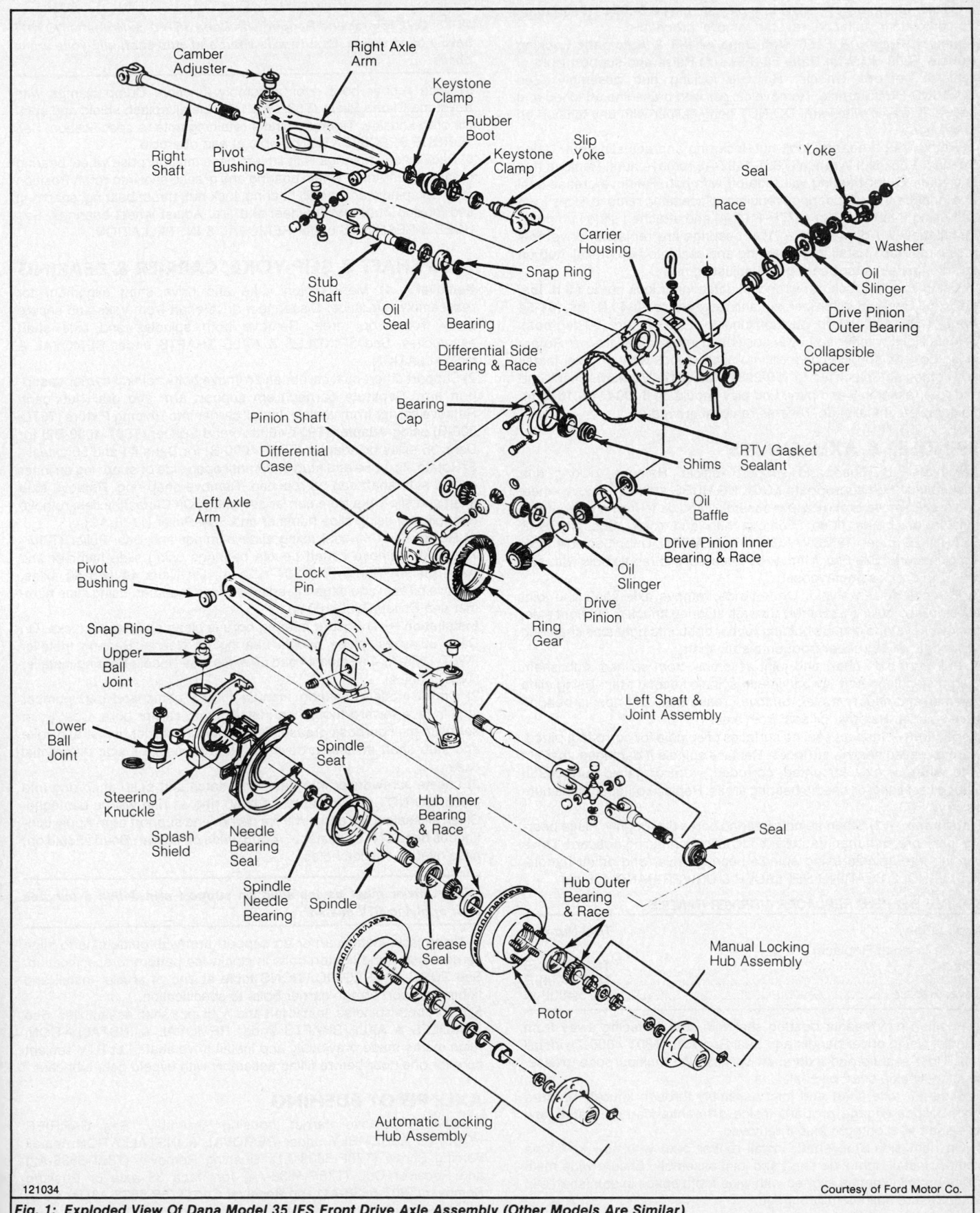

Camber Adjuster — **Right Axle Arm** — **Keystone Clamp** — **Rubber Boot** — **Keystone Clamp** — **Slip Yoke** — **Yoke** — **Seal** — **Race** — **Washer** — **Oil Slinger** — **Drive Pinion Outer Bearing** — **Collapsible Spacer**

Right Shaft — **Pivot Bushing** — **Stub Shaft** — **Oil Seal** — **Bearing** — **Snap Ring** — **Carrier Housing**

Differential Side Bearing & Race — **Bearing Cap** — **Shims** — **RTV Gasket Sealant** — **Oil Baffle** — **Drive Pinion Inner Bearing & Race**

Pinion Shaft — **Differential Case** — **Left Axle Arm** — **Pivot Bushing** — **Lock Pin** — **Oil Slinger** — **Drive Pinion** — **Ring Gear**

Snap Ring — **Upper Ball Joint** — **Lower Ball Joint** — **Steering Knuckle** — **Splash Shield** — **Needle Bearing Seal** — **Spindle Needle Bearing** — **Spindle** — **Spindle Seat** — **Grease Seal** — **Hub Inner Bearing & Race** — **Rotor** — **Hub Outer Bearing & Race** — **Left Shaft & Joint Assembly** — **Seal** — **Manual Locking Hub Assembly**

Automatic Locking Hub Assembly

121034

Courtesy of Ford Motor Co.

Fig. 1: Exploded View Of Dana Model 35 IFS Front Drive Axle Assembly (Other Models Are Similar)

and rotor assembly end play. End play should be **0-.004" (0-.10 mm)**. To complete installation, reverse removal procedure.

Removal (Bronco & F150 With Dana 44 IFS & Automatic Locking Hubs & F250 HD With Dana 50 IFS) – **1)** Raise and support front of vehicle. Remove wheels. Remove locking hub assembly. See LOCKING HUBS article. Remove caliper with brake line attached and secure to frame with wire. DO NOT hang caliper with any tension on brake hose.

2) Remove hub bearing lock nut, lock ring and adjusting nut. Using Spanner Lock Nut Wrench (T85T-1197-A), remove nuts. Remove hub and rotor. Outer bearing will slide off with hub. Remove grease seal and inner bearing. If bearings require replacement, remove races from hub using Internal Puller (T77F-1102-A) and attached slide hammer.

Installation & Adjustment – **1)** If bearings are replaced, drive new races into hub. Install inner bearing and seal into hub. Install hub on spindle. Install outer bearing and adjusting nut.

2) Using spanner lock nut wrench, tighten inner lock nut to **50 ft. lbs. (68 N.m)**. Back off inner lock nut and retighten to **30-40 ft. lbs. (41-54 N.m)**. While rotating hub, back off inner lock nut 1/4 turn (90 degrees).

3) Install lock washer so key is positioned into spindle groove. Rotate inner lock nut so pin is aligned into nearest lock washer hole. Install and tighten outer lock nut to **160-205 ft. lbs. (217-278 N.m)**. Check hub and rotor assembly end play. End play should be **0-.004" (0-.10 mm)**. To complete installation, reverse removal procedure.

SPINDLES & AXLE SHAFTS

Removal – **1)** Raise and support vehicle. Remove locking hub assemblies. See appropriate LOCKING HUBS article. Remove wheel and tire. Remove brake caliper assembly and tie to frame without any tension on brake hose. Remove hub and rotor. See HUBS & BEARINGS under REMOVAL & INSTALLATION. Unbolt spindle from knuckle studs. *See Fig. 1* It may be necessary to tap spindle with soft mallet to break spindle loose.

2) Remove splash shield. On left side, remove axle shaft and joint assembly by pulling assembly through steering knuckle. On right side, remove keystone clamps holding rubber boot onto right axle shaft and stub shaft. Slide rubber boot onto stub shaft.

3) Pull right axle shaft and joint assembly from splined stub shaft. Clamp spindle in soft-jawed vise on spindle second step. Using slide hammer and seal remover, remove grease seal and needle bearing from spindle. Remove oil seal from axle.

Inspection – Inspect sealing surfaces of spindle for corroded, pitted, worn or galled sealing surfaces. Replace spindle if damaged. Inspect outer shaft of axle for pitted, corroded, worn or galled surfaces in inner oil seal and/or needle bearing areas. Replace outer shaft as necessary.

Installation – **1)** Clean spindle bearing bores thoroughly. Place bearing into bore with manufacturer's identification facing outward. Drive bearing into spindle using spindle bearing driver and driver handle. See SPINDLE BEARING REPLACER & DRIVER HANDLE table.

SPINDLE BEARING REPLACER & DRIVER HANDLE

Application	Tool Number
Spindle Bearing Replacer	
Dana 35 & 44	T80T-4000-S
Dana 50	T80T-4000-R
Driver Handle	T80T-4000-W

2) Position new needle bearing seal with seal lip facing away from spindle. Using driver handle and Seal Replacer (T80T-4000-T), install seal. Coat seal lip and axle shaft splines with multipurpose grease. Install new axle shaft oil seal.

3) Slide left axle shaft and joint assembly through knuckle. Ensure shaft splines engage properly inside differential carrier. Install new axle shaft seal on right axle if removed.

4) On right side stub shaft, install rubber boot with new keystone clamps. Install right axle shaft and joint assembly. Ensure wide male spline on axle shaft is aligned with wide tooth space in stub shaft slip yoke. Ensure splines fully engage.

NOTE: On Explorer and Ranger with Dana 35 IFS, axle shafts DO NOT have a blind spline. Ensure axle shaft and stub shaft slip yoke are in phase.

5) Slide rubber boot over assembly junction. Crimp clamps with Keystone Clamp Pliers (T63P-9171-A). Install splash shield and spindle onto knuckle. Tighten spindle retaining nuts to specification. See TORQUE SPECIFICATIONS table at end of article.

6) Pack wheel bearings with lithium base multipurpose wheel bearing grease. Install inner wheel bearing and grease seal into rotor. Position rotor on spindle and install bearing, lock nut, thrust bearing, snap ring and locking hub. Install wheel and tire. Adjust wheel bearings. See HUBS & BEARINGS under REMOVAL & INSTALLATION.

STUB SHAFT & SLIP YOKE, CARRIER & BEARING

Removal – **1)** Mark pinion yoke and drive shaft alignment for reassembly reference. Disconnect drive shaft from yoke and secure away from work area. Remove both spindles and axle shaft assemblies. See SPINDLES & AXLE SHAFTS under REMOVAL & INSTALLATION.

2) Support differential carrier and remove bolts holding carrier to support arm. Separate carrier from support arm and drain lubricant. Remove carrier from vehicle. Install carrier into Holding Fixture (T57L-500-B) using Adapter (T90T-4000-A) and Spacer (T80T-4000-B2) for Dana 35 axles or Adapter (T80T-4000-B) for Dana 44 and 50 axles.

3) Rotate slip yoke and stub shaft until open side of snap ring on inner end of stub shaft can be reached. Remove snap ring. Remove stub shaft and slip yoke from carrier assembly. On Dana 35 axles, remove right oil seal using slide hammer and Seal Puller (1175-AC).

4) Remove left oil seal using slide hammer and Seal Puller (T74P-77248-A). Remove caged needle bearings using slide hammer and Axle Bearing Remover (T90T-1225-A). On Dana 44 and 50 axles, remove oil seal and caged needle bearings together, using slide hammer and Collet (D80L-100-A).

Installation – **1)** Ensure bearing bore is clean and has no nicks. On Dana 35 axles, place needle bearing on Needle Bearing Installer (T90T-1175-A). On Dana 44 and 50 axles, use Needle Bearing Installer (T83T-1244-A).

2) On all models, bearing manufacturer's name and part number should face toward tool when installed into carrier bore. Coat lip of seal with multipurpose grease. Drive seal into carrier. Install slip yoke and stub shaft so that groove on shaft is visible inside differential case.

3) Locate screwdriver into snap ring notch and push snap ring into place. DO NOT tap on center of snap ring as ring will be damaged. Clean all sealant, oil and dirt from carrier and support arm. Apply continuous bead of RTV sealant 1/4-3/8" wide on carrier. Bead should not pass over or outside holes.

NOTE: Carrier must be installed on support arm within 5 minutes after applying RTV sealant.

4) Using jack, install carrier on support arm with guide pins to align carrier. Install and tighten bolts in clockwise pattern to specification. See TORQUE SPECIFICATIONS table at end of article. Install and tighten support arm-to carrier bolts to specification.

5) Install both spindles. Install left and right axle shaft assemblies. See SPINDLES & AXLE SHAFTS under REMOVAL & INSTALLATION. Align marks made previously and install drive shaft. Let RTV sealant cure for one hour before filling assembly with hypoid gear lubricant.

AXLE PIVOT BUSHING

Removal – Remove carrier housing assembly. See CARRIER HOUSING ASSEMBLY under REMOVAL & INSTALLATION. Install Forcing Screw (T78P-5638-A1), Bushing Remover (T80T-5638-A2) and Receiver Cup (T78P-5638-A4) for Dana 35 axle or Bushing Remover (T80T-5638-A1) and Receiver Cup (T78P-5638-A3) for Dana 44 and 50 axle on pivot bushing. Turn forcing screw to remove pivot bushing.

Installation – 1) Place new pivot bushing into carrier housing. On Dana 35 axle, using Receiver Cup (T78P-5638-A4), forcing screw and Bushing Replacer (T82T-3006-A), install bushing. On Dana 44 and 50 axles, using Receiver Cup (T78P-5638-A2), forcing screw and Bushing Replacer (T80T-6538-A2), install bushing.

2) On Dana 35 axles, bushings must be flared to prevent movement after installation. Use forcing screw, Receiver Cup (T83T-3006-A1) and Flaring Flange (T83T-3006-A) to flare bushing lip. To complete installation, reverse removal procedure.

CARRIER HOUSING ASSEMBLY

Removal (Coil Spring Models) – 1) Raise vehicle on hoist. Place safety stands under radius arm brackets. Mark drive shaft position for installation reference. Disconnect drive shaft at pinion yoke and tie out of way. Remove wheels and brake calipers. Support caliper to side with no weight on brake hose. Disconnect steering linkage from steering knuckles.

2) On Explorer, remove left stabilizer bar link from radius arm bracket. On all models, place jack under axle arm assembly and compress coil spring slightly. On Dana 35 axle, remove nut which holds lower part of spring to axle arm. On Dana 44 axle, remove upper spring retainers.

3) On all models, lower jack. Remove coil spring, spring cushion, lower spring seat and stud. Disconnect shock absorber at radius arm bracket. Remove radius arm bracket and radius arm. Disconnect vent tube fitting (if equipped) and install 1/8" pipe plug into fitting hole. Remove pivot bolt holding right side axle arm assembly to crossmember.

4) Remove and discard keystone clamps. Remove right axle shaft assembly from slip joint. Lower jack and remove right axle arm assembly. Place jack under differential housing. Unbolt left axle arm assembly from crossmember. Remove left axle arm assembly.

Installation – To install, reverse removal procedure. Check alignment and adjust, if necessary.

Removal (Leaf Spring Models) – 1) Raise and support vehicle. Remove tires and wheels. Remove brake calipers. Support caliper to side with no tension on brake hose. Place jack under right axle arm assembly. Remove 2 "U" bolts holding shock absorber mounting plate and leaf springs to tube and yoke assembly.

2) Disconnect vent tube. Remove vent fitting and install 1/8" pipe plug. Remove pivot bolt holding right axle arm to crossmember. Remove keystone clamps from rubber boot. Move rubber boot off axle shaft assembly onto slip joint. Remove right axle arm assembly.

3) Pull right axle shaft out of slip joint. Place jack under left axle arm assembly. Remove 2 "U" bolts holding shock absorber mounting plate and leaf springs to tube and yoke assembly. Place jack under differential housing. Remove pivot bolt holding left axle arm assembly to crossmember. Remove left axle arm assembly.

Installation – To install, reverse removal procedure. Check alignment and adjust, if necessary.

OVERHAUL

DIFFERENTIAL ASSEMBLY

Disassembly – 1) With carrier housing removed from vehicle, remove differential carrier from axle arm. Note matched numbers or letters on differential bearing caps for reassembly reference. Remove bearing caps. Install Housing Spreader (4000-E) and Spreader Adapter (T80T-4000-B). *See Fig. 2.*

2) Rotate slip yoke and shaft assembly so open side of snap ring on shaft is exposed. Remove snap ring from shaft. Remove slip yoke and shaft assembly from carrier. Mount dial indicator on carrier housing to measure amount of spread.

CAUTION: *DO NOT spread carrier housing more than .010" (.25 mm). Permanent damage to housing could result.*

---

3) Spread carrier housing to a maximum of **.010" .25 mm.** Remove dial indicator. Carefully pry differential assembly out of housing. Remove spreader immediately so that housing does not distort permanently.

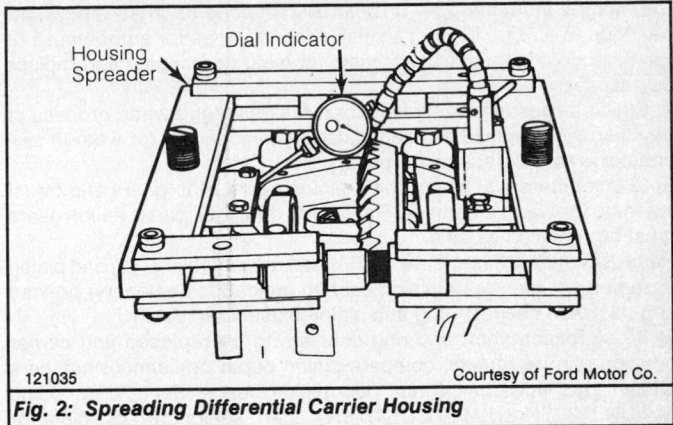

Fig. 2: *Spreading Differential Carrier Housing*

4) Place carrier assembly into holding device. Using Yoke Holder (T57T-4851-B) for Dana 35 axle or Yoke Holder (T78P-4851-A) for Dana 44 and 50 axles, hold yoke while removing drive pinion nut and washer.

5) Using Yoke Remover (T77F-4220-B1) for Dana 35 axle or Yoke Remover (T65L-4851-B) for Dana 44 and 50 axles, remove yoke from drive pinion. If yoke shows wear in seal contact area, replace yoke. Remove drive pinion by tapping with soft-faced mallet.

NOTE: *Pinion bearing adjusting shims may remain on pinion shaft, stick to bearing or fall loose. Collect shims and save for reassembly.*

---

6) Remove and discard drive pinion oil seal. Remove pinion outer bearing and oil slinger. On Dana 35 axle, remove collapsible spacer. On all models, drive out drive pinion inner bearing race using pinion bearing race remover and driver handle. See PINION BEARING RACE REMOVER & DRIVER HANDLE table.

7) Remove shims and oil baffle from bearing bore. Mark and keep shims and baffle together. Turn carrier over and drive out pinion outer bearing race using bearing race remover and driver handle. See PINION BEARING RACE REMOVER & DRIVER HANDLE table.

PINION BEARING RACE REMOVER & DRIVER HANDLE

Application	Tool Number
Driver Handle	
Dana 35	T80T-4000-W
Dana 44 & 50	D81L-4000-W
Pinion Bearing Race Remover	
Inner Bearing Race	
Dana 35	T86T-4628-AH
Dana 44	D81T-4628-C
Dana 50	D81T-4628-D
Outer Bearing Race	
Dana 35	T86T-4628-BH
Dana 44 & 50	D81T-4628-D

NOTE: *If oil baffle or slinger are damaged during disassembly procedure, measure them and replace with new units during reassembly. Baffle and slinger affect pinion depth and preload adjustments and are included in shim pack thickness.*

---

8) Place Universal Bearing Remover (D81L-4220-A) into vise to secure tool while removing differential side bearings. On Dana 35 axle, use Step Plate (D80L-630-4) under bearing to protect bearing from puller. On Dana 44 and 50 axles, use Step Plate (D80L-630-5). On all models, keep bearings, bearing races and shims in sets, marked as to location on carrier.

9) Place differential case into vise with rags underneath to protect ring gear. Remove and discard ring gear bolts. Tap ring gear with soft-faced mallet to remove ring gear from case. Using drift and hammer, drive out pinion shaft lock pin. Remove pinion shaft.

10) Rotate side gears until pinion gears are aligned with case opening. Remove pinion gears and spherical washers. Remove side gears with thrust washers.

Cleaning & Inspection – 1) Clean all components in solvent. Allow bearings to air dry. Inspect all machined surfaces for smoothness or raised edges. Inspect all gear teeth for wear or chipping and replace as necessary.

2) Check all bearings and races for nicks, roller end wear, grooves or any damage. Replace as needed. Check pinion yoke for wear in seal contact area. Replace as necessary.

3) Check differential pinion shaft, pinion gears, side gears and thrust washers for wear or damage. Replace all defective parts. Pinion gears must be replaced as sets.

Reassembly & Adjustments – 1) When reassembling ring and pinion assembly, pinion depth, pinion bearing preload, side bearing preload and backlash between ring and pinion must be adjusted.

2) If only pinion shaft and ring gear are to be replaced and carrier housing can be reused, compare pinion depth adjustment numbers etched into faces of old and new pinion heads. *See Fig. 3.* Using PINION DEPTH SHIM ADJUSTMENT chart, select correct shims for new pinion shaft depth adjustment.

NOTE: Old pinion shaft shim pack dimensions MUST be determined accurately to use PINION DEPTH SHIM ADJUSTMENT chart procedure. If original shim pack dimension cannot be determined or if the carrier housing is new, see DRIVE PINION DEPTH under OVERHAUL.

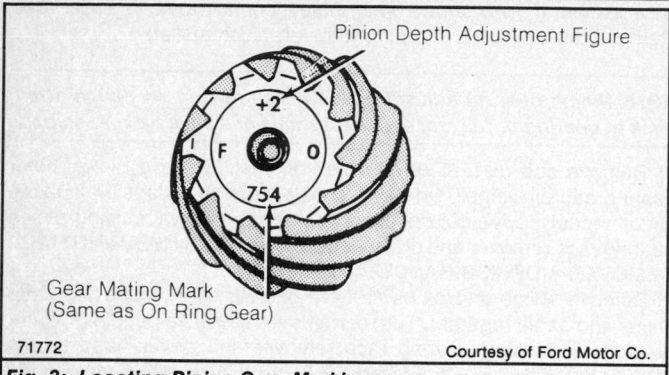

Pinion Depth Adjustment Figure

Gear Mating Mark
(Same as On Ring Gear)

71772   Courtesy of Ford Motor Co.

Fig. 3: Locating Pinion Gear Markings

3) The pinion depth adjustment number is determined by manufacturer at time of assembly. Number represents nominal distance that pinion shaft deviates from distance between pinion gear face and centerline of axle. Nominal distance is measured from centerline of ring gear to face of gear on drive pinion shaft.

4) Ring gear and pinion gear are supplied in matched sets only. Matching numbers are etched on ring and pinion gears. If new gearset is being used, verify matching gearset numbers. *See Fig. 3.*

5) Pinion Depth Gauge Set (T80T-4020-A) allows shim pack adjustment without having to remove and replace differential bearings when setting up shim packs. *See Fig. 4.*

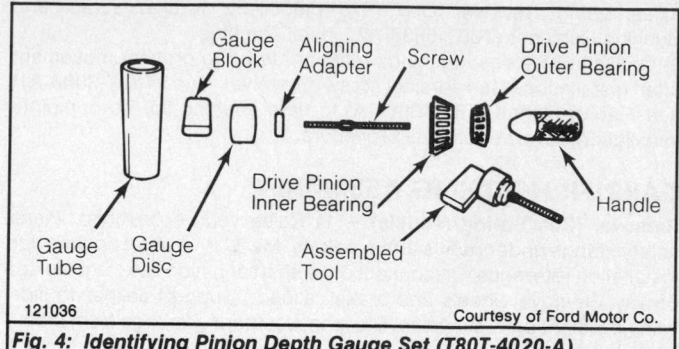

Gauge Block   Aligning Adapter   Screw   Drive Pinion Outer Bearing

Drive Pinion Inner Bearing

Gauge Tube   Gauge Disc   Assembled Tool   Handle

121036   Courtesy of Ford Motor Co.

Fig. 4: Identifying Pinion Depth Gauge Set (T80T-4020-A)

DIFFERENTIAL CASE

1) Place differential case into vise. Use multipurpose grease to lubricate side gears, pinion gears and all thrust washers. Install components into differential case. Rotate side gears until holes in pinion gears and washers line up with holes in case.

2) Install differential pinion shaft. Install lock pin. Using a punch and hammer, peen metal of differential case over lock pin at 2 locations, 90 degrees to the left and right of lock pin slot.

3) Install ring gear and tighten new bolts evenly to specification. See TORQUE SPECIFICATIONS table at end of article. Install master differential bearings on differential case. See MASTER DIFFERENTIAL BEARINGS table.

MASTER DIFFERENTIAL BEARINGS

Application	Bearing Number
Dana 35	T86T-4222-AH
Dana 44	D81T-4222-B
Dana 50	D81T-4222-C

4) Install case (without shims) into carrier housing. Install side bearing caps. Mount dial indicator with indicator tip at 90 degrees to flat surface on head of ring gear bolt or flat machined surface of ring gear. Measure and record amount of end play of differential case by moving case back and forth with screwdriver. *See Fig. 5.*

5) This measurement is total differential case end play and will be used later to determine proper shim pack dimension. Remove case from housing. Leave master bearings on case at this time.

PINION DEPTH SHIM ADJUSTMENT CHART (INCHES)

Old Pinion Marking	New Pinion Marking								
	-4	-3	-2	-1	0	+1	+2	+3	+4
+4	+0.008	+0.007	+0.006	+0.005	+0.004	+0.003	+0.002	+0.001	0
+3	+0.007	+0.006	+0.005	+0.004	+0.003	+0.002	+0.001	0	-0.001
+2	+0.006	+0.005	+0.004	+0.003	+0.002	+0.001	0	-0.001	-0.002
+1	+0.005	+0.004	+0.003	+0.002	+0.001	0	-0.001	-0.002	-0.003
0	+0.004	+0.003	+0.002	+0.001	0	-0.001	-0.002	-0.003	-0.004
-1	+0.003	+0.002	+0.001	0	-0.001	-0.002	-0.003	-0.004	-0.005
-2	+0.002	+0.001	0	-0.001	-0.002	-0.003	-0.004	-0.005	-0.006
-3	+0.001	0	-0.001	-0.002	-0.003	-0.004	-0.005	-0.006	-0.007
-4	0	-0.001	-0.002	-0.003	-0.004	-0.005	-0.006	-0.007	-0.008

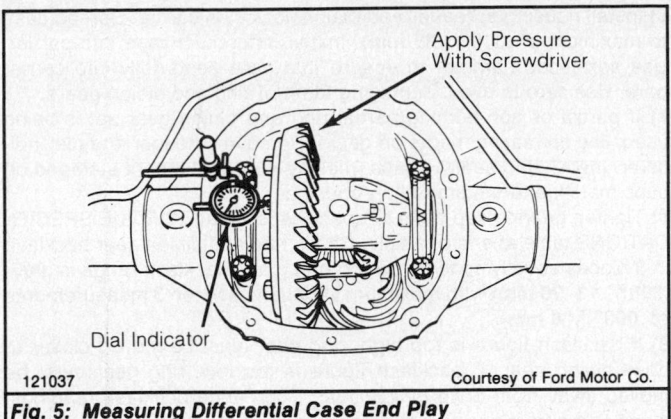

Fig. 5: *Measuring Differential Case End Play*

121037   Courtesy of Ford Motor Co.

DRIVE PINION BEARING RACE INSTALLATION

1) Place pinion inner and outer bearing races into bores of carrier. Place inner race installer on inner bearing race. *See Fig. 6.* See PINION BEARING RACE INSTALLER & FORCING SCREW table.

2) Place outer race installer on outer bearing race. Install forcing screw through bearings. Tighten screw until both bearing races are seated in carrier bore.

PINION BEARING RACE INSTALLER & FORCING SCREW

Application	Tool Number
Forcing Screw	T75T-1176-A
Pinion Bearing Race Installer	
Inner Bearing Race	
Dana 35	T60K-4616-A
Dana 44	T80T-4000-D
Dana 50	T80T-4000-F
Outer Bearing Race	
Dana 35	T71P-4616-A
Dana 44 & 50	T80T-4000-E

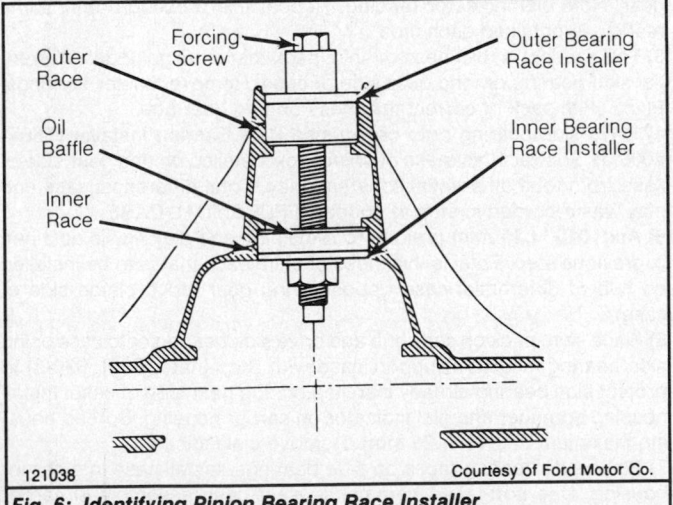

Fig. 6: *Identifying Pinion Bearing Race Installer*

121038   Courtesy of Ford Motor Co.

DRIVE PINION DEPTH

1) Put new drive pinion inner bearing on aligning adapter and assemble using gauge disc. *See Fig. 4.* See PINION DEPTH GAUGE table. Put pinion outer bearing (new or good used) into race. Place depth gauge assembly into housing with screw extending through outer bearing.

NOTE: Tools in Pinion Depth Gauge Set (T80T-4020-A) must be checked before each use for nicks or damage. Any high spots on tools must be removed to ensure accurate readings.

PINION DEPTH GAUGE

Application	Tool Number
Aligning Adapter	T75P-4020-A2
Gauge Block	
Dana 35	T76P-4020-A10
Dana 44 & 50	T80T-4020-F42
Gauge Disc	
Dana 35	PS88B878-1
Dana 44	T80T-4020-F44
Dana 50	T80T-4020-F40
Gauge Tube	
Dana 35	D80T-4020-F49
Dana 44	D80T-4020-F47
Dana 50	T80T-4020-F41
Handle	T76P-4020-A11
Screw	
Dana 35	T76P-4020-A9
Dana 44 & 50	T80T-4020-F43

2) Thread handle onto screw finger tight. Using 3/8" drive torque wrench in square drive on handle, tighten handle until preload on bearings is **15-25 INCH lbs. (1.7-2.8 N.m)** on Dana 35 axle or **20-40 INCH lbs. (2.3-4.5 N.m)** on Dana 44 and 50 axles. Center gauge tube in side bearing bore. Install side bearing caps and tighten bolts to specification. See TORQUE SPECIFICATIONS table at end of article.

3) Place gauge block on top of face of drive pinion underneath gauge tube. Determine clearance between gauge block and gauge tube using feeler gauge. Correct feeler gauge will give feeling of slight drag as gauge passes between tube and block.

4) On Dana 35 axles, thickness of correct feeler gauge is thickness of selective oil slinger that is to be installed between drive pinion head and pinion inner bearing, if drive pinion has zero marking.

5) On Dana 44 and 50 axles, thickness of correct feeler gauge is thickness of shim pack that is to be installed under inner bearing race, if drive pinion has zero marking.

6) On all models, if drive pinion has plus (+) marking on face, subtract that number from thickness dimension. If drive pinion has minus (−) marking on face, add that number to thickness dimension.

NOTE: Pinion inner bearing used during depth measurement procedure MUST be used for final assembly. Oil slinger and/or baffle (if equipped) are to be measured as part of shim pack.

7) On Dana 35 axle, using a micrometer, measure oil slinger to verify size. Place oil slinger on drive pinion. Press drive pinion inner bearing and oil slinger on drive pinion, using Axle Bearing/Seal Plate (T75L-1165-B), appropriate Pinion Bearing Replacer and arbor press. See PINION BEARING REPLACER table.

8) On Dana 44 and 50 axles, remove pinion inner bearing race and install shim pack with oil baffle (if equipped) into carrier bearing bore. Reinstall inner bearing race into carrier.

9) Press drive pinion inner bearing and oil slinger (if equipped) on drive pinion, using Axle Bearing/Seal Plate (T75L-1165-B), appropriate Pinion Bearing Replacer and arbor press. See PINION BEARING REPLACER table.

PINION BEARING REPLACER

Application	Tool Number
Dana 35	T85M-4621-B
Dana 44	T53T-4621-B
Dana 50	T70P-4625

DRIVE PINION BEARING PRELOAD & FINAL DEPTH CHECK

Dana 35 Axle – **1)** Install drive pinion into carrier. Install new collapsible spacer. Install pinion outer bearing and thrust washer. Lubricate and install drive pinion oil seal. Install pinion yoke, washer and new nut on pinion shaft.

2) Using Yoke Installer (T85T-4851-AH), install pinion yoke. Tighten pinion yoke nut until rotational torque necessary to turn pinion is **15-25 INCH lbs. (1.7-2.8 N.m)**. If reading exceeds **25 INCH lbs (2.8 N.m)**, collapsible washer must be replaced.

CAUTION: Always use NEW collapsible spacer when reassembling drive pinion. NEVER tighten pinion yoke nut more than 350 ft. lbs. (475 N.m) as collapsible spacer will be compressed too far.

Dana 44 & 50 Axles – **1)** Measure original preload shim pack and replace with new shims of equal thickness. Install drive pinion into carrier. Install new preload shim pack on pinion shaft. Install outer bearing and oil slinger. Install drive pinion yoke with washer, deflector, slinger and new nut, using Yoke Installer (T78T-4851-A).

2) Tighten pinion yoke nut to **200-220 ft. lbs. (271-298 N.m)**. Using torque wrench, check rotational torque necessary to turn drive pinion. Torque reading should be **20-40 INCH lbs. (2.3-4.5 N.m)** if preload is correct. If preload reading is too low, remove preload shims from drive pinion. If preload reading is too high, add preload shims to drive pinion.

3) Install appropriate gauge tube. Install side bearing caps and tighten bolts to specification. See TORQUE SPECIFICATIONS table at end of article. With drive pinion at correct depth, remove pinion yoke with holder and yoke remover. Coat pinion yoke oil seal with hypoid gear oil. Install seal using Oil Seal Replacer (T80T-4000-C).

4) Ensure spring behind lip of seal does not jump out while seal is being installed. If spring does jump out, remove and replace seal. Install drive pinion yoke and tighten nut.

RING & PINION GEAR BACKLASH

Dana 35 Axle – **1)** With drive pinion depth and preload adjustments properly made, install differential case into housing. Differential master bearings should still be on case. Force differential case away from drive pinion gear so that case is fully seated into cross bores of carrier.

2) Set dial indicator so that tip is against head of ring gear bolt at 90 degrees to bolt. Rock ring gear so that teeth of ring gear mesh fully with drive pinion gear teeth. Force ring gear teeth against drive pinion gear teeth and zero dial indicator. Force ring gear and case away from drive pinion gear. Repeat this procedure until same reading is obtained each time.

3) This reading, less **.008" (.20 mm)** for backlash, is thickness of shim pack that must go under differential side bearing on ring gear side of case. Remove case from carrier. Remove master bearings from case. Place correct shim pack on ring gear hub of case. Place side bearing on hub of case. Drive bearing onto case using Step plate (D80L-630-4), Side Bearing Replacer (T85M-4221-A) and Handle (T80T-4000-W).

4) To determine the correct amount of shims to place on pinion gear side hub, subtract thickness of shim pack installed on ring gear side of case from total of differential case end play. Total differential case end play was recorded in step **4)** under DIFFERENTIAL CASE. Add a preload of **.002" (.05 mm)** to figure calculated for shim pack thickness on side opposite ring gear.

5) Place required thickness shim pack on hub of case opposite ring gear. Place step plate on ring gear side bearing to protect bearing. Drive remaining side bearing onto case with side bearing replacer. Install side bearing races on side bearings.

6) Install housing spreader and dial indicator on carrier. Spread case to maximum of **.010" (.25 mm)**. Install differential case into carrier. Use soft-faced hammer to ensure that case seats fully into carrier bore. Use care to avoid damaging teeth of ring and pinion gears.

7) If partial or non-hunting/partial ring and pinion gear set is being used, line up mating marks on gears. Remove spreader and dial indicator. Install side bearing caps, making sure that letters stamped on caps match letters stamped on housing.

8) Tighten bearing cap bolts to specification. See TORQUE SPECIFICATIONS table at end of article. Check ring and pinion gear backlash in 3 places equally spaced around ring gear. Backlash range is **.005-.008" (.13-.20 mm)** with maximum variation between 3 measurements of **.003" (.08 mm)**.

9) If backlash figure is too high, ring gear must be moved closer to drive pinion gear. If backlash figure is too low, ring gear must be moved away from drive pinion gear. To change backlash readings, move shims from one side of differential case to other. Total thickness of end play shim packs must not change.

10) When backlash adjustment is completed, check tooth contact pattern. See GEAR TOOTH CONTACT PATTERNS article in GENERAL INFORMATION. Pattern will be correct if assembly and adjustments have been done properly.

11) When backlash is correct, apply bead of sealant to mating surfaces of carrier mounting face support arm. Bead should be 1/8" to 1/4" high and 1/4" to 1/2" wide. Install carrier on left axle arm assembly, using 2 carrier bolts as guide pins and being careful not to smear sealant.

12) Install remaining carrier bolts and tighten to specification in clockwise pattern. Install and tighten carrier shear bolt and nut. Allow one hour curing time for sealant. Fill assembly with hypoid lubricant.

Dana 44 & 50 Axles – **1)** With drive pinion depth and preload adjustments properly made, install differential case into housing. Differential master bearings should still be on case. Ensure differential case is fully seated in carrier bores. Set dial indicator so that tip is against head of ring gear mounting bolt at 90 degrees to bolt.

2) Rock ring gear so that teeth of ring gear mesh fully with drive pinion gear teeth. Force ring gear teeth against drive pinion gear teeth and zero dial indicator. Force ring gear and case away from drive pinion gear. Note dial indicator reading. Repeat this procedure until same reading is obtained each time.

3) This reading is thickness of shim pack that must go under differential side bearing on ring gear side of case. Remove master bearings. Place shim pack of correct thickness on ring gear hub.

4) Drive side bearing onto case using Side Bearing Installer (T80T-4000-J). Subtract thickness of shim pack installed on ring gear side of case from total differential case end play. Total differential case end play was recorded in step **4)** under DIFFERENTIAL CASE.

5) Add **.010" (.25 mm)** preload to remaining end play figure obtained in previous step. Total is thickness of shim pack that is to be installed on hub of differential case opposite ring gear (drive pinion side of case).

6) Place shim pack on case hub and drive side bearing onto case using side bearing installer. Support case with Step Plate (D80L-630-5) to protect side bearing already installed on ring gear side of case. Install housing spreader and dial indicator on carrier housing. Spread housing maximum of **.010" (.25 mm)**. Remove dial indicator.

7) Place side bearing races on side bearings. Install case into carrier housing. Use soft-faced hammer to seat case assembly in carrier bore. If partial or non-hunting/partial ring and pinion gear set is being used, line up mating marks on gears. Remove housing spreader and dial indicator.

8) Install side bearing caps. Ensure letters stamped on caps match letters stamped on housing. Tighten bearing cap bolts to specification. See TORQUE SPECIFICATIONS table at end of article. Check ring and pinion gear backlash in 3 places equally spaced around ring gear. Backlash range is **.005-.009"** **(.13-.23 mm)** with maximum variation between 3 measurements of **.003"** **(.08 mm)**.

9) To change backlash readings, move shims from one side of differential case to other. Total thickness of end play shim packs must not change. When backlash adjustment is completed, check tooth contact pattern. See GEAR TOOTH CONTACT PATTERNS article in GENERAL INFORMATION.

10) When backlash is correct, apply bead of sealant to mating surfaces of carrier mounting face support arm. Bead should be 1/8" to 1/4" high and 1/4" to 1/2" wide. Using 2 guide pins, install carrier on left axle arm assembly.

11) Use new carrier bolts with adhesive-treated threads or clean old bolts and apply locking compound. Tighten carrier bolts. Install and tighten support arm tab bolts on side of carrier. Allow one hour curing time for sealant. Fill assembly with hypoid lubricant.

TORQUE SPECIFICATIONS

TORQUE SPECIFICATIONS

Application	Ft. Lbs. (N.m)
Axle Pivot Bolt	120-150 (163-203)
Axle Pivot Bracket-To-Frame Nut	70-92 (95-125)
Differential Carrier-To-Carrier Housing Bolt	
Dana 35	40-50 (54-68)
Dana 44 & 50	30-40 (41-54)
Pinion Shaft Yoke Nut	
Dana 35	[1] 200-350 (271-475)
Dana 44 & 50	200-220 (271-298)
Ring Gear Bolt	
Dana 35	70-90 (95-122)
Dana 44 & 50	
Grade 8	50-60 (68-81)
Grade 9	75-85 (102-115)
Side Bearing Cap Bolt	
Dana 35	47-67 (64-91)
Dana 44 & 50	80-90 (108-122)
Spindle-To-Knuckle Nut	
Dana 35	40-50 (54-68)
Dana 44 & 50	50-60 (68-81)
Support Arm-To-Carrier Housing Bolt	
Dana 35	75-95 (102-129)
Dana 44 & 50	85-100 (115-136)
Wheel Lug Nuts	
All Except Bronco, Ranger & F150	140 (190)
Bronco, Ranger & F150	100 (136)

[1] – See DRIVE PINION BEARING PRELOAD & FINAL DEPTH CHECK.

1992 DRIVE AXLES
Dana Limited-Slip Differential

**Bronco Front Axle,
E250/350 Rear Axle,
Pickup Front Axle**

NOTE: Limited-slip and conventional axle assemblies are identical except for differential case. Most information in this article is related to differential case overhaul. For all other information, see DANA IFS FRONT AXLE or DANA 60, 70 & 80 DIFFERENTIALS article.

DESCRIPTION & OPERATION

Limited-slip differential has the same power flow as the conventional differential. Dana models 44 IFS, 44 IFS-HD and 60-1U (2-pinion) differential are Trac-Lok differentials. *See Fig. 4.* Dana model 70 (4-pinion) differential is a Power-Lok differential. *See Fig. 8.*

Limited slip differential uses clutch packs to automatically provide more direct power flow to drive wheels as driving conditions demand. Clutch packs permit regular differential action for turning corners and transmit equal torque to both wheels when driving straight ahead. If one wheel begins to slip because of reduced traction, clutch packs automatically provide more torque to wheel with greater traction.

AXLE RATIO & IDENTIFICATION

Axle can be identified by axle code on Safety Certification Label on left door pillar. See AXLE RATIO IDENTIFICATION article. Also, a metal identification tag, stamped with gear ratio and diameter, is attached to axle housing. *See Fig. 1.* Limited-slip differential is identified by "L-S" on tag.

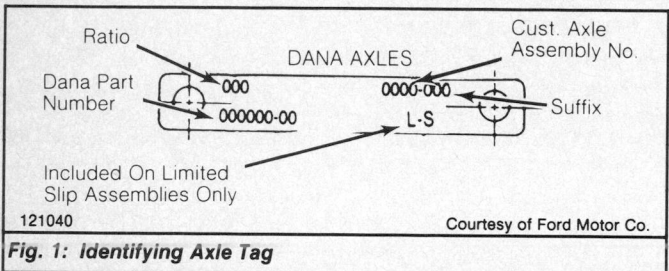

Fig. 1: Identifying Axle Tag

LUBRICATION

CAPACITY

LUBRICANT CAPACITY [1]

Application	Pts. (L)
Model 44 IFS & 44 IFS-HD	3.9 (1.8)
Model 60-1U	
Front	5.8 (2.7)
Rear	6.3 (3.0)
Model 70	6.6 (3.1)

[1] – Add an additional 2 oz. (front axle) or 8 oz. (rear axle) of Friction Modifier (C8AZ-19B546-A).

FLUID TYPE

Use Hypoid Gear Lubricant (C6AZ-19580-E or ESW-M2C105-A) and Friction Modifier (C8AZ-19B546-A).

DRAINING & REFILLING

CAUTION: DO NOT clean internal components of differential case with solvent. Clean components with lint-free shop towel only.

Model 44 IFS & 44 IFS-HD – Information is not available from manufacturer.
Model 60-1U & 70 – 1) Drive vehicle until lubricant is warm. Remove housing cover to drain lubricant. Remove gasket. Clean all lubricant from gasket surfaces. Install new gasket. Apply continuous bead of silicone sealant to housing, ensuring bead is inside of bolt hole pattern. Install housing cover within 15 minutes of silicone application.

2) Tighten bolts to specification. See TORQUE SPECIFICATIONS table at end of article. Allow at least 1 hour for sealant to cure before filling housing. Fill housing with lubricant until fluid level is at bottom of fill hole. Drive vehicle for 10 miles, making 10 or more figure-8 turns to flush old lubricant from clutch packs.
3) Drain and refill housing again. If slight noise or roughness remains after vehicle has been driven an additional 100 miles (to flush old lubricant from clutch packs), disassemble and repair differential.

TROUBLE SHOOTING

See TROUBLE SHOOTING article in GENERAL INFORMATION.

REMOVAL & INSTALLATION

See DANA IFS FRONT AXLE or DANA 60, 70 & 80 DIFFERENTIALS article.

OVERHAUL

DIFFERENTIAL CASE

NOTE: When overhauling differential case, it is not necessary to remove differential case bearings. An axle shaft, secured in a vise with the splines extending about 3" above the jaws, can be used as a holding fixture for differential case after it is removed.

Disassembly (Models 44 IFS, 44 IFS-HD & 60-1U) – 1) Remove ring gear. Remove roll pin or lock screw retaining cross shaft. Remove cross shaft using hammer and drift (by hand on 60-1U). Position Step Plate (T83T-4205-A4) onto bottom side gear. *See Fig. 2.* Apply grease to centering hole of step plate.
2) Install Forcing Nut (T83T-4205-A2) and Forcing Screw (T83T-4205-A3) into differential case. *See Fig. 3.* Guide forcing screw into step plate. Lightly tighten forcing screw. This will move side gears away from pinion gears and relieve the normal loaded condition. Using a **.030" (.76 mm)** thick shim or piece of gauge stock, push out spherical thrust washers. *See Fig. 5.*
3) Momentarily loosen forcing screw (this is very important as it relieves pressure on clutch pack). Retighten forcing screw until a very slight movement of pinion gears is seen. Insert Handle (T83T-4205-A1) into pinion mate shaft bore. Handle is used to rotate differential case.
4) Rotate differential case until pinion gears can be removed through large opening of differential case. When attempting to rotate side gear, it may be necessary to tighten or loosen forcing screw to permit gear movement.
5) While holding top side gear and clutch pack in case by hand, remove forcing screw and handle. Remove top side gear and clutch pack. Keep clutch pack discs and plates in exact order. Turn differential case over so ring gear side is up.
6) Remove step plate, other side gear and clutch pack. Remove retainer clips from both clutch packs. Separate discs and plates for cleaning and inspection. Replace complete clutch pack, even if only one component is defective.
Cleaning & Inspection – DO NOT clean clutch plates or discs with solvent; clean parts with a shop towel only. Inspect plates, discs and clips for excessive wear or scoring. Inspect gears for extreme wear, cracks or chips. Inspect case for scoring, wear or metal pick-up on machined surfaces.

NOTE: If any clutch pack component needs replacing, replace entire clutch pack for both sides. If any gear(s) needs replacing, replace all gears and thrust washers.

NOTE: Model 60-1U discs of newer coated design (without grooves) must be soaked for 20 minutes in Friction Modifier (C8AZ-19B546-A) before reassembly.

Reassembly (Models 44 IFS, 44 IFS-HD & 60-1U) – 1) Lubricate thrust face of side gear, discs and plates with gear lubricant or friction modifier. Assemble discs and plates onto side gear splines. *See Fig.*

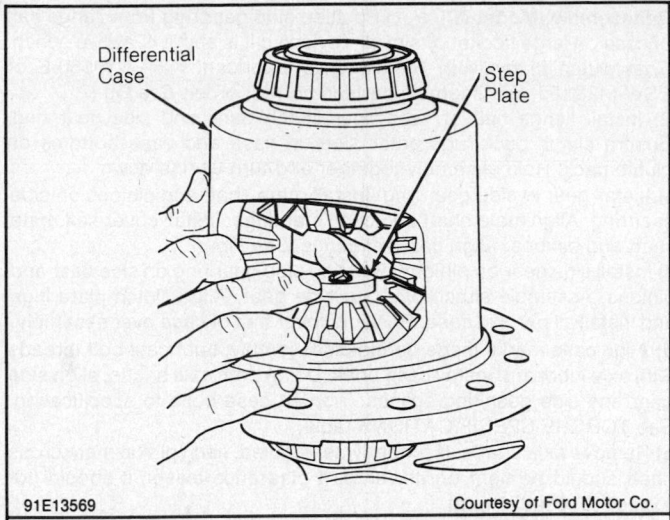

91E13569   Courtesy of Ford Motor Co.

Fig. 2: Installing Step Plate (Models 44 IFS, 44 IFS-HD & 60-1U)

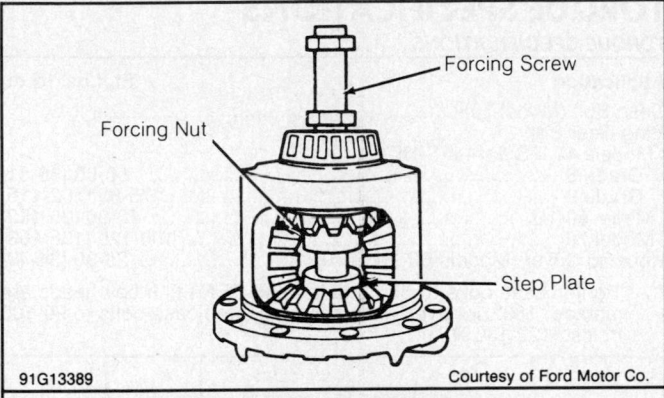

91G13389   Courtesy of Ford Motor Co.

Fig. 3: Installing Forcing Nut & Forcing Screw (Models 44 IFS, 44 IFS-HD & 60-1U)

4. Install retainer clips to ears of plates. Assemble clutch pack and side gear into differential case.

2) Hold clutch pack in place by hand. Reposition case and assemble step plate into side gear. Apply lubricant to centering hole of step plate. Assemble other clutch pack and side gear. Ensure retainer clips are fully seated in pockets of differential case.

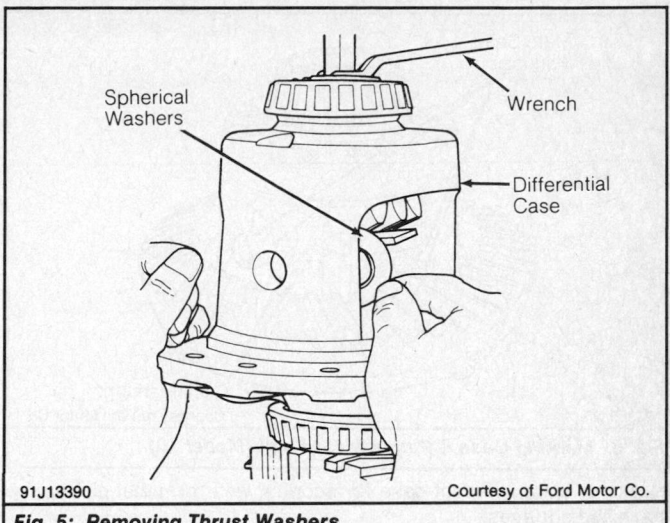

91J13390   Courtesy of Ford Motor Co.

Fig. 5: Removing Thrust Washers

3) Install step plate on top of side gear. Insert forcing screw through top of case. Install forcing nut onto threads. Position pinion gears in place and hold in place by hand. Tighten forcing screw to move side gears away from pinion gears. While holding pinion gears in place, use Handle (T83T-4205-A1) inserted into pinion mate shaft hole to rotate case.

4) Pinion gears should rotate into differential case. Tighten forcing screw to increase clearance for spherical washers. Remove forcing screw, forcing nut, step plate and handle.

Disassembly (Model 70) – 1) Mark both halves (flange half and cover half) of differential case, and mark pinion mate shafts and ramps for reassembly reference. *See Fig. 6.* Clamp differential in a soft-jawed vise. Loosen, but DO NOT remove, bolts holding case halves together. Place case assembly on bench with ring gear side down.

2) Insert axle shaft into top of case to aid removal of case bolts. Remove case bolts. Remove cover half of case. Remove pinion mate gear, side gear ring and clutch pack. Keep these parts in cover half of case so they will be assembled in their original positions. Remove other parts from flange half of case.

Cleaning & Inspection – DO NOT clean clutch discs or plates with solvent; clean parts with clean shop towel. Inspect plates, discs and clips for excessive wear or scoring. Inspect gears for extreme wear,

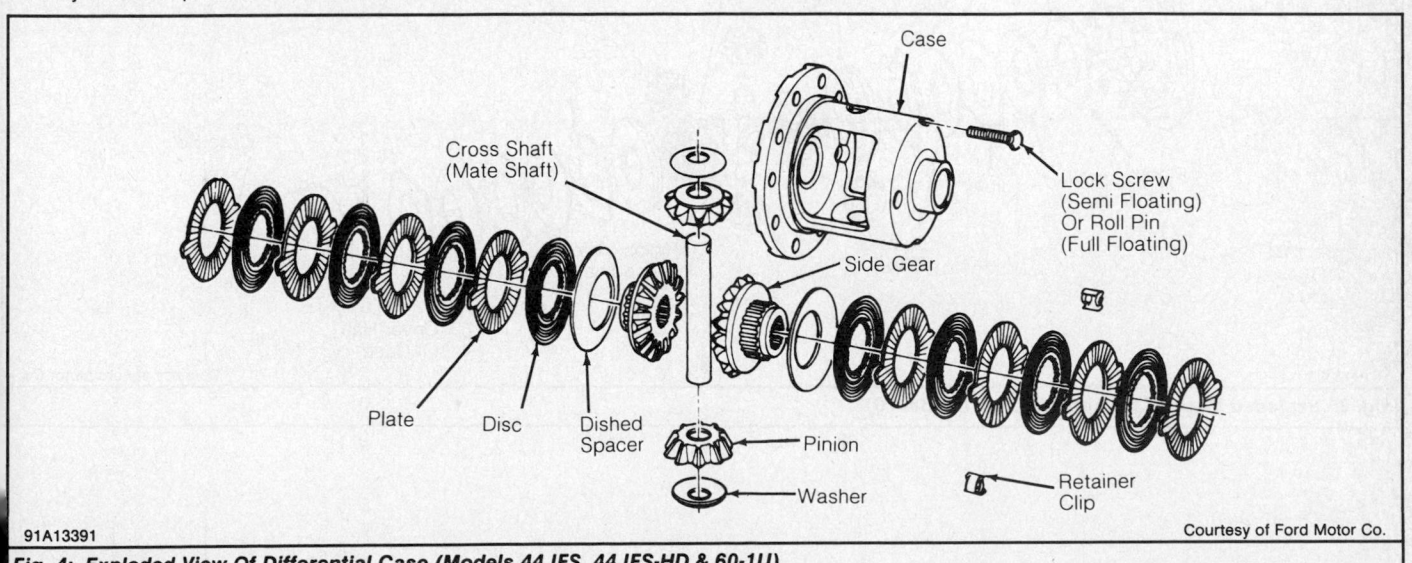

91A13391   Courtesy of Ford Motor Co.

Fig. 4: Exploded View Of Differential Case (Models 44 IFS, 44 IFS-HD & 60-1U)

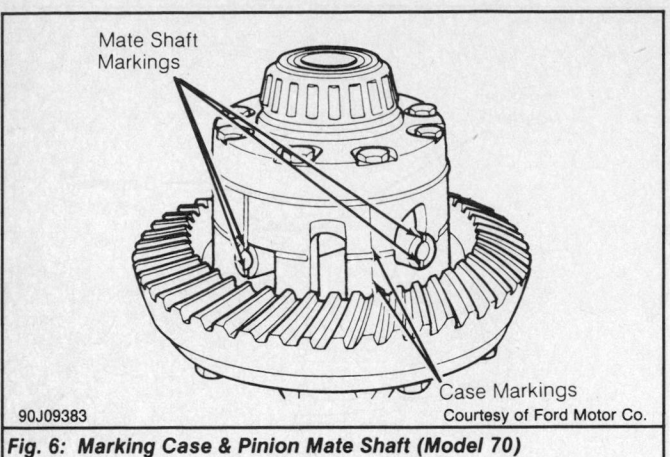

Fig. 6: Marking Case & Pinion Mate Shaft (Model 70)

cracks or chips. Inspect case for scoring, wear or metal pick-up on machined surfaces.

NOTE: If any clutch pack component needs replacing, replace entire clutch pack for both sides. If any gear(s) needs replacing, replace all gears and thrust washers.

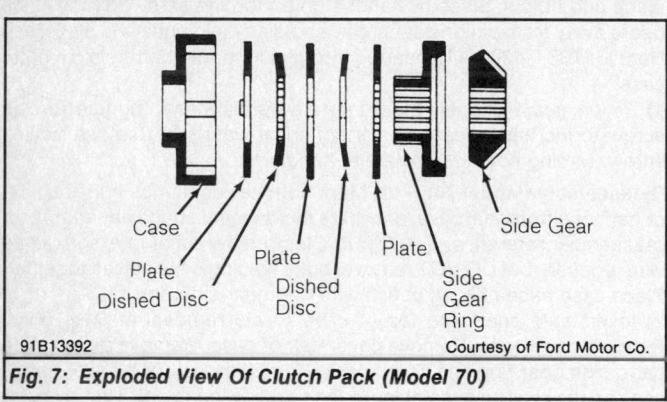

Fig. 7: Exploded View Of Clutch Pack (Model 70)

Reassembly (Model 70) – **1)** Position side gear ring from flange half of case on large socket or similar device so it is about 4" above bench. Coat clutch plates with Hypoid Gear Lubricant (C6AZ-19580-E or ESW-M2C105-A). Assemble parts in correct order. See Fig. 7.

2) Install flange half of case over clutch pack and side gear ring. Ensure clutch pack lugs enter slots in case and case bottoms on clutch pack. Hold assembly together and turn upside down.

3) Install gear in side gear ring. Install mate shaft and pinions on side gear ring. Align mate shaft and case markings. Install cover half mate shaft and pinions. Align case markings. See Fig. 6.

4) Install side gear on pinions. Position side gear ring on side gear and pinions. Assemble clutch pack on side gear. Align clutch plate lugs and install all parts in case. Position cover half of case over assembly.

5) Align case marks made during disassembly. Lubricate bolt threads with axle lubricant. Install case bolts. Using both axle shafts, align side gear and side gear ring splines. Tighten case bolts to specification. See TORQUE SPECIFICATIONS table.

6) Remove axle shafts. If properly assembled, each pinion mate cross shaft should be tight on its ramp. If clearance exists, it should not exceed .010" (.254 mm).

TORQUE SPECIFICATIONS
TORQUE SPECIFICATIONS

Application	Ft. Lbs. (N.m)
Case Bolt (Model 70)	[1]
Ring Gear Bolt	
Models 44 IFS & 44 IFS-HD	
Grade 8	50-60 (68-81)
Grade 9	75-85 (102-116)
Model 60-1U	70-90 (95-122)
Model 70	100-120 (136-163)
Housing Cover (Models 60-1U & 70)	25-35 (34-47)

[1] – Tighten case bolts to 65-70 ft. lbs. (88-95 N.m). If bolt heads are marked "180" or have 7 radial lines, tighten case bolts to 90-100 ft. lbs. (122-136 N.m).

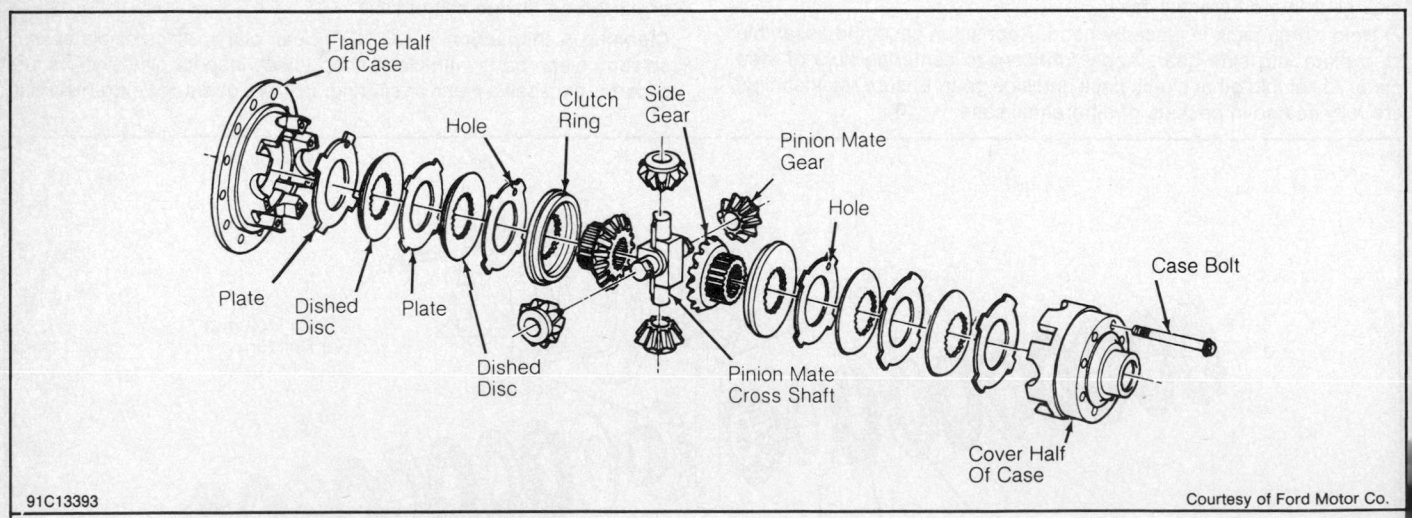

Fig. 8: Exploded View Of Differential Case (Model 70)

F250/350

DESCRIPTION

NOTE: Limited-slip and conventional rear axle assemblies are identical except for differential case. Most information in this article is related to differential case overhaul. For all other information, see 8 3/4" & 10 1/4" RING GEAR DIFFERENTIALS article.

Limited-slip differential case employs 2 sets of multiple disc clutches to control differential action. Side gear mounting distance is controlled by a clutch pack on each side gear. Each clutch pack includes 5 splined plates, 5 stationary plates and one Belleville spring plate.

AXLE RATIO & IDENTIFICATION

Axle can be identified by axle code on Safety Certification Label on left door pillar. See AXLE RATIO IDENTIFICATION table in AXLE RATIO IDENTIFICATION article. Also, a metal identification tag stamped with gear ratio and diameter is secured to housing by rear cover bolt.

LUBRICATION

CAPACITY

Capacity is **6.5 pts. (3.0L)** with axle assembly installed in vehicle, or **7.5 pts. (3.5L)** with axle assembly out of vehicle. In addition to normal lubricant, add 8 ozs. (.23L) of friction modifier.

FLUID TYPE

Use Ford Hypoid Gear Lubricant (E0AZ-19580-AA or ESP-M2C154-A) and Friction Modifier (C8AZ-19B546-A or EST-M2C118-A).

DRAINING & REFILLING

CAUTION: DO NOT clean internal components of differential case with solvent. Clean components with lint-free shop towel only.

Drive vehicle until lubricant is warm. Remove rear cover to drain lubricant. Remove gasket. Clean all lubricant from gasket surfaces. Install new gasket. Apply continuous bead of silicone sealant to housing, ensuring bead is inside of bolt holes. Install rear cover within 15 minutes of silicone application. Tighten bolts to specification. See TORQUE SPECIFICATIONS table at end of article. Fill housing with specified gear lubricant until fluid level is at bottom of fill hole.

TROUBLE SHOOTING

See TROUBLE SHOOTING article in GENERAL INFORMATION.

NOTE: A slight stick-slip noise in differential on tight turns after extended highway driving is considered acceptable and has no detrimental effect.

REMOVAL & INSTALLATION

Because conventional and limited-slip rear axle assemblies are identical except for differential case, removal and installation procedures for both axles are the same. See 8 3/4" & 10 1/4" RING GEAR DIFFERENTIALS article.

OVERHAUL

NOTE: It is not necessary to remove differential bearings to overhaul case.

DISASSEMBLY

1) Remove differential case. Remove ring gear from differential case. Remove pinion shaft lock bolt. Install Differential Case Holder (D83T-4205-A) in a vise. Install differential case onto holder with ring gear side of case facing up.

2) Using a drift, drive pinion shaft from differential case. Install Step Plate (D83T-4205-C2) in bore of right side gear (on bottom as mounted in vise). *See Fig. 2.* Apply a small amount of grease to centering hole of step plate. Install Nut (part of D83T-4205-C) in left side gear. Hold nut in position while installing Hex Head Screw (part of D83T-4205-C). *See Fig. 3.*

3) Install Dowel Bar (part of D83T-4205-C) into hole of nut to keep nut from turning. Tighten hex head screw to force side gears away from pinion mating gears. Using a proper size feeler gauge, push pinion gear thrust washers out from between pinion gears and case.

4) Remove thrust washers. Back off hex head screw until loose (about one turn). Ensure vise is tightened securely. Insert Rotating Handle (T86T-4205-A) into pinion shaft bore. Turn case to "walk" pinion gears out of differential case windows.

CAUTION: When separating clutch plates, note disassembly sequence. Reassemble clutch plates in the same sequence. DO NOT clean clutch components with solvent. Dry clutch components with a lint-free shop towel only.

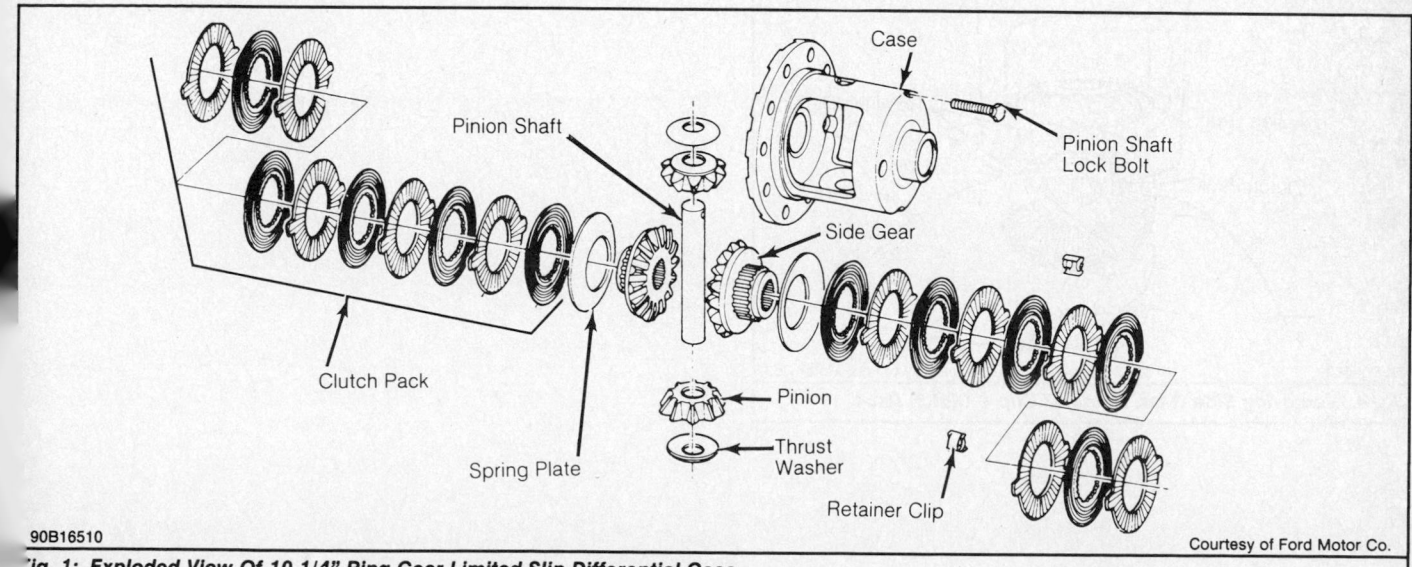

Fig. 1: Exploded View Of 10 1/4" Ring Gear Limited-Slip Differential Case

90B16510

Courtesy of Ford Motor Co.

FORD
7-40

1992 DRIVE AXLES
Limited-Slip 10 1/4" Ring Gear Differential (Cont.)

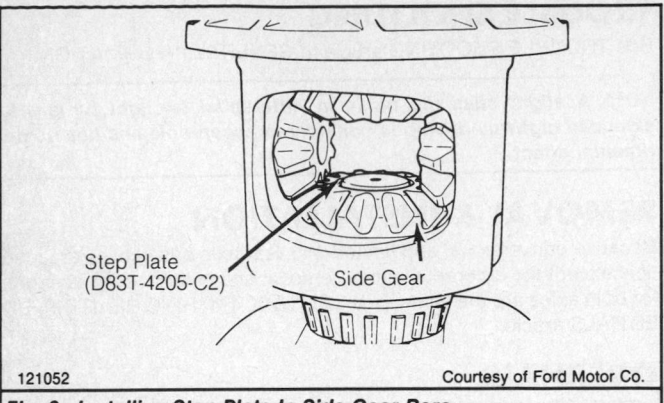

Fig. 2: Installing Step Plate In Side Gear Bore

Step Plate
(D83T-4205-C2)

Side Gear

121052

Courtesy of Ford Motor Co.

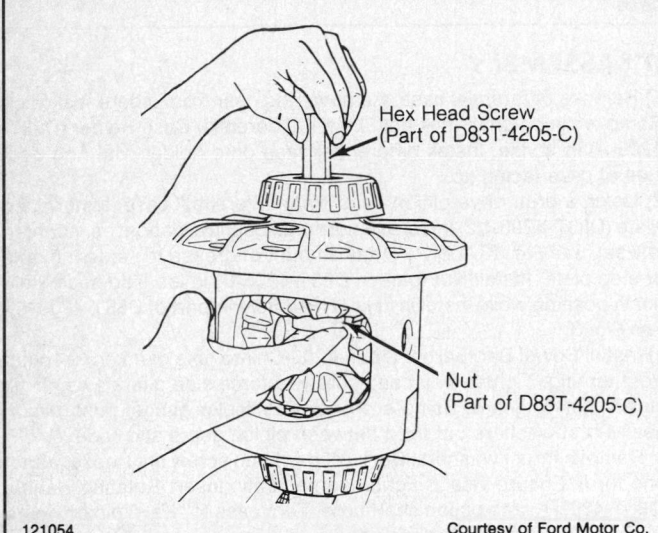

Fig. 3: Positioning Hex Head Screw & Nut

Hex Head Screw
(Part of D83T-4205-C)

Nut
(Part of D83T-4205-C)

121054

Courtesy of Ford Motor Co.

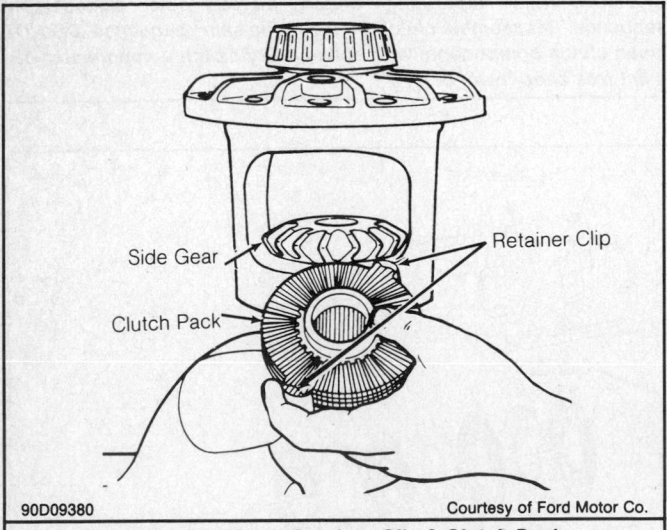

Fig. 4: Removing Side Gear, Retainer Clip & Clutch Pack

Side Gear

Retainer Clip

Clutch Pack

90D09380

Courtesy of Ford Motor Co.

5) Remove hex head screw and step plate. Remove side gears, retainer clips and clutch pack assemblies. *See Fig. 4.* Remove retainer clips from both clutch packs. Separate, clean and inspect clutch plates.

INSPECTION

Inspect clutch plates and discs for uneven or extreme wear. Plates must be free from burrs, nicks and scratches. Check discs for condition of material. Replace discs if spline teeth are worn. Replace plates if scored or if thickness is less than .058" (1.5 mm).

REASSEMBLY

1) To reassemble, reverse disassembly procedure. Lubricate clutch plates with Friction Modifier (C8AZ-19B546-A or EST-M2C118-A). Lubricate side gear thrust face and thrust washers with Hypoid Gear Lubricant (E0AZ-19580-A or ESP-M2C154-A).
2) Ensure thrust washers are installed with concave side facing inward. Ensure clutch plate retainer clips are completely assembled and seated into clutch plate ears. *See Fig. 1.*
3) Apply Loctite Thread Sealer (E0AZ-19554-B) to ring gear bolts and pinion shaft lock bolt. Tighten bolts to specification. See TORQUE SPECIFICATIONS table.

TORQUE SPECIFICATIONS
TORQUE SPECIFICATIONS

Application	Ft. Lbs. (N.m)
Differential Case Bearing Cap Bolt	80-95 (108-129)
Filler Plug	15-30 (20-41)
Pinion Nut	160 (217)
Pinion Shaft Lock Bolt	[1] 15-30 (20-41)
Rear Cover Bolt	25-35 (34-47)
Ring Gear Bolt	[1] 100-120 (136-163)
Wheel Lug Nut	140 (190)

[1] – Apply Loctite Thread Sealer (E0AZ-19554-B) to bolt threads.

Aerostar, Bronco, E150, F150, Ranger

DESCRIPTION

NOTE: Traction-lok and conventional rear axle assemblies are identical except for differential case. Most information in this article is related to differential case overhaul. For all other information, see 7 1/2" RING GEAR DIFFERENTIALS article or 8 3/4" & 10 1/4" RING GEAR DIFFERENTIALS article.

Traction-lok differential has limited-slip function (7 1/2" ring gear on Aerostar and Ranger; 8 3/4" ring gear on Bronco, E150 and F150). *See Fig. 1.* Two sets of multiple disc clutches control differential action.

On 7 1/2" ring gear, side gear mounting distance is controlled by 7 plates on each side: 3 steel, 4 friction and a maximum of 2 steel shims selectively fit to control side gear position. On 8 3/4" ring gear, side gear mounting distance is controlled by 7 plates on each side: 4 steel, 3 friction and one steel shim selectively fit to control side gear position.

Plates are stacked on side gear hubs and housed in differential case. An "S"-shaped preload spring between side gears applies initial force to clutch packs.

AXLE RATIO & IDENTIFICATION

Axle can be identified by axle code on the Safety Certification Label on left door pillar. See AXLE RATIO IDENTIFICATION article. Also, a metal identification tag, stamped with gear ratio and ring gear diameter, is attached to rear cover bolt.

LUBRICATION

CAPACITY

LUBRICANT CAPACITY [1]

Application	Pts. (L)
Aerostar	3.5 (1.7)
Bronco, E150 & F150	5.5 (2.6)
Ranger	5.0 (2.4)

[1] – If refilling, add 4 ounces (.12L) of friction modifier in addition to normal lubricant.

FLUID TYPE

Use Ford Hypoid Gear Lubricant (E0AZ-19580-AA or ESP-M2C154-A) and Friction Modifier (C8AZ-19B546-A or EST-M2C118-A).

DRAINING & REFILLING

CAUTION: DO NOT clean internal components of differential case with solvent. Clean components with lint-free shop towel only. On Aerostar with plastic rear cover, replace rear cover when removed.

Drive vehicle until lubricant is warm. Remove rear cover to drain lubricant. Remove gasket. Clean all lubricant from gasket surfaces. Install new gasket. Apply continuous bead of silicone sealant to axle housing, ensuring bead is inside of bolt hole pattern. Install rear cover within 15 minutes of silicone application. Tighten bolts to specification. See TORQUE SPECIFICATIONS table at end of article. Fill axle housing with lubricant until level with bottom of fill hole.

TROUBLE SHOOTING

NOTE: See TROUBLE SHOOTING article in GENERAL INFORMATION.

NOTE: A slight stick-slip noise in differential on tight turns after extended highway driving is considered acceptable and has no detrimental effect.

ON-VEHICLE TESTING

NOTE: Torque required to rotate wheel may decrease when wheel is turning.

1) Raise one wheel off ground, leaving opposite wheel firmly on ground. Install Traction-Lok Torque Adapter (T59L-4204-A) on mounting studs of raised wheel. Shift transmission into Neutral. Attach traction-lok torque adapter to torque wrench.

2) Using torque wrench to rotate wheel, note torque required to keep wheel rotating through several revolutions. If break-away torque (torque required to start wheel rotating) is not at least 20 ft. lbs. (27 N.m), and wheel does not turn smoothly without slipping, adjust clutch pack preload (part of clutch pack removal and installation procedure). See CLUTCH PACKS under REMOVAL & INSTALLATION.

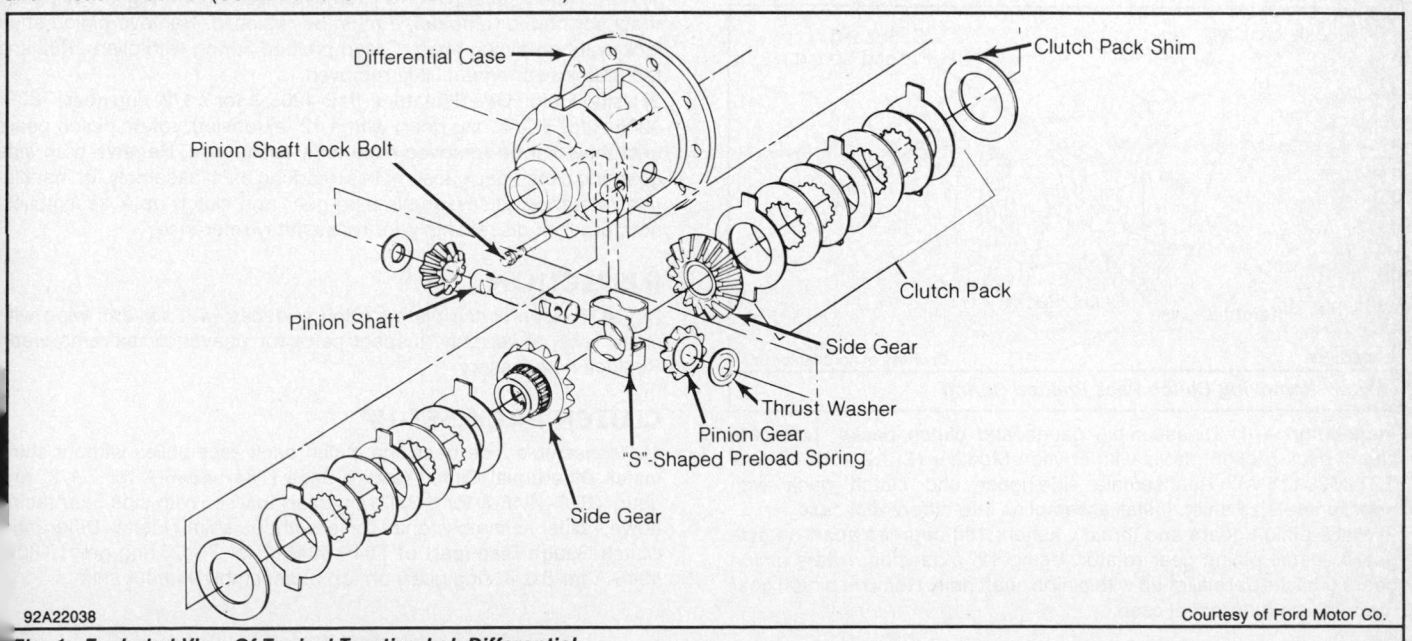

92A22038

Courtesy of Ford Motor Co.

Fig. 1: Exploded View Of Typical Traction-Lok Differential

FORD
7-42

1992 DRIVE AXLES
Traction-Lok 7 1/2" & 8 3/4" Differentials (Cont.)

REMOVAL & INSTALLATION

NOTE: Because traction-lok and conventional rear axle assemblies are identical except for differential case, removal and installation procedures for both axle assemblies are the same. For removal and installation of components other than clutch packs, see 7 1/2" RING GEAR DIFFERENTIALS article or 8 3/4" & 10 1/4" RING GEAR DIFFERENTIALS article.

CLUTCH PACKS

CAUTION: Carefully remove axle shafts to avoid damaging axle seals. Axle shafts must be completely removed from axle housing. DO NOT interchange clutches or shims. DO NOT clean clutch discs or plates with solvent; use shop towel only.

WARNING: Preload spring is under pressure; remove carefully.

Removal – 1) Remove axle shafts. Using drift, drive "S"-shaped preload spring half-way out of differential case. *See Fig. 2.* Rotate differential case 180 degrees. Grasp preload spring with pliers. Pull and tap preload spring until it is removed.

2) Using Pinion Gear Rotator (T84P-4205-A for 7 1/2" ring gear; T80P-4205-A for 8 3/4" ring gear) with a 12" extension, rotate pinion gears until they can be removed from differential case. Remove both side gear and clutch pack assemblies, marking each assembly for installation reference.

Adjusting Clutch Pack Preload – 1) Disassemble clutch packs, noting order of disassembly for reassembly reference. DO NOT clean clutch plate friction surfaces with solvent; wipe with clean shop towel only. Inspect clutch plates. Replace plates if they are uneven or extremely worn. Reassemble side gear and clutch pack assembly without shim.

2) Install Differential Clutch Gauge Base (T84P-4946-A for 7 1/2" ring gear; T87P-4946-A for 8 3/4" ring gear) in vise. With side gear facing down, slide assembly onto base without shim. Install Differential Clutch Gauge Disc (part of T84P-4946-A for 7 1/2" ring gear; T80P-4946-A for 8 3/4" ring gear) on top of assembly without shim. *See Fig. 3.*

3) Install nut on threaded end of gauge base. Tighten nut to **60 INCH lbs. (6.7 N.m).** Using feeler gauge, select thickest blade that will enter between clutch gauge and clutch pack. This reading will be thickness of new shim for that clutch pack. Repeat procedure for opposite clutch pack.

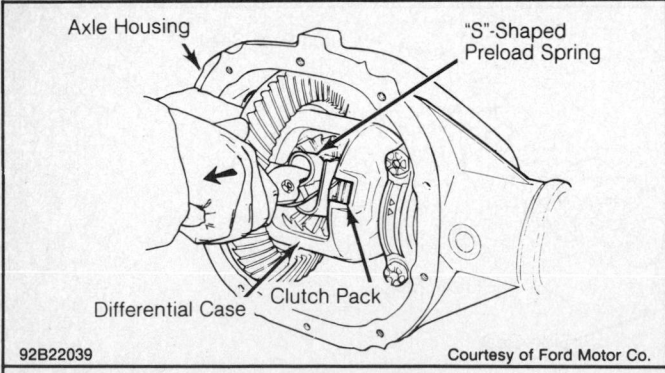

92B22039   Courtesy of Ford Motor Co.

Fig. 2: *Removing Clutch Pack Preload Spring*

Installation – 1) Disassemble gauge and clutch packs. Lubricate clutch pack friction plates with Friction Modifier (C8AZ-19B546-A or EST-M2C118-A). Reassemble side gear and clutch pack with appropriate size shim. Install assemblies into differential case.

2) Place pinion gears and thrust washers 180 degrees apart on side gears. Install pinion gear rotator. Using 12" extension, rotate pinion gears until they are aligned with pinion shaft hole. Remove pinion gear rotator from differential case.

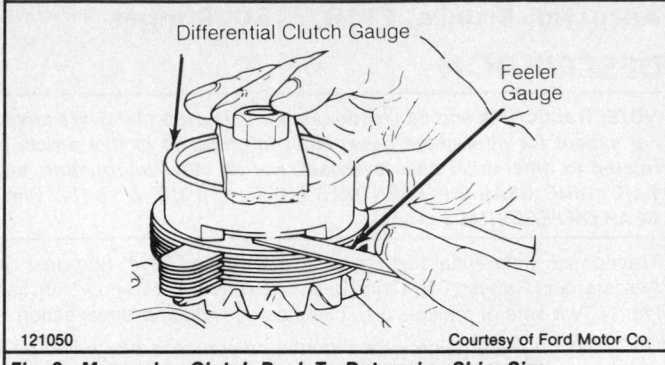

121050   Courtesy of Ford Motor Co.

Fig. 3: *Measuring Clutch Pack To Determine Shim Size*

3) Using soft-faced hammer, drive "S"-shaped preload spring into position. Ensure spring is undamaged. Install axle shafts and "C" locks. Push axle shaft as far outboard as possible. Apply Thread Lock & Sealer (E0AZ-19554-B) to pinion shaft lock bolt. Install pinion shaft lock bolt. Tighten to specification. See TORQUE SPECIFICATIONS table at end of article.

4) Install rear drums and wheels. Perform ON-VEHICLE TESTING to ensure unit is set up correctly. Apply continuous bead of silicone sealant to axle housing inside of bolt hole pattern. Install rear cover within 15 minutes of silicone application. Tighten bolts to specification. See TORQUE SPECIFICATIONS table. Fill axle housing with lubricant until level with bottom of fill hole.

OVERHAUL

NOTE: This procedure involves overhauling differential case with case removed from axle housing. Also, it is not necessary to remove differential bearings to overhaul differential case.

DISASSEMBLY

WARNING: Preload spring is under pressure; remove carefully.

CAUTION: DO NOT clean clutch plate friction surfaces with solvent; wipe with clean shop towel only. DO NOT interchange clutches or shims.

1) Remove ring gear. DO NOT remove ABS sensor ring (if equipped). If sensor ring is removed, it must be replaced. Remove pinion shaft lock bolt and pinion shaft. Grasp preload spring with pliers. Pull and tap preload spring until it is removed.

2) Using Pinion Gear Rotator (T84P-4205-A for 7 1/2" ring gear; T80P-4205-A for 8 3/4" ring gear) with a 12" extension, rotate pinion gears until they can be removed from differential case. Remove both side gear and clutch pack assemblies, marking each assembly for installation reference. Disassemble side gear and clutch pack assemblies; note order of disassembly for reassembly reference.

INSPECTION

DO NOT clean clutch plate friction surfaces with solvent; wipe with clean shop towel only. Inspect parts for uneven or extreme wear. Replace if necessary.

CLUTCH PACK SET-UP

1) Reassemble side gear and clutch pack assemblies without shim. Install Differential Clutch Gauge Base (T84P-4946-A for 7 1/2" ring gear; T87P-4946-A for 8 3/4" ring gear) in vise. With side gear facing down, slide assembly onto base without shim. Install Differential Clutch Gauge Disc (part of T84P-4946-A for 7 1/2" ring gear; T80P-4946-A for 8 3/4" ring gear) on top of assembly without shim.

1992 DRIVE AXLES
Traction-Lok 7 1/2" & 8 3/4" Differentials (Cont.)

FORD
7-43

2) Install nut on threaded end of gauge base. Tighten nut to **60 INCH lbs. (6.7 N.m)**. Using feeler gauge, select thickest blade that will enter between clutch gauge and clutch pack. *See Fig. 3*. This reading will be thickness of new shim for that clutch pack. Repeat procedure for opposite assembly. Disassemble gauge and assembly.

REASSEMBLY

1) Lubricate friction plates with Friction Modifier (C8AZ-19B546-A or EST-M2C118-A). Reassemble side gear and clutch pack assemblies with appropriate size shim. Install assemblies into cavity of differential case.

2) Place pinion gears and thrust washers 180 degrees apart on side gears. Install pinion gear rotator with 12" extension. Rotate pinion gears until they are aligned with pinion shaft hole. Remove pinion gear rotator from differential case.

3) Using soft-faced hammer, drive "S"-shaped preload spring into position. Ensure spring is not damaged. Install pinion shaft and pinion shaft lock bolt. DO NOT tighten pinion shaft lock bolt. Before installing differential case in axle housing, bench-test differential case clutch packs using Traction-Lok Torque Adapter (T59L-4204-A). *See Fig. 4.*

4) This checks torque required to rotate one side gear while other is held stationary. If break-away torque (torque required to rotate side gear) is not at least 20 ft. lbs. (27 N.m) and rotation is not smooth, different shim must be installed in clutch pack.

5) If break-away torque is as specified and rotation is smooth, tighten pinion shaft lock bolt to specification. See TORQUE SPECIFICATIONS table at end of article.

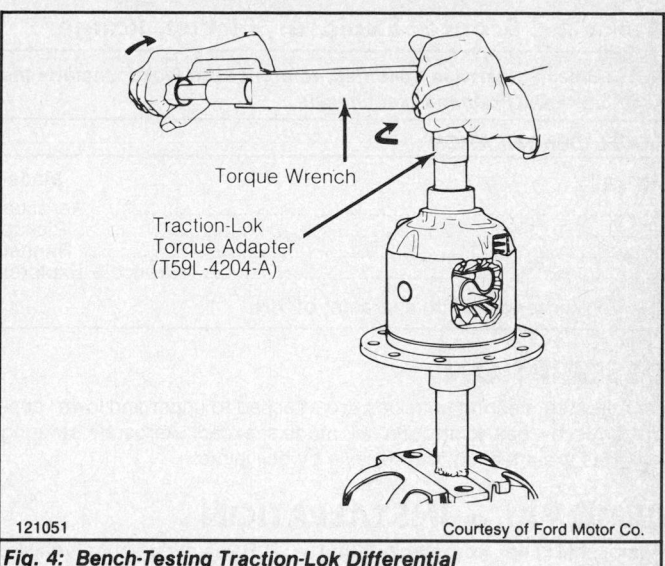

Torque Wrench

Traction-Lok
Torque Adapter
(T59L-4204-A)

121051   Courtesy of Ford Motor Co.

Fig. 4: Bench-Testing Traction-Lok Differential

TORQUE SPECIFICATIONS
TORQUE SPECIFICATIONS

Application	Ft. Lbs. (N.m)
Filler Plug	15-30 (20-41)
Pinion Shaft Lock Bolt	15-30 (20-41)
Rear Cover Bolt	25-35 (34-47)
Ring Gear Bolt	70-85 (95-115)

Aerostar, Bronco, Explorer, Pickup, Ranger

NOTE: Unless otherwise specified, references to Pickup include the F350 Super Duty commercial chassis.

MODEL IDENTIFICATION

Series [1]	Model
"A"	Aerostar
"F"	Pickup
"R"	Ranger
"U"	Bronco & Explorer

[1] – Vehicle series is fifth character of VIN.

DESCRIPTION

On Aerostar, steering knuckles are attached to upper and lower control arms by ball joints. On all models except Aerostar, steering knuckles are attached to front axle by ball joints.

REMOVAL & INSTALLATION

Removal (Except Aerostar & F350) – 1) Raise and support vehicle. Remove wheel and tire assemblies. Remove spindle and axle shaft. See SPINDLES & AXLE SHAFTS under REMOVAL & INSTALLATION in DANA IFS FRONT AXLE article. Disconnect steering linkage (as necessary). Disconnect tie-rod from knuckle.

2) On F150 and 250, remove upper ball joint cotter pin. Loosen upper and lower ball joint stud nuts. Remove stud nuts. On Explorer and Ranger, remove upper ball joint snap ring and remove ball joint pinch bolt. Loosen lower ball joint stud nut.

3) On all models, break ball joints loose from axle housing and separate components. Remove camber adjuster. Remove knuckle. To remove ball joints, place steering knuckle in vise and remove snap ring from bottom ball joint socket (if equipped). Remove lower ball joint first, and then upper ball joint.

NOTE: Install lower ball joint first.

Installation – Install lower and upper ball joints in steering knuckle (if removed). Install NEW nut on lower ball joint. Place knuckle onto axle arm. Install camber adjuster in same position as when removed. Install nuts and snap rings onto ball joints. To complete installation, reverse removal procedure.

CAUTION: If proper tightening sequence is not followed, excessive steering knuckle turning effort may result. See TORQUE SPECIFICATIONS table at end of article. When aligning ball joint nut to install cotter pin, always tighten nut to align. Never loosen nut to align hole.

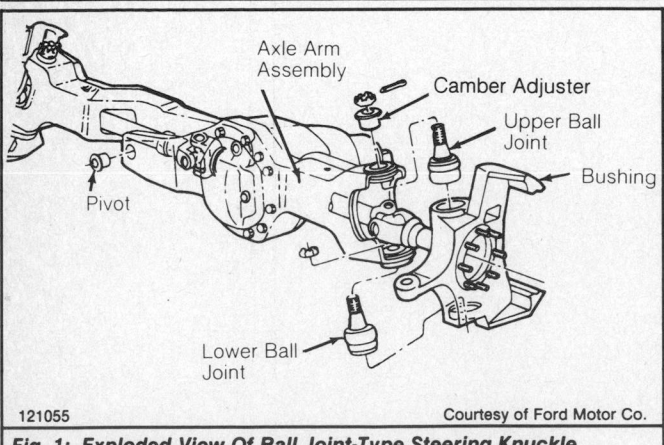

121055   Courtesy of Ford Motor Co.

Fig. 1: Exploded View Of Ball Joint-Type Steering Knuckle (Except Aerostar & F350)

Removal (Aerostar) – 1) Position front wheels in straight-ahead position. Raise vehicle with weight resting on lower control arms to keep chassis springs compressed. Remove wheel and tire assem-

blies. Remove wheel cover, hub nut and washer. Remove brake caliper and rotor. See REMOVAL & INSTALLATION in appropriate BRAKES article.

WARNING: DO NOT remove nut from lower control arm ball joint unless chassis spring is compressed by weight of vehicle resting on lower control arm.

2) Remove cotter pin and nut from tie rod end. *See Fig. 2.* Disconnect tie rod end from steering knuckle. Using Hub Remover/Installer (T81P-1104-A and C) with Hub Knuckle Adapters (T83P-1104-BH1 and T88P-1104-A1) or equivalent, free outer axle shaft from splines in center of hub and bearing assembly.

3) Remove cotter pin and nut from lower control arm ball joint at steering knuckle. Separate lower control arm from steering knuckle. Remove bolt and nut retaining steering knuckle to upper control arm ball joint. Separate and remove steering knuckle from upper control arm ball joint. Wire axle shaft to body to maintain in level position.

Installation – 1) With hub attached to steering knuckle, position hub over outer axle shaft. Ensure outer axle shaft splines are aligned in center of hub. Position steering knuckle over lower ball joint stud on lower control arm. Install lower ball joint nut and tighten to specification. See TORQUE SPECIFICATIONS table at end of article.

2) Install cotter pin. Install washer and hub nut. Lightly tighten hub nut to seat CV joint on back side of steering knuckle. DO NOT tighten to specification at this time.

3) Position steering knuckle to upper control arm ball joint stud. Install bolt and nut and tighten to specification. See TORQUE SPECIFICATIONS table. Connect tie rod end to steering knuckle. Tighten nut and install cotter pin.

4) Tighten hub nut to **170-210 ft. lbs. (230-285 N.m)**. Install rotor and caliper. Install wheel and tire assemblies. Install wheel lug nuts and tighten to specification. Lower vehicle.

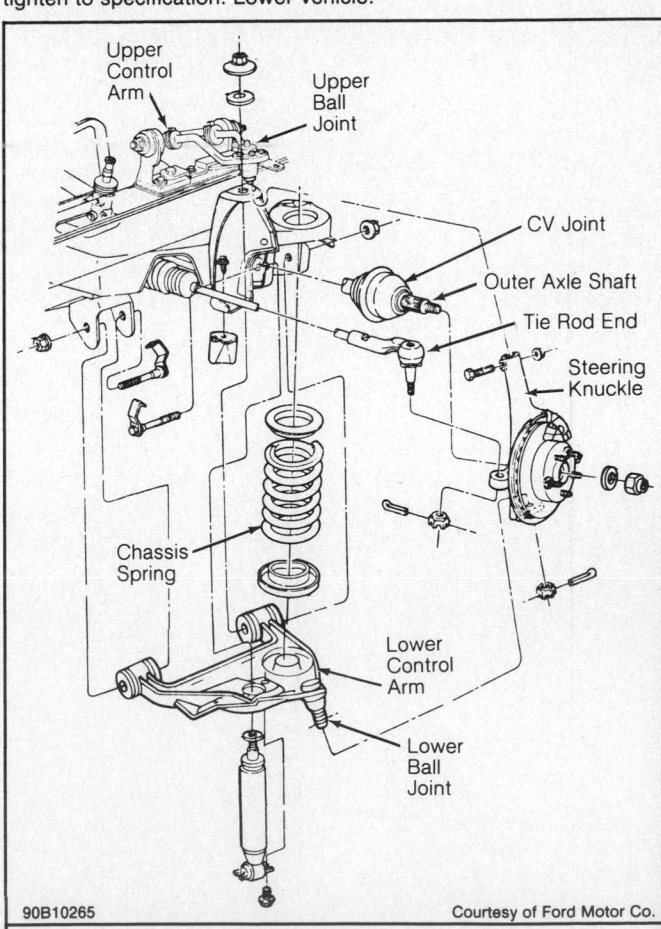

90B10265   Courtesy of Ford Motor Co.

Fig. 2: Exploded View Of Ball Joint-Type Steering Knuckle Assembly (Aerostar)

Removal (F350) – **1)** Raise and support vehicle. Remove wheel and tire assemblies. Remove brake caliper. See REMOVAL & INSTALLATION in appropriate BRAKES article. Remove locking hub. See LOCKING HUBS article.

2) Remove hub and rotor assembly. See REMOVAL & INSTALLATION in appropriate BRAKES article. Remove spindle and axle. See HUB, BEARING & AXLE SHAFTS under REMOVAL & INSTALLATION in DANA 60, 70 & 80 DIFFERENTIALS article.

3) Disconnect steering linkage at steering knuckle. Remove cotter pin from upper ball joint stud. Loosen both upper and lower ball joint stud nuts. Remove stud nut. Brake top ball joint loose from tube yoke. Remove lower ball joint stud nut. Remove knuckle from tube yoke.

Installation – **1)** Coat grease retainer-to-lower kingpin contact surface with RTV sealant. Install grease retainer in axle housing with concave portion toward upper kingpin.

2) Install bearing cup until it bottoms on grease retainer. Pack bearing and axle housing area with grease and install bearing. Using Seal Installer (T86T-3110-AH), install NEW grease seal.

3) Install upper kingpin and tighten to specification. Install steering knuckle and tapered bushing. Install lower kingpin and retainer. Evenly tighten retainer bolts to specification. See TORQUE SPECIFICATIONS table.

4) Install retainer, compression spring and spindle cap. Tighten spindle cap bolts to specification. Lubricate upper and lower kingpins through grease fittings.

TORQUE SPECIFICATIONS
TORQUE SPECIFICATIONS

Application	Ft. Lbs. (N.m)
Ball Joint Nut	
Aerostar	
Lower	59-81 (80-110)
Upper	27-37 (37-50)
Bronco & F150/250	
Lower	90-110 (122-149)
Upper	100 (136)
Explorer & Ranger	
Lower	80-120 (108-163)
Upper	27-37 (37-50)
F350	
Lower	35 (47)
Upper	150 (203)
Tie Rod End Nut	
Aerostar	52-74 (70-100)
All Others	50-75 (68-102)
Wheel Lug Nut	
Aerostar, Explorer & Ranger	100 (136)
Bronco & F150	100 (136)
F250/350	140 (190)

1992 DRIVE AXLES
Locking Hubs

Bronco, Explorer, Pickup, Ranger

DESCRIPTION

NOTE: Unless otherwise specified, references to Pickup include the F350 Super Duty commercial chassis.

MODEL IDENTIFICATION

Series [1]	Model
"F"	Pickup
"R"	Ranger
"U"	Bronco & Explorer

[1] – Vehicle series is fifth character of VIN.

The front driving axle hub locks are either automatically or manually actuated. When actuated, hub lock assembly locks hub, wheel and tire assembly to front drive axle.

When released, front drive axle is disengaged from hub assembly. Tire and wheel assembly rotate freely on spindle. Two opposed tapered roller bearings allow hub and wheel and tire assembly to rotate on spindle. A hub seal is installed behind inner bearing to prevent wheel bearing lubricant from contaminating brake pads and rotor surfaces.

OPERATION

AUTOMATIC LOCKING HUBS

When using 2WD, shift transfer case into 2H position by pushing selector LOW RANGE and/or 4 X 4 push buttons until both Amber indicator lights are off. To disengage automatic locking hubs, move vehicle in opposite direction (forward or reverse) and drive a minimum of 10 feet in a straight line. Always disengage hub locks before driving vehicle on dry, hard pavement.

Shifting Between 2H & 4H – Transfer case can be shifted between 2H and 4H with vehicle stopped or at normal road speed by depressing selector 4 X 4 button. The Amber indicator light will illuminate when vehicle is in 4WD.

Shifting Between High/Low Ranges – Stop vehicle and shift transmission to Neutral. On manual transmission models, disengage the clutch before depressing LOW RANGE button. On all models, LOW RANGE light should illuminate. DO NOT attempt to shift from or to low range with vehicle in motion.

MANUAL LOCKING HUBS

CAUTION: DO NOT shift to or from 4L when vehicle is in motion or gear clash will damage transfer case. Also, transfer case will be damaged if shifted from 2H to 4H with hub locks in the FREE position when vehicle is in motion.

When using 2WD, shift transfer case into 2H position and manually turn hub lock selector knob counterclockwise to FREE position. When using 4WD, lock both hubs by turning selector knob clockwise to LOCK position. If hub teeth do not engage with knob in this position, a slight movement of wheel in either direction will complete locking procedure.

If vehicle is stopped, place transmission in Neutral and select transfer case shift position. If vehicle is moving, transfer case may be shifted between 2H and 4H only, providing hub locks are in LOCK position. Shifting to or from 4L position requires vehicle be fully stopped and transmission in Neutral. Both hubs must be set in same function to avoid excess front differential wear on non-traction-lock front axles or steering pull on traction-lock front axles.

ADJUSTMENTS

FRONT WHEEL BEARINGS

Bronco & F150 W/Dana 44 IFS/HD & Manual Locking Hubs – 1) Raise and support front of vehicle. Remove front wheels. Remove locking hubs. See MANUAL LOCKING HUBS under REMOVAL & INSTALLATION.

2) Using a torque wrench and Spanner Lock Nut Wrench (T86T-1197-A), unlock wheel bearing adjusting nut locking splines by applying inward pressure. Tighten adjusting nut to **70 ft. lbs. (95 N.m)** while turning wheel back and forth. *See Fig. 1.*

NOTE: Adjusting nut will not tighten past 70 ft. lbs. (95 N.m). Threaded portion of nut will ratchet in assembly.

3) Applying inward pressure to spanner lock nut wrench to disengage locking splines, back off adjusting nut approximately 90 degrees. Retighten adjusting nut to **15-20 ft. lbs. (20-27 N.m)**.

4) Final end play of hub and rotor assembly should be zero. Install locking hub and wheels. Install wheels and tighten wheel lug nuts to specification. See TORQUE SPECIFICATIONS table at end of article.

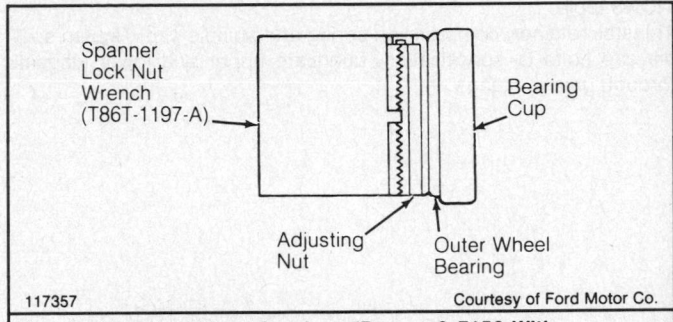

Spanner Lock Nut Wrench (T86T-1197-A)

Bearing Cup

Adjusting Nut

Outer Wheel Bearing

117357   Courtesy of Ford Motor Co.

Fig. 1: Adjusting Wheel Bearings (Bronco & F150 With Dana 44 IFS/HD & Manual Locking Hubs)

Bronco & F150 W/Dana 44-IFS & Automatic Locking Hubs, F250 W/ Dana 50-IFS & F350 W/Dana 60 Monobeam & Manual Locking Hubs – 1) Raise and support front of vehicle. Remove wheels. Remove locking hub assembly. See AUTOMATIC LOCKING HUBS or MANUAL LOCKING HUBS under REMOVAL & INSTALLATION.

2) Remove outer lock nut with Spanner Lock Nut Wrench (D85T-1197-A). *See Fig. 2.* Remove lock washer. Tighten inner lock nut to **50 ft. lbs. (68 N.m)**. Back off inner lock nut and retighten to **30-40 ft. lbs. (41-54 N.m)**. While rotating hub, back off inner lock nut 90 degrees.

3) Install lock washer so key is positioned in spindle groove. Rotate inner lock nut so pin is aligned in nearest lock washer hole. Install and tighten outer lock nut to **160-205 ft. lbs. (217-278 N.m)**. Final end play of hub and rotor assembly should be **0-.004" (0-.10 mm)**.

4) If end play is beyond specification remove hub and bearing assembly and inspect components for excessive wear or damage. Replace hub and/or bearing assemblies as necessary, then reinstall components. Install hub locks. Install wheels and tighten wheel lug nuts to specification. See TORQUE SPECIFICATIONS table at end of article.

Explorer & Ranger W/Dana 35-IFS & Automatic Locking Hubs
1) Raise and support vehicle. Remove wheels and tires. Remove retaining washers from wheel lug nut studs. *See Fig. 3.*

2) Remove automatic locking hub assemblies. Remove snap ring and axle shaft spacer. Carefully pull plastic cam assembly from bearing adjusting nut. Remove 2 plastic thrust washers from adjusting nut.

CAUTION: Before removing adjusting nut, remove locking key from spindle keyway. Failure to clear keyway will result in thread damage on spindle.

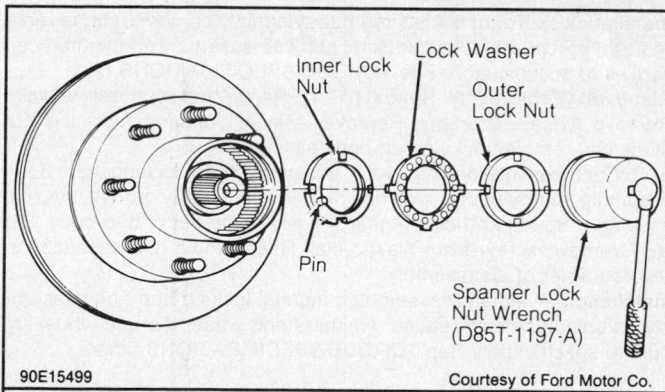

Fig. 2: Adjusting Wheel Bearings (Bronco & F150 W/Dana 44-IFS & Auto. Hubs, F250 W/Dana 50-IFS & F350 W/Dana-60 Monobeam

3) Using magnet, remove locking key from spindle keyway. It may be necessary to rotate adjusting nut slightly to relieve pressure for locking key removal. Loosen adjusting nut with 2 3/8" Hex Socket (T70T-4252-B).

4) Tighten adjusting nut to **35 ft. lbs. (47 N.m)** while turning hub back and forth to seat bearings. Spin hub and back off adjusting nut 90 degrees. Retighten adjusting nut to **16 INCH lbs. (1.8 N.m)**.

5) Align nearest hole in adjusting nut with center of spindle keyway slot. Advance nut to next lug, if necessary. Install locking key in spindle keyway under adjusting nut. Install 2 thrust washers. Press plastic cam assembly onto adjusting nut while lining up key in fixed cam with spindle keyway.

6) Install axle shaft spacer. Clip snap ring onto end of spindle. Install automatic locking hub assembly with 3 legs of hub assembly inserted into 3 pockets of cam assembly. Install retaining washers, wheel and tire. Check hub and rotor assembly end play. End play should be 0-.003" (0-.08 mm).

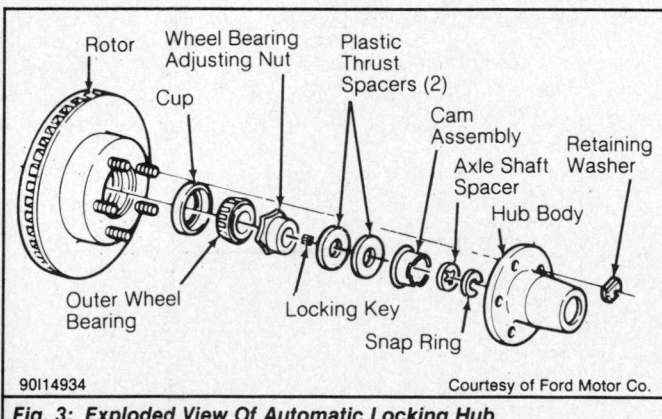

Fig. 3: Exploded View Of Automatic Locking Hub (Explorer & Ranger)

Explorer & Ranger W/Dana 35-IFS & Manual Locking Hubs – 1) Raise and support vehicle. Remove wheels and tires. Remove retaining washers from wheel lug nut studs. See Fig. 4. Remove manual locking hub assemblies.

2) Remove snap ring and axle shaft spacer from spindle. Remove outer bearing lock nut using Spanner Lock Nut Wrench (T86T-1197-B). Remove lock nut washer from spindle. Using spanner wrench, loosen inner wheel bearing lock nut.

3) It may be necessary to rotate adjusting nut slightly to relieve pressure for locking key removal. Loosen adjusting nut with 2 3/8" Hex Socket (T70T-4252-B). Tighten adjusting nut to **35 ft. lbs. (47 N.m)** while turning hub back and forth to seat bearings.

4) Spin hub and back off adjusting nut 90 degrees. Install lock washer on spindle. Mount lock washer over pin on adjusting nut, turning nut slightly if necessary to align pin. Install and tighten outer lock nut to **150 ft. lbs. (203 N.m)** using spanner lock nut wrench.

5) Install axle shaft spacer. Install snap ring on end of spindle. Install manual hub assembly. Install retaining washers, wheel and tire. Check hub and rotor assembly end play. End play should be **0-.003" (0-.08 mm)**.

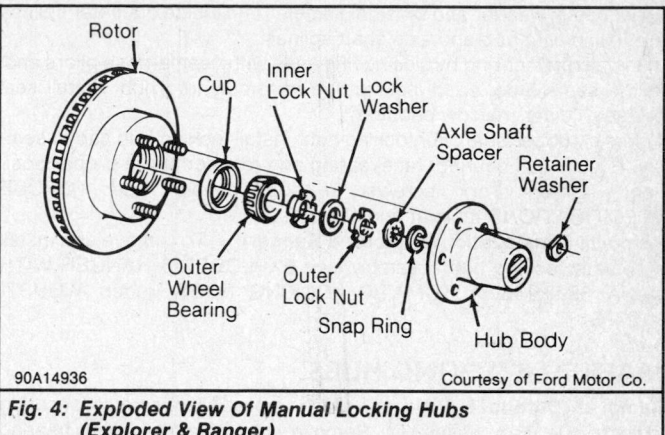

Fig. 4: Exploded View Of Manual Locking Hubs (Explorer & Ranger)

REMOVAL & INSTALLATION
AUTOMATIC LOCKING HUBS

Removal (Bronco & F150) – 1) Raise vehicle and install safety stands. Using T25 Torx bit, remove locking hub cap assembly-to-body assembly screws. Remove cap assembly and bearing components. *See Fig. 5.*

NOTE: DO NOT drop ball bearing, race, spring retainer or spring during disassembly.

2) Remove rubber seal. Remove seal bridge retainer (small metal stamping) from spring retainer ring space. Remove retainer ring by closing ends with needle-nose pliers while pulling hub lock from wheel hub.

3) If wheel hub and spindle are to be removed, remove "C" washer from stub shaft groove. Remove splined spacer from shaft.

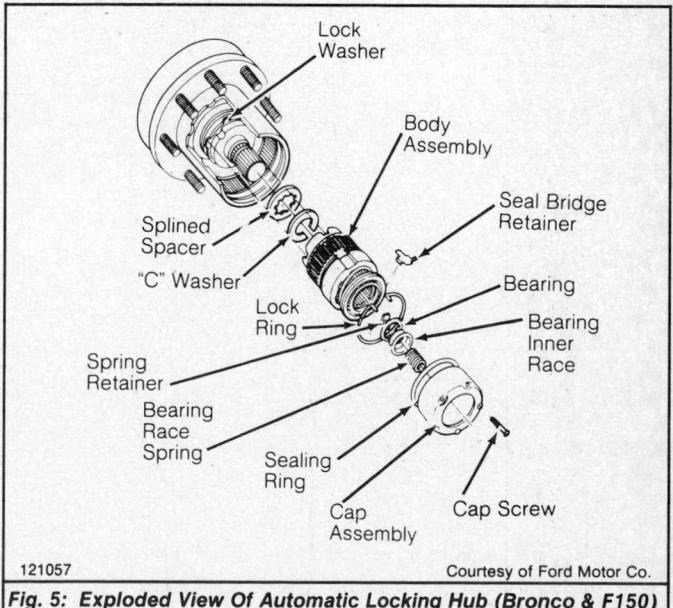

Fig. 5: Exploded View Of Automatic Locking Hub (Bronco & F150)

Inspection – Wash locking hub cap bearing, race and retainer in clean solvent. Inspect components for excessive wear or damage. Replace components as needed. Thoroughly blow dry parts with compressed air. Repack bearing with lithium grease. Position bearing assembly in race.

Installation – 1) Install splined spacer and "C" washer onto axle shaft. Remove excess grease from hub lock and hub splines before installation.

2) Start locking hub assembly into hub. Ensure large tangs are lined up with lock washer and outside diameter and inside diameter splines are in line with hub and axle shaft splines.

3) Install retainer ring by closing ring ends with needle-nose pliers and, at the same time, push locking hub assembly into hub. Install seal bridge retainer (narrow end first).

4) Install rubber seal over locking hub. Install locking hub cap assembly. Ensure ball bearing, race, spring and retainer are in proper position. Tighten Torx screws to specification. See TORQUE SPECIFICATIONS table at end of article.

Removal & Installation (Explorer & Ranger) – To remove and install automatic locking hub assembly, see EXPLORER & RANGER WITH DANA 35-IFS & AUTOMATIC LOCKING HUBS under ADJUSTMENTS.

MANUAL LOCKING HUBS

Removal (Bronco & Pickup) – 1) Remove Allen screws securing locking hub cap assembly. Remove cap assembly and bearing components. Remove snap ring (retainer ring) from end of axle shaft.

2) Remove lock ring (seated in groove of wheel hub). Slide hub body assembly out of wheel hub. If necessary, install 2 cap screws and pull body from hub.

NOTE: DO NOT pack grease into cap assembly. Excess grease can cause an increase in dialing effort.

Installation – To install locking hub assembly components, reverse removal procedure. Install locking hub cap assembly and tighten cap screws to specification. See TORQUE SPECIFICATIONS table.

Removal (Explorer & Ranger) – 1) Raise and support vehicle. Remove wheel assembly. Remove retainer washers from lug nut studs and remove locking hub body assembly.

2) To remove internal hub lock assembly from locking hub body assembly, remove outer lock ring seated in hub body groove. Internal assembly, spring and clutch gear will now slide out of hub body. DO NOT remove screw from plastic dial. Reassemble hub assembly in reverse order of disassembly.

Installation – Install reassembled manual locking hub body assembly on spindle. Install retainer washers and wheel. Torque wheel lug nuts to specification. See TORQUE SPECIFICATIONS table.

TORQUE SPECIFICATIONS

TORQUE SPECIFICATIONS

Application	Ft. Lbs. (N.m)
Wheel Lug Nuts	
F250/350	140 (190)
Except F250/350	100 (136)
	INCH Lbs. (N.m)
Locking Cap Assembly Screws [1]	
Bronco & Pickup	
Automatic Locking Hub	40-50 (4.5-5.6)
Manual Locking Hub	40-60 (4.5-6.8)

[1] – Tighten in a circular pattern.

DESCRIPTION

Aerostar 4WD front axle assembly uses 2 half-shafts and 2 inner axle shafts that are integral with differential assembly. The 2 outer half-shafts (consisting of 2 axle shafts with 4 Constant Velocity (CV) joints and dust boots) are bolted to inner axle shaft flanges. A CV joint is attached to both ends of each half-shaft. A fixed CV joint is used on outer end of each half-shaft. A plunging CV joint is used on inner end of each half-shaft. *See Fig. 1.*

Half-shafts are splined into inner CV joints and secured by snap rings. Half-shafts are fixed in non-serviceable outer CV joints.

Inner axle shafts are retained in axle housing by "C" clips in differential case. For additional information on inner axle shafts, see DANA 28-2 FRONT AXLE – AEROSTAR article.

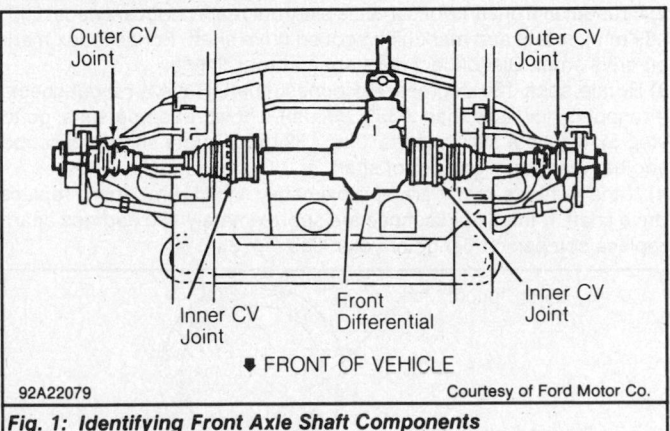

Fig. 1: Identifying Front Axle Shaft Components

TROUBLE SHOOTING

NOTE: See TROUBLE SHOOTING article in GENERAL INFORMATION.

REMOVAL, DISASSEMBLY, REASSEMBLY & INSTALLATION

INNER AXLE SHAFTS

NOTE: To remove axle shafts, remove axle housing assembly from vehicle. See DANA 28-2 FRONT AXLE – AEROSTAR article.

HALF-SHAFT ASSEMBLY

Removal – 1) Raise and support vehicle. Remove front wheels. Remove hub nut and washer. Discard hub nut. Mark differential inner axle shaft flange-to-half-shaft flange position for installation reference. Disconnect half-shaft from inner axle shaft flange and wire aside.

CAUTION: DO NOT allow half-shaft to hang unsupported; damage to outboard CV joint may occur. Once half-shaft(s) has been removed, DO NOT allow vehicle weight to be supported by hub bearing.

2) Remove lower shock absorber bolts. Position shock out of way. Remove rubber jounce bumper. To prevent rotor from turning, insert steel rod into rotor vent slot and rotate counterclockwise until rod contacts steering knuckle. Remove and discard hub nut and washer. Using Front Hub Remover/Installer (T81P-1104-C and T81P-1104-A) and Hub Adapters (T83P-1104-BH1 and T86P-1104-A1), separate outer CV joint stub axle shaft from hub and rotor assembly. Remove half-shaft assembly from vehicle.

Disassembly – 1) Secure half-shaft in soft-jawed vise. Remove inner CV joint boot clamps. *See Fig. 2.* Remove inner CV joint assembly bolts. Separate spacer and grease cap from joint. Remove snap ring from inner CV joint and discard. Slide inner CV joint from shaft.

Remove Belleville washer from shaft and discard. Remove inner CV joint boot from shaft and discard.

2) Clean inner CV joint parts in cleaning solvent. Inspect CV joint components for excessive wear, pitting, rust and broken parts. If any CV joint components are faulty, replace complete inner CV joint.

3) Outer CV joint cannot be overhauled. Outer boot can be changed if inner CV joint is remove and inner boot is also replaced. If outer CV joint is defective, remove inner CV joint and replace entire outer joint and interconnecting shaft as an assembly.

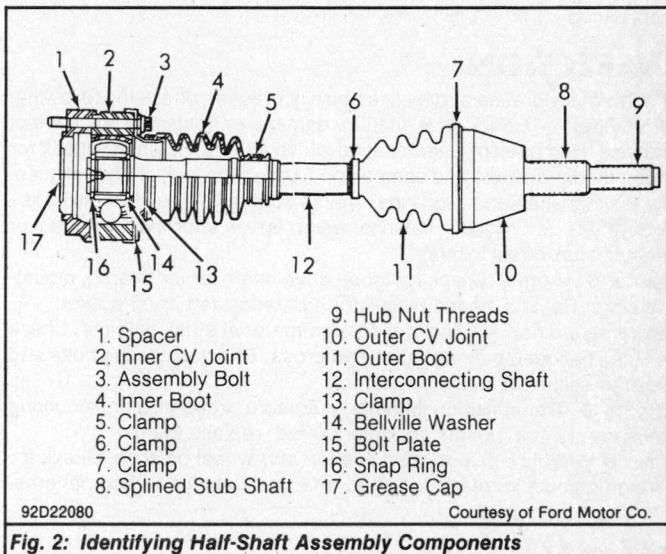

1. Spacer	9. Hub Nut Threads
2. Inner CV Joint	10. Outer CV Joint
3. Assembly Bolt	11. Outer Boot
4. Inner Boot	12. Interconnecting Shaft
5. Clamp	13. Clamp
6. Clamp	14. Bellville Washer
7. Clamp	15. Bolt Plate
8. Splined Stub Shaft	16. Snap Ring
	17. Grease Cap

Fig. 2: Identifying Half-Shaft Assembly Components

Reassembly – 1) If outer CV joint has been cleaned and is being repacked, fill outer CV joint area around balls with approximately 2.8 ounces of CV joint grease. Spread approximately 1.4 ounces of CV joint grease evenly inside large boot. Assemble large outer CV boot onto outboard shaft and joint assembly.

2) Ensure boot is seated in grooves. Tighten clamp using crimping pliers. Slide small inner CV boot and clamps onto outboard shaft and joint assembly. DO NOT tighten clamps at this time. Coat spline end of outboard shaft and joint assembly using Long-Life Lubricant (C1AZ-19590-BA).

3) Slide NEW Belleville washer onto shaft. Insert shaft spline end into inner CV joint. Install NEW snap ring. Spread approximately 1.4 ounces of CV joint grease into inner CV joint boot. Slip boot into place, and ensure boot is seated in grooves. Crimp NEW boot clamps in place with crimping pliers.

4) Fill spacer and grease cap with approximately 1.4 ounces of CV JOINT grease. DO NOT allow grease to enter bolt holes. Install spacer and grease cap onto inner CV joint. Install assembly bolts and tighten to **19-25 ft. lbs. (26-34 N.m).**

Installation – 1) With splines aligned, install outboard CV stub shaft into hub and rotor assembly. Install NEW washer and hub nut. To prevent rotor from turning, insert steel rod into rotor vent slot and rotate clockwise until rod contacts steering knuckle.

2) Tighten hub nut to **170-210 ft. lbs. (230-285 N.m).** Noting alignment marks made previously, install half-shaft flange to differential axle shaft flange. Install and tighten flange bolts to specification. See TORQUE SPECIFICATIONS table. To complete installation, reverse removal procedure.

TORQUE SPECIFICATIONS
TORQUE SPECIFICATIONS

Application	Ft. Lbs. (N.m)
Axle Hub Nut	170-210 (230-285)
Flange Bolts	22-29 (30-39)
Spacer & Grease Cap Bolts	19-25 (26-34)
Wheel Lug Nuts	85-115 (115-156)

1992 DRIVE AXLES
Drive Shafts

Aerostar, Bronco, Explorer
Pickup, Ranger, Van

NOTE: Unless otherwise specified, references to Pickup include the F350 Super Duty commercial chassis.

DESCRIPTION

Drive shaft assemblies may have one shaft, 2 shafts or 3 shafts, depending on application. Locations of slip joints vary with model application.

INSPECTION

If abnormal vibration or driveline noise is present, check the following:

Drive Shaft – Check drive shaft for damage or dents that could affect balance. Remove any undercoating which adheres to shaft. Check for index marks on yoke and companion flange. If marks are not aligned, disconnect shaft and align index marks so they are as close as possible. Check for missing balance weight(s) or improperly seated or defective universal joint(s).

Center Bearing – Check for loose drive shaft center bearing mounting bolts. Replace bearing insulator if deteriorated or oil soaked.

Universal Joints – Check for foreign material stuck in joints. Check for play between bearing races and cross. Check for loose bolts and worn or seized bearings.

Engine & Transmission Mounts – Ensure transmission mounting bolts are tight. If mounts are deteriorated, replace them.

Tires & Wheels – Check tire inflation and wheel balance. Check for foreign objects in tread, damaged tread, mismatched tread patterns, or incorrect tire size.

MAINTENANCE

Whenever drive shaft is removed from vehicle, clean yoke with solvent. Lubricate inside diameter of seal with hydraulic seal lubricant, and outside diameter of seal with transmission fluid.

ADJUSTMENTS

DRIVE SHAFT PHASING

Except 2-Piece Shafts – Ensure yoke on each end of drive shaft is in same plane. Check for arrows on slip joint and drive shaft to aid in alignment. When drive shaft is correctly installed, center line of yokes at each end of individual shafts will be parallel. *See Fig. 2.* If center lines are not in same plane, remove drive shaft. Install drive shaft with center lines aligned.

2-Piece Shafts – This type drive shaft has a "blind" spline on the slip joint which makes it impossible to assemble the shaft with incorrect phasing.

DRIVE SHAFT BALANCE

1) Raise and support vehicle. Remove drive wheels. Reinstall lug nuts. Rotate shaft by turning brake drum or rotor. Use dial indicator to measure runout. If runout at front and/or center of shaft exceeds .035" (.89 mm), replace drive shaft.

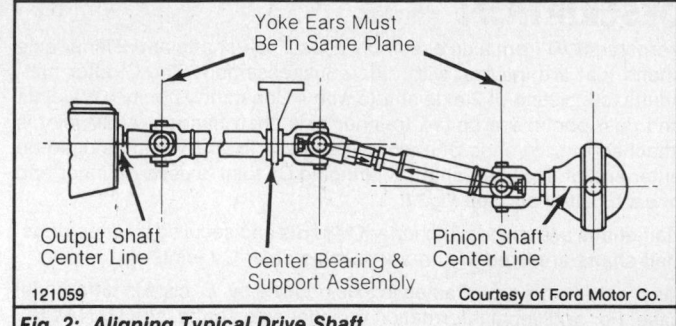

Fig. 2: Aligning Typical Drive Shaft

2) If runout at front and/or center is okay but rear runout exceeds .035" (.89 mm), rotate and mark high spot on drive shaft. Scribe index mark on drive shaft. Disconnect drive shaft at rear flange.

3) Rotate shaft 180 degrees. Reconnect shaft. Repeat runout check. If runout is now less than .035" (.89 mm), but vibration persists, go to step 5). If runout still exceeds .035" (.89 mm), rotate shaft and scribe another mark on high spot of shaft.

4) If the 2 marks made are approximately 1" (25 mm) apart, replace drive shaft. If the 2 marks made are approximately 180 degrees apart, replace companion flange or yoke. *See Fig. 3.*

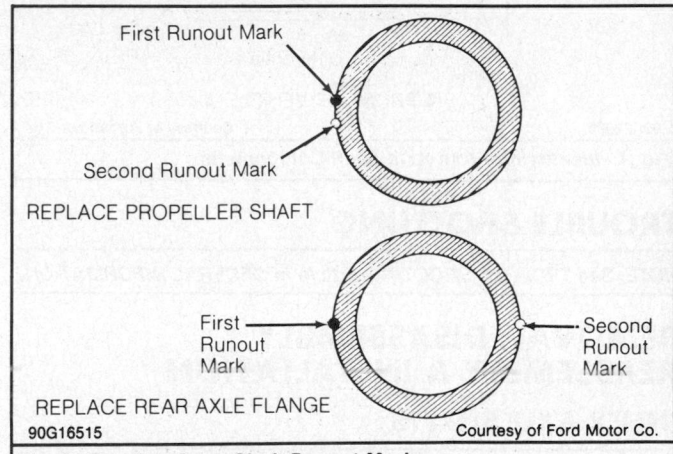

Fig. 3: Reading Drive Shaft Runout Marks

5) If drive shaft is within specification, but still vibrates, place 4 marks approximately 6" forward of weld at rear end of shaft, spaced equally around shaft. Label marks 1, 2, 3 and 4. Place screw-type hose clamp so clamp head is in No. 1 position. Start engine. Spin drive shaft at road speed.

6) If there is little or no change, move clamp head to No. 2 position, and repeat test. Continue procedure until vibration is at lowest level. If no difference is noted with clamp head moved to all 4 positions, vibration may not be drive shaft imbalance.

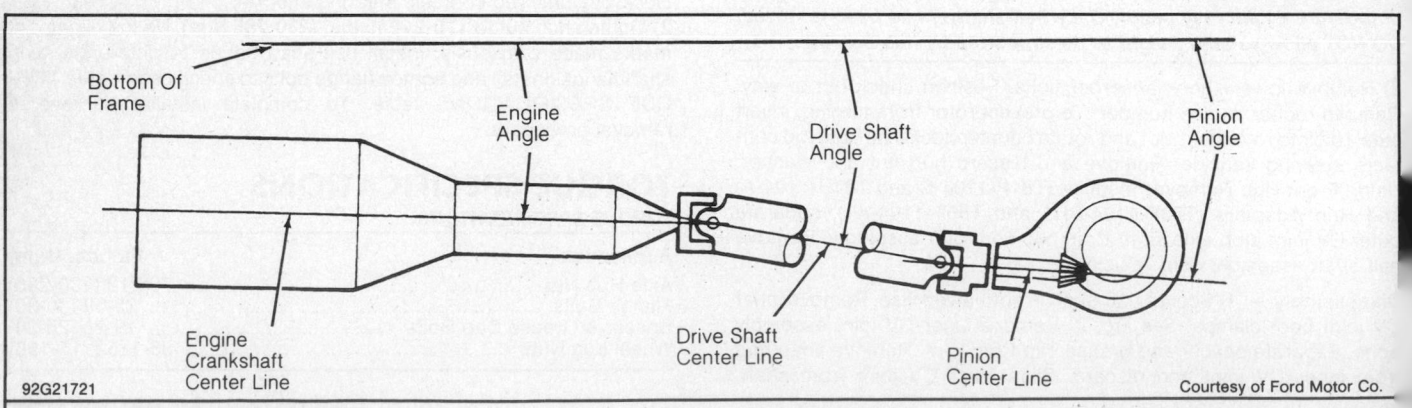

Fig. 1: Identifying Drive Line Angles

7) If vibration is lessened but not completely gone, place 2 clamps at that point, and run test again. Combined weight of clamps in one position may increase vibration. If vibration is increased, rotate clamps approximately 1/2" (13 mm) apart, above and below best position, and repeat test.

8) Continue to rotate clamps as necessary, until vibration is at lowest point. If vibration level is still unacceptable, leave rear clamp(s) in position and repeat procedure at front end of drive shaft. If vibration cannot be reduced to acceptable range using this procedure, replace drive shaft.

DRIVELINE ANGULARITY

Driveline angularity is the angular relationship between engine crankshaft, drive shaft, and drive axle pinion. Driveline angles are given in relation to a zero-degree frame rail angle and are specified for individual components and models. *See Fig. 1.*

RIDE HEIGHT

Measure distance between points specified in RIDE HEIGHT MEASUREMENT LOCATIONS table. This distance is ride height.

FRAME ANGLE

Install bubble protractor (spirit level) on bottom of level portion of frame, below driver seat. Measure angle. Repeat measurement on other side of vehicle. Average readings from both sides to obtain a more accurate reading. Average of both readings is frame angle.

ENGINE ANGLE

1) Rotate drive shaft until transmission slip yoke ear is parallel to floor. Place protractor flush against ear on slip yoke. If slip yoke is not machined, place protractor against bottom of starter. *See Fig. 4.* Measure and record reading. Subtract frame angle from reading obtained in this step to obtain engine angle.

2) If engine angle is greater than specification by one degree or more, loosen but DO NOT remove engine and transmission mount fasteners. See *Figs. 5-18.* Tighten engine and transmission mount fasteners. Repeat step 1). If angle is still out of specification, install shims under transmission mount and rear crossmember until correct angle is obtained.

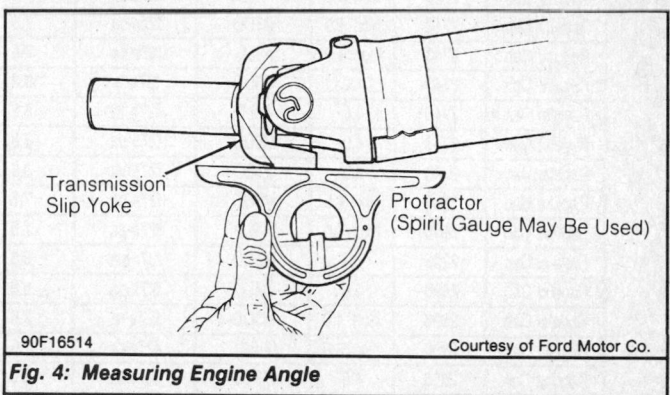

Transmission Slip Yoke

Protractor (Spirit Gauge May Be Used)

90F16514
Courtesy of Ford Motor Co.

Fig. 4: Measuring Engine Angle

RIDE HEIGHT MEASUREMENT LOCATIONS

Model	Measurement Location
Aerostar	Top Of Rear Axle Tube And Bottom Of Frame Rail
Bronco	Top Of Front Axle Tube And Bottom Of Spring Tower, Measured At Center Face Of Jounce Bumper
Explorer	Top Of Rear Axle Tube And Bottom Of Jounce Bumper
Pickup	
2WD	Top Of Front Axle And Bottom Of Spring Tower, Measured At Center Face Of Jounce Bumper
F250 4WD	Top Of Front Axle Tube And Bottom Of Frame
F350 4WD	Top Of Front Spring Spacer Plate And Bottom Of Bottom Of Jounce Stop Metal
F350 Super Duty	Top Of Front Spring Plate At Center Of Spring And Bottom Of Frame
Ranger	Top Of Rear Axle Tube And Bottom Of Jounce Bumper
Van	Top Of "A" Frame To Bottom Of Spring Tower

MODEL	WHEEL-BASE	ENGINE	TRANS-MISSION	SPRING CAPACITY	RING GEAR	RIDE HEIGHT	ENGINE ANGLE	DRIVE SHAFT ANGLE	PINION ANGLE
4x2	3022	3.0L	M50D	All	7.5"	5.9"	4.0°	4.8°	2.9°
4x2	3022	3.0L	A4LD	All	7.5"	5.9"	4.0°	4.9°	2.9°
4x2	3022	4.0L	A4LD	All	8.8"	5.9"	4.0°	5.3°	3.0°
E-4WD Rear	3022	4.0L	A4LD	All	7.5"	6.3"	4.0°	5.6°	3.1°
E-4WD Front	3022	4.0L	A4LD	All	N/A	N/A	4.0°	2.7°	0.0°

92H22852
Courtesy of Ford Motor Co.

Fig. 5: Determining Rear Driveline Angles (Aerostar)

MODEL	WHEEL BASE	ENGINE (L)	TRANS-MISSION	REAR SPRING	REAR AXLE		RIDE HEIGHT (mm)	ENGINE ANGLE	COUPLING SHAFT ANGLE	DRIVE SHAFT ANGLE	PINION ANGLE
					RING GEAR	GVW					
Bronco (4x4)	2660	4.9/5.0	M5OD	E3TA-AN	8.8	3800	155.65	5.5	—	11.9	10.8
	2660	4.9	M5OD-HD	E3TA-AN	8.8	3800	155.65	5.5	—	11.9	10.8
	2660	4.9/5.0/5.8	E4OD	E3TA-AN	8.8	3800	155.65	5.5	—	12.5	10.8
	2660	5.0	AOD	E3TA-AN	8.8	3800	155.65	5.5	—	11.4	10.8
	2660	5.0	C6	E3TA-AN	8.8	3800	155.65	5.5	—	11.2	10.8
	2660	4.9/5.0	T-18	E3TA-AN	8.8	3800	155.65	5.5	—	11.2	10.8

92H21722
Courtesy of Ford Motor Co.

Fig. 6: Determining Rear Driveline Angles (4WD Bronco)

1992 DRIVE AXLES
Drive Shafts (Cont.)

MODEL	WHEEL BASE (mm)	ENGINE (L)	TRANS- MISSION	REAR SPRING	RING GEAR	RIDE HEIGHT (mm)	ENGINE ANGLE	COUPLING SHAFT ANGLE	REAR D/S ANGLE	PINION ANGLE	FRONT D/S ANGLE
Ranger 4x2											
Regular Cab	2743	Non 4.0	M5OD	f27a-pa	7.5	193	5.5	—	7.4	6.7	—
Regular Cab	2743	Non 4.0	A4LD	f27a-pa	7.5	193	5.5	—	7.5	6.7	—
Regular Cab	2743	4.0	M5OD	f27a-pa	8.8	193	5.5	—	7.9	6.7	—
Regular Cab	2743	4.0	A4LD	f27a-pa	8.8	193	5.5	—	8.1	6.7	—
Regular Cab	2743	Non 4.0	M5OD	f27a-ra	7.5	198	5.5	—	7.6	6.8	—
Regular Cab	2743	Non 4.0	A4LD	f27a-ra	7.5	198	5.5	—	7.8	6.8	—
Regular Cab	2743	Non 4.0	M5OD	f27a-sa	7.5	196	5.5	—	7.5	6.7	—
Regular Cab	2743	Non 4.0	A4LD	f27a-sa	7.5	196	5.5	—	7.7	6.7	—
Regular Cab	2743	4.0	M5OD	f27a-ta	8.8	200	5.5	—	8.6	5.0	—
Regular Cab	2743	4.0	A4LD	f27a-ta	8.8	200	5.5	—	8.9	5.0	—
Regular Cab	2743	4.0	M5OD	f27a-ua	8.8	205	5.5	—	8.9	5.1	—
Regular Cab	2743	4.0	A4LD	f27a-ua	8.8	205	5.5	—	9.1	5.1	—
Regular Cab	2896	Non 4.0	M5OD	f27a-pa	7.5	193	5.5	—	6.6	6.7	—
Regular Cab	2896	Non 4.0	A4LD	f27a-pa	7.5	193	5.5	—	6.7	6.7	—
Regular Cab	2896	4.0	M5OD	f27a-pa	8.8	193	5.5	—	7.1	6.7	—
Regular Cab	2896	4.0	A4LD	f27a-pa	8.8	193	5.5	—	7.2	6.7	—
Regular Cab	2896	Non 4.0	M5OD	f27a-ra	7.5	198	5.5	—	6.8	6.8	—
Regular Cab	2896	Non 4.0	A4LD	f27a-ra	7.5	198	5.5	—	6.9	6.8	—
Regular Cab	2896	4.0	M5OD	f27a-ta	8.8	200	5.5	—	7.7	5.0	—
Regular Cab	2896	4.0	A4LD	f27a-ta	8.8	200	5.5	—	7.9	5.0	—
Regular Cab	2896	4.0	M5OD	f27a-ua	8.8	205	5.5	—	7.9	5.1	—
Regular Cab	2896	4.0	A4LD	f27a-ua	8.8	205	5.5	—	8.1	5.1	—
SuperCab	3177	Non 4.0	M5OD	f27a-pa	7.5	193	5.5	5.6	5.5	6.7	—
SuperCab	3177	Non 4.0	A4LD	f27a-pa	7.5	193	5.5	5.6	5.5	6.7	—
SuperCab	3177	4.0	M5OD	f27a-pa	8.8	193	5.5	5.6	6.1	6.7	—
SuperCab	3177	4.0	A4LD	f27a-pa	8.8	193	5.5	5.6	6.1	6.7	—
Ranger 4x4											
Regular Cab	2743	Non 4.0	M5OD	f27a-pa	7.5	181	5.5	—	12.0	9.0	1.87
Regular Cab	2743	4.0	M5OD	f27a-pa	8.8	181	5.5	—	12.7	9.0	1.87
Regular Cab	2896	Non 4.0	M5OD	f27a-pa	7.5	182	5.5	—	11.2	6.0	1.87
Regular Cab	2896	4.0	M5OD	f27a-pa	8.8	182	5.5	—	11.8	6.0	1.87
Regular Cab	2896	4.0	M5OD	f27a-pa	8.8	182	5.5	—	11.8	6.0	1.87
SuperCab	3177	Non 4.0	M5OD	f27a-pa	7.5	182	5.5	8.9	7.9	6.0	1.87
SuperCab	3177	4.0	M5OD	f27a-pa	8.8	182	5.5	8.9	8.5	6.0	1.87
Explorer 4x2											
2-Door	2593	4.0	M5OD	f17a-fd	8.8	122	5.5	—	8.3	5.7	—
2-Door	2593	4.0	A4LD	f17a-fd	8.8	122	5.5	—	8.5	5.7	—
2-Door	2593	4.0	A4LD	f17a-fd	8.8	122	5.5	—	8.5	5.7	—
4-Door	2842	4.0	M5OD	f17a-ed	8.8	129	5.5	—	7.1	5.9	—
4-Door	2842	4.0	A4LD	f17a-ed	8.8	129	5.5	—	7.2	5.9	—
4-Door	2842	4.0	M5OD	f17a-dc	8.8	124	5.5	—	6.9	5.8	—
4-Door	2842	4.0	A4LD	f17a-dc	8.8	124	5.5	—	7.0	5.8	—
Explorer 4x4											
2-Door	2593	4.0	M5OD	f17a-ed	8.8	129	5.5	—	9.5	5.9	1.87
2-Door	2593	4.0	M5OD	f17a-ed	8.0	129	5.5	—	9.5	5.9	1.87
2-Door	2593	4.0	M5OD	f17a-ed	8.8	129	5.5	—	9.5	5.9	1.87
2-Door	2593	4.0	M5OD	f17a-fd	8.8	122	5.5	—	9.1	5.7	1.87
4-Door	2842	4.0	M5OD	f17a-dc	8.8	124	5.5	—	7.2	5.8	1.87
4-Door	2842	4.0	M5OD	f17a-ed	8.8	129	5.5	—	7.4	5.9	1.87

92I22853

Fig. 7: Determining Rear Driveline Angles (Explorer & Ranger)

1992 DRIVE AXLES
Drive Shafts (Cont.)

MODEL	WHEEL BASE	ENGINE (L)	TRANS-MISSION	REAR SPRING	REAR AXLE RING GEAR	REAR AXLE GVW	RIDE HEIGHT (mm)	ENGINE ANGLE	COUPLING SHAFT ANGLE	REAR D/S ANGLE	PINION ANGLE
F-150 (4x4)	2967	4.9/5.0	M5OD	E3TA-KA	8.8	3800	186.08	5.5	—	13.3	4.9
	2967	4.9/5.0/5.8	E4OD	E3TA-KA	8.8	3800	186.08	5.5	—	13.9	4.9
	2967	4.9	M5OD-HD	E3TA-KA	8.8	3800	186.08	5.5	—	13.6	4.9
	2967	5.0	AOD	E3TA-KA	8.8	3800	186.08	5.5	—	13.2	4.9
	2967	4.9/5.0	T-18	E3TA-KA	8.8	3800	186.08	5.5	—	13.1	4.9
	3378	4.9/5.0	M5OD	E3TA-KA	8.8	3800	186.08	5.5	—	9.3	4.9
	3378	4.9	M5OD-HD	E3TA-KA	8.8	3800	186.08	5.5	—	9.3	4.9
	3378	5.0	AOD	E3TA-KA	8.8	3800	186.08	5.5	—	9.2	4.9
	3378	4.9/5.0	T-18	E3TA-KA	8.8	3800	186.08	5.5	—	9.2	4.9
	3378	4.9/5.0/5.8	E4OD	E3TA-KA	8.8	3800	186.08	5.5	—	9.5	4.9
	3378	4.9/5.0	M5OD	FOTA-LA	8.8	3800	181.52	5.5	—	9.1	4.9
	3378	4.9	M5OD-HD	FOTA-LA	8.8	3800	181.52	5.5	—	9.1	4.9
	3378	5.0	AOD	FOTA-LA	8.8	3800	181.52	5.5	—	9.0	4.9
	3378	4.9/5.0	T-18	FOTA-LA	8.8	3800	181.52	5.5	—	9.0	4.9
	3378	4.9/5.0/5.8	E4OD	FOTA-LA	8.8	3800	181.52	5.5	—	9.3	4.9
	3526	4.9/5.0	M5OD	FOTA-LA	8.8	3800	181.52	5.5	—	8.2	4.9
	3526	5.0	AOD	FOTA-LA	8.8	3800	181.52	5.5	—	8.1	4.9
	3526	5.0/5.8	E4OD	FOTA-LA	8.8	3800	181.52	5.5	—	8.3	4.9
	3526	4.9/5.0	T-18	FOTA-LA	8.8	3800	181.52	5.5	—	8.1	4.9
	3937	4.9/5.0	M5OD	FOTA-LA	8.8	3800	181.52	5.5	4.7	7.9	4.9
	3937	5.0	AOD	FOTA-LA	8.8	3800	181.52	5.5	4.8	7.9	4.9
	3937	5.0/5.8	E4OD	FOTA-LA	8.8	3800	181.52	5.5	4.6	7.9	4.9
	3937	4.9/5.0	T-18	FOTA-LA	8.8	3800	181.52	5.5	4.8	7.9	4.9

92H21722

Courtesy of Ford Motor Co.

Fig. 8: Determining Rear Driveline Angles (F150 4WD)

1992 DRIVE AXLES
Drive Shafts (Cont.)

| MODEL | WHEEL BASE | ENGINE (L) | TRANS-MISSION | REAR SPRING | REAR AXLE | | RIDE HEIGHT (mm) | ENGINE ANGLE | COUPLING SHAFT ANGLE | REAR D/S ANGLE | PINION ANGLE |
					RING GEAR	GVW					
F-150 (4x2) REG. CAB	2967	4.9/5.0	M5OD	E7TA-RA	8.8	3800	185.8	5.5	—	8.4	6.0
	2967	4.9/5.8	E4OD	E7TA-RA	8.8	3800	185.8	5.5	—	8.9	6.0
	2967	5.0	AOD	E7TA-RA	8.8	3800	185.8	5.5	—	8.4	6.0
	2967	4.9/5.0	T-18	E77A-RA	8.8	3800	185.8	5.5	—	8.4	6.0
	3378	4.9/5.0	M5OD	E7TA-RA	8.8	3800	185.8	5.5	—	6.4	6.0
	3378	4.9/5.0	M5OD	E7TA-RA	8.8	3800	185.8	5.5	5.0	7.6	6.0
	3378	4.9	M5OD-HD	E7TA-RA	8.8	3800	185.8	5.5	5.1	7.6	6.0
	3378	4.9/5.0/5.8	E4OD	E7TA-RA	8.8	3800	185.8	5.5	—	6.5	6.0
	3378	4.9/5.0	T-18	E7TA-RA	8.8	3800	185.8	5.5	—	6.4	6.0
	3378	5.0	AOD	E7TA-RA	8.8	3800	185.8	5.5	—	6.4	6.0
	3378	5.0/5.8	C6	E7TA-RA	8.8	3800	185.8	5.5	—	6.5	6.0
	3378	4.9/5.0	M5OD	E7TA-NA	8.8	3800	192.1	5.5	—	6.6	6.1
	3378	4.9/5.0	M5OD	E7A-NA	8.8	3800	192.1	5.5	5.0	7.9	6.1
	3378	4.9	M5OD-HD	E7TA-NA	8.8	3800	192.1	5.5	5.1	7.9	6.1
	3378	4.9/5.0/5.8	E4OD	E7TA-NA	8.8	3800	192.1	5.5	—	6.7	6.1
	3378	4.9/5.0	T-18	E7TA-NA	8.8	3800	192.1	5.5	—	6.6	6.1
	3378	5.0	AOD	E7TA-NA	8.8	3800	192.1	5.5	—	6.6	6.1
	3378	5.0/5.8	C6	E7TA-NA	8.8	3800	192.1	5.5	—	6.7	6.1
F-150 4x2 SUPERCAB	3526	4.9/5.0	M5OD	E7TA-NA	8.8	3800	192.1	5.5	4.6	7.6	6.1
	3526	4.9/5.0/5.8	E4OD	E7TA-NA	8.8	3800	192.1	5.5	4.3	7.7	6.1
	3526	5.0	AOD	E7TA-NA	8.8	3800	192.1	5.5	4.6	7.6	6.1
	3526	4.9/5.0	T-18	E7TA-NA	8.8	3800	192.1	5.5	4.6	7.6	6.1
	3937	4.9/5.0	M5OD	E7TA-NA	8.8	3800	192.1	5.5	3.8	6.7	6.1
	3937	4.9/5.0/5.8	E4OD	E7TA-NA	8.8	3800	192.1	5.5	3.5	6.8	6.1
	3937	5.0	AOD	E7TA-NA	8.8	3800	192.1	5.5	3.8	6.7	6.1
	3937	4.9/5.0	T-18	E7TA-NA	8.8	3800	192.1	5.5	3.8	6.7	6.1

92J21724

Courtesy of Ford Motor Co.

Fig. 9: Determining Rear Driveline Angles (F150 2WD)

1992 DRIVE AXLES
Drive Shafts (Cont.)

MODEL	WHEEL BASE	ENGINE (L)	TRANS-MISSION	REAR SPRING	REAR AXLE RING GEAR	REAR AXLE GVW	RIDE HEIGHT (mm)	ENGINE ANGLE	COUPLING SHAFT ANGLE	REAR D/S ANGLE	PINION ANGLE
F-250 (4x2) REG. CAB	3378	4.9/5.0	M5OD	E4TA-EA	10.25	5300	190.64	5.5	—	7.1	7.2
	3378	4.9/5.0	M5OD	E4TA-EA	10.25	5300	190.64	5.5	5.3	8.6	7.2
	3378	4.9	M5OD-HD①	E4TA-EA	10.25	5300	190.64	5.5	5.4	8.6	7.2
	3378	4.9/5.8	E4OD	E4TA-EA	10.25	5300	190.64	5.5	—	7.3	7.2
	3378	5.0	AOD	E4TA-EA	10.25	5300	190.64	5.5	—	7.1	7.2
	3378	4.9/5.0	T-18	E4TA-EA	10.25	5300	190.64	5.5	—	7.1	7.2
	3378	4.9	C6	E4TA-EA	10.25	5300	190.64	5.5	—	7.2	7.2
	3378	4.9/5.8/7.5	M5OD-HD①	E7TA-FA	10.25	6250	199.07	5.5	5.4	10.4	6.3
	3378	7.3	M5OD-HD②	E7TA-FA	10.25	6250	199.07	5.5	5.4	10.4	6.3
	3378	5.0/7.3/7.5	E4OD	E7TA-FA	10.25	6250	199.07	5.5	—	8.4	6.3
	3378	4.9/5.8	C6	E7TA-FA	10.25	6250	199.07	5.5	—	8.2	6.3
	3378	5.8/7.5	M5OD-HD①	E4TA-SA	10.25	6250	173.35	5.5	5.4	9.7	5.9
	3378	7.3	M5OD-HD②	E4TA-SA	10.25	6250	173.35	5.5	5.4	9.7	5.9
	3937	5.8/7.3/7.5	E4OD	E7TA-FA	10.25	6250	199.07	5.5	4.4	8.4	6.3
	3937	4.9/5.8	C6	E7TA-FA	10.25	6250	199.07	5.5	4.5	8.3	6.3
	3937	5.8/7.5	M5OD-HD①	E7TA-FA	10.25	6250	199.07	5.5	4.6	8.3	6.3
	3937	7.3	M5OD-HD②	E7TA-FA	10.25	6250	199.07	5.5	4.7	8.3	6.3
	3937	5.8/7.5	M5OD-HD①	E4TA-SA	10.25	6250	173.35	5.5	4.6	7.6	5.9
	3937	7.3	M5OD-HD②	E4TA-SA	10.25	6250	173.35	5.5	4.7	7.6	5.9

① - Wide ratio
② - Close ratio

92A21725

Courtesy of Ford Motor Co.

Fig. 10: Determining Rear Driveline Angles (F250 2WD)

MODEL	WHEEL BASE	ENGINE (L)	TRANS-MISSION	REAR SPRING	REAR AXLE RING GEAR	REAR AXLE GVW	RIDE HEIGHT (mm)	ENGINE ANGLE	COUPLING SHAFT ANGLE	REAR D/S ANGLE	PINION ANGLE
F-250 (4x4)	3378	4.9	M5OD-HD	E4TA-EA	10.25	5300	190.7	5.5	—	10.2	7.3
	3378	5.0	M5OD	E4TA-EA	10.25	5300	190.7	5.5	—	10.2	7.3
	3378	5.0	AOD	E4TA-EA	10.25	5300	190.7	5.5	—	10.0	7.3
	3378	5.8	E4OD	E4TA-EA	10.25	5300	190.7	5.5	—	10.5	7.3
	3378	4.9/5.0	T-18	E4TA-EA	10.25	5300	190.7	5.5	—	10.0	7.3
	3937	5.8/7.3/7.5	E4OD	E7TA-FA	10.25	6250	188.55	5.5	7.9	11.6	6.4
	3937	5.8/7.5	M5OD-HD①	E7TA-FA	10.25	6250	188.55	5.5	7.7	11.7	6.4
	3937	7.3	M5OD-HD②	E7TA-FA	10.25	6250	188.55	5.5	7.5	11.7	6.4
	3937	5.8/7.3/7.5	C6	E7TA-FA	10.25	6250	188.55	5.5	7.4	11.5	6.4
	3378	5.8/7.5	M5OD-HD①	E7TA-FA	10.25	6250	188.55	5.5	—	14.0	6.4
	3378	5.0/7.3/7.5	E4OD	E7TA-FA	10.25	6250	188.55	5.5	—	14.4	6.4
	3378	5.8/7.5	C6	E7TA-FA	10.25	6250	188.55	5.5	—	13.4	6.4
	3378	7.3	M5OD-HD②	E7TA-FA	10.25	6250	188.55	5.5	—	13.7	6.4

① - Wide ratio
② - Close ratio

92B21726

Courtesy of Ford Motor Co.

Fig. 11: Determining Rear Driveline Angles (F250 4WD)

1992 DRIVE AXLES
Drive Shafts (Cont.)

MODEL	WHEEL BASE	ENGINE (L)	TRANS-MISSION	REAR SPRING	REAR AXLE		RIDE HEIGHT (mm)	ENGINE ANGLE	COUPLING SHAFT ANGLE	REAR D/S ANGLE	PINION ANGLE
					RING GEAR	GVW					
F-350 4x2 REGULAR CAB	3937	5.8/7.3/7.5	E4OD	E7TA-FA	10.25	6250	199.07	5.5	4.4	8.4	6.3
	3937	4.9/5.8	C6	E7TA-FA	10.25	6250	199.07	5.5	4.5	8.3	6.3
	3937	5.8/7.5	M5OD-HD①	E7TA-FA	10.25	6250	199.07	5.5	4.6	8.3	6.3
	3937	7.3	M5OD-HD②	E7TA-FA	10.25	6250	199.07	5.5	4.7	8.3	6.3
	3937	5.8/7.5	M5OD-HD①	E4TA-SA	10.25	6250	173.35	5.5	4.6	7.6	5.9
	3937	7.3	M5OD-HD②	E4TA-SA	10.25	6250	173.35	5.5	4.7	7.6	5.9
	3378	5.8/7.3/7.5	E4OD	E4TA-SA	10.25	7400	173.35	5.5	—	8.0	5.9
	3378	5.8/7.5	C6	E4TA-SA	10.25	7400	173.35	5.5	—	7.9	5.9
	3378	5.8/7.5	M5OD-HD①	E4TA-SA	10.25	7400	173.35	5.5	5.4	9.8	5.9
	3378	7.3	M5OD-HD②	E4TA-SA	10.25	7400	173.35	5.5	5.4	9.8	5.9
F-350 4x2 CREW CAB	4278	5.8/7.3/7.5	E4OD	E7TA-FA	10.25	6250	199.07	5.5	4.4	6.1	6.3
	4278	5.8/7.3/7.5	C6	E7TA-FA	10.25	6250	199.07	5.5	4.5	6.1	6.3
	4278	5.8/7.3/7.5	M5OD-HD	E7TA-FA	10.25	6250	199.07	5.5	4.6	6.0	6.3
	4278	5.8/7.3/7.5	M5OD-HD	E7TA-FA	10.25	6250	199.07	5.5	4.7	6.0	6.3
	3475	4.9/5.8/7.3/7.5	M5OD-HD①	E7TA-YA	10.25	8250	156.74	5.5	5.2	7.7	4.6
	3475	4.9/5.8	C6	E7TA-YA	10.25	8250	156.74	5.5	5.1	7.7	4.6
	3475	5.8/7.3/7.5	E4OD	E7TA-YA	10.25	8250	156.74	5.5	5.0	7.8	4.6
	3475	7.3	M5OD-HD②	E7TA-YA	10.25	8250	156.74	5.5	5.3	7.7	4.6
	4085	4.9/5.0/7.3/7.5	M5OD-HD①	E7TA-YA	11.25	8250	156.74	5.5	4.4	5.7	4.6
	4085	4.9/5.8	C6	E7TA-YA	11.25	8250	156.74	5.5	4.1	5.8	4.6
	4085	5.8/7.3/7.5	E4OD	E7TA-YA	11.25	8250	156.74	5.5	4.0	5.8	4.6
	4085	7.3	M5OD-HD②	E7TA-YA	11.25	8250	156.74	5.5	4.4	5.7	4.6
F-350 4x2 SUPER CAB	3937	7.3/7.5	E4OD	E7TA-FA	10.25	7400	199.07	5.5	4.4	8.7	6.3
	3937	7.3/7.5	M5OD-HD	E7TA-FA	10.25	7400	199.07	5.5	4.6	8.6	6.3
	3937	7.3/7.5	M5OD-HD	E7TA-FA	10.25	7400	199.07	5.5	4.7	8.6	6.3
	3937	7.3/7.5	C6	E7TA-FA	10.25	7400	199.07	5.5	4.5	8.7	6.3

① – Wide ratio
② – Close ratio

92C21727

Courtesy of Ford Motor Co.

Fig. 12: Determining Rear Driveline Angles (F350 2WD)

MODEL	WHEEL BASE	ENGINE (L)	TRANS-MISSION	REAR SPRING	REAR AXLE		RIDE HEIGHT (mm)	ENGINE ANGLE	COUPLING SHAFT ANGLE	REAR D/S ANGLE	PINION ANGLE
					RING GEAR	GVW					
F-350 (4x4)	3378	5.8/7.3/7.5	E4OD	E4TA-SA	10.25	6250	183.92	5.5	—	11.2	5.9
	3378	5.8/7.5	C6	E4TA-SA	10.25	6250	183.92	5.5	—	10.5	5.9
	3378	5.8/7.5	M5OD-HD①	E4TA-SA	10.25	6250	183.92	5.5	—	10.9	5.9
	3378	7.3	M5OD-HD②	E47A-SA	10.25	6250	183.92	5.5	—	10.7	5.9

① – Wide ratio
② – Close ratio

92D21728

Courtesy of Ford Motor Co.

Fig. 13: Determining Rear Driveline Angles (F350 4WD)

MODEL	WHEEL BASE	ENGINE (L)	TRANS-MISSION	REAR SPRING	REAR AXLE		RIDE HEIGHT (mm)	ENGINE ANGLE	COUPLING SHAFT ANGLE	REAR D/S ANGLE	PINION ANGLE
					RING GEAR	GVW					
F-SUPER DUTY	3475	7.3/7.5	ZF	E7TA-YA	11.25	11000	156.74	5.5	7.0	5.9	4.6
	3475	7.3/7.5	E4OD	E7TA-YA	11.25	11000	156.74	5.5	7.5	5.8	4.6
	4085	7.3/7.5	ZF	E7TA-YA	11.25	11000	156.74	5.5	5.4	3.8	4.6
	4085	7.3/7.5	E4OD	E7TA-YA	11.25	11000	156.74	5.5	5.4	3.8	4.6

92J22847

Courtesy of Ford Motor Co.

Fig. 14: Determining Rear Driveline Angles (F350 Super Duty)

MODEL	WHEELBASE		ENGINE	REAR AXLE	TRANS-MISSION	SPRING RATING (LBS.)	DRIVE SHAFT ANGLE	RIDE HEIGHT	
	mm	INCH						INCHES	mm
E-150	3505	138	4.9L	All	AOD	1250	4 1/2°	5.08	129
			5.0L	Ford	C6	1685	4 3/4°	6.72	171
			5.8L	8.8	E40D				
E-250	3505	138	4.9L	5400	C6	1830	6°	7.52	191
			5.8L	Dana	E40D	2353	5 1/4°	7.20	183
E-350	3505	138	All	6340 Dana	C6 E40D	2452	5 3/4°	9.54	242
						2777	6°	8.12	206
						3461	6°	7.50	190
E-350	3505	138	All	7800 Dana	C6 E40D	3461	6°	TBD	TBD
						3307	6 1/4°	TBD	TBD
E-350	4013	158	All	6340 Dana	C6/E40D	3461	5 1/4°	7.50	190
E-350	4013	158	All	7800 Dana	C6 E40D	3461	5 1/2°	TBD	TBD
E-350	4470	176	All	7800 Dana	C6/E40D	3461	4°	7.50	190

92A22848

Courtesy of Ford Motor Co.

Fig. 15: Determining Rear Driveline Angles (Van)

MODEL	WHEEL BASE	ENGINE	TRANS-MISSION	FRONT AXLE		ENGINE ANGLE	FRONT D/S ANGLE	PINION ANGLE
				TYPE	GVW			
Bronco and F150 (4x4)	All	All	C6	Twin I-Beam W/Coil Spring	3800#	5.5	0.03	4.39
			T-18			5.5	0.01	4.39
			ZF-HD			5.5	−0.04	4.39
			AOD			5.5	−0.14	4.39
			ZF-LD/R2			5.5	−0.46	4.39
			E4OD			5.5	−0.09	4.39
F-250 (4x4)	All	All	C6	Twin I-Beam w/Leaf Spring	4600#	5.5	2.79	6.73
			T-18			5.5	2.77	6.73
			ZF-HD			5.5	2.69	6.73
			AOD			5.5	2.54	6.73
			ZF-LD/R2			5.5	2.06	6.73
			E4OD			5.6	2.45	6.73
F-350 (4x4)	All	All	All	Mono-Beam	5000#	5.5	2.50	4.50

92B22849

Courtesy of Ford Motor Co.

Fig. 16: Determining Front Driveline Angles (4WD Pickup)

| MODEL | WHEELBASE | | ENGINE | AXLE RATIO | TRANS-MISSION | ANGLE |
	mm	INCHES				
E-350	4013	158	4.9L	4.10	C6	3-1/2°
			5.8L	3.54/4.10		
			7.3L	3.54/4.10	E40D	3-1/4°
			7.5L	3.07/3.54/4.10		
E-350	4470	176	7.3L	3.54/4.10	C6	3-1/2°
			7.5L		E40D	3-1/4°

92F22850   Courtesy of Ford Motor Co.

Fig. 17: Determining Coupling Shaft Angles (E350)

| MODEL | WHEELBASE | | SPRING CAPACITY | | SPRING PART NO. | CURB LOAD EMPTY | |
	mm	INCHES	LBS.	kg		RATIO	ANGLE
E-150	3150	124	1250	566	E1TA-ACA	3.55	5°
			1450	658	E1TA-ADA	3.55	5°
			1685	764	D9TA-AVA	3.55	5°
			1750	794	E1TA-AGA	3.55	5-1/4°
E-150	3505	138	1250	566	E1TA-AEA	3.55	6-1/2°
			1450	658	E1TA-AFA	3.55	6-1/2°
			1685	764	D9TA-AYA	3.55	7°
			1750	794	E1TA-AHA	3.55	6-1/2°
E-250	3505	138	1825	828	D9TA-HA	3.54/3.73	5°
			2100	952	D9TA-JA	3.54/3.73	5°
			2365	1072	E4UA-RA	3.07/3.54/4.10	4°
			2450	111	D9TA-KA	3.54/3.73	5°
			2700	1224	D9TA-MA	3.07/3.54/4.10	5°
E-350	3505	138	2850	1292	E0TA-BVA	3.07/3.54/4.10	4-1/2
			2950	1338	D9TA-LA	3.07/3.54/4.10	4-3/4°
			3300	1496	E1TA-ALA	3.07/3.54/4.10	5°
E-350	4013	158	3300	1496	E1TA-ALA	3.07/3.54/4.10	5°
E-350	4470	176	3300	1496	E1TA-ALA	3.54/4.10	5°

92G22851   Courtesy of Ford Motor Co.

Fig. 18: Determining Pinion Angles (Van)

DRIVE SHAFT ANGLE

1) Measure ride height. See RIDE HEIGHT. Vehicle must be at curb weight (unloaded) condition. Specified pinion angles correspond to measured ride height. See *Figs. 5-18*. Place protractor at any location along bottom of drive shaft. *See Fig. 19.*

2) Read and record angle. Subtract frame angle to obtain drive shaft angle. On Bronco, Pickup, and Van, adjust drive shaft angle by installing tapered shims between rear springs and rear spring seats. Information is not available from manufacturer for adjustment procedure on Aerostar, Explorer and Ranger.

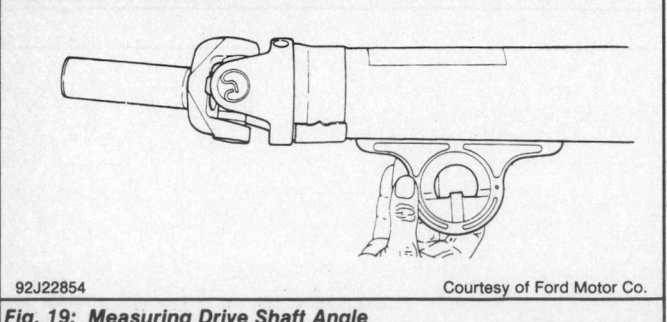

92J22854   Courtesy of Ford Motor Co.

Fig. 19: Measuring Drive Shaft Angle

PINION ANGLE

Aerostar – 1) Position protractor in vertical position, flush against 2 differential cover retaining bolts. Rotate protractor bubble indicator so that 90-degree mark aligns with indexing mark. Read protractor and calculate pinion angle. For example, if protractor indicates 85 degrees, pinion angle is 5 degrees.

2) If necessary, adjust pinion angle by installing new upper control arm bushing. Install bushing so that notch is at 12 o'clock, 9 o'clock or 3 o'clock position as necessary. *See Fig. 20.*

Except Aerostar – 1) Place protractor in vertical position, flush against 2 differential cover retaining bolts. Rotate protractor bubble indicator so that 90-degree mark aligns with indexing mark.

2) Read protractor and calculate pinion angle. For example, if protractor indicates 85 degrees, pinion angle is 5 degrees. Adjust pinion angle by installing tapered shims between rear springs and spring seats.

OVERHAUL

NOTE: Universal joints should not be disassembled unless external leakage or damage has occurred.

CAUTION: DO NOT clamp drive shaft in vise or similar holding fixture; damage may occur.

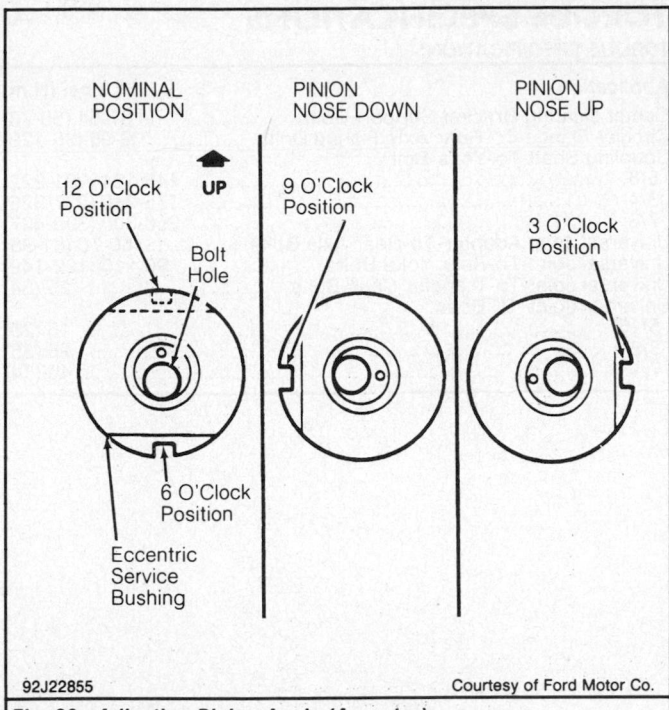

Fig. 20: Adjusting Pinion Angle (Aerostar)

SINGLE CARDAN UNIVERSAL JOINTS

Removal & Disassembly – 1) Mark drive shaft and differential companion flange or yoke for reassembly reference. Remove drive shaft from vehicle. Scribe alignment marks on yoke and shaft for reassembly reference. If joints are rusted or corroded, apply penetrating oil before pressing out bearing races or trunnion pin. Disconnect yoke or flange bolts.

NOTE: DO NOT use pry bar to hold drive shaft while loosening bolts; damage to bearing seals may result.

2) Remove retaining strap (if equipped). Remove bushing retainers from yoke. Press out rollers and bearings. Remove last roller and bushing assembly by pressing on end of cross.
3) Remove cross from yoke. DO NOT remove seal retainers from cross. Cross and retainers are serviced as an assembly.
Reassembly & Installation – 1) Coat roller and bearing assemblies with lubricant, and fill reservoirs in ends of cross. Install cross into drive shaft yoke. Install roller and bushing assemblies into position.
2) Press both bushing assemblies into yoke until retainers can be installed, keeping cross aligned in center of bushings. Install retainers. Repeat procedure for remaining bushings. Install strap (if equipped). Install drive shaft into vehicle, aligning scribe marks.

DOUBLE CARDAN UNIVERSAL JOINTS

NOTE: When handling drive shaft after removal, support shafts on both sides when moved horizontally. DO NOT allow shaft to hang freely or bend at sharp angle.

Removal & Disassembly – 1) Mark drive shaft and differential companion flange or yoke for reassembly reference. Remove drive shaft from vehicle. If joints are rusted or corroded, apply penetrating oil before pressing out bearing races or cross.

NOTE: To obtain correct clearance, cross must be installed onto bosses in original positions.

2) Place drive shaft assembly onto workbench. Mark position of cross, center yoke and centering socket yoke in relation to drive shaft tube. *See Fig. 21.* Cross MUST be installed with bosses in original position to provide proper clearance

3) Remove snap rings. Using "U" Joint Remover and Installer (T745P-4635-C), press cross until bearing protrudes 3/8" (10 mm). Clamp protruding part of bearing in vise. Tap center yoke with hammer until bearing is free of yoke.
4) Using this method, remove all bearings from cross. Remove cross from center yoke. Remove centering socket yoke and seal from centering ball stud. Remove snap rings from center yoke and drive shaft yokes.

NOTE: Centering ball is located inside center yoke socket. If centering ball replacement is required, replace center yoke socket.

5) Install "U" Joint Remover and Installer. Press bearing outward until inside of center yoke almost contacts slinger ring. Clamp exposed end of bearing in vise. Tap center yoke with soft mallet until bearing is free.
6) Press cross to remove remaining bearing. Remove center yoke from cross. Clean all serviceable parts in solvent.

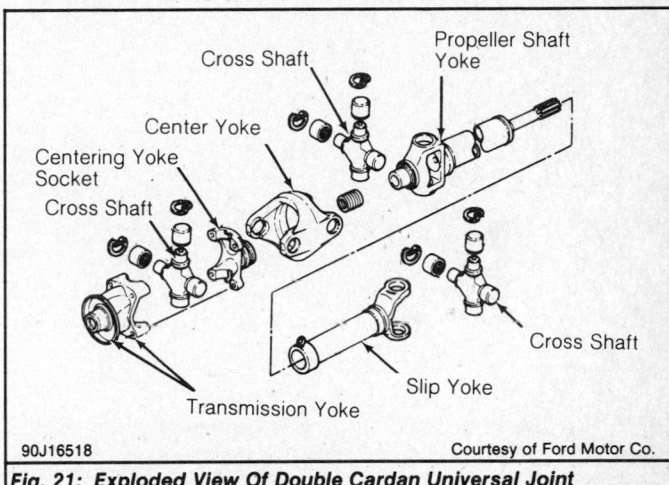

Fig. 21: Exploded View Of Double Cardan Universal Joint

Reassembly – 1) Install cross into drive shaft yoke. Ensure cross bosses (or lubrication plugs in kits) are installed in original position. Using "U" Joint Remover and Installer, press in bearings. Install snap rings. Fill center socket and coat centering ball with grease.
2) Position center yoke over cross. Press in bearings. Install snap rings. Install new seal onto centering ball stud. Install centering socket over stud. Install front cross into yoke. Ensure cross bosses (or lubrication plugs) are installed in original position.
3) Position cross loosely onto center stop. Press first set of bearings into center yoke, then install second set. Install snap rings. Apply pressure to center yoke socket and install remaining bearing cup. If replacement kit is used, remove plugs, lubricate "U" joints, and reinstall plugs.

NOTE: Install drive shaft assembly so yoke ears at each end of shaft are on same plane.

Installation (1-Piece Shaft – Front) – 1) Clean yoke. Inspect machined surface for scratches, nicks, or burrs. Check for arrows on slip joint and drive shaft to aid in alignment.
2) Connect single end of drive shaft to front axle. Install "U" bolts and tighten nuts. Connect double cardan joint end to transfer case. Install "U" bolts.
Installation (1-Piece Shaft – Rear) – 1) Clean yoke. Inspect machined surface for scratches, nicks, or burrs. Check for arrows on slip joint and drive shaft to aid in alignment. Lubricate yoke splines and install into transmission output shaft.
2) Connect drive shaft to rear companion flange. On all models except E350, install "U" bolts and tighten to **15 ft. lbs. (20 N.m)**. On E350, connect drive shaft flange to rear axle flange, and tighten bolts to **70-95 ft. lbs. (95-129 N.m)**.
Installation (2-Piece & 3-Piece Shafts) – 1) Rotate transmission until yoke ears are on a horizontal plane. Clean yoke. Inspect machined surface for scratches, nicks, or burrs. Lubricate splines.

2) Provide support for drive shaft during installation to prevent damage to universal joints. Align marks noted during removal. Connect front joint coupling shaft to transmission yoke. Tighten bolts to specification. See TORQUE SPECIFICATIONS table.

3) Ensure center bearing does not twist in support plate. Connect front and rear coupling shaft (if equipped). Attach universal joint to rear axle flange. Tighten nuts to specification. See TORQUE SPECIFICATIONS table.

TORQUE SPECIFICATIONS
TORQUE SPECIFICATIONS

Application	Ft. Lbs. (N.m)
Center Bearing Bracket Support Bolts	37-54 (50-73)
Circular Flange-To-Rear Axle Flange Bolts	70-95 (95-129)
Coupling Shaft-To-Yoke Bolt	
5/8"	148-164 (201-222)
3/4"	175-240 (237-325)
7/8"	250-300 (339-407)
Universal Joint Adapter-To-Rear Axle Bolts	60-70 (81-95)
Universal Joint-To-Rear Yoke Bolts	90-110 (122-149)
Universal Joint-To-Transfer Case Bolts	25 (34)
Universal Joint "U" Bolts	
5/16"	15 (20)
3/8"	26 (35)
7/16"	40 (54)

**Aerostar, Bronco, Explorer,
Pickup, Ranger, Van**

DESCRIPTION & OPERATION

The Rear Anti-Lock Brake System (RABS) is designed to prevent rear brake lock-up by controlling hydraulic fluid pressure to the rear wheel cylinders. The system consists of 2 warning lights (Red BRAKE and Yellow REAR ANTI-LOCK), a computer module, an electro-hydraulic (RABS) valve, speed sensor and exciter ring.

The control module monitors rear wheel speed continuously. If impending lock-up occurs, the control module energizes the RABS valve. The RABS valve closes an internal isolation valve to prevent rear brake pressure from increasing.

If deceleration is still too great, control module activates dump solenoid. Dump solenoid bleeds rear wheel cylinder fluid into RABS valve accumulator. This allows rear wheels to spin back up to vehicle speed. Dump and isolation valves will continue to be pulsed in a way that allows rear wheels to rotate, while maintaining maximum deceleration during braking.

NOTE: For more information on brake system, see DISC & DRUM article in BRAKES.

CAUTION: See ANTI-LOCK BRAKE SAFETY PRECAUTIONS article in GENERAL INFORMATION.

BLEEDING BRAKE SYSTEM

Hydraulic system bleeding is necessary whenever air enters system. If master cylinder lines have been disconnected, or master cylinder has run dry, bleed master cylinder and brakes at all 4 wheels. Bleed brakes with pressure bleeding equipment or by pumping brake pedal. Always bleed brake lines in sequence. See BLEEDING SEQUENCE.

MANUAL BLEEDING

CAUTION: DO NOT allow reservoir to run dry during bleeding operation. If brake fluid is spilled onto vehicle paint, rinse off immediately with water.

NOTE: Manufacturer does not specify manual bleeding procedure for Bronco, Pickup and Van.

Aerostar, Explorer & Ranger – **1)** Clean master cylinder cap and surrounding area. Remove cap. On Explorer and Ranger, bleed primary and secondary systems separately. Loosen primary or secondary master cylinder hydraulic line fitting.
2) On Aerostar, loosen either master cylinder hydraulic line. On all vehicles, wrap a cloth around brake lines to absorb escaping brake fluid. Press brake pedal down slowly, forcing air out. With pedal fully down, tighten fitting. Release pedal.
3) Loosen fitting. Repeat procedure until air is completely purged from master cylinder. When all air has been purged, tighten fitting while pedal is down. Release pedal and press again. Pedal should be firm. If pedal is not firm, repeat bleeding procedure.
4) On Aerostar, attach a rubber drain hose to bleeder fitting on front of master cylinder. Submerge other end of hose in small container half filled with clean brake fluid. Open bleeder fitting about 3/4 turn. Slowly press brake pedal completely down.
5) Close bleeder fitting. Allow pedal to return to fully released position. Repeat procedure until all air is purged from master cylinder. On all models, repeat procedure at bleeder fitting on RABS valve and at each wheel cylinder. See BLEEDING SEQUENCE. When bleeding is complete, refill master cylinder.

PRESSURE BLEEDING

1) Clean master cylinder cap and surrounding area. Remove cap. With bleeder tank at least half full of fluid and charged to 10-30 psi (.7-2.0

kg/cm²), connect tank to master cylinder. Follow equipment manufacturer's instructions.

CAUTION: DO NOT charge pressure bleeder to greater than 50 psi (3.5 kg/cm²).

2) Open pressure bleeder valve. On Aerostar, attach one end of rubber drain tube to master cylinder bleeder fitting. Open bleed fitting. On all vehicles, bleed master cylinder primary and secondary hydraulic lines one at a time. Put shop towels in place to catch brake fluid.
3) Open line. On all models, allow brake fluid to flow out until all air is purged. Close bleeder fitting and hydraulic line. Close pressure bleeder valve. Attach rubber drain hose to first wheel cylinder bleeder valve to be serviced. See BLEEDING SEQUENCE.
4) Submerge other end of hose in clean glass jar partially filled with clean brake fluid. Open pressure bleeder valve. Open bleeder fitting. Close bleeder fitting when fluid flows free of bubbles. Repeat procedure on remaining wheel cylinders in sequence. See BLEEDING SEQUENCE.
5) When bleeding operation is complete, close pressure bleeder valve. Remove pressure bleeder. Check brake pedal operation. Ensure master cylinder is full of fluid.

BLEEDING SEQUENCE

Before bleeding system, exhaust all vacuum from power unit by pressing brake pedal several times. Bleed master cylinder first, followed in sequence by RABS valve, rear wheel cylinders and front calipers. See BLEEDING SEQUENCE table.

BLEEDING SEQUENCE

Application	Sequence
All Models	Master Cylinder, RABS Valve
	Wheel Cylinders: RR, LR, RF, LF

ADJUSTMENTS

MASTER CYLINDER PUSH ROD

Aerostar – DO NOT adjust push rod.
All Other Vehicles – Remove master cylinder. See appropriate DISC & DRUM article. Fabricate a gauge with dimensions shown. *See Fig. 1.* Ensure vacuum hose remains connected to booster. Start engine. Place gauge against booster. Turn push rod adjuster screw until end of screw just touches gauge.

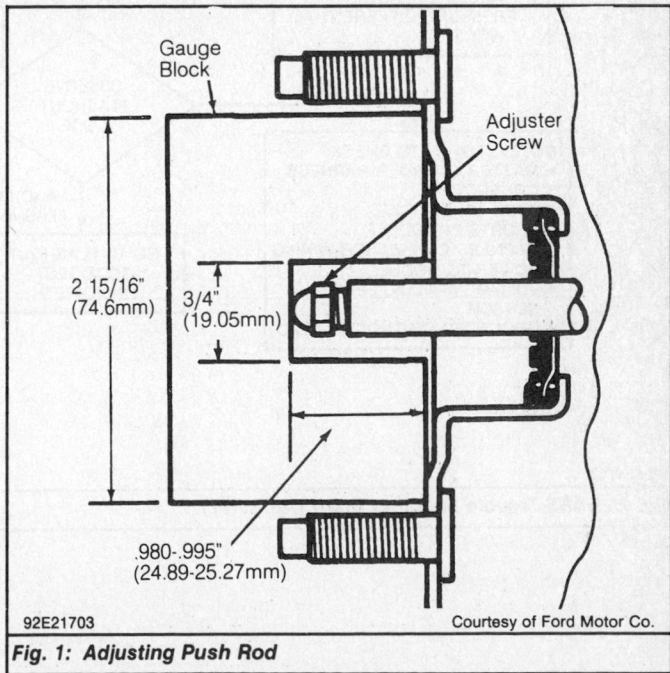

Gauge Block

Adjuster Screw

2 15/16" (74.6mm)

3/4" (19.05mm)

.980-.995" (24.89-25.27mm)

92E21703   Courtesy of Ford Motor Co.

Fig. 1: Adjusting Push Rod

1992 BRAKES
Anti-Lock – RABS (Cont.)

TROUBLE SHOOTING

Refer to appropriate trouble shooting chart. *See Fig. 2 or 3.*

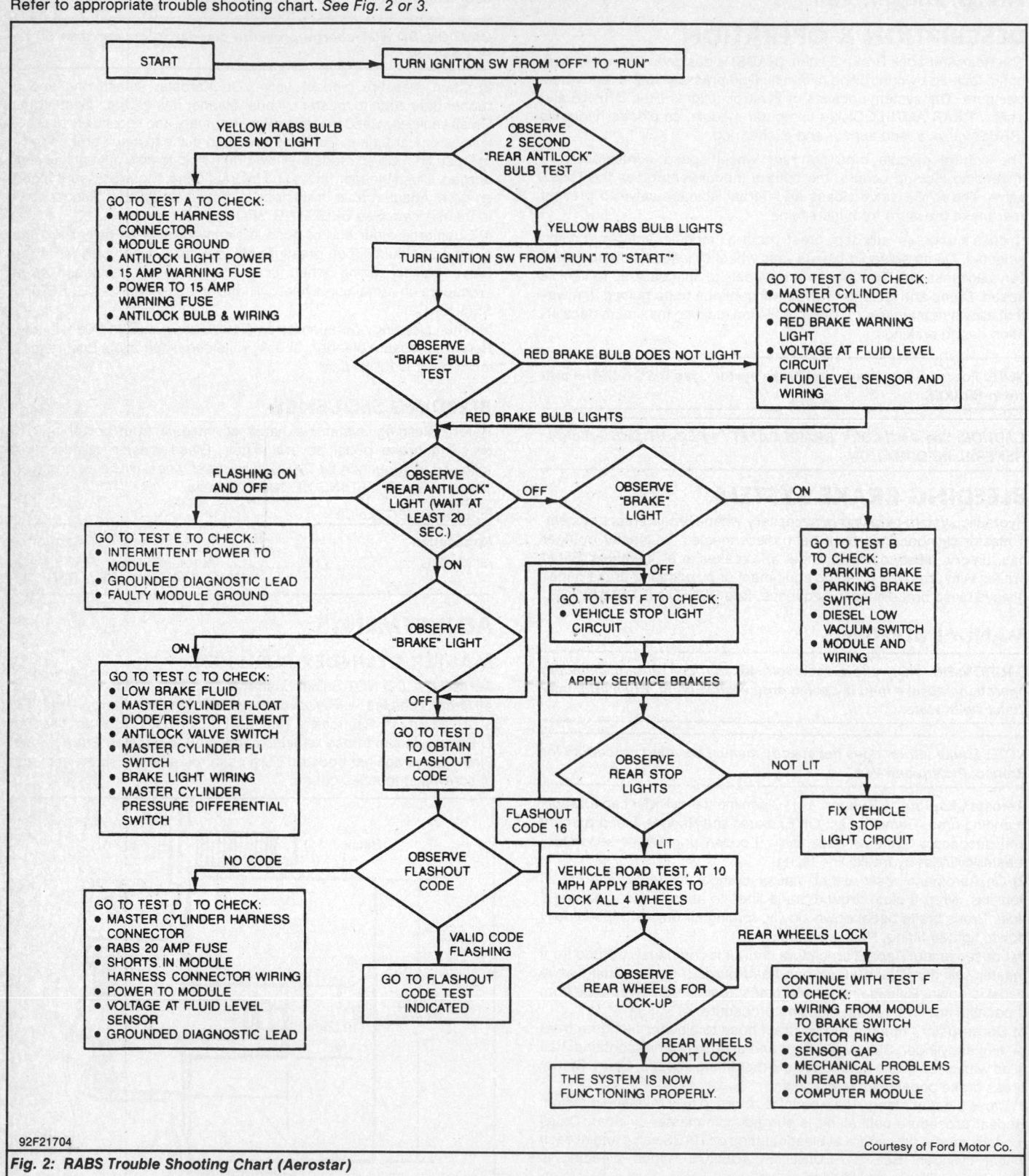

92F21704

Courtesy of Ford Motor Co.

Fig. 2: RABS Trouble Shooting Chart (Aerostar)

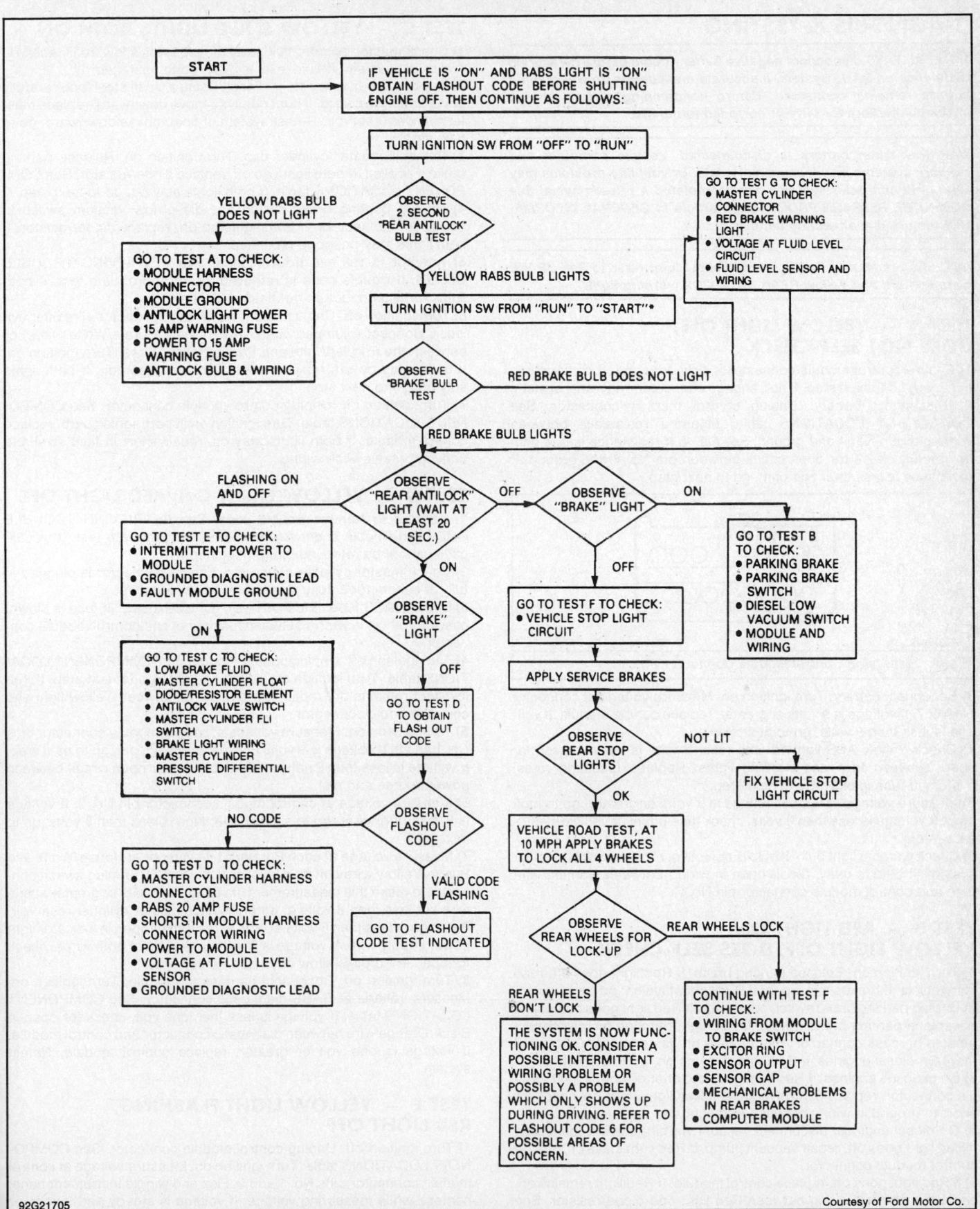

Courtesy of Ford Motor Co.

Fig. 3: RABS Trouble Shooting Chart (Bronco, Explorer, Pickup, Ranger & Van)

DIAGNOSIS & TESTING

NOTE: ALWAYS disconnect negative battery cable before measuring resistance on RABS system. Inaccurate measurements will result if battery remains connected. Before condemning circuit, always check connectors for dirty or corroded terminals.

WARNING: When battery is disconnected, vehicle computer and memory systems may lose memory data. Driveability problems may exist until computer systems have completed a relearn cycle. See COMPUTER RELEARN PROCEDURES article in GENERAL INFORMATION before disconnecting battery.

NOTE: References to Red light and Yellow light refer to Red BRAKE warning light and Yellow REAR ANTI-LOCK warning light.

TEST A – YELLOW LIGHT OFF, DOES NOT SELF-CHECK

1) Ensure control module connector is fully engaged. If connector is engaged, go to next step. If not, engage connector and retest system.
2) Disconnect battery. Unplug control module connector. See COMPONENT LOCATIONS table. Measure resistance between connector pin No. 4 and ground. *See Fig. 4.* If resistance is one ohm or greater, check for open circuit between pin No. 4 and ground. If resistance is less than one ohm, go to next step.

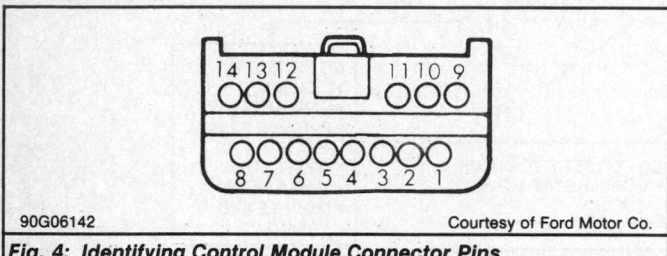

90G06142   Courtesy of Ford Motor Co.

Fig. 4: Identifying Control Module Connector Pins

3) Reconnect battery. Turn ignition on. Measure voltage at connector pin No. 7. If voltage is 9 volts or greater, replace control module. If voltage is less than 9 volts, go to next step.
4) Check Yellow ABS light 15-amp fuse. If fuse is blown, check for short between fuse and warning lights. Replace fuse and retest system. If fuse is okay, go to next step.
5) Measure voltage at fuse. If voltage is 9 volts or greater, go to next step. If voltage is less than 9 volts, check fuse panel or vehicle electrical system.
6) Check warning light bulb. If bulb is defective, replace bulb and retest system. If bulb is okay, repair open in wiring between warning light fuse and control module connector pin No. 7.

TEST B – RED LIGHT ON, YELLOW LIGHT OFF, DOES SELF-CHECK

1) Turn ignition on. Release parking brake. If Red light goes off, road test vehicle. If brakes lock up, or if Red light stays on, go to next step.
2) Unplug parking brake switch connector. If Red light goes out, adjust or replace parking brake switch. If Red light remains on, disconnect module harness connector from module on gas engines. Go to next step. On diesel engines, if Red light remains on, go to step 4).
3) On gasoline engines, if Red light goes out after disconnecting module connector, replace control module. If Red light stays on, check for short to ground in wiring between Red light and diode/resistor.
4) On diesel engines, disconnect vacuum warning switch connector. If Red light goes off, repair vacuum pump. If Red light stays on, unplug control module connector.
5) If Red light goes off, replace control module. If Red light remains on, check for shorted wiring between Red light and diode/resistor. See COMPONENT LOCATIONS table.

TEST C – YELLOW & RED LIGHTS BOTH ON

1) Check master cylinder fluid level. If fluid level is low, refill reservoir and retest system. If fluid level is okay, go to next step.
2) Remove cap from master cylinder. Using a clean steel tool, carefully press float downward. If float does not move downward, replace master cylinder reservoir. Retest system. If float moves downward, go to next step.
3) Reinstall master cylinder cap. Turn ignition on. Release parking brake if applied. If both lights go off, replace diode/resistor. See COMPONENT LOCATIONS table. If both lights stay on, go to next step.
4) Unplug parking brake switch and diesel low vacuum switch (if equipped) connectors. If both lights go off, replace diode/resistor. If both lights stay on, go to next step.
5) Attempt to retrieve trouble code. See RETRIEVING TROUBLE CODES. If trouble code is retrieved, go to appropriate test. If both lights remain on but do not flash, go to next step.
6) Turn ignition off. Unplug fluid level sensor connector at master cylinder. Connect a jumper wire between the 2 Purple/White wires, or between the Purple/White and Purple/Yellow wires. Turn ignition on. If both lights go off, replace master cylinder reservoir. If both lights stay on, go to next step.
7) Turn ignition off. Unplug control module connector. See COMPONENT LOCATIONS table. Turn ignition on. If both lights go off, replace control module. If both lights stay on, repair short in fluid level and parking brake switch wiring.

TEST D – YELLOW LIGHT ON, RED LIGHT OFF

1) Attempt to retrieve trouble code. See RETRIEVING TROUBLE CODES. If trouble code is retrieved, see appropriate test. If trouble code cannot be retrieved, go to next step.
2) Check master cylinder connector. Ensure connector is plugged in fully. If connector is fully plugged in, go to next step.
3) Check RABS fuse. If fuse is okay, go to next step. If fuse is blown, check for short in wiring between fuse panel and control module connector.
4) Turn ignition off. Unplug control module. See COMPONENT LOCATIONS table. Turn ignition on. If light goes off, go to next step. If Yellow light remains on, repair short in wiring between Yellow light and control module connector.
5) Turn ignition on. Measure voltage at control module connector pins No. 1 and 9. If voltage is 9 volts or greater at each pin, go to next step. If voltage is less than 9 volts at either pin, repair open circuit between power source and pin.
6) Measure voltage at control module connector pin No. 2. If voltage is 8 volts or greater, go to step 8). If voltage is less than 8 volts, go to next step.
7) Measure voltage at each Purple/White wire, or at Purple/White and Purple/Yellow wires, at fluid level switch. DO NOT unplug switch connector to make this measurement. If voltage is 8 volts or greater at one wire but less than 8 volts at other, replace master cylinder reservoir. If voltage is less than 8 volts at both wires, repair open in indicator light power supply wire. If voltage is 8 volts or greater at both wires, check for open in Purple/Yellow or Purple/White wires.
8) Turn ignition off. Reconnect harness to module. Turn ignition on. Measure voltage at RABS diagnostic connector. See COMPONENT LOCATIONS table. If voltage is less than one volt, check for open in Black/Orange wire between diagnostic connector and control module. If voltage is one volt or greater, replace control module. Retest system.

TEST E – YELLOW LIGHT FLASHING, RED LIGHT OFF

1) Turn ignition off. Unplug control module connector. See COMPONENT LOCATIONS table. Turn ignition on. Measure voltage at control module connector pins No. 1 and 9. Flex and wiggle instrument panel harness while measuring voltage. If voltage is steady and 9 volts or greater, go to next step. If voltage varies or is less than 9 volts, check for open in wiring between fuse panel and connector pins No. 1 and 9.

2) Turn ignition off. Disconnect battery. Measure resistance between control module connector pin No. 12 and ground. Flex and wiggle module harness while measuring resistance. If resistance is 100,000 ohms or greater and steady, go to next step. If resistance is less than 100,000 ohms or varies, repair Black/Orange wire between diagnostic connector and module connector.

3) Measure resistance between module connector pin No. 4 and ground. Flex and wiggle module harness while measuring resistance. If resistance is one ohm or greater, repair open in Black/White wire between module connector pin No. 4 and body ground. If resistance is less than one ohm and is steady, replace control module.

TEST F – REAR WHEELS LOCK UP, BOTH LIGHTS FUNCTION NORMALLY

1) Ensure stoplights are working properly. If stoplights are working properly, go to next step. If stoplights are not working properly, repair stoplights and retest.

2) Drive vehicle at approximately 10 MPH in an area free of traffic. Apply brakes to attempt lock-up of all wheels. Have assistant observe left rear wheel operation. If rear wheels lock up, go to next step. If rear wheels do not lock up, system is operating properly at this time. Intermittent wiring problem may be occurring during normal driving conditions. Go to CODE 6 for testing.

3) Turn ignition off. Unplug control module connector. See COMPONENT LOCATIONS table. Measure voltage at module connector pin No. 11 while pressing brake pedal. If voltage is 9 volts or greater, go to next step. If voltage is less than 9 volts, repair open in Red/Light Green wire on Aerostar, or Light Green wire on all others, between stoplight switch and module connector pin No. 11.

4) Turn ignition off. Remove speed sensor. See COMPONENT LOCATIONS table. Check for presence of exciter ring and condition of teeth. If exciter ring is okay, reinstall speed sensor and go to next step. If damage to any component exists, replace damaged component. Retest system.

WARNING: Use care when working around rotating wheels.

---

5) Raise and support rear wheels clear of floor. Block front wheels. On 4WD models, set transfer case mode to 2WD mode. Remove cap from speed sensor test connector. See COMPONENT LOCATIONS table. Start engine. With wheels rotating at 5 MPH, measure voltage between test connector pins. If voltage is 650 mV or greater, reinstall sensor test connector cap and go to step **7)**. If voltage is less than 650 mV, replace speed sensor and retest system. If voltage is still low after replacing speed sensor, go to next step.

6) Turn engine off. Remove speed sensor. Measure distance between sensor pole piece and mounting flange. Distance should be **1.070-1.080"** (27.18-27.43 mm). Measure distance between top of exciter ring teeth and sensor mounting face of carrier. Difference between measurements is sensor gap. Gap should be **.050"** (1.27 mm). If gap is less than specification, go to next step. If gap is greater than specification, check for defective sensor or carrier housing.

7) Check rear brakes for mechanical problems such as grabbing, locking and pulling. Repair brakes as necessary. If rear brakes are okay, replace control module. Retest system.

TEST G – YELLOW LIGHT SELF-CHECKS, RED LIGHT DOES NOT SELF-CHECK

1) Check connector on brake fluid level switch, at master cylinder. If connector is plugged in fully, go to next step. If connector is not fully engaged, fully engage connector and retest.

2) Apply parking brake. Observe Red warning light. If Red warning light does not come on, check for defective bulb or open in light circuit. If light comes on, go to step **6)** of TEST D – YELLOW LIGHT ON, RED LIGHT OFF.

RETRIEVING TROUBLE CODES

Rear Anti-Lock Brake System (RABS) has self-test capability. There are 2 warning lights, located on instrument panel, to inform driver of malfunction. Red BRAKE warning light indicates low fluid level, parking brake on or low vacuum (diesel models). Yellow REAR ANTI-LOCK warning light comes on when control module detects a malfunction and/or anti-lock brake system is inoperative. Both lights should come on for approximately 2 seconds when ignition is turned on or when cranking engine. *See Fig. 2 or 3.*

When Yellow REAR ANTI-LOCK warning light comes on during normal operation, a trouble code can be retrieved from control module. Code will be lost if ignition is turned off before code is retrieved. In some cases, code may reappear when vehicle is restarted. In other cases, vehicle may have to be driven to reproduce problem.

WARNING: Block front and rear wheels to prevent vehicle from moving while retrieving trouble codes.

NOTE: If multiple system faults exist, only first fault code detected can be retrieved. First fault must be repaired before next code, if any, can be retrieved.

If Red BRAKE warning light is on because of low brake fluid level, together with Yellow REAR ANTI-LOCK warning light, Yellow warning light will not flash trouble code, but will glow steadily. System faults concerning brake fluid level switch and power loss to control module will cause anti-lock brake system to deactivate. Yellow warning light will glow, but control module will not generate a trouble code.

Before retrieving trouble code, ensure vehicle is on a level area. Transmission should be in Park or Neutral. For future reference, note if Red BRAKE warning light is on. Apply parking brake. Keep ignition on so code will not be lost. Locate RABS diagnostic connector. See COMPONENT LOCATIONS table.

Connect jumper wire to diagnostic connector terminal (Black/Orange wire). Momentarily ground other end of jumper wire. When ground circuit is completed, then broken, Yellow REAR ANTI-LOCK warning light will flash trouble code. Code will repeat until ignition is turned off. Code consists of a number of short flashes and one long flash. Count each flash, short and long, to determine code number. For example: short, short, long is Code 3. First code displayed may be erroneous and should be ignored. Perform appropriate code test after retrieving code.

NO CODES

Some system faults light REAR ANTI-LOCK warning light but do not set a trouble code. See RETRIEVING TROUBLE CODES. If trouble code should be set but cannot be retrieved, refer to RABS trouble shooting chart. *See Fig. 2 or 3.* Ensure a good momentary ground is made at diagnostic connector.

CODE 1

Code 1 is not a valid code. Perform RETRIEVING TROUBLE CODES again. If Code 1 appears again, go to TEST E – YELLOW LIGHT FLASHING, RED LIGHT OFF under DIAGNOSIS & TESTING.

CODE 2 (OPEN ISOLATION CIRCUIT)

1) Turn ignition off. Disconnect negative battery cable. Unplug control module harness connector. See COMPONENT LOCATIONS table. Measure resistance between harness connector pin No. 13 and ground. *See Fig. 4.* If resistance is greater than 6 ohms, go to next step. If resistance is 6 ohms or less, replace control module and retest system.

2) Disconnect negative battery cable. Unplug RABS valve connector. See COMPONENT LOCATIONS table. On Bronco, Pickup and Van, go to next step. On all other vehicles, go to step **4)**.

3) Measure resistance between harness connector ground pin and ground. *See Fig. 5.* If resistance is one ohm or greater, repair open in ground circuit. If resistance is less than one ohm, go to next step.

4) Measure resistance between isolation solenoid pin and ground pin on valve. If resistance is 6 ohms or less, repair open between isolation solenoid valve and control module. If resistance is greater than 6 ohms, replace valve.

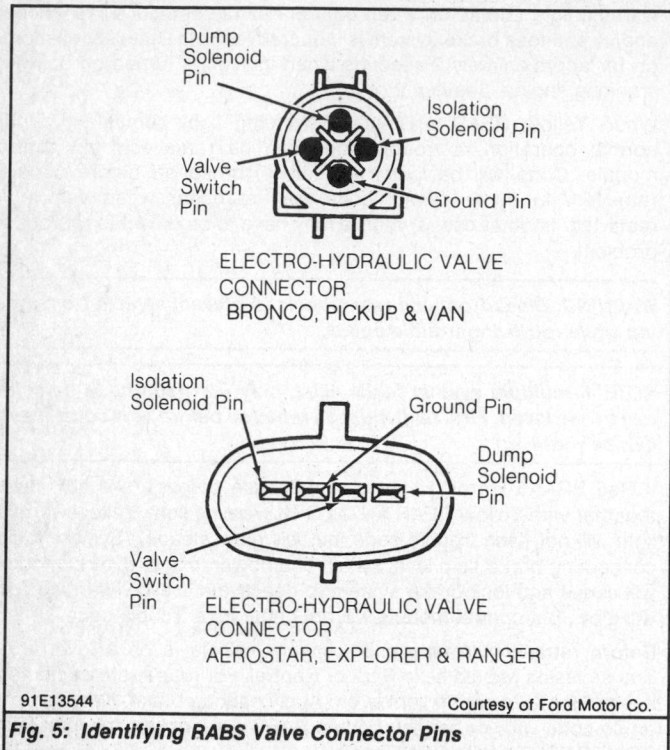

ELECTRO-HYDRAULIC VALVE
CONNECTOR
BRONCO, PICKUP & VAN

ELECTRO-HYDRAULIC VALVE
CONNECTOR
AEROSTAR, EXPLORER & RANGER

91E13544   Courtesy of Ford Motor Co.

Fig. 5: Identifying RABS Valve Connector Pins

CODE 3 (OPEN DUMP CIRCUIT)

1) Unplug control module connector. See COMPONENT LOCATIONS table. Measure resistance between harness connector pin No. 8 and ground, and between harness connector pin No. 14 and ground. See Fig. 4. If resistance is 3 ohms or greater, go to next step. If resistance is less than 3 ohms, replace control module.

2) Unplug RABS valve connector. See COMPONENT LOCATIONS table. Measure resistance between dump solenoid pin and ground pin on valve. See Fig. 5. If resistance is less than 3 ohms, repair open between dump valve connector and control module. If resistance is 3 ohms or greater, replace RABS valve.

CODE 4 (CLOSED RABS VALVE SWITCH)

Bronco, Pickup & Van – 1) Turn ignition off. Disconnect negative battery cable. Unplug RABS valve connector. See COMPONENT LOCATIONS table. Measure resistance between switch pin on valve and valve body. See Fig. 5. If resistance is 10,000 ohms or greater, go to next step. If resistance is less than 10,000 ohms, replace RABS valve.

2) Measure resistance between switch pin and ground pin on valve. If resistance is greater than 10,000 ohms, go to next step. If resistance is 10,000 ohms or less, replace RABS valve.

3) Unplug control module connector. See COMPONENT LOCATIONS table. Measure resistance between module harness connector pin No. 6 and ground. See Fig. 4. If resistance is 100,000 ohms or greater, replace control module. If resistance is less than 100,000 ohms, repair short between valve and control module.

CODE 4 (CLOSED VALVE SWITCH OR OPEN DUMP VALVE)

Aerostar, Explorer & Ranger – 1) Turn ignition off. Disconnect battery. Unplug RABS valve connector. See COMPONENT LOCATIONS table. Measure resistance between valve switch pin and valve body. See Fig. 5. If resistance is 10,000 ohms or greater, go to next step. If resistance is less than 10,000 ohms, replace RABS valve.

2) Measure resistance between switch pin and ground pin on valve. If resistance is 18,000 to 26,000 ohms, go to next step. If resistance is greater than 26,000 ohms or less than 18,000 ohms, replace RABS valve.

3) Measure resistance between valve switch pin and valve body, with hydraulic pressure applied for a minimum of 30 seconds. If resistance is 10,000 ohms or greater, go to next step. If resistance is less than 10,000 ohms, replace RABS valve.

4) Measure resistance between harness connector ground pin and chassis ground. If resistance is less than one ohm, go to next step. If resistance is one ohm or greater, repair open in isolation solenoid ground wire.

5) Reconnect wiring to valve. Unplug control module connector. See COMPONENT LOCATIONS table. Measure resistance between module harness connector pins No. 4 and 6. See Fig. 4. If resistance is greater than 26,000 ohms or less than 18,000 ohms, repair valve switch wiring between RABS valve and control module. If resistance is 18,000-26,000 ohms, replace control module.

CODE 5 (SYSTEM DUMPS TOO MANY TIMES)

1) If problem occurred with 2WD vehicle, or 4WD vehicle while in 2WD, go to next step. If problem occurred while in 4WD, go to step **3)**.

2) Unplug control module connector to disable system. See COMPONENT LOCATIONS table. Drive vehicle in 2WD mode. Make several normal stops to check rear brake operation. If rear brakes operate properly, replace RABS valve and retest system. If rear brakes grab or lock up easily, repair mechanical problem with rear brake system.

3) Unplug control module connector. Turn ignition on. Shift transfer case into 4WD mode. Measure voltage between module harness connector pin No. 5 and chassis ground. See Fig. 4. If voltage is less than one volt, replace RABS valve. If voltage is one volt or greater, repair or replace 4WD indicator switch, located on transfer case.

CODE 6 (SPEED SENSOR SIGNAL CUTS IN & OUT RAPIDLY)

1) Turn ignition off. Disconnect battery. Unplug module connector. See COMPONENT LOCATIONS table. Measure resistance between module connector pins No. 3 and 10, while flexing and wiggling wiring harness between speed sensor and module connector. See Fig. 4. If resistance is 1000-2000 ohms and steady, go to next step. If reading is erratic, repair loose connection in sensor circuit.

2) Remove speed sensor. See COMPONENT LOCATIONS table. Inspect for build-up of metal chips on sensor pole. If no metal chips are present, go to next step. If metal chips are present, drain and clean differential.

3) Rotate exciter ring. Inspect exciter ring for broken or damaged teeth. If teeth are okay and no lateral runout is visible, reinstall speed sensor. If teeth are damaged and lateral runout is visible, repair differential.

4) To check for low or erratic sensor output, raise and support vehicle so rear wheels can spin freely. Start engine. With rear wheels rotating at 5 MPH, measure voltage between speed sensor test connector pins (Light Green/Black and Red/Pink wires). See COMPONENT LOCATIONS table. If voltage is 650 mV or greater and steady, replace control module. If voltage is less than 650 mV and/or is erratic, replace speed sensor. Retest system.

CODE 7 (NO ISOLATION VALVE SELF-TEST)

1) Turn ignition off. Unplug RABS valve connector. See COMPONENT LOCATIONS table. Measure resistance between isolation solenoid pin and ground pin at valve. See Fig. 5. If resistance is 3 ohms or greater, go to next step. If resistance is less than 3 ohms, replace valve.

2) With RABS valve connector still unplugged, unplug control module connector. See COMPONENT LOCATIONS table. Measure resistance between module harness connector pin No. 13 and chassis ground. See Fig. 4. If resistance is 20,000 ohms or greater, replace control module. If resistance is less than 20,000 ohms, repair short in harness between RABS valve and control module.

CODE 8 (NO DUMP VALVE SELF-TEST)

) Turn ignition off. Disconnect negative battery cable. Unplug RABS valve connector. See COMPONENT LOCATIONS table. Measure resistance between dump solenoid pin and ground pin at valve. See Fig. 5. If resistance is one ohm or greater, leave connector unplugged, go to next step. If resistance is less than one ohm, replace RABS valve.

) Unplug control module connector. See COMPONENT LOCATIONS table. Measure resistance between module connector pins No. 8 and ground, and between pin No. 14 and ground. See Fig. 4. If resistance 20,000 ohms or greater, replace control module. If resistance is less than 20,000 ohms, repair short in harness between RABS valve and control module.

CODE 9 (HIGH SENSOR RESISTANCE)

) Turn ignition off. Disconnect negative battery cable. Unplug speed sensor connector. See COMPONENT LOCATIONS table. Measure resistance between sensor pins. If resistance is less than 2500 ohms, go to next step. If resistance is 2500 ohms or greater, replace sensor.

) Reconnect speed sensor. Unplug control module connector. See COMPONENT LOCATIONS table. Measure resistance between module connector pins No. 3 and 10. See Fig. 4. If resistance is less than 500 ohms, replace control module. If resistance is 2500 ohms or greater, repair open between speed sensor and control module.

NOTE: If jumper harness between speed sensor and frame rail is defective, replace ONLY with original equipment High Flex Wire. Splice Connector (E6EB-14488-AA) MUST be used.

CODE 10 (LOW SENSOR RESISTANCE)

) Turn ignition off. Disconnect negative battery cable. Unplug speed sensor connector. See COMPONENT LOCATIONS table. Measure resistance between sensor pins. If resistance is 1000 ohms or less, replace sensor. If resistance is greater than 1000 ohms, leave sensor connector unplugged. Go to step 2).

) Unplug control module connector. See COMPONENT LOCATIONS table. Measure resistance between module pin No. 10 and chassis ground. See Fig. 4. If resistance is greater than 20,000 ohms, go to next step. If resistance is less than 20,000 ohms, repair short between speed sensor and control module.

) Measure resistance between module connector pins No. 3 and 10. resistance is 20,000 ohms or greater, replace control module. If resistance is less than 20,000 ohms, repair short between speed sensor wires.

CODE 11 (STOPLIGHT SWITCH CIRCUIT)

) Check stoplight operation. If stoplights are okay, go to next step. If stoplights do not operate, repair stoplight circuit, then retest system.

) Unplug control module connector. See COMPONENT LOCATIONS table. Measure voltage at module connector pin No. 11 while pressing brake pedal. See Fig. 4. If voltage is less than 9 volts, repair open between stoplight switch and control module. If voltage is 9 volts or greater, check 4-way flasher and wiring. A problem with 4-way flasher or wiring could cause feedback through stoplight circuit.

CODE 12 (FLUID LEVEL SWITCH CLOSED DURING RABS STOP)

Bronco, Pickup & Van – When code sets, Red BRAKE warning light will be on. For test procedure, see TEST C under DIAGNOSIS & TESTING. Skip step 5).

CODE 12 (LOSS OF BRAKE FLUID FOR ONE SECOND DURING STOP)

Aerostar, Explorer & Ranger – 1) When code sets, Red BRAKE warning light comes on. Check brake fluid level. If fluid level is okay, go to next step. If fluid level is low, check entire system for leaks. Repair as necessary. Refill master cylinder.

2) Unplug harness connector from master cylinder. Connect jumper wire between Purple/White wires, or between Purple/White and Purple/Yellow wires, on harness connector. If Yellow and Red warning lights stay on, go to next step. If Yellow and Red warning lights go out, replace master cylinder reservoir.

3) Turn ignition off. Unplug harness connector from module. See COMPONENT LOCATIONS table. Turn ignition on. If Yellow light stays on and Red light goes off, repair short in wiring between diode/resistor and master cylinder, or between master cylinder and warning light. See COMPONENT LOCATIONS table. If both warning lights go out, replace module.

CODE 13 (SPEED PROCESSOR CHECK)

This code indicates control module failure. Replace control module.

CODE 14 (PROGRAM CHECK)

This code indicates control module program check sum failure was detected during self-test. This code will set on Explorer and Ranger only. Replace control module.

CODE 15 (MEMORY FAILURE)

This code indicates control module RAM failure was detected during self-test. This code will set on Explorer and Ranger only. Replace control module.

CODE 16

This code should not occur. Recheck flashing sequence. If codes continue to occur, replace control module.

REMOVAL & INSTALLATION

WARNING: When battery is disconnected, vehicle computer and memory systems may lose memory data. Driveability problems may exist until computer systems have completed a relearn cycle. See COMPUTER RELEARN PROCEDURES article in GENERAL INFORMATION before disconnecting battery.

RABS VALVE

Removal & Installation – Disconnect and plug brake lines connected to RABS valve. See COMPONENT LOCATIONS table. Unplug electrical connector. Remove retaining bolts. Remove valve. To install, reverse removal procedure. Bleed brakes. See BLEEDING BRAKE SYSTEM.

SPEED SENSOR

Removal & Installation – Unplug speed sensor connector. See COMPONENT LOCATIONS table. Remove hold-down bolt and sensor. To install, ensure "O" ring is positioned on sensor and sensor tip is clean of all metal particles. Lightly lubricate "O" ring with engine oil. Install sensor. DO NOT use force to install sensor. Install hold-down bolt.

CONTROL MODULE

Removal & Installation – Disconnect negative battery cable. On van, remove parking brake actuator assembly. On all models, remove module retaining screws and control module. See COMPONENT LOCATIONS table. To install, reverse removal procedure.

EXCITER RING

Removal & Installation – Remove differential case from axle housing. See appropriate article in DRIVE AXLES. Press exciter ring from differential case. Discard exciter ring upon removal. Use only NEW exciter ring upon reassembly. To install, reverse removal procedure.

TORQUE SPECIFICATIONS

TORQUE SPECIFICATIONS

Application	Ft. Lbs. (N.m)
Hydraulic Fittings	
1/2"-20	10-17 (14-23)
7/16"-24	10-15 (14-20)
3/8"-24	10-15 (14-20)
RABS Valve Mounting Bolts	
Aerostar	11-14 (15-19)
Bronco & Pickup	12-17 (16-23)
Explorer & Ranger	11-14 (15-19)
Van	19-24 (26-32)
Speed Sensor Hold-Down Bolt	25-30 (34-41)

COMPONENT LOCATIONS

COMPONENT LOCATIONS

Component	Location
Diode/Resistor	
Aerostar	Behind Left Side Of Instrument Panel, Taped To Harness
Bronco & Pickup	Left Rear Of Engine Compartment, Taped To Wiring Harness
Explorer	Behind Washer Reservoir, In Wiring Harness
Ranger	Left Side Of Engine Compartment, Above Wheel Well, Taped In Harness
Van	Behind Left Side Of Instrument Panel, Taped To Harness
RABS Diagnostic Connector	
Aerostar	Behind Left Side Of Instrument Panel, Taped To Main Harness
Bronco & Pickup	Far Right Side Of Instrument Panel, Below Bottom Right Corner Of Glove Box
Explorer	Left Side Of Engine Compartment, On Fender Apron
Ranger	Behind Left Side Of Instrument Panel, Taped To Main Harness, Near Parking Brake
Van	Left Side Of Upper Radiator Support, Forward Of Battery
RABS Module	
Aerostar	Behind Lower Center Of Instrument Panel, Below Ashtray
Bronco & Pickup	Behind Glove Box
Explorer	Behind Instrument Panel, To Left Of Center.
Ranger	Behind Lower Center Of Instrument Panel, To Left Of Ashtray.
Van	Instrument Panel Lower Brace, Near Windshield Wiper Control Module
RABS Valve	
All Vehicles	Left Frame Rail, Toward Rear Of Engine Compartment
Speed Sensor Test Connector	
Aerostar	Relay Bracket At Left Rear Of Engine Compartment
Bronco & Pickup	Bracket At Left Rear Of Engine Compartment
Explorer	Fender Apron At Left Rear Of Engine Compartment
Ranger	Top Of Left Fender Apron
Van	Left Front Of Engine Compartment, Near Relay Panel
Speed Sensor	
All Vehicles	Threaded Into Differential Housing

WIRING DIAGRAMS

For anti-lock brake system wiring diagrams, see Figs. 6-9. Also refer to appropriate chassis wiring diagram in WIRING DIAGRAMS.

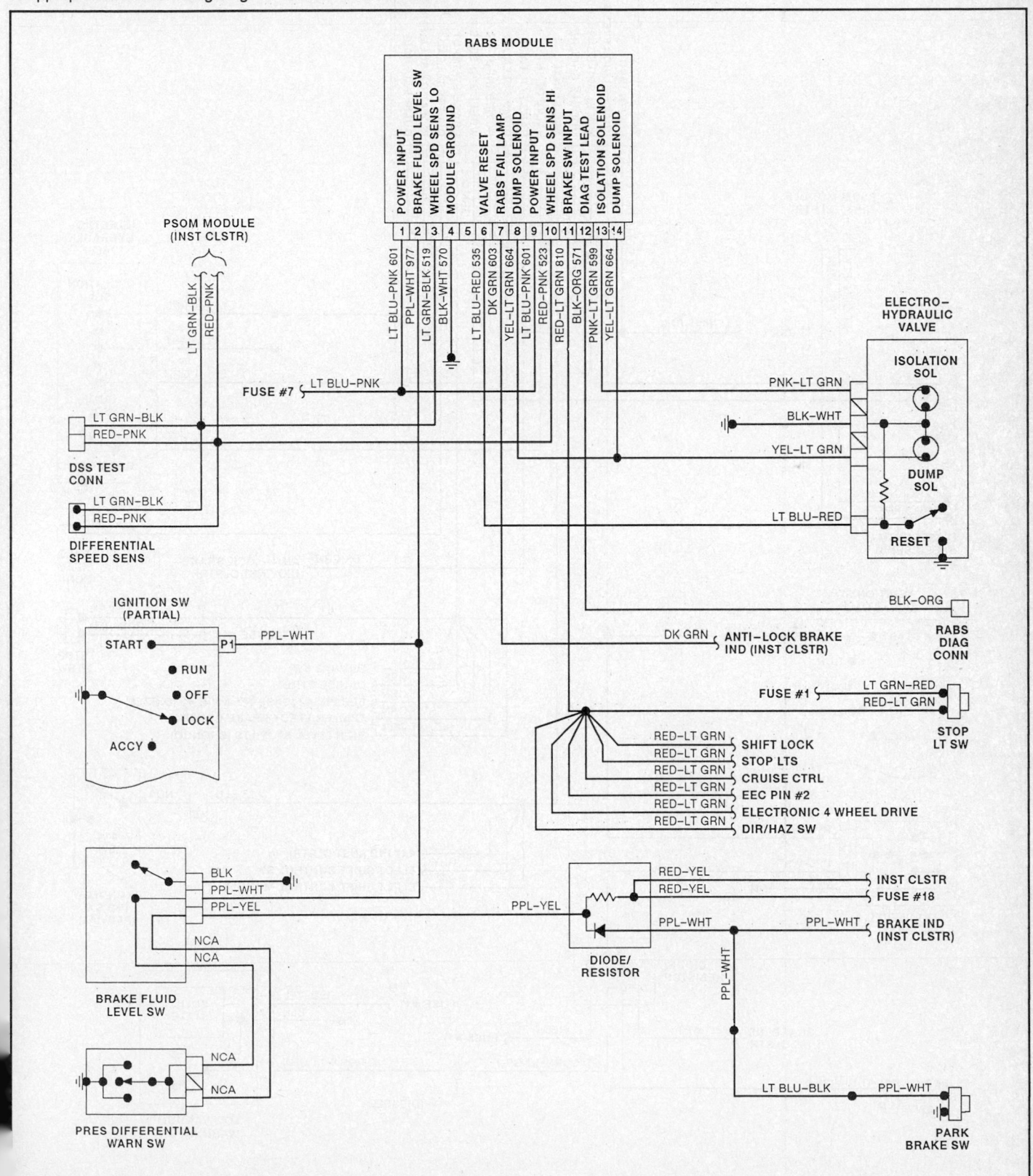

92H21805

Fig. 6: Rear Anti-Lock Brake System (RABS) Wiring Diagram (Aerostar)

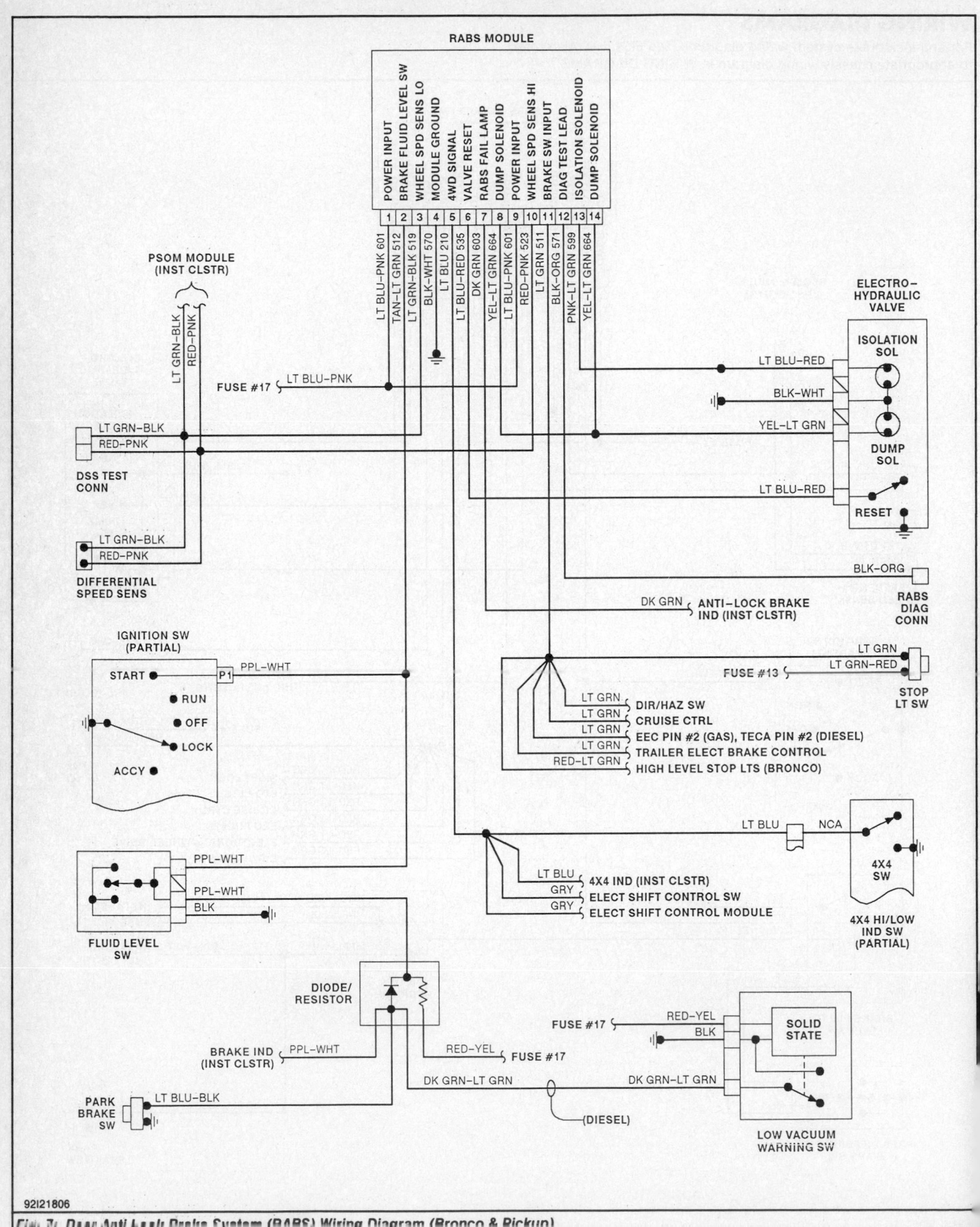

Fig. 7: Rear Anti-Lock Brake System (RABS) Wiring Diagram (Bronco & Pickup)

92I21806

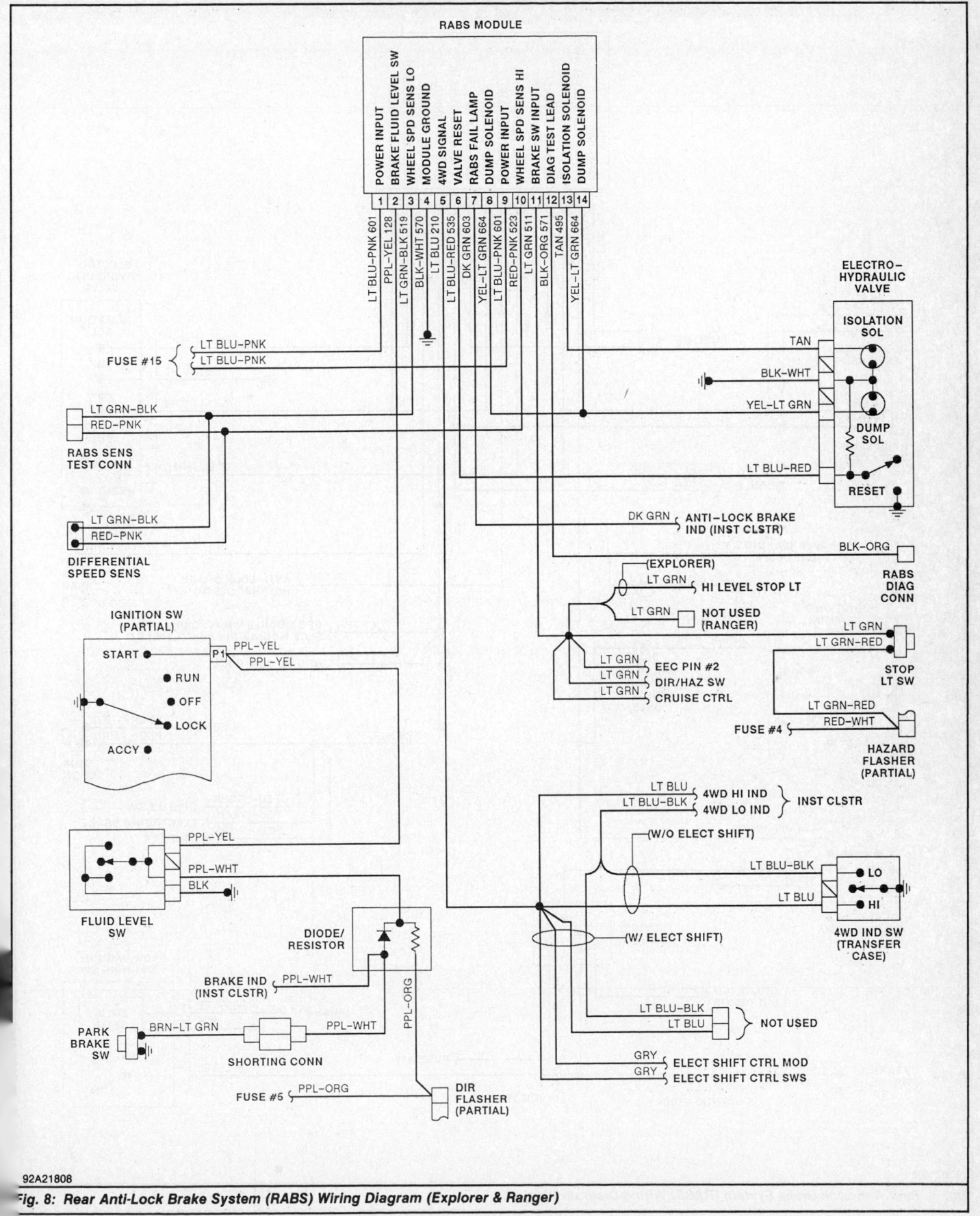

Fig. 8: Rear Anti-Lock Brake System (RABS) Wiring Diagram (Explorer & Ranger)

92A21808

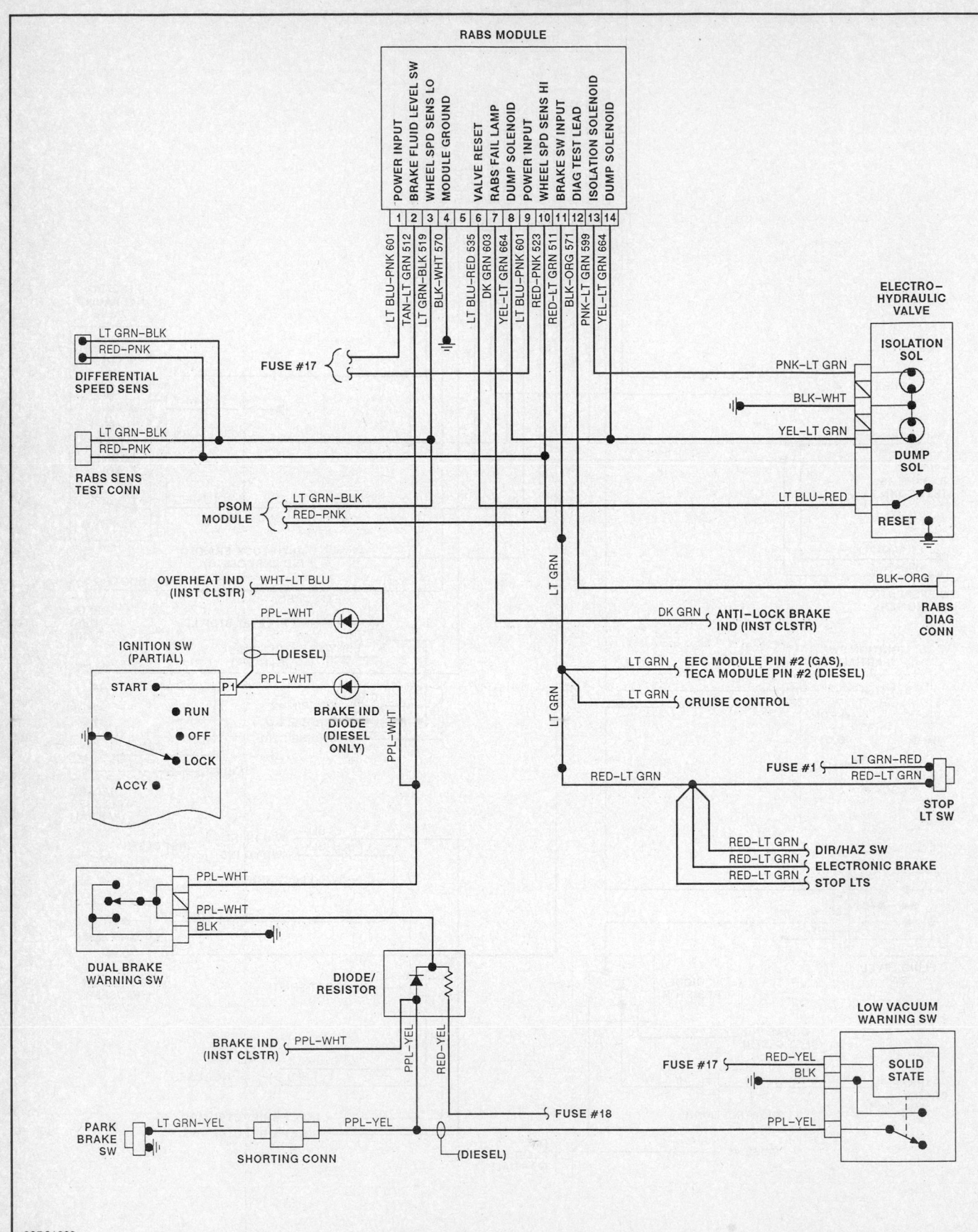

Fig. 9: Rear Anti-Lock Brake System (RABS) Wiring Diagram (Van)

92B21809

Aerostar, Bronco, Explorer, Pickup, Ranger, Van

NOTE: Unless otherwise specified, references to Pickup include the F350 Super Duty commercial chassis.

MODEL IDENTIFICATION

Series [1]	Model
"A"	Aerostar
"E"	RWD Van
"F"	Pickup
"R"	Ranger
"U"	Bronco & Explorer

[1] – Vehicle series is fifth character of VIN.

DESCRIPTION & OPERATION

Front disc and rear drum brakes are standard on all models except "F" Series Super Duty, which comes with front and rear disc brakes. A single anchor, dual piston brake assembly is used on E250/350, F250/350 and front and rear on "F" Series Super Duty. All other models use a single piston, pin rail sliding caliper front disc brake system. Rear drum brake assembly consists of a support plate, 2 brake shoes, return springs, automatic adjuster components and one dual piston wheel cylinder. On Aerostar, Explorer and Ranger, brake drums are available in 9" and 10" sizes.

On rear drum brake models, parking brake is actuated by a cable, which pulls the parking brake lever located inside rear brake assembly. The lever pivots parking brake strut between brake shoes. This movement pushes outward on brake shoes. The brake shoe linings are made of asbestos-free fiberglass material.

"F" Series Super Duty, equipped with rear disc brakes, uses a cable actuated, transmission mounted parking brake. Transmission mounted parking brake is situated on transmission extension housing, and consists of a case assembly and cable actuated 9" x 3" Bendix brake assembly. See Fig. 1. Case assembly consists of roller bearings, companion flange and mainshaft, assembled in a one-piece aluminum housing. Case assembly has a lubrication supply separate from transmission.

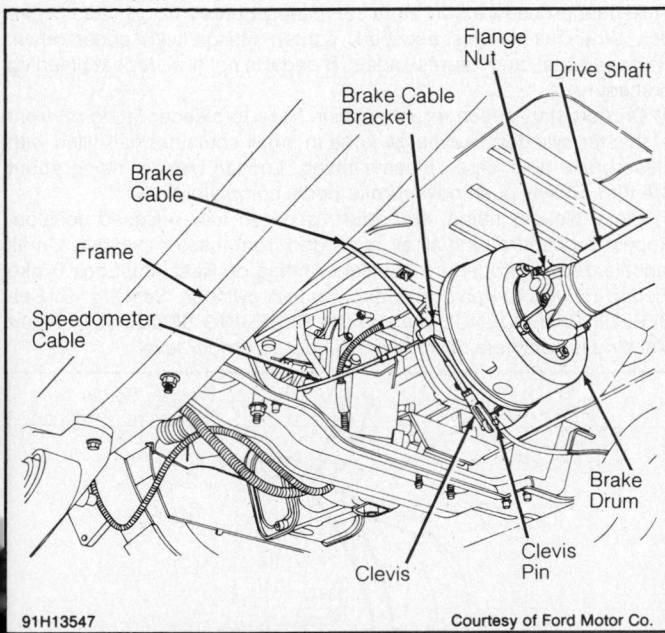

Flange Nut
Drive Shaft
Brake Cable Bracket
Brake Cable
Frame
Speedometer Cable
Clevis
Clevis Pin
Brake Drum

91H13547   Courtesy of Ford Motor Co.

Fig. 1: Locating Transmission Mounted Parking Brake ("F" Series Super Duty)

Aerostar is equipped with a cartridge master cylinder and vacuum booster. The cartridge-type master cylinder has, in addition to the standard primary and secondary pistons, a by-pass proportioning valve and differential pressure switch.

Bronco, Explorer, Ranger and "E" & "F" Series models are equipped with dual master cylinder and vacuum booster. The dual master cylinder has primary and secondary pistons and separate primary and secondary fluid reservoirs. "F" Series Super Duty model uses a dual master cylinder and hydro-boost. On all models, caliper is secured to steering knuckle by 2 caliper retaining pins. Aerostar, Explorer and Ranger use a dual-diaphragm vacuum booster; all others use single or dual-diaphragm vacuum booster.

The single and dual-diaphragm (tandem) vacuum boosters are self-contained, vacuum power brake units. The booster assists in actuating master cylinder push rod. Booster contains either a single or dual vacuum-suspended diaphragm which uses engine manifold vacuum or atmospheric pressure for power. Diesel powered vehicles use a belt-driven vacuum pump to provide vacuum for booster actuation.

A mechanically operated booster check valve controls power brake application and release in relation to foot pressure applied to check valve operating rod. Booster check valve is the only serviceable component of brake booster assembly. The "F" Series Super Duty hydro-boost is hydraulically operated by the power steering pump and provides a variable power assist regulated by brake pedal pressure.

Hydro-boost has a reserve system (compressed gas accumulator) which stores enough fluid under pressure to provide at least 2 power-assisted brake applications if power steering pump fluid flow stops. Brakes can also be operated manually if reserve system is lost.

Hydro-boost power units in normal condition produce certain noises. These noises occur when brakes are used more than usual. In general, these noises are hissing, clunks, clicks and chattering. Hydro-boost hisses when greater than normal braking effort is used. Hissing increases when pedal effort and operating temperatures increase. Loud hissing at normal pedal effort of 25-35 lbs. (11-16 kg.) or less should be investigated. Clunk, chatter and clicking noises are heard when brake pedal is quickly released from hard braking.

A fluid level indicator is located in the plastic reservoir of each master cylinder. It is not serviced separately. It consists of a float, magnet assembly and reed switch. The magnet operates the reed switch when fluid is low and activates a dash-mounted warning light.

WARNING: Hydro-boost unit should not be carried by accumulator. DO NOT drop hydro-boost on accumulator. Snap ring should be checked for proper seating before booster is used. Accumulator contains high pressure nitrogen gas and can be dangerous if mishandled. Before disposing of boosters, drill a 1/16" (1.6mm) hole in end of accumulator can to relieve gas pressure.

The cartridge-type master cylinder on Aerostar uses a pressure differential warning switch. This switch lights brake warning light on dash if pressure in either front or rear brake system becomes too low.

Aerostar and some Bronco and "E" & "F" Series vehicles use a proportioning valve integral with master cylinder. See Fig. 2. This proportioning valve has a by-pass feature. The proportioning valve restricts hydraulic pressure to the rear brakes to prevent lock-up. The by-pass feature allows full hydraulic pressure to the rear brakes in case of front brake system failure.

"F" Series Super Duty vehicles are equipped with a height sensing proportioning valve. See Fig. 3. The height sensing proportioning valve monitors changes in vehicle height. This valve automatically provides optimum front-to-rear brake balance, regardless of vehicle load. The valve controls pressure to rear brakes by sensing vehicle load conditions through movement between rear axle and body. As vehicle load increases (resulting in decreased vehicle height), higher brake line pressure to rear brakes is allowed. The valve is located on No. 5 crossmember.

CAUTION: If height sensing proportioning valve linkage is disconnected, proper indexing will be lost. A new sensing valve must be installed. The new sensing valve will have the shaft pre-set and secured internally. If shaft turns freely, DO NOT USE.

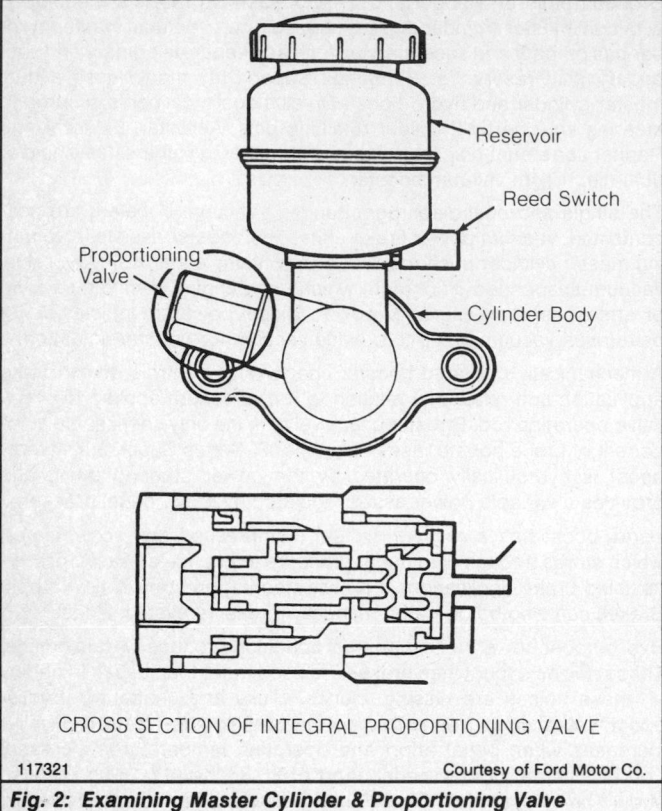

CROSS SECTION OF INTEGRAL PROPORTIONING VALVE

117321   Courtesy of Ford Motor Co.

Fig. 2: Examining Master Cylinder & Proportioning Valve (Bronco, "E" & "F" Series)

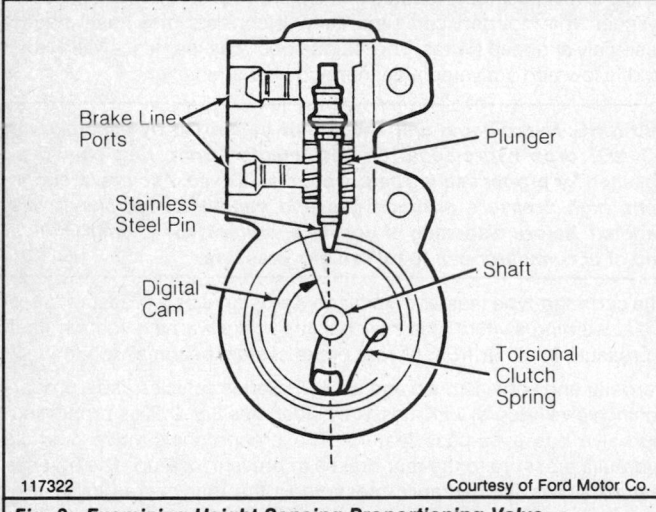

117322   Courtesy of Ford Motor Co.

Fig. 3: Examining Height Sensing Proportioning Valve ("F" Series Super Duty)

CAUTION: *Aftermarket load leveling kits, air shocks or modifications which change curb ride height and/or spring deflection rate provide false readings to height sensing proportioning valve. These modifications may result in unsatisfactory brake performance, which in turn could result in an accident.*

BLEEDING BRAKE SYSTEM

Bleed hydraulic system whenever air has been introduced into system. Bleed master cylinder and brakes at all 4 wheels if master cylinder lines have been disconnected or master cylinder has run dry. Bleed brakes with pressure bleeding equipment or by manually pumping brake pedal while using bleeder tubes. Always bleed brake lines in sequence. See BLEEDING SEQUENCE.

NOTE: *Do not allow reservoir to run dry during bleeding operation.*

MANUAL BLEEDING

NOTE: *Manual bleeding procedures for Bronco and "E" & "F" Series vehicles are not available from manufacturer, but should be similar to other manual bleeding procedures.*

1) Clean master cylinder cap and surrounding area. Remove cap. Explorer and Ranger models are equipped with dual-type master cylinder. Aerostar has a cartridge-type master cylinder. On Explorer and Ranger, bleed primary and secondary systems separately. On Explorer and Ranger, loosen primary or secondary master cylinder hydraulic line fitting. *See Fig. 4.*

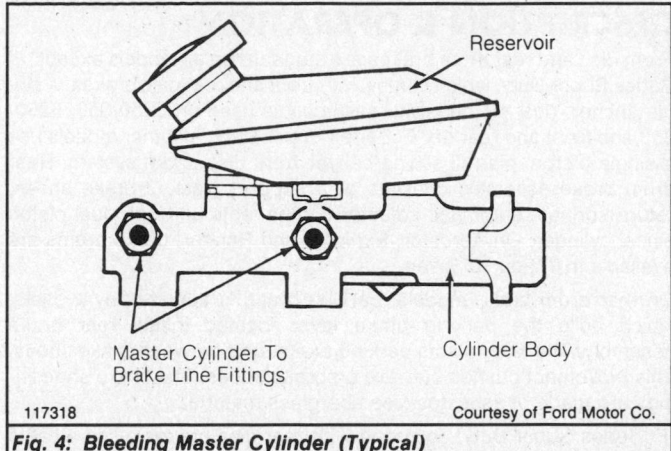

117318   Courtesy of Ford Motor Co.

Fig. 4: Bleeding Master Cylinder (Typical)

2) On Aerostar, loosen either master cylinder hydraulic line. On all models, wrap a cloth around brake lines to absorb escaping brake fluid (on Aerostar, bleed longest line first). Slowly push brake pedal down to force out air. With pedal fully depressed, tighten fittings to prevent air from being sucked into master cylinder when pedal is released. Release pedal.
3) Repeat procedure until air is completely purged from master cylinder. When all air has escaped, tighten fittings with pedal down. Release pedal, and depress again. If pedal is not firm, repeat bleeding procedure.
4) On Aerostar, attach a rubber drain hose to bleeder fitting on front of master cylinder. Submerge hose in small container half-filled with clean brake fluid. Open bleeder fitting. Loosen bleeder fitting about 3/4 turn. Slowly push down brake pedal completely.
5) Close bleeder fitting, and return pedal to fully released position. Repeat procedure until all air is purged from master cylinder. On all models, repeat procedure at bleeder fitting on Rear Anti-Lock Brake Electro-Hydraulic Valve and each wheel cylinder. *See Fig. 5.* See BLEEDING SEQUENCE table under BLEEDING SEQUENCE. When bleeding is complete, fill master cylinder to proper level.

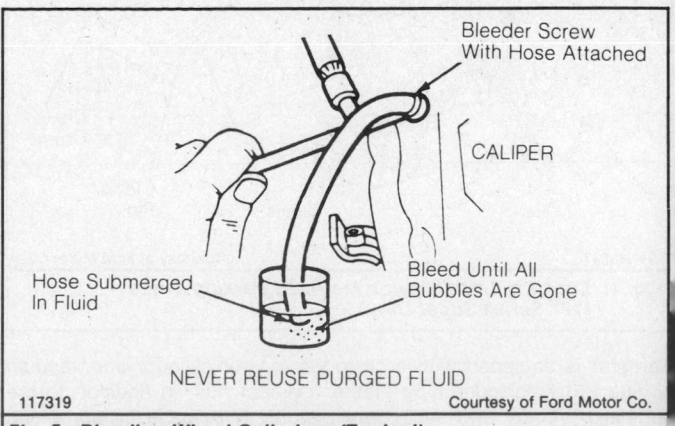

NEVER REUSE PURGED FLUID

117319   Courtesy of Ford Motor Co.

Fig. 5: Bleeding Wheel Cylinders (Typical)

PRESSURE BLEEDING

1) Clean master cylinder cap and surrounding area. Remove cap. With pressure tank at least 1/2 full of specified fluid and charged between 10-30 psi (.7-2.0 kg/cm²), use adapters to connect tank to master cylinder. Follow equipment manufacturer's pressure instructions.

CAUTION: NEVER exceed 50 psi (3.5 kg/cm²) during bleeding.

2) Open pressure bleeder valve. On Aerostar, attach one end of rubber drain tube to master cylinder bleeder fitting. Open bleed fitting. On all others, bleed master cylinder primary and secondary hydraulic lines individually. Put shop towels in place to catch brake fluid.
3) Open lines. On all models, allow brake fluid to flow out until all air is purged. Close bleed fitting and hydraulic line. Close pressure bleeder valve. Attach rubber drain hose to first wheel cylinder bleeder valve to be serviced. *See Fig. 5.* See BLEEDING SEQUENCE table under BLEEDING SEQUENCE.
4) Place other end of hose in clean glass jar partially filled with clean brake fluid so end of hose is submerged in fluid. Open pressure bleeder valve. Open bleeder fitting. Close bleeder fitting when fluid flow is free of bubbles. Repeat procedure on remaining wheel cylinders in sequence. See BLEEDING SEQUENCE table.
5) When bleeding operation is complete, close pressure bleeder valve, and remove tank hose from adapter fitting. Check brake pedal operation. Ensure master cylinder is full of fluid.

BLEEDING SEQUENCE

Before bleeding system, remove all vacuum from power unit by depressing brake pedal several times. Bleed master cylinder first, followed in sequence by rear wheel cylinders, anti-lock system components (if equipped) and calipers. See BLEEDING SEQUENCE table.

BLEEDING SEQUENCE

Application	Sequence
All Models	RR, LR, ABS Valve (if equipped), RF, LF

BLEEDING HYDRO-BOOST UNIT

"F" Series Super Duty – 1) Fill power steering pump reservoir with Motorcraft MERCON multipurpose automatic transmission fluid. Crank engine several seconds with coil wire disconnected. Check and add fluid if necessary. Start engine. Turn wheels from lock-to-lock twice.
2) Turn engine off. Depress brake pedal several times to discharge accumulator. Start engine, and turn wheels from lock-to-lock twice. If foaming occurs, stop engine, and allow foam to dissipate. Repeat lock-to-lock procedure until all air is removed from system.

NOTE: Hydro-boost is generally self-bleeding. Listed procedure will normally bleed air from system. Normal vehicle operation will remove any additional air.

ADJUSTMENTS

VACUUM POWER BOOSTER PUSH ROD

NOTE: Brake booster push rod on Aerostar should not be readjusted.

1) Push rod has an adjustment screw to maintain correct distance between booster push rod and master cylinder piston. If push rod is adjusted too long, it prevents master cylinder piston from completely releasing hydraulic pressure, causing brakes to drag. If push rod is adjusted too short, it causes excessive pedal travel and an undesirable clunk in booster area.
2) Remove master cylinder to gain access to push rod. To check screw adjustment, fabricate a gauge. *See Fig. 6.*
3) Place gauge against master cylinder mounting surface of booster. Adjust push rod screw by turning it until end of screw just touches inner edge of gauge slot.

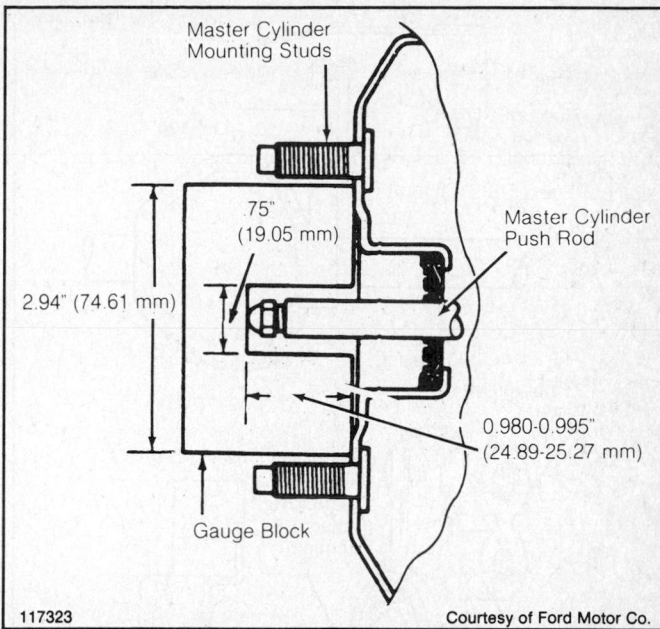

Fig. 6: Adjusting Brake Booster Push Rod
(All Models Except Aerostar & "F" Series Super Duty)

BRAKE PEDAL LINKAGE

"F" Series Super Duty – Remove spring clip and washer from lower end of brake pedal rod. Remove lower end of rod from bellcrank pin. Loosen jam nut. Hold brake pedal against rubber stop. Turn brake rod into clevis until lower hole lines up with pin on bellcrank. Slide brake rod onto pin of bellcrank, and attach washer and spring clip. *See Fig. 7.*

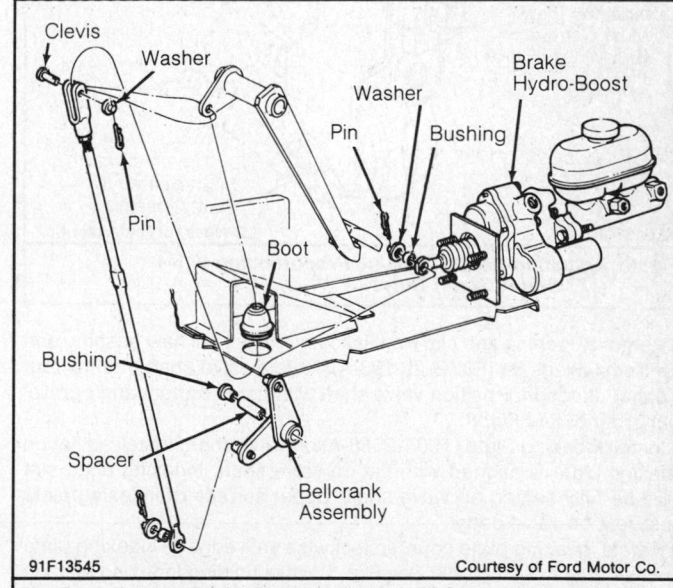

Fig. 7: Adjusting Brake Pedal Linkage ("F" Series Super Duty)

HEIGHT SENSING PROPORTIONING VALVE

"F" Series Super Duty – 1) Raise rear of vehicle using body jacks to gain a clearance of 6 5/8" (168 mm) between bottom surface of each rubber jounce bumper and rear axle housing. *See Fig. 8.* Remove nut from valve shaft, and remove leading arm.

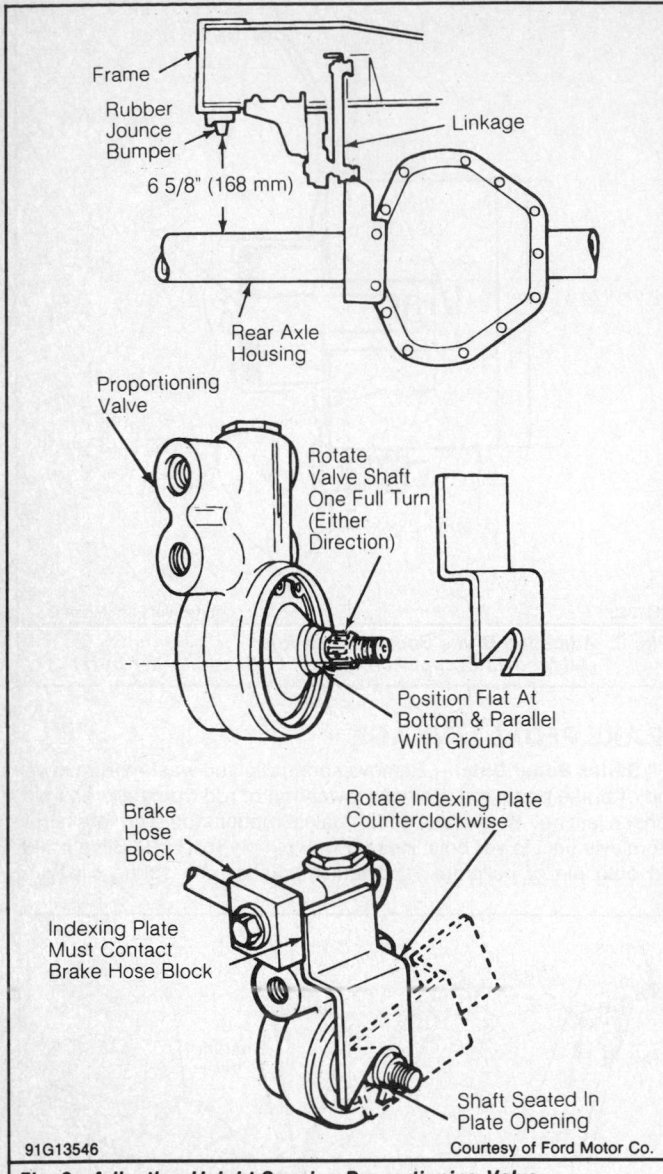

Fig. 8: Adjusting Height Sensing Proportioning Valve ("F" Series Super Duty)

2) Remove bushing and clip from leading arm. Install new bushing and clip from linkage kit (E8TZ-2L 193-A). Rotate valve shaft one full turn in either direction. Position valve shaft with flat at bottom and parallel with ground. *See Fig. 8.*

3) Install Indexing Plate (T90T-2588-A) on valve shaft. Install so flat on indexing plate is aligned with flat on valve shaft. Indexing plate slot must be fully seated on valve shaft. Upper surface of indexing plate must rest on valve body.

4) Rotate indexing plate counterclockwise until edge of indexing plate touches brake hose block. *See Fig. 8.* While holding indexing plate in position, install leading arm of linkage over splined part of valve shaft. Fully seat leading arm onto splines. Reinstall valve shaft nut. Remove indexing plate.

PARKING BRAKE

NOTE: Aerostar parking brake system is self-adjusting and requires no adjustment. On all other models except "F" Series Super Duty, initial adjustment procedure must be performed if tension limiter is replaced. If tensioner limiter has not been replaced, use field adjustment to remove cable slack.

Field Adjustment (Explorer & Ranger) – 1) Adjust service brakes before adjusting parking brake cable. Ensure brake drums are cold. Apply parking brake to fully depressed position. Grip threaded rod to prevent it from spinning.

2) Thread equalizer nut 6 full turns past its original position on threaded rod. Check cable tension at rear of equalizer assembly using Cable Tension Gauge (021-00018). If tension is not 400-600 lbs. (182-272 kg), repeat step 2).

3) Release pedal, and check rear wheel drag. If drag is noted, remove drums, and check for clearance between parking brake lever and cam plate. Cables should be tight enough to allow full application of rear brakes and loose enough to allow full release of rear brakes.

NOTE: Tension limiter will reset parking brake tension any time system is disconnected if distance between bracket and cinch strap hook is reduced during adjustment. When adjustment has been performed so cinch strap contacts bracket, system tension will increase greatly. This may cause an over-tension condition. When available adjustment travel has been used, replace tension limiter.

NOTE: If rear brake shoes are removed for any reason, parking brake cable tension should be checked and adjusted.

Initial Adjustment (Bronco, "E" & "F" Series) – 1) Adjust rear brakes before adjusting parking brake cables. Press parking brake lever to last detent position. On models with hand-operated (Orschein) parking brake, turn handle adjustment knob clockwise to end of travel. Apply parking brake. On all models, grip tension limiter housing to prevent it from spinning.

2) On Bronco and F150/350, thread equalizer nut 2.78-3.02" (70.6-76.7 mm) up rod. On E150/350, thread equalizer nut 2.98-3.22" (75.7-81.8 mm) up rod. Ensure cinch strap has slipped so less than 1.50" (38.1 mm) remains exposed. *See Fig. 9.*

3) On models with Orschein parking brake, release parking brake. Turn handle adjustment knob counterclockwise to obtain a minimum tension of 350 lbs. (159 kg) on Cable Tension Gauge (021-00018) with parking brake fully applied.

Field Adjustment (Bronco, "E" & "F" Series) – 1) Adjust rear brakes before adjusting parking brake cables. Use this procedure to correct slack in cable. Ensure brake drums are cold. Press parking brake to fully applied position. On models with Orschein parking brake, apply parking brake. On all models, grip tension limiter housing to prevent it from spinning.

2) Thread equalizer nut 6 turns past original position until cinch strap begins to slip. Check cable tension at rear of equalizer assembly using Cable Tension Gauge (021-00018). Tension should be at least 310 lbs. (140 kg) on models with Orschein parking brake and 350 lbs. (159 kg) on all others. If tension is below specifications, adjust equalizer nut again.

3) Release parking brake pedal or parking brake handle, and check for rear wheel drag. If drag is noted, remove drums, and check for clearance between parking brake lever and cam plate. Clearance should be .015" (.38 mm) with parking brake fully released. If clearance is incorrect, readjust parking brake cable.

NOTE: Tension limiter will reset parking brake tension any time system is disconnected if distance between bracket and cinch strap hook is reduced during adjustment. When adjustment has been performed so cinch strap contacts bracket, system tension will increase greatly. This may cause an over-tension condition. When available adjustment travel has been used, replace tension limiter.

Field Adjustment For Tight System (Bronco, "E" & "F" Series) – 1
Ensure brake drums are cold. Press parking brake pedal to floor. Release parking brake. Apply and release once again. Pressing parking brake pedal to floor causes tension limiter to automatically set cable tension and pedal feel.

2) Release parking brake lever. Install Cable Tension Gauge (021-00018) on cable, 2 1/2" behind equalizer. Apply parking brake. Cable tension should be a minimum of 350 lbs. (159 kg). If tension is below specification, repeat procedure.

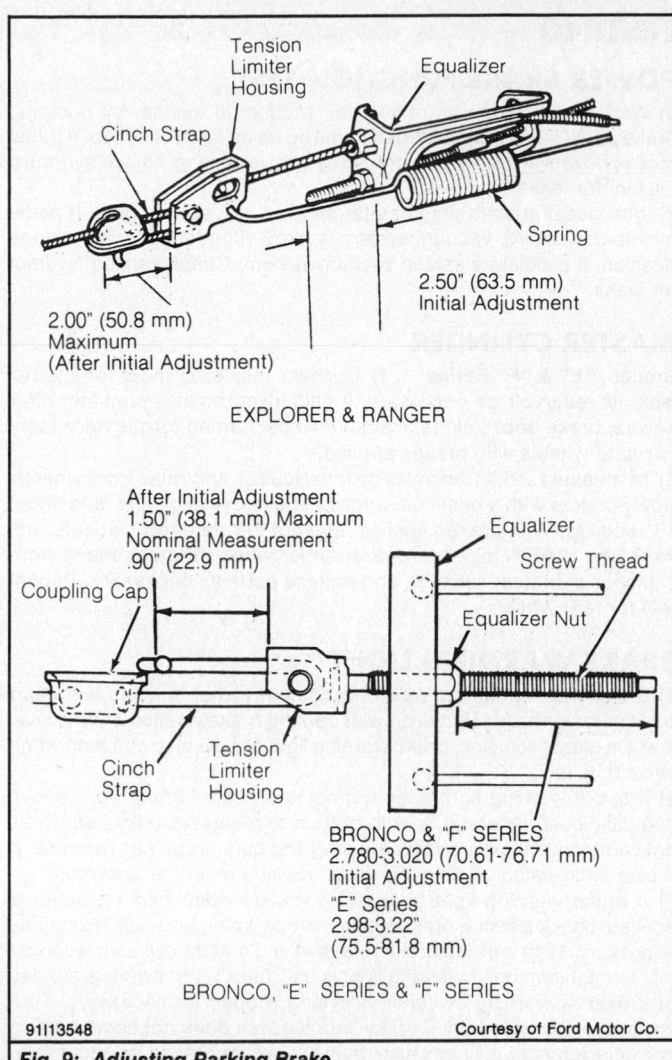

Fig. 9: *Adjusting Parking Brake
(Except Aerostar & "F" Series Super Duty)*

91I13548 — Courtesy of Ford Motor Co.

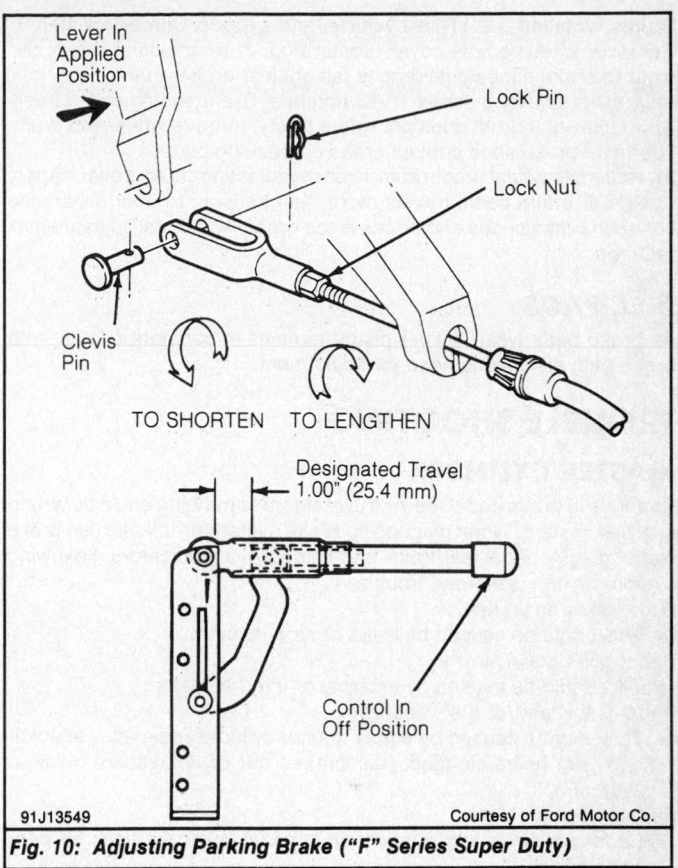

91J13549 — Courtesy of Ford Motor Co.

Fig. 10: *Adjusting Parking Brake ("F" Series Super Duty)*

Transmission Mounted Parking Brake Field Adjustment ("F" Series Super Duty) – **1)** Use this procedure to correct excess parking brake actuation lever travel. On foot actuated lever, raise vehicle and set on jack stands. Shift transmission to Neutral, and release parking brake. Loosen parking brake clevis adjusting jam nut several turns.

2) Remove lock pin and clevis pin from clevis. *See Fig. 10.* Hold lever and cable, removing slack. Screw adjusting clevis onto threaded end of cable until parking brake lever hole and clevis hole meet. Rotate clevis about 10 turns. Tighten jam nut. Rotate driveshaft to ensure rear brakes are not dragging. Lower vehicle to ground. Check parking brake for proper operation.

3) On vehicles with Orschein hand-actuated parking brake lever, turn handle adjustment knob to obtain one inch of travel. *See Fig. 10.* Release parking brake. Loosen parking brake clevis adjusting jam nut several times. Install parking brake cable into parking brake mounting bracket.

4) Hold parking brake actuation lever in applied position. Screw adjusting clevis onto threaded end of cable until parking brake lever hole and clevis hole meet. Rotate clevis about 10 turns. Tighten jam nut. Assemble clevis to parking brake actuation lever. Check parking brake for proper operation. Turn adjustment knob on parking brake actuation lever for additional adjustment.

BRAKE SHOES

NOTE: Rear brake shoes are automatically adjusted when vehicle is driven forward and backward and brakes are applied sharply. Manual adjustment is required if brakes do not self-adjust or after brake shoes have been removed or replaced.

Drums Removed – **1)** Adjust with brake drums cold and parking brake correctly adjusted. Measure brake drum inside diameter using brake shoe adjustment gauge. *See Fig. 11.*

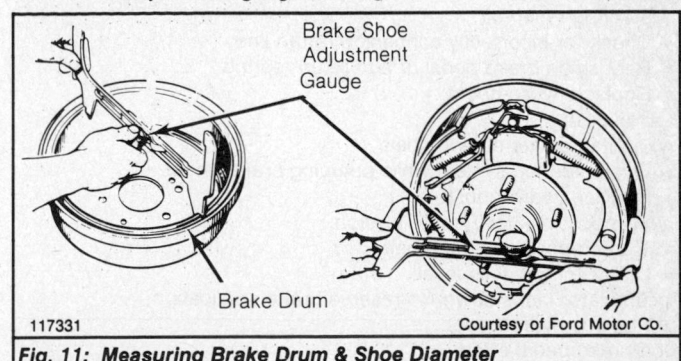

117331 — Courtesy of Ford Motor Co.

Fig. 11: *Measuring Brake Drum & Shoe Diameter*

2) Reverse adjustment gauge. Apply gauge to brake shoes on a line parallel to ground and through center of axle. Hold adjusting lever away from adjusting screw. Turn screw until outside diameter of shoes contacts gauge. *See Fig. 11.*

3) Install brake drum and wheel assembly. Complete adjustment by applying brakes quickly several times while driving vehicle alternately forward and backward. Check brake operation by stopping often while driving forward.

Drums Installed – 1) Raise vehicle, and support with safety stands. Remove adjusting hole cover rubber plug. Turn adjusting screw and expand brake shoes until drag is felt against brake drum.

2) Loosen adjusting screw 10-12 notches. Drum should rotate freely without drag. If drum does not rotate freely, remove wheel and drum. Lubricate brake shoe contact areas on backing plate.

3) Reinstall wheel and drum. Install adjusting hole cover. Apply brakes. If brake pedal travels more than halfway to floor, clearance between brake shoes and drums is too great. Additional adjustment is required.

DISC PADS

As brake pads wear, caliper piston remains in constant contact with brake pad, eliminating need for adjustment.

TROUBLE SHOOTING
MASTER CYLINDER

Changes in brake pedal feel or travel signal something could be wrong in brake system. When diagnosing brake system problems, use brake warning light, pedal feel/travel and fluid level as indicators. Following symptoms indicate brake trouble:

Pedal goes down fast.
- This could be caused by leaks or air in system.

Pedal goes down slowly.
- This could be caused by external or internal leaks.

Pedal is low and/or feels spongy.
- This may be caused by empty master cylinder reservoir, reservoir cap vent holes clogged, rear brakes out of adjustment or air in system.

Pedal effort too high.
- Check for binding or obstruction in pedal linkage. Check for poor booster assist.

Brake warning light is on.
- Check for low fluid level, ignition wires too close to fluid level indicator assembly, damaged indicator float, low vacuum (diesel) or applied parking brake.

HYDRO-BOOST UNIT

Use following list of symptoms to aid in diagnosing hydro-boost problems:

Brake pedal returns slowly.
- Check for restriction in return line between hydro-boost and power steering reservoir.
- Check for incorrectly connected return line.
- Reposition brake pedal or add return spring.
- Replace hydro-boost.

Brakes grab.
- Tighten power steering belt.
- Flush steering system while pumping brake pedal.
- Replace hydro-boost.

Hydro-boost chatter/Pedal vibration.
- Tighten power steering belt.
- Check for low fluid level.

Accumulator leaks down/No reserve brake application.
- Replace hydro-boost.

High brake pedal effort.
- Tighten or replace power steering belt.
- Low fluid level.
- Replace hydro-boost.

Brakes apply by themselves.
- Restriction in return line.
- Return line not connected correctly.
- Replace hydro-boost.

TESTING
POWER BRAKE FUNCTION TEST

1) With engine stopped, remove all vacuum in system by pumping brake pedal several times. Push pedal down as far as it will go. If pedal moves downward slowly, hydraulic system is leaking. Check hydraulic system for leaks.

2) With pedal pushed down as far as it will go, start engine. If pedal moves downward, vacuum system is okay. If pedal does not change position, a problem exists in vacuum system. Check vacuum system for leaks.

MASTER CYLINDER

Bronco, "E" & "F" Series – 1) To check master cylinder for internal leak, fill reservoir as necessary. If fluid level remains constant after several brake applications, measure wheel turning torque necessary to rotate wheels with brakes applied.

2) To measure, shift transmission into Neutral, and raise front wheels. Apply brakes with a minimum force of 100 lbs. (45 kg), and hold about 15 seconds. With brakes applied, attempt to rotate front wheels with 75 ft. lbs. (102 N.m) of torque. If either wheel rotates, check front chamber of master cylinder, and replace parts as necessary. Repeat test for rear wheels.

BRAKE WARNING LIGHT

1) Brake warning light should only come on when ignition is in start position or when ignition is on with parking brake applied or fluid level low. On diesel vehicles, brake warning light should also come on when vacuum is low.

2) If brake warning light does not come on when brake fluid is low, manually push reservoir float to bottom of reservoir. If light still does not come on, check circuit fuse, wiring and bulb. Repair as necessary. If bulb and related circuitry are okay, replace reservoir assembly.

3) If brake warning light does not come on when parking brake is applied, check parking brake switch, circuit wiring and bulb. Repair as necessary. With parking brake released and master cylinder reservoir full, turn ignition on. If warning light is on, check for shorted, grounded or defective warning switches or wiring. Repair as necessary. Turn ignition to start position. If brake warning light does not come on as a bulb check function, check fuse, bulb and wiring. Repair as necessary.

BRAKE PEDAL RESERVE

1) If complaint is low or bottoming out brake pedal, run engine at idle with transmission in Park or Neutral. Lightly depress brake pedal 3 or 4 times. Wait 15 seconds for vacuum to build in booster. Depress brake pedal until it stops moving downward.

2) While holding pedal down, raise engine speed to about 2000 RPM. Release accelerator pedal. Brake pedal should move downward as engine speed returns to idle. If results are correct, system has proper pedal reserve. If results are not correct, check for adequate vacuum. If vacuum is okay, replace vacuum booster.

HYDRO-BOOST RESERVE

Charge system with pressure by holding steering wheel on steering stop or by holding brake pedal down with 100 lbs. (45 kg) of force for 5 seconds with engine idling. Turn engine off. After 8-12 hours, depress brake pedal with engine off. If power reserve is not present, replace hydro-boost unit.

CAUTION: DO NOT hold brake pedal with 100 lbs. (45 kg) of force for longer than 5 seconds at a time.

VACUUM POWER BOOSTER

1) With a "T" fitting, connect vacuum gauge into vacuum line between engine and power brake booster. With engine at operating temperature, gauge should read 15-19 in. Hg (51-64 kPa) at idle with transmission in Neutral. If reading is below specifications, stop engine, disconnect vacuum hose at power brake booster and cap open end of hose and open port of vacuum "T".

2) Start engine, and allow it to idle. If vacuum reading is still less than 15-19 in. Hg (51-64 kPa), engine is producing low vacuum and problem must be corrected. If vacuum is to specification, check plastic check valve, rubber grommet and vacuum hose connection at power brake booster.

3) With low engine vacuum corrected and/or leaking components replaced, start engine, and allow it to idle. Stop engine, and depress brake pedal, holding down a few seconds. If vacuum drops to zero, booster is leaking and requires replacement.

REMOVAL & INSTALLATION

DISC BRAKE CALIPERS & PADS

Removal – 1) To prevent master cylinder overflow when caliper piston is depressed, remove and discard some brake fluid from master cylinder. Raise vehicle, and support with safety stands.

2) Remove front wheel assembly. Place a large "C" clamp on caliper. Tighten clamp to bottom piston in cylinder bore. Remove clamp.

3) Remove dirt around caliper pin tabs. Tap upper caliper pin toward inboard side of vehicle until pin tabs touch spindle face.

4) Insert screwdriver into slot provided behind pin tabs on inboard side of pin. Using pliers, compress end of pin while using screwdriver to pry until tabs slip into spindle groove.

5) Place a 7/16" diameter punch on end of pin, and drive caliper pin out of caliper slide groove. Repeat procedure for lower pin. Remove caliper from rotor. Remove outer brake pad. Compress anti-rattle spring clip, and remove inner brake pad. Support caliper aside.

6) On Aerostar, Explorer and Ranger, replace pads if lining is less than .12" (3.0 mm) thick at any point. On Bronco, E150 and F150, replace pads if lining is less than .06" (1.5 mm) above backing plate at any point. On E250/350, F250/350 and "F" Series Super Duty, replace pads if lining is less than .03" (.8 mm) above backing plate at any point.

CAUTION: During installation, DO NOT tap caliper pin too far into spindle groove. If this happens, tap pin in other direction until tabs snap back into place. Tabs on each end of caliper pin must be free to catch on spindle flanks.

Installation – Use "C" clamp to push caliper piston into piston bore until it bottoms out. To install, reverse removal procedure. Bleed air from brake system.

BRAKE SHOES

Removal (Except E250/350 & F250/350) – 1) Remove wheel assembly and drum. Place a wheel cylinder clamp over ends of wheel cylinder. Disengage adjusting lever from adjusting screw by pulling backwards on lever cable. *See Fig. 12.*

2) Move outboard side of adjusting screw upward, and back off pivot nut as far as possible. Pull adjusting lever, cable and adjusting spring down and toward rear to unhook pivot hook from large hole in secondary shoe. DO NOT pry pivot hook from hole.

3) Remove adjusting spring and adjusting lever. Remove secondary shoe-to-anchor spring. Remove primary shoe-to-anchor spring. Unhook cable anchor, and remove anchor pin plate.

4) Remove cable guide, shoe hold-down springs, brake shoes, adjusting screw, pivot nut and socket. Remove parking brake link spring and link. Note color and position of springs for reassembly.

5) Disconnect parking brake cable from lever. Remove secondary shoe. Disassemble parking brake lever from shoe by removing retaining clip and spring washer.

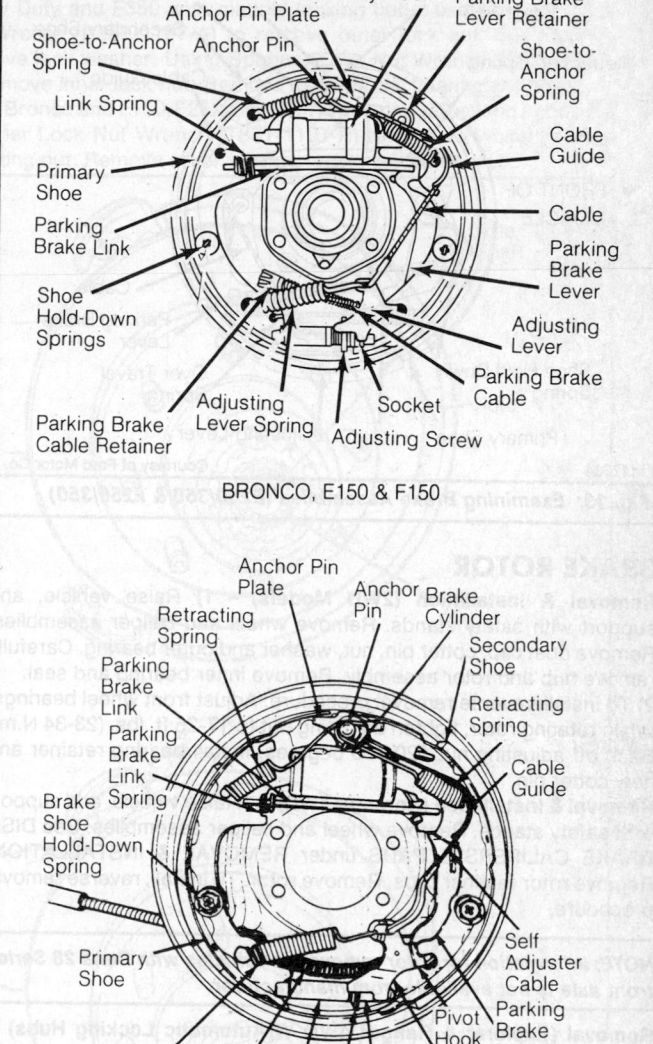

BRONCO, E150 & F150

AEROSTAR, EXPLORER & RANGER

117333   Courtesy of Ford Motor Co.

Fig. 12: Examining Rear Brake Assemblies (Except E250/350 & F250/350)

Installation – Clean and sand brake shoe contact points on backing plate. Apply a light coating of lithium base grease to contact points. Lubricate adjusting cable eye and anchor pin area. Lubricate adjusting screw, pivot and socket. To install, reverse removal procedure.

Removal (E250/350 & F250/350) – 1) Remove wheel assembly and brake drum. Remove parking brake lever assembly retaining nut from backing plate. Remove parking brake lever assembly. *See Fig. 13.* Remove adjusting cable assembly from anchor pin, cable guide and adjusting lever.

2) Remove brake shoe return springs, hold-down springs and brake shoes. Remove and disassemble adjusting screw assembly.

Installation – Clean and sand brake shoe contact points on backing plate. Apply a light coating of lithium base grease to contact points. Lubricate adjusting cable eye and anchor pin area. Lubricate adjusting screw, pivot and socket. To install, reverse removal procedure.

Resetting Cable Tension (Aerostar) – Connect parking brake cables to equalizer. Remove steel pin from spring lock-out hole, keeping fingers clear. Remove steel pin from pawl lock-out hole, restoring tension to parking brake cable. Apply and release parking brake several times to set cable tension.

Resetting Control Assembly Spring Tension (Aerostar) – **1)** Parking brake control assembly spring tension is lost when coil spring unwinds and disengages from tab on wheel. This occurs when a cable breaks, when servicing system without inserting lock pin or if lock pin is removed before brake cables are connected.

2) Remove parking brake control lever assembly. Hook end of coil spring on wheel tab. See Fig. 24. Insert a steel pin through pawl lock-out pin holes. Insert pin from inboard side at a slightly upward and forward angle and sweep downward and rearward to move self-adjusting pawl. This procedure locks out self-adjusting pawl.

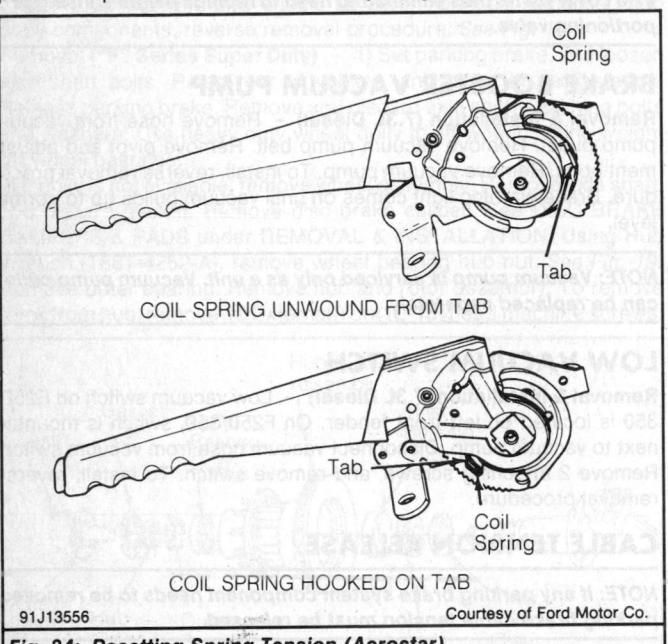

COIL SPRING UNWOUND FROM TAB

COIL SPRING HOOKED ON TAB

91J13556   Courtesy of Ford Motor Co.

Fig. 24: Resetting Spring Tension (Aerostar)

3) Slip a spare front cable around pulley. Insert cable anchor pin into pivot hole in ratchet plate assembly. With cable on floor, place foot on cable, or clamp end of cable in a vise.

4) Pull on brake control assembly, holding mounting bracket tightly against body of control assembly. Pull until cable tension rotates cable track in order to fully insert lock pin. Insert lock pin so control assembly is in released position. Install parking brake control lever assembly.

OVERHAUL

DISC BRAKE CALIPER

NOTE: Use same disassembly procedures for single and dual piston calipers.

Disassembly – **1)** Remove caliper. See DISC BRAKE CALIPERS & PADS under REMOVAL & INSTALLATION. Drain fluid from caliper. Secure caliper in a vise. Place a block of wood between caliper and piston(s). See Fig. 25. Apply low air pressure to brake hose inlet. Air pressure forces piston(s) outward.

CAUTION: DO NOT place fingers between wood and piston as piston leaves caliper.

2) If piston is jammed or seized and does not come out easily, use a brass hammer to lightly tap caliper while applying air pressure. DO NOT pry piston from bore. After piston comes out, remove seal and dust boot. Discard seals and boots.

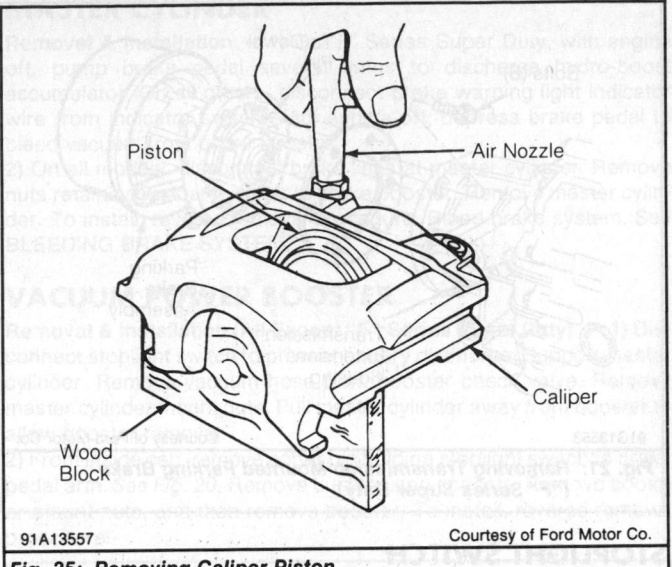

91A13557   Courtesy of Ford Motor Co.

Fig. 25: Removing Caliper Piston

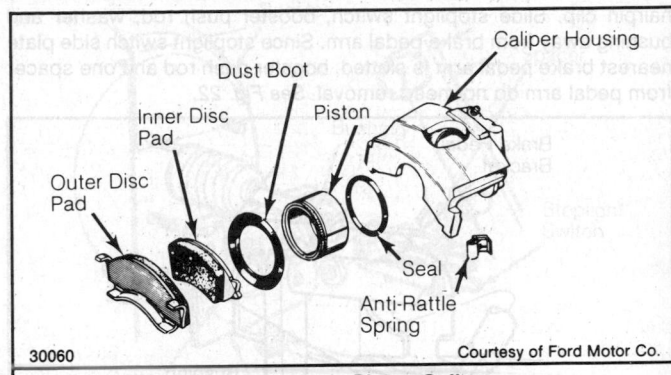

30060   Courtesy of Ford Motor Co.

Fig. 26: Exploded View Of Single Piston Caliper (Bronco, E150 & F150; Others Similar)

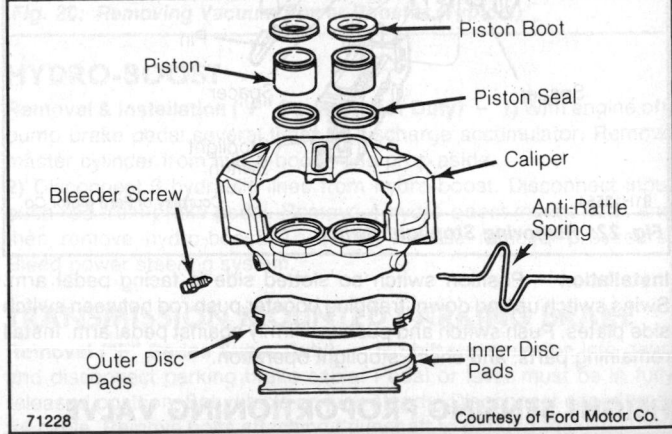

71228   Courtesy of Ford Motor Co.

Fig. 27: Exploded View Of Dual Piston Caliper (E250/350 & F250/350; "F" Series Super Duty Similar)

Cleaning & Inspection – **1)** Carefully clean rust and corrosion from caliper machined surfaces using a wire brush. DO NOT get wire brush in cylinder bores. Clean all components with isopropyl alcohol, and dry with compressed air.

2) Inspect cylinder bore, seal grooves and boot grooves for wear or damage. If bores are scored, corroded or worn, replace caliper. Replace anti-rattle clip, caliper support spring and key.

Reassembly – **1)** Lubricate piston seal with clean brake fluid, and install in cylinder bore groove. Lubricate cylinder with clean brake fluid. Coat piston and outside beads of dust boot with clean brake fluid.

2) Push piston through boot until boot is around bottom (closed end) of piston. *See Figs. 26 and 27.* Position piston and boot directly over cylinder bore. Spread dust boot over piston as it is installed.

3) With bead seated in groove, carefully press straight down on piston until it bottoms in cylinder bore. DO NOT cock or jam piston in cylinder. If necessary, use a "C" clamp and a block of wood to bottom piston in cylinder.

MASTER CYLINDER

NOTE: Aerostar recessed cartridge master cylinder cannot be overhauled; replace complete assembly if excessive wear or damage is apparent.

Disassembly – 1) Remove master cylinder. Clean outside of master cylinder. Remove filler cap and diaphragm. Drain any remaining fluid from cylinder. On dual master cylinder used on Bronco and "E" & "F" Series vehicles, remove stop bolt from bottom of master cylinder.

2) On all models, remove proportioning valve (if equipped). Depress piston, and remove snap ring from end of master cylinder bore. *See Figs. 28 and 29.* Remove piston assembly from cylinder bore. Carefully apply air pressure in outlet port of cylinder to remove remaining piston assembly from bore.

NOTE: Manufacturer does not recommend honing of cylinder bore.

Inspection – Clean all parts with isopropyl alcohol, and blow dry with compressed air. Ensure all ports and vents are open and free of foreign matter. Inspect master cylinder bore and all parts for excessive wear or damage. If bore is damaged, replace master cylinder.

Reassembly – Lubricate all components, including cylinder bore, with clean brake fluid. Install new grommets and plastic reservoir. Carefully insert piston assembly into master cylinder bore. If cylinder is equipped with piston stop pin, depress piston, and install pin. Install other piston assembly into cylinder. Depress piston, and install snap ring in groove.

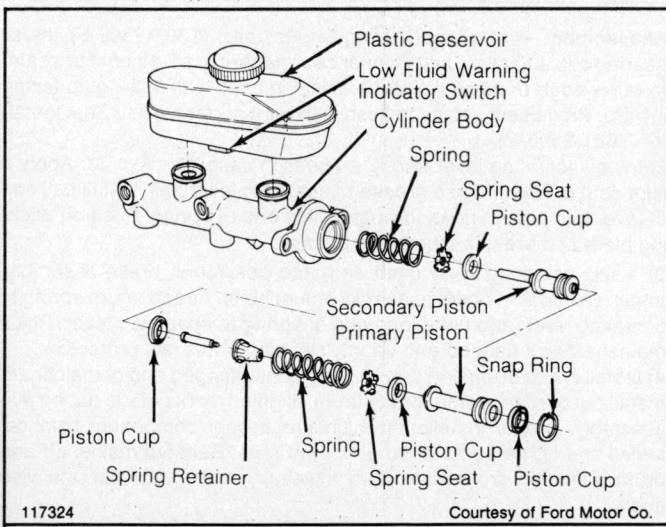

Fig. 28: Exploded View Of Master Cylinder Assembly (Aerostar, Explorer & Ranger)

ROTOR

Lateral Runout (Front & Rear Disc) – 1) On front disc brakes, tighten wheel bearing adjusting nut to eliminate bearing end play. Ensure rotor can be rotated by hand. When checking runout on rear disc brakes ("F" Series Super Duty only), make sure rear axle bearings are adjusted properly.

2) Once adjusted, do not change rear bearing setting. Attach dial indicator to suspension, with indicator tip set one inch from outer edge of rotor face. Set dial indicator to zero, and slowly turn rotor. Take read-

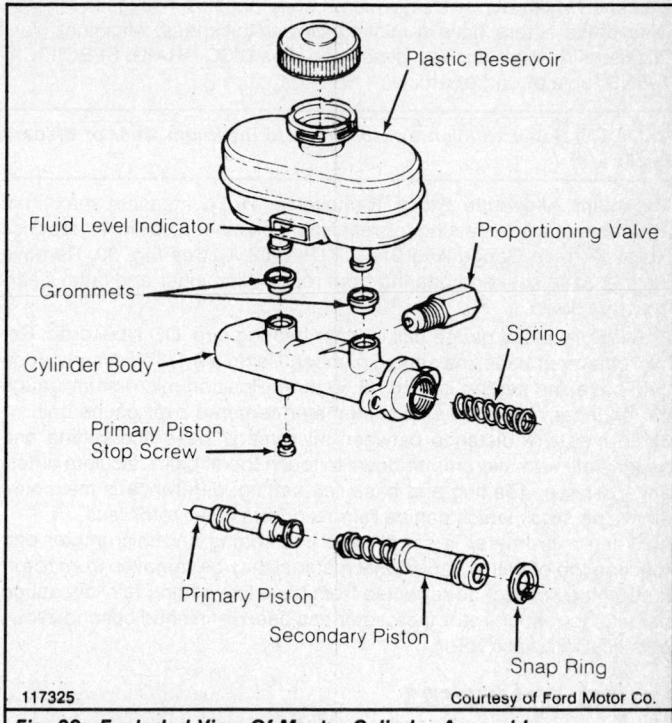

Fig. 29: Exploded View Of Master Cylinder Assembly (Bronco, "E" & "F" Series)

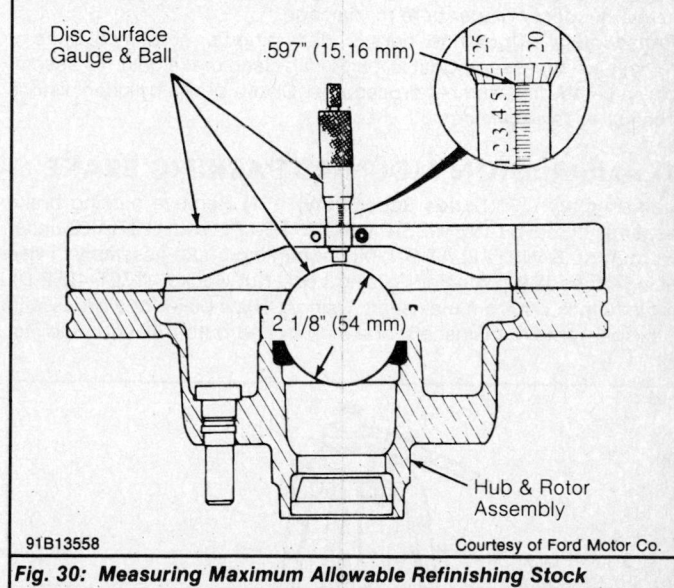

Fig. 30: Measuring Maximum Allowable Refinishing Stock

ing within a 6.00" (152.4 mm) radius on rotor. Runout must not exceed specification. See DISC BRAKE SPECIFICATIONS table at end of article. Resurface or replace rotor as required.

Parallelism – 1) Parallelism can be tested by 2 testing procedures. Using a micrometer, measure rotor thickness at 12 points, approximately 30 degrees apart and 1.00" (25.4 mm) from outer edge of rotor. Difference must not exceed specification. See DISC BRAKE SPECIFICATIONS table at end of article. Resurface or replace rotor as required.

2) Mount rotor on a brake lathe. Attach 2 dial indicators, one on each side of rotor, with tip of indicators contacting rubbing surface of rotor directly opposite each other and 1.00" (25.4 mm) from outer edge of rotor. Zero both indicators, and rotate rotor. Note indicator reading. If reading exceeds specification, resurface or replace as required. See DISC BRAKE SPECIFICATIONS table.

Discard Thickness – Using micrometer, measure thickness of rotor. Disc brake rotors have a minimum wear thickness. Minimum wear thickness is not refinishing dimension. See DISC BRAKE SPECIFICATIONS table at end of article.

CAUTION: Never refinish a rotor down to minimum wear or discard thickness.

Maximum Allowable Stock Removal – **1)** To measure maximum allowable stock remaining for refinishing on inner rotor face, use Disc Rotor Surface Gauge And Ball (T71P-1102-A). *See Fig. 30.* Remove inner grease seal and bearing from rotor. Wipe inner and outer bearing cups clean.

2) Carefully place gauge ball in inner bearing cup. DO NOT drop. Set micrometer at base line setting number. Using a 2 1/8" (54 mm) gauge ball, base line setting is .256" (6.50 mm). Position micrometer gauge bar on inner rotor face with micrometer centered over gauge ball.

3) To measure distance between micrometer base line setting and gauge ball, turn micrometer down to touch top of ball. Calculate difference between reading and base line setting; difference is maximum allowable stock which can be removed from inner rotor face.

4) When micrometer is set at base line setting and micrometer end touches top of ball, no additional material may be removed from rotor. If micrometer must be retracted from base line setting to allow gauge bar legs to rest on rotor face, rotor has been refinished beyond allowable limit. Replace rotor.

WHEEL CYLINDERS

Disassembly – With wheel cylinder removed from vehicle, remove rubber boots from ends of cylinders. Remove pistons, piston cups, return spring and piston expander from cylinder. Remove bleeder screw. Inspect cylinder bore for damage.

Reassembly – If cylinder bore is lightly pitted or scratched, hone or replace as necessary. Coat all parts with clean brake fluid. To assemble, reverse disassembly procedures. Clamp brake cylinder pistons against ends of cylinder.

TRANSMISSION MOUNTED PARKING BRAKE

Disassembly ("F" Series Super Duty) – **1)** Remove parking brake assembly. See TRANSMISSION MOUNTED PARKING BRAKE under REMOVAL & INSTALLATION. Mount parking brake assembly in vise using brass jaw protectors. Using Lock Nut Socket (T70T-4252-D), remove lock nut from mainshaft. Using a 3-jaw puller or a press with Adapter, remove mainshaft, brake drum and output flange. *See Fig. 31.*

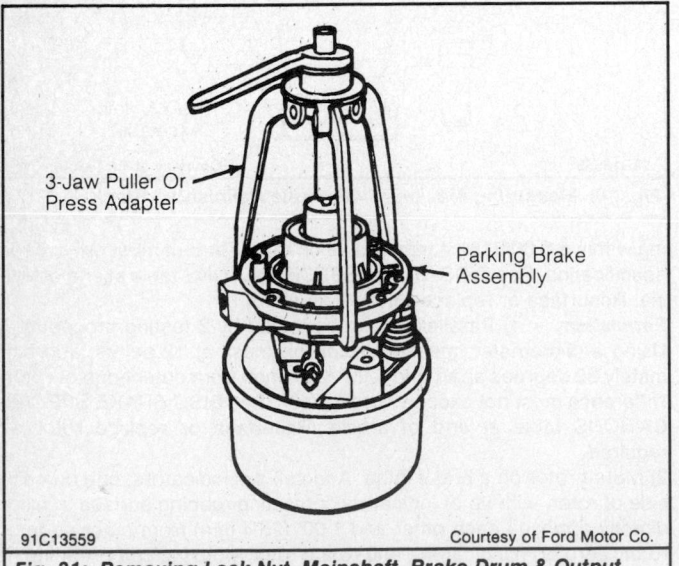

3-Jaw Puller Or Press Adapter

Parking Brake Assembly

91C13559   Courtesy of Ford Motor Co.

Fig. 31: Removing Lock Nut, Mainshaft, Brake Drum & Output Flange ("F" Series Super Duty)

2) Remove snap ring holding speedometer drive gear onto shaft, and then remove speedometer drive gear. Using Puller (D80L-1002-L) with Bearing Cone Remover (D79L-4621-A) and Step Plate (D80L-630-6), remove inner bearing cone from mainshaft.

3) Remove parking brake assembly from vise. Turn brake assembly over, and mount threaded end of mainshaft in vise using brass jaw protectors. Remove 4 nuts attaching output flange and brake drum to output shaft. Remove brake drum and flange from output shaft.

NOTE: Drum, flange and mainshaft are balanced as a unit. They must be marked to ensure parts are assembled in same position.

---

4) Using Bearing Cup Puller (T77F-1102-A), remove output shaft oil seal, spacer, "O" ring, bearing and bearing cup from input shaft end of case. Remove splash shield and brake assembly from case. *See Fig. 32.* Remove brake actuating lever and lever spring from case.

5) Using Bearing Cup Puller (T77F-1102-A), remove outer bearing cup. Unscrew and remove vent from case.

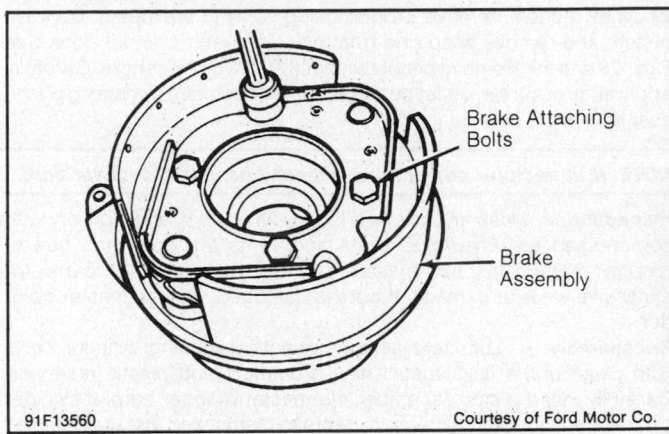

Brake Attaching Bolts

Brake Assembly

91F13560   Courtesy of Ford Motor Co.

Fig. 32: Removing Splash Shield & Brake Assembly ("F" Series Super Duty)

Reassembly – **1)** Using Bearing Cup Installer (T88T-2598-E), install bearing cup into case. Install inner bearing. Apply a light coat of sealer to outer edge of oil seal. Place oil seal in case with sealing lip facing inward. Press seal into case flush with bore surface using Seal Installer (T88T-2598-C).

2) Install actuating lever spring on boss in case. *See Fig. 33.* Apply a light coat of lithium base grease to actuating lever ball. Install ball end of lever into hole in boss through coiled end of spring. Position backing plate and brake assembly onto case.

3) Insert actuating lever (cam end) into position in brake assembly. Install and tighten brake assembly mount bolts. Attach return spring to actuating lever, and bend long end of spring to snap over lever. Place mainshaft with flanged end up in vise using brass jaw protectors.

4) Install brake drum and output flange onto flanged end of mainshaft. Install output flange onto brake drum, aligning marks made during disassembly. Proper installation maintains proper component balance. Install and tighten output flange mount nuts. Remove mainshaft and drum assembly from vise. Turn assembly over, and clamp in vise again.

5) Install case onto mainshaft, guiding shaft through oil seal and bearing. Using Bearing Installer (T88T-2598-F), seat output bearing onto mainshaft. Install speedometer drive gear and snap ring onto mainshaft. Using Bearing Cup Installer (T88T-2598-D), install input bearing cup into housing.

NOTE: Mainshaft shim determines end play. Shims are available in thicknesses of .0019" (.048 mm).

---

6) Install shim on mainshaft. Install inner bearing onto mainshaft. To measure end play, install bearing spacer, without "O" ring, onto mainshaft. Clamp case assembly and mainshaft in vise. Use Lock Nut Socket (T70T-4252-D) to screw hex nut onto mainshaft.

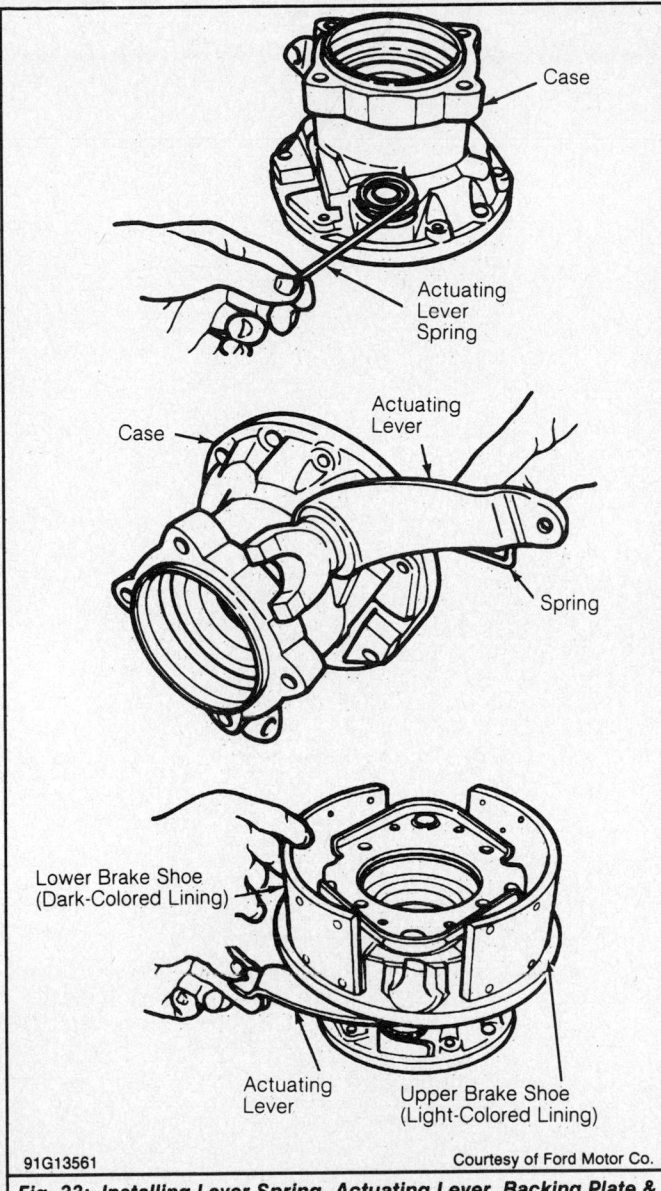

91G13561   Courtesy of Ford Motor Co.

Fig. 33: Installing Lever Spring, Actuating Lever, Backing Plate & Brake Assembly ("F" Series Super Duty)

Bearing Spacer

"O" Ring

91H13562   Courtesy of Ford Motor Co.

Fig. 34: Installing "O" Ring & Bearing Spacer ("F" Series Super Duty)

7) Mount a dial indicator between mainshaft and case. While rotating case assembly on mainshaft to center bearings, apply up and down pressure to take a reading. End play should be .0019-.0039" (.048-.099 mm). Select proper shim to reach specified end play.

8) Coat outer surface of new input oil seal with sealant. Install oil seal into case with sealing lip facing inward. Press seal in until it is fully seated. Install a new "O" ring in notch of bearing spacer. *See Fig. 34.* Install "O" ring and bearing spacer onto mainshaft until spacer butts against input bearing.

9) Use Lock Nut Socket (T70T-4252-D) to install a new lock nut onto shaft. Screw vent into case. Remove parking brake assembly from vise. Install onto vehicle. Fill case with Motorcraft MERCON multipurpose automatic transmission fluid. Fill to bottom of fill hole. To install remaining components, reverse removal procedure.

TORQUE SPECIFICATIONS
TORQUE SPECIFICATIONS

Application	Ft. Lbs. (N.m)
Backing Plate-to-Axle Bolt	
Aerostar, Explorer & Ranger	25-35 (34-47)
Bronco, E150 & F150	20-40 (27-54)
F250/350	50-70 (68-95)
Booster-To-Dash	13-25 (18-34)
Height Sensing Proportioning Valve	
Flex Hose Bolt	28-34 (38-46)
Linkage Arm	8-10 (11-14)
Mounting Bolts	12-18 (16-24)
Hydraulic Tube Nuts	
3/8" & 7/16"	10-15 (14-20)
1/2" & 9/16"	10-17 (14-23)
Master Cylinder-To-Booster	13-25 (18-34)
Pressure Differential Valve [1]	13-16 (18-22)

[1] – On Ranger only.

DISC BRAKE SPECIFICATIONS
DISC BRAKE SPECIFICATIONS

Application	In. (mm)
Lateral Runout [1]	
Aerostar, Explorer & Ranger	.003 (.08)
Bronco & F150 Integral (4WD)	.003 (.08)
Bronco & F150 2-Piece (4WD)	.005 (.13)
E150 & F150 (2WD)	.003 (.08)
E250/350 & F250/350 (2WD)	
Integral (Single Rear Wheels)	.003 (.08)
E350 & F350 (2WD)	
2-Piece (Dual Rear Wheels)	.005 (.13)
F250/350 (4WD)	.005 (.13)
"F" Series Super Duty	.008 (.20)
Parallelism	
Aerostar, Explorer & Ranger	[2]
Bronco & F150 Integral (4WD)	.0005 (.013)
Bronco & F150 2-Piece (4WD)	.0007 (.018)
E150 & F150 (2WD)	.0005 (.013)
E250/350 & F250/350 (2WD)	
Integral (Single Rear Wheels)	.0007 (.018)
E350 & F350 (2WD)	
2-Piece (Dual Rear Wheels)	.0010 (.025)
F250/350 (4WD)	.0010 (.025)
"F" Series Super Duty	.0010 (.025)
Discard Thickness	
Aerostar, Explorer & Ranger	.810 (20.60)
Bronco & E150/F150	1.120 (28.45)
E250/350 & F250/350	1.180 (29.97)
"F" Series Super Duty	1.43 (36.3)

[1] – Maximum runout before resurfacing is .010" (.25 mm). Maximum runout after resurfacing is .003" (.08 mm).

[2] – Information not available from manufacturer.

1992 BRAKES
Disc & Drum (Cont.)

DRUM BRAKE SPECIFICATIONS

DRUM BRAKE SPECIFICATIONS

Application	In. (mm)
Drum Diameter	
Aerostar, Explorer & Ranger (9")	9.00 (228.6)
Aerostar, Explorer & Ranger (10")	10.00 (254.0)
Bronco, E150 & F150	11.00 (279.4)
E250/350 [1] & F250 [1]/350 [2]	12.00 (304.8)
Maximum Drum Refinish Diameter	
Aerostar, Explorer & Ranger (9")	9.060 (230.10)
Aerostar, Explorer & Ranger (10")	10.060 (255.50)
Bronco, E150 & F150	11.060 (280.92)
E250/350 [1] & F250 [1]/350 [2]	12.060 (306.32)
Discard Thickness	
Aerostar, Explorer & Ranger (9")	9.090 (230.89)
Aerostar, Explorer & Ranger (10")	10.090 (256.29)
Bronco, E150 & F150	11.090 (281.69)
E250/350 [1] & F250 [1]/350 [2]	12.090 (307.09)

[1] – Includes Heavy Duty.
[2] – Includes "F" Series Super Duty.

Aerostar, Bronco, Explorer, Pickup, Ranger, Van

NOTE: Unless otherwise specified, references to Pickup include the F350 Super Duty commercial chassis.

NOTE: Prior to performing wheel alignment, perform visual and mechanical inspection of wheels, tires and suspension components. See PRE-ALIGNMENT INSTRUCTIONS in WHEEL ALIGNMENT THEORY & OPERATION article in GENERAL INFORMATION.

RIDING HEIGHT ADJUSTMENT

Before adjusting alignment, check riding height. Riding height must be checked with vehicle on level floor and tires properly inflated. Bounce vehicle several times and allow suspension to settle. Visually inspect vehicle for signs of abnormal height from front to rear or side to side. Check passenger compartment or vehicle bed for extra heavy items and remove if present.

Ride height is measured at center of front and rear wheel house opening. *See Fig. 1.* Maximum front side-to-side height difference is 5/8" (16 mm). Maximum rear side-to-side height difference is 3/4" (19 mm). If riding height is not as specified, check, repair or replace suspension components as necessary.

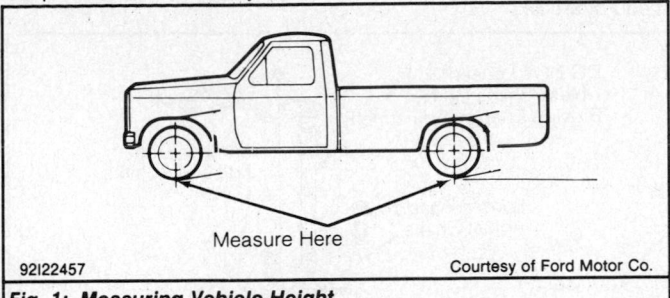

Measure Here

92122457   Courtesy of Ford Motor Co.

Fig. 1: Measuring Vehicle Height

JACKING & HOISTING

FLOOR JACK

Aerostar – To raise front of vehicle, position floor jack under horizontal portion of underbody frame member, behind front wheel of side to be lifted. *See Fig. 2.* To raise rear of vehicle, position floor jack under horizontal portion of underbody frame member, ahead of wheel on side to be lifted. Floor jack may also be used under front suspension lower control arms or rear axle.

All Other Models – Floor jack may be used under front suspension lower control arms or rear axle. *See Figs. 3-8.* Observe following precautions:

- Never use jack on any part of underbody.
- DO NOT raise entire vehicle at side rail, with jack midway between front and rear wheels, or permanent body damage may result.
- DO NOT allow lifting plate fingers to contact axle cover plate when lifting at rear axle housing.
- If vehicle is equipped with a stabilizer bar, DO NOT lift at rear axle housing.

AXLE CONTACT HOIST

Ensure hoist contacts lower control arms or front crossmember, and rear axle.

FRAME CONTACT HOIST

Aerostar – Vehicle may be raised on single-post or twin-post swiveling arm, or ramp-type drive hoist. If using single-post hoist, ensure lifting arms, pads or ramps are positioned at proper lifting points, and adequate underbody clearance is maintained. To ensure underbody clearance, place wooden blocks between lifting pads and frame at lift points. *See Fig. 2.*

If vehicle is raised on a twin-post hoist, use caution not to damage suspension, rear axle cover and/or steering linkage components. Front end adapters should be carefully positioned, as near wheels as possible, to ensure maximum contact under center of lower suspension arms or spring supports.

Rear suspension hoist adapters (forks) should be placed under rear axle tubes. These adapters must not interfere with lower control arm mounting brackets or hydraulic brake tubes. To avoid damage, DO NOT allow hoisting forks to contact axle housing rear cover, stabilizer bar or brackets.

All Other Models – Vehicle may be raised on single-post or twin-post swiveling arm, or ramp-type drive hoist as long as wide hoist adapters are used. If using single-post hoist, ensure lifting arms, pads or ramps are positioned at proper lifting points, and adequate underbody clearance is maintained.

If vehicle is to be raised on a twin-post hoist, use caution not to damage suspension, rear axle cover and/or steering linkage components. DO NOT allow lift pads to contact exhaust system components. *See Figs. 3-8.*

CAUTION: If single-post hoist is being used, add additional weight on rear end of vehicle before removing rear axle, fuel tank, spare tire or liftgate. This will prevent vehicle from tipping as center of gravity changes.

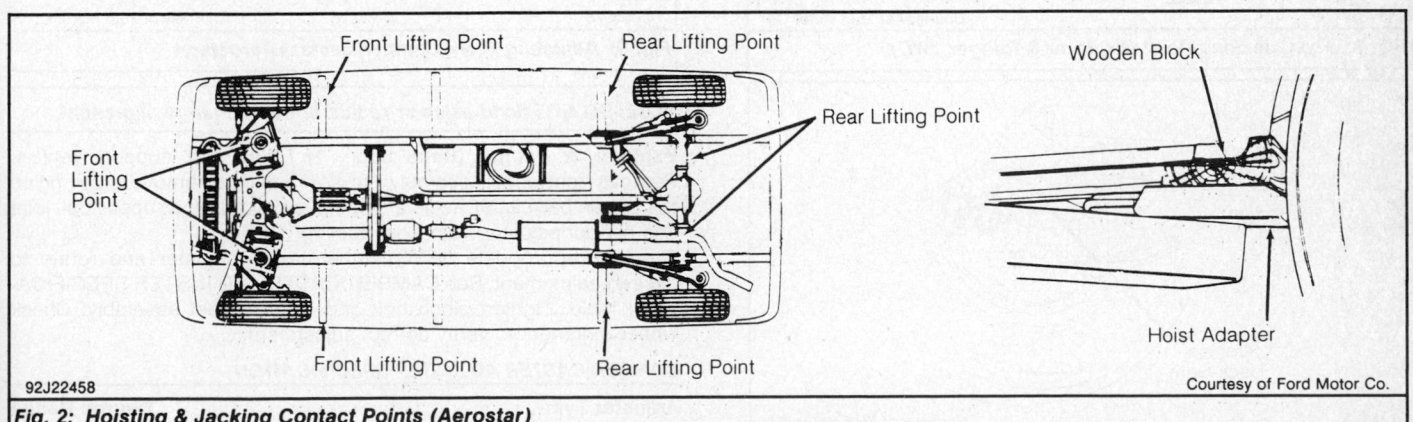

Front Lifting Point   Rear Lifting Point   Rear Lifting Point   Wooden Block

Front Lifting Point

Front Lifting Point   Rear Lifting Point

Hoist Adapter

92J22458   Courtesy of Ford Motor Co.

Fig. 2: Hoisting & Jacking Contact Points (Aerostar)

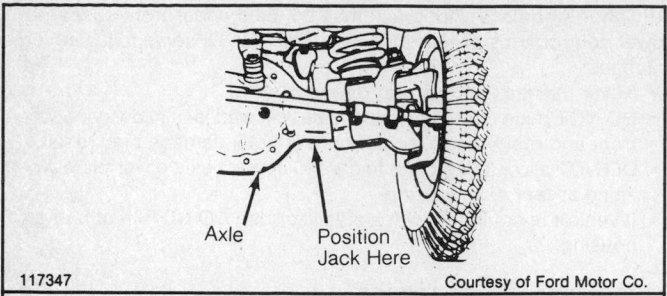

Axle

Position
Jack Here

117347   Courtesy of Ford Motor Co.

Fig. 3: Front Jacking Point (Bronco & F150/350 4WD)

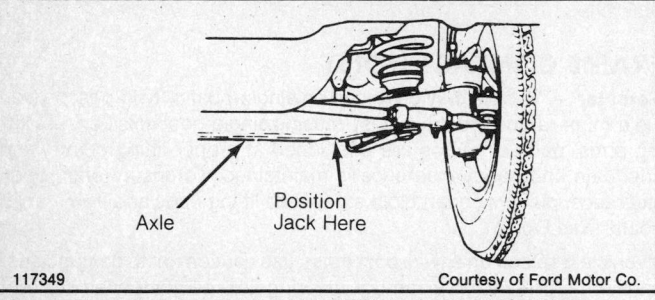

Axle

Position
Jack Here

117349   Courtesy of Ford Motor Co.

Fig. 4: Front Jacking Point (E150/250/350 & F250/350 2WD)

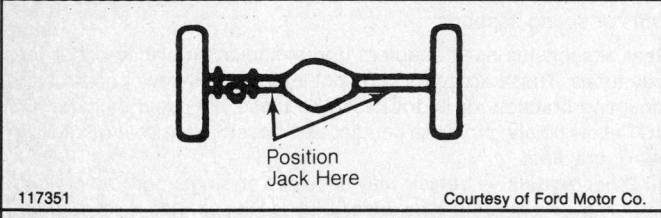

Position
Jack Here

117351   Courtesy of Ford Motor Co.

Fig. 5: Rear Jacking Point (E150/350 & F150/350 2WD & 4WD)

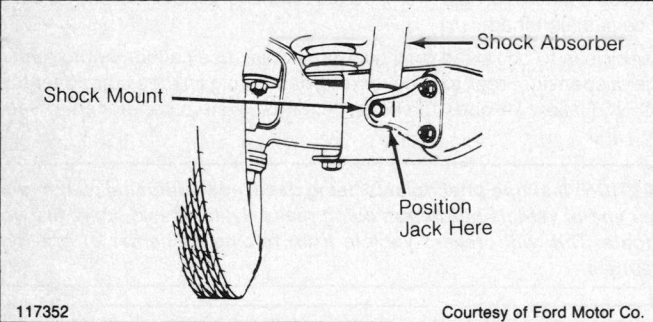

Shock Absorber

Shock Mount

Position
Jack Here

117352   Courtesy of Ford Motor Co.

Fig. 6: Front Jacking Point (Explorer & Ranger 2WD)

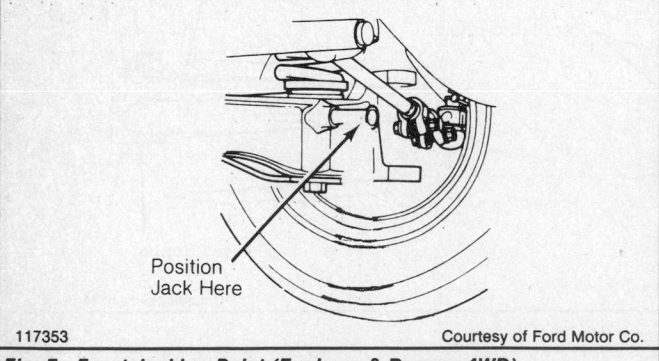

Position
Jack Here

117353   Courtesy of Ford Motor Co.

Fig. 7: Front Jacking Point (Explorer & Ranger 4WD)

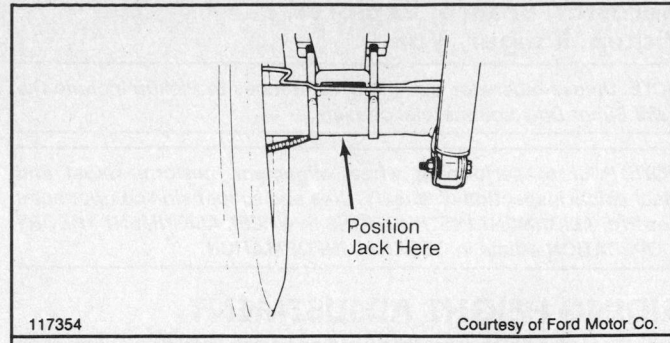

Position
Jack Here

117354   Courtesy of Ford Motor Co.

Fig. 8: Rear Jacking Point (Bronco, Explorer & Ranger)

WHEEL ALIGNMENT PROCEDURES

CAMBER & CASTER ADJUSTMENT

Aerostar – To adjust front camber, loosen 2 upper control arm nuts. Add or remove equal amount of shims from shim pack. Adding or removing an unequal amount of shims from shim pack will change caster. *See Fig. 9.* Tighten upper control arm nuts to specification when adjustment is complete. See TORQUE SPECIFICATIONS table at end of article.

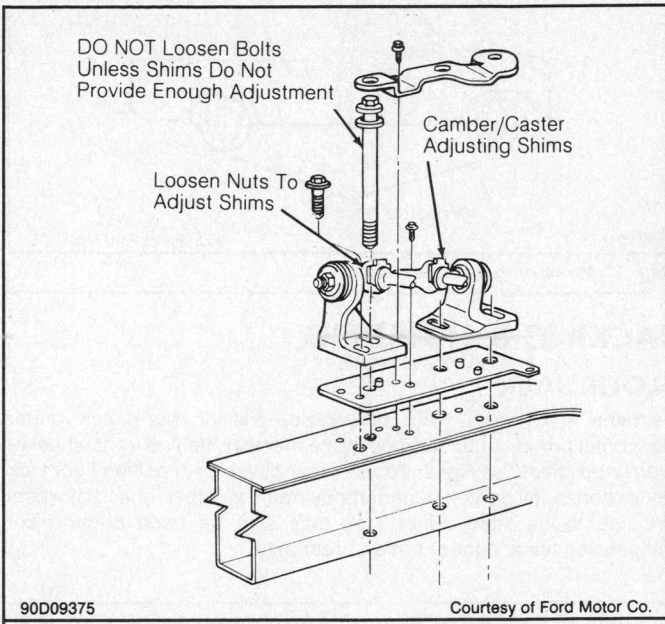

DO NOT Loosen Bolts
Unless Shims Do Not
Provide Enough Adjustment

Camber/Caster
Adjusting Shims

Loosen Nuts To
Adjust Shims

90D09375   Courtesy of Ford Motor Co.

Fig. 9: Adjusting Front Camber/Caster (Aerostar)

NOTE: DO NOT bend axles or radius arms to change alignment.

Explorer & Ranger (Dana 35) – 1) Raise and support vehicle. Remove front wheel assembly. On 4WD vehicles, remove snap ring on top of camber/caster adjuster. Remove pinch bolt at upper ball joint and pry out adjuster from axle. *See Fig. 10.*

2) Install appropriate NEW camber/caster adjuster and rotate to desired adjustment. See CAMBER/CASTER ADJUSTER SPECIFICATION table. Tighten pinch bolt and install wheel assembly. Check wheel alignment to verify correct adjustment.

CAMBER/CASTER ADJUSTER SPECIFICATION

Adjuster Type	Degree Range
0.5°	0.75
1.0°	2.0
1.5°	3.0

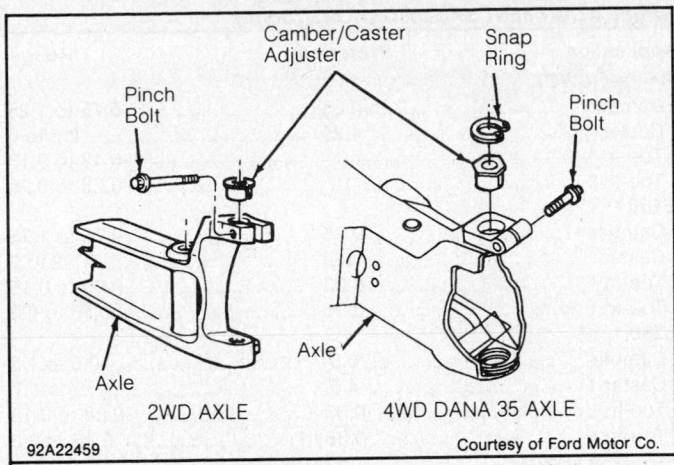

Fig. 10: *Adjusting Camber/Caster
(Explorer & Ranger 2WD & 4WD)*

92A22459   Courtesy of Ford Motor Co.

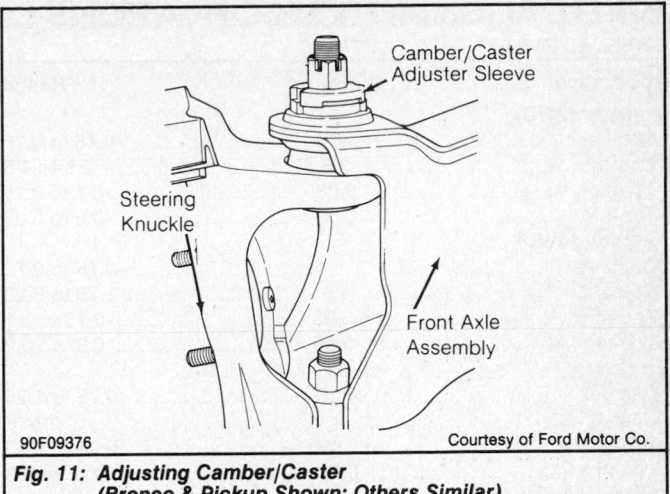

Fig. 11: *Adjusting Camber/Caster
(Bronco & Pickup Shown; Others Similar)*

90F09376   Courtesy of Ford Motor Co.

E150/350 & F150/350 – 1) Measure camber and caster to determine adjustment required. Record specifications for use in selection of camber/caster adjusters. To adjust, raise and support vehicle. Remove wheel assembly. Loosen pinch bolt at top of upper ball joint and pry adjuster out of axle.

2) Install appropriate NEW camber/caster adjuster and rotate to desired adjustment. See CAMBER/CASTER ADJUSTER SPECIFICATION table. Tighten pinch bolt to specification. See TORQUE SPECIFICATIONS table at end of article. Install wheel assembly. Check wheel alignment to verify correct adjustment.

Bronco & F150/350 – 1) Camber and caster can be adjusted by changing the upper ball joint mounting sleeve. If adjustment is required, raise vehicle and remove front wheel assembly.

2) Remove caliper. Remove upper ball joint cotter pin and nut. *See Fig. 11.* Loosen lower ball joint nut to end of stud. Break spindle loose from ball joint studs. Remove camber adjuster sleeve. Install replacement ball joint mounting sleeve.

3) If increased camber is required, point arrow on mounting sleeve outward. If decreased camber is required, point arrow on mounting sleeve inward. Install spindle. Apply Loctite and partially tighten lower ball joint nut.

4) Install NEW upper ball joint nut and tighten upper and lower ball joint nuts to specification. See TORQUE SPECIFICATIONS table at end of article. Install caliper and wheel assembly. Check alignment to verify correct adjustment.

F250 & F350 (4WD) – 1) Caster is adjustable on vehicles with leaf spring suspension systems. Adjustment is performed by inserting shims between spring and axle. Shims are available in zero, 1 and 2 degree increments. Zero degree shim is used to adjust side-to-side height. To adjust caster, raise vehicle and support front axle.

CAUTION: Caster should always be adjusted on right front axle to avoid changing front driveshaft alignment.

2) Loosen "U" bolt nuts and separate spring from axle. Install caster shim between spring and axle. Position thin edge of shim to front of vehicle to increase caster. Position thin edge of shim to rear of vehicle to decrease caster. Tighten "U" bolt nuts to specification. See TORQUE SPECIFICATIONS table at end of article. Check alignment to verify correct adjustment.

F350 (4WD) – Camber and caster are not adjustable on 4WD and F350 Super Duty monobeam-design vehicles.

TOE-IN ADJUSTMENT

Aerostar – Start engine. Center steering wheel. Secure steering wheel with holder and turn engine off. Loosen tie rod end lock nut. Loosen steering gear dust boot clamp(s) at tie rod end. Turn tie rod end to obtain correct toe-in. Tighten lock nut to specification. See TORQUE SPECIFICATIONS table at end of article. Ensure steering gear dust boot is straight after adjustment. Tighten dust boot clamp.

All Other Models – 1) Measure toe-in with front wheels straight ahead, and steering wheel locked in a centered position. Adjust toe-in by loosening clamps, and adjusting sleeve to obtain correct specification and maintain steering wheel in centered position.

2) If steering wheel is not centered prior to wheel alignment, determine which wheel assembly is out of adjustment, and compensate that side to center steering wheel. Multiple attempts may be necessary to properly center steering wheel.

3) When tightening clamps, ensure clamp bolts are positioned so there will be no interference with other parts throughout entire travel of steering linkage.

WHEEL ALIGNMENT SPECIFICATIONS

WHEEL ALIGNMENT SPECIFICATIONS

Application	Preferred	Range
Aerostar (2WD)		
Camber [1]	0	-0.75 to 0.75
Caster [1]	3.5	2.5 to 4.5
Toe-In [2]	0.03	-0.1 to 0.16
Toe-In [1]	0.06	-0.2 to 0.32
Aerostar (4WD)		
Camber [1]	0	-0.75 to 0.75
Caster [1]	4.5	3.75 to 5.25
Toe-In [2]	-0.03	-0.16 to 0.1
Toe-In [1]	-0.06	0.32 to 0.2
Bronco [3]		
Camber [1]	0.25	-0.75 to 1.25
Caster [1]	4	2 to 6
Toe-In [2]	0.03	-0.08 to 0.15
Toe-In [1]	0.06	0.16 to 0.3
Explorer (2WD)		
Camber [1]	0.25	-0.75 to 1.25
Caster [1]	5	4 to 6
Toe-In [2]	0	-0.13 to 0.13
Toe-In [1]	0	-0.25 to 0.25
Explorer (4WD)		
Camber [1]	0.25	-0.75 to 1.25
Caster [1]	4.25	2.5 to 6
Toe-In [2]	0	-0.13 to 0.13
Toe-In [1]	0	-0.25 to 0.25
Ranger (2WD)		
Camber [1]	0.25	-0.75 to 1.25
Caster [1]	4.75	3.5 to 6
Toe-In [2]	0	-0.13 to 0.13
Toe-In [1]	0	-0.25 to 0.25

WHEEL ALIGNMENT SPECIFICATIONS (Cont.)

Application	Preferred	Range
Ranger (4WD)		
Camber [1]	0.25	-0.75 to 1.25
Caster [1]	4.25	2.5 to 6
Toe-In [2]	0	-0.13 to 0.13
Toe-In [1]	0	-0.25 to 0.25
E150 [3]		
Camber [1]	0.25	-0.75 to 1.25
Caster [1]	4.5	2 to 7
Toe-In [2]	0.03	-0.08 to 0.15
Toe-In [1]	0.06	0.16 to 0.3
E250 [3]		
Camber [1]	0.5	-0.5 to 1.5
Caster [1]	4.5	2 to 7
Toe-In [2]	0.03	-0.08 to 0.15
Toe-In [1]	0.06	0.16 to 0.3
F150/250 (2WD) [3]		
Camber [1]	0.25	-0.75 to 1.25
Caster [1]	4	2 to 6
Toe-In [2]	0.03	-0.08 to 0.15
Toe-In [1]	0.06	-0.16 to 0.3
F150 (4WD) [3]		
Camber [1]	0.25	-0.75 to 1.25
Caster [1]	4	2 to 6
Toe-In [2]	0.03	-0.08 to 0.15
Toe-In [1]	0.06	-0.16 to 0.3
F250 (4WD)		
Camber [1]	0.25	-0.75 to 1.25
Caster [1]	3.5	2 to 5
Toe-In [2]	0.03	-0.08 to 0.15
Toe-In [1]	0.06	-0.16 to 0.3

[1] – Measurement in degrees.
[2] – Measurement in inches.
[3] – Specifications are for vehicles without aftermarket modifications. For vehicles with aftermarket modifications, *see Figs. 12-14.*

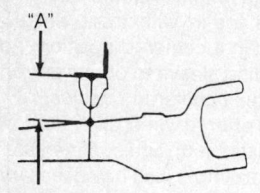

EXPLORER (2WD – RIGHT & LEFT)
RANGER (2WD – LEFT)

Bottom Of Spring Tower To Top Of Axle; Measured At Center Front Face Of Jounce Bumper

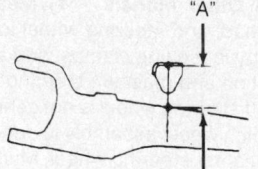

RANGER (2WD – RIGHT)

Bottom Of Spring Tower To Top Of Axle; Measured At Center Front Face Of Jounce Bumper

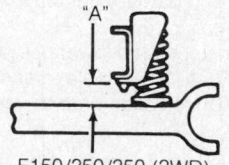

F150/250/350 (2WD)

Bottom Of Spring Tower To Top Front Face Of Axle; Measured At Center Of Jounce Bumper

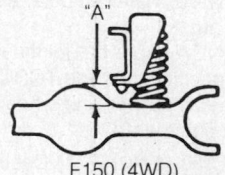

F150 (4WD)

Bottom Of Spring Tower To Top Of Axle; Measured At Center Front Face Of Jounce Bumper

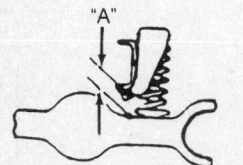

EXPLORER & RANGER (4WD)

Bottom Of Spring Tower At Top Of Axle; Measured At Outboard Front Face Of Jounce Bumper

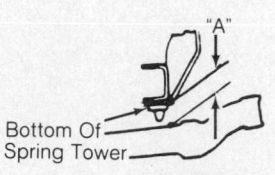

Bottom Of Spring Tower

E150/250/350

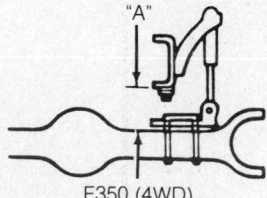

F250 (4WD)

Bottom Of Frame To Top Of Axle

F350 (4WD)

Monobeam Bottom Of Metal Jounce Stop To Top Of Spacer Front Spring Plate

92D22460   92E22461   92F22462   92G22463   92H22464   92I22465   92J22466   92A22467

Courtesy of Ford Motor Co.

Fig. 12: Measuring Front Axle Gap

NOTE: All graphs show the preferred specification. The tolerance from any specification is one degree (1°).

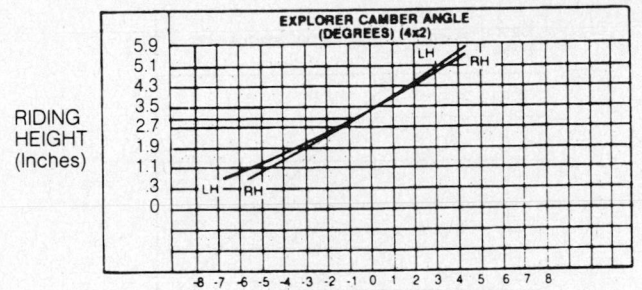

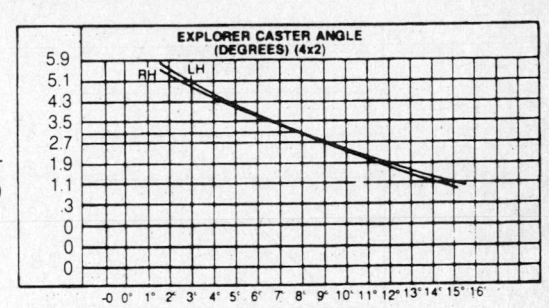

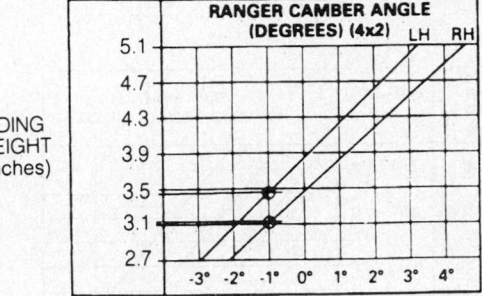

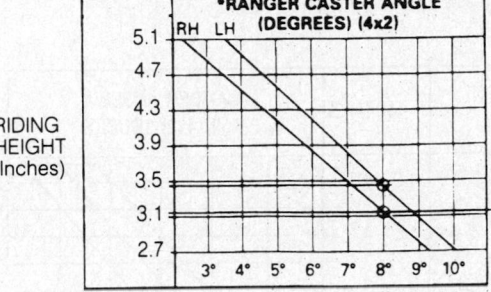

EXPLORER & RANGER (2WD)

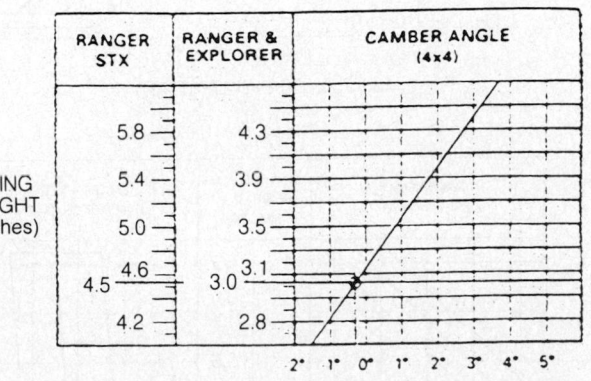

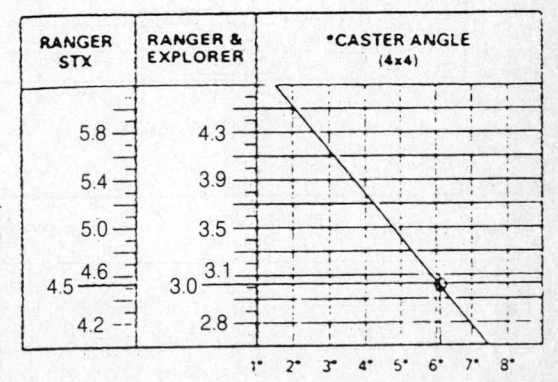

EXPLORER & RANGER (4WD)

92B22468   92C22469   92F22470   92G22471   92H22472   92I22473

Courtesy of Ford Motor Co.

Fig. 13: Camber/Caster Specification Graphs (Explorer & Ranger With Aftermarket Modifications)

1992 WHEEL ALIGNMENT
Specifications & Procedures (Cont.)

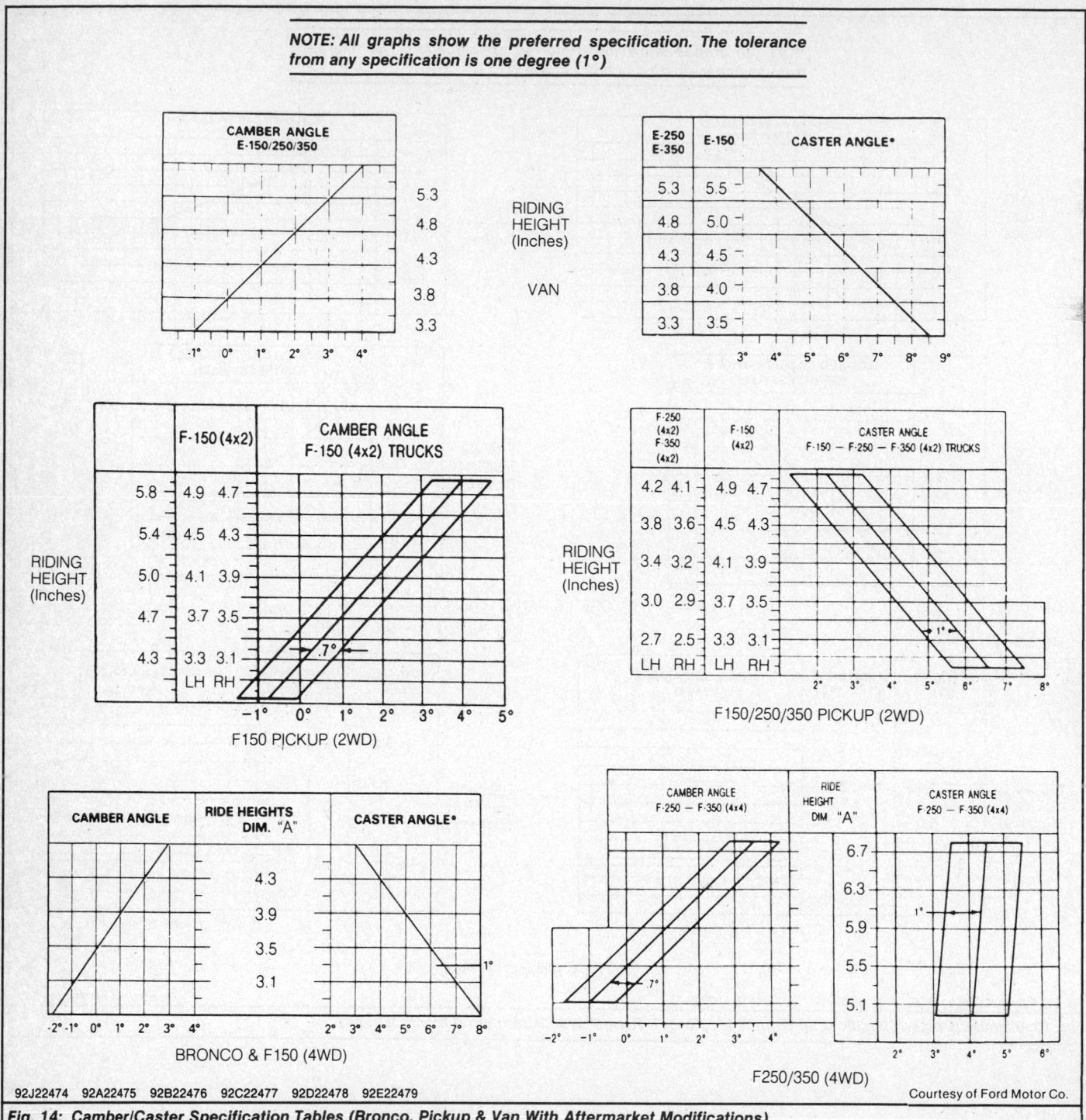

NOTE: All graphs show the preferred specification. The tolerance from any specification is one degree (1°)

92J22474   92A22475   92B22476   92C22477   92D22478   92E22479

Courtesy of Ford Motor Co.

Fig. 14: *Camber/Caster Specification Tables (Bronco, Pickup & Van With Aftermarket Modifications)*

TORQUE SPECIFICATIONS
TORQUE SPECIFICATIONS

Application	Ft. Lbs. (N.m)
Camber Adjuster Pinch Nut	48-65 (65-88)
Control Arm Nut	70-100 (95-136)
Lower Ball Joint Nut	95-110 (129-149)
Tie Rod End Clamp Nut	30-42 (41-57)
Tie Rod Lock Nut	43-50 (58-68)
"U" Bolt Nut	105 (142)
Upper Ball Joint Nut	85-100 (115-136)

DESCRIPTION

Front suspension is an unequal length control arm system. System consists of spindles, upper and lower control arms, ball joints, bushings, adjustment shims, coil springs, shock absorbers and a stabilizer bar. *See Fig. 1.*

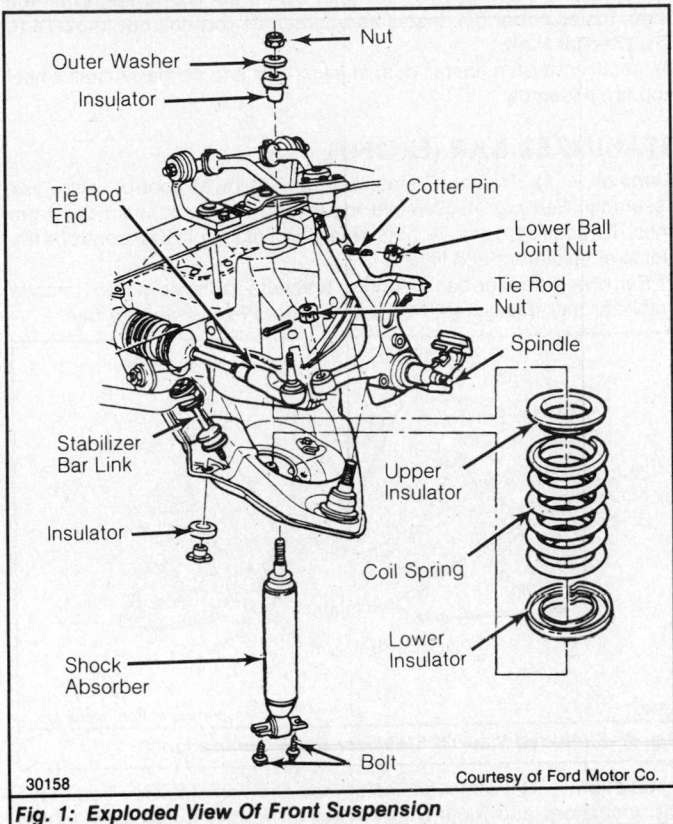

30158   Courtesy of Ford Motor Co.

Fig. 1: Exploded View Of Front Suspension

ADJUSTMENTS & INSPECTION

WHEEL ALIGNMENT SPECIFICATIONS & PROCEDURES

NOTE: See *SPECIFICATIONS & PROCEDURES article in WHEEL ALIGNMENT.*

WHEEL BEARING ADJUSTMENT

1) Raise and support vehicle. Remove wheel cover and grease cap. Remove cotter pin and retainer. Loosen adjusting nut 3 turns. Back off disc brake pads to obtain running clearance between rotor and pads.
2) While rotating wheel assembly, tighten adjusting nut to **17-25 ft. lbs. (23-34 N.m)** to seat bearing. Loosen adjusting nut 1/2 turn (180 degrees). Retighten to **18-20 INCH lbs. (2.0-2.3 N.m).**
3) Align retainer with cotter pin hole and place on adjusting nut. Install cotter pin. Install grease cap and wheel cover. Before driving vehicle, pump brake pedal several times to restore normal pedal position.

BALL JOINT CHECKING

Lower & Upper Ball Joint – Raise and support vehicle under axle. Move lower edge of tire in and out while watching lower spindle arm and lower part of axle jaw. If movement exceeds **1/32" (.794 mm)**, replace lower ball joint. To check upper ball joint, move upper edge of tire in and out. If movement between upper spindle arm and upper axle exceeds **1/32" (.794 mm)**, replace upper ball joint.

REMOVAL & INSTALLATION

NOTE: *Any time the steering linkage must be disconnected from the spindle, center the steering wheel and linkage.*

COIL SPRING

Removal – 1) Place steering wheel and steering system in the centered position. Raise vehicle on hoist. Remove tire and wheel assembly. Disconnect stabilizer bar link bolt from lower control arm.
2) Remove 2 shock absorber-to-lower control arm bolts. Remove upper nut and washer retaining shock absorber. Remove shock absorber.
3) Support vehicle with safety stands under vehicle jacking pads. Using Spring Compressor (D78P-5310-A), compress coil spring.
4) Loosen 2 lower control arm pivot bolts. Remove cotter pin. Loosen but DO NOT remove nut attaching lower ball joint to spindle.
5) Using Pitman Arm Puller (T64P-3590-F), loosen lower ball joint. Remove puller. Support lower control arm with a jack and remove ball joint nut. Lower control arm and remove spring.
Installation – Compress coil spring. Position coil spring assembly into lower control arm. To complete installation, reverse removal procedure.

LOWER CONTROL ARM

Removal – 1) Place steering wheel and steering system in centered position. Raise and support vehicle with safety stands under frame.
2) Remove coil spring. See COIL SPRING under REMOVAL & INSTALLATION. Remove lower control bolts. Remove lower control arm. Replace entire lower control arm assembly to service bushings.
Installation – 1) Position lower control arm in crossmember. Ensure bolts are installed in proper direction. *See Fig. 2.* Install nut and tighten until snug. DO NOT tighten nut to specified torque at this time.
2) Inspect lower ball joint boot seal for damage and replace if required. Install coil spring. With vehicle in normal ride height position, tighten lower control arm-to-crossmember bolts to **100-140 ft. lbs. (136-190 N.m).**

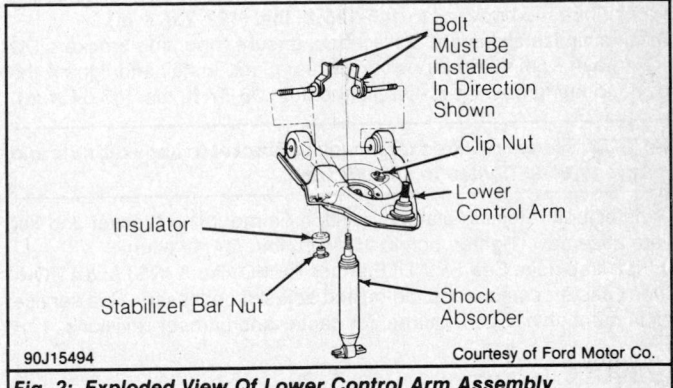

90J15494   Courtesy of Ford Motor Co.

Fig. 2: Exploded View Of Lower Control Arm Assembly

UPPER CONTROL ARM, BALL JOINT & MOUNTING BRACKETS

WARNING: *When servicing upper control arm and ball joint assemblies, service one side of vehicle at a time. DO NOT service both sides at the same time.*

Removal – 1) Place steering wheel and steering system in centered position. Raise and support vehicle with safety stands under body rail.
2) Remove spindle. See SPINDLE under REMOVAL & INSTALLATION. Remove bolt retaining bolt retainer plate and remove plate. Mark position of control arm mounting brackets on flat plate. *See Fig. 3.*

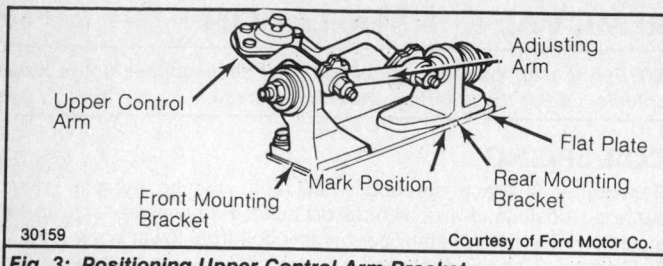

Fig. 3: Positioning Upper Control Arm Bracket

30159 — Courtesy of Ford Motor Co.

3) Remove bolt and washer retaining front mounting bracket to flat plate. From beneath frame rail, remove 3 nuts from bolts retaining 2 upper control arm mounting brackets to body rail.

4) Remove 3 long mounting bracket-to-body rail bolts by rotating upper control arm out of position. Remove upper control arm, adjusting arm, mounting bracket and flat plate from vehicle.

5) If servicing upper control arm/upper ball joint assembly or mounting bracket/adjusting arm assembly, remove nuts retaining upper control arm to adjusting arm.

6) Note exact position and number of shims on each control arm stud. Remove upper control arm from adjusting arm. Adjusting arm and mounting brackets are serviced as an assembly. Upper control arm and ball joint are serviced as an assembly.

Installation – 1) Install adjusting arm to control arm. Install shims, as removed, on control arm studs. Install and tighten nuts retaining shims to control arm.

2) Install boot seal on upper and/or lower ball joint. Place flat plate for mounting brackets in position on body rail. Install and tighten bolt to **10-14 ft. lbs. (14-18 N.m).**

3) Place mounting brackets and upper control arm assembly in position on flat plate. Install 3 long mounting bracket-to-body rail bolts.

4) Rotate or rock upper control arm and mounting bracket assembly until bolt heads rest against mounting bracket. Ensure studs extend through body rail.

5) Place mounting brackets in position marked on flat plate during removal. Install and tighten nuts and washers retaining mounting bracket bolts to body rail to **145-195 ft. lbs. (197-264 N.m).**

6) To minimize alignment corrections, ensure mounting brackets DO NOT move from marked position on flat plate. Install and tighten the front mounting bracket-to-flat plate bolt to **35-47 ft. lbs. (47-64 N.m).**

CAUTION: Torque required for mounting bracket to body rail nuts and bolts is critical. Tighten to specification.

7) Install bolt retaining plate in position on mounting bracket and flat plate assembly. Tighten bolt to **10-14 ft. lbs. (14-19 N.m).**

8) Install spindle. See SPINDLE under REMOVAL & INSTALLATION. Check caster, camber and toe-in, and adjust if necessary. Use service adjustment shims, as required, for caster and camber revisions.

SPINDLE

NOTE: When disconnecting steering linkage from spindle, place steering wheel in centered position.

Removal – 1) Raise and support vehicle with safety stands under the frame. Remove wheel and tire assembly. Remove caliper, rotor and dust shield from spindle. Remove cotter pin and tie rod end-to-spindle lower arm nut.

2) Using Pitman Arm Puller (T64P-3590-F), disconnect tie rod end. Ensure floor jack is supporting lower control arm. Remove cotter pin and loosen spindle-to-lower control arm joint nut.

WARNING: Use extreme caution in step 3) when lowering control arm. Coil spring may quickly expand with dangerous force.

3) Using Pitman Arm Puller (T64P-3590-F), loosen lower ball joint. Remove puller and ball joint retaining nut. With vehicle body supported on safety stands, slowly lower control arm until lower ball joint is disengaged from spindle.

4) Remove bolt and nut retaining spindle to upper control arm ball joint. Remove spindle from vehicle.

Installation – 1) Position spindle on upper ball joint. Install and tighten spindle nut and bolt to **27-37 ft. lbs. (37-50 N.m).** Inspect upper and lower ball joint boot seals for damage and replace (if necessary).

2) Install and tighten lower ball joint nut to **80-120 ft. lbs. (109-163 N.m).** Install cotter pin. Install and tighten tie rod end nut to **52-74 ft. lbs. (71-100 N.m).**

3) Install cotter pin. Install dust shield, rotor and caliper. Install wheel and tire assembly.

STABILIZER BAR (FRONT)

Removal – 1) Remove stabilizer bar-to-lower-control arm link assembly. *See Fig. 4.* Remove insulators and disconnect bar from links. If required, remove nuts retaining links to lower control arm. Remove insulators and links.

2) Remove stabilizer bar mounting brackets-to-frame bolts. Remove stabilizer bar. If required, remove insulators from stabilizer bar.

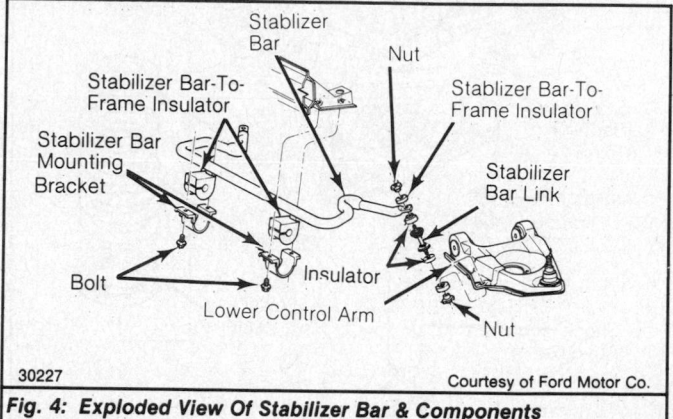

30227 — Courtesy of Ford Motor Co.

Fig. 4: Exploded View Of Stabilizer Bar & Components

Installation – 1) If removed, install insulators on stabilizer bar. Place bar, insulators and mounting bracket on frame. Install and tighten bolts to **16-24 ft. lbs. (22-33 N.m).**

2) Connect link and insulators to lower control arm. Connect links and insulators to stabilizer bar. Install and tighten nuts to **108-143 INCH lbs. (12-16 N.m).**

TORQUE SPECIFICATIONS
TORQUE SPECIFICATIONS

Application	Ft. Lbs. (N.m)
Bolt Retainer-To-Frame Bolt	10-14 (14-19)
Jounce Bumper-To-Frame Bolt	24-33 (33-45)
Lower Control Arm-To-No. 1	
Crossmember Bolt	[1] 100-140 (136-190)
Mounting Bracket-To-Frame	
Rail Bolt	145-195 (197-264)
Rebound Bumper-To-Frame Bolt	15-21 (20-27)
Shock Absorber	
To Lower Control Arm Bolt	16-24 (22-33)
To Upper Spring Seat Stud Nut	25-35 (34-47)
Spindle-To-Lower Ball Joint Nut	[2] 80-120 (109-163)
Spindle-To-Upper Ball Joint Nut	27-37 (37-50)
Stabilizer Bar Mounting	
Bracket-To-Frame Bolt	16-24 (22-33)
Tie Rod End-To-Spindle Arm Nut	[2] 52-74 (71-100)
Upper Control Arm-To-Adjusting	
Arm Nut	70-100 (95-136)
Wheel Lug Nut	100 (136)

	INCH Lbs. (N.m)
Stabilizer Bar-To-Lower Control Arm Nut	108-143 (12-16)
Stabilizer Bar-To-Stabilizer Link Nut	108-143 (12-16)

[1] – Tighten to specification with vehicle in normal ride height position and all other fasteners tightened to specification.

[2] – Tighten to specification and, if required, advance to next castellation to install cotter pin.

DESCRIPTION

Front suspension is coil spring, twin "I" beam-type. Suspension consists of coil spring, "I" beam axle arms, radius arm, upper and lower ball joint, spindle, tie rod, shock absorber and optional stabilizer bar. One end of each axle is attached to spindle and radius arm assembly. Other end is attached to a frame pivot bracket.

Spindle is connected to axle by upper and lower ball joints. Ball joints are sealed and do not require lubrication. Spindle movement is controlled by tie rods and steering linkage.

ADJUSTMENTS & INSPECTION

WHEEL ALIGNMENT SPECIFICATIONS & PROCEDURES

NOTE: See SPECIFICATIONS & PROCEDURES article in WHEEL ALIGNMENT.

WHEEL BEARING ADJUSTMENT

1) Raise and support vehicle. Remove wheel cover and grease cap. Remove cotter pin and retainer.

2) Loosen adjusting nut 3 turns. Obtain running clearance between brake rotor surface and lining by rocking entire wheel assembly several times to push caliper and brake pads away from rotor.

3) An alternate method of obtaining running clearance is to lightly tap on brake caliper housing. Do not tap on any area that may damage the rotor and lining. DO NOT pry on brake caliper piston.

4) Running clearance must be maintained throughout bearing adjustment procedure. If proper clearance cannot be maintained, brake caliper must be removed.

5) While rotating wheel, tighten adjusting nut to **17-25 ft. lbs. (23-34 N.m)**. Back off adjusting nut 1/2 turn (180 degrees). Tighten adjusting nut to **18-20 INCH lbs. (2.0-2.3 N.m)**. Install lock cap and new cotter pin.

6) Place retainer on adjusting nut. Align nut with cotter pin hole in spindle. If retainer will not align, remove retainer and reposition on adjusting nut. DO NOT turn adjusting nut to align cotter pin holes.

7) Install cotter pin. Check front wheel rotation. If wheel rotates properly, install grease cap and wheel cover.

8) If rotation is noisy or rough, remove, inspect and lubricate bearings. Before driving vehicle, pump brake pedal several times to restore normal pedal position.

BALL JOINT CHECKING

Lower & Upper Ball Joint – Raise and support vehicle under axle. Move lower edge of tire in and out while watching lower spindle arm and lower part of axle jaw. If movement exceeds 1/32" (.8 mm), replace lower ball joint. To check upper ball joint, move upper edge of tire in and out. If movement between upper spindle arm and upper axle exceeds 1/32" (.8 mm), replace upper ball joint.

REMOVAL & INSTALLATION

AXLE

Removal – 1) Remove spindle, coil spring and stabilizer bar (if equipped). See SPINDLE, COIL SPRING and STABILIZER BAR under REMOVAL & INSTALLATION.

2) Remove spring lower seat from radius arm. Remove stabilizer bar bracket and radius arm-to-front axle bolt. Remove axle-to-frame pivot bolt and remove axle.

Installation – 1) Install axle and axle-to-frame pivot bolt finger tight. See Fig. 1. Install opposite end of axle on radius arm. Install axle-to-radius arm bolt from underneath bracket and tighten to specification.

2) Install lower spring seat on radius arm. Ensure spring seat hole indexes over radius arm-to-axle bolt. Install remaining components. Tighten axle-to-frame pivot bolt to specification with vehicle at normal operating height. See TORQUE SPECIFICATIONS table at end of article.

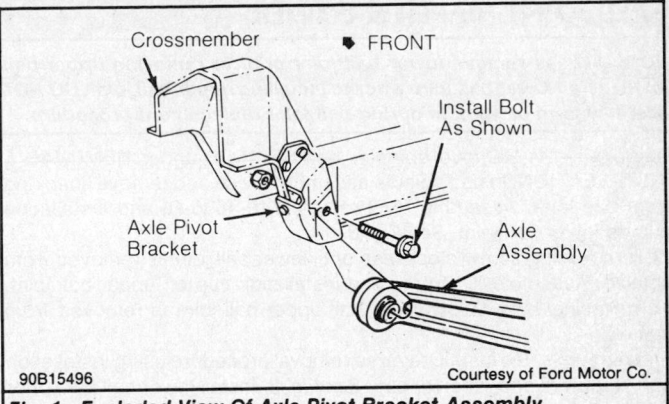

Fig. 1: Exploded View Of Axle Pivot Bracket Assembly

AXLE PIVOT BRACKET

Removal – Remove spindle and front axle. See SPINDLE and AXLE under REMOVAL & INSTALLATION. Remove axle pivot bracket bolts and bracket.

Installation – 1) Install axle pivot bracket on the frame. Install front and rear mounting bolts and retainers from inside of pivot bracket out through crossmember. See Fig. 1.

2) Loosely install nuts on outside of crossmember. Tighten nuts to specification. To complete installation, reverse removal procedure.

NOTE: Special nuts are used for this application to provide proper clearance. Use proper nuts or install a 0.20" (5.1 mm) thick hardened washer under each nut if standard nuts are used.

AXLE PIVOT BUSHING

Removal – 1) Remove coil spring. See COIL SPRING under REMOVAL & INSTALLATION. If left axle bushing is to be replaced, remove axle pivot bolt. Pull pivot end of axle downward until bushing is exposed.

2) If pivot bushing in right axle is to be removed, axle must be removed to gain access to pivot bushing. Remove axle. See AXLE under REMOVAL & INSTALLATION.

3) Install Forcing Screw (T78P-5638-A1), Bushing Remover (T80T-5638-A2) and Receiver Cup (T78P-5638-A3) onto pivot bushing. Turn forcing screw and remove pivot bushing. See Fig. 2.

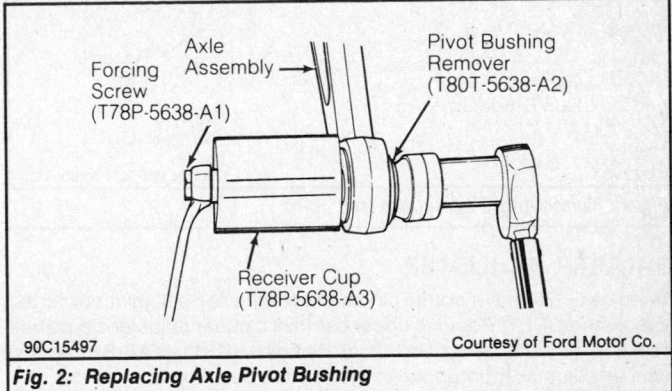

Fig. 2: Replacing Axle Pivot Bushing

Installation – Install bushing in axle using receiver cup, forcing screw and installation cup. To complete installation, reverse removal procedure. Lower vehicle. With weight on suspension, tighten pivot bushing nut to specification. See TORQUE SPECIFICATIONS table at end of article.

BALL JOINT (UPPER & LOWER)

NOTE: Always remove lower ball joint prior to removing upper ball joint. Install lower ball joint prior to installing upper ball joint. DO NOT heat ball joint or spindle during ball joint replacement procedure.

Removal – 1) Remove spindle. See SPINDLE under REMOVAL & INSTALLATION. Install spindle assembly in vise and remove snap ring from ball joint. Assemble "C" Frame (T74P-4635-C) and installation cup on lower ball joint. *See Fig. 3.*

2) Turn forcing screw clockwise until lower ball joint is removed from spindle. Assemble "C" frame and installation cup on upper ball joint. Turn forcing screw clockwise until upper ball joint is removed from spindle.

Installation – To install, reverse removal procedure using installation cup, adapters and receiver cup. *See Fig. 3.* Install lower ball joint prior to installing upper ball joint. Install spindle.

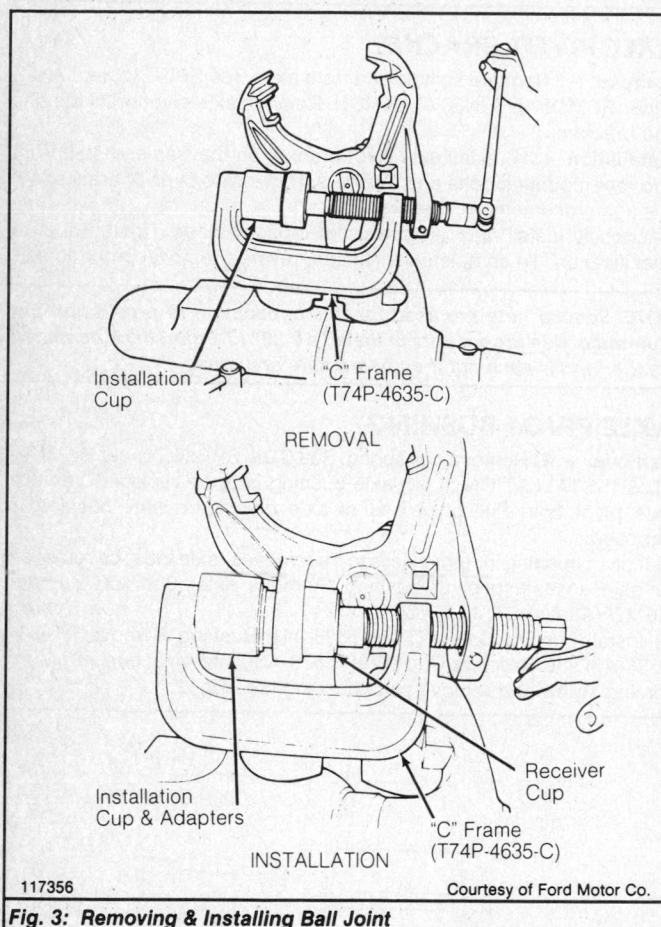

Fig. 3: Removing & Installing Ball Joint

CAMBER ADJUSTER

Removal – Remove cotter pin and loosen lower ball joint nut to the end of stud ONLY. Remove upper ball joint camber adjuster clamp bolt from top of axle. Using Ball Joint Remover (D81T-3010-B), remove camber adjuster from upper ball joint stud. *See Fig. 4.*

Installation – Install camber adjuster into axle. Ensure slot of adjuster aligns with axle. Install adjuster on upper ball joint stud. Install clamp bolt in axle and tighten to specification. Tighten lower ball joint nut to specification. See TORQUE SPECIFICATIONS table at end of article.

COIL SPRING

Removal & Installation – 1) Raise and support front of vehicle with safety stands under frame and place a jack under axle. Disconnect shock absorber from lower bracket. Remove nut holding lower retainer to spring seat. Remove lower retainer.

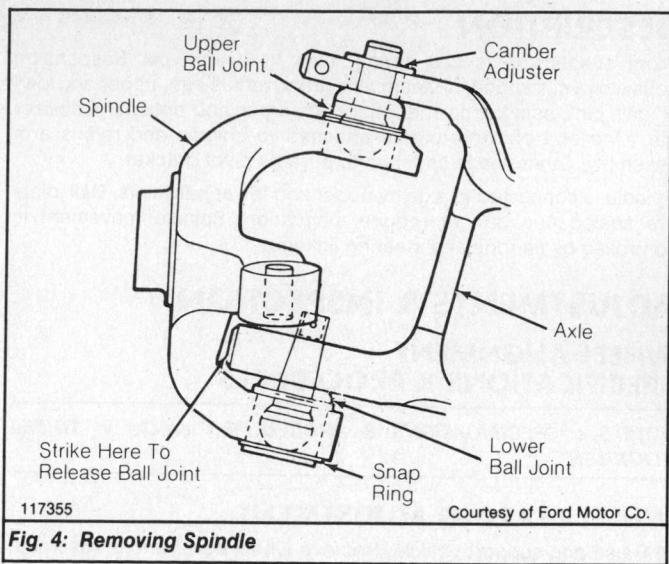

Fig. 4: Removing Spindle

NOTE: Axle must be supported by jack during removal and installation procedure. If brake hose length does not permit adequate clearance, remove brake caliper or compress spring with Spring Compressor (T81P-5310-A).

2) Lower axle as far as possible without stretching brake hose. Using pry bar, lift coil spring over bolt that passes through lower spring seat. Rotate spring so retainer on upper spring seat is cleared and remove spring. To install, reverse removal procedure.

RADIUS ARM

Removal & Installation – 1) Remove coil spring. See COIL SPRING under REMOVAL & INSTALLATION. Loosen axle pivot bolt. Remove lower spring seat from radius arm. Remove radius arm-to-axle bolt. *See Fig. 5.*

2) Remove nut and radius arm bushing from rear of radius arm. Remove inner bushing and retainer from radius arm stud. *See Fig. 5.* To install, reverse removal procedure.

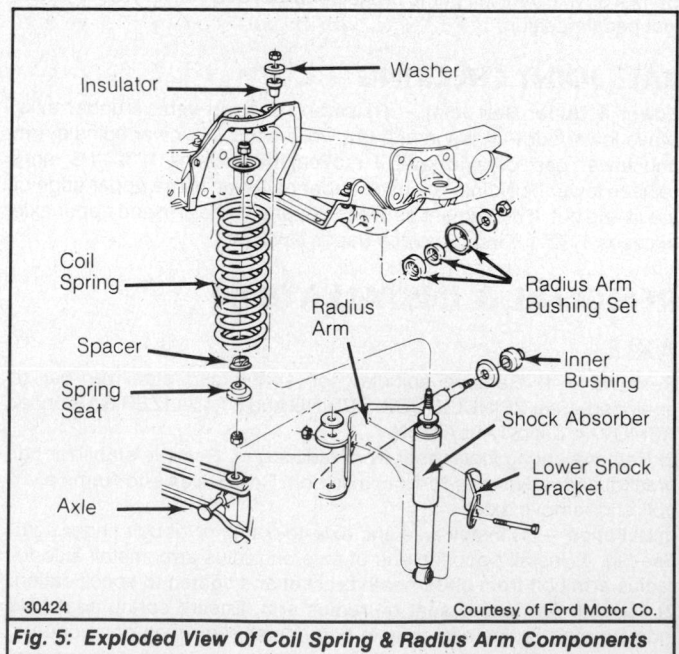

Fig. 5: Exploded View Of Coil Spring & Radius Arm Components

RADIUS ARM BUSHING

Removal & Installation – 1) Loosen radius arm-to-axle pivot bolt. Loosen upper shock absorber bolt and compress shock. Remove nut and washer attaching radius arm to radius arm bracket.

2) Remove bushing and components from rear of radius arm. Move radius arm and axle assembly forward, out of radius arm bracket. Remove inner bushing and retainer. To install, reverse removal procedure.

SHOCK ABSORBER

Removal & Installation – Remove nut and washer attaching shock absorber to spring seat. Remove nut and bolt retaining shock absorber to radius arm and lower shock bracket. Compress and remove shock absorber. To install, fully extend shock absorber and reverse removal procedure.

SPINDLE

Removal – 1) Raise and support front of vehicle. Remove wheel and tire assembly. Remove brake caliper from rotor and wire it to underbody to prevent damage to brake hose.

2) Remove dust cap, cotter pin, nut retainer, nut, washer and outer bearing. Remove rotor from spindle. Remove inner bearing and seal. Discard seal. Remove brake dust shield.

3) Remove tie rod end from spindle arm with Tie Rod End Remover (Tool-3290-D). Remove cotter pin from lower ball joint stud. Remove axle clamp bolt from axle. Note position of camber adjuster on top of axle.

4) Using Ball Joint Remover (D81T-3010-B), remove camber adjuster from upper ball joint stud and axle. Strike inside area of axle to release lower ball joint. See Fig. 4. Remove spindle and ball joint assembly from axle.

CAUTION: DO NOT use pickle fork to separate ball joint. This will damage the seal and ball joint socket.

Installation – 1) Ensure upper and lower ball joint seals are in place. Install spindle and ball joints in axle. Install camber adjuster in upper spindle over upper ball joint stud. Ensure slot of adjuster aligns with axle. See Fig. 6.

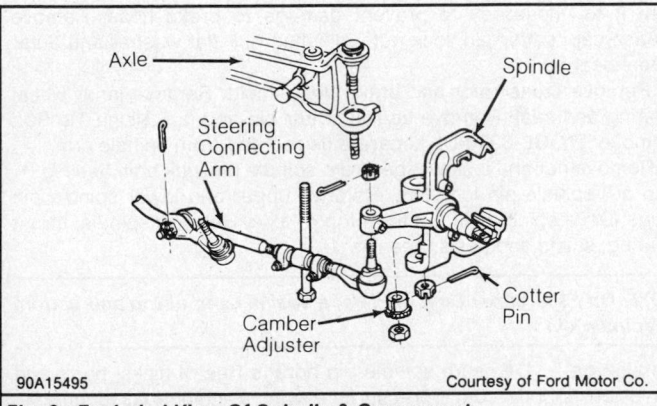

90A15495   Courtesy of Ford Motor Co.

Fig. 6: Exploded View Of Spindle & Components

2) If camber adjustment is required, special adapters must be installed. Install and tighten lower ball joint nut to specification. See TORQUE SPECIFICATIONS table at end of article. Continue tightening castellated nut until it lines up with hole in stud. Install cotter pin.

3) Install axle clamp bolt and tighten to specification. Install dust shield. Pack wheel bearings with bearing grease. Install hub and rotor on spindle. Install outer bearing, washer and nut.

4) Adjust wheel bearings. See WHEEL BEARING ADJUSTMENT under ADJUSTMENTS & INSPECTION. Install brake caliper. Connect tie rod end to spindle and tighten nut to specification. See TORQUE SPECIFICATIONS table.

STABILIZER BAR

CAUTION: Note direction of link installation between stabilizer bar and axle. Protrusion side of link must be installed facing outward.

Removal & Installation (Explorer) – Remove stabilizer link-to-front axle nut. Remove stabilizer mounting bolts. Remove stabilizer bar. To install, reverse removal procedure.

Removal & Installation (Ranger) – Remove "U" bolts and mount bolts retaining stabilizer bar bushing and shock absorber bracket to radius arm. Remove retainers, stabilizer bar and bushings. To install, reverse removal procedure.

TORQUE SPECIFICATIONS

TORQUE SPECIFICATIONS

Application	Ft. Lbs. (N.m)
Axle Clamp Bolt	48-65 (65-88)
Axle Pivot Bolt [1]	120-150 (163-203)
Axle Pivot Bracket-To-Frame Bolt	
Explorer	77-110 (104-149)
Ranger	70-92 (95-125)
Axle-To-Radius Arm Bolt	191-231 (258-312)
Ball Joint Stud Nut [2]	104-146 (141-198)
Explorer	95-110 (129-149)
Ranger	104-146 (141-198)
Bumper-To-Spring Seat Bolt	11-19 (15-26)
Radius Arm Bracket-To-Frame Bolt	77-110 (104-149)
Radius Arm-To-Frame Nut	81-120 (110-163)
Shock Absorber-To-Radius Arm Nut	40-63 (54-85)
Shock Absorber-To-Spring Seat Nut	25-35 (34-47)
Stabilizer Bar	
Explorer	
Mount Bolt	35-50 (47-68)
Stabilizer Link-To-Axle Bracket Bolt	29-44 (39-60)
Stabilizer Link-To-Stabilizer Bar Nut	40-60 (54-81)
Ranger	
Mount Bolt	35-50 (47-68)
Stabilizer Bar "U" Bolt	35-50 (47-68)
Stabilizer Link-To-Stabilizer Bar Nut	30-44 (41-60)
Tie Rod Nut [2]	51-75 (69-102)

[1] – Tighten to specification with vehicle in normal ride height position and all other fasteners tightened to specification.

[2] – Tighten to specification and, if required, advance to next castellation to install cotter pin.

1992 SUSPENSION
Front – Pickup & Van 2WD

NOTE: Unless otherwise specified, references to Pickup include the F350 Super Duty commercial chassis.

DESCRIPTION

On all models except F350 Super Duty, front suspension consists of a coil spring, twin "I" beam-type front axle assembly. "I" beams are mounted to a frame pivot bracket at one end, and to spindle and a radius arm at the other. Springs are mounted between frame spring pocket and axle.

F350 Super Duty models use leaf springs with a solid "I" beam axle. Springs are attached to fixed bracket on the rear and movable shackle on the front.

ADJUSTMENTS & INSPECTION

WHEEL ALIGNMENT SPECIFICATIONS & PROCEDURES

NOTE: See SPECIFICATIONS & PROCEDURES article in WHEEL ALIGNMENT.

WHEEL BEARING ADJUSTMENT

Pickup & Van Except F350 Super Duty Stripped Chassis – 1) Raise and support vehicle. Remove wheel cover and grease cap. Remove cotter pin and retainer. Loosen adjusting nut 3 turns.
2) Obtain running clearance between brake rotor surface and lining by rocking entire wheel assembly several times to push caliper and brake pads away from rotor.
3) An alternate method of obtaining running clearance is to lightly tap on brake caliper housing. DO NOT tap on any area which may damage rotor and lining. DO NOT pry on brake caliper piston.
4) Running clearance must be maintained throughout bearing adjustment procedure. If proper clearance cannot be maintained, caliper must be removed.
5) Tighten adjusting nut to **17-25 ft. lbs. (23-34 N.m)** while rotating brake rotor in opposite direction. Back off adjusting nut 120-180 degrees. Install retainer and NEW cotter pin without loosening retaining nut. Bearing end play should be **.00025-.005" (.006-.127 mm)**. Bend ends of cotter pin around castellated flange of lock nut.
F350 Super Duty Stripped Chassis – 1) Raise and support vehicle. Remove wheel cover and grease cap. Remove cotter pin and retainer. Loosen adjusting nut 3 turns.
2) Obtain running clearance between brake rotor surface and lining by rocking entire wheel assembly several times to push caliper and brake pads away from rotor.
3) An alternate method of obtaining running clearance is to lightly tap on brake caliper housing. DO NOT tap on any area which may damage rotor and lining. DO NOT pry on brake caliper piston.
4) Running clearance must be maintained throughout bearing adjustment procedure. If proper clearance cannot be maintained, caliper must be removed.
5) Tighten adjusting nut to **17-25 ft. lbs. (23-34 N.m)** while rotating brake rotor in opposite direction. Back off adjusting nut 120-180 degrees. Tighten adjusting nut to **18-20 INCH lbs. (2.03-2.26 N.m)** while rotating brake rotor. Install retainer and NEW cotter pin without loosening retaining nut. Bearing end play should be **.00025-.005" (.006-.127 mm)**. Torque required to turn hub should be **10-25 INCH lbs. (1.13-2.82 N.m)**. Bend ends of cotter pin around castellated flange of lock nut.

BALL JOINT & SPINDLE PIN CHECKING

Raise and support vehicle. Ensure wheel bearings are properly adjusted. Grasp lower edge of tire and move wheel in and out while watching for spindle movement. Spindle movement must not exceed **1/32" (.794 mm)** at upper or lower arms, relative to axle. If movement exceeds limit, replace ball joints or install new spindle pins and bushings.

REMOVAL & INSTALLATION

FRONT WHEEL BEARINGS

Removal & Installation – 1) Raise front of vehicle, and remove wheels. Remove brake caliper, and wire it to underbody to prevent damage to brake hose.
2) Remove grease cap from hub. Remove cotter pin, lock nut, adjusting nut and flat washer from spindle. Remove outer wheel bearing. Pull hub and rotor from spindle. Remove grease seal and inner wheel bearing.
3) Clean bearings, inspect for damage and replace as necessary. Fill inside of hub, flush with inside diameter of beading cones, with Lithium-base grease. To complete installation, reverse removal procedure. Adjust wheel bearings. See WHEEL BEARING ADJUSTMENT under ADJUSTMENTS & INSPECTION.

SHOCK ABSORBER

Removal & Installation (Van) – Remove upper shock retaining nut. Disconnect shock absorber from lower bracket. Remove shock absorber, washers and rubber insulators. To install, reverse removal procedure using NEW rubber bushings. See appropriate TORQUE SPECIFICATIONS table at end of article.
Removal (Pickup Except F350 Super Duty) – Hold upper shock retaining nut. Loosen stud by turning hex on exposed lower part of stud. Disconnect shock absorber from lower bracket. Compress shock absorber and remove shock absorber. Cut bushing from upper spring seat. See appropriate TORQUE SPECIFICATIONS table at end of article.
Installation – To install, reverse removal procedure. Coat upper spring seat with soap solution and install NEW insulator.
Removal & Installation (F350 Super Duty) – 1) Remove shock absorber-to-upper bracket nut. Remove shock absorber-to-spring spacer nut and remove shock absorber.
2) To install, reverse removal procedure. Coat upper spring seat with soap solution and install NEW bushing.

SPINDLE

Removal (Van & F350 Super Duty) – 1) Raise vehicle and support under front axle. Remove wheel assembly. Remove brake caliper, and wire it to underbody to prevent damage to brake hose. Remove grease cap, cotter pin, lock nut, adjusting nut, flat washer and outer wheel bearing.
2) Remove brake rotor and brake dust shield. Remove inner wheel bearing and seal. Remove tie rod cotter pin and nut. Using Tie Rod Remover (TOOL-3290-D), separate tie rod end from spindle arm.
3) Remove nut and lock washer from spindle pin lock bolt. See Fig. 1. Tap out spindle pin lock bolt. Remove upper and lower spindle pin plugs. Drive spindle pin out from top of axle. Remove spindle, thrust bearing, shims and seals. See Fig. 1.

NOTE: On F350 Super Duty models, a seal is used at top and bottom of spindle pin.

Installation – 1) Ensure spindle pin bore is free of nicks, burrs and corrosion. Lightly coat bore surface with a lithium-based grease. Install spindle pin seal with metal backing facing toward the bushing.
2) Press seal into position. Use care not to bend seal casing. Install NEW thrust bearing with lip flange facing toward lower bushing. Install thrust bearing until firmly seated against spindle surface.
3) Lightly coat bushing surface with lithium-based grease and place spindle in position on axle. Hold spindle and thrust bearing tightly against axle and measure distance between spindle and top of axle. Select proper thickness shim(s) and install.
4) Install spindle pin with "T" marking toward top, and notch in pin aligned with spindle pin lock bolt hole in axle. Drive spindle pin through bushings from top of axle until spindle pin notch aligns with spindle pin lock bolt hole. Install spindle pin lock bolt with threads pointing forward and groove facing spindle pin notch.

5) Firmly drive spindle pin lock bolt into position, and install lock washer and nut. Tighten nut to specification. Install upper and lower plugs and tighten to specification. See appropriate TORQUE SPECIFICATIONS table at end of article.

6) Lubricate spindle pin and bushings through grease fittings until grease seeps past upper seal at top and from thrust bearing slip joint at bottom. If grease fails to appear, recheck installation procedure.

7) To complete installation, reverse removal procedure. Adjust wheel bearings. See WHEEL BEARING ADJUSTMENT under ADJUSTMENTS & INSPECTION. Check and adjust toe-in.

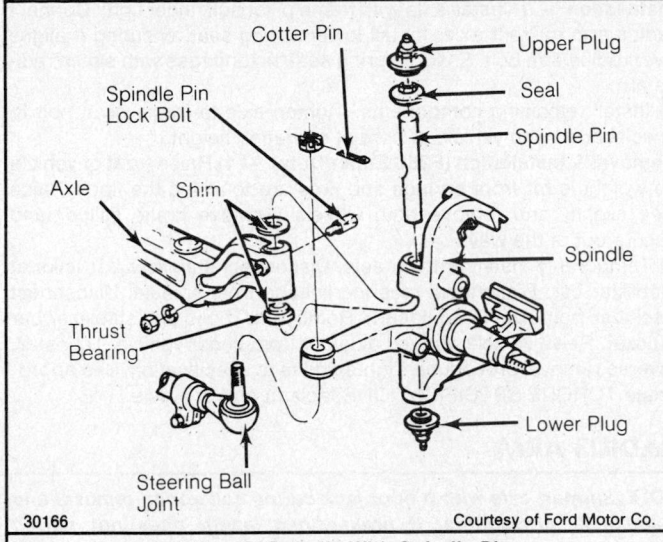

Fig. 1: Exploded View Of Spindle With Spindle Pin Assembly (Typical)

Removal (Pickup Except F350 Super Duty) – 1) Raise vehicle and support under front axle. Remove wheel assembly. Remove brake caliper, and wire it to underbody to prevent damage to brake hose. Remove grease cap, cotter pin, lock nut, adjusting nut, flat washer and outer wheel bearing.

2) Remove brake rotor and brake dust shield. Remove inner bearing and seal. Remove cotter pin and nut from tie rod end. Using Tie Rod Remover (TOOL-3290-D), remove tie rod end from spindle arm.

3) Remove cotter pin and nut from lower ball joint. Remove nut from axle clamp bolt and remove bolt. Note position of camber adjuster on top of axle. See Fig. 2. Remove camber adjuster from upper ball joint.

4) Strike axle to break lower ball joint loose from axle. See Fig. 2. Remove spindle assembly.

CAUTION: DO NOT use pickle fork to separate ball joint from spindle, as seal and ball joint socket will be damaged.

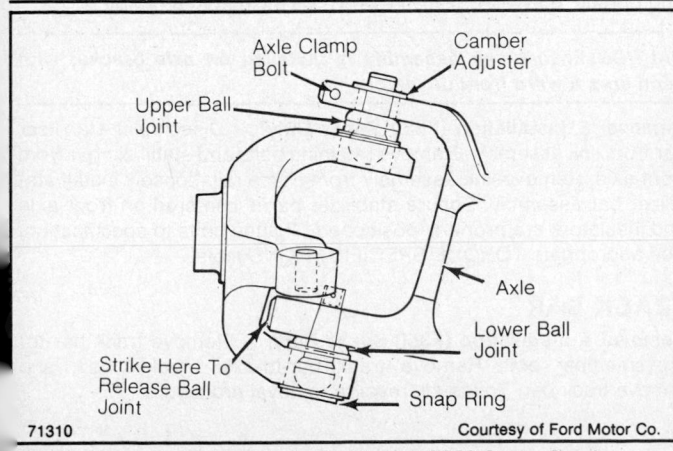

Fig. 2: Removing Pickup Spindle (Except F350 Super Duty)

Installation – 1) Ensure ball joint seals are in position. Place spindle and ball joints into axle. Install lower ball joint nut and tighten to specification. See appropriate TORQUE SPECIFICATIONS table at end of article.

2) Install camber adjuster over upper ball joint stud. Ensure camber adjuster is properly aligned. If camber adjustment is required, special camber adjusters must be installed. Tap camber adjuster into spindle. Tighten upper ball joint nut to specification.

3) Install cotter pin. Install axle clamp bolt and tighten to specification. To complete installation, reverse removal procedure. Adjust wheel bearings. See WHEEL BEARING ADJUSTMENT under ADJUSTMENTS & INSPECTION. Check and adjust toe-in. See SPECIFICATIONS & PROCEDURES article in WHEEL ALIGNMENT.

SPINDLE PIN BUSHINGS

Removal & Installation (Van & F350 Super Duty) – 1) Remove spindle. See SPINDLE under REMOVAL & INSTALLATION. Install spindle in a vise.

2) On E150 models, use Reamer (T53T-3110-DA), Bushing Remover/Installer Driver (D82T-3110-G) and Driver Handle (D82T-3110-C) for bushing service.

3) On E250/350 models, use Reamer (D82T-3110-A), Bushing Remover/Installer Driver (D82T-3110-B) and Driver Handle (D82T-3110-C) for bushing service.

4) On F350 Super Duty models, use Reamer (D88T-3110-BH), Bushing Remover/Installer Driver (D88T-3110-AH) and Driver Handle (T80T-4000-W) for bushing service.

5) On all applications, each side of bushing remover/installer driver is marked with "T" or "B". Use "T" side to install top spindle bushing and "B" side for bottom spindle bushing. Remove seal from bottom of upper bushing bore. Top spindle bushing should be removed first. Install driver handle through bottom bore.

6) Position new bushing on "T" side of bushing remover/installer driver so bushing open end grooves will face outward when installed. Position new bushing and remover/installer driver over old bushing. Drive old bushing out, while installing new bushing. Install bushing until remover/installer driver is seated.

7) Bushing must be installed minimum distance of .080" (2.03 mm) from bottom of upper spindle boss. Using "B" side, repeat procedure and install bottom bushing. Proper minimum depth of bottom bushing is 0.130" (3.30 mm) from top of lower spindle boss. Using reamer, ream bushings I.D. to be .001-.003" (.03-.08 mm) larger than diameter of new spindle pin. Ream top bushing first.

8) Install smaller diameter of reamer through top bore and into bottom bore until cutting blades are positioned in top bushing. Rotate reamer until cutting blades clear top bushing.

9) Ream bottom bushing. Larger diameter portion of reamer acts as a pilot in top bushing to properly ream bottom bushing. Remove all metal shavings and lubricate bushings and spindle pins.

10) Install a new seal on bushing remover/installer driver on side marked with "T" stamping. Using handle and remover/installer driver, install seal in bottom of top bushing bore. To complete installation, reverse removal procedure.

BALL JOINTS

Removal (Pickup Except F350 Super Duty) – 1) Remove spindle. See SPINDLE under REMOVAL & INSTALLATION. Install spindle in a vise. Remove snap ring from lower ball joint.

2) Using "C" Frame (T74P-4635-C) and Receiver Cup (D81T-3010-A4), rotate forcing screw clockwise until ball joint is removed from spindle. Repeat procedure to remove upper ball joint. See Fig. 3.

CAUTION: DO NOT heat ball joint or spindle when replacing ball joint.

Installation – 1) Lower ball joint must be installed first. Install lower ball joint squarely in spindle. Using "C" Frame, Receiver Cup, Installation Cup and Adapters (D81T-3010-A1 and D81T-3010-A3), install ball joint until firmly seated.

2) Repeat procedure for upper ball joint installation. Install snap rings. To complete installation, reverse removal procedure. Tighten bolts/

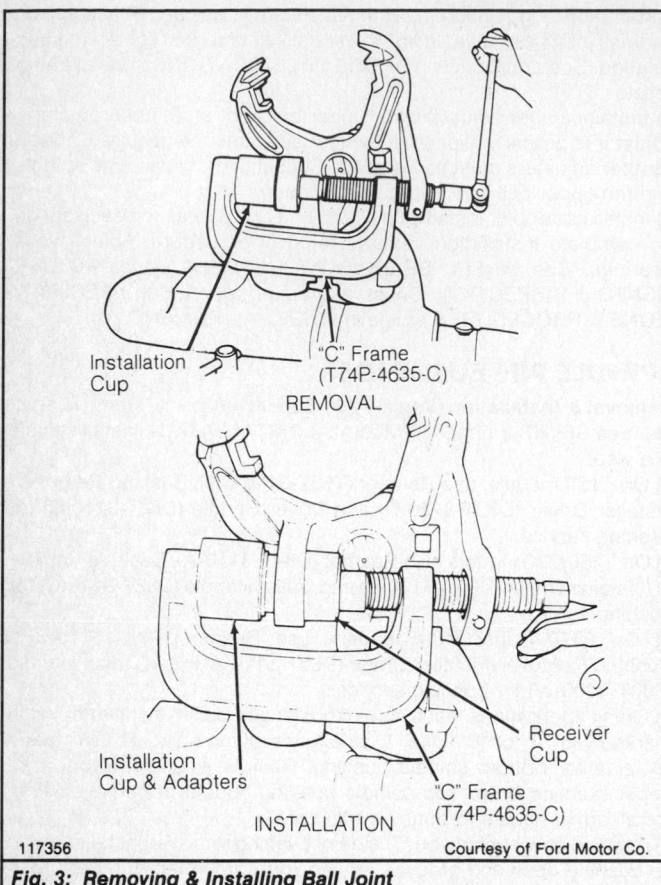

Installation Cup

"C" Frame (T74P-4635-C)

REMOVAL

Installation Cup & Adapters

Receiver Cup

"C" Frame (T74P-4635-C)

INSTALLATION

117356   Courtesy of Ford Motor Co.

Fig. 3: Removing & Installing Ball Joint (Pickup Except F350 Super Duty)

nuts to specifications. See appropriate TORQUE SPECIFICATIONS table at end of article.

COIL SPRING

NOTE: Support axle with a floor jack during coil spring removal and installation procedures. If brake hose length does not permit adequate clearance, remove brake caliper.

Removal (Pickup & Van Except F350 Super Duty) – Raise front of vehicle with jack stands under frame and floor jack under axle. Disconnect shock absorber from lower bracket. Remove upper spring retainer bolts and remove retainer. Remove lower spring retainer-to-spring seat and axle. Lower floor jack and remove spring.

Installation – Place spring in position and slowly raise front axle. Position spring lower retainer over stud, lower insulator (if equipped), and lower seat. Position upper retainer over spring coil and against spring upper seat. Tighten bolts/nuts to specification. See appropriate TORQUE SPECIFICATIONS table at end of article. To complete installation, reverse removal procedure.

LEAF SPRING

Removal (F350 Super Duty) – 1) Raise front of vehicle so weight is off front springs and tires are touching the floor. Support axle with jack to release weight from spring "U" bolts.

2) Disconnect shock absorber from spring spacer. Spacer is located below "U" bolts. Remove front and rear spring shackle bolts and stabilizer bar bracket. Remove "U" bolts and leaf spring.

Installation – To install, reverse removal procedure. Apply Lubricant (C1AZ-19590-BA) to spring bushings prior to shackle bolt installation.

Ensure spring is aligned with spring seat and axle. Tighten bolts to specification. See appropriate TORQUE SPECIFICATIONS table at end of article.

FRONT AXLE

Removal (Pickup & Van Except F350 Super Duty) – Remove spindle. See SPINDLE under REMOVAL & INSTALLATION. Remove coil spring and stabilizer bar (if equipped). Remove lower spring seat from radius arm. Remove radius arm-to-front axle bolt. Remove axle-to-frame pivot bolt and remove axle.

Installation – 1) Install axle with frame pivot bolt finger tight. Connect radius arm to front axle. Install lower spring seat, ensuring it aligns over radius arm bolt. Ensure spring seat pin engages with slot in radius arm.

2) Install remaining components. Tighten axle-to-frame pivot bolt to specification with vehicle at normal operating height.

Removal & Installation (F350 Super Duty) – 1) Raise front of vehicle so weight is off front springs and tires are touching the floor. Raise axle slightly and remove both wheels. Remove brake caliper and secure out of the way.

2) Temporarily install both wheels. Disconnect stabilizer bar links at stabilizer bar. Disconnect steering linkage from spindle. Disconnect track bar from axle (if equipped). Remove "U" bolts and stabilizer bar bracket. Raise vehicle and roll axle out from under vehicle. To install, reverse removal procedure. Tighten bolts to specification. See appropriate TORQUE SPECIFICATIONS table at end of article.

RADIUS ARM

NOTE: Support axle with a floor jack during coil spring removal and installation procedures. If brake hose length does not permit adequate clearance, remove brake caliper.

Removal (Pickup & Van Except F350 Super Duty) – 1) Raise and support vehicle with safety stands under frame and jack under axle. Remove wheels. Disconnect link from stabilizer bar (if equipped).

2) Disconnect shock absorber from lower bracket. Remove coil spring. See COIL SPRING under REMOVAL & INSTALLATION. Remove lower spring seat from radius arm.

3) Remove radius arm-to-axle bolt. Remove nut, washer, insulator and spacer from rear radius arm mount. Remove radius arm.

Installation – To install, reverse removal procedure. Tighten bolts to specification. See appropriate TORQUE SPECIFICATIONS table at end of article.

STABILIZER BAR

Removal & Installation (Pickup & Van Except F350 Super Duty) – Disconnect stabilizer bar from link assembly. Remove retaining bolts and stabilizer bar. Remove link assembly from axle brackets. To install, reverse removal procedure. Tighten bolts to specification. See appropriate TORQUE SPECIFICATIONS table at end of article.

CAUTION: Ensure link assembly is installed on axle bracket with bend area toward front of vehicle.

Removal & Installation (F350 Super Duty) – Disconnect stabilizer bar from link assembly. Remove retaining bolts and stabilizer bar from front axle. Remove link assembly from frame rail. Loosely install stabilizer bar assembly. Ensure stabilizer bar is centered on front axle and insulators are properly positioned. Tighten bolts to specification. See appropriate TORQUE SPECIFICATIONS table.

TRACK BAR

Removal & Installation (F350 Super Duty) – Remove track bar-to-crossmember bolt. Remove track bar-to-axle bracket bolt, and remove track bar. To install, reverse removal procedure.

TORQUE SPECIFICATIONS

TORQUE SPECIFICATIONS (Van)

Application	Ft. Lbs. (N.m.)
Axle Pivot Bracket-To-Frame Bolt	50-70 (68-95)
Axle-To-Pivot Bracket Bolt	120-150 (163-203)
Axle-To-Radius Arm Bolt	240-320 (326-433)
Coil Spring-To-Lower Retainer Nut	70-100 (95-136)
Coil Spring Upper Retainer-To-Spring Seat Bolt	20-30 (27-41)
Jounce Bumper-To-Frame Bolt	20-30 (27-41)
Radius Arm-To-Rear Bracket Nut	80-120 (109-163)
Radius Arm Rear Bracket-To-Frame Bolt	75-105 (102-142)
Shock Absorber Bracket-To-Radius Arm Bolt	70-95 (95-129)
Shock Absorber-To-Lower Bracket Bolt	40-60 (54-81)
Shock Absorber-To-Upper Spring Seat Nut	18-28 (24-38)
Spindle Lock Pin Nut	35-50 (47-68)
Spindle Upper & Lower Plugs	35-50 (47-68)
Stabilizer Bar Link-To-Bracket Bolt	40-60 (54-81)
Stabilizer Bar Link-To-Stabilizer Bar	18-28 (24-38)
Stabilizer Bar Retainer Mount Bolt	15-25 (20-34)
Tie Rod End-To-Spindle Nut	70-100 (95-136)

TORQUE SPECIFICATIONS (Pickup Except F350 Super Duty)

Application	Ft. Lbs. (N.m.)
Axle Clamp Bolt	48-65 (65-88)
Axle Pivot Bracket-To-Frame Bolt	77-109 (104-148)
Axle-To-Pivot Bracket Bolt	120-150 (163-203)
Axle-To-Radius Arm Bolt	269-329 (364-446)
Ball Joint-To-Spindle Nut	95-110 (129-149)
Coil Spring-To-Lower Retainer Nut	70-100 (95-136)
Coil Spring Upper Retainer-To-Spring Seat Nut	13-18 (18-24)
Jounce Bumper-To-Frame Bolt	14-22 (19-30)
Radius Arm-To-Rear Bracket Nut	80-120 (109-163)
Radius Arm Rear Bracket-To-Frame Bolt	77-100 (104-136)
Shock Absorber Bracket-To-Radius Arm Bolt	27-37 (37-50)
Shock Absorber-To-Lower Bracket Bolt	52-74 (71-100)
Shock Absorber-To-Upper Spring Seat Nut	25-35 (34-47)
Stabilizer Bar Link-To-Bracket	52-74 (71-100)
Stabilizer Bar Link-To-Stabilizer Bar	52-74 (71-100)
Stabilizer Bar Retainer-To-Frame Crossmember Mounting Bracket Bolt	27-37 (37-50)
Tie Rod End-To-Spindle Nut	70-100 (95-136)

TORQUE SPECIFICATIONS (F350 Super Duty)

Application	Ft. Lbs. (N.m.)
Axle-To-Spring "U" Bolt	150-210 (203-285)
Jounce Bumper Bracket Mounting Nut	18-30 (24-41)
Jounce Bumper Bracket "U" Bolt Nut	52-74 (71-100)
Shock Absorber Retaining Nut	52-74 (71-100)
Spindle Lock Pin Nut	38-62 (52-84)
Spindle Upper & Lower Plugs	35-50 (47-68)
Spring Shackle-To-Frame Nut	150-210 (203-285)
Spring-To-Shackle Nut	
Front	120-150 (163-203)
Rear	150-210 (203-285)
Stabilizer Bar Link Bracket Nut	35-50 (47-68)
Stabilizer Bar Link-To-Stabilizer Bar Nut	15-25 (20-34)
Steering Linkage-To-Spindle Nut	52-74 (71-100)
Track Bar Bolt	120-150 (163-203)
Track Bar Mounting Bracket Bolt	120-150 (163-203)

ing hub assembly legs are aligned with 3 cam assembly pockets. Final end play of hub on spindle should be .00-.003" (.00-.08 mm). Torque required to turn hub and rotor assembly should not exceed 25 INCH lbs. (2.8 N.m).

MANUAL LOCKING HUBS

Removal & Installation (Bronco & F150) – 1) Remove Allen head bolts and remove manual locking hub cover. Remove snap ring retaining axle shaft in hub body assembly. Remove locking hub body-to-wheel hub lock ring.

2) Install 2 bolts to remove locking hub body. See Fig. 7. To install locking hub, reverse removal procedure. Tighten Allen head bolts to 40-60 INCH lbs. (4-6 N.m). DO NOT pack locking hub cover with grease.

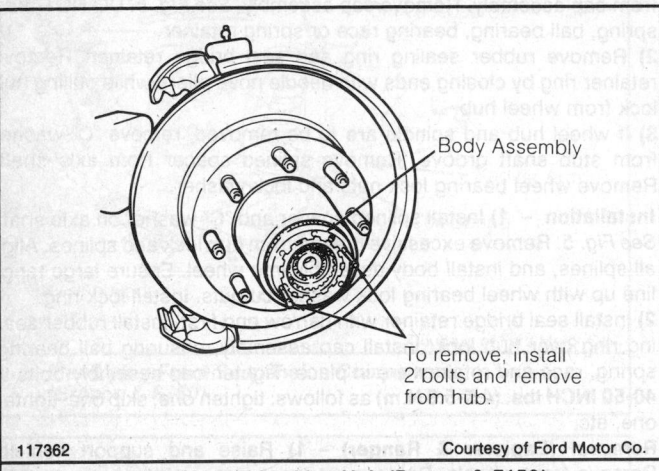

117362   Courtesy of Ford Motor Co.

Fig. 7: Removing Manual Locking Hub (Bronco & F150)

Removal (Explorer & Ranger) – 1) Raise and support vehicle. Remove front wheels. Remove retainer washers from lug nut studs. Remove manual locking hub assembly from spindle. See Fig. 8.

2) Remove snap ring from end of spindle. Remove axle shaft spacer, needle thrust bearing and bearing spacer from spindle.

Installation – To install hub assembly, reverse removal procedure. Final end play of hub on spindle should be .00-.003" (.00-.08 mm). Torque required to turn hub and rotor assembly should not exceed 25 INCH lbs. (2.8 N.m).

SHOCK ABSORBER

Removal & Installation – Remove nut and washer holding shock absorber to upper spring seat. Remove lower shock absorber-to-radius arm retaining bolts. Remove shock absorber from lower bracket. Compress shock absorber and remove. To install, reverse removal procedure.

QUAD SHOCK ABSORBERS

Removal & Installation (Bronco & F150) – Remove nut, washer and rubber bushings from upper end of shock absorbers. Remove nut from lower end of shock absorber, and remove shock absorber. Replace rubber bushings when replacing shock absorbers. To install reverse removal procedure.

SPINDLE & SHAFT ASSEMBLY

Removal – 1) Raise and support vehicle. Remove wheel assembly. Remove caliper from rotor. Remove locking hub. See AUTOMATIC LOCKING HUBS or MANUAL LOCKING HUBS under REMOVAL & INSTALLATION.

2) Remove wheel bearings, lock nuts, hub and rotor. Remove spindle-to-steering knuckle nuts. Tap spindle with plastic hammer to free spindle from steering knuckle. See Fig. 9. Remove spindle, spindle seat (if equipped) and splash shield.

3) On right side applications, remove and discard keystone clamp from shaft assembly and stub shaft. Slide rubber boot onto stub shaft. Remove shaft assembly from right axle. See Fig. 9.

4) Remove left shaft assembly (if required). On all applications, wrap spindle in protective cloth and place second step of spindle in soft jawed vise.

5) Remove oil seal using slide hammer and Seal Remover (TOOL 1175-AC) for Explorer and Ranger, or Cup Puller (T77F-1102-A) for all others. Remove needle bearing from spindle. Press seal (Explorer and Ranger) or "V" seal and slinger (all others) from shaft assembly. See Fig. 9.

Installation – 1) Clean all dirt and grease from spindle bearing bore. Ensure bearing bore is free of nicks and burrs. On Explorer and Ranger, install seal on shaft assembly using press and Seal Installer (T83T-3132-A).

2) On all other models, press slinger on shaft assembly. Install "V" seal on shaft assembly, with seal lip toward spindle. Install plastic spacer (located against "V" seal) on shaft assembly, with chamfered edge against shaft assembly.

3) On right side applications, install rubber boot and NEW keystone clamps on stub shaft. Install right shaft assembly into stub shaft, with stub shaft missing spline aligned with shaft assembly.

4) Ensure splines are fully engaged. Install rubber boot over assembly and tighten keystone clamps. On left axle applications, install shaft assembly through steering knuckle, and engage in splines.

5) Install needle bearing in spindle, with manufacturer identification mark facing away from spindle bore. For bearing installation, use Handle (T80T-4000-W), and Bearing/Seal Installer (T83T-3123-A) for Explorer and Ranger, or (T80T-4000-S) for all others.

CAUTION: Install spindle needle bearing with manufacturer's identification mark away from spindle bore.

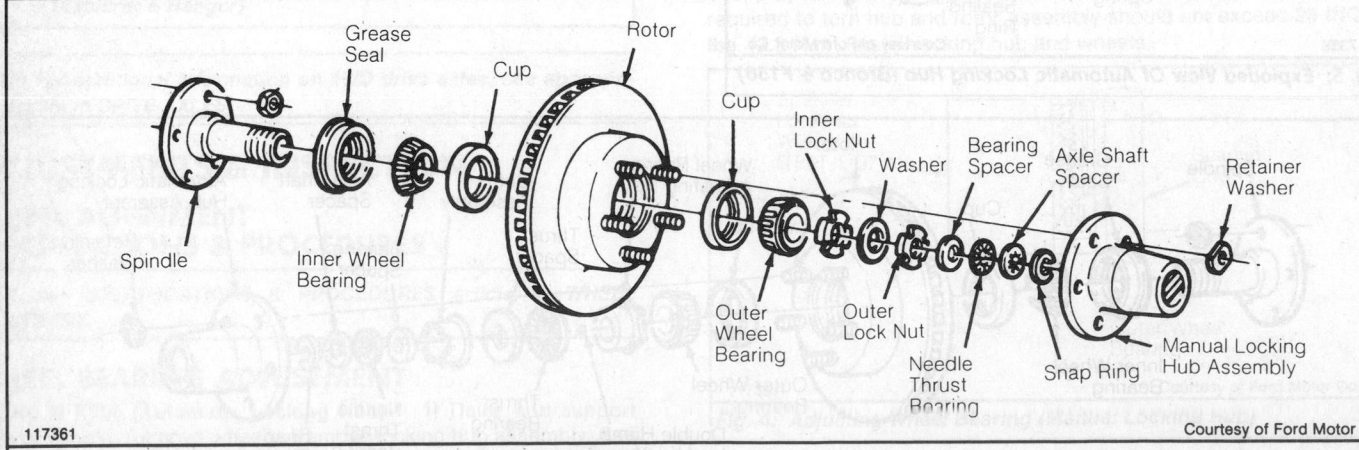

117361   Courtesy of Ford Motor Co.

Fig. 8: Exploded View Of Manual Locking Hub (Explorer & Ranger)

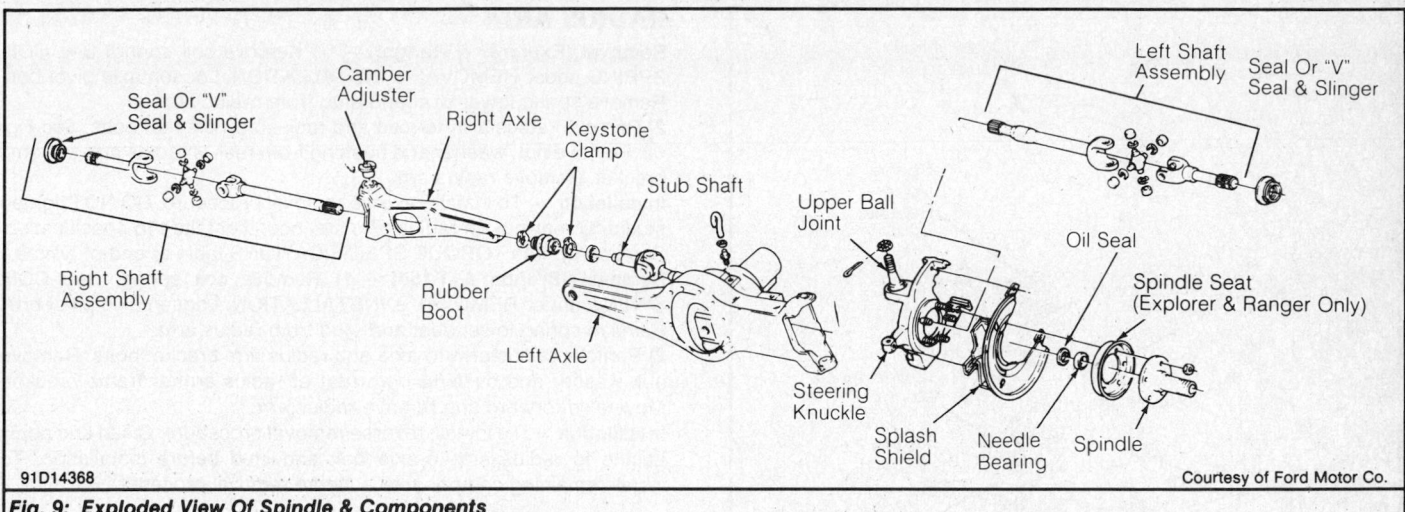

Fig. 9: Exploded View Of Spindle & Components

6) Using Bearing/Seal Installer (T83T-3123-A) for Explorer and Ranger, or (T80T-4000-T) for all others, install seal in spindle with seal lip facing away from spindle. Coat seal lip with multipurpose grease. Install spindle and splash shield.

7) To install remaining components, reverse removal procedure. Adjust wheel bearings. See WHEEL BEARING ADJUSTMENT under ADJUSTMENTS & INSPECTION.

STEERING KNUCKLE

Removal – 1) Remove spindle and shaft assembly. See SPINDLE & SHAFT ASSEMBLY under REMOVAL & INSTALLATION. Disconnect steering linkage from steering knuckle.

2) Remove cotter pin and loosen ball joint nuts. Strike steering knuckle near ball joint to release ball joint. Remove ball joint nuts. Note position of camber adjuster on top of axle. See Fig. 9. Remove camber adjuster and steering knuckle.

CAUTION: Camber adjuster must be installed in original location to maintain proper wheel alignment.

Installation – To install, reverse removal procedure. Ensure camber adjuster is installed in original position. Install NEW nuts on ball joints. Install remaining components.

BALL JOINT

NOTE: Always remove lower ball joint before removing upper ball joint. Install lower ball joint before installing upper ball joint. DO NOT heat ball joint or axle to aid in installation.

Removal – 1) Remove steering knuckle. See STEERING KNUCKLE under REMOVAL & INSTALLATION. Remove snap ring from bottom ball joint socket.

2) Assemble "C" Frame (T74P-4635-C) and Receiver Cup (T83T-3050-A for Explorer and Ranger, or D81T-3010-A4 for all others) on the lower ball joint. See Fig. 10.

3) Turn forcing screw clockwise until lower ball joint is removed from spindle. Repeat procedure to remove upper ball joint. See Fig. 10.

Installation – 1) Lower ball joint must be installed first. Assemble "C" Frame, Receiver Cup (T80T-3010-A for Explorer and Ranger, or T80T-3010-A3 for all others), and Installation Cup (T83T-3050-A for Explorer and Ranger, or D81T-3010-A for all others). See Fig. 10.

2) Turn forcing screw to install ball joint. Ensure ball joint is fully seated. To install upper ball joint, assemble "C" Frame, Receiver Cup (T80T-3050-A for Explorer and Ranger, or T80T-3010-A3 for all others), and Installation Cup (T83T-3050-A for Explorer and Ranger, D81T-3010-A for all others). See Fig. 10.

3) Turn forcing screw to install ball joint. Ensure ball joint is fully seated. Install snap ring on ball joints, and install steering knuckle.

COIL SPRING

NOTE: Axle must be supported by jack during removal and installation procedure. If brake hose length does not permit adequate clearance, remove brake caliper.

Removal (Bronco & F150) – Raise and support vehicle under frame rails and support axle with jack. Remove shock absorber-to-lower shock mount bolt. Remove lower spring retainer nut. Remove spring

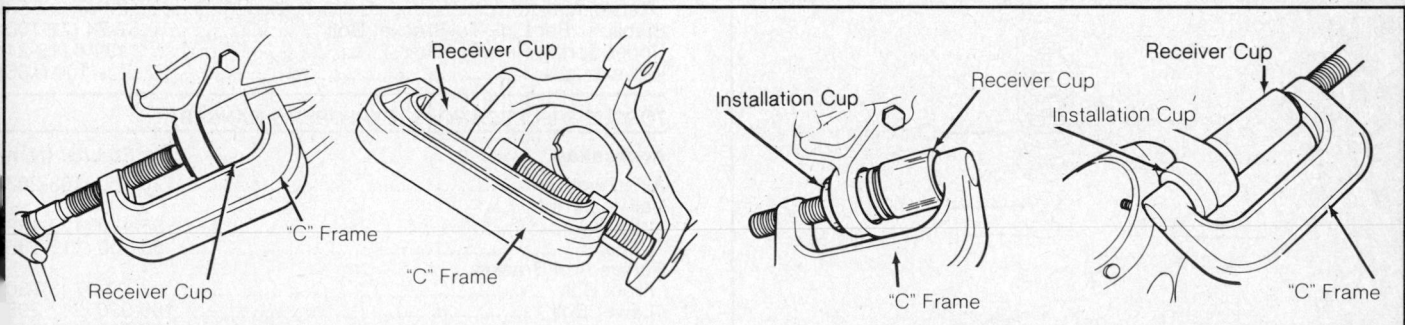

LOWER BALL JOINT REMOVAL   UPPER BALL JOINT REMOVAL   LOWER BALL JOINT INSTALLATION   UPPER BALL JOINT INSTALLATION

Fig. 10: Removing & Installing Ball Joint

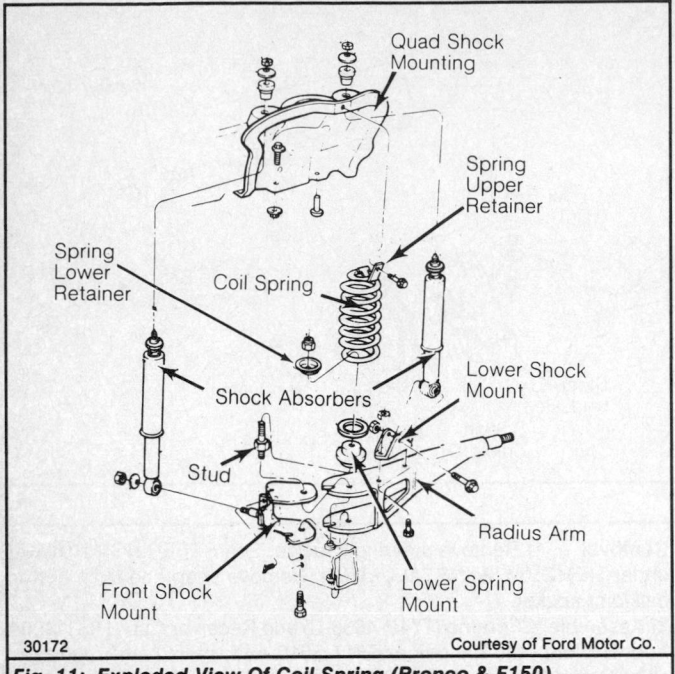

30172   Courtesy of Ford Motor Co.

Fig. 11: Exploded View Of Coil Spring (Bronco & F150)

upper retainer. *See Fig. 11.* Lower axle to relieve spring tension. Remove coil spring and lower spring mount.

Installation – Place spring into position. Ensure top of coil is correctly seated in upper spring seat. To complete installation, reverse removal procedure.

Removal (Explorer & Ranger) – 1) Raise and support vehicle. Support axle with jack. Disconnect shock absorber from radius arm.
2) Remove coil spring-to-axle nut and remove retainer. *See Fig. 12.* Lower axle until spring tension is removed and adequate clearance exists for spring removal.
3) Remove spring by rotating upper coil out of tabs in upper spring seat. Remove spacer and lower seat. Stud in axle may need to be removed to provide clearance.

Installation – Install stud in axle (if removed). Install lower seat and spacer over stud bolt. Position upper end of spring coil in spring stop area of upper spring seat. To complete installation, reverse removal procedure.

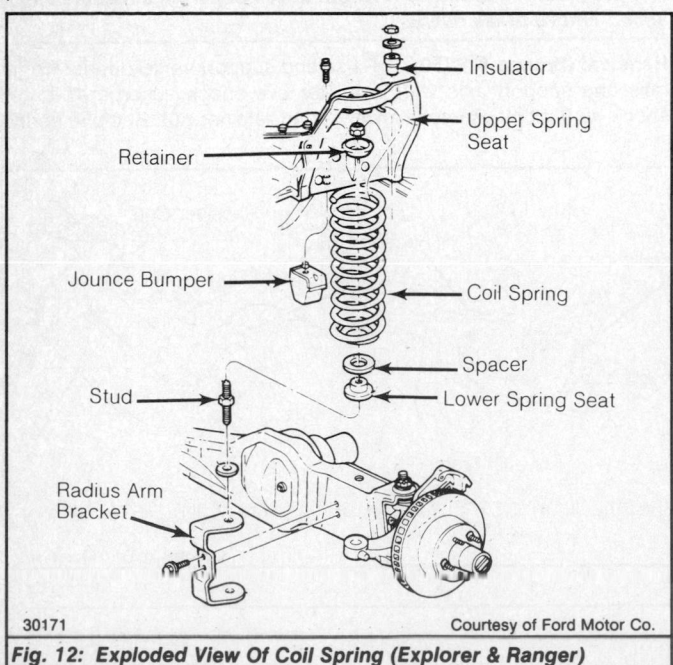

30171   Courtesy of Ford Motor Co.

Fig. 12: Exploded View Of Coil Spring (Explorer & Ranger)

RADIUS ARM

Removal (Explorer & Ranger) – 1) Remove coil spring. See COIL SPRING under REMOVAL & INSTALLATION. Loosen axle pivot bolt. Remove spring lower seat and stud from radius arm.
2) Remove radius arm-to-axle and radius arm bracket bolts. *See Fig. 12.* Remove nut, washer and bushing from rear of radius arm at frame bracket. Remove radius arm.
Installation – To install, reverse removal procedure. DO NOT tighten stud until rear nut on radius arm has been tightened to specification. See appropriate TORQUE SPECIFICATIONS table at end of article.
Removal (Bronco & F150) – 1) Remove coil spring. See COIL SPRING under REMOVAL & INSTALLATION. Loosen axle pivot bolt. Remove spring lower seat and stud from radius arm.
2) Remove radius arm-to-axle and radius arm bracket bolts. Remove nut, washer and bushing from rear of radius arm at frame bracket. Move axle forward and remove radius arm.
Installation – To install, reverse removal procedure. Clean and apply Loctite to radius arm-to-axle bolt and stud before installation. To install remaining components, reverse removal procedure.

FRONT AXLE ASSEMBLY

Removal & Installation – For removal and installation procedure, see appropriate article in DRIVE AXLES.

STABILIZER BAR

Removal & Installation (Explorer & Ranger) – Remove bolts and retainers from center and right end of stabilizer bar. Remove stabilizer bar-to-stabilizer bar link bolt. Remove stabilizer bar and bushings. To install, reverse removal procedure.
Removal & Installation (Bronco & F150) – Remove stabilizer bar-to-stabilizer link bolts. Remove stabilizer bar retainer bolts. Remove stabilizer bar and bushings. To install, reverse removal procedure.

TORQUE SPECIFICATIONS

TORQUE SPECIFICATIONS (BRONCO & F150)

Application	Ft. Lbs. (N.m)
Axle Pivot Bracket-To-Frame Bolt	77-110 (104-149)
Ball Joint Nut	
Lower	90-110 (122-149)
Upper	100 (136)
Lower Spring Retainer Nut	70-100 (95-136)
Radius Arm Bracket-To-Frame Bolt	77-110 (104-149)
Radius Arm-To-Axle Lower Bolt	320-340 (434-461)
Radius Arm-To-Axle Upper Stud	240-260 (325-353)
Rear Radius Arm Nut	80-120 (109-163)
Shock Absorber Mounting Bolt	
Lower	52-74 (71-100)
Upper	25-35 (34-47)
Spindle-To-Steering Knuckle Bolt	50-60 (68-81)
Stabilizer Bar	
To Stabilizer Link	52-74 (71-100)
Retaining Nut	27-37 (37-50)
Stabilizer Bar Link-To-Bracket Bolt	52-74 (71-100)
Upper Spring Retainer Bolt	13-18 (18-24)
Wheel Lug Nut	100 (136)

TORQUE SPECIFICATIONS (EXPLORER & RANGER)

Application	Ft. Lbs. (N.m)
Axle Pivot Bolt	120-150 (163-203)
Ball Joint Nut	
Lower	95-110 (129-149)
Upper	85-100 (115-136)
Radius Arm Bracket	
Front Bolt	27-37 (37-50)
Lower Bolt	160-220 (217-298)
Upper Stud	190-230 (258-312)
Radius Arm-To-Frame Bracket Nut	80-120 (109-163)
Shock Absorber-To-Radius Arm Bolt	41-63 (56-85)
Shock Absorber-To-Upper Seat Bolt	25-35 (34-47)
Spindle-To-Steering Knuckle Bolt	40-50 (54-68)
Spring Retainer Nut	70-100 (95-136)
Stabilizer Bar Retainer Bolt	35-50 (47-68)
Stabilizer Bar "U" Bolt Nut	35-50 (47-68)
Wheel Lug Nut	100 (136)

Aerostar

DESCRIPTION

The independent front suspension consists of steering knuckles, upper and lower control arms, coil springs, shock absorbers and stabilizer bar. *See Fig. 1.* Integral ball joints and bushings are mounted in the control arms. Movement of upper control arm provides for adjustment of caster and camber. Individual axle shafts are splined into the hub assembly. The 4WD hubs are constantly engaged and cannot be disengaged.

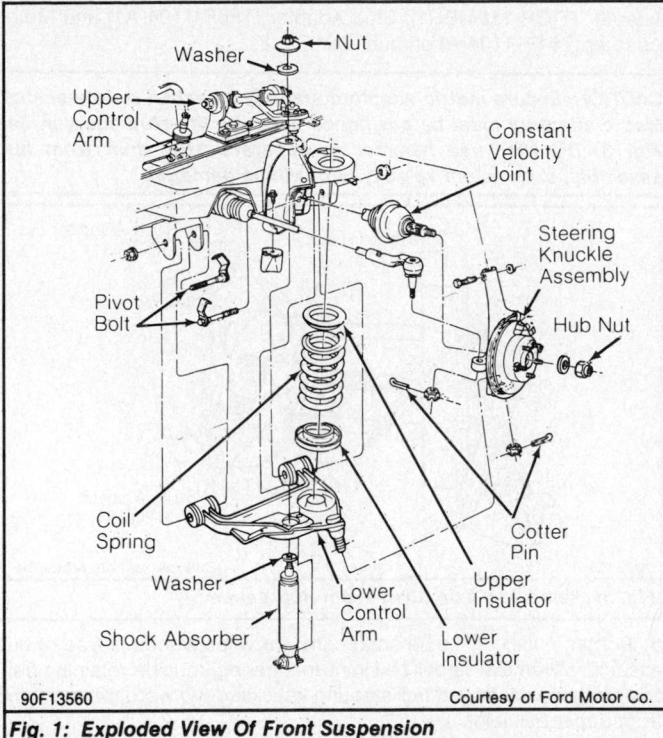

Fig. 1: Exploded View Of Front Suspension

ADJUSTMENTS & INSPECTION

WHEEL ALIGNMENT SPECIFICATIONS & PROCEDURES

NOTE: See SPECIFICATIONS & PROCEDURES article in WHEEL ALIGNMENT.

WHEEL BEARING ADJUSTMENT

Front wheel bearings are not adjustable. If service is required, bearings and hub assembly are replaced as a unit.

BALL JOINT CHECKING

Lower & Upper Ball Joint – Raise and support vehicle under lower control arm. Move lower edge of tire in and out while watching lower steering knuckle arm and lower part of lower control arm. If movement exceeds 1/32" (.794 mm), replace lower control arm. To check upper ball joint, move upper edge of tire in and out. If movement between upper steering knuckle arm and upper control arm exceeds 1/32" (.794 mm), replace upper control arm.

REMOVAL & INSTALLATION

NOTE: Any time the steering linkage is disconnected from the steering knuckle, the steering system must be placed in the centered position.

AXLE SHAFT

Removal – **1)** Place wheels in straight-ahead position. Raise and support vehicle. Remove wheel assembly. Install steel rod through hole in brake rotor. Rotate rotor until steel rod contacts steering knuckle, preventing rotor and hub from moving. Remove hub nut and washer from axle shaft.

2) Place reference mark on axle shaft flange and drive axle flange for reassembly reference. Remove axle shaft flange-to-drive axle flange bolts. Separate axle shaft from drive axle flange.

CAUTION: Support axle shaft when disconnected from drive axle flange. DO NOT allow axle shaft to hang unsupported, or constant velocity joint on axle shaft will be damaged.

3) Remove shock absorber-to-lower control arm bolts. *See Fig. 1.* Move shock absorber aside. Remove bumper from front drive axle crossmember. Install Puller (T81P-1104-C), Metric Stud Adapter (T83P-1104-BH1), Stud Adapter (T86P-1104-A1) and Metric Adapter (T81P-1104-A) on hub. *See Fig. 3.*

CAUTION: Ensure metric adapters are fully threaded on wheel stud. Metric adapters must be positioned opposite the stud adapter. See Fig. 3. DO NOT use hammer to separate axle shaft from hub assembly, or constant velocity joint will be damaged.

4) Tighten puller until axle shaft constant velocity joint is free of hub assembly. Remove axle shaft assembly. **Installation** – **1)** Install axle shaft in hub assembly. Push axle shaft in hub assembly as far as possible. Install rotor on hub (if removed) with 2 wheel lug nuts. Install steel rod through rotor. Rotate rotor until steel rod contacts steering knuckle.

CAUTION: Always install NEW hub nut. DO NOT reuse old hub nut.

2) Install NEW hub nut and tighten to specification. DO NOT use impact to tighten hub nut. To install remaining components, reverse removal procedure. Ensure reference marks are aligned on axle shaft flange and drive axle flange. Tighten bolts to specification. See TORQUE SPECIFICATIONS table at end of article.

BALL JOINT

Ball joint is not serviced separately. If ball joint is defective, control arm must be replaced as a unit.

COIL SPRING

Removal – **1)** Place wheels in centered position. Raise and support vehicle. Remove wheels. Disconnect stabilizer bar link-to-lower control arm bolt. *See Fig. 2.* Remove shock absorber.
2) Using Spring Compressor (D78P-5310-A), compress coil spring. Loosen lower control arm pivot bolts. *See Fig. 1.* Remove cotter pin from lower ball joint-to-steering knuckle nut and loosen nut. DO NOT remove nut.
3) Using Pitman Arm Puller (T64P-3590-F), loosen lower ball joint from steering knuckle. Remove puller. Support lower control arm with floor jack. Remove nut from ball joint.

CAUTION: Ensure lower control arm is supported with floor jack before removing nut from lower ball joint.

4) Separate lower ball joint from lower control arm. Release floor jack and allow lower control arm to move downward. Remove coil spring with upper and lower insulators. *See Fig. 1.*

NOTE: If new coil spring is to be installed, measure compressed length of coil spring removed. Adjust new coil spring compressed length to that of coil spring removed for installation purposes.

Installation – **1)** To install, reverse removal procedure. Install lower ball joint nut and tighten to specification. Install cotter pin. It may be necessary to advance ball joint nut for cotter pin installation. DO NOT back nut off.

2) Tighten pivot bolts to specification with vehicle on the ground at normal operating height. See TORQUE SPECIFICATIONS table at end of article.

HUB & BEARING ASSEMBLY

NOTE: Wheel bearings and hub assembly are not individually serviceable. If wheel bearings are defective, replace wheel bearings and hub assembly as a unit.

Removal & Installation – 1) Remove steering knuckle. See STEERING KNUCKLE under REMOVAL & INSTALLATION.
2) Remove 3 hub-to-steering knuckle bolts. Remove hub assembly and dust shield. To install, reverse removal procedure.

LOWER CONTROL ARM

CAUTION: Before removing lower control arm, vehicle should be supported under the front crossmember.

Removal – Remove coil spring. See COIL SPRING under REMOVAL & INSTALLATION. Note direction of pivot bolt installation. See Fig. 1. Remove pivot bolts and lower control arm. Lower control arm assembly must be replaced if ball joint or bushings are defective.
Installation – To install, reverse removal procedure. Ensure pivot bolts are installed in proper direction. See Fig. 1.

CAUTION: Pivot bolts must be tightened to specification with vehicle on the ground and at normal operating height.

SHOCK ABSORBER

Removal & Installation – Remove nut and washer from top of shock absorber. Remove shock absorber-to-lower control arm bolts. Remove shock absorber. To install, reverse removal procedure. Tighten bolts/nuts to specification. See TORQUE SPECIFICATIONS table at end of article.

STABILIZER BAR

Removal & Installation – Remove stabilizer bar-to-link assembly at lower control arms. See Fig. 2. Remove link assembly from lower control arm if necessary. Remove mounting bracket bolts and mounting brackets. Remove stabilizer bar with frame insulators. To install, reverse removal procedure. Tighten bolts to specification. See TORQUE SPECIFICATIONS table at end of article.

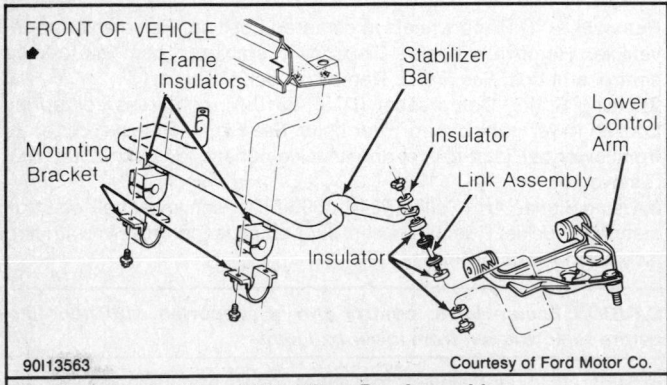

90I13563   Courtesy of Ford Motor Co.
Fig. 2: Exploded View Of Stabilizer Bar Assembly

STEERING KNUCKLE

Removal – 1) Place wheels in straight-ahead position. Remove hub nut and washer from axle shaft. See Fig. 1. Raise vehicle on twin post hoist. Place jack stands under frame. Twin post hoist is used to maintain pressure on coil spring.
2) Remove wheel assembly. Remove brake caliper retaining pins and brake caliper. Support brake caliper aside. Remove rotor. Remove

cotter pin from tie rod-to-steering knuckle nut and remove nut. Using Puller (T64P-3590-F), separate tie rod from steering knuckle.

CAUTION: Ensure twin post hoist is supporting lower control arm to maintain pressure on the coil spring.

3) Remove cotter pin from lower ball joint-to-steering knuckle nut and loosen nut. DO NOT remove nut. Using puller, loosen lower ball joint from steering knuckle. Remove puller and nut.
4) Pull downward on lower control arm. Disengage lower ball joint from steering knuckle. Install Puller (T81P-1104-C), Metric Stud Adapter (T83P-1104-BH1), Stud Adapter (T86P-1104-A1) and Metric Adapter (T81P-1104-A) on hub. See Fig. 3.

CAUTION: Ensure metric adapters are fully threaded on wheel stud. Metric adapters must be positioned opposite the stud adapter. See Fig. 3. DO NOT use hammer to separate axle shaft from hub assembly, or constant velocity joint will be damaged.

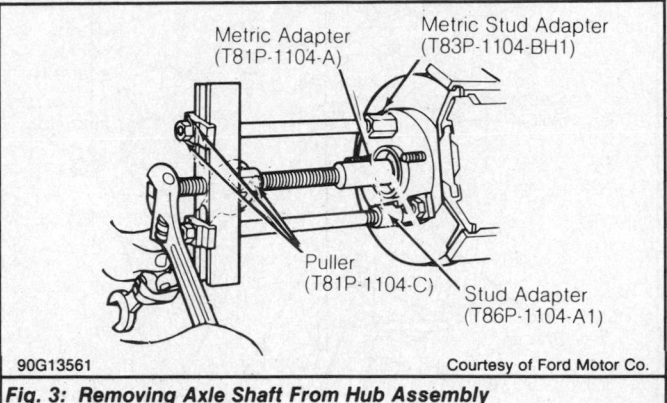

90G13561   Courtesy of Ford Motor Co.
Fig. 3: Removing Axle Shaft From Hub Assembly

5) Tighten puller until axle shaft constant velocity joint is free of hub assembly. Remove upper ball joint-to-steering knuckle retaining bolt. Support axle shaft, and pull steering knuckle downward, disengaging from upper ball joint.
6) Separate steering knuckle from axle shaft. Wire axle shaft to body to maintain axle shaft in a level position.
Installation – 1) Install steering knuckle over axle shaft and onto lower ball joint. Ensure axle shaft splines are engaged with hub assembly. Install lower ball joint nut, and tighten to specification. See TORQUE SPECIFICATIONS table at end of article.
2) Install cotter pin. If necessary, advance ball joint nut for cotter pin installation. DO NOT back nut off. Install rotor on hub (if removed) with 2 wheel lug nuts. Install steel rod through rotor. Rotate rotor until steel rod contacts steering knuckle.

CAUTION: Always install NEW hub nut. DO NOT reuse hub nut.

3) Install NEW hub nut and tighten nut just enough to seat constant velocity joint of the axle shaft. DO NOT tighten hub nut to specification at this time. Install upper ball joint in steering knuckle. Install and tighten retaining bolt to specification. See TORQUE SPECIFICATIONS table at end of article.
4) Install tie rod on steering knuckle. Tighten tie rod nut to specification. It may be necessary to advance tie rod nut for cotter pin installation. DO NOT back nut off.
5) Tighten hub nut to specification. DO NOT use impact to tighten hub nut. It will be necessary to use steel rod installed in step 2) to hold hub from turning. To install remaining components, reverse removal procedure.

UPPER CONTROL ARM

CAUTION: When servicing upper control arm components, service ONLY one side at a time. DO NOT service both sides at the same time. Manufacturer recommends that steering knuckle be removed during service procedure.

Removal – 1) Place wheels in straight-ahead position. Raise vehicle on twin post hoist. Place jack stands under body rail. Twin post hoist is used to maintain pressure on the coil spring.
2) Remove steering knuckle. See STEERING KNUCKLE under REMOVAL & INSTALLATION. Remove bolt retainer bracket. *See Fig. 4.*

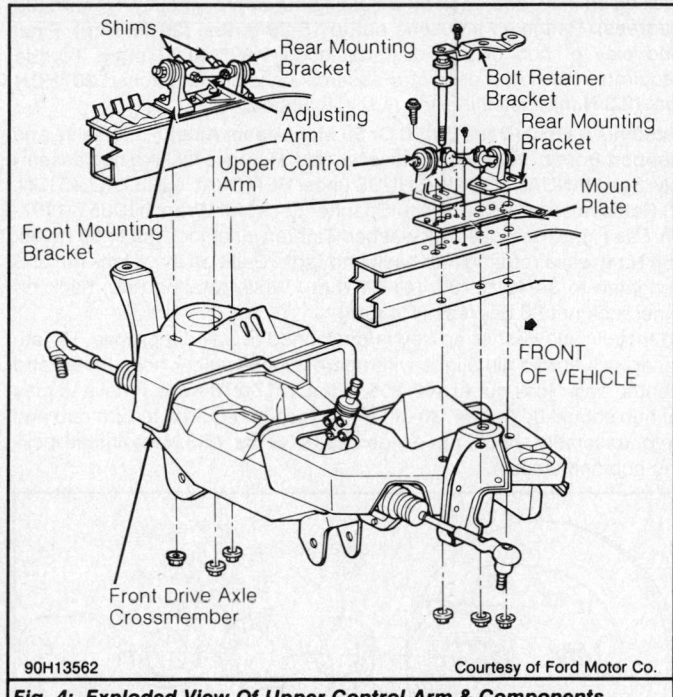

90H13562   Courtesy of Ford Motor Co.

Fig. 4: Exploded View Of Upper Control Arm & Components

CAUTION: Front and rear mounting bracket position on mounting plate must be marked before removing upper control arm.

3) Mark position of front and rear mounting brackets on mounting plate. *See Fig. 4.* Remove front and rear mounting bracket bolts. Remove upper control arm assembly and mounting plate.

4) If upper control arm is to be removed from adjusting arm, note location and number of shims. *See Fig. 4.* Remove upper control arm-to-adjusting arm nuts. Separate upper control arm from adjusting arm. Mounting brackets and adjusting arm are serviced as a complete unit.

CAUTION: Before removing upper control arm from adjusting arm, note location and number of shims installed at adjusting arm. See Fig. 4. Shims must be installed in original location to maintain wheel alignment.

Installation – To install, reverse removal procedure. Install mounting brackets in original position. Ensure mounting brackets do not move when bolts are tightened to specification. See TORQUE SPECIFICATIONS table. Check and adjust wheel alignment. See SPECIFICATIONS & PROCEDURES article in WHEEL ALIGNMENT.

TORQUE SPECIFICATIONS

TORQUE SPECIFICATIONS

Application	Ft. Lbs. (N.m)
Axle Shaft-To-Drive Axle Flange Bolt	19-26 (26-35)
Bolt Retainer Bracket Bolt	10-14 (14-19)
Bumper-To-Crossmember Bolt	24-33 (33-45)
Control Arm Front Mount Bracket-To-Mount Plate Bolt	35-47 (47-64)
Control Arm Mount Bracket-To-Frame Rail Bolt	145-195 (197-264)
Hub Nut [1]	170-210 (230-285)
Link Assembly Bolt	10-12 (14-16)
Lower Ball Joint Nut	80-120 (109-163)
Mount Plate-To-Frame Rail Bolt	10-14 (14-19)
Pivot Bolt [2]	100-140 (136-190)
Shock Absorber Lower Bolt	16-24 (22-33)
Upper Nut	25-35 (34-47)
Stabilizer Bar Mount Bracket Bolt	16-24 (22-33)
Tie Rod-To-Steering Knuckle Nut	52-74 (71-100)
Upper Ball Joint Bolt	27-37 (37-51)
Upper Control Arm-To-Adjusting Arm Nut	70-100 (95-136)
Wheel Lug Nut	100 (136)

[1] – Use NEW nut. DO NOT tighten with impact.
[2] – Tighten to specification with vehicle on ground and at normal operating height.

F250/350

DESCRIPTION

The standard F250 uses a Dana 44IFS (Independent Front Suspension) axle and F250 Heavy Duty (HD) uses a Dana 50IFS axle. Suspension system consists of a 2-piece drive axle with ball joint-supported steering knuckle. F350 uses a Dana 60 Monobeam axle system, consisting of a solid drive axle with kingpin-supported steering knuckles. All drive axles are suspended by semi-elliptic leaf-type springs.

FRONT AXLE IDENTIFICATION

Application	Axle
F250	[1] Dana 44IFS
F250 HD	[1] Dana 50IFS
F350	Dana 60 Monobeam

[1] – IFS is Independent Front Suspension.

NOTE: For additional information on 4WD drive axles, see appropriate article in DRIVE AXLES.

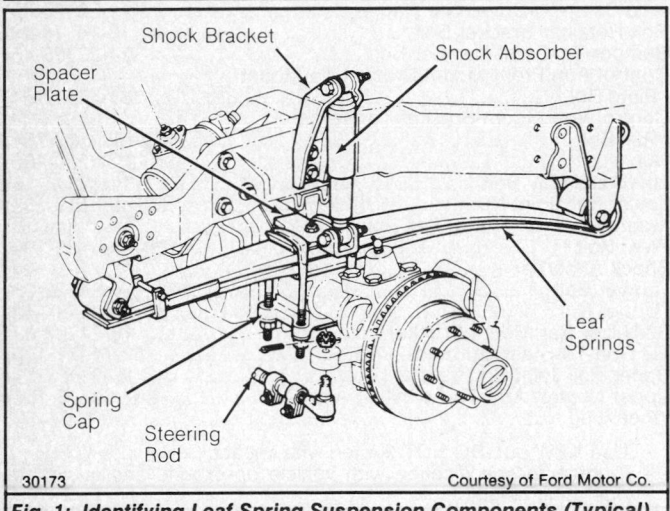

Fig. 1: Identifying Leaf Spring Suspension Components (Typical)

ADJUSTMENTS & INSPECTION

WHEEL ALIGNMENT SPECIFICATIONS & PROCEDURES

NOTE: See SPECIFICATIONS & PROCEDURES article in WHEEL ALIGNMENT.

WHEEL BEARING ADJUSTMENT

F250 (Dana 44IFS Axle) – 1) Raise and support front of vehicle. Remove front wheels. Remove locking hubs. See MANUAL LOCKING HUBS under REMOVAL & INSTALLATION.

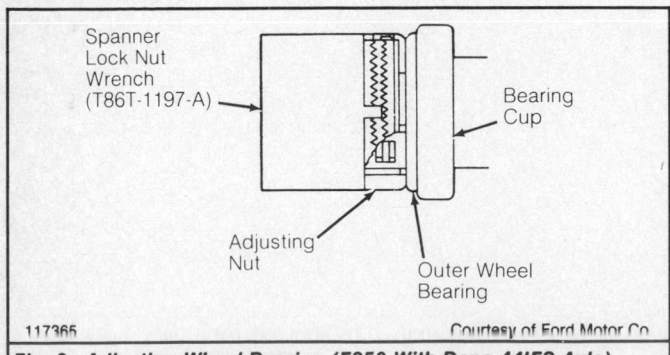

Fig. 2: Adjusting Wheel Bearing (F250 With Dana 44IFS Axle)

2) Use a torque wrench and Spanner Lock Nut Wrench (T86T-1197-A) to unlock locking splines of wheel bearing adjusting nut by applying inward pressure. *See Fig. 2.* Tighten adjusting nut to **70 ft. lbs. (95 N.m)** while turning hub and rotor back and forth to seat bearing.

3) Apply inward pressure to spanner lock nut wrench to disengage locking splines, and back off adjusting nut approximately 1/4 turn (90 degrees). Retighten adjusting nut to **15-20 ft. lbs. (20-27 N.m)**. Final end play of hub on spindle should be **0.00" (0.00 mm)**. Torque required to turn hub and rotor assembly should not exceed **20 INCH lbs. (2.3 N.m)**. Install locking hub and wheels.

F250 HD & F350 (Dana 50IFS Or 60 Monobeam Axle) – 1) Raise and support front of vehicle. Remove wheels. Remove locking hub assembly. See MANUAL LOCKING HUBS under REMOVAL & INSTALLATION.

2) Remove outer lock nut with Spanner Lock Nut Wrench (D85T-1197-A). *See Fig. 3.* Remove lock washer. Tighten inner lock nut to **50 ft. lbs. (68 N.m)** while rotating hub back and forth. Back off inner lock nut and retighten to **30-40 ft. lbs. (41-54 N.m)**. While rotating hub, back off inner lock nut 90 degrees (1/4 turn).

3) Install lock washer so key is positioned in spindle groove. Rotate inner lock nut so pin aligns with nearest lock washer hole. Install and tighten outer lock nut to **160-205 ft. lbs. (217-278 N.m)**. Final end play of hub should be **0-.004" (0-.11 mm)**. Torque required to turn hub and rotor assembly should not exceed **20 INCH lbs. (2.3 N.m)**. Install locking hub and wheels.

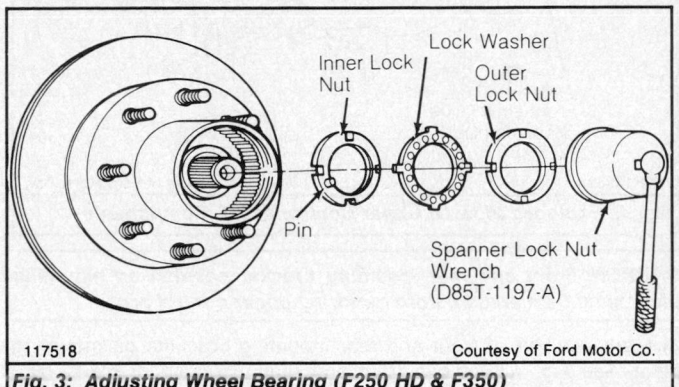

Fig. 3: Adjusting Wheel Bearing (F250 HD & F350)

BALL JOINT CHECKING

F250 – 1) Raise and support vehicle. Ensure wheel bearings are properly adjusted. See WHEEL BEARING ADJUSTMENT under ADJUSTMENTS & INSPECTION. Hold tire at top and bottom. Move wheel and watch for movement of spindle assembly.

2) If spindle assembly moves more than 1/32" (.794 mm) at upper or lower arms (relative to axle), replace upper and/or lower ball joint as necessary.

KINGPIN CHECKING

F350 – Information is not available from manufacturer.

REMOVAL & INSTALLATION
MANUAL LOCKING HUBS

Removal – Remove 6 Allen head bolts and remove manual locking hub cover. Remove snap ring retaining axle shaft in hub body assembly. Remove locking hub body-to-wheel hub lock ring. Install 2 bolts to remove locking hub body. *See Fig. 4.*

Installation – To install locking hub, reverse removal procedure. Tighten Allen head bolts to **35-53 INCH lbs. (4-6 N.m)**. DO NOT pack locking hub cover with grease.

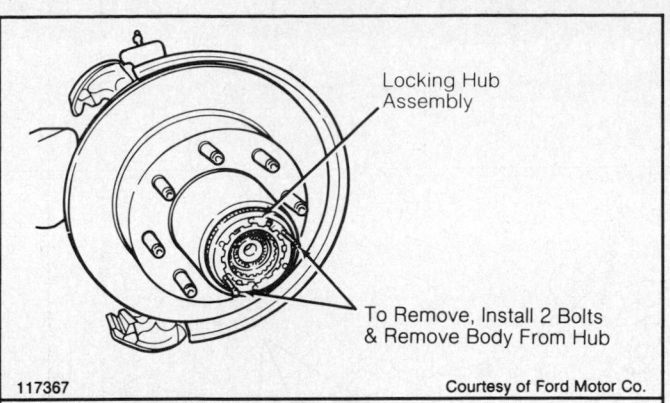

Locking Hub
Assembly

To Remove, Install 2 Bolts
& Remove Body From Hub

117367   Courtesy of Ford Motor Co.

Fig. 4: Removing Manual Locking Hub

SHOCK ABSORBERS

WARNING: Shock absorbers are gas filled. DO NOT puncture or apply heat to shock absorber.

Removal & Installation – Remove upper and lower shock absorber bolts. Compress shock absorber and remove. Remove upper shock bushing. To install, reverse removal procedure.

SPINDLE & SHAFT ASSEMBLY

Removal (F250/250 HD) – 1) Raise and support vehicle. Remove wheel and tire assembly. Remove locking hub. See MANUAL LOCKING HUBS under REMOVAL & INSTALLATION. Using Spanner Lock Nut Wrench (D85T-1197-A), remove outer lock nut, lock ring and adjusting nut. *See Figs. 3 and 5.*

2) Remove brake caliper and support aside. DO NOT hang by flexible brake hose. Wire caliper to frame. Remove hub and rotor assembly. Remove spindle-to-steering knuckle nuts. Tap spindle with plastic hammer to free spindle from steering knuckle. *See Fig. 5.* Remove spindle and splash shield.

3) On right side applications, remove and discard keystone clamp from stub shaft assembly and stub shaft. Slide rubber boot onto stub shaft. Remove shaft assembly from right axle.

4) Remove left shaft assembly (if required). Wrap spindle in protective cloth and place second step of spindle in soft-jawed vise. Using slide hammer and Cup Puller (T77F-1102-A), remove oil seal and needle bearing from spindle. Press "V" seal and slinger from shaft assembly. *See Fig. 5.*

Installation – 1) Clean dirt and grease from spindle bearing bore. Press slinger on shaft assembly. Install "V" seal on shaft assembly with seal lip toward spindle. Install plastic spacer (located against "V" seal) on shaft assembly, with chamfered edge against shaft assembly.

2) On right side applications, install rubber boot and NEW keystone clamps on stub shaft. Align right shaft assembly into stub shaft, so stub shaft missing spline is aligned with gapless male shaft assembly. Install shaft assembly.

3) Ensure splines are fully engaged. Install rubber boot over assembly and tighten keystone clamps. On left axle applications, install shaft assembly through steering knuckle and engage in splines.

CAUTION: Install spindle needle bearing so manufacturer's identification mark is away from spindle bore.

4) Using Bearing/Seal Installer (T80T-4000-S) and Handle (T80T-4000-W) for Dana 44IFS axles, or Bearing/Seal Installer (T80T-4000-R) for Dana 50IFS axles, install needle bearing in spindle, with manufacturer identification mark facing away from spindle bore.

5) Using Bearing/Seal Installer (T80T-4000-T), install oil seal in spindle, with seal lip facing away from spindle. Coat seal lip with multipurpose grease. Install spindle and splash shield. To install remaining components, reverse removal procedure.

6) Tighten bolts/nuts to specification. See appropriate TORQUE SPECIFICATIONS table at end of article. Adjust wheel bearings. See WHEEL BEARING ADJUSTMENT under ADJUSTMENTS & INSPECTION.

Removal (F350) – 1) Raise and support vehicle. Remove front wheels. Remove locking hub. See MANUAL LOCKING HUBS under REMOVAL & INSTALLATION. Using Spanner Lock Nut Wrench (D85T-1197-A), remove wheel bearing outer lock nut, lock washer and adjusting nut. *See Fig. 6.*

2) Remove brake caliper, and support aside. DO NOT hang by flexible brake hose. Remove hub and rotor assembly. Remove spindle-to-steering knuckle nuts. Tap spindle with plastic hammer to free spindle from steering knuckle. *See Fig. 6.*

3) Remove spindle and splash shield. Remove seal from spindle. Using puller, remove needle bearing from spindle. Pull shaft assembly from axle housing. Remove bronze spacer from axle shaft (if required).

Installation – 1) Clean dirt and grease from spindle bearing bore. Install shield and "V" seal on shaft assembly. *See Fig. 6.* Coat seal lip and "V" seal on shaft assembly with multipurpose grease. Install shaft assembly.

CAUTION: Install spindle needle bearing so manufacturer's identification mark is away from spindle bore.

2) Ensure shaft splines are fully engaged. Install bronze spacer on shaft assembly, with chamfered side against shaft assembly. Using Bearing/Seal Installer (T80T-4000-R) and Handle (T80T-4000-W), install needle bearing in spindle, with manufacturer identification mark facing away from spindle bore.

3) Pack bearing with grease. Install seal in spindle. Install spindle and splash shield. To complete installation, reverse removal procedure. Adjust wheel bearings. See WHEEL BEARING ADJUSTMENT under ADJUSTMENTS & INSPECTION.

STEERING KNUCKLE

Removal (F250/250 HD) – 1) Remove spindle and shaft assembly. See SPINDLE & SHAFT ASSEMBLY under REMOVAL & INSTALLATION. Disconnect steering linkage from steering knuckle.

2) Remove cotter pin and loosen ball joint nuts. Strike steering knuckle near ball joint to release ball joint. Remove nuts from ball joint studs. Note position of camber adjuster on top of axle. *See Fig. 5.* Remove camber adjuster and steering knuckle.

CAUTION: Camber adjuster must be installed in original location to maintain proper wheel alignment.

Installation – Ensure camber adjuster is installed in original position. Install NEW nuts on ball joints, and tighten to specification. See appropriate TORQUE SPECIFICATIONS table at end of article. To complete installation, reverse removal procedure.

Removal (F350) – 1) Remove spindle and shaft assembly. See SPINDLE & SHAFT ASSEMBLY under REMOVAL & INSTALLATION. Alternately remove spindle cap bolts. *See Fig. 6.*

CAUTION: Use care when removing spindle cap, as cap is under spring pressure.

2) Remove spindle cap, compression spring, retainer and gasket. Remove lower kingpin and retainer. Remove tapered bushing from top of upper kingpin. Remove steering knuckle from axle housing.

3) Using a 7/8" hex bar stock, remove upper kingpin from axle housing. *See Fig. 7.* Using 2-jaw puller and Step Plate (D80L-630-7), remove grease seal, bearing, bearing cup and grease retainer. *See Fig. 6.*

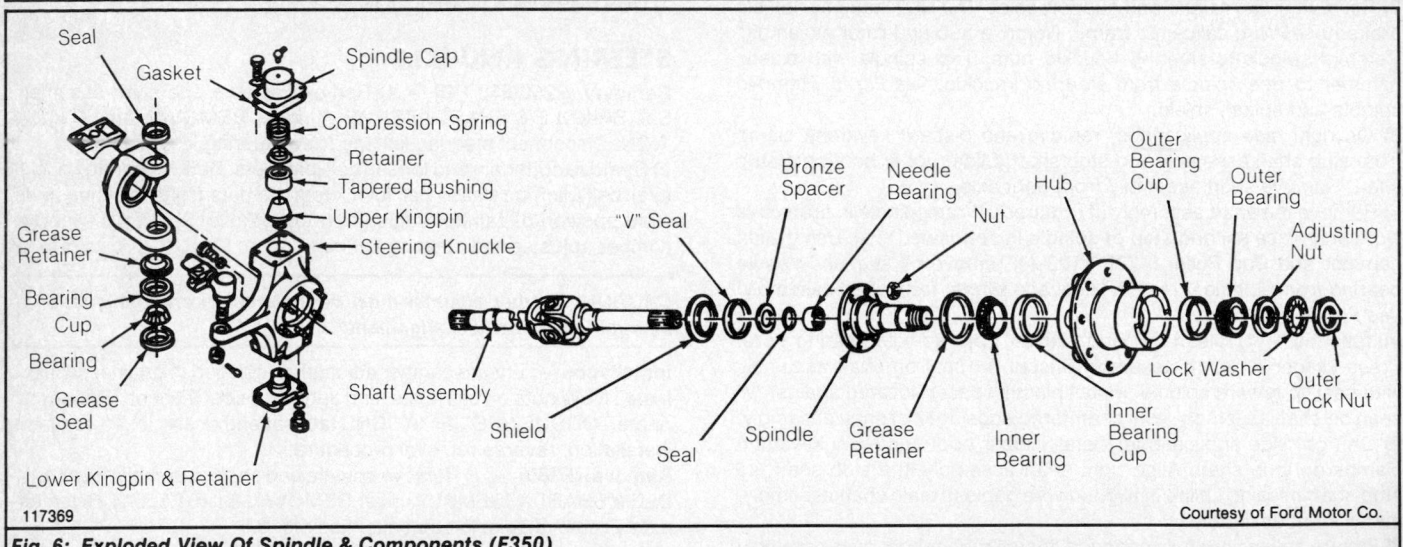

"V" Seal & Slinger
Camber Adjuster
Right Axle
Keystone Clamp
Stub Shaft
Right Shaft Assembly
Rubber Boot
Axle Pivot Bolt
Left Axle
Left Shaft Assembly
"V" Seal & Slinger
Upper Ball Joint
Splash Shield
Oil Seal
Needle Bearing
Spindle
Inner Wheel Bearing Assembly
Rotor
Universal Joint
Race
Hub
Steering Knuckle
Grease Seal
Race
Adjusting Nut
Lock Ring
Outer Lock Nut
Outer Wheel Bearing Assembly

117368
Courtesy of Ford Motor Co.

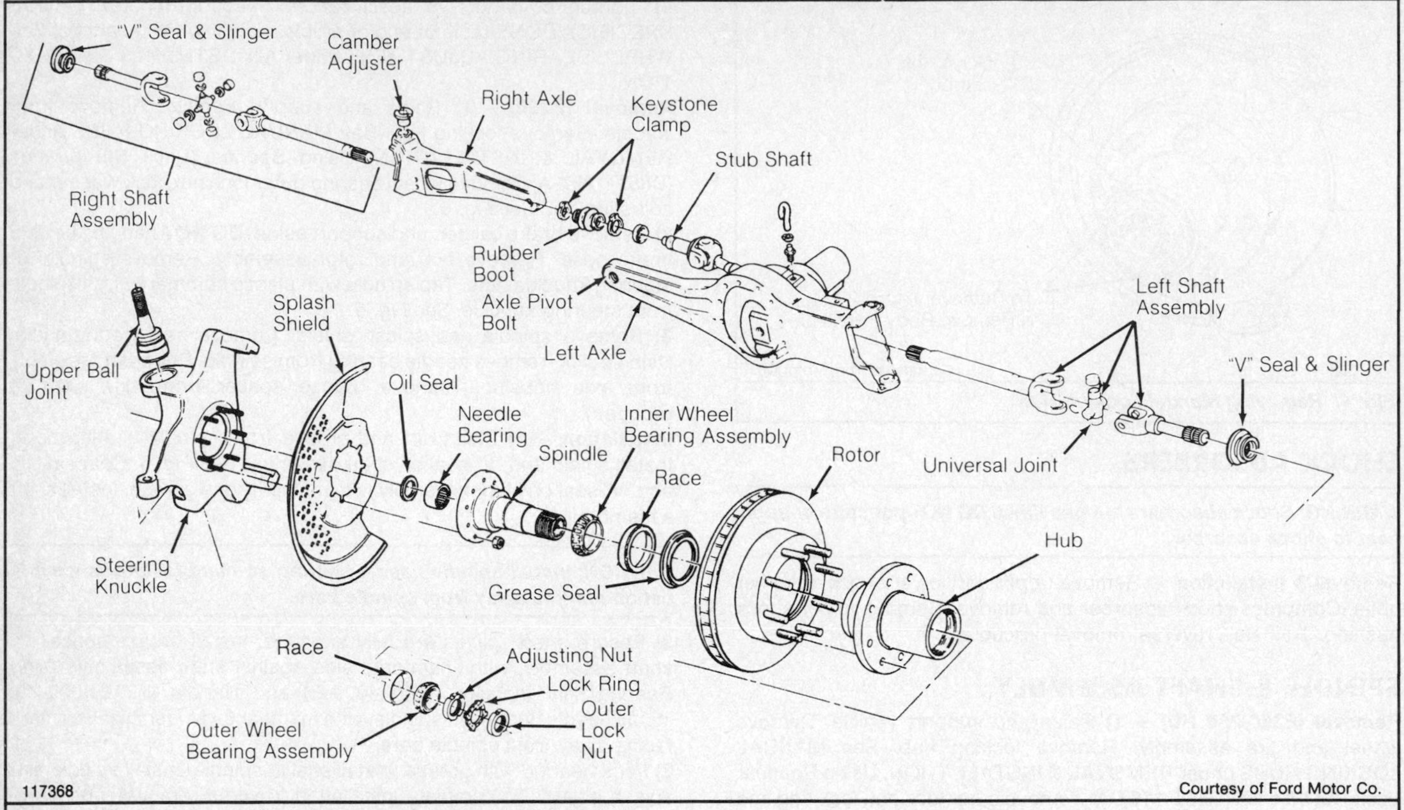

Fig. 5: Exploded View Of Spindle & Components (F250/250 HD)

Seal
Gasket
Spindle Cap
Compression Spring
Retainer
Tapered Bushing
Upper Kingpin
Bronze Spacer
Needle Bearing
Hub
Outer Bearing Cup
Outer Bearing
"V" Seal
Nut
Adjusting Nut
Grease Retainer
Bearing Cup
Steering Knuckle
Bearing
Grease Seal
Shaft Assembly
Shield
Seal
Spindle
Grease Retainer
Inner Bearing
Inner Bearing Cup
Lock Washer
Outer Lock Nut
Lower Kingpin & Retainer

117369
Courtesy of Ford Motor Co.

Fig. 6: Exploded View Of Spindle & Components (F350)

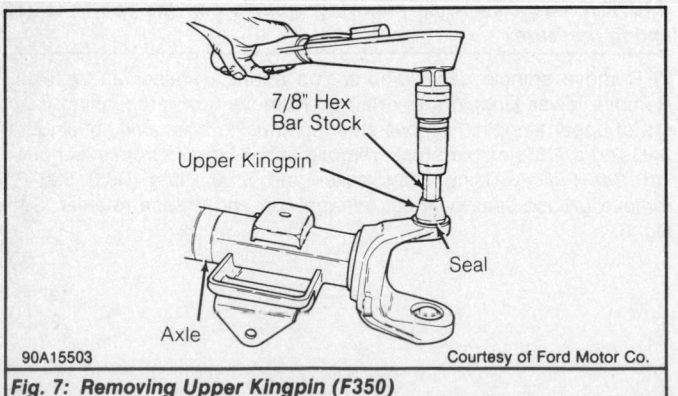

7/8" Hex Bar Stock
Upper Kingpin
Seal
Axle

90A15503
Courtesy of Ford Motor Co.

Fig. 7: Removing Upper Kingpin (F350)

Installation – 1) Coat grease retainer-to-lower kingpin contact surface with silicon-type sealant. Install grease retainer in axle housing, with concave portion toward upper kingpin.

2) Install bearing cup until it bottoms on grease retainer. Pack bearing and axle housing area with grease and install bearing. Using Seal Installer (T86T-3110-AH), install NEW grease seal.

3) Install upper kingpin and tighten to specification. See appropriate TORQUE SPECIFICATIONS table at end of article. Install steering knuckle and tapered bushing. Install lower kingpin and retainer. Alternately tighten bolts to specification.

4) Install retainer, compression spring, and spindle cap. Tighten spindle cap bolts to **70-90 ft. lbs. (95-122 N.m)**. To complete installation, reverse removal procedure. Lubricate upper kingpin through grease fitting. Lubricate lower kingpin through flush-type fitting on bottom of kingpin.

BALL JOINT

NOTE: Always remove lower ball joint before removing upper ball joint. Install lower ball joint before installing upper ball joint. DO NOT heat ball joint or axle to aid in installation.

Removal (F250/250 HD) – 1) Remove steering knuckle. See STEERING KNUCKLE under REMOVAL & INSTALLATION. Remove snap ring from bottom ball joint socket.
2) Remove plug from "C" Frame Assembly (T74P-4635-C), and replace with Plug (T80T-3010-A4). *See Fig. 8.* Assemble "C" frame assembly and Receiving Cup (T80T-3010-A2) on lower ball joint. *See Fig. 9.*
3) Turn forcing screw clockwise until lower ball joint is removed from spindle. Repeat procedure to remove upper ball joint. *See Fig. 9.*

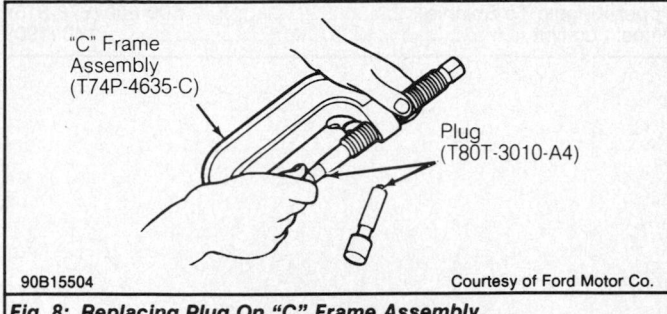

"C" Frame Assembly (T74P-4635-C)

Plug (T80T-3010-A4)

90B15504   Courtesy of Ford Motor Co.

Fig. 8: Replacing Plug On "C" Frame Assembly

Installation – 1) Install lower ball joint first. Assemble "C" frame assembly, Receiving Cup (T80T-3010-A3) and Installing Cup (D81T-3010-A) on lower ball joint. *See Fig. 9.* Turn forcing screw to install ball joint. Ensure ball joint is fully seated.
2) To install upper ball joint, assemble "C" frame, Receiving Cup (T80T-3010-A3) and Replacer (T80T-3010-A1). Turn forcing screw to install ball joint. Ensure ball joint is fully seated. Install snap ring on lower ball joints and install steering knuckle. See STEERING KNUCKLE under REMOVAL & INSTALLATION.

LEAF SPRING ASSEMBLY

Removal – 1) Raise and support vehicle frame, with weight off front springs and wheels touching ground. Support drive axle to prevent axle rotation. Remove lower shock absorber bolts.
2) On F350, remove track bar bolts from spring cap and track bar mounting bracket. On all models, remove "U" bolts, spring cap and spacer plate. *See Fig. 1.* Remove spring-to-hanger bolts, and remove spring.
Installation – To install, reverse removal procedure. On F350, track bar must be installed with vehicle at normal operating height.

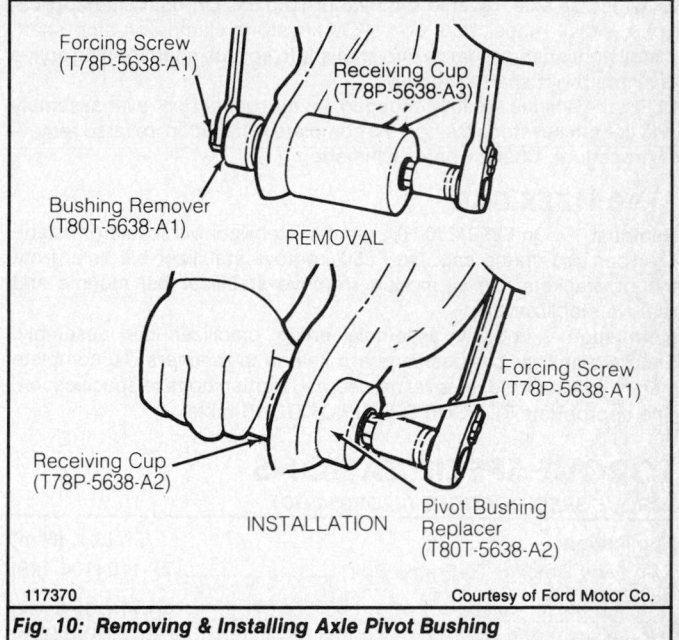

Forcing Screw (T78P-5638-A1)

Receiving Cup (T78P-5638-A3)

Bushing Remover (T80T-5638-A1)

REMOVAL

Forcing Screw (T78P-5638-A1)

Receiving Cup (T78P-5638-A2)

INSTALLATION

Pivot Bushing Replacer (T80T-5638-A2)

117370   Courtesy of Ford Motor Co.

Fig. 10: Removing & Installing Axle Pivot Bushing

AXLE PIVOT BUSHING

Removal (F250/250 HD) – 1) Front axle must be removed. Raise and support vehicle. Remove front wheels and brake calipers. DO NOT let brake caliper hang by flex hose. Disconnect steering linkage at steering knuckles. Support right axle with jack.
2) Remove leaf spring "U" bolts. Disconnect axle vent tube and plug opening. Remove right axle pivot bolt. Remove keystone clamps and rubber boot from shaft assembly. *See Fig. 5.* Remove right axle assembly while pulling shaft assembly from stub shaft.
3) For left axle applications, disconnect drive shaft from differential. Place jack under left axle and differential. Remove leaf spring "U" bolts. Remove left axle pivot bolt. Lower jack and remove axle.
4) Install Forcing Screw (T78P-5638-A1), Bushing Remover (T80T-5638-A1) and Receiving Cup (T78P-5638-A3) onto pivot bushing. *See Fig. 10.* Turn forcing screw and remove pivot bushing.
Installation – 1) Place new pivot bushing in axle housing bore. Install Receiving Cup (T78P-5638-A2), Forcing Screw (T78P-5638-A1) and Pivot Bushing Replacer (T80T-5638-A2) onto axle housing. *See Fig. 10.* Turn forcing screw to press bushing into bore.

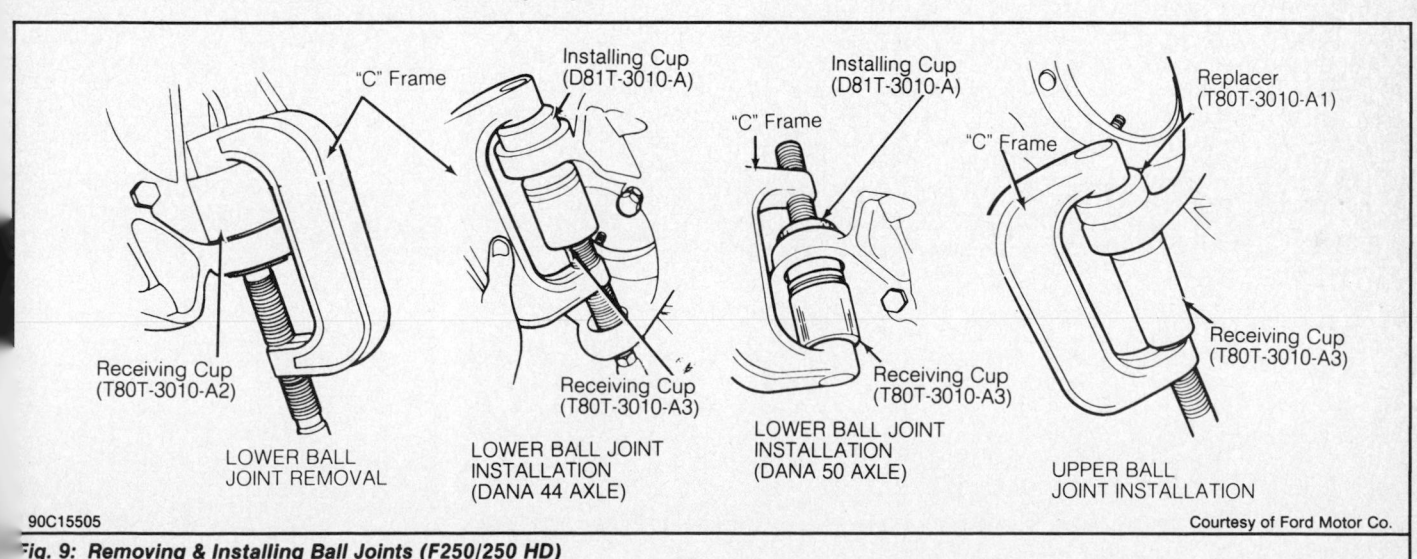

"C" Frame

Installing Cup (D81T-3010-A)

Installing Cup (D81T-3010-A)

"C" Frame

Replacer (T80T-3010-A1)

"C" Frame

Receiving Cup (T80T-3010-A2)

Receiving Cup (T80T-3010-A3)

Receiving Cup (T80T-3010-A3)

Receiving Cup (T80T-3010-A3)

LOWER BALL JOINT REMOVAL

LOWER BALL JOINT INSTALLATION (DANA 44 AXLE)

LOWER BALL JOINT INSTALLATION (DANA 50 AXLE)

UPPER BALL JOINT INSTALLATION

90C15505   Courtesy of Ford Motor Co.

Fig. 9: Removing & Installing Ball Joints (F250/250 HD)

2) To install axle, reverse removal procedure. On right side applications, install rubber boot and NEW keystone clamps on stub shaft. Install right shaft assembly into stub shaft, so stub shaft missing spline is aligned with shaft assembly.

3) Ensure splines are fully engaged. Install rubber boot over assembly and tighten keystone clamps. To complete installation, reverse removal procedure. Check wheel alignment.

STABILIZER BAR

Removal – On F250/250 HD, remove stabilizer bar links from stabilizer bar and spring cap. On F350, remove stabilizer bar links from mount brackets. On all models, remove stabilizer bar mounts and remove stabilizer bar.

Installation – Loosely assemble entire stabilizer bar assembly. Ensure stabilizer bar bushings are seated in retainers. To complete installation, reverse removal procedure. Tighten bolts to specification. See appropriate TORQUE SPECIFICATIONS table.

TORQUE SPECIFICATIONS

TORQUE SPECIFICATIONS (F250/250 HD)

Application	Ft. Lbs. (N.m)
Axle Pivot Bracket-To-Frame Bolt	77-110 (104-149)
Ball Joint Nut	
Lower	90-110 (122-149)
Upper	100 (136)
Front Leaf Spring "U" Bolt Nut	85-120 (115-163)
Shock Absorber Bolt	52-74 (71-100)
Shock Absorber Bracket-To-Frame Bolt	52-74 (71-100)
Spindle-To-Steering Knuckle Nut	50-60 (68-81)
Spring Hanger-To-Frame Bracket Bolt	150-210 (203-285)
Spring-To-Spring Hanger Bolt	120-150 (163-203)
Stabilizer Bar Link-To-Spring Cap Bolt	52-74 (71-100)
Stabilizer Bar Retainer-To-Frame Bolt	27-37 (37-50)
Stabilizer Bar-To-Link Nut	15-25 (20-34)
Tie Rod End-To-Spindle Nut	52-74 (71-100)
Wheel Lug Nut	140 (190)

TORQUE SPECIFICATIONS (F350)

Application	Ft. Lbs. (N.m)
Front Leaf Spring "U" Bolt Nut	85-120 (115-163)
Lower Kingpin Bolt	70-90 (95-122)
Shock Absorber Bolt	52-74 (71-100)
Shock Absorber Bracket-To-Frame Bolt	52-74 (71-100)
Spring Hanger-To-Frame Bracket Bolt	150-210 (203-285)
Spring-To-Spring Hanger Bolt	120-150 (163-203)
Stabilizer Bar Link Bracket-To-Frame Bolt	35-50 (47-68)
Stabilizer Bar Link-To-Mount Bracket Bolt	52-74 (71-100)
Stabilizer Bar Retainer-To-Frame Bolt	27-37 (37-50)
Stabilizer Bar-To-Link Nut	15-25 (20-34)
Steering Linkage-To-Steering Knuckle Nut	70-100 (95-136)
Tie Rod End-To-Spindle Nut	52-74 (71-100)
Track Bar Mount Bracket-To-Frame Bolt	77-110 (104-149)
Track Bar-To-Mount Bolt	120-150 (163-203)
Upper Kingpin To Spindle	500-600 (678-813)
Wheel Lug Nut	140 (190)

Aerostar, Bronco, Explorer, Pickup, Ranger, Van

NOTE: Unless otherwise specified, references to Pickup include the F350 Super Duty commercial chassis.

MODEL IDENTIFICATION

Series [1]	Model
"A"	Aerostar
"E"	RWD Van
"F"	Pickup
"R"	Ranger
"U"	Bronco & Explorer

[1] – Vehicle series is fifth character of VIN.

DESCRIPTION

All steering columns are energy-absorbing and collapse upon frontal impact. On Explorer and Ranger, steering column is available in standard and tilt column models.

Aerostar, Bronco, Pickup and Van are equipped with tilt steering wheel. Aerostar and Van are equipped with air bag. Wiper/washer, turn signal/hazard and horn/dimmer operate using a multifunction switch. Multifunction and ignition switches are mounted on steering column.

WARNING: On models with Supplemental Restraint System (SRS), observe the following precautions. Before any repairs are performed, disconnect and shield battery ground. Disconnect SRS connector at control unit. Use caution when working around steering column (air bag could deploy).

AIR BAG SERVICE PRECAUTIONS

The following precautions should be observed when working with air bag systems.

- Disable air bag system before servicing any air bag system or steering column components. Failure to do so may result in accidental air bag deployment and cause personal injury. See DISABLING AIR BAG SYSTEM.
- Back-up power supply will hold a deployment charge for approximately one minute after battery positive cable is disconnected. Servicing SRS before one-minute period may cause accidental air bag deployment and possible personal injury.
- Because of critical system operating requirements, DO NOT service sensors, clockspring, monitor, or air bag module. Corrections are made by replacement only.
- Always wear safety glasses whenever servicing an air bag equipped vehicle or handling an air bag.
- When carrying a live air bag module, ensure air bag module and trim cover are pointed away from your body. This minimizes chance of injury in event of an accidental deployment.
- When placing a live air bag module on a bench or other surface, always face air bag module and trim cover up, away from surface. This will reduce motion of module if it is accidentally deployed.
- After deployment, air bag surface may contain deposits of sodium hydroxide, which may irritate skin. Sodium hydroxide is a product of gas generant combustion. Always wear gloves and safety glasses when handling a deployed air bag. Wash your hands using mild soap and water. Follow correct disposal procedures.
- If a part is replaced and new part does not correct condition, reinstall original part and perform diagnostic procedure again.
- Never probe connectors on air bag module. Doing so may cause air bag deployment and/or personal injury.
- The instruction to DISCONNECT always refers to a connector. DO NOT disconnect a component from vehicle when instructed to DISCONNECT.
- After repairs, ensure AIR BAG warning light does not indicate any other faults.

DISABLING AIR BAG SYSTEM

WARNING: Back-up power supply will hold a deployment charge for approximately one minute after battery positive cable is disconnected. Servicing SRS before one-minute period may cause accidental air bag deployment and possible personal injury.

WARNING: When battery is disconnected, vehicle computer and memory systems may lose memory data. Driveability problems may exist until computer systems have completed a relearn cycle. See COMPUTER RELEARN PROCEDURES article in GENERAL INFORMATION before disconnecting battery.

NOTE: The following disabling procedure should be used for component replacement purposes only. If vehicle was involved in a collision and air bag did not deploy, or SRS is not functioning properly, and vehicle needs to be driven, complete system deactivation is required.

Disconnect battery negative and then positive cables. Shield both cables. Air bag system contains a back-up power supply built into the air bag diagnostic monitor. Wait a minimum of one minute before servicing any air bag system components. System is now disabled.

REMOVAL & INSTALLATION

WARNING: When battery is disconnected, vehicle computer and memory systems may lose memory data. Driveability problems may exist until computer systems have completed a relearn cycle. See COMPUTER RELEARN PROCEDURES article in GENERAL INFORMATION before disconnecting battery.

STEERING WHEEL & AIR BAG

Removal & Installation (Aerostar & Van) – 1) Set front wheels in straight-ahead position. Disconnect and shield battery negative and positive cables. Wait at least one minute to deplete charge in air bag back-up power supply. Remove air bag module-to-steering wheel retaining nuts. Remove air bag from steering wheel and disconnect air bag module electrical connector.

2) Disconnect horn switch and speed control (if equipped) electrical connectors. Mark steering wheel-to-steering shaft position for installation reference. Remove steering wheel retaining bolt. Using Steering Wheel Remover (T67L-3600-A), remove steering wheel.

3) To install, reverse removal procedure. Tighten steering wheel retaining bolt and air bag retaining nuts to specification. See TORQUE SPECIFICATIONS table at end of article.

STEERING WHEEL & HORN PAD

Removal & Installation (Bronco, Explorer, Pickup, Ranger & Van) – 1) Set front wheels in straight-ahead position. Disconnect battery negative cable. On Explorer and Ranger, remove horn pad retaining screws. Disconnect horn switch electrical connector and remove horn pad. On Bronco, Pickup and Van, grasp sides of horn pad and pull upward to unclip retainers. Disconnect horn switch electrical connector and remove horn pad.

2) Mark steering wheel-to-steering shaft position for installation reference. Remove steering wheel retaining bolt. Using Steering Wheel Remover (T67L-3600-A), remove steering wheel.

3) To install, reverse removal procedure. Tighten steering wheel retaining bolt and horn pad retaining screws (if equipped) to specification. See TORQUE SPECIFICATIONS table at end of article.

MULTIFUNCTION SWITCH

Removal & Installation – Disconnect battery negative cable. Remove upper and lower steering column shrouds. Remove 2 multifunction switch retaining screws. Disconnect multifunction switch electrical connector and remove multifunction switch from steering column. To install, reverse removal procedure.

LOCK CYLINDER

Removal (With Key) – **1)** Disconnect battery negative cable. Remove steering wheel. See STEERING WHEEL & AIR BAG or STEERING WHEEL & HORN PAD under REMOVAL & INSTALLATION. Remove upper and lower steering column shrouds. Disconnect key warning switch electrical connector. Using key, turn lock cylinder to RUN position.

2) On Ranger and Explorer A/T models, shift selector must be in Park. On all models, place a 1/8" (3.17 mm) diameter pin in hole located in outer edge of lock cylinder housing. Depress retaining pin and pull out lock cylinder. *See Fig. 1.*

Installation – **1)** To install, lubricate lock cylinder with grease. Turn lock cylinder to RUN position. Depress retaining pin. Insert lock cylinder into housing. Ensure tab on end of lock cylinder aligns with slot in ignition drive gear.

2) Using key, turn lock cylinder to OFF position to engage cylinder retaining pin into cylinder housing hole. To complete installation, reverse removal procedure. Check lock cylinder functions. Ensure column locks when switch is in LOCK position.

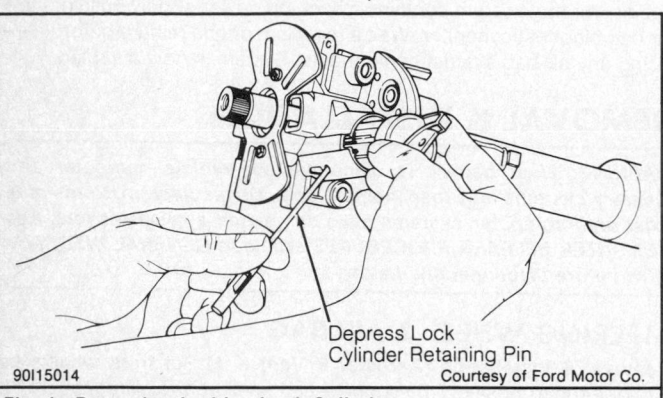

Depress Lock
Cylinder Retaining Pin

90I15014   Courtesy of Ford Motor Co.

Fig. 1: Removing Ignition Lock Cylinder

Removal (Without Key) – **1)** Use this procedure to remove ignition lock cylinder if key is missing or cylinder lock is frozen. Disconnect battery negative cable. Remove steering wheel. See STEERING WHEEL & AIR BAG or STEERING WHEEL & HORN PAD under REMOVAL & INSTALLATION. Remove upper and lower steering column shrouds. Disconnect key warning switch electrical connector. Use a 1/8" (3.17 mm) drill bit to drill out retaining pin. DO NOT drill deeper than 1/2" (12.7 mm).

2) Place a chisel at base of lock cylinder cap. Using a hammer, strike chisel with sharp blows to break cap away from lock cylinder. Using a 3/8" (9.52 mm) drill bit, drill out center of lock cylinder key slot. Drill down approximately 1 3/4" (44 mm) until lock cylinder breaks away from base of lock cylinder.

3) Remove metal shavings from lock cylinder housing. Remove bearing retainer, bearing and ignition drive gear from lock cylinder. Thoroughly clean all metal shavings and other foreign materials from housing. Carefully inspect housing for damage. If damage is apparent, replace housing.

Installation – **1)** Install ignition drive gear, bearing and bearing retainer. Lubricate cylinder cavity with lock cylinder lubricant. Turn ignition switch to RUN position. Depress retaining pin and insert NEW lock cylinder into housing.

2) Ensure tab on end of lock cylinder aligns with slot in ignition drive gear. Using key, turn lock cylinder to OFF position to engage cylinder retaining pin into cylinder housing hole. To complete installation, reverse removal procedure. Check lock cylinder functions. Ensure column locks when switch is in LOCK position.

IGNITION SWITCH

Removal & Installation (Aerostar, Bronco, Pickup & Van) – **1)** Set front wheels in straight-ahead position. Disable air bag (if equipped). See DISABLING AIR BAG SYSTEM. Remove steering wheel. See STEERING WHEEL & AIR BAG or STEERING WHEEL & HORN PAD

under REMOVAL & INSTALLATION. Remove steering column. See STEERING COLUMN under REMOVAL & INSTALLATION. Remove 2 ignition switch retaining screws. Disconnect ignition switch electrical connector and remove ignition switch from steering column.

2) Install ignition switch onto steering column. Ensure actuator pin on ignition switch is aligned with slot in actuator housing. Ensure slot in actuator housing is aligned with mark on steering column casting. Ignition switch should be in RUN position. Connect ignition switch electrical connector and tighten retaining screws to specification. See TORQUE SPECIFICATIONS table at end of article. To complete installation, reverse removal procedure.

Removal & Installation (Explorer & Ranger) – **1)** Disconnect battery negative cable. Remove steering wheel. See STEERING WHEEL & HORN PAD under REMOVAL & INSTALLATION. Remove lower steering column shroud. On tilt columns, unscrew and remove tilt lever. Remove steering column collar by squeezing it at 6 and 12 o'clock positions. On all models, remove upper steering column shroud. On A/T models, remove selector indicator cable by removing screw and plastic plug from column casting.

2) On all models, remove screws attaching toe plate to body panel. Support steering column. Remove bolts holding steering column to bracket. Turn column to right. Disconnect ignition switch electrical connector. Remove ignition switch retaining nuts and remove ignition switch from steering column.

3) Before ignition switch is installed, turn ignition lock cylinder to LOCK position. To preset ignition switch, place a wire in opening in side of switch. Using actuator rod, move switch through positions until wire drops down into slot in bottom of switch where actuator rod is to be inserted. Place actuator rod on switch and switch on column studs while aligning rod hole with rod. Tighten retaining nuts to specification. See TORQUE SPECIFICATIONS table at end of article. Remove wire from hole in ignition switch.

4) Ensure switch is operating smoothly and all functions are engaged. Turn key through each position from LOCK to START. To complete installation, reverse removal procedure.

STEERING COLUMN

Removal & Installation (Aerostar, Bronco, Pickup & Van) – **1)** Set front wheels in straight-ahead position. Disable air bag (if equipped). See DISABLING AIR BAG SYSTEM. Remove steering wheel. See STEERING WHEEL & AIR BAG or STEERING WHEEL & HORN PAD under REMOVAL & INSTALLATION. Remove right and left instrument panel lower moldings. Remove instrument panel lower trim cover.

2) Remove screws from lower steering column shroud. Remove lower steering column shroud by pulling shroud down and toward rear of vehicle. Disconnect air bag clockspring contact assembly electrical connectors (if equipped). Place tape across contact assembly stator and rotor to prevent accidental rotation (if equipped). Remove clockspring contact assembly retaining screws and remove contact assembly from steering column (if equipped).

3) Unscrew and remove tilt lever from column. Using key, turn lock cylinder to RUN position. Place a 1/8" (3.17 mm) diameter pin in hole located in outer edge of lock cylinder housing. Depress retaining pin and pull out lock cylinder. Remove upper steering column shroud from column. Remove 6 instrumental panel lower reinforcement brace retaining bolts and remove reinforcement brace.

4) Remove PRND21 cable retaining screw and disconnect cable from actuator housing. Disconnect PRND21 cable loop from shift tube hook. Remove 2 screws attaching multifunction switch to steering column. Disconnect multifunction switch electrical connector and remove switch.

5) Remove bolt attaching intermediate shaft to steering column shaft. Disconnect shift cable from selector lever pivot. Push in tab on shift cable and slide cable off shaft cable bracket. Disconnect ignition switch electrical connector. Support steering column assembly and remove 4 steering column-to-support bracket retaining nuts. Carefully remove column from vehicle.

6) To install steering column, reverse removal procedure. Tighten all nuts and bolts to specifications. See TORQUE SPECIFICATIONS table at end of article.

Removal & Installation (Explorer & Ranger) – 1) Disconnect battery negative cable. On A/T models, place transmission in Neutral. On all models, remove bolt attaching intermediate shaft-to-steering column shaft. Compress intermediate shaft until clear of steering column shaft.

2) On A/T models, remove nuts attaching shift cable bracket to steering column bracket. Disconnect shift cable from column lever. On tilt columns, ensure steering wheel is in full-up position before removing steering wheel.

3) On all models, remove steering wheel. See STEERING WHEEL & HORN PAD under REMOVAL & INSTALLATION. On tilt columns, unscrew and remove tilt lever. Remove steering column collar by squeezing it at 6 and 12 o'clock positions.

4) On all models, remove screws attaching panel trim cover and remove trim cover. Remove screws from lower steering column shroud. Remove lower steering column shroud by pulling shroud down and toward rear of vehicle. Remove upper steering column shroud from column.

5) On A/T models, disconnect selector indicator actuation cable by removing screw from column casting and plastic plug at end of cable.

To remove plastic plug from shift lever socket casting, push on nose of plug until head clears casting, and then pull plug from casting.

6) On all models, remove plastic clip holding multifunction switch wiring to steering column bracket. Remove screws attaching multifunction switch. Remove multifunction switch from column, leaving wiring connected to switch. Position switch and wiring aside.

7) Disconnect key warning buzzer electrical connector from horn brush. Remove screw holding horn brush electrical connector to column. Disconnect horn brush electrical connector. Remove screws attaching toe plate to body panel. Loosen toe plate clamp bolt.

8) Support steering column. Remove bolts holding steering column to bracket. Disconnect ignition switch wiring connector. Carefully remove column from vehicle.

9) To install steering column, reverse removal procedure. Tighten all nuts and bolts to specifications. See TORQUE SPECIFICATIONS table at end of article.

OVERHAUL

When overhauling steering columns, refer to exploded view illustrations. *See Figs. 2-6.*

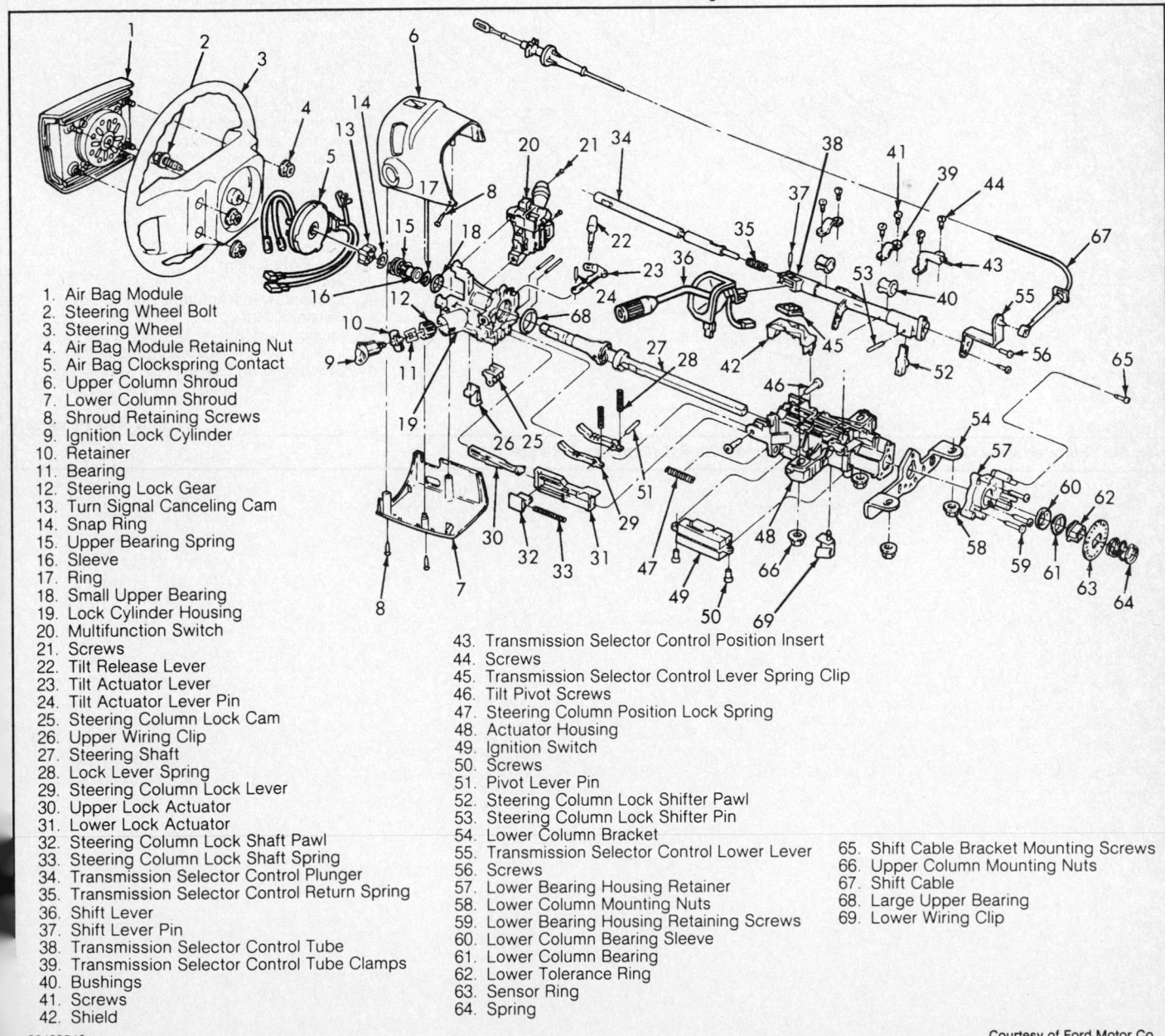

1. Air Bag Module
2. Steering Wheel Bolt
3. Steering Wheel
4. Air Bag Module Retaining Nut
5. Air Bag Clockspring Contact
6. Upper Column Shroud
7. Lower Column Shroud
8. Shroud Retaining Screws
9. Ignition Lock Cylinder
10. Retainer
11. Bearing
12. Steering Lock Gear
13. Turn Signal Canceling Cam
14. Snap Ring
15. Upper Bearing Spring
16. Sleeve
17. Ring
18. Small Upper Bearing
19. Lock Cylinder Housing
20. Multifunction Switch
21. Screws
22. Tilt Release Lever
23. Tilt Actuator Lever
24. Tilt Actuator Lever Pin
25. Steering Column Lock Cam
26. Upper Wiring Clip
27. Steering Shaft
28. Lock Lever Spring
29. Steering Column Lock Lever
30. Upper Lock Actuator
31. Lower Lock Actuator
32. Steering Column Lock Shaft Pawl
33. Steering Column Lock Shaft Spring
34. Transmission Selector Control Plunger
35. Transmission Selector Control Return Spring
36. Shift Lever
37. Shift Lever Pin
38. Transmission Selector Control Tube
39. Transmission Selector Control Tube Clamps
40. Bushings
41. Screws
42. Shield

43. Transmission Selector Control Position Insert
44. Screws
45. Transmission Selector Control Lever Spring Clip
46. Tilt Pivot Screws
47. Steering Column Position Lock Spring
48. Actuator Housing
49. Ignition Switch
50. Screws
51. Pivot Lever Pin
52. Steering Column Lock Shifter Pawl
53. Steering Column Lock Shifter Pin
54. Lower Column Bracket
55. Transmission Selector Control Lower Lever
56. Screws
57. Lower Bearing Housing Retainer
58. Lower Column Mounting Nuts
59. Lower Bearing Housing Retaining Screws
60. Lower Column Bearing Sleeve
61. Lower Column Bearing
62. Lower Tolerance Ring
63. Sensor Ring
64. Spring

65. Shift Cable Bracket Mounting Screws
66. Upper Column Mounting Nuts
67. Shift Cable
68. Large Upper Bearing
69. Lower Wiring Clip

Courtesy of Ford Motor Co.

92J22540

Fig. 2: Exploded View Of Steering Column With Air Bag (Aerostar & Van Shown – Bronco, Pickup & Van Without Air Bag Are Similar)

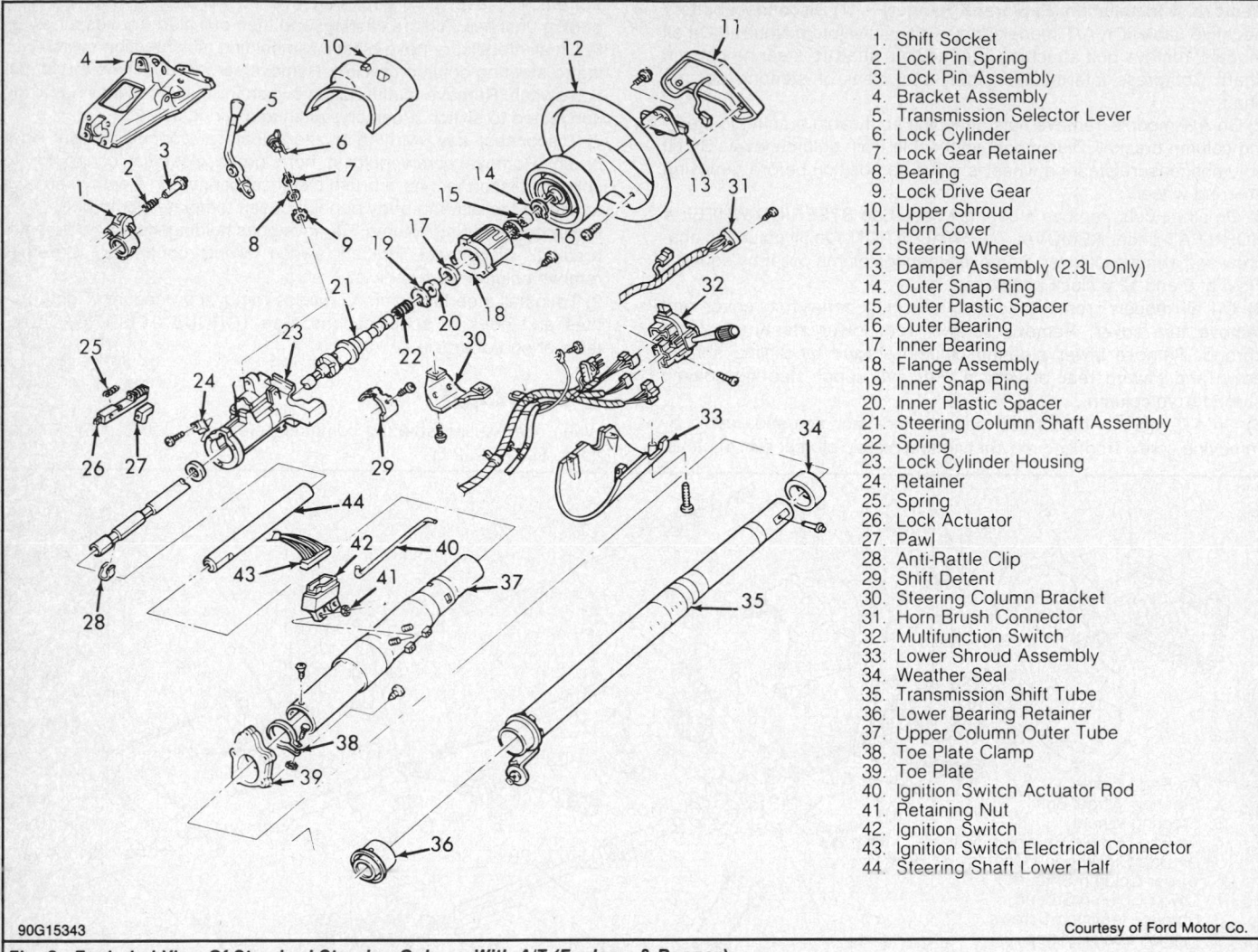

1. Shift Socket
2. Lock Pin Spring
3. Lock Pin Assembly
4. Bracket Assembly
5. Transmission Selector Lever
6. Lock Cylinder
7. Lock Gear Retainer
8. Bearing
9. Lock Drive Gear
10. Upper Shroud
11. Horn Cover
12. Steering Wheel
13. Damper Assembly (2.3L Only)
14. Outer Snap Ring
15. Outer Plastic Spacer
16. Outer Bearing
17. Inner Bearing
18. Flange Assembly
19. Inner Snap Ring
20. Inner Plastic Spacer
21. Steering Column Shaft Assembly
22. Spring
23. Lock Cylinder Housing
24. Retainer
25. Spring
26. Lock Actuator
27. Pawl
28. Anti-Rattle Clip
29. Shift Detent
30. Steering Column Bracket
31. Horn Brush Connector
32. Multifunction Switch
33. Lower Shroud Assembly
34. Weather Seal
35. Transmission Shift Tube
36. Lower Bearing Retainer
37. Upper Column Outer Tube
38. Toe Plate Clamp
39. Toe Plate
40. Ignition Switch Actuator Rod
41. Retaining Nut
42. Ignition Switch
43. Ignition Switch Electrical Connector
44. Steering Shaft Lower Half

90G15343

Courtesy of Ford Motor Co.

Fig. 3: Exploded View Of Standard Steering Column With A/T (Explorer & Ranger)

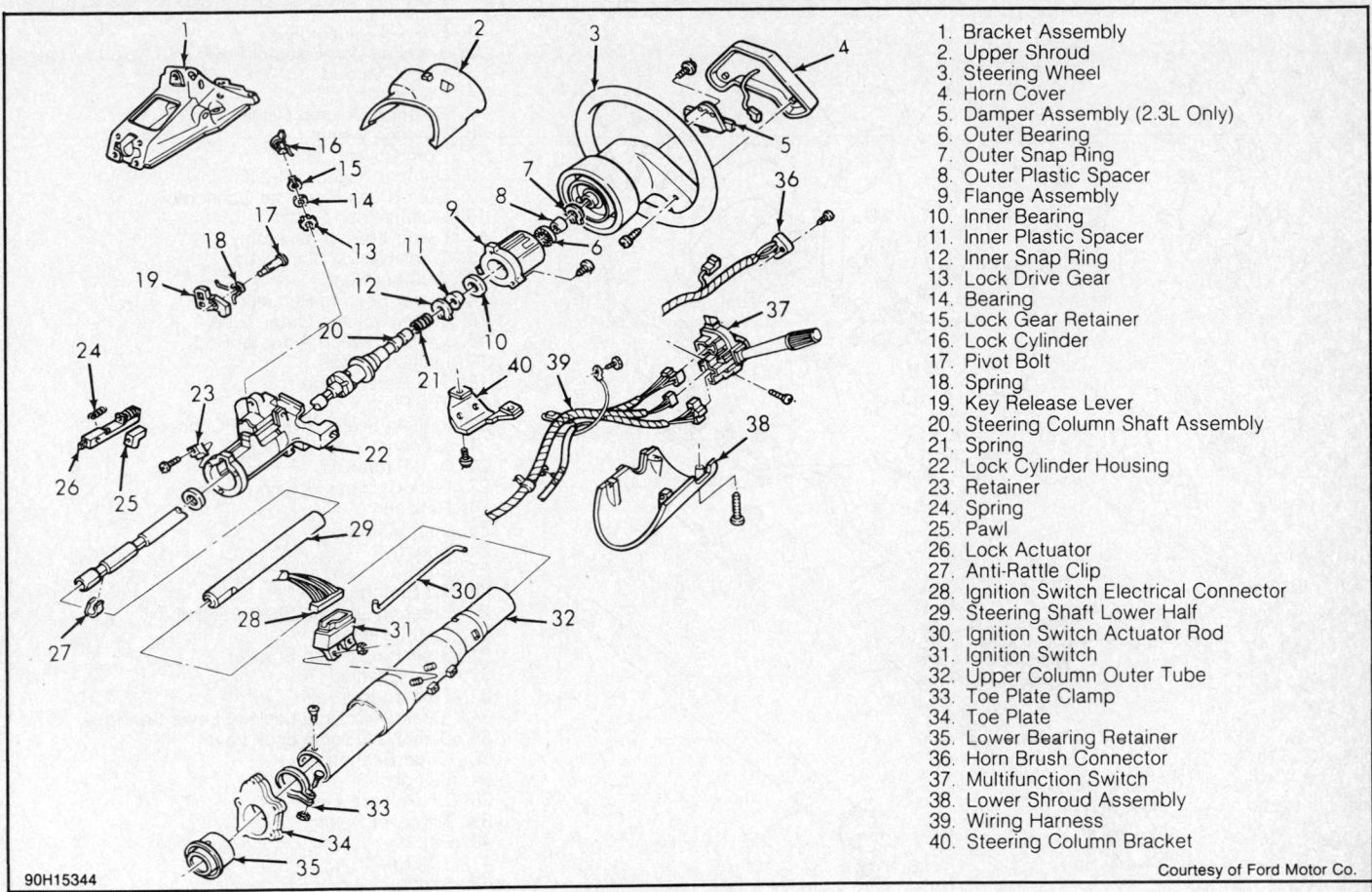

1. Bracket Assembly
2. Upper Shroud
3. Steering Wheel
4. Horn Cover
5. Damper Assembly (2.3L Only)
6. Outer Bearing
7. Outer Snap Ring
8. Outer Plastic Spacer
9. Flange Assembly
10. Inner Bearing
11. Inner Plastic Spacer
12. Inner Snap Ring
13. Lock Drive Gear
14. Bearing
15. Lock Gear Retainer
16. Lock Cylinder
17. Pivot Bolt
18. Spring
19. Key Release Lever
20. Steering Column Shaft Assembly
21. Spring
22. Lock Cylinder Housing
23. Retainer
24. Spring
25. Pawl
26. Lock Actuator
27. Anti-Rattle Clip
28. Ignition Switch Electrical Connector
29. Steering Shaft Lower Half
30. Ignition Switch Actuator Rod
31. Ignition Switch
32. Upper Column Outer Tube
33. Toe Plate Clamp
34. Toe Plate
35. Lower Bearing Retainer
36. Horn Brush Connector
37. Multifunction Switch
38. Lower Shroud Assembly
39. Wiring Harness
40. Steering Column Bracket

Courtesy of Ford Motor Co.

90H15344

Fig. 4: Exploded View Of Standard Steering Column With M/T (Explorer & Ranger)

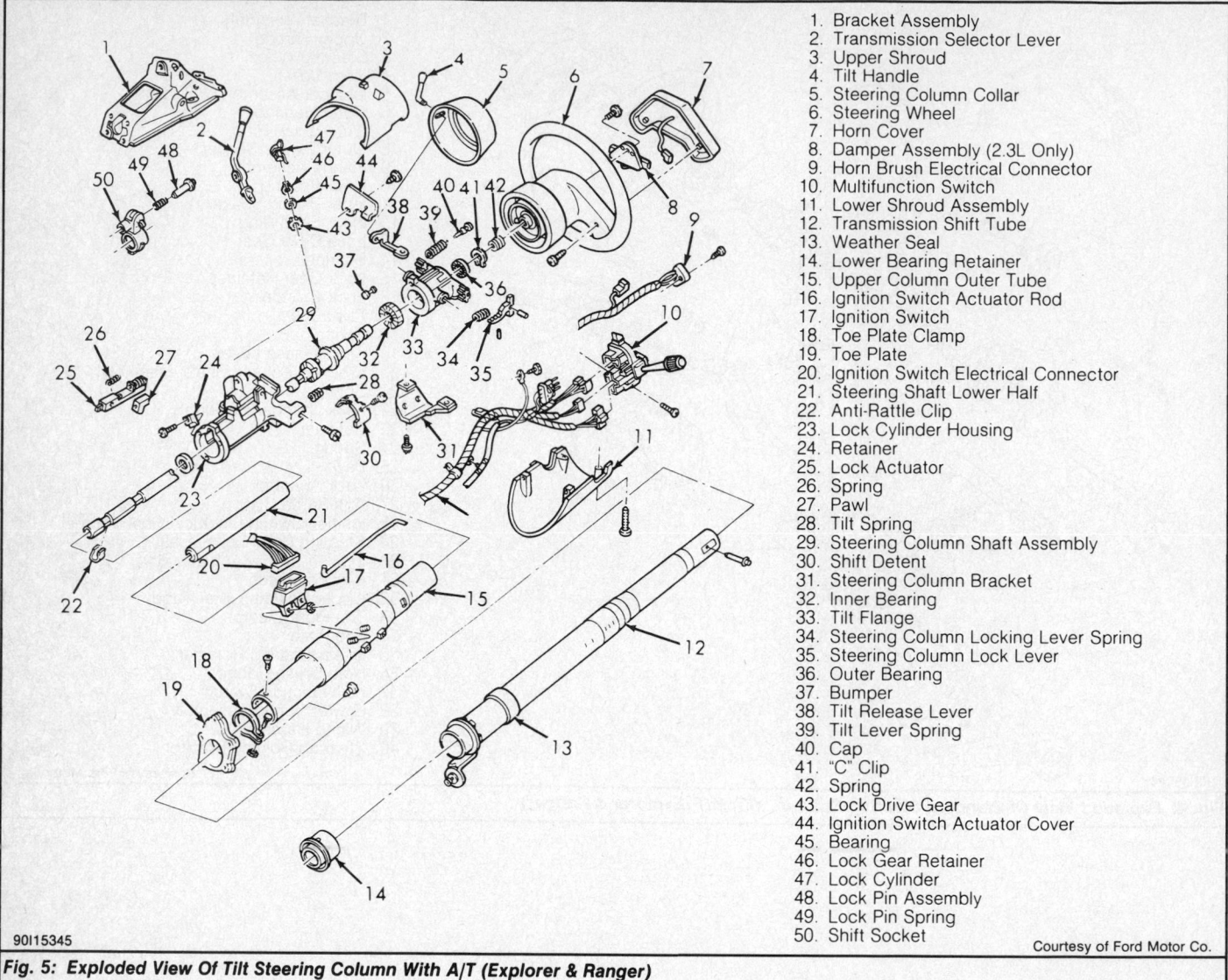

1. Bracket Assembly
2. Transmission Selector Lever
3. Upper Shroud
4. Tilt Handle
5. Steering Column Collar
6. Steering Wheel
7. Horn Cover
8. Damper Assembly (2.3L Only)
9. Horn Brush Electrical Connector
10. Multifunction Switch
11. Lower Shroud Assembly
12. Transmission Shift Tube
13. Weather Seal
14. Lower Bearing Retainer
15. Upper Column Outer Tube
16. Ignition Switch Actuator Rod
17. Ignition Switch
18. Toe Plate Clamp
19. Toe Plate
20. Ignition Switch Electrical Connector
21. Steering Shaft Lower Half
22. Anti-Rattle Clip
23. Lock Cylinder Housing
24. Retainer
25. Lock Actuator
26. Spring
27. Pawl
28. Tilt Spring
29. Steering Column Shaft Assembly
30. Shift Detent
31. Steering Column Bracket
32. Inner Bearing
33. Tilt Flange
34. Steering Column Locking Lever Spring
35. Steering Column Lock Lever
36. Outer Bearing
37. Bumper
38. Tilt Release Lever
39. Tilt Lever Spring
40. Cap
41. "C" Clip
42. Spring
43. Lock Drive Gear
44. Ignition Switch Actuator Cover
45. Bearing
46. Lock Gear Retainer
47. Lock Cylinder
48. Lock Pin Assembly
49. Lock Pin Spring
50. Shift Socket

90I15345

Courtesy of Ford Motor Co.

Fig. 5: Exploded View Of Tilt Steering Column With A/T (Explorer & Ranger)

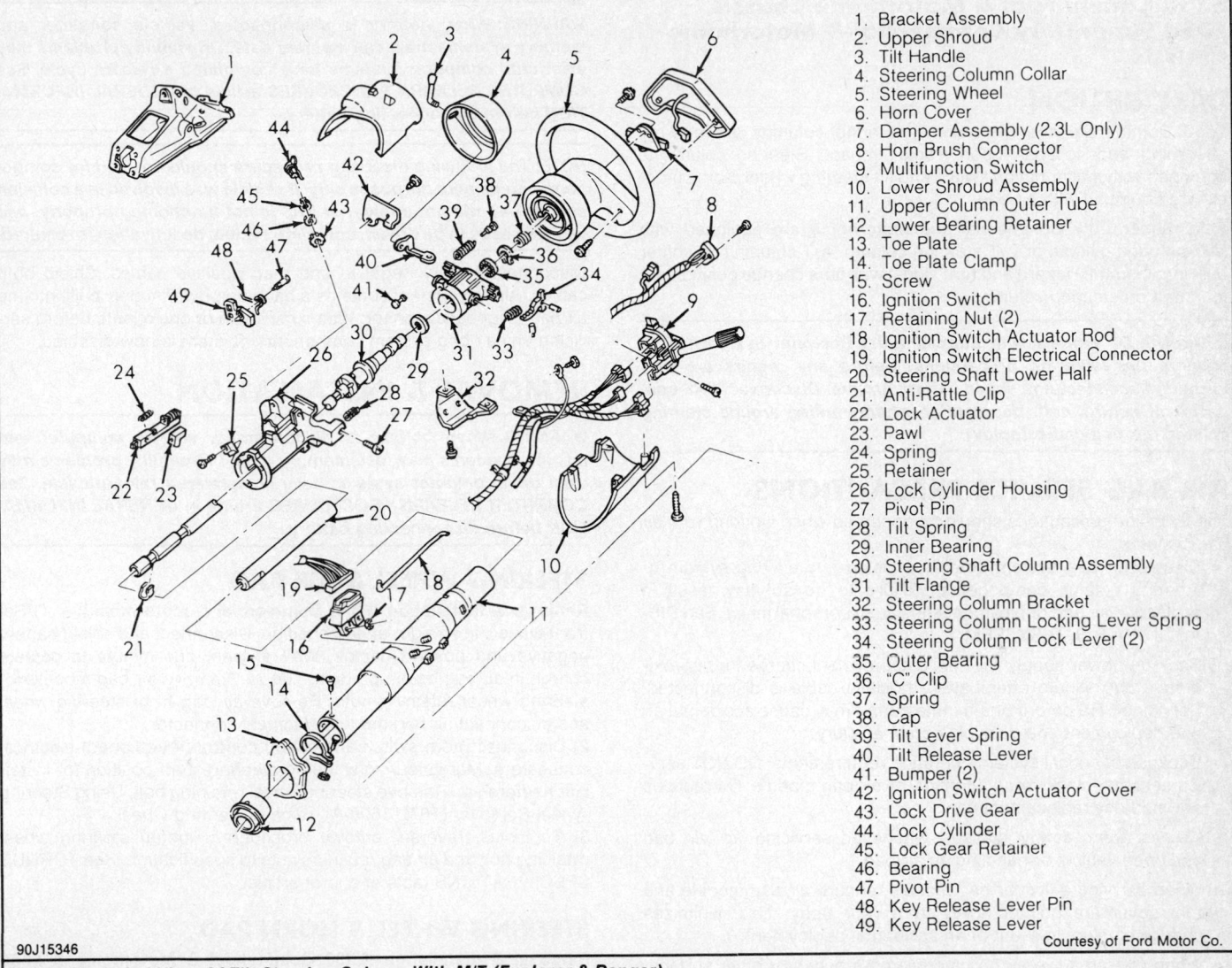

1. Bracket Assembly
2. Upper Shroud
3. Tilt Handle
4. Steering Column Collar
5. Steering Wheel
6. Horn Cover
7. Damper Assembly (2.3L Only)
8. Horn Brush Connector
9. Multifunction Switch
10. Lower Shroud Assembly
11. Upper Column Outer Tube
12. Lower Bearing Retainer
13. Toe Plate
14. Toe Plate Clamp
15. Screw
16. Ignition Switch
17. Retaining Nut (2)
18. Ignition Switch Actuator Rod
19. Ignition Switch Electrical Connector
20. Steering Shaft Lower Half
21. Anti-Rattle Clip
22. Lock Actuator
23. Pawl
24. Spring
25. Retainer
26. Lock Cylinder Housing
27. Pivot Pin
28. Tilt Spring
29. Inner Bearing
30. Steering Shaft Column Assembly
31. Tilt Flange
32. Steering Column Bracket
33. Steering Column Locking Lever Spring
34. Steering Column Lock Lever (2)
35. Outer Bearing
36. "C" Clip
37. Spring
38. Cap
39. Tilt Lever Spring
40. Tilt Release Lever
41. Bumper (2)
42. Ignition Switch Actuator Cover
43. Lock Drive Gear
44. Lock Cylinder
45. Lock Gear Retainer
46. Bearing
47. Pivot Pin
48. Key Release Lever Pin
49. Key Release Lever

Courtesy of Ford Motor Co.

Fig. 6: Exploded View Of Tilt Steering Column With M/T (Explorer & Ranger)

90J15346

TORQUE SPECIFICATIONS

TORQUE SPECIFICATIONS

Application	Ft. Lbs. (N.m)
Intermediate Shaft-To-Steering Column Shaft Bolt	
Aerostar, Bronco, Pickup & Van	30-42 (41-57)
Explorer & Ranger	25-35 (34-47)
Shift Cable Bracket Bolt	
Explorer & Ranger	13-22 (18-30)
Steering Column-To-Bracket Bolts	
Explorer & Ranger	19-27 (26-37)
Steering Column-To-Support Bracket Retaining Nuts	
Aerostar, Bronco, Pickup & Van	10-14 (14-19)
Steering Wheel Retaining Bolt	23-33 (31-45)

TORQUE SPECIFICATIONS (Cont.)

Application	INCH Lbs. (N.m)
Air Bag Clockspring Contact Assembly Retaining Screws	
Aerostar & Van	18-26 (2-3)
Air Bag-To-Steering Wheel Retaining Nuts	
Aerostar & Van	35-53 (4-6)
Column Toe Plate Clamp Bolt	
Explorer & Ranger	71-159 (8-18)
Column Toe Plate-To-Body Screws	
Explorer & Ranger	60-96 (7-11)
Horn Pad Retaining Screws	
Explorer & Ranger	8-11.5 (.9-1.3)
Ignition Switch Retaining Nuts	
Explorer & Ranger	40-64 (4.5-7.2)
Ignition Switch Retaining Screws	
Aerostar, Bronco, Pickup & Van	47-64 (5.3-7.2)
Lock Cylinder Housing-To-Column Screws	
Explorer & Ranger	71-97 (8-11)
Multifunction Switch Screws	18-26 (2-3)
PRND21 Cable Retaining Screw	
Aerostar, Bronco, Pickup & Van	60-96 (7-11)

**E350 Commercial & Motorhome Chassis,
F350 Super Duty Commercial & Motorhome
Chassis**

DESCRIPTION

E350 Commercial and Motorhome steering columns are energy-absorbing and collapse upon frontal impact. Steering column is equipped with multifunction switch and tilt steering wheel. Some models are equipped with air bag.

F350 Super Duty Commercial and Motorhome are equipped with M/T steering column or A/T steering column. A/T column has shifter built into column. Hazard and turn signal with lane change position are mounted on steering column.

WARNING: On models with Supplemental Restraint System (SRS), observe the following precautions. Before any repairs are performed, disconnect and shield battery ground. Disconnect SRS connector at control unit. Use caution when working around steering column (air bag could deploy).

AIR BAG SERVICE PRECAUTIONS

The following precautions should be observed when working with air bag systems.

- Disable air bag system before servicing any air bag system or steering column components. Failure to do so may result in accidental air bag deployment and cause personal injury. See DISABLING AIR BAG SYSTEM.

- Back-up power supply will hold a deployment charge for approximately one minute after battery positive cable is disconnected. Servicing SRS before one-minute period may cause accidental air bag deployment and possible personal injury.

- Because of critical system operating requirements, DO NOT service sensors, clockspring, monitor, or air bag module. Corrections are made by replacement only.

- Always wear safety glasses whenever servicing an air bag equipped vehicle or handling an air bag.

- When carrying a live air bag module, ensure air bag module and trim cover are pointed away from your body. This minimizes chance of injury in event of an accidental deployment.

- When placing a live air bag module on a bench or other surface, always face air bag module and trim cover up, away from surface. This will reduce motion of module if it is accidentally deployed.

- After deployment, air bag surface may contain deposits of sodium hydroxide, which may irritate skin. Sodium hydroxide is a product of the gas generant combustion. Always wear gloves and safety glasses when handling a deployed air bag. Wash your hands using mild soap and water. Follow correct disposal procedures.

- If a part is replaced and new part does not correct condition, reinstall original part and perform diagnostic procedure again.

- Never probe connectors on air bag module. Doing so may cause air bag deployment and/or personal injury.

- The instruction to DISCONNECT always refers to a connector. DO NOT disconnect a component from vehicle when instructed to DISCONNECT.

- After repairs, ensure AIR BAG warning light does not indicate any other faults.

DISABLING AIR BAG SYSTEM

WARNING: Back-up power supply will hold a deployment charge for approximately one minute after battery positive cable is disconnected. Servicing SRS before one-minute period may cause accidental air bag deployment and possible personal injury.

WARNING: When battery is disconnected, vehicle computer and memory systems may lose memory data. Driveability problems may exist until computer systems have completed a relearn cycle. See COMPUTER RELEARN PROCEDURES article in GENERAL INFORMATION before disconnecting battery.

NOTE: The following disabling procedure should be used for component replacement purposes only. If vehicle was involved in a collision and air bag did not deploy, or SRS is not functioning properly, and vehicle needs to be driven, complete system deactivation is required.

Disconnect battery negative and then positive cables. Shield both cables. Air bag system contains a back-up power supply built into the air bag diagnostic monitor. Wait a minimum of one minute before servicing any air bag system components. System is now disabled.

REMOVAL & INSTALLATION

WARNING: When battery is disconnected, vehicle computer and memory systems may lose memory data. Driveability problems may exist until computer systems have completed a relearn cycle. See COMPUTER RELEARN PROCEDURES article in GENERAL INFORMATION before disconnecting battery.

STEERING WHEEL & AIR BAG

Removal & Installation (E350 Commercial & Motorhome) – 1) Set front wheels in straight-ahead position. Disconnect and shield battery negative and positive cables. Wait at least one minute to deplete charge in air bag back-up power supply. Remove air bag module-to-steering wheel retaining nuts. Remove air bag from steering wheel and disconnect air bag module electrical connector.

2) Disconnect horn switch and speed control (if equipped) electrical connectors. Mark steering wheel-to-steering shaft position for installation reference. Remove steering wheel retaining bolt. Using Steering Wheel Remover (T67L-3600-A), remove steering wheel.

3) To install, reverse removal procedure. Tighten steering wheel retaining bolt and air bag retaining nuts to specification. See TORQUE SPECIFICATIONS table at end of article.

STEERING WHEEL & HORN PAD

Removal & Installation (E350 Commercial & Motorhome & F350 Super Duty Commercial & Motorhome) – 1) Set front wheels in straight-ahead position. Disconnect battery negative cable. On F350 Super Duty models, remove horn pad retaining screws. Disconnect horn switch electrical connector and remove horn pad. On E350 models, grasp sides of horn pad and pull upward to unclip retainers. Disconnect horn switch electrical connector and remove horn pad.

2) Mark steering wheel-to-steering shaft position for installation reference. Remove steering wheel retaining bolt. Using Steering Wheel Remover (T67L-3600-A), remove steering wheel.

3) To install, reverse removal procedure. Tighten steering wheel retaining bolt and horn pad retaining screws (if equipped) to specification. See TORQUE SPECIFICATIONS table at end of article.

MULTIFUNCTION SWITCH

Removal & Installation (E350 Commercial & Motorhome) – Disconnect battery negative cable. Remove upper and lower steering column shrouds. Remove 2 multifunction switch retaining screws. Disconnect multifunction switch electrical connector and remove multifunction switch from steering column. To install, reverse removal procedure.

LOCK CYLINDER

Removal (With Key) – 1) Disconnect battery negative cable. Remove steering wheel. See STEERING WHEEL & AIR BAG or STEERING WHEEL & HORN PAD under REMOVAL & INSTALLATION. Remove upper and lower steering column shrouds (if equipped). Disconnect key warning switch electrical connector. Using key, turn lock cylinder to RUN position.

2) Place a 1/8" (3.17 mm) diameter pin in hole located in outer edge of lock cylinder housing. Depress retaining pin and pull out lock cylinder.

Installation – 1) To install, lubricate lock cylinder with grease. Turn lock cylinder to RUN position. Depress retaining pin. Insert lock cylinder into housing. Ensure tab on end of lock cylinder aligns with slot in ignition drive gear.

2) Using key, turn lock cylinder to OFF position to engage cylinder retaining pin into cylinder housing hole. To complete installation, reverse removal procedure. Check lock cylinder functions. Ensure column locks when switch is in LOCK position.

Removal (Without Key) – 1) Use this procedure to remove ignition lock cylinder if key is missing or cylinder lock is frozen. Disconnect battery negative cable. Remove steering wheel. See STEERING WHEEL & AIR BAG or STEERING WHEEL & HORN PAD under REMOVAL & INSTALLATION. Remove upper and lower steering column shrouds (if equipped). Disconnect key warning switch electrical connector. Use a 1/8" (3.17 mm) drill bit to drill out retaining pin. DO NOT drill deeper than 1/2" (12.7 mm).

2) Place a chisel at base of lock cylinder cap. Using a hammer, strike chisel with sharp blows to break cap away from lock cylinder. Using a 3/8" (9.52 mm) drill bit, drill out center of lock cylinder key slot. Drill down approximately 1 3/4" (44 mm) until lock cylinder breaks away from base of lock cylinder.

3) Remove metal shavings from lock cylinder housing. Remove bearing retainer, bearing and ignition drive gear from lock cylinder. Thoroughly clean all metal shavings and other foreign materials from housing. Carefully inspect housing for damage. If damage is apparent, replace housing.

Installation – 1) Install ignition drive gear, bearing and bearing retainer. Lubricate cylinder cavity with lock cylinder lubricant. Turn ignition switch to RUN position. Depress retaining pin and insert NEW lock cylinder into housing.

2) Ensure tab on end of lock cylinder aligns with slot in ignition drive gear. Using key, turn lock cylinder to OFF position to engage cylinder retaining pin into cylinder housing hole. To complete installation, reverse removal procedure. Check lock cylinder functions. Ensure column locks when switch is in LOCK position.

IGNITION SWITCH

Removal & Installation (E350 Commercial & Motorhome) – 1) Set front wheels in straight-ahead position. Disable air bag (if equipped). See DISABLING AIR BAG SYSTEM. Remove steering wheel. See STEERING WHEEL & AIR BAG or STEERING WHEEL & HORN PAD under REMOVAL & INSTALLATION. Remove steering column. See STEERING COLUMN under REMOVAL & INSTALLATION.

2) Remove 2 ignition switch retaining screws. Disconnect ignition switch electrical connector and remove ignition switch from steering column.

3) Install ignition switch onto steering column. Ensure actuator pin on ignition switch is aligned with slot in actuator housing. Ensure slot in actuator housing is aligned with mark on steering column casting. Ignition switch should be in RUN position.

4) Connect ignition switch electrical connector and tighten retaining screws to specification. See TORQUE SPECIFICATIONS table at end of article. To complete installation, reverse removal procedure.

Removal & Installation (F350 Super Duty Commercial & Motorhome) – 1) Disconnect battery negative cable. Remove steering wheel. See STEERING WHEEL & HORN PAD under REMOVAL & INSTALLATION. Remove steering column. See STEERING COLUMN under REMOVAL & INSTALLATION.

2) Remove 2 ignition switch retaining screws. Disconnect ignition switch electrical connector and remove ignition switch from steering column.

3) Before ignition switch is installed, turn ignition lock cylinder to LOCK position. To preset ignition switch, place actuation rod on switch and switch on column studs while aligning rod hole in ignition switch with actuator rod.

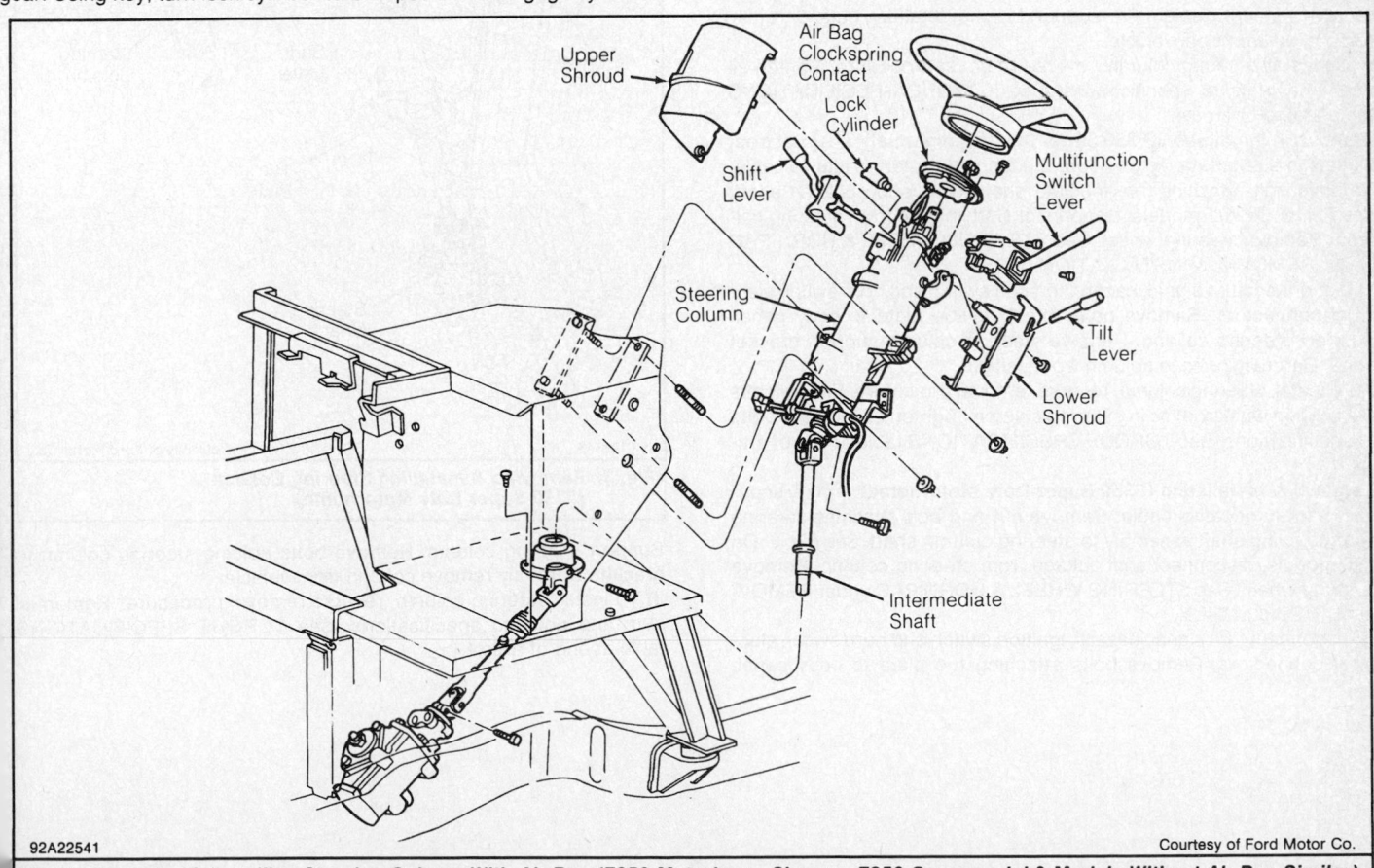

92A22541

Courtesy of Ford Motor Co.

Fig. 1: Removing & Installing Steering Column With Air Bag (E350 Motorhome Shown – E350 Commercial & Models Without Air Bag Similar)

4) Tighten retaining nuts to specification. See TORQUE SPECIFICATIONS table at end of article. Ensure switch is operating smoothly and all functions are engaged. To complete installation, reverse removal procedure.

STEERING COLUMN

Removal & Installation (E350 Commercial & Motorhome) – 1) Set front wheels in straight-ahead position. Disable air bag (if equipped). See DISABLING AIR BAG SYSTEM. Remove steering wheel. See STEERING WHEEL & AIR BAG or STEERING WHEEL & HORN PAD under REMOVAL & INSTALLATION. Remove instrument panel lower trim cover (if equipped).

2) Remove screws from lower steering column shroud (if equipped). *See Fig. 1.* Remove lower steering column shroud by pulling shroud down and toward rear of vehicle (if equipped). Disconnect air bag clockspring contact assembly electrical connectors (if equipped). Place tape across contact assembly stator and rotor to prevent accidental rotation (if equipped). Remove clockspring contact assembly retaining screws and remove contact assembly from steering column (if equipped).

3) Unscrew and remove tilt lever from column. Using key, turn lock cylinder to RUN position. Place a 1/8" (3.17 mm) diameter pin in hole located in outer edge of lock cylinder housing. Depress retaining pin and pull out lock cylinder. Remove upper steering column shroud from column.

4) Remove PRND21 cable retaining screw and disconnect cable from actuator housing. Disconnect PRND21 cable loop from shift tube hook. Remove 2 screws attaching multifunction switch to steering column. Disconnect multifunction switch electrical connector and remove switch.

5) Remove bolt attaching intermediate shaft to steering column shaft. Disconnect shift cable from selector lever pivot. Push in tab on shift cable and slide cable off shaft cable bracket. Disconnect ignition switch electrical connector. Support steering column assembly and remove 4 steering column-to-support bracket retaining nuts. Carefully remove column from vehicle.

6) To install steering column, reverse removal procedure. Tighten all nuts and bolts to specifications. See TORQUE SPECIFICATIONS table at end of article.

Removal & Installation (F350 Super Duty Commercial) – 1) Set front wheels in straight-ahead position. Disconnect battery negative cable. Remove bolt attaching intermediate shaft to steering column shaft. *See Fig. 2.* On A/T models, disconnect shift linkage from steering column. Remove steering wheel. See STEERING WHEEL & HORN PAD under REMOVAL & INSTALLATION.

2) Disconnect turn signal, hazard, ignition switch and horn switch electrical connectors. Remove bolts attaching toe plate to body panel. Support steering column. Remove steering column support bracket bolts. Carefully remove column from vehicle.

3) To install steering column, reverse removal procedure. Ensure bolts are aligned with grooves in steering column. Tighten all nuts and bolts to specifications. See TORQUE SPECIFICATIONS table at end of article.

Removal & Installation (F350 Super Duty Motorhome) – 1) Disconnect battery negative cable. Remove nut and bolt attaching steering gear coupling shaft assembly to steering column shaft. *See Fig. 3.* On A/T models, disconnect shift linkage from steering column. Remove steering wheel. See STEERING WHEEL & HORN PAD under REMOVAL & INSTALLATION.

2) Disconnect turn signal, hazard, ignition switch and horn switch electrical connectors. Remove bolts attaching toe plate to body panel.

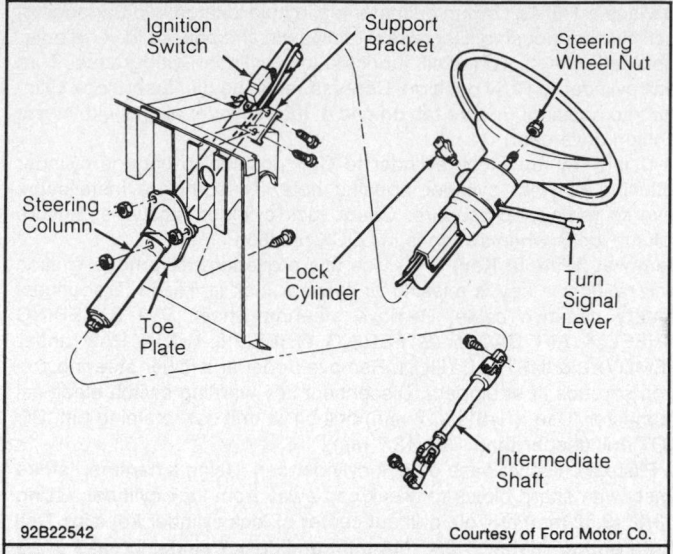

92B22542   Courtesy of Ford Motor Co.

Fig. 2: Removing & Installing Steering Column (F350 Super Duty Commercial)

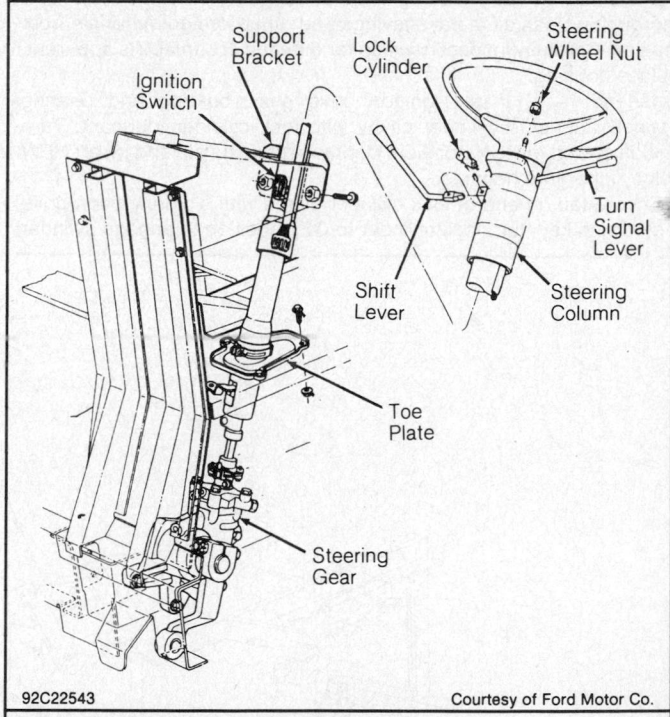

92C22543   Courtesy of Ford Motor Co.

Fig. 3: Removing & Installing Steering Column (F350 Super Duty Motorhome)

Support steering column. Remove bolts holding steering column to bracket. Carefully remove column from vehicle.

3) To install steering column, reverse removal procedure. Tighten all nuts and bolts to specifications. See TORQUE SPECIFICATIONS table at end of article.

OVERHAUL

When overhauling steering columns, refer to exploded view illustrations. *See Figs. 4-6.*

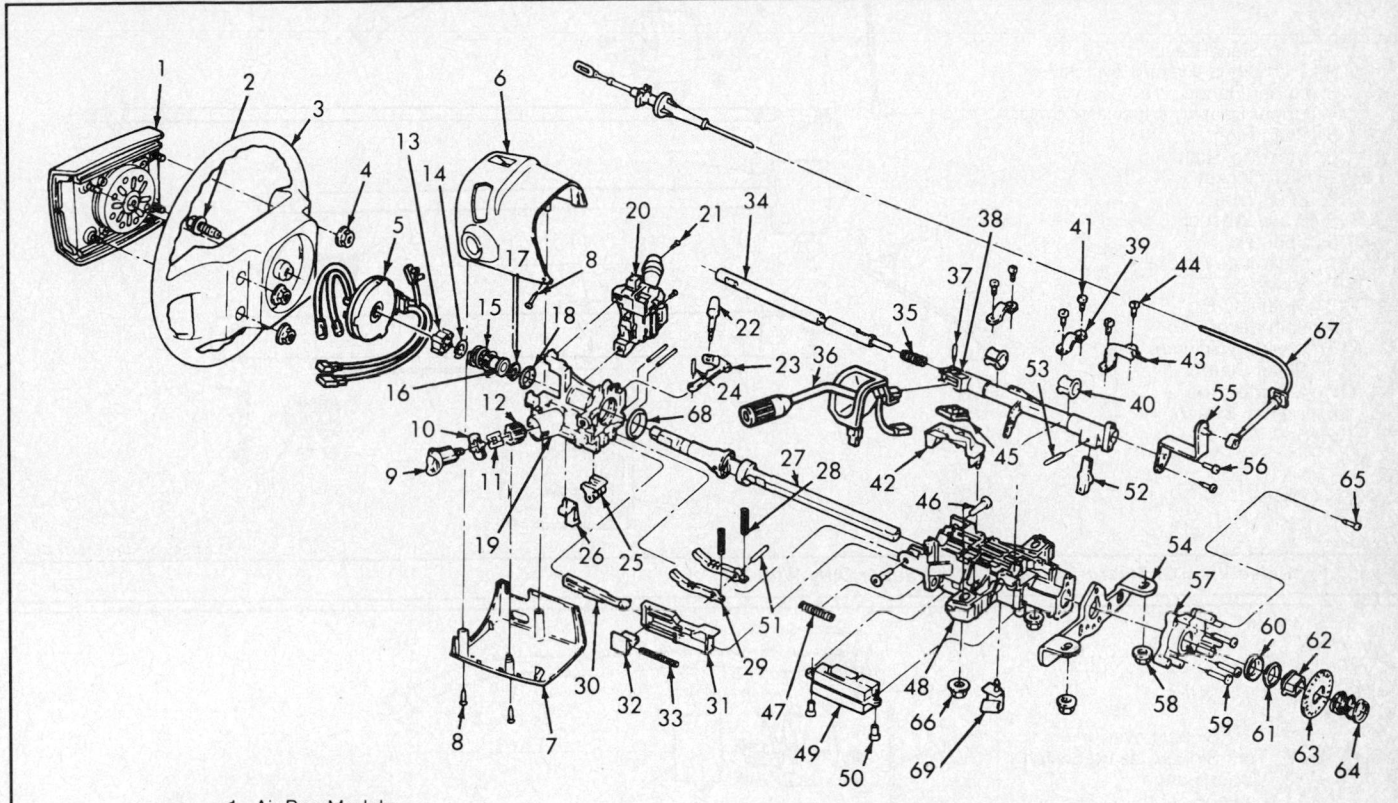

1. Air Bag Module	36. Shift Lever
2. Steering Wheel Bolt	37. Shift Lever Pin
3. Steering Wheel	38. Transmission Selector Control Tube
4. Air Bag Module Retaining Nut	39. Transmission Selector Control Tube Clamps
5. Air Bag Clockspring Contact	40. Bushings
6. Upper Column Shroud	41. Screws
7. Lower Column Shroud	42. Shield
8. Shroud Retaining Screws	43. Transmission Selector Control Position Insert
9. Ignition Lock Cylinder	44. Screws
10. Retainer	45. Transmission Selector Control Lever Spring Clip
11. Bearing	46. Tilt Pivot Screws
12. Steering Lock Gear	47. Steering Column Position Lock Spring
13. Turn Signal Canceling Cam	48. Actuator Housing
14. Snap Ring	49. Ignition Switch
15. Upper Bearing Spring	50. Screws
16. Sleeve	51. Pivot Lever Pin
17. Ring	52. Steering Column Lock Shifter Pawl
18. Small Upper Bearing	53. Steering Column Lock Shifter Pin
19. Lock Cylinder Housing	54. Lower Column Bracket
20. Multifunction Switch	55. Transmission Selector Control Lower Lever
21. Screws	56. Screws
22. Tilt Release Lever	57. Lower Bearing Housing Retainer
23. Tilt Actuator Lever	58. Lower Column Mounting Nuts
24. Tilt Actuator Lever Pin	59. Lower Bearing Housing Retaining Screws
25. Steering Column Lock Cam	60. Lower Column Bearing Sleeve
26. Upper Wiring Clip	61. Lower Column Bearing
27. Steering Shaft	62. Lower Tolerance Ring
28. Lock Lever Spring	63. Sensor Ring
29. Steering Column Lock Lever	64. Spring
30. Upper Lock Actuator	65. Shift Cable Bracket Mounting Screws
31. Lower Lock Actuator	66. Upper Column Mounting Nuts
32. Steering Column Lock Shaft Pawl	67. Shift Cable
33. Steering Column Lock Shaft Spring	68. Large Upper Bearing
34. Transmission Selector Control Plunger	69. Lower Wiring Clip
35. Transmission Selector Control Return Spring	

92J22540

Fig. 4: Exploded View Of Steering Column With Air Bag (E350 Motorhome Shown – E350 Commercial & Models Without Air Bag Similar)

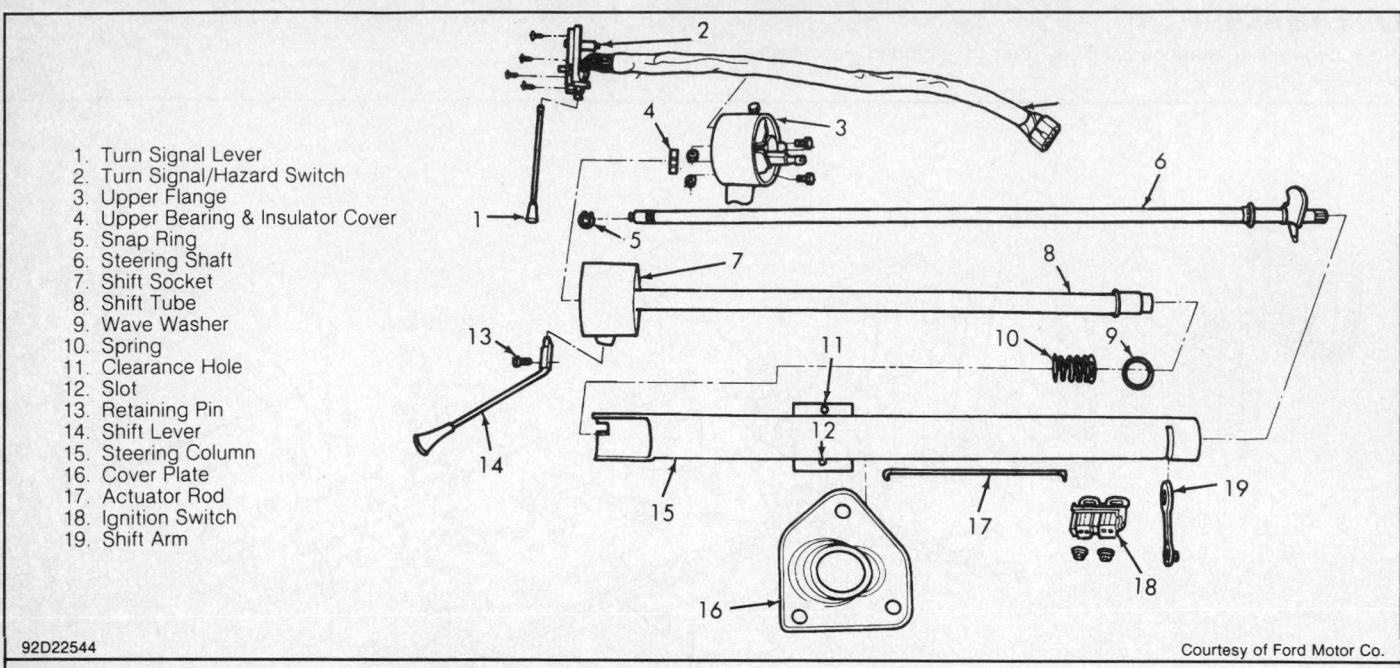

1. Turn Signal Lever
2. Turn Signal/Hazard Switch
3. Upper Flange
4. Upper Bearing & Insulator Cover
5. Snap Ring
6. Steering Shaft
7. Shift Socket
8. Shift Tube
9. Wave Washer
10. Spring
11. Clearance Hole
12. Slot
13. Retaining Pin
14. Shift Lever
15. Steering Column
16. Cover Plate
17. Actuator Rod
18. Ignition Switch
19. Shift Arm

92D22544

Courtesy of Ford Motor Co.

Fig. 5: Exploded View Of Steering Column (F350 Super Duty With A/T)

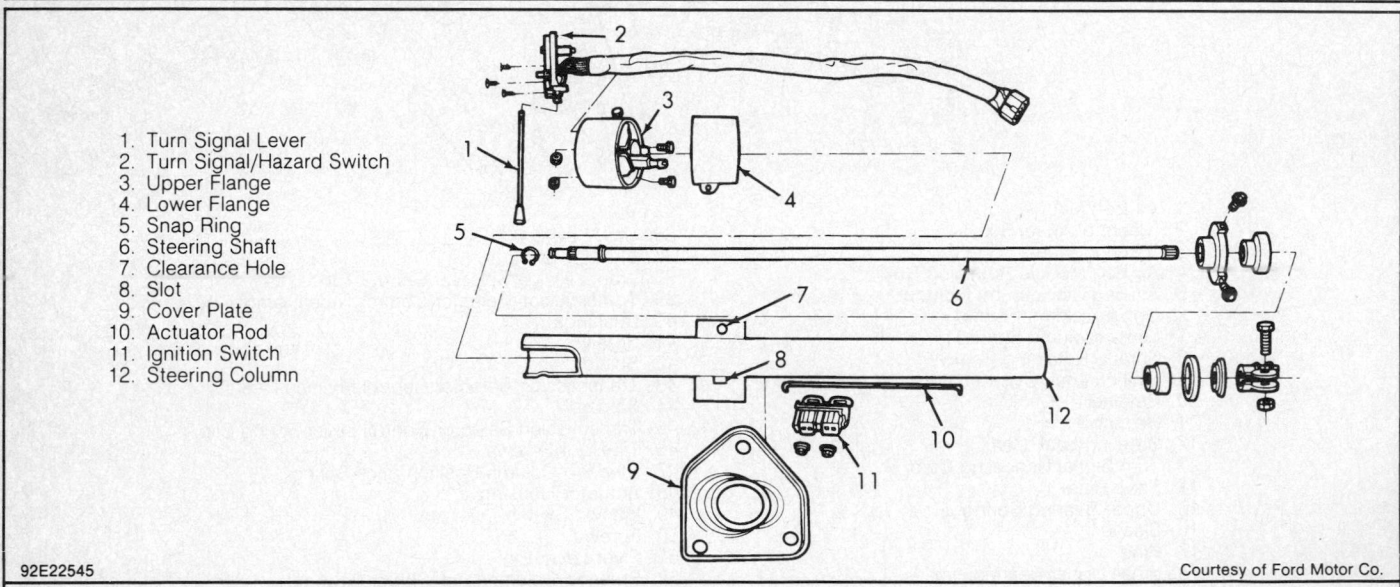

1. Turn Signal Lever
2. Turn Signal/Hazard Switch
3. Upper Flange
4. Lower Flange
5. Snap Ring
6. Steering Shaft
7. Clearance Hole
8. Slot
9. Cover Plate
10. Actuator Rod
11. Ignition Switch
12. Steering Column

92E22545

Courtesy of Ford Motor Co.

Fig. 6: Exploded View Of Steering Column (F350 Super Duty With M/T)

TORQUE SPECIFICATIONS
TORQUE SPECIFICATIONS

Application	Ft. Lbs. (N.m)
Intermediate Shaft-To-Steering Column Shaft Bolt	
E350 Commercial & Motorhome	30-42 (41-57)
F350 Super Duty Commercial	20-35 (27-47)
Steering Column Support Bracket Bolts	
F350 Super Duty Commercial	19-27 (25-36)
Steering Column-To-Support Bracket Bolts	
F350 Super Duty Motorhome	19-27 (25-36)
Steering Column-To-Support Bracket Retaining Nuts	
E350 Commercial & Motorhome	10-14 (14-19)
Steering Gear-To-Steering Column Shaft Bolt	
F350 Super Duty Motorhome	20-35 (27-47)
Steering Wheel Retaining Bolt	
F350 Super Duty Commercial & Motorhome	30-42 (41-57)
E350 Commercial & Motorhome	23-33 (31-45)

TORQUE SPECIFICATIONS (Cont.)

Application	INCH Lbs. (N.m)
Air Bag Clockspring Contact Assembly Retaining Screws	
E350 Commercial & Motorhome	18-26 (2-3)
Air Bag-To-Steering Wheel Retaining Nuts	
E350 Commercial & Motorhome	35-53 (4-6)
Column Toe Plate-To-Body Bolts	
F350 Super Duty Commercial	96-133 (11-15)
F350 Super Duty Motorhome	35-53 (4-6)
Horn Pad Retaining Screws	
F350 Super Duty Commercial & Motorhome	7-11 (.8-1.2)
Ignition Switch Retaining Nuts	
F350 Super Duty Commercial & Motorhome	40-64 (4.5-7.2)
Ignition Switch Retaining Screws	
E350 Commercial & Motorhome	60-96 (7-11)
Multifunction Switch Screws	
E350 Commercial & Motorhome	18-26 (2-3)
PRND?1 Cable Retaining Screw	
E350 Commercial & Motorhome	60-96 (7-11)

Ranger

DESCRIPTION

The steering gear is a worm and recirculating ball type. Needle bearing and bushing support the sector shaft in the housing. The worm shaft spiral groove floats on 2 continuous rows of ball bearings recirculating through the ball nut via return guide tubes. Teeth on the ball nut mate with the sector shaft.

INSPECTION & ADJUSTMENTS

PRELOAD & MESHLOAD IN-VEHICLE CHECK

NOTE: Before checking preload or meshload, ensure steering column is properly aligned and intermediate shaft flex coupling is not distorted.

1) Place reference mark on pitman arm and sector shaft for reassembly. Remove pitman arm retaining nut and lock washer. Using Pitman Arm Puller (T64P-3590-F), remove pitman arm from sector shaft.
2) Lubricate worm shaft seal with a drop of power steering fluid. Remove horn pad from steering wheel. Turn steering wheel slowly against one stop. Place INCH lb. torque wrench on steering wheel nut.
3) Measure torque (preload) required to rotate steering wheel at a constant speed, approximately 1 1/2 turns. If preload is not **2-6 INCH lbs. (.22-.68 N.m)**, readjust preload. See PRELOAD & MESHLOAD ADJUSTMENT. If preload is within specifications, check meshload.
4) Rotate steering wheel from stop-to-stop, noting total number of revolutions. Turn steering wheel back half way, to center position. Using an INCH lb. torque wrench, measure highest torque required to rotate steering wheel back and forth 90 degrees through center position.
5) Meshload must be within **4-10 INCH lbs. (.45-1.13 N.m)** and at least **2 INCH lbs. (.23 N.m)** over the measured preload reading. If meshload is not within specification, readjust meshload. See PRELOAD & MESHLOAD ADJUSTMENT. Meshload can be set while steering gear is on vehicle.

NOTE: Adjust worm preload with steering gear off vehicle.

PRELOAD & MESHLOAD ADJUSTMENT

1) Remove steering gear from vehicle. See STEERING GEAR under REMOVAL & INSTALLATION. Ensure sector shaft cover bolts are tightened to specification. See TORQUE SPECIFICATIONS table at end of article. Loosen worm bearing adjuster lock nut. Tighten worm bearing adjuster until all end play is removed. *See Fig. 1.*
2) Lubricate worm shaft seal with a drop of power steering fluid. Carefully turn worm shaft to right stop. Using an INCH lb. torque wrench, measure torque (preload) required to rotate wormshaft to left, in a constant motion, for approximately 1 1/2 turns. Tighten or loosen worm bearing adjuster until preload of **5-6 INCH lbs. (.56-.68 N.m)** is reached.

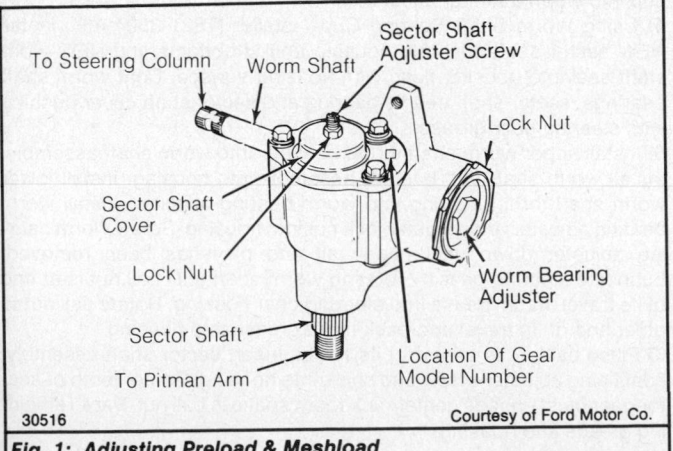

To Steering Column
Worm Shaft
Sector Shaft Adjuster Screw
Lock Nut
Sector Shaft Cover
Lock Nut
Worm Bearing Adjuster
Sector Shaft
To Pitman Arm
Location Of Gear Model Number

30516
Courtesy of Ford Motor Co.

Fig. 1: Adjusting Preload & Meshload

3) Tighten worm bearing adjuster lock nut to specification. See TORQUE SPECIFICATIONS table. To adjust meshload, rotate worm shaft from stop-to-stop, counting total number of turns, then turn back halfway. Worm shaft should be centered in steering gear. Using an INCH lb. torque wrench, observe highest reading while worm shaft is turned approximately 90 degrees either way across center. If highest reading (meshload) is not within **9-11 INCH lbs. (102-124 N.m)** and at least **4 INCH lbs. (.45 N.m)** over preload, turn sector shaft adjuster screw as required.
4) Tighten lock nut to specification while holding sector shaft adjuster screw. Reverse removal procedures to install remaining components. Ensure reference mark is aligned on pitman arm and sector shaft. Tighten pitman arm retaining nut to specification. See TORQUE SPECIFICATIONS table.

REMOVAL & INSTALLATION

STEERING GEAR

Removal – 1) Separate flex coupling shield from steering gear input shaft shield and slide flex coupling shield up intermediate shaft. Remove flex coupling-to-steering gear pinch bolt. Remove steering gear input shaft shield.
2) Place reference mark on pitman arm and sector shaft for reassembly. Remove pitman arm retaining nut and lock washer. Using Pitman Arm Puller (T64P-3590-F), remove pitman arm from sector shaft. Remove steering gear-to-frame bolts. Remove steering gear from vehicle.
Installation – 1) Rotate worm shaft from stop to stop, counting number of turns. Turn back exactly half way. Worm shaft should be centered in steering gear. Install steering gear input shaft shield. Install flex coupling, ensuring flat on worm gear shaft faces straight up and aligns with flat on flex coupling.
2) Install steering gear on frame. Tighten bolts to specification. See TORQUE SPECIFICATIONS table at end of article. To complete installation, reverse remaining removal procedure. Align 2 blocked teeth on pitman arm with 4 missing teeth on sector shaft. Tighten pitman arm nut to specification.

OVERHAUL

STEERING GEAR

Disassembly – 1) Remove steering gear. See STEERING GEAR under REMOVAL & INSTALLATION. Place steering gear in vise. Rotate worm shaft from stop to stop, counting number of turns. Turn back exactly half way. Worm shaft should be centered in steering gear.
2) Remove sector shaft cover bolts. *See Fig. 2.* Remove sector shaft and sector shaft cover assembly from housing. Loosen sector shaft adjuster lock nut. Rotate adjuster screw clockwise to remove sector shaft cover from sector shaft. DO NOT lose shim located on adjuster screw.
3) Using Lock Wrench (T82T-3504-BH), loosen worm bearing adjuster lock nut. Remove worm bearing adjuster and lower worm shaft thrust bearing. Remove worm shaft and ball nut assembly from housing. Remove upper worm shaft thrust bearing.

NOTE: Worm shaft and ball nut are NOT serviceable. If damaged or worn, replace complete assembly.

CAUTION: DO NOT allow ball nut to rotate down worm shaft, as ball guides may be damaged.

4) Using a screwdriver, remove worm shaft seal and sector shaft seal from housing, and discard. Using Puller (T58L-101-B), remove lower worm shaft thrust bearing cup from worm bearing adjuster. *See Fig. 3.* Using a bearing driver or socket and hammer, remove upper worm shaft thrust bearing cup from housing.

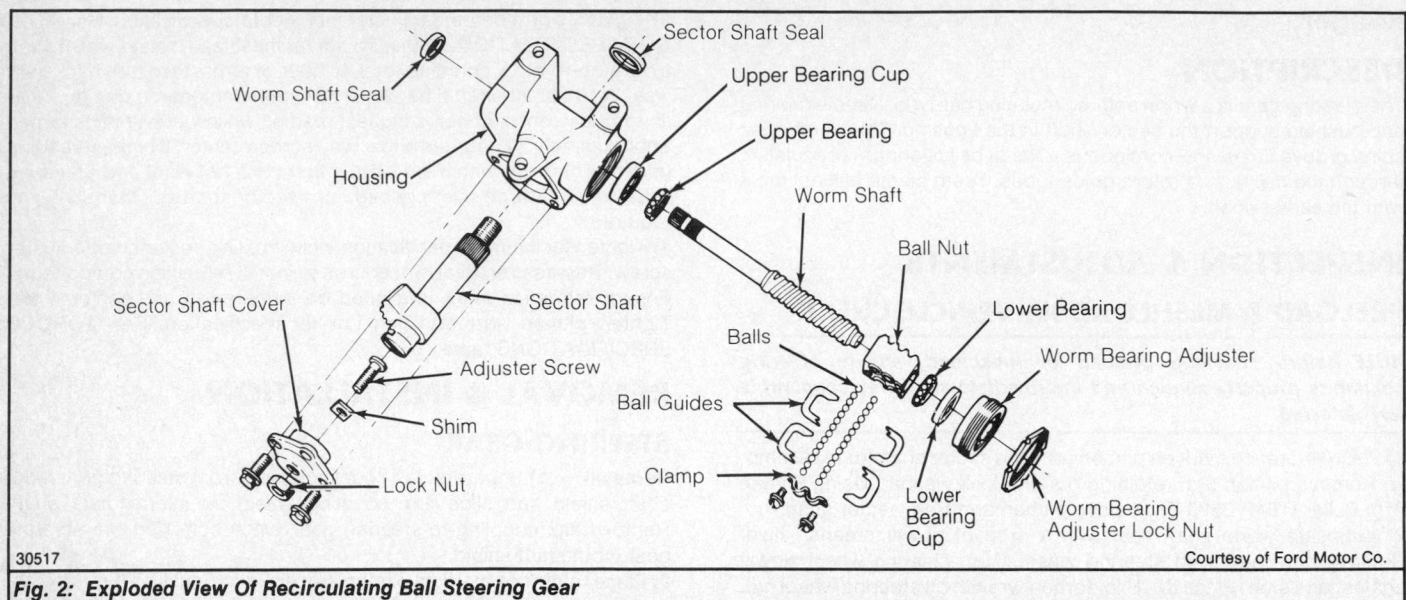

30517   Courtesy of Ford Motor Co.

Fig. 2: Exploded View Of Recirculating Ball Steering Gear

NOTE: Sector shaft cover bushing and sector shaft needle bearing are NOT serviceable. Cover or housing must be replaced if component is defective.

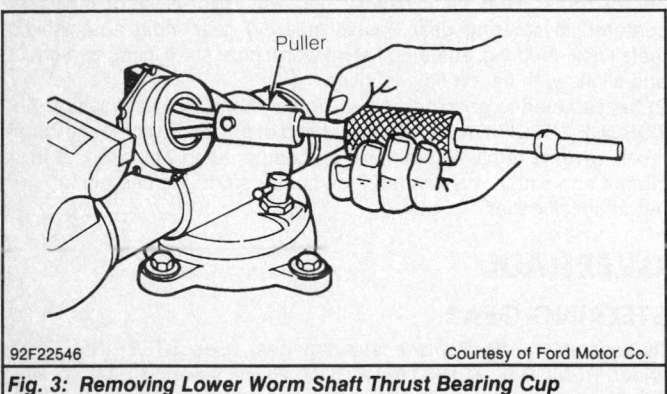

92F22546   Courtesy of Ford Motor Co.

Fig. 3: Removing Lower Worm Shaft Thrust Bearing Cup

Cleaning & Inspection – 1) Clean components with solvent and dry with compressed air. Inspect bearings and bearing cups for signs of damage or wear. Inspect ball nut and worm shaft for wear, pitting or chips. Rotate worm shaft in ball nut and check for binding or tightness. Replace worm shaft and ball nut as an assembly if damaged.

NOTE: Worm shaft and ball nut are NOT serviceable. If damaged or worn, replace complete assembly.

2) Inspect sector shaft fit into sector shaft cover bushing assembly. If bushing is defective, replace sector shaft cover and bushing as an assembly. Inspect sector shaft needle bearing for damage. Replace needle bearing and housing as an assembly if needle bearing is damaged.

NOTE: Sector shaft cover bushing and sector shaft needle bearing are NOT serviceable. Sector shaft cover or housing must be replaced if component is defective.

3) Inspect housing for cracks or damage. Inspect sector gear teeth for chipping or excessive wear. Replace components as necessary.
Reassembly – 1) Install sector shaft adjuster screw and shim into sector shaft. Using feeler gauge, measure clearance between adjuster screw and bottom of sector shaft "T" slot. *See Fig. 4.*

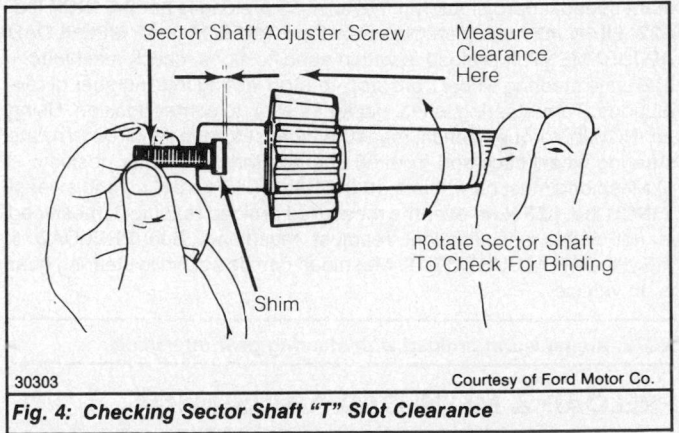

30303   Courtesy of Ford Motor Co.

Fig. 4: Checking Sector Shaft "T" Slot Clearance

2) The adjuster screw clearance should be .004" (.10 mm) or less. If clearance is greater than specification, install NEW shim from steering gear lash adjuster kit as necessary to reduce clearance to specification.
3) Once correct shim is determined, install shim and adjuster screw. Hold sector shaft adjuster screw while turning sector shaft. If sector shaft does not turn freely, recheck shim clearance. Lubricate all seals, bearings and sector shaft before installation. Using Worm Shaft Bearing Cup Installer (T82T-3504-AH), install NEW upper worm shaft thrust bearing cup into housing and NEW lower worm shaft thrust bearing cup into worm bearing adjuster.
4) Using Worm Shaft Bearing Cup Installer (T82T-3504-AH), install NEW sector shaft seal into housing until it bottoms and NEW worm shaft seal into housing flush with housing surface. Coat worm shaft bearings, sector shaft needle bearing and sector shaft cover bushing with steering gear grease.
5) Install upper worm shaft thrust bearing onto worm shaft assembly. Install worm shaft and ball nut assembly into housing. Install lower worm shaft thrust bearing into worm bearing adjuster. Install worm bearing adjuster and adjuster lock nut into housing. Screw worm bearing adjuster down until nearly all end play has been removed. Lubricate steering gear by rotating worm shaft until ball nut is at end of its travel. Pack grease into steering gear housing. Rotate ball nut to other end of its travel and pack more grease into housing.
6) Place ball nut in center of its travel. Insert sector shaft assembly, containing adjuster screw and shim, into housing. Center tooth of sector gear must engage center rack tooth space in ball nut. Pack remaining grease into housing.

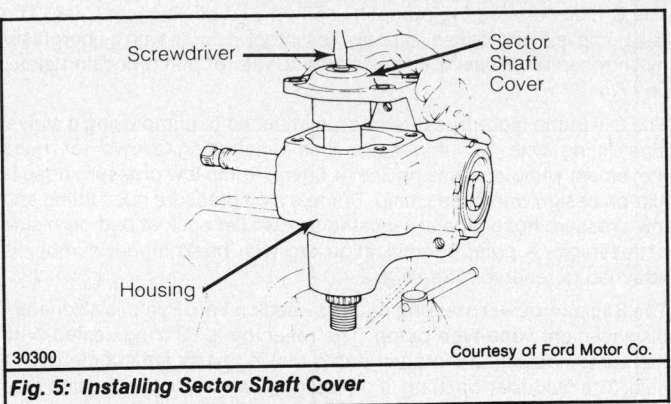

Screwdriver

Sector Shaft Cover

Housing

30300

Courtesy of Ford Motor Co.

Fig. 5: Installing Sector Shaft Cover

7) Apply a thin bead of sealant to sector shaft cover. Using a screwdriver through the center hole of sector shaft cover, align adjuster screw and install cover on sector shaft. *See Fig. 5.* Turn adjuster screw counterclockwise until sector shaft cover is flush with housing.

8) Coat sector shaft cover bolts with non-hardening sealant. Install sector shaft cover retaining bolts. Tighten only if there is lash between sector shaft and worm shaft. Lash can be obtained by turning sector shaft adjuster screw counterclockwise. Tighten sector shaft cover bolts to specification. See TORQUE SPECIFICATIONS table at end of article. Install sector shaft lock nut. Perform adjustments on steering gear. See INSPECTION & ADJUSTMENTS.

TORQUE SPECIFICATIONS

TORQUE SPECIFICATIONS

Application	Ft. Lbs. (N.m)
Adjuster Screw Lock Nut	14-25 (19-34)
Flex Coupling Pinch Bolt	25-35 (34-47)
Pitman Arm Nut	170-230 (230-312)
Sector Shaft Cover Bolts	32-40 (43-54)
Steering Gear-To-Frame Bolts	50-62 (68-84)
Worm Bearing Adjuster Lock Nut	166-187 (225-254)

1992 STEERING
Integral Power Steering

Bronco, Explorer, Pickup, Ranger, Van

NOTE: Unless otherwise specified, references to Pickup include the F350 Super Duty commercial chassis.

DESCRIPTION

Integral power steering unit consists of a rotary hydraulic control valve housing, input shaft/worm gear/valve sleeve assembly, sector shaft, and 1-piece piston containing 27-29 recirculating balls. The 1-piece piston's teeth are meshed to sector shaft teeth. Sector shaft is connected to Pitman arm. Rotary hydraulic control valve assembly contains upper input shaft/valve sleeve, sleeve Teflon seals, and internal torsion bar. The input shaft/control valve sleeve is retained inside control valve housing by bearing and lock nut. Hydraulic action is generated by relative rotary motion between input shaft/control valve sleeve and worm/piston assembly. *See Figs. 1 and 7.*

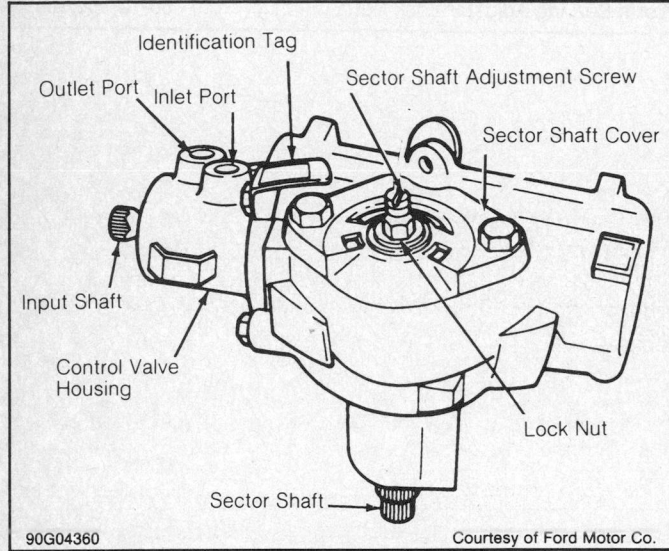

90G04360   Courtesy of Ford Motor Co.

Fig. 1: Identifying Steering Gear Unit Components

The C-II power steering pump is used on all models except Van. The C-II pump is a belt-driven, slipper-type integral pump with a fiberglass/nylon reservoir. Reservoir is attached to rear of pump housing plate. *See Fig. 2.*

The C-II pump high-pressure hose is attached to pump using a swivel type fitting with "O" ring seal. This type fitting allows for hose movement without stressing line or fitting. Pump low pressure hose is slip-on design with hose clamp. Pump's high pressure hose fitting and low pressure hose pipe are located below filler neck at outboard side of reservoir. A pump identification tag with basic model number is attached to reservoir. *See Fig. 2.*

The Saginaw power steering pump is used on Van. Pump is a constant displacement vane-type pump. The reservoir is "O" ring sealed onto the pump housing. All integral pump moving parts are submerged in fluid. The fluid filler opening is on top of reservoir, unless engine type requires alternate remote reservoir. Pump reservoir cap is sealed when using remote reservoir.

Rectangular pump vanes are mounted into rotor and cam, and are driven by main pump shaft. Vanes move fluid from reservoir into cam ring. Fluid is pressurized by vanes in cam ring, then forced into cavities of thrust plate and through flow control valve. The flow control valve, regulates pressurized fluid to the steering gear unit. *See Fig. 3.*

LUBRICATION

FLUID TYPE

Use Ford Premium Power Steering Fluid (E6AZ-19582-AA) or use Type "F" ATF fluid.

FLUID LEVEL CHECK

Fluid level may be checked when fluid is either hot or cold. If fluid is cold, below 75°F (24°C), check fluid level using the COLD full mark on dipstick. If fluid is hot, about 177°F (77°C), check fluid level using the HOT full mark on dipstick. If fluid is low, add small amount of fluid through dipstick opening and recheck fluid level. DO NOT overfill. On some van applications, check remote reservoir for proper fluid level. Remote reservoir has "full" and "low" lines on side of reservoir.

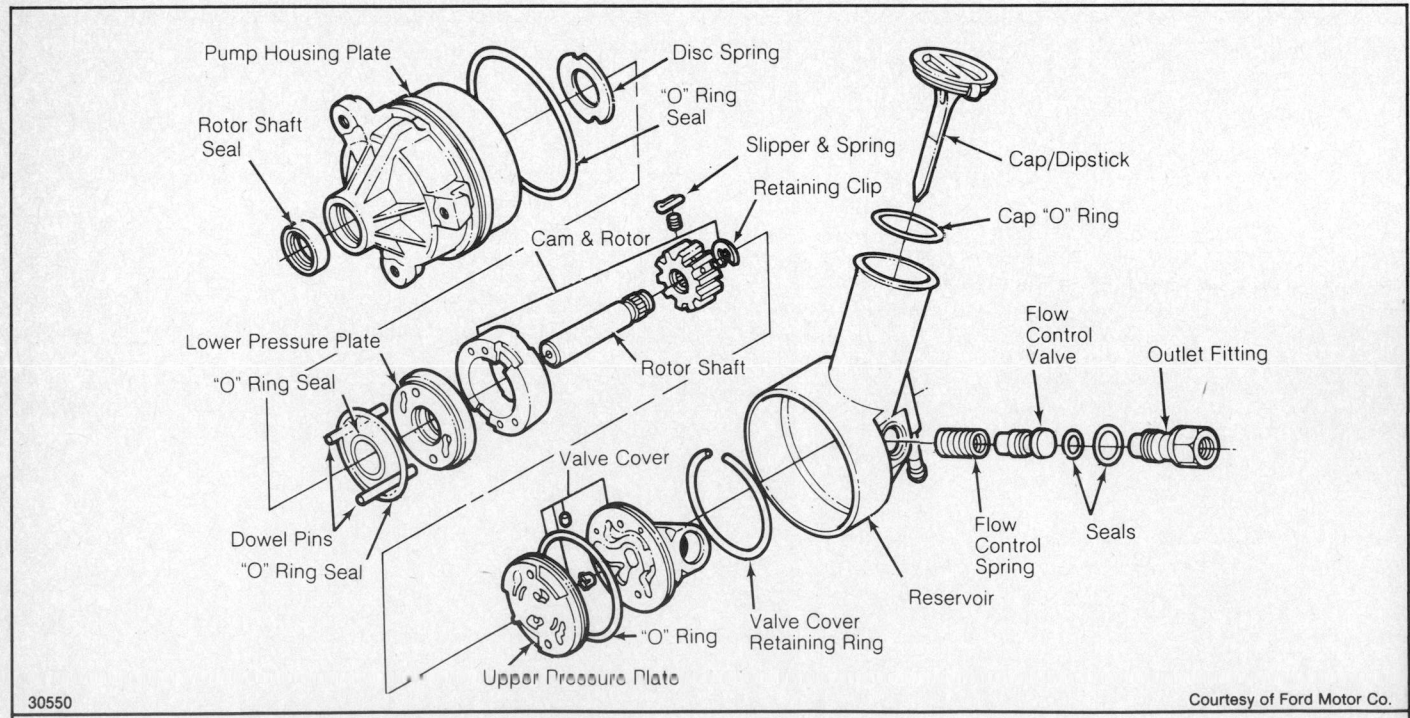

30550   Courtesy of Ford Motor Co.

Fig. 2: Exploded View Of C-II Power Steering Pump (Except Van)

3) Apply lifting pressure to tension... pulley. Ensure proper belt routing... SPECIFICATIONS in ENGINE PE... adjustment bracket, adjust belt and... bolts to specification.

4) Install hoses to pump. Tighten pre... See TORQUE SPECIFICATIONS ta... with new fluid. Start engine and let i... to bleed air from system. Recheck r...

SAGINAW POWER STEER...
SHAFT SEAL

Removal – 1) Remove pump from... PUMP. Drain fluid from reservoir... removed, remove pulley using Pulle... *Fig. 4.* DO NOT use conventional typ... damage will result.

2) Insert sharp, strong tool between... ing. DO NOT insert tool between sha... face will result in fluid leak. Pry out se... from shaft.

Installation – 1) Install new seal onto... outward (toward pulley end of shaft... seal installer. Tap seal installer lightly... erly seated flush with housing.

2) If required, install pump assembly t... ling pulley to pump shaft. Also if requ... to-support bracket and tighten all bolt... SPECIFICATIONS table at end of arti...

3) Install pulley to pump shaft using F... *See Fig. 4.* Pulley must be within .010"... to align with other pulleys for prope... installation, see POWER STEERING... INSTALLATION.

STEERING GEAR

Removal – 1) Place drain pan under... unit. Disconnect hydraulic lines at pow... Quickly cap lines and gear unit ports... loss of fluid. Remove splash shield fro... flex coupling. Remove coupling clamp b...

2) Mark relation of pitman arm to... reference. Remove pitman arm nut an... Puller (T64P-3590-F), remove pitman ar...

3) Remove steering gear-to-frame attach... free of flex coupling splines and remov... Use care not to damage flex coupling ma... spread coupling clamp slightly to remov...

Installation – 1) Center steering whe... splash shield over upper gear unit inpu... input shaft with indexing flat facing dov... shaft into position in flex coupling. Insta... tighten bolts to **50-62 ft. lbs. (68-84 N.m...** and tighten to **26-34 ft. lbs. (35-46 N.m).**

2) With wheels in straight-ahead positio... marks, install pitman arm on sector sha... pitman arm. Tighten to **170-228 ft. lbs. (2...** shaft splash shield to flex coupling. Co... lines to steering gear control valve hous... **20-30 ft. lbs. (27-41 N.m).**

3) Fill reservoir to proper level. Disconnec... wires and isolate them from ground. Cran... ing wheel left to right to distribute fluid... needed. Check for fluid leaks. If no leaks ... secondary coil wires. Start vehicle and ble... IC SYSTEM BLEEDING under LUBRICAT...

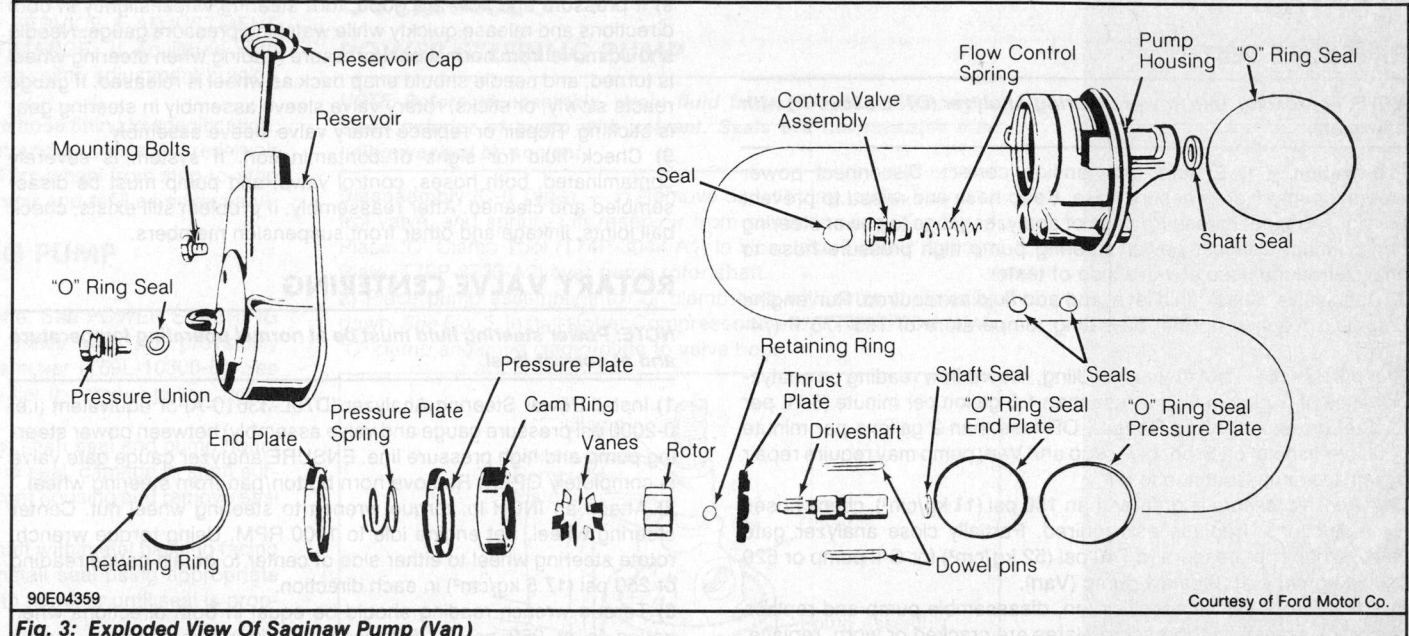

Fig. 3: Exploded View Of Saginaw Pump (Van)

90E04359

Courtesy of Ford Motor Co.

HYDRAULIC SYSTEM BLEEDING

1) Raise front wheels off surface and support vehicle. Fill reservoir to specified level. Run engine until power steering fluid reaches normal operating temperature, about 165-175°F (74-79°C). Recheck fluid level in reservoir and top off as necessary. With engine running, eliminate trapped air in system by turning steering wheel from lock-to-lock until fluid level no longer decreases and no bubbles exist in reservoir.

2) DO NOT hold steering wheel against lock (in far left or far right position). This action will create extremely high pressure and damage pump. Recheck fluid level in reservoir and top off as necessary.

ADJUSTMENTS

STEERING GEAR MESHLOAD

1) Reference mark pitman arm to sector shaft. Using Pitman Arm Puller (T64P-3590-F), remove pitman arm from sector shaft. Disconnect fluid return line at pump reservoir. Cap reservoir return line pipe. Place end of return line in suitable container.

2) Turn steering wheel in both directions several times to drain fluid. DO NOT reuse this fluid. Remove horn button from steering wheel to access steering wheel nut. Turn steering wheel until positioned 45 degrees from left or right steering stop.

3) Using an INCH lb. torque wrench on steering wheel nut, record torque required to turn steering shaft 1/8 turn toward top center from present 45 degrees position. (This is torque required to "start" steering wheel to move.)

4) Turn steering gear to center position. (This is steering wheel normal center position, half way between lock-to-lock.) Using an INCH lb. torque wrench on steering wheel nut, record torque required to move steering wheel and shaft, back and forth across top center position. Compare the two readings.

5) If vehicle is new (less than 5000 miles), center reading should be 12-24 INCH lbs. (1.4-2.7 N.m). Adjust as required, go to step **6)**. If vehicle has more than 5000 miles or sector shaft has been replaced, compare over center torque reading with torque recorded in step **3)**. If centering torque is greater than or less than recorded "starting" torque by **10 INCH lbs. (1.1 N.m)**, adjust to **9-13 INCH lbs. (1.0-1.5 N.m)**. To adjust, go to next step.

6) To adjust meshload, loosen sector shaft lock nut, turn sector shaft adjustment screw until proper torque reading across center position is obtained. Repeat Steps **3)** -**5)**. *See Fig. 1.* Tighten lock nut while holding adjusting screw in place.

7) Install horn button/pad. Attach pitman arm nut and tighten to specifications. See TORQUE SPECIFICATIONS table at end of article. Reconnect pump hose. Add fluid and bleed system. See HYDRAULIC SYSTEM BLEEDING under LUBRICATION.

BELT ADJUSTMENT

NOTE: For proper serpentine belt routing, see SERVICE & ADJUSTMENT SPECIFICATIONS article in ENGINE PERFORMANCE.

BELT ADJUSTMENT

Application	New Belt Lbs. (kg)	[1] Used Belt Lbs. (kg)
2.3L		
Fixed	150-190 (68-86)	140-160 (64-73)
With Tensioner [2]	150-190 (68-86)	140-160 (64-73)
2.9L	120-160 (54-73)	110-130 (50-59)
3.0L		
Fixed	120-160 (54-73)	110-130 (50-59)
With Tensioner [2]	150-190 (68-86)	140-160 (64-73)
4.0L With Tensioner [2]	108-132 (49-60)	108-132 (49-60)
4.9L With Tensioner [2]	[3]	[3]
5.0L With Tensioner [2]	[4]	[4]
5.8L With Tensioner [2]	[4]	[4]
7.3L Except Ambulance		
Vac. Pump W/ 3/8" Belt	90-130 (41-59)	65-85 (30-39)
Vac. Pump W/ 1/2" Belt	110-150 (50-68)	75-95 (34-43)
All Other W/ 1/2" Belt	140-180 (64-82)	95-115 (43-52)
7.3L Ambulance		
Alternator	140-160 (64-73)	140-160 (64-73)
Vac. Pump	90-130 (41-59)	65-85 (30-39)
A/C & P/S	140-180 (64-82)	95-115 (43-52)
7.5L		
With Tensioner [2]	[5]	[5]
Alt. & Air Pump	160-200 (73-91)	110-130 (50-59)

[1] – Any belt operated for 10 minutes.

[2] – Tension is correct if tensioner is within indicator marks.

[3] – 90 lbs. (41 kg) minimum for vehicles with 60- and 75-amp alternators. 117 lbs. (53 kg) minimum for vehicles with 100-amp alternators.

[4] – 77 lbs. (35 kg) minimum for vehicles with 60 and 75-amp alternators. 111 lbs. (50 kg) minimum for vehicles with 100-amp alternators.

[5] – 94 Lbs. (43 kg) minimum tension.

1992 STEERING
Integral Power Steering (Cont.)

In[t:

TESTING

PRESSURE TEST

*NOTE: For testing, use Power Ste___
flow meter.*

Preparation – 1) Ensure belt t___
steering pump high pressure hos___
fluid loss. Connect pressure hose___
pump fitting. Connect power ste___
analyzer gauge hose at valve side___
2) Open valve. Check fluid level a___
until fluid reaches normal operat___
79°C).

Pressure Test – 1) With engine i___
er gauge. If minimum flow is less ___
minute) on Explorer and Ranger, ___
(7.6L per minute) on Bronco, Picku___
or replacement. Continue test.
2) At idle, if pressure is greater th___
for restrictions. Replace as requ___
valve to build up pressure to 740 ___
psi (44 kg/cm²) on Saginaw pump___
3) If flow drops below specificatic___
cam pack assembly. If pressure p___
4) DO NOT close analyzer gate va___
pletely close and partially open ___
reading each time. If pressure is h___
or replace flow control valve or ___
SPECIFICATIONS table.

PRESSURE TEST SPECIFICATION___

Application	Idle Pr___ psi (k___
Explorer & Ranger	
Ford C-II Pump	
Model HBC	7___ (5___
Ranger 3.0L	
Ford C-II Pump	7___ (5___
Bronco, Pickup & Van	
Saginaw Pump	
Model HBA-HA/HB	6___ (4___
Ford C-II Pump	
Model HBC-JX	7___ (5___
Ford C-II Pump	
Model HBC-JY	7___ (5___

¹ – Engine idle RPM must be se___
obtain idle pressure.

5) Set engine speed at 1500 RPM___
than 1 gallon (3.8L) per minute fr___
flow control valve in pump must be___
6) Turn steering wheel to left and r___
3 seconds. Pressure should be n___
pressure. See PRESSURE TES___
should drop below .5 gallon (1.9L___
7) If pressure and flow are not as ___
internally. Remove steering gear___
Repair or replace damaged parts.___
age. See STEERING GEAR UNIT ___

Reassembly – 1) Place rotor onto rotor shaft splines, with rotor's large counterbore facing upward. Install retaining ring in rotor shaft groove. Place insert cam over rotor with recessed flat facing toward reservoir.
2) With rotor held half way out of cam, insert spring into rotor spring pocket. Use a slipper to compress spring. Install slipper with narrow groove facing cam. Slippers must be installed with narrow groove rail spacing facing cam, otherwise pump will not function.
3) Hold cam stationary. Turn rotor one space at a time and install all 10 rotor springs and slippers. Ensure springs and slippers do not fall out when turning rotor.
4) Using a plastic mallet and Seal Driver (T78P-3733-A3), install a new rotor shaft seal to housing by driving seal and then seal retainer into bore until bottomed. Turn pump housing over and position pump housing plate on a flat surface with pulley/seal side down. *See Fig. 2.*
5) Insert 2 dowel pins and disc spring (dished surface upward) into housing plate. Lubricate lower pressure plate "O" ring seals with power steering fluid. Install seals to lower pressure plate.
6) Insert lower pressure plate with "O" ring seals toward front of pump, into bottom of pump housing plate and over dowel pins. Place pump housing plate assembly into "C" clamp using lower support plate on pump rotor shaft to protect new seal. *See Fig. 5.* Place Driver (T78P-3733-A3) in center rotor shaft hole.
7) Tighten "C" clamp to press driver and lower plate lightly until it is "felt" to be bottomed in pump plate housing. This operation will seat lower pressure plate "O" ring. Install cam/rotor assembly (containing cam, rotor, slippers, and rotor shaft), into pump housing plate over dowel pins.

NOTE: When installing cam/rotor assembly, stepped holes must be used for dowel pins. Recessed notch in cam insert must face reservoir and be about 180° opposite square pump mounting boss.

8) Place upper pressure plate over dowel pins. Side of plate with square recessed notch must face reservoir end and be positioned 180° opposite the pump's square mounting boss. Place new "O" ring seal on valve cover. Lubricate with power steering fluid.

NOTE: Ensure plastic baffle is securely in place in valve cover. If not, apply petroleum jelly to baffle. Install baffle.

9) Place valve cover over dowel pins. Ensure valve cover outlet fitting hole is directly in line with square mounting boss of pump housing plate.
10) Place entire pump housing assembly in "C" clamp tool. Install upper compressor plate to valve cover and tighten "C" clamp to compress valve cover into pump housing plate, until retaining ring groove is exposed in pump housing plate.
11) Install valve cover retaining ring with ends near access hole in pump housing plate. *See Fig. 6.* Remove pump assembly from "C" clamp tool. Place new large "O" ring seal on outside of pump housing plate. Lubricate "O" ring seal with power steering fluid. Install power steering reservoir to pump housing, aligning outlet fitting hole in reservoir with threaded fitting hole in valve cover. *See Fig. 2.*
12) Install flow control spring and flow control valve into valve cover. Place new "O" ring seals on outlet fitting. Lubricate seals with power steering fluid.
13) Install pump outlet fitting into valve cover. Tighten fitting to specification. See TORQUE SPECIFICATIONS table at end of article.

CAUTION: When clamping pump cast iron housing in vise, be careful not to exert excessive force on front hub or pump. Hammering on ANY pump components during assembly/disassembly may cause damage.

Disassembly (Saginaw Type) – 1) Drain pump reservoir. Clean exterior of unit with solvent. Remove mounting bracket(s). If pulley was not previously removed, remove pulley using Pulley Remover (T69L-10300-B). *See Fig. 4.* DO NOT use conventional type puller to remove pulley, pulley damage will result.

2) Turn pump over to point pulley shaft down. Clamp square boss of pump shaft housing in a soft jawed vise. Remove high pressure line union fitting and "O" ring seal from rear of reservoir. Remove reservoir mounting bolts and studs. *See Fig. 3.*
3) Using plastic hammer, tap against filler tube and around reservoir beaded edge to loosen and remove reservoir from pump body. Remove and discard large "O" ring seal.
4) Using 1/8" punch, tap end plate retaining ring around until end of ring is near hole in pump body. *See Fig. 6.* Inserting punch into hole, disengage ring from groove in pump bore. Using a screwdriver, pry ring from body.
5) Tap end plate with a soft-faced hammer to loosen. Spring tension will push plate up. Remove pressure plate spring. Remove pump from vise. *See Fig. 3.*
6) Remove end plate "O" ring. Invert pump and place on flat surface. Using soft-faced hammer, tap end of drive shaft to loosen and remove pressure plate, cam ring and rotor vanes. Remove rotor and shaft assembly by pushing end of shaft through pump housing while lifting pump housing.
7) Lift pump housing off rotor and shaft assembly. Flow control valve and spring should slide out of bore. Clamp rotor drive shaft in soft-jawed vise, with rotor and thrust plate facing up. Pry rotor retaining ring from shaft. Use care not to nick shaft or rotor. Slide rotor and thrust plate off shaft. Remove shaft from vise.
8) Remove both dowel pins from housing. Remove pressure plate "O" ring from pump housing bore and discard. Using a screwdriver, pry drive shaft oil seal from pump housing.
Cleaning & Inspection – 1) Clean all pump components in clean solvent. Blow dry. Inspect flow control valve assembly for wear, scoring, burrs or other damage. Inspect seal bore for burrs, nicks, or score marks that would allow oil to by-pass outer seal surface.
2) Check all machined surfaces of body for scratches or burrs which might allow leaks. Check "O" ring mating surfaces. Inspect pump housing drive shaft bushing for excessive wear.
3) If replacement is required, replace pump and bushing as an assembly. Inspect end plate "O" ring mating surface for nicks and burrs. Polish with oil stone (if required).
4) Inspect rotor ring for roughness or irregularities. Use oil stone to correct minor irregularities. Replace ring if outside cam surface is worn or scored.
5) Check thrust plate and pressure plate for scoring and wear. To remove light scoring, lap with crocus cloth until surface is smooth and flat. Clean thoroughly. Check that vanes slide freely but fit snugly into slots. Replace as required.
6) If vanes are loose in rotor slots, replace rotor and/or vanes. Scoring on rotor may be removed with crocus cloth. Clean all components thoroughly.
Reassembly – 1) Lubricate all "O" rings, seals and seal surfaces with power steering fluid, or petroleum jelly. With pump on flat surface, drive new shaft seal in until it bottoms on bore shoulder.
2) Clamp pump housing in vise with shaft pointing down. Install pressure plate "O" ring in housing bore and into third groove from end of housing. Remove housing from vise.
3) Clamp shaft, splined end up, in soft-jawed vise. Install thrust plate with smooth, ported side upward, onto shaft. Slide rotor over shaft splines with counter bore down toward thrust plate. Install new rotor retaining ring to shaft. Ensure ring is seated in groove.
4) Install 2 dowel pins into holes in pump housing bore. Lubricate shaft with power steering fluid. Insert drive shaft, rotor, and thrust plate assembly into pump bore. Align thrust plate locating holes with dowel pins. Ensure thrust plate slides properly on dowel pins.
5) Slide cam ring over rotor and onto dowel pins, with arrow on cam ring facing toward rear of housing. Install vanes in rotor slots with rounded edge of vane facing out towards cam ring inner surface. Vanes should slide freely in rotor.
6) Lubricate pressure plate with power steering fluid. Position pressure plate on dowel pins with circular spring depression facing rear of housing. Narrow slots in plate should engage dowel pins. Using a 1 1/4" socket in groove of pressure plate, press down on socket with both thumbs to seat plate assembly over "O" ring in pump___

housing bore. Lubricate end plate "O" ring with power steering fluid and install in second groove from end of housing.

7) Place pressure plate spring in groove in pressure plate. Lubricate end plate with power steering fluid. Place end plate over spring. Using thumb pressure or arbor press, press end plate down to just slightly below retaining ring groove. Seat retaining ring in groove. Take care to prevent cocking end plate in bore or distorting assembly. Release pressure on end plate.

8) Using a punch, tap retaining ring ends around in groove until opening is opposite flow control valve bore. This ensures maximum retention of retaining ring. Install flow control valve spring in hole. Install flow control valve assembly with screened end towards front of housing.

9) Install new large "O" ring to outside of pump housing. Install "O" ring seals to countersunk holes for mounting studs and flow control valve. Lubricate inside edge of reservoir and install reservoir onto pump housing, aligning mounting stud holes. Install studs and snug tighten.

10) If necessary, tap reservoir down on pump housing using a soft-faced hammer. Install new "O" ring on pressure union groove next to hex head of fitting.

CAUTION: DO NOT install "O" ring in lower groove on pressure union fitting. This will restrict relief outlet orifice.

---

11) Install pressure union fitting to pump housing and tighten to **11-16 ft. lbs. (15-22 N.m).** Tighten mounting studs to **35 ft. lbs. (47 N.m).** Remove pump from vise. Install mounting bracket and pulley. See POWER STEERING PUMP under REMOVAL & INSTALLATION.

STEERING GEAR UNIT

Disassembly – 1) Remove steering gear unit. See STEERING GEAR under REMOVAL & INSTALLATION. Drain steering gear by holding gear unit upside down and turning input shaft several times. Mount gear in a soft-jawed vise with sector shaft cover upward. See Fig. 1.

2) Remove lock nut from sector shaft adjusting screw. Center steering gear by turning input shaft lock-to-lock while counting turns, then divide by two. From lock, turn shaft number of turns required to center sector shaft. If properly centered, flat surface on input shaft should be facing down.

3) Remove sector shaft cover bolts. Tap lower end of sector shaft with a soft faced hammer to loosen shaft in housing bore. Lift shaft and cover assembly from housing. Discard cover "O" ring. Remove sector shaft adjusting screw from cover.

4) Remove control valve housing attaching bolts and identification tag. Lift control valve housing and piston assembly from gear housing. Discard housing gasket. Remove Teflon ring and "O" ring from piston assembly. See Fig. 7.

5) Hold piston assembly over a clean container. Remove ball guide clamp screws, let guide tubes and balls fall into container. Rotate input shaft lock to lock until all 27-29 balls fall from piston into container. Remove worm and valve assembly from piston. Ensure that all balls have been removed from piston.

6) Install valve body assembly in bench mounted Holding Fixture (T57L-500-B) or soft jawed vise. Loosen Allen head race nut screw from valve housing. Remove worm bearing race nut using Wrench (T66P-3553-B), and Valve Housing-to-Piston Spacer (T66P-3553-C). See Fig. 8. Carefully slide input shaft, and worm and valve assembly out of control valve housing.

NOTE: Before reassembly, worm and valve sleeve, and control valve housing must be rebuilt. See WORM & VALVE SLEEVE, and CONTROL VALVE HOUSING under OVERHAUL. Also sector shaft seals must be replaced. See SECTOR SHAFT SEALS under OVERHAUL.

Reassembly – 1) Mount control valve housing in Holding Fixture (T57L-500-B) or vise with flanged end up. Using power steering fluid, lightly lubricate inside control housing bore and Teflon rings on valve sleeve. Carefully install input shaft and valve sleeve into control housing bore.

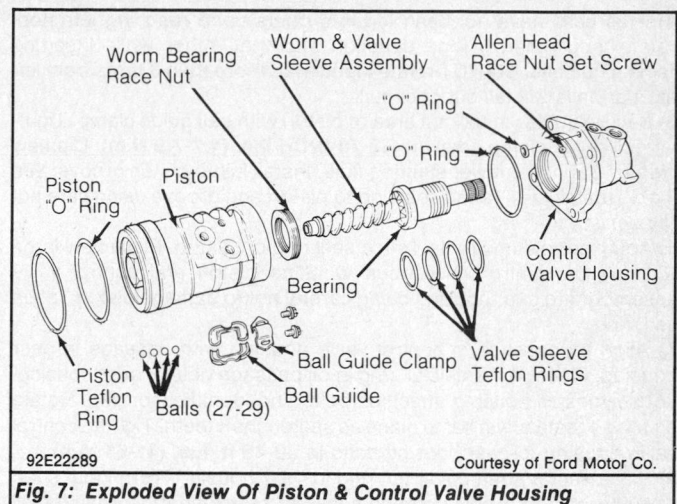

Fig. 7: Exploded View Of Piston & Control Valve Housing

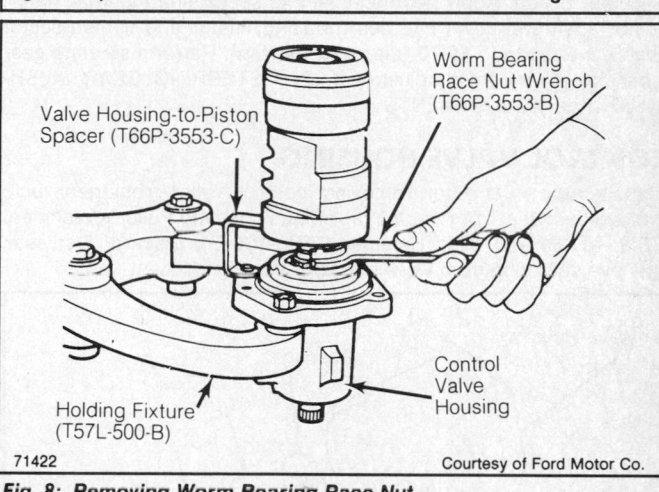

Fig. 8: Removing Worm Bearing Race Nut

2) Install worm bearing race nut to housing. Tighten nut to **55-90 ft. lbs. (75-122 N.m).** Install Allen head race nut set screw into control housing and tighten to **15-25 INCH lbs. (1.7- 2.8 N.m).**

3) Place piston on bench with ball guide holes facing up. See Fig. 9. Insert worm shaft into piston so first part of worm groove lines up with first hole in center of piston. Place ball guide in piston. Place 27-29 ball bearings in ball guide while turning worm counterclockwise as viewed from input end of shaft.

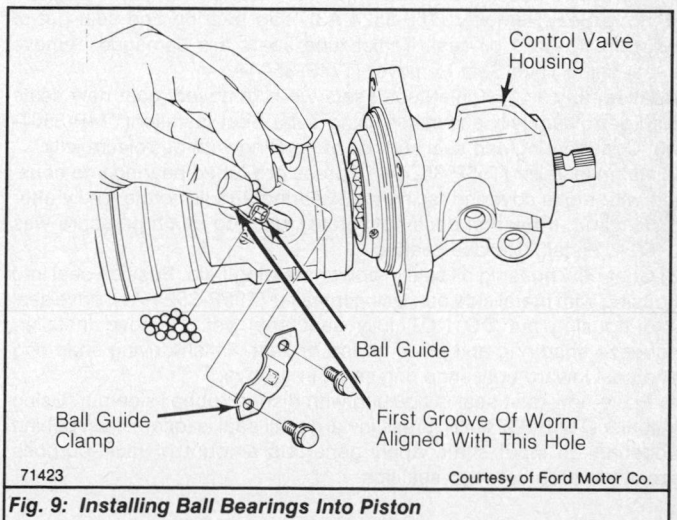

Fig. 9: Installing Ball Bearings Into Piston

4) If all balls have not been fed into guide upon reaching left stop, rotate input shaft in one direction and then other while inserting remaining balls. DO NOT rotate input shaft more than 3 turns from left stop or balls will fall out of circuit.

5) Secure guides in ball nut area of piston with ball guide clamp. Tighten ball guide clamp screw to **42-70 INCH lbs. (4.7-7.9 N.m).** Dip new piston "O" ring in power steering fluid. Install it into piston groove. *See Fig. 7.* Install new Teflon seal ring to piston end groove using care not to over-stretch ring.

6) Apply petroleum jelly to Teflon seal ring on piston. Place new large "O" ring on control valve housing. Slide piston and control valve assembly into gear housing being careful not to damage piston Teflon seal ring.

7) Align oil passage in control valve housing with passage in gear housing. Place new small "O" ring in oil passage hole of gear housing. Loosely install housing attaching bolts and identification tag. Rotate piston so teeth are in same plane as sector shaft teeth. Tighten control valve housing-to-gear housing bolts to **30-45 ft. lbs. (41-61 N.m).**

8) Place sector shaft cover "O" ring in gear housing. Turn input shaft to center piston. Apply petroleum jelly to sector shaft journal. Install sector shaft and cover into gear housing. Install and tighten sector shaft cover bolts to **55-70 ft.lbs. (75-95 N.m).** Perform steering gear meshload over-center adjustment. See STEERING GEAR MESHLOAD under ADJUSTMENTS.

CONTROL VALVE HOUSING

Disassembly – 1) After removing control valve from gear unit, remove dust seal from rear of valve housing using Puller Attachment (T58L-101-B) and Slide Hammer (T59L-100-B). Discard dust seal. Remove snap ring from valve housing. *See Fig. 10.*

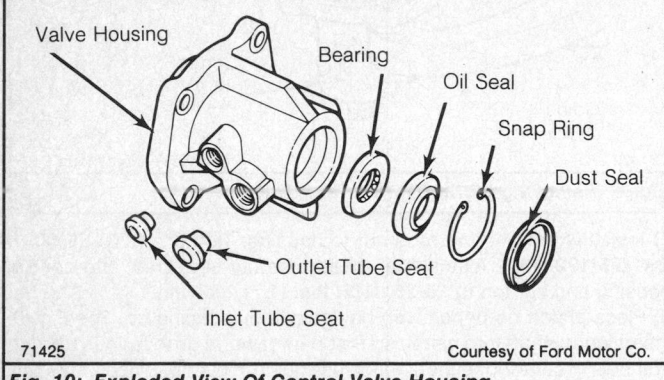

71425　　　　　Courtesy of Ford Motor Co.

Fig. 10: Exploded View Of Control Valve Housing

2) Turn valve housing over. Insert Driver Handle (T65P-3524-A2) and Bearing/Seal Remover (T65-3524-A3). Tap bearing and seal out of housing. Discard oil seal. If inlet tube seats are damaged, remove seats using Tube Seat Remover (T74P-3504-L).

Reassembly – 1) If inlet tube seats were removed, coat new seats with petroleum jelly and install using Tube Seat Installer (T74P-3504-M). Coat bearing and seal surface of housing with petroleum jelly.

2) Using Installer (T65P-3524-A1), press pre-lubed bearing into housing with metal covering facing out. Bearing should rotate freely after installation. If bearing does not rotate freely, to much pressure was used to install. Replace bearing.

3) Coat new housing oil seal in power steering fluid. Position seal into housing with metal side out. Using Installer (T65P-3524-A1), drive seal into housing but DO NOT fully seat seal yet. Remove Installer, squeeze snap ring and place on top of seal. Finish driving snap ring and seal inward until snap ring seats in groove.

4) Place new dust seal in housing with dished rubber side out. Using Installer (T65P-3524-A1), press inward until seal is located just behind undercut on input shaft. Apply generous amount of multi-purpose grease to area between seal lips.

SECTOR SHAFT SEALS

Disassembly – After sector shaft has been removed from gear unit housing, remove snap ring from lower end of gear housing (sector shaft seal end). Using Puller Attachment (T58L-101-B) and Slide Hammer (T59L-100-B), remove dust seal and pressure seal from housing. Discard seals.

Reassembly – 1) Lubricate new seals and seal bore with multi-purpose grease (Ford DOAZ-19584-AA). Place dust seal on Seal Installer (T77L-3576-A) so raised lip of seal faces installer. Place pressure seal on installer so lip faces away from installer. Flat side of each seal should be against each other. *See Fig. 11.*

2) Insert installer into sector shaft bore. Drive seals into bore until seals just clear snap ring groove. DO NOT bottom seals against bearing. Seals will not function properly if bottomed against bearing. Install snap ring into bore. Apply grease lightly to area between seal lips.

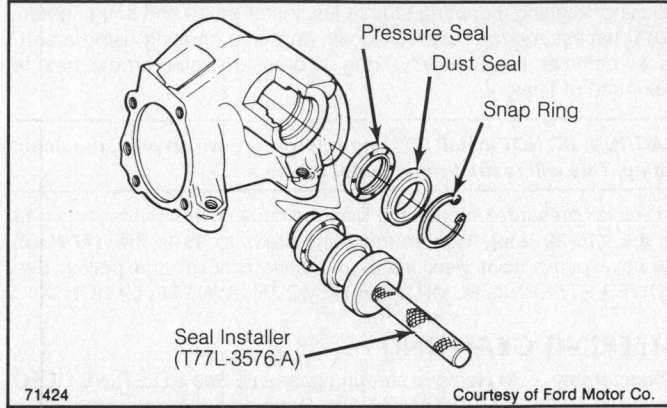

71424　　　　　Courtesy of Ford Motor Co.

Fig. 11: Installing Steering Gear Sector Shaft Seals

WORM & VALVE SLEEVE

NOTE: Use only Seal Installation Set (T75L-3517-A) to install Teflon sealing ring to sleeve. Failure to use proper installation tools will cause damage to sealing rings and result in internal fluid leaks.

Disassembly & Reassembly – 1) Remove Teflon sealing rings from valve sleeve using small-bladed knife. *See Fig. 7.* DO NOT scratch sleeve seal grooves. Wrap worm end of sleeve in shop towel and mount in soft-jawed vise. Place Mandrel (T75L-3517-A1) on sleeve. Install one valve sleeve Teflon ring over mandrel.

2) Using Pusher (T75L-3517-A2), rapidly push down on pusher forcing Teflon ring down mandrel cone and into fourth groove of valve sleeve. Repeat procedure for 3 more rings, adding another Spacer (T75L-3517-A3) under mandrel for each ring to line up with next open groove.

3) After all sleeve rings are installed, remove installation tools. Apply a light coat of power steering fluid to sleeve and Teflon rings. Reinstall one Spacer (T75L-3517-A3) on input shaft as a pilot for Sizing Tube (T75L-3517-A4). Slide sizing tube carefully over valve sleeve Teflon rings. Ensure rings are NOT being deformed when tube is slid over rings.

4) Allow sizing tube to sit over rings for minimum 5 minutes to help contract Teflon rings. Remove sizing tube. Check that rings turn freely in grooves. Install sleeve into control valve assembly soon after removing sizing tube.

TORQUE SPECIFICATIONS

TORQUE SPECIFICATIONS

Application	Ft. Lbs. (N.m)
Control Valve Housing-To-Gear Housing Bolts	35-50 (47-68)
Flex Coupling Bolt	25-34 (34-46)
Mesh Load Adjusting Screw Lock Nut	35-45 (47-61)
Piston End Cap	70-110 (95-149)
Pitman Arm Nut	190-230 (258-312)
Pressure Hose-to-Gear Fitting	16-25 (22-34)
Pump Bracket Brace nuts	13-17 (18-23)
Pump Mounting Bracket Bolts	23-30 (31-41)
Pump Outlet Fitting (C-II)	30-40 (41-54)
Pump Pressure Union Outlet Fitting (Saginaw)	11-16 (15-22)
Pump-To-Bracket Bolts	30-40 (41-54)
Return Hose-to-Gear Unit Fitting	17-32 (23-43)
Sector Shaft Cover Bolts	55-70 (75-95)
Steering Gear-to-Frame Bolts	50-62 (68-84)
Worm Bearing Race Nut	55-90 (75-122)

	INCH Lbs. (N.m)
Allen Head Race Nut Set Screw	15-25 (1.7-2.8)
Ball Guide Clamp Screw	42-70 (4.7-7.9)

1992 STEERING
Power Rack & Pinion

Aerostar

DESCRIPTION

Power rack and pinion has gear and valve housings cast into a 1-piece aluminum unit. *See Fig. 1*. Steering gear is a hydraulic mechanical type, which uses internal valving to direct hydraulic fluid flow and pressure. Gear contains a rotary hydraulic fluid control valve integrated to input shaft and a boost cylinder integrated with rack.

C-II power steering pump is a belt-driven, slipper-type integral pump with a fiberglass/nylon reservoir. Reservoir is attached to rear of pump housing plate. *See Fig. 2*. Pump body is encased within housing and reservoir.

Hoses are attached with quick disconnect fittings, located below filler neck at outboard side of reservoir. An identification tag with basic model number is attached to reservoir.

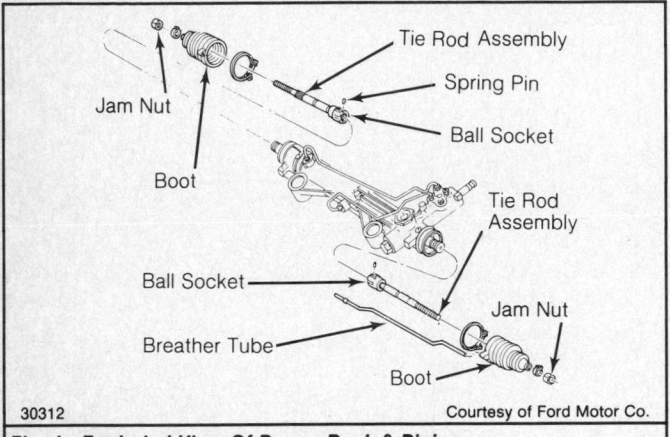

30312   Courtesy of Ford Motor Co.

Fig. 1: Exploded View Of Power Rack & Pinion

LUBRICATION

CAPACITY

Power steering fluid capacity including pump is 2.5 pts. (1.2 L).

FLUID TYPE

Use Ford Premium Power Steering Fluid (E6AZ-19582-AA) or Type F ATF fluid.

FLUID LEVEL CHECK

Fluid level may be checked when fluid is either hot or cold. If fluid is cold, approximately 75°F (24°C), check fluid level using the cold full mark on dipstick. If fluid is hot, approximately 177°F (77°C), check fluid level using the hot full mark on dipstick. Add fluid through dipstick opening as necessary and recheck. DO NOT overfill.

HYDRAULIC SYSTEM BLEEDING

Raise and support vehicle. Fill reservoir to specified level. Run engine until power steering fluid reaches normal operating temperature, approximately 165-175°F (74-79°C). Turn steering wheel from lock-to-lock until fluid level no longer decreases and no bubbles exist. DO NOT hold steering wheel in far left or right position. Check fluid level in reservoir and fill as necessary.

ADJUSTMENTS

POWER STEERING PUMP BELT

BELT ADJUSTMENT

Application	New Belt Lbs. (kg)	[1] Used Belt Lbs. (kg)
3.0L	100-140 (45-64)	80-100 (36-45)
4.0L With Tensioner [2]	108-132 (49-60)	108-132 (49-60)

[1] – Any belt operated for 5 minutes.
[2] – Tension is correct if tensioner is within indicator marks.

RACK YOKE PLUG PRELOAD

1) Remove steering gear. See POWER RACK & PINION STEERING GEAR under REMOVAL & INSTALLATION. Drain power steering fluid by rotating input shaft lock-to-lock twice, using Pinion Shaft Torque Adapter (T74P-3504-R). Cover ports on valve housing.

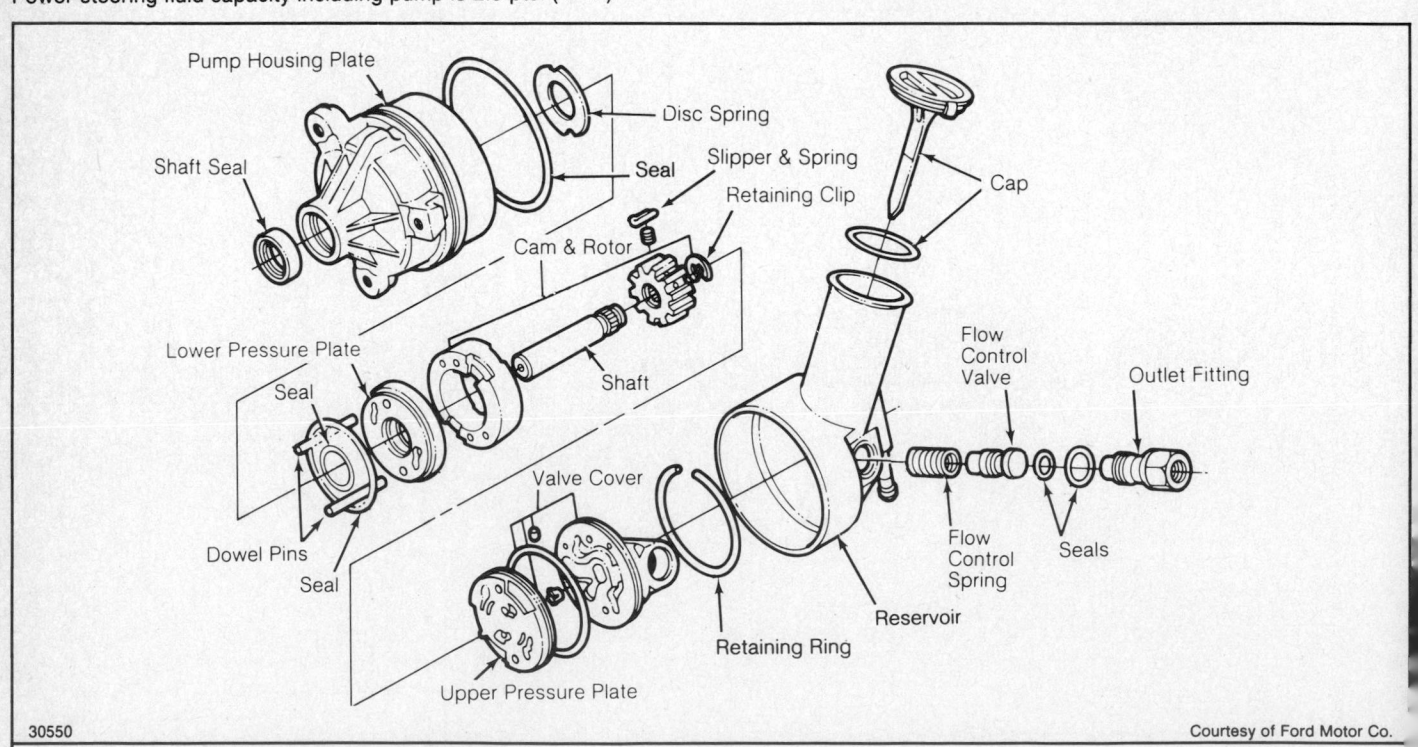

30550   Courtesy of Ford Motor Co.

Fig. 2: Exploded View Of C-II Power Steering Pump

2) Place pinion shaft torque adapter and an INCH-pound torque wrench on pinion shaft. Using Pinion Yoke Lock Nut Wrench (T78P-3504-H), loosen yoke plug lock nut. Loosen yoke plug using socket. Center rack by counting number of complete revolutions of input shaft and dividing by 2. Tighten yoke plug to **45-50 INCH lbs. (5.0-5.6 N.m).**

3) Back off yoke plug 1/8 turn (44 degrees minimum and 54 degrees maximum) until torque required to turn input shaft is **7-18 INCH lbs. (.78-2.03 N.m).** Hold yoke plug and tighten yoke plug lock nut to **44-66 ft. lbs. (60-89 N.m).** Do not allow yoke plug to move while tightening lock nut. Recheck input shaft torque after tightening lock nut.

TESTING

PRESSURE TEST

Pre-Test Preparation – 1) With belt tension correct, disconnect power steering pump pressure hose. Keep hose end raised to prevent fluid loss. Connect pressure hose of Power Steering Analyzer (D79L-33610-A) to power steering pump fitting. Connect other hose from valve side of analyzer to steering gear inlet.

2) Open valve. Run engine until fluid reaches normal operating temperature of **165-175°F (74-79°C).** Check fluid level. Add fluid as necessary.

Pressure Test – 1) Start engine and idle for approximately 2 minutes. Record flow. If flow is less than 1.6 gallons per minute (6.1L per minute), pump may require repair. Continue test.

2) If pressure is greater than 150 psi (10.5 kg/cm²), check hoses for restrictions. Partially close valve to build up pressure to 740 psi (52 kg/cm²).

3) If flow drops below specification, disassemble pump and replace cam pack. Inspect pressure plate for cracks or wear. Replace as necessary.

4) Completely close and partially open gate valve 3 times. Do not close valve for more than 5 seconds. Record highest reading each time. If pressure is higher or lower than specified, repair or replace flow control valve. Refer to PRESSURE TEST SPECIFICATIONS table.

PRESSURE TEST SPECIFICATIONS

Application	Idle Pressure psi (kg/cm²)	¹ Relief Pressure psi (kg/cm²)
Aerostar		
Ford C-II Pump		
Model HBC	740	1400-1530
	(52)	(98-108)

¹ – Measure with steering wheel turned to extreme right or left position.

5) Increase engine speed to 1500 RPM. Record flow. If flow varies more than one gallon (3.8L) per minute from pressure measured in step **1)**, repair or replace flow control valve in pump.

6) Turn steering wheel to left and right stops. Pressure should be nearly the same as maximum relief pressure. Flow should drop below .5 gallon (1.9L) per minute.

7) If pressure and flow are not as specified, steering gear is leaking internally. Remove steering gear. Remove flow control valve. Repair or replace damaged parts. Check rack piston and valve seals for damage.

8) If pressure and flow are good, turn steering wheel slightly in both directions and release quickly while watching pressure gauge. Needle should move from normal backpressure reading and snap back as wheel is released.

9) If gauge reacts slowly, or sticks, rotary valve in steering gear is sticking. Repair or replace rotary valve.

10) If system is severely contaminated, disassemble and clean both hoses, control valve and pump. If problem still exists, check ball joints, linkage and other front suspension components.

TURNING EFFORT CHECK

NOTE: Ensure front wheels are properly aligned and tire pressures are correct before checking turning effort.

1) Park vehicle on a dry, concrete surface and set parking brake. Run engine at idle for 2-3 minutes. Turn steering wheel to far left and right positions several times to warm fluid to 110-120°F (43-48°C). DO NOT hold steering wheel in far left or right position.

2) With engine running, attach a pull scale to steering wheel rim. Measure pull required to turn steering wheel one complete revolution in each direction. Effort required to turn steering wheel one complete revolution in each direction should be **29-39 INCH lbs. (3.3-4.4 N.m).** If turning effort is not within specification, repair or replace power steering gear or pump as necessary.

REMOVAL & INSTALLATION

POWER STEERING PUMP & PULLEY

Removal – 1) Disconnect fluid return hose at reservoir and drain fluid. Remove pressure hose and power steering pressure switch (if equipped) from pump. On 3.0L engine, loosen idler pulley adjustment bolts to loosen drive belt tension. On 4.0L engine, lift tensioner pulley in a counterclockwise direction to loosen drive belt tension. Remove belt from under tensioner. On all models, remove drive belt from steering pump pulley.

2) Remove pump and adjustment bracket from support bracket. Using Pulley Remover (T69L-10300-B), remove pulley from pump. Remove pump.

Installation – 1) Install adjustment bracket on pump. Tighten bolts to specification. See TORQUE SPECIFICATIONS table at end of article. Using Pulley Installer (T65P-3A733-C), install pulley on pump. Ensure pulley is within .010" (.25 mm) of end of pump shaft.

2) Place pump assembly on support bracket. Install and tighten adjustment bracket-to-support bracket bolts to specification. Install and adjust belt on pulley. Tighten adjustment bracket bolts to specification.

3) Install hoses to pump. Tighten to specification. Fill reservoir. Start engine. Turn wheel from stop-to-stop to bleed air from system. Recheck reservoir. Refill reservoir (as necessary).

POWER RACK & PINION STEERING GEAR

Removal (2WD Models) – 1) Place steering gear, steering wheel and front wheels in straight-ahead position. Raise and support vehicle. Remove steering column lower intermediate shaft-to-steering gear bolt. Disconnect intermediate shaft from steering gear. Disconnect and plug pressure and return lines at gear valve housing. *See Fig. 3.*

2) Remove and discard tie rod end cotter pin. Remove tie rod end castle nut. Using Tie Rod End Remover (T64P-3590-F), separate tie rod end from spindle arm. Support steering gear and remove nuts, bolts and washers retaining steering gear to crossmember. Remove steering gear. Remove front and rear insulators from steering gear housing (as necessary).

Installation – Install insulators (if removed). Position steering gear on crossmember. Place steering gear, steering wheel and front wheels in straight-ahead position. To complete installation, reverse removal procedure. Tighten bolts to specification. See TORQUE SPECIFICATIONS table at end of article.

Removal (4WD Models) – 1) Place steering gear, steering wheel and front wheels in straight-ahead position. Raise and support vehicle. Remove front wheel and tire assemblies. Remove steering column lower intermediate shaft-to-steering gear bolt. Disconnect intermediate shaft from steering gear. Disconnect and plug pressure and return lines at gear valve housing. *See Fig. 3.*

2) Remove and discard tie rod end cotter pin. Remove tie rod end castle nut. Using Tie Rod End Remover (T64P-3590-F), separate tie rod end from spindle arm. Remove shock absorber-to-crossmember bracket retaining nut, washer and insulator. Remove shock absorber-to-lower control arm retaining bolts. Remove shock absorber through lower control arm.

3) Remove front stabilizer bar. Compress and secure coil springs for removal of lower control arm pivot bolts. Loosen lower control arm pivot bolts. Remove lower control arm ball joint cotter pin. Loosen ball joint nut. Using Tie Rod End Remover (T64P-3590-F), loosen ball joint from steering knuckle. Remove ball joint nut and separate ball joint from steering knuckle. Lower control arm and remove coil spring.

4) Remove 5 crossmember lower plate nuts from front of plate. Remove left rear crossmember lower plate nut from plate. Remove right rear and center rear crossmember lower plate bolts from plate. Remove crossmember lower plate.

5) Support steering gear and remove bolts, spacers and bushings retaining steering gear to crossmember. Remove steering gear. Remove front insulators from steering gear housing (as necessary).

Installation – Install insulators (if removed). Position steering gear on crossmember. Place steering gear, steering wheel and front wheels in straight-ahead position. To complete installation, reverse removal procedure. Tighten bolts and nuts to specification. See TORQUE SPECIFICATIONS table at end of article.

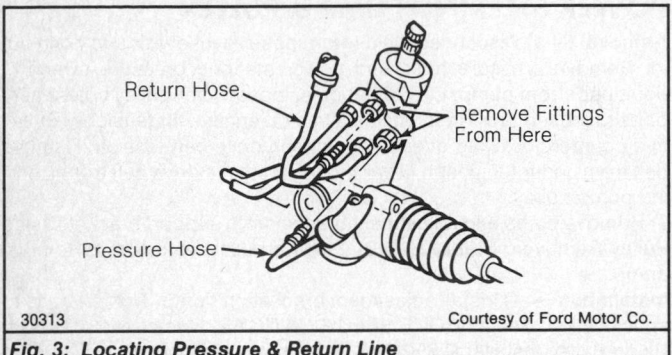

30313   Courtesy of Ford Motor Co.

Fig. 3: Locating Pressure & Return Line

OVERHAUL

POWER STEERING PUMP

Disassembly – 1) Remove adjustment bracket and pulley from pump, if not previously removed. Remove outlet fitting, flow control valve, spring and reservoir from pump housing. See Fig. 2.

2) Place a "C" clamp in vise. Install Lower Support Plate (T78P-3733-A2) over pump rotor shaft. See Fig. 4. Install Upper Compressor Plate (T78P-3733-A1) into "C" clamp. Place pump assembly into "C" clamp with rotor shaft facing down.

3) Tighten "C" clamp until slight bottoming of valve cover is felt. Insert small drift through hole in side of pump housing plate. Push valve cover retaining ring inward and remove ring. See Fig. 5.

4) Remove pump from "C" clamp. Remove valve cover and "O" ring seal. Push on rotor shaft. Remove rotor shaft, rotor and slippers and upper plate. Remove cam insert and 2 dowel pins.

5) Tap housing on flat surface to remove lower plate and disc spring. Remove "O" ring. Using a screwdriver, remove rotor shaft seal and seal retainer.

Reassembly – 1) Place rotor on rotor shaft splines, with large rotor counterbore facing upward. Install retaining ring in groove in end of rotor shaft. Place insert cam over rotor with recessed flat facing toward reservoir.

2) With rotor extended half way out of cam, insert spring into rotor spring pocket. Work it into rotor cavity directly below recessed flat on cam. Use a slipper to compress spring. Install slipper with groove facing cam.

3) Hold cam stationary. Turn rotor either direction, one space at a time. Install another spring and slipper until all 10 rotor cavities are filled. Ensure previously installed springs and slippers do not fall out when turning rotor.

4) Using Seal Driver (T78P-3733-A3), install a NEW rotor shaft seal. Using a plastic mallet, drive seal and then seal retainer into bore until bottomed. Place pump housing plate on a flat surface with pulley side down.

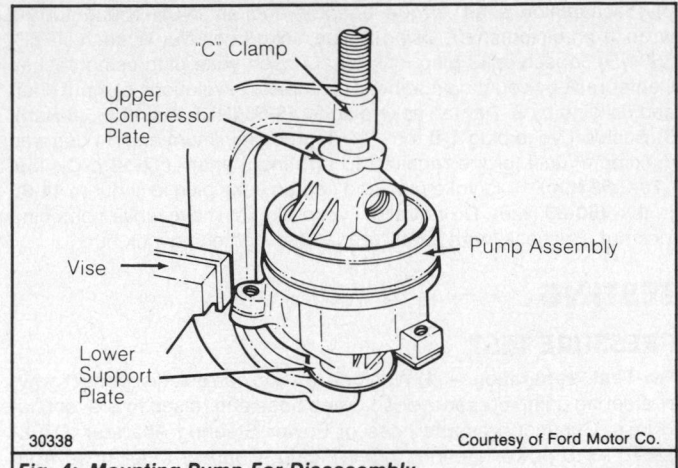

30338   Courtesy of Ford Motor Co.

Fig. 4: Mounting Pump For Disassembly

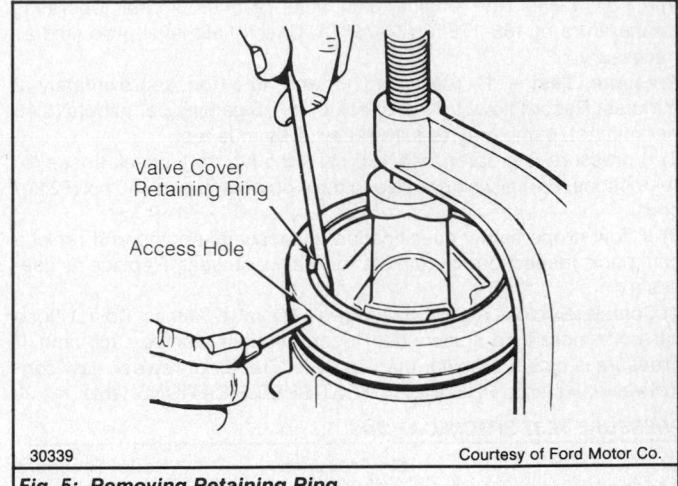

30339   Courtesy of Ford Motor Co.

Fig. 5: Removing Retaining Ring

5) Insert 2 dowel pins and disc spring (dished surface upward) into housing plate. Lubricate "O" ring seals with power steering fluid. Install seals on lower pressure plate. Insert pressure plate into pump housing plate and over dowel pins with seals facing front of pump.

6) Place assembly into "C" clamp. Using Driver (T78P-3733-A3) in rotor shaft hole, press lower plate lightly until bottomed in pump plate housing, seating "O" ring. Install cam, rotor and slippers and rotor shaft assembly into pump housing plate over dowel pins.

NOTE: When installing assembly, stepped holes must be used for dowel pins. Ensure recessed notch in cam insert faces reservoir and is approximately opposite square pump mounting boss.

7) Place upper pressure plate over dowel pins. Ensure side of plate with square recessed notch faces reservoir and is positioned opposite square pump mounting boss. Place NEW "O" ring seal on valve cover. Lubricate with power steering fluid.

NOTE: Ensure plastic baffle is securely in place in valve cover. If not, apply petroleum jelly to baffle and reinstall.

8) Place valve cover over dowel pins. Ensure valve cover outlet fitting hole is in line with square mounting boss of pump housing plate.

9) Place entire assembly in "C" clamp. Compress valve cover into pump housing plate, until retaining ring groove is exposed in pump housing plate.

10) Install valve cover retaining ring with ends near access hole in pump housing plate. Remove pump assembly from "C" clamp. Place NEW "O" ring seal on pump housing plate. Lubricate seal with power steering fluid. Install power steering reservoir.

11) Install flow control spring and flow control valve in valve cover. Place NEW "O" ring seals on outlet fitting. Lubricate seals with power steering fluid.

12) Install pump outlet fitting into valve cover. Tighten to specification. Install adjustment bracket on pump. Tighten bolts to specification. See TORQUE SPECIFICATIONS table at end of article. Using Pulley Installer (T65P-3A733-C), install pulley onto pump.

POWER RACK & PINION STEERING GEAR

Disassembly – 1) Remove steering gear from vehicle. See POWER RACK & PINION STEERING GEAR under REMOVAL & INSTALLATION. Clean exterior of steering gear. Mount gear in Holding Fixture (T57L-500-B) or soft-jawed vise. Loosen tie rod jam nut. Mark position of tie rod ends to tie rod for assembly reference. Remove tie rod ends from tie rod, counting and noting number of turns required for removal. Remove tie rod jam nuts.

2) Remove boot retaining clamps, boots and breather tube. Remove outer input shaft dust seal. Using Lock Nut Wrench (T78P-3504-H), remove yoke plug lock nut. See Fig. 13. Remove yoke plug and spring. Grip guide post of yoke with pliers and remove yoke from housing. Remove pinion bearing plug. To remove pinion bearing lock nut, install Torque Adapter (T74P-3504-R) over input shaft. See Fig. 6.

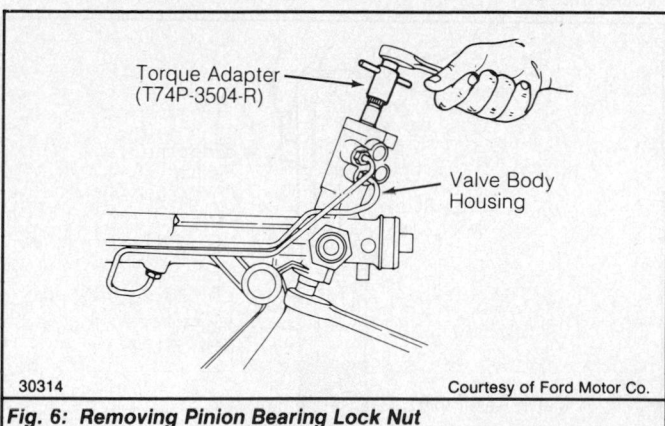

Fig. 6: Removing Pinion Bearing Lock Nut

NOTE: DO NOT allow rack to reach full travel when loosening pinion bearing lock nut.

---

3) Using an awl, pry inner input shaft dust seal from housing. DO NOT scratch housing inner surface. Remove input shaft snap ring. Using Valve Body Puller (T78P-3504-B), tighten nut on tool to remove input shaft seal, bearing plug and input shaft/valve assembly. See Fig. 7.

4) To remove lower input shaft seal, insert Seal Remover (T78P-3504-E2) and Spacer Collet (T86P-3504-J) until spacer and remover bottom out. Hold large nut while tightening small nut on tool, until expander tightens. See Fig. 8.

5) Insert slide hammer into rear of seal remover. Pull lower input shaft seal from housing. Inspect lower pinion bearing (remove only if necessary). Use slide hammer and Puller Attachment (T58L-101-B) to pull lower pinion bearing from housing. Using small knife, cut 4 valve "O" rings off of valve sleeve, being careful so as not to damage sleeve (remove only if necessary).

6) Thread point of Lock Nut Pin Remover (D81P-3504-N) into spring pin in ball socket. Finger tighten lock nut pin remover. Tighten nut on lock nut pin remover. Remove and discard spring pin. See Fig. 9.

7) Pull rack out to expose several teeth. Hold rack with adjustable wrench and loosen ball socket nuts with Socket Wrench (T74P-3504-J). Remove ball socket and tie rod assembly. Push right side of rack into housing far enough to access and remove snap ring. Using hammer and brass drift, carefully drive rack and bushing retainer out of housing from right side.

8) Insert Rack Oil Seal Remover (T78P-3504-J) into housing until remover bottoms in housing. Tighten nut on tool until expander tightens. Install slide hammer onto end of seal remover and pull rack seal

from housing. Discard seal. Remove plastic and rubber "O" rings from housing using "O" Ring Remover (T71P-19703-C).

9) To remove rack bushing retainer seal from rack bushing retainer, place seal in vise and squeeze, being careful so as not to damage bushing retainer. Pry distorted seal from bushing retainer with screwdriver.

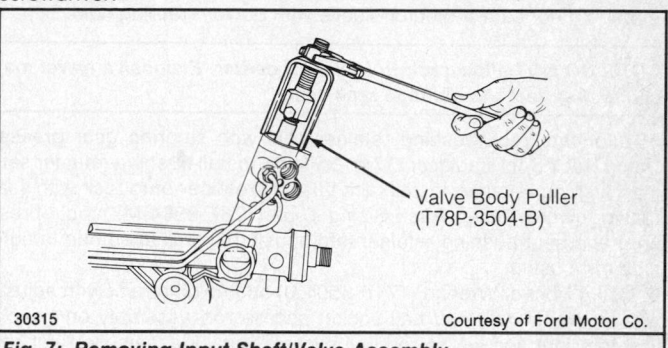

Fig. 7: Removing Input Shaft/Valve Assembly

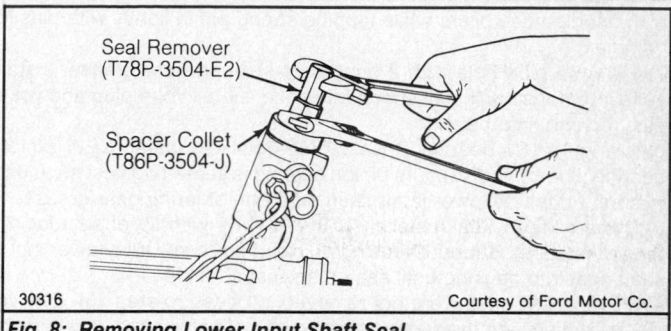

Fig. 8: Removing Lower Input Shaft Seal

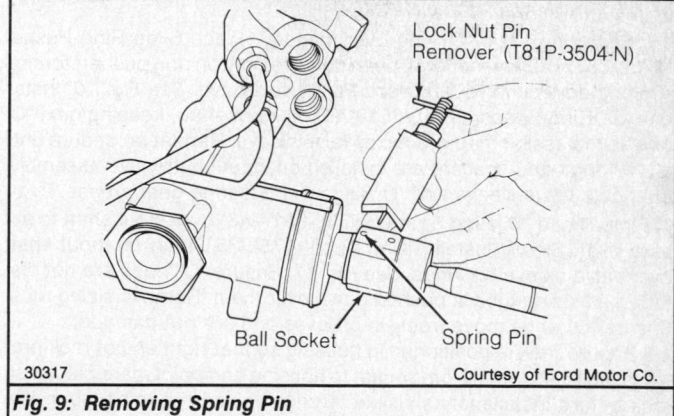

Fig. 9: Removing Spring Pin

Cleaning & Inspection – Examine parts for wear and contamination. Replace as necessary. Inspect yoke to ensure that insert is seated flush with yoke body. If pinion teeth are pitted or worn, or if upper bearing is damaged or binding, replace entire steering gear assembly as a unit.

Reassembly – 1) Mark center tooth of rack (eleventh tooth) with paint so that mark will be visible in valve bore of housing. Slide Ring Spacer (T74P-3504-G) onto rack until spacer seats on rack piston. Install rubber "O" ring onto rack and seat in groove of rack piston. Install plastic "O" ring onto rack over tool and seat in rack piston groove over rubber "O" ring.

2) Remove plastic insert from NEW rack seal. Install Rack Seal Protector (T85L-3504-B) over rack teeth. Lubricate protector with power steering fluid. Install rack seal with seal lip facing rack piston against piston. Remove seal protector. Install plastic insert in rack seal.

3) Pack rack teeth with steering gear grease. Lightly lubricate back of rack with steering gear grease. Lubricate rack seal with power steering fluid. Install Rack Sizing Tube (T78P-3504-M) into end of housing.

Carefully push rack assembly into housing until assembly bottoms in housing. Seat rack seal onto rack using brass drift and rubber mallet to tap end of rack.

4) Using Socket Wrench (T74P-3504-U) and holding rack with adjustable pliers, install left ball socket and tie rod assembly onto rack. Install Rack Seal Protector Sleeve (T74P-3504-J) over right side rack threads. Lubricate protector sleeve with power steering fluid.

NOTE: DO NOT allow rack to travel off center. Excessive travel may cause rack teeth to damage rack seal.

---

5) Lubricate rack bushing retainer seal with steering gear grease. Using Rack Seal Replacer (T74P-3504-F), install bushing retainer seal into bushing retainer. Install rack bushing retainer onto rack with seal facing inward. Using Rack Sizing Tube (T78P-3504-M), apply pressure and seat bushing retainer into housing. Install snap ring in right side of housing.

6) Using Socket Wrench (T74P-3504-U) and holding rack with adjustable pliers, install right ball socket and tie rod assembly onto rack. Tighten right and left tie rod ball sockets to rack assembly. Rest ball socket on wooden block. To install NEW spring pin, hold spring pin with needle-nose pliers while tapping spring pin in lightly with plastic hammer.

7) Fill yoke plug hole with 2 ounces of steering gear grease. Install yoke into housing. Install spring into yoke. Install yoke plug and yoke plug lock nut into housing.

8) Using Pinion Bearing Driver (T78P-3504-G), install NEW pinion bearing (if removed). Ensure pinion bearing is seated against shoulder in bore. Lubricate lower input shaft seal with steering gear grease.

9) Place seal on Seal Installer (T78P-3504-F), with lip of seal facing toward installer. Support housing on clean surface. Drive lower input shaft seal into housing until seated against shoulder.

10) If valve "O" rings were not removed, proceed to step **13)**. If valve "O" rings were removed, mount pinion end of valve assembly in soft-jawed vise. Lubricate Mandrel (T75L-3517-A1) with power steering fluid. Install mandrel over valve assembly.

11) Slide one valve "O" ring over mandrel. Place Slide Ring Pusher (T75L-3517-A2) on mandrel, push down rapidly on ring pusher, forcing "O" ring down into fourth groove of valve sleeve. See Fig. 10. Install one "O" Ring Spacer (T75L-3517-A3) on input shaft, keeping next "O" ring from passing third groove of valve sleeve. Repeat procedure until all "O" rings and spacers are installed on input shaft/valve assembly. Lubricate valve sleeve and "O" rings with steering gear grease.

12) Install one "O" Ring Spacer (T75L-3517-A3) over input shaft to act as a pilot. Slowly install Sizing Tube (T75L-3517-A4) on input shaft over valve sleeve "O" rings. See Fig. 11. Ensure "O" rings are not distorted as sizing tube is pushed down over them. Remove sizing tube. Ensure "O" rings move freely in grooves and are not damaged.

13) Ensure rack is positioned in housing so that right end of rack protrudes 9/16" (14 mm) from socket to housing and paint mark placed on rack before installation is visible through valve bore in housing. See Fig. 12. Place Valve Body Inserter (T78P-3504-C) into top of valve housing. Lubricate input shaft/valve assembly and install into housing. Align "D" shaped flat spot on input shaft facing backward (180° from yoke nut). Ensure input shaft teeth mesh with rack teeth. Push valve assembly in by hand until fully seated.

14) Install Pinion Shaft Torque Adapter (T74P-3504-R) onto input shaft. Install lock nut onto pinion end of valve assembly. Hold pinion shaft with torque adapter. Tighten lock nut to **30-44 ft. lbs. (40-55 N.m)**. To ensure pinion is centered, count input shaft turns from center to stops. If unequal, remove input shaft, rotate 60° (one tooth) in direction that requires least amount of turns. Reinstall input shaft. Repeat procedure until input shaft is centered.

15) Slide input shaft bearing over shaft and into valve bore. Using Bearing Installer (T78P-3504-D), firmly seat bearing into bore. Lightly lubricate input shaft seal with steering gear grease. Install seal with lip facing housing. Drive seal into housing until fully seated. Install snap ring.

16) Slide Input Shaft Dust Seal Installer (T85T-3504-CH1) over input shaft. Lubricate inner input shaft dust seal contact area with multipurpose grease. Install inner input shaft dust seal with Seal Installer (T85T-3504-CH2). Remove seal installer from shaft.

17) Install and tighten pinion bearing plug to **50 ft. lbs. (67 N.m)**. Pack outer input shaft dust seal with multipurpose grease. Place outer input shaft dust seal on input shaft and push down until ridge on inside of seal seats in groove on input shaft. Wipe away any excess grease.

18) Adjust rack yoke plug preload. See RACK YOKE PLUG PRELOAD under ADJUSTMENTS. To complete reassembly, reverse disassembly procedure. Apply steering gear grease to groove in tie rod where rubber boot is fastened with clamp. Install NEW boot clamps. Install boot clamps on crossmember side of gear with clamp screw axis parallel with yoke plug lock nut.

19) Lubricate tie rod end threads with disc brake caliper slide grease before installation on tie rod. Ensure tie rod ends are installed to tie rod using same number of turns required during disassembly procedure.

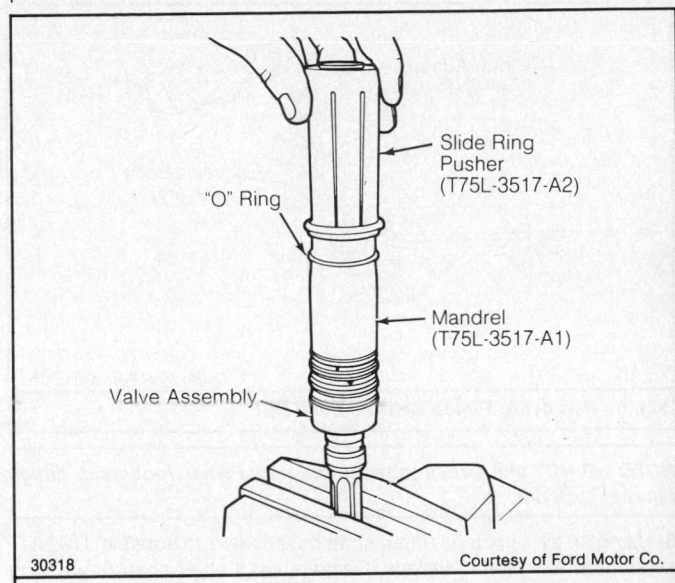

30318　　　　　　　　　　　　　　　　Courtesy of Ford Motor Co.

Fig. 10: Installing Valve "O" Rings

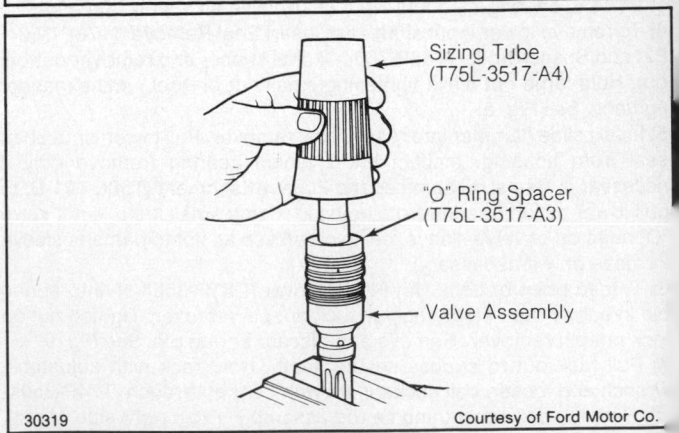

30319　　　　　　　　　　　　　　　　Courtesy of Ford Motor Co.

Fig. 11: Installing "O" Ring Sizing Tube

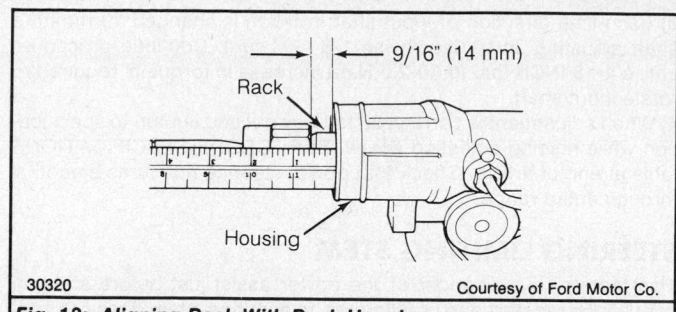

Fig. 12: Aligning Rack With Rack Housing

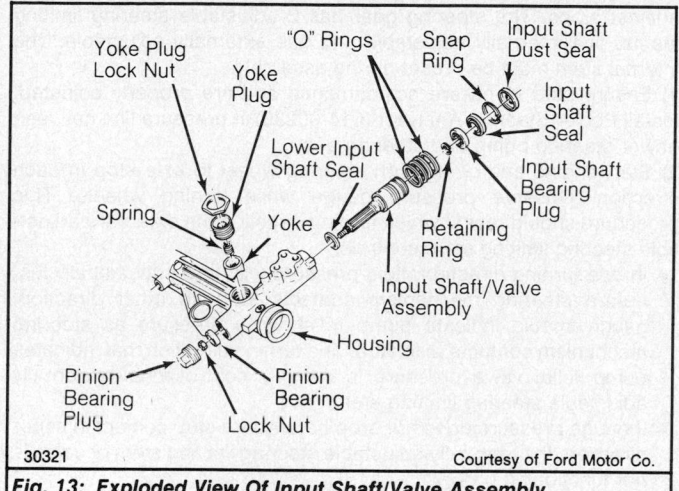

Fig. 13: Exploded View Of Input Shaft/Valve Assembly

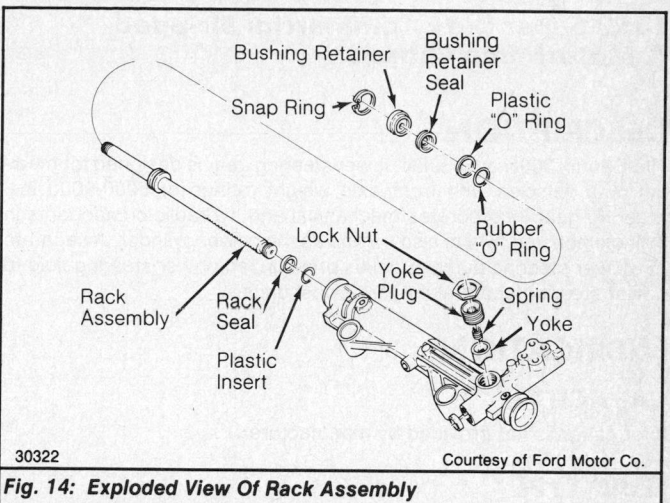

Fig. 14: Exploded View Of Rack Assembly

TORQUE SPECIFICATIONS

TORQUE SPECIFICATIONS

Application	Ft. Lbs. (N.m)
Adjustment Bracket-To-Support Bracket Bolts	35-47 (47-64)
Ball Joint-To-Steering Knuckle Nut	60-80 (81-108)
Lower Control Arm Pivot Bolts	100-140 (136-190)
Pinion Bearing Plug	50 (68)
Pinion Lock Nut	30-40 (41-54)
Pressure & Return Line Fittings [1]	10-14 (15-20)
Pump Outlet Fitting	25-40 (34-54)
Pump Quick Connect Fitting	30-40 (41-54)
Pump-To-Adjustment Bracket Bolts	
3.0L	30-45 (41-61)
4.0L	35-47 (47-64)
Shock Absorber-To-Crossmember Bracket Nuts	25-34 (34-47)
Shock Absorber-To-Lower Control Arm Bolts	16-25 (22-33)
Steering Column Lower Intermediate Shaft-To-Gear Bolt	30-42 (41-56)
Steering Gear-To-Crossmember	
2WD Models	80-105 (108-142)
4WD Models	61-82 (83-111)
Tie Rod Ball Socket-To-Rack	55-60 (75-81)
Tie Rod End-To-Spindle Nut	52-73 (71-99)
Tie Rod Jam Nut	35-50 (48-68)
Yoke Plug Lock Nut	44-66 (60-89)
	INCH Lbs. (N.m)
Yoke Plug [2]	45-50 (5.0-5.6)

[1] – Remove only at gear valve housing.
[2] – Tighten, then back off 1/8 turn.

1992 STEERING
Bendix Power Steering

F350 Super Duty Commercial Stripped & Motorhome Chassis

DESCRIPTION

The Bendix 300N or C-300N power steering gear is designed for medium duty vehicles with front axle weight ratings of 6000-9000 lbs. Steering gear incorporates mechanical and hydraulic components in a single housing, which also serves as the power cylinder. A separate ZF power steering pump supplies pressurized power steering fluid to power steering and brake hydro-boost units.

LUBRICATION

CAPACITY

Information is not provided by manufacturer.

FLUID TYPE

Use MERCON-II automatic transmission fluid or equivalent.

FLUID LEVEL CHECK

If fluid is cold, approximately 75°F (24°C), check fluid level using the cold full mark on dipstick. If fluid is hot, approximately 177°F (81°C), check fluid level using the hot full mark on dipstick. Fluid level must be maintained between ADD and FULL marks. Add fluid through dipstick opening, if needed, and recheck. DO NOT overfill.

HYDRAULIC SYSTEM BLEEDING

Diesel Engines – Fill reservoir. Start engine. Turn steering wheel from stop to stop several times. Stop engine. Check fluid level and refill reservoir as necessary.
Gasoline Engines – 1) Disconnect coil wire. Fill reservoir. Crank engine with starter until fluid level remains constant. Avoid overheating starter. Refill reservoir.
2) Reconnect coil wire. Start engine and allow it to run several minutes. Turn steering from stop to stop. Stop engine. Check fluid level and add fluid as necessary.

ADJUSTMENTS

POWER STEERING PUMP BELT

BELT ADJUSTMENT

Application	New Belt Lbs. (kg)	[1] Used Belt Lbs. (kg)
5.8L With Tensioner [2]	[3]	[3]
7.3L With 1/2" Belt	140-180 (64-82)	95-115 (43-52)
7.5L With Tensioner [2]	[4]	[4]

[1] – Any belt operated for 5 minutes or longer.
[2] – Tension is correct if tensioner is within indicator marks.
[3] – 77 lbs. (35 kg) minimum for vehicles with 60 & 75-amp alternators. 111 lbs. (50 kg) minimum for vehicles with 100-amp alternators.
[4] – 94 lbs. (43 kg) minimum tension.

OUTPUT SHAFT BACKLASH

Backlash is correct when 4-18 INCH lbs. (0.50-2.0 N.m) increase in torque occurs as input shaft is rotated and piston passes through midpoint of its travel. This torque increase will occur only as piston travels through midpoint of its travel and should disappear as piston moves past midpoint.
1) Ensure adjusting screw is turned counterclockwise as far as it will go. Rotate input shaft as far as possible in each direction. Count total turns in either direction and at same time measure average torque required to rotate shaft.
2) Rotate input shaft 180 degrees in both directions past midpoint of piston travel. The midpoint of piston travel is approximately one half the number of input shaft revolutions possible in a single direction.

3) Each time direction of input shaft rotation is changed, turn output shaft adjusting screw clockwise 1/8 - 1/4 turn. Continue procedure until a 4-18 INCH lbs. (0.50-2.0 N.m) increase in torque is required to rotate input shaft.
4) When adjustment is correct, install lock nut and tighten to specification while holding adjusting screw. See TORQUE SPECIFICATIONS table at end of article. Check that power steering unit turns smoothly through entire range.

STEERING LIMITING STEM

This feature relieves most of the power assist just before steering gear piston reaches end of full travel, to ensure system does not contact axle stops with full hydraulic assist when wheels are turned against stops. The steering gear has 2 adjustable steering limiting stems: one internally adjustable and one externally adjustable. The internal stem must be preset during assembly.
1) Ensure axle stops are not damaged and are properly adjusted. Install Power Steering Analyzer (014-00230) in pressure line between power steering pump and steering gear.
2) Start engine and gently turn steering wheel to axle stop in each direction. Observe pressure gauge while turning wheels. This procedure should reveal which turning direction the externally adjustable steering limiting stem controls.
- In one turning direction, fluid pressure will drop substantially just before steering mechanism contacts stop. In other direction, gauge should indicate pump relief valve pressure as steering mechanism contacts axle stop. The turning direction that indicates pump relief valve pressure is the one controlled by externally adjustable steering limiting stem.
- If gauge pressure does not drop before axle stop contact in either direction, the internally adjustable steering limiting stem or valve is not functioning properly.
- If gauge pressure drops prior to axle stop contact in both directions, turn externally adjustable steering limiting stem counterclockwise and repeat test until system operates properly.

3) Return steering to straight-ahead position. Turn externally adjustable steering limiting stem clockwise to its full travel. Gently turn steering wheel in direction controlled by internally adjustable stem until steering contacts axle stop. Pressure indication on gauge should be relatively low.
4) With steering wheel held to maintain axle stop contact, turn steering limiting stem counterclockwise until gauge pressure just begins to increase. After adjustment, install plug in stem bore in housing.

TESTING

PREPARATION

1) Ensure drive belt is in good condition and tension is properly adjusted. See POWER STEERING PUMP BELT under ADJUSTMENTS. Repair any external leaks before continuing with pressure test. Disconnect pressure line from connector at pump. Connect Power Steering Analyzer (014-00230). *See Fig. 1.*
2) Open shutoff valve fully. Start engine and purge air from system by turning steering wheel fully left and right several times. Turn engine off and check connections for leaks.
3) Check for proper fluid level at reservoir and add or remove fluid as necessary. Start engine. Partially close shutoff valve and observe pressure gauge. If pressure gauge needle vibration is excessive, repeat step 2) to bleed air. Place thermometer into reservoir and connect tachometer to engine.
4) Ensure shutoff valve is fully open. Place front wheels in straight-ahead position. Place transmission in Neutral position. Ensure parking brake is applied.
5) Start engine and partially close shutoff valve until gauge indicates **800-1000 psi (56-70 kg/cm²)**. When temperature of power steering fluid reaches 120°F (49°C), open shutoff valve fully and turn engine off

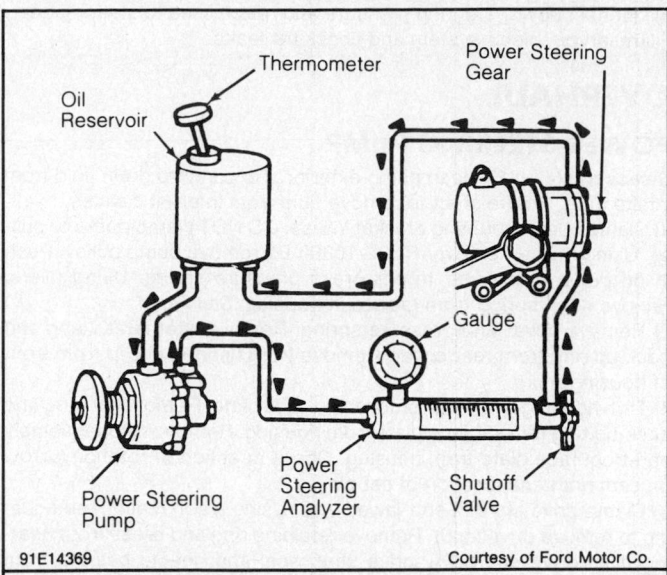

Fig. 1: Connecting Power Steering Analyzer

SYSTEM BACKPRESSURE CHECK

1) Ensure shutoff valve is fully open. Start engine and increase speed to 2200 RPM. When fluid temperature reaches 130°F (55°C), record flow rate and pressure.

2) If flow is less than 3.5 gallons (13.2L) per minute, verify correct pump is installed. If correct pump is installed, continue test.

3) If pressure exceeds 80 psi (5.6 kg/cm²), check lines for kinks or obstructions. If none are found and pressure remains high, proceed to MINIMUM PUMP FLOW TEST.

MINIMUM PUMP FLOW TEST

1) Decrease engine speed to 600 RPM. Slowly close shutoff valve to increase pressure to 1200 psi (84.4 kg/cm²). Record flow rate at 130°F (54°C).

2) If flow rate is less than 2.2 gallons (8.3L) per minute, pump may need service, especially if flow rate at 2200 RPM is less than specification.

PUMP RELIEF PRESSURE TEST

CAUTION: DO NOT close shutoff valve for longer than 5 seconds or damage to pump may result.

1) With engine speed at 600 RPM, close shutoff valve and observe pressure gauge. Flow rate should be zero. Open shutoff valve quickly after reading gauge and note flow rate return to normal. If pressure is not between 203 psi (14.3 kg/cm²) and 255 psi (18 kg/cm²), repair or replace relief valve.

2) Allow power steering fluid to cool to 130°F (55°C). With engine at full governed RPM, close shutoff valve. Flow should read zero. Quickly open shutoff valve; flow rate should immediately return to normal. Repeat this test once, but DO NOT allow fluid temperature to exceed 200°F (93°C).

3) If flow rate does not immediately return to normal, repair or replace pump.

STEERING GEAR RELIEF PRESSURE & INTERNAL LEAKAGE TEST

WARNING: Failure to follow these procedures carefully can result in serious injury or damage to equipment.

1) Place a steel block between the axle stop and adjusting screw. The block should be a minimum of 1" (25.4 mm) thick and long enough to be inserted without danger of pinching fingers. Ensure block is squared to contact points. *See Fig. 2.*

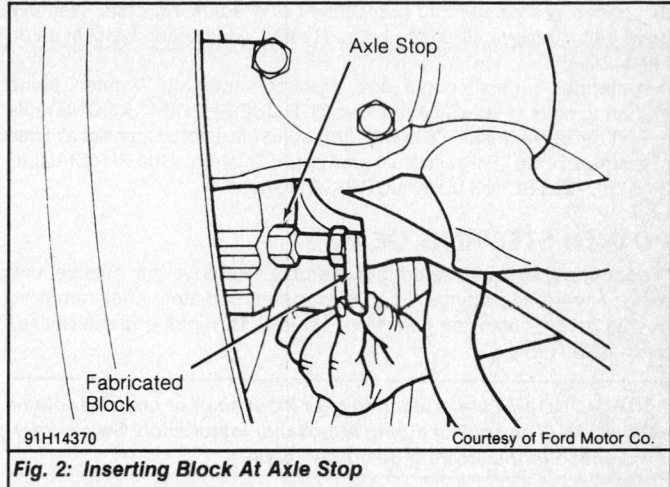

Fig. 2: Inserting Block At Axle Stop

2) Check fluid temperature in reservoir. Temperature should be approximately 130°F (55°C) at start of test. Shutoff valve must be fully open.

3) Run engine at idle. Turn steering wheel until axle stop contacts spacer block. *See Fig. 2.* Apply sufficient torque to steering wheel to ensure power steering gear control valve is completely open. Pressure gauge should indicate pressure relief setting. If pressure is not **1900-2100 psi (134-148 kg/cm²)**, adjust or repair relief valve as necessary.

CAUTION: When performing this test, DO NOT hold torque on steering wheel for more than 5 seconds beyond time pressure relief setting of steering gear has been measured.

4) Temporarily set steering gear by-pass valve setting higher than setting of power steering pump relief valve. Turn engine off. Remove plug from steering gear valve body. *See Fig. 3.* Insert 3/8" O.D. washer into socket portion of plug to increase by-pass valve setting. Generally, 1/8-1/4" of additional shim thickness is sufficient.

5) Run engine at idle. Turn steering wheel until axle stop contacts spacer block. *See Fig. 2.* Apply sufficient torque to steering wheel to ensure power steering gear control valve is completely open.

6) Pressure gauge indication should be the same as power steering pump relief pressure. See PUMP RELIEF PRESSURE TEST. With system pressure at pump relief, read flow meter. If flow is greater than 3.5 quarts (3.3L) per minute, internal leakage is excessive and steering gear requires repair.

7) Repeat steps **5)** and **6)**, turning steering in opposite direction. Remove shims installed in step **4)** and reinstall plug.

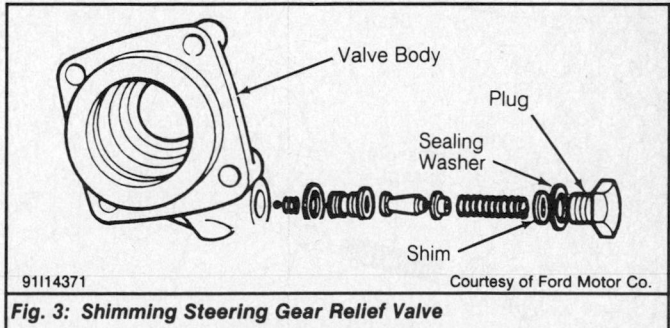

Fig. 3: Shimming Steering Gear Relief Valve

REMOVAL & INSTALLATION

POWER STEERING PUMP

Removal – 1) Using a suction gun, remove as much fluid as possible from reservoir through filler opening, or remove return hose to drain reservoir.

2) Disconnect both hoses from power steering pump. Raise both hoses, or plug disconnected hose ends to prevent fluid from draining.

3) Loosen power steering pump pivot and adjusting bolts. Remove drive belt. Remove mounting bolts. Remove pump and bracket as an assembly.

Installation – Install pump and bracket assembly. Tighten pump mounting bolts to specification. See TORQUE SPECIFICATIONS table at end of article. Install drive belt and adjust tension. Connect all lines to correct ports. Fill reservoir and bleed system. See HYDRAULIC SYSTEM BLEEDING under LUBRICATION.

POWER STEERING GEAR

Precautions – Drain steering assembly. Remove all outside dirt, especially around fittings. Plug all ports immediately after removing hoses, before removing gear from vehicle. Tag inlet and return lines for reinstallation.

CAUTION: DO NOT strike steering gear input shaft or steering column coupling with any object during removal or installation. Severe internal damage to the steering gear may result.

Removal – **1)** Disconnect hoses from steering gear. Mark relationship of pitman arm and shaft. Remove pitman arm retaining bolt. Using Pitman Arm Puller (T64P-3590-F), remove pitman arm.

2) Remove bolt and nut securing flange and insulator to steering gear input shaft. Remove retaining bolts and steering gear.

Installation – **1)** Install steering gear. Tighten bolts to specification. See TORQUE SPECIFICATIONS table at end of article. Install intermediate shaft-to-input shaft "U" joint and tighten bolt to specification.

2) Place pitman arm on steering gear sector shaft, ensuring marks are aligned. Spread pitman arm with a chisel while sliding it onto sector shaft. Install bolt and nut into pitman arm and tighten to specification.

CAUTION: DO NOT use hammer to force pitman arm onto sector shaft. Damage to sector shaft bearings and loss of gear preload may result.

---

3) Connect power steering pressure and return lines to steering gear. Fill reservoir, bleed system and check for leaks.

OVERHAUL

POWER STEERING PUMP

Disassembly – **1)** Clean pump exterior. Tip pump to drain fluid from intake tube. Rotate shaft to remove fluid from internal cavities.

2) Clamp pump mounting bracket in vise. DO NOT clamp pump or pulley. Using Pulley Remover (T69L-10300-B), remove pump pulley. Push in on pump rear cover to compress pressure spring. Using pliers, remove hook spring from groove in housing. *See Fig. 4.*

3) Remove cover and pressure spring. Remove internal "O" ring and back-up ring from rear cover. Remove front bearing circlip from front of housing.

4) Turn housing over and remove rear face plate. Remove "O" ring and back-up ring for rear face plate from housing. Remove rotor assembly and front face plate from housing. Check direction of rotation (arrow on cam ring) and location of set pin.

5) Clamp drive shaft in soft-jawed vise. Using a soft mallet, tap housing to remove drive shaft. Remove retaining ring and press front bearing from drive shaft. Pry drive shaft seal and needle bearing from housing.

Reassembly – **1)** Press NEW needle bearing into housing. Install NEW drive shaft seal into housing. Press NEW front bearing onto drive shaft and install retaining ring. Install drive shaft and bearing into housing and install circlip.

2) Install "O" ring and back-up ring onto rear face plate. Install set pin, front face plate and rotor assembly into housing. Rotor cam ring must be installed with arrow pointed in direction of rotation.

3) Install "O" ring and back-up ring into rear cover housing. Place pressure spring into rear face plate. Position rear cover into housing. Press rear cover downward and install hook spring into housing groove. Using Pulley Installer (T65P-3A733-C), install pulley.

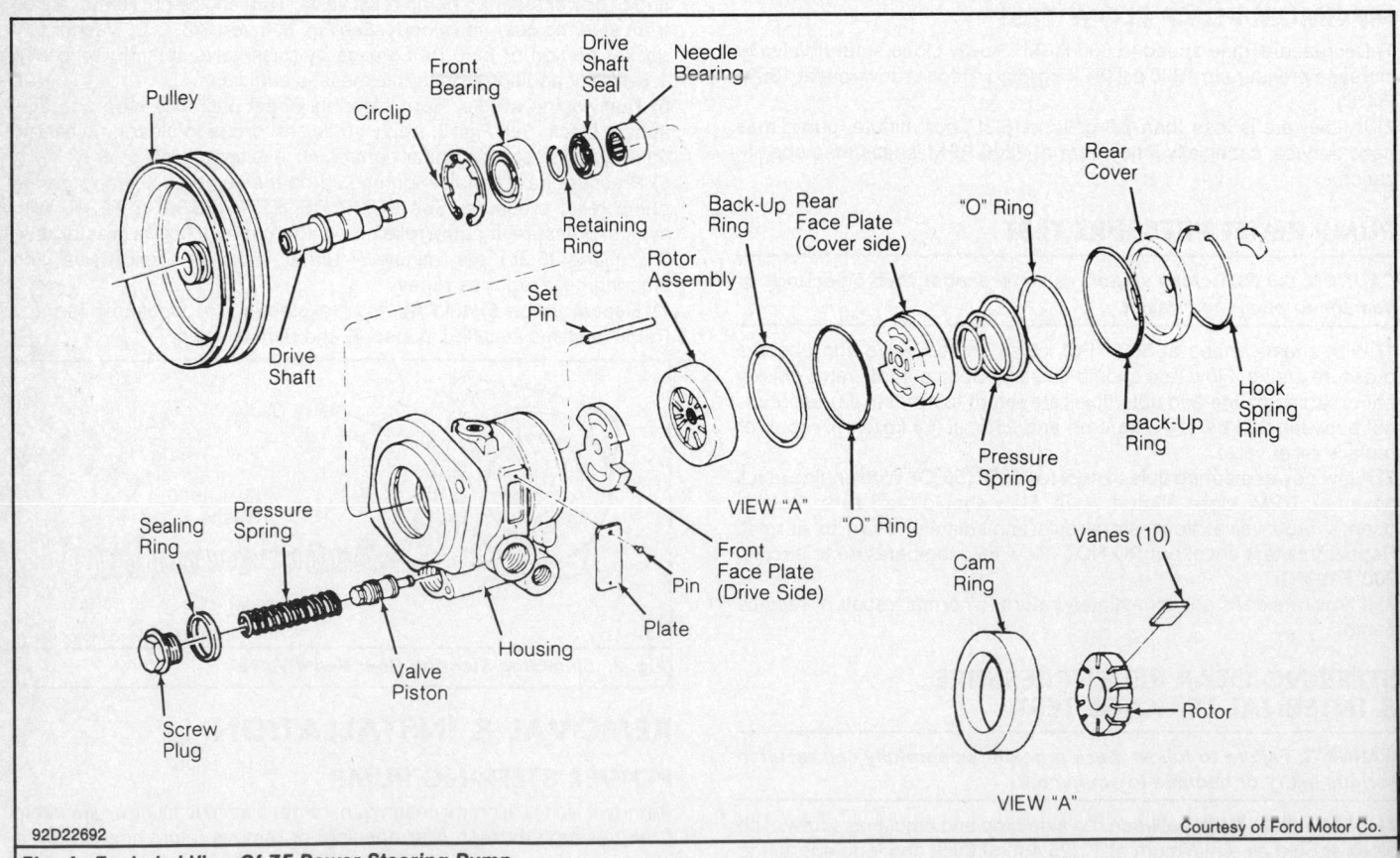

92D22692 Courtesy of Ford Motor Co.

Fig. 4: Exploded View Of ZF Power Steering Pump

POWER STEERING GEAR

NOTE: Several maintenance kits are available that do not require full disassembly of the steering gear. If installing one of these kits, follow the instructions provided with the kit.

Disassembly – **1)** Clamp steering gear across mounting bolt bosses in soft-jawed vise. Remove dust boot from spindle assembly. Mark relationship of valve body to housing. Remove valve body retaining bolts.

2) While holding or rotating input shaft, rotate output shaft with pitman arm to separate valve body from housing. Continue to separate valve body from housing until both "O" rings on valve body can be seen. Mark relationship of pitman arm to output shaft. Remove pitman arm.

3) Remove output shaft dust boot. Remove dirt and corrosion from exposed portion of output shaft to facilitate removal. Remove lock nut from adjusting screw on side cover. Mark relationship of side cover to housing. Remove side cover bolts.

4) Separate side cover from housing by turning adjusting screw clockwise. When side cover is removed, 17 rollers in side cover bearing will fall out. These rollers MUST NOT be interchanged with rollers in housing bearing. *See Fig. 5.*

CAUTION: DO NOT attempt to remove outer race of roller bearing from side cover.

5) Loosely install pitman arm and use it to center piston and output shaft gear teeth inside side cover opening. Remove pitman arm. Remove output shaft by tapping gently on splined end with soft mallet. When output shaft is removed from housing, 17 rollers in housing bearing will fall out. These rollers MUST NOT be interchanged with rollers in side cover bearing.

CAUTION: DO NOT attempt to remove outer race of roller bearing from housing.

6) While preventing rotation of input shaft end of spindle assembly, pull valve body and piston from housing. Remove retaining ring, ball tube cover, ball tube and 7 of 26 balls from piston. Remove sealing ring from piston.

7) To remove remaining balls from piston, rotate input shaft in whichever direction (clockwise or counterclockwise) that threads the spindle assembly out of piston. Separate valve body and spindle from piston. Check inside of piston for any balls that may not have been removed. There should be a total of 26 balls.

8) Remove sealing ring and "O" ring from groove in piston. Remove either steering limiting valve seat and sealing washer from piston. Remove one of 2 balls, spring and remaining ball. Remove remaining steering limiting valve seat and sealing washer from other end of piston.

9) Remove steering limiting stem protective plug from housing. Remove stroke limiting valve stem from housing. Separate "O" ring from stem.

10) Remove "O" ring from side cover. Remove seal and split nylon back-up ring from side cover bore. DO NOT remove outer race of roller bearing from side cover. Carefully pry dust seal from housing. Reaching through side cover opening of housing, remove output shaft seal and nylon back-up ring. DO NOT remove outer race of roller bearing from housing.

11) Remove input shaft dust seal from valve nut. Using a punch, unblock safety point between valve nut and valve body. Using Bendix Spanner Wrench (106234), remove valve nut from valve body. Grasp input shaft end of spindle and lift spindle assembly, ball cage, 17 balls and 1/2 of outer race out of valve body. Separate outer race, ball cage and 17 balls from spindle assembly. DO NOT remove outer half of ball bearing outer race in valve body.

12) Remove retaining ring and seal from valve nut. Remove 2 outside "O" rings from valve body. Remove Teflon rings and "O" rings from spindle bore. If equipped with steering limiting feature, check condition of limiting stem in valve body. If limiting stem is in good condition, DO NOT remove it. Limiting stem may be removed, if necessary, by heating poppet stem to soften Loctite, then turning counterclockwise.

13) Remove retaining ring, adjusting screw spacer and adjusting screw from output shaft. Begin disassembly of pressure relief valve by removing plug and sealing washer from valve body. Remove spring, spring seat adjusting shim and valve piston. Remove valve seat and sealing washer.

CAUTION: DO NOT attempt disassembly of spindle assembly. Individual replacement parts are NOT available. Replace spindle assembly as a single component.

Inspection – **1)** Wash all parts individually in clean solvent and dry thoroughly. Discard all non-metallic parts. Replace broken, cracked, distorted, excessively pitted or scored parts.

2) Inspect all parts, paying particular attention to:

* Hardness, pitting, flaking or cracks in bearing surfaces. If outer races of the roller bearings in housing or side cover are not serviceable, replace housing or side cover. If outer bearing races in valve body are not serviceable, replace entire valve body.
* Gear teeth in output shaft and piston may show signs of polishing and slight wear; however, pitting, flaking or cracks should not be present.
* Output and input shaft splines.
* Ball rolling surfaces on exterior of spindle and interior of piston for cracks, pitting, flaking or brinelling.
* Exterior of piston and interior of housing bore. Minor scuffing of piston exterior and housing bore is normal, but those parts must be replaced if there is deep scoring. DO NOT attempt to hone or bore these parts.
* Pitman arm.
* Exterior of housing and mounting lugs.
* Valve body and porting.

Reassembly – **1)** Install sealing washer around pressure relief valve seat. Install seat into valve body. Tighten valve seat to specification. See TORQUE SPECIFICATIONS table at end of article. Install pressure relief valve piston spring seat and spring into valve body. Install pressure adjusting shims and seal washer onto plug. Install plug into valve body and tighten to specification.

NOTE: When installing pressure adjusting shims, use those removed during disassembly. It may be necessary to add or subtract shims to adjust pressure relief valve after a complete rebuild.

2) Install "O" rings and Teflon rings into grooves in valve body. Form "O" rings and Teflon rings into their grooves by pushing Bendix Ring Seating Tool (297676) through bore of valve body. Lubricate tool with light film of lithium grease. The spindle assembly may be used to assist pushing tool through bore.

3) Apply Loctite 222 to limiting stem threads. Screw limiting stem into valve body until stem height is **0.735" (18.7 mm)** above valve body surface. DO NOT allow Loctite to contact other surfaces of valve body. Allow sufficient time for Loctite to cure. Install "O" rings onto valve body.

4) Install ball cage onto input end of spindle assembly. Using Ford Long Life Lubricant (C1AZ-19590-BA) to hold balls in place, install 17 balls into cage. Install outer ball bearing race half over input end of spindle assembly. Insert spindle assembly through Bendix Ring Seating Tool (297676). Insert spindle and tool into valve body until tool completely emerges from other side and balls of bearing assembly rest against outer race in valve body.

5) Position pressure side of seal in bore of non-pressure side of valve nut. Using round brass stock with a diameter of 1.55" (39.4 mm), carefully drive seal into bore until retaining ring groove within bore is visible. Install retaining ring, ensuring it is completely seated in groove. Gently tap seal from opposite side until it rests squarely against retaining ring.

6) Apply primer and Loctite 222 sealant to threads of valve nut. Without damaging seal, carefully install valve nut over input shaft end of spindle assembly and into valve body. Using Spanner Wrench (D89T-12458-R) or Bendix Tool (106243), tighten valve nut to specification. See TORQUE SPECIFICATIONS table at end of article. Using a punch, reset safety point between valve nut and valve body. Carefully install dust seal into valve nut. DO NOT damage seal.

7) Install one steering limiting valve seat and sealing washer into piston. Insert one ball and valve seat into piston from opposite end. Install remaining ball, sealing washer and remaining valve seat into piston. Carefully tighten each valve seat to specification. See TORQUE SPECIFICATIONS table at end of article.

8) Install "O" ring into groove in piston. Use a heat lamp or similar device to heat sealing ring to **285-320°F (140-160°C)**. DO NOT use an open flame. Install heated sealing ring over "O" ring in piston groove. DO NOT distort sealing ring more than necessary during installation. Using a piston ring compressor or a smooth piece of sheet metal and a large hose clamp, reshape sealing ring into piston groove. Allow approximately 10 minutes cooling time before removing compressor tool from piston.

9) Install "O" ring into groove in ball return opening of piston. Insert valve body and spindle assembly completely into piston. Ensure stroke limiting stem is not damaged and that it mates with valve seat in piston. Insert 19 balls individually into one recirculating tube hole in ball return opening in piston. Rotate input shaft end of spindle slightly after each ball is inserted. Rotate spindle in one direction only.

NOTE: *When this procedure is performed correctly, spindle and valve body should screw out of piston, and balls inserted in one recirculating tube hole should appear at opposite hole. Before proceeding, ensure balls are at equal depth in both holes of piston.*

10) Insert remaining 7 balls into recirculating tube halves, using lithium-base grease to hold balls in tube. Seat assembled tube halves into recirculating tube holes in piston. Lightly grease sealing surfaces of tube cover. Install tube into piston. Install retaining ring into piston to secure tube cover. After assembly, check for smooth rotation of spindle assembly in both directions.

11) Reaching through side cover opening of housing, install seal with pressure side toward interior of housing. DO NOT distort seal more than necessary for installation. Install split nylon back-up ring into groove formed by back side of seal and housing. Ensure split surfaces of ring mate properly. Install dust seal into housing with sealing lip toward outside of housing.

12) Install "O" ring into groove around steering limiting stem. Screw stem into housing 5-6 full turns. Install 17 rollers into outer bearing race in housing, using a heavy coating of Ford Long Life Lubricant (C1AZ-19590-BA) to hold rollers in place. Rollers must be same rollers removed from this bearing during disassembly.

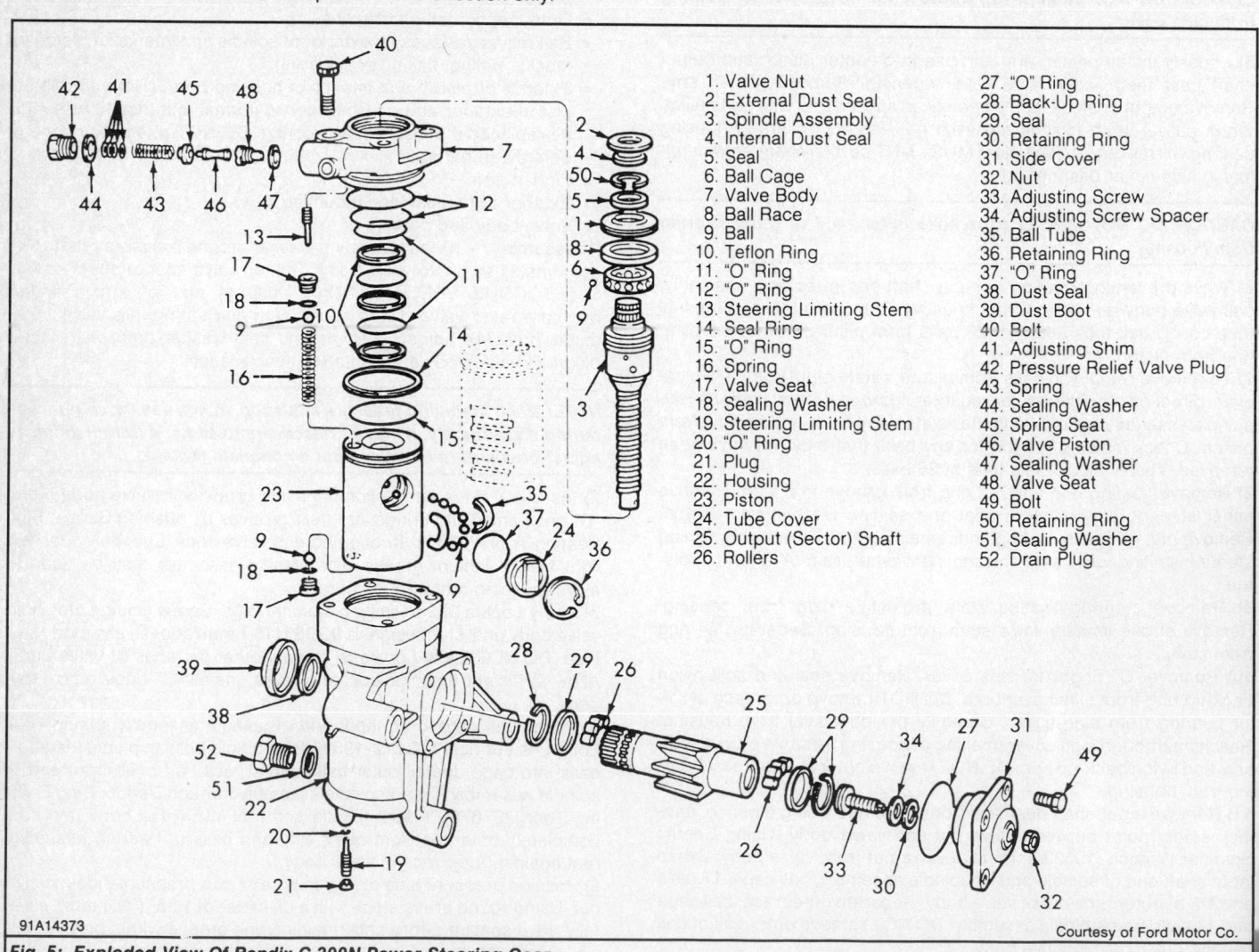

1. Valve Nut
2. External Dust Seal
3. Spindle Assembly
4. Internal Dust Seal
5. Seal
6. Ball Cage
7. Valve Body
8. Ball Race
9. Ball
10. Teflon Ring
11. "O" Ring
12. "O" Ring
13. Steering Limiting Stem
14. Seal Ring
15. "O" Ring
16. Spring
17. Valve Seat
18. Sealing Washer
19. Steering Limiting Stem
20. "O" Ring
21. Plug
22. Housing
23. Piston
24. Tube Cover
25. Output (Sector) Shaft
26. Rollers
27. "O" Ring
28. Back-Up Ring
29. Seal
30. Retaining Ring
31. Side Cover
32. Nut
33. Adjusting Screw
34. Adjusting Screw Spacer
35. Ball Tube
36. Retaining Ring
37. "O" Ring
38. Dust Seal
39. Dust Boot
40. Bolt
41. Adjusting Shim
42. Pressure Relief Valve Plug
43. Spring
44. Sealing Washer
45. Spring Seat
46. Valve Piston
47. Sealing Washer
48. Valve Seat
49. Bolt
50. Retaining Ring
51. Sealing Washer
52. Drain Plug

91A14373

Courtesy of Ford Motor Co.

Fig. 5: Exploded View Of Bendix C-300N Power Steering Gear

13) Align steering limiting stem into valve body with steering limiting valve seat in piston. Insert piston into housing so rack teeth of piston are visible through side cover opening of housing. Ensure valve body is oriented so reference marks align. Carefully slide piston and valve body assembly into housing. DO NOT damage piston guide ring and valve body "O" rings. Mount valve body to housing. Tighten bolts to specification. Rotate input shaft of spindle until rack teeth of piston are centered in side cover opening.

14) Install adjusting spacer over adjusting screw and secure both into output shaft with retaining ring. Maximum end play should be **0.002"** **(0.05 mm)**. If end play is excessive, install a different adjusting spacer. Adjusting spacers are available in 8 different thicknesses. Install seal into side cover with pressure side toward outer race of side cover roller bearing. DO NOT distort seal more than necessary for installation.

15) Install split nylon back-up ring by winding it into groove formed by side cover and back side of seal. Ensure split ring is completely seated and that diagonal split surfaces mate properly. Install "O" ring into groove in side cover.

16) Install 17 rollers into side cover outer race. Use lithium grease to hold rollers in place. The rollers must be those removed from this bearing during disassembly. Lightly lubricate seals in housing and side cover with lithium grease. Lubricate sealing surface of output shaft adjusting screw end. Install side cover assembly onto output shaft adjuster screw. Screw assembly on as far as it will go, then back it off 1/8 turn.

17) Wrap a single layer of masking tape around splines of output shaft to protect housing seal. Lubricate exterior of tape with lithium-base grease and insert shaft and side cover assembly into housing with a twisting motion. Remove tape from output shaft.

18) Ensure side cover is positioned so reference marks align. Install side cover and tighten bolts to specification. See TORQUE SPECIFICATIONS table at end of article. Pack input and output cavities with lithium-base grease. Install dust boot onto output shaft and dust seal onto input shaft.

TORQUE SPECIFICATIONS
TORQUE SPECIFICATIONS

Application	Ft. Lbs. (N.m)
Input Shaft Valve Nut	221-257 (300-348)
Intermediate Shaft-To-Input Shaft Bolt	50-70 (68-95)
Output Shaft Adjustment Screw Lock Nut	74-88 (100-119)
Pitman Arm-To-Gear Output Shaft Nut	220-300 (298-407)
Pressure Relief Valve Plug	66-73 (89-99)
Pressure Relief Valve Seat	15-18 (20-24)
Pump Mounting Bolts	30-45 (41-61)
Side Cover Bolts	81-88 (110-119)
Steering Gear-To-Frame Rail Bolts	150-205 (203-278)
Valve Body-To-Housing Bolts	81-88 (110-119)
	INCH Lbs. (N.m)
Steering Limiting Valve Seats	88-132 (10-15)

Aerostar, Bronco, Explorer, Pickup, Ranger, Van

NOTE: Unless otherwise specified, references to Pickup include the F350 Super Duty commercial chassis.

IDENTIFICATION

AUTOMATIC TRANSMISSION APPLICATIONS

Model	[1] Transmission
Aerostar, Explorer & Ranger	A4LD
Bronco	AOD & E4OD
Pickup & Van	AOD, C-6 & E4OD

[1] – Transmission may be identified by oil pan gasket. *See Figs. 1-4.*

MANUAL TRANSMISSION APPLICATIONS

Model	Transmission
Aerostar, Explorer & Ranger	
5-Speed	Mazda M5OD
5-Speed	[1] Mitsubishi FM146
Bronco	
4-Speed	Borg-Warner T18
5-Speed	Mazda M5OD
Pickup	
4-Speed	Borg-Warner T18
5-Speed [2]	
GVWR Less Than 8500 Lbs. (3855 kg)	Mazda M5OD
GVWR Greater Than 8500 Lbs. (3855 kg)	ZF S5-42

[1] – Used on Ranger models with 2.9L only.
[2] – Note vehicle Gross Vehicle Weight Rating (GVWR) for identifying transmission application. The GVWR is listed on safety compliance label on driver's door pillar.

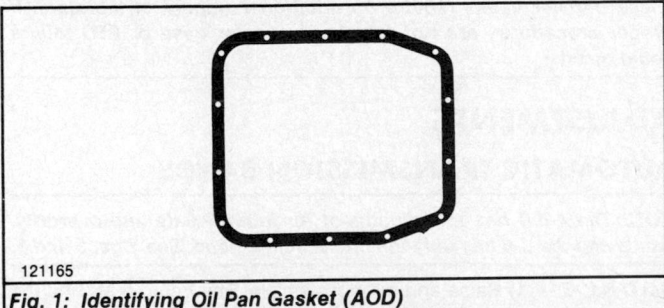

121165

Fig. 1: Identifying Oil Pan Gasket (AOD)

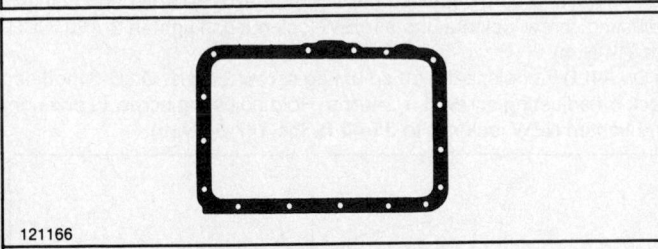

121166

Fig. 2: Identifying Oil Pan Gasket (A4LD)

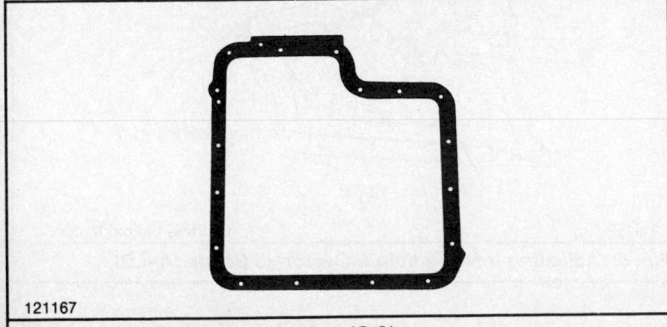

121167

Fig. 3: Identifying Oil Pan Gasket (C-6)

TRANSFER CASE APPLICATIONS

Model	Transfer Case
Aerostar	Dana TC-28
Bronco & Pickup	[1] [2] Borg-Warner 1356
Explorer & Ranger	[1] Borg-Warner 1354

[1] – Available with mechanical or electronic shift.
[2] – Some F350 Pickups may be equipped with a Power Take-Off (PTO) unit.

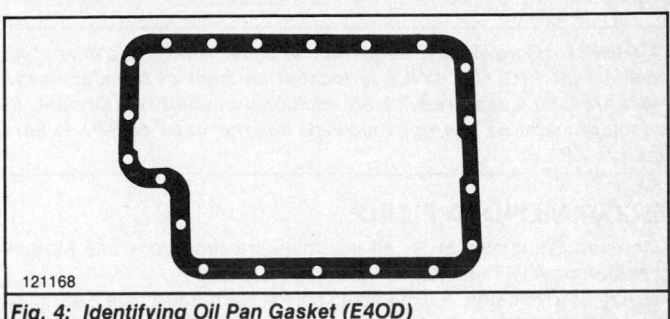

121168

Fig. 4: Identifying Oil Pan Gasket (E4OD)

LUBRICATION

SERVICE INTERVALS

Automatic Transmission – Vehicles used in normal service do not require regularly scheduled maintenance. Fluid level should be checked whenever underhood maintenance is performed or if leakage is detected. Adjust clutch bands on A4LD and C-6 when quality of shifts deteriorates or improper band adjustment is indicated.

On vehicles used for fleet service or those operated under severe conditions (such as police, taxi or towing), regular transmission fluid change is required every 30,000 miles or when fluid appears discolored.

Manual Transmission – Under normal driving conditions, replace transmission fluid every 60,000 miles. Perform service every 30,000 miles if vehicle is operated under the following severe driving conditions:

- Heavy loads in hilly terrain
- In hot weather greater than 90°F (32°C)
- Maximum loads
- Operating a transmission mounted PTO unit
- Towing trailer or carrying a slide-in camper

Transfer Case – Under normal driving conditions, replace transfer case fluid every 60,000 miles. Under heavy 4WD driving conditions, replace fluid more frequently.

CHECKING FLUID LEVEL

NOTE: Pickup F350 Super Duty commercial chassis have a parking brake assembly mounted on rear of the transmission. Parking brake assembly contains a separate reservoir and fluid level must be checked separately from the transmission. See PARKING BRAKE ASSEMBLY under CHECKING FLUID LEVEL.

Automatic Transmission – 1) With vehicle on level surface, start engine and operate until engine and transmission are at normal operating temperature. Apply parking brake. With engine idling, shift transmission through all gear ranges, ending in Park.

WARNING: On 4WD models, ensure transfer case is in any gear range EXCEPT Neutral before checking transmission fluid level.

2) Check transmission fluid level. Fluid level should be within the crosshatched area on the dipstick. Add fluid through filler tube as needed. DO NOT overfill.

CAUTION: DO NOT drive vehicle if fluid level is below bottom hole on dipstick and outside temperature is greater than 50°F (10°C).

Manual Transmission – Check lubricant level at filler plug hole on side of transmission. Fluid level should be even with bottom of filler plug hole. Add lubricant as needed.

Parking Brake Assembly (Pickup F350 Super Duty Commercial Chassis) – Check lubricant level at filler plug hole on side of parking brake assembly mounted on rear of transmission. Fluid level should be even with bottom of filler plug hole. Add lubricant as needed.

Transfer Case – Remove filler plug. Fluid level should be even with bottom of filler plug hole. Add lubricant as needed.

CAUTION: On Borg-Warner 1356 transfer cases with PTO, a filler plug labeled FOR PTO FILL ONLY is located on front of transfer case. These transfer cases require an additional amount of lubricant. If proper procedures are not followed, transfer case or PTO failure could result.

RECOMMENDED FLUID

Automatic Transmission – All automatic transmissions use Motorcraft Mercon ATF (XT-2-QDX).

Manual Transmission – On Mitsubishi FM146 models, use SAE 80W Gear Lube (D8DZ-19C547-A). On all other models, use Motorcraft Mercon ATF (XT-2-QDX).

Parking Brake Assembly (Pickup F350 Super Duty Commercial Chassis) – Use Motorcraft Mercon ATF (XT-2-QDX).

Transfer Case – All transfer cases use Motorcraft Mercon ATF (XT-2-QDX).

FLUID CAPACITIES

NOTE: Approximate fluid capacities are listed. Determine correct fluid level by mark on dipstick or by gauging fluid level at filler plug hole.

AUTOMATIC TRANSMISSION REFILL CAPACITIES [1][2]

Application	Qts. (L)
AOD Transmission	12.3 (11.6)
A4LD Transmission	
2WD	9.7 (9.2)
4WD	10.0 (9.5)
C-6 Transmission	
2WD Models	11.7 (11.1)
4WD Models	13.5 (12.8)
E4OD Transmission	
2WD Models	15.7 (14.9)
4WD Models	16.2 (15.3)

[1] – Includes torque converter, cooler and lines.

[2] – Pickup F350 Super Duty commercial chassis have parking brake assembly mounted on rear of transmission. Fluid level must be checked separately from the transmission. See PARKING BRAKE ASSEMBLY under CHECKING FLUID LEVEL. Parking brake assembly capacity is 3.8 ounces (.11L).

MANUAL TRANSMISSION REFILL CAPACITIES [1]

Application	Pts. (L)
Borg-Warner T18 4-Speed	7.0 (3.3)
Mazda M5OD 5-Speed Overdrive	
Aerostar, Explorer & Ranger	5.6 (2.6)
Bronco & Pickup	7.6 (3.6)
Mitsubishi FM146 5-Speed Overdrive	4.8 (2.3)
ZF S5-42 5-Speed	7.0 (3.3)

[1] – Pickup F350 Super Duty commercial chassis have parking brake assembly mounted on rear of transmission. Fluid level must be checked separately from the transmission. See PARKING BRAKE ASSEMBLY under CHECKING FLUID LEVEL. Parking brake assembly capacity is 3.8 ounces (.11L).

TRANSFER CASE REFILL CAPACITIES

Application	Pts. (L)
Borg-Warner 1354	2.5 (1.2)
Borg-Warner 1356	
With PTO	8.1 (3.8)
Without PTO	4.0 (1.9)
Dana TC-28	4.5 (2.1)

DRAINING & REFILLING

Automatic Transmission – 1) Raise and support vehicle. Loosen oil pan bolts. Tap oil pan to break gasket seal, allowing fluid to drain. Remove retaining bolts, oil pan and gasket.

2) Remove retaining bolt (if equipped), oil filter/screen and gasket. Install NEW gasket, oil filter/screen and oil pan. Tighten retaining bolt to specification. See TORQUE SPECIFICATIONS table at end of article.

3) On A4LD applications, add 3 quarts (2.8L) of ATF or 5 quarts (4.7L) on all other applications of ATF to transmission. Use Motorcraft Mercon ATF (XT-2-QDX).

4) Check fluid level. See CHECKING FLUID LEVEL under LUBRICATION. When filling transmission, refer to AUTOMATIC TRANSMISSION REFILL CAPACITIES table. Recheck fluid level when transmission is at normal operating temperature. DO NOT overfill.

Manual Transmission – Raise and support vehicle. Remove drain plug and drain fluid. Install drain plug. Remove filler plug. Refill transmission with proper fluid to bottom of filler plug hole. See RECOMMENDED FLUID under LUBRICATION. When filling transmission, refer to MANUAL TRANSMISSION REFILL CAPACITIES table. Install filler plug.

Parking Brake Assembly (Pickup F350 Super Duty Commercial Chassis) – No servicing information is available from manufacturer.

Transfer Case – Raise and support vehicle. Remove drain plug and drain fluid. Install drain plug. Remove filler plug. Refill transfer case with proper fluid to bottom of filler plug hole. See RECOMMENDED FLUID under LUBRICATION. When filling transfer case, refer to TRANSFER CASE REFILL CAPACITIES table. Install filler plug.

CAUTION: On Borg-Warner 1356 transfer cases with PTO, a filler plug labeled FOR PTO FILL ONLY is located on front of transfer case. These transfer cases require an additional amount of lubricant. If proper procedures are not followed, transfer case or PTO failure could result.

ADJUSTMENTS

AUTOMATIC TRANSMISSION BANDS

NOTE: The A4LD has an adjustment for intermediate and overdrive bands and the C-6 has only the intermediate band. See Figs. 5 and 6.

A4LD & C-6 – 1) Raise and support vehicle. Ensure area around the band adjusting screw is clean. *See Fig. 5 or 6.* Remove and discard adjusting screw lock nut. Install NEW lock nut and tighten to 120 INCH lbs. (14 N.m).

2) On A4LD models, back off adjusting screw 2 turns. On C-6 models, back off adjusting screw 1 1/2 turns. Hold adjusting screw in position and tighten NEW lock nut to **35-40 ft. lbs. (47-54 N.m)**.

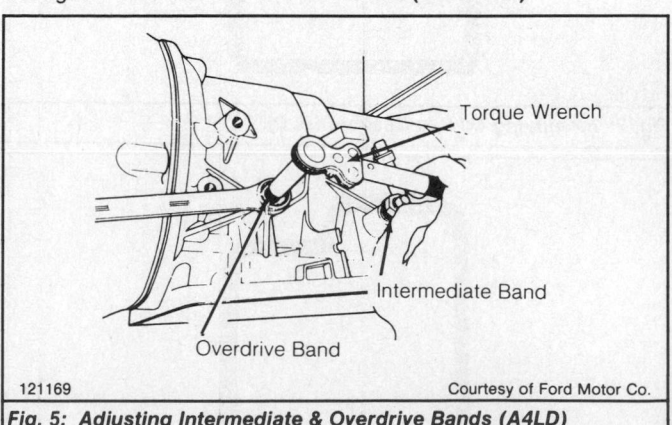

121169　　　　　　　　　　　　Courtesy of Ford Motor Co.

Fig. 5: Adjusting Intermediate & Overdrive Bands (A4LD)

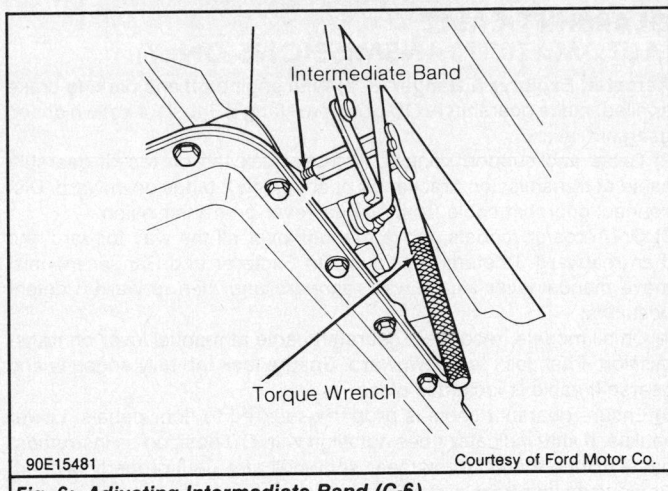

Fig. 6: Adjusting Intermediate Band (C-6)

KICKDOWN CONTROL CABLE (A4LD)

NOTE: Kickdown control cable self-adjusts after installation by depressing accelerator pedal to the floor. If kickdown cable is removed, it may need to be initially reset and then readjusted.

Initial Resetting Procedure & Adjustment – If kickdown cable has been removed it must be reset when installing. From under the hood, depress adjustment D-flat while pulling the cable conduit out from the body. *See Fig. 7.* Adjust kickdown cable by depressing accelerator pedal to floor.

NOTE: If transmission kickdown is difficult to achieve at wide open throttle, ensure accelerator pedal travel is not restricted by floor mats.

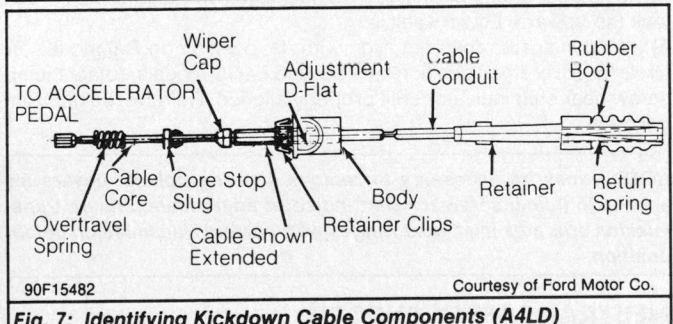

Fig. 7: Identifying Kickdown Cable Components (A4LD)

THROTTLE VALVE (T.V.) CONTROL CABLE (AOD TRANSMISSIONS)

NOTE: The T.V. control cable is locked to proper length during initial assembly. Control cable may require adjustment if throttle body, control cable or transmission is replaced.

Cable Adjustment With Engine Off – 1) Apply parking brake and place transmission in Neutral. DO NOT place transmission in Park. On F150/250 and Bronco models, remove cable linkage protective cover. On all models, ensure throttle lever is resting against idle stop. DO NOT adjust idle stop.
2) Ensure T.V. control cable is properly routed, free of sharp bends and operates freely. Using small screwdriver, pry lock tab outward to release T.V. control cable at throttle body. *See Fig. 8.*
3) Install a return spring on T.V. control lever at the transmission and hook spring on rear of transmission case. Ensure T.V. control lever is held in idle position (fully rearward toward rear of transmission).

NOTE: It may be necessary to use 2 return springs to retain T.V. control lever in position.

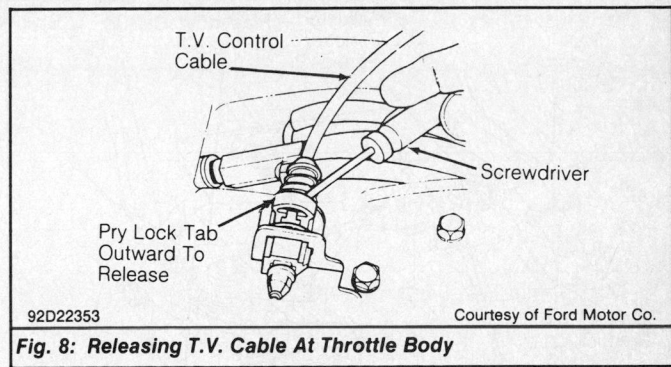

Fig. 8: Releasing T.V. Cable At Throttle Body

4) With T.V. cable lock tab released and return spring in place, rotate T.V. control lever at transmission approximately 10-30 degrees and return slowly. Push lock tab downward on T.V. control cable at throttle body until lock tab is flush. Remove return spring.
T.V. Pressure Check & Adjustment With Engine On – 1) Remove plug and install Pressure Gauge (T86L-70002-A) in T.V. pressure tap on side of transmission case. *See Fig. 9.* Remove cover from T.V. control cable linkage.
2) Insert tapered end of T.V. Cable Control Pressure Gauge Adjuster (T86L-70332-A) between slug on end of cable and plastic fitting attached to throttle lever. *See Fig. 10.*
3) Push T.V. cable control pressure gauge adjuster inward as far as possible, forcing slug away from plastic fitting. Start engine and operate until engine and transmission are at normal operating temperature.

NOTE: Transmission fluid temperature should be 100-150°F (37-65°C) when checking T.V. pressure. DO NOT perform T.V. pressure check unless transmission fluid temperature is correct.

4) Apply parking brake. Place transmission in Neutral. DO NOT check T.V. control pressure with transmission in Park. With engine idling, note that T.V. control pressure is 28-38 psi (1.97-2.67 kg/cm²).
5) If T.V. control pressure is not within specification, T.V. control cable must be adjusted. To adjust T.V. control cable, pry up on T.V. control cable locking tab at throttle body. *See Fig. 10.*
6) The adjuster preload spring should cause adjusting slider to move away from throttle body, causing T.V. control pressure to increase. Push on adjusting slider from behind throttle body bracket until T.V. control pressure is 33 psi (2.3 kg/cm²). *See Fig. 10.*
7) While holding slider, push T.V. control cable locking tab downward as far as possible to lock slider into position. Remove T.V. cable control pressure gauge adjuster. Allow engine to return to idle.
8) With engine idling and transmission in Neutral, T.V. control pressure should be less than 5 psi (.3 kg/cm²), preferably near zero. If T.V. control pressure is not as specified, readjust. Remove pressure gauge. Install and tighten plug to specification. See TORQUE SPECIFICATIONS table at end of article.

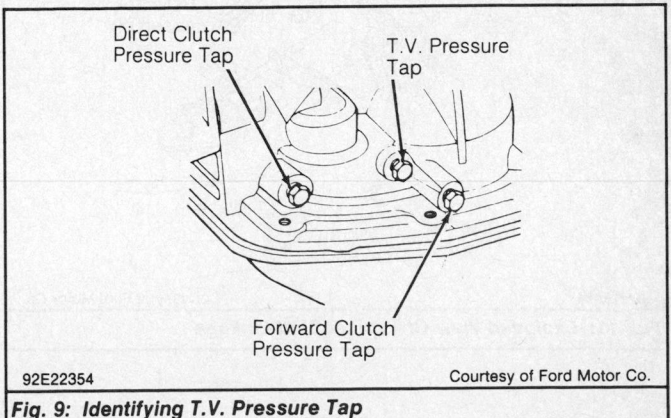

Fig. 9: Identifying T.V. Pressure Tap

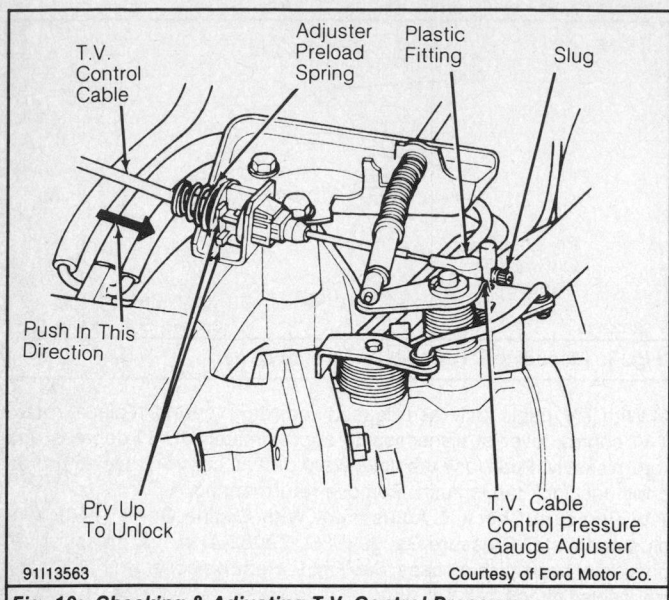

T.V. Control Cable

Adjuster Preload Spring

Plastic Fitting

Slug

Push In This Direction

Pry Up To Unlock

T.V. Cable Control Pressure Gauge Adjuster

91I13563

Courtesy of Ford Motor Co.

Fig. 10: Checking & Adjusting T.V. Control Pressure

GEARSHIFT LINKAGE (AUTOMATIC TRANSMISSIONS ONLY)

Bronco, Pickup & Van – **1)** Apply parking brake. On models with C-6 transmissions, place gearshift in "D" position. On models with AOD or E4OD transmissions, place gearshift in the circle "D" (overdrive) position.
2) On all models, hold gearshift lever against stop by hanging a 3-lb. (1.4 kg) weight on gearshift lever. Loosen shift rod-to-bellcrank assembly retaining nut. *See Fig. 11.*
3) Move manual lever on transmission to fully rearward position. Move manual lever forward to "D" position on C-6 models or circle "D" (overdrive) position on AOD and E4OD models.
4) With gearshift lever and manual lever on transmission in "D" or circle "D" (overdrive) position, tighten retaining nut to specification. See TORQUE SPECIFICATIONS table at end of article. Remove weight from gearshift lever. Check for normal operation in all selected positions.

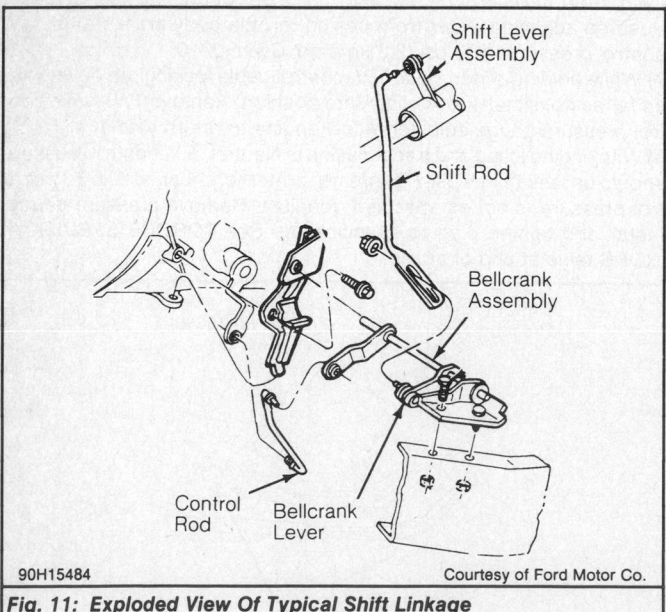

Shift Lever Assembly

Shift Rod

Bellcrank Assembly

Control Rod

Bellcrank Lever

90H15484

Courtesy of Ford Motor Co.

Fig. 11: Exploded View Of Typical Shift Linkage

GEARSHIFT CABLE (AUTOMATIC TRANSMISSIONS ONLY)

Aerostar, Explorer & Ranger – **1)** With engine off and parking brake applied, place gearshift in OD position. Hang a 3-lb. (1.4 kg) weight on gearshift lever.
2) Raise and support vehicle. Release lock tab on top of gearshift cable at transmission bracket by pushing the 2 tangs downward. Disconnect gearshift cable from manual lever on transmission.
3) On Aerostar models, move manual lever all the way forward and then rearward 3 detent positions. On Explorer and Ranger models, move manual lever all the way rearward and then forward 3 detent positions.
4) On all models, reconnect gearshift cable at manual lever on transmission. Push lock tab downward. Ensure lock tab fully engages and gearshift cable is locked in place.
5) Ensure gearshift cable is properly secured to floor panels. Lower vehicle. If shift indicator does not align with OD position on instrument panel, rotate thumb screw near shift indicator until properly aligned. Remove weight from gearshift.

NOTE: It may be necessary to remove steering column covers for access to thumb screw for shift indicator adjustment. Ensure transmission operates in all gear ranges with correct transmission detent position.

Bronco, Pickup & Van – **1)** Apply parking brake. On models with C-6 transmissions, place gearshift in "D" position. On models with AOD or E4OD transmissions, place gearshift in the circle "D" (overdrive) position.
2) On all models, raise and support vehicle. Disconnect gearshift cable from manual lever on transmission. Pull downward on lock tab on gearshift cable at transmission bracket.
3) Move manual lever on transmission to fully forward position. Move manual lever backward 4 detent positions to "D" position on C-6 models or circle "D" (overdrive) position on AOD and E4OD models.
4) Reconnect gearshift cable to manual lever on transmission. Push lock tab upward. Lower vehicle.
5) If shift indicator does not align with "D" position on C-6 models or circle "D" (overdrive) position on AOD and E4OD models, rotate thumb screw near shift indicator until properly aligned. Remove weight from gearshift.

NOTE: It may be necessary to remove steering column covers for access to thumb screw for shift indicator adjustment. Ensure transmission operates in all gear ranges with correct transmission detent position.

NEUTRAL SAFETY SWITCH

AOD & A4LD – Neutral safety switch is located on side of transmission case and is non-adjustable. Use Socket (T74P-77247-A) when replacing neutral safety switch or neutral safety switch will be damaged.

MANUAL LEVER POSITION SENSOR (MLPS)

C-6 – **1)** Ensure gearshift cable or linkage is properly adjusted. See GEARSHIFT CABLE or GEARSHIFT LINKAGE under ADJUST-MENTS. Apply parking brake. Place gearshift in Neutral.
2) Loosen MLPS retaining screws. Install MLPS Aligner (T92P-70010-AH) in 3 slots on switch and actuator plate of MLPS. *See Fig. 12.*

CAUTION: Ensure each leg of MLPS aligner engages with each slot of MLPS.

3) Tighten MLPS retaining screws to specification. See TORQUE SPECIFICATIONS table at end of article. Remove MLPS aligner.
4) Proper adjustment can be confirmed by ensuring etched line in actuator and housing are aligned with gearshift in Neutral. Ensure vehicle starts only in Park and Neutral and back-up lights operate in Reverse.

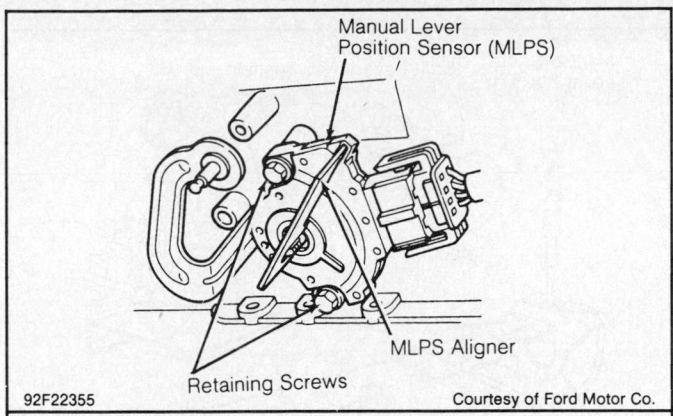

Fig. 12: *Adjusting Manual Lever Position Sensor (C-6)*

E4OD – Remove shift linkage from transmission. Loosen MLPS retaining screws. Using MLPS Aligner (T89T-70010-J), align manual lever position sensor for Neutral gear. *See Fig. 13.* Tighten retaining bolts to specification. See TORQUE SPECIFICATIONS table at end of article. Install shift linkage.

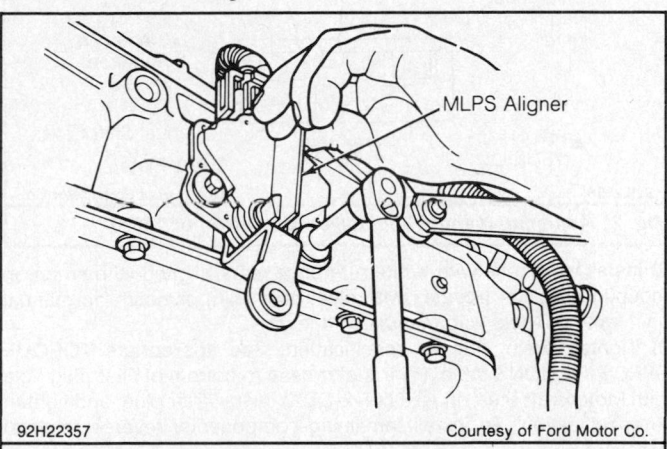

Fig. 13: *Adjusting Manual Lever Position Sensor (E4OD)*

FUEL INJECTION PUMP LEVER (FIPL) SENSOR (DIESEL)

NOTE: *Checking and adjusting FIPL requires a STAR Tester (007-00004) and Adapter Cable (007-00010).*

Checking FIPL Sensor Operation – 1) Perform Key On Engine Off (KOEO) Self-Test. See KOEO SELF-TEST in appropriate SELF-DIAGNOSTICS – EEC-IV article in ENGINE PERFORMANCE. During KOEO self-test, hold throttle to wide open position until fault codes have been displayed.
2) After last fault code has been displayed, press Overdrive Cancel Switch (OCS) to initiate FIPL sensor adjustment mode. In the adjustment mode, this will allow Star Tester to be used as an audible guide in checking and adjusting FIPL sensor.

NOTE: *Star tester will remain in adjustment mode for 10 minutes. Steps 3) and 4) must be done within this time frame. If time limit is exceeded, procedure must be repeated starting at step 1).*

3) Remove throttle cable from throttle lever on right side of fuel injection pump. Place a .515" (13.08 mm) Gauge Block (T83T-7B200-AH) between gauge boss and maximum throttle travel screw. *See Fig. 14.* Hold throttle lever open against gauge block.
4) A steady tone from Star Tester indicates proper FIPL sensor adjustment. If FIPL sensor setting is too low, Star tester will emit a slow beeping sound (one beep per second). If FIPL sensor setting is too high, Star tester will emit a fast beeping sound (4 beeps per second). Adjust FIPL sensor if necessary.

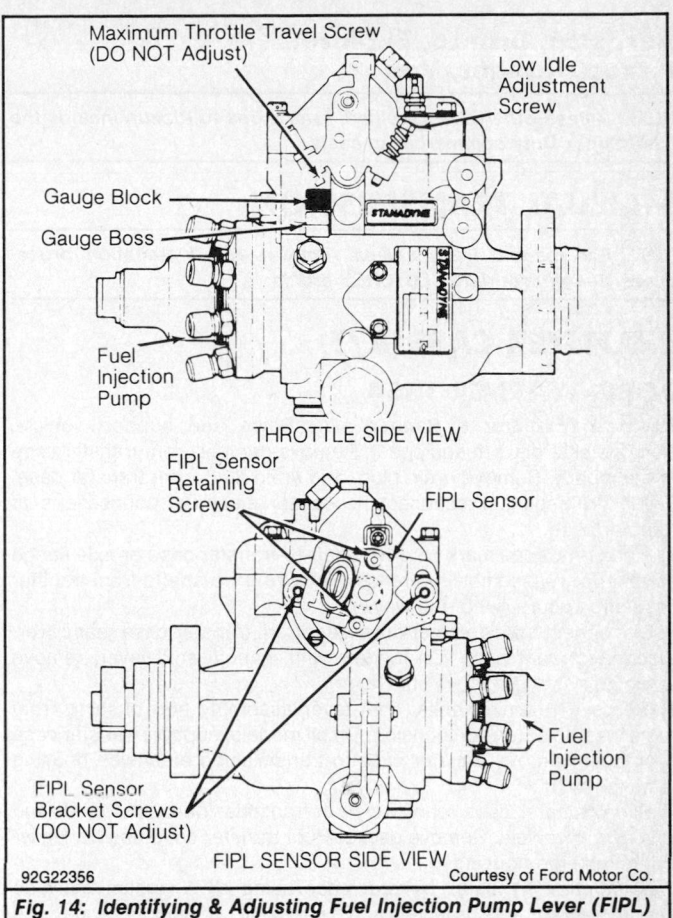

Fig. 14: *Identifying & Adjusting Fuel Injection Pump Lever (FIPL) Sensor*

Adjusting FIPL Sensor – 1) To adjust FIPL sensor, loosen FIPL sensor retaining screws. *See Fig. 14.* Rotate FIPL sensor until steady tone is heard from Star tester. A steady tone indicates FIPL sensor is properly adjusted.

CAUTION: *FIPL sensor bracket is permanently attached to fuel injection pump with tamper-proof screws. DO NOT loosen FIPL sensor bracket screws or move bracket to adjust FIPL sensor.*

2) If FIPL sensor cannot be adjusted to obtain a steady tone, replace FIPL sensor and repeat adjustment procedure.
3) Remove gauge block. Open throttle to wide open position 5 times. Reinstall gauge block and recheck FIPL sensor adjustment. Readjust if necessary. Remove gauge block. Attach throttle cable. Start engine. Check throttle and transmission shift operation.

CAUTION: *DO NOT alter maximum throttle travel screw setting. This screw has been preset and should not be adjusted.*

TORQUE SPECIFICATIONS

TORQUE SPECIFICATIONS

Application	Ft. Lbs. (N.m)
Band Adjusting Screw Lock Nut	35-40 (47-54)
Oil Pan Bolt	10-11 (14-15)
Shift Rod-To-Bellcrank Assembly Nut	12-18 (16-24)

	INCH Lbs. (N.m)
Manual Lever Position Sensor Screw	55-75 (6.2-8.5)
Neutral Safety Switch Bolt	96-132 (10.8-14.9)
Oil Filter/Screen Bolt	
AOD	80-120 (9.0-13.6)
A4LD	71-97 (8.0-10.9)
C6	40-55 (4.5-6.2)
T.V. Pressure Tap Plug	72-144 (8.1-16.2)

Aerostar, Bronco, Explorer, Pickup, Ranger, Van

NOTE: Unless otherwise specified, references to Pickup include the F350 Super Duty commercial chassis.

MANUAL TRANSMISSION

NOTE: For manual transmission removal and installation procedures, see appropriate CLUTCHES article.

TRANSFER CASE (A/T)

BORG-WARNER 1354

Removal (Explorer & Ranger) – 1) Raise and support vehicle. Remove skid plate (if equipped). Remove damper from transfer case (if equipped). Remove drain plug, and drain fluid from transfer case. Install drain plug. Disconnect necessary electrical connections at transfer case.

2) Place reference mark on drive shaft-to-transfer case or axle flange or yoke for reassembly reference. Remove drive shafts from transfer case and secure out of the way.

3) Disconnect speedometer drive gear from transfer case rear cover. Disconnect vent hose. On models with manual shift lever, remove retaining nut and remove shift lever.

4) Remove retaining bolts, shift lever assembly and bushing from transmission extension housing. On all models, support transfer case with jack. Remove transfer case-to-transmission extension housing retaining bolts.

5) Slide transfer case rearward from transmission output shaft and lower from vehicle. Remove gasket from transfer case and transmission extension housing.

Installation – 1) Install transfer case using NEW gasket between transfer case and transmission extension housing. It may be necessary to use grease to hold gasket in place.

2) Tighten transfer case-to-transmission extension housing bolts to specification in sequence. See Fig. 1. See appropriate TORQUE SPECIFICATIONS table at end of article.

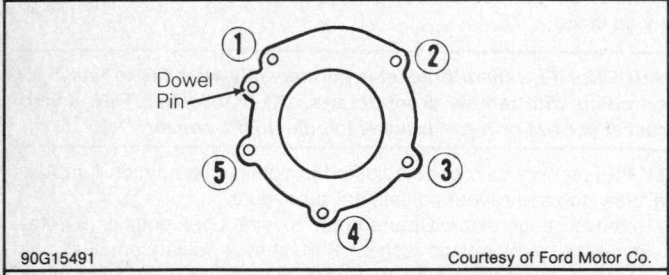

90G15491   Courtesy of Ford Motor Co.

Fig. 1: Transfer Case-To-Transmission Extension Housing Bolt Tightening Sequence (Borg-Warner 1354 & Dana TC-28)

3) On models with manual shift lever, install shift lever assembly with retaining bolts loosely installed. Raise manual shift lever boot for access to cam plate. See Fig. 2.

4) Place transfer case shift lever in 4L position. Rotate cam plate around bolt "A" clockwise until bottom chamfered corner of neutral lug contacts forward right edge of manual shift lever at point "C". See Fig. 2.

5) Hold cam plate in this position. Tighten bolt "A" to 70-90 ft. lbs. (95-122 N.m) and then bolt "B" to 31-42 ft. lbs. (42-57 N.m). Move manual shift lever into all gear positions and check for proper engagement.

6) Ensure clearance exists between manual shift lever and cam plate in 2H and 4H positions and no more than .13" (3.3 mm) exists when in 4L position. See Fig. 2. Install manual shift lever boot.

7) On all models, install speedometer driver gear. Install front and rear drive shafts. Ensure reference marks are aligned on drive shaft flanges.

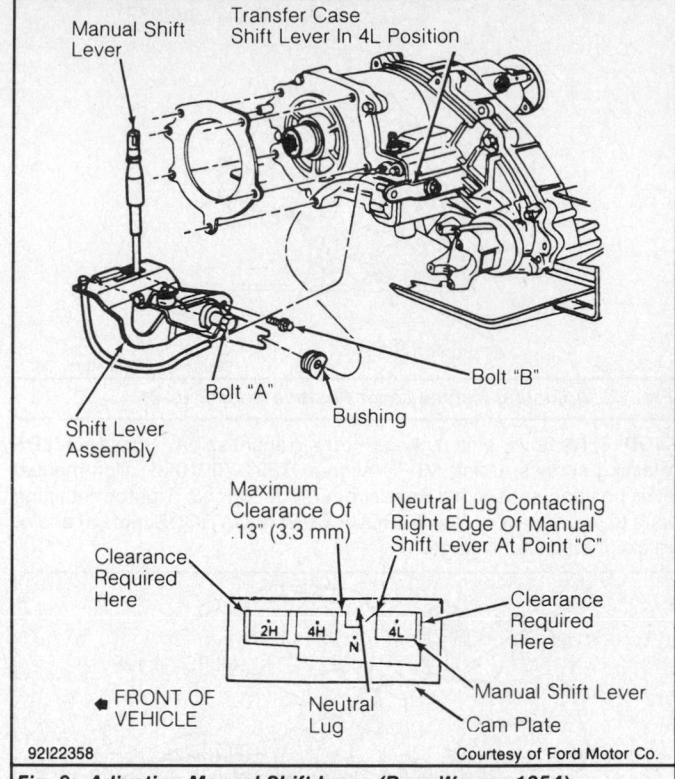

92I22358   Courtesy of Ford Motor Co.

Fig. 2: Adjusting Manual Shift Lever (Borg-Warner 1354)

8) Install vent hose with White reference mark aligned with notch on mounting bracket (models with electronic shift) or notch on manual shift lever (models with manual shift lever).

9) Tighten drain plug to specification. See appropriate TORQUE SPECIFICATIONS table. Fill transfer case to bottom of filler plug hole with Motorcraft Mercon ATF (XT-2-QDX). Install filler plug, and tighten to specification. To install remaining components, reverse removal procedure.

BORG-WARNER 1356

Removal (Bronco & Pickup) – 1) Raise and support vehicle. Remove skid plate (if equipped). Remove drain plug, and drain fluid from transfer case. Install drain plug. Disconnect necessary electrical connections at transfer case.

2) Place reference mark on drive shaft-to-transfer case or axle flange or yoke for reassembly reference. Remove drive shafts from transfer case and secure out of the way. Disconnect vent hose.

3) On models with manual shift lever, disconnect shift rod between transfer case shift lever and manual shift control lever assembly. On all models, support transfer case with jack.

4) Remove transfer case-to-transmission extension housing retaining bolts. Slide transfer case rearward from transmission output shaft and lower from vehicle. Remove gasket from transfer case and transmission extension housing.

Installation – 1) To install, reverse removal procedure using NEW gasket between transfer case and transmission extension housing. It may be necessary to use grease to hold gasket in place.

2) Tighten transfer case-to-transmission extension housing bolts to specification in sequence. See Fig. 3. See appropriate TORQUE SPECIFICATIONS table at end of article.

3) When installing front and rear drive shafts, ensure reference marks are aligned on drive shaft flanges. Tighten drain plug to specification. See appropriate TORQUE SPECIFICATIONS table.

4) Fill transfer case to bottom of filler plug hole with Motorcraft Mercon ATF (XT-2-QDX). Install filler plug, and tighten to specification. To install remaining components, reverse removal procedure.

CAUTION: *On Borg-Warner 1356 transfer cases with PTO, a filler plug labeled FOR PTO FILL ONLY is located on front of transfer case. These transfer cases require an additional 4.1 pts. (1.9L) of lubricant. If proper amount of lubricant is not installed, transfer case or PTO failure could result.*

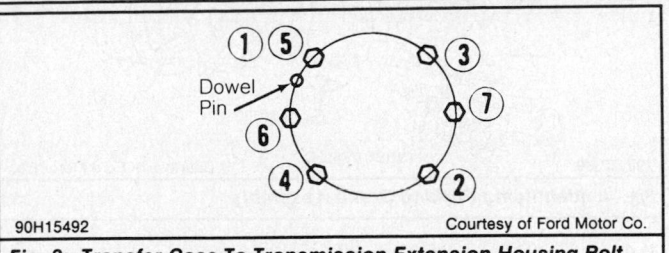

90H15492   Courtesy of Ford Motor Co.

Fig. 3: Transfer Case-To-Transmission Extension Housing Bolt Tightening Sequence (Borg-Warner 1356)

DANA TC-28

Removal (Aerostar) – 1) Raise and support vehicle. Remove drain plug, and drain fluid from transfer case. Install drain plug. Disconnect necessary electrical connections at transfer case by squeezing lock tabs together and pulling from socket.

2) Remove front drive shaft dust boot retaining clamp at transfer case. Pull dust boot from transfer case. Place reference mark on drive shaft-to-axle flange or yoke for reassembly reference.

3) Remove retaining bolts. Pull drive shafts from transfer case. Remove retaining bolts and transfer case-to-cylinder block strut. Support transfer case with jack.

4) Remove transfer case-to-transmission extension housing retaining bolts. Slide transfer case rearward from transmission output shaft and lower from vehicle. Remove gasket from transfer case and transmission extension housing.

Installation – 1) To install, reverse removal procedure using NEW gasket between transfer case and transmission extension housing. It may be necessary to use grease to hold gasket in place.

2) Tighten transfer case-to-transmission extension housing bolts to specification in sequence. *See Fig. 1.* See appropriate TORQUE SPECIFICATIONS table at end of article.

3) Apply light coat of grease on front drive shaft splines and inner edge of dust boot area on transfer case before installing. When installing front and rear drive shafts, ensure reference marks are aligned on drive shafts and flanges.

4) Install and crimp NEW clamp to retain front drive shaft dust boot on transfer case. Tighten drain plug to specification. See appropriate TORQUE SPECIFICATIONS table.

5) Fill transfer case to bottom of filler plug hole with Motorcraft Mercon ATF (XT-2-QDX). Install filler plug, and tighten to specification. To install remaining components, reverse removal procedure.

AUTOMATIC TRANSMISSION

A4LD TRANSMISSION

WARNING: *When battery is disconnected, vehicle computer and memory systems may lose memory data. Driveability problems may exist until computer systems have completed a relearn cycle. See COMPUTER RELEARN PROCEDURES article in GENERAL INFORMATION before disconnecting battery.*

Removal (Aerostar, Explorer & Ranger) – 1) Disconnect negative battery cable. Raise and support vehicle. Loosen oil pan bolts, allowing fluid to drain. When fluid stops draining, remove all but 2 bolts at the front of oil pan. Allow oil pan to drop down and drain remaining fluid. Reinstall bolts to hold oil pan in place.

NOTE: *On Explorer models, it may be necessary to pry lower clips on transmission heat shield back slightly for access to oil pan bolts.*

2) Remove torque converter access cover. Remove starter motor. Remove torque converter-to-drive plate retaining nuts. Rotate engine clockwise (viewed from front of engine) for access to retaining nuts.

CAUTION: *On 2.3L models, DO NOT rotate engine counterclockwise (viewed from front of engine) or engine damage may result.*

3) Place reference mark on drive shaft-to-axle flange or yoke for reassembly reference. Remove drive shaft. Disconnect speedometer cable, vacuum hoses, electrical connections and shift cable at transmission.

4) Disconnect kickdown cable from ball stud lever. Depress tabs on kickdown cable and disengage from bracket. Using floor jack, slightly raise transmission.

5) Remove transmission mount-to-crossmember nuts. Remove retaining bolts and crossmember. Lower floor jack, allowing transmission to hang downward.

6) On Explorer and Ranger models, using floor jack and a piece of wood, slightly raise front of engine. This must be done for access to the 2 upper transmission-to-cylinder block bolts.

7) On all models, disconnect oil cooler lines at transmission. Plug all oil cooler line openings. Remove lower transmission-to-cylinder block bolts. Remove transmission filler tube.

8) Secure transmission to floor jack with safety chain. Remove upper transmission-to-cylinder block bolts. Move transmission rearward and lower from vehicle.

NOTE: *If transmission is to be removed for a long period of time, support engine with safety stand and a wooden block.*

Installation – 1) Reverse removal procedure. Ensure torque converter is fully seated and reference marks on drive shaft and axle flange or yoke are aligned. Tighten bolts/nuts to specification. See appropriate TORQUE SPECIFICATIONS table at end of article.

2) Fill transmission with Motorcraft Mercon ATF (XT-2-QDX). For fluid capacity and proper control cable adjustment, see appropriate TRANSMISSION SERVICING article.

AOD TRANSMISSION

WARNING: *When battery is disconnected, vehicle computer and memory systems may lose memory data. Driveability problems may exist until computer systems have completed a relearn cycle. See COMPUTER RELEARN PROCEDURES article in GENERAL INFORMATION before disconnecting battery.*

Removal (Bronco, Pickup & Van) – 1) Disconnect negative battery cable. Raise and support vehicle. Loosen oil pan bolts, allowing fluid to drain. When fluid stops draining, remove all but 2 bolts at the front of oil pan. Allow oil pan to drop down and drain remaining fluid. Reinstall bolts to hold oil pan in place.

2) Remove torque converter cover. Remove drain plug from torque converter (if equipped) and drain torque converter. Reinstall drain plug. Remove torque converter-to-drive plate nuts.

3) Place reference mark on drive shaft-to-axle flange or yoke for reassembly reference. Remove drive shaft. Remove starter motor. Disconnect speedometer cable, necessary electrical connections and control cables at transmission.

4) On 4WD, remove transfer case. See TRANSFER CASE (A/T). On all models, support transmission using floor jack. Remove transmission mount-to-crossmember nuts and crossmember-to-frame bolts. Remove retaining bolts and transmission mount from transmission extension housing.

5) Remove crossmember and transmission mount. Disconnect oil cooler lines and filler tube from transmission. Plug all oil cooler line openings. Secure transmission to floor jack using safety chain.

6) Remove transmission-to-cylinder block bolts. Move transmission rearward, and lower it from vehicle.

Installation – 1) Reverse removal procedure using NEW "O" ring on filler tube. Ensure torque converter is fully seated and reference marks on drive shaft and axle flange or yoke are aligned.

2) Tighten torque converter drain plug and all bolts/nuts to specification. See appropriate TORQUE SPECIFICATIONS table at end of article. Fill transmission with Motorcraft Mercon ATF (XT-2-QDX). For fluid capacity and proper control cable adjustment, see appropriate TRANSMISSION SERVICING article.

C-6 TRANSMISSION

WARNING: When battery is disconnected, vehicle computer and memory systems may lose memory data. Driveability problems may exist until computer systems have completed a relearn cycle. See COMPUTER RELEARN PROCEDURES article in GENERAL INFORMATION before disconnecting battery.

Removal (Pickup & Van) – 1) Disconnect negative battery cable. Raise and support vehicle. On Van models, remove engine cover. Remove flexible hose from air cleaner heat tube (V8 models only). On all models, loosen oil pan bolts, allowing fluid to drain.
2) When fluid stops draining, remove all but 2 bolts at the front of oil pan. Allow oil pan to drop down and drain remaining fluid. Reinstall bolts to hold oil pan in place.
3) Remove torque converter cover. Remove drain plug from torque converter (if equipped) and drain torque converter. Reinstall drain plug. Remove torque converter-to-drive plate nuts.
4) Place reference mark on drive shaft-to-axle flange or yoke for reassembly reference. Remove drive shaft. Remove starter motor. Disconnect speedometer cable, necessary electrical connections and control cables or rods at transmission.
5) On Pickup 4WD models, remove transfer case. See TRANSFER CASE (A/T) in this article. On all models, support transmission with floor jack. Remove transmission mount-to-crossmember nuts and crossmember-to-frame bolts. Remove retaining bolts and transmission mount from transmission extension housing.
6) Remove crossmember and transmission mount. Disconnect oil cooler lines and filler tube from transmission. Plug all oil cooler line openings. Secure transmission to floor jack with safety chain.
7) Remove transmission-to-cylinder block bolts. Move transmission rearward and lower from vehicle.
Installation – 1) To install, reverse removal procedure using NEW "O" ring on filler tube. Ensure torque converter is fully seated and reference mark on drive shaft and axle flange or yoke are aligned.
2) Tighten torque converter drain plug and all bolts/nuts to specification. See appropriate TORQUE SPECIFICATIONS table at end of article. Fill transmission with Motorcraft Mercon ATF (XT-2-QDX). For fluid capacity and proper control cable or linkage adjustment, see appropriate TRANSMISSION SERVICING article.

E4OD TRANSMISSION

WARNING: When battery is disconnected, vehicle computer and memory systems may lose memory data. Driveability problems may exist until computer systems have completed a relearn cycle. See COMPUTER RELEARN PROCEDURES article in GENERAL INFORMATION before disconnecting battery.

Removal (Bronco, Pickup & Van) – 1) Disconnect negative battery cable. Raise and support vehicle. Remove dipstick. Place transmission in Neutral. Remove skid plate (if equipped). Place reference mark on drive shaft-to-axle flange or yoke for reassembly reference. Remove drive shaft(s).
2) On F350 Super Duty commercial chassis, disconnect speedometer cable from parking brake assembly mounted on rear of transmission. *See Fig. 4.* Loosen lock nut on parking brake cable at the clevis.
3) Remove clevis pin, clevis and lock nut from parking brake cable. Remove parking brake cable from bracket on parking brake assembly.

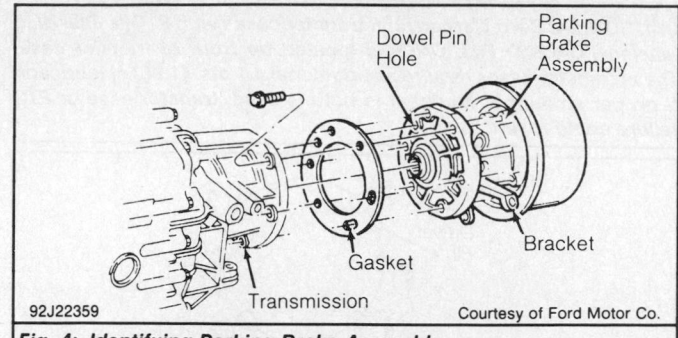

Fig. 4: Identifying Parking Brake Assembly

4) On all models, disconnect control cables, shift linkages, speedometer cable from transmission. On 4WD models, remove shift linkage from transfer case (manual shift models) or disconnect electrical connector at transfer case (models with electronic shift). Disconnect 4WD switch connector from transfer case. Disconnect wiring harness from retainers on the frame rail.
5) On all models, remove necessary heat shields for access to electrical connectors. Disconnect electrical connector from Manual Lever Position Sensor (MLPS), mounted at shift lever on transmission. Disconnect electrical connector from solenoid assembly on side of transmission.

CAUTION: Remove electrical connector from MLPS by squeezing tabs together and pulling connector from MLPS. Remove electrical connector from solenoid assembly by pushing inward on center tab. DO NOT pry on tab(s) with screwdriver.

6) Loosen oil pan bolts, allowing fluid to drain. When fluid stops draining, remove all but 2 bolts at the front of oil pan. Allow oil pan to drop down and drain remaining fluid. Reinstall bolts to hold oil pan in place.
7) Remove torque converter covers. Remove starter motor. Remove torque converter-to-drive plate nuts. Support transmission with floor jack. Remove transmission mount-to-crossmember nuts and crossmember-to-frame bolts.
8) Remove crossmember. Disconnect oil cooler lines and filler tube from transmission. Plug all oil cooler line openings. Secure transmission to floor jack with safety chain. Remove transmission-to-cylinder block bolts. Move transmission rearward and lower from vehicle.
9) On F350 Super Duty commercial chassis if necessary to remove parking brake assembly, remove retaining bolts, parking brake assembly and gasket. *See Fig. 4.*

CAUTION: Store parking brake assembly with breather assembly facing upward to prevent oil leakage onto the brake shoes.

Installation – 1) Reverse removal procedure using NEW "O" ring on filler tube. Ensure torque converter is fully seated and reference marks on drive shaft and axle flange or yoke are aligned.
2) On F350 Super Duty commercial chassis, use NEW gasket and retaining bolts when installing parking brake assembly. DO NOT reuse bolt. On all models, tighten all bolts/nuts to specification. See appropriate TORQUE SPECIFICATIONS table at end of article.

CAUTION: Pickup F350 Super Duty commercial chassis parking brake assembly contains a reservoir separate from transmission. Check lubricant level at filler plug hole on side of parking brake assembly. Fluid lever should be even with bottom of filler plug hole. Add Motorcraft Mercon ATF (XT-2-QDX) as needed.

3) Fill transmission with Motorcraft Mercon ATF (XT-2-QDX). For fluid capacity and proper control cable or linkage adjustment, see appropriate TRANSMISSION SERVICING article.

TORQUE SPECIFICATIONS

TORQUE SPECIFICATIONS (TRANSFER CASE)

Application	Ft. Lbs. (N.m)
Damper Bolt	
Borg-Warner 1354	25-35 (34-47)
Drain & Filler Plug	
Borg-Warner 1356	10-14 (14-19)
All Others	12-20 (16-27)
Shift Lever Assembly Bolt	
Borg-Warner 1354	
Bolt "A" [1]	70-90 (95-122)
Bolt "B" [1]	31-42 (42-57)
Transfer Case-To-Cylinder Block Strut Bolt/Nut	
Dana TC-28	
Cylinder Block Side	45-60 (61-81)
Transfer Case Side	55-65 (75-88)
Transfer Case-To-Transmission Extension	
Housing Bolt	
Borg-Warner 1354 [2]	25-35 (34-47)
Borg-Warner 1356 [3]	25-43 (34-58)
Dana TC-28 [2]	25-35 (34-47)

[1] – Bolt "A" is large bolt and bolt "B" is the small bolt. *See Fig. 2.*
[2] – Tighten bolts to specification in sequence. *See Fig. 1.*
[3] – Tighten bolts to specification in sequence. *See Fig. 3.*

TORQUE SPECIFICATIONS (TRANSMISSION)

Application	Ft. Lbs. (N.m)
A4LD	
Crossmember-To-Frame Bolt	
2.9L & 3.0L	65-85 (88-115)
Crossmember-To-Frame Through Bolt	
4.0L	37-52 (51-71)
2.3L	65-85 (88-115)
Oil Pan Bolt	[1]
Torque Converter-To-Drive Plate Nut	20-34 (27-46)
Transmission Mount-To-Crossmember Nut	71-85 (96-115)
Transmission-To-Cylinder Block Bolt	
3.0L	33-44 (45-60)
All Others	28-38 (38-52)
AOD	
Crossmember-To-Frame Bolt	43-57 (58-77)
Oil Pan Bolt	[1]
Torque Converter Drain Plug	10-28 (14-38)
Torque Converter-To-Drive Plate Nut	20-34 (27-46)
Transmission Mount-To-Crossmember Nut	60-80 (81-109)
Transmission Mount-To-Transmission Extension	
Housing Bolt	60-80 (81-109)
Transmission-To-Cylinder Block Bolt	40-50 (54-68)
C6	
Crossmember-To-Frame Bolt	40-60 (54-81)
Oil Pan Bolt	10-12 (14-16)
Torque Converter Drain Plug	10-28 (14-38)
Torque Converter-To-Drive Plate Nut	20-30 (27-41)
Transmission Mount-To-Crossmember Nut	50-70 (68-95)
Transmission Mount-To-Transmission Extension	
Housing Bolt	60-80 (81-109)
Transmission-To-Cylinder Block Bolt	40-50 (54-68)
E4OD	
Crossmember-To-Frame Bolt	43-57 (58-77)
Oil Pan Bolt	10-12 (14-16)
Parking Brake Assembly Filler Plug	25-30 (34-41)
Parking Brake Assembly-To-Transmission Bolt [2]	25-43 (34-58)
Torque Converter-To-Drive Plate Nut	20-30 (27-41)
Transmission Mount-To-Crossmember Nut	60-80 (81-109)
Transmission-To-Cylinder Block Bolt	40-50 (54-68)

[1] – Tighten bolts to 97-115 INCH lbs. (11.0-13.0 N.m).
[2] – Always use NEW bolts. DO NOT reuse bolts.

GENERAL MOTORS

1992 MODEL COVERAGE

MODEL	BODY CODE	ENGINE [1]	ENGINE ID	FUEL SYSTEM	IGNITION SYSTEM
Astro & Safari	M, L	4.3L (LB4)	Z	TBI	Magnetic
		4.3L (L35)	W	CPI	Magnetic
Blazer & Yukon	K	5.7L (LO5)	K	TBI	Magnetic
		6.2L (LH6) [2]	C	Diesel	.....
		6.2L (LL4) [3]	J	Diesel	.....
Lumina APV, Silhouette & Trans Sport	U	3.1L (LG6)	D	TBI	Magnetic
		3.8L (L27)	L	PFI	C³I
Parcel/Delivery Commercial Van & Motorhome	P	4.3L (LB4)	Z	TBI	Magnetic
		5.7L (LO5)	K	TBI	Magnetic
		6.2L (LL4) [3]	J	Diesel	.....
		7.4L (L19)	N	TBI	Magnetic
Pickup (C/K 10/35) & Sierra	C, K	4.3L (LB4)	Z	TBI	Magnetic
		5.0L (LO3)	H	TBI	Magnetic
		5.7L (LO5)	K	TBI	Magnetic
		5.7L (LO5)	K	CNG [4]	Magnetic
		6.2L (LH6) [2]	C	Diesel	.....
		6.2L (LL4) [3]	J	Diesel	.....
		6.5L (L65)	F	Turbo Diesel	.....
		7.4L (L19)	N	TBI	Magnetic
Suburban	C, K	5.0L (LO3)	H	TBI	Magnetic
		5.7L (LO5)	K	TBI	Magnetic
		6.2L (LH6) [2]	C	Diesel	.....
		6.2L (LL4) [3]	J	Diesel	.....
		7.4L (L19)	N	TBI	Magnetic
S/T Series Blazer, Bravada, Jimmy, Pickup, Sonoma, Syclone & Typhoon	S, T	2.5L (L38) [5]	A	TBI	Magnetic
		2.8L (LL2)	R	TBI	Magnetic
		4.3L (LB4)	Z	TBI	Magnetic
		4.3L (LB4)	Z	PFI Turbo	Magnetic
		4.3L (L35)	W	CPI	Magnetic

[1] – Engine code is stamped on engine block. See ENGINE CODE LOCATION.
[2] – Light Duty emissions.
[3] – Heavy Duty emissions.
[4] – Compressed natural gas, limited information available.
[5] – 2WD only.

1992 ENGINE PERFORMANCE
General Motors Introduction (Cont.)

1992 MODEL COVERAGE (Cont.)

MODEL	BODY CODE	ENGINE [1]	ENGINE ID	FUEL SYSTEM	IGNITION SYSTEM
Van (10/35), Rally Van & Vandura	G	4.3L (LB4)	Z	TBI	Magnetic
		5.7L (LO5)	K	TBI	Magnetic
		6.2L (LH6) [2]	C	Diesel	.....
		6.2L (LL4) [3]	J	Diesel	.....
		7.4L (L19)	N	TBI	Magnetic

[1] – Engine code is stamped on engine block. See ENGINE CODE LOCATION.
[2] – Light Duty emissions.
[3] – Heavy Duty emissions.
[4] – Compressed natural gas, limited information available.
[5] – 2WD only.

VIN DEFINITION

2GCDC14K1NR100001
① ② ③ ④ ⑤ ⑥ ⑦⑧ ⑨⑩ ⑪ ⑫⑬⑭⑮⑯⑰

① Indicates Nation of Origin.
② Indicates Manufacturer.
③ Indicates Vehicle Division.
④ Indicates Carline Code.
⑤ Indicates Carline/Series.
⑥ Indicates Body Type.
⑦ Indicates Restraint System.
⑧ **Indicates Engine Code.**
⑨ Indicates Check Digit.
⑩ **Indicates Model Year.**
⑪ Indicates Assembly Plant.
⑫⑬⑭⑮⑯⑰ Indicates Plant Sequential Number.

MODEL YEAR VIN CODE APPLICATION

VIN Code	Model Year
L	1990
M	1991
N	1992

ENGINE CODE LOCATION [1]

LB4, LO3, LO5, L19 & L35 – On front of engine block, on right side above timing gear cover **OR** on left side of engine block, on engine-to-transmission mating flange.

L38 – On left side of engine block, at rear below cylinder head **OR** on left side of engine block, on engine-to-transmission mating flange.

LL2 – On front of engine block, on left side above timing gear cover **OR** on right side of engine block above engine mount.

LH6, LL4 & L65 – On front of engine block, right side of timing gear housing casting **OR** on top of engine block, near left cylinder head-to-engine block mating surface, at front **OR** on left side of engine block, on engine-to-transmission mating flange.

LG6 & L27 – On left side of engine block, on engine-to-transmission mating flange.

[1] – See ENGINE in 1992 MODEL COVERAGE table for engine code prefix.

1992 ENGINE PERFORMANCE
Emission Applications

1992 GENERAL MOTORS

Engine & Fuel System	Emission Control Systems & Devices

Light Duty Emissions

2.5L (151") 4-Cyl. TBI .... **PCV, TAC, EVAP, TWC, FR, EGR, SPK, O₂, CEC, SES,**
EVAP-VC, EGR-CS, SPK-EST

2.8L (170") V6 TBI .... **PCV, TAC, EVAP, TWC, FR, EGR, SPK, AP, O₂, CEC, SES,**
EGR-CS, AP-ACV, SPK-EST, SPK-ESC

3.1L (190") V6 TBI .... **PCV, TAC, EVAP, OC, TWC, FR, EGR, SPK, O₂, CEC, SES,**
EVAP-VC, EVAP-CPTVS, EGR-CS, SPK-EST, SPK-ESC

3.8 (231") V6 PFI .... **PCV, EVAP, TWC, FR, EGR, SPK, O₂, CEC, SES,**
EVAP-VC, EVAP-CPCS, EVAP-TPCV, EGR-CS, SPK-EST, SPK-ESC

4.3L (262") V6 CPI .... **PCV, EVAP, TWC, FR, EGR, SPK, O₂, CEC, SES,**
EVAP-VC, EVAP-CPCS, SPK-EST, SPK-ESC

4.3L (262") V6 TBI .... **PCV, TAC, EVAP, TWC, FR, EGR, SPK, ² ³ AP, O₂, CEC, SES,**
EVAP-VC, EGR-CS, AP-ACV, SPK-EST, SPK-ESC

4.3L (262") V6 Turbo .... **PCV, EVAP, TWC, FR, EGR, SPK, O₂, CEC, SES,**
EVAP-VC, EGR-EVRV, SPK-EST

5.0L (305") V8 TBI .... **PCV, TAC, EVAP, TWC, FR, EGR, SPK, ⁴ AP, O₂, CEC, SES,**
EVAP-VC, EGR-CS, AP-ACV, SPK-EST, SPK-ESC

5.7L (350") V8 TBI .... **PCV, TAC, EVAP, TWC, FR, EGR, SPK, ⁴ AP, O₂, CEC, SES,**
EVAP-VC, EGR-CS, AP-ACV, SPK-EST, SPK-ESC

6.2L (378") V8 Diesel .... **PCV, EGR, CEC, SES**
CD-REGVLV, EGR-CS, EGR-EPR, EGR-EVRV

6.5L (396") V8 Diesel .... **PCV, EGR, CEC, SES**
CD-REGVLV, EGR-CS, EGR-EPR, EGR-EVRV

7.4L (454") V8 TBI .... **PCV, TAC, EVAP, OC, FR, EGR, SPK, O₂, CEC, SES,**
EVAP-VC, EGR-CS, AP-ACV, SPK-EST, SPK-ESC

Heavy Duty Emissions ⁵

4.3L (262") V6 TBI .... **PCV, TAC, EVAP, OC, FR, EGR, SPK, O₂, CEC, SES,**
EVAP-VC, EGR-CS, SPK-EST, SPK-ESC

5.7L (350") V8 TBI .... **PCV, TAC, EVAP, OC, FR, EGR, SPK, O₂, CEC, SES,**
EVAP-VC, EGR-CS, SPK-EST, SPK-ESC

6.2L (378") V8 Diesel .... **PCV, EGR,**
CD-REGVLV, EGR-EPR

6.5L (396") V8 Diesel .... **PCV, EGR, CEC, SES**
CD-REGVLV, EGR-CS, EGR-EPR, EGR-EVRV

7.4L .... **PCV, TAC, EVAP, OC, FR, EGR, SPK, O₂, CEC, SES,**
EVAP-VC, EGR-CS, SPK-EST, SPK-ESC

¹ – Vehicles up to 8500 GVW.
² – Except Fed. & High Alt. (A/T).
³ – Except "S" & "T" Series.
⁴ – M/T only.
⁵ – Vehicles over 8500 GVW.

NOTE: For quick reference, major emission control systems and devices are listed in bold type; components and other related devices are listed in light type.

AP – Air Injection Pump System
AP-ACV – AP Air Control Valve
CD-REGVLV – Crankcase Depression Regulator Valve
CEC – Computerized Engine Controls
CPI – Central Port Injection
EGR – Exhaust Gas Recirculation
EGR-CS – EGR Control Solenoid
EGR-EPR – EGR Exhaust Pressure Regulator Valve
EGR-EVRV – EGR Electronic Vacuum Regulator Valve
EVAP – Evaporative Emission Control
EVAP-CPCS – EVAP Canister Purge Control Solenoid
EVAP-CPTVS – EVAP Canister Purge Thermal Valve Switch

EVAP-TPCV – EVAP Tank Pressure Control Valve
EVAP-VC – EVAP Vapor Canister
FR – Fill Pipe Restrictor
OC – Oxidation Catalyst
O₂ – Oxygen Sensor
PCV – Positive Crankcase Ventilation
PFI – Port Fuel Injection
SES – SERVICE ENGINE SOON Light
SPK – Spark Controls
SPK-ESC – SPK Electronic Spark Control
SPK-EST – SPK Electronic Spark Timing
TAC – Thermostatic Air Cleaner
TBI – Throttle Body Injection
TWC – Three-Way Catalyst

1992 ENGINE PERFORMANCE
Service & Adjustment Specifications

Astro, Bravada, Commercial Van, Jimmy, Lumina APV, Safari, Sierra, Silhouette, Sonoma, Suburban, Syclone, Trans Sport, Typhoon, Van, Yukon, "C" & "K" Series Blazer & Pickup, "S" & "T" Series Blazer & Pickup

INTRODUCTION

Use this article to quickly find specifications related to servicing and on-vehicle adjustments. This article may be used for quick reference when you are familiar with proper adjustment procedures and only need a specification.

MODEL IDENTIFICATION

Vehicle model can be identified by fifth character of Vehicle Identification Number (VIN), stamped on metal pad on top of left end of instrument panel, near windshield. See MODEL IDENTIFICATION table.

MODEL IDENTIFICATION

Series [1]	Model
"C"	2WD Pickup, Sierra & Suburban
"G"	RWD Van
"K"	4WD Blazer, Pickup, Sierra, Suburban & Yukon
"L"	All-Wheel Drive Astro & Safari
"M"	2WD Astro & Safari
"P"	Commercial Van/Motorhome
"S"	2WD Blazer, Jimmy, Pickup & Sonoma
"T"	Bravada, 4WD Blazer, Jimmy, Pickup, Sonoma, Syclone & Typhoon
"U"	Lumina APV, Silhouette & Trans Sport

[1] – Vehicle series is fifth character of VIN.

CAPACITIES

BATTERY SPECIFICATIONS

Application	Cold Crank Amps @ 0°F (-18°C)	Reserve Capacity Minutes
2.5L (VIN E)	525	90
2.8L (VIN R)	525	90
3.1L (VIN D)	525	90
3.8L (VIN L)	630	90
4.3L (VIN W & Z)	630	115
5.0L (VIN H)	630	115
5.7L (VIN K)	630	115
6.2L (VIN C & J)	570	90
6.5L (VIN F)	630	115
7.4L (VIN N)	630	115

FLUID CAPACITIES

Application	[1] Quantity Qts. (L)
Crankcase	
2.5L (VIN E)	[2] 3.5 (3.3)
2.8L (VIN R)	[2] 4.0 (3.8)
3.1L (VIN D)	[2] 4.0 (3.8)
3.8L (VIN L)	[2] 4.0 (3.8)
4.3L (VIN W & Z)	[2][3] 4.0 (3.8)
5.0L (VIN H)	[2] 4.0 (3.8)
5.7L (VIN K)	[2] 4.0 (3.8)
6.2L (VIN C & J)	7.0 (6.6)
6.5L (VIN F)	7.0 (6.6)
7.4L (VIN N)	[2] 6.0 (5.7)
Cooling System (Includes Heater) [4]	
2.5L (VIN E)	11.5 (11.0)
2.8L (VIN R)	10.5 (10.0)
3.1L (VIN D)	13.0 (12.3)
3.8L (VIN L)	12.0 (11.3)
4.3L (VIN W & Z)	
W/Rear Heater	16.5 (15.6)
W/O Rear Heater	13.5 (12.8)

[1] – Fluid capacities listed are approximate. Always fill to FULL mark.
[2] – Does not include oil filter capacity.
[3] – Use of synthetic 10W-30 motor oil is required on Turbo models.
[4] – Add 3 qts. (2.8L) coolant for models equipped with rear heater.

FLUID CAPACITIES (Cont.)

Application	[1] Quantity Qts. (L)
5.0L (VIN H)	18.0 (17.0)
5.7L (VIN K)	
Standard	18.0 (17.0)
Heavy Duty	27.0 (26.0)
6.2L (VIN C & J)	25.0 (23.5)
6.5L (VIN F)	27.0 (26.0)
7.4L (VIN N)	
Standard	23.0 (22.0)
Heavy Duty	27.0 (26.0)
Automatic Transaxle (Dexron-II) [5]	
3.1L (VIN D)	4.0 (3.8)
3.8L (VIN L)	6.0 (5.7)
Automatic Transmission (Dexron-II) [5]	
2.5L (VIN E)	5.0 (4.7)
2.8L (VIN R)	5.0 (4.7)
4.3L (VIN W & Z)	5.0 (4.7)
V8 Engines	5.0 (4.7)
Manual Transmission	
2.5L (VIN E)	[6] 2.2 (2.0)
2.8L (VIN R)	[9] 2.0 (1.9)
4.3L (VIN W & Z)	[9] 2.0 (1.9)
V8 Engines	
4-Speed	[7] 4.0 (3.8)
5-Speed	[8] 2.2 (2.0)

[5] – Drain and refill capacity only. Does not include torque converter.
[6] – Dexron-II.
[7] – GL-4.
[8] – Manual Transmission Fluid (T2850).
[9] – Manual Transmission Fluid (T2732).

QUICK-SERVICE

SERVICE INTERVALS & SPECIFICATIONS
REPLACEMENT INTERVALS

Component	Interval (Miles)
Air Filter	30,000
Coolant	30,000
Fuel Filter	[1] 60,000
Oil & Filter	[2][3] 7500
Spark Plugs	30,000

[1] – On diesel engines, replace every 30,000 miles.
[2] – On diesel engines, replace every 5000 miles.
[3] – On turbo engines, replace every 3000 miles.

BELT TENSION
BELT ADJUSTMENT

Application	[1] Tension Lbs. (kg)
All Models	

[1] – Serpentine belt tension is maintained automatically by a spring tensioned idler pulley. No adjustment is necessary.

MECHANICAL CHECKS

ENGINE COMPRESSION
COMPRESSION SPECIFICATIONS

Application	Compression Ratio
2.5L (VIN E)	8.3
2.8L (VIN R)	8.9
3.1L (VIN D)	8.9
3.8L (VIN L)	8.5
4.3L	
VIN W	9.1
VIN Z	9.3
VIN Z Turbo	8.35
5.0L (VIN H)	9.3
5.7L (VIN K)	[1] 9.1
6.2L Diesel (VIN C & J)	21.3
6.5L Turbo Diesel (VIN F)	21.0
7.4L (VIN N)	7.9

[1] – 8.3:1 – Over 8500 lbs. GVW.

VALVE CLEARANCE

NOTE: All models are equipped with hydraulic lifters. No adjustments are required.

IGNITION SYSTEM

IGNITION COIL
PICK-UP COIL RESISTANCE

Application	Ohms
All Models	500-1500

HIGH TENSION WIRE RESISTANCE
HIGH TENSION WIRE RESISTANCE

Application	Ohms
All Models	30,000 Maximum

SPARK PLUGS
SPARK PLUG TYPE

Application	AC
2.5L (VIN E)	R43CTS6
2.8L (VIN R)	R43TSK
3.1L (VIN D)	R43TS
3.8L (VIN L)	41-600
4.3L	
VIN W & Z	CR43TS
VIN Z Turbo	CR42TS
5.0L (VIN H)	CR43TS
5.7L (VIN K)	CR43TS
7.4L (VIN N)	CR43TS

SPARK PLUG SPECIFICATIONS

Application	Gap In. (mm)	Torque Ft. Lbs. (N.m)
2.5L (VIN E)	.060 (1.52)	17 (23)
2.8L (VIN R)	.045 (1.14)	22 (30)
3.1L (VIN D)	.045 (1.14)	18 (24)
3.8L (VIN L)	.060 (1.52)	20 (27)
4.3L		
VIN W	.045 (1.14)	22 (30)
VIN Z	.035 (0.89)	22 (30)
VIN Z Turbo	.045 (1.14)	11 (15)
5.0L (VIN H)	.035 (0.89)	22 (30)
5.7L (VIN K)	.035 (0.89)	22 (30)
7.4L (VIN N)	.035 (0.89)	22 (30)

FIRING ORDER & TIMING MARKS

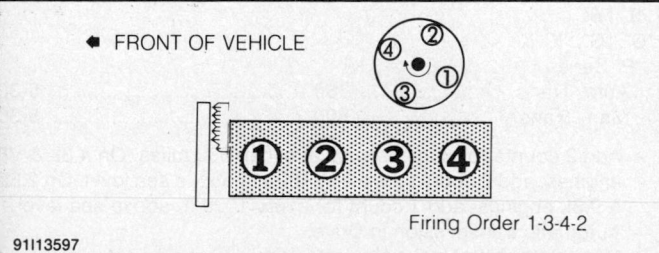

91I13597

Fig. 1: Firing Order & Timing Marks (2.5L)

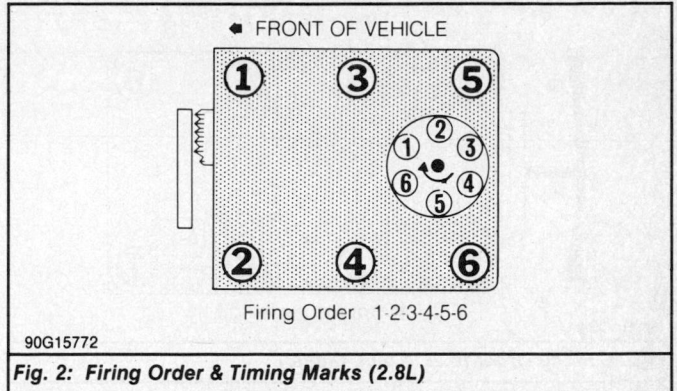

90G15772

Fig. 2: Firing Order & Timing Marks (2.8L)

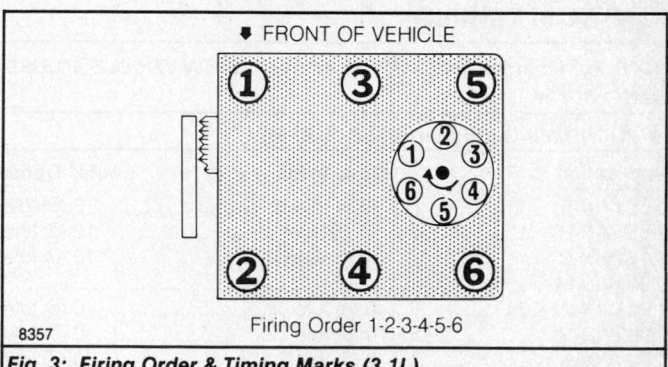

8357

Fig. 3: Firing Order & Timing Marks (3.1L)

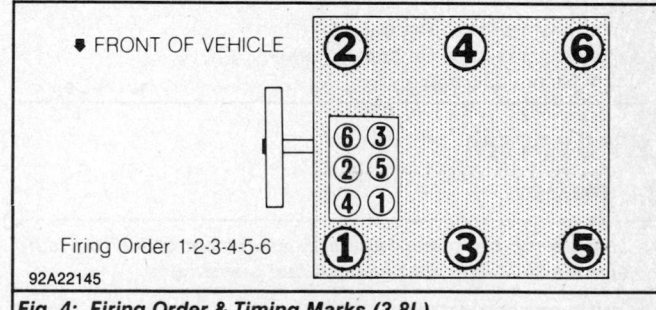

92A22145

Fig. 4: Firing Order & Timing Marks (3.8L)

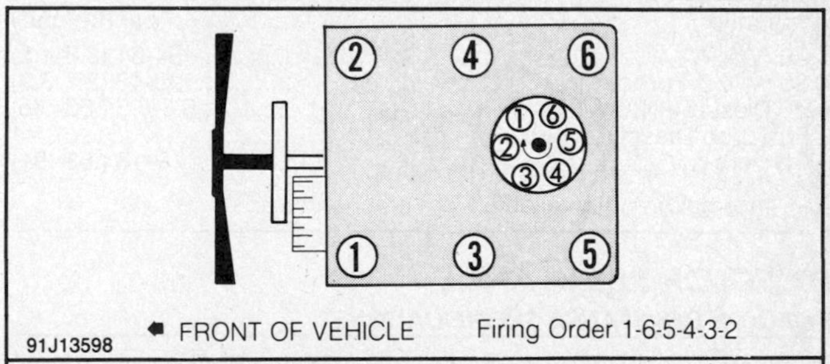

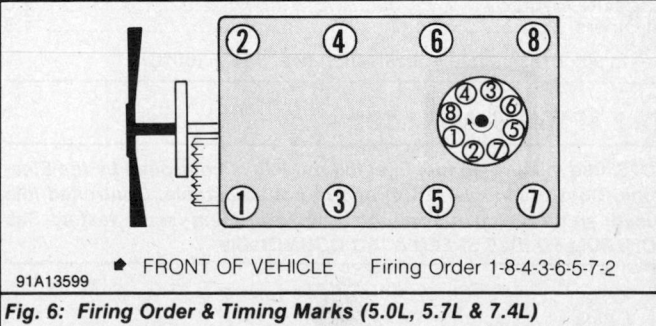

91J13598

Fig. 5: Firing Order & Timing Marks (4.3L)

91A13599

Fig. 6: Firing Order & Timing Marks (5.0L, 5.7L & 7.4L)

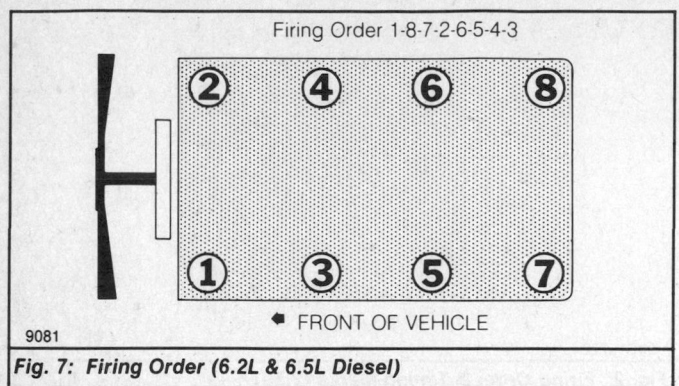

Firing Order 1-8-7-2-6-5-4-3

⟵ FRONT OF VEHICLE

9081

Fig. 7: Firing Order (6.2L & 6.5L Diesel)

IGNITION TIMING

NOTE: For timing adjustment procedures, see ON-VEHICLE ADJUSTMENTS article.

IGNITION TIMING (Degrees BTDC @ RPM)

Application	[1] Man. Trans.	[2] Auto. Trans.
2.5L (VIN E)	8 @ Idle	8 @ Idle
2.8L (VIN R)	10 @ Idle	10 @ Idle
3.1L (VIN D)	10 @ Idle	10 @ Idle
3.8L (VIN L)	[3]	[3]
4.3L (VIN W & Z)	0 @ Idle	0 @ Idle
5.0L (VIN H)	0 @ Idle	0 @ Idle
5.7L (VIN K)	0 @ Idle	0 @ Idle
7.4L (VIN N)	4 @ Idle	4 @ Idle

[1] – With transmission in Neutral.
[2] – With transmission in Neutral or Park.
[3] – Timing is not adjustable.

FUEL SYSTEM

FUEL PUMP

NOTE: Fuel pump performance is a measurement of fuel pressure and volume availability, not regulated fuel pressure.

FUEL PUMP PERFORMANCE

Application	psi (kg/cm²)
4.3L (VIN W)	54-64 (3.8-4.5)
4.3L (VIN Z Turbo)	38-43 (2.7-3.3)
6.2L Diesel (VIN C & J)	5.5-6.5 (.38-.45)
6.5L Turbo Diesel (VIN F)	[1]
All Others	9-13 (.63-.91)

[1] – Information not available from manufacturer.

INJECTOR RESISTANCE
INJECTOR RESISTANCE SPECIFICATIONS

Application	[1] Resistance (Ohms)
3.1L (VIN D)	1.2
4.3L (VIN Z Turbo)	2.0
All Others	1.3

[1] – Injector resistance specification is at 140°F (60°C).

IDLE SPEED & MIXTURE

NOTE: Idle mixture on fuel injected models is controlled by the Electronic Control Module (ECM) and is not adjustable. Controlled idle speed and IAC count can be checked using scan tester. See CONTROLLED IDLE SPEED & IAC COUNT table.

CONTROLLED IDLE SPEED & IAC COUNT

Application	Idle RPM	[1] IAC Counts
2.5L TBI		
"S" Series		
Auto. Trans. [2]	800	15-40
Man. Trans. [3]	900	5-20
2.8L TBI		
"S" Series		
Auto. Trans. [2]	800	5-20
3.1L TBI		
"U" Series		
Auto. Trans. [2]	600-700	5-15
3.8L PFI		
"U" Series		
Auto. Trans. [2]	650-750	16-20
4.3L CPI		
"L" Series		
Auto. Trans. [2]	625	5-50
"M", "S" & "T" Series		
Auto. Trans. [2]	550	5-40
4.3L PFI Turbo		
"S" & "T" Series		
Auto. Trans. [2]	[4]	1-50
4.3L TBI		
"C" & "K" Series		
Auto. Trans. [2][5]	537	5-30
Auto. Trans. [2][5]	650	20-35
Man. Trans. [3]	550	2-20
"G" Series		
Auto. Trans. [2]	538	5-30
Man. Trans. [3]	650	5-30
"L" Series		
Auto. Trans. [2]	625	5-50
Man. Trans. [3]	600	3-30
"M" Series		
Auto. Trans. [2]	538	5-30
"P" Series		
Auto. Trans. [2]	650	20-35
5.0L TBI		
"C" & "K" Series		
Auto. Trans. [2]	500	5-30
Man. Trans. [3]	600	5-30
5.7L TBI		
"C", "G", "K" & "P" Series		
(Under 8500 GVW)		
Auto. Trans. [2]	525	5-30
Man. Trans. [3]	600	5-30
(Over 8500 GVW)		
Auto. Trans. [2]	550	5-30
Man. Trans. [3]	600	5-30
7.4L TBI		
"C", "G", "K" & "P" Series		
Auto. Trans. [2]	750	5-30
Man. Trans. [3]	800	5-30

[1] – Add 2 counts for engines with less than 500 miles. On 4.3L & V8 engines, add 2 counts for every 1000 ft. above sea level. On 2.5L & 2.8L engines, add 1 count for every 1000 ft. above sea level.
[2] – Automatic transmission in Drive.
[3] – Manual transmission in Neutral.
[4] – Set to ±50 RPM from desired idle speed in Drive.
[5] – Calibration identification not given by manufacturer. IAC count and actual RPM should correspond to one of these calibrations

MINIMUM IDLE SPEED

NOTE: Minimum idle speed adjustment can only be performed on the 7.4L engines. For minimum idle speed adjustment procedures, see ON-VEHICLE ADJUSTMENTS article.

MINIMUM IDLE SPEED [1]

Application	RPM
7.4L	
Auto. Trans. [2]	600-650
Man. Trans. [3]	675-725

[1] – Idle speed with seated IAC is lower than specified, if engine has less than 500 miles or when checked at altitudes above 1500 feet.
[2] – Automatic transmission in Drive.
[3] – Manual transmission in Neutral.

THROTTLE POSITION SENSOR (TPS)

NOTE: TPS is adjustable only on 2.8L (VIN R) and 6.2L Diesel engines. For further testing, see appropriate SELF-DIAGNOSTICS article.

TPS ADJUSTMENT VOLTAGE

Application	[1] Voltage
2.8L (VIN R)	.42-.45
6.2L Diesel (VIN C & J)	[2] .63

[1] – At idle RPM or closed throttle.
[2] – This is a TPS voltage ratio. For adjustment procedure, see ON-VEHICLE ADJUSTMENTS article.

1992 ENGINE PERFORMANCE
On-Vehicle Adjustments

Astro, Bravada, Commercial Van, Jimmy, Lumina APV, Safari, Sierra, Silhouette, Sonoma, Suburban, Syclone, Trans Sport, Typhoon, Van, Yukon, "C" & "K" Series Blazer & Pickup, "S" & "T" Series Blazer & Pickup

ENGINE MECHANICAL

Before performing any on-vehicle adjustments to fuel or ignition systems, ensure engine mechanical condition is okay.

VALVE CLEARANCE

NOTE: All models use hydraulic lifters. No adjustments are required.

IGNITION TIMING (GASOLINE)

4-CYLINDER IGNITION TIMING

2.5L (VIN E) – 1) Set parking brake, block drive wheels and place transmission in Neutral or Park. Warm engine to normal operating temperature. Turn A/C off (if equipped). Ensure SERVICE ENGINE SOON light is off.

2) Connect jumper between ALDL connector terminals "A" and "B". SERVICE ENGINE SOON light should begin flashing. Connect timing light.

3) Note average timing of cylinders No. 1 and 4 and adjust to specification, if necessary. See 4-CYLINDER IGNITION TIMING table. Remove jumper from ALDL connector. Ensure SERVICE ENGINE SOON light is off.

4-CYLINDER IGNITION TIMING (DEGREES BTDC @ RPM)

Application	Man. Trans.	Auto. Trans.
2.5L (VIN E)	8 @ Idle	8 @ Idle

V6 IGNITION TIMING

All Models (Except 3.8L – VIN L) – 1) Set parking brake, block drive wheels and place transmission in Neutral or Park. Warm engine to normal operating temperature. Turn A/C off (if equipped). Ensure SERVICE ENGINE SOON light is off.

2) Disconnect Tan/Black Electronic Spark Timing (EST) by-pass connector wire. On 4.3L, by-pass connector is on wiring harness conduit near distributor. On other models, by-pass connector is located near heater housing in passenger compartment. On all models, DO NOT disconnect 4-wire connector at distributor.

3) Connect timing light to No. 1 spark plug wire. Check timing and adjust if necessary. See V6 IGNITION TIMING table. Reconnect EST by-pass connector, and clear ECM trouble code.

V6 IGNITION TIMING (DEGREES BTDC @ RPM)

Application	Man. Trans.	Auto. Trans.
2.8L (VIN R)	10 @ Idle	10 @ Idle
3.1L (VIN D)	10 @ Idle	10 @ Idle
3.8L (VIN L)	[1]	[1]
4.3L (VIN W & Z)	0 @ Idle	0 @ Idle

[1] – Ignition timing is not adjustable (DIS).

V8 IGNITION TIMING

All Models (Except Diesel) – 1) Set parking brake, block drive wheels and place transmission in Neutral or Park. Warm engine to normal operating temperature. Turn A/C off (if equipped). Ensure SERVICE ENGINE SOON light is not on.

2) Disconnect Tan/Black Electronic Spark Timing (EST) by-pass connector wire located near distributor. DO NOT disconnect 4-wire connector at distributor.

3) Connect timing light to No. 1 spark plug wire. Check timing and adjust if necessary. See V8 IGNITION TIMING table. Reconnect EST by-pass connector, and clear ECM trouble code.

V8 IGNITION TIMING (DEGREES BTDC @ RPM)

Application	Man. Trans.	Auto. Trans.
5.0L (VIN H)	0 @ Idle	0 @ Idle
5.7L (VIN K)	0 @ Idle	0 @ Idle
7.4L (VIN N)	4 @ Idle	4 @ Idle

INJECTION PUMP TIMING (DIESEL)
6.2L & 6.5L

1) Original factory injection pump timing is set by using static timing mark (a circle scribed across both pump flange and front housing) or static timing mark (straight line scribed across both pump flange and front housing).

NOTE: A service/replacement pump will not be marked with dynamic timing mark (circle) and should be timed using the static timing mark (line).

2) To properly set timing, 2 halves of dynamic timing mark (circle) or static timing mark (line) must be aligned. Engine must not be running while injection timing is set.

3) Check alignment of injection pump timing marks on top of engine front cover and injection pump flange. If timing marks are not aligned, loosen 3 retaining nuts and align mark on injection pump with mark on front cover. Tighten nuts to **30 ft. lbs. (41 N.m)**. Adjust throttle linkage.

IDLE SPEED & MIXTURE
IDLE SPEED & MIXTURE (GASOLINE)

NOTE: DO NOT attempt to adjust idle mixture and idle speed, which are controlled by the Electronic Control Module (ECM). Incorrect idle speeds are normally caused by dirty throttle plate or vacuum leaks. Ensure all vacuum components are functioning properly.

NOTE: Controlled idle speed and IAC count can be checked using scan tester. See CONTROLLED IDLE SPEED & IAC COUNT table. Minimum idle speed adjustment can only be performed on the 7.4L engines. See MINIMUM IDLE SPEED ADJUSTMENT (7.4L ONLY).

Controlled Idle Speed Check – 1) Ensure no trouble code(s) are present, IAC system has been checked and ignition timing is correct. Block drive wheel and apply parking brake. Connect scan tester to ALDL connector with scan tester in "Open Mode".

2) Start engine and bring to normal operating temperature. Check for correct state of Park/Neutral switch on scan tester. Check if idle speed and IAC valve pintle position (counts) are as specified. See CONTROLLED IDLE SPEED & IAC COUNT table.

3) If idle speed is not within specification, refer to TROUBLE SHOOTING – NO CODES article. On 7.4L engines, perform MINIMUM IDLE SPEED ADJUSTMENT.

CONTROLLED IDLE SPEED & IAC COUNT

Application	Idle RPM	[1] IAC Counts
2.5L TBI		
"S" Series		
Auto. Trans. [2]	800	15-40
Man. Trans. [3]	900	5-20
2.8L TBI		
"S" Series		
Auto. Trans. [2]	800	5-20
3.1L TBI		
"U" Series		
Auto. Trans. [2]	600-700	5-15
3.8L PFI		
"U" Series		
Auto. Trans. [2]	650-750	16-20

[1] – Add 2 counts for engines with less than 500 miles. On 4.3L & V engines, add 2 counts for every 1000 ft. above sea level. On 2.5 & 2.8L engines, add 1 count for every 1000 ft. above sea level.
[2] – Automatic transmission in Drive.
[3] – Manual transmission in Neutral.

CONTROLLED IDLE SPEED & IAC COUNT (Cont.)

Application	Idle RPM	[1] IAC Counts
4.3L CPI		
"L" Series		
Auto. Trans. [2]	625	5-50
"M", "S" & "T" Series		
Auto. Trans. [2]	550	5-40
4.3L PFI Turbo		
"S" & "T" Series		
Auto. Trans. [2]	[4]	1-50
4.3L TBI		
"C" & "K" Series		
Auto. Trans. [2][5]	537	5-30
Auto. Trans. [2][5]	650	20-35
Man. Trans. [3]	550	2-20
"G" Series		
Auto. Trans. [2]	538	5-30
Man. Trans. [3]	650	5-30
"L" Series		
Auto. Trans. [2]	625	5-50
Man. Trans. [3]	600	3-30
"M" Series		
Auto. Trans. [2]	538	5-30
"P" Series		
Auto. Trans. [2]	650	20-35
5.0L TBI		
"C" & "K" Series		
Auto. Trans. [2]	500	5-30
Man. Trans. [3]	600	5-30
5.7L TBI		
"C", "G", "K" &		
"P" Series		
(Under 8500 GVW)		
Auto. Trans. [2]	525	5-30
Man. Trans. [3]	600	5-30
(Over 8500 GVW)		
Auto. Trans. [2]	550	5-30
Man. Trans. [3]	600	5-30
7.4L TBI		
"C", "G", "K" &		
"P" Series		
Auto. Trans. [2]	750	5-30
Man. Trans. [3]	800	5-30

[1] – Add 2 counts for engines with less than 500 miles. On 4.3L & V8 engines, add 2 counts for every 1000 ft. above sea level. On 2.5L & 2.8L engines, add 1 count for every 1000 ft. above sea level.
[2] – Automatic transmission in Drive.
[3] – Manual transmission in Neutral.
[4] – Set to ±50 RPM from desired idle speed in Drive.
[5] – Calibration identification not given by manufacturer. IAC count and actual RPM should correspond to one of these calibrations.

Minimum Idle Speed Adjustment (7.4L Only) – 1) Check controlled idle speed and perform IAC system check first. Refer to CONTROLLED IDLE SPEED CHECK. Set parking brake and block drive wheels. Start engine and operate to normal operating temperature, about 185-212°F (85-100°C). Turn engine off.
2) Remove air cleaner, adapter and gaskets. Ensure that throttle lever is not binding TV or cruise control cables. Using a jumper, ground ALDL diagnostic connector. Turn ignition on (engine off). Wait for at least 10 seconds (this allows IAC pintle to extend and seat in throttle body).
3) Disconnect IAC harness connector. Remove jumper from ALDL diagnostic connector. Connect scan tester to ALDL diagnostic connector. Place scan tester in "Open Mode". Place transmission in neutral. Start engine and allow engine RPM to stabilize. Check engine RPM. See MINIMUM IDLE SPEED table. Disregard IAC count on scan tester with IAC disconnected.
If idle speed is not as specified, remove stop screw plug by using a awl. With engine at normal operating temperature, adjust stop screw to obtain nominal RPM with seated IAC valve. Turn ignition off.

Reconnect IAC harness connector. Disconnect scan tester. Reseal stop screw hole and reinstall air cleaner assembly.
5) Reset IAC valve. To reset IAC valve, turn ignition on (engine off) for 5 seconds. Turn ignition off for 10 seconds. Start engine and check for proper idle operation. Repeat procedure if proper idle operation is not obtained.

MINIMUM IDLE SPEED [1]

Application	RPM
7.4L	
Auto. Trans. [2]	600-650
Man. Trans. [3]	675-725

[1] – Idle speed with seated IAC is lower than specified, if engine has less than 500 miles or when checked at altitudes above 1500 feet.
[2] – Automatic transmission in Drive.
[3] – Manual transmission in Neutral.

IDLE SPEED (DIESEL)

Curb Idle – Set parking brake and block drive wheels. Warm engine to normal operating temperature. Install Tachometer (J-26925). Ensure air cleaner is in place and all accessories are turned off. Adjust curb (low) idle speed to specifications by turning curb idle speed screw on fuel injection pump. See Fig. 1. See IDLE SPEED (RPM) specifications table.

Fast Idle – 1) Set parking brake and block drive wheels. Warm engine to normal operating temperature. Install Tachometer (J-26925). Ensure air cleaner is in place and all accessories must turned off.
2) Remove connector from fast idle solenoid. See Fig. 1. To energize solenoid, connect jumper wire from battery positive terminal to fast idle solenoid terminal. Open throttle momentarily to energize and fully extend fast idle solenoid plunger.
3) Adjust extended fast idle solenoid plunger by turning plunger hex head to obtain fast idle speed. See IDLE SPEED (RPM) specifications table. Turn off engine. Remove jumper wire and test equipment. Install fast idle solenoid connector.

IDLE SPEED (RPM)

Application	Curb Idle	Fast Idle
6.2L	650	800
6.5L	700	800

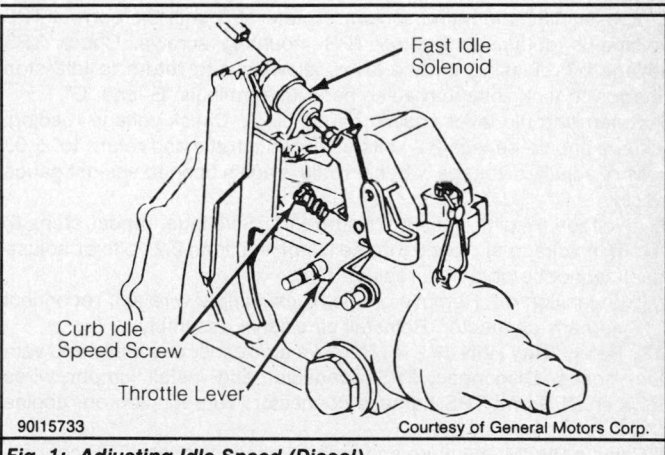

90I15733   Courtesy of General Motors Corp.

Fig. 1: Adjusting Idle Speed (Diesel)

THROTTLE POSITION SENSOR (TPS)

TPS ADJUSTMENT (GASOLINE)

NOTE: On all models except 2.8L engine (VIN R), Throttle Position Sensor (TPS) is NOT adjustable. Resistance values given in TPS OUTPUT VOLTAGE table are for reference only. If resistance value is not as specified, replace TPS. For testing procedures, refer to appropriate SELF-DIAGNOSTICS or SYSTEM & COMPONENT TESTING article.

2.8L (VIN R) – Throttle Position Sensor (TPS) can also be adjusted using a scan tester. Perform this check only when throttle body parts have been replaced or after minimum airflow has been adjusted.

1) Install 3 jumper wires between TPS and TPS wiring harness connector. Jumpers can be made using the following General Motors parts: Terminals No. 1214836 and 12014837.

2) Turn ignition switch to ON position. DO NOT start engine. Using a DVOM, connect test leads to Dark Blue and Black wire terminals. With throttle at closed position, TPS voltage should be **.42-.45 volt.**

3) If voltage reading is not as specified, rotate TPS until specified voltage is obtained. See TPS OUTPUT VOLTAGE table. If specified voltage cannot be obtained, replace TPS.

4) Tighten screws and recheck readings. Turn ignition off. Remove jumper wires and reconnect harness connector to TPS.

TPS OUTPUT VOLTAGE (GASOLINE)

Application	[1] Voltage
2.5L (VIN E) [2]	1.25 or less
2.8L (VIN R)	.42-.45
3.1L (VIN D) [2]	1.25 Or Less
4.3L (VIN W & Z) [2]	1.25 Or Less
5.0L (VIN H) [2]	1.25 Or Less
5.7L (VIN K) [2]	1.25 Or Less
5.7L CNG (VIN K) [2]	1.25 Or Less
7.4L (VIN N) [2]	1.25 Or Less

[1] – At idle RPM or closed throttle.
[2] – Not adjustable.

TPS ADJUSTMENT (DIESEL)

6.2L Light Duty (VIN C) – **1)** Remove air cleaner assembly and vacuum hoses. Disconnect TPS connector and install jumper wires between TPS and TPS harness connector. Turn ignition on, engine off.

2) Install .646 Gauge Block (J-33043-2) between gauge boss on injection pump and WOT stop screw on throttle shaft. See Fig. 2. Rotate throttle lever and hold the WOT stop screw against the gauge block.

3) Using a DVOM, measure and record voltage between TPS connector terminals "A" and "C". This is the TPS reference voltage. Measure and record voltage between TPS terminals "B" and "C". This is TPS voltage.

4) The TPS voltage should be within ±3 volts of TPS reference voltage. If voltage reading is not within tolerance, adjust TPS.

5) Loosen TPS mounting screws. Rotate TPS until the correct TPS voltage is obtained. Tighten TPS mounting screws. Check TPS voltage by releasing throttle lever, allowing it to return to idle stop position. Check voltage reading between terminals "B" and "C".

6) Return throttle lever against gauge block. Check voltage reading. Voltage should be less 2.2 volts at closed throttle and return to ±.03 volts of adjusted voltage, when throttle is again opened against gauge block.

7) If voltage reading does not return to TPS voltage, repeat steps **5)** and **6)**. If voltage at closed throttle is not less than 2.2 volts or adjustment cannot be obtained, replace TPS.

8) Turn ignition off. Remove gauge block, jumper wire and reconnect TPS harness connector. Reinstall air cleaner assembly.

6.2L Heavy Duty (VIN J) – **1)** Remove air cleaner assembly and vacuum hoses. Disconnect TPS connector and install jumper wires between TPS and TPS harness connector. Turn ignition on, engine off.

2) Using a DVOM, measure and record voltage between TPS connector terminals "A" and "C". This is the TPS reference voltage. Perform the following calculations:

• Reference voltage x 0.33 = Desired TPS voltage setting. Record the desired TPS voltage setting.

3) Insert a .646" Gauge Block (J-33043-2) between gauge boss on pump and WOT stop screw on throttle lever. See Fig. 2. Rotate throttle lever towards the WOT position, so gauge block is held firmly in place.

4) Measure voltage between TPS terminals "B" and "C". This is the TPS voltage. Voltage must be within ±1 percent of the desired TPS voltage setting from step **2)**. If TPS voltage is within tolerance,

proceed to step **6)**. If TPS voltage setting is not within tolerance, go to next step.

5) To adjust TPS, loosen TPS mounting screws and rotate TPS until desired TPS voltage is obtained. Tighten TPS mounting screws and recheck voltage reading. Replace TPS assembly, if adjustment is not possible.

NOTE: Switch point must be set only while rotating TPS body in clockwise direction.

6) Release throttle lever and allow lever to return to idle position. Open throttle lever back against gauge block and check if TPS voltage is within TPS reference voltage, see step **2)**. If reading is not within tolerance, replace TPS assembly.

7) Turn ignition off. Remove gauge block, jumper from TPS and wiring harness, and reconnect TPS harness connector. Reinstall air cleaner assembly.

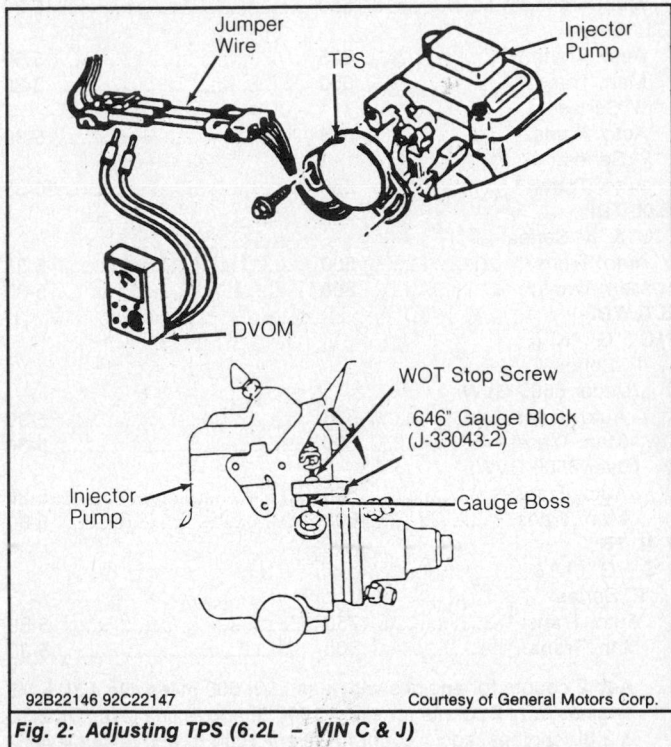

92B22146 92C22147   Courtesy of General Motors Corp.

Fig. 2: Adjusting TPS (6.2L – VIN C & J)

WASTEGATE ACTUATOR ADJUSTMENT (TURBO)

CAUTION: Improper wastegate actuator adjustment can severely limit performance or cause overboost, resulting in fuel shutoff.

4.3L PFI (VIN Z) – **1)** Remove passenger side wheelwell panel, retaining wire from actuator pin and boost control hose from wastegate actuator.

2) Install Turbocharger Pressure Gauge (J-35691) to hose connection on wastegate actuator. Ensure dial reads zero.

3) Install Dial Indicator (J-8001-3) on end of wastegate actuator lever. Ensure dial reads zero. Apply **4.5-5.0 psi (.31-.35 kg/cm²)** air pressure to Pressure Gauge (J-35691). Check dial indicator.

4) If dial indicator reads greater than **0.02-0.06" (0.5-1.5 mm)**, readjust rod by shortening it a half-turn at rod end. If dial indicator reads less than **0.02-0.06" (0.5-1.5 mm)**, readjust rod by lengthening it a half-turn at rod end.

5) Recheck actuator travel at **4.5-5.0 psi (.31-.35 kg/cm²)** air pressure. Repeat adjustment until specifications are met. Replace wastegate actuator if specifications cannot be met or if wastegate does not open at all.

Astro, Bravada, Commercial Van, Jimmy, Lumina APV, Safari, Sierra, Silhouette, Sonoma, Suburban, Syclone, Trans Sport, Typhoon, Van, Yukon, "C" & "K" Series Blazer & Pickup, "S" & "T" Series Blazer & Pickup

INTRODUCTION

This article covers basic description and operation of engine performance-related systems and components. Read this article before diagnosing vehicles or systems with which you are not completely familiar.

AIR INDUCTION SYSTEM

TURBOCHARGER (4.3L)

The turbocharger is basically an air compressor or air pump. Its major parts include a turbine wheel, shaft, compressor wheel, turbine housing, compressor housing and center housing. The center housing contains a turbine seal, compressor seal and bearings.

The internal combustion engine is an air-breathing machine. The amount of power produced by the engine is determined not by the amount of fuel it uses, but by the amount of air it breathes in a certain period of time. Air must mix with fuel to complete the combustion cycle. When the air/fuel ratio reaches a certain point, additional fuel produces only black smoke, not more power; the denser the smoke, the more the engine is being overfueled.

The turbocharger increases the quantity and density of air in the engine combustion chambers. The increased volume of air allows more fuel to be used while maintaining the proper air/fuel ratio. The increased air and fuel allows the engine to produce more horsepower than a non-turbocharged engine.

The turbocharger uses the normally wasted energy in the engine exhaust gas. As load on the engine is increased and the throttle is opened wider, more air/fuel mixture flows into the combustion chambers. The increased flow is burned and produces a larger volume of exhaust gas. The gas enters the exhaust manifolds, flows through the turbocharger turbine housing and turns the turbine wheel and shaft. The shaft is coupled to the compressor wheel. The compressor wheel compresses the air it receives and sends it to the intake manifold. The higher pressure in the intake manifold allows a denser charge to enter the combustion chambers.

Intake manifold pressure, or "boost", is controlled by an exhaust by-pass valve, or wastegate. The wastegate is operated by a spring-loaded diaphragm-type actuator which responds to boost pressure. The actuator, which is controlled by the wastegate solenoid, opens the wastegate to allow exhaust gases to by-pass the turbine wheel, thereby maintaining the correct boost level. The wastegate solenoid is controlled by the ECM through a turbo boost relay.

CAUTION: On a turbocharged engine, any alteration to the air intake or exhaust system which upsets the air flow balance may result in serious damage to the engine.

The rotating assembly in the turbocharger can reach speeds of 130,000-140,000 RPM. An adequate supply of clean engine oil is essential for cooling and lubrication. Whenever a basic engine bearing has been damaged or the turbocharger is replaced, the oil and oil filter should be changed and the turbocharger flushed with clean engine oil.

CAUTION: Interruption or contamination of the oil supply to the turbocharger bearings can result in major turbocharger damage.

Charge Air Cooler – Before entering the combustion chambers, the air from the turbocharger is routed through an air-to-water charge air cooler. As the turbocharger compresses air, the air's temperature rises. The heated, compressed air then flows through the charge air cooler core, where it is cooled by coolant passing through the charge air cooler. The cooler, denser air allows a denser air/fuel charge to enter the combustion chambers, producing significantly more power.

The hot coolant is then routed through the charge air cooler radiator, where it releases the heat it absorbed at the charge air cooler. An electric pump mounted to the charge air cooler radiator circulates coolant through the system. Pump is controlled by the ECM through a charge air cooler air pump relay.

AIRFLOW SENSING

Mass Airflow (3.8L) – Sensor measures flow of air entering the engine in grams per second. This measurement of airflow is a reflection of engine load (throttle opening and air volume), similar to the relationship of engine load to MAP or vacuum sensor signal. Mass Airflow (MAF) signal should remain relatively constant at cruise, gradually changing with throttle angle and rapidly changing on sudden acceleration.

The ECM uses MAF information to control fuel delivery. Sensor produces a frequency signal which cannot be easily measured in testing (32-150 Hertz). This varying signal is proportional to airflow.

Speed Density (Except 3.8L) – All gasoline vehicles except 3.8L are equipped with a MAP sensor, and use the speed density method to compute the airflow rate. ECM uses manifold pressure to calculate the airflow rate. The MAP sensor responds to manifold vacuum changes due to engine load and speed changes. The ECM sends a voltage signal to the MAP sensor. Manifold pressure changes result in resistance changes in the MAP sensor.

By monitoring MAP sensor signal voltage, the ECM determines manifold pressure. If MAP sensor fails, the ECM supplies a fixed MAP value, and uses the TPS to control fuel.

2.5L and 4.3L turbo models also use a Manifold Air Temperature (MAT) sensor. Sensor allows ECM to determine intake air temperature. ECM uses signal to delay EGR until intake air temperature reaches about 40°F (5°C). If intake air temperature becomes excessively high, ECM compensates by slightly retarding timing.

COMPUTERIZED ENGINE CONTROLS (GASOLINE)

The computerized engine control system monitors and controls a variety of engine/vehicle functions. The computerized engine control system is primarily an emission control system designed to maintain a 14.7:1 air/fuel ratio under most operating conditions. When the ideal air/fuel ratio is maintained, the 3-way catalytic converter can control oxides of nitrogen (NOx), hydrocarbon (HC) and carbon monoxide (CO) emissions.

The computerized engine control system consists of Electronic Control Module (ECM), input devices (sensor and switch input signals) and output signals.

ELECTRONIC CONTROL MODULE (ECM)

NOTE: Some models use a Powertrain Control Module (PCM). The difference between an ECM and PCM is the PCM also controls electronic transmission internals and cruise control system. Unless stated otherwise, references to ECM also apply to PCM-equipped vehicles.

ECM is located in passenger compartment. For exact location of ECM, see ECM LOCATION in appropriate SELF-DIAGNOSTICS article or under COMPONENT LOCATIONS in SYSTEM & COMPONENT TESTING article. The ECM consists of the Arithmetic Logic Unit (ALU), Central Processing Unit (CPU), power supply and system memories.

The ECM has a "learning" ability which allows it to make minor corrections for fuel system variations. If battery power is interrupted, a vehicle performance change may be noticed. ECM corrects itself, and normal performance returns if vehicle is allowed to "relearn" optimum control conditions. "Relearning" occurs when vehicle is driven at normal operating temperature under part throttle, moderate acceleration and idle conditions.

Arithmetic Logic Unit (ALU) – This internal component of the ECM converts electrical signals received from various engine sensors into digital signals for use by the CPU.

Central Processing Unit (CPU) – CPU uses digital signals to perform all mathematical computations and logic functions necessary to deliver proper air/fuel mixture. CPU also calculates spark timing and idle speed. The CPU controls operation of emission control, "closed loop" fuel control and diagnostic system.

Power Supply – Power for ECM reference output signals (5 volts) and control devices (12 volts) is received from the battery through ignition circuit when ignition switch is in ON position. Keep-alive memory power is received directly from the battery.

Memories – ECM uses 5 types of memory:

* **Read Only Memory (ROM)** – ROM is programmed information which only ECM can read. The ROM program cannot be changed. If battery voltage is removed, ROM information is retained.

* **Random Access Memory (RAM)** – RAM is the scratch pad for the CPU. Data input, diagnostic codes and results of calculations are constantly updated and temporarily stored in RAM. If battery voltage is removed from ECM, all information stored in RAM is lost.

* **Programmable Read Only Memory (PROM)** – PROM is factory programmed engine calibration data which "tailors" ECM for specific transmission, engine, emission, vehicle weight and rear axle ratio application. The PROM can be removed from ECM. If battery voltage is removed, PROM information is retained.

* **Calibration Package (CALPAC)** – Some models use a PROM and a CALPAC. CALPAC provides fuel delivery back-up so engine runs in case of PROM or ECM failure. Any time ECM is replaced, PROM and CALPAC must both be installed into replacement ECM. If battery voltage is removed, CALPAC information is retained.

* **Memory Calibration (MEM-CAL)** – Some vehicles may use a ECM containing a MEM-CAL unit. This assembly contains functions of PROM and CALPAC. If power to ECM is removed, MEM-CAL information is retained. MEM-CAL also contains an internal ESC module on models equipped with ESC.

NOTE: Components are grouped into 2 categories. The first category is INPUT DEVICES, consisting of components which control or produce voltage signals monitored by the control unit. The second category is OUTPUT SIGNALS, consisting of components controlled by the control unit.

INPUT DEVICES

Vehicles are equipped with different combinations of input devices. Not all devices are used on all models. To determine the input device usage on a specific model, see appropriate wiring diagram in WIRING DIAGRAMS article in ENGINE PERFORMANCE. The available input signals include:

A/C On (A/C Request) Signal – The air conditioner "on" switch is mounted in instrument panel. This switch provides a simple "on" ("A/C request") signal, which is monitored by the ECM. The ECM uses this signal to determine control of the A/C clutch relay (if equipped) and to adjust idle speed when air conditioner compressor clutch is engaged. On some models, ECM may also activate radiator cooling fan when this signal is present. If this signal is not present on A/C equipped vehicles, vehicle may idle rough when A/C compressor cycles. To check function of the A/C switch, perform functional check of switch. See SYSTEM & COMPONENT TESTING article.

Battery Voltage – Battery voltage is monitored by ECM. If battery voltage swings low, a weak spark or improper fuel control may result. To compensate for low battery voltage, ECM may increase idle speed, advance ignition timing, increase ignition dwell or enrich the air/fuel mixture. If voltage swings high, ECM may set a charging system fault code and turn on SERVICE ENGINE SOON light. If voltage signal swings excessively low (less than 9 volts) or excessively high (16 volts, most models), ECM shuts down for as long as condition exists. If condition is short-term, SERVICE ENGINE SOON light flickers and vehicle may stumble. Vehicle stalls if condition lasts long enough.

Brake Switch Feedback – On models equipped with cruise control systems, ECM may monitor the brake switch circuit to determine when to engage and disengage cruise control. On vehicles equipped with a Torque Converter Clutch (TCC), one circuit of brake switch is in series with the power supply for the TCC solenoid located in automatic transmission.

Coolant Temperature Sensor (CTS) – The CTS is a thermistor (temperature sensitive resistor) located in an engine coolant passage. The ECM supplies and monitors a 5-volt signal to CTS. This monitored 5-volt signal is then modified by resistance of the CTS. When coolant temperatures are low, CTS resistance is high and the ECM sees a high monitored voltage signal. When coolant temperatures are high, CTS resistance is low and the ECM sees a low monitored voltage. When fully warmed, CTS should reflect a temperature of at least 185°F (85°C).

Coolant temperature input is used in the control of fuel delivery, ignition timing, idle speed, emission control devices and converter clutch application. A CTS which is out of calibration will not set a trouble code, but can cause fuel delivery and driveability problems. A coolant sensor circuit problem should set a related trouble code.

Crankshaft Position Sensor – Crankshaft position sensor, used on 3.8L engine, utilizes a Hall Effect switch mounted near vibration damper. The sensor monitors vibration damper position (crankshaft position) and sends signals to ignition module. These signals provide ECM with a TDC position reference for each piston, as well as supplying an engine speed (RPM) signal. This allows ECM to compute crankshaft position and RPM and fire appropriate ignition coil at the proper time. Crankshaft position sensor signal is also used in conjunction with the camshaft position sensor signal to determine triggering of the sequentially-fired fuel injectors. For additional information, see COMPUTER CONTROLLED COIL IGNITION (C³I) under IGNITION SYSTEM (GASOLINE).

Cranking Signal – Cranking signal is a 12-volt signal monitored by the ECM. Signal is present when ignition switch is in the START position. The ECM uses signal to determine the need for starting enrichment. ECM also cancels diagnostics until engine is running and 12-volt signal is no longer present.

Digital Ratio Adapter Controller (DRAC) – DRAC compensates for various axle and tire ratios by monitoring the Vehicle Speed Sensor (VSS) signal and modifying it before passing it on to the ECM and speedometer unit. On models equipped with a DRAC, VSS buffer is an internal part of DRAC.

Fuel Pump Feedback – ECM monitors fuel pump circuit between fuel pump relay/oil pressure switch and fuel pump. This enables the ECM to determine if fuel pump is being energized by fuel pump relay or back-up oil pressure switch. A failure in this monitored circuit results in the setting of a related trouble code in ECM memory.

Gear Switches – Gear switches are located inside automatic transmission. Switches may be normally open or closed and change status depending upon internal hydraulic pressures. ECM uses high gear switch information in controlling emission components and engagement of Torque Converter Clutch (TCC).

Knock Sensor – The knock sensor is a piezoelectric device which detects abnormal engine vibrations (spark knock) in the engine. This vibration results in the production of a very low AC signal, which is sent from the knock sensor to the ESC controller or the MEM-CAL portion of the ECM (on models equipped with 4L80-E transmission). The ECM then retards ignition timing until the engine knock ceases. Two knock sensors are used on 4.3L CPI engines.

For additional information on knock sensor operation, see ESC DETONATION RETARD OPERATION under IGNITION TIMING CONTROL SYSTEMS (GASOLINE).

A fault in the ESC circuit may set a related trouble code. When a related trouble code is not present and the ESC system is the suspected cause of a driveability problem, perform functional check of ESC system. See SYSTEM & COMPONENT TESTING article.

Manifold Absolute Pressure (MAP) Sensor (Except 3.8L) – The MAP sensor measures changes in manifold pressure. Changes in manifold pressure result from engine load and speed changes. The MAP sensor converts these changes in manifold pressure into a voltage output signal to ECM (1.5 volts at idle to about 4.5 volts at WOT)

The ECM can monitor these signals and adjust air/fuel ratio and ignition timing under various operating conditions.

If MAP sensor fails, the ECM substitutes a fixed MAP value, and uses the TPS to control fuel delivery. A fault in the MAP circuit should set a related trouble code. If a related trouble code is not present and MAP sensor is suspected of causing a driveability problem, perform functional check of MAP sensor. See SYSTEM & COMPONENT TESTING article.

Manifold Air Temperature (MAT) Sensor (2.5L & 4.3L Turbo) – MAT sensor is a thermistor (temperature sensitive resistor) mounted in the intake manifold. Low intake air temperature produces high internal sensor resistance, while high temperature causes low internal sensor resistance. The ECM supplies and monitors a 5-volt signal to sensor through a pull-down resistor in ECM.

MAT sensor, also known as an intake air temperature sensor, allows ECM to determine intake air temperature. ECM uses signal to delay EGR until intake air temperature reaches about 40°F (5°C). If intake air temperature becomes excessively high, ECM compensates by slightly retarding ignition timing. After a vehicle has sat overnight, MAT and CTS signals (resistance and temperature) should be close to same reading. Failure in MAT sensor circuit should set a related trouble code.

Mass Airflow (MAF) Sensor (3.8L) – The MAF sensor measures flow of air entering the engine in grams per second. This measurement of airflow is a reflection of engine load (throttle opening and air volume), similar to the relationship of engine load to a MAP or vacuum sensor signal. MAF signal should remain relatively constant at cruise, gradually changing with throttle angle and rapidly changing on sudden acceleration. The ECM uses this information to control fuel delivery.

This frequency generator type MAF sensor produces a frequency signal that cannot be easily measured in testing (32-150 Hertz). This varying signal is proportional to airflow. A fault in the MAF sensor circuit should set a related trouble code.

CAUTION: Measure O_2 sensor voltage with a Digital Volt-Ohmmeter (minimum 10-megohm impedance) only. Current drain of a conventional voltmeter could damage sensor.

Oxygen (O_2) Sensor – The O_2 sensor is mounted in the exhaust system and monitors oxygen content of exhaust gases. The oxygen content causes the Zirconia/Platinum-tipped O_2 sensor to produce a voltage signal which is proportional to exhaust gas oxygen concentration (0-3%) compared to outside oxygen (20-21%). This voltage signal is low (about .1 volt) when a lean mixture is present and high (about 1.0 volt) when a rich mixture is present. As ECM compensates for a lean or rich condition, this voltage signal constantly fluctuates between high and low, crossing a .45-volt reference voltage supplied by ECM on the O_2 sensor signal line. This is referred to as "cross counts".

The O_2 sensor does not function properly (produce voltage) until its temperature reaches 600°F (316°C). At temperatures less than the normal operating range of the sensor, vehicle functions in "open loop" mode, and ECM does not make air/fuel adjustments based upon O_2 sensor signals, but uses TPS and MAP or MAF values to determine air/fuel ratio from a table built into memory. When ECM reads a voltage signal greater than .45 volt from the O_2 sensor, ECM begins to alter commands to injector to produce either a leaner or richer mixture.

Once vehicle has entered "closed loop", a fault in the O_2 circuit (cooled-down sensor or open or shorted O_2 sensor circuit) is the only thing which can return vehicle to open loop. A problem in the O_2 sensor circuit should set a related trouble code.

On 4.3L engines, O_2 sensor uses an internal heating element. Heating element allows O_2 sensor to warm more quickly, allowing fuel system to enter closed loop operation sooner. Heating element also prevents fuel system from re-entering open loop operation, which would be a normal response to prolonged idling.

Park/Neutral (P/N) Switch – This switch is connected to transmission gear selector and signals ECM when transmission is in Park or Neutral. ECM uses this information for determining control of ignition

timing, converter clutch and idle speed. To check function of P/N switch, perform functional check of switch. See SYSTEM & COMPONENT TESTING article.

Power Steering (P/S) Pressure Switch (2.5L) – This switch informs ECM of engine load conditions which exist when steering wheel is turned from center to full lock position. ECM uses this information to help control idle speed. To check function of P/S switch, perform functional check of switch. See SYSTEM & COMPONENT TESTING article.

Pressure Switch Manifold (PSM) (4L80-E Transmission) – The PSM is actually 5 pressure switches combined into a single unit mounted on the transmission valve body. The PCM supplies battery voltage on 3 separate wires to PSM. By grounding one or more of the switches in various combinations, PCM detects what gear range the vehicle operator has selected.

RPM Reference Signal – ECM monitors RPM through ignition module tach/pulse signals (on circuit No. 430) produced by the HEI module (RPM reference line of 4-wire EST connector) or Hall Effect camshaft and crankshaft sensors (3.8L). ECM uses signal to determine control of timing, fuel delivery (fuel pump relay energizing), EGR function and idle speed. ECM also uses signal to trigger fuel injectors.

Throttle Position Sensor (TPS) – The TPS is a variable mechanical resistor connected directly to the throttle shaft linkage. The TPS has 3 wires connected to it. One is connected to a 5-volt reference voltage supply from ECM, another is connected to ECM ground and the third is the signal return which is monitored by ECM. The voltage signal from the TPS varies from closed throttle (.5-1.0 volt) to wide open throttle (4.5-5 volts). ECM uses this signal to determine control of fuel, idle speed, spark timing and converter clutch. A problem in the TPS circuit may set a related trouble code.

Transmission Temperature Sensor (TTS) (4L80-E Transmission) – TTS is a thermistor (temperature sensitive resistor) mounted to the transmission valve body. The PCM supplies and monitors a 5-volt signal to TTS. This monitored 5-volt signal is then modified by resistance of TTS. When transmission fluid temperatures are low, TTS resistance is high and PCM sees a high monitored voltage signal. When transmission fluid temperatures are high, TTS resistance is low and PCM sees a low monitored voltage.

PCM uses transmission fluid temperature input in control of converter clutch application and shift quality. Sensor circuit problem should set a related trouble code.

Vehicle Speed Sensor (VSS) – VSS is a Permanent Magnet (PM) generator mounted in transmission or transfer case. The VSS sends a pulsing signal to either the ECM or Digital Ratio Adapter Controller (DRAC), which passes the signal on to the ECM. ECM then converts this signal into Miles Per Hour (MPH) by monitoring the time interval between pulses. ECM uses this sensor input in controlling converter clutch engagement.

On all models except 3.1L, 3.8L and 4WD equipped with 4L80-E transmission, a VSS buffer is built into the DRAC. On 3.1L, a VSS buffer is located between VSS and ECM. On 3.8L and 4WD equipped with 4L80-E transmission, VSS buffer is built into ECM.

OUTPUT SIGNALS

NOTE: Vehicles are equipped with different combinations of computer-controlled components. Not all listed components are used on every vehicle. For theory and operation of components, refer to indicated system.

A/C Clutch Relay – MISCELLANEOUS ECM CONTROLS.
Air Injection Control Solenoid – EMISSION SYSTEMS.
Charge Air Cooler Pump Relay (4.3L Turbo) – TURBOCHARGER.
Computer Controlled Coil Ignition (C³I) – IGNITION SYSTEM.
Cooling Fan Relay (3.1L) – MISCELLANEOUS ECM CONTROLS.
SERVICE ENGINE SOON Light – SELF-DIAGNOSTIC SYSTEM.
EGR Control Solenoid Valve – EMISSION SYSTEMS.
ESC Timing Retard – IGNITION SYSTEM.
EVRV Solenoid – EMISSION SYSTEMS.
Fuel Injectors – FUEL CONTROL.

Fuel Module – FUEL DELIVERY.
Fuel Pump & Fuel Pump Relay – FUEL DELIVERY.
HEI-EST Ignition – IGNITION SYSTEM.
Idle Air Control (IAC) Valve – IDLE SPEED.
Self-Diagnostics – SELF-DIAGNOSTIC SYSTEM.
Serial Data – SELF-DIAGNOSTIC SYSTEM.
Shift Solenoids (4L80-E Transmission) – MISCELLANEOUS ECM CONTROLS.
Torque Converter Clutch – MISCELLANEOUS ECM CONTROLS.
Transmission Shift Light (Manual Transmission) – MISCELLANEOUS ECM CONTROLS.
Turbo Boost Relay (4.3L Turbo) – TURBOCHARGER.
Wastegate Solenoid (4.3L Turbo) – TURBOCHARGER.

COMPUTERIZED ENGINE CONTROLS (DIESEL)

6.2L Diesel engine with light duty emissions uses Diesel Electronic Control (DEC) system. DEC system consists of Electronic Control Module (ECM), input devices and output signals. DEC system electronically controls EGR system operation, Torque Converter Clutch (TCC) engagement, cold advance and glow plug system.

ELECTRONIC CONTROL MODULE (ECM)

Electronic Control Module (ECM) is located in passenger compartment, behind glove box. It constantly monitors information from various sensors to control EGR, TCC, cold advance and glow plug systems. ECM processes input signals from sensors and then sends necessary electrical responses to control these systems.

The ECM performs the diagnostic function of the DEC system. It can recognize operational problems, alert driver through the SERVICE ENGINE SOON light and store codes which identify problem areas to technicians making system repairs.

Memories – ECM uses 3 types of memory:

- **Read Only Memory (ROM)** – ROM is programmed information which only ECM can read. ROM program cannot be changed. If battery voltage is removed, ROM information is retained.
- **Random Access Memory (RAM)** – RAM is the scratch pad for the CPU. Data input, diagnostic codes and results of calculations are constantly updated and temporarily stored in RAM. If battery voltage is removed from ECM, all information stored in RAM is lost.
- **Programmable Read Only Memory (PROM)** – PROM is factory programmed engine calibration data which "tailors" ECM for specific transmission, engine, emission, vehicle weight and rear axle ratio application. PROM can be removed from ECM. If battery voltage is removed, PROM information is retained.

INPUT DEVICES

Each sensor or switch furnishes electronic (voltage) signals to ECM. The ECM uses these input signals to control EGR, TCC, cold advance and glow plug systems. Various models are equipped with different combinations of input devices. Not all devices are used on all models. To determine the input usage on a specific model, see appropriate wiring diagram in WIRING DIAGRAMS article in ENGINE PERFORMANCE. The available input signals include:

Coolant Temperature Sensor (CTS) – CTS is a thermistor (temperature sensitive resistor). A coolant temperature of -40°F (-40°C) produces a high resistance (100,000 ohms), while a coolant temperature of 266°F (130°C) produces a low resistance (70 ohms).

ECM supplies a 5-volt reference signal through an internal resistor to CTS and measures return voltage. Voltage is high when coolant temperature is low, and low when coolant temperature is hot. By measuring voltage, ECM knows engine coolant temperature. Engine coolant temperature affects cold advance and glow plug systems.

Manifold Absolute Pressure (MAP) Sensor – MAP sensor, mounted on left side of cowl, monitors vacuum in the EGR system. It senses the actual vacuum in the EGR vacuum line and sends a signal to the ECM.

The signal is compared to the EGR duty cycle calculated by the ECM. If there is a minor difference in the vacuum value sensed and the ECM

command, the ECM corrects. When a major difference is sensed, the ECM recognizes a fault and sends a full EGR signal.

Throttle Position Sensor (TPS) – TPS, mounted on the injection pump, is a variable resistor monitoring throttle opening angle for the ECM. The sensor is connected to a 5-volt reference signal and has a high resistance value when throttle is closed. At wide open throttle, the TPS resistance value is low, and output to the ECM will be near 5 volts.

Engine Speed Sensor – The engine speed sensor is a camshaft driven pick-up and is mounted at center rear of engine. The sensor receives a 5-volt reference signal and allows the ECM to measure engine RPM by the number of times reference voltage is pulsed. The engine speed sensor pulses 4 times per revolution.

Vehicle Speed Sensor (VSS) – Mounted on the transmission, VSS sends a pulsing signal to ECM for vehicle speed calculation. This calculation is used to control TCC engagement.

OUTPUT SIGNALS

NOTE: Output signals are regulated by the ECM to maintain correct driveability and exhaust emissions. For theory and operation of components, refer to indicated system.

Electronic Controller/Glow Plug Relay – FUEL CONTROL.
Cold Advance Control – FUEL CONTROL.
Torque Converter Clutch – MISCELLANEOUS ECM CONTROLS.
Exhaust Gas Recirculation System – EMISSION SYSTEMS (DIESEL).

FUEL SYSTEM (GASOLINE)

FUEL DELIVERY

Fuel Module (7.4L, 5.7L G Van & 5.7L Over 8500 GVWR) – Fuel module overrides the ECM 2-second timer and fuel pump runs 20 seconds before shutting off when vehicle is not started. This added circuit corrects hot restart problems which could cause vapor lock during high ambient temperatures.

Fuel Pump – An in-tank electric fuel pump delivers fuel to injector(s) through an in-line fuel filter. The pump is designed to supply fuel pressure in excess of vehicle requirements. The pressure relief valve in the fuel pump controls maximum fuel pump pressure.

On TBI fuel systems, pressure regulator is mounted on throttle body. On Port Fuel Injection (PFI) systems, pressure regulator is mounted on the fuel rail. Regulator keeps fuel available to injector(s) at a constant pressure. Excess fuel is returned to fuel tank through pressure regulator return line.

When ignition switch is turned to ON position, ECM turns on electric fuel pump by energizing fuel pump relay. ECM keeps pump on if engine is running or cranking (ECM is receiving reference pulses from ignition module). If there are no reference pulses and vehicle is not equipped with a fuel module, ECM turns pump off within 2 seconds after key is turned on. For additional information, see FUEL PUMP RELAY and FUEL MODULE under FUEL DELIVERY.

Fuel Pressure Regulator (CPI) – A constant fuel pressure of 54-64 psi (3.8-4.5 kg/cm²) is maintained by a factory preset, nonadjustable, spring loaded diaphragm contained within CPI assembly. Spring tension maintains a constant fuel pressure to injector regardless of engine load.

Fuel Pressure Regulator (TBI) – A constant fuel pressure of 9-13 psi (.6-9 kg/cm²) is maintained by a factory preset, nonadjustable, spring loaded diaphragm contained within throttle body. Spring tension maintains a constant fuel pressure to injector regardless of engine load.

Fuel Pressure Regulator (4.3L Turbo PFI) – Fuel pressure regulator is a diaphragm-operated relief valve with injector pressure on one side and manifold pressure (vacuum) on the other. Pressure regulator compensates for engine load by increasing fuel pressure when low manifold vacuum is experienced.

During periods of high manifold vacuum, regulator-to-fuel tank return orifice is fully open, keeping fuel pressure on the low side of its regulated range. As throttle valve opens, vacuum to regulator diaphragm decreases, allowing spring tension to gradually close off return passage. At wide open throttle (when vacuum is at its lowest), return orifice is restricted, providing maximum fuel volume and maintaining constant fuel pressure to injectors.

Fuel Pump Relay – When ignition switch is turned to ON position, ECM turns electric fuel pump on by energizing fuel pump relay. ECM keeps relay energized if engine is running or cranking (ECM is receiving reference pulses from ignition module). If there are no reference pulses, ECM turns pump off within 2 seconds after key on. See FUEL MODULE under FUEL DELIVERY.

As a back-up system to fuel pump relay, the oil pressure switch also activates fuel pump. The oil pressure switch is normally open until oil pressure reaches approximately 4 psi (.28 kg/cm²). If fuel pump relay fails, the oil pressure switch closes when oil pressure is obtained, and operates the fuel pump. An inoperative fuel pump relay may result in extended cranking times due to the time required to build up oil pressure. Oil pressure switch may be combined into a single unit with an oil pressure gauge sending unit or sensor.

ECM monitors fuel pump circuit between fuel pump relay/oil pressure switch and fuel pump, enabling ECM to determine if fuel pump is being energized by fuel pump relay or oil pressure switch. A failure in this monitored circuit results in the setting of a related trouble code in ECM memory.

For additional information on fuel pump activation, see BASIC DIAGNOSTIC PROCEDURES and SYSTEM & COMPONENT TESTING articles.

FUEL CONTROL

The ECM, using input signals, determines adjustments to the air/fuel mixture to provide the optimum ratio for proper combustion under all operating conditions. Fuel control systems can operate in the "open loop" or "closed loop" mode.

Open Loop – When engine is cold and engine speed is greater than 400 RPM, ECM operates in open loop mode. In open loop, ECM calculates air/fuel ratio based upon coolant temperature and MAP or MAF sensor readings. Engine remains in open loop operation until O_2 sensor reaches operating temperature, coolant temperature reaches preset temperature and a specific period of time has elapsed after engine starts.

Closed Loop – When O_2 sensor reaches operating temperature, coolant temperature reaches a preset temperature and a specific period of time has passed since engine start-up, ECM operates in closed loop. In closed loop, ECM controls air/fuel ratio based upon O_2 sensor signals (in addition to other input parameters) to maintain as close to a 14.7:1 air/fuel ratio as possible. If O_2 sensor cools off (due to excessive idling) or a fault occurs in the O_2 sensor circuit, vehicle once again enters open loop mode.

On 4.3L engines, oxygen sensor is equipped with an internal heating element. This element enables system to reach "closed loop" sooner and maintain closed loop even during periods of extended idle.

Central Port Injection (CPI) – CPI is one of 3 fuel systems used on 4.3L engines. The non-repairable injector assembly consists of a fuel meter body, fuel pressure regulator, fuel injector and 6 poppet nozzles with fuel tubes. CPI assembly is housed in the lower manifold assembly. Fuel pump and pressure regulator maintain fuel pressure at 54-64 psi (3.8-4.5 kg/cm²) under all operating modes.

When injector is energized, pressurized fuel passes down fuel distribution tubes to poppet nozzles located at rear of intake valves. Fuel pressure forces poppet valves open, spraying fuel into cylinders when intake valves are open. As fuel pressure drops (due to all poppets opening or injector de-energizing), poppet nozzle spring pressure closes poppet nozzle until pressure again builds high enough to overcome poppet nozzle spring pressure. Excess fuel is returned to the fuel tank via the fuel return line.

Throttle Body Injection – Injectors are located in throttle body unit. All models except 2.5L use 220 Series dual injector throttle body. 2.5L models use 700 Series single injector throttle body. Battery voltage is supplied to injector when ignition is on. ECM energizes injector sole-noid by providing a ground path through its internal circuitry. By regulating injector ground circuit, ECM controls injector "on" time (pulse width) to provide proper amount of fuel to engine.

Pressure regulator maintains pressure to injector at 9-13 psi (.6-.9 kg/cm²). Excess fuel passes through pressure regulator and returns to fuel tank.

In the "run" mode, ECM uses tach (RPM) signal to determine when to pulse injector. Fuel injectors are pulsed once for each engine revolution; each spray provides 1/2 the fuel required for the combustion process. Thus, 2 injections of fuel (2 rotations of crankshaft) are mixed with incoming air to produce the fuel charge for each combustion cycle. On models equipped with dual injectors in the throttle body, injectors are pulsed alternately.

Port Fuel Injection (PFI) – Individual, electrically pulsed injectors (one per cylinder) are located in intake manifold fuel rails. These injectors are next to intake valves in cylinder head.

The 4.3L Turbo PFI system features simultaneous double-fire injection. Fuel injectors are pulsed once for each engine revolution; each spray provides 1/2 the fuel required for the combustion process. Thus, 2 injections of fuel (2 rotations of crankshaft) are mixed with incoming air to produce the fuel charge for each combustion cycle.

The 3.8L engine uses Sequential Fuel Injection (SFI). Injectors on these models are pulsed sequentially in spark plug firing order. Main differences between sequential and simultaneous systems are injectors, wiring and the ECM.

On both systems, constant fuel pressure is maintained to the injectors. Air/fuel mixture is regulated by amount of time injector stays open (pulse width). Various sensors provide information to the ECM to control pulse width. The ECM controls pulse width using information provided by various sensors.

Fuel System Operating Modes – Internal ECM calibration controls fuel delivery during starting, clear flood mode, deceleration and heavy acceleration.

- **Starting** – During engine starts, ECM delivers one injector pulse for each distributor reference pulse received (synchronized mode). Injector pulse width is based upon coolant temperature and throttle position. ECM determines air/fuel ratio when throttle position is less than 80 percent open. Engine starting air/fuel ratio ranges from 1.5:1 at -33°F (-36°C) to 14.7:1 at 201°F (94°C). At lower coolant temperatures, injector pulse width is wider (richer air/fuel mixture ratio). When coolant temperature is high, injector pulse width becomes narrower (leaner air/fuel ratio).

- **Clear Flood** – If engine is flooded, driver must depress accelerator pedal to Wide Open Throttle (WOT) position. At this position, ECM adjusts injector pulse width equal to an air/fuel ratio of 20:1. This air/fuel ratio is maintained as long as throttle remains in wide open position and engine speed is less than 600 RPM. If throttle position becomes less than 80 percent open and/or engine speed exceeds 600 RPM, ECM changes injector pulse width to that used during engine starting (based upon coolant temperature and manifold vacuum).

- **Heavy Acceleration** – ECM provides fuel enrichment during heavy acceleration. Sudden opening of throttle valve causes rapid increase in MAP signal. Pulse width is directly related to MAP, throttle position and coolant temperature. Higher MAP and wider throttle angles give wider injector pulse width (richer mixture). During enrichment, injector pulses are not in proportion to distributor reference signals (non-synchronized). Any reduction in throttle angle cancels fuel enrichment.

- **Deceleration** – During normal deceleration, fuel output is reduced. This reduction in available fuel serves to remove residual fuel from intake manifold. During sudden deceleration, when MAP, throttle position and engine speed are reduced to preset levels, fuel flow is cut off completely. This deceleration fuel cut-off overrides normal deceleration mode. During either deceleration mode, injector pulses are not in proportion to distributor reference signals.

- **Battery Voltage Correction** – ECM compensates for low battery voltage by increasing injector pulse width and increasing idle RPM. ECM is able to perform these commands because of a built-in memory/learning function.
- **Fuel Cut-Off** – When ignition is turned off, injectors are de-energized to prevent dieseling. Injectors are not energized if RPM reference pulses are not received by the ECM, even with ignition on. This prevents flooding before starting. Fuel cut-off also occurs at high engine RPM to prevent internal damage to engine. Some models may also cut off fuel injector signals during periods of sudden, closed throttle deceleration (when fuel is not needed).

IDLE SPEED (GASOLINE)

ECM controls engine idle speed depending upon engine operating conditions. The ECM senses engine operating conditions and determines the best idle speed.

Idle Air Control (IAC) Valve – The IAC valve controls engine idle speed to prevent stalling during engine load changes. The IAC valve is mounted on throttle body and controls the amount of air by-passed around the throttle plate. The IAC valve controls engine idle speed by moving its pintle in and out in steps referred to as "counts" (0 counts, fully seated; 255 counts, fully retracted). Counts can be measured by plugging a Scan tester into the Assembly Line Data Link (ALDL).

If engine RPM is too low, pintle is retracted and more air is by-passed around the throttle plate to increase engine RPM. If engine RPM is too high, pintle is extended and less air is by-passed around the throttle plate to decrease engine RPM. Normal counts on an idling engine should be 4-60. When engine is idling, ECM determines proper positioning of IAC valve based on battery voltage, coolant temperature, engine load and engine RPM.

If IAC valve is disconnected or reconnected with engine running, IAC loses its reference point and must be reset. On some models, IAC is reset by turning ignition on and off. Other models require driving vehicle at normal operating temperature over 35 MPH with circuit properly connected. Problems in IAC circuit should set a related code.

The IAC valve affects only the idle system. If valve is stuck fully open, excessive airflow into the manifold creates a high idle speed. Valve stuck closed allows insufficient airflow, resulting in low idle speed. For calibration purposes, several different IAC valves are used. Ensure replacement valve is proper design.

FUEL SYSTEM (DIESEL)

FUEL DELIVERY

A mechanical pump is mounted on the right side of engine block. Camshaft eccentric drives pump. Pump pulls fuel from the fuel tank through a primary filter. The fuel is then pumped through a secondary filter, mounted on firewall (pickups) or rear of air cleaner (vans), and to the injection pump.

The 6.2L diesel engine uses a mechanical, high pressure rotary diesel injection pump, which is gear-driven by camshaft at camshaft speed. Pump injects a precisely metered amount of fuel to each cylinder at the proper time.

High pressure fuel lines carry the fuel to an injection nozzle in each cylinder. All fuel lines are the same length to ensure no variance in timing. A rotary fuel metering valve controls engine RPM. As the accelerator pedal is depressed, throttle linkage opens fuel metering valve to allow increased fuel delivery.

Diesel Injection Pump – The high pressure diesel injection pump is mounted at top of engine, below intake manifold. The pump is gear-driven by camshaft. Pump precisely governs time and amount of fuel injection.

A built-in fuel pressure regulator and transfer pump picks up fuel at pump inlet, pushing it through a passage to the pump head. The pump head distributes fuel at transfer pump pressure 8-12 psi (.5-.8 kg/cm²) to metering valve, governor and automatic advance mechanisms. Fuel then passes to rotary fuel metering valve and into a charging passage. As pump shaft rotates, fuel is directed at high pressure through each delivery pipe to an injector. *See Fig. 1*

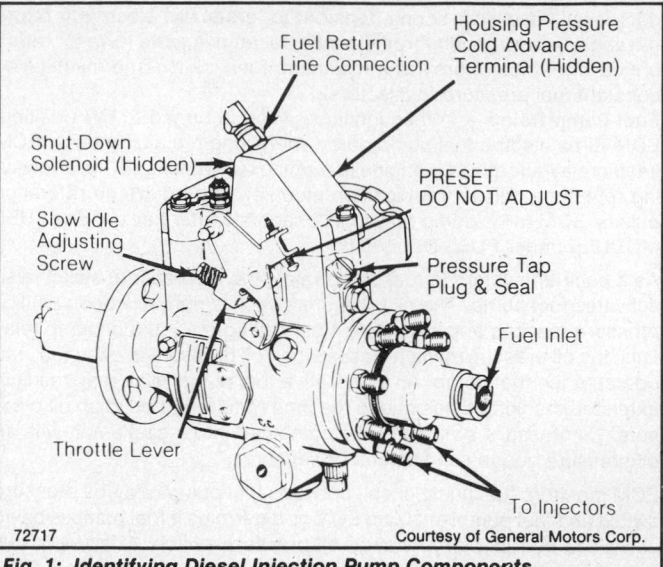

Fig. 1: Identifying Diesel Injection Pump Components

Courtesy of General Motors Corp.

Fuel Injection Lines – Eight high pressure fuel injection lines are routed from the injection pump to an injector in each cylinder. The lines are of equal length to prevent a difference in timing between cylinders. Lines are not interchangeable and are pre-bent by the manufacturer.

FUEL CONTROL

Electronic Controller/Glow Plug Relay – The electronic controller/glow plug relay is mounted at rear of left cylinder head. It monitors and controls glow plug operation. Controller uses four pins to determine glow plug operating requirements. Pin "B" senses voltage at starter motor solenoid. Pin "C" senses glow plug voltage. Pin "D" supplies 12 volts, through cold advance relay, to operate controller when coolant temperature is less than 80°F (27°C). Pin "E" is controller ground.

A normally operating system works as follows: at room temperature and with ignition on and engine off, the glow plugs come on for 4-6 seconds and then go off for about 4.5 seconds. The glow plugs then cycle on for about 1.5 seconds and off for about 4.5 seconds, for a total start sequence of about 20 seconds. If the engine is cranked during or after start sequence, the glow plugs will cycle on and off for a total of 25 seconds after the ignition switch is returned from the crank position, whether engine starts or not.

Glow Plugs – Glow plugs are small 6-volt heaters, powered by 12 volts to give rapid heating. Electronic controller operates glow plugs, which cycle on when ignition switch is turned to the RUN position (prior to starting the engine). The glow plugs remain pulsing a short time after engine starting, then automatically turn off.

The glow system for the LH6 (light duty emissions version) is different than the system for the LL4 (heavy duty emissions version). The LH6 system has the same glow plugs, glow plug controller and WAIT light. However, there is no temperature inhibit switch. Instead, the ECM, which receives temperature information from the coolant temperature sensor located in the water crossover of the engine, controls glow plug temperature inhibit.

The computer transposes this temperature information into a voltage signal, which it sends to the cold advance relay, ignition circuit and glow plug controller. The cold advance relay is located at the junction block in the engine compartment on the right side of the cowl. For diagnostic information on computer controlled system, see SELF-DIAGNOSTICS – DIESEL article.

CAUTION: Using a jumper wire on by-pass relay causes glow plug failure.

Glow Plug Inhibit Switch – The LL4 (heavy duty emissions version of 6.2L engine) is equipped with a glow plug inhibit switch. The inhibit switch is calibrated to open above 125°F (51.5°C) to prevent glow plug operation above this temperature.

Two types of inhibit switches are used. Switches can be identified by their cap color. A switch with a Black cap is a temperature-controlled switch. The other switch (with a non-Black cap) is an optional switch which is always closed to allow for more frequent cycling of glow plugs.

Glow Plug After-Start – Glow plug controller provides glow plug operation after starting a cold engine. This after-start operation is initiated when ignition switch is returned to RUN from START position.

Injection Nozzles – Each of the 8 combustion chambers is equipped with an injection nozzle. The injection nozzle has a single fuel inlet fitting and 2 fuel return fittings (one on each side of fuel inlet fitting). The nozzle is threaded into the cylinder head. Injection nozzles are spring loaded and calibrated to open at a specified fuel line pressure. The combustion chamber end of the nozzle has a replaceable compression seal and carbon stop seal.

Housing Pressure Cold Advance (HPCA) – The HPCA circuit is used to improve cold starting and aid in emission control. On light duty emissions (LH6 models), an ECM signal activates the HPCA circuit. On heavy duty emissions (LL4 models), a coolant temperature switch located on rear of right cylinder head controls the HPCA circuit. The circuit advances injection timing about 4 degrees when engine is cold.

When engine temperature is less than 80°F (27° C), the circuit decreases housing pressure from 10 psi (.7 kg/cm²) to zero. Meanwhile, the fast idle solenoid is activated. When the temperature switch opens, the HPCA circuit is de-energized and housing pressure rises, retarding pump timing. The temperature switch closes again when engine temperature falls to less than 85°F (30°C).

Cold Advance Control – The cold advance control circuit is designed to advance injection pump timing about 4 degrees during cold engine operation. ECM activates this circuit through the cold advance relay to energize the cold advance solenoid. The ECM opens the circuit when coolant temperature is greater than 95°F (35°C).

When coolant temperature is less than the switching point and with ignition on, the cold advance solenoid is continuously energized without the engine running. When coolant temperature is less than the switching point and with the engine running, injection pump housing pressure is decreased from 10 psi (.7 kg/cm²) to zero, which advances injection pump timing by about 4 degrees. As engine warms, the cold advance solenoid is de-energized and the injection pump housing pressure is returned to 10 psi (.70 kg/cm²).

IDLE SPEED (DIESEL)

Curb Idle Speed – Curb idle is controlled by mechanical adjustment of the low idle speed screw. For idle speed adjustment procedure, see CURB IDLE under IDLE SPEED (DIESEL) in ON-VEHICLE ADJUSTMENTS article.

Fast Idle Speed – Fast idle solenoid controls fast idle. For adjustment of fast idle speed, see FAST IDLE under IDLE SPEED (DIESEL) in ON-VEHICLE ADJUSTMENTS article.

IGNITION SYSTEM (GASOLINE)

WARNING: High Energy Ignition Electronic Spark Timing (HEI-EST) system can produce more than 50,000 volts.

High Energy Ignition Electronic Spark Timing (HEI-EST) Distributor – The Delco-Remy HEI-EST system consists of distributor housing, rotor, cap, 7 or 8-terminal ignition module, magnetic pick-up, pole piece, pick-up coil, connecting harness and the EST portion of the ECM. The distributor is connected to the EST system by a 4-wire connector leading to Electronic Control Module (ECM).

No vacuum or centrifugal advance mechanisms are used. Based upon monitored input signals, ECM controls all spark timing changes. Some models use an additional Electronic Spark Control (ESC) system, which retards timing in case of engine detonation (knock). Most models are equipped with sealed ignition coil and ignition module connectors.

When the external teeth on the timing core approach, align with and pass the pick-up coil windings, an alternating current is produced in the pick-up coil windings. In the cranking mode, this alternating current signals switching transistors in the HEI module to make or break the ignition coil primary ground circuit. Once the engine starts, ECM takes control of primary ground circuit (EST mode).

When the primary ground circuit is removed, the magnetic field created by the flow of current in the primary windings collapses across the primary and secondary windings of the coil. This induces a high-voltage surge in the secondary windings of the coil. Secondary voltage is then discharged to the rotor, which distributes voltage to the appropriate spark plug terminal. Depending on application, the distributor module may have either a 7-terminal or an 8-terminal (sealed connector) ignition module.

Computer Controlled Coil Ignition (C³I) – The Computer Controlled Coil Ignition (C³I) system, used on the 3.8L engine, eliminates the need for a mechanical distributor. The C³I ignition system consists of a coil pack (3 coils), ignition module, camshaft and crankshaft sensors, wiring harness and the Electronic Spark Timing (EST) portion of the Electronic Control Module (ECM).

In the C³I system, each cylinder is paired with the cylinder that is opposite it in the firing order. Cylinder No. 1 is paired with 4, 2 with 5, and 3 with 6. Spark occurs simultaneously in the cylinder approaching the compression stroke and in the cylinder approaching the exhaust stroke. The cylinder on the exhaust stroke requires less voltage for the spark plug to fire. This leaves the bulk of the available voltage to fire the spark plug for the cylinder on the compression stroke. The process is repeated when the cylinders reverse roles. Each cylinder pair is fired by its own ignition coil.

Input from the Hall Effect cam and crank sensors is used by the ignition module to determine when to trigger the appropriate coil pack. Module passes on camshaft sync-pulse signal to the ECM to initialize sequential fuel injector timing.

- **Type II Ignition Coil Pack** – On Type II ignition coil pack, 3 separate twin tower coils are independently mounted over the C³I ignition module. Each coil provides the spark for 2 simultaneously paired spark plugs. Each coil can be replaced separately.

- **Camshaft Position Sensor** – The 3.8L Hall Effect camshaft sensor is located on the timing cover, behind and below water pump. The ECM uses camshaft "sync-pulse" signals (passed to ECM by the ignition module) to determine the exact position of the No. 1 piston. Signal is used by ECM to properly initialize fuel injector timing. If camshaft sensor signal is lost, Code 41 may be set. Engine can be restarted and will run in sequential mode; however, odds are 1 in 6 that injectors will spray correctly without camshaft signal. This provides "walk home" protection against cam sensor failure.

- **Combination 3X & 18X Crankshaft Sensor** – In addition to the camshaft sensor, the 3.8L uses a Hall Effect crankshaft sensor containing 2 interrupter rings. The outside ring contains 18 evenly spaced interrupters, producing 18 pulses per crankshaft revolution. The inner ring has 3 interrupters spaced at irregular intervals (10, 20 and 30 degrees apart).
  The ignition module monitors signals generated by the 2 interrupter rings. The 18X ring will change state once during the 10-degree gap of the 3X ring, twice during the 20-degree gap and 3 times during the 30-degree gap. The changing relationship between the 2 rings allows the ignition module to identify the correct ignition coil to fire within the first 120 degrees of crankshaft rotation. This system provides for a faster start and a more accurate measurement of crankshaft sensor signals.
  If the 3X signal to ignition module is lost while the engine is running, the fuel injection system will continue to run in sequential mode; however, loss of 3X or 18X signal will prevent vehicle from restarting.

- **Fuel Control Signal** – In addition to the RPM reference (18X) signal and fuel sync (camshaft) signals generated by the ignition module on 3.8L, a fuel control reference signal must also be passed on to the ECM in order to inform ECM proper signals are being generated to the ignition module. The fuel control signal is generated by the C³I module from calculations involving signals from the crankshaft sensor 18X and the 3X pulse rings.

IGNITION TIMING CONTROL SYSTEMS (GASOLINE)

Ignition Timing Advance – At engine speeds less than 400 RPM, ignition module controls spark advance by triggering coil(s) at a predetermined interval based on engine speed only. At engine speeds greater than 400 RPM (EST mode), ECM controls ignition timing.

ECM controls ignition timing based upon input signals from engine RPM reference line (ignition module), coolant temperature sensor, manifold air temperature sensor, throttle position sensor, knock sensor, vehicle speed sensor, gear position switch and MAP or MAF sensor.

The PROM portion of the ECM has a programmed spark advance curve based on engine speed. ECM calculates spark timing whenever an ignition pulse is present. Spark advance is controlled only when engine is running (not during cranking). ECM uses input signal values to modify PROM information, increasing or decreasing spark advance to achieve maximum performance with minimum emissions. To check ignition system operation, see BASIC DIAGNOSTIC PROCEDURES or SYSTEM & COMPONENT TESTING article.

- **Reference (RPM)** – On all engines, ignition module converts signals from pick-up coil or Hall Effect sensors to digital signals which are used to trigger ignition coil. Since the signal on this circuit is also used as an injector trigger reference on fuel injected vehicles, engine will not run if circuit is open or grounded.
- **By-Pass** – When the ECM receives an engine speed signal of approximately 400 RPM, it considers engine to be running and applies 5 volts to the ignition module on the by-pass wire. This causes ignition module to switch timing control over to the variable timing control circuit in the ECM. On some models, this by-pass wire contains a connector located between the 4-wire connector and the ECM. This is disconnected when adjusting base timing. On all models, an open or grounded by-pass circuit sets a related trouble code in ECM memory. The engine runs at base timing plus a small amount of advance built into the HEI module.
- **EST** – When 5 volts is present on by-pass circuit and ignition module has turned control of engine timing over to ECM, ECM advances or retards spark on this circuit based on calculations involving reference signal and other sensor input signals. If base timing is incorrectly set, entire advance curve will be incorrect.
- **Ground** – This is the reference ground circuit. It is grounded at distributor and ECM, ensuring there is no voltage drop in the EST circuit which could affect ignition operation.

ESC Detonation Retard Operation – Some models use an Electronic Spark Control (ESC) retard system along with the HEI-EST system. System consists of a knock (detonation) sensor, a high energy ignition system, an ESC controller (some models) and the ECM. On some models, the function of the ESC controller is built into the Memory Calibration (MEM-CAL) unit of the ECM.

When engine knock (detonation) occurs, knock sensor produces a low voltage AC signal. This signal goes to the ESC controller or directly to the MEM-CAL unit inside the ECM, depending upon application.

On models using an ESC controller, controller supplies the ECM with a 12-volt signal. When detonation occurs, controller grounds the 12-volt signal to the ECM, pulling the signal down to near zero volts. The ECM interprets this as a signal to retard timing. The ECM then retards spark timing until the ESC controller returns the 12-volt signal. If signal wire becomes open or grounded on models using ESC controller, ECM continuously provides full ignition timing retard.

On vehicles using ECMs containing MEM-CAL units, the ECM supplies a 5-volt DC reference signal on the knock sensor signal line. Internal circuitry of the knock sensor pulls this voltage down to about 2.5 volts. When knock occurs, the knock sensor produces an AC voltage signal which rides on the 2.5-volt DC signal to the ECM. The voltage and frequency of this signal depend upon knock signals received by the sensor. The ECM retards spark timing until signals from detonation sensor cease. Two knock sensors are used on 4.3L CPI engines.

A malfunction in the ESC circuit should set a related trouble code. If a code is not present and ESC system is suspected cause of driveability problems, perform functional check of ESC system. See SYSTEM & COMPONENT TESTING article.

EMISSION SYSTEMS (GASOLINE)

AIR INJECTION SYSTEM

Air Injection Reaction (AIR) system is used to reduce carbon monoxide (CO) and hydrocarbon (HC) emissions. The AIR system provides additional oxygen to continue combustion process after exhaust gases leave the combustion chamber. This added air also brings catalytic converter up to operating temperature more quickly when engine is cold. The AIR system diverts air either to the exhaust manifold ports or to the air cleaner.

The system consists of an air pump, an Electric Air Control (EAC) valve (2.8L engine) or an electric air control valve with relief tube (4.3L and V8 engines), solenoid, check valve(s) and plumbing. *See Fig. 2 or 3.*

NOTE: On EAC valve, divert and signal tube locations are reversed from previous model year.

Electric Air Control (EAC) Valves With Relief Tube - When engine is cold or at wide open throttle, ECM energizes solenoid on valve, and air is directed to exhaust manifold ports. When coolant temperature increases, solenoid is de-energized and air goes into air cleaner.

At higher engine speeds, air is directed to air cleaner through pressure relief valve (if equipped), even though solenoid may be energized. Air should not be entering exhaust manifold during closed loop mode.

During deceleration, the increased manifold vacuum signal directs air to air cleaner. Check valve on air injection pipe prevents exhaust gases from entering air pump. Solenoid is de-energized under rich mixture condition or if SERVICE ENGINE SOON light is on.

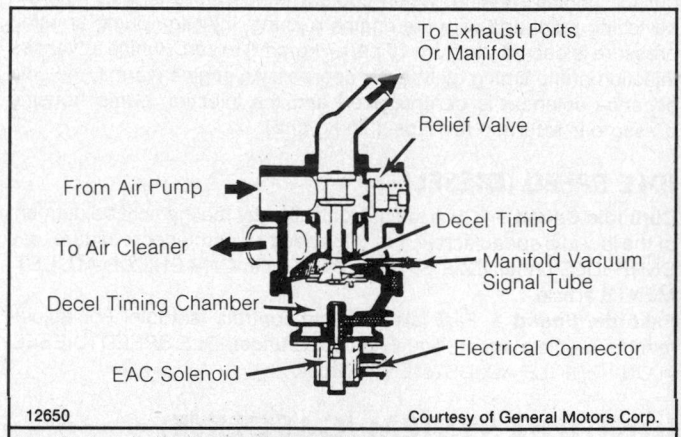

12650   Courtesy of General Motors Corp.

Fig. 2: Cross-Sectional View Of EAC Valve

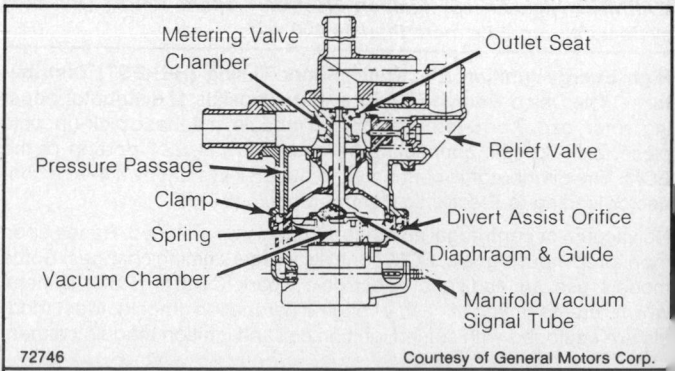

72746   Courtesy of General Motors Corp.

Fig. 3: Cross-Sectional View Of EAC Valve With Relief Tube

Air Pump – The air pump is a belt-driven, positive displacement vane-type pump. A centrifugal filter mounted behind the pulley purges air drawn into pump of dirt and contaminants. The air pump is permanently lubricated and requires no periodic service.

CAUTION: To prevent liquid from entering air pump, always cover centrifugal filter fan before cleaning engine. DO NOT oil air pump.

Check Valves – Check valves prevent the backflow of exhaust gases into the air injection system. Check valves close when exhaust gas pressure in exhaust manifold exceeds pressure delivered by pump. This occurs when air pump by-passes at high speeds, when air delivery is switched to catalytic converter, when air is diverted to either atmosphere or air cleaner or when air pump malfunctions.

Air Management System – When ECM energizes electronic air control solenoid on a cold vehicle, air is allowed to flow through control valve to exhaust manifold. As coolant temperature increases or system enters closed loop, ECM opens solenoid ground circuit, de-energizing control solenoid. Air is then routed to air cleaner.

CATALYTIC CONVERTER

A 3-way catalytic converter with dual bed is used to reduce exhaust emissions. This type of converter can reduce hydrocarbons (HC), carbon monoxide (CO) and oxides of nitrogen (NOx).

The upstream section of the converter contains a reducing/oxidizing bed to reduce NOx while oxidizing HC and CO. An air supply pipe from the AIR system injects air between the beds of the converter. Thus, the second converter bed oxidizes any remaining HC and CO to efficiently reduce exhaust emissions.

EXHAUST GAS RECIRCULATION (EGR)

The Exhaust Gas Recirculation (EGR) system is designed to reduce oxides of nitrogen (NOx) emissions by lowering combustion temperatures. A metered amount of exhaust gas is recirculated into the intake manifold and mixed with the air/fuel mixture.

There are 2 types of EGR systems used. Port EGR is used on 2.8L, 3.1L, 4.3L ("S" and "T" Series), 7.4L and 5.7L (over 8500 GVWR). Negative backpressure EGR is used on 2.5L, 4.3L (except "S" and "T" Series), 5.0L and 5.7 (under 8500 GVWR).

Port EGR – Port EGR valve is controlled by manifold vacuum regulated by an ECM-controlled solenoid. Vehicles equipped with 4L80-E transmissions use a pulse width-modulated EGR vacuum control solenoid, referred to as an Electronic Vacuum Regulator Valve (EVRV).

Negative Backpressure EGR – Vacuum is applied to upper EGR diaphragm via a hose connected to intake manifold vacuum. Manifold vacuum is also applied to lower EGR diaphragm (through intake port at base of EGR valve).

When manifold vacuum in lower chamber is insufficient to overcome spring tension on lower diaphragm, bleed valve closes, allowing vacuum in upper chamber to open EGR valve. With engine at idle or under light load, high manifold vacuum applied to lower chamber opens air bleed valve in lower diaphragm. This bleeds off vacuum in upper chamber, keeping the EGR valve closed.

EVAPORATIVE EMISSION CONTROL

All vehicles use carbon canister storage for evaporative fuel control. Evaporative emission control system stores gasoline fumes from fuel tank in a carbon canister until fumes can be drawn into engine for burning during combustion process.

The 4 basic components which may be used in evaporative emission system are activated carbon canister (all models, open at top or bottom for fresh air intake), vacuum operated canister control valve (4.3L and V8 high altitude, mounted remotely), thermostatic vacuum switch (2.8L and 3.1L, mounted in coolant passage in intake manifold) and tank pressure control valve (4.3L and V8 high altitude, mounted in hose between canister and fuel tank). For specific component application and vacuum hose routing, see VACUUM DIAGRAMS article.

Carbon Canister – Evaporative fumes from fuel tank are vented through hose(s) into a canister containing activated carbon. Activated carbon absorbs and holds fuel vapors when engine is not operating. When engine is started and engine speed is greater than idle (purge at idle would cause too rich a mixture), engine vacuum draws fuel vapors from canister into engine. A vacuum canister purge valve or thermostatic vacuum switch regulates vapors through this purge line.

Carbon canisters are open in design. When the engine is started, engine vacuum draws outside air into canister either through the top or bottom, and then through a filter in bottom of canister. This helps to purge vapors from the activated carbon.

Canister Control Valve (CCV) (High Altitude – 4.3L Except "S" & "T" Series & V8) – CCV is vacuum operated. When the engine is not running, vapor from the fuel tank is stored in the carbon canister. When the vehicle is started, vacuum to the upper port draws in the internal vacuum diaphragm, opening the port between the canister and purge valve. When engine is off, internal spring pressure closes valve diaphragm, preventing vapor from venting to atmosphere.

The canister control valve acts as both vapor vent valve and purge valve. When engine is running, manifold vacuum from PCV system pulls lower diaphragm upward. When engine is operating at greater than idle speed, control vacuum pulls upper diaphragm upward. This allows purging of canister through PCV system.

Thermostatic Vacuum Switch (2.8L & 3.1L) – A wax pellet-type thermostatic vacuum switch is installed in the engine coolant passage in the intake manifold. Two vacuum fittings on switch connect to charcoal canister and the TBI unit. When coolant temperature is less than 115°F (46°C), switch closes, preventing purging of canister. When coolant temperature increases to greater than 115°F (46°C), switch opens, allowing purging of canister.

Fuel Tank Pressure Control Valve (High Altitude – 4.3L Except "S" & "T" Series & V8) – Fuel tank pressure control valve allows vapors to flow from the fuel tank into the EEC system. When fuel tank pressure exceeds the spring pressure on the valve diaphragm, the valve opens and allows vapors to either enter canister or, when purge is enabled, go directly to the engine.

The tank pressure control valve is located inside the gas cap on the 3.1L, in the engine compartment on "C" and "K" Series and near the fuel tank on other models.

POSITIVE CRANKCASE VENTILATION (PCV)

The PCV system provides more effective elimination of crankcase vapors. Fresh air from the air filter housing is supplied to the crankcase, where it is mixed with blow-by gases and passed through a PCV valve into the intake manifold. This mixture is then passed into the combustion chamber and burned.

The PCV valve provides primary control in this system by metering the flow (according to manifold vacuum) of the blow-by vapors. When manifold vacuum is high (at idle), the PCV restricts the flow to maintain a smooth idle condition.

Under conditions in which abnormal amounts of blow-by gases are produced (such as worn cylinders or rings), system is designed to allow excess gases to flow back through crankcase vent hose into air inlet.

Spring pressure holds PCV valve closed when engine is not running. This prevents hydrocarbon fumes from collecting in the intake manifold, a condition which could result in hard starting.

During engine operation, manifold vacuum pulls the valve open against spring pressure, permitting crankcase fumes to enter the intake manifold. Should the engine backfire, the PCV valve closes to prevent ignition of fumes in crankcase.

THERMOSTATIC AIR CLEANER (TAC)

Many models are equipped with a system for preheating the air entering the throttle body during cold engine operation.

This system maintains incoming air temperature to a point where fuel injection system can maintain lean air/fuel ratios to reduce hydrocarbon (HC) and carbon monoxide (CO) emissions. TAC systems are either vacuum motor controlled or wax pellet controlled.

Vacuum Motor Controlled (2.8L & 3.1L) –This system consists of an air cleaner assembly with integral air control door, vacuum control temperature sensor, vacuum motor, heat shroud (on exhaust manifold), heated air tube and vacuum hoses.

- **Vacuum Control Temperature Sensor** – The vacuum control temperature sensor controls the operation of the air control door. During initial start-up situations, this valve directs engine vacuum to the air control vacuum motor. The motor closes the air intake door, allowing the intake of heated manifold air. When the intake air temperature reaches a pre-calibrated value, this valve opens, allowing the intake of cooler outside air.

- **Air Control Door** – The air control door temperature sensor closes when the temperature of air entering the air cleaner is less than the calibrated temperature of the temperature sensor. This allows engine vacuum to operate the air control door vacuum motor, and warm manifold air to be routed to the throttle body.

- **Vacuum Motor** – When engine vacuum is applied to the vacuum motor, the air control door stops the intake of outside air. The air cleaner then draws in air from around the exhaust manifold.

As air inside the air cleaner warms, the temperature sensor begins to open, bleeding off vacuum to the vacuum motor. As vacuum to vacuum motor decreases, the air control door begins to open.

As air control door opens, outside air is allowed to enter air cleaner assembly. When air entering air cleaner reaches a predetermined temperature, the air control door opens completely and stops the intake of heated air.

Wax Pellet Controlled (Except 2.8L & 3.1L) –A self-contained, wax pellet actuated assembly mounted in the air cleaner controls the air regulator damper (hot/cold air delivery door). When incoming air is cold, wax material sealed in the actuator is in a solid contracted state. As incoming air warms, wax material expands by changing to a liquid state. This forces piston outward, repositioning air regulator damper and allowing air (either a mix of hot and cold or all cold) to enter engine.

EMISSION SYSTEMS (DIESEL)

EXHAUST GAS RECIRCULATION (EGR)

NOTE: For additional information on 6.2L light duty emission EGR system, see SELF-DIAGNOSTICS – DIESEL article.

The Exhaust Gas Recirculation (EGR) system limits formation of oxides of nitrogen (NOx) emissions by reducing peak combustion chamber temperatures in which NOx is formed. EGR system consists of EGR valve, Exhaust Pressure Regulator (EPR) valve, EPR and EGR vent solenoids and EGR fault detection. A vacuum pump is required to provide a vacuum source to operate the EGR system.

EGR Valve – EGR valve reintroduces a small amount of exhaust gas into combustion chamber, diluting air/fuel mixture and reducing combustion chamber peak temperatures, thereby reducing NOx formation.

EPR Valve – The EPR valve is mounted between the exhaust manifold and the exhaust pipe. Valve increases exhaust backpressure during idle, which increases exhaust flow through EGR system. EPR valve resembles the EFE or heat riser type valves of earlier, carbureted vehicles. A vacuum diaphragm-type actuator opens and closes valve. An ECM-controlled EGR/EPR solenoid regulates actuator.

EGR/EPR Solenoids – EGR/EPR solenoids are mounted at rear of engine as a single assembly. Using input from engine speed sensor and TPS, ECM controls EGR by controlling amount of "on" and "off" time of EGR solenoid. When EGR is not needed, ECM energizes EGR vent solenoid to vent vacuum. Vacuum which controls EGR valve controls EPR valve. ECM energizes EPR solenoid to close EPR valve at idle to increase exhaust backpressure.

EGR Fault Detection – The ECM uses input from the MAP sensor to measure amount of absolute pressure in EGR vacuum line. If a minor variation between calculated EGR and actual EGR is monitored by ECM, the ECM corrects. If variation is too great for ECM to correct, an error is detected. The ECM then enters default mode and sets a related trouble code in memory.

Vacuum Pump – A vacuum pump is mounted on the engine and provides vacuum for operating emission controls (light duty emissions), transmission modulator (heavy duty emissions with M40 automatic transmission), cruise control and heater and A/C servos. The vacuum pump is either belt- or gear-driven.

The belt-driven vacuum pump is bracket mounted to the right front of the engine. Except for the pulley, the vacuum pump is replaced as an assembly.

The gear-driven pump is mounted at the top rear of the engine and contains a permanently-mounted speed sensor. Pump is driven by a cam inside the drive assembly to which it mounts. On the lower end of the drive housing assembly is a drive gear which meshes with the camshaft gear in the engine. The drive gear causes the cam in the drive housing to rotate.

CAUTION: The vacuum pump drives the engine oil pump. DO NOT run engine with gear-driven vacuum pump removed.

CRANKCASE DEPRESSION REGULATOR (CDR)

The CDR valve, located on the right valve cover, is used on both light and heavy duty diesel engines. Valve prevents crankcase pressure from accumulating during idle by regulating (metering) crankcase pressure back into the engine. Intake manifold vacuum acts against a spring-loaded diaphragm to control flow of crankcase gases. Higher intake manifold vacuum levels pull diaphragm closer to the top of the outlet tube, reducing amount of gases drawn from crankcase. As intake manifold vacuum drops, spring pressure pushes diaphragm away from top of outlet, allowing more gases to flow from crankcase into intake manifold.

Optimum pressure in crankcase is one inch of water (as measured with a manometer) at idle to 3-4 inches at full load. Too little vacuum causes oil leaks; too much vacuum pulls oil into the air crossover.

SELF-DIAGNOSTIC SYSTEM

The ECM is equipped with a self-diagnostic system which detects system failures or abnormalities. When a malfunction occurs, ECM illuminates the SERVICE ENGINE SOON light located on instrument panel. When malfunction is detected and light is turned on, a corresponding trouble code is stored in ECM memory. Malfunctions are designated as either "hard failures" or "intermittent failures". For procedures on retrieving stored codes, see appropriate SELF-DIAGNOSTICS article.

"Hard Failures" – Hard failures cause SERVICE ENGINE SOON light to glow and remain on until malfunction is repaired. If light comes on and remains on during vehicle operation, cause of malfunction must be determined using diagnostic charts located in SELF-DIAGNOS-TICS article. If a sensor fails, ECM uses a substitute value in its calculations to continue engine operation. Although vehicle is functional in this condition, driveability will probably be adversely affected.

"Intermittent Failures" – Intermittent failures cause SERVICE ENGINE SOON light to flicker or illuminate and go out about 10 seconds after intermittent fault goes away. However, ECM retains corresponding trouble code in memory. If related fault does not reoccur within 50 engine restarts, related trouble code is erased from ECM memory. Sensor, connector or wiring related problems may cause intermittent failures. See TROUBLE SHOOTING – NO CODES article.

SERVICE ENGINE SOON LIGHT

As a bulb and system check, SERVICE ENGINE SOON light glows when ignition switch is turned to ON position and engine is not running. When engine is started, light should go out. If not, a malfunction has been detected in computerized engine control system or SERVICE ENGINE SOON light circuit is faulty.

To verify proper operation of SERVICE ENGINE SOON light on gasoline vehicles, see DIAGNOSTIC CIRCUIT CHECK in BASIC DIAGNOS-TIC PROCEDURES article. To verify proper operation of SERVICE ENGINE SOON light and retrieve trouble codes on diesel vehicles, see DIAGNOSTIC CIRCUIT CHECK chart in SELF-DIAGNOSTICS – DIESEL article.

SERIAL DATA

ECM is equipped with a serial data line. Serial data is a stream of electrical impulses which can be interpreted by special testers of other control modules. Serial data must be accessed by connecting special Scan testers to the Assembly Line Data Link (ALDL) connector. Update intervals and information contained within the data stream vary with model application.

MISCELLANEOUS ECM CONTROLS

NOTE: Although not considered true Engine Performance-related systems, some controlled devices may affect driveability if they malfunction.

A/C CLUTCH

On many models, ECM regulates operation of the A/C clutch through an ECM-controlled relay. The ECM disengages the A/C compressor when compressor load on engine may cause driveability problems (i.e. during hot restart, idle, low speed steering maneuvers and wide open throttle operation) or if A/C freon pressure drops to less than or rises to greater than normal operating levels.

Freon pressure is sensed through the monitoring of high and low pressure switches or a pressure sensor which registers either high or low pressure levels. Power steering load is monitored through a power steering pressure switch (2.5L). Hot restart is monitored through the coolant temperature sensor. For component application and related wiring, see wiring schematics under MISCELLANEOUS ECM CONTROLS in SYSTEM & COMPONENT TESTING article.

A/C Pressure Switches – A/C high and low pressure switches may be used in the A/C compressor clutch or compressor clutch relay circuit. Switches are normally closed, completing the circuit which energizes the compressor clutch. When system freon pressure increases beyond a certain point, high side switch opens, causing compressor clutch to disengage.

If system freon level decreases (causing freon pressure to drop), low side pressure switch opens, preventing compressor damage by causing compressor clutch to disengage.

COOLING FAN (3.1L & 3.8L)

ECM regulates operation of the electric cooling fan through an ECM controlled relay which controls the ground or power circuit for the cooling fan. ECM operates the cooling fan based upon engine temperature. Most systems engage electric cooling fan whenever the A/C clutch is engaged, regardless of engine temperature. As a back-up system, many models use a coolant override switch, which engages the cooling fan in case the ECM fails to energize the cooling fan relay or if the cooling fan relay malfunctions. A malfunction of the cooling fan causes engine overheating and possible detonation.

For component application and related wiring, see wiring schematics under MISCELLANEOUS ECM CONTROLS in SYSTEM & COMPONENT TESTING article.

TRANSMISSION

Converter Clutch – The transmission/transaxle converter clutch eliminates power loss of torque converter stage when vehicle is in a cruise condition, allowing driver convenience of automatic transmission and fuel economy of a manual transmission. Fused battery ignition is supplied to converter solenoid through a brake switch.

On some models, 2nd, 3rd and 4th gear hydraulic apply switches (located within transmission) may also be in series with solenoid power or ground circuit. On other models, switch status may only be monitored by ECM, without sharing power or ground with converter solenoid. For wiring reference, see wiring schematics under MISCELLANEOUS ECM CONTROLS in SYSTEM & COMPONENT TESTING article.

Converter clutch engages when vehicle is moving faster than a pre-calibrated speed, engine is at normal operating temperature, throttle position sensor output is not changing (indicating a steady road speed) and transmission 3rd gear or high gear switch (if equipped) and brake switch are closed.

When vehicle speed is great enough (about 20-45 MPH as indicated by the vehicle speed sensor), ECM energizes converter clutch solenoid mounted in transmission, allowing torque converter to directly connect engine to the transmission. When operating conditions indicate transmission should operate as normal, converter clutch solenoid is de-energized, allowing transmission to return to normal automatic operation. Since power for the converter solenoid is delivered through the brake switch, transmission also returns to normal automatic operation when brake pedal is depressed. To check function of converter clutch system, perform functional check of system. See MISCELLANEOUS ECM CONTROLS in SYSTEM & COMPONENT TESTING article.

Electronic Transmission (4L80-E) – On gasoline vehicles equipped with 4L80-E transmission, Powertrain Control Module (PCM) controls transmission and other vehicle functions. On diesel vehicles, Transmission Control Module (TCM) controls electronic transmission, but no other components. PCM/TCM monitors a number of engine/vehicle functions and uses data to control shift solenoid "A", shift solenoid "B", TCC and the force motor and regulate TCC engagement, upshift pattern, downshift pattern and line pressure (shift quality).

- **Shift Solenoid "A"** – Shift solenoid "A" is attached to the valve body and is a normally open exhaust valve. PCM/TCM activates solenoid by grounding it through an internal quad-driver. Solenoid "A" is on in 1st and 4th gears, but off in 2nd and 3rd. When on, solenoid redirects fluid to act on the shift valves. Solenoid "A" is Blue. Code 82 is associated with solenoid "A".

- **Shift Solenoid "B"** – Shift solenoid "B" is attached to the valve body and is a normally open exhaust valve. PCM/TCM activates solenoid by grounding it through an internal quad-driver. Solenoid "B" is on in 3rd and 4th gears, but off in 1st and 2nd. When on, solenoid redirects fluid to act on the shift valves. Solenoid "B" is Red. Codes 81, 86 and 87 are associated with solenoid "B".

- **Force Motor** – Force motor is attached to the valve body and controls line pressure by moving a pressure regulator valve against spring pressure. Force motor replaces the throttle valve or vacuum modulator used on past transmissions. PCM/TCM varies line pressure based upon engine load. Engine load is calculated from various inputs, especially the TPS.

  Line pressure is actually varied by changing the amperage applied to the force motor from zero (high pressure) to 1.1 amps (low pressure). The force motor is periodically pulsed to prevent fluid contamination from causing pressure regulator valve to stick.

Shift Light – Shift light may be used on vehicles equipped with manual transmission. Light indicates best transmission shift point for maximum fuel economy. Power for light is supplied through GAUGES fuse. Light illuminates when ECM supplies a ground circuit for bulb. For wiring reference, see wiring schematics under MISCELLANEOUS ECM CONTROLS in SYSTEM & COMPONENT TESTING article.

1992 ENGINE PERFORMANCE
Basic Diagnostic Procedures

Astro, Bravada, Commercial Van, Jimmy,
Lumina APV, Safari, Sierra, Silhouette,
Sonoma, Suburban, Syclone, Trans Sport,
Typhoon, Van, Yukon,
"C" & "K" Series Blazer & Pickup,
"S" & "T" Series Blazer & Pickup

INTRODUCTION

The following diagnostic steps help prevent overlooking simple problems and begin diagnosis for no-start conditions.

The first step in diagnosing any driveability problem is verifying the customer's complaint by test driving vehicle under the conditions in which the problem reportedly occurred.

Before entering self-diagnostics, perform a careful and complete visual inspection. Most engine control problems result from mechanical breakdowns, poor electrical connections or damaged/misrouted vacuum hoses. Before condemning the computerized system, perform each test listed in this article.

NOTE: Unless otherwise instructed in test procedures, perform all voltage tests using a Digital Volt-Ohmmeter (DVOM) with a minimum 10-megohm input impedance.

PRELIMINARY INSPECTION & ADJUSTMENTS

VISUAL INSPECTION

Visually inspect all electrical wiring. Look for chafed, stretched, cut or pinched wiring. Ensure electrical connectors fit tightly and are not corroded. Ensure vacuum hoses are properly routed and not pinched or cut. If necessary, see VACUUM DIAGRAMS article to verify routing and connections. Inspect air induction system for possible vacuum leaks.

MECHANICAL INSPECTION

Compression – Check engine mechanical condition using a compression gauge, vacuum gauge or engine analyzer capable of performing a relative compression test. If using engine analyzer, see engine analyzer instruction manual for availability and description of relative compression feature.

WARNING: Because fuel injectors on many models are triggered by ignition switch during cranking mode, DO NOT use ignition switch during compression tests on fuel injected vehicles. Use a remote starter to crank engine to prevent fire hazard or engine's oiling system contamination.

Exhaust System Backpressure – Before replacing any components, check exhaust system for restrictions. Use a vacuum gauge or a low pressure (1-5 psi) pressure gauge to check exhaust system.

If using a vacuum gauge, connect gauge to intake manifold vacuum, and start engine. Observe gauge while holding throttle steady at 2000-2500 RPM. If vacuum gauge reading slowly drops after stabilizing, exhaust system may be restricted.

- **Check at AIR Pipe** – Remove rubber hose at exhaust manifold AIR pipe check valve, and remove check valve. Install pressure gauge to hose and nipple via Propane Enrichment Device (J26911). Nipple should be inserted into exhaust manifold AIR pipe.
- **Check at O$_2$ Sensor** – Remove O$_2$ sensor. Install backpressure tester in place of O$_2$ sensor. After test is completed, coat O$_2$ sensor threads with anti-seize compound.
- **Diagnosis – 1)** Start engine, and bring to operating temperature. Increase engine speed to 2000-2500 RPM. Note gauge. Exhaust system is restricted if reading exceeds **1.25 psi (.09 kg/cm^2)**.
  2) Check exhaust system for collapsed pipe, heat distress and possible internal muffler failure. If none of these conditions exists, check for restricted catalytic converter. Replace as required.

A-3, NO-START DIAGNOSIS

NOTE: For diesel information, see SELF-DIAGNOSTICS – DIESEL and TROUBLE SHOOTING – NO CODES articles.

Definition – No-start is defined as engine cranks okay, but does not start. Engine may fire a few times.

NOTE: Before performing following tests, check battery condition, engine cranking speed and fuel supply.

NO START – ENGINE CRANKS OKAY (EXCEPT 3.8L WITH C^{3}I)

General Inspection – 1) Ensure proper starting procedure is being used.

IMPORTANT: The following table provides the location of commonly used diagnostic information. These former "A" and "C" charts are now written in text and inserted into the appropriate location in the new Engine Performance workflow. To familiarize yourself with the Engine Performance workflow, see HOW TO USE THE ENGINE PERFORMANCE SECTION in GENERAL INFORMATION.

GENERAL MOTORS "A" & "C" CHART REFERENCE TABLE

System or Component	Diagnostic Information Location
DIAGNOSTIC CIRCUIT CHECK	See DIAGNOSTIC CIRCUIT CHECK in BASIC DIAGNOSTIC PROCEDURES
A-1 & A-2, SERVICE ENGINE SOON Light	See DIAGNOSTIC CIRCUIT CHECK in BASIC DIAGNOSTIC PROCEDURES
A-3, No-Start	See NO-START DIAGNOSIS in BASIC DIAGNOSTIC PROCEDURES
A-5, Fuel Pump Relay	See RELAYS, SOLENOIDS, MOTORS & MODULES in SYSTEM & COMPONENT TESTING
A-6 & A-7, Fuel System Diagnosis	See BASIC FUEL SYSTEM CHECKS in BASIC DIAGNOSTIC PROCEDURES
C-1, MAP Sensor	See ENGINE SENSORS & SWITCHES in SYSTEM & COMPONENT TESTING
C-1, Power Steering Pressure Switch	See ENGINE SENSORS & SWITCHES in SYSTEM & COMPONENT TESTING
C-1, Park/Neutral Switch	See ENGINE SENSORS & SWITCHES in SYSTEM & COMPONENT TESTING
C-2, Injector Balance Test (4.3L)	See FUEL CONTROL in SYSTEM & COMPONENT TESTING
C-2, IAC Motor	See IDLE CONTROL SYSTEM in SYSTEM & COMPONENT TESTING
C-3, Canister Purge System	See EMISSION SYSTEMS & SUB-SYSTEMS in SYSTEM & COMPONENT TESTING
C-4, EST Ignition Check	See BASIC IGNITION SYSTEM CHECKS in BASIC DIAGNOSTIC PROCEDURES
C-5, ESC Ignition Check	See IGNITION SYSTEM in SYSTEM & COMPONENT TESTING
C-6, Air Injection System	See EMISSION SYSTEMS & SUB-SYSTEMS in SYSTEM & COMPONENT TESTING
C-7, EGR System	See EMISSION SYSTEMS & SUB-SYSTEMS in SYSTEM & COMPONENT TESTING
C-8, Torque Converter Clutch	[1] See MISCELLANEOUS ECM CONTROLS in SYSTEM & COMPONENT TESTING
C-8, Manual Transmission Shift Lights	[1] See MISCELLANEOUS ECM CONTROLS in SYSTEM & COMPONENT TESTING
C-10, A/C Clutch Control	See MISCELLANEOUS ECM CONTROLS in SYSTEM & COMPONENT TESTING
C-12, Electric Cooling Fan Control	[2] See MISCELLANEOUS ECM CONTROLS in SYSTEM & COMPONENT TESTING

[1] – Complete coverage in MITCHELL® 1991-92 TRANSMISSION SERVICE & REPAIR manual for domestic vehicles.
[2] – Complete coverage in ENGINE COOLING in MITCHELL® 1992 DOMESTIC LIGHT TRUCKS & VANS SERVICE & REPAIR manual, 1992 ENGINE, CLUTCH & DRIVE AXLE supplement.

2) Visually check vacuum hoses for splits, kinks and improper connections. See underhood emission control information label. Check ignition wires for cracking, hardness and improper connections at both distributor cap and spark plugs.

3) Remove spark plugs. Check and replace as necessary.

4) Remove distributor cap and check for moisture, dust, cracks, burns and arcing to ground through coil mounting screws or rotor.

5) Try to turn distributor shaft by hand. Drive gear pin may be broken.

6) If vehicle has been exposed to very cold temperatures, ensure oil is proper viscosity and not contaminated with gasoline.

Ignition System – 1) Disconnect tachometer wire at distributor tachometer terminal (if equipped). A shorted tachometer or tachometer circuit prevents vehicle from starting. Ensure TPS and coolant sensor codes are not present and sensors are not out of calibration.

2) Check for battery voltage at "+" terminal of ignition coil with ignition on. *See Figs. 1-6.* Repair as necessary.

3) Connect ST-125 spark tester to end of one plug wire and crank engine. If spark is present, check fuel delivery.

4) If spark does not occur, disconnect 4-wire EST connector at distributor and check for spark at ignition coil tower using ST-125. If spark now occurs, check cap and rotor for damage or wear. Check for opens in coil wires.

5) If spark does not occur, reconnect EST connector. Leave ST-125 connected to coil tower for remainder of testing. Disconnect ignition coil Black 2-wire connector and check voltage on "C" and "+" terminals with ignition on.

6) If voltage on both terminals is 10 volts or greater, go to step 7). If voltage on both terminals is less than 10 volts, repair wire from module "+" terminal to "B" terminal on coil Black 2-wire connector. If voltage is less than 10 volts on terminal "C" only, check for open or short to ground in circuit from ignition module terminal "C" to ignition coil. If circuit is okay, problem is faulty coil or coil connections.

7) If voltage reading on both terminals is greater than 10 volts, connect voltmeter between ground and tachometer terminal at coil with ignition on. Tachometer terminal may be taped back against harness. If voltage is greater than 10 volts, go to step 9).

8) If voltage is 1-10 volts, replace ignition module and check for spark at coil tower using Spark Tester (ST-125). If Voltage is less than one volt, repair open in tachometer lead or tachometer connector. After repairs, recheck voltage at tachometer terminal.

9) Connect test light between ground and tachometer terminal. Crank engine. If test light remains on (steady), go to next step. If test light flashes, replace ignition coil with a known good unit and recheck for spark. If spark does not occur, reinstall original ignition coil and replace ignition module.

10) Disconnect distributor 4-wire connector. Remove distributor cap. Unplug ignition module pick-up coil connector. Connect voltmeter between ground and tachometer terminal. Turn ignition on. Using jumper wires, connect positive end of a known good 1.5 volt battery to terminal "P" of module. Observe voltmeter at tachometer terminal as negative end of test battery is momentarily grounded to distributor housing.

11) If voltage at tachometer terminal does not drop, check ignition module ground, and check for open in wires from ignition coil to module. If all is okay, replace ignition module.

12) If voltage at tachometer terminal drops, check for spark at spark tester as jumper is removed from terminal "P". If spark does not occur, go to next step. If spark occurs, check pick-up coil connections and check for 500-1500 ohms resistance at pick-up coil leads and ensure leads are not shorted to ground. Repair as necessary.

13) If spark does not occur, test ignition module with module tester. If module tests okay, check ignition coil wire. If module tester is not available, replace ignition coil, and touch terminal "P" again. If spark occurs, system is okay. If spark does not occur, reinstall original ignition coil and check coil wire from distributor cap. If no problem is found, replace ignition module.

Fuel System (TBI) – 1) Before checking fuel system for a no-start condition, check ignition for adequate spark. Check for proper fuel pump pressure (9-13 psi) and capacity (one pint in 30 seconds). See A-7, BASIC FUEL SYSTEM CHECKS (GASOLINE).

2) Crank engine, and watch for injector spray. If injector spray occurs, go to step 5). If no spray occurs, disconnect injector harness, and check for battery voltage at harness. Battery voltage should be present on one injector terminal. If battery voltage is not present, check for blown injector power fuse. If battery voltage is present on both terminals, check for wires shorted to one another.

3) If battery voltage is present on only one terminal, connect injector test light (also called a "node" light) to injector harness. Crank engine, and note light. If light flashes, check for stored ECM codes. See DIAGNOSTIC CIRCUIT CHECK. If no codes are present, refer to HARD START symptom in TROUBLE SHOOTING – NO CODES article. If light does not flash, momentarily touch test light from battery voltage to ECM RPM reference terminal (circuit No. 430).

4) Each time test light is removed from ECM RPM reference terminal, injector test light should flash. If test light does not flash, check for open in RPM reference wire or injector drive (ground) circuit. If wiring is okay, replace faulty ECM. Prior to replacing ECM, check ECM power and ground circuits.

5) If injector spray occurred while cranking engine, disconnect injector harness, and crank engine. If injector spray or leakage occurs, a no-start condition could be caused by excessive fuel being delivered during cranking. Repair faulty injector or injector seal. If no spray or leakage occurs, refer to HARD START symptom in TROUBLE SHOOTING – NO CODES article.

Fuel System (4.3L CPI) – Before checking fuel system for a no-start condition, check ignition for adequate spark. For fuel system testing, see CPI (4.3L) under A-7, BASIC FUEL SYSTEM CHECKS (GASOLINE).

Fuel System (4.3L Turbo PFI) – 1) Before checking fuel system for a no-start condition, check ignition for adequate spark. Check for proper fuel pump pressure and capacity. See A-7, BASIC FUEL SYSTEM CHECKS (GASOLINE).

2) Disconnect injector harness. Turn ignition on, and check for battery voltage at each injector harness. Battery voltage should be present on one side of each injector. If battery voltage is not present, check for blown injector power fuse. If battery voltage is present on both injector terminals, check for wires shorted together.

3) If battery voltage is present on only one terminal, connect injector test light to injector harness. Crank engine, and note light. Repeat on other injector connectors. If light flashes, check for stored ECM codes. If no codes are present, refer to HARD START symptom in TROUBLE SHOOTING – NO CODES article.

4) If light does not flash, disconnect distributor 4-wire HEI-EST connector. Momentarily touch test light from battery voltage to ECM RPM reference wire (circuit No. 430) of 4-wire connector. Each time test light is removed from ECM RPM reference terminal, injector test light should flash. If test light does not flash, check for open in RPM reference wire or injector drive (ground) circuit. If wiring is okay, replace faulty ECM.

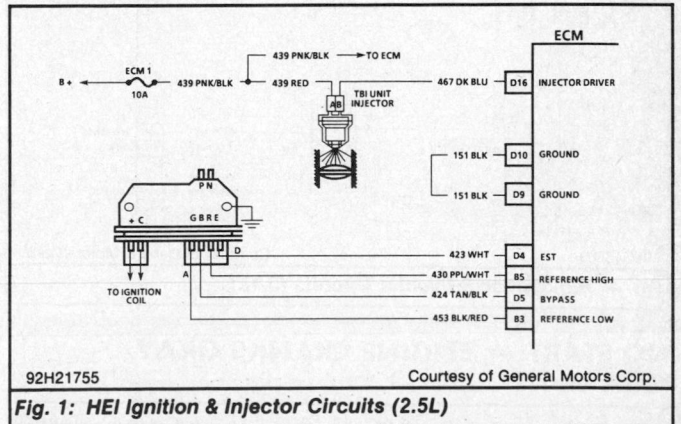

92H21755   Courtesy of General Motors Corp.

Fig. 1: HEI Ignition & Injector Circuits (2.5L)

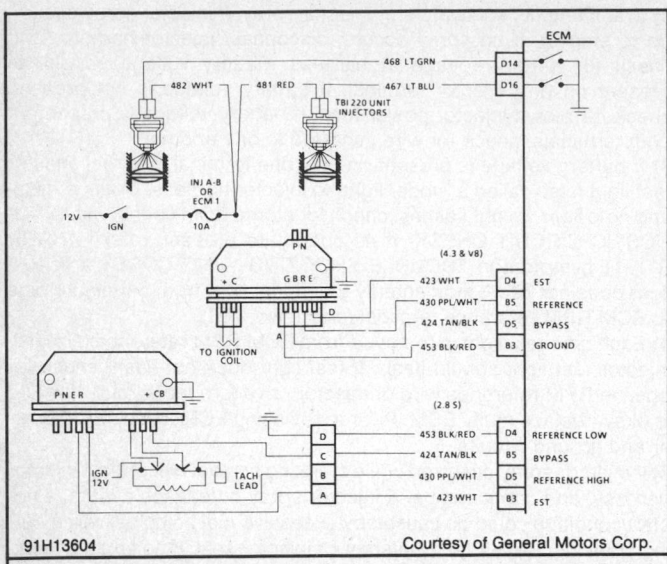

Fig. 2: HEI Ignition & Injector Circuits (2.8L, 4.3L TBI, 5.0L, 5.7L & 7.4L Without 4L80-E Transmission)

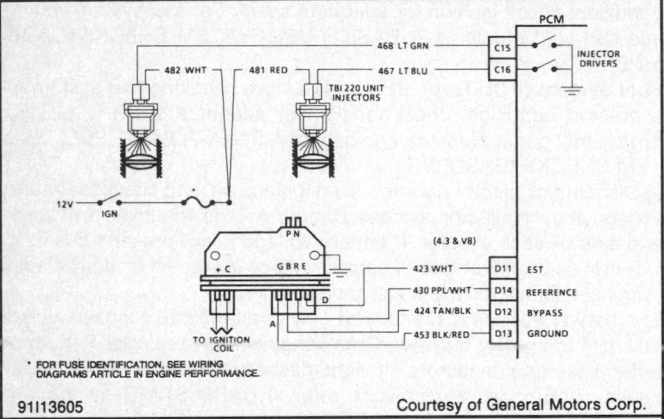

Fig. 3: HEI Ignition & Injector Circuits (2.8L, 4.3L TBI, 5.0L, 5.7L & 7.4L With 4L80-E Transmission)

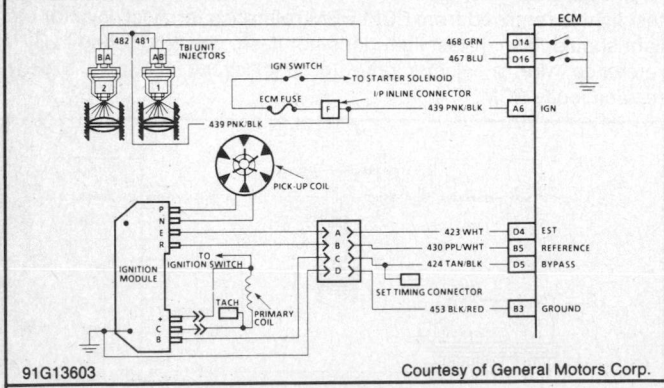

Fig. 4: HEI Ignition & Injector Circuits (3.1L)

NO START – ENGINE CRANKS OKAY
(3.8L WITH C³I)

NOTE: Before performing following tests, check battery condition, engine cranking speed and for adequate fuel in tank.

General Inspection – 1) Ensure proper starting procedure is being used. Visually check vacuum hoses for splits, kinks and proper connections, as shown on Vehicle Emission Control Information label.

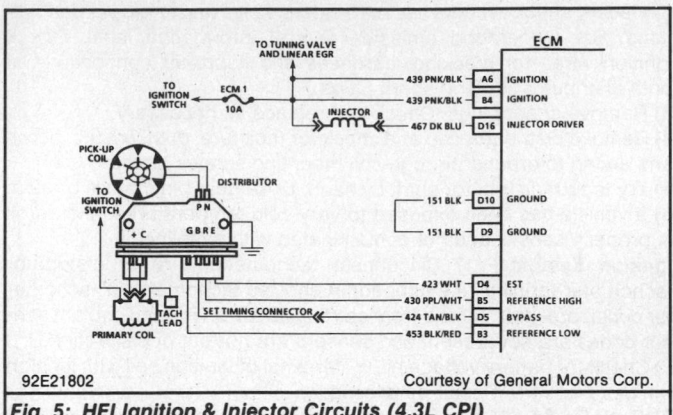

Fig. 5: HEI Ignition & Injector Circuits (4.3L CPI)

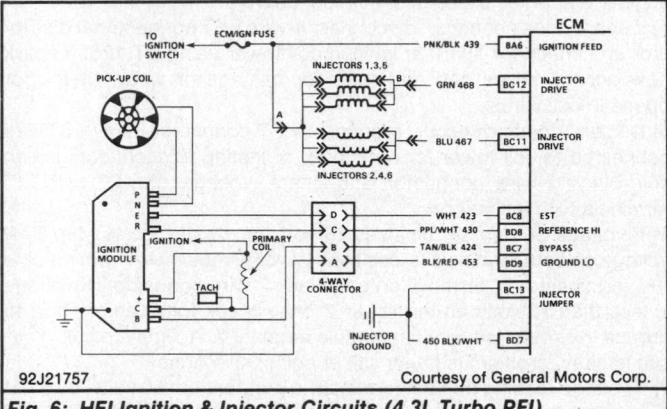

Fig. 6: HEI Ignition & Injector Circuits (4.3L Turbo PFI)

Check ignition wires for cracking, hardness and proper connections at both coil pack and spark plugs.
2) Remove spark plugs. Check and replace as necessary. In very cold temperatures, ensure oil is proper viscosity and not contaminated with gasoline.
Ignition System (3.8L) – 1) Ensure TPS scans less than 2.5 volts. If not, see Code 21 chart in appropriate SELF-DIAGNOSTICS article. Check for stored trouble codes. See appropriate SELF-DIAGNOSTICS article. If engine has not been started for at least 8 hours, MAT sensor scan temperature should be close to CTS scan temperature. Disconnect cam sensor and attempt to start engine. If engine starts, see Code 41 chart in appropriate SELF-DIAGNOSTICS article.
2) Reconnect cam sensor connector. Compare scanned CTS temperature with actual coolant temperature. If they are not close, replace coolant sensor. Depress accelerator pedal approximately 25 percent. Attempt to start engine. If engine does not start, go to next step. If engine starts, check IAC counts on scan tester. Check for stored Code 35. Check for blocked IAC passages.
3) Disconnect all injector connectors and install injector test light in each injector harness connector. All lights should be off and should blink as engine is cranked. If any injector lights are on, go to step **6)**. If lights do not blink at all while cranking, go to step **7)**. If all lights are off and they blink as engine is cranked, check for adequate spark using Spark Tester (ST-125). Check for spark on plug wires No. 1, 3 and 5 (one at a time). Leave matching plug wire connected while checking for spark. If spark jumped tester on all plug wires, check for fouled spark plugs or for fuel system as cause of no start. See BASIC FUEL SYSTEM CHECKS. If spark did not occur on any plug wire, ignition module connection is poor or ignition module is faulty.
4) If spark did not jump tester on all plug wires, verify that plug wire resistance is less than 30,000 ohms. Verify that ignition coils secondary resistance is **5000-6500 ohms** at room temperature. Replace as necessary. If wires and coils are okay, remove coil that did not fire. Verify primary resistance of **.3-.5 ohm**. Replace coil if necessary. If coil is okay, connect a test light across ignition module terminals for problem coil.

5) Crank engine. If test light flashes, check for poor coil to module connections. If connections are okay, replace faulty coil. If test light does not flash, replace ignition module.

6) Turn ignition off. Disconnect PCM Black C-D connector. Turn ignition on. If all lights are now off, replace PCM. If any lights are still on, repair short to ground in that injector drive circuit.

7) Check ignition module power supply (20-amp INJ fuse and circuit). Repair as necessary. Disconnect fuel injector connector. Turn ignition on. With a test light connected to ground, check for battery voltage on Pink/Black wire of injector harness. If test light is on, go to next step. If test light is off, check injector harness between injector connectors and 20-amp INJ fuse. If fuse is blown, repair short to ground and replace fuse. If fuse is okay, check power supply to fuse and circuit between fuse and the injector harness connector.

8) Turn ignition off. Disconnect ignition module connector. Turn ignition on. Install injector test light in any injector harness connector. Connect test light to battery voltage, and repeatedly touch terminal "D" of ignition module harness connector. See Fig. 7. Injector test light should flash each time test light is touched to terminal "D". If injector test light flashes, go to step **10)**.

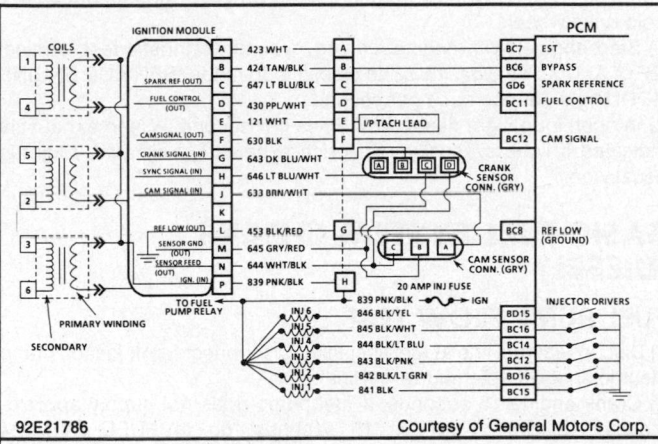

92E21786   Courtesy of General Motors Corp.

Fig. 7: 3.8L PFI Ignition System

9) If injector test light does not flash, check injector drive circuit between PCM and injector harness connector for open or short to voltage. Repair as necessary. If injector drive circuit is okay, check for open, short to ground or short to voltage on fuel control circuit No. 430. If circuit is okay, problem is faulty connection at PCM fuel control terminal or faulty PCM.

10) Turn ignition off. Using proper jumper adaptor from Adaptor Kit (J 35616), connect a fused jumper between ignition module harness connector terminal "N" and battery voltage. Connect a second jumper between ignition module harness connector terminals "M" and ground. Connect DVOM between ignition module harness connector terminal "H" and battery voltage. Observe voltmeter while cranking engine. Voltmeter should read approximately 1.7 volts.

11) If voltage is high, check circuit No. 646 for open or short to ground. If open or short to ground is not present, replace faulty crank sensor. If voltage is low, check circuit No. 646 for an open or short to voltage, circuit No. 645 for an open and circuit No. 644 for an open or short to ground. If all circuits are okay, replace faulty crank sensor.

12) If voltage is approximately 1.7 volts, move DVOM lead from terminal "H" to terminal "G". Crank engine and once again monitor voltage. Voltmeter should read about 5.5 volts. If voltage is correct, go to next step. If voltage is less than 5.5 volts, check for open or short to voltage in circuit No. 643. If voltage is greater than 5.5 volts, check for a short to ground on circuit No. 643. If no problem is found, crank sensor is faulty.

13) If voltage is close to 5.5 volts, turn ignition on. Probe ignition module harness connector terminals "P" with a DVOM connected to ground. If battery voltage is not present, repair open in ignition module power supply circuit. If battery voltage is present, problem is poor ignition module connections or faulty ignition module.

A-7, BASIC FUEL SYSTEM CHECKS (GASOLINE)

FUEL SYSTEM PRESSURE RELIEF

Model 700 TBI Unit (2.5L) – Place transmission gear selector in Park (Neutral on manual transmissions). Set parking brake, and block drive wheels. Loosen fuel filler cap to relieve tank pressure. Disconnect 3-terminal electrical connector at fuel tank. Start engine, and allow to run until engine stalls due to lack of fuel. Crank engine 3 seconds to remove any fuel pressure left in fuel lines. Fuel lines are now safe for servicing.

Model 220 TBI Unit (Except 2.5L) – Fuel pressure is relieved and drops to zero when ignition is turned off. To minimize risk of fire and personal injury, cover area to be disconnected with a shop rag.

CPI & Port Fuel Injection (4.3L CPI & 4.3L Turbo) – Fuel system is under pressure. Pressure must be relieved prior to servicing fuel system. Fuel pressure may be relieved by one of following methods.

- Disconnect fuel pump at rear body connector. Start engine, and run it until it stalls. Crank starter 3 seconds to remove remaining fuel from fuel lines. Reconnect rear body connector.
- Install Fuel Pressure Gauge (J-34730-1) on fuel pressure connector of fuel rail. Wrap shop towel around pressure connection when installing fuel pressure gauge to absorb fuel leakage. Install gauge bleed hose in container. Open bleed valve to bleed fuel pressure.

FUEL SYSTEM PRESSURE TEST

WARNING: Begin fuel system trouble shooting and diagnosis with fuel system pressure test. Relieve fuel system pressure before disconnecting any components or installing fuel pressure gauge.

TBI – 1) Turn ignition off for 10 seconds. Turn ignition on, and listen at fuel tank for fuel pump operation. Pump should run 2 seconds (20 seconds on models equipped with fuel module). If fuel pump runs, go to next step. If fuel pump does not run, go to step **7)**.

2) If fuel pump runs, turn ignition off. Verify fuel tank has fuel. Relieve fuel pressure. See FUEL SYSTEM PRESSURE RELIEF. Remove air cleaner, and plug air cleaner vacuum ports (if equipped). Disconnect fuel line between throttle body and fuel filter. Install Fuel Pressure Gauge (J-29658A) and Adapter (J-2968A-85) between steel fuel line and flexible hose, ahead of in-line fuel filter.

3) Turn ignition on, and note reading on pressure gauge. If fuel pressure is **9-13 psi (.63-.91 kg/cm²)**, no problems are present. If pressure is less than 9 psi (.63 kg/cm²), go to step **5)**. If pressure is greater than 13 psi (.91 kg/cm²), turn ignition off, and bleed fuel pressure. Disconnect fuel return line downstream of pressure gauge. Insert return line into a gasoline container.

4) Turn ignition on. If pressure is now 9-13 psi (.63-.91 kg/cm²), correct restriction in fuel return line between disconnected point and fuel tank. If fuel pressure is greater than 13 psi (.91 kg/cm²), check for restricted return line (including fuel filter) downstream of pressure gauge. If no restrictions are present, replace fuel pressure regulator (TBI 700) or fuel meter cover/pressure regulator (TBI 220).

5) If fuel pressure was less than 9 psi (.63 kg/cm²), check for restricted line between in-tank fuel pump and pressure regulator. If fuel line is okay, disconnect injector connector. Turn ignition on. Gradually pinch fuel pressure gauge outlet hose. Note pressure.

CAUTION: DO NOT pinch off fuel return line completely. DO NOT allow fuel pressure build-up to exceed specification, as damage to fuel pressure regulator may occur.

6) If pressure is greater than 13 psi (.91 kg/cm²), replace fuel pressure regulator (TBI 700) or fuel meter cover/pressure regulator (TBI 220). If pressure is less than 9 psi (.63 kg/cm²), check for faulty fuel pump or incorrect part. Check fuel pump coupling hose and pump inlet filter in fuel tank. On models with dual fuel tanks, check for faulty fuel selector valve and meter switch.

7) If fuel pump did not run in step **1)**, apply 12 volts to fuel pump test connector. For fuel pump test connector location, see underhood engine component views under COMPONENT LOCATIONS in SYSTEM & COMPONENT TESTING article. If fuel pump now runs, repair open in fuel pump relay drive or power circuit or repair faulty fuel pump relay. To test relay, see FUEL PUMP RELAY in SYSTEM & COMPONENT TESTING article.

8) If fuel pump does not run with 12 volts applied to fuel pump test connector, repair open in fuel pump power or ground circuit or repair faulty fuel pump.

CPI (4.3L) – 1) Relieve fuel pressure. See FUEL PRESSURE RELIEF. Connect Fuel Pressure Gauge (J-34730-1) to fuel pressure connector on fuel rail. Turn ignition on. With ignition on and engine off, pressure should be **54-64 psi (3.8-4.5 kg/cm²)** and should hold steady. If pressure is within specification and holds, go to next step. If pressure does not hold, go to step **3)**. If no fuel pressure is present, go to step **6)**. If pressure is greater than specification, go to step **8)**.

2) Start engine. With engine at operating temperature, open throttle quickly and note fuel pressure. If pressure does not approach 64 psi (4.5 kg/cm²), replace CPI assembly. If pressure does approach 64 psi (4.5 kg/cm²), no problem is present.

3) If pressure is within specification but does not hold, check for leaking injectors or fittings by pinching off fuel return line. If pressure does not hold, replace CPI assembly. If pressure does hold, check for faulty in-tank fuel pump or pump connections.

4) If pressure is present but less than specification, check for restricted delivery line or fuel filter. Repair as necessary. If no restriction is evident, apply battery voltage to fuel pump test connector using a 10-amp fused jumper wire. For location of fuel pump test connector, see COMPONENT LOCATIONS in SYSTEM & COMPONENT TESTING article.

5) Gradually pinch off flexible fuel return line between CPI assembly and fuel tank. If fuel pressure increases to within specifications, pressure regulator is faulty. Replace CPI assembly. If fuel pressure does not increase with line pinched, check for faulty in-tank fuel pump, loose pump connections or partial blocked fuel strainer.

6) Use a 10-amp fused jumper wire to apply battery voltage to fuel pump test connector. For location of fuel pump test connector, see COMPONENT LOCATIONS in SYSTEM & COMPONENT TESTING article. Observe fuel pressure reading. If fuel pressure is still not present, check wiring between test connector and fuel pump. If wiring is okay, replace fuel pump.

7) If fuel pressure is present with voltage applied to test connector, test fuel pump relay and voltage supply to relay. See SYSTEM & COMPONENT TESTING article.

8) Relieve fuel pressure. Disconnect flexible fuel return line. Attach 5/16 ID flexible fuel line to CPI side of fuel line. Route hose into appropriate container. Turn ignition on and note fuel pressure. If fuel pressure is within specification, locate and repair restriction in fuel return line.

9) If fuel pressure is still greater than specification, replace CPI assembly.

PFI (4.3L Turbo) – 1) Relieve fuel pressure. See FUEL PRESSURE RELIEF. Connect Fuel Pressure Gauge (J-34730-1) to fuel pressure connector on fuel rail. Turn ignition on. With ignition on and engine off, pressure should be **35-38 psi (2.46-2.67 kg/cm²)**. If no fuel pressure is present, go to step **5)**.

2) Start engine. Pressure should drop 3-10 psi (.21-.70 kg/cm²). Turn ignition off. Pressure should hold. If pressure does not hold, check for leaking injectors or fittings. If injectors or fittings are not leaking, replace pressure regulator.

3) If pressure is present but less than specification, check for restricted delivery line or fuel filter. Repair as necessary. If no restriction is evident, apply battery voltage to fuel pump test connector using a 10-amp fused jumper wire. For location of fuel pump test connector, see COMPONENT LOCATIONS in SYSTEM & COMPONENT TESTING article.

4) Gradually pinch off fuel delivery line between gauge and fuel rail. If fuel pressure increases to within specifications, replace fuel pressure regulator. If fuel pressure does not increase with line pinched, check for faulty in-tank fuel pump or partial blocked fuel strainer.

5) Use a 10-amp fused jumper wire to apply battery voltage to fuel pump test connector. For location of fuel pump test connector, see COMPONENT LOCATIONS in SYSTEM & COMPONENT TESTING article. Observe fuel pressure reading. If fuel pressure is still not present, check wiring between test connector and fuel pump. If wiring is okay, replace fuel pump.

6) If fuel pressure is present with voltage applied to test connector, test fuel pump relay and voltage supply to relay. See SYSTEM & COMPONENT TESTING article.

FIELD SERVICE MODE CHECK

NOTE: O₂ sensor may cool off while engine idles, causing system to enter open loop. To restore closed loop mode, run engine at part throttle several minutes and accelerate from idle to part throttle several times.

This test confirms proper fuel system operation and verifies closed loop operation. Clear codes and perform this test after any repair is completed. When performing this test, always engage parking brake and block DRIVE wheels. Parking brake on FWD models does NOT hold drive wheels.

1) Start engine. With engine running, ground diagnostic test terminal "B" of ALDL. See Figs. 10-12. In closed loop mode, SERVICE ENGINE SOON light flashes once per second.

2) In open loop, light flashes 2.5 times per second. A lean exhaust is indicated if light is usually off. A rich exhaust is indicated if light is usually on.

BASIC FUEL SYSTEM CHECKS (DIESEL)

FUEL PUMP FLOW TEST

1) Disconnect fuel line at fuel filter inlet. Disconnect fuel injection pump electric shut-off solenoid wire (Pink).

2) Crank engine 15 seconds. If fuel pump does not supply approximately 1/2 pint of fuel in 15 seconds, go to FUEL SYSTEM PRESSURE TEST.

FUEL SYSTEM PRESSURE TEST

CAUTION: Begin fuel system trouble shooting and diagnosis with fuel system pressure test. Relieve fuel system pressure before disconnecting any components or installing fuel pressure gauge.

1) Turn engine off. Disconnect fuel line at inlet to fuel filter assembly. Install low pressure fuel gauge to fuel line.

2) Crank or run engine 10-15 seconds. If fuel pressure is not **5.8-8.7 psi (.41-.61 kg/cm²)**, check fuel lines and fuel tank sending unit for restriction. If fuel lines and sending unit are okay, replace fuel pump.

C-4, BASIC IGNITION SYSTEM CHECKS (GASOLINE)

HEI-EST DISTRIBUTOR

NOTE: Only basic ignition timing is adjustable in HEI/EST ignition system.

Spark – 1) If factory tachometer is connected to ignition coil tachometer terminal, disconnect it before performing tests. When removing spark plug wire from spark plug, twist and pull on boot. DO NOT pull on wire.

2) Using Spark Tester (ST-125), check for spark at coil wire (if applicable) and at each spark plug wire. Check spark plug wire resistance on suspect wires. Resistance should not be greater than 30,000 ohms.

Ignition Coil Power Source – Turn ignition on. Use voltmeter to check voltage between terminal "B" of ignition coil and ground. If battery voltage does not exist, check for open circuit, blown ignition fuse or defective ignition switch.

Ignition Coil Resistance – **1)** Remove coil connectors and secondary coil wire. In test "A", use high ohmmeter scale. Resistance value should be very high (infinite). *See Fig. 8*. If reading is not infinite, replace coil.

2) In test "B", use low ohmmeter scale. Reading should be very low (near zero ohms). If reading is not near zero ohms, replace coil. In test "C", use high ohmmeter scale. If no continuity exists, replace coil.

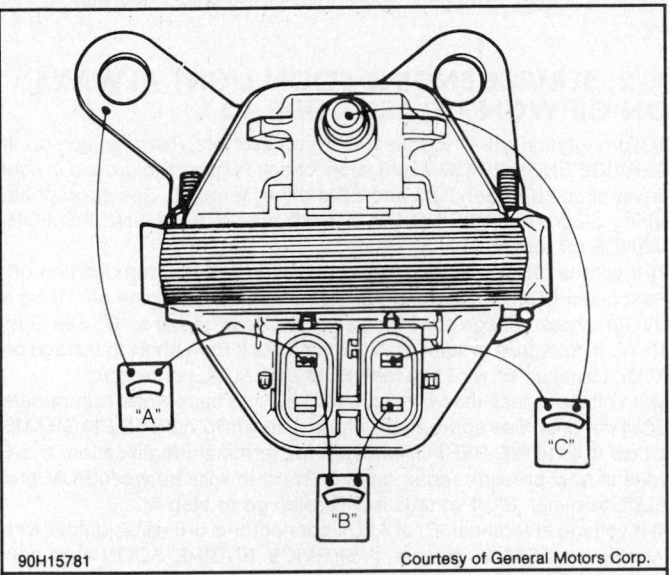

Courtesy of General Motors Corp.

Fig. 8: Testing Ignition Coil Resistance

Distributor Pick-Up Coil Short & Resistance Checks – **1)** Disconnect pick-up coil leads from HEI-EST module terminals "N" and "P". Set ohmmeter to middle scale, and connect one lead to either pick-up coil lead and other lead to distributor housing. *See Fig. 9*. Flex pick-up coil leads by hand to check for intermittent shorts to ground. If reading is not always infinite, replace pick-up coil.

2) Connect ohmmeter between both pick-up coil leads. Check for intermittent opens by flexing wires and connectors. If resistance is not **500-1500 ohms**, replace pick-up coil.

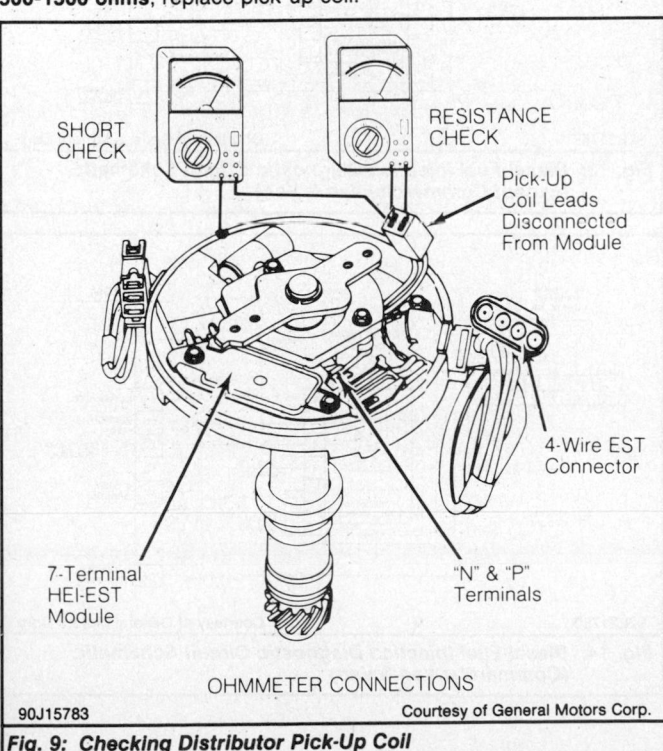

OHMMETER CONNECTIONS

Courtesy of General Motors Corp.

Fig. 9: Checking Distributor Pick-Up Coil

Tach Pulse (RPM) Signal – Use a Scan tester connected to ALDL connector of vehicle to check for a tach pulse signal. RPM should be indicated on tester when engine is being cranked or is running. Tach pulse (RPM reference) is indicated as a voltage signal when a DVOM (minimum 10-megohm input impedance) is touched to circuit No. 430 ECM terminal. *See Figs. 1-7*.

3.8L WITH C³I

Spark – Disconnect tachometer wire if equipped. A shorted tachometer will prevent vehicle from starting. Disconnect cam sensor, and attempt to start engine. If engine starts, see appropriate cam sensor trouble code in appropriate SELF-DIAGNOSTICS article. Check for adequate spark using Spark Tester (ST-125). Check for spark on plug wires No. 1, 3 and 5 (one at a time). Leave matching plug wire connected while checking for spark. When removing spark plug wire from spark plug, twist and pull on boot. DO NOT pull on wire.

Ignition Coil Power Source – Turn ignition on. Check for battery voltage on Pink/Black wire to ignition module. If battery voltage is not present, check for blown ignition fuse. If fuse is not blown, check for open between fuse and ignition module.

Ignition Coil Resistance – Disconnect ignition coil leads. Use an ohmmeter to check ignition coil resistance. Primary resistance should be **.5-.9 ohm**. Secondary resistance should be **5000-8000 ohms**. Replace ignition coil if not within specification.

Tach Pulse (RPM Reference) Signal – Connect scan tester to ALDL diagnostic connector. RPM should be indicated on tester when engine is cranked or running. Tach pulse (RPM reference) will be indicated as a voltage signal when a DVOM (with a minimum 10-megohm input impedance) is used to backprobe circuit No. 430 ECM terminal. For circuit and terminal reference, see appropriate schematic in NO START – ENGINE CRANKS OKAY.

IDLE SPEED & IGNITION TIMING (GASOLINE)

Ensure idle speed and ignition timing are set to specifications. For adjustment procedures, see ON-VEHICLE ADJUSTMENTS article.

DIAGNOSTIC CIRCUIT CHECK (GASOLINE)

Diagnostic Circuit Check determines:
- If SERVICE ENGINE SOON light works.
- If ECM is operating and can recognize a fault.
- If any codes are stored.

After performing basic diagnostic procedures listed under PRELIMINARY INSPECTION & ADJUSTMENTS, A-7, BASIC FUEL SYSTEM CHECKS and C-4, BASIC IGNITION SYSTEM CHECKS, use self-diagnostic system for determining computer-related problems. *See Fig. 15*.

After performing necessary tests in diagnostic circuit check and if no codes are indicated and driveability problems still exist, see TROUBLE SHOOTING – NO CODES article and SCAN TESTER USAGE in SELF-DIAGNOSTICS – GASOLINE article.

1) Check SERVICE ENGINE SOON light operation. Turn ignition on with Scan tester not connected, ALDL test terminal not grounded and engine not running. SERVICE ENGINE SOON light should be on steady. If light illuminates and stays on steady, go to next step. If light does not illuminate, go to A-1, SERVICE ENGINE SOON LIGHT INOPERATIVE. If light flashes, go to step **3)**.

2) Grounding ALDL diagnostic test terminal "B" now should cause SERVICE ENGINE SOON light to flash a Code 12, followed by any codes stored in ECM memory. If light goes from bright to dim or if light remains on and does not flash Code 12, see A-2, SERVICE ENGINE SOON LIGHT ALWAYS ON OR WON'T FLASH CODE 12.

3) If light begins to flash as soon as ignition is turned on, check for a short to ground on diagnostic test terminal wire between ALDL diagnostic terminal "B" and ECM terminal. *See Figs. 10-12*. If circuit is okay, replace ECM.

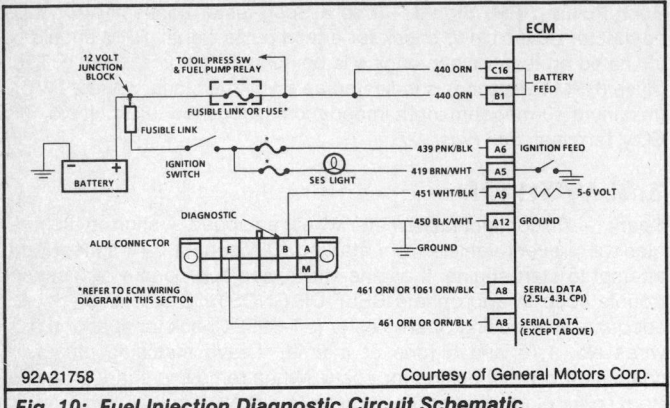

Fig. 10: *Fuel Injection Diagnostic Circuit Schematic*
(Except 4.3L Turbo & Models With 4L80-E Transmission)

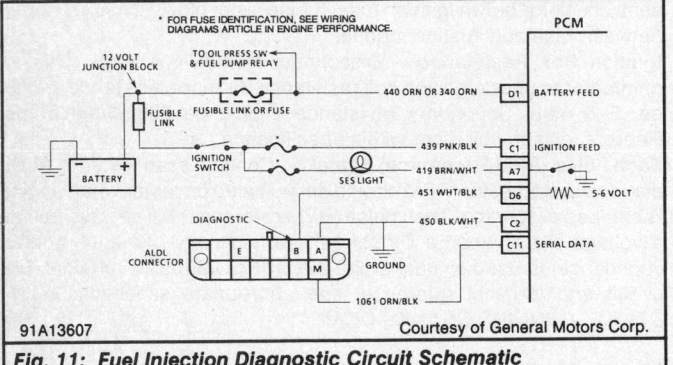

Fig. 11: *Fuel Injection Diagnostic Circuit Schematic*
(Models With 4L80-E Transmission)

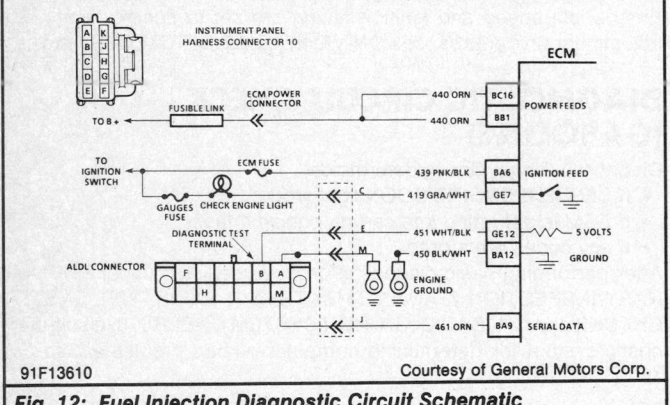

Fig. 12: *Fuel Injection Diagnostic Circuit Schematic*
(4.3L Turbo PFI)

A-1, SERVICE ENGINE SOON LIGHT INOPERATIVE

1) If SERVICE ENGINE SOON light does not illuminate with ignition on and engine off, attempt to start engine. If engine starts, go to step 3). If engine does not start, check fusible links at battery. Also check ECM fuse. If fusible links or ECM fuse are blown, repair short to ground.
2) If fusible links and ECM fuse are okay, turn ignition on, and check power circuits to ECM, including keep-alive memory and ignition feed. See appropriate wiring diagram in WIRING DIAGRAMS article in ENGINE PERFORMANCE for power terminal identification. If power is not available to power terminals of ECM, check for opens in power circuits. If power is available to ECM power terminals, check for poor ECM ground circuits. If circuits are okay, replace faulty ECM.
3) If engine starts and SERVICE ENGINE SOON light does not illuminate, turn ignition off. Disconnect ECM connectors. Turn ignition on, and jumper ECM SERVICE ENGINE SOON light driver terminal to

ground using a test light. See appropriate wiring diagram in WIRING DIAGRAMS article in ENGINE PERFORMANCE for power terminal identification.
4) If light is now on, repair light driver terminal connections at ECM or replace faulty ECM. If light stays off when test light is used to ground light driver terminal, check for blown instrument panel fuse, faulty bulb, open in light driver circuit between ECM and bulb, short in driver circuit to voltage or open in ignition feed to SERVICE ENGINE SOON light.

A-2, SERVICE ENGINE SOON LIGHT ALWAYS ON OR WON'T FLASH CODE 12

1) Turn ignition off. Disconnect ECM connectors. Turn ignition on. If SERVICE ENGINE SOON light is on, check for short to ground in light driver circuit between light and ECM driver terminal. See appropriate wiring diagram in WIRING DIAGRAMS article in ENGINE PERFORMANCE for terminal identification.
2) If light is off with ECM connectors disconnected, turn ignition off. Reconnect ECM connectors. Turn ignition on with engine off. Using a DVOM, check voltage at ALDL diagnostic "test" terminal "B". *See Figs. 10-12.* If voltage is greater than 9 volts, check for a short to voltage on ALDL terminal "B" wire between ECM and ALDL connector.
3) If voltage is less than 5 volts, use DVOM to backprobe appropriate ECM terminal. See appropriate wiring diagram in WIRING DIAGRAMS article in ENGINE PERFORMANCE for terminal identification. If 5-6 volts is now present, repair open or short in wire between ECM and ALDL terminal "B". If voltage is 5-6 volts, go to step 4).
4) If voltage at terminal "B" of ALDL connector is 5-6 volts, jumper wire terminal at ECM to ground. If SERVICE ENGINE SOON light now flashes a Code 12 and ALDL terminal "A" was used when previously grounding terminal "B", check terminal "A" for open circuit.

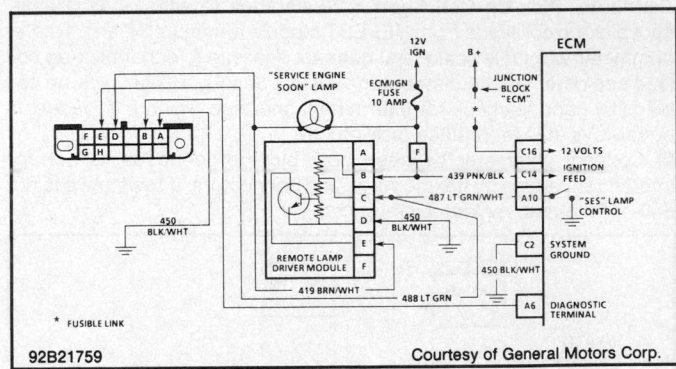

Fig. 13: *Diesel Fuel Injection Diagnostic Circuit Schematic*
(Except Commercial Van & Van)

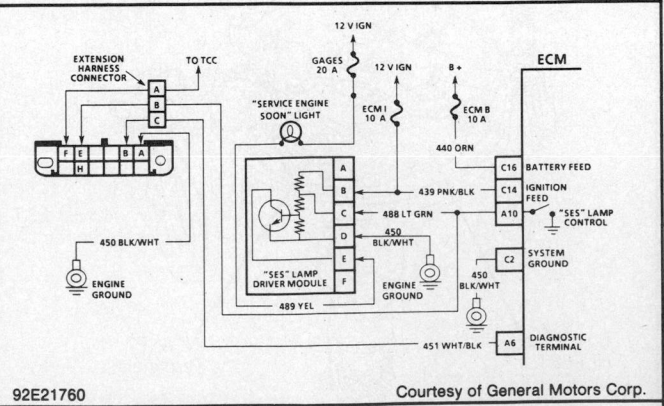

Fig. 14: *Diesel Fuel Injection Diagnostic Circuit Schematic*
(Commercial Van & Van)

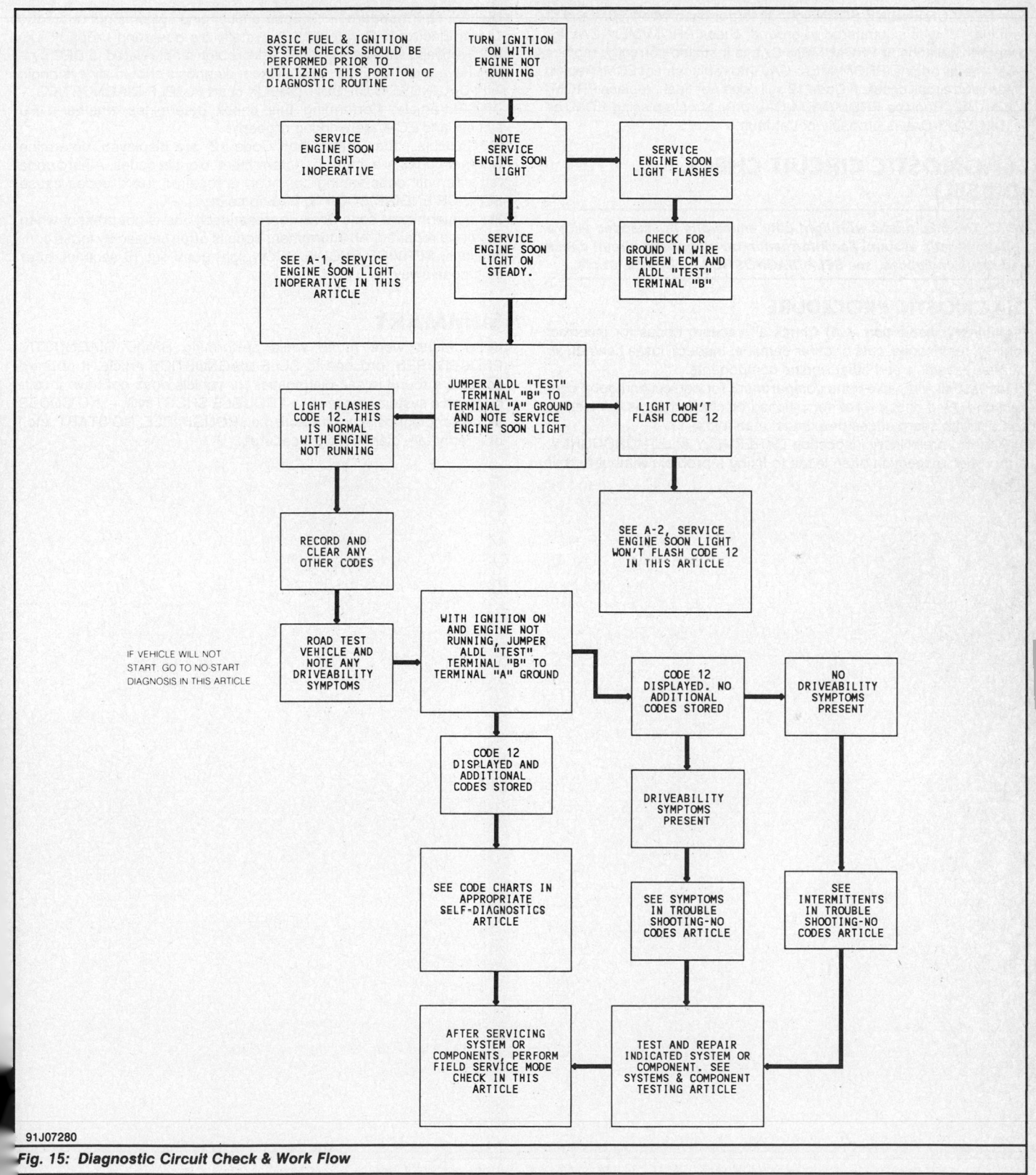

Fig. 15: Diagnostic Circuit Check & Work Flow

91J07280

5) If SERVICE ENGINE SOON light does not flash when ECM end of terminal "B" wire is jumpered to ground, check PROM/MEM-CAL for proper installation. If PROM/MEM-CAL is installed correctly, replace ECM. Install original PROM/MEM-CAL into replacement ECM. Repeat diagnostic circuit check. If Code 12 still does not flash, replace PROM/MEM-CAL. Replace PROM/MEM-CAL only after replacing ECM, as PROM/MEM-CAL is probably not at fault.

DIAGNOSTIC CIRCUIT CHECK (DIESEL)

NOTE: The 6.2L model with light duty emissions is equipped with a self-diagnostic system. For information on diagnostic circuit check and retrieving codes, see SELF-DIAGNOSTICS – DIESEL article.

DIAGNOSTIC PROCEDURE

Preliminary Inspection – 1) Check all vacuum hoses for incorrect routing, restrictions, cuts or other damage. Inspect hoses beneath air cleaner assembly and other engine components.

2) Inspect all wires in engine compartment for correct and good connections. Also check wires for pinched or chaffed spots, as well as contact with sharp edges or exhaust manifolds.

3) Perform preliminary inspection CAREFULLY and THOROUGHLY. A thorough inspection often leads to fixing a problem without further diagnosis.

Diagnostic Procedure – 1) Ensure all engine systems not related to Diesel Electronic Control (DEC) system are operating properly. DO NOT proceed with testing unless all problems not related to DEC system have been repaired. DEC system diagnosis should always begin with DIAGNOSTIC CIRCUIT CHECK chart in SELF-DIAGNOSTICS – DIESEL article. Performing this check determines whether DEC system and ECM are working properly.

2) If trouble codes (other than Code 12) are displayed, determine whether codes are "hard" or "intermittent" trouble codes. A hard code remains until code-setting condition is repaired. Hard codes cause SERVICE ENGINE SOON light to come on.

3) An intermittent code does not reset itself and is not present when vehicle is repaired. An intermittent code is often caused by loose connections. SERVICE ENGINE SOON light goes out 10 seconds after fault goes away.

SUMMARY

If no faults were found while performing BASIC DIAGNOSTIC PROCEDURES, proceed to SELF-DIAGNOSTICS article. If no hard codes are found in self-diagnostics, or vehicle does not have a self-diagnostic system, proceed to TROUBLE SHOOTING – NO CODES article for diagnosis by symptom (i.e., ROUGH IDLE, NO START, etc.) or intermittent diagnostic procedures.

Astro, Bravada, Commercial Van, Jimmy,
Lumina APV, Safari, Sierra, Silhouette,
Sonoma, Suburban, Syclone, Trans Sport,
Typhoon, Van, Yukon,
"C" & "K" Series Blazer & Pickup,
"S" & "T" Series Blazer & Pickup

INTRODUCTION

Most engine control problems result from mechanical failures, poor electrical connections or damaged vacuum hoses. Before condemning the computer system, perform checks and inspections covered in BASIC DIAGNOSTIC PROCEDURES article. Failure to do so may result in lost diagnostic time.

If no faults were found while performing BASIC DIAGNOSTIC PROCEDURES, proceed with DIAGNOSTIC PROCEDURE. If no fault codes or only a non-running Code 12 is present and driveability problems exist, proceed to TROUBLE SHOOTING – NO CODES article for diagnosis by symptom (i.e. ROUGH IDLE, NO START, etc.). If only intermittent codes are present, see INTERMITTENTS in TROUBLE SHOOTING – NO CODES article.

SELF-DIAGNOSTIC SYSTEM

SELF-DIAGNOSTICS DIRECTORY

Application	Page
Trouble Code Charts	1-34

All vehicle are equipped with either an Electronic Control Module (ECM) or Powertrain Control Module (PCM). Unless specifically stated, references to ECM also apply to PCM equipped vehicles.

The ECM is equipped with a self-diagnostic system, which detects system failures or abnormalities. When a malfunction occurs, ECM will illuminate the SERVICE ENGINE SOON light located on instrument panel. When malfunction is detected and light is turned on, a corresponding trouble code will be stored in ECM memory. To retrieve stored codes, see READING TROUBLE CODES. Malfunctions are recorded as HARD FAILURES or as INTERMITTENT FAILURES.

Hard Failures – Hard failures cause SERVICE ENGINE SOON light to illuminate and remain on until the malfunction is repaired. If light comes on and remains on (light may flash) during vehicle operation, cause must be found using diagnostic (code) charts. If a sensor fails, control unit will use a substitute value in its calculations to continue engine operation. In this condition, vehicle is functional, but driveability can be poor.

Intermittent Failures – Intermittent failures cause SERVICE ENGINE SOON light to flicker or illuminate and go out about 10 seconds after the intermittent fault goes away. The corresponding trouble code; however, will be retained in ECM memory. If related fault does not reoccur within 50 engine restarts, it will be erased from ECM memory. Intermittent failures may be caused by faulty sensor, connector or wiring. See INTERMITTENTS in TROUBLE SHOOTING – NO CODES article.

DIAGNOSTIC PROCEDURE

Diagnosis of the computerized engine control system should be performed in the following order:

1) Ensure all engine systems not related to the computer are operating properly. DO NOT proceed with testing unless all other problems have been repaired. Perform diagnostic circuit check before using trouble code charts. See BASIC DIAGNOSTIC PROCEDURES article.

2) If trouble codes were displayed (other than Code 12), determine whether codes are hard or intermittent. Hard codes cause SERVICE ENGINE SOON light to illuminate continuously with engine running. See HARD OR INTERMITTENT TROUBLE CODE DETERMINATION. For diagnosing hard codes, proceed to appropriate trouble code chart. For diagnosing intermittent codes, proceed to INTERMITTENTS in TROUBLE SHOOTING – NO CODES article. Exceptions

are Code 13, 15, 24, 44 and 45 charts, which can help diagnose intermittent codes.

3) If trouble codes were not displayed and a driveability problem exists, refer to SYMPTOMS in TROUBLE SHOOTING – NO CODES article. From there you will be sent to the appropriate area in SYSTEM & COMPONENT TESTING article.

4) After repairs are made, clear trouble codes and perform FIELD SERVICE MODE check in BASIC DIAGNOSTIC PROCEDURES article.

RETRIEVING CODES (NON-SCAN)

1) Turn ignition on with engine off. SERVICE ENGINE SOON light should glow. Locate Assembly Line Data Link (ALDL) connector, attached to ECM wiring harness. Most ALDL connectors are located under dash on driver's side of vehicle. For exact location of ALDL, see appropriate COMPONENT LOCATIONS illustration in SYSTEM & COMPONENT TESTING article. Turn ignition on. Insert jumper wire from terminal "B" (diagnostic test terminal) to terminal "A" (ground) of ALDL connector. See Fig. 1.

NOTE: Inserting jumper wire into test and ground terminals of ALDL connector with engine running will cause fuel-injected vehicles to enter field service mode and codes will not flash. See FIELD SERVICE MODE in BASIC DIAGNOSTIC PROCEDURES article.

A – Ground	F – TCC (If Used)
B – Test Terminal	G – Fuel Pump (If Used)
C – Air Injection (If Equipped)	H – Brake Sense Speed Input
E – Serial Data	M – Serial Data (P-4 If Used)

90B01199   Courtesy of General Motors Corp.

Fig. 1: Identifying ALDL Diagnostic Connector Terminals

2) SERVICE ENGINE SOON light should flash codes. Each code is flashed 3 times. If codes DO NOT flash, perform DIAGNOSTIC CIRCUIT CHECK in BASIC DIAGNOSTIC PROCEDURES article. To exit diagnostic mode, turn ignition off and remove jumper wire from ALDL connector.

READING TROUBLE CODES

NOTE: Trouble codes retrieved from ECM/PCM may be related to either engine or transmission. For engine related codes, use this article. For transmission related codes, see the SELF-DIAGNOSTICS — ELECTRONIC TRANSMISSION article. To identify which codes relate to transmission or engine, see TROUBLE CODE IDENTIFICATION table.

The ECM stores component failure information under a related trouble code which can be recalled for diagnosis and repair. Read trouble codes by counting SERVICE ENGINE SOON light flashes or with diagnostic scan tester connected to the ALDL connector. The tester is faster, and capable of reading information which would require testing individual ECM and sensor/solenoid connector terminals with a digital voltmeter. See SCAN TESTER DATA table and SCAN TESTER USAGE.

NOTE: When using a scan tester, there is a time delay between serial data updates. For instantaneous response, a digital voltmeter must be used.

If scan tester is not available, SERVICE ENGINE SOON light flashes can be read by grounding ALDL diagnostic terminal with ignition on and engine off. For example, FLASH, FLASH, pause, FLASH, longer pause, indicates Code 21. The first series of flashes are the first digit of trouble code. The second series of flashes are the second digit of trouble code. Trouble codes are displayed starting with the lowest code. Each code is displayed 3 times and will continue as long as ALDL is grounded.

NOTE: Trouble codes will be recorded at various operating times. Some codes require sensor or switch operation for 5 seconds and others may require longer under certain conditions. Some codes may not set in a service bay operational mode.

TROUBLE CODE IDENTIFICATION

Code	Probable Cause
12 [1]	No Engine Speed Sensor Reference Pulse To PCM/TCM
13 [1]	Open Oxygen Sensor Circuit
14 [1]	CTS Voltage Low (Sensor Or Signal Line Grounded)
16 [1]	System Voltage High/Low (3.8L)
17 [1]	RPM Signal Problem (3.8L)
18 [1]	Cam/Crank Error (3.8L)
15 [1]	CTS Voltage High (Sensor, Connections, Or Wires Open)
21 [1]	TPS Voltage High (Open Circuit Or Misadjusted TPS)
22 [1]	TPS Voltage Low (Circuit Grounded)
23 [1]	Intake Air Temperature Sensor Voltage High
24 [1]	Vehicle Speed Sensor Circuit Open Or Grounded
25 [1]	Intake Air Temperature Sensor Voltage Low
26 [1]	Quad-Driver "B" Fault (3.8L)
28	Pressure Switch Manifold Range Circuit Open Or Shorted
31 [1]	Turbocharger Wastegate Overboost
31 [1]	Park/Neutral Switch Circuit (3.8L)
32 [1]	EGR Error (Improper Vacuum Signal)
33 [1]	MAP Voltage High (Circuit Open Or Short To Voltage)
34 [1]	MAP Voltage Low (Circuit Open Or Short To Ground)
34 [1]	MAL Sensor Signal Voltage Low (3.8L)
35 [1]	IAC System Fault
36 [1]	Shift Control Problem (3.8L)
38 [1]	Brake Switch Circuit (3.8L)
39	TCC Stuck Off (Faulty TCC Solenoid)
41 [1]	Cam Sensor Circuit (3.8L)
42 [1]	EST Circuit Fault
43 [1]	ESC Fault
44 [1]	Lean Exhaust Indicated
45 [1]	Rich Exhaust Indicated
51 [1]	Improperly Installed/Faulty PROM/MEM-CAL
52 [1]	Fuel CAL-PAC Missing
53 [1]	System Voltage High (Charging System Problem)
54 [1]	Fuel Pump Circuit Voltage Low
55 [1]	Faulty ECM
56 [1]	Quad-Driver "B" Fault (3.8L)
58	TTS High Temperature (Sensor Or Signal Line Grounded)
59	TTS Low Temperature (Sensor, Connections, Or Wires Open)
61 [1]	Cruise Vent Solenoid (3.8L)
62 [1]	Cruise Vacuum Solenoid (3.8L)
63 [1]	Cruise System Problem (3.8L)
65 [1]	Cruise Servo Position (3.8L)
66 [1]	Low A/C Refrigerant Charge (3.8L)
67 [1]	Cruise Engage Switches (3.8L)
68	Overdrive Ratio Error (Engine RPM Greater Than Input Speed)
68 [1]	Cruise System Problem (3.8L)
69 [1]	A/C Head Pressure Switch (3.8L)
73	Force Motor Commanded Amperage Differs From Return
75	System Voltage Low (Charging System Problem)
81	QDM Solenoid "B" Monitored Voltage Differs From Commanded
82	QDM Solenoid "A" Monitored Voltage Differs From Commanded
83	QDM TCC Monitored Voltage Differs From Commanded
85	Undefined Gear Ratio (Input Or Output Sensor Failure)
86	Shift Solenoid "B" Stuck On (Commanded Gear Not Engaged)
87	Shift Solenoid "B" Stuck Off (Commanded Gear Not Engaged)

[1] – Engine code. For transmission code diagnosis, see SELF-DIAGNOSTICS – ELECTRONIC TRANSMISSION article.

NOTE: Trouble code charts should only be used if SERVICE ENGINE SOON light is illuminated (indicating a current problem exists). Exceptions are Code 13, 15, 24, 44 and 45 charts, which may be used to help diagnose intermittent codes. Anytime Codes 51, 52 or 55 are displayed with another code, start with 50-series code first and proceed to low profile numbered codes.

HARD OR INTERMITTENT TROUBLE CODE DETERMINATION

During any diagnostic procedure, determine if codes are due to hard or intermittent failure. Diagnostic charts will not usually help diagnose intermittent codes. To determine hard codes and intermittent codes, proceed as follows:
1) MANUALLY enter diagnostic mode. Read and record all stored trouble codes. Exit diagnostic mode and clear trouble codes. See CLEARING TROUBLE CODES.
2) Apply parking brake and place transmission in Neutral or Park. Block drive wheels and start engine. SERVICE ENGINE SOON light should go out. Run warm engine at specified curb idle for 2 minutes and note SERVICE ENGINE SOON light.
3) If SERVICE ENGINE SOON light comes on, manually enter diagnostic mode. Read and record trouble codes. This reveals hard failure codes. Codes 13, 15, 24, 44, 45 and 55 may require a road test to reset hard failure after trouble codes were cleared.
4) If SERVICE ENGINE SOON light does not come on, all stored trouble codes were intermittent failures. Exceptions are noted under DIAGNOSTIC PROCEDURE.

CLEARING TROUBLE CODES

Turn ignition switch to ON position and ground diagnostic test terminal "B" at ALDL connector. Turn ignition switch to OFF position and remove ECM fuse from fuse block for 10 seconds. Replace fuse. Remove diagnostic terminal ground lead.

ECM LOCATION

For ECM locations, see appropriate COMPONENT LOCATIONS illustration in SYSTEM & COMPONENT TESTING article.

DIAGNOSTIC MATERIALS

Diagnostic Aids – Diagnostic aids (located in many trouble code charts) are provided as additional tips to help with diagnosis when inspected circuit is okay.

Field Service Mode Check – SERVICE ENGINE SOON light indicates operational mode of engine if ALDL is grounded while engine is running. Light response confirms proper fuel system operation and verifies closed loop operation. Clear codes and perform this test after any repair is completed. Field service mode check can be found by proceeding to FIELD SERVICE MODE CHECK in BASIC DIAGNOSTIC PROCEDURES article.

SPECIAL TOOLS (DIAGNOSTIC)

NOTE: A special scan tester, plugged into the ALDL, can read trouble codes, check system voltages on the serial data line and save a great deal of time. For additional information, see tester owner's manual. Also, see SCAN TESTER USAGE and SCAN DATA.

The computerized engine control system is most easily diagnosed using a scan tester. However, other tools may aid in diagnosing problems if a scan tester is unavailable. These tools are a tachometer, test light, ohmmeter, digital voltmeter with 10-megohm input impedance (minimum), vacuum pump, vacuum gauge, fuel injector test lights and 6 jumper wires 6" long (one wire with female connectors at both ends, one wire with male connector at both ends and 4 wires with male and female connectors at opposite ends). A test light, rather than a voltmeter, must be used when indicated by a diagnostic chart.

SCAN TESTER USAGE

NOTE: Before connecting scan tester, check diagnostic system and ensure accurate information is received by scan tester. Perform DIAGNOSTIC CIRCUIT CHECK in BASIC DIAGNOSTIC PROCEDURES article. If vehicle does not pass diagnostic circuit check, information received by scan tester may be invalid.

The scan tester is a specialized tester which can diagnose on-board computer control systems by providing almost instant access to circuit voltage information without crawling under dash or hood to back-probe sensors and connectors. scan testers reduce diagnostic time by furnishing input data (voltage signals) which can be compared to specification parameters. See SCAN TESTER DATA table.

Scan testers also furnish information on output device (solenoids and motors) status. However, status parameters are only an indication output signals have been sent to devices by the ECM. They do not indicate whether devices respond properly to that signal. This must be verified at output device using a voltmeter or test light.

NOTE: Code 12 should always exist when ALDL is grounded with key on and engine off, but it may not be indicated by all makes of scan tester.

If trouble codes are not present, a problem may still exist. Driveability-related problems with codes displayed occur about 20 percent of the time, while driveability problems without codes occur about 80 percent of the time. Out-of-calibration sensors WILL NOT set a trouble code, but WILL cause driveability problems. A scan tester is the easiest method of checking sensor specifications and other data parameters. Tester is also useful in finding intermittent wiring problems by wiggling wiring harnesses and connections (key on, engine off) while observing data parameters. See SCAN TESTER DATA table.

NOTE: Information obtained by scan tester is only as accurate as the tester itself. If erroneous voltage signals are suspected, verify tester information using a digital voltmeter and wiring schematic. If non-existent codes are displayed, turn ignition off and remove tester. Turn ignition on and ground ALDL test terminal. If same codes are not flashed by SERVICE ENGINE SOON light as were indicated by scan tester, tester cannot be used on vehicle and information obtained by it will not be guaranteed accurate.

SCAN DATA

NOTE: Information contained in the following table is typical of readings taken on vehicle with engine idling, upper radiator hose hot, throttle closed, transmission in Park or Neutral, closed loop status achieved and all accessories off (except as noted in tables). Data parameters are updated every 1 1/2 seconds. Not all devices and systems are used on all models. For additional information, see tester owner's manual.

SCAN TESTER DATA

Tester Position	Units Measured	Nominal Data Value
A/C Clutch	On/Off	Off (On With A/C)
A/C Request	Yes/No	No/Yes (With Request)
Battery Voltage	Volts	13.5-14.5
Block Learn	Counts	118-138 (128 Normal)
Clear Flood	On/Off	***See Tester Manual***
Coolant Temp.	°C	85-105° (Norm. Temperature)
Crank RPM	RPM	100-900
Cross Counts	Counts	0-255
Desired RPM	RPM	ECM Desired RPM
EGR Duty Cycle	0-100%	0/Closed-100/Fully Open
IAC	Counts	0-50
Injector Pulse Width	Mil./Sec	.8-3.0
INT (Integrator)	Counts	110-145 (128 Normal)
Knock Retard (ESC)	Counts	0-255
Knock Signal	Yes/No	Yes When Knock Exists
MAT	°C	10-90°
MAP	Volts	1 (idle) To 4.5 (WOT)
Open/Closed Loop Status	Ol/Cl	Closed/Open During Extended Idle
O₂ Sensor	Millivolts	100 (Lean) To 999 (Rich)
P/N Switch	P/N/RDL	Park/Neutral
P/S Switch	Norm/Hi	Normal
PROM I.D.	PROM #	Original Factory Number
RPM	RPM	Spec. ±25 RPM Drive (A/T) Spec. ±50 RPM Neut. (M/T)
TCC	On/Off	Off (On With Command)
TPS	Volts	1.25 (Idle) To 5.0 (WOT)
Throttle Angle	0-100%	0 (Idle) To 100 (WOT)
Trouble Codes	Code #	No codes
Upshift Light (Man. Trans.)	On/Off	Off
VSS Or MPH	MPH	0-Actual
4th Gear Switch	On/Off	On/4th Gear

SUMMARY

If hard fault codes are not present and driveability symptoms or intermittent codes exist, proceed to TROUBLE SHOOTING – NO CODES article for diagnosis by symptom (i.e. ROUGH IDLE, NO START, etc.), or intermittent diagnostic procedures.

NOTE: The following diagnostic flow charts and mini-schematics are supplied courtesy of General Motors Corp.

TROUBLE CODES

CODE 13, OPEN OXYGEN SENSOR CIRCUIT (EXCEPT 4.3L TURBO)

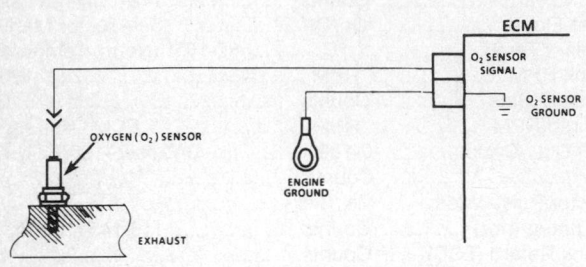

CODE 13 ECM TERMINAL & CIRCUIT WIRING IDENTIFICATION

Application	ECM Terminal	Wire Color
All With 4L80-E Transmission		
Oxygen Sensor Signal	C14	Purple
Oxygen Sensor Ground	C13	Tan
All Others Except 3.8L		
Oxygen Sensor Signal	D7	Purple
Oxygen Sensor Ground	D6	Tan
3.8L		
Oxygen Sensor Signal	D3	Purple
Oxygen Sensor Ground	D2	Tan

When exhaust temperature is less than 600°F (316°C), O_2 sensor is open and produces no voltage. An open sensor circuit or cold sensor will not allow system to entire closed loop.

NOTE: Test numbers refer to test numbers on diagnostic chart.

1) Code 13 will set at normal operating temperature if at least 2 minutes have passed since engine start, Code 21 or 22 is not present, O_2 signal voltage is steady at .35-.55 volt and throttle position sensor signal is greater than idle. All conditions must be met for at least one minute.
2) This determines if fault is in O_2 sensor, ECM or wiring.
3) Use only a high-impedance Digital Volt-Ohmmeter (DVOM) while checking for continuity in signal and ground circuits. If ground circuit is open, voltage on signal circuit will be greater than .6 volt.

NOTE: Models equipped with 4.3L Central Port Injection (CPI) use 2 oxygen sensors. Perform test procedures on both sensors on these models.

DIAGNOSTIC AIDS

Verify a clean, tight connection for ground circuit No. 413. An open circuit at sensor signal terminal or ground terminal will result in a Code 13.

91H07378 91B07281

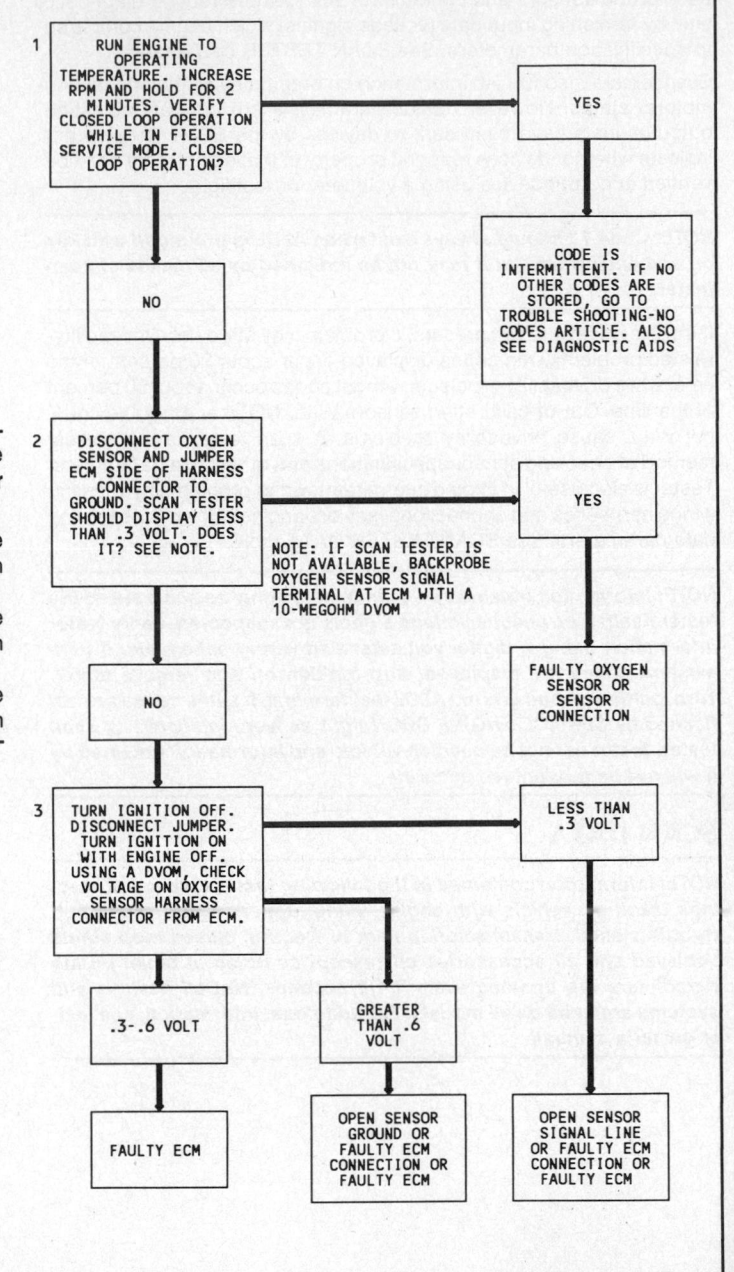

CODE 13, OPEN OXYGEN SENSOR CIRCUIT (4.3L TURBO)

ECM
OXYGEN SENSOR
BLK
WHT
WHT
C
B
A
HEATING ELEMENT
PPL 412
BLK/WHT 450
PNK/BLK 439
TAN 413 B
GE14
OXYGEN O₂ SENSOR SIGNAL
GE15
OXYGEN O₂ SENSOR GROUND
TO B+
ORN 440
ECM B FUSE
ENGINE GROUND
BA6

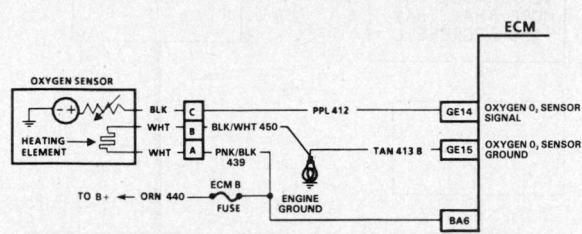

When exhaust temperature is less than 600°F (316°C), O_2 sensor is open and produces no voltage. An open sensor circuit or cold sensor will not allow system to entire closed loop.

NOTE: Test numbers refer to test numbers on diagnostic chart.

1) Code 13 will set at normal operating temperature if at least 2 minutes have passed since engine start, O_2 signal voltage is steady between .35-.55 volt and throttle position sensor signal is greater idle. All conditions must be met for at least one minute.
2) This checks oxygen sensor heating element. Resistance should be 3.5-14 ohms at 662°F (350°C).
3) This determines if fault is in O_2 sensor, ECM or wiring.
4) Use only a high-impedance Digital Volt-Ohmmeter (DVOM) while checking for continuity in signal and ground circuits. If ground circuit is open, voltage on signal circuit will be greater than .6 volt.

DIAGNOSTIC AIDS

Verify a clean, tight connection for ground circuit No. 413. An open circuit at sensor signal terminal or ground terminal will result in a Code 13. Both oxygen sensor and heating element must be functioning properly to enable closed loop operation.

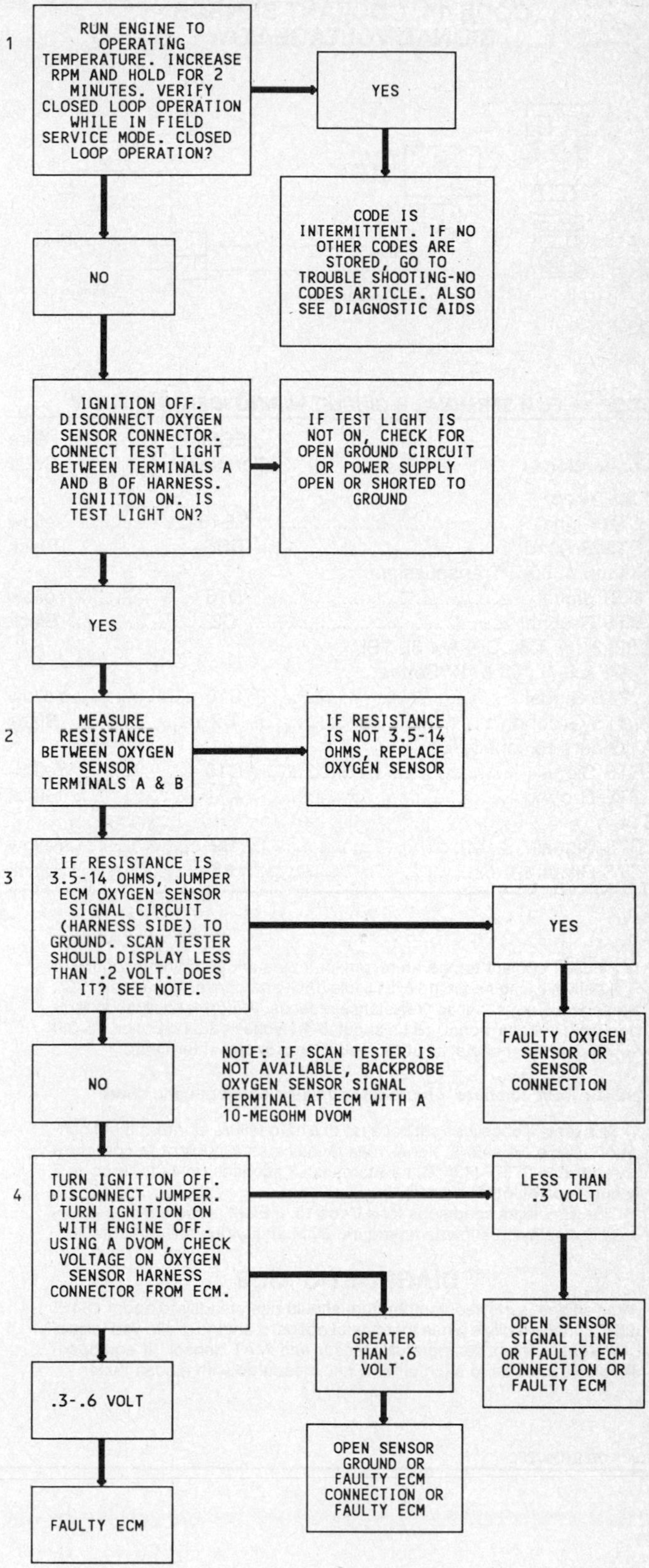

1
RUN ENGINE TO OPERATING TEMPERATURE. INCREASE RPM AND HOLD FOR 2 MINUTES. VERIFY CLOSED LOOP OPERATION WHILE IN FIELD SERVICE MODE. CLOSED LOOP OPERATION?
YES
CODE IS INTERMITTENT. IF NO OTHER CODES ARE STORED, GO TO TROUBLE SHOOTING-NO CODES ARTICLE. ALSO SEE DIAGNOSTIC AIDS
NO
IGNITION OFF. DISCONNECT OXYGEN SENSOR CONNECTOR. CONNECT TEST LIGHT BETWEEN TERMINALS A AND B OF HARNESS. IGNIITON ON. IS TEST LIGHT ON?
IF TEST LIGHT IS NOT ON, CHECK FOR OPEN GROUND CIRCUIT OR POWER SUPPLY OPEN OR SHORTED TO GROUND
YES
2
MEASURE RESISTANCE BETWEEN OXYGEN SENSOR TERMINALS A & B
IF RESISTANCE IS NOT 3.5-14 OHMS, REPLACE OXYGEN SENSOR
3
IF RESISTANCE IS 3.5-14 OHMS, JUMPER ECM OXYGEN SENSOR SIGNAL CIRCUIT (HARNESS SIDE) TO GROUND. SCAN TESTER SHOULD DISPLAY LESS THAN .2 VOLT. DOES IT? SEE NOTE.
YES
FAULTY OXYGEN SENSOR OR SENSOR CONNECTION
NO
NOTE: IF SCAN TESTER IS NOT AVAILABLE, BACKPROBE OXYGEN SENSOR SIGNAL TERMINAL AT ECM WITH A 10-MEGOHM DVOM
4
TURN IGNITION OFF. DISCONNECT JUMPER. TURN IGNITION ON WITH ENGINE OFF. USING A DVOM, CHECK VOLTAGE ON OXYGEN SENSOR HARNESS CONNECTOR FROM ECM.
LESS THAN .3 VOLT
OPEN SENSOR SIGNAL LINE OR FAULTY ECM CONNECTION OR FAULTY ECM
GREATER THAN .6 VOLT
OPEN SENSOR GROUND OR FAULTY ECM CONNECTION OR FAULTY ECM
.3-.6 VOLT
FAULTY ECM

91E13734 91G13710

CODE 14, COOLANT SENSOR SIGNAL VOLTAGE LOW

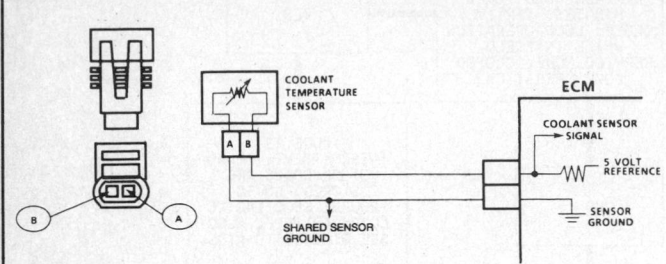

CODE 14 ECM TERMINAL & CIRCUIT WIRING IDENTIFICATION

Application	ECM Terminal	Wire Color
4.3L Turbo		
CTS Signal	GE16	Yellow
CTS Ground	BB6	Black
All With 4L80-E Transmission		
CTS Signal	D16	Yellow
CTS Ground	D3	Black
2.8L, 3.1L, 4.3L CPI & 4.3L TBI, 5.0L & 5.7L "C" & "K" Series		
CTS Signal	C10	Yellow
CTS Ground	D2	Black
All Others Except 3.8L		
CTS Signal	C10	Yellow
CTS Ground	A11	Black
3.8L		
CTS Signal	B9	Yellow
CTS Ground	A8	Black

1 DOES SCAN TESTER INDICATE TEMPERATURE OF MORE THAN THAN 130 DEGREES C → NO

YES

2 DISCONNECT COOLANT TEMPERATURE SENSOR CONNECTOR. DOES SCAN TESTER DISPLAY COOLANT TEMPERATURE LESS THAN -30 DEGREES C?

CODE IS INTERMITTENT. IF NO OTHER CODES WERE STORED, SEE TROUBLE SHOOTING-NO CODES ARTICLE. ALSO, SEE DIAGNOSTIC AIDS

YES → NO

REPLACE COOLANT TEMPERATURE SENSOR

COOLANT TEMPERATURE SENSOR SIGNAL LINE SHORTED TO GROUND OR FAULTY ECM

ECM uses coolant temperature sensor inputs in determining control of fuel delivery, engine timing (EST), idle (IAC) and converter clutch (TCC). As engine warms, sensor resistance reduces. At normal operating temperature, voltage signal will be about .5-1.1 volts (4.3L Turbo) or 1.5-2.0 volts (all other models) at ECM coolant sensor signal terminal.

NOTE: Test numbers refer to test numbers on diagnostic chart.

1) This tests if code was set because of a hard failure or intermittent condition. Code 14 sets if signal voltage indicates a coolant temperature greater than 275°F (135°C) for more than 3 seconds on 4.3L Turbo or 6 seconds on all other models.
2) This simulates conditions for a Code 15. If ECM recognizes open circuit by displaying a low temperature, ECM and wiring are not at fault.

DIAGNOSTIC AIDS

After engine is started, temperature should rise steadily to about 194°F (90°C), then stabilize when thermostat opens. If engine is allowed to cool overnight, coolant temperature sensor and MAT sensor (if equipped) should read close to each other, when measured with a scan tester.

TEMPERATURE-TO-RESISTANCE VALUES [1] [2]

°F (°C)	Ohms
210 (100)	185
160 (70)	450
100 (38)	1800
70 (20)	3400
40 (4)	7500
20 (–7)	13,500
0 (–18)	25,000
–40 (–40)	100,700

[1] – Measure resistance across sensor terminals.
[2] – Temperatures are approximates.

91J07379 91D07282

CODE 15, COOLANT SENSOR SIGNAL VOLTAGE HIGH

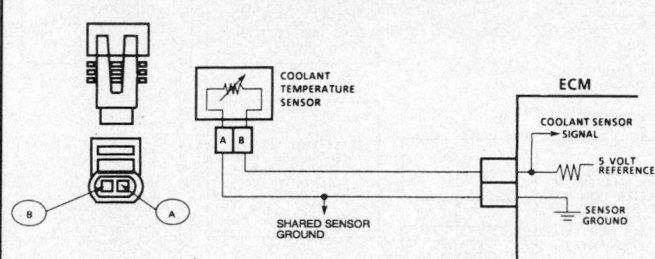

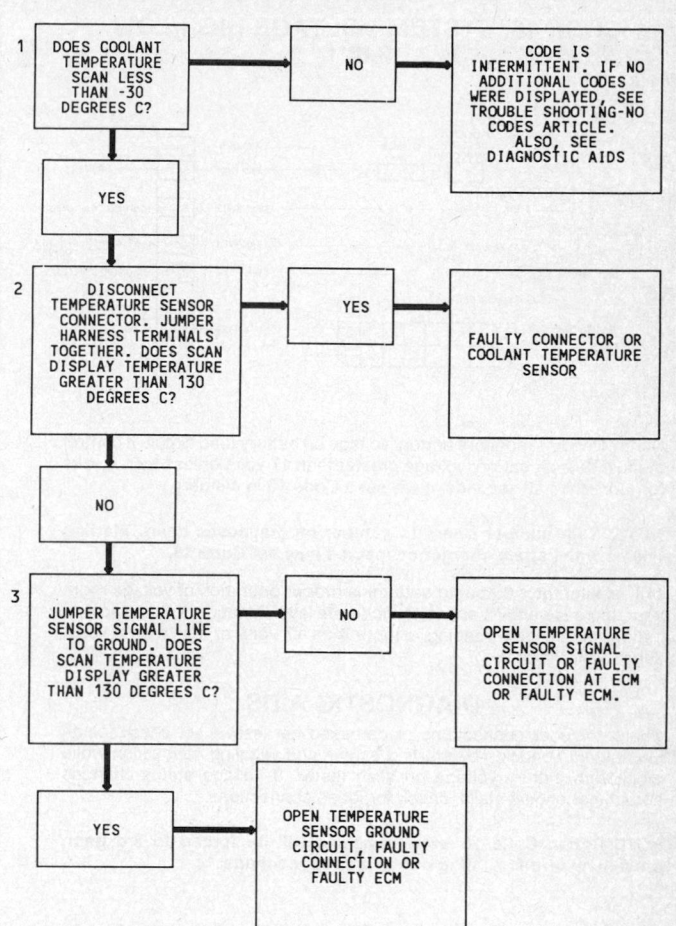

CODE 15 ECM TERMINAL & CIRCUIT WIRING IDENTIFICATION

Application	ECM Terminal	Wire Color
4.3L Turbo		
CTS Signal	GE16	Yellow
CTS Ground	BB6	Black
All With 4L80-E Transmission		
CTS Signal	D16	Yellow
CTS Ground	D3	Black
2.8L, 3.1L, 4.3L CPI & 4.3L TBI,		
5.0L & 5.7L "C" & "K" Series		
CTS Signal	C10	Yellow
CTS Ground	D2	Black
All Others Except 3.8L		
CTS Signal	C10	Yellow
CTS Ground	A11	Black
3.8L		
CTS Signal	B9	Yellow
CTS Ground	A8	Black

As engine warms, sensor resistance reduces and voltage drops. At normal operating temperature, voltage signal will be about .5-1.1 volts (4.3L Turbo) or 1.5-2.0 volts (all other models) at ECM coolant sensor signal terminal. If sensor signal circuit opens, ECM will see -40°F (-40°C) and deliver fuel for this temperature.

NOTE: Test numbers refer to test numbers on diagnostic chart.

1) This checks if code was set as a result of a hard failure or intermittent condition. Code 15 will set if engine is running for more 50 seconds and signal voltage indicates a coolant temperature less than -22°F (-30°C) for more than 30 seconds.
2) This simulates conditions for a Code 14. If ECM recognizes grounded circuit and displays a high temperature, ECM and wiring are okay.
3) This determines if problem is ECM or wiring. There should be 5 volts present at sensor when measured with a DVOM.

DIAGNOSTIC AIDS

After engine starts, temperature should rise steadily to about 194°F (90°C) and stabilize when thermostat opens. If engine is allowed to cool overnight, coolant temperature sensor and MAT sensor (if equipped) should read close to each other when measured with a scan tester. Code 15 will also set if sensor signal or ground circuit is open.

TEMPERATURE-TO-RESISTANCE VALUES [1] [2]

°F (°C)	Ohms
210 (100)	185
160 (70)	450
100 (38)	1800
70 (20)	3400
40 (4)	7500
20 (–7)	13,500
0 (–18)	25,000
–40 (–40)	100,700

[1] – Measure resistance across sensor terminals.
[2] – Temperatures are approximates.

91J07379 91F07283

CODE 16, SYSTEM VOLTAGE HIGH/LOW 3.8L

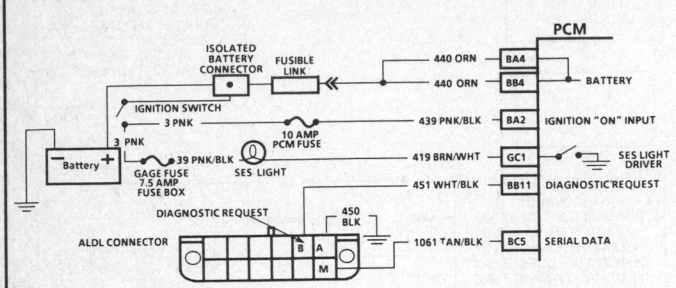

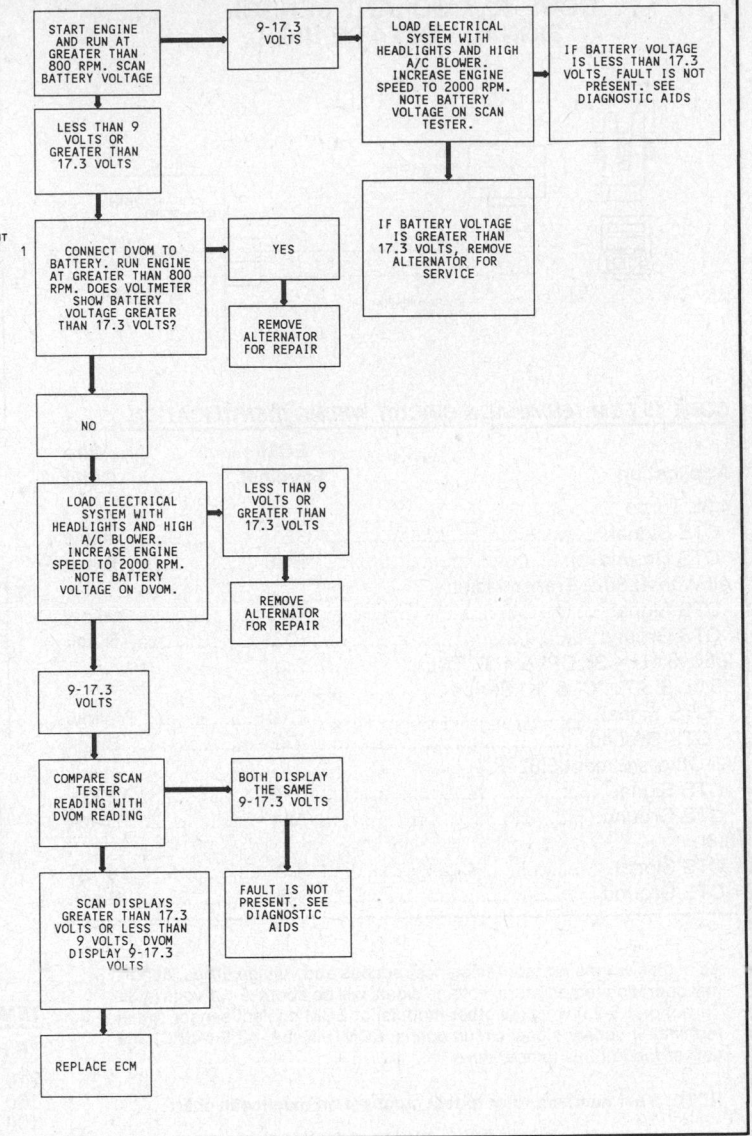

Control module monitors battery voltage on battery feed circuit. If control module detects battery voltage greater than 17 volts or less than 9 volts for more than 10 seconds, it will set a Code 16 in memory.

NOTE: Test number refers to number on diagnostic chart. Starting engine with battery charger connected may set Code 16.

1) Test alternator output to determine proper operation of voltage regulator. Increase engine speed to moderate level. Measure voltage across battery terminals. If reading is more than 17 volts or less than 9 volts, service alternator.

DIAGNOSTIC AIDS

Check for poor connections or damaged harness. Also, check for an intermittent condition by starting engine and wiggling connection while monitoring battery voltage on scan tester. If voltage status changes abruptly or engine stalls, check for loose connections.

NOTE: When Code 16 sets, transaxle will be forced to 3rd gear, preventing erratic shifting due to improper voltage.

92D21785 91A07285

CODE 17, RPM SIGNAL PROBLEM
3.8L

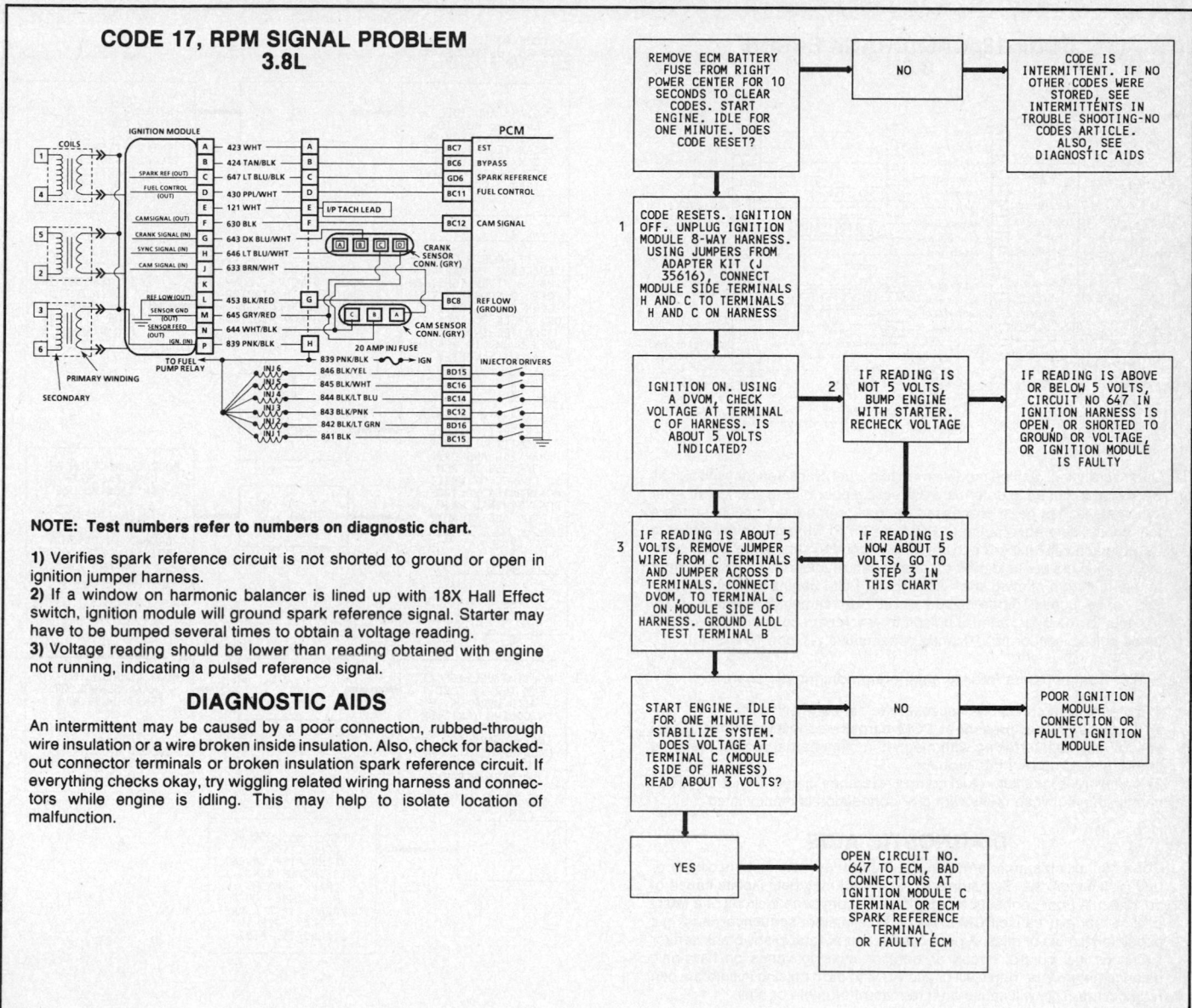

NOTE: Test numbers refer to numbers on diagnostic chart.

1) Verifies spark reference circuit is not shorted to ground or open in ignition jumper harness.

2) If a window on harmonic balancer is lined up with 18X Hall Effect switch, ignition module will ground spark reference signal. Starter may have to be bumped several times to obtain a voltage reading.

3) Voltage reading should be lower than reading obtained with engine not running, indicating a pulsed reference signal.

DIAGNOSTIC AIDS

An intermittent may be caused by a poor connection, rubbed-through wire insulation or a wire broken inside insulation. Also, check for backed-out connector terminals or broken insulation spark reference circuit. If everything checks okay, try wiggling related wiring harness and connectors while engine is idling. This may help to isolate location of malfunction.

92E21786 91C07286

CODE 18, CAM/CRANK ERROR
3.8L

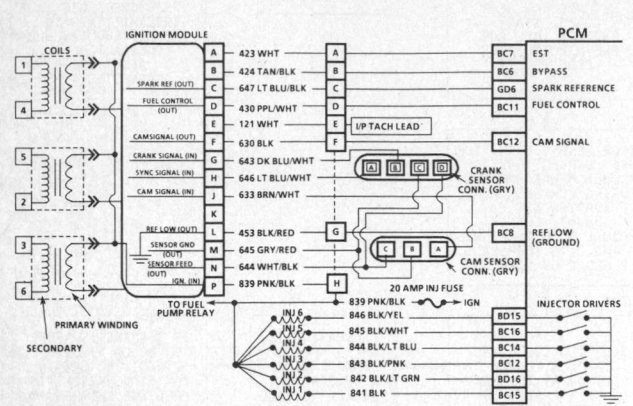

During cranking, ignition module monitors dual crank sensor sync signal. Sync signal is used to determine correct cylinder pair to spark first. After synch signal has been processed by ignition module, module sends a fuel control reference pulse to PCM. When PCM receives this pulse, it will command all 6 injectors to fire for one priming shot of fuel. After priming, all injectors are held off for 2 crankshaft revolutions to allow cylinder to use fuel from priming shot. After firing, PCM begins to operate injectors in sequential mode based upon true camshaft position. PCM expects to see 6 fuel control pulses for each cam pulse. If sequence of these pulses is incorrect 10 times consecutively, Code 18 will set.

NOTE: Test numbers refer to numbers on diagnostic chart.

1) Determines if conditions necessary to set code still exist.
2) If 5 volts are not present at PCM harness connector terminal, cam sensor may be interfacing with magnet in camshaft sprocket. Bumping starter should correct this problem.
3) If a failure is induced in fuel control reference circuit, 5 volts on circuit should change when faulty wiring or connection is manipulated.

DIAGNOSTIC AIDS

Code 18 indicates an intermittent fault and may not set immediately or under all conditions. Symptoms experienced may help isolate cause of condition. A poor connection or fault in any cam sensor circuit or a faulty cam sensor may cause PCM to re-initialize injector sequence, causing a possible stumble or miss. A poor connection or fault in any crank sensor circuit or fuel control circuit or bent or missing vanes on harmonic balancer interrupter rings will cause PCM to stop pulsing injectors when fault occurs. This will cause an intermittent stumble or stall.

92E21786 92I04295

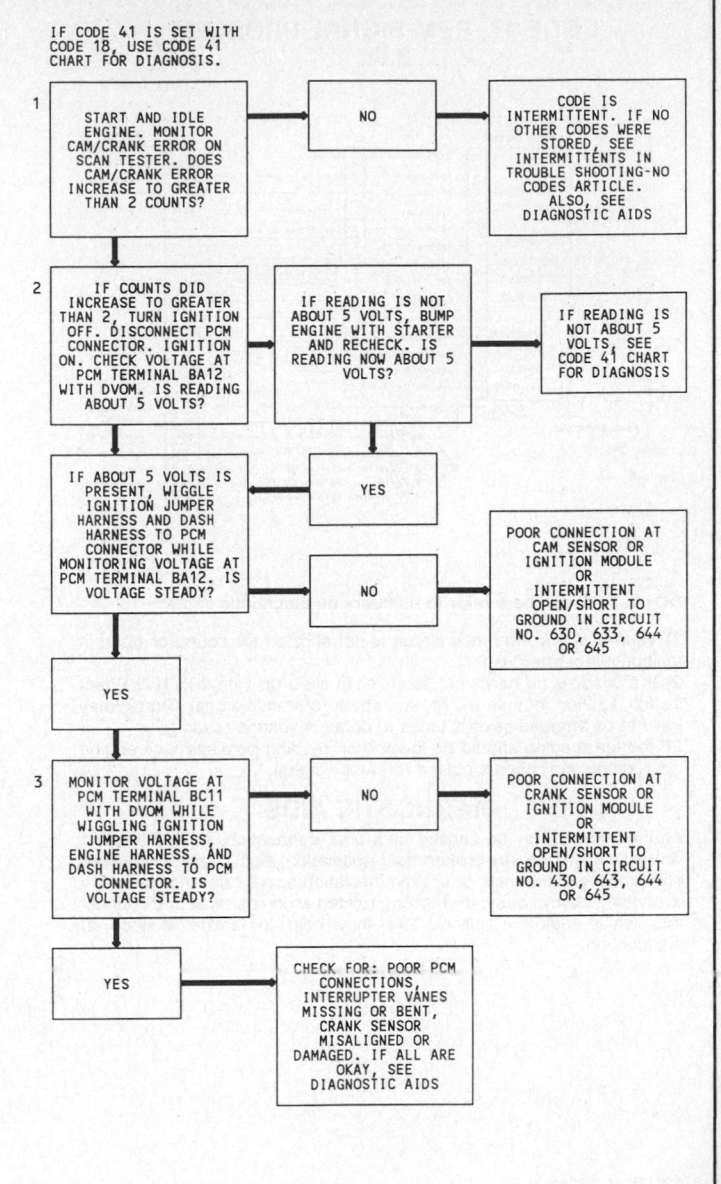

IF CODE 41 IS SET WITH CODE 18, USE CODE 41 CHART FOR DIAGNOSIS.

1 START AND IDLE ENGINE. MONITOR CAM/CRANK ERROR ON SCAN TESTER. DOES CAM/CRANK ERROR INCREASE TO GREATER THAN 2 COUNTS?

NO → CODE IS INTERMITTENT. IF NO OTHER CODES WERE STORED, SEE INTERMITTENTS IN TROUBLE SHOOTING-NO CODES ARTICLE. ALSO, SEE DIAGNOSTIC AIDS

2 IF COUNTS DID INCREASE TO GREATER THAN 2, TURN IGNITION OFF. DISCONNECT PCM CONNECTOR. IGNITION ON. CHECK VOLTAGE AT PCM TERMINAL BA12 WITH DVOM. IS READING ABOUT 5 VOLTS?

IF READING IS NOT ABOUT 5 VOLTS, BUMP ENGINE WITH STARTER AND RECHECK. IS READING NOW ABOUT 5 VOLTS?

IF READING IS NOT ABOUT 5 VOLTS, SEE CODE 41 CHART FOR DIAGNOSIS

IF ABOUT 5 VOLTS IS PRESENT, WIGGLE IGNITION JUMPER HARNESS AND DASH HARNESS TO PCM CONNECTOR WHILE MONITORING VOLTAGE AT PCM TERMINAL BA12. IS VOLTAGE STEADY?

YES

NO → POOR CONNECTION AT CAM SENSOR OR IGNITION MODULE OR INTERMITTENT OPEN/SHORT TO GROUND IN CIRCUIT NO. 630, 633, 644 OR 645

YES

3 MONITOR VOLTAGE AT PCM TERMINAL BC11 WITH DVOM WHILE WIGGLING IGNITION JUMPER HARNESS, ENGINE HARNESS, AND DASH HARNESS TO PCM CONNECTOR. IS VOLTAGE STEADY?

NO → POOR CONNECTION AT CRANK SENSOR OR IGNITION MODULE OR INTERMITTENT OPEN/SHORT TO GROUND IN CIRCUIT NO. 430, 643, 644 OR 645

YES → CHECK FOR: POOR PCM CONNECTIONS, INTERRUPTER VANES MISSING OR BENT, CRANK SENSOR MISALIGNED OR DAMAGED. IF ALL ARE OKAY, SEE DIAGNOSTIC AIDS

CODE 21, TPS SIGNAL VOLTAGE HIGH

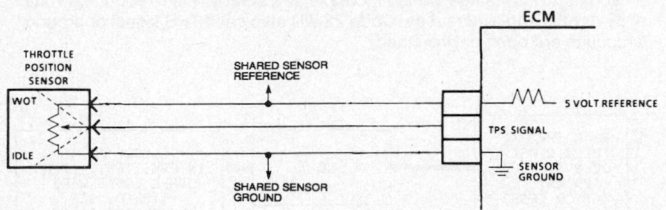

CODE 21 ECM TERMINAL & CIRCUIT WIRING IDENTIFICATION

Application	ECM Terminal	Wire Color
4.3L Turbo		
TPS Signal	GF13	Dark Blue
TPS Ground	BB5	Black
TPS Reference	BA5	Gray
All With 4L80-E Transmission		
TPS Signal	C5	Dark Blue
TPS Ground	D3	Black
TPS Reference	C4	Gray
2.8L, 3.1L & 4.3L Except Turbo, 5.0L & 5.7L "C" & "K" Series		
TPS Signal	C13	Dark Blue
TPS Ground	D2	Black
TPS Reference	C14	Gray
All Others Except 3.8L		
TPS Signal	C13	Dark Blue
TPS Ground	A11	Black
TPS Reference	C14	Gray
3.8L		
TPS Signal	B10	Dark Blue
TPS Ground	A8	Black
TPS Reference	B3	Gray

Throttle Position Sensor (TPS) provides a varying voltage signal depending on throttle valve angle. Signal voltage varies from about .50 volt at idle to 4.5 volts at wide open throttle. On models with non-adjustable TPS, each time TPS voltage drops to less than 1.25 volts and stops, ECM assumes this is zero degrees throttle angle and measures throttle percentage angle from this point.

NOTE: Test numbers refer to test numbers on diagnostic chart.

1) This test confirms Code 21 and checks if fault is a hard failure or an intermittent condition. Code 21 will set if TPS voltage is greater than 2.5 volts 2-10 seconds with engine running. On 2.8L, Code 21 may set if MAP sensor signal less than 2 volts.

2) This test simulates conditions for Code 22. If ECM recognizes low voltage signal and sets Code 22, ECM and power and signal circuits are not at fault.

3) This step isolates a faulty sensor, ECM or an open ground circuit.

DIAGNOSTIC AIDS

A scan tester displays throttle position in volts. Closed throttle voltage should be less than 1.0 volt (4.3L Turbo) or less than 1.25 volts (all other models). TPS voltage should increase at a steady rate to about 4.5 volts as throttle angle increases. Code 21 will also result if ground circuit is open or TPS signal circuit is shorted to voltage.

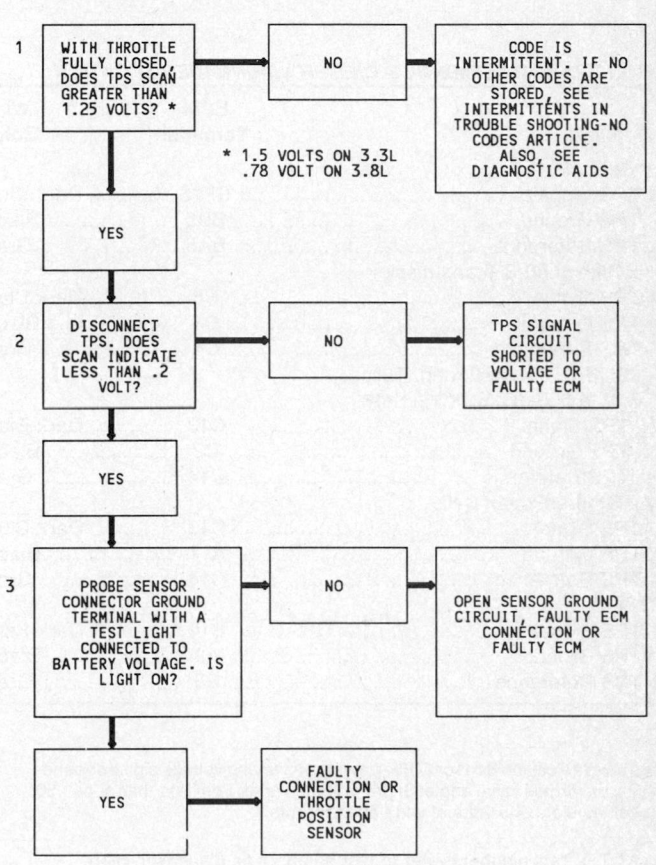

91C07385 91E07287

CODE 22, TPS SIGNAL VOLTAGE LOW

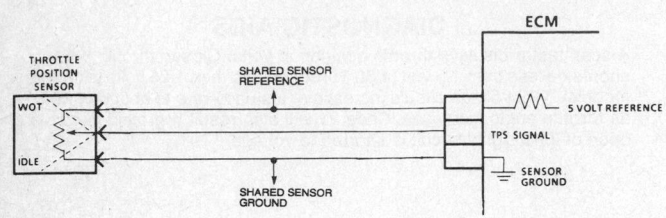

CODE 22 ECM TERMINAL & CIRCUIT WIRING IDENTIFICATION

Application	ECM Terminal	Wire Color
4.3L Turbo		
TPS Signal	GF13	Dark Blue
TPS Ground	BB5	Black
TPS Reference	BA5	Gray
All With 4L80-E Transmission		
TPS Signal	C5	Dark Blue
TPS Ground	D3	Black
TPS Reference	C4	Gray
2.8L, 3.1L & 4.3L Except Turbo,		
5.0L & 5.7L "C" & "K" Series		
TPS Signal	C13	Dark Blue
TPS Ground	D2	Black
TPS Reference	C14	Gray
All Others Except 3.8L		
TPS Signal	C13	Dark Blue
TPS Ground	A11	Black
TPS Reference	C14	Gray
3.8L		
TPS Signal	B10	Dark Blue
TPS Ground	A8	Black
TPS Reference	B3	Gray

Throttle Position Sensor (TPS) provides a varying voltage signal depending on throttle valve angle. Signal voltage varies from less than about .50 volt at idle to 4.5 volts at wide open throttle.

NOTE: Test numbers refer to test numbers on diagnostic chart.

1) This test confirms Code 22 and tests if fault is a hard failure or an intermittent condition. Code 22 will set if engine is running, TPS voltage is less than .2 volt for 2-4 seconds.
2) This simulates Code 21. If ECM recognizes a high voltage signal and sets Code 21, ECM and wiring are not at fault. On 2.8L, check and adjust TPS. On all others, replace TPS.
3) This simulates a high voltage signal to check for on open TPS signal circuit.

91C07385 91G07288

DIAGNOSTIC AIDS

A scan tester displays throttle position in volts. Closed throttle voltage should be less than 1.0 volt (4.3L Turbo) or less than 1.25 volts (all other models). TPS voltage should increase at a steady rate to about 4.5 volts as throttle angle increases. Code 22 will also set if TPS signal or ground circuits are open or grounded.

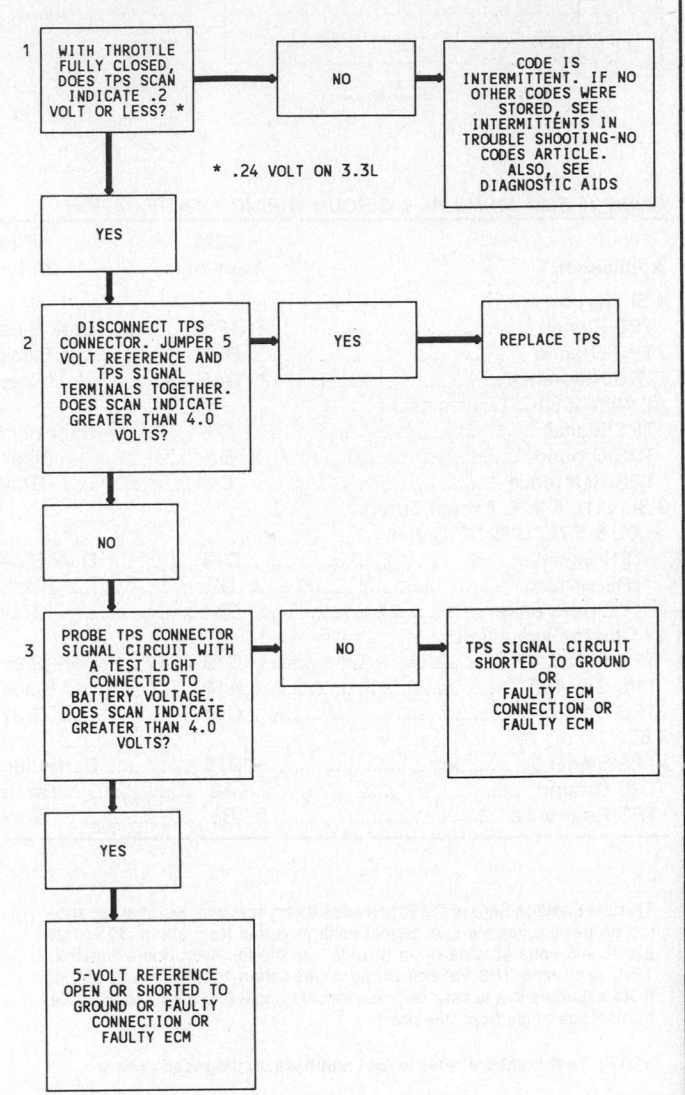

CODE 24, VEHICLE SPEED S...
3.8L

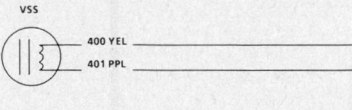

Speed sensor, which is a Permanent Magnet ...
control module with vehicle speed information.
in transmission, produces a pulsing AC voltage ...
speed is greater than 3 MPH. Voltage level a...
vehicle speed. Control module converts pulsin...
is used by control module to calculate vehicle a...

NOTE: Test numbers refer to numbers on dia...

1) PM generator only produces a voltage signal ...
ing greater than 3 MPH.
2) Before replacing control module, MEM-CAL ...
correct application.

DIAGNOSTIC AID...

A faulty or misadjusted park/neutral switch may ...
scan tester to check for proper signal in Drive...
Code 24 may set if vehicle is power braked (bra...
depressed) for more than 10 seconds. Check c...
for proper connections.

91D07395 91E07292

CODE 23, MAT SENSOR TEMP. LOW
(2.5L & 4.3L TURBO)

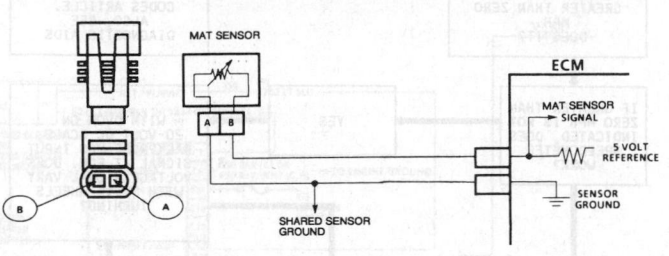

CODE 23 ECM TERMINAL & CIRCUIT WIRING IDENTIFICATION

Application	ECM Terminal	Wire Color
2.5L		
Signal	C12	Tan
MAT Ground	D2	Black/Orange
4.3L CPI		
Signal	C12	Tan
MAT Ground	A11	Black
4.3L Turbo		
Signal	GF16	Tan
MAT Ground	BB5	Black

ECM supplies and monitors a voltage signal (4-6 volts) to sensor. When temperatures are low, sensor resistance is high and ECM will see a high-monitored voltage signal. As temperature increases, sensor resistance decreases and voltage sensed by ECM drops.

NOTE: Test numbers refer to test numbers on diagnostic chart.

1) This checks if Code 23 is a hard failure or an intermittent condition. Code 23 will set if engine is running for one minute, MAT sensor temperature is less than -22°F (-30°C) for 12 seconds and speed sensor signal is not present.
2) This simulates conditions for a Code 25. If scan tester displays a high temperature, ECM and wiring are not at fault.
3) This checks for continuity of sensor signal and ground circuits.

DIAGNOSTIC AIDS

If engine is allowed to cool overnight, coolant and MAT sensors should read close to each other, when measured with a scan tester. A Code 23 will also result if signal and ground circuits become open.

91E07386 91I07289

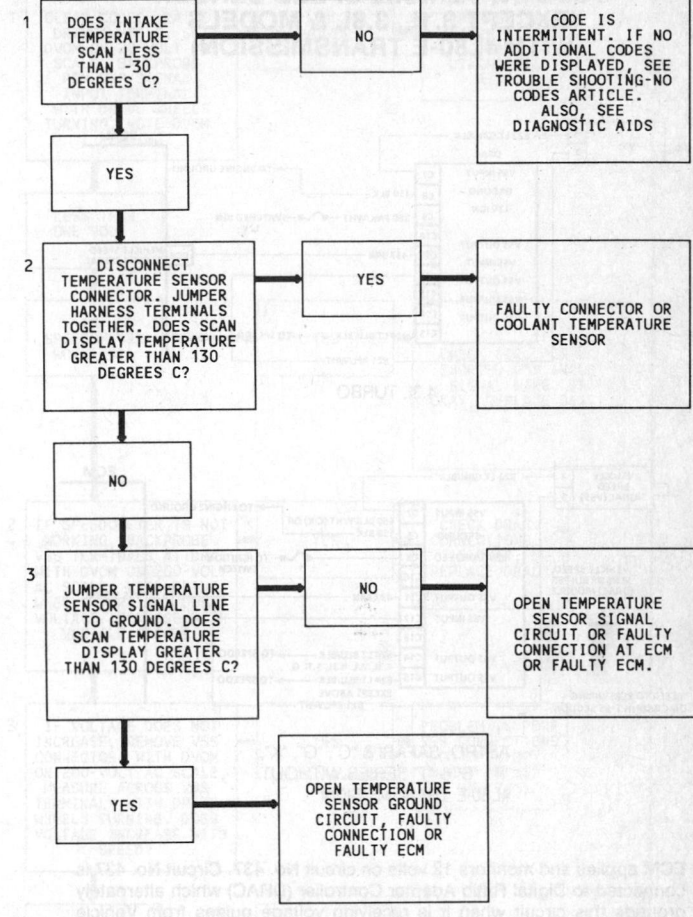

TEMPERATURE-TO-RESISTANCE VALUES [1] [2]

°F (°C)	Ohms
210 (100)	185
160 (70)	450
100 (38)	1800
70 (20)	3400
40 (4)	7500
20 (-7)	13,500
0 (-18)	25,000
-40 (-40)	100,700

[1] – Measure resistance across sensor terminals.
[2] – Temperatures are approximates.

GM
1-46

199

Self-Di

GM
1-48

1992 ENGINE PERFORMANCE
Self-Diagnostics – Gasoline (Cont.)

CODE 24, VEHICLE SPE
(4WD WITH 4L80-E TRA

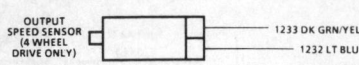

VSS output sensor is a magnetic induction ty
outside diameter of output carrier assem
current in sensor when drive wheels are turn
taken from transfer case on 4WD vehicles, c
on these units goes directly to PCM. Code 2
not in Park or Neutral, engine speed is at le
speed is less than 200 RPM for at least 1.5 s

NOTE: Test numbers refer to test numbers

1) Test verifies VSS voltage at PCM.
2) Test verifies VSS signal at sensor.

DIAGNOSTIC A

Check all connections, especially those a
connector. If code is intermittent, see INTE
SHOOTING – NO CODES article. While Coo
display an RPM derived from input speed. If
operational at start-up, this can cause VSS t

91G13736 91F13669

CODE 24, VEHICLE SPE
(3.1L)

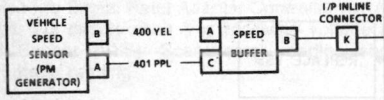

ECM applies and monitors a 12-volt signal o
Speed Sensor (VSS). VSS is connected to s
alternately grounds and opens circuit No. 43
This pulsing action takes place about 2000 ti
and pulses increase with vehicle speed. ECN
to MPH. ECM uses VSS information in calcul
adjustments. Scan tester reading should cl
reading when wheels are turning.

NOTE: Test numbers refer to test numbers

1) A Code 24 sets when MPH is less than 2 N
Park or Neutral, engine speed is greater than
than 5 percent, circuit No. 437 voltage is cons
tions are met for 30 seconds. These conditi
load deceleration.
2) A steady 8-12 volts at ECM connector indic
speed sensor is faulty. A voltage of less tha
indicates circuit No. 437 wire is shorted to g
speed sensor connector. If voltage is now gr
speed sensor buffer is faulty. If voltage rema
is grounded. If circuit is not grounded, check
or ECM. Before replacing ECM, PROM sho
application.

91D13741 91I13670

CODE 25, MAT SENSOR TEMP. HIGH
(2.5L & 4.3L TURBO)

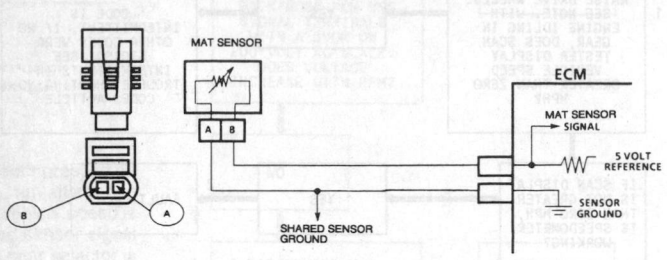

CODE 25 ECM TERMINAL & CIRCUIT WIRING IDENTIFICATION

Application	ECM Terminal	Wire Color
2.5L		
Signal	C12	Tan
MAT Ground	D2	Black/Red
4.3L Turbo		
Signal	GF16	Tan
MAT Ground	BB5	Black

ECM applies and monitors a voltage signal (4-6 volts) to MAT sensor. When manifold air is cold, sensor resistance is high and ECM sees a high signal voltage. As air warms, resistance decreases and voltage sensed by ECM drops. Sensor resistance can be measured at sensor terminals with harness disconnected.

NOTE: Test numbers refer to test numbers on diagnostic chart.

1) This checks if code is a hard failure or an intermittent condition. Code 25 will set if a VSS signal is present (2.5L) and monitored MAT sensor temperature is greater than 302°F (150°C) for 2.5L or 275°F (135°C) for 4.3L Turbo.
2) This simulates conditions for a Code 23. If scan tester displays a low temperature, ECM and wiring are not at fault.

DIAGNOSTIC AIDS

If engine is allowed to cool overnight, coolant temperature sensor and MAT sensor should read close to each other, when measured with a scan tester. A Code 25 will also result if sensor signal circuit is shorted to ground.

91E07386 91I07294

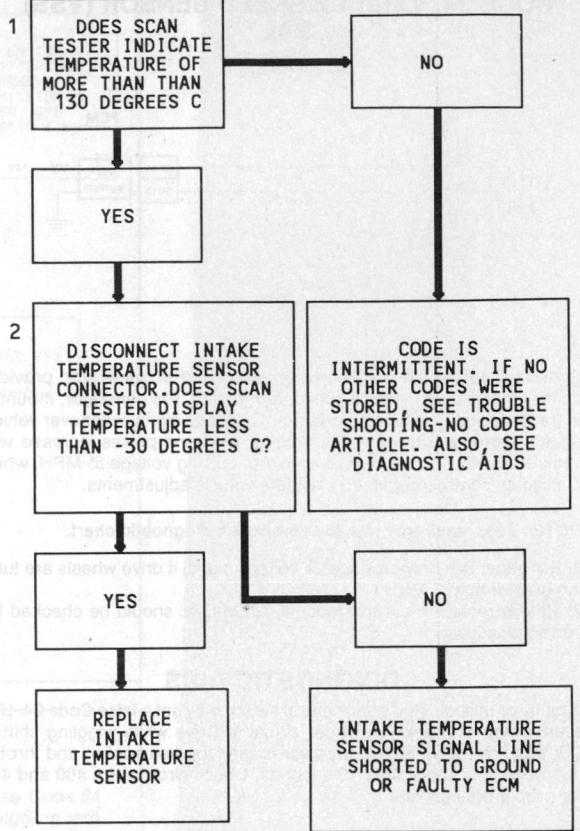

TEMPERATURE-TO-RESISTANCE VALUES [1] [2]

°F (°C)	Ohms
210 (100)	185
160 (70)	450
100 (38)	1800
70 (20)	3400
40 (4)	7500
20 (–7)	13,500
0 (–18)	25,000
–40 (–40)	100,700

[1] – Measure resistance across sensor terminals.
[2] – Temperatures are approximates.

CODE 26, QUAD-DRIVER CIRCUIT
3.8L (1 OF 3)

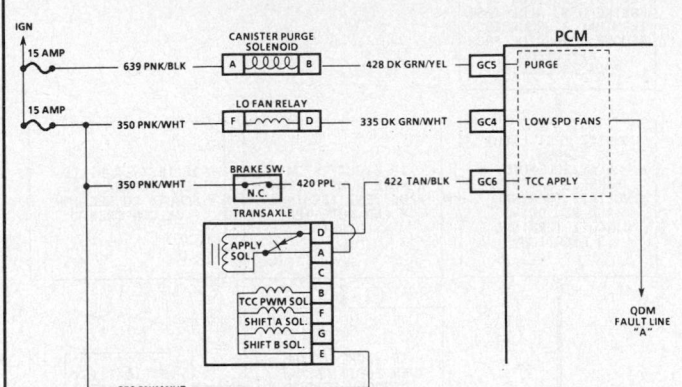

Each PCM Quad-Driver Module (QDM) has a fault line which is monitored by PCM. PCM compares voltage values of fault line with acceptable values in PCM memory. If PCM senses values other than accepted values, a Code 26 will set.

Some QDM circuits will normally cycle between high and low, such as depressing brake pedal. Some scan testers may set a false Code 26 if engine is running, tester is installed and brake pedal is depressed for more than 30 seconds.

NOTE: Test number refers to number on diagnostic chart.

1) PCM does not know which controlled circuit set Code 26, so this chart checks each circuit to determine which is at fault. This step tests SERVICE ENGINE SOON light driver and circuit.

92F21787 92A04673

QDM Symptoms:
- HOT light on all the time but off during bulb check.
- Cooling fan always on low speed or will not come on at all.
- Poor driveability due to 100 percent canister purge.

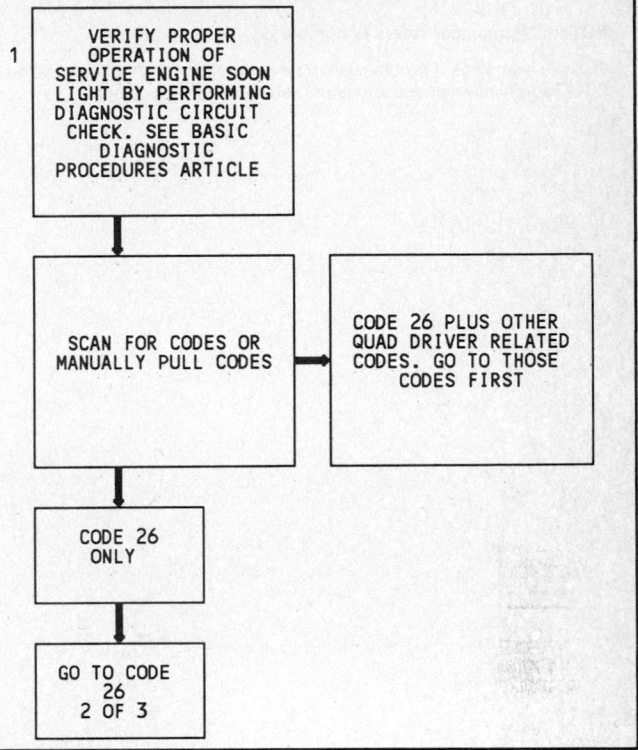

CODE 26, QUAD-DRIVER CIRCUIT
3.8L (2 OF 3)

NOTE: Test number refers to number on diagnostic chart.

2) This determines which circuit is out of specification. All terminals except GC7 should have battery voltage with ignition on, engine not running and ALDL test terminal not grounded.

DIAGNOSTIC AIDS

Monitor voltage of each terminal while moving related harness connectors, including PCM harness. If fault is induced, voltage will change. This may help locate intermittent problems. If code reappears with no apparent problems, replace PCM.

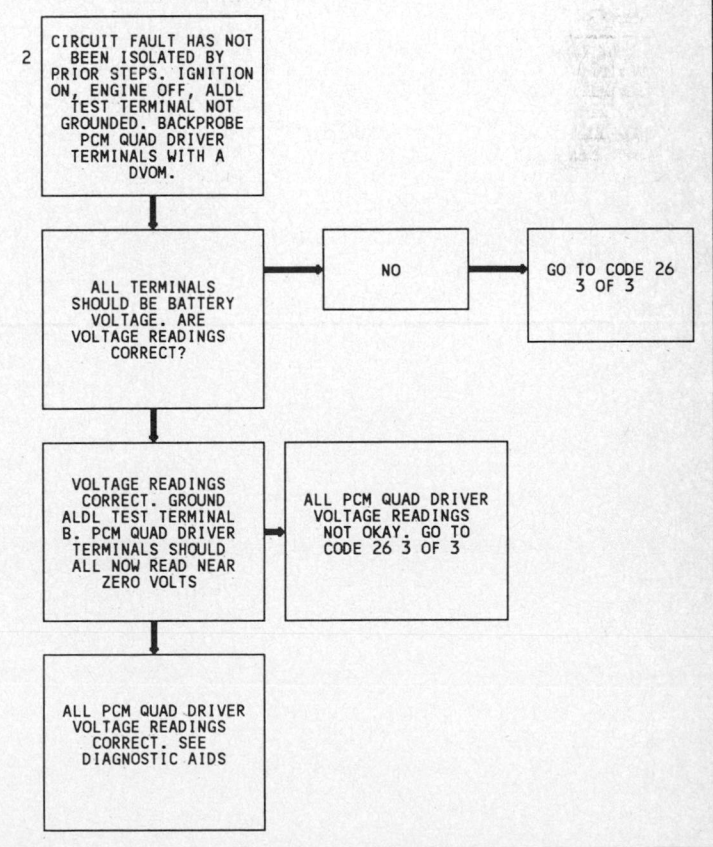

92G21788

CODE 26, QUAD-DRIVER CIRCUIT
3.8L (3 OF 3)

NOTE: **Test number refers to number on diagnostic chart.**

3) This determines if problem is circuit or component. Factory-installed PCM has an internal fuse and is unlikely to need replacement.

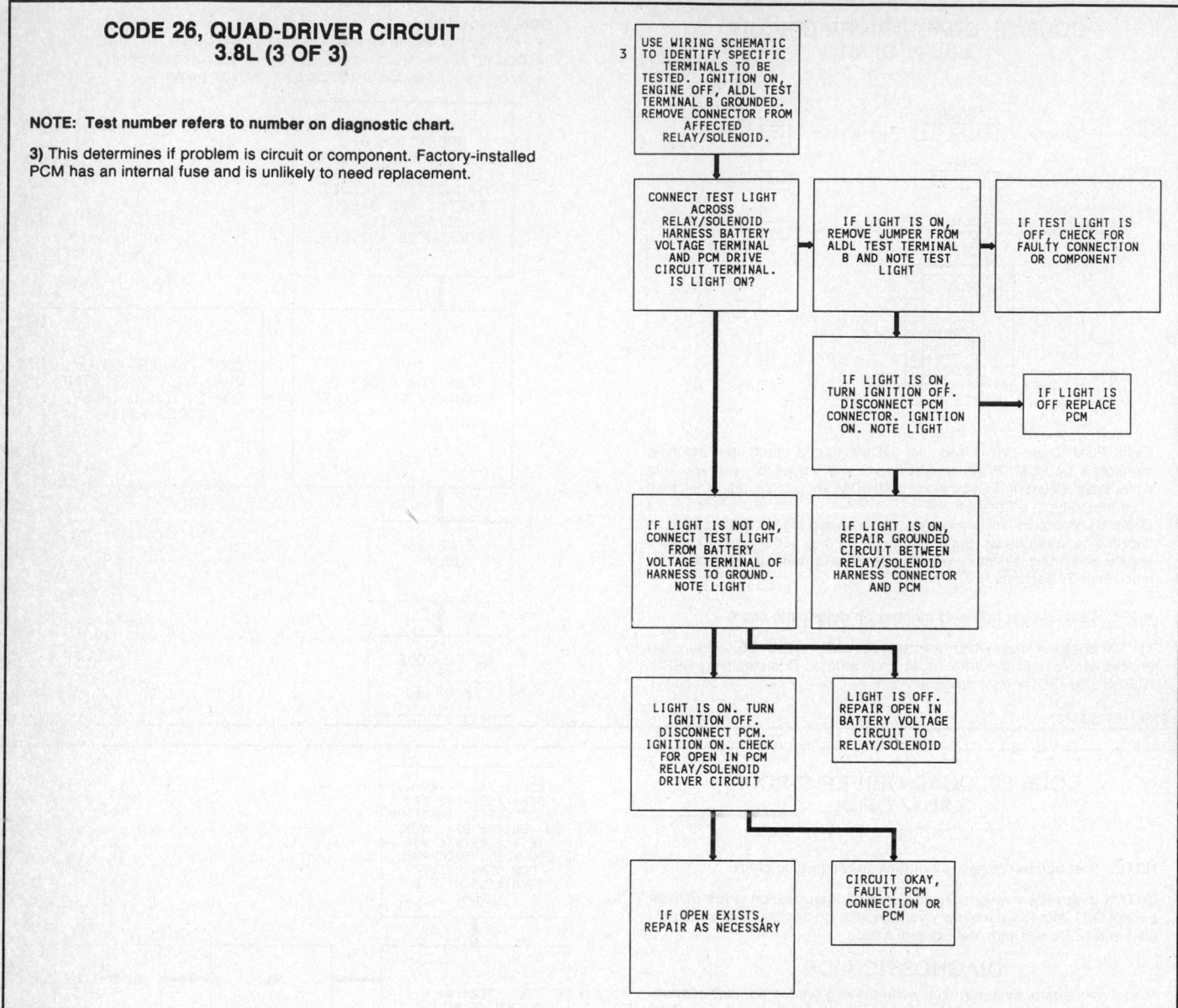

3 USE WIRING SCHEMATIC TO IDENTIFY SPECIFIC TERMINALS TO BE TESTED. IGNITION ON, ENGINE OFF, ALDL TEST TERMINAL B GROUNDED. REMOVE CONNECTOR FROM AFFECTED RELAY/SOLENOID.

CONNECT TEST LIGHT ACROSS RELAY/SOLENOID HARNESS BATTERY VOLTAGE TERMINAL AND PCM DRIVE CIRCUIT TERMINAL. IS LIGHT ON?

IF LIGHT IS ON, REMOVE JUMPER FROM ALDL TEST TERMINAL B AND NOTE TEST LIGHT

IF TEST LIGHT IS OFF, CHECK FOR FAULTY CONNECTION OR COMPONENT

IF LIGHT IS ON, TURN IGNITION OFF. DISCONNECT PCM CONNECTOR. IGNITION ON. NOTE LIGHT

IF LIGHT IS OFF REPLACE PCM

IF LIGHT IS NOT ON, CONNECT TEST LIGHT FROM BATTERY VOLTAGE TERMINAL OF HARNESS TO GROUND. NOTE LIGHT

IF LIGHT IS ON, REPAIR GROUNDED CIRCUIT BETWEEN RELAY/SOLENOID HARNESS CONNECTOR AND PCM

LIGHT IS ON. TURN IGNITION OFF. DISCONNECT PCM. IGNITION ON. CHECK FOR OPEN IN PCM RELAY/SOLENOID DRIVER CIRCUIT

LIGHT IS OFF. REPAIR OPEN IN BATTERY VOLTAGE CIRCUIT TO RELAY/SOLENOID

IF OPEN EXISTS, REPAIR AS NECESSARY

CIRCUIT OKAY, FAULTY PCM CONNECTION OR PCM

91J07317

CODE 31, PARK/NEUTRAL SWITCH CIRCUIT 3.8L

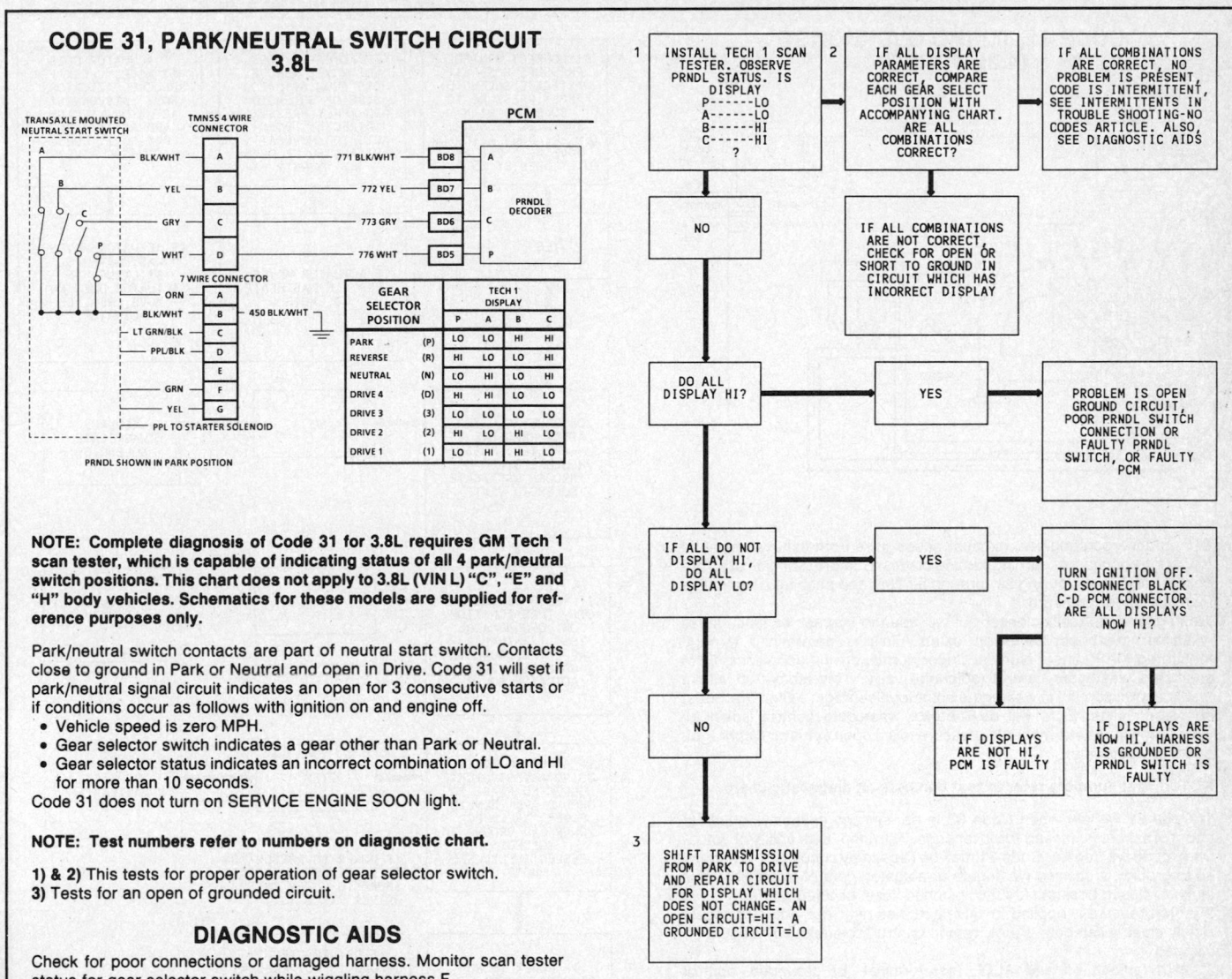

NOTE: Complete diagnosis of Code 31 for 3.8L requires GM Tech 1 scan tester, which is capable of indicating status of all 4 park/neutral switch positions. This chart does not apply to 3.8L (VIN L) "C", "E" and "H" body vehicles. Schematics for these models are supplied for reference purposes only.

Park/neutral switch contacts are part of neutral start switch. Contacts close to ground in Park or Neutral and open in Drive. Code 31 will set if park/neutral signal circuit indicates an open for 3 consecutive starts or if conditions occur as follows with ignition on and engine off.
- Vehicle speed is zero MPH.
- Gear selector switch indicates a gear other than Park or Neutral.
- Gear selector status indicates an incorrect combination of LO and HI for more than 10 seconds.

Code 31 does not turn on SERVICE ENGINE SOON light.

NOTE: Test numbers refer to numbers on diagnostic chart.

1) & 2) This tests for proper operation of gear selector switch.

3) Tests for an open of grounded circuit.

DIAGNOSTIC AIDS

Check for poor connections or damaged harness. Monitor scan tester status for gear selector switch while wiggling harness.F

92H21789 92A21790

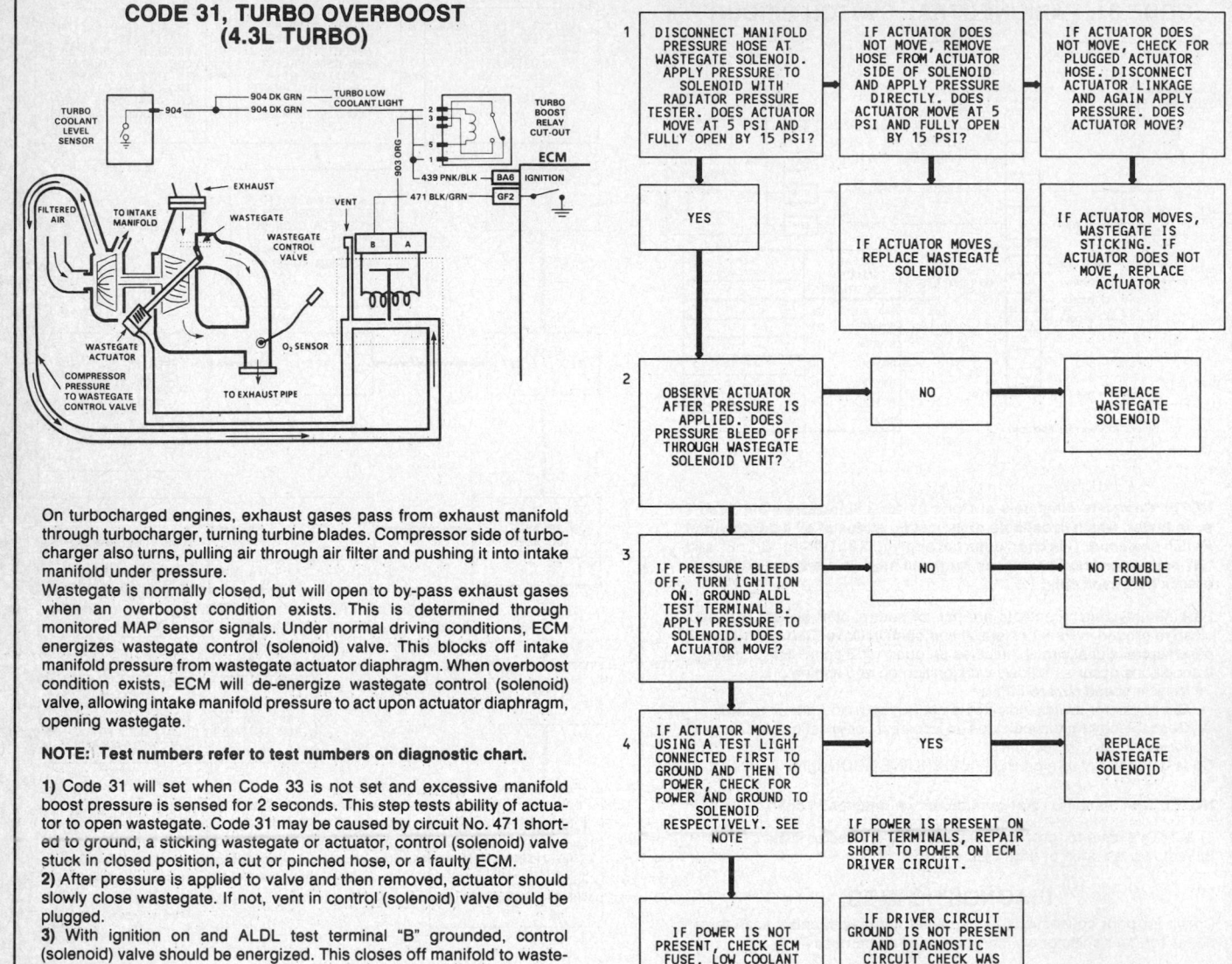

CODE 31, TURBO OVERBOOST
(4.3L TURBO)

On turbocharged engines, exhaust gases pass from exhaust manifold through turbocharger, turning turbine blades. Compressor side of turbocharger also turns, pulling air through air filter and pushing it into intake manifold under pressure.

Wastegate is normally closed, but will open to by-pass exhaust gases when an overboost condition exists. This is determined through monitored MAP sensor signals. Under normal driving conditions, ECM energizes wastegate control (solenoid) valve. This blocks off intake manifold pressure from wastegate actuator diaphragm. When overboost condition exists, ECM will de-energize wastegate control (solenoid) valve, allowing intake manifold pressure to act upon actuator diaphragm, opening wastegate.

NOTE: Test numbers refer to test numbers on diagnostic chart.

1) Code 31 will set when Code 33 is not set and excessive manifold boost pressure is sensed for 2 seconds. This step tests ability of actuator to open wastegate. Code 31 may be caused by circuit No. 471 shorted to ground, a sticking wastegate or actuator, control (solenoid) valve stuck in closed position, a cut or pinched hose, or a faulty ECM.

2) After pressure is applied to valve and then removed, actuator should slowly close wastegate. If not, vent in control (solenoid) valve could be plugged.

3) With ignition on and ALDL test terminal "B" grounded, control (solenoid) valve should be energized. This closes off manifold to wastegate actuator.

4) This checks electrical control portion of system. With ignition on and engine not running, solenoid should not be energized.

91E13742 91H13711

CODE 32, EGR SYSTEM ERROR
(4.3L "C", "G" "K" & "P" SERIES
WITH 4L80-E TRANSMISSION)

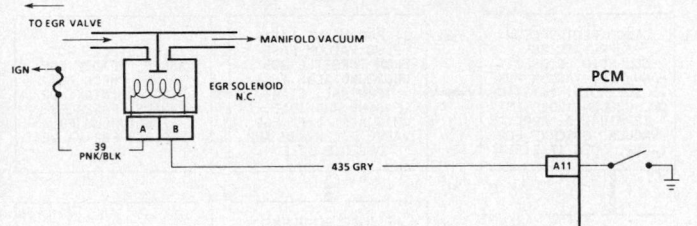

PCM controls a solenoid regulating vacuum to EGR valve. Normally closed solenoid prevents vacuum from passing until it is energized by PCM. A properly operating EGR will directly affect fuel integrator counts. With EGR valve open, integrator counts will be less than without EGR operation. If monitored integrator counts do not change with EGR commanded, Code 32 will set.

NOTE: Test numbers refer to test numbers on diagnostic chart.

1) When test terminal "B" of ALDL connector is grounded, EGR solenoid should be energized, allowing vacuum to EGR valve. Vacuum should hold.
2) When jumper wire is removed from terminal "B", vacuum to EGR valve should bleed through a vent in solenoid and EGR valve should close. Vacuum gauge may or may not bleed off vacuum, however, this does not indicate a problem.
3) Determines if fault lies in electrical control part of system, connector or solenoid.
4) This system uses a negative backpressure EGR valve. Valve should hold vacuum with engine off.
5) When engine is started, backpressure should cause vacuum to bleed off and valve should fully close.

DIAGNOSTIC AIDS

Prior to replacing PCM, check resistance of all PCM-controlled solenoids and relays. Replace any with a resistance value less than 20 ohms.

PRIOR TO USING THIS CHART, ENSURE THAT VACUUM HOSES ARE FREE OF LEAKS AND RESTRICTIONS AND THAT AT LEAST 7 IN. OF VACUUM IS BEING SUPPLIED TO SOLENOID FROM VACUUM SOURCE AT 2000 RPM.

1 IGNITION ON, ENGINE OFF. DISCONNECT EGR SOLENOID VACUUM HARNESS. GROUND ALDL TEST TERMINAL B. APPLY 10 IN. VACUUM TO MANIFOLD SIDE OF SOLENOID. VACUUM SHOULD HOLD

3 IF VACUUM HOLDS, PLUG EGR VACUUM SIDE OF SOLENOID. UNGROUND ALDL. DOES VACUUM BLEED OFF?

IF VACUUM DOES NOT BLEED OFF. DISCONNECT SOLENOID ELECTRICAL CONNECTOR. IF VACUUM DROPS, REPAIR SHORT TO GROUND IN CIRCUIT NO. 435. IF VACUUM DOES NOT BLEED OFF, REPLACE SOLENOID

2 IF 10 IN. VACUUM WILL NOT HOLD, DISCONNECT SOLENOID ELECTRICAL HARNESS. CONNECT TEST LIGHT ACROSS HARNESS TERMINALS. IS LIGHT ON?

4 IF VACUUM BLEEDS OFF, CONNECT VACUUM PUMP TO EGR VALVE. APPLY VACUUM. DIAPHRAGM SHOULD LIFT AND VACUUM SHOULD HOLD FOR AT LEAST 20 SECONDS. DOES IT?

IF DIAPHRAGM DOES NOT LIFT OR VACUUM DOES NOT HOLD FOR AT LEAST 20 SECONDS, REPLACE EGR VALVE

IF LIGHT IS ON, SOLENOID OR SOLENOID CONNECTIONS ARE FAULTY.

5 IF VACUUM HOLDS, START ENGINE. THIS IS A NEGATIVE BACKPRESSURE VALVE. VACUUM SHOULD IMMEDIATELY DROP AND EGR VALVE SHOULD SEAT. DOES IT?

IF VALVE DOES NOT SEAT AND VACUUM DOES NOT DROP, REMOVE VALVE AND CHECK FOR CARBON BUILD-UP. IF VALVE IS NOT PLUGGED, REPLACE VALVE.

IF LIGHT IS OFF, PROBE EACH HARNESS TERMINAL WITH TEST LIGHT CONNECTED TO GROUND

IF VACUUM DROPS AND VALVE SEATS, NO PROBLEM IS FOUND

LIGHT ON ONE TERMINAL. GROUND CIRCUIT BETWEEN SOLENOID AND ECM IS OPEN OR ECM IS FAULTY

LIGHT OFF ON BOTH. REPAIR OPEN IN IGNITION FEED CIRCUIT TO SOLENOID

LIGHT ON ON BOTH TERMINALS. REPAIR SHORT TO VOLTAGE ON GROUND CIRCUIT BETWEEN SOLENOID AND ECM

91J13747 91B07323

CODE 32, EGR SYSTEM ERROR
(ALL ENGINES WITH 4L80-E TRANSMISSION
EXCEPT 4.3L)

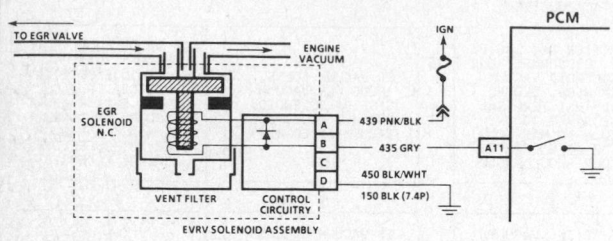

PCM controls a solenoid that regulates vacuum to EGR valve. The normally closed solenoid prevents vacuum from passing until it is energized by PCM. A properly operating EGR will directly affect fuel integrator counts. With EGR valve open, integrator counts will be less than without EGR operation. If monitored integrator counts do not change with EGR commanded, Code 32 will set.
ECM checks EGR operation when engine speed is greater than 1600 RPM, MAP sensor signal indicates cruise condition and throttle position are constant.

NOTE: Test numbers refer to test numbers on diagnostic chart.

1) With ignition on and engine off, solenoid should not be energized or allow vacuum to pass to EGR valve. When test terminal "B" of ALDL connector is grounded, EGR solenoid should be energized, allowing vacuum to EGR valve. Vacuum should hold.
2) Checks for plugged EGR passages. If passages are plugged, engine may have severe detonation on acceleration.
3) Vehicle must be driven during this test to produce sufficient load to operate EGR. Lightly accelerating (approximately 1/4 throttle) will produce a large and stable enough reading to determine if ECM is commanding system on.

DIAGNOSTIC AIDS

Prior to replacing PCM, check resistance of all PCM-controlled solenoids and relays. Replace any with a resistance value less than 20 ohms.

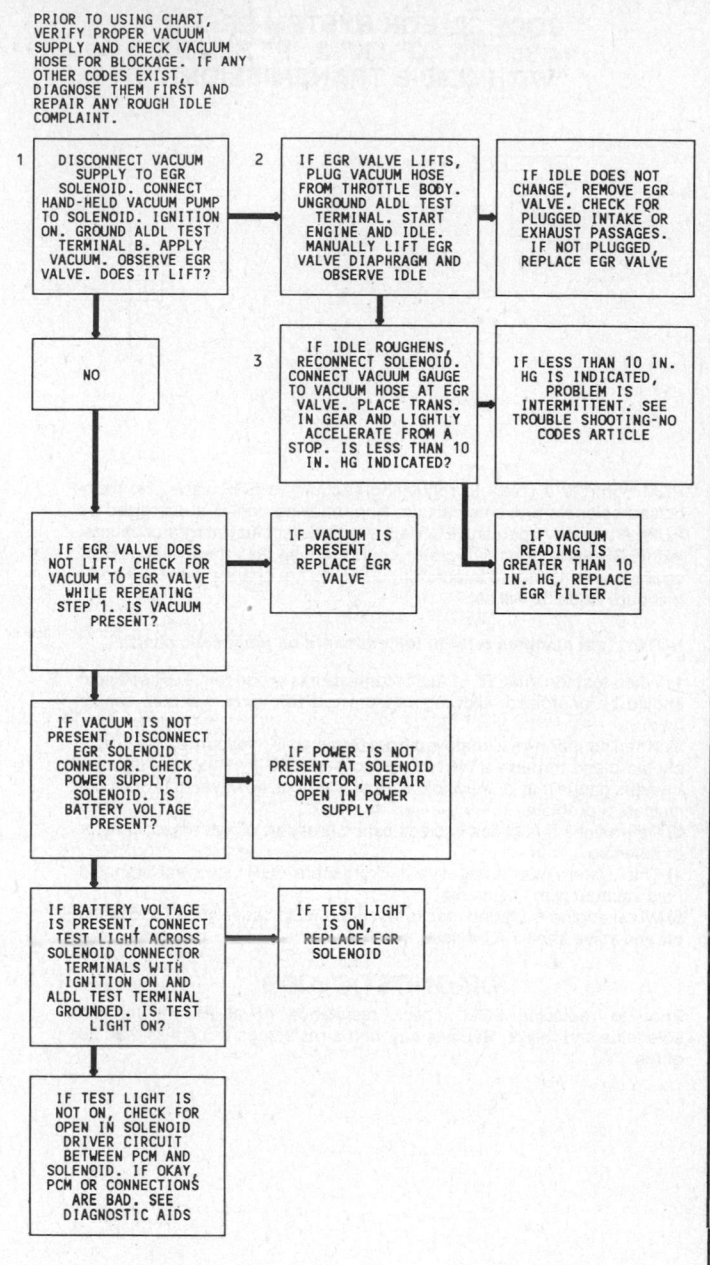

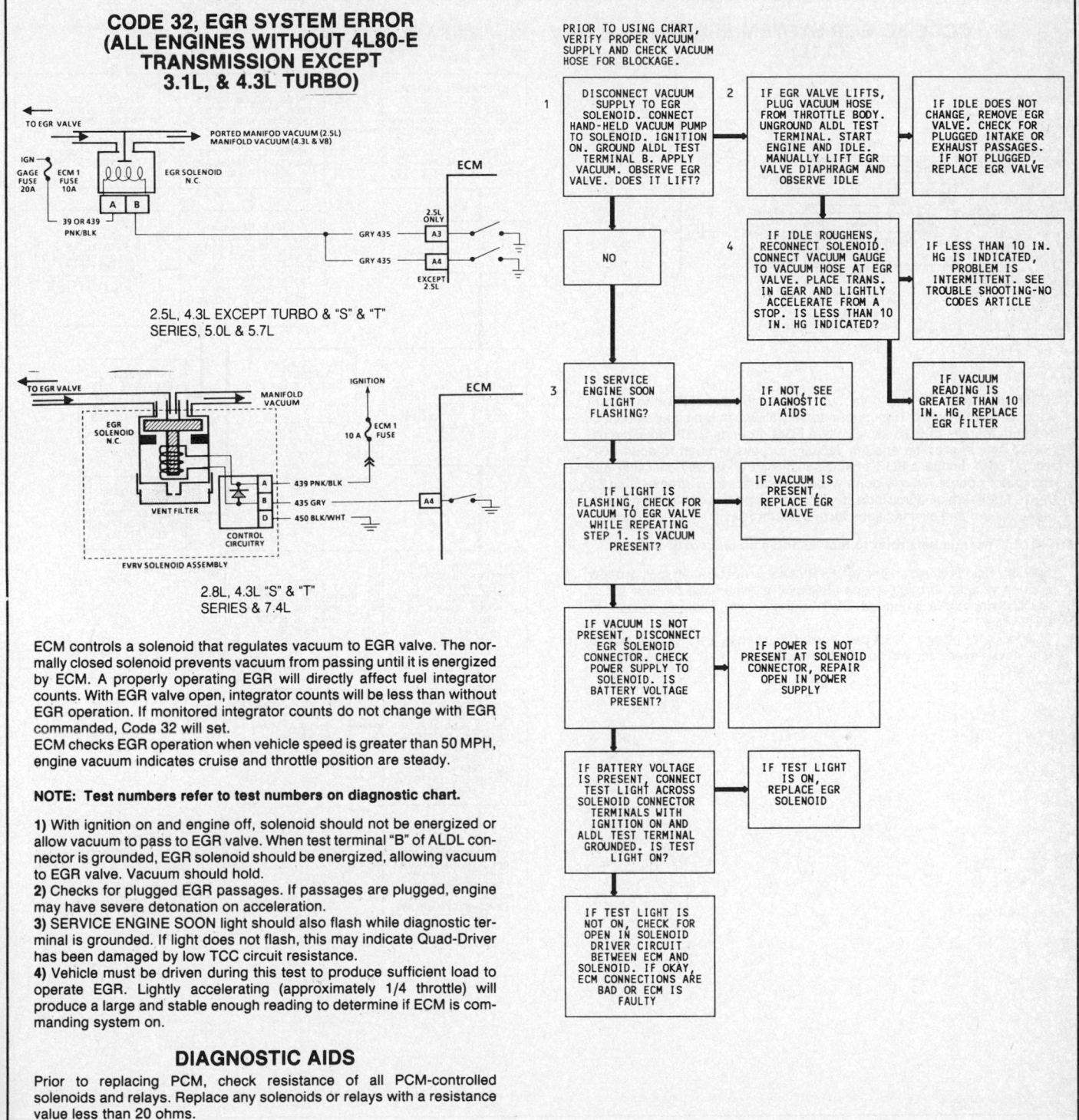

CODE 32, EGR SYSTEM ERROR (ALL ENGINES WITHOUT 4L80-E TRANSMISSION EXCEPT 3.1L, & 4.3L TURBO)

2.5L, 4.3L EXCEPT TURBO & "S" & "T" SERIES, 5.0L & 5.7L

2.8L, 4.3L "S" & "T" SERIES & 7.4L

ECM controls a solenoid that regulates vacuum to EGR valve. The normally closed solenoid prevents vacuum from passing until it is energized by ECM. A properly operating EGR will directly affect fuel integrator counts. With EGR valve open, integrator counts will be less than without EGR operation. If monitored integrator counts do not change with EGR commanded, Code 32 will set.

ECM checks EGR operation when vehicle speed is greater than 50 MPH, engine vacuum indicates cruise and throttle position are steady.

NOTE: Test numbers refer to test numbers on diagnostic chart.

1) With ignition on and engine off, solenoid should not be energized or allow vacuum to pass to EGR valve. When test terminal "B" of ALDL connector is grounded, EGR solenoid should be energized, allowing vacuum to EGR valve. Vacuum should hold.

2) Checks for plugged EGR passages. If passages are plugged, engine may have severe detonation on acceleration.

3) SERVICE ENGINE SOON light should also flash while diagnostic terminal is grounded. If light does not flash, this may indicate Quad-Driver has been damaged by low TCC circuit resistance.

4) Vehicle must be driven during this test to produce sufficient load to operate EGR. Lightly accelerating (approximately 1/4 throttle) will produce a large and stable enough reading to determine if ECM is commanding system on.

DIAGNOSTIC AIDS

Prior to replacing PCM, check resistance of all PCM-controlled solenoids and relays. Replace any solenoids or relays with a resistance value less than 20 ohms.

CODE 32, EGR SYSTEM ERROR
(3.1L)

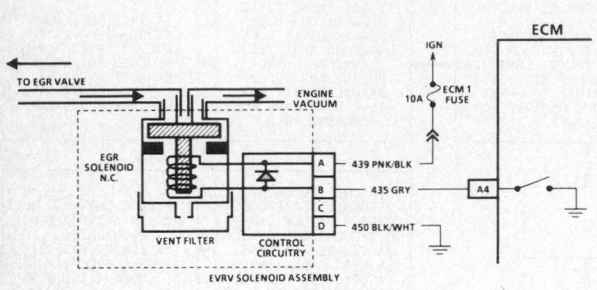

ECM operates a Electronic Vacuum Regulator Valve (EVRV) to control vacuum to EGR valve. Regulator normally allows only a small amount of vacuum to pass to EGR valve. When ECM grounds EVRV drive circuit, EVRV opens, allowing enough vacuum to pass through to open EGR valve. ECM monitors EGR effectiveness by periodically checking fuel integrator counts. This is done when vehicle speed is greater than 50 MPH, MAP sensor signal indicates cruise condition and throttle position are constant and all conditions have been met twice for 60 seconds.

NOTE: Test numbers refer to test numbers on diagnostic chart.

1) With ignition on and engine off, EVRV should not be energized or allow enough vacuum through to open EGR valve. When test terminal "B" of ALDL connector is grounded, EVRV will energize, allowing vacuum to EGR valve.

2) Checks for plugged EGR passages. If passages are plugged, engine may have severe detonation on acceleration.

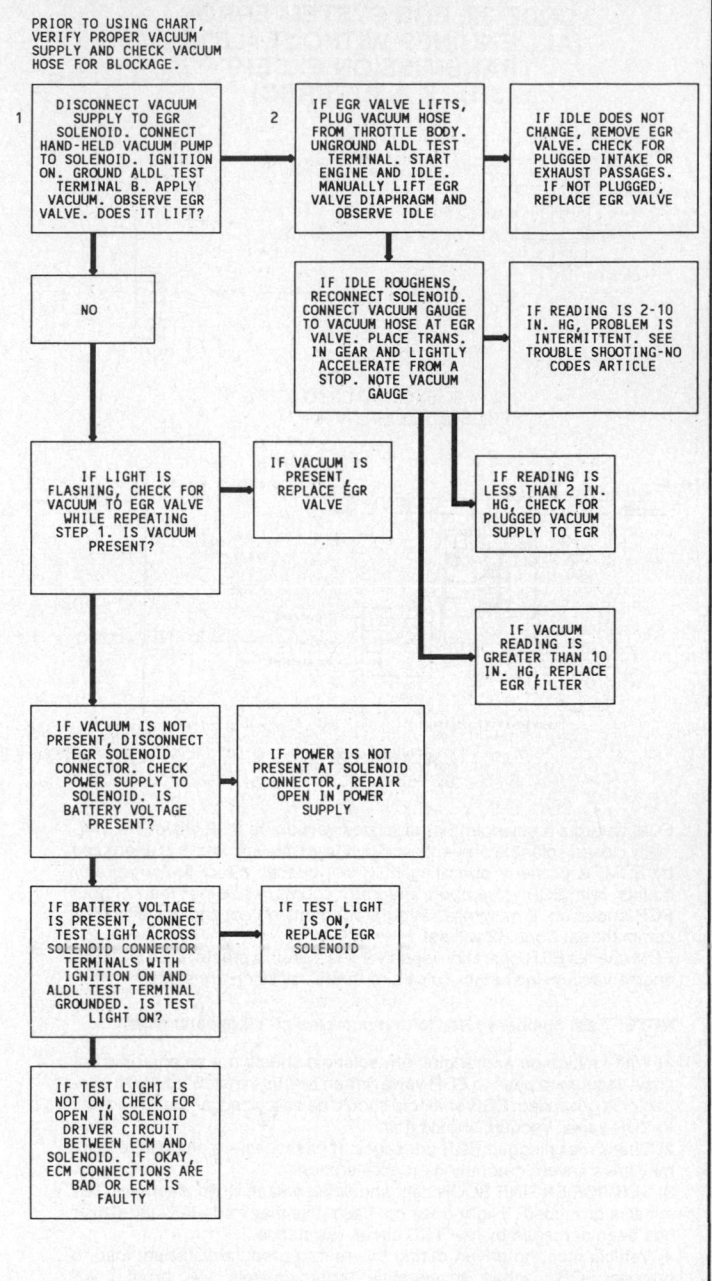

CODE 32, EGR SYSTEM ERROR
(4.3L TURBO)

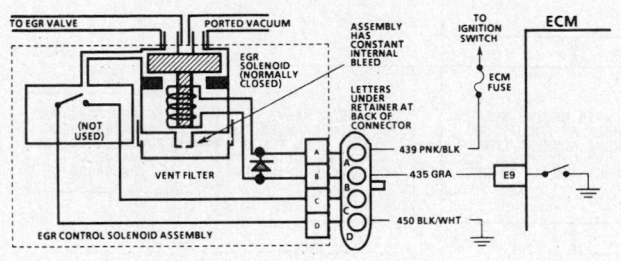

ECM controls a solenoid that regulates vacuum to EGR valve. The normally closed solenoid prevents vacuum from passing until it is energized by ECM. A properly operating EGR will directly affect fuel integrator counts. With EGR valve open, integrator counts will be less than without EGR operation. If monitored integrator counts do not change with EGR commanded, Code 32 will set.

Diagnostic chart covers checks for entire EGR system. If no trouble is found while performing chart routine, fault is an intermittent electrical problem or a sticky EGR valve.

DIAGNOSTIC AIDS

Vacuum switch in EGR solenoid is not used. If EGR valve sticks open, a rough idle will result. If EGR solenoid vent filter becomes plugged, EGR valve will remain open or close slowly. An inoperative check valve in ported vacuum supply line will result in faulty EGR system operation.

PRIOR TO USING CHART, VERIFY AT LEAST 20 IN. HG TO EGR SOLENOID AT 2000 RPM. IF VACUUM IS NOT ADEQUATE, CHECK HOSE AND VACUUM PORT FOR BLOCKAGE.

DISCONNECT VACUUM HOSE FROM EGR VALVE. START ENGINE. APPLY VACUUM TO EGR VALVE. DOES EGR VALVE HOLD VACUUM?

NO → REPLACE EGR VALVE

IF EGR VALVE HOLDS VACUUM, DID APPLICATION OF VACUUM CAUSE ROUGH IDLE OR STALLING?

IF VACUUM APPLICATION DID NOT CAUSE ROUGH IDLE OR STALLING, STOP ENGINE. TOUCH UNDERSIDE OF EGR VALVE. APPLY AND RELEASE VACUUM TO VALVE. DOES VALVE DIAPHRAGM MOVE?

IF VACUUM CAUSES VALVE DIAPHRAGM TO MOVE, REMOVE EGR VALVE AND CHECK FOR BLOCKED EGR VALVE PASSAGES

YES

IF VACUUM DID NOT CAUSE DIAPHRAGM TO MOVE, REPLACE EGR VALVE

IF TEST LIGHT IS ON, EGR SOLENOID DRIVE CIRCUIT IS SHORTED TO GROUND BETWEEN ECM AND EGR SOLENOID

STOP ENGINE. DISCONNECT EGR VACUUM HOSE AT THROTTLE BODY. CONNECT VACUUM PUMP TO VACUUM HOSE TO EGR SOLENOID. TURN IGNITION ON. APPLY VACUUM. DOES EGR DIAPHRAGM MOVE?

IF DIAPHRAGM MOVES, DISCONNECT EGR SOLENOID CONNECTOR. CONNECT TEST LIGHT ACROSS TERMINALS A & B. IS TEST LIGHT ON?

IF TEST LIGHT IS OFF, REPLACE EGR SOLENOID

IF DIAPHRAGM DOES NOT MOVE, GROUND ALDL TEST TERMINAL B AND APPLY AND RELEASE VACUUM. DOES DIAPHRAGM MOVE?

IF DIAPHRAGM MOVES, NO FAULT IS CURRENTLY PRESENT. CHECK FOR INTERMITTENT ELECTRICAL CONNECTIONS

IF DIAPHRAGM DOES NOT MOVE, VERIFY POWER AND GROUND SUPPLY TO EGR SOLENOID CONNECTOR. IS POWER AND GROUND PRESENT?

YES

CHECK FOR VACUUM LEAKS BETWEEN THROTTLE BODY AND EGR VALVE. CHECK SOLENOID ELECTRICAL CONNECTIONS. CHECK FOR PLUGGED EGR FILTER. IF OKAY, REPLACE EGR SOLENOID

IF POWER OR GROUND IS NOT PRESENT, REPAIR OPEN IN POWER OR GROUND CIRCUIT TO SOLENOID

CODE 32, EGR SYSTEM ERROR
4.3L CPI WITH LINEAR EGR

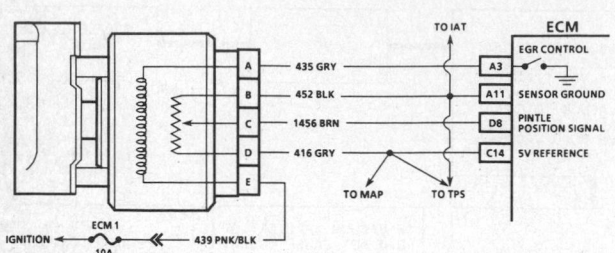

ECM regulates linear EGR valve to control exhaust gas recirculation by providing a ground control for internal pintle (solenoid). Pintle will pull away from its seat when energized. ECM controls linear EGR valve based upon coolant temperature and throttle position.

NOTE: Test numbers refer to test numbers on diagnostic chart.

1) Checks pintle's ability to be commanded to desired position.
2) Checks for voltage to linear EGR valve to verify if problem is in ignition feed circuit.
3) Checks ECM control circuit by jumpering across circuits No. 435 and 439 with a test light and grounding ALDL test terminal "B" to command EGR on.

DIAGNOSTIC AIDS

Before replacing ECM, use an ohmmeter and check EGR valve resistances. Resistance between terminals "A" and "E" should be 9.5-10.5 ohms. Resistance between terminals "B" and "D" should be greater than 3000 ohms. Resistance between terminals "B" and "C" should start at 700 ohms and increase to about 4000 ohms as pintle is slowly moved inward.

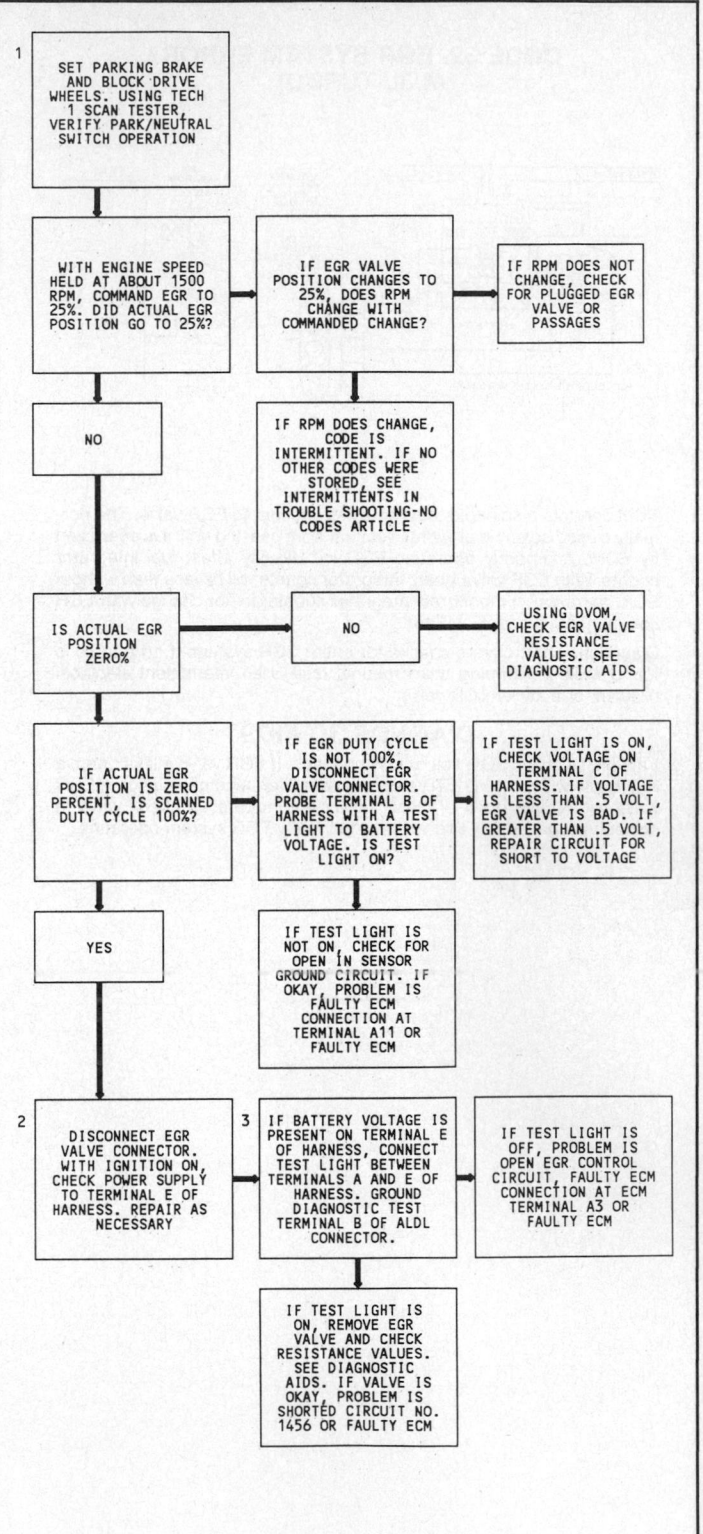

CODE 33, MAP SENSOR SIGNAL VOLTAGE HIGH

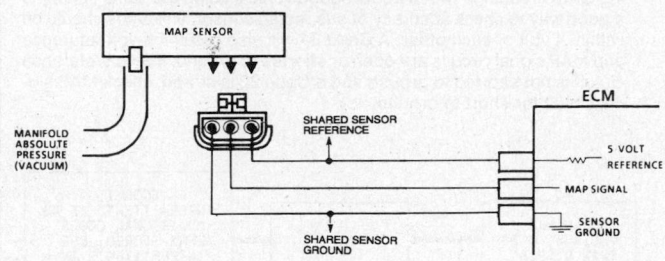

CODE 33 ECM TERMINAL & CIRCUIT WIRING IDENTIFICATION

Application	ECM Terminal	Wire Color
Astro & Safari 4.3L TBI & 2.5L & 4.3L TBI "S" & "T" Series		
MAP Signal	C11	[1] Light Green
MAP Ground	D2	Black/Red
MAP Reference	C14	Gray
All With 4L80-E Transmission		
MAP Signal	C10	Light Green
MAP Ground	D2	Purple
MAP Reference	D4	Gray
2.8L, 3.1L & 4.3L & V8 "C" & "K" Series		
MAP Signal	C11	[1] Light Green
MAP Ground	A11	Purple
MAP Reference	C14	Gray
4.3L Turbo		
MAP Signal	GF15	Light Green
MAP Ground	BB6	Black
MAP Reference	BA4	Gray
4.3L CPI & 4.3L TBI & 5.7L "G" & "P" Series		
MAP Signal	C11	[1] Light Green
MAP Ground	D2	Purple
MAP Reference	C14	Gray

[1] – May have a Black trace.

Manifold Absolute Pressure (MAP) sensor responds to changes in manifold pressure (vacuum). If MAP sensor fails, ECM will substitute a fixed MAP value and use TPS input to control fuel delivery.

NOTE: Test numbers refer to test numbers on diagnostic chart.

1) This test confirms Code 33 and determines if it is a hard failure or an intermittent condition. Code 33 will set when voltage signal reading is too high and TPS voltage indicates throttle is closed.

2) This step simulates conditions for a Code 34. If ECM recognizes and indicates low MAP signal, ECM and 5-volt reference and MAP signal circuits are not at fault.

DIAGNOSTIC AIDS

With ignition switch in ON position and engine off, manifold pressure is equal to atmospheric pressure and signal voltage is high. Comparing BARO readings from a known good vehicle using the same sensor is a good way to check accuracy of suspected sensor. Readings should be within .4 volt of each other. Code 33 will also result if ground circuit is open or MAP signal circuit is shorted to voltage or to 5-volt reference circuit.

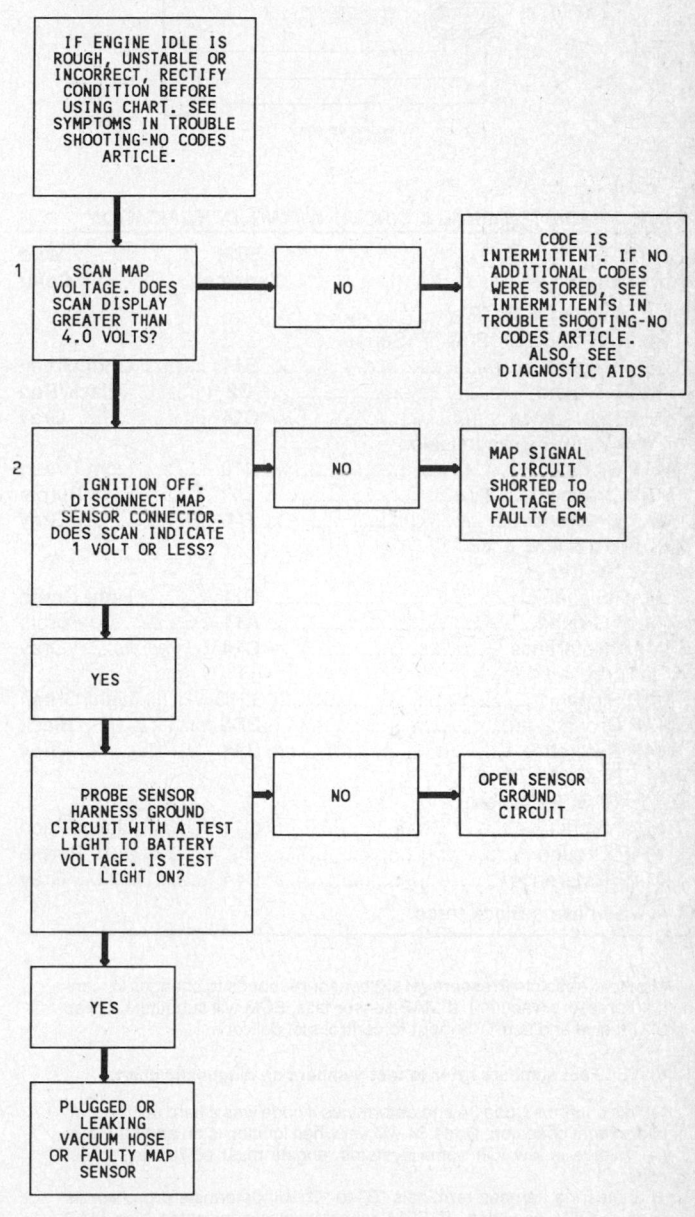

91D07423 91G07330

CODE 34, MAP SENSOR SIGNAL VOLTAGE LOW

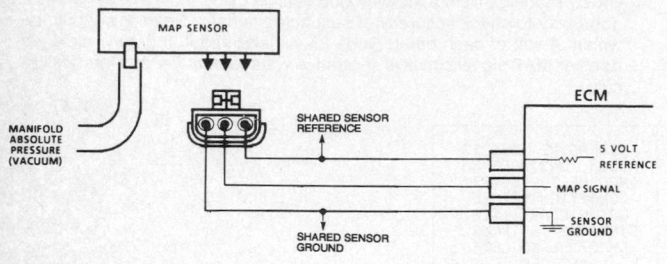

CODE 34 ECM TERMINAL & CIRCUIT WIRING IDENTIFICATION

Application	ECM Terminal	Wire Color
Astro & Safari 4.3L TBI & 2.5L & 4.3L TBI "S" & "T" Series		
MAP Signal	C11	¹ Light Green
MAP Ground	D2	Black/Red
MAP Reference	C14	Gray
All With 4L80-E Transmission		
MAP Signal	C10	Light Green
MAP Ground	D2	Purple
MAP Reference	D4	Gray
2.8L, 3.1L & 4.3L & V8 "C" & "K" Series		
MAP Signal	C11	¹ Light Green
MAP Ground	A11	Purple
MAP Reference	C14	Gray
4.3L Turbo		
MAP Signal	GF15	Light Green
MAP Ground	BB6	Black
MAP Reference	BA4	Gray
4.3L CPI & 4.3L TBI & 5.7L "G" & "P" Series		
MAP Signal	C11	¹ Light Green
MAP Ground	D2	Purple
MAP Reference	C14	Gray

¹ – May have a Black trace.

Manifold Absolute Pressure (MAP) sensor responds to changes in manifold pressure (vacuum). If MAP sensor fails, ECM will substitute a fixed MAP value and use TPS input to control fuel delivery.

NOTE: Test numbers refer to test numbers on diagnostic chart.

1) This confirms Code 34 and determines if code was a hard failure or an intermittent condition. Code 34 will set when ignition is on and MAP signal voltage is low. On some systems, engine must be running to set code.

2) Jumpering harness terminals "B" to "C" will determine if problem is sensor, ECM or wiring. If ECM recognizes and indicates high MAP signal, ECM and wiring are okay.

3) Scan tester may not display 12 volts. The important thing is that the ECM recognizes voltage as greater than 4 volts (high MAP voltage signal), indicating ECM and MAP signal circuit are not at fault.

DIAGNOSTIC AIDS

With ignition switch in ON position and engine off, manifold pressure is equal to atmospheric pressure and signal voltage will be high. Comparing BARO readings with a known good vehicle using the same sensor is a good way to check accuracy of suspected sensor. Readings should be within .4 volt of each other. A Code 34 will also result if 5-volt reference and MAP signal circuits are open or shorted to ground. If 5-volt reference circuit is not shorted to ground and a Code 22 is stored, check MAP signal circuit for short to ground.

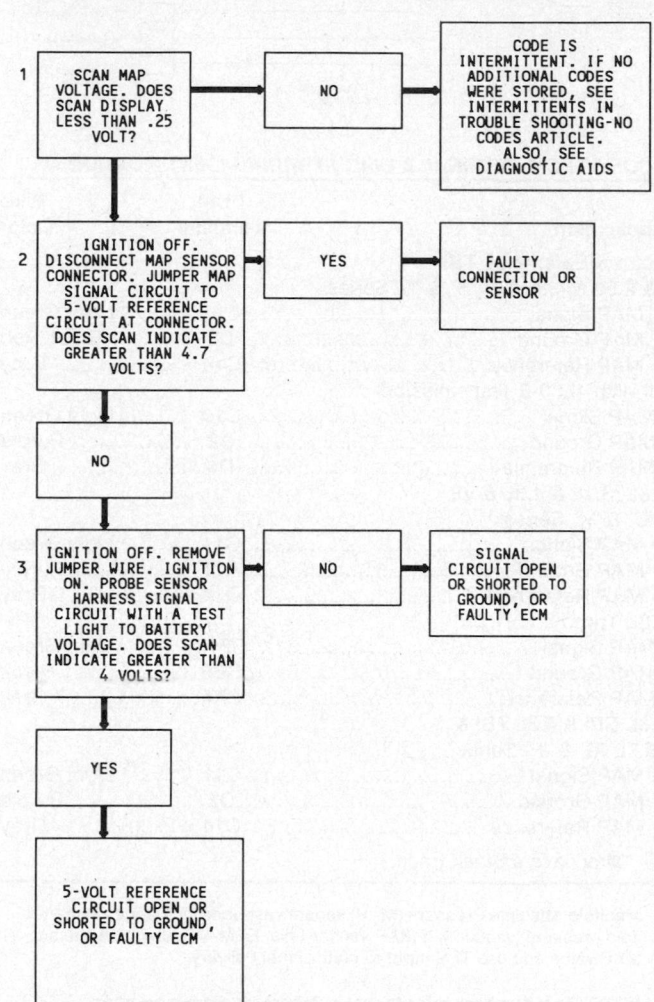

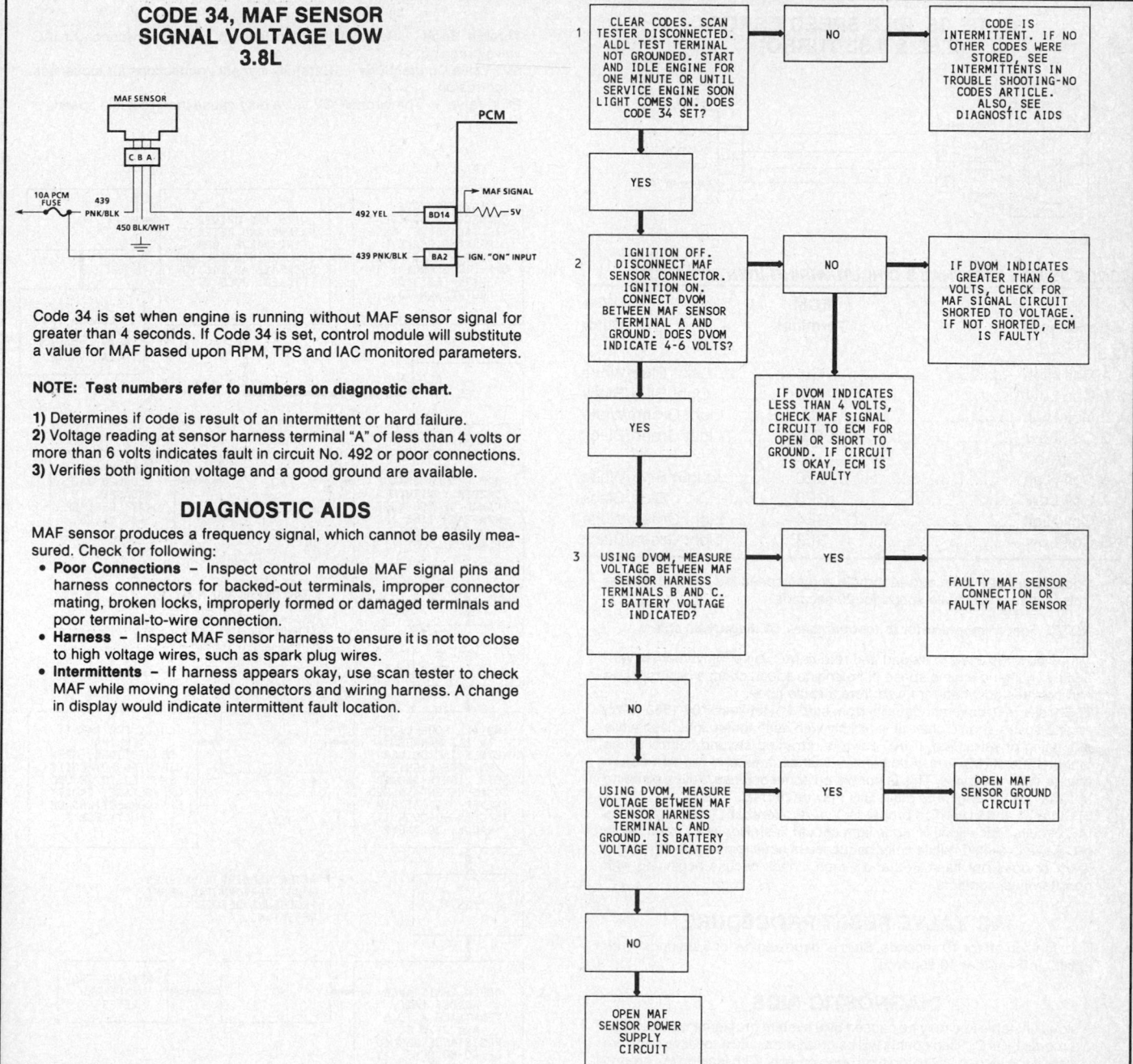

CODE 34, MAF SENSOR SIGNAL VOLTAGE LOW 3.8L

Code 34 is set when engine is running without MAF sensor signal for greater than 4 seconds. If Code 34 is set, control module will substitute a value for MAF based upon RPM, TPS and IAC monitored parameters.

NOTE: Test numbers refer to numbers on diagnostic chart.

1) Determines if code is result of an intermittent or hard failure.
2) Voltage reading at sensor harness terminal "A" of less than 4 volts or more than 6 volts indicates fault in circuit No. 492 or poor connections.
3) Verifies both ignition voltage and a good ground are available.

DIAGNOSTIC AIDS

MAF sensor produces a frequency signal, which cannot be easily measured. Check for following:

- **Poor Connections** – Inspect control module MAF signal pins and harness connectors for backed-out terminals, improper connector mating, broken locks, improperly formed or damaged terminals and poor terminal-to-wire connection.
- **Harness** – Inspect MAF sensor harness to ensure it is not too close to high voltage wires, such as spark plug wires.
- **Intermittents** – If harness appears okay, use scan tester to check MAF while moving related connectors and wiring harness. A change in display would indicate intermittent fault location.

92B21791 91A07332

CODE 35, IDLE SPEED ERROR
(2.5L & 4.3L TURBO)

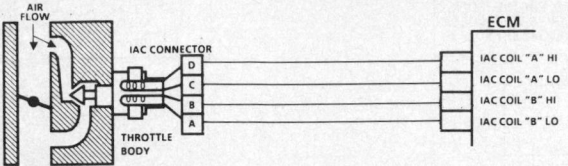

CODE 35 ECM TERMINAL & CIRCUIT WIRING IDENTIFICATION

Application	ECM Terminal	Wire Color
2.5L		
A Coil High	C5	Light Blue/White
A Coil Low	C6	Light Blue/Black
B Coil High	C4	Light Green/White
B Coil Low	C3	Light Green/Black
4.3L Turbo		
A Coil High	GE6	Light Blue/White
A Coil Low	GE5	Blue/Black
B Coil High	GE4	Light Green/White
B Coil Low	GE3	Light Green/Black

Code 35 will set when closed throttle engine speed is 150 RPM greater or less than correct idle speed for 20 seconds.

NOTE: Test numbers refer to test numbers on diagnostic chart.

1) IAC driver is used to extend and retract IAC valve. Movement is verified by changing engine speed. If no engine speed change occurs, valve can be retested when removed from throttle body.

2) Checks IAC movement quality from step **1)**. Between 700-1500 RPM, engine speed should change smoothly with each tester light flash while extending or retracting. If IAC valve is retracted beyond control range (about 1500 RPM), it may take many flashes in extend position before engine speed reduces. This is normal on some engines. Fully extending IAC may cause engine to stall. This may be normal.

3) Steps **1)** and **2)** verified proper IAC valve operation. This step checks IAC circuits. Each light on node light should flash Red and Green, while IAC valve is cycled. While color sequence is not important, if either light is off or does not flash Red and Green, check circuits beginning with poor terminal contacts.

IAC VALVE RESET PROCEDURE

Turn ignition off for 10 seconds. Start and run engine for 5 seconds. Turn ignition off another 10 seconds.

DIAGNOSTIC AIDS

A slow, unstable idle may be caused by a system problem that cannot be overcome by IAC. Scan counts will be greater than 60 if too low, and zero counts if too high. If idle is too high, stop engine. With ignition on, ground ALDL test terminal "B". Wait 45 seconds for IAC to seat, then disconnect IAC. Start engine. If idle speed is greater than 800 RPM, inspect vehicle for vacuum leaks.

System Too Lean – If air/fuel ratio is too lean, idle speed may be either too high (check for vacuum leaks) or too low. Engine speed may vary and disconnecting IAC may not help. Scan tester and/or digital voltmeter (10 megohm) will read an oxygen sensor output less than 300 mv (.3 volt). Check for low fuel pressure or water in fuel.

System Too Rich – If air/fuel ratio is too rich, idle speed will be too low and scan tester counts will usually be greater than 80. The system may be obviously rich with Black smoke from tailpipe. Scan tester and/or voltmeter will read an oxygen sensor voltage signal fixed greater than 800 mv (.8 volt). Look for high fuel pressure or leaking/sticky injectors. Remove IAC and inspect bore for foreign material or evidence of IAC valve dragging bore. A silicone-contaminated oxygen sensor will produce lean air/fuel mixture. Oxygen sensor output would be fixed greater than 800 mv (.8 volt). This may also set Code 45.

Throttle Body – Remove IAC and inspect bore for evidence of IAC valve dragging.
IAC Valve Connections – Carefully inspect connections for looseness or corrosion.
PCV Valve – The wrong PCV valve may cause incorrect idle speed.

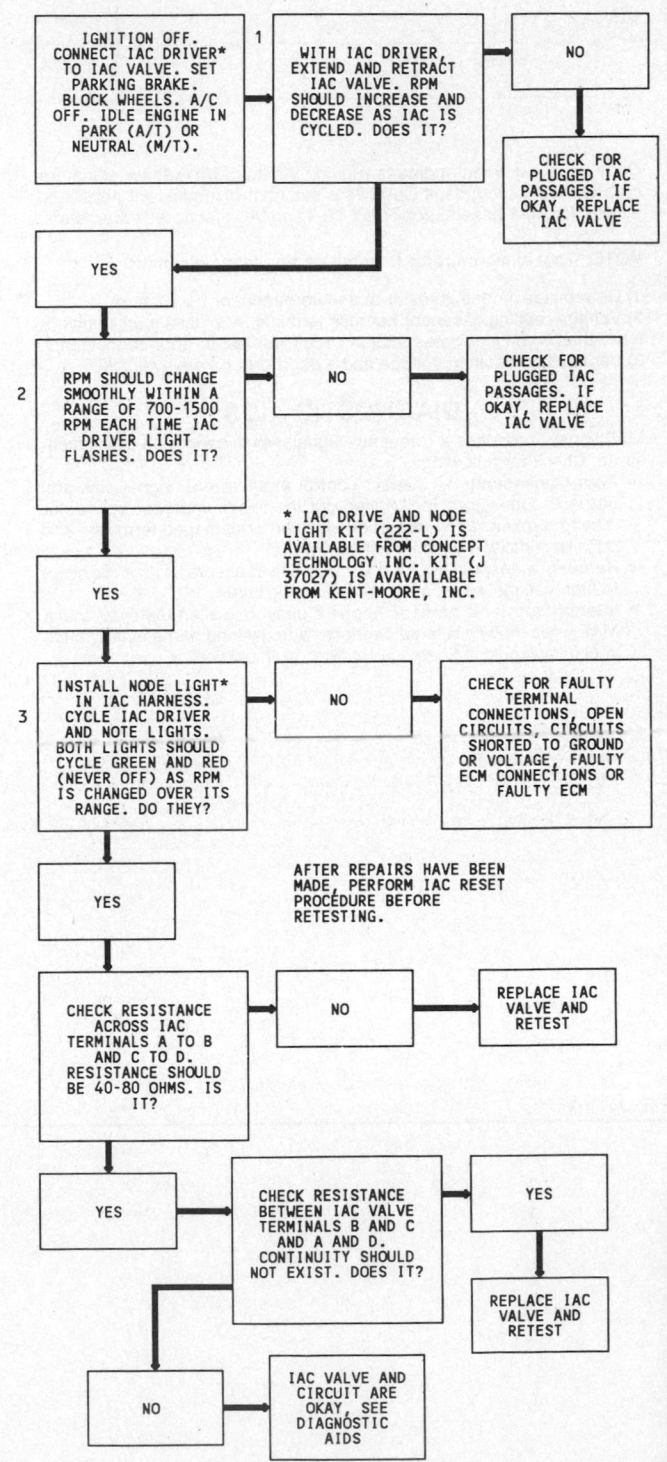

CODE 36, SHIFT CONTROL PROBLEM
(3.8L)

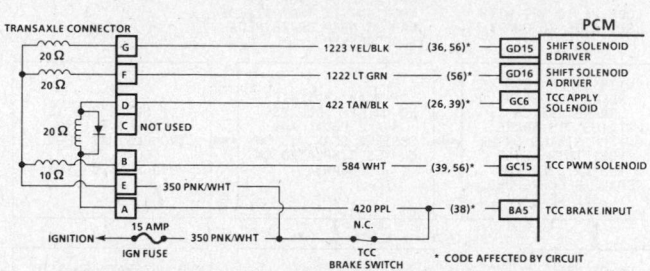

4T60E transaxle is electronically shifted. Within transaxle are 4 solenoids. Solenoid "A" is used for 1st and 4th gear operation only. Solenoid "B" is used for 1st and 2nd gear operation. Remaining 2 solenoids are for TCC operation only. All PRNDL indications are ignored as far as transaxle shifting is concerned except manual low. Code 36 will set if solenoid "B" failed in OFF position, which will cause transaxle to be in 4th gear, and desired gear is 1st, TPS is greater than 40 percent, engine speed is greater than 2000 RPM, VSS is 3-20 MPH and Codes 21, 22 and 24 are not present. Code will also set if solenoid "B" failed in ON position, which will cause transaxle to be in 1st gear, and desired gear is 4th, PRNDL is in 3rd or 4th, TPS is greater than 10 percent and Codes 31, 21 and 22 are not present. Code 36 does not turn on SERVICE ENGINE SOON light.

DIAGNOSTIC AIDS

When Code 36 is set, transaxle will be forced into 3rd gear. If code sets due to a grounded circuit No. 1223, only 1st and 2nd gear operation will be available. If circuit No. 1223 is open, only 3rd and 4th gear operation will be available. If fault goes away, normal operation will be resumed for duration of key cycle.

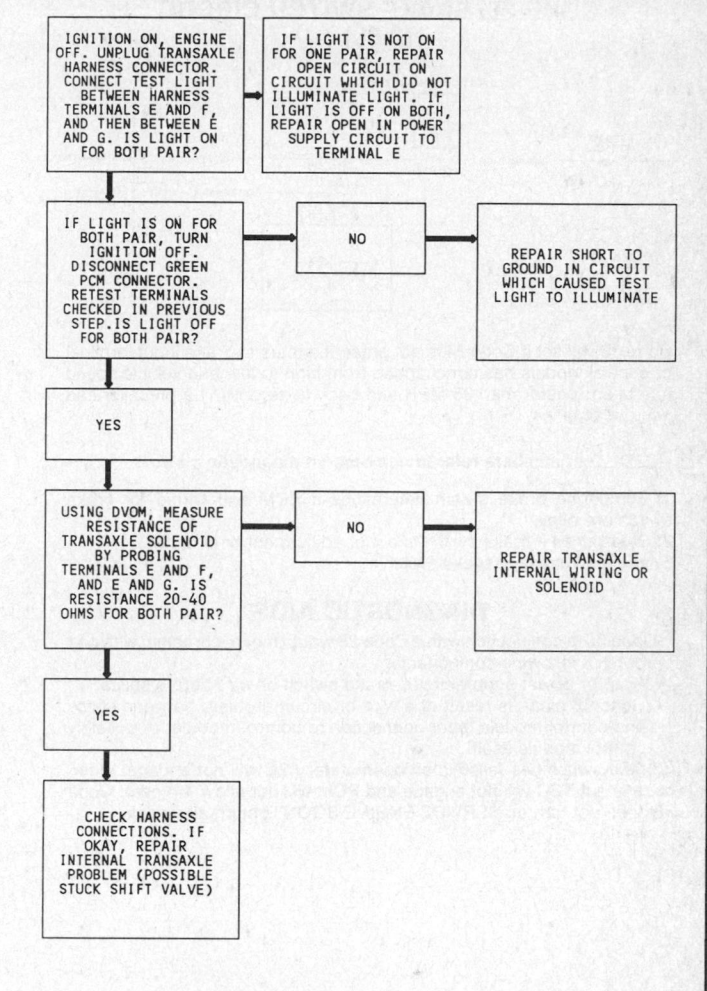

92H21797 91H07335

CODE 38, BRAKE SWITCH CIRCUIT
(3.8L)

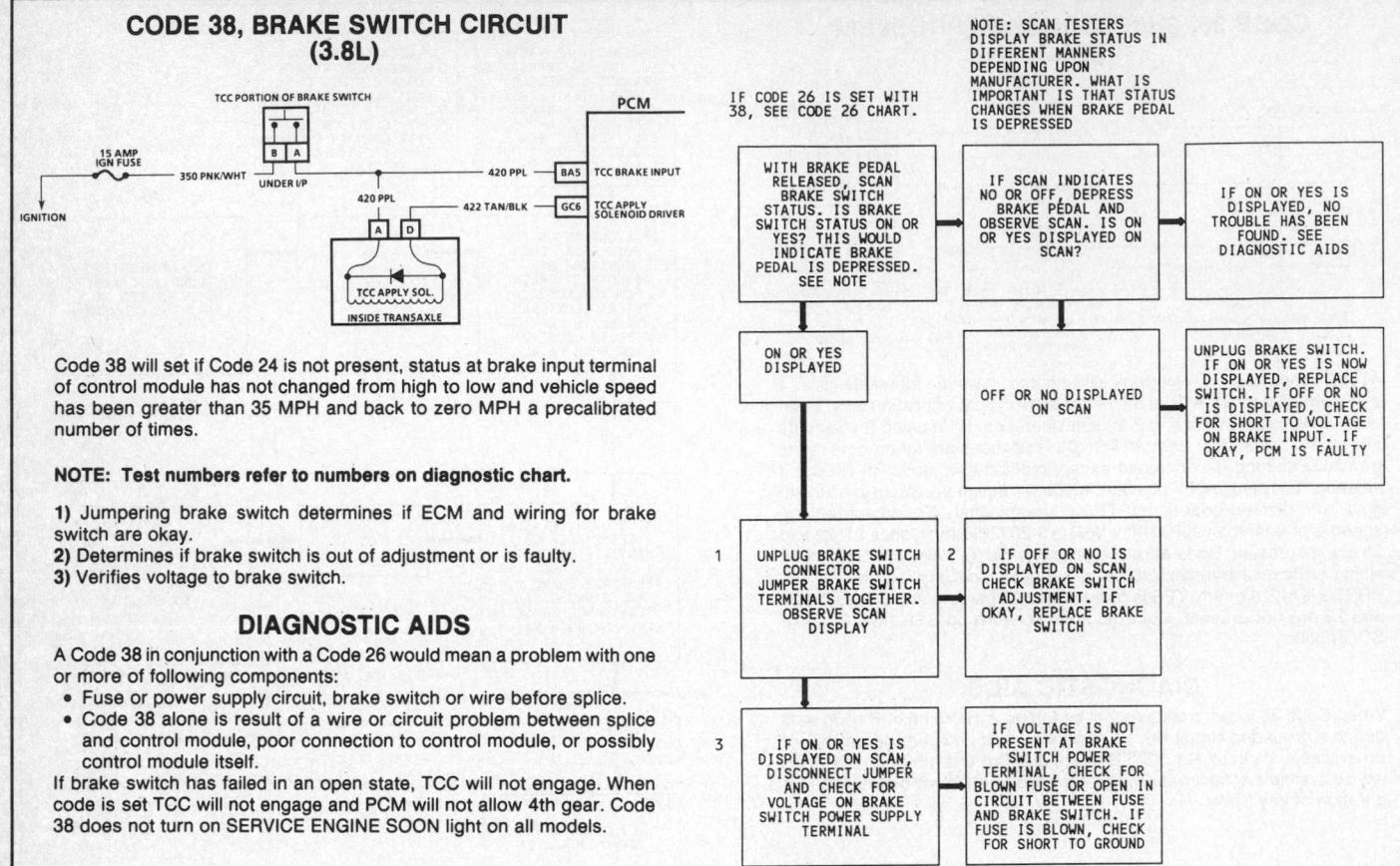

Code 38 will set if Code 24 is not present, status at brake input terminal of control module has not changed from high to low and vehicle speed has been greater than 35 MPH and back to zero MPH a precalibrated number of times.

NOTE: Test numbers refer to numbers on diagnostic chart.

1) Jumpering brake switch determines if ECM and wiring for brake switch are okay.
2) Determines if brake switch is out of adjustment or is faulty.
3) Verifies voltage to brake switch.

DIAGNOSTIC AIDS

A Code 38 in conjunction with a Code 26 would mean a problem with one or more of following components:

• Fuse or power supply circuit, brake switch or wire before splice.
• Code 38 alone is result of a wire or circuit problem between splice and control module, poor connection to control module, or possibly control module itself.

If brake switch has failed in an open state, TCC will not engage. When code is set TCC will not engage and PCM will not allow 4th gear. Code 38 does not turn on SERVICE ENGINE SOON light on all models.

92I21798 91J07336

CODE 39, TCC CIRCUIT
(3.8L)

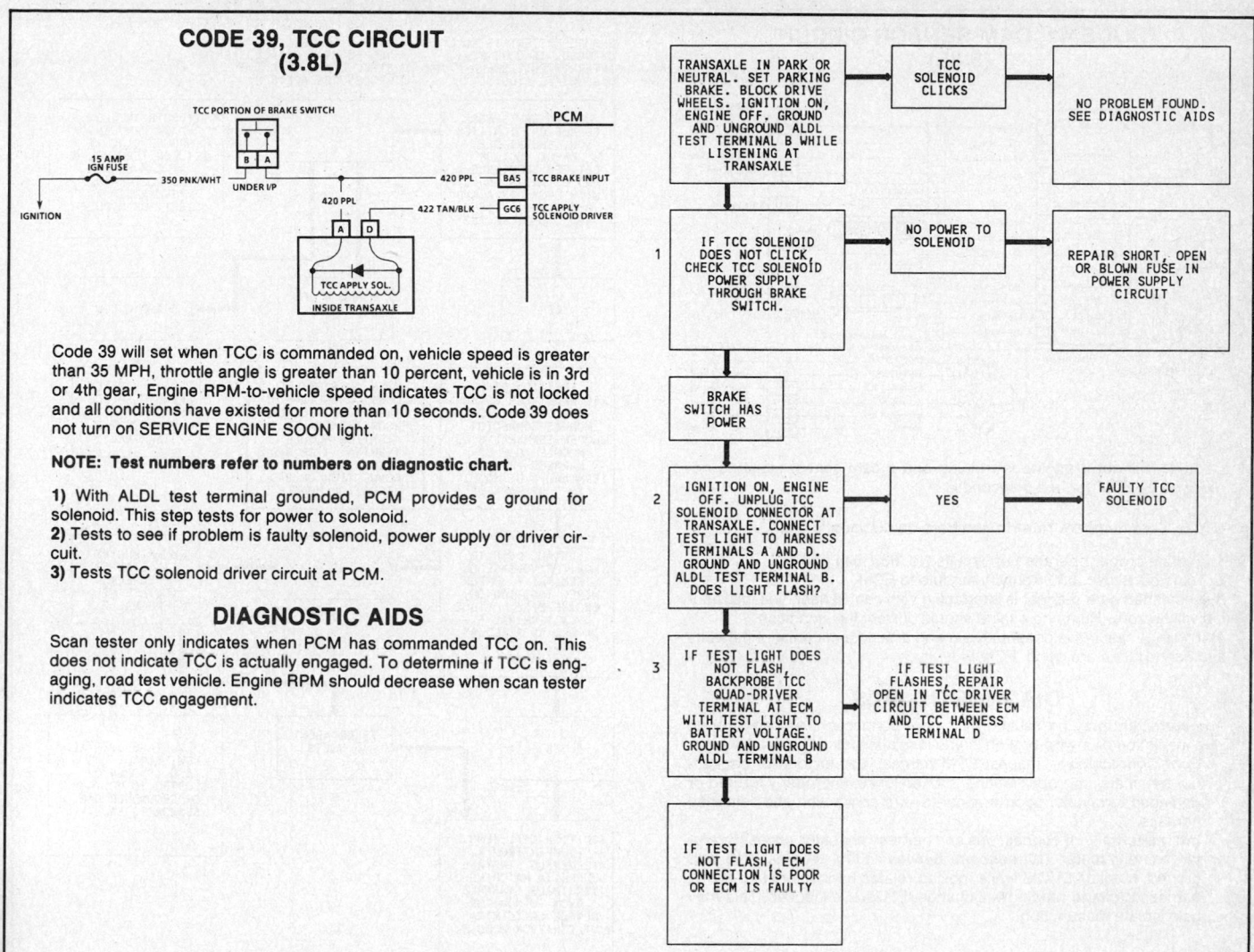

Code 39 will set when TCC is commanded on, vehicle speed is greater than 35 MPH, throttle angle is greater than 10 percent, vehicle is in 3rd or 4th gear, Engine RPM-to-vehicle speed indicates TCC is not locked and all conditions have existed for more than 10 seconds. Code 39 does not turn on SERVICE ENGINE SOON light.

NOTE: Test numbers refer to numbers on diagnostic chart.

1) With ALDL test terminal grounded, PCM provides a ground for solenoid. This step tests for power to solenoid.
2) Tests to see if problem is faulty solenoid, power supply or driver circuit.
3) Tests TCC solenoid driver circuit at PCM.

DIAGNOSTIC AIDS

Scan tester only indicates when PCM has commanded TCC on. This does not indicate TCC is actually engaged. To determine if TCC is engaging, road test vehicle. Engine RPM should decrease when scan tester indicates TCC engagement.

92I21798 91F07339

CODE 41, CAM SENSOR CIRCUIT
(3.8L)

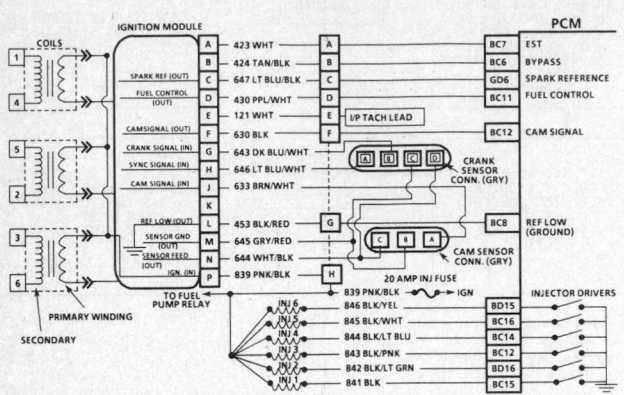

Code 41 will set if engine is running and a cam sensor signal is not received by ECM for last 5 seconds.

NOTE: Test numbers refer to numbers on diagnostic chart.

1) Verifies proper operation of circuits No. 633, 644 and 645.
2) Tests circuit No. 630 from C³I module to ECM.
3) If camshaft gear magnet is interfacing with cam sensor, voltage reading will be zero. Bumping engine should correct this condition.
4) If voltage reading is constantly varying around a midpoint of 4.6 volts and connections are good, PCM is faulty.

DIAGNOSTIC AIDS

An intermittent may be caused by a poor connection, rubbed-through wire insulation or a wire broken inside insulation. Check for following:

• **Poor Connection** – Inspect ECM harness connectors for backed-out terminals, improper mating, broken locks, improperly formed or damaged terminals, poor terminal-to-wire connection and damaged harness.
• **Intermittents** – If connections and harness are okay, connect a digital volt-ohmmeter (10-megohm) between ECM terminal R10 and ground. Monitor DVOM while moving related connectors and wiring harness. Voltage reading will change if failure is induced. This may help isolate malfunction.

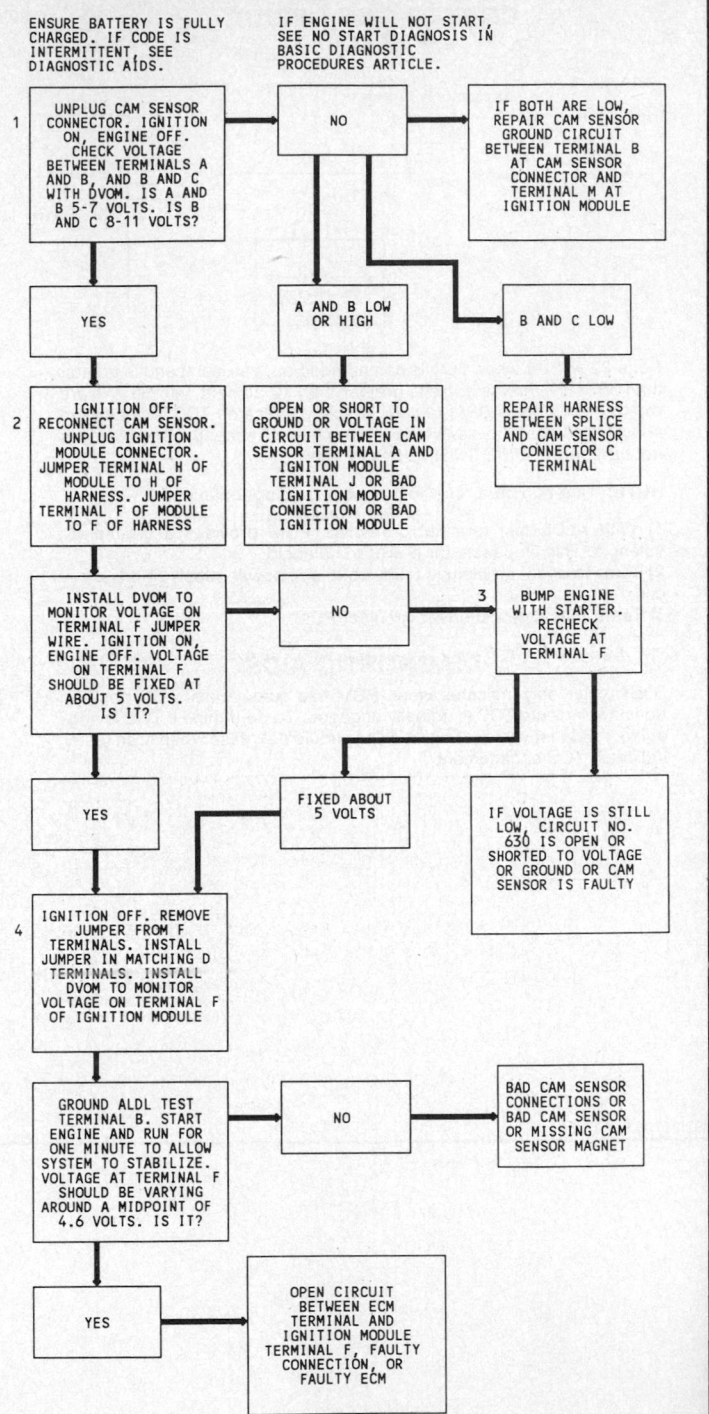

92E21786 91B07342

CODE 42, ELECTRONIC SPARK TIMING
(EXCEPT 3.8L)

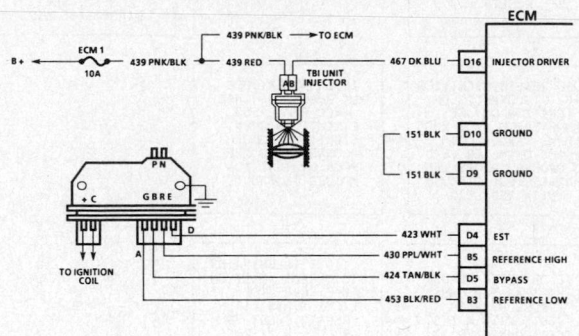

2.5L

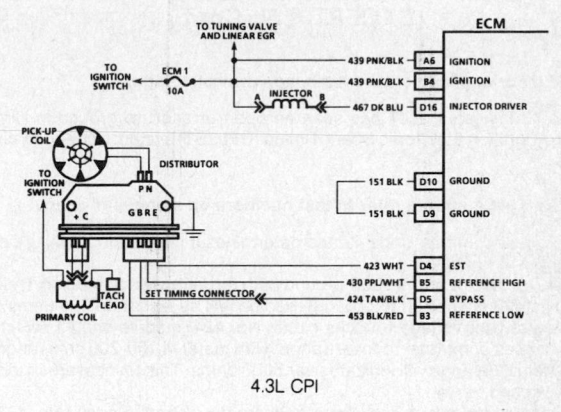

4.3L CPI

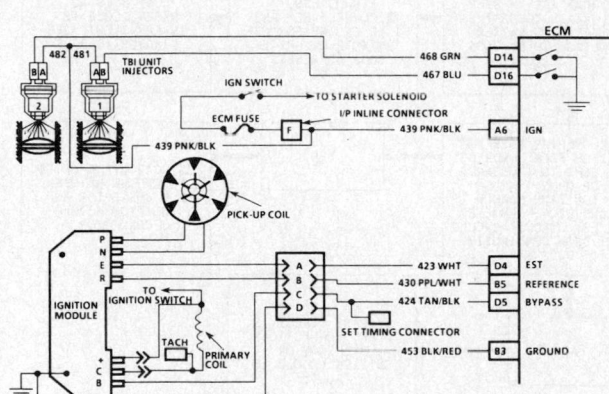

3.1

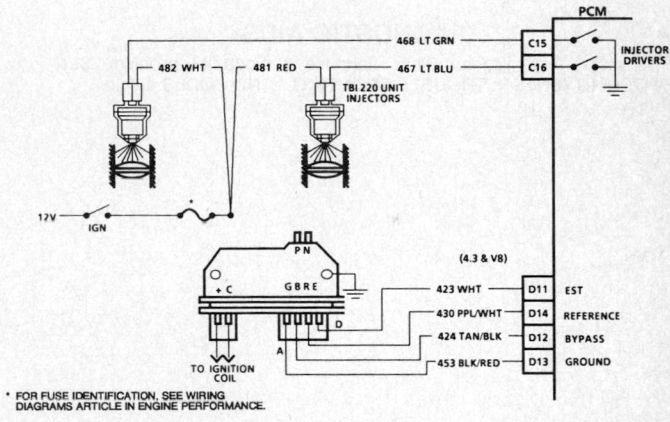

* FOR FUSE IDENTIFICATION, SEE WIRING
DIAGRAMS ARTICLE IN ENGINE PERFORMANCE.

ALL ENGINES WITH 4L80-E TRANSMISSION

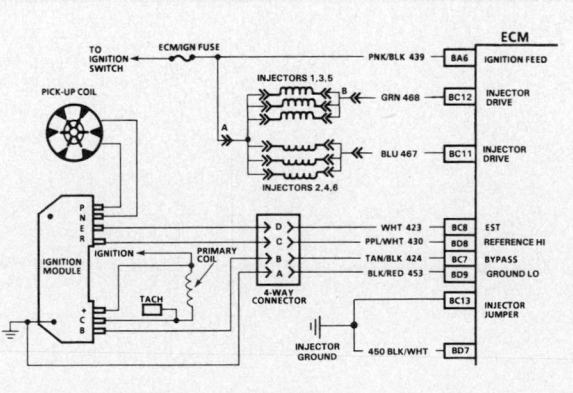

4.3L TURBO

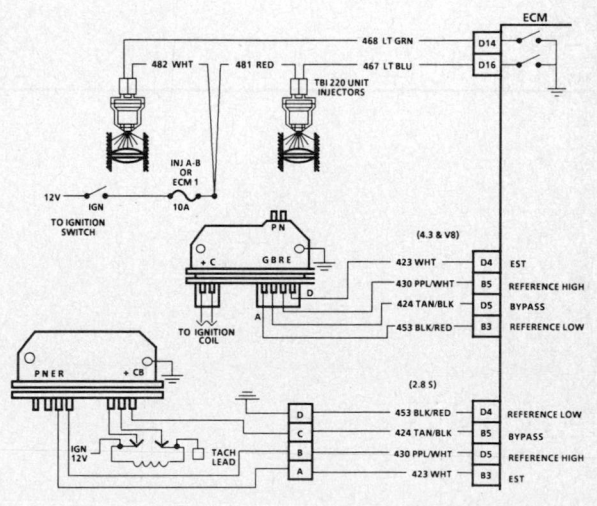

ALL ENGINES WITHOUT 4L80-E TRANSMISSION
EXCEPT 2.5L, 3.1L & 4.3L TURBO & CPI

CODE 42, ELECTRONIC SPARK TIMING
(EXCEPT 3.8L Cont.)

NOTE: For applicable schematic, see previous page.

Code 42 indicates ECM has seen an open or short to ground in High Energy Ignition Electronic Spark Timing (HEI EST) system or by-pass circuits.

NOTE: Test numbers refer to test numbers on diagnostic chart.

1) This test confirms Code 42 and determines if fault is a hard failure or intermittent condition.

2) This tests for a normal EST ground path through ignition module. If circuit No. 423 is shorted to ground, reading will be less than 500 ohms.

3) As test light voltage touches circuit No. 424, module should switch. This causes ohmmeter to "over-range" with meter in 100-200 ohm range. A higher ohm range will indicate over 5000 ohms. This test assures module switched.

4) If module did not switch, this step tests for a short in circuit No. 423, an open in circuit No. 424 and a faulty ignition module connection or module.

5) This step confirms Code 42 is a faulty ECM and not an intermittent problem in circuits No. 423 and 424.

DIAGNOSTIC AIDS

The scan tester cannot help diagnose a Code 42 problem. See INTERMITTENTS in TROUBLE SHOOTING – NO CODES article.

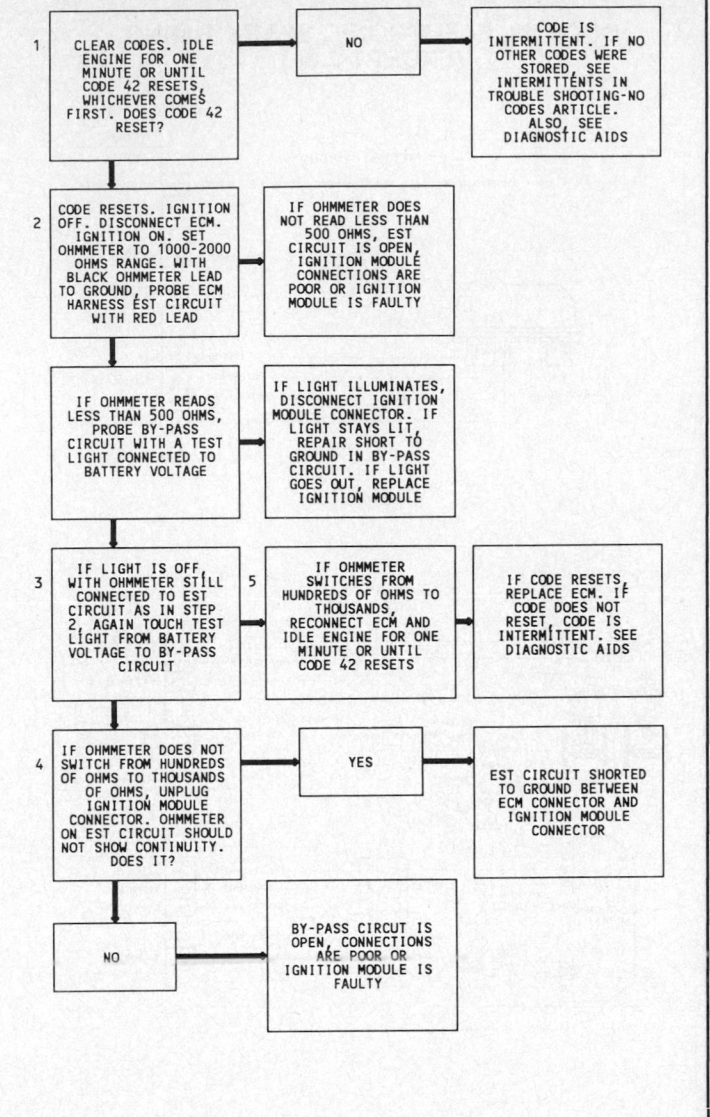

91I07345

CODE 42, ELECTRONIC SPARK TIMING
(3.8L)

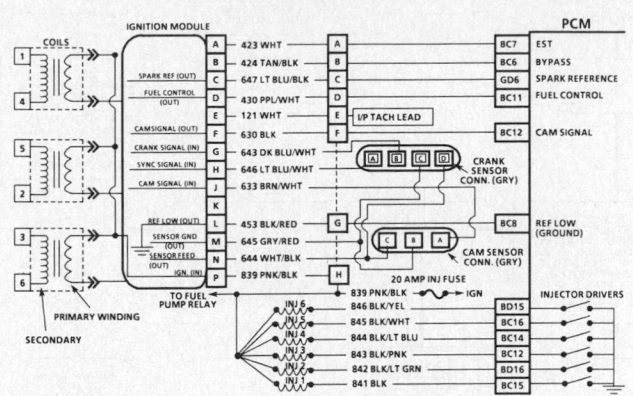

Code 42 will set if EST or by-pass circuit is open or grounded at time of engine start-up.

NOTE: Test numbers refer to numbers on diagnostic chart.

1) Tests if ECM recognizes a problem. If ECM does not set Code 42 at this point, problem is intermittent. Check for a loose connection.

2) With ECM disconnected, digital volt-ohmmeter should indicate less than 200 ohms. This is normal EST circuit resistance through ignition module. A higher resistance would indicate a fault in circuit No. 423, a poor Ignition module connection or a faulty ignition module.

3) If test light was on when connected from 12 volts to ECM harness by-pass circuit, either circuit No. 424 is shorted to ground or ignition module is faulty.

4) Tests if ignition module switches when by-pass circuit is energized by 12 volts through test light. If ignition module switches, resistance reading should switch from less than 200 ohms to more than 6000 ohms.

5) Disconnecting ignition module should make ohmmeter indicate as if it were monitoring an open circuit (infinite reading). Otherwise, circuit No. 423 is shorted to ground.

DIAGNOSTIC AIDS

An intermittent may be caused by a poor connection, rubbed-through wire insulation or a wire broken inside insulation. Inspect ECM harness connectors for backed-out terminals, improper mating, broken locks, improperly formed or damaged terminals, poor terminal-to-wire connection and damaged harness.

If connections and harness are okay, connect a digital volt-ohmmeter between affected terminal to ground, and monitor meter while moving related connectors and wiring harness. If failure is induced, voltage reading will change.

92E21786 91C07347

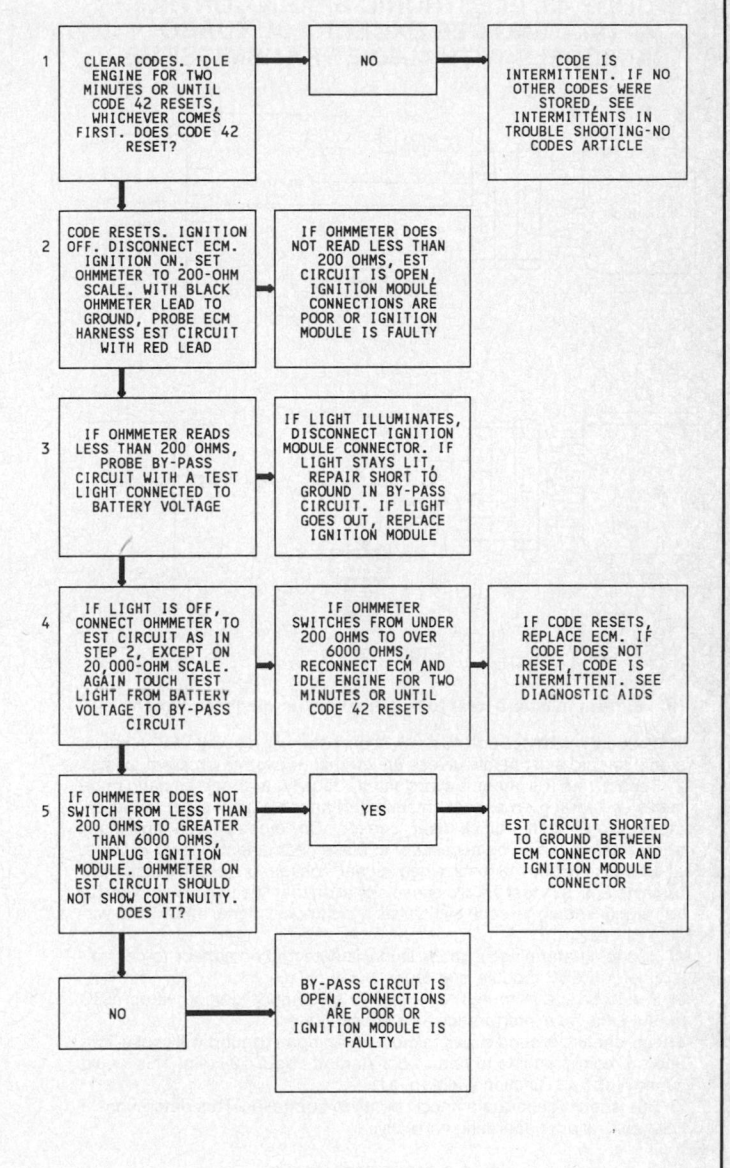

CODE 43, ELECTRONIC SPARK CONTROL (ALL ENGINES EXCEPT 4.3L TURBO & MODELS WITH 4L80-E TRANSMISSION)

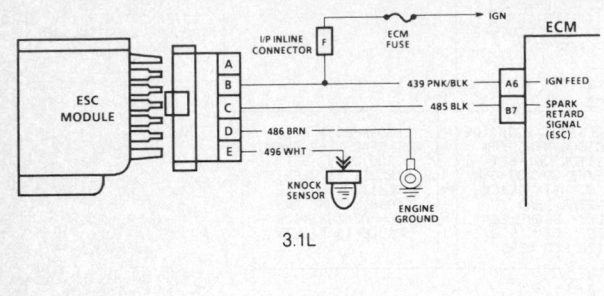

3.1L

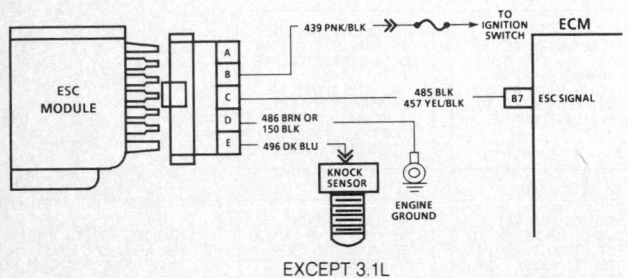

EXCEPT 3.1L

NOTE: Test numbers refer to test numbers on diagnostic chart.

1) If conditions for a Code 43 exist, scan tester will display YES. A knock signal should exist at idle unless an internal or system problem exists.

2) Determines if system is functioning. Usually, a knock signal can be made by tapping on exhaust manifold. If knock signal is not made, try tapping on engine block near sensor. On models with automatic transmission, it may be necessary to place gear selector lever in Drive.

3) Because Code 43 sets when signal voltage on spark retard line remains low, this test should cause signal on that line to go high. The 12-volt signal should be seen by ECM as a "no knock" signal if ECM and wiring are okay.

4) This test determines if knock signal is detected on sensor-to-controller line or if ESC module is at fault.

5) If sensor line is routed too close to secondary ignition wires, ESC module may see interference as a knock signal.

6) This checks ground circuit to module. An open ground will cause voltage on monitored line to remain constant at about 12 volts. This would cause Code 43 functional test to fail.

7) This should generate a knock signal to controller. This determines if ESC controller is operating correctly.

DIAGNOSTIC AIDS

Code 43 can be caused by a faulty knock sensor connection at ESC module or ECM. Also, check controller-to-ECM signal line for an open or short to ground.

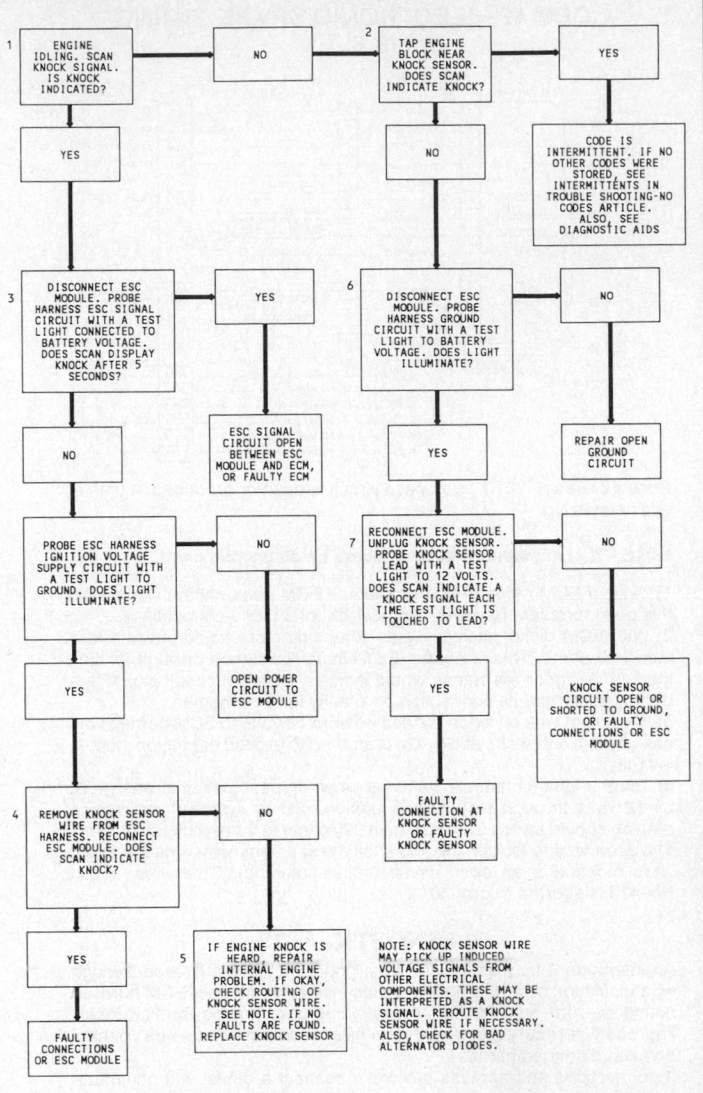

CODE 43, ELECTRONIC SPARK CONTROL (4.3L TURBO & MODELS WITH 4L80-E TRANSMISSION)

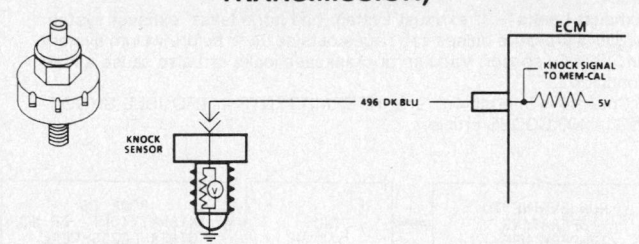

CODE 43 ECM TERMINAL & CIRCUIT WIRING IDENTIFICATION

Application	ECM Terminal	Wire Color
4.3L Turbo		
Knock Signal GF9		Dark Blue
All With 4L80-E Transmission		
Knock Signal D5		Dark Blue

ECM/PCM applies and monitors a 5-volt DC signal to knock sensor. Internal knock sensor circuitry pulls this DC signal down to about 2.5 volts. When knock sensor detects detonation, it generates an AC signal which rides back on DC signal to ECM/PCM. Knock signal intensity is dependent upon knock signal level.

NOTE: Test numbers refer to test numbers on diagnostic chart.

1) Code 43 will set when vehicle reaches normal operating temperature (but not overheating), high engine load is indicated by MAP sensor and voltage on circuit No. 496 is greater than 3.5 volts DC or less than 1.5 volts DC. This step determines if system is functioning properly at current time.

2) This step determines state of 5-volt reference signal applied to sensor.

3) Checks knock sensor internal resistance.

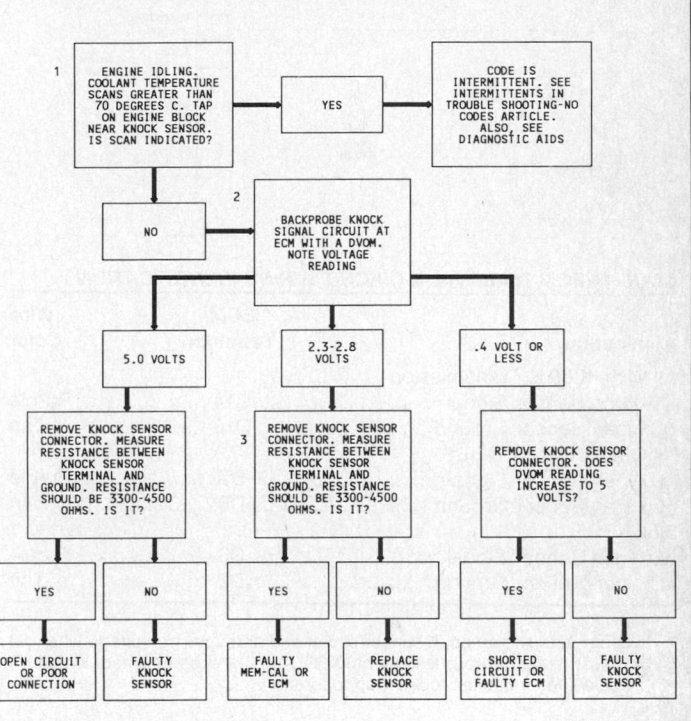

91A07445 91E07348

CODE 44, LEAN EXHAUST INDICATION
(EXCEPT 4.3L TURBO)

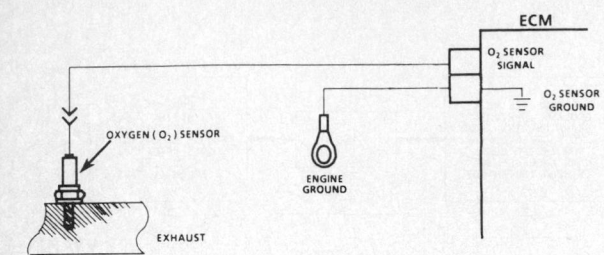

CODE 44 ECM TERMINAL & CIRCUIT WIRING IDENTIFICATION

Application	ECM Terminal	Wire Color
All With 4L80-E Transmission		
Oxygen Sensor Signal	C14	Purple
Oxygen Sensor Ground	C13	Tan
All Others Except 3.8L		
Oxygen Sensor Signal	D7	Purple
Oxygen Sensor Ground	D6	Tan
3.8L		
Oxygen Sensor Signal	D3	Purple
Oxygen Sensor Ground	D2	Tan

Sensor acts like an open sensor circuit and produces no voltage when exhaust temperature is less than 600°F (316°C). An open sensor circuit or cold sensor causes "open loop" operation.

NOTE: Test numbers refer to test numbers on diagnostic chart.

1) Code 44 sets when O_2 sensor signal remains low for a precalibrated period and system is operating in "closed loop".

DIAGNOSTIC AIDS

Using scan tester, observe Block Learn Memory (BLM) value at different RPMs. If Code 44 conditions exist, block learn value will be around 150-172.

O^2 Sensor Wire – O_2 sensor wire may be mispositioned and touching exhaust manifold. Check for ground between sensor and wire connector.

Fuel Contamination – Water, even small amounts, near in-tank fuel pump inlet can reach fuel injector, causing a lean exhaust and setting Code 44.

Fuel Pressure – System will be lean if fuel pressure is low. It may be necessary to monitor fuel pressure while driving vehicle. For fuel pressure checking procedure, see BASIC DIAGNOSTIC PROCEDURES article.

Exhaust Leaks – If exhaust system has large leaks, exhaust system negative pressure pulses can cause outside air to be drawn into system and past O_2 sensor. Vacuum or crankcase leaks can also cause a lean condition.

If Code 44 is intermittent, see INTERMITTENTS in TROUBLE SHOOTING – NO CODES article.

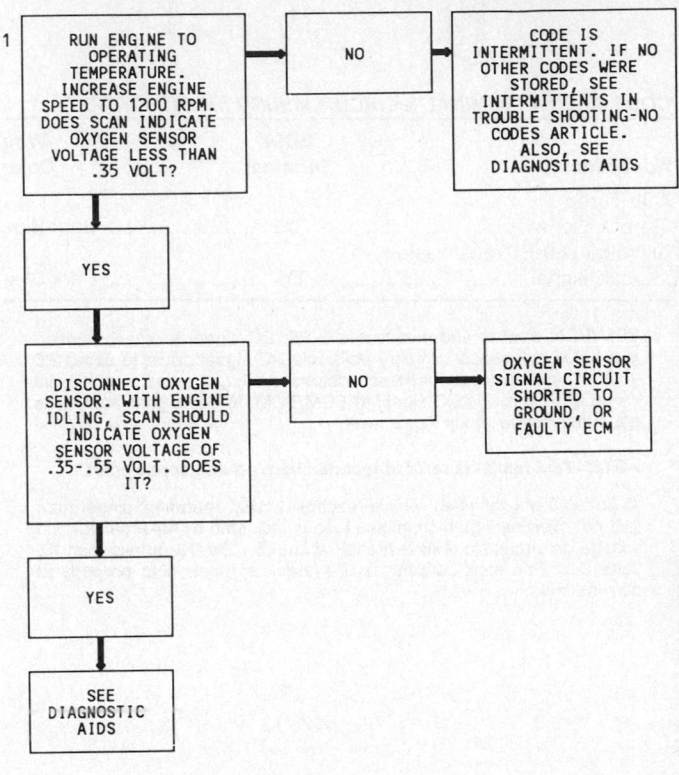

CODE 44, LEAN EXHAUST INDICATION
(4.3L TURBO)

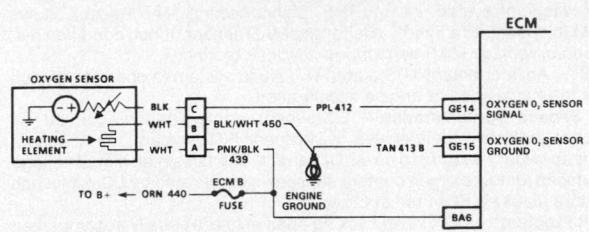

Sensor acts like an open sensor circuit and produces no voltage when exhaust temperature is less than 600°F (316°C). An open sensor circuit or cold sensor causes "open loop" operation.

NOTE: Test numbers refer to test numbers on diagnostic chart.

1) This tests oxygen sensor heating element. Heating element resistance should be 3.5 ohms at 68°F (20°C) and 14 ohms at 562°F (350°C).
2) Code 44 sets when O_2 sensor signal at ECM is less than .2 volt for at least 2 minutes and system is operating in "closed loop".

DIAGNOSTIC AIDS

Using scan tester, observe Block Learn Memory (BLM) value at different RPMs. If Code 44 conditions exist, block learn value will be around 150.
O^2 Sensor Wire – O_2 sensor wire may be mispositioned and touching exhaust manifold. Check for ground between sensor and wire connector.
Fuel Contamination – Water, even small amounts, near in-tank fuel pump inlet can reach fuel injector, causing a lean exhaust and setting Code 44.
Fuel Pressure – System will be lean if fuel pressure is low. It may be necessary to monitor fuel pressure while driving vehicle. For fuel pressure checking procedure, see BASIC DIAGNOSTIC PROCEDURES article.
Exhaust Leaks – If exhaust system has large leaks, exhaust system negative pressure pulses can cause outside air to be drawn into system and past O_2 sensor. Vacuum or crankcase leaks can also cause a lean condition.
If Code 44 is intermittent, see INTERMITTENTS in TROUBLE SHOOTING – NO CODES article.

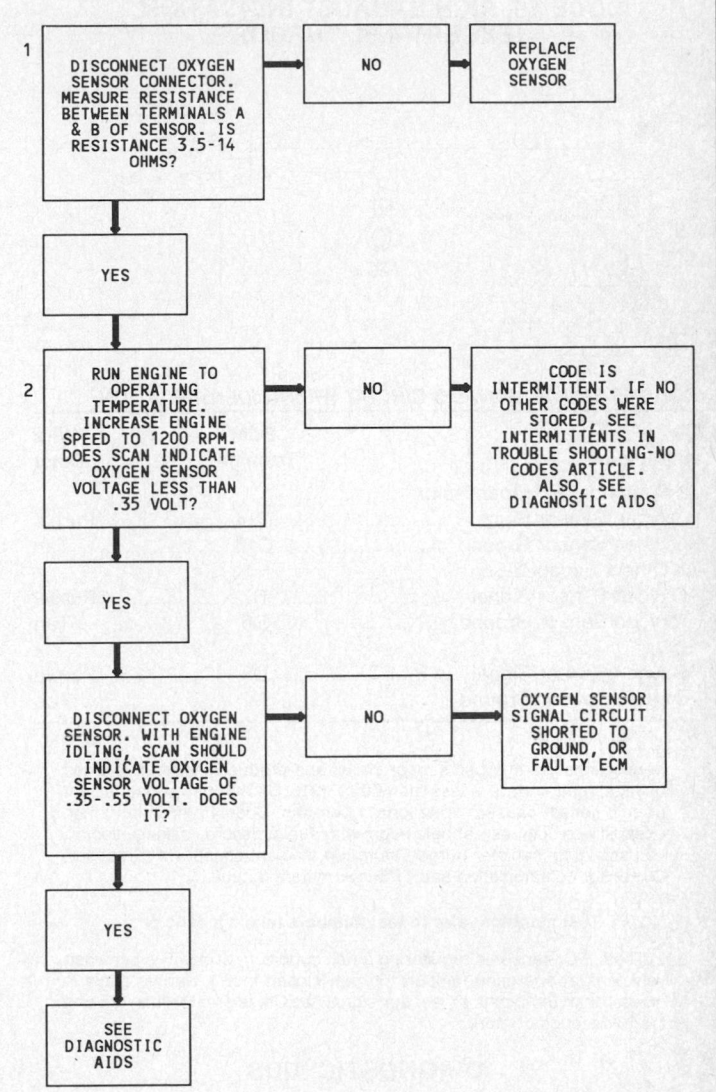

91E13734 91J13713

CODE 45, RICH EXHAUST INDICATION (EXCEPT 4.3L TURBO)

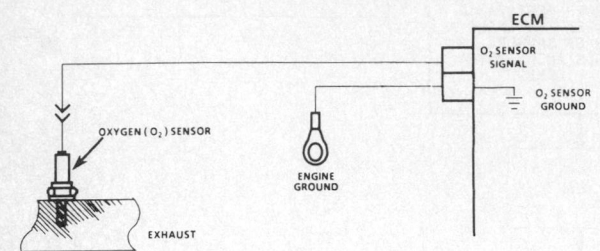

CODE 45 ECM TERMINAL & CIRCUIT WIRING IDENTIFICATION

Application	ECM Terminal	Wire Color
All With 4L80-E Transmission		
Oxygen Sensor Signal	C14	Purple
Oxygen Sensor Ground	C13	Tan
All Others Except 3.8L		
Oxygen Sensor Signal	D7	Purple
Oxygen Sensor Ground	D6	Tan
3.8L		
Oxygen Sensor Signal	D3	Purple
Oxygen Sensor Ground	D2	Tan

Sensor acts like an open sensor circuit and produces no voltage when exhaust temperature is less than 600°F (316°C). An open sensor circuit or cold sensor causes "open loop" operation. Code 45 indicates a rich exhaust and diagnosis should begin with: fuel pressure, leaking injector, HEI shielding, canister purge saturation, coolant sensor, MAP sensor, O_2 sensor contamination and TPS intermittent output.

NOTE: Test numbers refer to test numbers on diagnostic chart.

1) Tests if O_2 sensor is registering a rich condition. Code 45 is set when vehicle is at operating temperature (in "closed loop"), throttle angle is greater than 5 percent, O_2 sensor signal at ECM is greater than .75 volt for 60 seconds or more.

DIAGNOSTIC AIDS

Code 45, rich exhaust, is most likely caused by one of the following:
Fuel Pressure High – If fuel pressure is too high, air/fuel ratio will be rich. For fuel pressure checking procedure, see BASIC DIAGNOSTIC PROCEDURES article. The ECM can compensate for slight increases but if air/fuel ratio becomes too rich a Code 45 will be set.
Ignition Ground – If an open occurs at circuit No. 453, HEI induced electrical "noise" may result, causing simulated reference pulses picked up by ECM on EST harness reference line. Additional pulses result in a higher than actual engine speed signal. The ECM will increase injector pulse width ("on" time) to match increased RPM signal. Scan tester will show higher than actual RPM, which can help diagnose problem.

Fuel Canister – Charcoal canister fuel saturation will cause a rich air/fuel ratio. If full of fuel, check canister control and hoses.
MAP Sensor – If ECM senses higher than normal manifold pressure (low vacuum) system can go rich. Disconnecting MAP sensor allows ECM to substitute a fixed value for the MAP sensor. If rich condition disappears, replace MAP sensor and continue testing.
TPS – An intermittent TPS output will cause system to operate rich due to a false indication of engine acceleration.
O_2 Sensor Contamination – O_2 sensor contamination, caused by silicone in certain fuels or use of improper RTV sealant, may cause a White-powdery coating to cover O_2 sensor. The false high signal voltage produced (or low oxygen content sensed) is interpreted by ECM as a rich mixture, causing ECM to set Code 45.
EGR Problem – EGR valve sticking open at idle is usually accompanied by a rough idle and/or stalling. If Code 45 is intermittent, see INTERMITTENTS in TROUBLE SHOOTING – NO CODES article.

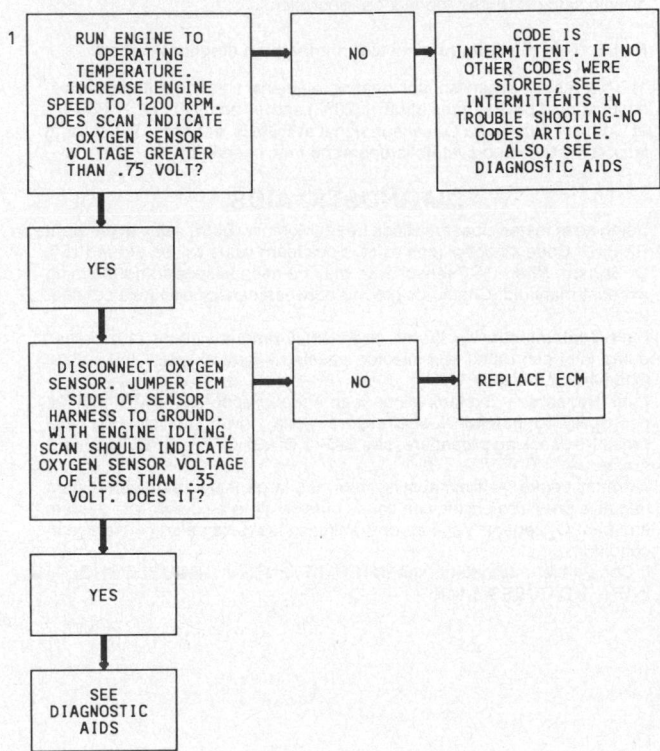

CODE 45, RICH EXHAUST INDICATION
(4.3L TURBO)

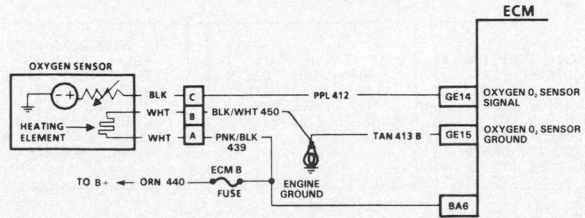

Sensor acts like an open sensor circuit and produces no voltage when exhaust temperature is less than 600°F (316°C). An open sensor circuit or cold sensor causes "open loop" operation. Code 45 indicates a rich exhaust and diagnosis should begin with: fuel pressure, leaking injector, HEI shielding, canister purge saturation, coolant sensor, MAP sensor, O_2 sensor contamination and TPS intermittent output.

NOTE: Test numbers refer to test numbers on diagnostic chart.

1) Tests if O_2 sensor is registering a rich condition. Code 45 is set when vehicle is at operating temperature (in "closed loop"), throttle angle is greater than 5 percent, O_2 sensor signal at ECM is greater than .75 volt for 50 seconds or more.

DIAGNOSTIC AIDS

Code 45, rich exhaust, is most likely caused by one of the following:

Fuel Pressure High – If fuel pressure is too high, air/fuel ratio will be rich. For fuel pressure checking procedure, see BASIC DIAGNOSTIC PROCEDURES article. The ECM can compensate for slight increases but if air/fuel ratio becomes too rich a Code 45 will be set.

Ignition Ground – If an open occurs at circuit No. 453, HEI induced electrical "noise" may result, causing simulated reference pulses picked up by ECM on EST harness reference line. Additional pulses result in a higher than actual engine speed signal. The ECM will increase injector pulse width ("on" time) to match increased RPM signal. Scan tester will show higher than actual RPM, which can help diagnose problem.

Fuel Canister – Charcoal canister fuel saturation will cause a rich air/fuel ratio. If full of fuel, check canister control and hoses.

MAP Sensor – If ECM senses higher than normal manifold pressure (low vacuum) system can go rich. Disconnecting MAP sensor allows ECM to substitute a fixed value for MAP sensor. If rich condition disappears, replace MAP sensor and continue testing.

TPS – An intermittent TPS output will cause system to operate rich due to a false indication of engine acceleration.

O_2 Sensor Contamination – O_2 sensor contamination, caused by silicone in certain fuels or use of improper RTV sealant, may cause a White-powdery coating to cover O_2 sensor. The false high signal voltage produced (or low oxygen content sensed) is interpreted by ECM as a rich mixture, causing ECM to set Code 45.

91E13734 91A13714

EGR Problem – EGR valve sticking open at idle is usually accompanied by a rough idle and/or stalling. If Code 45 is intermittent, see INTERMITTENTS in TROUBLE SHOOTING – NO CODES article.

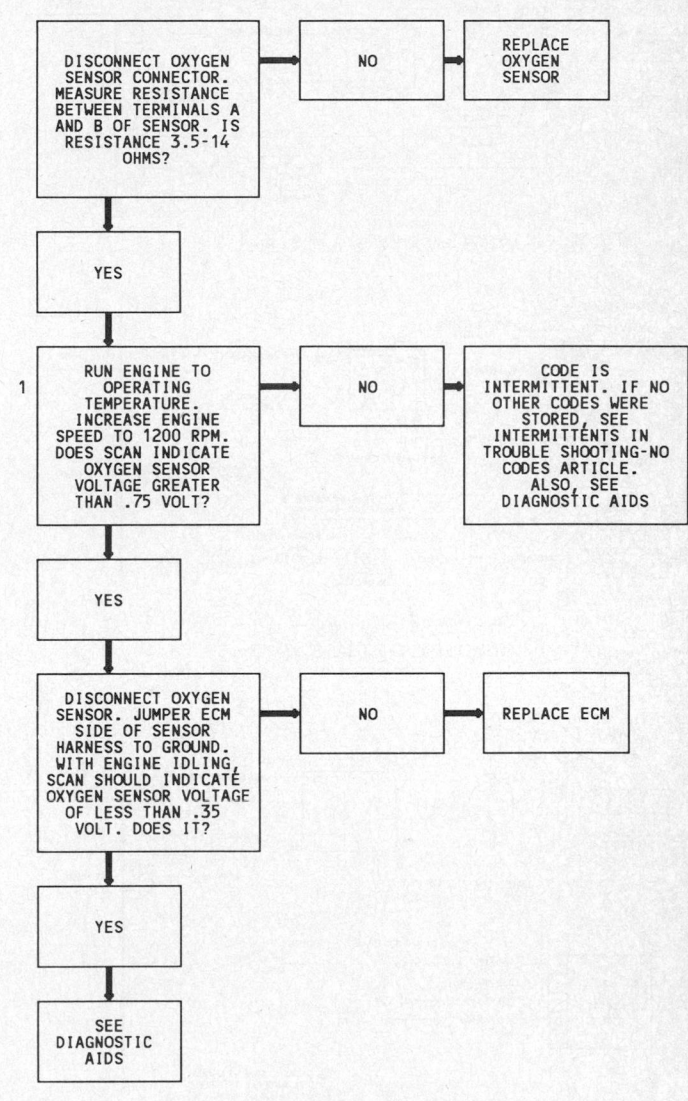

CODE 51, FAULTY PROM/MEM-CAL

Ensure all pins are fully inserted in socket. If okay, replace PROM/MEM-CAL, clear memory and recheck. If Code 51 reappears, replace ECM.

CODE 52, FAULTY CALPAK
(EXCEPT 2.5L)

Ensure all pins are fully inserted in socket. If okay, replace CALPAK, clear memory and recheck. If Code 51 reappears, replace ECM.

CODE 53, SYSTEM OVERVOLTAGE
(2.5L)

This code indicates a basic charging system problem. Code 53 will set when voltage at ECM terminal is greater than 17.1 volts for 2 seconds. Check and repair charging system.

CODE 55, ECM/PCM ERROR
(EXCEPT 2.5L)

Ensure ECM grounds are good and MEM-CAL is properly latched. If okay, replace ECM/PCM. Clear codes and confirm closed loop operation. Check operation of SERVICE ENGINE SOON light.

CODE 54, FUEL PUMP CIRCUIT

Code 54 will set if ECM does not see 12 volts on fuel pump signal voltage monitor during the first 2 seconds after ignition is turned on.

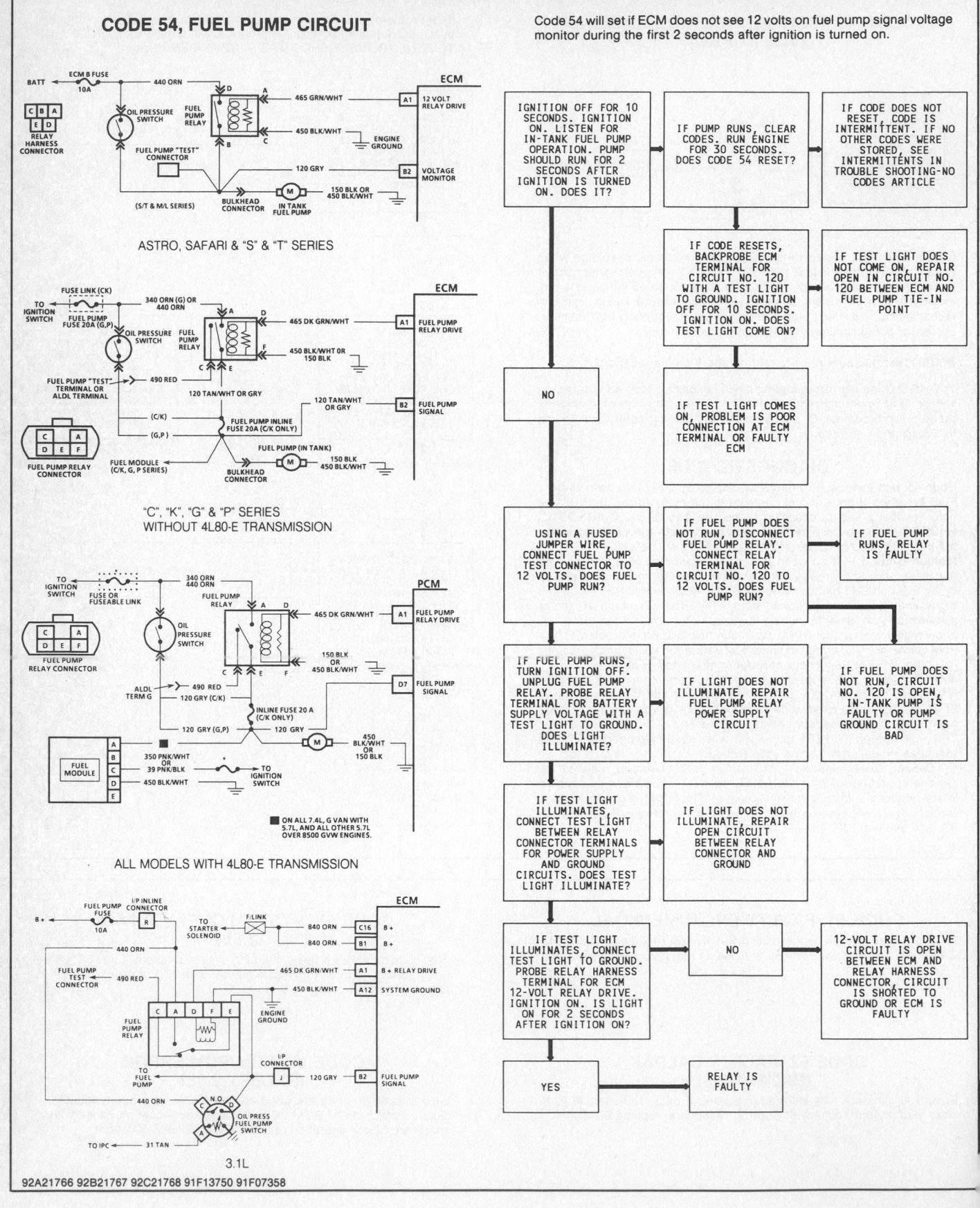

ASTRO, SAFARI & "S" & "T" SERIES

"C", "K", "G" & "P" SERIES
WITHOUT 4L80-E TRANSMISSION

ALL MODELS WITH 4L80-E TRANSMISSION

3.1L

92A21766 92B21767 92C21768 91F13750 91F07358

CODE 56, QUAD-DRIVER "B" FAULT
3.8L (1 OF 2)

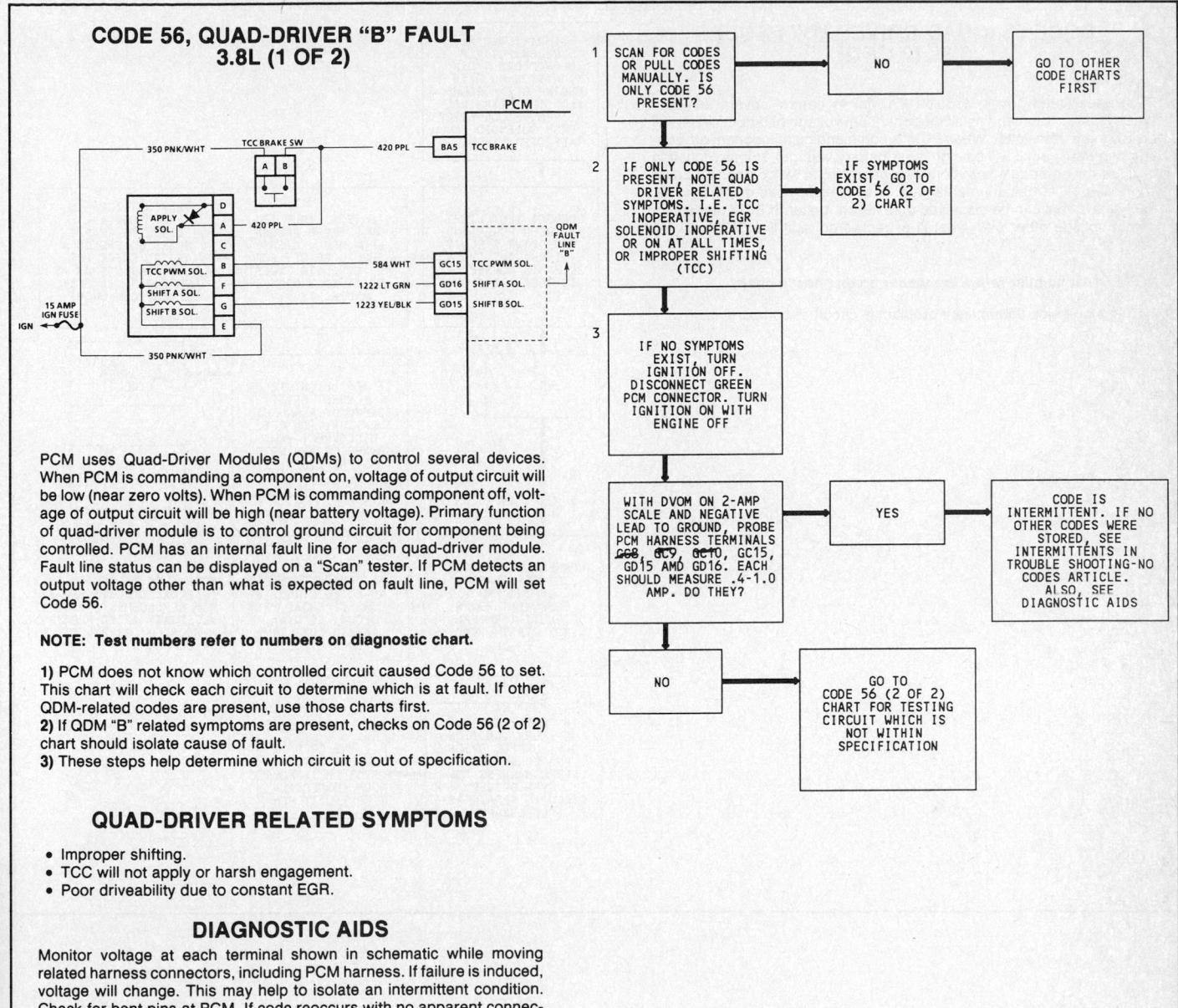

PCM uses Quad-Driver Modules (QDMs) to control several devices. When PCM is commanding a component on, voltage of output circuit will be low (near zero volts). When PCM is commanding component off, voltage of output circuit will be high (near battery voltage). Primary function of quad-driver module is to control ground circuit for component being controlled. PCM has an internal fault line for each quad-driver module. Fault line status can be displayed on a "Scan" tester. If PCM detects an output voltage other than what is expected on fault line, PCM will set Code 56.

NOTE: Test numbers refer to numbers on diagnostic chart.

1) PCM does not know which controlled circuit caused Code 56 to set. This chart will check each circuit to determine which is at fault. If other QDM-related codes are present, use those charts first.
2) If QDM "B" related symptoms are present, checks on Code 56 (2 of 2) chart should isolate cause of fault.
3) These steps help determine which circuit is out of specification.

QUAD-DRIVER RELATED SYMPTOMS

- Improper shifting.
- TCC will not apply or harsh engagement.
- Poor driveability due to constant EGR.

DIAGNOSTIC AIDS

Monitor voltage at each terminal shown in schematic while moving related harness connectors, including PCM harness. If failure is induced, voltage will change. This may help to isolate an intermittent condition. Check for bent pins at PCM. If code reoccurs with no apparent connection problem, replace PCM.

92J21799 92B04353

CODE 56, QUAD-DRIVER "B" FAULT
3.8L (2 OF 2)

PCM uses Quad-Driver Modules (QDMs) to control several devices. When PCM is commanding a component on, voltage of output circuit will be low (near zero volts). When PCM is commanding component off, voltage of output circuit will be high (near battery voltage). Primary function of quad-driver module is to control ground circuit for component being controlled. PCM has an internal fault line for each quad-driver module. Fault line status can be displayed on a "Scan" tester. If PCM detects an output voltage other than what is expected on fault line, PCM will set Code 56.

NOTE: Test number refers to number on diagnostic chart.

4) This step helps determine if problem is circuit or component.

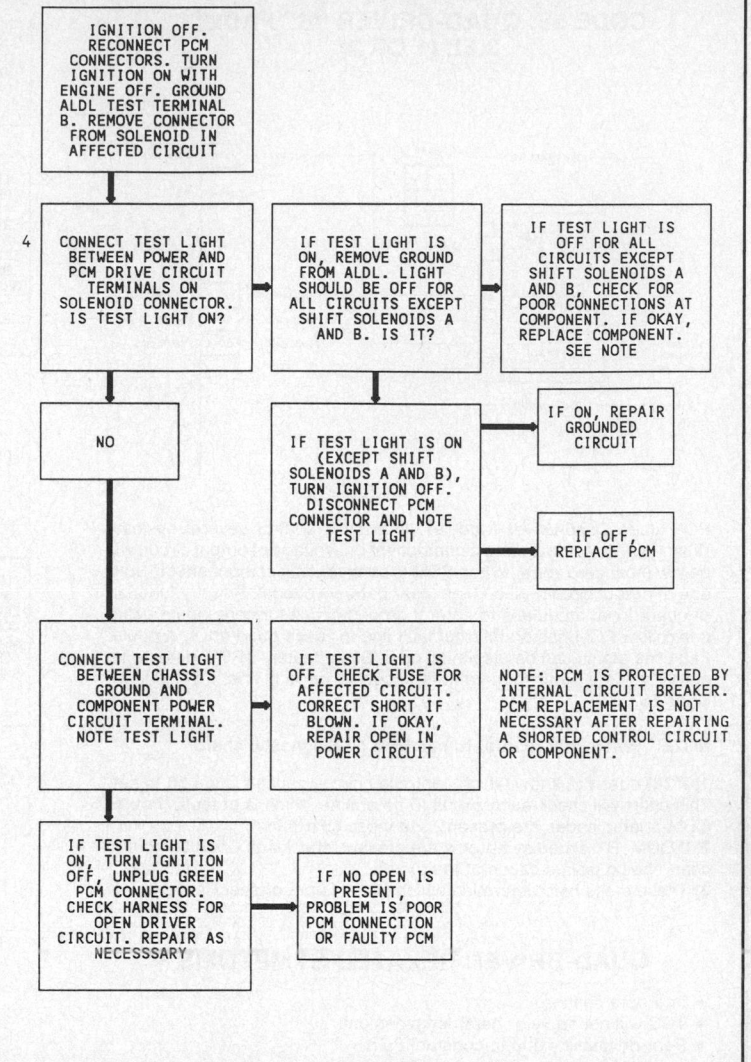

92D04354

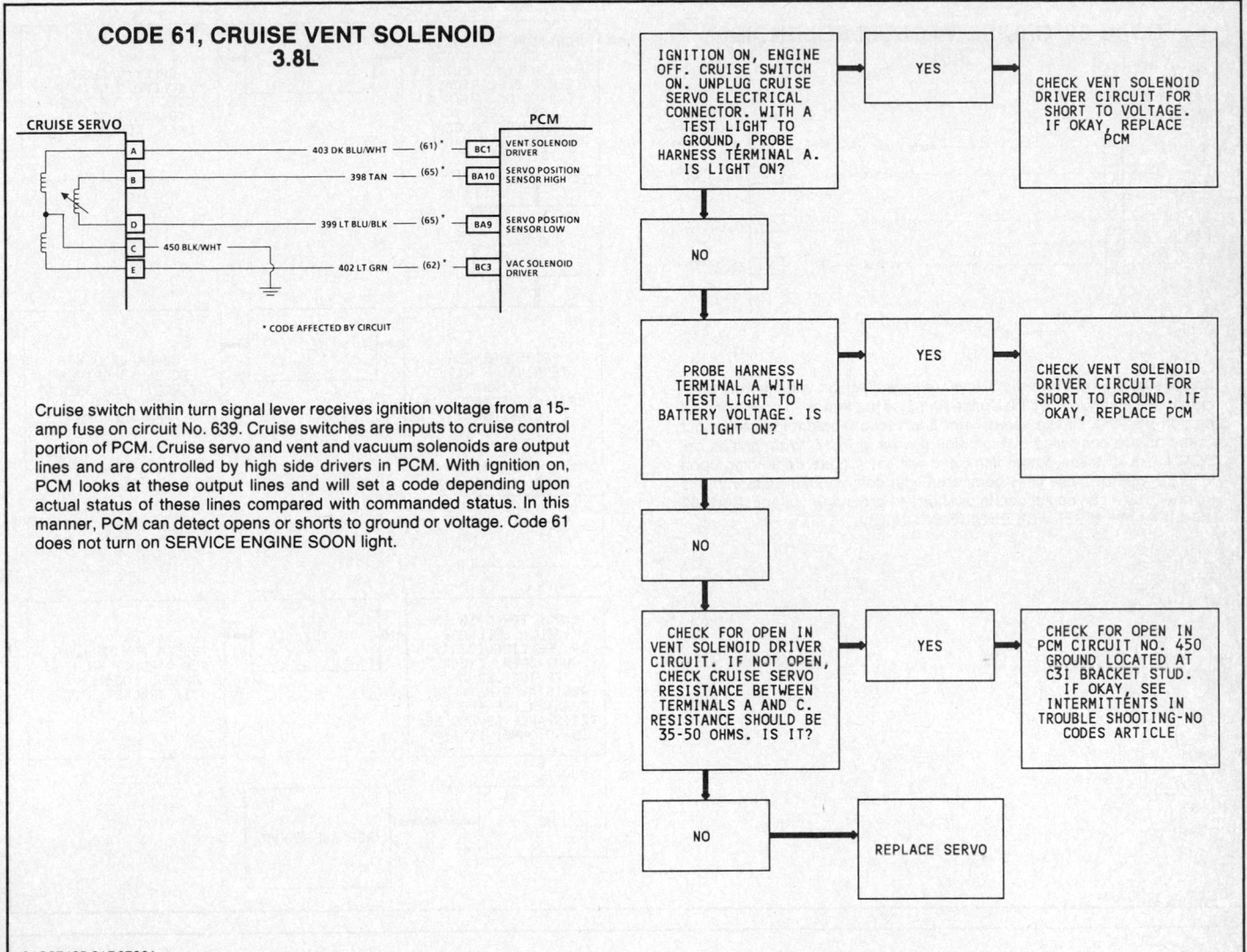

CODE 61, CRUISE VENT SOLENOID 3.8L

Cruise switch within turn signal lever receives ignition voltage from a 15-amp fuse on circuit No. 639. Cruise switches are inputs to cruise control portion of PCM. Cruise servo and vent and vacuum solenoids are output lines and are controlled by high side drivers in PCM. With ignition on, PCM looks at these output lines and will set a code depending upon actual status of these lines compared with commanded status. In this manner, PCM can detect opens or shorts to ground or voltage. Code 61 does not turn on SERVICE ENGINE SOON light.

CRUISE SERVO

A	403 DK BLU/WHT	(61) *	BC1	VENT SOLENOID DRIVER
B	398 TAN	(65) *	BA10	SERVO POSITION SENSOR HIGH
D	399 LT BLU/BLK	(65) *	BA9	SERVO POSITION SENSOR LOW
C	450 BLK/WHT			
E	402 LT GRN	(62) *	BC3	VAC SOLENOID DRIVER

PCM

* CODE AFFECTED BY CIRCUIT

IGNITION ON, ENGINE OFF. CRUISE SWITCH ON. UNPLUG CRUISE SERVO ELECTRICAL CONNECTOR. WITH A TEST LIGHT TO GROUND, PROBE HARNESS TERMINAL A. IS LIGHT ON? → YES → CHECK VENT SOLENOID DRIVER CIRCUIT FOR SHORT TO VOLTAGE. IF OKAY, REPLACE PCM

NO ↓

PROBE HARNESS TERMINAL A WITH TEST LIGHT TO BATTERY VOLTAGE. IS LIGHT ON? → YES → CHECK VENT SOLENOID DRIVER CIRCUIT FOR SHORT TO GROUND. IF OKAY, REPLACE PCM

NO ↓

CHECK FOR OPEN IN VENT SOLENOID DRIVER CIRCUIT. IF NOT OPEN, CHECK CRUISE SERVO RESISTANCE BETWEEN TERMINALS A AND C. RESISTANCE SHOULD BE 35-50 OHMS. IS IT? → YES → CHECK FOR OPEN IN PCM CIRCUIT NO. 450 GROUND LOCATED AT C3I BRACKET STUD. IF OKAY, SEE INTERMITTENTS IN TROUBLE SHOOTING-NO CODES ARTICLE

NO ↓

REPLACE SERVO

91C07465 91B07361

CODE 62, CRUISE VACUUM SOLENOID
3.8L

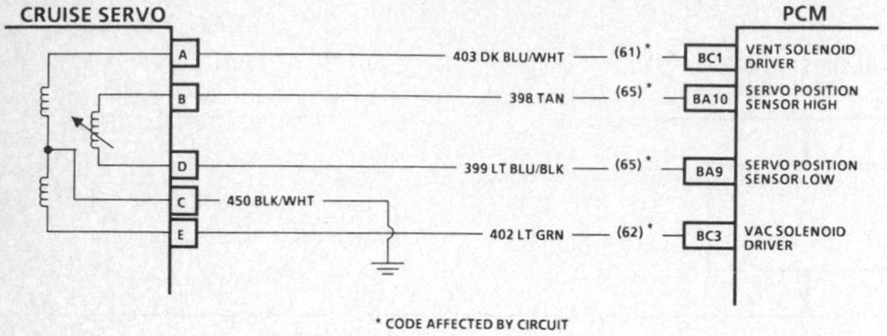

CRUISE SERVO | PCM

A	403 DK BLU/WHT	(61) *	BC1	VENT SOLENOID DRIVER
B	398 TAN	(65) *	BA10	SERVO POSITION SENSOR HIGH
D	399 LT BLU/BLK	(65) *	BA9	SERVO POSITION SENSOR LOW
C	450 BLK/WHT			
E	402 LT GRN	(62) *	BC3	VAC SOLENOID DRIVER

* CODE AFFECTED BY CIRCUIT

Cruise switch within turn signal lever receives ignition voltage from a 15-amp fuse on circuit No. 639. Cruise switches are inputs to cruise control portion of PCM. Cruise servo, vent and vacuum solenoids are output lines and are controlled by high side drivers in PCM. With ignition on, PCM looks at these output lines and will set a code depending upon actual status of these lines compared with commanded status. In this manner, PCM can detect opens or shorts to ground or voltage. Code 62 does not turn on SERVICE ENGINE SOON light.

```
IGNITION ON, ENGINE OFF. CRUISE SWITCH
ON. UNPLUG CRUISE SERVO ELECTRICAL
CONNECTOR. WITH A TEST LIGHT TO
GROUND, PROBE HARNESS TERMINAL E.
IS LIGHT ON?
        │
       YES ──────► CHECK VACUUM SOLENOID DRIVER
        │          CIRCUIT FOR SHORT TO VOLTAGE. IF
       NO          OKAY, REPLACE PCM
        │
PROBE HARNESS TERMINAL E WITH
TEST LIGHT TO BATTERY VOLTAGE. IS
LIGHT ON?
        │
       YES ──────► CHECK VACUUM SOLENOID DRIVER
        │          CIRCUIT FOR SHORT TO GROUND. IF OKAY,
       NO          REPLACE PCM
        │
CHECK FOR OPEN IN VACUUM SOLENOID
DRIVER CIRCUIT. IF NOT OPEN, CHECK
CRUISE SERVO RESISTANCE BETWEEN
TERMINALS E AND C. RESISTANCE SHOULD BE
35-50 OHMS. IS IT?
        │
       YES ──────► CHECK FOR OPEN IN PCM CIRCUIT NO. 450
        │          GROUND LOCATED AT C3I BRACKET STUD.
       NO
        │
REPLACE SERVO
```

91C07465 91H07364

CODE 63, CRUISE SYSTEM PROBLEM
3.8L

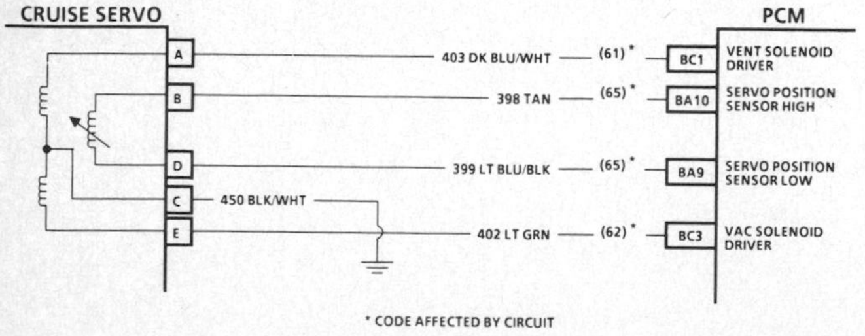

CRUISE SERVO | PCM

A	403 DK BLU/WHT	(61) *	BC1	VENT SOLENOID DRIVER
B	398 TAN	(65) *	BA10	SERVO POSITION SENSOR HIGH
D	399 LT BLU/BLK	(65) *	BA9	SERVO POSITION SENSOR LOW
C	450 BLK/WHT			
E	402 LT GRN	(62) *	BC3	VAC SOLENOID DRIVER

* CODE AFFECTED BY CIRCUIT

PCM monitors cruise control system servo position to ensure desired cruise position and actual cruise position are equal to each other. If servo position is low when maximum servo position is commanded, PCM will set Code 63. Code 63 does not turn on SERVICE ENGINE SOON light. If Code 61, 62 or 65 is set with Code 63, repair other code before using this flow chart.

```
TURN IGNITION ON WITH ENGINE OFF. SCAN
SERVO POSITION. MANUALLY COMPRESS
SERVO. DOES SERVO SCAN INCREASE AND
DECREASE AS SERVO IS COMPRESSED AND
RELEASED?
        │
       NO ──────► SEE CODE 65 CHART
        │
       YES
        │
IDLE ENGINE FOR 30 SECONDS. TURN
IGNITION OFF. TURN IGNITION ON WITH
ENGINE OFF. USING TECH 1 SCAN TESTER,
STROKE C/C SERVO TO 90%. NOTE SERVO
        │
        ├─► SERVO DOES NOT STROKE TO
        │   COMMANDED POSITION AND HOLD ──────►
        │   CHECK VACUUM LINES TO SERVO AND
        │   PROGRAMMER. CHECK VACUUM TANK AND
        │   CHECK VALVES FOR LEAKS. IF OKAY,
        │   REPLACE C/C SERVO
        │
SERVO STROKES TO COMMANDED POSITION
AND HOLDS ──────► REPLACE C/C SERVO
```

91C07465 92E21794

CODE 65, CRUISE SERVO POSITION
3.8L

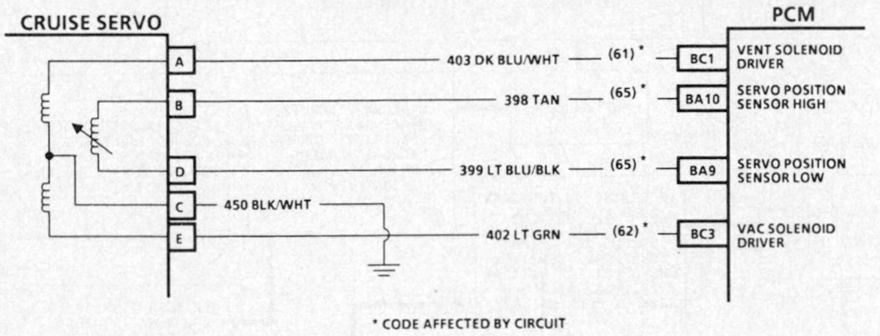

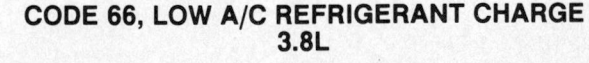

CRUISE SERVO | PCM

A	403 DK BLU/WHT	(61)*	BC1	VENT SOLENOID DRIVER
B	398 TAN	(65)*	BA10	SERVO POSITION SENSOR HIGH
D	399 LT BLU/BLK	(65)*	BA9	SERVO POSITION SENSOR LOW
C	450 BLK/WHT			
E	402 LT GRN	(62)*	BC3	VAC SOLENOID DRIVER

* CODE AFFECTED BY CIRCUIT

PCM supplies 5 volts to cruise control servo position sensor. Depending upon actual servo position, voltage on servo position sensor circuit will indicate to PCM position of servo. Code 65 will be set if circuit No. 399 is open or if circuit No. 398 is open or shorted to ground or voltage. Code 65 does not turn on SERVICE ENGINE SOON light.

91C07465 91I07369

IGNITION ON, ENGINE OFF. SCAN CRUISE CONTROL SERVO POSITION. MANUALLY COMPRESS SERVO. DOES SCANNED VALUE CHANGE AS SERVO IS COMPRESSED?

→ YES → CODE IS INTERMITTENT. IF NO OTHER CODES WERE STORED, SEE INTERMITTENTS IN TROUBLE SHOOTING-NO CODES ARTICLE

↓ NO

UNPLUG SERVO WIRING HARNESS. MEASURE VOLTAGE AT HARNESS TERMINAL B. IS READING ABOUT 5 VOLTS?

→ IF READING IS NOT ABOUT 5 VOLTS, BACKPROBE PCM TERMINAL BA10 WITH DVOM. IS MEASUREMENT NOW ABOUT 5 VOLTS?

→ IF VOLTAGE IS STILL NOT ABOUT 5 VOLTS, CHECK FOR SHORT TO GROUND IN SERVO POSITION SENSOR CIRCUIT BETWEEN SERVO AND TERMINAL BA10 AT PCM. IF OKAY, REPLACE PCM

↓ YES

IF READING IS NOW ABOUT 5 VOLTS, PROBLEM IS OPEN IN SERVO POSITION SENSOR CIRCUIT BETWEEN SERVO AND PCM TERMINAL BA10

CONNECT DVOM BETWEEN SERVO HARNESS TERMINALS B AND D. DOES VOLTMETER DISPLAY SAME VOLTAGE?

→ NO → PROBLEM IS OPEN OR SHORT TO VOLTAGE IN SERVO POSITION SENSOR CIRCUIT BETWEEN SERVO AND PCM TERMINAL BA9, OR FAULTY PCM CONNECTION OR FAULTY PCM.

↓ YES → CHECK SERVO CONNECTIONS. IF OKAY, REPLACE SERVO

CODE 66, LOW A/C REFRIGERANT CHARGE
3.8L

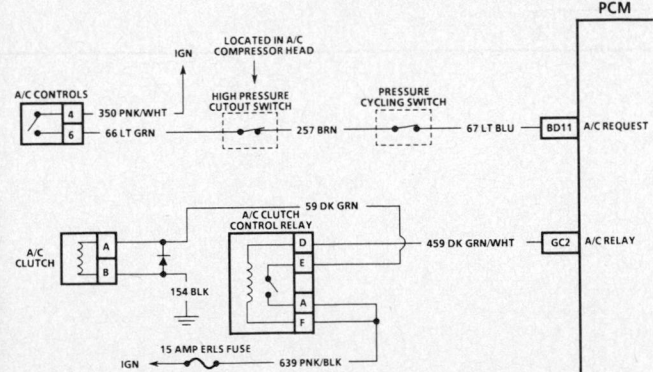

PCM

	67 LT BLU	BD11	A/C REQUEST
	459 DK GRN/WHT	GC2	A/C RELAY

A/C CONTROLS 4 / 6 — 350 PNK/WHT — IGN
66 LT GRN — 257 BRN (HIGH PRESSURE CUTOUT SWITCH / PRESSURE CYCLING SWITCH) LOCATED IN A/C COMPRESSOR HEAD

A/C CLUTCH A / B — 154 BLK
A/C CLUTCH CONTROL RELAY D/E/A/F — 59 DK GRN
15 AMP ERLS FUSE — 639 PNK/BLK — IGN

PCM monitors A/C request and completes ground for A/C relay when an A/C mode is selected at control head and refrigerant pressure is sufficient to close pressure cycling switch. If A/C pressure is low and clutch cycles too often, PCM will protect compressor by disabling A/C relay and setting Code 66. Relay will be disabled until next ignition cycle. If Code 66 is set during 3 consecutive ignition cycles, A/C relay will be disabled until Code 66 is cleared from memory. Code 66 does not illuminate SERVICE ENGINE SOON light. Code 66 will set if A/C request signal lasts less than 1.5 seconds for 10 or more consecutive compressor "on" cycles within a 15 minute period.

92C21800 91G07373

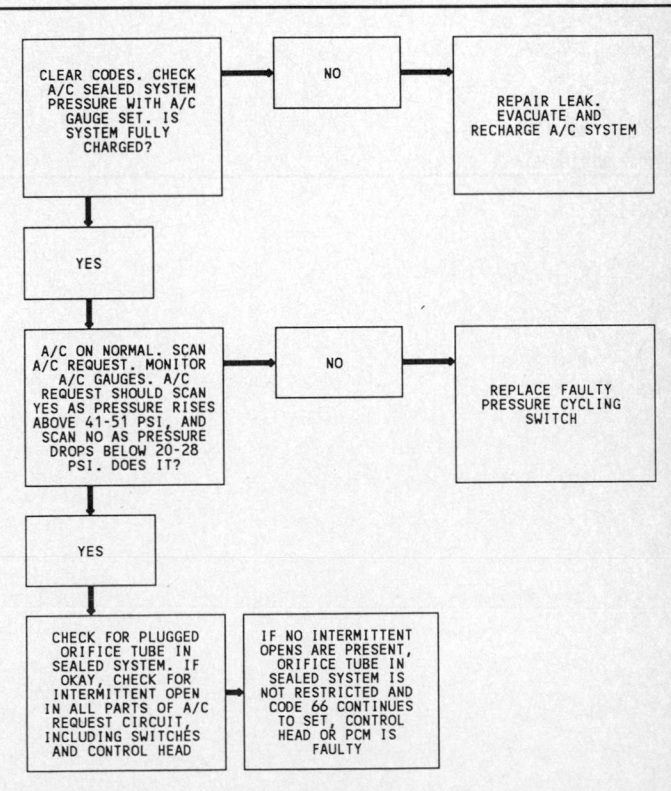

CLEAR CODES. CHECK A/C SEALED SYSTEM PRESSURE WITH A/C GAUGE SET. IS SYSTEM FULLY CHARGED?

→ NO → REPAIR LEAK. EVACUATE AND RECHARGE A/C SYSTEM

↓ YES

A/C ON NORMAL. SCAN A/C REQUEST. MONITOR A/C GAUGES. A/C REQUEST SHOULD SCAN YES AS PRESSURE RISES ABOVE 41-51 PSI, AND SCAN NO AS PRESSURE DROPS BELOW 20-28 PSI. DOES IT?

→ NO → REPLACE FAULTY PRESSURE CYCLING SWITCH

↓ YES

CHECK FOR PLUGGED ORIFICE TUBE IN SEALED SYSTEM. IF OKAY, CHECK FOR INTERMITTENT OPEN IN ALL PARTS OF A/C REQUEST CIRCUIT INCLUDING SWITCHES AND CONTROL HEAD

IF NO INTERMITTENT OPENS ARE PRESENT, ORIFICE TUBE IN SEALED SYSTEM IS NOT RESTRICTED AND CODE 66 CONTINUES TO SET, CONTROL HEAD OR PCM IS FAULTY

CODE 67, CRUISE ENGAGE SWITCHES
3.8L

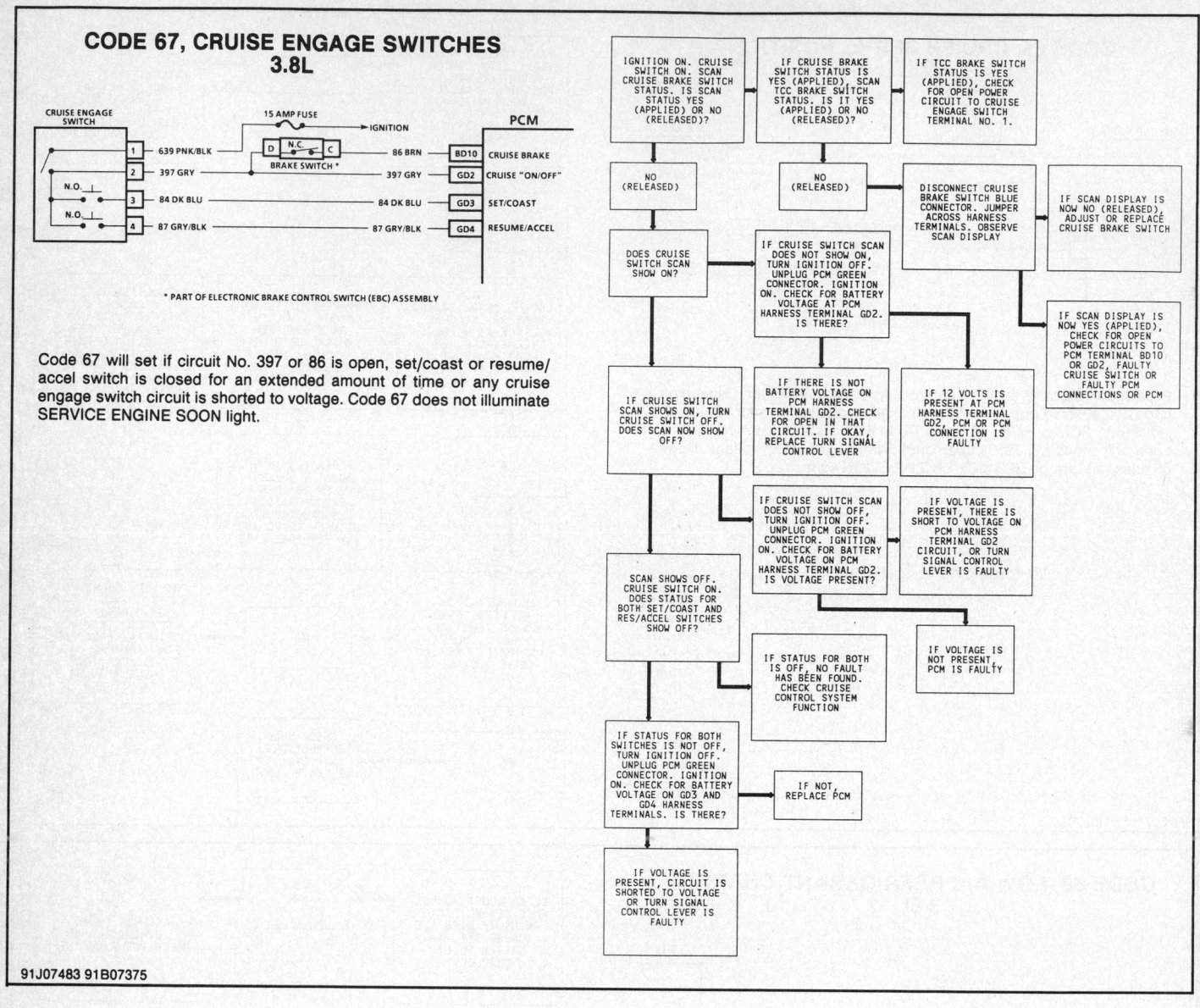

Code 67 will set if circuit No. 397 or 86 is open, set/coast or resume/accel switch is closed for an extended amount of time or any cruise engage switch circuit is shorted to voltage. Code 67 does not illuminate SERVICE ENGINE SOON light.

91J07483 91B07375

CODE 68, CRUISE SYSTEM PROBLEM USING TECH 1 3.8L

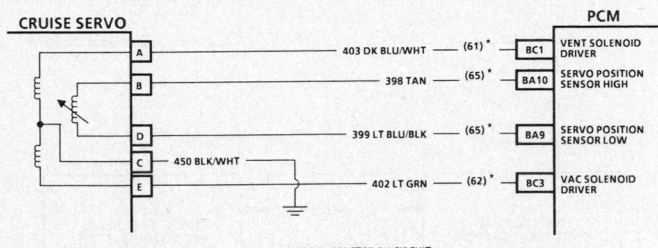

CRUISE SERVO / PCM

A	403 DK BLU/WHT	(61) *	BC1	VENT SOLENOID DRIVER
B	398 TAN	(65) *	BA10	SERVO POSITION SENSOR HIGH
D	399 LT BLU/BLK	(65) *	BA9	SERVO POSITION SENSOR LOW
C	450 BLK/WHT			
E	402 LT GRN	(62) *	BC3	VAC SOLENOID DRIVER

* CODE AFFECTED BY CIRCUIT

PCM-integrated cruise control system is designed to monitor itself to ensure desired cruise position and actual cruise position are equal to each other. Code 68 sets when actual servo position sensor signal is 15 percent greater than desired servo position sensor signal for .6 second. Code 68 does not illuminate SERVICE ENGINE SOON light. If Code 68 is current, vehicle will operate in "power management" mode. During this mode, PCM will shut of fuel to 3 cylinders to avoid overrevving engine in case of throttle being held open by cruise system malfunction. Power management mode may be perceived as a severe engine miss of lack of power.

NOTE: Test number refers to number on diagnostic chart.

1) Most VAC solenoids leak a small amount of vacuum when closed. However, they should not leak enough to allow WOT in 15 seconds with vent closed.
2) When VAC solenoid is forced on, vacuum will be vented to atmosphere unless vent valve is stuck closed.

DIAGNOSTIC AIDS

An intermittently binding or sticking throttle cable cam cause a Code 68 to set. Code can also be set by manually compressing servo to increase engine RPM. Outside interference such as CB antenna lead near PCM wiring harness may cause false servo position sensor signal and set Code 68.

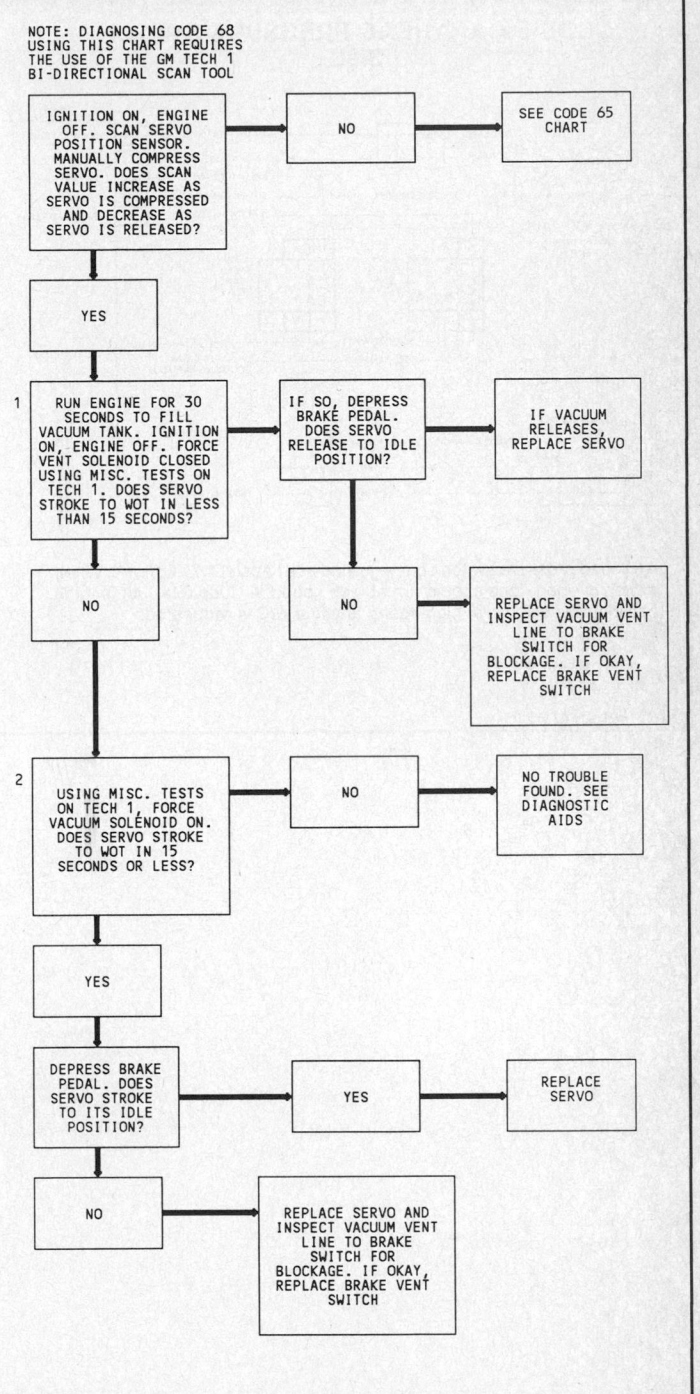

NOTE: DIAGNOSING CODE 68 USING THIS CHART REQUIRES THE USE OF THE GM TECH 1 BI-DIRECTIONAL SCAN TOOL

IGNITION ON, ENGINE OFF. SCAN SERVO POSITION SENSOR. MANUALLY COMPRESS SERVO. DOES SCAN VALUE INCREASE AS SERVO IS COMPRESSED AND DECREASE AS SERVO IS RELEASED? → NO → SEE CODE 65 CHART

YES

1. RUN ENGINE FOR 30 SECONDS TO FILL VACUUM TANK. IGNITION ON, ENGINE OFF. FORCE VENT SOLENOID CLOSED USING MISC. TESTS ON TECH 1. DOES SERVO STROKE TO WOT IN LESS THAN 15 SECONDS? → IF SO, DEPRESS BRAKE PEDAL. DOES SERVO RELEASE TO IDLE POSITION? → IF VACUUM RELEASES, REPLACE SERVO

NO / NO → REPLACE SERVO AND INSPECT VACUUM VENT LINE TO BRAKE SWITCH FOR BLOCKAGE. IF OKAY, REPLACE BRAKE VENT SWITCH

2. USING MISC. TESTS ON TECH 1, FORCE VACUUM SOLENOID ON. DOES SERVO STROKE TO WOT IN 15 SECONDS OR LESS? → NO → NO TROUBLE FOUND. SEE DIAGNOSTIC AIDS

YES

DEPRESS BRAKE PEDAL. DOES SERVO STROKE TO ITS IDLE POSITION? → YES → REPLACE SERVO

NO → REPLACE SERVO AND INSPECT VACUUM VENT LINE TO BRAKE SWITCH FOR BLOCKAGE. IF OKAY, REPLACE BRAKE VENT SWITCH

91C07465 91D07376

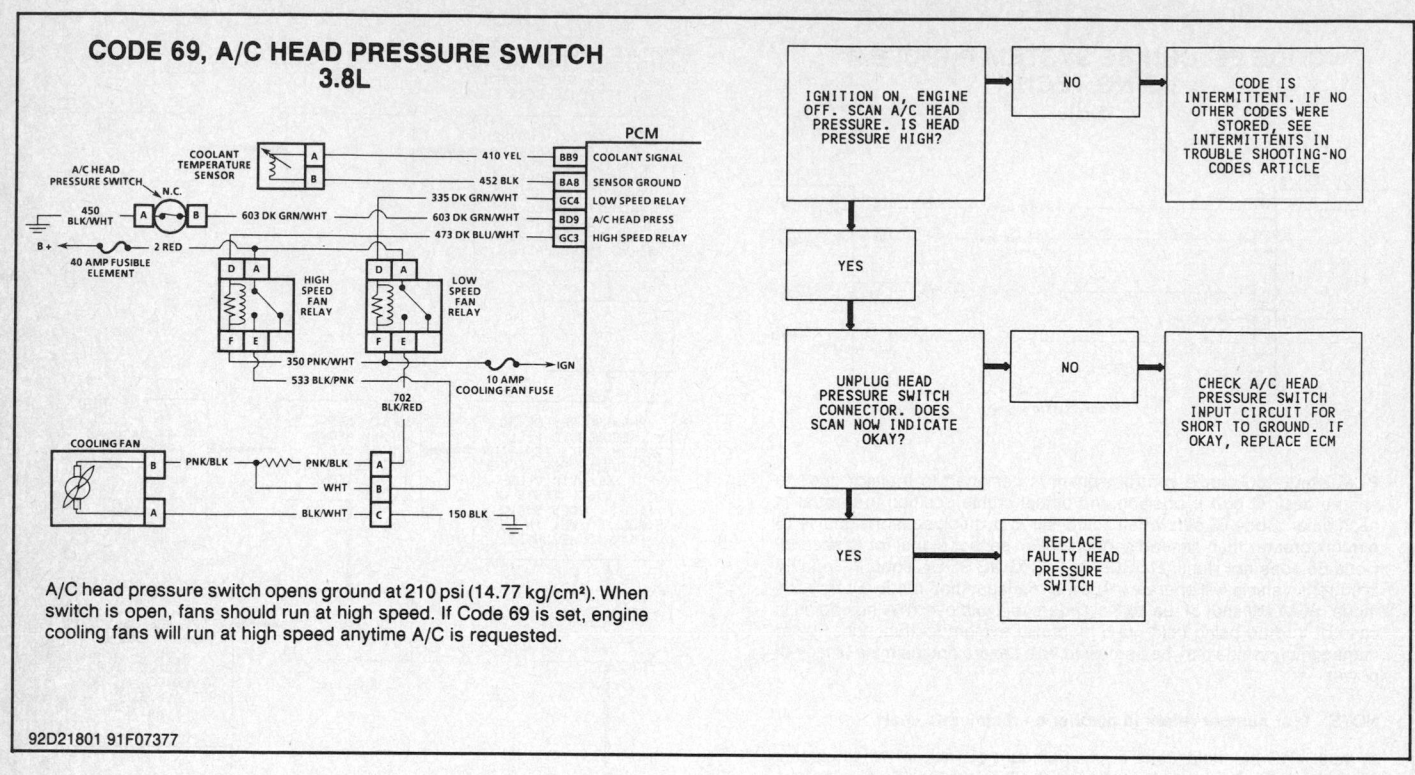

CODE 69, A/C HEAD PRESSURE SWITCH 3.8L

A/C head pressure switch opens ground at 210 psi (14.77 kg/cm²). When switch is open, fans should run at high speed. If Code 69 is set, engine cooling fans will run at high speed anytime A/C is requested.

92D21801 91F07377

Blazer, Commercial Van With Light Duty Emissions, Jimmy, Sierra, Suburban, Yukon, "C" & "K" Series Pickup, "G" Series Van

INTRODUCTION

The Diesel Electronic Control (DEC) system, on 6.2L with light duty emissions, electronically controls EGR system operation, Torque Converter Clutch (TCC) engagement, cold advance and glow plug operation.

Most engine control problems are NOT computer related, but result from mechanical breakdowns, poor electrical connections, or damaged vacuum hoses. Before condemning the computer system, carefully perform visual and mechanical inspections. Failure to perform these inspections can result in lost diagnostic time.

SELF-DIAGNOSTIC SYSTEM

SELF-DIAGNOSTIC DIRECTORY

The 6.2L light duty emissions system includes a self-diagnostic system which can determine input signal circuit malfunctions. Input signal circuits determine engine function control.

DIAGNOSTIC PROCEDURE

Preliminary Inspection – 1) Check all vacuum hoses for correct routing, restrictions, cuts or other damage. Inspect difficult-to-see vacuum hoses beneath air cleaner assembly and other engine components.
2) Inspect all engine compartment wiring for proper connections. Also check wires for pinched or chafed spots, as well as contact with sharp edges or exhaust manifolds.
3) The preliminary inspection is very important and should be performed carefully and thoroughly, as it can often fix a problem without requiring further diagnosis.
Diagnostic Procedure – 1) Ensure all engine systems NOT related to the Diesel Electronic Control (DEC) system are operating properly. DO NOT proceed with testing unless all non-DEC system problems are repaired.
2) ALWAYS begin diagnosis with checking diagnostic circuit to determine if DEC system and ECM are working properly. See DIAGNOSTIC CIRCUIT CHECK chart. Refer to SELF-DIAGNOSTIC DIRECTORY table for location of chart. If trouble codes (other than Code 12) are displayed, determine if they are hard or intermittent trouble codes.
3) A hard code is present while working on vehicle, and problem condition persists. Hard codes will cause SERVICE ENGINE SOON light to come on.
4) An intermittent code does not reset itself and is NOT present while working on vehicle. Intermittent codes are often caused by loose connections. SERVICE ENGINE SOON light will go out 10 seconds after fault goes away. For intermittent diagnostic procedures, see TROUBLE SHOOTING – NO CODES article.

ENTERING OR EXITING DIAGNOSTIC MODE

1) With key on and engine off, connect a jumper wire between ALDL terminal "B" (diagnostic terminal) and terminal "A" (ground). See Fig. 1. The Diesel Electronic Control (DEC) system will enter diagnostic mode.
2) In this mode, ECM will display Code 12 by flashing the SERVICE ENGINE SOON light once, followed by a short pause, then 2 flashes in quick succession.
3) Code 12 will be displayed 3 times. If no other codes are stored, Code 12 will continue to flash until diagnostic terminal is ungrounded. To exit diagnostic mode, turn ignition off and remove jumper from ALDL connector.

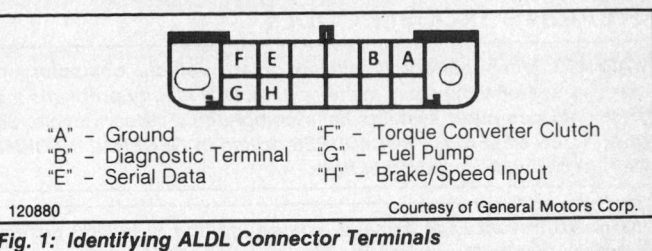

"A" – Ground
"B" – Diagnostic Terminal
"E" – Serial Data
"F" – Torque Converter Clutch
"G" – Fuel Pump
"H" – Brake/Speed Input

120880   Courtesy of General Motors Corp.

Fig. 1: Identifying ALDL Connector Terminals

TROUBLE CODE IDENTIFICATION

NOTE: Trouble codes retrieved from PCM/TCM may be either engine or transmission related. Engine-related codes are covered in this article. For transmission-related codes, see SELF-DIAGNOSTICS – ELECTRONIC TRANSMISSION article. See TROUBLE CODE IDENTIFICATION table to determine if code is engine or transmission related.

1) The DEC system codes indicate failure of a specific sensor and/or circuit. Sensor/circuit diagnosis may indicate replacement of ECM. Code 51 indicates PROM is either improperly installed or has failed.
2) Code 52 indicates ECM has failed and must be replaced. If condition is still not corrected after replacing ECM, the following may be the cause:

- An incorrect ECM or PROM application may cause a malfunction, which may or may not set a code.
- The ECM connector may be the problem. Connector terminals may have to be removed from connector to be checked properly.
- PROM failure. Although the PROM rarely fails, it could be the cause of the problem.
- Replacement ECM may be faulty.
- Intermittent problem. Make a careful physical inspection of affected sensor/circuit.
- A shorted solenoid, coil relay, or harness may be the cause of ECM failure. Use Short Circuit Tester (J-34636) to check for short circuits.

TROUBLE CODE IDENTIFICATION

Code	Probable Cause
12 [1]	No Engine Speed Sensor Reference Pulse To PCM/TCM
14 [1]	CTS Voltage Low (Sensor Or Signal Line Grounded)
15 [1]	CTS Voltage High (Sensor, Connections, Or Wires Open)
21 [1]	TPS Voltage High (Open Circuit Or Misadjusted TPS)
22 [1]	TPS Voltage Low (Circuit Grounded)
23 [1]	TPS Not Calibrated (.25-1.3 Volts At Curb Idle)
24 [1]	Vehicle Speed Sensor Circuit Open Or Grounded
28	Pressure Switch Manifold Range Circuit Open Or Shorted
31 [1]	MAP Voltage Low (Circuit Open Or Shorted To Ground)
32 [1]	EGR Error (Improper Vacuum Signal)
33 [1]	MAP Voltage High (Circuit Open Or Shorted To Ground)
39	TCC Stuck Off (Faulty TCC Solenoid)
51 [1]	Improperly Installed/Faulty PROM
52 [1]	ECM Fault
53 [1]	Voltage Reference Overload
58	TTS High Temperature (Sensor Or Signal Line Grounded)
59	TTS Low Temperature (Sensor, Connections, Or Wires Open)
68	Overdrive Ratio Error (Engine RPM Greater Than Input Speed)
73	Force Motor Commanded Amperage Differs From Return
75	System Voltage Low (Charging System Problem)
81	QDM Solenoid "B" Monitored Voltage Differs From Commanded
82	QDM Solenoid "A" Monitored Voltage Differs From Commanded
83	QDM TCC Monitored Voltage Differs From Commanded
85	Undefined Gear Ratio (Input Or Output Sensor Failure)
86	Shift Solenoid "B" Stuck On (Commanded Gear Not Engaged)
87	Shift Solenoid "B" Stuck Off (Commanded Gear Not Engaged)

[1] – Code is engine related. For information on transmission related codes, see SELF-DIAGNOSTICS – ELECTRONIC TRANSMISSION article.

CLEARING TROUBLE CODES

WARNING: When battery is disconnected, vehicle computer and memory systems may lose memory data. Driveability problems may exist until computer systems have completed a relearn cycle. See COMPUTER RELEARN PROCEDURES article in GENERAL INFORMATION before disconnecting battery.

NOTE: To prevent ECM damage, ensure ignition is in OFF position when disconnecting or reconnecting power to ECM.

Trouble codes should be cleared after repairs have been completed. Also, some diagnostic charts require codes to be cleared before using diagnostic chart. To clear codes, remove power to ECM for 30 seconds by either disconnecting battery cable and ECM pigtail to battery, or removing ECM "B" fuse.

If no hard fault codes are present (only intermittent codes exist), proceed to TROUBLE SHOOTING – NO CODES article for intermittent diagnostic procedures.

ECM LOCATION

The ECM is located under passenger's seat riser ("G" Series), or behind right side of dash (all other models).

SPECIAL TOOLS (DIAGNOSTIC)

Special scan testers, plugged into the ALDL connector, may be used to read trouble codes, and check voltages in system on serial data line. These testers can save a great deal of time. For additional information, see owner's manual included with tester.

TEST EQUIPMENT

A tachometer, test light, Digital Volt-Ohmmeter (DVOM) with a minimum 10-megohm input impedance, a vacuum gauge, and jumper wires are required to test and diagnose Diesel Electronic Control (DEC) system. A scan tester may also be used to access data parameters. Tester will supply a visual reading of most inputs, and some outputs, to ECM.

DIAGNOSTIC CHARTS

The following diagnostic flow charts and circuit schematics are provided courtesy of General Motors.

DIAGNOSTIC CIRCUIT CHECK

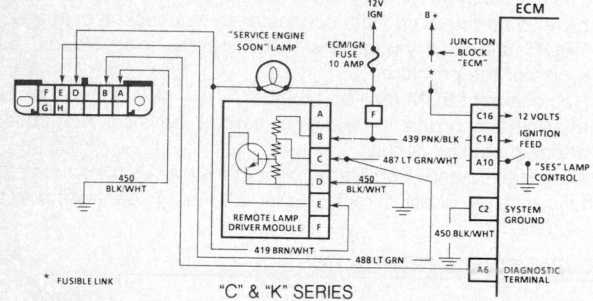

"C" & "K" SERIES

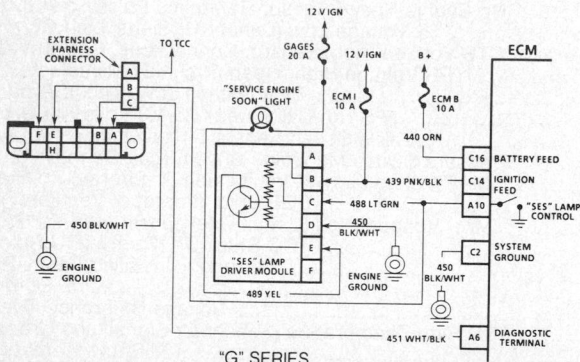

"G" SERIES

The ECM provides diagnostic logic to detect faults in Diesel Electronic Control (DEC) system. When ECM recognizes a fault, it turns on SERVICE ENGINE SOON light and stores codes. If condition is corrected, SERVICE ENGINE SOON light will go off. ECM recognizes errors in engine speed and EGR vacuum, as well as electrical faults involving 5-volt reference circuit. ECM controls the following:
- Exhaust Gas Recirculation (EGR)
- Exhaust Pressure Regulation (EPR)
- Torque Converter Clutch (TCC)
- System Diagnosis
- Cold Advance & Glow Plugs

To allow proper engine control, ECM monitors the following inputs:
- Engine RPM
- Manifold Absolute Pressure (MAP)
- Throttle Position Sensor (TPS)
- Vehicle Speed Sensor (VSS)
- Coolant Temperature Sensor (CTS)

Begin all diagnosis with diagnostic circuit check. After any DEC system repair, repeat diagnostic circuit check.

92B21759 90I13969 92E21760

NOTE: Test numbers refer to numbers on diagnostic chart.

1) This tests SERVICE ENGINE SOON light operation. With ignition on and engine off, light should be on.
2) Grounding ALDL diagnostic terminal "B" allows ECM to flash Code 12 and any stored codes. Light must flash on and off to be considered a proper code. If light just goes from bright to dim, it is not considered a code.

- ENGINE AT NORMAL OPERATING TEMPERATURE.
- MAKE PHYSICAL INSPECTION OF ENGINE COMPARTMENT.
- MAKE CERTAIN ALL ELECTRICAL COMPONENTS ARE CORRECTLY CONNECTED.
- CHECK ALL VACUUM HOSES THAT MAY BE DISCONNECTED, PINCHED OR BURNED.
- CHECK EGR VALVE FOR VACUUM LEAK AND FREE MOVEMENT.
- CHECK FOR PLUGGED EGR VENT FILTER AND REPLACE IF REQUIRED.

(1)
- KEY "ON," ENGINE STOPPED, DIAGNOSTIC TERMINAL NOT GROUNDED.
- NOTE "SERVICE ENGINE SOON" LIGHT.

| LIGHT "ON" STEADY | LIGHT FLASHES INTERMITTENTLY OR A CODE | LIGHT "OFF" |

(2)
GROUND DIAGNOSTIC TERMINAL AND NOTE "SERVICE ENGINE SOON" LIGHT

CHECK FOR GROUNDED CKT 451 TO ECM TERMINAL "A6". IF CKT OK, IT'S A FAULTY ECM.

SEE "SERVICE ENGINE SOON" LIGHT INOPERATIVE CHART

- FLASHES CODE 12 AND ANY OTHER CODE.
- REMOVE DIAGNOSTIC TERMINAL GROUND.
- START ENGINE, AND RUN FOR 2 MINUTES OR UNTIL THE "SERVICE ENGINE SOON" LIGHT COMES "ON."

DOES NOT FLASH CODE 12

GO TO "ECM CHECK" CHART

| NO LIGHT | "SERVICE ENGINE SOON" LIGHT "ON" |

NO LIGHT:
- CODE SYSTEM OK.
- KEY "OFF."
- INSTALL VACUUM GAGE IN PLACE OF EGR VALVE.
- START AND RUN ENGINE AT 850 RPM IN PARK OR NEUTRAL.
- NOTE VACUUM GAGE.

"SERVICE ENGINE SOON" LIGHT "ON":
- CHECK CODE.
- IF THERE IS CODE 51, 52, OR 53, GO TO THAT CODE CHART FIRST.
- FOR ANY OTHER CODE, START WITH LOWEST NUMBER CODE CHART.

| VACUUM ABOVE 41 kPa (12"). | VACUUM PULSES OR NO VACUUM |

VACUUM ABOVE 41 kPa (12"):
- VEHICLE IN PARK OR NEUTRAL.
- QUICKLY FLASH THROTTLE.
- OBSERVE VACUUM GAGE MOVEMENT.

VACUUM PULSES OR NO VACUUM:
CHECK VACUUM HOSE ROUTINGS FOR LEAKS OR RESTRICTIONS

| VACUUM GAGE DROPS FROM ABOVE 41 kPa (12") TO NEAR ZERO. | VACUUM GAGE DROPS ONLY ABOUT 1/2 DISTANCE FROM FULL VACUUM |

VACUUM GAGE DROPS FROM ABOVE 41 kPa (12") TO NEAR ZERO:
- KEY "OFF."
- RECONNECT EGR VACUUM HOSE.
- CONNECT VACUUM GAGE IN PLACE OF EPR VALVE.
- START ENGINE.
- OBSERVE VACUUM GAGE MOVEMENT.
- VACUUM SHOULD BE ABOVE 50 kPa (15"), WITH THE SOLENOID ELECTRICAL CONNECTOR IN PLACE, 0 kPa (0") WITH IT DISCONNECTED. IS IT?

VACUUM GAGE DROPS ONLY ABOUT 1/2 DISTANCE FROM FULL VACUUM:
CHECK VACUUM HOSE ROUTINGS FOR LEAKS OR RESTRICTIONS. IF OK, REPLACE THE EGR VENT SOLENOID FILTER.

| YES | NO |

YES:
ECM CONTROLS SYSTEM IS OK.

NO:
GO TO "EPR SOLENOID ELECTRICAL CHECK" CHART

SERVICE ENGINE SOON LIGHT INOPERATIVE

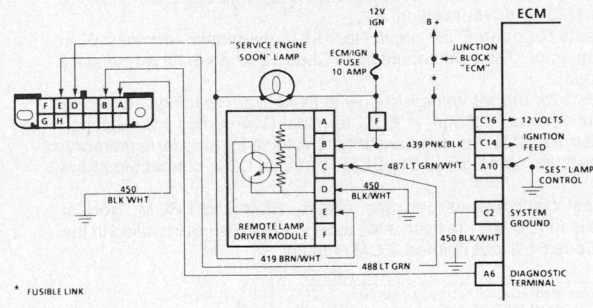

"C" & "K" SERIES

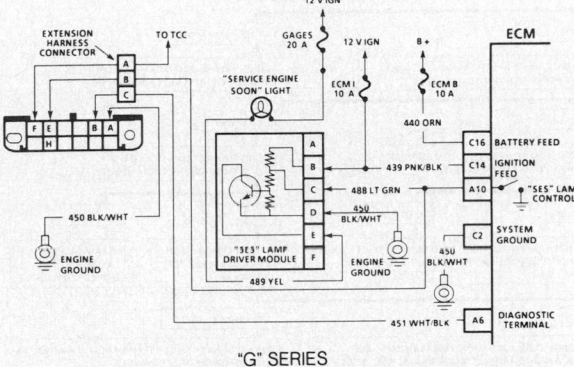

"G" SERIES

When engine is started, ECM grounds terminal A10 to turn off SERVICE ENGINE SOON light. When ALDL terminal "B" is grounded, ECM alternately grounds and opens terminal A10 to flash a code.

NOTE: Test numbers refer to numbers on diagnostic chart.

1) This tests for an open ECM fuse or an open in SERVICE ENGINE SOON light circuit, including instrument panel connector and printed circuit board. Light on is normal response.

2) This tests for a shorted ECM. A grounded ECM terminal A10 will cause SERVICE ENGINE SOON light to go off. If light comes on after disconnecting ECM, ECM is shorted. Light on is normal response.

3) This tests for a grounded circuit between terminal "C" of remote lamp driver and ECM terminal A10. It also checks for an open circuit No. 439 to terminal "B" of remote lamp driver module, a bad ground, or a faulty

remote lamp driver. Because of voltage drop through remote lamp driver upper resistor, a normal voltage reading should be **6-11 volts**. If voltage is greater than 11 volts, there is no voltage drop in remote lamp driver module due to bad ground or faulty module.

4) This tests for an open wire to remote lamp driver terminal "B". Normal reading should be close to battery voltage.

5) This tests for a grounded circuit between terminal "C" of remote lamp driver and ECM terminal A10. Light on is normal response.

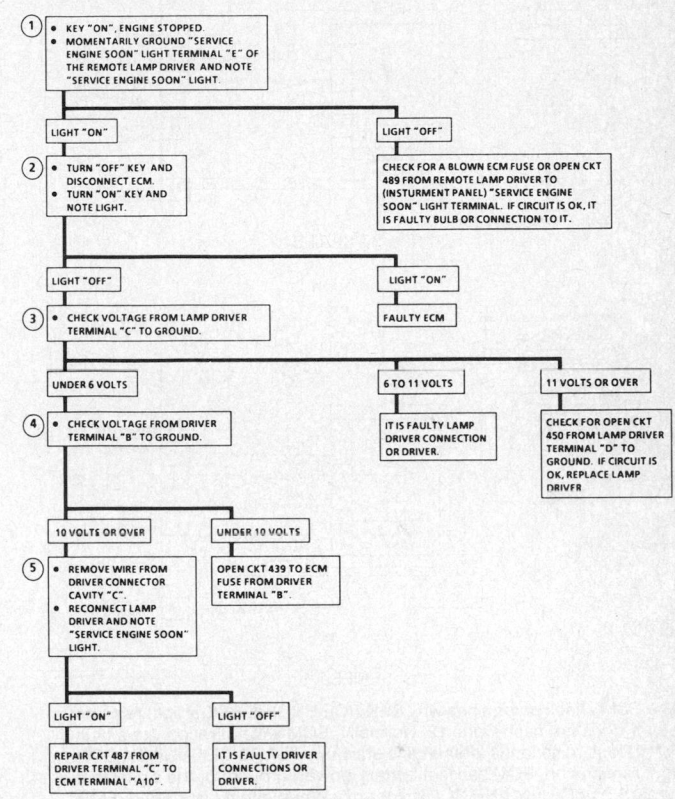

92B21759 90B13970 92E21760

Courtesy of General Motors Corp.

ECM CHECK, SERVICE ENGINE SOON LIGHT ON AT ALL TIMES OR WON'T FLASH CODE 12

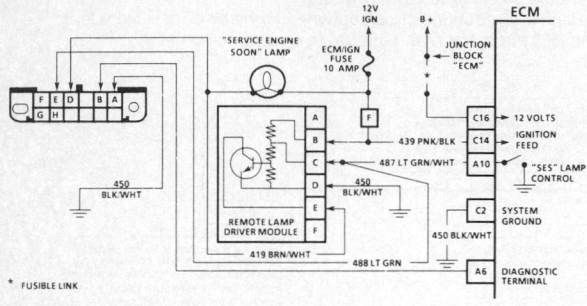

"C" & "K" SERIES

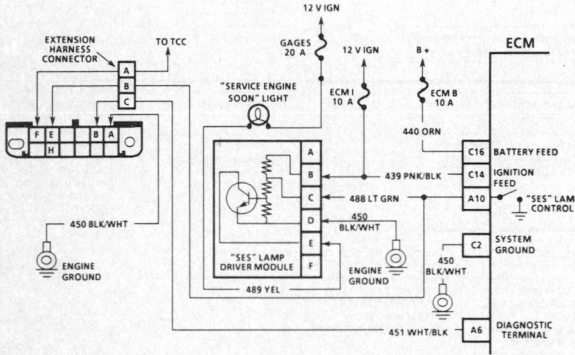

"G" SERIES

The ECM check determines why SERVICE ENGINE SOON light remains on, or does not flash Code 12. Normally, ECM will not recognize a fault for at least 10 seconds after engine start-up. If SERVICE ENGINE SOON light remains on, ECM has lost battery power, ground, or the signal that turns SERVICE ENGINE SOON light off. When engine is started, ECM grounds terminal A10 to turn off SERVICE ENGINE SOON light. ECM alternately grounds and opens terminal A10 to flash trouble code.

NOTE: Test numbers refer to numbers on diagnostic chart.

1) This tests for a short to battery voltage in wire to remote lamp driver terminal "C", or a faulty remote lamp driver. Normal reading is **9-11 volts**.
2) This tests if problem is related to ECM, or remote lamp driver. Normally, grounding remote lamp driver terminal "C" should turn light off. If light goes out when terminal "C" is grounded, problem is related to ECM and its wiring. If light does not go out, problem is related to remote lamp driver and its wiring.

3) Normally, grounding ECM terminal A10 should turn light off. If light stays on, there is an open in circuit between ECM harness terminal A10 and remote lamp driver terminal "C".
4) This tests for open ECM circuit No. 451 to diagnostic terminal "B" in ALDL connector. The light should flash Code 12 when ECM terminal A6 is grounded.
5) This tests for proper voltage supply to ECM. Both readings should be more than **9 volts**. Voltage to ECM terminal C14 comes from ignition switch. Terminal C16 has constant battery voltage for long term memory.
6) This tests for a bad ground to ECM. Terminal C2 is connected in the ECM.
7) This test distinguishes between a faulty ECM and PROM. Normal response is for Code 51 to flash even though PROM is not installed in the ECM. If Code 51 is not flashed, ECM is faulty.

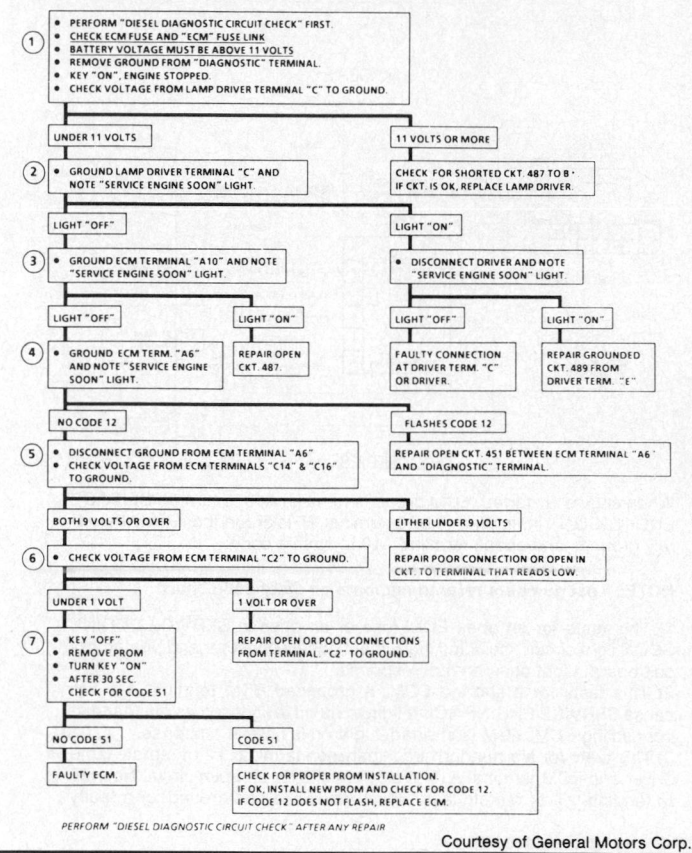

PERFORM "DIESEL DIAGNOSTIC CIRCUIT CHECK" AFTER ANY REPAIR

92B21759 90C13971 92E21760

Courtesy of General Motors Corp.

* FUSIBLE LINK

EPR SOLENOID ELECTRICAL CHECK

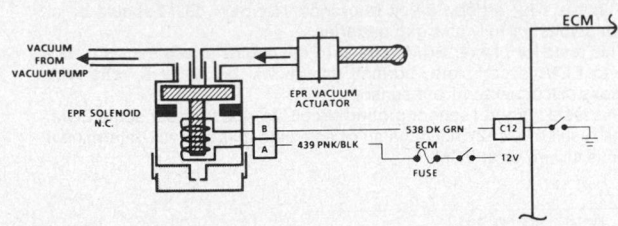

The Exhaust Pressure Regulation (EPR) solenoid controls vacuum to EPR valve. When energized, EPR solenoid allows vacuum to close EPR valve, increasing exhaust backpressure for proper EGR operation. The solenoid is supplied with 12 volts by ignition switch. ECM completes ground circuit to energize solenoid, and turn EPR on when needed (EGR operation command).

NOTE: Test numbers refer to numbers on diagnostic chart.

1) This tests for short to ground, or a faulty ECM signal to EPR solenoid. Test light should normally be off.
2) This tests for signal to energize EPR solenoid with engine at idle. If test light is on, electrical circuits to solenoid are okay.
3) This tests for voltage, or open circuit from terminal "B" of EPR solenoid to ECM terminal C12.

* PERFORM DIESEL DIAGNOSTIC CHECK FIRST.
* CHECK FOR PLUGGED EGR VENT FILTER.

(1)
* KEY "ON" AND ENGINE "OFF."
* DISCONNECT EPR SOLENOID CONNECTOR.
* CONNECT TEST LIGHT ACROSS CONNECTOR TERMINALS.
* NOTE TEST LIGHT. LIGHT SHOULD BE "OFF." IS IT?

YES / NO

(2)
* START ENGINE.
* NOTE LIGHT AT IDLE.
* LIGHT SHOULD BE "ON." IS IT?

* CHECK FOR GROUND IN CKT 538. IF NOT GROUNDED: ⚠
* REPLACE ECM.

NO / YES

(3)
* CONNECT TEST LIGHT FROM CONNECTOR TERMINAL "A" (PNK/BLK) TO GROUND.

* ELECTRICAL CIRCUIT OK.
* REINSTALL CONNECTOR.

* SEE EPR VACUUM CHECK CHART.

TEST LIGHT "ON" / TEST LIGHT "OFF"

* CHECK FOR OPEN IN CKT 538. IF NOT OPEN:
* CHECK FOR POOR CONTACT AT ECM TERMINAL "C12."
* IF GOOD CONTACT, REPLACE ECM. ⚠

* REPAIR OPEN IN CKT 439

⚠ PRIOR TO REPLACING ECM, CHECK RESISTANCE OF APPLICABLE SOLENOID. IF UNDER 20 OHMS, ALSO REPLACE SOLENOID.

Courtesy of General Motors Corp.

92J21781 90D13972

EPR VACUUM CIRCUIT CHECK

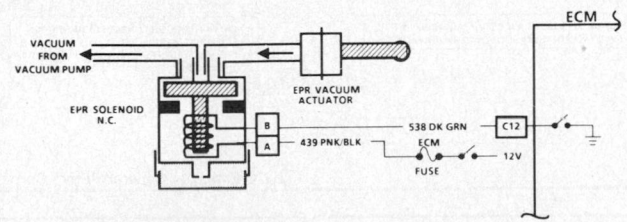

The Exhaust Pressure Regulation (EPR) solenoid controls vacuum to EPR valve. When energized, EPR solenoid allows vacuum to close EPR valve, increasing exhaust backpressure for proper EGR operation.

NOTE: Test numbers refer to numbers on diagnostic chart.

1) This tests for normal EPR vacuum at idle. Since electrical circuit was already proven okay in EPR SOLENOID ELECTRICAL CHECK chart, absence of vacuum is due to no vacuum source (vacuum pump), or a restriction or leak in vacuum hose to valve, including a leak in solenoid.
2) EPR solenoid is de-energized, no vacuum should be present.
3) This tests for normal operation of EPR valve. When vacuum is applied to vacuum valve, valve actuator should move and hold.

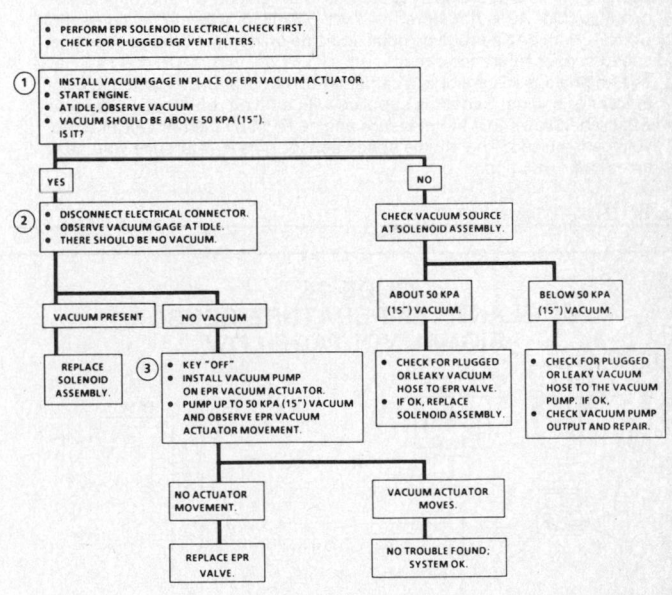

* PERFORM EPR SOLENOID ELECTRICAL CHECK FIRST.
* CHECK FOR PLUGGED EGR VENT FILTERS.

(1)
* INSTALL VACUUM GAGE IN PLACE OF EPR VACUUM ACTUATOR.
* START ENGINE.
* AT IDLE, OBSERVE VACUUM
* VACUUM SHOULD BE ABOVE 50 KPA (15"). IS IT?

YES / NO

(2)
* DISCONNECT ELECTRICAL CONNECTOR.
* OBSERVE VACUUM GAGE AT IDLE.
* THERE SHOULD BE NO VACUUM.

CHECK VACUUM SOURCE AT SOLENOID ASSEMBLY.

VACUUM PRESENT / NO VACUUM

ABOUT 50 KPA (15") VACUUM. / BELOW 50 KPA (15") VACUUM.

REPLACE SOLENOID ASSEMBLY.

(3)
* KEY "OFF"
* INSTALL VACUUM PUMP ON EPR VACUUM ACTUATOR.
* PUMP UP TO 50 KPA (15") VACUUM AND OBSERVE EPR VACUUM ACTUATOR MOVEMENT.

* CHECK FOR PLUGGED OR LEAKY VACUUM HOSE TO EPR VALVE.
* IF OK, REPLACE SOLENOID ASSEMBLY.

* CHECK FOR PLUGGED OR LEAKY VACUUM HOSE TO THE VACUUM PUMP. IF OK,
* CHECK VACUUM PUMP OUTPUT AND REPAIR.

NO ACTUATOR MOVEMENT. / VACUUM ACTUATOR MOVES.

REPLACE EPR VALVE. / NO TROUBLE FOUND; SYSTEM OK.

Courtesy of General Motors Corp.

92J21781 90E13973

CODE 12,
NO REFERENCE PULSE

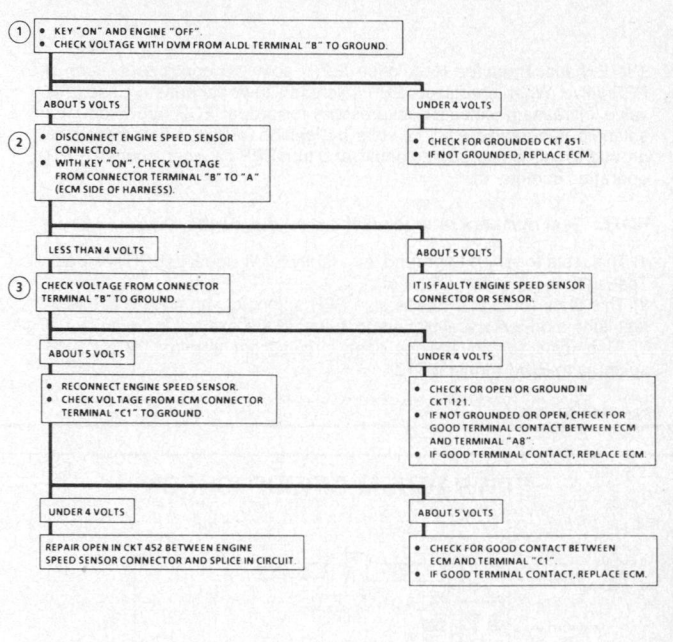

"C" & "K" SERIES

"G" SERIES

Code 12 indicates ECM is on, and sees no reference pulse from engine speed sensor. Code display is normal with ignition on and engine not running. Code 12 is not stored and will only flash when fault is present. Code 12 with engine running could indicate an open or ground in engine speed sensor reference circuit.

The engine speed sensor is a camshaft-driven pick-up, mounted at center rear of engine. Sensor is supplied with a 5-volt reference voltage by ECM, and allows ECM to measure engine RPM by the number of times voltage is pulsed. The engine speed sensor pulses reference voltage 4 times per revolution.

92H21771 92A21782 90F13974

NOTE: Test numbers refer to numbers on diagnostic chart.

1) This tests for a good 5-volt reference. Normally, ECM should be at about 5 volts for fully charged batteries.

2) This tests for proper ECM voltage to the engine speed sensor. If circuit to ECM is complete, normal voltage will be about **5 volts** with harness disconnected from sensor.

3) This tests for good sensor ground circuit No. 452 from sensor to ECM. Since result of test **2)** indicates an open exists, this test will determine if open is in wire or at ECM.

Courtesy of General Motors Corp.

CODE 14,
COOLANT TEMPERATURE SENSOR
SIGNAL VOLTAGE LOW

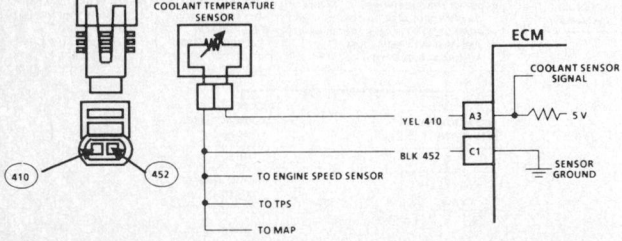

The coolant temperature sensor uses a thermistor to control signal voltage to ECM. The ECM applies and monitors voltage over circuit No. 410 to sensor. When engine is cold, sensor resistance is high. The ECM will sense a high signal voltage. As engine warms, sensor resistance becomes less and voltage drops. At normal engine operating temperature, voltage will be **1.5-2.0 volts**.

NOTE: Test numbers refer to numbers on diagnostic chart.

1) Code 14 will set if signal voltage indicates a coolant temperature greater than 275°F (135°C) for 3 minutes.

2) This test determines if circuit No. 410 is shorted to ground, causing conditions for Code 14.

DIAGNOSTIC AIDS

Check circuit No. 410 routing for a potential short to circuit No. 452, or ground. Scan tester displays engine temperature in degrees Celsius. After starting engine, temperature should rise to about 90°C and stabilize when thermostat opens. Test coolant sensor at various temperature levels. See COOLANT SENSOR TEMPERATURE TO RESISTANCE VALUES chart. An out-of-calibration sensor can cause poor driveability.

90I18844 90G13975

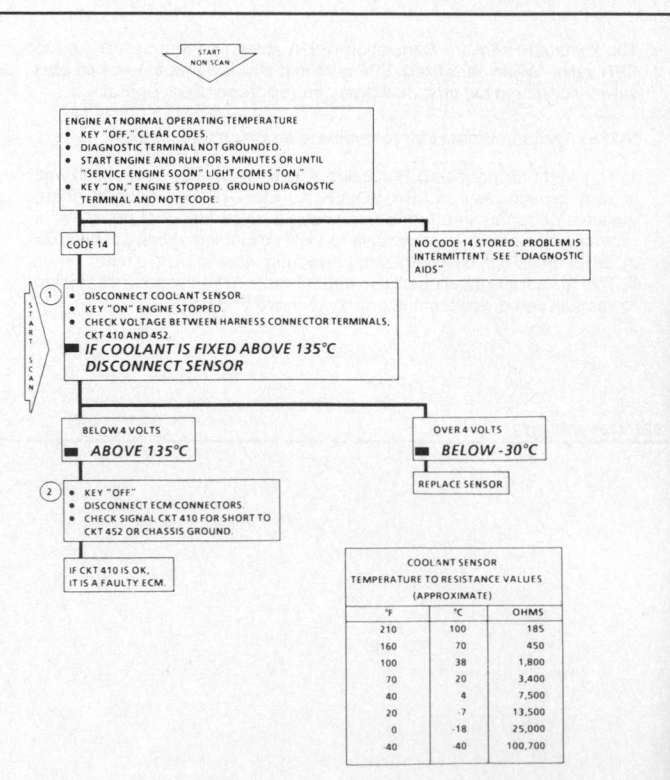

COOLANT SENSOR TEMPERATURE TO RESISTANCE VALUES (APPROXIMATE)		
°F	°C	OHMS
210	100	185
160	70	450
100	38	1,800
70	20	3,400
40	4	7,500
20	-7	13,500
0	-18	25,000
-40	-40	100,700

CLEAR CODES AND CONFIRM NO "SERVICE ENGINE SOON" LIGHT

Courtesy of General Motors Corp.

CODE 15, COOLANT TEMPERATURE SENSOR SIGNAL VOLTAGE HIGH

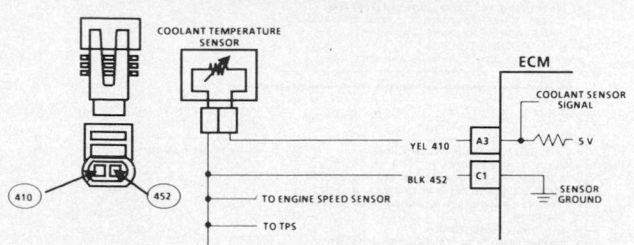

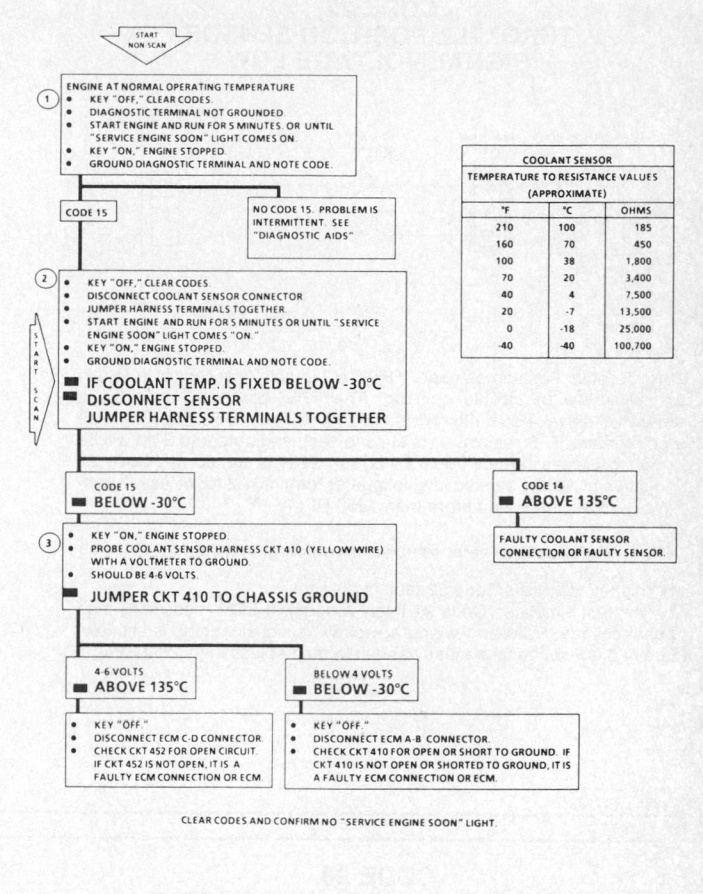

COOLANT SENSOR TEMPERATURE TO RESISTANCE VALUES (APPROXIMATE)		
°F	°C	OHMS
210	100	185
160	70	450
100	38	1,800
70	20	3,400
40	4	7,500
20	-7	13,500
0	-18	25,000
-40	-40	100,700

The coolant temperature sensor uses a thermistor which controls signal voltage to the ECM. The ECM applies and monitors voltage over circuit No. 410 to sensor. When engine is cold, sensor resistance is high. The ECM will sense a high signal voltage. As engine warms, sensor resistance reduces and voltage drops. At normal engine operating temperature, voltage should be **1.5-2.0 volts**.

NOTE: Test numbers refer to numbers on diagnostic chart.

1) Code 15 will set if engine has run for more than 5 minutes and coolant temperature is less than –22°F (–30°C).
2) This test simulates Code 14. If ECM recognizes low signal voltage (high temperature), and scan tester reads 130°C or greater, ECM and wiring are okay.
3) This test determines if circuit No. 410 is open. Voltage at sensor connector should be **5 volts** when measured with a DVOM.

DIAGNOSTIC AIDS

Scan tester displays engine temperature in degrees Celsius. After starting engine, temperature should rise to about 90°C and stabilize when thermostat opens. If Code 12 or 21 is also set, check circuit No. 452 for faulty wiring or connections. Check terminals at sensor connector. Test COOLANT SENSOR TEMPERATURE TO RESISTANCE VALUES chart. An out-of-calibration sensor can cause poor driveability.

90I18844 90H13976

Courtesy of General Motors Corp.

CODE 21, THROTTLE POSITION SENSOR SIGNAL VOLTAGE HIGH

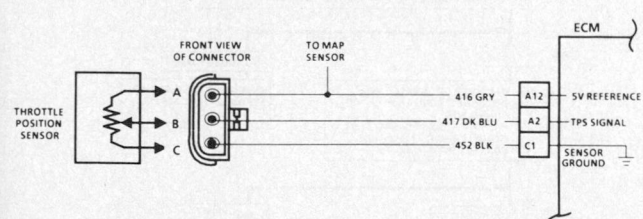

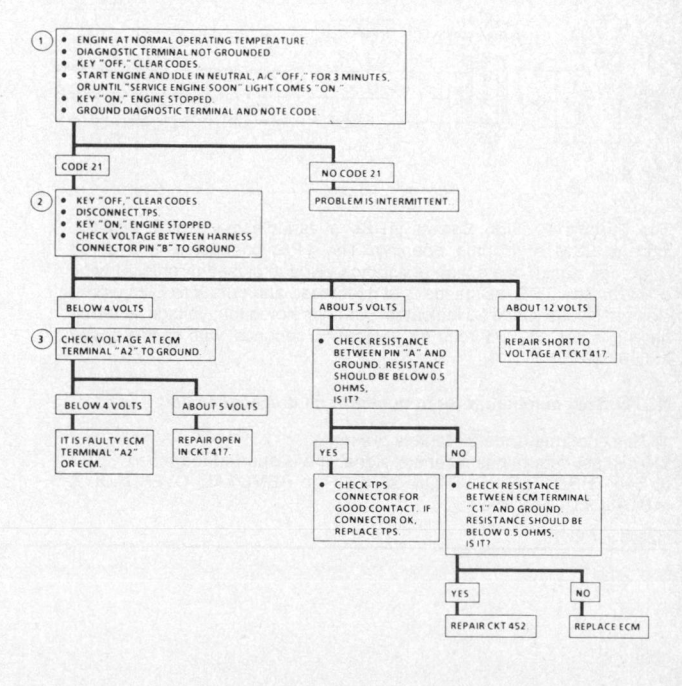

The Throttle Position Sensor (TPS), a variable mechanical resistor, informs ECM of throttle opening. The TPS, connected to a 5-volt reference signal, has a high resistance value at closed throttle. At wide open throttle, TPS resistance is at its lowest, and output to ECM will be close to 5 volts. When Code 21 is set, EPR is turned off. Code 21 indicates ECM has sensed high voltage at terminal A2 for at least 2 minutes, with engine speed less than 1120 RPM.

NOTE: Test numbers refer to numbers on diagnostic chart.

1) This test confirms Code 21 fault is present.
2) This tests for 5-volt reference signal at TPS harness connector, and separates an electrical circuit problem from a faulty TPS. If circuit is okay, normal voltage reading will be **5 volts**.
3) This checks if low reference voltage is due to an open wire, or ECM.

90J18845 90I13977

Courtesy of General Motors Corp.

CODE 22,
THROTTLE POSITION SENSOR SIGNAL VOLTAGE LOW

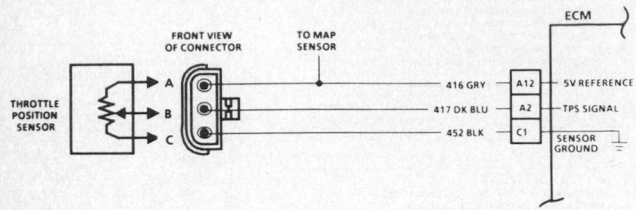

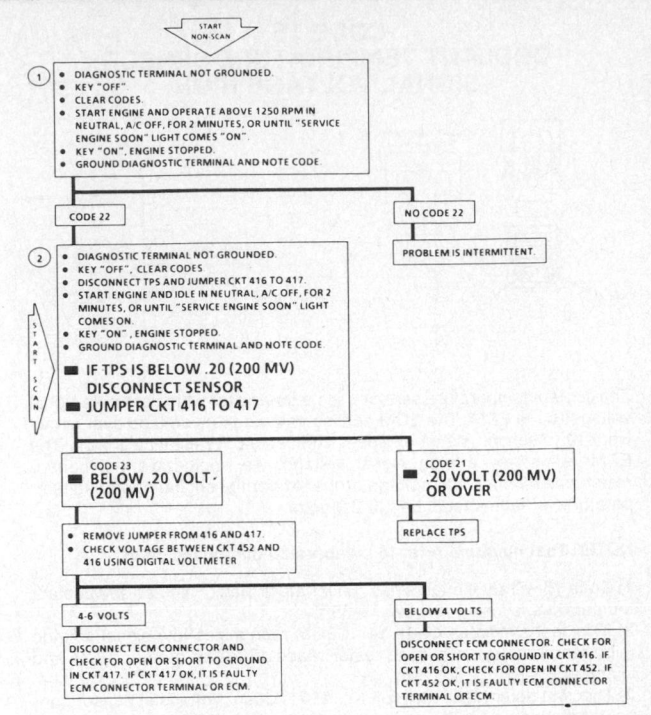

The Throttle Position Sensor (TPS), a variable mechanical resistor, informs ECM of throttle opening. The TPS, connected to a 5-volt reference signal, has a high resistance value at closed throttle. At wide open throttle, TPS resistance is at its lowest, and output to ECM will be close to 5 volts. When Code 21 is set, EPR is turned off. Code 22 indicates ECM has sensed low voltage at terminal A2 for at least 2 minutes, with engine speed more than 1250 RPM.

NOTE: Test numbers refer to numbers on diagnostic chart.

1) This test confirms Code 22 fault is present.
2) This test simulates Code 21 (high voltage). If ECM recognizes high signal voltage, ECM and wiring are okay. If signal voltage is still low, Code 23 will set because test was performed at less than 1250 RPM.

CLEAR CODES AND CONFIRM "CLOSED LOOP" OPERATION AND NO "SERVICE ENGINE SOON" LIGHT.

90J18845 90J13978

Courtesy of General Motors Corp.

CODE 23,
THROTTLE POSITION SENSOR MISADJUSTED

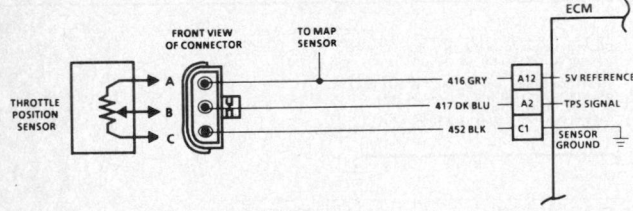

The Throttle Position Sensor (TPS), a variable mechanical resistor, informs ECM of throttle opening. The TPS, connected to a 5-volt reference signal, has a high resistance value at closed throttle. At wide open throttle, TPS resistance is at its lowest, and output to ECM will be close to 5 volts. Code 23 indicates ECM has noted that voltage, at terminal A2, is not .25-1.35 volts for at least 30 seconds, with engine speed at 550-650 RPM.

NOTE: Test numbers refer to numbers on diagnostic chart.

1) This confirms Code 23 fault is present.
2) This test determines if sensor signal line is shorted to ground.
3) See THROTTLE POSITION SENSOR in REMOVAL, OVERHAUL & INSTALLATION article.

90J18845 90A13979

DIAGNOSTIC AIDS

Disregard Code 23 if SERVICE ENGINE SOON light goes out when throttle is returned to idle.

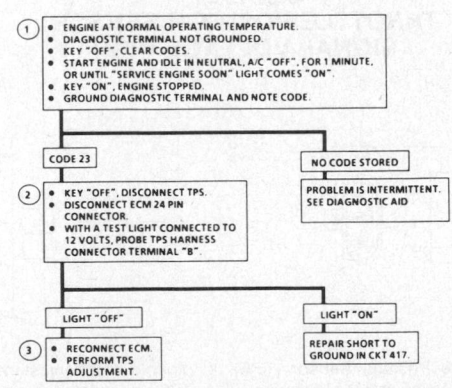

Courtesy of General Motors Corp.

CODE 24,
VEHICLE SPEED SENSOR CIRCUIT

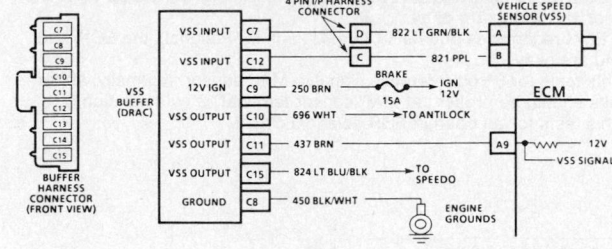

"C" & "K" SERIES

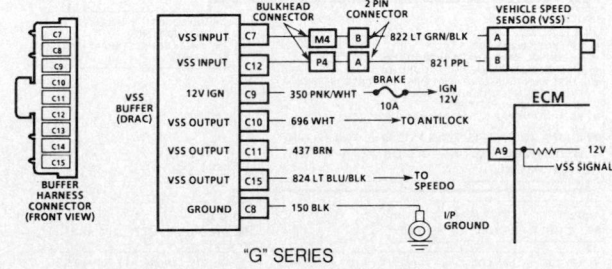

"G" SERIES

The ECM applies and monitors 12 volts on circuit No. 437. Circuit No. 437 connects to Digital Ratio Adapter Controller (DRAC), which alternately grounds and opens circuit No. 437 when drive wheels are turning. The circuit is opened and closed approximately 2000 times per mile when drive wheels are turning. ECM calculates vehicle speed based on the time between pulses. Scan tester reading should closely match speedometer reading with drive wheels turning.

Code 24 will set after the following conditions are met for at least 10 seconds: circuit No. 437 is constant, engine speed is more than 2000 RPM, vehicle speed signal at ECM terminal A9 is less than 5 MPH.

NOTE: Test numbers refer to numbers on diagnostic chart.

1) This test monitors ECM voltage on circuit No. 437. With wheels turning, the pulsating action causes varying voltage. Voltage variation will be greater at low wheel speeds, and an average of 4-6 volts at about 20 MPH.

2) Less than one volt at ECM connector indicates circuit No. 437 wire is shorted to ground. Disconnect circuit No. 437 at DRAC. If voltage now reads more than 10 volts, the DRAC is faulty. If voltage remains less than 10 volts, then circuit No. 437 wire is grounded. If circuit No. 437 is not grounded, check for a faulty ECM connector or ECM.

3) A steady 8-12 volts reading at the ECM connector indicates that circuit No. 437 is open or DRAC is faulty.

4) Normal voltage indicates a possible intermittent condition.

DIAGNOSTIC AIDS

With drive wheels turning, scan tester and speedometer reading should closely match.

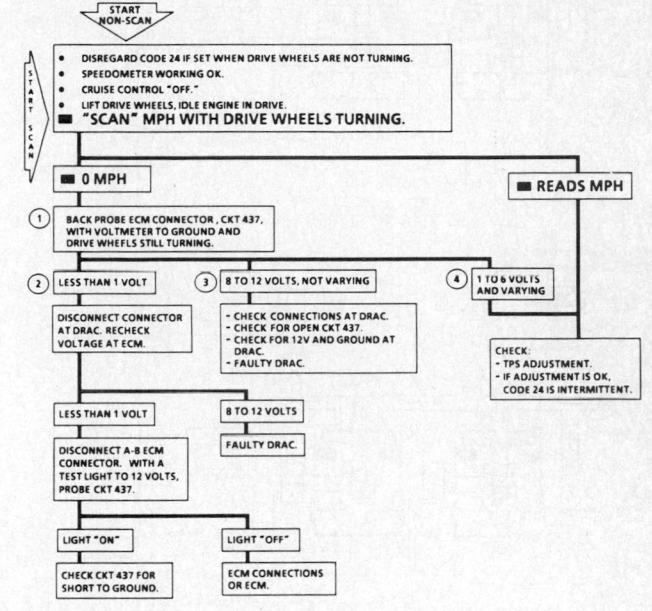

CODE 31,
MANIFOLD ABSOLUTE PRESSURE
SENSOR SIGNAL VOLTAGE LOW

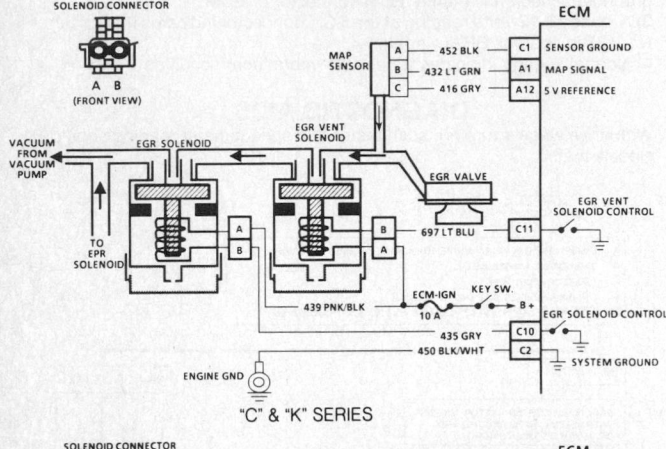

SOLENOID CONNECTOR

"C" & "K" SERIES

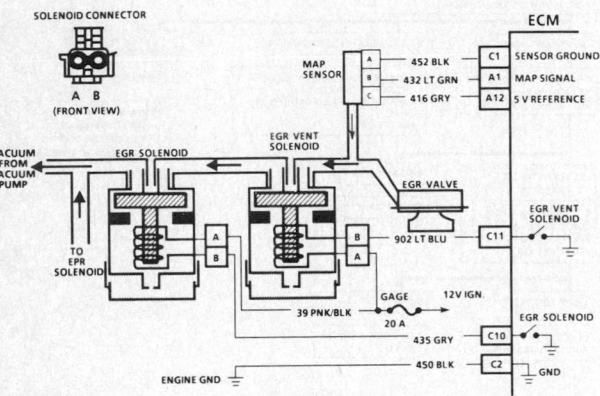

SOLENOID CONNECTOR

"G" SERIES

The Manifold Absolute Pressure (MAP) sensor monitors vacuum in EGR circuit. It senses actual vacuum in EGR vacuum line and sends a signal back to ECM. The signal is compared to EGR duty cycle calculated by ECM. If there is a difference in ECM command and what vacuum is at EGR valve as sensed by MAP sensor, ECM makes minor adjustments. When a major difference is sensed, ECM recognizes a fault and sends a full EGR signal.

NOTE: Test numbers refer to numbers on diagnostic chart.

1) This confirms Code 31 fault is present.
2) If ECM recognizes and sets Code 33 (high MAP signal), the ECM, MAP sensor and wiring are okay.
3) If ECM recognizes and sets Code 33 (high MAP signal), the ECM and wiring are okay.
4) This tests for 5-volt reference signal to MAP sensor. Normally, about 5 volts should be present at MAP sensor terminal "C" with ignition on.
5) This tests for an open in EGR solenoid circuit.

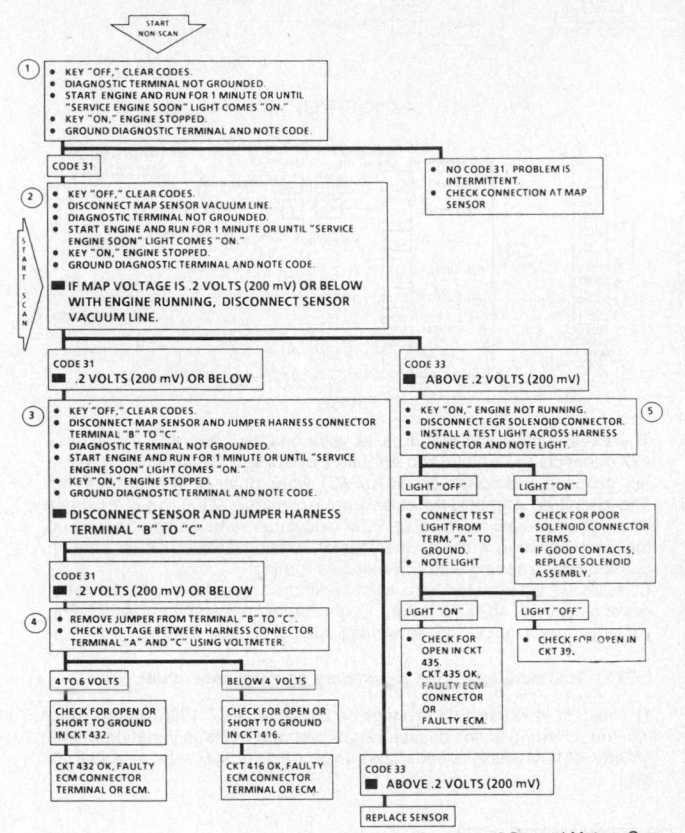

Courtesy of General Motors Corp.

CODE 32,
EGR CIRCUIT LOOP ERROR

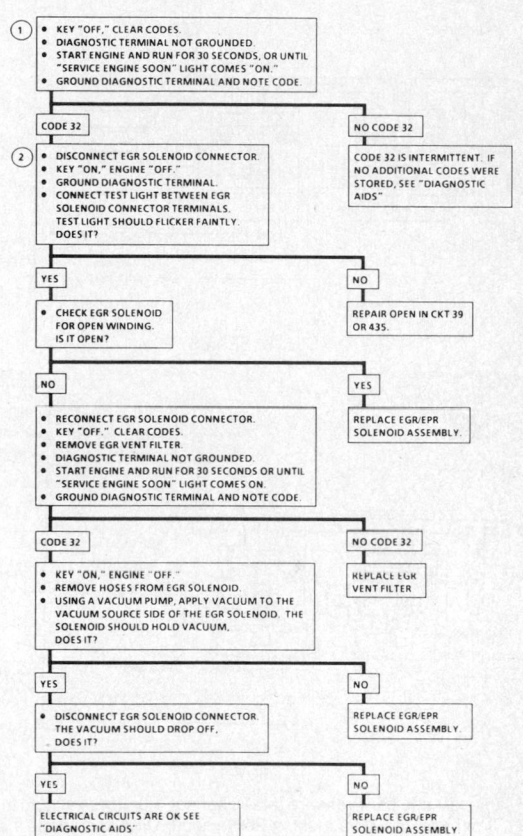

"C" & "K" SERIES

"G" SERIES

During normal operation, the ECM compares its EGR duty cycle signal with Manifold Absolute Pressure (MAP) signal and makes adjustments in duty cycle. If actual EGR control pressure (line vacuum) varies from what ECM has previously determined pressure should be, and this variance continues for 10 seconds or more, a Code 32 will be set and ECM will shut down EGR.

NOTE: Test numbers refer to numbers on diagnostic chart.

1) This determines if Code 32 can reset.
2) This tests EGR solenoid electrical control circuit. Test light should flicker faintly if ECM harness and connections are okay. A faintly flickering light is a slightly pulsating glow as opposed to a bright steady glow from a continuous ground path.

DIAGNOSTIC AIDS

A vacuum leak may cause a Code 32. Check all vacuum hoses and components connected to vacuum hoses for leaks. Also check cruise control and A/C systems vacuum hoses and components.

① • KEY "OFF," CLEAR CODES.
• DIAGNOSTIC TERMINAL NOT GROUNDED.
• START ENGINE AND RUN FOR 30 SECONDS, OR UNTIL "SERVICE ENGINE SOON" LIGHT COMES "ON."
• GROUND DIAGNOSTIC TERMINAL AND NOTE CODE.

CODE 32

NO CODE 32

② • DISCONNECT EGR SOLENOID CONNECTOR.
• KEY "ON," ENGINE "OFF."
• GROUND DIAGNOSTIC TERMINAL.
• CONNECT TEST LIGHT BETWEEN EGR SOLENOID CONNECTOR TERMINALS. TEST LIGHT SHOULD FLICKER FAINTLY. DOES IT?

CODE 32 IS INTERMITTENT. IF NO ADDITIONAL CODES WERE STORED, SEE "DIAGNOSTIC AIDS"

YES

NO

• CHECK EGR SOLENOID FOR OPEN WINDING. IS IT OPEN?

REPAIR OPEN IN CKT 39 OR 435.

NO

YES

• RECONNECT EGR SOLENOID CONNECTOR.
• KEY "OFF," CLEAR CODES.
• REMOVE EGR VENT FILTER.
• DIAGNOSTIC TERMINAL NOT GROUNDED.
• START ENGINE AND RUN FOR 30 SECONDS OR UNTIL "SERVICE ENGINE SOON" LIGHT COMES ON.
• GROUND DIAGNOSTIC TERMINAL AND NOTE CODE.

REPLACE EGR/EPR SOLENOID ASSEMBLY.

CODE 32

NO CODE 32

• KEY "ON," ENGINE "OFF."
• REMOVE HOSES FROM EGR SOLENOID.
• USING A VACUUM PUMP, APPLY VACUUM TO THE VACUUM SOURCE SIDE OF THE EGR SOLENOID. THE SOLENOID SHOULD HOLD VACUUM. DOES IT?

REPLACE EGR VENT FILTER

YES

NO

• DISCONNECT EGR SOLENOID CONNECTOR. THE VACUUM SHOULD DROP OFF. DOES IT?

REPLACE EGR/EPR SOLENOID ASSEMBLY.

YES

NO

ELECTRICAL CIRCUITS ARE OK SEE "DIAGNOSTIC AIDS"

REPLACE EGR/EPR SOLENOID ASSEMBLY

92A21774 91F13636 91D13634

CODE 33,
MANIFOLD ABSOLUTE PRESSURE
SENSOR SIGNAL VOLTAGE HIGH

CHECK FOR POOR CONNECTION, PLUGGED, DISCONNECTED, OR LEAKING MAP SENSOR VACUUM HOSE. REPAIR AS REQUIRED.

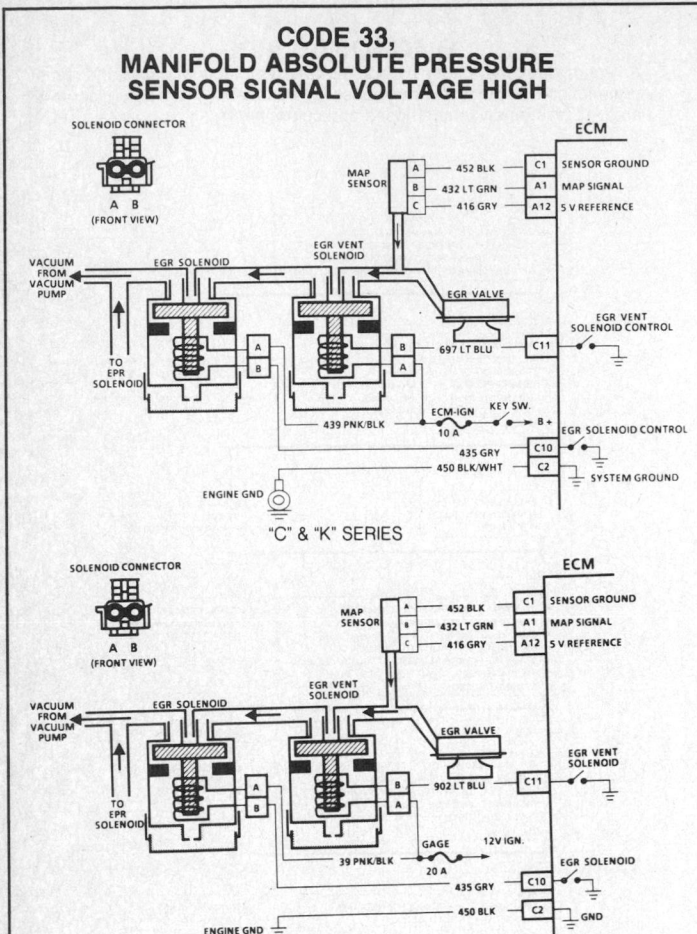

"C" & "K" SERIES

"G" SERIES

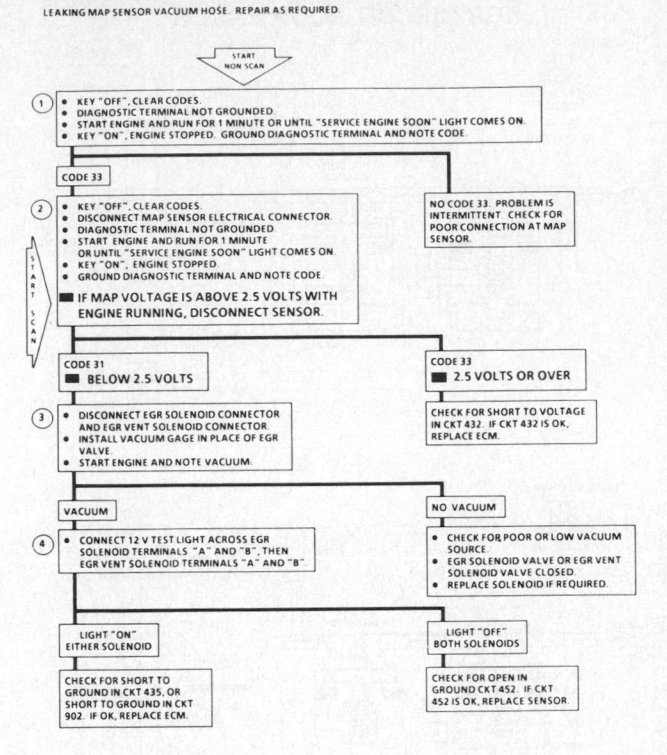

START NON SCAN

① • KEY "OFF", CLEAR CODES.
• DIAGNOSTIC TERMINAL NOT GROUNDED.
• START ENGINE AND RUN FOR 1 MINUTE OR UNTIL "SERVICE ENGINE SOON" LIGHT COMES ON.
• KEY "ON", ENGINE STOPPED. GROUND DIAGNOSTIC TERMINAL AND NOTE CODE.

CODE 33

② • KEY "OFF", CLEAR CODES.
• DISCONNECT MAP SENSOR ELECTRICAL CONNECTOR.
• DIAGNOSTIC TERMINAL NOT GROUNDED.
• START ENGINE AND RUN FOR 1 MINUTE OR UNTIL "SERVICE ENGINE SOON" LIGHT COMES ON.
• KEY "ON", ENGINE STOPPED.
• GROUND DIAGNOSTIC TERMINAL AND NOTE CODE.
■ IF MAP VOLTAGE IS ABOVE 2.5 VOLTS WITH ENGINE RUNNING, DISCONNECT SENSOR.

START SCAN

NO CODE 33: PROBLEM IS INTERMITTENT. CHECK FOR POOR CONNECTION AT MAP SENSOR.

CODE 31
■ BELOW 2.5 VOLTS

CODE 33
■ 2.5 VOLTS OR OVER

CHECK FOR SHORT TO VOLTAGE IN CKT 432. IF CKT 432 IS OK, REPLACE ECM.

③ • DISCONNECT EGR SOLENOID CONNECTOR AND EGR VENT SOLENOID CONNECTOR.
• INSTALL VACUUM GAGE IN PLACE OF EGR VALVE.
• START ENGINE AND NOTE VACUUM.

VACUUM

NO VACUUM
• CHECK FOR POOR OR LOW VACUUM SOURCE.
• EGR SOLENOID VALVE OR EGR VENT SOLENOID VALVE CLOSED.
• REPLACE SOLENOID IF REQUIRED.

④ • CONNECT 12 V TEST LIGHT ACROSS EGR SOLENOID TERMINALS "A" AND "B", THEN EGR VENT SOLENOID TERMINALS "A" AND "B".

LIGHT "ON"
EITHER SOLENOID

CHECK FOR SHORT TO GROUND IN CKT 435, OR SHORT TO GROUND IN CKT 902. IF OK, REPLACE ECM.

LIGHT "OFF"
BOTH SOLENOIDS

CHECK FOR OPEN IN GROUND CKT 452. IF CKT 452 IS OK, REPLACE SENSOR.

CLEAR CODES AND CONFIRM NO "SERVICE ENGINE SOON" LIGHT WITH ENGINE RUNNING.

The Manifold Absolute Pressure (MAP) sensor monitors vacuum in EGR circuit. It senses actual vacuum in EGR vacuum line and sends a signal back to ECM. The signal is compared to EGR duty cycle calculated by ECM. If there is a difference in ECM command and what vacuum is at EGR valve as sensed by MAP sensor, the ECM makes minor adjustments. When a major difference is sensed, the ECM recognizes a fault and sends a full EGR signal.

NOTE: Test numbers refer to numbers on diagnostic chart.

1) This step confirms Code 33 fault is present.
2) If ECM recognizes and sets Code 33 (low MAP signal), ECM and wiring are okay.
3) This determines if solenoids are stuck closed.
4) This determines whether a short circuit to ground exists in solenoid circuit, or if ECM is faulty.

92A21774 90G13983 91D13634

CODE 51,
PROM PROBLEM

Ensure all pins are fully inserted in socket. If pins are fully inserted, replace PROM and recheck. If problem is not corrected, replace ECM.

- CHECK THAT ALL PINS ARE FULLY INSERTED IN THE SOCKET.
- IF OK, REPLACE PROM AND RECHECK.
- IF PROBLEM NOT CORRECTED, REPLACE ECM.

CODE 52,
ECM FAULT

Ensure ECM connectors are fully inserted. Clear ECM memory. Start engine and check for SERVICE ENGINE SOON light. If light and Code 52 reappear, replace ECM. After repairs, clear ECM memory to confirm no SERVICE ENGINE SOON light.

- CHECK THAT ECM CONNECTORS ARE FULLY INSERTED.
- CLEAR MEMORY.
- START ENGINE AND CHECK FOR "SERVICE ENGINE SOON" LIGHT.
- IF LIGHT REAPPEARS, AND CODE 52, REPLACE ECM.

CODE 53,
VOLTAGE REFERENCE OVERLOAD

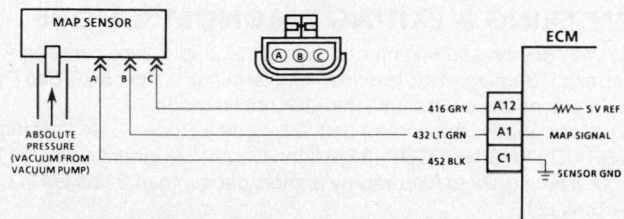

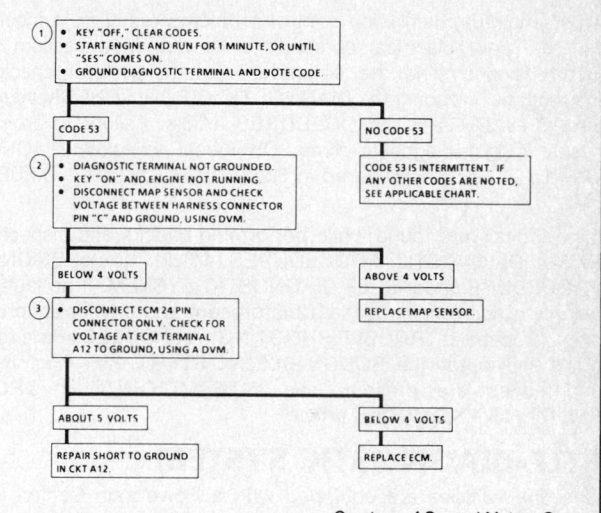

The 5-volt reference circuit is overloaded (grounded circuit). It takes 10 seconds before Code 53 will set.

NOTE: **Test numbers refer to numbers on diagnostic chart.**

1) This confirms Code 53 is still present.
2) This confirms 5-volt reference signal from ECM.
3) This tests if a short circuit to ground exists in circuit No. 416 or ECM.

92B21783 90H13984

Courtesy of General Motors Corp.

Commercial Van, Sierra, Suburban, Van, "C" & "K" Series Blazer & Pickup

INTRODUCTION

On gasoline vehicles with the 4L80-E transmission, transmission is controlled by the Powertrain Control Module (PCM). PCM controls other vehicle functions as well as the transmission. Electronic transmission is controlled by the Transmission Control Module (TCM) on diesel vehicles. TCM controls no other components. The PCM/TCM monitors a number of engine/vehicle functions and uses the data to control shift solenoid "A", shift solenoid "B", TCC, and the force motor to regulate TCC engagement, upshift pattern, downshift pattern and line pressure (shift quality).

Most engine/transmission control problems result from mechanical failures, poor electrical connections or damaged vacuum hoses. Before condemning the computer system, perform checks and inspections, including the DIAGNOSTIC CIRCUIT CHECK, covered in BASIC DIAGNOSTIC PROCEDURES article. Failure to do so may result in lost diagnostic time. On diesel vehicles, DIAGNOSTIC CIRCUIT CHECK is covered in SELF-DIAGNOSTICS – DIESEL article.

If no faults were found while performing checks and inspections in BASIC DIAGNOSTIC PROCEDURES article, go to DIAGNOSTIC PROCEDURE under SELF-DIAGNOSTIC SYSTEM. If no fault codes or only a non-running Code 12 is present and driveability problems exist, proceed to TROUBLE SHOOTING – NO CODES article for diagnosis by symptom (i.e. ROUGH IDLE, NO START, etc.). If only intermittent codes are present, see INTERMITTENTS in TROUBLE SHOOTING – NO CODES article.

SELF-DIAGNOSTIC SYSTEM

Gasoline vehicles are equipped with a Powertrain Control Module (PCM). The PCM controls engine/emission functions, and electronic-controlled transmission functions. For additional information on self-diagnostic system for gasoline vehicles, see THEORY & OPERATION and SELF-DIAGNOSTICS – GASOLINE articles.

Diesel vehicles are equipped with a Transmission Control Module (TCM). TCM controls only the electronic transmission. Unless specifically stated otherwise, references to PCM also apply to TCM-equipped vehicles.

Control module is equipped with a self-diagnostic system, which detects system failures or abnormalities. When a malfunction occurs, control module will illuminate the SERVICE ENGINE SOON light located on instrument panel. When malfunction is detected and light is turned on, a corresponding trouble code will be stored in control module memory. To retrieve stored codes, see ENTERING & EXITING DIAGNOSTIC MODE in this article. Malfunctions are recorded as either hard failures or intermittent failures.

SELF-DIAGNOSTICS DIRECTORY

DIAGNOSTIC PROCEDURE

Preliminary Inspection – 1) Check all vacuum hoses for correct routing, restrictions, cuts or other damage. Inspect difficult-to-see vacuum hoses beneath the air cleaner assembly and other engine components.
2) Inspect all engine compartment wiring for proper connections. Also check wires for pinched or chaffed spots, as well as contact with sharp edges or exhaust manifolds.
3) The preliminary inspection is very important and should be performed carefully and thoroughly, as it can often lead to fixing a problem without further diagnosis.
Diagnostic Procedure – 1) Ensure all non-controlled systems not related to engine or transmission control system are operating properly. DO NOT proceed with testing unless all other non-controlled system problems are repaired.

2) ALWAYS begin system diagnosis with checking diagnostic circuit. On gasoline vehicles, see DIAGNOSTIC CIRCUIT CHECK in BASIC DIAGNOSTIC PROCEDURES article. On diesel vehicles, DIAGNOSTIC CIRCUIT CHECK is covered in SELF-DIAGNOSTICS – DIESEL article. The diagnostic circuit check determines if the computer-controlled system is working properly. If trouble codes are displayed (other than Code 12), determine if codes are hard or intermittent trouble codes.
3) A hard code is one which is present while working on vehicle, and problem still exists. Hard codes will cause the SERVICE ENGINE SOON light to come on.
4) An intermittent code is one which does not reset itself and is NOT present while working on vehicle. Intermittent codes are often caused by loose connections. The SERVICE ENGINE SOON light will go out 10 seconds after fault goes away. For intermittent diagnosis procedures, see TROUBLE SHOOTING – NO CODES article.

ENTERING & EXITING DIAGNOSTIC MODE

1) With key on and engine off, connect a jumper wire between ALDL terminal "B" (diagnostic terminal) and terminal "A" (ground). *See Fig. 1.* This places the control unit into diagnostic mode.
2) In this mode, the control unit will display Code 12 by flashing the SERVICE ENGINE SOON (SES) light. Code 12 is identified by the SES light flashing once, followed by a short pause, then 2 flashes in quick succession.
3) Code 12 will be displayed 3 times. If no other codes are stored, Code 12 will continue to flash until the diagnostic terminal is ungrounded. To exit diagnostic mode, turn ignition off and remove jumper wire from ALDL connector.

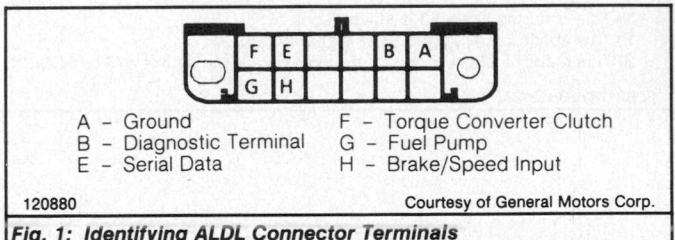

A – Ground	F – Torque Converter Clutch
B – Diagnostic Terminal	G – Fuel Pump
E – Serial Data	H – Brake/Speed Input

120880   Courtesy of General Motors Corp.

Fig. 1: Identifying ALDL Connector Terminals

TROUBLE CODE IDENTIFICATION

NOTE: Trouble codes retrieved from PCM/TCM may be related to either engine or transmission. Transmission-related codes are covered in this article. For engine-related codes, see appropriate SELF-DIAGNOSTICS article. See TROUBLE CODE IDENTIFICATION table to determine if code is transmission or engine related.

1) The system codes indicate failure of a specific sensor and/or circuit. Sensor/circuit diagnosis may indicate replacement of the control unit. Code 51 indicates PROM/MEM-CAL is installed improperly or has failed.
2) Code 52 indicates PCM/TCM has failed and must be replaced. If the condition is still not corrected after replacing PCM/TCM, the cause may be as follows:

- An incorrect PCM/TCM or PROM/MEM-CAL application may cause a malfunction, which may or may not set a code.
- The PCM/TCM connector may be the problem. Connector terminals may have to be removed from the connector to be properly checked.
- PROM/MEM-CAL failure. Although the PROM/MEM-CAL rarely fails, it could be the cause of the problem.
- Replacement PCM/TCM may be faulty.
- Intermittent problem. Make a careful physical inspection of affected sensor/circuit.
- A shorted solenoid, coil relay, or harness may be the cause of PCM/TCM failure. Use Short Circuit Tester (J-34636) to check for short circuits.

TROUBLE CODE IDENTIFICATION

Code	Probable Cause
12 [1]	No Engine Speed Sensor Reference Pulse To PCM/TCM
13 [1]	Open Oxygen Sensor Circuit (Gasoline)
14 [1]	CTS Voltage Low (Sensor Or Signal Line Grounded)
15 [1]	CTS Voltage High (Sensor, Connections, Or Wires Open)
21 [1]	TPS Voltage High (Open Circuit Or Misadjusted TPS)
22 [1]	TPS Voltage Low (Circuit Grounded)
23 [1]	TPS Not Calibrated (Diesel – .25-1.3 Volts At Curb Idle) Intake Air Temperature Sensor Voltage High (Gasoline)
24 [1]	Vehicle Speed Sensor Circuit Open Or Grounded
25 [1]	Intake Air Temperature Sensor Voltage Low (Gasoline)
28	Pressure Switch Manifold Range Circuit Open Or Shorted
31 [1]	MAP Voltage Low (Diesel) Turbocharger Wastegate Overboost (Gasoline)
32 [1]	EGR Error (Improper Vacuum Signal)
33 [1]	MAP Voltage High
34 [1]	MAP Voltage Low (Gasoline)
35 [1]	IAC System Fault (Gasoline)
39	TCC Stuck Off (Faulty TCC Solenoid)
42 [1]	EST Circuit Fault (Gasoline)
43 [1]	ESC Fault (Gasoline)
44 [1]	Lean Exhaust Indicated (Gasoline)
45 [1]	Rich Exhaust Indicated (Gasoline)
51 [1]	Improperly Installed/Faulty PROM/MEM-CAL
52 [1]	PCM/TCM Fault
53	System Voltage High (Gasoline – Charging Problem) Voltage Reference Overload (Diesel)
54 [1]	Fuel Pump Circuit Voltage Low (Gasoline)
55 [1]	Faulty ECM (Gasoline)
58	TTS High Temperature (Sensor Or Signal Line Grounded)
59	TTS Low Temperature (Sensor, Connections, Or Wires Open)
68	Overdrive Ratio Error (Engine RPM Greater Than Input Speed)
73	Force Motor Commanded Amperage Differs From Return
75	System Voltage Low (Charging System Problem)
81	QDM Solenoid "B" Monitored Voltage Differs From Commanded
82	QDM Solenoid "A" Monitored Voltage Differs From Commanded
83	QDM TCC Monitored Voltage Differs From Commanded
85	Undefined Gear Ratio (Input Or Output Sensor Failure)
86	Shift Solenoid "B" Stuck On (Commanded Gear Not Engaged)
87	Shift Solenoid "B" Stuck Off (Commanded Gear Not Engaged)

[1] – Code is engine related. For information on engine-related trouble codes, see appropriate SELF-DIAGNOSTICS article.

CLEARING TROUBLE CODES

Trouble codes should be cleared after repairs have been completed. Also, some diagnostic charts require that codes be cleared before using diagnostic chart. To clear codes, remove PCM/TCM memory battery voltage for 30 seconds.

If no hard fault codes are present (only intermittent codes exist), proceed to TROUBLE SHOOTING – NO CODES article for intermittent diagnostic procedures.

PCM/TCM LOCATION

The ECM is located under the passenger's seat riser ("G" Series Van), or behind right side of dash (all other models).

SPECIAL TOOLS (DIAGNOSTIC)

Special scan testers are plugged into the ALDL may be used to read trouble codes, and check voltages in system on serial data line. These testers can save a great deal of time. For additional information, see manual included with tester.

TEST EQUIPMENT

A tachometer, test light, Digital Volt-Ohmmeter (DVOM) with a minimum 10-megohm input impedance, vacuum gauge, and jumper wires are required to test and diagnose electronic transmission control system. A scan tester may also be used to access data parameters. Tester will supply a visual reading of most inputs, and some outputs, to the PCM/TCM. Some diagnostic flow charts require the use of a bidirectional (Tech 1) scan tester.

TROUBLE CODE CHARTS

The following diagnostic flow charts and circuit schematics are provided courtesy of General Motors Corp.

NOTE: Some charts require the use of a bidirectional (Tech 1) scan tester. If a bidirectional scan tester is not available, the PCM/TCM-controlled relays and solenoids may be energized by grounding ALDL test terminal "B" with ignition on and engine off.

CODE 28, PRESSURE SWITCH MANIFOLD FAULT

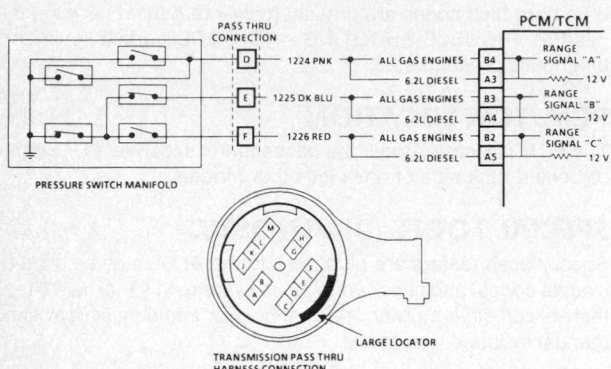

PRESSURE SWITCH MANIFOLD

TRANSMISSION PASS THRU HARNESS CONNECTION

LARGE LOCATOR

The Pressure Switch Manifold (PSM) is actually 5 pressure switches combined into one unit and mounted on the transmission valve body. The PCM/TCM supplies battery voltage to the PSM on 3 separate wires. By grounding one or more of these circuits through various combinations of the pressure switches inside the pressure switch manifold, the PCM/TCM detects what gear range has been selected by the vehicle operator.

NOTE: Test numbers refer to test numbers on diagnostic chart.

1) This test compares the indicated range to the range actually selected.
2) This test checks for correct voltage from the PCM/TCM to the transmission pass-thru connector.
3) This test will detect a short to ground in any one of the 3 PSM range circuits.

DIAGNOSTIC AIDS

Code 28 will set if PCM/TCM detects one of 2 "illegal" PSM combinations. See VALID PSM COMBINATION table for various combinations. Check pass-thru connector for good contact.

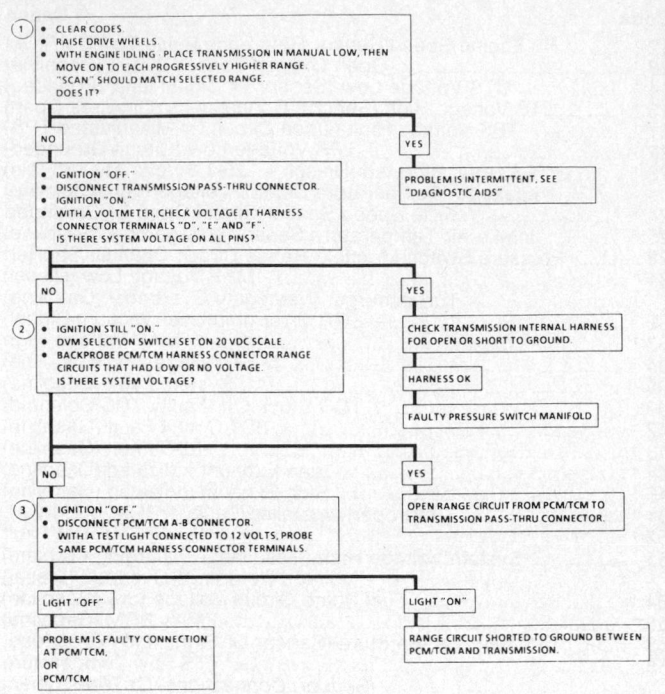

VALID PSM COMBINATION CHART

	A	B	C
Park	12	0	12
Reverse	0	0	12
Neutral	12	0	12
4th	12	0	0
3rd	12	12	0
2nd	12	12	12
1st	0	12	12
Illegal	0	12	0
Illegal	0	0	0

CODE 39, TORQUE CONVERTER CLUTCH STUCK "OFF"

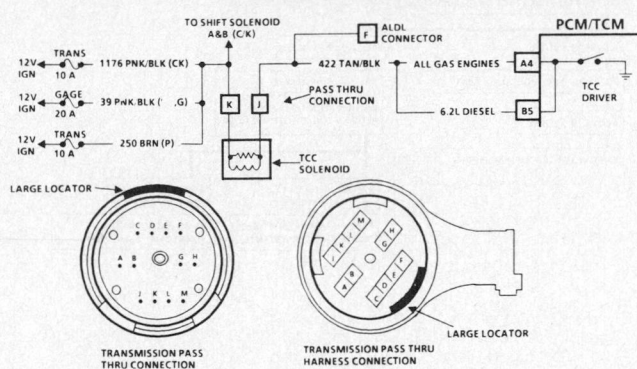

TRANSMISSION PASS THRU CONNECTION

TRANSMISSION PASS THRU HARNESS CONNECTION

The purpose of the automatic transmission Torque Converter Clutch (TCC) feature is to eliminate power loss of the torque converter stage when vehicle is in a cruise condition. This allows the convenience of the automatic transmission, and fuel economy of a manual transmission. Fused battery ignition voltage is supplied to the TCC solenoid, which is used inside the valve body to shift a spool valve to modulate pressure to the TCC. This modulated pressure normally allows some slight slippage of TCC.

The PCM/TCM will engage TCC by grounding circuit No. 422, energizing the solenoid.

Code 39 will set under the following conditions.
- TCC is engaged.
- TCC "slip" is greater than 65 RPM for 2 seconds.
- 2nd or 3rd gear is selected or indicated.

NOTE: Test numbers refer to test numbers on diagnostic chart.

1) This test determines if transmission is receiving a TCC command from the pass-thru connector. If bidirectional scan tester is not available, TCC may be activated by grounding ALDL test terminal "B" with ignition on and engine off.

2) This test checks for power to transmission.

3) This test determines if PCM/TCM is commanding TCC to be on.

DIAGNOSTIC AIDS

Clear codes and re-check for Code 39. If code resets, problem could be internal to the transmission. Code 39 will only set in 3rd gear. TCC slip in 4th gear will set Code 68.

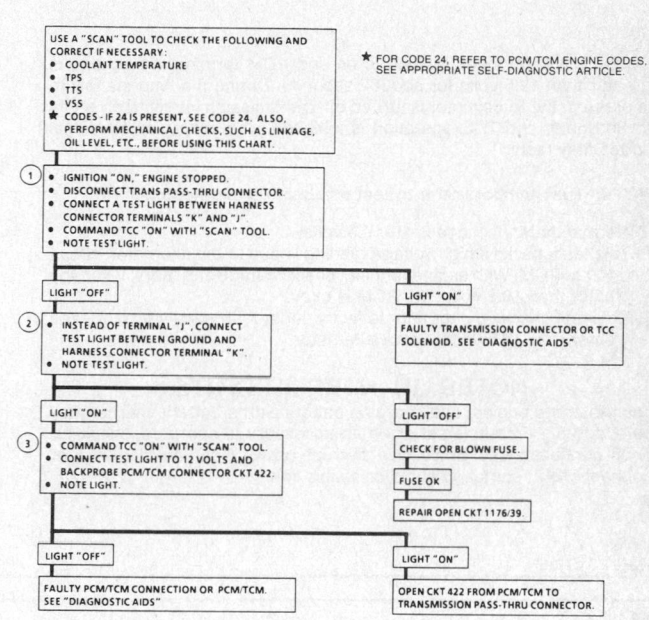

CODE 53, SYSTEM VOLTAGE HIGH

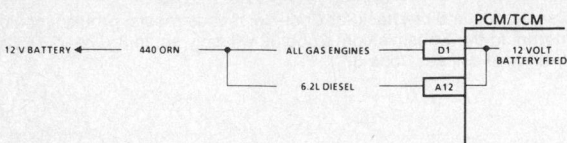

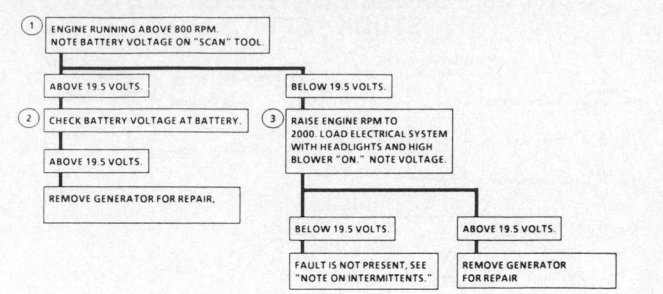

Code 53 will set when ignition is on and PCM terminal D1 voltage is greater than 19.5 volts for about 2 seconds. During the time the failure is present, the force motor is turned off, transmission immediately shifts to 2nd gear, and TCC operation is inhibited. The setting of additional codes may result.

NOTE: Test numbers refer to test numbers on diagnostic chart.

1) Normal battery voltage is 10-17.0 volts.
2) This test checks if high voltage reading is due to the alternator, circuit No. 440 or PCM. With engine running, check voltage at battery. If voltage is greater than 19.5 volts, the PCM is okay.
3) This test checks if alternator is faulty under load condition. If voltage is greater than 19.5 volts, check alternator.

NOTES ON INTERMITTENTS
Jump-starting engine, and charging battery with a battery charger may set Code 53. If code is set when an accessory is operated, check for poor connections or excessive current draw. Also, check for poor connections at starter solenoid or fusible link.

91F13677 91G13678

CODE 58, TRANSMISSION TEMPERATURE SENSOR CIRCUIT (HIGH TEMPERATURE INDICATED)

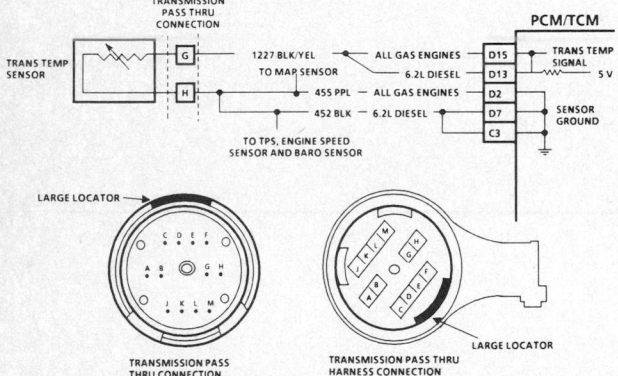

The transmission temperature sensor is a thermistor which controls the signal voltage to the PCM/TCM. The PCM/TCM applies and monitors voltage on circuit No. 1227 to the sensor. When transmission is cold, sensor resistance is high; therefore, the PCM/TCM will see high signal voltage. As the transmission warms up, sensor resistance and voltage will drop. At normal transmission operating temperature of 212°F (100°C), voltage will be about 1.5-2.0 volts.

NOTE: Test numbers refer to test numbers on diagnostic chart.

1) Code 58 will set if signal voltage indicates a transmission temperature greater than 309°F (154°C) for one second.
2) This test determines if circuit No. 1227 is shorted to ground, which will result in conditions for Code 58.

DIAGNOSTIC AIDS
Check harness routing for a potential short to ground in circuit No. 1227. Scan tester displays transmission temperature in degrees Centigrade. After transmission is running, the temperature display should rise steadily to about 100°C then stabilize. Test the transmission sensor at various temperature levels to determine if sensor is out of calibration. See TRANSMISSION SENSOR – TEMPERATURE TO RESISTANCE chart. An out-of-calibration sensor could result in delayed shifts, or TCC enabled complaint.

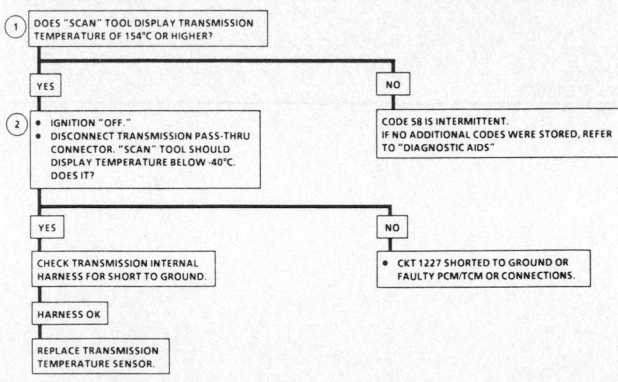

°C	°F	MINIMUM RESISTANCE	NOMINAL RESISTANCE	MAXIMUM RESISTANCE
-40°C	-40°F	80965	100544	120123
-30°C	-20°F	42701	52426	62151
-20°C	-4°F	23458	28491	33524
-10°C	14°F	13366	16068	18770
0°C	32°F	7871	9370	10869
10°C	50°F	4771	5640	6508
20°C	68°F	2981	3500	4018
30°C	86°F	1915	2232	2550
40°C	104°F	1260	1460	1660
50°C	122°F	848.8	977.1	1105
60°C	140°F	584.1	668.7	753.4
70°C	158°F	410.3	467.2	524.2
80°C	176°F	293.7	332.7	371.7
90°C	194°F	213.9	241.0	268.2
100°C	212°F	158.1	177.4	196.8
110°C	?	118.8	132.6	146.5
120°C	?	90.40	100.6	110.8
130°C	?	69.48	77.29	85.11
140°C	?	53.96	60.13	66.29
150°C	?	42.43	47.31	52.20

TRANSMISSION SENSOR – TEMPERATURE TO RESISTANCE (APPROX.)

91H13679 91A13680

CODE 59, TRANSMISSION TEMPERATURE SENSOR CIRCUIT
(LOW TEMPERATURE INDICATED)

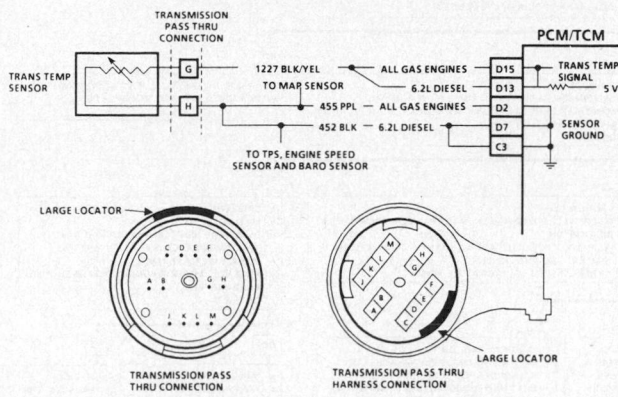

TRANSMISSION PASS THRU CONNECTION

TRANSMISSION PASS THRU HARNESS CONNECTION

The transmission temperature sensor is a thermistor which controls signal voltage to PCM/TCM. The PCM/TCM applies and monitors 5 volts to the sensor on circuit No. 1227. When transmission is cold, sensor resistance is high; therefore, the PCM/TCM will see high signal voltage. As transmission temperature warms up, sensor resistance and voltage drop. At normal transmission operating temperature of 212°F (100°C), voltage will be about 1.5-2.0 volts.

NOTE: Test numbers refer to test numbers on diagnostic chart.

1) Code 59 will set if signal voltage indicates a transmission temperature less than –54°F (–48°C) for one second.
2) This test simulates Code 58. If PCM/TCM recognizes the low signal voltage (high temperature) and scan tester reads 304°F (151°C) or greater, the PCM/TCM and wiring are okay.
3) This test determines if circuit No. 1227 is open. There should be 5 volts present at the sensor connector if measuring with a DVOM.

DIAGNOSTIC AIDS

Scan tester displays transmission temperature in degrees Centigrade. After transmission is running, the displayed temperature should rise steadily to about 212°F (100°C) then stabilize. A faulty connection or an open in circuit No. 455/452 or circuit No. 1227 will result in a Code 59. Test the coolant sensor at various temperature levels to determine if sensor is out of calibration. See TRANSMISSION SENSOR – TEMPERATURE TO RESISTANCE chart. An out-of-calibration sensor could result in firm shifts, or TCC enabled complaint.

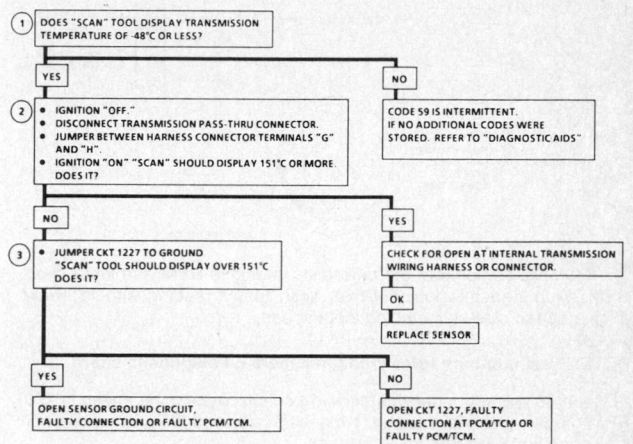

TRANSMISSION SENSOR - TEMPERATURE TO RESISTANCE (APPROX.)

°C	°F	MINIMUM RESISTANCE	NOMINAL RESISTANCE	MAXIMUM RESISTANCE
-40°C	-40°F	80965	100544	120123
-30°C	-20°F	42701	52426	62151
-20°C	-4°F	23458	28491	33524
-10°C	14°F	13366	16068	18770
0°C	32°F	7871	9370	10869
10°C	50°F	4771	5640	6508
20°C	68°F	2981	3500	4018
30°C	86°F	1915	2232	2550
40°C	104°F	1260	1460	1660
50°C	122°F	848.8	977.1	1105
60°C	140°F	584.1	668.7	753.4
70°C	158°F	410.3	467.2	524.2
80°C	176°F	293.7	332.7	371.7
90°C	194°F	213.9	241.0	268.2
100°C	212°F	158.1	177.4	196.8
110°C	?	118.8	132.6	146.5
120°C	?	90.40	100.6	110.8
130°C	?	69.48	77.29	85.11
140°C	?	53.96	60.13	66.29
150°C	?	42.43	47.31	52.20

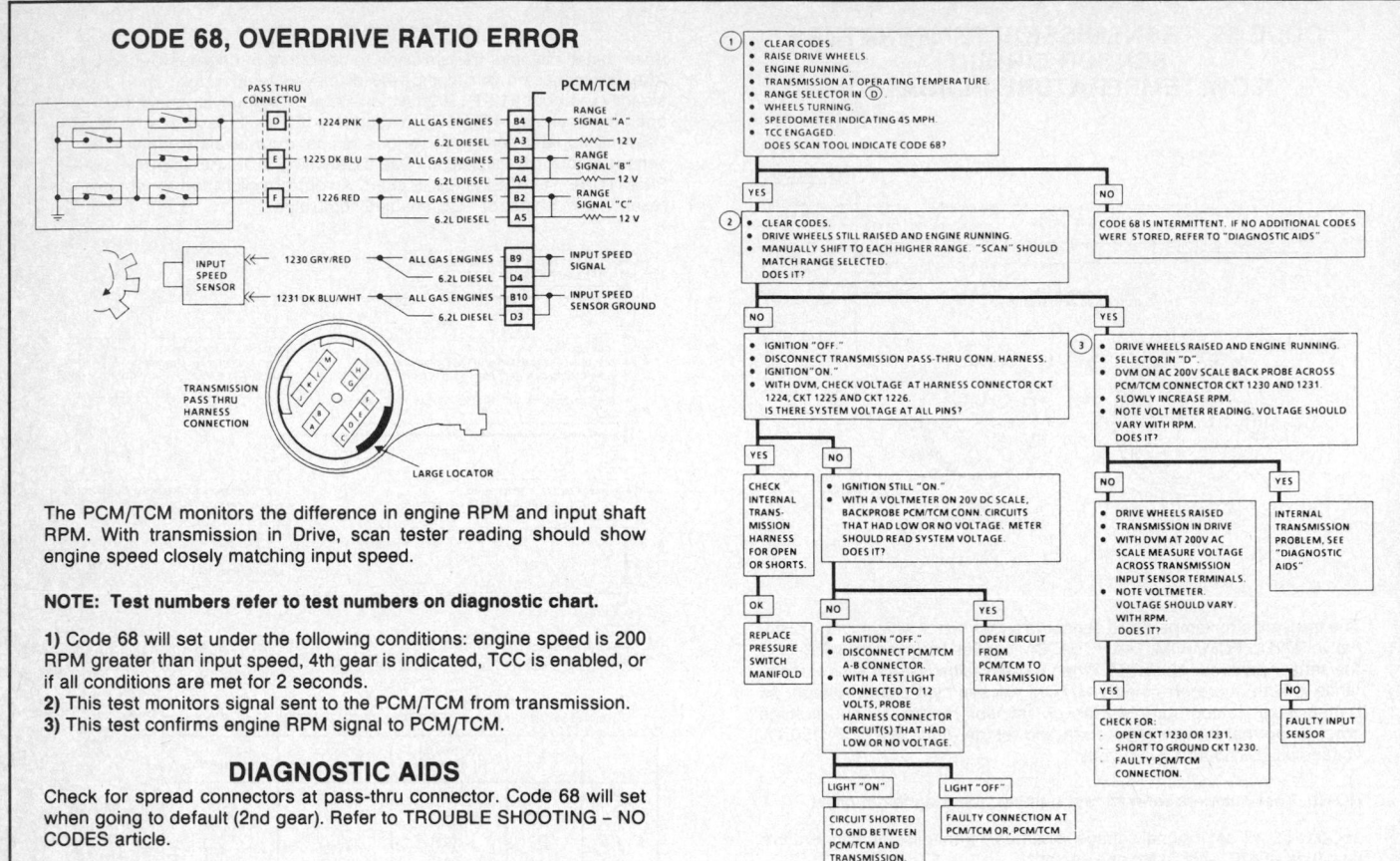

CODE 68, OVERDRIVE RATIO ERROR

The PCM/TCM monitors the difference in engine RPM and input shaft RPM. With transmission in Drive, scan tester reading should show engine speed closely matching input speed.

NOTE: Test numbers refer to test numbers on diagnostic chart.

1) Code 68 will set under the following conditions: engine speed is 200 RPM greater than input speed, 4th gear is indicated, TCC is enabled, or if all conditions are met for 2 seconds.

2) This test monitors signal sent to the PCM/TCM from transmission.

3) This test confirms engine RPM signal to PCM/TCM.

DIAGNOSTIC AIDS

Check for spread connectors at pass-thru connector. Code 68 will set when going to default (2nd gear). Refer to TROUBLE SHOOTING – NO CODES article.

91C13682 91D13683

CODE 73, FORCE MOTOR CURRENT (CURRENT ERROR)

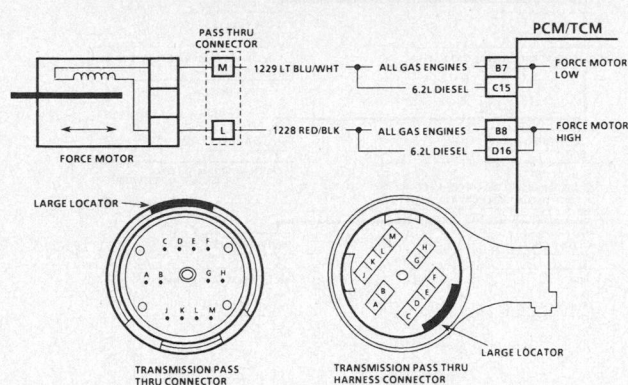

NOTE: This flow chart requires the use of a bidirectional (Tech 1) scan tester.

The force motor is a PCM/TCM-controlled device used to regulate transmission line pressure. The PCM/TCM looks at TPS voltage, engine RPM and other inputs to determine appropriate line pressure for a given load, then regulates the pressure by applying a varying amperage. The applied amperage can vary from 1-1.1 amps.

The PCM/TCM then monitors amperage at the return line. If the return amperage varies more than .16 amp from the commanded amperage for the duration of at least one second, Code 73 will set. Once Code 73 is set, the force motor is disabled and full line pressure will be applied until the next time the ignition switch is cycled. Code 73 will remain stored, but the force motor will resume normal function until the conditions for Code 73 re-occur.

NOTE: Test numbers refer to test numbers on diagnostic chart.

1) Checks the PCM and TCM's ability to command the force motor.
2) Checks for voltage at PCM/TCM.
3) Checks internal transmission harness and force motor for low resistance.
4) Checks for short to ground.
5) Checks internal transmission harness and force motor for high resistance.

DIAGNOSTIC AIDS

Check for poor connections at PCM/TCM and transmission pass-thru connector.

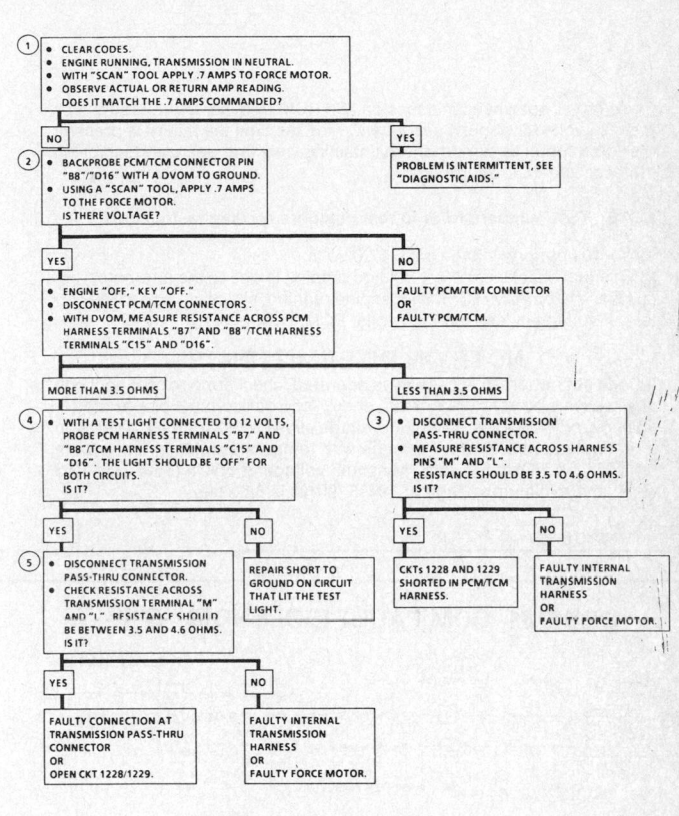

CODE 75, SYSTEM VOLTAGE LOW

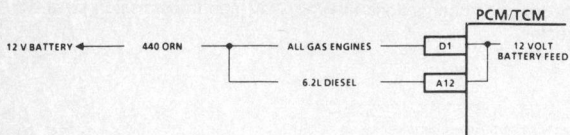

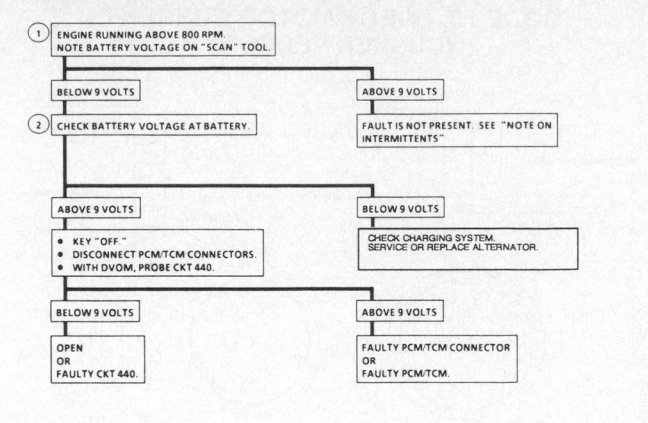

Code 75 will set when ignition is on and PCM terminal D1 voltage is less than 8.6 volts for about 4 seconds. During the time the failure is present, the force motor is turned off, maintaining only 2nd gear, and inhibiting 4th gear and TCC operation.

NOTE: Test numbers refer to test numbers on diagnostic chart.

1) Normal battery voltage is 10-17.0 volts.
2) This test checks if the low voltage reading is due to the alternator, circuit No. 440 or PCM/TCM. With engine running, check voltage at the battery. If voltage is less than 8.6 volts, PCM/TCM is okay.

NOTE ON INTERMITTENTS

If Code sets when an accessory is operated, check for poor connections or excessive current draw. Also, check for poor connections at starter solenoid or fusible link. Minimum voltage allowed for Code 75 to set is on a graduated scale, and will change with temperature. Minimum voltage at –40°F (–40°C) is 6.7 volts. Minimum voltage at 304°F (150°C) is 10.5 volts, and minimum voltage at 194°F (90°C) is 8.6 volts.

91F13677 91G13686   Courtesy of General Motors Corp.

CODE 81, QDM FAULT (SOLENOID "B")

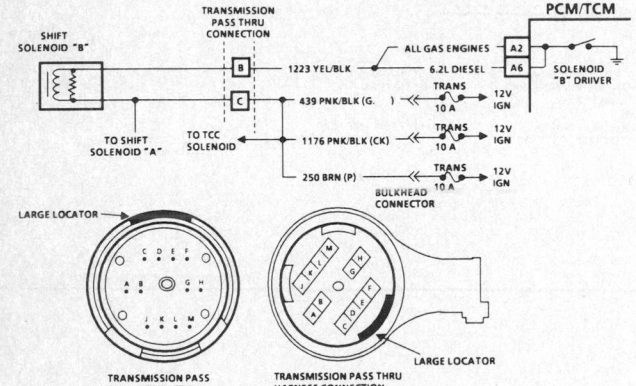

The PCM/TCM continually monitors voltage on each circuit connected to the quad driver, looking for either low or high voltage, depending on the commanded state of the devices connected to it. Code 81 will set if a fault has been detected on the shift solenoid "B" circuit. For example, if shift solenoid "B" is commanded on by the PCM/TCM, voltage on that circuit should drop when solenoid is grounded. If voltage stays up for at least .5 second, Code 81 will set. The opposite is also true. If shift solenoid "B" is off, voltage on the circuit should remain high. If voltage drops for more than .5 second, Code 81 will set.

NOTE: Test numbers refer to test numbers on diagnostic chart.

1) This procedure checks shift solenoid "B" and internal transmission wiring for shorts.
2) This test checks for power, from the ignition through transmission fuse, to the shift solenoid "B".
3) This test ensures circuit No. 1223 is not shorted to ground.
4) This test checks PCM/TCM's ability to ground or control shift solenoid "B". If bidirectional scan tester is not available, solenoid may be activated by grounding ALDL test terminal "B" with ignition on and engine off.
5) This test ensures circuit No. 1223 is not shorted to ground.

DIAGNOSTIC AIDS

Check all connections, especially those at the transmission pass-thru connector. If code is intermittent, see INTERMITTENTS in TROUBLE SHOOTING – NO CODES article.

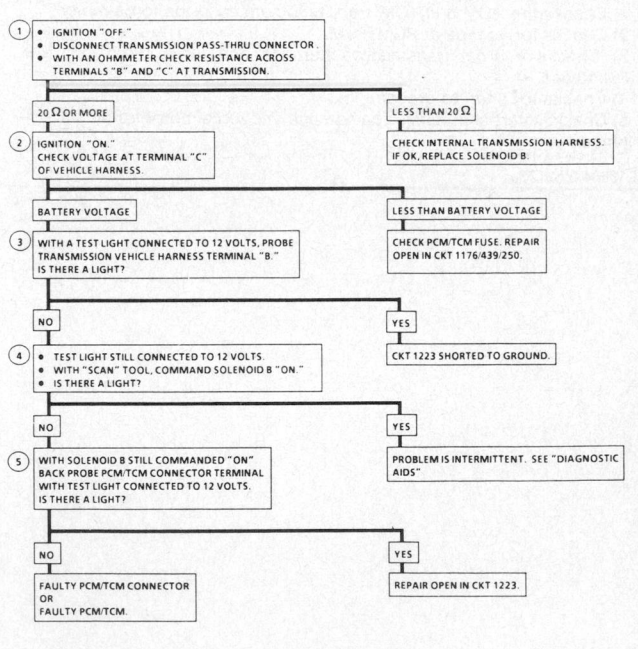

91H13687 91J13689   Courtesy of General Motors Corp.

CODE 82, QDM FAULT (SOLENOID "A")

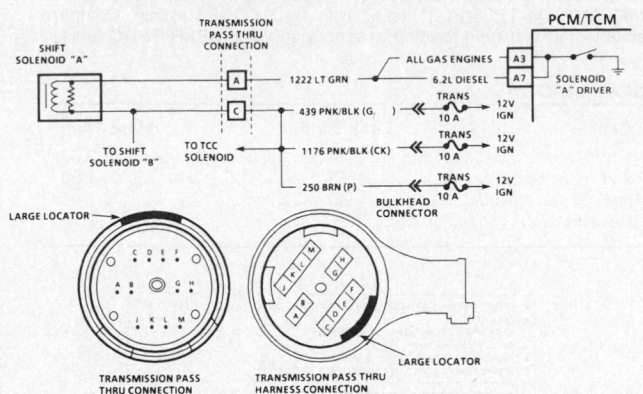

The PCM/TCM continually monitors each circuit connected to the quad driver for either low or high voltage, depending on the commanded state of the device connected to it. Code 82 will set if there is a fault detected on the shift solenoid "A" circuit. For example, if shift solenoid "A" is commanded on by the PCM/TCM, then voltage on circuit should drop as soon as solenoid is grounded.

However, if voltage remains high for 2 seconds after the "on" command is given, Code 82 will set. The opposite is also true. If shift solenoid "A" is off, voltage on the circuit should be high. If voltage drops for .5 second or longer, Code 82 will set.

NOTE: Test numbers refer to test numbers on diagnostic chart.

1) This procedure checks shift solenoid "A" and internal transmission wiring harness for shorts.
2) This test checks for power, from the ignition through the fuse, to the shift solenoid.
3) This test checks circuit No. 1222 for short to ground.

91I13688 91C13690

4) This test checks PCM/TCM's ability to ground or control shift solenoid "A". If bidirectional scan tester is not available, solenoid may be activated by grounding ALDL test terminal "B" with ignition on and engine off.

DIAGNOSTIC AIDS

Check all connections, especially at the transmission pass-thru connector. If code is intermittent, see INTERMITTENTS in TROUBLE SHOOTING – NO CODES article.

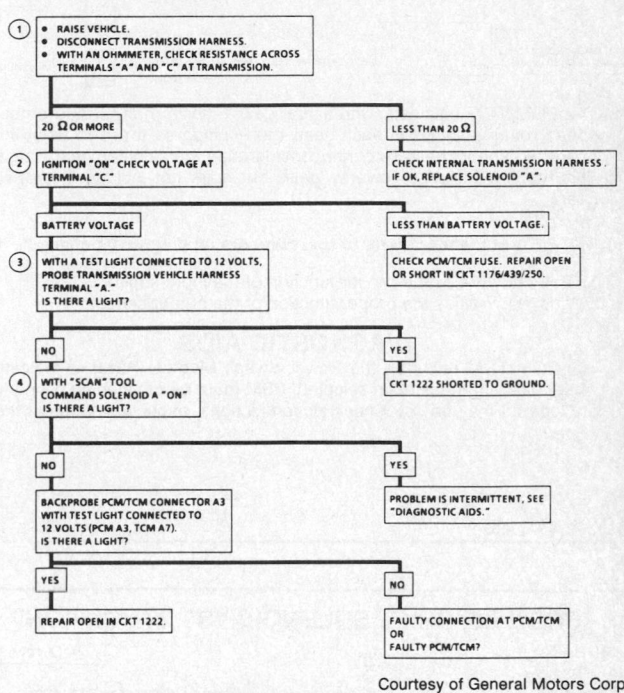

Courtesy of General Motors Corp.

CODE 83, TCC QDM FAULT

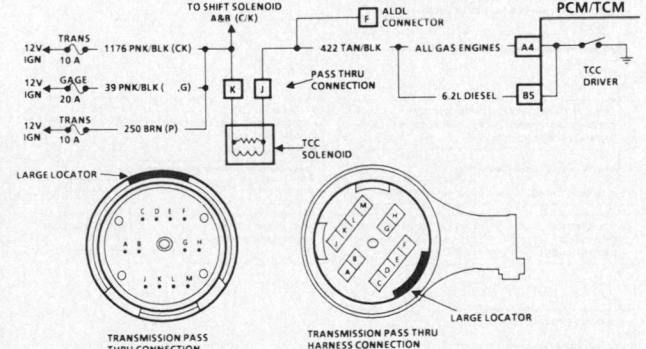

The PCM/TCM continually monitors voltage on each circuit connected to the quad driver for either low or high voltage, depending on the commanded state of the device connected to it. Code 83 will set if PCM/TCM detects an inappropriate reading on the TCC circuit. For example, if the TCC duty cycle is zero, but voltage on the TCC circuit drops as if the solenoid were on, then Code 83 will set. The TCC solenoid, because of its large current draw, is connected to 2 terminals of a single quad driver.

NOTE: Test numbers refer to test numbers on diagnostic chart.

1) This test checks for low resistance in the solenoid or internal transmission harness. This test also determines which circuit triggered the fault. If bidirectional scan tester is not available, TCC may be activated by grounding ALDL test terminal "B" with ignition on and engine off.

91D13675 91D13691

DIAGNOSTIC AIDS

Check all connections, especially those at the transmission pass-thru connector. If code is intermittent, see INTERMITTENTS in TROUBLE SHOOTING – NO CODES article.

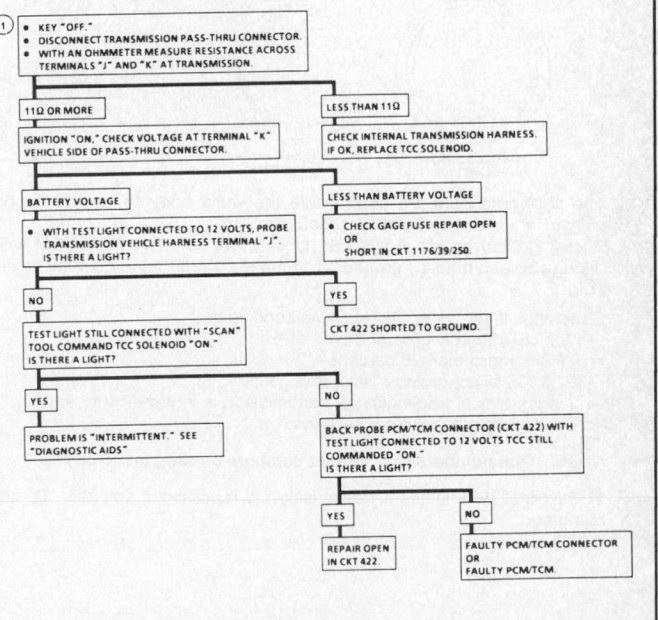

Courtesy of General Motors Corp.

CODE 85, UNDEFINED RATIO

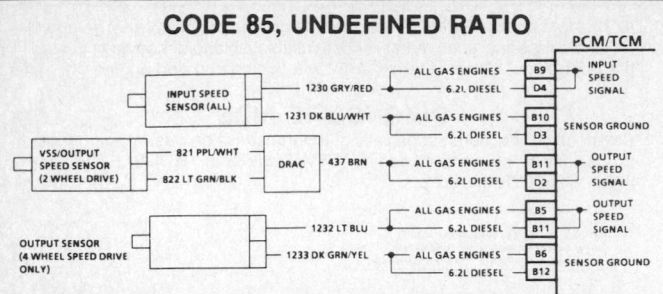

The PCM/TCM calculates the actual gear ratio from input and output speed readings while in each gear, then compares these to what the gear ratio should be, taking into consideration the selected gear range. This monitor includes Reverse gear, but does not include Overdrive gear.

NOTE: Test numbers refer to test numbers on diagnostic chart.

1) This test verifies the proper function of the input sensor.
2) This test verifies the proper function of the output sensor.

DIAGNOSTIC AIDS

The PCM/TCM relies on the Power Switch Module (PSM) to indicate what gear range has been selected. PSM must be functioning properly or Code 85 may be set. Check all connections, especially those at the transmission pass-thru connector. If code is intermittent, see INTER-MITTENTS in TROUBLE SHOOTING – NO CODES article. Compare scan tester gear ratio reading to specifications in GEAR RATIO table.

GEAR RATIO

Gear	Less Than	More Than
1st	2.38	2.63
2nd	1.43	1.58
3rd	.95	1.05
Reverse	1.97	2.17

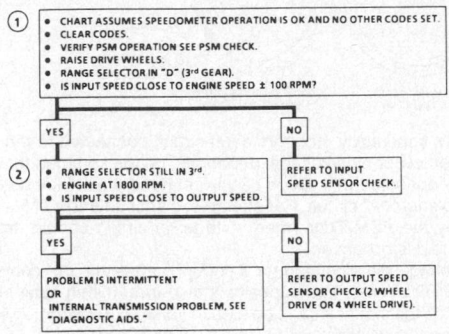

CODE 86, SHIFT SOLENOID "B" STUCK "ON"

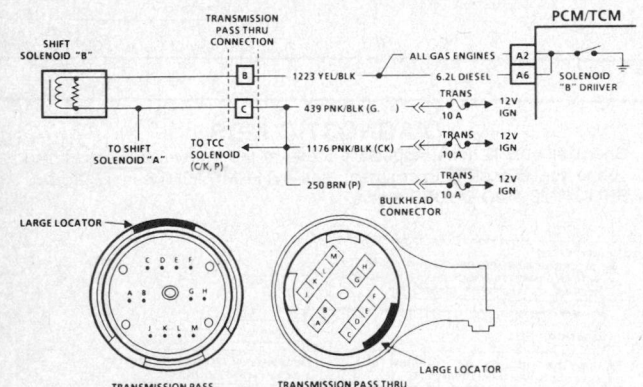

The shift solenoids are used inside the valve body to control spool valves, which determine the transmission gear.
Fused ignition power is supplied to solenoid "B". The PCM/TCM will engage solenoid "B" by grounding circuit No. 1223 to energize the solenoid.

Code 86 will set under the following conditions.
- Vehicle speed is greater than 7 MPH.
- TPS is more than 25 percent.
- PCM/TCM commands 1st or 2nd gear.
- Transmission ratio indicates transmission is in 3rd or 4th gear.
- Conditions are met for 6 seconds.

NOTE: Test numbers refer to test numbers on diagnostic chart.

1) This test determines if transmission is receiving a solenoid "B" on command.

DIAGNOSTIC AIDS

If code is intermittent, see INTERMITTENTS in TROUBLE SHOOTING – NO CODES article.

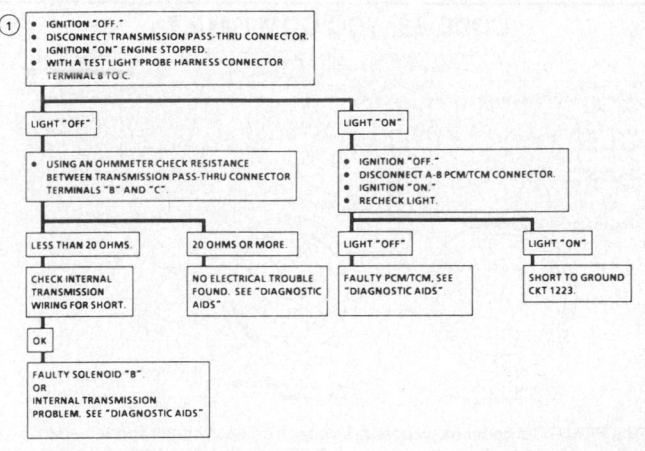

CODE 87, SHIFT SOLENOID "B" STUCK "OFF"

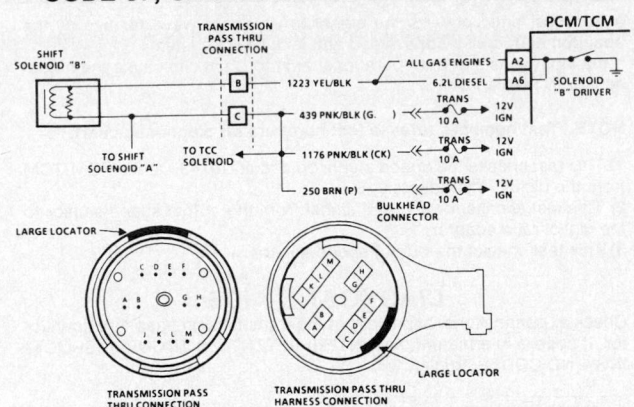

The shift solenoids are used inside the valve body to control spool valve position, which determines the transmission gear.

Fused ignition power is supplied to solenoid "B." The PCM/TCM will engage solenoid "B" by grounding circuit No. 1223 to energize the solenoid.

Code 87 will set under the following conditions.
- Vehicle speed is greater than 7 MPH.
- TPS is more than 25 percent.
- PCM/TCM commands 3rd or 4th gear.
- Transmission ratio indicates transmission is in 1st or 2nd gear.
- Conditions are met for 6 seconds.

NOTE: Test numbers refer to test numbers on diagnostic chart.

1) This test checks PCM/TCM's ability to ground or control solenoid "B". If bidirectional scan tester is not available, solenoid may be activated by grounding ALDL test terminal "B" with ignition on and engine off.

2) This test checks the power supply and circuit No. 1223.

3) This test checks the internal transmission harness and solenoid "B".

DIAGNOSTIC AIDS

Check all connections, especially those at the transmission pass-thru connector. Fault may be an internal transmission problem.

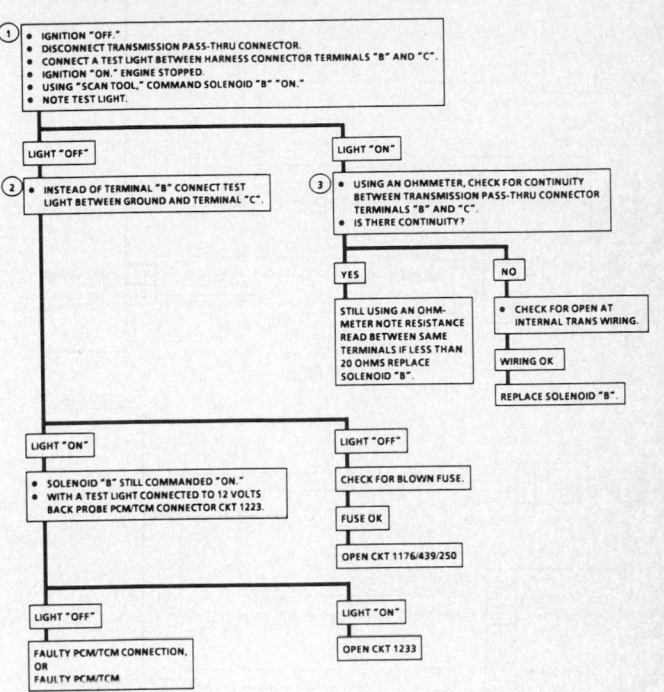

91H13687 91H13695

COMPONENT CHECK CHARTS

OUTPUT SPEED SENSOR CIRCUIT CHECK (2WD)

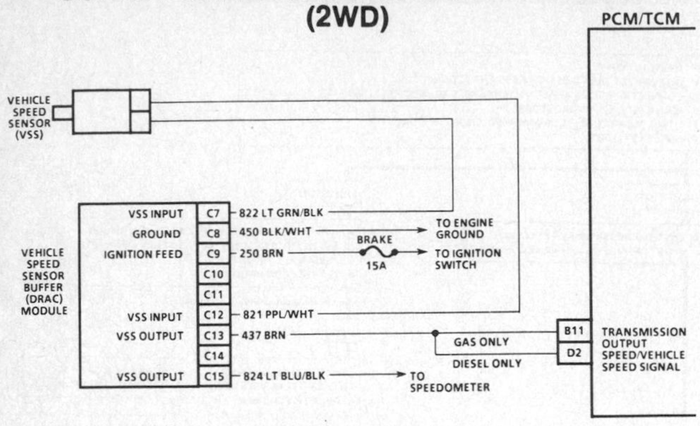

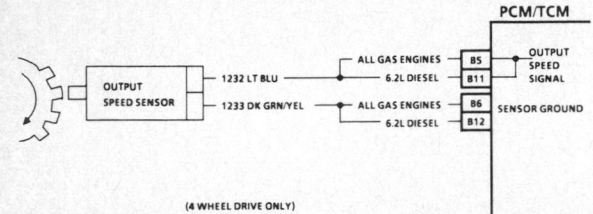

axle ratios, and converts the signal to a square wave for use by the speedometer, cruise control and anti-lock brake system.
If the input sensor is not operational at start up, it can cause the output sensor to read zero.

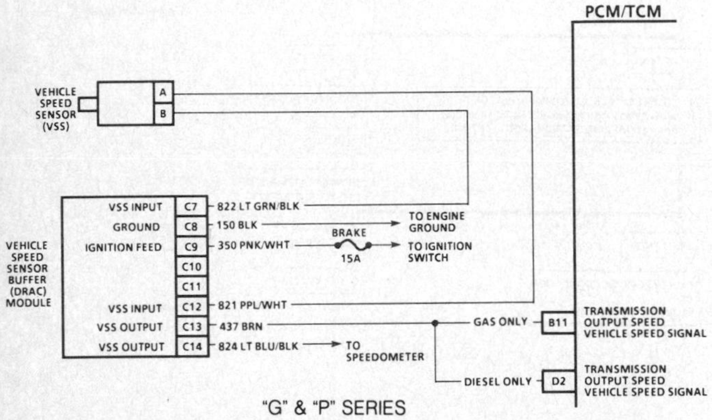

NOTE: Test numbers refer to test numbers on diagnostic chart.

1) This test checks the speed signal on circuit No. 437 at the PCM/TCM from the digital ratio adapter.
2) This test checks for a speed signal from the output speed sensor to the digital ratio adapter.
3) This test checks the output speed sensor.

DIAGNOSTIC AIDS
Check all connections, especially at the transmission pass-thru connector. If code is intermittent, see INTERMITTENTS in TROUBLE SHOOTING – NO CODES article.

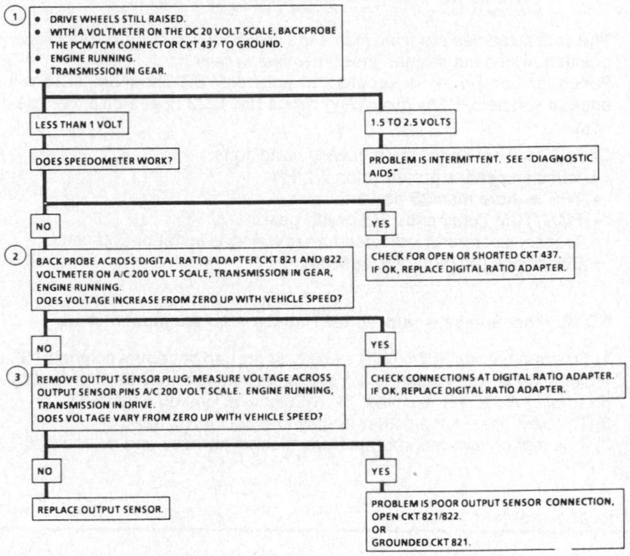

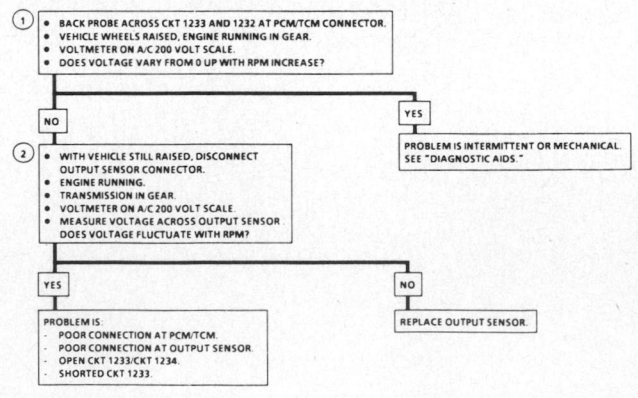

The output sensor circuit consists of a magnetic induction-type sensor, digital ratio adapter, and wiring. Gear teeth pressed on the outside diameter of the output carrier assembly induce an alternating current in the sensor.
This current is transmitted to a digital ratio adapter, where it is passed on to the PCM/TCM. The digital ratio adapter compensates for various

92D21777 92E21778 91J13697

Courtesy of General Motors Corp.

OUTPUT SPEED SENSOR CIRCUIT CHECK (4WD)

The output sensor is a magnetic induction type. Gear teeth pressed on the outside diameter of the output carrier assembly induce an alternating current in the sensor. Since vehicle speed is taken from the transfer case on 4WD drive vehicles, the transmission output sensor signal on these units goes directly to the PCM/TCM. If input sensor is not operational at start up, it can cause the output sensor to read zero.

NOTE: Test numbers refer to test numbers on diagnostic chart.

1) This test checks for a speed signal at the PCM/TCM.
2) This test checks the output sensor directly.

DIAGNOSTIC AIDS
Check all connections, especially at the transmission pass-thru connector. If code is intermittent, see INTERMITTENTS in TROUBLE SHOOTING – NO CODES article.

91E13700 91F13701

Courtesy of General Motors Corp.

INPUT SPEED SENSOR CIRCUIT CHECK

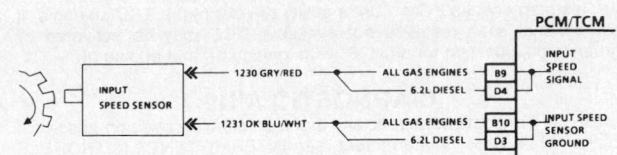

INPUT SPEED SENSOR

	PCM/TCM	
1230 GRY/RED	ALL GAS ENGINES	B9	INPUT SPEED SIGNAL
	6.2L DIESEL	D4	
1231 DK BLU/WHT	ALL GAS ENGINES	B10	INPUT SPEED SENSOR GROUND
	6.2L DIESEL	D3	

The input sensor is of the magnetic induction type and is located on the left side of the transmission, forward of center. Serrations in the forward clutch housing induce a small A/C current as they pass by the input sensor. While there is no specific code for an input sensor problem, the PCM/TCM uses input sensor readings to calculate gear ratio, turbine speed, TCC slip, and determine if the engine is running.

NOTE: Test numbers refer to test numbers on diagnostic chart.

1) This test checks the input sensor circuit up to the PCM/TCM.
2) This test checks the sensor output.

91G13702 91H13703

DIAGNOSTIC AIDS

Check all connectors. If code is intermittent, see INTERMITTENTS in TROUBLE SHOOTING – NO CODES article.

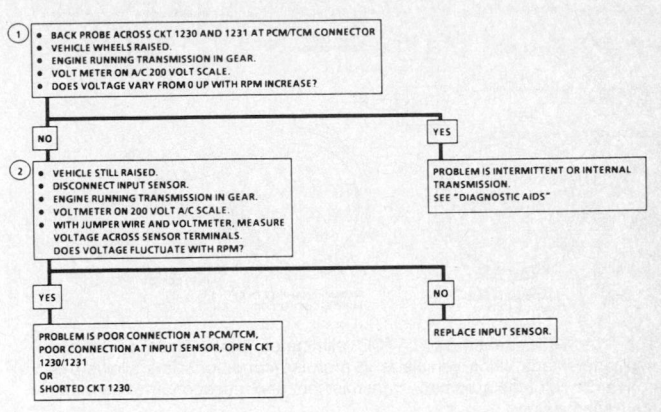

1)
- BACK PROBE ACROSS CKT 1230 AND 1231 AT PCM/TCM CONNECTOR
- VEHICLE WHEELS RAISED.
- ENGINE RUNNING TRANSMISSION IN GEAR.
- VOLT METER ON A/C 200 VOLT SCALE.
- DOES VOLTAGE VARY FROM 0 UP WITH RPM INCREASE?

NO → 2)
- VEHICLE STILL RAISED.
- DISCONNECT INPUT SENSOR.
- ENGINE RUNNING TRANSMISSION IN GEAR.
- VOLTMETER ON 200 VOLT A/C SCALE.
- WITH JUMPER WIRE AND VOLTMETER, MEASURE VOLTAGE ACROSS SENSOR TERMINALS. DOES VOLTAGE FLUCTUATE WITH RPM?

YES → PROBLEM IS INTERMITTENT OR INTERNAL TRANSMISSION. SEE "DIAGNOSTIC AIDS"

YES → PROBLEM IS POOR CONNECTION AT PCM/TCM, POOR CONNECTION AT INPUT SENSOR, OPEN CKT 1230/1231 OR SHORTED CKT 1230.

NO → REPLACE INPUT SENSOR.

Courtesy of General Motors Corp.

BRAKE SIGNAL CIRCUIT CHECK

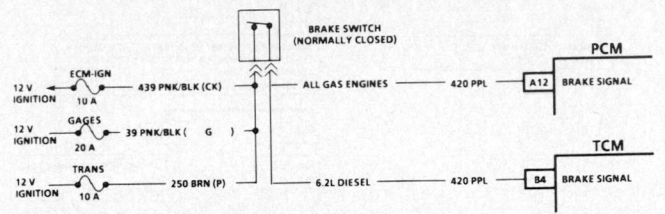

		BRAKE SWITCH (NORMALLY CLOSED)		PCM	
12 V IGNITION	ECM-IGN 10 A	439 PNK/BLK (CK)	ALL GAS ENGINES	420 PPL	A12	BRAKE SIGNAL
12 V IGNITION	GAGES 20 A	39 PNK/BLK (G)			TCM	
12 V IGNITION	TRANS 10 A	250 BRN (P)	6.2L DIESEL	420 PPL	B4	BRAKE SIGNAL

The normally closed brake switch supplies a 12-volt signal on circuit No. 420 to the PCM/TCM. The signal voltage is removed when brakes are applied. An incorrect brake signal may affect TCC operation.

NOTE: Test numbers refer to test numbers on diagnostic chart.

1) This test checks for voltage at brake switch.
2) This test simulates closed brake switch (brakes off).
3) This test checks circuit No. 420 from brake switch to PCM/TCM.
4) This test opens circuit No. 420 and simulates condition of brakes being applied.

DIAGNOSTIC AIDS

If code is intermittent, see INTERMITTENTS in TROUBLE SHOOTING – NO CODES article. Check customer driving habits and/or unusual traffic conditions (i.e. stop and go expressway traffic).

- INSTALL "SCAN" TOOL.
- IGNITION SWITCH "ON," ENGINE STOPPED.
- APPLY BRAKES.
- DOES "SCAN" DISPLAY BRAKES "ON," AND THEN DISPLAY "OFF" WHEN RELEASED?

NO → ALWAYS DISPLAYS "ON" / ALWAYS DISPLAYS "OFF"

YES → NO TROUBLE FOUND. REFER TO "DIAGNOSTIC AIDS" ON FACING PAGE.

ALWAYS DISPLAYS "ON"
1)
- IGNITION STILL "ON."
- DISCONNECT BRAKE SWITCH.
- WITH A TEST LIGHT CONNECTED TO GROUND, PROBE HARNESS CKT 39/439 250

LIGHT "ON" → 2)
- JUMPER BETWEEN HARNESS CKT 39/439 AND CKT 420. "SCAN" SHOULD INDICATE BRAKES "OFF". DOES IT?

LIGHT "OFF" → REPAIR OPEN CKT 39/439 250

NO → 3)
- JUMPER STILL INSTALLED.
- WITH A TEST LIGHT CONNECTED TO GROUND, BACKPROBE PCM/TCM CKT 420.

YES → BRAKE SWITCH OUT OF ADJUSTMENT OR FAULTY BRAKE SWITCH.

LIGHT "ON" → FAULTY PCM/TCM CONNECTION CKT 420 OR FAULTY PCM/TCM.

LIGHT "OFF" → OPEN CKT 420.

ALWAYS DISPLAYS "OFF"
4)
- IGNITION STILL "ON."
- DISCONNECT BRAKE SWITCH. "SCAN" TOOL SHOULD INDICATE BRAKES "ON." DOES IT?

NO → WITH TEST LIGHT CONNECTED TO GROUND PROBE HARNESS CKT 420.

YES → BRAKE SWITCH OUT OF ADJUSTMENT OR FAULTY BRAKE

LIGHT "ON" → CHECK FOR 12 VOLTS SHORTED TO CKT 420. CKT 420 OK. FAULTY PCM/TCM.

LIGHT "OFF" → FAULTY PCM/TCM.

91I13704 91J13705

Courtesy of General Motors Corp.

TORQUE CONVERTER CLUTCH (TCC) CIRCUIT CHECK

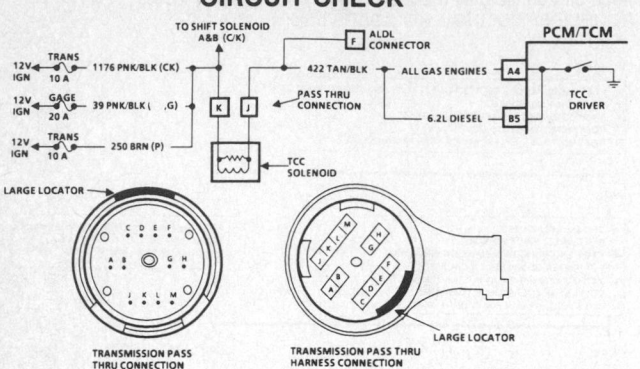

TRANSMISSION PASS THRU CONNECTION

TRANSMISSION PASS THRU HARNESS CONNECTION

The automatic transmission TCC eliminates power loss of torque converter stage when vehicle is in a cruise condition. This allows the convenience of the automatic transmission, and fuel economy of a manual transmission.

Fused battery ignition is supplied to the TCC solenoid, located inside valve body, to shift a spool valve in order to modulate pressure to the TCC.

The PCM/TCM will engage TCC by grounding circuit No. 422 to energize the solenoid.

TCC will engage under the following conditions.
- Vehicle speed is greater than 30 MPH (48 km/h).
- Engine at normal operating temperature greater than 149°F (65°C).
- Transmission at normal operating temperature of 195°F (91°C).
- Throttle position sensor output is not changing, indicating a steady road speed.
- Brake switch is closed.
- 4th gear is indicated.
- No codes are stored.

NOTE: Test numbers refer to test numbers on diagnostic chart.

1) This step checks for a shorted internal transmission harness or TCC solenoid.

91D13675 91A13706

2) This step verifies power supply to the TCC solenoid.
3) This step checks circuit No. 422 for a short to ground.
4) This step checks PCM/TCM's ability to control the TCC solenoid. If bidirectional scan tester is not available, TCC may be activated by grounding ALDL test terminal "B" with ignition on and engine off.

DIAGNOSTIC AIDS
Check all connections, especially those at the transmission pass-thru connector. If code is intermittent, see INTERMITTENTS in TROUBLE SHOOTING – NO CODES article. The TCC solenoid is pulse width modulated, and is designed to keep the TCC right at the point of engagement. Therefore, some slight slippage is normal.

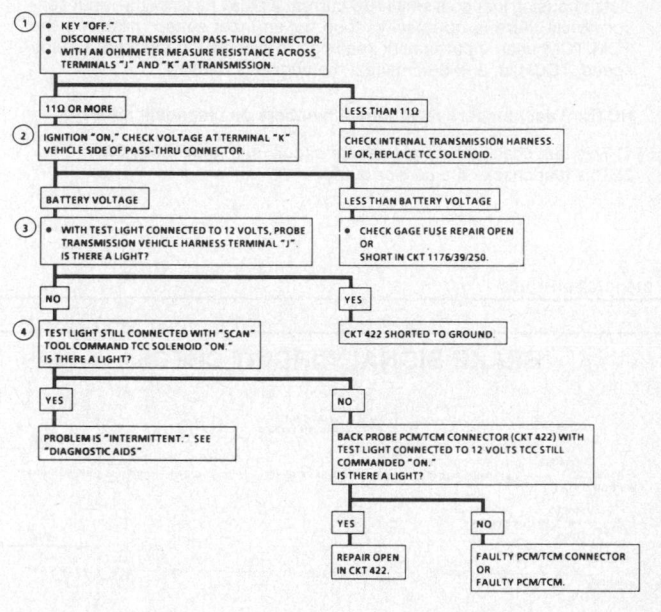

SHIFT SOLENOID "A" CIRCUIT CHECK

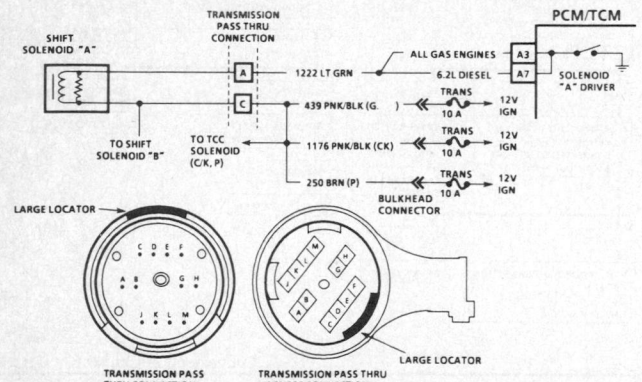

TRANSMISSION PASS THRU CONNECTION

TRANSMISSION PASS THRU HARNESS CONNECTION

Shift solenoid "A" is attached to the valve body and is a normally open exhaust valve. The PCM/TCM activates the solenoid by grounding it through an internal quad driver. Solenoid "A" (Blue) is on in 1st and 4th gears, but is off in 2nd and 3rd gears. When solenoid is on, it redirects fluid to act on the shift valves.

NOTE: Test numbers refer to test numbers on diagnostic chart.

1) This test checks shift solenoid "A" and the internal transmission wiring harness for shorts.
2) This test checks for power, from the ignition switch through the fuse, to the shift solenoid.
3) This test checks circuit No. 1222 for a short to ground.
4) This test checks PCM/TCM's ability to ground or control the shift solenoid "A". If bidirectional scan tester is not available, TCC may be activated by grounding ALDL test terminal "B" with ignition on and ongine off.

91I13688 91B13707

DIAGNOSTIC AIDS
Check all connections, especially those at the transmission pass-thru connector. If code is intermittent, see INTERMITTENTS in TROUBLE SHOOTING – NO CODES article.

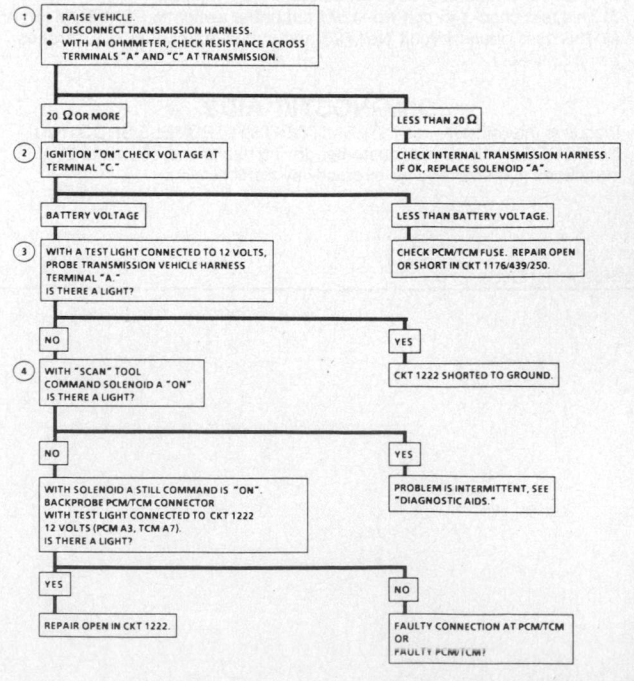

SHIFT SOLENOID "B" CIRCUIT CHECK

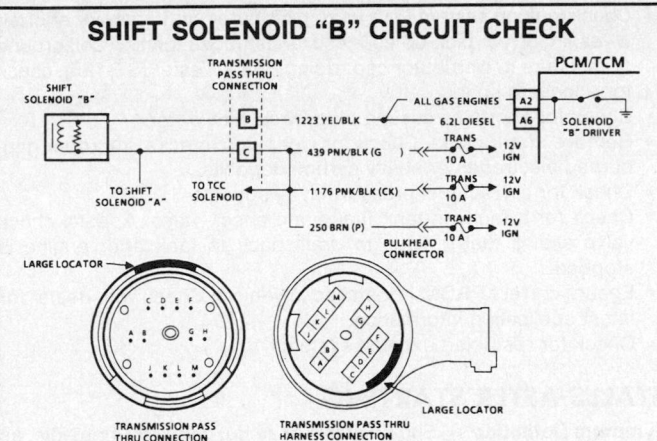

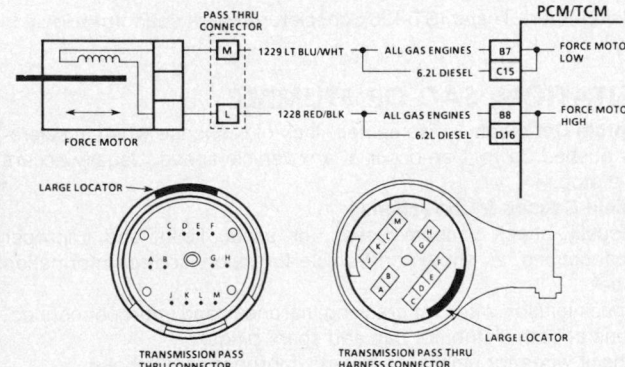

The shift solenoids are used inside the valve body to control the spool valves, which determine the transmission gear. Fused ignition is supplied to solenoid "B". The PCM/TCM will engage solenoid "B" by grounding circuit No. 1223 to energize the solenoid.

NOTE: Test numbers refer to test numbers on diagnostic chart.

1) This test checks shift solenoid "B" and the internal transmission wiring for shorts.
2) This test checks for power, from the ignition through the transmission fuse, to the shift solenoid "B".
3) This test checks PCM/TCM's ability to ground or control the shift solenoid "B".
3) This test ensures circuit No. 1223 is not shorted to ground.
4) This test checks PCM/TCM's ability to ground or control the shift solenoid "B". If bidirectional scan tester is not available, TCC may be activated by grounding ALDL test terminal "B" with ignition on and engine off.

91H13687 91C13708

5) This test ensures circuit No. 1223 is not shorted to ground.

DIAGNOSTIC AIDS

Check all connections, especially those at the transmission pass-thru connector. If code is intermittent, see INTERMITTENTS in TROUBLE SHOOTING – NO CODES article.

FORCE MOTOR CIRCUIT CHECK

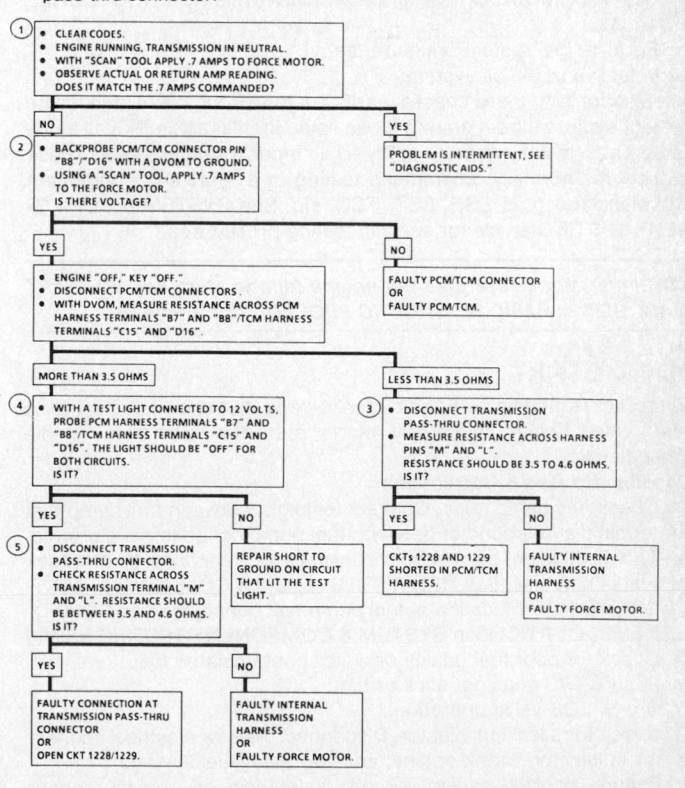

NOTE: This flow chart requires the use of a bidirectional (Tech 1) scan tester.

The force motor is a PCM/TCM-controlled device used to regulate transmission line pressure. The PCM/TCM looks at TPS voltage, engine RPM, and other inputs to determine the appropriate line pressure for a given load, then regulates the pressure by applying a variable amperage to the force motor. The applied amperage varies from .1-1.1 amps.

NOTE: Test numbers refer to test numbers on diagnostic chart.

1) Checks the PCM and TCM's ability to command the force motor.
2) Checks for voltage at PCM/TCM.
3) Checks internal transmission harness and force motor for low resistance.
4) Checks for short to ground.
5) Checks internal transmission harness and force motor for high resistance.

91E13684 92F21779

DIAGNOSTIC AIDS

Check for poor connections at PCM/TCM, especially at transmission pass-thru connector.

1992 ENGINE PERFORMANCE
Trouble Shooting – No Codes

Astro, Bravada, Commercial Van, Jimmy, Lumina APV, Safari, Sierra, Silhouette, Sonoma, Suburban, Syclone, Trans Sport, Typhoon, Van, Yukon, "C" & "K" Series Blazer & Pickup, "S" & "T" Series Blazer & Pickup

INTRODUCTION

Before diagnosing symptoms or intermittent faults, perform steps in BASIC DIAGNOSTIC PROCEDURES article and appropriate SELF-DIAGNOSTICS article. Use this article to diagnose driveability problems if a hard fault code is not present or if vehicle is not equipped with a self-diagnostic system.

Symptom checks are intended to direct the technician to malfunctioning component(s) for further diagnosis. A symptom should lead to either specific component or system testing or an adjustment specification. Use intermittent test procedures to locate driveability problems which DO NOT occur when the vehicle is being tested.

NOTE: For specific testing procedures, see SYSTEM & COMPONENT TESTING article. For specifications, see ON-VEHICLE ADJUSTMENTS or SERVICE & ADJUSTMENT SPECIFICATIONS article.

SYMPTOMS (GASOLINE)

NOTE: See SYMPTOMS (DIESEL) if necessary.

HOW TO USE THIS SECTION

Use this portion of article only AFTER performing these checks:

- Ensure on-vehicle diagnostics work (if equipped). Perform DIAGNOSTIC CIRCUIT CHECK in BASIC DIAGNOSTIC PROCEDURES article.
- Ensure ECM and SERVICE ENGINE SOON light function properly.
- Ensure no trouble codes, except intermittent ones, are stored.
- Ensure fuel control system operates properly. Perform FIELD SERVICE MODE CHECK in BASIC DIAGNOSTIC PROCEDURES article.
- Perform fuel system pressure test.
- Visually inspect all systems.

After performing these checks, verify customer complaint, and locate correct symptom from among those listed in this article. Not all items listed under each symptom apply to all models and systems. These procedures normally recommend testing of a system or component on vehicle, such as EGR, EST, TCC, etc. See SYSTEM & COMPONENT TESTING article for specific testing procedures.

NOTE: If ECM displays data but engine fails to start, see NO-START DIAGNOSIS in BASIC DIAGNOSTIC PROCEDURES article.

HARD START

Symptom Definition – Engine cranks okay, but does not start for a long time. Engine eventually starts and may run okay or die immediately.

Possible Causes & Corrections:

- Check fuel pump relay. Connect test light between fuel pump test terminal and ground or between fuel pump connector and ground. Turn ignition on. Light should illuminate for 2 seconds. If not, check fuel pump relay. See RELAYS in SYSTEM & COMPONENT TESTING article. For location of fuel pump test connector, see COMPONENT LOCATIONS in SYSTEM & COMPONENT TESTING article.
- Check for poor fuel quality or water-contaminated fuel.
- Ensure TPS does not stick or bind.
- Check EGR valve operation.
- Check for a leaking injector. Disconnect injector electrical connector at injector. Crank engine, and watch for fuel leakage.
- Ensure coolant sensor circuit resistance or coolant sensor resistance is not too high. See SENSOR OPERATING RANGE CHARTS article or CODE 15 chart in SELF-DIAGNOSTICS article.

- Check ignition system for a worn distributor shaft, bare or shorted wires, incorrect pick-up coil resistance, loose ignition coil ground or moisture in distributor cap. Using Spark Tester (ST-125), check for adequate spark.
- Check for shorts by misting plug wires with water.
- Remove spark plugs. Check for wet plugs, cracks, improper gap, burned electrodes or heavy carbon deposits.
- Check for correct fuel pressure at all speeds.
- Check for a faulty in-tank fuel pump check valve. A faulty check valve allows fuel in lines to drain back to tank after engine is stopped.
- Ensure correct PROM is installed in vehicle. Check with dealer for latest application information.
- Check for restricted exhaust system.

STALLS AFTER STARTING

Symptom Definition – Engine starts okay but dies after brief idle, as soon as any load is placed on engine (such as turning on air conditioner or engaging transmission) or on initial drive-away.

Possible Causes & Corrections:

- Ensure hot air tube is connected to air cleaner.
- Check thermostatic air cleaner for proper operation.
- Check Idle Air Control (IAC) system for proper operation.
- Check PCV valve for proper operation.
- Unplug MAP sensor. ECM substitutes a default value for sensor signal. If stall condition is eliminated, replace sensor.
- Check EGR system for proper operation.
- If stall occurs when air conditioner is turned on, check for air conditioner clutch signal to ECM terminal. Voltage at A/C terminal of ECM should be battery voltage when air conditioner compressor clutch is engaged. A high voltage surge due to a shorted compressor clutch diode could cause ECM shutdown.
- Check for an overcharged A/C system.
- Check for plugged or restricted fuel lines.
- If engine starts but then immediately stalls, open distributor by-pass circuit. If engine now starts and runs okay, replace distributor pick-up coil.
- Using Spark Tester (ST-125), check for a weak spark from ignition coil.

HESITATION, SAG OR STUMBLE

Symptom Definition – Momentary lack of response when accelerator is pushed down. Can occur at any vehicle speed. Usually occurs after a stop.

Possible Causes & Corrections:

- Visually check vacuum hoses for splits, kinks and improper connections, as shown on Vehicle Emission Control Information label.
- Check ignition wires for cracking, hardness and improper connections at both distributor cap and spark plugs.
- Check wires for pinches, cuts and improper connections.
- Ensure fuel pressure is correct in all speed ranges. Also check for poor fuel quality or water-contaminated fuel.
- Check for fouled spark plugs.
- Ensure correct PROM is installed in vehicle. Check with dealer for latest application information.
- Ensure TPS does not bind or stick.
- Ensure initial ignition timing is properly set.
- Ensure ECM-controlled idle speed is correct.
- Check EGR system for proper operation.
- Disconnect fuel injector electrical connectors. Crank engine, and check for injector leaks.
- Check for an open in HEI ground circuit.
- Check canister purge system for proper operation.
- Check charging system output. Repair charging system if voltage is less than 9 volts or more than 16 volts.

VEHICLE SURGES

Symptom Definition – Engine power varies under steady throttle or cruise. Feels like vehicle speeds up and slows down even though accelerator pedal position remains constant.

Possible Causes & Corrections:

- Check thermostatic air cleaner damper door for proper operation.
- Ensure park/neutral switch is properly adjusted.
- Check for intermittent open or short to ground in Torque Converter Clutch (TCC) or HEI by-pass circuits.
- Check canister purge system for proper operation.
- Check ESC system for proper operation.
- Check EGR system for proper operation.
- Ensure initial ignition timing is properly set.
- Using Spark Tester (ST-125), check for adequate spark output.
- Check O_2 sensor for lead or RTV sealant contamination. Such contamination causes a false high voltage signal to ECM, which responds by leaning air/fuel ratio.
- Check in-line fuel filter. Replace if dirty or clogged.
- Check fuel for water contamination. Ensure fuel system pressure is correct at all engine speeds.
- Remove spark plugs, and check for wet plugs, cracks, improper gap, burned electrodes or heavy carbon deposits. Also check condition of distributor cap, rotor and spark plug wires.
- Check A/C for excessive charge.
- Check for restricted exhaust system.

LACK OF POWER OR SLUGGISH

Symptom Definition – Engine delivers less power than expected. Little or no increase in speed when accelerator is pushed down.

Possible Causes & Corrections:

- Check air filter and fuel filter. Replace if necessary. Check for incorrect fuel pressure.
- Check injector wires for short to ground at air cleaner.
- Check thermostatic air cleaner damper door for proper operation.
- Ensure initial ignition timing is properly set.
- Check TCC system for proper operation.
- Check ECM grounds.
- Check ESC system for excessive retard.
- Check EST system for proper operation.
- Ensure EGR valve is not always open.
- Check exhaust system for restrictions, such as a damaged or collapsed pipe, muffler or catalytic converter. See EXHAUST SYSTEM BACKPRESSURE under MECHANICAL INSPECTION in BASIC DIAGNOSTIC PROCEDURES article.
- Check charging system output. Repair charging system if voltage is less than 9 volts or more than 16 volts.
- Check MAP sensor output.
- Using Spark Tester (ST-125), check for available secondary voltage.
- Check engine valve timing and compression.
- Check engine for a worn camshaft.

ENGINE BACKFIRES

Symptom Definition – Fuel ignites in intake manifold or in exhaust system, making a loud popping noise.

Possible Causes & Corrections:

- Ensure EGR valve is not always open.
- Check for proper valve timing.
- Check for engine vacuum leaks. Ensure engine is tuned to specifications.
- Check for faulty air injection diverter valve or check valve.
- Check engine for sticking or leaking valves.
- Check for fuel or water in vacuum hose to MAP sensor. Also check for restricted hose.
- Using Spark Tester (ST-125), check available output voltage of ignition coil.
- Check for crossfire between spark plugs, distributor cap and spark plug wires.
- Check for an intermittent ignition system problem.

- Check for erratic spark timing or distributor reference (RPM) signal.
- Ensure initial ignition timing is properly set.

CUTS OUT, MISSES

Symptom Definition – Cuts out, misses is defined as a steady pulsation or jerking following engine speed, usually more pronounced as engine load increases. Exhaust may have a steady spitting sound at idle or low speed. Perform careful visual inspection as described in BASIC DIAGNOSTIC PROCEDURES article.

Possible Causes & Corrections:

- Check ignition wires for short or faulty insulation.
- Check distributor cap for moisture, dust or cracks. Finely mist spark plug wires with water to check for shorts.
- Connect Spark Tester (ST-125) to spark plug, and check for adequate spark.
- Check ignition system for faulty grounds.
- Ensure EST wiring harness is not routed too close to wiring. EST wiring harness routed too close to wiring may cause induced voltage signals.
- Check ignition coil connections.
- Remove spark plugs, and check for incorrect heat range, wear, cracks, wetness, improper gap or heavy deposits.
- Check for poor or contaminated fuel.
- Check for improper fuel pressure.
- Ensure EGR valve does not stick open.
- Check ECM for proper ground circuits.
- Ensure TPS does not stick or bind. TPS voltage should be less than 1.25 volts at idle.
- Check for proper pick-up coil (HEI distributor) resistance.
- Check for restricted exhaust system. See EXHAUST SYSTEM BACKPRESSURE under MECHANICAL INSPECTION in BASIC DIAGNOSTIC PROCEDURES article.
- Check for bent push rods, broken valve springs or worn camshaft lobes.

CAUTION: Grounding spark plug wire for extended periods may cause catalytic converter overheating.

Misfire Isolation – 1) Start engine. Disconnect IAC motor. Using insulated pliers, remove one spark plug wire from a spark plug, and ground it against engine.

2) Note engine RPM as wire is grounded. Reconnect spark plug wire. Repeat procedure for all cylinders. Stop engine, and reconnect IAC motor.

3) If engine speed dropped equally (within 50 RPM) on all cylinders, refer to ROUGH, UNSTABLE OR INCORRECT IDLE symptom. If there was no engine RPM drop or no excessive variation on one or more cylinders, check spark on respective cylinder(s).

ROUGH, UNSTABLE OR INCORRECT IDLE

Symptom Definition – Engine runs unevenly at idle. If bad enough, vehicle will shake. Idle RPM may vary. Engine idles at incorrect RPM.

Possible Causes & Corrections:

- Ensure throttle linkage and/or TPS do not stick or bind.
- Ensure initial ignition timing is properly set.
- Check engine idle speed (both base and ECM idle).
- Check Idle Air Control (IAC) system. Check for foreign material in IAC bore. See DIAGNOSTIC AIDS in CODE 35 chart in appropriate SELF-DIAGNOSTICS article.
- Check EGR system for proper operation.
- Check park/neutral switch circuit. Ensure park/neutral switch is properly adjusted.
- Check power steering pressure switch circuit.
- Check exhaust system for restrictions, such as a damaged or collapsed pipe, muffler or catalytic converter. See EXHAUST SYSTEM BACKPRESSURE under MECHANICAL INSPECTION in BASIC DIAGNOSTIC PROCEDURES article.
- If rough idle occurs only when engine is hot, check PCV valve for proper operation. Check evaporative emission control system. Check for proper spark plug gap and engine compression.

voltage is not present, check for blown fuse or open fusible link. If okay, check for open in wire between ECM terminal and power source.

2) Turn ignition switch on. Using a voltmeter, check for battery voltage between ECM ignition power terminals and ground. If battery voltage is not present, check IGN fuse. If fuse is okay, check for an open in wire between battery and ignition switch, and between ignition switch and ECM terminal. If okay, check for a defective ignition switch.

3) Connect voltmeter between ground and ECM starter (crank) signal terminal. On vehicles with manual transmission/transaxle, depress clutch pedal. Turn ignition switch to START position. Battery voltage should be present ONLY when ignition switch is in the START position.

4) If voltage is not present, check CRANK fuse or fusible link between ignition switch and ECM terminal. If fuse or fusible link is okay, check for an open in wire between ignition switch and ECM terminal, or check for a defective ignition switch.

Quad-Driver Check (Except 3.1L & 4.3L Turbo) – 1) Remove ECM from vehicle. Using DVOM on 100/200 k/ohm scale, measure resistance between ECM case and each ECM quad-driver terminal. Touch negative DVOM lead to case and positive lead to ECM terminal. See appropriate ECM QUAD-DRIVER TERMINAL IDENTIFICATION table.

2) Each terminal should have at least 50 k/ohms resistance. If all quad-driver terminals have greater than 50 k/ohms resistance, go to step **4)**. If any terminal has less than 50 k/ohms resistance, locate driven component(s) for the quad-driver with the lowest resistance. Disconnect component from circuit and check circuit for short to voltage.

ing ECM to prevent recurring ECM failure. See appropriate ECM QUAD-DRIVER TERMINAL IDENTIFICATION table.

4) Using a fused ammeter capable of measuring at least 2 amps, turn ignition on with engine off. Connect one lead of ohmmeter to chassis ground. Connect remaining lead to each ECM harness quad-driver circuit. Measure each circuit for sustained current flow for at least 2 minutes.

NOTE: TCC solenoid cannot be easily tested for current draw, since completed circuit depends upon internal transmission oil pressure switches.

5) If no circuit has more than .75 amp sustained current flow, replace ECM. If any circuit has more than .75 amp sustained current flow, check for short to voltage in that circuit. If short to voltage is not present, replace related solenoid or relay.

ECM QUAD-DRIVER TERMINAL IDENTIFICATION (2.5L)

QDR No.	ECM Terminal	Component
1	A2	Shift Light (M/T)
		TCC Solenoid (A/T)
	A4	A/C Relay
	A5	SES Light
	C1	Not Used
2	A3	EGR Solenoid
	A7	Not Used
	C2	Not Used
	D12	Not Used

ECM QUAD-DRIVER TERMINAL IDENTIFICATION (2.8L WITHOUT 4L80-E TRANSMISSION)

QDR No.	ECM Terminal	Component
1	A2	A/C Relay
	A3	Not Used
	C1	Not Used
	C2	EAC Solenoid
2	A4	EGR Or EVRV Solenoid
	A5	SES Light
	A7	TCC Solenoid (A/T)
		Shift Light (M/T)

ECM QUAD-DRIVER TERMINAL IDENTIFICATION (3.8L WITH 4T60-3 TRANSAXLE)

QDR	PCM Terminal	Component
A	GC4	Cooling Fan (Low Speed)
	GC5	Purge Solenoid
	GC6	TCC Solenoid
B	GC15	TCC [1] PWM Solenoid
	GD15	Shift Solenoid "B"
	GD16	Shift Solenoid "A"

[1] – Pulse Width Modulated (PWM).

ECM QUAD-DRIVER TERMINAL IDENTIFICATION (4.3L CPI WITHOUT 4L80-E TRANSMISSION)

QDR No.	ECM Terminal	Component
1	A2	TCC Solenoid (A/T)
	A4	Not Used
	A5	SES Light
	C1	Not Used
2	A3	EGR Control
		Intake Tuning Valve
	C2	Not Used
	D12	Not Used

ECM QUAD-DRIVER TERMINAL IDENTIFICATION (4.3L TBI & V8 WITHOUT 4L80-E TRANSMISSION)

QDR No.	ECM Terminal	Component
1	A2	Not Used
	A3	Not Used
	C1	Not Used
	C2	EAC Solenoid
2	A4	EGR Or EVRV Solenoid
	A5	SES Light
	A7	TCC Solenoid (A/T)
		Shift Light (M/T)
	B4	Not Used

ECM QUAD-DRIVER TERMINAL IDENTIFICATION (ALL VEHICLES WITH 4L80-E TRANSMISSION)

QDR No.	ECM Terminal	Component
1	A2	Shift Solenoid B
	A3	Shift Solenoid A
	A4	TCC Solenoid
2	A7	SES Light
3	A11	EGR Or EVRV Solenoid

ENGINE SENSORS & SWITCHES

A/C ON Switch/System Test – 1) Turn ignition switch to RUN position. Move mode selector switch to OFF position. With A/C control assembly connected, measure voltage between mode selector switch Dark Green wire (Dark Green/White on "L", "M" & "U" Series) and ground. For wiring schematics, see mini-schematics in A/C CLUTCH under MISCELLANEOUS ECM CONTROLS.

2) Battery voltage should be present. If battery voltage is present, mode selector switch is operating normally. If battery voltage is not present, check wire from selector switch to fuse for an open circuit. Also check A/C high and low pressure switches for open.

3) Check voltage between mode selector Dark Green or Dark Green/White wire and ground. Voltage should not be present. If voltage was present, replace mode selector switch.

Brake Switch – Disconnect brake switch harness connector. Using an ohmmeter, check continuity between brake switch terminals. Continuity should be present. Depress brake pedal or activate brake switch, continuity should not be present.

Coolant Temperature Sensor (CTS) – If a coolant sensor-related code is present, see appropriate SELF-DIAGNOSTICS article. An out-of-calibration sensor may not set a trouble code. Use following procedure to test sensor calibration. Disconnect coolant temperature sensor connector. Measure resistance between sensor terminals. Resistance should be high when engine is cold and drop as engine warms up. See CTS RESISTANCE VALUES table.

CTS RESISTANCE VALUES

Temperature °F (°C)	Resistance (Ohms)
212 (100)	177
158 (70)	467
100 (38)	1800
68 (20)	3520
23 (-5)	12,300
0 (-18)	25,000
-40 (-40)	100,700

Knock Sensor – 1) Disconnect knock sensor harness connector. Using an ohmmeter, measure knock sensor resistance between sensor terminal and engine block. Resistance should be 3300-4500 ohms. Connect voltmeter between sensor terminal and ground. Set voltmeter to 2-volt AC scale.

2) Start and idle engine. Tap on engine block near sensor. A signal should be indicated on voltmeter. If no signal is indicated, replace knock sensor. Also see TIMING CONTROL SYSTEMS in this article.

Manifold Absolute Pressure (MAP) Sensor – 1) A malfunction in the MAP sensor circuit should set a related code in ECM memory. *See Fig. 1.* If a code is present, see appropriate SELF-DIAGNOSTICS article. An out-of-calibration sensor may not set a trouble code. Use following procedure to test sensor calibration. If driveability problems exist, MAP sensor failure is suspected, and no MAP code is present, disconnect MAP sensor connector. If driveability condition improves, check MAP vacuum hose for splits, kinks, proper routing and blockage. If no problems are found, replace MAP sensor.

blockage. If no problems are found, replace MAP sensor.

2) With ignition on and engine off, check MAP sensor parameter using a scan tester connected to the ALDL connector. Voltage should be as specified in MAP SENSOR VOLTAGE RANGE table. If MAP sensor voltage is as specified, go to next step. If voltage is not as specified, check for 5-volt reference supplied to sensor. Check harness integrity. If no problems are evident, replace MAP sensor.

3) Using a hand-held vacuum pump, apply 10 in. Hg to MAP sensor and note voltage change. Voltage should drop to about 1.0-2.5 volts less than specified in table. If voltage is not as specified or voltage reading does not immediately follow vacuum change, MAP sensor is faulty.

MAP SENSOR VOLTAGE RANGE

Altitude (Ft.)	Range (Volts)
Below 1000	3.8-5.5
1000-2000	3.6-5.3
2000-3000	3.5-5.1
3000-4000	3.3-5.0
4000-5000	3.2-4.8
5000-6000	3.0-4.6
6000-7000	2.9-4.5
7000-8000	2.8-4.3
8000-9000	2.6-4.2
9000-10,000	2.5-4.0

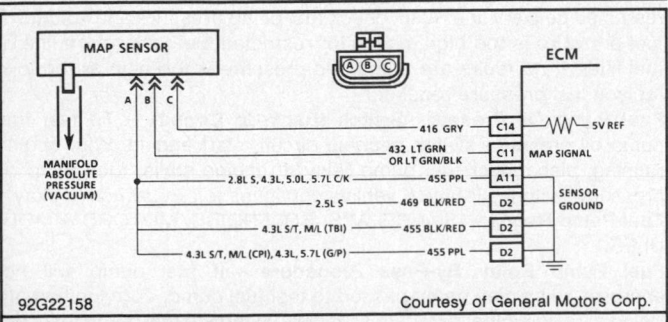

Fig. 1: Typical MAP Sensor Circuit

Manifold Air Temperature (MAT) Sensor – If a MAT sensor-related code is present, see appropriate SELF-DIAGNOSTICS article. An out-of-calibration sensor may not set a trouble code. Use following procedure to test calibration. Disconnect MAT sensor harness connector. Connect ohmmeter between sensor terminals. Sensor resistance should be as specified. See MAT SENSOR RESISTANCE table. With vehicle sitting overnight, MAT sensor and coolant sensor should have close to the same resistance reading.

MAT SENSOR RESISTANCE

Temperature °F (°C)	Resistance (Ohms)
210 (100)	185
160 (70)	450
100 (38)	1800
70 (20)	3400
40 (4)	7500
20 (-7)	13,500
0 (-18)	25,000
-40 (-40)	100,700

Oxygen (O_2) Sensor – 1) Start engine and warm to operating temperature. Disconnect oxygen sensor. Connect a DVOM between Purple lead of oxygen sensor and ground. Place meter on the 2-volt scale.

2) Using another DVOM on the 20-volt scale, connect voltmeter in series between Purple wire from the ECM and the positive post of battery. This will simulate a rich condition, causing ECM to respond by leaning mixture. Reading on voltmeter connected to oxygen sensor should decrease to less than .3 volt.

3) Move voltmeter lead from battery positive post to battery negative post. This will simulate a lean condition, causing ECM to respond by richening mixture. Reading on voltmeter connected to oxygen sensor should increase to greater than .8 volt. If reading does not change as specified, replace O_2 sensor.

4) If a second DVOM is not available, install a jumper in Purple wire from the ECM. Hold jumper in one hand and touch positive post of battery with other hand to simulate a rich condition. Touch negative post of battery to simulate a lean condition. For additional testing procedures, see appropriate SELF-DIAGNOSTICS article.

Oxygen Sensor Heating Element (4.3L Turbo PFI) – Disconnect 3-wire connector at oxygen sensor. Measure resistance between White wire terminals on sensor side of connector. Resistance should be 3.5-14 ohms at 68°F (20°C). If resistance is not 3.5-14 ohms, replace oxygen sensor.

Park/Neutral (P/N) Switch – Disconnect P/N switch (located on transmission) harness connector. Connect ohmmeter between P/N switch terminals. *See Fig. 2.* Continuity should be present only when gear shift selector is in Park or Neutral. If continuity is not present, check P/N switch adjustment or replace defective P/N switch.

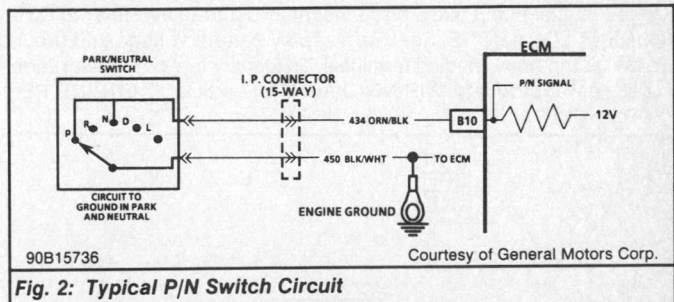

Fig. 2: Typical P/N Switch Circuit

Power Steering Pressure Switch (2.5L) – Disconnect P/S pressure switch harness connector. Connect ohmmeter between P/S pressure switch terminals. Start engine. With no load on power steering, continuity should not be present. Turn steering wheel to full stop, continuity should now be present. If readings are not as specified, replace defective P/S pressure switch.

Throttle Position Sensor (TPS) – 1) Install jumper wires to enable connection of a DVOM in parallel between TPS harness connectors. Connect DVOM positive lead to Dark Blue wire terminal. Connect negative lead to Black wire terminal. *See Fig. 3.*

2) Turn ignition on, engine off. Signal voltage should gradually change from less than one volt at closed throttle to about 5.0 volts at wide open throttle position. If reading is not as specified, adjust or replace TPS. See ON-VEHICLE ADJUSTMENTS article.

3) A malfunction in the TPS circuit should set a related trouble code. For further information, see appropriate SELF-DIAGNOSTICS article. Also see appropriate TPS ADJUSTMENT in ON-VEHICLE ADJUSTMENTS article.

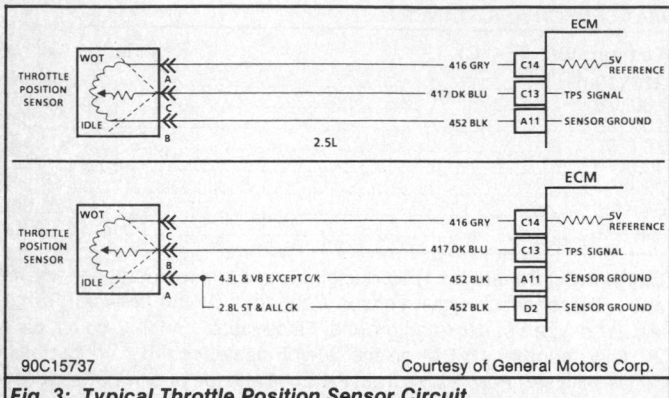

90C15737   Courtesy of General Motors Corp.

Fig. 3: Typical Throttle Position Sensor Circuit

Vehicle Speed Sensor (PM Generator) – Disconnect vehicle speed sensor harness connector (located in transmission/transaxle). Place gear selector in Neutral. Raise vehicle drive wheels off the ground. Turn drive wheels by hand (greater than 3 MPH). Measure AC signal voltage between sensor terminals. Voltage reading should be varying from 0.1-0.5 volt AC as the wheel is turned. If reading is not as specified, replace vehicle speed sensor. If a code is set, refer to appropriate SELF-DIAGNOSTICS article.

RELAYS, SOLENOIDS, MOTORS & MODULES

RELAYS

A/C Relays – See MISCELLANEOUS ECM CONTROLS.
Cold Advance Relay (6.2L Diesel) – See DIESEL COLD ADVANCE SYSTEM CHECK under FUEL SYSTEM (DIESEL).
Fuel Pump Relay – **1)** If a prolonged crank is required to start vehicle, fuel pump relay may be faulty. To verify this, start engine. With engine running, disconnect oil pressure switch (fuel pump back-up circuit). If engine stalls, fuel pump relay is faulty. If vehicle continues to run, relay is okay. Check for other causes of prolonged crank.
2) To test fuel pump relay, disconnect fuel pump relay. Refer to COMPONENT LOCATIONS. See Fig. 4. Apply battery voltage and ground to fuel pump relay winding terminals. To identify fuel pump relay terminals, see appropriate WIRING DIAGRAMS article in ENGINE PERFORMANCE.

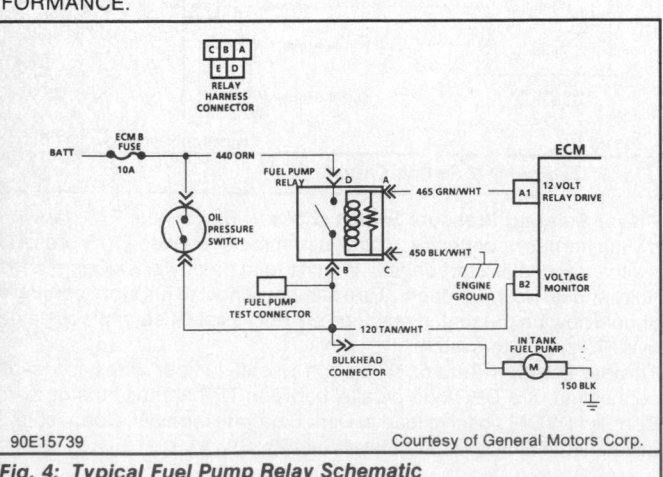

90E15739   Courtesy of General Motors Corp.

Fig. 4: Typical Fuel Pump Relay Schematic

3) Using an ohmmeter, check continuity between fuel pump relay power and fuel pump relay drive terminals. Continuity should exist. If continuity does not exist, fuel pump relay is defective.
4) To by-pass fuel pump relay on vehicle (fuel pump not operating), turn ignition off. Disconnect fuel pump relay connector. Using a fused jumper wire, connect fuel pump test connector to positive side of battery. Fuel pump should run.
5) If fuel pump runs, check for faulty connections to relay or replace defective relay. To locate fuel pump test connector, refer to COMPONENT LOCATIONS.

SOLENOIDS

NOTE: All ECM-controlled solenoids should have at least 20 ohms of resistance (except fuel injectors).

Canister Purge Solenoid – See EMISSION SYSTEMS & SUB-SYSTEMS.
Electronic Air Control (EAC) Solenoid – See EMISSION SYSTEMS & SUB-SYSTEMS.
EGR Control Solenoid – See EMISSION SYSTEMS & SUB-SYSTEMS.
Torque Converter Clutch (TCC) Solenoid – See MISCELLANEOUS ECM CONTROLS.
Wastegate Solenoid (4.3L Turbo PFI) – See AIR INDUCTION SYSTEMS.

MOTORS

Charge Air Cooler Pump (4.3L Turbo) – See AIR INDUCTION SYSTEMS.
Idle Air Control (IAC) Motor – See IDLE CONTROL SYSTEM under FUEL SYSTEM (GASOLINE).

FUEL SYSTEM (GASOLINE)

FUEL DELIVERY

NOTE: For fuel system pressure testing, see BASIC DIAGNOSTIC PROCEDURES article.

Fuel Pressure Regulator (PFI) – Fuel pressure regulator is a vacuum-controlled diaphragm type, which uses manifold vacuum to modify fuel pressure to compensate for engine load fuel requirements. Connect fuel pressure gauge to fuel pressure service port. Start engine and note fuel pressure. Disconnect vacuum hose from fuel pressure regulator. Fuel pressure should increase 4-10 psi (.28-.70 kg/cm²). If pressure does not increase 4-10 psi (.28-.70 kg/cm²), check for presence of manifold vacuum at signal line. If vacuum is not present, check for kinked, cut or split vacuum hose or plugged throttle body vacuum port. If vacuum is present and no pressure change occurred, replace fuel pressure regulator.

Fuel Pressure Regulator (TBI) – Fuel pressure regulator is mechanically controlled by internal spring pressure. Regulator is adjusted at factory and is not serviceable. If fuel pressure is too low, check for restricted delivery line. Also, check fuel pump pressure and volume. If fuel pressure is too high, check for restricted fuel tank return line or fuel filter. If no faults are found and pressure is too high or too low, replace fuel pressure regulator.

Fuel Pump Oil Pressure Switch (Back-Up Circuit) – To test fuel pump oil pressure switch back-up circuit, start engine. With engine running, disconnect fuel pump relay. If engine stalls, fuel pump oil pressure switch is faulty. If vehicle continues to run, switch is okay.

Fuel Pump Relay – See RELAYS, SOLENOIDS, MOTORS & MODULES.

Fuel Pump Relay By-Pass Procedure – If fuel pump will not energize, relay may be by-passed to test fuel pump. Turn ignition off. Using a fused jumper wire, apply battery voltage to fuel pump test connector. Fuel pump should turn on. For fuel pump test connector location, refer to COMPONENT LOCATIONS.

FUEL CONTROL

Fuel Injector(s) – Disconnect fuel injector harness connector. Measure resistance across injector terminals. Resistance should be as specified. See FUEL INJECTOR RESISTANCE table.

FUEL INJECTOR RESISTANCE

Application	[1] Resistance (Ohms)
3.1L (VIN D)	1.2
4.3L (VIN Z Turbo PFI)	[2] 2.0
All Others	1.3

[1] – Injector resistance specification is at 140°F (60°C).
[2] – Minimum reading.

Oxygen Sensor – See ENGINE SENSORS & SWITCHES.

NOTE: If injectors are dirty, they should be cleaned using approved injector cleaning procedure before performing PFI INJECTOR BALANCE TEST.

PFI Injector Balance Test (C-2) – The injector balance test is used to pulse the injector for a precise amount of time, spraying a measured amount of fuel in the intake manifold. As each injector is pulsed, a drop in fuel rail pressure occurs. This pressure drop can be recorded and compared to other injectors. An injector with a pressure drop of 1.5 psi (.11 kg/cm²) or more, greater than or less than other injectors, should be considered faulty.

NOTE: Allow engine to cool down to avoid irregular readings due to "hot soak" fuel boiling. To prevent flooding, the PFI INJECTOR BALANCE TEST should not be repeated more than once without starting and running engine.

CAUTION: To avoid possible vehicle fire, wrap a shop towel around fitting to avoid fuel spillage.

1) With ignition off, connect Fuel Pressure Gauge (J-34730-1) to pressure tap. Unplug harness connector at all injectors. Connect Injector Tester (J-34730-3) to one of the injectors.
2) Follow manufacturer's instructions when installing adapter harness. Ignition should be turned off at least 10 seconds to complete ECM shutdown cycle.
3) Turn ignition on. Fuel pump should run at least 2 seconds after ignition is turned on. Bleed air from gauge and hose to ensure accurate gauge reading. Repeat this procedure until all air is bled from system. Turn ignition off for at least 10 seconds.
4) Turn ignition on again to bring fuel pressure to maximum. Record initial pressure reading. Energize tester one time and note pressure drop at lowest point.
5) Disregard any slight pressure drop after low point is reached. Subtracting second pressure reading from initial reading indicates amount of injector pressure drop.
6) Repeat step **4)** on each injector and compare pressure drop. Recheck injectors not within pressure drop range. Replace injector(s) failing second check.
7) If injectors are all okay, plug in harness connectors and review SYMPTOMS in TROUBLE SHOOTING – NO CODES article.

IDLE CONTROL SYSTEM

Idle Air Control (IAC) Motor – **1)** Disconnect harness connector to motor. Check resistance across IAC coil terminals "A" to "B" and "C" to "D". See Fig. 5. Resistance should be 40-80 ohms. If okay, go to next step. If resistance is not as specified, replace IAC motor.
2) Check resistance between IAC terminals "B" to "C" and "A" to "D". Resistance should be infinite. If resistance is not as specified, replace IAC motor.

NOTE: Functional testing of Idle Air Control (IAC) motor requires a scan tester capable of cycling ECM output devices (bidirectional) or a special IAC Driver and Node Light Set (222L or J-37027). Flow charts in the SELF-DIAGNOSTICS articles may refer to the Tech 1 tester, General Motors' bidirectional tester.

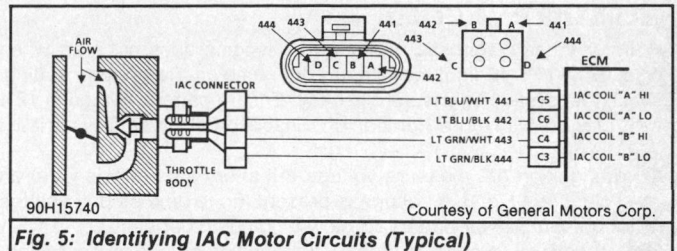

Fig. 5: Identifying IAC Motor Circuits (Typical)

90H15740 — Courtesy of General Motors Corp.

FUEL SYSTEM (DIESEL)

NOTE: The 6.2L light duty emissions engine (LH6) uses the Diesel Electronic Control (DEC) system. For complete system testing and diagnosis of DEC system, see SELF-DIAGNOSTICS – DIESEL article.

NORMAL GLOW PLUG CIRCUIT OPERATION

A normal functioning system should operate as follows:
1) With ignition switch in the ON position, engine not running and at room temperature, glow plugs are on for 4-6 seconds, then off for about 4.5 seconds. Following this on-and-off cycle, glow plugs are on for about 1.5 seconds and off for about 4.5 seconds. The glow plugs continue to cycle on and off in this time sequence for about 20 seconds.
2) If engine is cranked during or after the above sequence, glow plugs will cycle on and off for a total duration of 25 seconds after the ignition switch is returned from the crank position, whether engine starts or not. Engine does not have to be running to terminate glow plug cycling.

NOTE: Glow plug on-and-off times vary with engine temperature, system voltage and/or ambient temperature. Lower temperatures cause longer duration of cycling.

PRELIMINARY GLOW PLUG DIAGNOSIS

1) If system does not operate as described in NORMAL GLOW PLUG CIRCUIT OPERATION, ensure glow plug system is correctly installed. Ensure all connectors are properly attached, clean and tight. Inspect engine harness ground connection. Ensure nut securing 4-wire connector at controller is tightened to **96 INCH lbs. (11 N.m)**, with connector fully seated and latched.
2) Ensure controller copper stud upper nuts are tightened to **96 INCH lbs (11 N.m)**. DO NOT tighten lower nuts. Ensure temperature switch connector in water crossover near front of engine is tightened to **48 INCH lbs. (5.4 N.m)**. Inspect WAIT light on instrument panel for tight connection and operation.

INHIBIT SWITCH (BLACK CAP)

1) Remove connector from inhibit switch when engine temperature is less than 100°F (38°C). Inhibit switch is located in water crossover near front of engine. Set ohmmeter on low range. Test continuity across switch terminals. Switch should be closed (a reading of less than 1.0 ohm on meter.)
2) Test terminals for continuity to ground with a test light or ohmmeter on high scale. Light should be off. Meter should show greater than 1.0 megohm. Replace switch if results are not as specified.
3) Disconnect plug from switch terminals when engine temperature is greater than 125°F (52°C). Change ohmmeter setting to highest scale or use a self-powered test light. Test continuity across switch terminals. Test continuity from each terminal to ground. Switch should be open (test light off or high ohm reading of greater than 1.0 megohm on meter). Replace switch if it is closed. When installing replacement switch, tighten to **17 ft. lbs. (23 N.m)**.

GLOW PLUG SYSTEM DIAGNOSIS

Electrical Check – Turn ignition off. Disconnect all glow plug connectors. Using an ohmmeter, check resistance between each glow plug terminal and ground. Glow plug resistance should be greater than 2 ohms. Replace glow plug if resistance is not as specified.

NO START – COLD

Perform these diagnostic procedures if engine does not start when cold; GLOW PLUG light may or may not come on. Before proceeding, check fuel system to ensure it is okay. Ensure battery voltage is 12.4 volts or more with turned ignition off. Ensure cranking speed is at least 100 RPM.

1) With ignition off, measure voltage at battery stud (single wire) on glow plug. *See Fig. 6.* If voltage is present, go to next step. If voltage is not present, repair battery-to-glow plug controller circuit.

2) If voltage was present in step **1)**, turn ignition off and measure voltage at glow plug feed stud (twin lead) on glow plug controller. If battery voltage is present, go to next step. If battery voltage is not present, relay contacts are shorted. Replace controller and all glow plugs.

3) If voltage is present in step **2)**, disconnect harness from all glow plugs. Using an ohmmeter, measure resistance between glow plug terminals and engine block. Replace glow plug if resistance is greater than 2 ohms. Reconnect all glow plugs before continuing with diagnosis.

4) With all glow plugs reconnected, place ignition switch in RUN position. Remove controller connector and check voltage at harness connector terminal "D". *See Fig. 6.*

5) If no voltage is present, repair open in ignition feed circuit to controller. If voltage is present, measure resistance between terminal "E" of connector and engine block (ground). If measurement is greater than one ohm, repair ground circuit to controller.

6) With ground circuit working properly in step **4)**, measure resistance between terminals "C" and "E" of connector. If reading is greater than 2 ohms, go to next step. If reading is less than 2 ohms, go to step **8)**.

7) If reading in step **6)** is greater than 2 ohms, check for excessive resistance in voltage sense circuit to controller. Repair as necessary.

8) If reading in step **5)** was less than 2 ohms, reconnect controller harness connector and ensure complete engagement. Connector locking latch should click over controller locking tab. With controller connector harness correctly connected, measure voltage at glow plug feed stud (twin lead) on glow plug controller, while turning ignition switch from OFF position to RUN position.

9) If no voltage is present, replace glow plug controller. If battery voltage is present, measure voltage at any one glow plug harness connector when turning ignition switch from OFF to RUN position. Test both right and left banks.

10) If no voltage was present in step **9)**, repair glow plug feed circuit to glow plugs. If battery voltage is present and instrument panel GLOW PLUG light does not come on, locate and repair bulb or circuit.

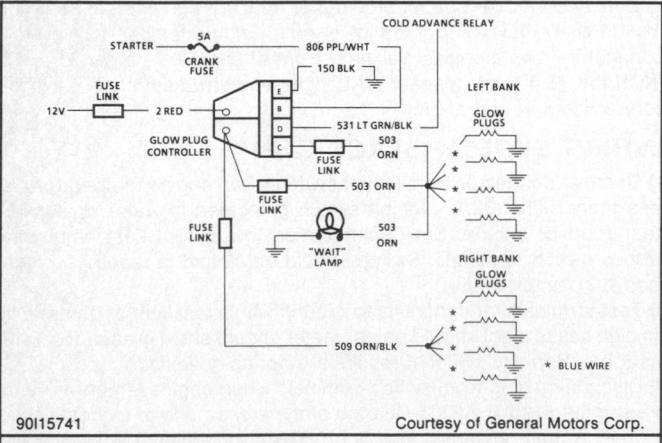

90I15741   Courtesy of General Motors Corp.

Fig. 6: Diesel Glow Plug Circuit

DIESEL COLD ADVANCE SYSTEM CHECK

With ignition on voltage is supplied to the cold advance relay through the 20-amp GAGES fuse. When coolant temperature is less than 80°F (27°C), as sensed by the coolant temperature sensor, the ECM provides a ground at terminal C6. *See Fig. 7.* Grounding terminal C6 energizes the cold advance relay, closing the relay contacts and sup-

plying 12 volts to the cold advance solenoid (in the injection pump), and the glow plug controller. The cold advance solenoid is now energized, causing injection pump timing to be advanced about 4 degrees.

Cold Advance Relay – 1) Disconnect harness connector to cold advance relay. Using an ohmmeter, check resistance between relay terminals "D" and "F". *See Fig. 7.* Continuity should be present or a resistance of 20 ohms. If not, replace cold advance relay.

2) Using an ohmmeter, check continuity between relay terminals "A" and "E". Continuity should not be present. If continuity is present, replace grounded cold advance relay.

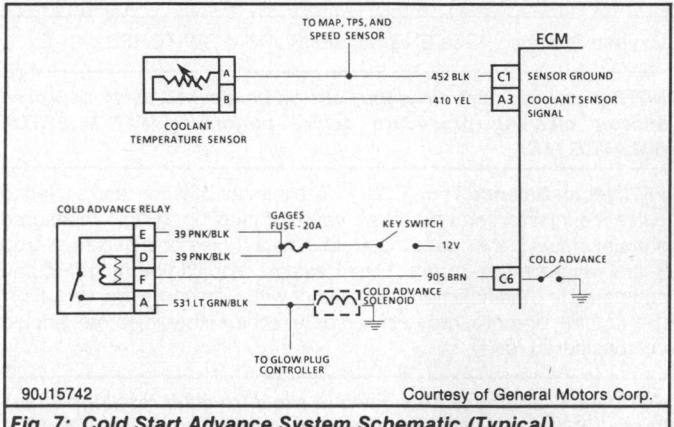

90J15742   Courtesy of General Motors Corp.

Fig. 7: Cold Start Advance System Schematic (Typical)

GLOW PLUG CONTROLLER

1) Ensure coolant temperature is less than 80°F (27°C) before beginning test. Place ignition switch in RUN position and allow glow plugs to cycle. After 2 minutes, crank engine for one second. It is NOT important that the engine starts. Return ignition switch to RUN position. Glow plugs should cycle on at least once.

2) If glow plugs do not cycle, disconnect controller (controller is located on top, rear of valve cover). Connect a 12-volt test light between Purple/White wire terminal of harness connector (terminal "B") and ground. *See Fig. 6.* With ignition switch in RUN position, test light should be off. Test light should glow when engine is cranked.

3) If test light does not glow as specified, repair short or open in engine harness Purple/White wire. If test light operates properly but glow plugs did not cycle, replace controller.

INJECTION PUMP HOUSING LEAKAGE TEST

1) Remove injection pump and drain all fuel. Connect an air supply line to fuel inlet fitting. Ensure air supply is clean and dry. Seal off return line fitting. Completely immerse pump assembly in a container of clean test oil.

2) Apply 20 psi (1.4 kg/cm²) to pump. Leave pump immersed for 10 minutes to allow trapped air to escape. Watch for leaks after 10 minutes. If no leaks are observed after 10 minutes, reduce air pressure to 2 psi (.14 kg/cm²) for 30 seconds.

3) If there are still no leaks, increase pressure to 20 psi (1.4 kg/cm²) again. If no leaks are observed, pump is ready for use. If leaks are noticed, pump must be replaced.

INJECTORS

Test Preparation – 1) Remove injector nozzles from engine. Clean carbon from tip area of nozzle with soft brass wire brush. DO NOT use steel brush or motorized brush to clean nozzle tip. Damage to nozzle tip may result.

CAUTION: Use Nozzle Socket (J-36142) to remove and replace injection nozzle. Attach socket to 30mm hex portion of nozzle. Failure to do so will result in damage to the injector nozzle.

2) Connect injector nozzle to injection nozzle tester. Place clear plastic tubing on both fuel return fittings to prevent bleed-off from being confused with leaks. Close tester shutoff valve to pressure gauge.

3) Fill tester with test fluid. Fill and flush nozzle assembly with test fluid by operating tester lever briskly and repeatedly. This purges air from injector nozzle and coats all parts with test fluid.

WARNING: When testing injectors, keep spray contained to avoid serious injury. DO NOT allow injector to release line pressure on hands, arms or any part of body. Pressure of atomized test spray has sufficient penetrating power to puncture flesh.

Opening Pressure Test – 1) Open tester shutoff valve 1/4 turn from closed position. Slowly depress tester lever and observe gauge. Note pressure at which needle of pressure gauge stops. Some injector nozzles may pop while other injector nozzles may drip (this is not a leak).

2) Injector opening pressure should not fall to less than 1500 psi (105 kg/cm²). Replace any injector nozzle that does not meet lowest acceptable pressure. Release tester pressure.

Leakage Test – 1) Open tester shutoff valve 3/4 to 1 3/4 turns from closed position. Blow dry injector nozzle tip. Slowly depress tester lever until pressure gauge reads 1400 psi (98 kg/cm²). Maintain pressure for 10 seconds and observe injector nozzle tip.

2) A drop may form on end of injector nozzle, but should not fall off within a 10 second period. Replace injector nozzle if a drop of test fluid falls from tip during the 10 second period. See Fig. 8. Release tester pressure.

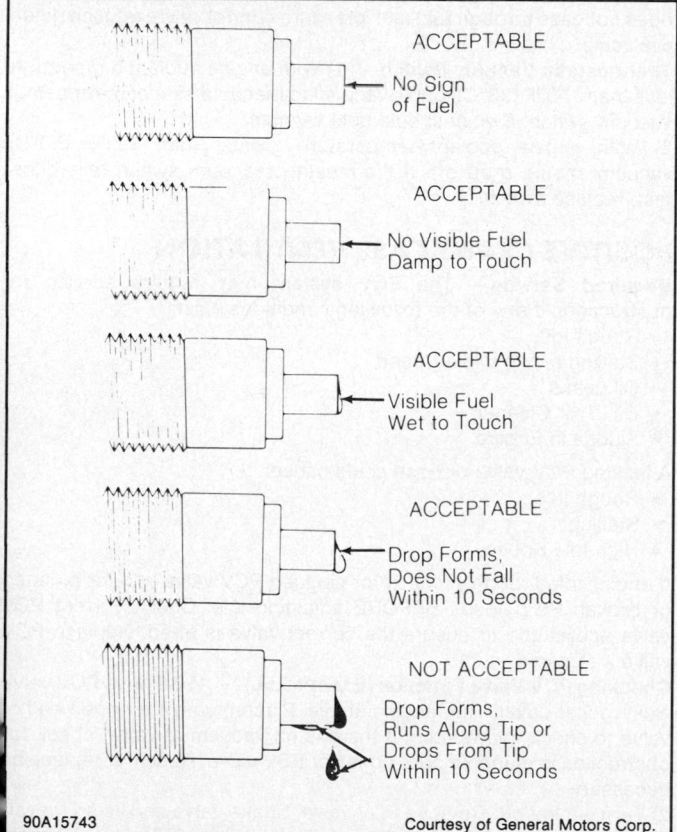

ACCEPTABLE
No Sign of Fuel

ACCEPTABLE
No Visible Fuel Damp to Touch

ACCEPTABLE
Visible Fuel Wet to Touch

ACCEPTABLE
Drop Forms, Does Not Fall Within 10 Seconds

NOT ACCEPTABLE
Drop Forms, Runs Along Tip or Drops From Tip Within 10 Seconds

90A15743   Courtesy of General Motors Corp.

Fig. 8: Injection Nozzle Leakage Test

Chatter Test – Chatter for new and used injector nozzles may vary. With some used injector nozzles, chatter is difficult to detect during slow actuation of tester lever. Some injector nozzles may chatter louder than others. As long as there is chatter, the injector nozzle is acceptable.

**) Close tester shutoff lever at pressure gauge. Slowly depress lever and note whether chatter can be heard. If no chatter is heard, increase speed of lever movement until it reaches a point at which injector nozzle chatters.

**) At fast lever movement, injector nozzle may emit a "hissing" or "squealing" sound rather than normal chatter. This is acceptable.

These sounds indicate that injector nozzle needle moves freely and injector nozzle seat, guide and pintle have no mechanical defects. Replace any injector nozzle assembly that does not chatter.

Spray Pattern Test – The injector nozzles used with this system have several features that make pattern testing difficult. These features include longer nozzle overlap, greater pintle-to-body clearances and an internal wave washer between injector nozzle nut and injector. Typical injector nozzle tester cannot deliver fuel with sufficient velocity to obtain proper spray patterns. DO NOT replace injector nozzle(s) based on spray pattern.

IGNITION SYSTEM

NOTE: For basic ignition system checks, see BASIC DIAGNOSTIC PROCEDURES article.

TIMING CONTROL SYSTEMS (C-4 & C-5)

C-4, Electronic Spark Timing (Gasoline Engines) – An open or short to ground in the Electronic Spark Timing (EST) or by-pass circuits will cause ECM to turn on SERVICE ENGINE SOON light and confirm fault causing Code 42 is present. Refer to SELF-DIAGNOSTICS – GASOLINE article.

C-5, Electronic Spark Control (ESC) Circuit (Gasoline Engines Except 2.5L, 4.3L Turbo & Vehicles With 4L80-E Transmission) – 1) An open or short circuit on ESC wire to ECM will cause a loss of 12-volt ESC controller signal. This will cause ECM to fully retard ignition timing.

2) If a scan tester is available, connect it to the ALDL connector. Using a metal object, tap on engine next to knock sensor and note knock parameter. Knock should be indicated on scan tester.

3) If a scan tester is not available, backprobe ECM ESC signal terminal with a DVOM. With engine idling, 8-12 volts should be present at this terminal. Using a metal object, tap on engine close to knock sensor. Voltage signal at ECM terminal should drop to zero volts, and return when knock signal ceases.

4) If signal does not respond as described, check knock sensor signal to controller signal. On vehicles equipped with automatic transmission, it may be necessary to place transmission in Drive for timing change to occur. See KNOCK SENSOR under ENGINE SENSORS & SWITCHES.

C-5, Electronic Spark Control (ESC) Circuit (4.3L Turbo & Vehicles With 4L80-E Transmission) – 1) An open or short circuit on the ESC wire to the ECM will set a related trouble code. A false detonation signal will not cause ECM to set a code.

2) If a scan tester is available, connect it to the ALDL connector. Tap on engine next to knock sensor and note "knock" parameter. Knock should be indicated on scan tester.

3) If a scan tester is not available, connect tachometer to engine. Start engine and hold RPM above idle. Using a metal object, tap on engine close to knock sensor. A noticeable decrease in engine RPM should occur. If no RPM decrease occurred, check knock sensor to ECM circuit.

4) On vehicles equipped with automatic transmission, it may be necessary to place transmission in Drive for timing change to occur. See KNOCK SENSOR under ENGINE SENSORS & SWITCHES.

EMISSION SYSTEMS & SUB-SYSTEMS (GASOLINE)

AIR INJECTION (C-6)

Air Pump – Accelerate engine to approximately 1500 RPM and observe airflow from hoses. If airflow increases as engine is accelerated, pump is working properly. If airflow does not increase, check system for plugged or restricted hoses, proper pump belt tension, leaky valves or defective air injection pump.

Check Valve – Allow engine to cool. Remove check valve from engine and blow through valve in direction of check valve flow (to cylinder head). Attempt to suck back. Replace valve if airflow is allowed against the direction of flow.

Electronic Air Control (EAC) Solenoid – 1) Turn ignition on, engine off. Disconnect EAC solenoid connector. Connect test light between solenoid connector terminals. *See Fig. 9.* If test light comes on, check for grounded wire from solenoid to ECM. If wire is not grounded, replace ECM. If test light does not turn on, go to next step.

2) Ground ALDL diagnostic connector. If test light comes on, check for faulty EAC solenoid connector. If connector is okay, replace EAC valve. If test light does not turn on, connect test light between harness terminal "A" and ground. *See Fig. 9.* If test light still did not turn on, check for open in fuse or wire to ignition.

3) If test light comes on, check for open in wire from solenoid to ECM. If wire is okay, check EAC solenoid resistance. If resistance is less than 20 ohms, replace EAC solenoid and perform ECM quad-driver check. See CONTROL UNIT under COMPUTERIZED ENGINE CONTROLS. If EAC solenoid resistance is greater than 20 ohms, replace ECM.

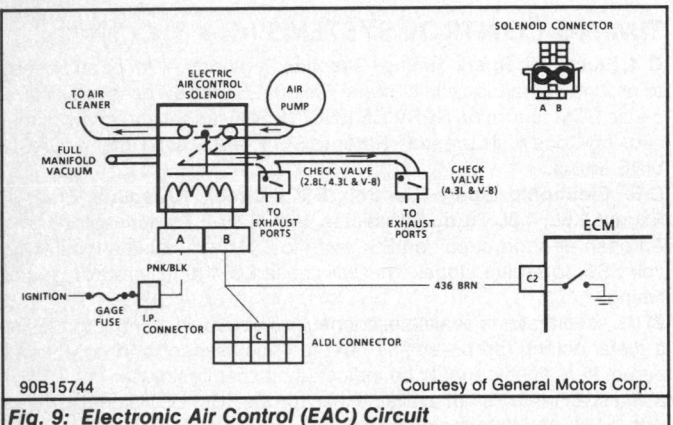

90B15744   Courtesy of General Motors Corp.

Fig. 9: Electronic Air Control (EAC) Circuit

EXHAUST GAS RECIRCULATION (C-7)

System Test – Start and run engine to normal operating temperature. With engine at idle, RPM should drop as EGR valve is opened by pushing up on underside of EGR diaphragm.

CAUTION: Wear gloves when handling hot EGR valve.

EGR Control Solenoid – 1) Disconnect EGR solenoid electrical harness connector and vacuum hoses. Connect a hand-held vacuum pump to solenoid vacuum source port. Connect vacuum gauge to solenoid EGR port. Pump up vacuum pump. Vacuum should not be present at port to EGR valve.

2) Activate EGR solenoid with a remote ground and 12-volt power supply. Vacuum should now be present at vacuum gauge. Solenoid should have at least 20 ohms of resistance.

Negative Backpressure EGR Valve – With engine off, disconnect vacuum hose to EGR valve. Connect vacuum pump to EGR and apply 10 in. Hg. If EGR diaphragm does not move up and stay up for 20 seconds, replace EGR valve.

Linear EGR Valve (4.3L CPI) – 1) Install scan tester. Ensure P/N switch is operating properly. See ENGINE SENSORS & SWITCHES. With engine at normal operating temperature, command EGR pintle position to 0%. Increase engine speed to 2000 RPM. If scan tester reads actual EGR pintle position at greater than 3%, EGR valve is stuck open. Replace EGR valve.

2) If scan tester reads actual EGR pintle position at 3% or less, command a 25% position step increase (i.e. 0-25%, 25-50%, 50-75%, etc.). Observe MAP reading and actual EGR pintle position for 3 seconds. EGR should increase by about 25% position and MAP reading should also increase.

3) If actual EGR pintle position is stable and within ±10% position of desired EGR pintle position command after 2 seconds, go to next step. If actual EGR pintle position is not as specified, go to step **5)**.

4) MAP reading should have increased when EGR pintle responded. If MAP did not respond, check EGR passages and EGR valve for

blockage. If MAP responded, set desired EGR pintle position to 100%. If EGR pintle position sets to 100%, EGR is okay. If not, replace EGR valve.

5) Turn engine off. Check EGR electrical circuit and connecting components. Turn ignition on, check for 5-volt reference voltage on harness connector terminal "D" (Gray wire). If 5-volt reference voltage is not present, check ECM. See CONTROL UNIT under COMPUTERIZED ENGINE CONTROLS. If circuits are okay, replace EGR valve.

FUEL EVAPORATION CONTROL (C-3)

Vapor Canister Purge Valve ("P" Series & 4.3L CPI) – 1) Install a short length of hose to lower port of purge valve. Blow into hose. Little or no air should pass into canister (a small amount of air will pass if the canister has a constant purge hole).

2) Using a hand-held vacuum pump, apply 15 in. Hg to vacuum control (upper) port. If vacuum does not hold for 20 seconds, replace canister.

3) With vacuum still applied, again try to blow through hose connected to lower port. An increased flow of air should be observed. If airflow does not increase, replace canister.

Fuel Tank Pressure Control Valve ("C", "G", "K" & "M" Series – High-Altitude) – 1) Connect a hand-held vacuum pump to "control vac" port of tank pressure control valve. Apply approximately 15 in Hg. to "control vac" port.

2) Attach a short piece of hose to fuel tank side of valve. Blow through hose. Air must pass through fuel tank pressure control valve. If air does not pass through fuel tank pressure control valve, replace defective valve.

Thermostatic Vacuum Switch – 1) With engine coolant temperature less than 100°F (38°C), apply vacuum to manifold side of thermostatic vacuum switch. Switch should hold vacuum.

2) With engine coolant temperature greater than 122°F (50°C), vacuum should drop off. If thermostatic vacuum switch fails either test, replace switch.

POSITIVE CRANKCASE VENTILATION

Required Service – The PCV system may require service for obstructions if any of the following conditions exist:
- Rough Idle
- Stalling or Slow Idle Speed
- Oil Leaks
- Oil in Air Cleaner
- Sludge in Engine

A leaking PCV valve or hose could cause:
- Rough Idle
- Stalling
- High Idle Speed

If engine idles roughly, check for clogged PCV valve and for plugged or broken PCV hoses BEFORE adjusting idle. Check correct PCV valve application to ensure the correct valve is fitted. Replace PCV valve if required.

Checking PCV Valve Function (Except 2.5L) – 1) Remove PCV valve from rocker cover. Run engine at idle. Place thumb over open end of valve to check for vacuum. If there is no vacuum at valve, check for obstruction in manifold port, hoses or PCV valve. Repair or replace as necessary.

2) Turn engine off. Remove PCV valve. Shake valve and listen for rattle of check valve inside PCV valve. If a clear rattle is not heard, replace PCV valve.

3) Visually inspect valve for varnish or deposits that may make PCV valve operation sticky, restricted or incompletely seated. Replace if necessary.

4) An engine must be sealed for the PCV system to function as designed. If leakage, sludging or dilution of oil is noted and the PCV system is functioning properly, check engine for cause, and repair as required to ensure PCV system will continue to function properly.

5) Since an engine operating without any crankcase ventilation can be damaged, it is important to replace PCV valve and air cleaner breather at regular intervals (at least every 30,000 miles). Check all hoses and clamps for failure or deterioration.

NOTE: The 2.5L engine does not use a conventional PCV valve. Valve consists of a fixed restricted orifice. To test valve, simply check for presence of vacuum with crankcase vent tube inlet end removed from rocker cover and engine running.

THERMOSTATIC AIR CLEANER

Temperature Sensor – Vacuum Motor Type (2.8L) – 1) Air cleaner temperature should be less than 86°F (30°C). Place thermometer as close as possible to sensor inside air cleaner. Start and idle engine. Damper door should close off outside air immediately.

2) When damper door starts to open snorkel passage, remove air cleaner cover and read thermometer temperature. Thermometer should read about 131°F (55°C).

3) If damper door does not open to outside air at the specified temperature, check vacuum motor diaphragm. If okay, replace defective thermostatic air cleaner temperature sensor.

Vacuum Motor Diaphragm (2.8L) – 1) Turn engine off. Disconnect vacuum hose to vacuum motor. Apply 7 in. Hg to vacuum motor. Damper door should close. If not, check if linkage is properly connected.

2) With vacuum still applied, trap vacuum in vacuum diaphragm motor by bending hose. Damper door should remain closed. If damper door does not remain closed, replace vacuum diaphragm motor assembly.

Damper Door – Wax Pellet Check (Except 2.8L) – 1) Remove air cleaner assembly from vehicle and allow to cool to less than 40°F (4°C). Damper door should be closed to outside (cold) air.

2) Reinstall air cleaner assembly. Start engine and observe damper door. As air cleaner assembly warms up, wax pellet should expand, closing off hot air delivery and opening cold air delivery.

3) If door does not respond as indicated, ensure door is not binding and calibrated damper spring is installed properly.

EMISSION SYSTEMS & SUB-SYSTEMS (DIESEL)

POSITIVE CRANKCASE VENTILATION

Crankcase Depression Regulator (CDR) – To test CDR valve, connect one hose of a water manometer to engine oil dipstick tube. Leave other hose of manometer open to atmosphere. Install air cleaner and run engine. CDR valve specification is one inch of water pressure at idle to 3-4 inches at full load. Add amount of distance water travels down one side of gauge to distance water travels up other side of gauge to obtain reading.

EXHAUST GAS RECIRCULATION (EGR)

EGR Valve Check – With engine off, disconnect vacuum hose to EGR valve. Connect vacuum pump to EGR and apply 10 in. Hg. EGR diaphragm should move up and stay up for at least 20 seconds. If not, replace EGR valve.

EXHAUST PRESSURE REGULATION (EPR) SYSTEM

NOTE: For testing of the EPR system, see appropriate chart in SELF-DIAGNOSTICS – DIESEL article.

VACUUM PUMP

Connect vacuum gauge to vacuum pump inlet (small fitting). DO NOT plug or disconnect outlet fitting. With engine idling, vacuum should be 8 in. Hg one minute after start. If not, check for belt slippage, vacuum leaks or other obvious defects. If no defects are present, replace vacuum pump.

MISCELLANEOUS ECM CONTROLS

NOTE: Although not considered true engine performance-related systems, some controlled devices may affect driveability if they malfunction.

TRANSMISSION (C-8)

NOTE: ECM transmission controls are also covered in greater detail in MITCHELL® TRANSMISSION SERVICE & REPAIR manual for domestic vehicles.

Torque Converter Clutch (TCC) Solenoid – Disconnect harness connector to TCC solenoid. Measure resistance between TCC solenoid terminals "A" and "D". See Figs. 10-14. Solenoid resistance should be greater than 20 ohms.

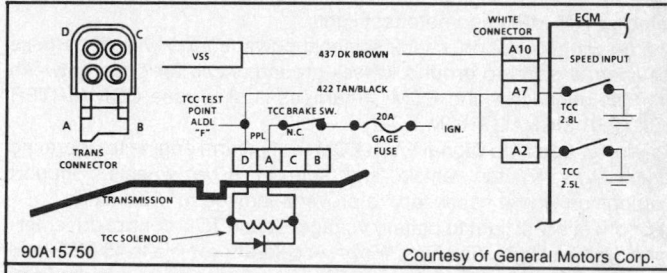

Fig. 10: Torque Converter Clutch Schematic (2.5L & 2.8L)

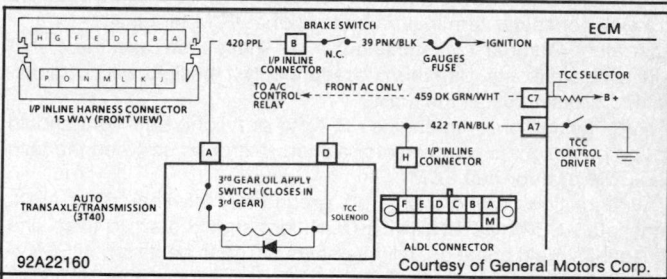

Fig. 11: Torque Converter Clutch Schematic (3.1L)

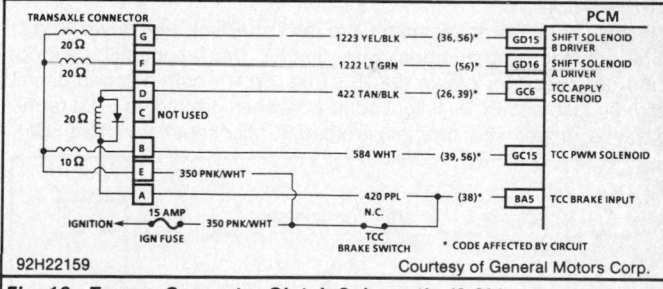

Fig. 12: Torque Converter Clutch Schematic (3.8L)

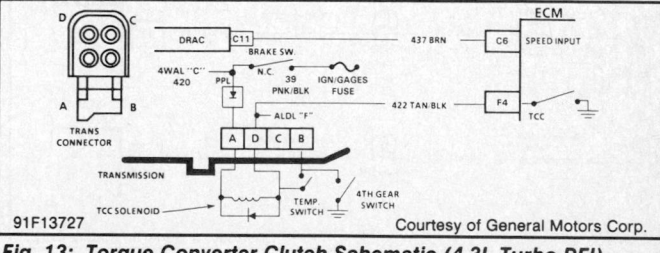

Fig. 13: Torque Converter Clutch Schematic (4.3L Turbo PFI)

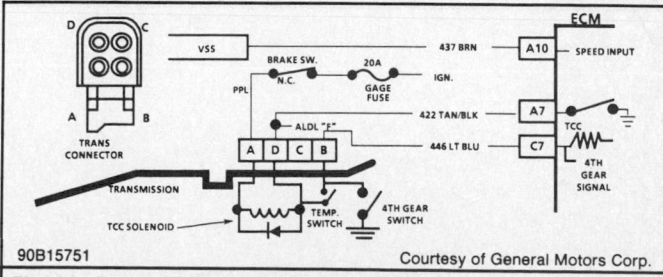

Fig. 14: Torque Converter Clutch Schematic (4.3L & V8 Without 4L80-E Transmission)

NOTE: Some solenoids have an internal pressure switch in series with the solenoid winding and will not show continuity until transmission hydraulic pressure is applied.

Converter Lock-Up Signal At Transmission – 1) Warm engine to operating temperature. Raise vehicle and support drive wheels. Support suspension where necessary to prevent damage to drive axles.

2) Disconnect converter clutch connector at transmission. Connect a test light across terminals "A" and "D" of converter clutch harness. *See Figs. 10-14.* Start engine and place transmission in Drive. Accelerate vehicle to 45 MPH and note test light.

3) If test light is not on, check solenoid power supply wire of harness for open or short to ground. Check ground circuit for open between harness connector and ECM. If harness is okay, see CONVERTER LOCK-UP SIGNAL FROM ECM.

Converter Lock-Up Signal From ECM – 1) Warm engine to operating temperature. Raise vehicle and support drive wheels. Support suspension where necessary to prevent damage to drive axles.

2) Connect a test light to battery voltage. Touch TCC control driver terminal with test light. *See Figs. 10-14.* Accelerate vehicle to 45 MPH and note test light. If test light does not illuminate, problem is a faulty ECM connector or ECM. On some models, lock-up signal may be checked at ALDL connector terminal "F" instead of at ECM terminal.

Shift Light (Manual Transmission) – 1) These tests assume a shift light problem exists. Use this procedure only if the light will not illuminate, or illuminates all the time.

2) Turn ignition on, with engine off. Note shift light. Shift light should not be on. If light is on, check for a short to ground between the bulb and ECM or a for bad ECM.

3) With ignition on and engine off, ground test terminal "B" of ALDL connector. SERVICE ENGINE SOON light should start to flash and shift light should come on. If light comes on, go to next step. If SERVICE ENGINE SOON light does not flash, perform DIAGNOSTIC CIRCUIT CHECK as described in BASIC DIAGNOSTIC PROCEDURES article.

4) If shift light does not come on, ground Tan/Black light driver wire at ECM terminal using a jumper wire. *See Fig. 15.* If light still does not come on, check for blown GAGES fuse, blown bulb or open circuit between fuse and ECM. If light comes on when grounding ECM terminal with a jumper wire, problem is a bad ECM connection or bad ECM.

A/C CLUTCH (C-10)

A/C Clutch Relay – 1) Disconnect A/C clutch relay harness connector. Using proper mini-schematic and an ohmmeter, check continuity between A/C clutch relay winding terminals. *See Figs. 16-21.* Continuity should exist. Check continuity between clutch drive circuit terminals of relay. Continuity should not exist.

2) Using jumper wires, apply ground and battery voltage to relay winding. Continuity should now exist between clutch drive circuit terminals of relay. Replace A/C clutch relay if continuity does not exist.

COOLING FAN (C-12)

NOTE: For additional information on electric cooling fans, see SPECIFICATIONS & ELECTRIC COOLING FANS article in ENGINE COOLING.

Cooling Fan Relay – 1) Disconnect cooling fan relay harness connector. Using an ohmmeter, check continuity of relay winding. *See Figs. 22-28.* Continuity should exist. Check continuity across power delivery terminals of relay. With relay not energized, continuity should not exist.

2) With ohmmeter still attached to power delivery terminals of relay, apply battery voltage and ground to energize relay winding. Continuity should now exist between cooling fan relay power delivery terminals. Replace cooling fan relay if continuity does not exist.

Cooling Fan Motor – Disconnect cooling fan motor harness connector. Apply battery voltage to one of the fan motor terminals and jumper the other terminal to ground. Fan motor should activate. If fan motor does not activate, replace faulty fan motor.

NOTE: For a more specific system testing, refer to the following C-10 or C-12 diagnostic charts. If any chart other than a C-10 or C-12 chart is referenced, see appropriate SELF-DIAGNOSTICS article.

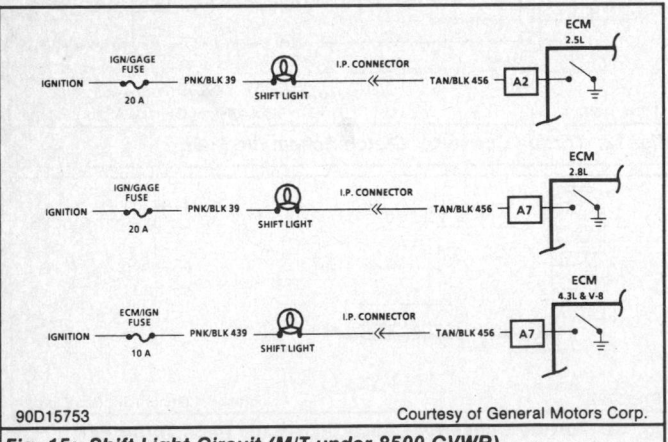

90D15753   Courtesy of General Motors Corp.

Fig. 15: Shift Light Circuit (M/T under 8500 GVWR)

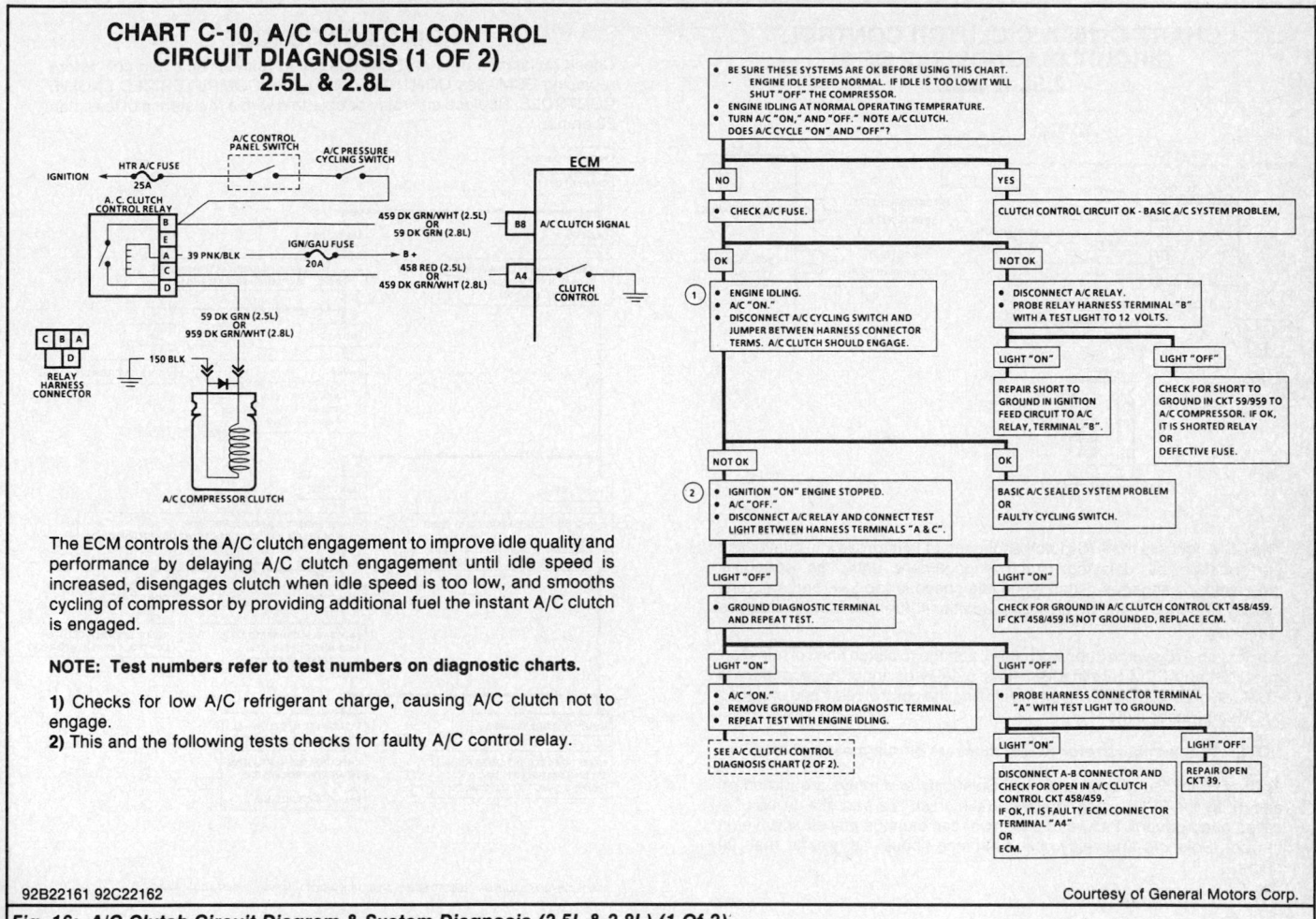

CHART C-10, A/C CLUTCH CONTROL CIRCUIT DIAGNOSIS (1 OF 2) 2.5L & 2.8L

The ECM controls the A/C clutch engagement to improve idle quality and performance by delaying A/C clutch engagement until idle speed is increased, disengages clutch when idle speed is too low, and smooths cycling of compressor by providing additional fuel the instant A/C clutch is engaged.

NOTE: Test numbers refer to test numbers on diagnostic charts.

1) Checks for low A/C refrigerant charge, causing A/C clutch not to engage.
2) This and the following tests checks for faulty A/C control relay.

92B22161 92C22162

Courtesy of General Motors Corp.

Fig. 16: A/C Clutch Circuit Diagram & System Diagnosis (2.5L & 2.8L) (1 Of 2)

CHART C-10, A/C CLUTCH CONTROL CIRCUIT DIAGNOSIS (2 OF 2) 2.5L & 2.8L

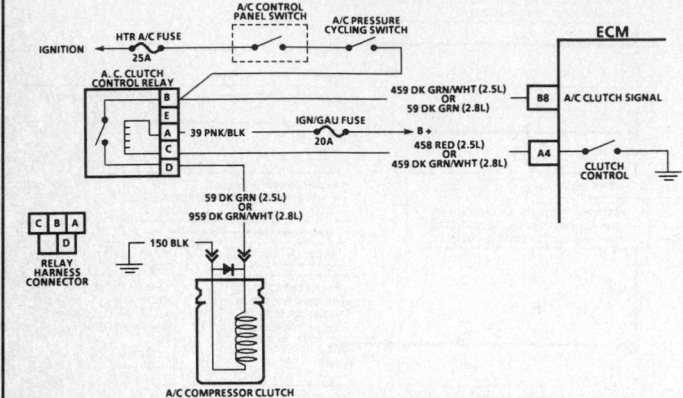

The ECM controls the A/C clutch engagement to improve idle quality and performance by delaying clutch engagement until idle speed is increased, disengages clutch when idle speed is too low, and smooths cycling of compressor by providing additional fuel the instant clutch is applied.

Turning on A/C switch supplies battery voltage to clutch control relay terminal "B" and ECM terminal B8. After a delay of about .5 seconds, the ECM will ground ECM terminal A4, closing the control relay and engages A/C compressor clutch.

NOTE: Test numbers refer to test numbers on diagnostic charts.

3) Checks for faulty cycling switch. Solenoids and relays are turned on and off by the ECM, using "drivers". Each driver is a part of a group of 4, called quad-drivers. Failure of one driver can damage any other driver in the set. Solenoid and relay coil resistance should be greater than 20 ohms.

DIAGNOSTIC AIDS

Check resistance of each ECM controlled relay or solenoid coil before replacing ECM. See CONTROL UNIT under COMPUTERIZED ENGINE CONTROLS. Replace any relay or solenoid with a resistance of less than 20 ohms.

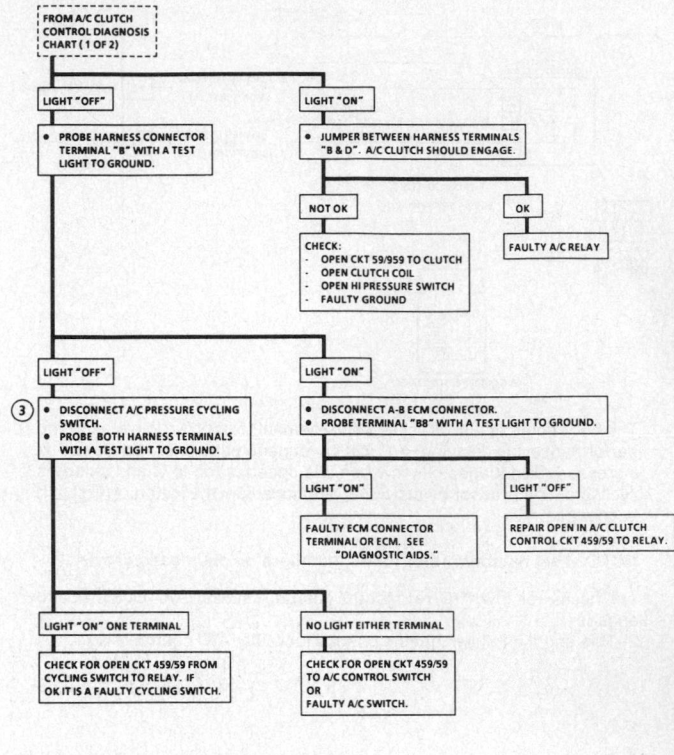

"AFTER REPAIRS," CONFIRM "CLOSED LOOP" OPERATION AND NO "SERVICE ENGINE SOON" LIGHT.

92B22161 92D22163

Fig. 17: A/C Clutch Circuit Diagram & System Diagnosis (2.5L & 2.8L) (2 Of 2)

CHART C-10, A/C CLUTCH CONTROL CIRCUIT DIAGNOSIS (FRONT A/C ONLY) (1 OF 2) 3.1L

FRONT A/C OPTION ONLY (C67)

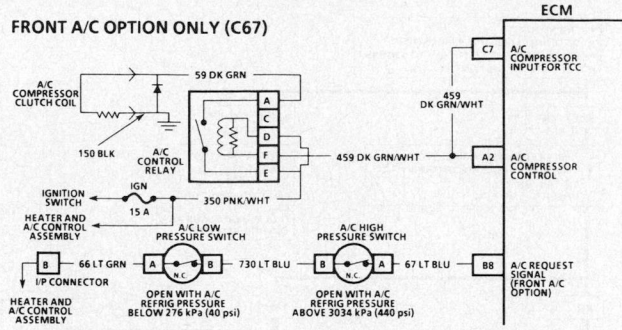

A/C clutch control circuit is ECM controlled to delay A/C clutch engagement approximately 8 seconds after engine is started. This allows the Idle Air Control Valve (IAC) to adjust engine RPM before A/C clutch engages. ECM also causes relay to disengage A/C clutch during Wide Open Throttle (WOT) operation or if engine is overheating.

A/C clutch control relay is energized when ECM provides a ground path for circuit No. 459. Low pressure switch will open if A/C pressure is less than 40 psi (2.8 kg/cm²); high pressure switch will open if A/C pressure is approximately 440 psi (30.9 kg/cm²).

Vehicles equipped with rear A/C option use a pressure cycling switch instead of a low pressure switch. A/C pressure cycling switch closes at pressure greater than 43-49 psi (3.0-3.4 kg/cm²) and opens at pressure of less than 23-25 psi (1.6-1.8 kg/cm²). An A/C refrigerant fan request switch opens to request fan(s) on, when A/C refrigerant pressure exceeds approximately 200 psi (14.1 kg/cm²).

NOTE: Test numbers refer to test numbers on diagnostic charts.

1) ECM will only energize A/C relay when engine is running. This test determines if relay or circuit No. 459 is faulty.
2) A/C compressor clutch should apply if the following conditions are met: On front A/C option only, low and high pressure switch must be closed so A/C request (12 volts) will be present at ECM. On rear A/C option only, A/C mode is requested via high pressure and pressure cycling switches, 12 volts is supplied to relay coil through high pressure switch. As compressor reduces evaporator pressure to approximately 25 psi (1.8 kg/cm²), pressure cycling switch will open and compressor clutch will disengage. As system equalizes and pressure cycling switch closes, compressor clutch will cycle on. This cycling continues and maintains evaporator discharge and temperature at approximately 33°F (1°C).

3) This step determines if signal is reaching ECM on circuit No. 66 from A/C control panel. Signal should only be present when A/C mode or defrost mode is selected.
4) With engine idling and A/C on, ECM should ground circuit No. 459, causing test light to illuminate.

DIAGNOSTIC AIDS

If complaint was insufficient cooling, problem may be caused by inoperative cooling fan(s) or faulty A/C refrigerant fan request switch. Engine cooling fan(s) should turn on when A/C pressure exceeds a value to open switch, causing ECM to energize cooling fan relay(s). See CHART C-12 for cooling fan diagnosis. If fan operates correctly, ensure A/C system refrigerant charge is okay.

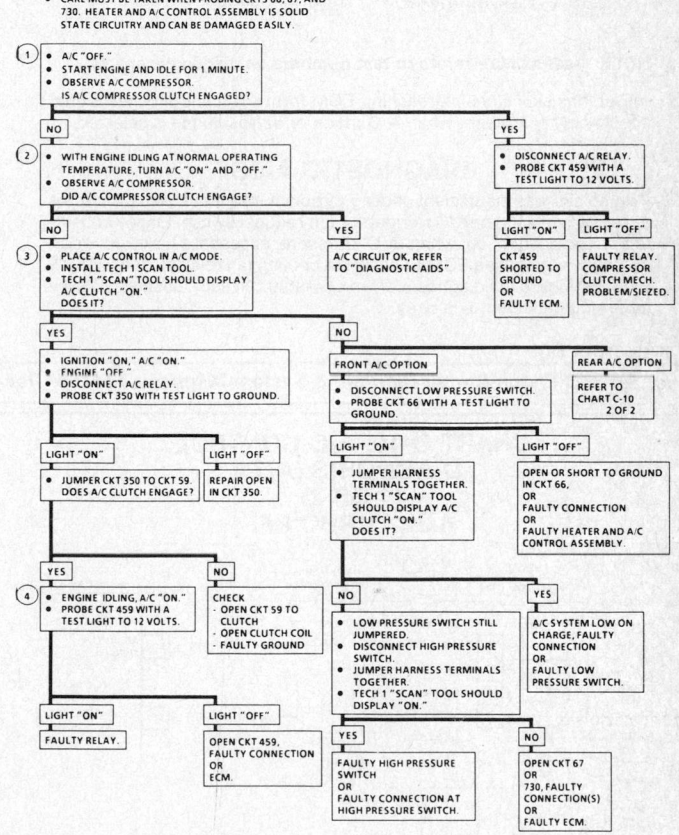

92I15915 92J15916

Courtesy of General Motors Corp.

Fig. 18: A/C Clutch Circuit Diagram & System Diagnosis (3.1L – Front A/C Only) (1 Of 2)

CHART C-10, A/C CLUTCH CONTROL CIRCUIT DIAGNOSIS (REAR A/C ONLY) (2 OF 2) 3.1L

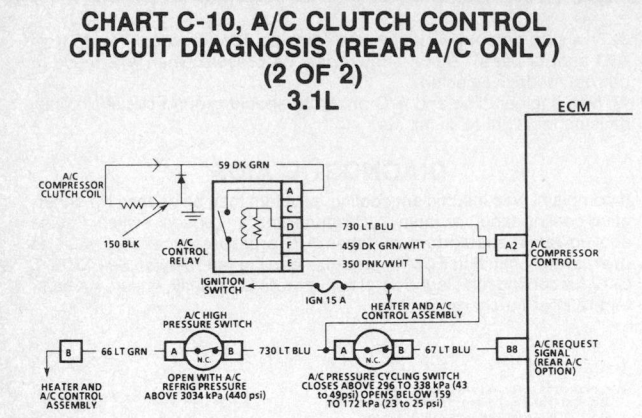

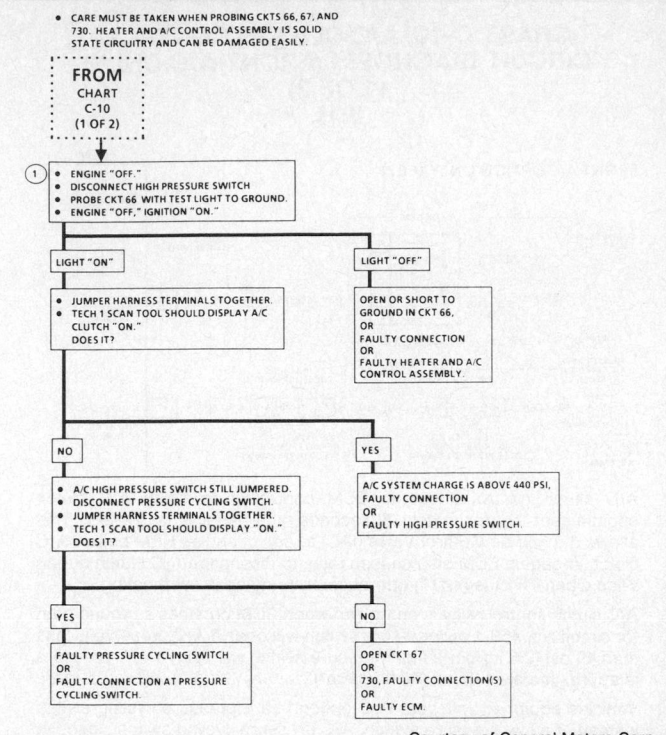

NOTE: Test number refers to test numbers on diagnostic charts.

1) Determines if signal is reaching ECM from A/C control panel. Signal should only be present when A/C mode or defrost mode is selected.

DIAGNOSTIC AIDS

If complaint was insufficient cooling, problem may be caused by inoperative cooling fan(s) or A/C refrigerant fan request switch. Engine cooling fan(s) should turn on when A/C pressure exceeds a value to open switch, which causes ECM to energize cooling fan relay(s). See CHART C-12 for cooling fan diagnosis. If fan operates correctly, ensure A/C system refrigerant charge is okay.

92I15881 92A15917

Courtesy of General Motors Corp.

Fig. 19: A/C Clutch Circuit Diagram & System Diagnosis (3.1L – Rear A/C Only) (2 Of 2)

CHART C-10, A/C CONTROL DIAGNOSIS (A/T) (1 OF 2) 4.3L TURBO PFI

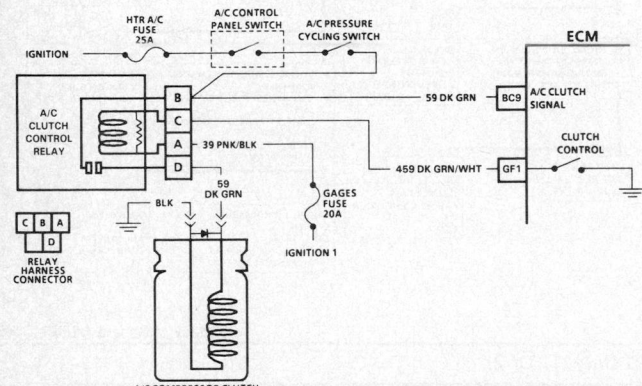

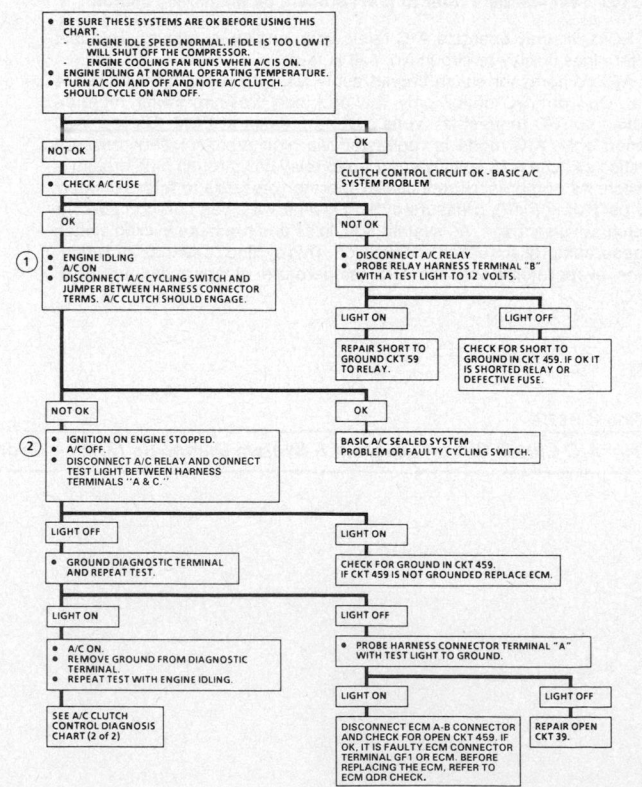

ECM controls operation of A/C clutch to improve idle quality and performance by:
- Delaying A/C clutch application until idle air rate is increased.
- Releasing A/C clutch when idle speed is too low.
- Releasing A/C clutch at wide open throttle operation.
- Smooths cycling of compressor by providing additional fuel the instant A/C clutch is applied.

Turning on A/C supplies battery voltage to clutch relay (circuit No. 59) and ECM terminal BC9. After a time delay of .5 seconds, the ECM grounds terminal GF1 (circuit No. 459), and closes control relay. A/C compressor clutch then engages.

NOTE: Test numbers refer to test numbers on diagnostic charts.

1) Checks for low refrigerant as cause for no A/C.
2) This step and the steps that follow checks for faulty A/C control relay. QUAD-DRIVER CHECK is located under COMPUTERIZED ENGINE CONTROLS.

92E22164 92F22165

Courtesy of General Motors Corp.

Fig. 20: A/C Clutch Circuit Diagram & System Diagnosis (4.3L Turbo PFI) (1 Of 2)

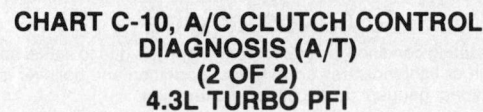

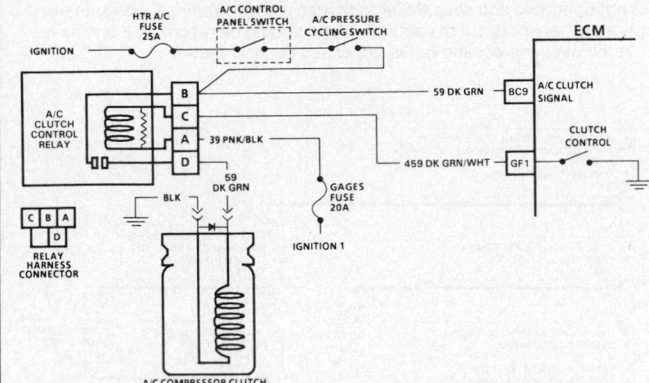

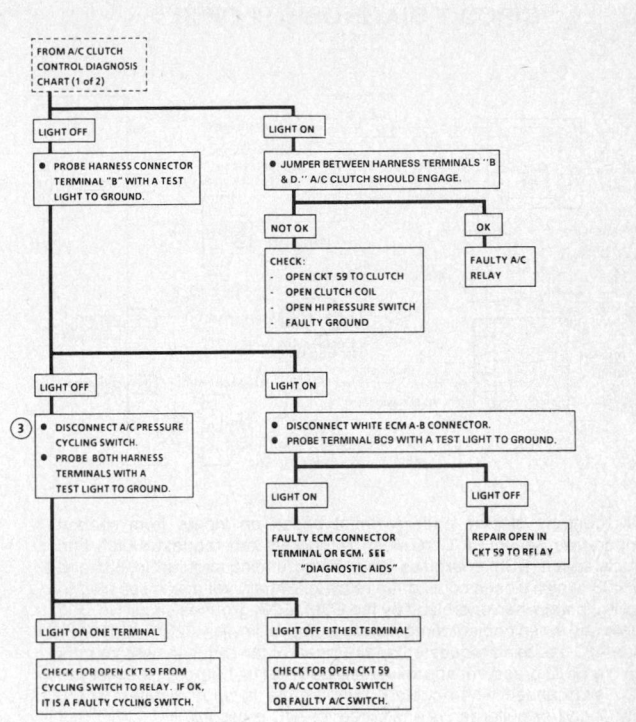

CHART C-10, A/C CLUTCH CONTROL DIAGNOSIS (A/T) (2 OF 2) 4.3L TURBO PFI

NOTE: Test numbers refer to test numbers on diagnostic charts.

3) Checks for faulty cycling switch. Solenoids and relays are turned on and off by the ECM, using "drivers". Each driver is a part of a group of 4, called quad-drivers. Failure of one driver can damage any other driver in the set. Solenoid and relay coil resistance should be greater than 20 ohms.

DIAGNOSTIC AIDS

Check resistance of each ECM controlled relay or solenoid before replacing ECM. See CONTROL UNIT under COMPUTERIZED ENGINE CONTROLS. Replace any relay or solenoid that measures less than 20 ohms.

92E22164 92G22166

Fig. 21: A/C Clutch Circuit Diagram & System Diagnosis (4.3L Turbo PFI) (2 Of 2)

CHART C-12, COOLING FAN CIRCUIT DIAGNOSIS (1 OF 2) 3.1L

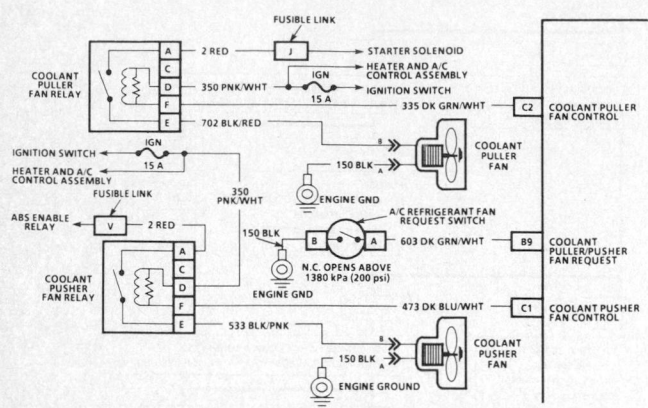

ECM controls electric cooling fan(s) based on inputs from coolant temperature sensor, A/C request, refrigerant fan request switch and vehicle speed. ECM energizes fan(s) by grounding circuits No. 335 and No. 473, which closes cooling fan relay(s). Battery voltage is supplied to cooling fan(s) when energized by the ECM. ECM grounds circuit No. 335 (puller fan) when coolant temperature is approximately 223°F (106°C) or when A/C has been requested and refrigerant fan request switch opens with high A/C pressure, approximately 200 psi (14.1 kg/cm²). Pusher fan relay is grounded when coolant temperature is approximately 217°F (103°C) and/or puller fan is energized for A/C pressure.

NOTE: Test numbers refer to test numbers on diagnostic charts.

1) With ALDL diagnostic terminal grounded, cooling fan driver closes and energizes fan control relay.
2) If A/C fan request switch or circuit is open, cooling fan operates whenever A/C is operating.
3) With A/C requested and 45 seconds after request is removed, A/C refrigerant fan request switch should open when A/C high pressure exceeds approximately 200 psi (14.1 kg/cm²). This signal should cause ECM to energize fan control relay(s).
4) This test checks if cooling puller and pusher fan relay(s) (circuits No. 335 and 473) are shorted to ground. This condition would cause fans to be energized continuously.

DIAGNOSTIC AIDS

If an overheating condition is suspected, verify if it is due to actual boilover. If gauge or light indicates an overheat condition and boilover is not evident, inspect gauge/light circuit for malfunction.

If vehicle is overheating and gauge or light indicates so, but cooling fan is not operating and scan tester indicates normal readings, coolant temperature sensor is out of calibration and should be replaced. If engine is overheating and cooling fan is on, check cooling system.

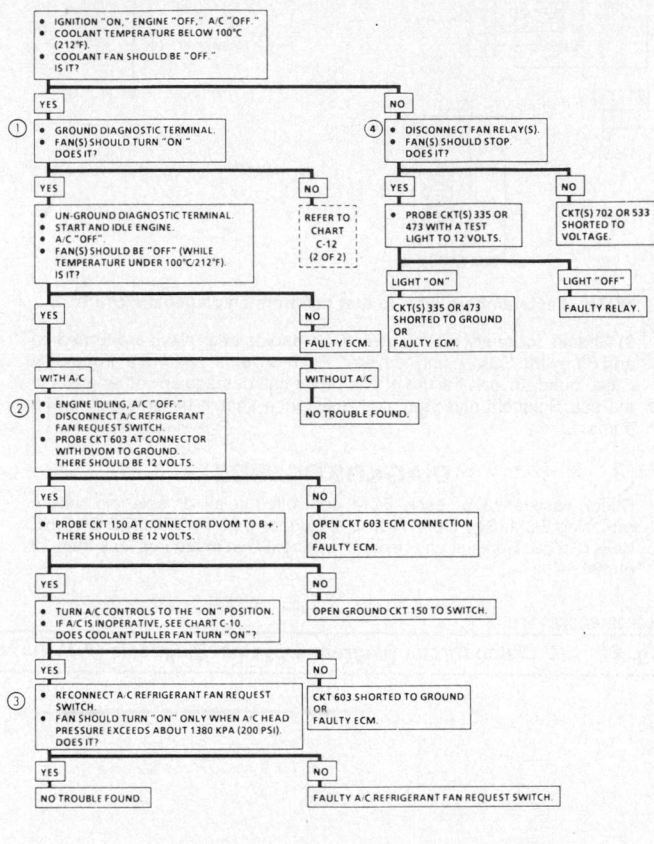

92F15912 92G15913

Fig. 22: Cooling Fan Circuit Diagram & System Diagnosis (3.1L) (1 Of 2)

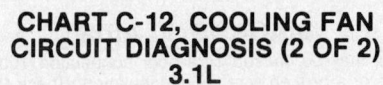

**CHART C-12, COOLING FAN
CIRCUIT DIAGNOSIS (2 OF 2)
3.1L**

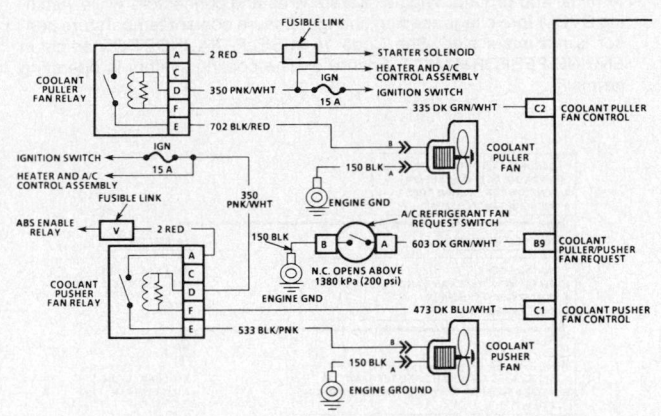

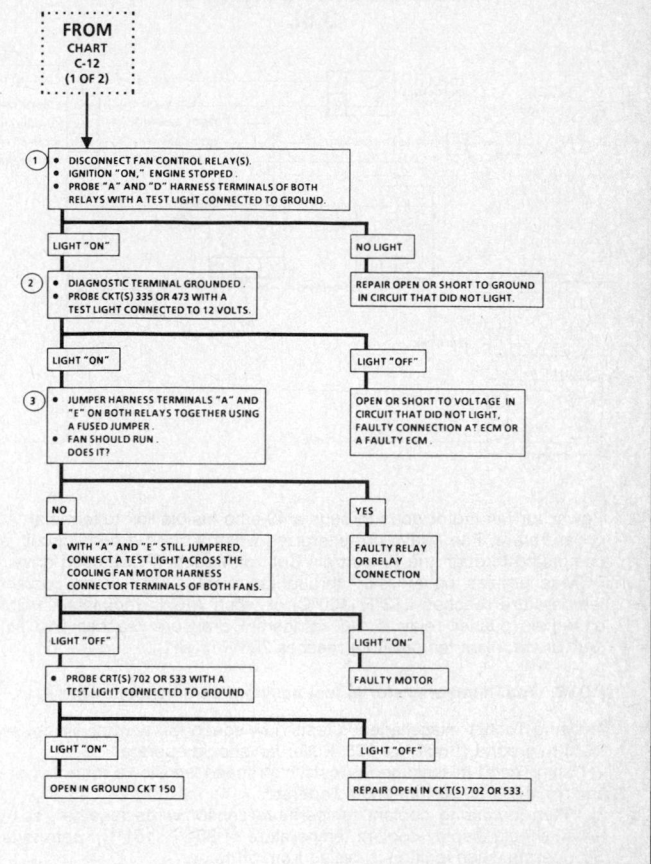

NOTE: Test numbers refer to test numbers on diagnostic charts.

1) Battery voltage should be available at cooling fan relay terminals "A" and "D" when ignition switch is in the ON position.
2) This checks ECM's ability to ground circuits No. 335 and 473. SERVICE ENGINE SOON light should be flashing at this point. If SERVICE ENGINE SOON light is not flashing, refer to SELF-DIAGNOSTICS article.
3) This test checks if cooling puller and pusher fan relays (circuits No. 533 and 702) are open. Jumpering relay terminals "A" and "E" by-passes relay, which should cause fans to operate, if motors and wiring are okay.

92F15912 92H15914

Courtesy of General Motors Corp.

Fig. 23: Cooling Fan Circuit Diagram & System Diagnosis (3.1L) (2 Of 2)

CHART C-12A, COOLING FAN CIRCUIT DIAGNOSIS (1 OF 4) 3.8L

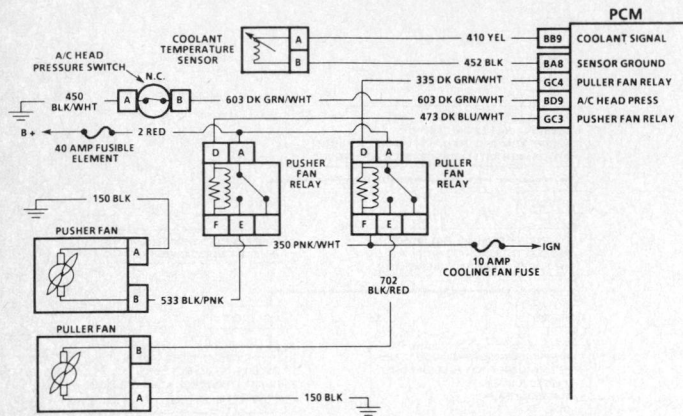

Power for fan motor goes through a 40-amp fusible link to terminal "A" of fan relays. Fan relays are energized when a good ground circuit is completed through the Powertrain Control Module (PCM) quad-driver. PCM energizes puller relay through terminal "GC4", when coolant temperature reaches 212°F (100°C) or when A/C is requested. PCM energizes pusher relay if A/C refrigerant pressure reaches 210 psi (99°C) or coolant temperature reaches 226°F (108°C).

NOTE: Test numbers refer to test numbers on diagnostic charts.

1) Using Tech 1 miscellaneous tests, low speed fan control will cause PCM to ground circuit No. 335. Puller fan should operate.
2) Using Tech 1 miscellaneous tests, high speed fan allows control of circuit No. 473. Pusher fan should operate.
3) When jumpering coolant temperature sensor wires together, scan tester should display coolant temperature of 304°F (151°C). Both fans will operate when ignition is cycled from off to on.
4) Opening A/C pressure switch will cause pusher fan to operate.

92B15918 92C15919

DIAGNOSTIC AIDS

An intermittent may be caused by a poor connection, rubbed-through wire insulation or a broken wire inside insulation. Check PCM harness connector for backed out terminals. Connect a DVOM between affected terminal and ground. Wiggle related wires and connectors while watching DVOM for voltage reading change. Ensure coolant temperature sensor is not mis-scaled. See Code 15 in SELF-DIAGNOSTICS article in ENGINE PERFORMANCE. Ensure engine cooling system is operating normally.

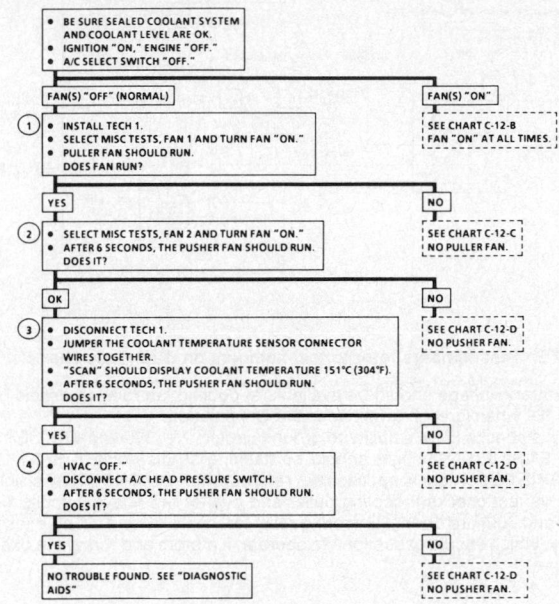

"AFTER REPAIRS," CONFIRM "CLOSED LOOP" OPERATION AND NO "SERVICE ENGINE SOON" LIGHT.

Courtesy of General Motors Corp.

Fig. 24: *Cooling Fan Circuit Diagram & System Diagnosis (3.8L) (1 Of 4)*

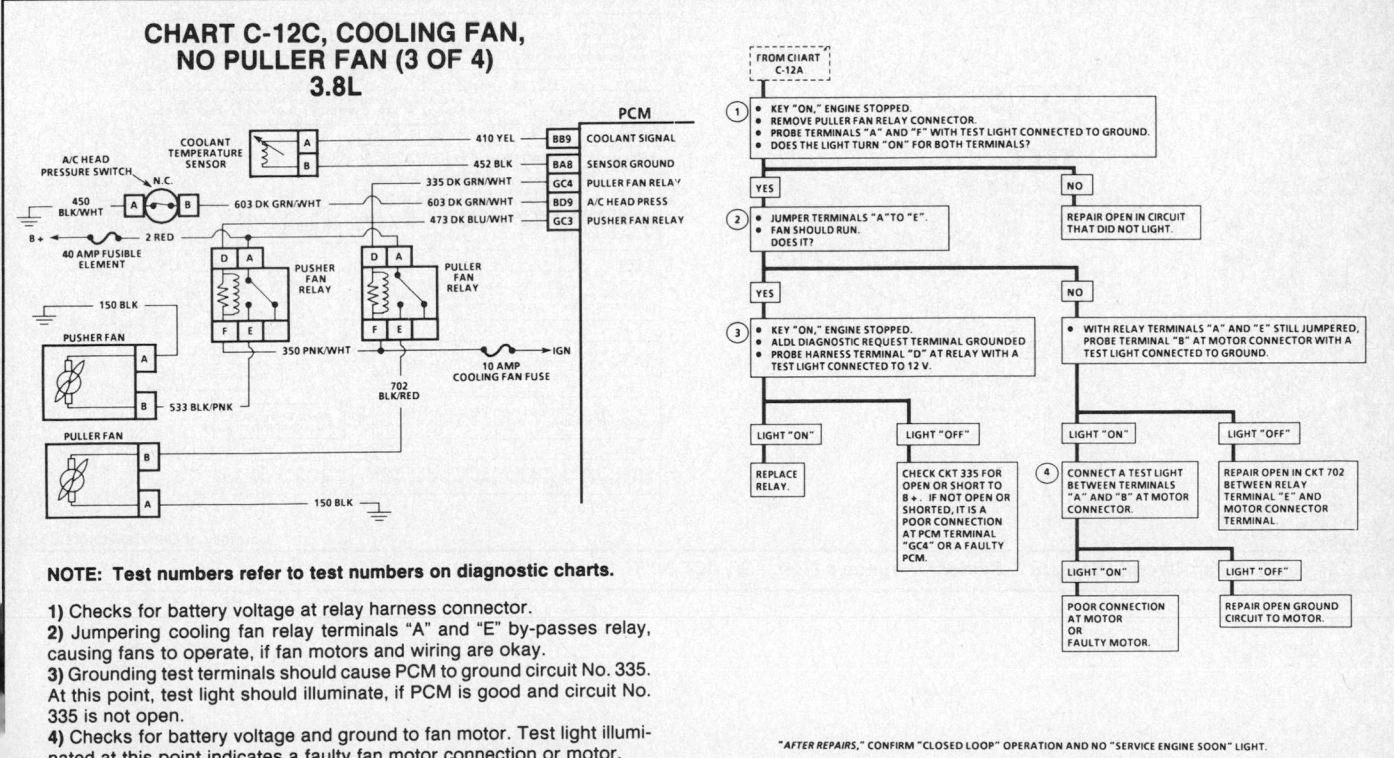

CHART C-12B, COOLING FAN, ON AT ALL TIMES (2 OF 4) 3.8L

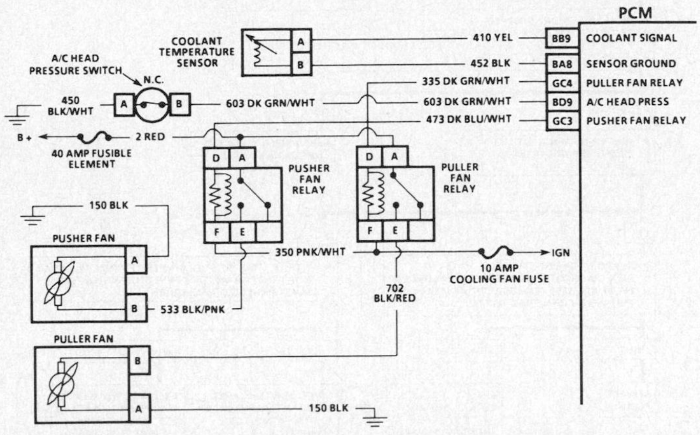

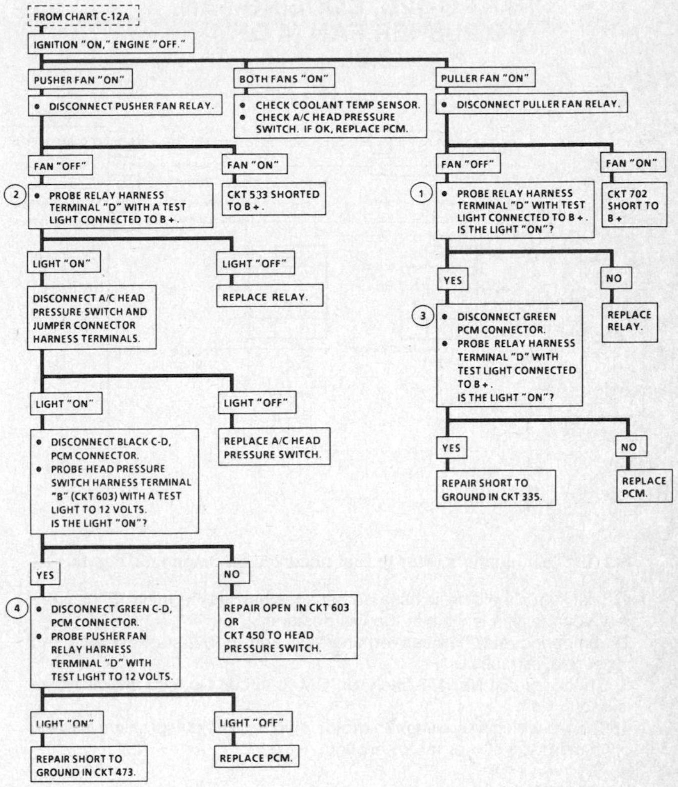

NOTE: Test numbers refer to test numbers on diagnostic charts.

1) Checks if circuit No. 335 is shorted to ground, keeping relay closed at all times.
2) Checks if circuit No. 473 is shorted to ground. An illuminated test light, indicates wire is shorted to ground.
3) If test light is off after disconnecting PCM, ensure circuit No. 335 is not shorted to B+. If circuit is not shorted to B+, PCM is shorted internally.
4) If test light is off after disconnecting PCM, ensure circuit No. 473 is not shorted to B+. If circuit is not shorted to B+, PCM is shorted internally.

92B15918 92F15920

Courtesy of General Motors Corp.

Fig. 25: Cooling Fan Circuit Diagram & System Diagnosis (3.8L) (2 Of 4)

CHART C-12C, COOLING FAN, NO PULLER FAN (3 OF 4) 3.8L

NOTE: Test numbers refer to test numbers on diagnostic charts.

1) Checks for battery voltage at relay harness connector.
2) Jumpering cooling fan relay terminals "A" and "E" by-passes relay, causing fans to operate, if fan motors and wiring are okay.
3) Grounding test terminals should cause PCM to ground circuit No. 335. At this point, test light should illuminate, if PCM is good and circuit No. 335 is not open.
4) Checks for battery voltage and ground to fan motor. Test light illuminated at this point indicates a faulty fan motor connection or motor.

"AFTER REPAIRS," CONFIRM "CLOSED LOOP" OPERATION AND NO "SERVICE ENGINE SOON" LIGHT.

92B15918 92G15921

Courtesy of General Motors Corp.

Fig. 26: Cooling Fan Circuit Diagram & System Diagnosis (3.8L) (3 Of 4)

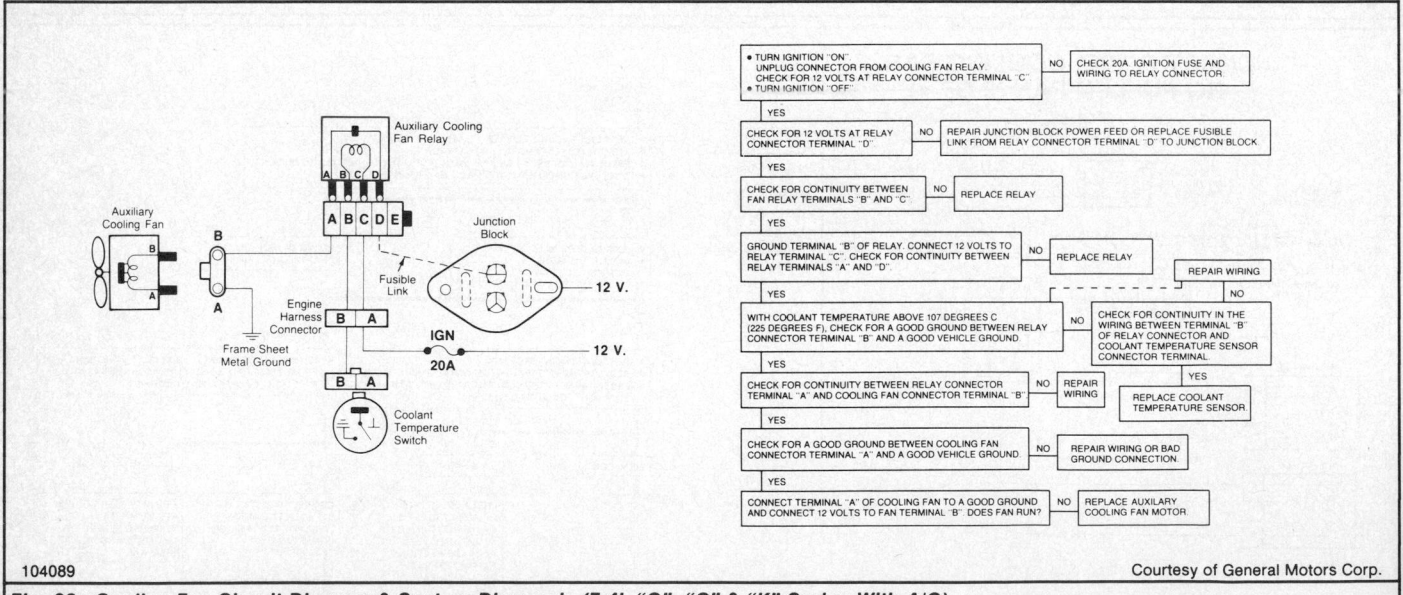

CHART C-12D, COOLING FAN, NO PUSHER FAN (4 OF 4) 3.8L

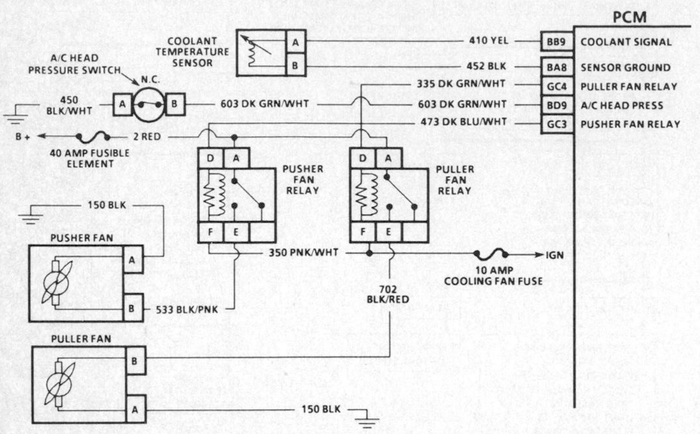

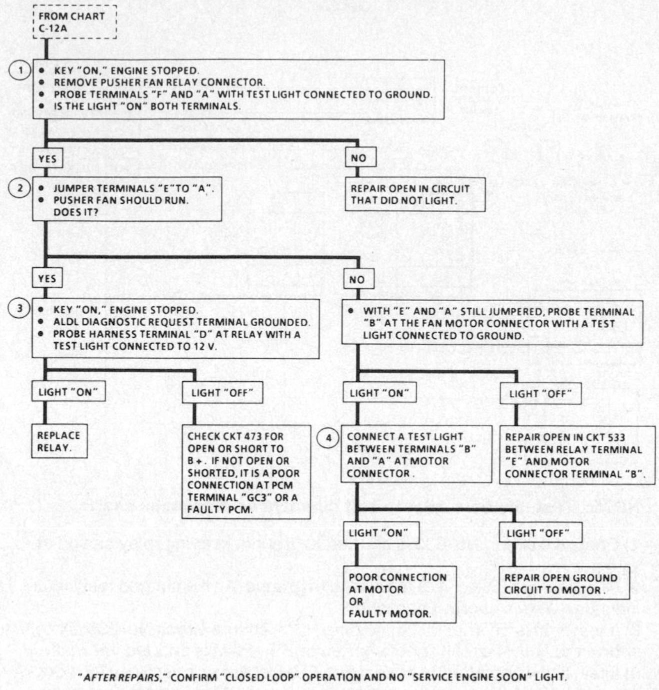

NOTE: Test numbers refer to test numbers on diagnostic charts.

1) Test light should be illuminated because harness terminal "F" has battery voltage with ignition in the ON position.

2) Jumpering relay harness terminals "A" and "E" by-passes relay. If fan runs, relay is faulty.

3) Checks circuit No. 473 back to PCM. If circuit No. 473 is okay, relay is bad.

4) Checks wiring to cooling fan motor. If wiring is okay, problem is in the connections, motor or motor ground.

"AFTER REPAIRS," CONFIRM "CLOSED LOOP" OPERATION AND NO "SERVICE ENGINE SOON" LIGHT.

92B15918 92H15922

Courtesy of General Motors Corp.

Fig. 27: Cooling Fan Circuit Diagram & System Diagnosis (3.8L) (4 Of 4)

104089

Courtesy of General Motors Corp.

Fig. 28: Cooling Fan Circuit Diagram & System Diagnosis (7.4L "G", "C" & "K" Series With A/C)

COMPONENT LOCATIONS

COMPUTER HARNESS
C1. Electronic Control Module (ECM)
C2. ALDL Diagnostic Connector
C3. SERVICE ENGINE SOON Light
C5. ECM Harness Ground
C6. Fuse Block
C8. Fuel Pump Prime/Test Connector

CONTROLLED DEVICES
1. Fuel Injector
2. Idle Air Control (IAC) Motor
3. Fuel Pump Relay
5. Torque Converter Clutch (TCC) Connector
6. Electronic Spark Timing (EST) Distributor
8. Oil Pressure Switch
12. EGR Vacuum Solenoid
13. A/C Clutch Control Relay

INFORMATION SENSORS/SWITCHES
A. Manifold Absolute Pressure (MAP) Sensor
B. Oxygen (O_2) Sensor
C. Throttle Position Sensor (TPS)
D. Coolant Temperature Sensor
F. Vehicle Speed Sensor (VSS)
G. Power Steering Pressure Switch (PSPS)
T. Manifold Air Temperature (MAT) Sensor

EMISSIONS SYSTEMS
(Not ECM Controlled)
N1. PCV Valve
N15. Fuel Vapor Canister

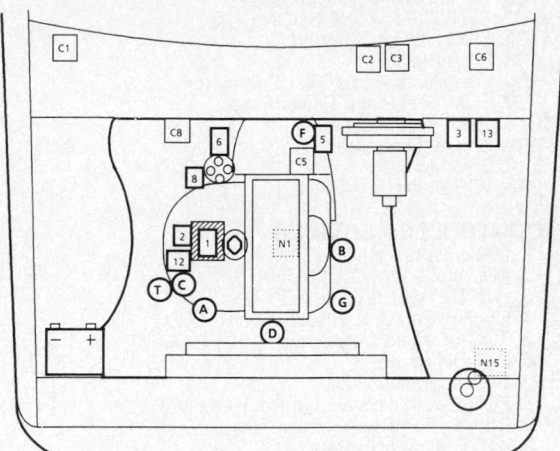

2.5L (VIN A) "S" SERIES

92JH21532

Courtesy of General Motors Corp.

Fig. 29: Component Location For 2.5L (VIN A) "S" Series

COMPUTER HARNESS
C1. Electronic Control Module (ECM)
C2. ALDL Diagnostic Connector
C3. SERVICE ENGINE SOON Light
C5. ECM Harness Ground
C6. Fuse Block
C8. Fuel Pump Prime/Test Connector
C9. Elapsed Timer Module

CONTROLLED DEVICES
1. Fuel Injector
2. Idle Air Control (IAC) Motor
3. Fuel Pump Relay
6. Electronic Spark Timing (EST) Distributor
6a. Remote Ignition Coil
7. Electronic Spark Control (ESC) Module
8. Oil Pressure Switch
9. Electronic Air Control (EAC) Solenoid
12. EGR Vacuum Solenoid
13. A/C Clutch Control Relay

INFORMATION SENSORS
A. Manifold Absolute Pressure (MAP) Sensor
B1. Oxygen (O_2) Sensor (Federal)
B2. Oxygen (O_2) Sensor (California)
C. Throttle Position Sensor (TPS)
D. Coolant Temperature Sensor
F. Vehicle Speed Sensor (VSS)
J. Knock Sensor

EMISSIONS SYSTEMS
(Not ECM Controlled)
N1. PCV Valve
N9. AIR Pump
N15. Fuel Vapor Canister

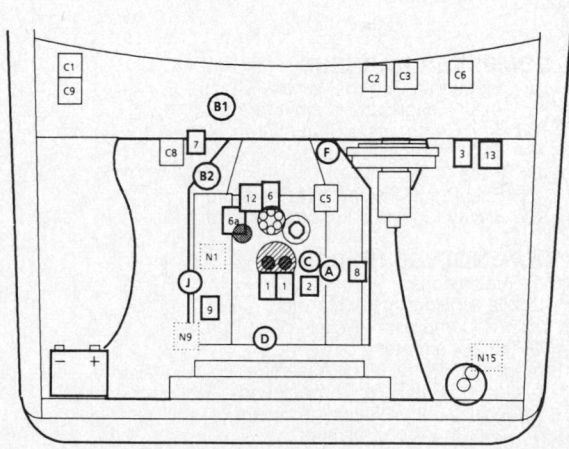

2.8L (VIN R) "S" SERIES

91A12187

Courtesy of General Motors Corp.

Fig. 30: Component Location For 2.8L (VIN R) "S" Series

COMPUTER HARNESS
C1. Electronic Control Module (ECM)
C2. ALDL Diagnostic Connector
C3. SERVICE ENGINE SOON Light
C5. ECM Harness Ground
C6. Fuse Block
C8. Fuel Pump Prime/Test Connector
C9. ECM/Fuel Pump Power Fuse
C10. Set Timing Connector
C11. Engine Grounds
C12. ESC Module
C13. VSS Buffer

CONTROLLED DEVICES
1. Fuel Injector
2. Idle Air Control (IAC) Motor
3. Fuel Pump Relay
4. Cooling Fan Relay (Pusher Fan)
5. TCC Solenoid Connector
6. EST Distributor
6a. Remote Ignition Coil
7. EGR Electronic Vacuum Regulator Valve
8. Cooling Fan Relay (Puller Fan)
9. A/C Compressor Relay

INFORMATION SENSORS/SWITCHES
A. Manifold Absolute Pressure (MAP) Sensor
B. Oxygen (O_2) Sensor
C. Throttle Position Sensor (TPS)
D. Coolant Temperature Sensor
F. Vehicle Speed Sensor (VSS)
G. Knock Sensor
H. Fuel Pump/Oil Pressure Switch
J. A/C Low Pressure Switch
K. A/C High Pressure Switch
L. A/C Refrigerant Fan Request Switch
M. A/C Pressure Cycling Switch

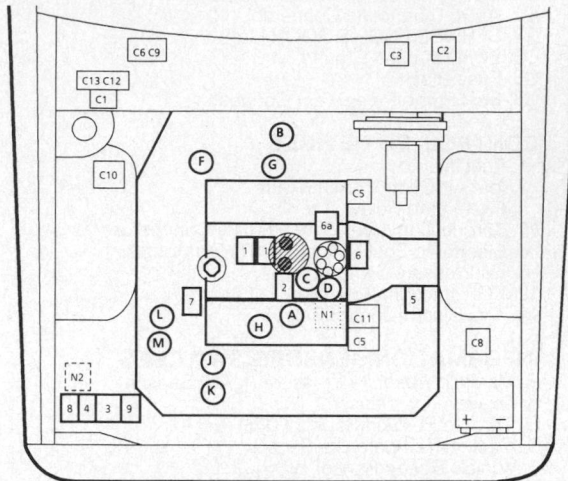

3.1L (VIN D) "U" SERIES

EMISSIONS SYSTEMS
(Not ECM Controlled)
N1. PCV Valve
N2. Fuel Vapor Canister

92H22167

Courtesy of General Motors Corp.

Fig. 31: *Component Location For 3.1L (VIN D) "U" Series*

COMPUTER HARNESS
C1. Electronic Control Module (ECM)
C2. ALDL Diagnostic Connector
C3. A/C Compressor Clutch Ground
C4. ECM Harness Ground
C5. Fuse Block
C6. Fuel Pump Prime/Test Connector
C7. 8-Way Ignition Jumper Connector

CONTROLLED DEVICES
1. Fuel Injector
2. Idle Air Control (IAC) Motor
3. A/C Compressor Relay
4. TCC Connector
5. Ignition Module/Coil Assembly
6. Cooling Fan Relay (Low Speed)
7. Cooling Fan Relay (High Speed)
8. Canister Purge Solenoid
9. Fuel Pump Relay
10. SERVICE ENGINE SOON Light

INFORMATION SENSORS/SWITCHES
A. Oxygen (O_2) Sensor
B. Throttle Position Sensor (TPS)
C. Coolant Temperature Sensor
D. Vehicle Speed Sensor (VSS)
E. Camshaft Position Sensor
F. Crankshaft Position Sensor
G. Knock Sensor
H. Mass Airflow Sensor
J. MAT Sensor
K. A/C High Pressure Switch
L. Transaxle Position Switch

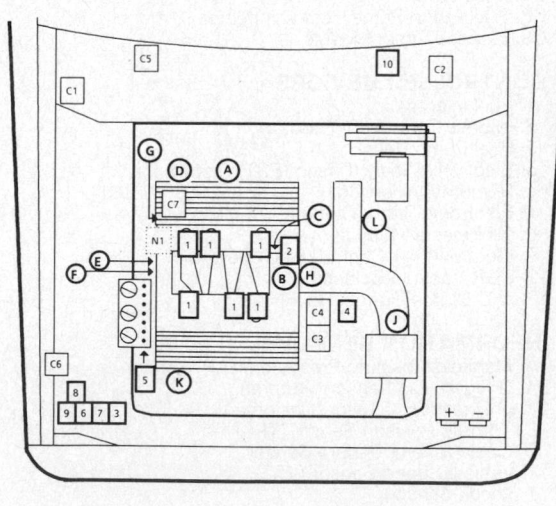

3.8L (VIN L) "U" SERIES

EMISSIONS SYSTEMS
(Not ECM Controlled)
N1. PCV Valve

92I21541

Courtesy of General Motors Corp.

Fig. 32: *Component Location For 3.8L (VIN L) "U" Series*

COMPUTER HARNESS
C1. Electronic Control Module (ECM)
C2. ALDL Diagnostic Connector
C3. SERVICE ENGINE SOON Light
C5. ECM Harness Ground
C6. Fuse Block
C8. Fuel Pump Prime/Test Connector

CONTROLLED DEVICES
1. Fuel Injector
2. Idle Air Control (IAC) Motor
3. Fuel Pump Relay
5. TCC Solenoid Connector
6. EST Distributor
6a. Remote Ignition Coil
7. Electronic Spark Control (ESC) Module
8. Fuel Pump/Oil Pressure Switch
9. Electric Air Control (EAC) Solenoid
12. EGR Vacuum Solenoid

INFORMATION SENSORS
A. Manifold Absolute Pressure (MAP) Sensor
B. Oxygen (O$_2$) Sensor
C. Throttle Position Sensor (TPS)
D. Coolant Temperature Sensor (CTS)
F. Vehicle Speed Sensor (VSS)
J. Knock Sensor

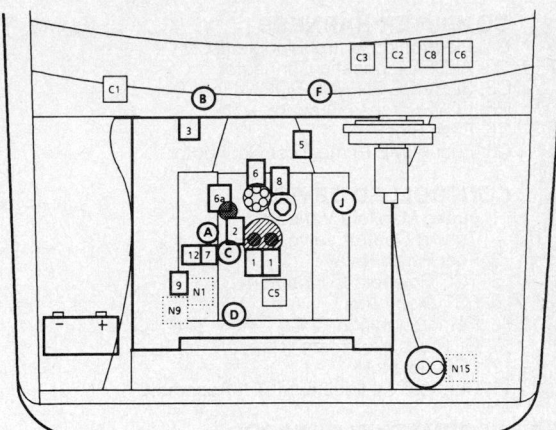

4.3L (VIN Z) "C" & "K" SERIES

EMISSIONS SYSTEMS
(Not ECM Controlled)
 N1. PCV Valve
 N9. AIR Pump
 N15. Fuel Vapor Canister

118220

Courtesy of General Motors Corp.

Fig. 33: Component Location For 4.3L (VIN Z) "C" & "K" Series

COMPUTER HARNESS
C1. Electronic Control Module (ECM)
C2. ALDL Diagnostic Connector
C3. SERVICE ENGINE SOON Light
C5. ECM Harness Ground
C6. Fuse Block
C8. Fuel Pump Prime/Test Connector

CONTROLLED DEVICES
1. Fuel Injector
2. Idle Air Control (IAC) Motor
3. Fuel Pump Relay
5. TCC Solenoid Connector
6. EST Distributor
6a. Remote Ignition Coil
7. ESC Module
8. Oil Pressure Switch
9. Electric Air Control (EAC) Solenoid
12. EGR Vacuum Solenoid

INFORMATION SENSORS
A. Manifold Absolute Pressure (MAP) Sensor
B. Oxygen (O$_2$) Sensor
C. Throttle Position Sensor (TPS)
D. Coolant Temperature Sensor
F. Vehicle Speed Sensor (VSS)
J. Knock Sensor

EMISSIONS SYSTEMS
(Not ECM Controlled)
 N1. PCV Valve
 N9. AIR Pump
 N15. Fuel Vapor Canister

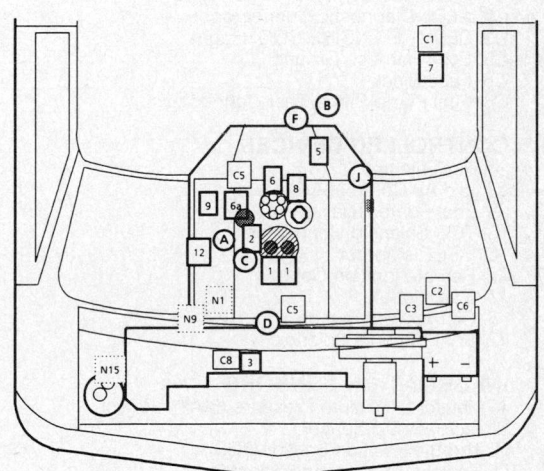

4.3L (VIN Z) "G" SERIES

90I15758

Courtesy of General Motors Corp.

Fig. 34: Component Location For 4.3L (VIN Z) "G" Series

COMPUTER HARNESS
C1. Electronic Control Module (ECM)
C2. ALDL Diagnostic Connector
C3. SERVICE ENGINE SOON Light
C5. ECM Harness Ground
C6. Fuse Block
C8. Fuel Pump Prime/Test Connector

CONTROLLED DEVICES
1. Intake Manifold Variable
   Tuning Control Valve
3. Fuel Pump Relay
5. TCC Solenoid Connector
6. EST Distributor
6a. Remote Ignition Coil
8. Oil Pressure Switch
12. EGR Solenoid
13. Central Port Injection (CPI) Assembly

INFORMATION SENSORS
A. Manifold Absolute Pressure (MAP) Sensor
B. Oxygen (O_2) Sensor
C. Throttle Position Sensor (TPS)
D. Coolant Temperature Sensor
F. Vehicle Speed Sensor (VSS)
J1. Knock Sensor No. 1
J2. Knock Sensor No. 2
T. MAT Sensor

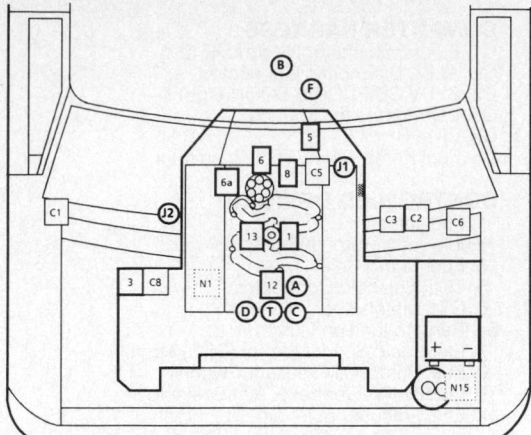

4.3L (VIN W) "L" & "M" SERIES

EMISSIONS SYSTEMS
(Not ECM Controlled)
N1. PCV Valve
N15. Fuel Vapor Canister

92E21539

Courtesy of General Motors Corp.

Fig. 35: *Component Location For 4.3L (VIN W) "L" & "M" Series*

COMPUTER HARNESS
C1. Electronic Control Module (ECM)
C2. ALDL Diagnostic Connector
C3. SERVICE ENGINE SOON Light
C5. ECM Harness Ground
C6. Fuse Block
C8. Fuel Pump Prime/Test Connector

CONTROLLED DEVICES
1. Fuel Injector
2. Idle Air Control (IAC) Motor
3. Fuel Pump Relay
5. TCC Solenoid Connector
6. EST Distributor
6a. Remote Ignition Coil
7. ESC Module
8. Oil Pressure Switch
12. EGR Vacuum Solenoid

INFORMATION SENSORS
A. Manifold Absolute Pressure (MAP) Sensor
B. Oxygen (O_2) Sensor
C. Throttle Position Sensor (TPS)
D. Coolant Temperature Sensor
F. Vehicle Speed Sensor (VSS)
J. Knock Sensor

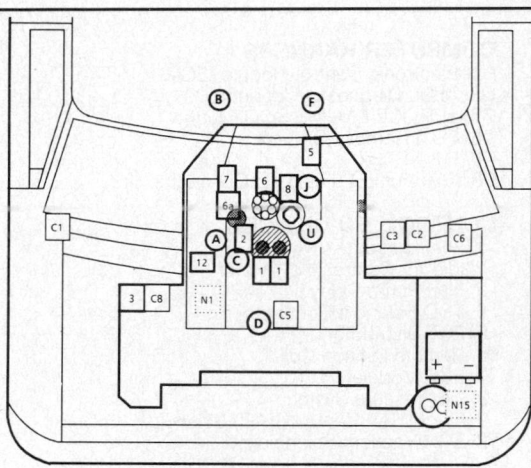

4.3L (VIN Z) "L" & "M" SERIES

EMISSIONS SYSTEMS
(Not ECM Controlled)
N1. PCV Valve
N15. Fuel Vapor Canister

91D12099

Courtesy of General Motors Corp.

Fig. 36: *Component Location For 4.3L (VIN Z) "L" & "M" Series*

COMPUTER HARNESS
C1. Electronic Control Module (ECM)
C2. ALDL Diagnostic Connector
C3. SERVICE ENGINE SOON Light
C5. ECM Harness Ground
C6. Fuse Block
C8. Fuel Pump Prime/Test Connector

CONTROLLED DEVICES
1. Fuel Injector
2. Idle Air Control (IAC) Motor
3. Fuel Pump Relay
5. TCC Solenoid Connector
6. EST Distributor
6a. Remote Ignition Coil
7. ESC Module
8. Oil Pressure Switch
12. EGR Vacuum Solenoid

INFORMATION SENSORS
A. Manifold Absolute Pressure (MAP) Sensor
B. Oxygen (O$_2$) Sensor
C. Throttle Position Sensor (TPS)
D. Coolant Temperature Sensor
F. Vehicle Speed Sensor (VSS)
J. Knock Sensor

EMISSIONS SYSTEMS
(Not ECM Controlled)
N1. PCV Valve
N2. Fuel Module
N15. Fuel Vapor Canister

92H21540

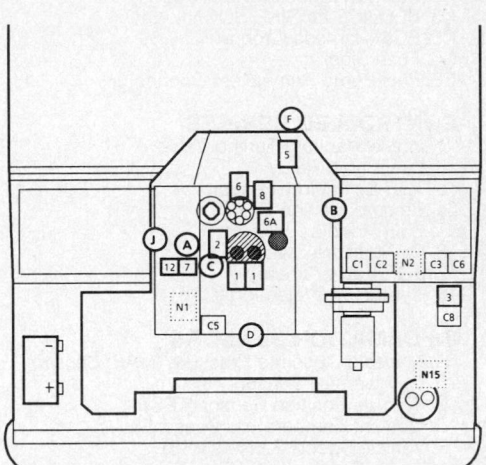

4.3L (VIN Z) "P" SERIES

Courtesy of General Motors Corp.

Fig. 37: Component Location For 4.3L (VIN Z) "P" Series

COMPUTER HARNESS
C1. Electronic Control Module (ECM)
C2. ALDL Diagnostic Connector
C3. SERVICE ENGINE SOON Light
C5. ECM Harness Ground
C6. Fuse Block
C8. Fuel Pump Prime/Test Connector

CONTROLLED DEVICES
1. Intake Manifold Tuning Valve
2. Idle Air Control (IAC) Motor
3. Fuel Pump Relay
4. A/C Clutch Control Relay
5. TCC Solenoid Connector
6. EST Distributor
6a. Remote Ignition Coil
7. ESC Module
8. Oil Pressure Switch
12. EVRV Valve

INFORMATION SENSORS
A. Manifold Absolute Pressure (MAP) Sensor
B. Oxygen (O$_2$) Sensor
C. Throttle Position Sensor (TPS)
D. Coolant Temperature Sensor
F. Vehicle Speed Sensor (VSS)
J. Knock Sensor

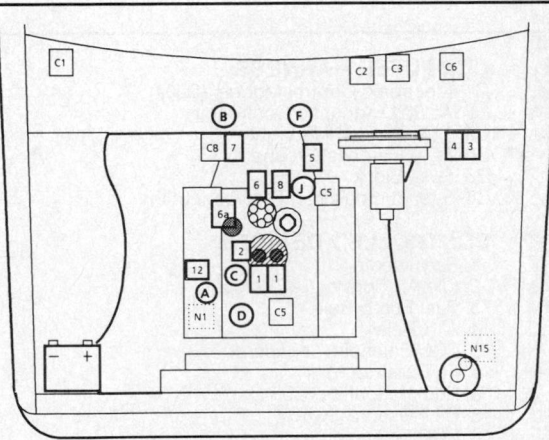

4.3L (VIN Z) "S" & "T" SERIES

EMISSIONS SYSTEMS
(Not ECM Controlled)
N1. PCV Valve
N15. Fuel Vapor Canister

91B12188

Courtesy of General Motors Corp.

Fig. 38: Component Location For 4.3L (VIN Z) "S" & "T" Series

COMPUTER HARNESS
C1. Electronic Control Module (ECM)
C2. ALDL Diagnostic Connector
C3. SERVICE ENGINE SOON Light
C5. ECM Harness Ground
C6. Fuse Block
C8. Fuel Pump Prime/Test Connector

CONTROLLED DEVICES
1. Intake Manifold Tuning Valve
3. Fuel Pump Relay
5. TCC Solenoid Connector
6a. Remote Ignition Coil
7. ESC Module
8. Oil Pressure Switch
12. EGR Valve (Linear)
13. Central Port Injection (CPI)

INFORMATION SENSORS
A. Manifold Absolute Pressure (MAP) Sensor
B. Oxygen (O₂) Sensor
C. Throttle Position Sensor (TPS)
D. Coolant Temperature Sensor
F. Vehicle Speed Sensor (VSS)
J1. Knock Sensor (Left Side)
J2. Knock Sensor (Right Side)
T. MAT Sensor

EMISSIONS SYSTEMS
(Not ECM Controlled)
N1. PCV Valve
N15. Fuel Vapor Canister

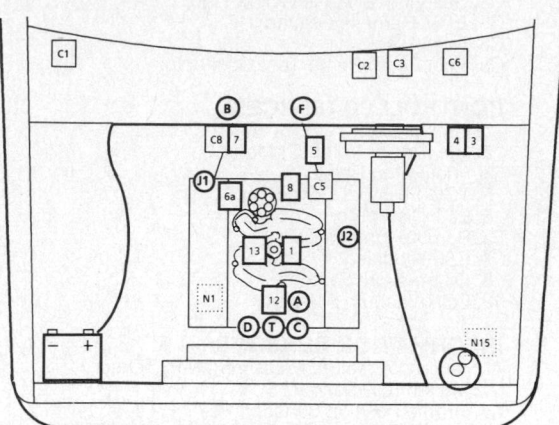

4.3L CPI (VIN W) "S" & "T" SERIES

92A21536

Courtesy of General Motors Corp.

Fig. 39: Component Location For 4.3L CPI (VIN W) "S" & "T" Series

---

COMPUTER HARNESS
C1. Electronic Control Module (ECM)
C2. ALDL Diagnostic Connector
C3. CHECK ENGINE Light
C5. ECM Harness Ground
C6. Fuse Block
C8. Fuel Pump Prime/Test Connector

CONTROLLED DEVICES
1. Fuel Injector
2. Idle Air Control (IAC) Motor
3. Fuel Pump Relay
4. A/C Relay
5. TCC Solenoid Connector
6. EST Distributor
6a. Remote Ignition Coil
8. Oil Pressure Switch
12. EGR Solenoid
13. Wastegate Solenoid
14. Turbo Boost Cut-Out Relay
15. Charge Air Cooler (CAC) Pump Control Relay
16. EGR Valve

INFORMATION SENSORS
A. Manifold Absolute Pressure (MAP) Sensor
B. Oxygen (O₂) Sensor
C. Throttle Position Sensor (TPS)
D. Coolant Temperature Sensor (CTS)
F. Vehicle Speed Sensor (VSS)
H. MAT Sensor
J. Knock Sensor (ESC)

EMISSIONS SYSTEMS
(Not ECM Controlled)
N1. PCV Valve
N15. Fuel Vapor Canister

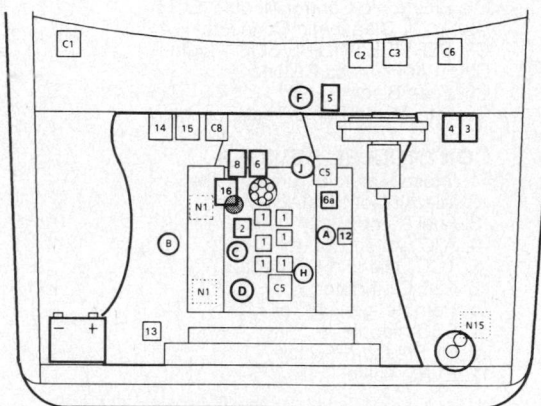

4.3L TURBO (VIN Z) "S" & "T" SERIES

92F22157

Courtesy of General Motors Corp.

Fig. 40: Component Location For 4.3L Turbo (VIN Z) "S" & "T" Series

COMPUTER HARNESS
C1. Electronic Control Module (ECM)
C2. ALDL Diagnostic Connector
C3. SERVICE ENGINE SOON Light
C5. ECM Harness Ground
C6. Fuse Block
C8. Fuel Pump Prime/Test Connector

CONTROLLED DEVICES
1. Fuel Injector
2. Idle Air Control (IAC) Motor
3. Fuel Pump Relay
5. TCC Solenoid Connector
6. EST Distributor
6a. Ignition Coil
7. ESC Module
8. Fuel Pump/Oil Pressure Switch
12. EGR Vacuum Solenoid
15. Fuel Pump In-Line Fuse

INFORMATION SENSORS
A. Manifold Absolute Pressure (MAP) Sensor
B. Oxygen (O_2) Sensor
C. Throttle Position Sensor (TPS)
D. Coolant Temperature Sensor (CTS)
F. Vehicle Speed Sensor (VSS)
J. Knock Sensor

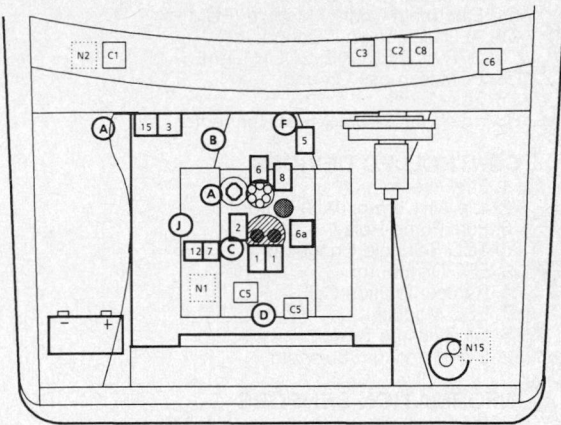

5.0L (VIN H) & 5.7L (VIN K) "C" & "K" SERIES

EMISSIONS SYSTEMS
(Not ECM Controlled)
N1. PCV Valve
N2. Fuel Module (5.7L HD)
N15. Fuel Vapor Canister

Courtesy of General Motors Corp.

91G12100

Fig. 41: Component Location For 5.0L (VIN H) & 5.7L (VIN K) "C" & "K" Series

COMPUTER HARNESS
C1. Electronic Control Module (ECM)
C2. ALDL Diagnostic Connector
C3. SERVICE ENGINE SOON Light
C5. ECM Harness Ground
C6. Fuse Block
C8. Fuel Pump Prime/Test Connector

CONTROLLED DEVICES
1. Fuel Injector
2. Idle Air Control (IAC) Motor
3. Fuel Pump Relay
5. TCC Solenoid Connector
6. EST Distributor
6a. Remote Ignition Coil
7. ESC Module
8. Oil Pressure Switch
9. EGR Solenoid (5.7L HD Only)

INFORMATION SENSORS
A. Manifold Absolute Pressure (MAP) Sensor
B. Oxygen (O_2) Sensor
C. Throttle Position Sensor (TPS)
D. Coolant Temperature Sensor (CTS)
F. Vehicle Speed Sensor (VSS)
J. Knock Sensor (ESC)

EMISSIONS SYSTEMS
(Not ECM Controlled)
N1. PCV Valve
N2. Fuel Module (5.7L HD Only)
N15. Fuel Vapor Canister

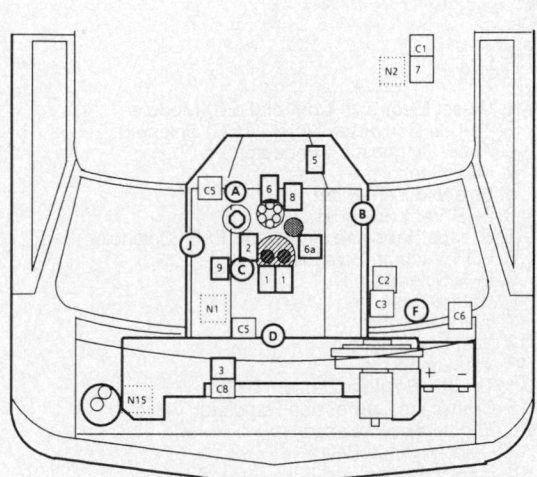

5.0L (VIN H) & 5.7L (VIN K) "G" SERIES

Courtesy of General Motors Corp.

92J21542

Fig. 42: Component Location For 5.0L (VIN H) & 5.7L (VIN K) "G" Series

COMPUTER HARNESS
C1. Electronic Control Module (ECM)
C2. ALDL Diagnostic Connector
C3. SERVICE ENGINE SOON Light
C5. ECM Harness Ground
C6. Fuse Block
C8. Fuel Pump Prime/Test Connector

CONTROLLED DEVICES
1. Fuel Injector
2. Idle Air Control (IAC) Motor
3. Fuel Pump Relay
5. TCC Solenoid Connector
6. EST Distributor
6a. Remote Ignition Coil
7. ESC Module
8. Oil Pressure Switch
12. EVRV Vacuum Solenoid

INFORMATION SENSORS
A. Manifold Absolute Pressure (MAP) Sensor
B. Oxygen (O_2) Sensor
C. Throttle Position Sensor (TPS)
D. Coolant Temperature Sensor (CTS)
F. Vehicle Speed Sensor (VSS)
J. Knock Sensor (ESC)
K. Vehicle Speed Sensor Buffer Module

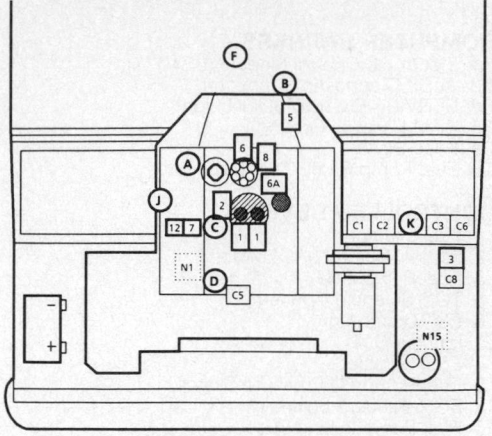

5.7L (VIN K) "P" SERIES

EMISSIONS SYSTEMS
(Not ECM Controlled)
N1. PCV Valve
N15. Fuel Vapor Canister

92A21543

Fig. 43: Component Location For 5.7L (VIN K) "P" Series

1. Diesel Electronic Control (DEC) Module
2. Torque Converter Clutch (TCC) Solenoid
3. ALDL Diagnostic Connector
4. MAP Sensor
5. Solenoid Vent/Filter
6. EGR Vent Solenoid
7. Exhaust Pressure Regulator (EPR) Solenoid
8. EGR Vacuum Solenoid
9. EPR Solenoid
10. Gauge Boss
11. Injection Pump
12. Fast Idle Solenoid
13. Vacuum Pump
14. Throttle Position Sensor (TPS)
15. Crankcase Depression Regulator Valve
16. Engine Speed Sensor
17. Cold Advance Relay
18. EGR Valve

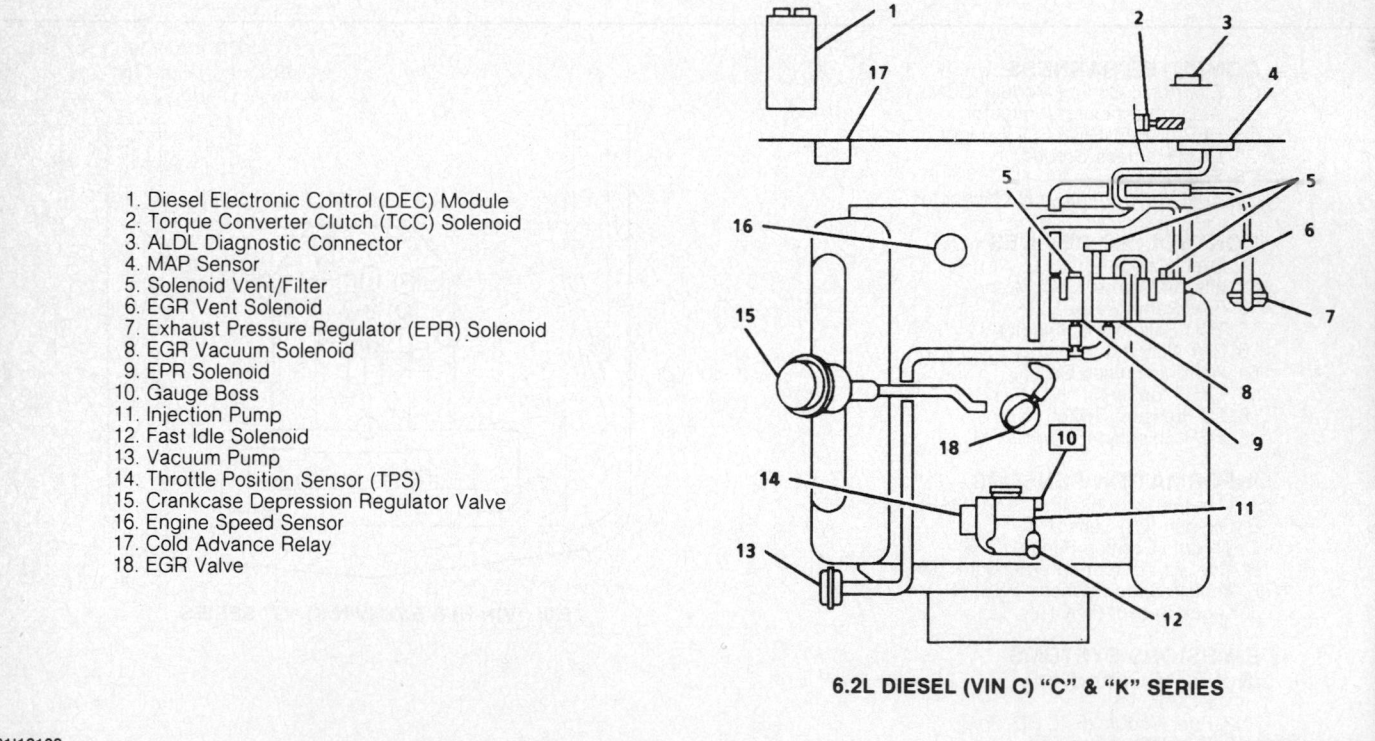

6.2L DIESEL (VIN C) "C" & "K" SERIES

91I12102

Fig. 44: Component Location For 6.2L Diesel (VIN C) "C" & "K" Series

1. Vacuum Pump
2. Crankcase Depression
3. EGR Valve
4. Engine Speed Sensor
5. Electronic Control Module (ECM)
6. Torque Converter Clutch (TCC) Solenoid
7. Vent Filter
8. ALDL Diagnostic Connector
9. Vehicle Speed Sensor (VSS)
10. Manifold
11. EGR Vent Solenoid
12. EPR Valve
13. EGR Vacuum Solenoid
14. EPR Solenoid
15. Injection Pump
16. Fast Idle Solenoid
17. Oil Filler Pipe
18. Throttle Position Sensor (TPS)
19. Cold Advance Control Relay
20. MAP Sensor

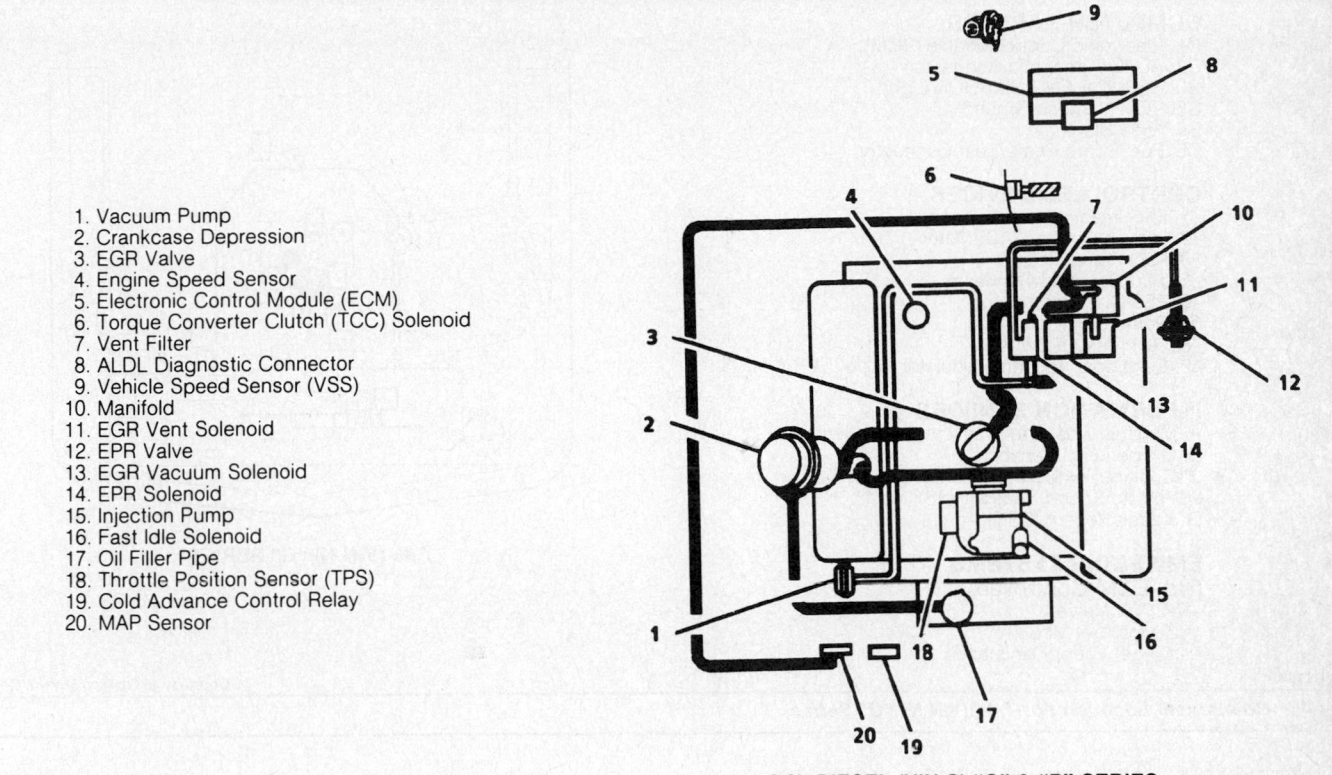

6.2L DIESEL (VIN C) "G" & "P" SERIES

92F21598

Courtesy of General Motors Corp.

Fig. 45: Component Location For 6.2L Diesel (VIN C) "G" & "P" Series

---

COMPUTER HARNESS
C1. Electronic Control Module (ECM)
C2. ALDL Diagnostic Connector
C3. SERVICE ENGINE SOON Light
C5. ECM Harness Ground
C6. Fuse Block
C8. Fuel Pump Prime/Test Connector

CONTROLLED DEVICES
1. Fuel Injector
2. Idle Air Control (IAC) Motor
3. Fuel Pump Relay
5. Transmission Connector
6. EST Distributor
6a. Ignition Coil
8. Oil Pressure Switch
9. Electric Air Control (EAC) Solenoid
12. EVRV Vacuum Regulator Solenoid
15. ESC Module

INFORMATION SENSORS
A. Manifold Absolute Pressure (MAP) Sensor
B. Oxygen (O$_2$) Sensor
C. Throttle Position Sensor (TPS)
D. Coolant Temperature Sensor
F. Vehicle Speed Sensor (VSS)
G. Knock Sensor

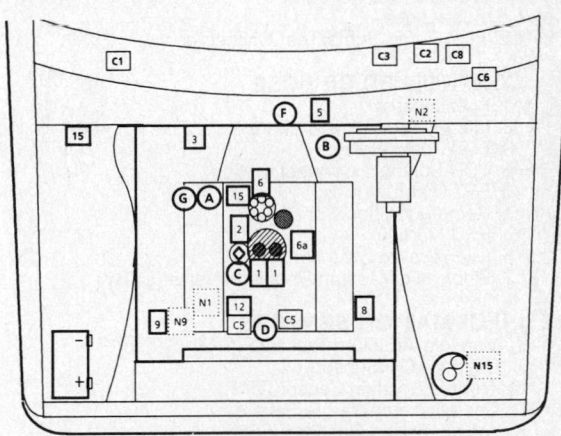

7.4L (VIN N) "C" & "K" SERIES

EMISSIONS SYSTEMS
(Not ECM Controlled)
N1. PCV Valve
N2. Fuel Module
N9. AIR Pump
N15. Fuel Vapor Canister

92B21544

Courtesy of General Motors Corp.

Fig. 46: Component Location For 7.4L (VIN N) "C" & "K" Series

COMPUTER HARNESS
C1. Electronic Control Module (ECM)
C2. ALDL Diagnostic Connector
C3. SERVICE ENGINE SOON Light
C5. ECM Harness Ground
C6. Fuse Block
C8. Fuel Pump Prime/Test Connector

CONTROLLED DEVICES
1. Fuel Injector
2. Idle Air Control (IAC) Motor
3. Fuel Pump Relay
5. TCC Solenoid Connector
6. EST Distributor
6a. Remote Ignition Coil
8. Oil Pressure Switch
12. Electronic Vacuum Regulator Valve (EVRV)

INFORMATION SENSORS
A. Manifold Absolute Pressure (MAP) Sensor
B. Oxygen (O_2) Sensor
D. Coolant Temperature Sensor
F. Vehicle Speed Sensor (VSS)
G. Knock Sensor (ESC)

EMISSIONS SYSTEMS
(Not ECM Controlled)
N1. PCV Valve
N2. Hot Fuel Module
N15. Fuel Vapor Canister

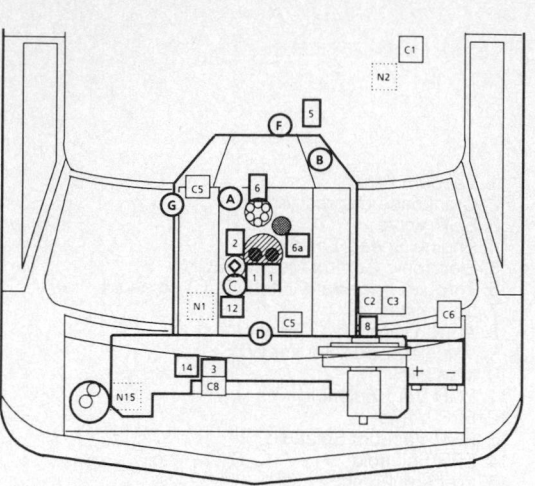

7.4L (VIN N) "G" SERIES

92C21545

Courtesy of General Motors Corp.

Fig. 47: Component Location For 7.4L (VIN N) "G" Series

COMPUTER HARNESS
C1. Electronic Control Module (ECM)
C2. ALDL Diagnostic Connector
C3. SERVICE ENGINE SOON Light
C5. ECM Harness Ground
C6. Fuse Block
C8. Fuel Pump Prime/Test Connector

CONTROLLED DEVICES
1. Fuel Injector
2. Idle Air Control (IAC) Motor
3. Fuel Pump Relay
5. TCC Solenoid Connector
6. EST Distributor
6a. Remote Ignition Coil
7. ESC Module
8. Oil Pressure Switch
12. Electronic Vacuum Regulator Valve (EVRV)

INFORMATION SENSORS
A. Manifold Absolute Pressure (MAP) Sensor
B. Oxygen (O_2) Sensor
C. Throttle Position Sensor (TPS)
D. Coolant Temperature Sensor
F. Vehicle Speed Sensor (VSS)
J. Knock Sensor (ESC)

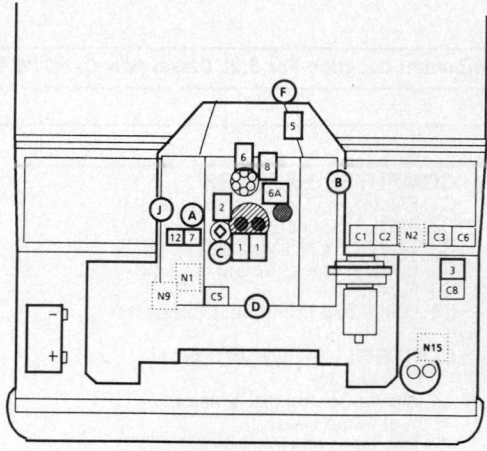

7.4L (VIN N) "P" SERIES

EMISSIONS SYSTEMS
(Not ECM Controlled)
N1. PCV Valve
N2. Hot Fuel Module
N9. AIR Pump
N15. Fuel Vapor Canister

92D21546

Courtesy of General Motors Corp.

Fig. 48: Component Location For 7.4L (VIN N) "P" Series

1992 ENGINE PERFORMANCE
Pin Voltage Charts

Astro, Bravada, Commercial Van, Jimmy, Lumina APV, Safari, Sierra, Silhouette, Sonoma, Suburban, Syclone, Trans Sport, Typhoon, Van, Yukon, "C" & "K" Series Blazer & Pickup, "S" & "T" Series Blazer & Pickup

MODEL IDENTIFICATION

Vehicle model can be identified by fifth character of Vehicle Identification Number (VIN), stamped on metal pad on top of left end of instrument panel, near windshield. See MODEL IDENTIFICATION table.

MODEL IDENTIFICATION

Series [1]	Model
"C"	2WD Pickup, Sierra & Suburban
"G"	RWD Van
"K"	4WD Blazer, Pickup, Sierra, Suburban & Yukon
"L"	All-Wheel Drive Astro & Safari
"M"	2WD Astro & Safari
"P"	Commercial Van/Motorhome
"S"	2WD Blazer, Jimmy, Pickup & Sonoma
"T"	Bravada, 4WD Blazer, Jimmy, Pickup, Sonoma, Syclone & Typhoon
"U"	Lumina APV, Silhouette & Trans Sport

[1] – Vehicle series is fifth character of VIN.

INTRODUCTION

PIN VOLTAGE CHARTS are supplied (when available) to reduce diagnostic time. Checking pin voltages at the electronic control unit determines if it is receiving and transmitting proper signals. Charts may also help determine if control unit harness is shorted or open.

NOTE: All voltage tests should be performed with a Digital Volt-Ohmmeter (DVOM) with a minimum 10-megohm input impedance, unless stated otherwise in testing procedures.

NOTE:
This ECM voltage chart along with digital voltmeter can help save diagnosis time. Voltage readings may vary slightly depending on battery voltage and alternator output.

The following conditions must be met before testing:
- Engine at operating temperature.
- Engine in closed loop operation.
- Engine idling (Engine Run column).
- ALDL "test" terminal NOT grounded.
- Scan tester NOT installed.

PIN	PIN FUNCTION	CKT #	WIRE COLOR	NORMAL VOLTAGE KEY "ON"	NORMAL VOLTAGE ENG RUN
A1	FUEL PUMP RELAY DRIVE	465	DK GRN/WHT	(1)	14
A2	SHIFT LIGHT (MT) TCC CONTROL (AT)	456 422	TAN/BLK	12	14
A3	EGR SOLENOID CONTROL	435	GRY	12	0
A4	A/C RELAY CONTROL	458	RED	(6)	(6)
A5	"SERVICE ENGINE SOON" LIGHT CONTROL	419	BRN/WHT	0	14
A6	IGN-ECM FUSE	439	PNK/BLK	12	14
A7	NOT USED	—	—	—	—
A8	SERIAL DATA	461	ORN	(2)	(2)
A9	DIAGNOSTIC TEST TERMINAL	451	WHT/BLK	5	5
A10	SPEED SENSOR SIGNAL	437	BRN	(3)	(3)
A11	CTS & TPS SENSOR GROUND	452	BLK	0	0
A12	SYSTEM GROUND	450	BLK/WHT	0	0

PIN	PIN FUNCTION	CKT #	WIRE COLOR	NORMAL VOLTAGE KEY "ON"	NORMAL VOLTAGE ENG RUN
B1	BATTERY 12 VOLTS	440	ORN	12	14
B2	FUEL PUMP SIGNAL	120	GRY	(1)	14
B3	EST REFERENCE LOW	453	BLK/RED	0	0
B4	NOT USED	—	—	—	—
B5	EST REFERENCE HIGH	430	PPL/WHT	0	1.6
B6	NOT USED	—	—	—	—
B7	NOT USED	—	—	—	—
B8	A/C SIGNAL	459	DK GRN/WHT	(4)	(4)
B9	NOT USED	451	WHT/BLK	5	5
B10	PARK/NEUTRAL SWITCH SIGNAL	434	ORN/BLK	(5)	(5)
B11	NOT USED	—	—	—	—
B12	NOT USED	—	—	—	—

(1) Battery voltage first two seconds.
(2) Varies from 2 volts to 5 volts.
(3) Varies from 0 to battery voltage depending on position of drive wheels.
(4) 0 volts A/C "OFF" battery voltage A/C "ON."
(5) 0 volts in neutral, battery voltage in gear.
(6) 0 volts A/C "ON," battery voltage A/C "OFF."

BACK VIEW OF CONNECTOR

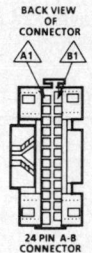

24 PIN A-B CONNECTOR

PIN	PIN FUNCTION	CKT #	WIRE COLOR	NORMAL VOLTAGE KEY "ON"	NORMAL VOLTAGE ENG RUN
C1	NOT USED	—	—	—	—
C2	NOT USED	—	—	—	—
C3	IAC "B" LOW	444	LT GRN/BLK	NOT USABLE	
C4	IAC "B" HIGH	443	LT GRN/WHT	NOT USABLE	
C5	IAC "A" HIGH	441	LT BLU/WHT	NOT USABLE	
C6	IAC "A" LOW	442	LT BLU/BLK	NOT USABLE	
C7	NOT USED	—	—	—	—
C8	P/S SWITCH	495	LT BLU/ORN	12.3	14.0
C9	CRANK SIGNAL	806	PPL/WHT	(1)	0
C10	COOLANT TEMP SIGNAL	410	YEL	(2)	(2)
C11	MAP SIGNAL	432	LT GRN	4.7	1.0
C12	IAT SIGNAL	472	TAN	(2)	(2)
C13	TPS SIGNAL	417	DK BLU	(3)	6
C14	5 VOLT REF MAP & TPS	416	GRY	5	5
C15	NOT USED	—	—	—	—
C16	BATTERY 12 VOLTS	440	ORN	12	14

PIN	PIN FUNCTION	CKT #	WIRE COLOR	NORMAL VOLTAGE KEY "ON"	NORMAL VOLTAGE ENG RUN
D1	SYSTEM GROUND	551	TAN/WHT	0	0
D2	MAP, IAT SENSOR GROUND	469	BLK/ORN	0	0
D3	NOT USED	—	—	—	—
D4	EST CONTROL	423	WHT	*	1.0
D5	EST BYPASS	424	TAN/WHT	*	4.75
D6	OXYGEN SENSOR GROUND	413	TAN	*	*
D7	OXYGEN SENSOR SIGNAL	412	PPL	(4)	(5)
D8	NOT USED	—	—	—	—
D9	GROUND	151	BLK	0	0
D10	GROUND	151	BLK	0	0
D11	NOT USED	—	—	—	—
D12	NOT USED	—	—	—	—
D13	NOT USED	—	—	—	—
D14	NOT USED	—	—	—	—
D15	NOT USED	—	—	—	—
D16	INJECTOR A	467	DK BLU	12	14

(1) Battery voltage when cranking.
(2) About 1.0 volt, varies with temperature.
(3) .6 volt to about 4.8 volts at Wide Open Throttle (WOT).
(4) .26 to .46 volts.
(5) Varies from .1 volt to .9 volt.
* Less than .5 volt.

BACK VIEW OF CONNECTOR

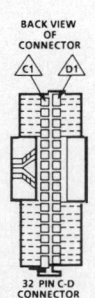

32 PIN C-D CONNECTOR

Courtesy of General Motors Corp.

Fig. 1: ECM Terminal Identification & Pin Voltages ("S" Series 2.5L)

NOTE:
This ECM voltage chart along with digital voltmeter can help save diagnosis time. Voltage readings may vary slightly depending on battery voltage and alternator output.

The following conditions must be met before testing:
- Engine at operating temperature.
- Engine in closed loop operation.
- Engine idling (Engine Run column).
- ALDL "test" terminal NOT grounded.
- Scan tester NOT installed.

PIN	PIN FUNCTION	CKT #	WIRE COLOR	NORMAL VOLTAGE KEY "ON"	NORMAL VOLTAGE ENG RUN
A1	FUEL PUMP RELAY DRIVE	465	DK GRN/WHT	(1)	14
A2	A/C RELAY CONTROL	459	DK GRN/WHT	(5)	(5)
A3	NOT USED	–	–	–	–
A4	EGR CONTROL	435	GRY	12	14
A5	"SERVICE ENGINE SOON" LIGHT CONTROL	419	BRN/WHT	0	14
A6	IGN-ECM FUSE	439	PNK/BLK	12	14
A7	MANUAL TRANS SHIFT LAMP	456	TAN/BLK	12	14
A8	SERIAL DATA	461	ORN	(2)	(2)
A9	DIAGNOSTIC TEST TERMINAL	451	WHT/BLK	5	5
A10	VEHICLE SPEED SENSOR SIGNAL	437	BRN	(3)	(3)
A11	MAP SENSOR GROUND	455	PPL	0	0
A12	SYSTEM GROUND	450	BLK/WHT	0	0

PIN	PIN FUNCTION	CKT #	WIRE COLOR	NORMAL VOLTAGE KEY "ON"	NORMAL VOLTAGE ENG RUN
B1	BATTERY 12 VOLTS	440	ORN	12	14
B2	FUEL PUMP SIGNAL	120	GRY	(1)	14
B3	EST REFERENCE "LOW"	453	BLK/RED	0	0
B4	NOT USED	–	–	–	–
B5	EST REFERENCE "HIGH"	430	PPL/WHT	0	1.6
B6	NOT USED	–	–	–	–
B7	ESC SIGNAL	485	BLK	9	9
B8	A/C SIGNAL	59	DK GRN	(4)	(4)
B9	NOT USED	–	–	–	–
B10	NOT USED	–	–	–	–
B11	NOT USED	–	–	–	–
B12	NOT USED	–	–	–	–

(1) Battery voltage first two seconds.
(2) Varies from 2 volts to 5 volts.
(3) Varies from 0 to battery voltage depending on position of drive wheels.
(4) 0 volts A/C "OFF," battery voltage A/C "ON."
(5) 0 volts A/C "ON," battery voltage A/C "OFF."

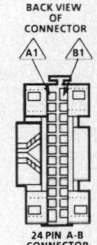

BACK VIEW OF CONNECTOR

24 PIN A-B CONNECTOR

PIN	PIN FUNCTION	CKT #	WIRE COLOR	NORMAL VOLTAGE KEY "ON"	NORMAL VOLTAGE ENG RUN
C1	NOT USED	–	–	–	–
C2	ELECTRONIC AIR CONTROL SOLENOID	436	BRN	B+	B+
C3	IAC "B" LOW	444	LT GRN/BLK	NOT	USABLE
C4	IAC "B" HIGH	443	LT GRN/WHT	NOT	USABLE
C5	IAC "A" HIGH	441	LT BLU/WHT	NOT	USABLE
C6	IAC "A" LOW	442	LT BLU/BLK	NOT	USABLE
C7	NOT USED	–	–	–	–
C8	NOT USED	–	–	–	–
C9	CRANK SIGNAL	806	PPL/WHT	(1)	0*
C10	COOLANT TEMP SIGNAL	410	YEL	(2)	(2)
C11	MAP SIGNAL	432	LT GRN	4.8	1.0†
C12	NOT USED	–	–	–	–
C13	TPS SIGNAL	417	DK BLU	(3)	.6
C14	5 VOLT REF MAP & TPS	416	GRY	5	5
C15	NOT USED	–	–	–	–
C16	BATTERY 12 VOLTS	440	ORN	B+	B+

PIN	PIN FUNCTION	CKT #	WIRE COLOR	NORMAL VOLTAGE KEY "ON"	NORMAL VOLTAGE ENG RUN
D1	SYSTEM GROUND	551	TAN/WHT	0*	0*
D2	TPS, CTS SENSOR GROUND	452	BLK	0*	0*
D3	NOT USED	–	–	–	–
D4	EST CONTROL	423	WHT	0*	1.0
D5	EST BYPASS	424	TAN/BLK	0*	4.75
D6	OXYGEN SENSOR GROUND	413	TAN	0*	0*
D7	OXYGEN SENSOR SIGNAL	412	PPL	(4)	(5)
D8	NOT USED	–	–	–	–
D9	NOT USED	–	–	–	–
D10	NOT USED	–	–	–	–
D11	NOT USED	–	–	–	–
D12	NOT USED	–	–	–	–
D13	NOT USED	–	–	–	–
D14	INJECTOR B	468	DK GRN	B+	B+
D15	NOT USED	–	–	–	–
D16	INJECTOR A	467	DK BLU	B+	B+

(1) Battery voltage when cranking.
(2) About 1.0 volt, varies with temperature.
(3) .6 volt to about 4.8 volts at Wide Open Throttle (WOT).
(4) .26 to .46 volts.
(5) Varies from .1 volt to .9 volt.
* Less than .5 volt.
† Varies with manifold pressure.

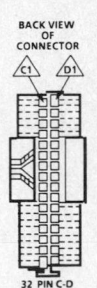

BACK VIEW OF CONNECTOR

32 PIN C-D CONNECTOR

Courtesy of General Motors Corp.

92C22170 92D22171

Fig. 2: ECM Terminal Identification & Pin Voltages ("S" Series 2.8L)

1992 ENGINE PERFORMANCE
Pin Voltage Charts (Cont.)

NOTE:
This ECM voltage chart along with digital voltmeter can help save diagnosis time. Voltage readings may vary slightly depending on battery voltage and alternator output.

The following conditions must be met before testing:

- Engine at operating temperature.
- Engine in closed loop operation.
- Engine idling (Engine Run column).
- ALDL "test" terminal NOT grounded.
- Scan tester NOT installed.

Note	VOLTAGE KEY "ON"	VOLTAGE ENG. RUN	CIRCUIT	PIN	WIRE COLOR
②	0	B+	FUEL PUMP RELAY DRIVE	A1	DK GRN/ WHT
	B+	B+	A/C CONTROL RELAY	A2	DK GRN/ WHT
			NOT USED	A3	
	B+	B+	EVRV	A4	GRY
	0	B+	"SERVICE ENGINE SOON" CONTROL	A5	BRN/ WHT
	B+	B+	IGN (ECM)	A6	PNK/ BLK
	B+	B+	TCC SOLENOID	A7	TAN/ BLK
	2-5	2-5	SERIAL DATA	A8	ORN
	5	5	DIAGNOSTIC TERMINAL	A9	WHT/ BLK
①	0 OR 12	0 OR 12	SPEED SENSOR SIGNAL	A10	BRN
	0	0	SENSOR GROUND	A11	PPL
	0	0	SYSTEM GROUND	A12	BLK/ WHT
	0	0	COOLING FAN CONTROL *	C1	DK BLU WHT
	B+	B+	COOLING FAN RELAY	C2	DK GRN/ WHT
	NOT USEABLE		IAC "B" LO	C3	LT GRN/ BLK
	NOT USEABLE		IAC "B" HI	C4	LT GRN/ WHT
	NOT USEABLE		IAC "A" HI	C5	LT BLU/ WHT
	NOT USEABLE		IAC "A" LO	C6	LT BLU BLK
	B+	B+	TCC SELECTOR	C7	DK GRN/ WHT
			NOT USED	C8	
⑦	0	0	CRANK DISCRETE	C9	PPL/WHT
⑤	1.6	1.6	COOLANT TEMP. SIGNAL	C10	YEL
③	4.75	1.1	MAP SIGNAL	C11	LT GRN
			NOT USED	C12	
	.7	.7	TPS SIGNAL	C13	DK BLU
	5	5	TPS 5 VOLT REFERENCE	C14	GRY
			NOT USED	C15	
	B+	B+	BATTERY	C16	ORN

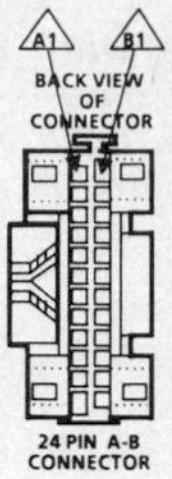
A1
B1
BACK VIEW OF CONNECTOR
24 PIN A-B CONNECTOR

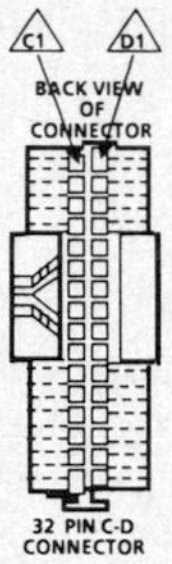
C1
D1
BACK VIEW OF CONNECTOR
32 PIN C-D CONNECTOR

WIRE COLOR	PIN	CIRCUIT	VOLTAGE KEY "ON"	VOLTAGE ENG. RUN	Note
ORN	B1	BATT 12 VOLTS	B+	B+	
GRY	B2	FUEL PUMP SIGNAL	0	B+	④
BLK/ RED	B3	REFERENCE GROUND	0	0	
	B4	NOT USED			
PPL/ WHT	B5	DISTRIBUTOR REFERENCE HIGH	0	1.3	
	B6	NOT USED			
BLK	B7	ESC SIGNAL	9.2	9.3	
LT BLU	B8	A/C REQUEST SIGNAL "OFF" / "ON"	0 / B+	0 / B+	
DK GRN/ WHT	B9	FAN REQUEST SIGNAL (A/C)			
ORN/ BLK	B10	PARK/NEUTRAL SW. SIGNAL (A/T)	0	0	⑥
	B11	NOT USED			
	B12	NOT USED			
TAN/ WHT	D1	SYSTEM GROUND	0	0	
BLK	D2	SENSOR GROUND	0	0	
	D3	NOT USED			
WHT	D4	EST CONTROL	0	1.3	
TAN/ BLK	D5	BYPASS	0	4.75	
TAN	D6	GROUND (O_2)	0	0	
PPL	D7	O_2 SENSOR SIGNAL	3.5	1.9	③
	D8	NOT USED			
	D9	NOT USED			
	D10	NOT USED			
	D11	NOT USED			
	D12	NOT USED			
	D13	NOT USED			
DK GRN	D14	INJECTOR #2	B+	B+	
	D15	NOT USED			
DK BLU	D16	INJECTOR #1	B+	B+	

① Varies from .60 to battery voltage, depending on position of drive wheels.
② 12 volts for first two seconds.
③ Varies.
④ 12 volts when fuel pump is running.
⑤ Varies with temperature.
⑥ Reads battery voltage in gear.
⑦ 12 volts, when engine is cranking.
* Front and rear A/C option.

92E22172

Courtesy of General Motors Corp.

Fig. 3: ECM Terminal Identification & Pin Voltages (Lumina APV, Silhouette & Trans Sport 3.1L)

NOTE:
This ECM voltage chart along with digital voltmeter can help save diagnosis time. Voltage readings may vary slightly depending on battery voltage and alternator output.

The following conditions must be met before testing:
- Engine at operating temperature.
- Engine in closed loop operation.
- Engine idling (Engine Run column).
- ALDL "test" terminal NOT grounded.
- Scan tester NOT installed.

NOTICE: Before checking voltages be sure PCM and engine grounds are clean and tight.

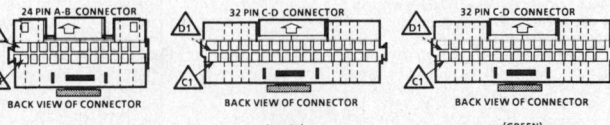

24 PIN A-B CONNECTOR   32 PIN C-D CONNECTOR   32 PIN C-D CONNECTOR

BACK VIEW OF CONNECTOR   BACK VIEW OF CONNECTOR   BACK VIEW OF CONNECTOR

(BLACK)   (BLACK)   (GREEN)

BLACK 32 PIN C-D CONNECTOR #1

VOLTAGE KEY "ON"	VOLTAGE ENG. RUN	CIRCUIT	PIN	WIRE COLOR	CKT #	CKT #	WIRE COLOR	PIN	CIRCUIT	VOLTAGE KEY "ON"	VOLTAGE ENG. RUN
0*	0*	C/C VENT SOLENOID	C1	DK BLU/WHT	403			D1			
3-5(2)	3-5(2)	SERIAL DATA	C2	ORN/BLK	1061	413	TAN	D2	O₂ GROUND REF	0*	0*
0*	0*	C/C VAC SOLENOID	C3	LT GRN	402	412	PPL	D3	O₂ SIGNAL	.3-5	.1-.9(2)
0*	B+	FUEL PUMP RELAY	C4	DK GRN/WHT	465			D4			
			C5			776	WHT	D5	PRNDL P	0*	0*
0*	5	BYPASS	C6	TAN/BLK	424	773	GRY	D6	PRNDL C	B+	B+
0*	2	EST	C7	WHT	423	772	YEL	D7	PRNDL B	B+	B+
0*	0*	REFERENCE LO	C8	BLK/RED	453	771	BLK/WHT	D8	PRNDL A	0*	0*
			C9			603	DK GRN/WHT	D9	A/C PRESSURE SWITCH	B+	B+
			C10			86	BRN	D10	CRUISE BRAKE	0*	0*
5	2.5	FUEL CONTROL	C11	PPL/WHT	430	67	LT BLU	D11	A/C REQUEST	0*	0*
B+	B+	INJECTOR 3	C12	BLK/PNK	843			D12			
0*	0*	INJECTOR GROUND	C13	BLK/WHT	450	450	BLK/WHT	D13	INJ GROUND	0*	0*
B+	B+	INJECTOR 4	C14	BLK/LT BLU	844	492	YEL	D14	MAF SIGNAL	5	5(2)
B+	B+	INJECTOR 1	C15	BLK	841	846	BLK/YEL	D15	INJECTOR 6	B+	B+
B+	B+	INJECTOR 5	C16	BLK/WHT	845	842	BLK/LT GRN	D16	INJECTOR 2	B+	B+

GREEN 32 PIN C-D CONNECTOR #3

VOLTAGE KEY "ON"	VOLTAGE ENG. RUN	CIRCUIT	PIN	WIRE COLOR	CKT #	CKT #	WIRE COLOR	PIN	CIRCUIT	VOLTAGE KEY "ON"	VOLTAGE ENG. RUN
0*	B+	SES LIGHT	C1	BRN/WHT	419			D1			
B+	B+	A/C RELAY	C2	DK GRN/WHT	459	397	GRY	D2	CRUISE "ON/OFF"	0*	0*
B+	B+	HI SPEED FAN	C3	DK BLU/WHT	473	84	DK BLU	D3	SET/COAST	0*	0*
B+	B+	LO SPEED FAN	C4	DK GRN/WHT	335	87	GRY/BLK	D4	RESUME/ACCL	0*	0*
B+	B+	CANISTER PURGE	C5	DK GRN/YEL	428			D5			
B+	B+	TCC APPLY SOLENOID	C6	TAN/BLK	422	647	LT BLU/BLK	D6	SPARK REFERENCE	0*	3
			C7					D7			
			C8					D8			
			C9					D9			
			C10					D10			
(2)	(2)	IACA HI	C11	LT BLU/WHT	441			D11			
(2)	(2)	IACA LO	C12	LT BLU/BLK	442			D12			
(2)	(2)	IACB LO	C13	LT GRN/BLK	444	401	PPL	D13	VSS LO	0*	0*
(2)	(2)	IACB HI	C14	LT GRN/WHT	443	400	YEL	D14	VSS HI	0*	0*
B+	B+	TCC PWM SOLENOID	C15	WHT	584	1223	YEL/BLK	D15	SHIFT B	0*	0*
			C16			1222	LT GRN	D16	SHIFT A	0*	0*

** VARIES AROUND 10 VOLTS   * LESS THAN .5v (500 mv)   (2) VARIES   ENGINE - 3800/L27

BLACK 24 PIN A-B CONNECTOR #2

VOLTAGE KEY "ON"	ENG. RUN	CIRCUIT	PIN	WIRE COLOR	CKT #	CKT #	WIRE COLOR	PIN	CIRCUIT	VOLTAGE KEY "ON"	ENG. RUN
			A1					B1			
B+	B+	IGNITION "ON" INPUT	A2	PNK/BLK	439			B2			
			A3			416	GRY	B3	5 VOLT REF.	5	5
B+	B+	BATTERY	A4	ORN	840	840	ORN	B4	BATTERY	B+	B+
B+	B+	TCC BRAKE	A5	PPL	420			B5			
0*	0*	PCM GROUND	A6	BLK/WHT	450	551	TAN/WHT	B6	PCM GND	0*	0*
0*	0*	IATS GROUND	A7	BLK/WHT	454	472	TAN	B7	IATS SIGNAL	(2)	(2)
0*	0*	SENSOR GROUND	A8	BLK	452	496	DK BLU	B8	ESC SIGNAL	2.4	2.4
0*	0*	SPS LOW	A9	LT BLU/BLK	399	410	YEL	B9	CTS SIGNAL	1.8 (2)	1.7 (2)
0*	0*	SPS HIGH	A10	TAN	398	417	DK BLU	B10	TPS SIGNAL	.33-.4G	.33-.4G
			A11			451	WHT/BLK	B11	DIAGNOSTIC REQ.	5	5
5	(2)	CAM HIGH	A12	BLK	630			B12			

*   Less than .5V (500 mV).
(1)   B + for first two seconds.
(2)   Varies.

NOTICE: Before closed loop operation can occur the following must take place:
- Coolant temperature above 75°C.
- O₂ Sensor voltage varying.
- Engine RPM greater than 800 for 15 consecutive seconds after 1 and 2 have occurred.

92F22173 92G22174 92H22175

Fig. 4: ECM Terminal Identification & Pin Voltages (Lumina APV, Silhouette & Trans Sport 3.8L)

NOTE:
This ECM voltage chart along with digital voltmeter can help save diagnosis time. Voltage readings may vary slightly depending on battery voltage and alternator output.

The following conditions must be met before testing:
- Engine at operating temperature.
- Engine in closed loop operation.
- Engine idling (Engine Run column).
- ALDL "test" terminal NOT grounded.
- Scan tester NOT installed.

PIN	CIRCUIT	CKT #	WIRE COLOR	VOLTAGE KEY "ON"	VOLTAGE ENG. RUN
A1	FUEL PUMP RELAY DRIVER	465	DK GRN WHT	(3)	B+
A2	TCC/CONTROL	422	TAN/BLK	B+	B+
A3	EGR CONTROL	435	GRY	B+	B+
A4	NOT USED			*	*
A5	S.E.S.	419	BRN/WHT	*0	B+
A6	IGNITION	439	PNK/BLK	B+	B+
A7	TUNING VALVE	1387	DK GRN WHT	B+	B+
A8	SERIAL DATA	461 1061	ORN ORN/BLK	(1)	(1)
A9	DIAG. TERMINAL	451	WHT/BLK	5	5
A10	DRAC/VSS	437	BRN	(2)	(2)
A11	TPS/IAT GND	452	BLK	*0	*0
A12	SYSTEM GND	450	BLK/WHT	*0	*0

PIN	CIRCUIT	CKT #	WIRE COLOR	VOLTAGE KEY "ON"	VOLTAGE ENG. RUN
B1	BATTERY	440	ORN	B+	B+
B2	FUEL PUMP SIGNAL	120	GRY	(3)	B+
B3	DIST. REF. LOW	453	BLK/RED	*0	*0
B4	IGNITION FEED	439	PNK/BLK	B+	B+
B5	DIST. REF. HIGH	430	PPL/WHT	*0	1.3
B6	NOT USED			-	-
B7	NOT USED				
B8	A/C SIGNAL	59	DK GRN	(4)	(4)
B9	HIGH GEAR	446	LT BLU	B+	B+
B10	P/N SW	434	ORN/BLK	(5)	(5)
B11	ESC SIGNAL	496	DK BLU	2.4	2.4
B12	NOT USED				

(1) Varies from 2 to 5 volts.
(2) Varies from 0 volts to battery voltage depending on position of drive wheels.
(3) Battery voltage for 2 seconds after ignition "ON."
(4) 0 volts A/C "OFF," battery voltage A/C "ON."
(5) 0 volts in P/N battery voltage in gear.
* Less than .5 volts.

BACK VIEW OF CONNECTOR

24 PIN A-B CONNECTOR

PIN	PIN FUNCTION	CKT #	WIRE COLOR	NORMAL VOLTAGE KEY "ON"	NORMAL VOLTAGE ENG RUN
C1	NOT USED	-	-	-	-
C2	NOT USED	-	-	-	-
C3	IAC "B" LOW	444	GRN/BLK	(2)	(2)
C4	IAC "B" HIGH	443	GRN/WHT	(2)	(2)
C5	IAC "A" HIGH	441	BLU/WHT	(2)	(2)
C6	IAC "A" LOW	442	BLU/BLK	(2)	(2)
C7	NOT USED	-	-	-	-
C8	NOT USED	-	-	-	-
C9	NOT USED	-	-	-	-
C10	CTS SIGNAL	410	YEL	(4)	(4)
C11	MAP SIGNAL	432	LT GRN	4.7	1.4 †
C12	IAT SIGNAL	472	TAN	(4)	(4)
C13	TPS SIGNAL	417	DK BLU	(5)	.6
C14	5V REF. (MAP, TPS)	416	GRY	5	5
C15	NOT USED	-	-	-	-
C16	BATTERY +	440	ORN	B+	B+

PIN	PIN FUNCTION	CKT #	WIRE COLOR	NORMAL VOLTAGE KEY "ON"	NORMAL VOLTAGE ENG RUN
D1	SYSTEM GROUND	450 551	BLK/WHT TAN/WHT	*0	*0
D2	SENSOR GROUND (MAP, CTS)	455	PPL	*0	*0
D3	NOT USED	-	-	-	-
D4	EST SIGNAL	423	WHT	*0	1.0
D5	EST BY-PASS	424	TAN/BLK	*0	4.6
D6	O₂ GROUND	413	TAN	*0	*0
D7	O₂ SIGNAL	412	PPL	(1)	(6)
D8	EGR (PINTLE SIGNAL)	1456	BRN	73	73
D9	DIRECT GROUND	151	BLK	*0	*0
D10	DIRECT GROUND	151	BLK	*0	*0
D11	NOT USED	-	-	-	-
D12	NOT USED	-	-	-	-
D13	NOT USED	-	-	-	-
D14	NOT USED	-	-	-	-
D15	NOT USED	-	-	-	-
D16	INJECTOR DRIVER	467	DK BLU	B+	B+

(1) .26 to .46 volt within 10 seconds the voltage goes near 0 volt as O₂ heater warms up.
(2) Not usable.
(3) Reads battery voltage for 2 seconds after ignition "ON," then should read 0 volt.
(4) Varies depending on temperature, about 1.3 volt.
(5) .6 volt to about 4.8 volts at Wide Open Throttle (WOT).
(6) Varies from .1 volt to .9 volt.
* Less than .5 volts.
† Varies with manifold pressure.

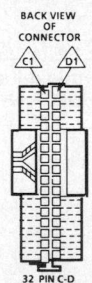

BACK VIEW OF CONNECTOR

32 PIN C-D CONNECTOR

ENGINE: 4.3L (L35) CPI

92I22176 92J22177

Courtesy of General Motors Corp.

Fig. 5: ECM Terminal Identification & Pin Voltages (Astro, Safari, & "S" & "T" Series 4.3L CPI)

NOTE:
This ECM voltage chart along with digital voltmeter can help save diagnosis time. Voltage readings may vary slightly depending on battery voltage and alternator output.

The following conditions must be met before testing:

- Engine at operating temperature.
- Engine in closed loop operation.
- Engine idling (Engine Run column).
- ALDL "test" terminal NOT grounded.
- Scan tester NOT installed.

PIN	PIN FUNCTION	CKT #	WIRE COLOR	KEY "ON"	ENG RUN
A1	FUEL PUMP RELAY DRIVE	465	DK GRN/WHT	(1)	14
A2	NOT USED	–	–	–	–
A3	NOT USED	–	–	–	–
A4	EGR CONTROL	435	GRY	12	14
A5	"SERVICE ENGINE SOON" LIGHT CONTROL	419	BRN/WHT	0	14
A6	IGN-ECM FUSED	439	PNK/BLK	12	14
A7	TCC CONTROL	422	TAN/BLK	12	14
A8	SERIAL DATA	461	ORN/BLK ORN	(2)	(2)
A9	DIAGNOSTIC TEST TERMINAL	451	WHT/BLK	5	5
A10	VEHICLE SPEED SENSOR SIGNAL	437	BRN	(3)	(3)
A11	TPS, CTS SENSOR GROUND	452	BLK	0	0
A12	SYSTEM GROUND	450	BLK/WHT	0	0

PIN	PIN FUNCTION	CKT #	WIRE COLOR	KEY "ON"	ENG RUN
B1	BATTERY 12 VOLT	440	ORN	12	14
B2	FUEL PUMP SIGNAL	120	GRY TAN/WHT	(1)	14
B3	EST REFERENCE LOW	453	BLK/RED	0	0
B4	NOT USED	–	–	–	–
B5	EST REFERENCE HIGH	430	PPL/WHT	0	1.6
B6	NOT USED	–	–	–	–
B7	ESC SIGNAL	485	BLK	9	9
B8	A/C SIGNAL	59	DK GRN	(4)	(4)
B9	NOT USED	–	–	–	–
B10	PARK/NEUTRAL SWITCH SIGNAL	434	ORN/BLK	(5)	(5)
B11	NOT USED	–	–	–	–
B12	NOT USED	–	–	–	–

(1) Battery voltage first 2 seconds.
(2) Varies from 2 volts to 5 volts.
(3) Varies from .01 to battery voltage depending on position of drive wheels.
(4) 0 volts A/C "OFF" battery voltage A/C "ON."
(5) 0 volts in neutral, battery voltage in gear.

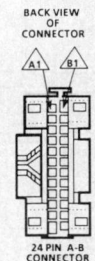

BACK VIEW OF CONNECTOR

24 PIN A-B CONNECTOR

PIN	PIN FUNCTION	CKT #	WIRE COLOR	KEY "ON"	ENG RUN
C1	NOT USED	–	–	–	–
C2	NOT USED	–	–	–	–
C3	IAC "B" LOW	444	LT GRN/BLK	NOT	USABLE
C4	IAC "B" HIGH	443	LT GRN/WHT	NOT	USABLE
C5	IAC "A" HIGH	441	LT BLU/WHT	NOT	USABLE
C6	IAC "A" LOW	442	LT BLU/BLK	NOT	USABLE
C7	HIGH GEAR SWITCH SIGNAL	446	LT BLU	12	14
C8	NOT USED	–	–	–	–
C9	CRANK SIGNAL	806	PPL PPL/WHT	(1)	0
C10	CTS SIGNAL	410	YEL	(2)	(2)
C11	MAP SENSOR SIGNAL	432	LT GRN LT GRN/BLK	4.8	1.0
C12	NOT USED	–	–	–	–
C13	TPS SIGNAL	417	DK BLU	(3)	.6
C14	MAP, TPS 5 VOLT REF.	416	GRY	5	5
C15	NOT USED	–	–	–	–
C16	BATTERY 12 VOLT	440	ORN	12	14

PIN	PIN FUNCTION	CKT #	WIRE COLOR	KEY "ON"	ENG RUN
D1	SYSTEM GROUND	450 551	BLK/WHT	0	0
D2	MAP SENSOR GROUND	455	PPL BLK/RED	0	0
D3	NOT USED	–	–	–	–
D4	EST	423	WHT	*	1.0
D5	EST BYPASS	424	TAN/BLK	*	4.75
D6	OXYGEN SENSOR GROUND	413	TAN	*	*
D7	OXYGEN SENSOR SIGNAL	412	PPL	(4)	(5)
D8	NOT USED	–	–	–	–
D9	NOT USED	–	–	–	–
D10	NOT USED	–	–	–	–
D11	NOT USED	–	–	–	–
D12	NOT USED	–	–	–	–
D13	NOT USED	–	–	–	–
D14	INJECTOR 2 DRIVER CONTROL	468	GRN	12	14
D15	NOT USED	–	–	–	–
D16	INJECTOR 1 DRIVER CONTROL	467	BLU	12	14

(1) Battery voltage when cranking.
(2) About 1.0 volt, varies with temperature.
(3) .6 Volt to about 4.8 volt at Wide Open Throttle (WOT).
(4) .26 to .46 volt within 10 seconds, the voltage goes near 0 volt as O₂ heater warms up.
(5) Varies from .1 volt to .9 volt.
* Less then .5 volt.

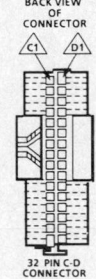

BACK VIEW OF CONNECTOR

32 PIN C-D CONNECTOR

92A22178 92B22179

Courtesy of General Motors Corp.

Fig. 6: ECM Terminal Identification & Pin Voltages (Astro, Safari, & "S" & "T" Series 4.3L TBI)

NOTE:
This ECM voltage chart along with digital voltmeter can help save diagnosis time. Voltage readings may vary slightly depending on battery voltage and alternator output.

The following conditions must be met before testing:
- Engine at operating temperature.
- Engine in closed loop operation.
- Engine idling (Engine Run column).
- ALDL "test" terminal NOT grounded.
- Scan tester NOT installed.

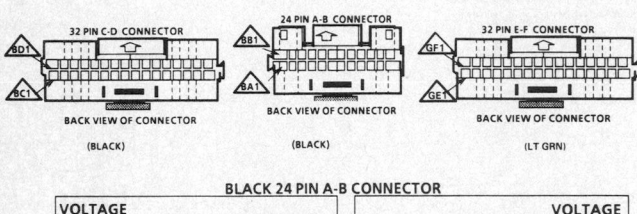

32 PIN C-D CONNECTOR — BACK VIEW OF CONNECTOR (BLACK)
24 PIN A-B CONNECTOR — BACK VIEW OF CONNECTOR (BLACK)
32 PIN E-F CONNECTOR — BACK VIEW OF CONNECTOR (LT GRN)

BLACK 32 PIN C-D CONNECTOR

KEY "ON"	ENG. RUN	CIRCUIT	PIN	WIRE COLOR	WIRE COLOR	PIN	CIRCUIT	KEY "ON"	ENG RUN
		NOT USED	BC1		TAN/WHT	BD1	ECM GROUND	0	0
		NOT USED	BC2			BD2	NOT USED		
		NOT USED	BC3			BD3	NOT USED		
		NOT USED	BC4			BD4	NOT USED		
		NOT USED	BC5			BD5	NOT USED		
B+	B+	DRAC SIGNAL	BC6	BRN		BD6	NOT USED		
0*	4.7	BYPASS	BC7	TAN/BLK	BLK/WHT	BD7	INJECTOR GROUND	0	0
0*	varies 1.2	EST	BC8	WHT	PPL/WHT	BD8	DIST. REFERENCE HI	0*	varies 1.0
0	0	A/C REQUEST	BC9	DK GRN	BLK/RED	BD9	DIST. REFERENCE LO	0*	0*
		NOT USED	BC10			BD10	NOT USED		
B+	B+	INJECTOR DRIVER	BC11	BLU		BD11	NOT USED		
B+	B+	INJECTOR DRIVER	BC12	GRN		BD12	NOT USED		
0*	0*	INJECTOR GROUND	BC13	BLK/WHT		BD13	NOT USED		
		NOT USED	BC14			BD14	NOT USED		
		NOT USED	BC15			BD15	NOT USED		
B+	B+	BATTERY	BC16	ORN	ORN/BLK	BD16	PARK/NEUTRAL	0*	0*

LIGHT GREEN 32 PIN E-F CONNECTOR

KEY "ON"	ENG. RUN	CIRCUIT	PIN	WIRE COLOR	WIRE COLOR	PIN	CIRCUIT	KEY "ON"	ENG RUN
		NOT USED	GE1		DK GRN/WHT	GF1	A/C CONTROL RELAY	B+	B+
		NOT USED	GE2		BLK/GRN	GF2	WASTEGATE SOL.	B+	.5
NOT USEABLE		IAC "B" LOW	GE3	LT GRN/WHT		GF3	NOT USED		
NOT USEABLE		IAC "B" HIGH	GE4	LT GRN/BLK	TAN/BLK	GF4	TCC SOLENOID	B+	B+
NOT USEABLE		IAC "A" LOW	GE5	BLU/BLK		GF5	NOT USED		
NOT USEABLE		IAC "A" HIGH	GE6	LT BLU/WHT		GF6	NOT USED		
.1	B+	CHECK ENGINE LAMP	GE7	GRA/WHT		GF7	NOT USED		
B+	B+	CAC PUMP CONTROL	GE8	YEL		GF8	NOT USED		
B+	.1	EVRV CONTROL	GE9	GRA	DK BLU	GF9	ESC SIGNAL	2.4	2.4
		NOT USED	GE10			GF10	NOT USED		
		NOT USED	GE11			GF11	NOT USED		
5.0	5.0	ALDL DIAG. ENABLE	GE12	WHT/BLK		GF12	NOT USED		
		NOT USED	GE13		DK BLU	GF13	TPS SIGNAL	.84	.84
.1-.3	varies .1-.9	0² SENSOR SIGNAL	GE14	PPL		GF14	NOT USED		
0*	0*	0² SENSOR GROUND	GE15	TAN	LT GRN	GF15	MAP SIGNAL	2.2	varies .8
varies 1.5	varies 1.5	COOLANT SIGNAL	GE16	YEL	TAN	GF16	MAT SIGNAL	varies 2.4	varies 2.2

* LESS THAN .5 VOLT   ▽ LESS THAN 1 VOLT   ① A/C, FAN OFF

BLACK 24 PIN A-B CONNECTOR

KEY "ON"	ENG. RUN	CIRCUIT	PIN	WIRE COLOR	WIRE COLOR	PIN	CIRCUIT	KEY "ON"	ENG RUN
		NOT USED	BA1		ORN	BB1	BATTERY	B+	B+
		NOT USED	BA2			BB2	NOT USED		
		NOT USED	BA3			BB3	NOT USED		
5.0	5.0	5 VOLTS REFERENCE	BA4	GRA		BB4	NOT USED		
5.0	5.0	5 VOLTS REFERENCE	BA5	GRA	BLK	BB5	MAT & TPS GROUND	0	0
B+	B+	IGN POWER	BA6	PNK/BLK	BLK	BB6	MAP & COOLANT GROUND	0	0
		NOT USED	BA7			BB7	NOT USED		
		NOT USED	BA8			BB8	NOT USED		
4.8	4.8	SERIAL DATA	BA9	ORN		BB9	NOT USED		
		NOT USED	BA10			BB10	NOT USED		
B+ 2 sec.	B+	FUEL PUMP RELAY	BA11	DK GRN/WHT		BB11	NOT USED		
0	0	ECM GROUND	BA12	BLK/WHT		BB12	NOT USED		

* Less than .5 Volt
▽ Less than 1 Volt
① A/C, Fan "OFF."

92E22180 92F22181

Courtesy of General Motors Corp.

Fig. 7: ECM Terminal Identification & Pin Voltages (Syclone & Typhoon 4.3L Turbo PFI)

NOTE:
This ECM voltage chart along with digital voltmeter can help save diagnosis time. Voltage readings may vary slightly depending on battery voltage and alternator output.

The following conditions must be met before testing:

- Engine at operating temperature.
- Engine in closed loop operation.
- Engine idling (Engine Run column).
- ALDL "test" terminal NOT grounded.
- Scan tester NOT installed.

PIN	PIN FUNCTION	CKT #	WIRE COLOR	NORMAL VOLTAGES KEY "ON"	NORMAL VOLTAGES ENG RUN
A1	FUEL PUMP RELAY DRIVE	465	DK GRN/WHT	(1)	B+
A2	NOT USED	–	–	–	–
A3	NOT USED	–	–	–	–
A4	EGR CONTROL	435	GRY	B+	B+
A5	"SERVICE ENGINE SOON" LIGHT CONTROL	419	BRN	0*	B+
A6	IGN ECM FUSED	439	PNK/BLK	B+	B+
A7	TCC CONTROL	422	TAN/BLK	B+	B+
A8	SERIAL DATA	461	ORN	(2)	(2)
A9	DIAGNOSTIC TEST TERMINAL	451	WHT/BLK	5	5
A10	VEHICLE SPEED SENSOR SIGNAL	437	BRN	(3)	(3)
A11	MAP SENSOR GROUND	455	PPL	0*	0*
A12	SYSTEM GROUND	450	BLK/WHT	0*	0*

PIN	PIN FUNCTION	CKT #	WIRE COLOR	NORMAL VOLTAGES KEY "ON"	NORMAL VOLTAGES ENG RUN
B1	BATTERY 12 VOLT	440	ORN	B+	B+
B2	FUEL PUMP SIGNAL	120	GRY	(1)	B+
B3	EST REFERENCE LOW	453	BLK/RED	0*	0*
B4	NOT USED	–	–	–	–
B5	EST REFERENCE HIGH	430	PPL/WHT	0*	1.6
B6	NOT USED	–	–	–	–
B7	ESC SIGNAL	457	YEL/BLK	9	9
B8	A/C SIGNAL	59	DK GRN	(4)	(4)
B9	NOT USED	–	–	–	–
B10	PARK/NEUTRAL SWITCH SIGNAL	434	ORN/BLK	(5)	(5)
B11	NOT USED	–	–	–	–
B12	NOT USED	–	–	–	–

(1) Battery voltage first 2 seconds.
(2) Varies from 2 to 5 volts.
(3) Varies from .01 to battery voltage depending on position of drive wheels.
(4) 0 volts A/C "OFF" battery voltage A/C "ON."
(5) 0 volts in P/N battery voltage in gear.
* Less then .5 volt.

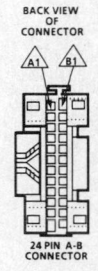

BACK VIEW OF CONNECTOR

24 PIN A-B CONNECTOR

PIN	PIN FUNCTION	CKT #	WIRE COLOR	NORMAL VOLTAGES KEY "ON"	NORMAL VOLTAGES ENG RUN
C1	NOT USED	–	–	–	–
C2	EAC SOLENOID	436	BRN	B+	B+
C3	IAC "B" LOW	444	LT GRN/BLK	NOT	USABLE
C4	IAC "B" HIGH	443	LT GRN/WHT	NOT	USABLE
C5	IAC "A" HIGH	441	LT BLU/WHT	NOT	USABLE
C6	IAC "A" LOW	442	LT BLU/BLK	NOT	USABLE
C7	HIGH GEAR SWITCH SIGNAL	446	LT BLU	B+	B+
C8	NOT USED	–	–	–	–
C9	CRANK SIGNAL	806	PPL/WHT	(1)	0*
C10	CTS SIGNAL	410	YEL	(2)	(2)
C11	MAP SIGNAL	432	LT GRN	4.8	1.0†
C12	NOT USED	–	–	–	–
C13	TPS SIGNAL	417	DK BLU	(3)	.6
C14	MAP & TPS 5 VOLT REF.	416	GRY	5	5
C15	NOT USED	–	–	–	–
C16	BATTERY 12 VOLT	440	ORN	B+	B+

PIN	PIN FUNCTION	CKT #	WIRE COLOR	NORMAL VOLTAGES KEY "ON"	NORMAL VOLTAGES ENG RUN
D1	SYSTEM GROUND	450	BLK/WHT	0*	0*
D2	TPS & CTS SENSOR GROUND	452	BLK	0*	0*
D3	NOT USED	–	–	–	–
D4	EST	423	WHT	0*	1.0
D5	EST BYPASS	424	TAN/BLK	0*	4.75
D6	OXYGEN SENSOR GROUND	413	TAN	0*	0*
D7	OXYGEN SENSOR SIGNAL	412	PPL	(4)	(5)
D8	NOT USED	–	–	–	–
D9	NOT USED	–	–	–	–
D10	NOT USED	–	–	–	–
D11	NOT USED	–	–	–	–
D12	NOT USED	–	–	–	–
D13	NOT USED	–	–	–	–
D14	INJECTOR 2 DRIVER	468	GRN	B+	B+
D15	NOT USED	–	–	–	–
D16	INJECTOR 1 DRIVER	467	BLU	B+	B+

(1) Battery voltage when cranking.
(2) About 1.0 volt, varies with temperature.
(3) .6 Volt to about 4.8 volt at Wide Open Throttle (WOT).
(4) Non-heated O_2 .26 to .46 volt, heated O_2 .26 to .46 volt within 10 seconds the voltage goes near 0 volt as O_2 heater warms up.
(5) Varies from .1 volt to .9 volt.
* Less than .5 volt.
† Varies with manifold pressure.

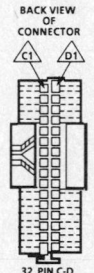

BACK VIEW OF CONNECTOR

32 PIN C-D CONNECTOR

92H22183 92I22184

Courtesy of General Motors Corp.

Fig. 8: ECM Terminal Identification & Pin Voltages ("C" & "K" Series 4.3L, 5.0L & 5.7L W/4L80-E Transmission)

NOTE:
This ECM voltage chart along with digital voltmeter can help save diagnosis time. Voltage readings may vary slightly depending on battery voltage and alternator output.

The following conditions must be met before testing:
- Engine at operating temperature.
- Engine in closed loop operation.
- Engine idling (Engine Run column).
- ALDL "test" terminal NOT grounded.
- Scan tester NOT installed.

PIN	PIN FUNCTION	CKT #	WIRE COLOR	NORMAL VOLTAGE KEY "ON"	NORMAL VOLTAGE ENG RUN
A1	FUEL PUMP RELAY DRIVE	465	DK GRN/WHT	(1)	B+
A2	NOT USED	-	-	-	-
A3	NOT USED	-	-	-	-
A4	EGR CONTROL	435	GRY	B+	B+
A5	"SERVICE ENGINE SOON" LIGHT CONTROL	419	BRN/WHT	0*	B+
A6	IGN-ECM FUSED	439	PNK/BLK	B+	B+
A7	TCC CONTROL	422	TAN/BLK	B+	B+
A8	SERIAL DATA	461	ORN	(2)	(2)
A9	DIAGNOSTIC TEST TERMINAL	451	WHT/BLK	5	5
A10	VEHICLE SPEED SENSOR SIGNAL	437	BRN	(3)	(3)
A11	CTS & TPS SENSOR GROUND	452	BLK	0*	0*
A12	SYSTEM GROUND	450	BLK/WHT	0*	0*

PIN	PIN FUNCTION	CKT #	WIRE COLOR	NORMAL VOLTAGE KEY "ON"	NORMAL VOLTAGE ENG RUN
B1	BATTERY 12 VOLTS	440	ORN	B+	B+
B2	FUEL PUMP SIGNAL	120	TAN/WHT	(1)	B+
B3	EST REFERENCE "LOW"	453	BLK/RED	0*	0*
B4	NOT USED	-	-	-	-
B5	EST REFERENCE "HIGH"	430	PPL/WHT	0*	1.6
B6	NOT USED	-	-	-	-
B7	ESC SIGNAL	485	BLK	9	9
B8	A/C SIGNAL	59	DK GRN	(4)	(4)
B9	NOT USED	-	-	-	-
B10	PARK/NEUTRAL SWITCH SIGNAL	434	ORN/BLK	(5)	(5)
B11	NOT USED	-	-	-	-
B12	NOT USED	-	-	-	-

(1) Battery voltage first two seconds.
(2) Varies from 2 to 5 volts.
(3) Varies from 0 to battery voltage depending on position of drive wheels.
(4) 0 volts A/C "OFF" battery voltage A/C "ON."
(5) 0 volts in P/N, battery voltage in gear.
* Less than .5 volt.

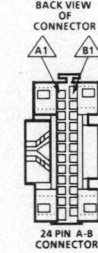

BACK VIEW OF CONNECTOR

24 PIN A-B CONNECTOR

PIN	PIN FUNCTION	CKT #	WIRE COLOR	NORMAL VOLTAGE KEY "ON"	NORMAL VOLTAGE ENG RUN
C1	NOT USED	-	-	-	-
C2	ELECTRONIC AIR CONTROL SOLENOID	436	BRN	B+	B+
C3	IAC "B" LOW	444	LT GRN/BLK	NOT USABLE	
C4	IAC "B" HIGH	443	LT GRN/WHT	NOT USABLE	
C5	IAC "A" HIGH	441	LT BLU/WHT	NOT USABLE	
C6	IAC "A" LOW	442	LT BLU/BLK	NOT USABLE	
C7	HIGH GEAR SWITCH SIGNAL	446	LT BLU	B+	B+
C8	NOT USED	-	-	-	-
C9	CRANK SIGNAL	806	PPL	(1)	0*
C10	COOLANT TEMP SIGNAL	410	YEL	(2)	(2)
C11	MAP SIGNAL	432	LT GRN	4.8	1.0†
C12	NOT USED	-	-	-	-
C13	TPS SIGNAL	417	DK BLU	(3)	6
C14	5 VOLTS REF MAP & TPS	416	GRY	5	5
C15	NOT USED	-	-	-	-
C16	BATTERY 12 VOLT	440	ORN	B+	B+

PIN	PIN FUNCTION	CKT #	WIRE COLOR	NORMAL VOLTAGE KEY "ON"	NORMAL VOLTAGE ENG RUN
D1	SYSTEM GROUND	450	BLK/WHT	0*	0*
D2	MAP SENSOR GROUND	455	PPL	0*	0*
D3	NOT USED	-	-	-	-
D4	EST CONTROL	423	WHT	0*	1.0
D5	EST BYPASS	424	TAN/BLK	0*	4.75
D6	OXYGEN SENSOR GROUND	413	TAN	0*	0*
D7	OXYGEN SENSOR SIGNAL	412	PPL	(4)	(5)
D8	NOT USED	-	-	-	-
D9	NOT USED	-	-	-	-
D10	NOT USED	-	-	-	-
D11	NOT USED	-	-	-	-
D12	NOT USED	-	-	-	-
D13	NOT USED	-	-	-	-
D14	INJECTOR 2 DRIVER	468	GRN	B+	B+
D15	NOT USED	-	-	-	-
D16	INJECTOR 1 DRIVER	467	BLU	B+	B+

(1) Battery voltage when cranking.
(2) About 1.0 volt, varies with temperature.
(3) .6 volt to about 4.8 volts at Wide Open Throttle (WOT).
(4) Non-heated O_2 .26 to .46 volt, heated O_2 .26 to .46 within 10 seconds the voltage goes near 0 volt as O_2 heater warms up.
(5) Varies from .1 volt to .9 volt.
* Less than .5 volt.
† Varies with manifold pressure.

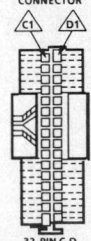

BACK VIEW OF CONNECTOR

32 PIN C-D CONNECTOR

Courtesy of General Motors Corp.

Fig. 9: ECM Terminal Identification & Pin Voltages ("G" Series 4.3L, 5.0L & 5.7L W/O 4L80-E Transmission)

NOTE:
This ECM voltage chart along with digital voltmeter can help save diagnosis time. Voltage readings may vary slightly depending on battery voltage and alternator output.

The following conditions must be met before testing:

- Engine at operating temperature.
- Engine in closed loop operation.
- Engine idling (Engine Run column).
- ALDL "test" terminal NOT grounded.
- Scan tester NOT installed.

PIN	PIN FUNCTION	CKT #	WIRE COLOR	KEY "ON"	ENG RUN
A1	FUEL PUMP RELAY CONTROL	465	DK GRN/WHT	(1)	14
A2	SHIFT SOLENOID "B" CONTROL	1223	YEL/BLK	B+	B+
A3	SHIFT SOLENOID "A" CONTROL	1222	LT GRN	B+	0*
A4	TCC SOLENOID CONTROL	422	TAN/BLK	B+	B+
A5	NOT USED	–	–	–	–
A6	EAC CONTROL (7.4L UNDER 8500 GVW)	436	BRN	B+	B+
A7	"SERVICE ENGINE SOON" LAMP CONTROL	419	BRN/WHT	0*	B+
A8	NOT USED	–	–	–	–
A9	NOT USED	–	–	–	–
A10	NOT USED	–	–	–	–
A11	EVRV (EGR) CONTROL	435	GRY	B+	B+
A12	BRAKE SIGNAL	420	PPL	(2)	(2)

PIN	PIN FUNCTION	CKT #	WIRE COLOR	KEY "ON"	ENG RUN
B1	NOT USED	–	–	–	–
B2	RANGE "C" SIGNAL	1226	RED	B+	B+
B3	RANGE "B" SIGNAL	1225	DK BLU	B+	0*
B4	RANGE "A" SIGNAL	1224	PNK	B+	B+
B5	TRANSMISSION OUTPUT SPEED SIGNAL (4WD)	1232	LT BLU	5	5
B6	TRANSMISSION OUTPUT SPEED SENSOR GROUND	1233	DK GRN/YEL	0*	0*
B7	FORCE MOTOR LOW	1229	LT BLU/WHT	0*	.85
B8	FORCE MOTOR HIGH	1228	RED/BLK	0*	3.62
B9	TRANSMISSION INPUT SPEED SIGNAL	1230	GRY/RED	0*	0*
B10	TRANSMISSION INPUT SPEED SENSOR GROUND	1231	DK BLU/WHT	0*	0*
B11	VEHICLE SPEED AND TRANSMISSION OUTPUT SPEED SIGNAL (2WD)	437	BRN	0*	0*
B12	A/C SIGNAL	59	DK GRN	(3)	(3)

(1) Battery voltage first 2 seconds.
(2) Battery voltage brakes "OFF,"
    0 Volts brakes "ON."
(3) 0 Volts A/C "OFF" battery voltage A/C "ON."
* Less than .50 volt.

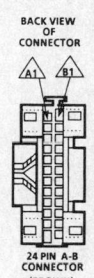

BACK VIEW OF CONNECTOR

24 PIN A-B CONNECTOR (BROWN)

PIN	PIN FUNCTION	CKT #	WIRE COLOR	KEY "ON"	ENG RUN
C1	FUSED IGNITION FEED	439	PNK/BLK	B+	B+
C2	SYSTEM GROUND	450	BLK/WHT	0*	0*
C3	SYSTEM GROUND	551	TAN/WHT	0*	0*
C4	TPS REFERENCE VOLTAGE	416	GRY	5	5
C5	TPS SIGNAL	417	DK BLU	(2)	6
C6	IAC COIL "A" HIGH	441	LT BLU/WHT	NOT	USE-ABLE
C7	IAC COIL "A" LOW	442	LT BLU/BLK	NOT	USE-ABLE
C8	IAC COIL "B" LOW	444	LT GRY/BLK	NOT	USE-ABLE
C9	IAC COIL "B" HIGH	443	LT GRN/WHT	NOT	USE-ABLE
C10	MAP SIGNAL	432	LT GRN	4.77	1.0†
C11	SERIAL DATA	1061	ORN/BLK	5	5
C12	NOT USED	–	–	–	–
C13	O₂ SENSOR GROUND	413	TAN	0*	0*
C14	O₂ SIGNAL	412	PPL	(3)	(4)
C15	INJECTOR #2 CONTROL	468	DK GRN	B+	B+
C16	INJECTOR #1 CONTROL	467	DK BLU	B+	B+

PIN	PIN FUNCTION	CKT #	WIRE COLOR	KEY "ON"	ENG RUN
D1	BATTERY VOLTAGE FEED	440	ORN	B+	B+
D2	MAP/TTS SENSOR GROUND	455	PPL	0*	0*
D3	TPS/CTS SENSOR GROUND	452	BLK	0*	0*
D4	MAP REFERENCE VOLTAGE	474	GRY	5.0	5.0
D5	ESC (KNOCK) SIGNAL	496	DK BLU	2.3	2.3
D6	DIAGNOSTIC TEST TERMINAL	451	WHT/BLK	5	5
D7	FUEL PUMP SIGNAL	120	GRY	(5)	B+
D8	NOT USED	–	–	–	–
D9	NOT USED	–	–	–	–
D10	NOT USED	–	–	–	–
D11	EST CONTROL	423	WHT	0*	1.4
D12	EST BYPASS	424	TAN/BLK	0*	4.64
D13	EST REFERENCE LOW	453	BLK/RED	0*	0*
D14	EST REFERENCE HIGH	430	PPL/WHT	0*	1.5
D15	TRANSMISSION TEMPERATURE SIGNAL	1227	BLK/YEL	2.24	2.0
D16	COOLANT TEMPERATURE SIGNAL	410	YEL	1.5	1.69

(2) .6 volt to about 4.5 volts at Wide Open Throttle (WOT).
(3) Non-heated O₂ .26 volt to .46 volt, on heated O₂ .26 volt to .46 volt within 10 seconds the voltage goes near 0 volt as O₂ heater warms up.
(4) Varies (toggles) .1 volt to .9 volt.
(5) Voltage for first 20 seconds.
* Less than .50 volt.
† Varies with manifold pressure.

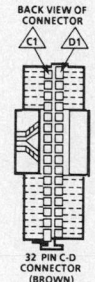

BACK VIEW OF CONNECTOR

32 PIN C-D CONNECTOR (BROWN)

92B22187 92C22188

Courtesy of General Motors Corp.

Fig. 10: ECM Terminal Identification & Pin Voltages (All Series 4.3L, 5.7L & 7.4L W/4L80-E Transmission)

NOTE:
This ECM voltage chart along with digital voltmeter can help save diagnosis time. Voltage readings may vary slightly depending on battery voltage and alternator output.

The following conditions must be met before testing:
- Engine at operating temperature.
- Engine in closed loop operation.
- Engine idling (Engine Run column).
- ALDL "test" terminal NOT grounded.
- Scan tester NOT installed.

	VOLTAGE				
	KEY "ON"	ENG. RUN	CIRCUIT	PIN	WIRE COLOR
	4.76	1.66	MAP SIGNAL	A1	LT GRN
	.2 - 2.2	.2 - 2.2	TPS SIGNAL	A2	DK BLU
(2)	1.9	1.7	COOLANT SENSOR	A3	YEL
			NOT USED	A4	
			NOT USED	A5	
	5.0	5.0	DIAGNOSTIC TERMINAL	A6	WHT/BLK
			NOT USED	A7	
	0 *	0 *	ENGINE SPEED SENSOR	A8	DK BLU/WHT
(1)	10.72	12.32	VEHICLE SPEED SENSOR	A9	BRN
	B +	.46	ECM TO LAMP DRIVER	A10	WHT/BLK
			NOT USED	A11	
	5.0	5.0	5 VOLT REFERENCE	A12	GRY
	0 *	0 *	SENSOR GROUND	C1	BLK
	0 *	0 *	GROUND	C2	BLK/WHT
			NOT USED	C3	
			NOT USED	C4	
	B +	B +	TCC SOLENOID	C5	TAN/BLK
	10.8	7.7	COLD ADVANCE	C6	DK BLU/WHT
			NOT USED	C7	
			NOT USED	C8	
			NOT USED	C9	
(2)	.90	B +	EGR SOLENOID	C10	GRY
	.89	B +	EGR VENT SOLENOID	C11	LT BLU
	B +	.87	EPR SOLENOID	C12	DK GRN
			NOT USED	C13	
	B +	B +	ECM FUSE KEY/SWITCH	C14	PNK/BLK
			NOT USED	C15	
	B +	B +	BATTERY/12 VOLTS	C16	ORN

1 Varies from .60 to battery voltage depending on position of drive wheels
2 Varies with temperature
* Less than .5 volts.

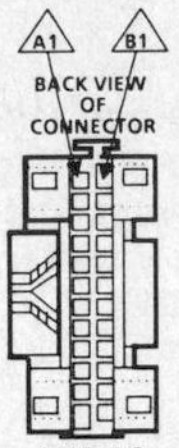

A1 B1

BACK VIEW OF CONNECTOR

24 PIN A-B CONNECTOR

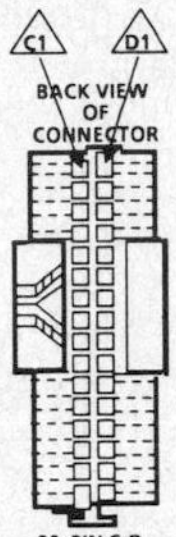

C1 D1

BACK VIEW OF CONNECTOR

32 PIN C-D CONNECTOR

WIRE COLOR	PIN	CIRCUIT	VOLTAGE	
			ENG. RUN	KEY "ON"
	B1	NOT USED		
	B2	NOT USED		
	B3	NOT USED		
	B4	NOT USED		
	B5	NOT USED		
	B6	NOT USED		
	B7	NOT USED		
	B8	NOT USED		
	B9	NOT USED		
	B10	NOT USED		
	B11	NOT USED		
	B12	NOT USED		
	D1	NOT USED		
	D2	NOT USED		
	D3	NOT USED		
	D4	NOT USED		
	D5	NOT USED		
	D6	NOT USED		
	D7	NOT USED		
	D8	NOT USED		
	D9	NOT USED		
	D10	NOT USED		
	D11	NOT USED		
	D12	NOT USED		
	D13	NOT USED		
	D14	NOT USED		
	D15	NOT USED		
	D16	NOT USED		

Courtesy of General Motors Corp.

91F13628

Fig. 11: ECM Terminal Identification & Pin Voltages ("C" & "K" Series 6.2L Diesel)

1992 ENGINE PERFORMANCE
Sensor Operating Range Charts

Astro, Bravada, Commercial Van, Jimmy, Lumina APV, Safari, Sierra, Silhouette, Sonoma, Suburban, Syclone, Trans Sport, Typhoon, Van, Yukon, "C" & "K" Series Blazer & Pickup, "S" & "T" Series Blazer & Pickup

INTRODUCTION

Sensor operating range information can help determine if a sensor is out of calibration. An out-of-calibration sensor may not set a trouble code, but it will cause driveability problems.

NOTE: Perform all voltage tests with a Digital Volt-Ohmmeter (DVOM) with a minimum 10-megohm input impedance, unless stated otherwise in testing procedures.

COOLANT TEMPERATURE RESISTANCE VALUES [1]

°F (°C)	Ohms
212 (100)	177
158 (70)	467
100 (38)	1800
68 (20)	3520
23 (-5)	12,300
0 (-18)	25,000
-40 (-40)	100,700

[1] – Measure resistance across sensor terminals.

MANIFOLD AIR TEMPERATURE (MAT) SENSOR RESISTANCE VALUES [1]

°F (°C)	Ohms
210 (100)	185
160 (70)	450
100 (38)	1800
70 (20)	3400
40 (4)	7500
20 (-7)	13,500
0 (-18)	25,000
-40 (-40)	100,700

[1] – Measure resistance across sensor terminals.

MAP SENSOR VOLTAGE RANGE [1]

Altitude (Ft.)	Volts
Below 1000	3.8-5.5
1000-2000	3.6-5.3
2000-3000	3.5-5.1
3000-4000	3.3-5.0
4000-5000	3.2-4.8
5000-6000	3.0-4.6
6000-7000	2.9-4.5
7000-8000	2.8-4.3
8000-9000	2.6-4.2
9000-10,000	2.5-4.0

[1] – Measured at sensor, or as seen on Scan tester.

OXYGEN SENSOR VOLTAGE TEST [1]

Condition	Volts
Lean	.1
Rich	.9

[1] – Measure voltage between O_2 sensor ground and signal terminals at ECM.

1992 ENGINE PERFORMANCE
Wiring Diagrams

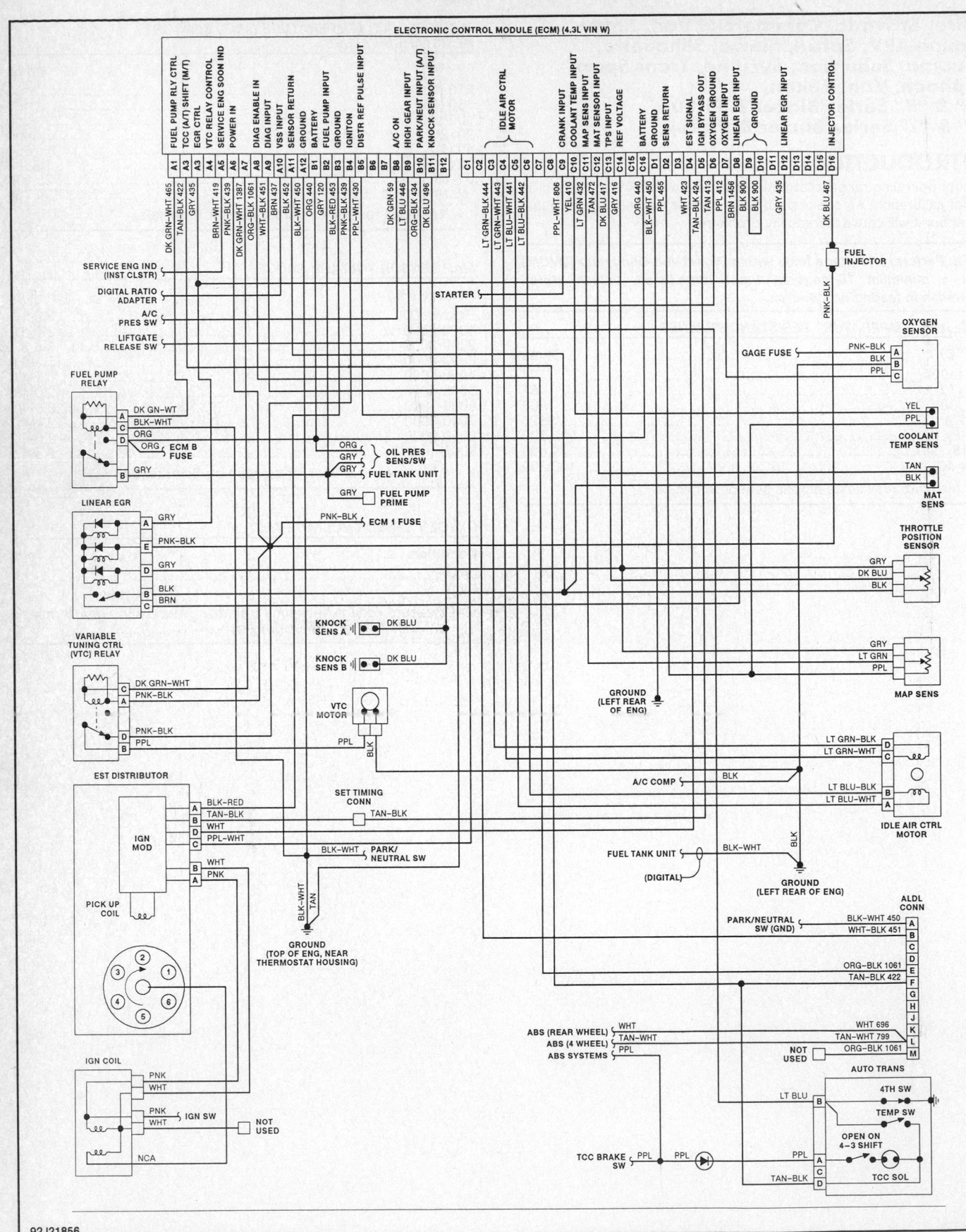

92J21856

Fig. 1: Wiring Diagram (Astro & Safari 4.3L CPI)

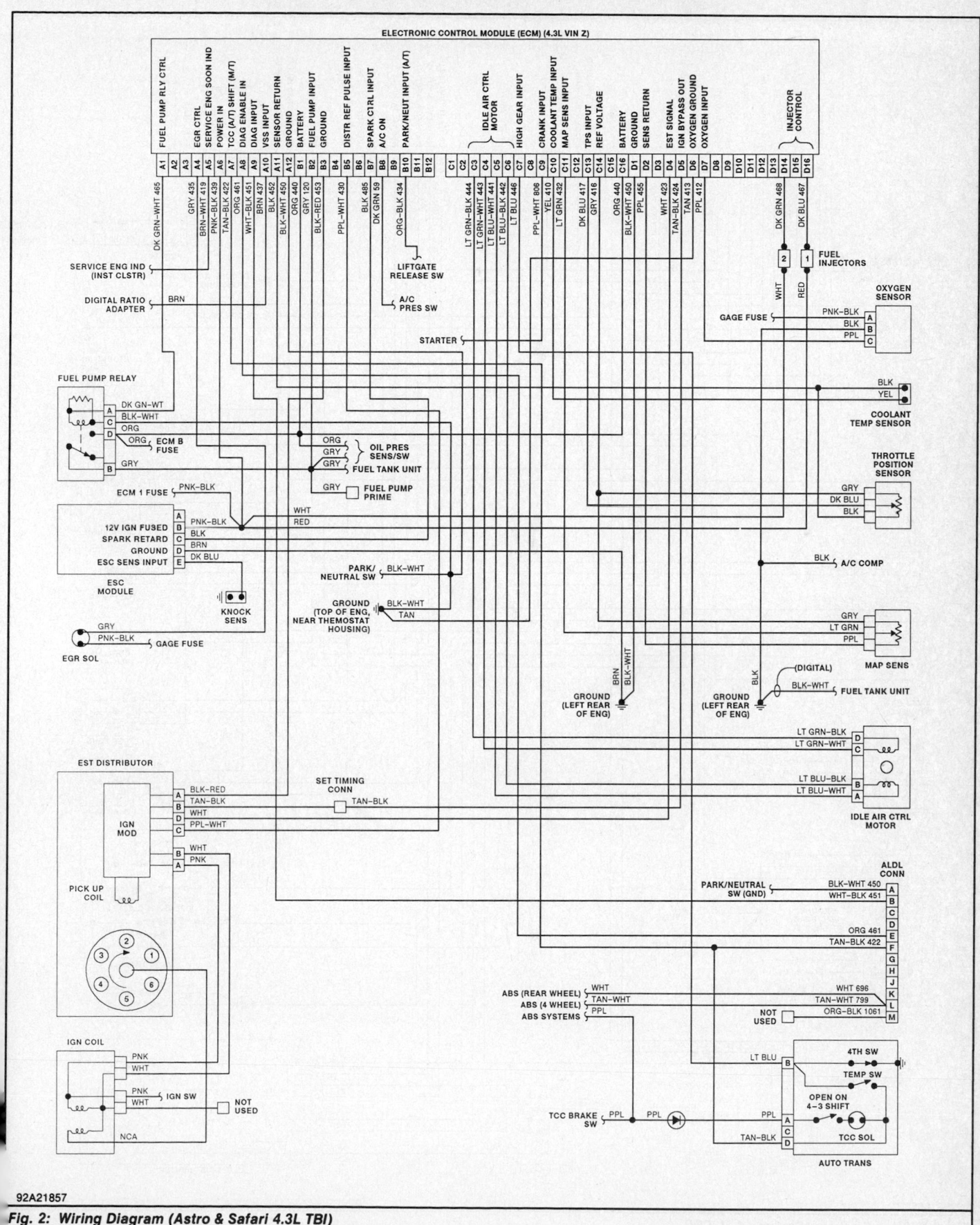

92A21857

Fig. 2: Wiring Diagram (Astro & Safari 4.3L TBI)

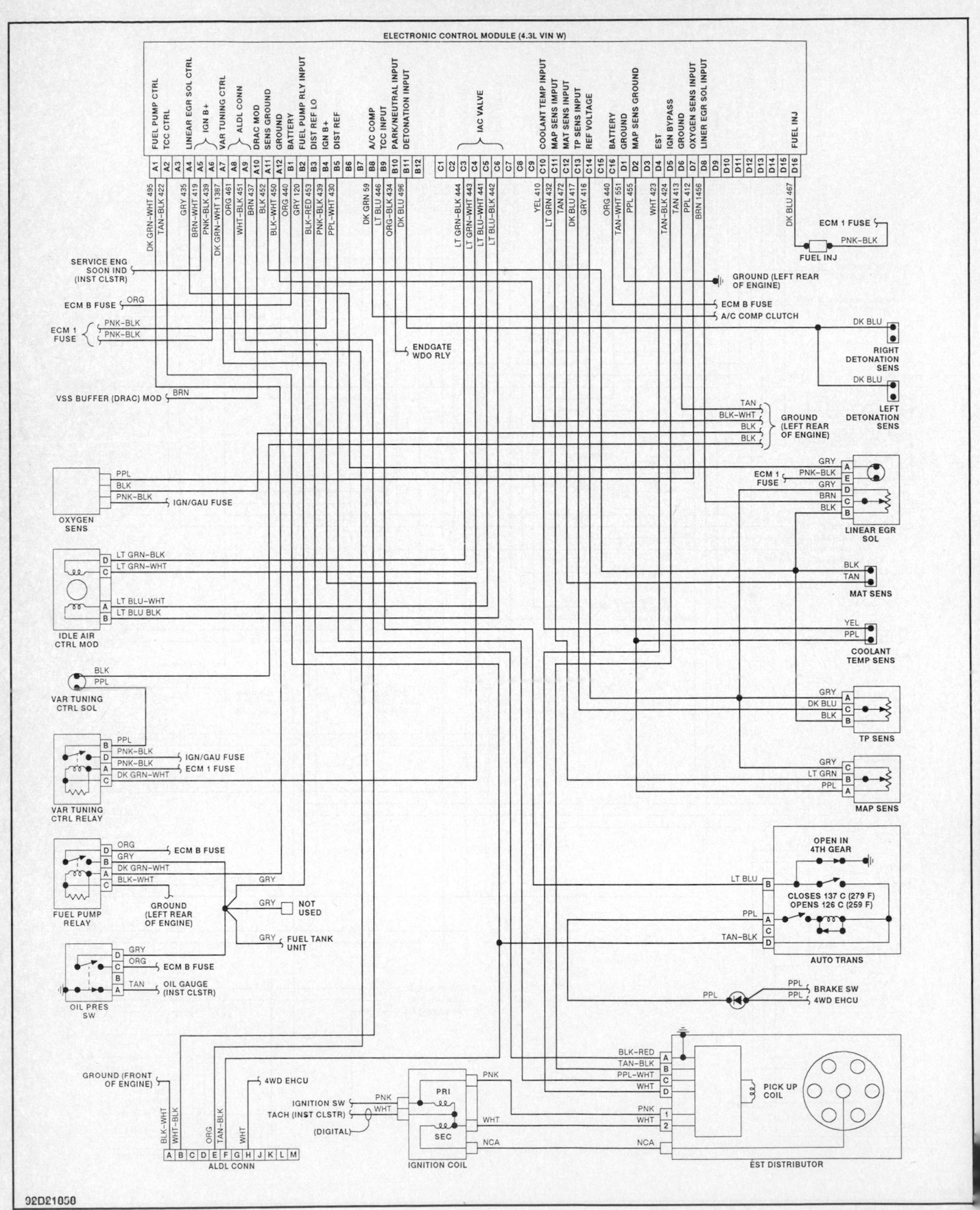

Fig. 3: *Wiring Diagram (Bravada 4.3L CPI)*

92D21050

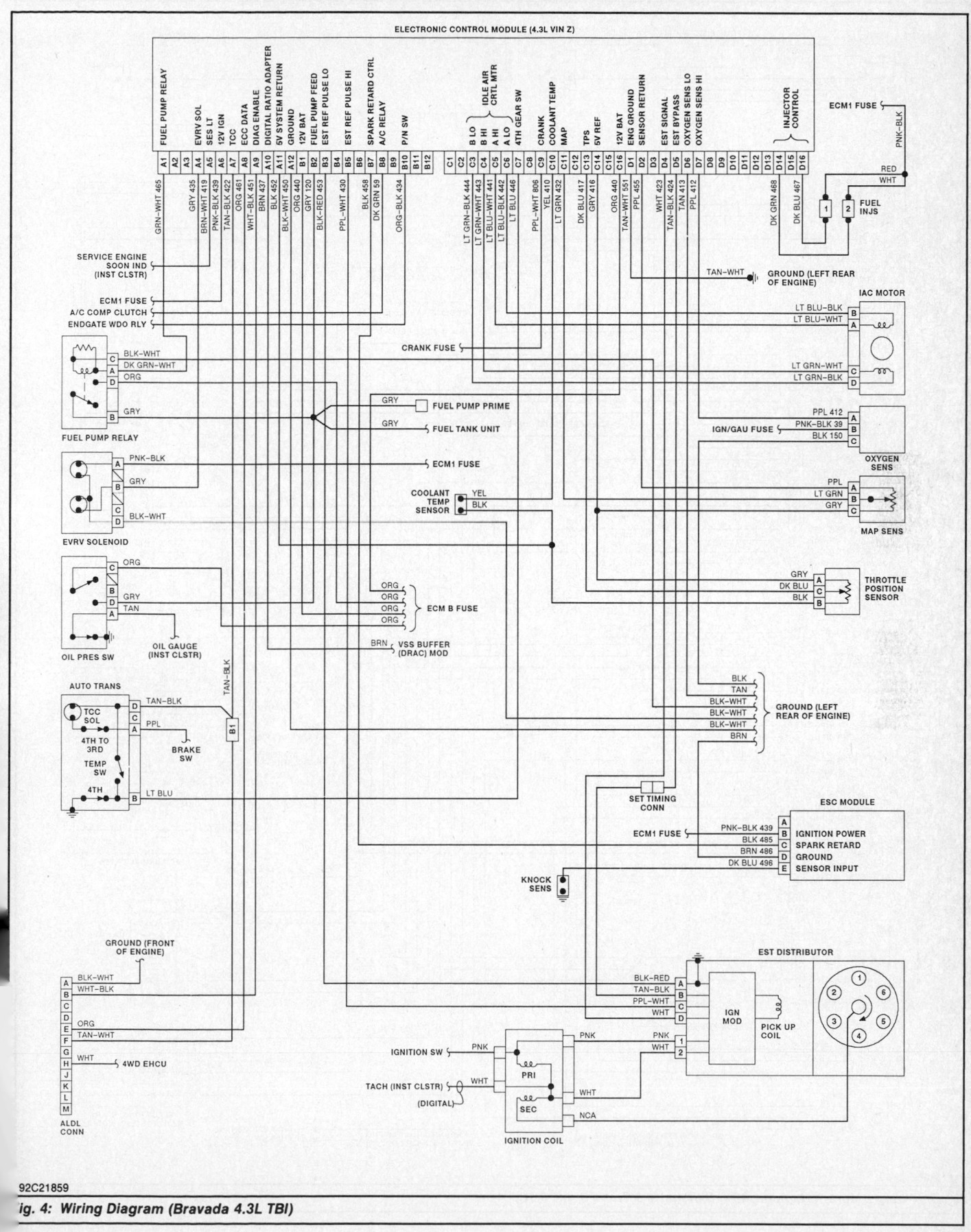

92C21859

Fig. 4: Wiring Diagram (Bravada 4.3L TBI)

1992 ENGINE PERFORMANCE
Wiring Diagrams (Cont.)

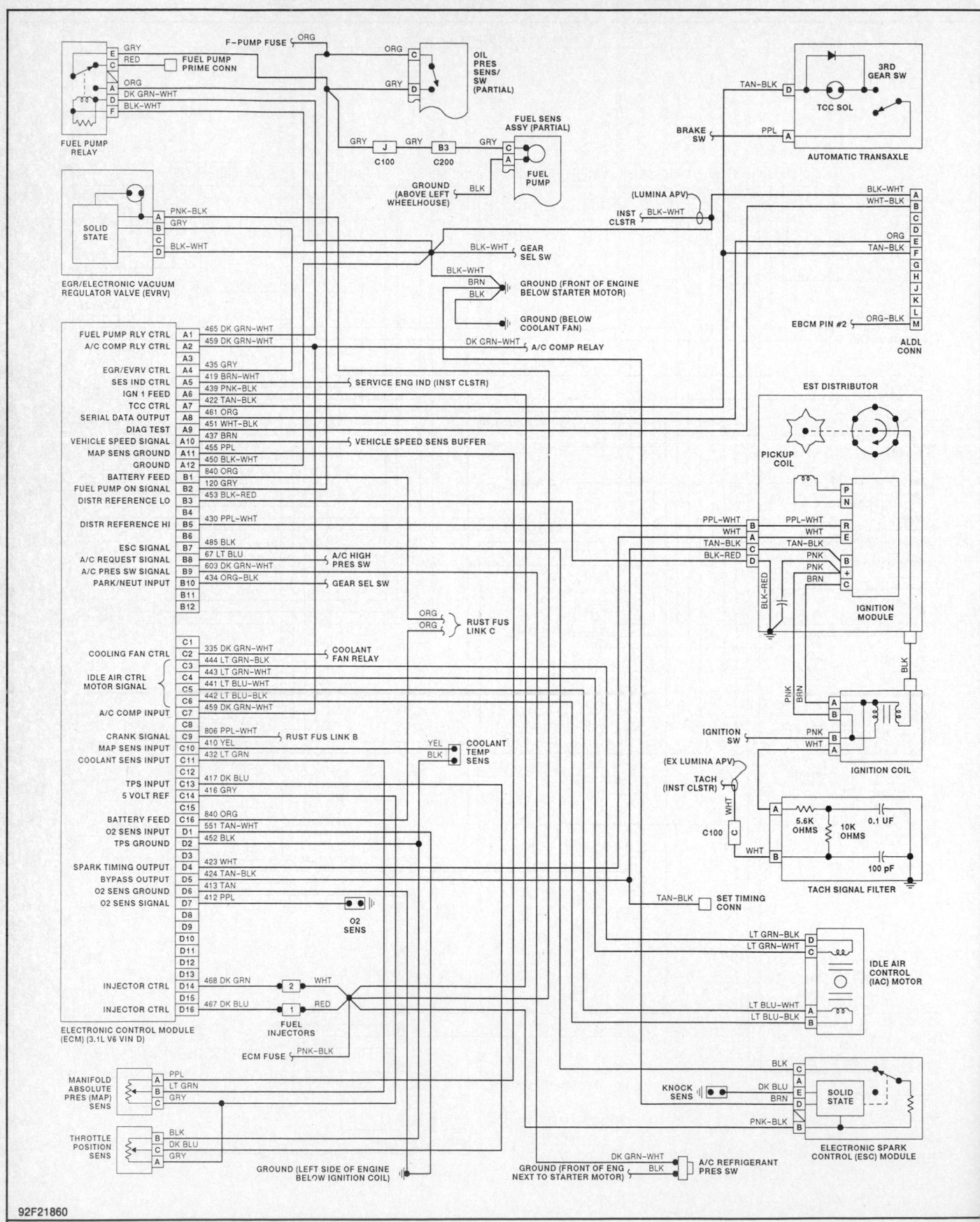

92F21860

Fig. 5: Wiring Diagram (Lumina APV, Silhouette & Trans Sport 3.1L)

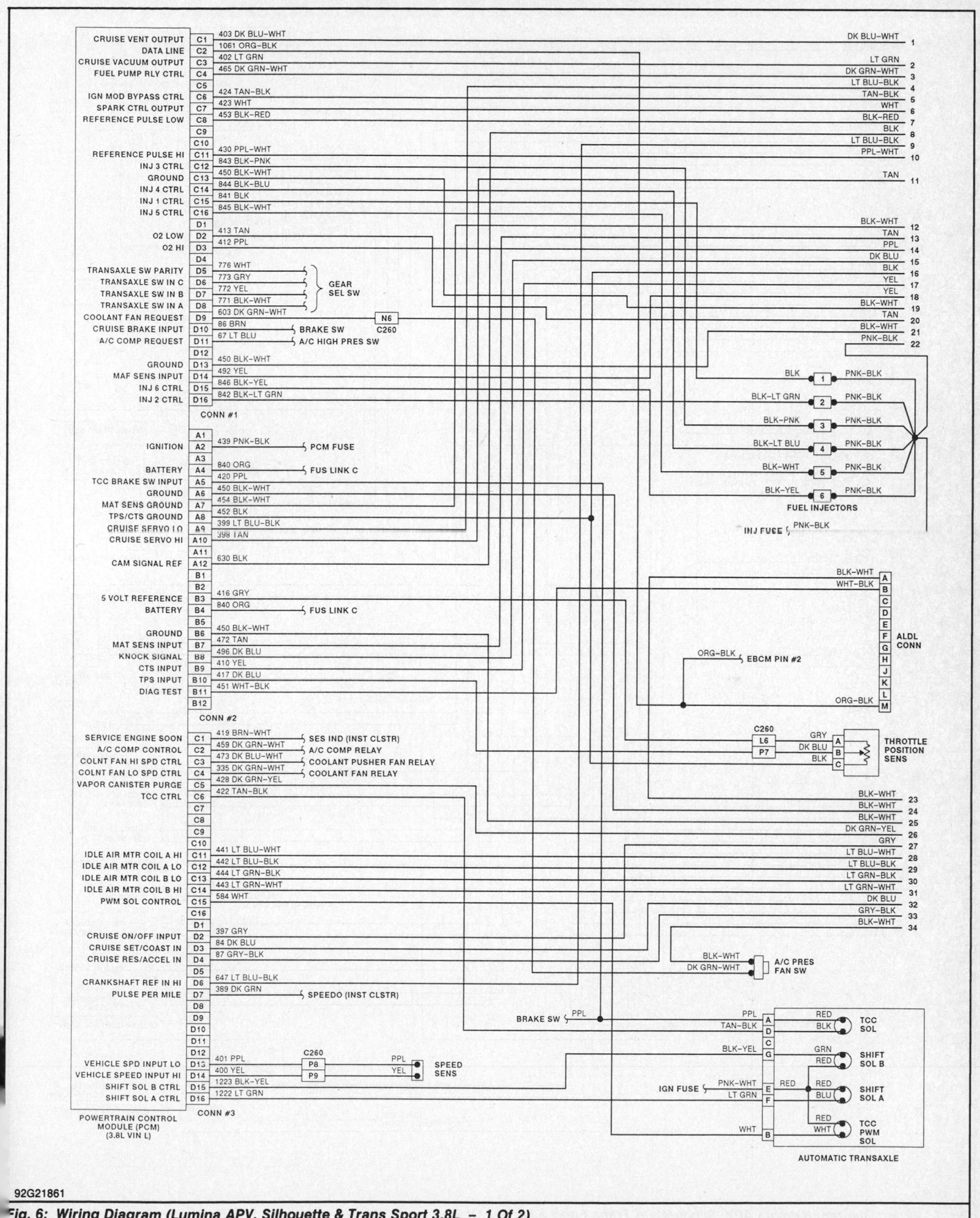

92G21861

Fig. 6: Wiring Diagram (Lumina APV, Silhouette & Trans Sport 3.8L – 1 Of 2)

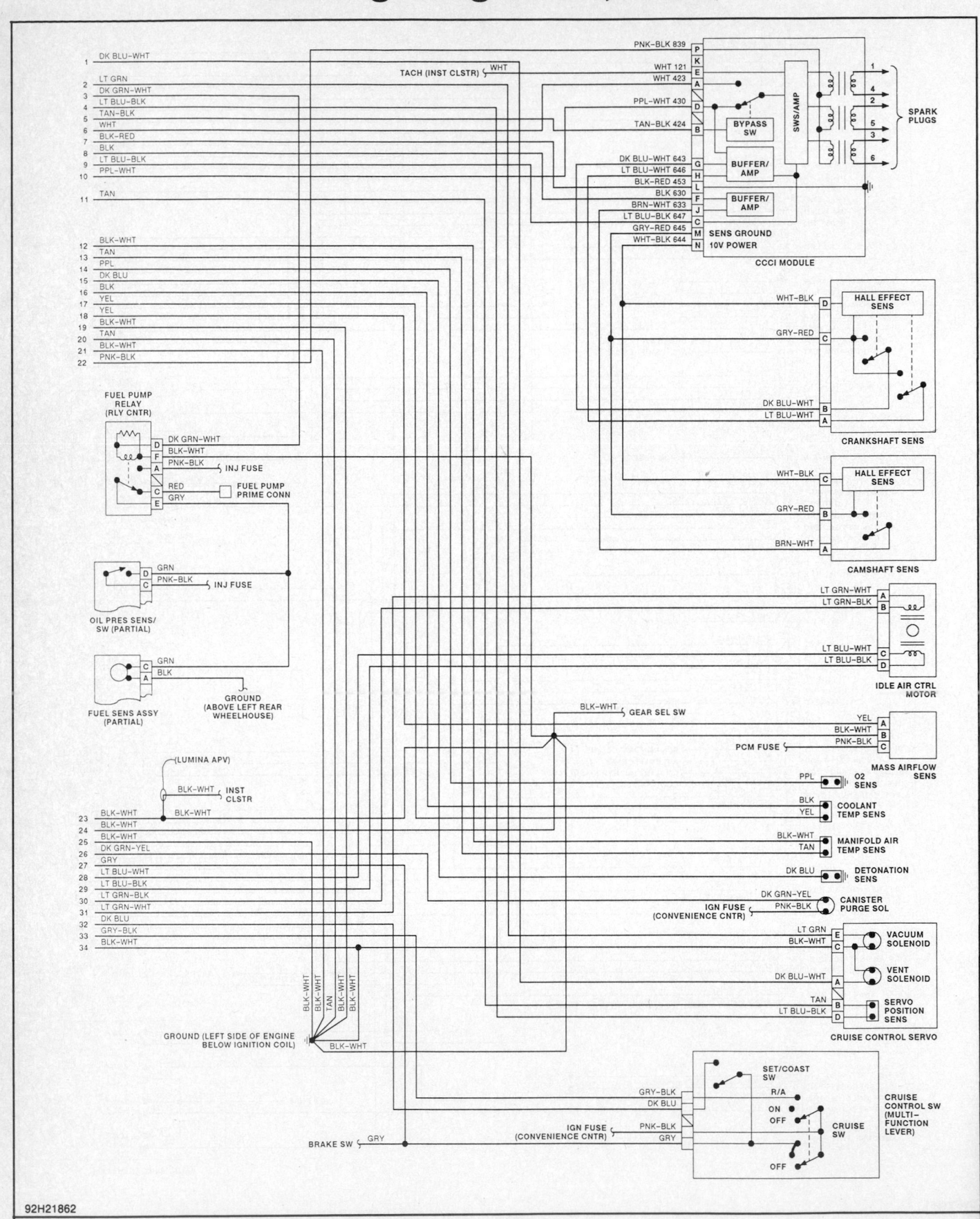

Fig. 7: Wiring Diagram (Lumina APV, Silhouette & Trans Sport 3.8L – 2 Of 2)

92H21862

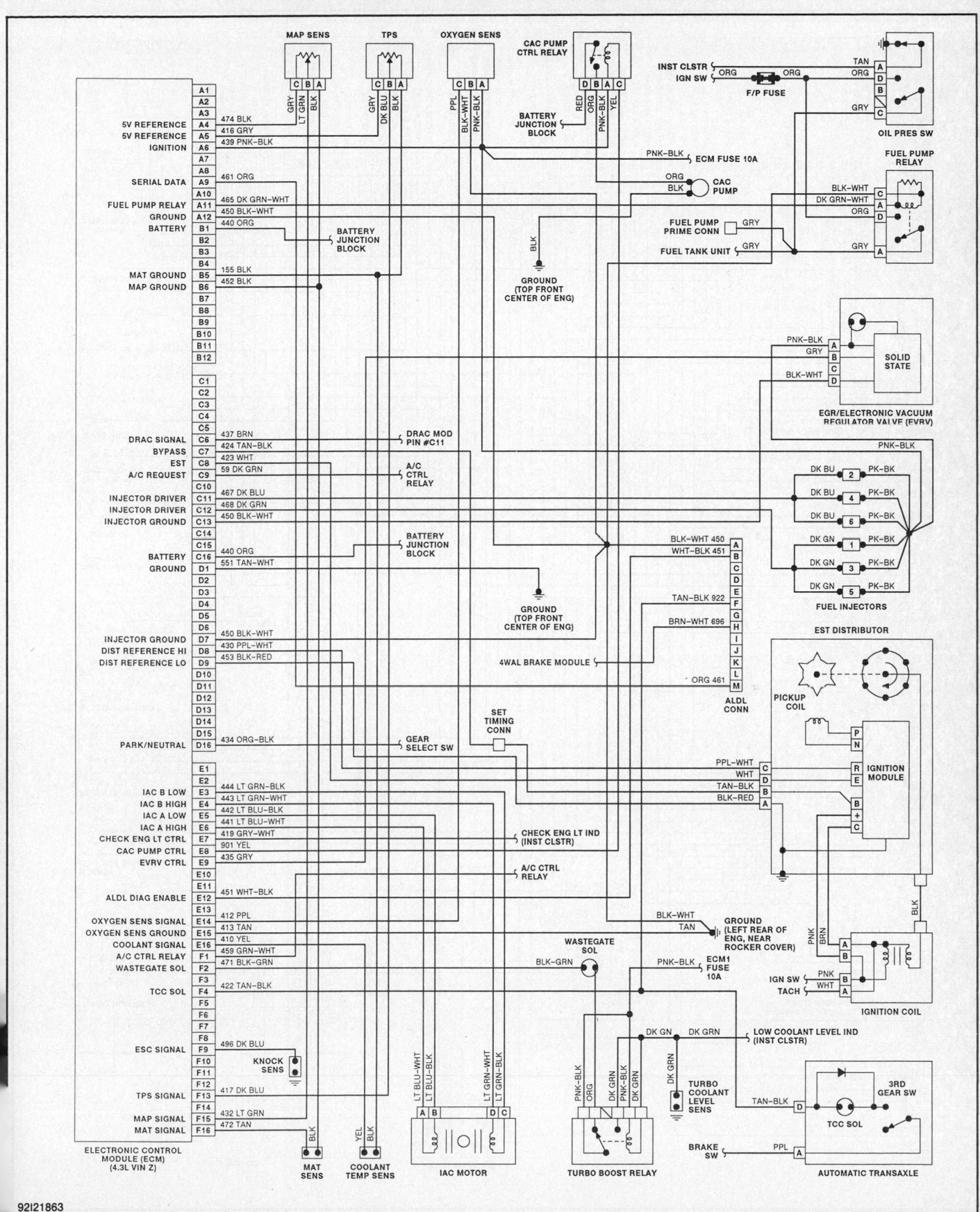

Fig. 8: Wiring Diagram (Syclone & Typhoon 4.3L Turbo)

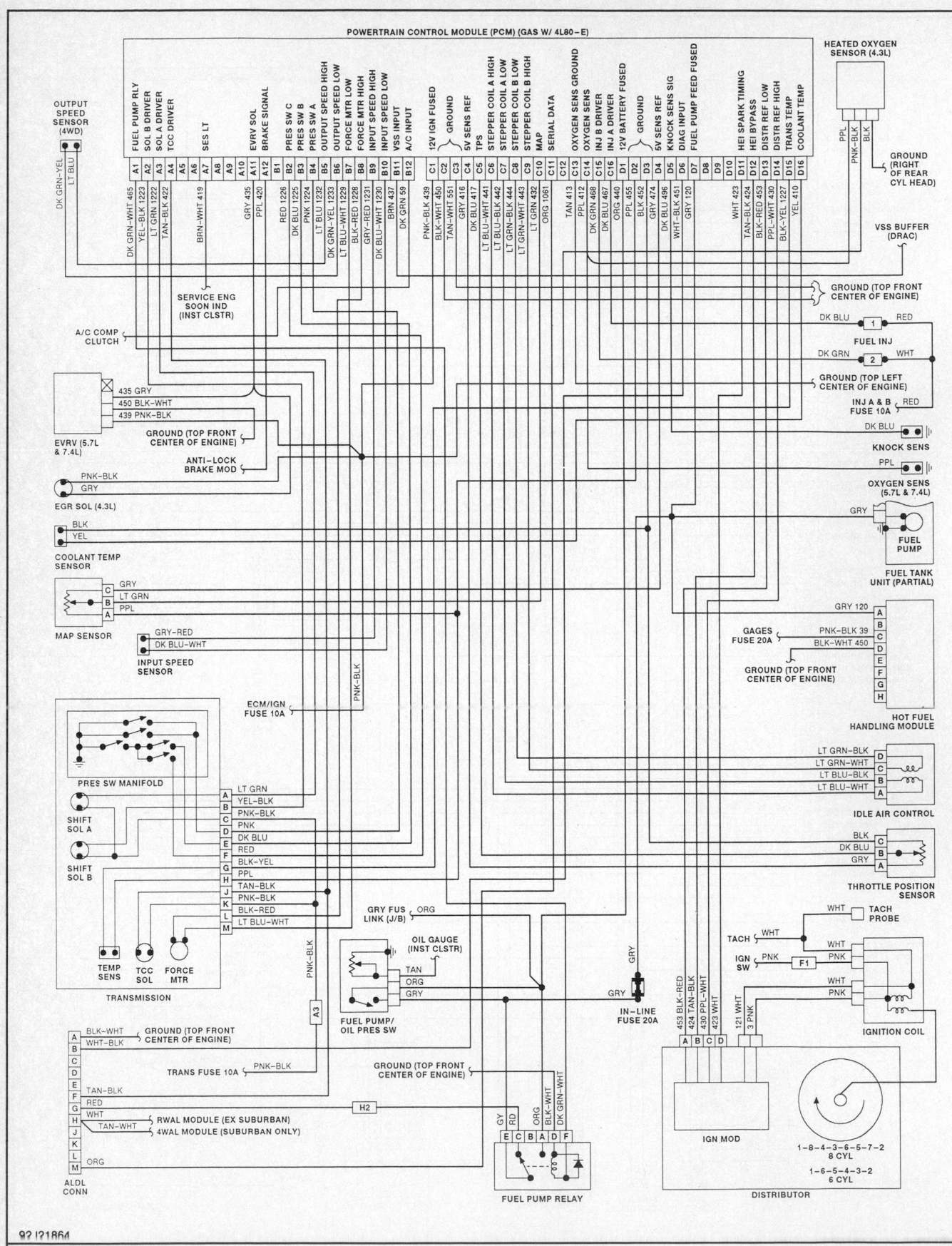

Fig. 9: *Wiring Diagram ("C" & "K" Series 4.3L, 5.7L & 7.4L With 4L80-E Transmission)*

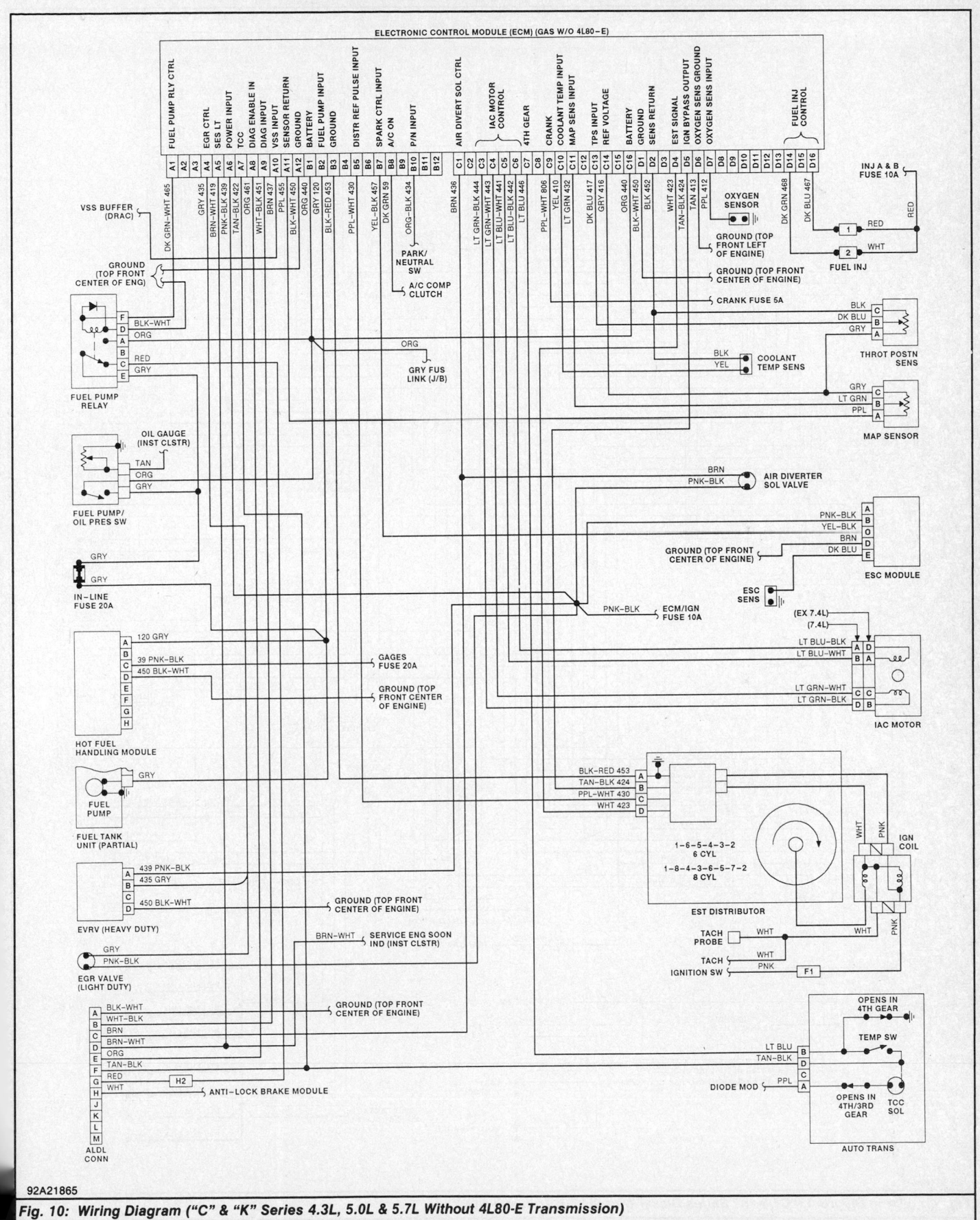

Fig. 10: Wiring Diagram ("C" & "K" Series 4.3L, 5.0L & 5.7L Without 4L80-E Transmission)

92A21865

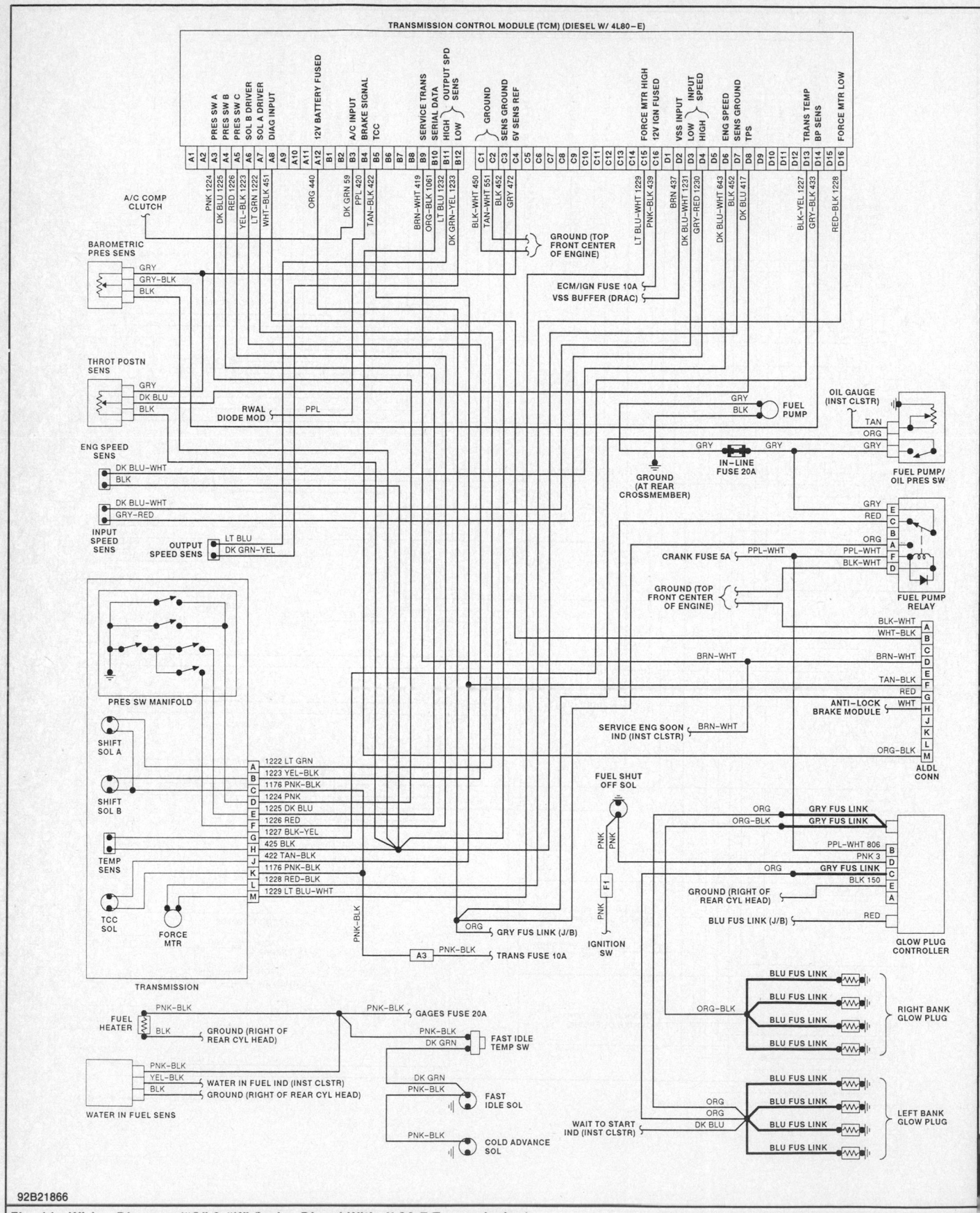

92B21866

Fig. 11: Wiring Diagram ("C" & "K" Series Diesel With 4L80-E Transmission)

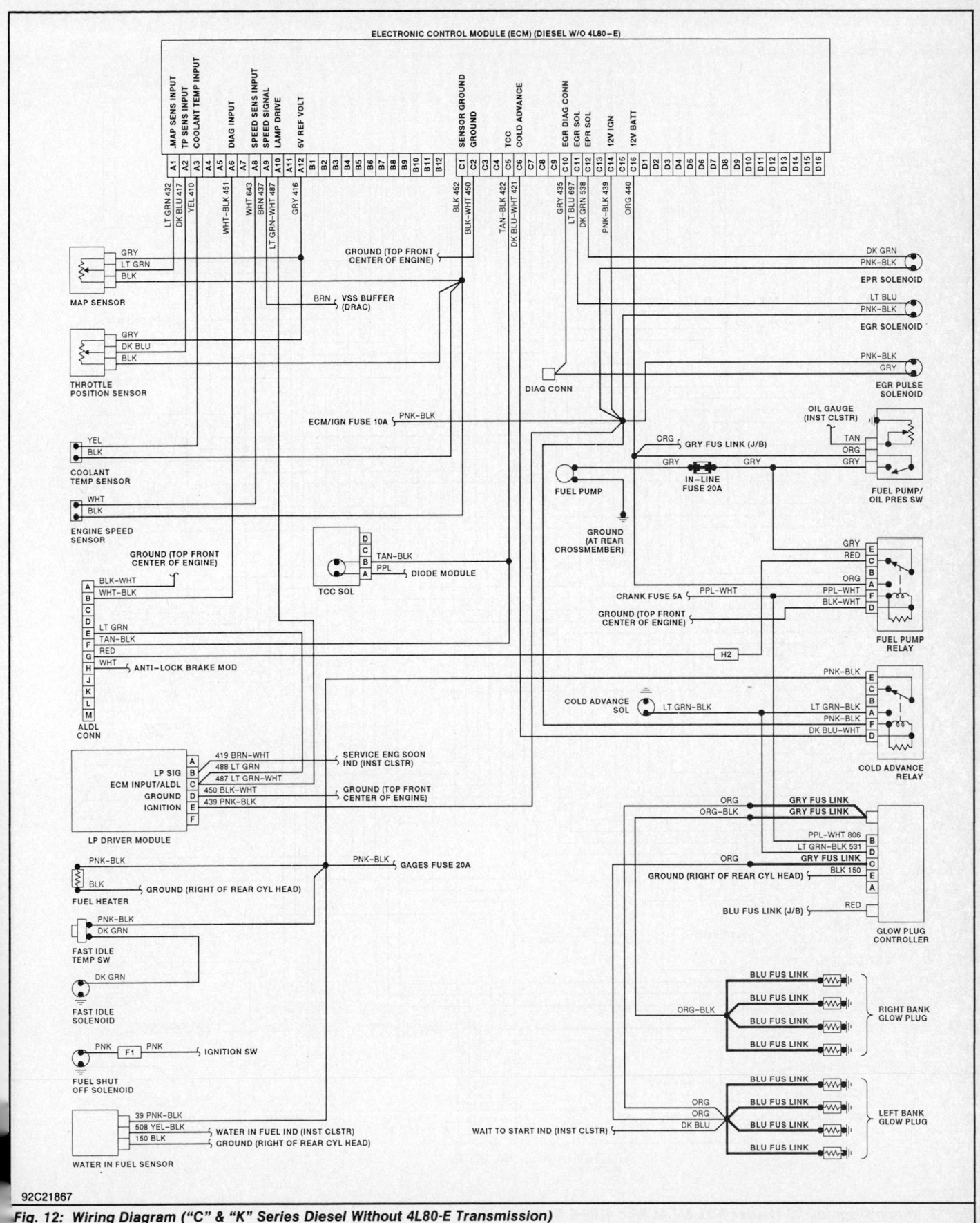

Fig. 12: Wiring Diagram ("C" & "K" Series Diesel Without 4L80-E Transmission)

92C21867

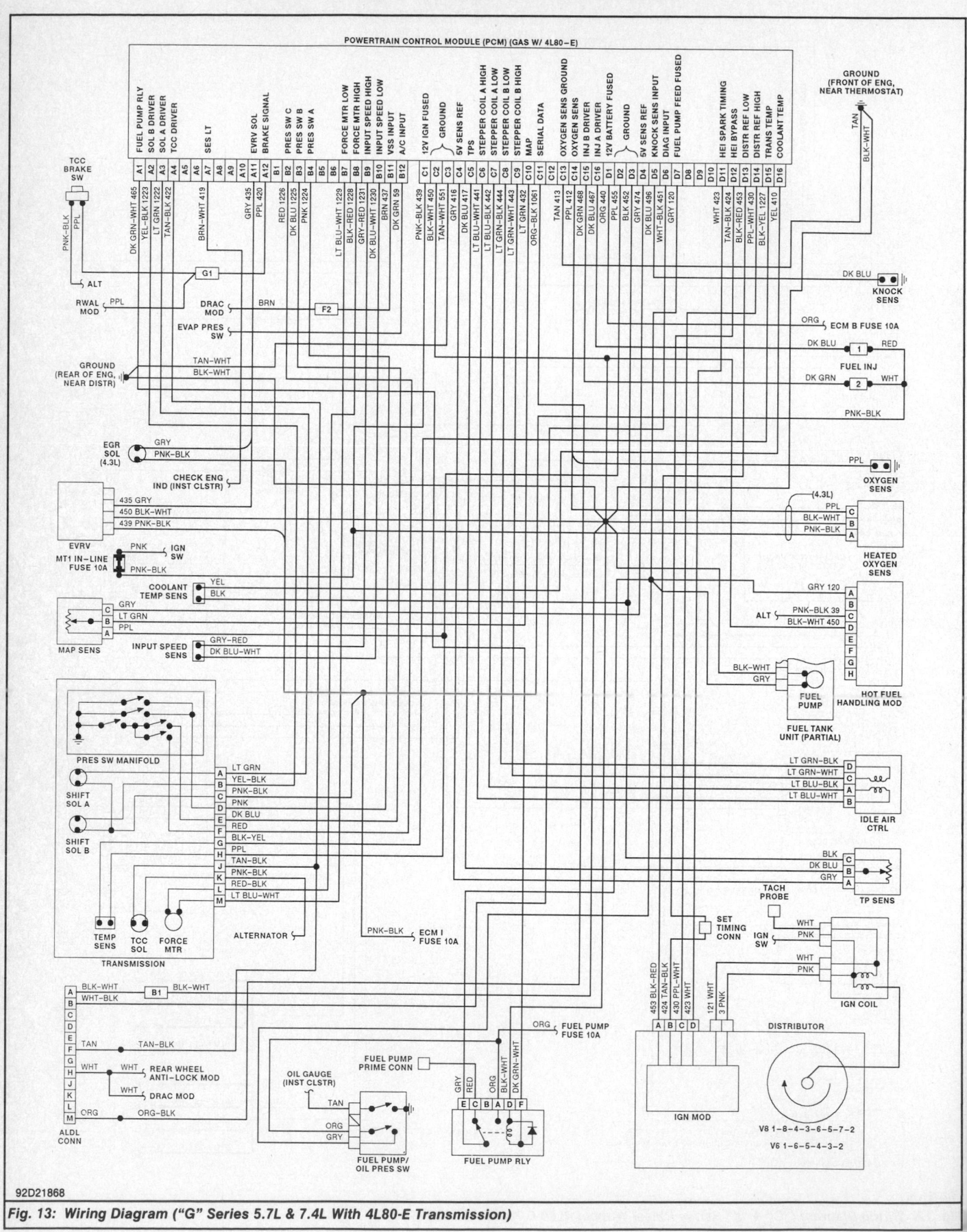

Fig. 13: *Wiring Diagram ("G" Series 5.7L & 7.4L With 4L80-E Transmission)*

92D21868

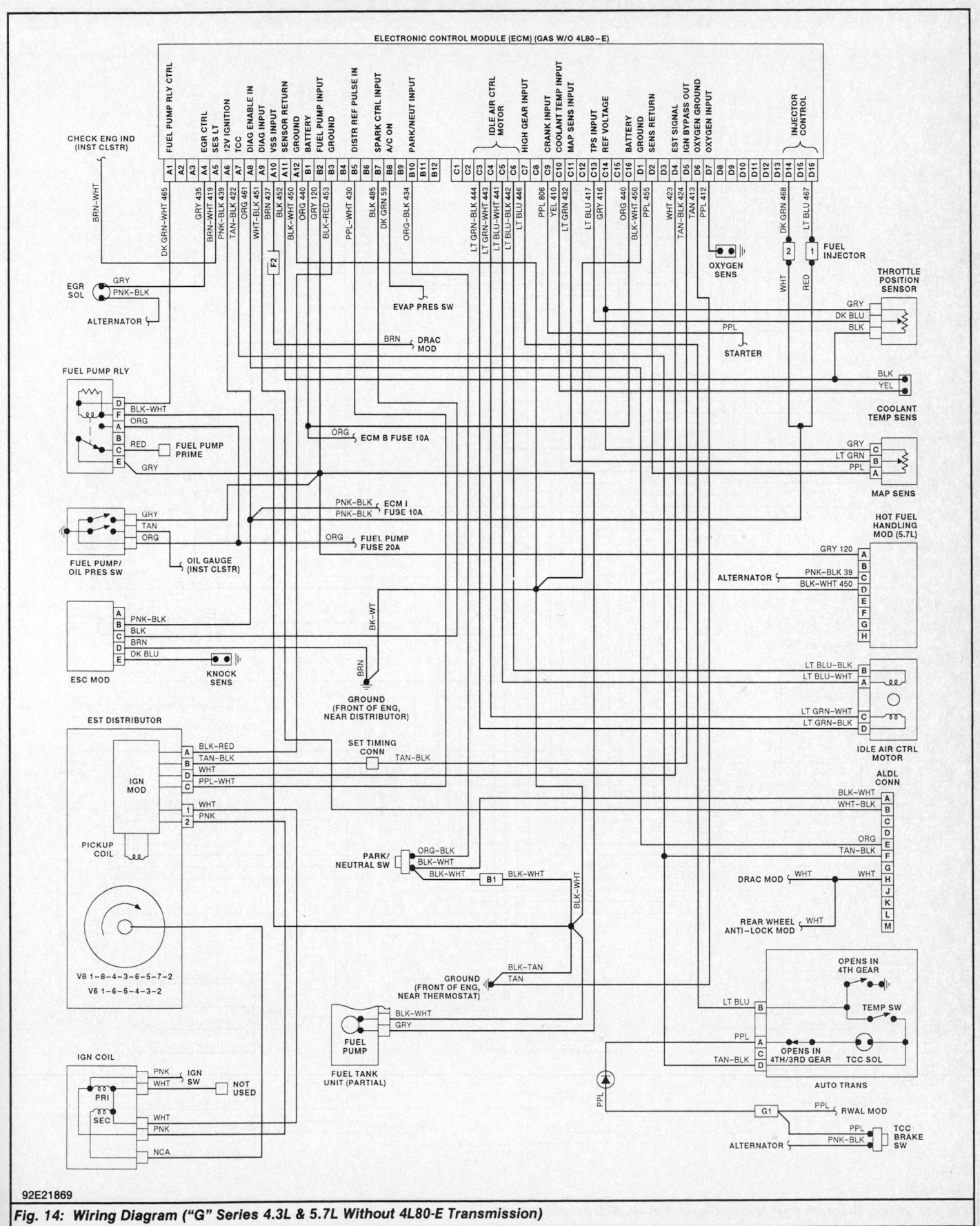

Fig. 14: Wiring Diagram ("G" Series 4.3L & 5.7L Without 4L80-E Transmission)

92E21869

1992 ENGINE PERFORMANCE
Wiring Diagrams (Cont.)

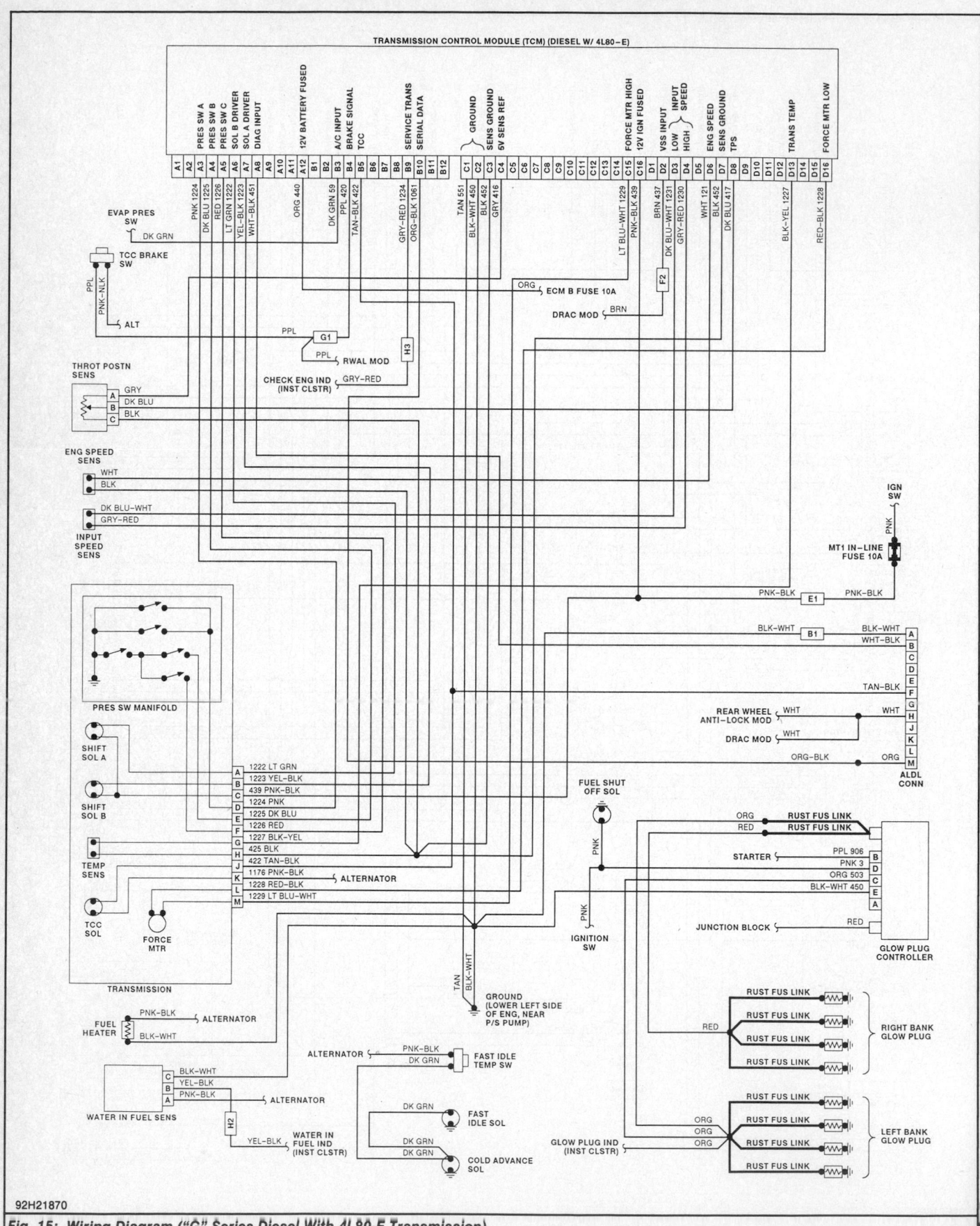

Fig. 15: Wiring Diagram ("G" Series Diesel With 4L80-E Transmission)

92H21870

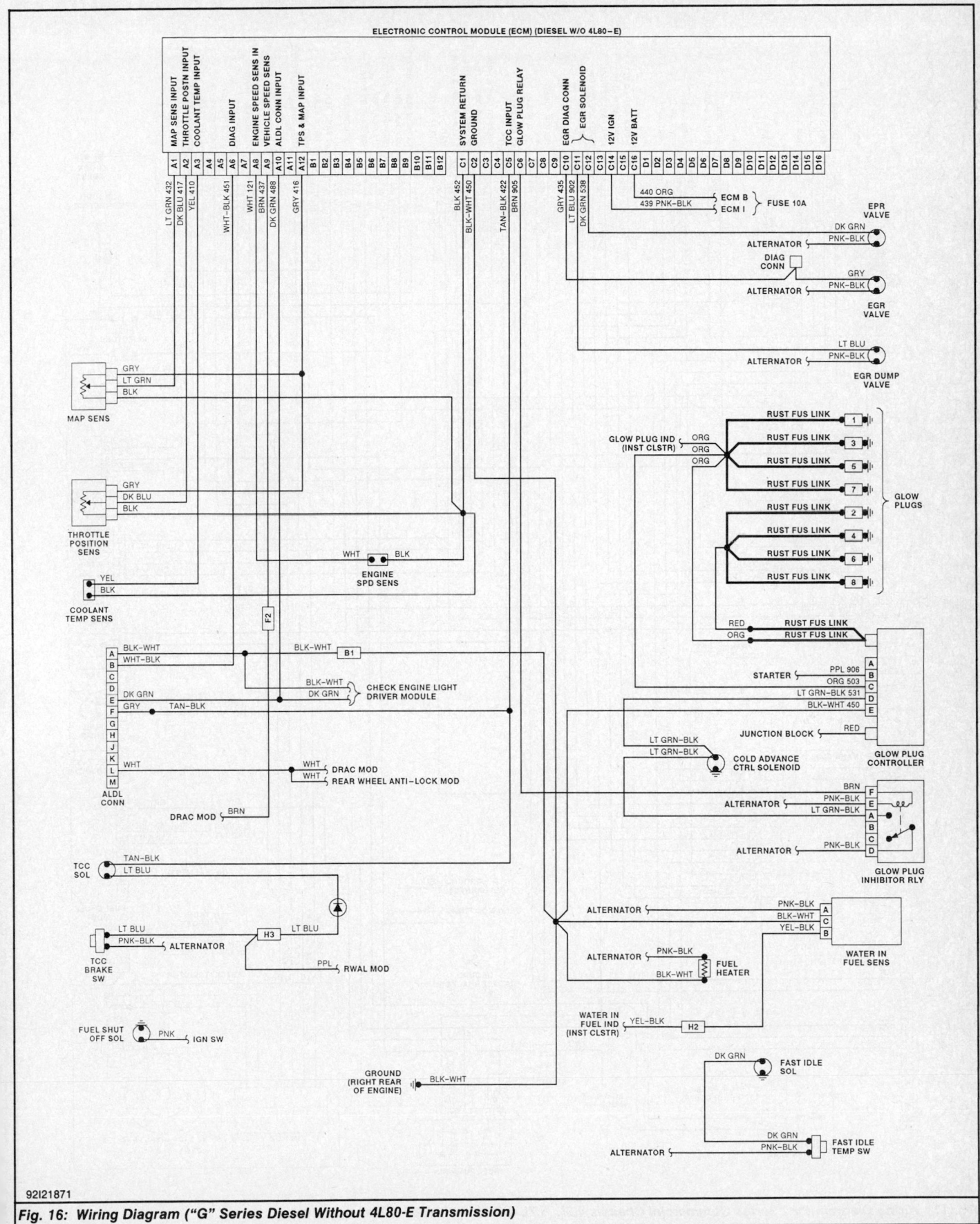

Fig. 16: Wiring Diagram ("G" Series Diesel Without 4L80-E Transmission)

92I21871

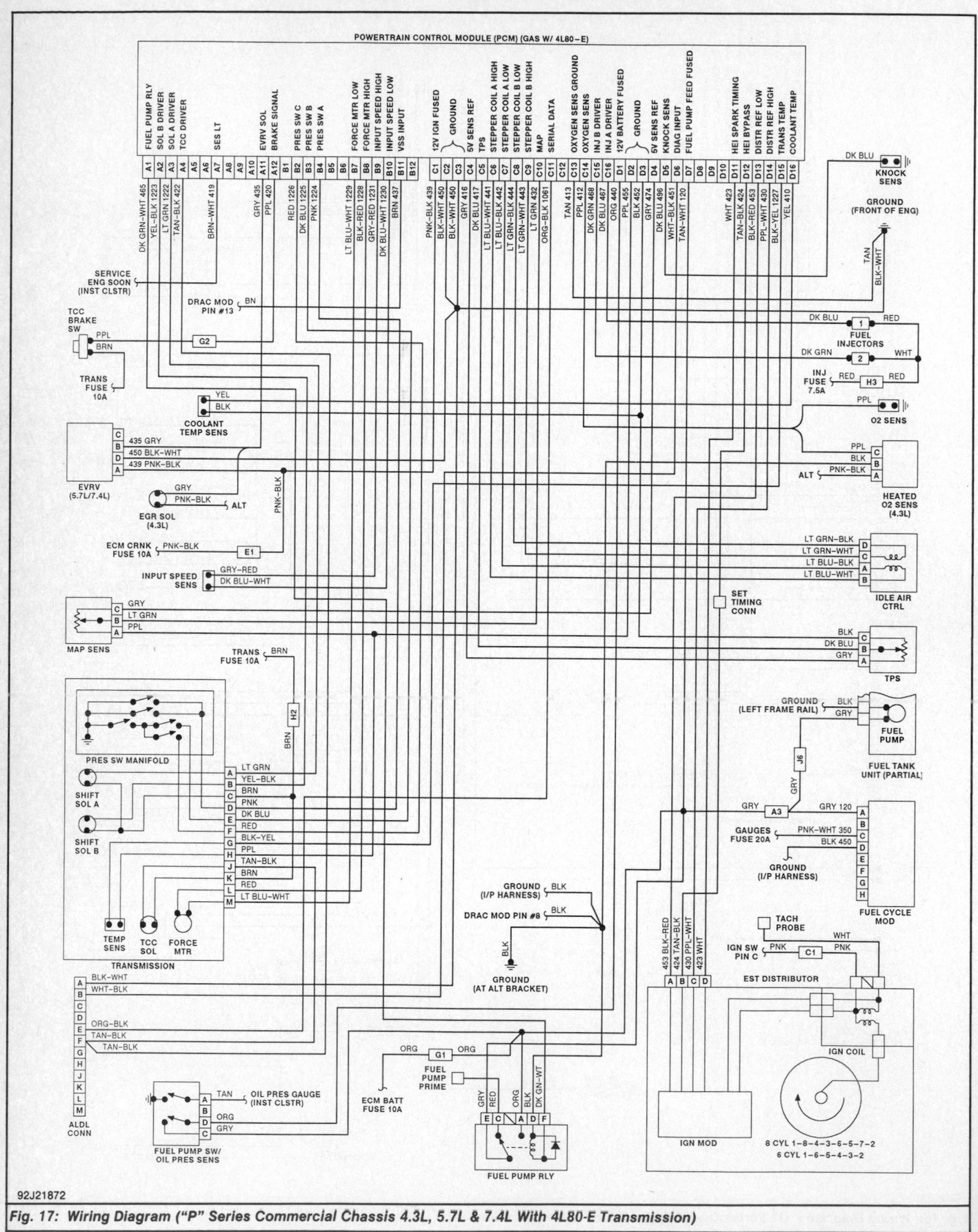

Fig. 17: Wiring Diagram ("P" Series Commercial Chassis 4.3L, 5.7L & 7.4L With 4L80-E Transmission)

92J21872

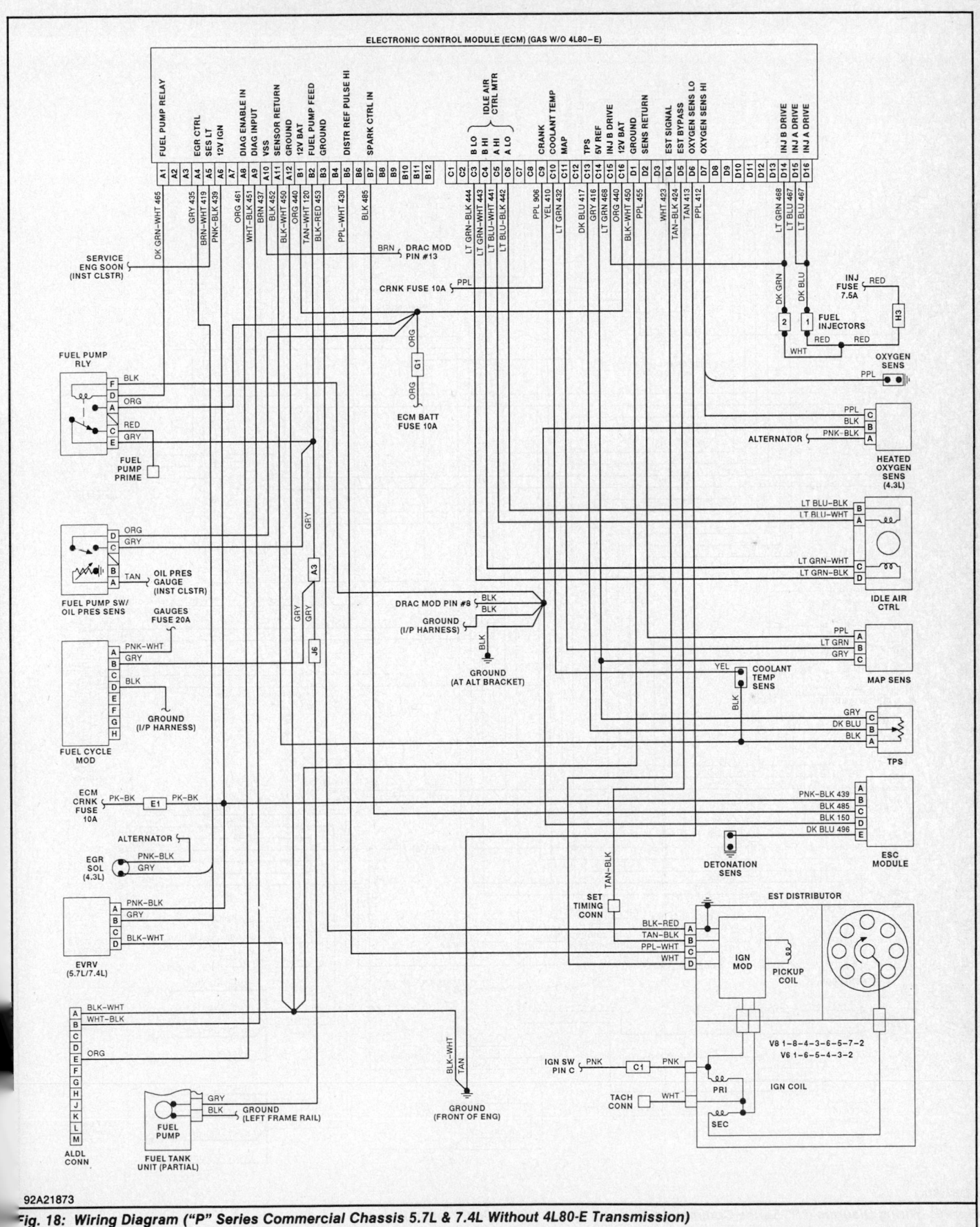

Fig. 18: Wiring Diagram ("P" Series Commercial Chassis 5.7L & 7.4L Without 4L80-E Transmission)

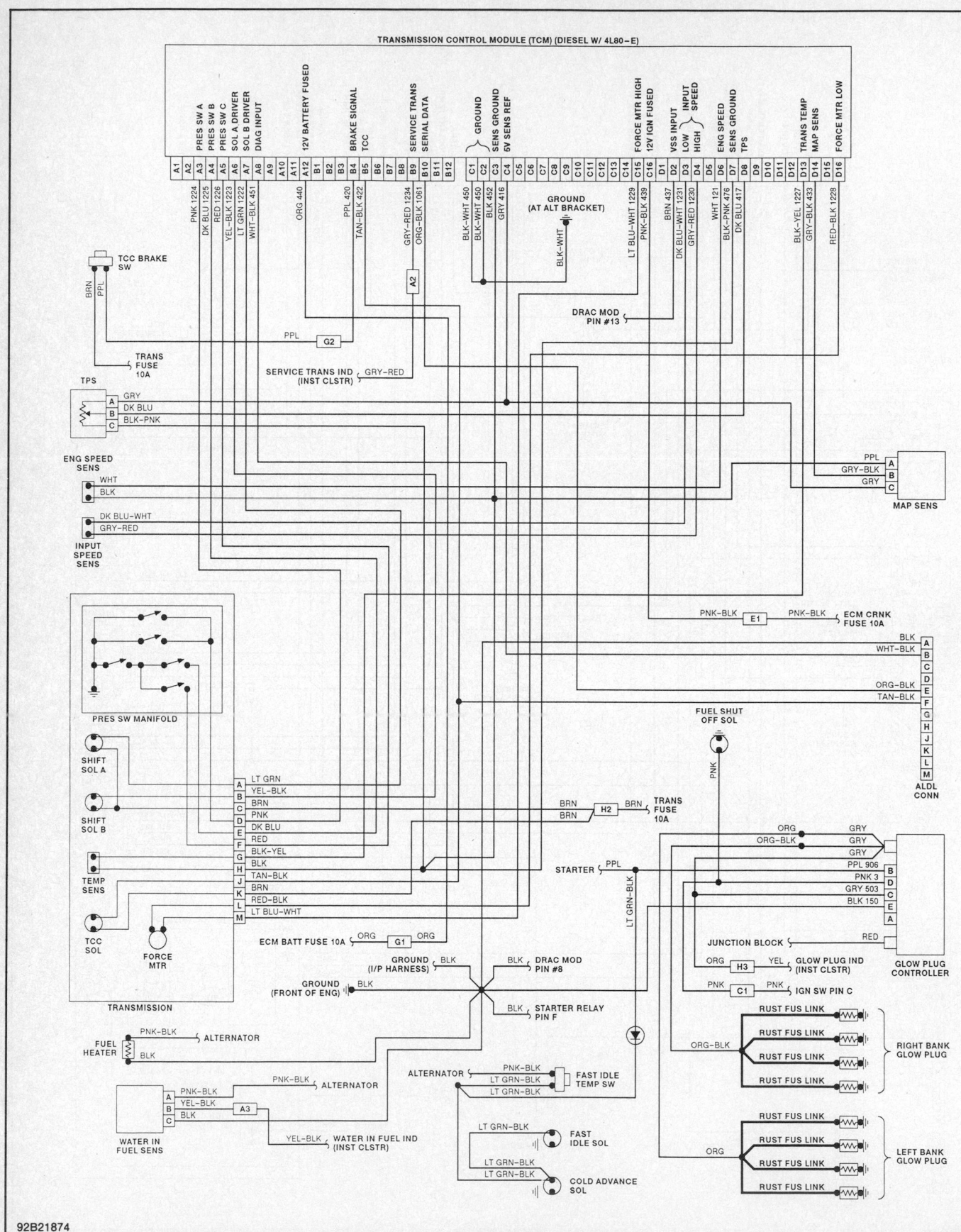

Fig. 19: Wiring Diagram ("P" Series Commercial Chassis Diesel With 4L80-E Transmission)

92B21874

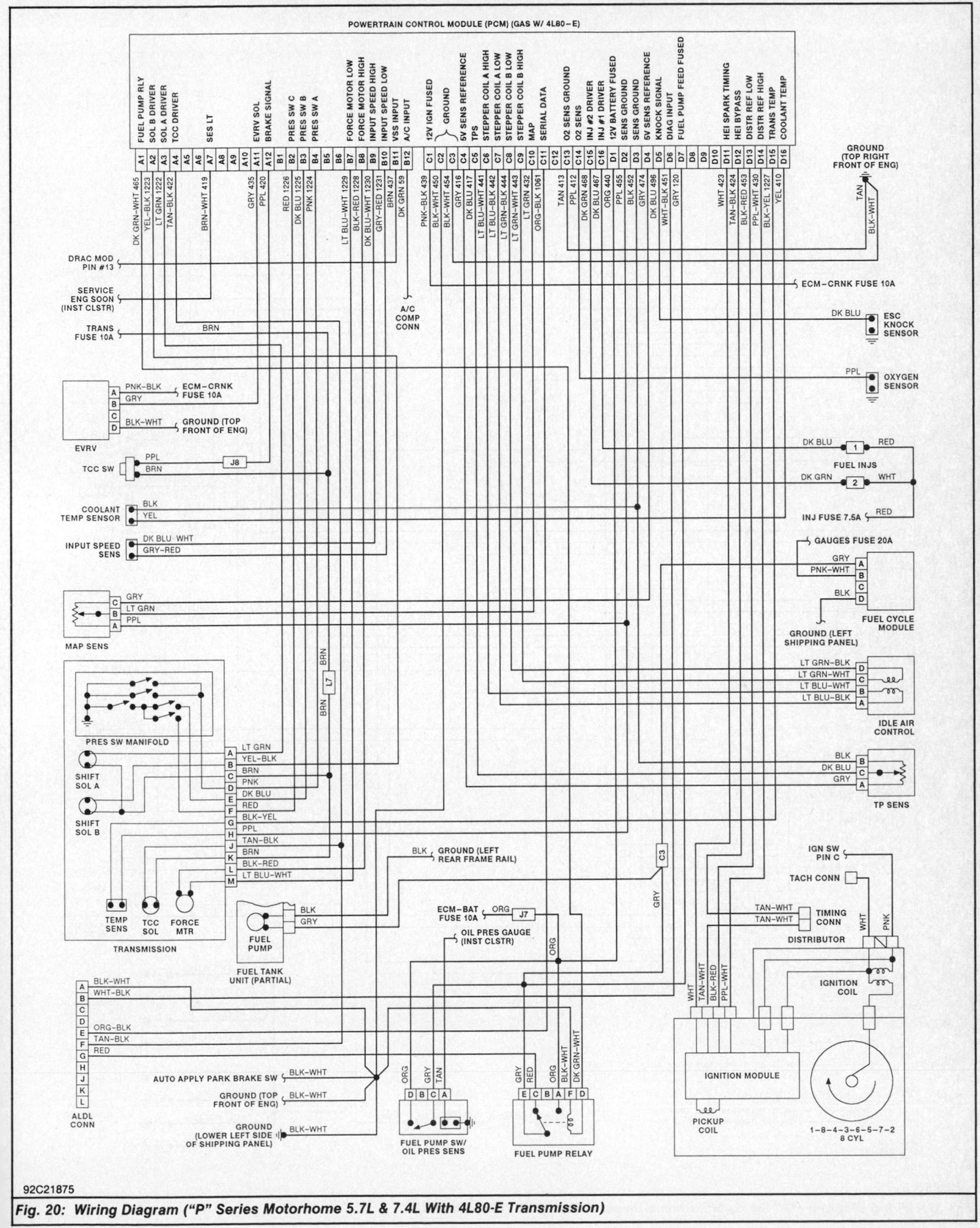

Fig. 20: Wiring Diagram ("P" Series Motorhome 5.7L & 7.4L With 4L80-E Transmission)

92C21875

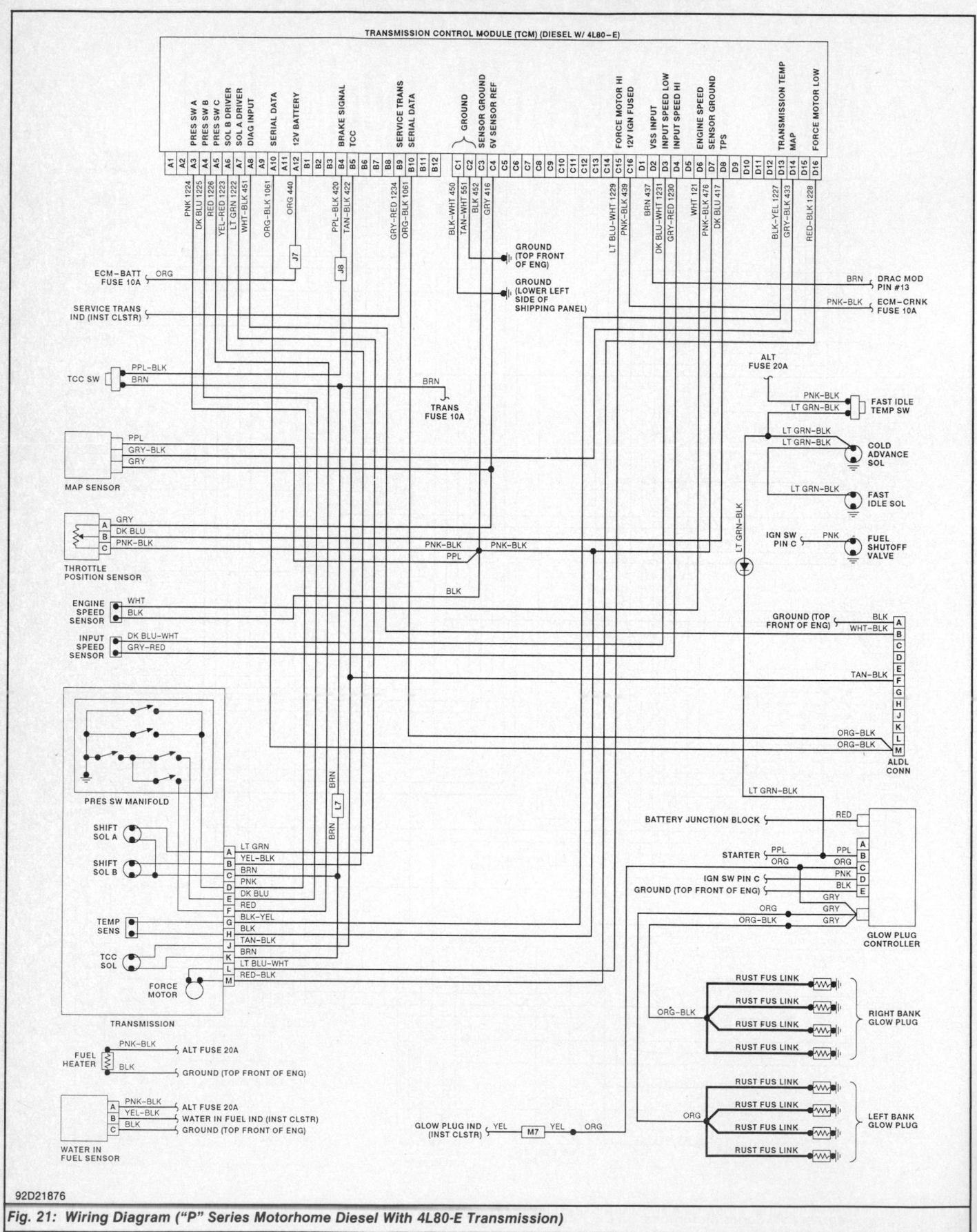

92D21876

Fig. 21: Wiring Diagram ("P" Series Motorhome Diesel With 4L80-E Transmission)

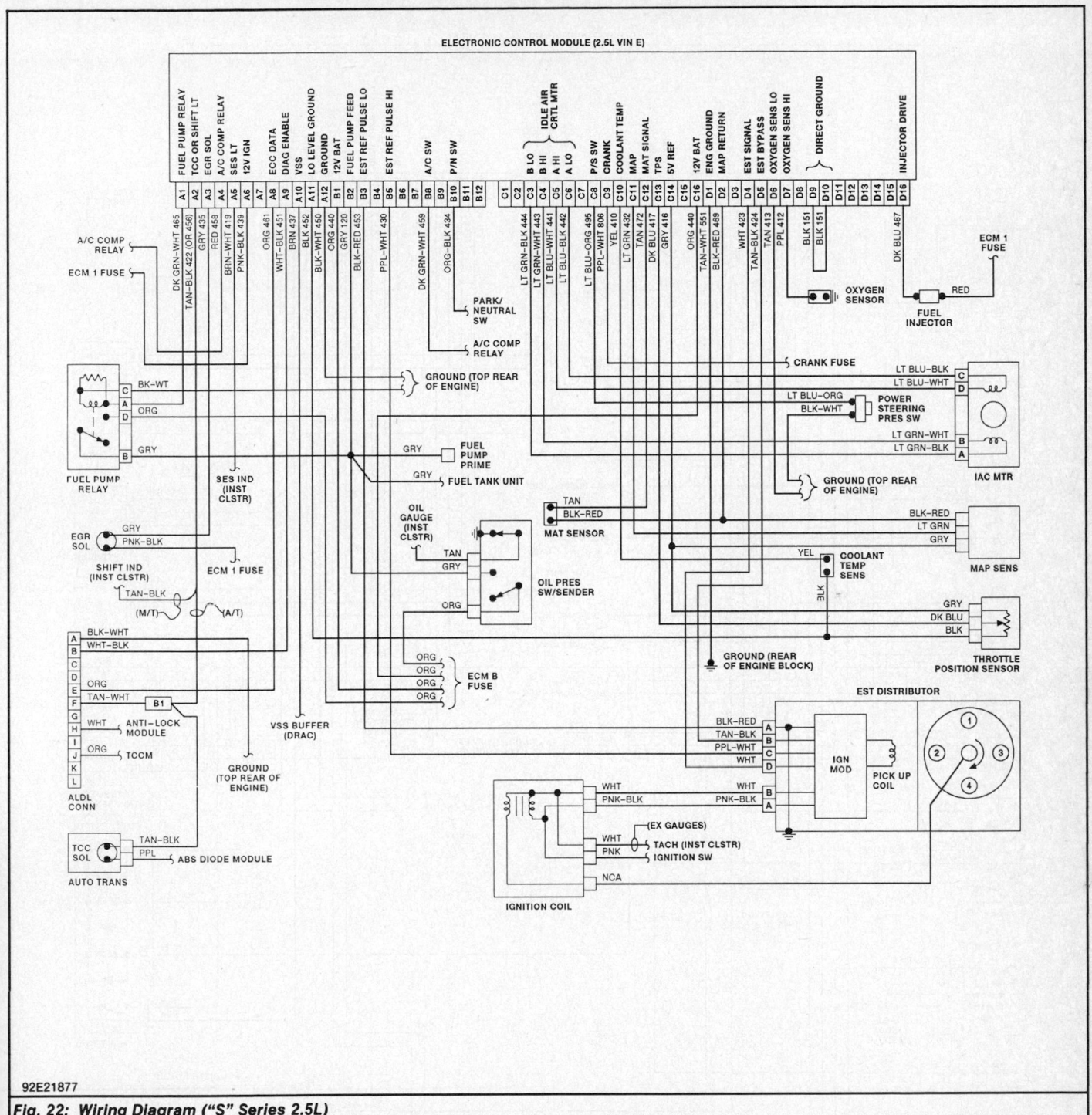

92E21877

Fig. 22: Wiring Diagram ("S" Series 2.5L)

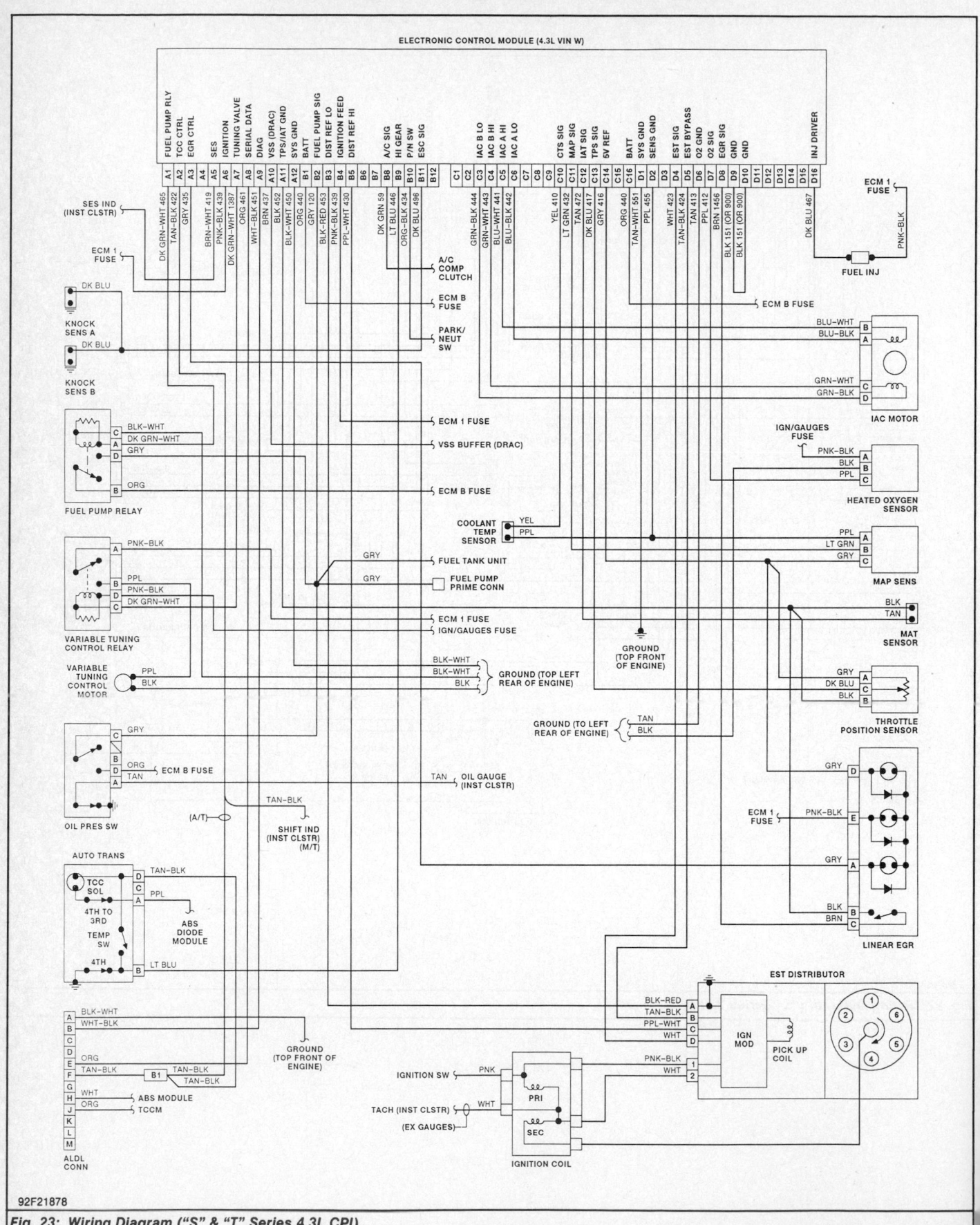

92F21878

Fig. 23: Wiring Diagram ("S" & "T" Series 4.3L CPI)

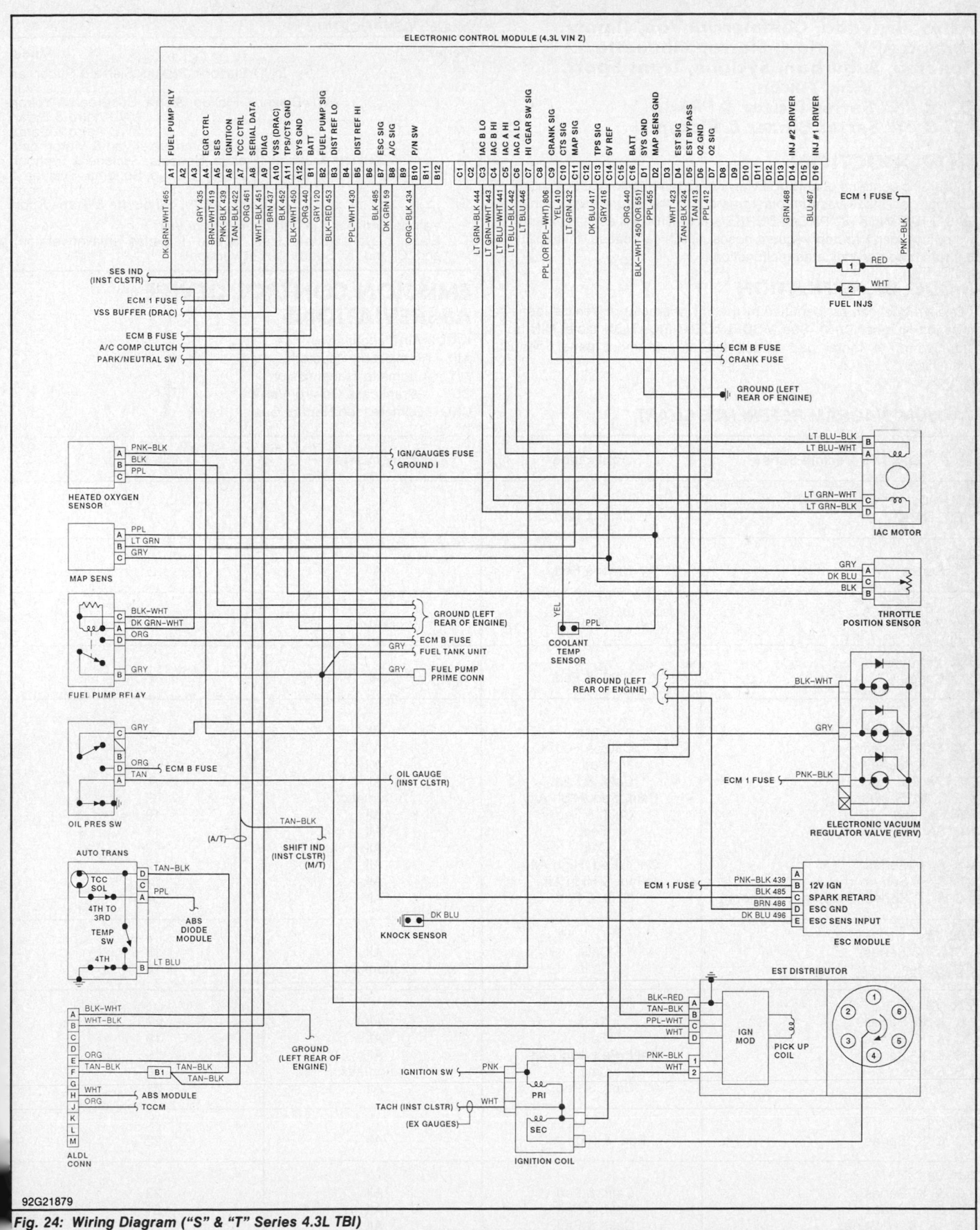

Fig. 24: Wiring Diagram ("S" & "T" Series 4.3L TBI)

92G21879

1992 ENGINE PERFORMANCE
Vacuum Diagrams

Astro, Bravada, Commercial Van, Jimmy, Lumina APV, Safari, Sierra, Silhouette, Sonoma, Suburban, Syclone, Trans Sport, Typhoon, Van, Yukon, "C" & "K" Series Blazer & Pickup, "S" & "T" Series Blazer & Pickup

INTRODUCTION

This article contains underhood views or schematics of vacuum hose routing. Use these vacuum diagrams during the visual inspection in BASIC DIAGNOSTIC PROCEDURES article. This will assist in identifying improperly routed vacuum hoses, which can cause driveability and/or computer-indicated malfunction.

MODEL IDENTIFICATION

Vehicle model can be identified by the fifth character of Vehicle Identification Number (VIN). See MODEL IDENTIFICATION table. VIN is stamped on a metal pad at top left of instrument panel, near windshield.

MODEL IDENTIFICATION

Series [1]	Model
"C"	2WD Blazer [2], Pickup, Sierra & Suburban
"G"	Van
"K"	4WD Blazer [2], Pickup, Sierra, Suburban & Yukon
"L"	AWD Astro & Safari
"M"	2WD Astro & Safari
"P"	Commercial Van & Motorhome
"S"	2WD Blazer [2], Jimmy, Pickup, Sonoma, Syclone & Typhoon
"T"	4WD Bravada, Blazer [2], Jimmy, Pickup, Sonoma, Syclone & Typhoon
"U"	Lumina APV, Silhouette & Trans Sport

[1] – Vehicle Series is the fifth character of VIN.
[2] – Blazer is available in 2 sizes: "S" and "T" Series (smaller version), and "C" and "K" Series (larger version).

EMISSION CONTROL DEVICE ABBREVIATIONS

A/CL – Air Cleaner
AIR – Air Injection Reactor
A/T – Automatic Transmission
CCV – Crankcase Control Valve
CNG – Compressed Natural Gas

VACUUM DIAGRAM REFERENCE CHART

Engine & Vehicle Series	Application	Transmission	Fig. No.
2.5L 4-Cyl.			
"S" Series	Calif. & Fed.	All	1
2.8L V6			
"S" Series	Calif. & Fed.	All	2
3.1L V6			
"U" Series	Fed.	All	3
3.8L V6			
"U" Series	Calif. & Fed.	All	4
4.3L V6			
"C" & "K" Series	Calif.	All	5
"C" & "K" Series	Calif. & Fed.	All	6
"C" & "K" Series	Fed.	All	7
"G" Series	Calif. & Fed.	All	8
"L" & "M" Series	Calif./Fed./High Alt.	Automatic	9
"P" Series	Calif. & Fed.	All	10
"P" Series	Fed.	All	11
"S" Series	Calif.	All	13
"S" & "T" Series	Calif./Fed./High Alt.	All	12
"S" & "T" Series	Fed. & High Alt.	All	13
"S" & "T" Series (Syclone & Typhoon)	Calif. & Fed.	All	14
5.0L V8			
"C" & "K" Series	Calif.	All	15
"G" Series	Calif.	Automatic	16
5.7L V8			
"C" & "K" Series	Calif.	All	17
"C" & "K" Series	Fed.	All	18
"C" & "K" Series	Calif./Fed./High Alt.	All	19
"G" Series	Calif.	Automatic	20
"P" Series	Calif. & Fed.	All	21
6.2L V8			
"C" & "K" Series	Fed. & High Alt.	All	22
7.4L V8			
"C" & "K" Series	Calif. & Fed.	All	23
"C" & "K" Series	Calif. & Fed.	All	24
"C", "K" & "P" Series	Calif. & Fed.	All	25
"C", "K" & "P" Series	Calif. & Fed.	All	26
"P" Series	Calif. & Fed.	All	27

CPI – Central Port Injection
DISTR – Distributor
DVTR – Diverter Valve
EFE – Early Fuel Evaporation
EGR – Exhaust Gas Recirculation
EGR SOL – EGR Solenoid
EPR – Exhaust Pressure Regulator
ESC – Electronic Spark Control
HVAC – Refers to A/C System
MAP – Manifold Air Pressure Sensor
M/T – Manual Transmission
MTR – Motor
PCV – Positive Crankcase Ventilation
PFI – Port Fuel Injection
TBI – Throttle Body Injection
TRC – Throttle Return Control
TVS – Thermal Vacuum Switch
VAC – Vacuum

VACUUM DIAGRAMS

NOTE: The following vacuum diagrams are courtesy of General Motors Corp. Information is not available for models not listed. Letters in parenthesis are the emission calibration code, located on underhood emissions label.

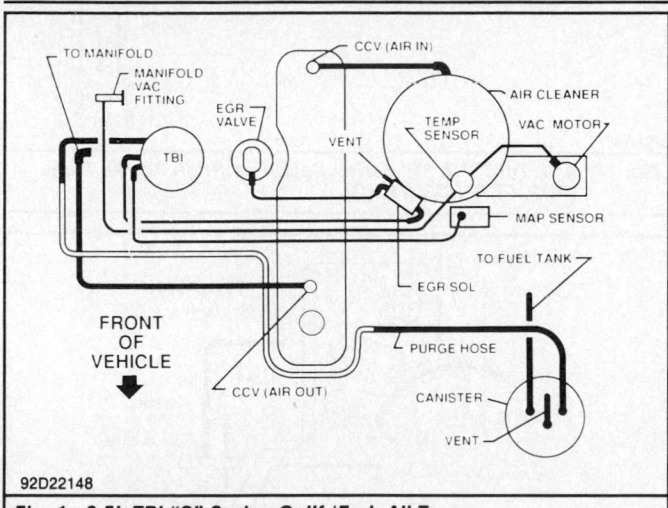

Fig. 1: 2.5L TBI "S" Series Calif./Fed. All Trans. (PDA, PDB & PDC)

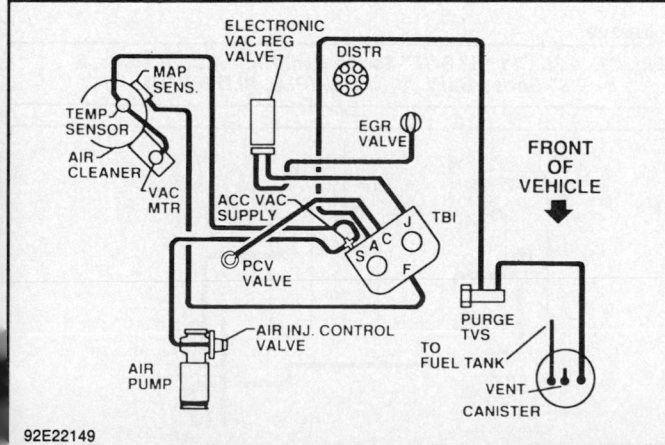

Fig. 2: 2.8L TBI "S" Series Calif./Fed. All Trans. (LDB & LDC)

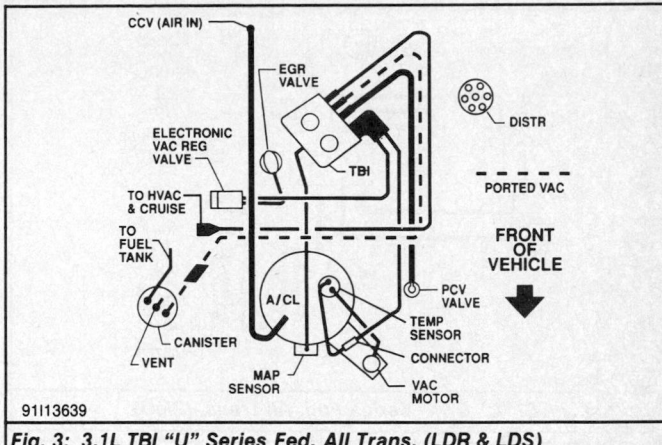

Fig. 3: 3.1L TBI "U" Series Fed. All Trans. (LDR & LDS)

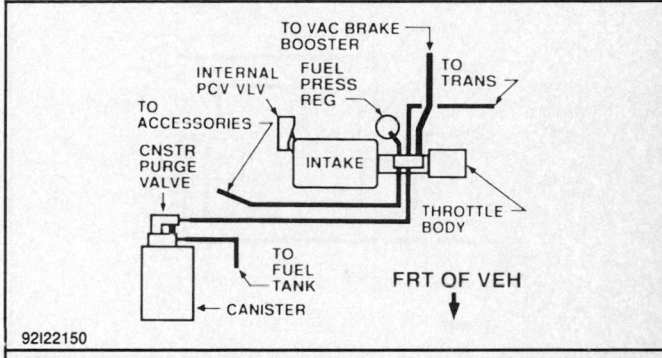

Fig. 4: 3.8L PFI "U" Series Calif./Fed. All Trans. (NLN & NLR)

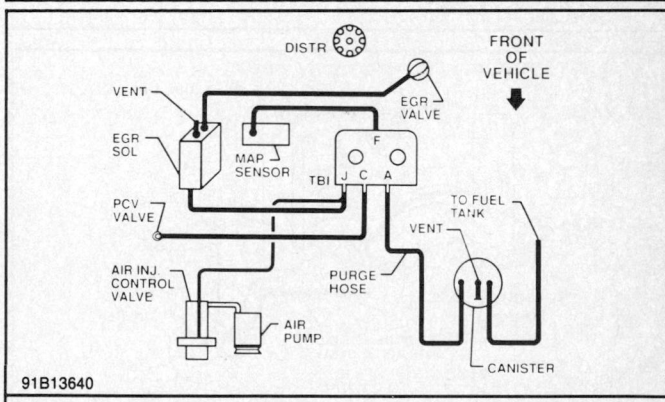

Fig. 5: 4.3L TBI "C" & "K" Series Calif. All Trans. (PDW & PMW)

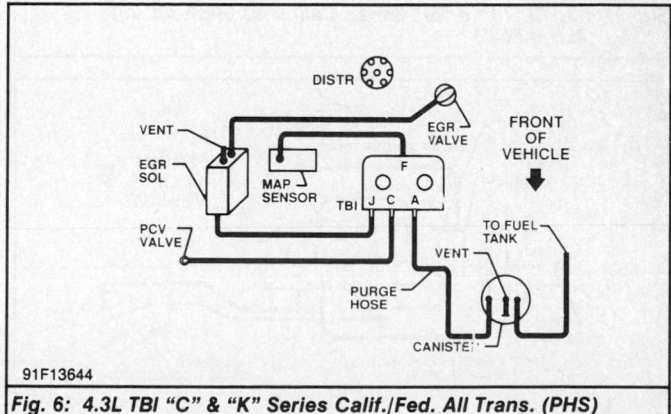

Fig. 6: 4.3L TBI "C" & "K" Series Calif./Fed. All Trans. (PHS)

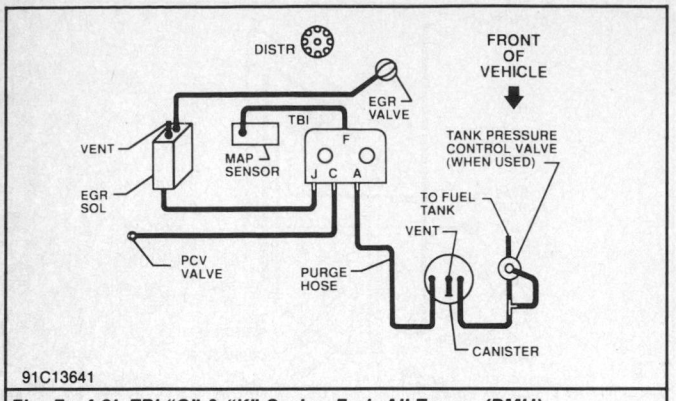

Fig. 7: 4.3L TBI "C" & "K" Series Fed. All Trans. (PMU)

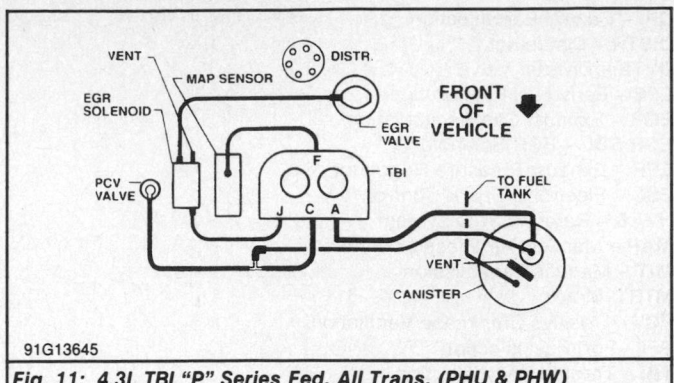

Fig. 11: 4.3L TBI "P" Series Fed. All Trans. (PHU & PHW)

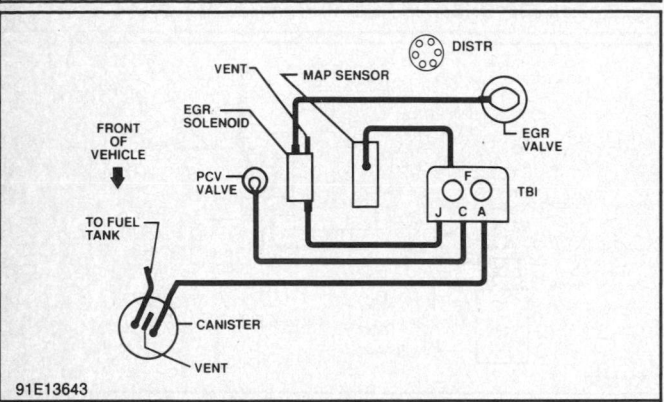

Fig. 8: 4.3L TBI "G" Series Calif./Fed. All Trans. (PFD, PLP & PNC)

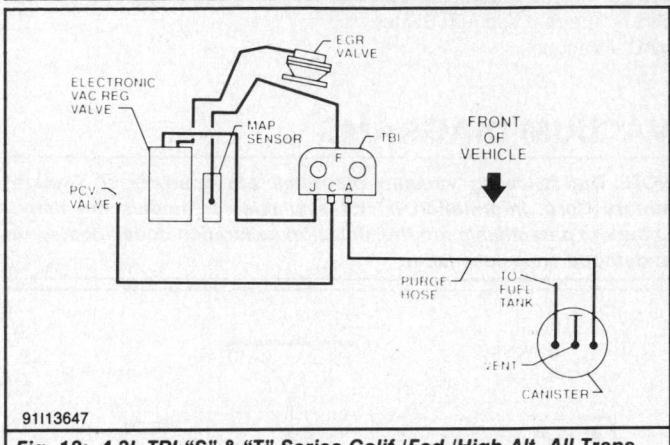

Fig. 12: 4.3L TBI "S" & "T" Series Calif./Fed./High Alt. All Trans. (PDP, PDR, PDS & PMC)

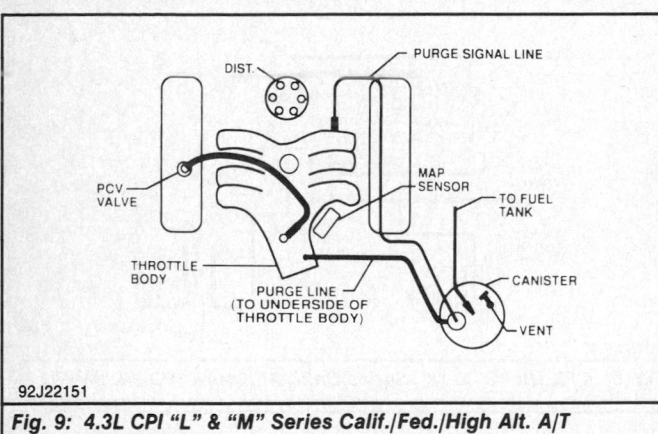

Fig. 9: 4.3L CPI "L" & "M" Series Calif./Fed./High Alt. A/T (PLH & PNK)

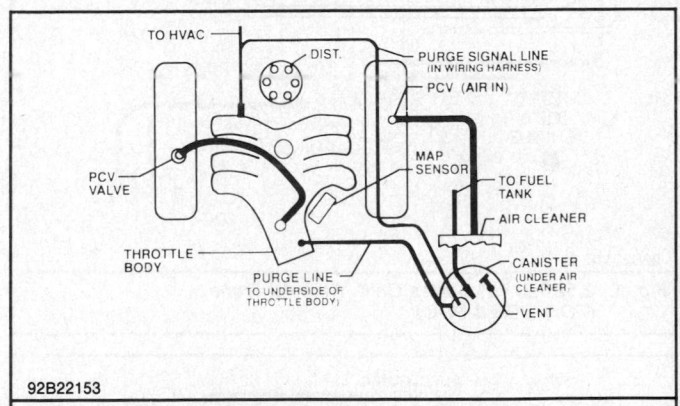

Fig. 13: 4.3L CPI "S" & "T" Series Fed./High Alt. All Trans. & "S" Series Calif. All Trans. (PLB, PLD & PFB)

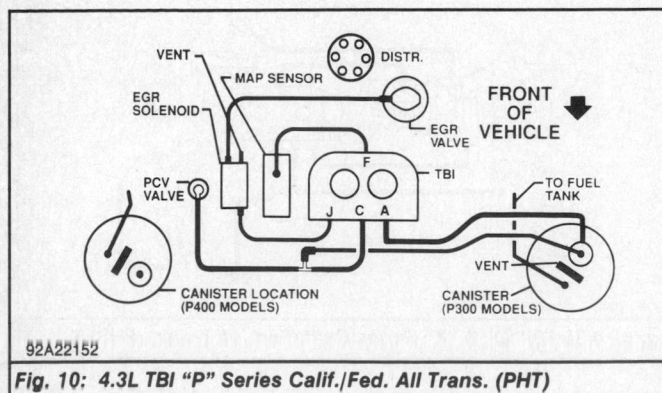

Fig. 10: 4.3L TBI "P" Series Calif./Fed. All Trans. (PHT)

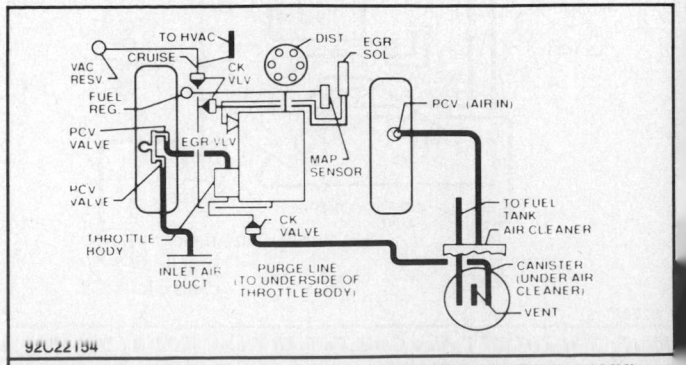

Fig. 14: 4.3L PFI Syclone & Typhoon Calif./Fed. All Trans. (JJK)

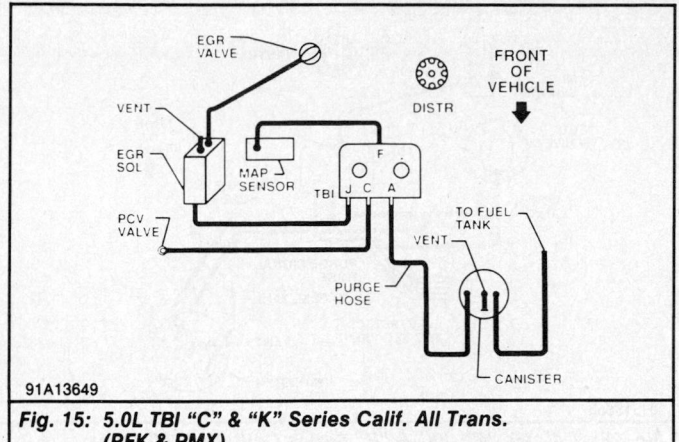

Fig. 15: 5.0L TBI "C" & "K" Series Calif. All Trans. (PFK & PMX)

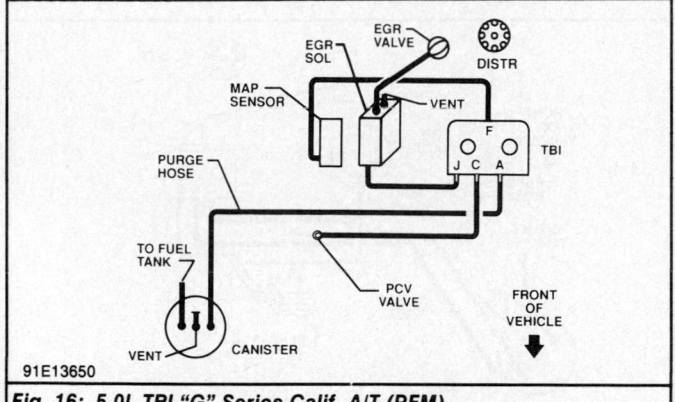

Fig. 16: 5.0L TBI "G" Series Calif. A/T (PFM)

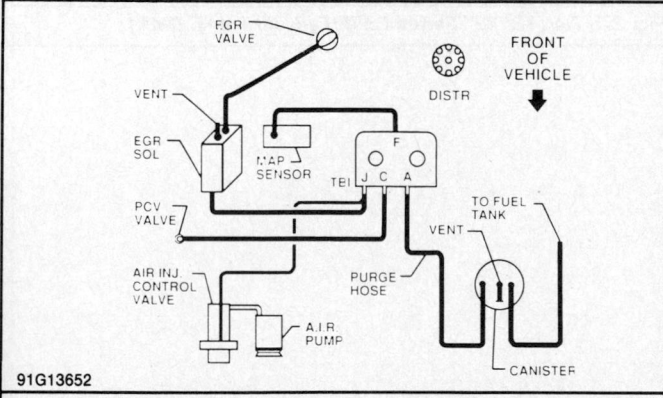

Fig. 17: 5.7L TBI "C" & "K" Series Calif. All Trans. (PFR & PFS)

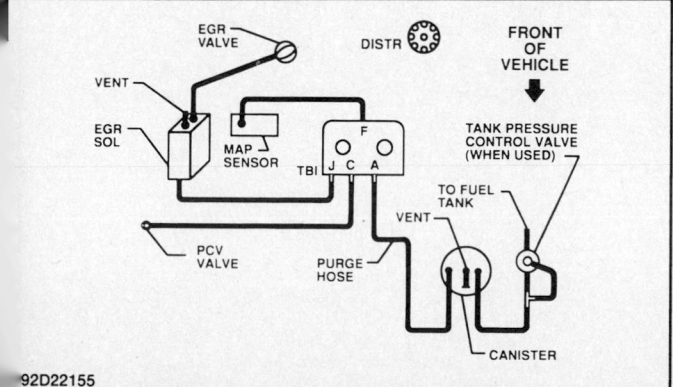

Fig. 18: 5.7L TBI "C" & "K" Series Fed. All Trans. (PMX & PMY)

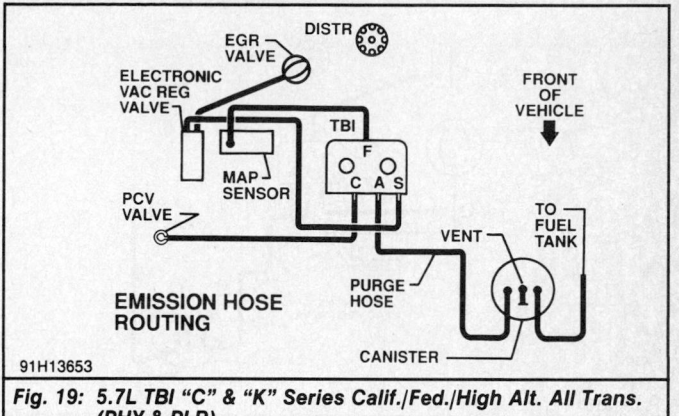

Fig. 19: 5.7L TBI "C" & "K" Series Calif./Fed./High Alt. All Trans. (PHY & PLR)

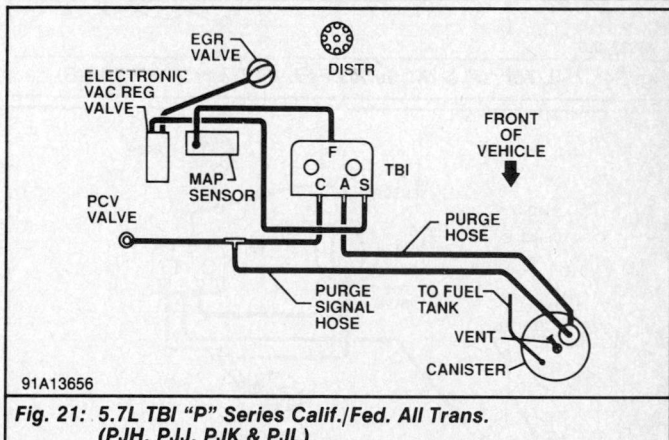

Fig. 20: 5.7L TBI "G" Series Calif. A/T (PFZ)

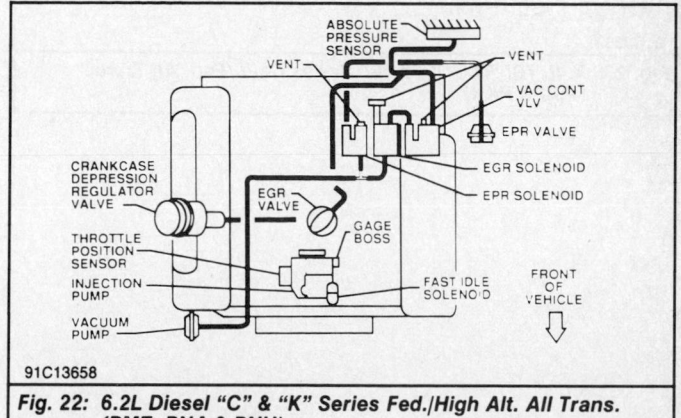

Fig. 21: 5.7L TBI "P" Series Calif./Fed. All Trans. (PJH, PJJ, PJK & PJL)

Fig. 22: 6.2L Diesel "C" & "K" Series Fed./High Alt. All Trans. (PMZ, PNA & PNH)

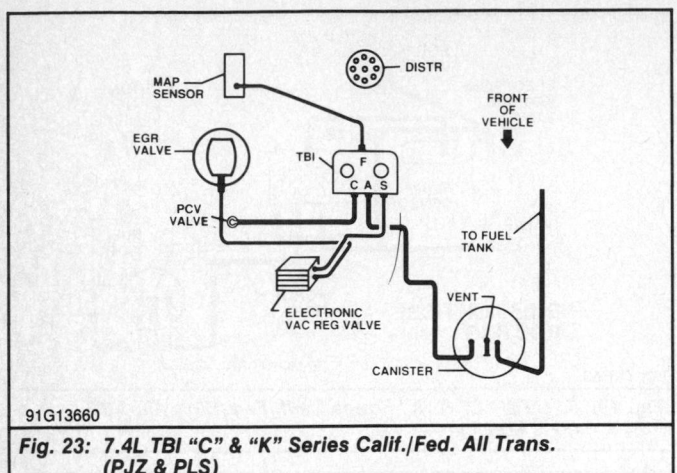

Fig. 23: 7.4L TBI "C" & "K" Series Calif./Fed. All Trans. (PJZ & PLS)

91G13660

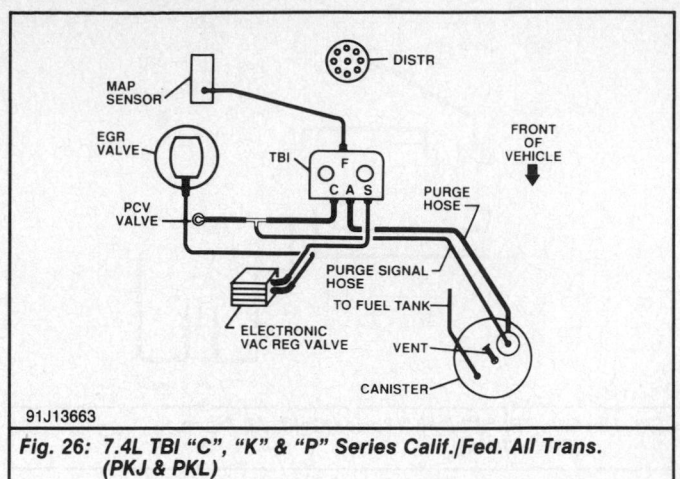

Fig. 26: 7.4L TBI "C", "K" & "P" Series Calif./Fed. All Trans. (PKJ & PKL)

91J13663

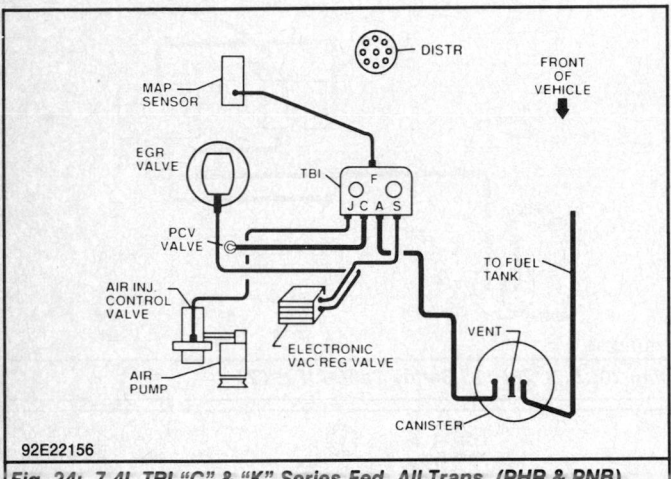

Fig. 24: 7.4L TBI "C" & "K" Series Fed. All Trans. (PHR & PNB)

92E22156

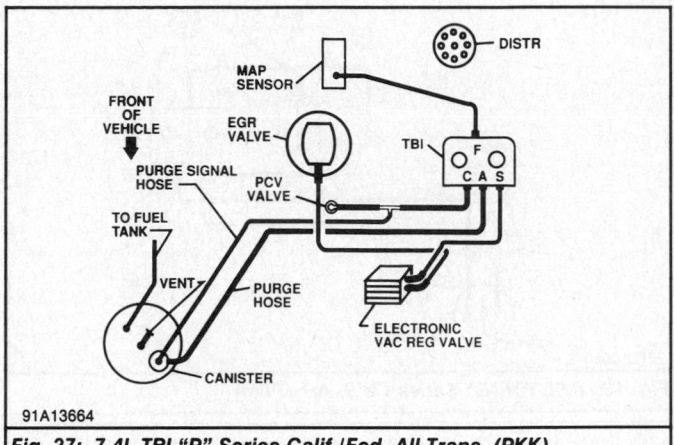

Fig. 27: 7.4L TBI "P" Series Calif./Fed. All Trans. (PKK)

91A13664

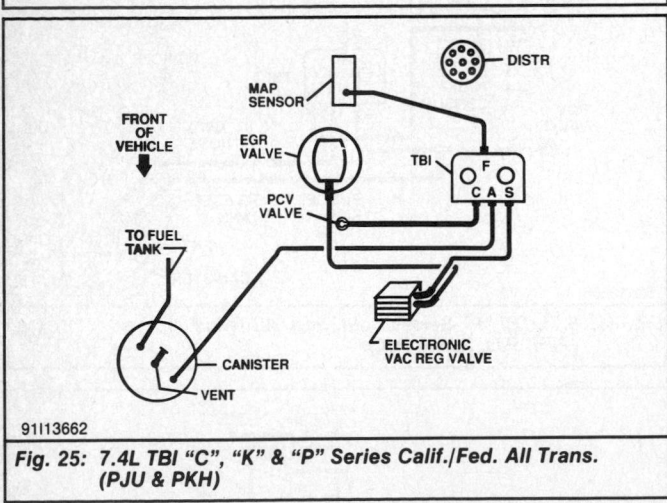

Fig. 25: 7.4L TBI "C", "K" & "P" Series Calif./Fed. All Trans. (PJU & PKH)

91I13662

Astro, Bravada, Commercial Van, Jimmy, Lumina APV, Safari, Sierra, Silhouette, Sonoma, Suburban, Syclone, Trans Sport, Typhoon, Van, Yukon, "C" & "K" Series Blazer & Pickup, "S" & "T" Series Blazer & Pickup

MODEL IDENTIFICATION

Vehicle model can be identified by fifth character of Vehicle Identification Number (VIN), stamped on metal pad on top of left end of instrument panel, near windshield. See MODEL IDENTIFICATION table.

MODEL IDENTIFICATION

Series [1]	Model
"C"	2WD Pickup, Sierra & Suburban
"G"	RWD Van
"K"	4WD Blazer, Pickup, Sierra, Suburban & Yukon
"L"	All-Wheel Drive Astro & Safari
"M"	2WD Astro & Safari
"P"	Commercial Van/Motorhome
"S"	2WD Blazer, Jimmy, Pickup & Sonoma
"T"	Bravada, 4WD Blazer, Jimmy, Pickup, Sonoma, Syclone & Typhoon
"U"	Lumina APV, Silhouette & Trans Sport

[1] – Vehicle series is fifth character of VIN.

INTRODUCTION

Removal, overhaul and installation procedures are covered in this article. If component removal and installation is primarily an unbolt and bolt-on procedure, only a torque specification may be furnished.

ON-VEHICLE ADJUSTMENTS

NOTE: For adjustments, see ON-VEHICLE ADJUSTMENTS article.

ELECTRONIC CONTROL MODULE (ECM)

CONTROL UNIT

CAUTION: When certain materials rub together, a transfer of electrons from one material to another may occur under special conditions. This causes electrostatic charge (static electricity) build up in one of the materials. When any conducting material comes in contact with the charged material, electrostatic discharge occurs, transferring electrons to the third material. Electronic components used in control systems are designed to carry very low voltages; a 30-volt charge created by static electricity can cause a total or degrading failure in ECM or other electronic components containing integrated circuits. Before servicing ECM, ground yourself, and ground the work area to discharge stored electricity.

STATIC CHARGE (VOLTS)

Movement	Relative Humidity 10-20%	Relative Humidity 65-90%
Walking Across Carpet	35,000	1500
Handling Clear Plastic Bag	20,000	1200
Sliding Across Velour Seat	15,000	400
Walking Across Tile/Vinyl	12,000	50
Handling Vinyl Envelope	7000	600

CAUTION: Static electricity can destroy integrated circuits within ECM. Before servicing ECM, ground yourself and the work area to discharge stored electricity.

CAUTION: DO NOT remove ECM from packaging until ready to install. Ground static-proof package BEFORE opening. DO NOT touch electrical terminals of components unless properly grounded. DO NOT lay electrical components on car seat, carpeting or dashboard. Use electrostatic protection mat and ground strap whenever possible. See Fig. 1.

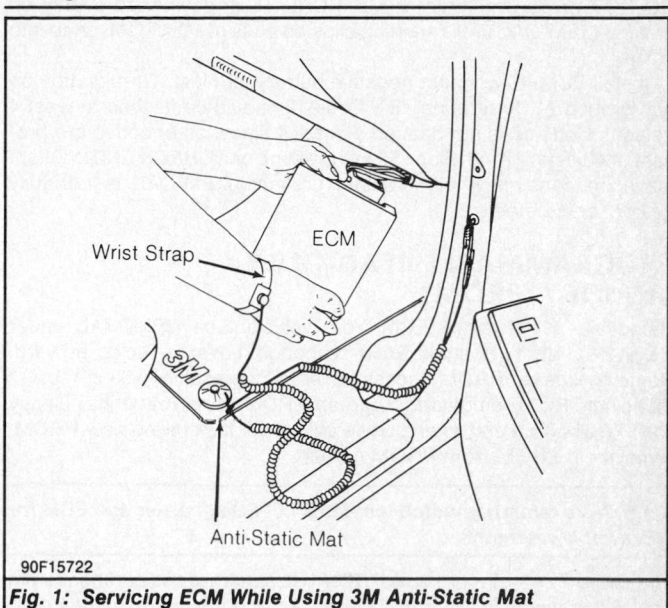

Fig. 1: Servicing ECM While Using 3M Anti-Static Mat

NOTE: Before replacing ECM, carefully inspect all wiring and control components. Ignition switch must be in OFF position when connecting or disconnecting ECM connector.

Removal – Disconnect negative battery terminal. Unplug connectors from ECM. See Fig. 1. Remove ECM from vehicle. Remove PROM and CALPAC (if equipped) or MEM-CAL from ECM. See CALPAC, MEM-CAL, or PROGRAMMABLE READ-ONLY MEMORY (PROM).

Installation – Install PROM and CALPAC (if equipped) or MEM-CAL in new ECM. See CALPAC, MEM-CAL, or PROGRAMMABLE READ-ONLY MEMORY (PROM). Install ECM into vehicle. Connect electrical connectors to ECM. Install access panels. Connect negative battery terminal to battery.

CALPAC

Removal & Installation – Some ECM's use a CALPAC as well as a PROM. See Fig. 2. The CALPAC must also be removed from old ECM and installed in new one. Removal and replacement procedures for CALPAC are same as for PROM. See PROGRAMMABLE READ-ONLY MEMORY (PROM) in this article. If units are installed improperly, grounding diagnostic test lead will set Code 52.

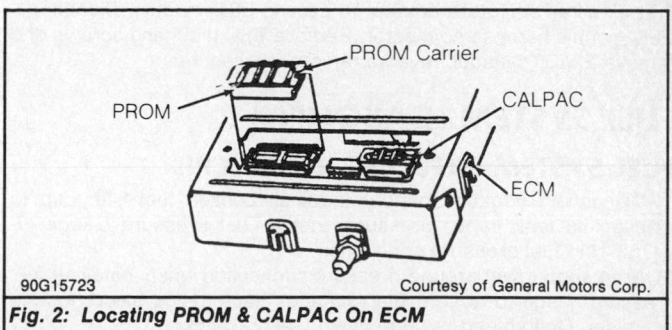

Courtesy of General Motors Corp.

Fig. 2: Locating PROM & CALPAC On ECM

MEM-CAL

Removal – Disconnect negative battery terminal. Remove ECM from vehicle. See REMOVAL under CONTROL UNIT. Using 2 fingers, push retaining clips back from MEM-CAL. At the same time, grasp it at both ends and lift out of socket. DO NOT remove MEM-CAL cover.

Installation – 1) Carefully align MEM-CAL pins with ECM pin holes. DO NOT press in middle of MEM-CAL. Push downward evenly on ends of MEM-CAL until retaining clips on ends of MEM-CAL snap into place.

2) Install ECM. Reconnect negative battery terminal. Turn ignition on and ground ALDL terminal "B". Code 12 should be flashed at least 4 times. If Code 12 is not flashed at least 4 times, other codes are present. If Code(s) 42, 43, 51 or 52 are present, or if CHECK ENGINE light stays on constantly with code(s) present, MEM-CAL is not fully seated, or is defective.

PROGRAMMABLE READ-ONLY MEMORY (PROM)

Removal – 1) Remove ECM from vehicle. See REMOVAL under CONTROL UNIT. Position ECM so bottom cover is facing upward. Remove slide-off PROM access cover by depressing locking tab.

2) Using PROM removal tool, grasp PROM at narrow ends. Gently rock PROM from end to end while pulling up. If installing new PROM, remove old PROM from PROM carrier.

NOTE: Note reference notch locations in PROM, carrier and ECM for reassembly reference.

Installation – 1) Ensure new PROM has same service number as old one. Place new PROM in PROM carrier, and position squarely over ECM PROM socket. Press on PROM carrier until PROM is firmly seated in ECM.

NOTE: Ensure reference notches in ECM and PROM are properly aligned. If PROM is installed backwards and ignition is turned on, PROM will be destroyed.

2) Install PROM access cover on ECM. Install ECM in vehicle. See INSTALLATION under CONTROL UNIT. Start engine, and ground ALDL terminal "B". Watch for trouble Code 51 or 52.

3) If this occurs, PROM is not fully seated in ECM, installed backwards, has bent pins, or is defective. If bent pins are cracked while straightening, replace PROM. If PROM is installed backwards or is defective, it must be replaced.

ELECTRONIC SPARK CONTROL (ESC) MODULE

NOTE: The ESC is located on a bracket behind the distributor, mounted to firewall.

Removal & Installation – Turn ignition off. Remove bracket-to-firewall screws. Rotate bracket to access ESC module. Disconnect ESC module harness connector. Remove ESC mounting screws and remove ESC. To install, reverse removal procedure.

FUEL SYSTEM (GASOLINE)

FUEL SYSTEM PRESSURE RELIEF (CPI)

1) Disconnect negative battery terminal. Loosen fuel filler cap to relieve fuel tank vapor pressure. Install Fuel Pressure Gauge (J-34730-1) to fuel pressure connection.

2) Wrap shop towel around pressure connection when installing fuel pressure gauge to absorb fuel leakage. Place gauge bleed hose in container. Open bleed valve to bleed fuel pressure.

FUEL SYSTEM PRESSURE RELIEF (PFI)

Fuel system is under pressure. Fuel pressure may be relieved by 2 different methods.

Method 1 – Disconnect fuel pump electrical connector. Start engine and allow to run until it stops. Operate starter for 3 seconds to relieve remaining fuel from fuel lines.

Method 2 – Install Fuel Pressure Gauge (J-34730-1) on fuel pressure connection. Wrap shop towel around pressure connection when installing fuel pressure gauge to absorb fuel leakage. Place gauge bleed hose in container. Open bleed valve to bleed fuel pressure.

FUEL SYSTEM PRESSURE RELIEF (TBI)

TBI Unit Model 700 – Place transmission gear selector in Park (Neutral on M/T). Set parking brake and block drive wheels. Loosen fuel filler cap to relieve tank pressure. Disconnect 3-terminal electrical connector at fuel tank. Start engine and allow to run until engine stalls. Crank engine for 3 seconds to relieve any residual pressure left in fuel lines. Fuel lines are now safe for servicing.

TBI Unit Model 220 – Fuel pressure is relieved and drops to zero when ignitions is turned off. To minimize risk of fire and personal injury, cover area to be disconnected with a shop rag.

FUEL PUMP

NOTE: When installing sending unit, DO NOT fold or twist strainer. This will restrict fuel flow.

Removal & Installation (All Models) – 1) Relieve fuel system pressure. See FUEL SYSTEM PRESSURE RELIEF (CPI, PFI or TBI) under FUEL SYSTEM (GASOLINE). Disconnect negative battery terminal. Raise vehicle and remove fuel tank. Remove sender unit and pump by turning cam lock counterclockwise using Tool (J-36608 or J-24187).

2) Remove fuel pump from sending unit by pulling pump up into attaching hose while pulling outward from the bottom support. DO NOT damage rubber insulator or strainer. To install, reverse removal procedure.

FUEL RAIL & INJECTORS (PFI)

Removal (3.8L) – 1) Relieve fuel pressure. See FUEL SYSTEM PRESSURE RELIEF (PFI) under FUEL SYSTEM (GASOLINE). Disconnect fuel supply and return lines from fuel rail by squeezing tabs and pulling them off. Remove vacuum line from fuel pressure regulator.

2) Disconnect electrical harness connector from injectors. Remove fuel rail hold-down bolts. Remove fuel rail from intake manifold by using equal force on both sides of fuel rail. Plug injector holes on intake manifold during service. To remove injector from fuel rail assembly, remove injector retaining clips.

CAUTION: DO NOT use compressed air to internally flush, clean or dry fuel rail. Fuel rail must not be immersed in solvent.

Installation – 1) To install, reverse removal procedure. Replace all injector "O" rings. Lubricate "O" rings with clean engine oil. Position fuel rail assembly on intake manifold and seat injectors by hand pressure.

2) Tighten fuel rail hold-down bolts to **84-177 INCH lbs. (10-20 N.m)**. Install fuel lines, fuel pressure regulator vacuum line and injector electrical harness connectors.

NOTE: On 4.3L Turbo, upper intake manifold must be removed in order to remove fuel rail and injectors.

Removal (4.3L Turbo) – 1) Move air cleaner and duct aside. Drain coolant from radiator. Drain charge air cooler radiator. Relief fuel pressure. See FUEL SYSTEM PRESSURE RELIEF (PFI) under FUEL SYSTEM (GASOLINE).

2) Disconnect negative battery terminal. Disconnect charge air cooler ducts and hoses. Remove charge air cooler center support bracket. Disconnect electrical connectors and hoses from EVRV solenoid, ignition coil and MAP sensor.

3) Remove multi-use bracket from lower intake manifold. Disconnect upper manifold electrical connectors and hoses. Remove throttle

body from upper manifold. See THROTTLE BODY (PFI) under FUEL SYSTEM (GASOLINE).

4) Remove upper intake manifold mounting bolts. Remove upper intake manifold assembly and gasket. Disconnect heater hose at lower intake manifold. Disconnect charge air cooler inlet pipe.

5) Disconnect fuel injector electrical connectors. Disconnect fuel line at fuel rail. Remove fuel rail retaining bolts. Remove fuel rail and injectors.

Installation – To install, reverse removal procedure. Lubricate injector "O" rings with clean engine oil. Tighten fuel rail retaining bolts. See appropriate TORQUE SPECIFICATIONS table at end of article.

IDLE AIR CONTROL (IAC) MOTOR

Removal (CPI & PFI) – Disconnect IAC harness connector. Remove IAC retaining screws and remove IAC from upper intake manifold assembly.

Installation – **1)** Inspect "O" ring for damage. Replace if necessary. If reusing IAC motor, DO NOT push or pull on pintle. Threads on worm gear will be damaged.

2) If replacing IAC motor, measure distance between tip of new IAC motor pintle and mounting flange. Distance should not exceed 1 1/8" (28 mm). If distance is greater than specified, use finger pressure to slowly retract pintle. Lubricate "O" ring with clean engine oil.

3) Apply thread locking compound (Loctite 262) to IAC motor retaining screw threads. Install IAC motor to throttle body. Tighten IAC retaining screws to **27 INCH lbs. (3 N.m)**. Connect IAC harness connector.

4) To reset IAC motor pintle position, turn ignition on for 5 seconds. Turn ignition off for 10 seconds. Start engine and check for proper idle operation. Repeat IAC resetting procedure if proper idle operation cannot be obtained.

Removal (TBI) – Remove air cleaner and related ducting. Remove Idle Air Control (IAC) electrical connector. On model 220, unscrew IAC motor. On model 700, remove IAC retaining screws and remove IAC motor. Replace if necessary.

Installation – **1)** Inspect gasket or "O" ring for damage. Replace if necessary. Measure distance from IAC contact flange to tip of pintle. Distance should not exceed 1 1/8" (28 mm). If valve is extended too far, damage to valve will result during installation.

2) To set IAC pintle length on a new IAC, use finger pressure to slowly retract pintle. Lubricate new "O" ring with ATF and install new gasket. Install IAC motor on throttle body. Tighten IAC valve to specification. See appropriate TORQUE SPECIFICATIONS table at end of article.

CAUTION: DO NOT extend or retract pintle if IAC has been in service, or damage to worm gear will result.

---

3) Connect electrical lead to IAC motor and install air cleaner. Start engine and allow it to reach normal operating temperature. Drive vehicle at 43 MPH minimum to allow ECM to reset idle speed. It may be necessary to cycle ignition off and restart vehicle before proper idle will be initialized.

NTAKE MANIFOLD TUNING VALVE (CPI)

Removal & Installation – **1)** Disconnect intake manifold tuning valve electrical harness connector. Remove intake manifold tuning valve retaining screws. Discard "O" ring. Use carburetor cleaner to remove carbon deposits. DO NOT soak tuning valve assembly in solvent.

2) To install, reverse removal procedure. Lubricate NEW "O" ring with clean engine oil. Apply thread locking compound (Loctite 262) to intake manifold tuning valve retaining screw threads. Tighten retaining screws to **18 INCH lbs. (2 N.m)**. Reconnect electrical harness connector.

THROTTLE BODY (PFI)

NOTE: Identification number is stamped on throttle body near throttle shaft. Identification number must be used for ordering replacement components.

Removal (3.8L) – **1)** Relieve fuel pressure. See FUEL SYSTEM PRESSURE RELIEF (TBI) under FUEL SYSTEM (GASOLINE). Disconnect negative battery terminal. Drain coolant from radiator. Remove air induction tube, throttle and cruise control cables.

2) Disconnect electrical harness connector from IAC, TPS and MAF sensor. Remove throttle body mounting bolts. Remove throttle body assembly.

Installation – **1)** To install, reverse removal procedure using new gasket. Ensure throttle and cruise control cables do not hold throttle valve open. Tighten retaining bolts to **11 ft. lbs. (15 N.m)**. Refill coolant. If IAC was removed or replaced, reset IAC motor pintle position.

2) To reset IAC motor pintle position, turn ignition on (engine off) and then turn ignition off. Start and allow engine to reach normal operating temperature. Check for proper idle operation.

Removal (4.3L Turbo) – **1)** Relieve fuel pressure. See FUEL SYSTEM PRESSURE RELIEF (PFI) under FUEL SYSTEM (GASOLINE). Disconnect negative battery terminal. Loosen charge air cooler mounting bolts, and reposition charge air cooler unit to access throttle body.

2) Disconnect electrical connectors, vacuum lines, accelerator cable, throttle valve cable, and cruise control cable (if equipped). Remove throttle body screws. Remove throttle body assembly from manifold.

Installation – **1)** To install, reverse removal procedure using new gasket. Ensure throttle and cruise control cables do not hold throttle valve open. Tighten retaining bolts to specification. See appropriate TORQUE SPECIFICATIONS table at end of article. Reset IAC motor pintle position.

2) To reset IAC motor pintle position, depress accelerator pedal slightly. Start and run engine for 5 seconds. Turn ignition off for 10 seconds. Restart engine and check for proper idle operation.

THROTTLE BODY (TBI)

Identification – An 8-digit unit identification number is stamped on throttle body assembly. On TBI model 220, number is stamped vertically on front of throttle body, at Throttle Position Sensor (TPS) side. On TBI model 700, number can be found on TPS side of mounting flange. Letter codes are stamped on throttle body at external tube locations to identify vacuum hose connections.

Removal – **1)** Disconnect air cleaner (THERMAC) hose from engine vacuum fitting (if equipped). Remove air cleaner, adapter, and gasket. Relieve fuel pressure. See FUEL SYSTEM PRESSURE RELIEF (TBI) under FUEL SYSTEM (GASOLINE).

2) Disconnect electrical leads at IAC motor, throttle position sensor, and fuel injector(s). Disconnect fuel lines from throttle body. Discard fuel line "O" rings. Disconnect grommet with wires from throttle body.

NOTE: On TBI model 220, squeeze plastic tabs on injectors and pull connector straight up.

---

3) Disconnect throttle linkage, return spring and cruise control linkage (if equipped). Label and disconnect all vacuum hoses from throttle body. Remove throttle body mount bolts/nut. Remove throttle body.

NOTE: Disassembling throttle body unit for immersion in cleaning solvent requires removal of throttle body cover or fuel meter assembly, TPS and IAC assembly. Throttle valve screws are staked in position and should NOT be removed.

WARNING: Pressure regulator spring is under heavy tension, and may cause personal injury if released. DO NOT immerse cover in any type of cleaning solvent.

Disassembly (Throttle Body Cover – Model 220) – **1)** Place throttle body on Holding Fixture (J-9789-118 or BT 30-15) to prevent damage to throttle valve. Remove cover-to-throttle body screws; note location of 2 short screws. Remove throttle body cover. *See Fig. 3.* Throttle body cover and pressure regulator are serviced as an assembly. DO NOT remove pressure regulator-to-cover screws.

2) Remove TPS, IAC, fuel injector, fuel filter, rubber parts, and diaphragms. Clean all remaining (metal) parts in a cold immersion-type cleaner such as Carbon X (X-55). Blow dry with compressed air. Inspect mating surfaces for damage which may prevent gasket sealing. Repair or replace faulty components.

Disassembly (Fuel Meter Assembly – Model 700) – 1) Remove fuel meter-to-throttle body retaining screws. Remove fuel meter assembly. *See Fig. 3.* Discard gasket. If fuel pressure regulator cover is removed, regulator diaphragm must be replaced to prevent fuel leaks.

2) Remove TPS, IAC, pressure regulator assembly, fuel injector, fuel filter, rubber parts, and diaphragms. Clean all remaining (metal) parts in a cold immersion-type cleaner such as Carbon X (X-55). Blow dry with compressed air. Inspect mating surfaces for damage which may prevent gasket sealing. Repair or replace faulty components.

Reassembly (Throttle Body Cover – Model 220) – 1) Install new dust seal into recess of throttle body. Install fuel outlet passage gasket on cover. Install throttle body cover gasket on throttle body. Install cover, making sure pressure regulator dust seal and cover gaskets are in place.

2) Apply thread locking compound to cover attaching screws. Install cover screws and lock washers. Tighten screws. Connect electrical lead to fuel injector, and install air cleaner.

Reassembly (Fuel Meter Assembly – Model 700) – 1) Install new fuel meter-to-throttle body assembly gasket. Match cutout portions of gasket with openings in throttle body assembly.

2) Place fuel meter assembly on throttle body. Install fuel meter-to-throttle body retaining screws and washers (screws should be coated with locking compound). Tighten screws to specification. See

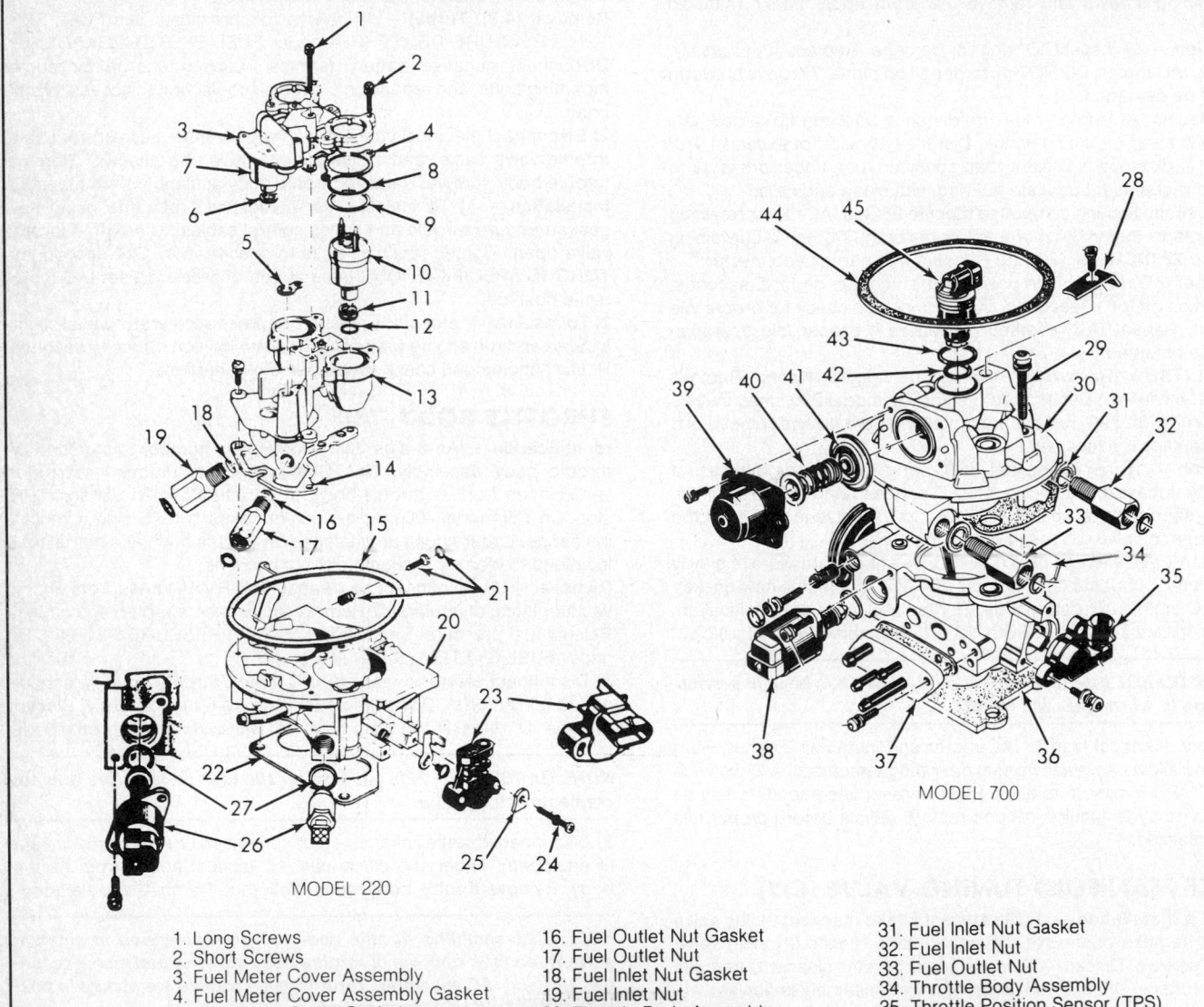

MODEL 220

MODEL 700

1. Long Screws	16. Fuel Outlet Nut Gasket	31. Fuel Inlet Nut Gasket
2. Short Screws	17. Fuel Outlet Nut	32. Fuel Inlet Nut
3. Fuel Meter Cover Assembly	18. Fuel Inlet Nut Gasket	33. Fuel Outlet Nut
4. Fuel Meter Cover Assembly Gasket	19. Fuel Inlet Nut	34. Throttle Body Assembly
5. Fuel Meter Outlet Gasket	20. Throttle Body Assembly	35. Throttle Position Sensor (TPS)
6. Pressure Regulator Dust Seal	21. Idle Stop Screw, Spring & Plug	36. Gasket
7. Pressure Regulator	22. Flange Gasket	37. Tube Assembly
8. "O" Ring–Upper	23. Throttle Position Sensor (TPS)	38. Idle Air Control (IAC) Motor
9. Washer	24. TPS Screw	39. Fuel Pressure Regulator Cover
10. Fuel Injector	25. TPS Screw Retainer	40. Spring
11. Injector Filter	26. Idle Air Control (IAC) Motor	41. Diaphragm
12. "O" Ring–Lower	27. IAC Motor Gasket	42. Lower "O" Ring
13. Fuel Meter Body Assembly	28. Injector Retainer	43. Upper "O" Ring
14. Fuel Meter Body Assembly Gasket	29. Long Screw	44. Gasket
15. Air Filter Gasket	30. Fuel Meter Assembly	45. Fuel Injector

Courtesy of General Motors Corp.

90H15724

Fig. 3: Exploded View Of Throttle Body Assemblies

appropriate TORQUE SPECIFICATIONS table at end of article.

3) Install new "O" rings on fuel lines. Using a back-up wrench on fuel fittings, tighten fuel line nuts to **20 ft. lbs. (27 N.m)**. To complete reassembly, reverse disassembly procedure.

Installation – To install, reverse removal procedure. Ensure throttle body and intake manifold sealing surfaces are clean. Always use new throttle body gasket and fuel line "O" rings. Check fuel system for leaks by turning ignition on, but DO NOT start engine.

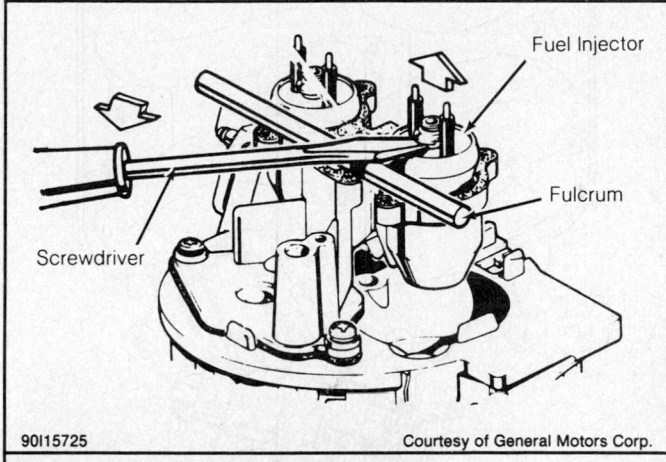

90I15725   Courtesy of General Motors Corp.

Fig. 4: Removing Throttle Body Injector

THROTTLE BODY INJECTOR (TBI)

Removal (Model 220) – **1)** Relieve fuel pressure. See FUEL SYSTEM PRESSURE RELIEF (TBI) under FUEL SYSTEM (GASOLINE).

Remove throttle body cover, leaving cover gasket in place. Using screwdriver and fulcrum, carefully pry injector out. *See Fig. 4.* Remove small "O" ring from nozzle end of injector.

2) Carefully rotate injector fuel filter back and forth to remove fuel filter from base of injector. Remove and discard throttle body cover gasket. Remove large "O" ring and steel back-up washer from top counterbore of throttle body injector cavity.

Installation – **1)** Install fuel filter on nozzle end of fuel injector. Ensure large end of filter faces injector so filter covers raised rib at base of injector. Lubricate small "O" ring with Automatic Transmission Fluid (ATF), and push "O" ring on nozzle end of injector until it presses against injector filter.

2) Install steel back-up washer in top counterbore of throttle body injector cavity. Lubricate large "O" ring with ATF, and install "O" ring directly over back-up washer. Ensure "O" ring is seated properly in cavity, and is flush with top of throttle body casting.

CAUTION: Install back-up washer and large "O" ring before installing injector. Improper seating of "O" ring will cause fuel leak.

---

3) Install "O" ring on injector. Install injector into cavity by aligning raised lug on injector base with cast-in notch of throttle body cavity. Push down on injector until fully seated. Electrical terminals of injector will be approximately parallel with throttle shaft. Install throttle body cover.

Removal (Model 700) – Relieve fuel pressure. See FUEL SYSTEM PRESSURE RELIEF (TBI) under FUEL SYSTEM (GASOLINE). Remove fuel injector retainer screw and retainer. Using screwdriver and fulcrum on side of injector opposite connector terminals, carefully pry injector out. *See Fig. 4.* Remove upper and lower "O" rings and discard.

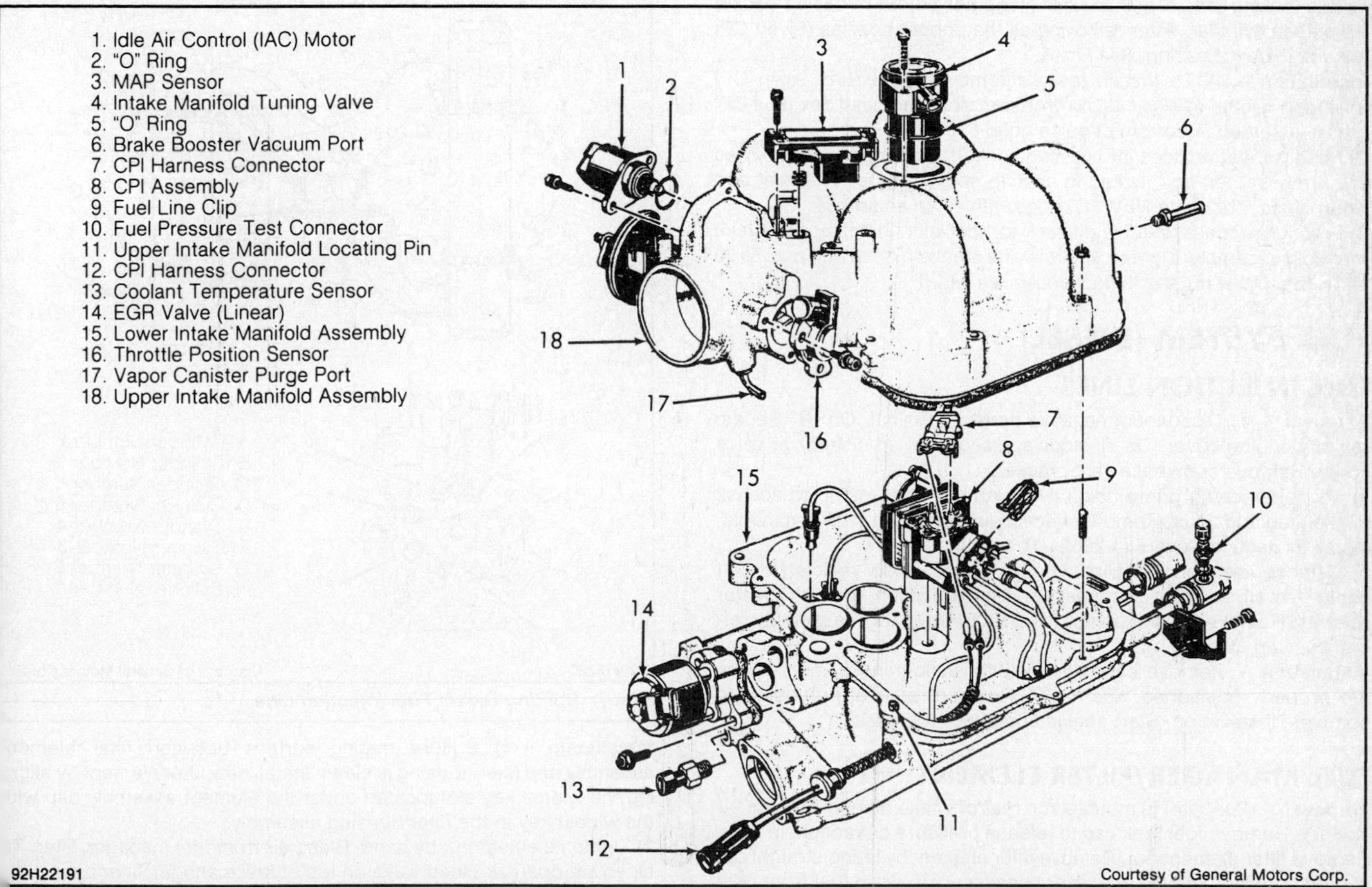

1. Idle Air Control (IAC) Motor
2. "O" Ring
3. MAP Sensor
4. Intake Manifold Tuning Valve
5. "O" Ring
6. Brake Booster Vacuum Port
7. CPI Harness Connector
8. CPI Assembly
9. Fuel Line Clip
10. Fuel Pressure Test Connector
11. Upper Intake Manifold Locating Pin
12. CPI Harness Connector
13. Coolant Temperature Sensor
14. EGR Valve (Linear)
15. Lower Intake Manifold Assembly
16. Throttle Position Sensor
17. Vapor Canister Purge Port
18. Upper Intake Manifold Assembly

92H22191   Courtesy of General Motors Corp.

Fig. 5: Exploded View Of Central Port Injection (CPI) Assembly

Installation – **1)** Lubricate new upper and lower "O" rings with engine oil and place them on injector. Ensure upper ring is in groove and lower ring is flush against filter.

2) Position injector in fuel meter assembly with electrical connector facing cutout for wire grommet.

3) Push injector down to seat in cavity. Install injector retainer. Coat injector retainer screw with thread locking compound and install. Tighten screw to **27 INCH lbs. (3.0 N.m)**.

UPPER INTAKE MANIFOLD & CPI ASSEMBLY

NOTE: Identification number is stamped on base of upper intake manifold or on fuel pressure regulator. Identification number must be used for ordering replacement components.

Removal – **1)** Relieve fuel pressure. See FUEL SYSTEM PRESSURE RELIEF (CPI) under FUEL SYSTEM (GASOLINE). Remove plastic cover on upper intake manifold. Disconnect wiring harness connector to TPS, IAC motor, MAP sensor and intake tuning valve assembly.

2) Disconnect throttle cable, TV linkage and cruise control cable from upper intake manifold. Remove ignition coil, PCV hose and related vacuum hoses. Remove air cleaner snorkel.

3) Mark location of all studs for proper reassembly. Remove upper intake manifold bolts and stud nuts. Remove upper intake manifold assembly. *See Fig. 5.*

NOTE: DO NOT attempt to disassemble CPI assembly. CPI unit is not serviceable and should be replaced as an assembly.

4) Remove wiring harness connector at CPI unit. Remove and discard fuel fitting clip. Disconnect fuel inlet and return lines, and fitting assembly. Discard "O" ring seal.

5) To remove CPI assembly from intake manifold, squeeze poppet nozzle locking tabs together while lifting nozzle out of casing socket from each cylinder. After removing all the poppet nozzles (6), lift CPI assembly out of casing. *See Fig. 5.*

Installation – **1)** To install, reverse removal procedure. Align CPI assembly grommet with casting grommet slots and push down on CPI until it is seated in bottom of guide hole. *See Fig. 5.*

2) Push poppet nozzles into casting sockets. Ensure poppet nozzles are firmly seated and locked in casting socket. Install fuel inlet and return lines. Lubricate NEW "O" rings with clean engine oil.

3) Pressurize fuel system and check for fuel leak. Install upper intake manifold assembly. Tighten upper intake manifold bolts and nuts to **90 INCH lbs. (10 N.m)** and in sequence. *See Fig. 6.*

FUEL SYSTEM (DIESEL)

FUEL INJECTION LINES

Removal – **1)** Disconnect negative battery terminal. On "G" Series, remove engine cover. On all models, disconnect air cleaner at valve cover. Remove crankcase vent bracket.

2) Loosen vacuum pump hold-down clamp. Rotate pump to access intake manifold bolts. Remove injection line clips and intake manifold. Install Protective Covers (J-29664-1) in intake ports.

3) Remove injection line clips. On "G" Series, raise vehicle (for left bank). On all models, disconnect and cap injection lines at injector nozzles. Remove lines at pump. Tag injector lines for reassembly reference. Cap all openings.

Installation – Remove caps and install injection lines. Ensure lines are properly positioned. *See Fig. 7.* Reverse removal procedure to complete installation. Start engine and check for leaks.

FUEL MANAGER/FILTER ELEMENT

Removal – Fuel filter is mounted on rear of intake manifold, under air cleaner. Remove fuel tank cap to release pressure or vacuum in tank. Remove filter element nut. Remove filter element by lifting straight out of filter housing. *See Fig. 8.* It is not necessary to drain fuel from filter housing when changing filter element.

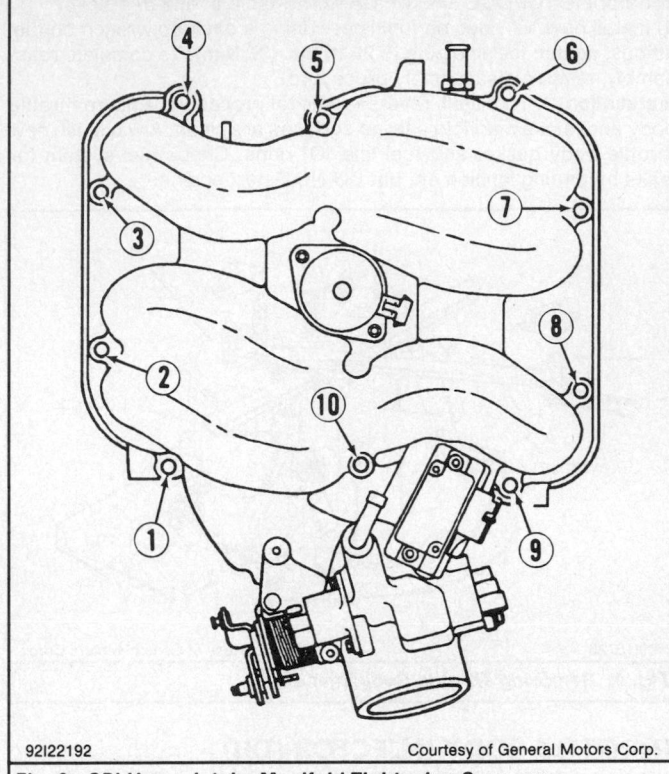

92I22192   Courtesy of General Motors Corp.

Fig. 6: CPI Upper Intake Manifold Tightening Sequence

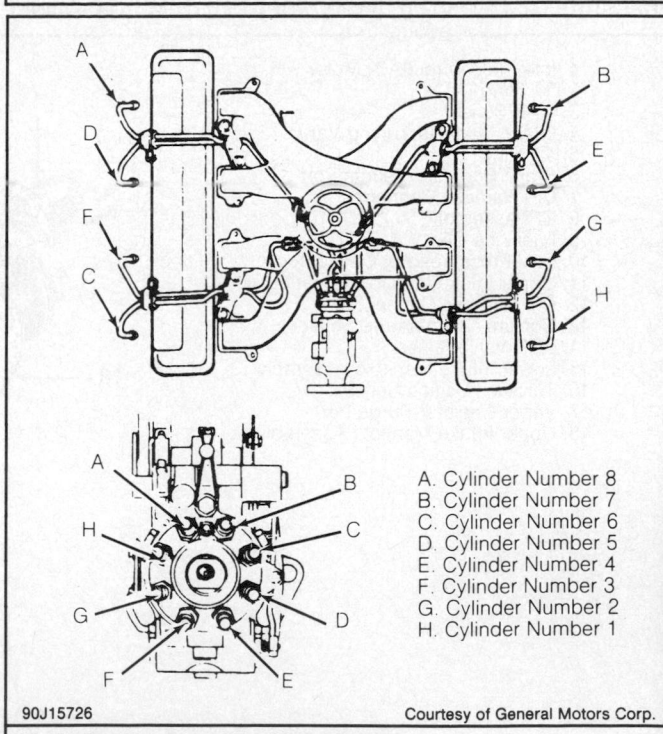

A. Cylinder Number 8
B. Cylinder Number 7
C. Cylinder Number 6
D. Cylinder Number 5
E. Cylinder Number 4
F. Cylinder Number 3
G. Cylinder Number 2
H. Cylinder Number 1

90J15726   Courtesy of General Motors Corp.

Fig. 7: Routing Diesel Fuel Injection Line

Installation – **1)** Ensure mating surface between filter element assembly and filter housing is clean. Install new filter element by aligning the widest key slot located under the element assembly cap with the widest key in the filter housing assembly.

2) Tighten element nut by hand. Bleed air from fuel manager/filter. To bleed air, open air bleed valve on top of fuel manager/filter assembly. Connect a hose to air bleed valve and place other end of hose in a container

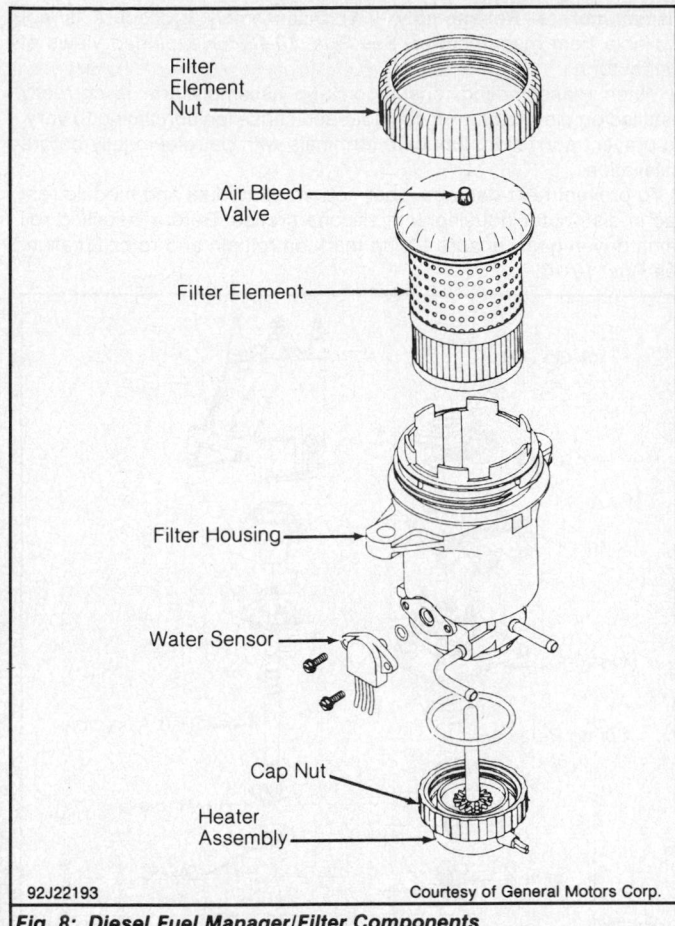

Fig. 8: Diesel Fuel Manager/Filter Components

92J22193   Courtesy of General Motors Corp.

3) Disconnect fuel injection pump shut-down solenoid wire. Crank engine for 10-15 seconds. Allow starter to cool down for one minute between cranking intervals. Repeat procedure until clear fuel is observed at the air bleed hose.

4) Close air bleed. Connect injection pump shut-down solenoid wire and reinstall fuel filler cap. Start engine and allow to idle for 5 minutes. Check fuel manager/filter for leaks.

FUEL PUMP

Removal & Installation – 1) Disconnect negative battery terminal. Disconnect electrical wiring from fuel pump and fuel pump support bracket.

2) Disconnect fuel lines from fuel pump. Remove support bracket screws and remove support bracket from fuel lines. Remove fuel pump and bracket from frame rail.

3) To install, reverse removal procedure. Check for fuel leak at fuel line fittings.

INJECTION PUMP

Removal ("C", "K" & "P" Series) – 1) Disconnect battery negative terminal. Remove intake manifold assembly. Install Protective Covers (J-29664-1) in intake ports. Remove fuel injection lines. Disconnect throttle cable and detent cable (if equipped). Disconnect wiring, fuel return line, fuel supply line, and fuel injection lines at pump. Cap all openings.

2) Remove A/C hose retainer bracket (if equipped). Remove oil filler tube and vent hose assembly. Remove grommet. Scribe or paint alignment mark on front cover and injection pump flange.

3) Rotate engine to remove injection pump-to-drive gear retaining bolts accessible through oil filler neck hole. Remove injection pump mount nuts. Remove injection pump and gasket. See Fig. 9.

Installation – 1) Install new injection pump gasket. Align locating pin on injection pump hub with slot in injection pump driven gear. At the same time, align injection pump timing marks. Cylinder No. 1 must be set at TDC.

2) Attach injection pump to front cover. Alignment marks made during removal must be aligned. Tighten nuts. Attach pump to drive gear and tighten bolts. Reverse removal procedure to complete installation. Check injection pump timing. See INJECTION PUMP TIMING (DIESEL) in ON-VEHICLE ADJUSTMENTS article.

Removal ("G" Series) – 1) Disconnect negative battery terminals. Remove engine cover and intake manifold. Rotate snorkel up, and remove air cleaner inlet hose. Remove hood latch. Disconnect cable and move aside.

2) Remove windshield washer bottle, fan shroud bolts, and upper fan shroud. Disconnect rubber hose from oil fill tube. Disconnect oil fill tube attaching nuts, and remove oil fill tube. Remove oil fill tube grommet.

3) Rotate engine as necessary and remove pump drive gear bolts. Remove fuel filter and bracket, including line to injection pump. Disconnect wire looms from injection lines, and injection lines at brackets.

4) Disconnect oil pan dipstick tube from left cylinder head. Disconnect electrical connections at injection pump. Disconnect detent cable (if equipped). Disconnect accelerator cable.

5) Remove injection lines. Tag lines for reassembly reference. Cap all openings. Disconnect fuel return line. Scribe or paint mark on front

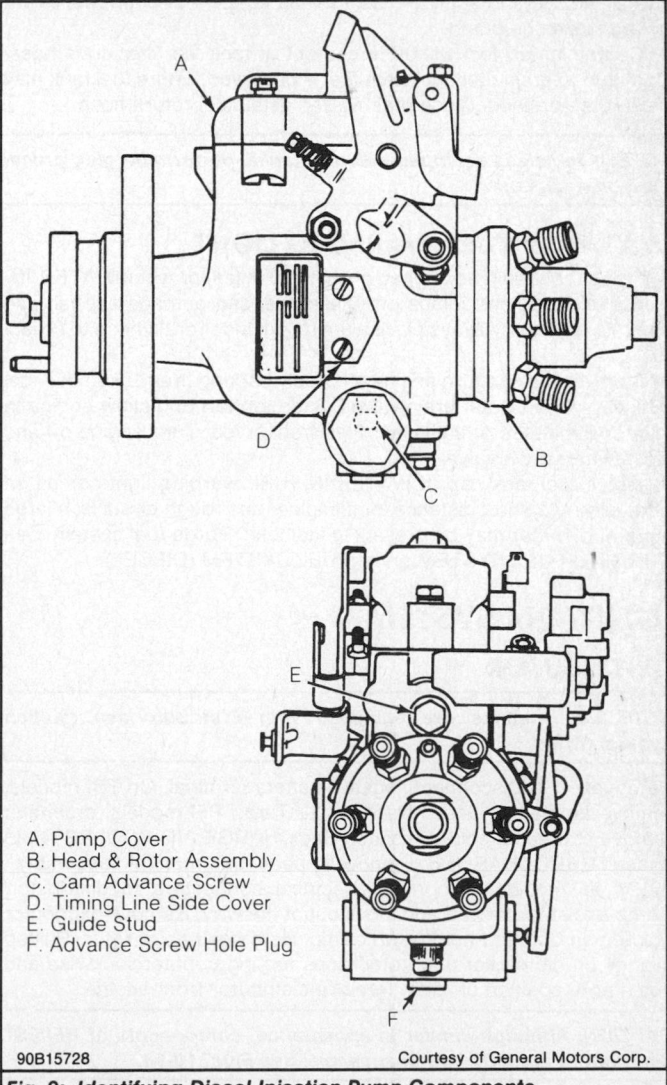

A. Pump Cover
B. Head & Rotor Assembly
C. Cam Advance Screw
D. Timing Line Side Cover
E. Guide Stud
F. Advance Screw Hole Plug

90B15728   Courtesy of General Motors Corp.

Fig. 9: Identifying Diesel Injection Pump Components

cover and pump flange. Remove injection pump mount nuts. Remove injection pump. *See Fig. 9.* Cap all openings.

Installation – 1) Install new injection pump gasket. Align locating pin on injection pump hub with slot in injection pump driven gear while aligning injection pump timing marks.

2) Attach injection pump to front cover. Alignment marks made during removal must be aligned. Tighten nuts. Attach pump to drive gear and tighten bolts. Reverse removal procedure to complete installation. Check injection pump timing. See INJECTION PUMP TIMING (DIESEL) in ON-VEHICLE ADJUSTMENTS article.

INJECTOR NOZZLES

Removal – Disconnect negative battery terminals. Disconnect fuel line clip. Remove fuel return line. Remove fuel injection line. Cap all openings. Using Injector Socket (J-29873), remove injector nozzles(s). Place socket on 1 3/16" (30 mm) hex flats of injector body to prevent damaging injector nozzle.

Installation – Remove caps from injector nozzles and fuel lines. Install injector nozzles(s). Install fuel line. Install fuel return line and fuel line clip. Connect battery terminals. Start engine and check for leaks.

PURGING FUEL SYSTEM

1) Park vehicle on a level surface. Place drain pan under drain hose to collect fuel. Open drain valve 3-4 turns. With fuel tank cap installed, use air nozzle and apply 3-5 psi (.21-.35 kg/cm²) through fuel return hose at injection pump.

2) Contaminated fuel will be forced out of tank via filter drain hose. Continue to drain fuel until clear fuel is observed. Entire fuel tank may have to be drained. Close drain valve. Install fuel return hose.

NOTE: If vehicle is equipped with dual tanks, perform purging procedure on each tank.

WATER-IN-FUEL WARNING LIGHT

1) Fuel filter should be drained every 5000 miles, or when WATER-IN-FUEL warning light comes on. Diesel fuel can damage asphalt and painted surfaces. Always place a drain pan under drain hose to collect fuel.

2) Stop vehicle and turn engine off. Apply parking brake. Remove fuel tank cap. Open water drain valve 2-3 turns. Start and allow engine to idle for 2 minutes or until clear fuel is observed. Turn engine off and close water drain valve.

3) Install fuel tank cap. If WATER-IN-FUEL warning light comes on after driving a short distance, or if engine runs rough or stalls, a large amount of water may be present in fuel tank. Purge fuel system. See PURGING FUEL SYSTEM under FUEL SYSTEM (DIESEL).

IGNITION SYSTEM

DISTRIBUTOR

NOTE: 3.8L engines are equipped with Distributorless Ignition System (DIS).

Removal – 1) Disconnect negative battery terminal. On TBI models, remove air cleaner assembly. On 4.3L Turbo PFI models, drain and remove charge air cooler radiator. See CHARGE AIR COOLER (4.3L) under TURBOCHARGER. Remove upper intake manifold assembly.

2) On all models, disconnect electrical connectors to distributor. Remove distributor cap and move out of the way. Remove distributor hold-down bolt and hold-down clamp. Note position of rotor. Pull up slightly on distributor until rotor stops turning counterclockwise and again note position of rotor. Remove distributor from engine.

CAUTION: Although similar in appearance, components of HEI/EST distributors are NOT interchangeable. See Figs. 10-13.

Disassembly & Reassembly – 1) Disassembly procedure is not available from manufacturer. *See Figs. 10-13* for exploded views of distributors.

2) When reassembling, ensure pick-up assembly arm is correctly installed on pin. If not, arm can float and cause ignition timing to vary. To prevent corrosion, lubricate terminals with petroleum jelly before installation.

3) To prevent heat damage, coat bottom of module and module rest pad in distributor housing with silicone grease. Before installing roll pin in driven gear, ensure timing mark on roll pin and rotor tip align. *See Figs. 10-13.*

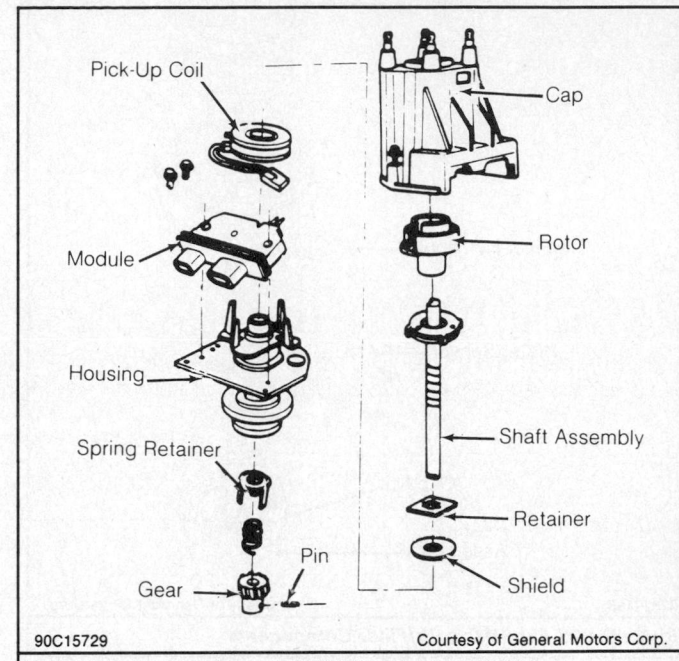

90C15729   Courtesy of General Motors Corp.

Fig. 10: Exploded View of HEI-EST Distributor (2.5L)

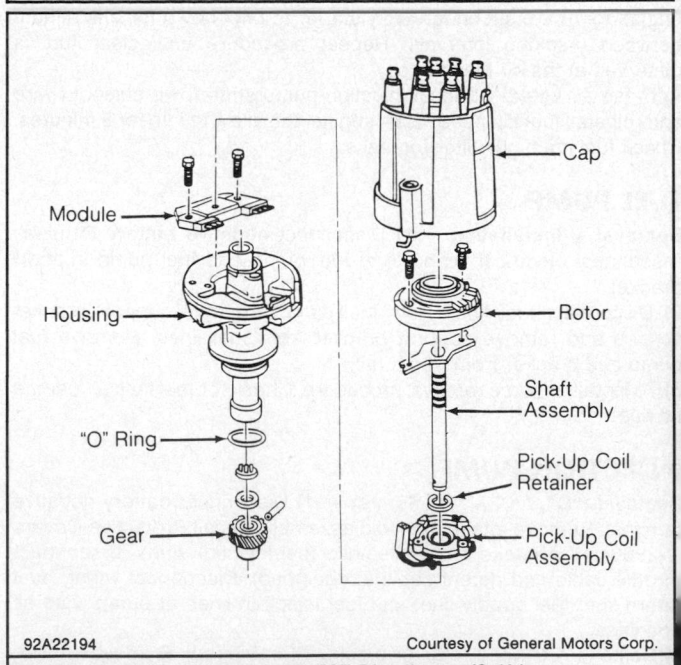

92A22194   Courtesy of General Motors Corp.

Fig. 11: Exploded View of HEI-EST Distributor (3.1L)

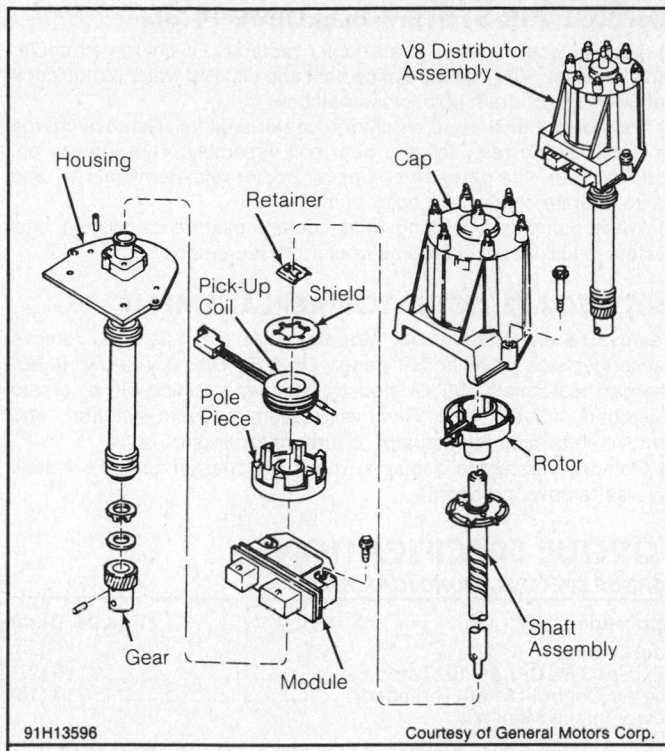

91H13596   Courtesy of General Motors Corp.

Fig. 12: Exploded View of HEI-EST Distributor (4.3L & V8)

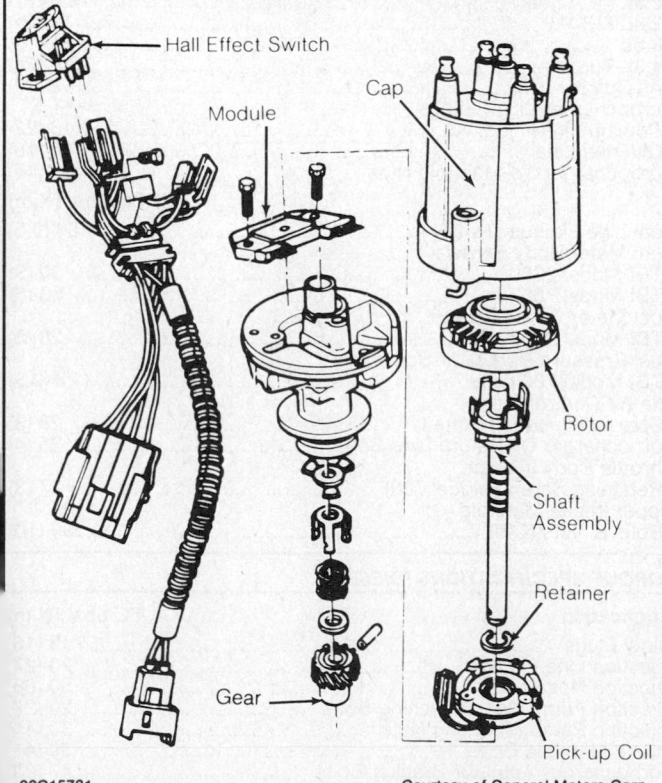

90G15731   Courtesy of General Motors Corp.

Fig. 13: Exploded View of HEI/EST Distributor with Hall Effect

Installation – 1) To install, reverse removal procedure. To insure correct timing of distributor, it must be installed with the rotor correctly positioned before distributor was removed.

2) If engine was cranked after distributor was removed, remove No. 1 spark plug. Place finger over No. 1 cylinder spark plug hole. Crank

engine slowly until compression is felt. Align timing mark on pulley to "0" on engine timing indicator. Turn rotor to point to cylinder No. 1 spark plug tower on distributor cap. Complete distributor installation. Start engine and check ignition timing.

THROTTLE POSITION SENSOR (TPS)

Removal & Installation (Except Diesel) – 1) Remove air cleaner assembly. Disconnect electrical lead from TPS. Remove attaching screws, lock washers, retainers, and TPS.

2) To install, reverse removal procedure. Adjust TPS to specification. See ON-VEHICLE ADJUSTMENTS article. When replacing a TPS, ensure correct part number is used. Use Loctite on TPS attaching screws.

Removal & Installation (Diesel) – 1) Remove air cleaner assembly and related hoses. Disconnect TPS connector. Remove 2 screws and throttle position sensor from injection pump. See Fig. 14.

2) To install, reverse removal procedure. Lightly tighten screws and adjust TPS. See ON-VEHICLE ADJUSTMENTS article.

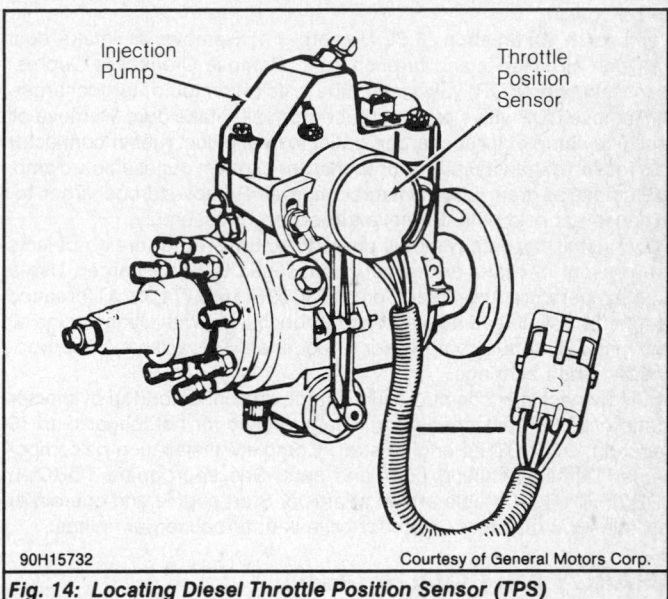

90H15732   Courtesy of General Motors Corp.

Fig. 14: Locating Diesel Throttle Position Sensor (TPS)

OXYGEN (O₂) SENSOR

CAUTION: O₂ sensor is equipped with a permanent pigtail, which must be protected to prevent damage when removing sensor.

Removal – 1) O₂ sensor is mounted in the exhaust pipe, below exhaust manifold. Ensure sensor is free of contaminants. DO NOT use cleaning solvents of any type. Sensor may be difficult to remove when engine temperature is less than 120°F (48°C). Excessive removal force may damage threads in exhaust manifold or pipe.

2) Disconnect negative battery terminal. Disconnect electrical connector from O₂ sensor. Carefully remove O₂ sensor from exhaust pipe.

CAUTION: Correct torque of O₂ sensor is critical to prevent crushing glass beads in graphite anti-seize compound. Crushing glass beads will cause sensor to seize in exhaust manifold. This may require replacement of exhaust manifold upon next removal.

Installation – 1) Whenever O₂ sensor is removed, coat threads with anti-seize compound before reinstalling. New O₂ sensors already have this compound applied to threads.

2) Install O₂ sensor in exhaust pipe and tighten sensor to **30 ft. lbs. (41 N.m)**. Reconnect electrical connector to O₂ sensor. Reconnect negative battery terminal.

TURBOCHARGER

NOTE: Turbocharger overhaul information is not available from man-ufacturer.

TURBOCHARGER REPLACEMENT

Removal & Installation (4.3L PFI) – 1) Drain coolant from radiator. Remove intake air duct and turbocharger air intake duct. Remove battery, battery tray, and vacuum reservoir tank.

2) Disconnect turbocharger oil feed line and electrical connector at solenoid. Remove turbocharger coolant return line assembly.

3) Raise and support vehicle. Remove wheel assembly. Remove right-hand wheelhouse panel. Remove turbocharger outlet pipe. Remove turbocharger oil return pipe, mounting nuts and coolant feed line assembly. Remove turbocharger assembly.

4) To install, reverse removal procedure. Ensure bolts and nuts are installed in same location from which they were removed. Tighten to specification. See appropriate TORQUE SPECIFICATIONS table at end of article.

Removal & Installation (6.5L Diesel) – 1) Remove air intake duct between air cleaner and turbocharger. Remove Crankcase Depression Regulator (CDR) valve vent tube bracket on top of turbocharger.

2) Remove CDR valve and vent tube from air intake duct. Remove oil feed line at top of turbocharger, outlet to intake duct rubber connector and loosen exhaust pipe-to-turbocharger exhaust outlet elbow clamp.

3) Remove oil drain tube from turbocharger. Remove turbocharger-to-exhaust manifold nuts. Remove turbocharger assembly.

4) To install, reverse removal procedure. Ensure no foreign objects are present in intake and exhaust passages to turbocharger. Use a high temperature Anti-Seize Compound (GM 1052771) on all threaded fasteners. Fill oil feed hole at top of turbocharger with clean engine oil and manually rotate compressor wheel/shaft. This will pre-lube turbocharger shaft bearings.

5) Disconnect injection pump fuel shutdown connector (top of injector pump or at harness connector). Crank engine for not longer than 15 seconds. DO NOT let engine start. Complete installation of components. Tighten retaining bolts and nuts. See appropriate TORQUE SPECIFICATIONS table at end of article. Start engine and operate at low idle for 3 minutes. Check for oil leak at turbocharger fittings.

CHARGE AIR COOLER (4.3L)

Removal & Installation – 1) Drain charge air cooler radiator. Remove hoses from charge air cooler. Remove charge air cooler assembly.

2) To install, reverse removal procedure. Fill charge air cooler radiator through the charge air cooler with a 56/44 mixture of coolant and distilled water. Bleed charge air cooling system. See CHARGE AIR SYSTEM BLEEDING (4.3L).

CHARGE AIR COOLER PUMP (4.3L)

Removal & Installation – 1) Drain charge air cooler radiator. Remove charge air cooler radiator. See CHARGE AIR COOLER RADIATOR (4.3L)

2) Remove charge air cooler pump mounting bolts, coolant hoses, and charge air cooler radiator bracket. Remove charge air cooler pump assembly.

3) To install, reverse removal procedure. Refill charge air system with 56/44 mixture of coolant and distilled water. Bleed charge air system. See CHARGE AIR SYSTEM BLEEDING (4.3L).

CHARGE AIR COOLER RADIATOR (4.3L)

Removal & Installation – 1) Drain charge air cooler radiator. Raise and support vehicle. Remove air deflector shield from front of vehicle. Disconnect electrical connectors.

2) Remove clamps and hoses from charge air cooler radiator and charge air cooler pump. Remove charge air cooler radiator.

3) To install, reverse removal procedure. Fill charge air cooler radiator with a 56/44 mixture of coolant and distilled water. Bleed charge air cooling system. See CHARGE AIR SYSTEM BLEEDING (4.3L).

CHARGE AIR SYSTEM BLEEDING (4.3L)

1) Open petcock on charge air cooler radiator. Fill charge air cooler radiator with a 56/44 mixture of coolant and distilled water. When coolant flows out of drain hole, close petcock.

2) Add coolant mixture to air charge cooler until full. Remove charge air cooler pump relay located near coil assembly. Turn ignition on. Install jumper wire between charge air cooler relay terminals "A" and "B" to operate charge air cooler pump.

3) While pump is operating, add coolant mixture to system until system is full. Install charge air cooler pressure cap.

WASTEGATE ACTUATOR REPLACEMENT

Removal & Installation (All Models) – 1) On 4.3L PFI, remove passenger side wheelhouse panel. On 6.5L Diesel, remove turbocharger heat shield. On all models, remove retaining pin or clip to wastegate actuator rod. Remove vacuum hose to actuator, and remove bolts securing actuator to turbocharger unit.

2) Remove wastegate actuator from turbocharger unit. To install, reverse removal procedure.

TORQUE SPECIFICATIONS
TORQUE SPECIFICATIONS (GASOLINE)

Application	Ft. Lbs. (N.m)
Fuel Line Nut	
Except 3.8L CPI & 4.3L Turbo	20 (27)
Idle Air Control Motor (Threaded)	13 (18)
Lower Intake Manifold	
Bolts (Turbo)	35 (47)
Oxygen Sensor	30 (41)
Throttle Body-To-Manifold Bolts	
2.5L	12.5 (17)
2.8L & 3.1L	18 (24)
3.8L	11 (15)
4.3L Turbo	18 (24)
All Others	12 (16)
Turbocharger Line Fittings	
Coolant Lines	16 (22)
Oil Feed Line	13 (18)
Turbocharger-To-Manifold Nuts	33 (45)
	INCH Lbs. (N.m)
Fuel Line Fittings (Turbo)	58 (6.5)
Fuel Meter Body Screws	
TBI Model 220	30 (3)
TBI Model 700	53 (6)
Fuel Meter Cover Screws	
TBI Model 220 Only	28 (3)
Fuel Pressure Regulator Screws	
TBI Model 700 Only	22 (2.5)
Idle Air Control Valve	
Screws (Flange Mounted)	28 (3)
Turbocharger Oil Return Line Bolt	35 (4)
Throttle Body Injector	
Retaining Screw (Model 700)	27 (3)
Upper Intake Manifold	
Bolts & Nuts (CPI)	90 (10)

TORQUE SPECIFICATIONS (DIESEL)

Application	Ft. Lbs. (N.m)
Glow Plugs	13 (18)
Injection Line Fittings	20 (27)
Injection Nozzles	50 (68)
Injection Pump Gear Attaching Bolts	20 (27)
Injection Pump Mounting Nuts	30 (41)
Intake Manifold Bolts	30 (41)
Turbocharger Actuator Bracket Bolts	47 (23)
Turbocharger-To-Exhaust	
Manifold Nuts	37 (50)
Turbocharger Oil Feed Line Fitting	13 (18)
	INCH Lbs. (N.m)
Advance Pin Hole Plug	90 (10)
Head Locating Screw	17 (23)
Injection Pump Cover Screws	33 (3.7)
Injection Pump Guide Stud	85 (9.5)
Side Cover Screws	18 (2)
Solenoid Terminal Nuts	12 (1.2)

Astro, Bravada, Commercial Van, Jimmy, Lumina APV, Safari, Sierra, Silhouette, Sonoma, Suburban, Syclone, Trans Sport, Typhoon, Van, Yukon, "C" & "K" Series Blazer & Pickup, "S" & "T" Series Blazer & Pickup

DESCRIPTION

The CS130 and CS144 (Charging System) alternators have a high amperage output. The 130 or 144 designation is the outside diameter of the stator laminations, measured in millimeters. This alternator series also has an integral regulator but does not have a diode trio. *See Fig. 1.* The delta wound stator, rectifier bridge, rotor with slip rings, and brushes are similar to other alternators. A conventional fan and pulley are used. An internal fan cools the slip rings, end frame, rectifier bridge and regulator.

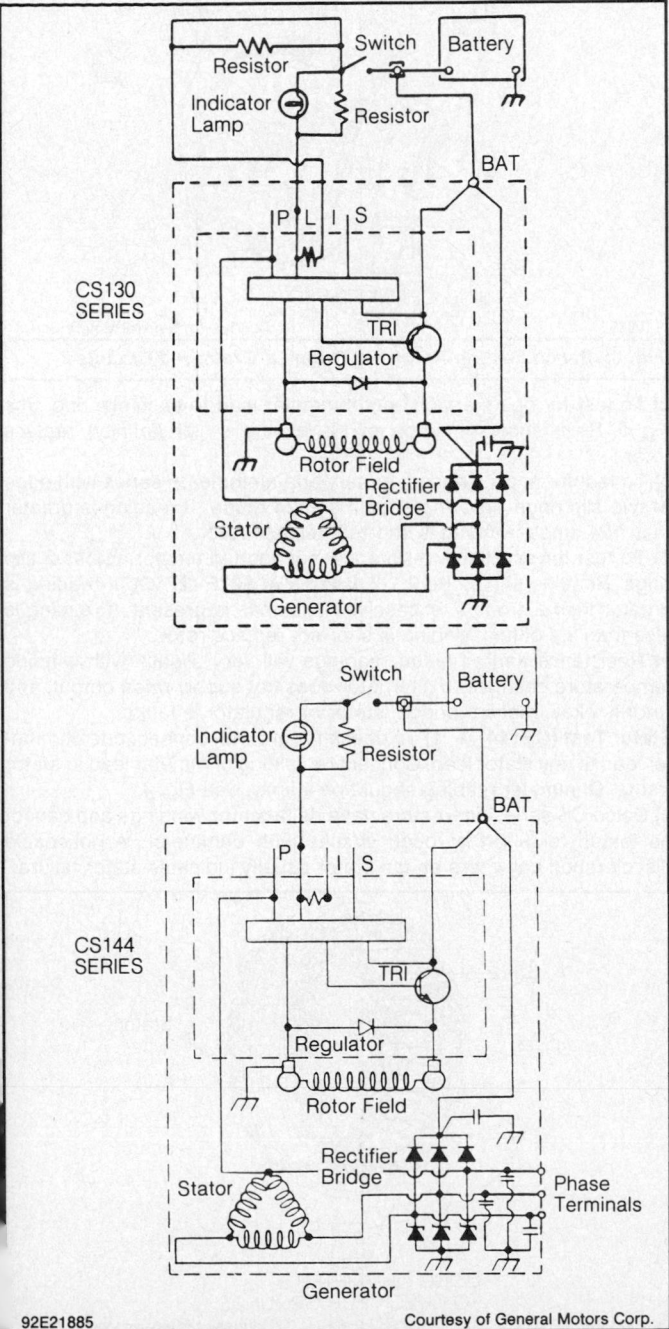

Fig. 1: Charging System Wiring Schematic

92E21885   Courtesy of General Motors Corp.

The CS130 alternator should not be disassembled for any reason. The alternator requires no periodic maintenance or adjustment and is serviceable only by complete replacement. The CS144, however, is serviceable. For model application, see ALTERNATOR IDENTIFICATION & OUTPUT table.

ALTERNATOR IDENTIFICATION & OUTPUT

Application	Alternator Part No.	Rated Output Amps
Astro & Safari		
CS130	1101616	85
CS130	1101617	100
CS130	1101637	105
Bravada		
CS130	10479802	100
Commercial Van		
CS130	1101571	105
CS130	1101806	105
CS130	1101807	105
CS130	1101815	85
CS130	1102629	85
CS130	1102631	105
CS144	1102635	124
CS130	10479883	105
CS144	10479884	124
Jimmy, Sonoma, Syclone, Typhoon & "S" & "T" Series Blazer & Pickup		
CS130	1101618	96
CS130	1101259	85
CS130	10479801	85
Lumina APV, Silhouette & Trans Sport		
CS144	10479891	140
CS130	10479895	105
CS130	10479905	100
Sierra, Suburban, Yukon & "C" & "K" Series Blazer & Pickup		
CS130	1101621	100
CS130	1101628	85
CS130	1101629	100
CS130	1101630	85
CS130	1101632	85
CS130	1101633	100
Van		
CS130	1101616	85
CS130	1101617	100
CS130	1101637	105
CS130	1102630	85

OPERATION

Regulator voltage varies to compensate for temperature. Voltage is regulated by controlling rotor field current. The regulator switches rotor field current on and off at a fixed frequency of approximately 400 cycles per second.

The regulator has 4 terminals: "P", "L", "I" and "S". *See Fig. 2.* The "L" terminal and/or the "I" terminal is used to turn on regulator and allows field current to flow when ignition switch is turned to START or RUN position. The "L" terminal is connected through a charging indicator light or resistor. The "I" terminal is connected to positive battery terminal either directly or through a resistor. These terminals are often used in parallel and are connected to 2 different vehicle circuits.

The "P" terminal is connected internally to the stator and may be wired to a tachometer or other device. The "S" terminal may be used to sense voltage at another vehicle location for voltage control. If "S" terminal is not used, alternator uses an internal sensor for voltage control.

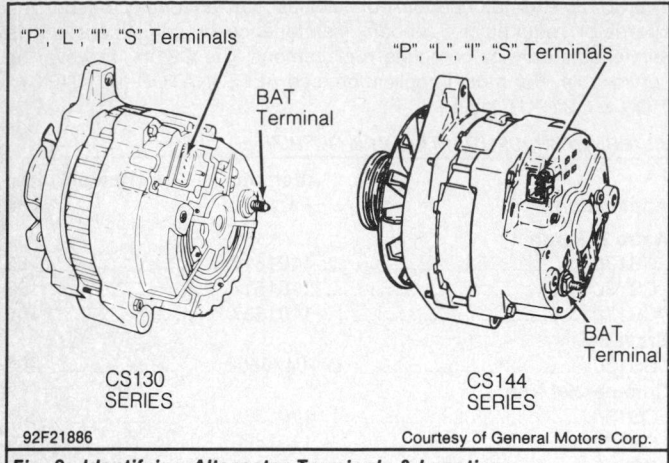

"P", "L", "I", "S" Terminals

BAT Terminal

"P", "L", "I", "S" Terminals

BAT Terminal

CS130 SERIES

CS144 SERIES

92F21886   Courtesy of General Motors Corp.

Fig. 2: Identifying Alternator Terminals & Locations

ADJUSTMENTS

BELT TENSION

BELT ADJUSTMENT

Application	Tension Lbs. (kg)
Commercial Van	
4.3L, 5.7L & 7.4L	
New Belt	135 (61.2)
Used Belt [2]	90 (40.8)
6.2L Diesel	
New Belt	146 (66.2)
Used Belt [2]	67 (30.4)
Except Commercial Van & Van	
2.5L, 2.8L, 3.1L, 3.8L, 4.3L, 5.0L,	
5.7L, 6.2L Diesel, 6.5L Diesel & 7.4L	[1]
Van	
4.3L, 5.0L, 5.7L & 7.4L	[1]
6.2L Diesel	
New Belt	146 (66.2)
Used Belt [2]	67 (30.4)

[1] – Serpentine single belt tension is maintained automatically by a spring tension idler pulley. No adjustment is necessary.

[2] – A used belt is one that has rotated one or more revolutions.

TROUBLE SHOOTING

NOTE: See TROUBLE SHOOTING article in GENERAL INFORMATION.

ON-VEHICLE TESTING

NOTE: Before making electrical checks, visually inspect all terminals for clean, tight connections. Check alternator mounting bolts and drive belt tension. Ensure battery is in good condition prior to testing charging system.

Overcharged Or Undercharged Battery – 1) If an overcharging condition is suspected, run engine at moderate speed. Connect voltmeter across battery terminals. If voltmeter indicates more than 16 volts, replace alternator.

2) If an undercharging condition is suspected, disconnect 4-wire connector from alternator. Turn ignition on with engine off. Connect a voltmeter between terminal "L" in wiring harness and ground. See Fig. 2. Record reading.

3) If terminal "I" is used, connect voltmeter between terminal "I" and ground. Record reading. If voltmeter reads battery voltage, circuits are okay. If voltmeter reads zero, this indicates an open circuit between terminal checked and battery. Repair as necessary.

Alternator Output Test – 1) Connect an ammeter in series with wire connected to BAT terminal of alternator. See Fig. 2. Turn on all available accessories. Connect a carbon pile across battery. Operate engine at 2000 RPM. Adjust carbon pile (as required) to obtain maximum current output while maintaining 13 volts or more.

2) Ampere output must be within 15 amps of rated output. If output is not within 15 amps of rated output, replace alternator. See ALTERNATOR IDENTIFICATION & OUTPUT table.

BENCH TESTING

NOTE: Internal components of CS130 alternator are not serviceable. Alternator replacement is required.

Rotor Field Winding Test (CS144) – 1) To check for ground, attach one ohmmeter lead to shaft and other lead to either slip ring. See Fig. 3. If reading is not infinity, replace rotor.

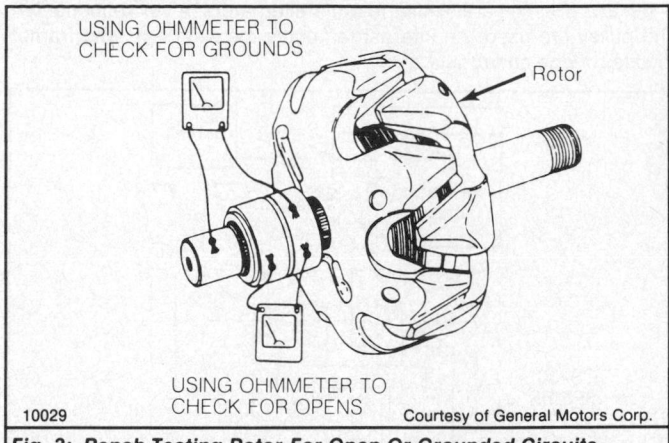

USING OHMMETER TO CHECK FOR GROUNDS

Rotor

USING OHMMETER TO CHECK FOR OPENS

10029   Courtesy of General Motors Corp.

Fig. 3: Bench Testing Rotor For Open Or Grounded Circuits

2) To test for open, attach one ohmmeter lead to each slip ring. See Fig. 3. Resistance should be low. If reading is high (infinity), replace rotor.

3) To test for short, connect battery and ammeter in series with edge of two slip rings. Reading should be **124 amps**. If reading is greater than 124 amps, winding is shorted, replace rotor.

4) To test for excessive resistance, connect ohmmeter across 2 slip rings. Reading should be **2.1-2.4 ohms at 80°F (27°C)**. If reading is greater than 2.4 ohms, excessive resistance is present. If reading is less than 2.1 ohms, winding is shorted, replace rotor.

5) Resistance and ammeter readings will vary slightly with winding temperature changes. If alternator does not supply rated output, and rotor is okay, rectifier bridge, stator or regulator is faulty.

Stator Test (CS144) – 1) To check for ground, connect one ohmmeter lead to any stator lead. Connect remaining ohmmeter lead to stator frame. Ohmmeter reading should be infinity. See Fig. 4.

2) Delco CS series alternators have delta stator windings and cannot be tested for short or open circuits with ohmmeter. A noticeable discoloration anywhere on the stator usually indicates stator failure.

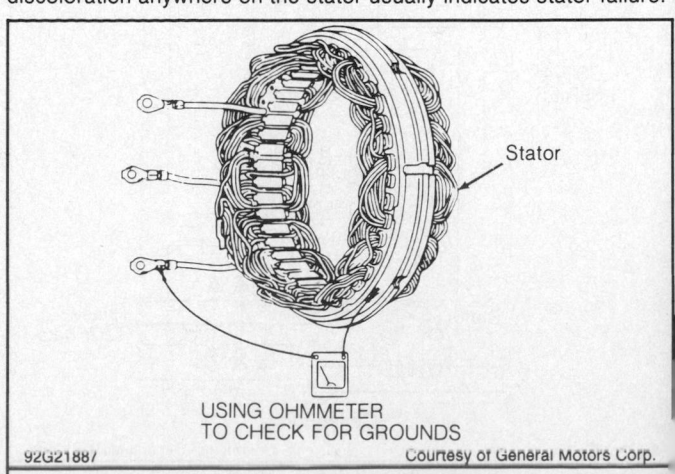

Stator

USING OHMMETER TO CHECK FOR GROUNDS

92G21887   Courtesy of General Motors Corp.

Fig. 4: Bench Testing Stator For Grounded Circuits

NOTE: *Some digital ohmmeters cannot be used to check diodes in rectifier bridge. Consult ohmmeter manufacturer to determine ohmmeter capabilities.*

Rectifier Bridge Test (CS144) – 1) Position ohmmeter with one lead touching grounded heat sink and other lead pressed firmly against flat metal clip on one of 3 terminals. Observe reading, and reverse test lead connections. *See Fig. 5.*

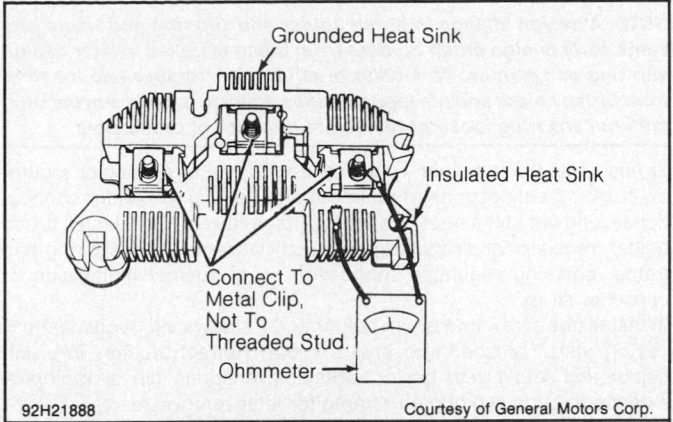

Fig. 5: **Bench Testing Rectifier Bridge**

2) If readings are same, replace rectifier bridge. A good bridge will give a high and low reading. Repeat tests for remaining terminals. There should be 6 tests altogether (2 tests at each terminal).

3) Connect test leads to insulated heat sink and one of the 3 terminals. *See Fig. 5.* Observe reading and reverse connections. Repeat tests for remaining terminals. There should be a total of 6 tests (2 at each terminal).

4) Testing is complete when all 12 tests have been made. If any terminals have same readings for both connections (leads reversed), replace rectifier bridge.

Regulator Test (CS144) – Regulator cannot be tested for short, open or grounded circuits. If rotor, stator and rectifier bridge are okay and alternator continues to produce greater than 16 volts or does not produce within 15 amps of rated output during alternator output test, replace regulator. See ALTERNATOR IDENTIFICATION & OUTPUT table.

REMOVAL & INSTALLATION

WARNING: *When battery is disconnected, vehicle computer and memory systems may lose memory data. Driveability problems may exist until computer systems have completed a relearn cycle. See COMPUTER RELEARN PROCEDURES article in GENERAL INFORMATION before disconnecting battery.*

Disconnect negative battery cable. Remove drive belt. Remove nut retaining positive battery terminal. Disconnect alternator electrical connector. Remove mounting bolts, nuts, braces and brackets. Remove other components as necessary. Remove alternator. To install, reverse removal procedure.

OVERHAUL

NOTE: *CS130 is not serviceable. Replacement is required.*

Disassembly (CS144) – 1) Clamp mounting flange of alternator in vise. Mark slip ring end frame and drive end frame for reassembly reference. *See Fig. 6.* Remove 4 through bolts. Separate rotor and drive end frame assembly from slip ring end frame.

2) Secure, but DO NOT overtighten, rotor and drive end frame assembly in vise. Remove pulley nut and washer from rotor shaft. Remove pulley, fan collar, fan and outside collar from rotor shaft. Remove drive end frame and inside collar from rotor shaft. Remove three screws and retainer from drive end frame.

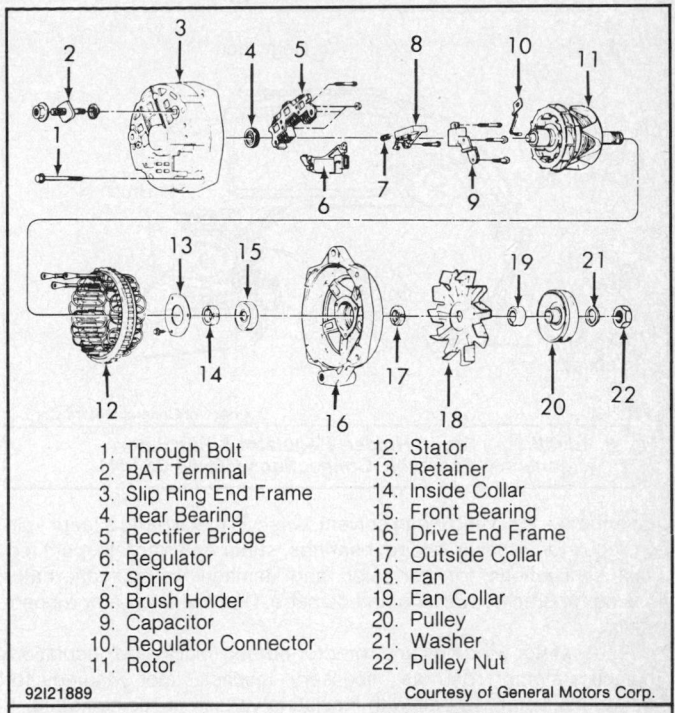

1. Through Bolt	12. Stator
2. BAT Terminal	13. Retainer
3. Slip Ring End Frame	14. Inside Collar
4. Rear Bearing	15. Front Bearing
5. Rectifier Bridge	16. Drive End Frame
6. Regulator	17. Outside Collar
7. Spring	18. Fan
8. Brush Holder	19. Fan Collar
9. Capacitor	20. Pulley
10. Regulator Connector	21. Washer
11. Rotor	22. Pulley Nut

Fig. 6: **Exploded View Of Alternator (Model CS144)**

3) Press front bearing from drive end frame. Using Bearing Remover (J-28509-A), remove rear bearing from rotor shaft. *See Fig. 7.* Remove 3 stator lead nuts and remove stator. Remove one screw from brush holder and 2 screws from regulator connector. Remove brush holder, regulator and regulator connector as an assembly from slip ring end frame.

NOTE: *If brush holder, regulator or regulator connector is faulty, components must be unsoldered from each other using as little heat as possible to prevent damage to regulator. See Fig. 8.*

4) Remove BAT terminal nut from insulated heat sink. Remove 2 screws and washers from grounded heat sink. Remove capacitor and rectifier bridge from slip ring end frame. Remove BAT terminal from outside of slip ring end frame.

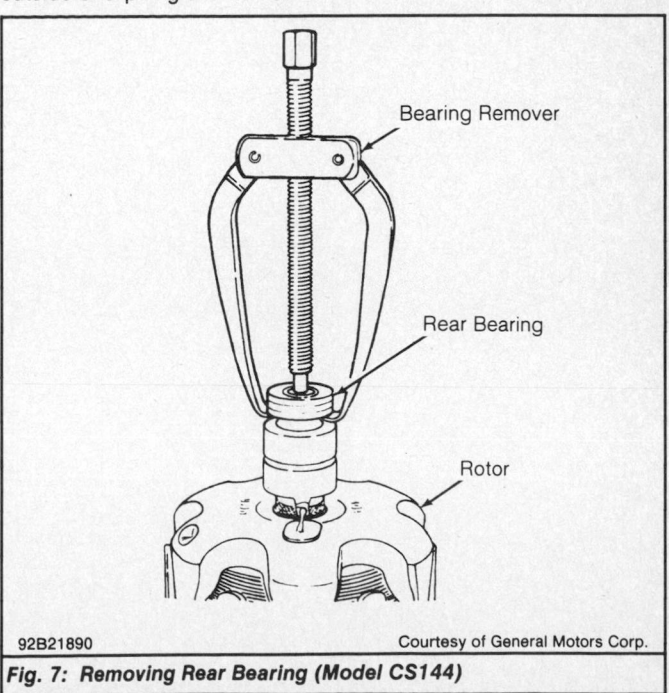

Fig. 7: **Removing Rear Bearing (Model CS144)**

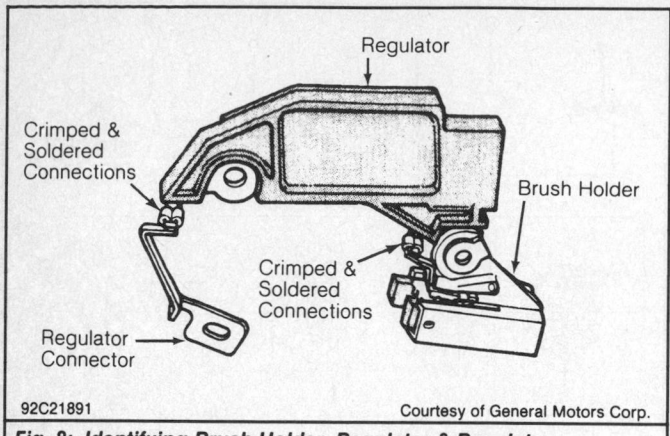

92C21891   Courtesy of General Motors Corp.

Fig. 8: Identifying Brush Holder, Regulator & Regulator Connector Assembly Connections (Model CS144)

Inspection – 1) Using clean solvent, wash all metal parts except voltage regulator, rectifier bridge, bearings, stator and rotor. Inspect terminal connections for corrosion and damage. Inspect alternator housing for cracks, warping and damage. Replace alternator as necessary.

2) Inspect stator windings and rotor for burned (blackened) insulation. Replace stator or rotor as necessary. Inspect stator windings for chipped insulation. Repair with insulating varnish or replace stator if damage is excessive.

3) Inspect rotor slip rings. They may be cleaned with 400 grit or finer polishing cloth while rotor is being rotated. Slip rings may be lathe turned to maximum indicator reading of .002" (.05 mm). Slip rings are not replaceable. Replace rotor if slip rings are excessively damaged. Inspect slip ring end of rotor shaft for overheating or scoring. Replace rotor as necessary.

4) Inspect front bearing for looseness, roughness and wear. Replace as necessary. Rear bearing must be replaced if alternator is disassembled.

5) Inspect brushes for wear. Replace if worn to less than 50 percent of original length. Inspect brush holder for damage. Inspect brush springs for corrosion or damage.

Reassembly – 1) Install BAT terminal onto outside of slip ring end frame. Install rectifier bridge and capacitor into slip ring end frame, ensuring insulated side of capacitor is against frame. Install 2 screws and washers through grounded heat sink. Install BAT terminal nut with flat side down to insulated heat sink.

NOTE: A design change in brush holder and slip ring end frame prevents early design brush holders from being installed in later design slip ring end frames. To modify brush holder, remove two locators from brush holder and file jagged edges down to level of surrounding material ensuring loose particles are kept out of brush slots.

2) Assemble brush holder, regulator and regulator connector together, crimping connections of components. *See Fig. 8.* Solder connections using very little heat to avoid damage to regulator. Install brush holder, regulator and regulator connector assembly into slip ring end frame, ensuring regulator connection rests against metal side of capacitor strap.

3) Install one screw into brush holder and 2 screws into regulator connector. Install brushes into brush holder. Retract brushes in brush holder and retain with pin or toothpick, ensuring pin or toothpick extends through slip ring end frame for later removal.

4) Install stator into slip ring end frame. Position 3 stator leads to 3 rectifier bridge terminals. Install and tighten 3 stator lead nuts. Install front bearing into drive end frame by pressing against outer race. Install retainer onto drive end frame using 3 screws.

5) Install NEW rear bearing onto rotor, pressing against inner race until stop is reached. Install rotor into drive end frame sliding rotor shaft through inside collar and drive end frame. Install outside collar, fan and fan collar onto rotor shaft. Install pulley, washer and pulley nut onto rotor shaft. Tighten pulley nut to **75 ft. lbs (100 N.m)**.

6) Assemble rotor and drive end frame assembly to slip ring end frame matching marks made during disassembly and carefully guiding rear bearing into slip ring end frame. Install and tighten 4 through bolts. Remove pin or toothpick retaining retracted brushes through slip ring end frame, enabling brushes to contact slip rings.

Astro, Bravada, Commercial Van, Jimmy, Lumina APV, Safari, Sierra, Silhouette, Sonoma, Suburban, Syclone, Trans Sport, Typhoon, Van, Yukon, "C" & "K" Series Blazer & Pickup, "S" & "T" Series Blazer & Pickup

DESCRIPTION

For identification, starter part numbers are stamped on the outside of the frame or on an identification label attached to the frame.

Six types of starters are used: SD-200/210/250/260/300 and 28MT series. The first series is designated SD (Straight Drive) because the pinion is driven directly by the armature shaft. Wound field coils energize pole pieces that are arranged around the armature. These are used on gasoline engines.

The 28MT starter has a pinion that is driven by a gear reduction system. This starter is used on diesel engines. The 28MT starter should not be dissembled for any reason and is serviceable only by complete replacement.

TROUBLE SHOOTING

NOTE: See TROUBLE SHOOTING article in GENERAL INFORMATION.

BENCH TESTING

WARNING: DO NOT operate starter motor for longer than 30 seconds without allowing a 2-minute cool-down period between cranking. Overheating will damage starter motor.

SOLENOID WINDING TESTS

NOTE: Tests are performed with all leads disconnected from solenoid. Complete tests as quick as possible to prevent solenoid from overheating.

NOTE: "S", "M" & BAT terminals are identified on solenoid. Terminal location may vary with different solenoids.

Hold-In Windings – 1) Connect an ammeter, voltmeter, carbon pile and battery into starter circuit. *See Fig. 1.* Using carbon pile, decrease battery voltage to 10 volts.
2) Refer to SOLENOID HOLD-IN WINDING SPECIFICATIONS table for correct amperage reading. A higher reading indicates windings are shorted or grounded; a lower reading indicates excessive resistance.

SOLENOID HOLD-IN WINDING SPECIFICATIONS

Part No.	Amps	Volts
1114520	13-19	10
1114530	13-19	10
1114531	10-20	10
1114563	14-18	10
1114577	13-19	10
10469039	[1] 13-15	10

[1] – 10-20 amps on Lumina APV, Silhouette and Trans Sport.

Pull-In Windings – Using solenoid test connections shown in illustration, decrease battery voltage to 5 volts (10 volts on Lumina APV, Silhouette and Trans Sport). *See Fig. 2.* Refer to SOLENOID PULL-IN WINDING SPECIFICATIONS table for correct amperage draw. A higher reading indicates windings are shorted or grounded; a lower reading indicates excessive resistance.

NOTE: To prevent overheating of pull-in windings, DO NOT energize for more than 15 seconds. Current draw will decrease as winding temperature increases.

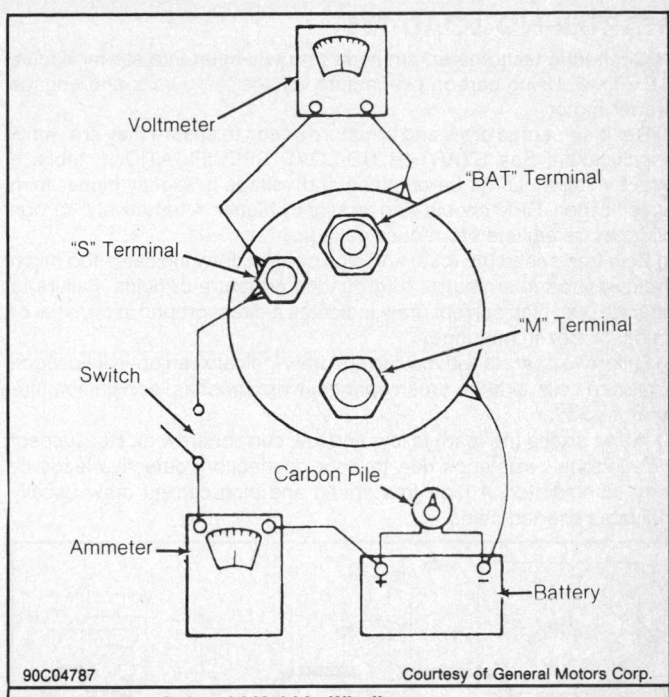

90C04787   Courtesy of General Motors Corp.

Fig. 1: Testing Solenoid Hold-In Windings

SOLENOID PULL-IN WINDING SPECIFICATIONS

Part No.	Amps	Volts
1114520	23-30	5
1114530	23-30	5
1114531	50-65	10
1114563	26-30	5
10469039	[1] 31-36	[2] 5

[1] – 50-65 amps on Lumina APV, Silhouette and Trans Sport.
[2] – 10 volts on Lumina APV, Silhouette and Trans Sport.

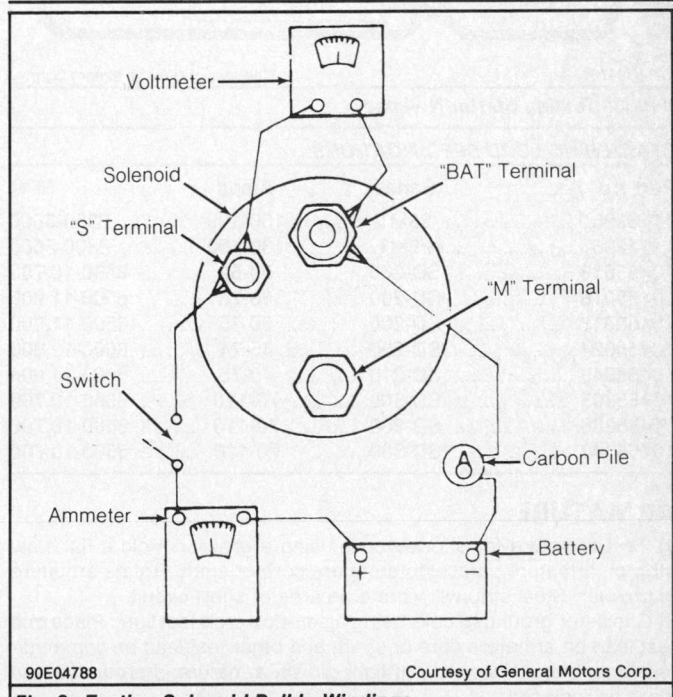

90E04788   Courtesy of General Motors Corp.

Fig. 2: Testing Solenoid Pull-In Windings

STARTER NO-LOAD TEST

1) Connect a tachometer, ammeter and voltmeter into starter circuit. *See Fig. 3.* Using carbon pile, adjust voltage to 10 volts and engage starter motor.

2) Read amperage draw and armature speed to ensure they are within specification. See STARTER NO-LOAD SPECIFICATIONS table. If exact voltage cannot be obtained and voltage is slightly higher than specification, RPM should also be slightly higher. Alternatively, carbon pile may be adjusted to reduce voltage.

3) Low free speed (no load) and high current draw indicates too much friction, shorted armature, or grounded armature or fields. Failure to operate with high current draw indicates a direct ground in terminal or fields, or frozen bearings.

4) Failure to operate with no current draw indicates an open field, open armature coils, broken brush springs, worn brushes, or high commutator insulation.

5) If free speed (no load) is low and low current draw exists, suspect high internal resistance due to poor connection, defective leads or dirty commutator. A high free speed and high current draw usually indicates shorted fields.

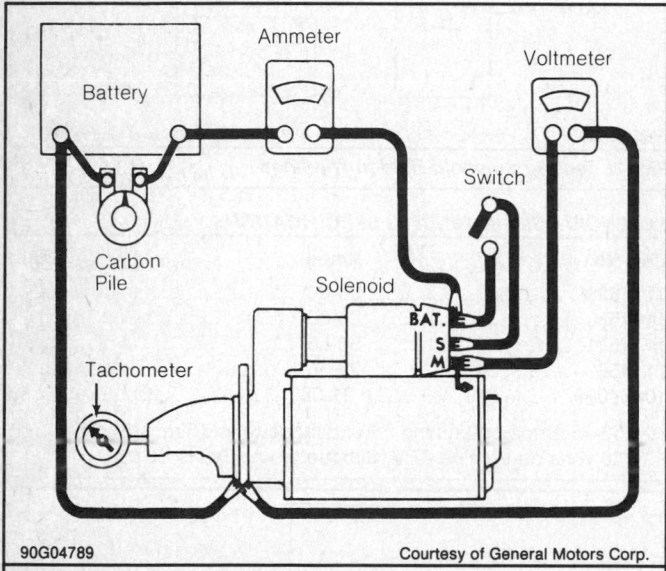

90G04789   Courtesy of General Motors Corp.

Fig. 3: Testing Starter No-Load

STARTER NO-LOAD SPECIFICATIONS

Part No.	Series	Amps	RPM
1113295	28MT	130-190	2300-5600
1113296	28MT	130-190	2300-5600
10455013	SD-260	50-62	8500-10,700
10455016	SD-200	50-75	6000-11,900
10455018	SD-200	50-75	6500-11,900
10455024	SD-250	45-74	8600-12,900
10455048	SD-210	45-77	6000-11,000
10455305	SD-300	70-110	6500-10,700
10455306	SD-300	70-110	6500-10,700
10455343	SD-300	70-110	6500-10,700

ARMATURE

1) Test armature for shorted coils using a growler. Hold a flat steel strip on armature parallel to armature core or shaft. Rotate armature in growler. Steel strip will vibrate on area of short circuit.

2) Check for grounded coils using a self-powered test light. Place one test lead on armature core or shaft, and other test lead on commutator. Light should not glow. If light glows, armature is grounded and must be replaced.

FIELD COILS (ENCLOSED HOUSING)

1) Disconnect field coil ground connections. Using self-powered test light, place one test lead on field coil frame and connect other test lead to field coil connector. If light glows, one or more coils are grounded and must be repaired or replaced.

2) Check for opens by placing test light across coil ends. Light should glow. If light does not glow, coils are open.

3) On SD-200 and SD-260 starters, coils cannot be replaced separately. Frame and fields must be replaced as a unit. On SD-300, a pole shoe spreader and pole shoe screwdriver should be used to replace a defective field coil. Assemble pole shoe with long lip (if equipped) facing direction of armature rotation.

BRUSHES, SPRINGS & HOLDERS

Replace brushes if worn to 1/2 original length, oil-soaked or pitted. Check brush spring tension and replace springs if weak or distorted.

NOTE: Entire frame and field assembly must be replaced for SD-210 and SD-260. Brushes and brush holders are integral parts of assembly.

DRIVE & PINION

Pinion should turn freely in overrun direction and should not slip in drive direction. Check spring for correct tension and drive collar for wear. These parts can be removed for replacement by forcing collar toward clutch and removing lock ring from end of tube. Replace drive assembly if pinion teeth are worn, chipped or cracked.

PINION CLEARANCE

1) Disconnect motor field coil connector from solenoid "M" terminal, and insulate it carefully. Connect a battery from solenoid "S" terminal to solenoid frame. Momentarily flash a jumper lead from "M" terminal to solenoid frame.

2) This shifts pinion into cranking position. Push pinion back toward commutator end to eliminate slack. Distance between pinion and pinion stop should be .010-.160" (.25-4.06 mm). *See Fig. 4.* Clearance is not adjustable. If clearance is not within specification, check for worn parts.

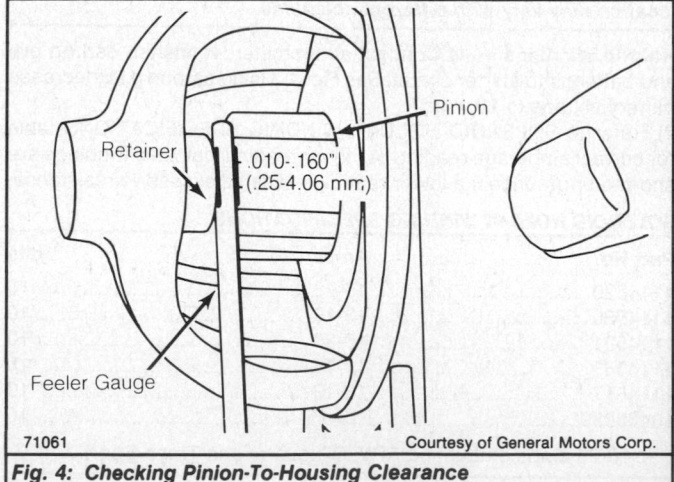

71061   Courtesy of General Motors Corp.

Fig. 4: Checking Pinion-To-Housing Clearance

REMOVAL & INSTALLATION

WARNING: When battery is disconnected, vehicle computer and memory systems may lose memory data. Driveability problems may exist until computer systems have completed a relearn cycle. See COMPUTER RELEARN PROCEDURES article in GENERAL INFORMATION before disconnecting battery.

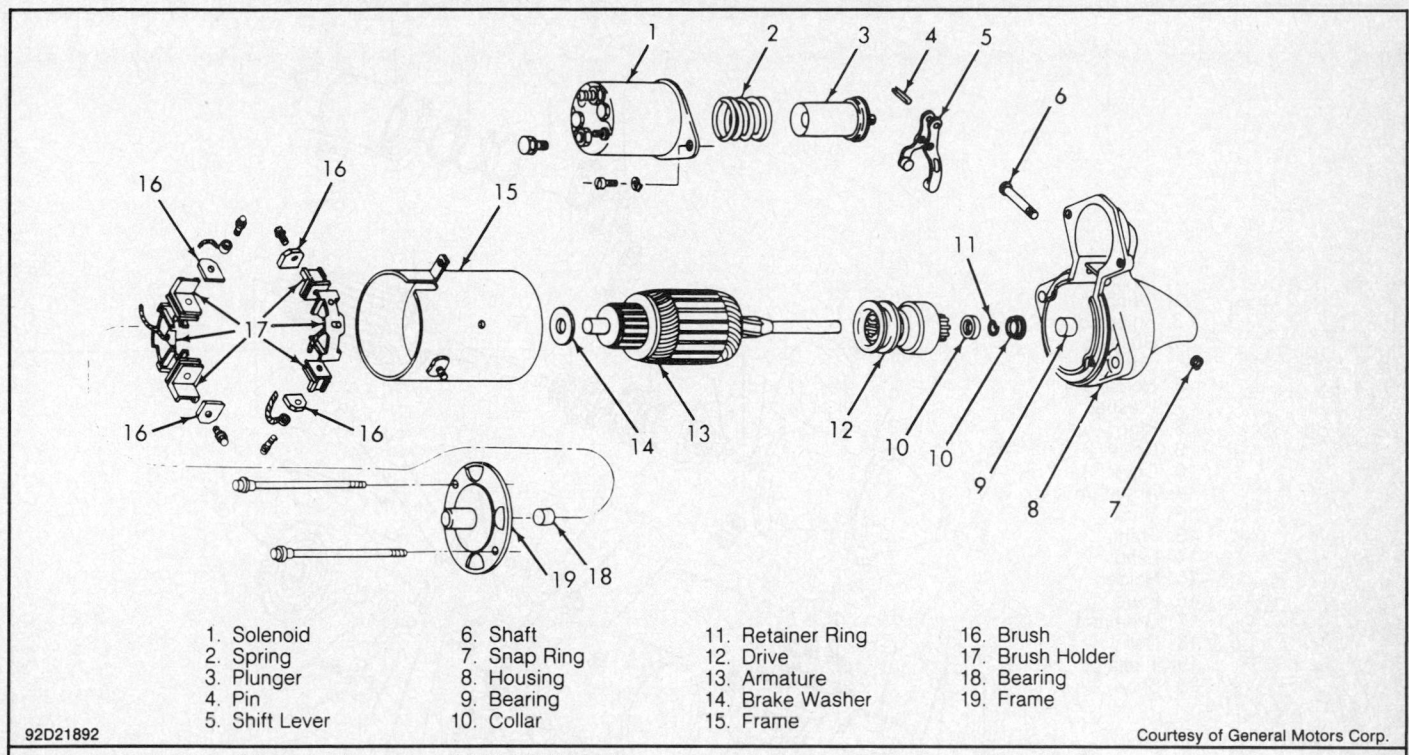

1. Solenoid
2. Spring
3. Plunger
4. Pin
5. Shift Lever
6. Shaft
7. Snap Ring
8. Housing
9. Bearing
10. Collar
11. Retainer Ring
12. Drive
13. Armature
14. Brake Washer
15. Frame
16. Brush
17. Brush Holder
18. Bearing
19. Frame

92D21892

Courtesy of General Motors Corp.

Fig. 5: Exploded View Of Starter Assembly (SD-200 & SD-250)

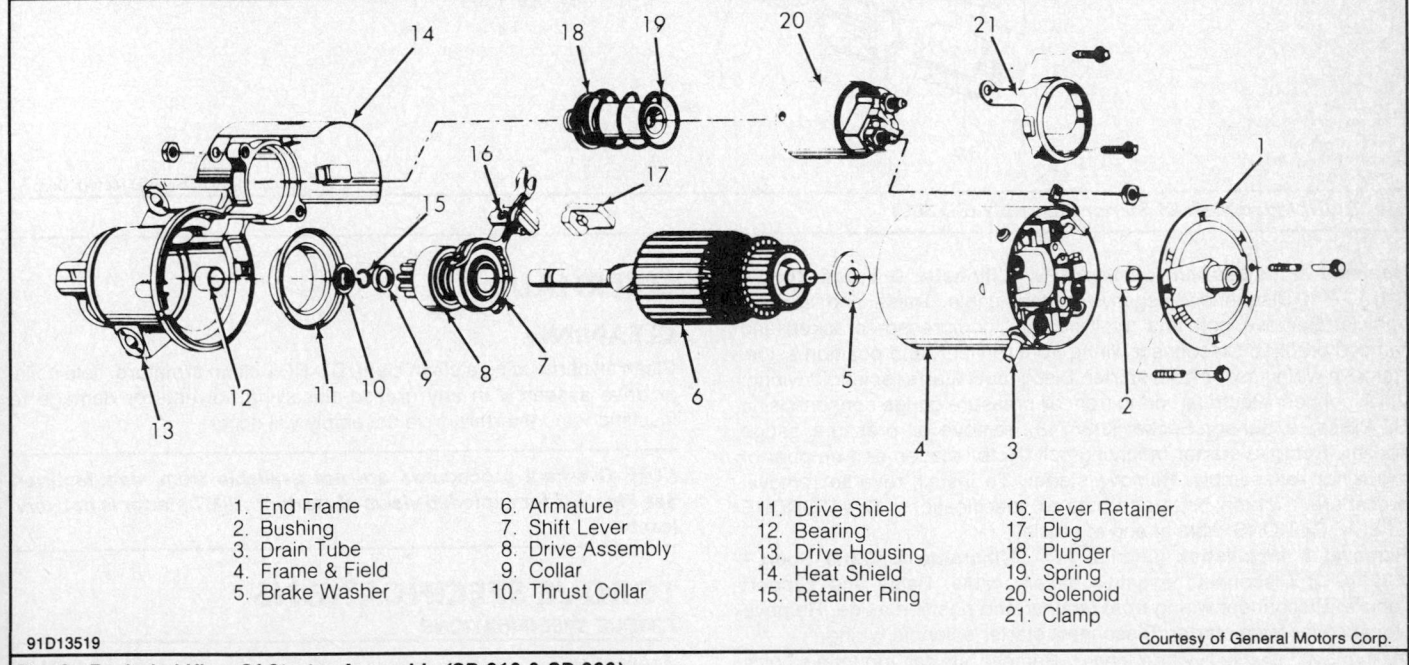

1. End Frame
2. Bushing
3. Drain Tube
4. Frame & Field
5. Brake Washer
6. Armature
7. Shift Lever
8. Drive Assembly
9. Collar
10. Thrust Collar
11. Drive Shield
12. Bearing
13. Drive Housing
14. Heat Shield
15. Retainer Ring
16. Lever Retainer
17. Plug
18. Plunger
19. Spring
20. Solenoid
21. Clamp

91D13519

Courtesy of General Motors Corp.

Fig. 6: Exploded View Of Starter Assembly (SD-210 & SD-260)

STARTER

NOTE: If shims are installed between starter and engine, note and record arrangement for installation reference.

Removal & Installation (Jimmy, Sonoma, Syclone, Typhoon & "T" Series Blazer & Pickup) – 1) Disconnect negative battery cable. Raise and support vehicle. Disconnect electrical wiring from starter solenoid. Remove mounting bracket and wiring from brush end of starter. Remove skid plate (if equipped). Remove 2 brake line-to-crossmember brackets.

2) Remove 6 crossmember bolts and remove crossmember. Remove transmission cooler line-to-flywheel housing bracket. Remove brace rod to flywheel housing. Remove lower flywheel housing cover (if necessary).

3) Remove starter bolts. Note location and number of shims for reassembly. Remove starter. To install, reverse removal procedure. Tighten bolts and nuts to specifications. See TORQUE SPECIFICATIONS table at end of article.

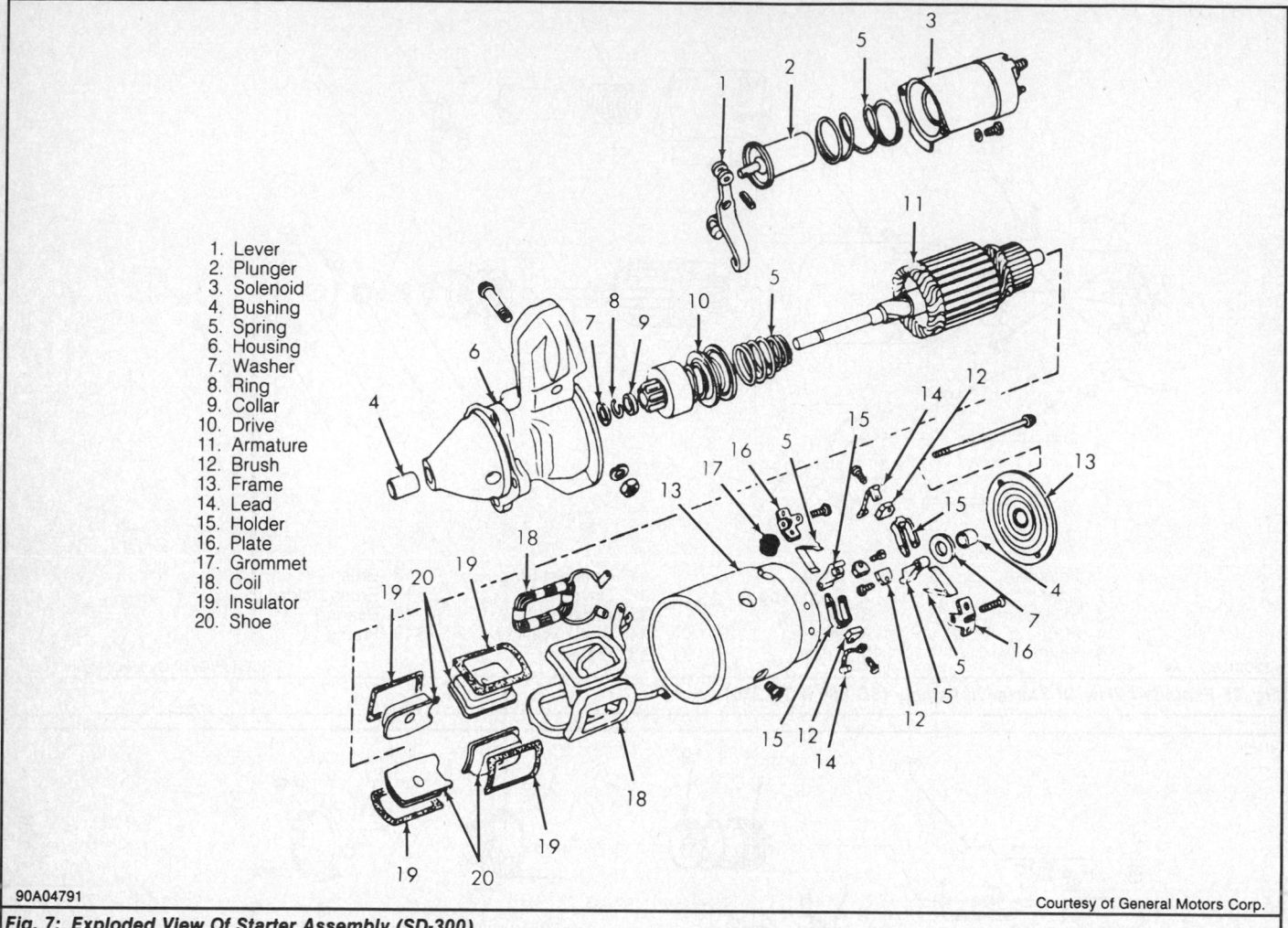

1. Lever
2. Plunger
3. Solenoid
4. Bushing
5. Spring
6. Housing
7. Washer
8. Ring
9. Collar
10. Drive
11. Armature
12. Brush
13. Frame
14. Lead
15. Holder
16. Plate
17. Grommet
18. Coil
19. Insulator
20. Shoe

90A04791   Courtesy of General Motors Corp.

Fig. 7: Exploded View Of Starter Assembly (SD-300)

Removal & Installation (Lumina APV, Silhouette & Trans Sport – 3.1L) – 1) Disconnect negative battery cable. Raise and support vehicle. Remove bolt and nut from A/C compressor bracket, and remove bracket. Disconnect wiring from retainer, and position aside. Remove wiring cover from starter. Disconnect starter solenoid wiring.

2) Disconnect electrical wiring from oil pressure gauge sensor. Using Oil Pressure Sensor Socket (J-35748), remove oil pressure gauge sensor. Remove starter mounting bolt. Note location and number of shims for reassembly. Remove starter. To install, reverse removal procedure. Tighten bolts and nuts to specifications. See TORQUE SPECIFICATIONS table at end of article.

Removal & Installation (Lumina APV, Silhouette & Trans Sport – 3.8L) – 1) Disconnect negative battery cable. Raise and support vehicle. Disconnect wiring from retainer and position aside. Remove wiring cover from starter. Disconnect starter solenoid wiring.

2) Remove plastic flywheel cover. Remove starter mounting bolts. Remove starter. To install, reverse removal procedure. Tighten bolts and nuts to specifications. See TORQUE SPECIFICATIONS table at end of article.

Removal & Installation (All Other Models) – 1) Disconnect negative battery cable. Raise and support vehicle. Remove starter brackets and shields (if equipped). Remove brush end mounting bracket (if equipped). Disconnect electrical wiring from starter solenoid.

2) Remove starter mounting bolts. Remove shims and note arrangement for reassembly. Remove starter. To install, reverse removal procedure. Ensure shims are installed in original location. Tighten bolts and nuts to specifications. See TORQUE SPECIFICATIONS table at end of article.

OVERHAUL

CLEANING

Clean all parts using a clean cloth. DO NOT clean armature, field coils, or drive assembly in any grease-dissolving solvents or damage to insulation and (starter) drive assembly will occur.

NOTE: Overhaul procedures are not available from manufacturer. See Figs. 5-7 for exploded views of starters. 28MT starter is not serviceable.

TORQUE SPECIFICATIONS
TORQUE SPECIFICATIONS

Application	Ft. Lbs. (N.m)
A/C Compressor Bracket Nut & Bolt	23 (31)
Crossmember-To-Frame Bolts	35 (47)
Starter Bracket-To-Block Bolt	24 (33)
Starter Mounting Bolts	
2.5L	31 (42)
2.8L, 4.3L, 5.0L, 5.7L, 6.2L & 7.4L	33 (45)
3.1L & 3.8L	32 (43)
5.7L & 7.4L [1]	24 (33)
	INCH Lbs. (N.m)
Bracket-To-Starter Nuts	75 (8)

[1] – Commercial Van only.

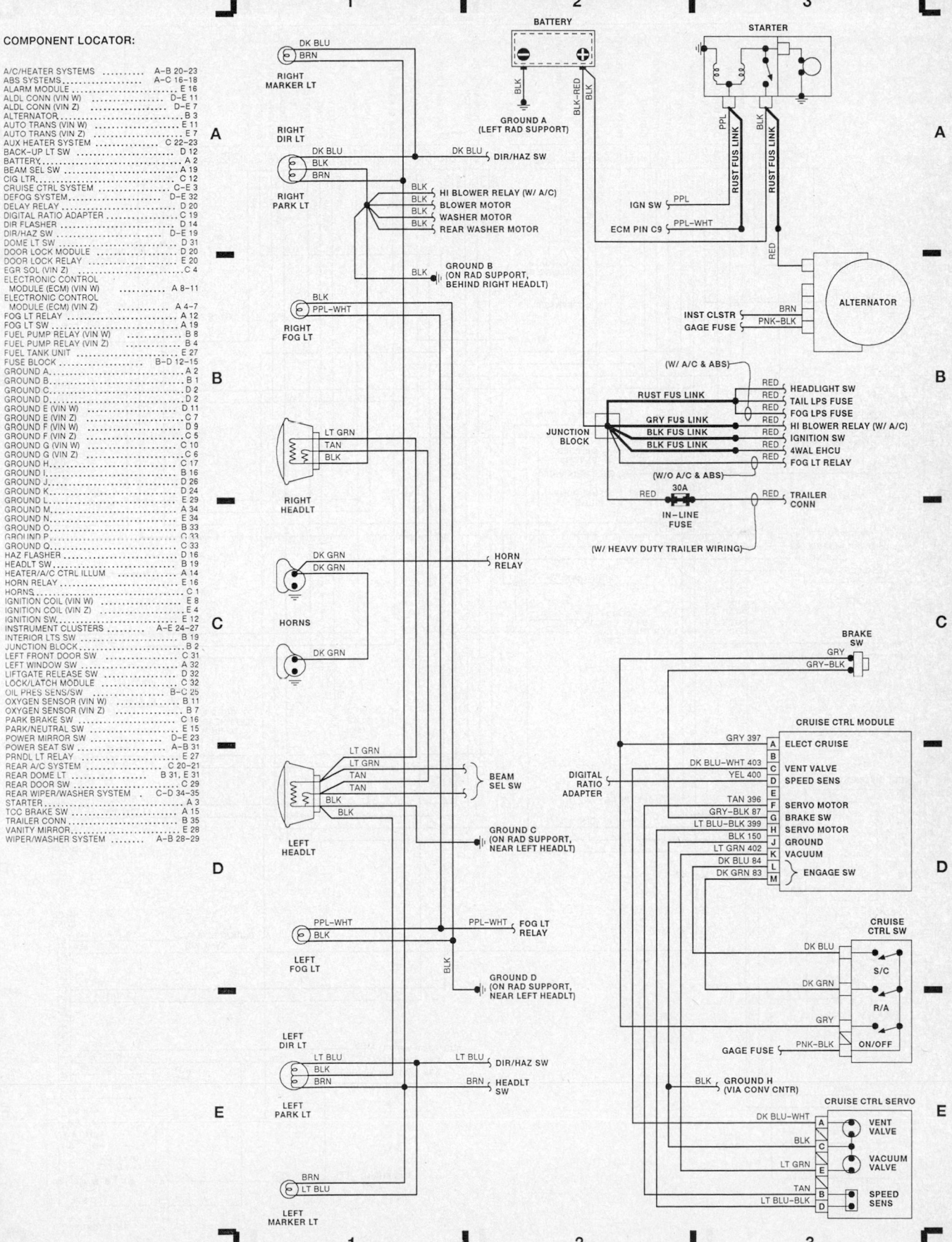

COMPONENT LOCATOR:

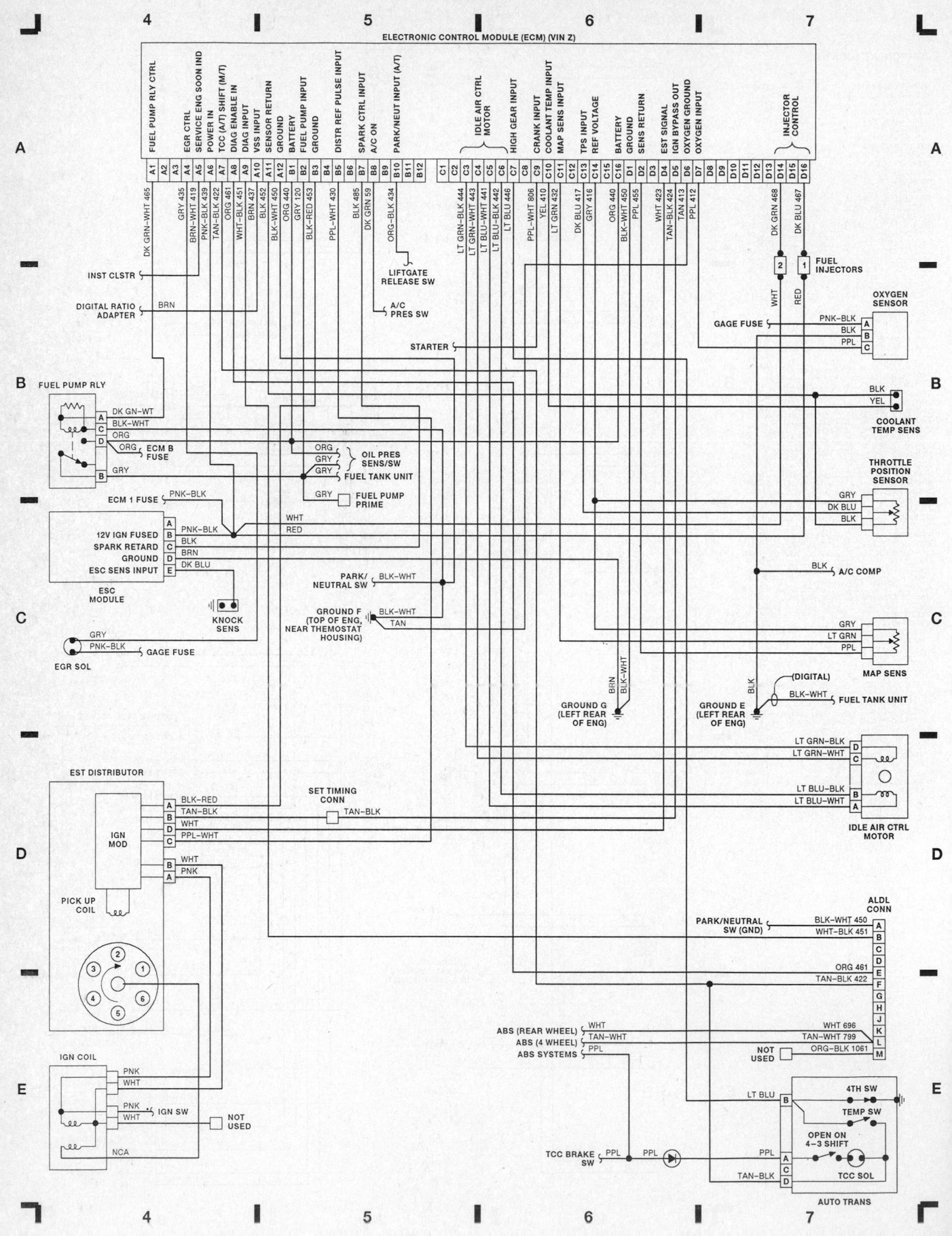

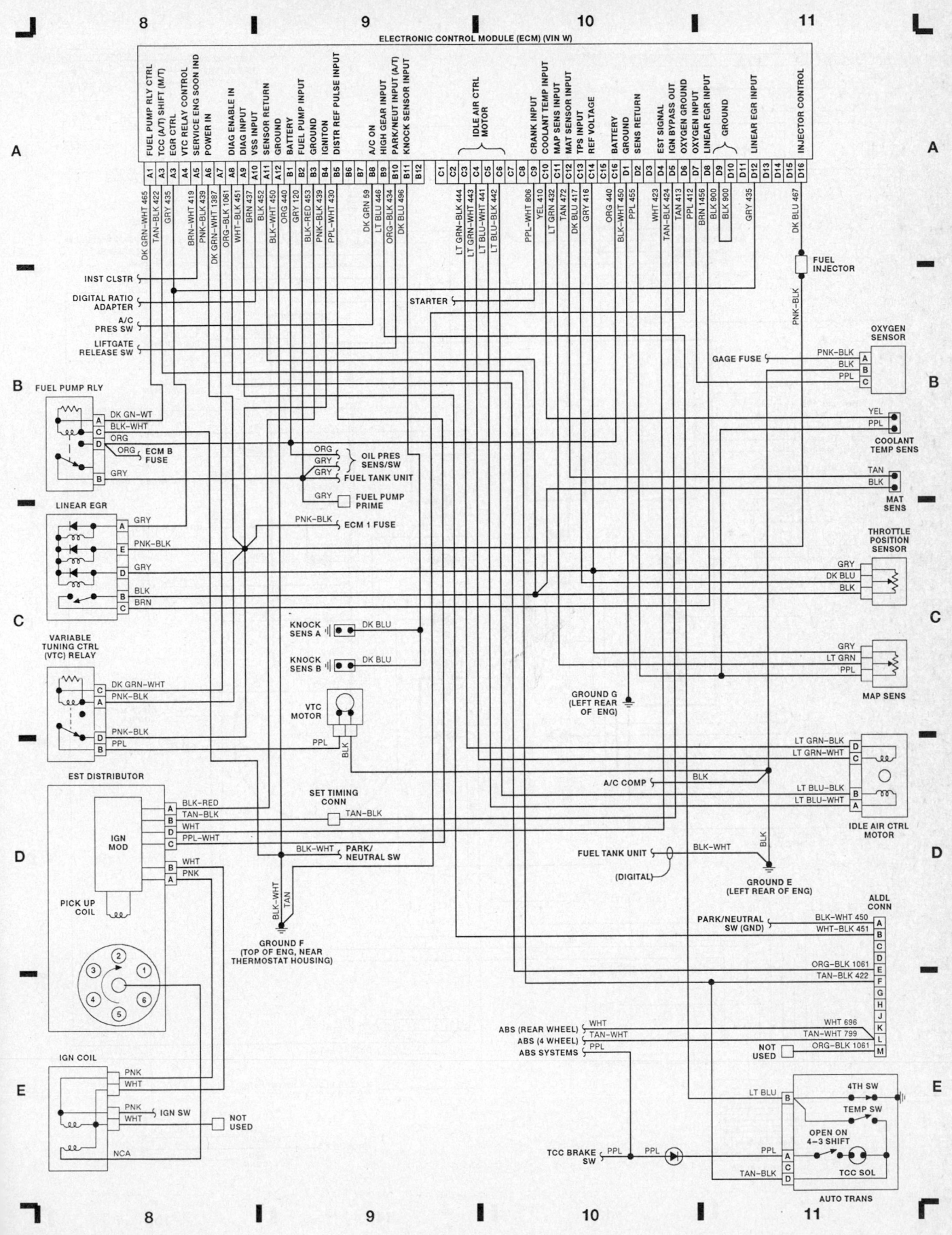

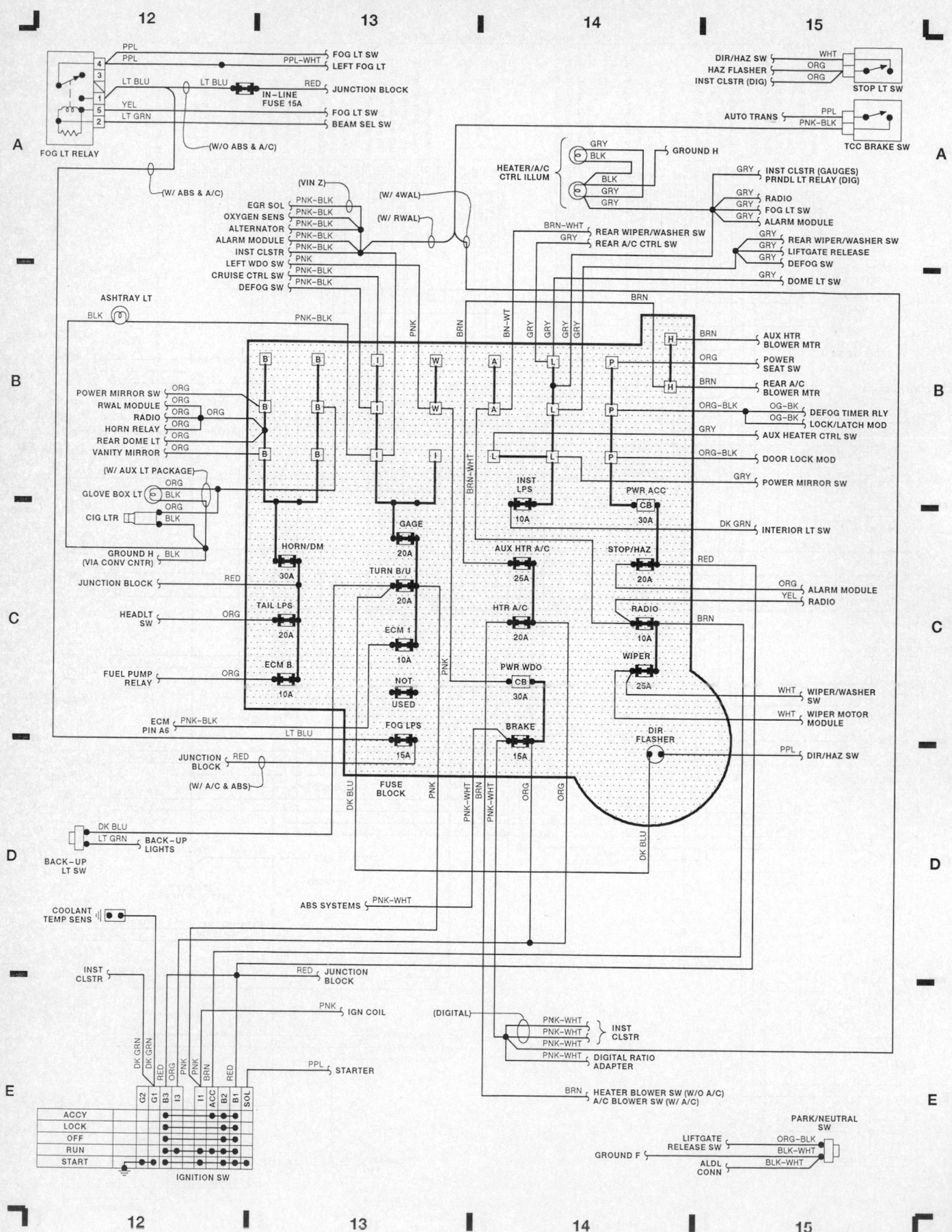

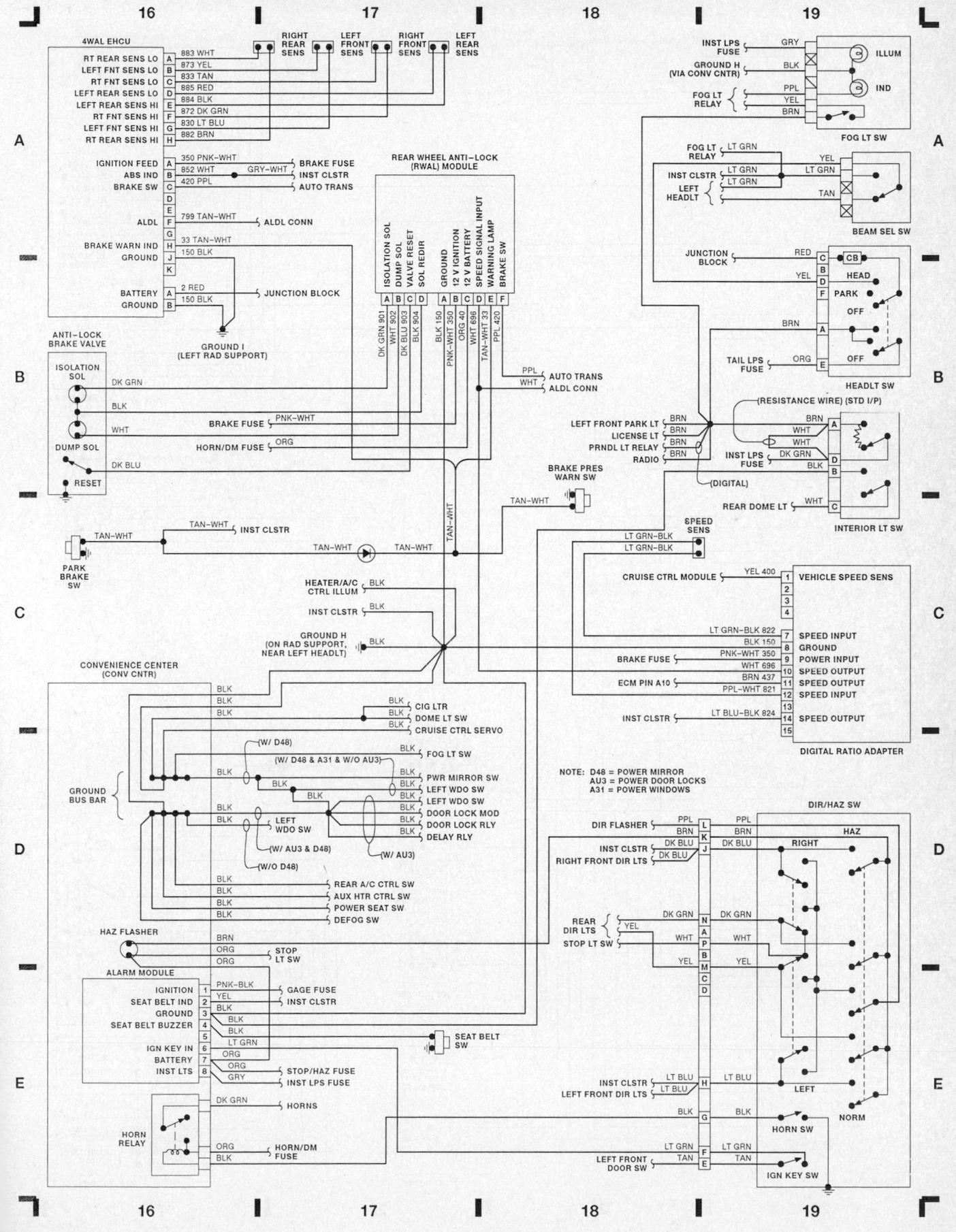

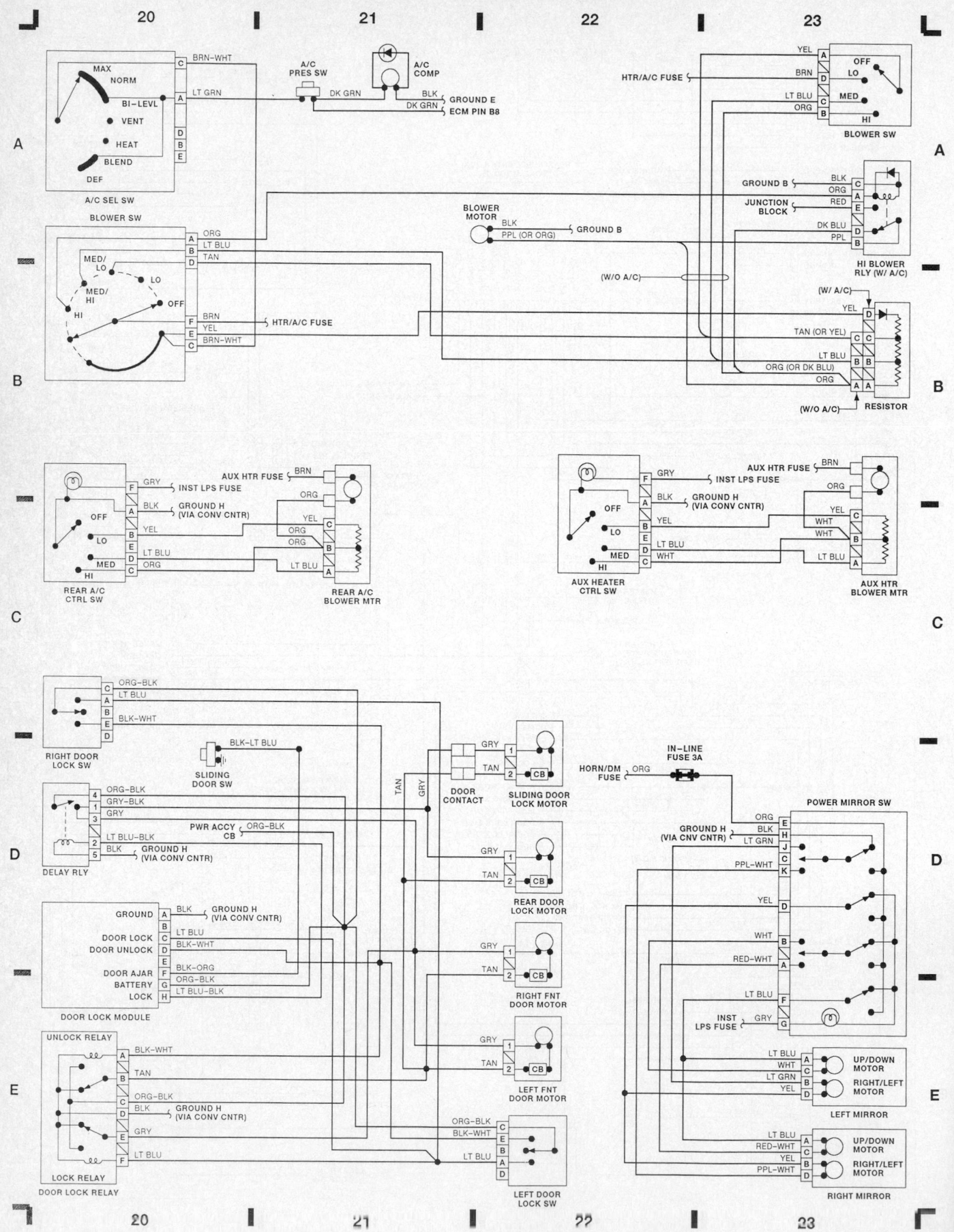

24   25   26   27

24   25   26   27

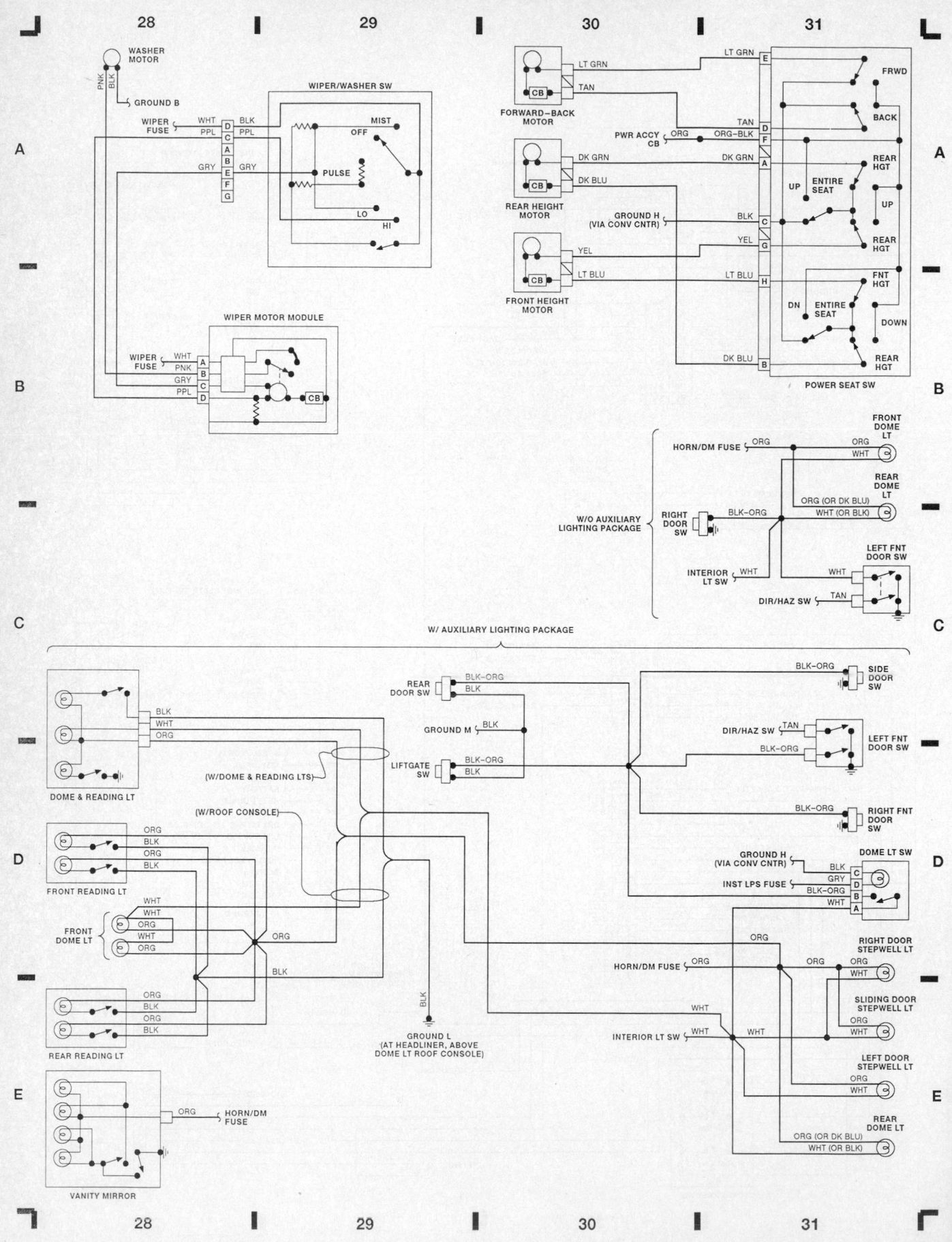

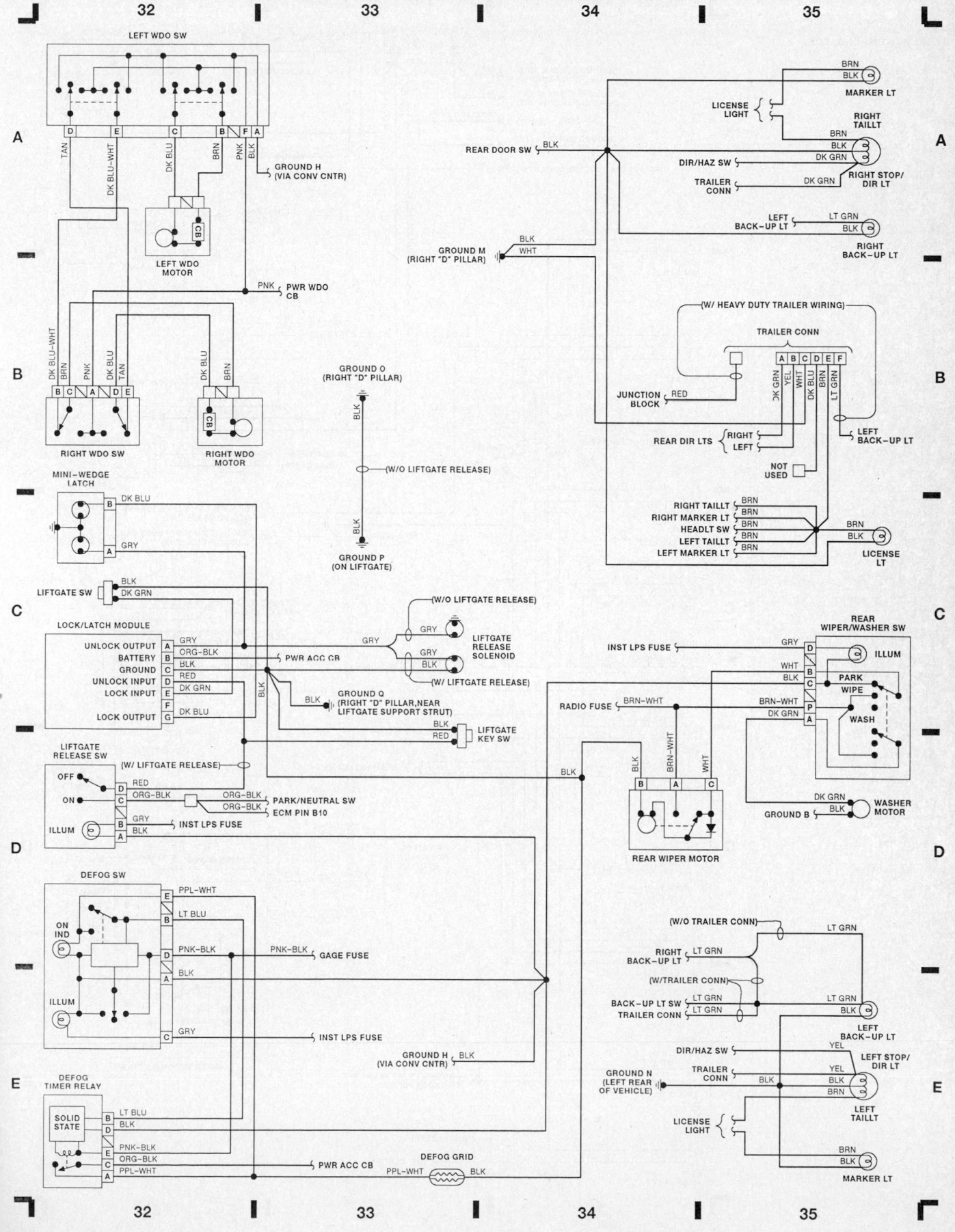

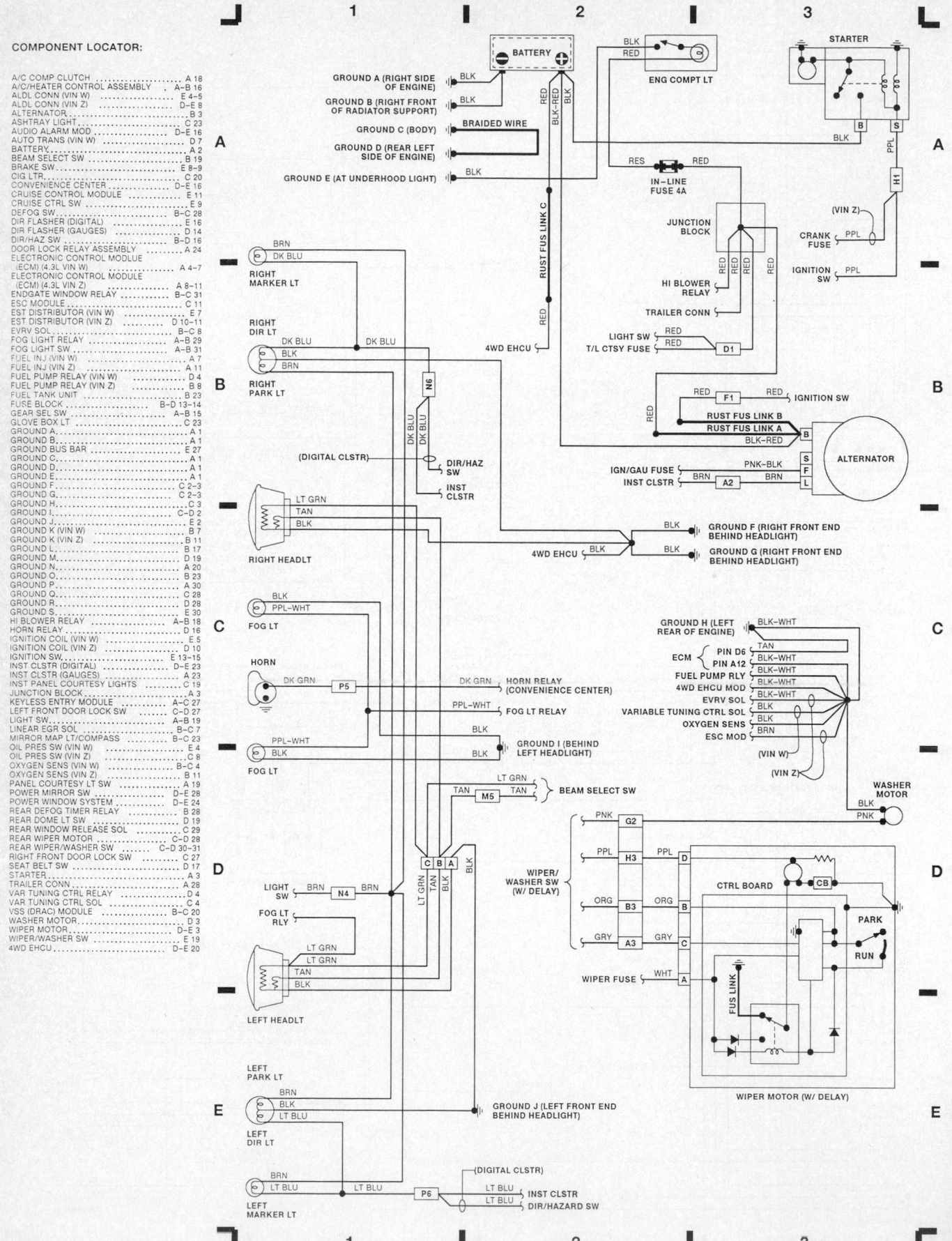

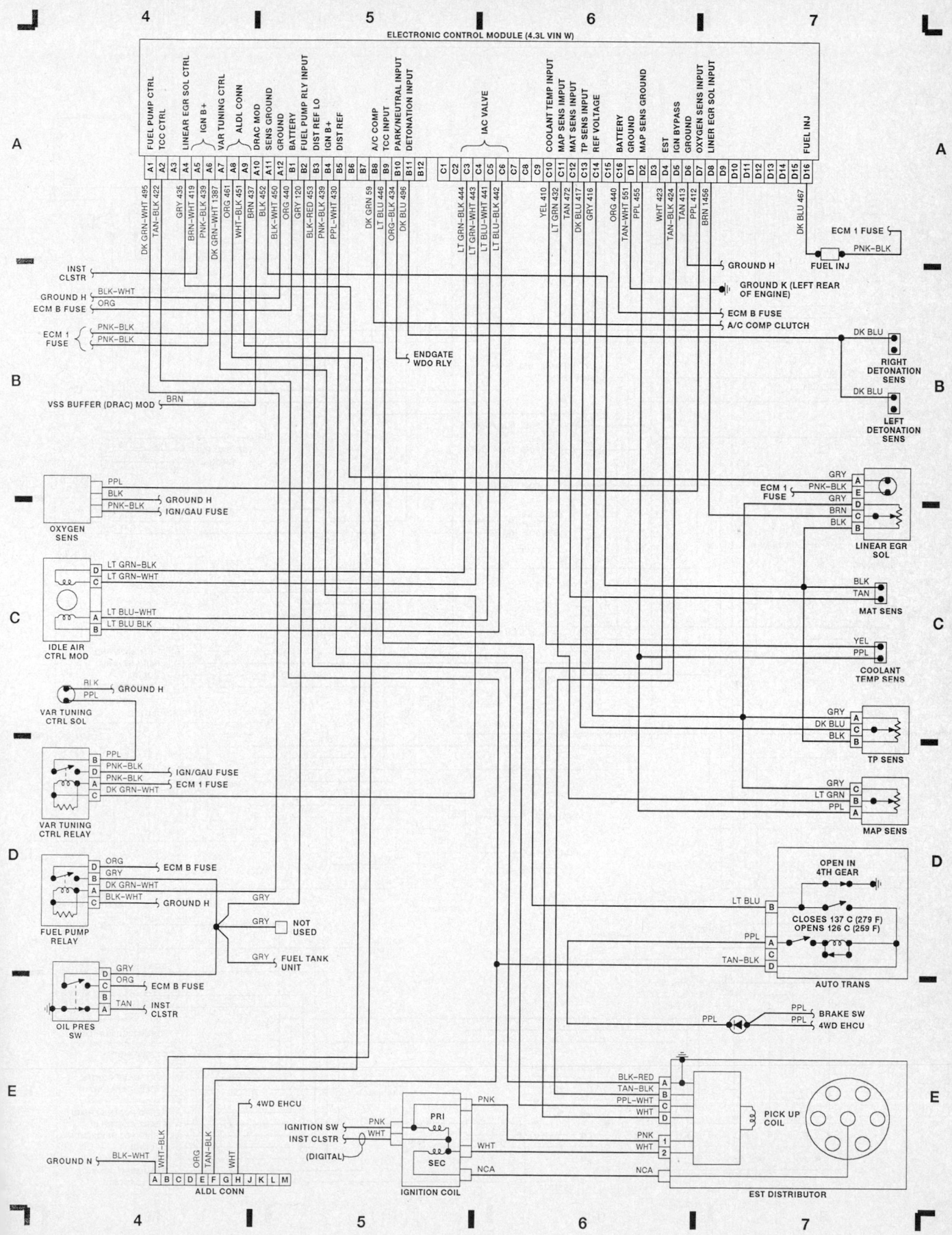

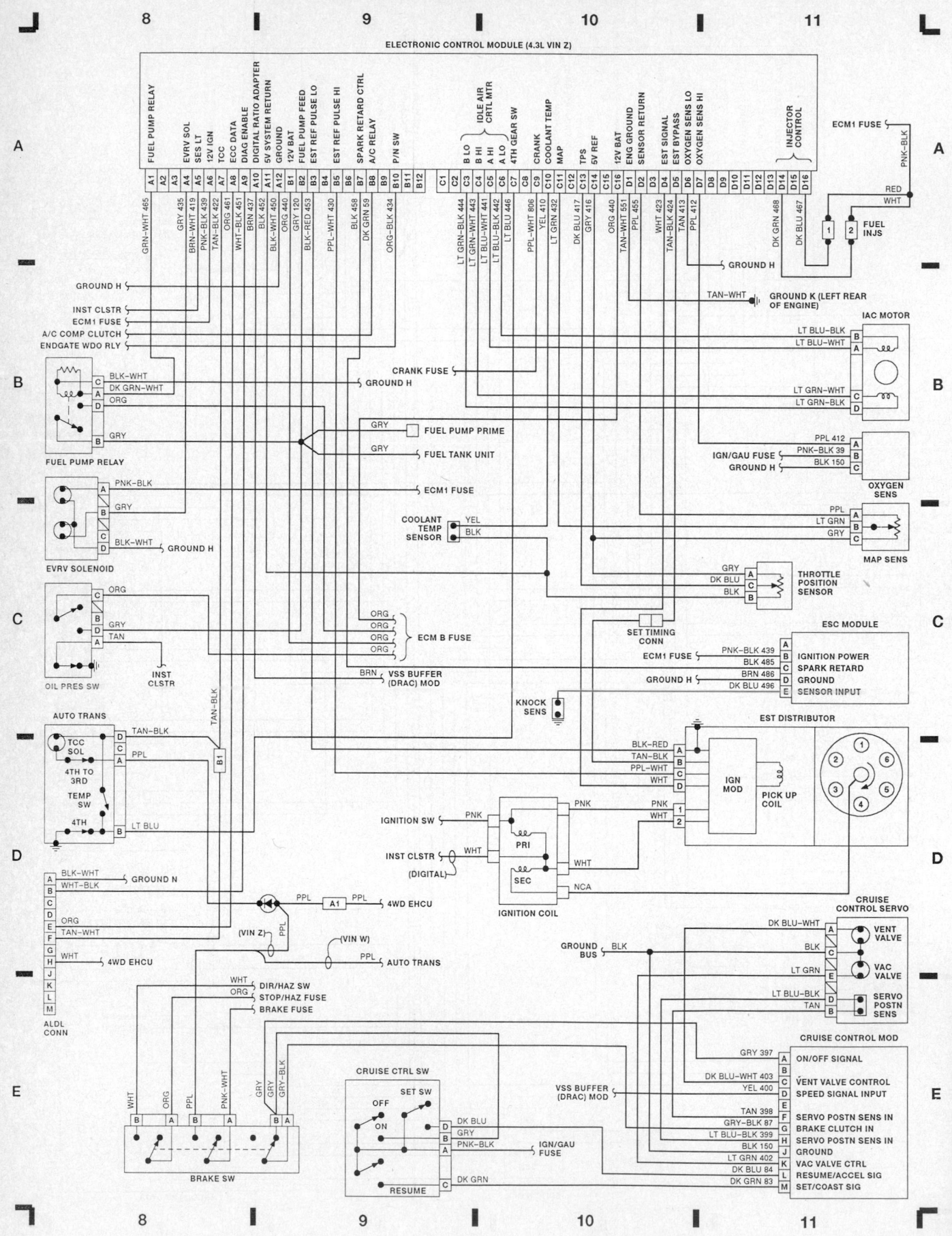

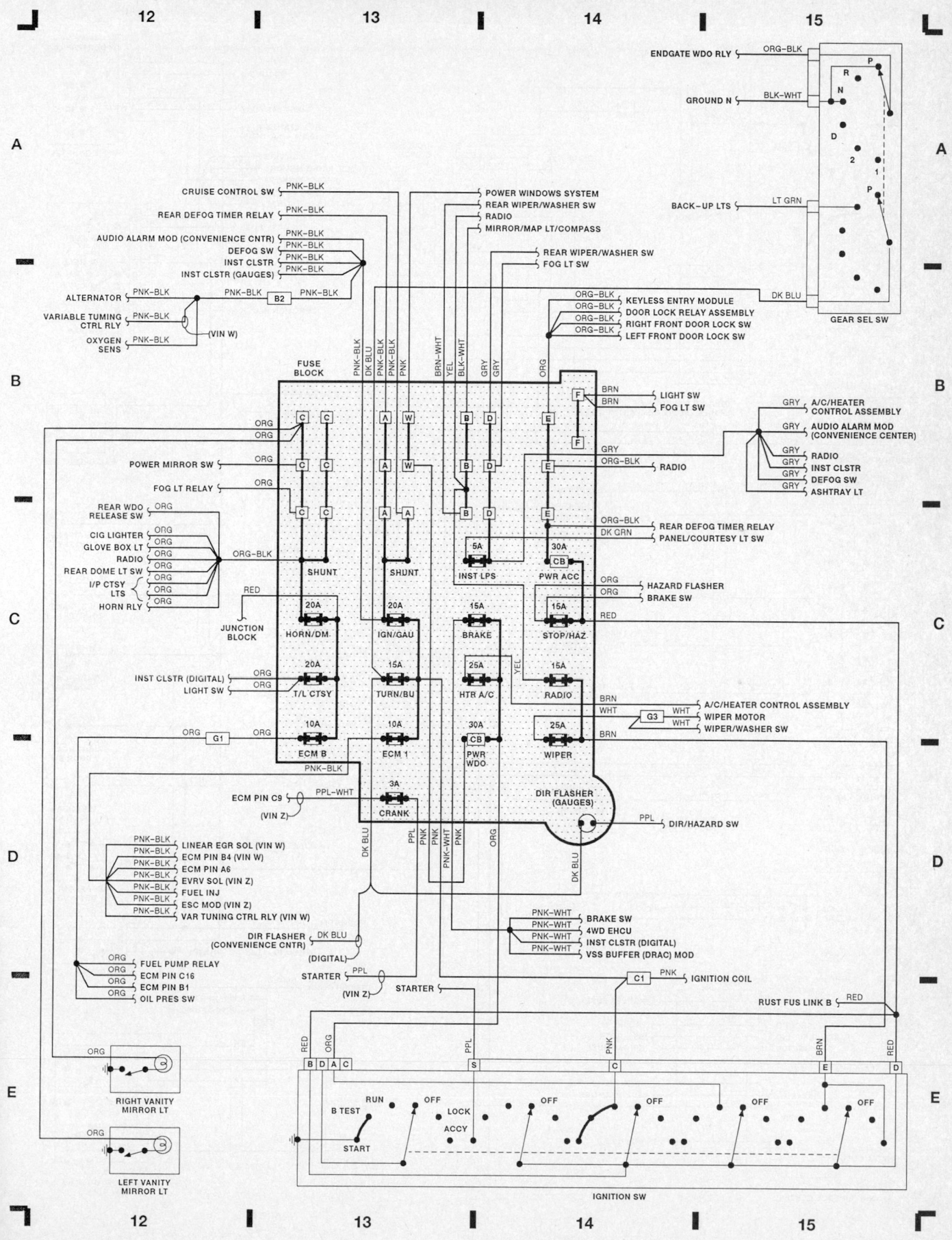

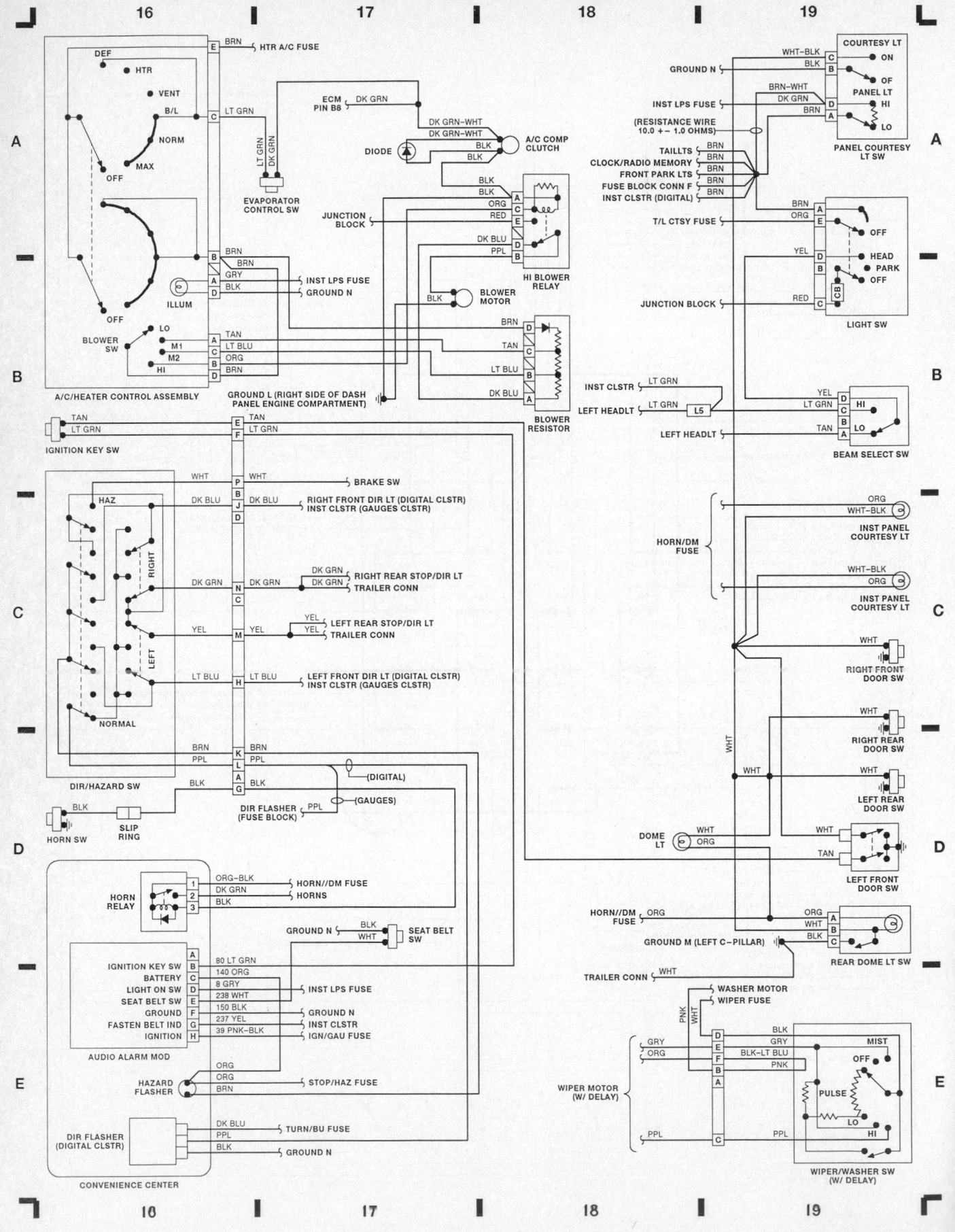

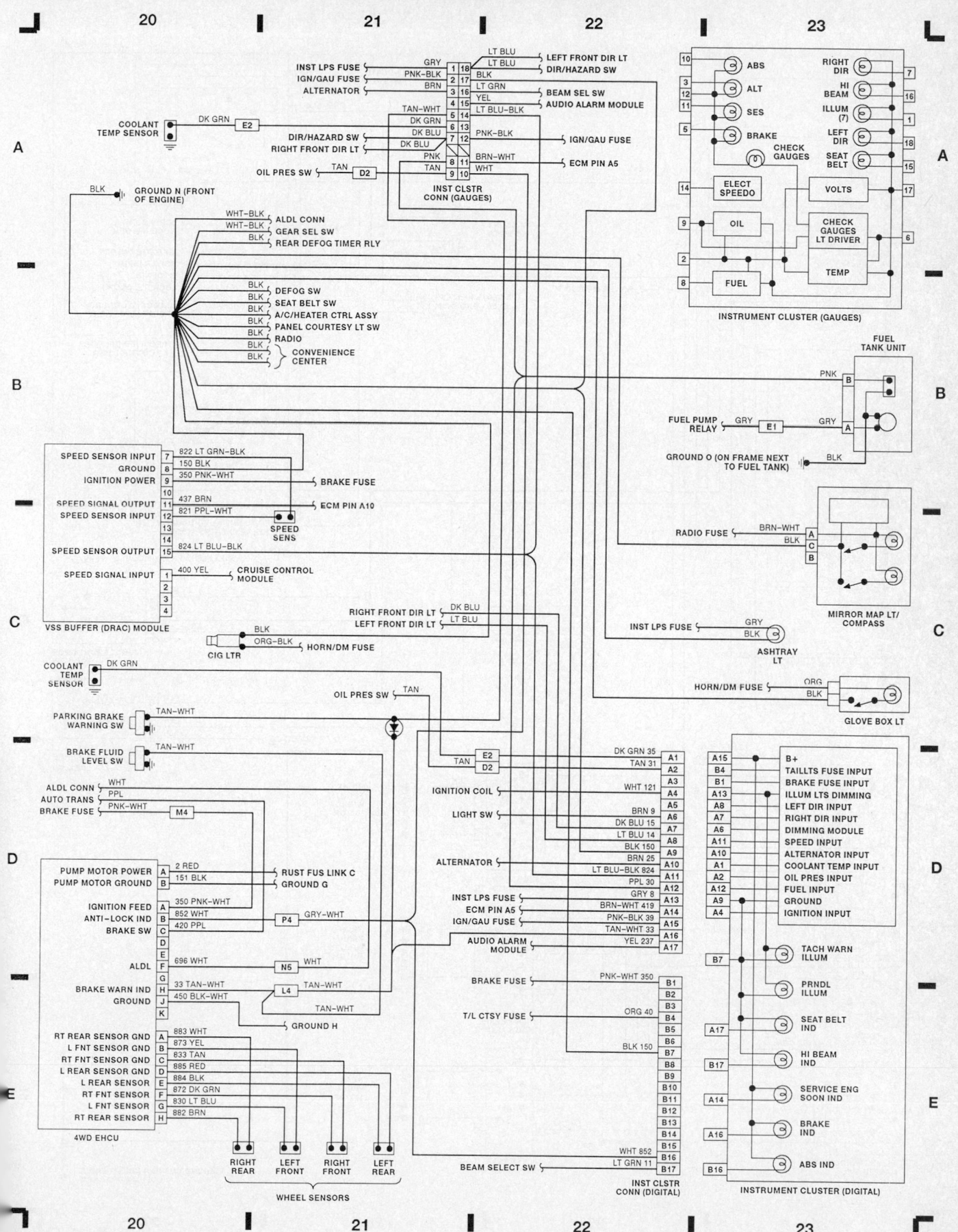

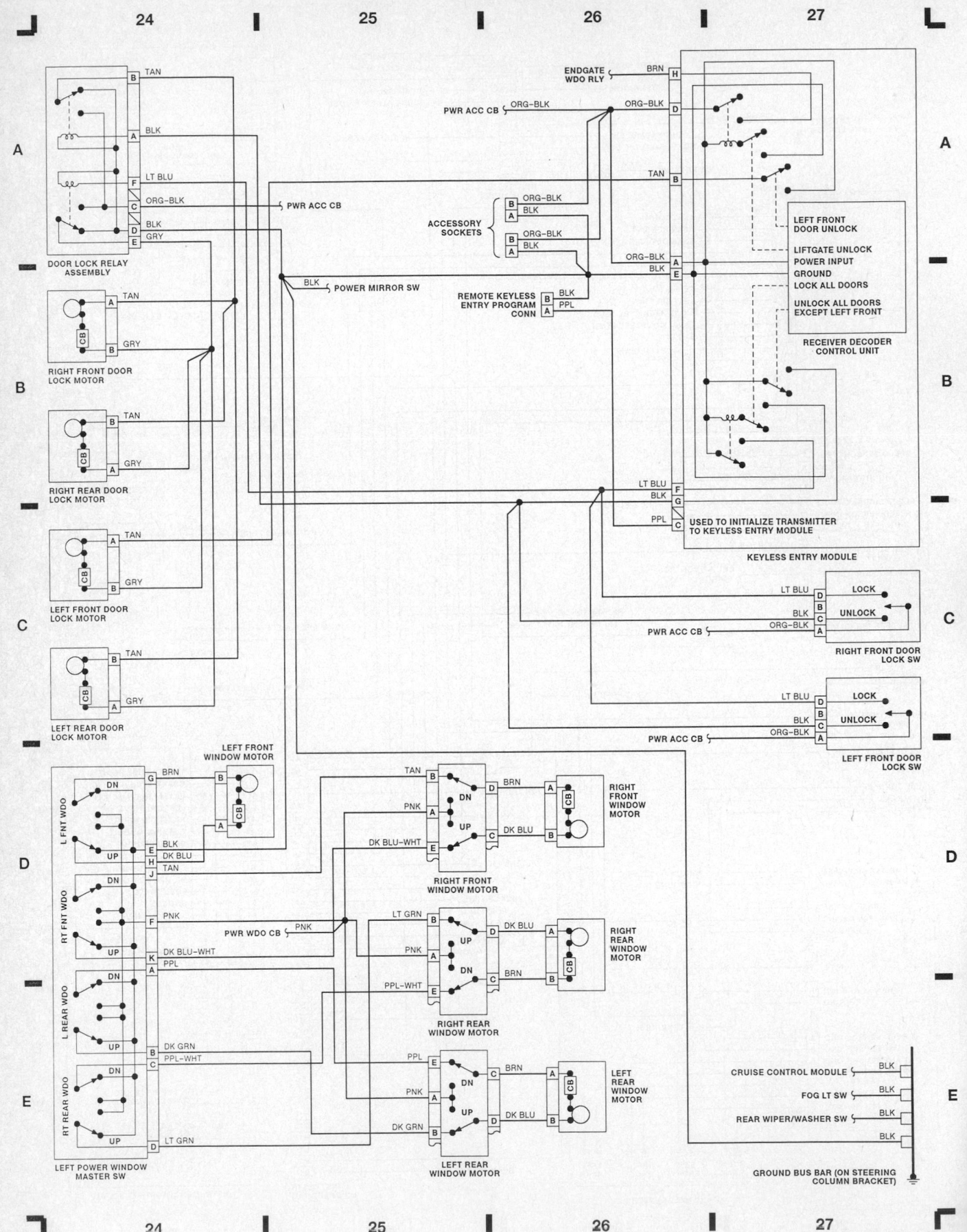

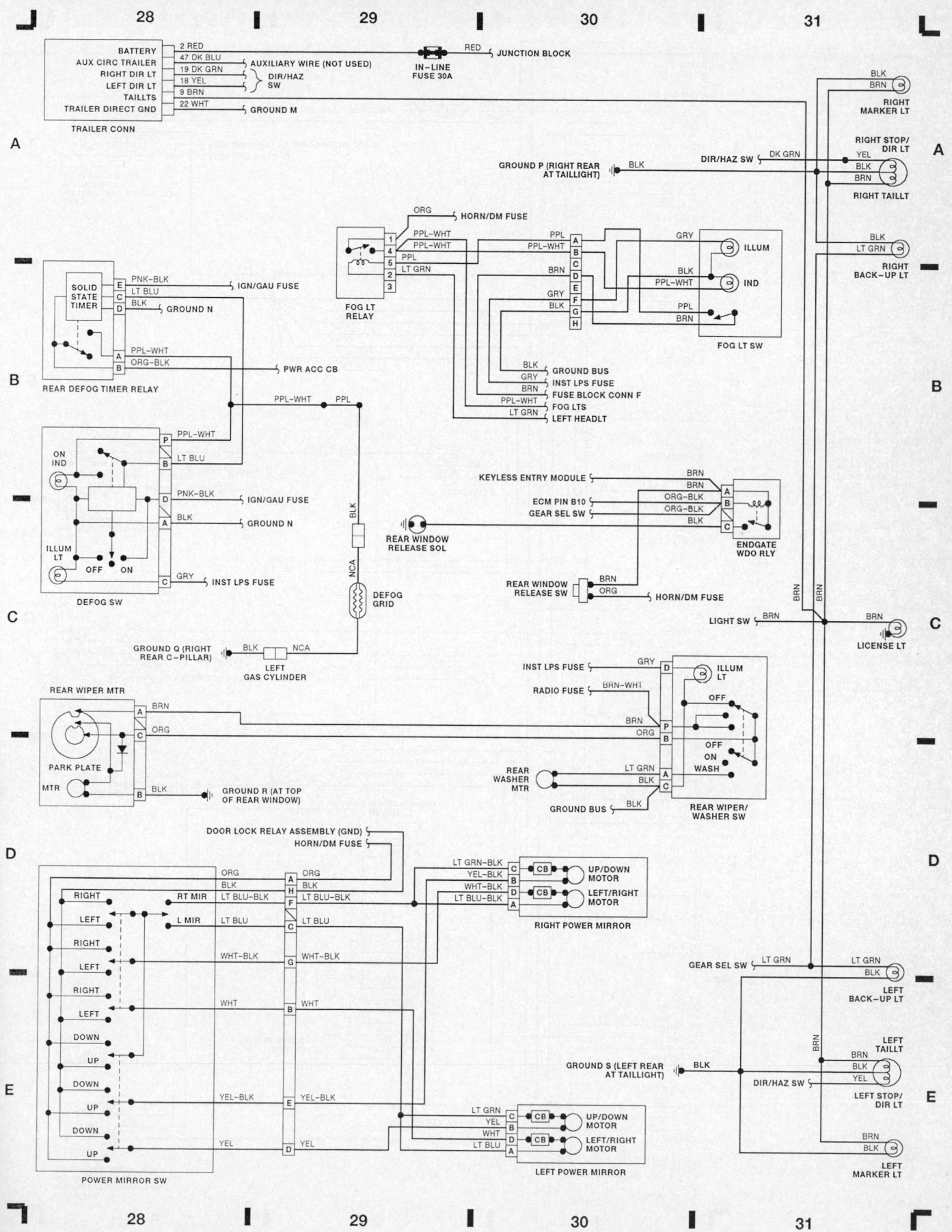

1992 WIRING DIAGRAMS
"C" & "K" Series

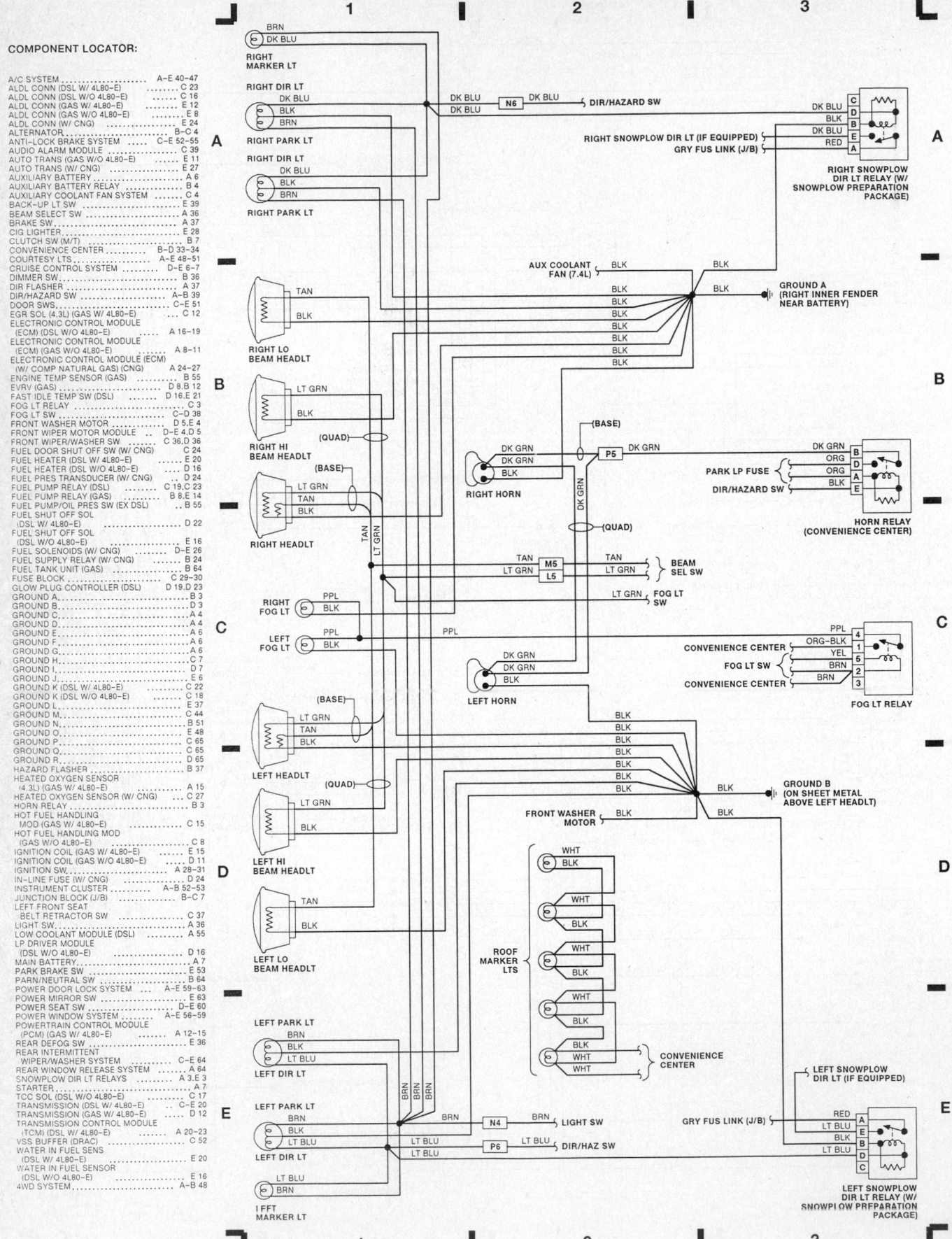

COMPONENT LOCATOR:

A/C SYSTEM .... A–E 40–47
ALDL CONN (DSL W/ 4L80–E) ..... C 23
ALDL CONN (DSL W/O 4L80–E) ..... C 16
ALDL CONN (GAS W/ 4L80–E) ..... E 12
ALDL CONN (GAS W/O 4L80–E) ..... E 8
ALDL CONN (W/ CNG) ..... E 24
ALTERNATOR ..... B–C 4
ANTI-LOCK BRAKE SYSTEM ..... C–E 52–55
AUDIO ALARM MODULE ..... C 39
AUTO TRANS (GAS W/O 4L80–E) ..... E 11
AUTO TRANS (W/ CNG) ..... E 27
AUXILIARY BATTERY ..... A 6
AUXILIARY BATTERY RELAY ..... B 4
AUXILIARY COOLANT FAN SYSTEM ..... C 4
BACK-UP LT SW ..... E 39
BEAM SELECT SW ..... A 36
BRAKE SW ..... A 37
CIG LIGHTER ..... E 28
CLUTCH SW (M/T) ..... B 7
CONVENIENCE CENTER ..... B–D 33–34
COURTESY LTS ..... A–E 48–51
CRUISE CONTROL SYSTEM ..... D–E 6–7
DIMMER SW ..... B 36
DIR FLASHER ..... A 37
DIR/HAZARD SW ..... A–B 39
DOOR SWS ..... C–E 51
EGR SOL (4.3L) (GAS W/ 4L80–E) ..... C 12
ELECTRONIC CONTROL MODULE
  (ECM) (DSL W/O 4L80–E) ..... A 16–19
ELECTRONIC CONTROL MODULE
  (ECM) (GAS W/O 4L80–E) ..... A 8–11
ELECTRONIC CONTROL MODULE (ECM)
  (W/ COMP NATURAL GAS) (CNG) ..... A 24–27
ENGINE TEMP SENSOR (GAS) ..... B 55
EVRV (GAS) ..... D 8,B 12
FAST IDLE TEMP SW (DSL) ..... D 16,E 21
FOG LT RELAY ..... C 3
FOG LT SW ..... C–D 38
FRONT WASHER MOTOR ..... D 5,E 4
FRONT WIPER MOTOR MODULE ..... D–E 4,D 5
FRONT WIPER/WASHER SW ..... C 36,D 36
FUEL DOOR SHUT OFF SW (W/ CNG) ..... C 24
FUEL HEATER (DSL W/ 4L80–E) ..... E 20
FUEL HEATER (DSL W/O 4L80–E) ..... D 16
FUEL PRES TRANSDUCER (W/ CNG) ..... D 24
FUEL PUMP RELAY (DSL) ..... C 19,C 23
FUEL PUMP RELAY (GAS) ..... B 8,E 14
FUEL PUMP/OIL PRES SW (EX DSL) ..... B 55
FUEL SHUT OFF SOL
  (DSL W/ 4L80–E) ..... D 22
FUEL SHUT OFF SOL
  (DSL W/O 4L80–E) ..... E 16
FUEL SOLENOIDS (W/ CNG) ..... D–E 26
FUEL SUPPLY RELAY (W/ CNG) ..... B 24
FUEL TANK UNIT (GAS) ..... B 64
FUSE BLOCK ..... C 29–30
GLOW PLUG CONTROLLER (DSL) ..... D 19,D 23
GROUND A ..... B 3
GROUND B ..... D 3
GROUND C ..... A 4
GROUND D ..... A 4
GROUND E ..... A 6
GROUND F ..... A 6
GROUND G ..... A 6
GROUND H ..... C 7
GROUND I ..... D 7
GROUND J ..... E 6
GROUND K (DSL W/ 4L80–E) ..... C 22
GROUND K (DSL W/O 4L80–E) ..... C 18
GROUND L ..... E 37
GROUND M ..... C 44
GROUND N ..... B 51
GROUND O ..... E 48
GROUND P ..... C 65
GROUND Q ..... C 65
GROUND R ..... D 65
HAZARD FLASHER ..... B 37
HEATED OXYGEN SENSOR
  (4.3L) (GAS W/ 4L80–E) ..... A 15
HEATED OXYGEN SENSOR (W/ CNG) ..... C 27
HORN RELAY ..... B 3
HOT FUEL HANDLING
  MOD (GAS W/ 4L80–E) ..... C 15
HOT FUEL HANDLING MOD
  (GAS W/O 4L80–E) ..... C 8
IGNITION COIL (GAS W/ 4L80–E) ..... E 15
IGNITION COIL (GAS W/O 4L80–E) ..... D 11
IGNITION SW ..... A 28–31
IN-LINE FUSE (W/ CNG) ..... D 24
INSTRUMENT CLUSTER ..... A–B 52–53
JUNCTION BLOCK (J/B) ..... B–C 7
LEFT FRONT SEAT
  BELT RETRACTOR SW ..... C 37
LIGHT SW ..... A 36
LOW COOLANT MODULE (DSL) ..... A 55
LP DRIVER MODULE
  (DSL W/O 4L80–E) ..... D 16
MAIN BATTERY ..... A 7
PARK BRAKE SW ..... E 53
PARN/NEUTRAL SW ..... B 64
POWER DOOR LOCK SYSTEM ..... A–E 59–63
POWER MIRROR SW ..... E 63
POWER SEAT SW ..... D–E 60
POWER WINDOW SYSTEM ..... A–E 56–59
POWERTRAIN CONTROL MODULE
  (PCM) (GAS W/ 4L80–E) ..... A 12–15
REAR DEFOG SW ..... E 36
REAR INTERMITTENT
  WIPER/WASHER SYSTEM ..... C–E 64
REAR WINDOW RELEASE SYSTEM ..... A 64
SNOWPLOW DIR LT RELAYS ..... A 3,E 3
STARTER ..... A 7
TCC SOL (DSL W/O 4L80–E) ..... C 17
TRANSMISSION (GAS W/ 4L80–E) ..... C–E 20
TRANSMISSION (GAS W/O 4L80–E) ..... D 12
TRANSMISSION CONTROL MODULE
  (TCM) (DSL W/ 4L80–E) ..... A 20–23
VSS BUFFER (DRAC) ..... C 52
WATER IN FUEL SENS
  (DSL W/ 4L80–E) ..... E 20
WATER IN FUEL SENSOR
  (DSL W/O 4L80–E) ..... E 16
4WD SYSTEM ..... A–B 48

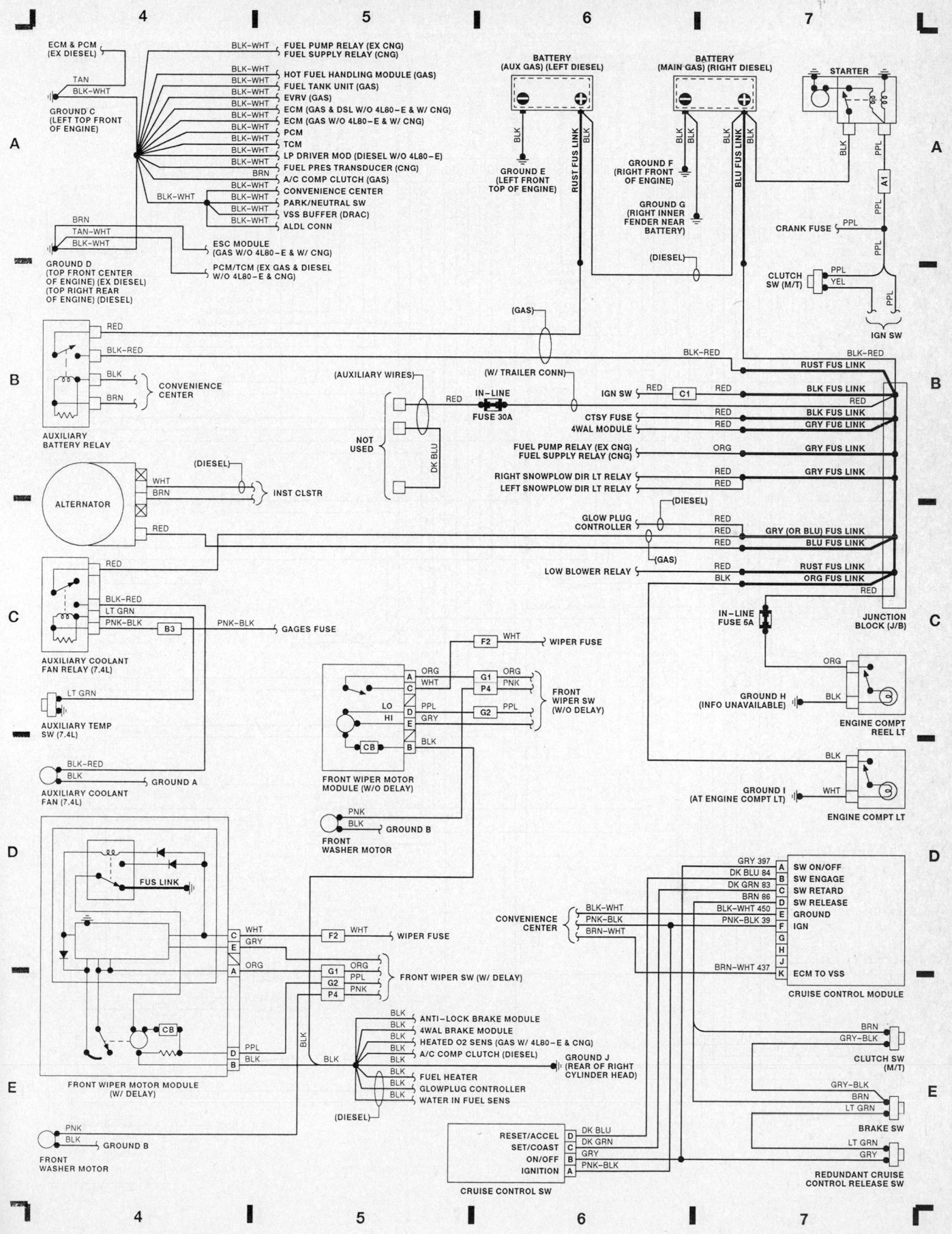

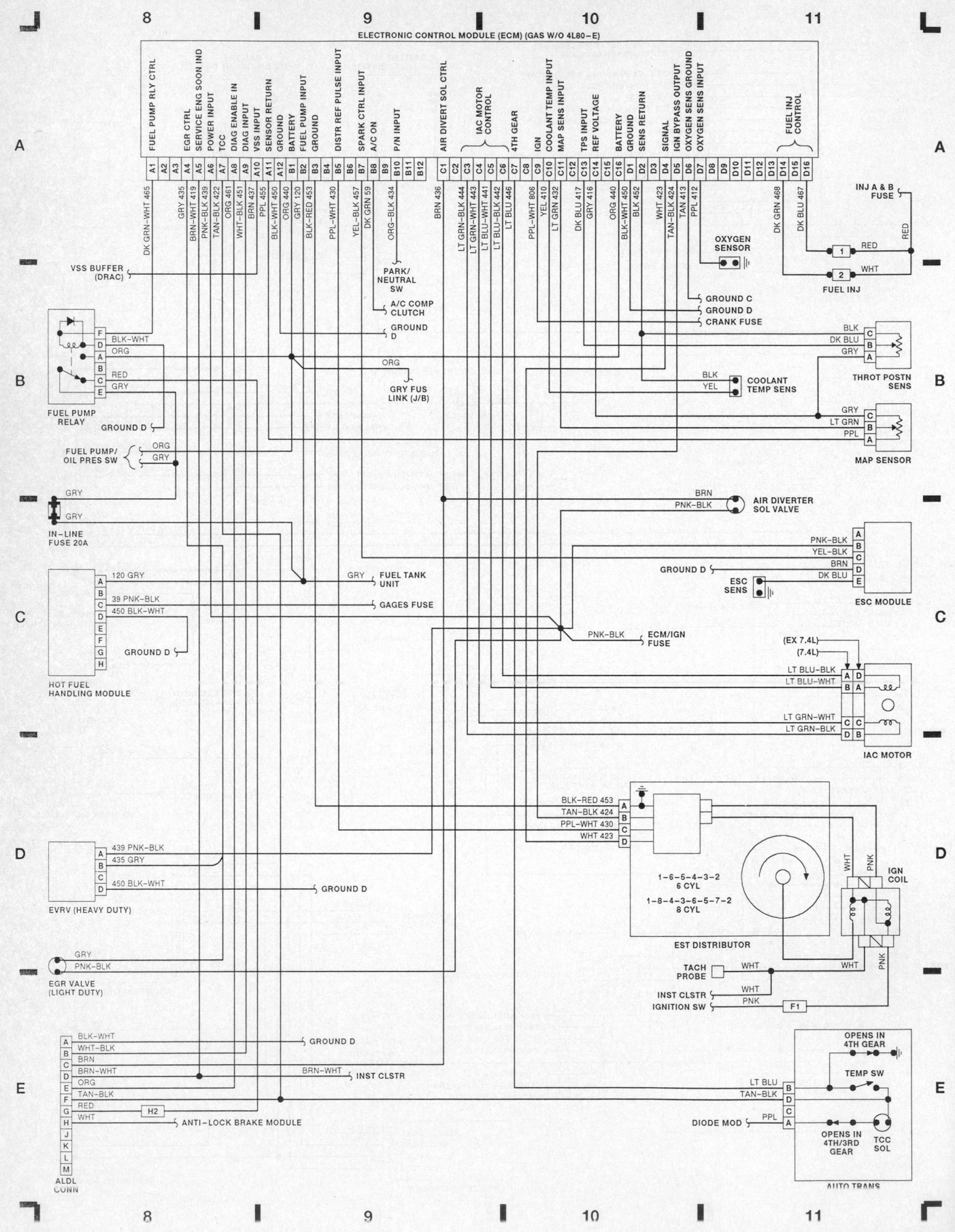

Electronic Control Module (ECM) (GAS W/O 4L80-E)

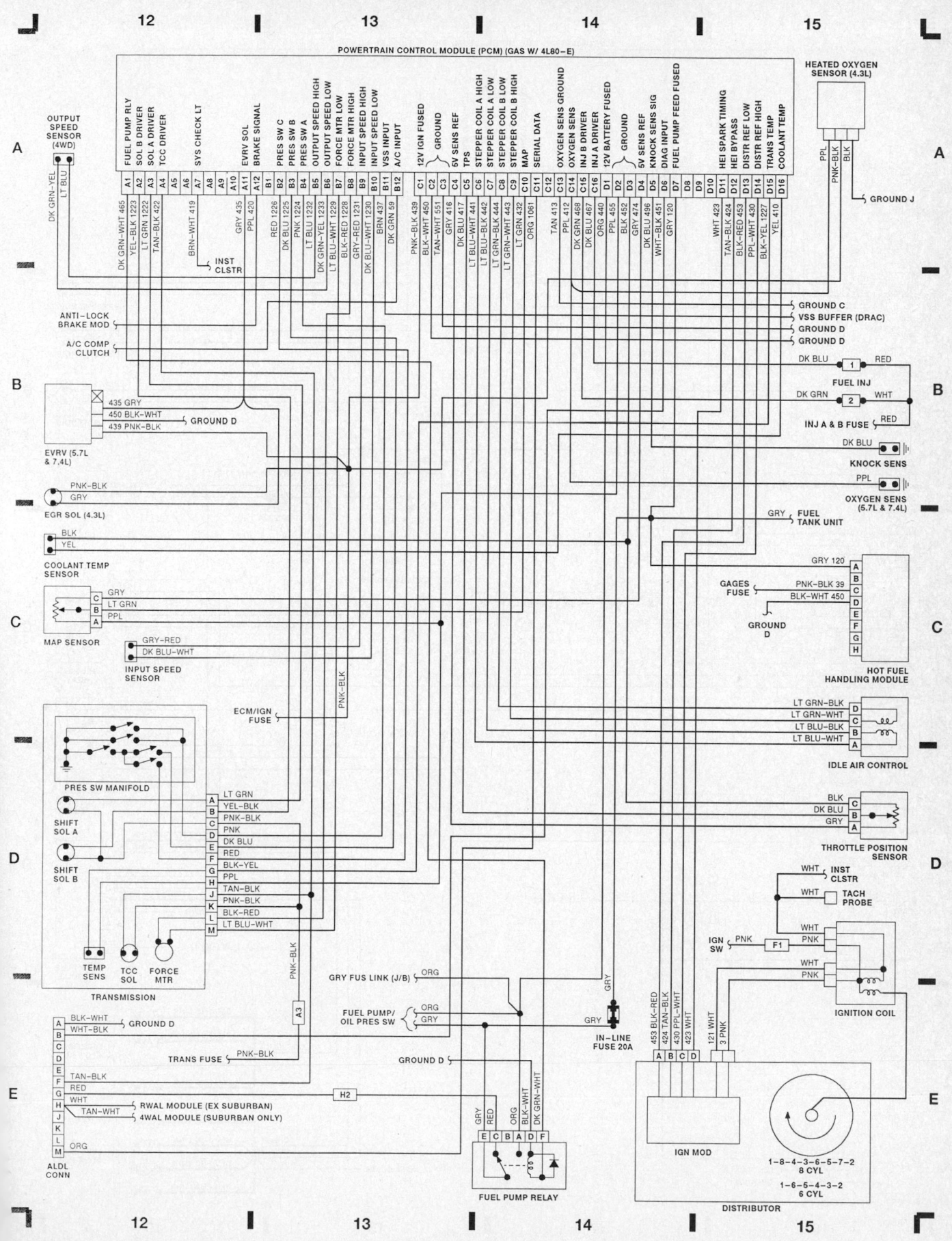

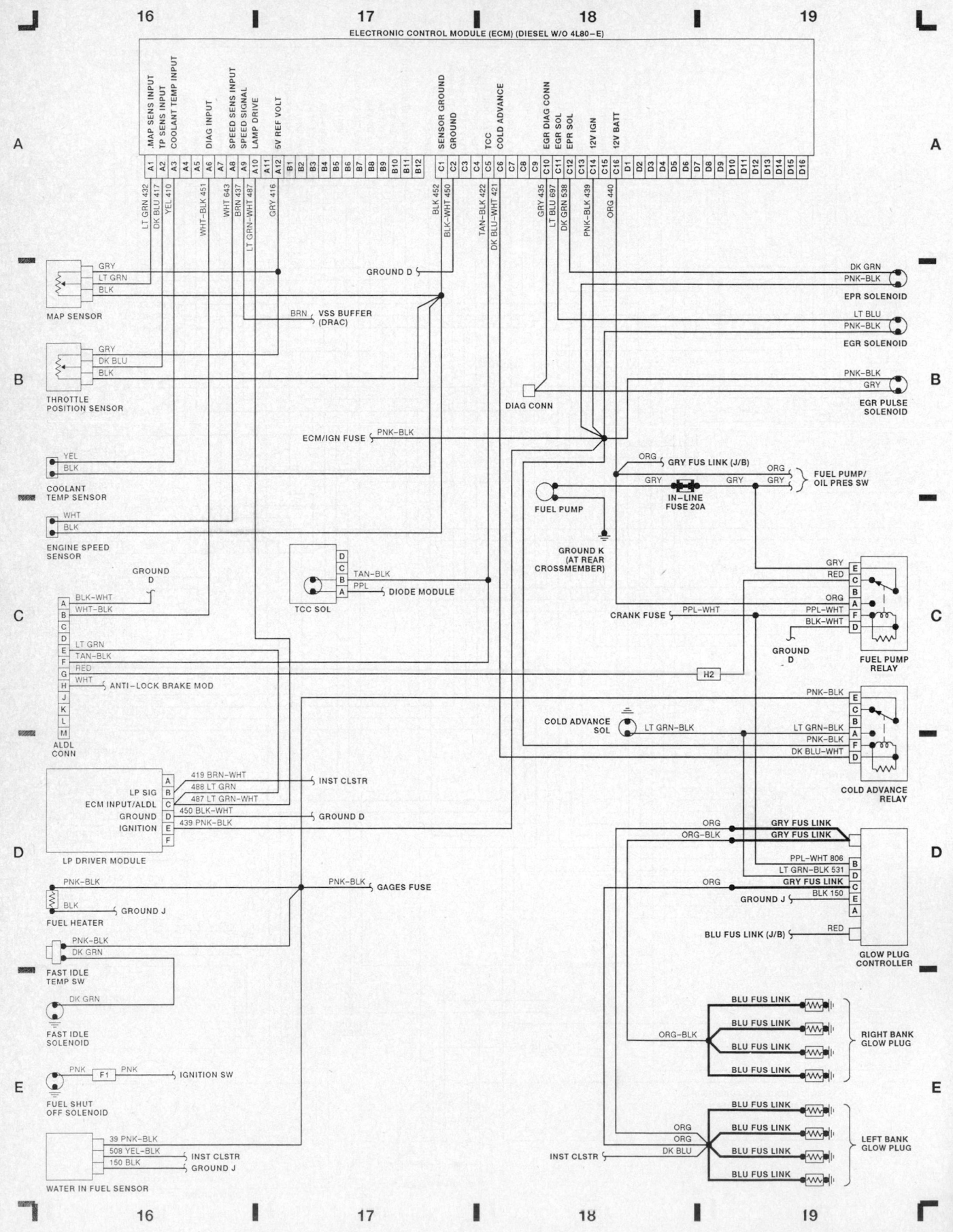

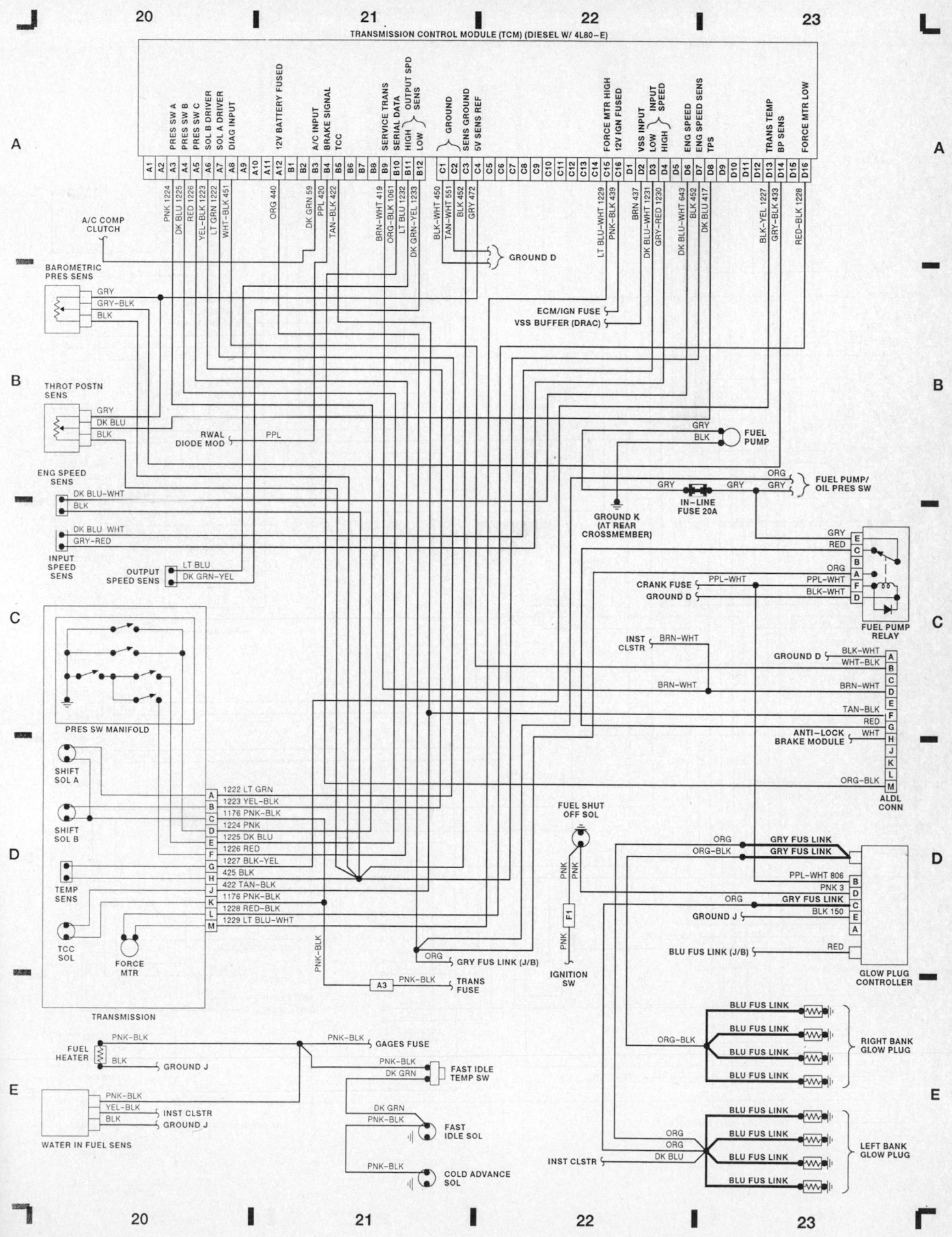

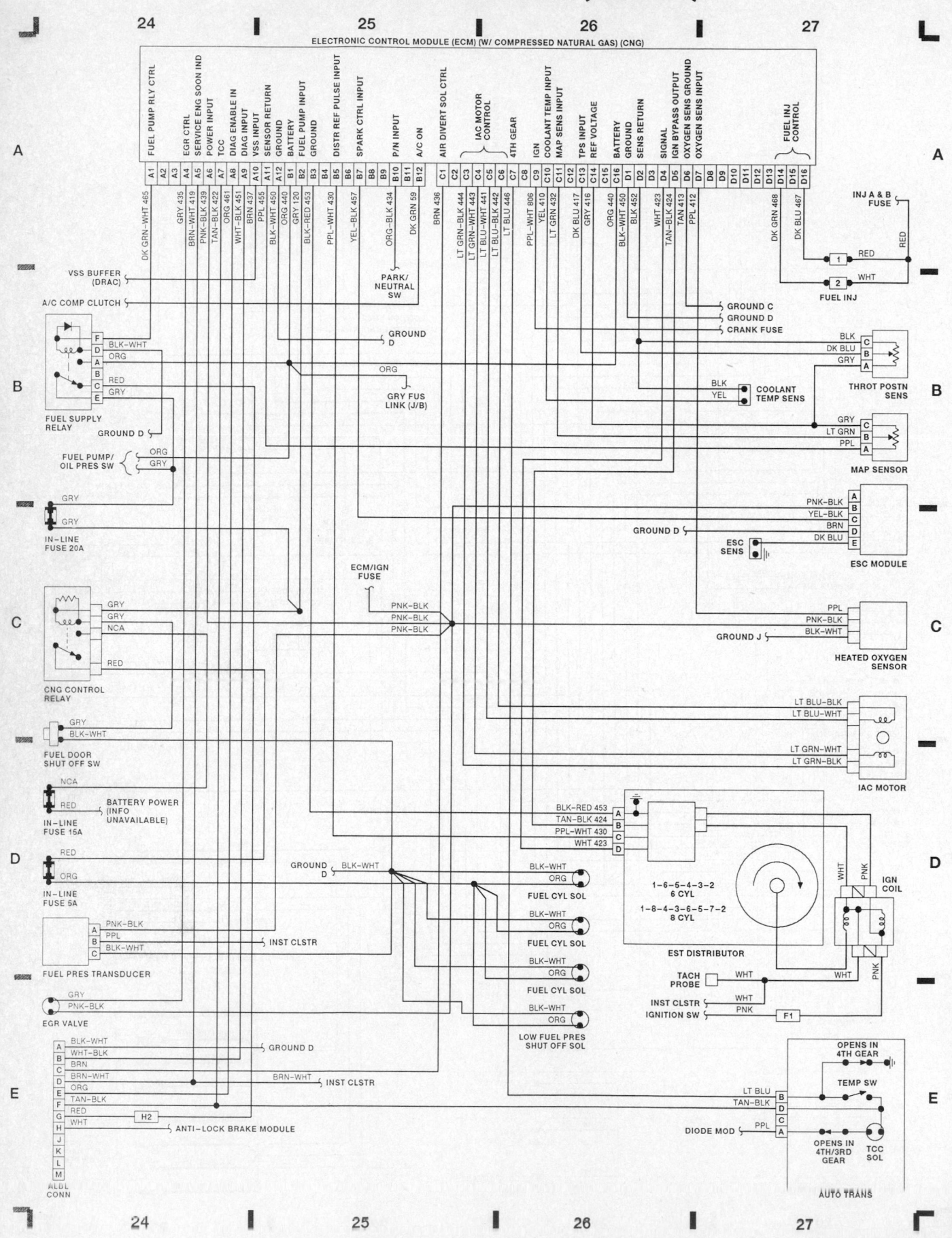

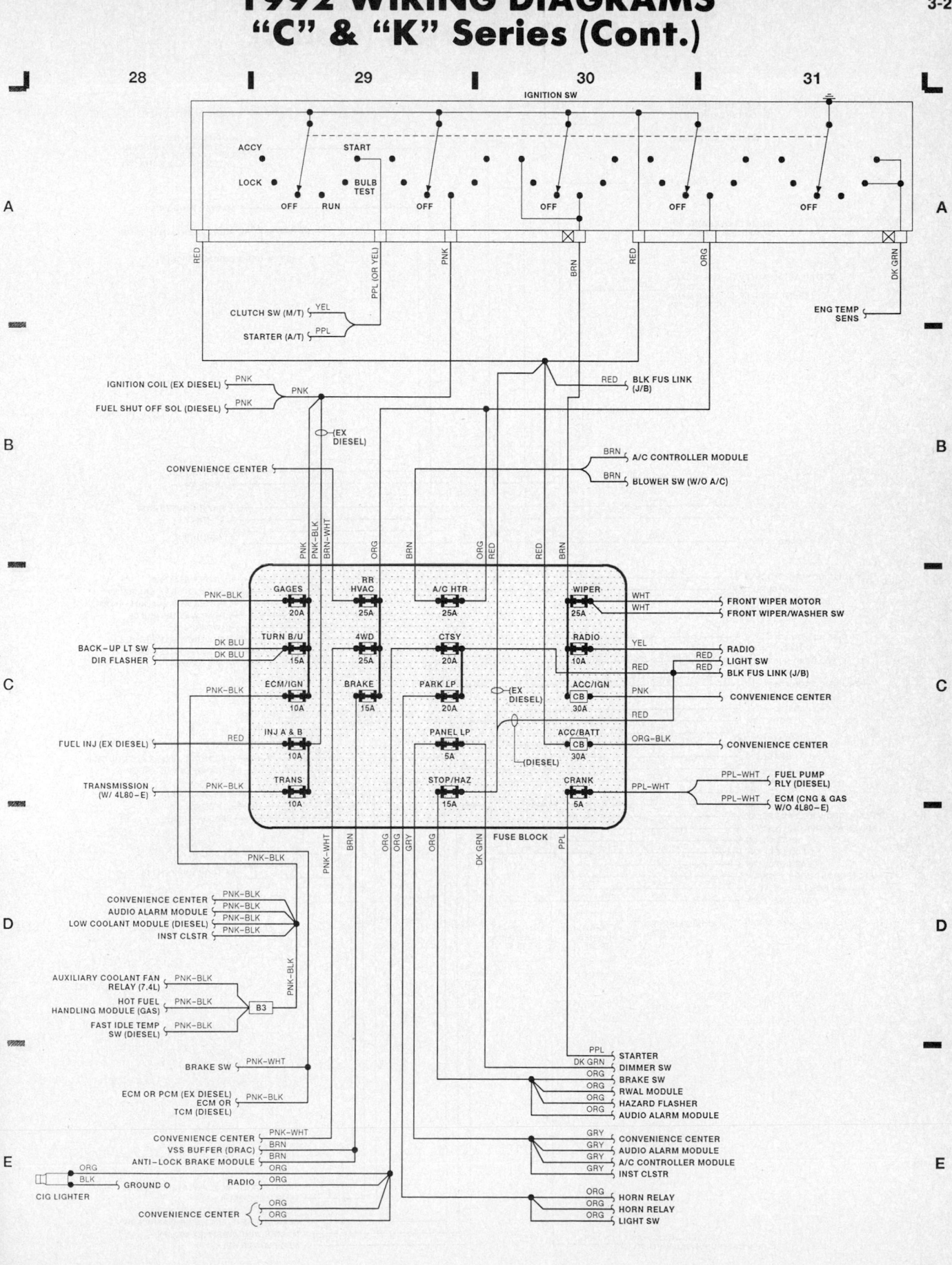

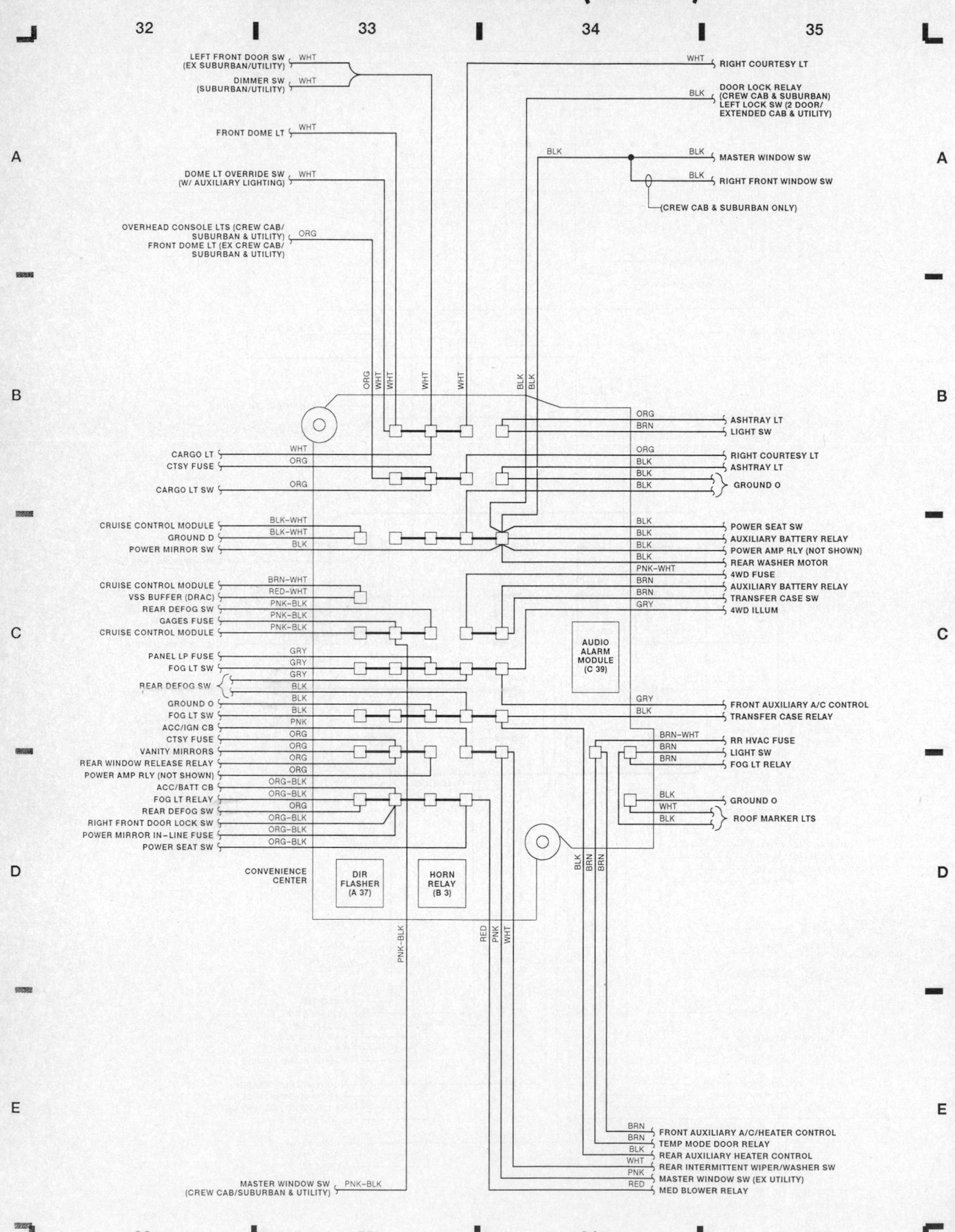

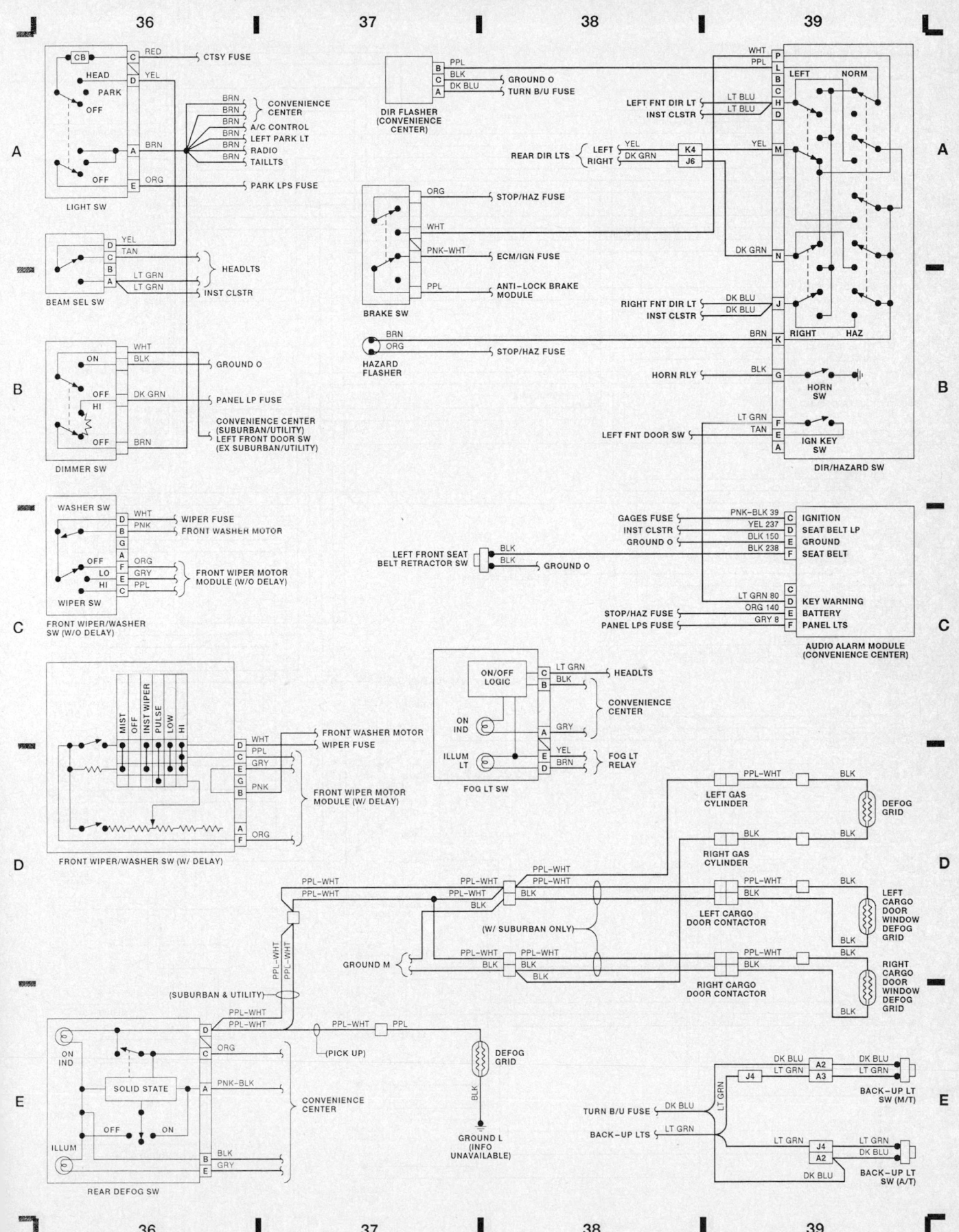

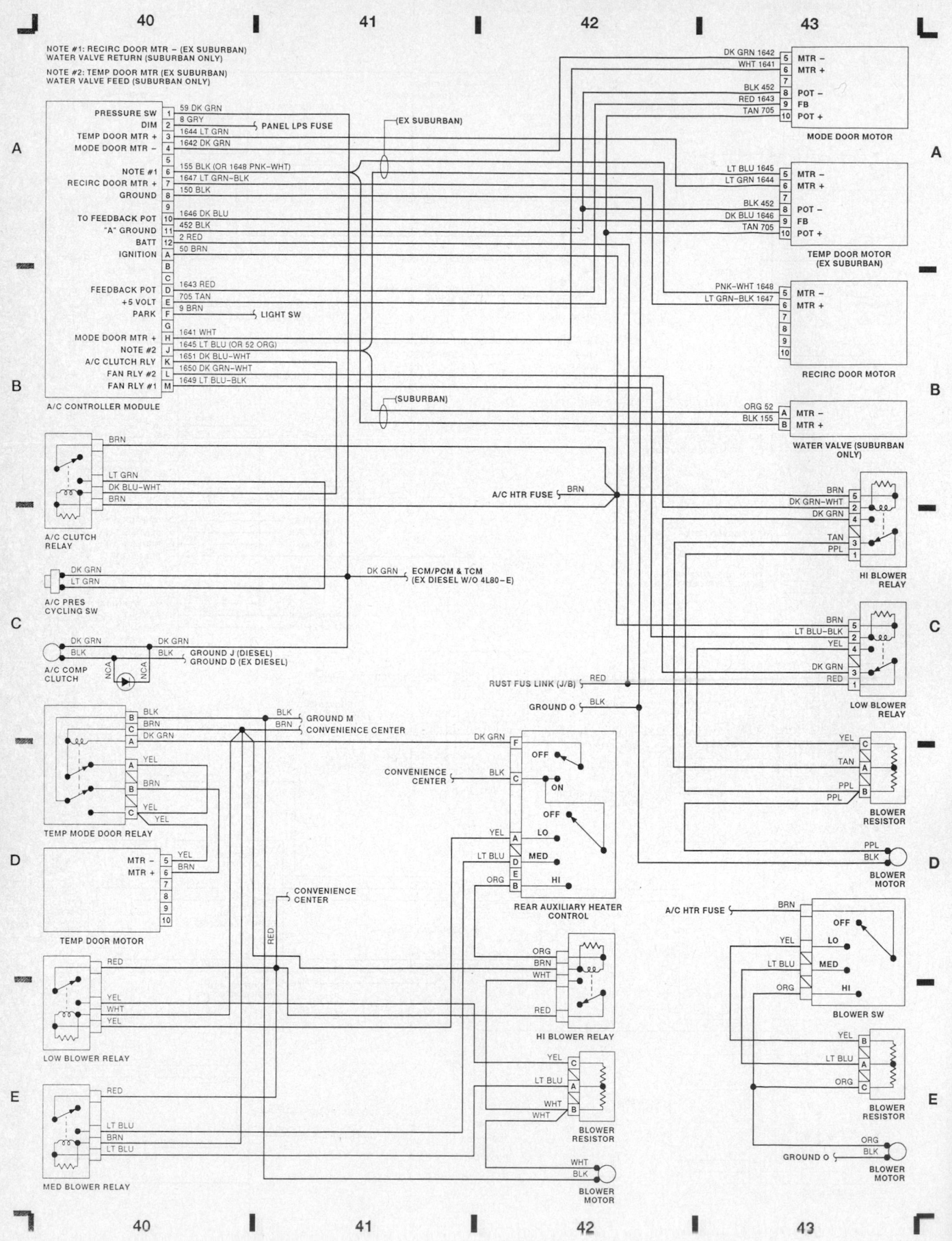

1992 WIRING DIAGRAMS
"C" & "K" Series (Cont.)

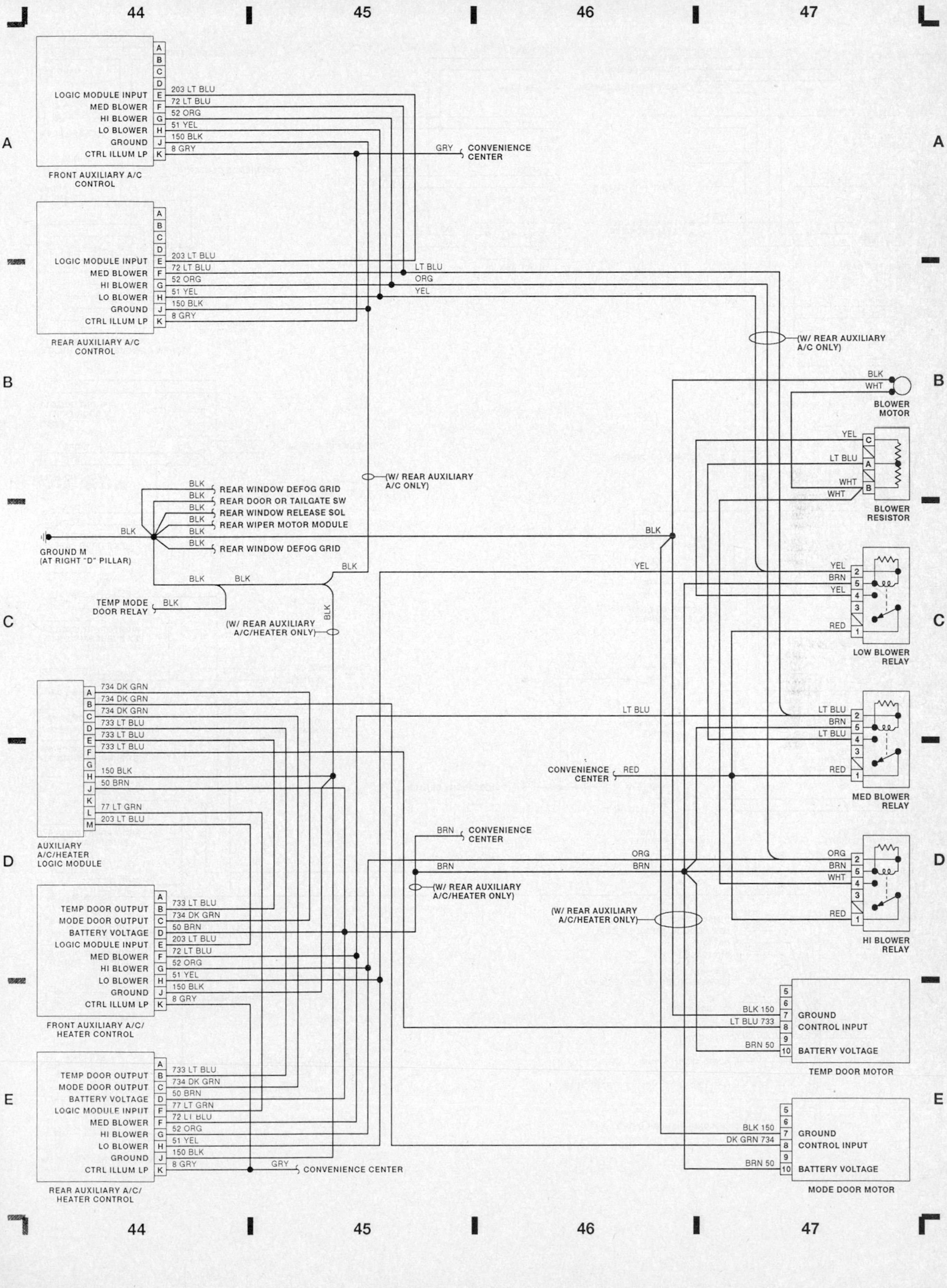

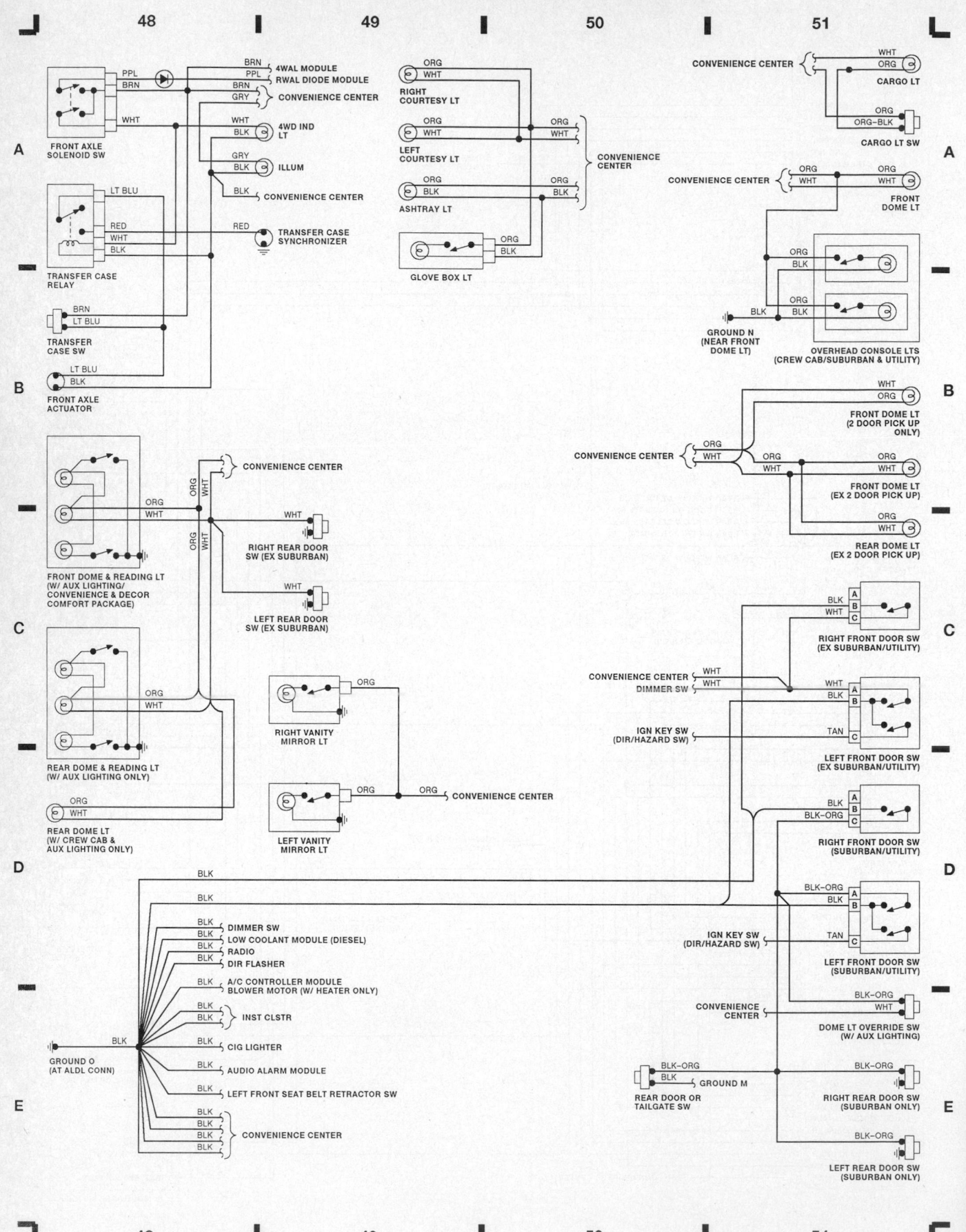

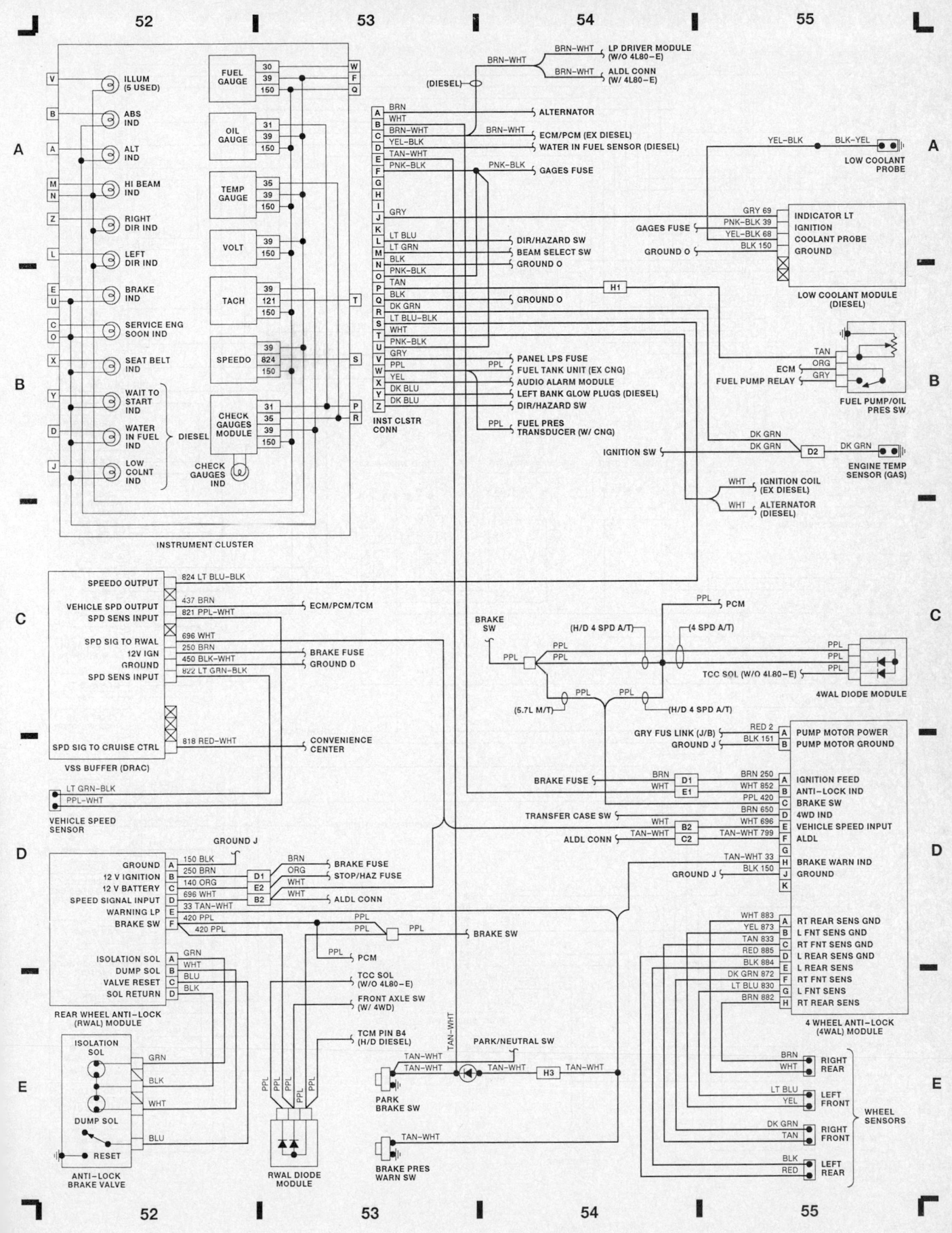

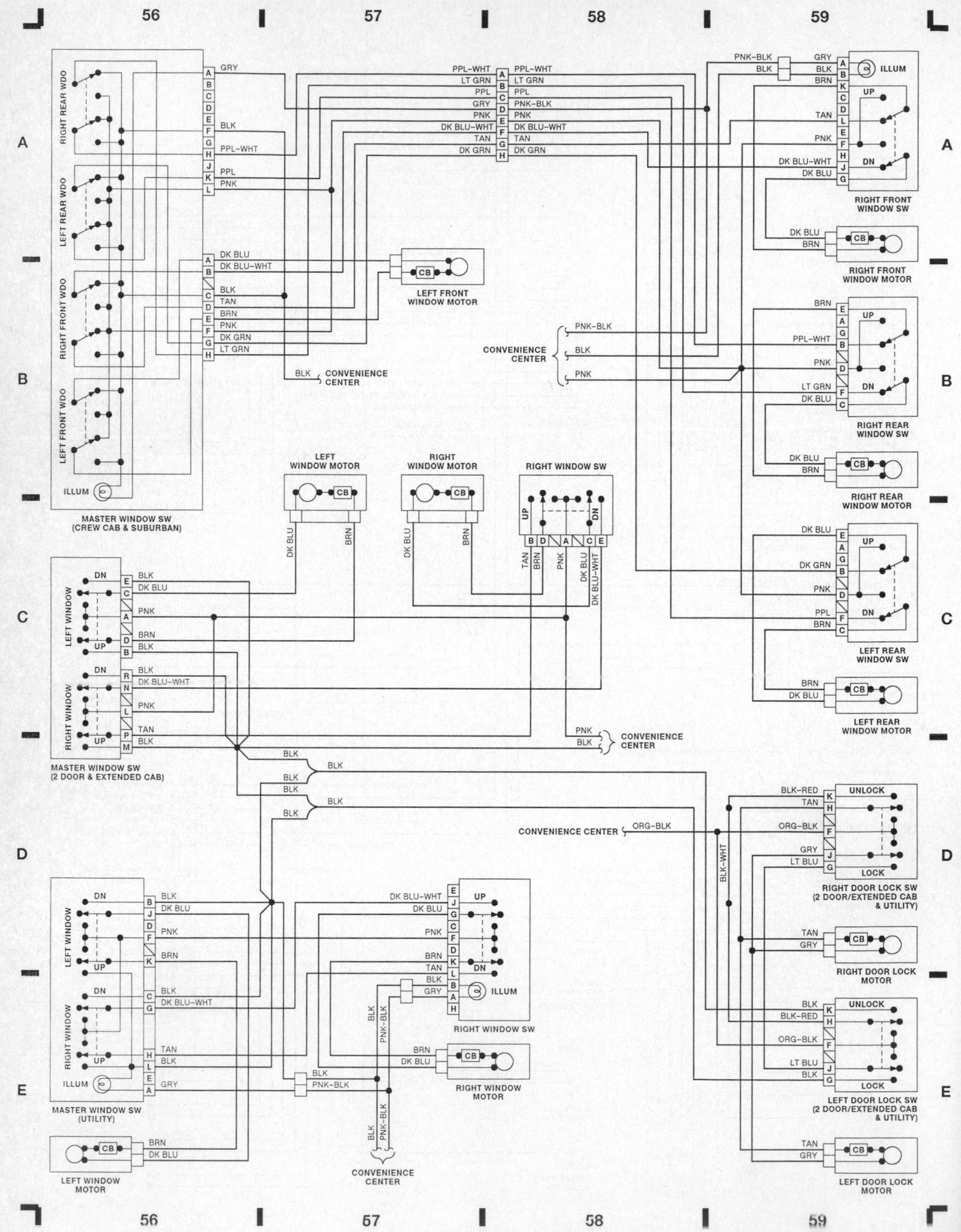

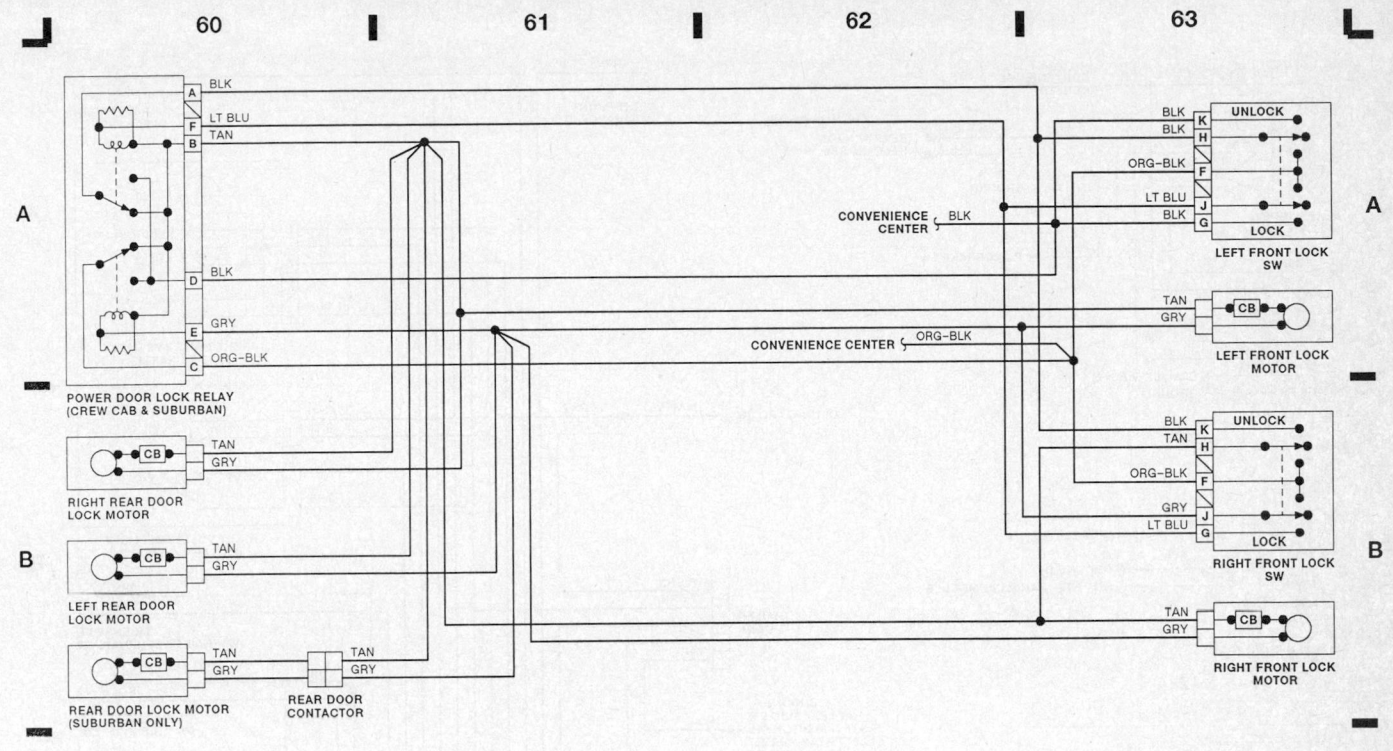

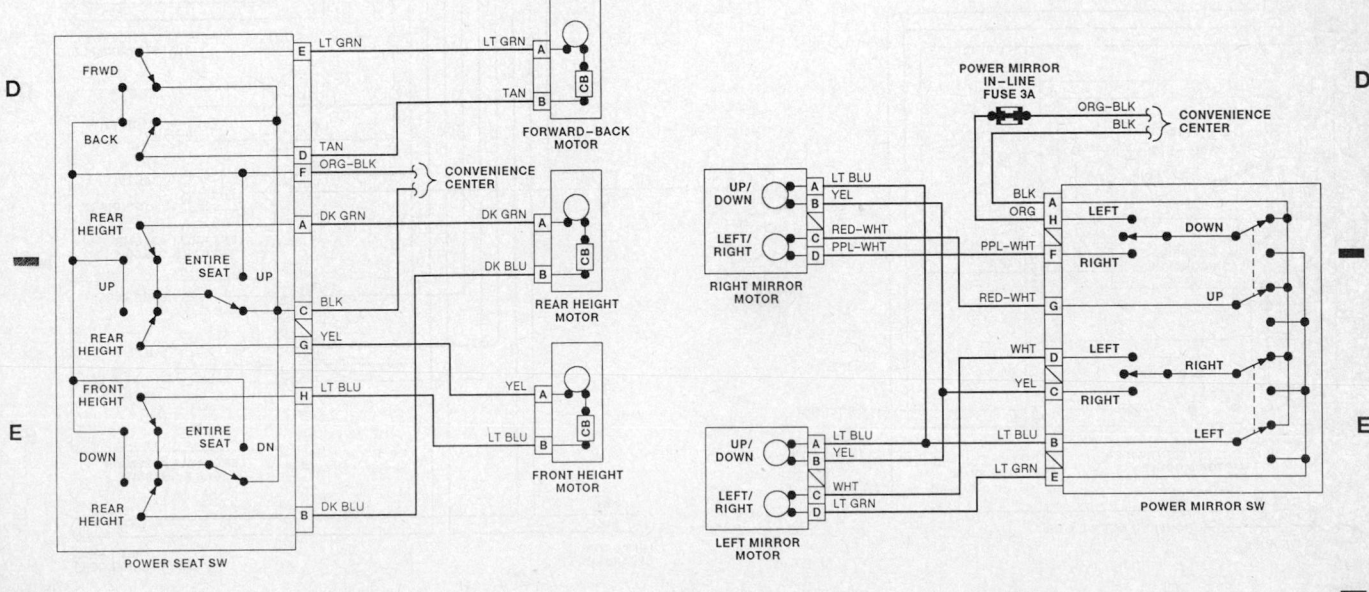

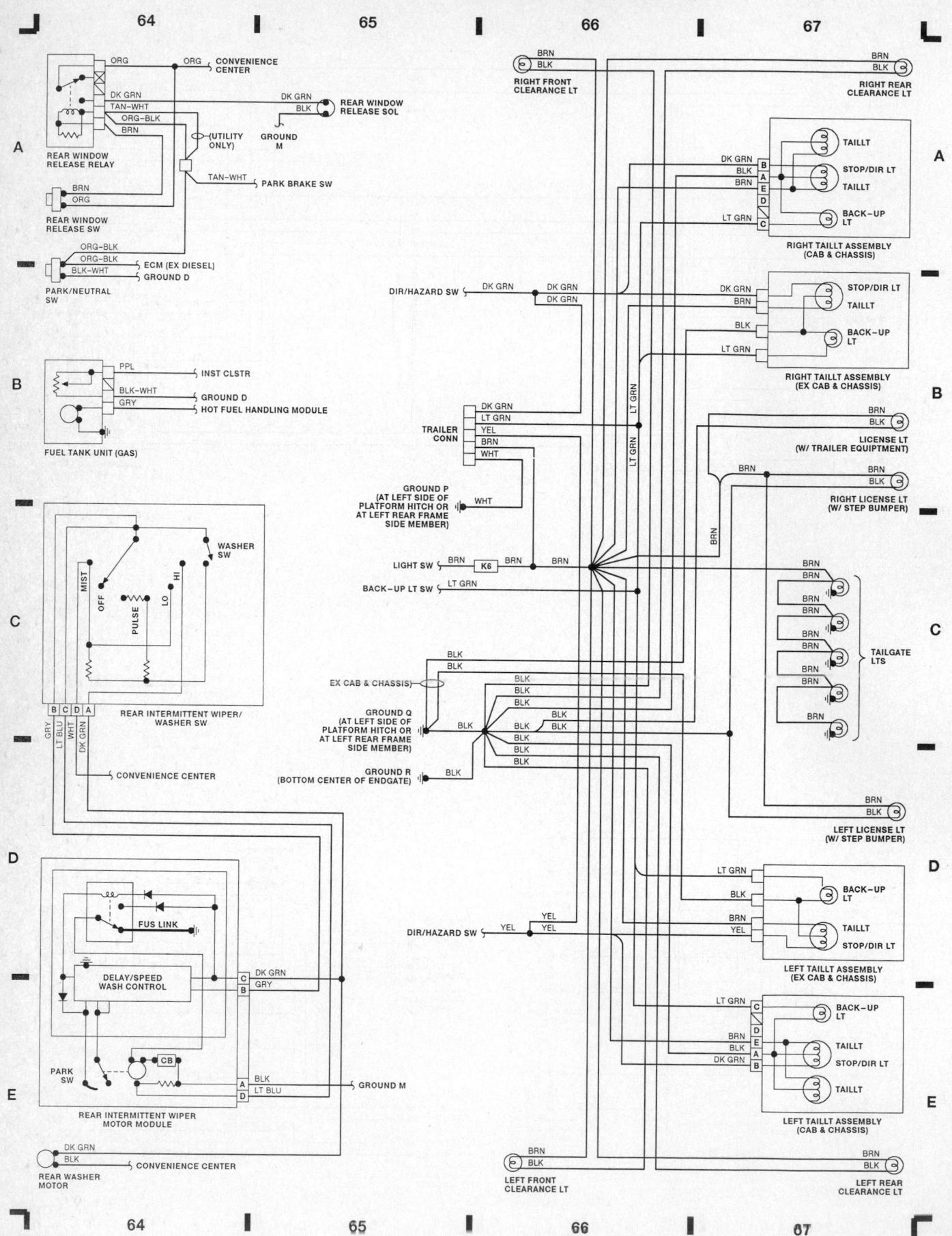

COMPONENT LOCATOR:

A/C SYSTEM .... D-E 36-38
ALARM MODULE .... D-E 28
ALDL CONN (DIESEL) ...... C-D 12, C-D 19
ALDL CONN (GAS) .... D 7, E 8
ALTERNATOR .... C 3
AUX BLOWER SYSTEM .... C 36
AUX COOLANT FAN RELAY .... E 3
BACK-UP LT SW .... C 39
BATTERY .... A 3
BEAM SEL SW .... D-E 24
BUZZER ASSEMBLY .... D 31
CHECK ENGINE LIGHT
   DRIVER MODULE .... E 20
CIG LTR. .... E 30
CRUISE CTRL SYSTEM .... D-E 25-27
DEFOG SYSTEM .... A 36-37
DIGITAL RATIO ADAPTER
   CONTROL (DRAC) MODULE ..... A 31
DIR/HAZ SW .... B-C 24
DOOR LOCK RELAY .... A 35, D 35
DOOR SWS. .... C 25
EGR DUMP VALVE (DIESEL
   W/O 4L80-E) .... B 15
EGR SOL (GAS W/O 4L80-E) ...... B 4
EGR VALVE (DIESEL W/O 4L80-E) . B 15
ELECTRONIC CONTROL MODULE
   (ECM) (DIESEL W/O 4L80-E) .. A 12-15
ELECTRONIC CONTROL MODULE
   (ECM) (GAS W/O 4L80-E) .... A 4-7
EPR VALVE (DIESEL W/O 4L80-E) . A 15
FAST IDLE TEMP SW (DIESEL) .. E 15, E 17
FUEL HEATER (DIESEL) .... E 15, E 16
FUEL PUMP RELAY (GAS) .... B 4, E 10
FUEL PUMP/OIL PRES SW (GAS) . C 4, E 9
FUEL SHUT OFF SOL
   (DIESEL W/ 4L80-E) .... D 18
FUEL SHUT OFF SOL (DIESEL) . E 12, D 18
FUEL TANK UNIT .... B 28
FUSE BLOCK .... B-D 21-22
GLOW PLUG CONTROLLER (DIESEL) .C 15, D 19
GLOW PLUG INHIBITOR RELAY
   (DIESEL W/ 4L80-E) .... D 15
GLOW PLUGS (DIESEL) ...... B-C 15, E 19
GLOW PLUGS IND .... E 28
GROUND A .... A 2
GROUND B .... A 3
GROUND C .... B 2
GROUND D .... B 3
GROUND E .... D 2
GROUND F (GAS W/ 4L80-E) ...... B 8
GROUND F (GAS W/O 4L80-E) ..... C 5
GROUND G (GAS W/ 4L80-E) ...... A 11
GROUND G (GAS W/O 4L80-E) ..... E 5
GROUND H (DIESEL W/ 4L80-E) ... E 17
GROUND H (DIESEL W/O 4L80-E) .. E 13
GROUND I .... E 29
GROUND J .... E 31
GROUND K .... C 35
GROUND L .... A 38
GROUND M .... B 38
GROUND N .... C 37
GROUND O .... E 36
GROUND P .... D 37
GROUND Q .... D 37
HEATER CTRL LT .... A 23
HEATER SW .... E 38
HORN RELAY .... B 27
HORNS .... D 2
HOT FUEL HANDLING MODULE (GAS) .C 7, C 11
IGNITION COIL (GAS) .... E 4, E 11
IGNITION SW .... A 20
INSTRUMENT CLUSTER .... B-D 30-31
JUNCTION BLOCK .... B 2
KEYLESS ENTRY MODULE .... A 32
LEFT POWER WINDOW SW .... A 28
LIGHT SW .... D 24
LOW COOLANT MODULE .... C 28
MT1 IN-LINE FUSE
   (DIESEL W/ 4L80-E) .... C 19
MT1 IN-LINE FUSE
   (GAS W/ 4L80-E) .... C 8
POWER ANTENNA SYSTEM .... B-C 36-37
POWER MIRROR SYSTEM .... B 36-38
POWERTRAIN CONTROL MODULE
   (PCM) (GAS W/ 4L80-E) ..... A 8-11
PRNDL LIGHT .... C 24
REAR BLOWER SW .... E 38
REAR WHEEL ANTI-LOCK
   (RWAL) MODULE .... A-B 27
STARTER .... A 2
TCC BRAKE SW (DIESEL) ..... D 12, B 16
TCC BRAKE SW (GAS) .... E 7, A 8
TRAILER CONN .... C 38
TRANSMISSION (DIESEL
   W/ 4L80-E) .... C-D 16
TRANSMISSION (GAS W/ 4L80-E) . D 8
TRANSMISSION CONTROL MODULE
   (TCM) (DIESEL W/ 4L80-E) .. A 16-19
WATER IN FUEL IND .... E 28
WATER IN FUEL SENSOR (DIESEL) .D 15, E 16
WIPER/WASHER SYSTEM .... A 24-26

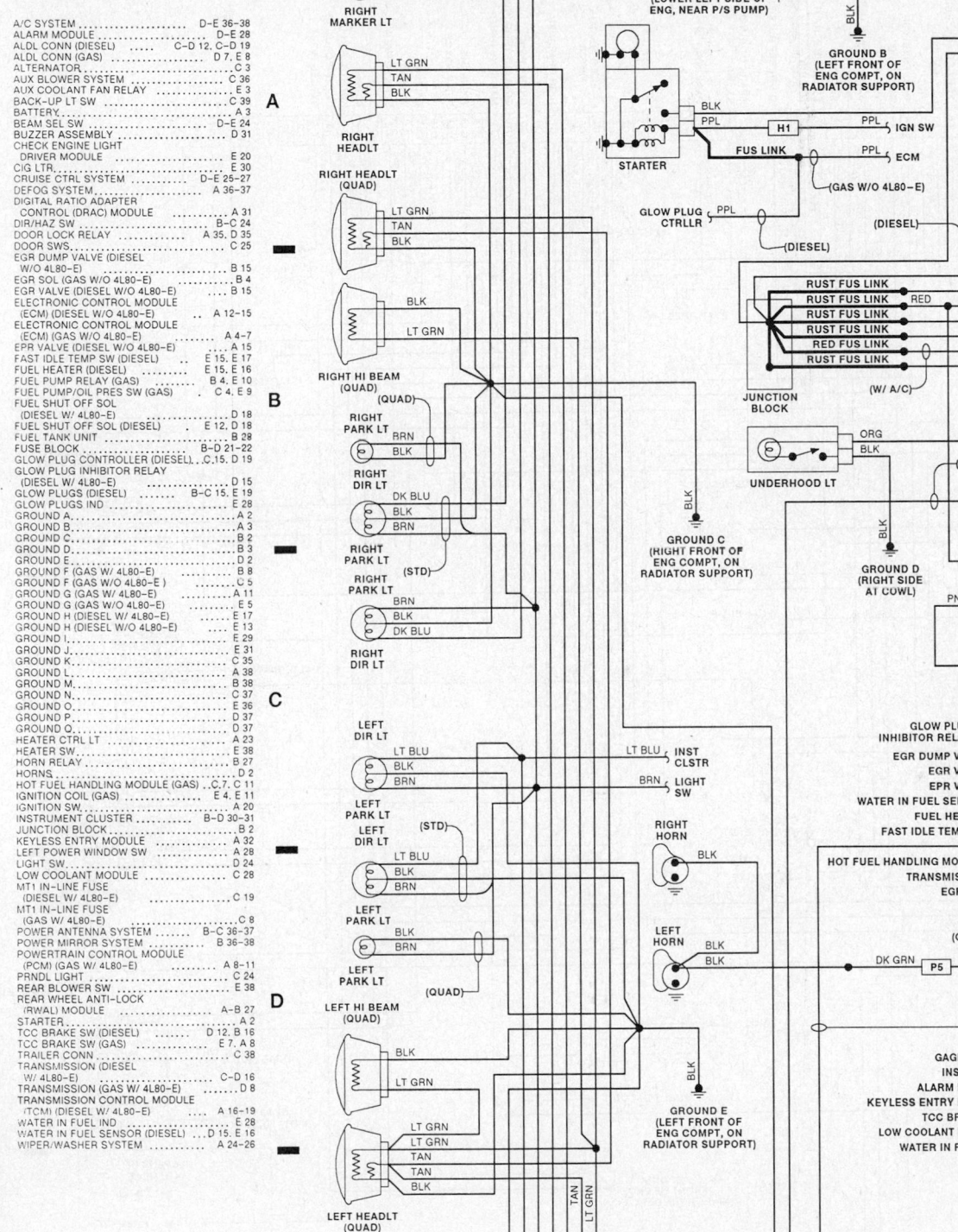

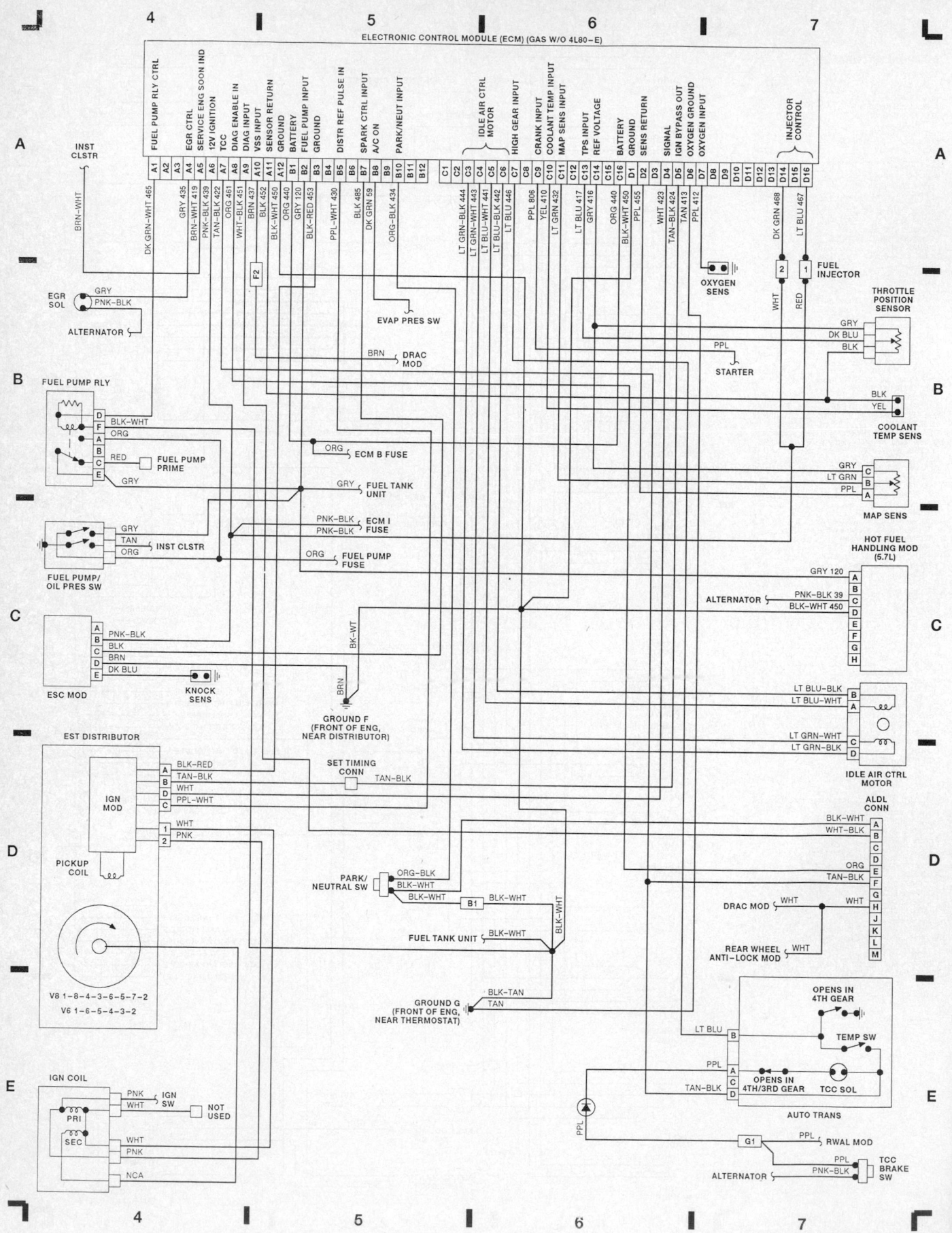

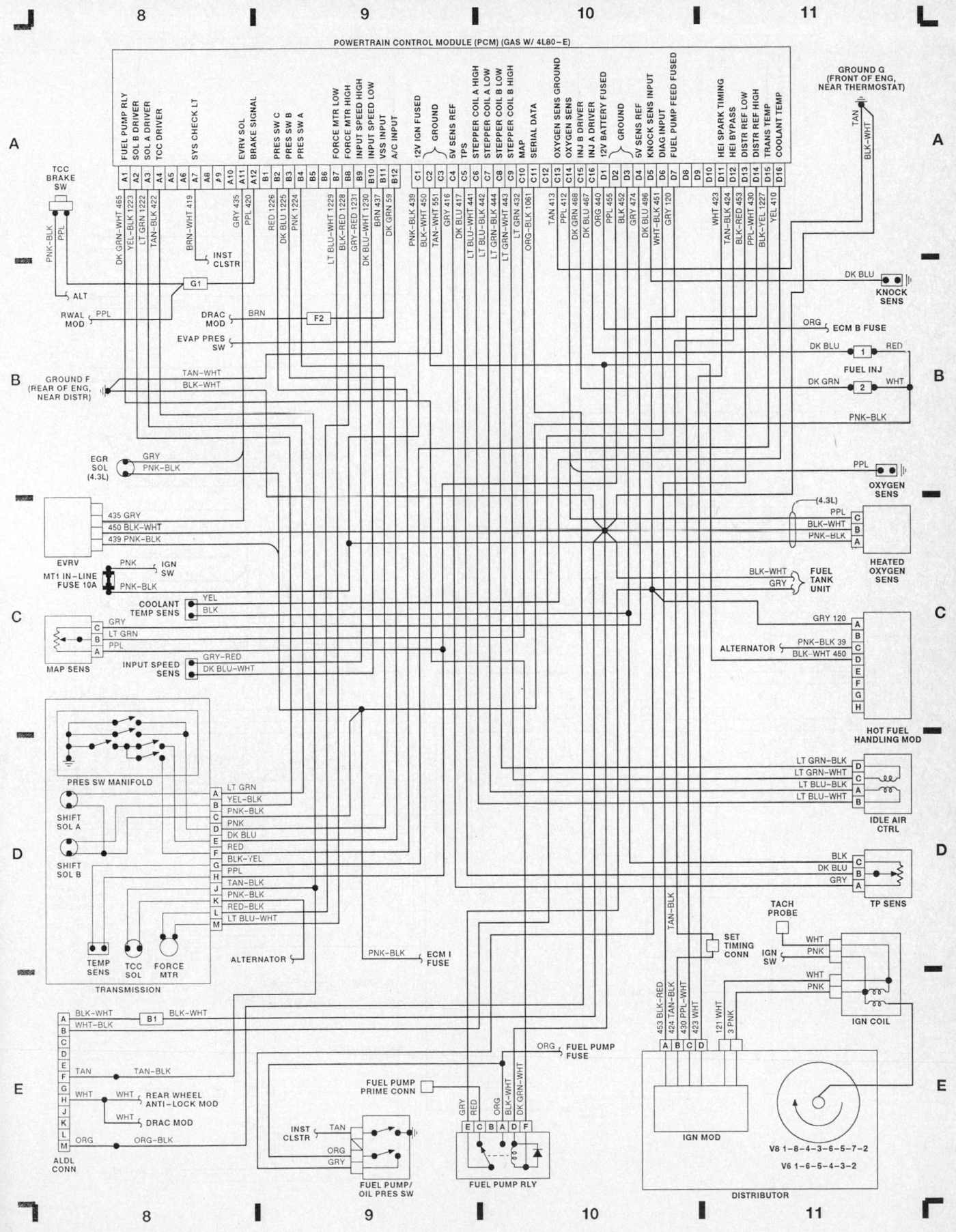

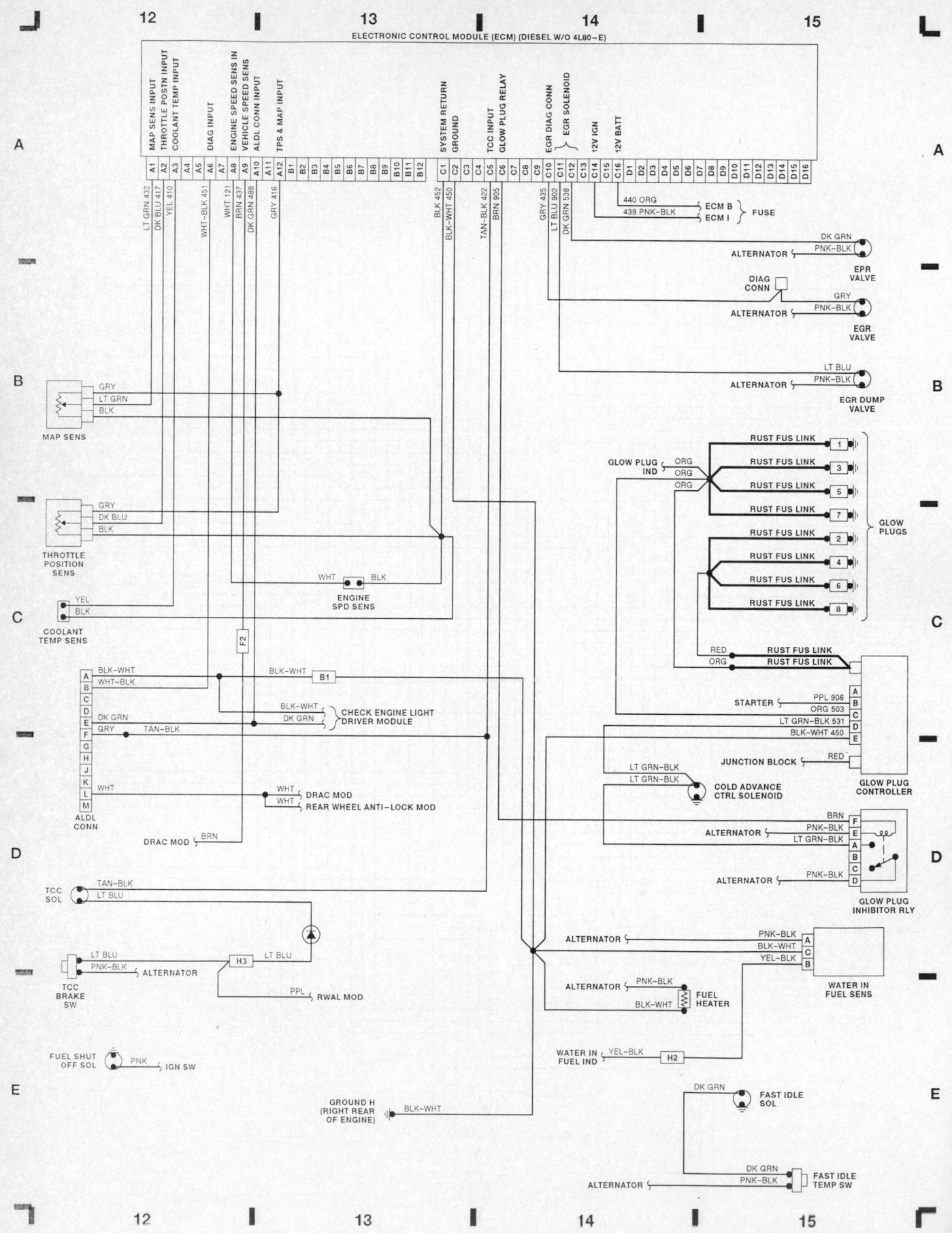

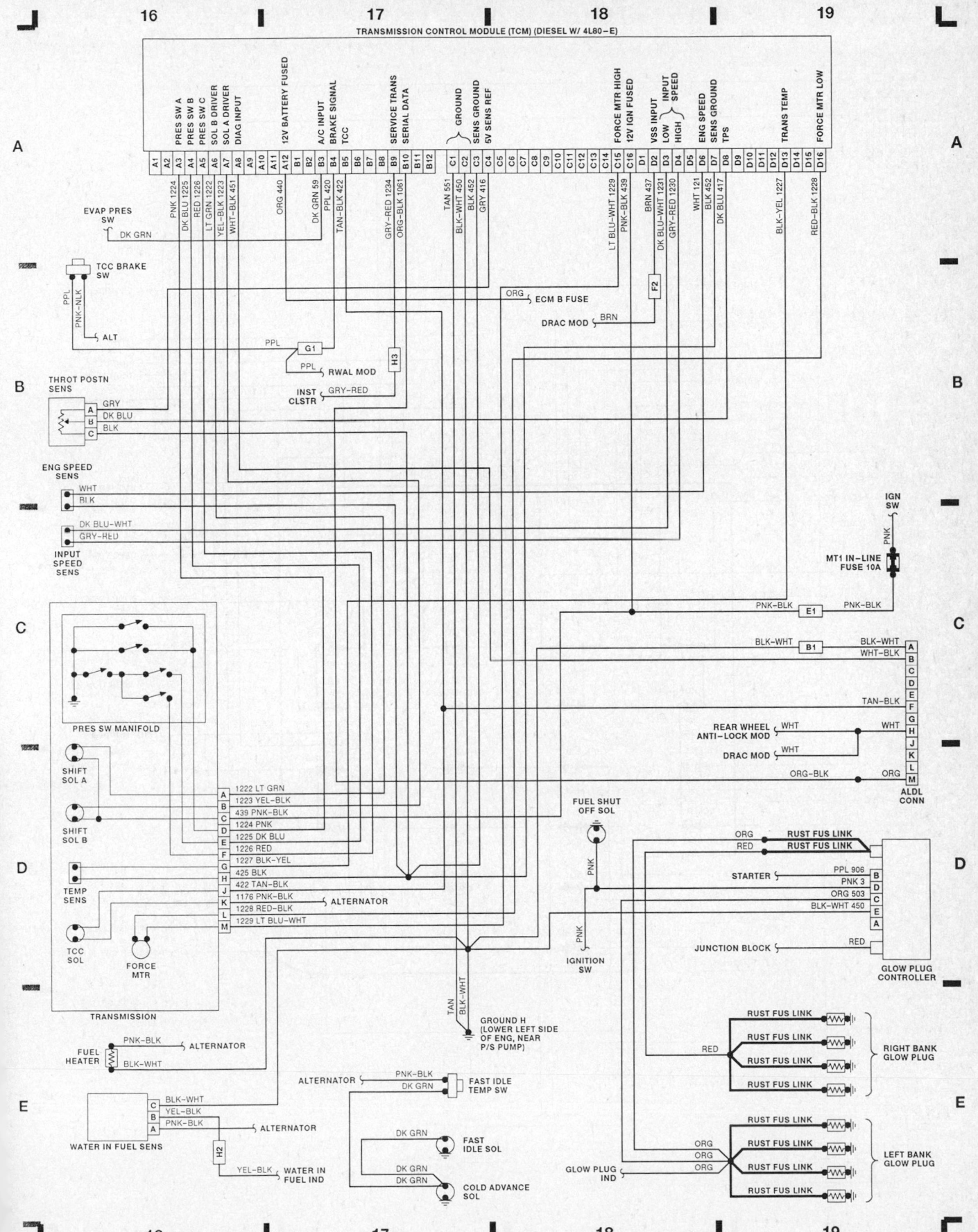

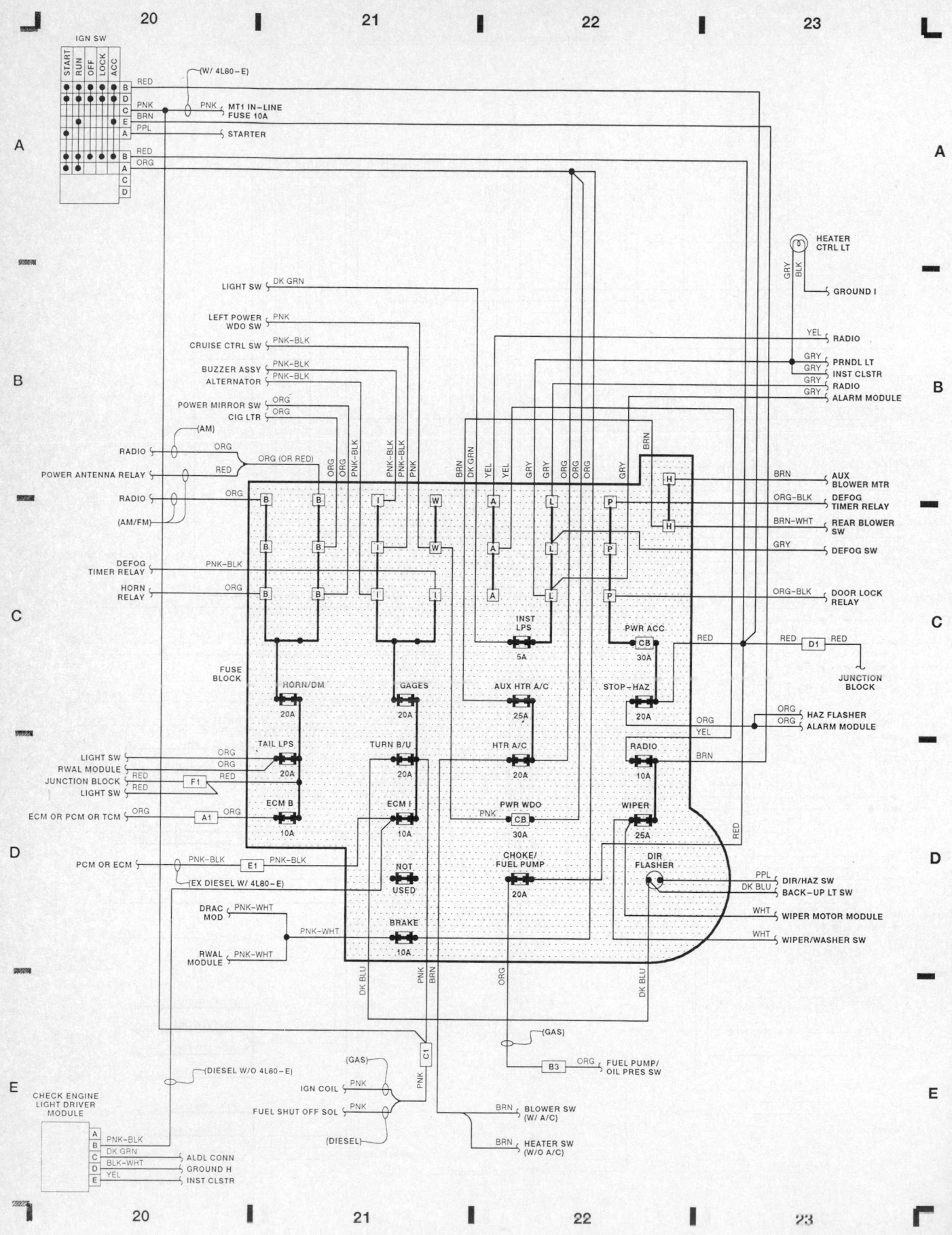

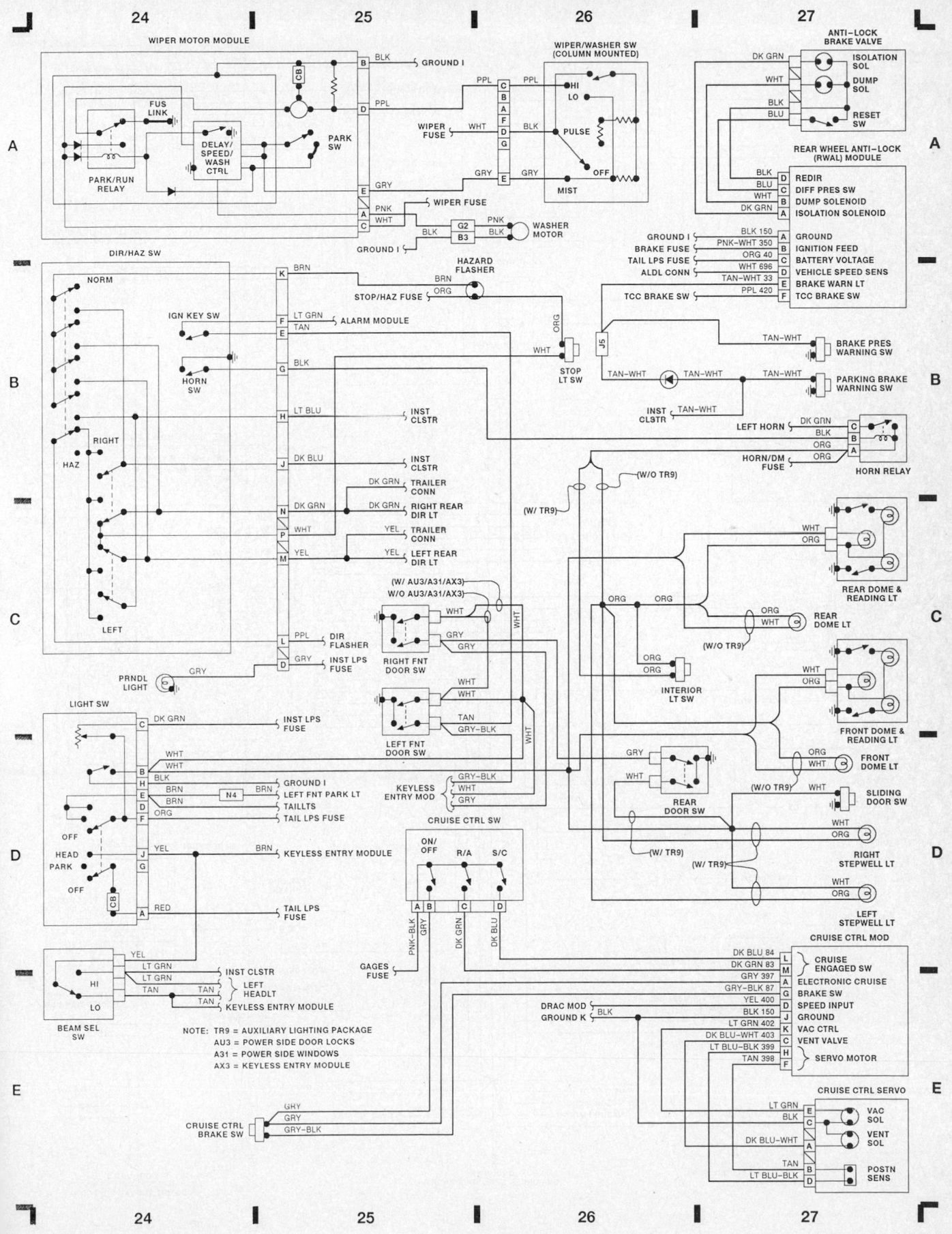

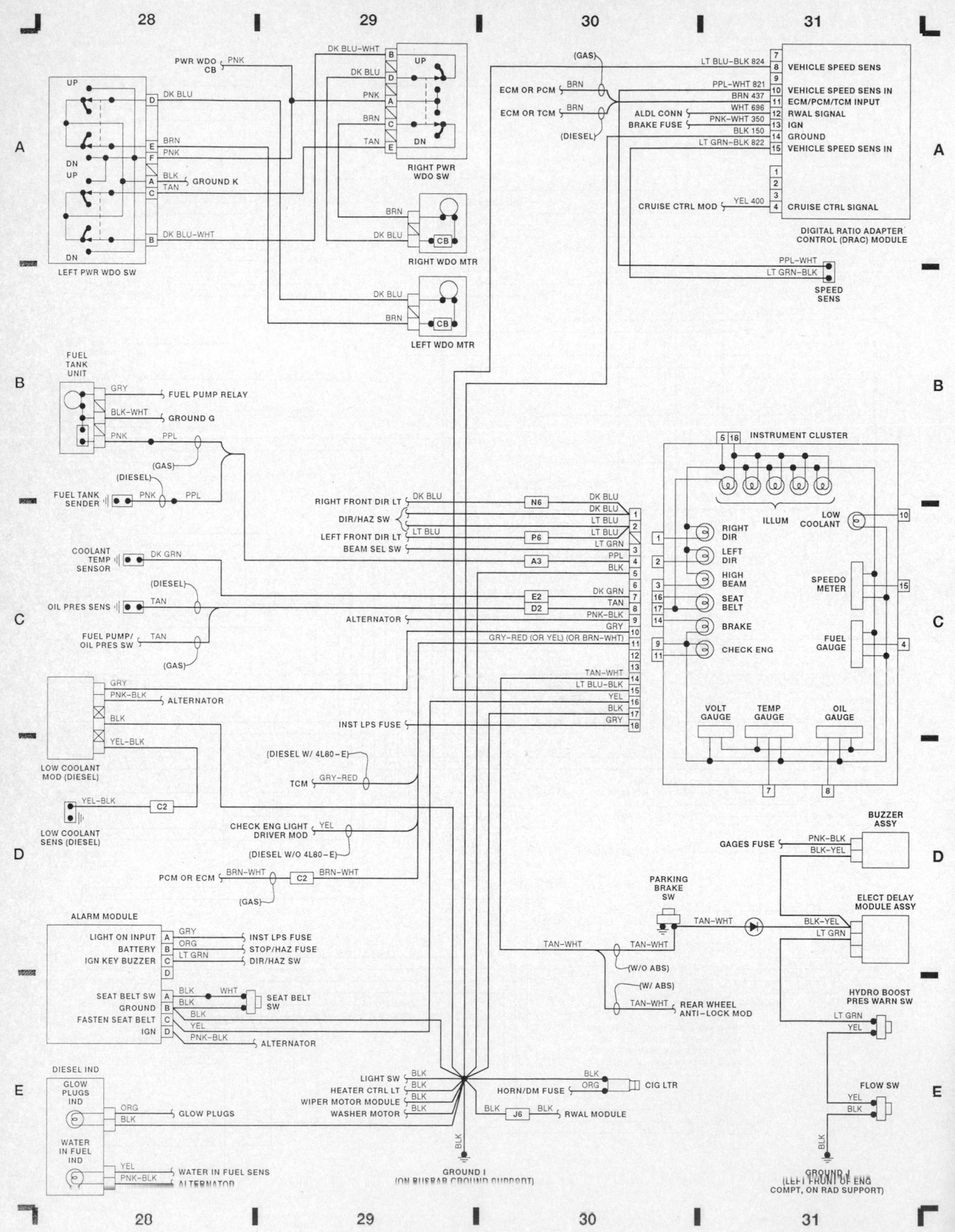

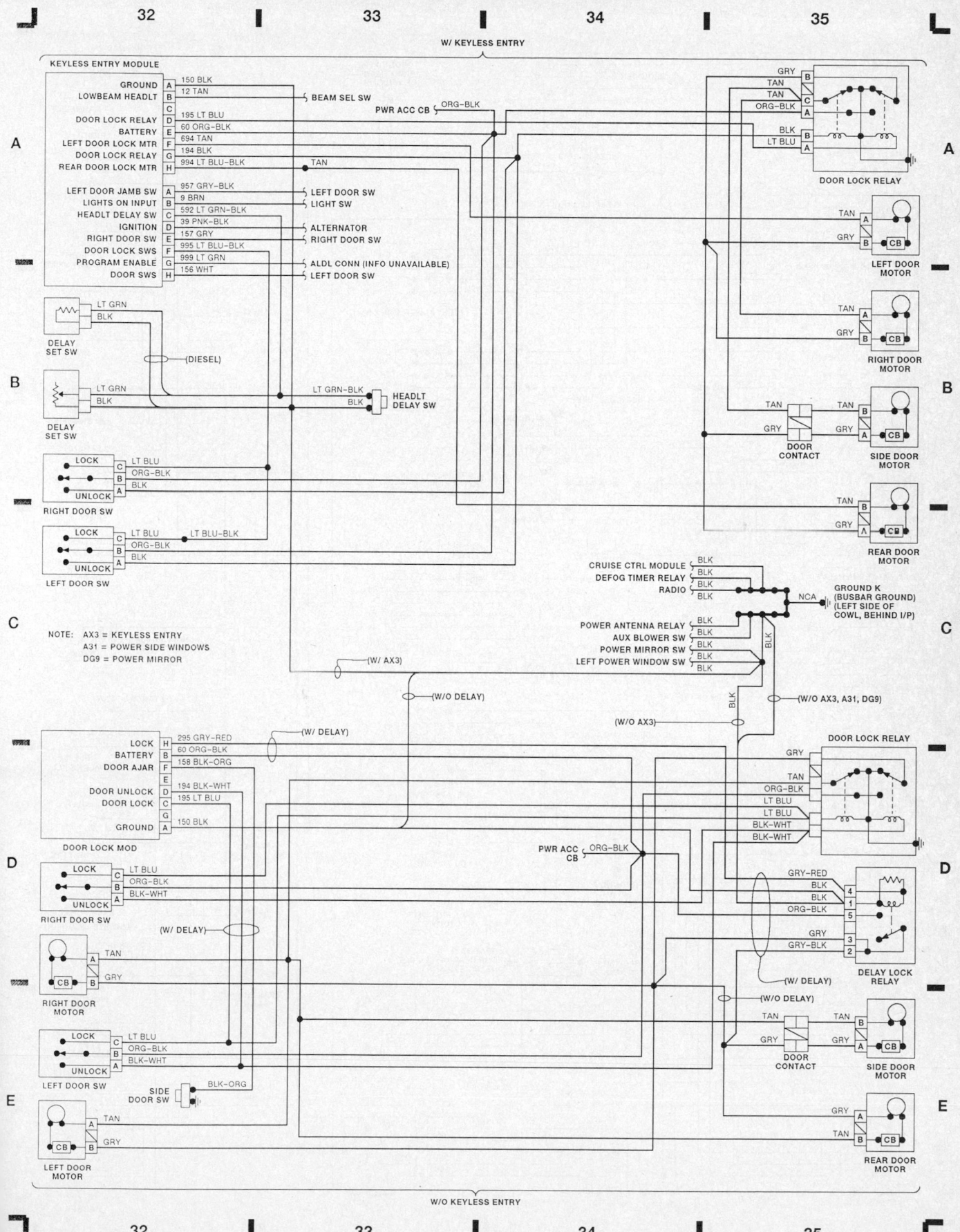

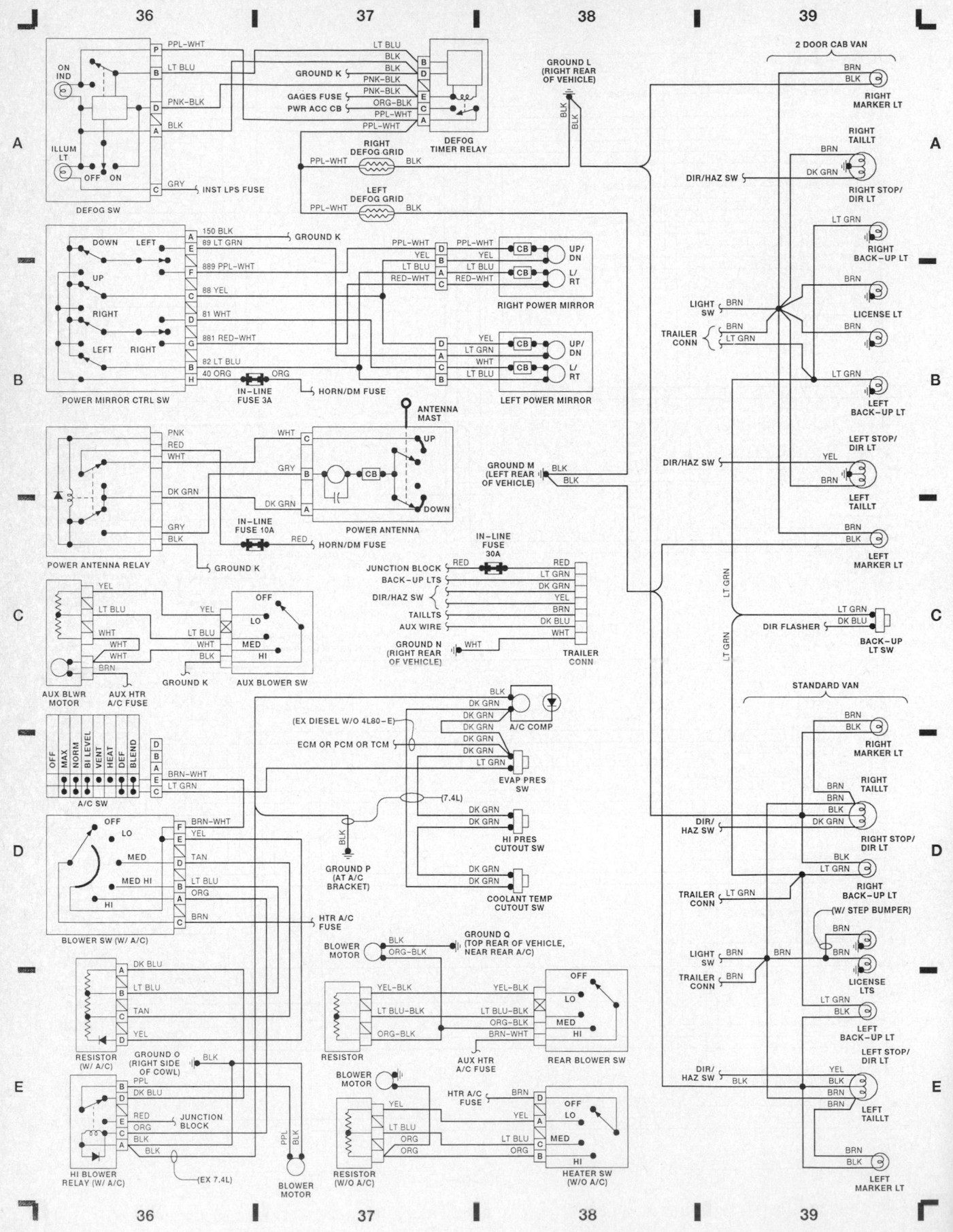

COMPONENT LOCATOR:

A/C COMP CLUTCH DIODE .... B-C 30
A/C COMP RELAY .... B 31
A/C HIGH PRES SW .... B 30
A/C REFRIGERANT PRES SW .... E 6
ABS ENABLE RELAY .... B-C 27
ABS LAMP DRIVER MODULE .... C 27
ALDL CONN (VIN D) .... A-B 7
ALDL CONN (VIN L) .... C 11
ALTERNATOR .... C 3
ASHTRAY LT .... C 43
AUDIO ALARM MODULE .... A 37
AUTOMATIC TRANSAXLE (VIN D) ... A 7
AUTOMATIC TRANSAXLE (VIN L) ... E 1
AUXILIARY BLOWER MOTOR RELAY .. D 31, C 35
AUXILIARY BLOWER MOTOR
  RELAY (EX C57) .... E 35
AUXILIARY BLOWER SW .... C 31, B 35
AUXILIARY BLOWER SW (EX C57) .. D-E 35
BATTERY .... A 2
BLOWER MOTOR HIGH SPEED RELAY A 35, A 31
BLOWER MOTOR LOW SPEED RELAY . B 38
BLOWER RESISTOR .... A 31, A 35
BRAKE SW .... D-E 37
CANISTER PURGE SOL .... D 15
CCCI MODULE (VIN L) .... A 15
CIG LIGHTER .... B 43
CONVENIENCE CENTER .... A-C 37-38
COOLANT FAN .... D 30
COOLANT FAN RELAY .... E 29
COOLANT PUSHER FAN RELAY .... C 33
COURTESY LIGHTS .... C 40-43
CRUISE CONTROL SERVO (VIN D) .. D-E 39
CRUISE CONTROL SW (VIN D) ...... E 36
CRUISE CONTROL SW (VIN L) ...... E 14-15
CRUISE MODULE (VIN D) .... E 39
DEFOG GRID .... B 36
DIR FLASHER .... B 16
DIR/HAZ SW .... C-D 36
DOOR LOCK SWS .... C 48
ELC COMP ASSY .... E 23
ELC HEIGHT SENS .... D-E 21-22
ELC INFLATION TIMER RELAY ..... C-D 21
ELC RELAY .... E 21
ELECTRONIC BRAKE CONTROL
  MODULE (EBCM) .... B-C 24
ELECTRONIC CONTROL
  MODULE (ECM) (VIN D) .... B-E 4
ENGINE COMPT LT .... A-B 43
EST DISTRIBUTOR (VIN D) .... B-C 7
FUEL INJ (VIN D) .... E 5
FUEL INJ (VIN L) .... B-C 11
FUEL PUMP RELAY (VIN D) .... A 4
FUEL PUMP RELAY (VIN L) .... B-C 12
FUEL SENS ASSY (VIN D) ...... A 6, C 45
FUEL SENS ASSY (VIN L) ...... C 12, C 45
FUS LINKS .... A-B 2-3
FUSE BLOCK .... A-D 18
GEAR SEL SW .... B-E 20
GROUND A .... A 2
GROUND B .... A 2
GROUND C .... A 2
GROUND D .... A 2
GROUND E .... A 2
GROUND F .... B 6
GROUND G .... B 6
GROUND H (VIN D) .... E 5
GROUND H (VIN L) .... E 13
GROUND I .... C-D 25
GROUND J .... E 26-27
GROUND K .... C 41
GROUND L .... D 40-41
GROUND M .... D 43
GROUND N .... B 50
GROUND O .... B 54
GROUND P .... C-D 53-54
HEADLT SW .... A-B 40
HEATER CONTROL ASSY .... A-E 28
HORN RELAY .... C 38
I/P COMP LT .... B 43
IGN COIL (VIN D) .... C-D 7
IGN KEY WARN SW .... A 36-37
IGNITION SW .... A 20-23
INFLATION SOL VALVE ASSY ..... C 23
INFLATION SW .... C-D 23
INST CLSTR (EX LUMINA APV) .... A-C 44
INST CLSTR (LUMINA APV) .... A-C 47
JUNCTION BLOCK .... B 3
KEYLESS ENTRY MODULE .... A 51
LEFT FRONT DOOR SW .... A 42
LIFTGATE JAMB SW .... D-E 47
OIL PRES SENS/SW (VIN D) .. A 5, C 45
OIL PRES SENS/SW (VIN L) ... C 12, C 45
OUSIDE MIRROR SW .... E 44
OUTSIDE AIR TEMP SENS .... D 44
OVERHEAD CONSOLE .... D-C 40, D 44
POWER DOOR LOCK RELAY ..... C-D 51
POWER SEAT SW .... D 52-53
POWER SLIDING DOOR LOCK RELAY .. D-E 51
POWER WDO SYS .... A-B 52
POWERTRAIN CONTROL
  MODULE (PCM) (VIN L) .... A-E 8
REAR READING LTS .... D 41
REAR WASHER MOTOR .... C 53
REAR WINDOW DEFOG RELAY .. B 37
REAR WIPER MOTOR MODULE .. B-C 53
REAR WIPER/WASHER
  SW (LUMINA APV) .... D 41-42
REMOTE DIMMER MODULE .... A 41
SEAT BELT SW .... A 36
SOLENOID BOX .... E 32, B 34
STARTER MOTOR .... A 3
TACH SIGNAL FILTER .... D 7
TEMP DOOR ACTUATOR ..... D 31, B 34
TEMP/COMPASS DISPLAY MODULE .. D 44
TRAILER CONN .... B 53-54
VEHICLE SPEED SENSOR
  BUFFER (VIN D) .... C-D 38
W/SHIELD WIPER/WASHER
  SW (LUMINA APV) .... D-E 42-43
WASHER MOTOR .... D 2
WATER CTRL SOLENOID (EX C57) .. E 33
WINDSHIELD WIPER MOTOR MODULE .. E 2-3
WINDSHIELD WIPER/WASHER
  SW (EX LUMINA) .... D-E 40-42

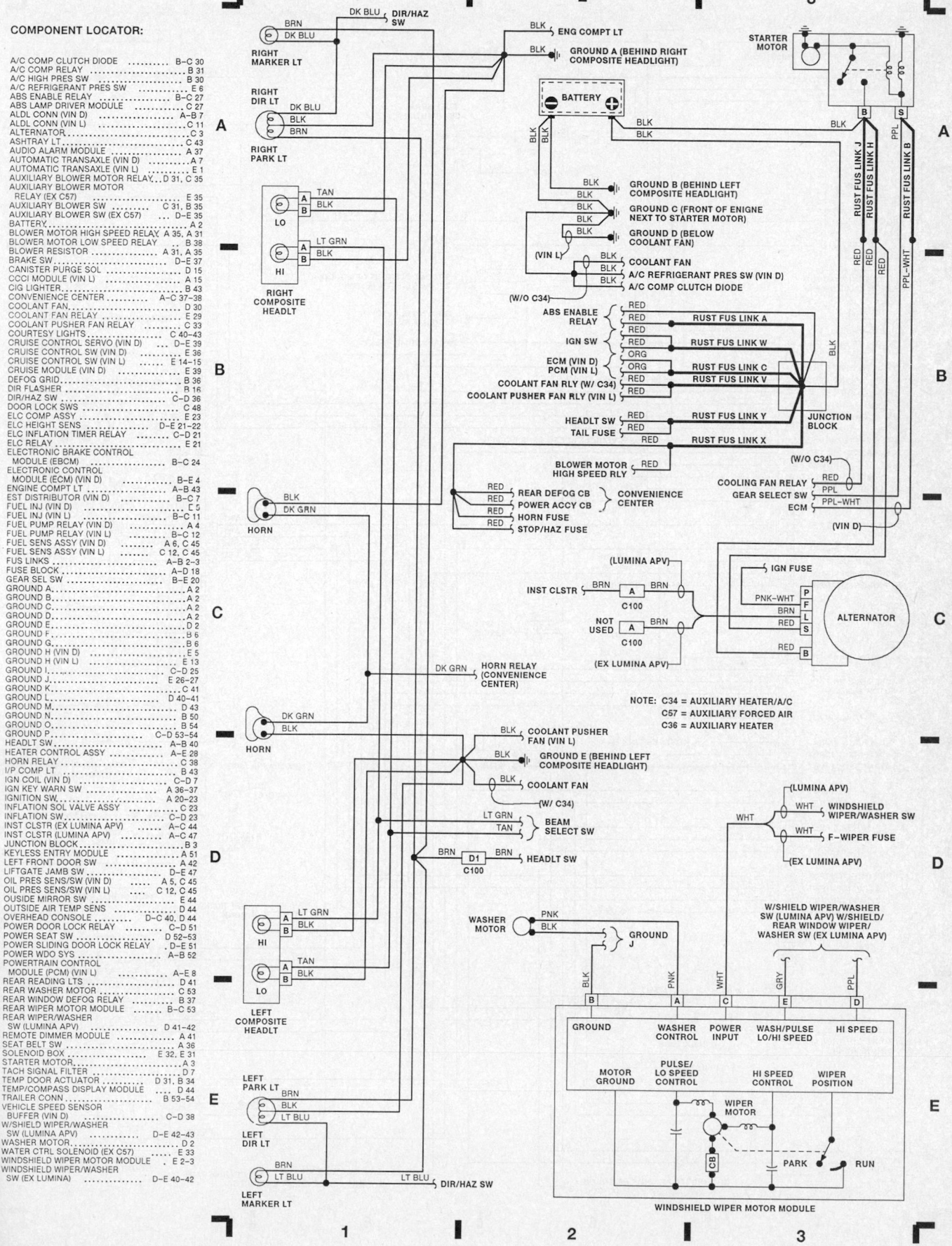

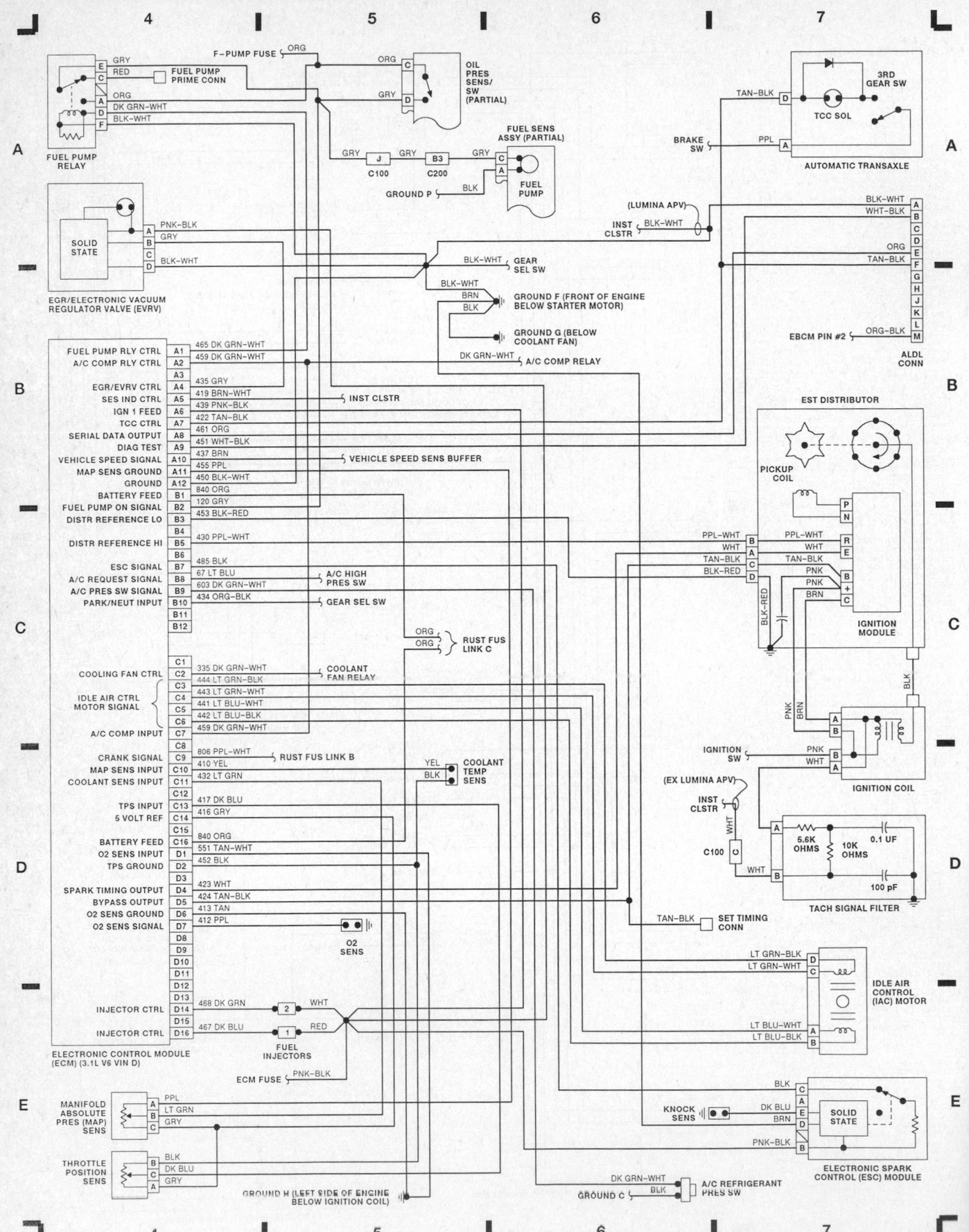

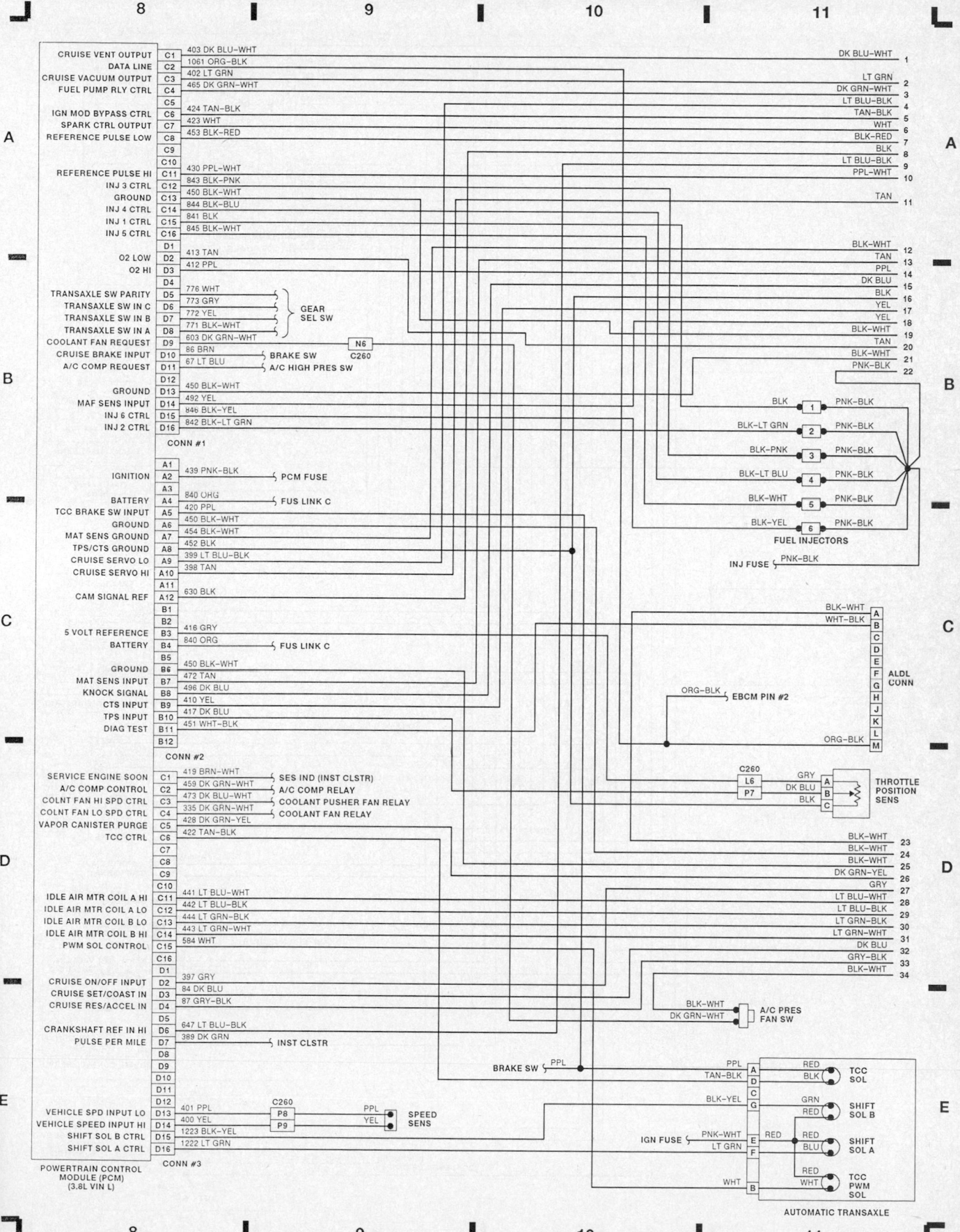

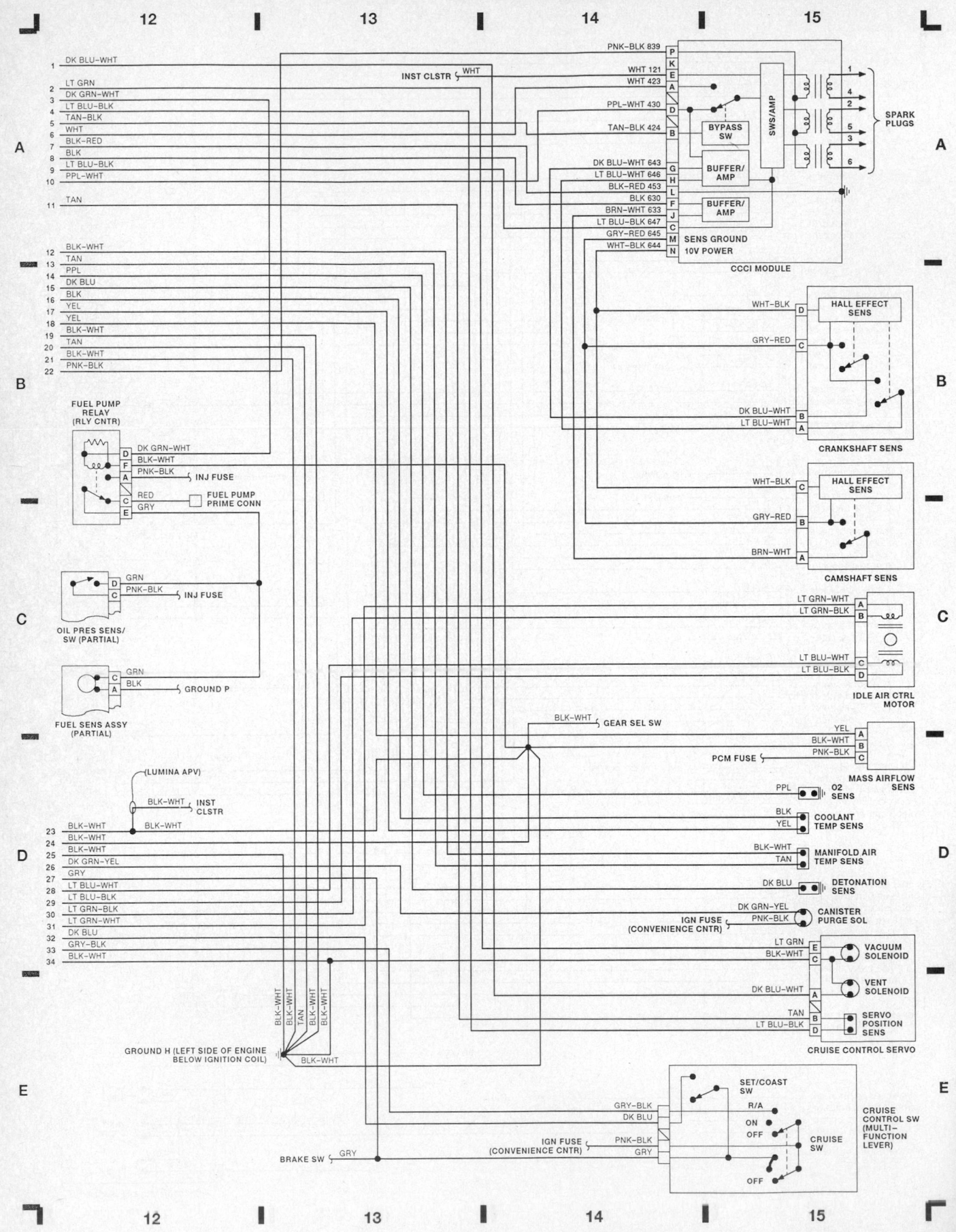

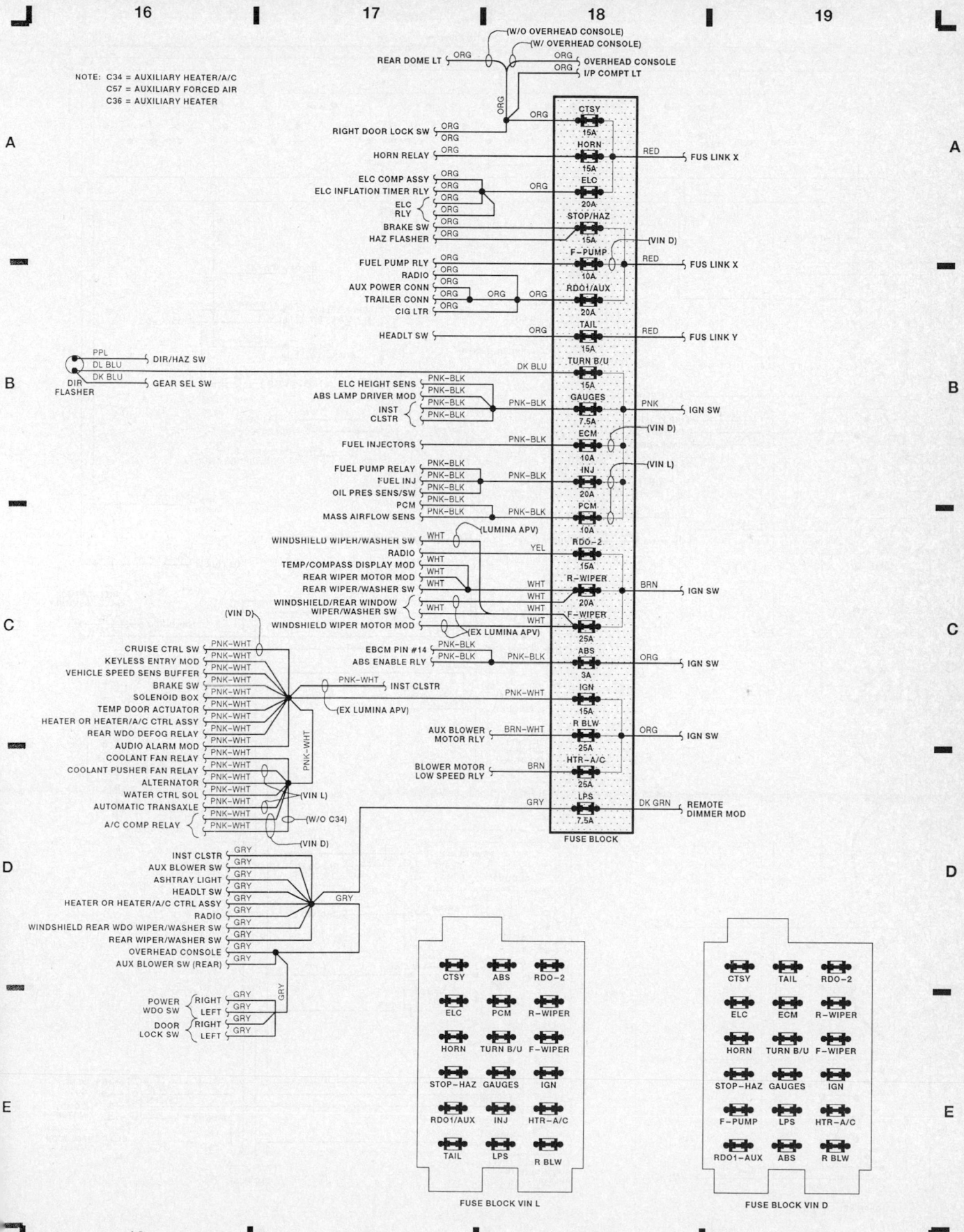

NOTE: C34 = AUXILIARY HEATER/A/C
C57 = AUXILIARY FORCED AIR
C36 = AUXILIARY HEATER

FUSE BLOCK VIN L

FUSE BLOCK VIN D

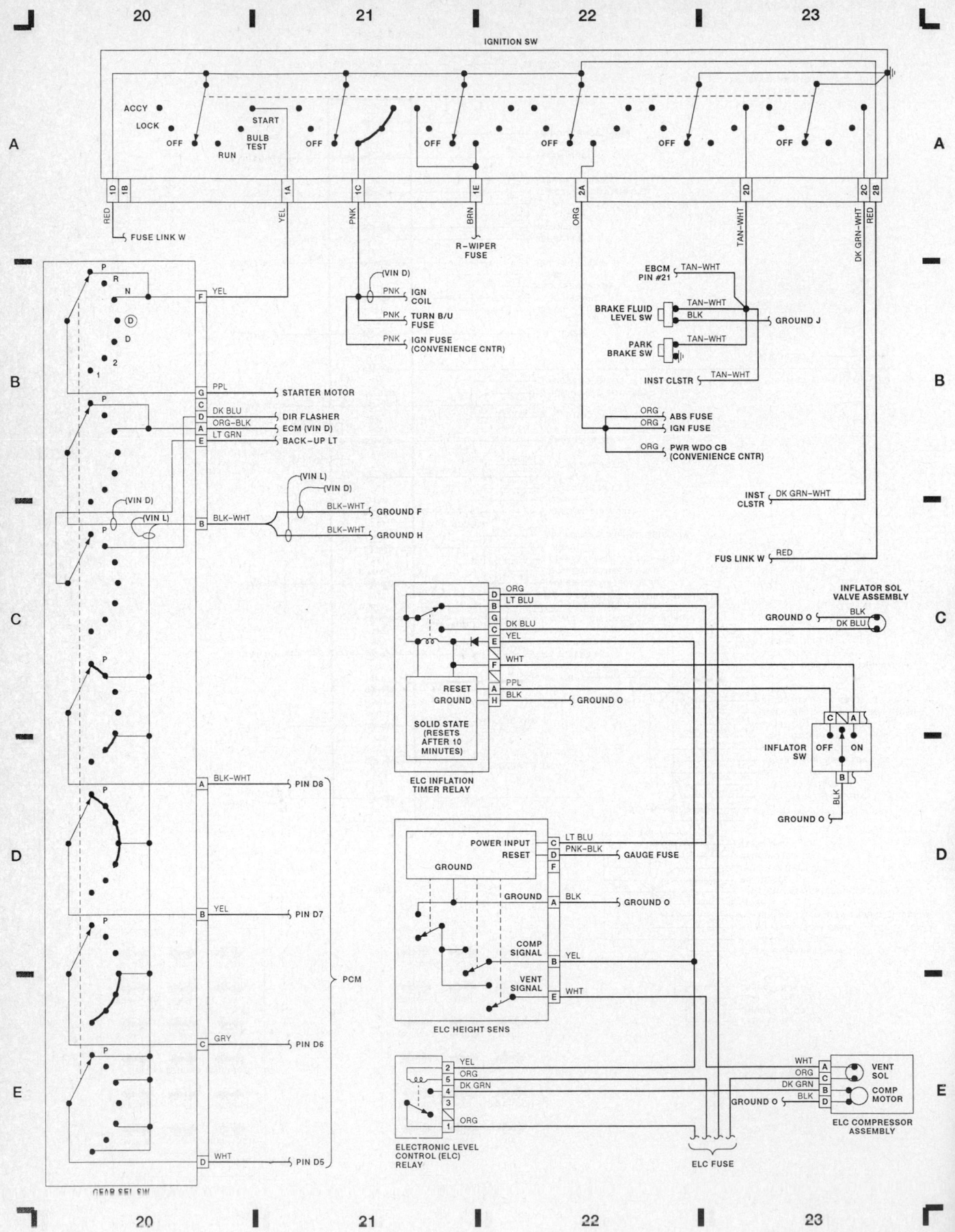

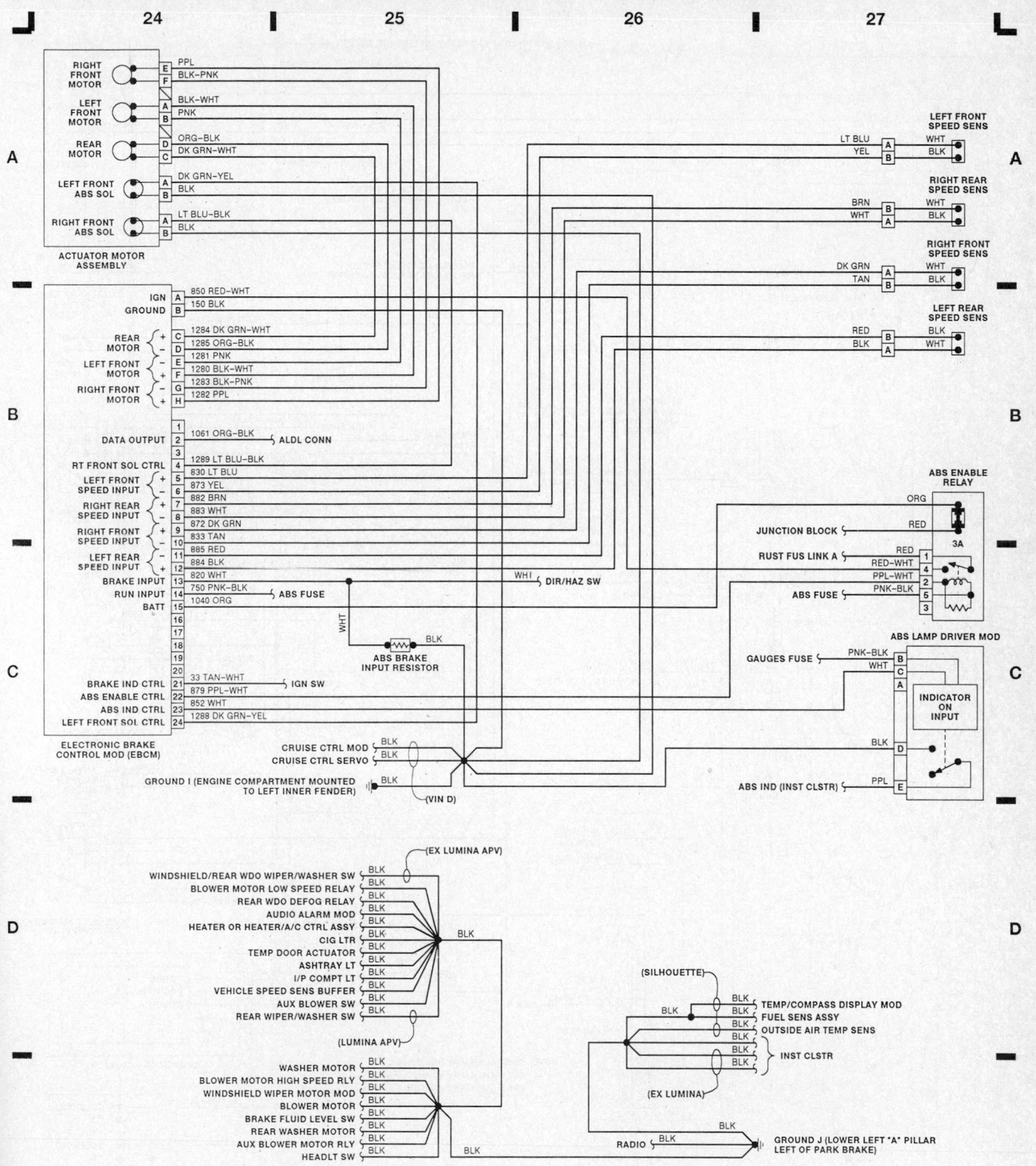

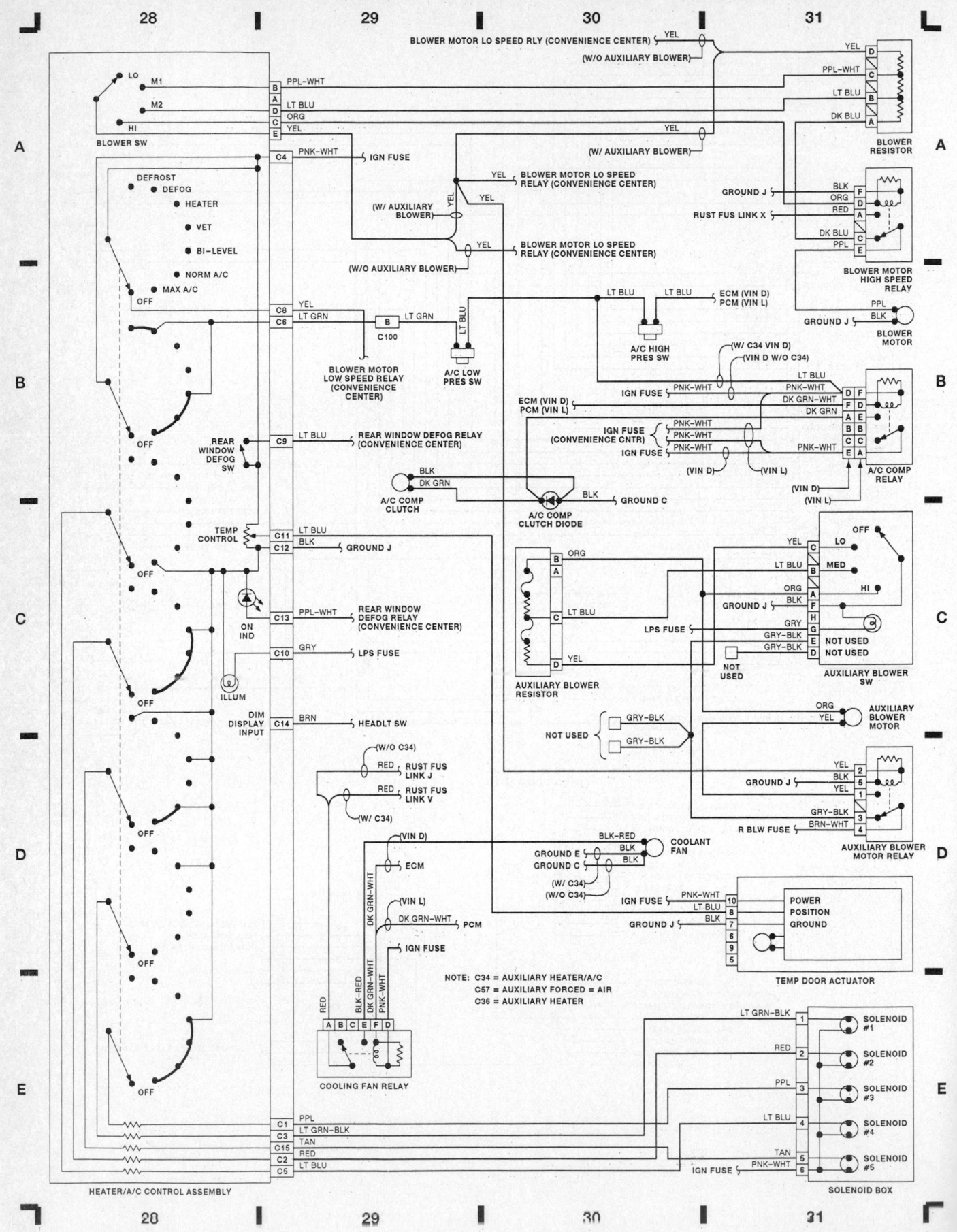

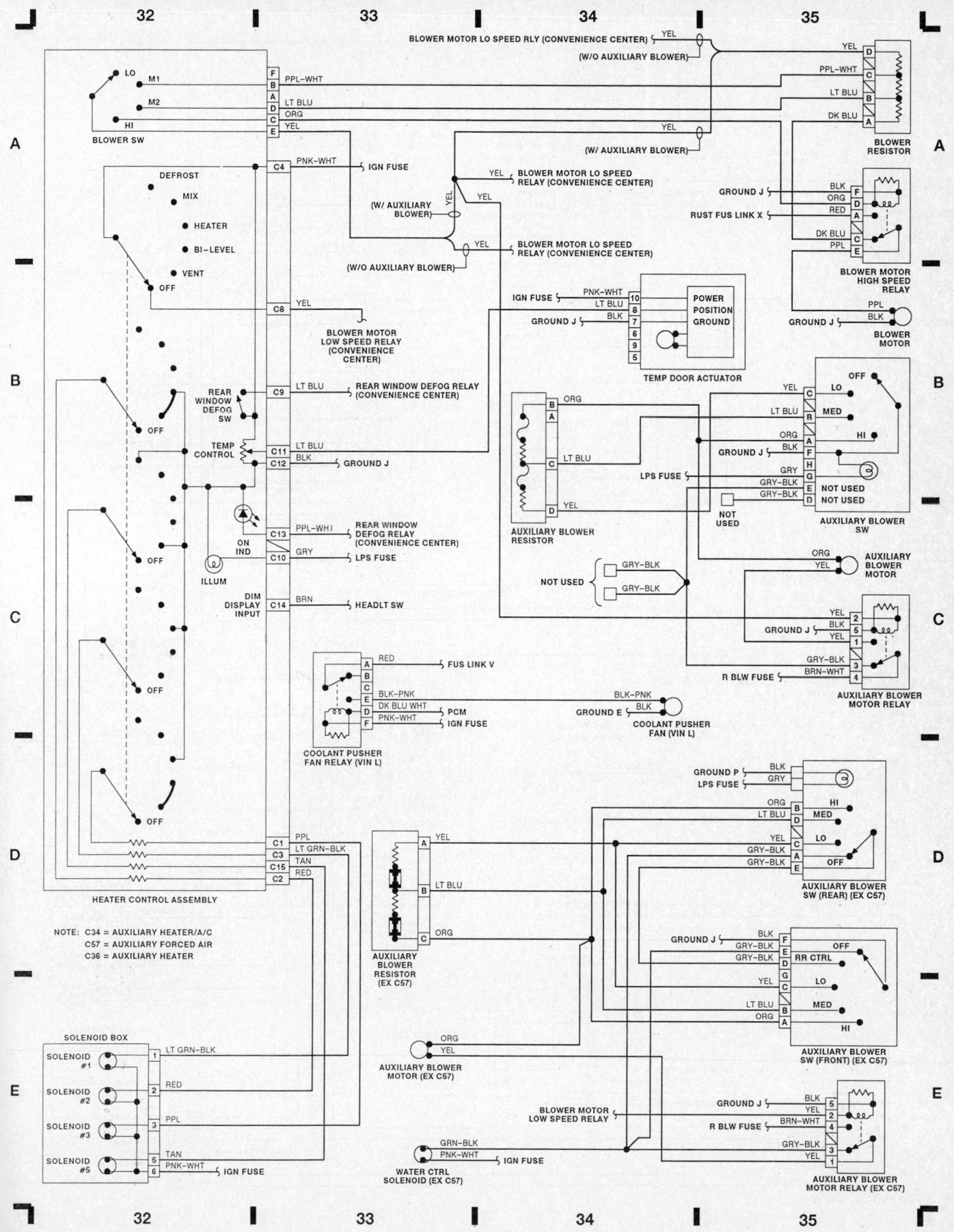

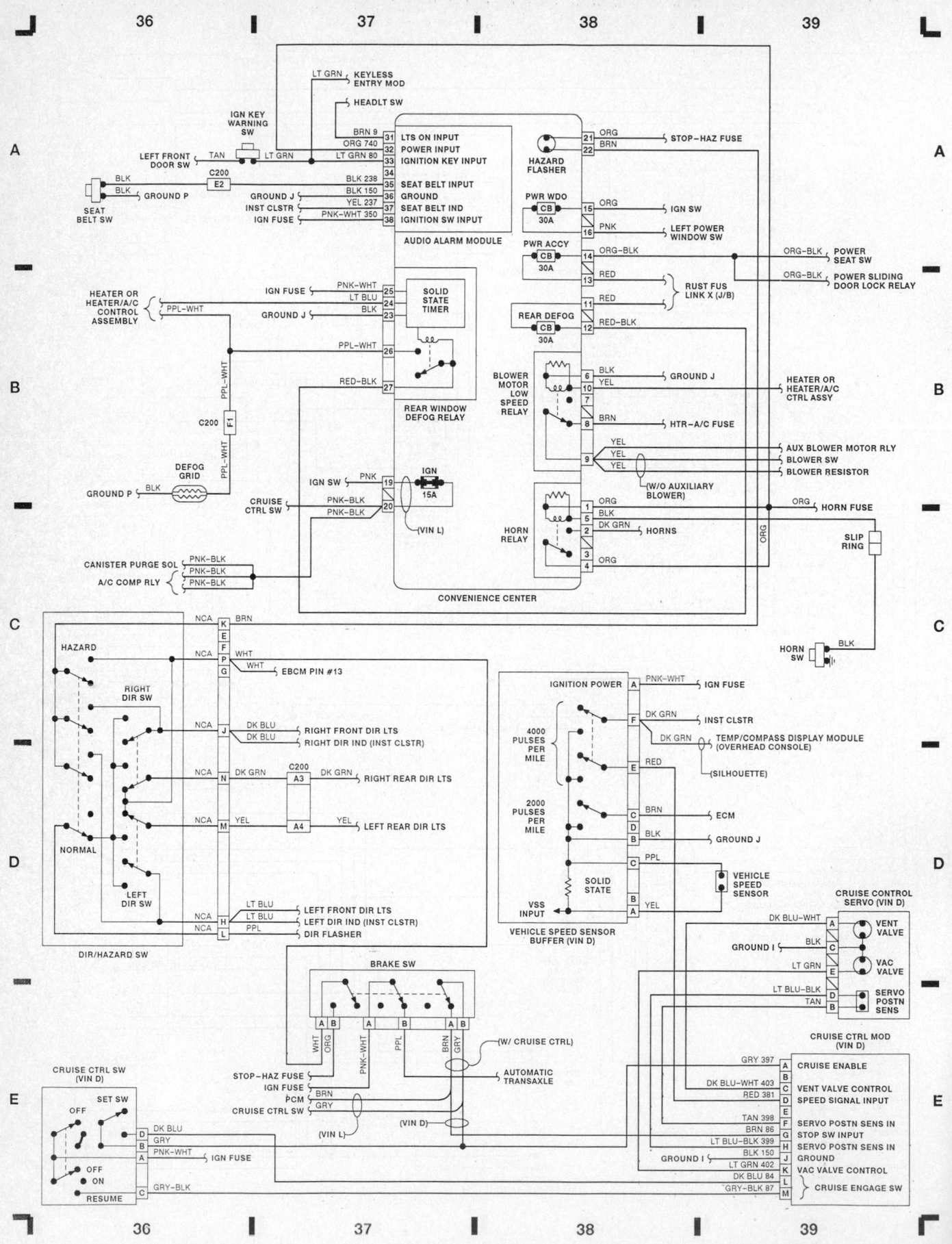

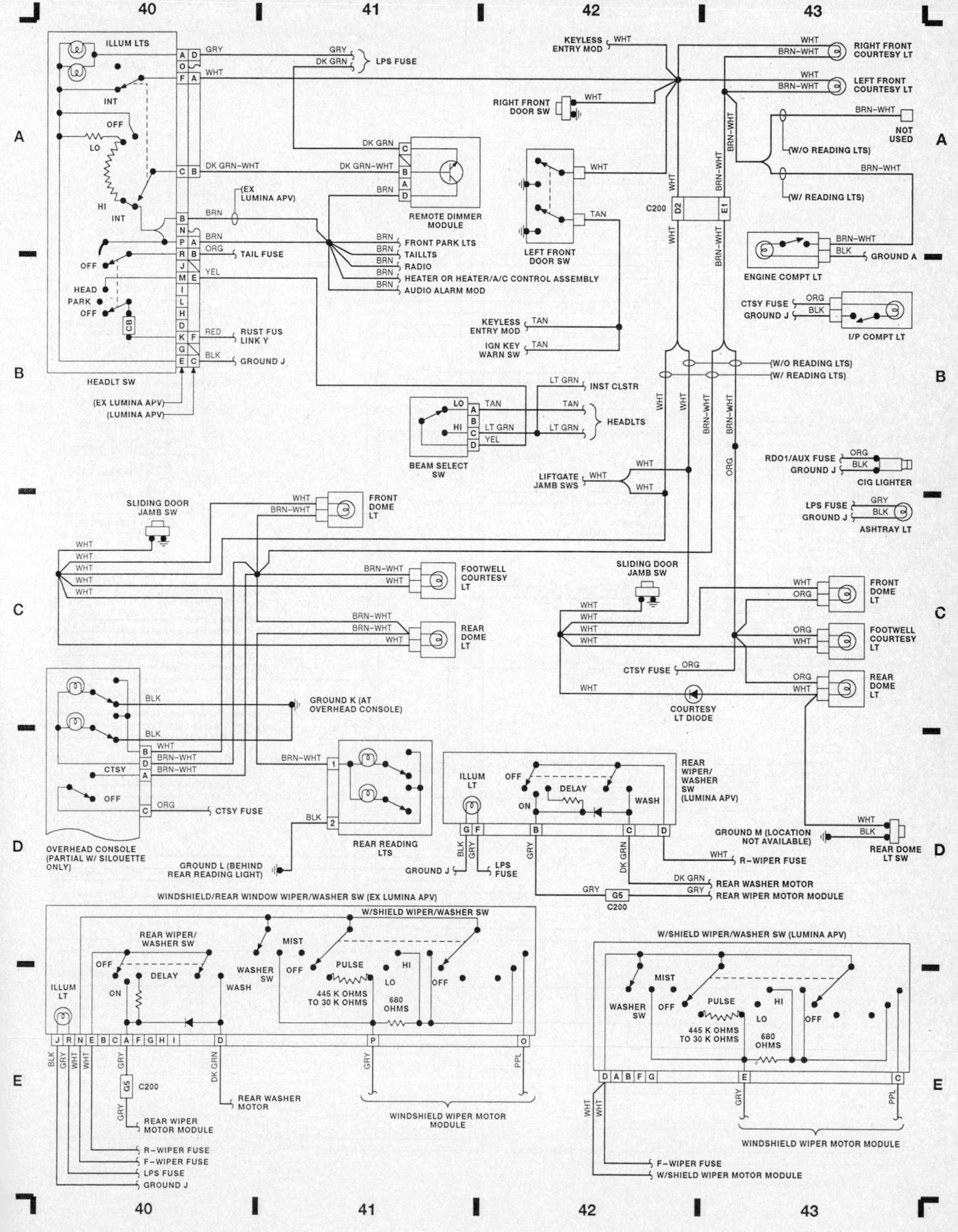

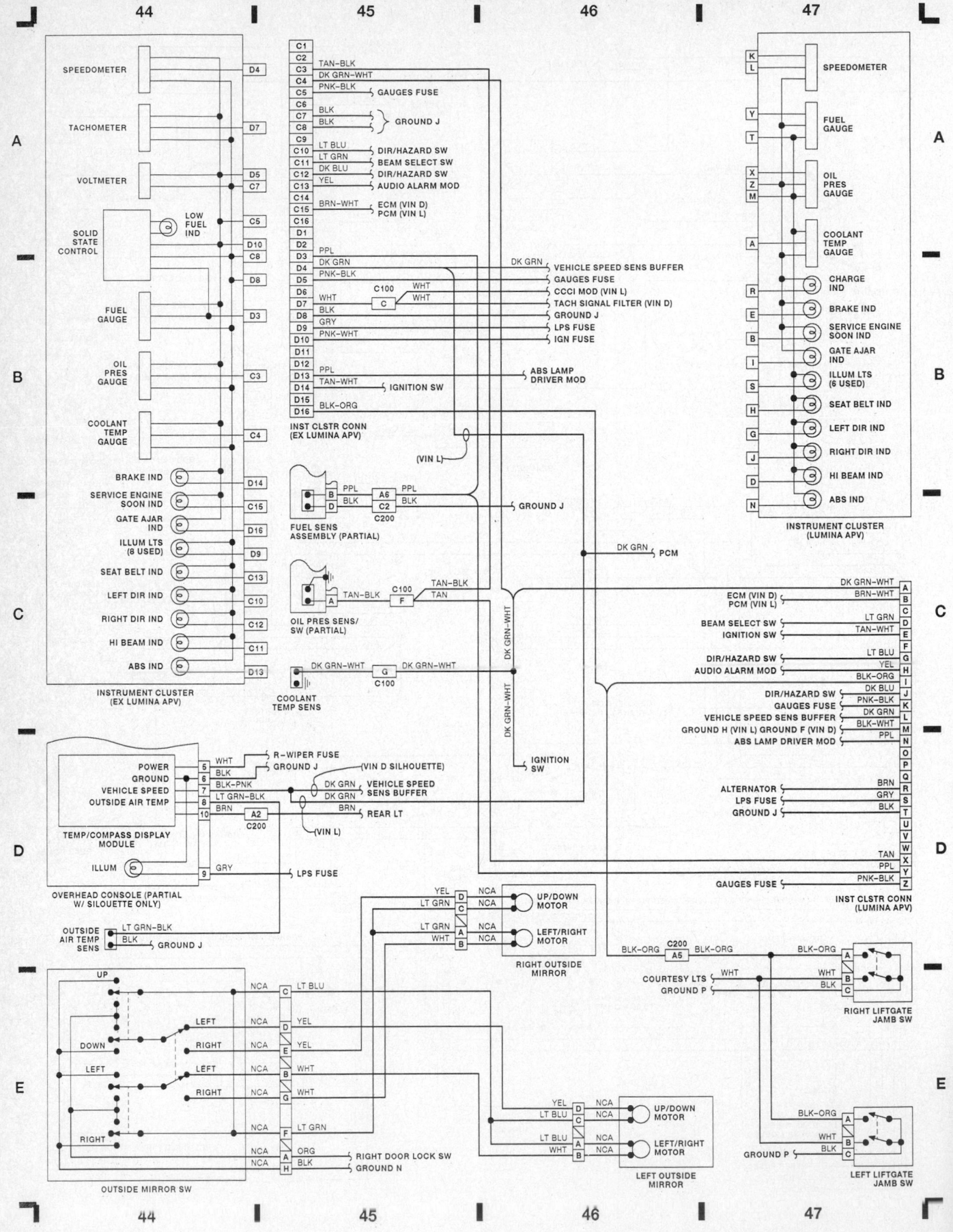

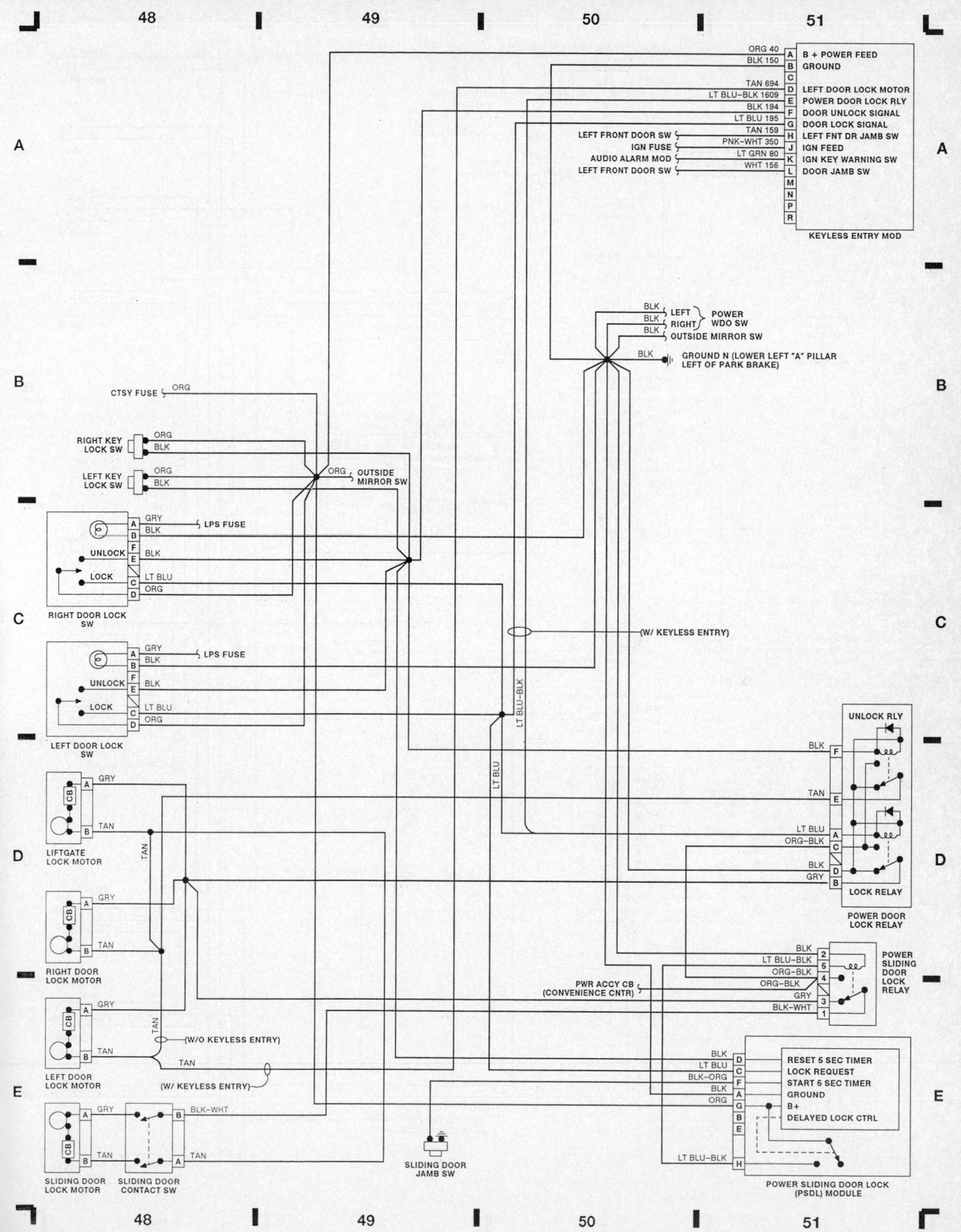

48   49   50   51

ORG 40 — A — B + POWER FEED
BLK 150 — B — GROUND
— C —
TAN 694 — D — LEFT DOOR LOCK MOTOR
LT BLU-BLK 1609 — E — POWER DOOR LOCK RLY
BLK 194 — F — DOOR UNLOCK SIGNAL
LT BLU 195 — G — DOOR LOCK SIGNAL
TAN 159 — H — LEFT FNT DR JAMB SW
LEFT FRONT DOOR SW — PNK-WHT 350 — J — IGN FEED
IGN FUSE — LT GRN 80 — K — IGN KEY WARNING SW
AUDIO ALARM MOD — WHT 156 — L — DOOR JAMB SW
LEFT FRONT DOOR SW — M — N — P — R —

KEYLESS ENTRY MOD

BLK — LEFT — POWER
BLK — RIGHT — WDO SW
BLK — OUTSIDE MIRROR SW
BLK — GROUND N (LOWER LEFT "A" PILLAR LEFT OF PARK BRAKE)

CTSY FUSE — ORG

RIGHT KEY LOCK SW — ORG / BLK
LEFT KEY LOCK SW — ORG / BLK

ORG — OUTSIDE MIRROR SW

RIGHT DOOR LOCK SW
A — GRY
B — BLK — LPS FUSE
F
E
UNLOCK — BLK
LOCK — LT BLU
C
D — ORG

LEFT DOOR LOCK SW
A — GRY
B — BLK — LPS FUSE
F
E
UNLOCK — BLK
LOCK — LT BLU
C
D — ORG

(W/ KEYLESS ENTRY)

LIFTGATE LOCK MOTOR
CB — A — GRY
B — TAN

RIGHT DOOR LOCK MOTOR
CB — A — GRY
B — TAN

LEFT DOOR LOCK MOTOR
CB — A — GRY
B — TAN
TAN — (W/O KEYLESS ENTRY)
TAN — (W/ KEYLESS ENTRY)

SLIDING DOOR LOCK MOTOR
CB — A — GRY
B — TAN

SLIDING DOOR CONTACT SW
B — BLK-WHT
A — TAN

SLIDING DOOR JAMB SW

LT BLU-BLK
LT BLU

UNLOCK RLY
BLK — F
TAN — E
LT BLU — A
ORG-BLK — C
BLK — D
GRY — B
LOCK RELAY
POWER DOOR LOCK RELAY

POWER SLIDING DOOR LOCK RELAY
BLK — 2
LT BLU-BLK — 5
ORG-BLK — 4
ORG-BLK —
GRY — 3
BLK-WHT — 1

PWR ACCY CB (CONVENIENCE CNTR)

POWER SLIDING DOOR LOCK (PSDL) MODULE
BLK — D — RESET 5 SEC TIMER
LT BLU — C — LOCK REQUEST
BLK-ORG — F — START 5 SEC TIMER
BLK — A — GROUND
ORG — G — B+
E — DELAYED LOCK CTRL
B
LT BLU-BLK — H

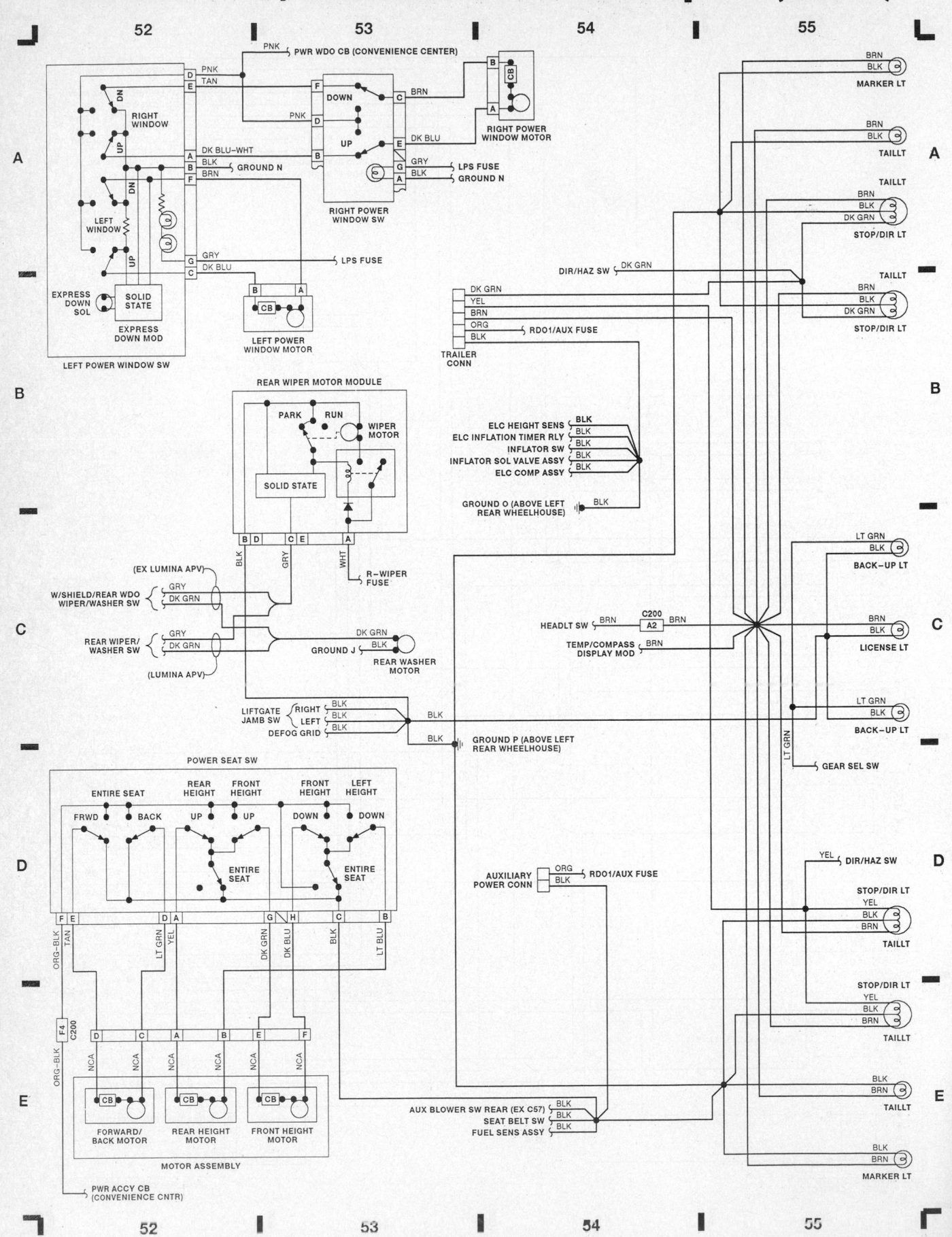

COMPONENT LOCATOR:

ALARM (SCHOOL BUS)	E 20
ALDL CONN (DIESEL W/ 4L80-E)	C-D 15
ALDL CONN (GAS W/ 4L80-E)	E 8
ALDL CONN (GAS W/O 4L80-E)	E 4
ALTERNATOR (DIESEL)	D 3
ALTERNATOR (GAS)	B 3
BACK-UP LT SW	A 26
BATTERY (DIESEL)	B 3
BATTERY (GAS)	A 3
BEAM SEL SW	B 24
BODY BUILDER JUNCTION	
BLOCK (DIESEL)	B 1
BODY BUILDER JUNCTION	
BLOCK (GAS)	A 1
CLUTCH SW (DIESEL)	C 2
CLUTCH SW (GAS)	B 1
DIGITAL RATIO ADAPTER	
CONTROLLER (DRAC) MOD	E 24
DIR FLASHER	D 18
DIR/HAZ SW	C-D 24
EGR SOL (4.3L)	
(GAS W/O 4L80-E)	D 4
EGR SOL (4.3L) (GAS W/ 4L80-E)	C 8
ELECTRONIC CONTROL UNIT	
(ECM) (GAS W/O 4L80-E)	A 4-7
EST DISTRIBUTOR	
(GAS W/ 4L80-E)	E 11
EST DISTRIBUTOR	
(GAS W/O 4L80-E)	E 7
FAST IDLE TEMP SW	
(DIESEL W/ 4L80-E)	E 14
FLASHER UNIT (SCHOOL BUS)	E 20
FUEL CYCLE MOD (GAS W/ 4L80-E)	C 11
FUEL CYCLE MOD	
(GAS W/O 4L80-E)	C 4
FUEL HEATER (DIESEL W/ 4L80-E)	E 12
FUEL INJECTORS (GAS W/ 4L80-E)	B 11
FUEL INJECTORS	
(GAS W/O 4L80-E)	B 7
FUEL PUMP RELAY	
(GAS W/ 4L80-E)	E 10
FUEL PUMP RELAY	
(GAS W/O 4L80-E)	B 4
FUEL PUMP SW/OIL PRES	
SENS (GAS W/ 4L80-E)	E 8
FUEL PUMP SW/OIL PRES	
SENS (GAS W/O 4L80-E)	C 4
FUEL TANK UNIT	C 23
FUSE BLOCK	B-D 16-19
GLOW PLUG CONTROLLER (DIESEL)	D 15
GROUND A (DIESEL)	C 3
GROUND A (GAS)	A 2
GROUND B (DIESEL)	C 3
GROUND B (GAS)	A 2
GROUND C (DIESEL)	C 3
GROUND D	D 2
GROUND E	D 1
GROUND F	E 1
GROUND G	E 1
GROUND H (DIESEL W/ 4L80-E)	E 13
GROUND H (GAS W/ 4L80-E)	E 10
GROUND H (GAS W/O 4L80-E)	C 5
GROUND I (DIESEL W/ 4L80-E)	A 14
GROUND I (GAS W/ 4L80-E)	A 11
GROUND I (GAS W/O 4L80-E)	A 5
GROUND J	E 19
GROUND K	D 20
GROUND L	C 22
GROUND M	B 27
HAZ FLASHER	C 26
HEATED OXYGEN SENS (4.3L)	
(GAS W/O 4L80-E)	B 7
HEATED OXYGEN SENS (4.3L)	
(GAS W/ 4L80-E)	C 11
HORN	E 2
HORN RELAY	D 24
IGNITION SW	A 16
INSTRUMENT CLUSTER	A–B 21-22
JUNCTION BLOCK (DIESEL)	C 2
JUNCTION BLOCK (GAS)	A 2
LIGHT SW	A 24
LOW COOLANT MOD (DIESEL)	C 21-22
POWERTRAIN CONTROL MODULE	
(PCM) (GAS W/ 4L80-E)	A 8-11
STARTER (DIESEL)	D 3
STARTER (GAS)	A 3
STARTER RELAY (DIESEL)	C 1
STOP LT SW	C 26
TCC BRAKE SW (DIESEL	
W/ 4L80-E)	B 12
TCC BRAKE SW (GAS W/ 4L80-E)	A 8
TRANSMISSION (DIESEL	
W/ 4L80-E)	C-D 12
TRANSMISSION (GAS W/ 4L80-E)	D 8
TRANSMISSION CONTROL MODULE	
(TCM) (DIESEL W/ 4L80-E)	A 12-15
WATER IN FUEL SENS	
(DIESEL W/ 4L80-E)	E 12
WIPER MOTOR	D 17, E 16-17
WIPER/WASHER SW	D 23, E 23

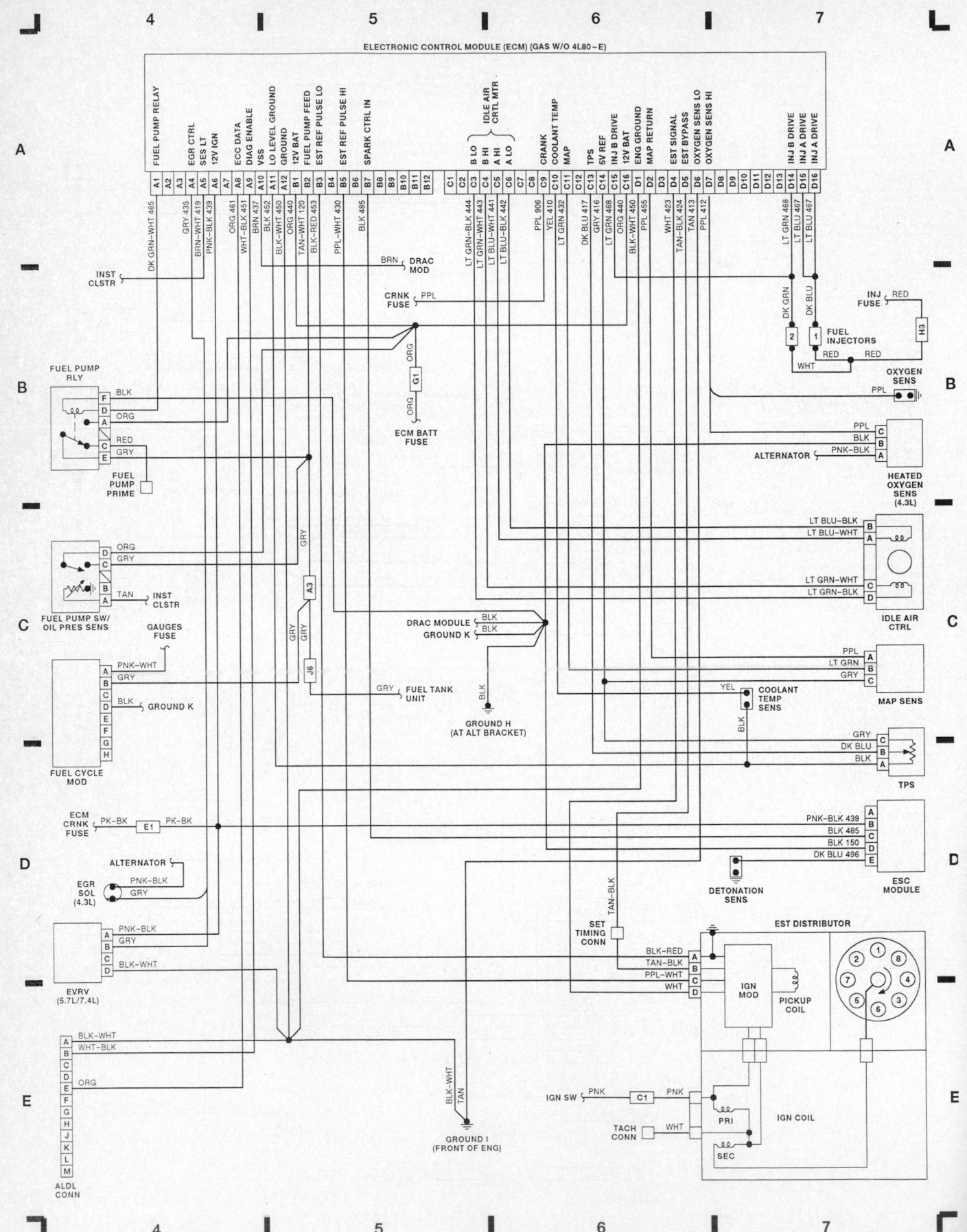

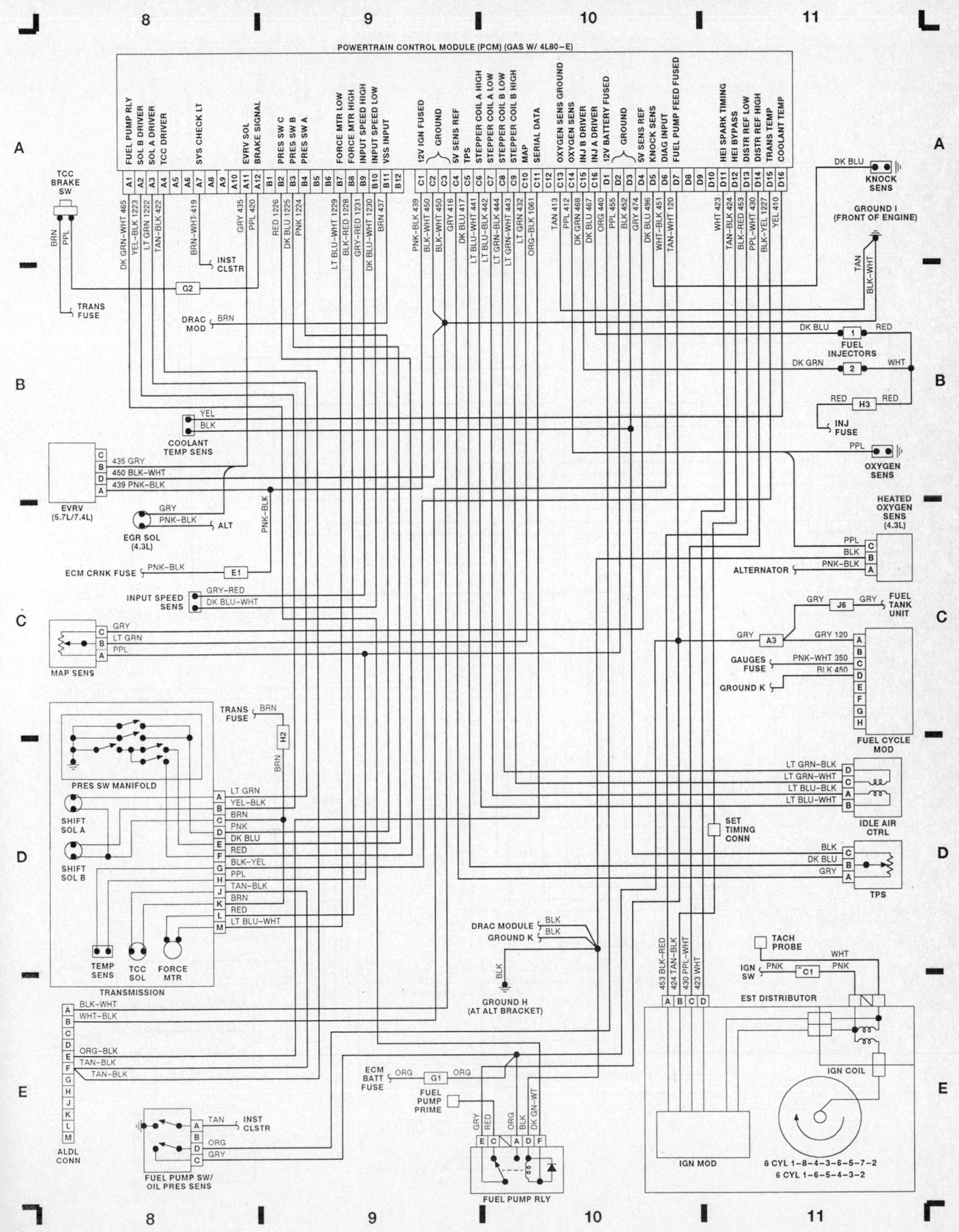

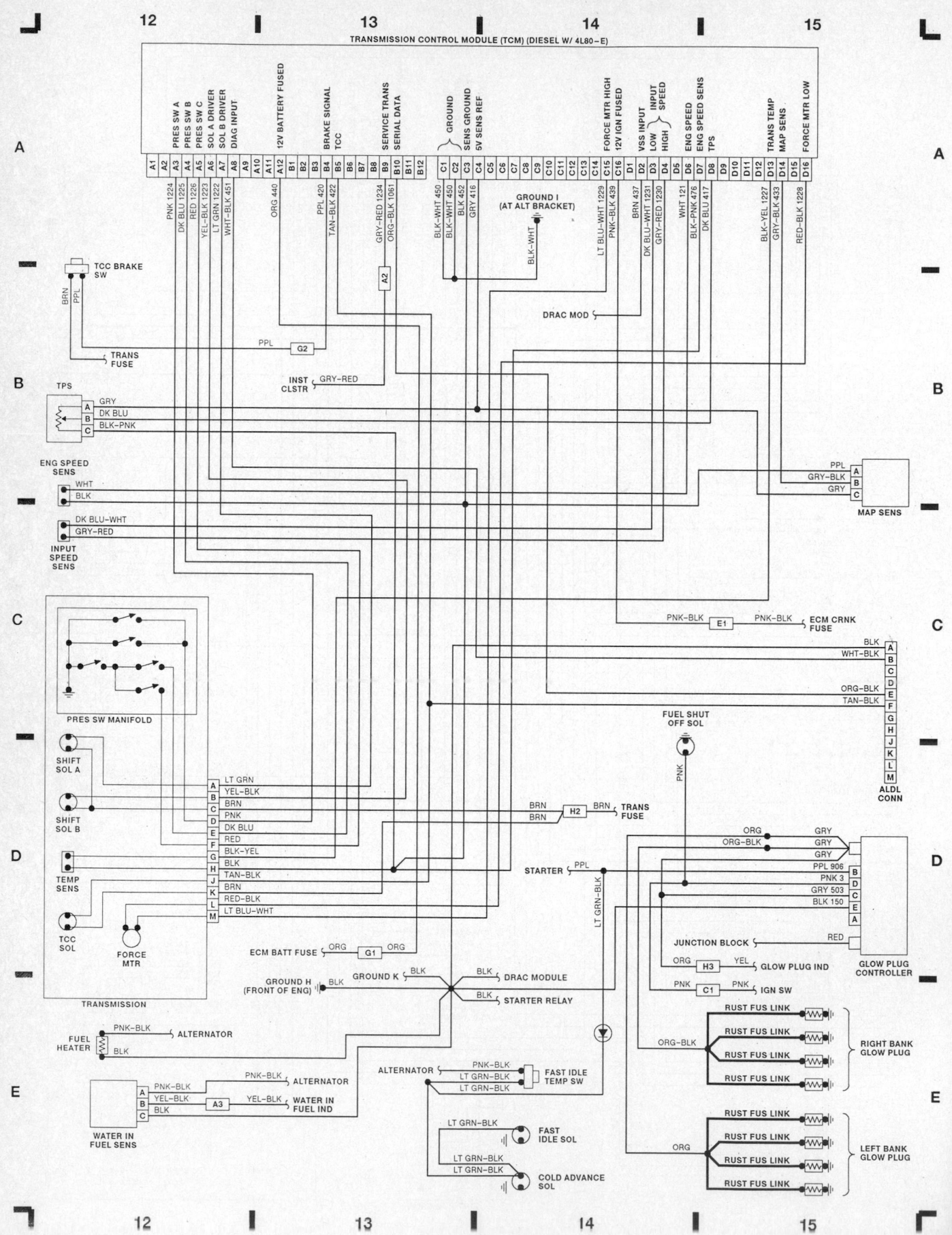

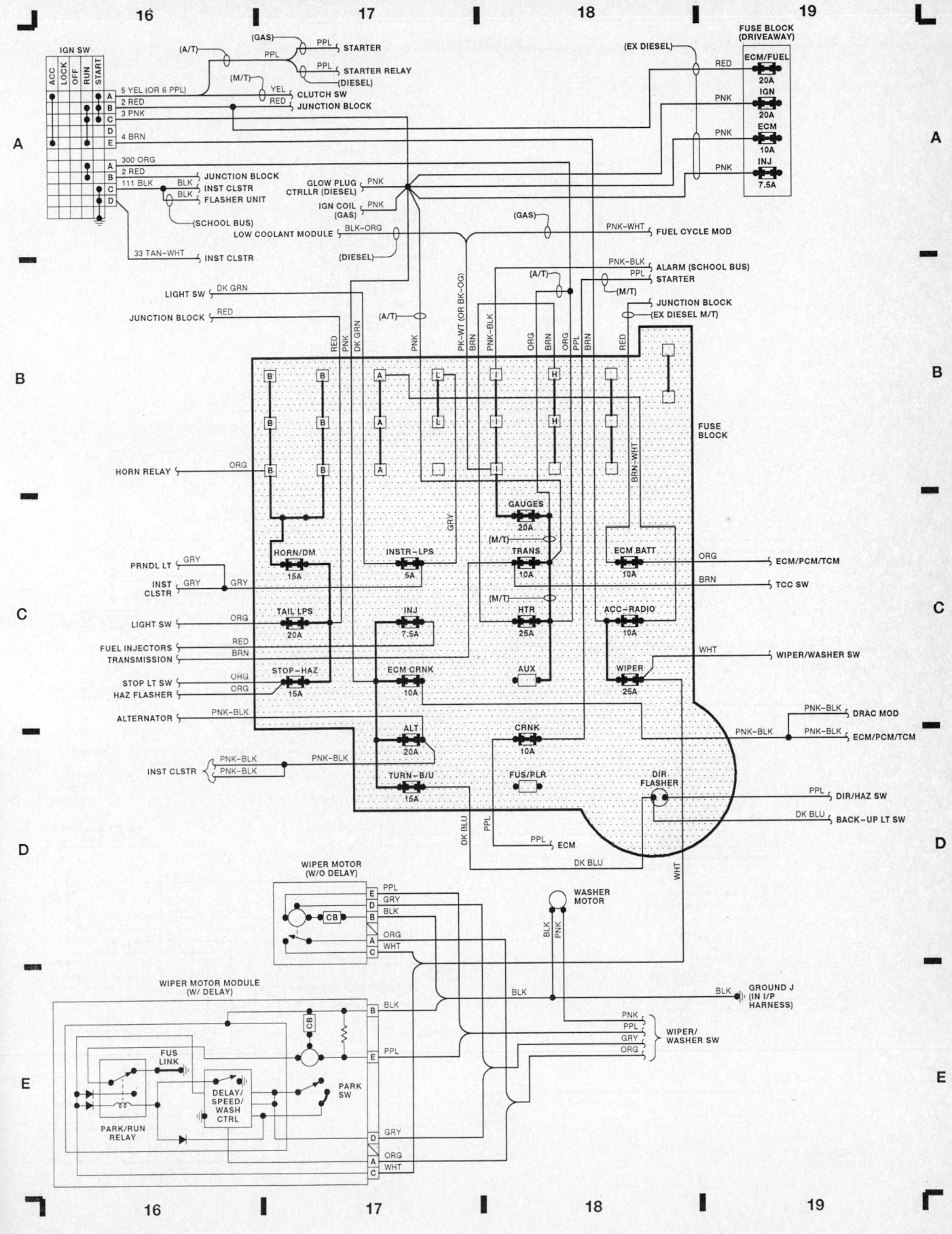

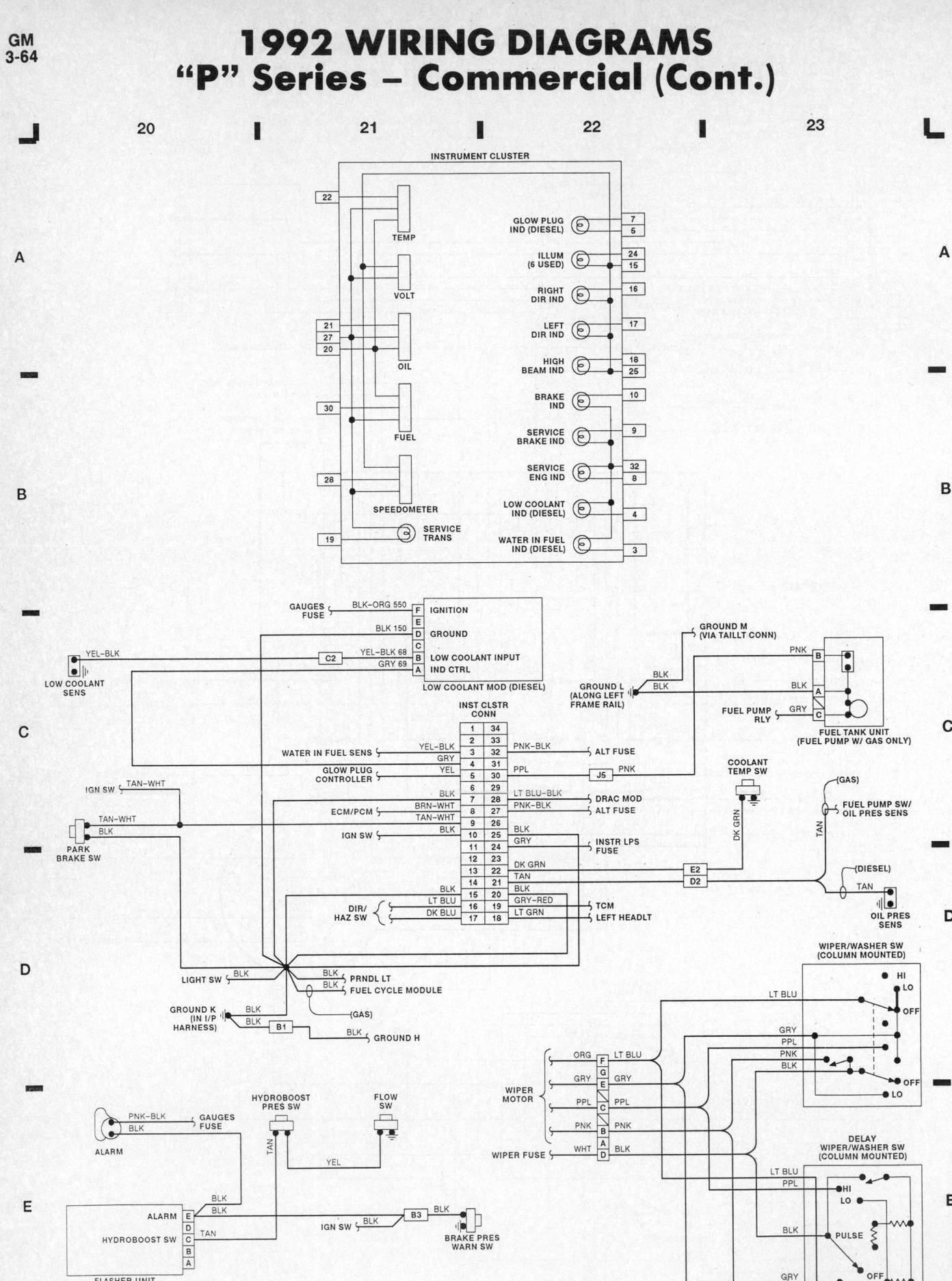

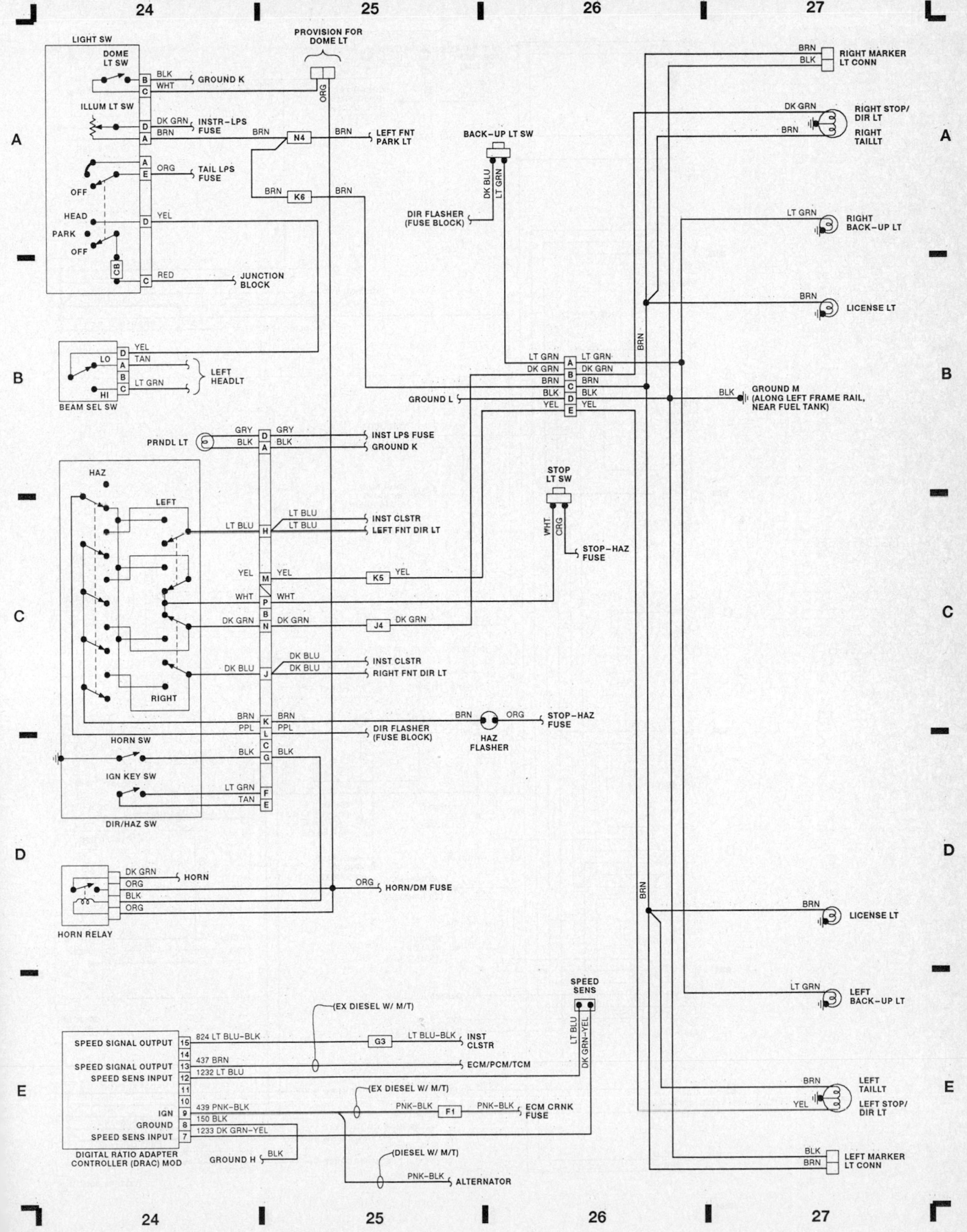

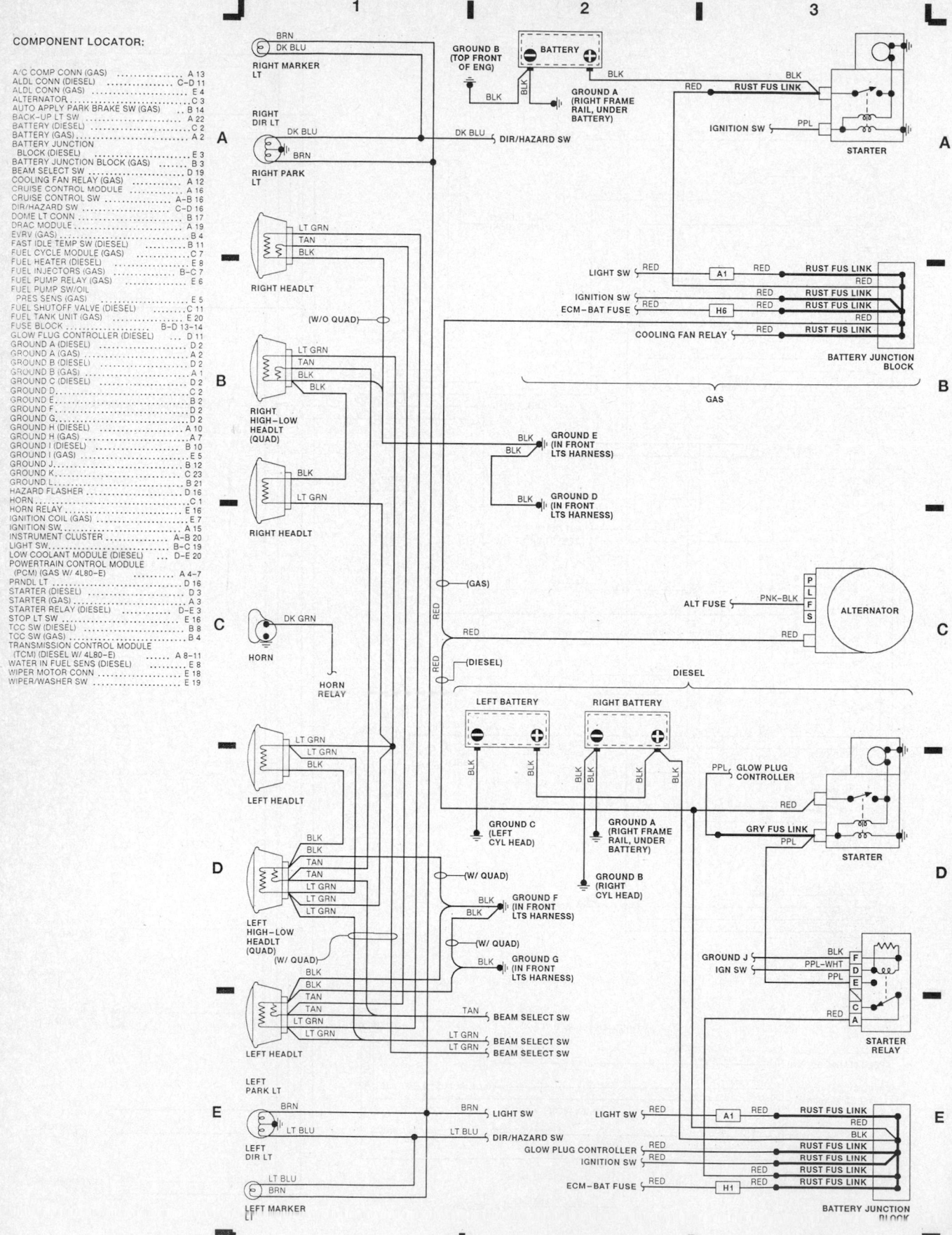

COMPONENT LOCATOR:

A/C COMP CONN (GAS)	A 13
ALDL CONN (DIESEL)	C-D 11
ALDL CONN (GAS)	E 4
ALTERNATOR	C 3
AUTO APPLY PARK BRAKE SW (GAS)	B 14
BACK-UP LT SW	A 22
BATTERY (DIESEL)	C 2
BATTERY (GAS)	A 2
BATTERY JUNCTION BLOCK (DIESEL)	E 3
BATTERY JUNCTION BLOCK (GAS)	B 3
BEAM SELECT SW	D 19
COOLING FAN RELAY (GAS)	A 12
CRUISE CONTROL MODULE	A 16
CRUISE CONTROL SW	A-B 16
DIR/HAZARD SW	C-D 16
DOME LT CONN	B 17
DRAC MODULE	A 19
EVRV (GAS)	B 4
FAST IDLE TEMP SW (DIESEL)	B 11
FUEL CYCLE MODULE (GAS)	C 7
FUEL HEATER (DIESEL)	E 8
FUEL INJECTORS (GAS)	B-C 7
FUEL PUMP RELAY (GAS)	E 6
FUEL PUMP SW/OIL PRES SENS (GAS)	E 5
FUEL SHUTOFF VALVE (DIESEL)	C 11
FUEL TANK UNIT (GAS)	E 20
FUSE BLOCK	B-D 13-14
GLOW PLUG CONTROLLER (DIESEL)	D 11
GROUND A (DIESEL)	D 2
GROUND A (GAS)	A 2
GROUND B (DIESEL)	D 2
GROUND B (GAS)	A 1
GROUND C (DIESEL)	D 2
GROUND C	C 2
GROUND E	B 2
GROUND F	D 2
GROUND G	D 2
GROUND H (DIESEL)	A 10
GROUND H (GAS)	A 7
GROUND I (DIESEL)	B 10
GROUND I (GAS)	E 5
GROUND J	B 12
GROUND K	C 23
GROUND L	B 21
HAZARD FLASHER	D 16
HORN	C 1
HORN RELAY	E 16
IGNITION COIL (GAS)	E 7
IGNITION SW	A 15
INSTRUMENT CLUSTER	A-B 20
LIGHT SW	B-C 19
LOW COOLANT MODULE (DIESEL)	D-E 20
POWERTRAIN CONTROL MODULE (PCM) (GAS W/ 4L80-E)	A 4-7
PRNDL LT	D 16
STARTER (DIESEL)	D 3
STARTER (GAS)	A 3
STARTER RELAY (DIESEL)	D-E 3
STOP LT SW	E 16
TCC SW (DIESEL)	B 8
TCC SW (GAS)	B 4
TRANSMISSION CONTROL MODULE (TCM) (DIESEL W/ 4L80-E)	A 8-11
WATER IN FUEL SENS (DIESEL)	E 8
WIPER MOTOR CONN	E 18
WIPER/WASHER SW	E 19

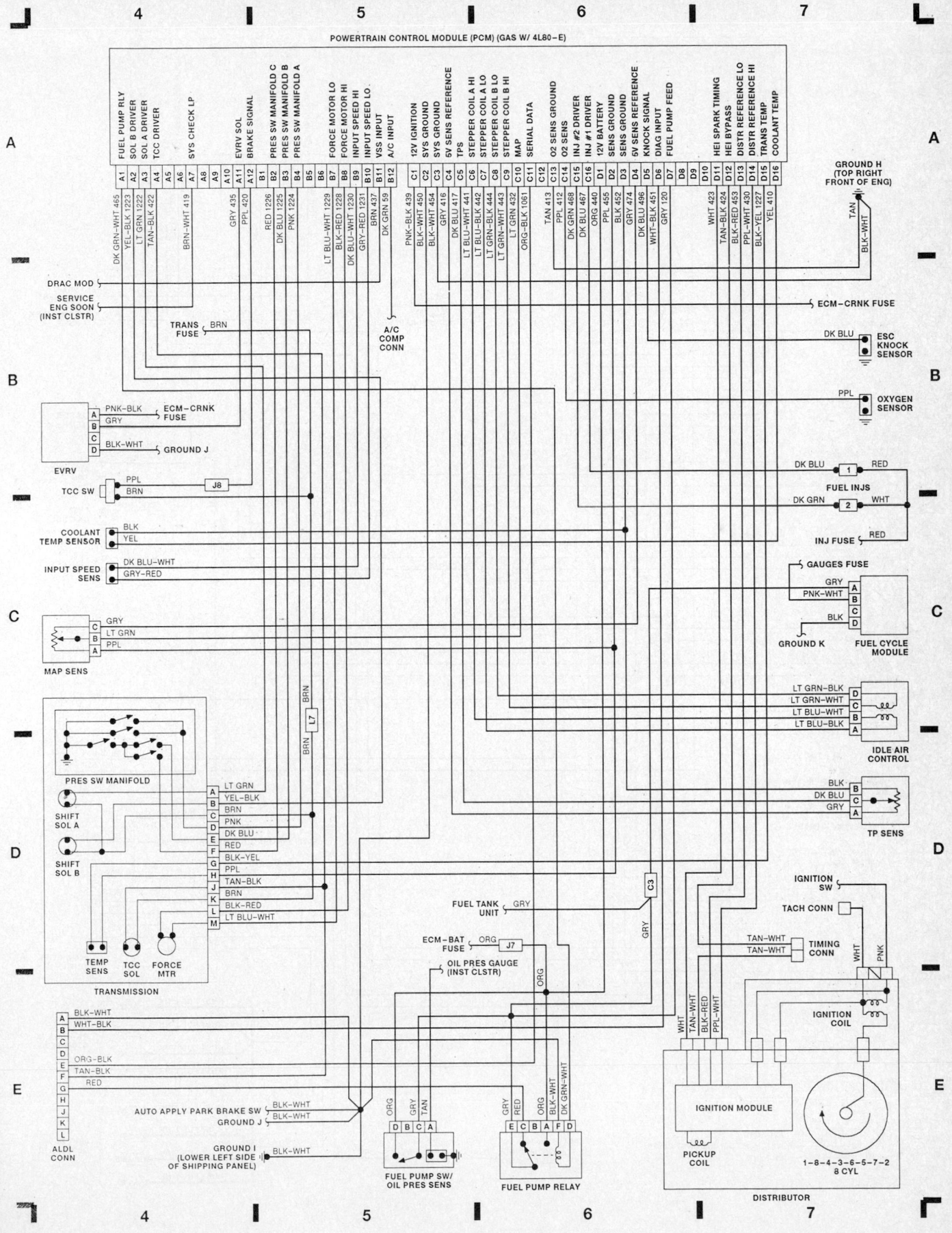

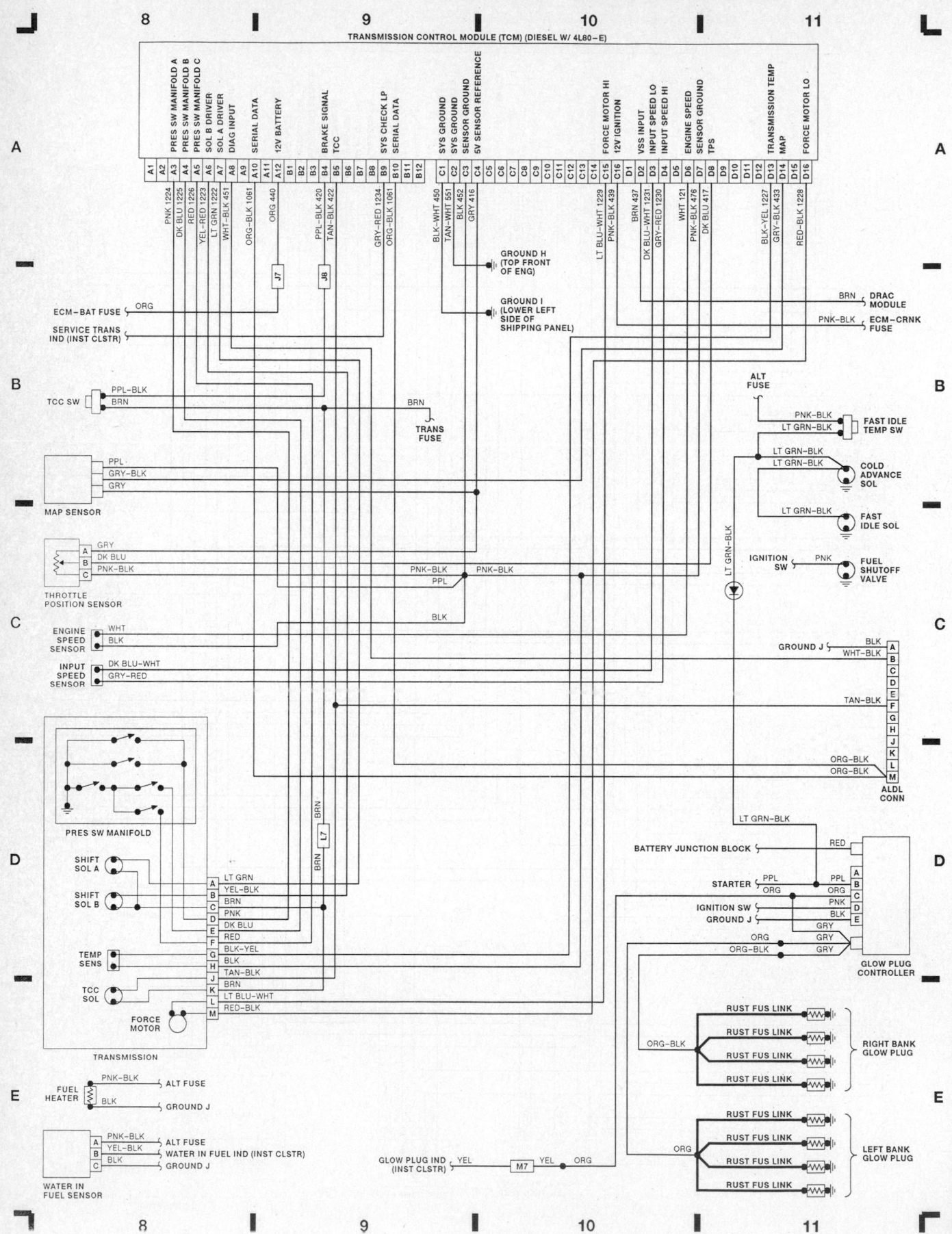

1992 WIRING DIAGRAMS
"P" Series – Motorhome (Cont.)

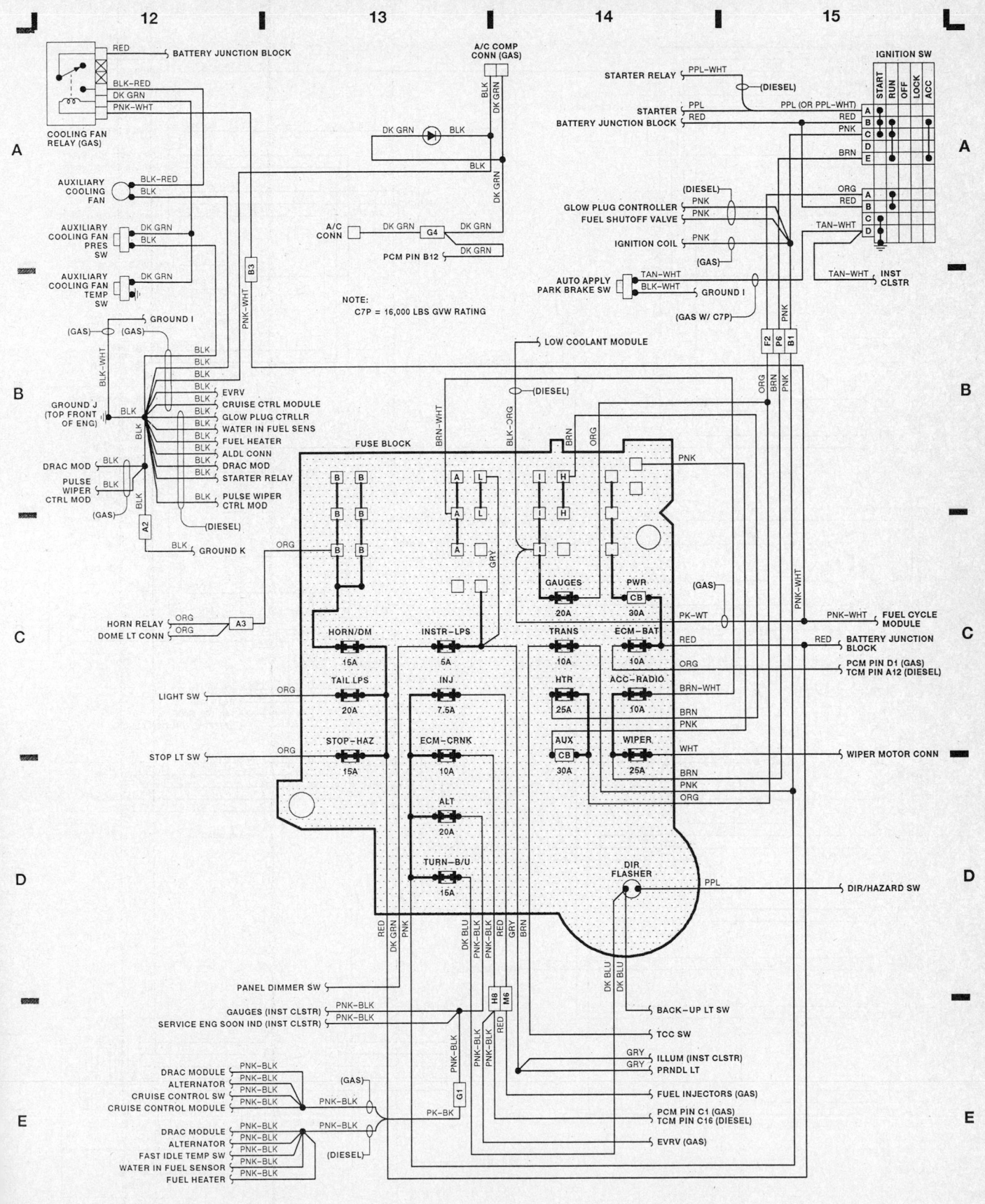

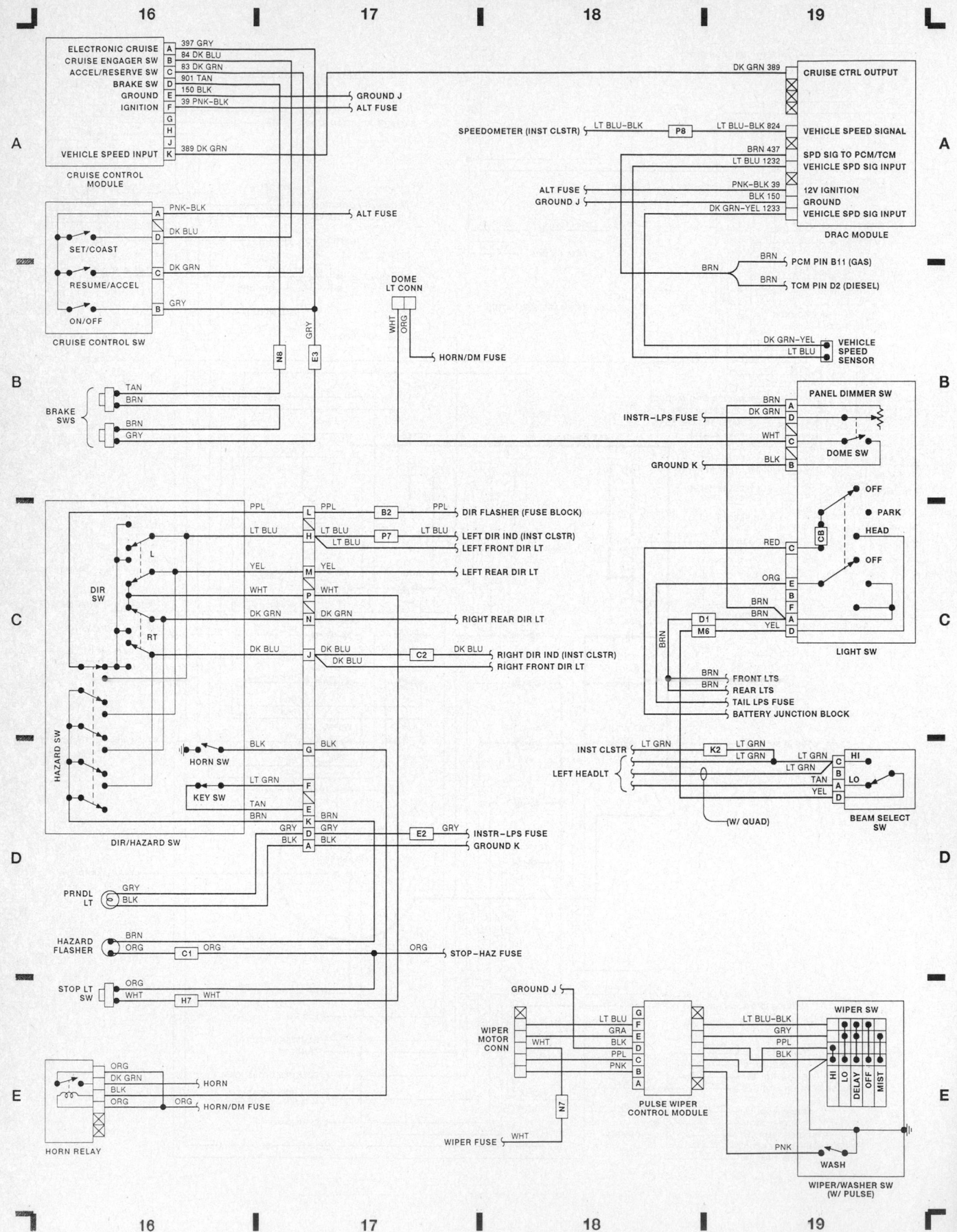

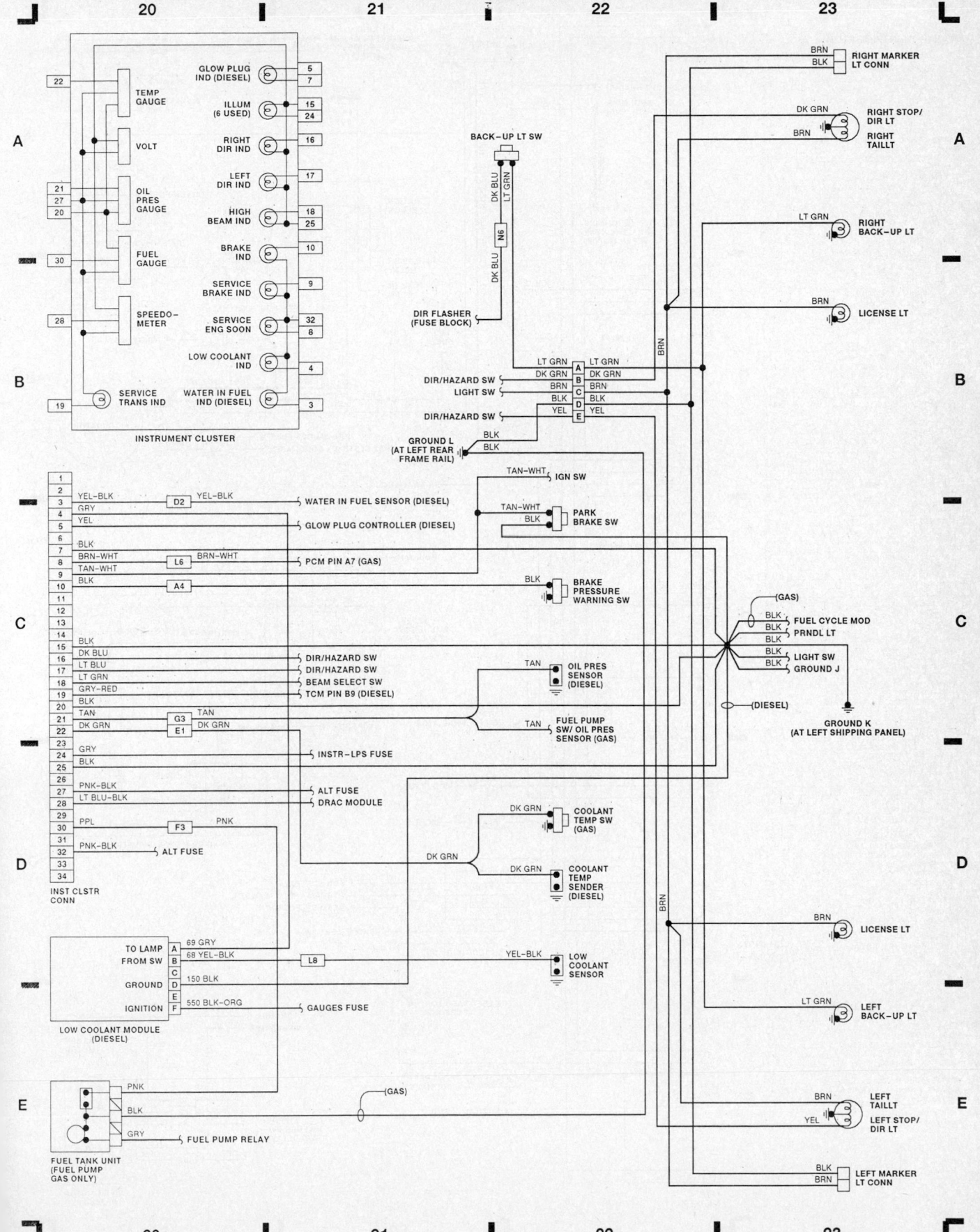

1992 WIRING DIAGRAMS
"S" & "T" Series Except Bravada

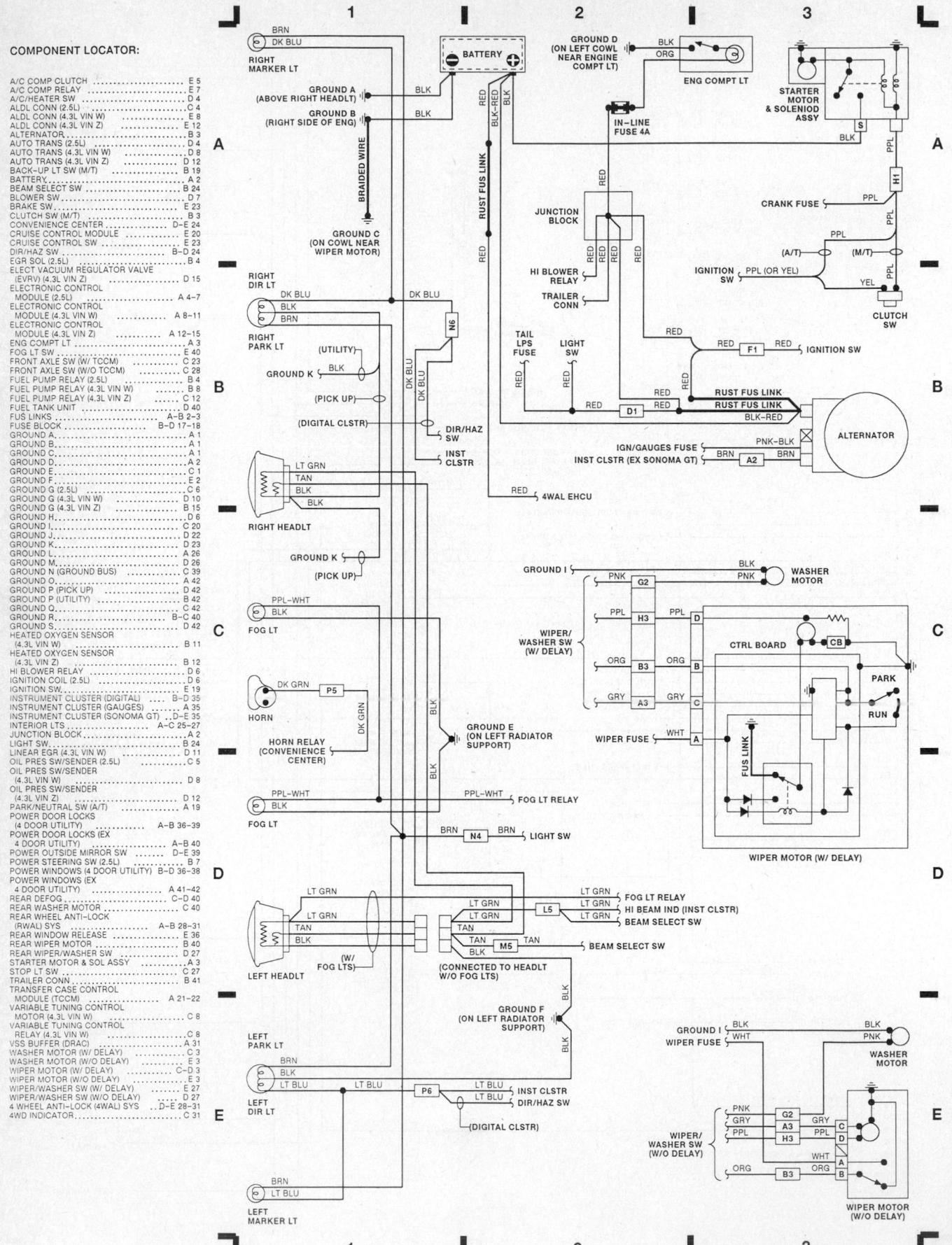

Component Locator:

A/C COMP CLUTCH	E 5
A/C COMP RELAY	E 7
A/C/HEATER SW	D 4
ALDL CONN (2.5L)	C 4
ALDL CONN (4.3L VIN W)	E 8
ALDL CONN (4.3L VIN Z)	E 12
ALTERNATOR	B 3
AUTO TRANS (2.5L)	D 4
AUTO TRANS (4.3L VIN W)	D 8
AUTO TRANS (4.3L VIN Z)	D 12
BACK-UP LT SW (M/T)	B 19
BATTERY	A 2
BEAM SELECT SW	B 24
BLOWER SW	D 7
BRAKE SW	E 23
CLUTCH SW (M/T)	B 3
CONVENIENCE CENTER	D-E 24
CRUISE CONTROL MODULE	E 20
CRUISE CONTROL SW	E 20
DIR/HAZ SW	B-D 24
EGR SOL (2.5L)	B 4
ELECT VACUUM REGULATOR VALVE	
(EVRV) (4.3L VIN Z)	D 15
ELECTRONIC CONTROL	
MODULE (2.5L)	A 4-7
ELECTRONIC CONTROL	
MODULE (4.3L VIN W)	A 8-11
ELECTRONIC CONTROL	
MODULE (4.3L VIN Z)	A 12-15
ENG COMPT LT	A 3
FOG LT SW	E 40
FRONT AXLE SW (W/TCCM)	C 23
FRONT AXLE SW (W/O TCCM)	C 28
FUEL PUMP RELAY (2.5L)	B 4
FUEL PUMP RELAY (4.3L VIN W)	B 8
FUEL PUMP RELAY (4.3L VIN Z)	C 12
FUEL TANK UNIT	D 40
FUS LINKS	A-B 2-3
FUSE BLOCK	B-D 17-18
GROUND A	A 1
GROUND B	A 1
GROUND C	A 1
GROUND D	A 2
GROUND E	C 1
GROUND F	E 2
GROUND G (2.5L)	C 6
GROUND G (4.3L VIN W)	D 10
GROUND G (4.3L VIN Z)	B 15
GROUND H	D 6
GROUND I	C 20
GROUND J	D 22
GROUND K	D 23
GROUND L	A 26
GROUND M	D 26
GROUND N (GROUND BUS)	C 39
GROUND O	A 42
GROUND P (PICK UP)	D 42
GROUND P (UTILITY)	B 42
GROUND Q	C 42
GROUND R	B-C 42
GROUND S	D 42
HEATED OXYGEN SENSOR	
(4.3L VIN W)	B 11
HEATED OXYGEN SENSOR	
(4.3L VIN Z)	B 12
HI BLOWER RELAY	D 6
IGNITION COIL (2.5L)	D 6
IGNITION SW	E 19
INSTRUMENT CLUSTER (DIGITAL)	B-D 35
INSTRUMENT CLUSTER (GAUGES)	A 35
INSTRUMENT CLUSTER (SONOMA GT)	D-E 35
INTERIOR LTS	A-C 25-27
JUNCTION BLOCK	A 2
LIGHT SW	B 24
LINEAR EGR (4.3L VIN W)	D 11
OIL PRES SW/SENDER (2.5L)	C 5
OIL PRES SW/SENDER	
(4.3L VIN W)	D 8
OIL PRES SW/SENDER	
(4.3L VIN Z)	D 12
PARK/NEUTRAL SW (A/T)	A 19
POWER DOOR LOCKS	
(4 DOOR UTILITY)	A-B 36-39
POWER DOOR LOCKS (EX	
4 DOOR UTILITY)	A-B 40
POWER OUTSIDE MIRROR SW	D-E 39
POWER STEERING SW (2.5L)	B 7
POWER WINDOWS (4 DOOR UTILITY)	B-D 36-38
POWER WINDOWS (EX	
4 DOOR UTILITY)	A 41-42
REAR DEFOG	C-D 40
REAR WASHER MOTOR	C 3
REAR WHEEL ANTI-LOCK	
(RWAL) SYS	A-B 28-31
REAR WINDOW RELEASE	E 36
REAR WIPER MOTOR	B 40
REAR WIPER/WASHER SW	D 27
STARTER MOTOR & SOL ASSY	A 3
STOP LT SW	C 27
TRAILER CONN	B 41
TRANSFER CASE CONTROL	
MODULE (TCCM)	A 21-22
VARIABLE TUNING CONTROL	
MOTOR (4.3L VIN W)	C 8
VARIABLE TUNING CONTROL	
RELAY (4.3L VIN W)	C 8
VSS BUFFER (DRAC)	A 31
WASHER MOTOR (W/ DELAY)	C 3
WASHER MOTOR (W/O DELAY)	E 3
WIPER MOTOR (W/ DELAY)	C-D 3
WIPER MOTOR (W/O DELAY)	E 3
WIPER/WASHER SW (W/ DELAY)	C 27
WIPER/WASHER SW (W/O DELAY)	D 27
4 WHEEL ANTI-LOCK (4WAL) SYS	D-E 28-31
4WD INDICATOR	C 31

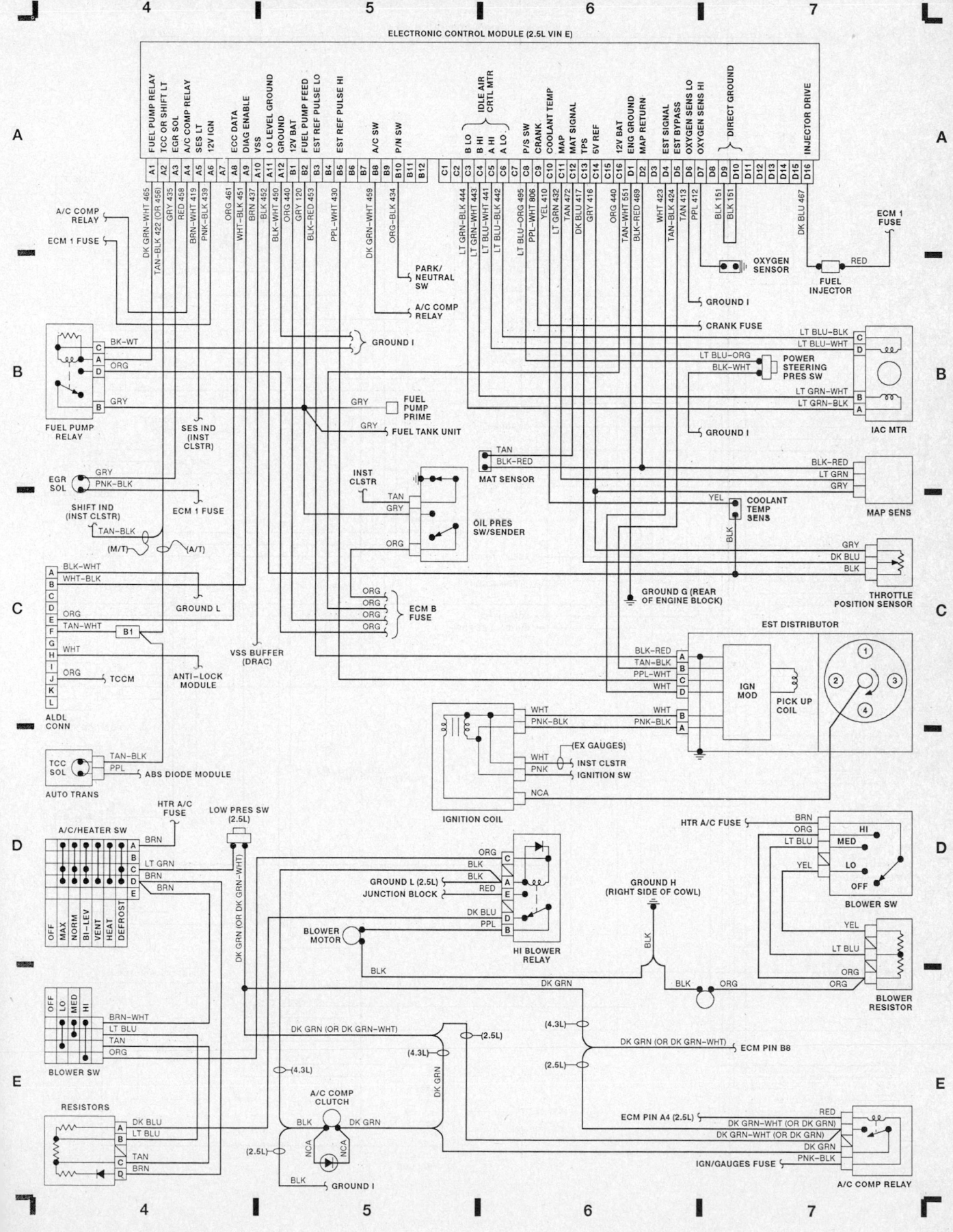

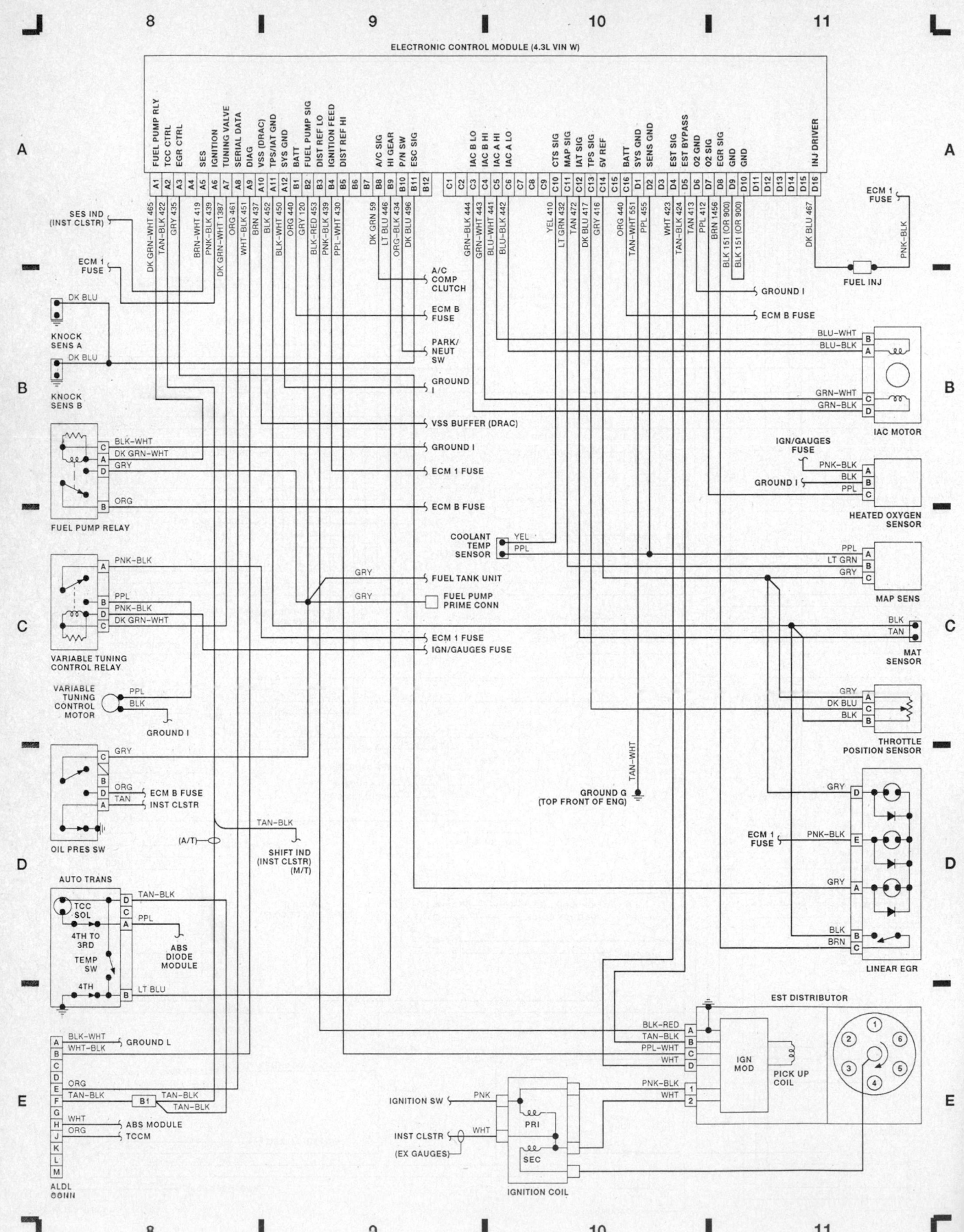

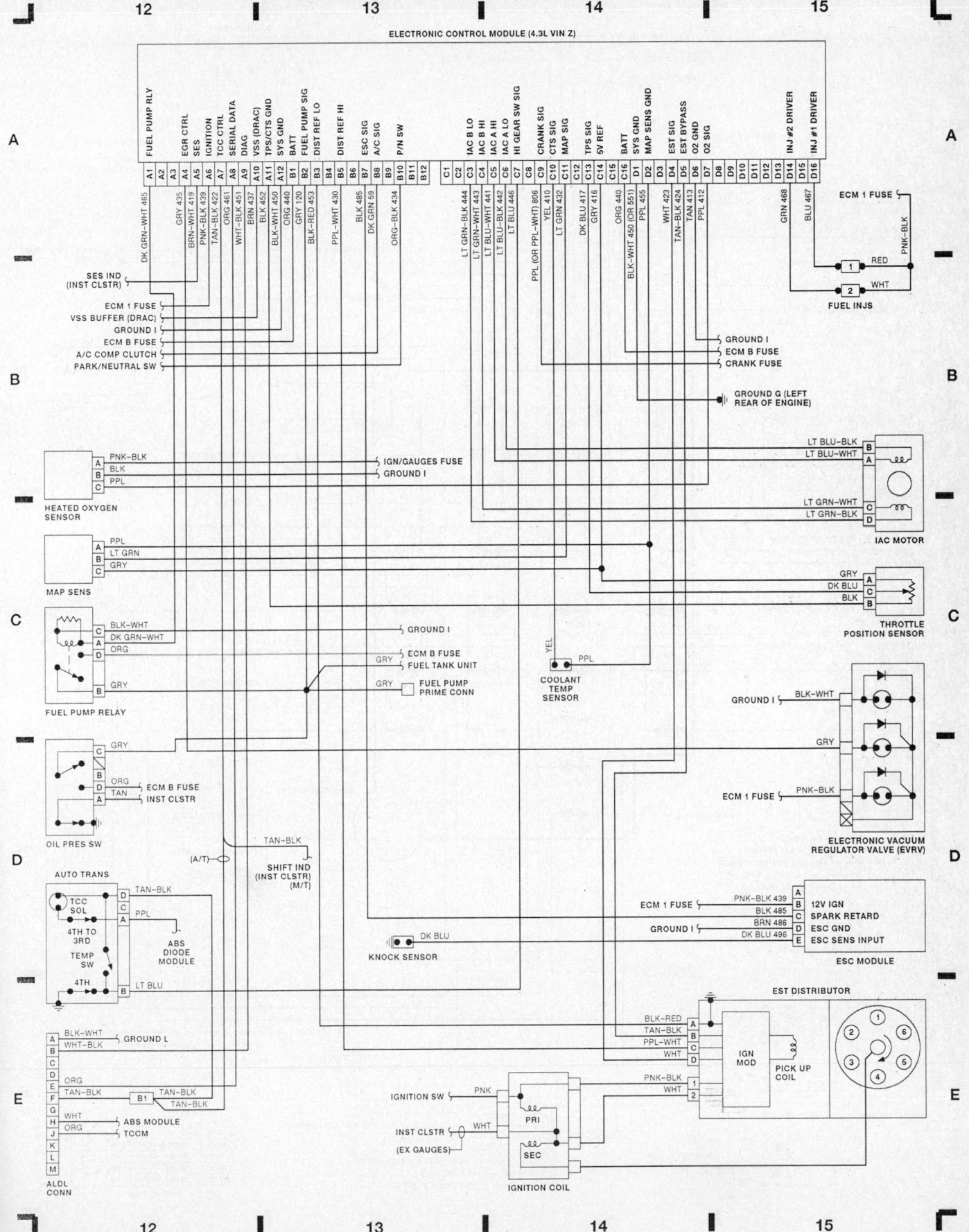

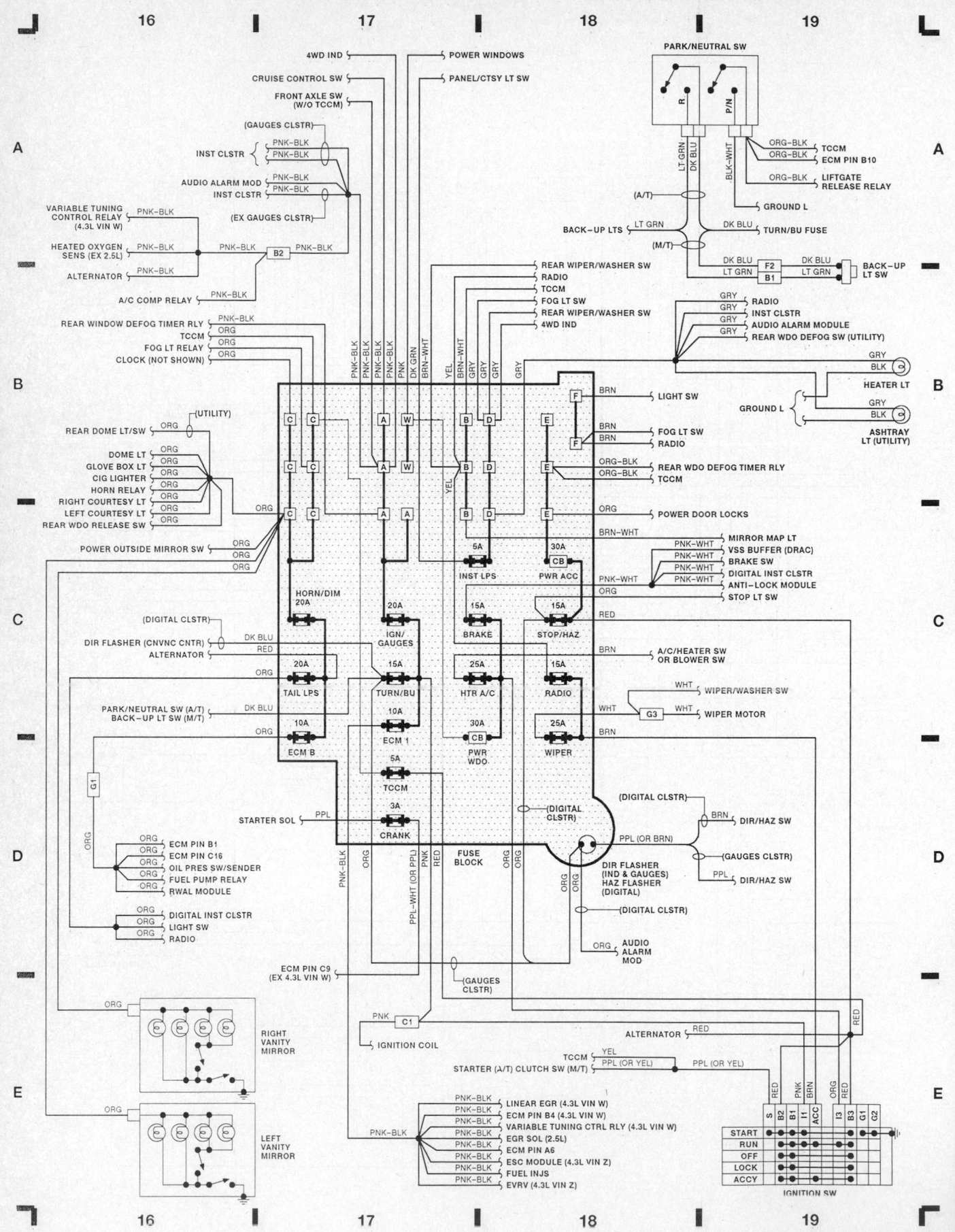

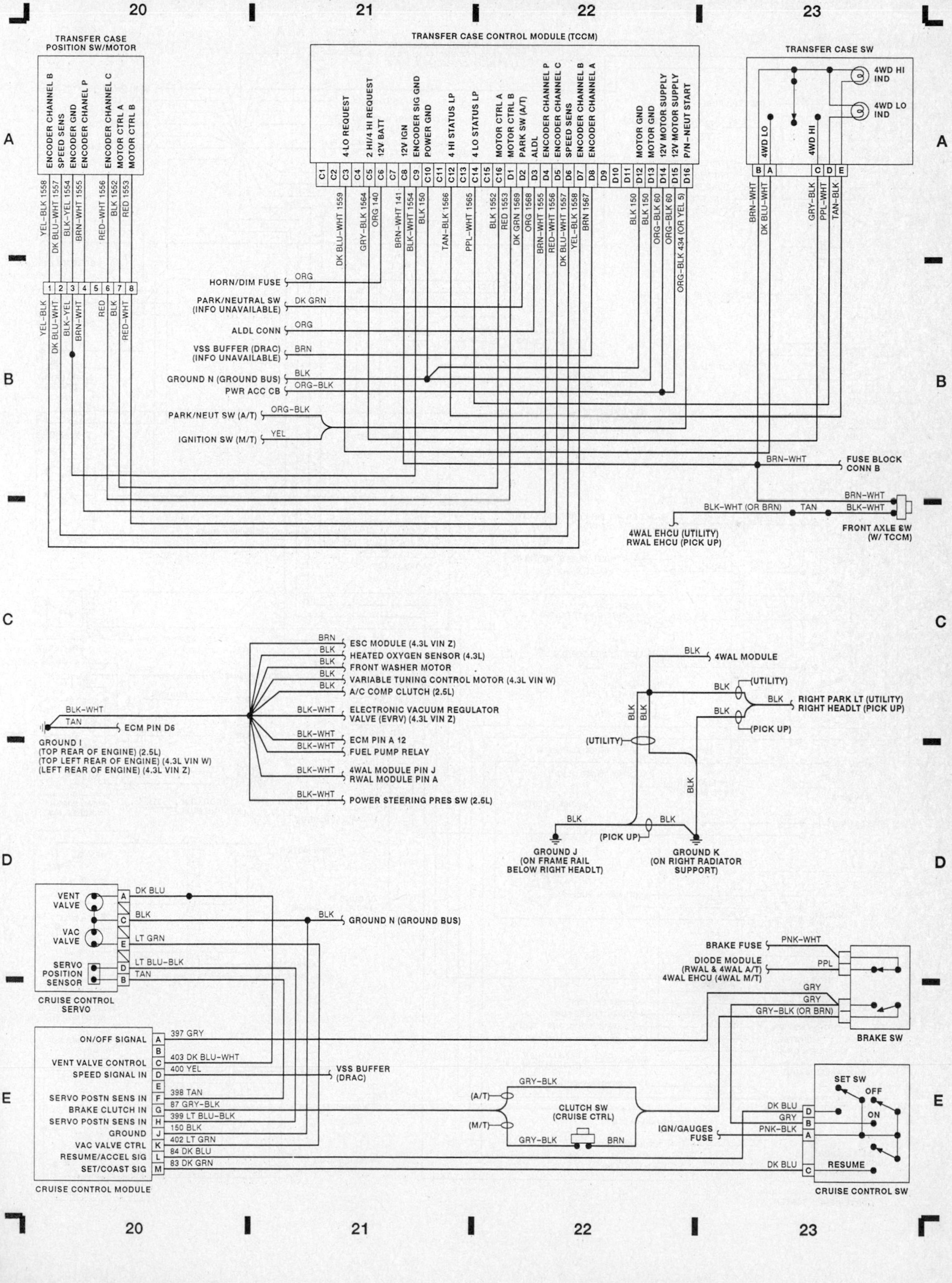

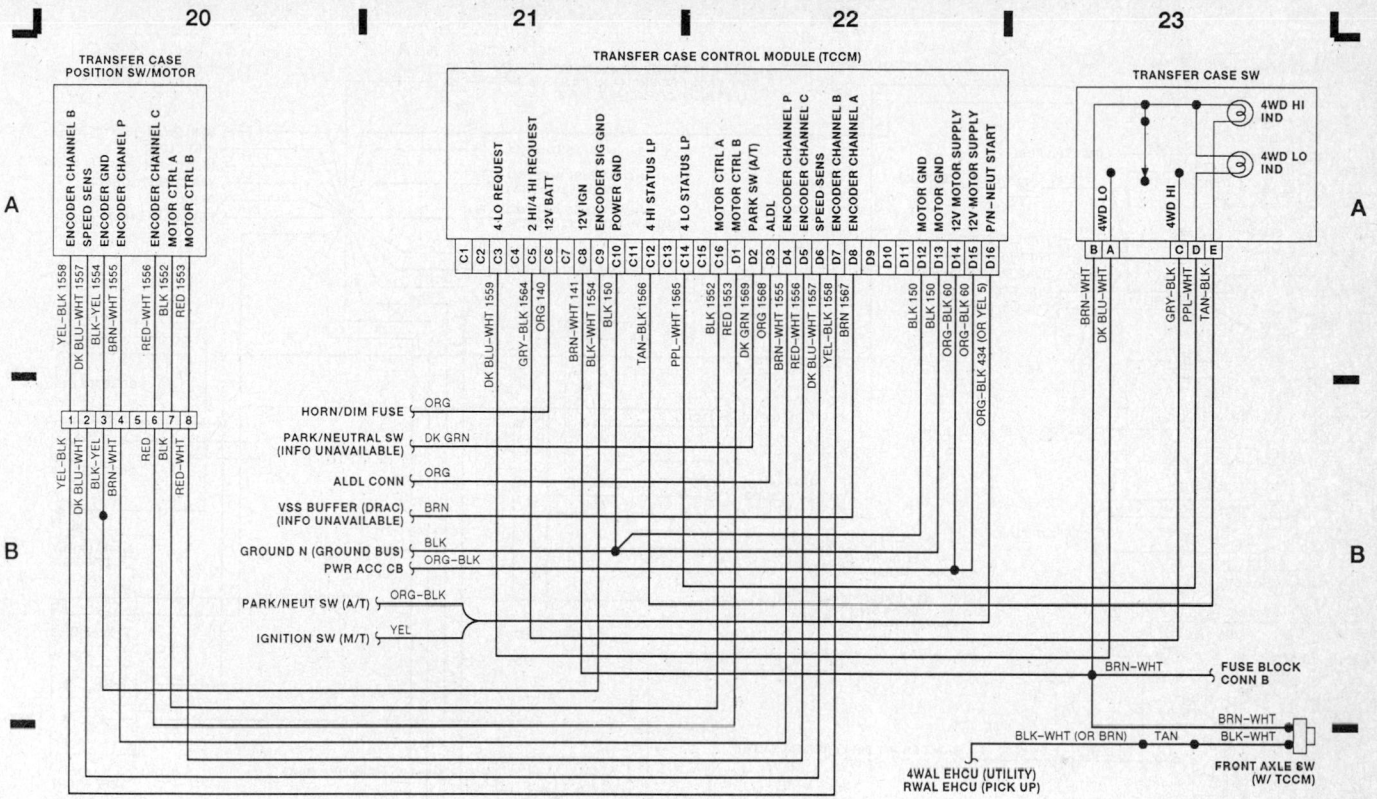

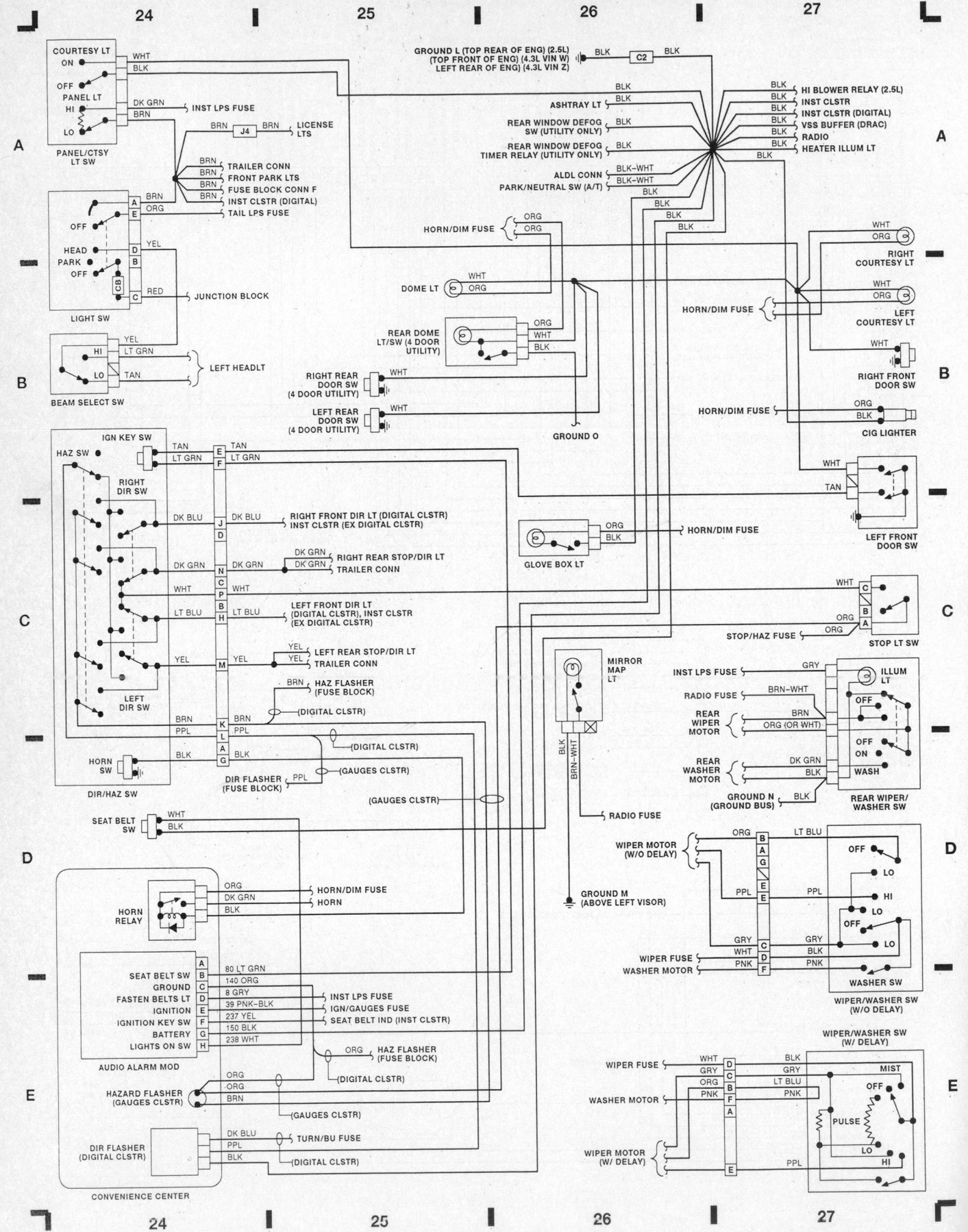

1992 WIRING DIAGRAMS
"S" & "T" Series Except Bravada (Cont.)

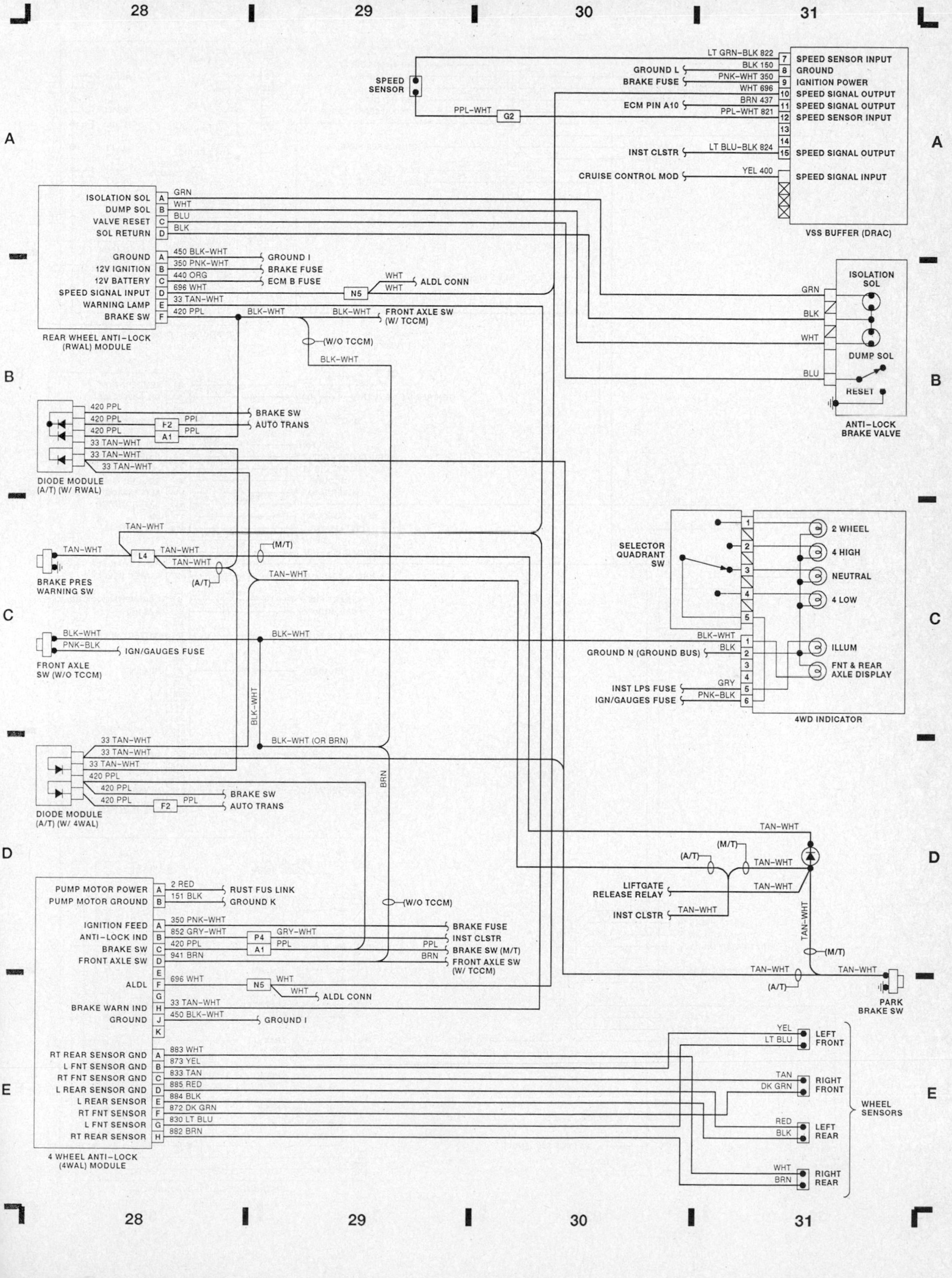

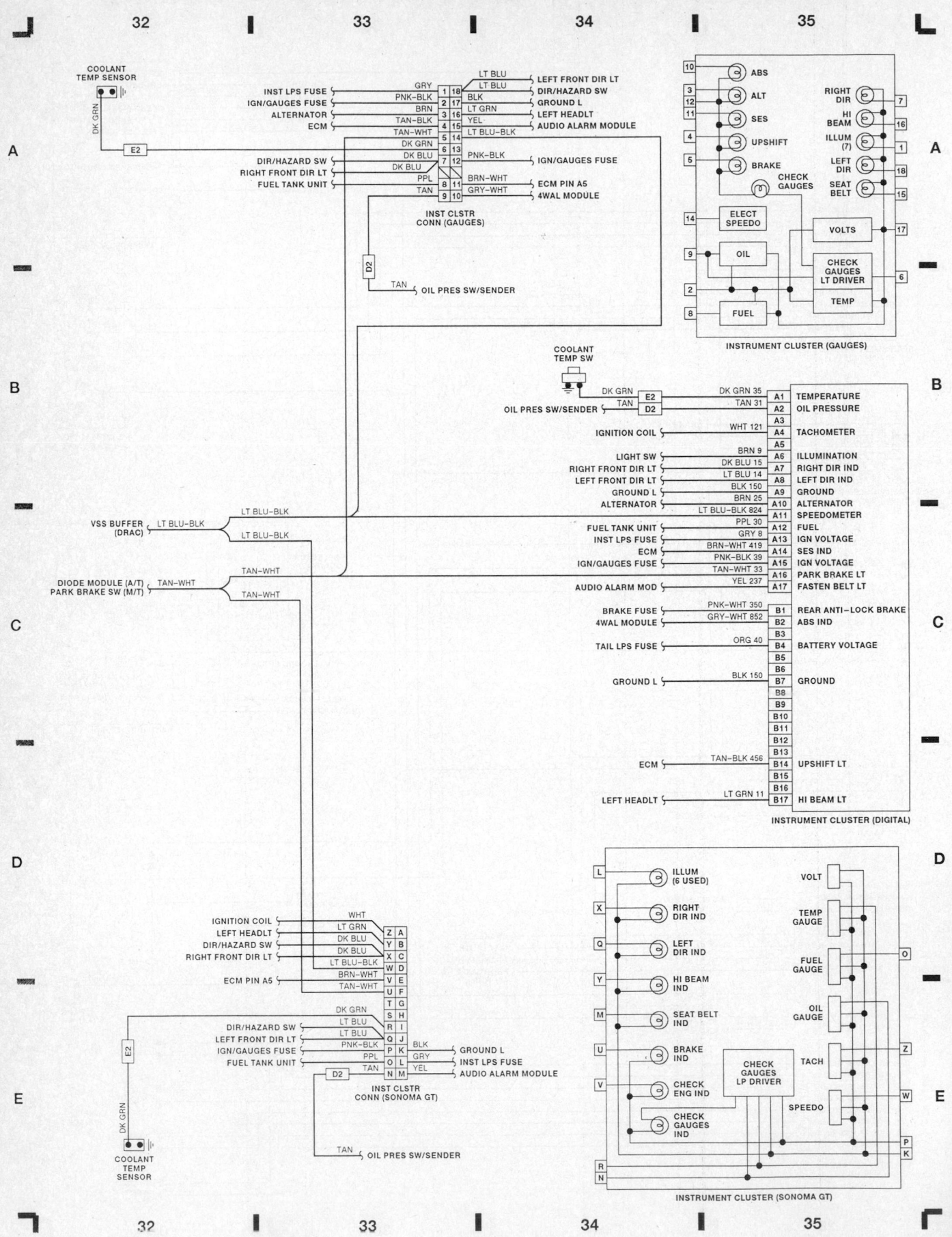

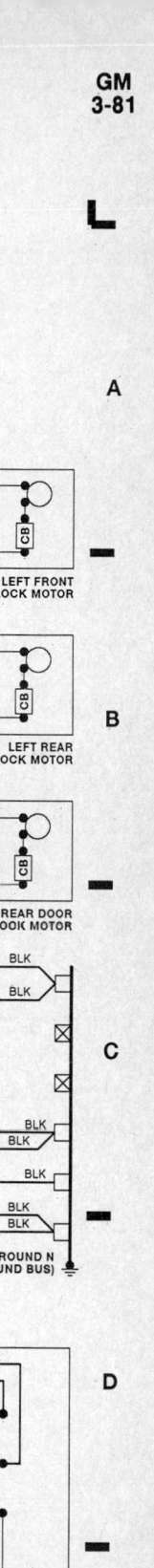

36

RIGHT FRONT DOOR LOCK MOTOR

RIGHT FRONT DOOR LOCK SW

DOOR LOCK RELAY (4 DOOR UTILITY)

37

38

39

A

GRY TAN

UNLOCK LOCK

LT BLU ORG-BLK BLK-WHT

B D C A F E

TAN BLK ORG BLK-WHT LT BLU GRY

TAN A
GRY B
CB

LEFT FRONT DOOR LOCK MOTOR

B

LOCK
BLK-WHT
ORG-BLK
LT BLU
UNLOCK

LEFT FRONT DOOR LOCK SW

ORG PWR ACC CB

TAN A
GRY B
CB

LEFT REAR DOOR LOCK MOTOR

C

LEFT FRONT WINDOW MOTOR

BRN G
A CB B

BLK E
DK BLU H
TAN J

PNK F
DK BLU-WHT K
PPL A

DK GRN B
PPL-WHT C

LT GRN D

MASTER POWER WINDOW SW (4 DOOR UTILITY)

TAN-WHT

PNK
PWR WDO CB

TAN B
PNK A
DK BLU-WHT E

BRN D
DK BLU C
A CB B

RIGHT FRONT WINDOW MOTOR

RIGHT FRONT WINDOW MOTOR

LT GRN B
PNK A
PPL-WHT E

DK BLU D
BRN C
A CB B

RIGHT REAR WINDOW MOTOR

RIGHT REAR WINDOW MOTOR

PPL B
PNK A
DK GRN E

DK BLU D
BRN C
A CB B

LEFT REAR WINDOW MOTOR

TAN A
GRY B
CB

RIGHT REAR DOOR LOCK MOTOR

(4 DOOR UTILITY) BLK
LEFT WINDOW SW BLK
BLK
LEFT DOOR LOCK SW BLK BLK
BLK
BLK

(PICK UP & 2 DOOR UTILITY)

CRUISE CONTROL MODULE BLK
REAR WIPER/WASHER SW BLK
4WD IND BLK
FOG LT SW BLK
TCCM BLK

GROUND N (GROUND BUS)

D

LEFT REAR WINDOW MOTOR

LT BLU LT BLU
L/RT WHT WHT
CB
LT GRN LT GRN
UP/DN YEL YEL
CB

LEFT POWER MIRROR MOTOR

HORN/DIM FUSE

ORG A
WHT B
LT BLU C
YEL D
YEL-BLK E
LT BLU-BLK F
WHT-BLK G
BLK H

WHT-BLK
WHT

E

GRN-BLK
TAN-WHT ORG-BLK PARK/NEUTRAL SW (A/T)
BLK PARK BRAKE SW
BRN (M/T)

LIFTGATE RELEASE RELAY

REAR WINDOW RELEASE SW BRN
ORG HORN/DIM FUSE

REAR WINDOW RELEASE SOL BLK

WHT-BLK WHT-BLK
L/RT LT BLU-BLK LT BLU-BLK
CB
YEL-BLK YEL-BLK
UP/DN LT GRN-BLK LT GRN-BLK
CB

RIGHT POWER MIRROR MOTOR

ORG
BLK
LT BLU L MIR
LT BLU-BLK RT MIR
YEL
YEL-BLK

POWER OUTSIDE MIRROR SW

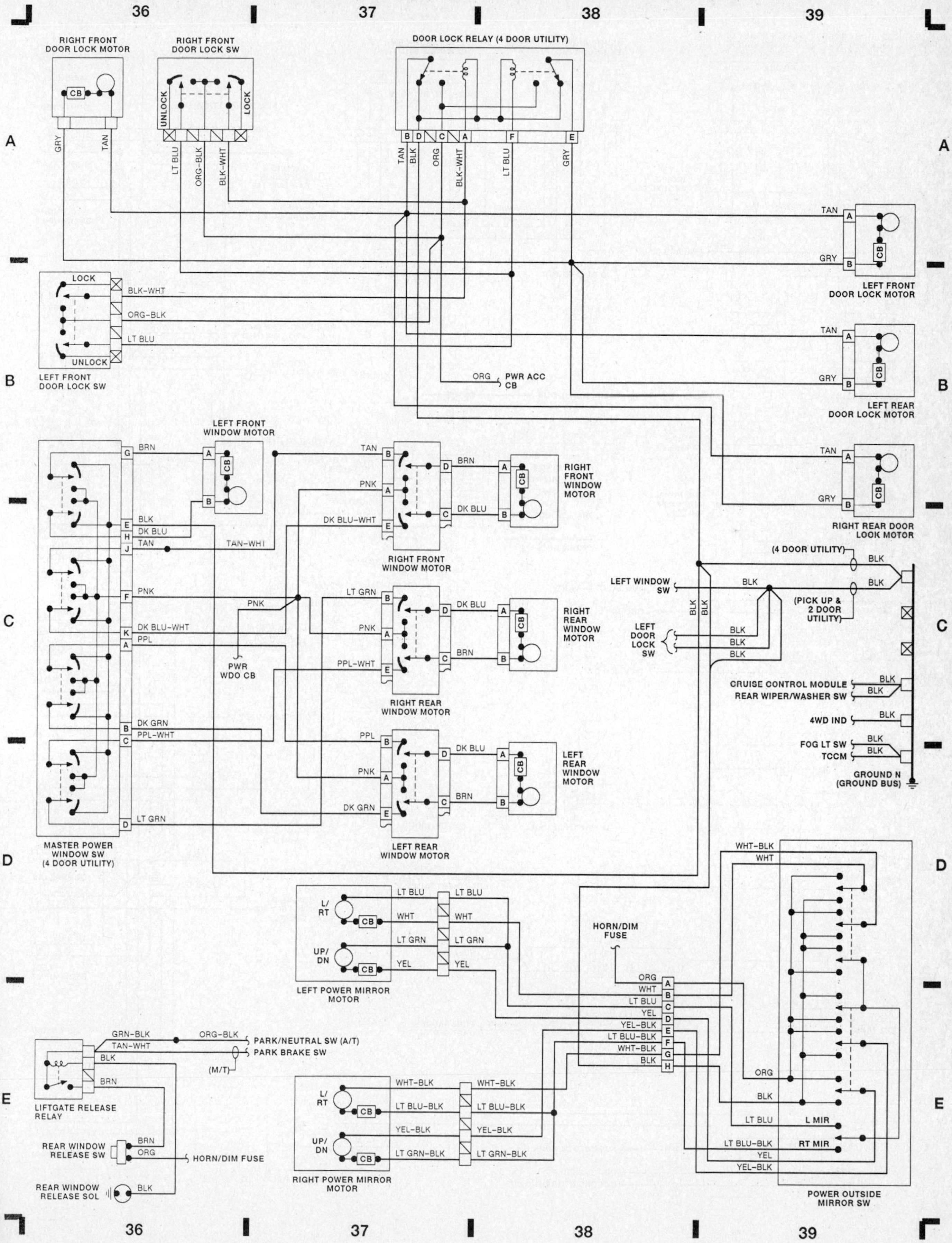

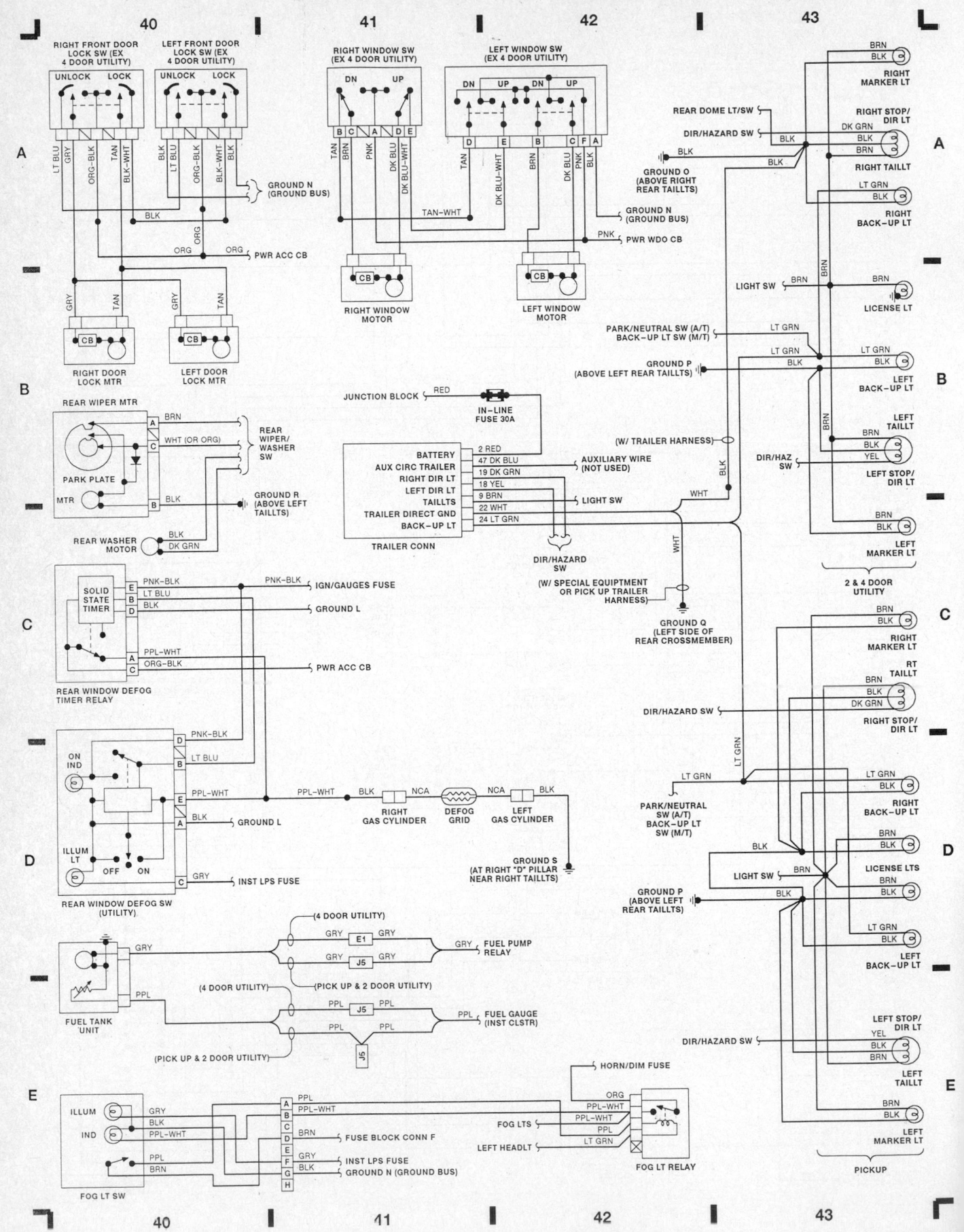

Astro, Bravada, Lumina APV, Safari, Silhouette, Sonoma, Suburban (1991), Syclone, Trans Sport, Typhoon, Van, "S" & "T" Series Blazer, Jimmy & Pickup, "R" & "V" Series Blazer, Jimmy & Pickup (1991)

NOTE: In 1991, "R" and "V" Series vehicles included Blazer, Jimmy, Pickup and Suburban. In 1992, body designations "R" and "V" were changed to "C" and "K". These 1992 vehicles include Blazer, Yukon, Pickup and Suburban. For information on these vehicles, see CRUISE CONTROL – ELECTRIC MOTOR SERVO article.

DESCRIPTION

System consists of cruise control module, cruise control switch, vacuum-actuated servo assembly, speed sensor, speed sensor buffer, brake release switch/valve and clutch release switch (M/T). On all models except Lumina APV, Silhouette and Trans Sport, speed sensor buffer is part of Digital Ratio Adaptor Controller (DRAC).

OPERATION

CRUISE CONTROL MODULE

Cruise control module monitors vehicle speed, servo diaphragm position, control switch position, brake switch position and clutch switch position. Based on these inputs, the module controls vacuum valves at the servo assembly. Module prevents system engagement at speeds of less than 25 MPH. Module is not serviceable. If defective, it must be replaced.

CRUISE CONTROL MODULE LOCATION

Application	Location
Astro & Safari	Behind Instrument Panel, Right Of Steering Column.
Bravada, Sonoma, Syclone, Typhoon & "S" & "T" Series Blazer, Jimmy & Pickup	Behind Left End Of Instrument Panel.
Lumina Apv, Silhouette, Trans Sport, Suburban & "R" & "V" Series Blazer, Jimmy & Pickup	Behind Instrument Panel, To Left Of Steering Column.
Van	Behind Instrument Panel, To Left Of Parking Brake Bracket.

CRUISE CONTROL SWITCH

Cruise control switch, located on end of (multifunction) turn signal lever, controls system operational modes.

SET/COAST – To set vehicle speed, turn control switch to ON position. With vehicle speed at 25 MPH or more, depress and release SET/COAST button. Vehicle will maintain set speed.

To increase speed during engaged cruise, accelerate to desired speed. Press and release SET/COAST button. Vehicle will maintain new set speed.

To decrease speed during engaged cruise, depress and hold SET/COAST button. System will disengage. When vehicle has slowed to desired speed, release SET/COAST button. Vehicle will maintain new set speed.

To decrease speed by one-MPH increments during engaged cruise, tap SET/COAST button (quickly depress and release button; DO NOT depress and hold button). Vehicle speed will decrease one MPH for each tap of the button.

RESUME/ACCEL – To resume set speed after system has been disengaged by braking, momentarily engage and release RESUME/ACCEL switch. Vehicle will return to set speed. If RESUME/ACCEL switch is engaged for more than one second, vehicle will begin to accelerate. To accelerate using cruise control system, engage and hold RESUME/ACCEL switch until desired speed is reached.

To increase speed by one-MPH increments during engaged cruise, tap RESUME/ACCEL switch (quickly move to RESUME/ACCEL position and release). Vehicle speed will increase one MPH for each tap of the switch. After 10 taps, system must be reset to a new speed to continue this function.

SERVO ASSEMBLY

Servo assembly consists of a vacuum diaphragm that actuates the throttle lever and 2 vacuum control solenoids (vacuum solenoid and vent solenoid). *See Fig. 1.* Vacuum and vent solenoids, responding to commands from cruise control module, regulate vacuum supply to diaphragm. Engine manifold vacuum (or vacuum pump on vehicles with diesel engine) provides vacuum source for diaphragm.

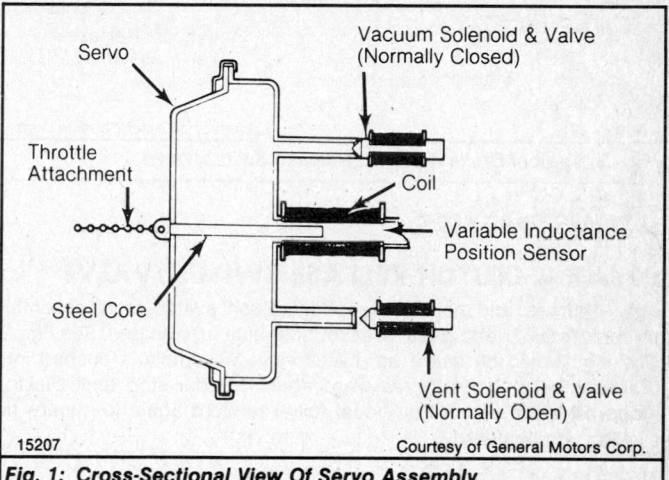

15207   Courtesy of General Motors Corp.

Fig. 1: Cross-Sectional View Of Servo Assembly

SPEED SENSOR & BUFFER

Astro, Bravada, Safari, Sonoma, Syclone, Typhoon & "S" & "T" Series Blazer, Jimmy & Pickup – Speed sensor consists of magnetic speed sensor, located in transmission (2WD) or transfer case (4WD), and speed sensor buffer (part of DRAC). DRAC is located:
- Behind instrument panel, on left side of radio (Astro and Safari)
- Behind instrument panel, at right end near ECM (all others)

Magnetic speed sensor sends signal representing vehicle speed to DRAC, which converts signal and sends it to cruise control module.

Suburban, Van & "R" & "V" Series Blazer, Jimmy & Pickup – Speed sensor consists of either an optical sensor in speedometer head or magnetic sensor in transmission, and speed sensor buffer (part of DRAC). DRAC is located:
- On parking brake bracket (Van)
- Behind instrument panel, to left of steering column (all others).

Speed sensor sends signal representing vehicle speed to DRAC, which converts signal and sends it to cruise control module.

Lumina APV, Silhouette & Trans Sport – Speed sensor consists of magnetic speed sensor, mounted on top of transaxle, and speed sensor buffer, located behind right end of instrument panel, above convenience center. Magnetic speed sensor sends signal representing vehicle speed to buffer, which converts signal and sends it to cruise control module.

BRAKE & CLUTCH RELEASE SWITCH/VALVE

These components, mounted on brake or clutch pedal bracket, disengage system when the respective pedal is depressed. *See Fig. 2.* Switch and vacuum valve may be combined, and may incorporate brakelight and torque converter clutch switch.

When pedal is depressed, switch interrupts electrical current to cruise control module, which then disengages the system. Vacuum valve vents servo assembly diaphragm to atmosphere when pedal is depressed, causing throttle to immediately return to closed position.

GM
4-2

1991-92 SAFETY EQUIPMENT
Cruise Control – Vacuum Servo – Except 3.8L (Cont.)

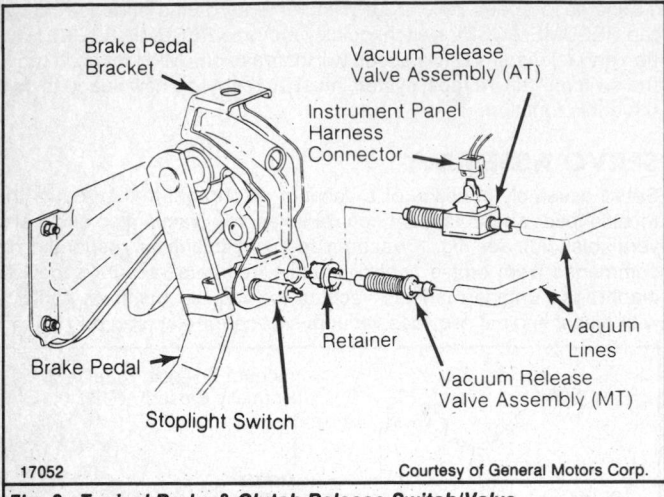

Fig. 2: Typical Brake & Clutch Release Switch/Valve

17052   Courtesy of General Motors Corp.

ADJUSTMENTS

BRAKE & CLUTCH RELEASE SWITCH/VALVE

Fully depress and hold brake pedal. Push switch/valve assembly through retainer and pedal bracket hole until fully seated. See Fig. 2. Clicking should be heard as switch/valve assembly is pushed into bracket. Pull pedal fully rearward against pedal stop until clicking stops. Release pedal. Pull pedal fully rearward again to ensure no clicking can be heard.

TESTING (ELECTRICAL SYSTEM)

NOTE: Intermittent or incorrect operation of system may be caused by a problem in vacuum system. However, perform electrical system testing first. If electrical system testing specifies replacement of component, perform vacuum system testing before replacing component. Also, if system operates intermittently, the cruise control switch wires may be pinched where they exit the multifunction lever. If wires are pinched, replace multifunction lever with a new service multifunction lever (25111290) designed to prevent pinching.

ASTRO, SAFARI, SONOMA, SYCLONE, TYPHOON & "S" & "T" SERIES BLAZER, JIMMY & PICKUP

NOTE: For 1991 cruise control system wiring diagram, see Figs. 3 and 4. For 1992 cruise control system wiring diagram, see appropriate chassis wiring diagram in WIRING DIAGRAMS.

Test system using Quick Check Box (J-34185). Operating instructions are provided with quick check box. If quick check box is not available, perform CRUISE CONTROL DIAGNOSIS test chart. See Fig. 9. This chart may lead to other test charts. See Figs. 10, 11 and 12.

BRAVADA

NOTE: For 1991 cruise control system wiring diagram, see Fig. 4. For 1992 cruise control system wiring diagram, see appropriate chassis wiring diagram in WIRING DIAGRAMS. For 1991-92 DRAC (speed sensor buffer) system wiring diagram, see appropriate chassis wiring diagram in WIRING DIAGRAMS. Check voltage and resistance using a DVOM. Unless specified otherwise, probe terminals on harness side of connector.

Cruise Control Does Not Engage – 1) Turn ignition switch to RUN position. Turn on cruise control. Check voltage at Pink/Black wire terminal of cruise control switch connector. If battery voltage is present, go to next step. If voltage is not present, replace IGN/GAU fuse or repair Pink/Black wire.

2) Check voltage at Gray wire terminal of cruise control switch connector. If voltage is not present, replace cruise control switch. If battery voltage is present, check voltage at Gray wire terminal of brakelight switch connector. If voltage is not present, check Gray wire and brakelight switch connector.

3) If battery voltage is present, check voltage at Gray wire terminal of cruise control module connector. If voltage is not present, repair Gray wire. If battery voltage is present, check voltage between Gray and Black wire terminals of cruise control module connector.

4) If voltage is not present, repair Black wire. If battery voltage is present, check voltage at Gray/Black wire terminal of brakelight switch connector. If battery voltage is present, go to next step. If voltage is not present, adjust brakelight switch. See BRAKE & CLUTCH RELEASE SWITCH/VALVE under ADJUSTMENTS. If brakelight switch cannot be adjusted, replace brakelight switch.

5) Check voltage at Gray/Black wire terminal of cruise control module connector. If voltage is not present, repair Gray/Black wire. If battery voltage is present, check voltage at Dark Blue wire terminal of cruise control switch connector.

6) If battery voltage is present, replace cruise control switch. If voltage is not present, check voltage at Dark Blue wire terminal of cruise control switch connector while depressing and holding SET switch. If voltage is not present, replace cruise control switch.

7) If battery voltage is present, check voltage at Dark Blue wire terminal of cruise control module connector while depressing and holding SET switch. If voltage is not present, repair Dark Blue wire. If battery voltage is present, check voltage at Dark Green wire terminal of cruise control switch connector while depressing and holding RESUME/ACCEL switch.

8) If voltage is not present, replace cruise control switch. If battery voltage is present, check voltage at Dark Green wire terminal of cruise control module connector while depressing and holding RESUME/ACCEL switch. If voltage is not present, repair Dark Green wire.

9) If battery voltage is present, disconnect cruise control module connector. Check resistance between Dark Blue/White and Black wire terminals of cruise control module connector. If resistance is greater than 55 ohms, go to next step. If resistance is less than 30 ohms, go to step 11). If resistance is 30-55 ohms, go to step 12).

10) Disconnect cruise control servo connector. Check resistance between Dark Blue/White and Black wire terminals of cruise control servo connector (servo side of connector). If resistance is greater than 55 ohms, replace cruise control servo. If resistance is less than 55 ohms, repair Dark Blue/White wire.

11) Disconnect cruise control servo connector. Check resistance between Dark Blue/White and Black wire terminals of cruise control servo connector (servo side of connector). If resistance is less than 30 ohms, replace cruise control servo. If resistance is greater than 30 ohms, repair Dark Blue/White wire.

12) Check resistance between Light Green and Black wire terminals of cruise control module connector. If resistance is greater than 55 ohms, go to next step. If resistance is less than 30 ohms, go to step 14). If resistance is 30-55 ohms, go to step 15).

13) Disconnect cruise control servo connector. Check resistance between Light Green and Black wire terminals of cruise control servo connector (servo side of connector). If resistance is greater than 55 ohms, replace cruise control servo. If resistance is less than 55 ohms, repair Light Green wire.

14) Disconnect cruise control servo connector. Check resistance between Light Green and Black wire terminals of cruise control servo connector (servo side of connector). If resistance is less than 30 ohms, replace cruise control servo. If resistance is greater than 30 ohms, repair Light Green wire.

15) Check resistance between Light Blue/Black and Tan wire terminals of cruise control module connector. If resistance is greater than 25 ohms, go to next step. If resistance is less than 15 ohms, go to step 17). If resistance is 15-25 ohms, go to step 18).

16) Disconnect cruise control servo connector. Check resistance between Light Blue/Black and Tan wire terminals of cruise control servo connector (servo side of connector). If resistance is greater than 25 ohms, replace cruise control servo. If resistance is less than 25 ohms, repair Light Blue/Black or Tan wire.

1991-92 SAFETY EQUIPMENT
Cruise Control – Vacuum Servo – Except 3.8L (Cont.)

GM
4-3

17) Disconnect cruise control servo connector. Check resistance between Tan and Black wire terminals of cruise control module connector. If resistance is greater than 15 ohms, replace cruise control servo. If resistance is less than 15 ohms, repair Tan wire.

18) Raise and support vehicle with drive wheels off of ground. Start engine. Shift transmission into Drive. Check AC voltage between Yellow and Black wire terminals of cruise control module connector. If AC voltage is present, repair vacuum leak in cruise control system. If voltage is not present, check DRAC. See DRAC (SPEED SENSOR BUFFER) INOPERATIVE.

DRAC (Speed Sensor Buffer) Inoperative – **1)** Turn ignition switch to RUN position. Disconnect DRAC connector. Check voltage at Pink/White wire terminal of DRAC connector. If voltage is not present, check fuse and Pink/White wire.

2) If battery voltage is present, check voltage between Pink/Black and Black wire terminals of DRAC connector. If voltage is not present, check Black wire. If battery voltage is present, raise and support vehicle with drive wheels off of ground.

3) Start engine. Place transmission in Drive. Check AC voltage between Purple/White and Light Green/Black wires of DRAC connector. If AC voltage is present, go to next step. If voltage is not present, check Purple/White and Light Green/Black wires. If wires are okay, replace speed sensor.

4) Turn ignition off. Connect DRAC connector. Start engine. Place transmission in Drive. Check AC voltage between Yellow and Black wire terminals of DRAC connector. If voltage is not present, replace DRAC. If battery voltage is present, repair Yellow wire.

Cruise Control Does Not Disengage Using Brake Pedal – **1)** Turn ignition switch to RUN position. Turn on cruise control. Press brake pedal. Using test light, check for voltage at Gray/Black wire terminal of brakelight switch connector.

2) If test light does not come on, go to next step. If test light comes on, adjust brakelight switch. See BRAKE & CLUTCH RELEASE SWITCH/VALVE under ADJUSTMENTS. If brakelight switch cannot be adjusted, replace brakelight switch.

3) Connect a 10-amp fused jumper wire between ground and Gray/Black wire terminal of cruise control module connector. Press brake pedal. If test light does not come on, replace cruise control module. If test light comes on, repair short to battery in Gray/Black wire.

LUMINA APV, SILHOUETTE & TRANS SPORT

NOTE: For 1991 cruise control system wiring diagram, see Fig. 5. For 1992 cruise control system wiring diagram, see appropriate chassis wiring diagram in WIRING DIAGRAMS. For speed sensor and buffer system wiring diagram, see appropriate chassis wiring diagram in WIRING DIAGRAMS.

Test system using Quick Check Box (J-34185-A). Operating instructions are provided with quick check box. If quick check box is not available, perform appropriate test chart. *See Figs. 15 and 16.* Chart may lead to the following test:

Speed Sensor & Buffer – **1)** Ensure IGN fuse is okay. If speedometer does not operate or operates inaccurately, go to step **4)**. If speedometer operates accurately, turn ignition switch to RUN position. Turn cruise control switch to ON position. Check voltage at Red wire terminal of speed sensor buffer.

2) If voltage is not present, go to next step. If about 5 volts is present, check for poor connection at Red wire terminal of speed sensor buffer. Repair as necessary. If connection is okay, replace speed sensor buffer.

3) Check for open or poor connection in Red wire circuit between speed sensor buffer and cruise control module. If circuit is okay, replace cruise control module.

4) Check for ECM Code 24. If ECM Code 24 is set, go to step **9)**. If ECM Code 24 is not set, raise and support vehicle. Disconnect speed sensor connector. Connect Signal Generator IP Tester (J-33431-B) to speed sensor connector. Set tester to 54 MPH.

5) Turn ignition switch to RUN position. If speedometer does not display 6 MPH, go to next step. If speedometer displays 6 MPH, check for

poor connection at speed sensor. If connection is okay, replace speed sensor.

6) Turn ignition off. Disconnect tester. Disconnect speed sensor buffer 2-wire connector. Connect tester to Dark Green wire terminal of speed sensor buffer connector. Set tester to 54 MPH. Turn ignition switch to RUN position.

7) If speedometer does not display 54 MPH, go to next step. If speedometer displays 54 MPH, check for poor connection at speed sensor buffer. If connection is okay, replace speed sensor buffer.

8) Check for open, poor connection, short to ground or short to voltage in Dark Green wire circuit between speed sensor buffer and instrument cluster. If circuit is okay, replace speedometer.

9) If ECM Code 24 is set as in step **4)**, turn ignition switch to RUN position. Check voltage at Pink/White wire terminal of speed sensor buffer connector. If voltage is not present, repair open in Pink/White wire.

10) If battery voltage is present, check voltage between Pink/White and Black wire terminals of speed sensor buffer connector. If voltage is not present, check for open in Black wire. If battery voltage is present, turn ignition switch to RUN position.

11) Shift transaxle into Neutral. Raise and support vehicle with drive wheels off of ground. While turning drive wheels by hand, check AC voltage between Yellow and Purple wire terminals of speed sensor buffer connector.

12) If voltmeter indicates zero volts constantly, go to next step. If voltage fluctuates from zero to one volt, check for poor connection at speed sensor buffer connector. If connector is okay, replace speed sensor buffer.

13) Check for open in Yellow or Purple wire between speed sensor and speed sensor buffer. If wires are okay, replace speed sensor buffer.

SUBURBAN, VAN & "R" & "V" SERIES BLAZER, JIMMY & PICKUP

NOTE: For 1991 cruise control system wiring diagram and terminal identification, see Figs. 6, 7 and 8. For 1992 cruise control system wiring diagram and terminal identification, see appropriate chassis wiring diagram in WIRING DIAGRAMS and Fig. 8.

Test system using Quick Check Box (J-34185). Operating instructions are provided with quick check box. If quick check box is not available, perform CRUISE CONTROL DIAGNOSIS test chart. *See Fig. 9.* This chart may lead to other test charts. *See Figs. 10, 13 and 14.*

TESTING (VACUUM SYSTEM)

Source Vacuum Check – Disconnect vacuum supply (small) hose from servo. Connect vacuum gauge to end of hose. Start engine. If gauge indicates at least 10 in. Hg, go to SERVO VACUUM VALVE CHECK. If gauge does not indicate at least 10 in. Hg, check for leaking or pinched hoses.

Servo Vacuum Valve Check – Turn engine off. Disconnect vacuum supply (small) hose from servo. Connect hand-held vacuum pump to vacuum supply hose fitting on servo. Apply 10-15 in. Hg to servo. If vacuum holds, go to SERVO VENT VALVE CHECK. If vacuum does not hold, or if vacuum decreases in less than 10 seconds, replace servo (in a good servo, vacuum will decrease in more than 30 seconds).

Servo Vent Valve Check – **1)** Disconnect servo cable from throttle lever. Disconnect servo electrical connector. Using a fused jumper wire, apply battery voltage to Dark Blue/White wire terminal of servo connector. Jumper Black wire terminal of servo connector to ground.

2) If vent solenoid is not heard clicking, replace servo. If vent solenoid is heard clicking, disconnect hose from large fitting on servo. Connect vacuum pump to large fitting on servo. Apply 10-20 in. Hg to diaphragm. If diaphragm moves in completely and vacuum does not decrease quickly, go to BRAKE RELEASE VALVE TEST. If diaphragm does not respond as specified, replace servo.

Brake Release Valve Test – Disconnect vacuum release hose (large hose) from servo. Connect vacuum pump to end of hose. Apply 10-20 in. Hg to hose. If vacuum does not hold, or if it leaks down slowly, check for leaking or misadjusted brake release valve. See BRAKE &

1991-92 SAFETY EQUIPMENT
Cruise Control – Vacuum Servo – Except 3.8L (Cont.)

CLUTCH RELEASE SWITCH/VALVE under ADJUSTMENTS. If brake release valve is okay, check for leaking hose between servo and brake release valve. If hose is okay, replace servo.

WIRING DIAGRAMS

NOTE: For 1992 cruise control system wiring diagrams, see appropriate chassis wiring diagram in WIRING DIAGRAMS.

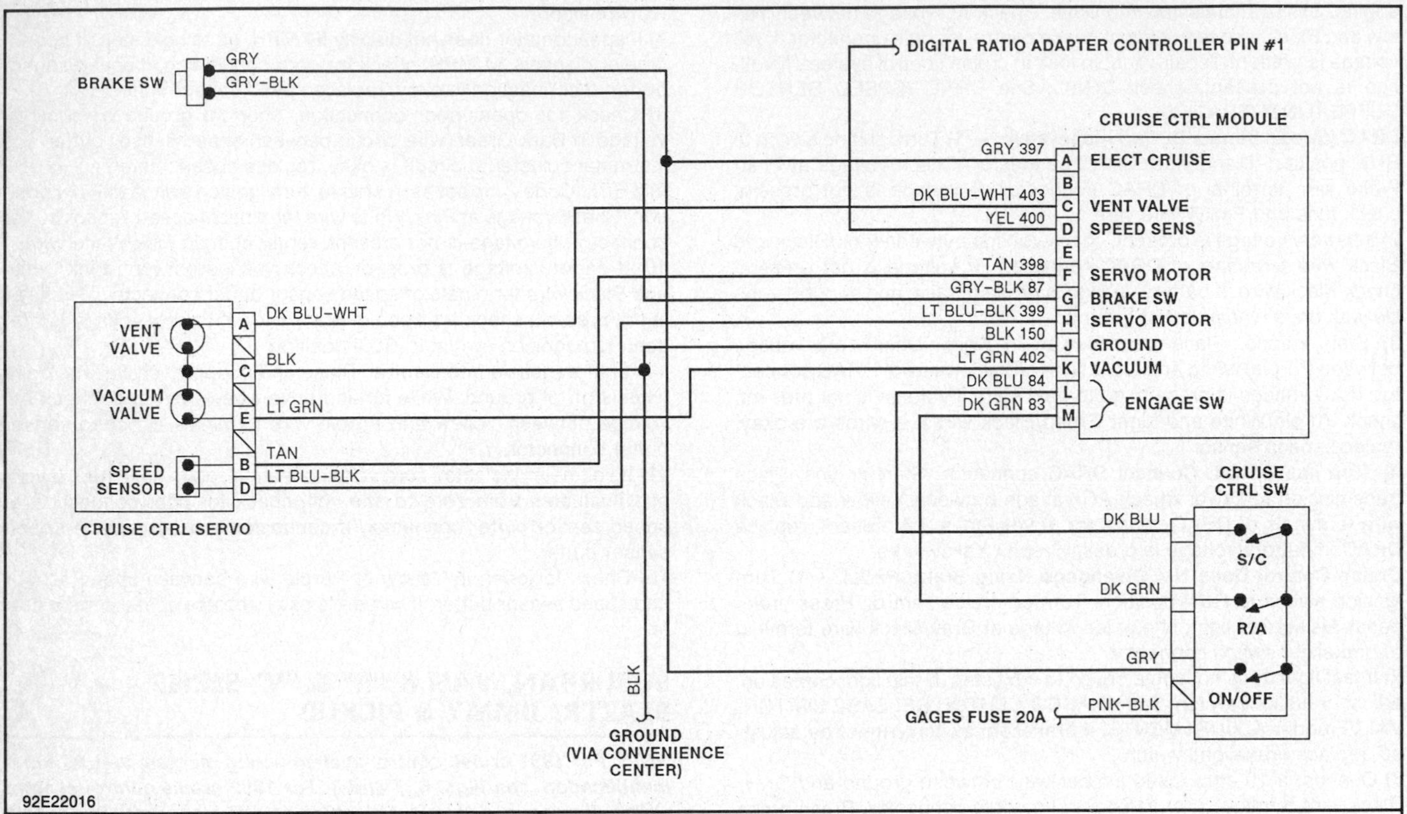

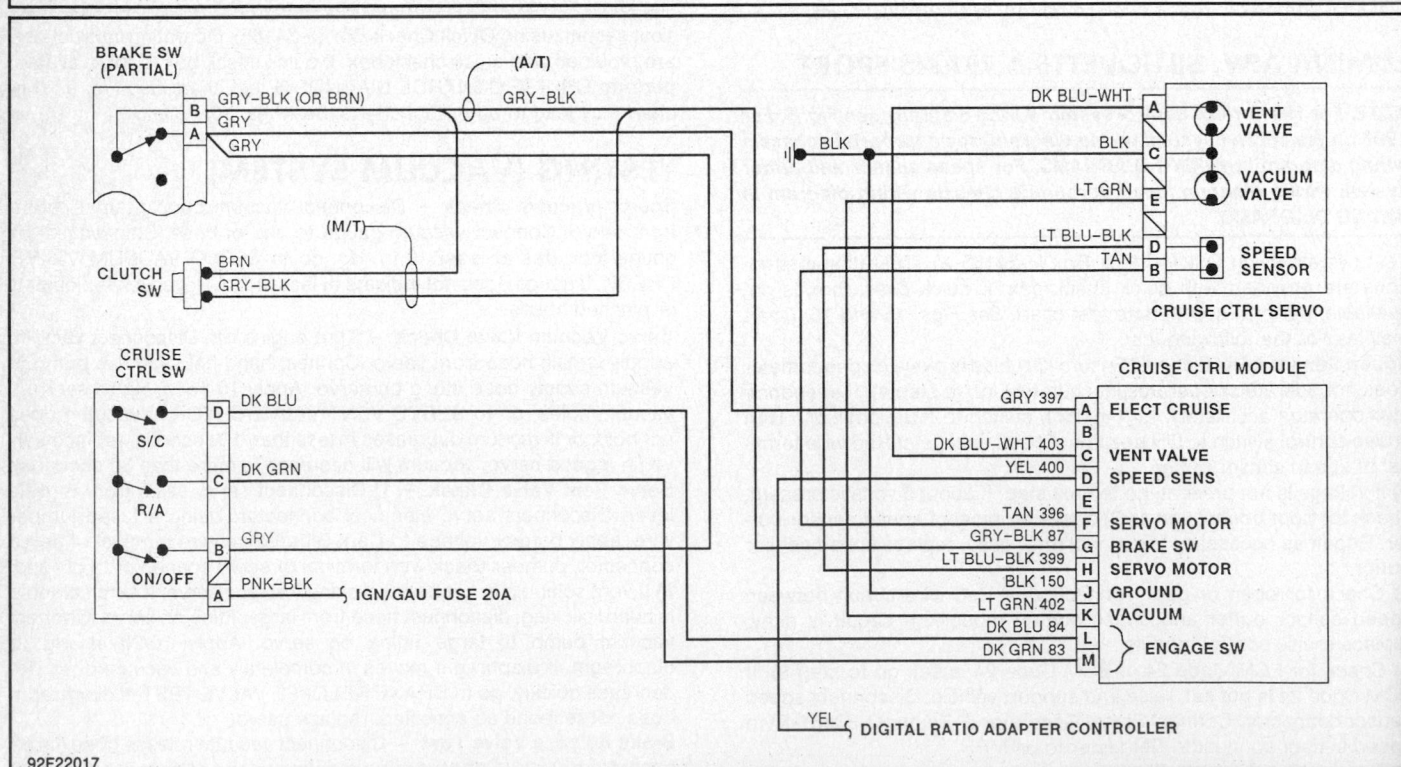

Fig. 3: 1991 Cruise Control System Wiring Diagram (Astro & Safari)

Fig. 4: 1991 Cruise Control System Wiring Diagram (Bravada, Sonoma, Syclone, Typhoon & "S" & "T" Series Blazer, Jimmy & Pickup)

1991-92 SAFETY EQUIPMENT
Cruise Control – Vacuum Servo – Except 3.8L (Cont.)

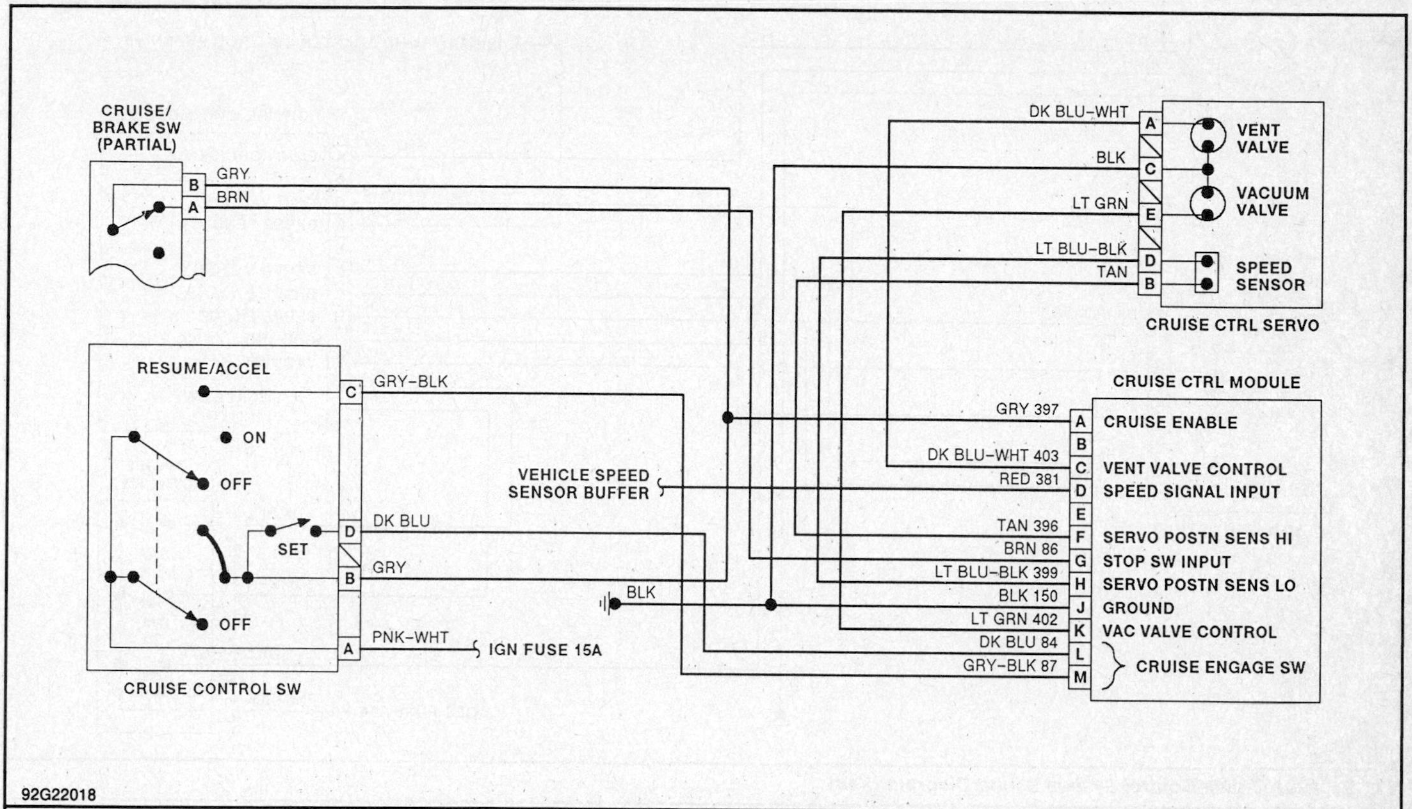

GM
4-5

Fig. 5: *1991 Cruise Control System Wiring Diagram (Lumina APV, Silhouette & Trans Sport)*

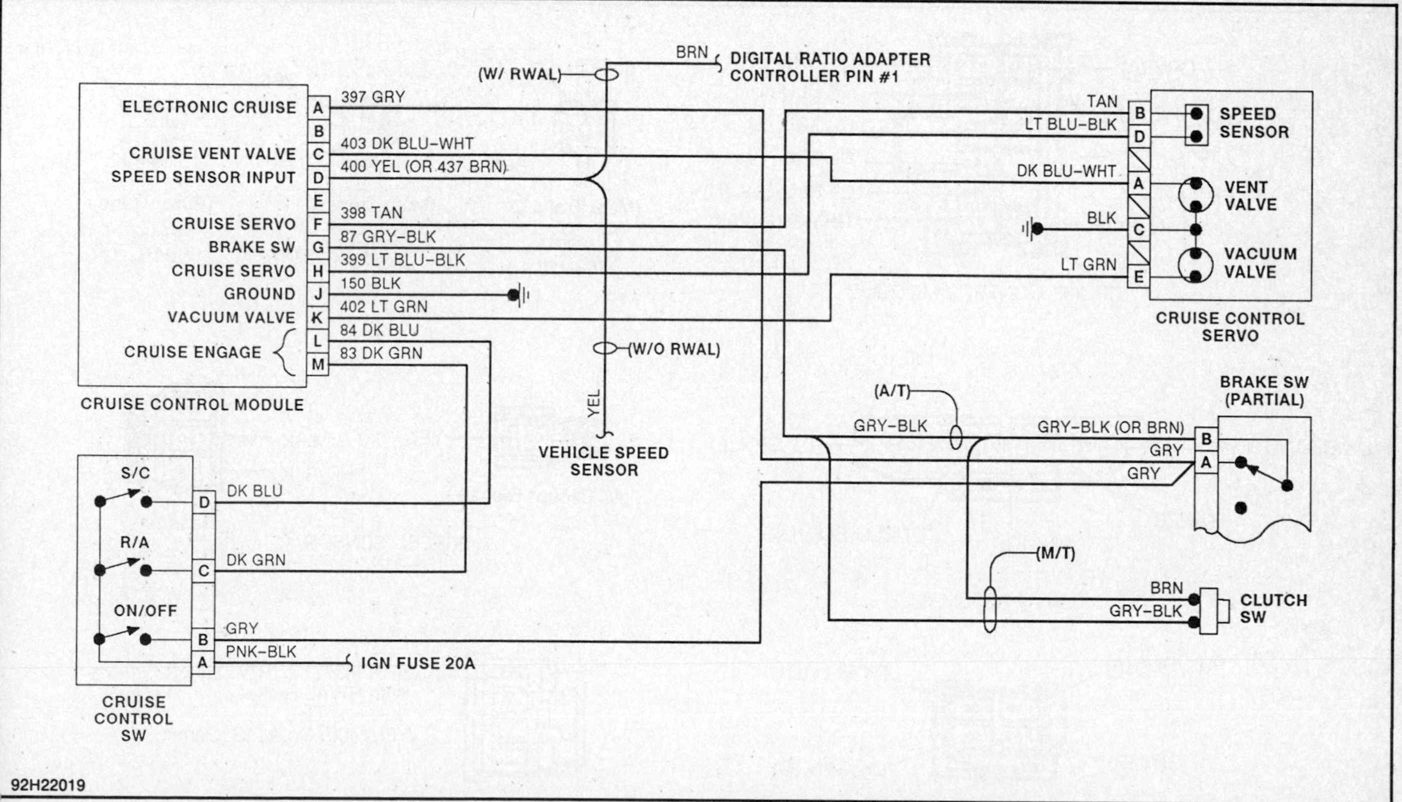

Fig. 6: *1991 Cruise Control System Wiring Diagram (Suburban & "R" & "V" Series Blazer, Jimmy & Pickup)*

GM
4-6

1991-92 SAFETY EQUIPMENT
Cruise Control – Vacuum Servo – Except 3.8L (Cont.)

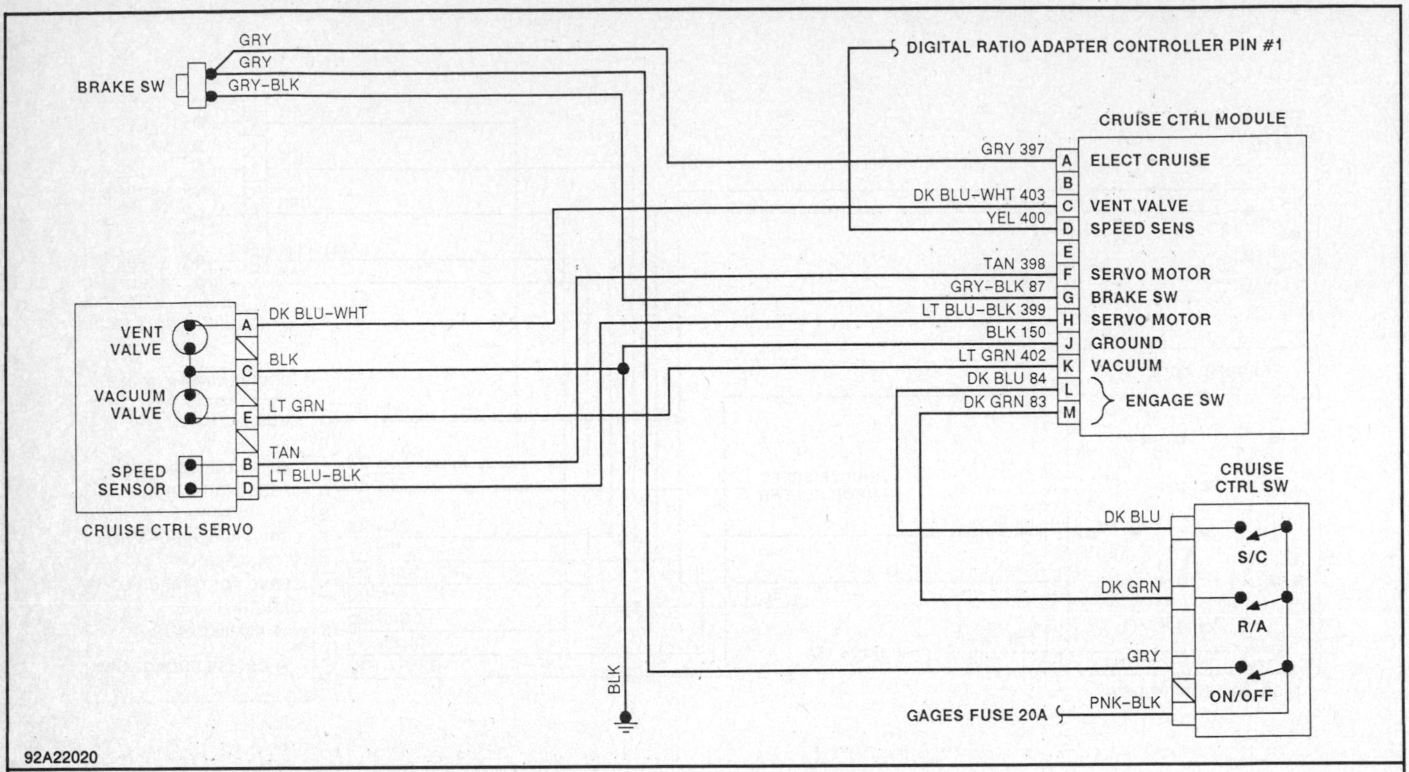

92A22020

Fig. 7: 1991 Cruise Control System Wiring Diagram (Van)

CRUISE CONTROL DIAGNOSIS

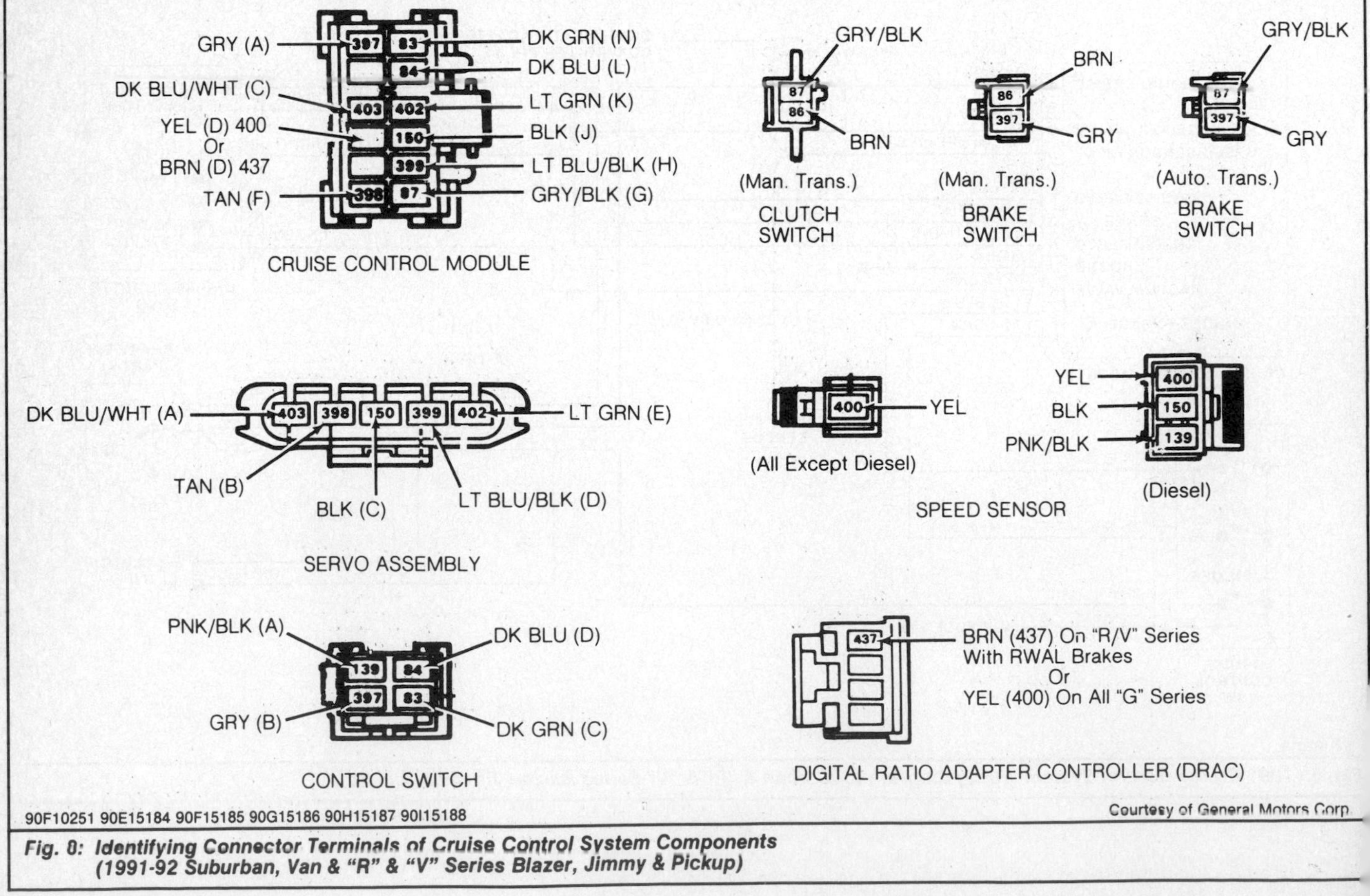

90F10251 90E15184 90F15185 90G15186 90H15187 90I15188

Courtesy of General Motors Corp.

**Fig. 8: Identifying Connector Terminals of Cruise Control System Components
(1991-92 Suburban, Van & "R" & "V" Series Blazer, Jimmy & Pickup)**

1991-92 SAFETY EQUIPMENT
Cruise Control – Vacuum Servo – Except 3.8L (Cont.)

GM
4-7

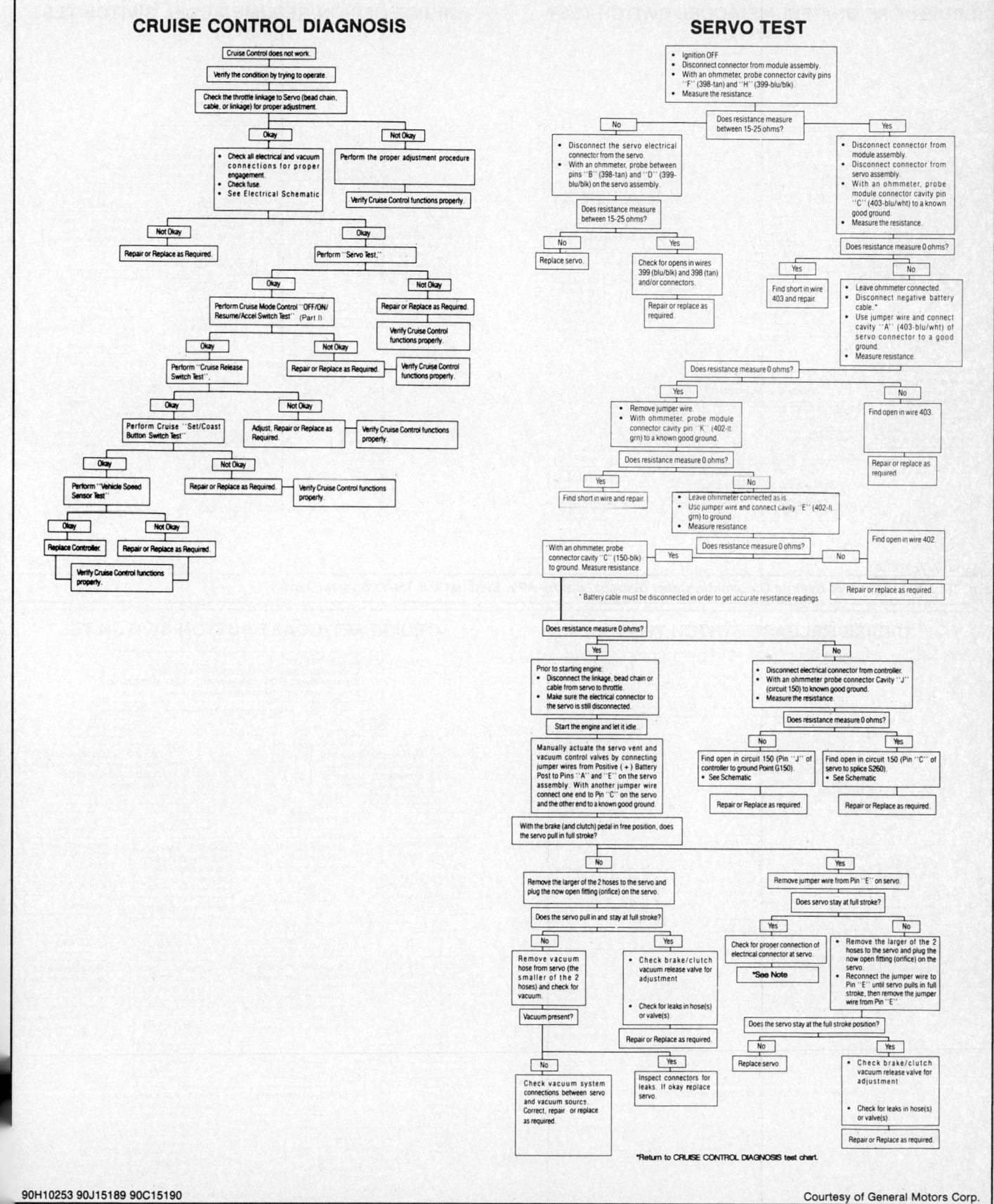

CRUISE CONTROL DIAGNOSIS

SERVO TEST

90H10253 90J15189 90C15190

Courtesy of General Motors Corp.

Fig. 9: Cruise Control System Diagnostic Charts (Except Lumina APV, Silhouette & Trans Sport)

GM
4-8

1991-92 SAFETY EQUIPMENT
Cruise Control – Vacuum Servo – Except 3.8L (Cont.)

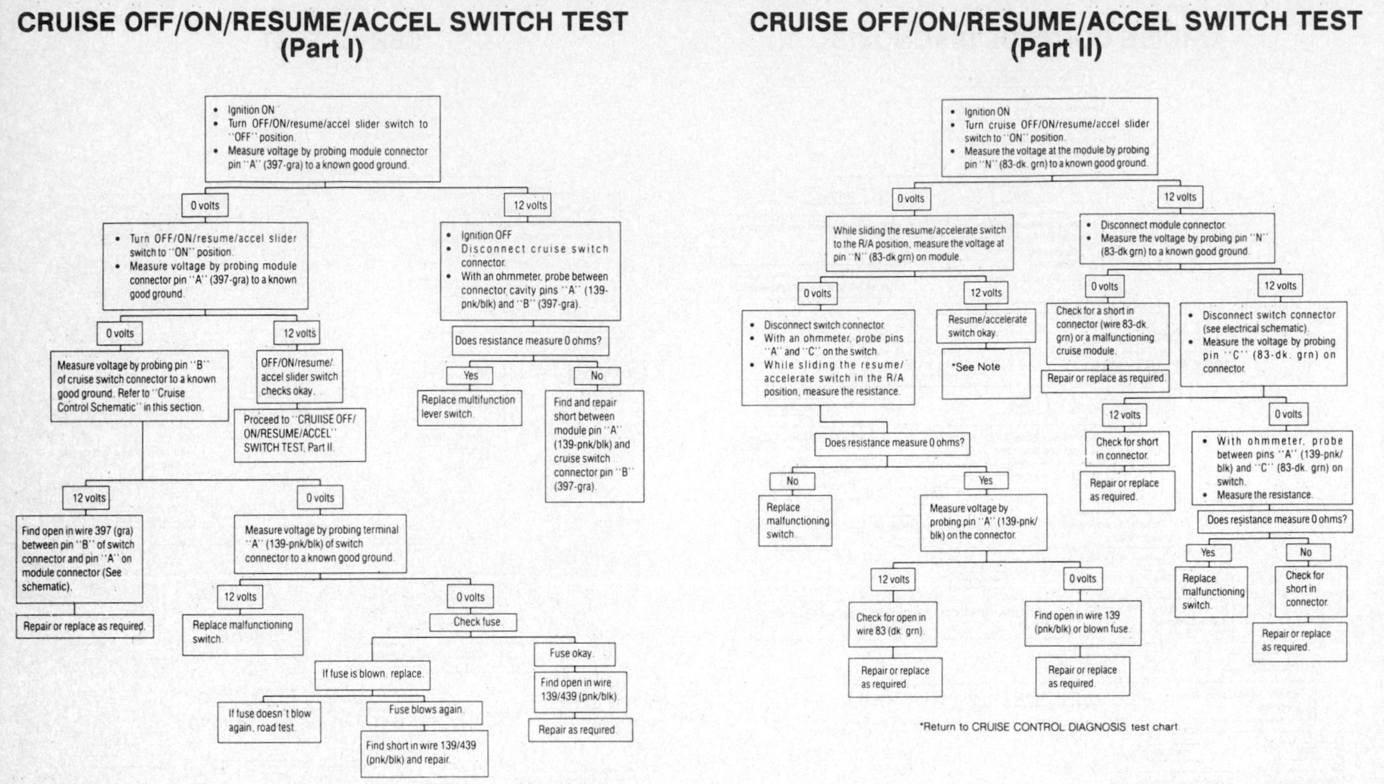

CRUISE OFF/ON/RESUME/ACCEL SWITCH TEST (Part I)

- Ignition ON
- Turn OFF/ON/resume/accel slider switch to "OFF" position.
- Measure voltage by probing module connector pin "A" (397-gra) to a known good ground.

0 volts

- Turn OFF/ON/resume/accel slider switch to "ON" position.
- Measure voltage by probing module connector pin "A" (397-gra) to a known good ground.

0 volts

Measure voltage by probing pin "B" of cruise switch connector to a known good ground. Refer to "Cruise Control Schematic" in this section.

12 volts

Find open in wire 397 (gra) between pin "B" of switch connector and pin "A" on module connector (See schematic).

Repair or replace as required.

0 volts — Measure voltage by probing terminal "A" (139-pnk/blk) of switch connector to a known good ground.

12 volts — Replace malfunctioning switch.

0 volts — Check fuse.

If fuse is blown, replace.

Fuse okay. — Find open in wire 139/439 (pnk/blk).

Repair as required.

If fuse doesn't blow again, road test.

Fuse blows again. — Find short in wire 139/439 (pnk/blk) and repair.

12 volts

OFF/ON/resume/accel slider switch checks okay.

Proceed to "CRUISE OFF/ON/RESUME/ACCEL" SWITCH TEST, Part II.

12 volts

- Ignition OFF
- Disconnect cruise switch connector.
- With an ohmmeter, probe between connector cavity pins "A" (139-pnk/blk) and "B" (397-gra).

Does resistance measure 0 ohms?

Yes — Replace multifunction lever switch.

No — Find and repair short between module pin "A" (139-pnk/blk) and cruise switch connector pin "B" (397-gra).

CRUISE OFF/ON/RESUME/ACCEL SWITCH TEST (Part II)

- Ignition ON
- Turn cruise OFF/ON/resume/accel slider switch to "ON" position.
- Measure the voltage at the module by probing pin "N" (83-dk. grn) to a known good ground.

0 volts

While sliding the resume/accelerate switch to the R/A position, measure the voltage at pin "N" (83-dk grn) on module.

0 volts
- Disconnect switch connector.
- With an ohmmeter, probe pins "A" and "C" on the switch.
- While sliding the resume/accelerate switch in the R/A position, measure the resistance.

Does resistance measure 0 ohms?

No — Replace malfunctioning switch.

Yes — Measure voltage by probing pin "A" (139-pnk/blk) on the connector.

12 volts — Check for open in wire 83 (dk. grn).

Repair or replace as required.

0 volts — Find open in wire 139 (pnk/blk) or blown fuse.

Repair or replace as required.

12 volts

Resume/accelerate switch okay.

*See Note

12 volts

- Disconnect module connector.
- Measure the voltage by probing pin "N" (83-dk grn) to a known good ground.

0 volts — Check for a short in connector (wire 83-dk. grn) or a malfunctioning cruise module.

Repair or replace as required.

12 volts

Check for short in connector.

Repair or replace as required.

12 volts — Disconnect switch connector (see electrical schematic). Measure the voltage by probing pin "C" (83-dk. grn) on connector.

0 volts
- With ohmmeter, probe between pins "A" (139-pnk/blk) and "C" (83-dk. grn) on switch.
- Measure the resistance.

Does resistance measure 0 ohms?

Yes — Replace malfunctioning switch.

No — Check for short in connector.

Repair or replace as required.

*Return to CRUISE CONTROL DIAGNOSIS test chart.

90D15191 92D22015

Courtesy of General Motors Corp.

Fig. 10: Cruise Control System Diagnostic Chart (Except Lumina APV, Silhouette & Trans Sport) (Cont.)

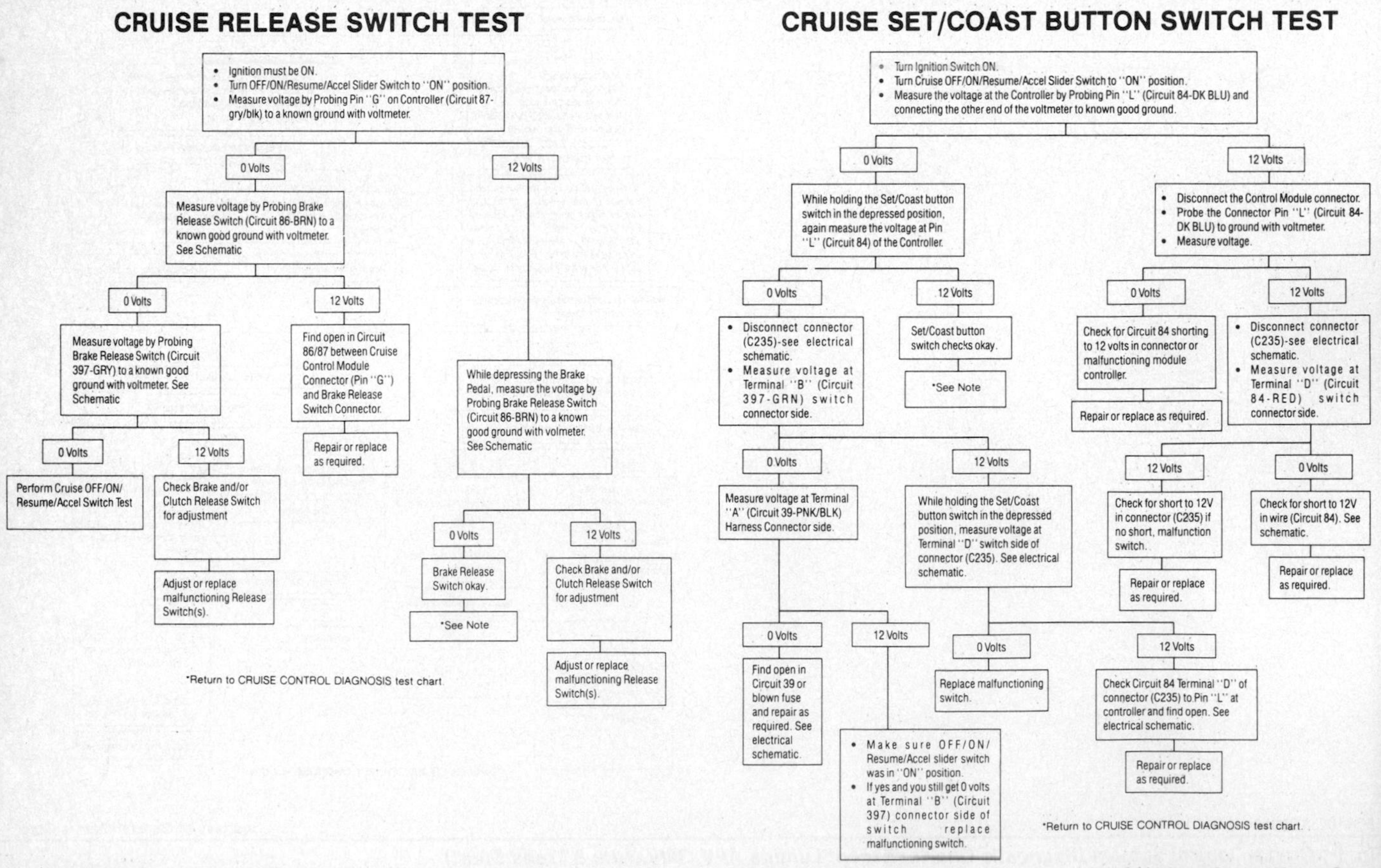

CRUISE RELEASE SWITCH TEST

- Ignition must be ON.
- Turn OFF/ON/Resume/Accel Slider Switch to "ON" position.
- Measure voltage by Probing Pin "G" on Controller (Circuit 87-gry/blk) to a known ground with voltmeter.

0 Volts

Measure voltage by Probing Brake Release Switch (Circuit 86-BRN) to a known good ground with voltmeter. See Schematic.

0 Volts — Measure voltage by Probing Brake Release Switch (Circuit 397-GRY) to a known good ground with voltmeter. See Schematic.

0 Volts — Perform Cruise OFF/ON/Resume/Accel Switch Test

12 Volts — Check Brake and/or Clutch Release Switch for adjustment

Adjust or replace malfunctioning Release Switch(s).

12 Volts — Find open in Circuit 86/87 between Cruise Control Module Connector (Pin "G") and Brake Release Switch Connector.

Repair or replace as required.

12 Volts

While depressing the Brake Pedal, measure the voltage by Probing Brake Release Switch (Circuit 86-BRN) to a known good ground with voltmeter. See Schematic

0 Volts — Brake Release Switch okay. *See Note

12 Volts — Check Brake and/or Clutch Release Switch for adjustment

Adjust or replace malfunctioning Release Switch(s).

*Return to CRUISE CONTROL DIAGNOSIS test chart.

CRUISE SET/COAST BUTTON SWITCH TEST

- Turn Ignition Switch ON.
- Turn Cruise OFF/ON/Resume/Accel Slider Switch to "ON" position.
- Measure the voltage at the Controller by Probing Pin "L" (Circuit 84-DK BLU) and connecting the other end of the voltmeter to known good ground.

0 Volts

While holding the Set/Coast button switch in the depressed position, again measure the voltage at Pin "L" (Circuit 84) of the Controller.

0 Volts
- Disconnect connector (C235)-see electrical schematic.
- Measure voltage at Terminal "B" (Circuit 397-GRN) switch connector side.

0 Volts — Measure voltage at Terminal "A" (Circuit 39-PNK/BLK) Harness Connector side.

0 Volts — Find open in Circuit 39 or blown fuse and repair as required. See electrical schematic.

12 Volts — While holding the Set/Coast button switch in the depressed position, measure voltage at Terminal "D" switch side of connector (C235). See electrical schematic.

0 Volts — Replace malfunctioning switch.

12 Volts
- Make sure OFF/ON/Resume/Accel slider switch was in "ON" position.
- If yes and you still get 0 volts at Terminal "B" (Circuit 397) connector side of switch replace malfunctioning switch.

12 Volts — Set/Coast button switch checks okay. *See Note

12 Volts

- Disconnect the Control Module connector.
- Probe the Connector Pin "L" (Circuit 84-DK BLU) to ground with voltmeter.
- Measure voltage.

0 Volts — Check for Circuit 84 shorting to 12 volts in connector or malfunctioning module controller.

Repair or replace as required.

12 Volts
- Disconnect connector (C235)-see electrical schematic.
- Measure voltage at Terminal "D" (Circuit 84-RED) switch connector side.

12 Volts — Check for short to 12V in connector (C235) if no short, malfunction switch.

Repair or replace as required.

12 Volts — Check Circuit 84 Terminal "D" of connector (C235) to Pin "L" at controller and find open. See electrical schematic.

Repair or replace as required.

0 Volts — Check for short to 12V in wire (Circuit 84). See schematic.

Repair or replace as required.

*Return to CRUISE CONTROL DIAGNOSIS test chart.

90I10254 90E15192

Courtesy of General Motors Corp.

Fig. 11: Cruise Control System Diagnostic Charts (Astro, Safari, Sonoma, Syclone, Typhoon & "S" & "T" Series Blazer, Jimmy & Pickup)

1991-92 SAFETY EQUIPMENT
Cruise Control – Vacuum Servo – Except 3.8L (Cont.)

GM
4-9

SPEED SENSOR TEST

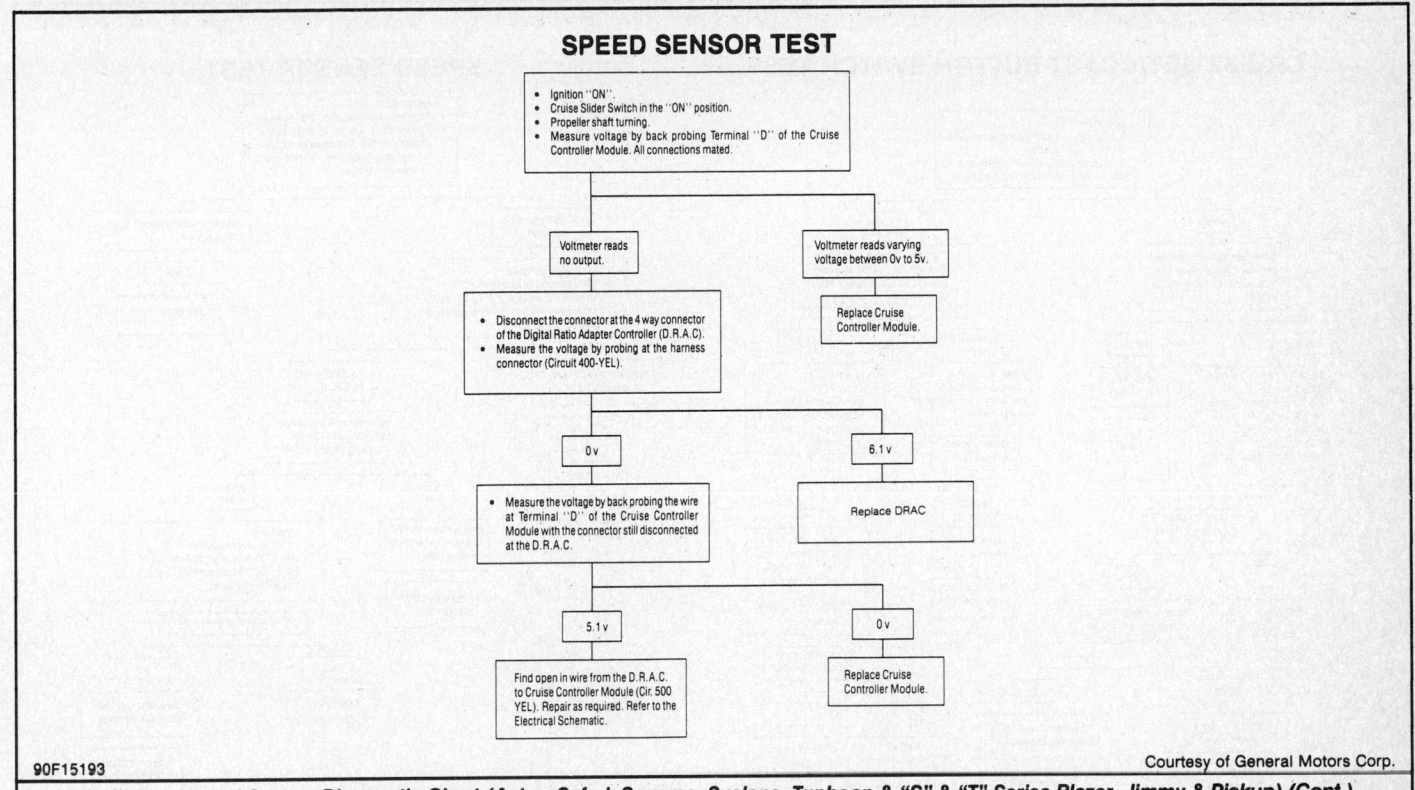

90F15193

Courtesy of General Motors Corp.

Fig. 12: Cruise Control System Diagnostic Chart (Astro, Safari, Sonoma, Syclone, Typhoon & "S" & "T" Series Blazer, Jimmy & Pickup) (Cont.)

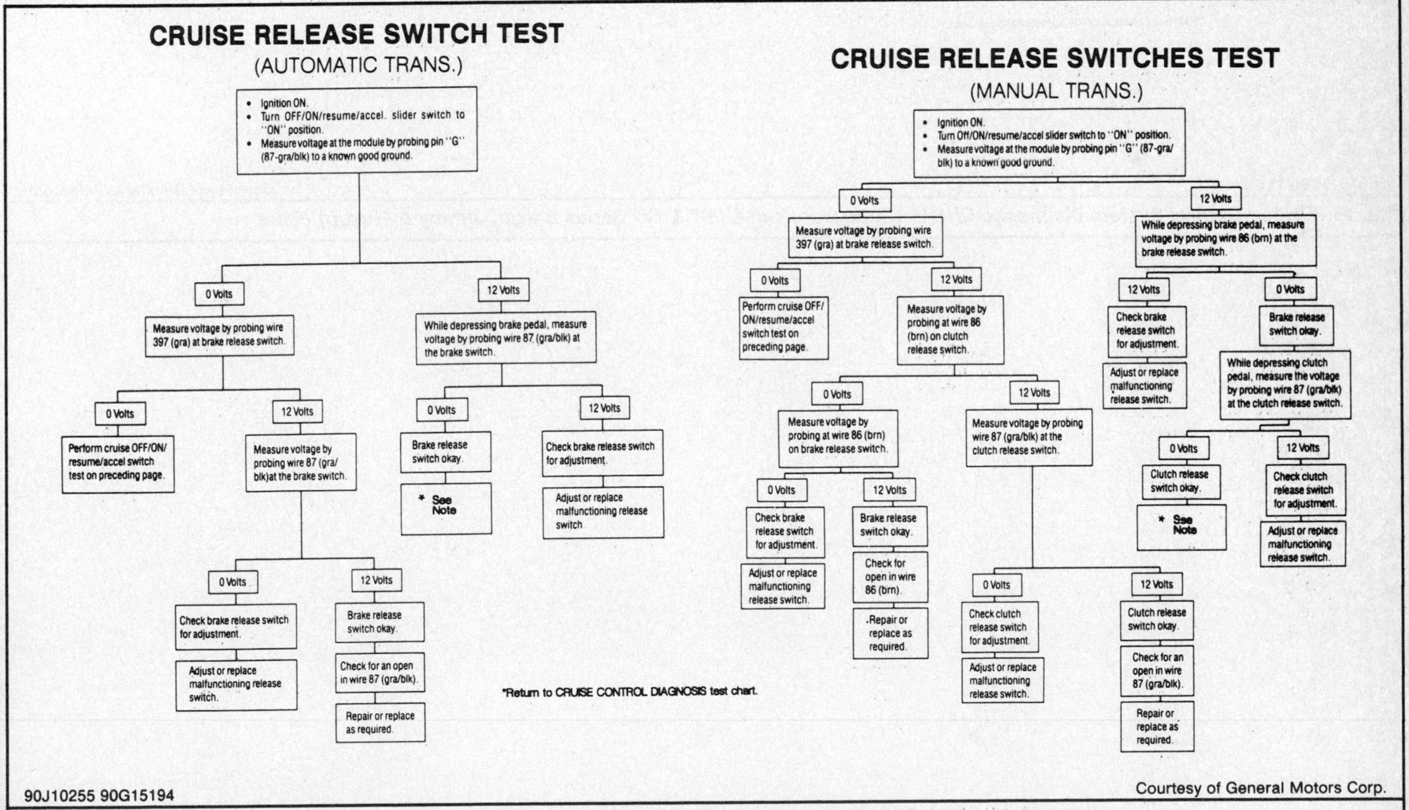

CRUISE RELEASE SWITCH TEST
(AUTOMATIC TRANS.)

- Ignition ON.
- Turn OFF/ON/resume/accel. slider switch to "ON" position.
- Measure voltage at the module by probing pin "G" (87-gra/blk) to a known good ground.

0 Volts

Measure voltage by probing wire 397 (gra) at brake release switch.

- **0 Volts** — Perform cruise OFF/ON/resume/accel switch test on preceding page.
- **12 Volts** — Measure voltage by probing wire 87 (gra/blk) at the brake switch.
  - **0 Volts** — Check brake release switch for adjustment. / Adjust or replace malfunctioning release switch.
  - **12 Volts** — Brake release switch okay. / Check for an open in wire 87 (gra/blk). / Repair or replace as required.

12 Volts

While depressing brake pedal, measure voltage by probing wire 87 (gra/blk) at the brake switch.

- **0 Volts** — Brake release switch okay. / * See Note
- **12 Volts** — Check brake release switch for adjustment. / Adjust or replace malfunctioning release switch

*Return to CRUISE CONTROL DIAGNOSIS test chart.

CRUISE RELEASE SWITCHES TEST
(MANUAL TRANS.)

- Ignition ON.
- Turn Off/ON/resume/accel slider switch to "ON" position.
- Measure voltage at the module by probing pin "G" (87-gra/blk) to a known good ground.

0 Volts

Measure voltage by probing wire 397 (gra) at brake release switch.

- **0 Volts** — Perform cruise OFF/ON/resume/accel switch test on preceding page.
- **12 Volts** — Measure voltage by probing at wire 86 (brn) on clutch release switch.
  - **0 Volts** — Measure voltage by probing at wire 86 (brn) on brake release switch.
    - **0 Volts** — Check brake release switch for adjustment. / Adjust or replace malfunctioning release switch.
    - **12 Volts** — Brake release switch okay. / Check for open in wire 86 (brn). / Repair or replace as required.
  - **12 Volts** — Measure voltage by probing wire 87 (gra/blk) at the clutch release switch.
    - **0 Volts** — Check clutch release switch for adjustment. / Adjust or replace malfunctioning release switch.
    - **12 Volts** — Clutch release switch okay. / Check for an open in wire 87 (gra/blk). / Repair or replace as required.

12 Volts

While depressing brake pedal, measure voltage by probing wire 86 (brn) at the brake release switch.

- **12 Volts** — Check brake release switch for adjustment. / Adjust or replace malfunctioning release switch.
- **0 Volts** — Brake release switch okay. / While depressing clutch pedal, measure the voltage by probing wire 87 (gra/blk) at the clutch release switch.
  - **0 Volts** — Clutch release switch okay. / * See Note
  - **12 Volts** — Check clutch release switch for adjustment. / Adjust or replace malfunctioning release switch.

90J10255 90G15194

Courtesy of General Motors Corp.

Fig. 13: Cruise Control System Diagnostic Charts (Suburban, Van & "R" & "V" Series Blazer, Jimmy & Pickup)

GM
4-10

1991-92 SAFETY EQUIPMENT
Cruise Control – Vacuum Servo – Except 3.8L (Cont.)

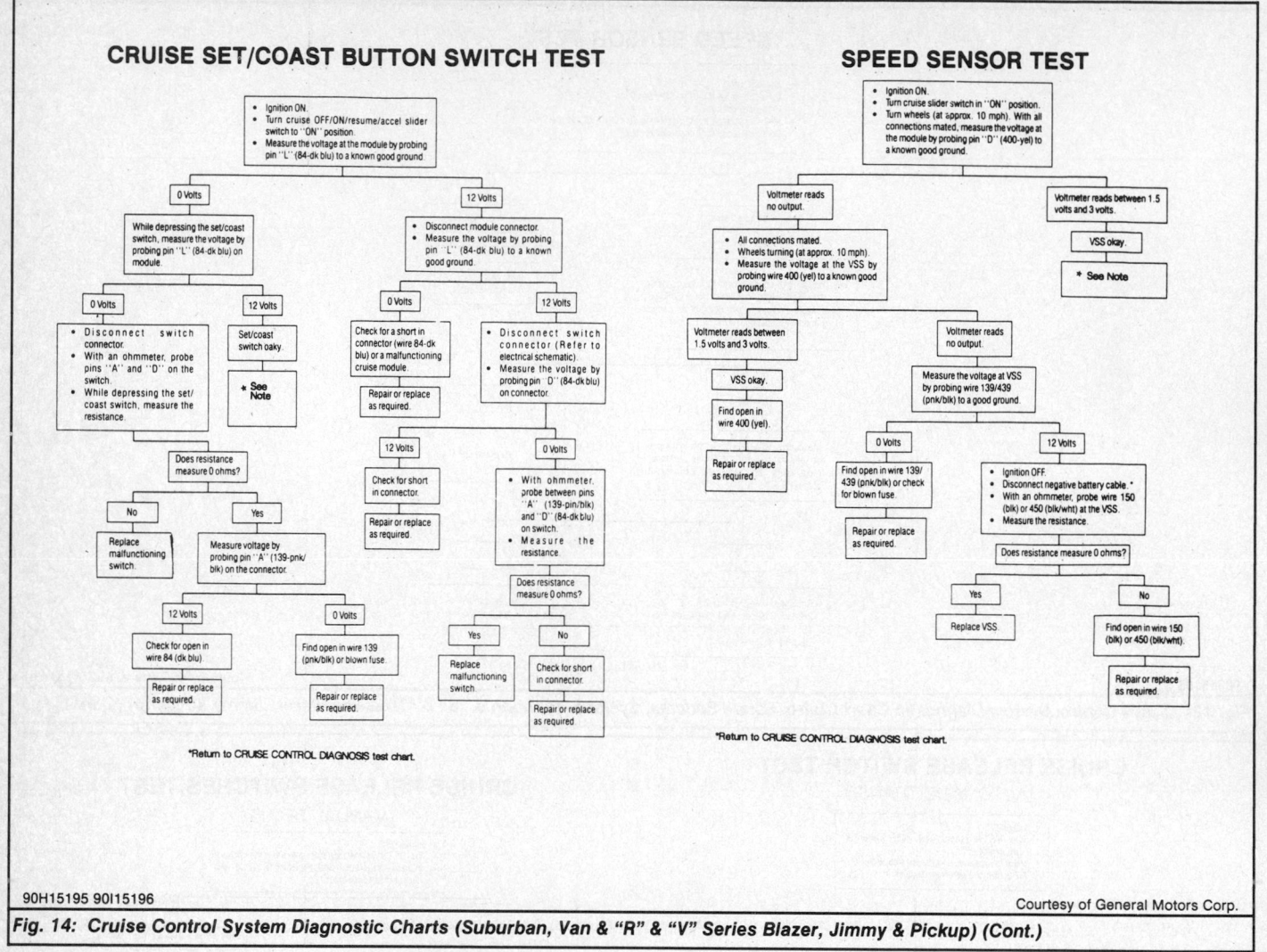

CRUISE SET/COAST BUTTON SWITCH TEST

SPEED SENSOR TEST

90H15195 90I15196

Courtesy of General Motors Corp.

Fig. 14: Cruise Control System Diagnostic Charts (Suburban, Van & "R" & "V" Series Blazer, Jimmy & Pickup) (Cont.)

1991-92 SAFETY EQUIPMENT
Cruise Control – Vacuum Servo – Except 3.8L (Cont.)

GM
4-11

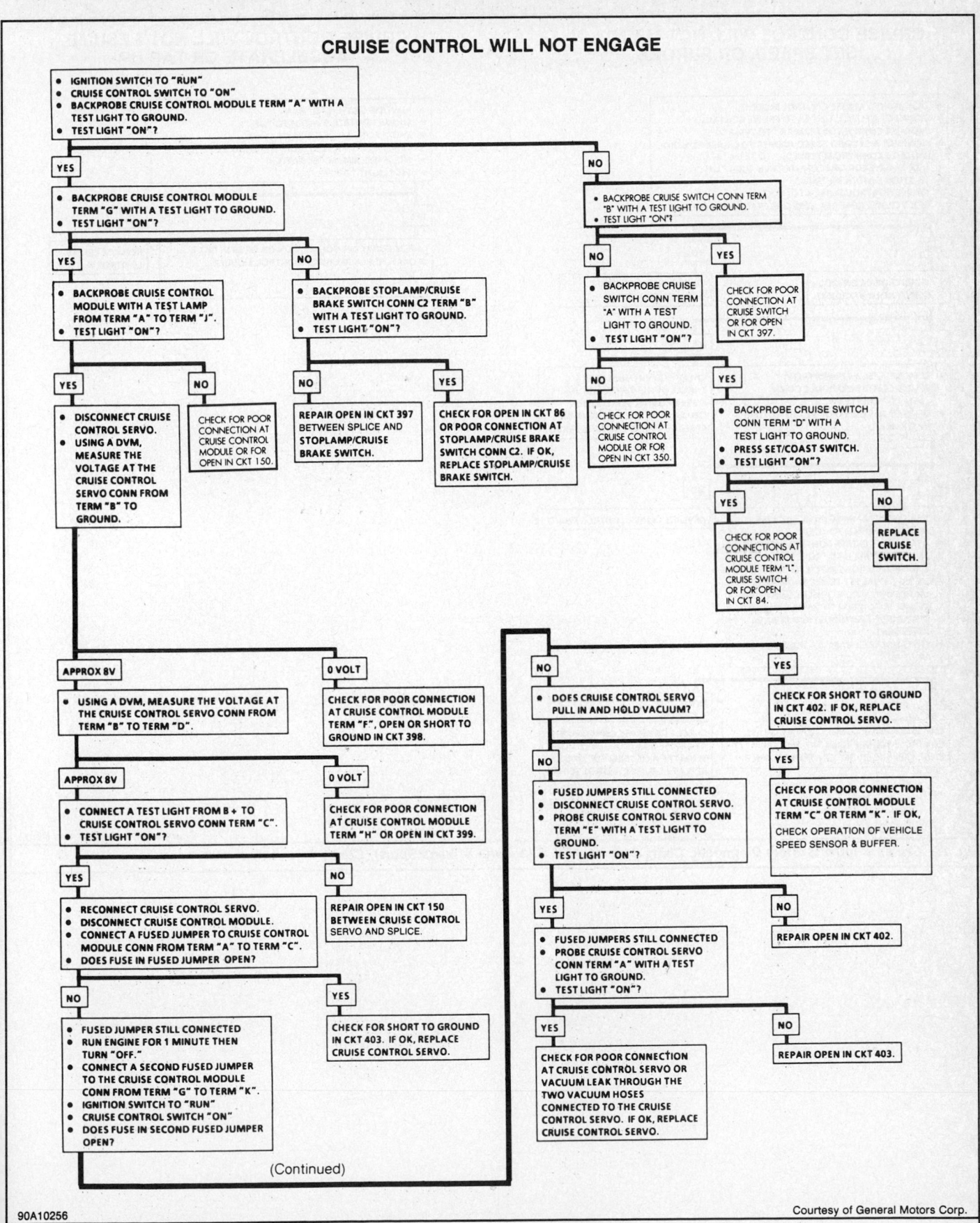

90A10256

Courtesy of General Motors Corp.

Fig. 15: Cruise Control System Diagnostic Chart (Lumina APV, Silhouette & Trans Sport)

GM
4-12

1991-92 SAFETY EQUIPMENT
Cruise Control – Vacuum Servo – Except 3.8L (Cont.)

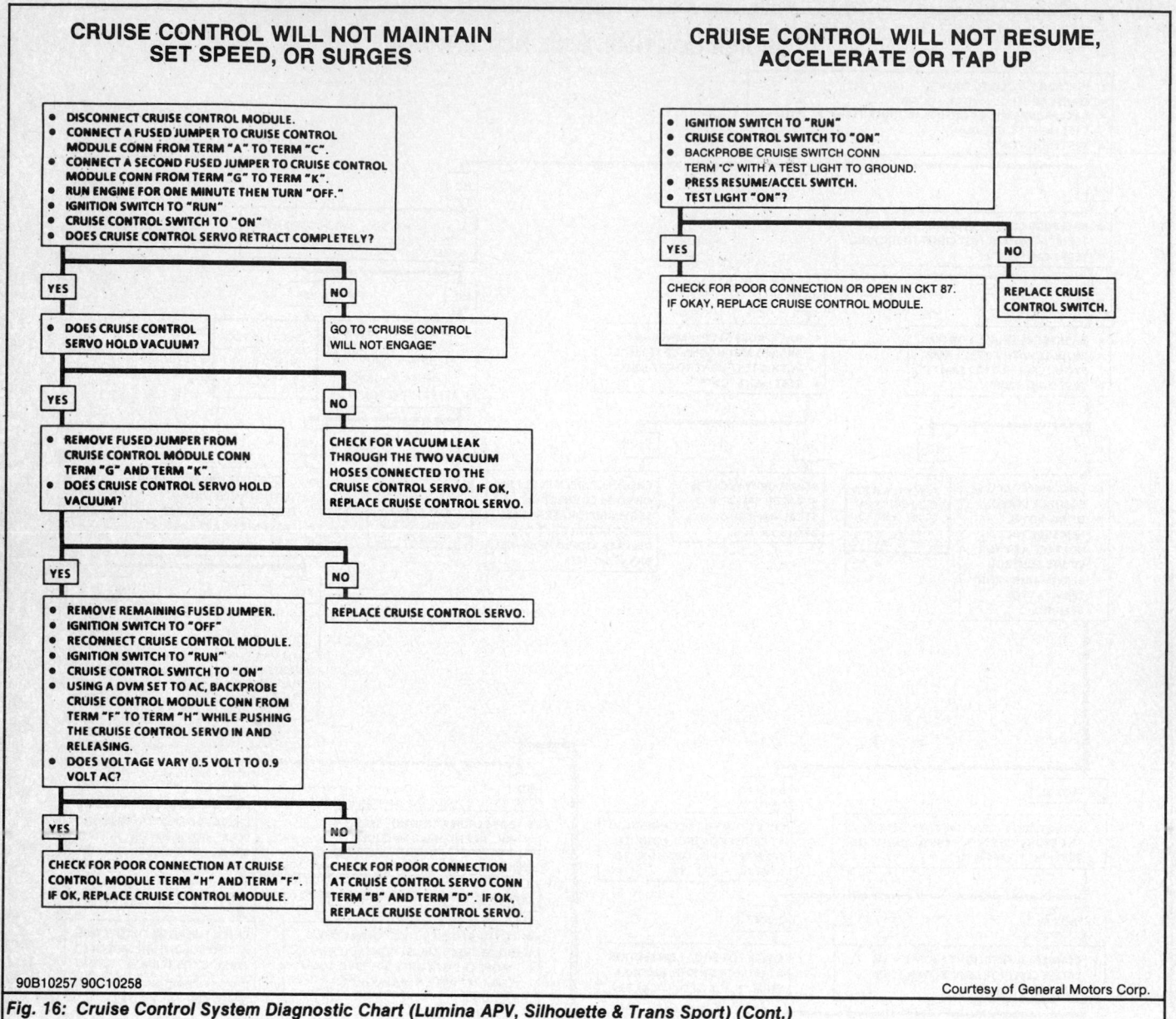

CRUISE CONTROL WILL NOT MAINTAIN SET SPEED, OR SURGES

- DISCONNECT CRUISE CONTROL MODULE.
- CONNECT A FUSED JUMPER TO CRUISE CONTROL MODULE CONN FROM TERM "A" TO TERM "C".
- CONNECT A SECOND FUSED JUMPER TO CRUISE CONTROL MODULE CONN FROM TERM "G" TO TERM "K".
- RUN ENGINE FOR ONE MINUTE THEN TURN "OFF."
- IGNITION SWITCH TO "RUN"
- CRUISE CONTROL SWITCH TO "ON"
- DOES CRUISE CONTROL SERVO RETRACT COMPLETELY?

YES
- DOES CRUISE CONTROL SERVO HOLD VACUUM?

NO
GO TO "CRUISE CONTROL WILL NOT ENGAGE"

YES
- REMOVE FUSED JUMPER FROM CRUISE CONTROL MODULE CONN TERM "G" AND TERM "K".
- DOES CRUISE CONTROL SERVO HOLD VACUUM?

NO
CHECK FOR VACUUM LEAK THROUGH THE TWO VACUUM HOSES CONNECTED TO THE CRUISE CONTROL SERVO. IF OK, REPLACE CRUISE CONTROL SERVO.

YES
- REMOVE REMAINING FUSED JUMPER.
- IGNITION SWITCH TO "OFF"
- RECONNECT CRUISE CONTROL MODULE.
- IGNITION SWITCH TO "RUN"
- CRUISE CONTROL SWITCH TO "ON"
- USING A DVM SET TO AC, BACKPROBE CRUISE CONTROL MODULE CONN FROM TERM "F" TO TERM "H" WHILE PUSHING THE CRUISE CONTROL SERVO IN AND RELEASING.
- DOES VOLTAGE VARY 0.5 VOLT TO 0.9 VOLT AC?

NO
REPLACE CRUISE CONTROL SERVO.

YES
CHECK FOR POOR CONNECTION AT CRUISE CONTROL MODULE TERM "H" AND TERM "F". IF OK, REPLACE CRUISE CONTROL MODULE.

NO
CHECK FOR POOR CONNECTION AT CRUISE CONTROL SERVO CONN TERM "B" AND TERM "D". IF OK, REPLACE CRUISE CONTROL SERVO.

CRUISE CONTROL WILL NOT RESUME, ACCELERATE OR TAP UP

- IGNITION SWITCH TO "RUN"
- CRUISE CONTROL SWITCH TO "ON"
- BACKPROBE CRUISE SWITCH CONN TERM "C" WITH A TEST LIGHT TO GROUND.
- PRESS RESUME/ACCEL SWITCH.
- TEST LIGHT "ON"?

YES
CHECK FOR POOR CONNECTION OR OPEN IN CKT 87. IF OKAY, REPLACE CRUISE CONTROL MODULE.

NO
REPLACE CRUISE CONTROL SWITCH.

90B10257 90C10258

Courtesy of General Motors Corp.

Fig. 16: Cruise Control System Diagnostic Chart (Lumina APV, Silhouette & Trans Sport) (Cont.)

Lumina APV, Silhouette, Trans Sport

DESCRIPTION

System consists of Powertrain Control Module (PCM), cruise control switch, vacuum-actuated servo, speed sensor, speed sensor buffer and brake release switch/valve.

OPERATION

POWERTRAIN CONTROL MODULE

Powertrain Control Module (PCM), located behind right end of instrument panel, receives inputs from vehicle speed sensor, servo diaphragm position sensor, cruise control switch and brake release switch. Based on these inputs, PCM controls vacuum valves at servo. PCM prevents system engagement at speeds of less than 25 MPH. PCM is not serviceable; if defective, it must be replaced. System faults are stored as codes in PCM memory.

CONTROL SWITCH

Control switch, located on end of multifunction switch (turn signal) lever, controls system operational modes.

SET/COAST – To set vehicle speed, turn control switch to ON position. With vehicle speed at 25 MPH or more, press and release SET/COAST button. Vehicle will maintain set speed.

To increase speed during engaged cruise, accelerate to desired speed. Press and release SET/COAST button. Vehicle will maintain new set speed.

To decrease speed during engaged cruise, press and hold SET/COAST button. System will disengage. When vehicle has slowed to desired speed, release SET/COAST button. Vehicle will maintain new set speed.

To decrease speed by one-MPH increments during engaged cruise, tap SET/COAST button (quickly press and release button; DO NOT press and hold button). Vehicle speed will decrease one MPH for each tap of the button.

RESUME/ACCEL – To resume set speed after system has been disengaged by braking, momentarily engage and release RESUME/ACCEL switch. Vehicle will return to set speed. If RESUME/ACCEL switch is engaged for more than one second, vehicle will begin to accelerate. To accelerate using cruise control system, engage and hold RESUME/ACCEL switch until desired speed is reached.

To increase speed by one-MPH increments during engaged cruise, tap RESUME/ACCEL switch (quickly move to RESUME/ACCEL position and release). Vehicle speed will increase one MPH for each tap of the switch. After 10 taps, system must be reset to a new speed to continue this function.

NOTE: If transmission is shifted into Park when ignition is on, cruise memory will not retain the set speed. When this occurs, cruise cannot be activated using the RESUME function until a new set speed is entered.

SERVO

Servo consists of a vacuum diaphragm that actuates the throttle lever, and 2 vacuum control solenoids (vacuum solenoid and vent solenoid). *See Fig. 1.* Vacuum and vent solenoids, responding to commands from cruise control module, regulate vacuum supply to diaphragm. Engine manifold vacuum and a reservoir provide vacuum source for diaphragm.

VEHICLE SPEED SENSOR (VSS)

VSS is a permanent magnet generator that generates AC voltage pulses that are monitored by the PCM. VSS is mounted on top of right end transaxle extension housing.

BRAKE RELEASE SWITCH/VALVE

Switch/valve assembly, mounted on brake pedal bracket, disengages system. When brake pedal is depressed, electrical current to PCM is

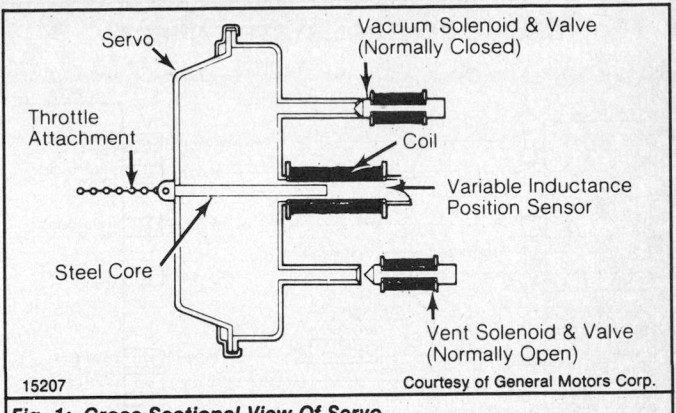

Fig. 1: Cross-Sectional View Of Servo

15207 — Courtesy of General Motors Corp.

interrupted, causing PCM to vent servo diaphragm to atmosphere. This releases servo cable, allowing throttle to close. Also, a vacuum hose is routed from servo to switch/valve assembly. When brake pedal is depressed, servo diaphragm is vented through brake switch.

ADJUSTMENTS

SERVO CABLE

Attach cable end to throttle lever. Attach cable housing clip to servo bracket. Pull servo end of cable toward servo without moving throttle lever. Align cable end stud with hole in servo tab. If stud does not align with hole, move cable away from servo enough to align stud with hole. Install cable end retainer on stud.

BRAKE RELEASE SWITCH/VALVE

Fully depress and hold brake pedal. Push switch/valve assembly through retainer and hole in pedal bracket until fully seated. Clicking sound should be heard as switch/valve assembly is pushed into pedal bracket. Pull pedal fully rearward against pedal stop until clicking stops. Release pedal. Pull pedal fully rearward again to ensure no clicking can be heard.

TESTING & TROUBLE SHOOTING

NOTE: For cruise control system wiring diagram, see appropriate chassis wiring diagram in WIRING DIAGRAMS.

Check fuse. Check for bare, broken or disconnected wires. Check for pinched, damaged, crossed or disconnected vacuum hoses. Ensure servo and throttle linkages operate freely. If cruise operation is erratic, check for loose ground wire at ground stud under coil pack. *See Fig. 2.* Tighten stud nut to **12 ft. lbs. (16 N.m)**. Test or trouble shoot cruise control system using CRUISE CONTROL SYSTEM CHECK chart.

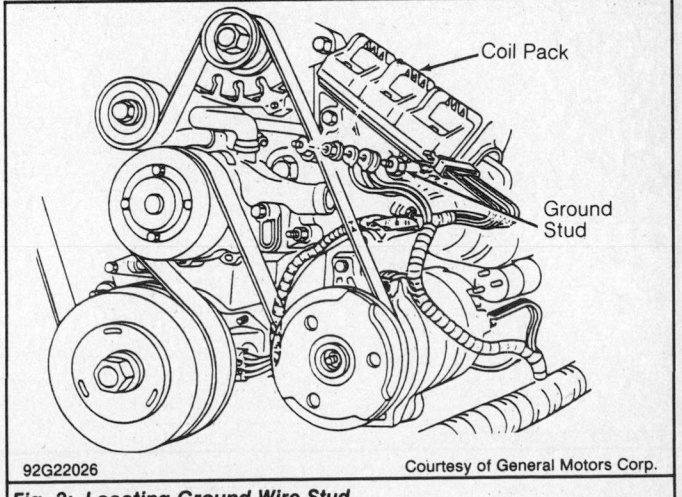

92G22026 — Courtesy of General Motors Corp.

Fig. 2: Locating Ground Wire Stud

GM
4-14

1992 SAFETY EQUIPMENT
Cruise Control – Vacuum Servo – 3.8L (Cont.)

CRUISE CONTROL SYSTEM CHECK

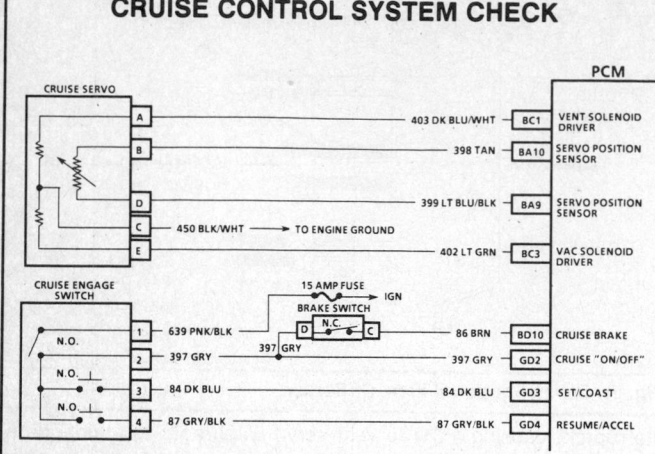

PCM		
403 DK BLU/WHT	BC1	VENT SOLENOID DRIVER
398 TAN	BA10	SERVO POSITION SENSOR
399 LT BLU/BLK	BA9	SERVO POSITION SENSOR
450 BLK/WHT → TO ENGINE GROUND		
402 LT GRN	BC3	VAC SOLENOID DRIVER

CRUISE SERVO — A, B, D, C, E

CRUISE ENGAGE SWITCH

15 AMP FUSE
BRAKE SWITCH
IGN

1 N.O.	639 PNK/BLK	86 BRN	BD10 CRUISE BRAKE
2 N.O.	397 GRY	397 GRY	GD2 CRUISE "ON/OFF"
3 N.O.	84 DK BLU	84 DK BLU	GD3 SET/COAST
4 N.O.	87 GRY/BLK	87 GRY/BLK	GD4 RESUME/ACCEL

Cruise control operation is controlled by Powertrain Control Module (PCM). PCM receives and processes inputs from cruise control (C/C) engage switch, brake switch, vehicle speed sensor, TPS and servo position sensor. Based on these inputs, PCM sends output signals to the vacuum and vent solenoids at servo. The vacuum and vent solenoids control amount of vacuum in servo diaphragm.

DIAGNOSTIC AIDS

If problem is intermittent, check for poor connections (especially at PCM harness connectors), chafed wiring or broken wires. If one or more of the following codes are stored, cruise control system may not operate. Before diagnosing system, repair conditions that cause the codes.

- Code 16 – System Voltage High Or Low
- Code 21 – TPS High
- Code 22 – TPS Low
- Code 24 – Vehicle Speed Sensor (VSS) Circuit
- Code 36 – Transaxle Shift Problem
- Code 38 – Torque Converter Clutch (TCC) Brake Switch
- Code 61 – Cruise Vent Solenoid
- Code 62 – Cruise Vacuum Solenoid
- Code 63 – Cruise Servo Position Sensor (SPS) Indicates Low
- Code 65 – Cruise Servo Position Sensor (SPS)
- Code 67 – Cruise Engage Switches
- Code 68 – Cruise System Problem

NOTE: Only Codes 16, 21, 22 and 24 will turn on the SERVICE ENGINE SOON light.

Flowchart:

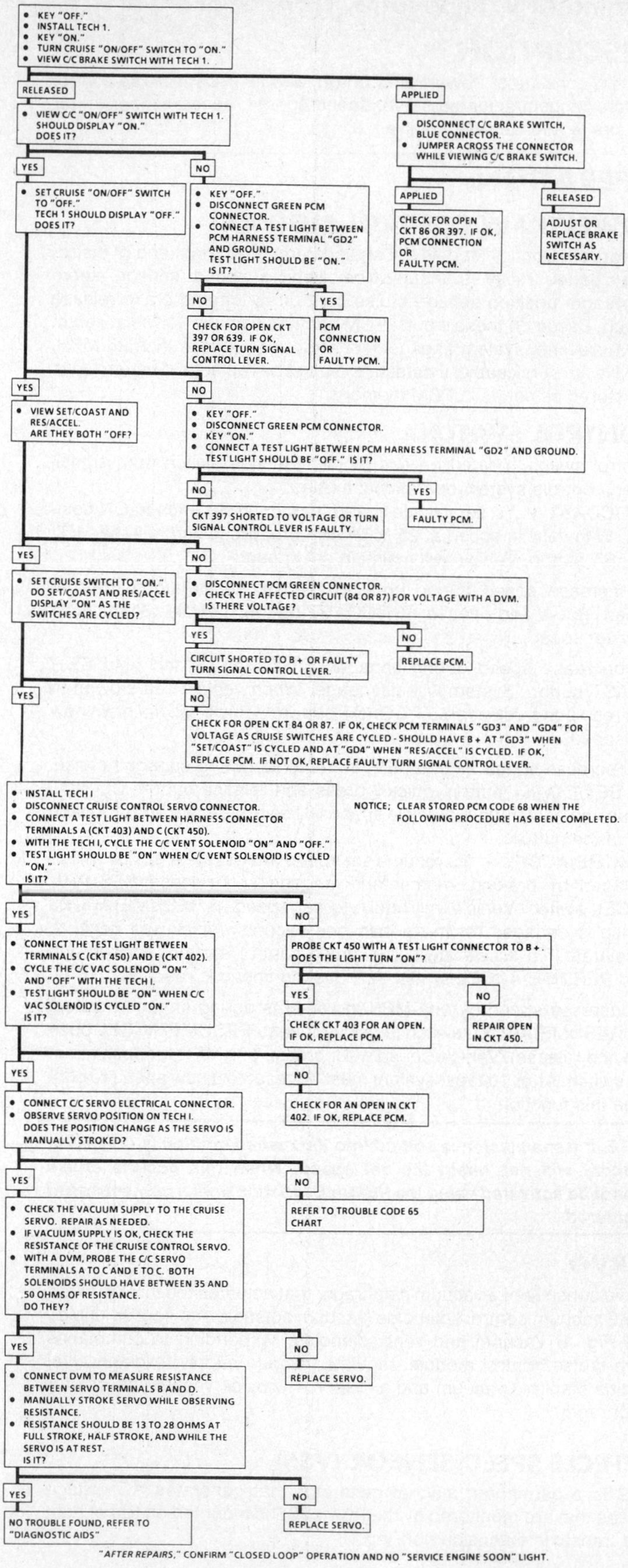

- KEY "OFF."
- INSTALL TECH 1.
- KEY "ON."
- TURN CRUISE "ON/OFF" SWITCH TO "ON."
- VIEW C/C BRAKE SWITCH WITH TECH 1.

RELEASED
- VIEW C/C "ON/OFF" SWITCH WITH TECH 1. SHOULD DISPLAY "ON." DOES IT?

  YES
  - SET CRUISE "ON/OFF" SWITCH TO "OFF." TECH 1 SHOULD DISPLAY "OFF." DOES IT?

    YES
    - VIEW SET/COAST AND RES/ACCEL. ARE THEY BOTH "OFF"?

      YES
      - SET CRUISE SWITCH TO "ON." DO SET/COAST AND RES/ACCEL DISPLAY "ON" AS THE SWITCHES ARE CYCLED?

    NO
    - KEY "OFF."
    - DISCONNECT GREEN PCM CONNECTOR.
    - KEY "ON."
    - CONNECT A TEST LIGHT BETWEEN PCM HARNESS TERMINAL "GD2" AND GROUND. TEST LIGHT SHOULD BE "OFF." IS IT?

      NO
      - CKT 397 SHORTED TO VOLTAGE OR TURN SIGNAL CONTROL LEVER IS FAULTY.

      YES
      - FAULTY PCM.

    NO
    - DISCONNECT PCM GREEN CONNECTOR.
    - CHECK THE AFFECTED CIRCUIT (84 OR 87) FOR VOLTAGE WITH A DVM. IS THERE VOLTAGE?

      YES
      - CIRCUIT SHORTED TO B + OR FAULTY TURN SIGNAL CONTROL LEVER.

      NO
      - REPLACE PCM.

  NO
  - KEY "OFF."
  - DISCONNECT GREEN PCM CONNECTOR.
  - CONNECT A TEST LIGHT BETWEEN PCM HARNESS TERMINAL "GD2" AND GROUND. TEST LIGHT SHOULD BE "ON." IS IT?

    NO
    - CHECK FOR OPEN CKT 397 OR 639. IF OK, REPLACE TURN SIGNAL CONTROL LEVER.

    YES
    - PCM CONNECTION OR FAULTY PCM.

APPLIED
- DISCONNECT C/C BRAKE SWITCH, BLUE CONNECTOR.
- JUMPER ACROSS THE CONNECTOR WHILE VIEWING C/C BRAKE SWITCH.

  APPLIED
  - CHECK FOR OPEN CKT 86 OR 397. IF OK, PCM CONNECTION OR FAULTY PCM.

  RELEASED
  - ADJUST OR REPLACE BRAKE SWITCH AS NECESSARY.

YES (from set/coast res/accel cycle)
- CHECK FOR OPEN CKT 84 OR 87. IF OK, CHECK PCM TERMINALS "GD3" AND "GD4" FOR VOLTAGE AS CRUISE SWITCHES ARE CYCLED - SHOULD HAVE B + AT "GD3" WHEN "SET/COAST" IS CYCLED AND AT "GD4" WHEN "RES/ACCEL" IS CYCLED. IF OK, REPLACE PCM. IF NOT OK, REPLACE FAULTY TURN SIGNAL CONTROL LEVER.

NOTICE: CLEAR STORED PCM CODE 68 WHEN THE FOLLOWING PROCEDURE HAS BEEN COMPLETED.

- INSTALL TECH 1
- DISCONNECT CRUISE CONTROL SERVO CONNECTOR.
- CONNECT A TEST LIGHT BETWEEN HARNESS CONNECTOR TERMINALS A (CKT 403) AND C (CKT 450).
- WITH THE TECH I, CYCLE THE C/C VENT SOLENOID "ON" AND "OFF."
- TEST LIGHT SHOULD BE "ON" WHEN C/C VENT SOLENOID IS CYCLED "ON." IS IT?

  YES
  - CONNECT THE TEST LIGHT BETWEEN TERMINALS C (CKT 450) AND E (CKT 402).
  - CYCLE THE C/C VAC SOLENOID "ON" AND "OFF" WITH THE TECH I.
  - TEST LIGHT SHOULD BE "ON" WHEN C/C VAC SOLENOID IS CYCLED "ON." IS IT?

    YES
    - CONNECT C/C SERVO ELECTRICAL CONNECTOR.
    - OBSERVE SERVO POSITION ON TECH I. DOES THE POSITION CHANGE AS THE SERVO IS MANUALLY STROKED?

      YES
      - CHECK THE VACUUM SUPPLY TO THE CRUISE SERVO. REPAIR AS NEEDED.
      - IF VACUUM SUPPLY IS OK, CHECK THE RESISTANCE OF THE CRUISE CONTROL SERVO.
      - WITH A DVM, PROBE THE C/C SERVO TERMINALS A TO C AND E TO C. BOTH SOLENOIDS SHOULD HAVE BETWEEN 35 AND 50 OHMS OF RESISTANCE. DO THEY?

        YES
        - CONNECT DVM TO MEASURE RESISTANCE BETWEEN SERVO TERMINALS B AND D.
        - MANUALLY STROKE SERVO WHILE OBSERVING RESISTANCE.
        - RESISTANCE SHOULD BE 13 TO 28 OHMS AT FULL STROKE, HALF STROKE, AND WHILE THE SERVO IS AT REST. IS IT?

          YES
          - NO TROUBLE FOUND, REFER TO "DIAGNOSTIC AIDS"

          NO
          - REPLACE SERVO.

        NO
        - REPLACE SERVO.

      NO
      - REFER TO TROUBLE CODE 65 CHART

    NO
    - CHECK FOR AN OPEN IN CKT 402. IF OK, REPLACE PCM.

  NO
  - PROBE CKT 450 WITH A TEST LIGHT CONNECTOR TO B +. DOES THE LIGHT TURN "ON"?

    YES
    - CHECK CKT 403 FOR AN OPEN. IF OK, REPLACE PCM.

    NO
    - REPAIR OPEN IN CKT 450.

"AFTER REPAIRS," CONFIRM "CLOSED LOOP" OPERATION AND NO "SERVICE ENGINE SOON" LIGHT.

1992 SAFETY EQUIPMENT
Cruise Control – Vacuum Servo – 3.8L (Cont.)

GM
4-15

CODE 24, VEHICLE SPEED SENSOR (VSS)

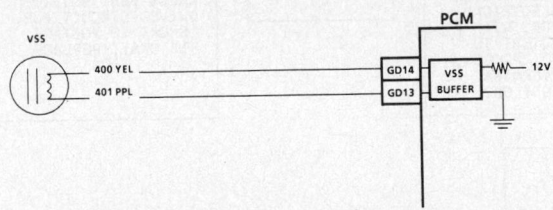

VSS, mounted on transaxle extension housing, is a permanent magnet generator that provides Powertrain Control Module (PCM) with pulsing AC voltage signals. VSS produces signals when vehicle speed is greater than 3 MPH. Voltage level and pulses increase with vehicle speed. PCM receives and converts signals.

NOTE: Test numbers refer to numbers on diagnostic chart.

1) VSS only produces a voltage signal if drive wheels are turning at speeds greater than 3 MPH.
2) Before replacing PCM, check MEM-CAL for correct application.

DIAGNOSTIC AIDS

A faulty or misadjusted Park/Neutral switch may set a false Code 24. Use Scan tester to check for proper signal in Drive while wiggling shifter. Code 24 may set if vehicle is power-braked (brakes applied and throttle depressed) for more than 10 seconds. Check circuits No. 400 and 401 for proper connections.

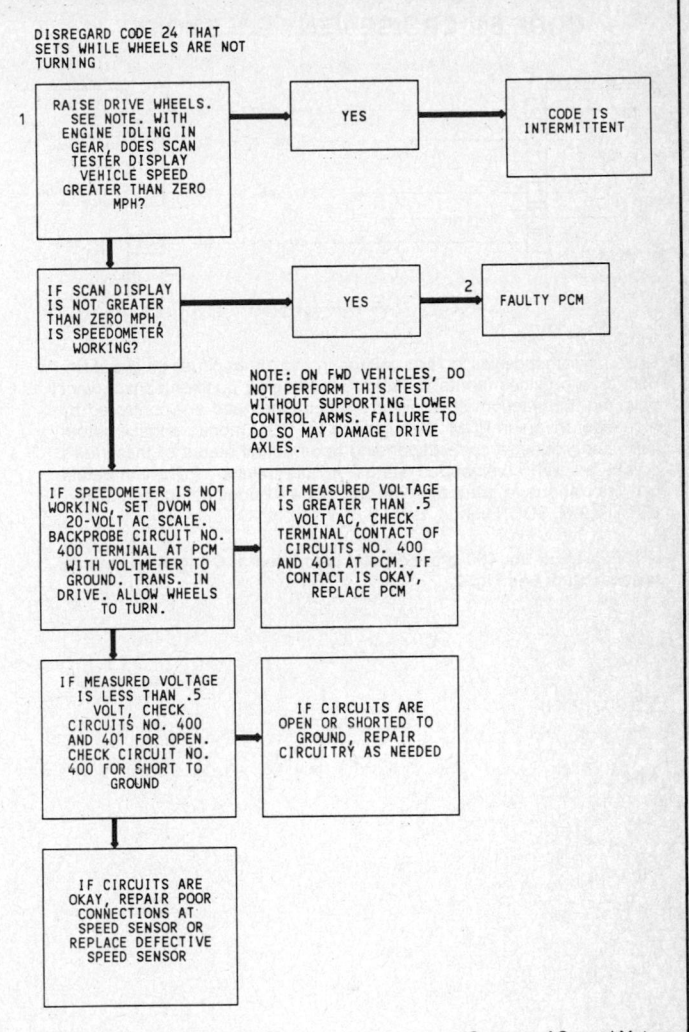

GM
4-16

1992 SAFETY EQUIPMENT
Cruise Control – Vacuum Servo – 3.8L (Cont.)

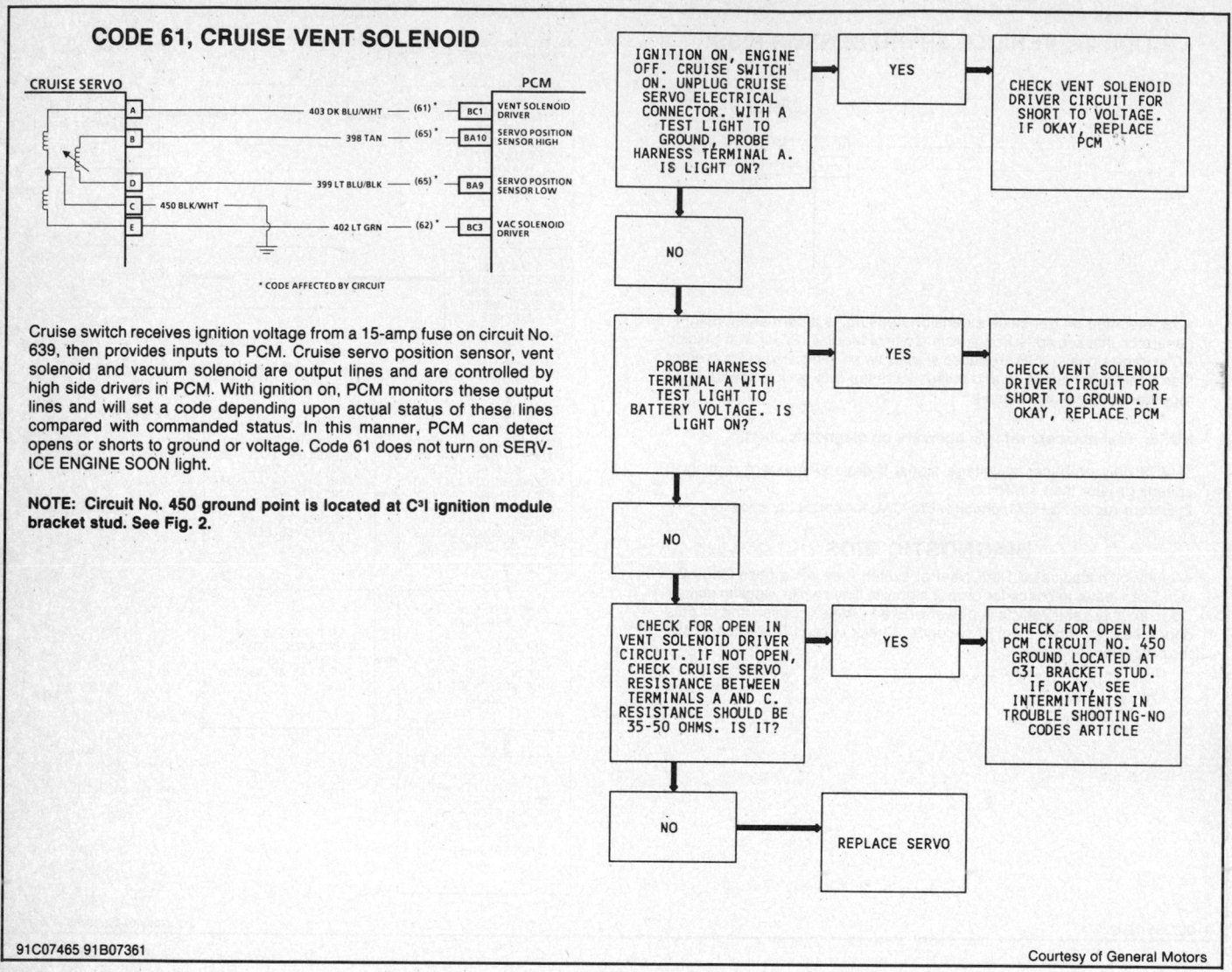

CODE 61, CRUISE VENT SOLENOID

Cruise switch receives ignition voltage from a 15-amp fuse on circuit No. 639, then provides inputs to PCM. Cruise servo position sensor, vent solenoid and vacuum solenoid are output lines and are controlled by high side drivers in PCM. With ignition on, PCM monitors these output lines and will set a code depending upon actual status of these lines compared with commanded status. In this manner, PCM can detect opens or shorts to ground or voltage. Code 61 does not turn on SERV-ICE ENGINE SOON light.

NOTE: Circuit No. 450 ground point is located at C³I ignition module bracket stud. See Fig. 2.

91C07465 91B07361

Courtesy of General Motors

1992 SAFETY EQUIPMENT
Cruise Control – Vacuum Servo – 3.8L (Cont.)

GM
4-17

CODE 62, CRUISE VACUUM SOLENOID

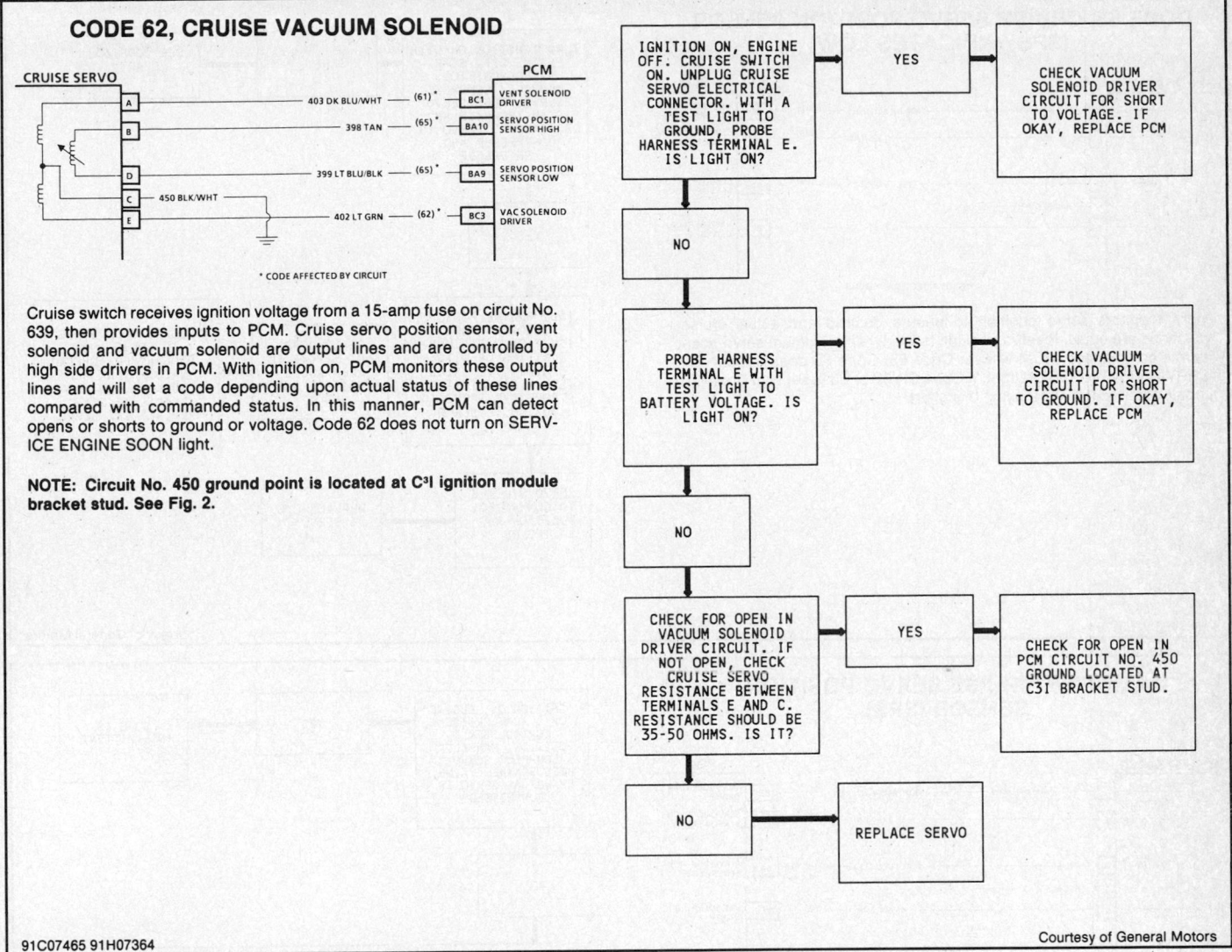

Cruise switch receives ignition voltage from a 15-amp fuse on circuit No. 639, then provides inputs to PCM. Cruise servo position sensor, vent solenoid and vacuum solenoid are output lines and are controlled by high side drivers in PCM. With ignition on, PCM monitors these output lines and will set a code depending upon actual status of these lines compared with commanded status. In this manner, PCM can detect opens or shorts to ground or voltage. Code 62 does not turn on SERVICE ENGINE SOON light.

NOTE: Circuit No. 450 ground point is located at C³I ignition module bracket stud. See Fig. 2.

GM
4-18

1992 SAFETY EQUIPMENT
Cruise Control – Vacuum Servo – 3.8L (Cont.)

CODE 63, CRUISE SERVO POSITION SENSOR (SPS) INDICATES LOW

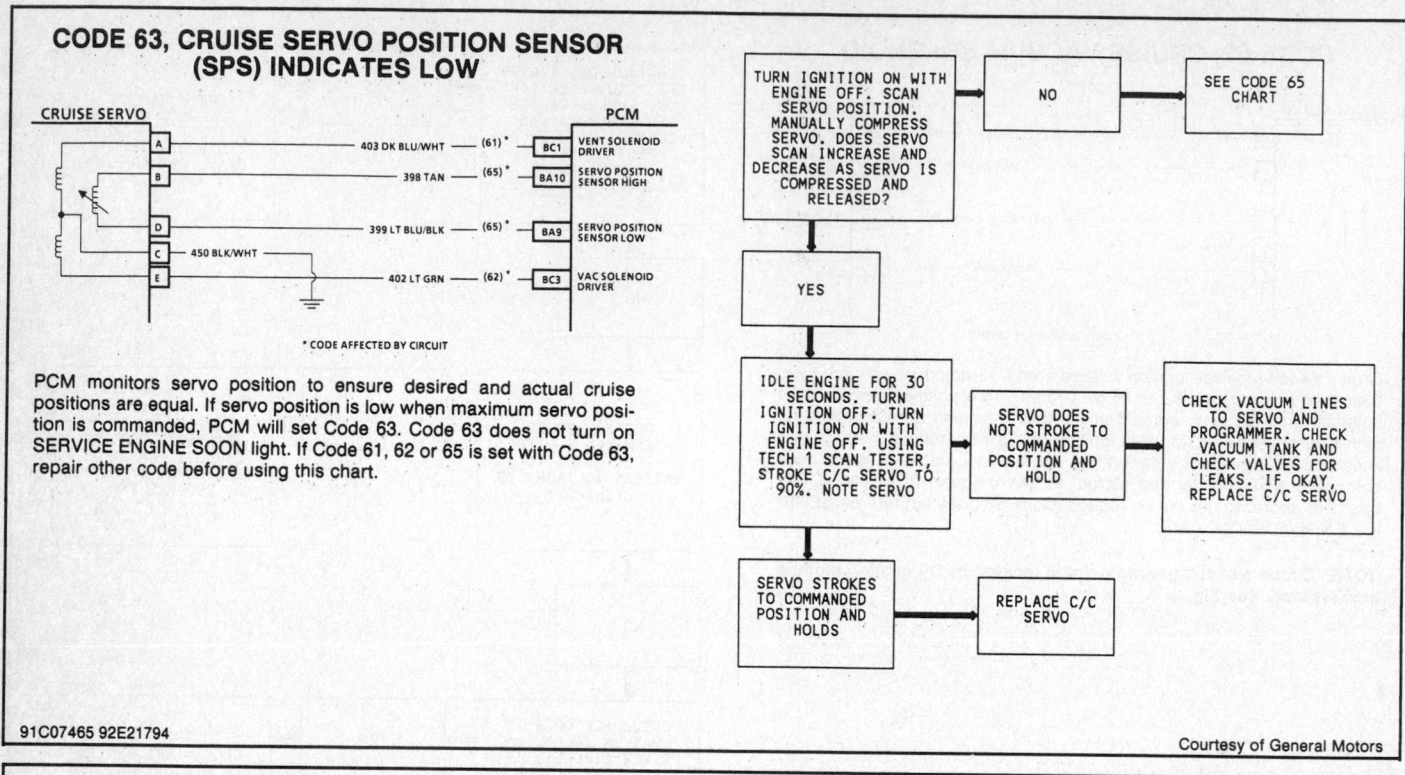

PCM monitors servo position to ensure desired and actual cruise positions are equal. If servo position is low when maximum servo position is commanded, PCM will set Code 63. Code 63 does not turn on SERVICE ENGINE SOON light. If Code 61, 62 or 65 is set with Code 63, repair other code before using this chart.

TURN IGNITION ON WITH ENGINE OFF. SCAN SERVO POSITION. MANUALLY COMPRESS SERVO. DOES SERVO SCAN INCREASE AND DECREASE AS SERVO IS COMPRESSED AND RELEASED?

NO → **SEE CODE 65 CHART**

YES →

IDLE ENGINE FOR 30 SECONDS. TURN IGNITION OFF. TURN IGNITION ON WITH ENGINE OFF. USING TECH 1 SCAN TESTER, STROKE C/C SERVO TO 90%. NOTE SERVO

SERVO DOES NOT STROKE TO COMMANDED POSITION AND HOLD → **CHECK VACUUM LINES TO SERVO AND PROGRAMMER. CHECK VACUUM TANK AND CHECK VALVES FOR LEAKS. IF OKAY, REPLACE C/C SERVO**

SERVO STROKES TO COMMANDED POSITION AND HOLDS → **REPLACE C/C SERVO**

91C07465 92E21794

Courtesy of General Motors

CODE 65, CRUISE SERVO POSITION SENSOR (SPS)

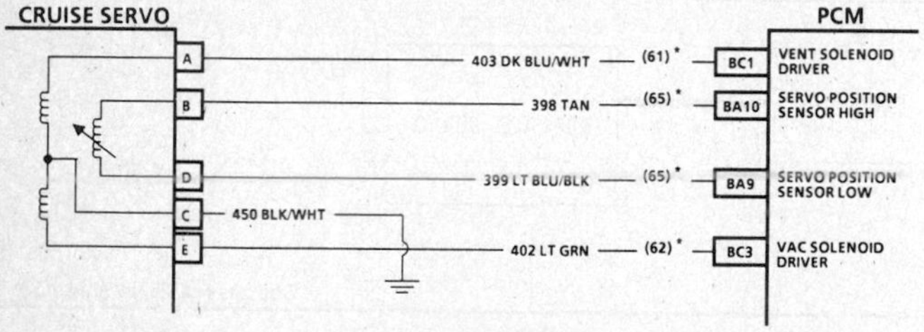

PCM supplies 5 volts to servo position sensor. Depending upon actual servo position, voltage on servo position sensor circuit will indicate position of servo to PCM. Code 65 will set if circuit No. 399 is open or if circuit No. 398 is open or shorted to ground or voltage. Code 65 does not turn on SERVICE ENGINE SOON light.

IGNITION ON, ENGINE OFF. SCAN CRUISE CONTROL SERVO POSITION. MANUALLY COMPRESS SERVO. DOES SCANNED VALUE CHANGE AS SERVO IS COMPRESSED?

YES → **CODE IS INTERMITTENT**

NO →

UNPLUG SERVO WIRING HARNESS. MEASURE VOLTAGE AT HARNESS TERMINAL B. IS READING ABOUT 5 VOLTS?

IF READING IS NOT ABOUT 5 VOLTS, BACKPROBE PCM TERMINAL B WITH DVOM. IS MEASUREMENT NOW ABOUT 5 VOLTS? → **IF VOLTAGE IS STILL NOT ABOUT 5 VOLTS, CHECK FOR SHORT TO GROUND IN SERVO POSITION SENSOR CIRCUIT BETWEEN SERVO AND TERMINAL BA10 AT PCM. IF OKAY, REPLACE PCM**

YES →

IF READING IS NOW ABOUT 5 VOLTS, PROBLEM IS OPEN IN SERVO POSITION SENSOR CIRCUIT BETWEEN SERVO AND PCM TERMINAL BA10

CONNECT DVOM BETWEEN SERVO HARNESS TERMINALS B AND D. DOES VOLTMETER DISPLAY SAME VOLTAGE?

NO → **PROBLEM IS OPEN OR SHORT TO VOLTAGE IN SERVO POSITION SENSOR CIRCUIT BETWEEN SERVO AND PCM TERMINAL BA9, OR FAULTY PCM CONNECTION OR FAULTY PCM.**

YES → **CHECK SERVO CONNECTIONS. IF OKAY, REPLACE SERVO**

91C07465 92C22022

Courtesy of General Motors

1992 SAFETY EQUIPMENT
Cruise Control – Vacuum Servo – 3.8L (Cont.)

GM
4-19

CODE 67, CRUISE ENGAGE SWITCHES

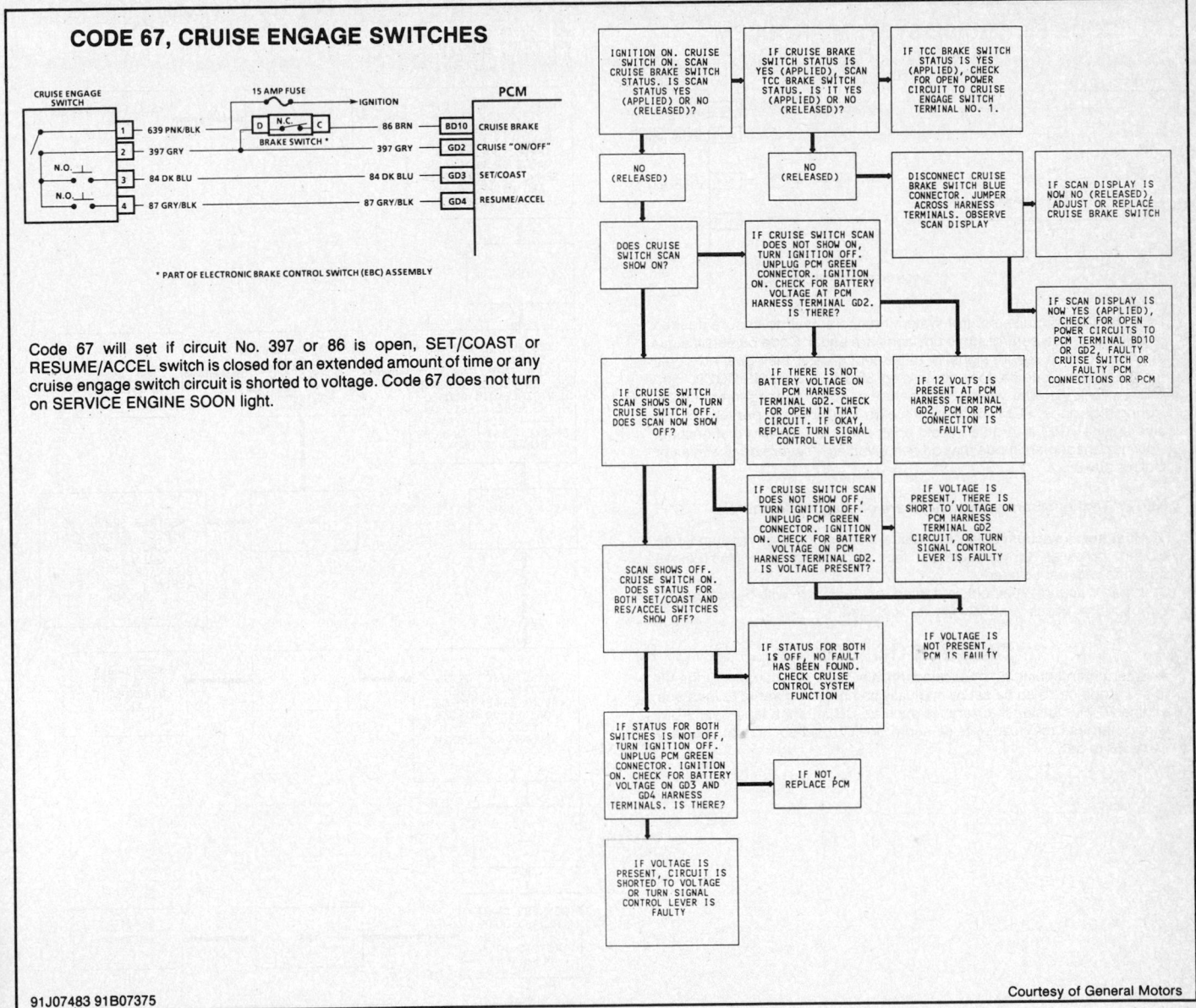

Code 67 will set if circuit No. 397 or 86 is open, SET/COAST or RESUME/ACCEL switch is closed for an extended amount of time or any cruise engage switch circuit is shorted to voltage. Code 67 does not turn on SERVICE ENGINE SOON light.

91J07483 91B07375

Courtesy of General Motors

GM
4-20

1992 SAFETY EQUIPMENT
Cruise Control – Vacuum Servo – 3.8L (Cont.)

CODE 68, CRUISE SYSTEM PROBLEM

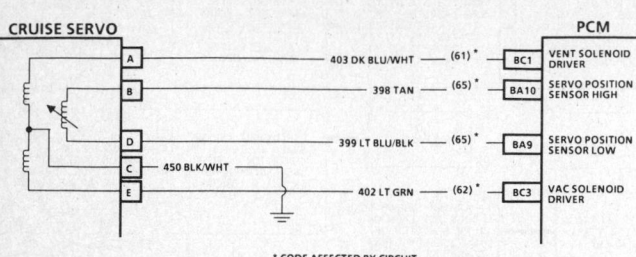

CRUISE SERVO

				PCM	
A	403 DK BLU/WHT	(61)*	BC1	VENT SOLENOID DRIVER
B	398 TAN	(65)*	BA10	SERVO POSITION SENSOR HIGH
D	399 LT BLU/BLK	(65)*	BA9	SERVO POSITION SENSOR LOW
C	450 BLK/WHT			
E	402 LT GRN	(62)*	BC3	VAC SOLENOID DRIVER

* CODE AFFECTED BY CIRCUIT

PCM-controlled cruise control system monitors itself to ensure desired and actual cruise control servo positions are equal. Code 68 sets if actual servo position sensor signal is 15 percent greater than desired signal for .6 second. Code 68 does not turn on SERVICE ENGINE SOON light. If Code 68 is current, vehicle will operate in power management mode. During this mode, PCM will shut off fuel to 3 cylinders to prevent excessive engine RPM if throttle is held open by cruise system malfunction. Power management mode may be perceived as a severe engine miss or lack of power.

NOTE: Test numbers refer to numbers on diagnostic chart.

1) Most servo vacuum solenoids leak a small amount of vacuum when closed, however, they should not leak enough to allow WOT in 15 seconds with vent closed.
2) When vacuum solenoid is forced on, vacuum will be vented to atmosphere unless vent valve is stuck closed.

DIAGNOSTIC AIDS

An intermittently-binding or sticking throttle cable can cause a Code 68 to set. Code can also be set by manually compressing servo to increase engine RPM. Outside interference such as CB antenna lead near PCM wiring harness may cause false servo position sensor signal, causing Code 68 to set.

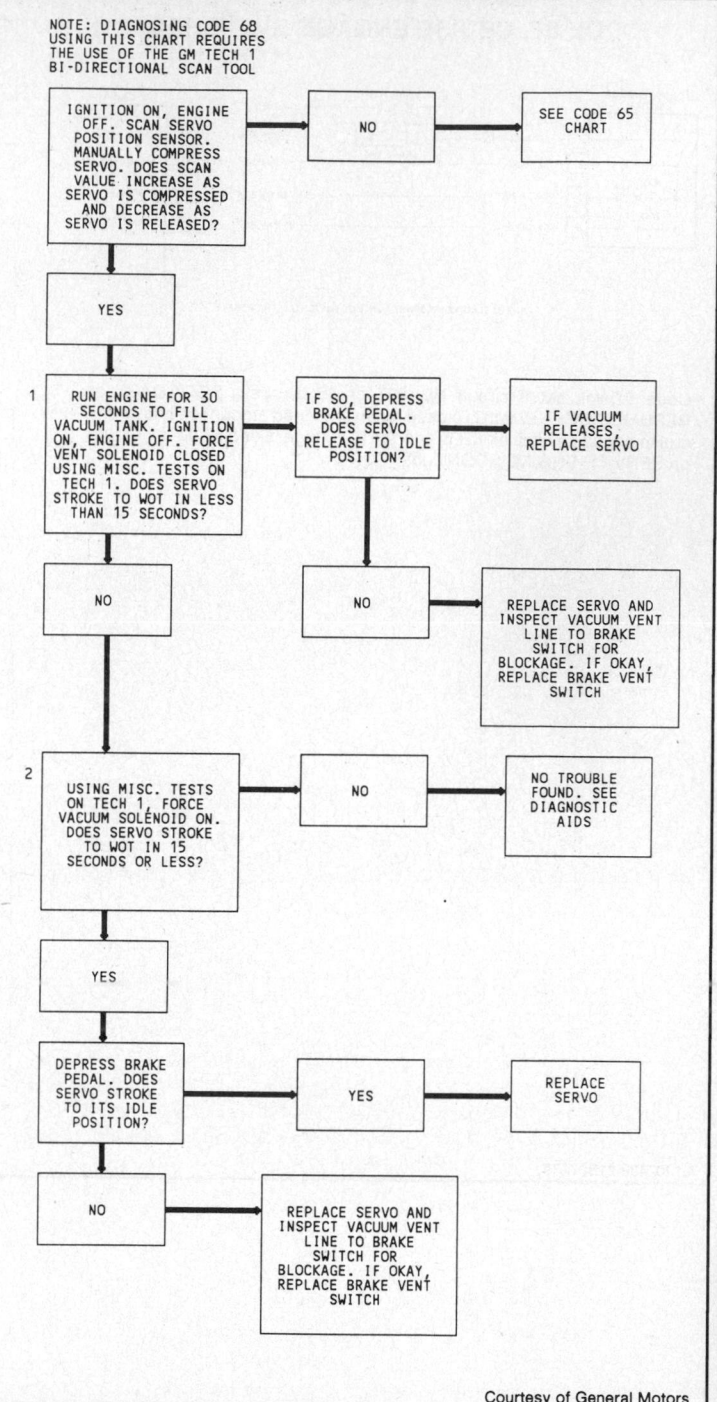

NOTE: DIAGNOSING CODE 68 USING THIS CHART REQUIRES THE USE OF THE GM TECH 1 BI-DIRECTIONAL SCAN TOOL

IGNITION ON, ENGINE OFF. SCAN SERVO POSITION SENSOR. MANUALLY COMPRESS SERVO. DOES SCAN VALUE INCREASE AS SERVO IS COMPRESSED AND DECREASE AS SERVO IS RELEASED? — NO → SEE CODE 65 CHART

YES

1 RUN ENGINE FOR 30 SECONDS TO FILL VACUUM TANK. IGNITION ON, ENGINE OFF. FORCE VENT SOLENOID CLOSED USING MISC. TESTS ON TECH 1. DOES SERVO STROKE TO WOT IN LESS THAN 15 SECONDS? — IF SO, DEPRESS BRAKE PEDAL. DOES SERVO RELEASE TO IDLE POSITION? → IF VACUUM RELEASES, REPLACE SERVO

NO (from test 1) ↓   NO (from brake pedal) → REPLACE SERVO AND INSPECT VACUUM VENT LINE TO BRAKE SWITCH FOR BLOCKAGE. IF OKAY, REPLACE BRAKE VENT SWITCH

2 USING MISC. TESTS ON TECH 1, FORCE VACUUM SOLENOID ON. DOES SERVO STROKE TO WOT IN 15 SECONDS OR LESS? — NO → NO TROUBLE FOUND. SEE DIAGNOSTIC AIDS

YES

DEPRESS BRAKE PEDAL. DOES SERVO STROKE TO ITS IDLE POSITION? — YES → REPLACE SERVO

NO → REPLACE SERVO AND INSPECT VACUUM VENT LINE TO BRAKE SWITCH FOR BLOCKAGE. IF OKAY, REPLACE BRAKE VENT SWITCH

Blazer & Suburban (1992), Motorhome, Sierra, Yukon, "C" & "K" Series Pickup

DESCRIPTION

Cruise control system components include cruise control module (control module and electric stepper motor servo combined), cruise control switch, vehicle speed sensor, and brake and clutch release switches. A vehicle speed sensor buffer is used on 1991 Motorhome and 1992 vehicles.

OPERATION

CRUISE CONTROL MODULE

Cruise control module is mounted on upper radiator support, to left of radiator (Motorhome), or next to master cylinder (all others). *See Fig. 1.* Module incorporates an electronic control module and an electric stepper motor servo. Servo regulates throttle position in response to control module commands. Module is not serviceable.

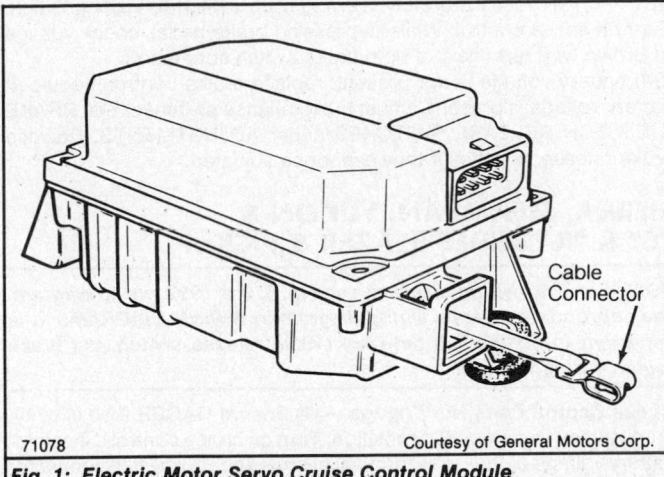

71078   Courtesy of General Motors Corp.

Fig. 1: Electric Motor Servo Cruise Control Module

CRUISE CONTROL SWITCH

Cruise control switch, mounted on end of multifunction (turn signal) lever, controls system operational modes.

SET/COAST – To set vehicle speed, turn control switch to ON position. With vehicle speed at 25 MPH or more, press and release SET/COAST button. Vehicle will maintain set speed.

To increase speed during engaged cruise, accelerate to desired speed. Press and release SET/COAST button. Vehicle will maintain new set speed.

To decrease speed during engaged cruise, press and hold SET/COAST button. System will disengage. When vehicle has slowed to desired speed, release SET/COAST button. Vehicle will maintain new set speed.

To decrease speed by one-MPH increments during engaged cruise, tap SET/COAST button (quickly press and release button; DO NOT hold button). Vehicle speed will decrease one MPH for each tap of the button.

RESUME/ACCEL – To resume set speed after system has been disengaged by braking, momentarily engage and release RESUME/ACCEL switch. Vehicle will return to set speed. If RESUME/ACCEL switch is engaged for more than one second, vehicle will begin to accelerate. To accelerate using cruise control system, engage and hold RESUME/ACCEL switch until desired speed is reached.

To increase speed by one-MPH increments during engaged cruise, tap RESUME/ACCEL switch (quickly move to RESUME/ACCEL position and release). Vehicle speed will increase one MPH for each tap of the switch. After 10 taps, system must be reset to a new speed to continue this function.

BRAKE RELEASE SWITCHES

Brake release switches allow current flow to module when brakes are applied. When module receives this signal it disengages servo. Switch may be combined with brakelight switch or may be a separate redundant switch. Switches are connected in series.

CLUTCH RELEASE SWITCH

Clutch release switch allows current flow to module when clutch pedal is depressed. When module receives this signal it disengages servo. Switch is connected in series with brake release switches.

VEHICLE SPEED SENSOR

Vehicle speed sensor, mounted in transmission (2WD) or transfer case (4WD), generates AC voltage pulses that represent vehicle speed. On 1991 vehicles (except Motorhome), these pulses are sent to speedometer. Speedometer converts pulses to DC voltage, then sends signals to cruise control module. On 1991 Motorhome and 1992 vehicles, AC pulses are sent to vehicle speed sensor buffer (Digital Ratio Adapter Controller, or DRAC).

VEHICLE SPEED SENSOR BUFFER

Vehicle speed sensor buffer receives and conditions AC voltage pulses, then sends them to cruise control module. Buffer is located behind left side of instrument panel (Motorhome) or behind instrument panel, above glove box (all others).

ADJUSTMENTS

BRAKE & CLUTCH RELEASE SWITCHES

NOTE: Brake release switch (type 1) is part of brakelight switch. See Fig. 2.

Brake Release Switch (Type 1) – Press and hold brake pedal. Pull lever on brake release switch backward until it stops. *See Fig. 2.* Pull brake pedal backward against pedal stop. Release brake pedal. Switch is adjusted if brake lights do not come on with pedal released.

Brake Release Switch (Type 2) & Clutch Release Switch – **1)** Fully depress and hold brake pedal. Push switch through retainer and pedal bracket hole until fully seated. Clicking can be heard as switch is pushed into bracket.

2) Pull pedal fully rearward against pedal stop until clicking stops. Release pedal. Pull pedal fully rearward again to ensure no clicking can be heard.

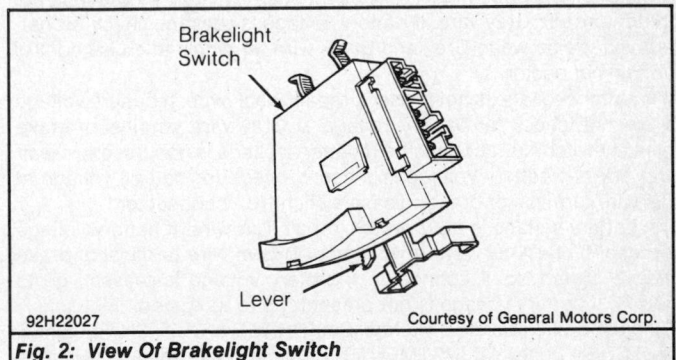

Brakelight Switch

Lever

92H22027   Courtesy of General Motors Corp.

Fig. 2: View Of Brakelight Switch

SERVO CABLE

NOTE: On vehicles with diesel engine, throttle lever refers to injection pump lever in this procedure.

1) Disconnect servo cable from throttle lever. Lightly pull cable end out of cable housing. If cable cannot be pulled out of cable housing, cable is adjusted. If cable can be pulled out of cable housing, connect cable end to throttle lever. Pull up locking button at end of cable housing. *See Fig. 3.*

GM
4-22

1991-92 SAFETY EQUIPMENT
Cruise Control – Electric Motor Servo (Cont.)

2) Pull cable housing until throttle lever begins to move off of idle stop screw. Move cable housing in opposite direction until throttle lever just contacts idle stop screw. While holding cable housing in this position, push down locking button.

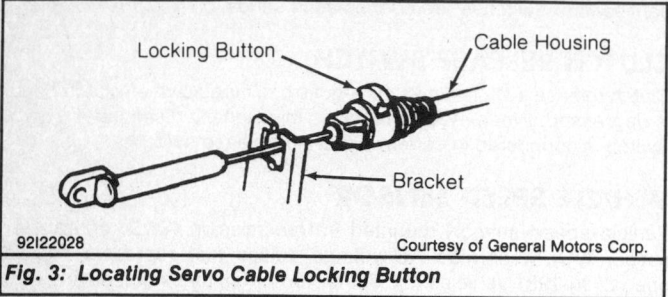

92122028   Courtesy of General Motors Corp.

Fig. 3: Locating Servo Cable Locking Button

TESTING & DIAGNOSIS

Ensure servo cable and throttle linkage move freely. Check servo cable adjustment. See SERVO CABLE under ADJUSTMENTS. Some problems may be related to vehicle speed sensor circuit. Check for Code 24, Vehicle Speed Sensor Circuit. See appropriate SELF-DIAGNOSTICS article in ENGINE PERFORMANCE.

MOTORHOME

NOTE: For 1991 wiring diagram, see Fig. 4. For 1992 wiring diagram, see appropriate chassis wiring diagram in WIRING DIAGRAMS.

NOTE: To distinguish between brake release switches No. 1 and 2, look at color of wires that terminate at each switch. Gray and Brown wires terminate at switch No. 1. Tan and Brown wires terminate at switch No. 2.

Cruise Control Does Not Engage – 1) Ensure ALT and IGN fuses are okay. Turn ignition switch to RUN position. Turn on cruise control. Check for battery voltage at Pink/Black wire terminal of cruise control switch connector and cruise control module connector.

2) If battery voltage is not present, repair Pink/Black wire. If battery voltage is present, check for battery voltage at Gray wire terminal of cruise control switch connector. If battery voltage is not present, replace cruise control switch.

3) If battery voltage is present, check for battery voltage at Gray wire terminal of cruise control module connector. If battery voltage is not present, repair Gray wire. If battery voltage is present, check for battery voltage between Gray and Black wire terminals at cruise control module connector.

4) If battery voltage is not present, repair Black wire. If battery voltage is present, check for battery voltage at Gray wire terminal of brake release switch No. 1 connector. If battery voltage is not present, repair Gray wire. If battery voltage is present, check for battery voltage at Tan wire terminal of brake release switch No. 2 connector.

5) If battery voltage is not present, repair Tan wire. If battery voltage is present, check for battery voltage at Brown wire terminal of brake release switch No. 2 connector. If battery voltage is present, go to step **7)**. If battery voltage is not present, go to next step.

6) Adjust brake release switches. See BRAKE & CLUTCH RELEASE SWITCHES under ADJUSTMENTS. Replace brake release switches if they cannot be adjusted.

7) Check for battery voltage at Brown wire terminal of brake release switch No. 1 connector. If battery voltage is present, go to next step. If battery voltage is not present, adjust brake release switches. See BRAKE & CLUTCH RELEASE SWITCHES under ADJUSTMENTS. Replace brake release switches if they cannot be adjusted.

8) Check for battery voltage at Dark Blue wire terminal of cruise control switch connector. If battery voltage is present, replace cruise control switch. If battery voltage is not present, check for battery voltage at Dark Blue wire terminal of cruise control switch connector while pressing SET switch.

9) If battery voltage is not present, replace cruise control switch. If battery voltage is present, check for battery voltage at Dark Blue wire terminal of cruise control module connector. If battery voltage is not present, repair Dark Blue wire.

10) If battery voltage is present, check for battery voltage at Dark Green wire terminal of cruise control switch connector while pressing RESUME/ACCEL switch. If battery voltage is not present, replace cruise control switch.

11) If battery voltage is present, check for battery voltage at Dark Green wire terminal of cruise control module connector. If battery voltage is not present, repair Dark Green wire.

12) If battery voltage is present, raise and support vehicle with drive wheels off of ground. While slowly turning drive wheels, check voltage between Pink/White and Dark Green wire terminals of cruise control module connector.

13) If voltage pulses between zero and battery voltage, replace cruise control module. If voltage does not pulse between zero and battery voltage, or if no voltage is present, check vehicle speed sensor circuit.

Cruise Control Does Not Disengage Using Brake Pedal – 1) Ensure ALT and IGN fuses are okay. Turn ignition switch to RUN position. Turn on cruise control. While depressing brake pedal, check voltage at Brown wire terminals of both brake switch connectors.

2) If battery voltage is not present, replace cruise control module. If battery voltage is present, adjust brake release switches. See BRAKE & CLUTCH RELEASE SWITCHES under ADJUSTMENTS. Replace brake release switches if they cannot be adjusted.

SIERRA, SUBURBAN, YUKON & "C" & "K" SERIES BLAZER & PICKUP

NOTE: For 1991 wiring diagram, see Fig. 5. For 1992 wiring diagram, see appropriate chassis wiring diagram in WIRING DIAGRAMS. It is important to distinguish between cruise release switch and brake switch during testing.

Cruise Control Does Not Engage – 1) Ensure GAGES fuse is okay. Turn ignition switch to RUN position. Turn on cruise control. Check for battery voltage at Pink wire terminal of cruise control switch connector and cruise control module connector.

2) If battery voltage is not present, repair Pink wire. If battery voltage is present, check for battery voltage at Gray wire terminal of cruise control switch connector. If battery voltage is not present, replace cruise control switch.

3) If battery voltage is present, check for battery voltage at Gray wire terminal of cruise control module connector. If battery voltage is not present, repair Gray wire. If battery voltage is present, check for battery voltage between Gray and Black/White wire terminals of cruise control module connector.

4) If battery voltage is not present, repair Black/White wire. If battery voltage is present, check for battery voltage at Gray wire terminal of cruise release switch connector. If battery voltage is not present, repair Gray wire. If battery voltage is present, check for battery voltage at Light Green wire terminal of cruise release switch connector while depressing brake pedal.

5) If battery voltage is present, go to next step. If battery voltage is not present, ensure brake pedal is not depressed and brake switch is not out of adjustment. See BRAKE & CLUTCH RELEASE SWITCHES under ADJUSTMENTS. If brake pedal is not depressed and brake switch is not out of adjustment, replace cruise release switch.

6) Check for battery voltage at Light Green wire terminal of brake switch connector while depressing brake pedal. If battery voltage is not present, repair Light Green wire. If battery voltage is present, check for battery voltage at Brown wire terminal of brake switch connector while depressing brake pedal.

7) If battery voltage is present on vehicles with automatic transmission, go to step **9)**. If battery voltage is present on vehicles with manual transmission, go to next step. If battery voltage is not present, adjust brake switch. See BRAKE & CLUTCH RELEASE SWITCHES under ADJUSTMENTS. Replace brake switch if it cannot be adjusted.

8) Check for battery voltage at Brown wire terminal of clutch switch connector while depressing brake pedal. If battery voltage is present,

1991-92 SAFETY EQUIPMENT
Cruise Control – Electric Motor Servo (Cont.)

GM
4-23

go to next step. If battery voltage is not present, adjust clutch switch. See BRAKE & CLUTCH RELEASE SWITCHES under ADJUST-MENTS. Replace clutch switch if it cannot be adjusted.

9) Check for battery voltage at Brown wire terminal of cruise control module connector while depressing brake pedal. If battery voltage is present, replace cruise control module. If battery voltage is not present, repair Brown wire.

Cruise Control Does Not Disengage Using Brake Or Clutch Pedal –
1) Ensure GAGES fuse is okay. Turn ignition switch to RUN position. Turn on cruise control. While depressing brake pedal, check for battery voltage at Brown wire terminal of brake switch connector.

2) If battery voltage is not present, replace cruise control module. If battery voltage is present, adjust brake switch. See BRAKE & CLUTCH RELEASE SWITCHES under ADJUSTMENTS. Replace brake switch if it cannot be adjusted. On vehicles with manual transmission, go to next step.

3) While depressing clutch pedal, check for battery voltage at Brown wire terminal of clutch switch connector. If battery voltage is not present, replace cruise control module. If battery voltage is present, adjust clutch switch. See BRAKE & CLUTCH RELEASE SWITCHES under ADJUSTMENTS. Replace clutch switch if it cannot be adjusted.

WIRING DIAGRAMS

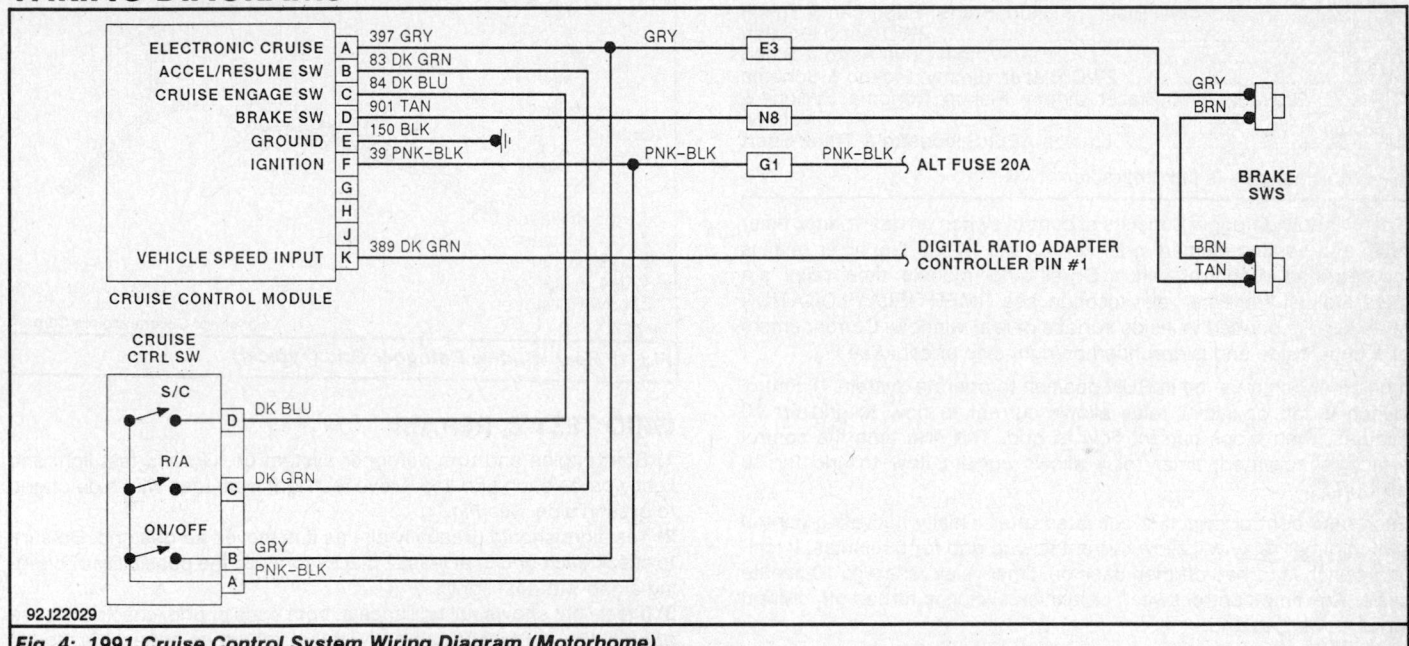

Fig. 4: 1991 Cruise Control System Wiring Diagram (Motorhome)

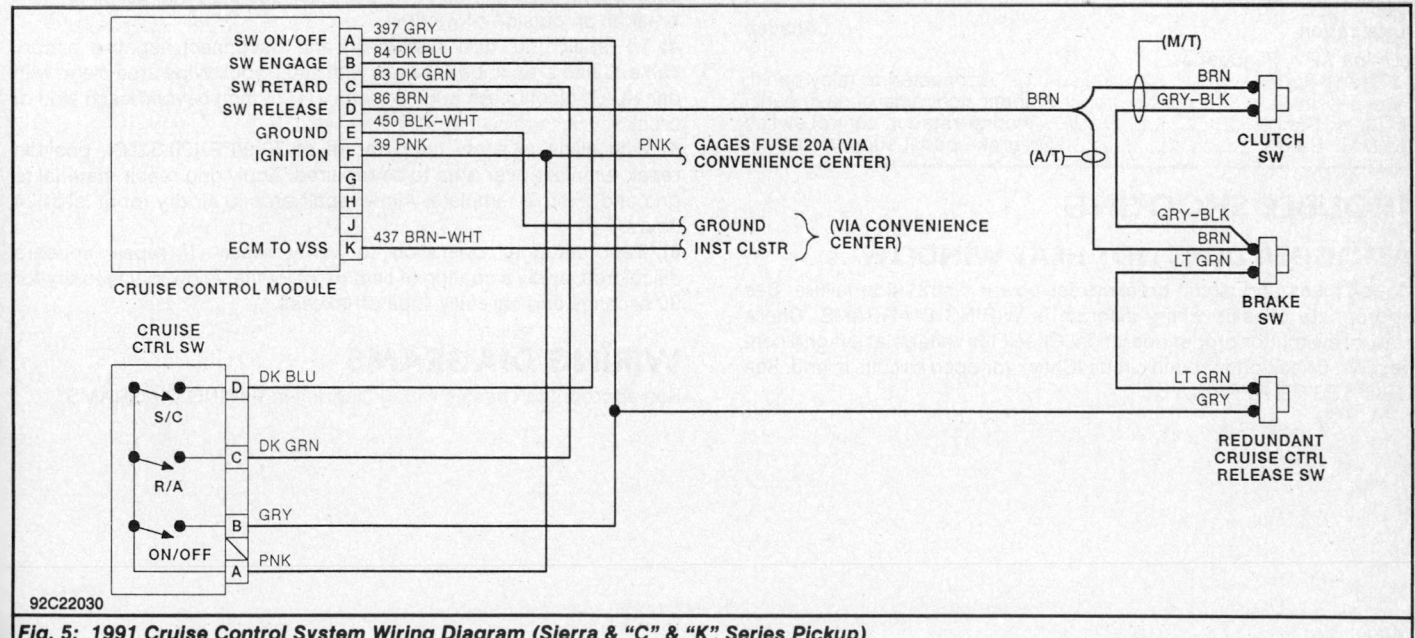

Fig. 5: 1991 Cruise Control System Wiring Diagram (Sierra & "C" & "K" Series Pickup)

Astro, Bravada, Jimmy, Lumina APV, Safari, Sierra, Silhouette, Sonoma, Suburban, Trans Sport, Typhoon, Van, Yukon, "C" & "K" Series Blazer & Pickup, "S" & "T" Series Blazer & Pickup

DESCRIPTION & OPERATION

MODEL IDENTIFICATION

Series [1]	Model
"C"	2WD Pickup, Sierra & Suburban
"K"	4WD Blazer, Pickup, Sierra, Suburban & Yukon
"L"	2WD Astro & Safari
"M"	All-Wheel Drive Astro & Safari
"S"	2WD Blazer, Jimmy, Pickup & Sonoma
"T"	Bravada, 4WD Blazer, Jimmy, Pickup, Sonoma, Syclone & Typhoon
"U"	Lumina APV, Silhouette & Trans Sport

[1] – Vehicle series is fifth character of VIN.

Rear window defogger consists of control switch on dash panel, timer relay and heating element grid. On "C" and "K" Series, timer relay is incorporated in control switch. On all other models, timer relay is a separate unit. For timer relay location, see TIMER RELAY LOCATION table. Grid is bonded to inside surface of rear window. Current enters grid on left side and is grounded on right side of cab. See Fig. 1.

Ignition switch must be in RUN position to operate system. If control switch is left on, timer relay allows current to flow to grid for 10 minutes, then stops current flow to grid. The first time the control switch is activated, timer relay allows current flow to grid for 10 minutes.

Each time control switch is activated after initially activating control switch, timer relay will allow current flow to grid for 5 minutes. If ignition switch is turned off then back on, timer relay resets to 10 minute cycle. Any time control switch or ignition switch is turned off, current stops flowing to grid.

TIMER RELAY LOCATION

Application	Location
Lumina APV, Silhouette & Trans Sport	Connected to relay panel, under right side of dash panel
"C" & "K" Series	Incorporated in control switch
"S" & "T" Series	On brake pedal support bracket

TROUBLE SHOOTING

DEFOGGER DOES NOT HEAT WINDOW

Check fuses and circuit breakers for power distribution failure. See appropriate chassis wiring diagram in WIRING DIAGRAMS. Check control switch for proper operation. Check for voltage at left grid connection. Check grid ground circuit. Check for open circuits in grid. See GRID TEST & REPAIR.

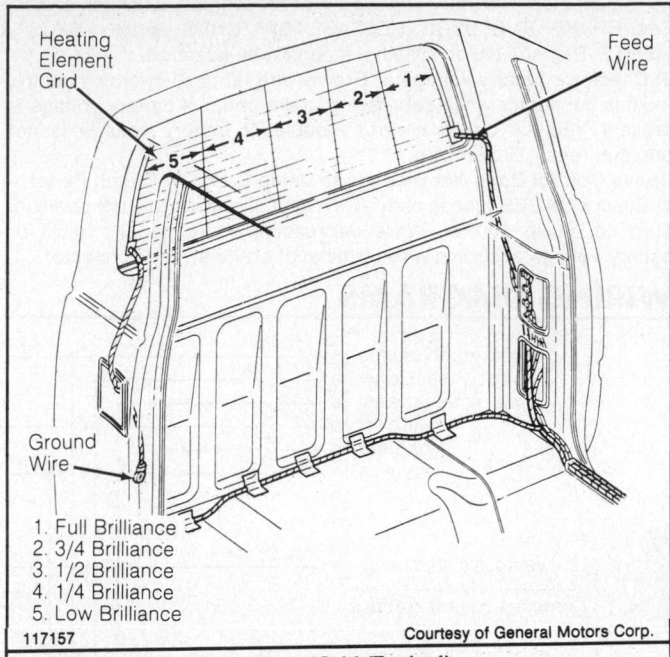

1. Full Brilliance
2. 3/4 Brilliance
3. 1/2 Brilliance
4. 1/4 Brilliance
5. Low Brilliance

117157

Courtesy of General Motors Corp.

Fig. 1: Rear Window Defogger Grid (Typical)

GRID TEST & REPAIR

1) Start engine and turn defogger system on. Ground test light and lightly probe each grid line. Move test light from feed wire side of grid to ground side. See Fig. 1.
2) Test light should gradually dim as it is moved across grid. Be sure to check each grid in at least 2 places to avoid the possibility of bridging a gap with test light.
3) If test light shows full brilliance at both ends of grid, check for loose ground wire contact at cab body. If test light goes out as it is moved across grid, a break has been detected. Use a grease pencil to mark break(s) on outside of window.
4) To repair grid, turn system off and disconnect negative battery cable. Clean area to be repaired with steel wool. Wipe area clean with denatured alcohol. Be sure to clean 1/4" (6 mm) beyond each side of break.
5) With glass at room temperature of 70-90°F (20-32°C), position repair template over area to be repaired. Apply grid repair material to grid and remove template. Allow repair area to air dry for at least 24 hours.
6) Test defogger operation to verify repair. If repair appears discolored, apply a coating of tincture of iodine. Allow iodine to dry for 30 seconds and carefully wipe off excess.

WIRING DIAGRAMS

See appropriate chassis wiring diagram in WIRING DIAGRAMS.

Blazer, Pickup, Sierra, Suburban, Yukon

DESCRIPTION
MODEL IDENTIFICATION

Series [1]	Model
"C"	2WD Pickup, Sierra & Suburban
"K"	4WD Blazer, Pickup, Sierra, Suburban & Yukon

[1] – Vehicle series is fifth character of VIN.

STANDARD INSTRUMENT PANELS

Standard mechanical instrument panels on all models are designed to permit the removal and installation of all control switches, gauges and illuminating bulbs from the driver's side. The standard instrument panels are equipped with gauges and warning lights only. Optional equipment instrument cluster comes with gauges and tachometer as well as standard and optional warning lights.

OPERATION

BRAKE WARNING LIGHT SYSTEM

Warning system consists of a warning light on instrument cluster/panel, a brake warning light/pressure differential switch (located on brake combination/proportioning valve) and a parking brake engagement telltale switch. Warning light illuminates if brake hydraulic system malfunctions or parking brake is NOT fully released.

CHARGING SYSTEM WARNING SYSTEM

Warning system consists of a battery symbol warning light on instrument cluster/panel. One side of warning light bulb is connected to alternator field circuit and other side of bulb is connected to ignition power circuit. Warning light illuminates if charging system malfunction is detected.

CHECK GAUGES LIGHT

This optional equipment warning light illuminates when engine coolant temperature is too high or when engine oil pressure is too low. Warning signals from engine coolant temperature and/or oil pressure switches are monitored by CHECK GAUGES light driver. Light driver is an integral part of coolant temperature gauge circuit board.

Warning light switches are separate units from gauge sending units. Coolant temperature warning system uses engine-mounted temperature switch. When coolant overheats, switch closes, and CHECK GAUGES warning light illuminates. Coolant switch closing temperature is 257°F (125°C).

Oil pressure warning system uses an oil pressure switch. When oil pressure drops below 4 psi (.28 kg/cm²), switch closes, activating CHECK GAGES warning light on instrument cluster. On vehicles equipped with gauges, oil pressure warning switch is mounted next to oil pressure sending unit. Warning switch is mounted in place of sending unit on vehicles not equipped with gauges.

COOLANT TEMPERATURE GAUGE

Coolant temperature gauge measures electrical current resistance from coolant temperature sending unit, mounted in cylinder head. Sending unit has a resistance of 53.4 ohms at 257°F (125°C) and 1200 ohms at 104°F (40°C). As coolant temperature increases, current flow through sending unit to gauge increases due to less resistance, causing gauge pointer to move toward HOT.

DIGITAL RATIO ADAPTER CONTROLLER (DRAC)

NOTE: Vehicle speed sensor buffer is an internal part of the DRAC and is not serviceable. References to buffer are referring to DRAC.

Digital Ratio Adapter Controller (DRAC) is a solid-state device used to change AC voltage signal from the VSS to a digital signal for speedometer operation.

The DRAC is matched to the final drive ratio of each vehicle. If the final drive ratio is changed for any reason (i.e., tires or gears), the DRAC must be replaced to maintain accurate speedometer/odometer reading. See SPEEDOMETER CALIBRATION.

NOTE: Incorrect speedometer calibration will affect operation of Rear Wheel Anti-Lock (RWAL) Brakes, Electronic Control Module (ECM) and Cruise Control Module (CCM).

FUEL GAUGE

Fuel gauge measures current flow through a variable-resistance fuel gauge sending unit in fuel tank. When fuel level in tank is high, fuel gauge sending unit resistance is high. Fuel sending unit is located on or near top of fuel tank. Some units use short connector lead, while others have harness connected directly to unit.

LOW COOLANT INDICATOR

Diesel – Warning system consists of radiator mounted sensor, low coolant module and instrument cluster warning light. When coolant level is low in radiator, sensor sends high resistance feedback to low coolant module. Module then activates LOW COOLANT warning light. As a bulb check, light illuminates when ignition is turned on. If no problem exists, light goes out when engine starts.

OIL PRESSURE GAUGE

Oil pressure gauge measures electrical current from variable resistance unit (oil pressure sending unit). Sending unit should register one ohm of resistance with engine off. It should register 44 ohms of resistance with oil pressure at 40 psi (2.8 kg/cm²). A change in resistance changes current flow through gauge electromagnetic coils, moving pointer toward appropriate reading. Sending unit is located on left rear side of engine.

SERVICE ENGINE SOON OR CHECK ENGINE WARNING LIGHT

Warning light is part of the computerized engine control system and illuminates if a malfunction or trouble code(s) exists. As a bulb check, light illuminates when ignition is turned on. If no problem exists, light goes out when engine starts.

SERVICE FUEL FILTER OR WATER IN FUEL WARNING LIGHT

Diesel – As a bulb check, light illuminates when ignition is turned on. If no problem exists, light goes out when engine starts. If light stays illuminated at any time, excessive water is in fuel filter. Filter should be serviced immediately.

SHIFT LIGHT

Manual Transmission – Depending on ECM/PCM prom calibration, shift light responds as follows: shows driver when to upshift for best fuel economy, indicates engine RPM greater than 4000, or is inoperative on models without this option. See SHIFT INDICATOR LIGHT APPLICATION table. Driver should disregard light during downshift.

SHIFT INDICATOR LIGHT APPLICATION

Application	Trans. Type	Indicator Option
Under 8500 GVW		
"C" Series	5LM60 5-Speed	Shift/Engine Rev.
"C" & "K" Series	4500 5-Speed	Engine Rev.
"K" Series	5LM60 5-Speed	Engine Rev.
Over 8500 GVW		
"C" & "K" Series	4500 5-Speed	Inoperative
C/K Series	4-Speed	Inoperative

SPEEDOMETER/ODOMETER

Speedometer uses disc-type dial indicator display, which is lighted by electronic quartz crystals. Odometer uses electronically driven numerical wheels to display mileage. Speedometer/odometer receives its signals from the Digital Ratio Adapter Controller (DRAC). The DRAC receives its input signals from the VSS, located in transmission tailshaft housing.

VEHICLE SPEED SENSOR

Vehicle Speed Sensor (VSS) is a permanent magnet signal generator, located in transmission tailshaft housing. A toothed rotor or tone wheel fastened to transmission tailshaft rotates near VSS magnetic sensor coil, producing AC voltage pulses which are sent to DRAC. This sensor assembly takes the place of speedometer cable and related gear hardware.

VOLTMETER

Voltmeter measures voltage of charging system with engine running and measures battery voltage with ignition on. Voltmeter uses an internal shunt.

WAIT OR GLOW PLUGS LIGHT

Diesel – Light illuminates when ignition is turned on, showing glow plugs are warming cylinder combustion area to ease starting. When light goes out, engine is ready to be started. During cranking or after starting, light normally cycles on and off a few times, showing glow plugs are still warming cylinder.

SPEEDOMETER CALIBRATION

CAUTION: DO NOT touch exposed terminals at back of instrument cluster with hands or tools, as immediate electrostatic discharge damage to cluster will result.

Calibration – The vehicle speed buffer is matched to the final drive and tire size of each vehicle. If final drive or tire size has been changed for any reason, buffer must also be changed. Speed buffer is an internal part of the Digital Ratio Adapter Controller (DRAC) and is not serviceable. If buffer is faulty, DRAC must be replaced. If buffer is faulty and is not changed, speedometer/odometer reading will be inaccurate. An incorrect buffer signal will also affect anti-lock brakes, engine and cruise control system operation.

TESTING & DIAGNOSIS

BRAKE WARNING SYSTEM

NOTE: For reference to wire colors, see appropriate chassis wiring diagram in WIRING DIAGRAMS.

Warning Light Does Not Illuminate During Bulb Check – If warning light does not illuminate when ignition is turned on with engine off and parking brake disengaged, check for burned-out bulb. If bulb is okay, check for open in circuit by removing wire connector from differential pressure switch on brake combination valve and touching connector to ground. If warning light does not illuminate, repair open in circuit. If light illuminates, circuit is okay. Replace differential pressure switch.

SPEEDOMETER & ODOMETER

NOTE: Vehicle speed sensor buffer is an internal part of the DRAC and is not serviceable. References to buffer are referring to DRAC.

Speedometer & Odometer Do Not Operate Properly – 1) Disconnect DRAC and turn ignition on. Check for 12 volts between Brown wire and ground. If 12 volts is present, go to next step. If voltage reading is less than 12 volts, check for open in Brown wire.
2) Check for 12 volts between Brown wire and Black/White wire at DRAC harness connector. If 12 volts is present, ground circuit is okay. If voltage reading is less than 12 volts, check for open in Black/White wire circuit.

3) Raise and support vehicle with drive wheels off of ground. Start engine and shift transmission to drive. Check for AC voltage between Purple/White and Light Green/Black wires of DRAC.
4) Voltage should change when wheel speed increases or decreases. If AC voltage is not present, check for short or open in Purple/White and Light Green/Black wires. If wiring is okay, replace speed sensor.
5) Raise and support vehicle. Start engine and shift transmission to drive. Check for AC voltage at DRAC speedometer output terminal by backprobing ECM/PCM connector terminal A10 (without 4L80-E transmission) or B11 (with 4L80-E transmission). Replace DRAC if AC voltage is not present.
6) Raise and support vehicle. Start engine and shift transmission to drive. Check for AC voltage between Light Blue/Black and Black/White wires at DRAC connector. If AC voltage changes with wheel speed, replace DRAC.

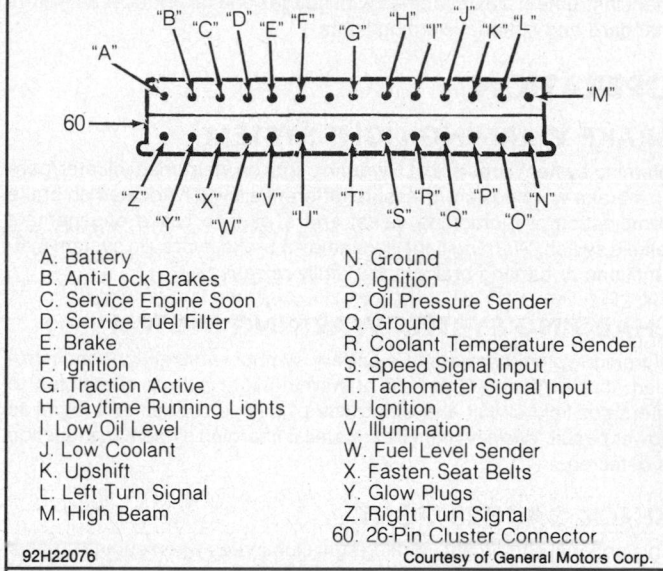

A. Battery
B. Anti-Lock Brakes
C. Service Engine Soon
D. Service Fuel Filter
E. Brake
F. Ignition
G. Traction Active
H. Daytime Running Lights
I. Low Oil Level
J. Low Coolant
K. Upshift
L. Left Turn Signal
M. High Beam
N. Ground
O. Ignition
P. Oil Pressure Sender
Q. Ground
R. Coolant Temperature Sender
S. Speed Signal Input
T. Tachometer Signal Input
U. Ignition
V. Illumination
W. Fuel Level Sender
X. Fasten Seat Belts
Y. Glow Plugs
Z. Right Turn Signal
60. 26-Pin Cluster Connector

92H22076 — Courtesy of General Motors Corp.

Fig. 1: Identifying Instrument Cluster Connector Terminals

CHECK GAUGES LIGHT

Light Inoperative With High Coolant Temperature – Check for burned bulb. Check for inoperative coolant temperature gauge and circuit. Repair/replace as necessary. If temperature gauge and circuit are okay, replace defective instrument cluster.
Light Inoperative With Low Oil Pressure – Check for burned bulb. Check for inoperative oil pressure gauge switch circuit. Repair or replace as necessary. If gauge and circuit are okay, replace defective instrument cluster.
Light Always On – Check for burned bulb. Check for inoperative coolant temperature and oil pressure gauge circuits. Replace coolant temperature and/or oil pressure gauge if necessary. If coolant temperature and oil pressure gauges and circuits are okay, replace defective instrument cluster.

COOLANT TEMPERATURE GAUGE

Gauge Reads Cold When Engine Is Hot – 1) Check for blown GAGES fuse. If fuse is okay, disconnect lead connector from coolant temperature sending unit, and turn ignition on. Connect sending unit lead to ground. Gauge should read 260°F.
2) If gauge reads 260°F, go to next step. If gauge does not read 260°F, check for open in sending unit lead circuit. If sending unit lead circuit is okay, replace gauge.
3) Reconnect connector to sending unit. If gauge now reads 100°F, ensure sending unit connection is correct. If connection is okay, replace sending unit. After replacing sending unit, if gauge still reads near 100°F with hot engine, gauge is also damaged. Replace gauge.
Gauge Reads Hot When Engine Is Cold – 1) Turn ignition on. Remove connector from temperature gauge sending unit. If gauge reading goes down to 100°F, replace externally shorted sending unit.

2) If temperature gauge continues to read 260°F, check for short to ground in wiring circuit between sending unit and gauge. If circuit is okay, replace temperature gauge.

Gauge Readings Are Inaccurate – 1) Check wiring for corroded or loose connections. Clean and tighten terminals and connections as necessary. Also check resistance in temperature sending unit ground circuit. If terminals, connections and ground circuit are okay, go to next step.

2) Disconnect lead connector from temperature gauge sending unit. Using an ohmmeter, test sending unit resistance. See TEMPERATURE GAUGE SENDING UNIT RESISTANCE table. If sending unit values are incorrect, replace temperature gauge sending unit.

TEMPERATURE GAUGE SENDING UNIT RESISTANCE

Degrees °F (°C)	Ohms
104 (40)	1200
257 (125)	53.4

FUEL GAUGE

Gauge Stays At EMPTY Position – Check for fuel in tank. Turn ignition on. Disconnect lead at fuel tank. If gauge now reads past FULL mark, replace fuel gauge sending unit. If gauge does not read past FULL mark, check for short to ground between gauge and fuel tank. Repair as necessary. If ground is okay, replace gauge.

Gauge Stays At FULL Position – 1) Turn ignition on. Check for open circuit between gauge and sending unit by disconnecting sending unit lead at fuel tank. Connect sending unit lead to ground and note gauge reading.

2) If fuel gauge now reads EMPTY, replace fuel gauge sending unit. If fuel gauge still reads FULL or beyond, repair open in wire between gauge and fuel tank.

Gauge Reading Is Inaccurate –1) Check wiring for corroded or loose connections. Clean and tighten as required. If wiring and connections are okay, remove fuel gauge sending unit. Using an ohmmeter, test sending unit resistance. See FUEL GAUGE SENDING UNIT RESISTANCE table.

2) If sending unit resistance values are correct, disconnect front body wiring harness connector at engine firewall. Connect Gauge Tester (J-24538-A) to instrument cluster terminal W. *See Fig. 1.*

3) Turn ignition on, and test gauge using tester. See FUEL GAUGE SENDING UNIT RESISTANCE table. If gauge reads accurately when connected to gauge tester, check wiring between fuel tank and front connector. If gauge reads between 1/4 and 1/2 full when tester is set at 90 ohms, replace fuel gauge.

FUEL GAUGE SENDING UNIT RESISTANCE

Position	Ohms
Empty	1
1/2	44
Full	88

OIL PRESSURE GAUGE

Gauge Reads Zero psi When Engine Running – 1) Check oil level, and add oil if necessary. Test oil pressure using manual gauge and adapter. If oil pressure reading is good on manual gauge tester, check for grounded gauge circuit by disconnecting lead at sending unit.

2) Turn ignition on. Oil pressure gauge should now read 80 psi. If gauge stays at zero, disconnect lead from gauge. If gauge now reads 80 psi, find and repair short to ground between gauge and sending unit.

3) If gauge still reads zero, replace gauge and test oil pressure gauge sending unit resistance. See OIL PRESSURE GAUGE SENDING UNIT RESISTANCE table. Replace sending unit if it reads one ohm with engine running.

OIL PRESSURE GAUGE SENDING UNIT RESISTANCE

Position	Ohms
Engine Off	1
Engine Running	[1] 44

[1] – With oil pressure at about 40 psi (2.8 kg/cm²).

Gauge Constantly Reads 80 Or More – 1) Check for open circuit between gauge and sending unit by disconnecting lead at sending unit. Connect lead to ground, and note reading on gauge.

2) If oil pressure gauge reads zero, replace oil pressure gauge sending unit. If oil pressure gauge still reads 80 psi or beyond, find open wire between gauge and sending unit.

Gauge Reading Inaccurate – Disconnect lead from oil pressure sending unit. Connect Gauge Tester (J-24538-A) to lead and ground. Turn ignition on. If gauge reads accurately when connected to tester, replace oil pressure sending unit. If gauge still reads inaccurately, replace oil pressure gauge.

VOLTMETER

Voltmeter Reads 9 Volts Or Less – 1) Measure voltage across battery terminals. Voltage should be about 12 volts. If battery is discharged, recharge battery, and perform load test. Repair cause of discharged battery.

2) With ignition on and battery terminals cleaned and connected, observe voltmeter with battery charger in operation. Voltmeter gauge should read 12 volts or more.

3) If gauge does not read 12 volts or more, check for high resistance in voltmeter gauge terminal connections. Clean and tighten connections.

4) If voltmeter reading is still low, apply 12 volts directly to positive terminal of gauge. If voltmeter does not respond accurately, replace gauge.

WIPER SWITCH

See appropriate WIPER/WASHER SYSTEMS article.

REMOVAL & INSTALLATION

WARNING: When battery is disconnected, vehicle computer and memory systems may lose memory data. Driveability problems may exist until computer systems have completed a relearn cycle. See COMPUTER RELEARN PROCEDURES article in GENERAL INFORMATION before disconnecting battery.

GAUGES

Removal & Installation – Remove instrument cluster. See INSTRUMENT CLUSTER under REMOVAL & INSTALLATION. Remove cluster case retainer screws and retainer (if equipped). Remove individual gauge mounting screws. Carefully remove gauge. To install, reverse removal procedure.

INSTRUMENT CLUSTER

CAUTION: Static electricity can destroy integrated circuits within instrument cluster. Before servicing, ground yourself and work area to discharge stored electricity.

Removal & Installation – 1) Disconnect battery negative cable. Remove cluster bezel. Remove radio and heater control units. Remove headlight switch. Remove cluster retaining screws. Remove gear shift indicator from steering column.

2) Touch hands to ground to discharge static electricity before removing instrument cluster. DO NOT touch circuit board pins. Remove cluster. To install, reverse removal procedure.

SPEEDOMETER

Removal & Installation – Remove instrument cluster. See INSTRUMENT CLUSTER under REMOVAL & INSTALLATION. Remove lens screws, lens, faceplate/applique and retainer. Remove speedometer head retainer screws and retainer. Carefully remove speedometer without touching circuitry. To install, reverse removal procedure.

VEHICLE SPEED SENSOR

Removal & Installation – Raise and support vehicle. At transmission tailshaft housing, unplug vehicle speed sensor harness. Remove hold-down bolt or unscrew vehicle speed sensor. Catch transmission fluid in suitable container. Remove "O" ring. To install, reverse removal procedure and recheck fluid level.

DESCRIPTION

INSTRUMENT PANELS

Standard instrument panels are designed to allow removal and installation of all control switches, gauges and illuminating bulbs from the driver's side. Instrument panels are equipped with gauges, analog speedometer and warning lights.

OPERATION

BRAKE WARNING LIGHT SYSTEM

Warning system consists of a warning light on instrument cluster/panel, a brake warning light/pressure differential switch (located on brake combination valve), and a parking brake engagement telltale switch. If brake hydraulic system malfunctions, or if parking brake is NOT fully released, warning light will illuminate.

CHARGING SYSTEM WARNING SYSTEM

Warning system consists of a battery symbol warning light on instrument cluster. One side of warning light bulb is connected to alternator field circuit, and other side of bulb is connected to ignition power circuit. If charging system malfunction is detected, warning light will illuminate.

COOLANT TEMPERATURE GAUGE

Coolant temperature gauge measures electrical current flow from coolant temperature sending unit mounted in cylinder head. Sending unit has a resistance of 55 ohms at 260°F (127°C), and 1400 ohms at 100°F (38°C). As coolant temperature increases, current flow through sending unit to gauge increases due to lower resistance, causing gauge pointer to move toward HOT position.

FUEL GAUGE

Fuel gauge is an electrical instrument that measures current flow from variable-resistance fuel gauge sending unit in fuel tank. When fuel level in tank is high, fuel gauge sending unit resistance is high. Fuel sending unit is located on, or near top of fuel tank. Some units use short connector lead, while others have harness connected directly to unit.

LOW COOLANT INDICATOR (6.2L DIESEL)

Warning system consists of radiator-mounted sensor, low coolant module, and instrument cluster warning light. When coolant level in radiator is low, sensor sends high resistance feedback to low coolant module. Module then illuminates LOW COOLANT warning light. Light will illuminate when ignition is turned on, and if no problem exists, it will go out when engine is started.

OIL PRESSURE GAUGE

Oil pressure gauge measures electrical current flow from variable-resistance oil pressure sending unit. Sending unit resistance is low when oil pressure is low, and is about 90 ohms when oil pressure is high. A change in resistance changes current flow through gauge electromagnetic coils, causing pointer to move from low to high. The oil pressure sender is located on left rear of engine.

PARK BRAKE WARNING LIGHT

Commercial Van (A/T) – Vehicles NOT equipped with Park position are equipped with warning light/buzzer system. If vehicle is stopped, shifted into Neutral, and parking brake is NOT immediately applied, warning light illuminates and buzzer sounds until parking brake is applied.

SERVICE ENGINE SOON

This warning light is part of computerized engine control system, and will flash when a malfunction or trouble code(s) exists. As a bulb

check, light will illuminate when ignition is turned on. If no problem exists, light will go out when engine is started.

SERVICE FUEL FILTER OR WATER IN FUEL WARNING LIGHT (6.2L DIESEL)

As a bulb check, light will illuminate when ignition is turned on. If no problem exists, light will go out when engine is started. If light stays on at any time, excessive water in fuel filter is indicated. Service filter immediately.

SPEEDOMETER/ODOMETER

Integrated circuits control needle-type air core speedometer, and stepper motor-driven odometer. Speedometer/odometer receives its signals from the Digital Ratio Adapter Controller (DRAC), which receives its input signals from the Vehicle Speed Sensor (VSS).

VEHICLE SPEED SENSOR (VSS)

The VSS is a permanent magnet signal generator located in transmission tailshaft housing. A toothed rotor, or tone wheel fastened to transmission tailshaft rotates near VSS magnetic sensor coil, producing AC voltage pulses that are sent to the DRAC. This sensor assembly takes the place of speedometer cable and related gear hardware.

VOLTMETER

Voltmeter gauge on instrument panel measures voltage of charging system with engine running, and measures battery voltage with ignition on and engine not running. When engine is running, state of charge should be higher than when engine is off. If indicator enters either Red zone, charging system malfunction is indicated.

WAIT OR GLOW PLUGS LIGHT (6.2L DIESEL)

Light will illuminate when ignition is turned on to indicate glow plugs are warming up the cylinder combustion area to ease starting. When light goes out, engine is ready to be started. During cranking or after starting, it is normal for light to cycle on and off a few times, indicating glow plugs are still operating to warm cylinder.

TESTING

BRAKE WARNING SYSTEM

If warning light does not illuminate with ignition switch on, engine off and parking brake NOT applied, check for burned out light bulb. If bulb is okay, check for open in circuit. Remove wire connector at differential pressure switch on brake combination valve, and touch connector to ground. If warning light DOES NOT illuminate, repair open in circuit. If light illuminates, circuit is okay. Replace differential pressure switch.

BRAKE WARNING ALARM

Alarm Inoperative – **1)** Connect test light between Pink/Black wire at alarm connector and ground. If test light does not light, repair open in Pink/Black wire between alarm and fuse block. If test light comes on, connect jumper between Black wire (Black/Yellow on Van) of alarm connector and ground.

2) If alarm does not sound, replace alarm. If alarm sounds, connect jumper between Black wire (Black/Yellow on Van) of delay module and ground. Delay module is located behind left side of dash. If alarm does not sound, repair open in Black wire (Black/Yellow on Van) between alarm connector and delay module connector. If alarm sounds, go to next step.

3) Connect jumper between Tan wire (Light Green on Van) of hydro-boost pressure switch and ground. If alarm does not sound, repair open in Tan wire (Black/Yellow on Van) between hydro-boost pressure switch connector and delay module connector. If wiring is okay, replace delay module.

Alarm Won't Shut Off (Van) – **1)** Disconnect delay module connector. If alarm continues to sound, repair short to ground in Black/Yellow wire between delay module and alarm connector. If alarm shuts off, disconnect hydro-boost pressure switch connector.

2) Connect test light between Light Green wire at hydro-boost pressure switch connector and positive side of battery. If test light does not light, replace delay module. If test light comes on, repair short to ground in Light Green wire between hydro-boost pressure switch connector and delay module connector.

COOLANT TEMPERATURE GAUGE (COMMERCIAL VAN)

Gauge Inaccurate – 1) Disconnect temperature gauge sending unit connector. Connect Red lead of Gauge Tester (J 33431-B) to sending unit connector Dark Green wire. Connect other wire to ground. Adjust tester resistance dials to **1400 ohms**, then adjust to **55 ohms**. See TEMPERATURE GAUGE RESISTANCE table.

2) Temperature gauge should read cold, then hot. If gauge responds correctly, replace temperature sending unit. If gauge does not respond as described, check for open circuit in Dark Green wire. If circuit is okay, replace temperature gauge.

TEMPERATURE GAUGE RESISTANCE

Temperature °F (°C)	Ohms
100 (38)	1400
260 (127)	55

Gauge Always Reads Cold – Disconnect temperature sending unit connector. Connect Dark Green wire to ground. If temperature gauge reads hot, replace temperature sending unit. If temperature gauge does not read hot, check for open circuit in Dark Green wire. If circuit is okay, replace temperature gauge.

Gauge Reads Too Hot – Disconnect temperature sending unit lead connector. Turn ignition on. If gauge reads cold, replace temperature sending unit. If gauge does not read cold, check for open circuit in Dark Green wire. If circuit is okay, see GAUGE INACCURATE under COOLANT TEMPERATURE GAUGE.

Temperature Indicator Stays On – Disconnect temperature sender and turn ignition on. Observe temperature indicator. If indicator stays on, repair short in Dark Green wire. If indicator goes out, replace temperature sender.

Check Gauges Indicator Inoperative With High Temperature – Inspect check gauges indicator bulb. Replace bulb if blown. If bulb is okay, check printed circuit for open between coolant temperature gauge and check gauges indicator. Replace printed circuit if necessary. If printed circuit is okay, replace instrument cluster.

COOLANT TEMPERATURE GAUGE (VAN)

Temperature Gauge Inoperative Or Inaccurate – 1) Disconnect temperature sender connector. Connect Gauge Tester (J24538-A) to sender wire connector and ground. Turn ignition on. If gauge responds okay, replace sender. If gauge reads beyond hot end of scale, go to step **4)**.

2) If gauge does not respond correctly, disconnect engine harness connector. Attach Gauge Tester (J24538-A) to temperature gauge wire terminal. If gauge responds okay, check wiring between sender connector and engine harness connector.

3) Repair as necessary. If gauge does not respond correctly, remove gauge. Check for loose gauge terminal nuts, loose cluster connector or open connections at gauge. Repair loose open connections as necessary. If connections are okay, replace gauge.

4) Remove gauge. Check for loose terminal nuts and/or lack of ground connection. Repair connections as necessary. If connections and ground are okay, replace gauge.

FUEL GAUGE (COMMERCIAL VAN)

Gauge Reading Is Inaccurate – 1) Disconnect fuel gauge sending unit wire. Connect Red lead of Gauge Tester (J 33431-B) to sending unit connector Pink wire. Connect other wire to ground. Adjust tester resistance dials to **zero ohm**, then to **90 ohms**.

2) Gauge should read empty, then full. If gauge responds correctly, check fuel tank ground wire for high resistance and repair if necessary. If ground circuit is okay, replace fuel tank sending unit.

3) If gauge does not respond correctly, check for high resistance in Pink wire. If Pink wire is okay, replace instrument cluster

Gauge Always Reads Empty – Disconnect fuel gauge sending unit wire. Turn ignition on. If gauge reads full, replace fuel gauge sending unit. If gauge reads empty, check for short circuit in Pink wire. If circuit is okay, replace instrument cluster.

Gauge Always Reads Full – 1) Disconnect fuel gauge sending unit wire. Turn ignition on. Connect a fused jumper wire from sending unit Pink wire to ground. If gauge reads full, check for short circuit in Pink wire. If wire is okay, replace instrument cluster.

2) If fuel gauge reads empty, connect a fused jumper between Pink and Black wires of fuel sending unit. If fuel gauge reads full, repair open in Black wire. If fuel gauge reads empty, replace fuel sending unit.

FUEL GAUGE (VAN)

Fuel Gauge Inoperative Or Inaccurate – 1) Disconnect fuel sender. Connect Gauge Tester (J24538-A) to sender wire and ground. Turn ignition on. If gauge responds okay, check fuel sender wires for shorts and connector for loose terminals.

2) Repair wires and connector as necessary. If wires and connector are okay, replace fuel sender. If gauge does not respond correctly, disconnect front body connector. Connect Gauge Tester (J24538-A) to fuel gauge wire in body connector.

3) With gauge tester set at 90 ohms, fuel gauge should read **1/4 to 1/2**. If reading is correct, check wiring to fuel sender for loose connections and chaffed insulation. Repair as necessary. If reading is incorrect, remove fuel gauge and check for loose terminal nuts.

4) Tighten nuts as necessary. If gauge connections are tight, replace fuel gauge. If gauge does not respond to 90 ohm application, disconnect front body connector. Connect Gauge Tester (J24538-A) to fuel gauge wire in body connector.

5) If gauge responds okay, check wiring between fuel sender and body connector. Repair as necessary. If gauge does not respond, remove gauge and check for loose or open connections at gauge terminals.

6) Check for loose instrument cluster connector. Repair connections as necessary. If connections are okay, replace fuel gauge.

OIL PRESSURE GAUGE (COMMERCIAL VAN)

Some Commercial Van models with gasoline engines may show high oil pressure. This occurs on upper range of oil pressure gauge. Oil pressure gauge will read correctly in mid and lower range.

Excessive oil pressure may be caused by an incorrect oil pressure sender. Some models are equipped with a 60 lb. sender instead of the correct 80 lb. sender. The incorrect sender is stamped with the No. 563. The correct sender is stamped with the No. 178.

Gauge Reads Low Or No Pressure – 1) Ensure oil level is correct. Test oil pressure with manual gauge and adapter. If oil pressure reading is good on manual gauge tester, disconnect lead at sending unit.

2) Turn ignition on. If gauge still reads low, check for short in Tan wire. If wire is okay, replace instrument cluster. If gauge reads high, replace sending unit.

Gauge Reads High Pressure – Disconnect lead at sending unit. Turn ignition on. Connect a fused jumper wire from sending unit Tan wire to ground. If gauge reads low pressure, replace oil pressure sending unit. If fuel gauge reads high pressure, check for open circuit in Tan wire. If circuit is okay, replace instrument cluster.

Gauge Reading Is Inaccurate – 1) Disconnect oil pressure sending unit connector. Connect Red lead of Gauge Tester (J 33431-B) to sending unit connector Tan wire. Connect other wire to ground. Adjust tester resistance dials to **zero ohm**, then adjust to **90 ohms**.

2) Oil pressure gauge should read low, then high pressure. If gauge responds correctly, replace oil pressure sending unit. If gauge does not respond as described, check for open circuit in Tan wire. If circuit is okay, replace instrument cluster.

OIL PRESSURE GAUGE (VAN)

Oil Pressure Gauge Inoperative Or Inaccurate – 1) Disconnect oil pressure sender. Connect Gauge Tester (J24538-A) to sender wire and ground. Turn ignition on. If gauge responds okay, replace oil pressure sender.

2) If gauge does not respond correctly, disconnect engine harness connector. Connect Gauge Tester (J24538-A) to oil pressure gauge wire in engine harness connector.

3) With gauge tester set at 90 ohms, oil pressure gauge should read slightly below mid-scale. If reading is correct, check wiring to oil pressure sender for loose connections and chaffed insulation. Repair as necessary. If reading is incorrect, remove oil pressure gauge and check for loose terminal nuts.

4) Tighten nuts as necessary. If gauge connections are tight, replace gauge. If gauge does not respond to 90 ohm application, disconnect engine harness connector. Connect Gauge Tester (J24538-A) to oil pressure gauge wire in engine harness connector.

5) If gauge responds okay, check wiring between oil sender and engine harness connector. Repair as necessary. If gauge does not respond, remove gauge and check for loose or open connections at gauge terminals.

6) Check for loose instrument cluster connector. Repair connections as necessary. If connections are okay, replace oil pressure gauge.

SPEEDOMETER/ODOMETER

Speedometer Inaccurate (Van) – Check for correct vehicle speed sensor buffer.

Speedometer Inoperative (Van) – 1) Disconnect vehicle speed sensor buffer. Turn ignition on. Check for voltage between Brown wire ground. If voltage is less than battery voltage, check for open or short in Brown wire.

2) If battery voltage is present, check for voltage between Pink/Black and Black/White wires. If voltage is less than battery voltage, check for open or short in Black/White wire. If voltage is okay, raise and support vehicle. Start engine and shift transmission into drive.

3) Check for AC voltage between Purple/White and Light Green/Black wires of vehicle speed sensor buffer. If AC voltage is not present, check for opens in Purple/White and Light Green/Black wires.

4) If wires are okay, replace vehicle speed buffer. If AC voltage is present between Purple/White and Light Green/Black wires, check for AC voltage between Light Green/Black and White wires.

5) If voltage is not present, replace vehicle speed buffer. If voltage is present, check for AC voltage between Yellow and Black/White wires. If voltage changes with rpm, replace digital ratio adapter.

Speedometer Does Not Work Properly (Commercial Van) – 1) Turn ignition on. Disconnect vehicle speed buffer. Connect voltmeter between Pink/Black wire and ground. If battery voltage is present, go to next step. If battery voltage is not present, check IGN fuse and replace if necessary. If fuse is okay, repair open in Pink/Black wire.

2) Connect voltmeter between Pink/Black and Black wires of buffer connector. If battery voltage is not present, repair open in Black wire between buffer connector and ground. If battery voltage is present, raise and support vehicle.

3) Start engine and shift transmission into drive. Connect DVOM between Dark Green/Yellow and Light Blue wires of speed buffer connector. If AC voltage is not present, check for open in Purple/White and Light Green/Black wires.

4) If wires are okay, replace speed sensor. If AC voltage is present, reconnect buffer connector. Connect DVOM between Light Blue/Black and Black wires of speed buffer connector. If AC voltage is still not present, replace speed sensor buffer.

5) If AC voltage is present, repair open in Light Blue/Black wire between speed buffer and instrument cluster. If wire is okay, replace instrument cluster.

VOLTMETER GAUGE

Voltmeter Not Accurate (Commercial Van) – Turn ignition on. Using voltmeter, measure voltage across battery terminals. If reading is the same as vehicle's voltmeter, gauge is okay. If reading is not the same

as vehicle's voltmeter, check instrument cluster connector Pink/Black and Black wires for open circuit. If circuits are okay, replace voltmeter.

Voltmeter Reads Below 9 Volts (Van) – 1) Check battery voltage. If battery voltage is greater than **9.6 volts**, check all voltmeter gauge connections. Ensure connections are clean and tight. If voltmeter gauge still reads below normal, apply 12 volts directly to voltmeter gauge.

2) If voltmeter does not respond correctly, replace voltmeter gauge. If battery voltage is below 9.6 volts, recharge battery. Observe voltmeter gauge while battery charger is working. Voltmeter gauge should read at least **12 volts**. Check charging system for proper operation.

Voltmeter Reads Too High (Van) – 1) If voltmeter gauge constantly reads in red area, check battery voltage. Check for overcharging condition. Repair charging system malfunction and recheck voltmeter gauge.

2) If battery voltage is normal, apply 12 volts directly to voltmeter gauge. If voltmeter does not respond correctly, replace voltmeter gauge.

WIPER SWITCH

See appropriate WIPER/WASHER SYSTEMS article.

REMOVAL & INSTALLATION
DIGITAL RATIO ADAPTER CONTROLLER (DRAC)

CAUTION: Static electricity can destroy integrated circuits within DRAC. Before servicing DRAC, ground yourself and the work area to discharge stored electricity.

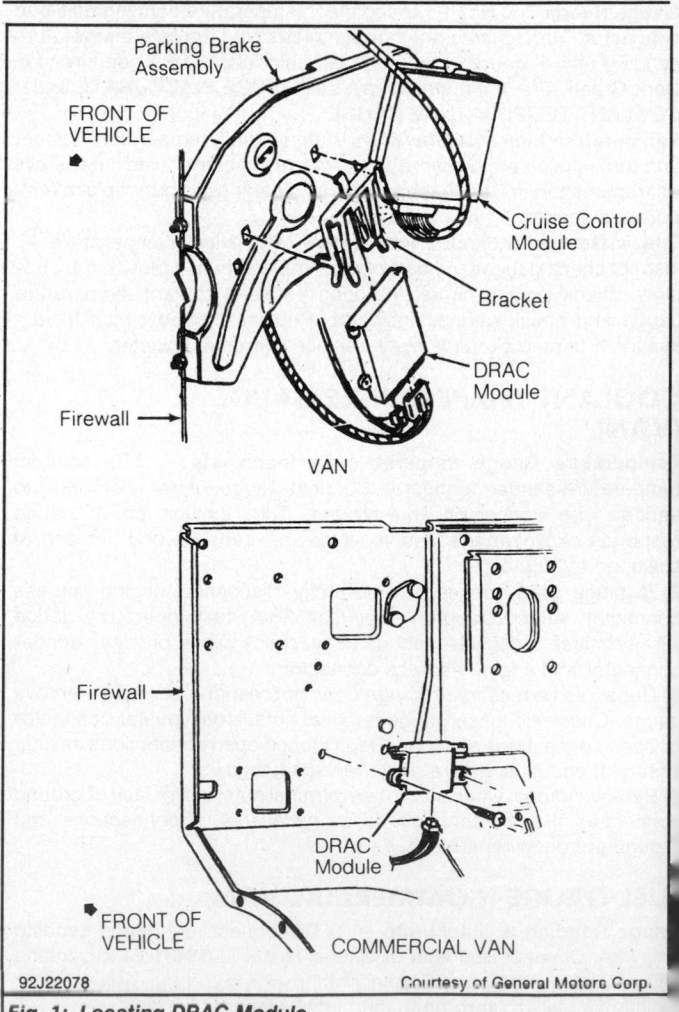

Fig. 1: Locating DRAC Module

Removal & Installation – On Commercial Van, DRAC module is located on left side of firewall in passenger compartment. On Van, DRAC module is located on parking brake assembly. To remove, disconnect negative battery terminal. Unplug instrument panel harness from DRAC. Remove DRAC retaining screws and remove DRAC. *See Fig. 1.* To install, reverse removal procedure.

GAUGES

Removal & Installation (Van) – Remove instrument cluster. See INSTRUMENT CLUSTER under REMOVAL & INSTALLATION. Remove instrument cluster lens and lens retainer. Remove printed circuit board. Remove nuts from gauge being serviced. Remove gauge(s). *See Fig. 2.* To install, reverse removal procedure.

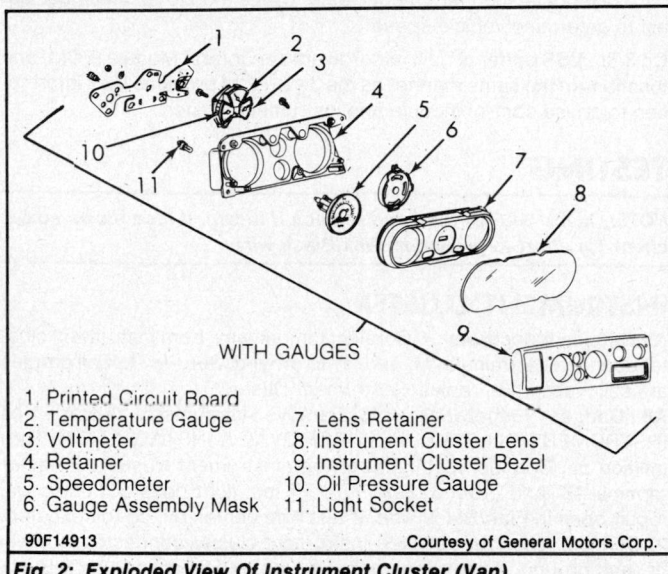

WITH GAUGES

1. Printed Circuit Board
2. Temperature Gauge
3. Voltmeter
4. Retainer
5. Speedometer
6. Gauge Assembly Mask
7. Lens Retainer
8. Instrument Cluster Lens
9. Instrument Cluster Bezel
10. Oil Pressure Gauge
11. Light Socket

90F14913   Courtesy of General Motors Corp.

Fig. 2: Exploded View Of Instrument Cluster (Van)

Removal & Installation (Commercial Van) – Remove instrument cluster. See INSTRUMENT CLUSTER under REMOVAL & INSTALLATION. Remove light socket assemblies. Remove printed circuit board. See PRINTED CIRCUIT under REMOVAL & INSTALLATION. Remove instrument cluster case retaining screws. Remove instrument cluster case from bezel. Remove screws from gauge being serviced. Remove gauge(s). To install, reverse removal procedure.

INSTRUMENT CLUSTER

Removal & Installation (Van) – **1)** Disconnect negative battery cable. Remove heater and fan control knobs. Remove interior light bezel. Remove headlight switch bezel. Remove instrument cluster bezel retaining screws and remove bezel. *See Fig. 2.*

2) Remove instrument cluster retaining screws. Pull top of cluster away from dash panel, and lift cluster out. Disconnect instrument cluster harness, and remove cluster. To install, reverse removal procedure.

Removal & Installation (Commercial Van) – Disconnect negative battery terminal. Disconnect instrument cluster harness connector. Remove instrument cluster bezel retaining screws, and remove bezel. Remove cluster. To install, reverse removal procedure.

PRINTED CIRCUIT

Removal & Installation – **1)** Remove instrument cluster. See INSTRUMENT CLUSTER under REMOVAL & INSTALLATION. Remove instrument cluster light sockets. Remove printed circuit board retaining screws.

2) Remove fuel, temperature and ammeter gauge terminal nuts. Remove printed circuit board. To install, reverse removal procedure. Ensure all gauge terminal nuts are tightened securely.

SPEEDOMETER

Removal & Installation (Van) – Remove instrument cluster. See INSTRUMENT CLUSTER under REMOVAL & INSTALLATION. Remove speedometer retaining screws. Remove 2 Torx head screws and rubber grommets securing speedometer assembly to cluster cover. Disconnect speedometer cable, and remove speedometer. To install, reverse removal procedure. *See Fig. 2.*

Removal & Installation (Commercial Van) – **1)** Remove instrument cluster. See INSTRUMENT CLUSTER under REMOVAL & INSTALLATION. Remove light sockets. Remove printed circuit retaining nuts. Remove printed circuit. Remove instrument cluster case retaining screws.

2) Remove instrument cluster case from bezel. Remove speedometer retaining screws. Disconnect speedometer cable, and remove speedometer. To install, reverse removal procedure.

WIRING DIAGRAMS

See appropriate chassis wiring diagram in WIRING DIAGRAM.

DESCRIPTION

INSTRUMENT PANELS

Standard mechanical instrument panels are designed to allow easy removal and installation of control switches, gauges, and illuminating bulbs. The instrument panels are equipped with gauges and analog speedometer, as well as warning lights.

OPERATION

ANTI-LOCK BRAKE WARNING LIGHT

The Electronic Brake Control Module (EBCM) monitors the anti-lock braking system. The anti-lock indicator lights for 3 seconds after ignition is turned to Run, Bulb Test or Start positions. If indicator light flashes, a problem is present but it will not immediately affect ABS system. Problem should be repaired as soon as possible. If indicator light remains on and does not flash, a problem is present and ABS system will not function properly.

BRAKE/PARK WARNING LIGHT SYSTEM

Warning system consists of a warning light on instrument cluster, a brake warning light switch (located on brake combination valve), and a parking brake engagement telltale switch. If brake hydraulic system malfunctions, or if parking brake is NOT fully released, warning light will illuminate. As a bulb check, light will illuminate when ignition is turned on and parking brake is released.

CHARGING SYSTEM WARNING LIGHT

Warning system consists of a battery symbol warning light on instrument cluster. One side of warning light bulb is connected to alternator field circuit, and other side of bulb is connected to ignition power circuit. If charging system malfunction is detected, warning light will illuminate. As a bulb check, light will illuminate when ignition is turned on.

COOLANT TEMPERATURE GAUGE

Coolant temperature gauge measures electrical resistance from coolant temperature sending unit mounted in cylinder head. As coolant temperature increases, the current flow through sending unit to gauge increases due to less resistance, causing gauge pointer to move toward HOT position.

FUEL GAUGE

Fuel gauge measures current flow from a fuel gauge sending unit with variable resistance. When fuel level in tank is high, fuel gauge sending unit resistance is high. Fuel gauge sending unit is located on, or near top of fuel tank.

OIL PRESSURE GAUGE

Oil pressure gauge measures electrical current from an oil pressure sending unit with variable resistance. Sending unit resistance is low when oil pressure is low, high when oil pressure is high. A change in resistance changes current flow through gauge electromagnetic coils, causing pointer to move from low to high. Sending unit is located at bottom left of engine block, on oil filter housing.

SERVICE ENGINE SOON LIGHT

This warning light is part of computer command control system, and will flash when a malfunction or trouble code(s) exists. As a bulb check, light will illuminate when ignition is turned on. If no problem exists, light will go out when engine is started.

SPEEDOMETER/ODOMETER

Integrated circuits control the needle-type air core speedometer and the stepper motor-driven odometer based upon Vehicle Speed Sensor (VSS) signal. On 3.1L engine, instrument cluster applies and monitors a battery voltage signal to the VSS buffer which received an AC voltage signal from VSS.

VSS buffer pulls monitored voltage signal to zero volts approximately 4000 times per mile. This pulsed signal is interpreted by the instrument cluster as vehicle speed. On 3.8L engine, VSS buffer is built into Powertrain Control Module (PCM) and functions in the same manner as the 3.1L engine.

VEHICLE SPEED SENSOR (VSS)

The VSS is a permanent magnet signal generator mounted in the transaxle. VSS produces an AC signal proportional to vehicle speed. This signal is amplified and converted to a DC signal by VSS buffer.

On 3.1L with externally-mounted VSS buffer, signal is transmitted to ECM, cruise control module and instrument cluster. The ECM, cruise control module and instrument cluster utilize monitored electrical signal to determine vehicle speed.

On 3.8L, VSS buffer is built into Powertrain Control Module (PCM) and functions in the same manner as the 3.1L. PCM provides VSS information to cruise control module and instrument cluster.

TESTING

NOTE: Check GAGES fuse and replace if blown. If fuse blows again, check for short to ground in Pink/Black wire.

INSTRUMENT CLUSTER

All Gauges Inaccurate – Connect jumper wire from instrument cluster connector terminals "M" and "T" to ground. *See Fig. 1.* If all gauges are still inaccurate, replace instrument cluster.

All Gauges Inoperative – 1) Remove instrument cluster. See INSTRUMENT CLUSTER under REMOVAL & INSTALLATION. Turn ignition on. Connect test light between instrument cluster connector terminal "Z" and ground. *See Fig. 1.* If test light does not come on, repair open in Pink/Black wire. If test light comes on, go to next step.
2) Connect test light between instrument cluster connector terminal "K" and ground. If light does not come on, repair open in Pink/Black wire. If test light comes on, connect test light between connector terminals "K" and "M". If test light does not comes on, repair open in Black/White wire. If test light comes on, go to next step.
3) Connect test light between instrument cluster connector terminals "K" and "T". If light does not come on, repair open in Black wire. If test light comes on, check for poor connections at instrument cluster. If connections are okay, replace instrument cluster.
Erratic Speedometer Or Instrument Cluster – Lumina APV models equipped with the 3.8L engines may experience intermittent speedometer or cluster operation. This problem is caused by a loose ground connection located under front ignition coil pack. Ensure nut is tightened to **12 ft. lbs. (16 N.m)**.

ANTI-LOCK BRAKE WARNING LIGHT

Indicator On Constantly – 1) Remove ABS light driver module circuit board. Light driver module is located behind park brake cable bracket. Turn ignition on. If ABS indicator light is on, repair short to ground in Purple wire circuit, connector terminal "N".
2) If ABS indicator light did not come on, use test light to back probe ABS light driver module terminal "B" to ground. If test light does not come on, repair open in Pink/Black wire circuit. If test light comes on, turn ignition off.
3) Reinstall ABS light driver module circuit board. Disconnect electronic brake control module connector C1. Using a fused jumper, connect terminal No. 23 to ground. Turn ignition on. If indicator light comes on, check for poor connection at ABS light driver module terminal "C" or for open in Dark Blue wire circuit.
4) If indicator light does not come on, check fused jumper. If fused jumper is blown, repair short in Dark Blue wire circuit. If fused jumper is not blown, check for poor connection at EBCM. If connection okay, replace EBCM.
Indicator Inoperative – 1) Remove ABS light driver module circuit board. Using a fused jumper, connect driver module terminal "E" to ground. Turn ignition on. If ABS indicator light does not come, che

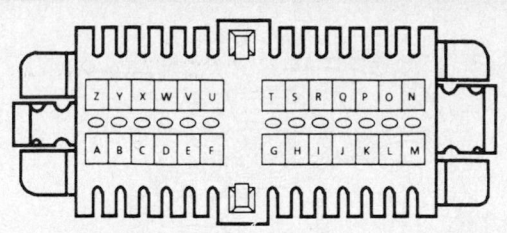

CAVITY	WIRE COLOR	CKT	DESCRIPTION	PAGE
A	DK GRN/WHT	135	COOLANT TEMPERATURE SIGNAL	8A-81-1
B	BRN/WHT	419	"SERVICE ENGINE SOON" INDICATOR	8A-20-4, 8A-21-2
D	LT GRN	11	HI BEAM INDICATOR (WITHOUT DRL) (WITH DRL)	8A-100-0 8A-104-1
E	TAN/WHT	33	"BRAKE" INDICATOR	8A-41-0
G	LT BLU	14	LEFT TURN INDICATOR	8A-110-4
H	YEL	237	FASTEN BELTS INDICATOR	8A-76-0
I	BLK/ORN	158	"GATE AJAR" INDICATOR	8A-81-1
J	DK BLU	15	RIGHT TURN INDICATOR	8A 110 4
K	PNK/BLK	39	IGNITION 1 – HOT IN RUN, BULB TEST OR START	8A-81-0, 8A-81-1
L	DK GRN	389	VEHICLE SPEED INPUT	8A-33-0, 1
M	BLK/WHT	450	GROUND	8A-81-0
N	PPL	865	"ANTI-LOCK" INDICATOR	8A-44-0
U	BRN	25	CHARGE INDICATOR CONTROL	8A-30-0
S	GRY	8	INSTRUMENT CLUSTER DIMMABLE BACKLIGHTING	8A-117-0
T	BLK	151	GROUND	8A-81-0
X	TAN	31	OIL PRESSURE SIGNAL	8A-81-0
Y	PPL	30	FUEL LEVEL SIGNAL	8A-81-0
Z	PNK/BLK	39	IGNITION 1 – HOT IN RUN, BULB TEST OR START	8A-81-0, 8A-81-1

92I22077   Courtesy of General Motors Corp.

Fig. 1: Identifying Instrument Cluster Connector Terminals

...or poor connection at terminal "B" of connector C215 located behind instrument panel grommet or terminal "N" of cluster connector. Also ...check for open in Purple wire circuit or for faulty indicator bulb. If connector, terminal, wiring and bulb are okay, replace instrument cluster.
...If ABS indicator light comes on, connect fused jumper between ABS ...ght driver module terminals "E" and "D". If indicator light does not ...ome on, repair open in Black wire circuit.
...If indicator light comes on, remove fused jumper. Using test light, ...ck probe driver module terminal "B" to ground. If test light does not

come on, check for poor connection at terminal "A" of connector C215 located behind instrument panel grommet. If connection is okay, repair open in Pink/Black wire circuit.
4) If test light comes on, turn ignition off. Disconnect electronic brake control module connector C1. Using test light, back probe between ABS light driver module terminals "B" and "C". Turn ignition on. If test light comes on, repair short to ground in Dark Blue wire circuit.
5) If test light does not come on, reinstall ABS light driver module circuit board. If ABS indicator light does not come, replace ABS light driver module. If ABS indicator light comes on, check for poor connection at EBCM. If connections are okay, replace EBCM.

BRAKE WARNING SYSTEM

If warning light does not illuminate with ignition switch on, engine off and parking brake NOT applied, check for burnt out light bulb. If bulb is okay, check for open in circuit. Remove wire connector from differential pressure switch on brake combination valve. Touch connector to ground. If warning light DOES NOT illuminate, repair open in circuit. If light illuminates, circuit is okay. Replace differential pressure switch.

COOLANT TEMPERATURE GAUGE

Gauge Inaccurate – 1) Disconnect coolant temperature sender. Use Signal Generator Instrument Cluster Tester (J-33431-B) to test gauge. Check coolant temperature gauge readings. See COOLANT TEMPERATURE GAUGE SPECIFICATIONS table.

COOLANT TEMPERATURE GAUGE SPECIFICATIONS

Temperature	Ohms
100°F (40°C)	1365
220°F (100°C)	92
260°F (125°C)	55

2) If gauge indicates correctly, replace sending unit. If gauge does not indicate correctly, check for high resistance in Dark Green/White wire between gauge and sender. If high resistance is not present, replace instrument cluster.

FUEL GAUGE

Gauge Inoperative Or Inaccurate – 1) Turn ignition on. If gauge does not read FULL at all times, go to step **4)**. If gauge reads FULL at all times, disconnect fuel sender assembly connector. Connect test light between battery positive and connector terminal "D" (Black wire). If test light comes on, go to next step. If test light does not come on, check for poor connection at fuel sender or for open in Black wire circuit.
2) Connect a fused jumper wire between fuel sender assembly connector terminal "B" (Purple wire) and ground. If fuel gauge reads EMPTY, check for poor connection at fuel sender assembly connector. If fuel sender assembly connection is okay, replace fuel lever meter.
3) If fuel gauge does not read EMPTY, check for poor connections at cluster connector or fuel sender connector or for open in Purple wire between fuel sender assembly and instrument cluster. If wire is okay, replace fuel gauge.
4) Does gauge read EMPTY at all times? If gauge does not read EMPTY at all times, go to step **6)**. If gauge reads EMPTY at all times, disconnect fuel sender assembly connector at fuel tank. If gauge now reads FULL, replace fuel level meter.
5) If gauge does not read FULL, disconnect instrument cluster connector. Connect test light between terminals "Y" (Purple wire) and "Z" (Pink/Black). See Fig. 1. If test light comes on, repair short to ground in Purple wire. If test light does not come on, replace fuel gauge.
6) If gauge does not read EMPTY at all times, note fuel level as indicated by fuel gauge. Disconnect instrument cluster connector. Using a Digital Volt Ohm Meter (DVOM), measure resistance at cluster connector terminal "Y" (Purple wire) to ground.
7) Compare previously noted fuel level indicated by fuel gauge and resistance reading from DVOM. See FUEL GAUGE SENDING UNIT

RESISTANCE table. If fuel level and resistance are close to specification, replace fuel gauge. If fuel level and resistance are not close to specification, replace fuel level meter.

FUEL GAUGE SENDING UNIT RESISTANCE

Position	Ohms
Empty	1
1/4 Full	33
1/2 Full	50
3/4 Full	83
Full	88

OIL PRESSURE GAUGE

Gauge Reads Low or No Pressure – Check oil level and add if necessary. If oil level was low and gauge still reads low or no pressure, disconnect oil pressure sender connector. If gauge indicates high pressure, replace oil pressure sender. If gauge does not indicate high pressure, check for short to ground in Tan wire circuit. If wire is okay, replace oil pressure gauge.

Gauge Reads High Pressure – Disconnect lead at sending unit. Using voltmeter, measure voltage between terminal "A" (Tan wire) and ground. If battery voltage is not present, check for poor connection at cluster connector or for open in Tan wire circuit. If wire is okay, replace oil pressure gauge. If battery voltage is present, check connection at oil pressure sending unit. If connection is okay, replace oil pressure sending unit.

SPEEDOMETER/ODOMETER

Speedometer Is Inoperative Or Inaccurate (3.8L Engine) – 1) If ECM Code 24 is set, proceed to SELF-DIAGNOSTICS – GASOLINE article in ENGINE PERFORMANCE. If ECM Code 24 is not set, go to next step.

2) Disconnect Powertrain Control Module (PCM) connector C3 from below right side of instrument panel, behind convenience center. Connect Signal Generator Instrument Panel Tester (J-33431-B) to PCM connector C3 terminal D7 (Dark Green wire). Set tester to 54 MPH. Turn ignition on. If speedometer does not reads 54 MPH, go to next step. If speedometer reads 54 MPH, check for poor connection at PCM connector C3. If connection is okay, replace PCM.

3) If speedometer does not read 54 MPH, check for open or short circuit in Dark Green wire or for poor connection at instrument cluster. If wire and connection are okay, replace speedometer.

Speedometer Is Inoperative Or Inaccurate (3.1L Engine) – 1) If ECM Code 24 is set, proceed to SPEEDOMETER IS INACCURATE & ECM CODE 24 IS SET test under SPEEDOMETER/ODOMETER. If ECM Code 24 is not set, go to next step.

2) Raise and support vehicle. Disconnect Vehicle Speed Sensor (VSS) from top of transaxle. Connect Signal Generator Instrument Panel Tester (J-33431-B) to VSS connector. Set tester to 54 MPH. Turn ignition on. If speedometer does not reads 6 MPH, go to next step. If speedometer reads 6 MPH, check for poor connection at VSS. If connection is okay, replace VSS.

3) Turn ignition off. Disconnect tester from VSS. Disconnect VSS buffer located behind instrument panel, above convenience center. See Fig. 2. Connect Signal Generator Instrument Panel Tester (J-33431-B) to terminal "F" (Dark Green wire) of VSS buffer connector C1. See Fig. 2.

4) Set tester to 54 MPH. Turn ignition on. If speedometer reads 54 MPH, check for poor connection at VSS buffer. If connection is okay, replace VSS buffer. If speedometer does not read 54 MPH, check for open or short circuit in Dark Green wire or for poor connection at instrument cluster. If wire and connection are okay, replace speedometer.

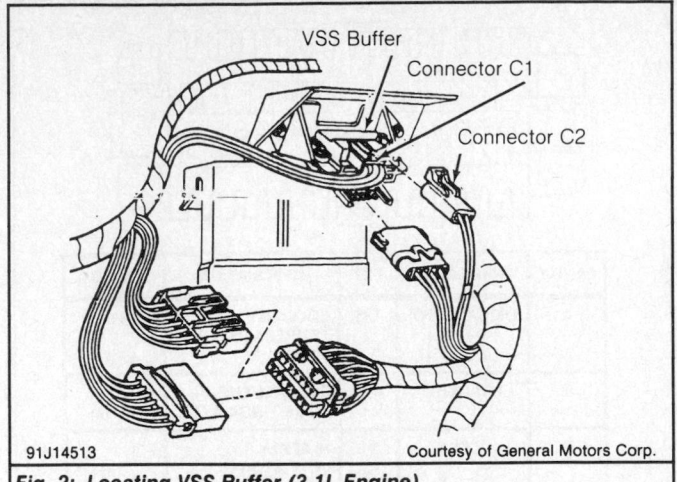

91J14513　　　　　Courtesy of General Motors Corp.

Fig. 2: Locating VSS Buffer (3.1L Engine)

Speedometer Is Inaccurate & ECM Code 24 Is Set (3.1L Engine) – 1) Turn ignition on. Connect voltmeter between terminal "A" (Pink/White wire) of VSS buffer connector C1 and ground. See Fig. 2. If battery voltage is present, go to next step. If battery voltage is not present, repair open in Pink/White wire.

2) Connect voltmeter between terminals "A" (Pink/White wire) and "B" (Black wire) of VSS buffer connector C1. If battery voltage is present, go to next step. If battery voltage is not present, repair open in Black wire.

3) Turn ignition on. Place transaxle in Neutral. Raise and support front wheels. Set voltmeter to AC scale. Measure voltage between terminals "A" (Yellow wire) and "C" (Purple wire) of VSS buffer connector C2 while rotating front wheels by hand. See Fig. 2. If voltage varies between zero and one volt, check for poor connections at VSS buffer connectors C1 and C2. If connections are okay, replace VSS buffer. If voltage remains zero, check for open in Yellow or Purple wire or for poor connections at VSS buffer connector C2. If wire and connections are okay, replace VSS.

WIPER SWITCH

See appropriate WIPER/WASHER SYSTEMS article.

REMOVAL & INSTALLATION

WARNING: When battery is disconnected, vehicle computer and memory systems may lose memory data. Driveability problems may exist until computer systems have completed a relearn cycle. See COMPUTER RELEARN PROCEDURES article in GENERAL INFORMATION before disconnecting battery.

INSTRUMENT CLUSTER

Removal & Installation – 1) Disconnect negative battery cable. Remove left and right switch pods by grasping in hand and pulling away from cluster. After pulling switch pods away from cluster, remove spring clips.

2) Disconnect pod electrical connectors. Remove 2 screws attaching trim to lower trim pad. Lift cluster housing up while pulling rearward to release tabs from slots in housing. Remove cluster. To install, reverse removal procedure.

DESCRIPTION

Instrument cluster is equipped with analog (needle-type) speedometer and gauges. Except for indicator lights, instrument cluster is not serviceable. If speedometer, gauges or printed circuit is faulty, entire cluster must be replaced.

NOTE: Manufacturer's dealer may be able to service cluster.

ELECTRICAL COMPONENT LOCATIONS

Component	Location
ABS Light Driver Module	Behind Parking Brake Cable Bracket.
Coolant Temp. Sending Unit	
3.1L	Below Ignition Coil, On End Of Cylinder Head. *See Fig. 3.*
3.8L	Between Throttle Body And Right Cylinder Head.
Electronic Brake Control Module (EBCM)	Behind Instrument Panel, To Left Of Brake Pedal Bracket.
Electronic Control Module (ECM – 3.1L)	Behind Right End Of Instrument Panel, Forward Of Convenience Center.
Fuse Block	Behind Left End Of Instrument Panel.
Oil Pressure Sending Unit	
3.1L	On Left Side Of Cylinder Block, Near Oil Filter.
3.8L	At Front Of Engine, Near Oil Filter.
Parking Brake Switch	On Parking Brake Bracket.
Powertrain Control Module (PCM – 3.8L)	Behind Right End Of Instrument Panel, Forward Of Convenience Center.
Tachometer Signal Filter	On Ignition Coil Bracket. *See Fig. 3.*
Turn Signal Flasher	On Instrument Panel Lower Trim Pad, To Right Of Steering Column.
Vehicle Speed Sensor (VSS)	On Transaxle, At End Of Right Extension Housing.
VSS Buffer (3.1L)	Behind Right End Of Instrument Panel, Above Convenience Center.

OPERATION

GAUGES

Coolant Temperature – Gauge responds to resistance of coolant temperature sending unit. Resistance of sending unit decreases as coolant temperature increases.

Fuel – Gauge responds to resistance of sending unit in fuel tank. Resistance of sending unit decreases as volume of fuel in tank decreases.

Oil Pressure – Gauge responds to resistance of oil pressure sending unit. When oil pressure is low, resistance is low. When oil pressure is high, resistance is about 90 ohms.

Tachometer – Tachometer receives an AC voltage signal from the ignition coil (3.1L) or computer controlled coil ignition module (3.8L). On 3.1L, signal is sent to tachometer signal filter, then to tachometer. *See Fig. 3.* On 3.8L, signal is sent directly to tachometer. On all vehicles, tachometer converts AC signal and displays it as engine speed.

Voltmeter – Voltmeter indicates battery voltage when engine is off, and charging system voltage when engine is running.

INDICATOR LIGHTS

ABS – Electronic Brake Control Module (EBCM) monitors Anti-Lock Brake System (ABS). If EBCM detects a fault in ABS, it signals an ABS light driver module which grounds the ABS light. EBCM also signals ABS light driver module to ground light for 3 seconds after ignition is turned on. If no faults exist, light will go out. If a fault exists, light will stay on solid or will flash.

BRAKE – Light comes on under the following conditions:

- Ignition switch is in BULB TEST or START position
- Parking brake switch is closed (indicates parking brake is on)
- Brake fluid level switch is closed (indicates reservoir is low)
- ECBM grounds light (indicates brake system problem exists).

GATE AJAR – When liftgate is open, left and right liftgate jamb switches are closed. These switches ground the GATE AJAR light.

Low Fuel – Solid state controller in instrument cluster turns on light when volume in fuel tank is about 3 gallons or less. Light also comes on with ignition on and engine off.

SERVICE ENGINE SOON – ECM (3.1L) or PCM (3.8L) provides ground for light. Light comes on when ignition is turned on, then goes out when engine is started if no problems exist in engine control system. If a problem exists, light stays on.

SPEEDOMETER/ODOMETER

Vehicle Speed Sensor (VSS) produces an AC signal proportional to transaxle rotation speed. Signal is sent to VSS buffer (3.1L) or PCM (3.8L) where it is conditioned for use by speedometer. Based on signals, integrated circuit in speedometer controls the speedometer needle and the stepper motor-driven odometer.

TESTING

NOTE: Ensure GAGES and IGN fuses are okay before testing.

INSTRUMENT CLUSTER

All Gauges Erratic (3.8L) – Check for poor connection at ground wire stud under coil pack. *See Fig. 1.* Tighten stud nut to 12 ft. lbs. (16 N.m). If ground wire connection is okay, check for poor connection at instrument panel connector. If instrument panel connector is okay, replace instrument cluster.

All Gauges Inaccurate – Connect jumper wire from ground to instrument cluster connector terminals C7, C8 and D8. *See Fig. 2.* If all gauges are accurate, repair instrument cluster ground circuits. If all gauges are still inaccurate, replace instrument cluster.

All Gauges Inoperative – 1) Remove instrument cluster. Turn ignition switch to RUN position. Connect test light between ground and instrument cluster connector terminal D10. *See Fig. 2.* If test light does not come on, repair open in Pink/White wire to connector terminal D10.

2) If test light comes on, connect test light between ground and connector terminal C5. If test light does not come on, repair open in Pink/Black wire to connector terminal C5. If test light comes on, connect test light between ground and connector terminal D5.

3) If test light does not come on, repair open in Pink/Black wire to connector terminal D5. If test light comes on, connect test light between connector terminals C7 and D10. If test light does not come on, repair open in Black wire to connector terminal C7.

4) If test light comes on, connect test light between connector terminals C8 and D10. If test light does not come on, repair open in Black wire to connector terminal C8. If test light comes on, connect test light between connector terminals D8 and D10.

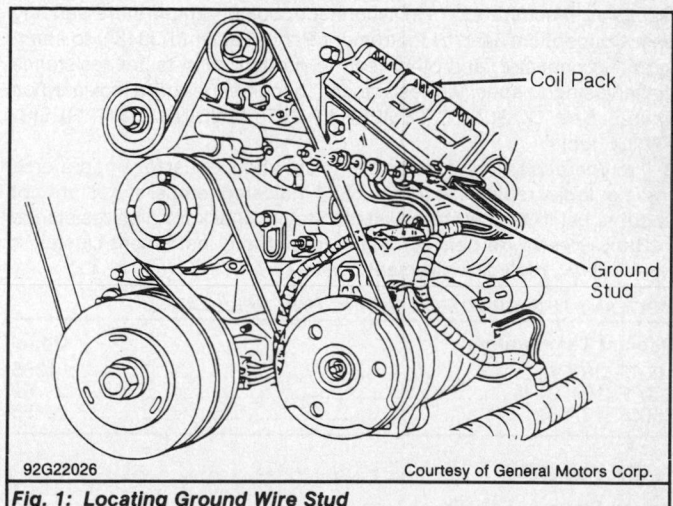

92G22026   Courtesy of General Motors Corp.

Fig. 1: Locating Ground Wire Stud

5) If test light does not come on, repair open in Black wire to connector terminal D8. If test light comes on, check for poor connection at instrument cluster connector. If connection is okay, replace instrument cluster.

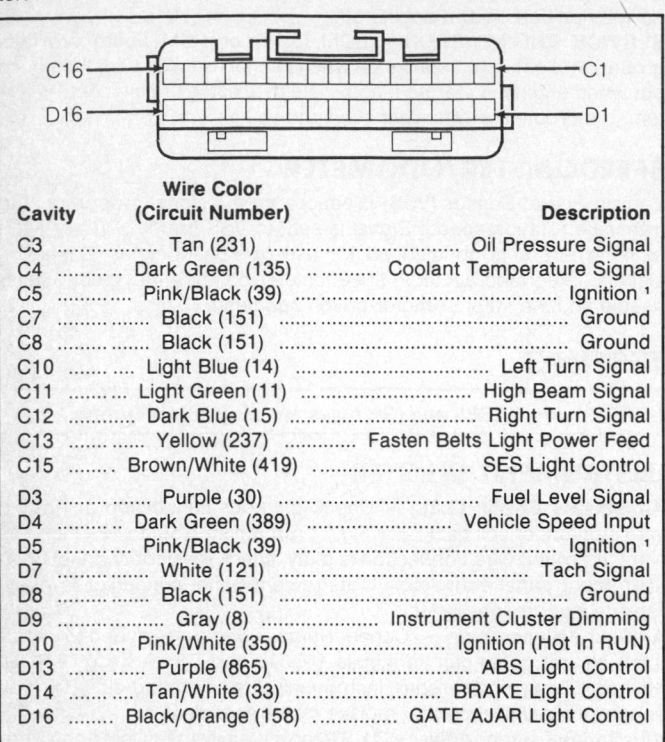

Cavity	Wire Color (Circuit Number)	Description
C3	Tan (231)	Oil Pressure Signal
C4	Dark Green (135)	Coolant Temperature Signal
C5	Pink/Black (39)	Ignition [1]
C7	Black (151)	Ground
C8	Black (151)	Ground
C10	Light Blue (14)	Left Turn Signal
C11	Light Green (11)	High Beam Signal
C12	Dark Blue (15)	Right Turn Signal
C13	Yellow (237)	Fasten Belts Light Power Feed
C15	Brown/White (419)	SES Light Control
D3	Purple (30)	Fuel Level Signal
D4	Dark Green (389)	Vehicle Speed Input
D5	Pink/Black (39)	Ignition [1]
D7	White (121)	Tach Signal
D8	Black (151)	Ground
D9	Gray (8)	Instrument Cluster Dimming
D10	Pink/White (350)	Ignition (Hot In RUN)
D13	Purple (865)	ABS Light Control
D14	Tan/White (33)	BRAKE Light Control
D16	Black/Orange (158)	GATE AJAR Light Control

[1] – Hot in RUN, BULB TEST and START position.

92122036 — Courtesy of General Motors Corp.

Fig. 2: Identifying Instrument Cluster Connector Terminals

COOLANT TEMPERATURE GAUGE

Gauge Reads High – Turn ignition switch to RUN position. Disconnect coolant temperature sending unit connector. If gauge reads low, replace sending unit. If gauge still reads high, check for short to ground in Dark Green wire between sending unit and instrument cluster. If wire is okay, replace instrument cluster.

Gauge Reads Low – Disconnect coolant temperature sending unit. Connect fused jumper wire between ground and sending unit connector. Turn ignition switch to RUN position. If gauge reads high, replace sending unit. If gauge still reads low, check for open in Dark Green wire between sending unit and instrument cluster. If wire is okay, replace instrument cluster.

Gauge Is Inaccurate – **1)** Disconnect coolant temperature sending unit. Connect one lead of Instrument Panel Tester (J-33431) to sending unit connector, and other lead to ground. With tester resistance dial adjusted to specified resistance, check temperature indicated on gauge. See COOLANT TEMPERATURE SENDING UNIT RESISTANCE table.

2) If temperatures indicated on gauge are about equal to temperatures listed in table, replace sending unit. If indicated temperatures are not about equal to temperatures listed in table, check for high resistance in Dark Green wire between sending unit and instrument cluster. If wire is okay, replace instrument cluster.

COOLANT TEMPERATURE SENDING UNIT RESISTANCE

Coolant Temperature	Ohms
100°F (38°C)	1365
220°F (104°C)	92
260°F (127°C)	55

FUEL GAUGE

Gauge Stays At EMPTY – Turn ignition switch to RUN position with engine off. Disconnect fuel gauge sending unit connector. If gauge reads FULL, replace sending unit. If gauge stays at EMPTY, disconnect instrument cluster connector. Connect test light between instrument cluster connector terminals D3 and D10. See Fig. 2. If test light comes on, repair short to ground in Purple wire. If test light does not come on, replace instrument cluster.

Gauge Stays At FULL – **1)** Turn ignition switch to RUN position with engine off. Disconnect fuel gauge sending unit connector. Connect test light between battery positive terminal and Black wire terminal of sending unit connector. If test light does not come on, repair open in Black wire.

2) If test light comes on, connect a fused jumper wire between ground and Purple wire terminal of sending unit connector. If gauge reads EMPTY, go to next step. If gauge does not read EMPTY, check for open in Purple wire between sending unit and instrument cluster. If wire is okay, replace instrument cluster.

3) If gauge reads EMPTY, check for poor connection at sending unit connector. If connector is okay, replace sending unit.

Gauge Is Inaccurate – Note fuel level indicated by gauge. Turn ignition off. Disconnect instrument cluster connector. Measure resistance between ground and Purple wire terminal of fuel gauge sending unit connector. If resistance is as specified in FUEL GAUGE SENDING UNIT RESISTANCE table, replace instrument cluster. If resistance is not as specified, replace fuel gauge sending unit.

FUEL GAUGE SENDING UNIT RESISTANCE

Position	Ohms
Empty	1
1/4 Tank	33
1/2 Tank	50
3/4 Tank	83
Full	88

INDICATOR LIGHTS

NOTE: Clear ABS codes before testing ABS light. See appropriate ANTI-LOCK article in BRAKES. Backprobe all wire terminals to prevent terminal damage.

ABS Light Always On – **1)** Disconnect ABS light driver module connector. Turn ignition switch to RUN position. If ABS light is on, repair short to ground in Purple wire between instrument cluster and ABS light driver module. If ABS light is off, check voltage at Pink/Black wire terminal of ABS light driver module connector.

2) If no voltage is present, repair open in Pink/Black wire between fuse and ABS light driver module. If battery voltage is present, turn off ignition. Connect ABS light driver module connector. Disconnect EBCM 24-cavity connector. Connect fused jumper wire between ground and Dark Blue wire terminal of EBCM 24-cavity connector.

3) Turn ignition switch to RUN position. If ABS light does not come on, go to next step. If ABS light comes on, check for open in Dark Blue wire between EBCM and ABS light driver module. If wire is okay, replace ABS light driver module.

4) If fuse in jumper wire blew, repair short to battery voltage in Dark Blue wire. If fuse in jumper wire did not blow, check for poor connection at Dark Blue wire terminal of EBCM connector. If connection is okay, replace EBCM.

ABS Light Inoperative – **1)** Disconnect ABS light driver module connector. Connect fused jumper wire between ground and Purple wire terminal of ABS light driver module connector. Turn ignition switch to RUN position.

2) If ABS light comes on, go to next step. If ABS light does not come on, check for open in Purple wire between instrument cluster and ABS light driver module. If wire is okay, check ABS light bulb. If bulb is okay, replace instrument cluster.

3) Connect fused jumper wire between Purple and Black wire terminals of ABS light driver module connector. If ABS light does not come on, repair open in Black wire between ABS light driver module and ground. If ABS light comes on, disconnect fused jumper wire.

4) Connect test light between ground and Pink/Black wire terminal of ABS light driver module connector. If test light does not come on, repair open in Pink/Black wire between fuse and ABS light driver module. If test light comes on, turn ignition off.

5) Disconnect EBCM 24-cavity connector. Connect test light between Pink/Black and Dark Blue wire terminals of ABS light driver module. Turn ignition switch to RUN position. If test light comes on, repair short to ground in Dark Blue wire between ABS light driver module and EBCM.

6) If test light does not come on, connect ABS light driver module connector. If ABS light does not come on, replace ABS light driver module. If ABS light comes on, check for poor connection at EBCM connector. If connection is okay, replace EBCM.

BRAKE Light Inoperative – 1) Turn ignition switch to RUN position. Connect test light between ground and instrument cluster connector terminal D5. See Fig. 2. If test light does not come on, repair open in Pink/Black wire between fuse and instrument cluster.

2) If test light comes on, connect test light between ground and instrument cluster connector terminal C5. If test light does not come on, repair open in Pink/Black wire between fuse and instrument cluster. If test light comes on, connect fused jumper wire between ground and instrument cluster connector terminal D14.

3) If BRAKE light comes on, repair open in Tan/White wire between instrument cluster and splice. If BRAKE light does not come on, check BRAKE light bulb. If bulb is okay, replace instrument cluster.

BRAKE Light Does Not Come On With Ignition On – 1) Turn ignition switch to RUN position. Apply parking brake. If BRAKE light does not come on, go to BRAKE LIGHT INOPERATIVE. If BRAKE light comes on, connect test light between battery positive terminal and Tan/White wire terminal of Black ignition switch connector with ignition switch in BULB TEST position (just past RUN position).

2) If test light comes on, repair open in Tan/White wire between instrument cluster and ignition switch. If test light does not come on, check for poor connection at Tan/White wire terminal of Black ignition switch connector. If connection is okay, replace ignition switch.

BRAKE Light Does Not Come On With Parking Brake Applied – 1) Turn ignition switch to BULB TEST position (just past RUN position). If BRAKE light does not come on, go to BRAKE LIGHT INOPERATIVE. If BRAKE light comes on, disconnect parking brake switch connector.

2) Connect fused jumper between ground and parking brake switch connector. Turn ignition switch to RUN position. If BRAKE light does not come on, repair open in Tan/White wire between parking brake switch and splice. If BRAKE light comes on, check for poor connection at parking brake switch connector. If connection is okay, replace parking brake switch.

BRAKE Light Stays On With Ignition On & Parking Brake Released – 1) Turn ignition switch to RUN position. Release parking brake. Disconnect brake fluid level switch connector. If BRAKE light is on, go to next step. If BRAKE light is off, check brake fluid level. If brake fluid level is okay, replace brake fluid level switch.

2) Disconnect parking brake switch connector. If BRAKE light is off, replace parking brake switch. If BRAKE light is on, repair short to ground in Tan/White wire between instrument cluster and the following components: parking brake switch, ignition switch, EBCM and brake fluid level switch.

Low Fuel Light Inoperative Or Stays On, Fuel Gauge Okay – Replace instrument cluster.

SERVICE ENGINE SOON Light Inoperative – Check for open in Brown/White wire, burned bulb or faulty instrument cluster. If these components are okay, problem exists in engine control system. See appropriate SELF-DIAGNOSTICS article in ENGINE PERFORMANCE.

SERVICE ENGINE SOON Light Stays On – Check for short to battery in Brown/White wire. If wire is okay, problem exists in engine control system. See appropriate SELF-DIAGNOSTICS article in ENGINE PERFORMANCE.

OIL PRESSURE GAUGE

Gauge Reads Low Or No Pressure – Turn ignition switch to RUN position with engine off. Disconnect oil pressure sending unit connector. If gauge reads high, replace sending unit. If gauge still reads low, check for short to ground in Tan wire. If wire is okay, replace instrument cluster.

Gauge Reads High – 1) Turn ignition switch to RUN position with engine off. Check voltage between ground and Tan wire terminal of oil pressure sending unit connector. If battery voltage is present, go to next step. If battery voltage is not present, check for open in Tan wire. If wire is okay, replace instrument cluster.

2) Check for poor connection at sending unit. If connection is okay, replace sending unit.

Gauge Is Inaccurate – Turn ignition off. Disconnect instrument cluster connector. Measure resistance between ground and instrument cluster connector terminal C3. If resistance is about one ohm, replace instrument cluster. If resistance is not about one ohm, replace sending unit.

SPEEDOMETER/ODOMETER

Speedometer Inoperative Or Inaccurate, No ECM Code 24 (3.1L) – 1) Raise and support vehicle. Disconnect VSS connector. Connect Instrument Panel Tester (J 33431-B) to VSS connector. Set tester to 54 MPH. Turn ignition switch to RUN position. If speedometer does not display 6 MPH, go to next step. If speedometer displays 6 MPH, check for poor connection at VSS. If connection is okay, replace VSS.

2) Turn ignition off. Disconnect tester from VSS. Disconnect VSS buffer 6-cavity connector. Connect tester to Dark Green wire terminal of VSS buffer 6-cavity connector. Set tester to 54 MPH. Turn ignition switch to RUN position.

3) If speedometer does not display 54 MPH, go to next step. If speedometer displays 54 MPH, check for poor connection at VSS buffer 6-cavity connector. If connection is okay, replace VSS buffer.

4) Check for open, short to ground or short to battery voltage in Dark Green wire, or poor connection at instrument cluster connector. If wire and connector are okay, replace instrument cluster.

Speedometer Inaccurate & ECM Code 24 Is Set (3.1L) – 1) Turn ignition switch to RUN position. Check voltage at Pink/White wire terminal of VSS buffer 6-cavity connector. If battery voltage is not present, repair open in Pink/White wire between fuse block and VSS buffer.

2) If battery voltage is present, check voltage between Pink/White and Black wire terminals of VSS buffer 6-cavity connector. If battery voltage is not present, repair open in Black wire between VSS buffer and ground.

3) If battery voltage is present, turn ignition switch to RUN position. Shift transaxle into Neutral. Raise and support vehicle with drive wheels off of ground. Measure AC voltage between Purple and Yellow wire terminals of VSS buffer 2-cavity connector while rotating drive wheels by hand.

4) If constant zero volts is present, go to next step. If voltage varies between zero and one volt, check for poor connection at VSS buffer connectors. If connections are okay, replace VSS buffer.

5) If voltage remains at zero volts, check for open in Yellow or Purple wire between VSS and VSS buffer, or missing or damaged VSS connector seal. If wires and seal are okay, replace VSS.

Speedometer Inoperative Or Inaccurate (3.8L) – 1) If PCM Code 24 is set, see appropriate SELF-DIAGNOSTICS article in ENGINE PERFORMANCE. If PCM Code 24 is not set, disconnect Orange (or Green) 32-cavity connector from PCM. Connect Instrument Panel Tester (J 33431-B) to terminal D7 (Dark Green wire) of PCM connector.

2) Set tester to 54 MPH. Turn ignition switch to RUN position. If speedometer does not indicate 54 MPH, go to next step. If speedometer indicates 54 MPH, check for poor connection at PCM connector. If connection is okay, replace PCM.

3) Check for open, short to ground or short to voltage in Dark Green wire, or poor connection at instrument cluster connector. If wire and connection are okay, replace instrument cluster.

TACHOMETER

NOTE: Two White wires terminate at tachometer signal filter connector. Terminal identification information for this connector is not available from manufacturer.

Tachometer Is Inoperative Or Inaccurate (3.1L) – 1) Disconnect tachometer signal filter connector. See Fig. 3. Turn ignition switch to RUN position. Check voltage between ground and terminal "A" of tachometer signal filter connector. If battery voltage is present, go to next step. If battery voltage is not present, check for open in White wire between tachometer signal filter and ignition coil. If wire is okay, replace ignition coil.

2) Turn ignition off. Connect tachometer signal filter connector. Disconnect instrument cluster connector. Turn ignition switch to RUN position. Measure voltage between ground and instrument cluster connector terminal D10. *See Fig. 2*. If battery voltage is not present, check for open circuit in Pink/White wire.

3) If battery voltage is present, measure voltage between ground and instrument cluster connector terminal D7. If battery voltage is present, go to next step. If battery voltage is not present, check for open in White wire between tachometer signal filter and instrument cluster. If White wire is okay, replace tachometer signal filter.

4) Check for poor connection at instrument cluster connector. If connector is okay, check printed circuit board. If printed circuit board is okay, replace tachometer. If printed circuit board is faulty, replace instrument cluster.

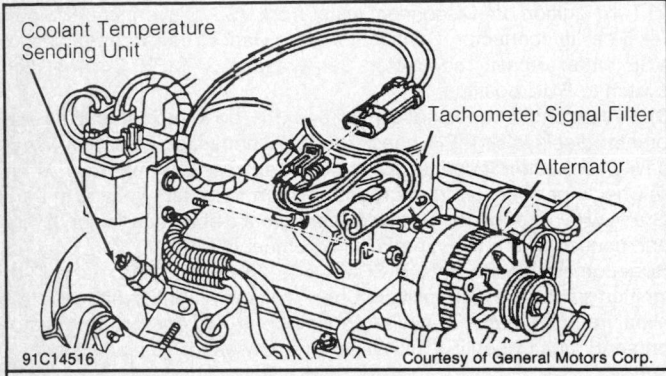

Coolant Temperature Sending Unit

Tachometer Signal Filter

Alternator

91C14516   Courtesy of General Motors Corp.

Fig. 3: Locating Tachometer Signal Filter

Tachometer Is Inoperative Or Inaccurate (3.8L – Using Instrument Panel Tester) – 1) Disconnect 8-cavity connector in engine harness near point where fuel injector harness breaks away from main engine harness. This connector leads to Computer Controlled Coil Ignition (CCCI) module. Connect one lead of Instrument Panel Tester to White wire terminal of 8-cavity connector, and other lead to ground.

2) Set tester to 60 Hz (54 MPH). Turn ignition switch to RUN position. If tachometer does not indicate about 1190 RPM, go to next step. If tachometer indicates about 1190 RPM, check for open in White wire

between 8-cavity connector and CCCI module. If White wire is okay, replace CCCI module.

3) Check for open or short to ground in White wire between instrument cluster and CCCI module. If White wire is okay, replace instrument cluster.

Tachometer Is Inoperative Or Inaccurate (3.8L – Not Using Instrument Panel Tester) – 1) Disconnect instrument cluster connector. Start engine. Check voltage between ground and instrument cluster connector terminal D7 (White wire). *See Fig. 2*. About 1.5 volts should be present at idle and voltage should increase with engine RPM.

2) If voltage is as specified, replace tachometer. If voltage is not as specified, check for open in White wire between instrument cluster and CCCI module. If White wire is okay, replace CCCI module.

WIPER SWITCH

See appropriate WIPER/WASHER SYSTEMS article.

REMOVAL & INSTALLATION

WARNING: When battery is disconnected, vehicle computer and memory systems may lose memory data. Driveability problems may exist until computer systems have completed a relearn cycle. See COMPUTER RELEARN PROCEDURES article in GENERAL INFORMATION before disconnecting battery.

INSTRUMENT CLUSTER

NOTE: Figure 4 shows trim pad removed from lower trim pad, but removing instrument cluster does not require removing trim pad.

1) Disconnect negative battery cable. Remove glove box door for access to screws. Remove 2 screws securing lower trim pad to trim pad (View "A" in illustration). *See Fig. 4*. Remove 2 screws securing cluster trim panel to trim pad.

2) Remove headlight switch-to-cluster trim panel screw. Remove headlight switch. Remove wiper switch-to-cluster trim panel screw. Remove wiper switch. Remove 2 screws (one behind each switch) securing cluster trim panel to cluster mounting brackets.

3) Remove filler panel from below steering column. Disconnect shift indicator cable clip. Disconnect instrument cluster connector. Remove 2 screws securing instrument cluster to brackets. Remove instrument cluster. To install, reverse removal procedure.

WIRING DIAGRAMS

See appropriate chassis wiring diagram in WIRING DIAGRAMS.

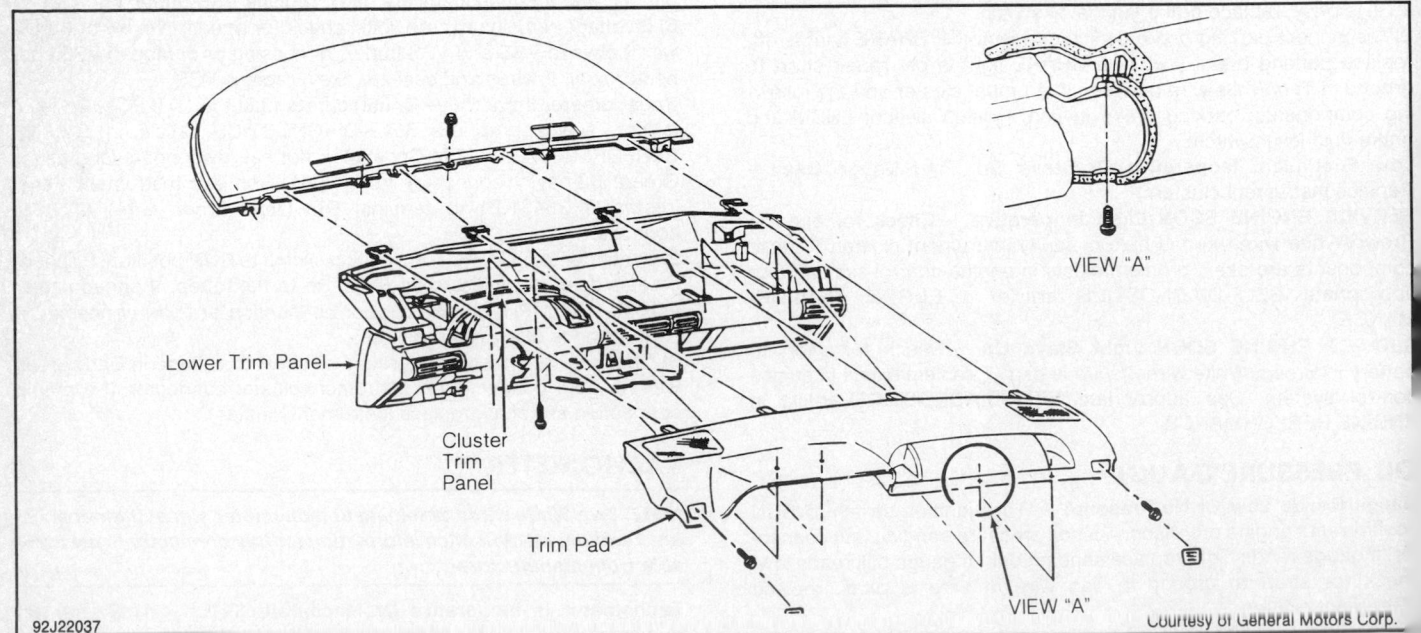

Lower Trim Panel

Cluster Trim Panel

Trim Pad

VIEW "A"

VIEW "A"

92J22037   Courtesy of General Motors Corp.

Fig. 4: Exploded View Of Instrument Panel

Astro, Bravada, Safari, Sonoma, Syclone, Typhoon, "S" & "T" Series Blazer, Jimmy & Pickup

DESCRIPTION

ANALOG INSTRUMENT CLUSTER

Instrument cluster uses analog (needle-type) speedometer and gauges. Indicator light bulbs, plugged into back of cluster, are serviceable, but no other components on cluster are serviceable. If any component on cluster is faulty, replace cluster.

ELECTRONIC INSTRUMENT CLUSTER

Solid-state instrument cluster uses vacuum fluorescent tubes to display vehicle speed and odometer reading in digital form, and gauge readings in bar graph form. Cluster is not serviceable; if faulty, replace cluster.

Odometer display is a separate board attached to main display board. If cluster is replaced, odometer board must be transferred to new cluster to keep vehicle mileage current. Buttons on cluster control the odometer tripmeter. Speedometer and odometer display can be changed from English to metric.

Indicator lights around symbol in bar graph area of each gauge are part of cluster; they cannot be replaced. All other indicator light bulbs are plugged into back of cluster and are serviceable.

ELECTRICAL COMPONENT LOCATIONS

ELECTRICAL COMPONENT LOCATIONS

Electrical Component	Location
Brake Press. Differential Switch	Below Master Cylinder, On Proportioning Valve.
Electronic Control Module (ECM)	
Except Astro & Safari	Behind Right End
Astro & Safari	Behind Right Kick Panel. Of Instrument Panel.
Electronic Hydraulic Control Unit (EHCU)	In Engine Compartment, On Left Inner Fender.
Fuse Block	Behind Left End Of Instrument Panel.
Oil Pressure Sending Unit	
2.5L	On Right Side Of Cylinder Block.
4.3L	To Left Of Distributor.
Parking Brake Switch	On Parking Brake Bracket.
Temp. Gauge Sending Unit	
2.5L	On Top Rear End Of Cylinder Head.
4.3L	On Right Side Of Right Cylinder Head.
Turbo Coolant Level Sensor	On Charge Air Cooler Radiator.
Vehicle Speed Sensor (VSS)	On Left Rear Side Of Transmission (2WD) Or Transfer Case (4WD).
Vehicle Speed Sensor Buffer	
Except Astro & Safari	Behind Right End Of Instrument Panel, To Left Of ECM.
Astro & Safari	Behind Instrument Panel, To Left Of Radio.

OPERATION

GAUGES

Coolant Temperature – Gauge responds to resistance of coolant temperature sending unit. As coolant temperature increases, sending unit resistance decreases.
Fuel – Gauge responds to resistance of fuel tank sending unit. As fuel level increases, sending unit resistance increases.
Oil Pressure – Gauge responds to resistance of oil pressure sending unit. As oil pressure increases, sending unit resistance increases.
Tachometer – Gauge (analog) or cluster (electronic) monitors engine RPM through ignition coil signal.
Turbo Boost – Gauge responds to voltage reference of Manifold Absolute Pressure (MAP) sensor circuit. Voltage is proportional to manifold pressure.
Voltmeter – Voltmeter indicates battery voltage (ignition on, engine off) or charging system voltage (engine on).

INDICATOR LIGHTS

ANTI-LOCK Or ABS – ANTI-LOCK or ABS light comes on when EHCU detects problem in electrical part of Anti-Lock Brake System (ABS). Light also comes on for 2 seconds after ignition is turned on, and engine is off (EHCU turns on light for 2-second system check). If light stays on after system check, brake system will still operate, but without anti-lock assistance.

WARNING: If BRAKE light is on, ensure brake hydraulic system is okay before driving vehicle.

BRAKE – When one or more of the following conditions exists, BRAKE light is grounded, turning on light:
- Parking brake switch is closed
- Brake pressure differential switch is closed (detects loss of hydraulic pressure)
- EHCU detects problem in hydraulic part of Anti-Lock Brake System (ABS). Light also comes on for 2 seconds after ignition is turned on, and engine is off (EHCU turns on light for 2-second system check).

Charging System (Analog) – One side of battery symbol light bulb is connected to alternator field circuit, and other side to ignition power circuit. When ignition is turned on, bulb is grounded through field circuit. When engine is started, field output equalizes voltage across bulb, turning off light. If charging system output is insufficient, light comes on.
Charging System (Electronic) – Cluster monitors charging system output through alternator field. If output is insufficient or excessive, cluster turns on flashing box around battery symbol in voltmeter bar graph area.
CHECK GAUGES – If coolant temperature exceeds 245°F (118°C) or oil pressure is 10 psi (.7 kg/cm²) or less, light comes on to alert driver of condition indicated by gauges. A CHECK GAUGES light driver (part of coolant temperature gauge) monitors signals from temperature gauge sending unit and oil pressure sending unit. If CHECK GAUGES light driver receives a signal from either sending unit, it grounds the light.
Coolant Temperature (Analog) – See CHECK GAUGES.
Coolant Temperature (Electronic) – Cluster monitors coolant temperature through sending unit. If coolant temperature exceeds 245°F (118°C), cluster turns on flashing box around thermometer symbol in temperature gauge bar graph area.
Low Fuel (Electronic) – Cluster monitors fuel level through fuel tank sending unit. When volume in fuel tank is about 3.0 gals. (11L) or less, cluster turns on flashing box around gas pump symbol in fuel gauge bar graph area.
TURBO COOLANT – Light comes on if coolant level sender is grounded, indicating low coolant level in charge air cooler radiator.
Oil Pressure (Analog) – See CHECK GAUGES.
Oil Pressure (Electronic) – Cluster monitors oil pressure through sending unit. If oil pressure is 10 psi (.7 kg/cm²) or less, cluster turns on flashing box around oil can symbol in oil pressure gauge bar graph area.
SERVICE ENGINE SOON (CHECK ENGINE) – If a problem occurs in engine control system, ECM grounds light. Light should come on when ignition is turned on, then go out when engine starts if no problems exist in engine control system.
Shift (M/T) – Light comes on to tell driver when to upshift for best fuel economy. ECM grounds light. Disregard light during downshift.

SPEEDOMETER & ODOMETER

Vehicle Speed Sensor (VSS) is a permanent magnet, AC signal generator. A toothed rotor (tone wheel) on transmission output shaft rotates near magnetic coil of VSS. VSS generates AC voltage pulses that are sent to a solid-state VSS buffer.

VSS buffer conditions AC voltage pulses and sends them to speedometer. VSS buffer is also known as Digital Ratio Adapter Controller (DRAC) because it is matched to final drive ratio of vehicle. If final drive ratio is changed for any reason (i.e., tire size change or rear axle gear change), VSS buffer must be replaced to maintain accurate speedometer/odometer readings.

Based on AC voltage pulses it receives from VSS buffer, an integrated circuit in the speedometer (analog cluster) or the cluster assembly (electronic cluster) controls the speedometer and odometer. On analog cluster, odometer is driven by a stepper motor.

NOTE: Incorrect VSS buffer calibration may adversely affect operation of ABS, engine control system and cruise control system.

TRIPMETER

Analog – Pressing button on cluster resets trip mileage to 0.
Electronic – Pressing TRIP button changes odometer display from total mileage to trip mileage. Pressing RESET button (with display in trip mode) resets trip mileage to 0. Pressing E/M (English/metric) button changes speedometer and odometer display from English (miles) to metric (kilometers).

TESTING

WARNING: When battery is disconnected, vehicle computer and memory systems may lose memory data. Driveability problems may exist until computer systems have completed a relearn cycle. See COMPUTER RELEARN PROCEDURES article in GENERAL INFORMATION before disconnecting battery.

CAUTION: Static electricity can destroy integrated circuits in instrument cluster and VSS buffer. Before servicing these components, ground yourself and work area to discharge static electricity.

NOTE: Check GAUGES or IGN/GAU fuse in passenger compartment fuse block before testing. If all components in cluster are inoperative, check instrument cluster power and ground circuits. If power and ground circuits are okay, replace instrument cluster.

COOLANT TEMPERATURE GAUGE

Gauge Indicates Cold When Engine Is Hot – Disconnect temperature gauge sending unit connector. Connect jumper between ground and Dark Green wire terminal of sending unit connector. Turn ignition on. If gauge indicates HOT, replace sending unit. If gauge does not indicate HOT, check Dark Green wire between sending unit and cluster. If wire is okay, replace instrument cluster.

Gauge Indicates Hot When Engine Is Cold – Disconnect temperature gauge sending unit connector. Turn ignition on. If gauge indicates COLD, replace sending unit. If gauge still indicates HOT, check Dark Green wire between sending unit and cluster. If wire is okay, replace instrument cluster.

Gauge Is Inaccurate – 1) Disconnect temperature gauge sending unit connector. Connect Red wire lead of Instrument Panel Tester (J-33431) to Dark Green wire terminal of sending unit connector, and connect other lead to ground. Turn ignition on.

2) Adjust tester dial to 1400 ohms, then 55 ohms. If gauge indicates COLD with dial at 1400 ohms, and HOT with dial at 55 ohms, replace sending unit. If gauge does not indicate as specified, check Dark Green wire between sending unit and cluster. If wire is okay, replace instrument cluster.

DISPLAY BRIGHTNESS CONTROL (ELECTRONIC)

NOTE: Replace electronic cluster if display is always dim.

Display Will Not Adjust From Bright To Dim – 1) Turn ignition and parking lights on. On all except Astro and Safari, check voltage at Brown wire terminal A6 of instrument cluster connector. *See Fig. 1.* On Astro and Safari, check voltage at Brown wire terminal A8 of large instrument cluster connector. *See Fig. 1.*

2) On all vehicles, if battery voltage is not present, repair Brown wire. If battery voltage is present, check voltage at same terminal while

rotating panel light dimmer wheel. If voltage varies between zero volts and battery voltage, replace instrument cluster.

3) If voltage does not vary between zero volts and battery voltage, check Gray wire between instrument cluster and fuse; repair as necessary. If wire is okay, replace panel light dimmer.

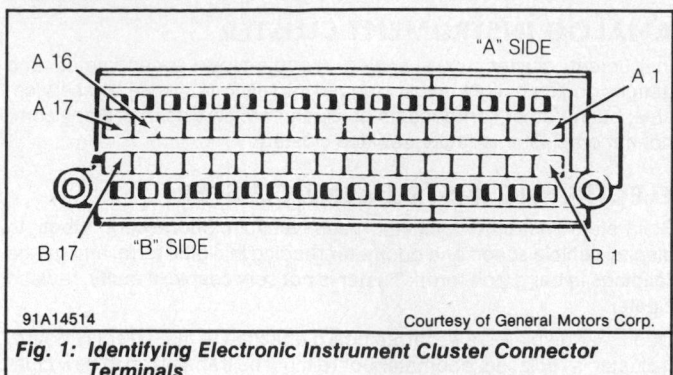

91A14514   Courtesy of General Motors Corp.

Fig. 1: Identifying Electronic Instrument Cluster Connector Terminals

FUEL GAUGE

Gauge Stays At EMPTY – Disconnect fuel tank sending unit connector. Turn ignition on. If gauge indicates FULL, replace sending unit. If gauge indicates EMPTY, check Purple wire between sending unit and cluster. If wire is okay, replace instrument cluster.

Gauge Stays At FULL – 1) Disconnect fuel tank sending unit connector. Turn ignition on. Connect fused jumper wire between ground and Purple wire terminal of sending unit connector. If gauge indicates EMPTY, go to next step. If gauge indicates FULL, check Purple wire between sending unit and cluster. If wire is okay, replace instrument cluster.

2) Connect fused jumper wire between sending unit ground and Purple wire terminal of sending unit connector. If gauge indicates EMPTY, replace sending unit. If gauge still indicates FULL, repair sending unit ground.

Gauge Is Inaccurate – 1) Disconnect fuel tank sending unit connector. Connect Red lead of Instrument Panel Tester (J-33431) to Purple wire terminal of sending unit connector, and connect other lead to ground. Turn ignition on.

2) Set tester dial to 0 ohms, then 90 ohms. If fuel gauge indicates EMPTY at 0 ohms and FULL at 90 ohms, check sending unit ground. If ground is okay, replace sending unit. If fuel gauge does not indicate as specified, check Purple wire between sending unit and cluster. If wire is okay, replace instrument cluster.

INDICATOR LIGHTS

NOTE: On electronic cluster, if fuel level, coolant temperature or oil pressure indicator light does not come on during warning condition, replace instrument cluster.

ANTI-LOCK (ABS) Light Does Not Come On During Warning Condition Or Bulb Check – Disconnect EHCU connector. Connect fused jumper wire between ground and White wire terminal of EHCU connector. If light comes on, repair ABS problem. See appropriate ANTI-LOCK article under BRAKES. If light does not come on, check for open in White wire between EHCU and instrument cluster. If wire is okay, replace instrument cluster.

BRAKE Light Is On With Parking Brake Off – 1) Disconnect parking brake switch connector. If light goes out, adjust parking brake switch. If light stays on, disconnect brake pressure differential switch connector. If light goes out, check for brake hydraulic system leak. If no leaks are found, replace brake pressure differential switch.

2) On vehicles without ABS, if light stays on, check for short to ground in circuit between instrument cluster and parking brake switch, and between instrument cluster and brake pressure differential switch. If wires are okay, replace instrument cluster.

3) On vehicles with ABS, if light stays on, disconnect EHCU connector. If light goes out, repair ABS problem. See appropriate ANTI-LOCK article under BRAKES. If light stays on, check for short to ground in each circuit between instrument cluster and the following components: parking brake switch, brake pressure differential switch and EHCU. If circuits are okay, replace instrument cluster.

BRAKE Light Does Not Come On During Warning Condition Or Bulb Check – 1) Disconnect parking brake switch connector. Connect fused jumper between parking brake switch connector and ground. If light comes on, adjust parking brake switch. If light does not come on, disconnect brake pressure differential switch connector.

2) Connect fused jumper wire between ground and Tan/White wire terminal of brake pressure differential switch connector. If light comes on, replace brake pressure differential switch. If light does not come on, disconnect EHCU connector. Connect fused jumper wire between ground and Tan/White wire terminal of EHCU connector.

3) If light comes on, repair ABS system. See appropriate ANTI-LOCK article under BRAKES. If light does not come on, check for open in each circuit between instrument cluster and the following components: parking brake switch, brake pressure differential switch and EHCU. If circuits are okay, replace instrument cluster.

CHECK GAUGES Light Inoperative With High Coolant Temperature – Inspect CHECK GAUGES bulb; replace if faulty. If bulb is okay, check for open in printed circuit between temperature gauge and CHECK GAUGES bulb. If printed circuit is open, replace instrument cluster. If printed circuit is okay, replace temperature gauge.

CHECK GAUGES Light Inoperative With Low Oil Pressure – Inspect CHECK GAUGES bulb; replace if faulty. If bulb is okay, check for open in printed circuit between oil pressure gauge and temperature gauge, and between temperature gauge and CHECK GAUGES bulb. If printed circuit is open, replace instrument cluster. If printed circuit is okay, replace temperature gauge.

TURBO COOLANT Light On, Coolant Level Okay – Disconnect turbo coolant level sensor. Turn ignition on. If light turns off, replace turbo coolant level sensor. If light stays on, check for short to ground in Dark Green wire. If wire is okay, replace instrument cluster.

TURBO COOLANT Light Inoperative – Disconnect turbo coolant level sensor connector. Connect fused jumper wire from ground to turbo coolant level sensor connector. If light comes on, replace turbo coolant level sensor. If light does not come on, check Dark Green wire between turbo coolant level sensor and instrument cluster. If wire is okay, check indicator light bulb. If bulb is okay, replace instrument cluster.

TURBO COOLANT Light Inoperative – Disconnect turbo coolant level sensor connector. Connect fused jumper wire from ground to turbo coolant level sensor connector. If light comes on, replace turbo coolant level sensor. If light does not come on, check Dark Green wire between turbo coolant level sensor and instrument cluster. If wire is okay, check indicator light bulb. If bulb is okay, replace instrument cluster.

OIL PRESSURE GAUGE

NOTE: If procedure specifies replacing oil pressure sending unit, replace with revised sending unit. Some older version sending units may cause gauge to indicate oil pressure higher than actual pressure, or may cause gauge fluctuations. Check with manufacturer for latest part number.

Gauge Indicates High When Pressure Is Okay – Disconnect oil pressure sending unit connector. Connect fused jumper wire between ground and Tan wire terminal of sending unit connector. Turn ignition on. If gauge indicates LOW, replace sending unit. If gauge indicates HIGH, check Tan wire between sending unit and cluster. If wire is okay, replace instrument cluster.

Gauge Indicates Low When Pressure Is Okay – Disconnect oil pressure sending unit connector. Turn ignition on. If gauge indicates HIGH, replace sending unit. If gauge indicates LOW, check Tan wire between sending unit and cluster. If wire is okay, replace instrument cluster.

Gauge Is Inaccurate – 1) Disconnect oil pressure sending unit connector. Connect Red wire lead of Instrument Panel Tester (J-33431) to Tan wire terminal of temperature sending unit connector, and connect other lead to ground. Turn ignition on.

2) Adjust tester dial to 0 ohms, then 90 ohms. If gauge indicates LOW at 0 ohms and HIGH at 90 ohms, replace sending unit. If gauge does not indicate as specified, check Tan wire between sending unit and cluster. If wire is okay, replace instrument cluster.

SPEEDOMETER & ODOMETER

NOTE: On electronic cluster, replace cluster if either or both of the following conditions exist:

* *Speedometer is inoperative or inaccurate, but odometer is okay*
* *Trip and/or total odometers are inoperative or inaccurate, but speedometer is okay.*

Speedometer & Odometer Are Inaccurate – Replace VSS buffer with unit that matches rear axle ratio.

Speedometer & Odometer Do Not Operate – 1) Check VSS and VSS buffer. See VEHICLE SPEED SENSOR & BUFFER under TESTING. If VSS and VSS buffer are okay, turn ignition off. Disconnect instrument cluster connector and VSS buffer connector.

2) Check resistance of Light Blue/Black wire between instrument cluster connector and VSS buffer connector. If resistance is not about 0 ohms, repair Light Blue/Black wire. If resistance is about 0 ohms, replace instrument cluster.

TRIPMETER

NOTE: If odometer is inoperative or inaccurate in trip and/or total modes, but speedometer is okay, replace instrument cluster.

Tripmeter Does Not Change From Total To Trip Mileage – 1) Disconnect instrument cluster connector. Check continuity between ground and Black wire terminal of tripmeter switch assembly connector. If there is no continuity, repair Black wire.

2) If there is continuity, measure resistance between ground and Light Green wire terminal of instrument cluster connector with TRIP button pressed and released. There should be no resistance with button in one position, and infinite resistance (open) with button in other position.

3) If resistance is as specified, replace instrument cluster. If resistance is not as specified, check Light Green wire between tripmeter switch assembly and instrument cluster connector. If wire is okay, replace tripmeter switch assembly.

Tripmeter Does Not Reset – 1) Disconnect instrument cluster connector. Check continuity between ground and Black wire terminal of tripmeter switch assembly connector. If there is no continuity, repair Black wire.

2) If there is continuity, measure resistance between ground and Light Green/Black wire terminal of instrument cluster connector with RESET button pressed and released. There should be no resistance with button in one position, and infinite resistance (open) with button in other position.

3) If resistance is as specified, replace instrument cluster. If resistance is not as specified, check Light Green/Black wire between tripmeter switch assembly and instrument cluster connector. If wire is okay, replace tripmeter switch assembly.

Display Does Not Change From English To Metric – 1) Disconnect instrument cluster connector. Check continuity between ground and Black wire terminal of tripmeter switch assembly connector. If there is no continuity, repair Black wire.

2) If there is continuity, measure resistance between ground and Light Blue wire terminal of instrument cluster connector with E/M button pressed and released. There should be no resistance with button in one position, and infinite resistance (open) with button in other position.

3) If resistance is as specified, replace instrument cluster. If resistance is not as specified, check Light Blue wire between tripmeter switch assembly and instrument cluster connector. If wire is okay, replace tripmeter switch assembly.

TURBO BOOST GAUGE

Turbo Boost Gauge Inoperative – Check for ECM Codes 33 and 34; repair cause of code(s) as necessary. See SELF-DIAGNOSTICS – GASOLINE article in ENGINE PERFORMANCE. If no codes are present, check Light Green wire (circuit No. 432) at ECM, or Dark Green wire (circuit No. 932) at instrument cluster. If circuits are okay, replace instrument cluster.

VEHICLE SPEED SENSOR & BUFFER

1) Disconnect VSS buffer connector. Turn ignition on. Check voltage at Pink/White wire terminal of VSS buffer connector. If battery voltage is not present, check Pink/White wire between VSS buffer and fuse.
2) If battery voltage is present, check voltage between Pink/White and Black wire terminals of VSS buffer connector. If battery voltage is not present, repair Black wire between VSS buffer and ground. If battery voltage is present, raise and support vehicle.
3) Check AC voltage between Purple/White and Light Green/Black wire terminals of VSS buffer connector with drive wheels turning in high gear. If pulsing AC voltage is present, go to next step. If pulsing AC voltage is not present, check Purple/White and Light Green/Black wires between VSS buffer and VSS. If wires are okay, replace VSS.
4) Check AC voltage between Light Blue/Black and Black wire terminals of VSS buffer connector with drive wheels turning in high gear. If AC voltage is not present, or if AC voltage is present but does not vary with engine RPM, replace VSS buffer.

VOLTMETER

Voltmeter Is Inaccurate – Turn ignition on. Check voltage across battery terminals. If battery voltage matches vehicle voltmeter, voltmeter is accurate. If battery voltage does not match vehicle voltmeter, check for resistance in Pink/Black wire between instrument cluster and fuse, and in Black wire between instrument cluster and ground. If wires are okay, replace instrument cluster.

REMOVAL & INSTALLATION

WARNING: When battery is disconnected, vehicle computer and memory systems may lose memory data. Driveability problems may exist until computer systems have completed a relearn cycle. See COMPUTER RELEARN PROCEDURES article in GENERAL INFORMATION before disconnecting battery.

CAUTION: Static electricity can destroy integrated circuits in instrument cluster and VSS buffer. Before servicing these components, ground yourself and work area to discharge static electricity.

INSTRUMENT CLUSTER

Removal & Installation (Except Astro & Safari) – **1)** Disconnect negative battery cable. Remove foglight switch (if equipped). Remove headlight switch trim plate. Disconnect headlight switch electrical connector. Remove power mirror adjust switch (if equipped). Remove A/C-heater control assembly. Disconnect A/C-heater control assembly electrical connector.
2) Remove filler panel (lower column trim plate). *See Fig. 2.* Disconnect shift indicator cable (A/T). Remove instrument cluster housing nuts and cluster. Disconnect cluster electrical connector. To install, reverse removal procedure.
Removal & Installation (Astro & Safari) – Disconnect negative battery cable. Remove lower column trim plate and instrument cluster trim plate. *See Fig. 3.* Remove instrument cluster. To install, reverse removal procedure.

TRIPMETER SWITCH ASSEMBLY

Removal & Installation (Elcotronic) – Disconnect negative battery terminal. Remove instrument cluster. Disconnect electrical connector from tripmeter switch assembly. Remove tripmeter switch assembly from cluster. To install, reverse removal procedure.

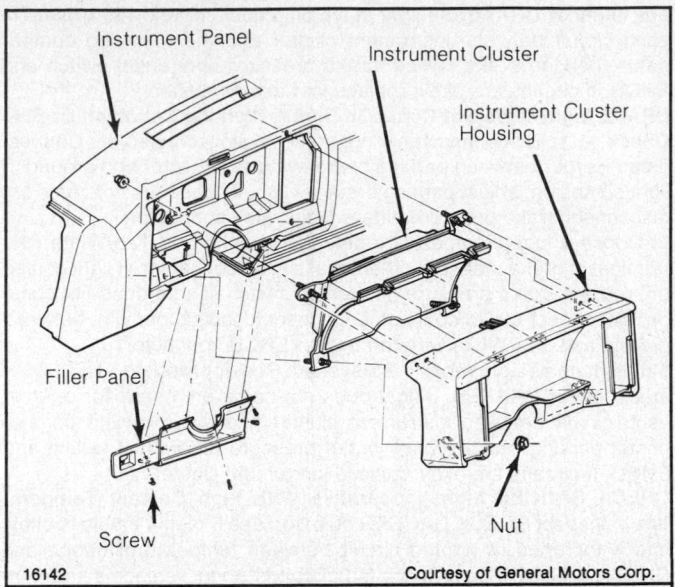

16142   Courtesy of General Motors Corp.

Fig. 2: Exploded View Of Instrument Cluster (Except Astro & Safari)

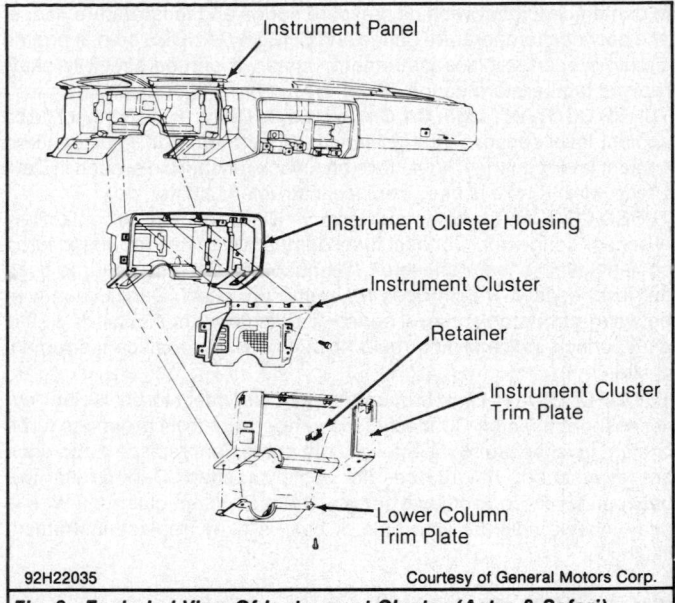

92H22035   Courtesy of General Motors Corp.

Fig. 3: Exploded View Of Instrument Cluster (Astro & Safari)

VEHICLE SPEED SENSOR

Removal & Installation – Raise and support vehicle. Disconnect VSS electrical connector. Prepare to catch transmission fluid in a container. Remove VSS. Remove "O" ring. To install, reverse removal procedure. Check transmission fluid level.

VEHICLE SPEED SENSOR BUFFER

Removal & Installation – Disconnect negative battery cable. Remove trim panel from instrument panel. Disconnect electrical connector from VSS buffer. Remove VSS buffer. To install, reverse removal procedure.

WIRING DIAGRAMS

See appropriate chassis wiring diagram in WIRING DIAGRAMS.

Astro, Bravada, Commercial Van, Jimmy, Lumina APV, Safari, Sierra, Silhouette, Sonoma, Suburban, Syclone, Trans Sport, Typhoon, Van, Yukon, "C" & "K" Series Blazer & Pickup, "S" & "T" Series Blazer & Pickup

TESTING

HAZARD WARNING SWITCH

1) Turn ignition on and operate turn signals. If turn signals operate, check if stop/hazard fuse is blown. If fuse is okay, go to next step. If fuse is blown, replace fuse.

2) Turn hazard warning switch On. Connect test light between Brown wire terminal of hazard flasher and ground. If test light does not light, go to next step. If test light lights, go to step **4)**.

3) Connect test light between Orange wire terminal of hazard flasher and ground. If test light lights, replace hazard flasher. If test light does not light, repair open in Orange wire between hazard flasher and fuse.

4) Connect test light between Brown wire terminal of turn/hazard switch and ground. If test light lights, replace turn/hazard switch. If test light does not light, repair open in Brown wire between hazard flasher and turn/hazard switch.

HORN

Horn Inoperative – 1) Disconnect horn relay. Connect jumper wire between Orange wire terminal and Dark Green wire terminal of horn relay. If horn does not sound, go to next step. If horn sounds, replace horn relay.

2) Connect test light between Orange wire terminal of horn relay and ground. If test light does not light, go to next step. If test light lights, reconnect horn relay and go to step **4)**.

3) Check if horn fuse is blown. If fuse is okay, repair open in Orange wire between horn relay and fuse. If fuse is blown, replace fuse.

4) Connect test light between Dark green wire terminal of horn connector and ground. If test light does not light, go to next step. If test light lights, check for clean and tight horn mounting bolts. If bolts are okay, replace horn.

5) Disconnect turn signal switch connector. Connect jumper wire between Black wire terminal of turn signal connector and ground. If horn sounds, replace horn switch. If horn does not sound, repair open in Black wire between turn signal connector and horn relay.

Horn Sounds Continuously – Disconnect turn signal switch connector. If horn stops, replace horn switch. If horn does not stop, disconnect horn relay. Check for short to ground in Dark Green wire and Black wire. If wires are okay, replace relay. If wires are not okay, replace or repair wires as necessary.

TURN SIGNAL SWITCH

One Side Inoperative – 1) Turn hazard warning system on. Observe turn signal lights on side that do not operate. If lights flash, go to next step. If lights do not flash, go to step **3)**.

2) Turn hazard warning system off. Turn ignition switch to RUN position and place turn signal lever in position of lights that do not operate. Connect test light between Light Blue wire terminal or Dark Blue wire terminal (depending on side that lights do not operate) of turn signal switch connector and ground. If test light lights, system is functioning properly. If test light do not light, replace turn signal switch.

3) Connect test light between Light Blue wire terminal or Dark Blue wire terminal (depending on side that lights do not operate) of park/turn signal light connector and ground. If test light lights, go to next step. If test light does not light, repair open in Light Blue wire or Dark Blue wire between park/turn signal light and turn signal switch.

4) Connect test light between Light Blue wire terminal or Dark Blue wire terminal (depending on side that lights do not operate) of park/turn signal light connector and Black wire terminal of park/turn signal light connector. If test light lights, check for faulty bulb sockets. If test light does not light, repair open in Black wire between park/turn signal light and ground.

Both Sides Inoperative – 1) Turn hazard warning system on. If turn signals flash, go to next step. If turn signals do not flash, replace turn signal flasher.

2) Turn hazard warning system off. Turn ignition switch to RUN position and place turn signal lever in LEFT TURN position. Connect test light between Purple wire terminal of turn signal switch connector and ground. If test light lights, replace turn signal switch. If test light does not light, check for blown turn signal fuse. If fuse is okay, go to next step. If fuse is blown, replace fuse.

3) Connect test light between Purple wire terminal of turn flasher connector and ground. If test light does not light, go to next step. If test light lights, repair open in Purple wire between turn signal switch and turn flasher.

4) Connect test light between Dark Blue wire terminal of turn flasher connector and ground. If test light lights, replace turn signal flasher. If test light does not light, repair open in Dark Blue wire between turn flasher and fuse.

WIPER SWITCH

For testing information on wiper switch, see appropriate WIPER/WASHER SYSTEMS article.

REMOVAL & INSTALLATION

WARNING: When battery is disconnected, vehicle computer and memory systems may lose memory data. Driveability problems may exist until computer systems have completed a relearn cycle. See COMPUTER RELEARN PROCEDURES article in GENERAL INFORMATION before disconnecting battery.

NOTE: Use only specified screws. Using screws that are too long may prevent column from compressing under impact.

STEERING WHEEL & HORN PAD

Removal – Disconnect battery negative cable. Remove horn pad. Remove snap ring and steering wheel retaining nut. Disconnect horn lead assembly (if equipped). Mark steering wheel and shaft for reassembly reference. Using Steering Wheel Puller (J-1859-03), remove steering wheel.

NOTE: Turn signal switch must be in neutral position prior to installing steering wheel to prevent damage to canceling cam and switch assembly.

Installation – Before installing steering wheel, ensure turn signal switch is in neutral position. Install steering wheel onto steering shaft aligning marks made during removal. DO NOT misalign steering wheel more than .79" (20 mm) from horizontal centerline. Connect horn lead assembly (if equipped). Install and tighten steering wheel retaining nut to 30 ft. lbs. (41 N.m). Install snap ring and horn pad. Connect battery negative cable.

IGNITION & DIMMER SWITCHES

NOTE: It is not necessary to remove steering wheel. Ignition and dimmer switches are mounted on top of steering column.

Removal – Remove steering column support bracket bolts and support bracket. Lower steering column. Disconnect dimmer switch electrical connector. Remove dimmer switch retaining screws and remove dimmer switch. Remove dimmer switch actuator rod. Remove ignition switch retaining screws. Disconnect ignition switch electrical connector. Remove ignition switch. See Fig. 1.

Installation – 1) On standard column, move ignition switch slider to far left position, then back 1 detent to right. On tilt column, move ignition switch slider to far right position, then back 1 detent to left. See Fig. 2. Ignition switch should now be in OFF/LOCK position.

NOTE: Install ignition switch with switch in OFF/LOCK position. NEW ignition switch will be pinned in OFF/LOCK position and plastic pin MUST be remove after installation of ignition switch to steering column.

2) Install ignition switch onto steering column. Ensure actuating rod is aligned with ignition switch. Install dimmer switch actuator rod. Connect dimmer switch to actuator rod. Place a 3/32" drill bit into hole on dimmer switch. Position dimmer switch onto steering column and push against actuator rod to remove lash.

3) Remove drill bit and tighten dimmer switch retaining screws. See TORQUE SPECIFICATIONS table at end of article. Connect ignition switch and dimmer switch electrical connectors.

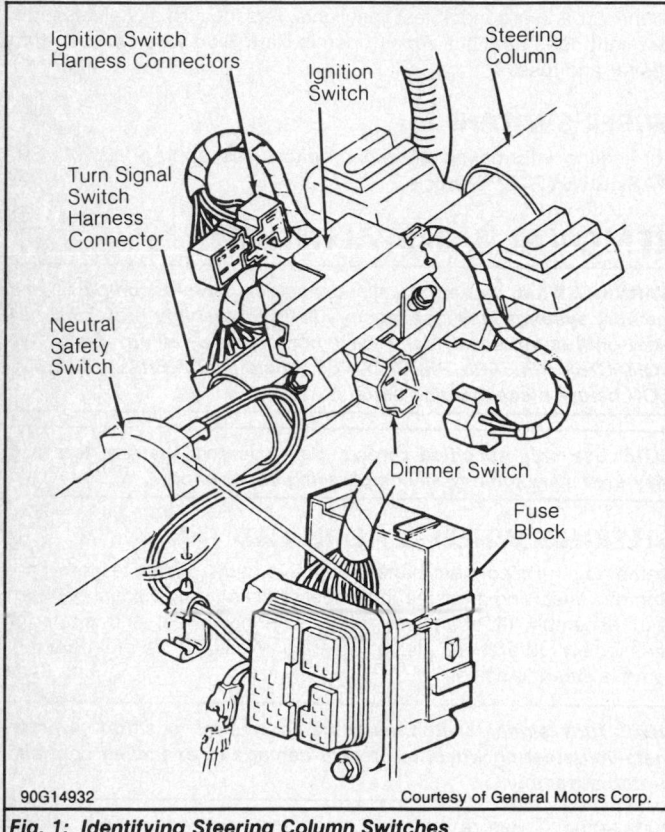

90G14932   Courtesy of General Motors Corp.

Fig. 1: Identifying Steering Column Switches

TURN SIGNAL SWITCH & LOCK CYLINDER

Removal – 1) Disconnect battery negative cable. Remove steering wheel. See STEERING WHEEL & HORN PAD under REMOVAL & INSTALLATION. Remove shaft lock cover. Using Lock Plate Compressor (J-23653-C), compress lock plate and pry retaining ring from groove in steering shaft. See Fig. 3. Discard retaining ring. Remove lock plate. Remove turn signal cancelling cam.

2) Remove upper bearing spring. Remove thrust washer. Place turn signal in up (right turn) position. Remove turn signal/combination switch lever and hazard switch lever. Remove switch actuator arm screw and remove switch actuator arm. Remove 3 turn signal switch retaining screws. Remove steering column support bracket bolts and support bracket.

3) Disconnect turn signal switch electrical connector. Remove 2 wiring protectors and carefully pull wiring through steering column. Remove turn signal switch and allow to hang free.

4) Remove buzzer switch. Place key in lock cylinder and turn to LOCK position. Remove lock retaining screw, being careful not to drop screw down column. See Fig. 4. Pull lock cylinder from housing.

Installation – 1) To install, reverse removal procedure. Install turn signal switch electrical connector through housing. Install 2 wiring protectors. Install steering column support bracket and support bracket bolts.

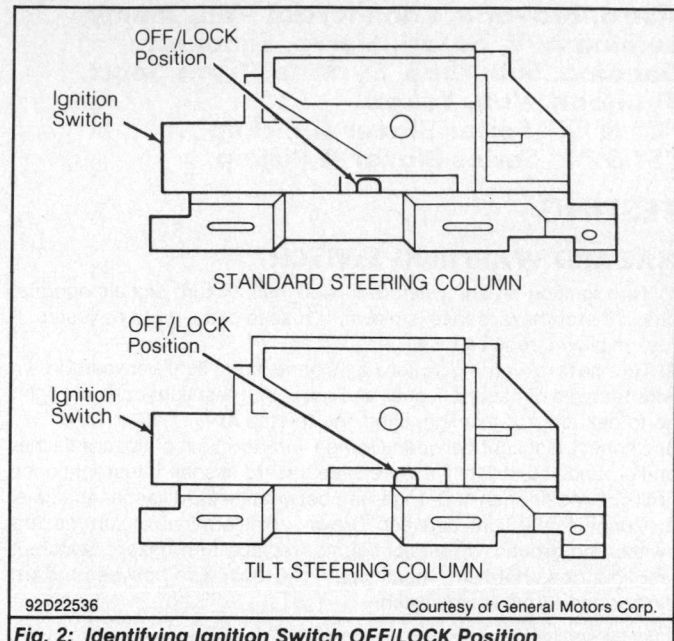

92D22536   Courtesy of General Motors Corp.

Fig. 2: Identifying Ignition Switch OFF/LOCK Position

2) To complete installation, reverse remaining removal procedure. Lubricate turn signal cancelling cam with synthetic grease before installation. Using Lock Plate Compressor (J-23653-C), install NEW shaft lock retaining ring. See Fig. 3. Ensure retaining ring is fully seated in groove on steering shaft.

3) Carefully pull down on turn signal electrical wiring to remove any possible kinks within steering column. Tighten bolts and screws to specifications. See TORQUE SPECIFICATIONS table at end of article.

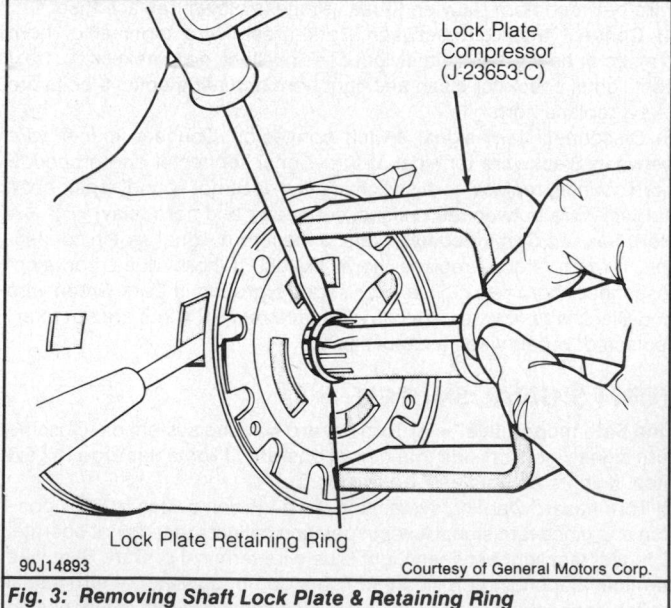

90J14893   Courtesy of General Motors Corp.

Fig. 3: Removing Shaft Lock Plate & Retaining Ring

WASHER/WIPER SWITCH

Removal – 1) Disconnect battery negative cable. Remove steering wheel. See STEERING WHEEL & HORN PAD under REMOVAL & INSTALLATION. Remove turn signal switch and lock cylinder. See TURN SIGNAL SWITCH & LOCK CYLINDER under REMOVAL & INSTALLATION.

2) Remove steering column housing-to-steering column retaining screws. Remove steering column housing from column. Remove housing cover end cap screw and housing cover end cap (if equipped). Remove washer/wiper switch actuator pivot pin. Remove wiper/washer switch.

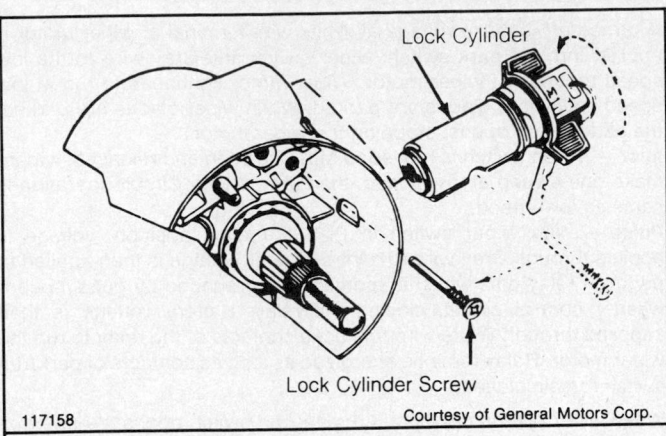

Lock Cylinder

Lock Cylinder Screw

117158

Courtesy of General Motors Corp.

Fig. 4: Removing Lock Cylinder Assembly

Installation – To install, reverse removal procedure. Tighten bolts and screws to specifications. See TORQUE SPECIFICATIONS table.

TORQUE SPECIFICATIONS

TORQUE SPECIFICATIONS

Application	Ft. Lbs. (N.m)
Steering Column Steering Column Support Bracket Bolts ...	22 (30)
Steering Wheel Retaining Nut	30 (41)

	INCH Lbs. (N.m)
Dimmer Switch Screw	35 (4)
Housing Cover End Cap Screw	17 (2)
Ignition Switch Screw	35 (4)
Lock Cylinder Screw	
Standard Column	40 (4.5)
Tilt Column	22 (2.5)
Steering Column Housing-To-Steering Column Screws	47 (5.3)
Turn Signal Actuator Arm Screw	20 (2.3)
Turn Signal Switch Screws	30 (3.4)

1992 SAFETY EQUIPMENT
Wiper/Washer Systems – Astro & Safari

DESCRIPTION

FRONT

System uses a positive park, 2-speed wiper motor. Combined wiper and washer switch, mounted on end of multifunction switch (turn signal) lever, controls system. *See Figs. 1 and 2.* Circuit breaker in wiper motor opens if current flow is excessive, then closes (resets) after it cools off. Motor contains a radio frequency interference suppressor.

System is either a base system or pulse system. In both systems, wiper motor can operate in high, low and mist mode. In addition to these modes, pulse system can operate in pulse mode. In pulse mode, wipers make single sweeps with an adjustable time interval between sweeps. A variable resistor (rheostat) in wiper switch provides input to a solid state pulse/speed/wash control board inside wiper motor housing cover. Control board controls the time interval (delay) between sweeps. Control board is replaceable. Washer pump motor is in right rear corner of engine compartment, inside washer fluid reservoir.

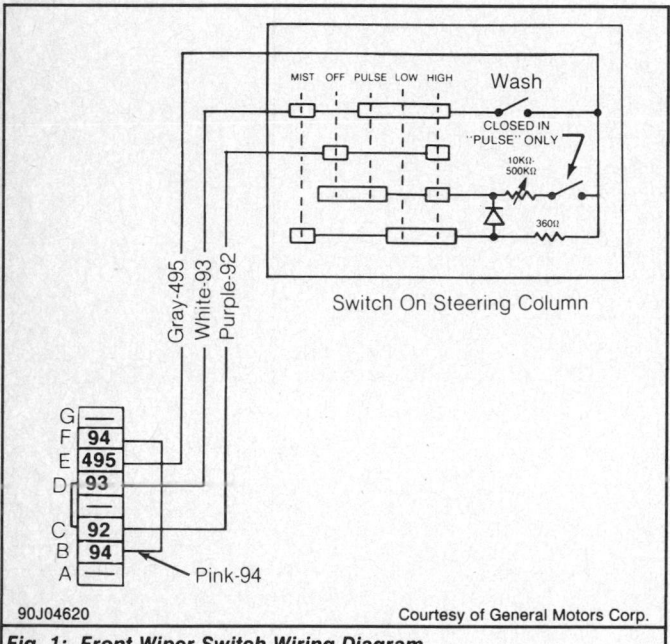

Switch On Steering Column

Pink-94

90J04620   Courtesy of General Motors Corp.

Fig. 1: Front Wiper Switch Wiring Diagram

REAR

System uses a positive park, single-speed wiper motor attached to rear door. In addition to ON and OFF positions, switch on instrument panel has momentary wash and wipe positions. Washer pump motor is in right rear corner of engine compartment, inside washer fluid reservoir.

OPERATION

FRONT

Low Speed (Base System) – Wiper switch completes circuit through Gray wire to low speed brushes of wiper motor.
Low Speed (Pulse System) – Wiper switch completes circuit through Gray wire to pulse/speed/wash control board. Control board provides ground for park/run relay. This energizes relay, supplying power to low speed brushes of wiper motor.
High Speed (Base System) – Wiper switch completes circuit through Purple wire to high speed brushes of wiper motor.
High Speed (Pulse System) – Wiper switch completes circuit through Purple wire to high speed brushes of wiper motor. When wiper switch is turned off, wipers complete last sweep at low speed before parking.
Park – Park switch is open when wiper blades are parked, and closed when wiper blades are out of park position. When wiper switch

is turned off, battery voltage at White wire terminal of wiper motor is applied through park switch, wiper switch and Gray wire to the low speed brushes of wiper motor. Wiper motor continues to run at low speed until wiper blades are parked. When wiper blades are parked, the park switch opens, stopping the wiper motor.
Mist – When switch is moved to MIST position and released, wipers make one sweep at low speed, then are parked. Circuit operation is same as low speed.
Pulse – With wiper switch in PULSE (delay) position, voltage is applied through Gray wire to control board. Voltage is then applied to park/run relay coil, which is momentarily grounded by pulse/speed/washer control circuit, closing the relay. Battery voltage is then supplied through White wire to closed contacts of the relay to run the wiper motor. Relay remains energized as long as contacts of park/run switch remain closed.

When wiper blades have parked, park/run switch opens, de-energizing the park/run relay. Wiper blades remain parked until control board grounds the park/relay coil to start another sweep. Delay time between sweeps is controlled by pulse delay resistors (rheostat) in wiper switch. Delay can be adjusted from zero to 43 seconds.
Washer (Base System) – When washer button is pushed, wiper switch is mechanically moved to LOW position, simultaneously starting wiper and washer motors.
Washer (Pulse System) – When washer button is pushed, voltage is applied to control board. Control board simultaneously supplies power to washer motor through Pink wire and starts wiper cycle through low speed brushes of wiper motor.

Washer continues to run as long as button is pushed. Control board keeps wipers on for about 6 seconds after washer goes off. If washer is turned on during delay operation, wipers run in low speed for 6 seconds. Wash cycle is completed before wipers return to delay operation.

REAR

With wiper switch on, power is supplied to wiper motor terminal "C". Wiper motor terminal "B" leads to ground through wiper switch. When wiper switch is turned off, voltage is applied to wiper motor terminal "A", completing circuit through park plate. Cam gear on plate opens circuit at park position, causing wipers to park at proper position.

TESTING

NOTE: Ensure WIPER fuse is okay before testing system.

FRONT

Wipers Inoperative In All Modes – 1) Turn ignition switch to ACC position. Connect test light between ground and White wire terminal of wiper switch connector. *See Fig. 2.* If test light does not come on, repair open in White wire between wiper switch and fuse.

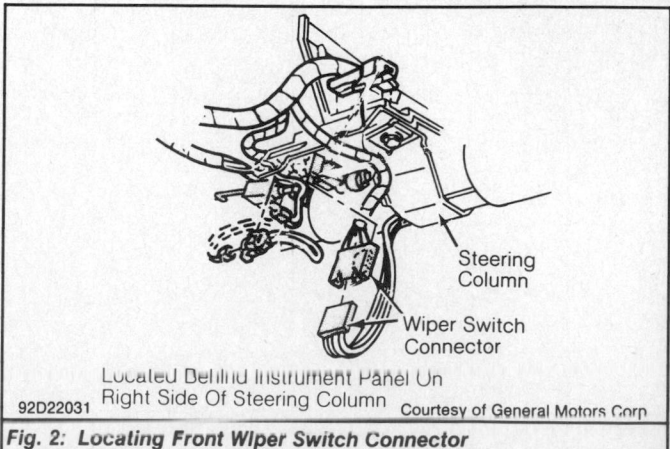

Steering Column

Wiper Switch Connector

Located Behind Instrument Panel On Right Side Of Steering Column

92D22031   Courtesy of General Motors Corp

Fig. 2: Locating Front Wiper Switch Connector

2) If test light comes on, connect test light between ground and Gray wire terminal of wiper switch connector with wiper switch in LOW position, and at Purple wire with wiper switch in HIGH position. If test light does not come on at one or both wires, replace wiper switch.

3) If test light comes on at both wires, disconnect wiper motor connector. Connect fused jumper wire between battery positive terminal and Gray wire terminal of wiper motor connector. If wipers do not operate, repair or replace wiper motor. If wipers operate, repair open in White or Purple wire between wiper switch and wiper motor.

Wipers Operate In Low Speed, But Not High – 1) Disconnect wiper motor connector. Turn ignition switch to ACC position. Turn wiper switch to HIGH position. Connect test light between ground and Purple wire terminal of wiper motor connector. If test light comes on, repair or replace wiper motor.

2) If test light does not come on, connect test light between ground and Purple wire terminal of wiper switch connector. *See Fig. 2.* If test light does not come on, replace wiper switch. If test light comes on, repair open in Purple wire between wiper switch and wiper motor.

Wipers Operate In High Speed, But Not Low – 1) Disconnect wiper motor connector. Turn ignition switch to ACC position. Turn wiper switch to LO position. Connect test light between ground and Gray wire terminal of wiper motor connector. If test light comes on, repair or replace wiper motor.

2) If test light does not come on, connect test light between ground and Gray wire terminal of wiper switch connector. *See Fig. 2.* If test light does not come on, replace wiper switch. If test light comes on, repair open in Gray wire between wiper switch and wiper motor.

Wipers Do Not Park – 1) Turn ignition switch to RUN position. Connect test light between ground and White wire terminal of wiper motor connector. If test light does not come on, repair open in White wire between wiper motor and fuse.

2) If test light comes on, connect test light between ground and Pink wire terminal of wiper motor connector. If test light comes on, replace wiper switch. If test light does not come on, repair or replace wiper motor.

Wipers Do Not Turn Off – 1) Disconnect wiper motor connector. Connect fused jumper wire between Pink and Gray wire terminals of wiper motor connector. Connect fused jumper wire between battery positive terminal and White wire terminal of wiper motor connector.

2) If wiper motor parks and turns off, replace wiper switch. If wiper motor does not turn off, repair or replace wiper motor.

No Delay In Pulse Mode – 1) Disconnect wiper switch connector. *See Fig. 2.* Turn wiper switch to PULSE position. Connect ohmmeter between Gray and White wire terminals of wiper switch. If reading is less than 670 ohms or greater than 690 ohms, replace wiper switch.

2) If reading is 670-690 ohms, move wiper switch through pulse range to maximum delay position. If readings do not increase in steps to about 450,000 ohms, replace wiper switch. If readings increase in steps to about 450,000 ohms, check for open in Gray or White wire between wiper switch and wiper motor. If wires are okay, replace wiper switch.

Washer Inoperative – 1) Disconnect washer pump motor connector. Turn ignition switch to RUN position. Connect test light between ground and Pink wire terminal of washer pump connector with WASH button pushed. If test light does not come on, go to step **3)**.

2) If test light comes on, connect test light between Pink and Black wire terminals of washer pump connector with WASH button pushed. If test light comes on, replace washer pump. If test light does not come on, repair open in Black wire between washer pump and ground.

3) Connect test light between ground and Gray wire terminal of wiper motor connector with WASH button pushed. If test light does not come on, replace wiper switch. If test light comes on, connect test light between ground and Pink wire terminal of wiper motor connector.

4) If test light comes on, repair open in Pink wire between wiper motor and washer pump. If test light does not come on, repair or replace wiper motor.

REAR

NOTE: Ensure RADIO and INST LPS fuses are okay before testing.

Wiper Inoperative – 1) Turn ignition switch to ACC position. Disconnect wiper switch connector. Connect test light between ground and Brown/White wire terminal of wiper switch connector. If test light does not come on, repair open in Brown/White wire between wiper switch and fuse.

2) If test light comes on, connect wiper switch connector. Turn wiper switch on. Connect test light between ground and White wire terminal of wiper switch connector. If test light does not come on, replace wiper switch. If test light comes on, connect test light between ground and White wire terminal of wiper motor connector.

3) If test light does not come on, repair open in White wire between wiper switch and motor. If test light comes on, connect test light between ground and Brown/White wire terminal of wiper motor connector. If test light does not come on, repair open in Brown/White wire between wiper motor and splice.

4) If test light comes on, connect test light between White and Black wire terminals of wiper motor connector. If test light comes on, replace wiper motor. If test light does not come on, repair open in Black wire between wiper motor and ground.

Washer Inoperative – 1) Disconnect washer pump motor connector. Turn ignition switch to ACC position. Connect test light between ground and Dark Green wire terminal of washer pump motor connector. Push and hold washer button. If test light comes on, go to next step. If test light does not come on, go to step **3)**.

2) Connect test light between Dark Green and Black wire terminals of washer pump motor connector. Push and hold washer button. If test light comes on, replace washer pump motor. If test light does not come on, repair open in Black wire between washer pump motor and ground.

3) Connect test light between ground and Dark Green wire terminal of wiper switch connector. Push and hold washer button. If test light does not come on, replace wiper switch. If test light comes on, repair open in Dark Green wire between wiper switch and washer pump motor.

REMOVAL & INSTALLATION

WARNING: When battery is disconnected, vehicle computer and memory systems may lose memory data. Driveability problems may exist until computer systems have completed a relearn cycle. See COMPUTER RELEARN PROCEDURES article in GENERAL INFORMATION before disconnecting battery.

WIPER MOTOR

Removal & Installation (Front) – Disconnect negative battery cable. Remove firewall vent grille. Disconnect wiper motor electrical connector. Remove transmission drive link from motor crank arm by prying or pulling link toward rear of vehicle. Remove wiper motor mounting bolts. Remove motor. To install, reverse removal procedure.

NOTE: To ease removal and installation of rear wiper motor, insert a 1/8" drift pin through wiper arm hinge to control spring detent.

Removal & Installation (Rear) – Disconnect negative battery cable. Remove rear door trim panels. Separate wiper arm from motor. Disconnect washer hose from wiper arm. Remove wiper motor mounting nuts and bolts. Remove wiper motor. To install, reverse removal procedure.

WIPER SWITCH

NOTE: Manufacturer gives wiper switch removal procedure with steering column removed from vehicle.

Removal & Installation (Front) – 1) Turn steering wheel to straight-ahead position. Disconnect negative battery cable. Remove instrument panel trim cover. Disconnect shift cable from steering column shift tube lever. Remove upper pinch bolt from column intermediate shaft. Mark intermediate shaft yoke in relation to steering shaft for reassembly reference.

2) Remove steering wheel. Disconnect electrical connectors as necessary. While supporting steering column, remove bolts from steering column upper support bracket. Remove steering column.

3) Remove lock plate cover. Screw center post of Lock Plate Compressor (J-23653-A) onto steering shaft as far as it will go. Compress lock plate by turning center post nut clockwise. *See Fig. 3.*

4) Pry snap ring out of shaft groove. Discard ring. Remove lock plate compressor. Remove lock plate. Remove turn signal cancel cam. Remove upper bearing spring and thrust washer. Turn multifunction lever upward (right turn position).

5) Pull multifunction lever straight out to remove. Remove hazard warning knob. Remove turn signal switch assembly mounting screws. Pull switch assembly and wiring harness out of column. Remove wire protector. Remove buzzer switch assembly. Remove lock cylinder retaining screw.

6) Remove lock cylinder set. Remove retaining ring from upper end of steering shaft. Slide steering shaft out of column assembly. Remove dimmer switch and actuator rod. Remove ignition switch. Remove 4 screws securing gear shift bowl to column housing. Remove upper bearing retainer. Separate gear shift bowl from column housing. Remove cover for access to wiper switch. Remove wiper switch.

7) To install, reverse removal procedure using new lock plate snap ring. Tighten intermediate shaft upper pinch bolt to **30 ft. lbs. (41 N.m).**

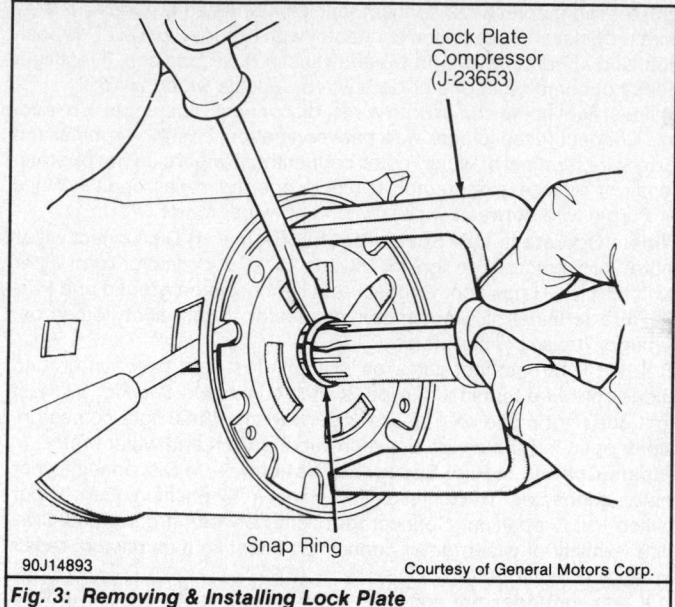

90J14893   Courtesy of General Motors Corp.

Fig. 3: Removing & Installing Lock Plate

WIRING DIAGRAMS

For rear wiring diagram and an additional front wiring diagram, see appropriate chassis wiring diagram in WIRING DIAGRAMS.

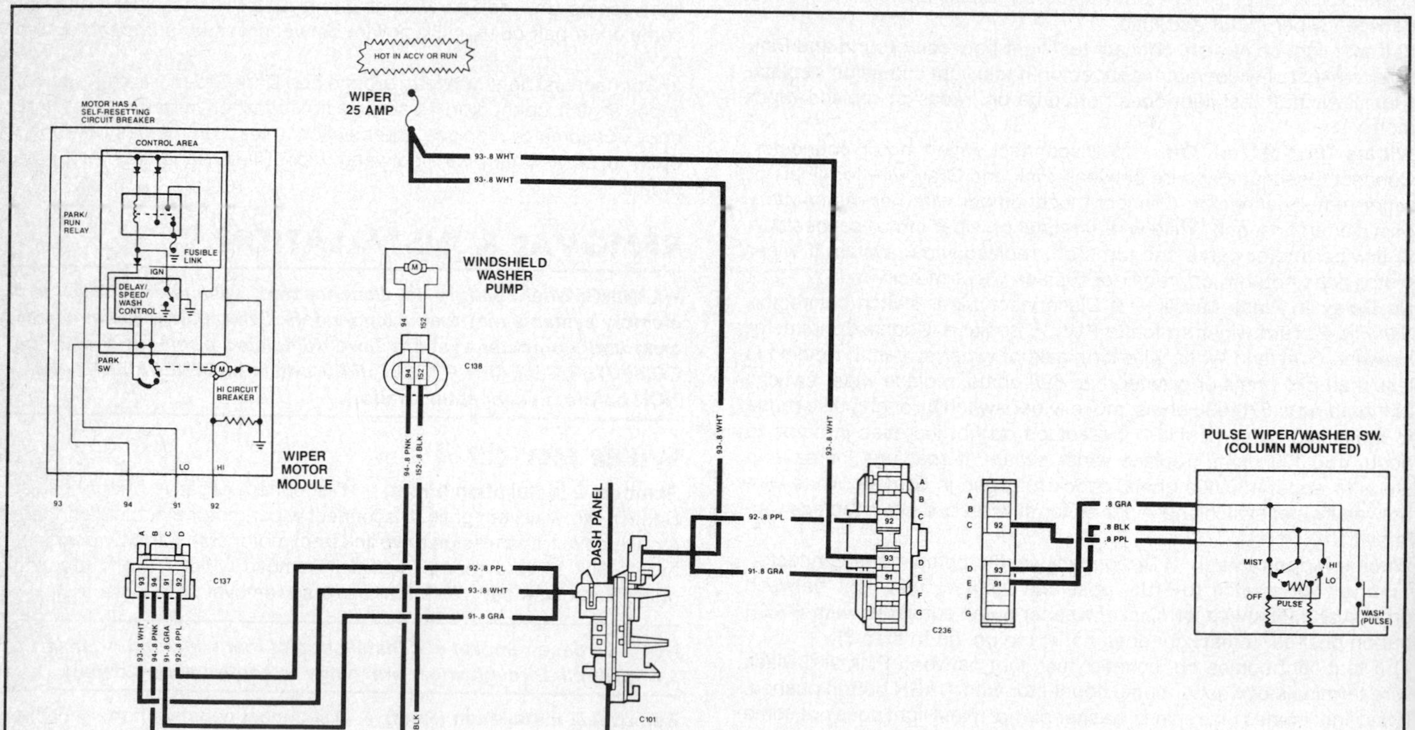

91B13715

Fig. 4: Front Wiper/Washer System Wiring Diagram (Astro & Safari)

**Blazer, Pickup, Sierra,
Suburban, Yukon**

DESCRIPTION

FRONT

System uses a permanent magnet, 2-speed, positive-park wiper motor. Motor drives a crank arm, which is attached to individual transmission links for left and right wipers. Wiper motor is sealed and not serviceable (except for delay module on pulse system). Washer pump motor is mounted on fluid reservoir.

System is either a base system or pulse (delay) system. Base system has high and low speeds. Pulse system is similar to base system, but with the addition of a delay function that causes the wipers to sweep once with a delay interval between sweeps. Variable resistor in wiper switch adjusts amount of current to a delay module attached to wiper motor. Delay module controls current to wiper motor.

REAR

In addition to high and low speeds, system has a pulse (delay) feature that causes the wipers to sweep once with a delay interval between sweeps. Variable resistor in wiper switch adjusts amount of current to delay module in wiper motor. Delay module controls current to wiper motor. Wiper motor (including delay module) is sealed and not serviceable.

TESTING

WARNING: When battery is disconnected, vehicle computer and memory systems may lose memory data. Driveability problems may exist until computer systems have completed a relearn cycle. See COMPUTER RELEARN PROCEDURES article in GENERAL INFORMATION before disconnecting battery.

FRONT

NOTE: Ensure WIPER fuse is okay before testing system. Front wiper switch connector is located near base of steering column.

Wipers Inoperative In All Modes – 1) Disconnect wiper switch connector. Connect test light between ground and White wire terminal of wiper switch connector. *See Fig. 2.* If test light does not come on, repair open in White wire between wiper switch and 25-amp WIPER fuse.
2) If test light comes on, reconnect wiper switch connector. Move wiper switch to LO position. Connect test light between ground and Gray wire terminal of wiper switch connector. If test light does not come on, replace wiper switch. If test light comes on, repair open in Gray wire between wiper switch and wiper motor.
Wipers Run At Low Speed Only – 1) Disconnect wiper motor connector. Turn ignition to ACC position and wiper switch to HI position. Connect test light between ground and Purple wire terminal of wiper motor connector. *See Fig. 2.* If test light comes on, replace wiper motor (replace delay module on pulse system).
2) If test light does not come on, connect test light between ground and Purple wire terminal of wiper switch connector. If test light does not come on, replace wiper switch. If test light comes on, repair open in Purple wire between wiper switch and wiper motor.
Wipers Run At High Speed Only – 1) Disconnect wiper motor connector. Turn ignition to ACC position and wiper switch to HI position. Connect test light between ground and Gray wire terminal of wiper motor connector. *See Fig. 2.* If test light comes on, replace wiper motor (replace delay module on pulse system).
2) If test light does not come on, connect test light between ground and Gray wire terminal of wiper switch connector. If test light does not come on, replace wiper switch. If test light comes on, repair open in Gray wire between wiper switch and wiper motor.
Wiper Motor Runs Continuously – 1) Disconnect wiper motor connector. Turn ignition to ACC position and wiper switch to LO position. Connect test light between ground and Gray wire terminal of wiper

er motor connector. *See Fig. 2.* If test light does not come on, repair open in Gray wire between wiper motor and wiper switch.
2) If test light comes on, move wiper switch to HI position. Connect test light between ground and Purple wire terminal of wiper motor connector. If test light does not come on, repair open in Purple wire between wiper motor and wiper switch.
3) If test light comes on, connect test light between ground and White wire terminal of wiper motor connector. If test light does not come on, repair open in White wire between ground and wiper motor. If test light comes on, replace delay module (pulse system), or go to next step (base system).
4) Turn ignition and wiper switches off. Disconnect negative battery cable. Connect ohmmeter between Orange and Gray wire terminals of wiper motor connector. If ohmmeter reads zero ohm, replace wiper motor. If ohmmeter reads greater than zero ohm, repair open in Orange wire between wiper motor and wiper switch.
No Delay In Pulse (Delay) Mode – 1) Disconnect wiper switch connector. Place wiper switch in LO position. Connect ohmmeter between Gray and White wire terminals of wiper switch connector. If ohmmeter reads decidedly less than or greater than 680 ohms, replace wiper switch.
2) If ohmmeter reads about **680 ohms**, move wiper switch through delay range to maximum delay position. If ohmmeter readings do not increase in steps to about 450,000 ohms, replace wiper switch. If ohmmeter readings increase in steps to about 450,000 ohms, check for open in Gray or White wire between wiper switch and wiper motor. *See Fig. 2.* If wires are okay, replace wiper switch.
Washer Inoperative (Base System) – 1) Disconnect washer pump motor connector. Turn ignition switch to ACC position and wiper switch to WASH position. Connect test light between ground and Pink wire terminal of washer pump motor connector. *See Fig. 2.* If test light glows, go to next step. If test light does not glow, go to step 3).
2) Connect test light between Pink and Black wire terminals of washer pump motor connector. If test light comes on, replace washer pump motor. If test light does not come on, repair open in Black wire between ground and washer pump motor.
3) Connect test light between ground and Pink wire terminal of wiper switch connector. If test light does not come on, replace wiper switch. If test light comes on, repair open in Pink wire between wiper switch and washer pump motor.
Washer Inoperative (Pulse System) – 1) Disconnect washer pump motor connector. Turn ignition switch to ACC position and wiper switch to WASH position. Connect test light between ground and Pink wire terminal of washer pump motor connector. *See Fig. 2.* If test light glows, go to next step. If test light does not glow, go to step 3).
2) Connect test light between Pink and Black wire terminals of washer pump motor connector. If test light comes on, replace washer pump motor. If test light does not come on, repair open in Black wire between ground and washer pump motor.
3) Connect test light between ground and Gray wire terminal of wiper motor connector. If test light comes on, go to next step. If test light does not come on, check for open in Gray wire between wiper motor and wiper switch. If wire is okay, replace wiper switch.
4) Connect test light between ground and Orange wire terminal of wiper motor connector. If test light does not come on, replace delay module. If test light comes on, check for open in Orange wire between wiper motor and wiper switch. If wire is okay, replace wiper switch.

REAR

NOTE: Ensure ACC-IGN circuit breaker is okay before testing system.

Wipers Inoperative In All Modes – 1) Turn ignition switch to ACC or RUN position. Connect test light between ground and White wire terminal of wiper switch connector. *See Fig. 3.* If test light does not come on, repair open in White wire between wiper switch and fuse block.
2) If test light comes on, connect test light between ground and Gray wire terminal of wiper switch connector with wiper switch in LO position, and Light Blue wire terminal with switch in HI position. If test light does not come on at one or both wires, replace wiper switch.

GM
4-50

1992 SAFETY EQUIPMENT
Wiper/Washer Systems – "C" & "K" Series (Cont.)

3) If test light comes on at both wires, disconnect wiper motor connector. Connect test light between ground and Gray wire terminal of wiper motor connector with wiper switch in LO position, and Light Blue wire terminal with switch in HI position.

4) If test light does not come on at one or both wires, repair open in Gray or Light Blue wire between wiper motor and wiper switch. If test light comes on at both wires, connect test light from Gray or Light Blue wire terminal to Black wire terminal of wiper motor connector. Turn wiper switch to LO position.

5) If test light comes on, replace wiper motor. If test light does not come on, repair open in Black wire between wiper motor and ground.

Wipers Run At Low Speed Only – 1) Turn wiper switch to HI position. Connect test light between ground and Dark Green wire terminal of wiper switch connector. *See Fig. 3.* If test light does not come on, replace wiper switch. If test light comes on, disconnect wiper motor connector.

2) Connect test light between ground and Light Blue wire terminal of wiper motor connector. Move wiper switch to HI position. If test light comes on, replace wiper motor. If test light does not come on, repair open in Light Blue wire between wiper motor and wiper switch.

Wipers Run At High Speed Only – 1) Turn wiper switch to LO position. Connect test light between ground and Gray wire terminal of wiper switch connector. *See Fig. 3.* If test light does not come on, replace wiper switch. If test light comes on, disconnect wiper motor connector. Turn wiper switch to LO position.

2) Connect test light between ground and Gray wire terminal of wiper motor connector. If test light comes on, replace wiper motor. If test light does not come on, repair open in Gray wire between wiper motor and wiper switch.

Wiper Motor Runs Continuously Or Will Not Park – 1) Turn ignition switch to ACC or RUN position. Turn off wiper switch. Connect test light between ground and Gray wire terminal of wiper motor connector. *See Fig. 3.* If test light comes on, replace wiper switch.

2) If test light does not come on, connect self-powered test light between ground and Black wire terminal of wiper motor connector. If test light comes on, replace wiper motor. If test light does not come on, repair open in Black wire between wiper motor and ground.

Washer Inoperative – 1) Turn ignition switch to ACC or RUN position. Turn wiper switch to WASH position. Connect test light between ground and Dark Green wire terminal of wiper switch. *See Fig. 3.* If test light does not come on, replace wiper switch.

2) If test light comes on, disconnect washer pump motor connector. Connect test light between ground and Dark Green wire terminal of washer pump motor connector. If test light does not come on, repair open in Dark Green wire between washer pump motor and wiper switch.

3) If test light comes on, connect test light between Dark Green and Black wire terminals of washer pump motor connector. If test light comes on, replace washer pump motor. If test light does not come on, repair open in Black wire between washer pump motor and ground.

REMOVAL & INSTALLATION

WARNING: When battery is disconnected, vehicle computer and memory systems may lose memory data. Driveability problems may exist until computer systems have completed a relearn cycle. See COMPUTER RELEARN PROCEDURES article in GENERAL INFORMATION before disconnecting battery.

WIPER SWITCH

NOTE: Manufacturer gives wiper switch removal procedure with steering column removed from vehicle.

Removal & Installation (Front) – 1) Turn steering wheel to straight-ahead position. Disconnect negative battery cable. Remove instrument panel trim cover. Disconnect shift cable from steering column shift tube lever. Remove upper pinch bolt from column intermediate shaft. Mark intermediate shaft yoke in relation to steering shaft for reassembly reference.

2) Remove steering wheel. Disconnect electrical connectors as necessary. While supporting steering column, remove bolts from steering column upper support bracket. Remove steering column.

3) Remove lock plate cover. Screw center post of Lock Plate Compressor (J-23653) onto steering shaft as far as it will go. Compress lock plate by turning center post nut clockwise. *See Fig. 1.*

4) Pry snap ring out of shaft groove. Discard ring. Remove lock plate compressor. Remove lock plate. Remove turn signal cancel cam. Remove upper bearing spring and thrust washer. Turn multifunction lever upward (right turn position).

5) Pull multifunction lever straight out to remove. Remove hazard warning knob. Remove turn signal switch assembly mounting screws. Pull switch assembly and wiring harness out of column. Remove wire protector. Remove buzzer switch assembly. Remove lock cylinder retaining screw.

6) Remove lock cylinder set. Remove retaining ring from upper end of steering shaft. Slide steering shaft out of column assembly. Remove dimmer switch and actuator rod. Remove ignition switch. Remove 4 screws securing gear shift bowl to column housing. Remove upper bearing retainer. Separate gear shift bowl from column housing. Remove cover for access to wiper switch. Remove wiper switch.

7) To install, reverse removal procedure using new lock plate snap ring. Tighten intermediate shaft upper pinch bolt to **30 ft. lbs. (41 N.m).**

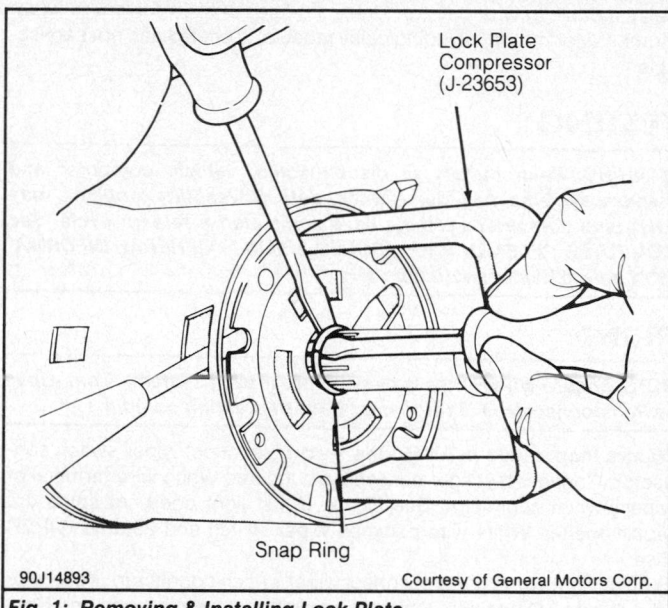

90J14893   Courtesy of General Motors Corp.
Fig. 1: Removing & Installing Lock Plate

WIPER MOTOR

NOTE: On vehicles with front pulse system, it is not necessary to remove wiper motor to remove delay module.

Removal & Installation (Front) – 1) Disconnect battery negative cable. Remove wiper arms. Remove cowl vent grille. Disconnect wiper motor electrical connector. Loosen drive link bracket nuts where motor crank arm is attached to transmission arm. DO NOT remove crank arm from motor.

2) Separate transmission arm from motor crank arm. Remove wiper motor mounting screws. Remove wiper motor. To install, reverse removal procedure. Lubricate contact point of motor crank arm and transmission arm before connecting components.

WIRING DIAGRAMS

For additional information, see appropriate chassis wiring diagram in WIRING DIAGRAMS.

1992 SAFETY EQUIPMENT
Wiper/Washer Systems – "C" & "K" Series (Cont.)

GM
4-51

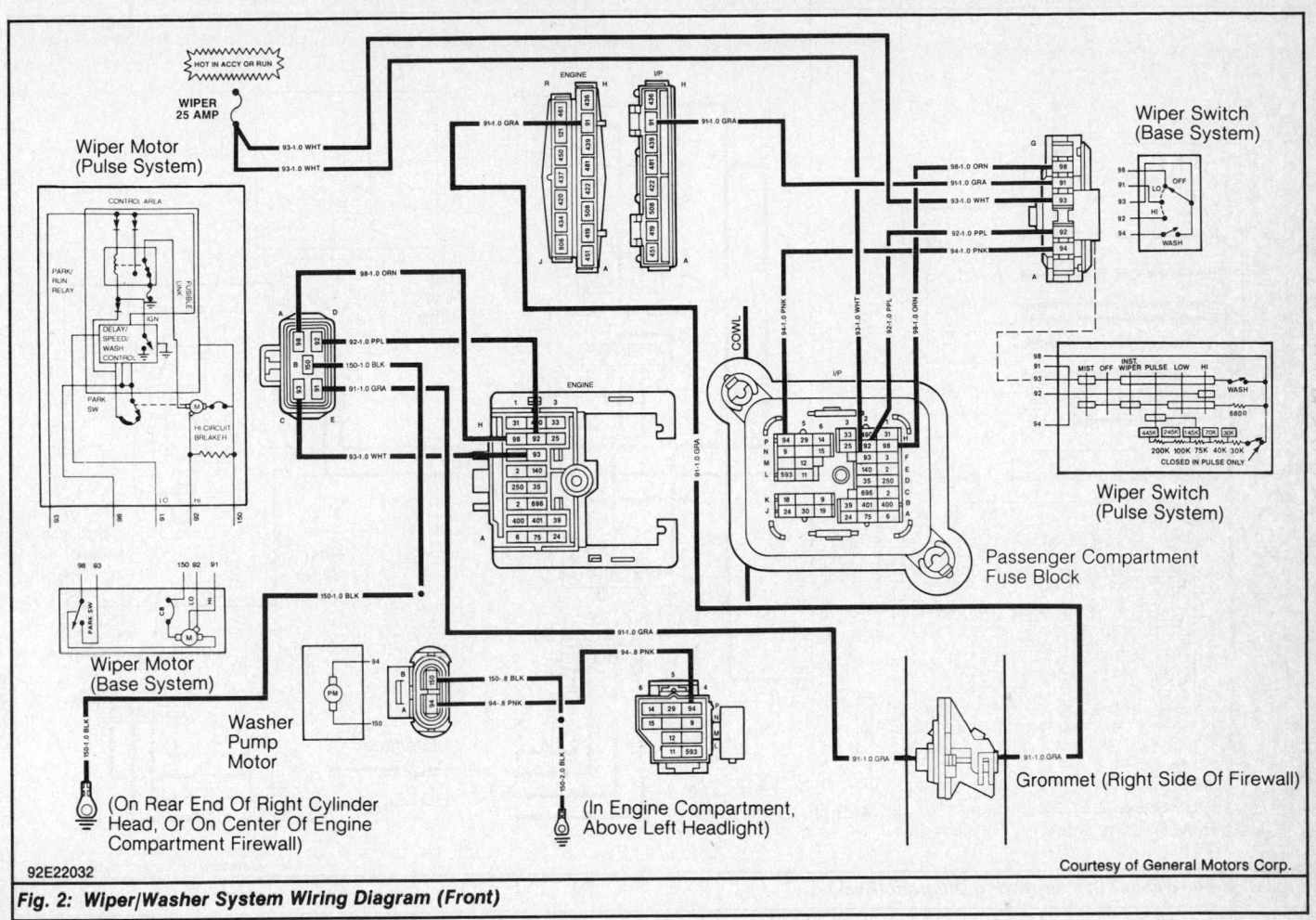

92E22032

Courtesy of General Motors Corp.

Fig. 2: Wiper/Washer System Wiring Diagram (Front)

GM
4-52

1992 SAFETY EQUIPMENT
Wiper/Washer Systems – "C" & "K" Series (Cont.)

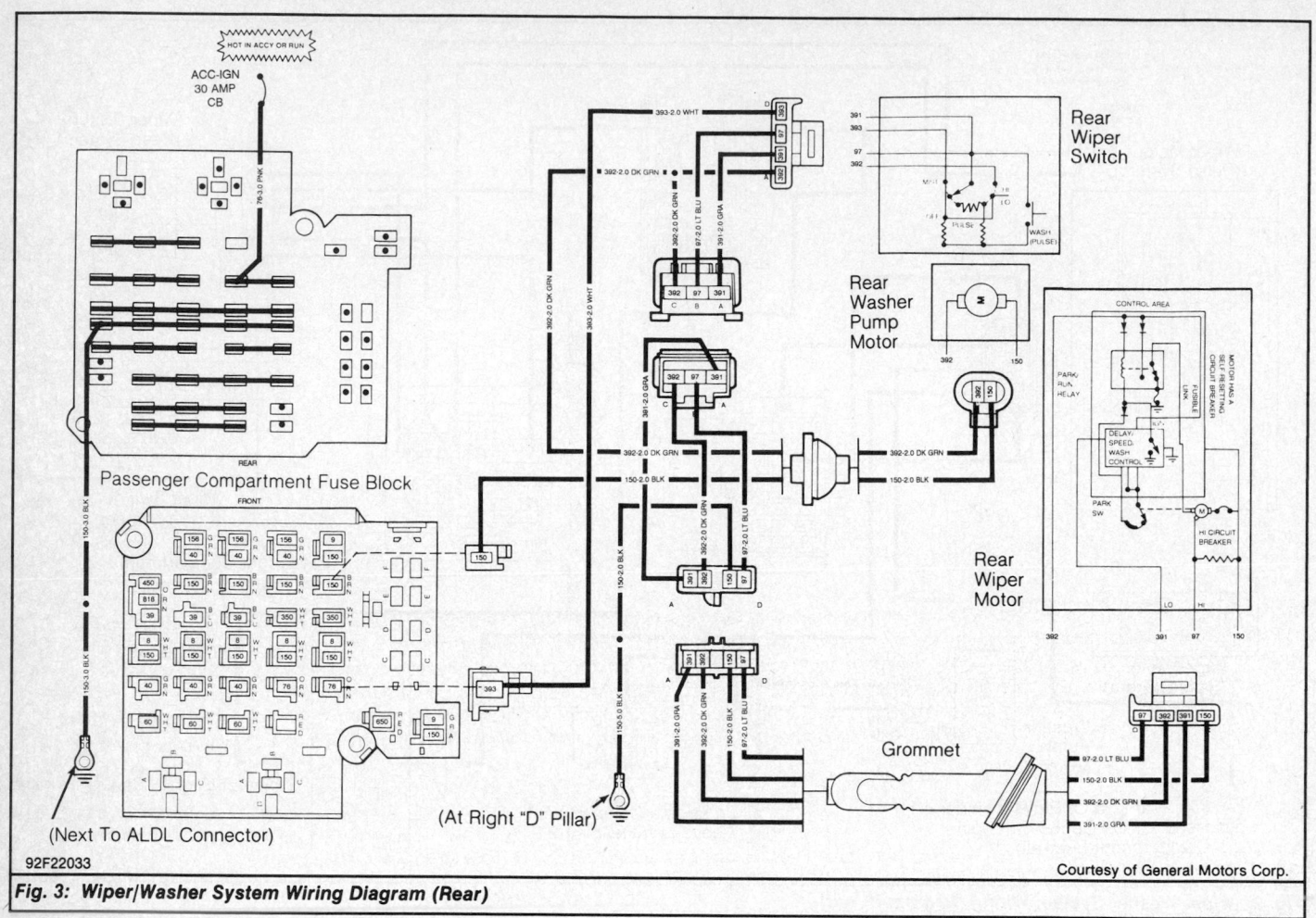

Fig. 3: Wiper/Washer System Wiring Diagram (Rear)

92F22033

Courtesy of General Motors Corp.

Blazer, Bravada, Jimmy, Pickup,
Sonoma, Syclone, Typhoon

DESCRIPTION

FRONT

System is either a base system or pulse system. Both systems include low, high, and mist modes. Pulse system includes a delay function that causes the wipers to sweep once with a delay interval between sweeps. Variable resistor in wiper switch adjusts amount of current to a delay module attached to wiper motor. Delay module controls current to wiper motor.

REAR

System uses a positive park, single-speed wiper motor. In addition to ON and OFF positions, switch on instrument panel has momentary WASH and WIPE positions. Washer pump motor is located in engine compartment, inside washer fluid reservoir.

TESTING

FRONT

NOTE: Ensure WIPER fuse is okay before testing system.

Wipers Inoperative In All Modes – 1) Turn ignition switch to ACC position. Check voltage at White wire terminal of wiper switch connector. See Fig. 4. If battery voltage is not present, repair open in White wire between wiper switch and fuse.

2) If battery voltage is present, check voltage at Gray wire terminal of wiper switch connector with wiper switch in LOW position, and at Purple wire with wiper switch in HIGH position. If battery voltage is not present at one or both wires, replace wiper switch.

3) If battery voltage is present at both wires, disconnect wiper motor connector. Connect fused jumper wire between battery positive terminal and Gray wire terminal of wiper motor connector. If wipers do not operate, replace delay module or wiper motor. If wipers operate, repair open in Gray or Purple wire between wiper switch and wiper motor.

Wipers Run In Low Speed Only – 1) Disconnect wiper motor connector. Turn ignition switch to ACC position. Turn wiper switch to HIGH position. Check voltage at Purple wire terminal of wiper motor connector. See Fig. 4. If battery voltage is present, replace delay module or wiper motor.

2) If battery voltage is not present, check voltage at Purple wire terminal of wiper switch connector. If battery voltage is not present, replace wiper switch. If battery voltage is present, repair open in Purple wire between wiper switch and wiper motor.

Wipers Run In High Speed Only – 1) Disconnect wiper motor connector. Turn ignition switch to ACC position. Turn wiper switch to LO position. Connect test light between ground and Gray wire terminal of wiper motor connector. See Fig. 4. If test light comes on, replace delay module or wiper motor.

2) If test light does not come on, connect test light between ground and Gray wire terminal of wiper switch connector. If test light does not come on, replace wiper switch. If test light comes on, repair open in Gray wire between wiper switch and wiper motor.

Wipers Will Not Park – 1) Turn ignition switch to RUN position. Connect test light between ground and White wire terminal of wiper motor connector. See Fig. 4. If test light does not come on, repair open in White wire between wiper motor and 25-amp WIPER fuse.

2) If test light comes on, connect test light between ground and Orange wire terminal of wiper motor connector. If test light does not come on, replace delay module or wiper motor. If test light comes on, disconnect wiper switch connector.

3) Connect test light between ground and Orange wire terminal of wiper motor connector. If test light comes on, replace wiper switch. If test light does not comes on, repair open in Orange wire between wiper motor and wiper switch.

Wipers Will Not Shut Off – 1) Disconnect wiper motor connector. Connect fused jumper wire between Orange and Gray wire terminals of wiper motor connector. See Fig. 4. Connect fused jumper wire between battery positive terminal and White wire terminal of wiper motor connector.

2) If wiper motor parks and turns off, replace wiper switch. If wiper motor does not turn off, replace delay module or wiper motor.

Washer Inoperative (Base System) – 1) Disconnect washer pump motor connector. Turn ignition switch to ACC position. Connect test light between ground and Pink wire terminal of washer pump connector with WASH button pushed. See Fig. 4. If test light does not come on, go to step 3).

2) If test light comes on, connect test light between Pink and Black wire terminals of washer pump connector with WASH button pushed. If test light comes on, replace washer pump. If test light does not come on, repair open in Black wire between washer pump and ground.

3) Connect test light between ground and Pink wire terminal of wiper motor connector with WASH button pushed. If test light does not come on, replace wiper switch. If test light comes on, repair open in Pink wire between wiper motor and washer pump.

Washer Inoperative (Pulse System) – 1) Disconnect washer pump motor connector. Turn ignition switch to ACC position. Connect test light between ground and Pink wire terminal of washer pump connector with WASH button pushed. See Fig. 4. If test light does not come on, go to step 3).

2) If test light comes on, connect test light between Pink and Black wire terminals of washer pump connector with WASH button pushed. If test light comes on, replace washer pump. If test light does not come on, repair open in Black wire between washer pump and ground.

3) Connect test light between ground and Gray wire terminal of wiper motor connector with WASH button pushed. If test light does not come on, replace wiper switch. If test light comes on, connect test light between ground and Orange wire terminal of wiper motor connector.

4) If test light does not come on, replace delay module or wiper motor. If test light comes on, check for open in Orange wire between wiper motor and wiper switch. If wire is okay, replace wiper switch.

REAR

NOTE: Ensure RADIO fuse is okay before testing.

Wiper Inoperative – 1) Turn ignition switch to ACC position. Disconnect wiper switch connector. Connect test light between ground and Brown/White wire terminal of wiper switch connector. If test light does not come on, repair open in Brown/White wire between wiper switch and fuse.

2) If test light comes on, connect wiper switch connector. Turn wiper switch on. Connect test light between ground and White wire terminal of wiper switch connector. If test light does not come on, replace wiper switch. If test light comes on, connect test light between ground and White wire terminal of wiper motor connector.

3) If test light does not come on, repair open in White wire between wiper switch and wiper motor. If test light comes on, connect test light between White and Black wire terminals of wiper motor connector. If test light comes on, replace wiper motor. If test light does not come on, repair open in Black wire between wiper motor and ground.

Washer Inoperative – 1) Disconnect washer pump motor connector. Turn ignition switch to ACC position. Connect test light between ground and Dark Green wire terminal of washer pump motor connector. Push and hold washer button. If test light comes on, go to next step. If test light does not come on, go to step 3).

2) Connect test light between Dark Green and Black wire terminals of washer pump motor connector. Push and hold washer button. If test light comes on, replace washer pump motor. If test light does not come on, repair open in Black wire between washer pump motor and ground.

3) Connect test light between ground and Dark Green wire terminal of wiper switch connector. Push and hold washer button. If test light does not come on, replace wiper switch. If test light comes on, repair open in Dark Green wire between wiper switch and washer pump motor.

GM
4-54

1992 SAFETY EQUIPMENT
Wiper/Washer Systems – "S" & "T" Series (Cont.)

REMOVAL & INSTALLATION

WARNING: When battery is disconnected, vehicle computer and memory systems may lose memory data. Driveability problems may exist until computer systems have completed a relearn cycle. See COMPUTER RELEARN PROCEDURES article in GENERAL INFORMATION before disconnecting battery.

WIPER MOTOR

Removal & Installation (Front) – 1) Disconnect negative battery cable. Remove wiper arms. *See Fig. 1.* Remove cowl vent grille and screen. Mark wiper motor crank arm in relation to motor shaft for reassembly reference.

2) Remove wiper motor crank arm. Disconnect wiper motor electrical connector. Remove motor mounting screws. Remove motor. To install, reverse removal procedure.

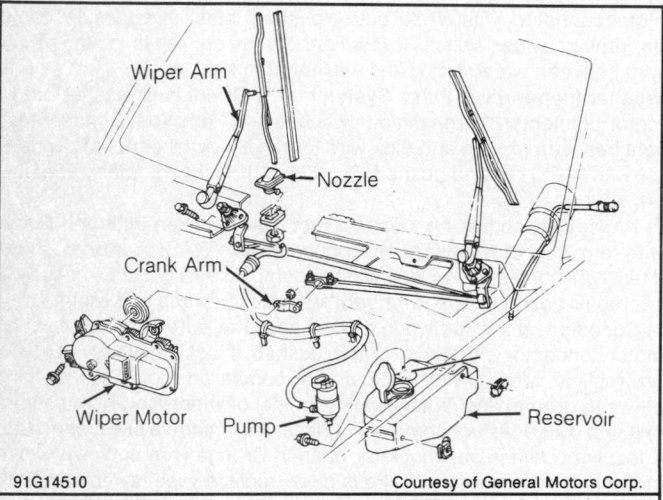

91G14510   Courtesy of General Motors Corp.

Fig. 1: Exploded View Of Front Wiper/Washer System

Removal & Installation (Rear) – 1) Disconnect battery negative cable. Remove wiper motor cover. *See Fig. 2.* Remove roof trim panel. Disconnect washer hose. Disconnect wiper motor electrical connector. To ease removal of wiper arm, install 1/8" drift pin through hole in wiper arm to hold detent spring. Remove wiper arm.

2) While supporting end gate glass, remove end gate glass support arm. Remove wiper motor mounting screws. Remove wiper motor/hinge bolt. Remove nuts, spacers and flat seals from wiper motor. Remove wiper motor. To install, reverse removal procedure.

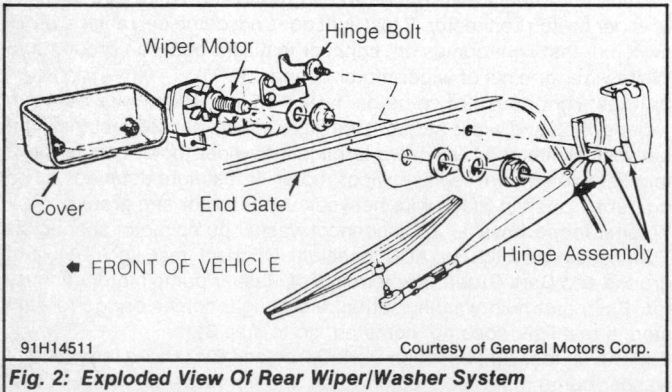

91H14511   Courtesy of General Motors Corp.

Fig. 2: Exploded View Of Rear Wiper/Washer System

WIPER MOTOR COVER (FRONT)

Removal & Installation – Remove wiper motor. See WIPER MOTOR under REMOVAL & INSTALLATION. From housing side, drill out 7 rivets holding cover to housing. Remove cover. To install, reverse removal procedure using self-tapping screws to attach cover to housing.

WIPER MOTOR HOUSING (FRONT)

Removal – 1) Remove wiper motor. See WIPER MOTOR under REMOVAL & INSTALLATION. Remove wiper motor cover. See WIPER MOTOR COVER (FRONT). Remove crank gear lock nut, crank arm, shaft seal, thrust collar and washer. Push end of gear shaft through housing to remove gear assembly and washer.

2) File burr from retaining ring groove and where crank arm seats on shaft. Remove intermediate gear and washers. Drill ends off 4 rivets holding bearings and bearing straps in place.

CAUTION: DO NOT let metal chips fall into wiper motor.

3) Remove screws holding brush assembly in place. Remove armature, brush and magnet as an assembly to avoid having to realign brushes.

Installation – To install, reverse removal procedure using new housing retaining ring and self-tapping screws. Position thrust pin casing with insert about 1/32" above rear of pin.

WIPER SWITCH (FRONT)

NOTE: Manufacturer gives wiper switch removal procedure with steering column removed from vehicle.

Removal & Installation – 1) Turn steering wheel to straight-ahead position. Disconnect negative battery cable. Remove instrument panel trim cover. Disconnect shift cable from steering column shift tube lever. Remove upper pinch bolt from column intermediate shaft. Mark intermediate shaft yoke in relation to steering shaft for reassembly reference.

2) Remove steering wheel. Disconnect electrical connectors if necessary. While supporting steering column, remove bolts from steering column upper support bracket. Remove steering column.

3) Remove lock plate cover. Screw center post of Lock Plate Compressor (J-23653) onto steering shaft as far as it will go. *See Fig. 3.* Compress lock plate by turning center post nut clockwise.

4) Pry snap ring out of shaft groove. Discard ring. Remove lock plate compressor. Remove lock plate. Remove turn signal cancel cam. Remove upper bearing spring and thrust washer. Turn multifunction lever upward (right turn position).

5) Pull multifunction lever straight out to remove. Remove hazard warning knob. Remove turn signal switch assembly mounting screws. Pull switch assembly and wiring harness out of column. Remove wire protector. Remove buzzer switch assembly. Remove lock cylinder retaining screw.

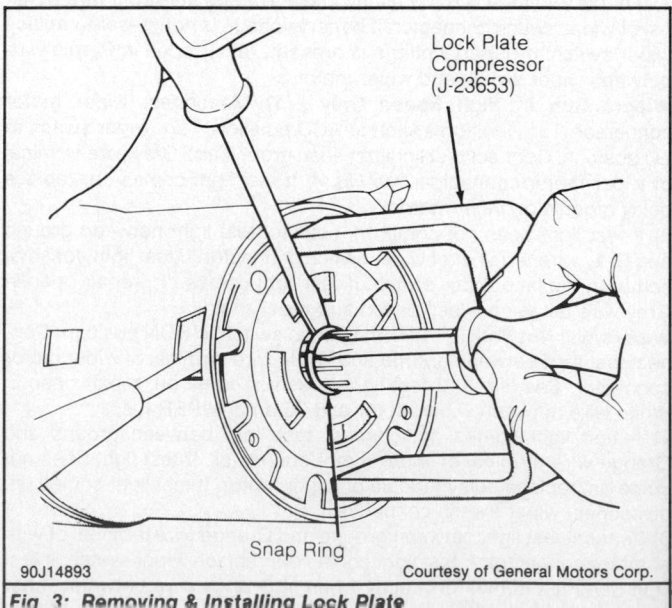

90J14893   Courtesy of General Motors Corp.

Fig 3: Removing & Installing Lock Plate

1992 SAFETY EQUIPMENT
Wiper/Washer Systems – "S" & "T" Series (Cont.)

GM
4-55

6) Remove lock cylinder set. Remove retaining ring from upper end of steering shaft. Slide steering shaft out of column assembly. Remove dimmer switch and actuator rod. Remove ignition switch. Remove 4 screws securing gear shift bowl to column housing. Remove upper bearing retainer. Separate gear shift bowl from column housing. Remove cover for access to wiper switch. Remove wiper switch.

7) To install, reverse removal procedure using new lock plate snap ring. Tighten intermediate shaft upper pinch bolt to **30 ft. lbs. (41 N.m)**.

WIRING DIAGRAMS

For rear wiper/washer system wiring diagram and an additional front wiper/washer system wiring diagram, see appropriate chassis wiring diagram in WIRING DIAGRAMS.

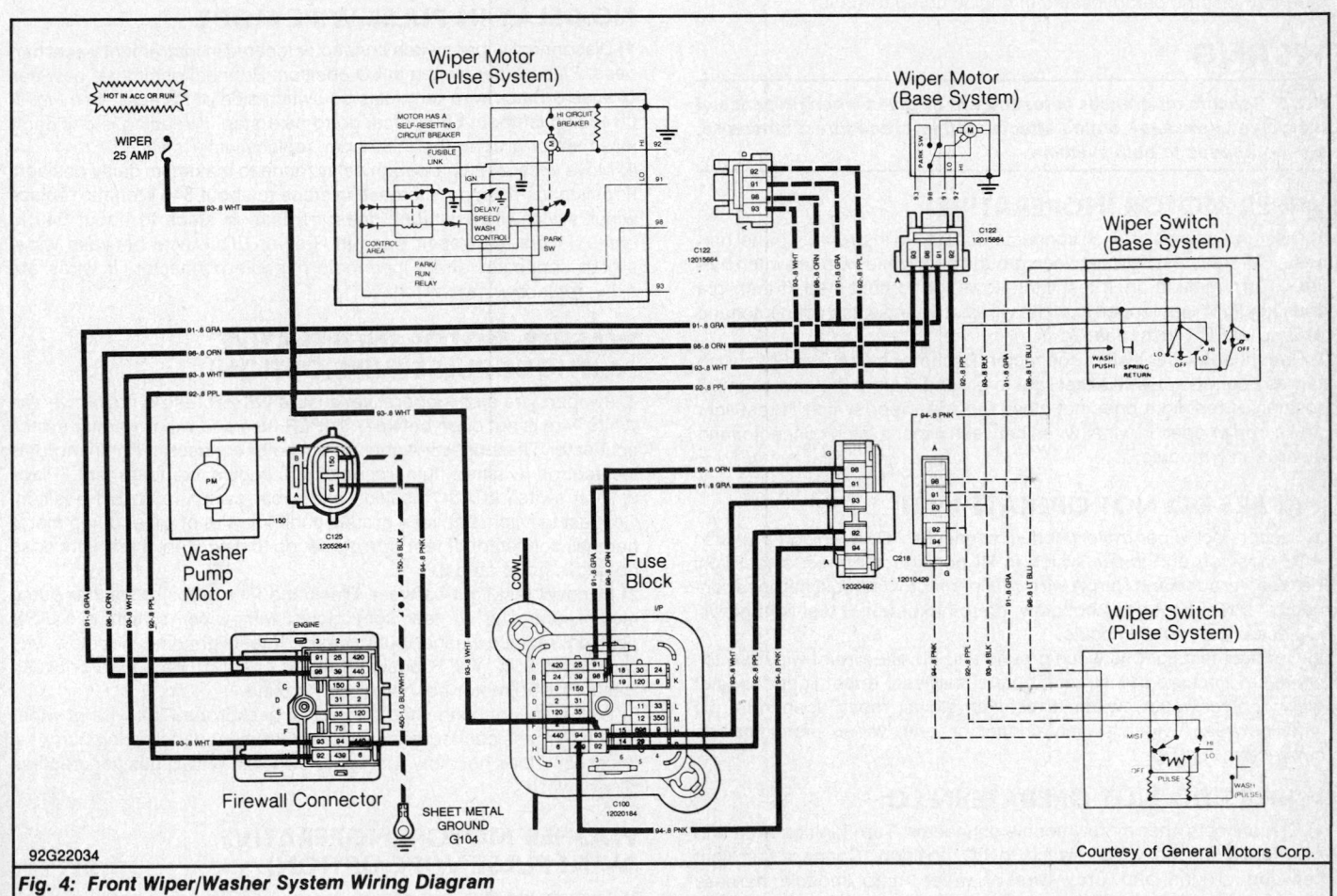

92G22034

Courtesy of General Motors Corp.

Fig. 4: Front Wiper/Washer System Wiring Diagram

DESCRIPTION

Wiper system consists of a 2-speed, permanent magnet motor enclosed in an upper and lower housing, a column-mounted wiper switch and a wiper motor mounted on the firewall. Vehicles equipped with an optional pulse wipe delay use a motor/module combination. Power for wiper/washer system is provided by a 25-amp WIPER fuse located in the fuse block. Motor/module is protected by an internal, self-resetting circuit breaker. Windshield washer is a reservoir-mounted electric pump located in engine compartment.

TESTING

NOTE: *Specific differences in testing will be given when presence of the pulse wipe delay option affects testing procedures; otherwise, testing applies to both systems.*

WIPER MOTOR INOPERATIVE

1) Disconnect wiper switch connector located in instrument panel harness. Connect test light between ground and White wire of switch harness. Turn ignition on. If test light glows, go to next step. If test light does not light repair open in White wire between switch connector and 20-amp WIPER fuse. See Fig. 1.
2) Reconnect wiper switch connector. Backprobe Gray wire of switch harness connector with a test light to ground. Turn wiper switch to LO position. If test light does not glow, replace wiper switch. If test light glows, repair open in wiper wires between wiper switch connector and wiper motor/module.

WIPERS DO NOT OPERATE IN HI

1) Disconnect wiper motor/module connector. Turn ignition switch to ACC position and wiper switch in HI position. Connect a test light between ground and Purple wire of wiper motor/module harness connector. If test light does not glow, go to next step. If test light glows, replace wiper motor/module.
2) Connect test light between ground and Purple wire of wiper switch connector located in instrument panel harness. If test light does not glow, replace wiper switch. If test light glows, repair open in Purple wire between wiper switch connector and wiper motor/module connector. See Fig. 1.

WIPERS DO NOT OPERATE IN LO

1) Disconnect wiper motor/module connector. Turn ignition switch to ACC position and wiper switch to LO position. Connect test light between ground and Gray wire of wiper motor/module harness connector. See Fig. 1. If test light does not glow, go to next step. If test light does glow, replace wiper motor/module.
2) Connect test light between ground and Gray wire of wiper switch connector located in instrument panel harness. If test light does not glow, replace wiper switch. If test light glows, repair open in Gray wire between wiper switch connector and wiper motor/module connector.

WIPERS WILL NOT SHUT OFF

1) Disconnect wiper motor/module connector. Turn ignition switch to ACC position and wiper switch to LO position. Connect test light between ground and Gray wire of wiper switch harness connector located in instrument panel harness. If test light glows, go to next step. If test light does not glow, repair open in Gray wire between wiper motor/module connector and wiper switch connector.
2) Place wiper switch in HI position. Connect test light between ground and Purple wire of wiper motor/module harness connector. If test light glows, go to next step. If test light does not glow, repair open in Purple wire between wiper motor/module connector and wiper switch connector.
3) Connect test light between ground and White wire of wiper motor/module harness connector. If test light does not glow, repair open in White wire between wiper motor/module connector and ground. If vehicle is equipped with pulse wipe delay option and test light glows,

replace wiper motor/module. If vehicle is not equipped with pulse wipe delay option and test light glows, go to next step.
4) Turn ignition and wiper switches to OFF position. Disconnect battery negative cable. Connect ohmmeter between Orange and Gray wires of wiper motor harness connector. If resistance reading is zero ohms, replace wiper motor. If resistance is greater than zero ohms, repair open in Orange wire between wiper motor connector and wiper switch connector.

NO DELAY IN PULSE WIPE MODE

1) Disconnect wiper switch connector located in instrument panel harness. Place wiper switch in LO position. Connect ohmmeter between Gray and Black wire terminals on switch side of harness. See Fig. 1. If reading is about 680 ohms, go to next step. If reading is decidedly less than or greater than 680 ohm, replace wiper switch.
2) Move wiper switch through delay range to maximum delay position. If resistance does not increase in steps to about 540 k/ohms, replace wiper switch. If resistance does increase in steps to about 540 k/ohms, locate and repair open in Gray or Black wire between wiper switch connector and wiper motor/module connector. If wires are okay, replace wiper switch.

WASHER MOTOR INOPERATIVE (WITHOUT PULSE WIPE OPTION)

1) If wipers are also inoperative, ensure WIPER fuse is not blown and White wire is not open between WIPER fuse and wiper washer switch connector. Disconnect washer pump motor connector. Pump motor is located on washer fluid reservoir in engine compartment. Place ignition switch in ACC position and wiper switch in WASH position. Connect test light between ground and Pink wire of wiper pump motor harness connector. If test light glows, go to next step. If test light does not glow, go to step 3).
2) Connect test light between Black and Pink wires of washer pump motor connector. If test light glows with wiper switch in WASH position, replace washer pump motor. If test light does not glow with wiper switch in WASH position, repair open in Black wire between washer pump motor connector and ground.
3) With test light connected to ground, backprobe Pink wire of wiper switch harness connector located in instrument panel wiring harness. If test light does not glow with wiper switch in WASH position, replace wiper switch.

WASHER MOTOR INOPERATIVE (WITH PULSE WIPE OPTION)

1) If wipers are also inoperative, ensure WIPER fuse is not blown and White wire is not open between WIPER fuse and wiper washer switch connector. Disconnect washer pump motor connector. Pump motor is located on washer fluid reservoir in engine compartment. Place ignition switch in ACC position and wiper switch in WASH position. Connect test light between ground and Pink wire of wiper pump motor harness connector. See Fig. 1. If test light glows, go to next step. If test light does not glow, go to step 3).
2) Connect test light between Black and Pink wires of washer pump motor connector. If test light glows with wiper switch in WASH position, replace washer pump motor. If test light does not glow with wiper switch in WASH position, repair open in Black wire between washer pump motor connector and ground.
3) Connect test light between ground and Gray wire of wiper motor/module harness connector. If test light glows, go to next step. If test light does not glow, locate and repair open in Gray wire between wiper motor/module and wiper switch connector. If wire is not open, replace wiper switch.
4) Connect test light between ground and Orange wire of wiper motor/module connector. If test light does not glow, replace wiper motor/module. If test light does glow, locate and repair open in Orange wire between wiper motor/module connector and wiper switch connector. If no open is present in Orange wire, replace wiper switch.

Fig. 3: Identifying Front Wiper M...

Rear Wiper/Washer Switch Test

tor at rear wiper motor module. U...
for voltage or continuity at design...
tor as specified. *See Fig. 4.*

2) Check for voltage with ignition...
with ignition off. If power is not pres...
ness. Repair as necessary. If switc...

REAR WIPER MOTOR MODULE TE...

Terminal

A ....
B ....
C ....

TERM.	SW ON	PULS...
A	B (+)	B (+...
B	Ground	Grou...
C	B (+)	B (+...

91A14506

Fig. 4: Rear Wiper/Washer Switch T...

SYSTEM TESTING

*NOTE: Check front wiper system ope...
system. See Fig. 1.*

Front Wipers Inoperative In All Mod...
a voltmeter, check for battery voltag...
"N") at front wiper switch and ground. I...
step. If voltage does not exist, chec...
White wire between fuse block and w...

2) Remove electrical connector from...
check for battery voltage between Wh...
tor and ground. If voltage exists, proce...
not exist, check for defective connec...
White wire between fuse block and wi...

3) Place wiper switch in LO position. Us...
etween Gray wire of wiper motor co...
voltage exists, proceed to next step. If...
check for open in Gray wire between...
motor. If wiring circuit is okay, replace...
4) Place wiper switch in high speed. Usi...
etween Purple wire of wiper motor co...
voltage exists, proceed to next step. If...

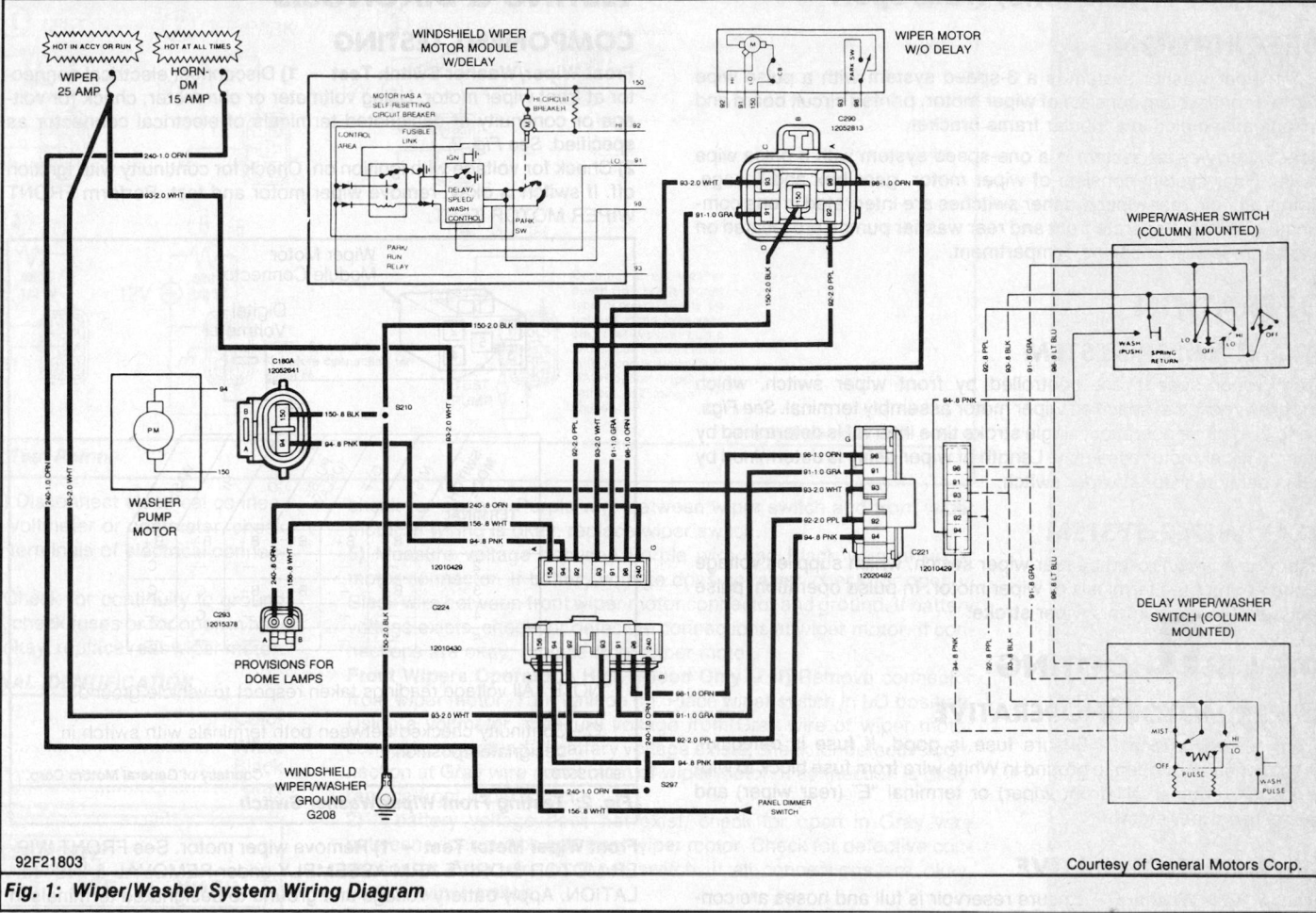

Fig. 1: Wiper/Washer System Wiring Diagram

Courtesy of General Motors Corp.

REMOVAL & INSTALLATION

WIPER MOTOR

NOTE: Wiper motor removal and installation information is not available from manufacturer since wiper motor is installed by individual body manufacturers.

OVERHAUL

Repairs to motor/gear box section of wiper assembly are limited to switch, plus external parts, crank arm, spacer and plastic seal, and output shaft seal. No other overhaul procedures are given by manufacturer.

WIRING DIAGRAMS

For additional information, see appropriate chassis wiring diagram in WIRING DIAGRAMS.

Wip

Lumina APV, Silhoue

DESCRIPTION

Front wiper/washer system is
mode. Front system consists
linkage assembled in a tubula

Rear wiper/washer system is
mode. Rear system consists
Both front and rear wiper/was
bination switch. Separate front
washer reservoir in engine co

OPERATION

FRONT WIPER SYSTE

Front wiper speeds are cor
supplies voltage to specified w
1 and 2. In pulse operation, sin
timer in wiper motor assembly.
pulse delay resistor in wiper s

REAR WIPER SYSTEM

Rear wiper is controlled by re
to the appropriate terminals of
module of motor controls wipe

TROUBLE SHOOTI

WIPER MOTOR INOP

Front & Rear Wipers – Ens
check for short or open to grou
er switch terminal "N" (front
respective wiper motor.

WASHER INOPERATI

Front & Rear Washers – Ens
nected. Check for clogged spr
aged connector seal at was
operate and wipers operate i
between front wiper switch an

W I P E R	M I S T	Wipe uous	
	O F F	Wipe posit	
S W I T C H P O S I T I O N	D E L A Y	Wipe wipe of 0- then	
	L O	Wipe	
	H I	Wipe	

90E13569

Fig. 1: Identifying Front Wipe

Front Washer Inoperative – **1)** Remove electrical connector at washer motor. Turn ignition on. Connect test light between Black wire and
Pink wire of washer motor connector.

2) Turn washer on and note test light. If voltage exists, replace washer
motor. If no voltage exists, connect test light between Black wire terminal of washer motor connector and ground.

3) Turn washer on and note test light. If voltage exists, repair open in
Black wire from washer motor to ground.

4) If voltage does not exist, install electrical connector on washer
motor. Remove connector from wiper motor. Connect test light
between Gray wire of wiper motor harness and ground. Turn washer
on and observe test light.

5) If voltage exists, check for open in Pink wire between wiper motor
and washer motor. If wire is okay, replace wiper motor. If voltage does
not exist, check for open in Gray wire between wiper switch terminal
"P" and wiper motor. If wire is okay, replace wiper switch.

Rear Wiper Inoperative In All Modes – **1)** Turn ignition on. Using test
light, check for battery voltage between terminal "E" (White wire) at
rear wiper switch and ground. If test light comes on, proceed to next
step. If test light does not come on, check for defective fuse or open
in White wire between fuse block and wiper switch terminal "E".

2) Place rear wiper switch in ON position. Using a test light, check for
voltage between terminal "A" (Gray wire) of wiper switch and ground.
If test light comes on, go to next step. If test light does not come on,
check connections at wiper switch terminals "E" (White wire) and "A"
(Gray wire). If connections are okay, replace wiper switch.

3) Using a test light, backprobe terminal "C" (Gray wire) of wiper motor
module connector to ground. If test light comes on, go to next step. If
test light does not come on, check for faulty connections or open in
Gray wire between wiper motor module connector terminal "C" and
wiper switch terminal "A". Repair as necessary.

4) Using a test light, backprobe terminal "A" (White wire) of wiper
motor module connector to ground. If test light comes on, go to next
step. If test light does not come on, check for faulty connections or
open in White wire between wiper motor module connector terminal
"A" and fuse block. Repair as necessary.

5) Using a test light, backprobe between terminals "A" (White wire) and
"B" (Black wire) of wiper motor module connector. If test light comes
on, check for faulty connection at wiper motor module. If connection
is okay, replace wiper motor module. If test light does not come on,
repair open in Black (ground) wire between wiper motor module connector terminal "B" and ground.

Rear Wiper Delay Operates Incorrectly Or Not At All – **1)** Remove
wiper switch from console and then reconnect electrical connector.
Place rear wiper switch in DELAY position. Using an ohmmeter, measure the resistance between terminals "A" and "E" of wiper switch.

2) If resistance is approximately 750,000 ohms, replace rear window
wiper motor module. If resistance is not as specified, replace wiper
switch.

Rear Washer Inoperative – **1)** Disconnect rear washer motor at
washer reservoir. Turn ignition on. Connect a test light between terminals "A" (Dark Green wire) and "B" (Black wire) of washer motor
harness connector. Activate wash switch while observing test light.

2) If test light does not come on while activating wash switch, go to
next step. If test light does come on while activating wash switch,
check for faulty connections at rear washer motor and repair as necessary. If connections are okay, replace washer motor.

3) Connect test light between terminal "A" (Dark Green wire) of rear
washer motor harness connector and ground. If test light does not
come on while activating wash switch, go to next step. If test light does
come on while activating wash switch, repair open in Black wire
between washer motor and ground.

4) Check for open or faulty connections in Dark Green wire between
washer motor and wiper switch. Repair as necessary. If Dark Green
wire is okay, replace wiper switch.

REMOVAL & INSTALLATION

FRONT WIPER ARMS

Removal – Disconnect washer hoses. Remove wiper arm retaining
nut. Lift wiper arm and insert a small pin through both holes next to
pivot area of wiper arm. Using Puller (J-22888-D), remove wiper arm.

Installation – **1)** Ensure wiper motor is in Park position. Install wiper
arm. Install retaining nut finger tight. Remove pin from pivot area of
wiper arm.

2) On driver side applications, measure from tip of wiper blade to bottom edge of windshield at the glass junction panel. Glass junction panel is located at bottom of windshield. Distance must be approximately
5.8" (147 mm). If distance is correct, tighten retaining nut to specification.

3) On passenger side applications, measure from tip of wiper blade to
bottom edge of windshield. Distance must be approximately 1.3" (33
mm). If distance is correct, tighten retaining nut to specification. On all
applications, reconnect washer hoses.

FRONT WIPER MOTOR
& DRIVE ARM ASSEMBLY

Removal – **1)** Remove wiper arms. See FRONT WIPER ARMS under
REMOVAL & INSTALLATION. Remove air cleaner. Remove electrical
connector from wiper motor.

2) Remove drive arm retaining bolts. Remove wiper motor assembly
retaining nuts. *See Fig. 5.* Remove wiper motor assembly with drive
arms. Disconnect wiper motor from drive arms.

Installation – To install, reverse removal procedure. Install center
nut on wiper motor frame first, followed by remaining wiper motor
frame retaining nuts. Install drive arm housing bolts last. Tighten bolts/
nuts to specification. See TORQUE SPECIFICATIONS table at end of
article.

FRONT WIPER LINKAGE

Removal – Remove wiper motor assembly. See FRONT WIPER
MOTOR & DRIVE ARM ASSEMBLY under REMOVAL & INSTALLA-
TION. Loosen bolts until linkage is released from ball on drive arms.
Remove bellcrank bolts. *See Fig. 5.*

Installation – To install, reverse removal procedure. Ensure linkage
is positioned correctly.

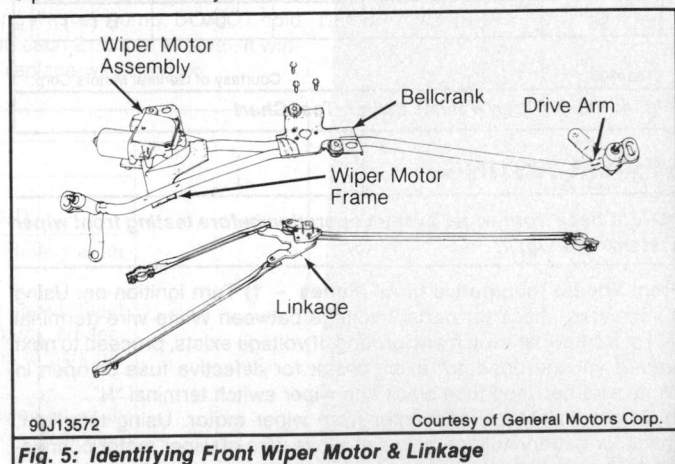

90J13572   Courtesy of General Motors Corp.

Fig. 5: Identifying Front Wiper Motor & Linkage

FRONT WIPER MOTOR
PRINTED CIRCUIT BOARD

NOTE: Remove front wiper motor assembly to service printed circuit
board (if necessary).

Removal & Installation – Disconnect electrical connector at front wiper motor. Remove cover retaining bolts on wiper motor. Lift circuit board from front wiper motor assembly. To install, reverse removal procedure.

REAR WIPER ARM

Removal – Lift wiper arm from back glass and pull retaining latch. Remove arm from wiper pivot shaft.

Installation – With wiper motor in PARK position, install head of wiper arm on serrated wiper pivot shaft in a position where wiper blade will rest in proper parked position. Install left arm extension and push in retaining latch when head is fully seated on pivot shaft.

REAR WIPER MOTOR

Removal & Installation – Disconnect motor electrical connector. Remove rear wiper arm. See REAR WIPER ARM under REMOVAL & INSTALLATION. Remove nut securing pivot shaft to back glass. Remove motor mounting screws from inside vehicle. Remove motor. To install, reverse removal procedure.

WIRING DIAGRAMS

See appropriate chassis wiring diagram in WIRING DIAGRAMS.

TORQUE SPECIFICATIONS

NOTE: Torque specifications for rear wiper/washer system components are not available from manufacturer.

TORQUE SPECIFICATIONS (FRONT WIPER/WASHER SYSTEM)

Application	Ft. Lbs. (N.m)
Wiper Arm Nut	30 (41)

Application	INCH Lbs. (N.m)
Drive Arm Housing Bolt	72-84 (8-9)
Linkage Bellcrank Bolt	48-72 (5-8)
Linkage-To-Ball Bolt	48-72 (5-8)
Linkage-To-Wiper Motor Bolt	48-72 (5-8)
Wiper Motor Bolt	48-72 (5-8)
Wiper Motor Frame Nut	72-84 (8-9)

DESCRIPTION

Wiper system consists of a 2-speed, permanent magnet motor enclosed in an upper and lower housing, a column-mounted wiper switch and a wiper motor/module mounted on the firewall. Vehicle is equipped with a pulse wipe delay. Power for wiper/washer system is provided by a 25-amp WIPER fuse located in the fuse block. Motor/module is protected by an internal, self-resetting circuit breaker. Windshield washer is a reservoir-mounted electric pump located in engine compartment.

TESTING

WIPER MOTOR INOPERATIVE

1) Disconnect wiper switch connector located under instrument panel, to left of steering column. Connect test light between ground and White wire of switch harness. Turn ignition on. If test light glows, go to next step. If test light does not light repair open in White wire between switch connector and 25-amp WIPER fuse. See Fig. 1.

2) Reconnect wiper switch connector. Place wiper switch in LO position and backprobe Gray wire of switch harness connector with a test light to ground. Place wiper switch in HI position and backprobe Purple wire of switch harness connector. If test light glows on both wires, go to next step. If test light does not glow on one or both wires, replace wiper switch.

3) Disconnect wiper motor/module connector. Using a jumper wire, connect terminal No. 150 (Black wire) of wiper motor to ground. Using a fused jumper wire, apply battery voltage to terminal No. 91 (Gray wire) of wiper motor.

4) If wipers do not operate, repair/replace wiper motor. If wipers operate, locate and repair open in White and/or Purple wires between wiper switch connector and motor/module harness connector.

WIPERS DO NOT OPERATE IN HI

1) Disconnect wiper motor/module connector. Turn ignition switch to ACC position and wiper switch in HI position. Connect a test light between ground and Purple wire of wiper motor/module harness connector. If test light does not glow, go to next step. If test light glows, repair/replace wiper motor/module.

2) Connect test light between ground and Purple wire of wiper switch connector located under instrument panel, to left of steering column. If test light does not glow, replace wiper switch. If test light glows, repair open in Purple wire between wiper switch connector and wiper motor/module connector. See Fig. 1.

WIPERS DO NOT OPERATE IN LO

1) Disconnect wiper motor/module connector. Turn ignition switch to ACC position and wiper switch to LO position. Connect test light between ground and Gray wire of wiper motor/module harness connector. See Fig. 1. If test light does not glow, go to next step. If test light does glow, repair/replace wiper motor/module.

2) Connect test light between ground and Gray wire of wiper switch connector located under instrument panel, to left of steering column. If test light does not glow, replace wiper switch. If test light glows, locate and repair open in Gray wire between wiper switch connector and wiper motor/module connector.

WIPERS WILL NOT PARK

1) Place ignition switch in RUN position. Connect test light between ground and White wire of wiper motor/module harness connector. If test light glows, go to next step. If test light does not glow, repair open in White wire between 25-amp WIPER fuse and wiper motor/module harness connector.

2) Connect test light between ground and Pink wire of wiper motor/module harness connector. If test light glows, replace wiper/washer switch. If test light does not glow, repair/replace wiper motor/module.

WIPERS WILL NOT SHUT OFF

Disconnect wiper motor/module connector. Connect jumper wire between terminals No. 94 and 91 of wiper motor. See Fig. 1. Connect fused jumper wire between battery voltage terminal No. 93 of wiper motor/module. If wiper motor parks and turns off, replace wiper switch. If motor continues to run, repair/replace motor.

NO DELAY IN PULSE WIPE MODE

1) Disconnect wiper switch connector located under instrument panel, to left of steering column. Place wiper switch in PULSE position. Connect ohmmeter between Gray and Black wire terminals on switch side of harness. See Fig. 1. If reading is about 680 ohms, go to next step. If reading is decidedly less than or greater than 680 ohm, replace wiper switch.

2) Move wiper switch through delay range to maximum delay position. If resistance does not increase in steps to about 540 k/ohms, replace wiper switch. If resistance does increase in steps to about 540 k/ohms, locate and repair open in Gray or Black wire between wiper switch connector and wiper motor/module connector. If wires are okay, replace wiper switch.

WASHER MOTOR INOPERATIVE

1) If wipers are also inoperative, ensure WIPER fuse is not blown and White wire is not open between WIPER fuse and wiper washer switch connector. Disconnect washer pump motor connector. Pump motor is located on washer fluid reservoir in engine compartment. Place ignition switch in ACC position and wiper switch in WASH position. Connect test light between ground and Pink wire of wiper pump motor harness connector. See Fig. 1. If test light glows, go to next step. If test light does not glow, go to step 3).

2) Connect test light between Black and Pink wires of washer pump motor connector. If test light glows with wiper switch in WASH position, replace washer pump motor. If test light does not glow with wiper switch in WASH position, repair open in Black wire between washer pump motor connector and ground.

3) Connect test light between ground and Gray wire of wiper motor/module harness connector. Place wiper switch in WASH position. If test light glows, go to next step. If test light does not glow, locate and repair open in Gray wire between wiper motor/module and wiper switch connector. If wire is not open, replace wiper switch.

4) Connect test light between ground and Pink wire of wiper motor/module connector. If test light does not glow, repair/replace wiper motor/module. If test light does glow, locate and repair open in Pink wire between wiper motor/module connector and wiper switch connector.

REMOVAL & INSTALLATION

WIPER MOTOR

Removal – 1) Ensure wipers are in park position. Disconnect negative battery cable. Remove wiper arms from wiper linkage. Remove cowl panel cover. Remove drive rod from wiper motor crank arm. Loosen nuts holding drive rod to wiper motor and remove drive rod. Disconnect wiring to motor.

2) Remove left defroster outlet from flex hose and position hose to one side. Remove screw securing left heater duct to engine cover shroud and slip heater duct down and out. Remove washer hoses. Remove screws securing wiper motor to firewall. Remove wiper motor.

Installation – To install, reverse removal procedure. Ensure wipers are in park position before installing. Lubricate wiper motor crank arm pivot prior to installation.

OVERHAUL

Repairs to motor/gear box section of wiper assembly are limited to switch, plus external parts, crank arm, spacer and plastic seal, and output shaft seal. No other overhaul procedures are given by manufacturer.

WIRING DIAGRAMS

For additional information, see appropriate chassis wiring diagram in WIRING DIAGRAMS.

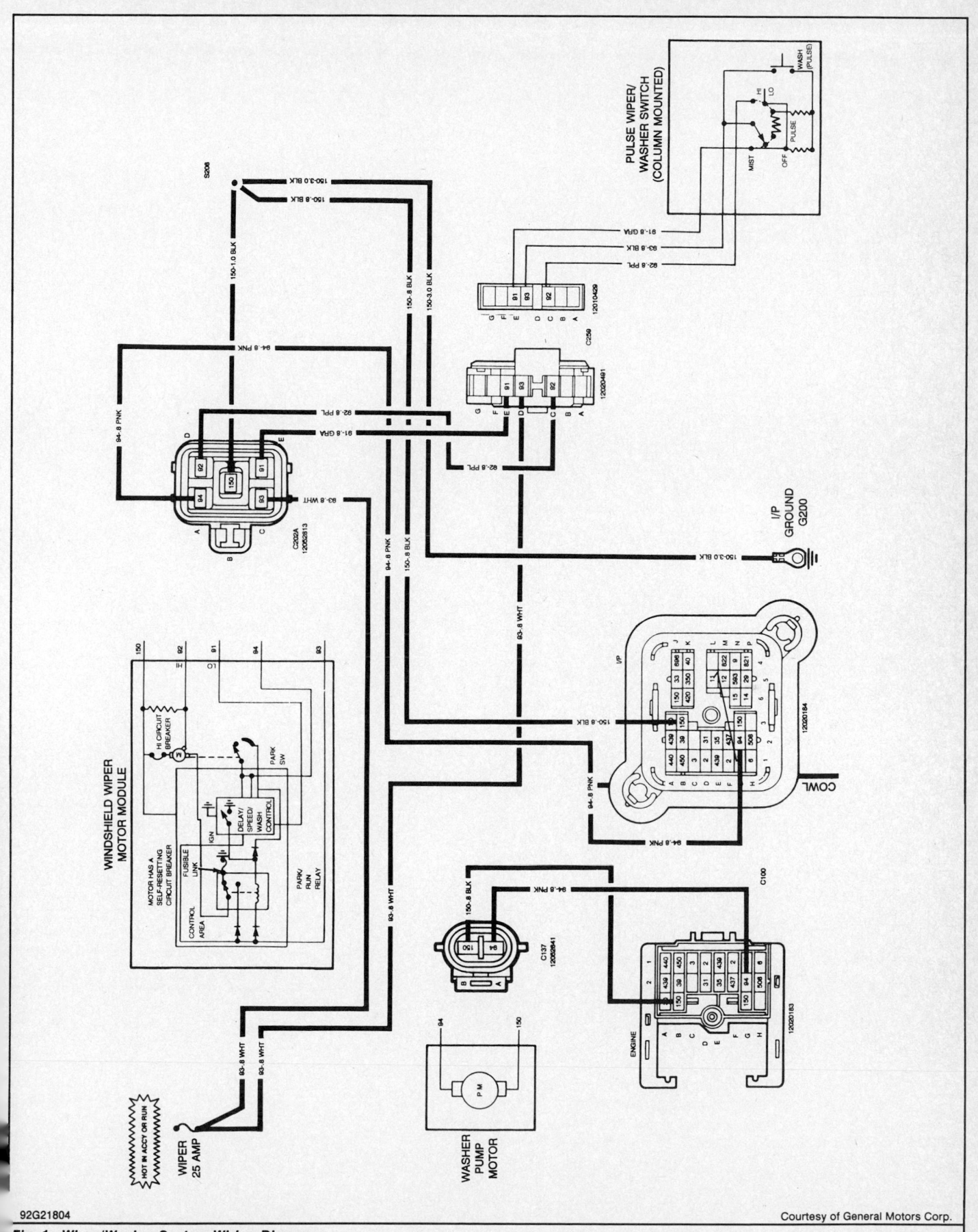

Fig. 1: Wiper/Washer System Wiring Diagram

92G21804

Sonoma, "S" Series Pickup

NOTE: For repair procedures not covered in this article, see ENGINE OVERHAUL PROCEDURES article in GENERAL INFORMATION.

ENGINE IDENTIFICATION

Engine can be identified by eighth character of Vehicle Identification Number (VIN). VIN is stamped on a metal tag on top left end of instrument panel, near windshield. See ENGINE IDENTIFICATION table.

Engine can also be identified by engine identification (ID) number, stamped on left side rear of cylinder block below cylinder head or on left side of cylinder block on engine-to-transmission mounting flange.

ENGINE IDENTIFICATION

Engine	VIN Code [1]	Engine ID No.
2.5L (151 CID) TBI	A	L38

[1] – Eighth character of Vehicle Identification Number (VIN).

ADJUSTMENTS

VALVE CLEARANCE ADJUSTMENT

Engine is equipped with hydraulic valve lifters and valve clearance is not adjustable.

REMOVAL & INSTALLATION

WARNING: When battery is disconnected, vehicle computer and memory systems may lose memory data. Driveability problems may exist until computer systems have completed a relearn cycle. See COMPUTER RELEARN PROCEDURES article in GENERAL INFORMATION before disconnecting battery.

NOTE: For reassembly reference, label all electrical connectors, vacuum hoses and fuel lines before removal. Also, place mating marks on engine hood and other assemblies before removal.

FUEL PRESSURE RELEASE

Loosen fuel tank filler cap to release tank pressure. Disconnect 3-wire electrical connector at fuel tank. Operate engine until it stalls. Crank engine for an additional 3 seconds. Turn ignition off. Connect 3-wire electrical connector.

ENGINE

Removal & Installation – 1) Release fuel pressure. See FUEL PRESSURE RELEASE. Remove hood. Disconnect negative battery cable. Drain cooling system.

2) Remove power steering reservoir from fan shroud (if equipped). Remove upper fan shroud, fan and radiator. Remove A/C compressor and power steering pump (if equipped) with hoses connected and lay aside. Remove air cleaner.

3) Remove fuel line bracket near fuel filter. Disconnect electrical connectors, vacuum lines, fuel lines and control cables as necessary. Disconnect heater hoses.

4) Raise vehicle with hoist and support with safety stands. Remove strut rod. Disconnect exhaust pipe from converter hanger and exhaust manifold. Remove flexplate/flywheel cover, drive belt splash shield (if equipped) and starter. Remove flexplate-to-converter bolts (A/T). Remove 2 outer air dam bolts (left side).

5) Remove lower fan shroud. For access to upper transmission-to-engine bolts, remove body-to-chassis mounting bolts (left side), raise left side of body and support with wood blocks. Remove upper transmission-to-engine bolts. Lower body.

6) Remove remaining transmission-to-engine bolts. Remove motor mount through bolts. Lower vehicle. Support transmission with jack and support engine with engine hoist. Pull engine forward slightly and turn sideways. Remove engine. To install, reverse removal procedure. Fill cooling system.

INTAKE MANIFOLD

Removal & Installation – 1) Release fuel pressure. See FUEL PRESSURE RELEASE. Disconnect negative battery cable. Remove air cleaner. Mark for reassembly and disconnect electrical connectors, vacuum lines, fuel lines and control cables as necessary.

2) Remove emissions sensor bracket from intake manifold. Drain cooling system. Disconnect water pump by-pass hose from intake manifold. Remove rear bracket from alternator. Disconnect heater hose from intake manifold. Remove intake manifold.

3) To install, reverse removal procedure using new intake manifold gasket. Tighten intake manifold bolts to **25 ft. lbs. (34 N.m)**. Fill cooling system.

EXHAUST MANIFOLD

Removal & Installation – 1) Disconnect negative battery cable. Remove air cleaner assembly and heat stove tube. Remove A/C compressor (if equipped) and brackets with hoses connected and lay aside.

2) Remove oil dipstick tube bracket bolt. Disconnect oxygen sensor electrical connector. Disconnect exhaust pipe from manifold. Remove exhaust manifold.

3) To install, reverse removal procedure using new exhaust manifold gasket. Tighten exhaust manifold bolts in sequence. *See Fig. 1.* Tighten bolts No. 1, 2 and 7 to **36 ft. lbs. (49 N.m)**. Tighten bolts No. 3, 4, 5 and 6 to **32 ft. lbs. (43 N.m)**.

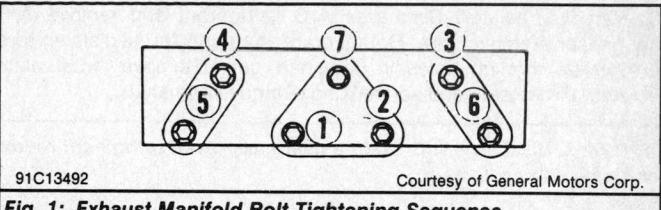

91C13492   Courtesy of General Motors Corp.

Fig. 1: Exhaust Manifold Bolt Tightening Sequence

CYLINDER HEAD

Removal – 1) Release fuel pressure. See FUEL PRESSURE RELEASE under REMOVAL & INSTALLATION. Disconnect negative battery cable. Drain cooling system. Remove air cleaner.

2) Remove A/C compressor (if equipped) and brackets with hoses connected and lay aside. Remove rocker arm cover. Loosen rocker arm nuts, rotate rocker arms to one side and remove push rods.

3) Mark for reassembly and disconnect electrical connectors, vacuum lines, fuel lines and control cables as necessary. Remove alternator and brackets. Disconnect water pump by-pass hose and heater hose from intake manifold. Disconnect exhaust pipe from exhaust manifold.

4) Remove upper radiator hose. Remove fuel filter and fuel line bracket from rear of cylinder head. Remove dipstick tube. Remove cylinder head bolts and cylinder head.

Installation – 1) Clean cylinder head bolt threads and cylinder block holes. Apply thread sealing compound (1052080) to cylinder head bolt No. 9. Install gasket over dowel pins and ensure all holes align with holes in cylinder block.

2) Install cylinder head with all bolts finger tight. Tighten all bolts in sequence to 18 ft. lbs. (24 N.m). *See Fig. 2.* Then tighten all bolts, EXCEPT bolt No. 9, to **26 ft. lbs. (35 N.m)**. Tighten bolt No. 9 to **18 ft. lbs. (24 N.m)**.

3) Repeat sequence, tightening all bolts an additional 1/4 turn (90 degrees). To install remaining components, reverse removal proce-

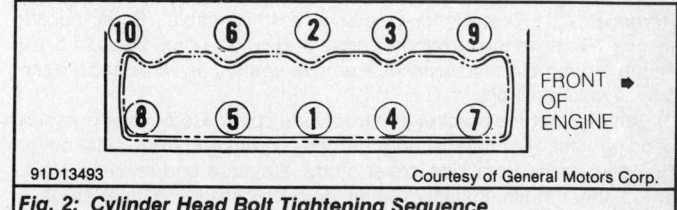

91D13493   Courtesy of General Motors Corp.

Fig. 2: Cylinder Head Bolt Tightening Sequence

dure. Tighten rocker arm bolts with lifter on base circle of camshaft. Fill cooling system.

FRONT CRANKSHAFT SEAL

Removal – Disconnect negative battery cable. Remove serpentine drive belt. Remove crankshaft damper hub bolt. Remove pulley and hub using puller. Replace hub if oil seal contact area is grooved or rough. Carefully pry out front crankshaft seal using large screwdriver (DO NOT distort timing gear cover).

Installation – Coat seal-to-hub sealing lip with oil. Install seal using Seal Installer (J-34995). Tighten crankshaft damper hub bolt to 160 ft. lbs. (217 N.m). To complete installation, reverse removal procedure.

TIMING GEARS & CAMSHAFT

NOTE: Camshaft gear is pressed onto camshaft. Camshaft gear and camshaft must be removed as an assembly.

Removal – **1)** Disconnect negative battery cable. Remove power steering reservoir from fan shroud (if equipped). Remove upper fan shroud. Remove serpentine drive belt, fan and water pump pulley. Remove crankshaft pulley and damper hub.
2) Remove timing gear cover. Remove distributor. Remove cover plate, bearing and oil pump drive shaft and gear assembly from right side of cylinder block. *See Fig. 3.* Remove hydraulic valve lifters. See HYDRAULIC VALVE LIFTERS under REMOVAL & INSTALLATION.
3) Remove radiator. Discharge A/C refrigerant and remove A/C condenser. Remove grille. Rotate crankshaft until thrust plate screws are visible through holes in camshaft gear. Remove thrust plate screws, thrust plate and spacer ring. Remove camshaft.

WARNING: Discharge A/C system using approved refrigerant recovery/recycling equipment.

Inspection – **1)** Measure camshaft end play. If end play exceeds .005" (.13 mm), replace thrust plate. If end play is less than .0015" (.038 mm), replace spacer ring.
2) Measure journal diameter and out-of-round. If journal diameter is not **1.869" (47.47 mm)** or out-of-round exceeds **.001" (.03 mm)**, replace camshaft.
Installation – Coat camshaft lobes and journals with engine oil supplement. Install camshaft, ensuring timing marks on camshaft gear and crankshaft gear are aligned. To install remaining components, reverse removal procedure. Fill cooling system. Evacuate and charge A/C refrigerant system.

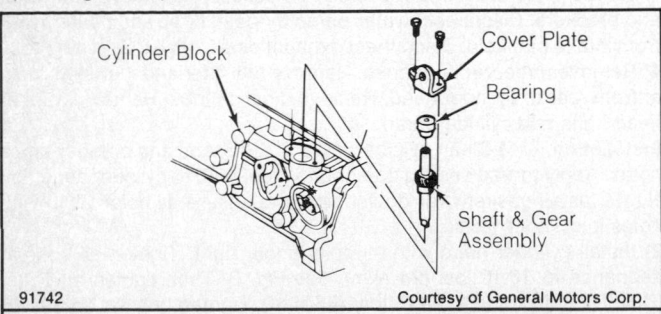

91742 Courtesy of General Motors Corp.

Fig. 3: Exploded View Of Oil Pump Drive Shaft Assembly

PUSH ROD SIDE COVER

Removal – **1)** Disconnect negative battery cable. Drain cooling system. Remove lower radiator hose and water pump by-pass hose. Remove alternator and bracket. Remove spark plug wires and bracket from intake manifold.
2) Remove fuel line bracket bolt from side cover. Remove oil pressure sending unit. Remove wiring harness brackets from side cover. Remove 4 nuts from side cover studs. Reverse and reinstall 2 nuts onto 2 inner studs. Install 2 remaining nuts onto same inner studs.
3) Using 2 wrenches, hold inner nut stationary. Jam 2 nuts tightly together. Using a wrench on inner nut, alternately unscrew studs until

side cover breaks loose. Remove jammed nuts from studs. Remove studs from side cover.
Installation – Clean side cover-to-cylinder block sealing surfaces. Replace damaged studs and rubber washers. Tighten studs to **90 INCH lbs. (10 N.m)**. Apply a 3/16" diameter (5 mm) bead of RTV sealant to side cover. Install side cover. To complete installation, reverse removal procedure. Tighten side cover studs/nuts to **90 INCH lbs. (10 N.m)**. Fill cooling system.

ROCKER ARMS & PUSH RODS

Removal – **1)** Disconnect negative battery cable. Remove air cleaner, PCV valve and crankcase ventilation pipe. Remove EGR valve. Disconnect vacuum lines as necessary. Remove spark plug wires and clip from cover.

CAUTION: To prevent sealing surface damage, DO NOT pry rocker arm cover from cylinder head.

---

2) Remove rocker arm cover bolts. Install Rocker Arm Cover Remover (J-34144-A) in place of each rocker arm cover bolt. Rotate rocker arm cover remover until rocker arm cover is lifted from cylinder head. Remove rocker arm cover.
3) Mark component location for reassembly reference. Remove rocker arm bolt and ball. Remove rocker arm, push rod and guide.

CAUTION: Push rod guides are different and must be installed in their original locations.

Installation – **1)** If installing new rocker arms or balls, coat components with Molykote. Install push rod guides, push rods, rocker arms, balls and rocker arm bolts. Ensure push rods seat in lifters. Tighten rocker arm bolt to **22 ft. lbs. (30 N.m)** with lifter on base circle of camshaft lobe.
2) Apply a 3/16" (5 mm) diameter bead of RTV sealant to rocker arm cover, inboard of bolt holes. DO NOT allow sealant to enter rocker arm cover bolt holes in cylinder head. Install rocker arm cover. Tighten rocker arm cover bolts to **75 INCH pounds (8 N.m)**. To install remaining components, reverse removal procedure.

HYDRAULIC VALVE LIFTERS

Removal – **1)** Remove rocker arms and push rods. See ROCKER ARMS & PUSH RODS under REMOVAL & INSTALLATION. Remove push rod side cover. See PUSH ROD SIDE COVER under REMOVAL & INSTALLATION.
2) Remove lifter retainer, guide and lifter. *See Fig. 4.* Mark component location for reassembly reference.

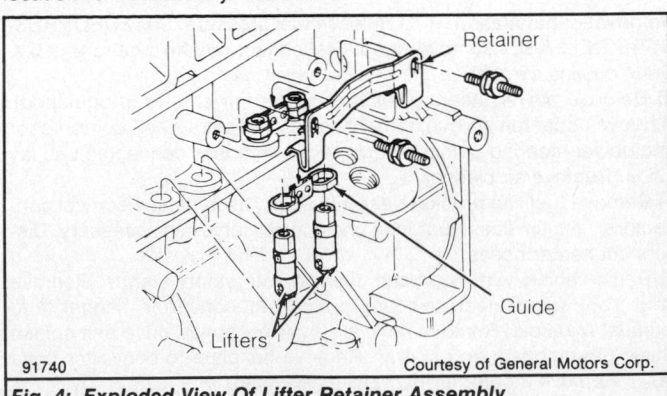

91740 Courtesy of General Motors Corp.

Fig. 4: Exploded View Of Lifter Retainer Assembly

Inspection – Measure lifter diameter and lifter bore diameter. Determine lifter oil clearance. Replace lifter if oil clearance is not within specification. See VALVE LIFTERS table under ENGINE SPECIFICATIONS at end of article.
Installation – Lubricate lifter surfaces with oil and install in bore. To install remaining components, reverse removal procedure. Tighten lifter retainer stud to **90 INCH lbs. (10 N.m)**.

REAR CRANKSHAFT SEAL

Removal – Remove transmission and flywheel/flexplate. See appropriate AUTOMATIC TRANSMISSION SERVICING article (A/T) in TRANSMISSION SERVICING or appropriate CLUTCHES article (M/T) in CLUTCHES. Note direction of seal for installation. Carefully pry seal from housing. DO NOT scratch sealing surface on crankshaft outer diameter.

Installation – Coat inner and outer seal surfaces with engine oil. Using Seal Installer (J-34924), install seal. To install remaining components, reverse removal procedure.

WATER PUMP

Removal – Drain cooling system. Remove serpentine belt. Remove upper fan shroud, fan/clutch assembly and water pump pulley. Disconnect hose(s) from water pump. Remove water pump bolts and water pump.

Installation – To install, reverse removal procedure. Apply Sealant (1052080) to water pump bolt threads. Tighten water pump bolts to **22 ft. lbs. (30 N.m)**. Fill cooling system.

OIL PAN

Removal – 1) Disconnect negative battery cable. Remove power steering fluid reservoir from fan shroud (if equipped). Remove upper fan shroud. Raise and support vehicle. Drain crankcase. Remove strut rods.

2) Disconnect exhaust pipe from manifold and catalytic converter as necessary. Remove flywheel/flexplate cover, starter and brace. Disconnect brake line bracket from crossmember. Remove front engine mount bolts. Remove oil pan.

Installation – 1) Apply a bead of RTV sealant to sealing surface of oil pan (inboard of oil pan bolt holes), rear main bearing cap-to-cylinder block junction and front cover-to-cylinder block junction. Install oil pan.

2) Tighten oil pan bolts to **90 INCH lbs. (10 N.m)**. To install remaining components, reverse removal procedure.

OVERHAUL

CYLINDER HEAD

Valve Springs – Replace valve spring if free length, installed height and pressure are not within specification. See VALVES & VALVE SPRINGS table under ENGINE SPECIFICATIONS at end of article.

Valve Stem Oil Seals – 1) Valve stem uses an upper "O" ring seal and a lower cone seal. To install valve stem oil seals, slide cone seal over valve stem until seated against cylinder head. Install spring/damper, shield and cap. Apply engine oil to "O" ring seal.

2) Compress valve spring. Install "O" ring seal in groove in valve stem, ensuring seal is not twisted. Install keepers (hold in place with grease if necessary). Decompress valve spring.

3) To test valve seal, lightly wet suction cup on Valve Stem Seal Tester (J-22330) with oil. Place suction cup on top of cap. Press on tester to create vacuum. If cup will not hold vacuum, seal is damaged or installed incorrectly.

Valve Guides – Valve guides are part of cylinder head (not replaceable). If valve stem-to-guide clearance is not .0010-.0025" (.025-.064 mm) on intake valves and .0013-.0030" (.033-.076 mm) on exhaust valves, ream valve guide and install oversized valve. Oversized intake valves are available in .003" (.08 mm) and .005" (.13 mm). Oversized exhaust valves are available in .003" (.08 mm).

Valve Seats – Valve seats are induction hardened. DO NOT remove an excessive amount of material from seat.

Valves – Replace valve if margin is less than 1/32" (.8 mm).

VALVE TRAIN

Hydraulic Valve Lifter – 1) To disassemble, press down on push rod seat with screwdriver and remove retainer. See Fig. 5. Remove push rod seat, metering valve, plunger and plunger spring. If plunger is stuck, turn lifter upside down and tap against flat surface to dislodge.

2) Using small screwdriver, pry check ball retainer from plunger. Remove check ball spring and check ball from plunger. Remove plunger spring from lifter body.

CAUTION: DO NOT interchange parts between lifters.

---

3) To assemble, turn plunger upside-down. Insert check ball, check ball spring and check ball retainer into plunger. Slide plunger spring over check ball retainer.

4) Insert plunger into lifter body, aligning oil feed holes in lifter body and plunger. Turn lifter upright. Fill lifter with 10W oil.

5) Insert end of 1/8" (3 mm) drift punch into top of plunger and press down firmly DO NOT force or pump plunger. Insert a 1/16" (1.5 mm) drift punch through both oil holes to hold plunger down against spring pressure. Remove 1/8" (3 mm) drift punch.

6) Refill lifter with 10W oil. Install metering valve, push rod seat and retainer. Push down on push rod seat using a push rod. Remove 1/16" (1.5 mm) drift punch.

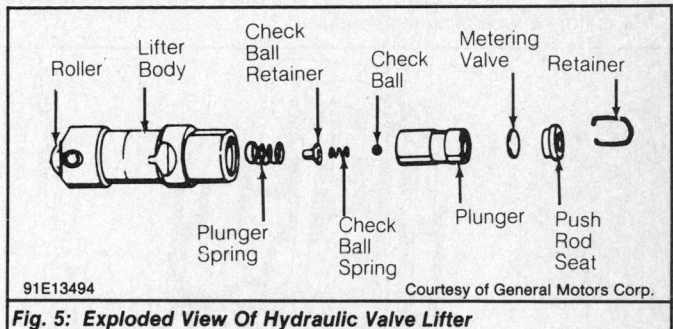

91E13494   Courtesy of General Motors Corp.

Fig. 5: Exploded View Of Hydraulic Valve Lifter

CYLINDER BLOCK ASSEMBLY

Piston & Rod Assembly – Mark piston position in relation to connecting rod before separating components. Install piston in cylinder block with mark on top of piston toward front of engine.

Fitting Pistons – Measure piston diameter at 90-degree angle to piston pin bore, on center line of piston pin bore (1 13/16" below top of piston). Measure cylinder bore diameter 2.25" (57.2 mm) from cylinder block deck surface.

Piston Rings – Install piston rings with end gaps properly spaced around circumference of piston. See Fig. 6.

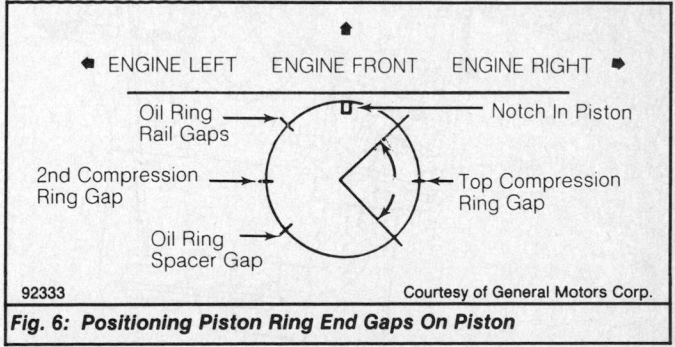

92333   Courtesy of General Motors Corp.

Fig. 6: Positioning Piston Ring End Gaps On Piston

CAUTION: Crankshaft is rolled fillet type. DO NOT grind crankshaft.

Rod Bearings – Bearings are available in standard and .001" (.025 mm) undersize.

Crankshaft & Main Bearings – Mark main bearing caps for reassembly reference. Bearings are available in standard and .001" (.025 mm) undersize.

Thrust Bearing – Rear main bearing is thrust bearing. To measure crankshaft end play, tighten main bearing cap bolts to **10 ft. lbs. (14 N.m)**. Tap end of crankshaft rearward then forward with lead hammer to align rear main bearing and crankshaft thrust surfaces. Tighten main bearing cap bolts to **65 ft. lbs. (88 N.m)**. Measure end play between front end of rear main bearing cap and crankshaft.

Cylinder Block – If cylinder block deck surface warpage exceeds .004" (.10 mm), machine surface. Replace cylinder block if more than .010" (.25 mm) material is removed from deck surface.

ENGINE OILING

ENGINE LUBRICATION SYSTEM

Oil pump is gear-driven from camshaft. See Fig. 7. Pump draws oil from pan, feeding it through oil filter and into passage along right side of block, where it intersects lifter bosses. Oil is then routed to camshaft and crankshaft bearings through smaller drilled passages. Oil is supplied to rocker arms through hydraulic lifters and push rods. By-pass valves are located in pick-up screen, oil filter mounting and oil pump. Oil returns to pan through return holes in cylinder head and cylinder block.

Crankcase Capacity – Oil capacity is approximately **3.5 qts. (3.3L)** with filter change.

Oil Pressure – Oil pressure is **36-41 psi (2.53-2.88 kg/cm²)** at 2000 RPM at normal operating temperature.

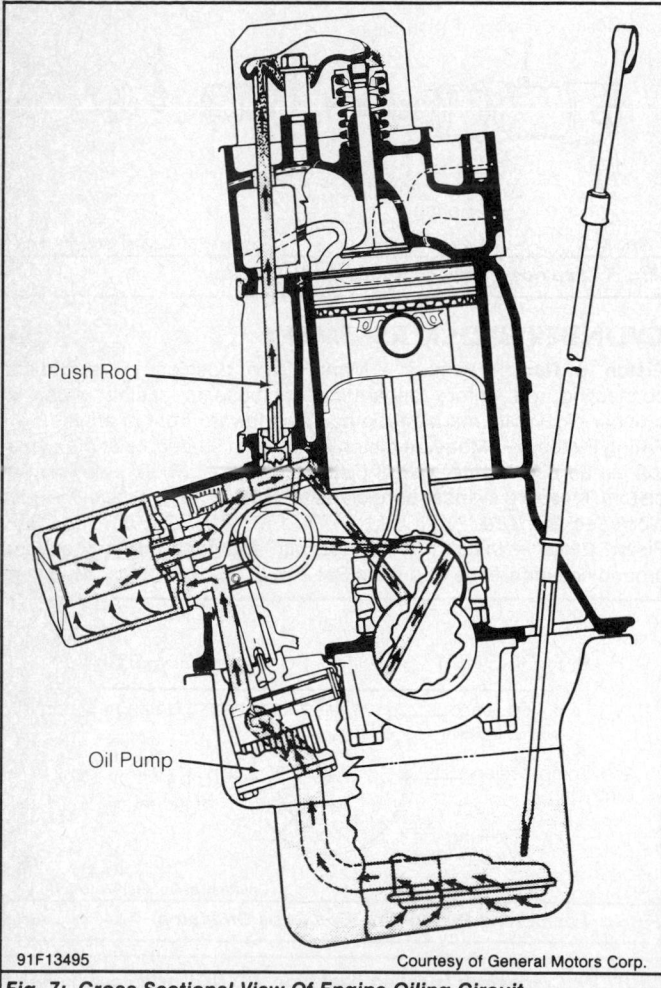

91F13495   Courtesy of General Motors Corp.

Fig. 7: Cross-Sectional View Of Engine Oiling Circuit

Push Rod

Oil Pump

OIL PUMP

Removal & Disassembly – **1)** Remove oil pan. See OIL PAN under REMOVAL & INSTALLATION. Remove oil pump bolts and pick-up tube nut. Remove oil pump.

2) Remove oil pump cover screws, cover and gasket. See Fig. 8. Mark gear teeth for reassembly reference. Remove drive gear and shaft. Remove idler gear. Remove spring retainer, pressure regulator spring and pressure regulator valve.

Inspection – **1)** Replace oil pump if pick-up tube is loose. Ensure pressure regulator valve slides freely in its bore. With gears removed,

measure gear length and diameter, and gear pocket depth and diameter.

2) Install gears. Measure gear lash, side clearance and end clearance. Replace oil pump if any measurements are not within specification. See OIL PUMP SPECIFICATIONS table.

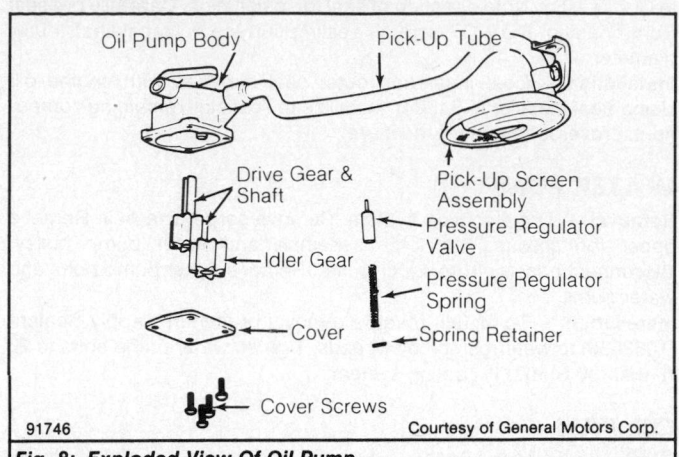

Oil Pump Body — Pick-Up Tube

Drive Gear & Shaft

Pick-Up Screen Assembly

Pressure Regulator Valve

Idler Gear

Pressure Regulator Spring

Cover

Spring Retainer

Cover Screws

91746   Courtesy of General Motors Corp.

Fig. 8: Exploded View Of Oil Pump

OIL PUMP SPECIFICATIONS

Application	Specification In. (mm)
Gear	
Diameter	1.496-1.500 (38.00-38.10)
End Clearance	.002-.005 (.05-.13)
Lash	.009-.015 (.23-.38)
Length	.999-1.002 (25.37-25.45)
Side Clearance (Maximum)	.004 (.10)
Gear Pocket	
Depth	.995-.998 (25.27-25.35)
Diameter	1.503-1.506 (38.18-38.25)

Reassembly & Installation – To reassemble, reverse disassembly procedure. Align marks on gears when installing in pump body. Tighten pump cover screws to **10 ft. lbs. (14 N.m)**. To install, reverse removal procedure. Tighten oil pump bolts to **18 ft. lbs. (24 N.m)**. Tighten pick-up tube nut to **22 ft. lbs. (30 N.m)**.

TORQUE SPECIFICATIONS

TORQUE SPECIFICATIONS

Application	Ft. Lbs. (N.m)
Connecting Rod Cap Nut	30 (40)
Crankshaft Damper Hub Bolt	162 (220)
Crankshaft Pulley-To-Damper Hub Bolt	25 (34)
Cylinder Head Bolt	[1]
Exhaust Manifold Bolt [2]	
Bolts No. 1, 2 & 7	37 (50)
Bolts No. 3, 4, 5 & 6	32 (43)
Flexplate Bolt (A/T)	55 (75)
Flywheel Bolt (M/T)	66 (90)
Intake Manifold Bolt	25 (34)
Main Bearing Cap Bolt	65 (88)
Oil Pump Cover Bolt	10 (14)
Oil Pump-To-Block Bolt	18 (25)
Oil Pump Pick-Up Tube Nut	31 (42)
Rocker Arm Bolt	22 (30)
Water Pump Bolt	17 (23)

[1] – See CYLINDER HEAD under REMOVAL & INSTALLATION for cylinder head bolt tightening procedures. Tighten bolts in sequence. See Fig. 2.

[2] – Tighten exhaust manifold bolts in sequence and to specification. See Fig. 1.

TORQUE SPECIFICATIONS (Cont.)

Application	INCH Lbs. (N.m)
Camshaft Thrust Plate Bolt	90 (10)
Front Timing Gear Cover Bolt	90 (10)
Lifter Retainer Bolt/Stud	90 (10)
Oil Pan Bolt	90 (10)
Push Rod Cover Nut & Stud	90 (10)
Rocker Arm Cover Bolt	75 (8.5)

ENGINE SPECIFICATIONS

GENERAL SPECIFICATIONS

Application	Specification
Displacement	151 Cu. In. (2.5L)
Bore	4.00" (101.6 mm)
Stroke	3.00" (76.2 mm)
Compression Ratio	8.3:1
Fuel System	TBI
HP @ RPM	105 @ 4800
Torque Ft. Lbs. @ RPM	135 @ 3200

CRANKSHAFT, MAIN & CONNECTING ROD BEARINGS

Application	In. (mm)
Crankshaft End Play	.005-.010 (.127-.254)
Main Bearings	
Journal Diameter	2.984-2.992 (58.38-58.40)
Journal Out-Of-Round	.0005 (.013)
Journal Taper	.0005 (.013)
Oil Clearance	.0005-.0022 (.013-.056)
Connecting Rod Bearings	
Journal Diameter	1.9963-2.0001 (50.71-50.80)
Journal Out-Of-Round	.0005 (.013)
Journal Taper	.0005 (.013)
Oil Clearance	.0005-.0030 (.013-.076)

CONNECTING RODS

Application	In. (mm)
Side Play	.002-.006 (.05-.15)

PISTONS, PINS & RINGS

Application	In. (mm)
Pistons	
Clearance	.0015-.0035 (.038-.089)
Pins	
Diameter	.927-.928 (23.55-23.57)
Piston Fit	.0004-.0006 (.010-.015)
Rod Fit	
Production	.0002-.0007 (.005-.018)
Service	.0002-.0023 (.005-.058)
Rings	
No. 1	
End Gap	.010-.015 (.25-.38)
Side Clearance	.002-.003 (.05-.08)
No. 2	
End Gap	.010-.020 (.25-.51)
Side Clearance	.001-.003 (.03-.08)
No. 3 (Oil)	
End Gap	.015-.055 (.38-1.40)
Side Clearance	.0005-.007 (.013-1.78)

CYLINDER BLOCK

Application	In. (mm)
Cylinder Bore	
Diameter	4.00 (101.6)
Maximum Taper	.005 (.13)
Maximum Out-Of-Round	.001 (.03)
Maximum Deck Warpage	.004 (.10)

VALVES & VALVE SPRINGS

Application	Specification
Intake Valves	
Face Angle	45°
Minimum Margin	1/32" (.8 mm)
Stem Diameter	.3131-.3138" (7.953-7.971 mm)
Exhaust Valves	
Face Angle	45°
Minimum Margin	1/32" (.8 mm)
Stem Diameter	.3129-3137" (7.948-7.963 mm)
Valve Springs	
Free Length	1.90" (48.3 mm)
Installed Height	1.679" (42.6 mm)

	Lbs. @ In. (kg @ mm)
Pressure	
Valve Closed	71-78 Lbs. @ 1.679 In. (33-35 kg @ 42.65 mm)
Valve Open	210-230 Lbs. @ 1.239 In. (93-104 kg @ 31.47 mm)

CYLINDER HEAD

Application	Specification
Valve Seats	
Intake Valve	
Seat Angle	46°
Seat Width	.050-.106" (1.27-2.69 mm)
Maximum Seat Runout	.002" (.05 mm)
Exhaust Valve	
Seat Angle	46°
Seat Width	.060-.116" (1.52-2.95 mm)
Maximum Seat Runout	.002" (.05 mm)
Valve Guides	
Intake Valve	
Valve Guide Oil Clearance	.0010-.0025" (.025-.064 mm)
Exhaust Valve	
Valve Guide Oil Clearance	.0013-.0030" (.033-.076 mm)

CAMSHAFT

Application	In. (mm)
End Play	.0015-.005 (.038-.13)
Journal Diameter	1.869 (47.47)
Lobe Lift (Intake & Exhaust)	.251 (6.38)
Oil Clearance	.0007-.0027 (.018-.069)

VALVE LIFTERS

Application	In. (mm)
Bore Diameter	.8435-.8445 (21.425-21.450)
Lifter Diameter	.8421-.8429 (21.389-21.409)
Oil Clearance	.0025 (.064)

1992 ENGINES
2.8L V6

Jimmy, Sonoma, "S" Series Blazer & Pickup

NOTE: For repair procedures not covered in this article, see ENGINE OVERHAUL PROCEDURES article in GENERAL INFORMATION.

WARNING: When battery is disconnected, vehicle computer and memory systems may lose memory data. Driveability problems may exist until computer systems have completed a relearn cycle. See COMPUTER RELEARN PROCEDURES article in GENERAL INFORMATION before disconnecting battery.

ENGINE IDENTIFICATION

Engine may be identified by eighth character of Vehicle Identification Number (VIN) on top of instrument panel, near lower left corner of windshield. Eighth character R identifies 2.8L TBI engine.

Engine may also be identified by engine identification number stamped on right side of cylinder block below cylinder No. 1 exhaust manifold port, or on front of cylinder block above timing chain cover (to left of center). Engine ID number LL2 identifies 2.8L TBI engine.

ADJUSTMENTS

VALVE CLEARANCE ADJUSTMENT

NOTE: Although valve clearance adjustment is not usually required (engine uses hydraulic valve lifters), perform following procedures after servicing valve train.

1) Remove rocker arm cover. Rotate crankshaft until cylinder No. 1 is at TDC of compression stroke. Grasp cylinder No. 1 intake valve push rod with thumb and forefinger, and attempt to rotate.

2) Loosen adjusting nut until push rod rotates freely. Continue to rotate push rod back and forth while slowly tightening adjusting nut. When resistance is felt while rotating push rod, stop tightening adjusting nut. Valve train is now at zero lash. Tighten adjusting nut 1 1/2 turns.

3) Repeat step **2)** for intake valves of cylinders No. 5 and 6, and exhaust valves of cylinders No. 1, 2 and 3. Rotate crankshaft one revolution (until cylinder No. 4 is at TDC of compression stroke).

4) Repeat step **2)** for intake valves of cylinders No. 2, 3 and 4, and exhaust valves of cylinders No. 4, 5 and 6. Install rocker arm cover and gasket.

REMOVAL & INSTALLATION

NOTE: For reassembly reference, label all electrical connectors, vacuum hoses and fuel lines before removal. Also, place mating marks on engine hood and other major assemblies before removal.

WARNING: When battery is disconnected, vehicle computer and memory systems may lose memory data. Driveability problems may exist until computer systems have completed a relearn cycle. See COMPUTER RELEARN PROCEDURES article in GENERAL INFORMATION before disconnecting battery.

FUEL PRESSURE RELEASE

Disconnect negative battery cable. Loosen fuel tank cap to relieve tank pressure. Internal constant bleed feature relieves fuel system pressure in fuel lines and TBI unit when ignition switch is turned off. No further pressure release is required.

ENGINE

Removal & Installation – 1) Release fuel pressure. See FUEL PRESSURE RELEASE. Disconnect negative battery cable. Remove hood. Drain cooling system. Disconnect upper radiator hose from radiator.

2) Remove coolant overflow hose, upper fan shroud, radiator and fan/clutch assembly. Remove air cleaner. Disconnect fuel lines, electrical connectors, vacuum hoses, coolant hoses and control cables as necessary. Remove distributor cap. Raise and support vehicle.

3) Remove exhaust pipe between converter and exhaust manifolds. Remove engine strut rods from bell housing. Remove flexplate/flywheel cover (if equipped). Remove torque converter bolts (A/T). Remove rear shield from converter.

4) Disconnect converter hanger at exhaust pipe. Remove lower fan shroud and 2 outer air dam bolts. Remove left body mount bolts. Raise body to access bell housing bolts. Remove bell housing bolts. Lower body. Remove motor mount through bolts.

5) Lower vehicle. Remove A/C compressor and Power Steering (P/S) pump with hoses connected and lay aside (if equipped). Support transmission and remove engine. To install, reverse removal procedure. Fill cooling system.

INTAKE MANIFOLD

Removal – 1) Release fuel pressure. See FUEL PRESSURE RELEASE. Drain cooling system. Disconnect negative battery cable. Remove air cleaner.

2) Disconnect fuel lines, electrical connectors, vacuum hoses, coolant hoses and control cables as necessary. Mark distributor position and remove distributor. Remove rocker arm covers. Remove intake manifold bolts and nuts. Remove intake manifold and gaskets.

Installation – 1) Inspect intake manifold-to-cylinder head gasket surface for warpage. If warpage exceeds .005" (.13 mm), replace intake manifold. Apply 3/16" (5 mm) bead of RTV sealant to front and rear intake manifold-to-cylinder block sealing surfaces; extend RTV sealant bead 1/4" (6 mm) beyond cylinder block-to-cylinder head junctions.

2) Position new intake manifold gaskets on cylinder heads, cutting gaskets as necessary to fit behind push rods. Ensure all holes are aligned. Install intake manifold. Tighten intake manifold bolts in sequence to 23 ft. lbs. (31 N.m). *See Fig. 1.* To install remaining components, reverse removal procedure.

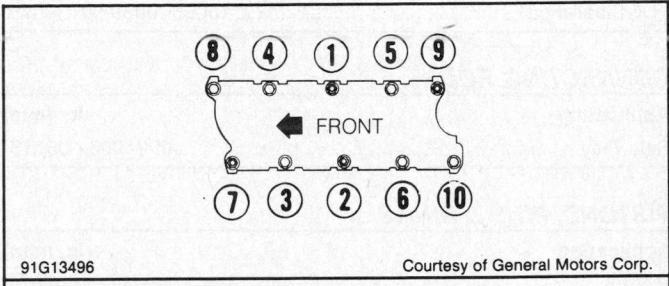

91G13496   Courtesy of General Motors Corp.

Fig. 1: Intake Manifold Bolt Tightening Sequence

EXHAUST MANIFOLDS

Removal – 1) Disconnect negative battery cable. Raise and support vehicle. Disconnect exhaust pipe from manifold. Remove 4 bolts from rear end of exhaust manifold. Lower vehicle.

2) For right manifold, remove heat shield, diverter valve, air pump and alternator brackets. For left manifold, remove heat stove pipe and P/S pump bracket. Remove remaining manifold bolts. Remove manifold and gasket.

Installation – Inspect exhaust manifold-to-cylinder head gasket surface for warpage. If warpage exceeds .005" (.13 mm), replace exhaust manifold. To install, reverse removal procedure using new gasket. Tighten exhaust manifold bolts to 25 ft. lbs. (34 N.m).

CYLINDER HEAD

Removal – 1) Remove intake manifold. See INTAKE MANIFOLD. Drain coolant from cylinder block. Raise and support vehicle. Disconnect exhaust pipe from manifold. Lower vehicle.

2) Remove oil dipstick tube (if removing left cylinder head). Disconnect fuel lines, electrical connectors, vacuum hoses, coolant hoses and control cables as necessary.

3) Remove serpentine belt, alternator and air pump with bracket (if removing right cylinder head). Remove rocker arm nuts, rocker arms, pivot balls and push rods. Keep components in order for reassembly. Remove cylinder head bolts. Remove cylinder head and gasket.

Installation – 1) Ensure cylinder head bolt threads and cylinder block holes are clean. Install cylinder head. Apply GM Sealant (1052080) to head bolt threads. Install head bolts and tighten in sequence to **40 ft. lbs. (54 N.m)**. *See Fig. 2.* Tighten head bolts in sequence an additional 90 degrees (1/4 turn).

2) To install remaining components, reverse removal procedure. Adjust valves. See VALVE CLEARANCE ADJUSTMENT under ADJUSTMENTS. Fill cooling system.

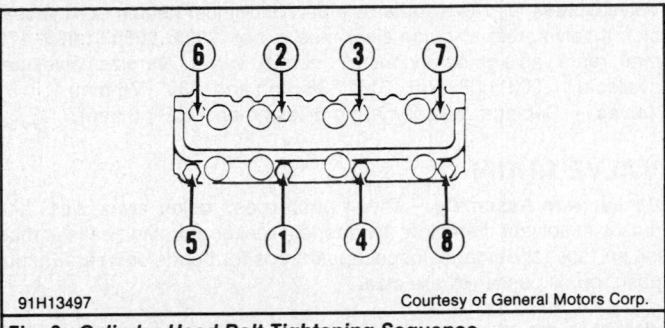

91H13497   Courtesy of General Motors Corp.

Fig. 2: Cylinder Head Bolt Tightening Sequence

FRONT CRANKSHAFT OIL SEAL

Removal – Disconnect negative battery cable. Remove serpentine belt. Remove crankshaft damper bolt. Remove pulley from damper. Raise and support vehicle. Remove damper using Crankshaft Damper Puller (J-24420-B) or (J-23523-E). Using large screwdriver, carefully pry out seal.

Installation – Coat sealing lip and damper surface with oil. Install seal using Seal Installer (J-35468). Clean damper key and keyway. Apply GM Sealant (1052336) to keyway. Install damper using Crankshaft Damper Installer (J-29113). Install damper bolt and tighten to **70 ft. lbs. (95 N.m)**. To complete installation, reverse removal procedure.

TIMING CHAIN & SPROCKETS

Removal – 1) Remove water pump. See WATER PUMP under REMOVAL & INSTALLATION. Remove Power Steering (P/S) pump bracket (if equipped). Remove crankshaft damper bolt. Remove pulley from damper. Raise and support vehicle.

2) Remove damper using Crankshaft Damper Puller (J-24420-B) or (J-23523-E). Disconnect lower radiator hose from timing chain cover. Remove timing chain cover bolts. Remove cover and gasket.

3) Rotate crankshaft until timing marks on camshaft and crankshaft sprockets align. *See Fig. 3.* Check timing chain deflection. If timing chain deflects more than 3/8" (9.5 mm) from timing chain damper, replace chain.

4) Remove camshaft sprocket bolts. Remove camshaft sprocket and timing chain. Remove crankshaft sprocket (if necessary).

Installation – 1) Install crankshaft sprocket (if removed). Apply Molykote to camshaft sprocket thrust surface. Install timing chain over camshaft sprocket. Hold sprocket vertically with chain hanging downward. Align timing marks. *See Fig. 3.*

2) Install timing chain and camshaft sprocket on camshaft, ensuring sprocket dowel pin hole aligns with camshaft dowel pin. Install and tighten camshaft sprocket bolts to **20 ft. lbs. (27 N.m)**. Lubricate timing chain with engine oil.

3) Lightly coat both sides of new timing chain cover gasket with anaerobic sealer. Install timing chain cover. Tighten cover bolts to **18 ft. lbs. (24 N.m)**. To install remaining components, reverse removal procedure. Fill cooling system.

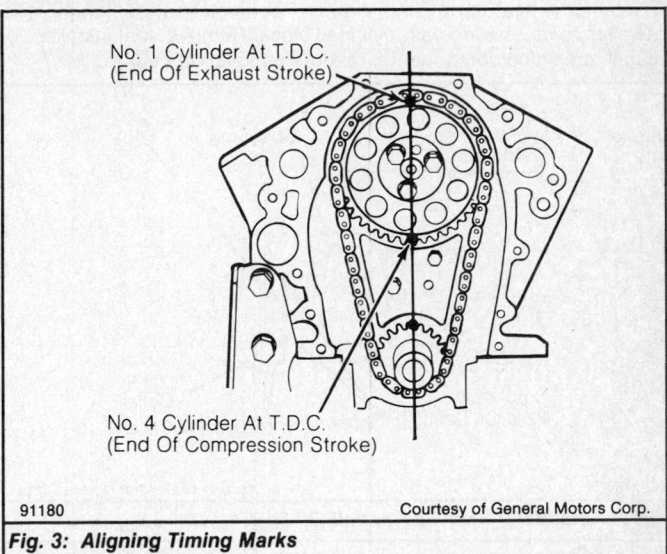

91180   Courtesy of General Motors Corp.

Fig. 3: Aligning Timing Marks

VALVE LIFTERS

Removal – Remove intake manifold. See INTAKE MANIFOLD under REMOVAL & INSTALLATION. Remove rocker arm nut. Remove rocker arm, pivot ball and push rods. Keep components in order for reassembly. Remove valve lifters.

NOTE: Some engines are equipped with standard and oversize valve lifters. Oversize lifter usage is indicated by small, White paint dot and/or ".25 mm O.S." stamped near lifter bore.

Installation – If installing new lifter, coat bottom of lifter with Molykote. Install lifter in original bore. To complete installation, reverse removal procedure. Adjust valves. See VALVE CLEARANCE ADJUSTMENT under ADJUSTMENTS.

CAMSHAFT

Removal – 1) Drain cooling system. Remove radiator. Remove upper fan shroud. Remove valve lifters. See VALVE LIFTERS.

2) Remove timing chain and camshaft sprocket. See TIMING CHAIN & SPROCKETS. Carefully remove camshaft.

Inspection – Measure camshaft journal diameter, lobe lift and oil clearance. See CAMSHAFT table under ENGINE SPECIFICATIONS at end of article. Replace components if measurements are not within specification.

Installation – 1) Lubricate camshaft bearings and camshaft lobes with GM Lubricant (1051396). Install camshaft. To install remaining components, reverse removal procedure. Ensure timing marks are aligned. *See Fig. 3.* Install valve lifters and push rods in original location.

2) Adjust valves. See VALVE CLEARANCE ADJUSTMENT under ADJUSTMENTS. If camshaft is replaced, add GM Engine Oil Supplement (1052367) to engine oil.

REAR CRANKSHAFT OIL SEAL

Removal – Remove transmission and flexplate/flywheel. Note direction of seal installation. Using screwdriver, carefully pry seal from housing in rear main bearing. DO NOT scratch crankshaft sealing surface.

Installation – 1) Coat inner and outer seal surfaces with engine oil. Install seal on mandrel of Seal Installer (J-34686) until dust lip bottoms against tool collar. *See Fig. 4.*

2) Align seal installer dowel pin with alignment hole of crankshaft. Install seal installer on crankshaft. Hand tighten seal installer bolts or torque to **35 INCH lbs. (4 N.m)**.

3) To install seal in housing, tighten seal installer handle until seal installer collar is even with cylinder block. Remove seal installer. To install remaining components, reverse removal procedure.

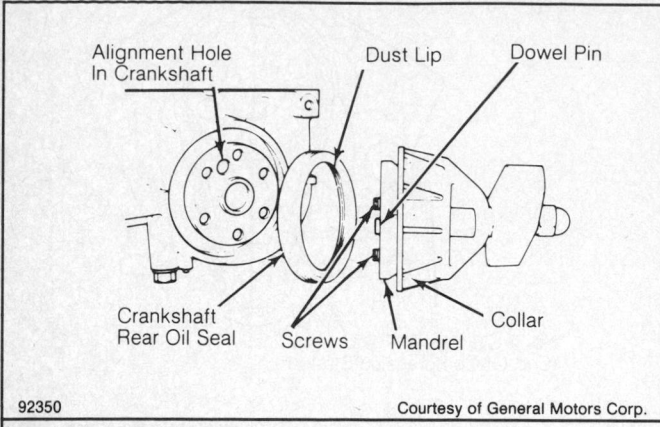

92350   Courtesy of General Motors Corp.

Fig. 4: Installing Rear Crankshaft Oil Seal

WATER PUMP

Removal – Disconnect negative battery cable. Drain coolant. Remove serpentine belt and upper fan shroud. Remove fan/clutch assembly and water pump pulley. Disconnect necessary coolant hoses. Remove water pump bolts and nut. Note bolt lengths and location. Remove water pump and gasket.

Installation – Apply GM Sealant (1052080) to bolts. To install, reverse removal procedure using new gasket. Tighten water pump bolts and nut to **22 ft. lbs. (30 N.m)**. Fill cooling system.

OIL PAN

Removal & Installation – 1) Remove engine. See ENGINE under REMOVAL & INSTALLATION. Remove oil pan bolts. Remove oil pan and gasket.

2) To install, apply GM Sealer (1052914) to half-round section at rear end of oil pan. Install oil pan with new gasket. Tighten 2 bolts at rear end of oil pan to **18 ft. lbs. (25 N.m)**. Tighten all other bolts to **89 INCH lbs. (10 N.m)**.

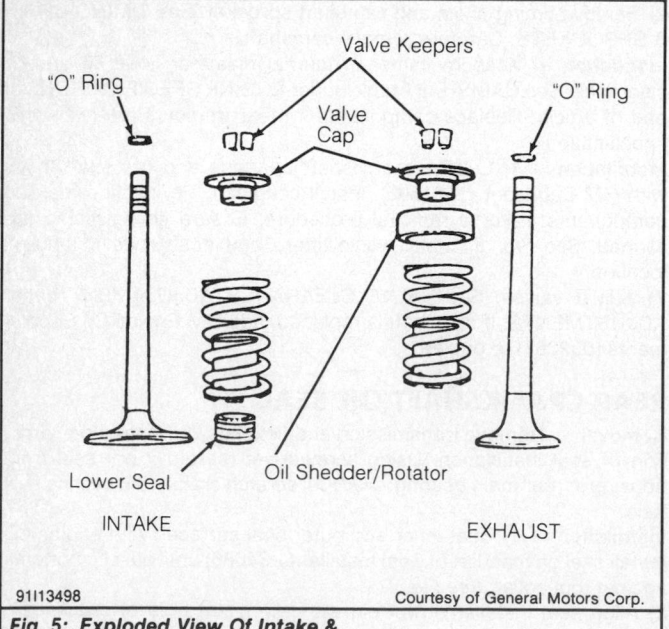

91113498   Courtesy of General Motors Corp.

Fig. 5: Exploded View Of Intake & Exhaust Valve/Spring Assemblies

OVERHAUL
CYLINDER HEAD

Valve Springs – Replace valve spring if free length, installed height and pressure are not within specification. Replace valve spring damper if free length is not within specification. See VALVES & VALVE SPRINGS table under ENGINE SPECIFICATIONS at end of article.

Valve Stem Oil Seals – Intake valve uses an upper "O" ring seal and a lower seal. See Fig. 5. Exhaust valve uses only an upper "O" ring seal and an oil shedder/rotator. When installing intake valve lower seal, slide seal over valve stem and valve guide boss. Coat "O" ring seal with engine oil before installation. Ensure seal is not twisted when installed.

Valve Guides – Valve guides are part of cylinder head (not replaceable). If valve stem-to-guide clearance is not **.0026-.0068" (.066-.172 mm)**, ream valve guide and install oversize valve. Oversize valves are available in .003" (.08 mm), .015" (.38 mm) and .030" (.76 mm).

Valves – Replace valve if margin is less than 1/32" (.8 mm).

VALVE TRAIN

Rocker Arm Assembly – Clean push rods, rocker arms, balls and nuts with solvent then blow dry. Inspect rocker arms and balls at mating surface for damage. Inspect push rods for bends or wear. Ensure push rod oil passages are clear.

CYLINDER BLOCK ASSEMBLY

Cylinder Block – If cylinder block deck surface warpage exceeds **.004" (.10 mm)**, machine surface. Replace cylinder block if more than **.010" (.25 mm)** material is removed from deck surface.

Piston & Rod Assembly – Mark piston position in relation to connecting rod before separating components. Replace piston and pin as matched set. Install piston in cylinder block, with mark on top of piston toward front of engine.

Fitting Pistons – 1) Mark piston and cylinder for reassembly reference. Remove rings from piston. Ensure piston and cylinder are clean. Insert piston into cylinder bore upside down.

2) Piston should free fall in cylinder bore when bottom of piston skirt is 1/2 - 1" (12-25 mm) from top of deck surface. Try piston in different bore if piston fails to free fall.

3) If piston free falls, correct fit must be determined. Install piston and a .0025" (.060 mm) feeler gauge for used pistons, or .0020" (.050 mm) feeler gauge for new pistons in cylinder bore. Feeler gauge must be at least 6" (152 mm) long and no more than 1/2" (12 mm) wide. Position feeler gauge at 90-degree angle to piston pin.

4) With piston 1/2 - 1" (12-25 mm) from top of deck surface, note if piston free falls. If piston fails to free fall, piston is correctly fitted for that cylinder. If piston free falls, select a larger diameter piston.

Piston Rings – Ensure ring end gap and side clearance are within specification. See PISTONS, PINS & RINGS table under ENGINE SPECIFICATIONS at end of article. Install rings with mark on top of ring facing top of piston, and with ring end gaps properly spaced around piston. See Fig. 6.

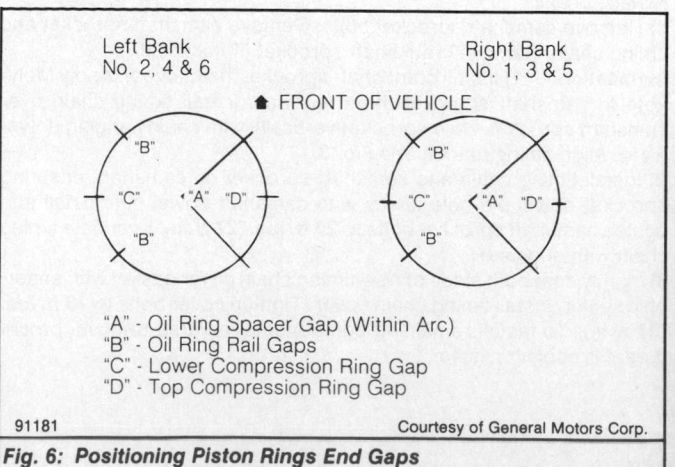

91181   Courtesy of General Motors Corp.

Fig. 6: Positioning Piston Rings End Gaps

Rod Bearings – Mark rods and rod bearing caps for reassembly reference. Rod bearings of .001" (.26 mm) undersize are available. Install rod bearing cap on rod, with bearing tang slot facing away from center of engine. Ensure rod side clearance is **.006-.025" (.16-.64 mm)**.

CAUTION: Crankshaft is rolled fillet type. DO NOT grind crankshaft. DO NOT scrape, shim or file bearings.

Crankshaft & Main Bearings – **1)** Mark main bearing caps for reassembly reference. Main bearings of .0006" (.016 mm) and .0013" (.032 mm) undersize are available.
2) Apply thin coats of GM Anaerobic Sealant (1052756) and RTV sealant to rear main bearing cap in specified areas. *See Fig. 7.* Install main bearing caps with arrows facing front of engine. Ensure crankshaft end play is **.002-.008" (.06-.21 mm)**. See THRUST BEARING.
Thrust Bearing – **1)** Main bearing cap No. 3 is thrust bearing. Tighten main bearing cap bolts, except No. 3 main bearing cap, to **70 ft. lbs. (95 N.m)**. Tighten No. 3 main bearing cap bolts to **11 ft. lbs. (15 N.m)**.
2) Using lead hammer, tap crankshaft toward rear of engine then toward front of engine to align crankshaft thrust surfaces. Tighten No. 3 main bearing cap bolts to **70 ft. lbs. (95 N.m)**. Measure crankshaft end play between front side of No. 3 main bearing and crankshaft thrust surface.
Valve Lifter Bores – Some engines may be equipped with oversize valve lifters. Oversize lifter usage is indicated by small, White paint dot and/or ".25 mm O.S." stamped near lifter bore.

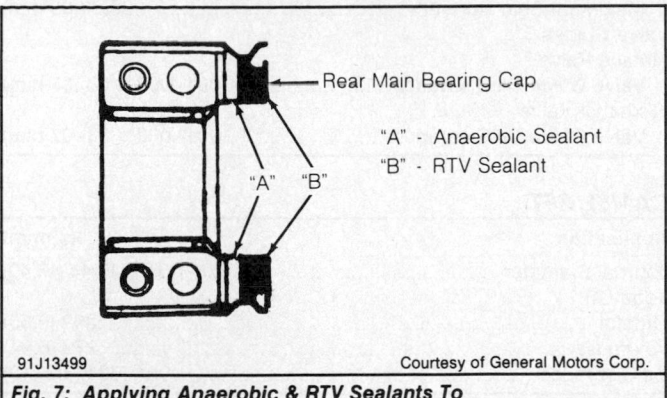

91J13499   Courtesy of General Motors Corp.

Rear Main Bearing Cap

"A" - Anaerobic Sealant
"B" - RTV Sealant

Fig. 7: Applying Anaerobic & RTV Sealants To Rear Main Bearing Cap

ENGINE OILING

ENGINE LUBRICATION SYSTEM

Camshaft-driven gear-type oil pump provides pressurized lubrication through oil filter, to main gallery above left side of camshaft center line. Main gallery provides lubrication to valve lifters on left bank, camshaft bearings, crankshaft bearings and right gallery.

Right gallery supplies oil to valve lifters on right bank. Rocker arms are lubricated by passages in the push rods. Slot in front camshaft bearing provides lubrication to timing chain. Pistons and piston pins are lubricated by oil splash. Pressure regulator valve is mounted in oil pump body.
Crankcase Capacity – Engine oil capacity is approximately **4.5 qts. (4.3L)** with filter change.
Oil Pressure – Normal oil pressure is **50-55 psi (3.5-3.9 kg/cm²)** at 2000 RPM.

OIL PUMP

Removal & Disassembly – **1)** Remove oil pan. See OIL PAN under REMOVAL & INSTALLATION. Remove oil pump bolt, oil pump and extension shaft from rear main bearing cap.

CAUTION: Pressure regulator valve spring is under pressure. Use care when removing to prevent personal injury.

---

2) Remove pump cover. Mark teeth on both gears for reassembly reference. Remove idler gear, drive gear and shaft from pump body. Remove pressure regulator valve retaining pin, valve and spring.
Inspection – Pump is serviced as an assembly. Replace pump if damaged or excessively worn. Replace pick-up screen tube if loose.

CAUTION: Use only original equipment oil pump cover gasket, as gasket thickness is critical.

Reassembly & Installation – Coat all internal components with engine oil. To reassemble, reverse disassembly procedure using new cover gasket. Ensure reference mark is aligned on gears. To install, reverse removal procedure. Ensure pump extension shaft is fully engaged.

TORQUE SPECIFICATIONS

TORQUE SPECIFICATIONS

Application	Ft. Lbs. (N.m)
Camshaft Sprocket Bolt	17 (23)
Connecting Rod Cap Nut	39 (53)
Crankshaft Damper Bolt	70 (95)
Cylinder Head Bolt	[1]
EGR Valve	18 (25)
Exhaust Manifold Bolt	25 (34)
Flexplate/Flywheel Bolt	52 (70)
Intake Manifold Bolt	[2] 15 (21)
Main Bearing Cap Bolt	70 (95)
Oil Filter Adapter Bolt	63 (85)
Oil Pan Bolt (Rear 2)	18 (25)
Oil Pump Bolt	30 (41)
Rocker Arm Stud	48 (65)
Timing Chain Cover Bolt	
10-mm	37 (50)
8-mm	22 (30)
Timing Chain Damper Bolt	15 (21)
Water Pump Bolt (8 mm)	18 (24)

	INCH Lbs. (N.m)
Oil Pan Bolt/Nut (Except Rear 2)	89 (10)
Rocker Arm Cover Bolt	71 (8)
Water Pump Bolt (6 mm)	89 (10)
Water Pump Nut [3]	89 (10)

[1] – Apply GM Sealant (1052080) to bolt threads. Tighten bolts in sequence to 40 ft. lbs. (54 N.m), then tighten in sequence an additional 90 degrees (1/4 turn). *See Fig. 2.*
[2] – Tighten in sequence to specification then repeat procedure. *See Fig. 1.*
[3] – Apply GM Sealant (1052080) to bolt threads.

ENGINE SPECIFICATIONS

GENERAL SPECIFICATIONS

Application	Specification
Displacement	173 Cu. In. (2.8L)
Bore	3.50" (89.0 mm)
Stroke	2.99" (76.0 mm)
Compression Ratio	8.9:1
Fuel System	TBI
Horsepower @ RPM	125 @ 4800
Torque Ft. Lbs. @ RPM	150 @ 2400

1992 ENGINES
2.8L V6 (Cont.)

CRANKSHAFT MAIN & CONNECTING ROD BEARINGS

Application	In. (mm)
Crankshaft End Play	.002-.008 (.06-.21)
Main Bearings	
Journal Diameter	
Dot 1	2.6479-2.6482 (67.257-67.265)
Dot 2	2.6476-2.6479 (67.249-67.257)
Dot 3	2.6473-2.6476 (67.241-67.249)
Journal Out-Of-Round	.0002 (.005)
Journal Taper	.0002 (.005)
Oil Clearance	.0013-.0027 (.032-.069)
Connecting Rod Bearings	
Journal Diameter	
Dot 1	1.9989-1.9994 (50.771-50.784)
Dot 2	1.9983-1.9989 (50.758-50.771)
Journal Out-Of-Round	.0002 (.005)
Journal Taper	.0002 (.005)
Oil Clearance	.0011-.0033 (.028-.083)

CONNECTING RODS

Application	In. (mm)
Side Play	.014-.022 (.36-.60)

PISTONS, PINS & RINGS

Application	In. (mm)
Pistons	
Clearance	.0007-.0017 (.017-.043)
Pins	
Diameter	.9053-.9056 (22.994-23.002)
Piston Fit	.0003-.0004 (.007-.009)
Rod Fit (Press)	.0007-.0020 (.019-.052)
Rings	
No. 1	
End Gap	.010-.020 (.25-.50)
Side Clearance	.001-.003 (.03-.07)
No. 2	
End Gap	.010-.020 (.25-.50)
Side Clearance	.002-.004 (.04-.10)
No. 3 (Oil)	
End Gap	.011-.049 (.27-1.25)
Side Clearance (Max.)	.008 (.20)

CYLINDER BLOCK

Application	In. (mm)
Cylinder Bore	
Diameter	3.504-3.507 (88.99-89.07)
Maximum Taper	.0008 (.02)
Maximum Out-Of-Round	.0008 (.02)

VALVES & VALVE SPRINGS

Application	Specification
Intake Valves	
Face Angle	45°
Exhaust Valves	
Face Angle	45°
Valve Springs	
Free Length	1.91" (48.5 mm)
Installed Height	1.57" (40.0 mm)
	Lbs. @ In. (kg @ mm)
Pressure	
Valve Closed	88 Lbs. @ 1.57 In. (40 kg @ 40.0 mm)
Valve Open	194 Lbs. @ 1.18 In. (88 kg @ 30.0 mm)

CYLINDER HEAD

Application	Specification
Valve Seats	
Intake Valve	
Seat Angle	46°
Seat Width	.049-.059" (1.25-1.50 mm)
Maximum Seat Runout	.002" (.05 mm)
Exhaust Valve	
Seat Angle	46°
Seat Width	.063-.075" (1.60-1.90 mm)
Maximum Seat Runout	.002" (.05 mm)
Valve Guides	
Intake Valve	
Valve Guide Oil Clearance	.001-.003" (.03-.07 mm)
Exhaust Valve	
Valve Guide Oil Clearance	.001-.003" (.03-.07 mm)

CAMSHAFT

Application	In. (mm)
Journal Diameter	1.868-1.870 (47.44-47.49)
Lobe Lift	
Intake	.262 (6.65)
Exhaust	.273 (6.94)
Oil Clearance	.001-.004 (.03-.10)

Lumina APV, Silhouette, Trans Sport

NOTE: For repair procedures not covered in this article, see ENGINE OVERHAUL PROCEDURES article in GENERAL INFORMATION.

ENGINE IDENTIFICATION

Engine may be identified by eighth character of Vehicle Identification Number (VIN) stamped on pad on top of instrument panel, near lower left corner of windshield. Eighth character, "D", identifies 3.1L TBI engine.

Engine may also be identified by engine identification (ID) number stamped on left side of cylinder block, on engine-to-transaxle mating flange. Engine ID number, LG6, identifies 3.1L TBI engine.

ADJUSTMENTS

VALVE CLEARANCE ADJUSTMENT

NOTE: Although valve clearance adjustment is not usually required (engine uses hydraulic valve lifters), perform following procedures after servicing valve train.

1) Remove rocker arm covers. Rotate crankshaft until cylinder No. 1 is at TDC of compression stroke.
2) Grasp cylinder No. 1 intake valve push rod with thumb and forefinger, and loosen adjusting nut until push rod rotates freely. Continue to rotate push rod back and forth while tightening adjusting nut. When push rod can no longer be rotated, stop tightening adjusting nut. Valve train is now at zero lash. Turn adjusting nut 1 1/2 turns more.
3) Repeat step 2) for intake valves of cylinders No. 5 and 6, and exhaust valves of cylinders No. 1, 2 and 3. Rotate crankshaft one revolution (until cylinder No. 4 is at TDC of compression stroke).
4) Repeat step 2) for intake valves of cylinders No. 2, 3 and 4, and exhaust valves of cylinders No. 4, 5 and 6. Install rocker arm covers and gaskets.

REMOVAL & INSTALLATION

WARNING: When battery is disconnected, vehicle computer and memory systems may lose memory data. Driveability problems may exist until computer systems have completed a relearn cycle. See COMPUTER RELEARN PROCEDURES article in GENERAL INFORMATION before disconnecting battery.

NOTE: For reassembly reference, label all electrical connectors, vacuum hoses and fuel lines before removal. Also, place mating marks on engine hood and other major assemblies before removal.

FUEL PRESSURE RELEASE

Disconnect negative battery cable. Loosen fuel tank cap to relieve tank pressure. Internal constant bleed feature relieves fuel system pressure in fuel lines and TBI unit when ignition switch is turned off. No further pressure release is required.

COOLING SYSTEM BLEEDING

CAUTION: On vehicles with rear heater, turn off rear blower switch while filling cooling system to ensure maximum coolant flow to rear heater system.

ENGINE

NOTE: Manufacturer's engine removal procedure states removing engine, transaxle and frame as an assembly.

Removal – 1) Release fuel pressure. See FUEL PRESSURE RELEASE. Disconnect battery cables. Drain cooling system.
2) Remove air intake tube from air cleaner and radiator support. Disconnect ECM electrical connectors from ECM, and push harness through hole in firewall, into engine compartment. Disconnect necessary harness-to-chassis fasteners. Lay harness on engine.
3) Disconnect engine harness from block connector near left hood hinge. Lay harness on engine. Disconnect fuel lines, electrical connectors, vacuum hoses, coolant hoses and control cables as necessary. Discharge A/C system using approved refrigerant recovery/recycling equipment.
4) Remove A/C compressor from mounting bracket with hoses attached. Disconnect refrigerant hoses from A/C compressor. Remove upper engine strut rod mount. Raise and support vehicle. Remove front wheels. Remove stabilizer shaft.
5) Disconnect tie rod ends from steering knuckles. Disconnect lower control arm ball joints from steering knuckles. Remove drive axles from transaxle, and wire aside. Remove intermediate steering shaft pinch bolt.
6) Remove starter, flexplate cover and torque converter bolts. Disconnect exhaust downpipe from right manifold. Support engine/transaxle/frame assembly. Remove frame bolts. Lower engine/transaxle/frame assembly from vehicle.
Installation – To install, reverse removal procedure. Fill cooling system. Evacuate and charge A/C system.

INTAKE MANIFOLD

Removal – 1) Release fuel pressure. See FUEL PRESSURE RELEASE. Drain cooling system. Disconnect negative battery cable. Remove air cleaner.
2) Disconnect fuel lines, electrical connectors, vacuum hoses, coolant hoses and control cables as necessary. Remove engine strut rod mount. Remove coolant by-pass tube between timing chain cover and thermostat housing. Remove Throttle Body Injection (TBI) unit. Remove left rocker arm cover.
3) Remove serpentine belt, alternator and alternator brackets. Remove right rocker arm cover. Remove P/S pump with hoses attached and lay aside. Remove distributor. Remove intake manifold.
Installation – 1) Apply 3/16" (5 mm) bead of RTV sealant to front and rear intake manifold-to-cylinder block sealing surfaces; extend RTV sealant 1/4" (6 mm) beyond cylinder block-to-cylinder head junctions. Position new intake manifold gaskets on cylinder heads.
2) Install intake manifold. Tighten intake manifold bolts in sequence to specification. See TORQUE SPECIFICATIONS table at end of article. See Fig. 1. To install remaining components, reverse removal procedure. Fill cooling system.

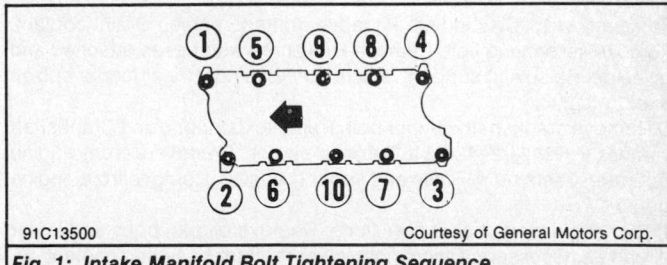

91C13500   Courtesy of General Motors Corp.

Fig. 1: Intake Manifold Bolt Tightening Sequence

EXHAUST MANIFOLDS

Removal (Left) – Disconnect negative battery cable. Remove serpentine belt. Remove A/C compressor with hoses attached and lay aside. Remove engine strut rod mount. Disconnect exhaust crossover pipe from manifold. Remove manifold.
Removal (Right) – Disconnect negative battery cable and oxygen sensor wire. Disconnect exhaust crossover pipe from manifold. Raise and support vehicle. Disconnect exhaust downpipe from manifold. Support rear center of frame. Remove rear center frame mount bolts. Lower frame 8-10" (203-254 mm). Remove manifold.
Installation (Left & Right) – Install manifold. Tighten manifold-to-cylinder head bolts to specification. See TORQUE SPECIFICATIONS table at end of article. To install remaining components, reverse removal procedure.

CYLINDER HEAD

Removal – 1) Remove intake manifold. See INTAKE MANIFOLD under REMOVAL & INSTALLATION. Remove exhaust manifold. See EXHAUST MANIFOLDS under REMOVAL & INSTALLATION.

2) Loosen push rod nuts enough to remove push rods. Keep components in order for reassembly. Remove cylinder head bolts. Remove cylinder head and gasket.

Installation – 1) Clean cylinder head bolt threads and cylinder block holes. Install cylinder head and new gasket. Apply GM Sealant (1052080) to head bolt threads. Install head bolts and tighten in sequence to specification. See TORQUE SPECIFICATIONS table at end of article. *See Fig. 2.*

2) To install remaining components, reverse removal procedure. Adjust valves. See VALVE CLEARANCE ADJUSTMENT under ADJUSTMENTS. Fill cooling system.

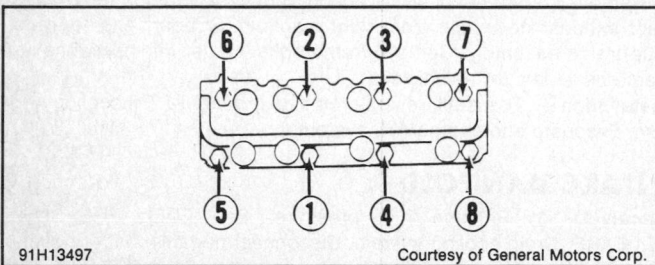

91H13497   Courtesy of General Motors Corp.

Fig. 2: Cylinder Head Bolt Tightening Sequence

FRONT CRANKSHAFT OIL SEAL

Removal – Disconnect negative battery cable. Remove serpentine belt. Raise and support vehicle. Remove right inner fender splash shield. Remove crankshaft damper bolt. Remove damper using Crankshaft Damper Puller (J-24420-B). Using large screwdriver, carefully pry out seal.

Installation – Coat sealing lip and damper surface with oil. Install seal using Seal Installer (J-35468). Clean damper key and keyway. Apply GM Sealant (1052336) to keyway. Install damper using Crankshaft Damper Installer (J-29113). Install damper bolt and tighten to specification. See TORQUE SPECIFICATIONS table at end of article. To complete installation, reverse removal procedure.

TIMING CHAIN & SPROCKETS

Removal – 1) Disconnect negative battery cable. Drain coolant. Remove serpentine belt. Remove P/S pump with hoses attached and lay aside. Raise and support vehicle. Remove right inner fender splash shield.

2) Remove crankshaft damper bolt. Remove damper using Crankshaft Damper Puller (J-24420-B). Remove starter. Remove 2 front engine mount-to-frame nuts. Raise and support engine. Remove front engine mount.

3) Remove timing chain cover bolts. Remove oil pan bolts and lower oil pan as necessary. Disconnect lower radiator hose and coolant bypass hose from timing chain cover. Remove serpentine belt pulley. Remove timing chain cover.

4) Rotate crankshaft until timing marks on camshaft and crankshaft sprockets align. *See Fig. 3.* Remove camshaft sprocket bolts. Remove camshaft sprocket and timing chain. Remove crankshaft sprocket (if necessary).

Installation – 1) If crankshaft sprocket was removed, install using Crankshaft Sprocket Installer (J-5590). Install timing chain over camshaft sprocket. Hold sprocket vertically with chain hanging down. Align timing marks. *See Fig. 3.*

2) Install timing chain and camshaft sprocket on camshaft, ensuring sprocket dowel pin hole aligns with camshaft dowel pin. Install and tighten camshaft sprocket bolts to specification. See TORQUE SPECIFICATIONS table at end of article. Lubricate timing chain with engine oil.

3) Apply GM Sealer (1052080) to timing chain cover-to-oil pan sealing surface. Install timing chain cover with new gasket. Tighten cover

bolts to specification. See TORQUE SPECIFICATIONS table at end of article. To install remaining components, reverse removal procedure. Fill cooling system.

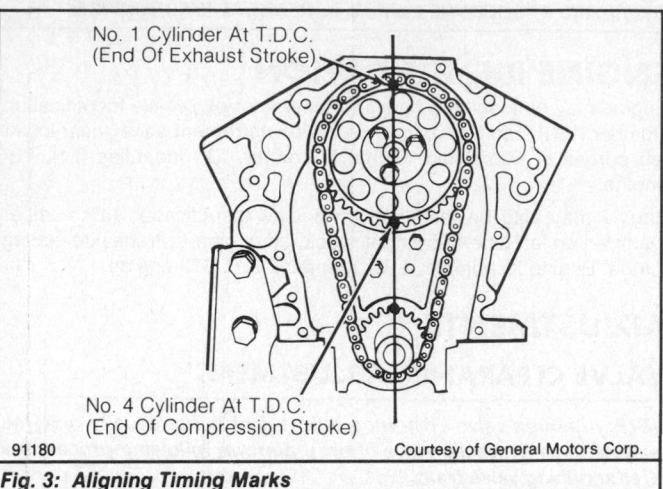

No. 1 Cylinder At T.D.C. (End Of Exhaust Stroke)

No. 4 Cylinder At T.D.C. (End Of Compression Stroke)

91180   Courtesy of General Motors Corp.

Fig. 3: Aligning Timing Marks

VALVE LIFTERS

Removal – Remove intake manifold. See INTAKE MANIFOLD under REMOVAL & INSTALLATION. Loosen rocker arm nuts, rotate rocker arms and remove push rods. Keep push rods in order for reassembly. Remove valve lifters.

NOTE: Some engines are equipped with standard and oversize valve lifters. Oversize lifter usage is indicated by small, White paint dot and/or ".25 mm O.S." stamped near lifter bore.

Installation – If installing new lifter, coat bottom of lifter with Molykote. Install lifter in original bore. To complete installation, reverse removal procedure. Adjust valves. See VALVE CLEARANCE ADJUSTMENT under ADJUSTMENTS.

CAMSHAFT

NOTE: To remove camshaft, engine must be removed from vehicle.

Removal – 1) Remove engine. See ENGINE under REMOVAL & INSTALLATION. Remove valve lifters. See VALVE LIFTERS.

2) Remove timing chain and camshaft sprocket. See TIMING CHAIN & SPROCKETS. Carefully remove camshaft.

Inspection – Measure camshaft journal diameter, lobe lift and oil clearance. Replace components if measurements are not within specification. See CAMSHAFT table under ENGINE SPECIFICATIONS at end of article.

Installation – 1) Lubricate camshaft bearings and camshaft lobes with GM Lubricant (1051396). Install camshaft. To install remaining components, reverse removal procedure. Ensure timing marks are aligned. *See Fig. 3.* Install valve lifters and push rods in original location.

2) Adjust valves. See VALVE CLEARANCE ADJUSTMENT under ADJUSTMENTS. If camshaft was replaced, add GM Engine Oil Supplement (1052367) to engine oil.

REAR CRANKSHAFT OIL SEAL

Removal – Remove transaxle and flexplate. Note direction of seal installation. Using screwdriver, carefully pry seal from housing in rear main bearing. DO NOT scratch sealing surface of crankshaft.

Installation – 1) Coat inner and outer seal surfaces with engine oil. Install seal on mandrel of Seal Installer (J-34686) until dust lip bottoms against tool collar. *See Fig. 4.*

2) Align seal installer dowel pin with alignment hole of crankshaft. Install seal installer on crankshaft. Hand tighten seal installer bolts, or torque to **36 INCH lbs. (4 N.m)**.

3) To install seal in housing, tighten seal installer handle until seal installer collar is even with cylinder block. Remove seal installer. To install remaining components, reverse removal procedure.

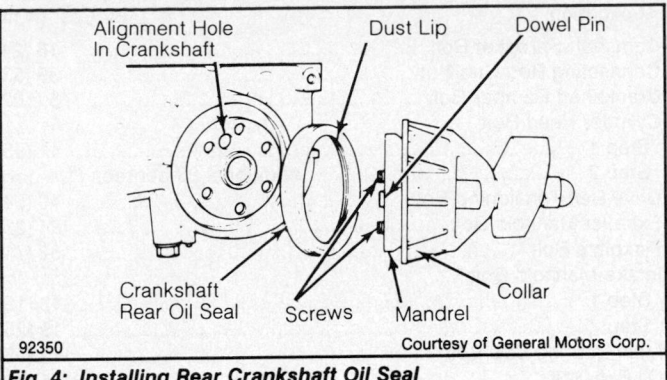

Fig. 4: Installing Rear Crankshaft Oil Seal

Courtesy of General Motors Corp.

WATER PUMP

Removal – Disconnect negative battery cable. Drain coolant. Remove serpentine belt. Remove water pump pulley. Note locator tab near 12 o'clock position at top of water pump housing for installation reference. Remove water pump and gasket.

Installation – Apply thread sealant to water pump bolts. Install water pump with new gasket, ensuring locator tab at top of water pump housing is positioned vertically.

OIL PAN

Removal – **1)** Disconnect negative battery cable. Remove serpentine belt. Raise and support vehicle. Remove right inner fender splash shield. Remove crankshaft damper bolt. Remove damper using Crankshaft Damper Puller (J-24420-B).

2) Drain crankcase. Remove flexplate cover and starter. Remove 2 front engine mount-to-frame nuts. Raise and support engine. Remove oil pan bolts. Remove oil pan and gasket.

Installation – Apply GM Sealer (1052914) to half-round section at rear end of oil pan. Install oil pan with new gasket.

OVERHAUL

CYLINDER HEAD

Valve Springs – Replace valve spring if free length, installed height and pressure are not within specification. See VALVES & VALVE SPRINGS table under ENGINE SPECIFICATIONS at end of article.

Valve Stem Oil Seals – Intake valve uses an upper "O" ring seal and a lower seal. See Fig. 5. Exhaust valve uses upper "O" ring seal only. When installing intake valve lower seal, slide seal over valve stem and valve guide boss. Exhaust valve uses oil shedder/rotator. Coat "O" ring seal with engine oil before installation; ensure seal is not twisted when installed.

VALVE TRAIN

Rocker Arm Assembly – Clean push rods, rocker arms, balls and nuts with solvent then blow dry. Inspect rocker arms and balls at mating surface for damage. Inspect push rods for bends or wear. Ensure push rod oil passages are clear.

CYLINDER BLOCK ASSEMBLY

Piston & Rod Assembly – Mark piston in relation to cylinder bore and rod for reassembly. Replace rod if bend exceeds .010" (.25 mm) per 3" (76.2 mm) of rod length.

Fitting Pistons – Measure piston diameter with pin removed. Measure diameter at 90-degree angle to pin on pin center line.

Piston Rings – Ensure ring end gap and side clearance are within specification. See PISTONS, PINS & RINGS table under ENGINE SPECIFICATIONS at end of article.

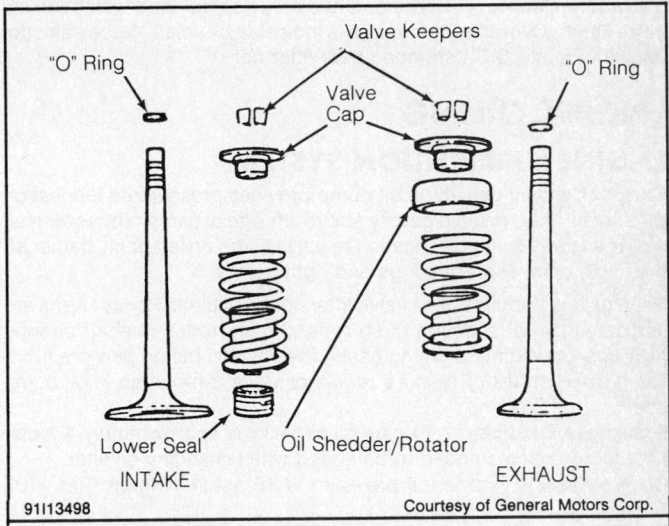

Fig. 5: Exploded View Of Intake & Exhaust Valve/Spring Assemblies

Courtesy of General Motors Corp.

Rod Bearings – Ensure rod side clearance is .014-.027" (.36-.68 mm).

Crankshaft & Main Bearings – Ensure crankshaft journal diameter, runout and taper are within specification. See CRANKSHAFT, MAIN & CONNECTING ROD BEARINGS under ENGINE SPECIFICATIONS at end of article.

Thrust Bearing – With main bearing cap bolts loosely tightened, pry crankshaft rearward to align main bearing caps. Pry crankshaft forward to align rear face of thrust bearing. Tighten main bearing cap bolts to specification, and measure crankshaft end play between thrust bearing rear face and crankshaft thrust surface. See TORQUE SPECIFICATIONS table at end of article.

CAUTION: If transaxle case mating surface is not flat, a broken flywheel may result.

Transaxle Case Mating Surface – **1)** Mount dial indicator gauge plate flat against crankshaft flange. Place dial indicator stem on lower left transaxle mounting bolt boss (flat area around bolt hole). See Fig. 6. **2)** Adjust dial indicator to zero. Record readings obtained on all mounting bolt hole bosses. If variation between mounting bolt bosses exceeds .010" (.25 mm), replace crankshaft or cylinder block as necessary.

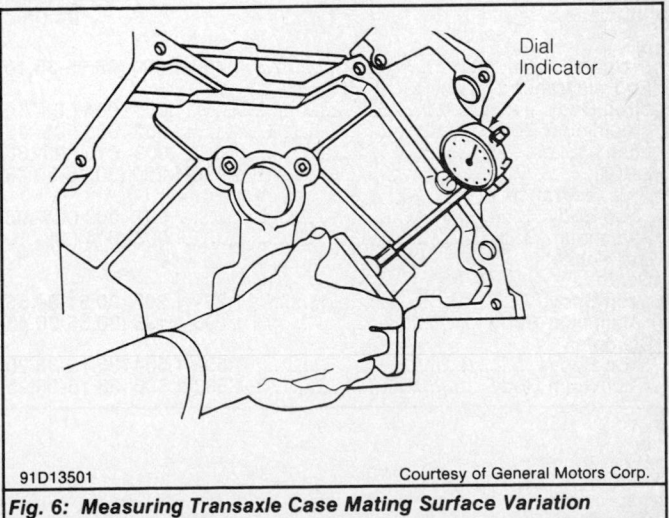

Fig. 6: Measuring Transaxle Case Mating Surface Variation

Courtesy of General Motors Corp.

Cylinder Block – Replace cylinder block if more than .010" (.25 mm) material needs to be removed from deck surface.

Valve Lifter Bores – Some engines may be equipped with oversize valve lifters. Oversize lifter usage is indicated by small, White paint dot and/or ".25 mm O.S." stamped near lifter bore.

ENGINE OILING

ENGINE LUBRICATION SYSTEM

Camshaft-driven gear-type oil pump provides pressurized lubrication through oil filter, to main gallery above left side of camshaft center line. Main gallery provides lubrication to valve lifters on left bank, camshaft bearings, crankshaft bearings and right gallery.

Right gallery supplies oil to valve lifters on right bank. Rocker arms are lubricated by passages in push rods. Slot in front camshaft bearing provides lubrication to timing chain. Pistons and piston pins are lubricated by oil splash. Pressure regulator valve is mounted in oil pump body.

Crankcase Capacity – Engine oil capacity is approximately **4.0 qts. (3.8L)**. More oil may need to be added when changing oil filter.

Oil Pressure – Normal oil pressure is **15 psi (1.1 kg/cm²)** at 1100 RPM.

OIL PUMP

WARNING: Pressure regulator valve spring is under pressure. Use care when removing to prevent personal injury.

Removal & Disassembly – **1)** Remove oil pan. See OIL PAN under REMOVAL & INSTALLATION. Remove oil pump mounting bolt. Remove oil pump and drive shaft extension.

2) Remove oil pump cover screws. Remove cover and gasket. Mark gear teeth for reassembly reference. Remove drive gear and idler gear. Remove spring retaining pin, spring and pressure relief valve.

Inspection – **1)** Replace pick-up tube if loose. Ensure pressure regulator valve slides freely in its bore. With gears removed, measure gear length and diameter, and measure gear pocket depth and diameter.

2) Install gears. Measure gear lash, side clearance and end clearance. Replace oil pump if any measurements are not within specification. See OIL PUMP SPECIFICATIONS table.

Reassembly & Installation – To reassemble, reverse disassembly procedure. Align marks on gears when installing in pump body. To install, reverse removal procedure. Tighten oil pump mounting bolt to specification. Tighten pick-up tube nut to specification. See TORQUE SPECIFICATIONS table.

OIL PUMP SPECIFICATIONS

Application	Specification In. (mm)
Gear	
Diameter	1.498-1.500 (38.05-38.10)
End Clearance	
Iron Body	.001-.004 (.03-.10)
Aluminum Body	.002-.005 (.05-.13)
Lash	.009-.015 (.23-.38)
Length	1.199-1.200 (30.45-30.48)
Side Clearance	
Iron Body	.001-.003 (.03-.08)
Aluminum Body	.003-.004 (.08-.10)
Gear Pocket	
Depth	
Iron Body	1.201-1.203 (30.51-30.56)
Aluminum Body	1.195-1.198 (30.35-30.43)
Diameter	
Iron Body	1.502-1.504 (38.15-38.20)
Aluminum Body	1.503-1.506 (38.18-38.25)

TORQUE SPECIFICATIONS

TORQUE SPECIFICATIONS

Application	Ft. Lbs. (N.m)
Camshaft Sprocket Bolt	18 (24)
Connecting Rod Cap Nut	39 (53)
Crankshaft Damper Bolt	75 (102)
Cylinder Head Bolt [1]	
Step 1	41 (55)
Step 2	Additional 90 degrees (1/4 turn)
Drive Belt Tensioning Bolt	40 (54)
Exhaust Manifold Bolt	24 (33)
Flexplate Bolt	52 (71)
Intake Manifold Bolt [2]	
Step 1	13 (18)
Step 2	19 (26)
Main Bearing Cap Bolt	72 (98)
Oil Pan Bolt	15 (20)
Oil Pump Bolt	30 (41)
Oil Pump Pick-Up Tube Nut	22 (30)
Rocker Arm Stud	48 (65)
Timing Chain Cover Bolt	
Small Diameter	20 (27)
Large Diameter	28 (38)
Timing Chain Damper Bolt	15 (20)

	INCH Lbs. (N.m)
Oil Pan Stud Nuts	89 (10)
Oil Pump Cover Bolt	89 (10)
Rocker Arm Cover Bolt	89 (10)
Water Pump Bolt	89 (10)

[1] – Apply thread sealant to bolts. Tighten bolts in sequence. *See Fig. 2.*

[2] – Tighten bolts in sequence. *See Fig. 1.*

ENGINE SPECIFICATIONS

GENERAL SPECIFICATIONS

Application	Specification
Displacement	189 Cu. In. (3.1L)
Bore	3.50" (89.0 mm)
Stroke	3.31" (84.0 mm)
Compression Ratio	8.9:1
Fuel System	TBI
Horsepower @ RPM	120 @ 4200
Torque Ft. Lbs. @ RPM	175 @ 2200

CRANKSHAFT, MAIN & CONNECTING ROD BEARINGS

Application	In. (mm)
Crankshaft End Play	.002-.008 (.06-.21)
Main Bearings	
Journal Diameter	2.6473-2.6479 (67.241-67.257)
Journal Out-Of-Round	.0002 (.005)
Journal Taper	.0002 (.005)
Oil Clearance	.0013-.0029 (.032-.074)
Connecting Rod Bearings	
Journal Diameter	1.9987-1.9994 (50.768-50.784)
Journal Out-Of-Round	.0002 (.005)
Journal Taper	.0002 (.005)
Oil Clearance	.0011-.0033 (.028-.083)

CONNECTING RODS

Application	In. (mm)
Maximum Bend	[1] .010 (.25)
Side Play	.014-.027 (.36-.68)

[1] – Specification is per 3" of rod length.

PISTONS, PINS & RINGS

Application	In. (mm)
Pins	
Diameter	.9052-.9054 (22.992-22.996)
Piston Fit	.0004-.0009 (.010-.022)
Rod Fit	.0006-.0018 (.015-.046)
Rings	
No. 1	
End Gap	.010-.020 (.25-.50)
Side Clearance	.002-.004 (.05-.10)
No. 2	
End Gap	.020-.028 (.50-.71)
Side Clearance	.002-.004 (.05-.10)
No. 3 (Oil)	
End Gap	.010-.030 (.25-.75)
Side Clearance (Max.)	.008 (.20)

CYLINDER BLOCK

Application	In. (mm)
Cylinder Bore	
Diameter	3.5036-3.5067 (88.992-89.070)
Maximum Taper	.0005 (.013)
Maximum Out-Of-Round	.0005 (.013)

VALVES & VALVE SPRINGS

Application	Specification
Intake Valves	
Face Angle	45°
Exhaust Valves	
Face Angle	45°
Valve Springs	
Free Length	1.91" (48.5 mm)
Installed Height	1.58" (40.0 mm)
Out-Of-Square	1/16" (1.6 mm)
	Lbs. @ In. (kg @ mm)
Pressure	
Valve Closed	81 Lbs. @ 1.57 In. (37 kg @ 40.0 mm)
Valve Open	192 Lbs. @ 1.18 In. (87 kg @ 30.0 mm)

CYLINDER HEAD

Application	Specification
Valve Seats	
Intake Valve	
Seat Angle	46°
Seat Width	.061-.073" (1.55-1.85 mm)
Maximum Seat Runout	.002" (.05 mm)
Exhaust Valve	
Seat Angle	46°
Seat Width	.067-.079" (1.70-2.00 mm)
Maximum Seat Runout	.002" (.05 mm)
Valve Guides	
Intake Valve	
Valve Guide Oil Clearance	.001-.003" (.03-.07 mm)
Exhaust Valve	
Valve Guide Oil Clearance	.001-.003" (.03-.07 mm)

CAMSHAFT

Application	In. (mm)
Journal Diameter	1.8677-1.8815 (47.440-47.790)
Lobe Lift	
Intake	.2306 (5.858)
Exhaust	.2620 (6.654)
Oil Clearance	.001-.004 (.03-.10)

Lumina APV, Silhouette, Trans Sport

NOTE: For repair procedures not covered in this article, see ENGINE OVERHAUL PROCEDURES article in GENERAL INFORMATION.

ENGINE IDENTIFICATION

Engine may be identified by using Vehicle Identification Number (VIN) stamped on metal tag, located near lower left corner of windshield. Eighth character identifies engine model. See ENGINE IDENTIFICATION CODES table.

Engine code, located on cylinder block, may be required when ordering replacement parts. *See Fig. 1.* See ENGINE IDENTIFICATION CODES table.

ENGINE IDENTIFICATION CODES

Engine	Code
8th Character Of VIN	L
Engine Code	L27

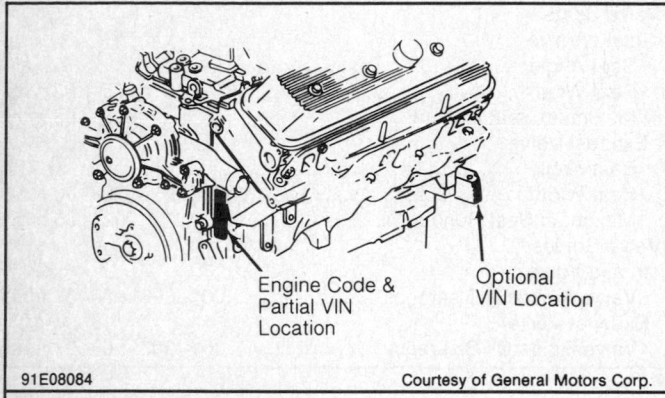

Engine Code & Partial VIN Location

Optional VIN Location

91E08084   Courtesy of General Motors Corp.

Fig. 1: Locating Engine Codes

ADJUSTMENTS

VALVE CLEARANCE ADJUSTMENT

Hydraulic valve lifters are used and no valve adjustment is required.

REMOVAL & INSTALLATION

WARNING: When battery is disconnected, vehicle computer and memory systems may lose memory data. Driveability problems may exist until computer systems have completed a relearn cycle. See COMPUTER RELEARN PROCEDURES article in GENERAL INFORMATION before disconnecting battery.

NOTE: For reassembly reference, label all electrical connectors, vacuum hoses and fuel lines before removal. Also place mating marks on engine hood and other major assemblies before removal.

FUEL PRESSURE RELEASE

Loosen fuel tank cap to release fuel tank pressure. Remove fuel pump fuse. Start engine and operate until engine stalls. Crank engine for an additional 3 seconds to release residual line pressure. Disconnect negative battery cable, and reinstall fuel pump fuse.

ENGINE

Removal – 1) Release fuel pressure. See FUEL PRESSURE RELEASE. Disconnect negative battery cable. Remove air cleaner and duct system. Remove fuel lines from fuel rail and mounting bracket. Drain cooling system. Remove throttle cables from throttle body and mounting bracket.
2) Remove radiator and heater hoses. Remove engine cooling fan. Remove transmission cooler lines to radiator. Remove torque strut and bracket. Remove radiator assembly.

3) Disconnect relay center wiring. Disconnect fuel vapor canister hoses. Remove battery cables to engine ground and starter assembly. Disconnect shift cables from transaxle. Disconnect ECM main wiring harness. Remove serpentine drive belt. Disconnect A/C compressor from mounting bracket and secure aside.
4) Disconnect P/S line attachment at lower right-hand rail. Disconnect engine wiring at left-hand rail. Raise vehicle and support. Remove front wheels. Remove stabilizer bar. Disconnect tie rod ends from steering knuckle. Lower control arm ball joints from steering knuckles. Disconnect drive axles from transaxle and wire up and aside.
5) Remove intermediate steering shaft pinch bolt. Remove starter assembly. Remove flywheel cover. Remove torque converter bolts. Disconnect exhaust pipe at rear manifold. Support engine/transaxle/frame assembly. Remove frame bolts. Lower engine/transaxle/frame assembly.
6) Support engine with engine hoist. Remove transaxle-to-engine mount bracket. Remove exhaust crossover. Remove left and right exhaust manifolds. Disconnect engine-to-frame front mount. Disconnect left and right engine-to-frame mounts. Remove transaxle bolts. Separate engine from transaxle and/or frame assembly. Lift engine from vehicle.

Installation – To install, reverse removal procedure. Fill cooling system and check engine fluids.

INTAKE MANIFOLD

Removal – 1) Disconnect negative battery cable. Remove plastic engine cover and air intake duct.
2) Remove spark plug wires and fuel rail. Remove exhaust crossover heat shield and power steering pump bracket. Remove serpentine belt, alternator and alternator bracket. Remove cable bracket, heater pipes and by-pass hose. Remove intake manifold bolts, manifold, gaskets and seals.
Installation – 1) Ensure sealing surfaces and bolt threads and holes are clean. Apply GM Sealant (12345336) at end of seals on cylinder block. Install manifold and gaskets. Coat bolt threads with thread sealant and install.
2) Tighten intake manifold bolts in sequence TWICE to specification. *See Fig. 2.* See TORQUE SPECIFICATIONS table at end of article. Lubricate coolant "O" rings with anti-freeze and fuel rail "O" rings with engine oil prior to installation. To install remaining components, reverse removal procedure. Fill cooling system.

NOTE: Apply thread sealant to intake manifold bolts before installation. Intake manifold bolts must be tightened in sequence TWICE to 88 INCH lbs. (10 N.m). See Fig. 2.

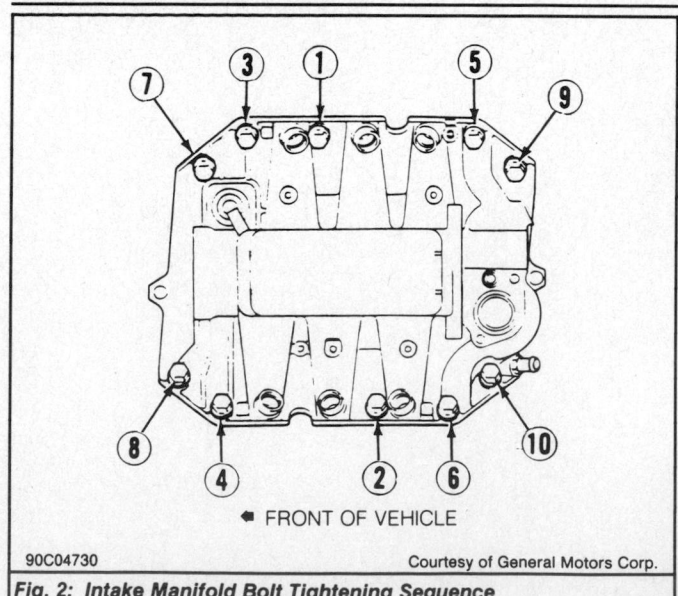

← FRONT OF VEHICLE

90C04730   Courtesy of General Motors Corp.

Fig. 2: Intake Manifold Bolt Tightening Sequence

EXHAUST MANIFOLDS

Removal & Installation (Left/Front) – **1)** Disconnect negative battery cable. Remove air inlet duct. Disconnect spark plug wires. Remove crossover pipe bolts from manifold.

2) On all engines, remove engine lift hook and manifold heat shield (if equipped). Remove oil dipstick and tube. Remove manifold bolts, manifold and gasket. To install, reverse removal procedure using new gasket.

Removal & Installation (Right/Rear) – **1)** Disconnect negative battery cable. Remove air inlet duct. Remove throttle cable from throttle body. Remove brake booster hose. Remove serpentine belt and power steering pump bracket with hoses attached and lay aside.

2) Drain cooling system. Disconnect spark plug wires and oxygen sensor. Disconnect crossover pipe and exhaust pipe from manifold.

3) Remove transaxle dipstick. Remove manifold heat shield (if equipped). Remove catalytic converter heat shield and pipe hanger. Remove exhaust pipe-to-manifold nuts. Remove engine lift bracket, manifold bolts, manifold and gasket. To install, reverse removal procedure. Use new gasket.

CYLINDER HEAD

Removal – **1)** Remove intake manifold. See INTAKE MANIFOLD under REMOVAL & INSTALLATION. Remove exhaust manifold. See EXHAUST MANIFOLDS under REMOVAL & INSTALLATION.

2) On front cylinder head, disconnect spark plug wires. Remove engine lift bracket and valve cover. Remove exhaust crossover pipe and cooling fan. Remove alternator, ignition coil and bracket. Remove A/C compressor bracket bolt.

3) On rear cylinder head, disconnect spark plug wires. Remove exhaust crossover pipe. Remove power steering pump with hoses attached and lay aside. Remove heater pipe from front cover housing. Remove transaxle fill tube.

4) Remove rocker arms, push rods and guide plates. See ROCKER ARMS & PUSH RODS under REMOVAL & INSTALLATION. Remove cylinder head bolts, cylinder head and gasket.

Inspection – Inspect cylinder head warpage. See CYLINDER HEAD under OVERHAUL.

Installation – **1)** Ensure cylinder head bolt threads and cylinder block holes are clean. Ensure all holes align with cylinder block.

2) Install cylinder head. Apply GM Sealant (1052080) to head bolt threads and install. Tighten all bolts to specification in proper sequence. See Fig. 3. See TORQUE SPECIFICATIONS table at end of article.

3) To install remaining components, reverse removal procedure. Coat rocker arm bolts with GM Threadlock (12345493) prior to installation.

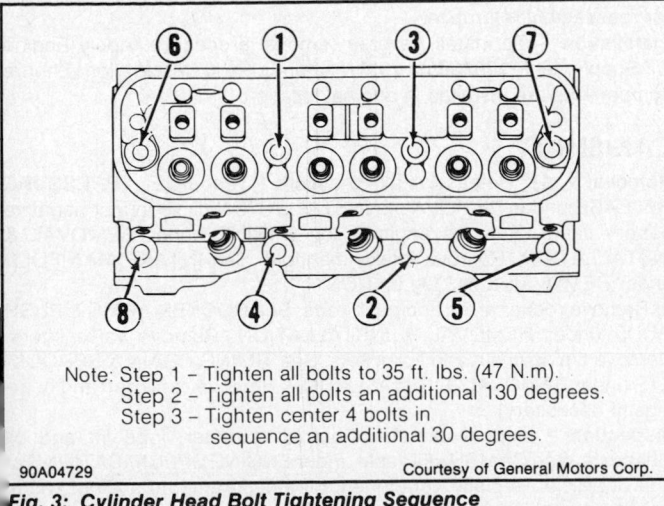

Note: Step 1 – Tighten all bolts to 35 ft. lbs. (47 N.m).
Step 2 – Tighten all bolts an additional 130 degrees.
Step 3 – Tighten center 4 bolts in sequence an additional 30 degrees.

90A04729   Courtesy of General Motors Corp.

Fig. 3: Cylinder Head Bolt Tightening Sequence

FRONT CRANKSHAFT SEAL

Removal – Disconnect negative battery cable. Remove serpentine belt. Raise and support vehicle. Remove right front wheel and inner splash shield. Remove crankshaft pulley/balancer bolt and crankshaft pulley/balancer. Pry seal from front timing case cover.

Installation – Coat outside surface of crankshaft pulley/balancer and seal with oil prior to installation. Using Seal Installer (J-35354) and crankshaft pulley/balancer bolt, install seal. Remove seal installer. To install remaining components, reverse removal procedure.

FRONT TIMING CASE COVER

Removal – **1)** Disconnect negative battery cable. Drain cooling system and crankcase oil. Remove serpentine belt. Remove water pump pulley. Disconnect heater pipes. Disconnect coolant hoses at case cover. Remove lower radiator hose.

2) Raise and support vehicle. Remove right front wheel and inner splash shield. Remove crankshaft pulley/balancer bolt and crankshaft pulley/balancer. Disconnect electrical connections at oil pressure sender, camshaft sensor and crankshaft sensor.

3) Remove oil pan-to-case cover bolts. Remove power steering pump, with hoses attached, and lay aside. Remove front timing case cover bolts, case cover and gasket. See Fig. 4.

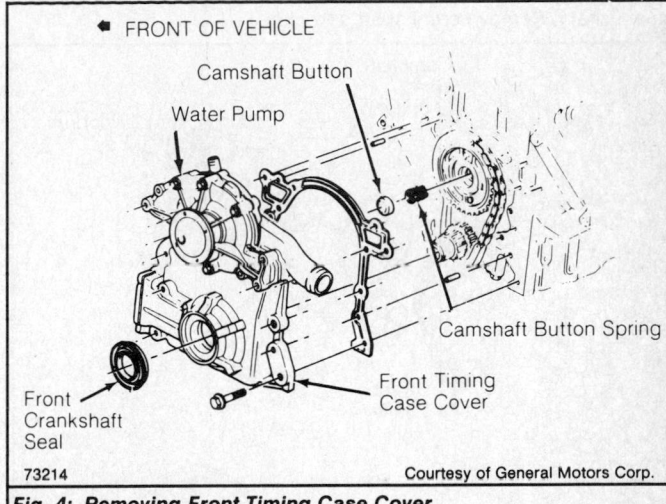

73214   Courtesy of General Motors Corp.

Fig. 4: Removing Front Timing Case Cover

Installation – **1)** Inspect timing chain and sprockets for wear. Timing chain slack should not exceed 1" (25.4 mm). Replace if necessary.

2) To install, reverse removal procedure using new gasket. Coat case cover bolts with thread sealant prior to installation. Crankshaft sensor must be adjusted.

3) With crankshaft sensor mounted loosely on mounting pedestal, install sensor and mounting pedestal on Crankshaft Sensor Adjuster (J-37089). See Fig. 5. Install crankshaft sensor adjuster and sensor assembly on crankshaft.

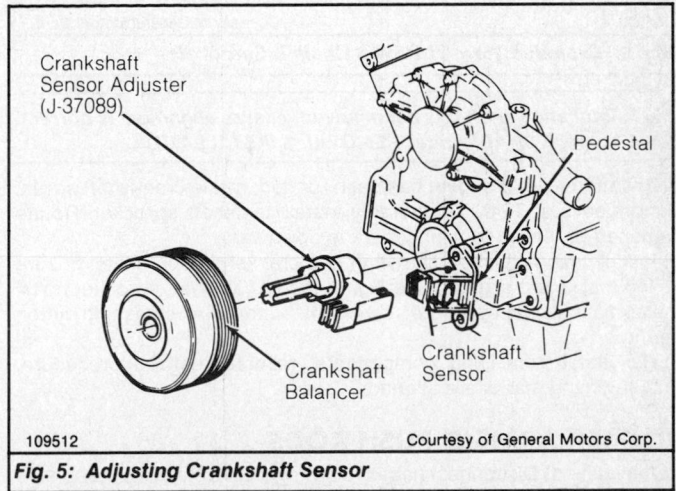

109512   Courtesy of General Motors Corp.

Fig. 5: Adjusting Crankshaft Sensor

4) Install mounting pedestal-to-cylinder block bolts and tighten to **14-28 ft. lbs. (19-38 N.m)**. Tighten sensor-to-mounting pedestal bolts to **30-35 INCH lbs. (3.3-3.9 N.m)**.

5) Remove crankshaft sensor adjuster from crankshaft. Place sensor adjuster inside crankshaft pulley/balancer. Rotate sensor adjuster. Replace crankshaft pulley/balancer if sensor adjuster contacts balancer at any point.

6) To install remaining components, reverse removal procedure. Coat outside surface of crankshaft pulley/balancer shaft and seal with oil prior to installation.

TIMING CHAIN & SPROCKETS

Removal – **1)** Remove front timing case cover. See FRONT TIMING CASE COVER. Remove camshaft button and camshaft button spring. *See Fig. 4.*

2) Inspect timing chain and sprockets for wear. Timing chain slack should not exceed 1" (25.4 mm). Replace timing chain if necessary.

3) Rotate crankshaft, and align timing marks on camshaft and crankshaft sprockets. *See Fig. 6.* Remove timing chain damper assembly.

4) Remove camshaft sprocket bolts. Remove camshaft sprocket and timing chain. Remove crankshaft sprocket.

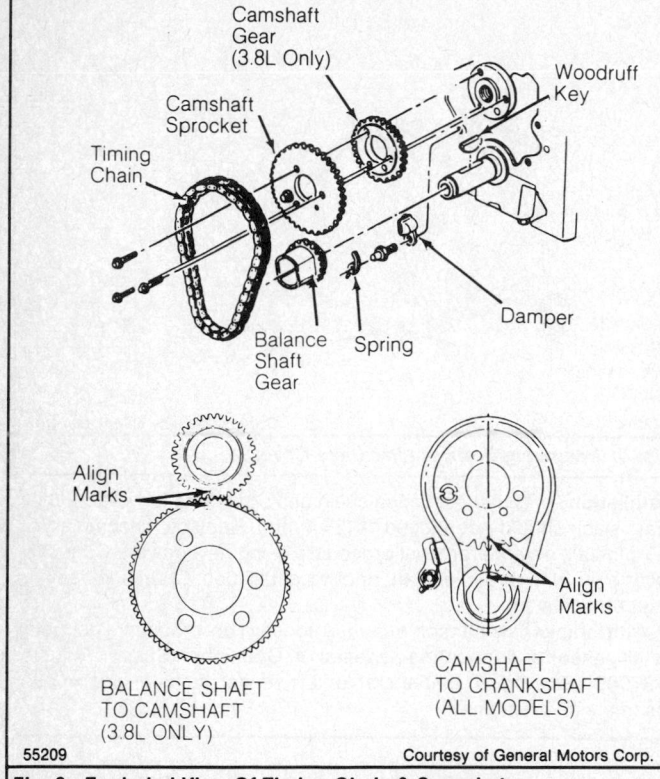

Fig. 6: Exploded View Of Timing Chain & Sprockets

NOTE: If balance shaft has been moved, ensure alignment is correct. See BALANCE SHAFT under REMOVAL & INSTALLATION.

Installation – **1)** If engine has been rotated, rotate crankshaft so No. 1 cylinder is at TDC. Temporarily install camshaft sprocket. Rotate camshaft sprocket so timing mark is downward.

2) Install timing chain on camshaft and crankshaft sprockets. Ensure timing marks are aligned. *See Fig. 6.* Install camshaft sprocket bolts. Install timing chain damper, camshaft button and camshaft button spring.

3) To install remaining components, reverse removal procedure. Ensure timing marks are aligned.

ROCKER ARMS & PUSH RODS

Removal – **1)** Disconnect negative battery cable. Remove serpentine belt. For left (front) valve cover removal, remove alternator bracket and spark plug wires.

2) For right (rear) valve cover removal, loosen power steering pump bolts, and move pump forward with hoses still attached. Remove power steering pump brackets.

3) Remove spark plug wires and valve cover. Remove rocker arm pivot bolts. Remove rocker arms and components. *See Fig. 7.* Mark component locations for reassembly reference.

NOTE: Mark location of all valve train components for reassembly reference. Components must be installed in original location.

Installation – To install, reverse removal procedure. Coat rocker arm bolts with GM Threadlock (12345493) prior to installation. Apply thread sealant to valve cover bolts prior to installation.

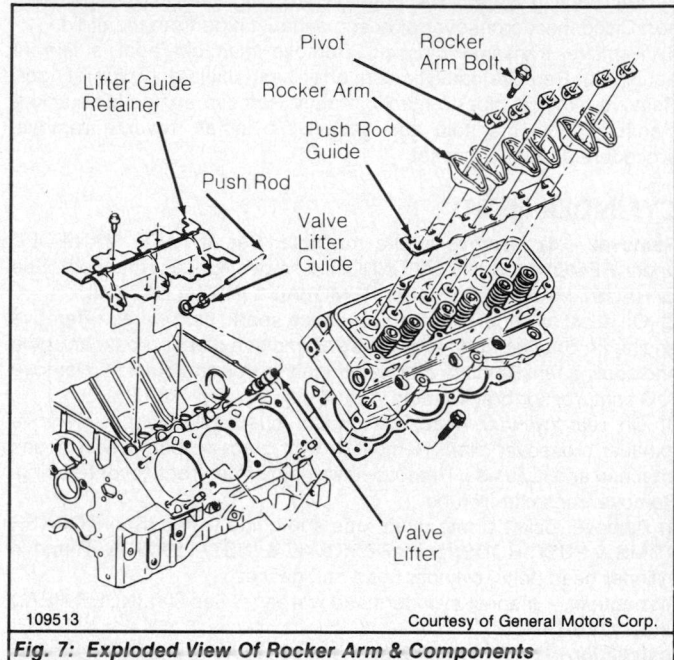

Fig. 7: Exploded View Of Rocker Arm & Components

VALVE LIFTERS

Removal – **1)** Remove intake manifold. See INTAKE MANIFOLD under REMOVAL & INSTALLATION. Remove rocker arms and push rods. See ROCKER ARMS & PUSH RODS.

2) Remove push rod guide bolts and push rod guide. *See Fig. 7.* Remove valve lifter guide and valve lifters. Mark component locations for reassembly reference.

Installation – To install, reverse removal procedure. Apply Engine Oil Supplement (1052365) to valve lifters prior to installation. Ensure components are installed in original location.

CAMSHAFT

Removal – **1)** Release fuel pressure. See FUEL PRESSURE RELEASE under REMOVAL & INSTALLATION. Disconnect negative battery cable. Remove engine. See ENGINE under REMOVAL & INSTALLATION. Remove intake manifold. See INTAKE MANIFOLD under REMOVAL & INSTALLATION.

2) Remove rocker arms and push rods. See ROCKER ARMS & PUSH RODS under REMOVAL & INSTALLATION. Remove valve lifters. Remove timing chain and sprockets. See TIMING CHAIN & SPROCKETS under REMOVAL & INSTALLATION. Remove camshaft and bearings (if necessary).

Inspection – Inspect camshaft journal diameter, lobe lift and oil clearance. See CAMSHAFT table under ENGINE SPECIFICATIONS at end of article. Replace components if measurements are not within specification.

NOTE: Lubricate camshaft bearings and camshaft lobes with GM Lubricant (1052365) prior to installation.

Installation – 1) Install camshaft bearings (if removed). Ensure oil holes are aligned. Apply Sealant (1052914) to rear camshaft plug prior to installation. Lubricate camshaft bearings and camshaft lobes with GM Lubricant (1052365) prior to installation. Install camshaft.

2) To install remaining components, reverse removal procedure. Ensure components are installed in original location and all timing marks are aligned.

BALANCE SHAFT

Removal – 1) Disconnect negative battery cable. Remove engine. See ENGINE under REMOVAL & INSTALLATION.

2) Remove flywheel. Remove intake manifold. See INTAKE MANIFOLD under REMOVAL & INSTALLATION. Remove lifter guide retainer. *See Fig. 7.*

3) Remove front timing case cover. See FRONT TIMING CASE COVER under REMOVAL & INSTALLATION. Remove balance shaft gear bolt. *See Fig. 8.* Remove camshaft sprocket and timing chain.

4) Remove balance shaft retainer bolts. *See Fig. 8.* Remove balance shaft retainer and balance shaft gear. Install Slide Hammer (J-6125-B) in front of balance shaft, and remove balance shaft. Remove balance shaft plug from rear of cylinder block.

5) Note direction of rear bearing installation. Using Rear Bearing Remover (J-36995-5), remove bearing from block. *See Fig. 9.*

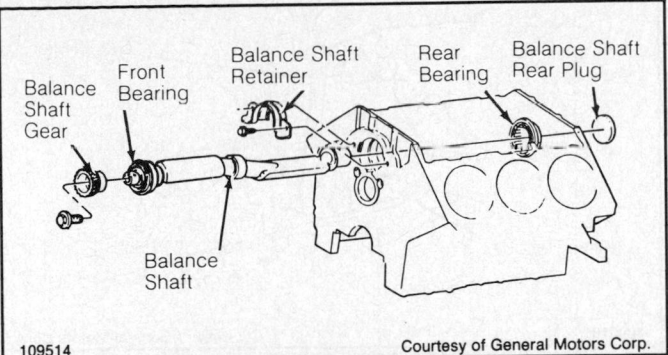

109514   Courtesy of General Motors Corp.

Fig. 8: Identifying Balance Shaft & Components

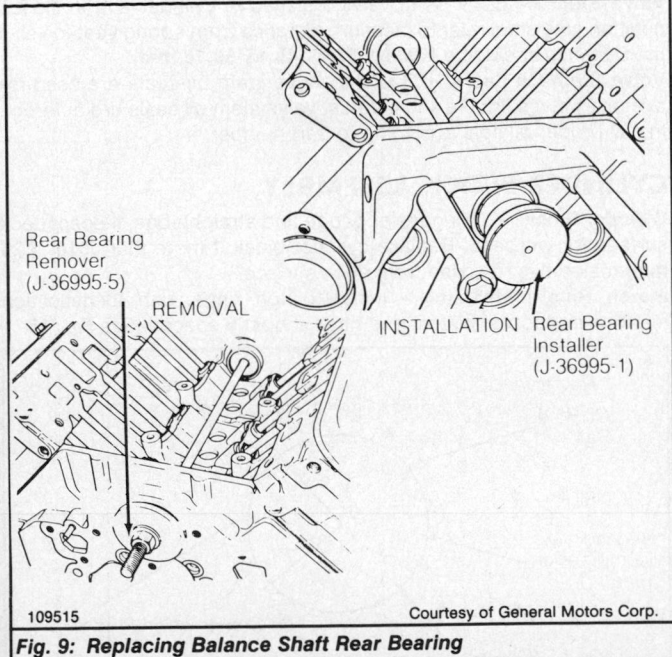

109515   Courtesy of General Motors Corp.

Fig. 9: Replacing Balance Shaft Rear Bearing

NOTE: *Balance shaft and bearings are serviced as a complete assembly only. Proper installation tools must be used to prevent balance shaft damage.*

Inspection – Inspect components for damage. Measure bearing bore I.D. Replace components if I.D. is not within specification. See BALANCE SHAFT SPECIFICATIONS table.

Installation – 1) Lubricate balance shaft bearings with engine oil. Install rear bearing with rolled edge facing inward, toward engine, and manufacturer's marking facing flywheel side of engine. Using Rear Bearing Installer (J-36995-1), install rear bearing. *See Fig. 9.*

NOTE: *Install balance shaft rear bearing with rolled edge facing inward, toward engine, and manufacturer's marking facing flywheel side of engine.*

2) Using Balance Shaft Installer (J-36996), install balance shaft. Temporarily install balance shaft retainer and bolts. Install balance shaft gear. Apply GM Threadlock (12345493) to gear retaining bolt, and install bolt. Tighten gear retaining bolt to specification. See TORQUE SPECIFICATIONS table at end of article.

3) Install balance shaft rear plug. Using dial indicator, measure balance shaft end play and radial clearance at front and rear of balance shaft. *See Fig. 10.* Replace components if measurements are not within specification. See BALANCE SHAFT SPECIFICATIONS table.

4) Rotate camshaft so timing mark is downward when sprocket is installed. With camshaft sprocket and gear removed, rotate balance shaft so timing mark on gear is downward.

5) Rotate balance shaft to align timing marks on camshaft gear and balance shaft gear, and install camshaft gear. *See Fig. 6.* Rotate crankshaft so No. 1 piston is at TDC. Install timing chain and sprocket. Ensure timing marks are aligned. *See Fig. 6.*

BALANCE SHAFT SPECIFICATIONS

Application	In. (mm)
Bearing Bore I.D.	
Front	2.0462-2.0472 (51.973-51.999)
Rear	1.950-1.952 (49.53-49.58)
End Play	0-.008 (0-.20)
Gear Lash	.002-.005 (.05-.13)
Radial Clearance	
Front	0-.0011 (0-.028)
Rear	.0005-.0047 (.013-.119)

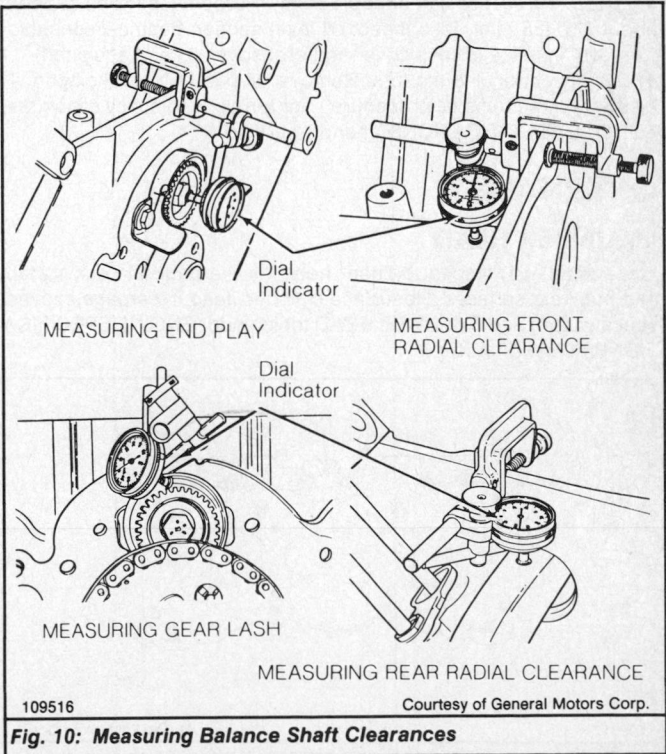

109516   Courtesy of General Motors Corp.

Fig. 10: Measuring Balance Shaft Clearances

6) Using dial indicator, measure gear lash at 4 places every 1/4 turn. Gear lash should be within specification. See BALANCE SHAFT SPECIFICATIONS table. If all measurements are within specification, tighten balance shaft retainer bolts to specification. See TORQUE SPECIFICATIONS table at end of article. To install remaining components, reverse removal procedure.

REAR CRANKSHAFT OIL SEAL

Removal – 1) For seal replacement, engine must be removed. See ENGINE under REMOVAL & INSTALLATION. Remove flywheel. Confirm rear seal leak.

2) To remove seal, pry around dust lip using a screwdriver. DO NOT damage crankshaft O.D. surface or chamfer. Ensure seal areas are clean.

Installation – 1) Apply engine oil to new seal. Install seal using Seal Installer (J-38196). Align dowel pin of installer with dowel pin hole in crankshaft. Tighten installer attaching screws to 60 INCH lbs. (5 N.m).

2) Rotate handle of installer until collar is tight against case. Reverse removal procedure for remaining components.

WATER PUMP

Removal & Installation – 1) Disconnect negative battery cable. Drain cooling system. Remove water pump drive belt. Disconnect necessary coolant hoses.

2) Remove water pump pulley bolts and pulley (access hole in body side rail for long bolt). Remove front engine mount. Remove water pump bolts, water pump and gasket. To install, reverse removal procedure using new gasket. Fill cooling system.

OIL PAN

Removal & Installation – 1) Disconnect negative battery cable. Raise and support vehicle. Drain crankcase, and remove oil filter. Remove right front wheel, lower flap and splash shield. Remove crankshaft pulley. Remove crank sensor cover.

2) Disconnect A/C compressor electrical connector. Remove A/C compressor and lay aside. Remove hose support from suspension support (if equipped). Remove bolts at front of right suspension support.

3) Loosen all suspension support bolts to drop suspension supports about 1.5" (38 mm). Disconnect oil level sensor electrical connector. Remove flexplate access cover and crossover pipe (if equipped).

4) Disconnect engine mounts. Remove oil pan bolts and oil pan. To install, reverse removal procedure. Tighten bolts to specification. See TORQUE SPECIFICATIONS at end of article.

OVERHAUL

CYLINDER HEAD

Inspection – 1) Inspect cylinder head for warpage at deck surface and manifold surfaces. Resurface cylinder head if warpage exceeds specification. See CYLINDER HEAD table under ENGINE SPECIFICATIONS at end of article.

2) Check amount of metal removed from cylinder head to determine if head can be reused. To determine amount removed, use depth micrometer, and measure distance from deck surface to 3 cast pads. See Fig. 11.

3) Distance should be **.054-.066"** (1.37-1.68 mm) on new cylinder heads. Minimum dimension is **.044"** (1.12 mm). Replace cylinder head if measurement is less than specified minimum dimension.

Valve Seats – No replacement procedure is given by manufacturer.

Valve Guides – Valve guides must be reamed for an oversize valve if valve stem oil clearance is not within specification. See CYLINDER HEAD table under ENGINE SPECIFICATIONS at end of article.

Seat Correction Angles – After grinding, if seat width is too wide, use 20-degree or 70-degree stone to reduce seat width. The 20-degree stone will lower seat, and the 70-degree stone will raise seat.

Valve Spring Installed Height – 1) Install valve, valve retainer and keepers. Pull upward on valve, and measure height from top of spring seat to spring side of valve retainer. See Fig. 12.

2) Ensure spring installed height is within specification. See VALVES & VALVE SPRINGS table under ENGINE SPECIFICATIONS at end of article. If measurement exceeds specification, add shims under valve spring to obtain correct height.

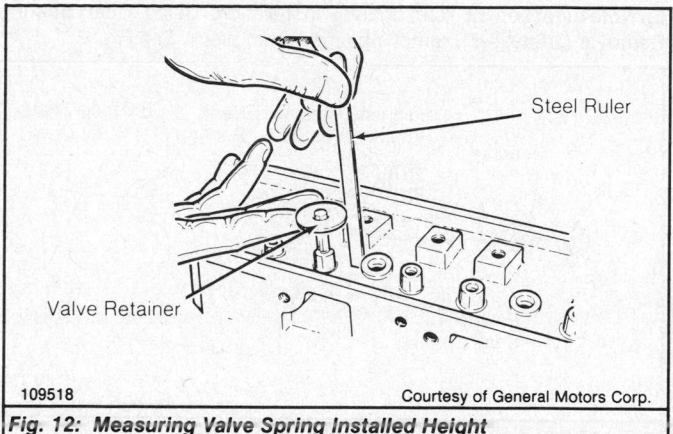

Steel Ruler

Valve Retainer

109518   Courtesy of General Motors Corp.

Fig. 12: Measuring Valve Spring Installed Height

Valve Stem Height – With valve installed in cylinder and in closed position, use steel ruler to measure distance from spring seat to valve tip. Distance should be **1.935-1.975"** (49.15-50.16 mm).

Valve Stem Oil Seals – Oversize valve stem oil seals are used for oversize valves. Intake and exhaust valve stem oil seals are different. Install proper oil seal according to part number.

CYLINDER BLOCK ASSEMBLY

Cylinder Block – Using feeler gauge and straightedge, inspect deck surface for warpage. Replace cylinder block if more than **.010"** (.25 mm) material is removed from deck surface.

Piston Ring Installation – Install piston rings with identification mark toward top of piston, and rings properly spaced. See Fig. 13.

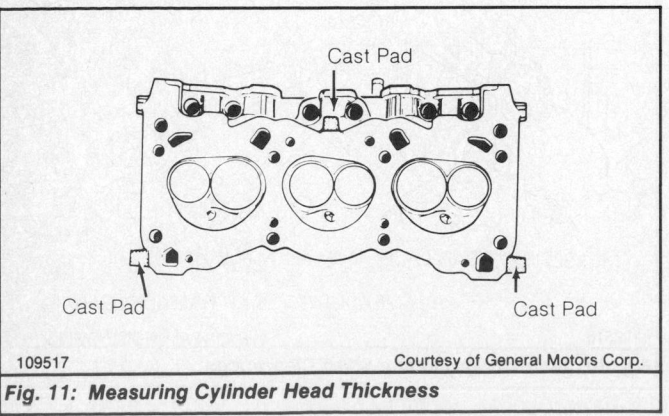

Cast Pad

Cast Pad   Cast Pad

109517   Courtesy of General Motors Corp.

Fig. 11: Measuring Cylinder Head Thickness

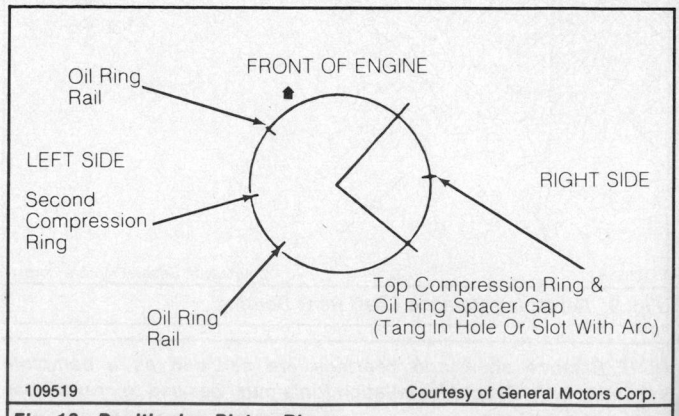

Oil Ring Rail

FRONT OF ENGINE

LEFT SIDE

Second Compression Ring

RIGHT SIDE

Oil Ring Rail

Top Compression Ring & Oil Ring Spacer Gap (Tang In Hole Or Slot With Arc)

109519   Courtesy of General Motors Corp.

Fig. 13: Positioning Piston Rings

Piston & Rod Assembly – Piston can be installed on connecting rod in either direction. Piston and connecting rod must be installed with 2 parallel ridges on bottom of pin boss toward front of engine.
Fitting Pistons – Piston diameter should be measured **1.73" (44 mm)** from top of piston.

NOTE: Oversize pistons must not be machined down, or engine balance will be affected.

CAUTION: Use soft-faced mallet to install main bearing caps. DO NOT pull into place with attaching bolts.

Crankshaft & Main Bearings – **1)** To align crankshaft thrust surfaces, install all bearings and main caps, and tighten all bolts evenly to specification. Loosen all bolts one turn. Using soft-faced mallet, carefully tap crankshaft forward and then backward to align thrust bearing. **2)** Retighten all bolts to specification. See TORQUE SPECIFICATIONS table at end of article.

NOTE: The No. 4 (rear) main bearing cap must be installed flush with, or .010" (.254 mm) forward of, the rear face of the cylinder block. Misalignment of the cap toward the transaxle may cause interference with the flywheel to converter bolt heads. Rear main bearing lip seal must be replaced whenever No. 4 (rear) main bearing cap is removed. Lip seal should be installed after bearing cap has been installed. Installing bearing cap with lip seal in place may cause pinching or misalignment of seal resulting in an oil leak.

CAUTION: Bearing inserts must not be shimmed, scraped or filed. DO NOT touch bearing surface with fingers.

Rod Bearings – **1)** Ensure bearing cap bolt holes and mating surfaces are clean and dry. Use connecting rod stud protector on all rod cap bolts. Install inserts in connecting rod and cap. Lubricate bearings and crank pin.
2) Install bearing cap. Tighten rod bearing cap bolts to specification. See TORQUE SPECIFICATIONS table at end of article.
Crankshaft Flange Runout – **1)** With engine removed and crankshaft installed, measure crankshaft flange runout. Mount dial indicator gauge plate flat against crankshaft flange. Place dial indicator stem on lower left transmission mounting bolt boss (flat area around bolt hole). Adjust dial indicator to zero.
2) Observe and record readings obtained on all mounting bolt hole bosses. Measurements should not vary more than .010" (.25 mm). If readings exceed specification, remount dial gauge plate, and recheck flange runout. Replace crankshaft if runout exceeds specification.

ENGINE OILING

LUBRICATION SYSTEM

Crankshaft driven gear-type oil pump provides pressurized lubrication to main gallery. *See Fig. 14.* Oil pump and pressure regulator valve are located in front timing case cover.
Crankcase Capacity – Engine oil capacity is approximately **4 qts. (3.7L)** with filter change. Recheck oil level after changing filter.
Normal Oil Pressure – With engine at normal operating temperature, oil pressure (with 5W-30 or 10W-30 engine oil) should be **60 psi (4.2 kg/cm²)** at 1850 RPM.

OIL PUMP

Removal & Disassembly – Remove front timing case cover. See FRONT TIMING CASE COVER under REMOVAL & INSTALLATION. Remove oil filter adapter, gasket, pressure regulator and valve from front timing case cover. Remove pump cover bolts, cover and gears from case cover.
Inspection – **1)** Inspect components for damage. Measure gear end clearance. Measure housing gear pocket depth and diameter. Measure tip clearance between gears and outer gear-to-housing clearance.

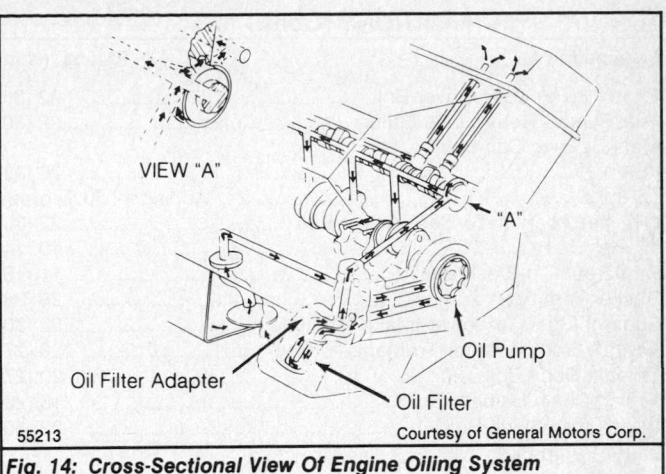

VIEW "A"

Oil Pump
Oil Filter Adapter
Oil Filter

55213   Courtesy of General Motors Corp.

Fig. 14: Cross-Sectional View Of Engine Oiling System

2) Check clearance between pressure regulator valve and bore. Replace components or pump assembly if measurements are not within specification. See OIL PUMP SPECIFICATIONS table.
Reassembly & Installation – To reassemble, reverse disassembly procedure. Lubricate all gears, and fill cavities with petroleum jelly. Install pump cover. To install, reverse removal procedure. Tighten cover screws to specification. Tighten oil filter adapter bolts to specification. See TORQUE SPECIFICATIONS table at end of article.

OIL PUMP SPECIFICATIONS

Application	In. (mm)
Gear End Clearance	.0010-.0035 (.025-.089)
Gear Tip Clearance	.006 (.15)
Housing Gear Pocket	
Depth	.4610-.4625 (11.709-11.748)
Diameter	3.508-3.512 (89.10-89.20)
Outer Gear-To-Housing Clearance	.008-.015 (.20-.38)
Pressure Regulator	
Valve-To-Bore Clearance	.0015-.0030 (.038-.076)

TORQUE SPECIFICATIONS

TORQUE SPECIFICATIONS

Application	Ft. Lbs. (N.m)
Balance Shaft Gear Bolt [1]	
Step 1	14 (19)
Step 2	Additional 35 Degrees
Balance Shaft Retainer Bolt	22 (30)
Camshaft Sprocket Bolt	
Step 1	74 (100)
Step 2	Additional 105 Degrees
Connecting Rod Bolt	
Step 1	20 (27)
Step 2	Additional 50 Degrees
Crankshaft Pulley/Balancer Bolt	
Step 1	111 (150)
Step 2	Additional 76 Degrees
Cylinder Head Bolts [1]	
Step 1	[2]
Step 2	[3]
Step 3	[4]
Exhaust Manifold Bolt	38 (52)
Flywheel Bolt	
Step 1	11 (15)
Step 2	Additional 50 Degrees

[1] – Apply thread sealant to bolt(s).
[2] – Tighten bolts in sequence to 35 ft. lbs. (47 N.m). *See Fig. 3.*
[3] – Tighten bolts in sequence an additional 130 degrees. *See Fig. 3.*
[4] – Tighten center 4 bolts in sequence an additional 30 degrees. *See Fig. 3.*
[5] – Tighten bolts TWICE in sequence. *See Fig. 2.*

TORQUE SPECIFICATIONS (Cont.)

Application	Ft. Lbs. (N.m)
Front Timing Case Cover Bolt	[1] 22 (30)
Fuel Feed & Return Line Fitting	22 (30)
Main Bearing Cap Bolt	
Step 1	26 (35)
Step 2	Additional 50 Degrees
Oil Filter Adapter-To-Case Cover Bolt	22 (30)
Oil Pan Bolt	[1] 10 (14)
Oil Screen-To-Block Bolt	11 (15)
Rocker Arm Bolt	[1] 28 (38)
Supercharger-To-Lower Intake Manifold	22 (30)
Throttle Body Adapter-To-Manifold Bolt	20 (27)
Throttle Body Bolt	20 (27)
Timing Chain Damper Bolt	16 (22)
Valve Lifter Guide Bolt	22 (30)
Water Pump Bolt	
Step 1	11 (15)
Step 2	Additional 80 Degrees

	INCH Lbs. (N.m)
Intake Manifold Bolt	[1] [5] 88 (10)
Oil Pump Cover Bolt	97 (11)
Valve Cover Bolt	[1] 88 (10)

[1] – Apply thread sealant to bolt(s).
[2] – Tighten bolts in sequence to 35 ft. lbs. (47 N.m). *See Fig. 3.*
[3] – Tighten bolts in sequence an additional 130 degrees. *See Fig. 3.*
[4] – Tighten center 4 bolts in sequence an additional 30 degrees. *See Fig. 3.*
[5] – Tighten bolts TWICE in sequence. *See Fig. 2.*

ENGINE SPECIFICATIONS

GENERAL SPECIFICATIONS

Application	Specification
Displacement	231 Cu. In. (3.8L)
Bore	3.80" (96.5 mm)
Stroke	3.40" (86.4 mm)
Compression Ratio	8.5:1
Fuel System	PFI
Horsepower @ RPM	165 @ 4300
Torque Ft. Lbs. @ RPM	220 @ 3200

CRANKSHAFT, MAIN & CONNECTING ROD BEARINGS

Application	In. (mm)
Crankshaft End Play	.003-.011 (.08-.28)
Main Bearings	
Journal Diameter	2.4988-2.4998 (63.469-63.495)
Journal Out-Of-Round	.0003 (.008)
Journal Taper	.0003 (.008)
Oil Clearance	.0008-.0022 (.020-.056)
Connecting Rod Bearings	
Journal Diameter	2.2487-2.2499 (57.117-57.147)
Journal Out-Of-Round	.0003 (.008)
Journal Taper	.0003 (.008)
Oil Clearance	.0008-.0022 (.020-.056)

CONNECTING RODS

Application	In. (mm)
Maximum Bend	[1] .005 (.13)
Maximum Twist	[1] .010 (.25)
Side Play	.003-.015 (.08-.38)

[1] – Bend or twist over total length.

PISTONS, PINS & RINGS

Application	In. (mm)
Pistons	
Clearance	.0004-.0022 (.010-.056)
Pins	
Diameter	.9053-.9055 (22.994-23.000)
Piston Fit	.0004-.0008 (.010-.020)
Rod Fit	.0007-.0017 (.018-.043)
Rings	
No. 1	
End Gap	.010-.025 (.25-.64)
Side Clearance	.0013-.0031 (.033-.079)
No. 2	
End Gap	.010-.025 (.25-.64)
Side Clearance	.0013-.0031 (.033-.079)
No. 3 (Oil)	
End Gap	.015-.055 (.38-1.40)
Side Clearance	.0081-.0110 (.206-.279)

CYLINDER BLOCK

Application	In. (mm)
Cylinder Bore	
Diameter	3.80 (96.5)
Maximum Taper	.0005 (.013)
Maximum Out-Of-Round	.0004 (.010)

VALVES & VALVE SPRINGS

Application	Specification
Intake & Exhaust Valves	
Face Angle	45°
Minimum Margin	.025" (.64 mm)
Valve Springs	
Installed Height	1.690-1.720" (42.93-43.69 mm)

	Lbs. @ In. (kg @ mm)
Pressure	
Valve Closed	80 @ 1.750 (36 @ 43.69)
Valve Open	210 @ 1.315 (94 @ 33.40)

CYLINDER HEAD

Application	Specification
Maximum Warpage	.010" (.25 mm)
Valve Seats	
Intake Valve	
Seat Angle	45°
Seat Width	.060-.080" (1.52-2.03 mm)
Exhaust Valve	
Seat Angle	45°
Seat Width	.090-.110" (2.29-2.79 mm)
Valve Guides	
Valve Guide Oil Clearance	
Intake Valve	.0015-.0035" (.038-.089 mm)
Exhaust Valve	.0015-.0032" (.038-.081 mm)

CAMSHAFT

Application	In. (mm)
Journal Diameter	1.785-1.786 (45.34-45.36)
Lobe Lift	
Intake	.250 (6.35)
Exhaust	.255 (6.48)
Oil Clearance	.0005-.0035 (.013-.089)

1992 ENGINES
4.3L V6, 5.0L, 5.7L & 7.4L V8

Astro, Bravada, Commercial Van, Jimmy, Safari, Sierra, Sonoma, Suburban, Syclone, Typhoon, Van, Yukon, "C" & "K" Series Blazer & Pickup, "S" & "T" Series Blazer & Pickup

NOTE: *For repair procedures not covered in this article, see ENGINE OVERHAUL PROCEDURES article in GENERAL INFORMATION.*

ENGINE IDENTIFICATION

Engine can be identified by eighth character of Vehicle Identification Number (VIN). VIN is stamped on a metal tag on top left end of instrument panel, near windshield. See ENGINE IDENTIFICATION table.

Engine can also be identified by engine identification (ID) number. Number is stamped on front of cylinder block, immediately forward of right cylinder head or on left side of cylinder block, on engine-to-transmission mating flange.

ENGINE IDENTIFICATION

Engine	[1] VIN Code	Engine ID No.
4.3L		
CPI	W	L35
TBI	Z	LB4
5.0L TBI	H	LO3
5.7L TBI	K	LO5
7.4L TBI	N	L19

[1] – Eighth character of VIN.

ADJUSTMENTS
VALVE CLEARANCE ADJUSTMENT

NOTE: *Although valve clearance adjustment is not usually required (engine uses hydraulic valve lifters), perform following procedures after servicing valve train.*

4.3L With Screw-In Rocker Studs & 4.3L VIN W – Tighten rocker arm nuts to 20 ft. lbs. (27 N.m).

Except 4.3L With Screw-In Rocker Studs & 4.3L VIN W – **1)** Rotate engine until No. 1 piston is on TDC of compression stroke. Go next step and adjust specified valves listed in appropriate VALVE CLEARANCE ADJUSTMENT table.

2) Loosen rocker arm adjusting nut until lash is present. Tighten adjusting nut until lash is removed (under this condition, push rod cannot be rotated with fingers). On all engines except 7.4L, tighten adjusting nut one full turn. On 7.4L, tighten adjusting nut 3/4 turn.

3) Rotate crankshaft 360 degrees to bring No. 4 piston (4.3L) or No. 6 piston (5.0L, 5.7L and 7.4L) to TDC of compression stroke. Adjust remaining valves. See appropriate VALVE CLEARANCE ADJUSTMENT table

VALVE CLEARANCE ADJUSTMENT (4.3L [1])

Piston At TDC	Intake	Exhaust
No. 1	No. 1, 2 & 3	No. 1, 5 & 6
No. 4	No. 4, 5 & 6	No. 2, 3 & 4

[1] – On VIN Z with screw-in rocker studs and all VIN W, simply tighten all rocker arm nuts to 20 ft. lbs. (27 N.m) to adjust.

VALVE CLEARANCE ADJUSTMENT (5.0L, 5.7L & 7.4L)

Piston AT TDC	Intake	Exhaust
No. 1	No. 1, 2, 5 & 7	No. 1, 3, 4 & 8
No. 6	No. 3, 4, 6 & 8	No. 2, 5, 6 & 7

REMOVAL & INSTALLATION

WARNING: *When battery is disconnected, vehicle computer and memory systems may lose memory data. Driveability problems may exist until computer systems have completed a relearn cycle. See COMPUTER RELEARN PROCEDURES article in GENERAL INFORMATION before disconnecting battery.*

NOTE: *For reassembly reference, label all electrical connectors, vacuum hoses and fuel lines before removal. Also place mating marks on engine hood and other major assemblies before removal.*

FUEL PRESSURE RELEASE

Disconnect battery terminals. Loosen fuel tank cap to relieve tank pressure. Internal constant bleed feature in injection unit relieves fuel system pressure when ignition switch is turned off. No further pressure relief is required.

ENGINE (4.3L)

CAUTION: *Minimal clearance exists between oil pump pick-up tube and bottom of oil pan. DO NOT place jack under oil pan, crankshaft pulley or any sheet metal when lifting engine.*

Removal & Installation (Astro & Safari) – **1)** Release fuel system pressure. See FUEL PRESSURE RELEASE under REMOVAL & INSTALLATION. Disconnect battery. Drain cooling system. Raise and support vehicle.

2) Disconnect exhaust pipes from manifolds. Remove flywheel cover, torque converter bolts (A/T), starter and oil filter. Disconnect engine wiring harness from transmission and frame.

3) Disconnect fuel lines from frame. Disconnect transmission fluid lines and engine oil cooler lines from radiator. Remove lower fan shroud bolts. Remove motor mount through-bolts. Lower vehicle.

4) Remove headlight bezels and grille. Remove lower radiator close-out panel, radiator support braces and radiator cross brace. Remove hood latch mechanism. Discharge A/C system (if equipped) using approved refrigerant recovery/recycling equipment. Remove master cylinder, upper fan shroud, upper radiator core support and radiator.

5) Remove radiator filler panels. Remove engine cover. Disconnect A/C hose from accumulator. Remove A/C compressor and bracket. Remove power steering pump.

6) Disconnect vacuum hoses as necessary. Disconnect engine wiring harness clips from firewall. Remove right kick panel. Disconnect engine wiring harness connector from ESC module. Push connector and harness through firewall. Remove distributor cap and A/C accumulator. Disconnect fuel line from injection unit.

7) Remove transmission dipstick tube. Disconnect heater hose from heater core. Remove horn. Support transmission. Support engine with adjustable jack. Remove bellhousing bolts. Lower engine from vehicle.

8) To install, reverse removal procedure. Fill crankcase and cooling system. Evacuate and charge A/C system.

Removal & Installation ("C" & "K" Series Pickup & Sierra) – **1)** Release fuel system pressure. See FUEL PRESSURE RELEASE under REMOVAL & INSTALLATION. Disconnect battery. Remove hood. Remove air cleaner, accessory drive belt, fan and water pump pulley.

2) Drain cooling system. Remove fan shroud and radiator. Disconnect heater hoses from engine. Disconnect fuel lines, electrical connectors, vacuum hoses, coolant hoses and control cables as necessary. Remove A/C compressor and power steering pump with hoses attached and position aside (if equipped).

3) Raise and support vehicle. Drain crankcase. Disconnect exhaust pipes from manifolds. Disconnect strut rods. Remove flywheel cover. Remove starter. Remove torque converter bolts (A/T). Lower vehicle.

4) Support transmission. Attach engine hoist. Remove bellhousing bolts. Remove front engine mount-to-frame bolts. Remove engine. To install, reverse removal procedure. Fill crankcase and cooling system. Evacuate and charge A/C system.

Removal & Installation (Van) – 1) Release fuel system pressure. See FUEL PRESSURE RELEASE under REMOVAL & INSTALLATION. Disconnect battery. Drain cooling system. Remove engine cover and air cleaner. Remove power steering fluid reservoir.

2) Remove upper fan shroud, fan, fan pulley, radiator and lower fan shroud. Discharge A/C system (if equipped) using approved refrigerant recovery/recycling equipment. Remove A/C condenser. Remove A/C compressor and brace. Remove alternator. Remove cruise control servo (if equipped).

3) Disconnect fuel lines, electrical connectors, vacuum hoses, coolant hoses and control cables as necessary. Remove injection unit. Remove distributor cap with wires attached. Remove diverter valve assembly and pipe.

4) Remove ignition coil and manifold absolute pressure sensor. Remove upper half of engine oil dipstick tube. Remove engine oil filler tube. Remove headlight bezels, grille and upper radiator support (sheet metal cross panel support).

5) Raise and support vehicle. Drain crankcase. Disconnect exhaust pipes from manifolds. Remove strut rods. Remove flywheel cover. Disconnect oil cooler lines from engine. Remove starter, torque converter bolts (A/T) and engine mount through-bolts.

6) Lower vehicle. Attach engine hoist. Remove bellhousing bolts. Support transmission. Remove engine. To install, reverse removal procedure. Fill crankcase and cooling system. Evacuate and charge A/C system.

NOTE: *On Commercial Van, engine and transmission are removed as an assembly through side door.*

Removal & Installation (Commercial Van) – 1) Release fuel system pressure. See FUEL PRESSURE RELEASE under REMOVAL & INSTALLATION. Disconnect battery. Drain cooling system. Remove engine cover and floor panel sections.

2) Remove air cleaner, duct and exhaust heat stove pipe. Remove distributor cap and position aside. Disconnect all engine harness electrical connectors and position aside. Disconnect fuel lines from injection unit. Remove fuel line clamps from transmission and position fuel lines aside.

3) Disconnect ground strap from rear end of left cylinder head. Disconnect all transmission harness electrical connectors and position harness aside. Remove transmission shifter (if necessary). Remove upper radiator hose, all accessory drive belts, fan, fan pulley, fan shroud and lower radiator hose.

4) Remove engine oil filler tube. Remove clutch adjuster rod, return spring and pivot arm assembly (M/T). Disconnect exhaust pipes from manifolds. Disconnect battery cable from clamp on cylinder block. Disconnect drive shaft from transmission. Remove transmission mount.

5) Disconnect oil cooler lines from oil filter adapter and oil cooler line clamps from engine. Attach engine hoist. Remove engine mount through-bolts. Remove engine and transmission assembly through side door. To install, reverse removal procedure. Fill crankcase and cooling system.

Removal & Installation ("S" Series Blazer & Pickup, Jimmy, Sonoma, Syclone & Typhoon – 2WD) –1) Release fuel system pressure. See FUEL PRESSURE RELEASE under REMOVAL & INSTALLATION. Disconnect battery. Remove hood. Drain cooling system.

2) Disconnect upper radiator hose from radiator. Remove coolant overflow hose and upper fan shroud. Disconnect transmission fluid lines and engine oil cooler lines (if equipped). Remove radiator and fan. Disconnect heater hoses. Remove air cleaner.

3) Disconnect fuel lines, electrical connectors, vacuum hoses, coolant hoses and control cables as necessary. Remove distributor cap. Raise and support vehicle. Disconnect exhaust pipe from converter and manifolds. Remove strut rods and flywheel cover.

4) Remove torque converter bolts (A/T). Remove shield from rear of catalytic converter. Disconnect converter hanger from exhaust pipe.

Remove 2 outer air dam bolts. Remove left body mount bolts, raise and support body and remove bellhousing bolts. Lower body.

5) Remove motor mount through-bolts. Lower vehicle. Remove A/C compressor and power steering pump with hoses attached and position aside (if equipped). Attach engine hoist. Support transmission. Remove engine. To install, reverse removal procedure. Fill crankcase and cooling system.

Removal & Installation ("T" Series Blazer & Pickup, Jimmy, Sonoma, Syclone & Typhoon – 4WD) – 1) Release fuel system pressure. See FUEL PRESSURE RELEASE under REMOVAL & INSTALLATION. Disconnect battery. Remove hood. Raise and support vehicle.

2) Loosen or remove body mount bolts. Raise and support body. Remove upper bellhousing bolts and front air dam end bolts. Lower body. Remove remaining bellhousing bolts. Remove No. 2 frame crossmember. Disconnect exhaust pipes from manifolds.

3) Disconnect catalytic converter hanger. Remove flywheel cover bolts. Disconnect front drive shaft from differential. Remove flywheel cover. Disconnect transmission cooler lines from engine clips. Remove motor mount bolts.

4) Remove torque converter bolts. Remove front splash shield and lower fan shroud bolts. Lower vehicle. Drain cooling system. Remove upper fan shroud. Disconnect radiator hoses from radiator. Disconnect oil filter pipe from remote oil filter.

5) Remove radiator, fan and air cleaner. Remove A/C compressor and power steering pump with hoses attached and position aside (if equipped). Disconnect fuel lines, electrical connectors, vacuum hoses, coolant hoses and control cables as necessary.

6) Support transmission. Attach engine hoist. Remove engine. To install, reverse removal procedure. Fill crankcase and cooling system.

Removal & Installation (Bravada) – 1) Release fuel system pressure. See FUEL PRESSURE RELEASE under REMOVAL & INSTALLATION. Disconnect battery. Remove hood. Raise and support vehicle. Drain cooling system and crankcase.

2) Disconnect exhaust pipes from manifolds. Disconnect drive shaft from front differential. Remove starter. Remove flywheel cover and torque converter bolts. Remove engine mount through-bolts. Remove oil filter adapter.

3) Remove strut rod. Remove bellhousing bolts. Disconnect transmission fluid cooler lines from clips. Lower vehicle. Remove air cleaner, upper fan shroud, accessory drive belt and fan/clutch assembly.

4) Remove A/C compressor with hoses attached and position aside (if equipped). Remove radiator. Disconnect power steering hoses from power steering pump. Disconnect fuel lines, electrical connectors, vacuum hoses, coolant hoses and control cables as necessary.

5) Remove alternator. Disconnect spark plug wires from distributor cap. Remove cap. Support transmission. Remove bracket from oil cooler. Attach engine hoist. Remove engine.

6) To install, reverse removal procedure. Fill crankcase and cooling system. Bleed power steering fluid system.

ENGINE (5.0L & 5.7L)

CAUTION: *Minimal clearance exists between oil pump pick-up tube and bottom of oil pan. DO NOT place jack under oil pan, crankshaft pulley or any sheet metal when lifting engine.*

Removal & Installation ("C" & "K" Series Blazer & Pickup, Sierra, Suburban & Yukon) – 1) Release fuel system pressure. See FUEL PRESSURE RELEASE under REMOVAL & INSTALLATION. Disconnect battery. Remove hood. Drain cooling system.

2) Remove air cleaner, accessory drive belt, fan and water pump pulley. Remove radiator and fan shroud. Disconnect heater hoses from engine. Disconnect fuel lines, electrical connectors, vacuum hoses, coolant hoses and control cables as necessary.

3) Remove A/C compressor and power steering pump with hoses attached and position aside (if equipped). Raise and support vehicle. Drain crankcase. Disconnect exhaust pipes from manifolds. Remove strut rods (if equipped). Remove flywheel cover and starter. Remove torque converter bolts (A/T).

4) Lower vehicle. Support transmission. Attach engine hoist. Remove bellhousing bolts. Remove engine mount through-bolts. Remove engine. To install, reverse removal procedure. Fill crankcase and cooling system.

NOTE: On Van, engine and transmission are removed as an assembly.

Removal & Installation (Van) – **1)** Release fuel system pressure. See FUEL PRESSURE RELEASE under REMOVAL & INSTALLATION. Disconnect battery negative cable. Drain cooling system.

2) Remove coolant recovery reservoir. Remove grille, lower grille valance and upper radiator support. Discharge A/C system (if equipped) using approved refrigerant recovery/recycling equipment. Remove A/C condenser and radiator. Remove power steering pump with hoses attached and position aside (if equipped).

3) Remove engine cover, air cleaner and injection unit. Disconnect fuel lines, electrical connectors, vacuum hoses, coolant hoses and control cables as necessary. Remove thermostat housing and oil filler tube. Raise and support vehicle. Disconnect exhaust pipes from manifolds.

4) Disconnect drive shaft from transmission. Disconnect transmission shift linkage and vehicle speed sensor connector from transmission. Drain crankcase. Remove transmission mount bolts. Support engine with jack.

5) Remove front engine mounts and place wood blocks between cylinder block and frame. Lower vehicle. Attach engine hoist. Remove engine and transmission as an assembly. To install, reverse removal procedure. Fill crankcase and cooling system. Evacuate and charge A/C system.

NOTE: On Commercial Van, engine and transmission are removed as an assembly through side door.

Removal & Installation (Commercial Van) – **1)** Release fuel system pressure. See FUEL PRESSURE RELEASE under REMOVAL & INSTALLATION. Disconnect battery. Drain cooling system. Remove engine cover and floor panel sections from inside vehicle.

2) Remove air cleaner, duct and exhaust heat stove pipe. Remove distributor cap and position aside. Disconnect all engine harness electrical connectors and position harness aside. Disconnect fuel lines from injection unit. Remove fuel line clamps from transmission and position fuel lines aside.

3) Disconnect hydraulic line from clutch slave cylinder. Disconnect ground strap from rear end of left cylinder head. Disconnect all transmission harness electrical connectors and position harness aside. Remove transmission shift lever (M/T).

4) Remove upper radiator hose, all accessory drive belts, fan, fan pulley, fan shroud and lower radiator hose. Remove engine oil filler tube. Raise and support vehicle. Disconnect exhaust pipes from manifolds. Disconnect battery cable from clamp on cylinder block.

5) Disconnect drive shaft from transmission. Remove transmission mount. Disconnect oil cooler lines from oil filter adapter. Disconnect oil cooler line clamps from engine. Attach engine hoist.

6) Remove engine mount through-bolts. Remove engine and transmission assembly through side door. To install, reverse removal procedure. Fill crankcase and cooling system.

ENGINE (7.4L)

CAUTION: Minimal clearance exists between oil pump pick-up tube and bottom of oil pan. DO NOT place jack under oil pan, crankshaft pulley or any sheet metal when lifting engine.

Removal & Installation ("C" & "K" Series Pickup, Commercial Van, Sierra & Suburban) – **1)** Release fuel system pressure. See FUEL PRESSURE RELEASE under REMOVAL & INSTALLATION. Disconnect battery. Remove hood. Drain cooling system.

2) Remove air cleaner, accessory drive belt, fan and water pump pulley. Remove radiator and fan shroud. Disconnect heater hoses from engine. Disconnect fuel lines, electrical connectors, vacuum hoses, coolant hoses and control cables as necessary.

3) Remove A/C compressor and power steering pump with hoses attached and position aside (if equipped). Raise and support vehicle. Drain crankcase. Disconnect exhaust pipes from manifolds. Remove starter. Remove flywheel cover. Remove torque converter bolts (A/T).

4) Remove bellhousing bolts and engine mount through-bolts. Lower vehicle. Support transmission. Attach engine hoist. Remove engine. To install, reverse removal procedure. Fill crankcase and cooling system.

Removal & Installation (Van) – **1)** Release fuel system pressure. See FUEL PRESSURE RELEASE under REMOVAL & INSTALLATION. Disconnect battery. Remove engine cover. Drain crankcase and cooling system.

2) Remove air intake duct and air cleaner. Disconnect fuel lines, electrical connectors, vacuum hoses, coolant hoses and control cables as necessary. Remove distributor cap, distributor and ignition coil.

3) Remove transmission and engine oil dipstick tubes. Remove EGR purge valve. Remove 2 A/C compressor brackets. Remove injection unit. Remove headlight bezels, grille, bumper filler panel and cruise control servo (if equipped). Remove hood latch, coolant reservoir and upper radiator brackets.

4) Remove front end sheet metal cross panel. Discharge A/C system (if equipped) using approved refrigerant recovery/recycling equipment. Remove A/C condenser, windshield washer fluid reservoir and washer pump. Remove upper fan shroud, engine oil cooler and transmission oil cooler. Remove radiator, lower fan shroud, fan, serpentine drive belt and water pump pulley.

5) Disconnect A/C refrigerant line from accumulator and alternator bracket. Remove A/C compressor and idler pulley. Remove alternator and belt tensioner. Remove exhaust crossover pipe from manifolds. Remove starter. Disconnect drive shaft and shift linkage from transmission.

6) Remove engine mount through-bolts. Support transmission. Remove transmission crossmember. Lower vehicle. Attach engine hoist. Remove engine and transmission as an assembly.

7) To install, reverse removal procedure. Fill crankcase and cooling system. Evacuate and charge A/C refrigerant system.

INTAKE MANIFOLD

Removal – **1)** Release fuel system pressure. See FUEL PRESSURE RELEASE under REMOVAL & INSTALLATION. Disconnect battery. Drain cooling system. Remove air cleaner.

2) Disconnect fuel lines, electrical connectors, vacuum hoses, coolant hoses and control cables as necessary. Remove alternator bracket, A/C compressor (with hoses attached), injection unit and cruise control servo as necessary.

3) Remove distributor cap. Mark distributor rotor in relation to distributor housing. Mark base of distributor housing in relation to intake manifold. Remove distributor. Remove intake manifold bolts, intake manifold and gaskets.

Installation – **1)** On all engines except 7.4L, install gaskets on cylinder heads. Apply a 3/16" (5 mm) bead of RTV silicone sealant to front and rear intake manifold-to-cylinder block mounting surfaces. *See Fig. 1.* Extend bead 1/2" (13 mm) beyond cylinder block-to-cylinder head junction.

2) On 7.4L, install front and rear intake manifold seals on cylinder block. Install gaskets on cylinder heads. *See Fig. 2.*

3) On all models, install intake manifold and bolts. Tighten bolts in sequence to specification. *See Fig. 3.* See TORQUE SPECIFICATIONS table at end of article. To complete installation, reverse removal procedure. Fill cooling system.

EXHAUST MANIFOLD

Removal – Remove heat stove tube. Remove all attached brackets and heat shields. If necessary, remove dip stick tube. Disconnect oxygen sensor electrical connector. Disconnect exhaust pipe from manifold. Remove exhaust manifold bolts and exhaust manifold.

Installation – Install manifold. Tighten bolts to specification. See TORQUE SPECIFICATIONS table at end of article. Bend lock tabs (if equipped). To complete installation, reverse removal procedure.

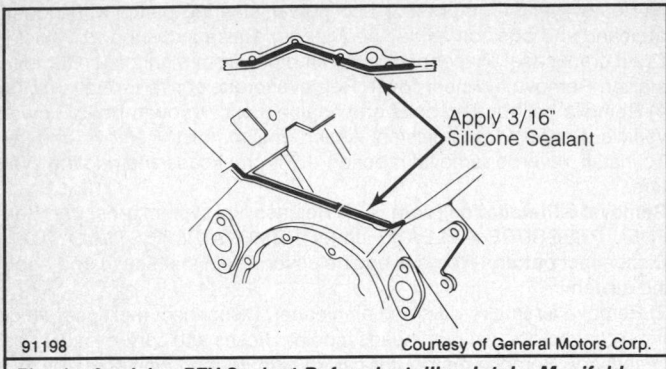

Fig. 1: Applying RTV Sealant Before Installing Intake Manifold (Except 7.4L)

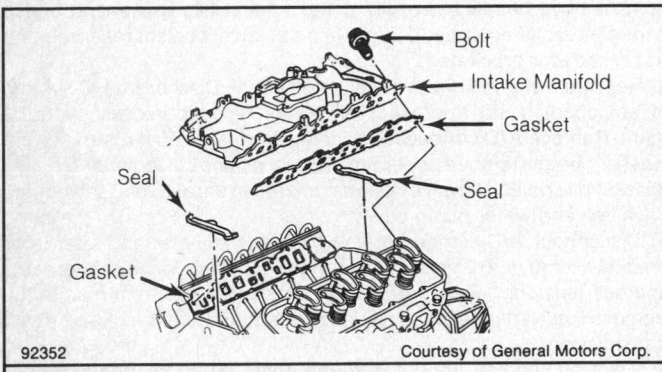

Fig. 2: Installing Intake Manifold (7.4L)

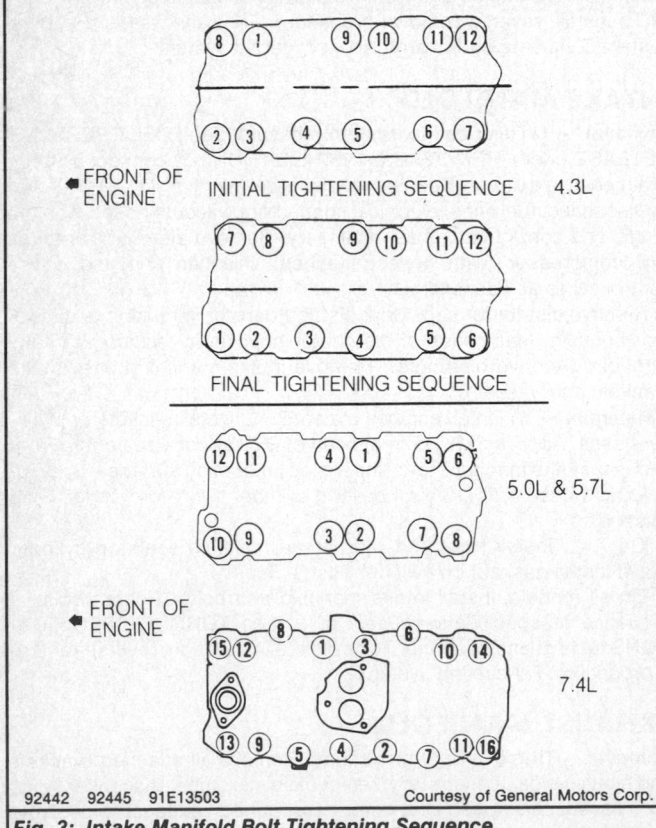

Fig. 3: Intake Manifold Bolt Tightening Sequence

CYLINDER HEAD

NOTE: On 7.4L, exhaust valve push rods are longer than intake valve push rods.

Removal – 1) Release fuel system pressure. See FUEL PRESSURE RELEASE under REMOVAL & INSTALLATION. Remove intake manifold. See INTAKE MANIFOLD under REMOVAL & INSTALLATION.

2) Remove exhaust manifold. See EXHAUST MANIFOLD under REMOVAL & INSTALLATION. Remove valve covers. Loosen rocker arm nuts. Rotate rocker arms aside. Remove push rods and mark for reassembly to original locations. Remove cylinder head bolts. Remove cylinder head.

Installation – 1) Clean gasket surfaces, bolt threads and bolt holes. If using steel head gasket, thinly coat both sides of gasket with sealant. DO NOT apply sealant to composition (steel/asbestos) head gaskets. Position head gasket on cylinder block. Ensure all holes align. Coat head bolt threads with GM Sealant (1052080).

2) Install cylinder head with bolts finger-tight. Tighten head bolts in sequence to specification. *See Fig. 4.* See TORQUE SPECIFICATIONS table at end of article. Lubricate valve tip, rocker arm pivot and push rod socket with Molykote.

3) To complete installation, reverse removal procedure. Adjust valves. See VALVE CLEARANCE ADJUSTMENT under ADJUSTMENTS.

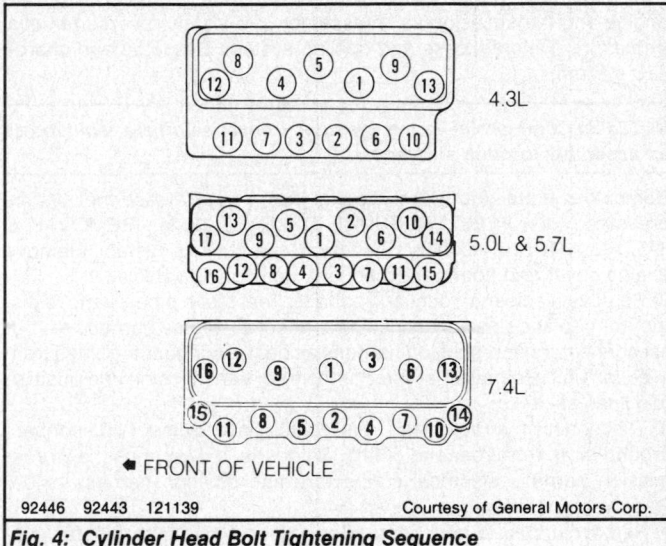

Fig. 4: Cylinder Head Bolt Tightening Sequence

FRONT COVER OIL SEAL

Removal – Remove accessory drive belt(s) and pulley. Remove crankshaft damper bolt. Using Damper Puller/Installer (J-23523-E), remove crankshaft damper. Carefully pry seal from cover with screwdriver. DO NOT distort front cover.

Installation – 1) Coat seal lip with engine oil. Using Seal Installer (J-22102) on 7.4L and (J-35468) on all others, install new seal in front cover with seal lip facing engine. Apply RTV sealant to Woodruff keyway in crankshaft damper.

2) Install crankshaft damper. Install crankshaft damper bolt and tighten to specification. See TORQUE SPECIFICATIONS table at end of article. To install remaining components, reverse removal procedure.

TIMING CHAIN & SPROCKETS

Removal – 1) Disconnect battery. Drain cooling system. If necessary, remove radiator shroud. Remove accessory drive belts, fan and pulley. Remove crankshaft damper bolt. Using Damper Puller/Installer (J-23523-E), remove crankshaft damper.

2) Remove all mounting brackets and coolant hoses attached to water pump. Remove water pump. Remove oil pan. See OIL PAN under REMOVAL & INSTALLATION. Remove front cover and gasket.

3) Rotate crankshaft until timing marks on camshaft and crankshaft sprockets are aligned. *See Fig. 5.* Remove camshaft sprocket and timing chain. To remove crankshaft sprocket, use Sprocket Puller (J-1619) on 7.4L and (J-5825-A) on all others.

Installation – 1) Install Woodruff key in crankshaft (if removed). Using Crankshaft Sprocket Installer (J-22102) on 7.4L and (J-5590) on all others, install crankshaft sprocket. Install camshaft sprocket and timing chain, ensuring timing marks on sprockets are aligned. *See Fig. 5.*

2) Install and tighten camshaft sprocket bolts to specification. See TORQUE SPECIFICATIONS table at end of article. Install gasket to front cover with gasket sealant. Install front cover and gasket.

3) Apply RTV sealant to Woodruff keyway in crankshaft damper. Install crankshaft damper. Install crankshaft damper bolt and tighten to specification. See TORQUE SPECIFICATIONS table. To install remaining components, reverse removal procedure.

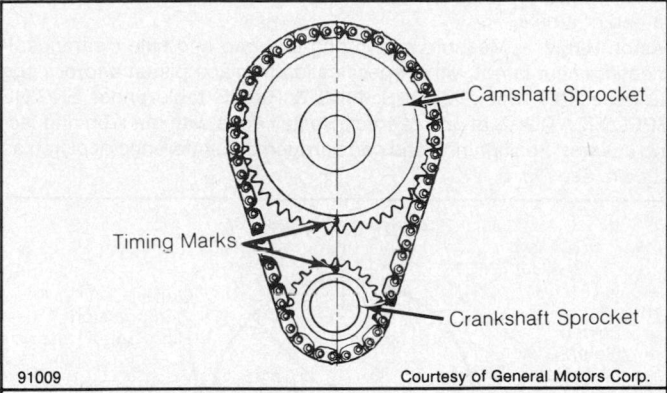

91009   Courtesy of General Motors Corp.

Fig. 5: Aligning Timing Marks

ROCKER ARM STUDS (EXCEPT 7.4L & 4.3L VIN W)

CAUTION: Ream rocker arm stud bore before installing oversize rocker arm stud, or cylinder head may be damaged.

Removal & Installation – 1) Rocker arm studs are pressed into cylinder head. Using Stud Remover (J-5802-01), place remover over stud. Install flat washer and nut. Tighten nut to remove stud from cylinder head.

2) If stud is loose in cylinder head, ream stud bore for oversize stud using Reamer (J-5715) for .003" (.08 mm) oversize stud and (J-6036) for .013" (.33 mm) oversize stud.

3) Coat press-fit area of stud with hypoid axle lubricant. Using Stud Driver (J-6880), drive stud into bore until driver bottoms against cylinder head.

VALVE LIFTERS

NOTE: On 7.4L, exhaust valve push rods are longer than intake valve push rods.

Removal – 1) Remove intake manifold. See INTAKE MANIFOLD under REMOVAL & INSTALLATION. Remove valve covers. Loosen all rocker arm nuts and rotate rockers aside.

2) Remove push rods, noting location for reassembly reference. On 4.3L, remove lifter retainer. On all engines, remove lifters, noting location for reassembly reference.

Installation – Coat lifter feet and body with High Viscosity Oil/Zinc (12345501). Install lifters in original location. To install remaining components, reverse removal procedure.

CAMSHAFT

Removal – Remove radiator, Discharge A/C system (if equipped) using approved refrigerant recovery/recycling equipment and remove A/C condenser (if equipped) and grille. Remove valve lifters. See

VALVE LIFTERS under REMOVAL & INSTALLATION. Remove timing chain and camshaft sprocket. See TIMING CHAIN & SPROCKETS under REMOVAL & INSTALLATION. If necessary, raise engine. Remove camshaft.

Installation – Coat camshaft lobes and bearing journals with High Viscosity Oil/Zinc (12345501). Install camshaft. To install remaining components, reverse removal procedure.

REAR CRANKSHAFT OIL SEAL

Removal – Remove transmission, clutch (M/T) and flywheel. Using screwdriver, pry seal from housing. DO NOT scratch crankshaft sealing surface. Note direction of seal lip.

Installation – 1) Lubricate inner and outer diameter of seal with engine oil. Place seal on Seal Installer (J-35621 for 4.3L, 5.0L and 5.7L; or J-38841 for 7.4L). Position seal installer against crankshaft.

2) Thread attaching screws into crankshaft flange and tighten with screwdriver. This squares seal with crankshaft. Rotate seal installer handle until it bottoms. Remove seal installer. Install flywheel, clutch (M/T) and transmission.

WATER PUMP

Removal – Disconnect battery. Drain cooling system. Remove all drive belts, coolant hoses and mounting brackets attached to water pump. If necessary, remove fan shroud. Remove fan and pulley. Remove water pump and gaskets.

Installation – Install water pump with new gaskets. Tighten water pump bolts to specification. See TORQUE SPECIFICATIONS table at end of article. To install remaining components, reverse removal procedure.

OIL PAN

CAUTION: Minimal clearance exists between oil pump pick-up tube and bottom of oil pan. DO NOT place jack under oil pan, crankshaft pulley or any sheet metal when lifting engine.

Removal (4.3L, 5.0L & 5.7L – Except "S" & "T" Series Pickup, Bravada, Jimmy, Sonoma & Syclone – 1) Disconnect battery. Raise and support vehicle. Drain crankcase. Remove exhaust crossover pipe, strut rods, strut rod brackets and flywheel cover.

2) Remove starter. Remove or disconnect engine oil cooler lines and/or transmission fluid lines as necessary. Remove oil pan bolts, oil pan and gasket.

Removal (Bravada) – 1) Disconnect battery. Remove engine oil dipstick. Raise and support vehicle. Remove accessory drive belt splash shield. Drain crankcase. Remove flywheel cover. Remove front engine mount through-bolts.

2) Raise engine. Support in place with wood blocks. Disconnect oil cooler line. Remove oil filter adapter. Remove pitman arm and idler arm. Remove front differential mount through-bolts. Remove front drive shaft. Roll differential forward. Remove starter. Remove oil pan bolts, oil pan and gasket.

CAUTION: On Pickup, Sierra and Suburban with 7.4L, disconnect oil pressure tube from side of engine to prevent damage to tube when engine is raised.

Removal ("C" & "K" Series Pickup, Sierra & Suburban – 7.4L) – 1) Disconnect battery. Remove fan shroud bolts. Move shroud rearward. Remove air cleaner and distributor cap. Raise and support vehicle. Drain crankcase. Remove starter (M/T). Remove flywheel cover and oil filter.

2) Disconnect oil pressure line from side of cylinder block. Remove front engine mount through-bolts. Raise and support engine. Remove oil pan bolts, oil pan and gasket.

Removal (Van – 7.4L) – 1) Disconnect battery. Remove engine cover. Raise and support vehicle. Drain crankcase. Disconnect front drive shaft from differential. Remove transmission. Remove flywheel and engine oil dipstick tube.

2) Remove front engine mount through-bolts. Raise engine enough to allow room for oil pan removal. Remove oil pan bolts (DO NOT remove oil pan). Remove oil pump and allow to rest in oil pan. Remove oil pump and oil pan.

CAUTION: On Commercial Van with 7.4L, disconnect oil pressure tube from side of engine to prevent damage to tube when engine is raised.

Removal (Commercial Van – 7.4L) –1) Disconnect battery. Disconnect oil pressure tube from side of engine. Raise and support vehicle. Drain crankcase. Remove strut rods and flywheel cover. Disconnect oil cooler lines from oil filter housing.

2) Disconnect vent hose from front differential (4WD). Remove starter. Remove front engine mount through-bolts. Raise and support engine. Remove oil pan bolts, oil pan and gasket.

Removal ("S" Series Pickup, Jimmy, Sonoma & Syclone – 2WD) – Raise and support vehicle. Drain crankcase. Remove engine. See ENGINE under REMOVAL & INSTALLATION. Remove oil pan bolts, oil pan and gasket.

Removal ("T" Series Pickup, Jimmy, Sonoma & Syclone – 4WD) – **1)** Disconnect battery. Remove engine oil dipstick and accessory drive belt splash shield. Raise and support vehicle. Drain crankcase. Remove front axle shield and transfer case shield. Remove brake line clips from crossmember.

2) Remove second crossmember. Remove converter hanger bolts and exhaust pipe clamp from converter. Disconnect exhaust pipes from manifolds. Slide exhaust pipe rearward. Disconnect front drive shaft from differential.

3) Remove flywheel cover. Remove starter motor. Remove idler arm-to-frame bolts. Remove differential housing mounting bolts from bracket (right side) and frame (left side).

4) Move differential housing forward. Remove front engine mount through-bolts. Raise and support engine. Remove oil pan bolts, oil pan and gasket.

Installation (All Models) – **1)** On all engines except 7.4L, apply RTV sealant to front cover-to-cylinder block junction and rear main bearing-to-cylinder block junction. On 7.4L, apply RTV sealant to both sides of oil pan gasket.

2) On all engines, install oil pan. Tighten oil pan bolts to specification. See TORQUE SPECIFICATIONS table at end of article. To install remaining components, reverse removal procedure. Fill crankcase.

OVERHAUL

CYLINDER HEAD

Valve Springs – **1)** Measure valve spring free length, installed height and pressure (tension). Replace valve spring if measurement is not within specification. See VALVES & VALVE SPRINGS table under ENGINE SPECIFICATIONS at end of article.

2) Measure installed height between cylinder head spring seat (or top of shim, if shimmed) and top of spring shield (top of spring on 7.4L). If installed height exceeds specification, install shims as necessary to bring installed height to specification. Ensure installed height is not less than specified.

Valve Stem Oil Seals – **1)** On 4.3L, intake valve uses upper "O" ring seal and lower umbrella seal; exhaust valve uses upper "O" ring seal. On 5.0L and 5.7L, intake and exhaust valves use upper "O" ring seal and lower umbrella seal. On 7.4L, intake and exhaust valves use lower umbrella seal.

2) When installing umbrella seal, seat seal against valve guide boss on cylinder head. Coat upper "O" ring seal with engine oil before installation and ensure seal is not twisted when installed.

Valve Guides – Valve guides are part of cylinder head (not replaceable). Measure valve guide oil clearance. See CYLINDER HEAD table under ENGINE SPECIFICATIONS at end of article. If not within specification, ream valve guide and install valves with oversize stems.

Valves – Replace valve if margin is less than 1/32" (.8 mm).

VALVE TRAIN

Rocker Arm Assembly – Clean push rods, rocker arms, balls and nuts with solvent and blow dry. Inspect rocker arms and balls at mating surface. Surface should be smooth and free of damage. Inspect push rods for bends or wear. Ensure oil passages are clear.

CYLINDER BLOCK ASSEMBLY

Piston & Rod Assembly – **1)** Mark piston in relation to cylinder bore before removal. Piston pin is press-fit in connecting rod. Mark piston in relation to connecting rod before separating components.

2) Replace piston and piston pin as matched set. Install piston in bore with notch (dimple on 7.4L) on top of piston toward front of engine.

Fitting Pistons – **1)** Measure piston diameter at 90-degree angle to piston pin, on piston pin center line. Measure cylinder bore diameter 2 1/2" below cylinder block deck. Determine piston clearance.

2) If piston clearance is not within specification, replace piston and/or machine cylinder bore as necessary. See CYLINDER BLOCK table and PISTONS, PINS & RINGS table under ENGINE SPECIFICATIONS at end of article.

Piston Rings – Measure piston ring end gap and side clearance. If measurement is not within specification, replace piston and/or rings as necessary. See PISTONS, PINS & RINGS table under ENGINE SPECIFICATIONS at end of article. Install rings with mark on ring facing upward. Position ring end gaps around circumference of piston as shown. *See Fig. 6.*

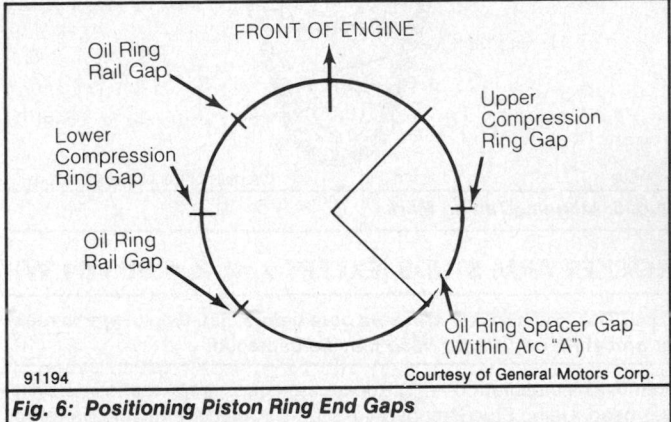

Fig. 6: Positioning Piston Ring End Gaps

Rod Bearings – **1)** Measure rod bearing journal out-of-round, taper and oil clearance. If measurement is not within specification, replace rod bearings and/or machine crankshaft. See CRANKSHAFT, MAIN & CONNECTING ROD BEARINGS table under ENGINE SPECIFICATIONS at end of article.

2) Ensure rod side play is within specification. See CONNECTING RODS table under ENGINE SPECIFICATIONS at end of article.

NOTE: On 7.4L, if rear main bearing cap is removed, replace rear crankshaft oil seal (transmission must be removed to replace seal).

Crankshaft & Main Bearings – **1)** Mark bearing caps for reassembly. Measure journal diameter, out-of-round, taper and oil clearance. If measurement is not within specification, replace main bearings and/or machine crankshaft. See CRANKSHAFT, MAIN & CONNECTING ROD BEARINGS table under ENGINE SPECIFICATIONS at end of article.

2) Align thrust bearing surfaces, and measure crankshaft end play. See THRUST BEARING.

NOTE: Distance between rear main bearing thrust faces on some 4.3L, 5.0L and 5.7L engines is .008" (.20 mm) wider than standard. When replacing rear main bearings on these engines (identified by .008" stamped on crankshaft rear counterweight), use only .008" (.20 mm) wider bearings.

Thrust Bearing – **1)** Install main bearing caps (except rear), and tighten cap bolts to specification. See TORQUE SPECIFICATIONS table at end of article. On 7.4L, apply anaerobic sealant to cap-to-cylinder block mating surfaces. On all engines, Install rear main bearing cap and tighten cap bolts to **10 ft. lbs. (14 N.m)**.
2) Tap crankshaft rearward then forward to align thrust surfaces. Tighten rear main bearing cap bolts to specification. Measure crankshaft end play at forward thrust surface of rear main bearing cap. See CRANKSHAFT, MAIN & CONNECTING ROD BEARINGS table under ENGINE SPECIFICATIONS at end of article.
Cylinder Block – Measure cylinder bore out-of-round and taper. If measurement is not within specification, machine cylinder bore and/or replace piston. See CYLINDER BLOCK table under ENGINE SPECIFICATIONS at end of article.

ENGINE OILING

ENGINE LUBRICATION SYSTEM

Gear-type oil pump delivers full pressure lubrication through full-flow oil filter to main oil gallery. Main oil gallery feeds crankshaft and camshaft bearings through drilled passages in block.

Valve lifter oil gallery feeds valve lifters. From lifters, oil is routed through hollow push rods to upper valve train components. Timing chain and sprockets are lubricated by oil drainage from No. 1 camshaft bearing. Pistons and piston pins are lubricated by oil splash. Non-adjustable oil pressure regulator is located in oil pump body.
Crankcase Capacity – See CRANKCASE CAPACITY table.

CRANKCASE CAPACITY [1]

Application	Qts. (L)
Except 7.4L	5 (4.7)
7.4L	7 (6.6)

[1] – Capacity includes oil filter.

Oil Pressure – Measure oil pressure with engine at operating temperature and specified RPM. See OIL PRESSURE SPECIFICATIONS table.

OIL PRESSURE SPECIFICATIONS [1]

Application	psi (kg/cm²)
7.4L	
500 RPM	10 (.7)
2000 RPM	40-60 (2.8-4.2)
Except 7.4L	
1000 RPM	6 (.4)
2000 RPM	18 (1.3)
4000 RPM	24 (1.7)

[1] – Minimum specification.

OIL PUMP

NOTE: On all engines except 7.4L, pick-up tube is serviceable, however, DO NOT remove tube from pump body unless tube is damaged. On 7.4L, pick-up tube and pump are serviced as an assembly.

Removal & Disassembly – **1)** Remove oil pan. See OIL PAN under REMOVAL & INSTALLATION. Remove oil pump bolt. Remove pump and extension shaft. On all engines except 7.4L, remove pick-up tube (if necessary).
2) Remove pump cover. Mark relationship between gears at a meshing point for reassembly. Remove gears. Remove pressure regulator valve retaining pin. Remove pressure regulator valve and spring.
Inspection – Inspect pump body and cover for cracks or excessive wear. Inspect pump gears for damage or wear. Check drive gear shaft for looseness in pump body. Check pressure regulator valve for fit in bore. Replace entire pump assembly if damaged. Inspect inlet tube and screen assembly for damage.
Reassembly & Installation – **1)** Install pump gears into pump body with marked gear teeth indexed. If pick-up tube was removed, apply sealant to tube end. Tap tube end into pump using plastic hammer. Reassemble remaining components in reverse order of disassembly.

2) Prime oil pump with engine oil. Install pump and extension shaft, ensuring slot on top of extension shaft engages with drive tang on end of distributor shaft. Tighten oil pump bolt to specification. See TORQUE SPECIFICATIONS table. Install oil pan.

TORQUE SPECIFICATIONS

TORQUE SPECIFICATIONS (4.3L, 5.0L & 5.7L)

Application	Ft. Lbs. (N.m)
Bellhousing Bolt	32 (43)
Camshaft Sprocket Bolt	21 (28)
Connecting Rod Cap Nut	
4.3L	[1]
5.0L & 5.7L	45 (61)
Crankshaft Damper Bolt	70 (95)
Cylinder Head Bolt [2]	
Step 1	25 (34)
Step 2	45 (61)
Step 3	65 (88)
Exhaust Manifold Bolt	
Center 2	26 (35)
All Others	20 (27)
Flywheel Bolt	75 (102)
Front Cover Bolt (4.3L)	10 (14)
Intake Manifold Bolt	[3] 35 (47)
Main Bearing Cap Bolt	
4.3L	75 (102)
5.0L & 5.7L	
Outer Bolts Of Caps No. 2, 3 & 4	70 (95)
All Others	80 (108)
Oil Filter Adapter Bolt (4.3L)	15 (20)
Oil Filter By-Pass Valve Bolt (5.0L & 5.7L)	20 (27)
Oil Pan Nut	17 (23)
Oil Pump Bolt	65 (88)
Rear Crankshaft Oil Seal Retainer Bolt	11 (15)
Valve Lifter Retainer Bolt (4.3L)	12 (16)
Water Pump Bolt	30 (41)

	INCH Lbs. (N.m)
Front Cover Bolt (5.0L & 5.7L)	97 (11)
Oil Pan Bolt	97 (11)
Oil Pump Cover Bolt	80 (9)
Valve Cover Bolt	89 (10)

[1] – Tighten nut to 20 ft. lbs. (27 N.m) then tighten an additional 60 degrees.
[2] – Apply GM Sealant (1052080) to head bolt threads. Tighten bolts in sequence. *See Fig. 4.*
[3] – Tighten bolts in sequence. *See Fig. 3.*

TORQUE SPECIFICATIONS (7.4L)

Application	Ft. Lbs. (N.m)
Bellhousing Bolt	30 (41)
Camshaft Sprocket Bolt	20 (27)
Connecting Rod Cap Nut	48 (65)
Crankshaft Damper Bolt	85 (115)
Cylinder Head Bolt [1]	
Step 1	30 (41)
Step 2	60 (81)
Step 3	80 (108)
Exhaust Manifold Bolt	40 (54)
Flywheel Bolt	65 (88)
Intake Manifold Bolt	[2] 30 (41)
Main Bearing Cap Bolt	100 (136)
Oil Pan Bolt	13 (18)
Oil Pump Bolt	65 (88)
Rocker Arm Bolt	40 (54)

[1] – Apply GM Sealant (1052080) to head bolt threads. Tighten bolts in sequence. *See Fig. 4.*
[2] – Tighten bolts in sequence. *See Fig. 3.*

TORQUE SPECIFICATIONS (7.4L – Cont.)

Application	Ft. Lbs. (N.m)
Water Pump Bolt	30 (41)

Application	INCH Lbs. (N.m)
Front Cover Bolt	97 (11)
Oil Pump Cover Bolt	80 (9)
Valve Cover Bolt	60 (7)

¹ – Apply GM Sealant (1052080) to head bolt threads. Tighten bolts in sequence. *See Fig. 4.*
² – Tighten bolts in sequence. *See Fig. 3.*

ENGINE SPECIFICATIONS

GENERAL SPECIFICATIONS

Application	Specification
4.3L	
Displacement	262 (4.3L)
Bore	4.00" (101.6 mm)
Stroke	3.48" (88.4 mm)
Compression Ratio	
VIN W	9.05:1
VIN Z	9.30:1
Fuel System	
VIN W	TBI
VIN Z	CPI
Horsepower @ RPM	
VIN W	155 @ 4000
VIN Z	195 @ 4500
Torque Ft. Lbs. @ RPM	
VIN W	235 @ 2400
VIN Z	260 @ 3600
5.0L	
Displacement	305 Cu. In. (5.0L)
Bore	3.74" (95.0 mm)
Stroke	3.48" (88.4 mm)
Compression Ratio	9.3:1
Fuel System	TBI
Horsepower @ RPM	175 @ 4000
Torque Ft. Lbs. @ RPM	260 @ 2400
5.7L	
Displacement	350 Cu. In. (5.7L)
Bore	4.00" (101.6 mm)
Stroke	3.48" (88.4 mm)
Compression Ratio	¹ 9.3:1
Fuel System	TBI
Horsepower @ RPM	¹ 210 @ 4000
Torque Ft. Lbs. @ RPM	¹ 300 @ 2800
7.4L	
Displacement	454 Cu. In. (7.4L)
Bore	4.25" (108.0 mm)
Stroke	4.00" (101.6 mm)
Compression Ratio	7.9:1
Fuel System	TBI
Horsepower @ RPM	230 @ 3600
Torque Ft. Lbs. @ RPM	385 @ 1600

¹ – On vehicles with GVW more than 8500 lbs., some specifications are different. Compression ratio is 8.6:1, horsepower is 190 @ 4000 RPM, and torque is 295 ft. lbs. @ 2400 RPM.

CRANKSHAFT, MAIN & CONNECTING ROD BEARINGS

Application	In. (mm)
4.3L	
Crankshaft End Play	.002-.006 (.05-.15)
Main Bearings	
Journal Diameter	
No. 1	2.4484-2.4493 (62.189-62.212)
No. 2 & 3	2.4481-2.4490 (62.182-62.205)
No. 4	2.4479-2.4488 (62.177-62.200)
Journal Out-Of-Round	.002 (.05)
Journal Taper	.001 (.03)
Oil Clearance	
Standard	
No. 1	.0008-.0020 (.020-.051)
No. 2 & 3	.0011-.0023 (.028-.059)
No. 4	.0017-.0032 (.043-.081)
Service Limit	
No. 1	.0010-.0015 (.025-.038)
No. 2 & 3	.0010-.0025 (.025-.064)
No. 4	.0025-.0035 (.064-.089)
Connecting Rod Bearings	
Journal Diameter	2.2487-2.2497 (57.117-57.142)
Journal Out-Of-Round	.002 (.05)
Journal Taper	.001 (.03)
Oil Clearance	.0013-.0035 (.033-.089)
5.0L & 5.7L	
Crankshaft End Play	.002-.006 (.05-.15)
Main Bearings	
Journal Diameter	
No. 1	2.4484-2.4493 (62.189-62.212)
No. 2, 3 & 4	2.4481-2.4490 (62.182-62.205)
No. 5	2.4479-2.4488 (62.177-62.200)
Journal Out-Of-Round	.001 (.03)
Journal Taper	.001 (.03)
Oil Clearance	
No. 1	.0010-.0015 (.025-.038)
No. 2, 3 & 4	.0010-.0025 (.025-.064)
No. 5	.0025-.0035 (.064-.089)
Connecting Rod Bearings	
Journal Diameter	2.0988-2.0998 (53.310-53.335)
Journal Out-Of-Round	.001 (.03)
Journal Taper	.001 (.03)
Oil Clearance	.0013-.0035 (.033-.089)
7.4L	
Crankshaft End Play	.006-.010 (.15-.25)
Main Bearings	
Journal Diameter	2.7482-2.7489 (69.804-69.822)
Journal Out-Of-Round	.001 (.03)
Journal Taper	.001 (.03)
Oil Clearance	
Standard	
No. 1, 2, 3 & 4	.0017-.0030 (.043-.076)
No. 5	.0025-.0038 (.064-.097)
Service Limit	
No. 1, 2, 3 & 4	.0010-.0030 (.025-.076)
No. 5	.0025-.0040 (.064-.102)
Connecting Rod Bearings	
Journal Diameter	2.1990-2.1996 (55.855-55.870)
Journal Out-Of-Round	.001 (.03)
Journal Taper	.001 (.03)
Oil Clearance	.0011-.0029 (.028-.074)

CONNECTING RODS

Application	In. (mm)
4.3L, 5.0L & 5.7L	
Side Play	.006-.014 (.15-.36)
7.4L	
Side Play	.013-.023 (.33-.58)

PISTONS, PINS & RINGS

Application	In. (mm)
4.3L, 5.0L & 5.7L	
Pistons	
Clearance	.0007-.0017 (.018-.043)
Pins	
Diameter	
4.3L	.9270-.9273 (23.546-23.553)
5.0L & 5.7L	.9269-.9271 (23.543-23.548)
Piston Fit	.0002-.0007 (.005-.018)
Rod Fit	.0008-.0016 (.020-.041) Interference
Rings	
No. 1	
End Gap	.010-.020 (.25-.51)
Side Clearance	.001-.003 (.03-.08)
No. 2	
End Gap	.010-.025 (.25-.64)
Side Clearance	.001-.003 (.03-.08)
No. 3 (Oil)	
End Gap	.015-.055 (.38-1.40)
Side Clearance	.002-.007 (.05-.18)
7.4L	
Pistons	
Clearance	[1] .003-.004 (.08-.10)
Pins	
Diameter	.9895-.9897 (2.513-2.514)
Piston Fit	.0002-.0007 (.005-.018)
Rod Fit	.0021-.0031 (.053-.079) Interference
Rings	
No. 1	
End Gap	.010-.018 (.25-.46)
Side Clearance	.001-.003 (.03-.07)
No. 2	
End Gap	.016-.024 (.41-.61)
Side Clearance	.001-.003 (.03-.07)
No. 3 (Oil)	
End Gap	.010-.030 (.25-.76)
Side Clearance	.005-.007 (.127-.178)

[1] – Maximum service limit is 005" (.13 mm).

CYLINDER BLOCK

Application	In. (mm)
4.3L	
Cylinder Bore	
Diameter	4.0007-4.0017 (101.618-101.643)
Maximum Taper	[1] .0005 (.013)
Maximum Out-Of-Round	[2] .001 (.03)
5.0L	
Cylinder Bore	
Diameter	3.7350-3.7385 (94.869-94.958)
Maximum Taper	[1] .0005 (.013)
Maximum Out-Of-Round	[2] .001 (.03)
5.7L	
Cylinder Bore	
Diameter	3.9995-4.0025 (101.587-101.664)
Maximum Taper	[1] .0005 (.013)
Maximum Out-of-Round	[2] .001 (.03)
7.4L	
Cylinder Bore	
Diameter	4.2500-4.2507 (107.950-107.968)
Maximum Taper	[1] .0005 (.013)
Maximum Out-Of-Round	[2] .001 (.03)

[1] – Specification is for thrust side. Relief side is .001" (.03 mm).

[2] – Production specification is given. Maximum service specification is .002" (.05 mm).

VALVES & VALVE SPRINGS (4.3L, 5.0L & 5.7L)

Application	Specification
Intake & Exhaust Valves	
Face Angle	45°
Minimum Margin	.031" (.79 mm)
Valve Springs	
Free Length	2.03" (51.6 mm)
Installed Height	1.69-1.75" (42.9-44.5 mm)
	Lbs. @ In. (Kg @ mm)
Pressure	
Valve Closed	76-84 @ 1.70 (34-38 @ 43.2)
Valve Open	194-206 @ 1.25 (88-93 @ 31.8)

VALVES & VALVE SPRINGS (7.4L)

Application	Specification
Intake & Exhaust Valves	
Face Angle	45°
Valve Springs	
Free Length	2.12 (53.8)
Installed Height	1.80 (45.7)
	Lbs. @ In. (Kg @ mm)
Pressure	
Valve Closed	74-86 @ 1.80 (34-39 @ 45.7)
Valve Open	195-215 @ 1.40 (88-98 @ 35.6)

CYLINDER HEAD

Application	Specification
Valve Seats	
Intake Valve	
Seat Angle	46°
Seat Width	.031-.063" (.79-1.60 mm)
Maximum Seat Runout	.002" (.05 mm)
Exhaust Valve	
Seat Angle	46°
Seat Width	.063-.094" (1.60-2.39 mm)
Maximum Seat Runout	.002" (.05 mm)
Valve Guides	
Intake & Exhaust Valves	
Valve Guide Oil Clearance	.001-.003" (.03-.08 mm)

CAMSHAFT

Application	In. (mm)
4.3L	
End Play	.004-.012 (.10-.30)
Journal Diameter	1.8682-1.8692 (47.452-47.478)
Lobe Lift	
VIN W	
Intake	[1] .288 (7.32)
Exhaust	[1] .294 (7.47)
VIN Z	
Intake	[1] .234 (5.94)
Exhaust	[1] .257 (6.53)
5.0L	
End Play	.004-.012 (.10-.30)
Journal Diameter	1.8682-1.8692 (47.452-47.478)
Lobe Lift	
Intake	[1] .2336 (5.933)
Exhaust	[1] .2565 (6.515)
5.7L	
End Play	.004-.012 (.10-.30)
Journal Diameter	1.8682-1.8692 (47.452-47.478)
Lobe Lift	
Intake	[1] .2565 (6.515)
Exhaust	[1] .2690 (6.833)
7.4L	
Journal Diameter	1.9482-1.9492 (49.484-49.510)
Lobe Lift	
Intake	[1] .2343 (5.951)
Exhaust	[1] .2530 (6.426)

[1] – Plus or minus .002" (.05 mm).

Commercial Van, Sierra, Suburban, Van, Yukon, "C" & "K" Series Blazer & Pickup

NOTE: For repair procedures not covered in this article, see ENGINE OVERHAUL PROCEDURES article in GENERAL INFORMATION.

ENGINE IDENTIFICATION

Engine can be identified by eighth character of Vehicle Identification Number (VIN). VIN is stamped on a metal plate on top left end of instrument panel, near windshield. See ENGINE IDENTIFICATION table.

Engine can also be identified by engine identification (ID) number, stamped on cylinder block in one of the following locations:
- On right side of timing chain case casting.
- On engine-to-transmission mating flange, near left cylinder head.
- At left front of engine block, near cylinder head-to-block mating surface.

ENGINE IDENTIFICATION

Application	VIN Code	Engine ID
6.2L		
Light Duty Emissions	C	LH6
Heavy Duty Emissions	J	LL4
6.5L	F	L65

ADJUSTMENTS

VALVE CLEARANCE ADJUSTMENT

Engine is equipped with hydraulic valve lifters. No valve adjustment is required.

REMOVAL & INSTALLATION

WARNING: When battery is disconnected, vehicle computer and memory systems may lose memory data. Driveability problems may exist until computer systems have completed a relearn cycle. See COMPUTER RELEARN PROCEDURES article in GENERAL INFORMATION before disconnecting battery.

NOTE: For reassembly reference, label all electrical connectors, vacuum hoses and fuel lines before removal. Also place mating marks on engine hood and other major assemblies before removal.

ENGINE

NOTE: Removal and installation information on Commercial Van ("P" Series) is not available from manufacturer.

Removal & Installation ("C" & "K" Series Blazer & Pickup, Sierra, Suburban & Yukon) – 1) Disconnect batteries. Raise and support vehicle. Remove flywheel cover. Remove torque converter bolts (A/T). Disconnect exhaust pipes from manifolds. Remove starter, bellhousing bolts and engine mount through bolts.
2) Disconnect cylinder block heater wires. Remove wiring harness, automatic transmission cooler lines and front battery cable from clamp on oil pan. Disconnect fuel return and oil cooler lines from engine. Lower vehicle. Remove hood. Drain cooling system.
3) Remove air cleaner. Disconnect alternator wires and clips. Disconnect injection pump wiring. Disconnect wiring from valve cover clips and glow plugs. Remove EGR/EPR solenoids, glow plug controller and temperature solenoid. Move harness aside. Disconnect engine-to-chassis ground strap.
4) Remove upper fan shroud and fan. Remove power steering pump and reservoir and lay aside. Disconnect control cables from injection pump. Disconnect heater hose from engine. Disconnect radiator hoses. Remove radiator. Support transmission. Remove engine. To install, reverse removal procedure. Fill cooling system.

Removal & Installation (Van) – 1) Disconnect batteries. Remove headlight bezels, grille, bumper and lower valance panel. Remove hood latch, coolant recovery bottle, upper fan shroud and tie bar. Remove engine cover. Discharge A/C system using approved refrigerant recovery/recycling equipment, disconnect A/C condenser lines and remove condenser (if equipped).
2) Drain cooling system. Remove radiator, fan and lower shroud. Remove intake manifold. See INTAKE MANIFOLD under REMOVAL & INSTALLATION. Remove injection pump. See INJECTION PUMP under REMOVAL & INSTALLATION.
3) Raise and support vehicle. Remove P/S pump with hoses attached and lay aside. Disconnect exhaust pipes from manifolds. Remove flywheel cover, torque converter bolts (A/T) and engine mount through bolts. Disconnect cylinder block heater wires.
4) Remove starter. Disconnect fuel line from fuel pump. Lower vehicle. Remove bellhousing bolts. Discharge A/C system using approved refrigerant recovery/recycling equipment and remove A/C compressor (if equipped). Remove oil filler tube upper bracket.
5) Disconnect engine harness electrical connectors and lay harness aside. Remove air cleaner resonator and bracket. Remove transmission dipstick tube. Disconnect heater hoses from engine. Remove alternator upper bracket.
6) Remove coolant crossover pipe. Attach Engine Lifting Fixture (J-33888) to center intake manifold bolt holes. Support transmission. Remove engine. To install, reverse removal procedure. Fill cooling system. Evacuate and charge A/C system.

INTAKE MANIFOLD

Removal – 1) Disconnect batteries. Remove air cleaner. Remove PCV and EGR hoses. Remove fuel line bracket and ground strap. Remove A/C compressor rear bracket (if equipped). On "C" and "K" Series Blazer and Pickup, Sierra, Suburban, Van and Yukon, remove EPR/EGR solenoids and bracket. On Van, remove crankcase depression relief valve.
2) On all models, loosen vacuum pump hold-down clamp (if equipped). Rotate pump to gain access to intake manifold bolt. Remove intake manifold bolts and fuel line clips. Remove intake manifold and gaskets.

CAUTION: Engines with light duty emissions rating (VIN C) use intake manifold gaskets that have openings for EGR ports; engines with heavy duty emissions rating (VIN J) DO NOT have openings. Use correct gaskets according to vehicle emissions rating.

Installation – 1) Install new manifold gaskets according to emissions rating. Install intake manifold. Tighten intake manifold bolts in sequence to specification. *See Fig. 1.* See TORQUE SPECIFICATIONS table at end of article.
2) To complete installation, reverse removal procedure. Rotate vacuum pump to correct position, and tighten hold-down clamp (if equipped). *See Fig. 2.*

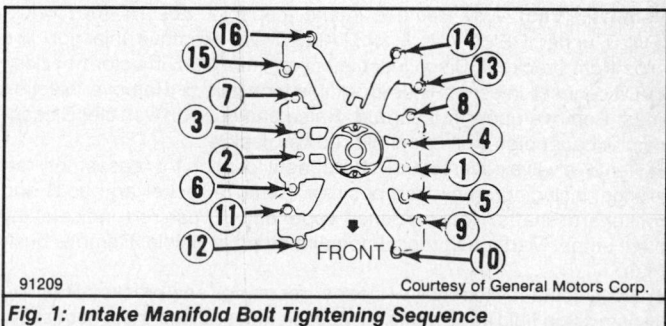

91209   Courtesy of General Motors Corp.

Fig. 1: Intake Manifold Bolt Tightening Sequence

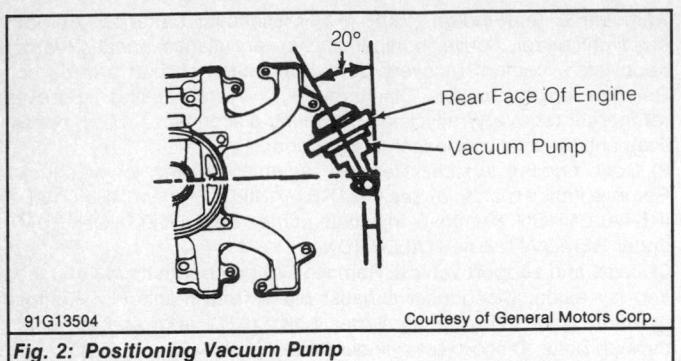

20°

Rear Face Of Engine

Vacuum Pump

91G13504   Courtesy of General Motors Corp.

Fig. 2: Positioning Vacuum Pump

EXHAUST MANIFOLD

Removal – Disconnect batteries. Raise vehicle. Disconnect exhaust pipe from manifold. Lower vehicle. On Commercial Van and Van, disconnect glow plug wires. Remove glow plugs. On all models, remove air cleaner duct bracket. If removing left manifold, remove dipstick tube (if necessary). Remove air conditioning bracket (if equipped). Remove exhaust manifold.

Installation – Install exhaust manifold. Tighten bolts to specification. See TORQUE SPECIFICATIONS table at end of article. To complete installation, reverse removal procedure.

CYLINDER HEAD

NOTE: Removal and installation information on Commercial Van is not available from manufacturer.

Removal (Except Van) – 1) Remove intake manifold. See INTAKE MANIFOLD under REMOVAL & INSTALLATION. Remove injection line clips from brackets. Disconnect injection lines from injector nozzles.

2) Disconnect injection lines from injection pump. Remove injection lines. Remove valve covers. Drain coolant. Raise and support vehicle. Disconnect exhaust pipe from manifold. Lower vehicle.

3) Discharge A/C system using approved refrigerant recovery/recycling equipment and remove A/C compressor. Remove ground strap from rear of cylinder head, power steering pump and alternator as necessary. Disconnect necessary wiring. Remove glow plug relay and dipstick tube.

4) Disconnect glow plug wires. Remove rocker arm bolts and rocker arm shafts. Mark component location for reassembly reference. Note hardened upper end of push rod, indicated by paint stripe. Mark push rods if no paint stripe is visible. Remove push rods.

5) Disconnect necessary coolant hoses and ground straps. Remove coolant crossover pipe. Remove cylinder head bolts (rear bolt in left cylinder head may need to remain in head during removal). Remove cylinder head.

Removal (Van) – 1) Remove intake manifold. See INTAKE MANIFOLD under REMOVAL & INSTALLATION. Remove injection line clips from brackets. Disconnect injection lines from injector nozzles.

2) Disconnect injection lines from injection pump. Remove injection lines. Remove upper fan shroud. Raise and support vehicle. Disconnect exhaust pipe from manifold. Lower vehicle.

3) Remove valve covers. Mark component location for reassembly reference, including crankshaft position. Remove rocker arm bolts and rocker arm shafts. Note hardened upper end of push rod, indicated by paint stripe. Mark push rods if no paint stripe is visible. Remove push rods.

4) Drain coolant. Remove air cleaner resonator and bracket. Remove transmission fluid and engine oil dipstick tubes. Disconnect necessary coolant hoses. Remove alternator and upper bracket. Remove coolant crossover pipe.

5) Disconnect necessary coolant hoses and ground straps. Remove coolant crossover pipe. Remove cylinder head bolts (rear bolt in left cylinder head may need to remain in head during removal). Remove cylinder head bolts, cylinder head and gasket.

Inspection (All Models) – See CYLINDER HEAD under OVERHAUL.
Installation (All Models) – 1) Clean cylinder head and cylinder block gasket surfaces. Clean cylinder head bolt thread and bolt holes. Apply Sealant (1052080) to head bolt threads and underside of bolt heads. DO NOT apply sealant to head gasket surface. Install rear head bolt in left cylinder head. Install cylinder head.

CAUTION: Install push rods with hardened end (indicated by paint stripe) upward to prevent damaging engine. To prevent valve and piston contact during rocker arm shaft installation, rotate crankshaft until positioned as noted in step 3) before tightening rocker arm shaft bolts.

2) Install head bolts and tighten in sequence to specification. See Fig. 3. See TORQUE SPECIFICATIONS table at end of article. Install push rods in original location with hardened end upward.

3) Rotate crankshaft until timing mark on crankshaft damper aligns with "0" mark on timing tab, then rotate crankshaft counterclockwise 3 1/2" (estimate this distance by aligning crankshaft damper mark with first lower water pump bolt). See Fig. 8.

4) Install rocker arm shafts, ensuring push rods are seated in rocker arms. Alternately tighten shaft bolts to specification. See TORQUE SPECIFICATIONS table at end of article. To complete installation, reverse removal procedure.

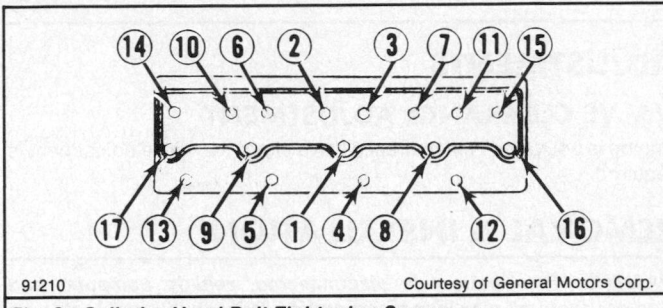

⑭ ⑩ ⑥ ② ③ ⑦ ⑪ ⑮

⑰ ⑬ ⑨ ⑤ ① ④ ⑧ ⑫ ⑯

91210   Courtesy of General Motors Corp.

Fig. 3: Cylinder Head Bolt Tightening Sequence

FRONT COVER OIL SEAL

Removal – Disconnect batteries. Remove drive belts. Raise and support vehicle. Remove crankshaft pulley bolts and pulley. Remove crankshaft damper bolt and washer. Using Damper Puller (J-23523-E), remove crankshaft damper. Pry seal from cover using screwdriver. Note direction of seal lip.

Installation – Ensure seal area is free of burrs. Coat seal lip and crankshaft damper sealing surface with engine oil. Install new seal using Seal Installer (J-22101). Install crankshaft damper, washer and bolt. Tighten crankshaft damper bolt to **200 ft. lbs. (269 N.m)**. To complete installation, reverse removal procedure.

TIMING CHAIN & SPROCKETS

NOTE: Adjust injection pump timing if timing chain, sprockets or injection pump gears are replaced.

Removal – 1) Disconnect batteries. Drain coolant. Remove water pump and plate. See WATER PUMP under REMOVAL & INSTALLATION. Remove intake manifold. See INTAKE MANIFOLD under REMOVAL & INSTALLATION.

2) Remove crankshaft pulley bolts and pulley. Remove crankshaft damper bolt and washer. Using Damper Puller (J-23523-E), remove crankshaft damper. Pry front cover oil seal from front cover using screwdriver.

3) Rotate crankshaft until mark on crankshaft damper aligns with "0" mark on timing tab with injection pump gear-to-camshaft gear timing marks aligned. See Fig. 4. Remove injection pump gear-to-injection pump bolts. Remove injection pump gear.

4) Remove baffle (if equipped). Scribe mark injection pump flange in relation to front cover (if unmarked). Remove injection pump mounting nuts. Pull pump from front cover and lay on cylinder block. Remove oil pan-to-front cover bolts and front cover-to-cylinder block bolts.

5) Remove front cover. Measure timing chain free play. See TIMING CHAIN FREE PLAY. Remove camshaft gear from camshaft sprocket. *See Fig. 5.* Note alignment of timing marks on crankshaft and camshaft sprockets. Remove camshaft sprocket and timing chain. Remove crankshaft sprocket (if necessary).

Timing Chain Free Play – 1) Position dial indicator on front of cylinder block with dial indicator tip in contact with center of timing chain between sprockets. Pull chain away from crankshaft and adjust dial indicator to zero.

2) Push chain toward crankshaft and note indicator reading. If chain deflection exceeds .80" (20.3 mm) on used parts or .50" (12.7 mm) on new parts, replace chain. Replace sprockets if worn.

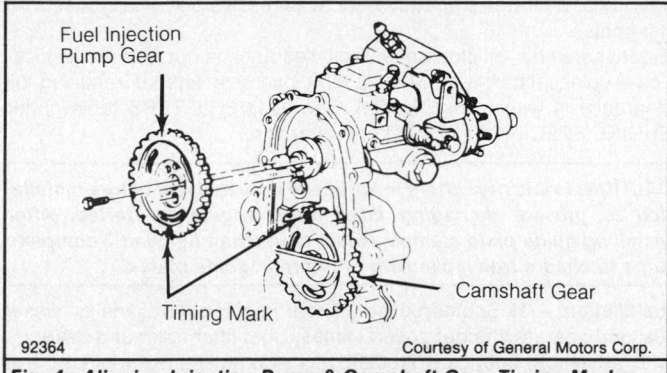

92364   Courtesy of General Motors Corp.

Fig. 4: Aligning Injection Pump & Camshaft Gear Timing Marks

91213   Courtesy of General Motors Corp.

Fig. 5: Aligning Crankshaft & Camshaft Sprocket Timing Marks

Installation – 1) Install crankshaft sprocket (if removed). Install camshaft sprocket and timing chain as an assembly, ensuring timing marks are aligned. *See Fig. 5.* Install camshaft gear, washer and bolt. Tighten camshaft gear bolt to specification. See TORQUE SPECIFICATIONS table at end of article.

2) Install new front cover oil seal using Seal Installer (J-22102). Coat seal lip and crankshaft damper sealing surface with engine oil. Apply 3/32" (2 mm) bead of anaerobic sealant to front cover at front cover-to-cylinder block sealing surface. Apply 3/16" (5 mm) bead of RTV sealant to front cover at front cover-to-oil pan sealing surface.

3) Install front cover. Tighten front cover bolts and oil pan bolts to specification. Install baffle (if equipped). If installing new front cover, place a timing mark on new front cover. See MARKING TDC ON FRONT COVER.

4) Install injection pump gasket and injection pump, aligning timing marks on injection pump flange and front cover. Install injection pump gear, ensuring timing marks on injection pump gear and camshaft gear are aligned. *See Fig. 4.* Tighten gear bolts to specification.

5) Ensure .040" (1.0 mm) minimum clearance exists between baffle and injection pump gear. To complete installation, reverse removal procedure. Fill cooling system. Adjust injection pump timing if timing chain, sprockets or injection pump gears were replaced.

Marking TDC On Front Cover – 1) Rotate crankshaft until cylinder No. 1 is on TDC of compression stroke (timing marks on injection pump gear and camshaft gear will be aligned, and slot in injection pump gear will be in 6 o'clock position). *See Figs. 4 and 6.*

2) Install Timing Fixture (J-33042) in place of injection pump without gasket. Install injection pump gear bolts to fasten gear to timing fixture. Install nut finger tight on upper front cover stud to secure timing fixture.

3) Tighten large bolt (18 mm head) on timing fixture to **35 ft. lbs. (47 N.m)**. Tighten nut on upper front cover stud. Ensure crankshaft did not rotate and timing fixture is not binding. Strike scriber with hammer to mark TDC indicator on front housing. Remove timing fixture.

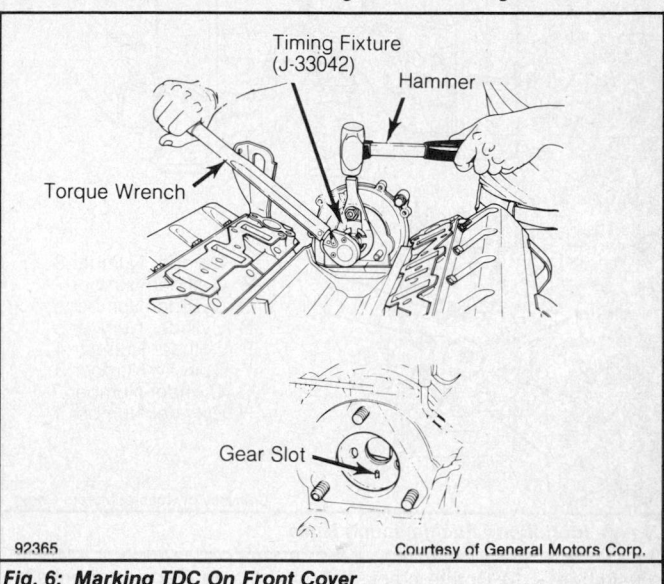

92365   Courtesy of General Motors Corp.

Fig. 6: Marking TDC On Front Cover

INJECTION PUMP

Removal – 1) Disconnect batteries. Remove intake manifold. See INTAKE MANIFOLD under REMOVAL & INSTALLATION. Remove fuel injection lines. Disconnect control cables from injection pump.

2) Disconnect wiring, fuel return line and fuel supply line from injection pump. Cap all fuel line openings. Remove A/C hose retainer bracket (if equipped). Remove oil filler tube and vent hose assembly. Remove grommet.

3) Scribe an alignment mark on front cover and injection pump flange. Remove injection pump gear-to-injection pump bolts, accessible through oil filler neck hole (rotate crankshaft as necessary). Remove injection pump mounting nuts. Remove injection pump and gasket.

Installation – 1) Install new injection pump gasket. Install injection pump, aligning locating pin on injection pump hub with slot in injection pump gear. Loosely install injection pump mounting nuts.

2) Align timing marks on injection pump flange and front cover. Tighten injection pump mounting nuts to specification. Install injection pump gear-to-injection pump bolts. Tighten bolts to specification. See TORQUE SPECIFICATIONS table at end of article.

3) To complete installation, reverse removal procedure. Ensure fuel lines are properly connected to ports on injection pump. *See Fig. 7.*

ROCKER ARM ASSEMBLY

Removal – 1) Remove intake manifold. See INTAKE MANIFOLD under REMOVAL & INSTALLATION. Remove fuel injection lines and valve covers.

2) Remove rocker arm shaft bolts and rocker arm shaft. Mark component location for reassembly reference. To disassemble rocker arm shaft, see VALVE TRAIN under OVERHAUL.

3) If removing push rods, note paint stripe on hardened end of push rod (end closest to rocker arm). If no paint stripe is present, mark hardened end of push rod for reassembly reference.

CAUTION: Follow installation procedure to prevent piston and valve damage.

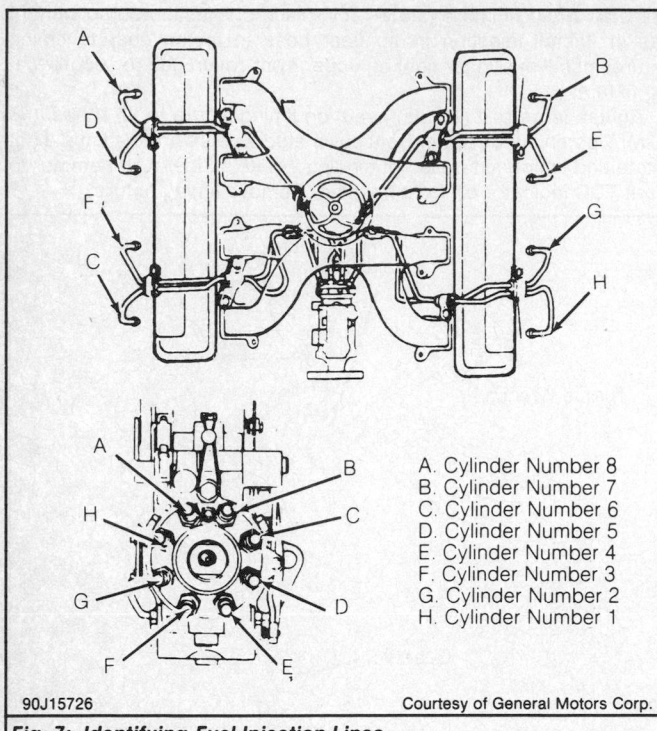

A. Cylinder Number 8
B. Cylinder Number 7
C. Cylinder Number 6
D. Cylinder Number 5
E. Cylinder Number 4
F. Cylinder Number 3
G. Cylinder Number 2
H. Cylinder Number 1

90J15726   Courtesy of General Motors Corp.

Fig. 7: Identifying Fuel Injection Lines

Installation – 1) Rotate crankshaft until timing mark on crankshaft damper aligns with "0" mark on timing tab. Rotate crankshaft counterclockwise 3 1/2" (estimate this distance by aligning crankshaft damper mark with first lower water pump bolt). *See Fig. 8.*

2) Install push rods with hardened end upward in original location (if removed). Install rocker arm assembly in original location, ensuring push rods are seated in rocker arms. Install rocker arm shaft bolts. Alternately tighten shaft bolts to specification. See TORQUE SPECIFICATIONS table at end of article. To complete installation, reverse removal procedure.

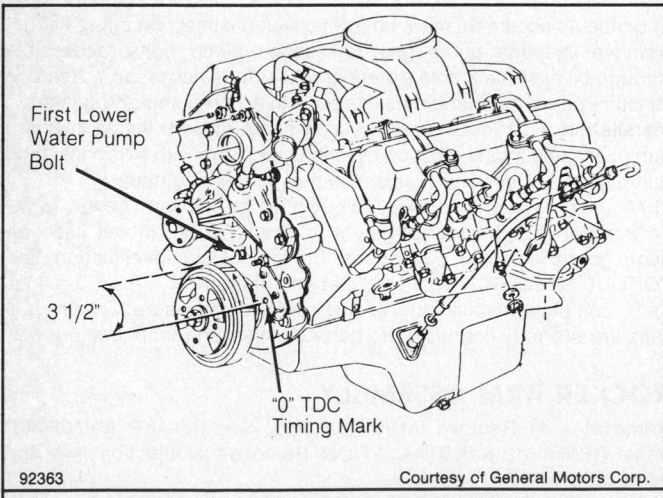

First Lower Water Pump Bolt

3 1/2"

"0" TDC Timing Mark

92363   Courtesy of General Motors Corp.

Fig. 8: Positioning Crankshaft Before Installing Rocker Arm Assembly

HYDRAULIC VALVE LIFTERS

Removal – 1) Remove intake manifold. See INTAKE MANIFOLD under REMOVAL & INSTALLATION. Remove rocker arm assembly. See ROCKER ARM ASSEMBLY under REMOVAL & INSTALLATION. On Van, remove cylinder head. Remove guide plate clamps, guide plates and lifters.

2) On all other models, remove guide plate clamps and guide plates through access holes in cylinder head using mechanical fingers. Remove lifters using Lifter Remover (J-29834) and magnet. Mark lifter location.

NOTE: Some engines are equipped with standard size and .010" (.25 mm) oversize diameter lifters. Bores fitted with oversize lifters are identified by O.S. stamped on cylinder block pad, adjacent to lifter bore, and on top rail of cylinder case, above lifter bore. Oversize lifters are identified by a number 10 stamped on side of lifter.

Inspection – 1) Check for nicks, burrs or scoring on parts. Ensure lifter roller operates smoothly without excessive play and contains no flat spots.
2) Measure lifter oil clearance. If oil clearance is not within specification, replace lifter with .010" (mm) oversize lifter if resulting oil clearance is within specification. See VALVE LIFTERS table under ENGINE SPECIFICATIONS at end of article.

CAUTION: Prime new lifters in kerosene or diesel fuel before installation to prevent damaging lifter when engine is started. After installing guide plate clamps, rotate crankshaft by hand 2 complete turns to ensure free movement of lifters in guide plates.

Installation – 1) Submerge new lifters in clean kerosene or diesel fuel and operate plunger several times. Coat lifter roller and bearings with Assembly Lubricant (1052365). Install lifter into original bore. Install guide plate and guide plate clamp. Tighten clamp bolts to specification. See TORQUE SPECIFICATIONS table at end of article.
2) After all clamps are installed, rotate crankshaft by hand 2 complete turns to ensure free movement of lifters in guide plates. If crankshaft will not rotate, lifter(s) may be binding in guide plate.
3) Install rocker arm assemblies in proper sequence to prevent piston and valve damage. See ROCKER ARM ASSEMBLY under REMOVAL & INSTALLATION. To complete installation, reverse removal procedure.

CAMSHAFT

Removal (Except Van) – 1) Disconnect batteries. Drain cooling system. Remove alternator, grille, A/C compressor, condenser, radiator and power steering pump as necessary. Remove vacuum pump, engine speed sensor or oil pump drive unit from top of engine.
2) Remove hydraulic valve lifters. See HYDRAULIC VALVE LIFTERS under REMOVAL & INSTALLATION. Remove timing chain and sprockets. See TIMING CHAIN & SPROCKETS under REMOVAL & INSTALLATION.
3) Remove front engine mount through-bolts. Raise and support engine to ease camshaft removal. Remove camshaft thrust plate and spacer. Remove camshaft.
Removal (Van) – 1) Disconnect batteries. Drain cooling system. Remove grille, bumper, lower valance, coolant bottle and upper tie bar. Remove engine cover. Remove A/C compressor, condenser, radiator, shroud and fan. Remove vacuum pump, oil pump drive or engine speed sensor. Remove cylinder heads. See CYLINDER HEAD under REMOVAL & INSTALLATION.
2) Remove timing chain and sprockets. See TIMING CHAIN & SPROCKETS under REMOVAL & INSTALLATION. Remove valve lifters. See HYDRAULIC VALVE LIFTERS under REMOVAL & INSTALLATION. Remove camshaft thrust plate and spacer (if equipped). Remove camshaft.
Inspection (All Models) – Inspect camshaft lobes for signs of flaking or flat spots. Measure camshaft journal diameter. Determine oil clearance. Replace camshaft and/or bearings as necessary if not within specification. See CAMSHAFT table under ENGINE SPECIFICATIONS at end of article.

NOTE: Replace hydraulic lifters if installing new camshaft.

Installation (All Models) – 1) If replacing camshaft bearings, see CAMSHAFT BEARINGS under REMOVAL & INSTALLATION. Coat camshaft journals with engine oil and lobes with High Viscosity Oil/Zinc (12345501). Install camshaft. Install thrust spacer with inside chamfer toward camshaft. Install thrust plate.

2) Ensure camshaft end play is **.002-.012" (.05-.31 mm)**. Install camshaft sprocket and timing chain, ensuring timing marks are aligned. See Fig. 5. To complete installation, reverse removal procedure.

CAMSHAFT BEARINGS

Removal – Remove rear camshaft plug. Remove inner camshaft bearings using Bearing Remover/Installer (J-6098-01) and Adapter (J-6098-10). Rear inner bearing must be removed with pilot fitted in rear camshaft bearing. Remove front and rear camshaft bearings.

CAUTION: Camshaft bearing bores are different sizes. Install bearings with bearing seam in upper half of bore (cylinder block). Install front bearing with notch on bearing facing front of cylinder block. Front bearing contains 2 oil holes. Ensure oil holes in all bearings align with oil holes in block.

Installation – Install rear camshaft bearings, then front camshaft bearings to act as guides for remover/installer pilot. Install inner camshaft bearings. Coat new rear camshaft bore plug with Loctite Sealer (592). Install plug from even with block surface to 1/32" (.8 mm) below surface.

REAR CRANKSHAFT OIL SEAL

Removal & Installation – 1) Remove oil pan and oil pump. See OIL PAN under REMOVAL & INSTALLATION. Remove rear main bearing cap. Remove lower half of seal from cap. Tap end of upper half of seal with a small drift punch to remove seal from block. Clean block surface and seal grooves.

2) Lubricate new crankshaft seal lips with engine oil. Carefully insert end of one half of new seal into block seal groove. Push this piece into groove until one end of seal extends 1/2" (13 mm) from block.

3) Insert other half of seal into block seal groove. Contact ends of seal halves will be at 4 o'clock and 10 o'clock positions, or 8 o'clock and 2 o'clock positions. This provides proper alignment of main cap with seal lips. Lightly coat seal groove of main bearing cap with Loctite (414).

4) Apply a thin film of anaerobic sealant to bearing cap in specified areas. See Fig. 9. Lightly oil cap bolt threads. Tap main bearing cap into place with brass or leather mallet. Install cap bolts and tighten to specification. See TORQUE SPECIFICATIONS table at end of article. To install remaining components, reverse removal procedure.

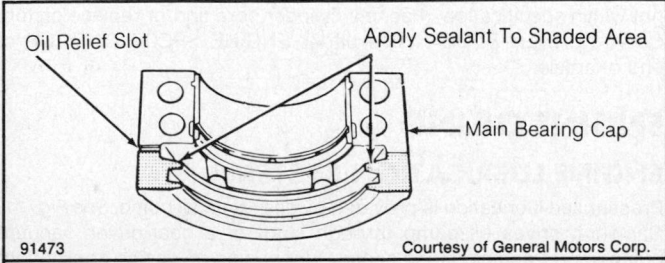

Oil Relief Slot

Apply Sealant To Shaded Area

Main Bearing Cap

91473

Courtesy of General Motors Corp.

Fig. 9: Applying Anaerobic Sealant To Rear Main Bearing Cap

WATER PUMP

Removal – 1) Disconnect batteries. Drain coolant. Remove accessory drive belts, fan, fan shroud and pulley. Remove alternator, power steering pump and related brackets as necessary.

2) Disconnect coolant by-pass hose and lower radiator hose from water pump. Remove water pump bolts. Remove water pump and water pump plate as an assembly. Remove water pump plate-to-water pump bolt. Separate water pump from plate.

Installation – 1) Apply anaerobic sealant to sealing surface of plate and water pump. Install plate to pump with new gasket. Coat water pump bolt threads with Sealant (1052080).

2) Install pump and plate assembly to front cover with new gasket. Tighten bolts to specification. See TORQUE SPECIFICATIONS table at end of article. To complete installation, reverse removal procedure.

OIL PAN

Removal ("C" & "K" Series Blazer & Pickup, Sierra, Suburban & Yukon) – Disconnect batteries. Raise and support vehicle. Drain crankcase. Remove flywheel cover. Disconnect exhaust pipes from manifolds. Remove front engine mount through-bolts. Raise and support engine. Remove oil pan bolts, oil pan and oil pan rear seal.

Removal (Van) – 1) Disconnect batteries. Remove engine cover. Remove engine oil dipstick and tube from valve cover. Raise and support vehicle. Remove flywheel cover. Drain crankcase. Disconnect engine oil cooler lines from cylinder block.

2) Remove starter. Remove battery cables, automatic transmission fluid lines and clamps from oil pan. Remove oil pan bolts. Lower oil pan from engine (DO NOT attempt to remove oil pan).

3) Rotate crankshaft until forward crankshaft throw for connecting rods No. 1 and 2 is up. Remove oil pump bolt. Allow oil pump and extension shaft to fall into oil pan. Remove oil pan and oil pump. Remove oil pan rear seal.

Removal (Commercial Van) – 1) Disconnect batteries. Raise and support vehicle. Drain crankcase. Remove oil filter. Remove flywheel cover. Remove left front engine mount through-bolt. Raise and support engine. Remove strut rods.

2) Remove battery cables, automatic transmission fluid cooler lines and clamps from oil pan. Move cylinder block heater wire aside (if equipped). Raise and support engine. Remove oil pan bolts, oil pan and oil pan rear seal.

Installation (All Models) – Apply 3/16" (5 mm) bead of RTV sealant to oil pan sealing surface, inboard of bolt holes. Install oil pan rear seal. Install oil pan. Lower engine. Tighten oil pan bolts to specification. See TORQUE SPECIFICATIONS table at end of article. To complete installation, reverse removal procedure.

OVERHAUL

WARNING: When battery is disconnected, vehicle computer and memory systems may lose memory data. Driveability problems may exist until computer systems have completed a relearn cycle. See COMPUTER RELEARN PROCEDURES article in GENERAL INFORMATION before disconnecting battery.

CYLINDER HEAD

Cylinder Head – 1) Replace cylinder head if surface warpage exceeds .006" (.15 mm) across its length or .003" (.08 mm) across its width. DO NOT machine cylinder head surface.

2) Inspect pre-chamber for facial cracks. Replace pre-chamber if facial crack length exceeds 3/16" or if crack reaches head gasket sealing mark. To remove pre-chamber from cylinder head, insert small nylon punch through injector hole. Drive pre-chamber from cylinder head.

3) To install pre-chamber, align pre-chamber with alignment notch in cylinder head. Using 1 1/4" (32 mm) socket and hammer, tap pre-chamber into bore.

4) Measure pre-chamber installed height in 2 or more locations where pre-chamber seats against head gasket shield and sealing ring. Ensure pre-chamber is even with cylinder head or does not protrude from cylinder head more than .002" (.05 mm). Pre-chamber must not be recessed in cylinder head.

5) Measure cylinder head thickness between valve cover gasket surface and cylinder head gasket surface. Replace cylinder head if thickness is less than 3.853" (97.87 mm).

Valve Springs – Measure valve spring pressure. Measure valve spring installed height between spring seat (or top of shim, if shimmed) and top of spring shield. Replace valve spring if pressure or installed height is not within specification. See VALVES & VALVE SPRINGS table under ENGINE SPECIFICATIONS at end of article.

Valve Stem Oil Seals – Intake valve uses upper "O" ring seal. Exhaust valve uses upper "O" ring seal and lower umbrella seal, seated against cylinder head.

Valve Guides – **1)** Valve guides are part of cylinder head (not replaceable). Measure valve stem-to-guide oil clearance. See CYLINDER HEAD table under ENGINE SPECIFICATIONS at end of article.

2) If oil clearance is not within specification, ream valve guides using Reamer Set (J-7049) and install oversize valves. Oversize valves are available in .003" (.08 mm) and .015" (.38 mm) oversize.

Valve Seat – No replacement procedure is available from manufacturer. Valve seats are induction hardened. Excessive removal of material may damage valve seat. Measure seat width and runout. See CYLINDER HEAD table under ENGINE SPECIFICATIONS at end of article.

Valves – Valves with .003" (.08 mm) and .015" (.38 mm) oversize stems are available for worn valve guides.

VALVE TRAIN

CAUTION: Note paint stripe on hardened end of push rod (end closest to rocker arm). If no paint stripe is present, mark hardened end of push rod for reassembly reference.

Rocker Arm Assembly – **1)** To disassemble rocker arm assembly, insert screwdriver into rocker arm shaft bore. Break off end of retainer. Pull out retainer with pliers. Mark rocker arms for reassembly to original location on shaft. Remove rocker arms from shaft.

2) Inspect rocker arms and rocker arm shaft at mating surface for damage. Inspect push rods for bend and wear. Ensure oil passages are clear.

3) To assemble rocker arm assembly, coat rocker arms with engine oil and install on shaft in original locations. Center rocker arms with their corresponding holes on shaft. Install retainers with a 1/2" (13 mm) minimum diameter drift punch.

Hydraulic Valve Lifters – Engine is equipped with roller type hydraulic valve lifters. Lifters are serviced as complete assemblies only. Parts are not interchangeable between lifters.

CYLINDER BLOCK ASSEMBLY

Piston & Rod Assembly – **1)** Mark piston and rod assembly for installation to original bore. Mark rod and cap in relation to piston. Assemble rod to piston with rod bearing tang on same side of piston as piston crown indent.

2) Properly position ring end gaps around circumference of piston. *See Fig. 10.* Install piston and rod assembly in bore with piston crown indent toward outside of engine.

Fitting Pistons – **1)** Measure cylinder bore diameter 2 1/2" (63.5 mm) below cylinder block deck surface. Measure piston diameter at 90-degree angle to piston pin, on pin center line. Determine piston clearance.

2) If clearance is not within specification, replace piston and/or machine cylinder bore. See CYLINDER BLOCK table and PISTON, PINS & RINGS table under ENGINE SPECIFICATIONS at end of article.

Piston Rings – Measure piston ring end gap and side clearance. If not within specification, replace piston and/or rings as necessary. See PISTONS, PINS & RINGS table under ENGINE SPECIFICATIONS at end of article. Install rings with mark on ring facing upward. Position ring end gaps around circumference of piston as shown. *See Fig. 10.*

CAUTION: Crankshaft is rolled fillet type. DO NOT machine crankshaft.

Rod Bearings – **1)** Mark rod caps in relation to rod for reassembly reference. Measure rod bearing journal out-of-round, taper and oil clearance. If measurement is not within specification, install new rod bearings. See CRANKSHAFT, MAIN & CONNECTING ROD BEARINGS table under ENGINE SPECIFICATIONS at end of article.

2) Undersize bearings may be used in combination with standard to produce correct clearance. If not within specification after installing new bearings, replace crankshaft. DO NOT machine crankshaft. Ensure rod side play is .007-.025" (.17-.63 mm).

NOTE: Some VIN C engines may contain both standard and .003" (.08 mm) oversize connecting rod bearings, identified by O.S. stamped on bearing cap lower end.

CAUTION: Crankshaft is rolled fillet type. DO NOT machine crankshaft.

Crankshaft & Main Bearings – **1)** Mark main bearing caps in relation to cylinder block. Measure main bearing journal diameter, out-of-round and taper. Determine main bearing oil clearance.

2) If measurement is not within specification, replace main bearings. DO NOT machine crankshaft. See CRANKSHAFT, MAIN & CONNECTING ROD BEARINGS table under ENGINE SPECIFICATIONS at end of article.

3) For rear main bearing installation, see REAR CRANKSHAFT OIL SEAL under REMOVAL & INSTALLATION. Align thrust bearing surfaces and measure crankshaft end play. See THRUST BEARING.

Thrust Bearing – **1)** Main bearing No. 3 is thrust bearing. Tighten all other main bearing caps to specification. Tighten thrust bearing to 10 ft. lbs. (14 N.m). Tap crankshaft rearward then forward.

2) Tighten thrust bearing cap to specification. Measure crankshaft end play at front face of thrust bearing. If crankshaft end play is not .004-.010" (.10-.25 mm), replace thrust bearing or crankshaft.

Cylinder Block – **1)** Measure cylinder block deck surface warpage. If warpage exceeds .006" (.15 mm) over its length or .003" (.08) across its width, replace cylinder block. DO NOT machine cylinder block deck surface.

2) Measure cylinder bore taper and out-of-round. If measurement is not within specification, machine cylinder bore and/or replace piston. See CYLINDER BLOCK table under ENGINE SPECIFICATIONS at end of article.

ENGINE OILING

ENGINE LUBRICATION SYSTEM

Pressurized lubrication is provided by gear-type oil pump. *See Fig. 11.* Camshaft drives oil pump through shaft of a gear-driven vacuum pump and/or engine speed sensor, depending on engine application. Lubrication flows through external oil cooler then into full-flow oil filter. Non-adjustable oil pressure regulator valve is located in oil pump body.

Main oil gallery supplies oil through drilled passages to camshaft and crankshaft bearings. Oil flows through galleries to valve lifters then through hollow push rods to rocker arms.

NOTE: Manufacturer recommends changing oil filter at EVERY oil change.

Crankcase Capacity – Crankcase capacity is **7 quarts (6.6L)** including oil filter change.

Oil Pressure – Normal oil pressure is **40-45 psi (2.81-3.16 kg/cm²)** at 2000 RPM.

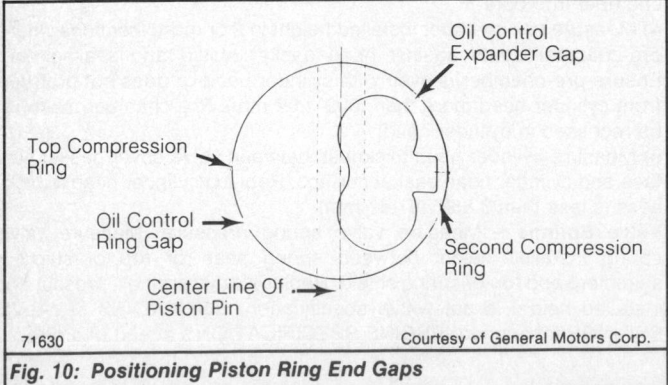

Oil Control Expander Gap

Top Compression Ring

Oil Control Ring Gap

Center Line Of Piston Pin

Second Compression Ring

71630   Courtesy of General Motors Corp.

Fig. 10: Positioning Piston Ring End Gaps

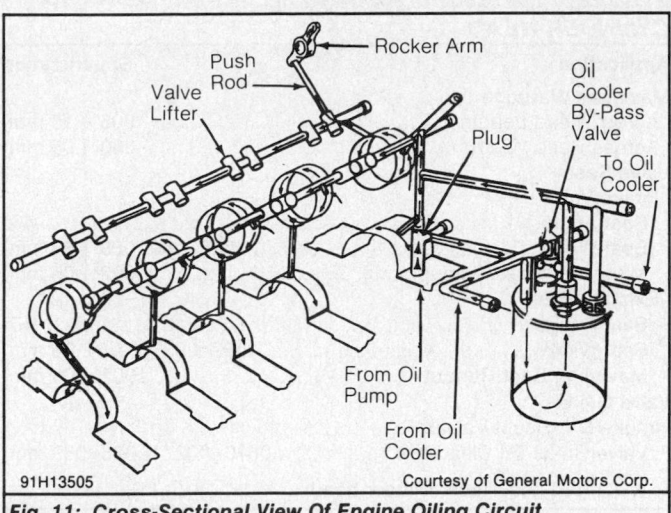

Push Rod — Rocker Arm
Valve Lifter
Oil Cooler By-Pass Valve
Plug
To Oil Cooler
From Oil Pump
From Oil Cooler

91H13505 — Courtesy of General Motors Corp.

Fig. 11: Cross-Sectional View Of Engine Oiling Circuit

OIL PUMP

Removal & Disassembly – 1) Remove oil pan, oil pump and extension shaft. See OIL PAN under REMOVAL & INSTALLATION. Remove pump cover screws and pump cover. Mark gears so they may be reassembled with same tooth indexed. Remove idler gear, drive gear and shaft from pump housing.

2) Remove pressure regulator valve retaining pin from pump cover. Remove regulator valve components from pump cover. Note order of removal. DO NOT disassemble pick-up screen and pipe. Screen and pipe are serviced only as an assembly with pump.

Inspection – 1) Inspect pump body and cover for cracks or excessive wear. Inspect pump gears for damage or wear. Check drive gear shaft for looseness in pump body.

2) Check pressure regulator valve for fit in bore. Inspect inlet tube and screen assembly for damage. Replace entire pump assembly if damaged.

Reassembly & Installation – 1) Install pump gears into pump body with marked gear teeth indexed. Reassemble remaining components in reverse order of disassembly. On Van, place pump and extension shaft inside oil pan. Position oil pan in place.

2) On all models, install pump and extension shaft on engine, ensuring slot on top of extension shaft engages with drive tang on end of pump drive or vacuum pump. Tighten mounting bolt to specification. See TORQUE SPECIFICATIONS table. Install oil pan.

TORQUE SPECIFICATIONS

TORQUE SPECIFICATIONS

Application	Ft. Lbs. (N.m)
Bellhousing Bolt	30 (40)
Camshaft Gear Bolt	74 (100)
Camshaft Thrust Plate Bolt	17 (23)
Connecting Rod Nut	48 (65)
Coolant Crossover Pipe Bolt	31 (42)
Crankshaft Damper Bolt	199 (270)
Crankshaft Pulley Bolt	30 (40)
Cylinder Head Bolt [1]	
Step 1	18 (25)
Step 2	48 (65)
Step 3	Tighten an additional 90 degrees.
Engine Speed Sensor Clamp Bolt	30 (40)
Exhaust Manifold Bolt	26 (35)
Flywheel Bolt	66 (90)
Front Cover Bolt	33 (45)
Injection Line Fitting	18 (25)

[1] – Tighten in sequence. See Fig. 3.
[2] – Tighten in sequence. See Fig. 1.

TORQUE SPECIFICATIONS (Cont.)

Application	Ft. Lbs. (N.m)
Injection Nozzle	52 (70)
Injection Pump Gear Baffle Bolt	33 (45)
Injection Pump Gear Bolt	17 (23)
Injection Pump Mounting Nut	31 (42)
Intake Manifold Bolt [2]	31 (42)
Main Bearing Cap Bolt	
Step 1 – Inner	111 (150)
Step 2 – Outer	100 (135)
Oil Pan Bolt (Rear 2)	17 (23)
Oil Pump Bolt	66 (90)
Oil Pump Drive Clamp Bolt	31 (42)
Rocker Arm Cover Bolt	16 (22)
Rocker Arm Shaft Bolt	41 (55)
Thermostat Housing-To-Coolant Crossover Pipe Bolt	31 (42)
Turbo Charger-To-Exhaust Manifold	37 (50)
Vacuum Pump Clamp Bolt	30 (40)
Valve Lifter Guide Plate Clamp Bolt	19 (26)
Water Pump Plate-To-Front Cover Bolt	17 (23)
Water Pump Plate-To-Pump Bolt	17 (23)
Water Pump-To-Cylinder Block Bolt	31 (42)

	INCH Lbs. (N.m)
Glow Plug	124 (14)
Oil Pan Bolt (Except Rear 2)	89 (10)

[1] – Tighten in sequence. See Fig. 3.
[2] – Tighten in sequence. See Fig. 1.

ENGINE SPECIFICATIONS

GENERAL SPECIFICATIONS

Application	Specification
Displacement	
6.2L	378 Cu. In.
6.5L	397 Cu. In.
Bore	
6.2L	3.98" (101 mm)
6.5L	4.06" (103 mm)
Stroke	3.82" (97 mm)
Compression Ratio	
6.2	21.3:1
6.5	21.0:1
Fuel System	Diesel
Horsepower @ RPM	
6.2L	140-155 @ 3600
6.5L	180-190 @ 3400
Torque Ft. Lbs. @ RPM	
6.2L	255-285 @ 2000
6.5L	360-380 @ 1700

CRANKSHAFT, MAIN & CONNECTING ROD BEARINGS

Application	In. (mm)
Crankshaft End Play	.004-.010 (.10-.25)
Main Bearings	
Journal Diameter	
Journals No. 1-4	2.9495-2.9504 (74.917-74.941)
Journal No. 5	2.9496-2.9502 (74.920-74.936)
Journal Out-Of-Round	.0002 (.005)
Journal Taper	.0002 (.005)
Oil Clearance	
Journals No. 1-4	.0018-.0033 (.045-.083)
Journal No. 5	.0022-.0037 (.055-.093)
Connecting Rod Bearings	
Journal Diameter	2.3981-2.3992 (60.913-60.939)
Journal Out-Of-Round	.0002 (.005)
Journal Taper	.0002 (.005)
Oil Clearance	.0018-.0039 (.045-.100)

1992 ENGINES
6.2L & 6.5L V8 Diesel (Cont.)

CONNECTING RODS

Application	In. (mm)
Side Play	.007-.025 (.17-.63)

PISTONS, PINS & RINGS

Application	In. (mm)
Pistons	
Clearance	
Bohn Pistons	
Journals No. 1-6	.0035-.0045 (.089-.115)
Journals No. 7 & 8	.0040-.0050 (.102-.128)
Pins	
Diameter	1.2203-1.2206 (30.996-31.004)
Piston Fit	.0003-.0012 (.008-.031)
Rod Fit	.0003-.0012 (.008-.031)
Rings	
No. 1	
End Gap	
6.2L	.012-.022 (.30-.55)
6.5L	.010-.020 (.26-.51)
Side Clearance	.0030-.0070 (.076-.178)
No. 2	
End Gap	.030-.040 (.75-1.00)
Side Clearance	.0015-.0031 (.039-.080)
No. 3 (Oil)	
End Gap	.010-.020 (.25-.51)
Side Clearance	.0016-.0038 (.040-.096)

CYLINDER BLOCK

Application	In. (mm)
Maximum Deck Warpage [1]	
Across Block Length	.006 (.15)
Across Block Width	.003 (.08)
Cylinder Bore	
Diameter	3.9759-3.9789 (100.987-101.065)
Maximum Taper	.0008 (.020)
Maximum Out-Of-Round	.0008 (.020)

[1] – DO NOT resurface cylinder block deck.

VALVES & VALVE SPRINGS

Application	Specification
Intake & Exhaust Valves	
Face Angle	45°
Valve Springs	
Installed Height	1.8" (46 mm)
Out-Of-Square	.062" (1.58 mm)

	Lbs. @ In. (kg @ mm)
Pressure	
Valve Closed	79 @ 1.81 (36 @ 46.0)
Valve Open	231 @ 1.39 (105 @ 35.3)

CYLINDER HEAD

Application	Specification
Maximum Warpage [1]	
Across Head Length	.006" (.15 mm)
Across Head Width	.003" (.08 mm)
Valve Seats	
Intake Valve	
Seat Angle	46°
Seat Width	.035-.060" (.89-1.53 mm)
Maximum Seat Runout	.002" (.05 mm)
Exhaust Valve	
Seat Angle	46°
Seat Width	.062-.093" (1.57-2.36 mm)
Maximum Seat Runout	.002" (.05 mm)
Valve Guides	
Intake & Exhaust Valves	
Valve Guide Oil Clearance	.0010-.0027" (.026-.069 mm)

[1] – DO NOT resurface cylinder head.

CAMSHAFT

Application	In. (mm)
End Play	.0020-.0120 (.051-.305)
Journal Diameter	
Journals No. 1-4	2.1642-2.1663 (54.970-55.025)
Journal No. 5	2.0067-2.0089 (50.970-51.025)
Lobe Lift	
Intake	[1] .2808 (7.133)
Exhaust	[1] .2808 (7.133)
Oil Clearance	.0010-.0046 (.025-.118)

[1] – Plus or minus .002" (.05 mm).

VALVE LIFTERS

Application	In. (mm)
Bore Diameter	
Standard	.923-.924 (23.45-23.47)
Oversize	.933-.934 (23.70-23.72)
Lifter Diameter	
Standard	.921-.922 (23.39-23.41)
Oversize	.931-.932 (23.64-23.66)
Oil Clearance [1]	.0016-.0031 (.040-.080)

[1] – Oversized lifter can be used to replace standard lifter if resulting clearance is within specification.

Astro, Bravada, Commercial Van, Jimmy, Lumina APV, Safari, Sierra, Silhouette, Sonoma, Suburban, Syclone, Trans Sport, Typhoon, Van, Yukon, "C" & "K" Series Blazer & Pickup, "S" & "T" Series Blazer & Pickup

MODEL IDENTIFICATION

Vehicle model can be identified by fifth character of Vehicle Identification Number (VIN), stamped on metal pad on top of left end of instrument panel, near windshield. See MODEL IDENTIFICATION table.

MODEL IDENTIFICATION

Series [1]	Model
"C"	2WD Pickup, Sierra & Suburban
"G"	RWD Van
"K"	4WD Blazer, Pickup, Sierra, Suburban & Yukon
"L"	AWD Astro & Safari
"M"	2WD Astro & Safari
"P"	Commercial Van/Motorhome
"S"	2WD Blazer, Jimmy, Pickup & Sonoma
"T"	Bravada, 4WD Blazer, Jimmy, Pickup, Sonoma, Syclone & Typhoon
"U"	Lumina APV, Silhouette & Trans Sport

[1] – Vehicle series is fifth character of VIN.

SPECIFICATIONS

BELT ADJUSTMENT

NOTE: For serpentine belt routing, see Figs. 1-6.

BELT ADJUSTMENT

Application	Tension Lbs. (kg)
2.5L, 2.8L, 3.1L & 3.8L	[1]
4.3L, 5.0L & 5.7L	
New Belt	135 (61.2)
Old Belt	90 (40.8)
6.2L & 6.5L Diesel	
New Belt	146 (66.2)
Old Belt	67 (30.4)
7.4L	
New Belt	129.4-140.6 (58.7-63.8)
Old Belt	84.4-95.6 (38.3-43.4)

[1] – Serpentine belt tension is maintained automatically by a spring-tensioned idler pulley. No adjustment is necessary.

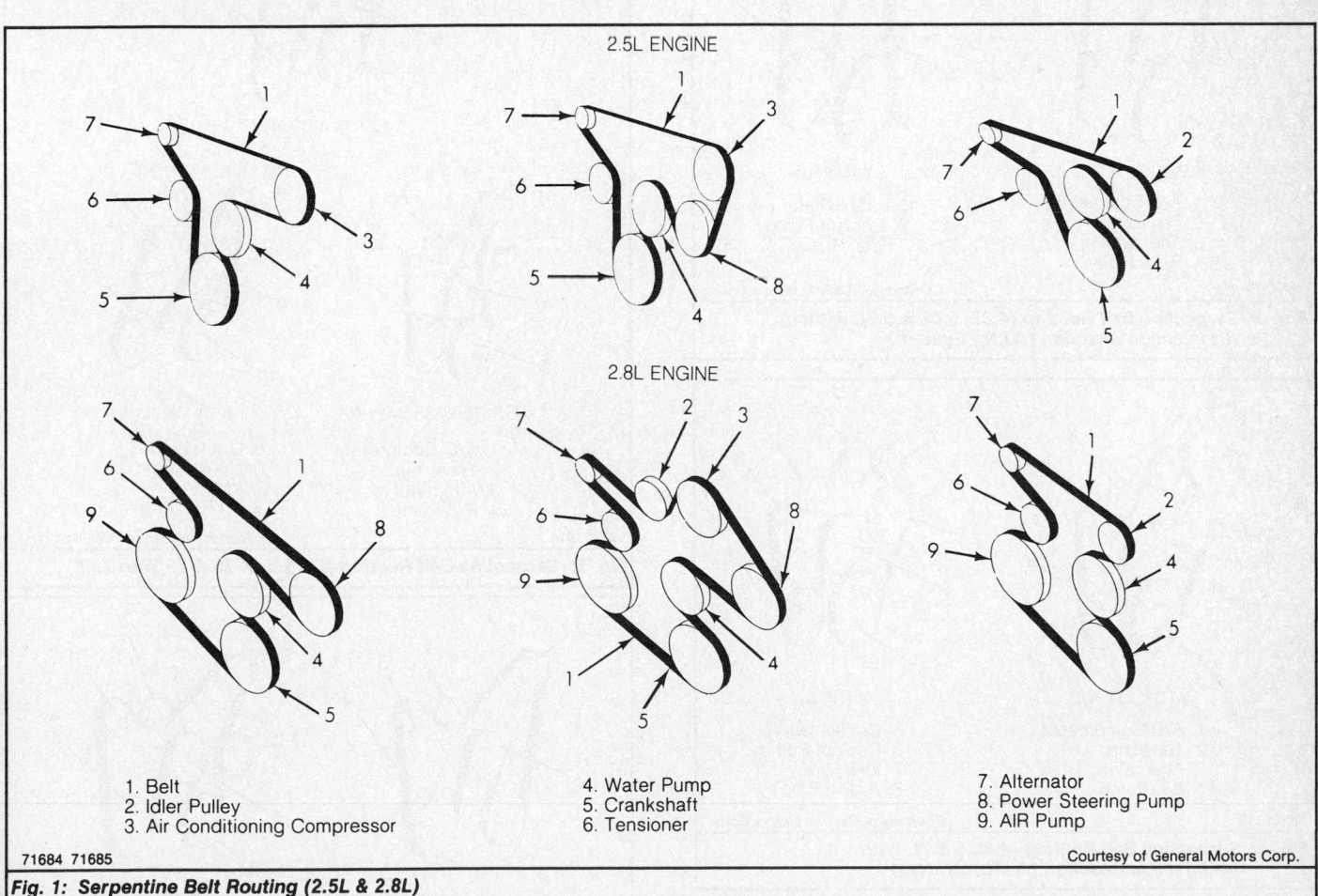

2.5L ENGINE

2.8L ENGINE

1. Belt
2. Idler Pulley
3. Air Conditioning Compressor
4. Water Pump
5. Crankshaft
6. Tensioner
7. Alternator
8. Power Steering Pump
9. AIR Pump

71684 71685

Courtesy of General Motors Corp.

Fig. 1: Serpentine Belt Routing (2.5L & 2.8L)

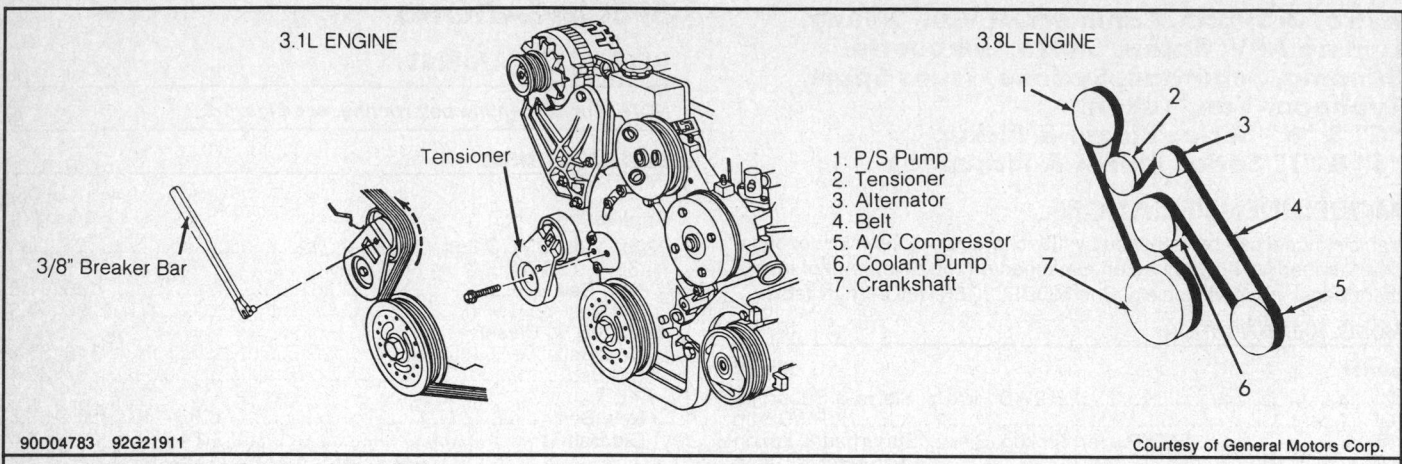

3.1L ENGINE

3.8L ENGINE

Tensioner

3/8" Breaker Bar

1. P/S Pump
2. Tensioner
3. Alternator
4. Belt
5. A/C Compressor
6. Coolant Pump
7. Crankshaft

90D04783   92G21911

Courtesy of General Motors Corp.

Fig. 2: Serpentine Belt Routing (3.1L & 3.8L)

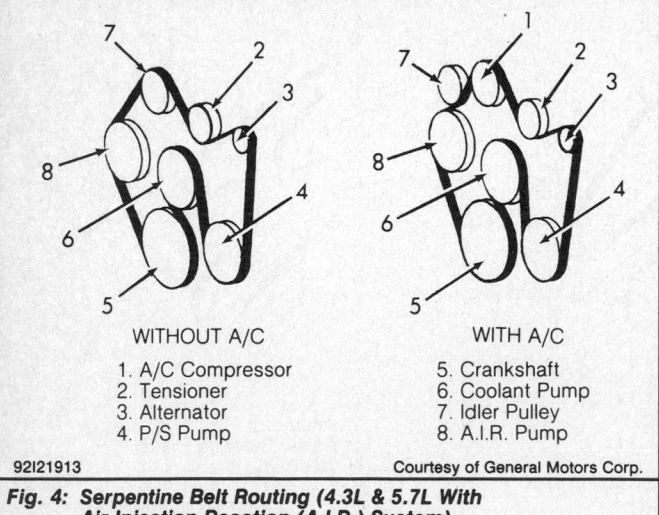

WITHOUT A/C

WITH A/C

1. A/C Compressor
2. Tensioner
3. Alternator
4. P/S Pump

5. Crankshaft
6. Coolant Pump
7. Idler Pulley

92H21912   Courtesy of General Motors Corp.

Fig. 3: Serpentine Belt Routing (4.3L, 5.0L & 5.7L Without Air Injection Reaction (A.I.R.) System)

WITHOUT A/C

WITH A/C

1. A/C Compressor
2. Tensioner
3. Alternator
4. P/S Pump

5. Crankshaft
6. Coolant Pump
7. Idler Pulley
8. A.I.R. Pump

92I21913   Courtesy of General Motors Corp.

Fig. 4: Serpentine Belt Routing (4.3L & 5.7L With Air Injection Reaction (A.I.R.) System)

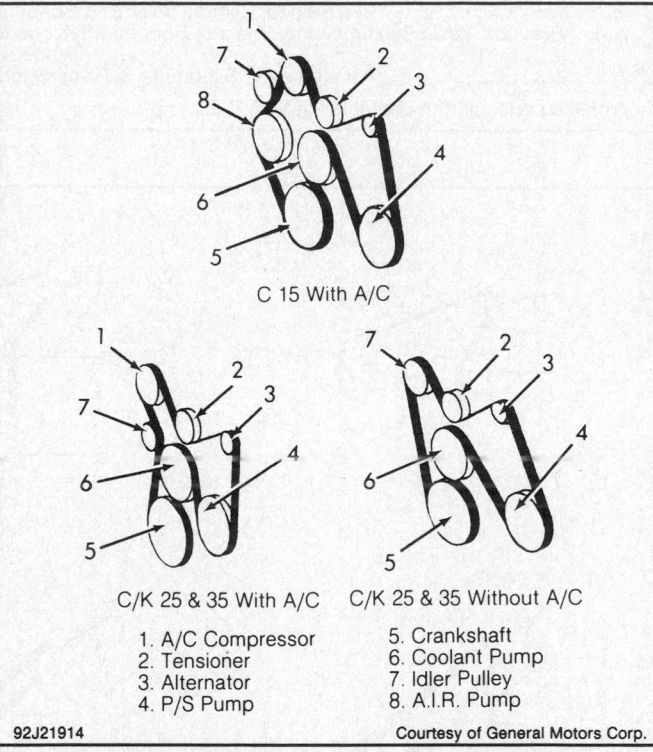

C 15 With A/C

C/K 25 & 35 With A/C   C/K 25 & 35 Without A/C

1. A/C Compressor
2. Tensioner
3. Alternator
4. P/S Pump

5. Crankshaft
6. Coolant Pump
7. Idler Pulley
8. A.I.R. Pump

92J21914   Courtesy of General Motors Corp.

Fig. 5: Serpentine Belt Routing (C 15, C/K 25 & 35 With 7.4L)

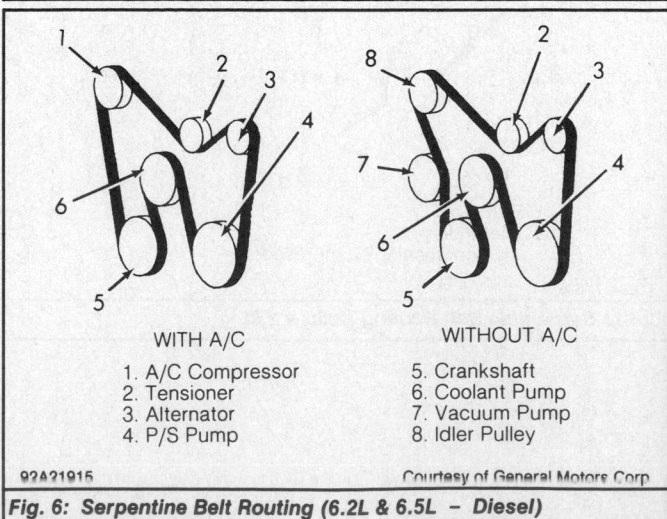

WITH A/C

WITHOUT A/C

1. A/C Compressor
2. Tensioner
3. Alternator
4. P/S Pump

5. Crankshaft
6. Coolant Pump
7. Vacuum Pump
8. Idler Pulley

92A21915   Courtesy of General Motors Corp.

Fig. 6: Serpentine Belt Routing (6.2L & 6.5L – Diesel)

COOLING SYSTEM SPECIFICATIONS

COOLING SYSTEM SPECIFICATIONS

Application	Specification
Coolant Replacement Interval	30,000 Miles
Pressure Cap	15 psi
Thermostat Opens	
Starts	188°F (87°C)
Fully Open	206° (97°C)

	Qts. (L)
Coolant Capacity [1]	
2.5L (VIN E)	11.5 (11.0)
2.8L (VIN R)	10.5 (10.0)
3.1L (VIN D)	[2] 13.0 (12.3)
3.8L (VIN L)	12.4 (11.7)
4.3L (VIN Z)	
"C" & "K" Series	10.9 (10.3)
Except "C" & "K" Series	13.5 (12.8)
5.0L (VIN H)	17.0 (16.0)
5.7L (VIN K)	17.0 (16.0)
6.2L (VIN C & J)	25.0 (23.5)
6.5L (VIN F)	26.5 (25.0)
7.4L (VIN N)	23.0 (22.0)

[1] – Specification is approximate and includes heater capacity.
[2] – On vehicles with rear heater, add 3 extra quarts (2.8L) of coolant.

COOLING SYSTEM BLEEDING

Lumina APV, Silhouette & Trans Sport With Rear Heater – Turn off rear blower switch while filling cooling system. This ensures maximum coolant flow to rear heater system.

ELECTRIC COOLING FAN

1992 ELECTRIC COOLING FAN APPLICATION

Application	Engine
Lumina APV, Silhouette & Trans Sport	3.1L & 3.8L
"C", "G" & "K" Series (A/C Equipped)	7.4L

DESCRIPTION

On Lumina APV, Silhouette and Trans Sport, electric cooling fan provides cooling for radiator and A/C condenser. On "C", "G" and "K" Series, electric cooling fan is an auxiliary unit providing cooling for A/C condenser.

OPERATION

Lumina APV, Silhouette & Trans Sport – ECM completes path to ground for cooling fan relay to activate cooling fan motor. Cooling fan relay is the center of 3 relays behind right headlight. A fusible link protects circuit. When engine cools, ECM opens relay, stopping fan operation. If coolant sensor fails, ECM commands constant fan operation.

CHART C-12, COOLING FAN CIRCUIT DIAGNOSIS (1 OF 2) 3.1L – VIN D ("U" SERIES)

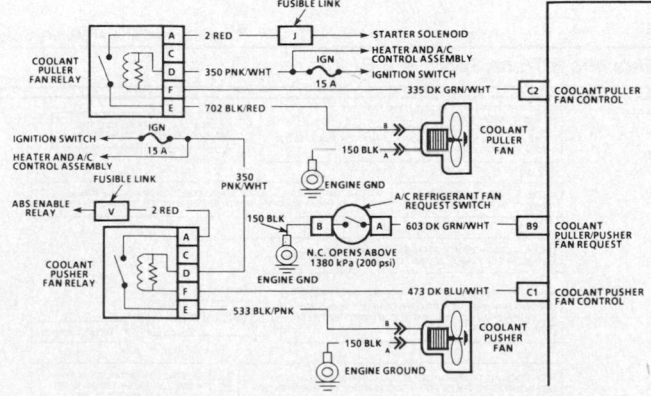

DIAGNOSTIC AIDS

If an overheating condition is suspected, verify if it is due to actual boilover. If gauge or light indicates an overheat condition and boilover is not evident, inspect gauge/light circuit for malfunction.

If vehicle is overheating and gauge or light indicates so but cooling fan is not operating and Scan tester indicates normal readings, coolant temperature sensor is out of calibration and should be replaced. If engine is overheating and cooling fan is on, check cooling system.

ECM controls electric cooling fan(s) based on inputs from coolant temperature sensor, A/C request, refrigerant fan request switch and vehicle speed. ECM energizes fan(s) by grounding circuits No. 335 and 473, which closes cooling fan relay(s). Battery voltage is supplied to cooling fan(s) when energized. ECM grounds circuit No. 335 (puller fan) when coolant temperature is approximately 223°F (106°C) or when A/C has been requested and refrigerant fan request switch opens with high A/C pressure, approximately 200 psi (14.1 kg/cm²). Pusher fan relay is grounded when coolant temperature is approximately 217°F (103°C) and/or puller fan is energized for A/C pressure.

NOTE: Test numbers refer to numbers on diagnostic charts.

1) With ALDL diagnostic terminal grounded, cooling fan driver closes and energizes fan control relay.
2) If A/C fan request switch or circuit is open, cooling fan operates whenever A/C is operating.
3) With A/C requested and 45 seconds after request is removed, A/C refrigerant fan request switch should open when A/C high pressure exceeds approximately 200 psi (14.1 kg/cm²). This signal should cause ECM to energize fan control relay(s).
4) This tests if cooling puller and pusher fan relay(s) (circuits No. 335 and 473) are shorted to ground. This condition would cause fans to be energized continuously.

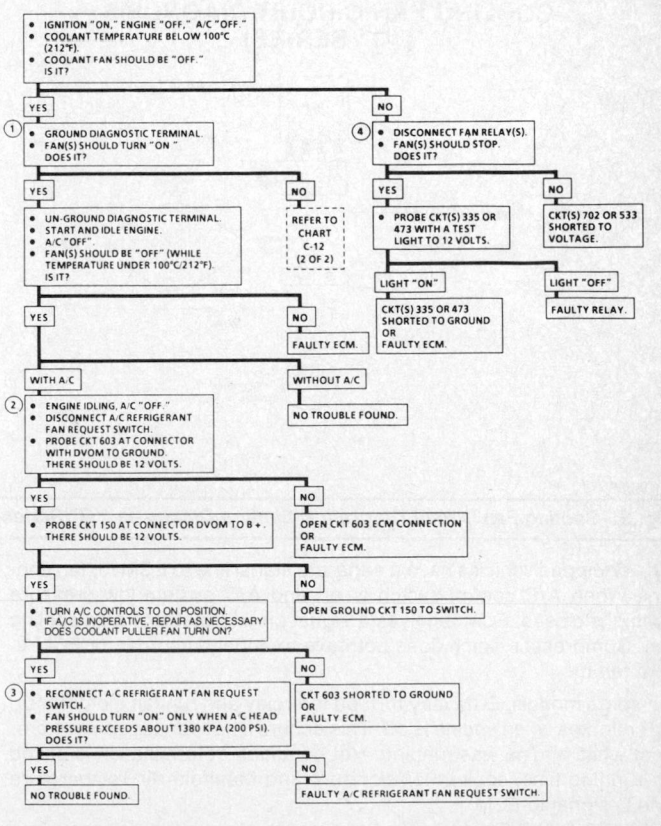

92F15912   92G15913

Courtesy of General Motors Corp.

Fig. 7: Cooling Fan Circuit Diagram & System Diagnosis (Lumina APV, Silhouette & Trans Sport – 1 Of 2)

CHART C-12, COOLING FAN CIRCUIT DIAGNOSIS (2 OF 2)
3.1L – VIN D ("U" SERIES)

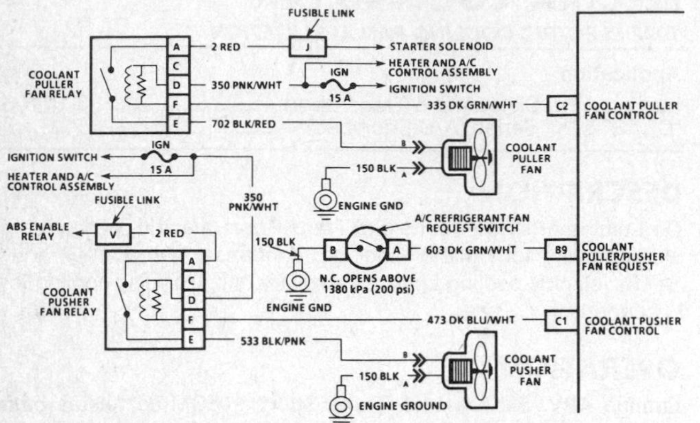

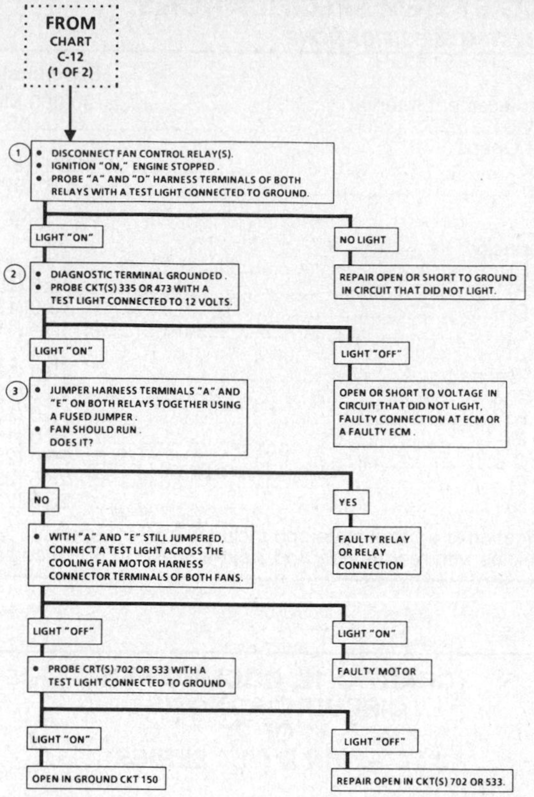

FROM CHART C-12 (1 OF 2)

① • DISCONNECT FAN CONTROL RELAY(S).
• IGNITION "ON," ENGINE STOPPED.
• PROBE "A" AND "D" HARNESS TERMINALS OF BOTH RELAYS WITH A TEST LIGHT CONNECTED TO GROUND.

LIGHT "ON" | NO LIGHT

NO LIGHT → REPAIR OPEN OR SHORT TO GROUND IN CIRCUIT THAT DID NOT LIGHT.

② • DIAGNOSTIC TERMINAL GROUNDED.
• PROBE CKT(S) 335 OR 473 WITH A TEST LIGHT CONNECTED TO 12 VOLTS.

LIGHT "ON" | LIGHT "OFF"

LIGHT "OFF" → OPEN OR SHORT TO VOLTAGE IN CIRCUIT THAT DID NOT LIGHT, FAULTY CONNECTION AT ECM OR A FAULTY ECM.

③ • JUMPER HARNESS TERMINALS "A" AND "E" ON BOTH RELAYS TOGETHER USING A FUSED JUMPER.
• FAN SHOULD RUN.
DOES IT?

NO | YES

YES → FAULTY RELAY OR RELAY CONNECTION

NO → • WITH "A" AND "E" STILL JUMPERED, CONNECT A TEST LIGHT ACROSS THE COOLING FAN MOTOR HARNESS CONNECTOR TERMINALS OF BOTH FANS.

LIGHT "OFF" | LIGHT "ON"

LIGHT "ON" → FAULTY MOTOR

LIGHT "OFF" → • PROBE CRT(S) 702 OR 533 WITH A TEST LIGHT CONNECTED TO GROUND

LIGHT "ON" | LIGHT "OFF"

LIGHT "ON" → OPEN IN GROUND CKT 150

LIGHT "OFF" → REPAIR OPEN IN CKT(S) 702 OR 533.

NOTE: Test numbers refer to numbers on diagnostic charts.

1) Battery voltage should be available at both terminals "A" and "D" when ignition switch is in ON position.

2) This checks ECM ability to ground circuits No. 335 and 473. SERVICE ENGINE SOON light should flash. If SERVICE ENGINE SOON light is not flashing, refer to appropriate article in ENGINE PERFORMANCE.

3) This tests if coolant puller and pusher fan relays (circuits No. 702 and 533) are open. Connecting jumper wire to terminals "A" and "E" by-passes relays, causing fans to run (provided motors and wiring are okay).

92F15912 92H15914

Courtesy of General Motors Corp.

Fig. 8: Cooling Fan Circuit Diagram & System Diagnosis (Lumina APV, Silhouette & Trans Sport – 2 Of 2)

COOLING FAN CIRCUIT DIAGNOSIS ("G" SERIES)

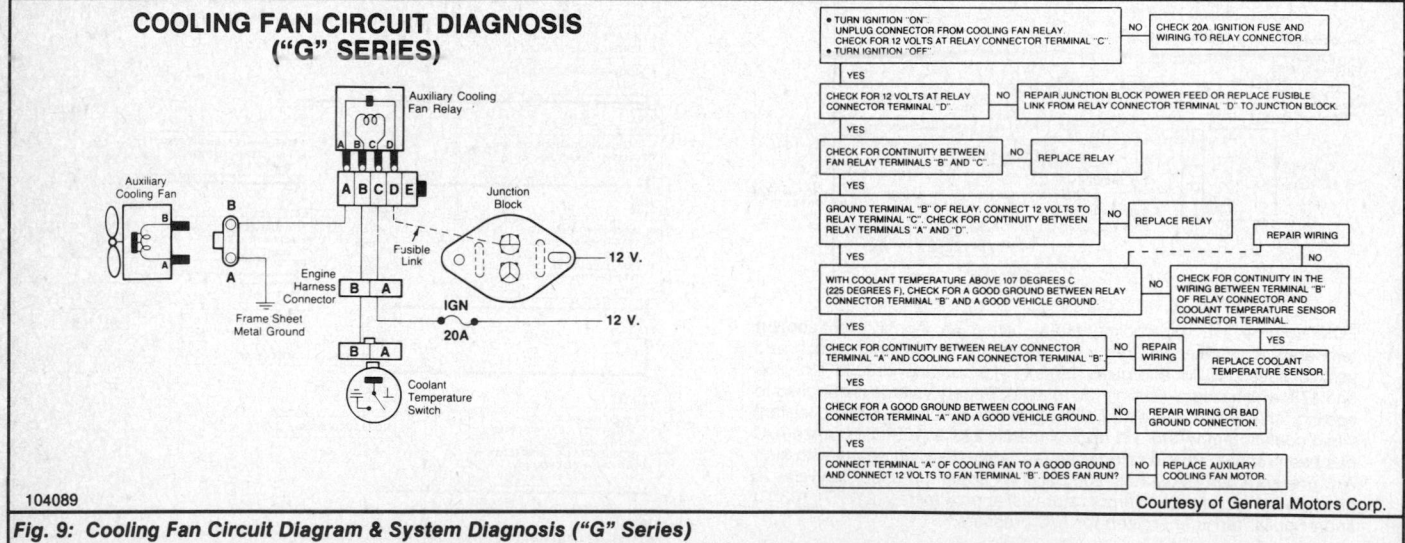

104089

Courtesy of General Motors Corp.

Fig. 9: Cooling Fan Circuit Diagram & System Diagnosis ("G" Series)

A/C-equipped vehicles have a separate signal line to ECM for fan control. When A/C control switch is on and A/C system low pressure switch is closed, ECM receives a signal on this line to turn on cooling fan. Compressor clutch does not have to engage in order for ECM to turn fan on.

On some models, ECM may turn on fan relay and run fan motor for up to 7 minutes when engine is off. This occurs if hot conditions were present while engine was running. Hot condition determination is based on running time, coolant temperature and Manifold Air Temperature (MAT) signal to ECM.

"C", "G" & "K" Series – Coolant temperature switch closes when predetermined temperature is reached. Relay contacts will close, completing circuit to fan motor.

Switch is located on right cylinder head, above center of exhaust manifold. On "G" Series, relay is located in engine compartment on center of firewall. On "C" and "K" Series, relay is mounted to left inner fender, near engine compartment firewall.

TROUBLE SHOOTING & TESTING

Trouble shooting and testing procedures for "C" and "K" Series are not available from manufacturer. For trouble shooting and testing procedures of all other applicable models, *see Figs. 7-9*.

NOTE: Some TROUBLE SHOOTING & TESTING procedures may include test charts for General Motors Computerized Engine Control (CEC) system. Only those charts required to test electric cooling fans are provided. For complete information on General Motors CEC systems, see appropriate article in ENGINE PERFORMANCE.

WIRING DIAGRAMS

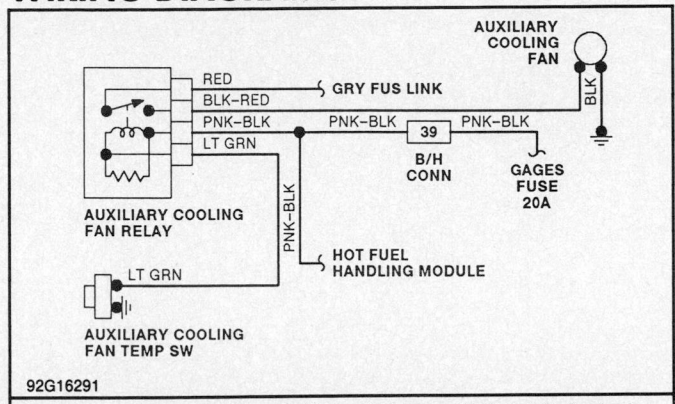

Fig. 10: Cooling Fan Circuit Wiring Diagram ("C" & "K" Series)

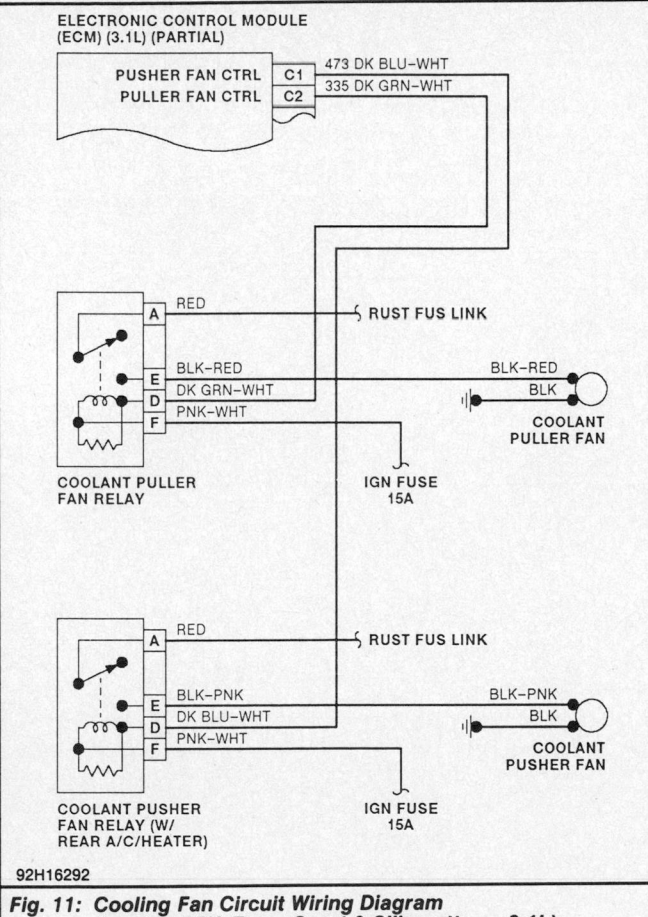

Fig. 11: Cooling Fan Circuit Wiring Diagram
(Lumina APV, Trans Sport & Silhouette – 3.1L)

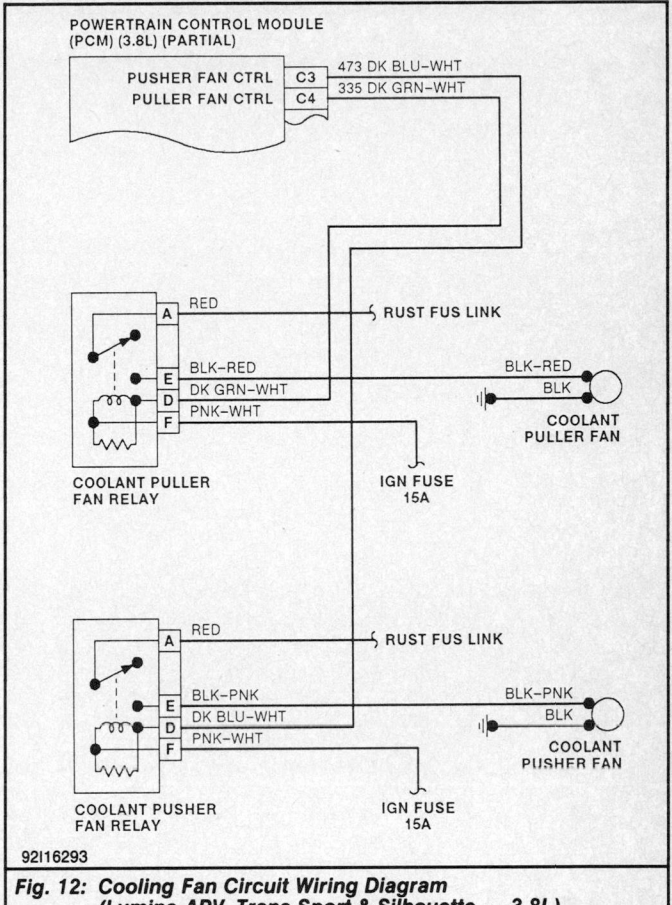

Fig. 12: Cooling Fan Circuit Wiring Diagram
(Lumina APV, Trans Sport & Silhouette – 3.8L)

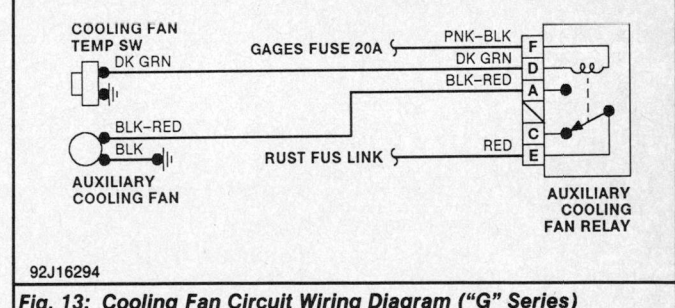

Fig. 13: Cooling Fan Circuit Wiring Diagram ("G" Series)

Commercial Van, Jimmy,
Sierra, Sonoma, Suburban, Yukon,
"C" & "K" Series Blazer & Pickup,
"S" & "T" Series Blazer & Pickup

DESCRIPTION

The hydraulic clutch consists of a clutch plate, pressure plate and pilot bearing. Hydraulic clutch has a master cylinder with a reservoir. Clutch pedal moves master cylinder push rod, and a slave cylinder at the bellhousing moves the clutch fork and release bearing. See Fig. 1.

TRANSMISSION APPLICATION

Vehicle Model	Transmission Model (RPO)
Commercial Van	NVG 4500 109 MM 5-Speed O/D (MT8)
Jimmy, Sonoma, & "S" & "T" Series Blazer & Pickup	Borg-Warner T5 77 MM 5-Speed (MW1) & NVG 5LM60 85 MM 5-Speed O/D (MY2)
Sierra, Suburban, Yukon, & "C" & "K" Series Blazer & Pickup	NVG 5LM60 85 MM 5-Speed O/D (MG5) & NVG 4500 109 MM 5-Speed O/D (MT8)

LUBRICATION

RECOMMENDED FLUID
RECOMMENDED FLUID

Application	Fluid Type
Borg-Warner T5 77 MM 5-Speed	[1] Dexron-IIE ATF
NVG 5LM60 85 MM 5-Speed O/D	API GL5 (SAE 80W-90)
NVG 4500 109 MM 5-Speed O/D	GM Man. Trans. Syn. Fluid (12345871)
Transfer Cases	[1] Dexron-IIE ATF

[1] – Although Dexron-IIE is recommended, Dexron-II may still be used. Dexron-II will eventually be replaced with Dexron-IIE.

ADJUSTMENTS

The hydraulic clutch system provides automatic adjustment; no manual adjustments are necessary.

IN-VEHICLE SERVICE

BLEEDING HYDRAULIC CLUTCH SYSTEM

NOTE: DO NOT reuse fluid that has been bled from system.

With Bleeder Screw – 1) Fill reservoir with clean DOT 3 brake fluid. Disconnect slave cylinder from bellhousing, leaving line attached. Hold slave cylinder at 45-degree angle with bleeder screw facing upward.

2) Have an assistant depress clutch pedal while opening bleeder screw. Close bleeder screw and release pedal. Repeat sequence until all air is removed from system. Ensure master cylinder reservoir stays full during bleeding process. Install slave cylinder.

Without Bleeder Screw – 1) Separate master cylinder push rod from clutch pedal. Disconnect slave cylinder from bellhousing, leaving line attached. Remove reservoir cap. Slowly depress slave cylinder push rod to bottom of cylinder bore. Hold slave cylinder push rod, and fill reservoir with clean DOT 3 brake fluid. Slowly release slave cylinder push rod.

2) Hold slave cylinder vertically with push rod end facing the ground. Hold slave cylinder push rod against palm of hand and position lower than master cylinder. Depress slave cylinder push rod into cylinder bore with short strokes while observing reservoir for air bubbles.

3) Repeat sequence until air bubbles are not longer present in reservoir fluid. Ensure master cylinder reservoir stays full during bleeding process. Install slave cylinder. Install reservoir cap. Re-attach master cylinder push rod to clutch pedal.

CHECKING HYDRAULIC CLUTCH SYSTEM

Clutch hydraulic system malfunctions can be verified by measuring travel of clutch slave cylinder push rod. On "C" and "K" Series Blazer and Pickup, Sierra, Suburban and Yukon, slave cylinder push rod travel at clutch fork should be at least 1" (25.4 mm) with clutch pedal pressed fully to floor stop.

On "S" and "T" Series Blazer and Pickup, Jimmy and Sonoma, slave cylinder push rod travel at clutch fork should be at least .75" (19 mm) with clutch pedal pressed fully to floor stop.

On Commercial Van, slave cylinder push rod travel at clutch fork should be at least 1.338" (34 mm) with clutch pedal pressed fully to floor stop. If slave cylinder push rod travel is not as specified, check reservoir fluid level. If fluid level is low, check hoses for cracks, wear or other damage. Check hydraulic cylinders for loose mounting and signs of leakage. Fill reservoir with fluid. See RECOMMENDED FLUID table under LUBRICATION. If necessary, bleed hydraulic system. See BLEEDING HYDRAULIC CLUTCH SYSTEM. Repair or replace clutch hydraulic system if fluid leakage is excessive.

REMOVAL & INSTALLATION

WARNING: When battery is disconnected, vehicle computer and memory systems may lose memory data. Driveability problems may exist until computer systems have completed a relearn cycle. See COMPUTER RELEARN PROCEDURES article in GENERAL INFORMATION before disconnecting battery.

TRANSFER CASE

Removal (BW-4401, BW-4470 & NP-241 – "K" Series Blazer & Pickup, Sierra, Suburban & Yukon) – 1) Disconnect battery negative cable. Place transfer case in 4H position. Raise and support vehicle. Remove skid plate (if equipped). Drain fluid from transfer case. Mark front output shaft yoke and drive shaft for reassembly reference. Remove front drive shaft. Remove left strut rod. Mark rear output shaft yoke and drive shaft for reassembly reference. Remove rear drive shaft.

2) Disconnect electrical connectors from transfer case. Disconnect shift rod from transfer case. Support transfer case with jack. Remove transfer case-to-transmission mount bolts and spring washers (if equipped). Slide transfer case rearward until free of transmission output shaft. Lower and remove transfer case. Remove and discard gasket.

Installation – To install, reverse removal procedure. Tighten transfer case-to-transmission mount bolts to **24 ft. lbs. (33 N.m)**. Fill transfer case with fluid. See RECOMMENDED FLUID table under LUBRICATION.

Removal (NP-231 & NP-233 – "T" Series Blazer & Pickup, Jimmy & Sonoma) – 1) Disconnect battery negative cable. Place transfer case in 4H position. Raise and support vehicle. Remove skid plate (if equipped). Drain fluid from transfer case. Mark front and rear output shaft yokes and drive shafts for reassembly reference. Remove front and rear drive shafts.

2) Disconnect vacuum lines and electrical connectors from transfer case (if equipped). Disconnect shift rod from transfer case. Support transfer case with jack. Remove transfer case-to-transmission mount bolts. Slide transfer case rearward until free of transmission output shaft. Lower and remove transfer case. Remove and discard gasket.

Installation – To install, reverse removal procedure. Tighten transfer case-to-transmission mount bolts to **24 ft. lbs. (33 N.m)**. Fill transfer case with fluid. See RECOMMENDED FLUID table under LUBRICATION.

TRANSMISSION

Removal ("C" & "K" Series Blazer & Pickup, Sierra, Suburban & Yukon) – 1) Disconnect battery negative cable. Remove shift lever retainer screws and retainer. Remove shift lever boot mounting screws and boot. Remove shift lever insulator. Remove shift lever. Raise and support vehicle. Drain transmission fluid.

2) Mark drive shaft for reassembly reference. Remove drive shaft. Carefully remove transfer case (if equipped). Remove parking brake

and cable (if equipped). Disconnect electrical connectors. Remove clutch slave cylinder. Support transmission.

3) Remove exhaust pipes, crossmember and other components as necessary for clearance. Remove dust cover bolts and dust cover (if equipped). Remove transmission mounting bolts. Pull transmission straight back on clutch hub splines, and remove transmission.

Installation – To install, shift transmission into Neutral, and reverse removal procedure. Lightly coat input shaft splines with high-temperature grease. Tighten bolts to specifications. See TORQUE SPECIFICATIONS table at end of article. Fill transmission with fluid. See RECOMMENDED FLUID table under LUBRICATION.

Removal ("S" & "T" Series Blazer & Pickup, Jimmy & Sonoma) – **1)** Disconnect battery negative cable. Shift transmission into Neutral. Remove shift lever knob and nut. Remove shift lever retainer screws and retainer (if equipped). Remove shift lever boot mounting screws and boot. Remove shift lever and nut.

2) Raise and support vehicle. Drain transmission fluid. Remove parking brake cable for clearance. Mark drive shaft for reassembly reference. Remove drive shaft. Remove skid plate (if equipped). Carefully remove transfer case (if equipped).

3) Disconnect electrical connectors. On 4.3L models, purge fuel system, and disconnect fuel lines at manifold. On all models, disconnect exhaust pipe. Remove clutch slave cylinder. Support transmission. Remove transmission mounting bolts as necessary. Remove catalytic converter hanger. Remove support braces. Remove crossmember. Remove transmission mounting bolts.

4) On 4.3L models, rotate transmission counterclockwise, then pull transmission straight back on clutch hub splines, and remove transmission. On 2.5L and 2.8L models, pull transmission straight back on clutch hub splines, and remove transmission.

Installation – **1)** To install, shift transmission into High gear, and reverse removal procedure. Lightly coat input shaft splines with high-temperature grease. On 4.3L models, rotate transmission clockwise onto clutch hub splines.

2) Before installing shift lever, shift transmission into Neutral gear. Tighten bolts to specifications. See TORQUE SPECIFICATIONS table at end of article. Fill transmission with fluid. See RECOMMENDED FLUID table under LUBRICATION.

Removal (Commercial Van) – **1)** Disconnect battery negative cable. Remove shift lever knob and nut. Remove shift lever boot. To remove shift lever, push down and turn shift lever retainer counterclockwise. Remove shift lever. Raise and support vehicle. Drain transmission fluid.

2) Mark drive shaft for reassembly reference. Remove drive shaft. Remove parking brake and cable (if equipped). Remove electrical harness bracket bolt. Disconnect electrical connectors. Support transmission.

3) Remove exhaust pipe and other components as necessary for clearance. Remove transmission mounting bolts and washers. Pull transmission straight back on clutch hub splines, and remove transmission.

Installation – To install, shift transmission into Neutral, and reverse removal procedure. Lightly coat input shaft splines with high-temperature grease. Tighten bolts to specifications. See TORQUE SPECIFICATIONS table at end of article. Fill transmission with fluid. See RECOMMENDED FLUID table under LUBRICATION.

CLUTCH ASSEMBLY & PILOT BEARING

NOTE: DO NOT use compressor air to clean clutch parts. The clutch plate contains asbestos which is harmful if inhaled.

Removal ("C" & "K" Series Blazer & Pickup, Sierra, Suburban & Yukon) – **1)** Remove transmission. See TRANSMISSION under REMOVAL & INSTALLATION. Remove slave cylinder from bellhousing. See Fig. 1. Remove bellhousing bolts and remove bellhousing.

2) Remove flywheel cover bolts and remove flywheel cover. Remove clutch fork spring, seat, clutch fork and release bearing. Remove ball stud. Install Clutch Aligner (J-5824-01) to support clutch plate. Mark flywheel, clutch plate and pressure plate for reassembly reference.

3) Evenly loosen pressure plate bolts 1-2 turns at a time until clutch plate spring tension is released. Remove clutch plate and pressure plate. Remove clutch aligner. Remove pilot bearing if worn or damaged using Pilot Bearing Puller (J-23907).

Inspection – **1)** Clean all components with water-dampened cloth to remove asbestos fibers. Clean clutch fork, bellhousing and ball stud with solvent. Release bearing is permanently packed with lubricant and should not be cleaned with solvent.

2) Inspect all components for wear or damage. Inspect all contact surfaces for scoring, warping and damage. Clutch plate runout must not be greater than .20" (5.08 mm). Inspect friction surfaces for excessive oil. Inspect splines for nicks, burrs and sliding fit. Bellhousing transmission pilot hole runout should not be greater than .015" (.38 mm).

Installation – **1)** On 4.3L, 5.0L and 5.7L models, use brass drift to install NEW pilot bearing into flywheel, if removed. On 6.2L and 6.5L diesel models, use Pilot Bearing Driver (J-34140) to install NEW pilot bearing into flywheel, if removed. On 4.3L, 5.0L and 5.7L models, lubricate pilot bearing with machine oil. On 6.2L and 6.5L diesel models, pilot bearing is sealed and does not require lubrication. See Fig. 1.

2) Install Clutch Aligner (J-5824-01) to support clutch plate. Install clutch plate and pressure plate to flywheel. Ensure reference marks are aligned. Install and tighten NEW spring washers and bolts evenly to avoid distortion. Remove clutch aligner.

3) Lubricate ball stud and clutch fork fingers with high-temperature grease. Lubricate O.D. groove and pack grease into I.D. recess of release bearing. Install ball stud, clutch fork, seat, clutch fork spring and release bearing. See Fig. 1. To complete installation, reverse removal procedure. Tighten bolts to specifications. See TORQUE SPECIFICATIONS table at end of article. Fill reservoir with fluid. See RECOMMENDED FLUID table under LUBRICATION. Bleed system. See BLEEDING HYDRAULIC CLUTCH SYSTEM under IN-VEHICLE SERVICE.

Removal ("S" & "T" Series Blazer & Pickup, Jimmy & Sonoma) – **1)** Remove transmission. See TRANSMISSION under REMOVAL & INSTALLATION. Remove slave cylinder from bellhousing. See Fig. 1. Remove bellhousing bolts and remove bellhousing.

2) Remove flywheel cover bolts and remove flywheel cover. Remove clutch fork and release bearing. Remove ball stud from clutch fork. Remove retainer from clutch fork if worn or damage. Install Clutch Aligner (J-33169) to support clutch plate. Mark flywheel, clutch plate and pressure plate for reassembly reference.

3) Evenly loosen pressure plate bolts 1-2 turns at a time until clutch plate spring tension is released. Remove clutch plate and pressure plate. Remove clutch aligner. Remove pilot bearing if worn or damaged using Pilot Bearing Puller (J-23907).

Inspection – **1)** Clean all components with water-dampened cloth to remove asbestos fibers. Clean clutch fork, bellhousing and ball stud with solvent. Release bearing is permanently packed with lubricant and should not be cleaned with solvent.

2) Inspect all components for wear or damage. Inspect all contact surfaces for scoring, warping and damage. Clutch plate runout must not be greater than .20" (5.08 mm). Inspect friction surfaces for excessive oil. Inspect splines for nicks, burrs and sliding fit.

Installation – **1)** Use Pilot Bearing Driver (J-1522) to install NEW pilot bearing into flywheel, if removed. See Fig. 1. Lubricate pilot bearing with machine oil. Install Clutch Aligner (J-33169) to support clutch plate. Install clutch plate and pressure plate to flywheel. Ensure reference marks are aligned.

2) Install and tighten NEW spring washers and bolts evenly to avoid distortion. Remove clutch aligner. Lubricate ball stud and clutch fork fingers with high-temperature grease. Lubricate O.D. groove and pack grease into I.D. recess of release bearing.

3) If replacing clutch fork retainer, install retainer so fingers and tabs fit into release bearing groove, and retainer wraps around flat side of ball stud. Install ball stud, clutch fork, retainer and release bearing. See Fig. 1.

4) To complete installation, reverse removal procedure. Tighten bolts to specifications. See TORQUE SPECIFICATIONS table at end of article. Fill reservoir with fluid. See RECOMMENDED FLUID table under

LUBRICATION. Bleed system. See BLEEDING HYDRAULIC CLUTCH SYSTEM under IN-VEHICLE SERVICE.

Removal (Commercial Van) – 1) Remove transmission. See TRANSMISSION under REMOVAL & INSTALLATION. Remove slave cylinder from bellhousing. See Fig. 1. Remove bellhousing bolts and remove bellhousing.

2) Remove flywheel cover bolts and remove flywheel cover. Remove clutch fork and release bearing. Remove ball stud. Install Clutch Aligner (J-5824-01) to support clutch plate. Mark flywheel, clutch plate and pressure plate for reassembly reference.

3) Evenly loosen pressure plate bolts 1-2 turns at a time until clutch plate spring tension is released. Remove clutch plate and pressure plate. Remove clutch aligner. Remove pilot bearing if worn or damaged; use Pilot Bearing Puller (J-23907) on 4.3L, 5.7L and 7.4L models or Pilot Bearing Puller (J-1448) on 6.2L diesel models.

Inspection – 1) Clean all components with water-dampened cloth to remove asbestos fibers. Clean clutch fork, bellhousing and ball stud with solvent. Release bearing is permanently packed with lubricant and should not be cleaned with solvent.

2) Inspect all components for wear or damage. Inspect all contact surfaces for scoring, warping and damage. Clutch plate runout must not be greater than .20" (5.08 mm). Inspect friction surfaces for excessive oil. Inspect splines for nicks, burrs and sliding fit.

Installation – 1) On 4.3L, 5.7L and 7.4L models, use brass drift to install NEW pilot bearing into flywheel, if removed. On 6.2L diesel models, use Pilot Bearing Driver (J-34140) to install NEW pilot bearing into flywheel, if removed. On 4.3L, 5.7L and 7.4L models, lubricate pilot bearing with machine oil. On 6.2L diesel models, pilot bearing is sealed and does not require lubrication. See Fig. 1.

2) Install Clutch Aligner (J-5824-01) to support clutch plate. Install clutch plate and pressure plate to flywheel. Ensure reference marks are aligned. Install and tighten NEW spring washers and bolts evenly to avoid distortion. Remove clutch aligner.

3) Lubricate ball stud and clutch fork fingers with high-temperature grease. Lubricate O.D. groove and pack grease into I.D. recess of release bearing. Install ball stud, clutch fork and release bearing. See Fig. 1.

4) To complete installation, reverse removal procedure. Tighten bolts to specifications. See TORQUE SPECIFICATIONS table at end of article. Fill reservoir with fluid. See RECOMMENDED FLUID table under LUBRICATION. Bleed system. See BLEEDING HYDRAULIC CLUTCH SYSTEM under IN-VEHICLE SERVICE.

MASTER CYLINDER & RESERVOIR

Removal ("C" & "K" Series Blazer & Pickup, Sierra, Suburban & Yukon) – 1) Disconnect battery negative cable. Remove steering column lower cover or panel. Remove A/C duct from lower left side of instrument panel as necessary. Remove nut retaining push rod to clutch pedal. Separate push rod from clutch pedal.

2) Disconnect slave cylinder hose from master cylinder and plug openings. Remove master cylinder retaining nuts. Remove master cylinder and reservoir assembly. Remove gasket from master cylinder and cowl.

Installation – To install, reverse removal procedure. Install NEW gasket. Tighten nuts to specifications. See TORQUE SPECIFICATIONS table at end of article. Fill reservoir with fluid. See RECOMMENDED FLUID table under LUBRICATION. Bleed system. See BLEEDING HYDRAULIC CLUTCH SYSTEM under IN-VEHICLE SERVICE.

Removal ("S" & "T" Series Blazer & Pickup, Jimmy & Sonoma) – 1) Disconnect battery negative cable. Remove steering column lower cover or panel. Remove A/C duct from lower left side of instrument panel as necessary. Remove cotter pin and washer retaining push rod to clutch pedal. Separate push rod from clutch pedal.

2) Disconnect reservoir hose and slave cylinder hose from master cylinder and plug openings. Remove master cylinder retaining nuts. Remove master cylinder. Remove gasket from master cylinder and cowl. Remove reservoir retaining bolts and remove reservoir.

Installation – To install, reverse removal procedure. Install NEW gasket. Tighten bolts and nuts to specifications. See TORQUE SPECIFICATIONS table at end of article. Fill reservoir with fluid. See RECOMMENDED FLUID table under LUBRICATION. Bleed system. See BLEEDING HYDRAULIC CLUTCH SYSTEM under IN-VEHICLE SERVICE.

Removal (Commercial Van) – 1) Disconnect battery negative cable. Remove nut retaining push rod to clutch pedal. Separate push rod from clutch pedal. Remove master cylinder retaining nuts. Remove master cylinder reservoir and slave cylinder hose coupling bracket retaining nuts and washers.

2) Separate master cylinder and reservoir assembly hose from coupling and plug openings. Remove master cylinder and reservoir assembly.

Installation – 1) To install, reverse removal procedure. Difficulty may be experienced in connecting master cylinder reservoir hose to coupling due to internal hydraulic pressure. Ensure push rods are fully retracted to assist in connection of master cylinder reservoir hose to coupling.

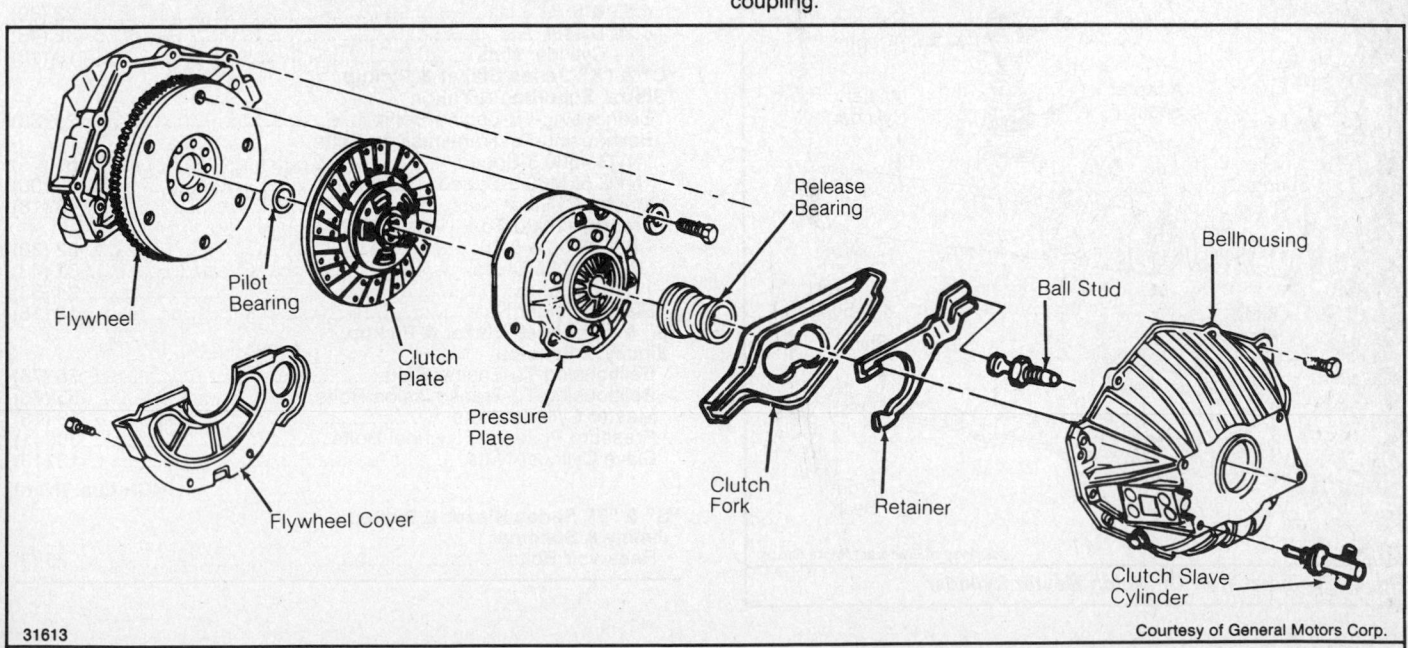

31613

Courtesy of General Motors Corp.

Fig. 1: Exploded View Of Clutch Assembly & Pilot Bearing ("S" & "T" Series Blazer & Pickup, Jimmy & Sonoma Shown – Others Similar)

2) Tighten nuts to specifications. See TORQUE SPECIFICATIONS table at end of article. Fill reservoir with fluid. See RECOMMENDED FLUID table under LUBRICATION. Bleed system. See BLEEDING HYDRAULIC CLUTCH SYSTEM under IN-VEHICLE SERVICE.

SLAVE CYLINDER

Removal – Disconnect battery negative cable. Raise and support vehicle. Disconnect slave cylinder hose from slave cylinder and plug openings. Remove slave cylinder retaining nuts and remove slave cylinder.

Installation – To install, reverse removal procedure. On commercial van, DO NOT remove plastic push rod retainer from slave cylinder. Retainer straps will break when clutch pedal is depressed. Tighten nuts to specifications. See TORQUE SPECIFICATIONS table at end of article. Bleed hydraulic system. See BLEEDING HYDRAULIC CLUTCH SYSTEM under IN-VEHICLE SERVICE.

OVERHAUL

NOTE: Information for Commercial Van not available from manufacturer.

MASTER CYLINDER

Disassembly & Inspection (Except Commercial Van) – 1) Pull out reservoir adapter and adapter seal. Pull back dust cover and remove snap ring from cylinder. See Fig. 2. Remove push rod. Remove plunger and spring assembly.

2) Remove spring from front of plunger. Remove seal support, front seal, shim and back seal from plunger. DO NOT damage plunger surface. Clean all parts with clean brake fluid.

3) Inspect cylinder bore and plunger for scratches, ridges or scoring. Inspect dust cover for wear or damage. Replace master cylinder if damaged.

Reassembly – 1) Lubricate NEW seals and cylinder bore with clean brake fluid. Fit NEW back seal into groove in plunger. See Fig. 2. Install shim and NEW front seal on plunger, with flat side against shim. Install seal support and spring.

2) Carefully install plunger assembly into cylinder bore. Depress plunger with push rod, and seat snap ring in groove. Lightly grease inside of dust cover and install. Install NEW adapter seal into master cylinder and press reservoir adapter into place.

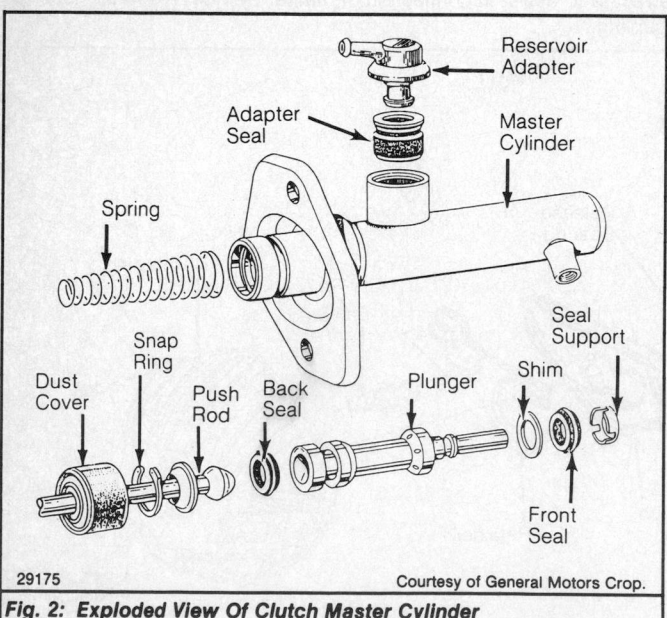

29175   Courtesy of General Motors Crop.

Fig. 2: Exploded View Of Clutch Master Cylinder

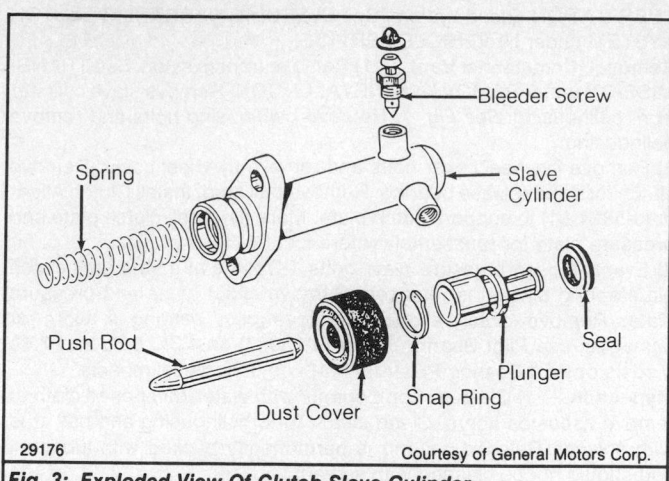

29176   Courtesy of General Motors Corp.

Fig. 3: Exploded View Of Clutch Slave Cylinder

SLAVE CYLINDER

Disassembly & Inspection (Except Commercial Van) – 1) Remove push rod and dust cover. See Fig. 3. Remove snap ring. Remove plunger and spring assembly from cylinder. Remove seal from plunger. DO NOT damage plunger surface.

2) Clean all parts with clean brake fluid. Inspect cylinder bore and plunger for scratches, ridges or scoring. Inspect dust cover for wear or damage. Replace slave cylinder if damaged.

Reassembly – Lubricate NEW seal and cylinder bore with clean brake fluid. Fit NEW seal into groove in plunger. See Fig. 3. Carefully install spring and plunger assembly into cylinder bore. Depress plunger with push rod, and seat snap ring in groove. Lightly grease inside of dust cover and install. Install push rod.

TORQUE SPECIFICATIONS

TORQUE SPECIFICATIONS

Application	Ft. Lbs. (N.m)
Commercial Van	
Bellhousing-To-Engine Bolts	29 (39)
Bellhousing-To-Transmission Bolts	74 (100)
Hose Coupling Bracket Nuts	29 (39)
Master Cylinder Nuts	13 (18)
Pressure Plate-To-Flywheel Bolts	
4.3L & 5.7L	22 (30)
6.2L Diesel	32 (43)
Slave Cylinder Nuts	13 (18)
"C" & "K" Series Blazer & Pickup,	
Sierra, Suburban & Yukon	
Bellhousing-To-Engine Bolts	29 (39)
Bellhousing-To-Transmission Bolts	
NVG 4500 5-Speed	55 (75)
NVG 5LM60 5-Speed	74 (100)
Master Cylinder Nuts	13 (18)
Pressure Plate-To-Flywheel Bolts	
4.3L, 5.0L & 5.7L	22 (30)
6.2L & 6.5L Diesel	32 (43)
7.4L	24 (33)
Slave Cylinder Nuts	13 (18)
"S" & "T" Series Blazer & Pickup,	
Jimmy & Sonoma	
Bellhousing-To-Engine Bolts	55 (75)
Bellhousing-To-Transmission Bolts	55 (75)
Master Cylinder Nuts	13 (18)
Pressure Plate-To-Flywheel Bolts	30 (41)
Slave Cylinder Nuts	13 (18)
	INCH Lbs. (N.m)
"S" & "T" Series Blazer & Pickup,	
Jimmy & Sonoma	
Reservoir Bolts	25 (3)

Astro, Bravada, Commercial Van, Jimmy, Safari, Sierra, Sonoma, Suburban, Syclone, Typhoon, Van, Yukon, "C" & "K" Series Blazer & Pickup, "S" & "T" Series Blazer & Pickup

MODEL IDENTIFICATION

Series [1]	Model
"C"	2WD Pickup, Sierra & Suburban
"G"	RWD Van
"K"	4WD Blazer, Pickup, Sierra, Suburban & Yukon
"L"	All-Wheel Drive Astro & Safari
"M"	2WD Astro & Safari
"P"	Commercial Van/Motorhome
"S"	2WD Blazer, Jimmy, Pickup & Sonoma
"T"	Bravada, 4WD Blazer, Jimmy, Pickup, Sonoma, Syclone & Typhoon

[1] – Vehicle series is fifth character of VIN.

CORPORATE BUILT AXLES

Axle identification code for rear axles is stamped on forward surface of right axle tube, 3-5" outboard of carrier (6-8" on 20 and 30 Series trucks). Location of identification code for front axles is not available from manufacturer.

DANA BUILT AXLES

Identification code is stamped on rear surface of right axle tube. In addition, the 3-digit axle code appears on tape strip attached to outboard end of axle tube.

ROCKWELL BUILT AXLES

Identification code is stamped on carrier assembly.

ASTRO & SAFARI REAR AXLE RATIO IDENTIFICATION

Application & Code	Ratio
7.625" Ring Gear	
RHB, RHC [1], RHL, RHP [1], SGF, SGG [1], SGS, SGT [1], SHD, SHF [1], SHR, SHS [1], ULT, UTM [1], UTT, UTU [1]	3.23:1
RHD, RHF [1], RHM, RHR [1], SGH, SGJ [1], SGU, SGW [1], SHG, SHH [1], SHT, SHU [1], UNT, UTP [1], UTW, UTX [1]	3.42:1
RHG, RHH [1], RHN, RHS [1], SGK, SGX, SGL [1], SGX, SGY [1], SHJ, SHK [1], SHW, SHX [1], UTR, UTS [1], UTY, UTZ [1]	3.73:1
PZK, PZL [1], RHT, RHU [1], SGM, SGN [1], SHL, SHM [1] SHY, SHZ [1]	4.10:1

[1] – With positive traction, limited slip differential.

NOTE: *Front axle on Astro/Safari is balanced with pinion flange modified to act as a harmonic member to reduce driveline vibration. If ring and pinion gear set, pinion flange assembly or pinion bearings need replacement, replace entire axle assembly using appropriate system balanced service axle assembly available from manufacturer.*

CAUTION: *Prior to replacement of axle assembly, it is essential that position of drive shaft relative to all driveline components be observed and marked for reassembly reference. Attach drive shaft to replacement axle first, then to transfer case, and road test. If vibration is noted, reindex drive shaft to transfer case and test drive again.*

"C" SERIES REAR AXLE RATIO IDENTIFICATION

Application & Code	Ratio
8.5" Ring Gear	
TWK, TWN [1], TWR [1], TWS, TWU [1], UUS, UUT [1], XNA, XND [1], XNH, XNK [1], XRS, XRT [1]	3.08:1
TWP [1], TWT, TWW, XNB, XNF [1], XNJ, XNL [1]	3.42:1
TWM, TWR [1], UUU, UUW [1], XNC, XNG [1], TGY	3.73:1
9.5" Ring Gear	
TXW, TXZ [1], RYA, RYF [1], RSY	3.42:1
TXX, TYA [1], RYB, RYG [1]	3.73:1
TYC [1], TYX, TYB [1], RYC, RYH [1], SJA	4.10:1
RYD, RYJ [1]	4.56:1
10.5" Ring Gear	
RYK, RYN [1]	3.42:1
RYL, RYP [1], RZJ, RZM [1], SJM, SZX [1], XUA, XUB [1]	3.73:1
RYM, RYR [1], SJR [1], SJT, SJW [1]	4.10:1
SJP, SJS [1], SJU, SJX [1]	4.56:1
12" Ring Gear	
UXF	4.63:1
UXG	5.13:1

[1] – With positive traction, limited slip differential.

"C/K" SERIES REAR AXLE RATIO IDENTIFICATION

Application & Code	Ratio
10.5" Ring Gear	
XUA, XUB [1], RZJ, RZM [1], SFB, SFF [1], SFJ, SFM, SJM, SZZ	3.73:1
RZH [1], XUC, RZK, RZN [1], SFC, SFG [1], SFK, SFN [1], SFX, SFY [1], SJW [1], SZS	4.10:1
RLK [1], RLZ, RZP [1], SFD, SFH [1], SFL, SFP [1], SFZ, SGA [1]	4.56:1

[1] – With positive traction, limited slip differential.

"G" SERIES REAR AXLE RATIO IDENTIFICATION

Application & Code	Ratio
8.5" Ring Gear	
RKF, RKG [1]	3.08:1
RKH, RKJ [1]	3.42:1
RKK, RKL [1]	3.73:1
9.5" Ring Gear	
RKM, RKU [1]	3.23:1
RKX, RKZ [1]	3.73:1
RKY [1], RLA	4.10:1
RKR, RKW [1]	4.56:1
10.5" Ring Gear	
RMU, RMX [1], SYK, SYP [1]	3.42:1
RMW, RMY [1], RMA, RMC [1], SYL, SYR [1], XSX, XSZ [1]	3.73:1
RLW, RLZ [1], RMB, RMD [1], SYM, SYS [1], XSY, XTA [1]	4.10:1
RMG, RMJ [1], SYN, SYT [1], XTB, XTC [1]	4.56:1

[1] – With positive traction, limited slip differential.

"K" SERIES REAR AXLE RATIO IDENTIFICATION

Application & Code	Ratio
8.5" Ring Gear	
TWX, TXA [1], TXD, TXG [1], TXJ, TXK [1], UUM, UUN [1], UUX, UUY [1], XMN, XNR [1], XNU, XNX [1], TYJ, USJ [1]	3.42:1
PFH, PFM, PFU, PFZ, PFK [1], PFR [1], PFX [1], PGA [1], PGB [1]	3.73:1
TWZ, TXC [1], XNP, XNT [1]	4.10:1
9.5" Ring Gear	
TXN, TXS [1], RYS, RYX [1]	3.42:1
TXP, TXT [1], RYT, RYY [1]	3.73:1
TXR, TXU [1], RYU, RYZ [1]	4.10:1
RYW, RZA [1]	4.56:1
10.5" Ring Gear	
RYK, RYN [1], RZB, RZF [1]	3.42:1
RZC, RZG [1]	3.73:1
RZD, RZH [1], RDN, RDR [1], RLG, RLH [1]	4.10:1
RDP, RDS [1], RLJ, RLK [1]	4.56:1

[1] – With positive traction, limited slip differential.

"K" SERIES FRONT AXLE RATIO IDENTIFICATION

Code	Ratio
ZBK, ZCP, ZGS, ZHW	3.42:1
ZBL, ZCR, ZGT, ZGX, ZHX	3.73:1
ZBM, ZCS, ZGU	4.10:1
ZHZ, ZGZ	4.56:1

"P" SERIES REAR AXLE RATIO IDENTIFICATION

Application & Code	Ratio
10.5" Ring Gear	
HJN, HJS [1], PXR, RPP, PXU [1], SDK, SDN [1], SDR, SDU [1], TJA, TJD [1], TJG [1], TJK [1]	3.73:1
HJP, PXS, RPR, SDL, SDS, SDX, TJB, TJH, TJN	4.10:1
HJR, HJT [1], PXT, PXW, RPS, RPU [1], SDM, SDP, SDT, SDW [1], SDY, SFA [1], SWT, SWX, TJC, TJF, TJJ, TJL [1], TJP, TJS [1]	4.56:1
SWU, SWY	4.88:1
PLX, SWW, RPT, SDZ	5.13:1
10.5" Ring Gear (Dana)	
SHL, THX, TZA	4.63:1
11.5" Ring Gear	
SLJ, TFT, TFU, THY, TZB	5.13:1
12.0" Ring Gear	
RLL, TFS, UZR	5.13:1

[1] – With positive traction, limited slip differential.

"S" & "T" SERIES REAR AXLE RATIO IDENTIFICATION

Application & Code	Ratio
7.5" Ring Gear	
GAJ, UUL	3.42:1
GAK, HZP [1], UBB, UBU	3.73:1
GAL, HZR [1], UBC, UBD [1]	4.11:1
7.625" Ring Gear	
RNB, TFY, THF	2.73:1
KUK, KUN, RNC, RND [1], RNH, RPW, RPZ, RRC, RRG, TFZ [1], TGA, TGB, TGC, TGD, THG, THH [1], THJ, THK, THL, UBJ, UBR, UBY, UCF	3.08:1
KUR, KUS [1], PLM [1], PMM, RNF, RNG, RNJ, RNK [1], RPX, RPY [1], RRA, RRB [1], RRD, RRF [1], RRH, TGF, TGH, TGJ, TGK, TGL, TGM, THM, THN [1], THP, THR [1], THS, THT [1], THU, THW [1], UBK, UBL [1], UBS, UBT [1], UBZ, UCA [1], UCG, UCH [1]	3.42:1

[1] – With positive traction, limited slip differential.

"T" SERIES FRONT AXLE RATIO IDENTIFICATION

Code	Ratio
ZAH	3.08:1
SKY, ZAD, ZAK, ZXC, ZYD, ZYH	3.42:1
SKZ, ZYF	3.73:1

Lumina APV, Silhouette, Trans Sport

DESCRIPTION

Drive axles are completely flexible assemblies consisting of an inner and an outer Constant Velocity (CV) joint connected by an axle shaft. *See Fig. 1* Inner tripot CV joint is capable of moving in and out. Outer ball/cage CV joint is flexible but cannot move in and out.

All drive axles, except left inboard end on A/T models, incorporate a male spline and interlock with transaxle gears through the use of barrel-type snap rings. Left inboard shaft attachment on A/T models uses a female spline. Female spline is installed over a stub shaft extending out from transaxle.

Drive axle spline end mating with knuckle and hub assembly is a helical spline. Spline provides a tight press fit and assures end play does not exist between hub bearing and drive shaft assembly. Intermediate shaft assemblies are used on M/T models.

REMOVAL & INSTALLATION

DRIVE AXLES

Removal & Installation – 1) Raise and support vehicle. Remove tire and wheel assembly. Remove tie rod end cotter pin and tie rod nut. Separate tie rod end from steering knuckle.

2) Remove axle nut and washer. Insert a long punch through brake caliper and into brake rotor fins to aid in axle nut removal. Discard axle nut. Remove lower ball joint pinch bolt. Install modified (inner tabs removed) Seal Protector (J-34754) over drive axle seal.

NOTE: Drive Axle Seal Protector (J-34754) should be modified and installed on any drive axle before performing services on or near drive axle. Failure to do so may result in seal damage and possible future joint failure.

---

3) Separate ball joint from steering knuckle. To remove axle shaft from hub/bearing assembly, press axle shaft inward using Axle Remover (J-28733). DO NOT allow axle shaft to drop or hang freely when removing from hub/bearing assembly.

4) Remove axle remover. Remove axle shaft from transaxle using slide hammer. To install axle shaft, reverse removal procedure. Seat drive axle into transaxle by placing screwdriver into groove on joint housing and tapping until axle is seated. Use a new axle shaft nut. Tighten all nuts and bolts to specification. See TORQUE SPECIFICATIONS table.

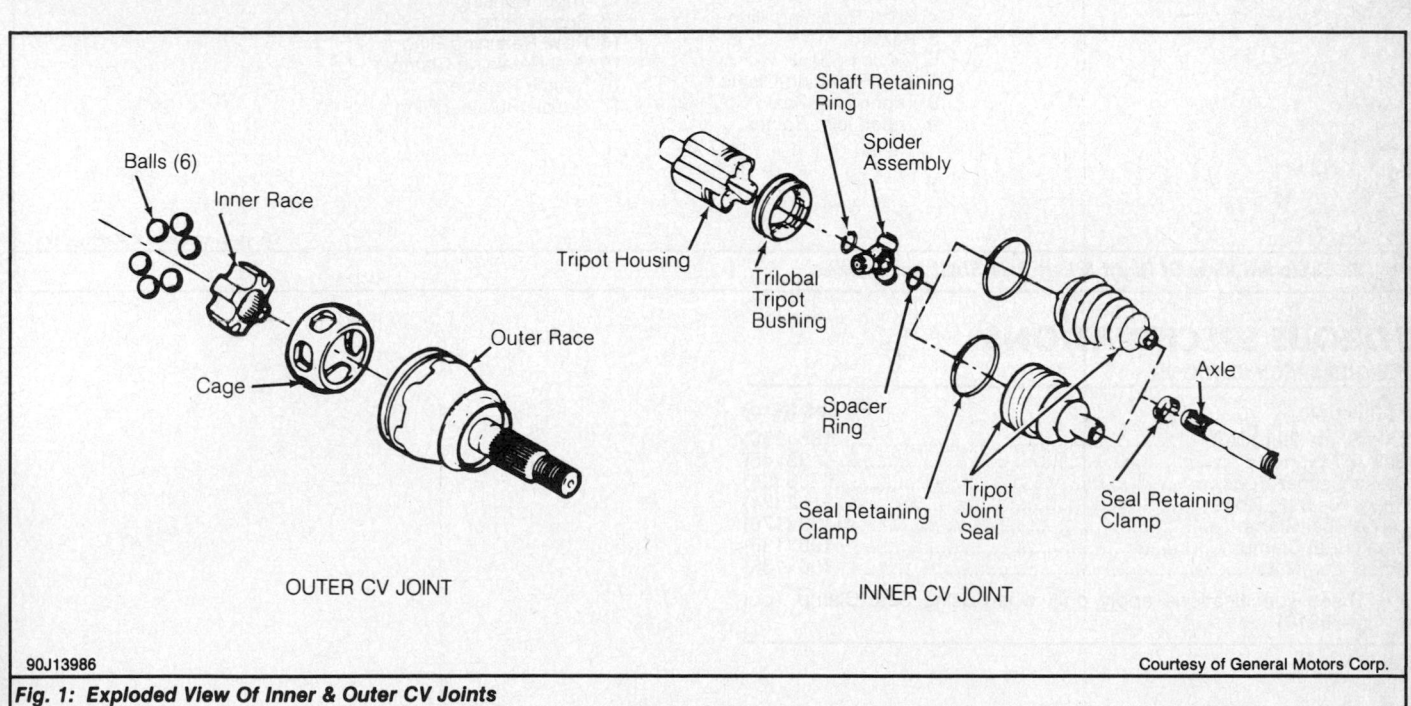

Fig. 1: Exploded View Of Inner & Outer CV Joints

90J13986

Courtesy of General Motors Corp.

OVERHAUL

NOTE: For exploded view of axle shaft assemblies, see Fig. 2.

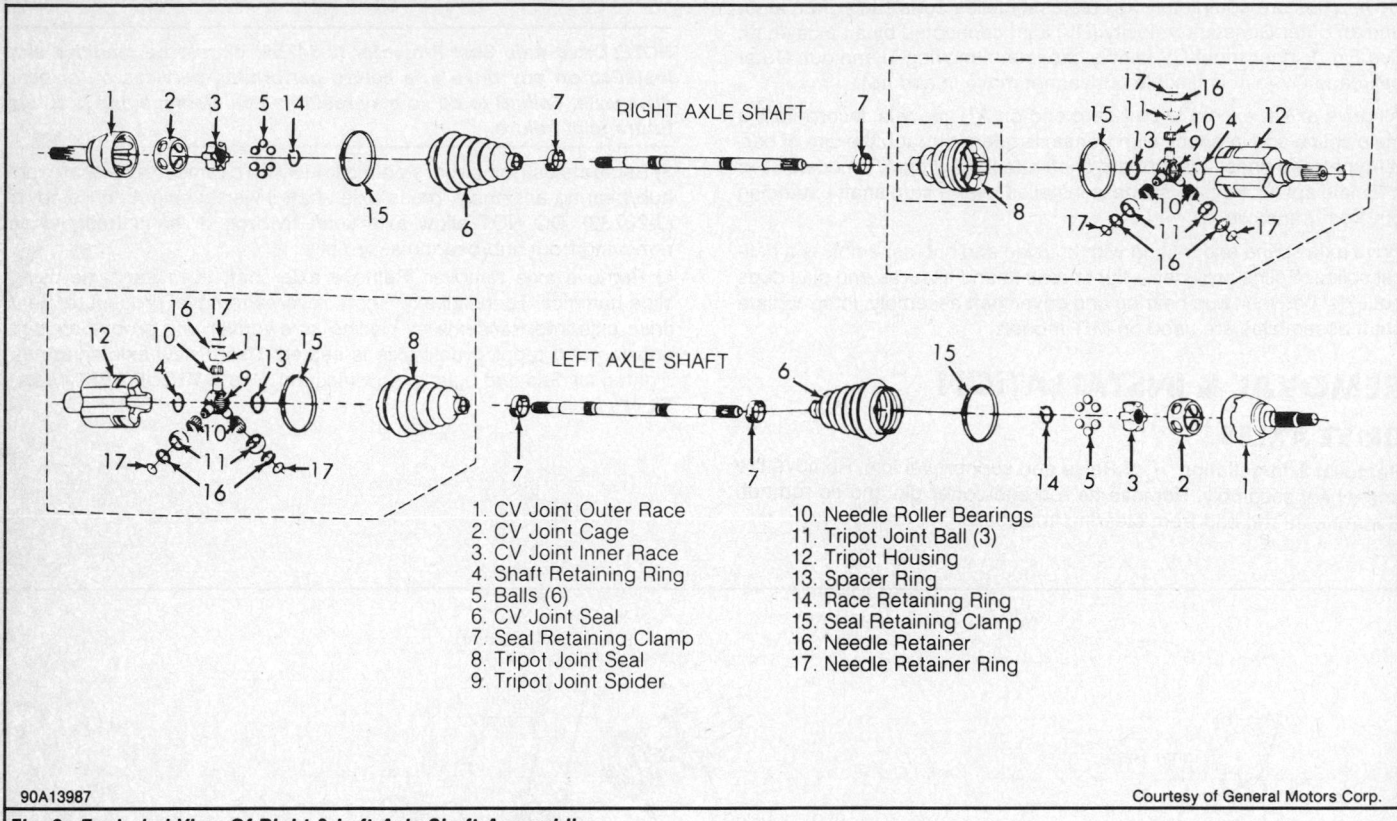

1. CV Joint Outer Race
2. CV Joint Cage
3. CV Joint Inner Race
4. Shaft Retaining Ring
5. Balls (6)
6. CV Joint Seal
7. Seal Retaining Clamp
8. Tripot Joint Seal
9. Tripot Joint Spider
10. Needle Roller Bearings
11. Tripot Joint Ball (3)
12. Tripot Housing
13. Spacer Ring
14. Race Retaining Ring
15. Seal Retaining Clamp
16. Needle Retainer
17. Needle Retainer Ring

90A13987

Courtesy of General Motors Corp.

Fig. 2: Exploded View Of Right & Left Axle Shaft Assemblies

TORQUE SPECIFICATIONS
TORQUE SPECIFICATIONS

Application	Ft. Lbs (N.m)
Axle Shaft (Hub) Nut	185 (250)
Ball Joint Pinch Bolt	33 (45)
Brake Caliper Bolts	38 (51)
Hub & Bearing Bolts	62 (84)
Large Seal Clamp	[1] 130 (176)
Small Seal Clamp	[1] 100 (136)
Wheel Lug Nuts	100 (136)

[1] – These specifications apply only when using Seal Clamp Tool (J-35910).

Blazer, Pickup, Sierra, Suburban, Yukon

DESCRIPTION

Front axle assembly on "K" Series models uses an 8 1/4" ring gear for K15/25, or 9 1/4" ring gear for K35. There are minor differences between the 2 assemblies.

Both front axle assemblies have an electric 4WD engage/disengage feature which allows shifting in or out of 4WD while vehicle is in motion (under most conditions). The 4WD feature is "shifted" by a thermal actuator solenoid mounted to right axle tube. See Fig. 4 or 5.

The 4WD thermal actuator solenoid contains a coil, fluid, and plunger. When coil is electrically heated by 4WD in/out switch, the fluid changes to a gas and extends plunger to engage front axle.

Right side of axle assembly consists of a solid axle shaft which rides inside of a stationary axle tube. A short stub shaft with CV joint attached is bolted to right inner axle shaft flange. Left drive axle shaft consists of a flexible drive shaft using an inner tripod joint and outer CV joint. Left axle tripod joint housing bolts to axle carrier output shaft drive flange. CV joint splined/threaded shaft on outer end of drive axle shaft slips through steering knuckle/hub assembly. See Fig. 2.

Front axle assembly differential uses a conventional ring and pinion gear set to transmit the driving force of engine to the front wheels. Ring and pinion gear set transfers driving force at a 90 degree angle from front drive shaft to drive axle shafts/CV joints.

AXLE RATIO & IDENTIFICATION

To identify vehicle differential ring gear size and drive axle ratio, see AXLE RATIO IDENTIFICATION article.

LUBRICATION

Fill differential with 80W or 80W-90 GL-5 gear lubricant to edge of filler hole when vehicle is in level, running height position.

LUBRICATION CAPACITIES

Series	Qts. (L)
K15/25	1.75 (1.66)
K35	2.25 (2.13)

TROUBLE SHOOTING

NOTE: See TROUBLE SHOOTING article in GENERAL INFORMATION.

REMOVAL & INSTALLATION

WARNING: When battery is disconnected, vehicle computer and memory systems may lose memory data. Driveability problems may exist until computer systems have completed a relearn cycle. See COMPUTER RELEARN PROCEDURES article in GENERAL INFORMATION before disconnecting battery.

CARRIER CASE MOUNTING BUSHINGS

Removal & Installation – Remove front axle assembly. See FRONT AXLE ASSEMBLY under REMOVAL & INSTALLATION. Using Carrier Bushing Remover/Installer (J-36616), press bushing out of carrier housing. See Fig. 1. To install, reverse tool and press new bushing into housing. Repeat procedure for other mounting bushing.

FRONT AXLE ASSEMBLY

Removal & Installation – 1) Disconnect battery negative cable. Raise and support vehicle. Remove wheels. Remove 6 right stub shaft-to-axle flange bolts. Remove 6 left axle shaft-to-output shaft flange bolts. Wire left axle shaft and right stub shaft aside.

2) Disconnect drive shaft at pinion yoke. Wrap tape around all "U"joint caps to secure in position. Wire drive shaft aside. Disconnect harness connectors for indicator light switch and actuator solenoid at right axle tube. Disconnect vent hose at axle. Remove bolts securing right axle tube to frame rail.

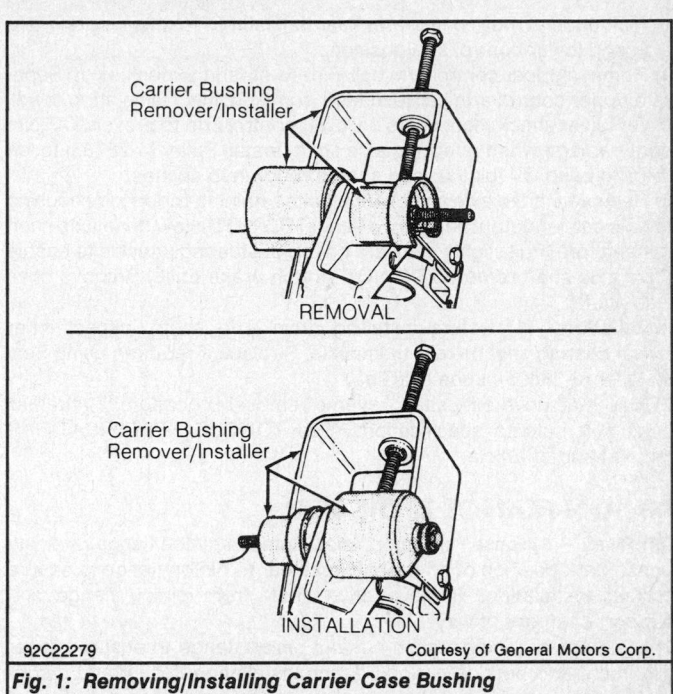

Carrier Bushing Remover/Installer

REMOVAL

Carrier Bushing Remover/Installer

INSTALLATION

92C22279

Courtesy of General Motors Corp.

Fig. 1: Removing/Installing Carrier Case Bushing

3) Remove lower mounting bolt from axle assembly. Disconnect right side inner tie rod from steering linkage rod. Remove engine oil filter (if necessary). Support axle assembly using appropriate transmission jack. Remove upper axle assembly mounting bolt. Lower transmission jack and remove axle assembly from vehicle.

4) To install axle assembly, reverse removal procedure. Tighten all nuts and bolts to specifications. See TORQUE SPECIFICATIONS table at end of article.

LEFT DRIVE AXLE SHAFT

Removal – 1) Raise and support vehicle. Remove skid plate (if equipped). Remove wheel. Remove stabilizer bar from lower control arm. If both ends of stabilizer bar are being removed, DO NOT mix left and right stabilizer bar components. See Fig. 2.

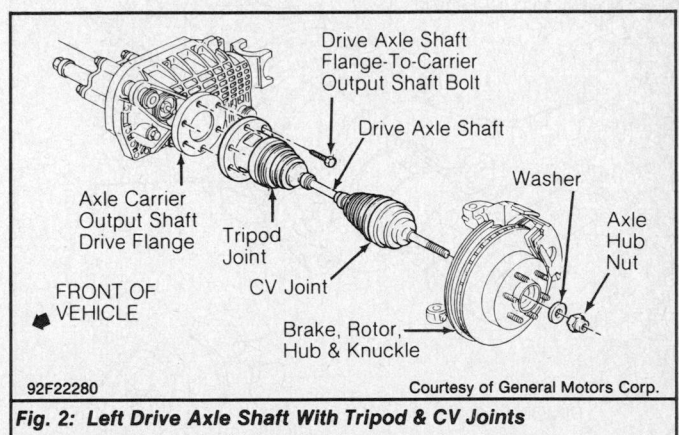

Drive Axle Shaft Flange-To-Carrier Output Shaft Bolt

Drive Axle Shaft

Washer

Axle Carrier Output Shaft Drive Flange

Tripod Joint

CV Joint

Axle Hub Nut

FRONT OF VEHICLE

Brake, Rotor, Hub & Knuckle

92F22280

Courtesy of General Motors Corp.

Fig. 2: Left Drive Axle Shaft With Tripod & CV Joints

CAUTION: DO NOT use wedge type remover tool on tie rod end. Damage to tie rod end will result.

2) Disconnect left outer tie rod end from steering knuckle using Steering Linkage Puller (J-24319-01 or J-6627-A). Wire tie rod end aside. Insert a long drift through caliper and into disc rotor vanes to prevent rotation. Remove axle hub nut and washer from drive axle shaft CV joint. Loosen 6 drive axle shaft flange bolts retaining tripod joint housing to axle carrier output shaft drive flange.

3) Remove brake line bracket from upper control arm. Remove shock absorber from lower control arm mounting bracket. Install floor stand

or jack under lower control arm near ball joint to maintain spring tension and lower control arm position.

4) Remove upper control arm ball joint-to-steering knuckle nut. Separate upper control arm ball joint stud from knuckle. Using shop towel, cover lower shock mount ears on lower control arm to prevent CV joint boot damage when removing axle shaft. Install Puller (J-28733) to left rotor to push CV joint splined shaft through hub splines.

5) Remove 6 drive axle shaft flange bolts retaining tripod joint housing to axle carrier output shaft drive flange. DO NOT allow drive axle shaft to hang free. Pull slightly outward on top of steering knuckle to enable drive axle shaft removal. DO NOT stretch brake hose. Remove drive axle shaft.

Installation – 1) Before installing drive axle shaft, inspect inner wheel bearing seal on rear of knuckle. Replace if required using Seal Installer (J-36605). Lube seal lip.

2) To install drive axle shaft, reverse removal procedure. Tighten all bolts and nuts to specifications. See TORQUE SPECIFICATIONS table at end of article.

PINION FLANGE & OIL SEAL

Removal – 1) Raise vehicle on hoist. Remove pinion flange retaining bolts. Mark position of drive shaft yoke ear to pinion flange to ensure correct installation. Remove drive shaft from pinion flange and support shaft out of way.

2) Scribe mark pinion, pinion nut and pinion flange to ensure proper alignment and bearing preload during installation. Count and record number of exposed threads on pinion. Using pinion flange holder of Pinion Flange Remover Set (J-8614-01), hold pinion flange stationary. Using large socket and wrench, remove pinion flange nut and washer.

3) Place drain pan under pinion area of differential carrier. Insert pinion flange remover through pinion flange holder and rotate 90°. Tighten bolt to remove pinion flange. *See Fig. 3.* Pry pinion seal from housing. DO NOT damage differential carrier or seal running surface on pinion when removing pinion oil seal.

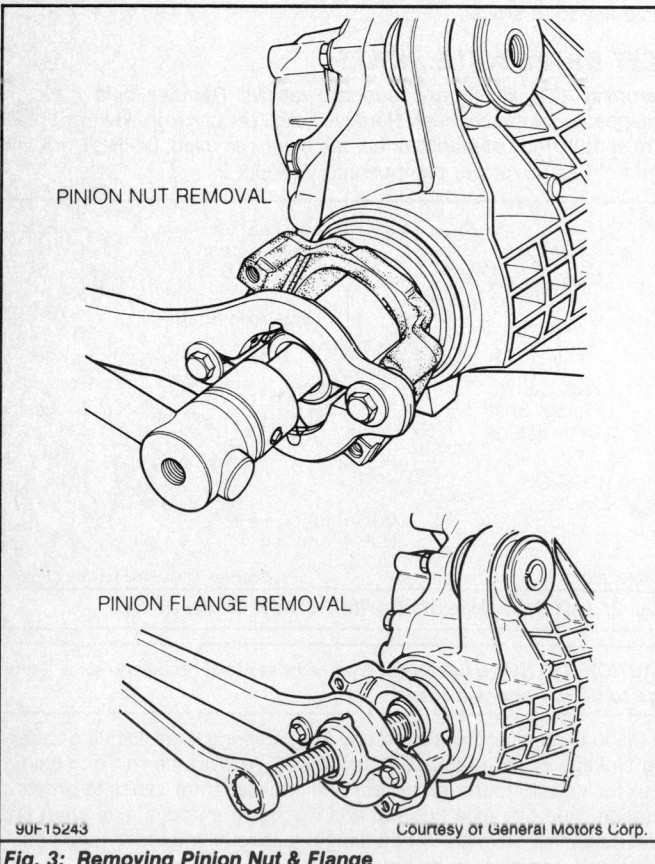

PINION NUT REMOVAL

PINION FLANGE REMOVAL

90F15243

Courtesy of General Motors Corp.

Fig. 3: Removing Pinion Nut & Flange

4) Clean pinion flange in solvent and inspect seal surface of pinion flange for nicks, burrs or damage such as a groove worn into pinion flange by oil seal. Repair or replace as necessary.

CAUTION: DO NOT use "hard-faced" hammer to drive/install flange onto pinion shaft. Ring gear, pinion and flange will be damaged.

Installation – 1) Lubricate pinion flange seal running surface. Lubricate lip of oil seal. Install oil seal using Seal Installer (J-39366). Ensure seal is driven in straight or aluminum housing will be severely damaged.

2) Install new dust deflector onto pinion flange and stake in 3 places. Install pinion flange onto pinion shaft aligning marks made before removal. If required, use only "soft" faced (rubber) hammer to tap flange onto pinion.

3) Install pinion nut and tighten to no more than position marked on pinion shaft and flange. Note number of threads exposed. Tighten pinion nut no more than 1/16" beyond alignment marks. If this marked position is exceeded by more than 1/16", remove pinion and install NEW collapsible sleeve. Install drive shaft and tighten bolts to **15 ft. lbs. (20 N.m)**. Check gear oil level.

RIGHT AXLE TUBE & INNER AXLE SHAFT

Removal – 1) Disconnect battery negative cable. Raise and support vehicle. Remove skid plate (if equipped). Remove wheel. Remove stabilizer bar from both lower control arms. DO NOT mix left and right stabilizer bar components.

2) Disconnect right outer tie rod end from steering knuckle using Steering Linkage Puller (J-24319-01 or J-6627-A). Wire right outer tie rod linkage aside.

3) Remove stub axle shaft flange bolts from inner axle shaft flange. Turn right wheel outward to loosen stub axle shaft from inner axle shaft flange. Push stub axle shaft toward front of vehicle and wire aside.

4) Disconnect harness connectors for indicator light switch and actuator solenoid at right axle tube. Place drain pan under drive axle. Remove drain plug to drain lubricant. Remove bolts retaining axle tube to right frame.

5) Remove bolts attaching axle tube to axle carrier. Remove axle tube by pulling away from axle carrier to clear shift shaft. While pulling axle tube away, note shifter fork spring location to keep from losing it off end of shifter shaft when removing axle tube. Ensure that open end of tube is pointed upward.

Installation – 1) If internal carrier components have been changed, see reassembly steps **4)** through **9)** of RIGHT AXLE TUBE ASSEMBLY under OVERHAUL. If internal carrier components have NOT been changed, clean mating surfaces thoroughly to remove any oil residue. Ensure shift shaft spring is in position.

2) Apply sealant (GM 1052942 or Loctite 518) to carrier sealing surfaces. Install axle tube to carrier housing. Install 6 axle tube retaining bolts and tighten to **30 ft. lbs. (40 N.m)**. Connect stub shaft to inner shaft flange and install 6 bolts. Using a criss-cross pattern, tighten bolts evenly to **59 ft. lbs. (80 N.m)**.

3) Raise axle tube and install frame-to-tube mounting bolts. On K15/25, tighten nuts to **75 ft. lbs. (102 N.m)**. On K35, tighten nuts to **110 ft. lbs. (149 N.m)**. Install tie rod end to steering knuckle. Tighten tie rod nut to **35 ft. lbs (48 N.m)**.

4) Install stabilizer bar and hardware. Tighten stabilizer bracket-to-frame bolts to **24 ft. lbs. (33 N.m)**. Tighten all remaining stabilizer hardware to **13 ft. lbs. (18 N.m)**.

5) Reconnect harness connectors for indicator light switch and actuator solenoid at right axle tube. Install differential carrier drain plug and tighten to **24 ft. lbs. (33 N.m)**. Remove differential carrier filler plug and fill drive axle to hole level with SAE 80W-90 GL5 gear lubricant. Tighten fill plug to **24 ft. lbs. (33 N.m)**. To complete installation, reverse removal procedure. Recheck gear oil when vehicle is on level ground.

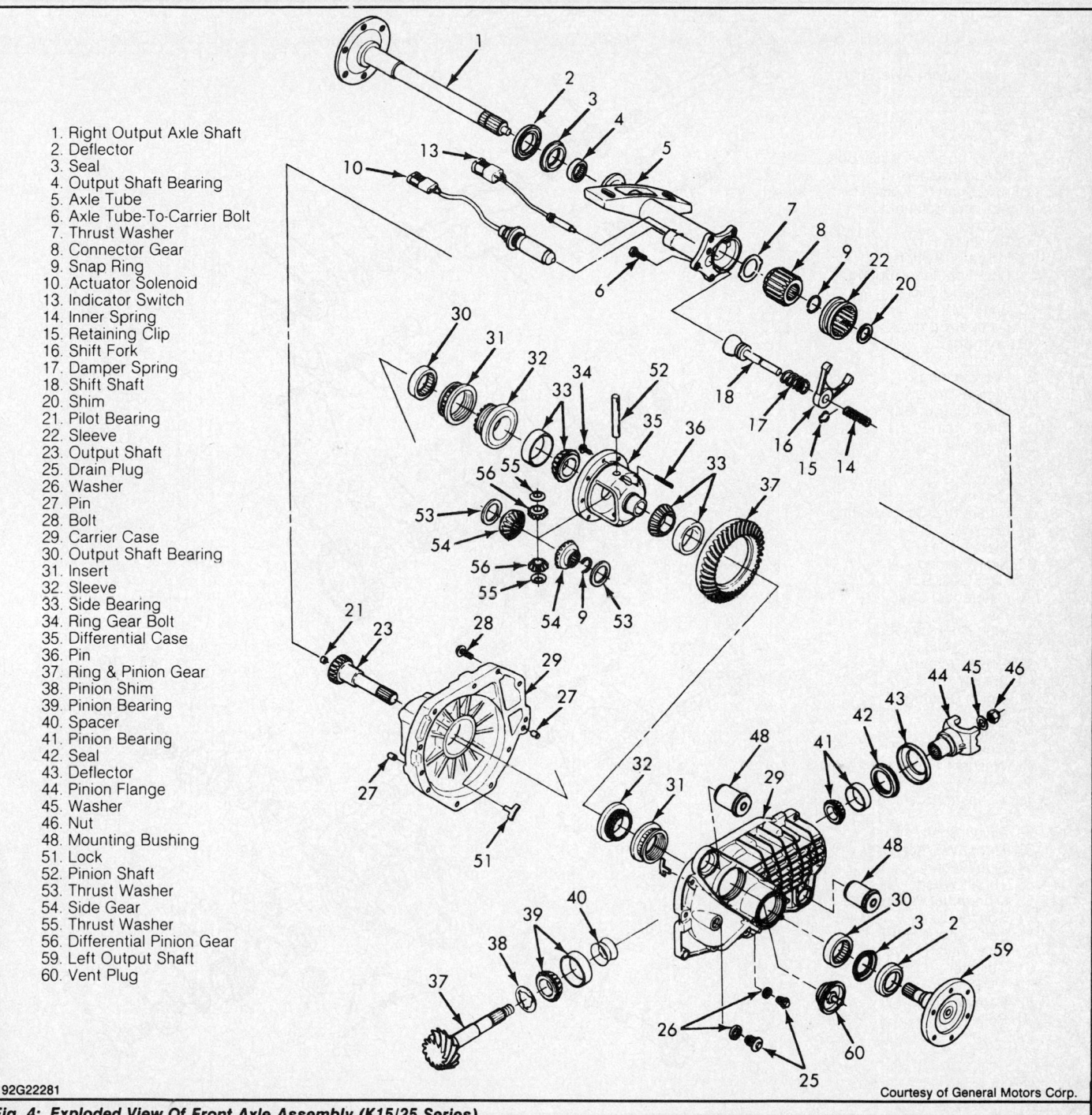

1. Right Output Axle Shaft
2. Deflector
3. Seal
4. Output Shaft Bearing
5. Axle Tube
6. Axle Tube-To-Carrier Bolt
7. Thrust Washer
8. Connector Gear
9. Snap Ring
10. Actuator Solenoid
13. Indicator Switch
14. Inner Spring
15. Retaining Clip
16. Shift Fork
17. Damper Spring
18. Shift Shaft
20. Shim
21. Pilot Bearing
22. Sleeve
23. Output Shaft
25. Drain Plug
26. Washer
27. Pin
28. Bolt
29. Carrier Case
30. Output Shaft Bearing
31. Insert
32. Sleeve
33. Side Bearing
34. Ring Gear Bolt
35. Differential Case
36. Pin
37. Ring & Pinion Gear
38. Pinion Shim
39. Pinion Bearing
40. Spacer
41. Pinion Bearing
42. Seal
43. Deflector
44. Pinion Flange
45. Washer
46. Nut
48. Mounting Bushing
51. Lock
52. Pinion Shaft
53. Thrust Washer
54. Side Gear
55. Thrust Washer
56. Differential Pinion Gear
59. Left Output Shaft
60. Vent Plug

92G22281

Courtesy of General Motors Corp.

Fig. 4: Exploded View Of Front Axle Assembly (K15/25 Series)

RIGHT SIDE OUTPUT SHAFT PILOT BEARING

Removal & Installation – Remove right axle tube and inner axle shaft assembly. See RIGHT AXLE TUBE & INNER AXLE SHAFT. Remove shim (No. 20). See Fig. 4 or 5. Remove pilot bearing using Pilot Bearing Remover (J-34011). Lubricate new pilot bearing with wheel bearing grease. Install pilot bearing using Pilot Bearing Installer (J-33842). Install shim (No. 20). To complete installation, reverse removal procedure.

OVERHAUL

RIGHT AXLE TUBE ASSEMBLY

Disassembly – **1)** Place mounting flange of axle tube assembly in a vise. Remove actuator and engagement switch from tube. Remove shift shaft, springs, shift fork, and differential sleeve (No. 22). See Fig. 4 or 5. Remove snap ring, connector gear and thrust washer from axle shaft.

2) Tap on flange end of axle shaft using a soft mallet to remove axle shaft from tube. DO NOT hammer on pilot bearing stem end of axle shaft, severe damage will result. Using a screwdriver, pry out oil seal.

3) To remove axle bearing from tube, use Bearing Remover (J-29369-1) for K15/25 or (J-29369-2) for K35. Using appropriate puller and slide hammer, remove axle bearing.

Cleaning & Inspection – Wash all parts in solvent and dry with compressed air. Inspect all parts for excessive wear and scoring. Inspect connector gear and axle shaft splines for wear, cracks and twisted splines.

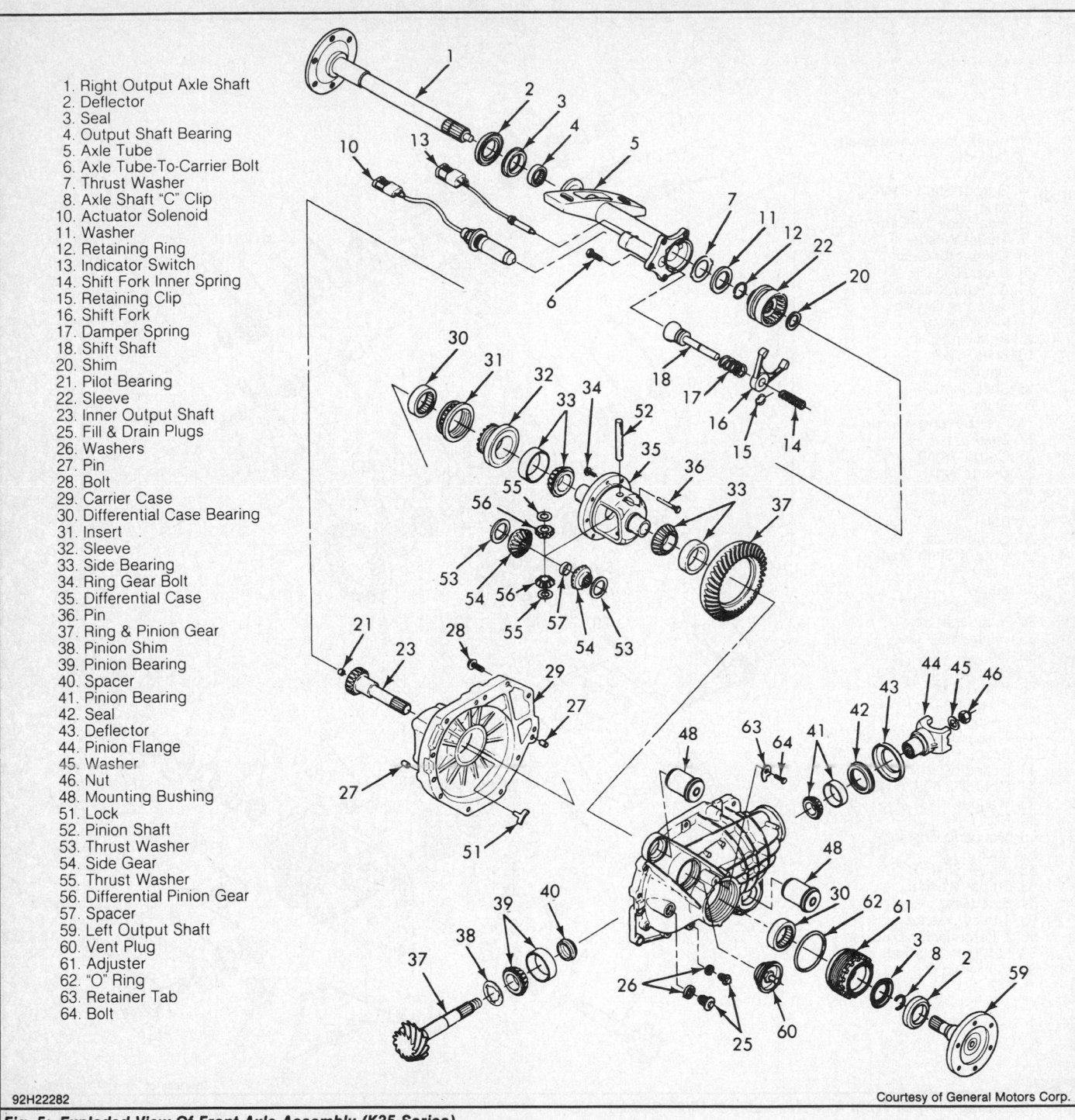

1. Right Output Axle Shaft
2. Deflector
3. Seal
4. Output Shaft Bearing
5. Axle Tube
6. Axle Tube-To-Carrier Bolt
7. Thrust Washer
8. Axle Shaft "C" Clip
10. Actuator Solenoid
11. Washer
12. Retaining Ring
13. Indicator Switch
14. Shift Fork Inner Spring
15. Retaining Clip
16. Shift Fork
17. Damper Spring
18. Shift Shaft
20. Shim
21. Pilot Bearing
22. Sleeve
23. Inner Output Shaft
25. Fill & Drain Plugs
26. Washers
27. Pin
28. Bolt
29. Carrier Case
30. Differential Case Bearing
31. Insert
32. Sleeve
33. Side Bearing
34. Ring Gear Bolt
35. Differential Case
36. Pin
37. Ring & Pinion Gear
38. Pinion Shim
39. Pinion Bearing
40. Spacer
41. Pinion Bearing
42. Seal
43. Deflector
44. Pinion Flange
45. Washer
46. Nut
48. Mounting Bushing
51. Lock
52. Pinion Shaft
53. Thrust Washer
54. Side Gear
55. Thrust Washer
56. Differential Pinion Gear
57. Spacer
59. Left Output Shaft
60. Vent Plug
61. Adjuster
62. "O" Ring
63. Retainer Tab
64. Bolt

92H22282

Courtesy of General Motors Corp.

Fig. 5: Exploded View Of Front Axle Assembly (K35 Series)

Reassembly – 1) Clean gasket surfaces on axle tube and carrier housing. Lubricate new bearing using wheel bearing grease. Using Bearing Installer J-36609, install axle bearing into tube. Lightly coat lip of new seal with grease. Install seal using Seal Installer (J-36600) for K15/25 or (J-22833) for K35.

2) Install deflector to axle shaft (if removed) and insert axle shaft into axle tube. Install thrust washer, ensuring tube slots align with tabs on washer. See Fig. 6. Use wheel bearing grease to hold thrust washer in place.

3) On K15/25, drive connector gear onto end of axle using a plastic hammer. Install snap ring. On K35, install washer and snap ring. Ensure snap ring seats properly in groove. On all models, an output shaft shim (No. 20) of proper thickness must be selected if any of the following parts have been changed. If no parts have been changed, go to step 6).

- Differential Case
- Carrier Connector (K15/25)
- Output Shaft
- Ring and Pinion
- Inner Shaft
- Axle Tube
- Carrier Case
- Bearings

4) If any of the listed parts have been changed, use grease to hold ORIGINAL shim in place. Assemble axle tube and inner shaft assembly to carrier. Use no sealer at this time. Tighten bolts to **30 ft. lbs. (40 N.m).**

5) Install dial indicator onto axle tube with dial indicator shaft at right angle to axle output shaft flange. Check axle shaft end play by pushing

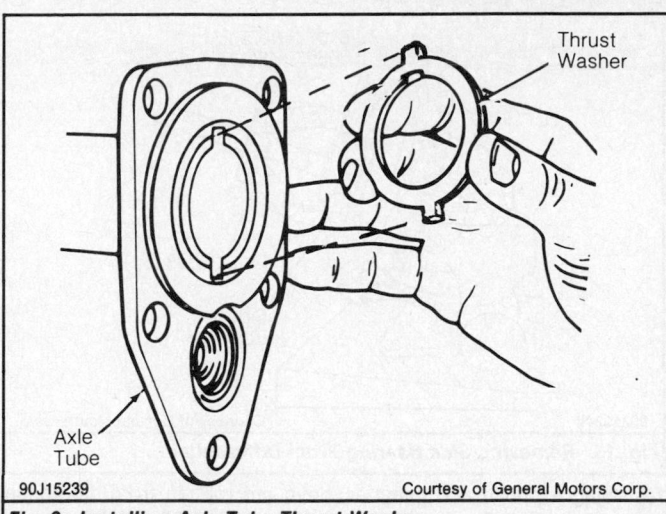

90J15239   Courtesy of General Motors Corp.

Fig. 6: Installing Axle Tube Thrust Washer

and pulling in and out on axle shaft. Maximum end play is .001-.020" (.03-.51 mm). If end play is incorrect, select shim as necessary to bring end play within specification. Remove axle tube from carrier.

6) Ensure axle tube and carrier case sealing surfaces are clean. Install correct shim onto output shaft using wheel bearing grease. Slip damper spring onto shift shaft. Slide shift fork onto shift shaft, ensuring damper spring fits into indentation in shift fork.

7) Install clip, ensuring clip seats properly in shift shaft indentation. Install fork tension spring on shift shaft. Insert shift fork into groove in differential sleeve. Install shift fork assembly into tube assembly at same time installing sleeve onto connector gear (K15/25) or axle shaft splines (K35).

8) Apply a bead of appropriate sealant (GM 1052942 or Loctite 518) to axle tube sealing surface. Assemble axle tube to carrier case. Install axle tube-to-carrier bolts and tighten to specifications. See TORQUE SPECIFICATIONS table at end of article.

9) Inspect shift mechanism operation by inserting a drift into shift actuator hole on axle tube. Rotate axle shaft flange while moving the shift mechanism back and forth with drift. Shift mechanism should work smoothly without binding.

10) Apply appropriate sealant (GM 1052942 or Loctite 518) to threads of actuator solenoid and install solenoid onto axle tube. Repeat procedure with switch assembly.

FRONT AXLE ASSEMBLY

Disassembly – 1) Remove axle carrier. See FRONT AXLE ASSEMBLY under REMOVAL & INSTALLATION. Remove actuator solenoid and indicator switch from right axle tube. Remove tube and inner axle shaft assembly. See RIGHT AXLE TUBE & INNER AXLE SHAFT under REMOVAL & INSTALLATION.

2) Remove shift shaft assembly consisting of sleeve, damper spring, shift fork, clip and inner spring. See Fig. 4 or 5. Remove shim (No.20) and output shaft from right side of carrier assembly. Remove left out-

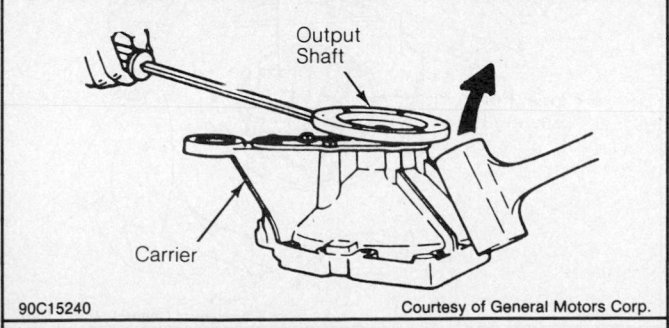

90C15240   Courtesy of General Motors Corp.

Fig. 7: Removing Left Output Flange

put flange from carrier assembly by prying on one side with a screwdriver while simultaneously tapping outward on other side with a soft faced hammer. See Fig. 7. Remove deflector from output flange.

3) Pry out left output flange seal with a screwdriver. Remove left and right output shaft bearings using Bearing Remover (J-29369-1) for K15/25 or (J-29369-2) for K35. Remove bolts holding carrier halves together. Tap on lugs provided to separate carrier halves.

4) Pry up on left and right side bearing locks (right side only on K35) and remove differential assembly from carrier. See Fig. 4. On K35, remove adjuster plug lock and bolt on outer left half of carrier. See Fig. 8.

5) Using Sleeve Adjuster (J-36599), rotate sleeve and push side bearings out of bores (do right side only on K35). See Fig. 9. On K35 left side bearing; remove adjuster plug, bearing and "O" ring from left side of carrier by rotating adjuster plug using Adjuster Plug Remover (J-36615). See Fig. 9.

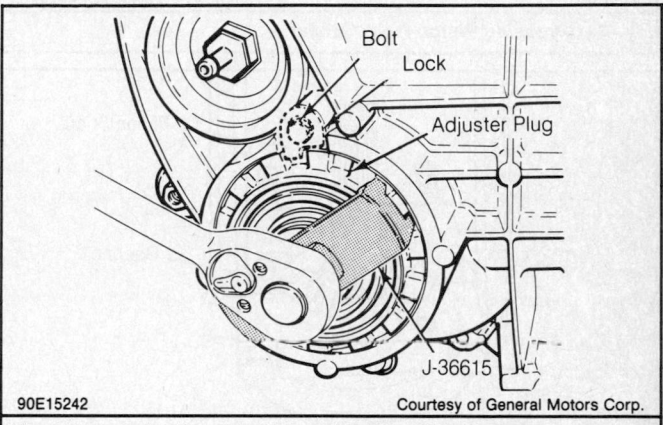

90E15242   Courtesy of General Motors Corp.

Fig. 8: Removing Bearing Using Adjuster Plug Remover

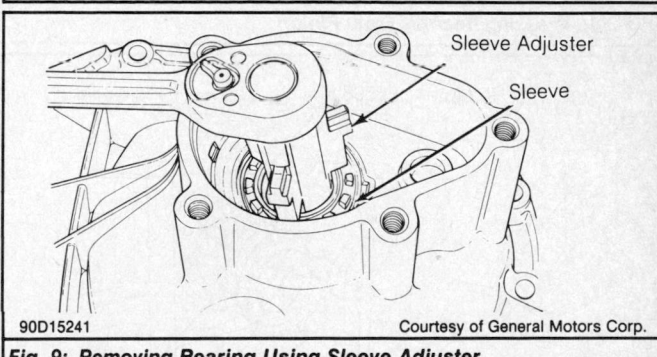

90D15241   Courtesy of General Motors Corp.

Fig. 9: Removing Bearing Using Sleeve Adjuster

6) Using Pinion Flange Remover Set (J-8614-01), hold pinion flange stationary and remove pinion nut, flat washer and pinion flange. See Fig. 3. Remove deflector from pinion. Mount left carrier case half in Holding Fixture from Pinion Service Tool Set (J-36598). See Fig. 10. Press pinion from case. Remove pinion with attached shim, inner bearing and spacer as an assembly. Remove collapsible spacer from pinion.

7) Using Pinion Bearing Remover (J-8612-B) for K15/25 or (J-36606) for K35, press bearing from pinion. See Fig. 11. Remove shim(s) from pinion, keeping shims in order.

8) Using holding fixture and Pinion Service Tool Set (J-36598), remove seal and outer bearing from left half of carrier. Use Adapter Plate (J-36598-6), remove bearing races using same service tool set. See Fig. 12.

9) Using Puller (J-22888-D) and Adapter (J-8107-2) for K15/25 or (J-36597) for K35, remove side bearings from differential case assembly. See Fig. 13. Remove ring gear bolts. Ring gear bolts are left-hand thread. Using a brass drift, drive ring gear from differential case. DO NOT pry ring gear from differential case. This will damage ring gear and differential case.

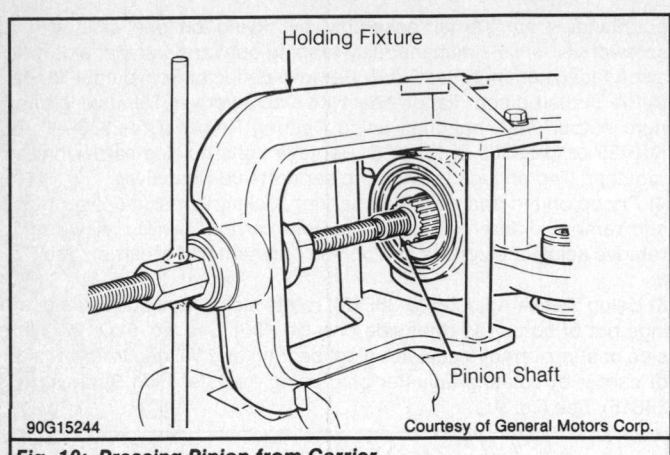

Fig. 10: Pressing Pinion from Carrier

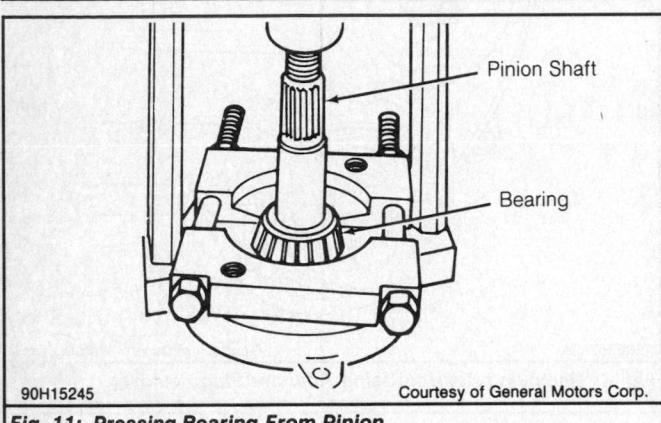

Fig. 11: Pressing Bearing From Pinion

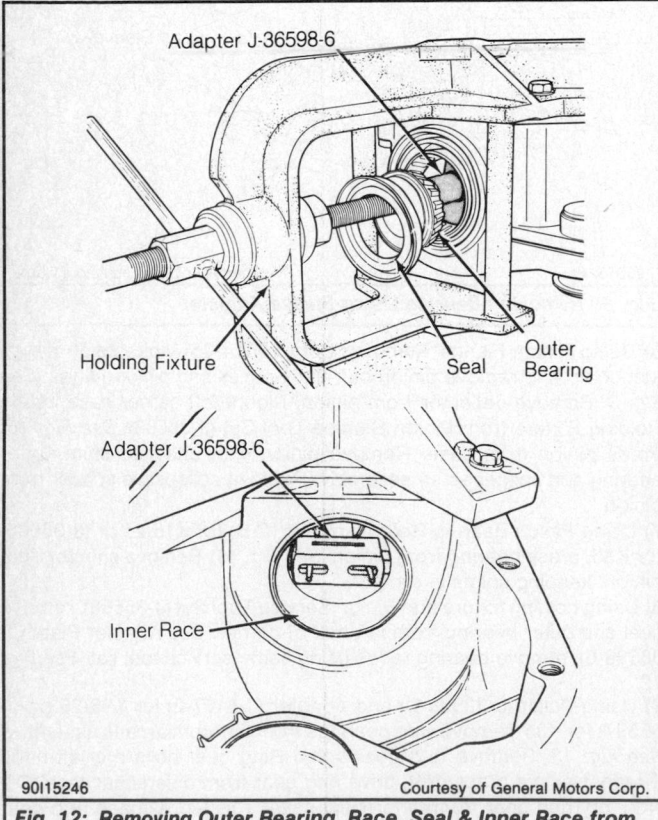

Fig. 12: Removing Outer Bearing, Race, Seal & Inner Race from Carrier

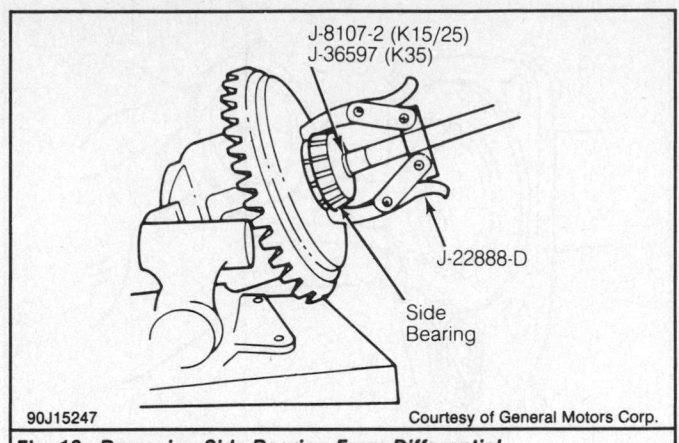

Fig. 13: Removing Side Bearing From Differential

10) Using a punch and hammer, drive out roll pin from differential pinion gear shaft. Remove pinion gear shaft. On K35, a bolt is used in place of a roll pin. Roll pinion gears and thrust washers out of differential case.

11) Remove side gears and thrust washers, marking side gears and differential case left and right for reassembly reference. On K35, remove spacer. Using a 6-point socket, remove vent plug. Upper and lower carrier mounting bushings should be replaced using Remover/Installer (J-36616).

Cleaning & Inspection – Clean all parts in cleaning solvent. Inspect all parts for excessive wear. Replace as required.

Reassembly – 1) To install pinion bearing races, install left carrier case to Holding Fixture from Pinion Service Set (J-36598). *See Fig. 14.* Lightly lubricate outer and inner pinion bearing races. Using race installer (J-36598-3) for K15/25 or (J-36598-4) for K35, press in outer pinion race and pull in inner pinion race until both are seated in housing. *See Fig. 14.* Lubricate inner and outer bearings. Set pinion depth. See DRIVE PINION DEPTH under ADJUSTMENTS.

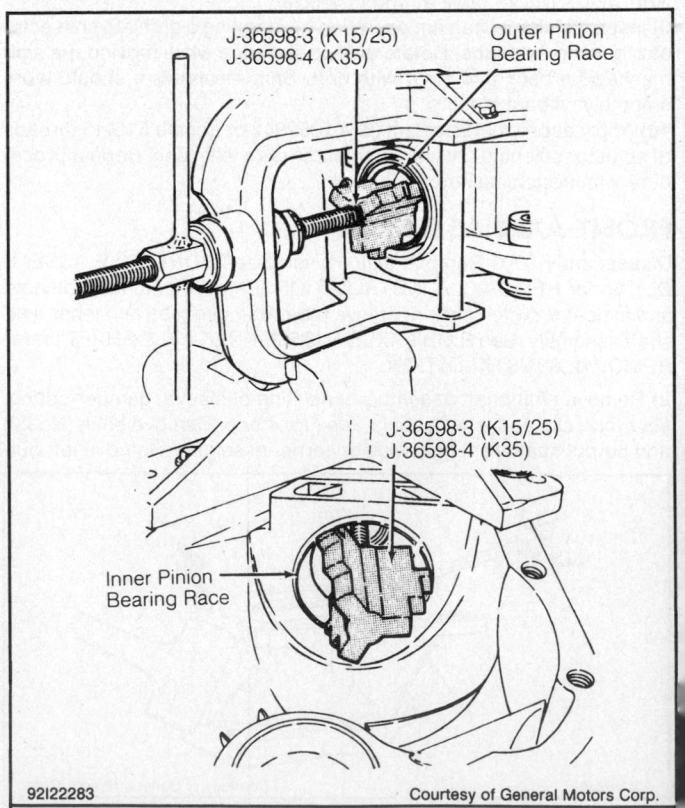

Fig. 14: Installing Pinion Races

2) Install appropriate shim size onto pinion. Shim size was previously determined during pinion depth adjustment. Using Pinion Bearing Installer (J-35512) for K15/25 or (J-36614) for K35, install inner pinion bearing onto pinion. Install NEW collapsible spacer onto pinion shaft. Lubricate outer pinion bearing and install bearing and pinion seal into carrier case using Seal Installer (J-33782). Insert pinion, with attached inner bearing and collapsible spacer, into carrier case.

3) Install deflector, pinion flange. Apply GM PST sealant to area where pinion threads meet pinion flange. Install pinion washer and nut. Install same flange holder previously used to remove pinion flange. Hold flange while slowly tightening nut and checking pinion flange until no end play is present. DO NOT tighten nut any further.

4) Rotate pinion several times to ensure bearings have been seated. Recheck end play. Set final pinion preload to **15-25 INCH lbs. (1.7-2.8 N.m)** by tightening pinion nut in small increments, rotating pinion between tightenings. Each tightening increases preload by several INCH pounds.

5) If preload specification is exceeded, remove pinion and install NEW collapsible spacer. Once preload has been obtained, rotate pinion several times to ensure bearings have seated and recheck preload.

6) Install side gears and thrust washers into differential case. On K35, install side gear spacer to left-hand side. If old side gears are being reinstalled, ensure they are placed in their original locations as marked during disassembly.

7) Position one pinion gear between side gears and rotate gears until pinion gear is directly opposite opening in case. Place remaining pinion gear between side gears. Ensure holes in both pinion gears line up. Rotate pinion gears toward opening just enough to allow installation of thrust washers.

8) Install differential pinion gear shaft. On K15/25, install roll pin through case and into pinion gear shaft. On K35, install pinion gear shaft bolt. Install ring gear onto differential assembly. Tighten NEW bolts alternately in progressive steps to **88 ft. lbs. (119 N.m)**. Ring gear uses left-hand thread bolts.

9) Press side bearings onto differential assembly using Adapter (J-8092) and Side Bearing Installer (J-22761) for K15/25 or (J-29710) for K35. Press bearings onto sleeves (and onto adjuster plug on left side of K35) using Adapter (J-8092) and Bearing Installer (J-36612) for K15/25 or (J-36613) for K35.

10) On K35, install NEW "O" ring to adjuster plug. Using same sleeve adjusting wrench used during disassembly, install sleeves into carrier case (except left side on K35). On K35, on left side of carrier, install adjuster plug using same adjuster plug wrench used during disassembly.

11) Install side bearing races into carrier using Adapter (J-8092) and Race Installer (J-36603). Place differential assembly into left carrier case half. On K15/25, turn left sleeve inward until backlash is felt between ring and pinion. On K35, turn left adjuster plug inward until backlash is felt between ring and pinion.

12) Remove carrier case from holding fixture and attach carrier halves together using 4 bolts. If halves DO NOT make complete contact, back out right sleeve. Install carrier case bolts and tighten to **35 ft. lbs. (47 N.m)**. Set ring gear backlash adjustment to specification. See RING GEAR BACKLASH under ADJUSTMENTS.

13) On K15/25, bend lock tabs over left and right sleeves. On K35, install left adjuster plug lock and bolt, and bend lock tab over right sleeve. On all models, remove 4 bolts holding axle carrier halves together and separate housing halves. Apply appropriate sealant (GM 1052942 or Loctite 518) to one carrier housing surface.

14) Reconnect axle carrier housing halves. Install 10 attaching bolts and tighten to specification. See TORQUE SPECIFICATIONS table at end of article. Using appropriate Seal Installer (J-36600) for K15/25 or J-22833) for K35, install/drive seal into left side of carrier case. Install deflector onto left output shaft and insert shaft into left side of carrier. Drive shaft into place with a soft-faced (brass or plastic) hammer.

15) Install new pilot bearing into right output shaft using Pilot Bearing Installer (J-33842). Insert right output shaft into right side of carrier. Apply appropriate sealant (GM 1052942 or Loctite 518) to threads of vent plug. Install vent plug into left side of carrier.

16) Install right axle tube and inner shaft assembly. See RIGHT AXLE TUBE & INNER AXLE SHAFT under REMOVAL & INSTALLATION.

LEFT DRIVE AXLE SHAFT

NOTE: For exploded view of left drive axle shaft, see Fig. 15.

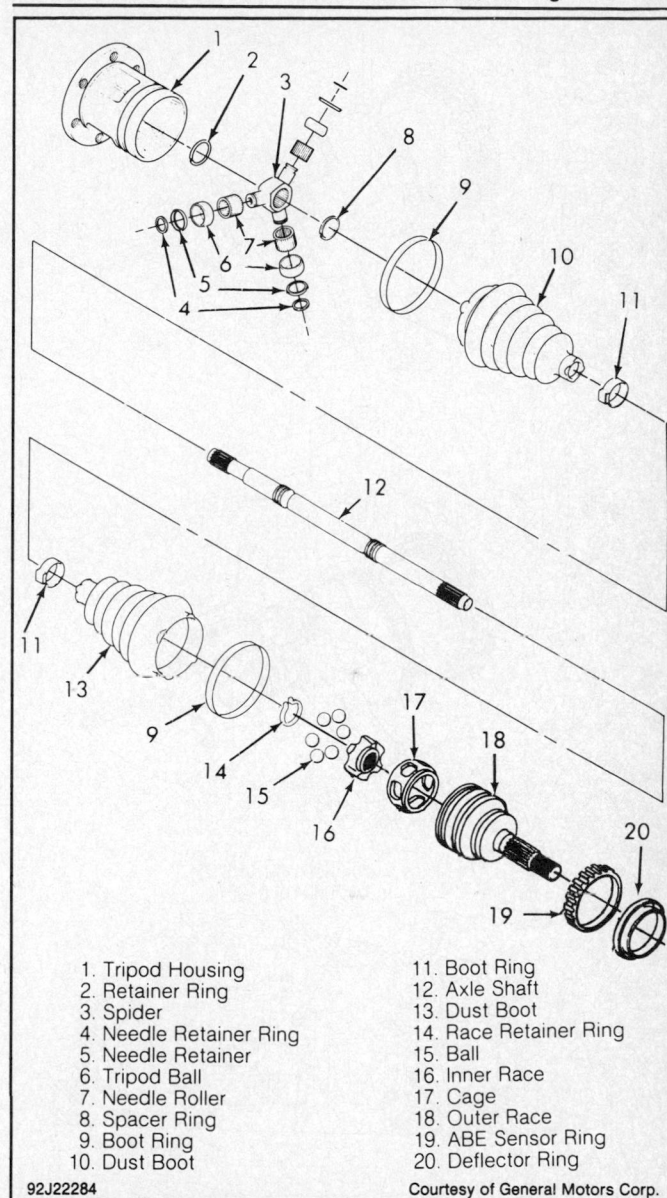

1. Tripod Housing	11. Boot Ring
2. Retainer Ring	12. Axle Shaft
3. Spider	13. Dust Boot
4. Needle Retainer Ring	14. Race Retainer Ring
5. Needle Retainer	15. Ball
6. Tripod Ball	16. Inner Race
7. Needle Roller	17. Cage
8. Spacer Ring	18. Outer Race
9. Boot Ring	19. ABE Sensor Ring
10. Dust Boot	20. Deflector Ring

92J22284   Courtesy of General Motors Corp.

Fig. 15: Exploded View Of Left Drive Axle Shaft

ADJUSTMENTS

DRIVE PINION DEPTH

1) Lubricate inner and outer pinion bearings liberally with gear oil. Hold pinion bearings in position and install Pinion Shim Setting Gauge (J-36601-4) for K15/25 or (J-36601-3) for K35. Install Dial Indicator (J-29763) onto gauge. See Fig. 16.

2) With gauge installed, preload inner and outer pinion bearings to **10-15 INCH lbs. (1.0-1.6 N.m)** by tightening shim setting gauge mounting bolt while also holding end of gauge shaft with a wrench. Rotate shaft several times to ensure bearings have seated. Recheck preload.

3) Push dial indicator downward until needle rotates about 3/4 of turn clockwise. Tighten dial indicator in this position. Set button of pinion shim setting gauge on differential bearing bore. See Fig. 16.

NOTE: The 4WD front axle drive pinion gears are nominal or zero, and are not marked on pinion head surface. Shim thickness will equal dial indicator gauge reading.

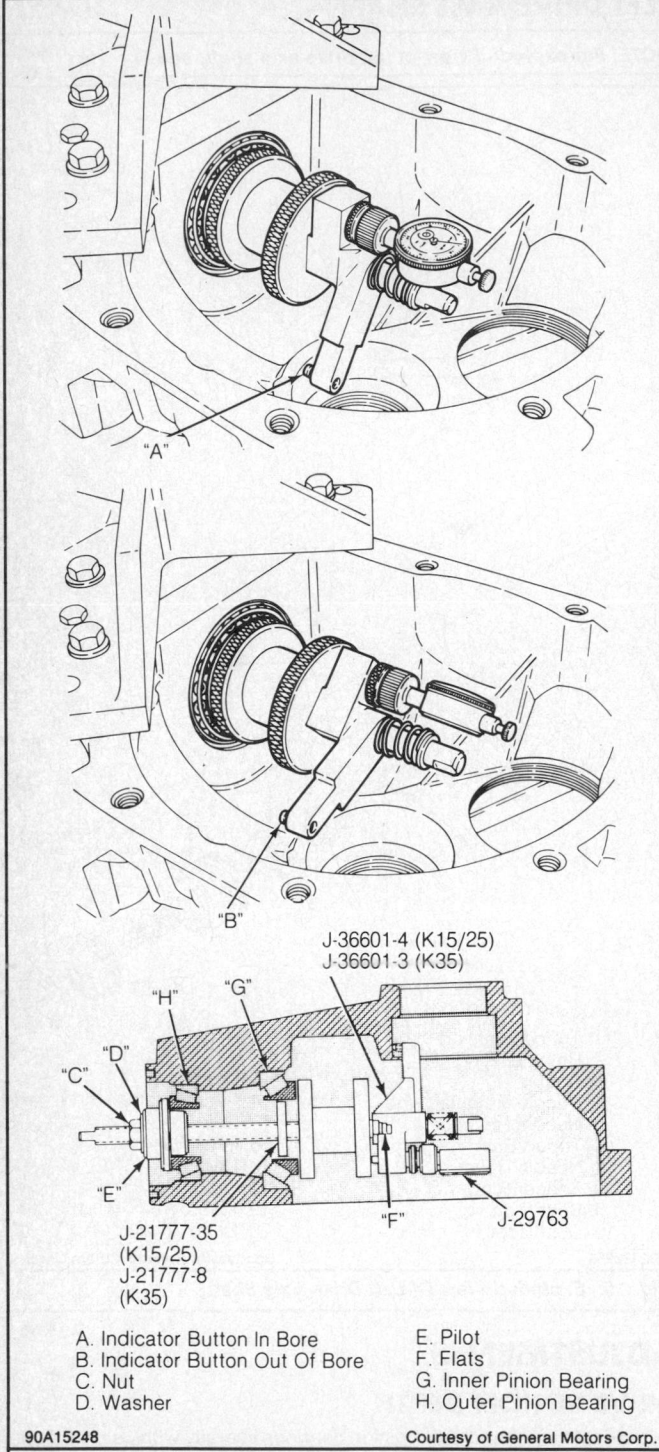

A. Indicator Button In Bore
B. Indicator Button Out Of Bore
C. Nut
D. Washer

E. Pilot
F. Flats
G. Inner Pinion Bearing
H. Outer Pinion Bearing

90A15248   Courtesy of General Motors Corp.

Fig. 16: Pinion Shim Setting Gauge & Dial Indicator Installation & Measurement

4) Rotate gauge slowly back and forth until dial indicator reads lowest point of bore. Set dial indicator to zero. Repeat rocking action of gauge to verify zero setting.

5) After satisfactory zero setting is obtained and verified, move gauge button out of differential side bearing bore. Record dial indicator reading. Use a shim that is exactly the same size as this indicator reading.

6) Remove dial indicator and gauge from carrier. Position correct shim on drive pinion. Install drive pinion bearing. Continue at step **2)** of REASSEMBLY in FRONT AXLE ASSEMBLY under OVERHAUL.

RING GEAR BACKLASH

1) Use Sleeve Adjusting Wrench (J-36599) and torque wrench to tighten right adjusting sleeve until no backlash is present. This torque measurement should be about **100 ft. lbs. (136 N.m)**.

2) Using Sleeve Adjusting Wrench (J-36599) for K15/25 or Adjuster Plug Wrench (J-36615) for K35, tighten left adjusting sleeve until no backlash is present. This torque measurement should be about **100 ft. lbs. (136 N.m)**.

3) Mark location of adjusting sleeves and adjuster plug (K35) in relation to carrier halves so notches can be counted when turned. On all models, turn right sleeve OUT 2 notches using sleeve adjusting wrench. On K15/25, turn left sleeve IN one notch. On K35, turn adjuster plug IN one notch. Rotate pinion several times to seat bearings.

4) Mount base clamp of Dial Indicator Set (J-8001) so gauge plunger button contact outer edge of pinion flange. Plunger must be at right angle to flange. See Fig. 17. Move pinion flange through its free play travel while holding differential carrier and ring gear stationary. Record dial indicator reading. Divide dial indicator reading by 2 to obtain backlash reading.

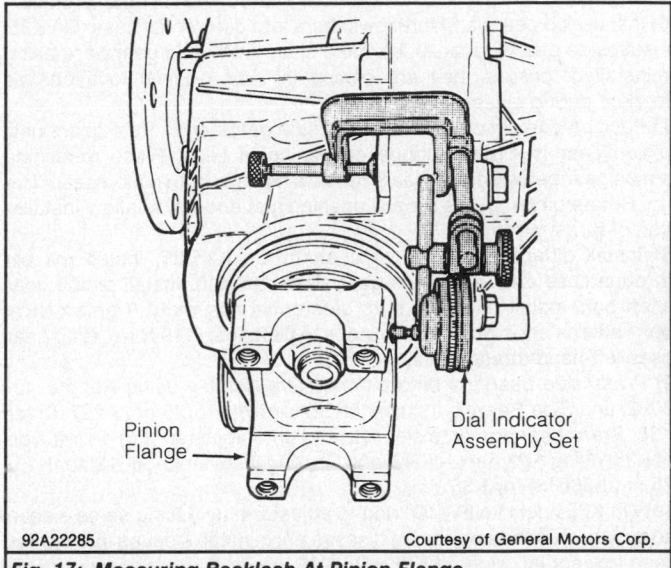

Pinion Flange

Dial Indicator Assembly Set

92A22285   Courtesy of General Motors Corp.

Fig. 17: Measuring Backlash At Pinion Flange

5) Gear backlash at pinion flange should be **.003-.010" (.08-.25 mm)**, with a preferred measurement of **.005-.007 (.13-.18 mm)**. If backlash is not within specification, equally turn right and left adjusting sleeves as necessary.

6) To increase backlash, turn left sleeve (adjuster plug on K35) in and turn right sleeve out an equal amount. To decrease backlash, turn right sleeve in and turn left sleeve (adjuster plug on K35) out an equal amount. Turning sleeve (or adjuster plug on K35) one notch will change backlash about .003" (.08 mm). DO NOT install/bend sleeve locks at this time.

7) When backlash is within specification, perform gear tooth contact pattern check. See GEAR TOOTH CONTACT PATTERNS article in GENERAL INFORMATION. When pattern is satisfactory, continue at step **13)** of REASSEMBLY in FRONT AXLE ASSEMBLY under OVERHAUL.

AXLE ASSEMBLY SPECIFICATIONS

AXLE ASSEMBLY SPECIFICATIONS

Application	In. (mm)
Ring Gear Backlash	[1] .003-.010 (.08-.25
Ring Gear Maximum Runout	.002 (.05
	INCH Lbs. (N.m
Pinion Bearing Preload	15-25 (1.7-2.8

[1] – Preferred backlash is .005-.007" (.13-.18 mm).

TORQUE SPECIFICATIONS

TORQUE SPECIFICATIONS

Application	Ft. Lbs. (N.m)
Actuator Solenoid	16 (22)
Axle Assembly Mounting Bolts	35 (47)
Axle Assembly Bushing Bolts	80 (108)
Axle Hub Nut	180 (245)
Ball Joint Nut (Upper)	61 (83)
Drain & Fill Plugs	24 (33)
Drive Axle-To-Output Flange Bolts	59 (80)
Front Drive Shaft Bolts	15 (20)
Right Axle Tube-To-Carrier Bolts	30 (41)
Right Axle Tube-To-Frame Bolts	
K15/25	75 (102)
K35	110 (149)
Ring Gear Attaching Bolts [1]	88 (119)
Shock Absorber Lower Mounting Bolt	54 (73)
Skid Plate Screws	25 (34)
Stabilizer Bar Hardware	13 (18)
Stabilizer Bar Bushing	
Bracket-To-Frame Bolts	24 (33)
Tie Rod Nut	35 (47)
Wheel Lug Nuts (Front)	120 (163)
	INCH Lbs. (N.m)
Switch Housing	45 (5.0)

[1] – Bolts are left-hand thread.

Blazer, Jimmy, Pickup, Sonoma

DESCRIPTION & OPERATION

NOTE: "T" Series Bravada is equipped with an All-Wheel Drive (AWD) front axle. For information on this axle, see ALL-WHEEL DRIVE FRONT AXLE article in DRIVE AXLES.

"T" Series (4WD) models use an independent front drive axle with a vacuum actuation system. Axle consists of a transfer case with a synchronized input shaft and a front axle unit with central locking clutch and vacuum operated cable shift control.

The vacuum actuation system consists of a vacuum switch and vacuum actuator. *See Fig. 1.* Shift mechanism in the transfer case triggers vacuum switch to apply engine vacuum to vacuum actuator after about a 3-second delay. The vacuum actuator, in turn, pulls on shift cable which pulls on shift fork in axle. This connects the right axle output shaft to the front axle differential. Torque is now available to front wheels.

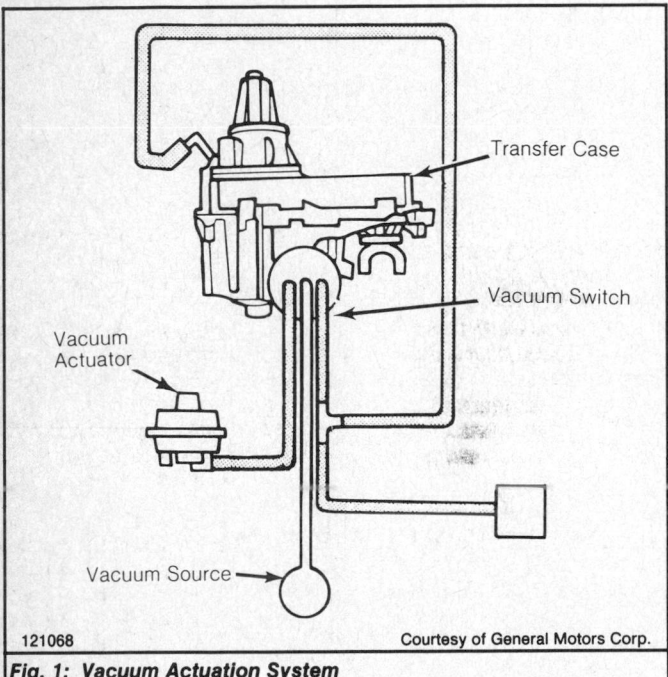

121068   Courtesy of General Motors Corp.
Fig. 1: Vacuum Actuation System

AXLE RATIO & IDENTIFICATION

To determine drive axle ratio, see AXLE RATIO IDENTIFICATION article.

REMOVAL & INSTALLATION

AXLE SHAFTS

Removal & Installation – 1) Raise and support vehicle on safety stands. Remove wheel and brake caliper and flex hoses at brackets. Remove tie rods at steering knuckle using Puller (J-24319). Remove shock lower bolts and push shocks aside.
2) Remove drive axle-to-axle tube bolts. Remove axle shaft cotter pin, nut and washer. Position inner part of drive axle forward and support away from frame. Remove shaft from hub using Puller (J-28733). Remove axle shaft from vehicle.
3) Install axle shaft into hub. Tighten nut and washer to specification. See TORQUE SPECIFICATIONS table at end of article. Install retainer and install cotter pin. To complete installation, reverse removal procedure.

RIGHT AXLE TUBE & INNER SHAFT

WARNING: When battery is disconnected, vehicle computer and memory systems may lose memory data. Driveability problems may exist until computer systems have completed a relearn cycle. See COMPUTER RELEARN PROCEDURES article in GENERAL INFORMATION before disconnecting battery.

Removal – 1) Disconnect battery negative cable. Remove shift cable from vacuum actuator by disengaging lock spring. Push in actuator diaphragm to release cable.
2) Unlock steering wheel. Raise and support vehicle. Remove front wheels, engine drive belt shield and front axle skid plate (if equipped).
3) Place a support under right lower control arm and disconnect right upper ball joint. Remove support so control arm can hang free. Disconnect right axle shaft from differential output shaft.
4) Remove 4WD indicator light connection from switch. Remove 3 bolts securing cable and switch housing. Pull housing away to gain access to cable locking spring. DO NOT unscrew cable coupling nut unless cable is being replaced. See SHIFT CABLE under REMOVAL & INSTALLATION.
5) Disconnect shift cable from shift fork shaft by lifting spring over slot in shift fork. Remove bolts securing tube bracket to frame bracket. Remove bolts securing tube assembly to carrier.
6) Remove tube assembly by working around drive axle. DO NOT allow sleeve, thrust washers, connector and output shaft to fall out of carrier while removing tube. *See Fig. 4.*
Installation – 1) Install sleeve, thrust washers, connector and output shaft in carrier. Apply Loctite (514) on axle tube to differential surface. Ensure thrust washer is installed with notch aligned with tab on washer. *See Fig. 2.*
2) Install tube and shaft assembly to differential and install one bolt at one o'clock position but DO NOT tighten. Pull assembly down and install cable, switch housing and remaining 4 bolts. Tighten bolts to specification. See TORQUE SPECIFICATIONS table at end of article.
3) Install 2 bolts securing tube to frame. Tighten bolts to specification. See TORQUE SPECIFICATIONS table at end of article. Check shift unit operation. To complete installation, reverse removal procedure.

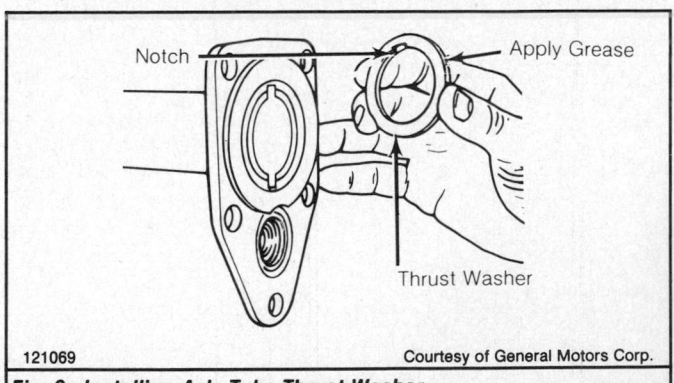

121069   Courtesy of General Motors Corp.
Fig. 2: Installing Axle Tube Thrust Washer

SHIFT CABLE

Removal – 1) Disengage shift cable from vacuum actuator by disengaging locking spring. Push actuator diaphragm in to release cable. Squeeze 2 locking fingers of cable with pliers. Pull cable out of bracket hole.
2) Raise and support vehicle. Remove bolts securing cable and switch housing to carrier. DO NOT unscrew coupling nut at this time. Remove shift cable housing from carrier assembly. Pull out about 3/4" (19 mm) of cable. Remove cable end from shift fork shaft. Bend tang of lock spring, then pull cable end from shift fork shaft.
3) Note cable routing for installation. Unscrew coupler nut and remove shift cable from shift cable housing. Remove cable from vehicle.
Installation – 1) Install cable and switch housing to carrier. Tighten mounting bolts to specification. See TORQUE SPECIFICATIONS table at end of article.

2) Guide cable though switch housing into fork shaft hole and push cable in. Cable will snap into place. Start coupling nut by hand to avoid cross threading. Tighten nut to specification. See TORQUE SPECIFICATIONS table at end of article. DO NOT overtighten nut.

3) Connect shift cable to vacuum actuator by pressing cable into bracket hole. Cable and housing will snap into place. Check cable operation.

VACUUM ACTUATOR

Removal & Installation – Disconnect vacuum line from actuator. Remove shift cable. See SHIFT CABLE under REMOVAL & INSTALLATION. Remove vacuum actuator bolts and actuator. To install, reverse removal procedure.

AXLE OUTPUT SHAFT PILOT BEARING

Removal & Installation – Remove right extension tube and inner axle shaft. See RIGHT AXLE TUBE & INNER SHAFT under REMOVAL & INSTALLATION. Remove pilot bearing using Output Shaft Pilot Bearing Remover (J-34011). Install new pilot bearing using Output Shaft Pilot Bearing Installer (J-33842). To complete installation, reverse removal procedure.

PINION FLANGE & OIL SEAL

Removal – **1)** Remove crossmember if necessary. Remove bolts and retainers from pinion flange. Mark position of drive shaft to pinion flange to ensure correct installation. Remove drive shaft from pinion flange and wire shaft aside.

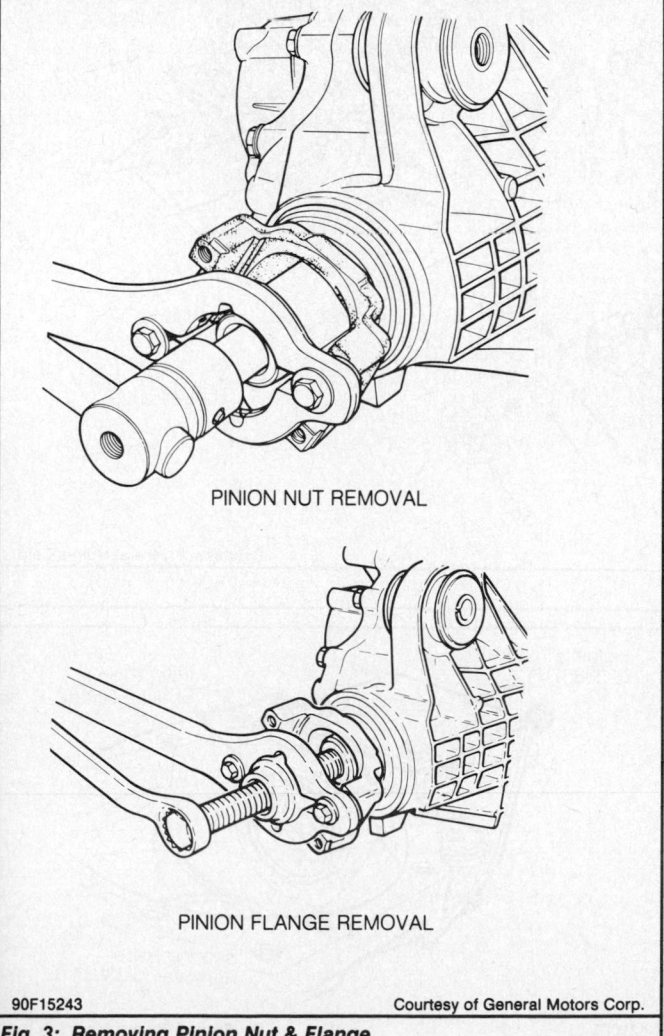

PINION NUT REMOVAL

PINION FLANGE REMOVAL

90F15243   Courtesy of General Motors Corp.

Fig. 3: Removing Pinion Nut & Flange

2) Mark pinion flange, pinion shaft and pinion nut to ensure alignment and bearing preload are maintained on installation. Using Pinion Flange Remover Set (J-8614-01), hold pinion flange stationary and remove pinion flange nut and washer. Remove pinion flange and oil seal. *See Fig. 3.*

3) Clean pinion flange in solvent and inspect seal surface of pinion flange for nicks, burrs or damage such as a groove worn into pinion flange by oil seal. Repair or replace as necessary.

Installation – **1)** Lubricate pinion flange surface and sealing lip of oil seal. Install oil seal using seal installer. Install pinion flange onto pinion shaft with marks aligned. Install pinion nut and tighten to position marked on pinion shaft.

2) Tighten nut 1/16" beyond alignment marks. Install drive shaft and tighten bolts to specification. See TORQUE SPECIFICATIONS table at end of article. Install crossmember if removed. Check fluid level.

FRONT AXLE ASSEMBLY

Removal & Installation – **1)** Raise and support vehicle. Remove right extension tube and inner axle. See RIGHT AXLE TUBE & INNER SHAFT. Remove steering stabilizer and idler arm bolts at vehicle frame. Pull steering linkage forward. Remove axle vent hose. Remove inner attaching bolts for left drive axle.

2) Mark front of drive shaft to ensure proper installation. Remove bolts and clamps. Working through hole in frame, remove axle-to-frame mounting bolts. Tip axle assembly counterclockwise while lifting to gain clearance from mounting ears and remove axle assembly. To install, reverse removal procedure. Tighten all bolts and nuts to specification. See TORQUE SPECIFICATIONS table at end of article.

OVERHAUL

AXLE SHAFTS

NOTE: For axle shaft overhaul, see Fig. 11.

AXLE UNIT

Disassembly – **1)** Remove axle output shaft and thrust washer. Remove left output shaft by prying between shaft flange and carrier bolt head with a screwdriver and simultaneously striking shaft flange with a soft-faced hammer.

2) Remove 6 cover-to-carrier bolts securing left side. Tap cover to loosen and remove. While supporting cover, drive out left seal using a punch.

3) Remove 10 bolts holding axle housing halves together. Insert screwdriver in slots provided (one next to fill plug, and 180 degrees from fill plug) and pry axle housing halves apart. *See Fig. 10.*

4) Remove differential from housing. Remove both side bearing adjusting locks. Remove race for both differential side bearings by turning side bearing adjusting sleeve with Side Bearing Adjuster Wrench (J-33792) until race is pushed out of carrier.

5) Using Pinion Flange Remover Set (J-8614-01), remove pinion flange nut. Install Holding Fixture (J-33837-1). Use bolts supplied with tool to install fixture on carrier and remove pinion and flange. *See Fig. 5.*

6) Install Bearing Race Remover (J-33837-6) on Holding Fixture (J-33837-1) and remove outer pinion bearing, race and pinion seal. *See Fig. 6.*

7) Remove inner pinion bearing race by pushing it out of housing with bearing race remover installed on Pinion Bearing Remover/Installer (J-33837). Remove inner drive pinion bearing using Differential Side/Pinion Bearing Remover (J-22912-01).

Cleaning & Inspection – Clean all parts in cleaning solvent. Inspect all parts for excessive wear.

1992 DRIVE AXLES
"T" Series 4WD Front Axle (Cont.)

1. Axle Shaft (Inner)
2. Deflector
3. Seal
4. Bearing
5. Tube
6. Bolt
7. Washer
8. Ring
9. Connector
10. Cable
11. Housing
12. Gasket
13. Switch
14. Spring
15. Seal
16. Spring
17. Shaft
18. Bolt
19. Lock
20. Washer
21. Bearing
22. Sleeve
23. Shaft
24. Washer
25. Plug
26. Washer
27. Pin
28. Bolt
29. Axle Housing
30. Bearing
31. Insert
32. Sleeve
33. Bearing
34. Bolt
35. Differential Housing
36. Screw
37. Ring & Pinion Gears
38. Shim Kit
39. Bearing
40. Spacer
41. Bearing
42. Seal
43. Deflector
44. Flange
45. Washer
46. Nut
47. Plug
48. Bushing
49. Housing
50. Ventilator
51. Connector
52. Shaft
53. Washer
54. Gear
55. Washer
56. Gear
57. Cover
58. Bolt
59. Left Axle Shaft (Inner)

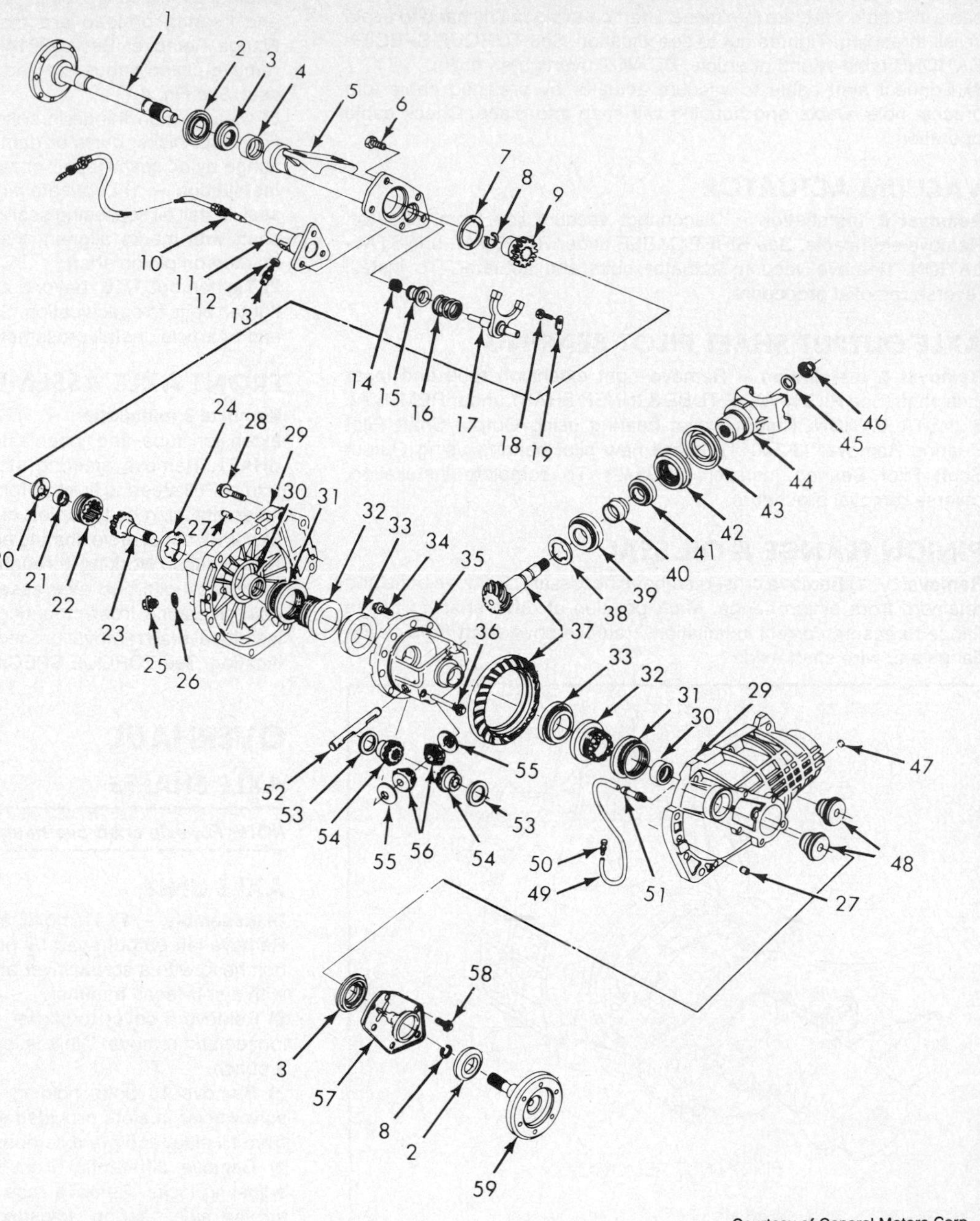

121070

Courtesy of General Motors Corp.

Fig. 4: Exploded View Of 4WD "T" Series Front Axle Assembly

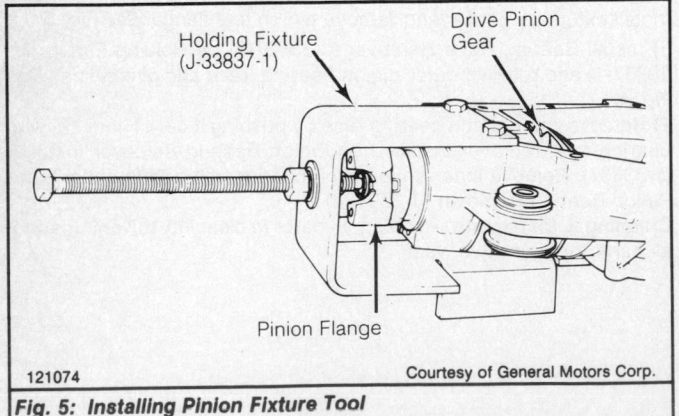

121074

Courtesy of General Motors Corp.

Fig. 5: Installing Pinion Fixture Tool

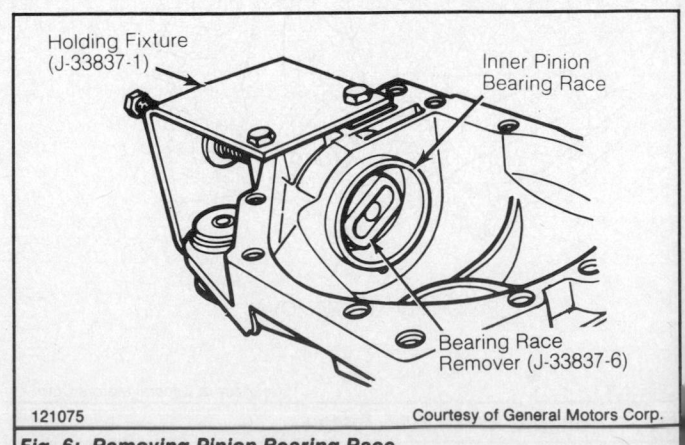

121075

Courtesy of General Motors Corp.

Fig. 6: Removing Pinion Bearing Race

Reassembly – 1) Lubricate outer pinion and inner bearing races. Install using Holding Fixture (J-33837-1) and Bearing Race Installer (J-33837-4) until races are seated in housing. *See Fig. 7.* Lubricate inner and outer bearings, then set pinion depth. See DRIVE PINION DEPTH under ADJUSTMENTS.

2) Install inner pinion bearing on shaft using Pinion Bearing Installer (J-33785). Install NEW collapsible spacer on pinion shaft and position assembly in carrier. Lubricate outer pinion bearing and install in housing.

3) Lubricate pinion bearing seal with axle lube. Using Pinion Seal Installer (J-33782), install seal. Install pinion flange, washer and nut.

4) Install Flange Holder (J-8614-01) on pinion flange and hold flange while tightening pinion flange nut. Tighten nut until no end play is present. Do not tighten further as preload specifications are being approached. For preload procedure, see DRIVE PINION DEPTH under ADJUSTMENTS.

5) Rotate pinion several times to ensure bearings have been seated. Set final preload to **15-25 INCH lbs. (1.7-2.8 N.m)**.

6) Assemble output shaft bearings and adjusting sleeves into inserts in carrier and finger tighten. Install differential side bearing race into housing using Differential Side Bearing Race Installer (J-23423-A).

7) Using new output shaft bearings, adjusting sleeve inserts and Output Shaft Bearing Installer (J-33788), press output shaft bearings into adjusting sleeves from inner side of sleeves.

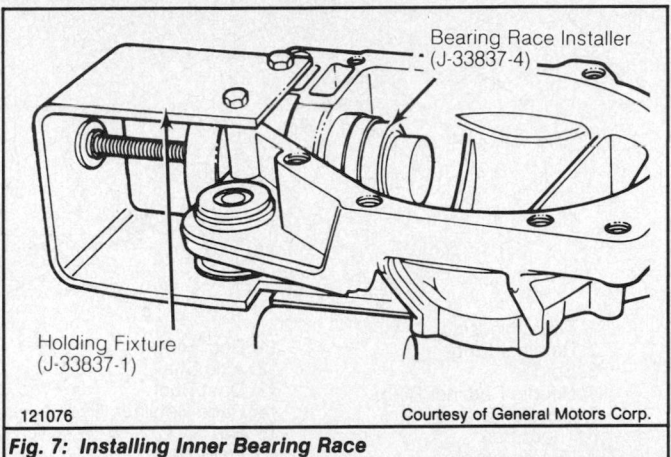

Bearing Race Installer (J-33837-4)

Holding Fixture (J-33837-1)

121076   Courtesy of General Motors Corp.

Fig. 7: Installing Inner Bearing Race

8) Install adjusting sleeve and bearing into insert and finger tighten. Using Differential Side Bearing Race Installer (J-23423-A), press assembly into axle housing.

9) Install differential into housing and set ring gear backlash adjustment to specification. See RING GEAR BACKLASH under ADJUSTMENTS.

10) Install left differential housing seal. Support housing to prevent distorting or bending of housing. Apply gasket sealer to housing surface and install housing cover.

DIFFERENTIAL HOUSING

Disassembly – 1) Using Differential Side/Pinion Bearing Remover (J-22912-01), remove side bearings. Remove pinion shaft lock screw and pinion. Remove pinions, side gears and thrust washers from housing. Mark side gears and housing for reassembly reference.

2) If ring gear is to be replaced and is tight on housing after removing right-hand thread bolts, drive off ring gear using a brass drift and hammer. DO NOT pry between ring gear and housing.

Reassembly – 1) Lubricate all parts with axle lubricant. Place side gear thrust washers over side gear hubs. Install side gears in housing. Ensure all reused parts are installed in original positions.

2) Position a pinion (with washer) between side gears and rotate gears until pinion is directly opposite opening in housing. Place other pinion between side gears so pinion shaft holes align. Rotate gears to make sure holes in pinions will line up with holes in housing.

3) Rotate pinions back toward opening just enough to permit sliding in pinion gear thrust washer. Install pinion shaft and lock screw. Install

2 NEW bolts into opposite sides of ring gear, then install ring gear onto housing. Tighten ring gear bolts to specification. See TORQUE SPECIFICATIONS table at end of article.

ADJUSTMENTS

DRIVE PINION DEPTH

1) Lubricate inner and outer pinion bearings liberally with axle lubricant. Hold pinion bearings in position and install Pinion Shim Setting Gauge (J-33838). With gauge installed, preload inner and outer pinion bearing to **15-25 INCH lbs. (1.7-2.8 N.m)** by tightening mounting bolt while holding end of gauge shaft with a wrench.

2) Using Dial Indicator (J-29763), set reading to zero, then position dial indicator on pinion shim setting gauge. Push dial indicator downward until needle rotates approximately 3 turns clockwise. Tighten dial indicator in this position. *See Fig. 8.*

NOTE: All "T" series 4WD front axle drive pinions are nominal or zero, and are not marked. Shim thickness will equal dial indicator gauge reading.

3) Set button of pinion shim setting gauge on differential bearing bore. Rotate gauge slowly back and forth until dial indicator reads lowest point of bore. Set dial indicator to zero. Repeat rocking action of gauge to verify zero setting.

4) After zero setting is obtained and verified, move gauge button out of differential side bearing bore. Record dial indicator reading. Use a shim that is exactly the same size as indicator reading.

5) Remove dial indicator and gauge from carrier. Position correct shim on drive pinion. Install drive pinion.

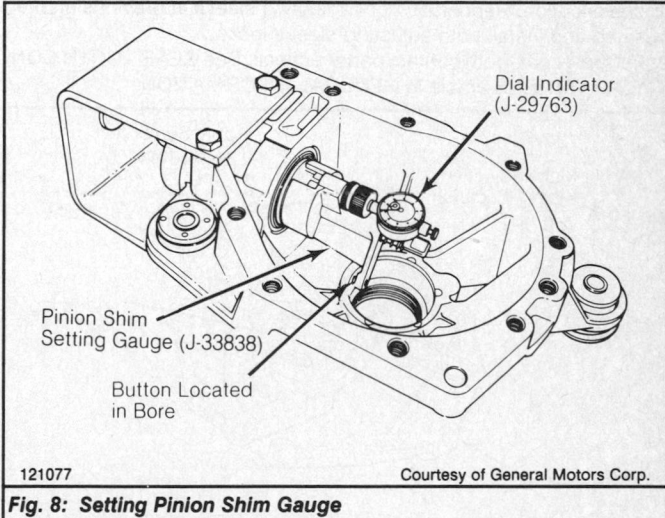

Dial Indicator (J-29763)

Pinion Shim Setting Gauge (J-33838)

Button Located in Bore

121077   Courtesy of General Motors Corp.

Fig. 8: Setting Pinion Shim Gauge

RING GEAR BACKLASH

1) Using Side Bearing Adjusting Wrench (J-33792), turn left adjusting sleeve in toward differential housing until backlash is felt between ring and pinion gears.

2) Ensure carrier mating surfaces are clean. Assemble carrier without using sealer. If axle housing halves will not make complete contact, back out right adjusting sleeve.

3) Install 4 axle housing bolts and tighten to specification. See TORQUE SPECIFICATIONS table at end of article. Using side bearing adjusting wrench, tighten right adjusting sleeve until no backlash is present, which is approximately **100 ft. lbs. (140 N.m)**. *See Fig. 9.*

4) Mark location of adjusting sleeves in relation to carrier halves so notches in adjusting sleeves can be counted when turned. Turn right adjusting sleeve out 2 notches using side bearing adjusting wrench. Turn left adjusting sleeve in one notch. *See Fig. 10.*

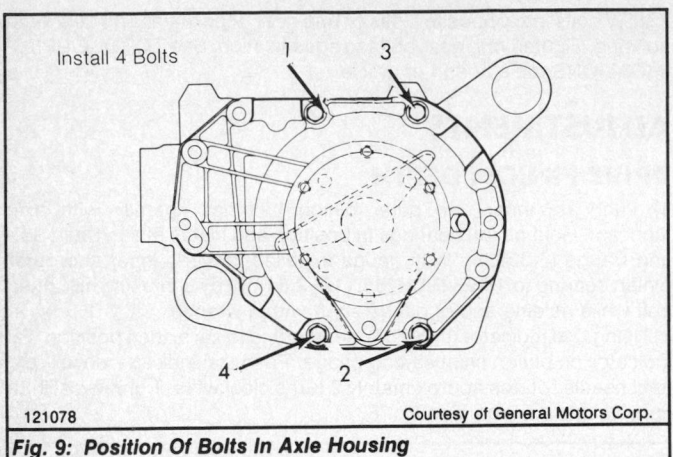

Install 4 Bolts

121078   Courtesy of General Motors Corp.

Fig. 9: Position Of Bolts In Axle Housing

5) Rotate axle housing several times to seat bearings, then mount dial indicator. Use a small button on indicator stem so contact can be made near heel end of tooth angle for accurate backlash reading. Set backlash to specification. See AXLE ASSEMBLY SPECIFICATIONS table at end of article.

6) If backlash is not within specification, readjust adjusting sleeves as necessary. DO NOT install adjusting sleeve locks at this time.

7) Mark right adjusting sleeve so it can be repositioned in same location and loosen sleeve to release right side bearing to differential housing contact. Remove 4 axle housing bolts and axle housing half. Apply Loctite (514) on one axle housing surface.

8) Reinstall axle housing halves. Install 10 attaching bolts and tighten to specification. Reposition right adjusting sleeve in previous marked position and install both adjusting sleeve locks.

9) Perform gear tooth contact pattern check. See GEAR TOOTH CONTACT PATTERNS article in GENERAL INFORMATION.

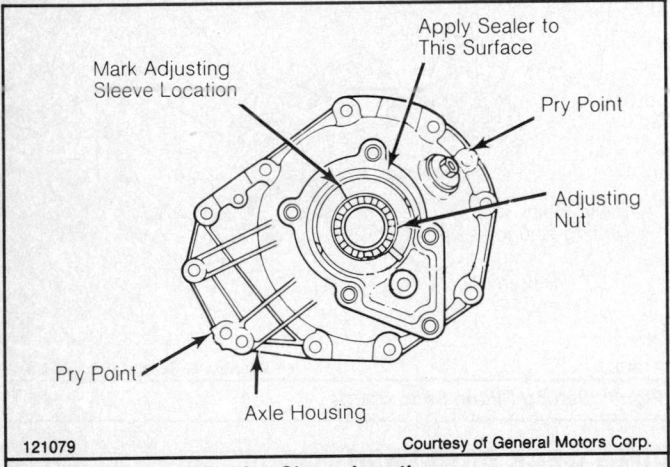

Apply Sealer to This Surface

Mark Adjusting Sleeve Location

Pry Point

Adjusting Nut

Pry Point

Axle Housing

121079   Courtesy of General Motors Corp.

Fig. 10: Marking Adjusting Sleeve Location

AXLE ASSEMBLY SPECIFICATIONS
AXLE ASSEMBLY SPECIFICATIONS

Application	In. (mm)
Ring Gear Backlash	.003-.010 (.08-.25)
Ring Gear Runout	.003 (.08)
	INCH Lbs. (N.m)
Pinion Bearing Preload	15-25 (1.7-2.8)

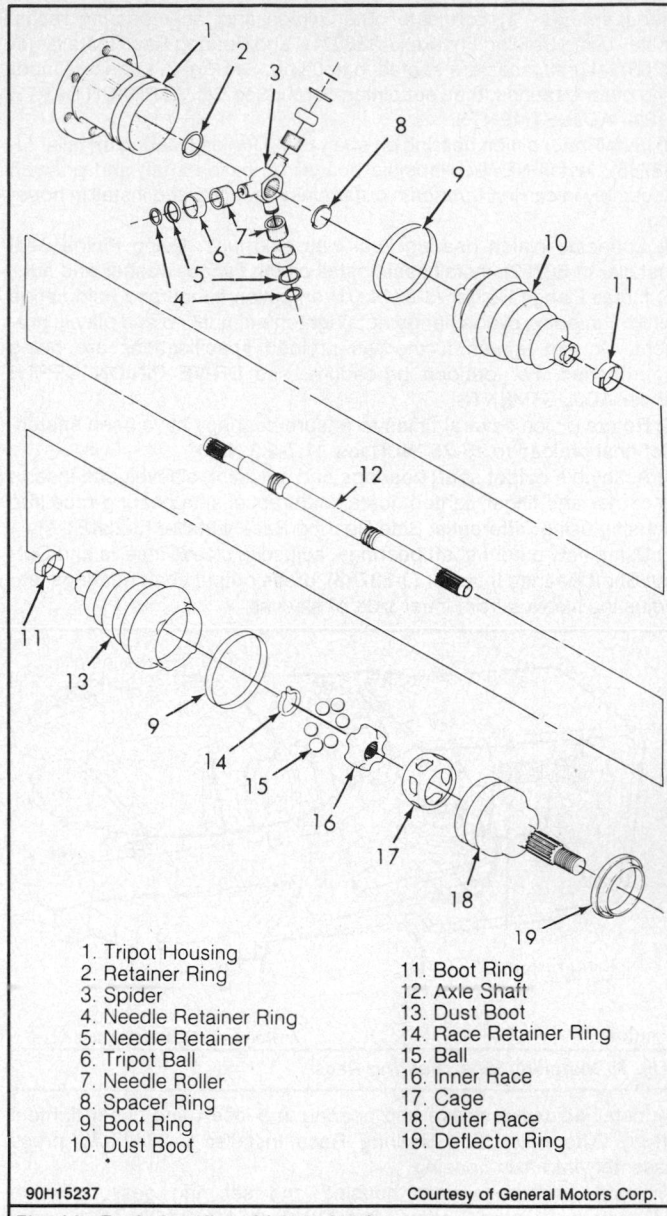

1. Tripot Housing
2. Retainer Ring
3. Spider
4. Needle Retainer Ring
5. Needle Retainer
6. Tripot Ball
7. Needle Roller
8. Spacer Ring
9. Boot Ring
10. Dust Boot
11. Boot Ring
12. Axle Shaft
13. Dust Boot
14. Race Retainer Ring
15. Ball
16. Inner Race
17. Cage
18. Outer Race
19. Deflector Ring

90H15237   Courtesy of General Motors Corp.

Fig. 11: Exploded View Of Axle Shaft

TORQUE SPECIFICATIONS
TORQUE SPECIFICATIONS

Application	Ft. Lbs. (N.m)
Adjusting Sleeve Lock Nut	14 (19)
Axle Housing Bolts	30-40 (41-54)
Axle Housing-To-Frame Bolts	65 (88)
Axle Hub Nut	160-200 (217-271)
Cable Switch Housing Bolts	30-40 (41-54)
Drive Axle-To-Output Flange Bolts	60 (81)
Front Propeller Shaft Bolts	15 (20)
Idler Arm-To-Frame Bolts	60 (81)
Lower Shock Bolt	54 (73)
Right Axle Tube-To-Housing Nuts	55 (75)
Ring Gear Attaching Bolts	52-66 (70-89)
Tie Rod Nut	35 (47)
Upper Ball Joint Nut	61 (83)
Wheel Lug Nuts	
Aluminum	90 (122)
Steel	73 (99)
	INCH Lbs. (N.m)
Shift Cable Coupling Nut	90 (10

Astro, Bravada, Safari, Syclone, Typhoon

DESCRIPTION & OPERATION

The 7 1/4" ring gear front axle is part of a full time all-wheel drive system. The all-wheel drive system does not have a disengagement feature. Differential case is supported in the axle housing by 2 tapered roller bearings. Pinion gear is supported by 2 tapered roller bearings. Drive axles are flexible assemblies made up of inner and outer constant velocity (CV) joints connected with an axle shaft. The inner CV joint is a tripot design. Outer CV joint is a Rzeppa design.

AXLE RATIO & IDENTIFICATION

To determine drive axle ratio, see AXLE RATIO IDENTIFICATION article.

REMOVAL & INSTALLATION

DRIVE AXLE SHAFTS

Removal & Installation – 1) Disconnect negative battery cable. Unlock steering column so linkage is free to move. Raise and support vehicle on safety stands. Remove wheel assembly. Mark drive axles for reassembly reference.
2) Support lower control arm. Insert a drift through opening in top of brake caliper into vanes of brake rotor (this will keep drive axle from turning). Remove cotter pin, retainer, axle nut and washer. *See Fig. 1.* Remove lower shock absorber nut and bolt. Remove drive axle to output shaft flange bolts.
3) Using a puller, push drive axle through wheel hub. Remove drive axle from vehicle. To install, reverse removal procedure. Torque drive axle to output shaft flange bolts and axle nut to specification. See TORQUE SPECIFICATIONS table at end of article.

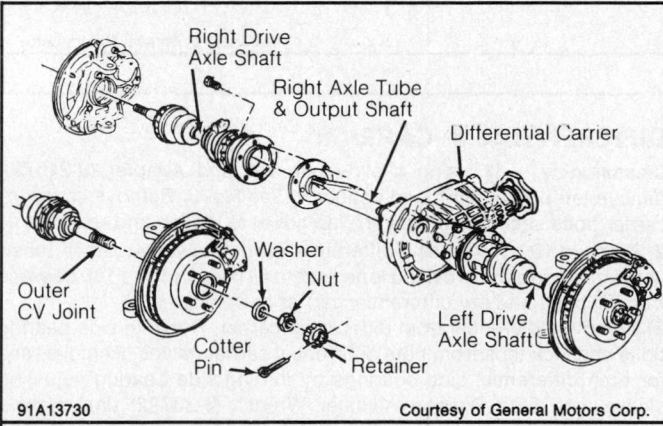

Right Drive Axle Shaft
Right Axle Tube & Output Shaft
Differential Carrier
Outer CV Joint
Washer
Nut
Cotter Pin
Retainer
Left Drive Axle Shaft

91A13730   Courtesy of General Motors Corp.

Fig. 1: Exploded View Of All-Wheel Drive Front Axle Assembly

RIGHT AXLE TUBE & OUTPUT SHAFT

NOTE: If differential fluid is not drained prior to removal of right axle tube, some differential fluid may spill out when axle tube is removed.

Removal – Remove right drive axle shaft. See DRIVE AXLE SHAFTS under REMOVAL & INSTALLATION. Remove right axle tube support bracket bolts and nuts from vehicle frame. Remove axle tube to differential carrier bolts. Remove right axle tube and output shaft from differential carrier.
Installation – Apply Loctite (514) on axle tube-to-differential surface. Align splines on output axle shaft-to-differential splines. Install right axle tube and output axle shaft to differential carrier. To complete installation, reverse removal procedure. Torque bolts and nuts to specification. See TORQUE SPECIFICATIONS table at end of article. Ensure differential fluid level is full.

RIGHT OUTPUT SHAFT SEAL & BEARING

Removal – 1) Remove right drive axle shaft. See DRIVE AXLE SHAFTS under REMOVAL & INSTALLATION. Remove right axle tube and output shaft. See RIGHT AXLE TUBE & OUTPUT SHAFT under REMOVAL & INSTALLATION.
2) Using a brass hammer, strike inside of output shaft flange to dislodge shaft. Remove output shaft with deflector and retaining ring from right axle tube. Use care when pulling output shaft splines through seal to avoid cutting seal. Using a slide hammer and Countershaft Roller Bearing Remover (J-29369-2), remove output shaft seal and bearing from right axle tube. *See Fig. 2.*

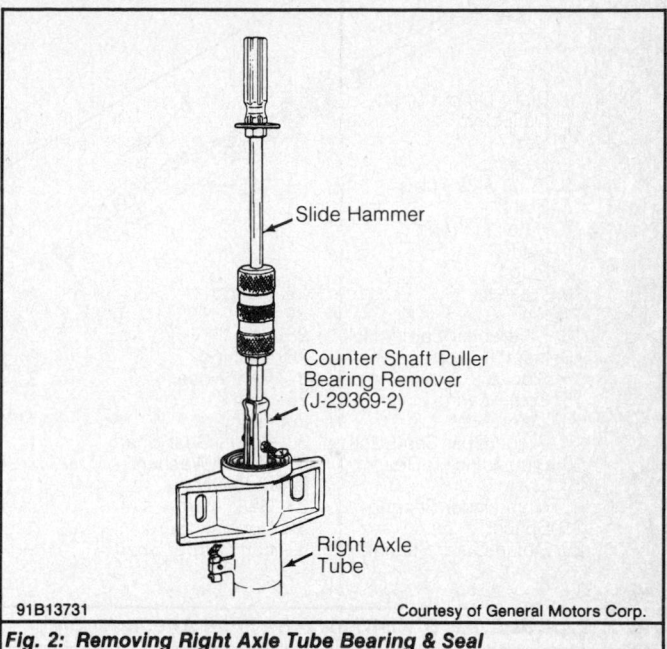

Slide Hammer
Counter Shaft Puller Bearing Remover (J-29369-2)
Right Axle Tube

91B13731   Courtesy of General Motors Corp.

Fig. 2: Removing Right Axle Tube Bearing & Seal

Installation – 1) Lubricate seal lips, bearings and bearing surfaces with axle lubricant. Using Axle Tube Bearing Installer (J-33844), install bearing into axle tube.
2) Using Output Shaft Seal Installer (J-33893), install seal into axle tube. Install axle shaft into axle tube. DO NOT cut seal with splines of axle shaft. To complete installation, reverse removal procedure.

PINION FLANGE & OIL SEAL

Removal – 1) Unlock steering column so linkage is free to move. Raise and support vehicle on safety stands. Place a reference mark on drive shaft and pinion flange for reassembly reference. Remove bolts from pinion flange. Remove drive shaft from pinion flange and wire shaft aside.
2) Using an INCH lb. torque wrench, check and record pinion preload. This measurement gives combined pinion bearing, seal, carrier bearing, axle bearing and seal preload.
3) Mark pinion flange, pinion shaft and pinion nut to ensure alignment and bearing preload can be maintained on installation. Using Pinion Flange Remover Set (J-8614-01), hold pinion flange stationary and remove pinion flange nut and washer. Place a container under pinion flange opening to catch differential fluid. Remove pinion flange and oil seal.
4) Clean pinion flange in solvent and inspect seal surface for nicks, burrs or damage such as a groove worn by oil seal. Repair or replace as necessary.

NOTE: If replacing original pinion flange, discard pinion and ring gear after removal. Replacement pinion, ring gear and pinion flange are balanced as an assembly.

Installation – 1) Lubricate pinion flange surface and sealing lip of oil seal. Using Seal Installer (J-33782), install pinion oil seal. Install pinion

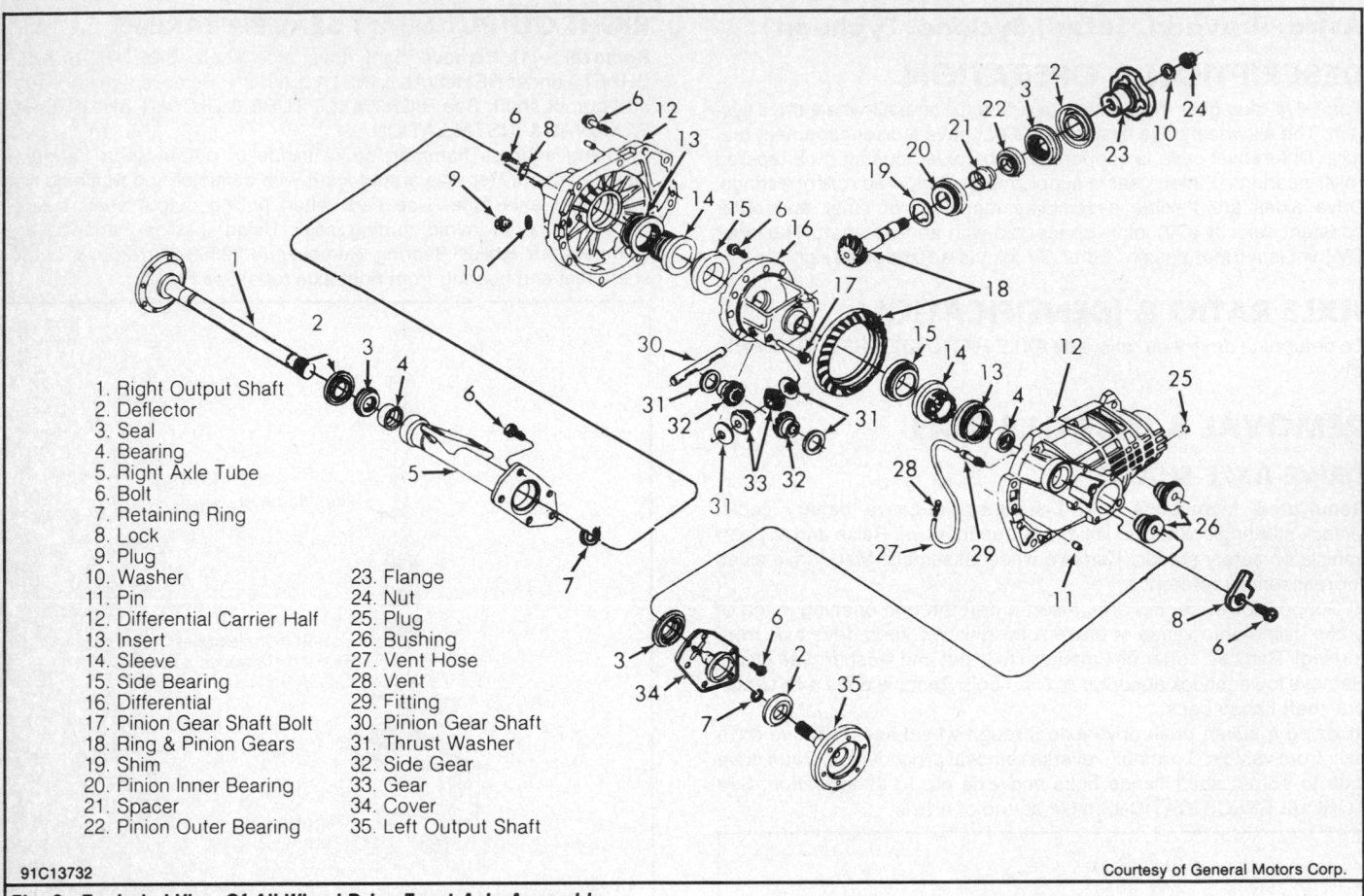

1. Right Output Shaft
2. Deflector
3. Seal
4. Bearing
5. Right Axle Tube
6. Bolt
7. Retaining Ring
8. Lock
9. Plug
10. Washer
11. Pin
12. Differential Carrier Half
13. Insert
14. Sleeve
15. Side Bearing
16. Differential
17. Pinion Gear Shaft Bolt
18. Ring & Pinion Gears
19. Shim
20. Pinion Inner Bearing
21. Spacer
22. Pinion Outer Bearing
23. Flange
24. Nut
25. Plug
26. Bushing
27. Vent Hose
28. Vent
29. Fitting
30. Pinion Gear Shaft
31. Thrust Washer
32. Side Gear
33. Gear
34. Cover
35. Left Output Shaft

91C13732

Courtesy of General Motors Corp.

Fig. 3: Exploded View Of All-Wheel Drive Front Axle Assembly

flange onto pinion shaft with marks aligned. Install pinion nut. Tighten pinion nut gradually. Turn pinion flange several times after each turn of pinion nut to ensure bearings are seated. Tighten pinion nut to position marked on pinion shaft.

2) Check pinion bearing preload. If preload is 3-5 INCH lbs. (.3-.6 N.m) more than preload recorded before disassembly, installation of pinion nut is complete. If preload is not 3-5 INCH lbs. (.3-.6 N.m) more than preload recorded before disassembly, tighten pinion nut until preload is 3-5 INCH lbs. (.3-.6 N.m) more than preload before disassembly. DO NOT overtighten pinion nut.

DIFFERENTIAL CARRIER

Removal & Installation – 1) Remove drive axle shafts. See DRIVE AXLE SHAFTS under REMOVAL & INSTALLATION. Remove right axle tube and output shaft. See RIGHT AXLE TUBE & OUTPUT SHAFT under REMOVAL & INSTALLATION.

2) Place a reference mark on drive shaft and pinion flange for reassembly reference. Remove bolts from pinion flange. Remove drive shaft from pinion flange and wire shaft aside.

3) Support differential carrier assembly. Remove upper mounting bolt and nut. Remove lower mounting bolt and nut. Slide front carrier assembly to right. Drop right side of carrier assembly and twist to clear mounting brackets, oil pan and steering linkage. Remove differential carrier assembly from vehicle.

OVERHAUL

NOTE: If replacing pinion and ring gear, discard original pinion flange after removal. Replacement pinion, ring gear and pinion flange are balanced as an assembly.

DIFFERENTIAL & CARRIER

Disassembly – 1) Using a slide hammer and Adapter (J-21579), remove left output shaft and deflector. *See Fig. 3.* Remove cover-to-carrier bolts securing left cover. Tap cover to loosen and remove.

2) Remove 10 bolts holding differential carrier halves together. Insert screwdriver in slots provided (one next to fill plug and one 180 degrees from fill plug) and pry differential carrier halves apart.

3) Remove differential from differential carrier. Remove side bearing bolts and lock tabs from both differential carrier halves. Remove race for both differential side bearings by turning side bearing adjusting sleeve with Side Bearing Adjuster Wrench (J-33792) until race is pushed out of carrier.

4) Using Pinion Flange Remover Set (J-8614-01), remove pinion flange nut and washer. Install Holding Fixture (J-33837-1) on left carrier case half. Thread Bolt (J-33837-3) into Fixture (J-33837-1). Turn Bolt (J-33837-3) to remove pinion flange and deflector.

5) Remove pinion shaft with spacer, pinion bearings and shim from left carrier half. Remove outer bearing and spacer from pinion shaft. Using a press, remove inner bearing and shim from pinion shaft.

6) Install Holding Fixture (J-33837-1) onto left carrier half. Thread Bolt (J-33837-3) into Fixture (J-33837-1). Place Driver (J-33837-6) in front of bearing race in left carrier half. *See Fig. 4.* Turn Bolt (J-33837-3) to press outer pinion shaft bearing race from carrier half.

7) Remove pinion gear shaft bolt. *See Fig. 3.* Remove pinion gear shaft. Remove pinion gears, side gears and thrust washers. Mark pinion gears and side gears for reassembly reference.

8) Remove ring gear bolts. Remove ring gear, using a brass drift and hammer if necessary. Using Side Bearing Remover (J-22912-01), remove side bearings. Using Bushing Remover (J-33791), remove side bearing bushings.

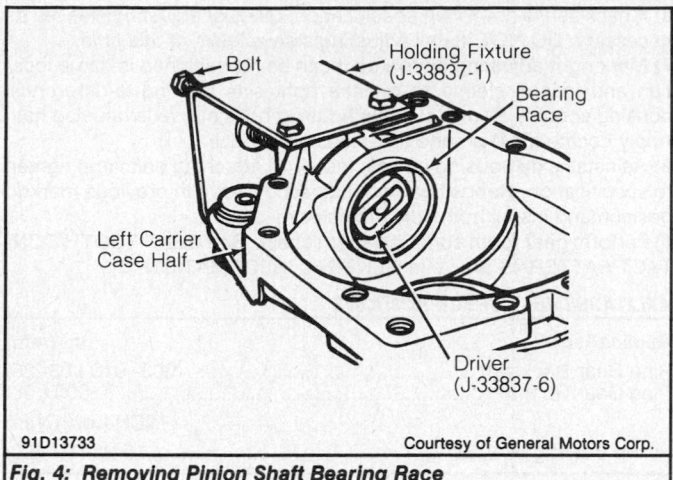

91D13733   Courtesy of General Motors Corp.

Fig. 4: Removing Pinion Shaft Bearing Race

Cleaning & Inspection – 1) Clean all parts in cleaning solvent. Inspect all bearings, bearing races and rollers for scoring, chipping or excessive wear. Inspect axle shaft and side gear splines for excessive wear.

NOTE: *DO NOT steam clean any parts having a ground and polished surface, such as bearings, gears and shafts.*

2) Inspect ring gear and pinion for scoring, cracking or chipping. Inspect differential case, pinion side gears, thrust washers and pinion shaft for cracks, scoring, galling or excessive wear.

Reassembly – 1) Lubricate pinion shaft bearing races. Install bearing races using Holding Fixture (J-33837-1) and Bearing Race Installer (J-33837-4) until races are seated in left differential carrier half. Lubricate inner and outer pinion shaft bearings.

2) Install inner pinion bearing on shaft using Pinion Bearing Installer (J-33785). Install NEW collapsible spacer on pinion shaft and position assembly in carrier. Lubricate outer pinion bearing and install in carrier.

3) Lubricate pinion bearing seal with axle lube. Using Pinion Seal Installer (J-33782), install seal. Install pinion flange, washer and nut.

4) Install Flange Holder (J-8614-01) on pinion flange and hold flange while tightening pinion flange nut. Tighten nut until no end play is present. Do not tighten further as preload specifications are being approached. For preload procedure, see DRIVE PINION DEPTH under ADJUSTMENTS.

5) Rotate pinion several times to ensure bearings have been seated. Set final preload to **15-25 INCH lbs. (1.7-2.8 N.m)**.

6) Assemble output shaft bearings and adjusting sleeves into inserts in carrier and finger tighten. Install differential side bearing race into housing using Differential Side Bearing Race Installer (J-23423-A).

7) Using new output shaft bearings, adjusting sleeve inserts and Output Shaft Bearing Installer (J-33788), press output shaft bearings into adjusting sleeves from inner side of sleeves.

8) Install adjusting sleeve and bearing into insert and finger tighten. Using Differential Side Bearing Race Installer (J-23423-A), press assembly into axle housing.

9) Lubricate all differential parts with axle lubricant. Place side gear thrust washers over side gear hubs. Install side gears in housing. Ensure all reused parts are installed in original positions.

10) Position a pinion (with washer) between side gears and rotate gears until pinion is directly opposite opening in housing. Place other pinion between side gears so pinion shaft holes align. Rotate gears to ensure holes in pinions will line up with holes in housing.

11) Rotate pinions back toward opening just enough to permit sliding in pinion gear thrust washer. Install pinion shaft and lock screw. Install 2 new bolts into opposite sides of ring gear, and install ring gear on housing. Tighten ring gear bolts to specification. See TORQUE SPECIFICATIONS table at end of article.

12) Install differential into housing and set ring gear backlash adjustment to specification. See RING GEAR BACKLASH under ADJUSTMENTS.

13) Install left differential housing seal. Support housing to prevent distorting or bending of housing. Apply gasket sealer to housing surface and install housing cover.

ADJUSTMENTS

DRIVE PINION DEPTH

1) Lubricate inner and outer pinion bearings liberally with axle lubricant. Hold pinion bearings in position and install Pinion Shim Setting Gauge (J-33838). With gauge installed, preload inner and outer pinion bearing to **15-25 INCH lbs. (1.7-2.8 N.m)** by tightening mounting bolt while holding end of gauge shaft with a wrench.

2) Using Dial Indicator (J-29763), set reading to zero, then position dial indicator on pinion shim setting gauge. Push dial indicator downward until needle rotates approximately 3 turns clockwise. Tighten dial indicator in this position. *See Fig. 5.*

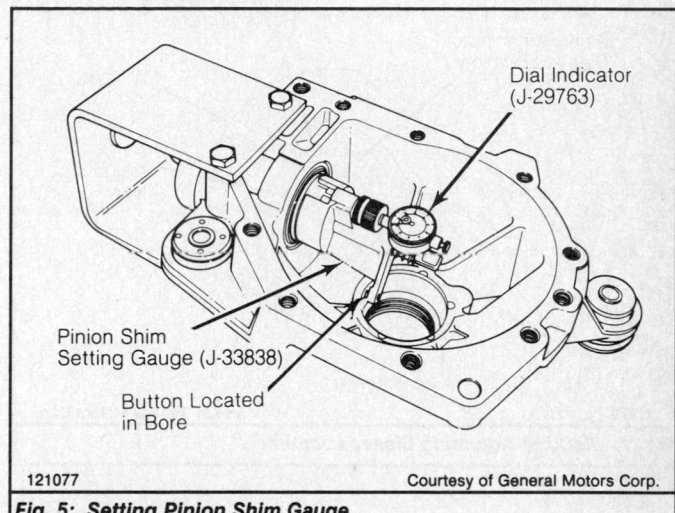

121077   Courtesy of General Motors Corp.

Fig. 5: Setting Pinion Shim Gauge

3) Set button of pinion shim setting gauge on differential bearing bore. Rotate gauge slowly back and forth until dial indicator reads lowest point of bore. Set dial indicator to zero. Repeat rocking action of gauge to verify zero setting.

4) After zero setting is obtained and verified, move gauge button out of differential side bearing bore. Record dial indicator reading. Use a shim that is exactly the same size as indicator reading.

5) Remove dial indicator and gauge from carrier. Position correct shim on drive pinion. Install drive pinion.

RING GEAR BACKLASH

1) Using Side Bearing Adjusting Wrench (J-33792), turn left side adjusting sleeve in toward differential housing until backlash is felt between ring and pinion gears.

2) Ensure carrier mating surfaces are clean. Assemble carrier halves without sealer. If housing halves do not make complete contact, back out right side adjusting sleeve.

3) Install 4 axle housing bolts and tighten to **37 ft. lbs. (50 N.m)**. Using side bearing adjusting wrench, tighten right adjusting sleeve approximately 100 ft. lbs. (136 N.m) until no backlash is felt. *See Fig. 6.*

4) Mark location of adjusting sleeves in relation to carrier halves so notches in adjusting sleeves can be counted when turned. Turn right adjusting sleeve out 2 notches using side bearing adjusting wrench. Turn left adjusting sleeve in one notch. *See Fig. 7.*

5) Rotate axle housing several times to seat bearings, then mount dial indicator. Use small button on indicator stem so contact can be made near heel of tooth for accurate backlash reading. Set backlash to specification. See AXLE ASSEMBLY SPECIFICATIONS table at end of article.

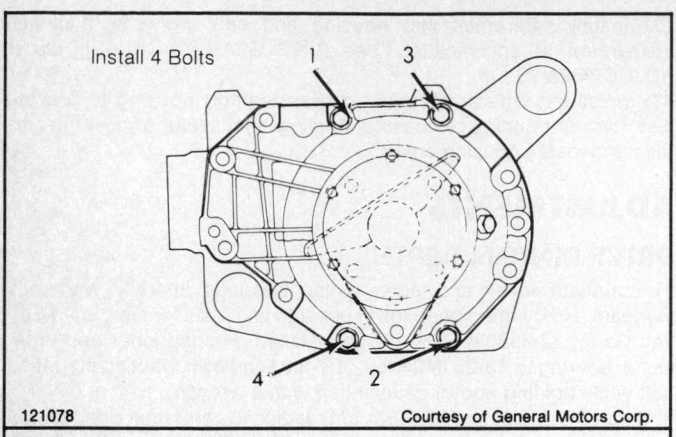

Install 4 Bolts

121078   Courtesy of General Motors Corp.

Fig. 6: Position of Bolts in Axle Housing

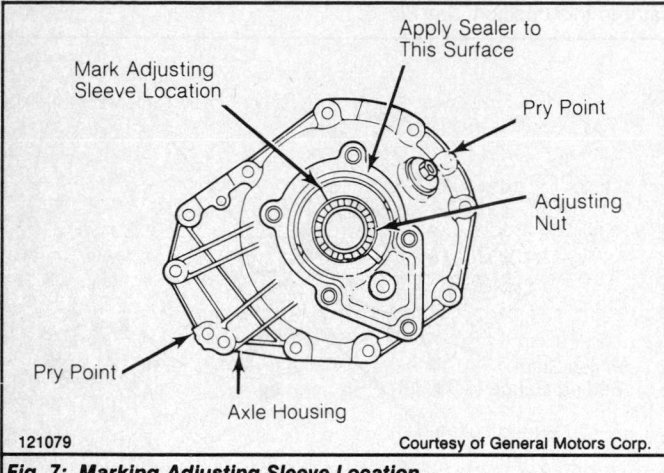

Mark Adjusting Sleeve Location

Apply Sealer to This Surface

Pry Point

Adjusting Nut

Pry Point

Axle Housing

121079   Courtesy of General Motors Corp.

Fig. 7: Marking Adjusting Sleeve Location

6) If backlash is not within specification, readjust adjusting sleeves as necessary. DO NOT install adjusting sleeve locks at this time.

7) Mark right adjusting sleeve so it can be repositioned in same location and loosen sleeve to release right side bearing-to-differential housing contact. Remove 4 axle housing bolts and axle housing half. Apply Loctite (514) on one axle housing surface.

8) Reinstall axle housing halves. Install 10 attaching bolts and tighten to specification. Reposition right adjusting sleeve in previous marked position and install both adjusting sleeve locks.

9) Perform gear tooth contact pattern check. See GEAR TOOTH CONTACT PATTERNS article in GENERAL INFORMATION.

AXLE ASSEMBLY SPECIFICATIONS

Application	In. (mm)
Ring Gear Backlash	.003-.010 (.08-.25)
Ring Gear Runout	.003 (.08)
	INCH Lbs. (N.m)
Pinion Bearing Preload	15-25 (1.7-2.8)

AXLE ASSEMBLY SPECIFICATIONS
AXLE ASSEMBLY SPECIFICATIONS

Application	In. (mm)
Ring Gear Backlash	.003-.010 (.08-.25)
Ring Gear Backlash Runout	.003 (.08)
	INCH Lbs. (N.m)
Pinion Bearing Preload	15-25 (1.7-2.8)

TORQUE SPECIFICATIONS
TORQUE SPECIFICATIONS

Application	Ft. Lbs. (N.m)
Differential Carrier Case Bolts	35 (47)
Drive Axle Nut	160-200 (217-271)
Drive Axle-To-Output Flange Bolts	60 (81)
Front Axle Mounting Bolts	65 (88)
Idler Arm-To-Frame Bolts	60 (81)
Lower Shock Bolt	18 (24)
Pinion Flange Bolts	55 (75)
Right Axle Tube-To-Differential Carrier Bolts	36 (49)
Right Axle Tube-To-Support Bracket Bolts	55 (75)
Ring Gear Attaching Bolts	60 (81)
Wheel Lug Nuts	90 (122)
	INCH Lbs. (N.m)
Adjusting Sleeve Lock Bolt	71 (8)

Astro, Bravada, Jimmy, Safari, Sierra, Sonoma, Suburban, Syclone, Typhoon, Van, Yukon, "C" & "K" Series Blazer & Pickup, "S" & "T" Series Blazer & Pickup

MODEL IDENTIFICATION

Vehicle model can be identified by fifth character of Vehicle Identification Number (VIN), stamped on metal pad on top of left end of instrument panel, near windshield. See MODEL IDENTIFICATION table.

MODEL IDENTIFICATION

Series [1]	Model
"C"	2WD Pickup, Sierra & Suburban
"K"	4WD Blazer, Pickup, Sierra, Suburban & Yukon
"L"	All-Wheel Drive Astro & Safari
"M"	2WD Astro & Safari
"S"	2WD Blazer, Jimmy, Pickup & Sonoma
"T"	Bravada, 4WD Blazer, Jimmy, Pickup, Sonoma, Syclone & Typhoon

[1] – Vehicle series is fifth character of VIN.

DESCRIPTION

NOTE: 8 1/2" ring gear differential is also used as front drive axle on K15/25 models. K15/25 models may also be equipped with a Dana front drive axle. See appropriate article in DRIVE AXLES.

NOTE: Some models are equipped with limited-slip or locking differentials. For testing and overhaul procedures for these units, see appropriate LOCKING DIFFERENTIAL article in DRIVE AXLES.

Drive axle assembly is hypoid gear type with integral carrier housing. This type assembly is used on Light Duty emission vehicles with semi-floating axles. Differential side bearing preload adjustment and drive pinion depth adjustment are made by using shims. Pinion bearing preload is made with a collapsible spacer.

A removable differential cover permits inspection and minor servicing of differential without removing axle assembly from vehicle. Service procedures are same for all assemblies, except for torque specifications and special tool numbers. Astro and Safari use 7 5/8" ring gear. "S" and "T" Series use 7 1/2" and 7 5/8" ring gears. All other models use 8 1/2" and 9 1/2" ring gears.

AXLE RATIO & IDENTIFICATION

To identify vehicle differential ring gear size and drive axle ratio, see AXLE RATIO IDENTIFICATION article.

LUBRICATION

Fill differential with 80W or 80W-90 GL-5 gear lubricant to 1/4" (6 mm) below edge of filler hole. On models equipped with limited-slip or locking differentials, add 4 ounces (.12 L) of limited slip additive.

TROUBLE SHOOTING

See TROUBLE SHOOTING article in GENERAL INFORMATION.

REMOVAL & INSTALLATION

AXLE SHAFT & BEARING

Removal – 1) Raise vehicle and support. Remove rear wheels and brake drums. Place drain pan below differential cover. Loosen but do not remove differential cover bolts. Break cover loose and catch lubricant in drain pan. Remove differential cover bolts and remove cover. Remove differential pinion shaft lock bolt.

2) On non-locking differential drive axle assemblies (without thrust block and clutch packs), remove differential pinion shaft. Push outer flanged end of axle shaft toward center of vehicle. Remove "C" lock from axle shaft groove and from counterbore recess in side gear. Remove axle shaft from axle housing.

3) On locking differential drive axle assemblies (with thrust block and clutch packs), partially remove pinion shaft from differential case. Rotate differential case until pinion shaft touches edge of carrier housing. See Fig. 1.

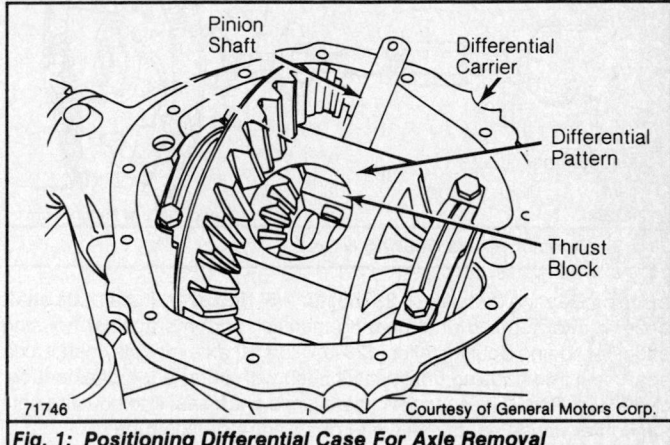

71746   Courtesy of General Motors Corp.
Fig. 1: Positioning Differential Case For Axle Removal

4) Reach into case with screwdriver and rotate "C" lock until its open end points directly inward toward thrust block and "C" lock is aligned with thrust block sides. See Fig. 2. When "C" lock is correctly positioned, push outer flanged end of axle shaft toward center of vehicle. This will move "C" lock out of counterbore recess in side gear and allow it to be removed from thrust block and from axle shaft groove. Remove axle shaft from axle housing. See Fig. 2.

CAUTION: DO NOT hammer on axle shaft flange. Axle shaft should slide inward easily when "C" lock is correctly aligned with thrust block. When removing pinion shaft from differential case on 9½" ring gear axle, be sure pinion gear thrust washer does not slip out.

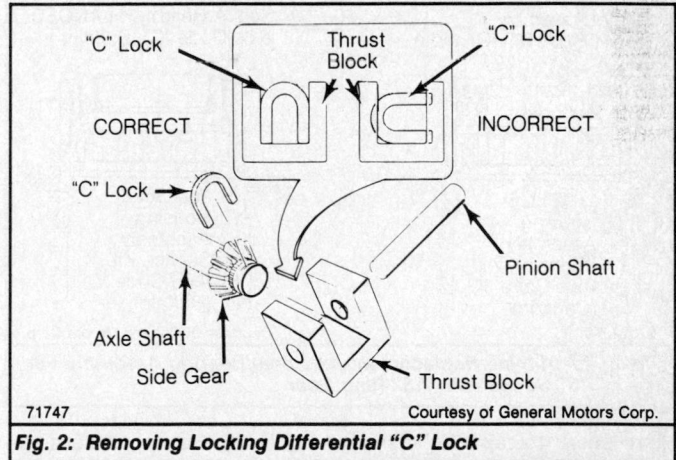

71747   Courtesy of General Motors Corp.
Fig. 2: Removing Locking Differential "C" Lock

5) On all assemblies, with axle shaft removed, insert Axle Bearing & Seal Remover (J-22813-01) for 7 1/2" and 7 5/8", (J-23689) for 8 1/2" or (J-29712) for 9 1/2" ring gears into axle housing behind bearing. Attach Slide Hammer (J-2619) and Adapter (J-2619-4) for 7 1/2" and 7 5/8" or (J-2619-01) for 8 1/2" and 9 1/2" ring gears to bearing remover. Remove axle bearing and axle seal. See Fig. 3.

CAUTION: On "S" Series with 7.5" ring gear, there are 2 different replacement seal/bearing assemblies available. These assemblies are not interchangeable.

Installation ("S" Series) – 1) On "S" Series with 7.5" ring gear assembly, there are 2 different seal/bearing assemblies available that are not interchangeable. If axle code fourth digit is a "K", use part numbers 26029139 (seal) and 26024326 (bearing kit). If axle code fourth digit is a "C", use part numbers 26029137 (seal) and 26023822 (bearing kit). See Fig. 4.

GM
7-24

1992 DRIVE AXLES
7 1/2", 7 5/8", 8 1/2" & 9 1/2" Ring Gears (Cont.)

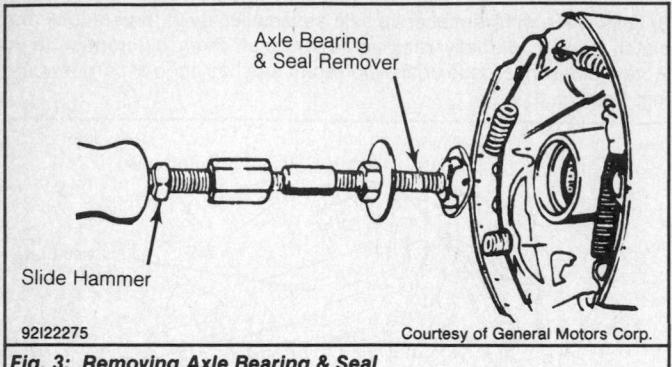

Fig. 3: Removing Axle Bearing & Seal

2) Using Bearing Installer (J-23765) for 7.5" ring gear, install axle shaft bearing into housing until bearing installer bottoms against housing shoulder. Using Seal Installer (J23771), on "K" axle models, install axle shaft seal into housing until seal is flush with outer edge of axle tube. See Fig. 4. On "C" axle models, install axle shaft seal into housing until seal outer flange seats itself with outer edge of axle tube.

3) Install axle shaft and "C" lock. Pull axle shaft outward to seat "C" lock into side gear counterbore recess. Install pinion shaft and pinion shaft lock bolt. Tighten bolt to specification. See TORQUE SPECIFICATIONS table at end of article. To complete installation, reverse removal procedure.

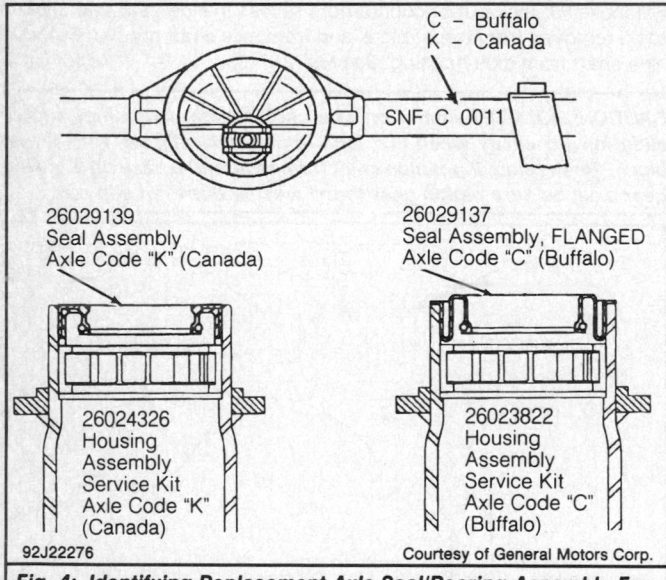

Fig. 4: Identifying Replacement Axle Seal/Bearing Assembly For "S" Series With 7.5" Ring Gear

Installation (Except "S" Series) – 1) Using Bearing Installer (J-23765) for 7 1/2" and 7 5/8", (J-23690) for 8 1/2" or (J-29709) for 9 1/2" ring gears, install axle shaft bearing into housing until bearing installer bottoms against housing shoulder.

2) Using Seal Installer (J-23771) for 7 1/2" and 7 5/8", (J-21128) for 8 1/2" or (J-29713) for 9 1/2" ring gears, install axle shaft seal into housing until seal is flush with outer edge of axle tube. Install axle shaft and "C" lock. Pull axle shaft outward to seat "C" lock into side gear counterbore recess.

3) Install pinion shaft and pinion shaft lock bolt. Tighten lock bolt to specification. See TORQUE SPECIFICATIONS table at end of article. To complete installation, reverse removal procedure.

PINION FLANGE & OIL SEAL

NOTE: If replacing pinion and ring gear, discard original pinion flange after removal. Replacement pinion, ring gear and pinion flange are balanced as an assembly.

Removal – 1) Raise vehicle and support. Allow rear hub and carrier assembly to hang free. Remove drive shaft from pinion flange. Wrap tape around all "U" joint caps to retain caps in place. Position drive shaft out of way.

2) Using an INCH lb. torque wrench with proper size socket connected to pinion flange nut, rotate pinion several revolutions. Stop and start rotation several times to note and record pinion bearing preload.

3) Ensure relationship of pinion-to-pinion flange nut-to-pinion flange is marked for reassembly purposes. Count and record number of exposed threads on pinion.

4) Hold pinion flange with Companion Flange Holder/Remover (J-8614-01 or J-8614-1). See Fig. 5. Remove pinion self-locking nut. Install Pinion Flange Remover (J-8614-1, -2 and -3) through companion flange holder and remover. Tighten pinion flange remover. Remove pinion flange from pinion. Pry pinion seal from housing. DO NOT damage differential carrier or seal running surface on pinion when removing pinion seal.

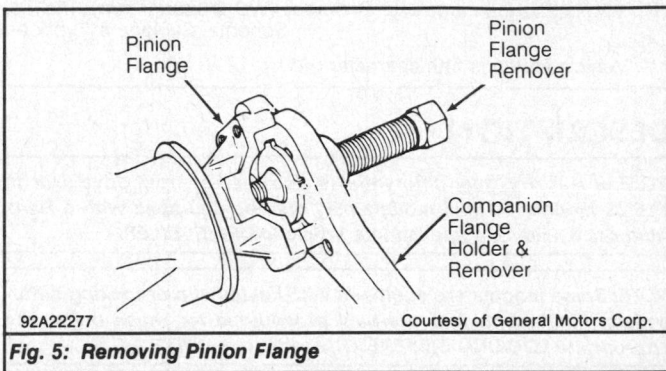

Fig. 5: Removing Pinion Flange

CAUTION: DO NOT hammer flange onto pinion shaft to install, as ring gear and pinion will be damaged.

Installation – 1) Inspect pinion flange oil seal surface, drive splines, flange ears and bearing contact surface. Replace pinion flange if damaged. Lubricate inside diameter of seal. Place pinion seal in housing bore.

2) Using Seal Installer (J-23911) for 7 1/2" and 7 5/8" ring gears, (J-23836) for 8 1/2" ring gear or (J-22388) for 9 1/2" ring gear, install pinion seal into bore until seal is flush with outer edge of housing. Ensure oil seal is square in housing.

3) Install a non-hardening sealer to pinion splines or internal splines of pinion flange. Install flange on pinion shaft, aligning scribe marks made previously. If required, use only soft-faced (rubber) hammer to tap flange onto pinion.

4) Install washer and self-locking nut to pinion, and snug tighten, taking note of scribe marks and number of exposed threads. Measure pinion preload. Using companion flange holder and remover, and socket/torque wrench assembly, tighten self-locking nut in small increments. Measure pinion preload until preload exceeds original figure by 3-5 INCH lbs. (.3-.6 N.m). If preload exceeds specification, remove pinion and replace collapsible sleeve. Install drive shaft. Add gear oil as needed.

REAR HUB & CARRIER ASSEMBLY

Removal & Installation – 1) Raise vehicle and support at frame. Allow rear hub and carrier assembly to hang free. Drain lubricant. Remove rear wheels and brake drums. Remove parking brake cable. Disconnect drive shaft and brake lines. Disconnect vent hose from vent fitting on axle housing. Support axle housing with floor jack under center of carrier assembly. Disconnect height sensing and brake proportional valve linkage (if equipped).

2) Disconnect shock absorbers at axle housing. Remove stabilizer shaft (if equipped) from housing. Remove "U" bolt nuts, washers, spacers and spring plates from axle assembly. Note angle position of wedge type spring plates (if equipped). Slowly lower floor jack. Remove axle assembly from vehicle.

1992 DRIVE AXLES
7 1/2", 7 5/8", 8 1/2" & 9 1/2" Ring Gears (Cont.)

GM
7-25

3) To install rear hub and carrier assembly, reverse removal procedure. Bleed brake system. Adjust height sensing and brake proportional valve linkage (if equipped).

OVERHAUL

DIFFERENTIAL ASSEMBLY

NOTE: Check and record ring gear backlash and pinion bearing preload before disassembly.

Disassembly – 1) Remove axle shafts. See AXLE SHAFT & BEARING under REMOVAL & INSTALLATION. Roll out differential pinions and thrust washers. Mark pinions and thrust washers (left and right) for reassembly purposes. Remove side gears and thrust washers. Mark side gears and thrust washers (left and right) for reassembly purposes.

2) Mark differential case side bearing caps and housing for reassembly purposes. Loosen bearing cap bolts and tap bearing cap surfaces to loosen caps. Remove caps, mark shims, spacers, and side bearing races. Using pry bar inserted into differential case, pry against housing at differential window to remove case.

CAUTION: Differential case side bearings are preloaded. Differential case will fall free after being pried past a certain point.

3) After removing differential case, place loose shims with appropriate left and right bearing races. Using Differential Side Bearing Puller/Remover (J-22888) and Adapter (J-8107-2) for 7 1/2" and 7 5/8" ring gears, (J-8107-4) for 8 1/2" or (J-8107-3) for 9 1/2" ring gears, remove differential case side bearings. DO NOT pull on bearing cage, pull on bearing cone.

4) Ring gear bolts have left-hand threads. Remove ring gear bolts. Tap ring gear off carrier using a soft drift and hammer. Using an INCH lb. torque wrench and proper socket, check torque required to rotate drive pinion. If no preload reading is obtained, check for looseness of pinion assembly. Looseness indicates pinion bearings and collapsible sleeve should be replaced.

5) Remove pinion flange. See PINION FLANGE & OIL SEAL under REMOVAL & INSTALLATION. Install pinion nut back onto pinion. Install rear differential cover using 2 bolts to keep pinion from falling out. Tap end of pinion (using soft drift and hammer) to remove pinion from front bearing.

CAUTION: Use care not to damage pinion bearings when removing pinion from differential housing.

6) Remove differential cover and pinion assembly. Remove pinion oil seal and front bearing from housing. Remove collapsible spacer from pinion. Remove inner bearing from pinion using a press and Bearing Remover Clamp (J-25320) for 7 1/2" and 7 5/8", (J-8612-B) for 8 1/2" or (J-22912-01) on 9 1/2" ring gears. Press bearing from pinion and remove shim.

7) Remove pinion bearing races from axle housing using hammer and punch. Inspect bearings and bearing races. Replace as required. Discard and replace pinion oil seal, pinion self-locking nut and collapsible spacer.

Cleaning & Inspection – Clean all parts in cleaning solvent. Inspect all bearings and races for chipping, cracks, brinelling or excessive wear. Inspect axle shaft splines, ring gear and pinion teeth for scoring, cracking or chipping. Inspect differential case side gears, thrust washers and pinion shaft for cracks or excessive wear. Inspect pinion flange oil seal surface, drive splines, flange ears and bearing contact surface. Replace components as required.

Reassembly – 1) If installing new ring gear and pinion, and/or pinion bearings, see DRIVE PINION DEPTH and SIDE BEARING PRELOAD under ADJUSTMENTS. After installing original pinion shims onto pinion, install inner pinion bearing onto pinion using Bearing Installer (J-5590). Drive bearing onto pinion until bearing is tightly seated against pinion shims.

2) Install a NEW collapsible spacer onto pinion. Lubricate pinion bearings. Install pinion into axle housing. Install outer bearing onto pinion using Bearing Installer (J-5590). Hold pinion in position from inside housing while driving bearing onto pinion. To install pinion oil seal and pinion flange, see PINION FLANGE & OIL SEAL under REMOVAL & INSTALLATION.

3) Install ring gear squarely onto differential case. Tighten ring gear bolts evenly and alternately to specification. Ring gear bolts are left-hand thread. See TORQUE SPECIFICATIONS table at end of article.

4) Lubricate pinion gears and side gears with gear oil. Install left and right side gears and thrust washers into case as marked in disassembly. Install one pinion gear onto side gears and rotate gears until pinion gear is exactly opposite. Place second pinion gear onto side gears so that pinion gear holes are exactly opposite each other.

5) Verify pinion shaft fits through both pinion gears for alignment purposes. Install pinion gear thrust washers. Hold pinion gears in position and carefully remove pinion shaft. Rotate side gears to position pinion gears in alignment with differential case holes. Install pinion shaft and pinion shaft lock bolt. Temporarily snug tighten lock bolt.

6) If side bearings were removed, install side bearings to differential case using Press or Bearing Installer (J-25299). Using Bearing Installer (J-25299), first install Adapter (J-8107-2) to opposite bearing end of differential case to protect case surface. Drive bearing onto case using hammer, Bearing Installer (J-25299) and Adapter (J-8092). Repeat for opposite side.

7) Lubricate side bearings and install races. Install differential case into carrier housing. Install spacer between each bearing race and housing with chamfered edge of spacer against housing. Install right bearing cap and loosely tighten bolts so that differential case is free to move but will not fall out of housing. To complete installation, see SIDE BEARING PRELOAD under ADJUSTMENTS.

ADJUSTMENTS

DRIVE PINION DEPTH

1) Drive pinion rear bearing shim thickness must be determined whenever a new axle housing, ring gear and pinion, or pinion bearings is installed. Shim pack thickness is determined by using Pinion Setting Gauge Set (J-21777). *See Fig. 6.*

2) Install pinion bearing races into housing (if previously removed). Install lubricated rear pinion bearing through rear of housing. Position Gauging Plate (J-23597-11) for 7 1/2" and 7 5/8", (J-21777-29) for 8 1/2" or (J-21777-85) for 9 1/2" ring gears to rear pinion bearing. Install stud bolt and washer through gauging plate and rear pinion bearing, pointing stud bolt toward front pinion bearing position. *See Fig. 6.*

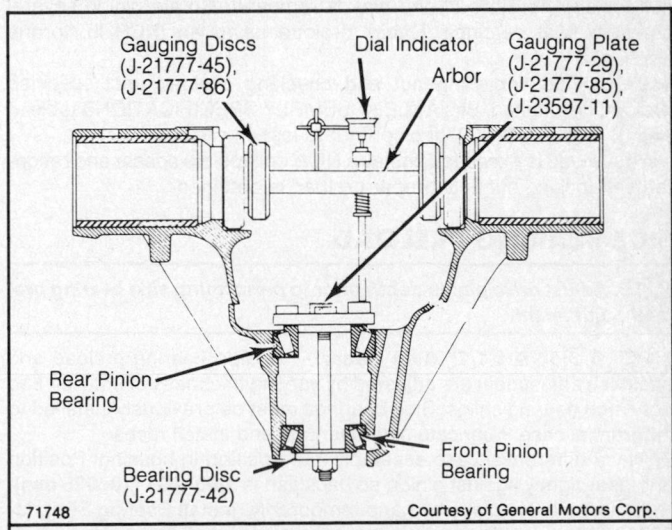

Gauging Discs
(J-21777-45),
(J-21777-86)

Dial Indicator

Gauging Plate
(J-21777-29),
(J-21777-85),
(J-23597-11)

Arbor

Rear Pinion
Bearing

Front Pinion
Bearing

Bearing Disc
(J-21777-42)

71748

Courtesy of General Motors Corp.

Fig. 6: Sectional View Of Pinion Setting Gauge Set

GM
7-26

1992 DRIVE AXLES
7 1/2", 7 5/8", 8 1/2" & 9 1/2" Ring Gears (Cont.)

3) Install lubricated front pinion bearing into race. Install Bearing Disc (J-21777-42) to outside of front pinion bearing. Install and tighten stud bolt hex nut until snug. Rotate gauge plate and bearings to insure proper seating, while snugging hex nut. Hold stud bolt head stationary with a wrench. Using INCH lb. torque wrench, tighten hex nut in small increments until **20 INCH lbs. (2.2 N.m)** of torque is required to rotate gauge plate and bearings. *See Fig. 6.*

4) Mount side bearing Gauging Discs (J-21777-45) for 7 1/2", 7 5/8" and 8 1/2" ring gears or (J-21777-86) for 9 1/2" ring gear on ends of arbor. Place arbor into carrier side bearing recesses making sure gauging discs are properly seated. Install side bearing caps and bolts. Snug tighten bolts to avoid arbor movement.

5) Position dial indicator on mounting post of arbor with contact button resting on top surface of plunger. Set dial indicator to zero. Push indicator down on indicator shaft until needle rotates 3 to 4 revolutions to right, then tighten in this position.

6) Place plunger onto gauging area of pinion gauge plate. Rock plunger rod slowly back and forth across gauging area until dial indicator reads greatest deflection.

7) At point of greatest deflection, set indicator to zero. Repeat rocking action several times to verify setting. Once zero reading is obtained, rotate gauge shaft to remove plunger from gauging area.

8) Dial indicator will now read required pinion shim thickness for nominal pinion setting. Record this reading. Check drive pinion for painted or stamped markings on pinion stems, or for a stamped code number on small end of pinion gear.

9) If marking is a plus (+), add that many thousandths of an inch to recorded indicator reading. If marking is a minus (–), subtract that many thousandths of an inch from indicator reading. This measurement will then be required thickness of rear pinion bearing shim pack.

NOTE: If no markings are found on pinion, use dial indicator reading as shim thickness.

10) Remove bearing caps and all gauging tools from housing. Place selected shim pack on pinion gear. Using a press, install lubricated pinion bearing onto pinion shaft.

11) Install a NEW collapsible spacer over pinion gear shaft. Install pinion assembly into position from rear of housing. While holding pinion in position, carefully drive front pinion bearing onto pinion gear shaft until a few threads are exposed.

12) Install pinion seal, pinion flange, washer and nut. Ensure pinion flange alignment mark is properly aligned with pinion shaft end mark. Using Companion Flange Holder/Remover (J-8614-01), tighten pinion self-locking nut until all end play is removed. Rotate pinion several times to seat bearings. Check preload using an INCH lb. torque wrench.

13) Continue tightening nut and checking preload until specified preload is obtained. See AXLE ASSEMBLY SPECIFICATIONS table at end of article. DO NOT back off nut to lessen preload.

14) If preload is exceeded, install a NEW collapsible spacer and retighten self-locking nut until proper preload is obtained.

SIDE BEARING PRELOAD

NOTE: Adjust drive pinion depth prior to performing side bearing preload adjustment.

7 1/2", 7 5/8" & 8 1/2" Ring Gears – 1) Side bearing preload and backlash adjustment are adjusted by varying thickness of both left and right side bearing shims. Side bearings must be previously installed to differential case. Lubricate side bearings and install races.

2) Place differential case assembly into position in housing. Position ring gear tightly against pinion so backlash is **.000-.001" (0-.025 mm)**. Hold assembly in place by hand temporarily. Install Bearing Strap (J-22799-6) to left side bearing race.

3) Install Side Bearing Backlash Gauge (J-22779) between left side bearing race and carrier housing. *See Fig. 7.* While moving gauge up and down, tighten gauge adjusting nut until a slight drag is felt. Tighten lock bolt on side of gauge and leave gauge in position.

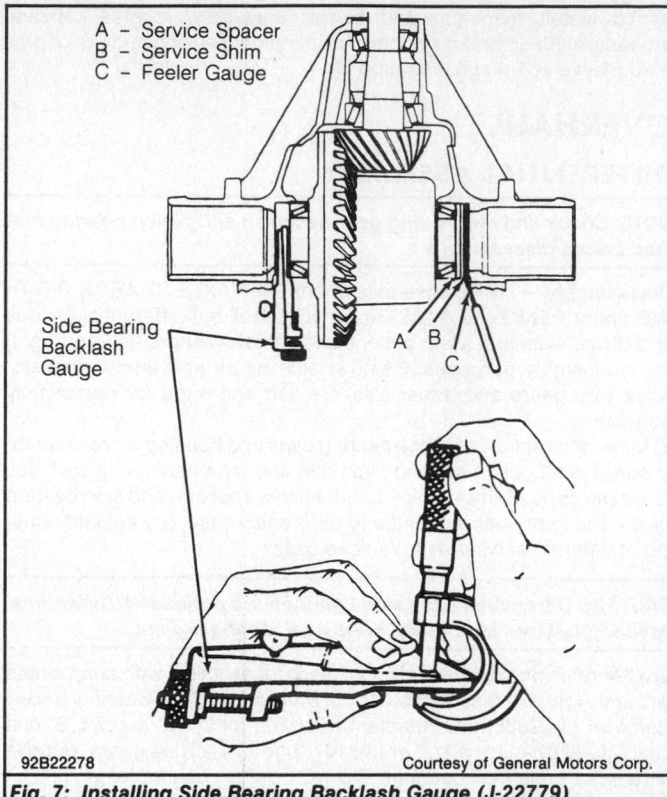

A – Service Spacer
B – Service Shim
C – Feeler Gauge

Side Bearing
Backlash
Gauge

92B22278   Courtesy of General Motors Corp.

Fig. 7: Installing Side Bearing Backlash Gauge (J-22779)

4) Install service adjustment spacer and shim between right bearing race and carrier housing. Determine bearing preload by inserting progressively larger feeler gauges between carrier and shim. The point just before feeler gauge drag begins is the correct feeler gauge thickness. This is the zero setting without preload.

5) Remove gauge from left side. Using a micrometer, measure gauge in 3 places and average readings. Record measurements.

6) Add together measurements of right side shim, spacer and feeler gauge. Subtract .010" (.25 mm) from ring gear (left) side measurement and add .010" (.25 mm) to opposite (right) side measurement. This allows for initial backlash adjustment.

7) To obtain correct preload, add .004" (.10 mm) to both measurements. The total measurement is correct shim pack thickness for each side.

Example:

Ring Gear Side (Left) Shim Pack

  .250" (Gauging Tool Measurement)

-.010" (Backlash Adjustment)

+.004" (Bearing Preload)

=.244" (Ring Gear Side Shim Pack)

Opposite Ring Gear Side (Right) Shim Pack

  .265" (Combined Measurement Total)

+.010" (Backlash Adjustment)

+.004" (Bearing Preload)

=.279" (Opposite Ring Gear Side Shim Pack)

NOTE: If shim is not chamfered enough and scrapes spacer when it is installed, file or grind chamfer before installation.

8) Install ring gear side shim first. Wedge opposite side shim between bearing cup and spacer. Install shim so chamfered side is against spacer. It may be necessary to partially remove differential case to install right side shim. If necessary, carefully tap shim into place with a soft-faced hammer. Tighten bearing cap bolts to specifications. See TORQUE SPECIFICATIONS table at end of article. Check backlash. See BACKLASH & FINAL ASSEMBLY.

9 1/2" Ring Gear – 1) Differential side bearing preload is adjusted by adjusting nut in right side differential bearing bore and by adjusting

1992 DRIVE AXLES
7 1/2", 7 5/8", 8 1/2" & 9 1/2" Ring Gears (Cont.)

GM
7-27

shims in left side bearing bore. Bore and bearing cap provide mating threads for preload adjusting nut.

2) Install bearing races to differential bearings. Install differential case into axle housing assembly and temporarily hold in position by hand. Install bearing shims so chamfered side is against spacer.

3) Push differential case away from pinion and install adjusting nut. Tighten right side preload adjusting nut using Spanner Wrench (J-24429). Turn pinion to seat differential case bearings.

4) Back off adjusting nut slightly. Install bearing caps and snug tighten bolts. Turn adjusting nut until nut contacts shim. Note nut position and tighten nut 3 additional slots.

5) Tighten bearing cap bolts to specification. Install adjusting nut lock bolt and tighten to specification. See TORQUE SPECIFICATIONS table at end of article. Check backlash adjustment. See BACKLASH & FINAL ASSEMBLY.

BACKLASH & FINAL ASSEMBLY

1) Rotate pinion and differential case several times to seat bearings. Using a dial indicator mounted to axle housing, check ring gear backlash at 4 different teeth locations around ring gear. Install indicator in line with gear rotation and perpendicular to tooth angle.

2) Pinion flange must be locked in position or held rigid while taking each backlash reading. The 4 backlash readings should not vary more than .002" (.05 mm).

3) Total backlash reading should be .005-.009" (.13-.23 mm). If backlash is incorrect, adjust side bearing shims as necessary. After backlash adjustment is completed, perform gear tooth contact pattern check. See GEAR TOOTH CONTACT PATTERNS article in GENERAL INFORMATION.

4) If pattern is incorrect, adjust pinion or ring gear as required. Install axle shafts, "C" locks, pinion shaft and lock bolt. Install rear housing cover and add gear oil. *See Fig. 8.*

NOTE: DO NOT change total shim pack thickness for each side bearing. If a shim is removed from one side, add same thickness shim to other side.

AXLE ASSEMBLY SPECIFICATIONS

AXLE ASSEMBLY SPECIFICATIONS

Application	Specification In. (mm)
Ring Gear Backlash	.005-.009 (.13-.23)
Side Bearing Preload	.008 (.20)

	INCH Lbs. (N.m)
Pinion Bearing Preload [1]	
7 1/2" & 7 5/8" Ring Gear	
New Bearings	24-32 (2.7-3.6)
Used Bearings	8-12 (1.0-1.4)
8 1/2" & 9 1/2" Ring Gear	
New Bearings	20-25 (2.3-2.8)
Used Bearings	10-15 (1.1-1.7)

[1] – Preload measurement is torque needed to turn pinion in housing without differential case and ring gear installed.

TORQUE SPECIFICATIONS

TORQUE SPECIFICATIONS

Application	Ft. Lbs. (N.m)
Differential Bearing	
Adjusting Nut Lock Bolt (9 1/2" Ring Gear)	22 (30)
Differential Cover Bolts	20 (27)
Drive Shaft-To-Pinion Flange Bolts	
Except "S" & "T" Series	[1]
"S" & "T" Series	27 (37)
Pinion Shaft Lock Bolt	25 (34)
Ring Gear-To-Differential Case Bolt [2]	
7 1/2" & 7 5/8" Ring Gear	90 (122)
8 1/2" Ring Gear	90 (122)
9 1/2" Ring Gear	105 (142)
Side Bearing Cap Bolt	
7 1/2" Ring Gear	55 (75)
8 1/2" Ring Gear	60 (81)
9 1/2" Ring Gear	60 (81)
Side Bearing Preload Adjusting Nut Lock Bolt	
9 1/2" Ring Gear	22 (30)
Spring U-Bolts ("S" & "T" Series)	
Inner Nuts	41 (56)
Outer Nuts	48 (65)

[1] – Information is not available.
[2] – Left-hand thread. Use new bolts.

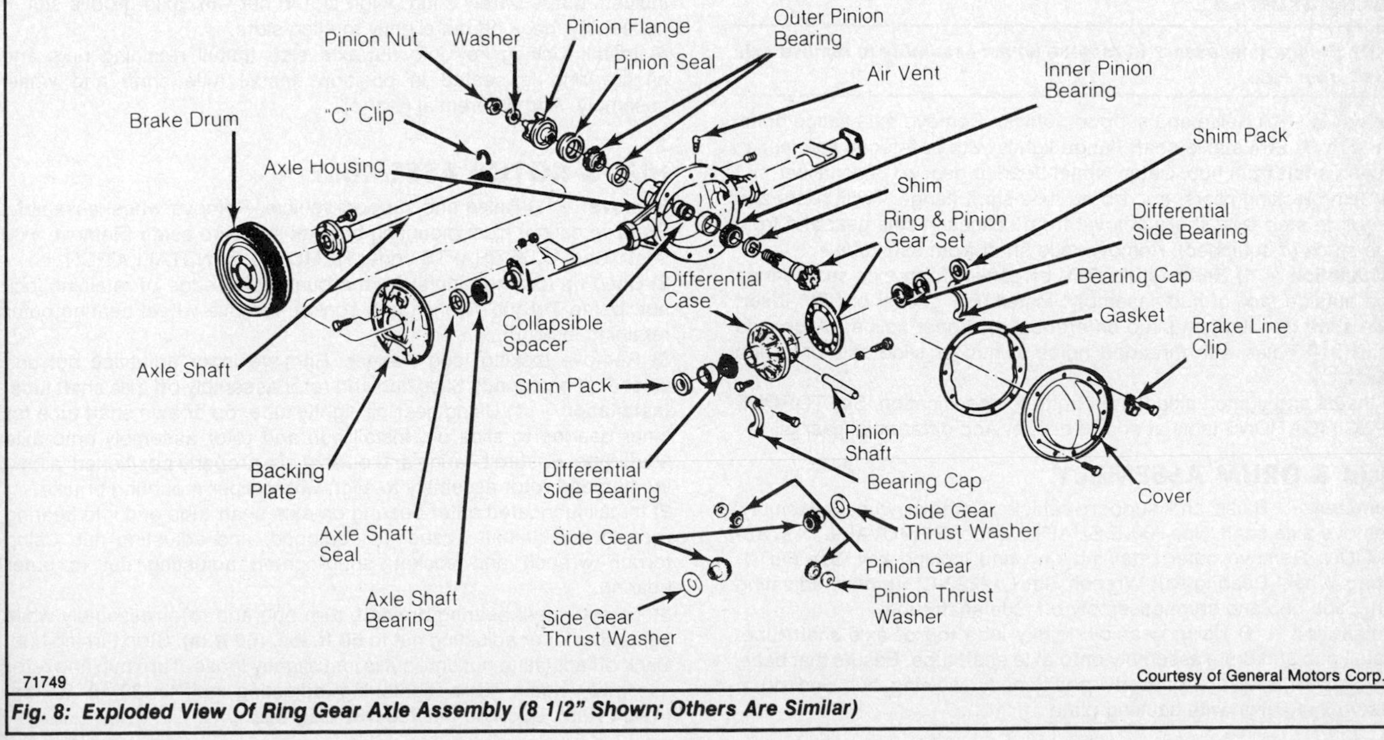

71749

Courtesy of General Motors Corp.

Fig. 8: Exploded View Of Ring Gear Axle Assembly (8 1/2" Shown; Others Are Similar)

1992 DRIVE AXLES
Dana 9 3/4" & 10 1/2" Full-Floating Axles

Commercial Van, Sierra, Suburban, Van, Yukon, "C" & "K" Series Blazer & Pickup

DESCRIPTION

MODEL IDENTIFICATION

Vehicle model can be identified by fifth character of Vehicle Identification Number (VIN), stamped on metal pad on top of left end of instrument panel, near windshield. See MODEL IDENTIFICATION table.

MODEL IDENTIFICATION

Series [1]	Model
"C"	2WD Pickup, Sierra & Suburban
"G"	RWD Van
"K"	4WD Blazer, Pickup, Sierra, Suburban & Yukon
"P"	Commercial Van/Motorhome

[1] – Vehicle series is fifth character of VIN.

The 9 3/4" and 10 1/2" ring gear rear axle assemblies use an integral carrier with conventional hypoid ring gear and pinion assembly. Full floating axle shaft is not supported by a bearing on wheel hub end. The axle shaft flange is bolted to outer wheel hub assembly. Wheel hub assembly is supported by bearings that mount to axle housing tube. The splined end of axle shaft is supported by differential side gear and case bearing.

AXLE RATIO & IDENTIFICATION

To identify vehicle differential ring gear size and drive axle ratio, see AXLE RATIO IDENTIFICATION article.

LUBRICATION

Fill differential with 80W or 80W-90 GL-5 gear lubricant to 1/4" (6 mm) below edge of filler hole.

TROUBLE SHOOTING

NOTE: See TROUBLE SHOOTING article in GENERAL INFORMATION.

REMOVAL & INSTALLATION

AXLE SHAFTS

NOTE: It is not necessary to remove wheel assembly to remove axle shaft from hub.

Removal – **1)** Raise and support vehicle. Remove axle flange bolts. See Fig. 1. Strike axle shaft flange lightly with soft-faced hammer to loosen shaft from hub. Catch wheel bearing gear oil in container.
2) Using locking pliers, grip rib on axle shaft flange. Twist pliers and flange to start axle shaft removal from splines in side gear and from hub studs (if equipped). Remove axle shaft from axle tube.
Installation – **1)** Remove old RTV or gasket from axle shaft flange and outside face of hub assembly. Install new gasket or RTV. Insert axle shaft into tube and into differential side gear splines. Align axle shaft bolt holes with threaded holes in hub or slide axle onto hub studs.
2) Install and tighten axle flange bolts to specification. See TORQUE SPECIFICATIONS table at end of article. Add differential gear oil.

HUB & DRUM ASSEMBLY

Removal – Raise and support vehicle. Remove wheel assembly. Remove axle shaft. See AXLE SHAFTS under REMOVAL & INSTALLATION. Remove outer retaining ring and locking key. See Fig. 1. Using Wheel Bearing Nut Wrench Set (J-2222-C), remove adjusting nut. Slide hub and drum assembly off axle shaft tube.
Installation – **1)** Using gear oil, lightly lube top of axle shaft tube. Install hub and drum assembly onto axle shaft tube. Ensure that bearing and oil seal are properly positioned, allowing hub and drum assembly to align with backing plate.

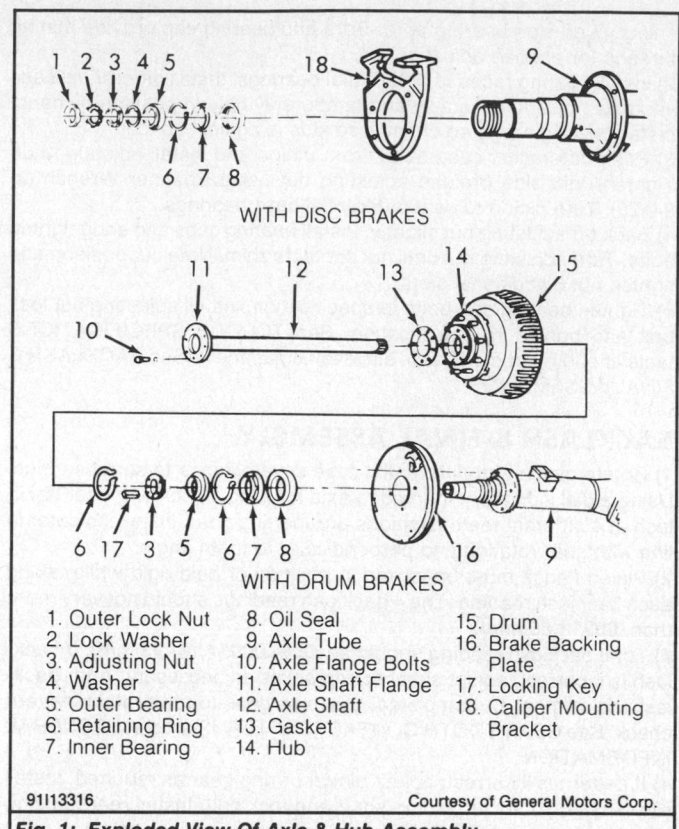

1. Outer Lock Nut
2. Lock Washer
3. Adjusting Nut
4. Washer
5. Outer Bearing
6. Retaining Ring
7. Inner Bearing
8. Oil Seal
9. Axle Tube
10. Axle Flange Bolts
11. Axle Shaft Flange
12. Axle Shaft
13. Gasket
14. Hub
15. Drum
16. Brake Backing Plate
17. Locking Key
18. Caliper Mounting Bracket

91I13316   Courtesy of General Motors Corp.

Fig. 1: Exploded View Of Axle & Hub Assembly

2) Install lubricated outer bearing on axle shaft tube and into bearing race in hub. Using torque wrench and socket from Wheel Bearing Nut Wrench Set (J-2222-C), install and tighten adjusting nut snugly to outer bearing.
3) To set wheel bearing preload, turn hub and drum assembly while tightening adjusting nut to **50 ft. lbs. (68 N.m)**. Stop turning hub. Back off adjusting nut until nut is just slightly loose. Tighten adjusting nut until nut just contacts bearing. Feeling at wrench handle should indicate nut is barely snug. Align slot in nut with axle groove slot. If necessary, back off nut slightly to align slots.
4) Install locking key into nut/axle slot. Install retaining ring, and ensure ring is seated in position. Install axle shaft and wheel assembly. Add differential gear oil.

HUB & ROTOR ASSEMBLY

Removal – **1)** Raise and support vehicle. Remove wheel assembly. Remove caliper from mounting bracket and wire aside. Remove axle shaft. See AXLE SHAFTS under REMOVAL & INSTALLATION.
2) Bend up locking tang(s) from around outer edge of retaining lock nut. Using Torque Wrench and socket, remove wheel bearing outer retaining lock nut.
3) Remove locking tang washer. Remove inner adjusting nut and washer (if equipped). Slide hub and rotor assembly off axle shaft tube.
Installation – **1)** Using gear oil, lightly lube top of axle shaft tube for inner bearing to slide on. Install hub and rotor assembly onto axle shaft tube. Ensure bearing and oil seal are properly positioned, allowing hub and rotor assembly to align with caliper mounting bracket.
2) Install lubricated outer bearing on axle shaft tube and into bearing race in hub. Install washer (if equipped) and adjusting nut. Using torque wrench and socket, snug-tighten adjusting nut to outer bearing.
3) To set wheel bearing preload, turn hub and rotor assembly while tightening inner adjusting nut to **50 ft. lbs. (68 N.m)**. Stop turning hub. Back off adjusting nut until nut is just slightly loose. Turn hub and rotor assembly again while tightening adjusting nut to **30-40 ft. lbs. (41-54 N.m)**. Back off nut **135-150 degrees**.

1992 DRIVE AXLES
Dana 9 3/4" & 10 1/2" Full-Floating Axles (Cont.)

GM
7-29

4) After completing adjustment, install locking tang washer and outer lock nut. Tighten lock nut to **65 ft. lbs. (88 N.m)**. Bend minimum of 2 locking tangs outward against flat surfaces or into notches of outer lock nut. Install axle shaft and wheel assembly. Add differential gear oil.

PINION FLANGE & PINION SEAL

NOTE: If replacing pinion and ring gear, discard original pinion flange after removal. Replacement pinion, ring gear and pinion flange are balanced as an assembly for vehicle drivetrain "harmonics" reasons.

Removal – 1) Raise vehicle and support. Allow rear axle housing assembly to hang free. Remove drive shaft from pinion flange. Wrap tape around all "U" joint caps to retain caps in place. Position drive shaft aside.

2) For reassembly reference, scribe mark across pinion, pinion flange nut, and pinion flange. Count number of exposed threads on pinion before removing nut.

3) Hold pinion flange with Companion Flange Holder/Remover (J-8614-01 or J-8614-1). *See Fig. 2.* Remove pinion self-locking nut and washer (if equipped). Install Pinion Flange Remover (J-8614-1, -2 and -3) through companion flange holder/remover. Tighten pinion flange remover. Remove pinion flange from pinion. Pry pinion seal from housing bore, being careful not to damage machined surfaces.

CAUTION: DO NOT hammer-force flange onto pinion shaft to install, as flange, ring gear and pinion will be damaged.

Installation – 1) Inspect pinion flange oil seal surface, drive splines, flange ears and bearing contact surface. Replace pinion flange if damaged. Thoroughly clean machined surfaces. Lubricate inside diameter of seal. Place pinion seal in housing bore.

2) Using Pinion Seal Installer (J-24384), drive oil seal into position in housing bore until flush with housing. Install a non-hardening sealer to pinion splines or to internal splines of pinion flange. Install flange on pinion shaft, aligning scribe marks made previously. If required, use only "soft" faced (rubber) hammer to tap flange onto pinion.

3) Install washer (if equipped) and self-locking nut to pinion, and snug tighten. Using companion flange holder and remover, hold pinion flange and tighten pinion nut. Take note of scribe alignment marks and number of exposed threads.

4) If scribe alignment marks are exceeded when tightening nut, remove pinion and install NEW collapsible sleeve. Install drive shaft. Add gear oil as needed.

REAR AXLE HOUSING ASSEMBLY

Removal – 1) Raise and support vehicle. Place jackstands under frame side rails. Allow rear axle housing assembly to hang free. Drain lubricant from differential. Remove drive shaft and wheel assemblies.

2) Remove hub and drum assembly or hub and rotor assembly. See HUB & DRUM ASSEMBLY or HUB & ROTOR ASSEMBLY under REMOVAL & INSTALLATION. On all models, disconnect parking brake cable from lever and at brake flange plates. Remove hydraulic brake lines. Detach height-sensing/brake proportioning valve linkage (if equipped). Remove shock absorbers.

3) Remove stabilizer bar (if equipped). Disconnect hose from axle vent fitting (if equipped). Support rear axle assembly with floor jack. Remove leaf spring "U" bolt nuts. Carefully lower rear axle assembly and remove from under vehicle.

Installation – Place rear axle assembly on floor jack. Raise rear axle assembly into position to align housing spring saddle holes with leaf spring center bolts. Install "U" bolts and nuts. To complete installation, reverse removal procedure. Add gear oil as needed. Bleed brake system.

DIFFERENTIAL ASSEMBLY

Removal & Installation – Removal and installation of differential assembly is covered as part of overhaul procedure. See DIFFERENTIAL ASSEMBLY under OVERHAUL.

OVERHAUL

DIFFERENTIAL ASSEMBLY

Disassembly – 1) Raise and support vehicle. Place jackstands under frame side rails. Allow rear axle housing assembly to hang free. Remove drive shaft. Remove wheel assemblies. Place drain pan under differential. Remove differential cover bolts and cover. Remove axle shafts. See AXLE SHAFTS under REMOVAL & INSTALLATION.

2) Note letters on bearing caps and drive axle housing for reassembly reference. Remove differential bearing caps. *See Fig. 4 or 5.* Mount dial indicator on differential housing. *See Fig. 3.* Preload dial indicator to .020" (.51 mm) and then return dial to zero.

3) Mount Drive Axle Housing Spreader (J-24385-01) to differential housing. *See Fig. 3.* Spread drive axle housing to maximum of **.015" (.38 mm)**. Using 2 pry bars, pry differential case out of housing.

CAUTION: DO NOT spread housing more than .015" (.38 mm) as housing will be damaged and require replacement.

4) Remove drive axle housing spreader. Using Differential Bearing Remover (J-29721), Adapters (J-29721-70), and Removal Plug (J-8107-03), remove differential case side bearings and shims. Mark bearing, race, and shims left or right side for reassembly reference.

5) Using shop towels, place differential case in soft-jawed vise. Remove ring gear bolts. Ring gear bolts may be left-hand thread. Using a soft-faced hammer, tap ring gear off differential case.

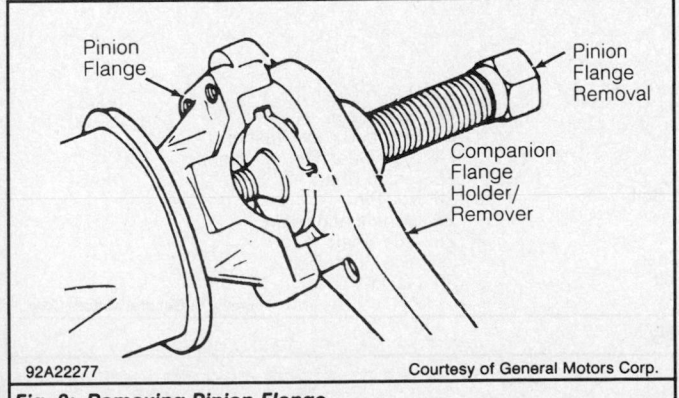

Pinion Flange

Pinion Flange Removal

Companion Flange Holder/ Remover

92A22277　　　Courtesy of General Motors Corp.

Fig. 2: Removing Pinion Flange

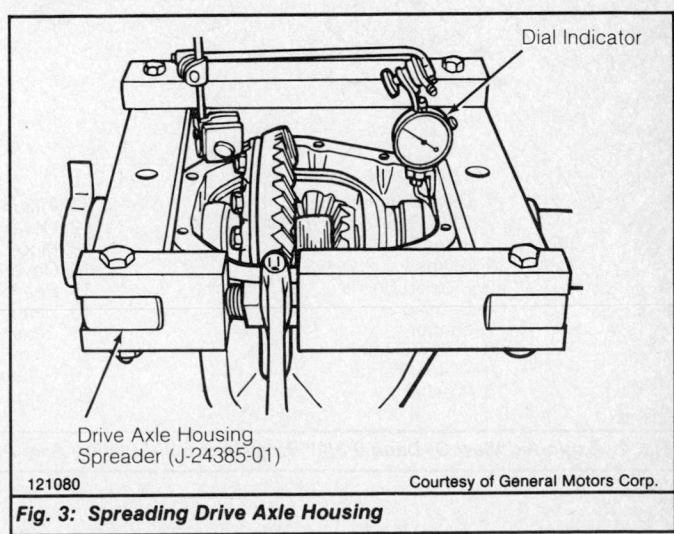

Dial Indicator

Drive Axle Housing Spreader (J-24385-01)

121080　　　Courtesy of General Motors Corp.

Fig. 3: Spreading Drive Axle Housing

GM
7-30

1992 DRIVE AXLES
Dana 9 3/4" & 10 1/2" Full-Floating Axles (Cont.)

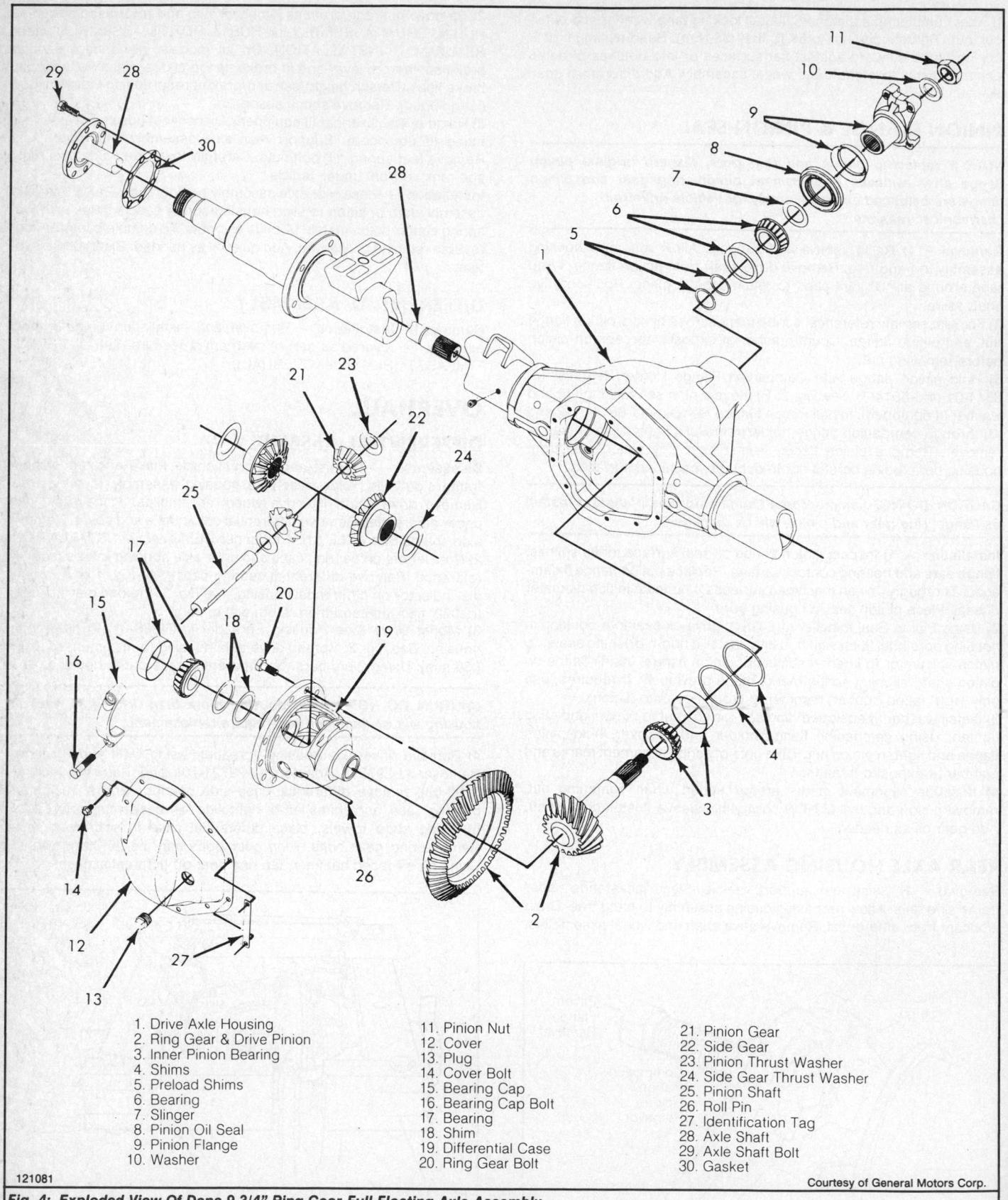

1. Drive Axle Housing	11. Pinion Nut	21. Pinion Gear
2. Ring Gear & Drive Pinion	12. Cover	22. Side Gear
3. Inner Pinion Bearing	13. Plug	23. Pinion Thrust Washer
4. Shims	14. Cover Bolt	24. Side Gear Thrust Washer
5. Preload Shims	15. Bearing Cap	25. Pinion Shaft
6. Bearing	16. Bearing Cap Bolt	26. Roll Pin
7. Slinger	17. Bearing	27. Identification Tag
8. Pinion Oil Seal	18. Shim	28. Axle Shaft
9. Pinion Flange	19. Differential Case	29. Axle Shaft Bolt
10. Washer	20. Ring Gear Bolt	30. Gasket

121081

Courtesy of General Motors Corp.

Fig. 4: Exploded View Of Dana 9 3/4" Ring Gear Full-Floating Axle Assembly

1992 DRIVE AXLES
Dana 9 3/4" & 10 1/2" Full-Floating Axles (Cont.)

GM
7-31

6) Using hammer and punch, remove pinion shaft lock roll pin from differential case. Pinion shaft is slightly press fit. Using hammer and punch, remove pinion shaft, pinion gears and thrust washers. Remove differential side gears and thrust washers. Mark all gears and washers in relation to differential case for reassembly reference.

7) Check drive pinion bearing preload using INCH lb. torque wrench and proper socket. Record amount of torque required to start pinion to rotate. Perform preload check several times to ensure accurate reading. If drive pinion moves noticeably in and out, bearings need to be replaced.

8) For reassembly reference, scribe mark pinion, pinion nut and pinion flange. Using Companion Flange Holder/Remover (J-8614-01), remove drive pinion nut. See Fig. 2. Install Pinion Flange Remover (J-8614-1, -2 and -3) through companion flange holder/remover. Tighten pinion flange remover. Remove pinion flange from pinion.

9) Install differential cover with 2 bolts to keep drive pinion from falling out of housing during removal. Install pinion nut and tap drive pinion out of differential housing. Remover cover and retrieve drive pinion and small diameter pinion preload shims. Save shims for reassembly.

10) Pry drive pinion oil seal from bore, being careful not to damage machined surfaces. Remove outer drive pinion bearing and oil slinger. Remove drive pinion bearing races from drive axle housing.

11) Remove drive pinion adjustment shims and baffle (if equipped). Keep shims and baffle together for reassembly. Using Differential Side Bearing Remover (J-29721) and 4 Adapters (J-29721-70), remove inner drive pinion bearing.

NOTE: DO NOT steam clean any parts having a ground and polished surface, such as bearings, gears and shafts.

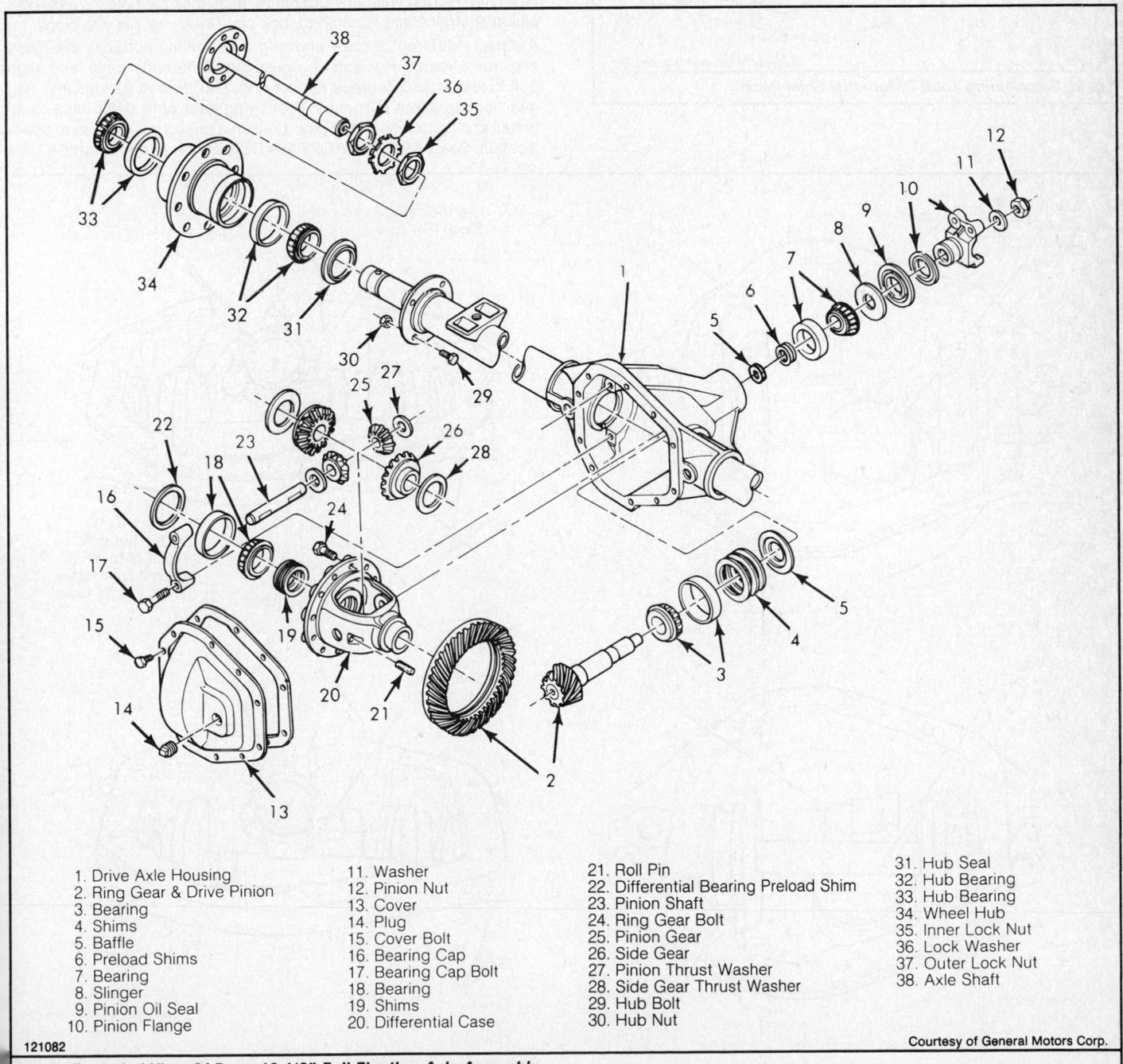

1. Drive Axle Housing	11. Washer	21. Roll Pin	31. Hub Seal
2. Ring Gear & Drive Pinion	12. Pinion Nut	22. Differential Bearing Preload Shim	32. Hub Bearing
3. Bearing	13. Cover	23. Pinion Shaft	33. Hub Bearing
4. Shims	14. Plug	24. Ring Gear Bolt	34. Wheel Hub
5. Baffle	15. Cover Bolt	25. Pinion Gear	35. Inner Lock Nut
6. Preload Shims	16. Bearing Cap	26. Side Gear	36. Lock Washer
7. Bearing	17. Bearing Cap Bolt	27. Pinion Thrust Washer	37. Outer Lock Nut
8. Slinger	18. Bearing	28. Side Gear Thrust Washer	38. Axle Shaft
9. Pinion Oil Seal	19. Shims	29. Hub Bolt	
10. Pinion Flange	20. Differential Case	30. Hub Nut	

121082

Fig. 5: Exploded View Of Dana 10 1/2" Full-Floating Axle Assembly

GM
7-32

1992 DRIVE AXLES
Dana 9 3/4" & 10 1/2" Full-Floating Axles (Cont.)

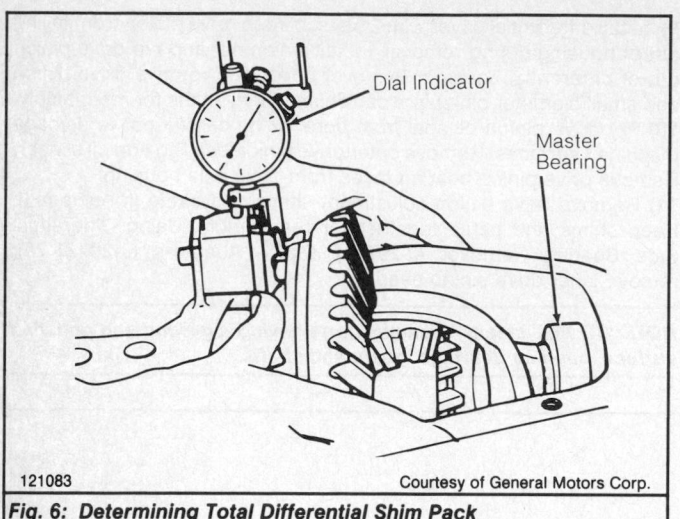

Fig. 6: Determining Total Differential Shim Pack

121083

Courtesy of General Motors Corp.

Cleaning & Inspection – **1)** DO NOT steam clean parts. Use cleaning solvent to rinse gears and bearings. Check bearing rollers for wear. Check pinion and flange splines for excessive wear. Inspect ring gear and pinion teeth for excessive or improper wear.

2) Check differential case for cracks. Check for scoring or wear of side gears, thrust washers and pinion thrust faces. Check fit of side gears to case and to axle shaft splines. Replace as required.

Differential Case Reassembly – **1)** Apply gear oil lubricant to all differential parts. Assemble new side gear thrust washers with side gears. Install side gear assembly in differential case. Ensure side gears are installed on same side as removed.

2) Place pinion gears onto side gears so that holes in pinion gears are 180 degrees apart. Rotate pinion gears into place and ensure pinion gears line up with pinion shaft holes.

3) Rotate pinion gears toward differential opening just enough to slide new pinion thrust washers into place. Align lock pin holes in case and pinion shaft. Install pinion shaft lock pin. Drive lock pin into place.

4) Ensure differential case and ring gear mating surfaces are clean and free of burrs. Position ring gear onto differential case, and align bolt holes. At 180 degrees across ring gear, thread 2 studs into ring gear for alignment purposes. Press ring gear onto differential case. Install and tighten new ring gear bolts in a crisscross pattern to specification. See TORQUE SPECIFICATIONS table at end of article.

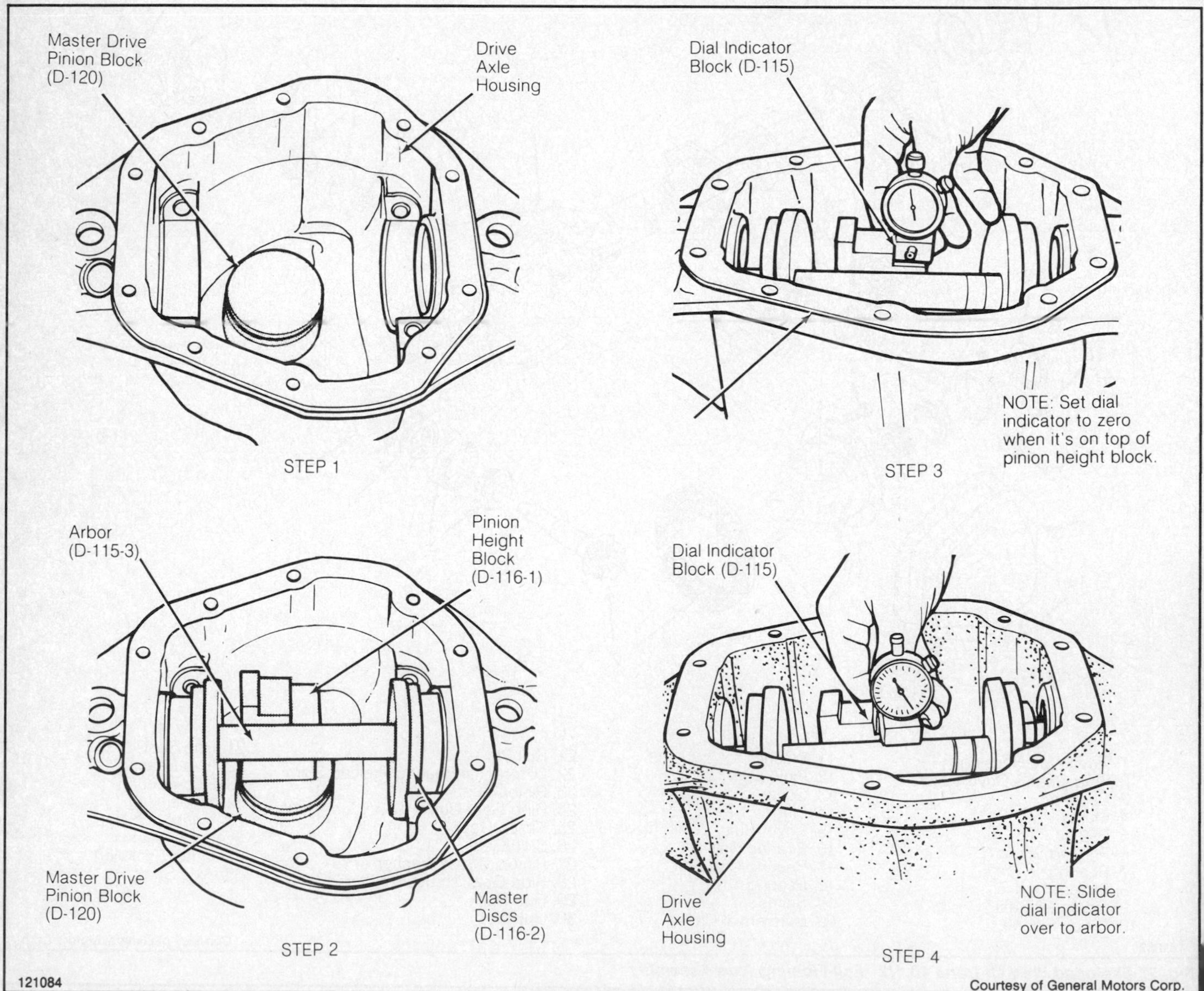

Master Drive
Pinion Block
(D-120)

Drive
Axle
Housing

STEP 1

Dial Indicator
Block (D-115)

NOTE: Set dial
indicator to zero
when it's on top of
pinion height block.

STEP 3

Arbor
(D-115-3)

Pinion
Height
Block
(D-116-1)

Master Drive
Pinion Block
(D-120)

Master
Discs
(D-116-2)

STEP 2

Dial Indicator
Block (D-115)

Drive
Axle
Housing

NOTE: Slide
dial indicator
over to arbor.

STEP 4

121084

Courtesy of General Motors Corp.

Fig. 7: Adjusting Pinion Depth

1992 DRIVE AXLES
Dana 9 3/4" & 10 1/2" Full-Floating Axles (Cont.)

GM
7-33

Determining Total Differential Shim Pack – 1) Ensure drive pinion is out of drive axle housing. On 9 3/4" drive axle, install Master Differential Bearings (D-117) to differential case. On 10 1/2" drive axle, install Master Differential Bearings (D-136) to differential case.

2) On all axles, install assembled differential case into drive axle housing. Mount dial indicator on ring gear bolt side of differential case. *See Fig. 6.* On 10 1/2" heavy duty drive axles, install outboard spacer between master bearing (ring gear side) and drive axle housing.

3) On all axles, force differential assembly toward dial indicator as far as possible. Preload dial indicator to one half of its travel. Place tip of dial indicator on a machined (flat) differential surface, just next to ring gear bolt. Mark this location with chalk. Reset preloaded dial indicator gauge dial to zero.

4) Force differential assembly away from dial indicator as far as assembly will forcibly go. Repeat this step until constant indicator reading is obtained. Record number of thousandths that dial indicator traveled, this is NOT the present reading on dial (dial may have gone completely around once).

5) On 9 3/4" and 10 1/2" light duty (model "B" and "U") drive axles, reading obtained in step **4)** will determine thickness of shim pack to be used without any bearing preload, which will be added later.

6) On 10 1/2" heavy duty drive axles, reading obtained in step **4)** plus spacer thickness will determine thickness of shims and spacer to be used.

7) On all axles, remove dial indicator from drive axle housing. Remove differential case from drive axle housing. DO NOT remove master bearings from differential case assembly at this time. Go to PINION DEPTH ADJUSTMENT.

Pinion Depth Adjustment – 1) Clean all drive axle housing bearing race bores. Ensure drive pinion bore is free of nicks and dirt. Install Master Drive Pinion Block (J-24771) for 9 3/4" drive axle or (D-120 or D-137) 10 1/2" heavy duty drive axle into pinion bore. *See Fig. 7.* Assemble Master Discs (D-116-2) onto Arbor (D-115-3). Install arbor and disc assembly into drive axle housing. *See Fig. 7.*

2) Place Pinion Height Block (D-116-1) on top of master drive pinion block and against arbor. *See Fig. 7.* Place Dial Indicator Block (D-115) on lowest step of pinion height block. While applying a downward pressure on dial indicator block, set dial indicator to zero.

3) Slide dial indicator block over to arbor. Move dial indicator block back and forth (perpendicular to arbor) to get highest reading. This reading, added together with the "plus or minus figure" etched on drive pinion head, is thickness of shim pack necessary for proper pinion depth adjustment. *See Fig. 8.*

4) Using a micrometer, measure each shim thickness separately. Add shim thicknesses together to obtain total shim pack thickness. If a baffle or slinger is used, its thickness must also be measured and included in shim pack total thickness.

NOTE: A positive (+) value figure on drive pinion head indicates the distance between ring gear centerline and drive pinion must be increased by the number of thousandths marked on pinion head. A negative (–) value figure indicates that distance must be decreased. A zero (0) figure etched on drive pinion means to use the shim thickness as determined by this procedure. See Fig. 8.

2) Use Pinion Bearing Race Installer (J-7818) and Handle (J-8092) to install drive pinion outer bearing race into drive axle housing. Use Pinion Bearing Installer (J-5590) to install inner bearing and oil slinger (if used) on drive pinion.

3) Install drive pinion in drive axle housing. Install outer drive pinion bearing and slinger (if used). DO NOT install preload shims and oil seal at this time.

4) Install drive pinion flange. Install washer and drive pinion nut. Using Pinion Flange Holder/Remover (J-8614-01), tighten drive pinion nut until a torque of **10 INCH Lbs. (1.13 N.m)** is required to rotate drive pinion. Rotate drive pinion several times to seat bearings.

5) Assemble Master Discs (D-116-2) onto Arbor (D-115-3). Install arbor and disc assembly into drive axle housing. *See Fig. 7.* Place Pinion Height Block (D-116-1) on top of drive pinion and against arbor. Place Dial Indicator Block (D-115) on lowest step of pinion height block. While applying a downward pressure on dial indicator block, set dial indicator to zero.

6) Slide dial indicator block over to arbor. *See Fig. 7.* Move dial indicator block back and forth (perpendicular to arbor) to get highest reading. If reading is within .002" (.05 mm) of drive pinion marking, drive pinion depth is set correctly.

7) If depth reading is not within drive pinion marking, change pinion depth shim pack by amount indicator needle is deflected away from drive pinion marking. Dial indicator needle will be moved to left if drive pinion has a positive (+) figure etched on it. Needle will be moved to right if pinion head has a negative (-) figure etched on it. *See Fig. 8.*

8) Remove drive pinion nut, washer, pinion flange and bearing. See PINION FLANGE & PINION SEAL under REMOVAL & INSTALLATION. Remove preload shims. Install original shims or measure original shims and replace them with new shims.

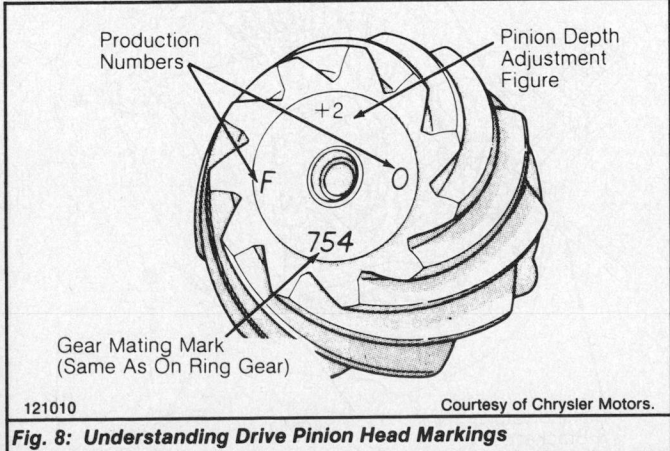

121010   Courtesy of Chrysler Motors.

Fig. 8: Understanding Drive Pinion Head Markings

Drive Pinion Assembly & Preload – 1) Place required shims and baffle (if used) in inner bearing bore. Use Pinion Bearing Race Installer (D-111 on 9 3/4" axles or C-4204 on 10 1/2" axles) and Handle (C-4171) to install drive pinion inner bearing race into drive axle housing. Ensure race is fully seated on shims.

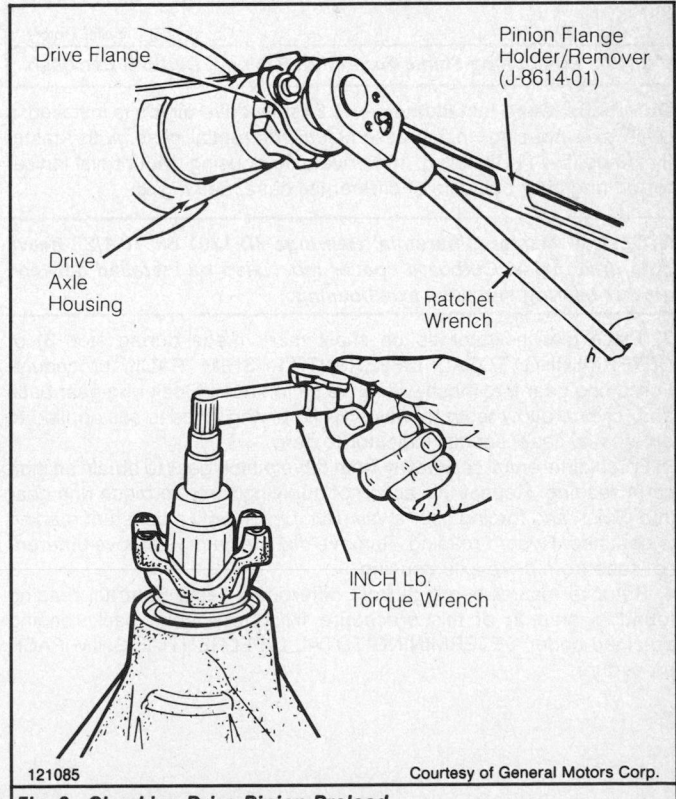

121085   Courtesy of General Motors Corp.

Fig. 9: Checking Drive Pinion Preload

GM
7-34

1992 DRIVE AXLES
Dana 9 3/4" & 10 1/2" Full-Floating Axles (Cont.)

9) Install outer drive pinion bearing and oil slinger (if used). Apply a light coat of lubricant to pinion seal lip. Use Seal Installer (D-163) to install drive pinion oil seal.

10) Install drive pinion flange. Install washer and new drive pinion nut. Using Pinion Flange Holder/Remover (J-8614-01), tighten drive pinion nut until a torque of **20-40 INCH lbs. (2.26-4.53 N.m)** is required to rotate pinion. See Fig. 9. If necessary, add small diameter shims to increase preload, or remove shims to decrease preload. See Fig. 10.

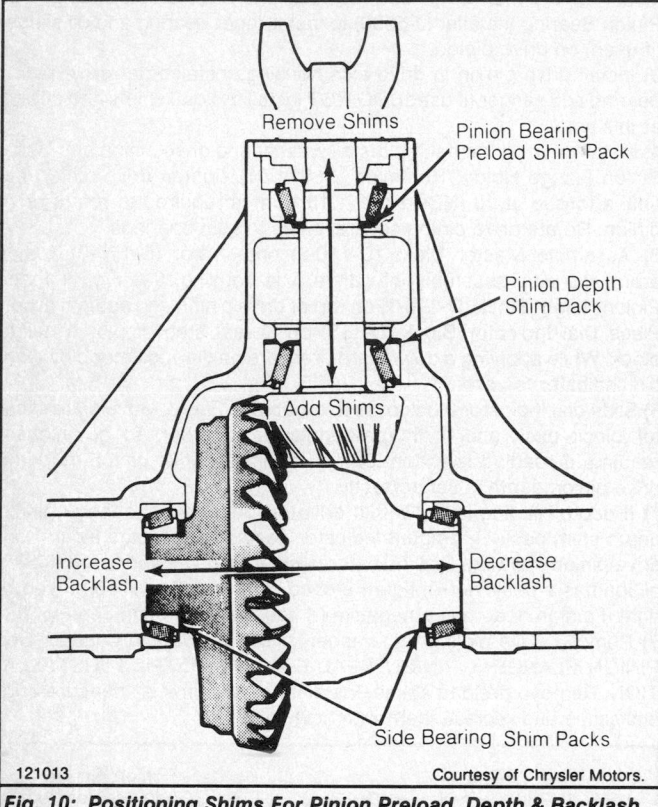

121013   Courtesy of Chrysler Motors.

Fig. 10: Positioning Shims For Pinion Preload, Depth & Backlash

Differential Case Installation – 1) Ensure drive pinion is installed in drive axle housing. Install assembled differential case, with Master Bearings (D-117) installed, into drive axle housing. Mount dial indicator on ring gear bolt side of differential case. See Fig. 6.

NOTE: Use Master Differential Bearings (D-136) on 10 1/2" heavy duty drive axles. Outboard spacer must also be installed between master bearing and drive axle housing.

2) Place dial indicator tip on chalk mark made during step 3) of DETERMINING TOTAL DIFFERENTIAL SHIM PACK procedure. Force ring gear into mesh with drive pinion gear. Rock ring gear back and forth to allow teeth to mesh. While prying force is still applied to differential case, set dial indicator to zero.

3) Force differential case away from drive pinion gear to obtain an indicator reading. Repeat this action of applying force to mesh ring gear into pinion and forcing gear away from pinion until a constant reading is obtained. Record reading. Remove dial indicator. Remove differential case from drive axle housing.

4) Remove master bearings from differential case. Subtract reading found in step 3) of this procedure from total shim pack reading obtained under DETERMINING TOTAL DIFFERENTIAL SHIM PACK procedure.

NOTE: Reading found in step 3) of this procedure will determine shim size to be used on ring gear side of differential case. Use remaining portion of shim pack on opposite side of differential case after adding an additional .015" (.38 mm) to preload the bearings.

5) Place proper amount of shims on differential bearing hub (ring gear side). Drive or press differential bearing onto hub using Differential Bearing Installer (J-23690) and Handle (J-8092).

6) Place calculated amount of shims on differential bearing hub (opposite to ring gear side). Drive or press differential bearing onto hub using differential bearing installer and handle.

7) Mount dial indicator on differential housing to measure housing spread, in order to install differential case. See Fig. 3. Preload dial indicator to .020" (.51 mm), then rotate gauge to zero dial. Use Drive Axle Housing Spreader (J-24385-01) to spread drive axle housing to .015" (.38 mm). DO NOT spread housing more than specified, as housing will be damaged and require replacement.

8) Remove dial indicator. Install races to differential case bearings. Install differential case into drive axle housing. If necessary, use a rawhide or rubber mallet to properly seat differential case into housing. On 10 1/2" heavy duty drive axles, use Preload Shim Installer (J-4205) and Handle (C-4171) to tap outboard spacer into place.

9) On all drive axles, remove drive axle housing spreader. Install bearing caps and tighten to specification. See TORQUE SPECIFICATIONS table at end of article.

Checking Ring Gear Backlash – 1) Mount dial indicator on drive axle housing. See Fig. 11. Place dial indicator tip at heel end of ring gear tooth. Check backlash at 3 equally spaced locations around ring gear.

2) Backlash should be .005-.009" (.13-.23 mm). Ensure variation between points checked is not more than .002" (.05 mm). High backlash is corrected by moving ring gear closer to drive pinion; low backlash is corrected by moving ring gear from pinion. See Fig. 10.

3) To adjust ring gear backlash, remove differential case from housing using housing spreader. Remove both differential case side bearings, and move proper amount of shims from one side to other.

4) When backlash adjustment is completed, check ring gear tooth contact pattern. See GEAR TOOTH CONTACT PATTERNS article in GENERAL INFORMATION. Pattern should be correct if assembly and adjustments were done properly.

5) With differential assembled and correctly adjusted, install new cover gasket and cover. Tighten cover bolts to specification. See TORQUE SPECIFICATIONS table at end of article. Install axle shafts. Fill drive axle with lubricant.

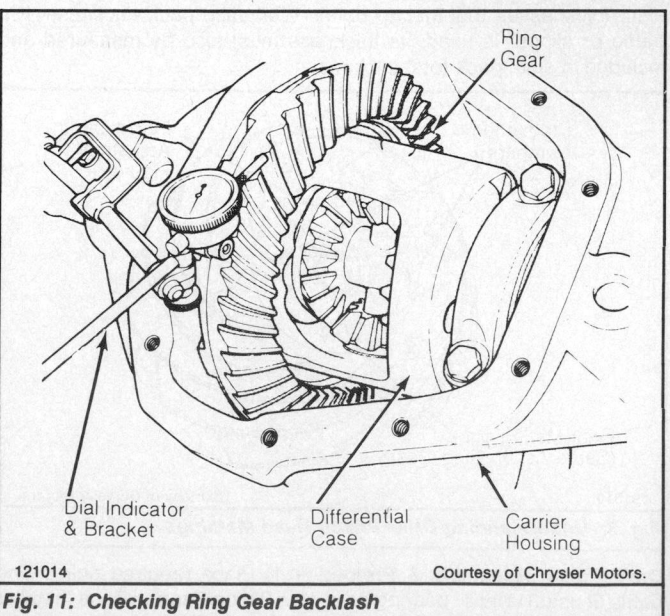

121014   Courtesy of Chrysler Motors.

Fig. 11: Checking Ring Gear Backlash

1992 DRIVE AXLES
Dana 9 3/4" & 10 1/2" Full-Floating Axles (Cont.)

GM
7-35

DRIVE AXLE ASSEMBLY SPECIFICATIONS

DRIVE AXLE ASSEMBLY SPECIFICATIONS [1]

Application	Specification
Ring Gear Backlash	.005-.009" (.13-.23 mm)
Pinion Bearing Preload	20-40 INCH lbs. (2.26-4.53 N.m)
10 1/2" Ring Gear	
Inner Pinion Bearing Width	
"B" & Heavy Duty Models	1.4375" (36.51 mm)
"U" Models	1.1875" (30.16 mm)
10 1/2" Ring Gear Differential Bearing Width	
"B" & "U" Models	1.0000" (25.40 mm)
Heavy Duty Models	1.1875" (30.16 mm)

[1] – Adjustment shims are available in .003" (.08 mm), .005" (.13 mm), .010" (.25 mm) and .030" (.76 mm) thicknesses.

TORQUE SPECIFICATIONS

TORQUE SPECIFICATIONS

Applications	Ft. Lbs. (N.m)
Axle Shaft-To-Hub Bolts/Nuts	115 (156)
Bearing Cap Bolts	85 (115)
Brake Backing Plate Bolts	105 (142)
Drive Shaft Bolt	15 (20)
Filler Plug	25 (34)
Housing Rear Cover Bolts	35 (47)
Leaf Spring "U" Bolt Nut	114 (155)
Lower Shock Mount Nut	75 (102)
Ring Gear Bolts	
9 3/4" Ring Gear	110 (150)
10 1/2" Ring Gear	105 (142)
Wheel Lug Nut	
Dual Real Wheels	140 (190)
Single Rear Wheels	120 (163)

**Commercial Van, Jimmy, Sierra,
Suburban, Van, Yukon,
"C" & "K" Series Blazer & Pickup**

NOTE: Van may also be equipped with a Dana drive axle. See appropriate article in DRIVE AXLES.

DESCRIPTION

MODEL IDENTIFICATION

Vehicle model can be identified by fifth character of Vehicle Identification Number (VIN), stamped on metal pad on top of left end of instrument panel, near windshield. See MODEL IDENTIFICATION table.

MODEL IDENTIFICATION

Series [1]	Model
"C"	2WD Pickup, Sierra & Suburban
"G"	RWD Van
"K"	4WD Blazer, Pickup, Sierra, Suburban & Yukon
"P"	Commercial Van/Motorhome

[1] – Vehicle series is fifth character of VIN.

The axle assembly is a hypoid gear type with integral carrier housing, which is used with full floating axles. The drive pinion bearing preload adjustment is made with a collapsible spacer. The differential side bearing preload adjustment is made with side bearing adjusting nuts. Pinion drive gear is supported in separate cage by 3 bearings: a pinion front bearing, a pinion rear bearing and a pilot bearing. Selective shims are used between pinion cage and axle housing to set pinion depth. A removable housing cover permits inspection and minor service of differential without removing from vehicle.

AXLE RATIO & IDENTIFICATION

See AXLE RATIO IDENTIFICATION article.

REMOVAL & INSTALLATION

AXLE SHAFT

Removal & Installation – 1) Raise vehicle and support with jack stands. Remove wheels on axle to be serviced. Remove 8 axle shaft bolts from axle flange. Tap flange on axle shaft with a soft-faced hammer to loosen shaft.
2) Grip rib on end of axle shaft flange with pliers and twist to begin removal. Remove axle from housing. To install shaft, reverse removal procedure. Use new flange gaskets. Tighten bolts to specification. See TORQUE SPECIFICATIONS table at end of article.

HUB & DRUM ASSEMBLY

Removal & Installation – 1) Remove axle shaft. See AXLE SHAFT under REMOVAL & INSTALLATION. Remove lock nut retainer ring, key and lock nut. Pull hub and drum assembly straight off axle housing.
2) Thoroughly clean seal contact area. Apply a thin coat of bearing lubricant to contact surface on outside of axle tube. To install, reverse removal procedure. See WHEEL BEARINGS for bearing adjustment procedure.

WHEEL BEARINGS

Removal – 1) Remove axle shaft and hub/drum assembly. See AXLE SHAFT and HUB & DRUM ASSEMBLY under REMOVAL & INSTALLATION. Use a long drift or punch to drive inner bearing, race, and oil seal from hub. Remove outer bearing retaining ring.

NOTE: Remove inner bearing race and outer bearing retaining ring before removing outer bearing race.

2) Use Driver Handle (J-8092) and Outer Bearing Race Remover/Installer (J-24426) to drive outer bearing and race out of hub. See Fig. 1.

Installation – 1) Lubricate bearings with gear oil. Place outer bearing race into hub from rear. Using Driver Handle (J-8092) and Bearing Race Installer (J-8608), drive race into hub beyond retaining ring groove.

NOTE: Ensure Bearing Race Installer (J-8608) is installed upside down on Driver Handle (J-8092) so chamfer does not contact bearing race.

2) Install outer bearing retaining ring. Using Outer Bearing Race Remover/Installer (J-24426), drive outer race back against retaining ring until seated. Place inner bearing race into hub. Using Driver Handle (J-8092) and Inner Bearing Race Installer (J-24427), drive race into hub until seated against hub shoulder.
3) Install inner bearing. Pack cavity between seal lips with high melting point wheel bearing lubricant. Position seal in hub bore. Using Seal Installer (J-24428), carefully drive seal into hub until seal is flush with edge of hub. Place hub assembly onto axle housing. Install outer bearing. Using Wheel Bearing Nut Wrench (J-2222L), install adjusting nut.
4) Tighten adjusting nut to **50 ft. lbs. (70 N.m)** while rotating hub. Ensure bearing cones are seated and in contact with spindle shoulder. Back off nut. Tighten finger tight against bearing. Install key and retaining ring.

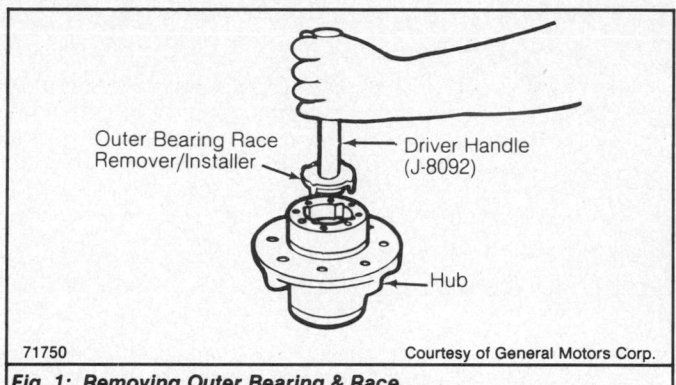

Outer Bearing Race Remover/Installer

Driver Handle (J-8092)

Hub

71750   Courtesy of General Motors Corp.

Fig. 1: Removing Outer Bearing & Race

PINION FLANGE & OIL SEAL

Removal & Installation – 1) Raise vehicle and remove pinion flange bolts. Position drive shaft aside. Count number of exposed threads and scribe a mark on pinion stem, nut, and pinion flange for reassembly reference.
2) Use Companion Flange Holder Set (J-8614-01) to hold flange. Remove pinion nut and pinion flange from pinion. Using care not to damage machined surfaces, pry oil seal from bore. Clean area thoroughly. Pack cavity between seal lips with high melting point bearing lubricant.
3) Place new seal into bore. Use Pinion Oil Seal Installer (J-24384) to drive seal in until it bottoms against inner shoulder. Install pinion flange and pinion nut to the scribe mark to ensure proper alignment. Install drive shaft. Tighten flange bolts to specification. See TORQUE SPECIFICATIONS table at end of article.

AXLE ASSEMBLY

Removal & Installation – 1) Raise vehicle, and support at frame side rails using jackstands. Remove rear wheels. Remove pinion flange bolts, and position drive shaft aside. Remove wheel hub. Disconnect parking brake cable at lever and at backing plate.
2) Disconnect hydraulic brake hose at connector on axle housing. Remove stabilizer bar (if equipped). Disconnect shock absorbers at axle brackets. Using floor jack, raise axle assembly slightly to relieve tension on springs. Remove spring "U" bolts, and lower floor jack.
3) Remove axle assembly from vehicle. To install axle assembly, reverse removal procedure. Tighten bolts to specification. See TORQUE SPECIFICATIONS table at end of article.

OVERHAUL

DIFFERENTIAL ASSEMBLY

Disassembly – 1) Place drain pan under differential carrier cover. Loosen housing cover bolts and drain lubricant. Remove housing cover and axle shafts. See AXLE SHAFT under REMOVAL & INSTALLATION. Remove pinion flange bolts and position drive shaft aside. Note and record ring gear backlash and pinion bearing preload for reassembly reference. Mark bearing caps for reassembly reference.

2) Remove adjusting nut locks and lock bolts from bearing caps. Remove bearing caps. Use Adjusting Nut Wrench (J-24429) to loosen side bearing adjusting nuts. Remove differential case assembly from axle housing. Remove differential side bearings using Puller (J-22888) and Plug (J-8107).

NOTE: Ensure jaws of Puller (J-22888) pull from beneath bearing cone, not cage.

3) Scribe mark across differential case halves. Remove left-hand thread ring gear bolts. Remove ring gear using brass drift if necessary. Split case halves. Remove differential side gears and thrust washers. Mark case halves and gears as left or right for reassembly.

4) Remove differential pinion spider gear. Remove pinion gears and thrust washers from spider. Check pinion bearing preload using an INCH lb. torque wrench. Looseness indicates excessive wear. See AXLE ASSEMBLY SPECIFICATIONS table.

5) Remove 6 pinion cage assembly bolts and washers. Remove pinion assembly. It may be necessary to tap on pinion gear with a brass drift to free cage. Remove pinion cage and cage shims. Ensure shims are marked as right or left for side identification. Set shims aside for later measurement.

6) Place pinion cage assembly in a soft-jawed vise. Using Companion Flange Holder Set (J-8614-01), remove pinion nut and flange. *See Fig. 2.* Place pinion cage in press and press pinion from cage. DO NOT let pinion fall to floor.

7) Remove collapsible spacer from pinion. Using Press and Bearing Remover (J-22912-01), press inner bearing from pinion. Using a hammer and punch, remove pinion seal from pinion cage. Remove outer bearing from pinion cage.

8) Remove bearing races from pinion cage. Using a hammer and brass drift, remove pilot bearing from axle housing.

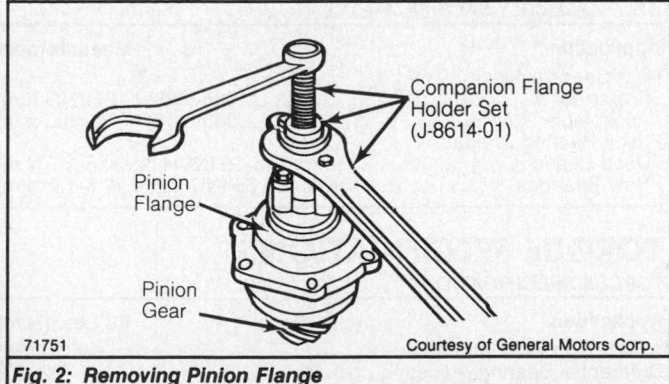

71751   Courtesy of General Motors Corp.

Fig. 2: Removing Pinion Flange

Cleaning & Inspection – 1) Clean all parts in cleaning solvent. Inspect all bearings, bearing races, and rollers for scoring, chipping or excessive wear. Inspect axle shaft and side gear splines for excessive wear.

2) Inspect ring gear and pinion for scoring, cracking or chipping. Inspect differential case, pinion side gears, thrust washers and pinion shaft for cracks, scoring or excessive wear.

NOTE: Rear axle ring and pinion sets are system balanced as an assembly. Assembly is balanced as a unit with pinion flange weighted as a harmonic balancer. If axle repairs dictate installation of new ring and pinion, a new pinion flange must also be used. Discard original flange and refer to appropriate GMSPO Parts Catalog for proper service flange.

Reassembly (Pinion Assembly) – 1) Lubricate all parts with hypoid gear oil. Using press and Pinion Bearing Installer (J-24433), press pinion inner bearing onto pinion. Using Driver Handle (J-8092) and Outer Bearing Race Installer (J-8608), install outer bearing race. Using driver and Inner Bearing Race Installer (J-24432), install inner race.

2) Install NEW collapsible spacer on pinion. Insert pinion into pinion cage. Press outer bearing onto pinion shaft. Install new pinion oil seal using driver handle and Seal Installer (J-24434). Install pinion flange oil deflector and pinion flange.

3) Install pinion washer and new pinion nut. Place pinion cage in soft-jawed vise. Install Companion Flange Holder Set (J-8614-01) to pinion flange. While rotating pinion gear, tighten pinion nut until there is no end play left at pinion. Rotate pinion several times and check pinion preload. Tighten pinion nut in small steps, rotating pinion between adjustments until preload is adjusted to specification. See AXLE ASSEMBLY SPECIFICATIONS table.

NOTE: If pinion preload limit is exceeded, remove pinion and install NEW collapsible spacer.

4) If reinstalling original ring and pinion gears, use new pinion shims of same number and thickness as those removed. If installing new gears, compare pinion depth code number of new pinion gear with that of original pinion gear. From these 2 codes, determine correction factor by referring to PINION DEPTH CODES table.

5) Combine correction factor with thickness of new shim pack. Place new shim pack onto carrier housing. Install new pinion pilot bearing into axle housing using driver handle and Pilot Bearing Installer (J-34943). Install pinion cage to axle housing. Tighten 6 cage retaining bolts to specification in a crosswise sequence. See TORQUE SPECIFICATIONS table at end of article.

PINION DEPTH CODES

Original Code	Service Code	Correction In. (mm)
+2	+2	0 (0)
+2	+1	−.001 (−.025)
+2	0	−.002 (−.050)
+2	−1	−.003 (−.074)
+2	−2	−.004 (−.098)
+1	+2	+.001 (+.025)
+1	+1	0 (0)
+1	0	−.001 (−.025)
+1	−1	−.002 (−.050)
+1	−2	−.003 (−.074)
0	+2	+.002 (+.050)
0	+1	+.001 (+.025)
0	0	0 (0)
0	−1	−.001 (−.025)
0	−2	−.002 (−.050)
−1	+2	+.003 (+.074)
−1	+1	+.002 (+.050)
−1	0	+.001 (+.025)
−1	−1	0 (0)
−1	−2	−.001 (−.025)
−2	+2	+.004 (+.098)
−2	+1	+.003 (+.074)
−2	0	+.002 (+.050)
−2	−1	+.001 (+.025)
−2	−2	0 (0)

Reassembly (Case Assembly) – 1) Lubricate all parts with hypoid gear oil. Place pinion gears and thrust washers on differential spider.

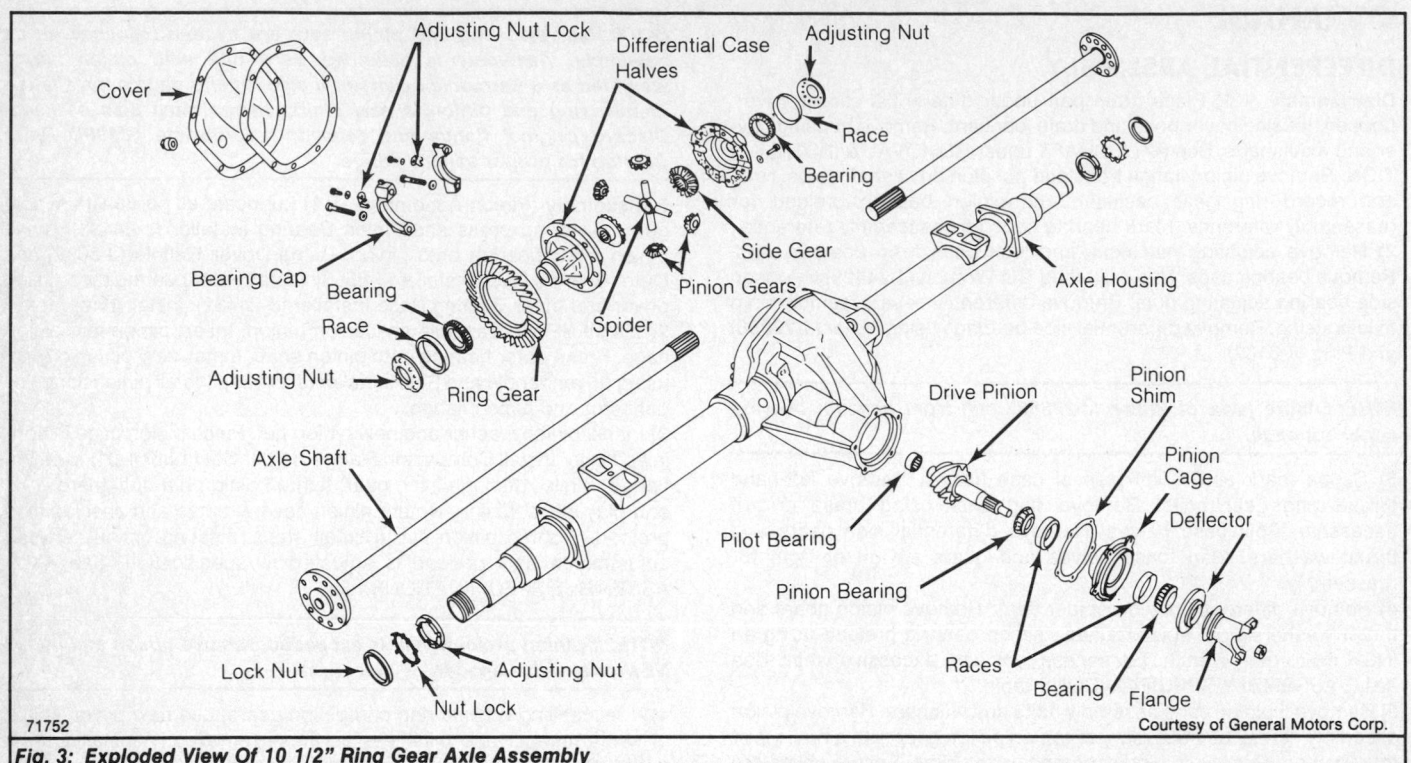

Fig. 3: Exploded View Of 10 1/2" Ring Gear Axle Assembly

71752

Courtesy of General Motors Corp.

Install side gears and thrust washers to case halves in their original locations. Install differential spider to differential.

2) Assemble case halves, aligning marks previously scribed on case. Obtain and install 2 left-hand threaded studs in ring gear, directly opposite each other to ease in alignment/installation process of ring gear.

3) Install ring gear onto studs. Tap ring gear lightly with soft-faced hammer until new ring gear attaching bolts can be installed. Tighten bolts evenly until ring gear is flush with case flange.

4) Remove threaded studs. Install 2 remaining bolts and tighten all ring gear bolts alternately and evenly to specification. See TORQUE SPECIFICATIONS table at end of article. Install differential side bearings using driver handle and Bearing Installer (J-24449).

ADJUSTMENTS

SIDE BEARING PRELOAD

1) Place lubricated bearing races onto differential side bearings in original locations Place differential assembly into carrier. Install bearing caps in their original positions. Tighten cap bolts until just snug.

2) Using Bearing Backlash Wrench (J-24429), loosen right side bearing adjusting nut. Tighten left side adjusting nut until ring gear just contacts drive pinion (zero lash point). Back off left adjusting nut 2 slots to locking position. Install left adjusting nut lock and lock bolt. DO NOT tighten bolt.

3) Tighten right adjusting nut until case is in firm contact with left adjusting nut. Loosen right adjusting nut until it is free of bearing. Retighten right nut until it just contacts bearing. Tighten right adjusting nut an additional 2 slots (used bearings) or 3 slots (new bearings) to properly preload differential side bearings. Install adjusting nut lock and lock bolt. DO NOT tighten bolt. Proceed with BACKLASH & FINAL ASSEMBLY.

BACKLASH & FINAL ASSEMBLY

1) Install a dial indicator (with indicator stem installed) at heel end of a tooth, in line with gear rotation and perpendicular to the tooth angle. With pinion stationary, measure ring gear backlash in at least 4 locations around ring gear. Backlash at each point should be the same, within .002" (.05 mm). See AXLE ASSEMBLY SPECIFICATIONS table.

2) Adjust to specification by moving adjusting nuts in or out as necessary. If one adjusting nut is loosened, other nut must be tightened an equal amount to maintain side bearing preload.

3) With backlash adjustment complete, install adjusting nut lock into slots in nuts. Install nut lock bolt and tighten to specification. Tighten bearing cap bolts to specification. See TORQUE SPECIFICATIONS table. Perform gear tooth contact pattern check. See GEAR TOOTH CONTACT PATTERNS article in GENERAL INFORMATION. Install drive axles. See AXLE SHAFT under REMOVAL & INSTALLATION. Install axle housing cover and lubricant.

AXLE ASSEMBLY SPECIFICATIONS

AXLE ASSEMBLY SPECIFICATIONS

Application	Measurement
Ring Gear Backlash	
Preferred	.005-.008" (.127-.203 mm)
Acceptable	.003-.008" (.076-.203 mm)
Pinion Bearing Preload	
Used Bearings	5-15 INCH Lbs. (.6-1.7 N.m)
New Bearings	23-35 INCH Lbs. (2.6-4.0 N.m)

TORQUE SPECIFICATIONS

TORQUE SPECIFICATIONS

Application	Ft. Lbs. (N.m)
Axle Shaft Retaining Bolts	115 (156)
Differential Bearing Adjusting Lock Bolts	22 (30)
Differential Cover Bolts	20 (27)
Differential Filler Plug	18 (24)
Drive Pinion Nut	[1]
Pinion Cage-To-Axle Housing Bolts	65 (88)
Propeller Shaft Flange Bolts	22 (30)
Ring Gear Bolts [2]	120 (163)
Shock Absorber Nuts	75 (102)
Side Bearing Cap Bolts	135 (183)
"U" Bolt Nuts	
"C" & "K" Series	109 (148)
"G" & "P" Series	
Bolts Facing Up	125 (169)
Bolts Facing Down	147 (199)

[1] – Tighten as necessary to obtain previously measured preload. Preload should be at or less than 25-35 INCH Lbs. (2.8-4.0 N.m)

[2] – Bolts have left-hand threads.

Commercial Van

DESCRIPTION

MODEL IDENTIFICATION

Vehicle model can be identified by fifth character of Vehicle Identification Number (VIN), stamped on metal pad on top of left end of instrument panel, near windshield. See MODEL IDENTIFICATION table.

MODEL IDENTIFICATION

Series [1]	Model
"P"	Commercial Van/Motorhome

[1] – Vehicle series is fifth character of VIN.

Rockwell 12" ring gear uses a full-floating axle. Axle shaft is supported by wheel hubs at the wheel ends of axle and is held in the axle housing by an axle cap bolted to the wheel hub. Splined end of the axle shaft is supported by the differential. Axle is sealed with a pinion seal, a gasket at each axle shaft end and a gasket between the axle housing and differential carrier.

AXLE RATIO & IDENTIFICATION

To determine drive axle ratio, see AXLE RATIO IDENTIFICATION article.

ADJUSTMENTS

HUB BEARINGS

1) Raise and support vehicle. Remove axle shaft. See AXLE SHAFT under REMOVAL & INSTALLATION. Remove wheel hub assembly nut and lock washer. See Fig. 1. Using Wheel Hub Bearing Nut Wrench (J-25510), tighten hub bearing adjusting nut to **50 ft. lbs. (68 N.m)** while rotating hub.
2) Ensure bearings are seated. Loosen adjusting nut 1/8 turn. Install lock washer and axle shaft nut. Tighten axle shaft nut to specification. Bend tang on lock washer. Install axle shaft and hub cover.

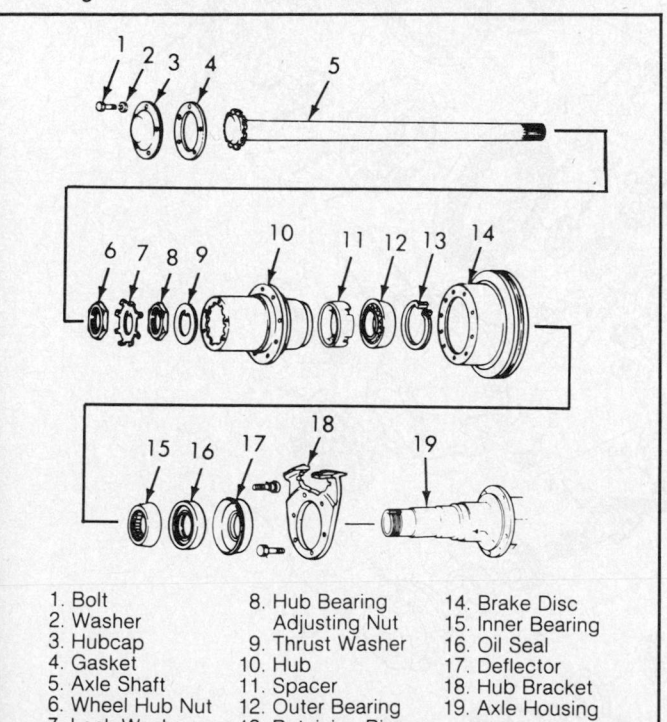

1. Bolt
2. Washer
3. Hubcap
4. Gasket
5. Axle Shaft
6. Wheel Hub Nut
7. Lock Washer
8. Hub Bearing Adjusting Nut
9. Thrust Washer
10. Hub
11. Spacer
12. Outer Bearing
13. Retaining Ring
14. Brake Disc
15. Inner Bearing
16. Oil Seal
17. Deflector
18. Hub Bracket
19. Axle Housing

91H13307   Courtesy of General Motors Corp.

Fig. 1: Exploded View Of Axle & Hub Assembly

REMOVAL & INSTALLATION

AXLE SHAFT

Removal – Raise and support vehicle. Remove axle shaft hubcap bolts and washers. Remove hubcap with gasket. See Fig. 1. Thread an adapter into wheel hub end of axle shaft. Attach a slide hammer to adapter. Using slide hammer, remove axle shaft from axle housing.
Installation – Index splines on axle shaft and wheel hub. Using a slide hammer, tap axle shaft into axle housing. Ensure old hubcap gasket material is removed from wheel hub assembly. Install a new hubcap gasket. Install hubcap with bolts and washers.

WHEEL HUB & SEAL

Removal & Installation – 1) Remove caliper and support with wire. Remove axle shaft. See AXLE SHAFT under REMOVAL & INSTALLATION. Using Wheel Hub Bearing Nut Wrench (J-25510), remove wheel hub assembly nut. See Fig. 1. Remove lock washer.
2) Using Wheel Hub Bearing Nut Wrench (J-25510), remove hub bearing adjusting nut and thrust washer. Remove hub and rotor assembly from axle housing. Remove deflector. Pry oil seal from wheel hub, using care not to damage bore surface. Thoroughly clean seal contact surface area.
3) To install, pack cavity between seal lips with high melting point wheel bearing lubricant. Using Seal Installer (J-24428), carefully press seal into hub until seal is flush with edge of hub. To complete installation, reverse removal procedure.

HUB BEARINGS

Removal & Installation – 1) Remove wheel hub assembly. See WHEEL HUB & SEAL under REMOVAL & INSTALLATION. Use a long drift or punch to drive inner bearing and race from hub. Remove outer bearing retaining ring. Drive outer bearing out of hub.

NOTE: Remove inner bearing race and outer bearing retaining ring before attempting to remove outer bearing.

2) To install, place outer bearing assembly into hub. Drive bearing past retaining ring groove in hub. Ensure chamfer of bearing race installer does not contact bearing race.
3) Install outer bearing retaining ring. Drive race into hub until seated. Drive inner race into hub until seated against shoulder. Install inner bearing and NEW oil seal. Place hub assembly onto axle housing. Install adjusting nut. Adjust hub bearing.

PINION FLANGE & OIL SEAL

Removal & Installation – 1) Disconnect drive shaft. Scribe a line down pinion nut, pinion stem and pinion flange for reassembly reference. Remove pinion nut cotter pin and pinion nut. Using a puller, remove pinion flange from stem. See Fig. 2.
2) Remove bolts securing oil seal retainer to differential carrier. Remove oil seal retainer. Pry oil seal from bore, using care not to damage machined surface.
3) Lubricate inside cavity of new oil seal with extreme pressure lubricant. Install new pinion oil seal into bore. Ensure seal bottoms against shoulder in bore. Install oil seal retainer and bolts to carrier.
4) Pack cavity between pinion stem and pinion flange with a non-hardening sealer such as Permatex type A. See Fig. 2. Discard old pinion shaft nut. Using reference marks scribed during removal, install pinion flange, new pinion nut, pinion nut cotter pin and drive shaft. Torque pinion nut to specification.

DIFFERENTIAL ASSEMBLY

Removal & Installation – 1) Drain differential. Remove axle shafts. See AXLE SHAFT under REMOVAL & INSTALLATION. Disconnect drive shaft. To prevent differential carrier from falling out during removal, loosen (but do not remove) 2 top carrier-to-housing bolts. Remove remaining carrier-to-housing bolts and washers.

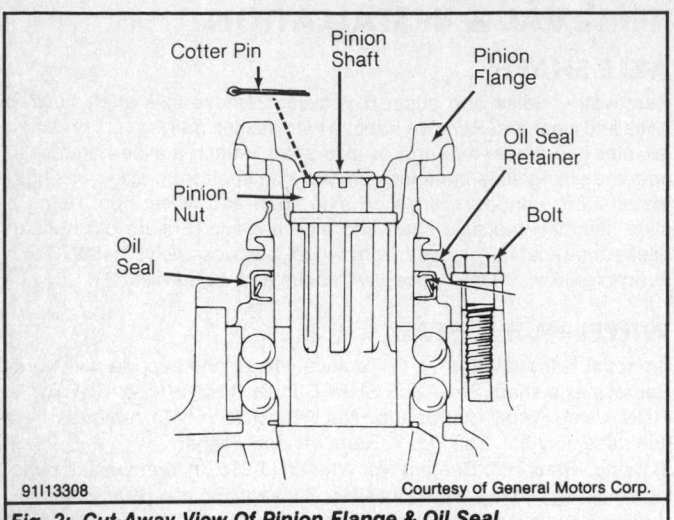

91I13308   Courtesy of General Motors Corp.

Fig. 2: Cut-Away View Of Pinion Flange & Oil Seal

2) Break carrier loose from axle housing with soft mallet. Remove 2 top bolts and washers and work carrier free. Use a roller jack to safely remove carrier from housing. To install, reverse removal procedure.

OVERHAUL
DIFFERENTIAL ASSEMBLY

NOTE: Before disassembly, check and record ring gear backlash and pinion bearing preload. See REASSEMBLY (DRIVE PINION & CAGE) and RING GEAR BACKLASH under OVERHAUL.

Disassembly (Differential Case & Gear) – 1) With carrier in holding fixture, loosen jam nut and back off thrust block adjusting screw. *See Fig. 3.* Center punch one differential carrier leg and bearing cap for reassembly reference.

2) Remove bearing cap bolts and bearing caps. Remove adjusting nuts. Remove differential and ring gear assembly from carrier. Scribe a reference mark across differential case halves.

3) Remove differential case bolts. *See Fig. 3.* Separate case halves. Remove pinion spider. Remove side gears with thrust washers and pinion gears with thrust washers from pinion spider. *See Fig. 3.*

4) Remove ring gear nuts and washers from differential case. Remove ring gear bolts. Separate ring gear from differential case. *See Fig. 3.* Using a press, remove differential side bearings. Identify bearings for reassembly reference.

Disassembly (Drive Pinion & Cage) – 1) Hold pinion flange and remove pinion nut and washer. Using a puller, remove flange. Remove pinion cage cover bolts. Using bolts from a puller, thread bolts into pinion cage holes to push cage away from carrier. *See Fig. 4.* Remove drive pinion cage. Wire shim pack together and save for reassembly reference.

1. Axle Housing
2. Axle Vent
3. Bolt
4. Washer
5. Bearing Cap
6. Bracket
7. Nut
8. Plug
9. Gasket
10. Pin
11. Adjusting Nut
12. Bearing
13. Differential Case
14. Side Gears
15. Pinion Thrust Washers
16. Pinion Gears
17. Side Gear Thrust Washer
18. Pinion Spider
19. Ring Gear Bolt
20. Carrier
21. Thrust Block Screw
22. Pinion Depth Shims
23. Retaining Ring
24. Pinion & Ring Gear Set
25. Pinion Cage
26. Pinion Oil Seal
27. Deflector
28. Pinion Flange
29. Pinion Pilot Bearing
30. Rear Pinion Bearing
31. Front Pinion Bearing
32. Bearing Race

91J13309   Courtesy of General Motors Corp.

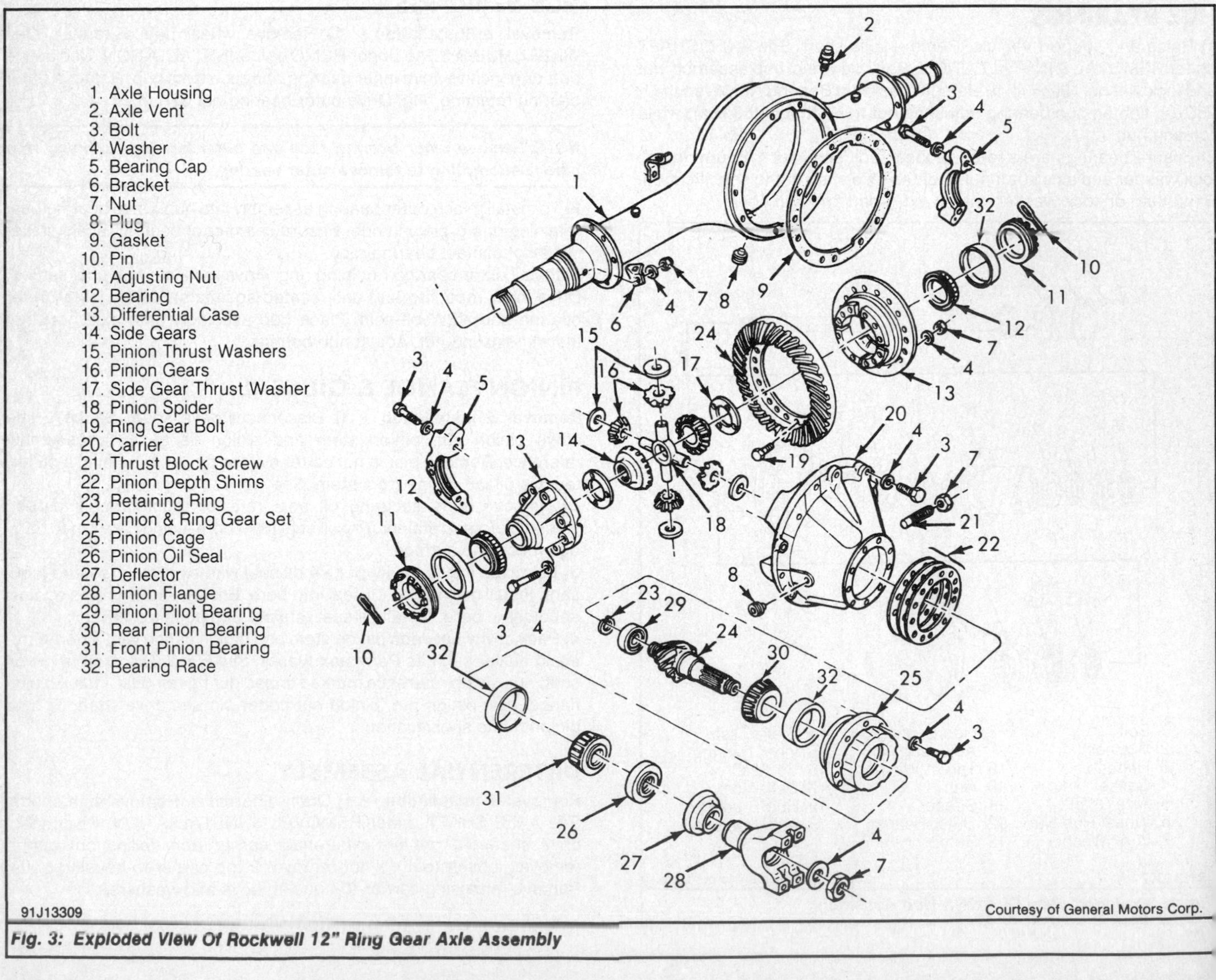

Fig. 3: Exploded View Of Rockwell 12" Ring Gear Axle Assembly

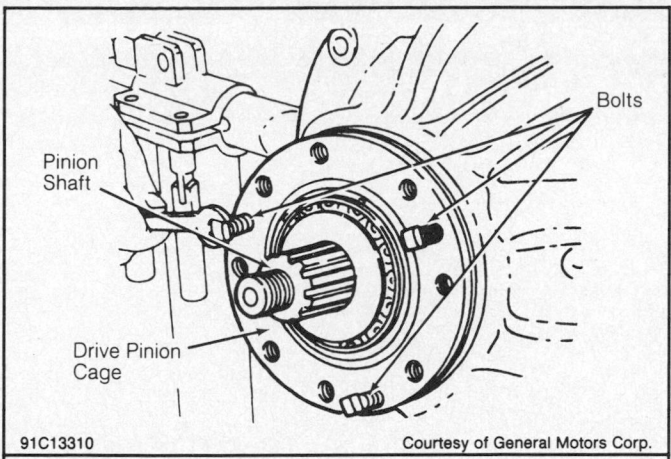

Fig. 4: Removing Pinion Cage

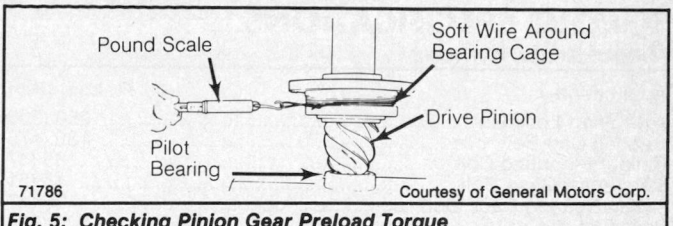

Fig. 5: Checking Pinion Gear Preload Torque

2) Using a press, remove pinion gear from cage. Remove pinion oil seal from cage. Remove outer bearing from cage. Using a press, remove inner bearing from cage. Remove pilot bearing retaining ring. Using a puller, remove pilot bearing from pinion gear.

Cleaning & Inspection – 1) Clean all parts in cleaning solvent. Inspect all bearings, bearing races and rollers for scoring, chipping and excessive wear. Inspect axle shaft and side gear splines for excessive wear.

NOTE: DO NOT steam clean any parts having a ground and polished surface, such as bearings, gears and shafts.

---

2) Inspect ring gear and pinion for scoring, cracking or chipping. Inspect differential case, pinion side gears, thrust washers and pinion shaft for cracks, scoring, galling or excessive wear.

NOTE: Rear axle ring and pinion sets are system balanced as an assembly. Assembly is balanced as a unit with pinion flange weighted as a harmonic balancer. If axle repairs dictate installation of new ring and pinion, a new pinion flange must also be used. Discard original flange and refer to appropriate GMSPO Parts Catalog for proper service flange

---

Reassembly (Drive Pinion & Cage) – 1) Lubricate bearings and races with axle lubricant. Using a press, install rear and pilot bearings firmly against pinion shoulders. *See Fig. 3.*

2) Using pliers, install pilot bearing snap ring and squeeze ring into pinion shaft groove. Insert pinion and bearing assembly in pinion cage and position spacer(s) over pinion shaft. Using a press, install front pinion gear bearing firmly against spacer(s).

3) Rotate cage several revolutions to ensure bearings seat. Using a press, apply 11 tons of pressure to pinion assembly. To check bearing preload torque, wrap soft wire around cage. Attach wire to a pound scale. Pull in horizontal line with pound scale. Record rotating torque, not starting torque. *See Fig. 5.*

4) Preload (rotating) torque should be 5-15 INCH lbs. (5.6-17.0 N.m). To determine INCH lbs. torque, determine diameter of pinion cage in inches. Divide diameter by 2 to find radius in inches. Multiply radius by number of pounds on scale. Use a thinner spacer to increase bearing preload, or a thicker spacer to decrease bearing preload.

5) Press pinion flange against forward bearing and install washer and old pinion shaft nut. Hold flange and tighten pinion shaft nut to **240 ft. lbs. (325 N.m)**. Recheck pinion bearing preload torque. If preload is within specification, go to step 7). If preload is not within specification, go to next step.

6) Hold flange and remove pinion shaft nut and flange. Add or remove spacers as necessary to achieve 5-15 INCH lbs. (5.6-17.0 N.m) of preload.

7) Discard old pinion shaft nut. Cover outer edge of seal body with a non-hardening sealing compound. Using a seal installer, drive pinion seal against cover shoulder. Install pinion flange deflector.

8) Press flange against outer bearing, and install washer and new pinion shaft nut. Torque pinion shaft nut to **240 ft. lbs. (325 N.m)**.

Reassembly (Differential Case & Gear) – 1) DO NOT press or drive ring gear onto differential case, or damage to components may result. Ensure ring gear is clean and free of burrs. Heat ring gear in water to **160-180°F (71-82°C)** for 10 minutes before assembly. Place ring gear onto differential case. Install NEW ring gear bolts. Torque ring gear bolts gradually in an alternating pattern to pull ring gear onto differential case.

2) Position thrust washers and side gears in case halves assembly. Place spider with pinions and thrust washers in position. Align scribe (reference) marks on differential case made during disassembly. Install differential case bolts. Torque to specification. Ensure differential case assembly rotates freely. Using a press, install bearings onto differential case.

3) Temporarily install bearing races, threaded adjusting rings and bearing caps. Tighten bearing cap bolts to specification. Bearing races must have a hand fit in bores. If bearing races do not have a hand fit in bores, use emery cloth on bearing bores until a hand fit is obtained.

4) Once races fit, remove bearing caps. Coat differential bearings and races with rear axle lubricant. Place bearing races over assembled differential bearing. Position differential assembly in carrier. Insert bearing adjusting nuts and turn hand tight against bearing races.

5) If bearing caps do not position properly, ensure adjusting nuts are not cross threaded. Remove caps and reposition adjusting nuts. Install bearing cap washers and bolts. Torque bearing cap bolts to specification. See TORQUE SPECIFICATIONS table at end of article.

Adjusting Pinion Gear Depth – To accurately install a new pinion and cage assembly into carrier, mathematically calculate the proper pinion cage shim pack thickness using variation number on pinion head of original and new drive pinion.

Example:

Original Pack Thickness	.030"
Original Variation Number (+2)	-.002"
Standard Pack Thickness	.028"
New Variation Number (+5)	+.005"
New Pack Thickness	.033"

Ring Gear Runout & Side Bearing Preload – 1) Use a dial indicator at back face of ring gear. Loosen bearing adjusting nut on side opposite ring gear, but only enough to notice end play on dial indicator. Tighten same adjusting nut until zero end play is obtained.

2) Rotate ring gear and check runout. If runout exceeds **.008" (.20 mm)**, remove differential and check for cause. Tighten adjusting nuts one notch each from zero end play to preload differential bearings.

Ring Gear Backlash – 1) If drive gear is not going to be replaced, use established backlash recorded before disassembly. For new gears, backlash should be set at **.008-.015" (.20-.38 mm)** initially.

2) Adjust backlash by moving ring gear only. Back off one adjusting nut and tighten opposite adjusting nut the same amount. *See Fig. 3.*

NOTE: Preload will change if adjusting nuts are not moved exactly the same amount.

---

3) Install adjusting nut pins. Install thrust block screw and lock nut. Torque thrust block screw sufficiently to place thrust block firmly against back face of ring gear.

4) To secure correct adjustment of **.008-.015" (.20-.38 mm)** clearance, loosen thrust block screw 1/4 turn and lock securely with nut. Recheck to ensure clearance is within specification during full rotation of ring gear.

TORQUE SPECIFICATIONS

TORQUE SPECIFICATIONS

Application	Ft. Lbs. (N.m)
Axle Shaft Lock Nut	250 (339)
Bearing Cap Bolt	130 (176)
Caliper Mounting Bolt	35 (47)
Differential Case Bolt	45 (61)
Pinion Bearing Cage Bolt	35 (47)
Pinion Shaft Nut	240 (325)
Ring Gear Bolt	100 (136)
Thrust Block Screw Nut	150-190 (203-257)
Wheel Hub Bearing Nut	50 (68)

Astro, Bravada, Jimmy, Safari, Sierra, Sonoma, Syclone, Typhoon, Yukon "K" & "T" Series Blazer & Pickup

MODEL IDENTIFICATION

Vehicle model can be identified by fifth character of Vehicle Identification Number (VIN), stamped on metal pad on top of left end of instrument panel, near windshield. See MODEL IDENTIFICATION table.

MODEL IDENTIFICATION

Series [1]	Model
"K"	4WD Blazer, Pickup, Sierra, Suburban & Yukon
"L"	All-Wheel Drive Astro & Safari
"T"	Bravada, 4WD Blazer, Jimmy, Pickup, Sonoma, Syclone & Typhoon

[1] – Vehicle series is fifth character of VIN.

ADJUSTMENTS

BALL JOINT TURNING EFFORT

NOTE: Front axle ball joint adjustment is only necessary when there is excessive play in steering, irregular wear on tire or persistent loosening of tie rod.

REMOVAL & INSTALLATION

STEERING KNUCKLE

Removal – 1) Raise and support vehicle. Remove wheel and tire assembly. Install Axle Shaft Boot Seal Protector (J-28712) on axle shaft boot to protect boot during repair. Depress brake caliper piston, detach brake caliper and wire aside. Remove brake rotor.

2) Remove cotter pin and retainer (if equipped) from axle shaft nut. Remove nut and washer from axle shaft. Remove cotter pin and tie rod end nut. Separate tie rod end from steering knuckle. *See Fig. 1.*

3) Attach puller to hub. Tighten pressure screw, and force axle shaft from hub and bearing assembly. Remove hub and bearing assembly from steering knuckle. Remove splash shield. Support lower control arm using floor jack or jackstand.

CAUTION: Support lower control arm with floor jack or jack stand to maintain tension on torsion bar.

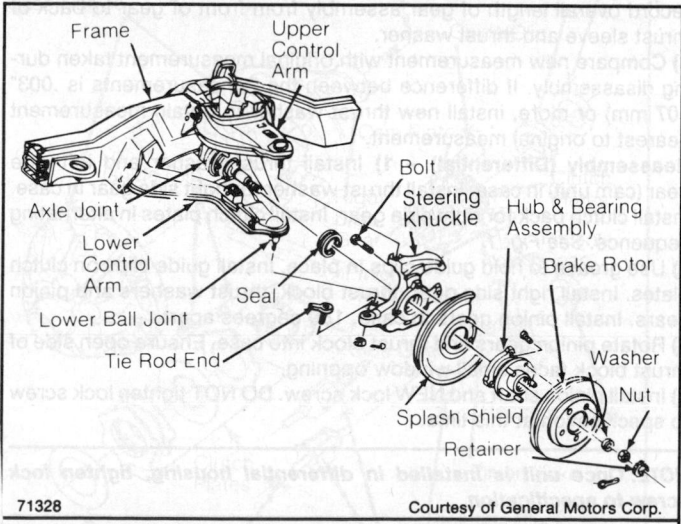

71328   Courtesy of General Motors Corp.

Fig. 1: Exploded View Of Hub & Steering Knuckle Assembly ("K" Series Shown; Others Similar)

4) Remove cotter pins from ball joint studs. On "T" Series, place Ball Joint Separator (J-34026) over upper or lower ball joint. *See Fig. 2.* Loosen ball joint nut. Back off until nut contacts ball joint separator. Continue backing off nut until nut forces ball stud out of steering knuckle.

5) On all other models, separate ball joint from steering knuckle using Ball Joint Separator (J-36607). On all models, remove steering knuckle from vehicle without damaging or moving axle shaft. Remove seal from steering knuckle.

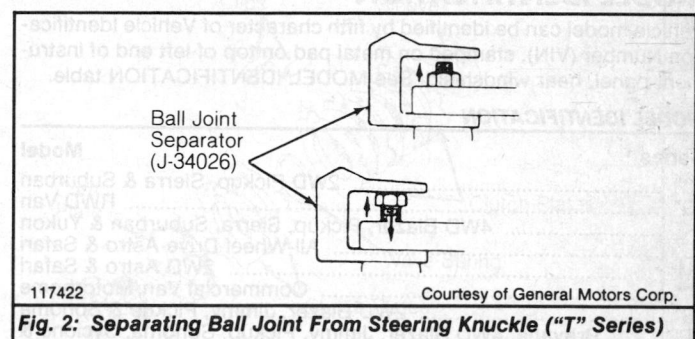

Ball Joint Separator (J-34026)

117422   Courtesy of General Motors Corp.

Fig. 2: Separating Ball Joint From Steering Knuckle ("T" Series)

Installation – 1) To install, reverse removal procedure. Using seal installer, install NEW seal in steering knuckle. Use Seal Installer (J-36605) for Astro, Safari, Syclone and Typhoon, (J-36606) for "K" Series or (J-28574) for "T" Series.

2) On "T" Series, ensure spacer is installed on steering knuckle at upper ball joint stud hole. On all models, tighten bolts/nuts to specification. See TORQUE SPECIFICATIONS table at end of article. If necessary, tighten tie rod and ball joint nuts to align cotter key hole. DO NOT loosen nuts for alignment. Remove boot protector from axle shaft.

TORQUE SPECIFICATIONS

TORQUE SPECIFICATIONS

Application	Ft. Lbs. (N.m)
Astro & Safari	
Axle Shaft Nut	173 (235)
Ball Joint Nut	94 (127)
Brake Caliper Bolt	37 (50)
Hub & Bearing Assembly Bolt	66 (89)
Splash Shield Bolt	12 (16)
Tie Rod Nut	35 (47)
Wheel Lug Nut	92 (125)
"K" Series	
Axle Shaft Nut	173 (235)
Ball Joint Nut	94 (127)
Brake Caliper Bolt	28 (38)
Hub & Bearing Assembly Bolt	66 (89)
Splash Shield Bolt	12 (16)
Tie Rod Nut	35 (47)
Wheel Lug Nut	
Dual Wheel	125 (169)
Single Wheel	90 (122)
"T" Series	
Axle Shaft Nut	181 (245)
Ball Joint Nut	
Lower	83 (113)
Upper	61 (83)
Brake Caliper Bolt	37 (50)
Hub & Bearing Assembly Bolt	86 (117)
Tie Rod Nut	35 (47)
Wheel Lug Nut	
Aluminum Wheel	90 (122)
Steel Wheel	73 (99)

4WAL SYMPTOM DIAGNOSIS

Symptom	Perform Chart
ANTILOCK Light On	ANTILOCK LIGHT ON (Fig. 8)
ANTILOCK Light Off	ANTILOCK LIGHT OFF (Fig. 9)
Brake Pedal Pulses [1]	BRAKE PEDAL PULSES (Fig. 10)
Wheel Pull During Hard Braking [1]	WHEEL PULL DURING HARD BRAKING (Fig. 11)

[1] – These conditions must exist with no fault codes stored.

4WAL FAULT CODES

Fault Code	Description
21, 25, 31 or 35 [1]	Speed Sensor Failure Or Open Circuit
22, 26, 32 Or 36 [2]	Missing Speed Signal
23, 27, 33 Or 37 [3]	Erratic Speed Sensor
28	Erratic Speed Sensor Signal (2 Dropouts Above 20 MPH)
29	Simultaneous Dropout Of All 4 Speed Sensors Above 8 MPH
35 [4]	Speed Sensor Failure Or Open Circuit
36 [4]	Missing Speed Sensor Signal
37 [4]	Erratic Speed Sensor Signal
38	Speed Sensor Error
41-54	Control Valves
61, 62 Or 63	Reset Switches
65 & 66	Motor Relay Open Or Shorted
67 [5]	Pump Motor Circuit Open Or EHCU Output Shorted
68 [5]	Pump Motor Locked Or Motor Circuit Shorted
71-74	Memory Errors
81	Brake Switch Circuit Open Or Shorted
86	ANTILOCK Light Shorted
88	BRAKE Light Shorted

[1] – "C" and "K" series vehicles will only display Codes 21 and 25.
[2] – "C" and "K" series vehicles will only display Codes 22 and 26.
[3] – "C" and "K" series vehicles will only display Codes 23 and 27.
[4] – Applies only to "C" and "K" series vehicles.
[5] – Codes 67 and 68 use the same trouble shooting flow chart.

CLEARING FAULT CODES

Turn ignition on. Using a jumper wire, connect ALDL connector terminal "H" to terminal "A" for 2 seconds. Remove jumper wire for one second. Again, jumper ALDL connector terminal "H" to "A" for 2 seconds. Remove jumper wire. Fault codes are cleared when ANTILOCK and BRAKE lights illuminate, then turn off. Turn ignition off. Check to verify codes are cleared. See RETRIEVING CODES.

REMOVAL & INSTALLATION

WARNING: When battery is disconnected, vehicle computer and memory systems may lose memory data. Driveability problems may exist until computer systems have completed a relearn cycle. See COMPUTER RELEARN PROCEDURES article in GENERAL INFORMATION before disconnecting battery.

ELECTRO-HYDRAULIC CONTROL UNIT (EHCU)

Removal (Astro & Safari) – 1) Turn ignition off. Bleed vacuum and hydraulic pressure from system by depressing brake pedal several times. Position front wheels straight ahead. Index upper and lower "U" joints on intermediate steering shaft. Remove pinch bolt from upper and lower "U" joint. Index steering gear position. Remove steering gear mounting bolts. DO NOT disconnect pitman arm from pitman shaft. Separate steering gear from frame rail.

2) Remove intermediate steering shaft. Disconnect hydraulic lines from bottom of combination valve. Disconnect electrical connector from combination valve. Remove master cylinder mounting bolts. Remove master cylinder and combination valve as an assembly.

3) Disconnect hydraulic lines from EHCU. Disconnect electrical connectors from EHCU. Remove EHCU bracket-to-body bolts and nuts. Remove EHCU and bracket from vehicle as an assembly. Remove bracket from EHCU.

Installation – 1) To install, reverse removal procedure. Align all index marks for steering components. Ensure intermediate steering shaft pinch bolts pass through shaft undercut.

2) Bleed brake system, including EHCU. See BLEEDING BRAKE SYSTEM. DO NOT overtighten EHCU-to-bracket bolts during installation. This may cause excessive noise transfer into vehicle. See TORQUE SPECIFICATIONS table.

Removal & Installation (Bravada & "S" & "T" Series) – 1) Disconnect hydraulic lines from bottom of combination valve. Disconnect electrical connector from combination valve. Disconnect hydraulic lines from EHCU. Disconnect electrical connectors from EHCU. Remove EHCU bracket-to-body bolts. Remove EHCU and bracket from vehicle as an assembly. Remove bracket from EHCU.

2) To install, reverse removal procedure. Bleed brake system, including EHCU. See BLEEDING BRAKE SYSTEM. DO NOT overtighten EHCU-to-bracket bolts during installation. This may cause excessive noise transfer into vehicle. See TORQUE SPECIFICATIONS table.

Removal & Installation ("C" & "K" Series) – 1) Disconnect hydraulic lines from EHCU. Disconnect electrical connectors from EHCU. Remove EHCU bracket-to-body bolts. Remove EHCU and bracket from vehicle as an assembly. Remove bracket from EHCU.

2) To install, reverse removal procedure. Bleed brake system, including EHCU. See BLEEDING BRAKE SYSTEM. DO NOT overtighten EHCU-to-bracket bolts during installation. This may cause excessive noise transfer into vehicle. See TORQUE SPECIFICATIONS table.

FRONT WHEEL SPEED SENSOR

NOTE: For installation purposes, note speed sensor wire routing before removing. Misrouted wiring may cause electromagnetic interference failures.

Removal & Installation (2WD Astro, Safari & "S" & "T" Series) – 1) Remove wheel and tire assembly. Remove brake caliper and wire aside. Remove hub and rotor assembly. Disconnect speed sensor electrical connector. Remove splash shield and speed sensor assembly. To install, reverse removal procedure. Tighten wheel bearing nut to 12 ft. lbs. (16 N.m), then back off until just loose.

2) Hand tighten wheel bearing nut. Back-off wheel bearing nut no more than 1/2 of a flat until hole in spindle aligns with slot in wheel bearing nut. If wheel bearing nut is adjusted properly, hub end play is .001-.005" (.03-.13 mm). If hub end play is not within specification, repeat procedure. Speed sensor air gap is non-adjustable. See TORQUE SPECIFICATIONS table.

Removal & Installation (AWD Astro, Bravada & Safari; 4WD "S" & "T" Series) – 1) Remove wheel and tire assembly. Remove brake caliper and wire aside. Remove drive axle nut. Disconnect speed sensor electrical connector. Remove speed sensor wire from clip on upper control arm. Remove bolts retaining hub and bearing assembly. Remove splash shield bolts. Using a puller, remove hub and bearing assembly.

2) Remove hub and bearing assembly, splash shield and speed sensor assembly. Remove speed sensor from hub and bearing assembly. Remove speed sensor wire harness from splash shield. To install, reverse removal procedure. Ensure drive axle nut is properly torqued.

3) DO NOT move drive axle nut more than 1/6 of a turn to align for cotter pin. If speed sensor is being replaced, drill out rivet in splash shield and replace rivet with a small bolt, nut and washer. Speed sensor air gap is non-adjustable. See TORQUE SPECIFICATIONS table.

Removal & Installation (2WD "C" & "K" Series) – 1) Remove wheel and tire assembly. Remove brake caliper and wire aside. Remove hub and rotor assembly. Disconnect speed sensor electrical connector. Remove speed sensor wire from clip on upper control arm. Remove splash shield and speed sensor assembly. To install, reverse removal procedure. Tighten wheel bearing nut to 12 ft. lbs. (16 N.m), then back off until just loose.

2) Back-off wheel bearing nut again no more than 1/4 of a turn until hole in spindle aligns with slot in wheel bearing nut. If wheel bearing

nut is adjusted properly, hub end play is .001-.008" (.03-.20 mm). If hub end play is not within specification, repeat procedure. Speed sensor air gap is non-adjustable. See TORQUE SPECIFICATIONS table.

Removal & Installation (4WD "C" & "K" Series) – 1) Remove wheel and tire assembly. Disconnect speed sensor electrical connector. Remove speed sensor wire from clip on upper control arm. Remove bolt attaching speed sensor wiring harness to vehicle frame.

2) Remove 2 bolts attaching speed sensor to back of steering knuckle. Remove speed sensor. To install, reverse removal procedure. Speed sensor air gap is non-adjustable. See TORQUE SPECIFICATIONS table.

REAR WHEEL SPEED SENSOR

Removal & Installation – Remove wheel assembly. Remove brake drum. Remove primary brake shoe. Remove necessary clips and bolts. Remove speed sensor by pulling speed sensor wire through backing plate. To install, reverse removal procedure.

VEHICLE SPEED SENSOR (VSS) BUFFER

CAUTION: VSS buffer is sensitive to Electrostatic Discharge (ESD). DO NOT touch VSS buffer terminals with hands or tools, or damage to VSS buffer may result from static electricity.

NOTE: VSS buffer is an internal portion of Digital Ratio Adapter Controller (DRAC); however, manufacturer now refers to DRAC as the VSS buffer.

Removal & Installation ("C" & "K" Series) – Ensure ignition is off. Disconnect negative battery cable. VSS buffer is located behind center of dashboard. Remove 4 screws mounting VSS buffer to dashboard. Disconnect 2 small electrical connectors from VSS buffer. Remove VSS buffer. To install, reverse removal procedure.

TORQUE SPECIFICATIONS

TORQUE SPECIFICATIONS

Application	Ft. Lbs. (N.m)
Brake Caliper Mounting Bolts	37 (50)
Brake Line Hydraulic Fittings	16 (22)
Drive Axle Nut	
Astro & Safari (AWD)	173 (234)
Bravada (AWD)	181 (245)
EHCU Mounting Bracket-To-Body Bolt	33 (45)
Hub & Bearing Assembly Mounting Bolts	
Astro & Safari (AWD)	12 (16)
Bravada (AWD) & "S" & "T" Series 4WD	86 (116)
Intermediate Steering Shaft	
"U" Joint Pinch Bolt	30 (41)
Speed Sensor Mounting Bolts	
Front [1]	11 (15)
Rear	26 (35)
Splash Shield Bolts	11 (15)
Steering Gear-To-Frame Bolts	55 (75)
Wheel Bearing Nut (2WD) [2]	12 (16)
Wheel Lug Nuts	90 (122)

	INCH Lbs. (N.m)
EHCU Internal Bleeder Screw	60 (7)
EHCU-To-Mounting Bracket Bolt	60 (7)

[1] – Not all models have speed sensor mounting bolts, some models have a speed sensor which is mounted onto a splash shield.

[2] – Refer to appropriate procedure in FRONT SPEED SENSOR under REMOVAL & INSTALLATION to ensure proper adjustment.

TROUBLE SHOOTING CHARTS

NOTE: See WIRING DIAGRAMS for circuit and terminal identification.

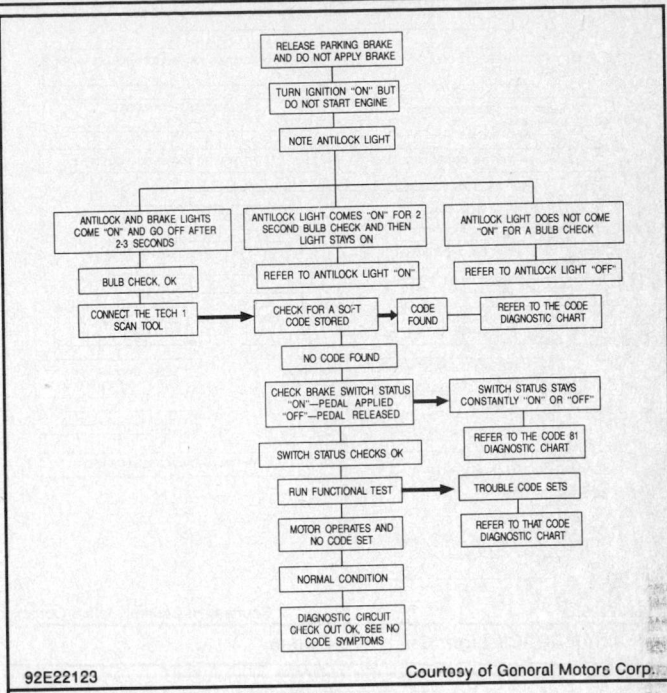

92E22123   Courtesy of General Motors Corp.

Fig. 7: Diagnostic Circuit Check

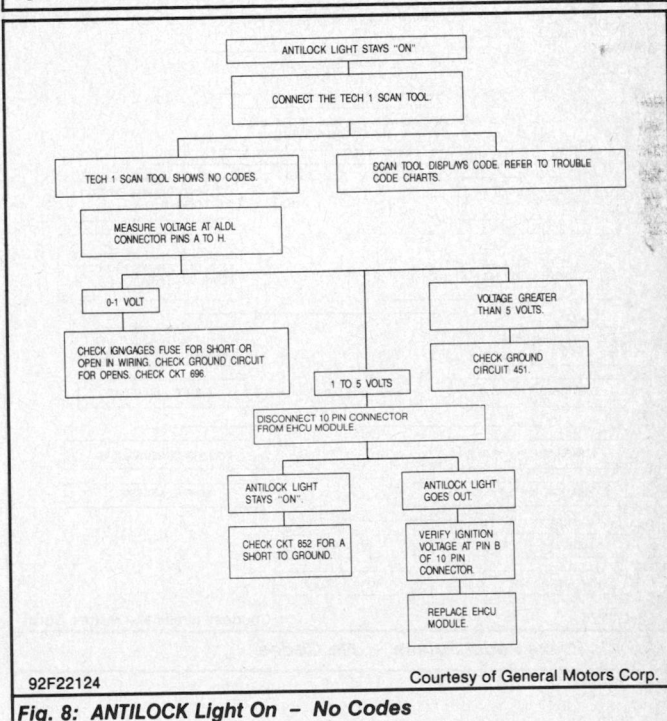

92F22124   Courtesy of General Motors Corp.

Fig. 8: ANTILOCK Light On – No Codes

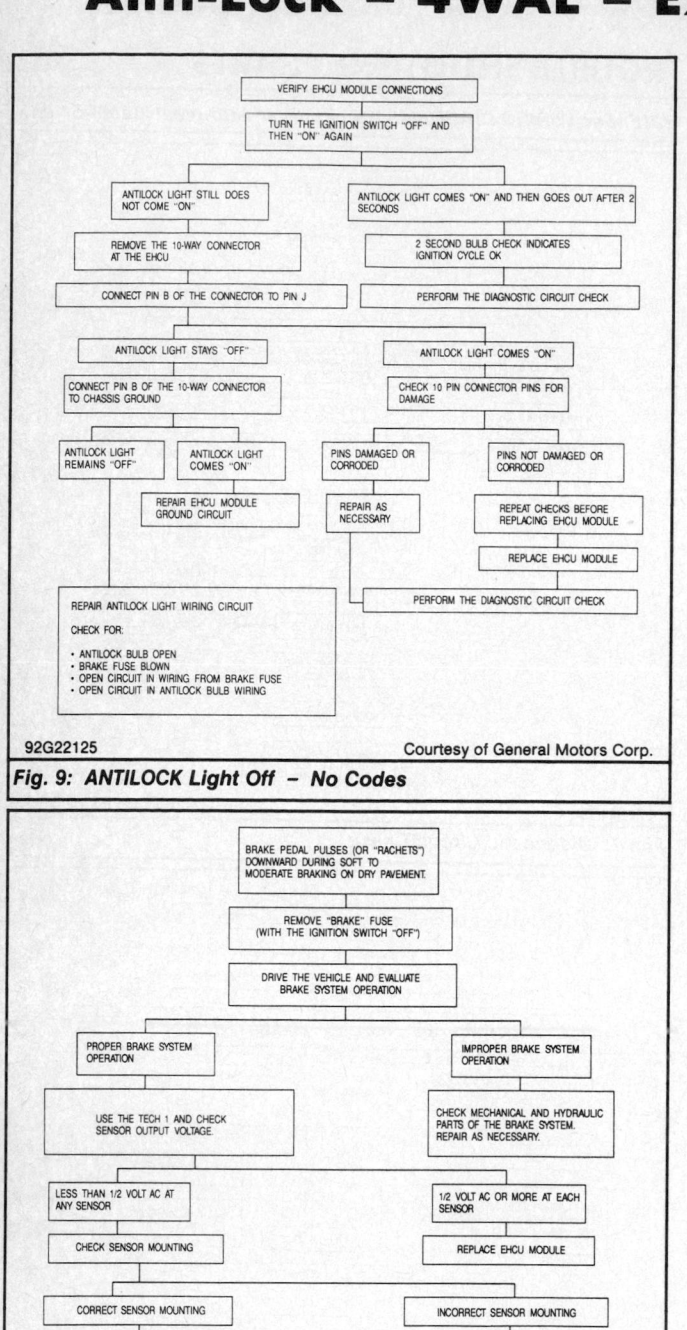

Fig. 9: ANTILOCK Light Off – No Codes

Fig. 10: Brake Pedal Pulses – No Codes

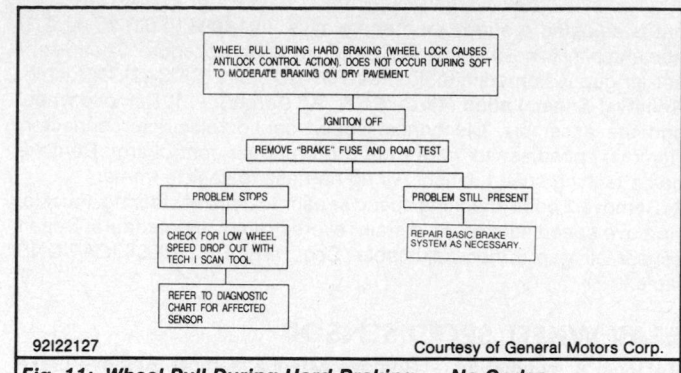

Fig. 11: Wheel Pull During Hard Braking – No Codes

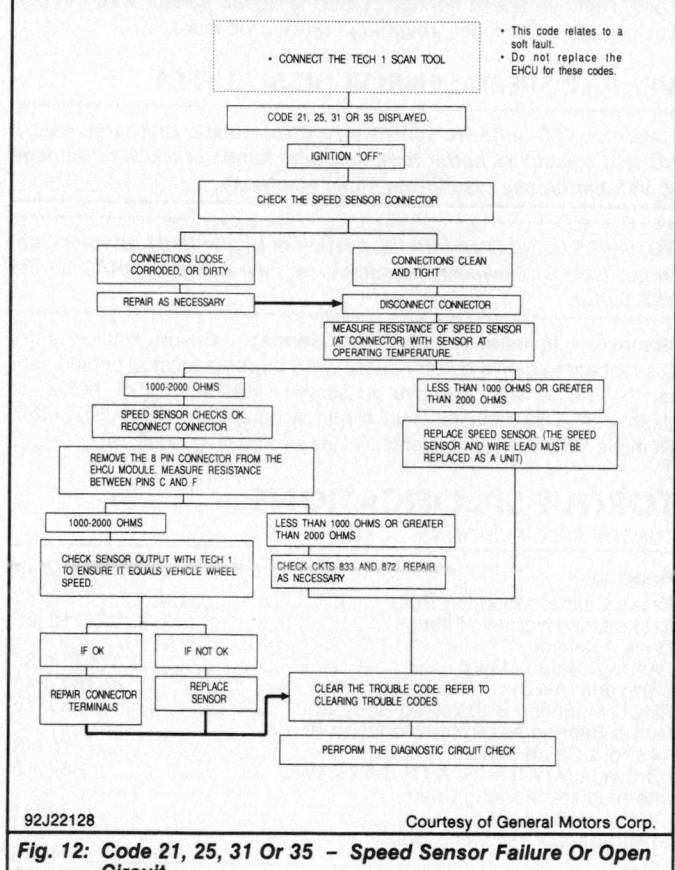

Fig. 12: Code 21, 25, 31 Or 35 – Speed Sensor Failure Or Open Circuit

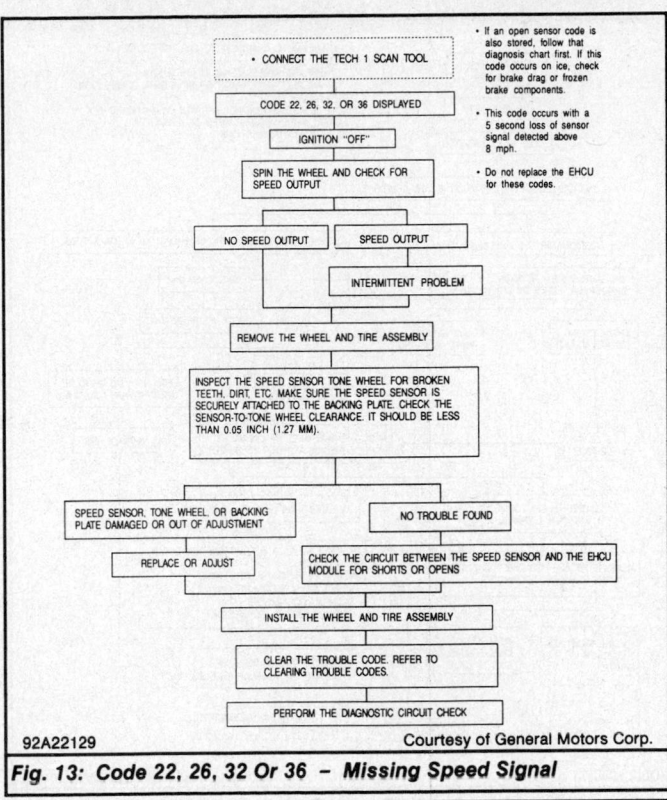

92A22129   Courtesy of General Motors Corp.

Fig. 13: Code 22, 26, 32 Or 36 – Missing Speed Signal

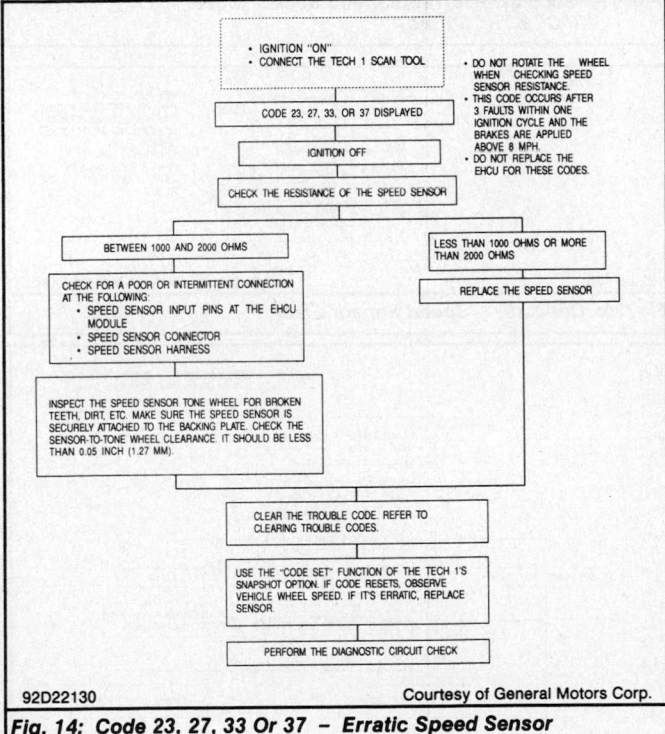

92D22130   Courtesy of General Motors Corp.

Fig. 14: Code 23, 27, 33 Or 37 – Erratic Speed Sensor

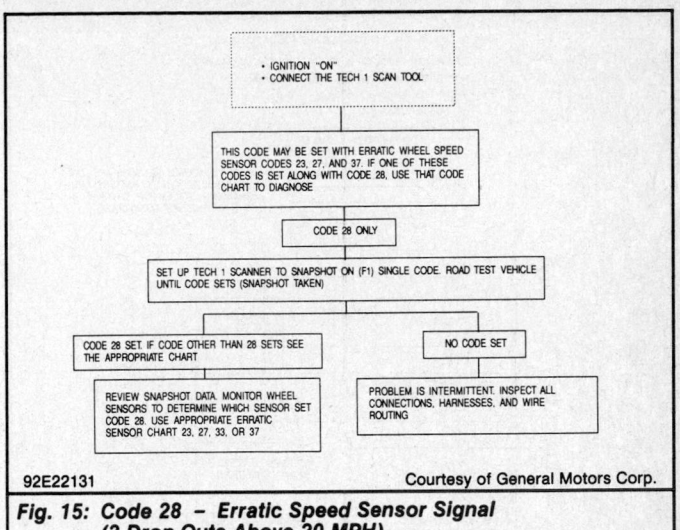

92E22131   Courtesy of General Motors Corp.

**Fig. 15: Code 28 – Erratic Speed Sensor Signal
(2 Drop-Outs Above 20 MPH)**

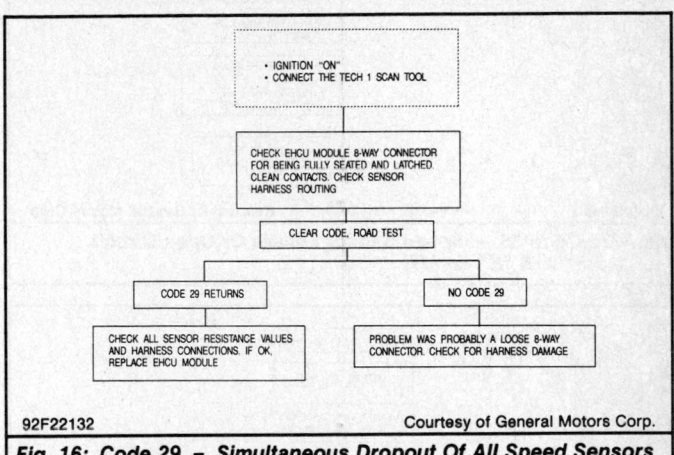

92F22132   Courtesy of General Motors Corp.

**Fig. 16: Code 29 – Simultaneous Dropout Of All Speed Sensors
Above 8 MPH**

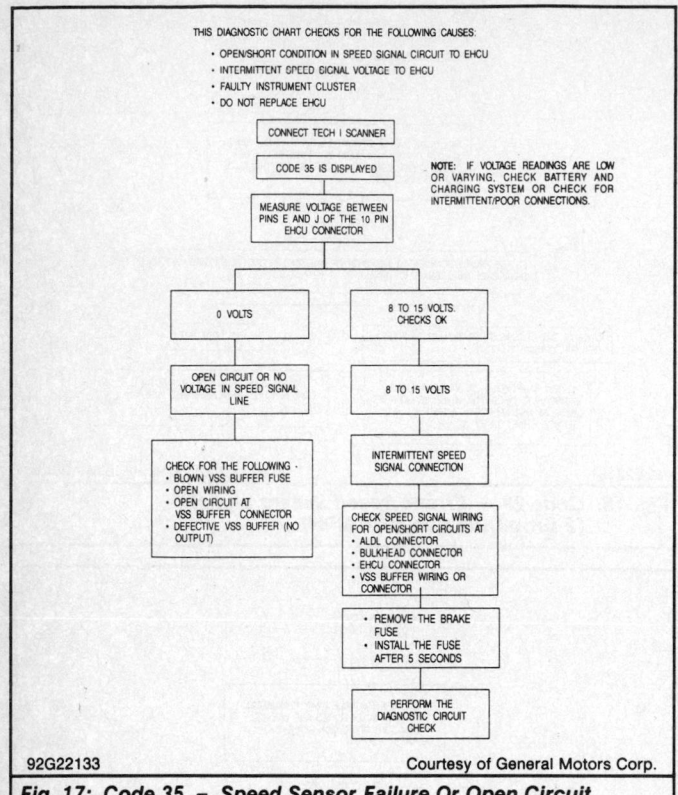

Fig. 17: Code 35 – Speed Sensor Failure Or Open Circuit ("C" & "K" Series)

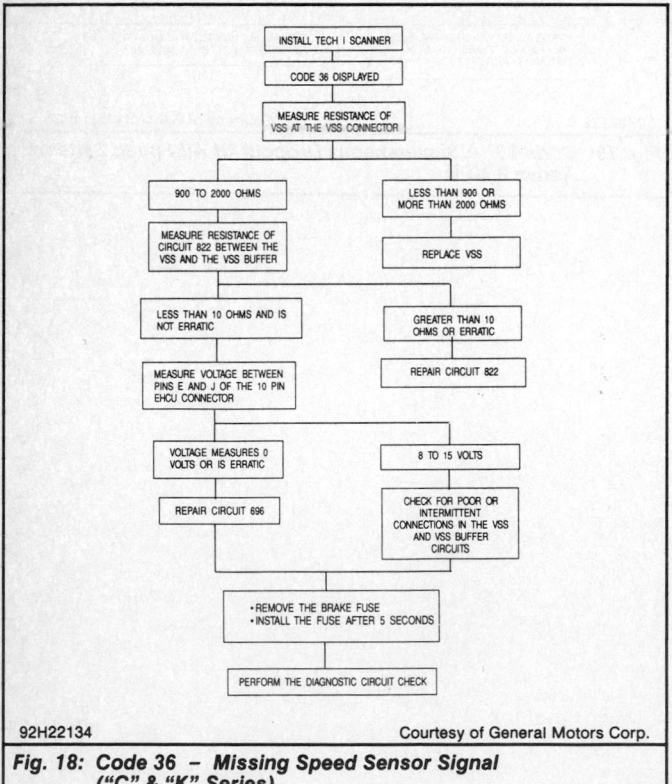

Fig. 18: Code 36 – Missing Speed Sensor Signal ("C" & "K" Series)

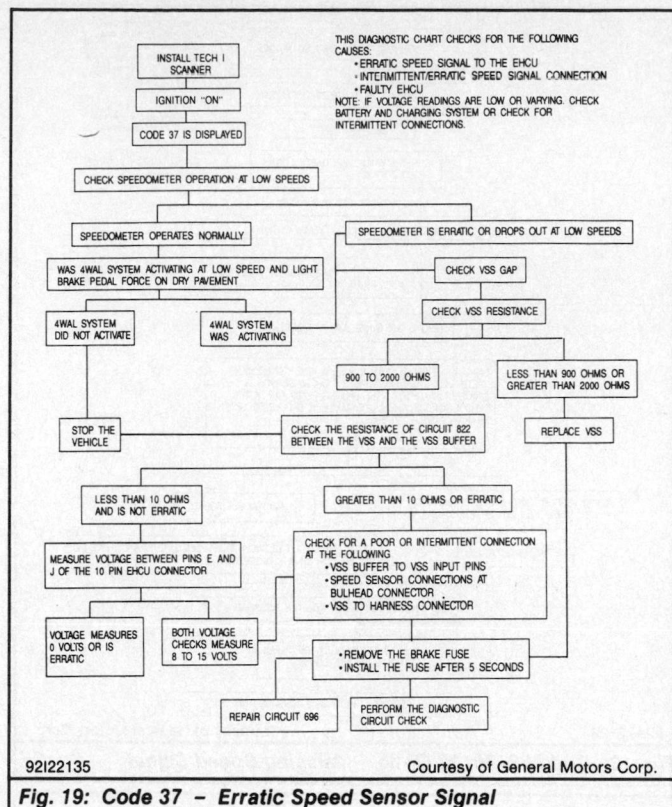

Fig. 19: Code 37 – Erratic Speed Sensor Signal ("C" & "K" Series)

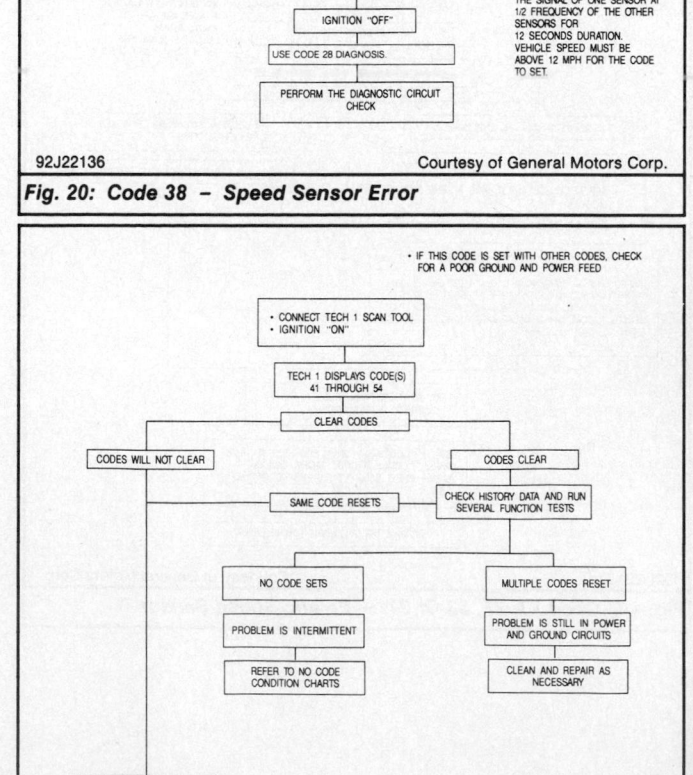

Fig. 20: Code 38 – Speed Sensor Error

Fig. 21: Codes 41-54 – Control Valves

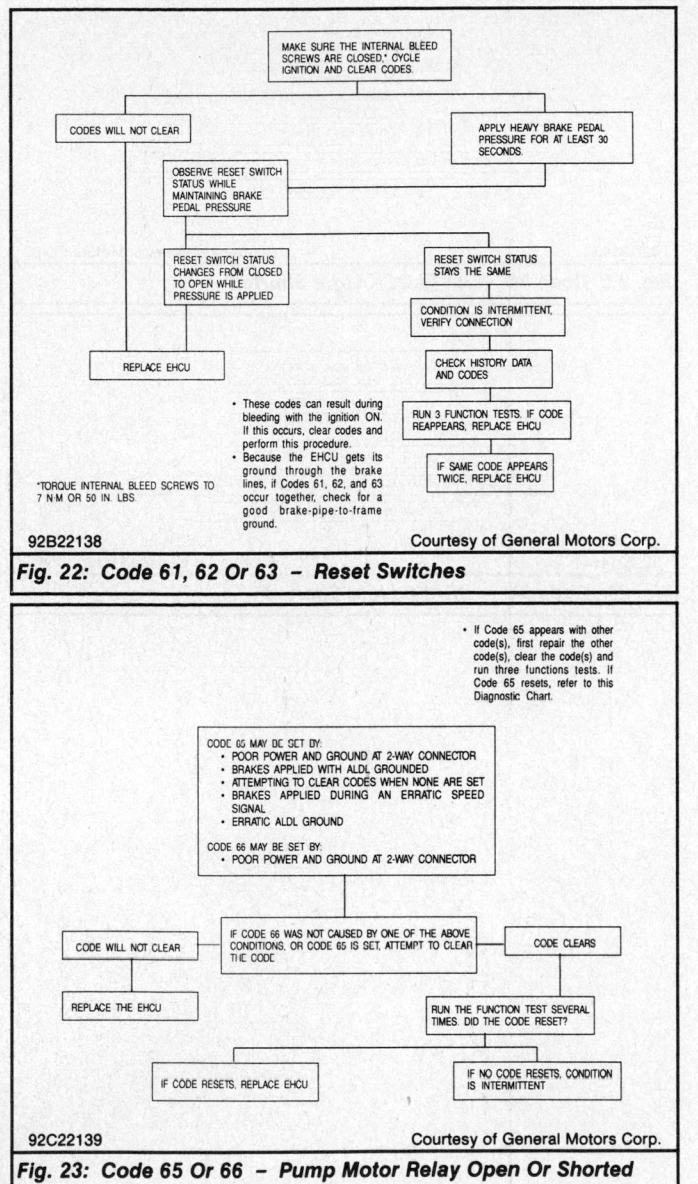

Fig. 22: Code 61, 62 Or 63 – Reset Switches

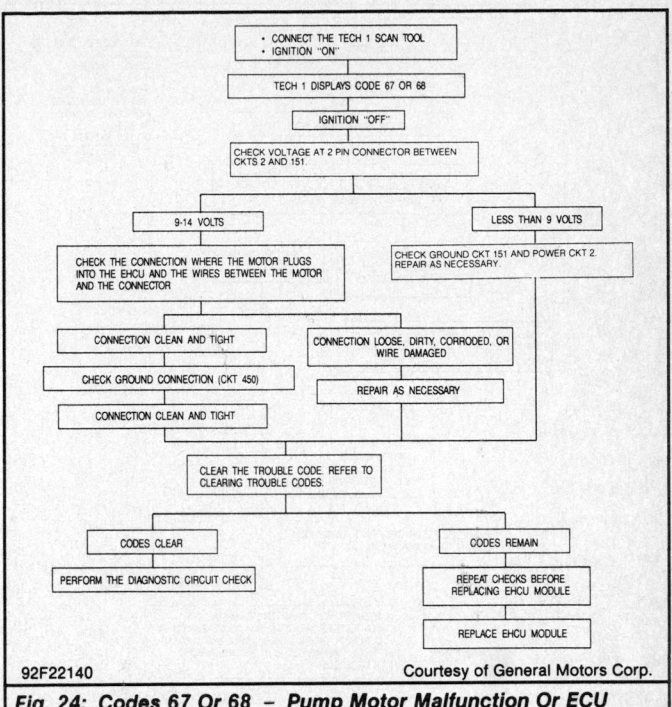

Fig. 24: Codes 67 Or 68 – Pump Motor Malfunction Or ECU Output Shorted (See 4WAL FAULT CODES Table)

Fig. 23: Code 65 Or 66 – Pump Motor Relay Open Or Shorted

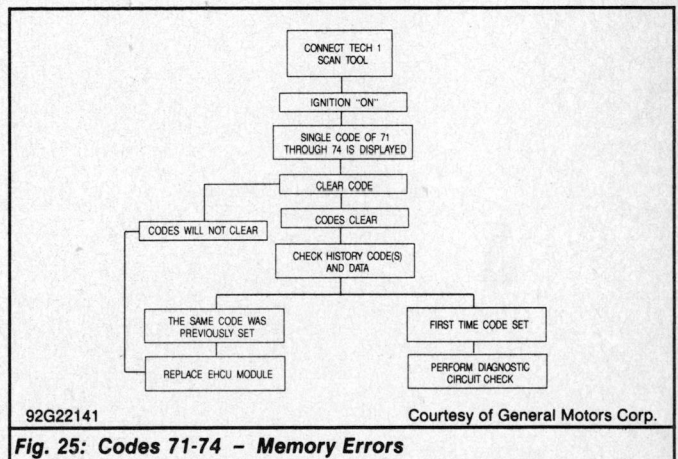

Fig. 25: Codes 71-74 – Memory Errors

1992 BRAKES
Anti-Lock – 4WAL – Except FWD Vans (Cont.)

92H22142 Courtesy of General Motors Corp.

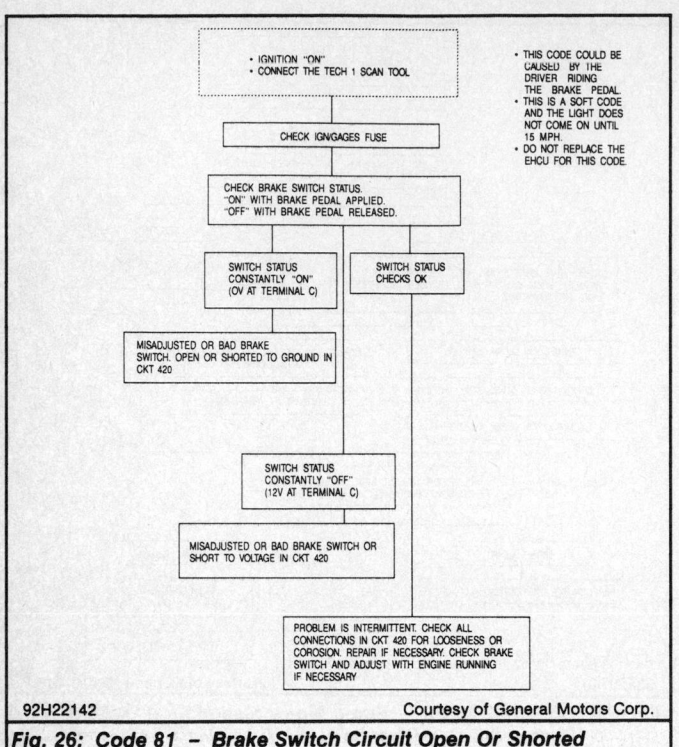

Fig. 26: Code 81 – Brake Switch Circuit Open Or Shorted

92I22143 Courtesy of General Motors Corp.

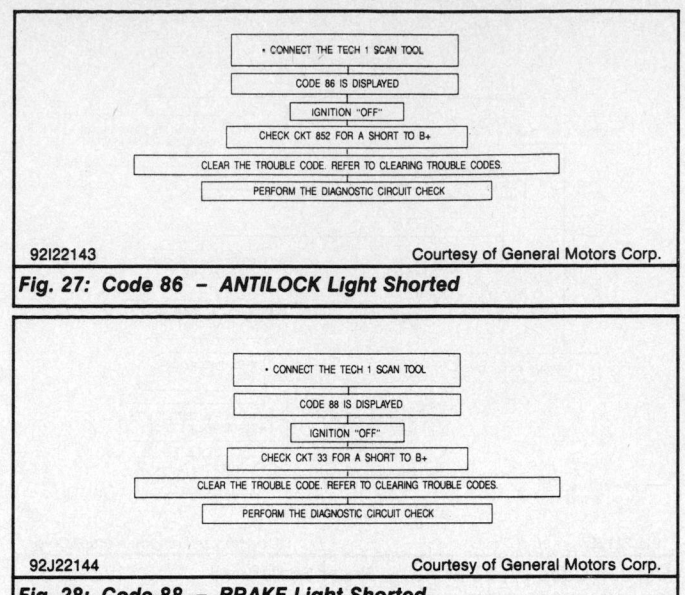

Fig. 27: Code 86 – ANTILOCK Light Shorted

92J22144 Courtesy of General Motors Corp.

Fig. 28: Code 88 – BRAKE Light Shorted

WIRING DIAGRAMS

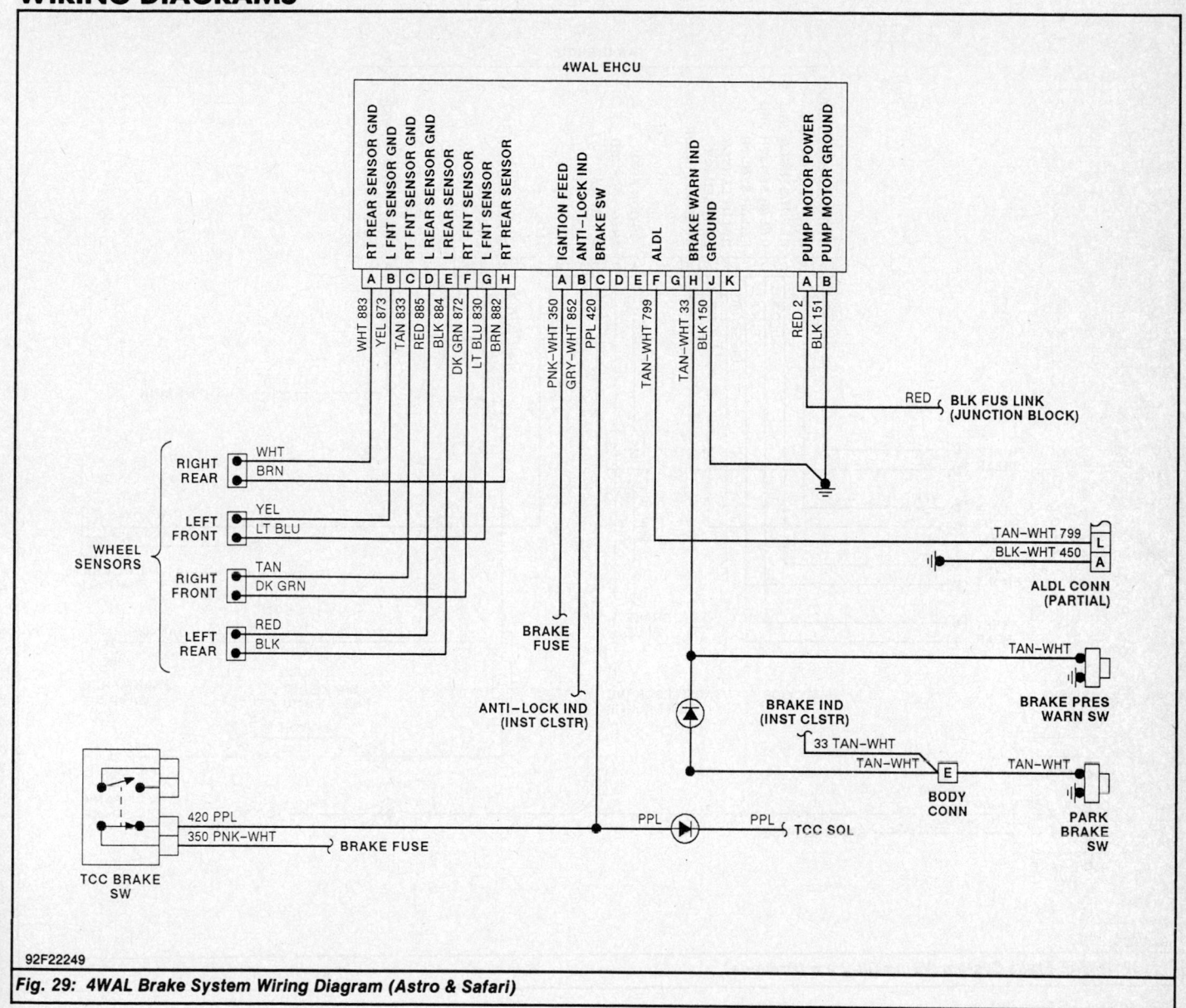

Fig. 29: 4WAL Brake System Wiring Diagram (Astro & Safari)

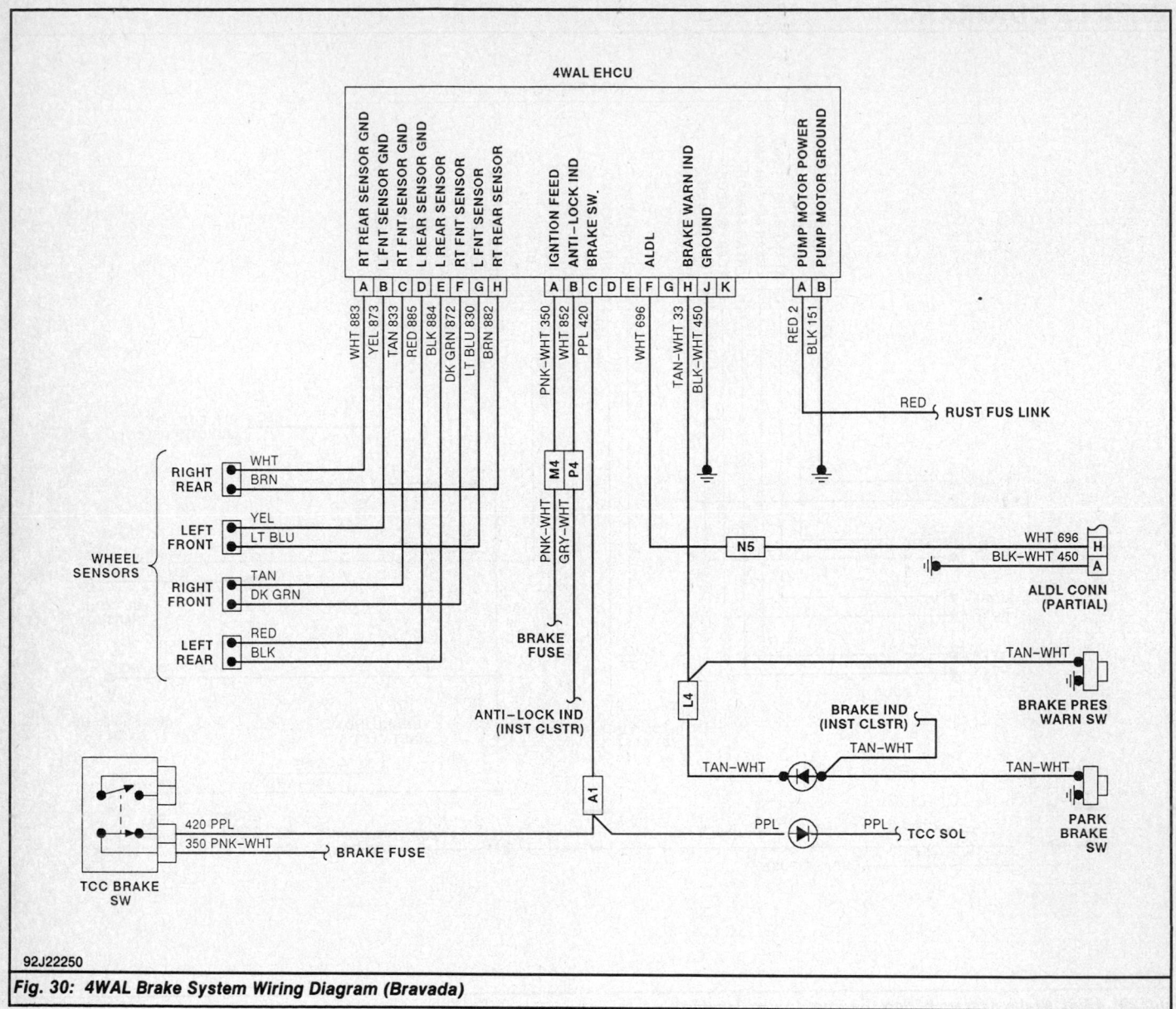

Fig. 30: *4WAL Brake System Wiring Diagram (Bravada)*

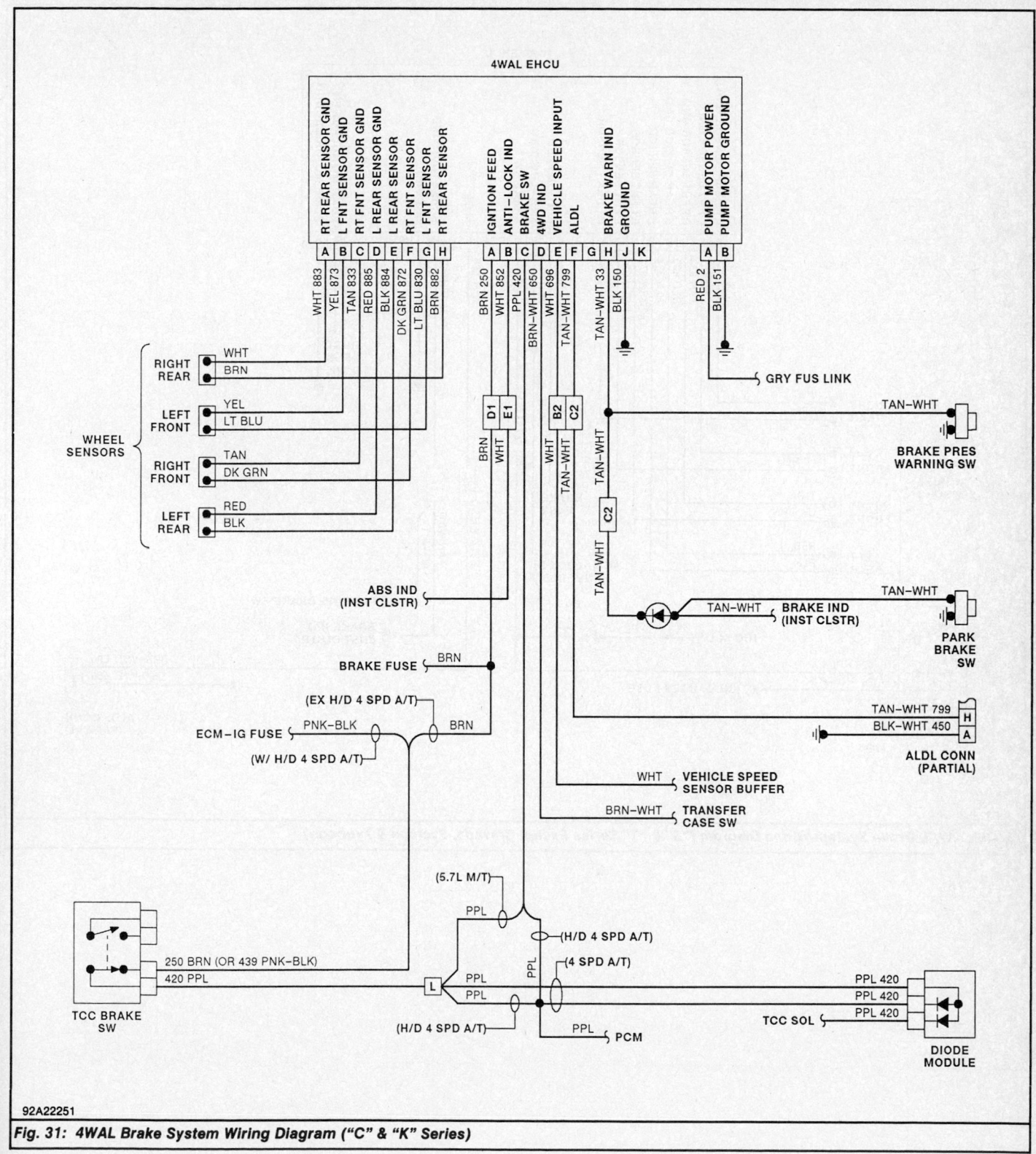

Fig. 31: 4WAL Brake System Wiring Diagram ("C" & "K" Series)

92A22251

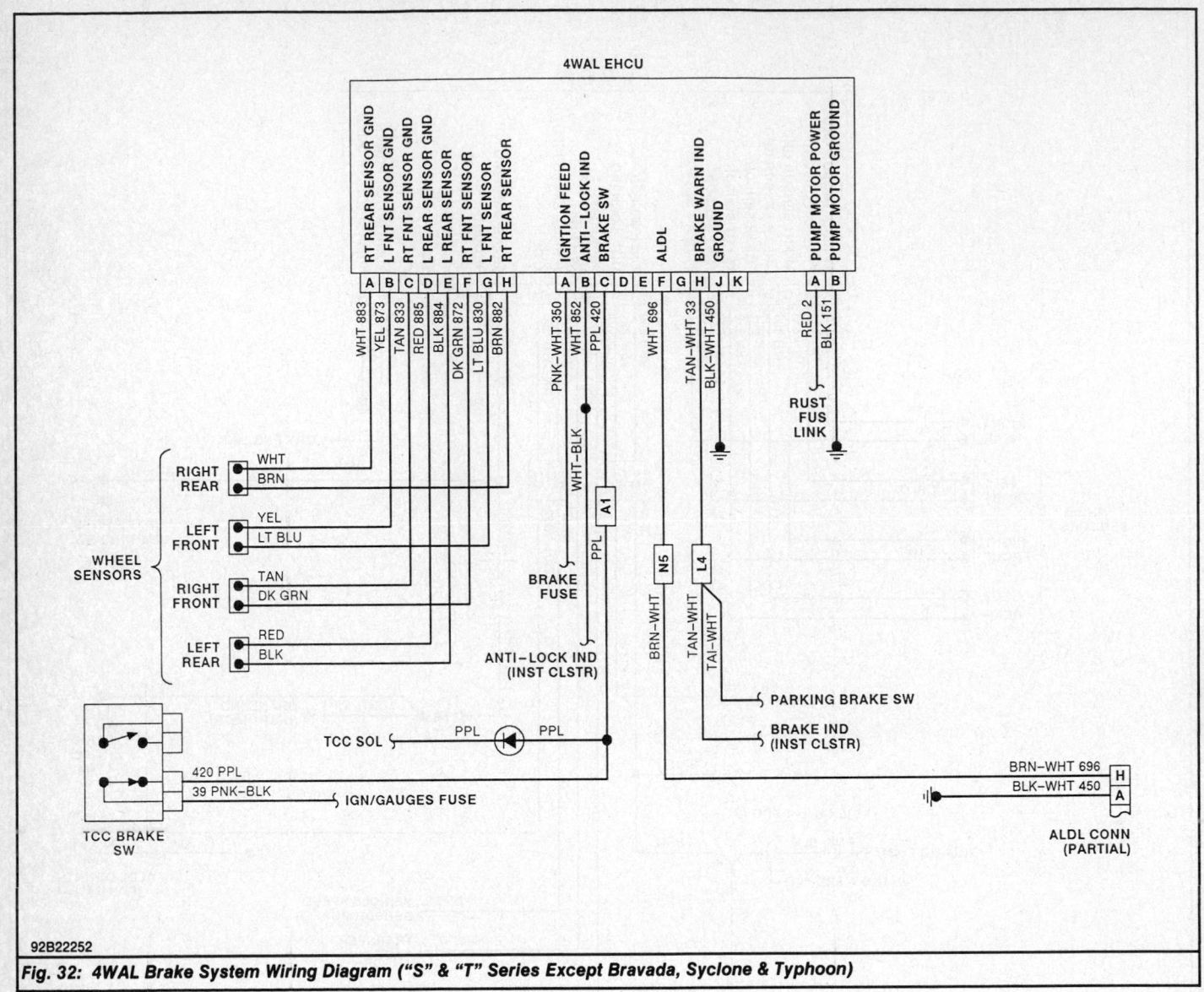

Fig. 32: 4WAL Brake System Wiring Diagram ("S" & "T" Series Except Bravada, Syclone & Typhoon)

92B22252

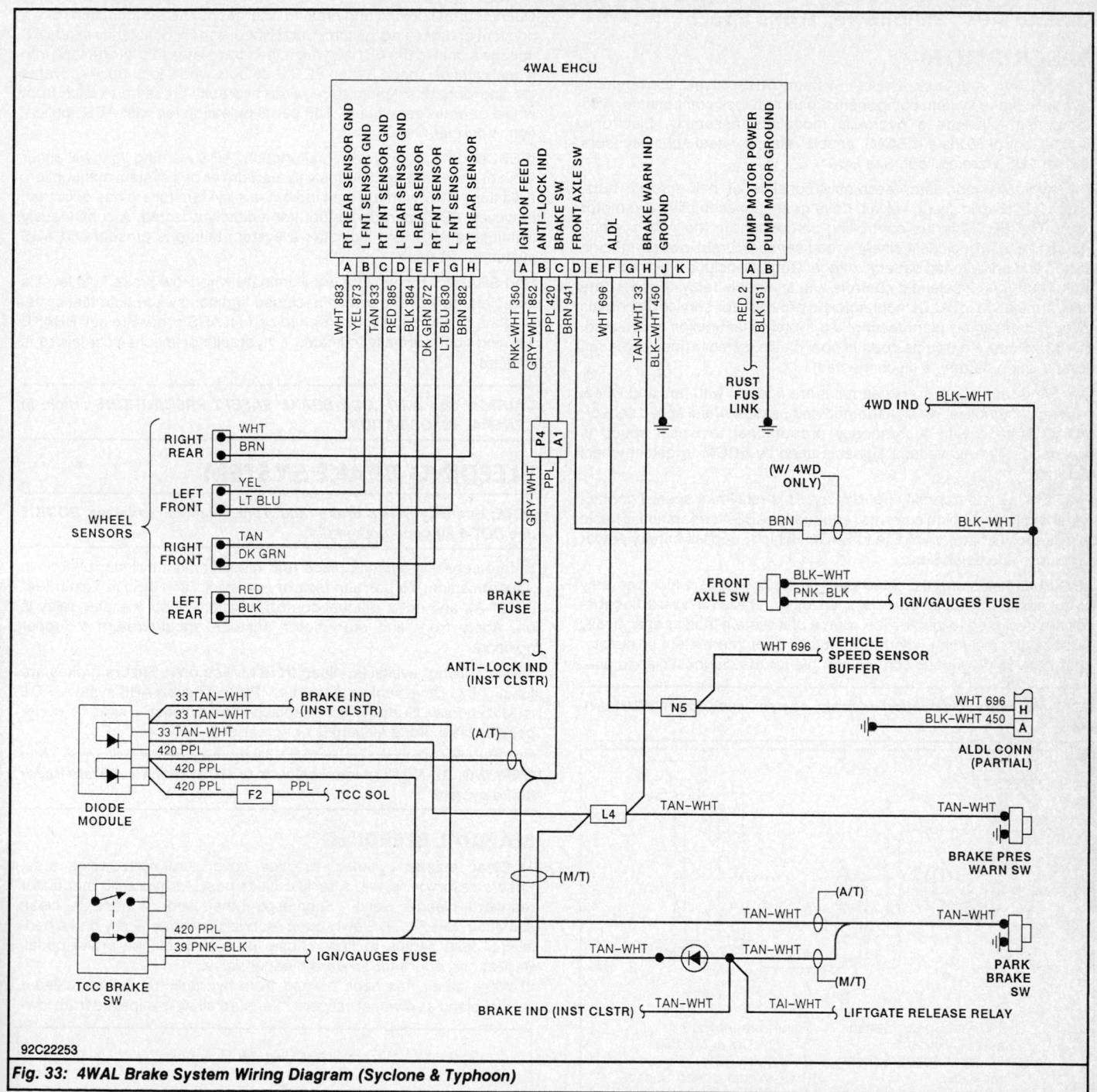

Fig. 33: 4WAL Brake System Wiring Diagram (Syclone & Typhoon)

92C22253

Lumina APV, Silhouette, Trans Sport

DESCRIPTION

The ABS-VI Anti-Lock Brake System (ABS) uses conventional hydraulic brake system components, plus anti-lock components. ABS components include a hydraulic modulator assembly, Electronic Brake Control Module (EBCM), enable relay, 4 wheel speed sensors and an ABS warning light. *See Fig. 1.*

The hydraulic modulator assembly consists of ball screws, nuts, pistons, hydraulic check valves, drive gear subassemblies and motor pack. The EBCM is the controlling component in the ABS system. Inputs to EBCM include 4 wheel speed sensors, brake switch, ignition switch and unswitched battery voltage. Outputs include 3 bidirectional motor controls, 2 solenoid controls and an enable relay. A serial data link (terminal "M" of ALDL connector) is provided for service diagnostic tools and assembly plant testing. If a system malfunction is detected, EBCM will store a trouble code in nonvolatile memory (memory is not erased when battery is disconnected).

Front and rear wheel speed sensors are integral with hub and wheel bearing assemblies. When a toothed ring passes wheel speed sensor, an AC voltage with a frequency proportional to wheel speed is produced. This AC voltage signal is used by EBCM to detect wheel lock-up.

Enable relay is a normally open relay. This relay has special contact material to handle high currents required for ABS-VI operation. Enable relay supplies battery voltage to EBCM, which supplies battery power to motors and solenoids.

ABS-VI contains sophisticated on-board diagnostics which can only be accessed with a bidirectional scan tester. These on-board diagnostics are designed to identify the source of a system fault as specifically as possible, including whether a fault code is intermittent or history. There are 58 diagnostic codes available for the diagnostician to use.

NOTE: For more information on brake system, see DISC & DRUM article.

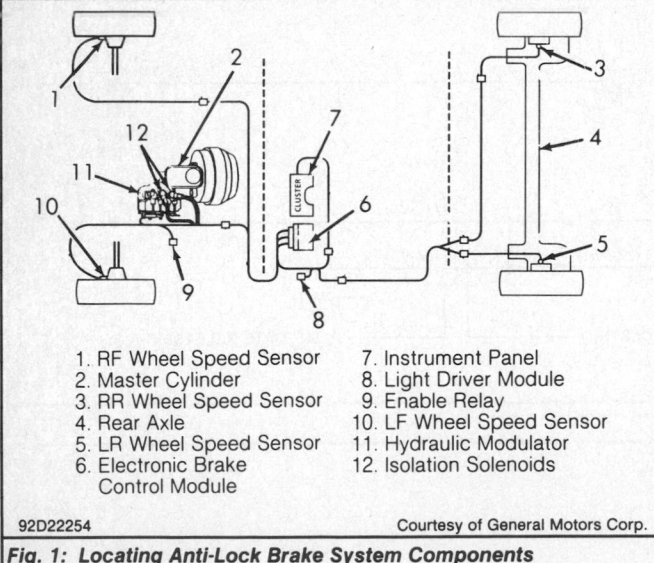

1. RF Wheel Speed Sensor
2. Master Cylinder
3. RR Wheel Speed Sensor
4. Rear Axle
5. LR Wheel Speed Sensor
6. Electronic Brake Control Module
7. Instrument Panel
8. Light Driver Module
9. Enable Relay
10. LF Wheel Speed Sensor
11. Hydraulic Modulator
12. Isolation Solenoids

92D22254   Courtesy of General Motors Corp.

Fig. 1: Locating Anti-Lock Brake System Components

OPERATION

ABS warning light will be on for approximately 3 seconds after ignition is turned on. ABS warning light will also be on for approximately 3 seconds after engine is started. A slight "click" may be heard during first part of system initialization. The rest of system initialization is run when vehicle accelerates past 3 MPH. If brake pedal is depressed when engine is started, system will not initialize until brake pedal is released. If brake pedal is depressed when system is initializing, system initialization will be interrupted and slight movement may be felt in brake pedal.

During normal driving and braking operations, ABS-VI functions like a conventional braking system. Each wheel sensor constantly sends AC voltage signal to the EBCM, which then translates this information into wheel rotation speed. When EBCM detects wheel lock-up, it activates the appropriate solenoid to regulate hydraulic pressure to each front wheel or both rear wheels. The pedal pulsation felt with ABS application is normal.

If EBCM detects a system malfunction, ABS warning light will either flash or illuminate continuously to alert driver of a system malfunction. A flashing ABS warning light indicates a system failure has occurred; however, ABS operation is not immediately affected. A continuously illuminated ABS light indicates a system failure is present and ABS system is disabled.

Red BRAKE warning light will illuminate when low brake fluid level is detected, park brake switch is closed, ignition switch bulb test cycle, or when EBCM turns light on when certain ABS codes are set. BRAKE warning light normally indicates a hydraulic or mechanical failure is present.

CAUTION: See ANTI-LOCK BRAKE SAFETY PRECAUTIONS article in GENERAL INFORMATION.

BLEEDING BRAKE SYSTEM

NOTE: Use only DOT 3 brake fluid from a sealed container. DO NOT use DOT 5 silicone brake fluid.

Before servicing system, place rear displacement cylinder pistons in upper position. To position pistons, connect Tech 1 Scan Tester (94-00101-A), and enter manual control function. Ensure enable relay is on. Apply front and rear motor. Pistons should return to upper position.

If Tech 1 is not available, bleed front brakes only. Ensure brakes are functioning. Drive vehicle at least 4 MPH to initialize ABS system. ABS initialization will return rear displacement cylinder piston to upper position. The brake system is now ready for service.

WARNING: DO NOT tap into vehicle's brake system to operate trailer brake system.

MANUAL BLEEDING

1) Clean master cylinder reservoir cover and surrounding area. Ensure reservoir is full. Attach a clear hose to hydraulic modulator rearward bleeder valve. Submerge other end of hose in clean container. *See Fig. 2.* Slowly open rearward bleeder. Apply brake pedal until fluid begins to flow. Close valve and release brake pedal. Repeat procedure for forward bleeder valve.

2) When all air has been purged from hydraulic modulator bleeder valves, bleed all 4 wheel calipers to ensure all air is expelled from low-

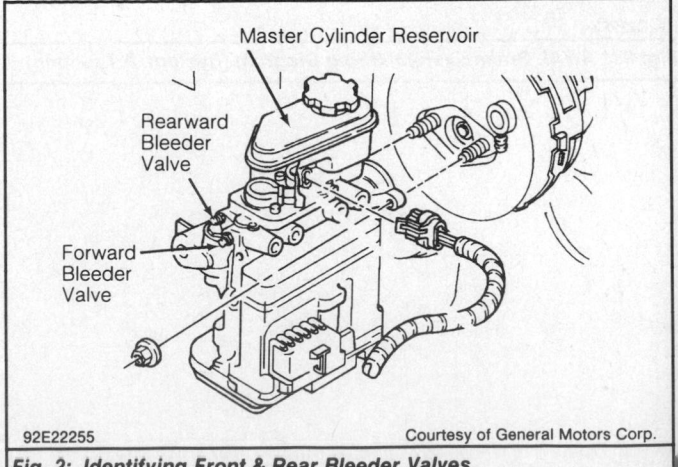

Master Cylinder Reservoir

Rearward Bleeder Valve

Forward Bleeder Valve

92E22255   Courtesy of General Motors Corp.

Fig. 2: Identifying Front & Rear Bleeder Valves

est part of brake system. Raise and support vehicle. Attach a clear hose to right rear caliper bleeder valve. Submerge other end of hose in container of brake fluid.

3) Open bleeder valve. Slowly depress brake pedal. Close bleeder valve and release brake pedal. Wait 5 seconds. Repeat process until no air bubbles are seen from hose. Repeat procedure on left rear, right front and left front bleeder valves. Ensure reservoir is full. Repeat procedure for bleeding hydraulic modulator and master cylinder assembly to bleed any remaining air from brake system.

PRESSURE BLEEDING

1) Clean master cylinder reservoir cover and surrounding area. Remove reservoir cap. Ensure reservoir is full. Attach Bleeder Adapter (J-35589) to reservoir. Attach bleeding equipment, and pressurize system to 10 psi (.7 kg/cm²) for 30 seconds to ensure there are no leaks.

2) Slowly increase pressure to 35 psi (2.5 kg/cm²). Attach a clear hose to hydraulic modulator rearward bleeder valve, and submerge other end of hose in clean container. *See Fig. 2.* Slowly open rearward bleeder. Allow fluid to flow until no air bubbles are seen from hose. Close valve and repeat procedure for forward bleeder valve.

CAUTION: DO NOT allow brake fluid to contact motor pack or electrical connectors. Premature failure of motor pack may result.

---

3) Position shop towel below 4 hydraulic modulator brake pipes. Using flare wrench, slightly open front upper brake pipe fitting at hydraulic modulator. DO NOT allow brake fluid to run down side of motor pack or onto electrical connector. Allow air to escape and tighten fitting. Repeat procedure for remaining 3 brake lines, working from front to rear.

4) Ensure master cylinder reservoir is full. Raise and support vehicle. Bleed all 4 wheel calipers. Attach a clear hose to right rear caliper bleeder valve and submerge other end of hose in container of brake fluid.

5) Open bleeder valve. Allow fluid to flow until no air bubbles are seen in hose. Tap lightly on cylinder/caliper housing to free trapped air. Close bleeder valve. Repeat process until no air bubbles are seen from hose. Repeat procedure on left rear, right front and left front bleeder valves. Ensure reservoir is full.

REMOVAL & INSTALLATION

ABS LIGHT DRIVER MODULE

Removal & Installation – Ensure ignition is off. Remove lower sound insulator panel located under steering column. Remove ABS light driver module from instrument panel harness located near parking brake assembly. *See Fig. 3.* To install, reverse removal procedure. Ensure ABS light driver module is taped in same location onto instrument panel harness.

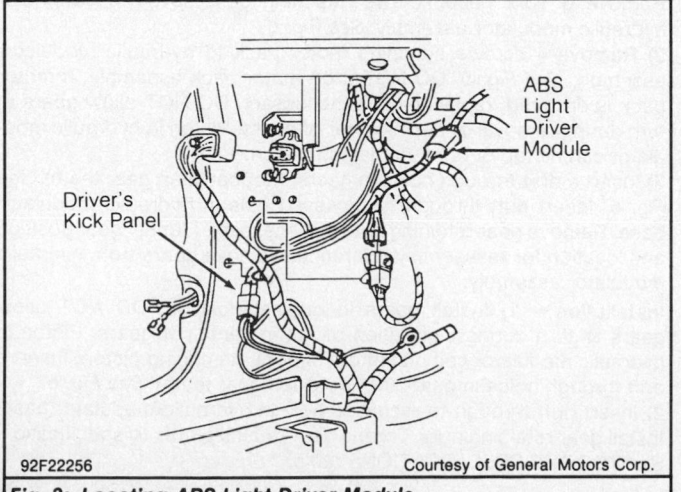

92F22256   Courtesy of General Motors Corp.

Fig. 3: Locating ABS Light Driver Module

ELECTRONIC BRAKE CONTROL MODULE (EBCM)

Removal & Installation – Ensure ignition is off. Remove lower sound insulator panel located under steering column. Remove 3 screws attaching EBCM to dash panel. Remove 3 electrical connectors from EBCM. Remove EBCM from vehicle. *See Fig. 4.* To install, reverse removal procedure. Ensure 3 plastic grommets are properly positioned prior to installing EBCM.

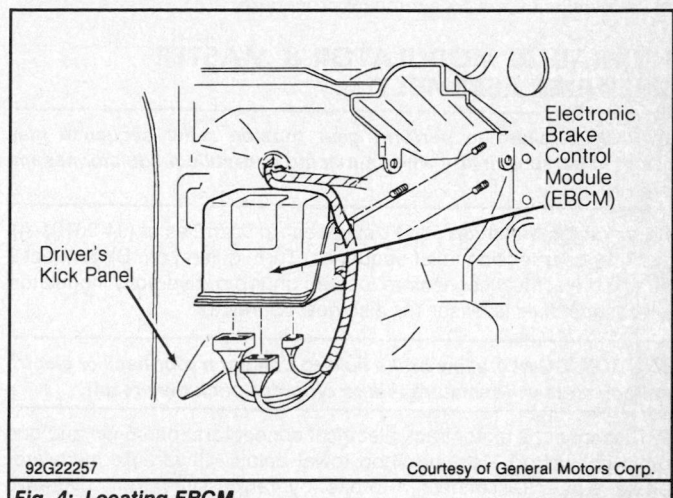

92G22257   Courtesy of General Motors Corp.

Fig. 4: Locating EBCM

ENABLE RELAY

Removal & Installation – Ensure ignition is off. Enable relay is located on front of left strut tower. Remove enable relay cover. Remove enable relay. To install, reverse removal procedure.

FLUID LEVEL SENSOR

Removal & Installation – Remove brake fluid from master cylinder reservoir to facilitate removal of fluid level sensor. Remove electrical connector from fluid level sensor. Using needle-nose pliers, compress fluid level sensor locking tabs on inboard side of master cylinder reservoir. Remove fluid level sensor. To install, reverse removal procedure. Ensure locking tabs snap into place when installing fluid level sensor. Fill master cylinder reservoir.

FRONT WHEEL SPEED SENSOR

Removal – 1) Remove wheel and tire assembly. Disconnect wheel speed sensor electrical connector located next to steering knuckle. Clean drive axle threads. Insert a drift punch through brake caliper into brake rotor vents. Remove drive axle nut and washer. Remove drift punch. Remove brake caliper and wire aside.

2) Remove brake rotor. Remove 3 hub and bearing assembly mounting bolts. Using Puller (J-28733), remove hub and bearing assembly. Discard "O" ring from hub and bearing assembly. Using a blunt screwdriver, remove wheel speed sensor from hub & bearing assembly.

NOTE: Factory hub and bearing seal is installed from engine side of steering knuckle. Install replacement hub and bearing seal from wheel side of steering knuckle.

---

3) Using a punch, tap hub and bearing seal in steering knuckle toward engine. When hub and bearing seal is removed from steering knuckle, cut seal from drive axle shaft.

NOTE: DO NOT reuse speed sensor after it has been removed from hub and bearing assembly. Speed sensor is damaged when removed.

Installation – 1) Install NEW hub and bearing seal from wheel side of steering knuckle. Install NEW "O" ring onto hub and bearing assembly. Lubricate hub and bearing assembly seal and "O" ring with grease. Install NEW wheel speed sensor onto hub and bearing assembly.

2) Install hub and bearing assembly into steering knuckle. Torque hub and bearing assembly bolts to specification. See TORQUE SPECIFICATIONS table. Install brake rotor. Install brake caliper. Torque brake caliper bolts to specification. See TORQUE SPECIFICATIONS table.

3) Install drive axle nut and washer. Insert a drift punch through brake caliper into brake rotor vents. Torque drive axle nut to specification. See TORQUE SPECIFICATIONS table. Remove drift punch. To complete installation, reverse removal procedure.

HYDRAULIC MODULATOR & MASTER CYLINDER ASSEMBLY

WARNING: Failure to perform gear tension relief sequence may result in personal injury when servicing hydraulic modulator assembly.

Removal & Installation – 1) Using Tech 1 Scan Tester (94-00101-A), perform gear tension relief sequence. Turn ignition off. Disconnect 2 solenoid electrical connectors located on top of hydraulic modulator. Disconnect fluid level sensor electrical connector.

CAUTION: DO NOT allow brake fluid to contact motor pack or electrical connectors. Premature failure of motor pack may result.

2) Disconnect 2 motor pack electrical connectors (one 6-pin and one 3-pin connector). Position shop towel below 4 hydraulic modulator brake pipes. Disconnect 4 brake hydraulic lines from hydraulic modulator. Plug open hydraulic lines to prevent fluid loss and contamination.

3) Remove 2 nuts attaching hydraulic modulator and master cylinder assembly to vacuum booster. It may be necessary to remove vacuum check valve from vacuum booster to access nut closest to check valve.

4) Remove hydraulic modulator and master cylinder assembly from vehicle. To install, reverse removal procedure. Bleed brake system. See BLEEDING BRAKE SYSTEM. If separation of hydraulic modulator from master cylinder is necessary, go to next step.

5) With hydraulic modulator and master cylinder assembly removed from vehicle, remove as much fluid as possible from master cylinder. Turn hydraulic modulator and master cylinder assembly upside down. Remove 6 Torx head screws attaching gear cover to bottom of hydraulic modulator assembly.

6) Remove 4 screws attaching motor pack to hydraulic modulator assembly. Remove motor pack assembly. *See Fig. 5.* DO NOT drop motor pack assembly. If motor pack is dropped, replacement is necessary. DO NOT allow hydraulic modulator gears to turn during procedure. Piston in hydraulic modulator can hit top or bottom of bore, damaging piston.

7) Temporarily install gear cover to bottom of hydraulic modulator assembly to prevent gears from turning. Remove 2 hydraulic modulator-to-master cylinder through bolts and "O" rings. Separate master cylinder from hydraulic modulator. Remove 2 transfer tubes and "O" rings from master cylinder or hydraulic modulator. *See Fig. 5.*

NOTE: DO NOT reuse transfer tubes or "O" rings. Install NEW components.

8) To assemble master cylinder and hydraulic unit, lubricate NEW transfer tube "O" rings and NEW through bolt "O" rings with clean brake fluid. Install NEW transfer tubes with NEW "O" rings into hydraulic modulator. Install NEW through bolt "O" rings into master cylinder and hydraulic modulator.

9) Clamp mounting flange of master cylinder in a soft-jawed vise. Assemble master cylinder to hydraulic unit. Ensure transfer tubes and "O" rings are not damaged during assembly. Torque hydraulic modulator to master cylinder through bolts to specification. See TORQUE SPECIFICATIONS table.

10) To complete assembly, reverse disassembly procedure. Ensure motor pack gears are aligned with hydraulic modulator gears. Bleed brake system. See BLEEDING BRAKE SYSTEM.

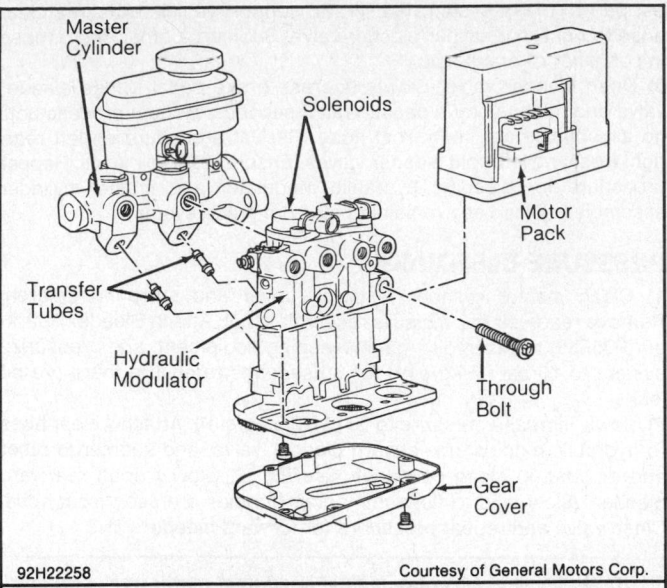

Fig. 5: Identifying Hydraulic Modulator & Master Cylinder Assembly Components

92H22258   Courtesy of General Motors Corp.

FRONT SPEED SENSOR JUMPER HARNESS

NOTE: Note speed sensor wire routing before removal for installation purposes. Misrouted wiring may cause failures due to electromagnetic interference.

Removal & Installation – 1) Ensure ignition is off. Disconnect front speed sensor electrical connector located near speed sensor at wheel. Remove speed sensor jumper wiring harness from retaining clips. Push speed sensor jumper harness through inner fender.

2) Disconnect speed sensor electrical connector located near strut tower in engine compartment. Remove speed sensor jumper wiring harness from vehicle. To install, reverse removal procedure. Ensure grommet is properly positioned in inner fender. Ensure speed sensor jumper wiring harness is routed correctly.

HYDRAULIC MODULATOR GEARS

WARNING: Keep fingers clear of gear set. Drive gears are under spring pressure and may turn during removal.

Removal – 1) Remove hydraulic modulator and master cylinder assembly from vehicle. See HYDRAULIC MODULATOR & MASTER CYLINDER ASSEMBLY under REMOVAL & INSTALLATION. Turn hydraulic modulator and master cylinder assembly upside down. Remove 6 Torx head screws attaching gear cover to bottom of hydraulic modulator assembly. *See Fig. 5.*

2) Remove 4 screws attaching motor pack to hydraulic modulator assembly. *See Fig. 5.* DO NOT drop motor pack assembly. If motor pack is dropped, replacement is necessary. DO NOT allow gears to turn during removal of nut in center of gears. Piston in hydraulic modulator can hit top of bore, damaging piston.

3) Insert a drift through holes in gears, (not between gear teeth). *See Fig. 6.* Insert drift through to recessed hole in hydraulic modulator base. Remove gear retaining nuts as necessary. Identify gear position and location for reassembly reference. Remove gears from hydraulic modulator assembly.

Installation – 1) Install gears in original position. DO NOT allow gears to turn during installation of nut in center of gears. Piston in hydraulic modulator can hit bottom of bore, damaging piston. Insert a drift through holes in gears (not between gear teeth). *See Fig. 6.*

2) Insert drift through to recessed hole in hydraulic modulator base. Install gear retaining nuts. Torque gear retaining nuts to specification. See TORQUE SPECIFICATIONS table.

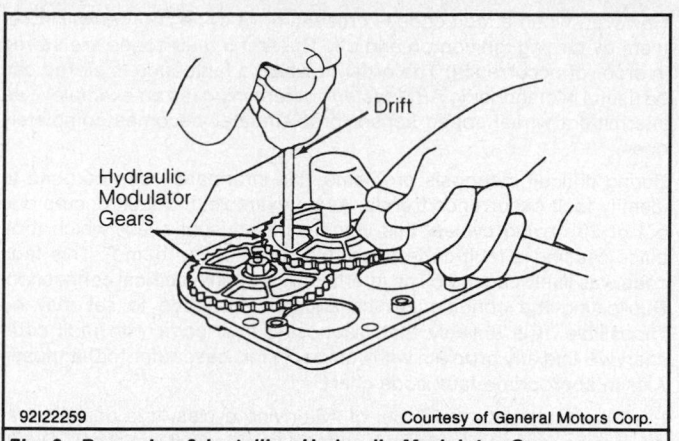

92I22259   Courtesy of General Motors Corp.

Fig. 6: Removing & Installing Hydraulic Modulator Gears

3) With hydraulic modulator and master cylinder assembly upside down (gears facing upward), rotate each gear counterclockwise until movement stops. Rotating gears counterclockwise will position pistons very close to top of hydraulic modulator bore, making brake bleeding easier.

4) Position motor pack onto hydraulic modulator, aligning 3 motor pack gears with hydraulic modulator gears. Install motor pack attaching screws. Torque motor pack screws to specification. See TORQUE SPECIFICATIONS table.

5) Install gear cover onto bottom of hydraulic modulator. Torque gear cover screws to specification. See TORQUE SPECIFICATIONS table. Install hydraulic modulator and master cylinder assembly onto vehicle. Bleed brake system. See BLEEDING BRAKE SYSTEM.

HYDRAULIC MODULATOR SOLENOID

Removal & Installation – Ensure ignition is off. Disconnect solenoid electrical connector. Note solenoid electrical connector position. Remove solenoid screws. Remove solenoid from hydraulic modulator. Ensure seal is removed when solenoid is removed from hydraulic modulator. To install, reverse removal procedure. Lubricate seal on solenoid assembly with clean brake fluid. Ensure solenoid electrical connector is positioned properly. Bleed brake system. See BLEEDING BRAKE SYSTEM.

REAR WHEEL BEARING & SPEED SENSOR ASSEMBLY

NOTE: Rear wheel speed sensor is integral with rear wheel bearing assembly.

Removal & Installation – 1) Remove wheel and tire assembly. Remove brake drum. Rotate axle flange to access rear speed sensor and wheel bearing mounting bolts. Remove 4 rear speed sensor and wheel bearing mounting bolts and nuts.

2) After removing 4 bolts and nuts, DO NOT move drum brake assembly. Only brake hydraulic line is holding drum brake assembly. Disconnect rear wheel speed sensor electrical connector. Remove rear wheel bearing and speed sensor assembly. To install, reverse removal procedure. See TORQUE SPECIFICATIONS table.

REAR WHEEL SPEED SENSOR JUMPER HARNESS

NOTE: Note speed sensor wire routing before removal for installation purposes. Misrouted wiring may cause failures due to electromagnetic interference.

Removal & Installation – 1) Ensure ignition is off. Disconnect right rear speed sensor electrical connector located near speed sensor at wheel. Remove speed sensor jumper wiring harness from retaining clips. Right rear speed sensor jumper wiring harness runs from right to left across bottom of vehicle. There is no jumper harness for left rear speed sensor.

2) Disconnect speed sensor electrical connector located near left wheel speed sensor. Remove speed sensor jumper wiring harness from vehicle. To install, reverse removal procedure. Ensure speed sensor jumper wiring harness is routed correctly.

DIAGNOSIS & TESTING

NOTE: Tech 1 Scan Tester (94-00101-A) and Adapter (T-100) are required to diagnose ABS-VI.

1) Before diagnosing ABS system for fault codes, perform pre-diagnostic visual inspection to detect obvious problems. See PRE-DIAGNOSTIC INSPECTION under DIAGNOSIS & TESTING. Repair problems as necessary.

2) Using Tech 1, read all current and history fault codes. Fault codes are stored in order of occurrence. If no fault codes are present, go to step 3). If fault codes are stored, note which codes are current and which codes are history. DO NOT clear fault codes.

3) Using Tech 1, review code history. Review fault codes stored and frequency of failure. Refer to ENHANCED DIAGNOSTICS under DIAGNOSIS & TESTING. DO NOT clear codes until ABS system repairs are complete. After reviewing ENHANCED DIAGNOSTICS, perform DIAGNOSTIC CIRCUIT CHECK under DIAGNOSTIC CHARTS. Reference ABS FAULT CODES table as necessary.

4) Using Tech 1, perform automated modulator test. Automated modulator test may isolate cause of problem. If failure is intermittent and not reproducible, test drive vehicle using snapshot feature of Tech 1. Drive vehicle in a normal manner, with normal acceleration, stopping and turning.

5) If vehicle test drive does not reproduce any failures, perform another test drive. On second test drive, perform an ABS stop from approximately 30-50 MPH. Check snapshot feature of Tech 1 to see if any faults were set.

6) If fault codes were set, perform DIAGNOSTIC CIRCUIT CHECK under DIAGNOSTIC CHARTS. Reference ABS FAULT CODES table as necessary. DO NOT clear codes until ABS system repairs are complete. If no faults were set and ABS warning light and/or BRAKE warning light is on, refer to CHART A or CHART B under DIAGNOSTIC CHARTS.

ABS FAULT CODES

Code	Definition
A011	ABS Warning Light Circuit Open Or Shorted To Ground
A013	ABS Warning Light Circuit Shorted To Battery
A014	Enable Relay Contacts Or Fuse Open
A015	Enable Relay Contacts Shorted To Battery
A016	Enable Relay Coil Circuit Open
A017	Enable Relay Coil Circuit Shorted To Ground
A018	Enable Relay Coil Circuit Shorted To Battery
A021	Left Front Wheel Speed Is Zero
A022	Right Front Wheel Speed Is Zero
A023	Left Rear Wheel Speed Is Zero
A024	Right Rear Wheel Speed Is Zero
A025	Excessive Left Front Wheel Speed Variation
A026	Excessive Right Front Wheel Speed Variation
A027	Excessive Left Rear Wheel Speed Variation
A028	Excessive Right Rear Wheel Speed Variation
A031	Two Wheel Speeds Are Zero
A032	Left Front Wheel Sensor Shorted To Battery Or Ground
A033	Right Front Wheel Sensor Shorted To Battery Or Ground
A034	Left Rear Wheel Sensor Shorted To Battery Or Ground
A035	Right Rear Wheel sensor Shorted To Battery or Ground
A036	System Voltage Low
A037	System Voltage High
A038	[1] Left Front ESB Will Not Hold Motor
A041	[1] Right Front ESB Will Not Hold Motor
A042	[1] Rear Axle ESB Will Not Hold Motor
A044	Left Front Channel Will Not Move
A045	Right Front Channel Will Not Move
A046	Rear Axle Channel Will Not Move
A047	Left Front Motor Spins Freely
A048	Right Front Motor Spins Freely
A051	Rear Axle Motor Spins Freely

[1] – Expansion Spring Brake (ESB), located inside motor pack assembly.

ABS FAULT CODES (Cont.)

Code	Definition
A052	Left Front Channel In Release Too Long
A053	Right Front Channel In Release Too Long
A054	Rear Axle Channel In Release Too Long
A055	Motor Driver Fault Detected
A056	Left Front Motor Circuit Open
A057	Left Front Motor Circuit Shorted To Ground
A058	Left Front Motor Circuit Shorted To Battery Or Motor Shorted
A061	Right Front Motor Circuit Open
A062	Right Front Motor Shorted To Ground
A063	Right Front Motor Shorted To Battery
A064	Rear Axle Motor Circuit Open
A065	Rear Axle Motor Circuit Shorted To Ground
A066	Rear Axle Motor Circuit Shorted To Battery Or Motor Shorted
A076	Left Front Solenoid Circuit Open Or Shorted To Battery
A077	Left Front Solenoid Circuit Shorted To Ground Or Driver Circuit Open
A078	Right Front Solenoid Circuit Open Or Shorted To Battery
A081	Right Front Solenoid Circuit Shorted To Ground Or Driver Circuit Open
A082	Calibration Memory Failure
A086	Red BRAKE Warning Light Activated By EBCM
A087	Red BRAKE Warning Light Circuit Open
A088	Red BRAKE Warning Light Circuit Shorted To Battery
A091	Open Brake Switch Contacts During Deceleration
A092	Open Brake Switch Contacts When ABS Was Required
A093	Code A091 Or A092 Set In Last Or Current Ignition Cycle
A094	Brake Switch Contacts Always Closed
A095	Brake Switch Circuit Open
A096	Brakelight Circuit Open

WARNING LIGHTS

Amber ABS Warning Light – With ignition on, a flashing ABS warning light indicates a system failure has occurred; however, ABS operation is not immediately affected. A continuously illuminated ABS light indicates a system failure is present and ABS system is disabled.
Red BRAKE Warning Light – With ignition on, Red BRAKE warning light will illuminate when low brake fluid level is detected, park brake switch is closed, ignition switch bulb test cycles, or when EBCM turns light on when certain ABS codes are set. BRAKE warning light normally indicates a hydraulic or mechanical failure is present.

PRE-DIAGNOSTIC INSPECTION

1) Check master cylinder reservoir for correct fluid level. Inspect ABS hydraulic modulator for leakage or wiring damage. Check caliper piston for activation and release. Check all brakes to verify no drag exists.
2) Check speed sensors for correct mounting and alignment. Inspect wire harness for correct routing. Ensure connectors are not damaged and have good contact.
3) Verify all wheel bearings are not worn, causing wheel wobble. Ensure outer CV joints are correctly aligned and no play exists. Ensure all tires are in good condition and properly inflated.

ENHANCED DIAGNOSTICS

The ENHANCED DIAGNOSTICS feature is used to analyze specific fault occurrence information. Fault occurrence information is stored for first 5 fault codes stored and very last fault code stored. Fault occurrence information stored consists of fault code number, number of failure occurrences and number of drive cycles since fault first and last occurred. A drive cycle occurs when ignition is turned on and vehicle is driven faster than 10 MPH.

However, when a fault code is present, drive cycle counter will increment by turning ignition on and off. The first 5 fault codes are stored in order of occurrence. The order in which a fault code is stored can be useful in diagnosing ABS system, determining (as an example) if an intermittent wheel speed sensor problem later becomes completely open.

During difficult diagnosis problems, this information can be used to identify fault occurrence trends. As an example, if a fault occurs one out of 20 driving cycles, this identifies a unusual event which took place causing a fault code to set (i.e. large speed bump). This fault code was likely caused by an intermittently open electrical connection. Duplicating the condition which caused fault code to set may be impossible. It is unlikely that diagnosing fault code with fault code chart will find any problem with vehicle. In this case refer to Diagnostic Aids in appropriate fault code chart.

Even if a fault occurred 3 out of 15 driving cycles, it is unlikely that diagnosing fault code with fault code chart will result in a repair. Duplicating the condition which caused fault code to set may be impossible. These intermittent fault codes will have to be diagnosed over time, referencing past customer visits and arranging future customer visits to identify cause of failure.

If a fault occurs 10 out of 20 driving cycles, there's a good chance that diagnosing fault code with fault code chart will result in a repair. Duplicating the condition which caused fault code to set may be easy.

If a fault occurred 10 out of 20 driving cycles, but has not reoccurred for the last 10 driving cycles, this means an environmental change occurred or customer had vehicle repaired 10 driving cycles ago. Diagnosis may not be necessary after confirming with customer that vehicle was repaired elsewhere.

INTERMITTENTS

Diagnostic charts can be used to identify problem(s), but fault must be present during testing in order to correctly locate problem. Most intermittent problems are caused by faulty electrical connections or wiring; however, a sticking relay or solenoid can cause a failure.

When intermittent failure is encountered, check for trouble codes stored in ABS module. If trouble codes are found, inspect related components and circuitry for poor connections. See ABS FAULT CODES table. If no trouble codes are found, inspect suspect circuits as follows:

- Check for poor mating of connector halves or terminals not fully seated in connector body (backed-out).
- Check for improperly formed or damaged terminals. Carefully reform all connector terminals of problem circuit to increase contact tension.
- Check for poor terminal-to-wire connection. This requires removing terminal and wire from connector body for inspection.

If inspection does not help locate intermittent problem, use ABS-VI self-diagnostic system to identify suspect circuit.
- Display and then clear ABS-VI trouble codes.
- Test drive vehicle, and attempt to duplicate conditions causing problem or complaint. Stop vehicle and record any codes set.

Program ABS-VI Snapshot feature to identify intermittent fault. Use the ENHANCED DIAGNOSTIC feature to analyze specific fault occurrence information. Determine how often and under what conditions fault occurs. Analyze ABS-VI snapshot data for unusual conditions.

USING TECH 1

NOTE: Tech 1 Scan Tester (94-00101-A), Adapter (T-100), 1988-92 Brake Systems Cartridge (TK-3030-B) and high-impedance (10-megohm minimum) multimeter are required to test parts of ABS system.

Insert brake systems cartridge in Tech 1 to perform ABS diagnostic procedures. Plug Tech 1 and adapter into ALDL connector before turning ignition on.

Selecting Model Year – Turn ignition switch to RUN position. Select appropriate model year using function keys.

Selecting Vehicle – After selecting model year, enter type of vehicle being tested. Press NO until "B" is flashing. Pressing EXIT will return Tech 1 to previous screen.

Selecting Test Mode – The following test modes are available for diagnosing ABS:

- **Mode F0 (Data List)** – Mode continuously displays the actual reading sent to EBCM by each wheel speed sensor, stoplight switch status and various other inputs and outputs are monitored.
- **Mode F1 (Code History)** – Mode displays fault code history data. Fault occurrence information is stored for first 5 fault codes stored and very last fault code stored. Fault occurrence information stored consists of fault code number, number of failure occurrences and number of drive cycles since fault first and last occurred.
- **Mode F2 (Trouble Codes)** – Mode displays ABS trouble codes stored by EBCM. Trouble codes can be cleared in this mode.
- **Mode F3 (ABS Snapshot)** – Mode helps isolate intermittent problems by capturing data before and after fault occurred. By selecting Manual Trigger, Tech 1 will wait for ENTER to be pressed before storing speed sensor information. All stored information can be displayed and examined for conditions that may indicate a problem.
- **Mode F4 (ABS Test)** – In this mode, Tech 1 performs hydraulic modulator assembly testing to help isolate problems during trouble shooting. Mode is also used for manual control of hydraulic modulator motors, which is used prior to bleeding brakes.

Scan Data Parameters – Only parameters listed in SCAN DATA PARAMETERS table should be used when diagnosing ABS. If other data is received, it should not be considered reliable, and scan tester should be repaired or replaced.

SCAN DATA PARAMETERS

Scan Position	Unit Displayed
ABS Batt Voltage	Volts
ABS Warning Light	On/Off/Flashing
Brakes Available	Anti-Lock/Base Brakes
Brake T-Tale CMD	On/Off
Brake Tell-Tale CMD	On/Off/Circuit Open
Brake Switch	On/Off/Circuit Open
Enable Relay CMD	On/Off
Front WHL Speeds	MPH-km/h
Left Front Solenoid	On/Off
Left Front Motor Command FWD/REV	Amps
Left Motor Feedback	Amps
Right Front Motor Command FWD/REV	Amps
Right Motor Feedback	Amps
Rear Motor Command FWD/REV	Amps
Rear Motor Feedback	Amps
Rear WHL Speeds	MPH-km/h
Right Front Solenoid	On/Off
Vehicle Speed	MPH-km/h

CLEARING CODES

Tech 1 – Connect Tech 1 to ALDL connector. Select F2 for trouble codes. After codes have been viewed, Tech 1 will display CLEAR ABS CODES message; select YES key. Tech 1 will now display the following message: DISPLAY CODE HIST. DATA? LOST IF CODES CLEARED. NO TO CLEAR CODES; select NO key to clear codes.

Ignition Cycle Default – If no fault codes occur for 100 driving cycles, any existing fault codes will be cleared from EBCM memory. A drive cycle occurs when ignition is turned on and vehicle is driven faster than 10 MPH. Ignition cycle counter will be reset to zero.

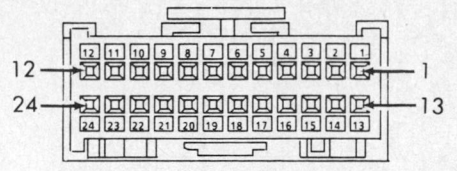

EBCM CONNECTOR (TERMINAL SIDE)

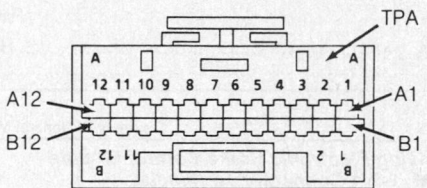

EBCM CONNECTOR (HARNESS SIDE)
WITH TEST PROBE ADAPTER (TPA) INSTALLED

EBCM 24-PIN CONNECTOR & TPA CAVITY IDENTIFICATION

Terminal	TPA Cavity	Wire Color
1	A12	Not Used
2	A11	Orange/Black
3	A10	Not Used
4	A9	Light Blue/Black
5	A8	Light Blue
6	A7	Yellow
7	A6	Brown
8	A5	White
9	A4	Dark Green
10	A3	Tan
11	A2	Red
12	A1	Black
13	B12	White
14	B11	Pink/Black
15	B10	Orange
16	B9	Not Used
17	B8	Not Used
18	B7	[1] Black
19	B6	Not Used
20	B5	Not Used
21	B4	Tan/White
22	B3	Purple/White
23	B2	Dark Blue
24	B1	Dark Green/Yellow

[1] – Vent tube.

92B22260   Courtesy of General Motors Corp.

Fig. 7: Identifying Electronic Brake Control Module (EBCM) 24-Pin Connector Terminals

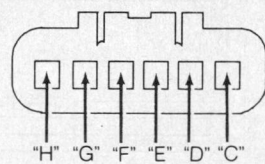

"H" "G" "F" "E" "D" "C"

EBCM 6-PIN CONNECTOR TERMINAL IDENTIFICATION

Terminal	Wire Color
"C"	Dark Green/White
"D"	Orange/Black
"E"	Pink
"F"	Black/White
"G"	Black/Pink
"H"	Purple

92C22261   Courtesy of General Motors Corp.

Fig. 8: Identifying Electronic Brake Control Module (EBCM) 6-Pin Connector Terminals

1992 BRAKES
Anti-Lock – 4WAL FWD Van (Cont.)

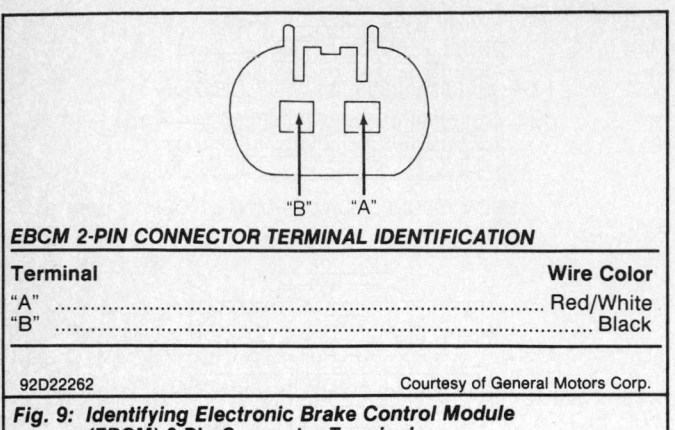

EBCM 2-PIN CONNECTOR TERMINAL IDENTIFICATION

Terminal	Wire Color
"A"	Red/White
"B"	Black

92D22262 Courtesy of General Motors Corp.

Fig. 9: Identifying Electronic Brake Control Module (EBCM) 2-Pin Connector Terminals

TORQUE SPECIFICATIONS

TORQUE SPECIFICATIONS

Application	Ft. Lbs. (N.m)
Brake Caliper Bolts	38 (52)
Drive Axle Nut	185 (115)
Hub & Bearing Assembly Bolts	70 (95)
Hydraulic Modulator-To-Master Cylinder Through Bolts	12 (16)
Modulator Hydraulic Lines	13 (18)
Rear Wheel Bearing and Speed Sensor Assembly Bolts	46 (62)
Wheel Lug Nuts	100 (136)
	INCH Lbs. (N.m)
Hydraulic Modulator Bleeder Valves	65 (7)
Hydraulic Modulator Drive Gear Nuts	75 (9)
Hydraulic Modulator Gear Cover Screws	12 (1)
Motor Pack-To-Hydraulic Modulator Screws	40 (5)

WIRING DIAGRAM

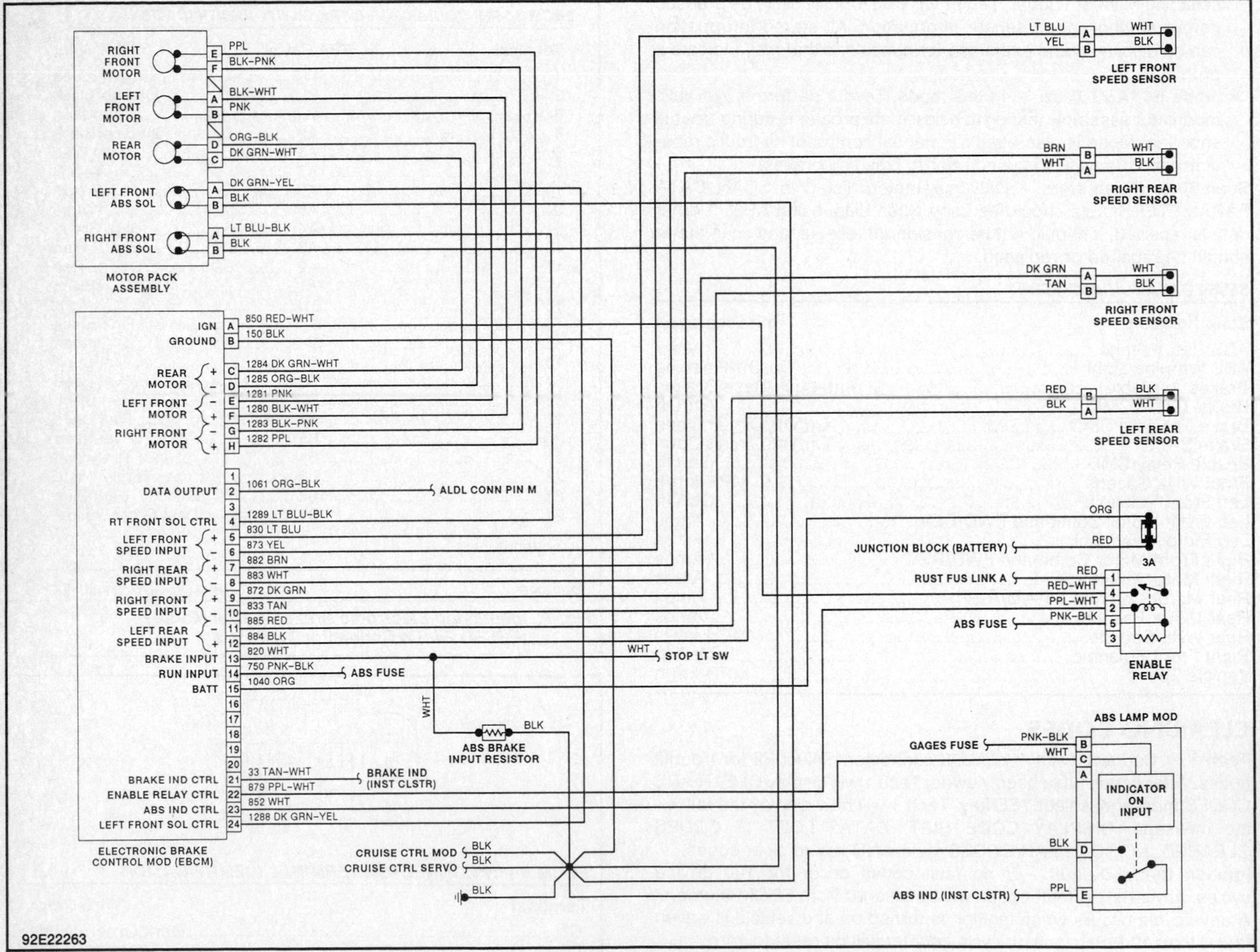

92E22263

Fig. 10: 4WAL Brake System Wiring Diagram (Lumina APV, Silhouette & Trans Sport)

DIAGNOSTIC CHARTS

NOTE: See Figs. 7-9 to identify connector terminals referenced in flow charts.

DIAGNOSTIC CIRCUIT CHECK

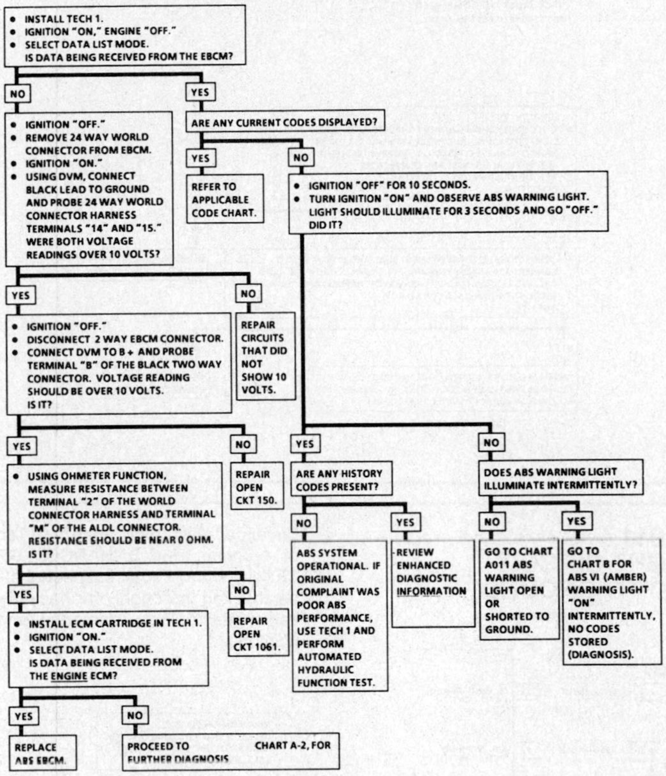

- INSTALL TECH 1.
- IGNITION "ON," ENGINE "OFF."
- SELECT DATA LIST MODE.
  IS DATA BEING RECEIVED FROM THE EBCM?

NO

- IGNITION "OFF."
- REMOVE 24 WAY WORLD CONNECTOR FROM EBCM.
- IGNITION "ON."
- USING DVM, CONNECT BLACK LEAD TO GROUND AND PROBE 24 WAY WORLD CONNECTOR HARNESS TERMINALS "14" AND "15." WERE BOTH VOLTAGE READINGS OVER 10 VOLTS?

YES

- IGNITION "OFF."
- DISCONNECT 2 WAY EBCM CONNECTOR.
- CONNECT DVM TO B + AND PROBE TERMINAL "B" OF THE BLACK TWO WAY CONNECTOR. VOLTAGE READING SHOULD BE OVER 10 VOLTS. IS IT?

YES

- USING OHMETER FUNCTION, MEASURE RESISTANCE BETWEEN TERMINAL "2" OF THE WORLD CONNECTOR HARNESS AND TERMINAL "M" OF THE ALDL CONNECTOR. RESISTANCE SHOULD BE NEAR 0 OHM. IS IT?

YES

- INSTALL ECM CARTRIDGE IN TECH 1.
- IGNITION "ON."
- SELECT DATA LIST MODE.
  IS DATA BEING RECEIVED FROM THE *ENGINE* ECM?

YES
REPLACE ABS EBCM.

NO
PROCEED TO CHART A-2, FOR FURTHER DIAGNOSIS

NO
REPAIR OPEN CKT 1061.

NO
REPAIR OPEN CKT 150.

YES
ARE ANY CURRENT CODES DISPLAYED?

YES
REFER TO APPLICABLE CODE CHART.

NO
- IGNITION "OFF" FOR 10 SECONDS.
- TURN IGNITION "ON" AND OBSERVE ABS WARNING LIGHT. LIGHT SHOULD ILLUMINATE FOR 3 SECONDS AND GO "OFF." DID IT?

NO
REPAIR CIRCUITS THAT DID NOT SHOW 10 VOLTS.

YES
ARE ANY HISTORY CODES PRESENT?

NO
ABS SYSTEM OPERATIONAL. IF ORIGINAL COMPLAINT WAS POOR ABS PERFORMANCE, USE TECH 1 AND PERFORM AUTOMATED HYDRAULIC FUNCTION TEST.

YES
REVIEW ENHANCED DIAGNOSTIC INFORMATION

NO
DOES ABS WARNING LIGHT ILLUMINATE INTERMITTENTLY?

NO
GO TO CHART A011 ABS WARNING LIGHT OPEN OR SHORTED TO GROUND.

YES
GO TO CHART B FOR ABS VI (AMBER) WARNING LIGHT "ON" INTERMITTENTLY, NO CODES STORED (DIAGNOSIS).

92F22652

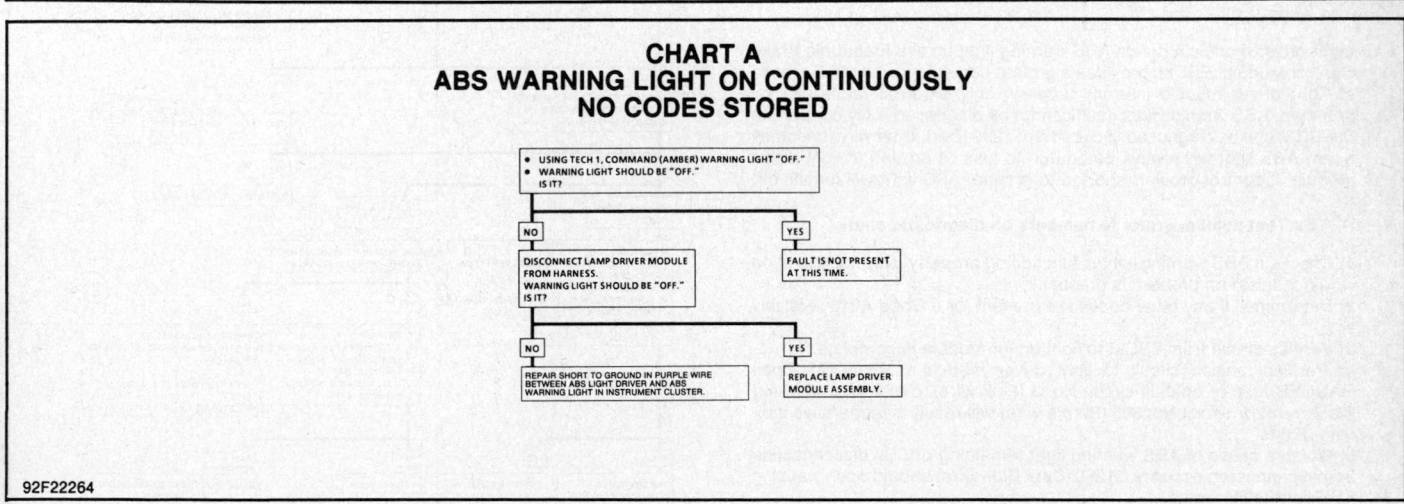

CHART A
ABS WARNING LIGHT ON CONTINUOUSLY
NO CODES STORED

- USING TECH 1, COMMAND (AMBER) WARNING LIGHT "OFF."
- WARNING LIGHT SHOULD BE "OFF." IS IT?

NO
DISCONNECT LAMP DRIVER MODULE FROM HARNESS. WARNING LIGHT SHOULD BE "OFF." IS IT?

YES
FAULT IS NOT PRESENT AT THIS TIME.

NO
REPAIR SHORT TO GROUND IN PURPLE WIRE BETWEEN ABS LIGHT DRIVER AND ABS WARNING LIGHT IN INSTRUMENT CLUSTER.

YES
REPLACE LAMP DRIVER MODULE ASSEMBLY.

92F22264

CHART B
ABS WARNING LIGHT ON INTERMITTENTLY
NO CODES STORED

NOTICE: DIAGNOSTIC CIRCUIT CHECK MUST BE COMPLETED FIRST BEFORE USING THIS CHART.

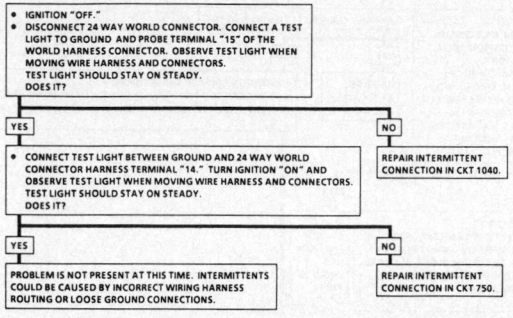

92G22265

CODE A011
ABS WARNING LIGHT CIRCUIT
OPEN OR SHORTED TO GROUND

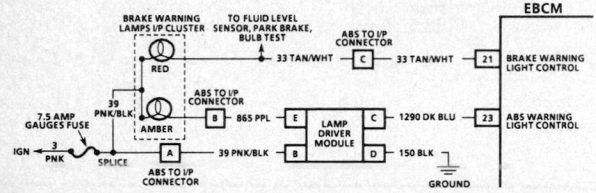

Light driver module turns on ABS warning light unless Electronic Brake Control Module (EBCM) provides a ground circuit to turn it off. Because of light driver module internal circuitry, only external faults can be detected. ABS warning light itself cannot be diagnosed, only control line to EBCM can be diagnosed. If circuit No. 1290 (Dark Blue wire) becomes open, ABS light will always be on due to loss of ground at light driver module. If control circuit is shorted to ground, ABS light will remain off.

NOTE: Test numbers refer to numbers on diagnostic chart.

1) Checks if ABS warning light is functioning properly. Normal operation would indicate no problem is present.
2) Determines if any other codes are present, or if Code A018 is falsely set.
3) Verifies circuit from EBCM to light driver module is complete.
4) Verifies ignition circuit to light driver module is okay. An open GAUGES fuse or open in circuit No. 3 (Pink wire), circuit No. 39 (Pink/Black wire) or circuit No. 865 (Purple wire) will result in inoperative indicator lights.
5) Isolates cause of ABS warning light remaining off. By disconnecting 24-pin connector, circuit No. 1290 (Dark Blue wire) should open, causing ABS light to illuminate.

DIAGNOSTIC AIDS

Intermittent problem may be caused by poor connection, rubbed-through wire insulation or broken wire inside insulation. Light Test feature of Tech 1 may be used to turn on ABS warning light while looking for intermittent problem in warning light circuit.

Enhanced Diagnostic feature of Tech 1 can be used to check frequency of problem. See ENHANCED DIAGNOSTICS under DIAGNOSIS & TESTING. Any circuit suspected of causing intermittent problem should be checked thoroughly for backed-out terminals, improper mating, broken connector locks, damaged terminals or poor terminal-to-wiring connections.

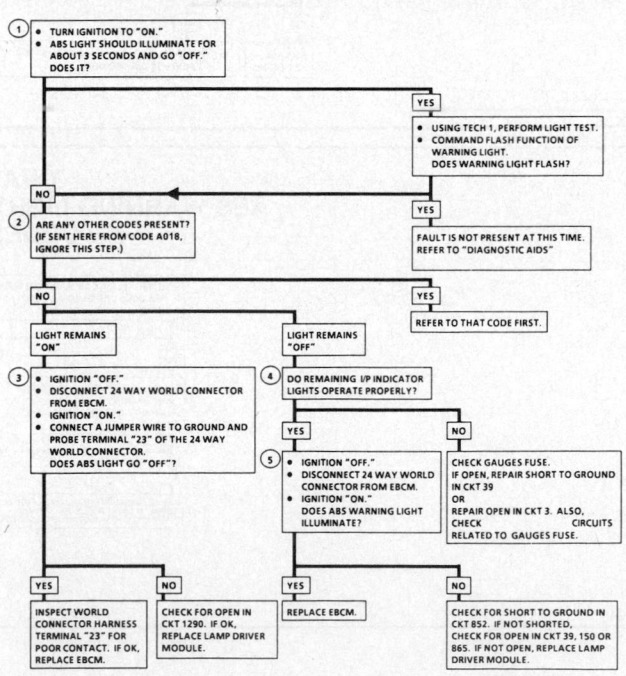

THIS CHART ASSUMES THAT A CURRENT CODE IS STORED INDICATING THAT THIS FAULT IS PRESENT.

92H22266 92I22267

CODE A013
ABS WARNING LIGHT CIRCUIT
SHORTED TO BATTERY

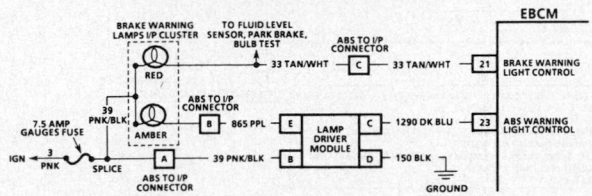

Light driver module turns on ABS warning light unless Electronic Brake Control Module (EBCM) provides a ground circuit to turn it off. Because of light driver module internal circuitry, only external faults can be detected. ABS warning light itself cannot be diagnosed, only control line to EBCM can be diagnosed. If circuit No. 1290 (Dark Blue wire) becomes shorted to battery voltage or EBCM control circuit is open, EBCM will be unable to turn off ABS warning light.

NOTE: Test numbers refer to numbers on diagnostic chart.

1) Checks if ABS warning light is functioning properly. Normal operation would indicate no problem is present.
2) After ignition is turned off, voltage to light driver module should be interrupted. If ABS warning light remains on, a short to battery voltage exists in circuit.
3) After removing 7.5-amp GAUGES fuse, voltage on circuit No. 1290 (Dark Blue wire) should be eliminated. If voltage is still present, there is a short to battery voltage between light driver module and EBCM.

92H22266   92A22269

DIAGNOSTIC AIDS

Intermittent problem may be caused by poor connection, rubbed-through wire insulation or broken wire inside insulation. If Code A013 is a history code, proceed with current codes before attempting to repair Code A013.
Enhanced Diagnostic feature of Tech 1 can be used to check frequency of problem. See ENHANCED DIAGNOSTICS under DIAGNOSIS & TESTING. Any circuit suspected of causing intermittent problem should be checked thoroughly for backed-out terminals, improper mating, broken connector locks, damaged terminals or poor terminal-to-wiring connections.

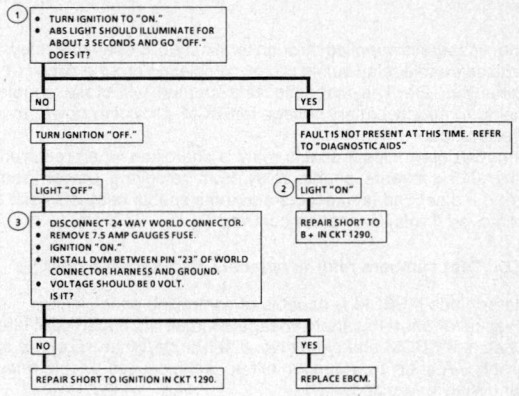

THIS CHART ASSUMES THAT A CURRENT CODE IS STORED INDICATING THAT THIS FAULT IS PRESENT.

CODE A014
ENABLE RELAY CONTACTS
OR FUSE OPEN

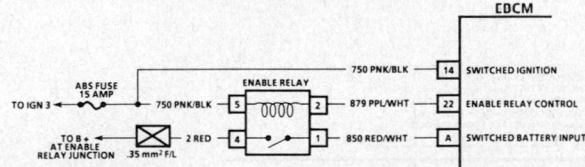

Ignition voltage is supplied through terminal No. 5 of enable relay. EBCM energizes enable relay pull-in coil by completing ground circuit at EBCM terminal No. 22. The magnetic field created will close enable relay contacts to supply battery voltage to EBCM, providing power to motors and solenoids.
This code monitors availability of voltage and current to motors and solenoids. Code A014 indicates voltage is not available, and ABS operation is not possible.

NOTE: Test numbers refer to numbers on diagnostic chart.

1) Determines whether enable relay and circuit are functional by checking if EBCM is sensing battery voltage through terminal "A" of enable relay contacts.
2) Checks for battery voltage at enable relay terminals No. 4 and 5.
3) Checks for continuity in enable relay pull-in coil.
4) Checks ability of EBCM to energize enable relay. An open circuit in EBCM or circuit No. 879 (Purple/White wire) would prevent enable relay from being energized.
5) Checks for open in circuit No. 850 (Red/White wire) between enable relay and EBCM.

DIAGNOSTIC AIDS

Intermittent problem may be caused by poor connection, rubbed-through wire insulation or broken wire inside insulation. Enhanced Diagnostic feature of Tech 1 can be used to check frequency of problem. See ENHANCED DIAGNOSTICS under DIAGNOSIS & TESTING.
Any circuit suspected of causing intermittent problem should be checked thoroughly for backed-out terminals, improper mating, broken connector locks, damaged terminals or poor terminal-to-wiring connections.

92D22270   92E22271

Check for vibration effects using Relay Test feature on Tech 1. With Relay Test activated, lightly tap top and sides of enable relay while monitoring relay voltage.
If relay voltage changes significantly, replace enable relay. If Code A014 is only set when vehicle is initially started in cold ambient temperatures less than 32°F (-0°C), replace enable relay.

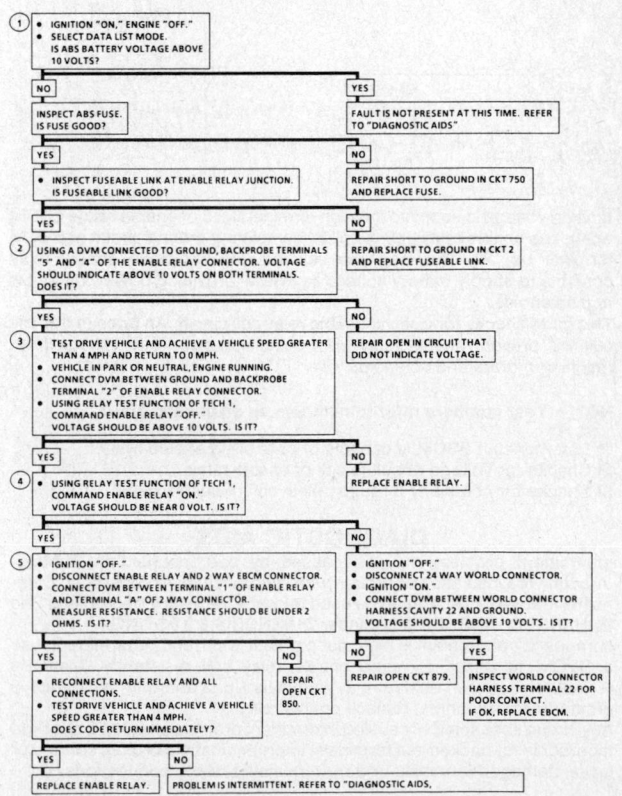

THIS CHART ASSUMES THAT A CURRENT CODE IS STORED INDICATING THAT THIS FAULT IS PRESENT.

CODE A015
ENABLE RELAY CONTACTS SHORTED TO BATTERY

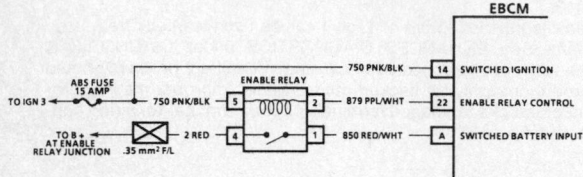

Ignition voltage is supplied through terminal No. 5 of enable relay. EBCM energizes enable relay pull-in coil by completing ground circuit at EBCM terminal No. 22. The magnetic field created will close enable relay contacts to supply battery voltage to EBCM, providing power to motors and solenoids.

This code determines if enable relay is energized when required. Fault Code A015 prevents enable relay from removing power from ABS system. If a second fault occurs and turns enable relay off, fault cannot be removed if relay cannot be controlled.

NOTE: Test numbers refer to numbers on diagnostic chart.

1) Determines if EBCM is capable of controlling enable relay.
2) Checks for short to battery voltage in circuit No. 850 (Red/White wire).
3) Checks if EBCM and circuit No. 879 (Purple/White wire) are shorted to ground. A short to ground in either circuit causes enable relay to be continuously energized.

DIAGNOSTIC AIDS

Intermittent problem may be caused by poor connection, rubbed-through wire insulation or broken wire inside insulation. Enhanced Diagnostic feature of Tech 1 can be used to check frequency of problem. See ENHANCED DIAGNOSTICS under DIAGNOSIS & TESTING.

92D22270   92G22273

Any circuit suspected of causing intermittent problem should be checked thoroughly for backed-out terminals, improper mating, broken connector locks, damaged terminals or poor terminal-to-wiring connections.

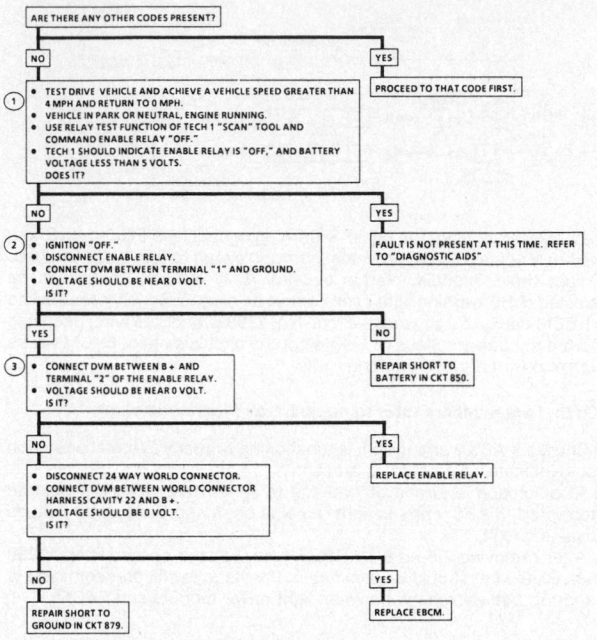

THIS CHART ASSUMES THAT A CURRENT CODE IS STORED INDICATING THAT THIS FAULT IS PRESENT.

CODE A016
ENABLE RELAY COIL CIRCUIT OPEN

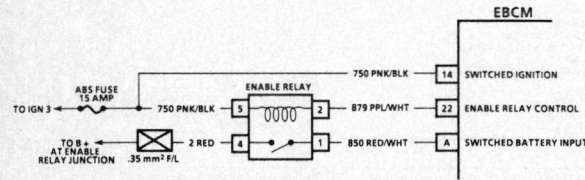

Ignition voltage is supplied through terminal No. 5 of enable relay. EBCM energizes enable relay pull-in coil by completing ground circuit at EBCM terminal No. 22. The magnetic field created will close enable relay contacts to supply battery voltage to EBCM, providing power to motors and solenoids.

This code checks for open in enable relay coil circuit. An open in this circuit will prevent enable relay from being energized and voltage from reaching motors and solenoids.

NOTE: Test numbers refer to numbers on diagnostic chart.

1) Determines if EBCM is capable of controlling enable relay.
2) Checks for voltage at pull-in coil of enable relay.
3) Checks for continuity through pull-in coil of enable relay.

DIAGNOSTIC AIDS

Intermittent problem may be caused by poor connection, rubbed-through wire insulation or broken wire inside insulation. Enhanced Diagnostic feature of Tech 1 can be used to check frequency of problem. See ENHANCED DIAGNOSTICS under DIAGNOSIS & TESTING.

If frequency of problem is high, but problem is currently intermittent, use a DVOM to check for high enable relay coil resistance. Measure resistance between enable relay terminals No. 2 and 5. If resistance is greater than 100 ohms, replace enable relay.

Any circuit suspected of causing intermittent problem should be checked thoroughly for backed-out terminals, improper mating, broken connector locks, damaged terminals or poor terminal-to-wiring connections.

92D22270   92F22561

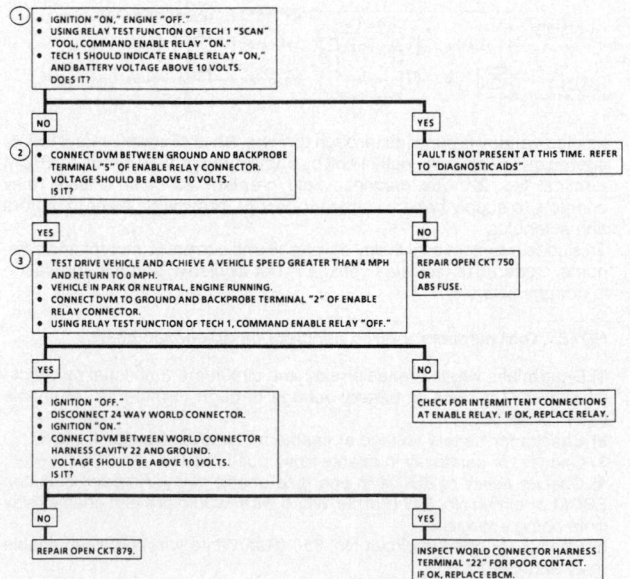

THIS CHART ASSUMES THAT A CURRENT CODE IS STORED INDICATING THAT THIS FAULT IS PRESENT.

CODE A017
ENABLE RELAY COIL CIRCUIT SHORTED TO GROUND

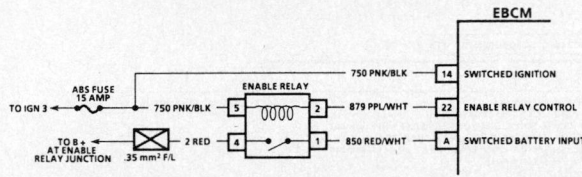

Ignition voltage is supplied through terminal No. 5 of enable relay. EBCM energizes enable relay pull-in coil by completing ground circuit at EBCM terminal No. 22. The magnetic field created will close enable relay contacts to supply battery voltage to EBCM, providing power to motors and solenoids.

This code checks if enable relay is energized when it should not be. Code A017 prevents enable relay from removing power from ABS system. If a second fault occurs and turns off enable relay, fault cannot be removed if relay cannot be controlled.

NOTE: Test numbers refer to numbers on diagnostic chart.

1) Determines if EBCM is capable of controlling enable relay.
2) Checks for short to ground in enable relay or control circuit No. 879 (Purple/White wire).
3) Checks if EBCM is internally shorted to ground. A grounded EBCM terminal No. 22 will cause enable relay to be energized whenever ignition is on.

92D22270   92H22563

DIAGNOSTIC AIDS

Intermittent problem may be caused by poor connection, rubbed-through wire insulation or broken wire inside insulation. Enhanced Diagnostic feature of Tech 1 can be used to check frequency of problem. See ENHANCED DIAGNOSTICS under DIAGNOSIS & TESTING. Any circuit suspected of causing intermittent problem should be thoroughly checked for backed-out terminals, improper mating, broken connector locks, damaged terminals or poor terminal-to-wiring connections.

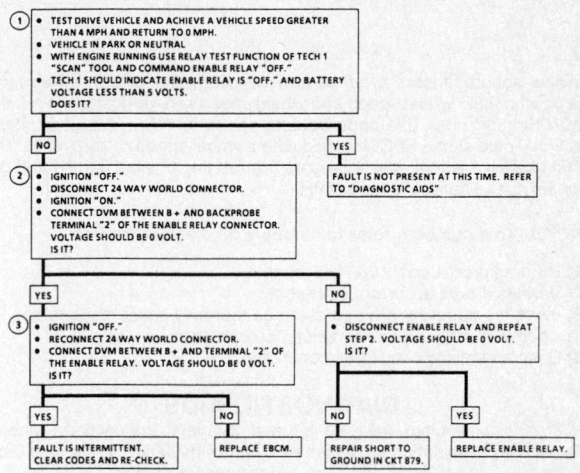

THIS CHART ASSUMES THAT A CURRENT CODE IS STORED INDICATING THAT THIS FAULT IS PRESENT.

CODE A018
ENABLE RELAY COIL CIRCUIT SHORTED TO BATTERY

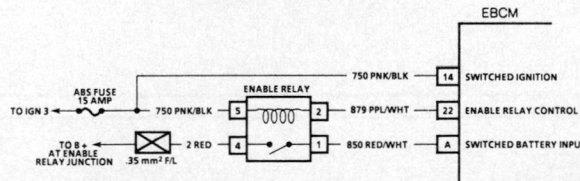

Ignition voltage is supplied through terminal No. 5 of enable relay. EBCM energizes enable relay pull-in coil by completing ground circuit at EBCM terminal No. 22. The magnetic field created will close enable relay contacts to supply battery voltage to EBCM, providing power to motors and solenoids.

This code checks availability of voltage and current to motors and solenoids. Code A018 will disable ABS function.

NOTE: Test numbers refer to numbers on diagnostic chart.

1) Determines if EBCM is capable of controlling enable relay.
2) Checks if voltage is present at enable relay connector terminal No. 2 with enable relay removed. If voltage is present, circuit No. 879 (Purple/White wire) is shorted to battery.
3) Checks for open circuit in EBCM quad driver.

DIAGNOSTIC AIDS

Intermittent problem may be caused by poor connection, rubbed-through wire insulation or broken wire inside insulation. Enhanced Diagnostic feature of Tech 1 can be used to check frequency of problem. See ENHANCED DIAGNOSTICS under DIAGNOSIS & TESTING. Any circuit suspected of causing intermittent problem should be thoroughly checked for backed-out terminals, improper mating, broken connector locks, damaged terminals or poor terminal-to-wiring connections.

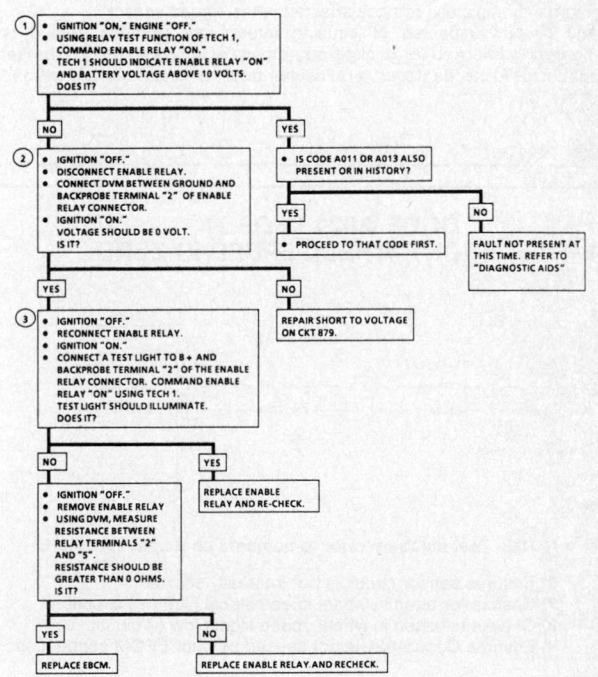

THIS CHART ASSUMES THAT A CURRENT CODE IS STORED INDICATING THAT THIS FAULT IS PRESENT.

92D22270   92J22565

CODE A021 (1 OF 2)
LEFT FRONT WHEEL SPEED IS ZERO

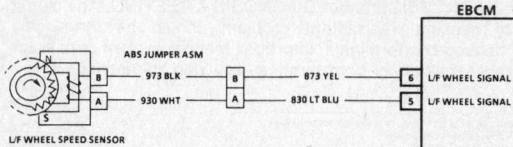

Wheel speed sensors produce an AC voltage signal with a frequency proportional to wheel speed and wheel speed sensor position in relation to a toothed ring. This code detects opens or a low output condition which would cause EBCM to calculate a wheel speed of zero MPH. This code sets if 3 wheel speed sensors are rotating at least 5 MPH and one wheel speed sensor is zero MPH.

NOTE: Test numbers refer to numbers on diagnostic chart.

1) Determines if Code A032 is present.
2) Verifies if fault is currently present.
3) Identifies apparent physical damage that may cause code to set.
4) Checks if sensor internal resistance is correct.
5) Ensures sensor circuit has continuity.

DIAGNOSTIC AIDS

Intermittent problem may be caused by poor connection, rubbed-through wire insulation or broken wire inside insulation. Enhanced Diagnostic feature of Tech 1 can be used to check frequency of problem. See ENHANCED DIAGNOSTICS under DIAGNOSIS & TESTING.

If ABS warning light only comes on during moist conditions, thoroughly check wheel speed sensor circuits for signs of water intrusion. To simulate moist conditions, spray affected wheel speed sensor with a 5 percent salt water solution (mix 2 teaspoons of salt with 12 ounces of water). Test drive vehicle. Vehicle speed must exceed 4 MPH. If code returns immediately, replace affected wheel speed sensor.

Any circuit suspected of causing intermittent problem should be thoroughly checked for backed-out terminals, improper mating, broken connector locks, damaged terminals or poor terminal-to-wiring connections.

92A22566   92B22567

IMPORTANT: WHEEL SPEED SENSOR INTERMITTENT PROBLEMS MAY BE DIFFICULT TO LOCATE. CARE SHOULD BE TAKEN NOT TO DISTURB ANY ELECTRICAL CONNECTIONS PRIOR TO AN INDICATED STEP OF THIS CHART. THIS WILL INSURE THAT AN INTERMITTENT CONNECTION WILL NOT BE CORRECTED BEFORE THE SOURCE OF THE PROBLEM IS FOUND.

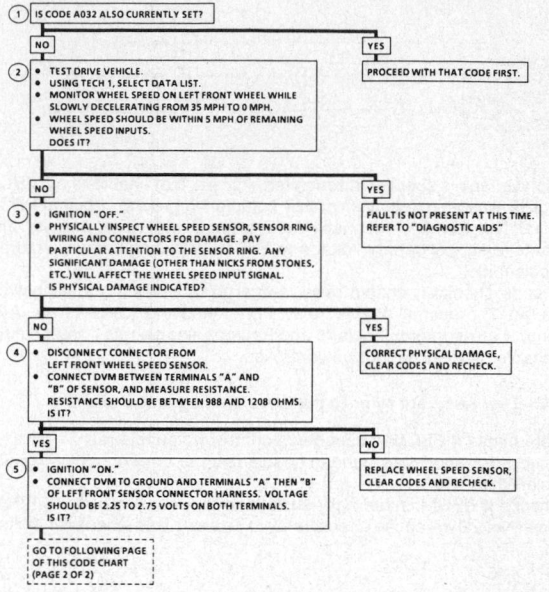

THIS CHART ASSUMES THAT A CURRENT CODE IS STORED INDICATING THAT THIS FAULT IS PRESENT.

CODE A021 (2 OF 2)
LEFT FRONT WHEEL SPEED IS ZERO

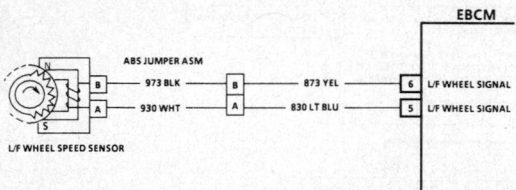

NOTE: Test numbers refer to numbers on diagnostic chart.

6) Ensures sensor circuit is not internally shorted.
7) Checks for open in wheel speed signal high (+) circuit.
8) Checks for open in wheel speed signal low (-) circuit.
9) Ensures Code A021 is not caused by poor EBCM connections.

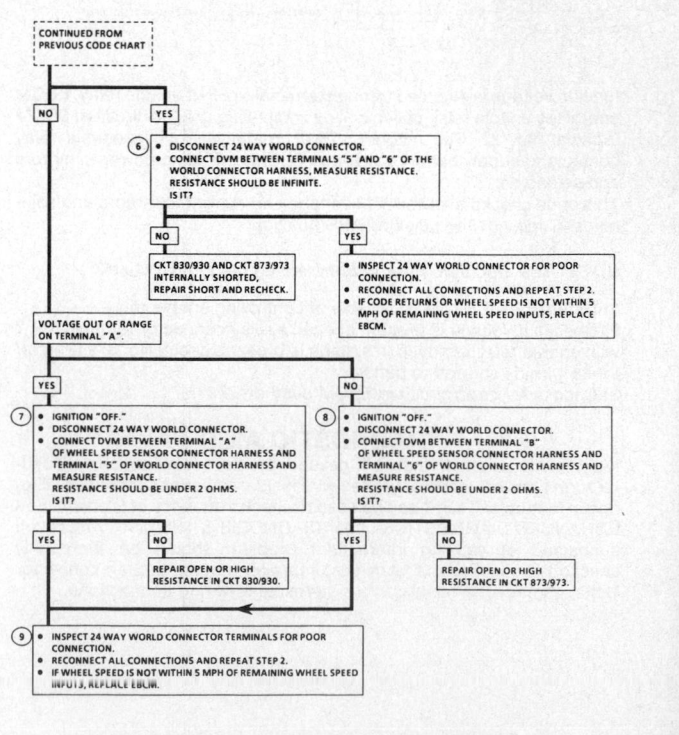

THIS CHART ASSUMES THAT A CURRENT CODE IS STORED INDICATING THAT THIS FAULT IS PRESENT.

92A22566   92C22568

CODE A022 (1 OF 2)
RIGHT FRONT WHEEL SPEED IS ZERO

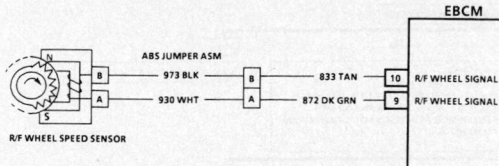

Wheel speed sensors produce an AC voltage signal with a frequency proportional to wheel speed and wheel speed sensor position in relation to a toothed ring. This code detects opens or a low output condition which would cause EBCM to calculate a wheel speed of zero MPH. This code sets if 3 wheel speed sensors are rotating at least 5 MPH and one wheel speed sensor is zero MPH.

NOTE: Test numbers refer to numbers on diagnostic chart.

1) Determines if Code A033 is present.
2) Verifies if fault is currently present.
3) Identifies apparent physical damage that may cause code to set.
4) Checks if sensor internal resistance is correct.
5) Ensures sensor circuit has continuity.

DIAGNOSTIC AIDS

Intermittent problem may be caused by poor connection, rubbed-through wire insulation or broken wire inside insulation. Enhanced Diagnostic feature of Tech 1 can be used to check frequency of problem. See ENHANCED DIAGNOSTICS under DIAGNOSIS & TESTING.
If ABS warning light only comes on during moist conditions, thoroughly check wheel speed sensor circuits for signs of water intrusion. To simulate moist conditions, spray affected wheel speed sensor with a 5 percent salt water solution (mix 2 teaspoons of salt with 12 ounces of water). Test drive vehicle. Vehicle speed must exceed 4 MPH. If code returns immediately, replace affected wheel speed sensor.
Any circuit suspected of causing intermittent problem should be thoroughly checked for backed-out terminals, improper mating, broken connector locks, damaged terminals or poor terminal-to-wiring connections.

92D22569   92G22570

IMPORTANT: WHEEL SPEED SENSOR INTERMITTENT PROBLEMS MAY BE DIFFICULT TO LOCATE. CARE SHOULD BE TAKEN NOT TO DISTURB ANY ELECTRICAL CONNECTIONS PRIOR TO AN INDICATED STEP OF THIS CHART. THIS WILL INSURE THAT AN INTERMITTENT CONNECTION WILL NOT BE CORRECTED BEFORE THE SOURCE OF THE PROBLEM IS FOUND.

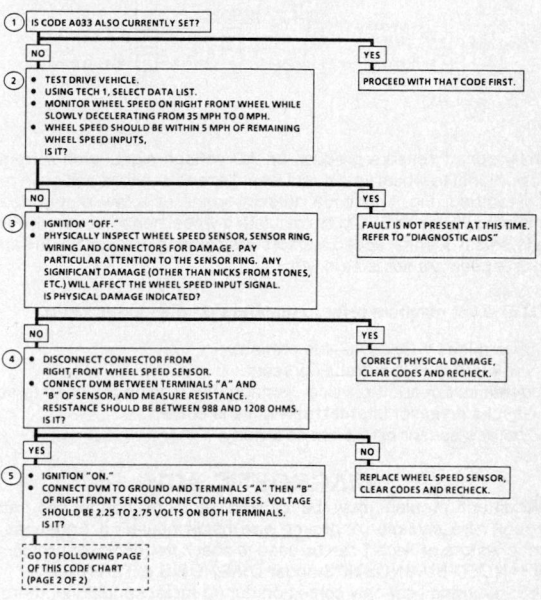

THIS CHART ASSUMES THAT A CURRENT CODE IS STORED INDICATING THAT THIS FAULT IS PRESENT.

CODE A022 (2 OF 2)
RIGHT FRONT WHEEL SPEED IS ZERO

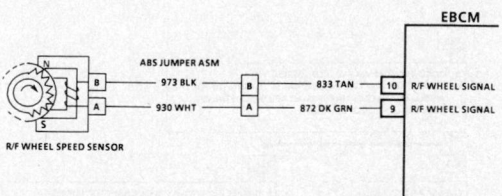

NOTE: Test numbers refer to numbers on diagnostic chart.

6) Ensures sensor circuit is not internally shorted.
7) Checks for open in wheel speed signal low (-) circuit.
8) Checks for open in wheel speed signal high (+) circuit.
9) Ensures Code A022 is not caused by poor EBCM connections.

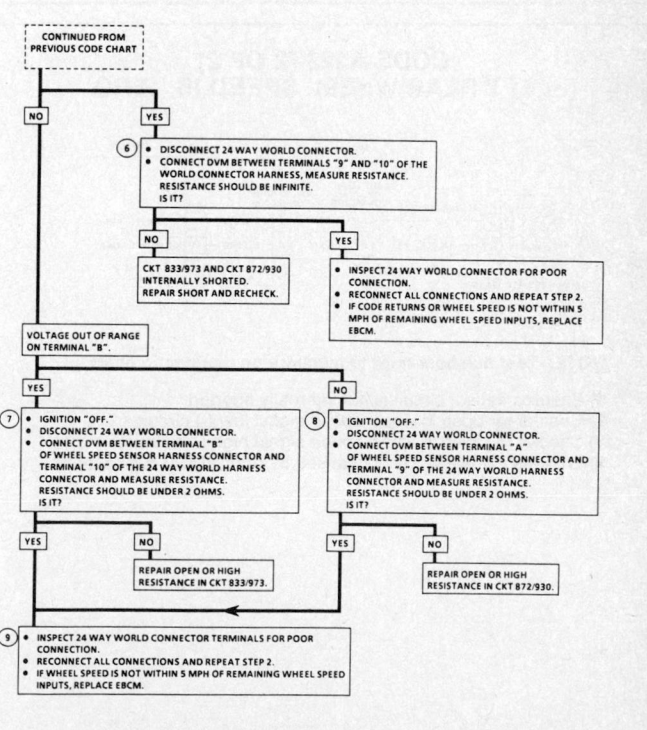

THIS CHART ASSUMES THAT A CURRENT CODE IS STORED INDICATING THAT THIS FAULT IS PRESENT.

92D22569   92H22571

CODE A023 (1 OF 2)
LEFT REAR WHEEL SPEED IS ZERO

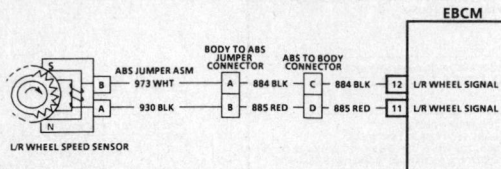

Wheel speed sensors produce an AC voltage signal with a frequency proportional to wheel speed and wheel speed sensor position in relation to a toothed ring. This code detects opens or a low output condition which would cause EBCM to calculate a wheel speed of zero MPH. This code sets if 3 wheel speed sensors are rotating at least 5 MPH and one wheel speed sensor is zero MPH.

NOTE: Test numbers refer to numbers on diagnostic chart.

1) Determines if Code A034 is present.
2) Verifies if fault is currently present.
3) Identifies apparent physical damage that may cause code to set.
4) Checks if sensor internal resistance is correct.
5) Ensures sensor circuit has continuity.

DIAGNOSTIC AIDS

Intermittent problem may be caused by poor connection, rubbed-through wire insulation or broken wire inside insulation. Enhanced Diagnostic feature of Tech 1 can be used to check frequency of problem. See ENHANCED DIAGNOSTICS under DIAGNOSIS & TESTING.

If ABS warning light only comes on during moist conditions, thoroughly check wheel speed sensor circuits for signs of water intrusion. To simulate moist conditions, spray affected wheel speed sensor with a 5 percent salt water solution (mix 2 teaspoons of salt with 12 ounces of water). Test drive vehicle. Vehicle speed must exceed 4 MPH. If code returns immediately, replace affected wheel speed sensor.

Any circuit suspected of causing intermittent problem should be thoroughly checked for backed-out terminals, improper mating, broken connector locks, damaged terminals or poor terminal-to-wiring connections.

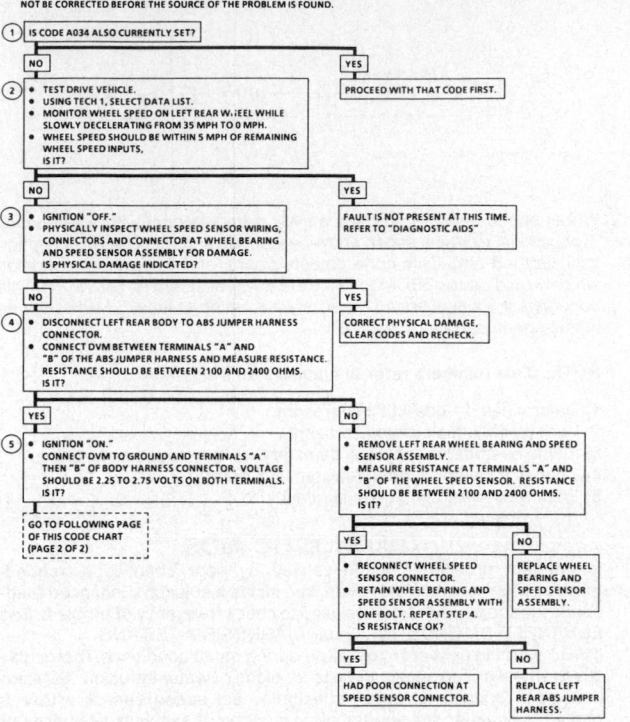

92I22572   92J22573

CODE A023 (2 OF 2)
LEFT REAR WHEEL SPEED IS ZERO

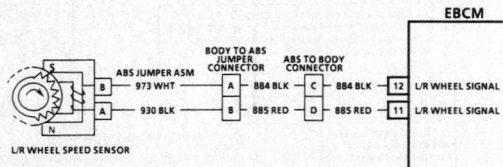

NOTE: Test numbers refer to numbers on diagnostic chart.

6) Ensures sensor circuit is not internally shorted.
7) Checks for open in wheel speed signal low (-) circuit.
8) Checks for open in wheel speed signal high (+) circuit.
9) Ensures Code A023 is not caused by poor EBCM connections.

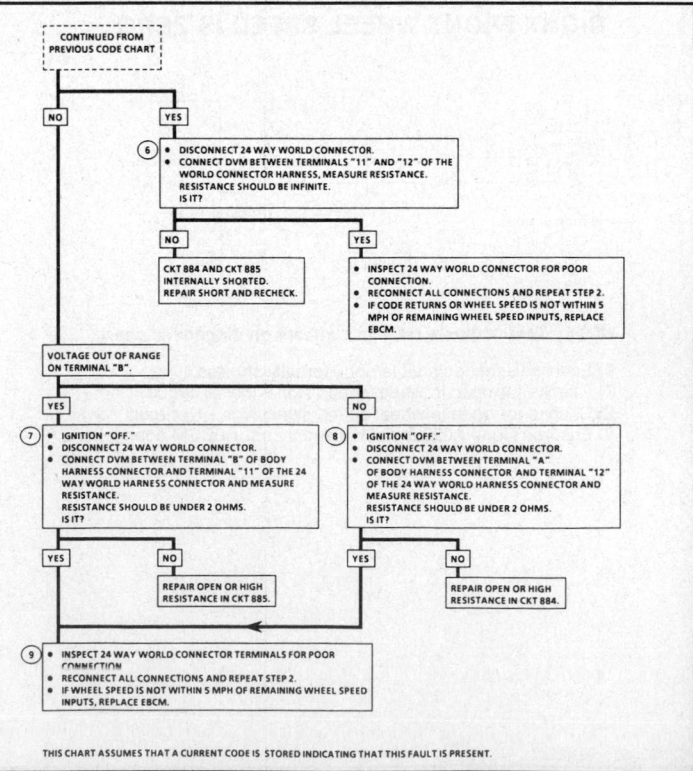

92I22572   92A22574

CODE A024 (1 OF 2)
RIGHT REAR WHEEL SPEED IS ZERO

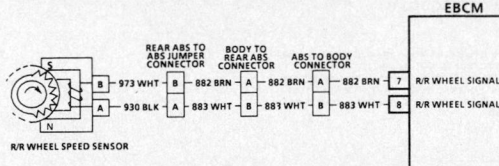

Wheel speed sensors produce an AC voltage signal with a frequency proportional to wheel speed and wheel speed sensor position in relation to a toothed ring. This code detects opens or a low output condition which would cause EBCM to calculate a wheel speed of zero MPH. This code sets if 3 wheel speed sensors are rotating at least 5 MPH and one wheel speed sensor is zero MPH.

NOTE: Test numbers refer to numbers on diagnostic chart.

1) Determines if Code A035 is present.
2) Verifies if fault is currently present.
3) Identifies apparent physical damage that may cause code to set.
4) Checks if sensor internal resistance is correct.
5) Ensures sensor circuit has continuity.

DIAGNOSTIC AIDS

Intermittent problem may be caused by poor connection, rubbed-through wire insulation or broken wire inside insulation. Enhanced Diagnostic feature of Tech 1 can be used to check frequency of problem. See ENHANCED DIAGNOSTICS under DIAGNOSIS & TESTING.

If ABS warning light only comes on during moist conditions, thoroughly check wheel speed sensor circuits for signs of water intrusion. To simulate moist conditions, spray affected wheel speed sensor with a 5 percent salt water solution (mix 2 teaspoons of salt with 12 ounces of water). Test drive vehicle. Vehicle speed must exceed 4 MPH. If code returns immediately, replace affected wheel speed sensor.

Any circuit suspected of causing intermittent problem should be thoroughly checked for backed-out terminals, improper mating, broken connector locks, damaged terminals or poor terminal-to-wiring connections.

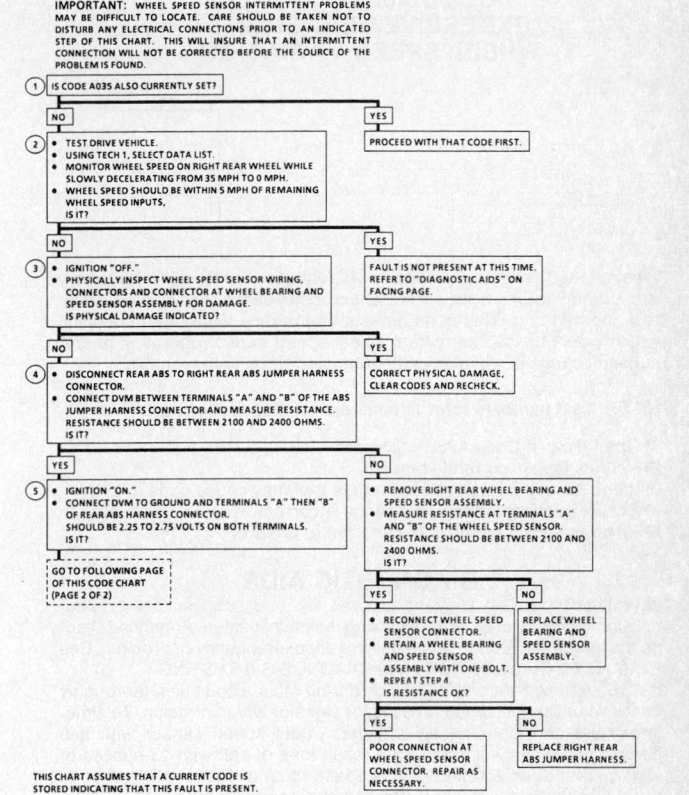

92B22575   92C22576

CODE A024 (2 OF 2)
RIGHT REAR WHEEL SPEED IS ZERO

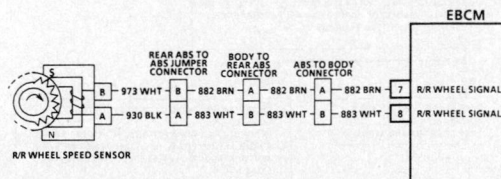

NOTE: Test numbers refer to numbers on diagnostic chart.

6) Ensures sensor circuit is not internally shorted.
7) Checks for open in wheel speed signal low (-) circuit.
8) Checks for open in wheel speed signal high (+) circuit.
9) Ensures Code A024 is not caused by poor EBCM connections.

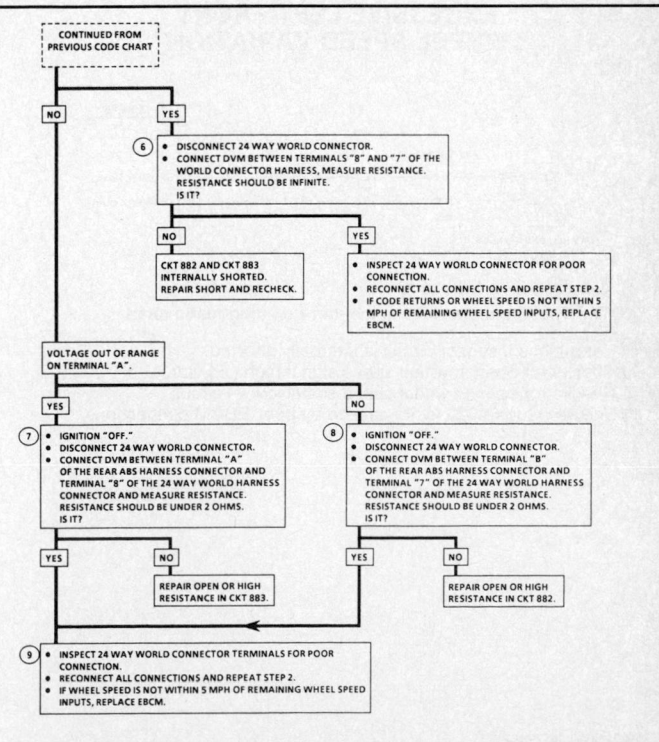

THIS CHART ASSUMES THAT A CURRENT CODE IS STORED INDICATING THAT THIS FAULT IS PRESENT.

92B22575   92D22577

CODE A025 (1 OF 2)
EXCESSIVE LEFT FRONT
WHEEL SPEED VARIATION

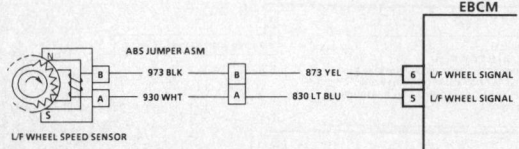

Wheel speed sensors produce an AC voltage signal with a frequency proportional to wheel speed and wheel speed sensor position in relation to a toothed ring. This code detects opens or a low output condition which would cause intermittent wheel speed sensor operation and/or sudden change in wheel speed determined to be unreasonable.

NOTE: Test numbers refer to numbers on diagnostic chart.

1) Determines if Code A032 is present.
2) Verifies fault is currently present.
3) Identifies apparent physical damage that may cause code to set.
4) Ensures sensor internal resistance is correct.
5) Ensures sensor circuit is not shorted to ground.

DIAGNOSTIC AIDS

Intermittent problem may be caused by poor connection, rubbed-through wire insulation or broken wire inside insulation. Enhanced Diagnostic feature of Tech 1 can be used to check frequency of problem. See ENHANCED DIAGNOSTICS under DIAGNOSIS & TESTING.
If ABS warning light only comes on during moist conditions, thoroughly check wheel speed sensor circuits for signs of water intrusion. To simulate moist conditions, spray affected wheel speed sensor with a 5 percent salt water solution (mix 2 teaspoons of salt with 12 ounces of water). Test drive vehicle. Vehicle speed must exceed 4 MPH. If code returns immediately, replace affected wheel speed sensor.
Any circuit suspected of causing intermittent problem should be thoroughly checked for backed-out terminals, improper mating, broken connector locks, damaged terminals or poor terminal-to-wiring connections.

Perform a careful visual inspection of wheel speed sensor, toothed ring and CV joint assembly for physical damage. Check wheel bearing for excessive play. If code sets at same vehicle speed (MPH) every time and wheel speed variation is noted above this speed on Tech 1, toothed ring is most likely damaged.

IMPORTANT: WHEEL SPEED SENSOR INTERMITTENT PROBLEMS MAY BE DIFFICULT TO LOCATE. CARE SHOULD BE TAKEN NOT TO DISTURB ANY ELECTRICAL CONNECTIONS PRIOR TO AN INDICATED STEP OF THIS CHART. THIS WILL INSURE THAT AN INTERMITTENT CONNECTION WILL NOT BE CORRECTED BEFORE THE SOURCE OF THE PROBLEM IS FOUND.

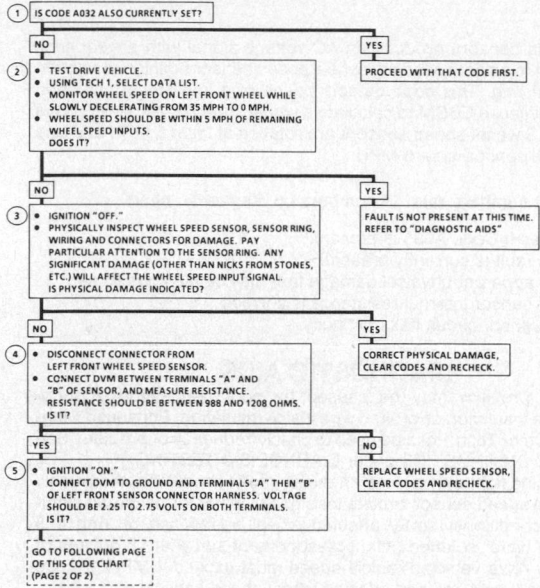

THIS CHART ASSUMES THAT A CURRENT CODE IS STORED INDICATING THAT THIS FAULT IS PRESENT.

92A22566   92F22579

CODE A025 (2 OF 2)
EXCESSIVE LEFT FRONT
WHEEL SPEED VARIATION

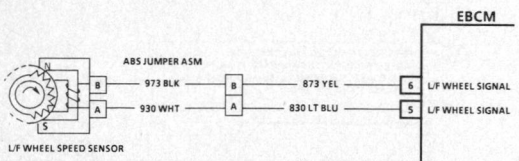

NOTE: Test numbers refer to numbers on diagnostic chart.

6) Determines if sensor circuit is internally shorted.
7) Checks for open in wheel speed signal high (+) circuit.
8) Checks for open in wheel speed signal low (-) circuit.
9) Ensures Code A025 is not caused by poor EBCM connections.

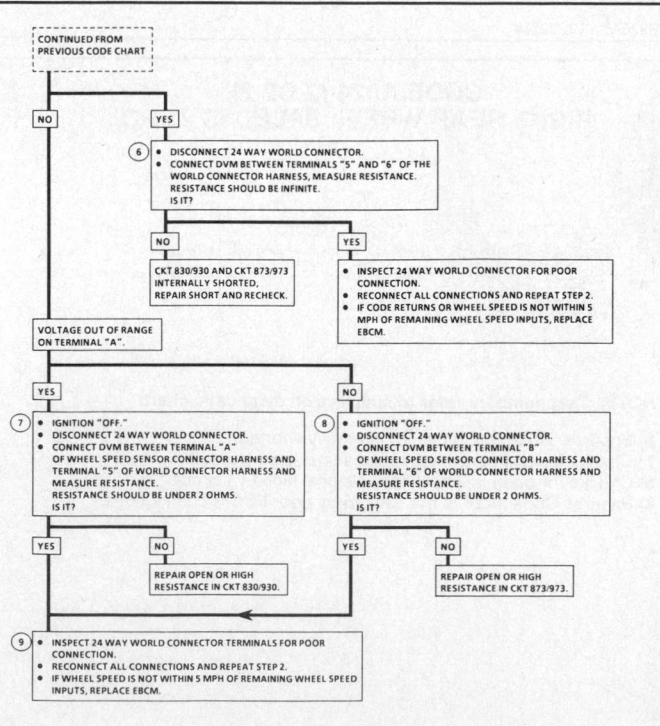

THIS CHART ASSUMES THAT A CURRENT CODE IS STORED INDICATING THAT THIS FAULT IS PRESENT.

92A22566   92I22580

CODE A026 (1 OF 2)
EXCESSIVE RIGHT FRONT
WHEEL SPEED VARIATION

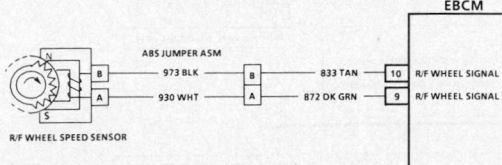

Wheel speed sensors produce an AC voltage signal with a frequency proportional to wheel speed and wheel speed sensor position in relation to a toothed ring. This code detects opens or a low output condition which would cause intermittent wheel speed sensor operation and/or sudden change in wheel speed determined to be unreasonable.

NOTE: Test numbers refer to numbers on diagnostic chart.

1) Determines if Code A033 is present.
2) Verifies fault is currently present.
3) Identifies apparent physical damage that may cause code to set.
4) Ensures sensor internal resistance is correct.
5) Ensures sensor circuit is not shorted to ground.

DIAGNOSTIC AIDS

Intermittent problem may be caused by poor connection, rubbed-through wire insulation or broken wire inside insulation. Enhanced Diagnostic feature of Tech 1 can be used to check frequency of problem. See ENHANCED DIAGNOSTICS under DIAGNOSIS & TESTING.
If ABS warning light only comes on during moist conditions, thoroughly check wheel speed sensor circuits for signs of water intrusion. To simulate moist conditions, spray affected wheel speed sensor with a 5 percent salt water solution (mix 2 teaspoons of salt with 12 ounces of water). Test drive vehicle. Vehicle speed must exceed 4 MPH. If code returns immediately, replace affected wheel speed sensor.
Any circuit suspected of causing intermittent problem should be thoroughly checked for backed-out terminals, improper mating, broken connector locks, damaged terminals or poor terminal-to-wiring connections.

Perform a careful visual inspection of wheel speed sensor, toothed ring and CV joint assembly for physical damage. Check wheel bearing for excessive play. If code sets at same vehicle speed (MPH) every time and wheel speed variation is noted above this speed on Tech 1, toothed ring is most likely damaged.

IMPORTANT: WHEEL SPEED SENSOR INTERMITTENT PROBLEMS MAY BE DIFFICULT TO LOCATE. CARE SHOULD BE TAKEN NOT TO DISTURB ANY ELECTRICAL CONNECTIONS PRIOR TO AN INDICATED STEP OF THIS CHART. THIS WILL INSURE THAT AN INTERMITTENT CONNECTION WILL NOT BE CORRECTED BEFORE THE SOURCE OF THE PROBLEM IS FOUND.

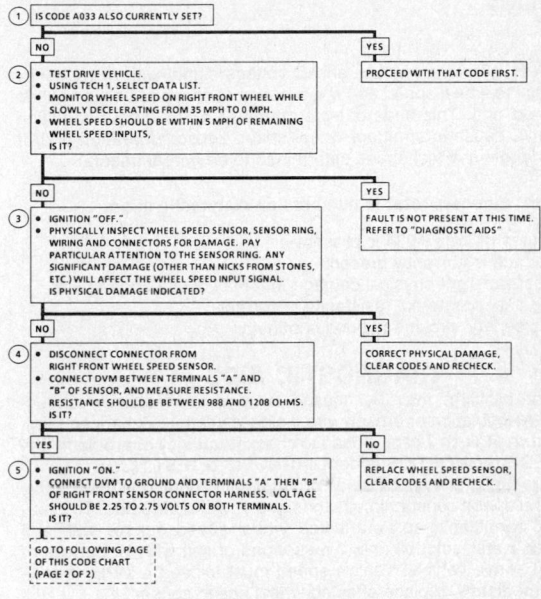

THIS CHART ASSUMES THAT A CURRENT CODE IS STORED INDICATING THAT THIS FAULT IS PRESENT.

92D22569   92A22582

CODE A026 (2 OF 2)
EXCESSIVE RIGHT FRONT
WHEEL SPEED VARIATION

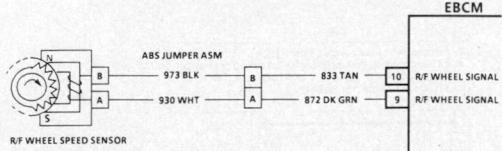

NOTE: Test numbers refer to numbers on diagnostic chart.

6) Determines if sensor circuit is internally shorted.
7) Checks for open in wheel speed signal low (-) circuit.
8) Checks for open in wheel speed signal high (+) circuit.
9) Ensures Code A026 is not caused by poor EBCM connections.

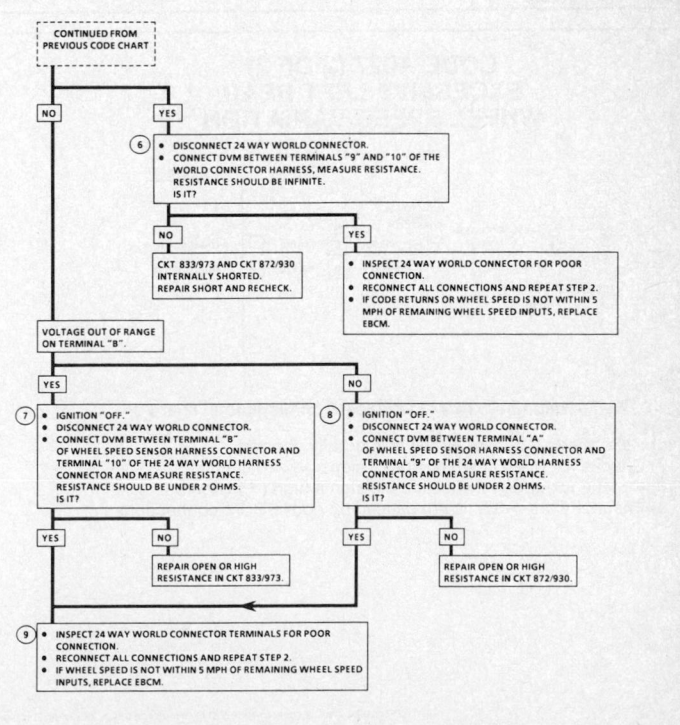

THIS CHART ASSUMES THAT A CURRENT CODE IS STORED INDICATING THAT THIS FAULT IS PRESENT.

92D22569   92B22583

CODE A027 (1 OF 2)
EXCESSIVE LEFT REAR
WHEEL SPEED VARIATION

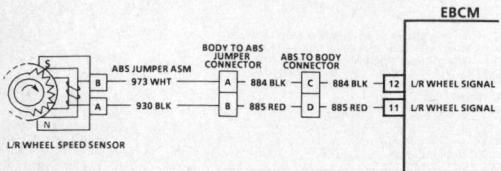

Wheel speed sensors produce an AC voltage signal with a frequency proportional to wheel speed and wheel speed sensor position in relation to a toothed ring. This code detects opens or a low output condition which would cause intermittent wheel speed sensor operation and/or sudden change in wheel speed determined to be unreasonable.

NOTE: Test numbers refer to numbers on diagnostic chart.

1) Determines if Code A034 is present.
2) Verifies fault is currently present.
3) Identifies apparent physical damage that may cause code to set.
4) Ensures sensor internal resistance is correct.
5) Ensures sensor circuit has good continuity.

DIAGNOSTIC AIDS

Intermittent problem may be caused by poor connection, rubbed-through wire insulation or broken wire inside insulation. Enhanced Diagnostic feature of Tech 1 can be used to check frequency of problem. See ENHANCED DIAGNOSTICS under DIAGNOSIS & TESTING.
If ABS warning light only comes on during moist conditions, thoroughly check wheel speed sensor circuits for signs of water intrusion. To simulate moist conditions, spray affected wheel speed sensor with a 5 percent salt water solution (mix 2 teaspoons of salt with 12 ounces of water). Test drive vehicle. Vehicle speed must exceed 4 MPH. If code returns immediately, replace affected wheel speed sensor.
Any circuit suspected of causing intermittent problem should be thoroughly checked for backed-out terminals, improper mating, broken connector locks, damaged terminals or poor terminal-to-wiring connections.
Excessive bearing end play can cause this code to set. Check wheel bearing for excessive play.

92I22572   92D22585

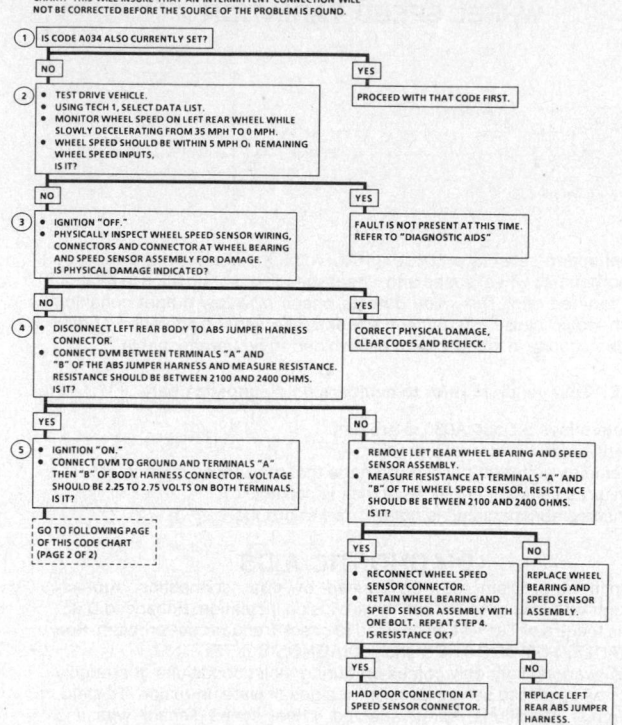

THIS CHART ASSUMES THAT A CURRENT CODE IS STORED INDICATING THAT THIS FAULT IS PRESENT.

CODE A027 (2 OF 2)
EXCESSIVE LEFT REAR
WHEEL SPEED VARIATION

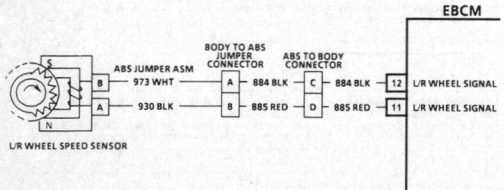

NOTE: Test numbers refer to numbers on diagnostic chart.

6) Determines if sensor circuit is internally shorted.
7) Checks for open in wheel speed signal low (-) circuit.
8) Checks for open in wheel speed signal high (+) circuit.
9) Ensures Code A027 is not caused by poor EBCM connections.

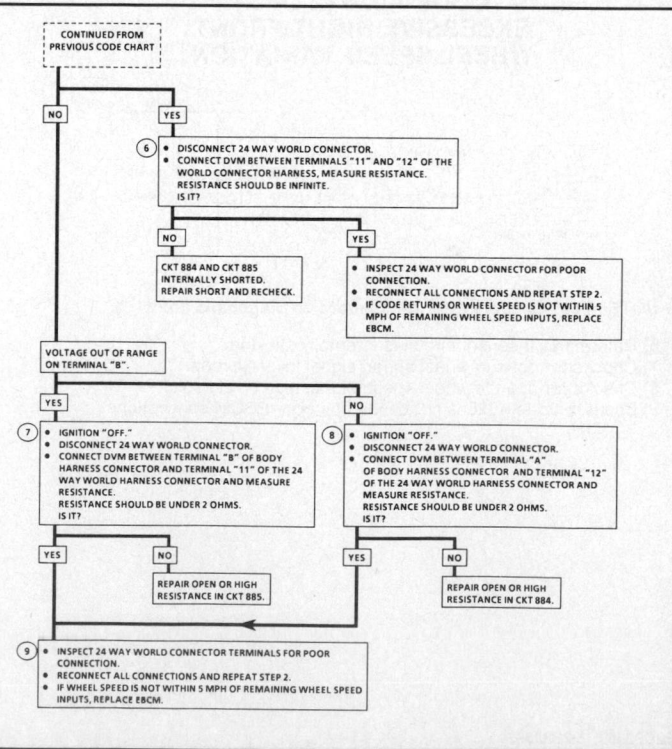

THIS CHART ASSUMES THAT A CURRENT CODE IS STORED INDICATING THAT THIS FAULT IS PRESENT.

92I22572   92E22586

CODE A028 (1 OF 2)
EXCESSIVE RIGHT REAR
WHEEL SPEED VARIATION

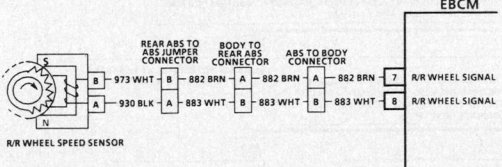

Wheel speed sensors produce an AC voltage signal with a frequency proportional to wheel speed and wheel speed sensor position in relation to a toothed ring. This code detects opens or a low output condition which would cause intermittent wheel speed sensor operation and/or sudden change in wheel speed determined to be unreasonable.

NOTE: Test numbers refer to numbers on diagnostic chart.

1) Determines if Code A035 is present.
2) Verifies fault is currently present.
3) Identifies apparent physical damage that may cause code to set.
4) Ensures sensor internal resistance is correct.
5) Ensures sensor circuit has good continuity.

DIAGNOSTIC AIDS

Intermittent problem may be caused by poor connection, rubbed-through wire insulation or broken wire inside insulation. Enhanced Diagnostic feature of Tech 1 can be used to check frequency of problem. See ENHANCED DIAGNOSTICS under DIAGNOSIS & TESTING.

If ABS warning light only comes on during moist conditions, thoroughly check wheel speed sensor circuits for signs of water intrusion. To simulate moist conditions, spray affected wheel speed sensor with a 5 percent salt water solution (mix 2 teaspoons of salt with 12 ounces of water). Test drive vehicle. Vehicle speed must exceed 4 MPH. If code returns immediately, replace affected wheel speed sensor.

Any circuit suspected of causing intermittent problem should be thoroughly checked for backed-out terminals, improper mating, broken connector locks, damaged terminals or poor terminal-to-wiring connections.

Excessive bearing end play can cause this code to set. Check wheel bearing for excessive play.

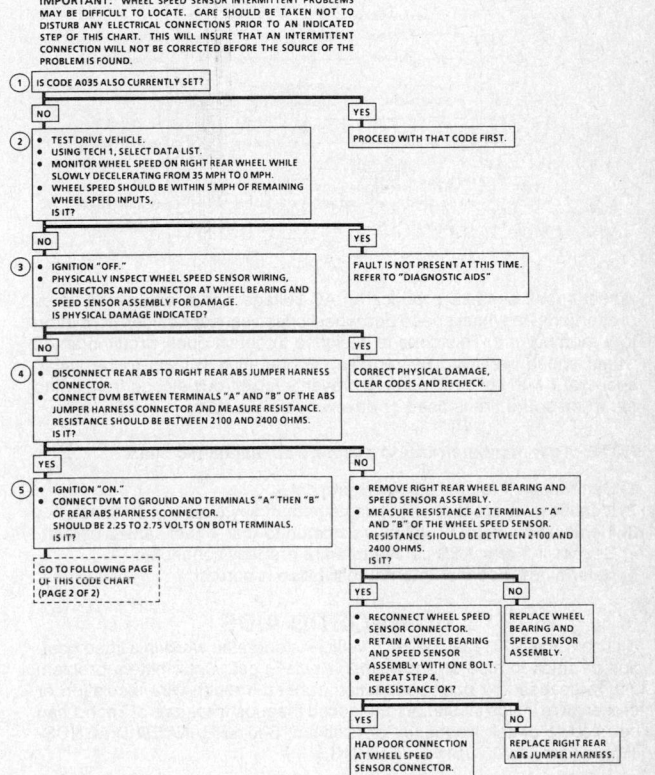

92B22575   92G22588

CODE A028 (2 OF 2)
EXCESSIVE RIGHT REAR
WHEEL SPEED VARIATION

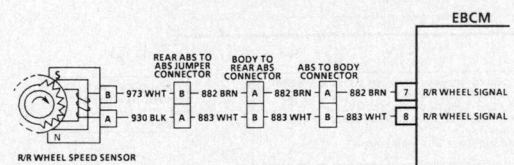

NOTE: Test numbers refer to numbers on diagnostic chart.

6) Determines if sensor circuit is internally shorted.
7) Checks for open in wheel speed signal low (-) circuit.
8) Checks for open in wheel speed signal high (+) circuit.
9) Ensures Code A028 is not caused by poor EBCM connections.

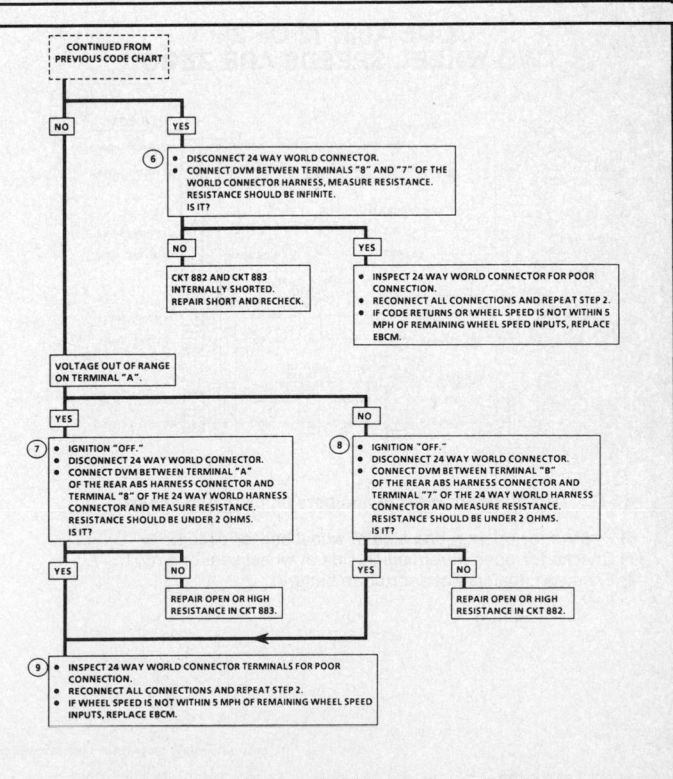

92B22575   92H22589

THIS CHART ASSUMES THAT A CURRENT CODE IS STORED INDICATING THAT THIS FAULT IS PRESENT.

CODE A031 (1 OF 2)
TWO WHEEL SPEEDS ARE ZERO

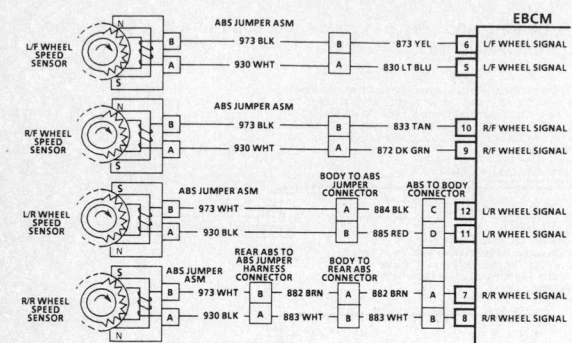

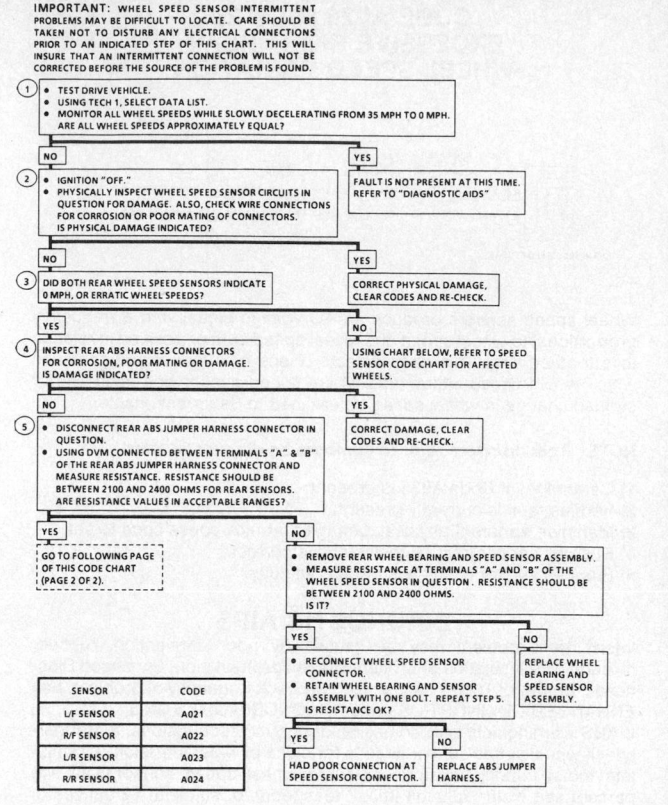

Wheel speed sensors produce an AC voltage signal with a frequency proportional to wheel speed and wheel speed sensor position in relation to a toothed ring. This code is designed to detect open circuit in any 2 wheel speed sensors. By requiring 2 operating wheels to be within speed of 7 MPH of each other, it prevents false trouble code from being set when spare tire is used or drive wheels are spun.

NOTE: Test numbers refer to numbers on diagnostic chart.

1) Determines if fault is currently present.
2) Identifies apparent physical damage that may cause code to set.
3) Identifies cause of problem is common to rear wheel sensor circuit.
4) Checks if 2 rear ABS connectors are properly connected.
5) Determines if sensor internal resistance is correct.

DIAGNOSTIC AIDS

A false Code A031 may be set if vehicle is operated while in a lifted position or stuck in mud or snow with vehicle in gear. Intermittent problem may be caused by poor connection, rubbed-through wire insulation or broken wire inside insulation. Enhanced Diagnostic feature of Tech 1 can be used to check frequency of problem. See ENHANCED DIAGNOSTICS under DIAGNOSIS & TESTING.

SENSOR	CODE
L/F SENSOR	A021
R/F SENSOR	A022
L/R SENSOR	A023
R/R SENSOR	A024

92A22590   92B22591

CODE A031 (2 OF 2)
TWO WHEEL SPEEDS ARE ZERO

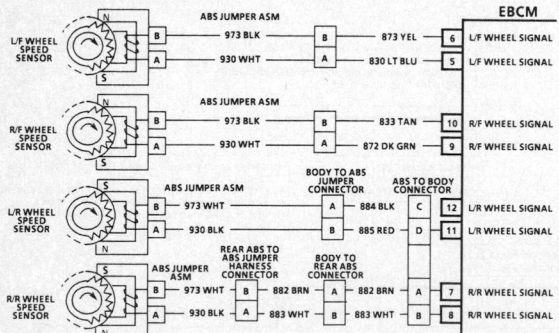

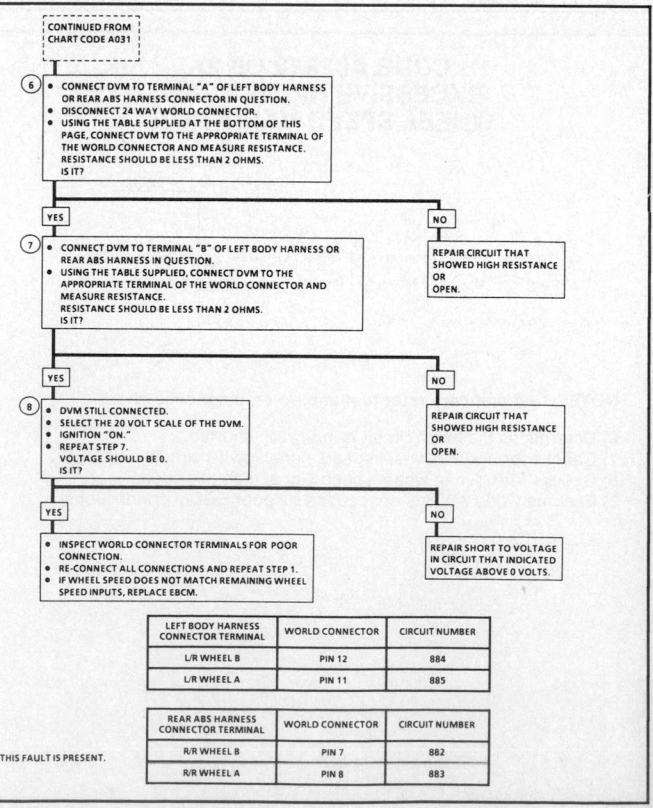

NOTE: Test numbers refer to numbers on diagnostic chart.

6) Checks for open in one side of wheel sensor circuit.
7) Checks for open in remaining side of wheel sensor circuit.
8) Ensures circuit is not shorted to battery.

LEFT BODY HARNESS CONNECTOR TERMINAL	WORLD CONNECTOR	CIRCUIT NUMBER
L/R WHEEL B	PIN 12	884
L/R WHEEL A	PIN 11	885

REAR ABS HARNESS CONNECTOR TERMINAL	WORLD CONNECTOR	CIRCUIT NUMBER
R/R WHEEL B	PIN 7	882
R/R WHEEL A	PIN 8	883

THIS CHART ASSUMES THAT A CURRENT CODE IS STORED INDICATING THAT THIS FAULT IS PRESENT.

92A22590   92C22592

CODE A032
LEFT FRONT WHEEL SENSOR
SHORTED TO BATTERY OR GROUND

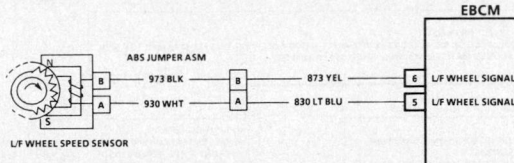

Wheel speed sensors produce an AC voltage signal with a frequency proportional to wheel speed and wheel speed sensor position in relation to a toothed ring. This code detects shorts to ground and shorts to battery voltage in wheel speed circuit sensed by EBCM.

NOTE: Test numbers refer to numbers on diagnostic chart.

1) Identifies whether code is due to short to battery voltage or short to ground.
2) Checks if wheel speed sensor is shorted to ground.
3) Checks if wheel speed sensor circuit is shorted to battery.
4) Ensures wheel speed sensor circuit has good continuity.
5) Checks for short to ground in wheel speed sensor wiring.
6) Checks for short to voltage in wheel speed sensor wiring.

DIAGNOSTIC AIDS

Intermittent problem may be caused by poor connection, rubbed-through wire insulation or broken wire inside insulation. Enhanced Diagnostic feature of Tech 1 can be used to check frequency of problem. See ENHANCED DIAGNOSTICS under DIAGNOSIS & TESTING.

If ADS warning light only comes on during moist conditions, thoroughly check wheel speed sensor circuits for signs of water intrusion. To simulate moist conditions, spray affected wheel speed sensor with a 5 percent salt water solution (mix 2 teaspoons of salt with 12 ounces of water). Test drive vehicle. Vehicle speed must exceed 4 MPH. If code returns immediately, replace suspected harness.

Any circuit suspected of causing intermittent problem should be thoroughly checked for backed-out terminals, improper mating, broken connector locks, damaged terminals or poor terminal-to-wiring connections.

IMPORTANT: WHEEL SPEED SENSOR INTERMITTENT PROBLEMS MAY BE DIFFICULT TO LOCATE. CARE SHOULD BE TAKEN NOT TO DISTURB ANY ELECTRICAL CONNECTIONS PRIOR TO AN INDICATED STEP OF THIS CHART. THIS WILL INSURE THAT AN INTERMITTENT CONNECTION WILL NOT BE CORRECTED BEFORE THE SOURCE OF THE PROBLEM IS FOUND.

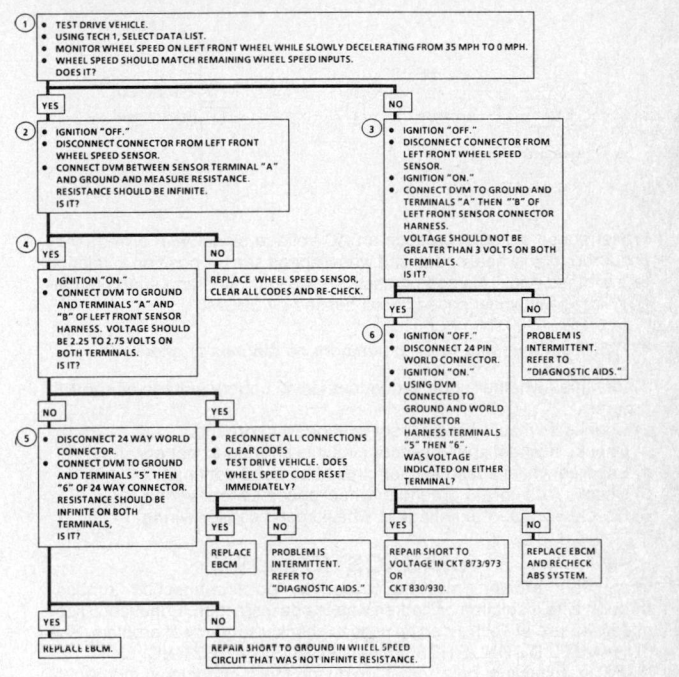

92A22566   92E22594

CODE A033
RIGHT FRONT WHEEL SENSOR
SHORTED TO BATTERY OR GROUND

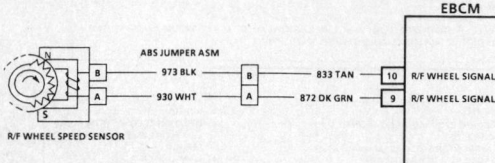

Wheel speed sensors produce an AC voltage signal with a frequency proportional to wheel speed and wheel speed sensor position in relation to a toothed ring. This code detects shorts to ground and shorts to battery voltage in wheel speed circuit sensed by EBCM.

NOTE: Test numbers refer to numbers on diagnostic chart.

1) Identifies whether code is due to short to battery voltage or short to ground.
2) Checks if wheel speed sensor is shorted to ground.
3) Checks if wheel speed sensor circuit is shorted to battery.
4) Ensures wheel speed sensor circuit has good continuity.
5) Checks for short to ground in wheel speed sensor wiring.
6) Checks for short to voltage in wheel speed sensor wiring.

DIAGNOSTIC AIDS

Intermittent problem may be caused by poor connection, rubbed-through wire insulation or broken wire inside insulation. Enhanced Diagnostic feature of Tech 1 can be used to check frequency of problem. See ENHANCED DIAGNOSTICS under DIAGNOSIS & TESTING.

If ABS warning light only comes on during moist conditions, thoroughly check wheel speed sensor circuits for signs of water intrusion. To simulate moist conditions, spray affected wheel speed sensor with a 5 percent salt water solution (mix 2 teaspoons of salt with 12 ounces of water). Test drive vehicle. Vehicle speed must exceed 4 MPH. If code returns immediately, replace suspected harness.

Any circuit suspected of causing intermittent problem should be thoroughly checked for backed-out terminals, improper mating, broken connector locks, damaged terminals or poor terminal-to-wiring connections.

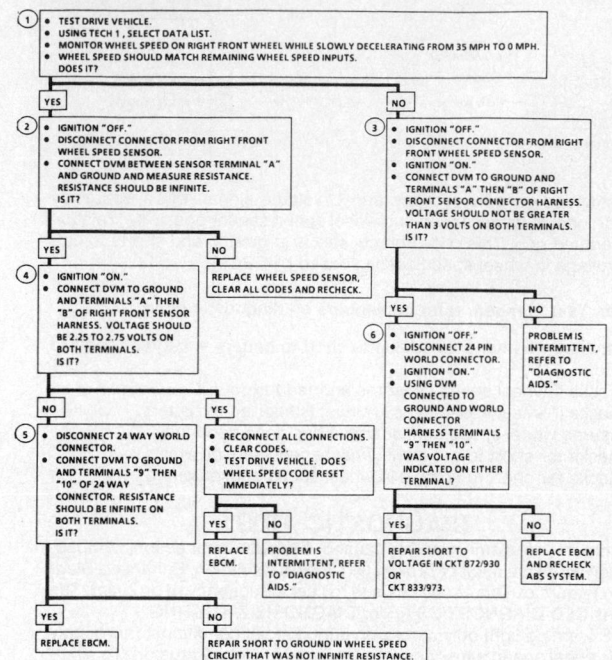

92D22569   92G22596

CODE A034
LEFT REAR WHEEL SENSOR
SHORTED TO BATTERY OR GROUND

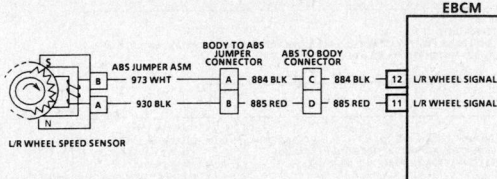

Wheel speed sensors produce an AC voltage signal with a frequency proportional to wheel speed and wheel speed sensor position in relation to a toothed ring. This code detects shorts to ground and shorts to battery voltage in wheel speed circuit sensed by EBCM.

NOTE: Test numbers refer to numbers on diagnostic chart.

1) Identifies whether code is due to short to battery voltage or short to ground.
2) Checks if wheel speed sensor is shorted to ground.
3) Checks if wheel speed sensor circuit is shorted to battery.
4) Ensures wheel speed sensor circuit has good continuity.
5) Checks for short to ground in wheel speed sensor wiring.
6) Checks for short to voltage in wheel speed sensor wiring.

DIAGNOSTIC AIDS

Intermittent problem may be caused by poor connection, rubbed-through wire insulation or broken wire inside insulation. Enhanced Diagnostic feature of Tech 1 can be used to check frequency of problem. See ENHANCED DIAGNOSTICS under DIAGNOSIS & TESTING.

If ABS warning light only comes on during moist conditions, thoroughly check wheel speed sensor circuits for signs of water intrusion. To simulate moist conditions, spray affected wheel speed sensor with a 5 percent salt water solution (mix 2 teaspoons of salt with 12 ounces of water). Test drive vehicle. Vehicle speed must exceed 4 MPH. If code returns immediately, replace suspected harness.

Any circuit suspected of causing intermittent problem should be thoroughly checked for backed-out terminals, improper mating, broken connector locks, damaged terminals or poor terminal-to-wiring connections.

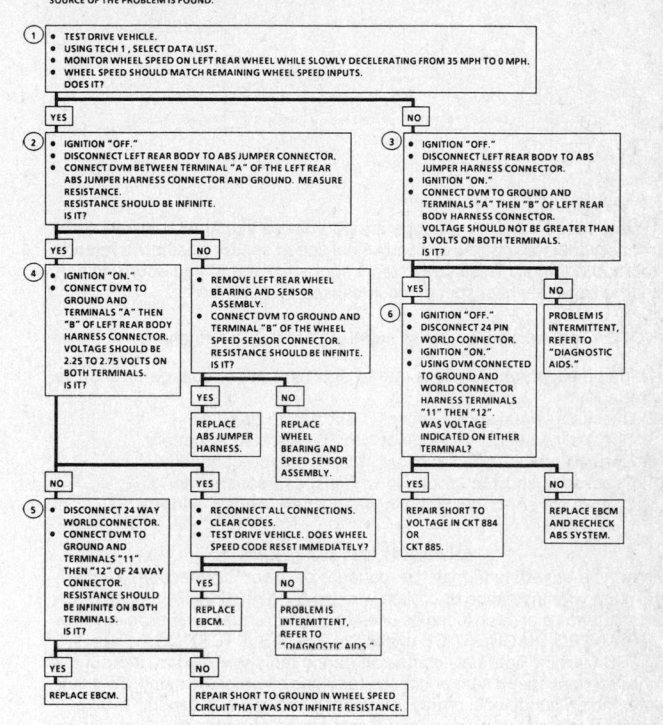

92122572   92122598

CODE A035
RIGHT REAR WHEEL SENSOR
SHORTED TO BATTERY OR GROUND

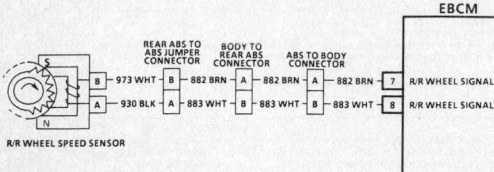

EBCM

Wheel speed sensors produce an AC voltage signal with a frequency proportional to wheel speed and wheel speed sensor position in relation to a toothed ring. This code detects shorts to ground and shorts to battery voltage in wheel speed circuit sensed by EBCM.

NOTE: Test numbers refer to numbers on diagnostic chart.

1) Identifies whether code is due to short to battery voltage or short to ground.
2) Checks if wheel speed sensor is shorted to ground.
3) Checks if wheel speed sensor circuit is shorted to battery.
4) Ensures wheel speed sensor circuit has good continuity.
5) Checks for short to ground in wheel speed sensor wiring.
6) Checks for short to voltage in wheel speed sensor wiring.

DIAGNOSTIC AIDS

Intermittent problem may be caused by poor connection, rubbed-through wire insulation or broken wire inside insulation. Enhanced Diagnostic feature of Tech 1 can be used to check frequency of problem. See ENHANCED DIAGNOSTICS under DIAGNOSIS & TESTING.

If ABS warning light only comes on during moist conditions, thoroughly check wheel speed sensor circuits for signs of water intrusion. To simulate moist conditions, spray affected wheel speed sensor with a 5 percent salt water solution (mix 2 teaspoons of salt with 12 ounces of water). Test drive vehicle. Vehicle speed must exceed 4 MPH. If code returns immediately, replace suspected harness.

Any circuit suspected of causing intermittent problem should be thoroughly checked for backed-out terminals, improper mating, broken connector locks, damaged terminals or poor terminal-to-wiring connections.

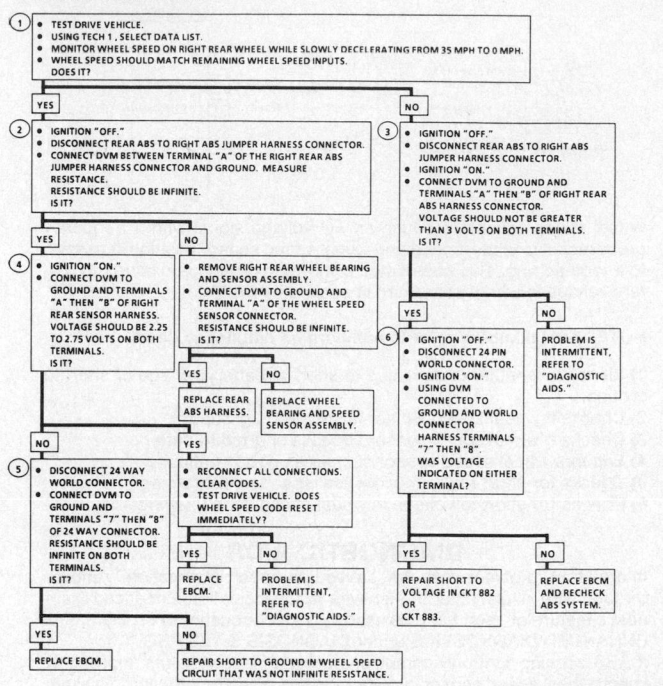

92B22575 92C22600

CODE A036
SYSTEM VOLTAGE LOW

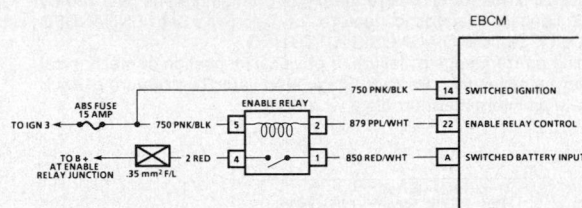

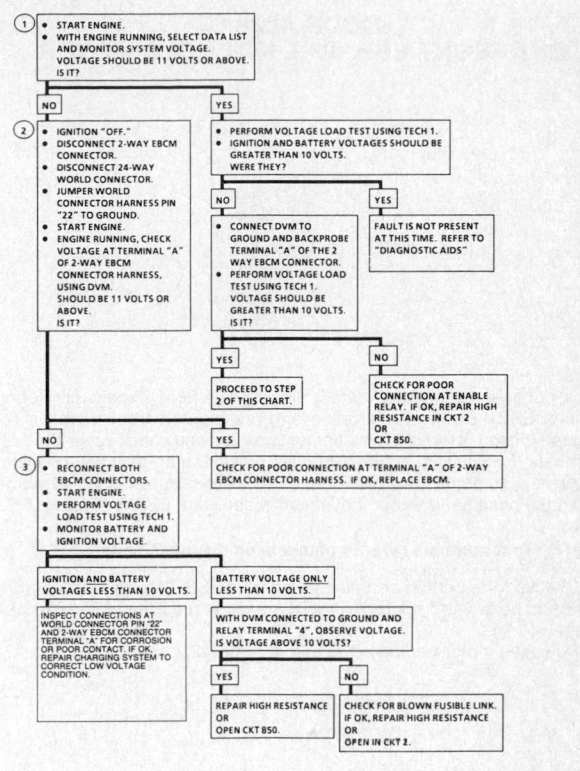

This code checks voltage available to EBCM. If voltage drops below 11 volts, ABS performance may be affected. During ABS operation, several current requirements will cause battery voltage to drop. Voltage is monitored prior to ABS activation and during ABS activation. Code A036 will set if voltage falls below minimum level required for adequate ABS performance.

NOTE: Test numbers refer to numbers on diagnostic chart.

1) Checks voltage available at EBCM terminal "A". If voltage is representative of a good charging system condition, fault is not present.
2) Isolates EBCM to check charging system performance.
3) Isolates low voltage condition to high circuit resistance or incorrect charging system operation.

DIAGNOSTIC AIDS

Intermittent problem may be caused by poor connection, rubbed-through wire insulation or broken wire inside insulation. Enhanced Diagnostic feature of Tech 1 can be used to check frequency of problem. See ENHANCED DIAGNOSTICS under DIAGNOSIS & TESTING.
Any circuit suspected of causing intermittent problem should be thoroughly checked for backed-out terminals, improper mating, broken connector locks, damaged terminals or poor terminal-to-wiring connections.
While performing voltage load test, if ONLY ignition voltage drops below acceptable voltage limits, check circuit No. 750 (Pink/Black wire) for high resistance or open circuit.

92D22270   92D22601

CODE A037
SYSTEM VOLTAGE HIGH

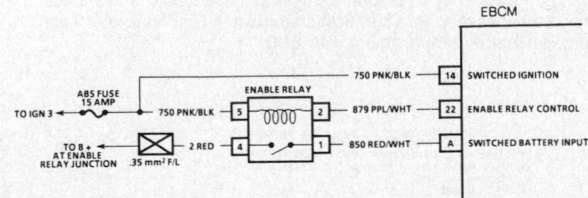

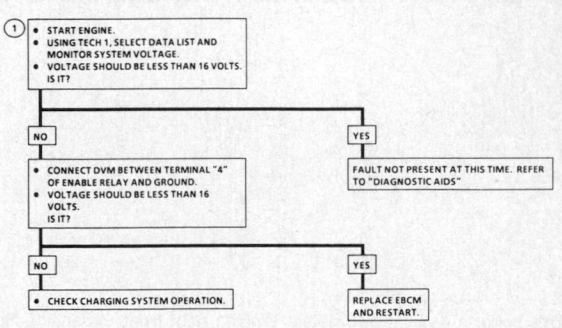

This code detects high vehicle voltage levels prior to any required ABS motor movement (i.e. initialization or ABS). If voltage is excessive, demagnetization of motor magnets may eventually affect or eliminate ABS operation.

NOTE: Test numbers refer to numbers on diagnostic chart.

1) Checks voltage level being received by EBCM. If high voltage is present, charging system malfunction is indicated.

DIAGNOSTIC AIDS

An intermittent problem may be caused by a poor connection, rubbed through wire insulation, or a wire that is broken inside insulation. Frequency of problem can be checked by using Enhanced Diagnostic feature of Tech 1. See ENHANCED DIAGNOSTICS under DIAGNOSIS & TESTING.
Any circuit that is suspected of causing intermittent problem should be checked thoroughly for backed-out terminals, improper mating, broken connector locks, damaged terminals, or poor terminal-to-wiring connections.

THIS CHART ASSUMES THAT A CURRENT CODE IS STORED INDICATING THAT THIS FAULT IS PRESENT.

92D22270   92J22268

CODE A038
LEFT FRONT ESB WILL NOT HOLD MOTOR

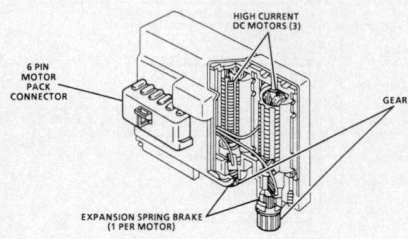

This code is designed to detect slipping left front Expansion Spring Brake (ESB). During initialization and braking, left front motor is re-homed (piston is moved to its upmost position and check valve lifted off its seat). If ESB slips, motor/piston will move. During next key-on initialization, a re-home of motor verifies motor/piston remained at home (upmost) position. If motor movement is detected, ESB is slipping.

NOTE: Test numbers refer to numbers on diagnostic chart.

1) Checks for a broken or defective left front ESB. This causes left front piston to be driven back by hydraulic pressure, resulting in pedal movement.
2) Releases motor pack tension before removal.

DIAGNOSTIC AIDS

An intermittent Code A038 may result from a mechanical part of system which sticks, binds, or slips. Frequency of problem can be checked by using Enhanced Diagnostic feature of Tech 1. See ENHANCED DIAGNOSTICS under DIAGNOSIS & TESTING.
Depending on frequency of failure, a physical inspection of mechanical parts may be necessary. Perform Static Modulator Test feature of Tech 1 to locate an intermittent problem with ESB.

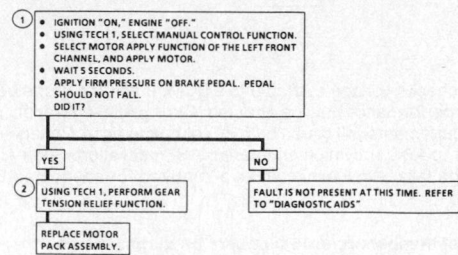

92F22272   92H22274

CODE A041
RIGHT FRONT ESB WILL NOT HOLD MOTOR

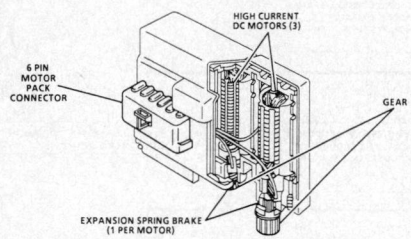

This code is designed to detect slipping right front Expansion Spring Brake (ESB). During initialization and braking, right front motor is re-homed (piston is moved to its upmost position and check valve lifted off its seat). If ESB slips, motor/piston will move. During next key-on initialization, a re-home of motor verifies motor/piston remained at home (upmost) position. If motor movement is detected, ESB is slipping.

NOTE: Test numbers refer to numbers on diagnostic chart.

1) Checks for a broken or defective right front ESB. This causes left front piston to be driven back by hydraulic pressure, resulting in pedal movement.
2) Releases motor pack tension before removal.

DIAGNOSTIC AIDS

An intermittent Code A041 may result from a mechanical part of system which sticks, binds, or slips. Frequency of problem can be checked by using Enhanced Diagnostic feature of Tech 1. See ENHANCED DIAGNOSTICS under DIAGNOSIS & TESTING.
Depending on frequency of failure, a physical inspection of mechanical parts may be necessary. Perform Static Modulator Test feature of Tech 1 to locate an intermittent problem with ESB.

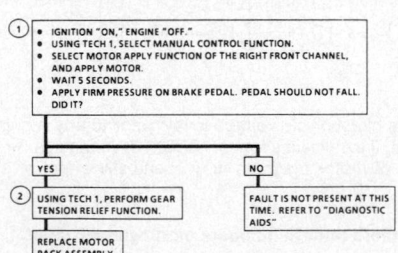

92F22272   92G22562

CODE A042
REAR AXLE ESB WILL NOT HOLD MOTOR

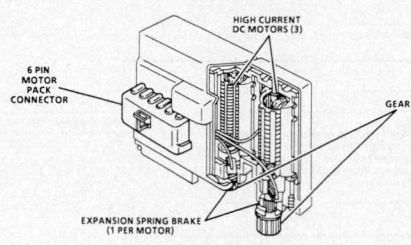

This code is designed to detect slipping rear axle Expansion Spring Brake (ESB). During initialization and braking, rear motor is re-homed (piston is moved to its upmost position and check valve lifted off its seat). If ESB slips, motor/piston will move. During next key-on initialization, a re-home of motor verifies motor/piston remained at home (upmost) position. If motor movement is detected, ESB is slipping.

NOTE: Test numbers refer to numbers on diagnostic chart.

1) Checks for a broken or defective rear axle ESB. This causes left front piston to be driven back by hydraulic pressure, resulting in pedal movement.
2) Releases motor pack tension before removal.

DIAGNOSTIC AIDS

An intermittent Code A042 may result from a mechanical part of system which sticks, binds, or slips. Frequency of problem can be checked by using Enhanced Diagnostic feature of Tech 1. See ENHANCED DIAGNOSTICS under DIAGNOSIS & TESTING.
Depending on frequency of failure, a physical inspection of mechanical parts may be necessary. Perform Static Modulator Test feature of Tech 1 to locate an intermittent problem with ESB.

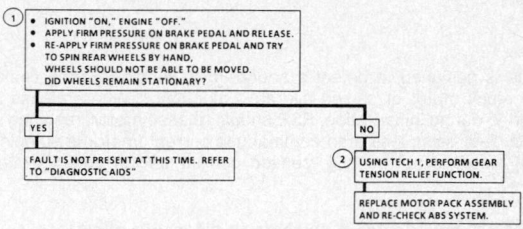

92F22272   92I22564

CODE A044
LEFT FRONT CHANNEL WILL NOT MOVE

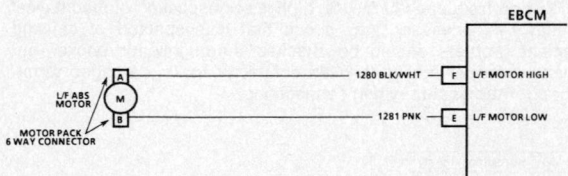

This code is designed to detect a bound-up Expansion Spring Brake (ESB), a stuck motor or seized hydraulic modulator. When release is commanded during initialization, ESB should release motor, resulting in sensed current being less than commanded current (motor is spinning freely). If motor is not moving, sensed current will be equal to stall current.

NOTE: Test numbers refer to numbers on diagnostic chart.

1) Checks for motor movement.
2) Releases motor pack tension before removal.
3) Isolates fault to either the motor pack or ABS hydraulic modulator.

DIAGNOSTIC AIDS

An intermittent Code A044 may result from a mechanical part of system which sticks, binds, or slips. Frequency of problem can be checked by using Enhanced Diagnostic feature of Tech 1. See ENHANCED DIAGNOSTICS under DIAGNOSIS & TESTING. Code A044 may set after modulator disassembly if modulator pistons are positioned at bottom of bore.

Any circuit that is suspected of causing intermittent problem should be checked thoroughly for backed-out terminals, improper mating, broken connector locks, damaged terminals, or poor terminal-to-wiring connections.

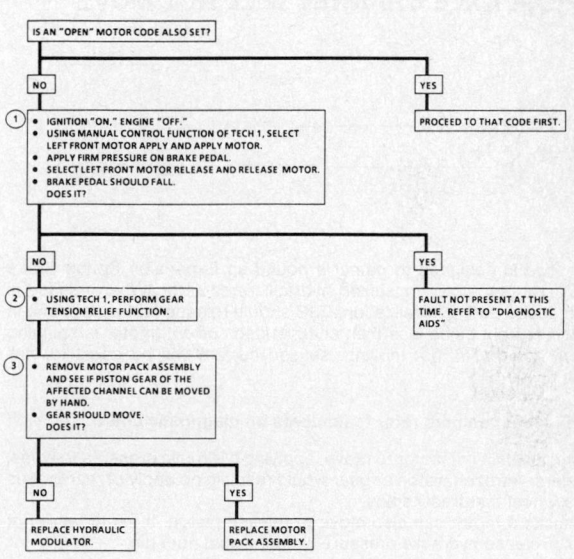

92E22578   92J22581

CODE A045
RIGHT FRONT CHANNEL WILL NOT MOVE

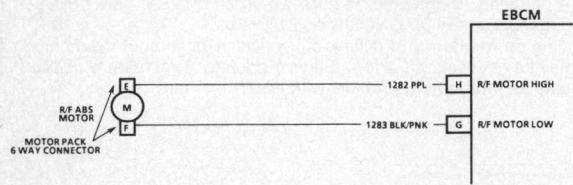

This code is designed to detect a bound-up Expansion Spring Brake (ESB), a stuck motor or seized hydraulic modulator. When release is commanded during initialization, ESB should release motor, resulting in sensed current being less than commanded current (motor is spinning freely). If motor is not moving, sensed current will be equal to stall current.

NOTE: Test numbers refer to numbers on diagnostic chart.

1) Checks for motor movement.
2) Releases motor pack tension before removal.
3) Isolates fault to either the motor pack or ABS hydraulic modulator.

DIAGNOSTIC AIDS

An intermittent Code A045 may result from a mechanical part of system which sticks, binds, or slips. Frequency of problem can be checked by using Enhanced Diagnostic feature of Tech 1. See ENHANCED DIAGNOSTICS under DIAGNOSIS & TESTING. Code A045 may set after modulator disassembly if modulator pistons are positioned at bottom of bore.

Any circuit that is suspected of causing intermittent problem should be checked thoroughly for backed-out terminals, improper mating, broken connector locks, damaged terminals, or poor terminal-to-wiring connections.

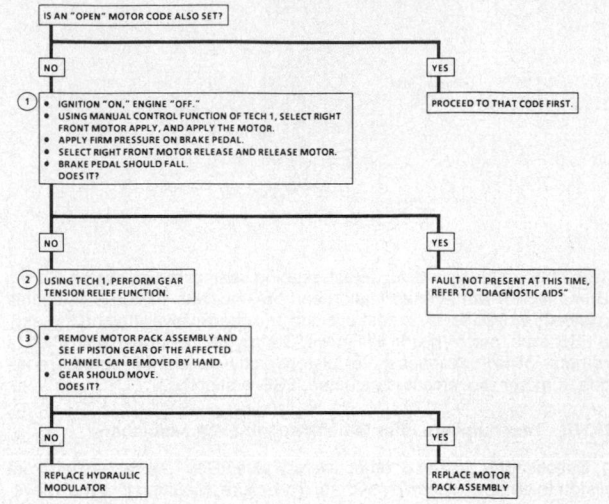

92C22584   92F22587

CODE A046
REAR AXLE CHANNEL WILL NOT MOVE

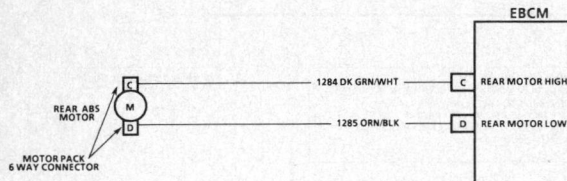

This code is designed to detect a bound-up Expansion Spring Brake (ESB), a stuck motor or seized hydraulic modulator. When release is commanded during initialization, ESB should release motor, resulting in sensed current being less than commanded current (motor is spinning freely). If motor is not moving, sensed current will be equal to stall current.

NOTE: Test numbers refer to numbers on diagnostic chart.

1) Checks ability of motor to move, applying hydraulic pressure to wheel cylinders. A frozen piston or gear would result in no apply of rear brakes and a wheel that freely spins.
2) Checks if motor can also move to release piston. If motor were not able to release hydraulic pressure, wheel would not spin.
3) Releases motor pack tension before removal.
4) Isolates fault to either the motor pack or ABS hydraulic modulator.

DIAGNOSTIC AIDS

An intermittent Code A046 may result from a mechanical part of system which sticks, binds, or slips. Frequency of problem can be checked by using Enhanced Diagnostic feature of Tech 1. See ENHANCED DIAGNOSTICS under DIAGNOSIS & TESTING. Code A046 may set after modulator disassembly if modulator pistons are positioned at bottom of bore.

Depending on frequency of failure, a physical inspection of mechanical parts may be necessary. Any circuit that is suspected of causing intermittent problem should be checked thoroughly for backed-out terminals, improper mating, broken connector locks, damaged terminals, or poor terminal-to-wiring connections.

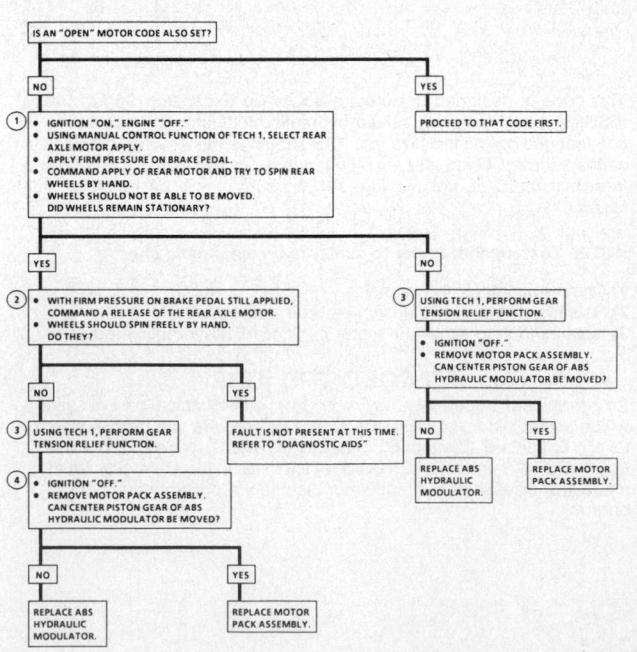

92D22593   92F22595

CODE A047
LEFT FRONT MOTOR SPINS FREELY

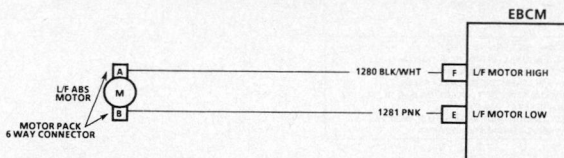

This code is designed to detect a stripped gear or nut assembly during initialization. During the homing sequence, piston should reach top of bore resulting in a stalled motor. If motor does not stall, motor must be free spinning with little or no resistance, indicating a nut, screw or gear failure.

NOTE: Test numbers refer to numbers on diagnostic chart.

1) Positions motor at bottom of its travel.
2) Determines if gear or nut is stripped. If either are stripped, hydraulic pressure applied from master cylinder will not overcome hydraulic ball screw, and brake pedal will not rise.
3) When ball screw reaches top of its travel during full application, motor should stall. If motor continues to run, this indicates a gear or nut is stripped.
4) Releases motor pack tension before removal.

DIAGNOSTIC AIDS

An intermittent Code A047 may result from a mechanical part of system which sticks, binds, or slips. Frequency of problem can be checked by using Enhanced Diagnostic feature of Tech 1. See ENHANCED DIAGNOSTICS under DIAGNOSIS & TESTING. If Code A047 only sets once and Code A056 also sets, go to Code A056 diagnostics.
If intermittent and enhanced diagnostics shows Code A047 sets during ABS operation, go to Code A056 diagnostics. Depending on frequency of code setting, perform a physical inspection of suspected mechanical parts.

92E22578   92H22597

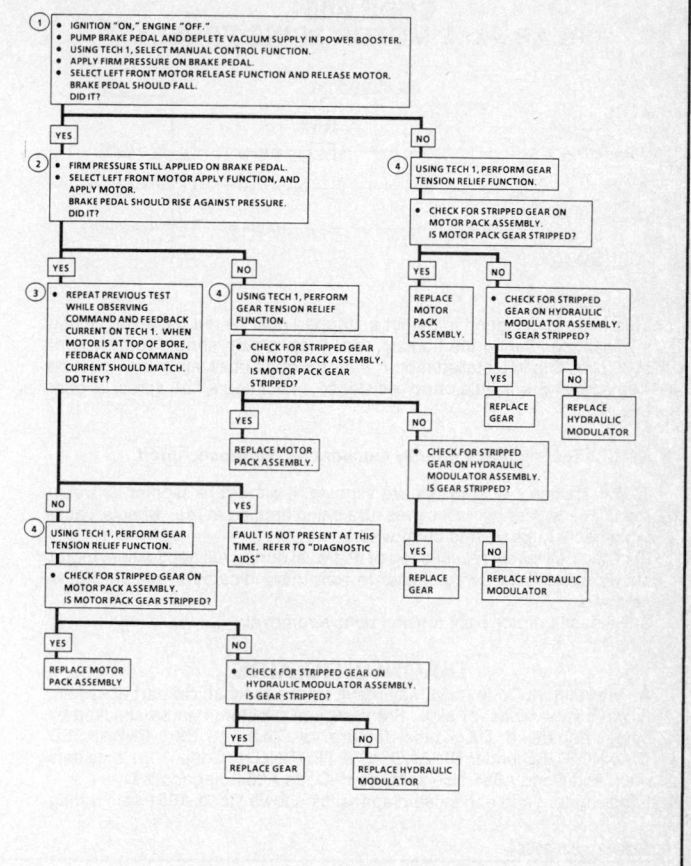

CODE A048
RIGHT FRONT MOTOR SPINS FREELY

ABS operation, go to Code A061 diagnostics. Depending on frequency of code setting, perform a physical inspection of suspected mechanical parts.

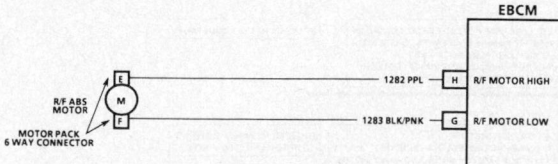

This code is designed to detect a stripped gear or nut assembly during initialization. During the homing sequence, piston should reach top of bore resulting in a stalled motor. If motor does not stall, motor must be free spinning with little or no resistance, indicating a nut, screw or gear failure.

NOTE: Test numbers refer to numbers on diagnostic chart.

1) Positions motor at bottom of its travel.
2) Determines if gear or nut is stripped. If either are stripped, hydraulic pressure applied from master cylinder will not overcome hydraulic ball screw, and brake pedal will not rise.
3) When ball screw reaches top of its travel during full application, motor should stall. If motor continues to run, this indicates a gear or nut is stripped.
4) Releases motor pack tension before removal.

DIAGNOSTIC AIDS

An intermittent Code A048 may result from a mechanical part of system which sticks, binds, or slips. Frequency of problem can be checked by using Enhanced Diagnostic feature of Tech 1. See ENHANCED DIAGNOSTICS under DIAGNOSIS & TESTING. If Code A048 only sets once and Code A061 also sets, go to Code A061 diagnostics.
If intermittent and enhanced diagnostics shows Code A048 sets during

92C22584   92J22599

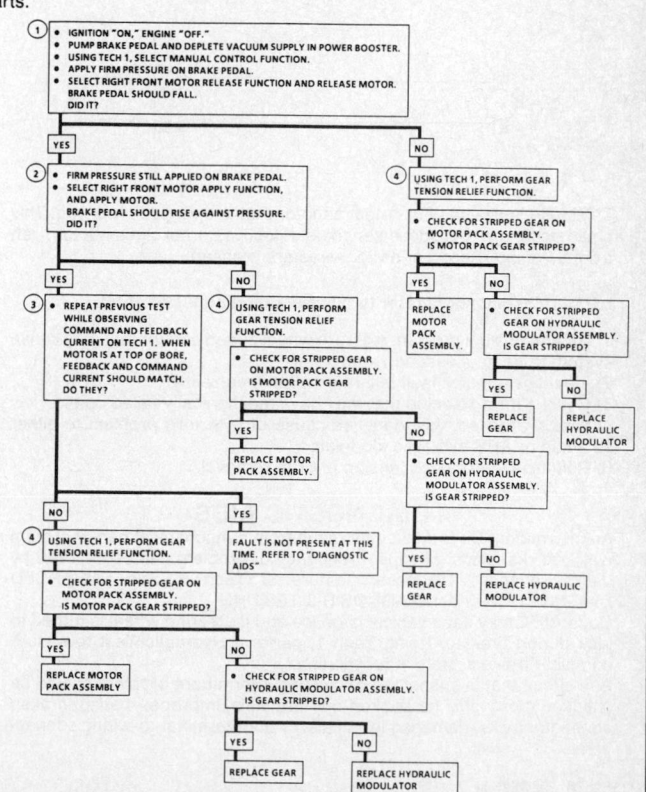

CODE A051
REAR AXLE MOTOR SPINS FREELY

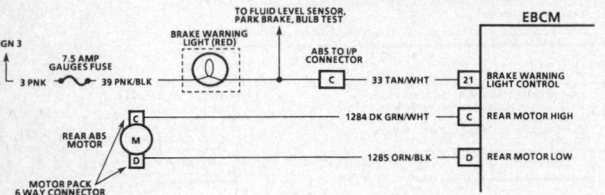

This code is designed to detect a stripped gear or nut assembly during initialization. During the homing sequence, piston should reach top of bore resulting in a stalled motor. If motor does not stall, motor must be free spinning with little or no resistance, indicating a nut, screw or gear failure.

NOTE: Test numbers refer to numbers on diagnostic chart.

1) Determines if gear or nut are slipping. If either are slipping, it would result in a lack of hydraulic pressure being applied at rear wheels, causing wheels to be able to be moved.
2) When ball screw reaches top of its travel during full application, motor should stall. If motor continues to run, this indicates a gear or nut is stripped.
3) Releases motor pack tension before removal.

DIAGNOSTIC AIDS

An intermittent Code A051 may result from a mechanical part of system which sticks, binds, or slips. Frequency of problem can be checked by using Enhanced Diagnostic feature of Tech 1. See ENHANCED DIAGNOSTICS under DIAGNOSIS & TESTING. If Code A051 only sets once and Code A064 also sets, go to Code A064 diagnostics. If intermittent and enhanced diagnostics shows Code A051 sets during

92E22602   92F22603

ABS operation, go to Code A064 diagnostics. Depending on frequency of code setting, perform a physical inspection of suspected mechanical parts.

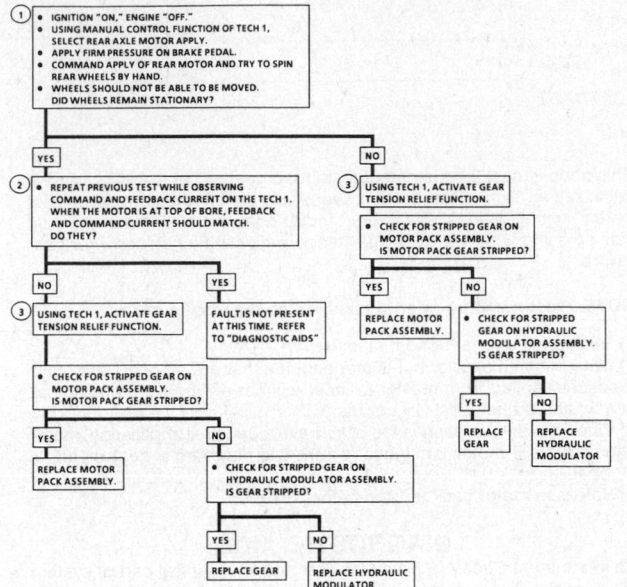

CODE A052
LEFT FRONT CHANNEL IN RELEASE TOO LONG

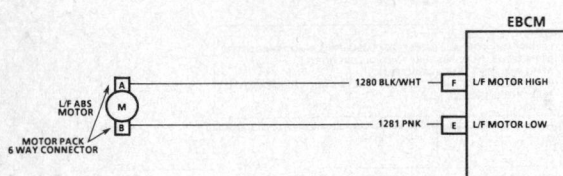

This code is designed to detect a motor that is energized too long. This could occur if wheel speed sensor is defective, motor does not turn, left front solenoid is open or motor wires are crossed.

NOTE: Test numbers refer to numbers on diagnostic chart.

1) Determines if a problem exists in wheel speed sensor that may cause system to be in release too long.
2) Identifies a motor fault failure or wired incorrectly.
3) Checks for a solenoid that may have mechanically failed open.
4) If step 3) failed, this identifies cause of hydraulic problem to either solenoid or ABS hydraulic modulator.
5) Releases motor pack tension prior to removal.

DIAGNOSTIC AIDS

An intermittent Code A052 may result from a mechanical part of system which sticks, binds, or slips. Frequency of problem can be checked by using Enhanced Diagnostic feature of Tech 1. See ENHANCED DIAGNOSTICS under DIAGNOSIS & TESTING.
Code A052 may set if vehicle is on ice and if steering wheel is turned to lock during braking. Using Tech 1, perform Hydraulic Test to ensure complete brake system is functioning.
Any circuit that is suspected of causing intermittent problem should be checked thoroughly for backed-out terminals, improper mating, broken connector locks, damaged terminals, or poor terminal-to-wiring connections.

92E22578   92G22604

CODE A053
RIGHT FRONT CHANNEL IN RELEASE TOO LONG

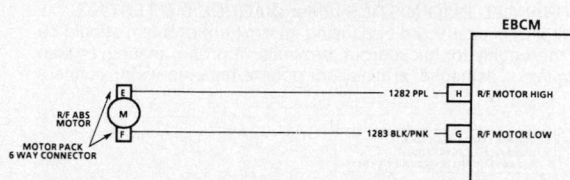

This code is designed to detect a motor that is energized too long. This could occur if wheel speed sensor is defective, motor does not turn, right front solenoid is open or motor wires are crossed.

NOTE: Test numbers refer to numbers on diagnostic chart.

1) Determines if a problem exists in wheel speed sensor that may cause system to be in release too long.
2) Identifies a motor fault failure or wired incorrectly.
3) Checks for a solenoid that may have mechanically failed open.
4) If step 3) failed, this identifies cause of hydraulic problem to either solenoid or ABS hydraulic modulator.
5) Releases motor pack tension prior to removal.

DIAGNOSTIC AIDS

An intermittent Code A053 may result from a mechanical part of system which sticks, binds, or slips. Frequency of problem can be checked by using Enhanced Diagnostic feature of Tech 1. See ENHANCED DIAGNOSTICS under DIAGNOSIS & TESTING.
Code A053 may set if vehicle is on ice and if steering wheel is turned to lock during braking. Using Tech 1, perform Hydraulic Test to ensure complete brake system is functioning.
Any circuit that is suspected of causing intermittent problem should be checked thoroughly for backed-out terminals, improper mating, broken connector locks, damaged terminals, or poor terminal-to-wiring connections.

92C22584   92H22605

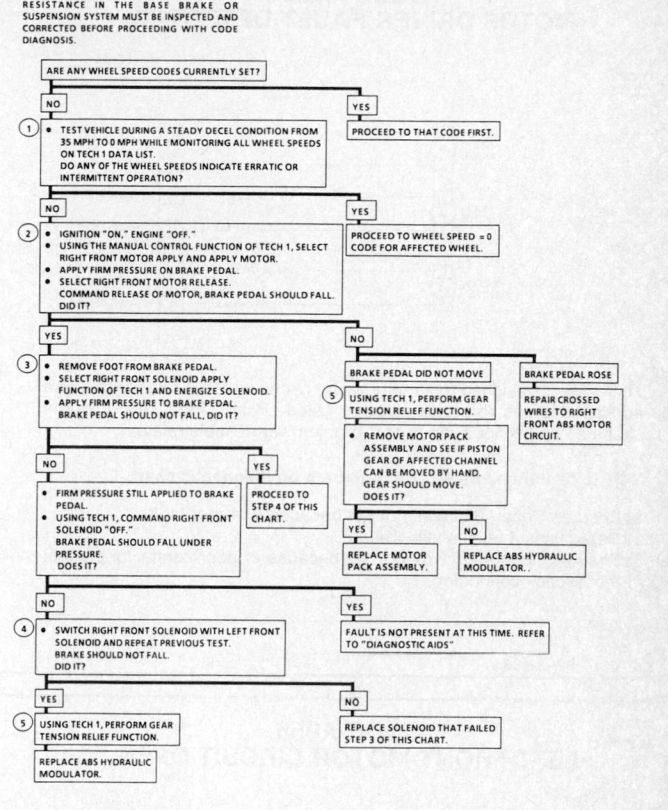

CODE A054
REAR AXLE CHANNEL IN RELEASE TOO LONG

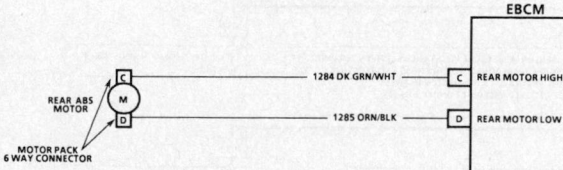

This code is designed to detect a motor that is energized too long. This could occur if wheel speed sensor is defective, motor does not turn or motor wires are crossed.

NOTE: Test numbers refer to numbers on diagnostic chart.

1) Determines if a problem exists in wheel speed sensor that may cause system to be in release too long.
2) Checks for a wheel speed sensor that may stick or bind due to mechanical fault.
3) Determines if motor is capable of moving and applying rear wheel hydraulic piston.
4) Ensures motor wiring is not crossed.
5) Releases motor pack tension before removal.
6) Determines if no-brake application fault is due to motor pack or hydraulic modulator.

DIAGNOSTIC AIDS

An intermittent Code A054 may result from a mechanical part of system which sticks, binds, or slips. Frequency of problem can be checked by using Enhanced Diagnostic feature of Tech 1. See ENHANCED DIAGNOSTICS under DIAGNOSIS & TESTING.
Any circuit that is suspected of causing intermittent problem should be checked thoroughly for backed-out terminals, improper mating, broken connector locks, damaged terminals, or poor terminal-to-wiring connections.

92D22593   92I22606

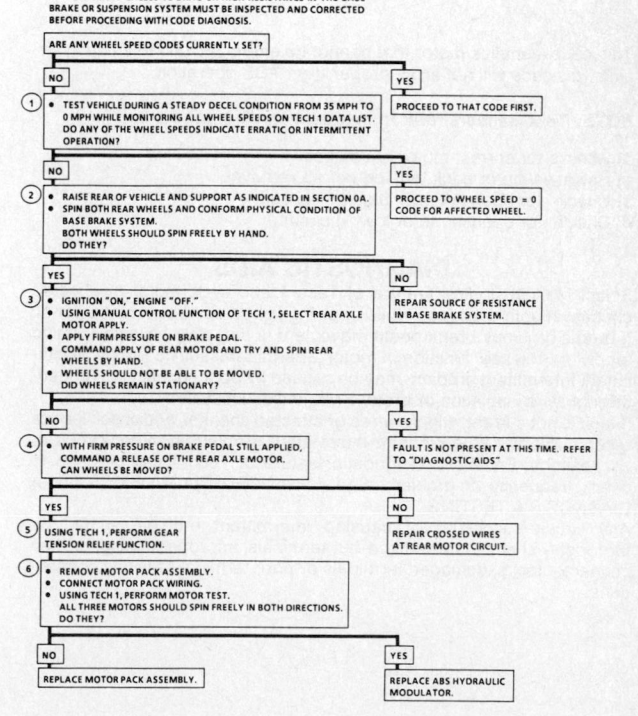

CODE A055
MOTOR DRIVER FAULT DETECTED

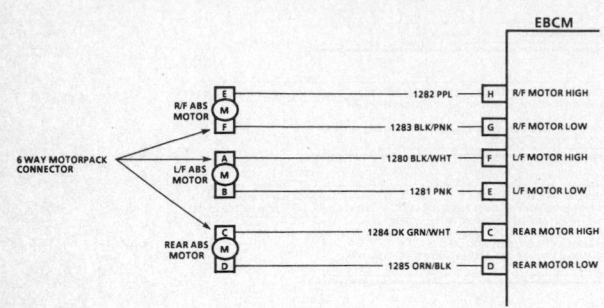

This code is designed to identify which circuit has failed and may cause additional codes to set to pinpoint failed circuit. Code A055 ensures cause of fault is not a result of a problem with enable relay.

NOTE: Test numbers refer to numbers on diagnostic chart.

1) Ensures Code A055 was not set because of motor fault.
2) Determines if fault is still present.
3) Ensures Code A055 was not set because of poor connector contact at motor pack connector.

92J22607   92A22608

DIAGNOSTIC AIDS

An intermittent problem may be caused by a poor connection, rubbed through wire insulation, or a wire broken inside insulation. Frequency of problem can be checked by using Enhanced Diagnostic feature of Tech 1. See ENHANCED DIAGNOSTICS under DIAGNOSIS & TESTING. Any circuit that is suspected of causing intermittent problem should be checked thoroughly for backed-out terminals, improper mating, broken connector locks, damaged terminals, or poor terminal-to-wiring connections.

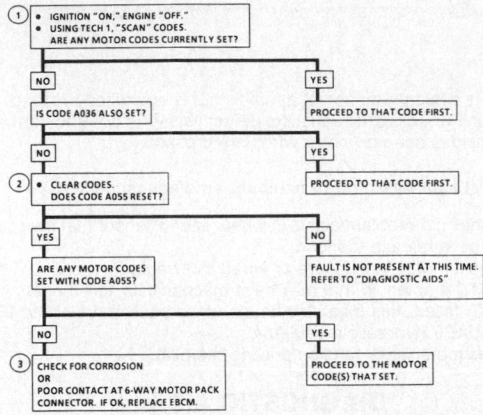

CODE A056
LEFT FRONT MOTOR CIRCUIT OPEN

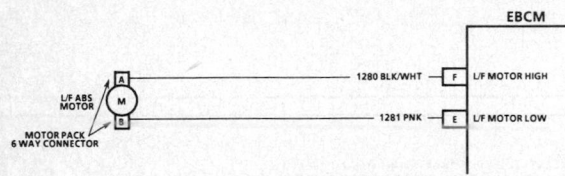

This code identifies motor that cannot be energized due to an open circuit. This code will not allow proper front ABS operation.

NOTE: Test numbers refer to numbers on diagnostic chart.

1) Checks for correct motor resistance.
2) Releases motor pack tension before removal.
3) Checks for open in motor high (+) circuit.
4) Checks for open in motor low (-) circuit.

DIAGNOSTIC AIDS

Select Manual Control feature of Tech 1 and cycle motor of affected channel in both directions while applying light pressure on brake pedal. If erratic or jumpy brake pedal movement is detected while performing "apply" or "release" function of motor, intermittent fault code may be indicated. Intermittent problem may be caused by poor connection, rubbed-through wire insulation or broken wire inside insulation.
If fault is not current, wiggle wires of affected channel, and check if code resets. This will help pinpoint intermittent problem in motor circuit or connections. Enhanced Diagnostic feature of Tech 1 can be used to check frequency of problem. See ENHANCED DIAGNOSTICS under DIAGNOSIS & TESTING.
Any circuit suspected of causing intermittent problem should be thoroughly checked for backed-out terminals, improper mating, broken connector locks, damaged terminals or poor terminal-to-wiring connections.

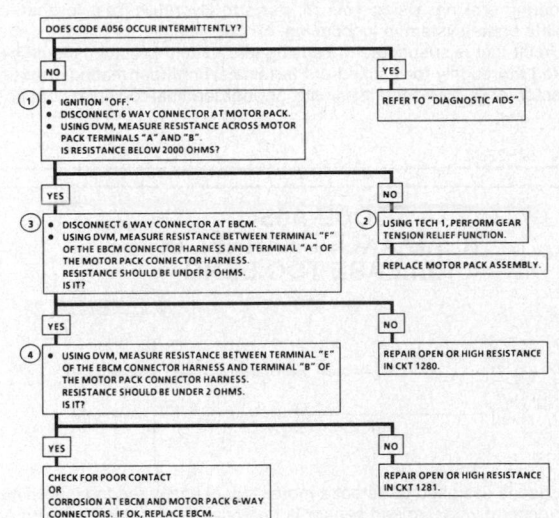

92E22578   92B22609

CODE A057
LEFT FRONT MOTOR CIRCUIT SHORTED TO GROUND

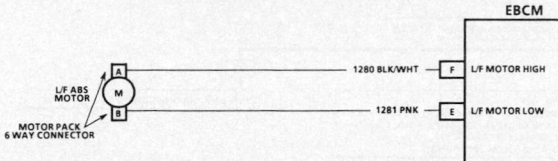

This code identifies motor circuit that is shorted to ground. Fault will not allow motor to be controlled at requested current rate or will cause driver circuit to allow current directly to ground.

NOTE: Test numbers refer to numbers on diagnostic chart.

1) Checks for short to ground in motor high (+) circuit.
2) Checks for short to ground in motor low (-) circuit.
3) Checks for motor internally shorted to ground.
4) Releases motor pack tension before removal.

DIAGNOSTIC AIDS

Select Manual Control feature of Tech 1 and cycle motor of affected channel in both directions while applying light pressure on brake pedal. If erratic or jumpy brake pedal movement is detected while performing "apply" or "release" function of motor, intermittent fault code may be indicated. Intermittent problem may be caused by poor connection, rubbed-through wire insulation or broken wire inside insulation.
If fault is not current, wiggle wires of affected channel, and check if code resets. This will help pinpoint intermittent problem in motor circuit or connections. Enhanced Diagnostic feature of Tech 1 can be used to check frequency of problem. See ENHANCED DIAGNOSTICS under DIAGNOSIS & TESTING.

92E22578   92E22610

Any circuit suspected of causing intermittent problem should be thoroughly checked for backed-out terminals, improper mating, broken connector locks, damaged terminals or poor terminal-to-wiring connections.

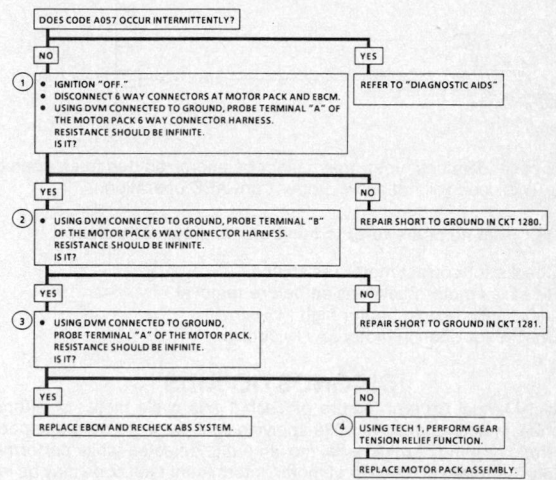

THIS CHART ASSUMES THAT A CURRENT CODE IS STORED INDICATING THAT THIS FAULT IS PRESENT.

CODE A058
LEFT FRONT MOTOR CIRCUIT SHORTED TO BATTERY OR MOTOR SHORTED

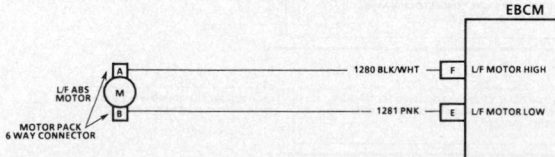

This code identifies motor circuit that is shorted to battery voltage, or motor with low or no resistance. Fault will not allow motor to be controlled at requested current rate, cause it to rotate in opposite direction or cause it to be inoperative.

NOTE: Test numbers refer to numbers on diagnostic chart.

1) Checks for short to battery voltage in motor high (+) circuit.
2) Checks for short to battery voltage in motor low (-) circuit.
3) Checks for motor internally shorted.
4) Releases motor pack tension before removal.

DIAGNOSTIC AIDS

Select Manual Control feature of Tech 1 and cycle motor of affected channel in both directions while applying light pressure on brake pedal. If erratic or jumpy brake pedal movement is detected while performing "apply" or "release" function of motor, intermittent fault code may be indicated. Intermittent problem may be caused by poor connection, rubbed-through wire insulation or broken wire inside insulation.
If fault is not current, wiggle wires of affected channel, and check if code resets. This will help pinpoint intermittent problem in motor circuit or connections. Enhanced Diagnostic feature of Tech 1 can be used to check frequency of problem. See ENHANCED DIAGNOSTICS under DIAGNOSIS & TESTING.

92E22578   92F22611

Any circuit suspected of causing intermittent problem should be thoroughly checked for backed-out terminals, improper mating, broken connector locks, damaged terminals or poor terminal-to-wiring connections.

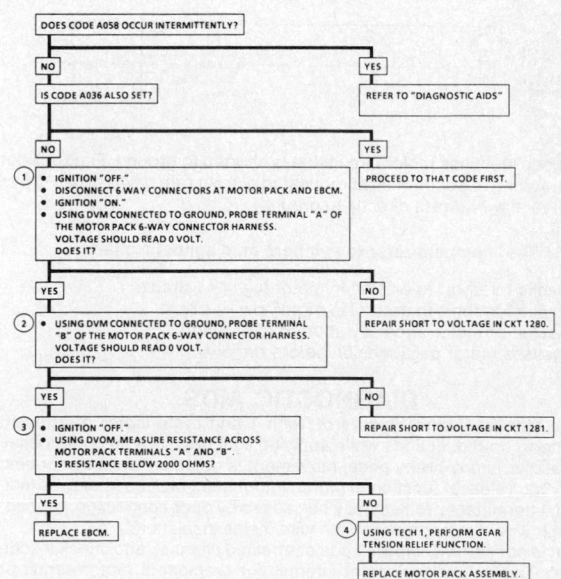

CODE A061
RIGHT FRONT MOTOR CIRCUIT OPEN

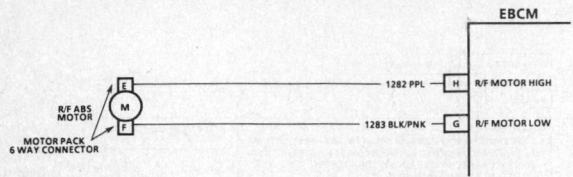

This code identifies motor that cannot be energized due to an open circuit. This code will not allow proper front ABS operation.

NOTE: Test numbers refer to numbers on diagnostic chart.

1) Checks for correct motor resistance.
2) Releases motor pack tension before removal.
3) Checks for open in motor high (+) circuit.
4) Checks for open in motor low (-) circuit.

DIAGNOSTIC AIDS

Select Manual Control feature of Tech 1 and cycle motor of affected channel in both directions while applying light pressure on brake pedal. If erratic or jumpy brake pedal movement is detected while performing "apply" or "release" function of motor, intermittent fault code may be indicated. Intermittent problem may be caused by poor connection, rubbed-through wire insulation or broken wire inside insulation.
If fault is not current, wiggle wires of affected channel, and check if code resets. This will help pinpoint intermittent problem in motor circuit or connections. Enhanced Diagnostic feature of Tech 1 can be used to check frequency of problem. See ENHANCED DIAGNOSTICS under DIAGNOSIS & TESTING.

Any circuit suspected of causing intermittent problem should be thoroughly checked for backed-out terminals, improper mating, broken connector locks, damaged terminals or poor terminal-to-wiring connections.

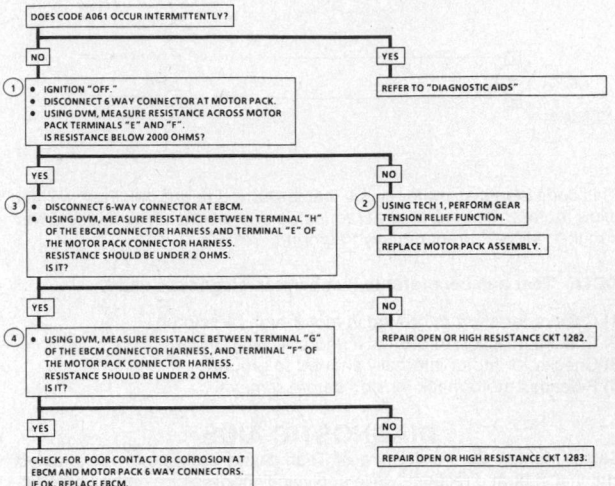

92C22584   92G22612

CODE A062
RIGHT FRONT MOTOR CIRCUIT
SHORTED TO GROUND

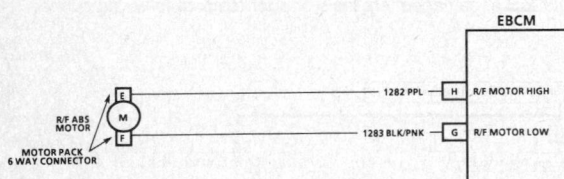

This code identifies motor circuit that is shorted to ground. Fault will not allow motor to be controlled at requested current rate or will cause driver circuit to allow current directly to ground.

NOTE: Test numbers refer to numbers on diagnostic chart.

1) Checks for short to ground in motor high (+) circuit.
2) Checks for short to ground in motor low (-) circuit.
3) Checks for motor internally shorted to ground.
4) Releases motor pack tension before removal.

DIAGNOSTIC AIDS

Select Manual Control feature of Tech 1 and cycle motor of affected channel in both directions while applying light pressure on brake pedal. If erratic or jumpy brake pedal movement is detected while performing "apply" or "release" function of motor, intermittent fault code may be indicated. Intermittent problem may be caused by poor connection, rubbed-through wire insulation or broken wire inside insulation.
If fault is not current, wiggle wires of affected channel, and check if code resets. This will help pinpoint intermittent problem in motor circuit or connections. Enhanced Diagnostic feature of Tech 1 can be used to check frequency of problem. See ENHANCED DIAGNOSTICS under DIAGNOSIS & TESTING.
Any circuit suspected of causing intermittent problem should be thoroughly checked for backed-out terminals, improper mating, broken connector locks, damaged terminals or poor terminal-to-wiring connections.

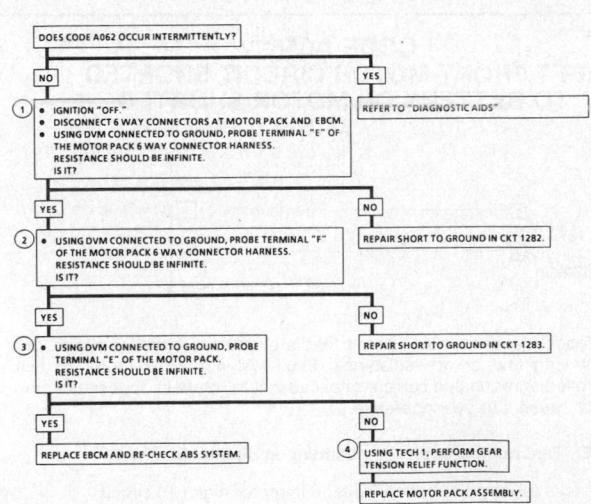

THIS CHART ASSUMES THAT A CURRENT CODE IS STORED INDICATING THAT THIS FAULT IS PRESENT.

92C22584   92H22613

CODE A063
RIGHT FRONT MOTOR CIRCUIT
SHORTED TO BATTERY

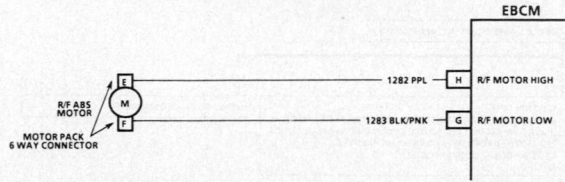

This code identifies motor circuit that is shorted to battery voltage, or motor with low or no resistance. Fault will not allow motor to be controlled at requested current rate, cause it to rotate in opposite direction or cause it to be inoperative.

NOTE: Test numbers refer to numbers on diagnostic chart.

1) Checks for short to battery voltage in motor high (+) circuit.
2) Checks for short to battery voltage in motor low (-) circuit.
3) Checks for motor internally shorted.
4) Releases motor pack tension before removal.

DIAGNOSTIC AIDS

Select Manual Control feature of Tech 1 and cycle motor of affected channel in both directions while applying light pressure on brake pedal. If erratic or jumpy brake pedal movement is detected while performing "apply" or "release" function of motor, intermittent fault code may be indicated. Intermittent problem may be caused by poor connection, rubbed-through wire insulation or broken wire inside insulation. If fault is not current, wiggle wires of affected channel, and check if code resets. This will help pinpoint intermittent problem in motor circuit or connections. Enhanced Diagnostic feature of Tech 1 can be used to check frequency of problem. See ENHANCED DIAGNOSTICS under DIAGNOSIS & TESTING.

Any circuit suspected of causing intermittent problem should be thoroughly checked for backed-out terminals, improper mating, broken connector locks, damaged terminals or poor terminal-to-wiring connections.

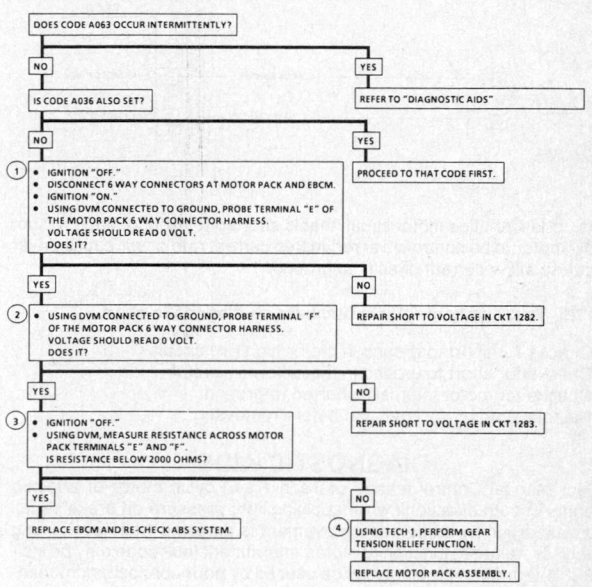

THIS CHART ASSUMES THAT A CURRENT CODE IS STORED INDICATING THAT THIS FAULT IS PRESENT.

92C22584   92I22614

CODE A064
REAR AXLE MOTOR CIRCUIT OPEN

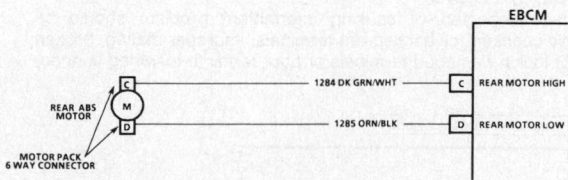

This code identifies motor that cannot be energized due to an open circuit. This code will not allow proper rear ABS operation.

NOTE: Test numbers refer to numbers on diagnostic chart.

1) Checks for correct motor resistance.
2) Releases motor pack tension before removal.
3) Checks for open in motor high (+) circuit.
4) Checks for open in motor low (-) circuit.

DIAGNOSTIC AIDS

Select Manual Control feature of Tech 1 and cycle motor of affected channel in both directions while applying light pressure on brake pedal. If erratic or jumpy brake pedal movement is detected while performing "apply" or "release" function of motor, intermittent fault code may be indicated. Intermittent problem may be caused by poor connection, rubbed-through wire insulation or broken wire inside insulation. If fault is not current, wiggle wires of affected channel, and check if code resets. This will help pinpoint intermittent problem in motor circuit or connections. Enhanced Diagnostic feature of Tech 1 can be used to check frequency of problem. See ENHANCED DIAGNOSTICS under DIAGNOSIS & TESTING.

Any circuit suspected of causing intermittent problem should be thoroughly checked for backed-out terminals, improper mating, broken connector locks, damaged terminals or poor terminal-to-wiring connections.

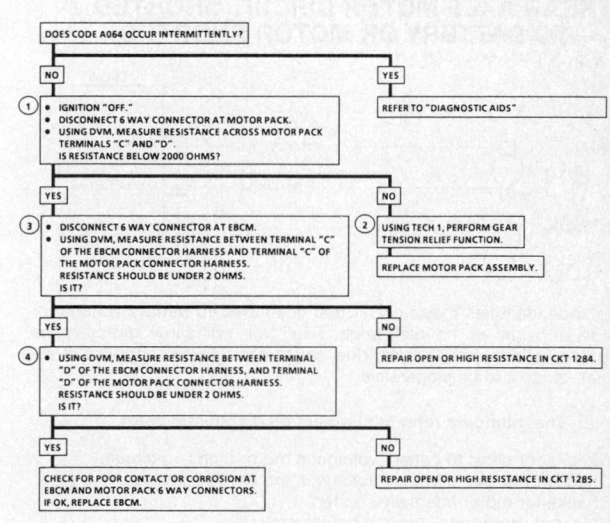

THIS CHART ASSUMES THAT A CURRENT CODE IS STORED INDICATING THAT THIS FAULT IS PRESENT.

92D22593   92J22615

CODE A065
REAR AXLE MOTOR CIRCUIT
SHORTED TO GROUND

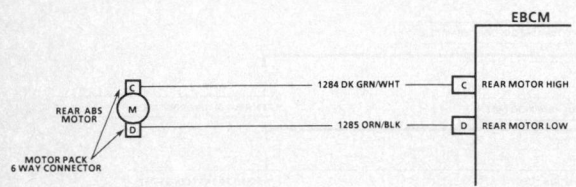

This code identifies motor circuit that is shorted to ground. Fault will not allow motor to be controlled at requested current rate or will cause driver circuit to allow current directly to ground.

NOTE: Test numbers refer to numbers on diagnostic chart.

1) Checks for short to ground in motor high (+) circuit.
2) Checks for short to ground in motor low (-) circuit.
3) Checks for motor internally shorted to ground.
4) Releases motor pack tension before removal.

DIAGNOSTIC AIDS

Select Manual Control feature of Tech 1 and cycle motor of affected channel in both directions while applying light pressure on brake pedal. If erratic or jumpy brake pedal movement is detected while performing "apply" or "release" function of motor, intermittent fault code may be indicated. Intermittent problem may be caused by poor connection, rubbed-through wire insulation or broken wire inside insulation.
If fault is not current, wiggle wires of affected channel, and check if code resets. This will help pinpoint intermittent problem in motor circuit or connections. Enhanced Diagnostic feature of Tech 1 can be used to check frequency of problem. See ENHANCED DIAGNOSTICS under DIAGNOSIS & TESTING.

92D22593   92A22616

Any circuit suspected of causing intermittent problem should be thoroughly checked for backed-out terminals, improper mating, broken connector locks, damaged terminals or poor terminal-to-wiring connections.

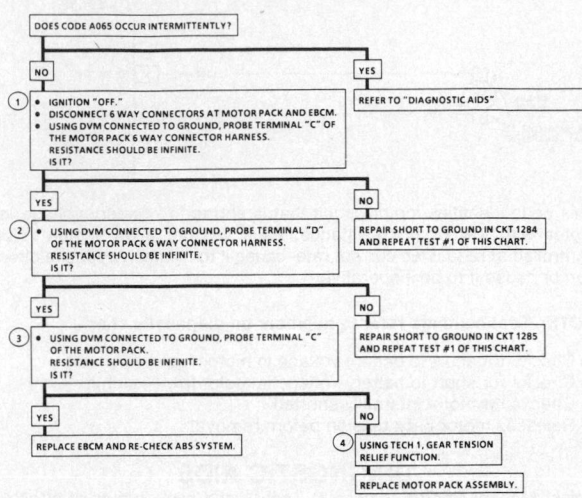

THIS CHART ASSUMES THAT A CURRENT CODE IS STORED INDICATING THAT THIS FAULT IS PRESENT.

CODE A066
REAR AXLE MOTOR CIRCUIT SHORTED
TO BATTERY OR MOTOR SHORTED

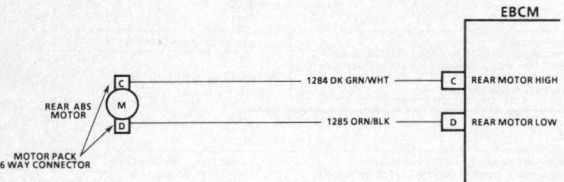

This code identifies motor circuit that is shorted to battery voltage, or motor with low or no resistance. Fault will not allow motor to be controlled at requested current rate, cause it to rotate in opposite direction or cause it to be inoperative.

NOTE: Test numbers refer to numbers on diagnostic chart.

1) Checks for short to battery voltage in motor high (+) circuit.
2) Checks for short to battery voltage in motor low (-) circuit.
3) Checks for motor internally shorted.
4) Releases motor pack tension before removal.

DIAGNOSTIC AIDS

Select Manual Control feature of Tech 1 and cycle motor of affected channel in both directions while applying light pressure on brake pedal. If erratic or jumpy brake pedal movement is detected while performing "apply" or "release" function of motor, intermittent fault code may be indicated. Intermittent problem may be caused by poor connection, rubbed-through wire insulation or broken wire inside insulation.

If fault is not current, wiggle wires of affected channel, and check if code resets. This will help pinpoint intermittent problem in motor circuit or connections. Enhanced Diagnostic feature of Tech 1 can be used to check frequency of problem. See ENHANCED DIAGNOSTICS under DIAGNOSIS & TESTING.
Any circuit suspected of causing intermittent problem should be thoroughly checked for backed-out terminals, improper mating, broken connector locks, damaged terminals or poor terminal-to-wiring connections.

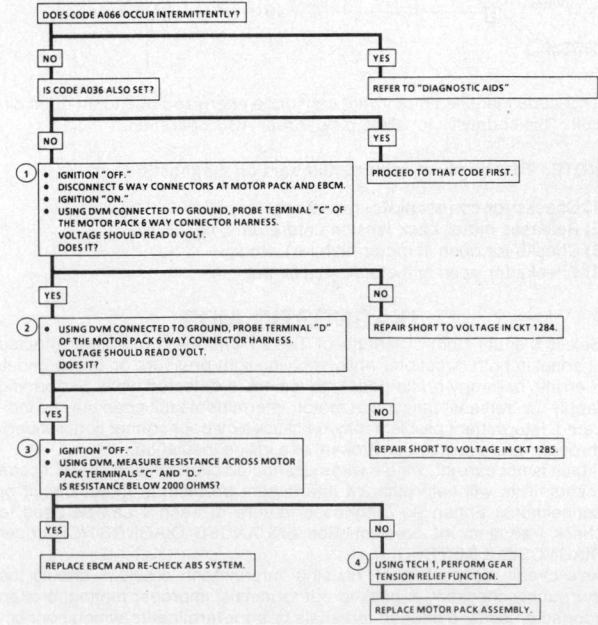

THIS CHART ASSUMES THAT A CURRENT CODE IS STORED INDICATING THAT THIS FAULT IS PRESENT.

92D22593   92B22617

CODE A076
LEFT FRONT SOLENOID CIRCUIT
OPEN OR SHORTED TO BATTERY

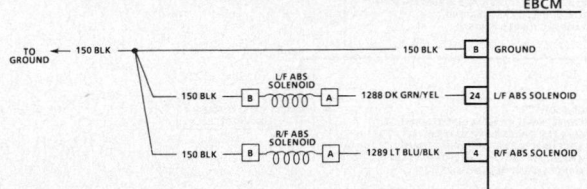

This code identifies a solenoid that cannot be energized due to an open circuit, or a solenoid that is always energized due to a short to battery voltage in circuit between driver and solenoid. An open will not allow proper ABS operation, but short to battery voltage simply turns on solenoid.

NOTE: Test numbers refer to numbers on diagnostic chart.

1) Checks for short to battery voltage in solenoid circuit.
2) Checks for open in solenoid circuit.
3) Isolates open to either solenoid or ground circuit.
4) Tests for intermittent problem in solenoid circuit due to poor connector terminal contact.

DIAGNOSTIC AIDS
An intermittent problem may be caused by a poor connection, rubbed through wire insulation, or a wire broken inside insulation. Frequency of problem can be checked by using Enhanced Diagnostic feature of Tech 1. See ENHANCED DIAGNOSTICS under DIAGNOSIS & TESTING. Any circuit that is suspected of causing intermittent problem should be checked thoroughly for backed-out terminals, improper mating, broken connector locks, damaged terminals, or poor terminal-to-wiring connections.

92C22618   92D22619

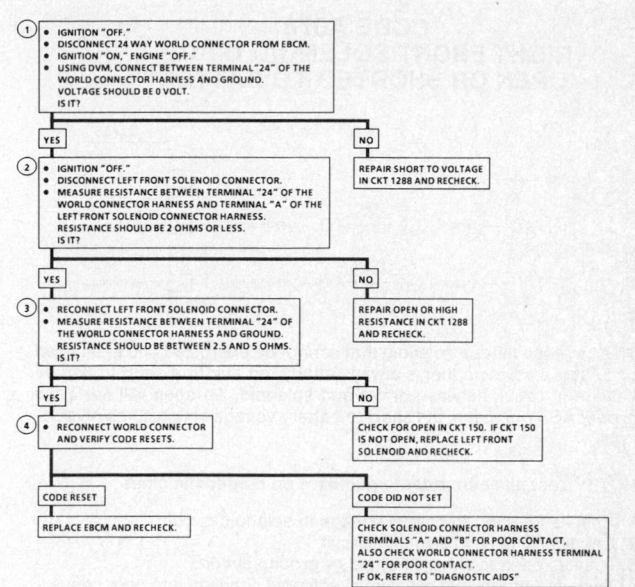

THIS CHART ASSUMES THAT A CURRENT CODE IS STORED INDICATING THAT THIS FAULT IS PRESENT.

CODE A077
LEFT FRONT SOLENOID CIRCUIT SHORTED
TO GROUND OR DRIVER CIRCUIT OPEN

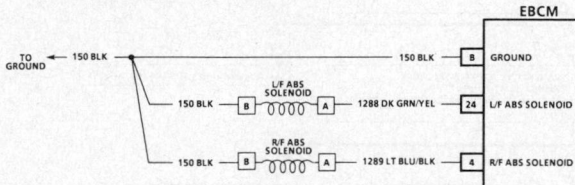

This code identifies a solenoid that cannot be energized due to an open in driver circuit, or a short to ground between solenoid driver and solenoid. These faults can affect ABS operation since flow of brake fluid to wheel cylinder cannot be stopped, making ABS operation for that channel impossible.

NOTE: Test numbers refer to numbers on diagnostic chart.

1) Checks for internal solenoid short.
2) Checks for incorrect solenoid resistance.
3) Tests for short to ground in solenoid circuit.
4) Tests for open in solenoid circuit.

DIAGNOSTIC AIDS
An intermittent problem may be caused by a poor connection, rubbed through wire insulation, or a wire broken inside insulation. Frequency of problem can be checked by using Enhanced Diagnostic feature of Tech 1. See ENHANCED DIAGNOSTICS under DIAGNOSIS & TESTING. Any circuit that is suspected of causing intermittent problem should be checked thoroughly for backed-out terminals, improper mating, broken connector locks, damaged terminals, or poor terminal-to-wiring connections.

92C22618   92G22620

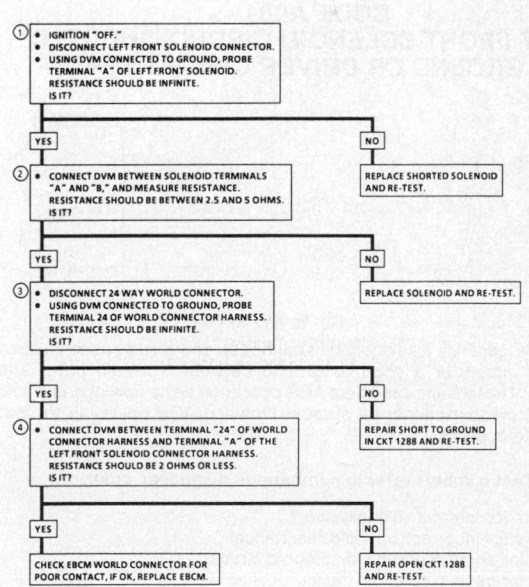

THIS CHART ASSUMES THAT A CURRENT CODE IS STORED INDICATING THAT THIS FAULT IS PRESENT.

CODE A078
RIGHT FRONT SOLENOID CIRCUIT
OPEN OR SHORTED TO BATTERY

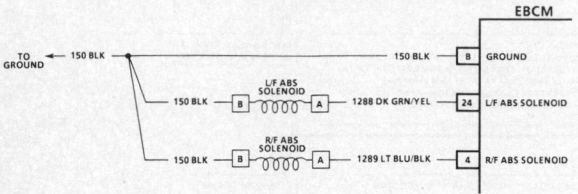

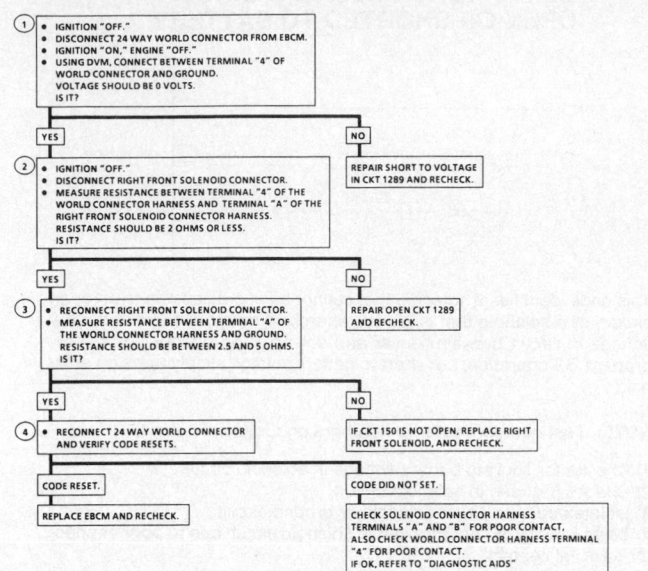

1 • IGNITION "OFF."
• DISCONNECT 24 WAY WORLD CONNECTOR FROM EBCM.
• IGNITION "ON," ENGINE "OFF."
• USING DVM, CONNECT BETWEEN TERMINAL "4" OF WORLD CONNECTOR AND GROUND. VOLTAGE SHOULD BE 0 VOLTS. IS IT?

YES → / NO → REPAIR SHORT TO VOLTAGE IN CKT 1289 AND RECHECK.

2 • IGNITION "OFF."
• DISCONNECT RIGHT FRONT SOLENOID CONNECTOR.
• MEASURE RESISTANCE BETWEEN TERMINAL "4" OF THE WORLD CONNECTOR HARNESS AND TERMINAL "A" OF THE RIGHT FRONT SOLENOID CONNECTOR HARNESS. RESISTANCE SHOULD BE 2 OHMS OR LESS. IS IT?

YES → / NO → REPAIR OPEN CKT 1289 AND RECHECK.

3 • RECONNECT RIGHT FRONT SOLENOID CONNECTOR.
• MEASURE RESISTANCE BETWEEN TERMINAL "4" OF THE WORLD CONNECTOR HARNESS AND GROUND. RESISTANCE SHOULD BE BETWEEN 2.5 AND 5 OHMS. IS IT?

YES → / NO → IF CKT 150 IS NOT OPEN, REPLACE RIGHT FRONT SOLENOID, AND RECHECK.

4 • RECONNECT 24 WAY WORLD CONNECTOR AND VERIFY CODE RESETS.

CODE RESET. / CODE DID NOT SET.

REPLACE EBCM AND RECHECK. / CHECK SOLENOID CONNECTOR HARNESS TERMINALS "A" AND "B" FOR POOR CONTACT, ALSO CHECK WORLD CONNECTOR HARNESS TERMINAL "4" FOR POOR CONTACT. IF OK, REFER TO "DIAGNOSTIC AIDS"

This code identifies a solenoid that cannot be energized due to an open circuit, or a solenoid that is always energized due to a short to battery voltage in circuit between driver and solenoid. An open will not allow proper ABS operation, but short to battery voltage simply turns on solenoid.

NOTE: Test numbers refer to numbers on diagnostic chart.

1) Checks for short to battery voltage in solenoid circuit.
2) Checks for open in solenoid circuit.
3) Isolates open to either solenoid or ground circuit.
4) Tests for intermittent problem in solenoid circuit due to poor connector terminal contact.

DIAGNOSTIC AIDS

An intermittent problem may be caused by a poor connection, rubbed through wire insulation, or a wire broken inside insulation. Frequency of problem can be checked by using Enhanced Diagnostic feature of Tech 1. See ENHANCED DIAGNOSTICS under DIAGNOSIS & TESTING. Any circuit that is suspected of causing intermittent problem should be checked thoroughly for backed-out terminals, improper mating, broken connector locks, damaged terminals, or poor terminal-to-wiring connections.

THIS CHART ASSUMES THAT A CURRENT CODE IS STORED INDICATING THAT THIS FAULT IS PRESENT.

92C22618   92H22621

CODE A081
RIGHT FRONT SOLENOID CIRCUIT SHORTED
TO GROUND OR DRIVER CIRCUIT OPEN

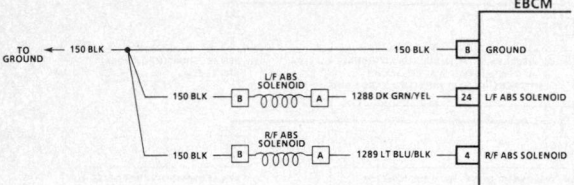

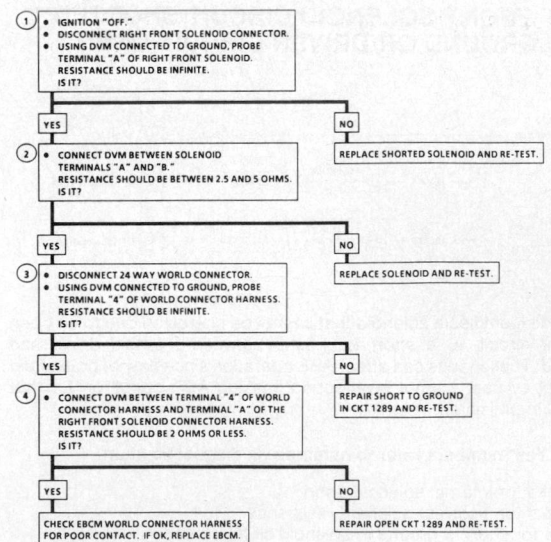

1 • IGNITION "OFF."
• DISCONNECT RIGHT FRONT SOLENOID CONNECTOR.
• USING DVM CONNECTED TO GROUND, PROBE TERMINAL "A" OF RIGHT FRONT SOLENOID. RESISTANCE SHOULD BE INFINITE. IS IT?

YES → / NO → REPLACE SHORTED SOLENOID AND RE-TEST.

2 • CONNECT DVM BETWEEN SOLENOID TERMINALS "A" AND "B." RESISTANCE SHOULD BE BETWEEN 2.5 AND 5 OHMS. IS IT?

YES → / NO → REPLACE SOLENOID AND RE-TEST.

3 • DISCONNECT 24 WAY WORLD CONNECTOR.
• USING DVM CONNECTED TO GROUND, PROBE TERMINAL "4" OF WORLD CONNECTOR HARNESS. RESISTANCE SHOULD BE INFINITE. IS IT?

YES → / NO → REPAIR SHORT TO GROUND IN CKT 1289 AND RE-TEST.

4 • CONNECT DVM BETWEEN TERMINAL "4" OF WORLD CONNECTOR HARNESS AND TERMINAL "A" OF THE RIGHT FRONT SOLENOID CONNECTOR HARNESS. RESISTANCE SHOULD BE 2 OHMS OR LESS. IS IT?

YES → / NO →

CHECK EBCM WORLD CONNECTOR HARNESS FOR POOR CONTACT. IF OK, REPLACE EBCM. / REPAIR OPEN CKT 1289 AND RE-TEST.

This code identifies a solenoid that cannot be energized due to an open in driver circuit, or a short to ground between solenoid driver and solenoid. These faults can affect ABS operation since flow of brake fluid to wheel cylinder cannot be stopped, making ABS operation for that channel impossible.

NOTE: Test numbers refer to numbers on diagnostic chart.

1) Checks for internal solenoid short.
2) Checks for incorrect solenoid resistance.
3) Tests for short to ground in solenoid circuit.
4) Tests for open in solenoid circuit.

DIAGNOSTIC AIDS

An intermittent problem may be caused by a poor connection, rubbed through wire insulation, or a wire broken inside insulation. Frequency of problem can be checked by using Enhanced Diagnostic feature of Tech 1. See ENHANCED DIAGNOSTICS under DIAGNOSIS & TESTING. Any circuit that is suspected of causing intermittent problem should be checked thoroughly for backed-out terminals, improper mating, broken connector locks, damaged terminals, or poor terminal-to-wiring connections.

THIS CHART ASSUMES THAT A CURRENT CODE IS STORED INDICATING THAT THIS FAULT IS PRESENT.

92C22618   92I22622

CODE A082
CALIBRATION MEMORY FAILURE

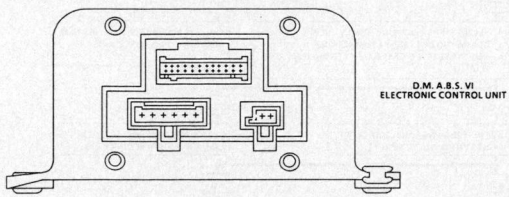

D.M. A.B.S. VI
ELECTRONIC CONTROL UNIT

This code allows EBCM to check for a calibration failure by comparing calibration value to a known value stored in EEPROM. This code is also used to prevent incorrect use of calibrations or changes to calibrations that may alter designed function of ABS.

NOTE: Test number refers to number on diagnostic chart.

1) Tests for fault during diagnosis. If fault is present, replace EBCM.

92J22623   92A22624

DIAGNOSTIC AIDS

An intermittent Code A082 may be caused by a bad cell in EEPROM that is sensitive to temperature changes. If Code A082 set more than once, but is intermittent, replace EBCM. Frequency of problem can be checked by using Enhanced Diagnostic feature of Tech 1. See ENHANCED DIAGNOSTICS under DIAGNOSIS & TESTING.

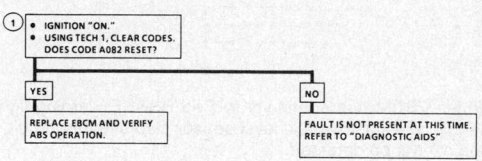

THIS CHART ASSUMES THAT A CURRENT CODE IS STORED INDICATING THAT THIS FAULT IS PRESENT.

CODE A086
RED BRAKE WARNING LIGHT
ACTIVATED BY EBCM

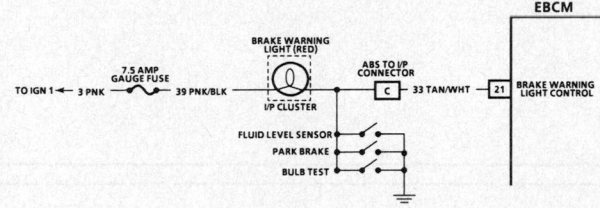

This code is used for information only. It reflects ability of EBCM to illuminate Red BRAKE warning light. If another code issues a command to illuminate Red BRAKE warning light, Code A086 will be stored in EEPROM as a history code.

NOTE: Test number refers to number on diagnostic chart.

1) Identifies if code other than Code A086 commanded illumination of Red BRAKE warning light.

92B22625   92C22626

DIAGNOSTIC AIDS

Any ABS mechanical code that issues a command to illuminate Red BRAKE warning light will also result in Code A086 being stored in EEPROM during shutdown. These codes are: A038, A041, A042, A046 and A051.

If motors are not in their home position, certain electrical codes will also command Red BRAKE warning light on. These codes are: A014, A016, A018, A055, A056, A057, A058, A061, A062, A063, A064, A065 and A066.

If any of these codes are indicated along with Code A086, correct them prior to repairing Code A086.

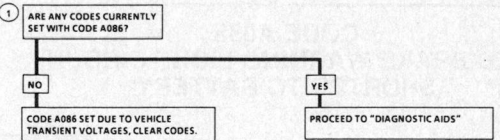

CODE A087
RED BRAKE WARNING LIGHT CIRCUIT OPEN

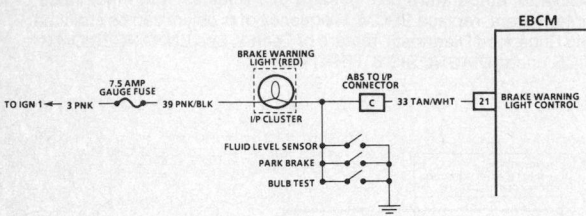

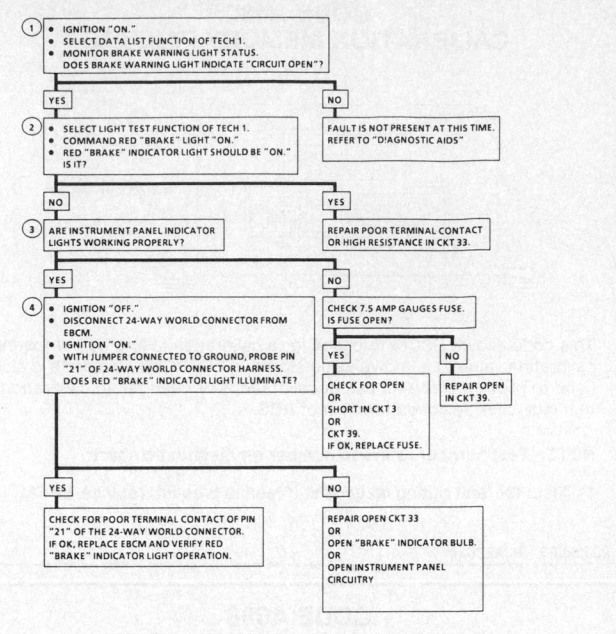

This code verifies EBCM has continuity to Red BRAKE warning light. Because parking brake and low fluid level sensor also use this circuit, a short to ground cannot be detected.

NOTE: Test number refers to number on diagnostic chart.

1) Determines if fault is still present.
2) Indicates if EBCM and circuit has ability to complete ground to Red BRAKE warning light.
3) Tests for circuit completion to instrument cluster.
4) Determines if open circuit is due to EBCM failure or BRAKE warning light circuit failure.

DIAGNOSTIC AIDS

An intermittent problem may be caused by a poor connection, rubbed through wire insulation, or a wire broken inside insulation. Frequency of problem can be checked by using Enhanced Diagnostic feature of Tech 1. See ENHANCED DIAGNOSTICS under DIAGNOSIS & TESTING. If Tech 1 is not available, BRAKE light operation and continuity of circuits No. 3 and 39 can be verified by lifting parking brake handle.

Any circuit that is suspected of causing intermittent problem should be checked thoroughly for backed-out terminals, improper mating, broken connector locks, damaged terminals, or poor terminal-to-wiring connections.

THIS CHART ASSUMES THAT A CURRENT CODE IS STORED INDICATING THAT THIS FAULT IS PRESENT.

92B22625   92D22627

CODE A088
RED BRAKE WARNING LIGHT CIRCUIT SHORTED TO BATTERY

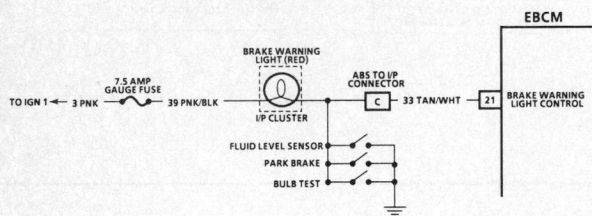

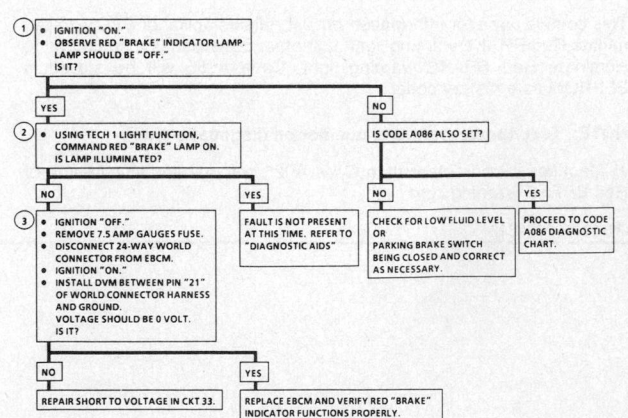

This code isolates a short to battery voltage between EBCM and Red BRAKE warning light or an open driver circuit that does not allow warning light to be illuminated by EBCM. This will only occur if an ABS failure is detected which may degrade base brake operation.

NOTE: Test number refers to number on diagnostic chart.

1) Identifies if ground circuit to Red BRAKE warning light is being completed by a source other than EBCM.
2) Determines if fault is still present.
3) By removing 7.5-amp GAUGES fuse, voltage source is eliminated. This test indicates if voltage is being supplied from a source other than GAUGES fuse.

DIAGNOSTIC AIDS

An intermittent problem may be caused by a poor connection, rubbed through wire insulation, or a wire broken inside insulation. Frequency of problem can be checked by using Enhanced Diagnostic feature of Tech 1. See ENHANCED DIAGNOSTICS under DIAGNOSIS & TESTING.

Any circuit that is suspected of causing intermittent problem should be checked thoroughly for backed-out terminals, improper mating, broken connector locks, damaged terminals, or poor terminal-to-wiring connections.

THIS CHART ASSUMES THAT A CURRENT CODE IS STORED INDICATING THAT THIS FAULT IS PRESENT.

92B22625   92E22628

CODE A091
OPEN BRAKE SWITCH CONTACTS
DURING DECELERATION

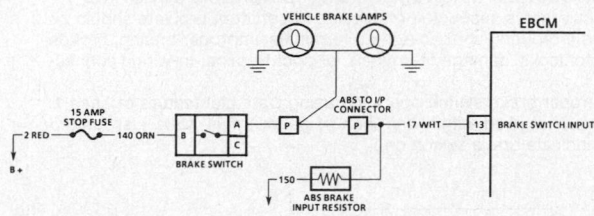

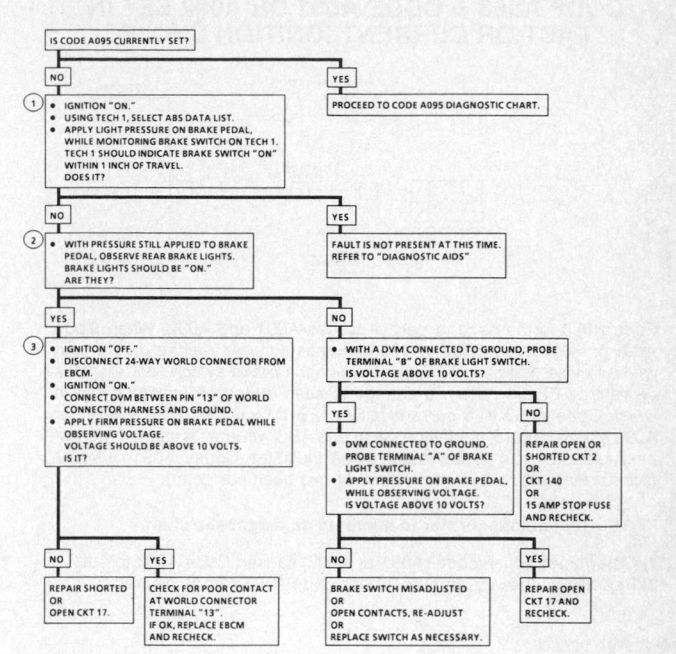

This code is used to detect an open brake switch in non-ABS mode. The EBCM looks for decel rates which would indicate a braking action and verifies this assumption by requiring several repeat detections. ABS braking action will not be available because EBCM does not see a brake switch signal.

NOTE: Test numbers refer to numbers on diagnostic chart.

1) Determines if brake switch signal is being received by EBCM.
2) Indicates if an open circuit exists in brake switch or brake lamp circuit.
3) Isolates open circuit to either brake switch input circuit or EBCM.

DIAGNOSTIC AIDS

An intermittent problem may be caused by a poor connection, rubbed through wire insulation, or a wire broken inside insulation. Frequency of problem can be checked by using Enhanced Diagnostic feature of Tech 1. See ENHANCED DIAGNOSTICS under DIAGNOSIS & TESTING. Any circuit that is suspected of causing intermittent problem should be checked thoroughly for backed-out terminals, improper mating, broken connector locks, damaged terminals, or poor terminal-to-wiring connections.

92F22629   92I22630

CODE A092
OPEN BRAKE SWITCH CONTACTS
WHEN ABS WAS REQUIRED

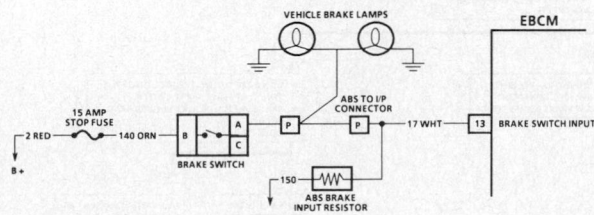

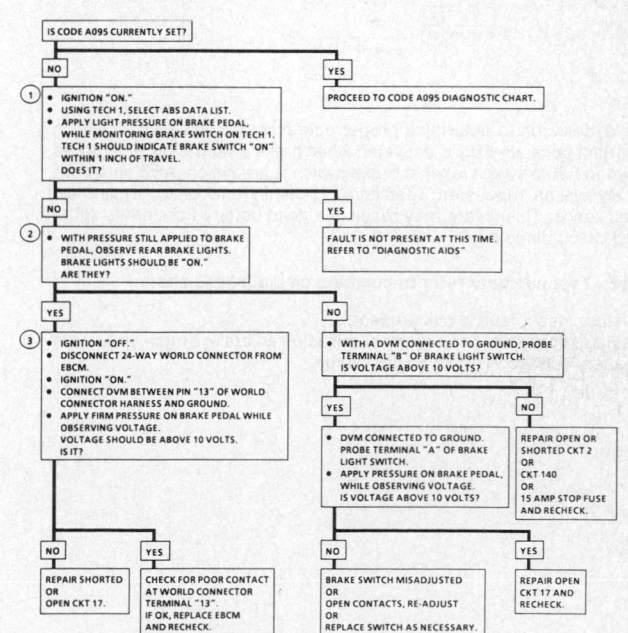

This code detects a brake switch fault. When brake pedal is applied, brake switch closes and a voltage signal is sent to EBCM. The EBCM looks for this signal to know when brake pedal has been applied. The EBCM cannot activate ABS without this signal. Code A092 will set only when conditions requiring ABS are present.

NOTE: Test numbers refer to numbers on diagnostic chart.

1) Determines if brake switch signal is being received by EBCM.
2) Isolates open circuit to either brake switch or brake light circuit.
3) Isolates open circuit to either brake switch input circuit or EBCM.

DIAGNOSTIC AIDS

An intermittent problem may be caused by a poor connection, rubbed through wire insulation, or a wire broken inside insulation. Frequency of problem can be checked by using Enhanced Diagnostic feature of Tech 1. See ENHANCED DIAGNOSTICS under DIAGNOSIS & TESTING. Any circuit that is suspected of causing intermittent problem should be checked thoroughly for backed-out terminals, improper mating, broken connector locks, damaged terminals, or poor terminal-to-wiring connections.

92F22629   92J22631

CODE A093 & CODE A091 OR A092 SET IN LAST OR CURRENT IGNITION CYCLE

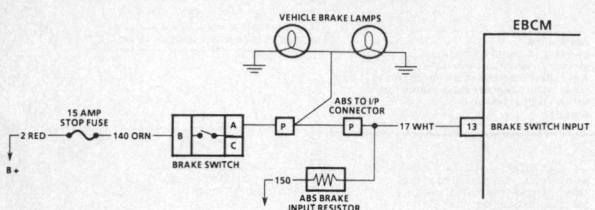

Code A093 is the second part of Codes A091 and A092. When Code A091 or A092 is set, Code A093 becomes a current failure during next ignition cycle, keeping ABS disabled until a brake switch "on" signal is sensed by EBCM. When a change is seen during an ignition cycle in which Code A093 is a current failure, EBCM will clear Code A091 or A092 at end of current ignition cycle and ABS will enable itself at start of next ignition cycle. Code A093 alone indicates Codes A091 or A092 failed previously, but is intermittent or has been corrected.

NOTE: Test numbers refer to numbers on diagnostic chart.

1) Determines which code (A091 or A092) caused Code A093 to set.
2) Perform necessary repairs so that Code A093 can be cleared.

92F22629   92A22632

DIAGNOSTIC AIDS

An intermittent problem may be caused by a poor connection, rubbed through wire insulation, or a wire broken inside insulation. Frequency of problem can be checked by using Enhanced Diagnostic feature of Tech 1. See ENHANCED DIAGNOSTICS under DIAGNOSIS & TESTING. Any circuit that is suspected of causing intermittent problem should be checked thoroughly for backed-out terminals, improper mating, broken connector locks, damaged terminals, or poor terminal-to-wiring connections.

Verify proper brake switch operation using Data List feature of Tech 1. As brake is applied within one inch of pedal travel, Data List feature should indicate brake switch on.

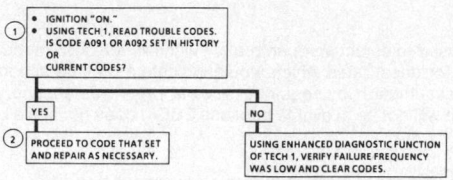

THIS CHART ASSUMES THAT A CURRENT CODE IS STORED INDICATING THAT THIS FAULT IS PRESENT.

CODE A094
BRAKE SWITCH CONTACTS ALWAYS CLOSED

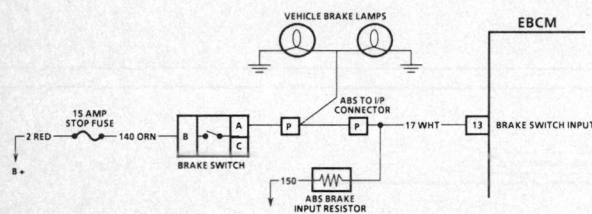

This code is run to determine proper operation of brake switch. This is important because ABS is activated when brake switch is on, and turned off when brake switch is off. If brake switch is always on, ABS operation will always be requested, resulting in potential modulator cycling on rough roads. This failure may result in a dead battery from brake lights being on continuously.

NOTE: Test numbers refer to numbers on diagnostic chart.

1) Determines if fault is still present.
2) Isolates fault to either a faulty or misadjusted brake switch, or a short to battery voltage in brake switch circuit.

DIAGNOSTIC AIDS

An intermittent problem may be caused by a poor connection, rubbed through wire insulation, or a wire broken inside insulation. Frequency of problem can be checked by using Enhanced Diagnostic feature of Tech 1. See ENHANCED DIAGNOSTICS under DIAGNOSIS & TESTING. Any circuit that is suspected of causing intermittent problem should be checked thoroughly for backed-out terminals, improper mating, broken connector locks, damaged terminals, or poor terminal-to-wiring connections.

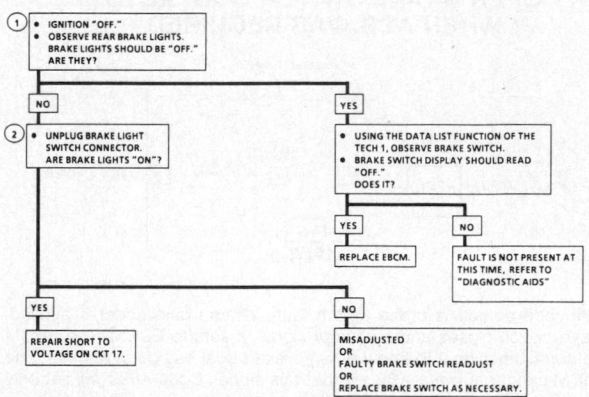

THIS CHART ASSUMES THAT A CURRENT CODE IS STORED INDICATING THAT THIS FAULT IS PRESENT.

92F22629   92B22633

CODE A095
BRAKE SWITCH CIRCUIT OPEN

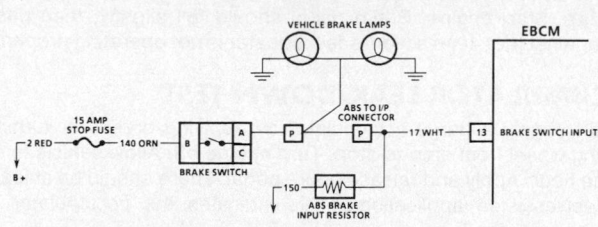

This code is used to identify open brake switch circuit preventing brake switch input to EBCM from changing when brakes are applied. This code is used in conjunction with Codes A091 and A092 to determine cause of open brake switch fault.

NOTE: Test numbers refer to numbers on diagnostic chart.

1) Confirms open circuit currently exists.
2) Determines if brake switch signal is being received by EBCM.
3) Isolates open circuit to either brake switch or brake light circuit.
4) Isolates open circuit to either brake switch input circuit or EBCM.

DIAGNOSTIC AIDS

An intermittent problem may be caused by a poor connection, rubbed through wire insulation, or a wire broken inside insulation. Frequency of problem can be checked by using Enhanced Diagnostic feature of Tech 1. See ENHANCED DIAGNOSTICS under DIAGNOSIS & TESTING. Any circuit that is suspected of causing intermittent problem should be checked thoroughly for backed-out terminals, improper mating, broken connector locks, damaged terminals, or poor terminal-to-wiring connections.

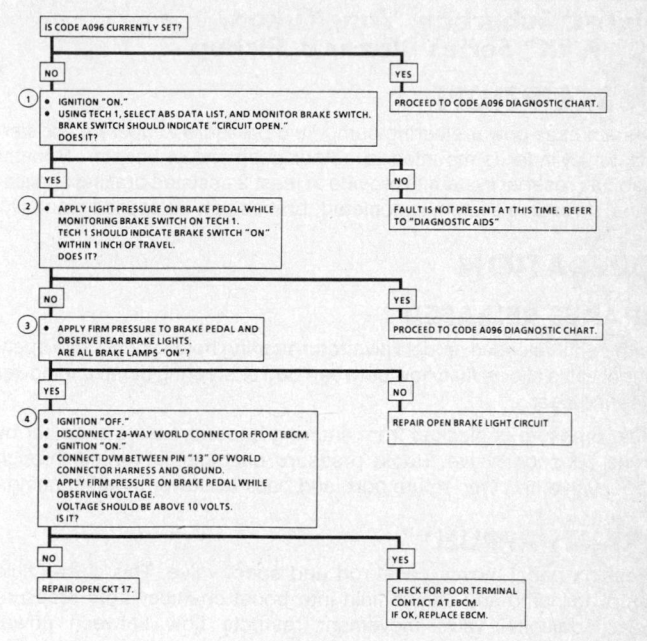

THIS CHART ASSUMES THAT A CURRENT CODE IS STORED INDICATING THAT THIS FAULT IS PRESENT.

92F22629   92C22634

CODE A096
BRAKELIGHT CIRCUIT OPEN

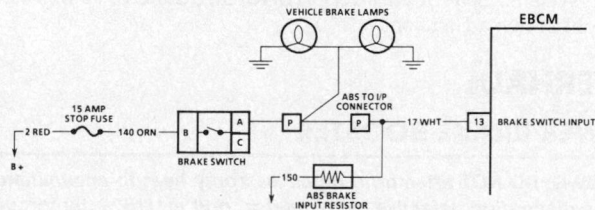

This code is used to identify cause of Code A095 failure and indicate to driver ABS is still available. If Code A095 appears with Code A096, then either brake lights are open, brake light ground is open, or ABS brake input resistor is open during 4-way flasher operation. Battery voltage at brake switch input indicates a valid brake switch input is still available.

NOTE: Test numbers refer to numbers on diagnostic chart.

1) A Code A096 may set due to other brake switch circuit malfunctions. If any other codes are present, proceed to that code first.
2) Confirms that fault is currently present in brake circuit.

DIAGNOSTIC AIDS

An intermittent problem may be caused by a poor connection, rubbed through wire insulation, or a wire broken inside insulation. Frequency of problem can be checked by using Enhanced Diagnostic feature of Tech 1. See ENHANCED DIAGNOSTICS under DIAGNOSIS & TESTING. Any circuit that is suspected of causing intermittent problem should be checked thoroughly for backed-out terminals, improper mating, broken connector locks, damaged terminals, or poor terminal-to-wiring connections.

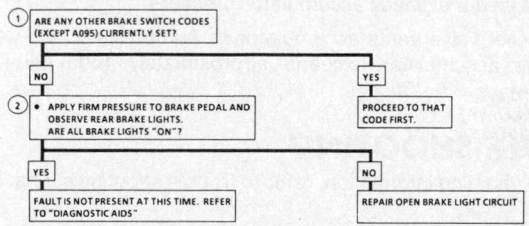

THIS CHART ASSUMES THAT A CURRENT CODE IS STORED INDICATING THAT THIS FAULT IS PRESENT.

92F22629   92D22635

Astro, Commercial Van, Safari, Sierra, Suburban, Van, Yukon, "C" & "K" Series Blazer & Pickup

DESCRIPTION

System uses power steering pump fluid pressure to operate booster. Master cylinder is mounted to output push rod of booster. Booster also has reserve system to provide at least 2 assisted braking applications. If reserve system is depleted, brakes can be applied manually.

OPERATION

BRAKES RELEASED

With pedal released, spool valve return spring holds spool valve open. Spool valve allows fluid flow between power steering pump and power steering gear.

Fluid pressure is blocked from entering boost pressure chamber by lands on spool valve. Boost pressure chamber is vented through spool valve, to pump return port, and back to power steering pump.

BRAKES APPLIED

Pressing pedal moves pedal rod and spool valve. This closes fluid return to pump and admits fluid into boost chamber from pressure port. Additional valve movement restricts flow between power steering pump and power steering gear.

As fluid pressure increases in boost chamber, it forces piston forward, actuating master cylinder piston and applying brakes. If steering is required while braking, power steering pump pressure will rise and spool valve will shift open, allowing more fluid to flow to power steering gear.

RESERVE SYSTEM

System consists of charging valve, accumulator valve and spring-loaded accumulator. Accumulator is integral with booster. System is open to pressure port of booster.

Charging valve has an orifice and ball check valve. Fluid from pump passes through orifice in valve, unseats ball check valve and enters accumulator. Ball check valve prevents reverse flow.

Accumulator valve is poppet-type valve held closed by accumulator pressure. If no pump pressure is available, an actuator on spool valve sleeve opens accumulator valve. Fluid pressure can also enter accumulator from boost chamber through accumulator valve, when boost chamber pressure exceeds accumulator pressure.

Pressure relief valve vents accumulator to pump return port when pressure in accumulator exceeds approximately 1600 psi (112 kg/cm²).

TROUBLE SHOOTING

For trouble shooting information, refer to trouble shooting charts. See Fig. 6.

TESTING

NOTE: Inoperative Hydro-Boost cannot cause noisy brakes, fading brake pedal or pulling brakes. If one of these conditions exists, other components of brake system are at fault.

PRELIMINARY CHECKS

1) Check engine idle speed. Check all power steering hoses and brake lines for leaks or restrictions. Fill master cylinder with brake fluid. Fill power steering pump reservoir with power steering fluid.
2) Check for air in power steering fluid reservoir. Check power steering belt tension and condition. Check power steering pump pressure.

BOOSTER FUNCTIONAL TEST

With engine off, press brake pedal several times to deplete accumulator reserve. Press and hold brake pedal with about 40 lbs. (18 kg) pressure. Start engine. Brake pedal should fall slightly, then push back against foot. If no action is felt, booster is not operating properly.

ACCUMULATOR LEAK-DOWN TEST

1) Start engine. Charge accumulator by applying brakes or turning steering wheel from stop-to-stop. Turn engine off. Allow vehicle to sit for one hour. Apply and release brake pedal. There should be at least 2 power-assisted applications. This indicates the accumulator is retaining a charge.
2) If accumulator does not retain charge for one hour but functions normally immediately after charging, replace accumulator valve. If accumulator can be heard charging and discharging but does not hold a charge, replace accumulator valve. See OVERHAUL.
3) Discharge accumulator by pressing brake pedal several times. Attempt to rotate accumulator can in respect to housing. If it is possible to rotate can, accumulator has lost its gas charge. Replace accumulator assembly.

REMOVAL & INSTALLATION

POWER BRAKE BOOSTER

Removal – 1) Press brake pedal several times to exhaust pressure from accumulator. Clean dirt from hydraulic line connections at booster and at master cylinder. Disconnect hydraulic lines from booster and plug all openings.

NOTE: In most cases, it is not necessary to disconnect master cylinder brake lines to remove booster.

2) Remove and support master cylinder. Disconnect booster push rod from brake pedal. Remove booster-to-firewall nuts from inside vehicle. Remove booster and gaskets.
Installation – To install, reverse removal procedure. Lubricate pedal rod and linkage pivot bolts, pins, sleeves and bushings. Bleed hydro-boost system. See BLEEDING HYDRO-BOOST SYSTEM. Check stoplight switch adjustment.

OVERHAUL

POWER BRAKE BOOSTER

WARNING: DO NOT attempt to repair or apply heat to accumulator. Before discarding defective accumulator, drill a 1/16" hole through end of accumulator can at end opposite of "O" ring.

Disassembly – 1) Install Accumulator Piston Compressor (J-26889) on master cylinder mounting stud and retain with nut. See Figs. 1 and 2. Compress accumulator using "C" clamp.
2) Insert punch into hole in housing. Release clamp and remove accumulator piston compressor. Remove accumulator and "O" ring. Remove retainer, spool plug, "O" ring and spool return spring from spool plug bore.
3) Remove baffle, output pushrod, spring and baffle retainer, piston return spring and spring retainer. Saw off eyelet on pedal rod. Remove pedal rod boot, bracket nut and bracket. Remove housing cover bolts. Separate cover from housing.
4) Remove seal from end of rod on piston assembly. Remove housing seal. Remove piston assembly and piston seal. Remove spool valve. Remove accumulator valve using wire hook. See Fig. 3. Remove return port fitting and "O" ring.
Cleaning & Inspection – 1) Clean all parts with power steering fluid. DO NOT use any other cleaner. If any accumulator valve components are damaged or lost, replace all valve components.
2) Inspect tube seats from burrs or nicks. If damaged, remove tube seat using a No. 4 bolt extractor. Install tube seat using hammer and Tube Seat Installer (J-6217). See Fig. 4.

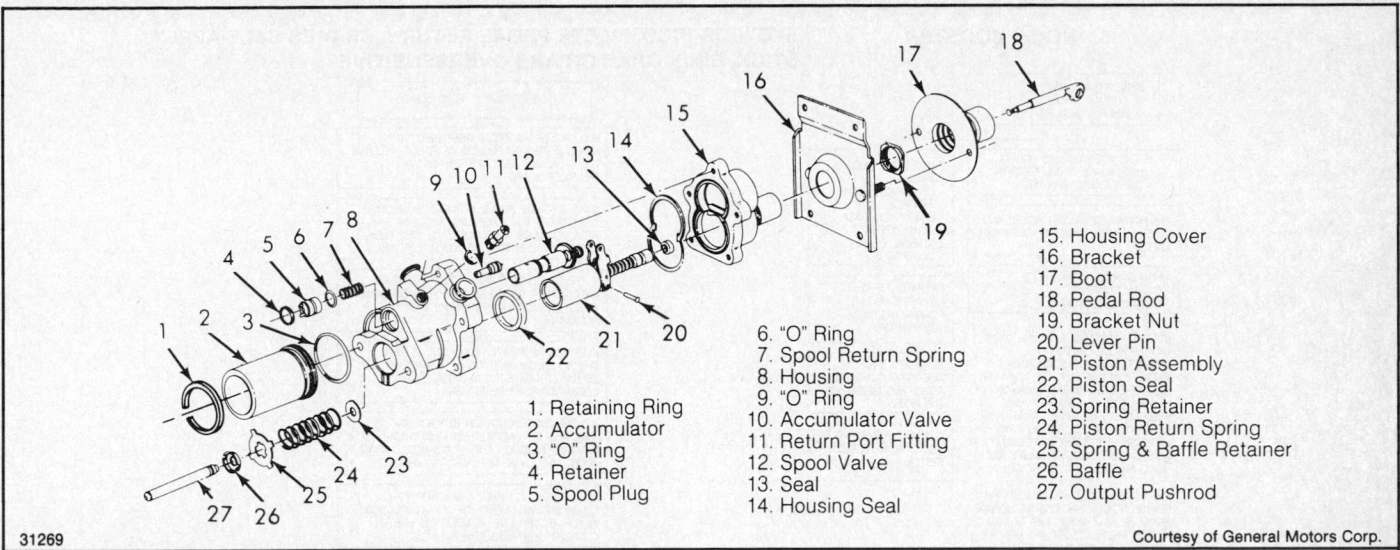

15. Housing Cover
16. Bracket
17. Boot
18. Pedal Rod
19. Bracket Nut
20. Lever Pin
21. Piston Assembly
22. Piston Seal
23. Spring Retainer
24. Piston Return Spring
25. Spring & Baffle Retainer
26. Baffle
27. Output Pushrod

6. "O" Ring
7. Spool Return Spring
8. Housing
9. "O" Ring
10. Accumulator Valve
11. Return Port Fitting
12. Spool Valve
13. Seal
14. Housing Seal

1. Retaining Ring
2. Accumulator
3. "O" Ring
4. Retainer
5. Spool Plug

31269
Courtesy of General Motors Corp.

Fig. 1: Exploded View Of Bendix Hydro-Boost Power Brake Booster

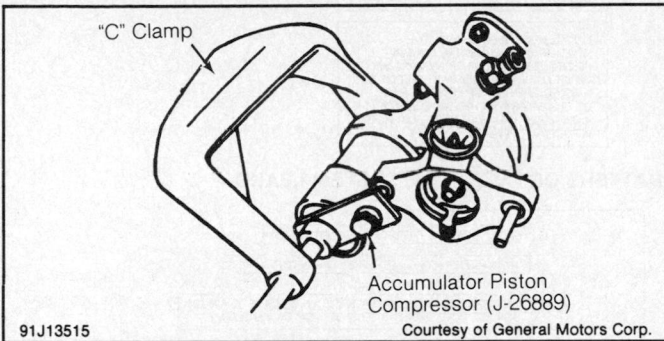

91J13515
Courtesy of General Motors Corp.

Fig. 2: Compressing Accumulator

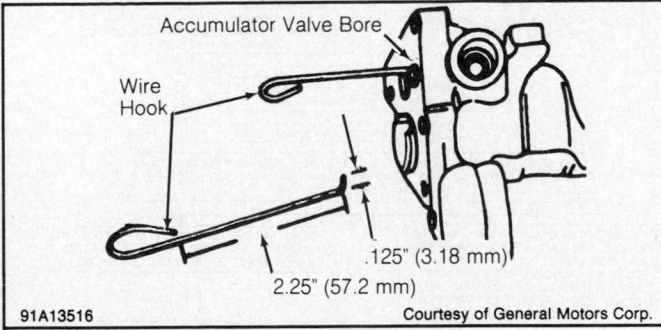

91A13516
Courtesy of General Motors Corp.

Fig. 3: Removing Accumulator Valve Using Fabricated Tool

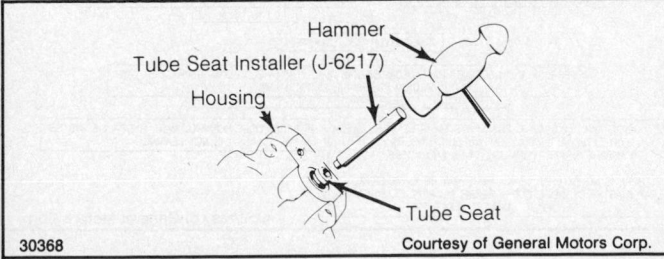

30368
Courtesy of General Motors Corp.

Fig. 4: Installing Tube Seat

Reassembly – 1) Lubricate all seals, "O" rings and metal friction points with power steering fluid. Install "O" ring and return port fitting. Install accumulator valve and spool valve.
2) Lubricate Seal Protector (J-24551-A) or (J-25083) with power steering fluid. Install piston seal and piston assembly. See Fig. 5. Install seal on end of piston assembly. Install housing seal in groove.

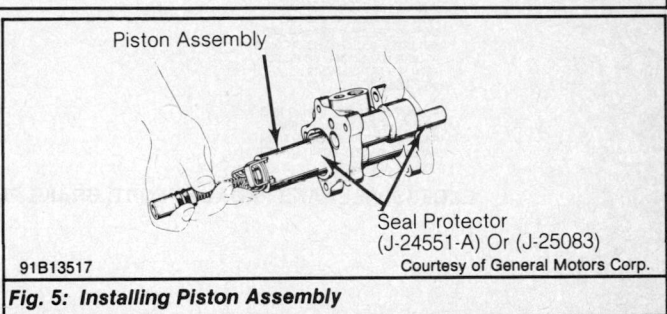

91B13517
Courtesy of General Motors Corp.

Fig. 5: Installing Piston Assembly

3) Mate housing to cover. Install housing-to-cover bolts and tighten to **22 ft. lbs. (30 N.m)**. Install bracket and bracket nut. Tighten bracket nut to **110 ft. lbs. (149 N.m)**. Install boot.
4) Install spring retainer, piston return spring, baffle and output push rod using seal protector. Install spring and baffle retainer. Install "O" ring on spool plug. Install spool return spring, spool plug and retainer in spool plug bore.
5) Install "O" ring on accumulator. Install accumulator using Accumulator Piston Compressor (J-26889) and "C" clamp. See Fig. 2. Install accumulator retaining ring. Install jam nut and eyelet from repair kit onto pedal rod.

BLEEDING HYDRO-BOOST SYSTEM

1) Fill power steering pump reservoir and leave undisturbed for at least 2 minutes. Start engine and run momentarily. Add fluid if necessary. Repeat until fluid level remains constant with engine running.
2) Stop engine. Raise front wheels off the ground. Turn steering wheel from stop-to-stop. Add fluid if necessary. Lower vehicle.
3) Start engine. Press brake pedal several times while turning steering wheel from stop-to-stop. Turn engine off. Press brake pedal several times to exhaust accumulator pressure. Check fluid level. Add fluid (if necessary).
4) If fluid is foamy, let vehicle stand for several minutes, then repeat step **3)**. Air in system will cause fluid level to rise with engine off. Continue to bleed system until all air is expelled. If all air is not expelled after bleeding system, check power steering system for problem.

TORQUE SPECIFICATIONS
TORQUE SPECIFICATIONS

Application	Ft. Lbs. (N.m)
Booster-To-Cowl Nut	20 (27)
Bracket Nut	110 (149)
Housing-To-Cover Bolts	22 (30)
Master Cylinder-To-Booster Nut	20 (27)
Power Steering-To-Booster Line	25 (34)

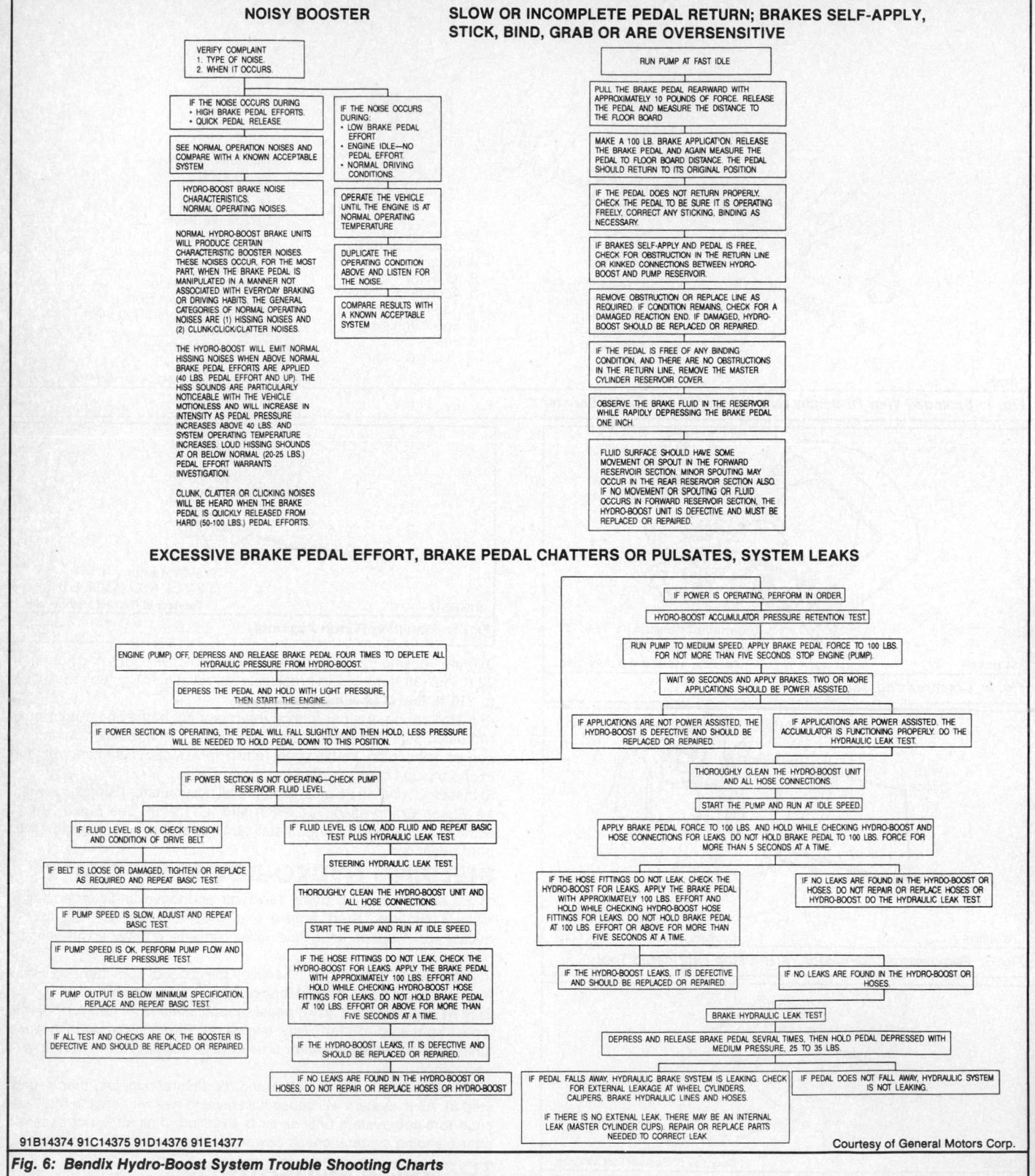

NOISY BOOSTER

VERIFY COMPLAINT
1. TYPE OF NOISE.
2. WHEN IT OCCURS.

IF THE NOISE OCCURS DURING
• HIGH BRAKE PEDAL EFFORTS.
• QUICK PEDAL RELEASE

SEE NORMAL OPERATION NOISES AND COMPARE WITH A KNOWN ACCEPTABLE SYSTEM

HYDRO-BOOST BRAKE NOISE CHARACTERISTICS. NORMAL OPERATING NOISES.

NORMAL HYDRO-BOOST BRAKE UNITS WILL PRODUCE CERTAIN CHARACTERISTIC BOOSTER NOISES. THESE NOISES OCCUR, FOR THE MOST PART, WHEN THE BRAKE PEDAL IS MANIPULATED IN A MANNER NOT ASSOCIATED WITH EVERYDAY BRAKING OR DRIVING HABITS. THE GENERAL CATEGORIES OF NORMAL OPERATING NOISES ARE (1) HISSING NOISES AND (2) CLUNK/CLICK/CLATTER NOISES.

THE HYDRO-BOOST WILL EMIT NORMAL HISSING NOISES WHEN ABOVE NORMAL BRAKE PEDAL EFFORTS ARE APPLIED (40 LBS. PEDAL EFFORT AND UP). THE HISS SOUNDS ARE PARTICULARLY NOTICEABLE WITH THE VEHICLE MOTIONLESS AND WILL INCREASE IN INTENSITY AS PEDAL PRESSURE INCREASES ABOVE 40 LBS. AND SYSTEM OPERATING TEMPERATURE INCREASES. LOUD HISSING SHOUNDS AT OR BELOW NORMAL (20-25 LBS.) PEDAL EFFORT WARRANTS INVESTIGATION.

CLUNK, CLATTER OR CLICKING NOISES WILL BE HEARD WHEN THE BRAKE PEDAL IS QUICKLY RELEASED FROM HARD (50-100 LBS.) PEDAL EFFORTS.

IF THE NOISE OCCURS DURING:
• LOW BRAKE PEDAL EFFORT.
• ENGINE IDLE—NO PEDAL EFFORT.
• NORMAL DRIVING CONDITIONS.

OPERATE THE VEHICLE UNTIL THE ENGINE IS AT NORMAL OPERATING TEMPERATURE

DUPLICATE THE OPERATING CONDITION ABOVE AND LISTEN FOR THE NOISE.

COMPARE RESULTS WITH A KNOWN ACCEPTABLE SYSTEM

SLOW OR INCOMPLETE PEDAL RETURN; BRAKES SELF-APPLY, STICK, BIND, GRAB OR ARE OVERSENSITIVE

RUN PUMP AT FAST IDLE

PULL THE BRAKE PEDAL REARWARD WITH APPROXIMATELY 10 POUNDS OF FORCE. RELEASE THE PEDAL AND MEASURE THE DISTANCE TO THE FLOOR BOARD

MAKE A 100 LB. BRAKE APPLICATION. RELEASE THE BRAKE PEDAL AND AGAIN MEASURE THE PEDAL TO FLOOR BOARD DISTANCE. THE PEDAL SHOULD RETURN TO ITS ORIGINAL POSITION

IF THE PEDAL DOES NOT RETURN PROPERLY, CHECK THE PEDAL TO BE SURE IT IS OPERATING FREELY, CORRECT ANY STICKING, BINDING AS NECESSARY.

IF BRAKES SELF-APPLY AND PEDAL IS FREE, CHECK FOR OBSTRUCTION IN THE RETURN LINE OR KINKED CONNECTIONS BETWEEN HYDRO-BOOST AND PUMP RESERVOIR.

REMOVE OBSTRUCTION OR REPLACE LINE AS REQUIRED. IF CONDITION REMAINS, CHECK FOR A DAMAGED REACTION END. IF DAMAGED, HYDRO-BOOST SHOULD BE REPLACED OR REPAIRED.

IF THE PEDAL IS FREE OF ANY BINDING CONDITION, AND THERE ARE NO OBSTRUCTIONS IN THE RETURN LINE, REMOVE THE MASTER CYLINDER RESERVOIR COVER.

OBSERVE THE BRAKE FLUID IN THE RESERVOIR WHILE RAPIDLY DEPRESSING THE BRAKE PEDAL ONE INCH.

FLUID SURFACE SHOULD HAVE SOME MOVEMENT OR SPOUT IN THE FORWARD RESERVOIR SECTION. MINOR SPOUTING MAY OCCUR IN THE REAR RESERVOIR SECTION ALSO. IF NO MOVEMENT OR SPOUTING OR FLUID OCCURS IN FORWARD RESERVOIR SECTION, THE HYDRO-BOOST UNIT IS DEFECTIVE AND MUST BE REPLACED OR REPAIRED.

EXCESSIVE BRAKE PEDAL EFFORT, BRAKE PEDAL CHATTERS OR PULSATES, SYSTEM LEAKS

ENGINE (PUMP) OFF, DEPRESS AND RELEASE BRAKE PEDAL FOUR TIMES TO DEPLETE ALL HYDRAULIC PRESSURE FROM HYDRO-BOOST.

DEPRESS THE PEDAL AND HOLD WITH LIGHT PRESSURE, THEN START THE ENGINE.

IF POWER SECTION IS OPERATING, THE PEDAL WILL FALL SLIGHTLY AND THEN HOLD, LESS PRESSURE WILL BE NEEDED TO HOLD PEDAL DOWN TO THIS POSITION.

IF POWER SECTION IS NOT OPERATING—CHECK PUMP RESERVOIR FLUID LEVEL.

IF FLUID LEVEL IS OK, CHECK TENSION AND CONDITION OF DRIVE BELT.

IF BELT IS LOOSE OR DAMAGED, TIGHTEN OR REPLACE AS REQUIRED AND REPEAT BASIC TEST.

IF PUMP SPEED IS SLOW, ADJUST AND REPEAT BASIC TEST.

IF PUMP SPEED IS OK, PERFORM PUMP FLOW AND RELIEF PRESSURE TEST.

IF PUMP OUTPUT IS BELOW MINIMUM SPECIFICATION, REPLACE AND REPEAT BASIC TEST.

IF ALL TEST AND CHECKS ARE OK, THE BOOSTER IS DEFECTIVE AND SHOULD BE REPLACED OR REPAIRED.

IF FLUID LEVEL IS LOW, ADD FLUID AND REPEAT BASIC TEST PLUS HYDRAULIC LEAK TEST.

STEERING HYDRAULIC LEAK TEST.

THOROUGHLY CLEAN THE HYDRO-BOOST UNIT AND ALL HOSE CONNECTIONS.

START THE PUMP AND RUN AT IDLE SPEED.

IF THE HOSE FITTINGS DO NOT LEAK, CHECK THE HYDRO-BOOST FOR LEAKS. APPLY THE BRAKE PEDAL WITH APPROXIMATELY 100 LBS. EFFORT AND HOLD WHILE CHECKING HYDRO-BOOST HOSE FITTINGS FOR LEAKS. DO NOT HOLD BRAKE PEDAL AT 100 LBS. EFFORT OR ABOVE FOR MORE THAN FIVE SECONDS AT A TIME.

IF THE HYDRO-BOOST LEAKS, IT IS DEFECTIVE AND SHOULD BE REPLACED OR REPAIRED.

IF NO LEAKS ARE FOUND IN THE HYDRO-BOOST OR HOSES, DO NOT REPAIR OR REPLACE HOSES OR HYDRO-BOOST.

IF POWER IS OPERATING, PERFORM IN ORDER.

HYDRO-BOOST ACCUMULATOR PRESSURE RETENTION TEST.

RUN PUMP TO MEDIUM SPEED. APPLY BRAKE PEDAL FORCE TO 100 LBS. FOR NOT MORE THAN FIVE SECONDS. STOP ENGINE (PUMP).

WAIT 90 SECONDS AND APPLY BRAKES. TWO OR MORE APPLICATIONS SHOULD BE POWER ASSISTED.

IF APPLICATIONS ARE NOT POWER ASSISTED, THE HYDRO-BOOST IS DEFECTIVE AND SHOULD BE REPLACED OR REPAIRED.

IF APPLICATIONS ARE POWER ASSISTED, THE ACCUMULATOR IS FUNCTIONING PROPERLY. DO THE HYDRAULIC LEAK TEST.

THOROUGHLY CLEAN THE HYDRO-BOOST UNIT AND ALL HOSE CONNECTIONS.

START THE PUMP AND RUN AT IDLE SPEED.

APPLY BRAKE PEDAL FORCE TO 100 LBS. AND HOLD WHILE CHECKING HYDRO-BOOST AND HOSE CONNECTIONS FOR LEAKS. DO NOT HOLD BRAKE PEDAL TO 100 LBS. FORCE FOR MORE THAN 5 SECONDS AT A TIME.

IF THE HOSE FITTINGS DO NOT LEAK, CHECK THE HYDRO-BOOST FOR LEAKS. APPLY THE BRAKE PEDAL WITH APPROXIMATELY 100 LBS. EFFORT AND HOLD WHILE CHECKING HYDRO-BOOST HOSE FITTINGS FOR LEAKS. DO NOT HOLD BRAKE PEDAL AT 100 LBS. EFFORT OR ABOVE FOR MORE THAN FIVE SECONDS AT A TIME.

IF NO LEAKS ARE FOUND IN THE HYDRO-BOOST OR HOSES. DO NOT REPAIR OR REPLACE HOSES OR HYDRO-BOOST. DO THE HYDRAULIC LEAK TEST.

IF THE HYDRO-BOOST LEAKS, IT IS DEFECTIVE AND SHOULD BE REPLACED OR REPAIRED.

IF NO LEAKS ARE FOUND IN THE HYDRO-BOOST OR HOSES.

BRAKE HYDRAULIC LEAK TEST.

DEPRESS AND RELEASE BRAKE PEDAL SEVRAL TIMES, THEN HOLD PEDAL DEPRESSED WITH MEDIUM PRESSURE, 25 TO 35 LBS.

IF PEDAL FALLS AWAY, HYDRAULIC BRAKE SYSTEM IS LEAKING. CHECK FOR EXTERNAL LEAKAGE AT WHEEL CYLINDERS, CALIPERS, BRAKE HYDRAULIC LINES AND HOSES.

IF THERE IS NO EXTENAL LEAK, THERE MAY BE AN INTERNAL LEAK (MASTER CYLINDER CUPS). REPAIR OR REPLACE PARTS NEEDED TO CORRECT LEAK.

IF PEDAL DOES NOT FALL AWAY, HYDRAULIC SYSTEM IS NOT LEAKING.

91B14374 91C14375 91D14376 91E14377

Courtesy of General Motors Corp.

Fig. 6: Bendix Hydro-Boost System Trouble Shooting Charts

Astro, Bravada, Commercial Van, Jimmy, Lumina APV, Safari, Sierra, Silhouette, Sonoma, Syclone, Trans Sport, Typhoon, Van, "C" & "K" Series Blazer & Pickup, "S" & "T" Series Blazer & Pickup

NOTE: Information in this article also applies to vehicles equipped with Anti-Lock Brake System (ABS); however, not all information on ABS is included in this article. See ANTI-LOCK – RWAL or ANTI-LOCK – 4WAL article.

DESCRIPTION & OPERATION

NOTE: On vehicles with full-floating axle, axle shaft and hub must be removed to remove brake disc or drum. See Figs. 10 and 11. On vehicles with semi-floating axle, brake drum can be removed without removing axle shaft.

MODEL IDENTIFICATION

Vehicle model can be identified by fifth character of Vehicle Identification Number (VIN), stamped on metal pad on top of left end of instrument panel, near windshield. See MODEL IDENTIFICATION table.

MODEL IDENTIFICATION

Series [1]	Model
"C"	2WD Pickup, Sierra & Suburban
"G"	RWD Van
"K"	4WD Blazer, Pickup, Sierra, Suburban & Yukon
"L"	2WD Astro & Safari
"M"	All-Wheel Drive Astro & Safari
"P"	Commercial Van/Motorhome
"S"	2WD Blazer, Jimmy, Pickup & Sonoma
"T"	Bravada, 4WD Blazer, Jimmy, Pickup, Sonoma, Syclone & Typhoon
"U"	Lumina APV, Silhouette & Trans Sport

[1] – Vehicle series is fifth character of VIN.

AUTOMATIC PARKING BRAKE

"P" Series Motorhome – On the automatic apply parking brake system, when shift lever is in Park, engine running, and manual parking brake foot lever in released position, fluid flows from steering gear to port SR on relay valve and out to port TW to the control valve supply port SC. *See Fig. 1.* Once the system is charged, pressure should range between 130-150 psi (9.1-10.5 kg/cm²). Any excess fluid will be discharged through port "R" and back to the pump. The supply port or charge port SC is blocked off due to control valve position in Park mode.

Any previously pressure built-up in control valve flows through control valve out port EC back through the relay valve, triggering release of pressure from port "D" of relay valve through port ER to reservoir. *See Fig. 1.* This allows the spring controlled actuator to apply parking brake. The spring will apply brake by travelling as far as the brake adjustment demand requires to balance brake apply and spring force.

When valve is released from Park position, fluid charge at shift control valve port SC is diverted to port DC. The shift control port EC is blocked off. Fluid charge at relay valve port SR is diverted to port "D", pressurizing parking brake system and actuator. *See Fig. 1.* Fluid pressure working against the spring pressure in actuator releases parking brake.

The manual foot lever should still be applied whenever vehicle is shifted into Park. This will alert operator of need for adjustment in the parking brake system.

BRAKE SHOE ASSEMBLY

Some "C" and "K" Series vehicles are equipped with leading/trailing brakes, identified by adjuster screw hole in backing plate, located above horizontal centerline of rear axle. All other "C" and "K" Series vehicles and all other models are equipped with dual-servo brakes, identified by adjuster screw hole at bottom of backing plate.

Brake assembly consists of backing plate, brake shoes, return springs, automatic adjusting assembly and a wheel cylinder.

Automatic adjusting assembly consists of an actuator lever, return spring, actuator link, adjusting screw and spring. Automatic adjustment is accomplished through movement of actuating lever and secondary shoe.

BRAKE WARNING LIGHT

Lumina APV, Silhouette & Trans Sport – Brake warning light is energized when ignition is on and parking brake is applied or when master cylinder fluid level is low. Brake warning light is not energized if hydraulic pressure is lost; system is not equipped with pressure differential switch.

Except Lumina APV, Silhouette & Trans Sport – Pressure differential warning switch in combination valve energizes brake warning light on instrument panel when front or rear brakes lose hydraulic

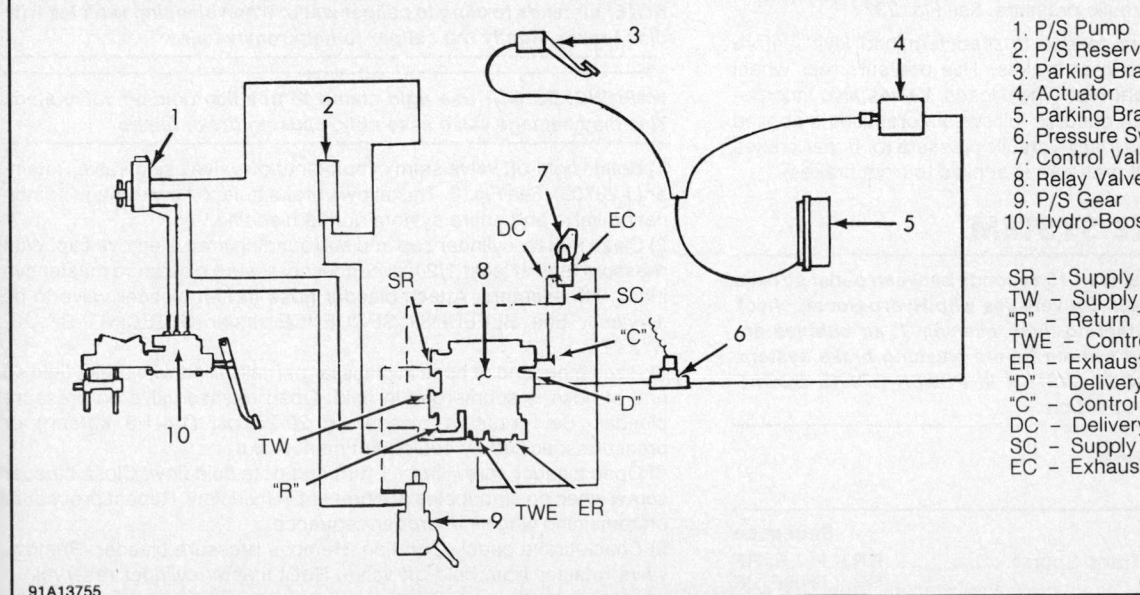

1. P/S Pump
2. P/S Reservoir
3. Parking Brake Pedal
4. Actuator
5. Parking Brake
6. Pressure Switch
7. Control Valve
8. Relay Valve
9. P/S Gear
10. Hydro-Boost Power Brake Booster

SR – Supply To Relay Valve
TW – Supply To Control Valve
"R" – Return To Pump
TWE – Control Valve Exhaust
ER – Exhaust To Reservoir
"D" – Delivery To Actuator
"C" – Control Signal
DC – Delivery From Control Valve
SC – Supply To Control Valve
EC – Exhaust From Control Valve

91A13755

Fig. 1: Schematic Of Automatic Parking Brake System ("P" Series Motorhome)

pressure. After repairing failed side of hydraulic system, depress brake pedal with moderate to heavy pressure to hydraulically center the piston. This will turn off brake warning light.

CALIPERS

Front brakes are floating caliper or sliding caliper design. *See Figs. 14 and 15.* Rear brakes are sliding caliper design. Caliper is attached to caliper mount. Caliper is mounted to steering knuckle or caliper adapter, depending on application. Caliper assembly slides back and forth in machined cut-outs.

HYDRAULIC CONTROL VALVES

Combination Valve (Except Lumina APV, Silhouette & Trans Sport) – System uses a combination valve to regulate brake system hydraulic pressure. Combination valve, located in brake lines between master cylinder and wheels, has 3 pressure control functions:

- **Metering** (or hold-off) section of valve limits pressure to front brakes until pressure of rear brake shoe retractor springs is overcome, then allows pressure to front brakes.
- **Proportioning** section of valve allows input pressure to rise to predetermined level before allowing output pressure to rear brakes. This prevents rear wheel lock-up on vehicles with light rear wheel loads.
- **By-Pass** section of valve ensures full system pressure is applied to rear brakes if front brakes loses hydraulic pressure (or if rear brakes lose hydraulic pressure, full pressure is applied to front brakes).

Combination valve also contains a pressure differential warning switch. See BRAKE WARNING LIGHT under DESCRIPTION & OPERATION.

Height-Sensing Proportioning Valve ("C" & "K" Series & "P" Series) – Valve senses vehicle load conditions through relative movement between rear axle and body. *See Figs. 4 and 5.* As vehicle load increases (resulting in decreased vehicle height), valve allows higher pressure to rear brakes, resulting in optimum front-to-rear brake pressure balance.

WARNING: On vehicles with height sensing proportioning valve, use of aftermarket load leveling kits, air shocks, or modifications that change axle-to-frame distance will provide a false reading to valve. False readings may result in unsatisfactory brake performance.

Proportioning Valves (Lumina APV, Silhouette & Trans Sport) – System uses 2 proportioning valves, threaded into master cylinder, to regulate brake system hydraulic pressure. *See Fig. 23.*

Valves allow input pressure to rise to predetermined level before allowing output pressure to rear brakes. This prevents rear wheel lock-up on vehicles with light rear wheel loads. Valves also incorporate a by-pass feature which ensures full system pressure is applied to rear brakes if front brakes lose hydraulic pressure (or if rear brakes lose hydraulic pressure, full pressure is applied to front brakes).

BLEEDING BRAKE SYSTEM

NOTE: On vehicles with ABS, wait 15 seconds between pedal strokes when bleeding brake system. On vehicles with Hydro-Boost, check for air bubbles in power steering fluid reservoir. If air bubbles are present, bleed Hydro-Boost system before bleeding brake system. See BLEEDING HYDRO-BOOST SYSTEM in POWER BRAKE BOOSTER – BENDIX HYDRO-BOOST article.

BLEEDING SEQUENCE
BLEEDING SEQUENCE

Application	Sequence
Lumina APV, Silhouette & Trans Sport	RR, LF, LR, RF
All Others	RR, LR, RF, LF

MASTER CYLINDER BLEEDING

NOTE: To prevent air from entering brake system, bench bleed master cylinder before installing.

1) Place master cylinder in soft-jawed vise. DO NOT overtighten vise. Install bleeder tubes in both outlets of master cylinder. *See Fig. 2.* Fill master cylinder reservoir. Ensure ends of bleeder tubes are submerged in brake fluid.

2) Using screwdriver or drift punch at end of master cylinder bore, press and release piston assembly until air bubbles are no longer present in fluid flow. Leave bleeder tubes installed on master cylinder. Install master cylinder.

3) Remove bleeder tubes. Connect brake lines at master cylinder. DO NOT fully tighten brake lines at this time. Slowly press brake pedal to floor and hold. Tighten brake lines. Release brake pedal. Bleed brake system. See MANUAL BLEEDING, PRESSURE BLEEDING or VACUUM BLEEDING.

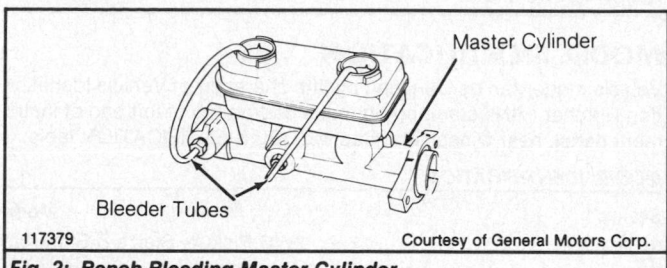

117379   Courtesy of General Motors Corp.

Fig. 2: Bench Bleeding Master Cylinder

MANUAL BLEEDING

NOTE: Air tends to cling to caliper walls. When bleeding vehicles with disc brakes, lightly tap caliper to help remove air.

1) Fill master cylinder. Install bleeder hose to bleeder screw at first wheel to be serviced. See BLEEDING SEQUENCE under BLEEDING BRAKE SYSTEM. Submerge other end of hose in glass jar partially filled with brake fluid.

2) Open bleeder screw 3/4 - 1 turn. Slowly press brake pedal to floor. Note fluid flow. Close bleeder screw. Release pedal. Repeat procedure until air bubbles are no longer present in fluid flow.

PRESSURE BLEEDING

NOTE: Air tends to cling to caliper walls. When bleeding vehicles with disc brakes, lightly tap caliper to help remove air.

WARNING: DO NOT use rigid clamp to position hold-off valve stem. This may damage valve assembly, causing brake failure.

1) Retain hold-off valve stem of combination valve using Valve Retainer (J-23709). *See Fig. 3.* This allows brake fluid to flow through combination valve and entire system during bleeding.

2) Clean master cylinder cap and surrounding area. Remove cap. With pressure tank at least 1/2 full, connect pressure bleeder to master cylinder with adapters. Attach bleeder hose to first bleeder valve to be serviced. See BLEEDING SEQUENCE under BLEEDING BRAKE SYSTEM.

3) Place other end of hose in glass jar partially filled with brake fluid so end of hose is submerged in fluid. Open release valve on pressure bleeder. Set pressure bleeder to 20-25 psi (1.4-1.8 kg/cm²) or pressure specified by equipment manufacturer.

4) Open bleeder screw 3/4 - 1 turn and note fluid flow. Close bleeder screw when no air bubbles are present in fluid flow. Repeat procedure on remaining wheels in proper sequence.

5) Check brake pedal operation. Remove pressure bleeder. Remove valve retainer from hold-off valve. Refill master cylinder reservoir, if necessary.

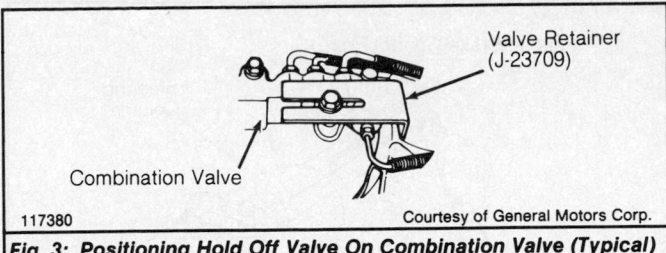

117380   Courtesy of General Motors Corp.

Fig. 3: Positioning Hold Off Valve On Combination Valve (Typical)

VACUUM BLEEDING

NOTE: Air tends to cling to caliper walls. When bleeding vehicles with disc brakes, lightly tap caliper to help remove air.

1) Fill master cylinder reservoir. Install vacuum bleed equipment to first bleeder valve to be serviced. See BLEEDING SEQUENCE under BLEEDING BRAKE SYSTEM.

2) Open bleeder valve 3/4 - 1 turn. Press vacuum pump to draw fluid into reservoir jar until no air bubbles are present in fluid flow. Close bleeder screw. Repeat procedure on remaining wheels in sequence.

ADJUSTMENTS

HEIGHT-SENSING PROPORTIONING VALVE

NOTE: If front wheel lock-up is experienced during braking when vehicle is near maximum GVWR, adjust height-sensing proportioning valve.

"C" & "K" Series – Ensure rear axle is hanging free and valve is securely bolted to frame when lever is attached to valve before height-sensing proportioning valve is adjusted. *See Fig. 4.*

"P" Series – 1) Raise vehicle at frame rails, allowing rear axle to hang free. Remove nut and lever from valve shaft. *See Fig. 5.* Select appropriate adjustment gauge (available from manufacturer). Rotate valve shaft to permit installation of gauge.

2) Install gauge with flat on valve shaft indexed to flat on gauge, and tang on gauge inserted in valve mounting hole. Install lever (DO NOT pull lever onto shaft using nut). Install nut. Break off tang on gauge. Lower and test-drive vehicle.

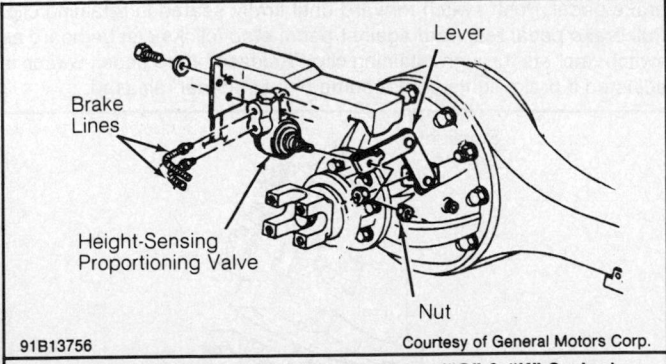

91B13756   Courtesy of General Motors Corp.

Fig. 4: Height-Sensing Proportioning Valve ("C" & "K" Series)

PARKING BRAKE

NOTE: On all models except "C" and "K" Series with leading/trailing brakes, ensure rear brake shoes are adjusted before adjusting parking brake. See REAR BRAKE SHOES under ADJUSTMENTS.

Astro & Safari – 1) Raise and support vehicle. Loosen parking brake cable adjusting nut. Apply parking brake pedal 2 notches from fully released position.

2) Tighten adjusting nut until left rear wheel can be turned rearward using 2 hands, but not forward. Release parking brake and ensure wheels rotate freely. Lower vehicle.

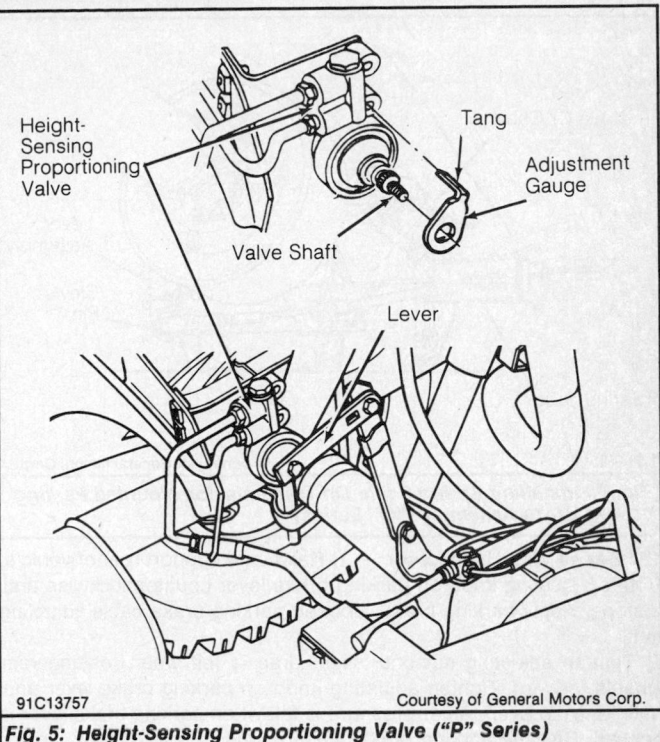

91C13757   Courtesy of General Motors Corp.

Fig. 5: Height-Sensing Proportioning Valve ("P" Series)

Lumina APV, Silhouette & Trans Sport – Apply parking brake pedal 3 notches from fully released position. Raise and support vehicle. Tighten parking brake cable adjusting nut until right rear wheel can be turned rearward but not forward. Release parking brake and ensure wheels rotate freely. Lower vehicle.

"C" & "K" Series With Leading/Trailing Brakes – 1) Raise and support rear of vehicle. Remove rear wheels. Remove brake drums. Rotate parking brake adjusting screw until clearance between brake drum and shoes is .010-.020" (.25-.51 mm). Use brake drum diameter gauge to determine clearance.

2) Ensure stop on parking brake lever is in contact with edge of brake shoe web. If parking brake cable is holding stops off of shoe web, loosen cable adjusting nut. Tighten cable adjusting nut until lever stop begins to move off of shoe web.

3) Loosen cable adjusting nut until lever stop moves back toward lever stop and barely contacts the stop. Clearance should be no more than .020" (.51 mm) between lever stop and shoe web.

4) Install brake drums and wheels. Apply and release service brake pedal 30-35 times with normal pedal force, pausing about one second between pedal applications. Apply parking brake pedal 6 notches from fully released position.

5) Rear wheels should not be able to be rotated. Release parking brake and ensure wheels rotate freely. Lower vehicle.

"C" Series with Transmission-Mounted Parking Brake –
1) Remove clevis pin from lever assembly. *See Fig. 6.* Apply parking brake pedal 4 notches from fully released position.

2) Using small length of cable or chain and a turnbuckle, install Spring Scale (J-35999) between lever assembly and vehicle frame. Tighten turnbuckle until spring scale indicates 50 lbs. (22.7 kg).

3) Loosen clevis nut (at cable end). Turn clevis until clevis pin slides freely into lever assembly with all slack removed from cable. Install clevis pin and retain with a cotter pin. Tighten clevis nut. Remove spring scale. Release parking brake.

"C" & "K" Series With Dual-Servo Brakes, "G" Series & "P" Series With Foot Pedal – Raise and support vehicle. Loosen parking brake cable adjusting nut. Apply parking brake pedal 4 notches from fully released position. Tighten adjusting nut until wheels rotate forward with moderate drag. Release parking brake and ensure wheels rotate freely. Lower vehicle.

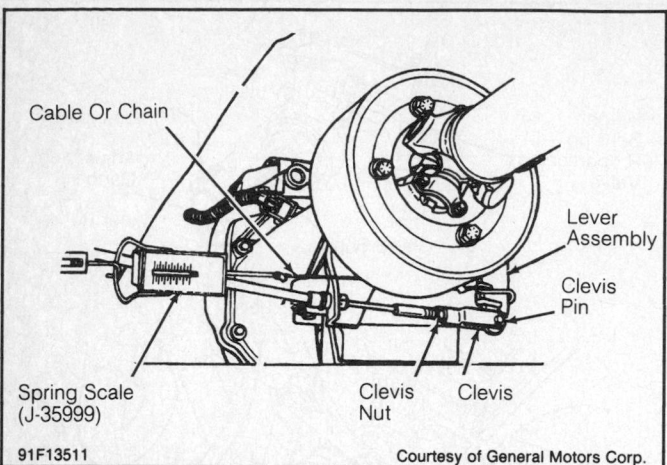

Fig. 6: Installing Spring Scale On Transmission-Mounted Parking Brake Assembly ("C" Series)

91F13511   Courtesy of General Motors Corp.

"P" Series With Hand Lever – 1) Raise and support rear of vehicle. Rotate adjusting knob on parking brake lever counterclockwise until it stops. Apply parking brake. Loosen parking brake cable adjusting nut.

2) Tighten adjusting nut until slight drag is felt when rotating rear wheels forward. Tighten adjusting knob on parking brake lever until definite snap-over-center pressure is felt when parking brake lever is applied. Release parking brake. Ensure wheels rotate freely. Lower vehicle.

"P" Series With Transmission-Mounted Parking Brake – 1) Raise and support rear of vehicle. For preferred method of adjustment, perform steps **2)** and **3)**. For alternate method of adjustment, perform step **4)**.

2) Remove drive shaft. Install parking brake drum over first rivet section of brake shoes. Insert .010" (.25 mm) shims between both shoes and drum, spaced 140-180 degrees apart.

3) Rotate adjuster screw until no clearance exists. Remove shims. Install drum and drive shaft. Drum should rotate freely with light drag.

4) Rotate adjuster screw through hole in backing plate until brake drum just locks up. Back off adjuster screw until drum spins freely with light drag. Lower vehicle.

"S" & "T" Series – 1) Raise and support vehicle. Loosen parking brake cable adjusting nut. Apply parking brake pedal 2 notches (2WD) or 3 notches (Bravada and 4WD) from fully released position.

2) Tighten adjusting nut until wheels will not rotate forward without excessive force. Back off adjusting nut until slight drag exists when wheels are rotated forward. Release parking brake and ensure wheels rotate freely. Lower vehicle.

PARKING BRAKE CONTROL ROD

"P" Series Motorhome – 1) Disconnect parking brake control rod from control valve lever and transmission control equalizer. See Fig. 7. Place control valve lever in park position. Place transmission selector in Park.

2) Connect parking brake control rod to control valve lever. Loosen parking brake control rod jam nuts. Rotate rod as necessary to align hole at end of rod with hole in transmission control equalizer lever. Install and tighten bolt.

REAR BRAKE SHOES

Lumina APV, Silhouette & Trans Sport – 1) Ensure parking brake is released. Raise and support vehicle. Remove rear wheels. Rotate adjusting screw until clearance between brake drum and shoes is .050" (1.27 mm). Use brake drum diameter gauge to determine clearance.

2) Install brake drum. Install wheels. Operate vehicle for several forward and reverse stops while firmly applying brakes. Repeat procedure until ample brake pedal reserve is obtained.

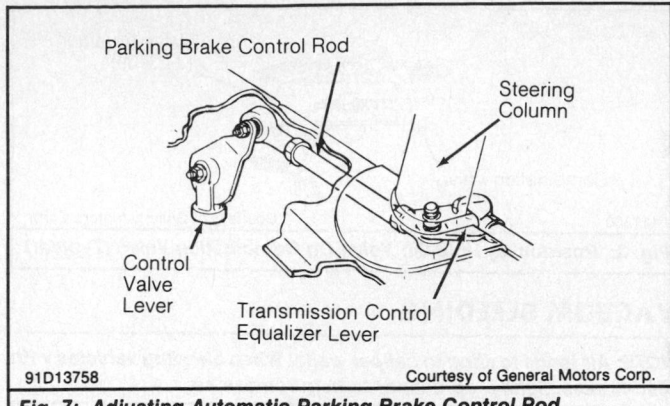

Fig. 7: Adjusting Automatic Parking Brake Control Rod ("P" Series Motorhome)

91D13758   Courtesy of General Motors Corp.

"C" & "K" Series With Leading/Trailing Brakes – Brake shoe adjustment is accomplished by adjusting parking brake. See PARKING BRAKE under ADJUSTMENTS.

Except "C" & "K" Series With Leading/Trailing Brakes – 1) Ensure parking brake is released. Raise and support vehicle. Knock out lanced area in backing plate with a punch (if not already removed) and remove from brake assembly.

2) Working through hole in backing plate, rotate adjusting screw until brake shoes expand and brake drums can just be turned by hand. Ensure drag is equal at both wheels. Back off adjusting screw 24 notches (Astro, Safari and "S" & "T" Series) or 33 notches (all others) at each wheel.

3) If heavy drag is present after adjusting screw is backed off 12 notches (Astro, Safari and "S" & "T" Series) or 15 notches (all others), check parking brake adjustment. See PARKING BRAKE under ADJUSTMENTS. To complete procedure, install plug in backing plate. Check parking brake adjustment.

STOPLIGHT SWITCH

"C" & "K" Series With Cruise Control – Depress and hold brake pedal. Pull lever on stoplight switch back to its stop. See Fig. 8. Pull brake pedal against pedal stop. Release brake pedal. Switch is adjusted if brake lights do not come on with pedal released.

Except "C" & "K" Series With Cruise Control – Depress and hold brake pedal. Push switch forward until firmly seated in retaining clip. Pull brake pedal rearward against pedal stop (clicks can be heard as switch ratchets through retaining clip). Release brake pedal. Switch is adjusted if brake lights do not come on with pedal released.

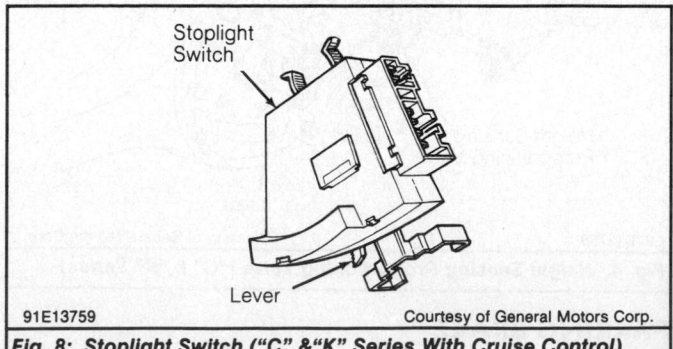

91E13759   Courtesy of General Motors Corp.

Fig. 8: Stoplight Switch ("C" &"K" Series With Cruise Control)

TESTING

BRAKE WARNING LIGHT

Electrical Circuit – Disconnect wire from switch terminal on combination valve. Connect wire to ground. Turn ignition on. If brake warning light does not come on, repair brake warning light bulb or wiring circuit. If light operates, brake warning light electrical circuit is okay.

NOTE: On Astro and Safari, system is not equipped with pressure differential switch.

Warning Light Switch – 1) Fill master cylinder reservoir. Attach bleeder hose to bleeder screw at either rear wheel. Immerse other end of hose in container of brake fluid. Turn ignition on.

2) While depressing brake pedal, open bleeder screw (close bleeder screw before releasing pedal). On all models except Astro and Safari, if light comes on, go to step **3)**. If light does not come on, switch is defective; replace combination valve.

3) Close bleeder screw. Depress brake pedal with moderate to heavy pressure. If light goes out, switch is okay. If light stays on, switch is defective, replace combination valve. Repeat test on front brake system. System should function in same manner as rear.

REMOVAL & INSTALLATION

AUTOMATIC PARKING BRAKE ("P" SERIES MOTORHOME)

NOTE: Adjust parking brake control rod after removing and installing control valve. See PARKING BRAKE CONTROL ROD under ADJUSTMENTS. Adjust parking brake after removing and installing actuator. See PARKING BRAKE under ADJUSTMENTS. If any parking brake system fluid lines are disconnected, bleed parking brake system.

System Bleeding – 1) Place transmission in Park to set control valve in Park mode. Start engine. Turn steering wheel from stop to stop to bleed power steering system. Place transmission in Neutral.

2) Open bleed screw on actuator until fluid flow is free of air, then close bleed screw (bleed screw is near fluid hose connection, on top of actuator). Loosen exhaust line fitting (port EC) at control valve. *See Fig. 1.* Place transmission in Park. Allow small amount of fluid to bleed from fitting, then tighten fitting.

3) Cycle the system. If noisy, repeat bleeding procedure. Check power steering fluid level with transmission in Neutral and parking brake applied manually. Fluid level should be 7.12" (180.9 mm) from top of reservoir.

FRONT BRAKE CALIPER

NOTE: For front disc pad removal and installation, perform FRONT BRAKE CALIPER removal and installation procedures but do not disconnect brake hose from caliper (hang caliper out of way with wire). Replace all pads on an axle if wear indicator on any pad contacts rotor or if pad is worn to within 1/32" (.8 mm) of pad backing.

Removal (Floating Caliper) – 1) Remove two-thirds of brake fluid from master cylinder. Raise and support vehicle. Remove wheel. Using "C" clamp or large pliers, compress caliper piston until it bottoms in its bore.

2) Disconnect brake hose from caliper. Remove caliper guide pins. *See Fig. 14.* Remove caliper. Remove pads from caliper. Note retainer spring on inner pad (some models) and remove if replacing pads.

Installation – 1) Remove caliper sleeves from caliper. *See Fig. 14.* Apply silicone grease to outer diameter of caliper sleeves and inner diameter of bushings. Insert caliper sleeves into bushings.

2) Install retainer spring on inner pad (if removed). Install pads in caliper. Install caliper. Install guide pins and tighten to specification. See TORQUE SPECIFICATIONS table at end of article.

3) Connect brake hose to caliper and tighten hose bolt to 32 ft. lbs. (43 N.m). Bleed brake system. See MANUAL BLEEDING, PRESSURE BLEEDING or VACUUM BLEEDING under BLEEDING BRAKE SYSTEM.

4) If outer pads are equipped with locking ears, bend ears toward caliper until ears touch caliper. This prevents movement of outer pad in caliper. *See Fig. 9.* Install wheel.

Removal (Sliding Caliper) – 1) Remove two-thirds of brake fluid from master cylinder. Raise and support vehicle. Remove wheel. Using "C"

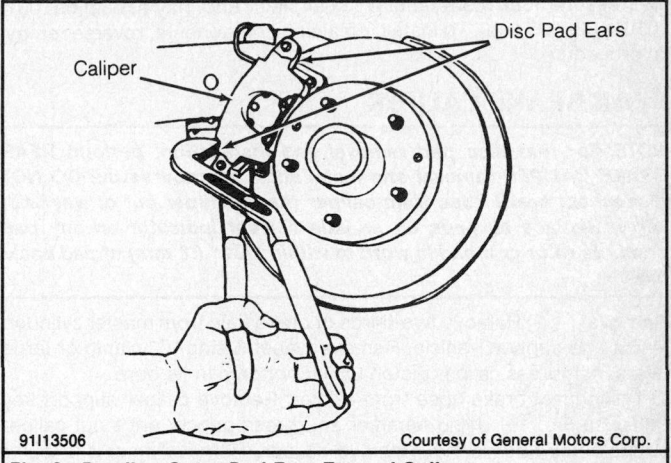

91113506   Courtesy of General Motors Corp.
Fig. 9: Bending Outer Pad Ears Toward Caliper

clamp or large pliers, compress caliper piston until it bottoms in its bore.

2) Disconnect brake hose from caliper. Remove caliper support key bolt. *See Fig. 15.* Using hammer and brass punch, drive out caliper support key and spring. Remove caliper. Remove inner and outer pads.

Installation – 1) Using wire brush, clean corrosion from machined ways on caliper and caliper mount. Apply silicone grease to these surfaces. Install inner pad and anti-rattle spring on caliper mount. *See Fig. 15.* Install outer pad in caliper. Place caliper on caliper mount.

2) Using a hammer and brass punch, install caliper support key and spring. Install caliper support key bolt, ensuring bolt boss fits into circular cutout on caliper support key. Tighten bolt to 15 ft. lbs. (20 N.m).

3) Connect brake hose to caliper and tighten hose bolt to specification. See TORQUE SPECIFICATIONS table at end of article. Bleed brake system. See MANUAL BLEEDING, PRESSURE BLEEDING or VACUUM BLEEDING under BLEEDING BRAKE SYSTEM. Install wheel.

FRONT BRAKE ROTOR

Removal (All 2WD Vehicles Except Lumina APV, Silhouette & Trans Sport) – Remove brake caliper (DO NOT disconnect brake hose). See FRONT BRAKE CALIPER under REMOVAL & INSTALLATION. Remove grease cap from end of hub. Remove cotter pin, nut, washer and outer bearing. Remove rotor and hub assembly.

Installation – 1) Clean and pack wheel bearings. Install rotor and hub assembly. Install outer bearing, washer and nut. Tighten nut to 12 ft. lbs. (16 N.m) while rotating rotor and hub assembly. This seats bearings.

2) Back off nut until it just begins to loosen. Finger-tighten nut. Back off nut until hole in spindle aligns with hole in nut (DO NOT back off more than 1/2 of a flat). Install new cotter pin, bend ends over and ensure ends will not contact grease cap when installed. To complete installation, reverse removal procedure.

Removal & Installation (AWD Astro & Safari, Bravada, Lumina APV, Silhouette, Trans Sport & All 4WD Vehicles) – Remove brake caliper (DO NOT disconnect brake hose). See FRONT BRAKE CALIPER under REMOVAL & INSTALLATION. Remove rotor. To install, reverse removal procedure.

Installation – 1) Install hub and rotor assembly. Install wheel bearing adjusting nut and tighten to 50 ft. lbs. (68 N.m) while turning hub and rotor assembly. This seats wheel bearings.

2) On vehicles with automatic locking hubs, back off adjusting nut then tighten to 35 ft. lbs. (47 N.m) while turning hub and rotor assembly. Back off adjusting nut 3/8 turn maximum.

3) On vehicles with manual locking hubs, back off adjusting nut then tighten to 50 ft. lbs. (68 N.m) while turning hub and rotor assembly. Back off adjusting nut enough to free bearing.

4) On all vehicles, install ring, ensuring hole in ring aligns with pin on adjusting nut (turn adjusting nut slightly, if necessary). Install lock nut and tighten to 160 ft. lbs. (217 N.m).

5) Measure hub/rotor end play (axial play). End play should be .001-.010" (.025-.25 mm). To install remaining components, reverse removal procedure.

REAR BRAKE CALIPER

NOTE: For rear disc pad removal and installation, perform REAR BRAKE CALIPER removal and installation procedures but DO NOT disconnect brake hose from caliper (hang caliper out of way with wire). Replace all pads on an axle if wear indicator on any pad contacts rotor or if pad is worn to within 1/32" (.8 mm) of pad backing.

Removal – 1) Remove two-thirds of brake fluid from master cylinder. Raise and support vehicle. Remove wheel. Using "C" clamp or large pliers, compress caliper piston until it bottoms in its bore.
2) Disconnect brake hose from caliper. Remove caliper support key bolt. *See Fig. 15.* Using hammer and brass punch, drive out caliper support key and spring. Remove caliper. Remove inner and outer pads.
Installation – 1) Using wire brush, clean corrosion from machined ways on caliper and caliper mount. Apply silicone grease to these surfaces. Install inner pad and anti-rattle spring on caliper mount. Install outer pad in caliper. Install caliper.
2) Using hammer and brass punch, install caliper support key and spring. Install caliper support key bolt, ensuring bolt boss fits into circular cutout on caliper support key. Tighten bolt to 15 ft. lbs. (20 N.m).
3) Connect brake hose to caliper and tighten hose bolt to specification. See TORQUE SPECIFICATIONS table at end of article. Bleed brake system. See MANUAL BLEEDING, PRESSURE BLEEDING or VACUUM BLEEDING under BLEEDING BRAKE SYSTEM. Install wheel.

REAR BRAKE ROTOR

Removal (9 3/4" & 10 1/2" Full-Floating Axle) – 1) Raise and support vehicle. Remove brake caliper (DO NOT disconnect brake hose). See REAR BRAKE CALIPER under REMOVAL & INSTALLATION. Remove bolts from end of axle shaft.
2) Lightly tap axle shaft flange with soft hammer to loosen shaft. Grip rib on axle shaft flange with locking pliers. Twist axle shaft to start shaft removal. Pull axle shaft from axle housing.
3) Bend lock washer tab away from lock nut. Using Wheel Bearing Nut Wrench (J-2222-C), remove lock nut. Remove lock washer. Remove adjusting nut and washer. Remove hub and rotor assembly.
Installation – 1) Install hub and rotor assembly. Install washer and adjusting nut. Using Wheel Bearing Nut Wrench (J-2222-C), tighten adjusting nut to 50 ft. lbs. (68 N.m) while turning hub and rotor assembly.

2) Back off adjusting nut and tighten to 30-40 ft. lbs. (41-54 N.m) while turning hub and rotor assembly. Back off adjusting nut 135-150 degrees. Install lock washer and lock nut finger tight. Bend lock washer tab over adjusting nut flat at a minimum angle of 30 degrees.
3) Tighten lock nut to 65 ft. lbs. (88 N.m) minimum. Bend lock washer tab over lock nut flat at a minimum angle of 60 degrees. To install remaining components, reverse removal procedure.
Removal (12" Full-Floating Axle) – 1) Raise and support vehicle. Remove brake caliper (DO NOT disconnect brake hose). See REAR BRAKE CALIPER under REMOVAL & INSTALLATION. Remove hub cap and gasket from hub. *See Fig. 10.* Install Adapter (J-2619-01) in tapped hole on axle shaft flange.
2) Using slide hammer and adapter, remove axle shaft. Bend lock washer tab away from lock nut. Using Wheel Bearing Nut Wrench (J-25510), remove lock nut. Remove lock washer, adjusting nut and washer. Remove hub and rotor assembly.
Installation – 1) Install hub and rotor assembly. Install washer and adjusting nut. *See Fig. 10.* Using Wheel Bearing Nut Wrench (J-25510), tighten adjusting nut to 50 ft. lbs. (68 N.m) while turning hub and rotor assembly. Back off adjusting nut 1/8 turn.
2) Install lock washer and lock nut finger tight. Bend lock washer tab over adjusting nut flat. Tighten lock nut to 250 ft. lbs. (339 N.m). Bend lock washer long tab over lock nut flat. To install remaining components, reverse removal procedure.

REAR BRAKE DRUM

Removal & Installation (Semi-Floating Axle) – Ensure parking brake is released. Raise and support rear of vehicle. Remove wheel. Remove brake drum (if necessary, back off adjuster wheel before removing brake drum). To install, reverse removal procedure. Adjust rear brake shoes. See REAR BRAKE SHOES under ADJUSTMENTS.
Removal (Full-Floating Axle) – 1) Ensure parking brake is released. Raise and support rear of vehicle. Remove wheel. Remove bolts from end of axle shaft. *See Fig. 11.*
2) Lightly tap axle shaft flange with soft hammer to loosen shaft. Grip rib on axle shaft flange with locking pliers. Twist axle shaft to start shaft removal. Pull axle shaft from axle housing.
3) Remove retaining ring and key. Using Wheel Bearing Nut Wrench (J-2222-C), remove adjusting nut. Remove washer. Remove hub and brake drum assembly (if necessary, back off adjuster wheel before removing brake drum).
Installation – 1) Apply light coat of bearing lubricant to axle tube. Install hub and brake drum assembly. Install washer and adjusting nut. Using Wheel Bearing Nut Wrench (J-2222-C), tighten adjusting nut 50 ft. lbs. (68 N.m), while turning hub and rotor assembly.
2) Back off adjusting nut until just loose, then tighten until nut's inboard face contacts outer bearing cone shoulder (torque on nut MUST be zero or finger-tight).

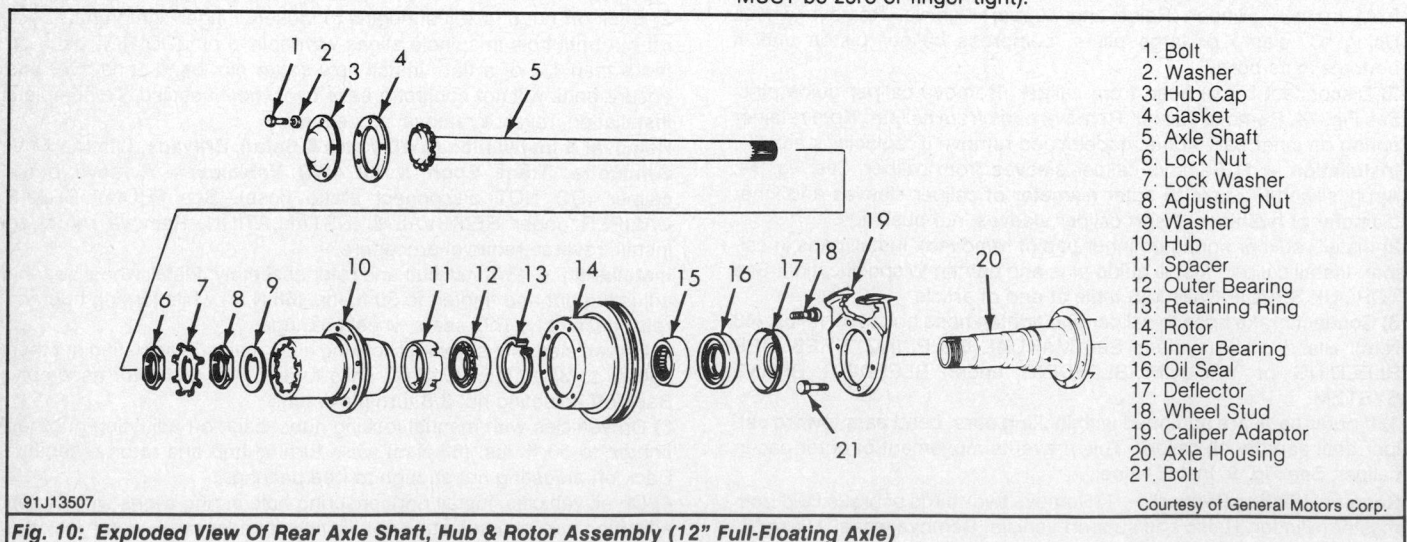

1. Bolt
2. Washer
3. Hub Cap
4. Gasket
5. Axle Shaft
6. Lock Nut
7. Lock Washer
8. Adjusting Nut
9. Washer
10. Hub
11. Spacer
12. Outer Bearing
13. Retaining Ring
14. Rotor
15. Inner Bearing
16. Oil Seal
17. Deflector
18. Wheel Stud
19. Caliper Adaptor
20. Axle Housing
21. Bolt

91J13507

Courtesy of General Motors Corp.

Fig. 10: Exploded View Of Rear Axle Shaft, Hub & Rotor Assembly (12" Full-Floating Axle)

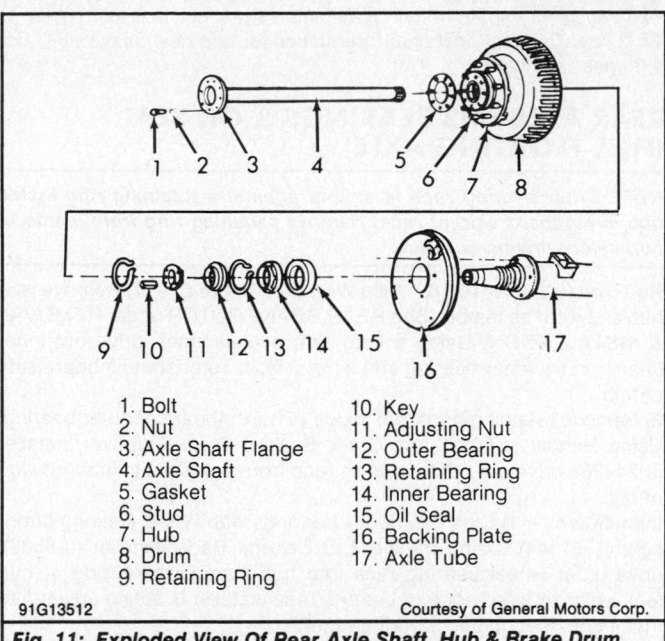

1. Bolt
2. Nut
3. Axle Shaft Flange
4. Axle Shaft
5. Gasket
6. Stud
7. Hub
8. Drum
9. Retaining Ring
10. Key
11. Adjusting Nut
12. Outer Bearing
13. Retaining Ring
14. Inner Bearing
15. Oil Seal
16. Backing Plate
17. Axle Tube

91G13512   Courtesy of General Motors Corp.

Fig. 11: Exploded View Of Rear Axle Shaft, Hub & Brake Drum Assembly (Full-Floating Axle)

3) Insert key into adjusting nut slot. If slot is in alignment with axle spindle keyway, loosen nut slightly but not more than one slot to align key. Install retaining ring. Install axle shaft and wheel. Lower vehicle.

REAR BRAKE SHOES

NOTE: For rear brake shoe removal and installation, see Figs. 16-18. DO NOT interchange left and right adjusting screw assemblies as one side is right-hand thread and other is left-hand thread.

WHEEL CYLINDER

Removal & Installation – Remove rear brake shoes. See REAR BRAKE SHOES under REMOVAL & INSTALLATION. Disconnect brake line from wheel cylinder. Remove brake cylinder retaining bolts and brake cylinder. To install, reverse removal procedure. Bleed brake system. See MANUAL BLEEDING, PRESSURE BLEEDING or VACUUM BLEEDING under BLEEDING BRAKE SYSTEM.

MASTER CYLINDER

Removal – **1)** With engine off, press brake pedal several times to release vacuum in power brake unit. Clean dirt and grease from master cylinder brake line fittings. Disconnect brake lines from master cylinder and plug line ends.

2) On vehicles with combination valve and bracket attached to master cylinder mounting studs, remove combination valve and bracket. On vehicles without power brake unit, disconnect brake pedal push rod at brake pedal. On all vehicles, remove master cylinder retaining nuts and master cylinder.

Installation – **1)** Bench bleed master cylinder before installing. See MASTER CYLINDER BLEEDING under BLEEDING BRAKE SYSTEM. Position master cylinder on mounting studs. Position combination valve and bracket on mounting studs (if applicable). Loosely install master cylinder retaining nuts. Connect brake lines to master cylinder but DO NOT tighten.

2) Tighten master cylinder retaining nuts. Tighten brake lines. Connect brake pedal push rod (if disconnected). Fill fluid reservoir. Bleed brake system. See MANUAL BLEEDING, PRESSURE BLEEDING or VACUUM BLEEDING under BLEEDING BRAKE SYSTEM.

POWER BRAKE BOOSTER

NOTE: For Hydro-Boost removal and installation, see POWER BRAKE BOOSTER – BENDIX HYDRO-BOOST article.

Removal & Installation – **1)** Remove master cylinder. See MASTER CYLINDER under REMOVAL & INSTALLATION. Ensure no brake fluid contacts ABS control unit (if equipped) or related electrical connectors and wiring.

2) Disconnect vacuum hose from booster. Disconnect booster push rod from brake pedal. Remove booster mounting nuts from inside vehicle. Remove booster and gasket.

3) To install, reverse removal procedure. Bleed brake system if lines were disconnected from master cylinder. See MANUAL BLEEDING, PRESSURE BLEEDING or VACUUM BLEEDING under BLEEDING BRAKE SYSTEM.

HEIGHT-SENSING PROPORTIONING VALVE

Removal & Installation ("C" & "K" Series) – **1)** Raise vehicle by frame, allowing rear axle to hang free. Remove bracket that covers valve. Remove nut and lever from valve shaft. *See Fig. 4.* Clean area around brake line fittings at valve. Disconnect brake lines from valve. Remove valve-to-frame bolts and valve.

2) To install, reverse removal procedure, ensuring rear axle is hanging free and valve is securely bolted to frame when lever is attached to valve (this ensures correct valve adjustment). Bleed brake system. See MANUAL BLEEDING, PRESSURE BLEEDING or VACUUM BLEEDING under BLEEDING BRAKE SYSTEM.

Removal & Installation ("P" Series) – **1)** Raise vehicle by frame, allowing rear axle to hang free. Clean area around brake line fittings at valve. *See Fig. 5.* Disconnect brake lines from valve. Remove nut and lever from valve shaft. Remove valve-to-frame bolts and valve.

2) To install, reverse removal procedure. If installing new valve, adjust the new valve. See HEIGHT-SENSING PROPORTIONING VALVE under ADJUSTMENTS. Bleed brake system. See MANUAL BLEEDING, PRESSURE BLEEDING or VACUUM BLEEDING under BLEEDING BRAKE SYSTEM.

COMBINATION VALVE

Removal – Disconnect brake warning light electrical connector from combination valve switch. Disconnect brake lines from valve. Cap brake line ends. Remove valve mounting bolts. Remove valve.

Installation – To install, reverse removal procedure. Bleed brake system. See MANUAL BLEEDING, PRESSURE BLEEDING or VACUUM BLEEDING under BLEEDING BRAKE SYSTEM. Center the brake warning light switch piston by applying moderate to heavy force on brake pedal.

REAR AXLE BEARING & OIL SEAL (SEMI-FLOATING AXLE)

Removal (Astro, Safari & "S" & "T" Series) – **1)** Raise and support vehicle. Remove wheels and brake drums. Loosen differential cover plate and drain lubricant from axle. Remove cover plate.

2) Remove pinion shaft lock bolt. *See Figs. 12 and 13.* Remove pinion shaft. Push axle shaft toward center of vehicle and remove "C" lock from end of axle shaft. Remove axle shaft.

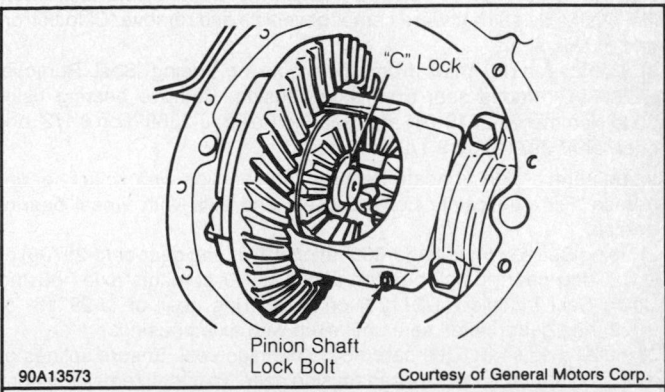

90A13573   Courtesy of General Motors Corp.

Fig. 12: Locating "C" Lock & Pinion Shaft Lock Bolt (Astro, Safari & "S" & "T" Series Shown; Others Similar)

3) Pry seal from axle housing. Using Slide Hammer (J-2619-01) and Axle Bearing Puller (J-22813-01), remove bearing from axle housing.
Installation – 1) Lubricate bearing with axle lubricant. Using Handle (J-8092) and Bearing Installer (J-23765), install bearing in axle housing until bearing installer bottoms against shoulder of axle housing.
2) Using Seal Installer (J-23771), install seal until even with surface of axle housing. Lubricate seal lips with axle lubricant. Install axle shaft and "C" lock. *See Figs. 12 and 13.* Pull axle shaft outward to ensure "C" lock seats in side gear.
3) Install pinion shaft. Install NEW pinion shaft lock bolt. Tighten lock bolt to 25 ft. lbs. (34 N.m). Install differential cover and new gasket. Fill drive axle with axle lubricant.

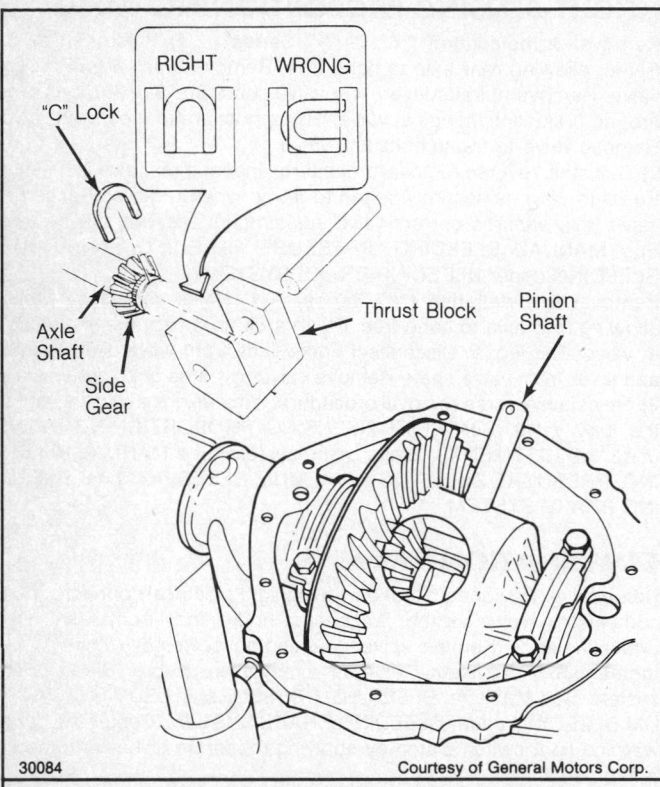

30084   Courtesy of General Motors Corp.

Fig. 13: Removing & Installing "C" Lock & Pinion Shaft On Locking Differential (Typical)

Removal (Except Astro, Safari & "S" & "T" Series) – 1) Raise and support vehicle. Remove wheel and brake drum. Loosen differential cover plate and drain lubricant from axle. Remove cover plate. Remove pinion shaft lock bolt. *See Figs. 12 and 13.*
2) On locking differential models, remove pinion shaft part way. Rotate differential case until pinion shaft contacts axle housing. Using screwdriver, rotate "C" lock until it aligns with thrust block. On all models, push axle shaft toward center of vehicle and remove "C" lock from end of axle shaft.
3) Remove axle shaft from axle housing. Using Seal Remover (J-23689), remove seal from axle housing. Remove bearing using Slide Hammer (J-2619-01) and Bearing Puller (J-23689) on 8 1/2" ring gear, or (J-29712) on 9 1/2" ring gear.
Installation – 1) Lubricate bearing and seal lips with wheel bearing grease. Fill axle cavity between seal and axle with wheel bearing grease.
2) Using Bearing Installer (J-23690) on 8 1/2" ring gear or (J-29709) on 9 1/2" ring gear, install bearing until installer contacts axle housing. Using Seal Installer (J-21128) on 8 1/2" ring gear or (J-29713) on 9 1/2" ring gear, install seal until even with axle housing.
3) Install axle shaft. Use care not to damage seal. Ensure splines on axle shaft engage with splines on side gear. To install remaining components, reverse removal procedure. Ensure "C" lock is fully seated or positioned in thrust block. *See Figs. 12 and 13.*

4) Install pinion shaft. Install NEW pinion shaft lock bolt and tighten to 25 ft. lbs. (34 N.m). Install differential cover and new gasket. Fill axle with gear lubricant.

REAR AXLE HUB BEARINGS & OIL SEAL (FULL-FLOATING AXLE)

NOTE: Outer bearing race is seated against a retaining ring inside hub, on inboard side of race. Remove retaining ring from inside of hub before driving out race.

Removal (9 3/4" & 10 1/2" Axle With Disc Brakes) – 1) Remove rear hub and rotor assembly. See REAR BRAKE ROTOR under REMOVAL & INSTALLATION. Using a long drift and hammer, drive out inner bearing race, inner bearing and oil seal from outboard to inboard side of hub.
2) Remove retaining ring from inside of hub, inboard of outer bearing. Using Handle (J-8092) and Outer Bearing Race Remover/Installer (J-24426), drive out outer bearing race from outboard to inboard side of hub.
Installation – 1) Clean and pack bearings with Wheel Bearing Lubricant (1051344). Using handle and Bearing Race Installer (J-8608), drive outer wheel bearing race into hub from inboard side of hub (ensure chamfered edge of bearing race installer is facing upward so that it does not contact bearing race).
2) Install retaining ring on inboard side of outer bearing race. Turn hub and rotor assembly inboard side down. Using Outer Bearing Race Remover/Installer (J-24426), seat outer bearing race against retaining ring.
3) Using Inner Bearing Race Remover/Installer (J-24427), drive inner bearing race into hub from inboard side of hub. Install inner bearing. Install new oil seal using Axle Shaft Seal Installer (J-24428).
4) To complete installation, reverse removal procedure. To adjust wheel bearings, follow REAR BRAKE ROTOR installation procedure under REMOVAL & INSTALLATION.
Removal (9 3/4" & 10 1/2" Axle With Drum Brakes) – 1) Remove rear hub and drum assembly. See REAR BRAKE DRUM under REMOVAL & INSTALLATION. Using a long drift and hammer, drive out inner bearing race, inner bearing and oil seal from outboard to inboard side of hub. *See Fig. 11.*
2) Remove retaining ring from inside of hub, inboard of outer bearing. Using Handle (J-8092) and Outer Bearing Race Remover/Installer (J-24426), drive out outer bearing race from outboard to inboard side of hub.
Installation – 1) Clean and pack bearings with Wheel Bearing Lubricant (1051344). Using handle and Bearing Race Installer (J-8608), drive outer wheel bearing race into hub from inboard side of hub (ensure chamfered edge of bearing race installer is facing upward so it does not contact bearing race). *See Fig. 11.*
2) Install retaining ring on inboard side of outer bearing race. Turn hub and rotor assembly inboard side down. Using Outer Bearing Race Remover/Installer (J-24426), seat outer bearing race against retaining ring.
3) Using Inner Bearing Race Remover/Installer (J-24427), drive inner bearing race into hub from inboard side of hub. Install inner bearing. Install new oil seal using Axle Shaft Seal Installer (J-24428).
4) To complete installation, reverse removal procedure. To adjust wheel bearing, follow REAR BRAKE DRUM installation procedure under REMOVAL & INSTALLATION.
Removal & Installation (12" Axle) – Remove rear hub and rotor assembly. See REAR BRAKE ROTOR under REMOVAL & INSTALLATION. Note how outer bearing race is seated against retaining ring inside hub, on inboard side of race. *See Fig. 10.* Hub bearing removal and installation procedure is not available from manufacturer.

OVERHAUL

NOTE: For overhaul of brake assemblies, See Figs. 14-23.

WARNING: DO NOT hone composite master cylinder bore. Honing destroys hardened surface, causing premature piston seal failure. If bore surface is rough or pitted, replace master cylinder.

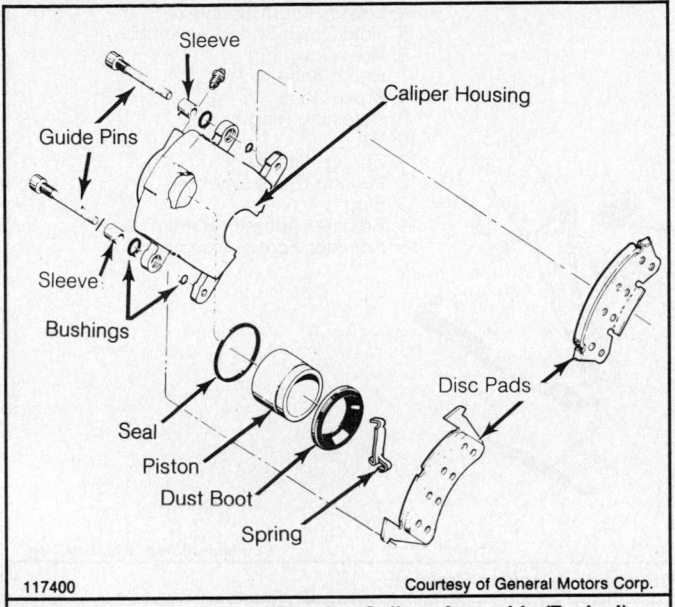

117400   Courtesy of General Motors Corp.

Fig. 14: Exploded View Of Floating Caliper Assembly (Typical)

30073   Courtesy of General Motors Corp.

Fig. 16: Exploded View Of Sliding Caliper Assembly (Typical)

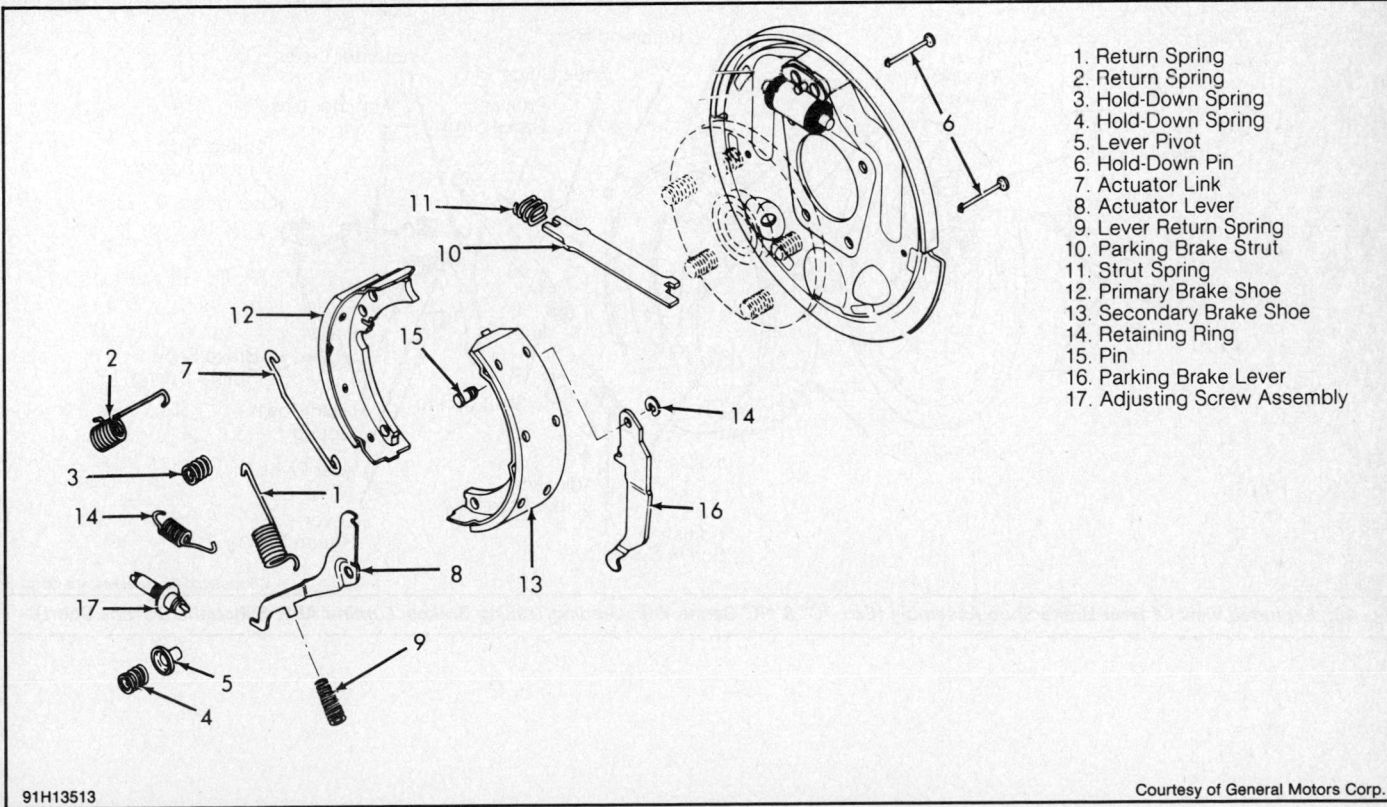

1. Return Spring
2. Return Spring
3. Hold-Down Spring
4. Hold-Down Spring
5. Lever Pivot
6. Hold-Down Pin
7. Actuator Link
8. Actuator Lever
9. Lever Return Spring
10. Parking Brake Strut
11. Strut Spring
12. Primary Brake Shoe
13. Secondary Brake Shoe
14. Retaining Ring
15. Pin
16. Parking Brake Lever
17. Adjusting Screw Assembly

91H13513   Courtesy of General Motors Corp.

Fig. 15: Exploded View Of Rear Brake Shoe Assembly (Lumina APV, Silhouette & Trans Sport)

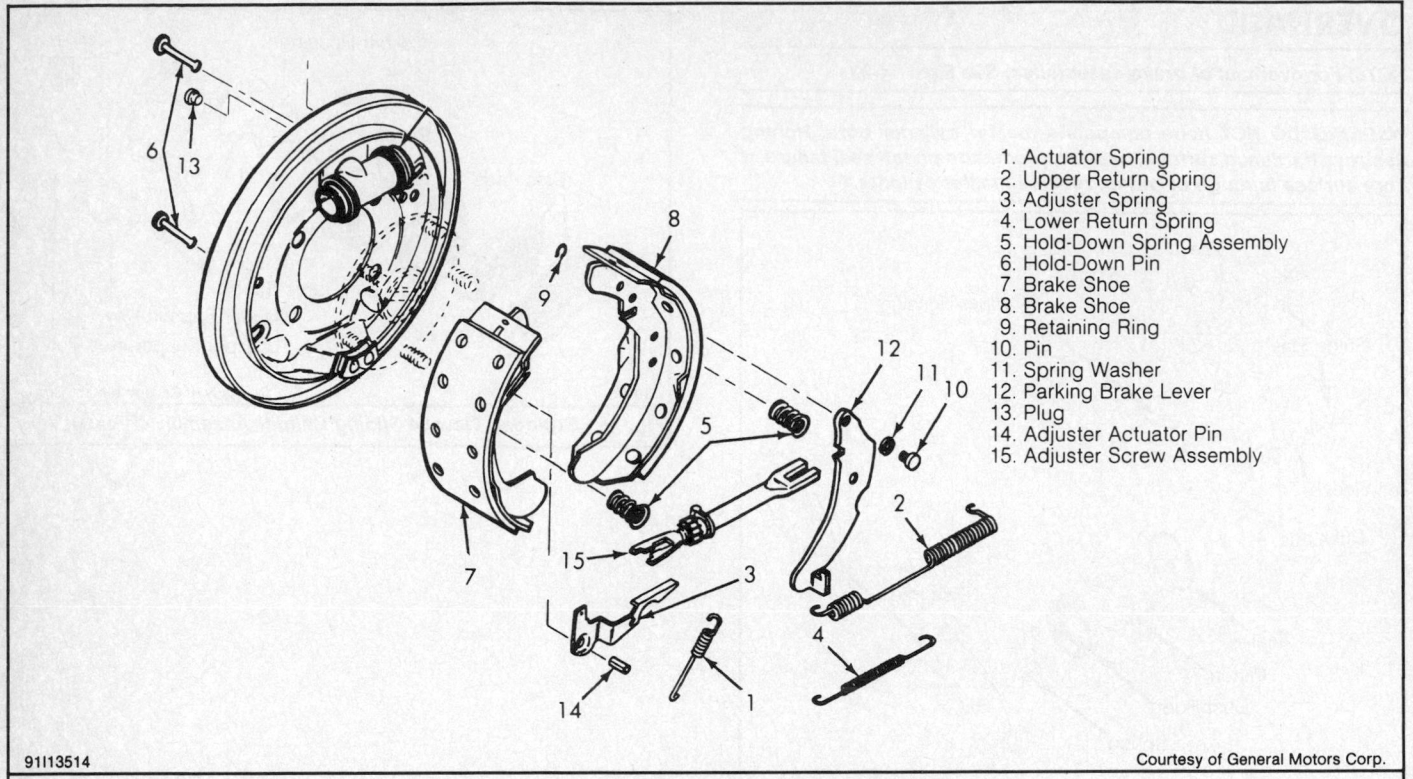

1. Actuator Spring
2. Upper Return Spring
3. Adjuster Spring
4. Lower Return Spring
5. Hold-Down Spring Assembly
6. Hold-Down Pin
7. Brake Shoe
8. Brake Shoe
9. Retaining Ring
10. Pin
11. Spring Washer
12. Parking Brake Lever
13. Plug
14. Adjuster Actuator Pin
15. Adjuster Screw Assembly

91I13514

Courtesy of General Motors Corp.

Fig. 17: Exploded View Of Rear Brake Shoe Assembly ("C" & "K" Series With Leading/Trailing Brakes)

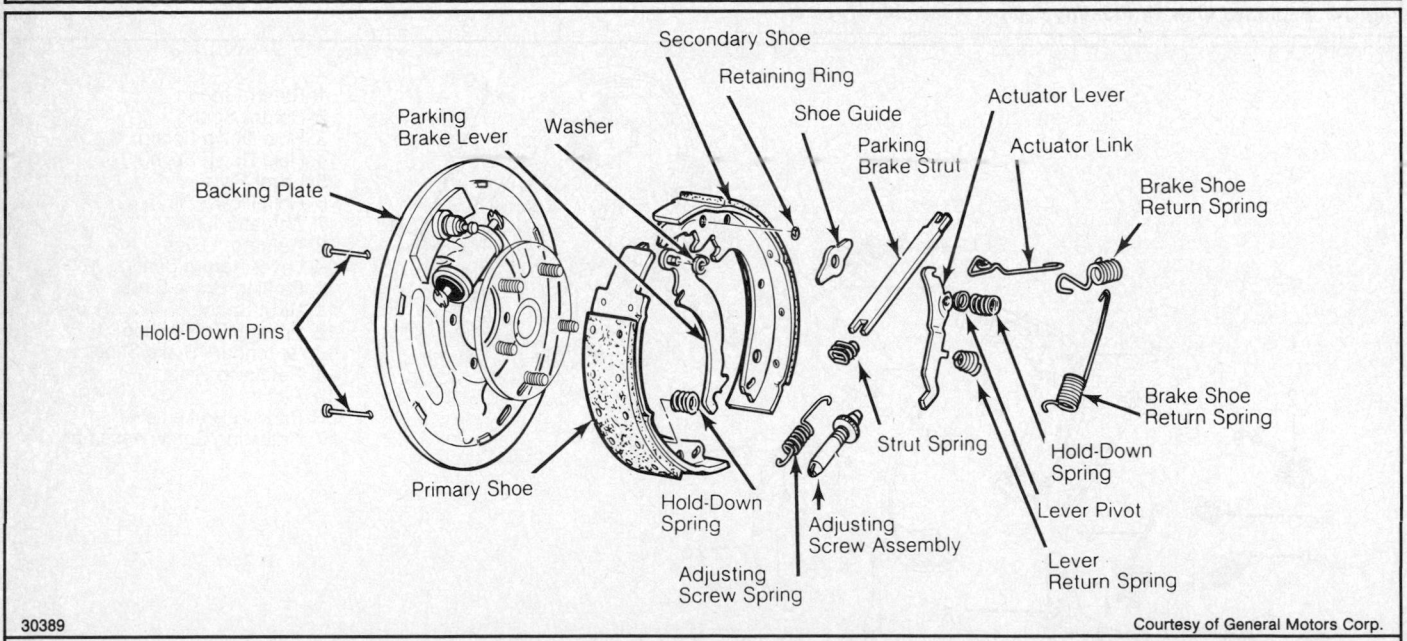

Secondary Shoe
Retaining Ring
Shoe Guide
Parking Brake Strut
Actuator Lever
Actuator Link
Parking Brake Lever
Washer
Brake Shoe Return Spring
Backing Plate
Brake Shoe Return Spring
Hold-Down Pins
Hold-Down Spring
Lever Pivot
Primary Shoe
Hold-Down Spring
Strut Spring
Lever Return Spring
Adjusting Screw Assembly
Adjusting Screw Spring

30389

Courtesy of General Motors Corp.

Fig. 18: Exploded View Of Rear Brake Shoe Assembly (Exc. "C" & "K" Series With Leading/Trailing Brakes, Lumina APV, Silhouette & Trans Sport)

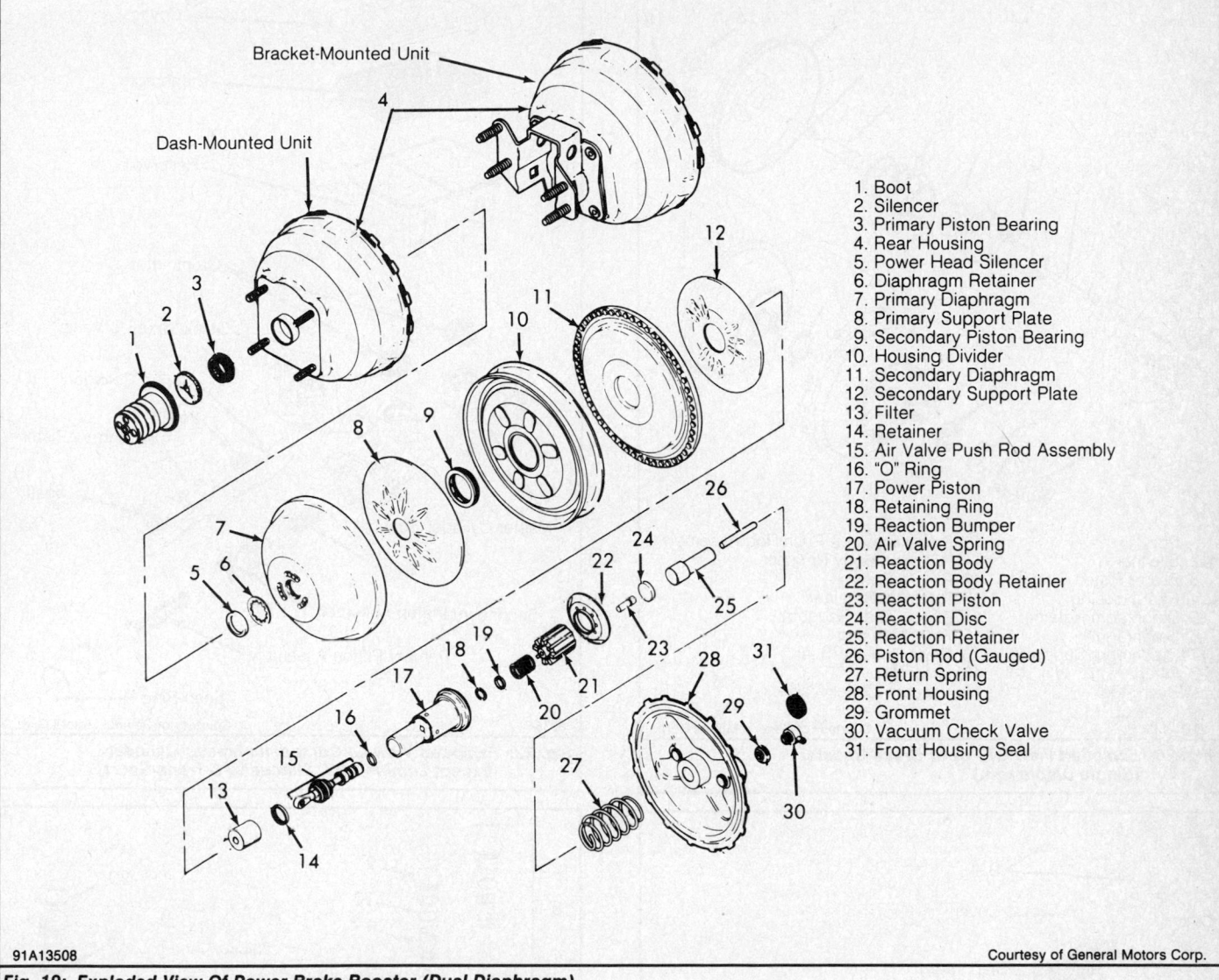

Bracket-Mounted Unit

Dash-Mounted Unit

1. Boot
2. Silencer
3. Primary Piston Bearing
4. Rear Housing
5. Power Head Silencer
6. Diaphragm Retainer
7. Primary Diaphragm
8. Primary Support Plate
9. Secondary Piston Bearing
10. Housing Divider
11. Secondary Diaphragm
12. Secondary Support Plate
13. Filter
14. Retainer
15. Air Valve Push Rod Assembly
16. "O" Ring
17. Power Piston
18. Retaining Ring
19. Reaction Bumper
20. Air Valve Spring
21. Reaction Body
22. Reaction Body Retainer
23. Reaction Piston
24. Reaction Disc
25. Reaction Retainer
26. Piston Rod (Gauged)
27. Return Spring
28. Front Housing
29. Grommet
30. Vacuum Check Valve
31. Front Housing Seal

91A13508

Courtesy of General Motors Corp.

Fig. 19: Exploded View Of Power Brake Booster (Dual Diaphragm)

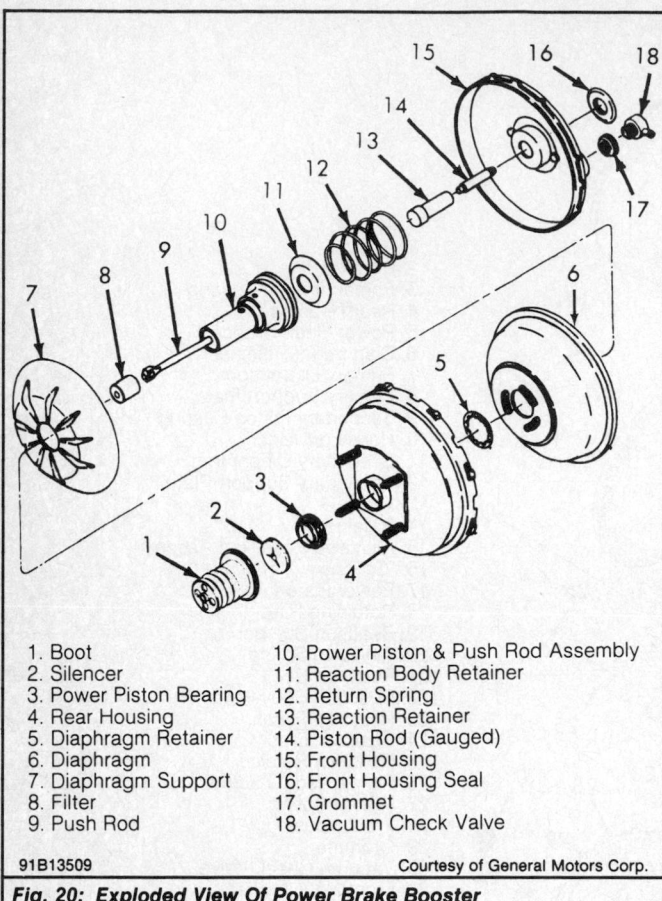

1. Boot
2. Silencer
3. Power Piston Bearing
4. Rear Housing
5. Diaphragm Retainer
6. Diaphragm
7. Diaphragm Support
8. Filter
9. Push Rod
10. Power Piston & Push Rod Assembly
11. Reaction Body Retainer
12. Return Spring
13. Reaction Retainer
14. Piston Rod (Gauged)
15. Front Housing
16. Front Housing Seal
17. Grommet
18. Vacuum Check Valve

91B13509   Courtesy of General Motors Corp.

Fig. 20: Exploded View Of Power Brake Booster (Single Diaphragm)

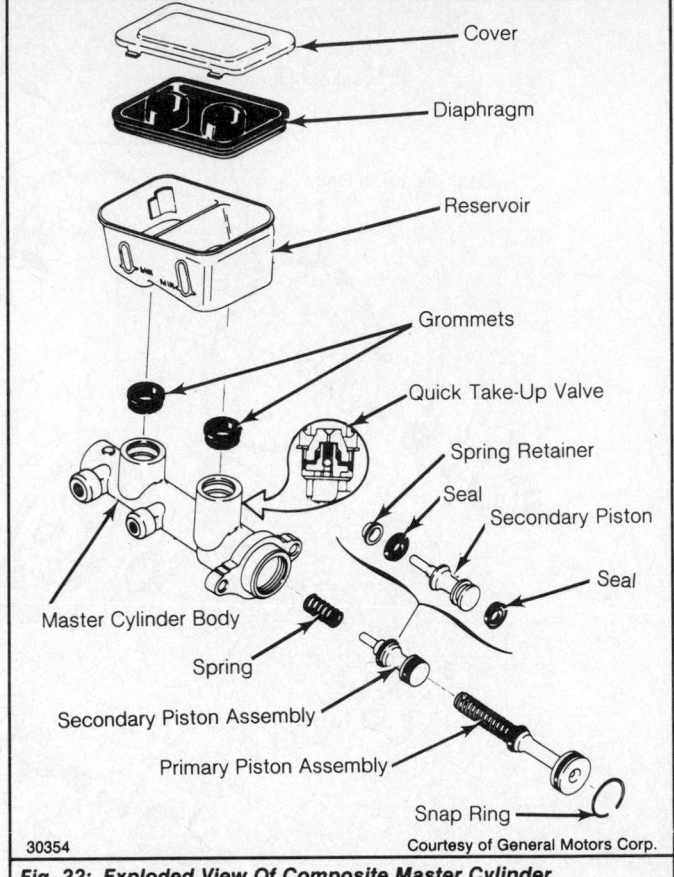

Cover
Diaphragm
Reservoir
Grommets
Quick Take-Up Valve
Spring Retainer
Seal
Secondary Piston
Seal
Master Cylinder Body
Spring
Secondary Piston Assembly
Primary Piston Assembly
Snap Ring

30354   Courtesy of General Motors Corp.

Fig. 22: Exploded View Of Composite Master Cylinder (Except Lumina APV, Silhouette & Trans Sport)

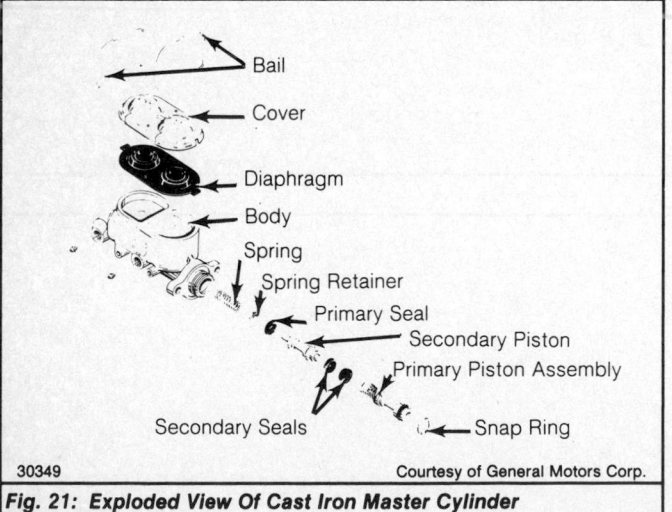

Bail
Cover
Diaphragm
Body
Spring
Spring Retainer
Primary Seal
Secondary Piston
Primary Piston Assembly
Secondary Seals
Snap Ring

30349   Courtesy of General Motors Corp.

Fig. 21: Exploded View Of Cast Iron Master Cylinder

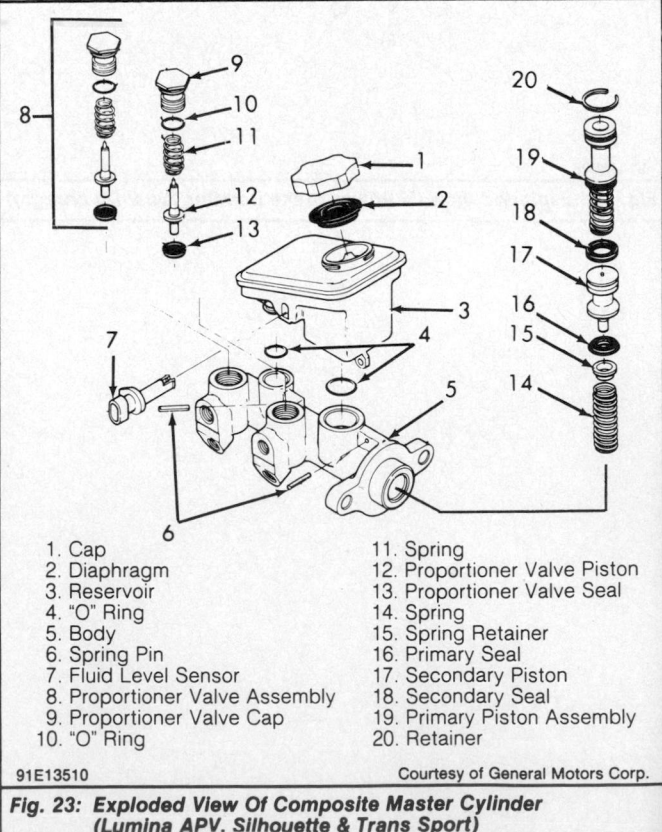

1. Cap
2. Diaphragm
3. Reservoir
4. "O" Ring
5. Body
6. Spring Pin
7. Fluid Level Sensor
8. Proportioner Valve Assembly
9. Proportioner Valve Cap
10. "O" Ring
11. Spring
12. Proportioner Valve Piston
13. Proportioner Valve Seal
14. Spring
15. Spring Retainer
16. Primary Seal
17. Secondary Piston
18. Secondary Seal
19. Primary Piston Assembly
20. Retainer

91E13510   Courtesy of General Motors Corp.

Fig. 23: Exploded View Of Composite Master Cylinder (Lumina APV, Silhouette & Trans Sport)

TORQUE SPECIFICATIONS

TORQUE SPECIFICATIONS

Application	Ft. Lbs. (N.m)
Axle Shaft-To-Hub Bolt (9 3/4" & 10 1/2" Ring Gear) 115 (156)	
Caliper Guide Pin (Floating Caliper)	
"C" & "K" Series 28 (38)	
Except "C" & "K" Series 37 (50)	
Caliper Support Key Bolt (Sliding Caliper) 15 (20)	
Differential Cover Bolt 20 (27)	
Front Brake Hose-To-Caliper Bolt 32 (43)	
Pinion Shaft Lock Bolt [1] 25 (34)	
Rear Wheel Bearing Lock Nut	
9 3/4" & 10 1/2" Ring Gear 65 (88)	
12" Ring Gear 250 (339)	
Wheel Lug Nut	
Astro, Bravada & Safari 90 (122)	
Lumina APV, Silhouette & Trans Sport 100 (136)	
"C" & "K" Series	
With Dual Rear Wheels	
Light Duty 140 (190)	
Heavy Duty 175 (237)	
With Single Rear Wheels 120 (163)	
"G" Series	
G15 & G25 .... 100 (136)	
G35	
With Dual Rear Wheels 140 (190)	
With Single Rear Wheels 120 (163)	
"P" Series	
With Dual Rear Wheels	
8 Lug 140 (190)	
10 Lug 175 (237)	
With Single Rear Wheels	
5 Lug 100 (136)	
6 Lug	
Aluminum Wheels 100 (136)	
Steel Wheels 88 (119)	
8 Lug 120 (163)	
"S" & "T" Series Except Bravada	
With Aluminum Wheels 90 (122)	
With Steel Wheels 73 (99)	

[1] – Use NEW pinion shaft lock bolt. DO NOT reuse bolt.

DRUM BRAKE SPECIFICATIONS

DRUM BRAKE SPECIFICATIONS

Application	In. (mm)
Astro, Safari & "S" & "T" Series	
Drum	
Original Diameter 9.50 (241.3)	
Discard Diameter 9.56 (242.8)	
Maximum Refinish Diameter 9.59 (243.6)	
Width 2.00 (50.8)	
Lumina APV, Silhouette & Trans Sport	
Drum	
Original Diameter 8.86 (225.0)	
Discard Diameter 8.91 (226.3)	
Maximum Refinish Diameter 8.89 (225.8)	
Wheel Cylinder Diameter .... .748 (19.00)	
All Others	
Drum	
Original Diameter 10.00 (254.0)	
11.15 (283.2)	
12.00 (304.8)	
13.00 (330.2)	
Discard Diameter	
10.00" Drum 10.09 (256.3)	
11.15" Drum 11.24 (285.5)	
12.00" Drum 12.090 (307.09)	
13.00" Drum 13.09 (332.5)	
Maximum Refinish Diameter	
10.00" Drum 10.05 (255.3)	
11.15" Drum 11.21 (284.7)	
12.00" Drum 12.060 (306.32)	
13.00" Drum 13.06 (331.7)	
Width	
10.00" Drum 2.25 (57.0)	
11.15" Drum 2.75 (69.9)	
12.00" Drum .... [1]	
13.00" Drum .... 2.50 (63.5) Or 3.50 (88.9)	

– Information is not available from manufacturer.

DISC BRAKE SPECIFICATIONS

DISC BRAKE SPECIFICATIONS

Application	In. (mm)
Lateral Runout	
All Models .... .004 (.10)	
Parallelism	
All Models .... .0005 (.013)	
Original Thickness	
Astro & Safari 1.04 (26.4)	
Lumina APV, Silhouette & Trans Sport 1.043 (26.49)	
"S" & "T" Series 1.03 (26.2)	
All Others	
11.57" Rotor	
4600 Lbs. GVW 1.00 (25.4)	
6400 & 7200 Lbs. GVW 1.25 (31.8)	
11.86" Rotor 1.29 (32.8)	
12.50" Rotor	
"C" & "K" Series 1.26 (32.0)	
Except "C" & "K" Series	
8400 Lbs. GVW 1.28 (32.5)	
10,000 Lbs. GVW 1.54 (39.1)	
13.75" Rotor 1.54 (39.1)	
14.25" Rotor 1.54 (39.1)	
Minimum Refinish Thickness [1]	
Astro, Safari & "S" & "T" Series .... .980 (24.89)	
Lumina APV, Silhouette & Trans Sport .... .972 (24.69)	
All Others	
11.57 X 1.00" Rotor .... .980 (24.89)	
11.57 X 1.25" Rotor 1.230 (31.24)	
11.86 X 1.29" Rotor 1.230 (31.24)	
12.50 X 1.26" Rotor 1.230 (31.24)	
12.50 X 1.28" Rotor 1.230 (31.24)	
12.50 X 1.54" Rotor 1.480 (37.59)	
13.75 X 1.54" Rotor 1.480 (37.59)	
14.25 X 1.54" Rotor 1.480 (37.59)	
Discard Thickness	
Astro, Safari & "S" & "T" Series .... .965 (24.51)	
Lumina APV, Silhouette & Trans Sport .... .957 (24.31)	
All Others	
11.57 X 1.00" Rotor .... .965 (24.51)	
11.57 X 1.25" Rotor 1.215 (30.86)	
11.86 X 1.29" Rotor 1.215 (30.86)	
12.50 X 1.26" Rotor 1.215 (30.86)	
12.50 X 1.28" Rotor 1.215 (30.86)	
12.50 X 1.54" Rotor 1.465 (37.21)	
13.75 X 1.54" Rotor 1.465 (37.21)	
14.25 X 1.54" Rotor 1.465 (37.21)	

[1] – Use specification stamped on rotor (if available).

1992 WHEEL ALIGNMENT
Specifications & Procedures

Astro, Bravada, Commercial Van, Jimmy, Lumina APV, Safari, Sierra, Silhouette, Sonoma, Suburban, Syclone, Trans Sport, Typhoon, Van, Yukon, "C" & "K" Series Blazer & Pickup, "S" & "T" Series Blazer & Pickup

MODEL IDENTIFICATION

Vehicle model can be identified by fifth character of Vehicle Identification Number (VIN), stamped on metal pad on top of left end of instrument panel, near windshield. See MODEL IDENTIFICATION table.

MODEL IDENTIFICATION

Series [1]	Model
"C"	2WD Pickup, Sierra & Suburban
"G"	RWD Van
"K"	4WD Blazer, Pickup, Sierra, Suburban & Yukon
"L"	All-Wheel Drive Astro & Safari
"M"	2WD Astro & Safari
"P"	Commercial Van/Motorhome
"S"	2WD Blazer, Jimmy, Pickup & Sonoma
"T"	Bravada, 4WD Blazer, Jimmy, Pickup, Sonoma, Syclone & Typhoon
"U"	Lumina APV, Silhouette & Trans Sport

[1] – Vehicle series is fifth character of VIN.

PRE-ALIGNMENT

VEHICLE CHECKS

Before making wheel alignment adjustments:

1) Tire pressure must be inflated to manufacturer's recommended specification. Tires should be equal in size and type. Runout must not be excessive. Tires and wheels should be in balance.

2) Wheel bearings must be properly adjusted. Steering linkage and suspension must not have excessive wear and/or looseness. Check for wear in tie rod ends and ball joints.

3) Steering gear box must not have excessive play. Check and adjust to manufacturer's specification.

4) Vehicle must be at correct ride height with full fuel load and spare tire in vehicle. No extra load should be on vehicle. See RIDE HEIGHT under ALIGNMENT PROCEDURES.

5) Vehicle must be level with floor and with suspension settled. Jounce front and rear of vehicle several times and allow it to settle to normal ride height.

6) Ensure steering wheel spokes are centered with front wheels in straight-ahead position. Correct by shortening one tie rod adjusting sleeve and lengthening opposite sleeve in equal amounts.

7) Ensure wheel lug nuts are tightened to proper specification. See TORQUE SPECIFICATIONS table at end of article.

JACKING & HOISTING

Vehicle may be raised by floor jack or vehicle hoist. Ensure hoist or jack supports vehicle at proper lifting points. *See Figs. 1-5.* If vehicle is to be raised on a twin-post hoist, use caution not to damage suspension, rear axle cover and/or steering linkage components.

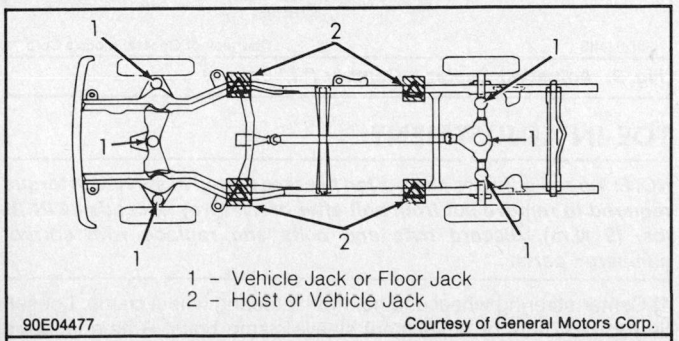

1 – Vehicle Jack or Floor Jack
2 – Hoist or Vehicle Jack

90E04477   Courtesy of General Motors Corp.

Fig. 1: Hoisting & Jacking Locations (Astro, Safari, "S" & "T" Series)

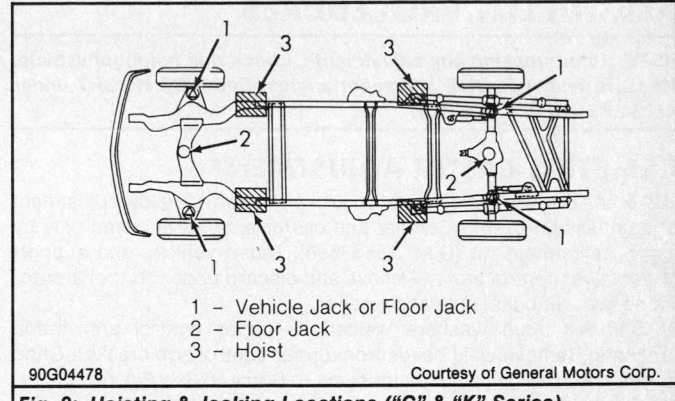

1 – Vehicle Jack or Floor Jack
2 – Floor Jack
3 – Hoist

90G04478   Courtesy of General Motors Corp.

Fig. 2: Hoisting & Jacking Locations ("C" & "K" Series)

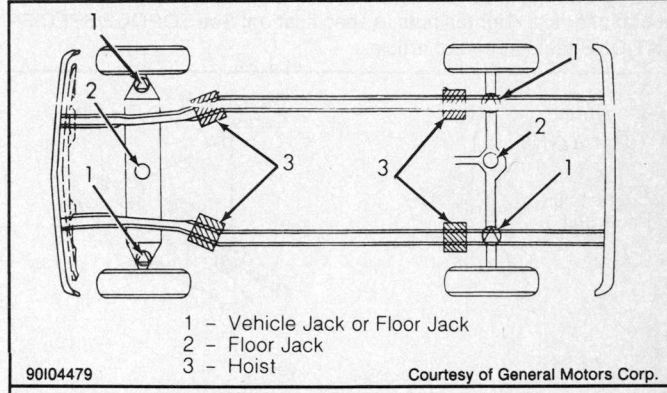

1 – Vehicle Jack or Floor Jack
2 – Floor Jack
3 – Hoist

90I04479   Courtesy of General Motors Corp.

Fig. 3: Hoisting & Jacking Locations (Commercial Van)

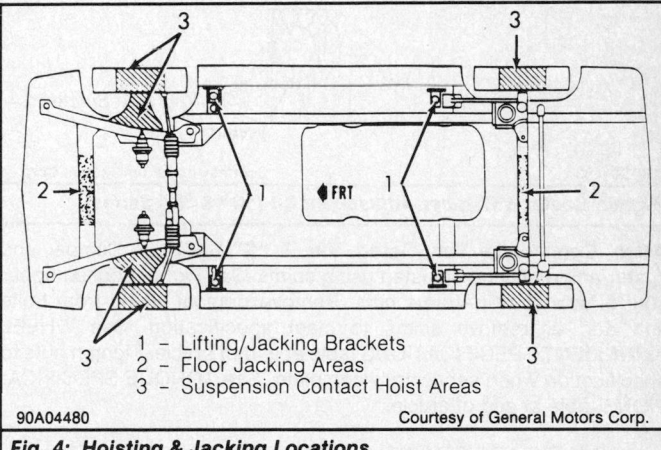

1 – Lifting/Jacking Brackets
2 – Floor Jacking Areas
3 – Suspension Contact Hoist Areas

90A04480   Courtesy of General Motors Corp.

Fig. 4: Hoisting & Jacking Locations (Lumina APV, Silhouette & Trans Sport)

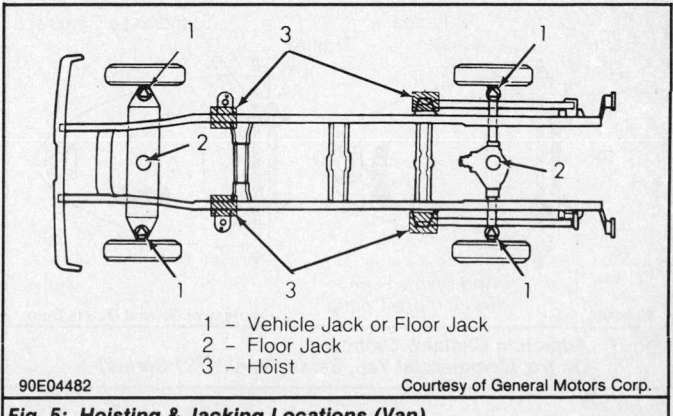

1 – Vehicle Jack or Floor Jack
2 – Floor Jack
3 – Hoist

90E04482   Courtesy of General Motors Corp.

Fig. 5: Hoisting & Jacking Locations (Van)

ALIGNMENT PROCEDURES

NOTE: Before making any adjustments, check ride height of vehicle. Measure and record all alignment angles. See RIDE HEIGHT under ALIGNMENT PROCEDURES.

CAMBER & CASTER ADJUSTMENT

"C" & "K" Series – 1) Original control arm does not allow adjustment of camber and caster. Camber and caster may be adjusted only by using Adjustment Kit (G.M. 15538596). Raise vehicle, and support under lower control arms. Remove and discard upper control arm-to-frame bracket bolts, nuts and washer.

2) Remove large washers welded to upper control arm frame brackets. Remove weld beads from upper control arm bracket. Grind area smooth. Install adjustment cams to bracket. *See Fig. 6.*

3) Install bolt. Adjust camber and caster to correct specifications by rotating bolt head. See WHEEL ALIGNMENT SPECIFICATIONS table at end of article. Tighten nuts to specification. See TORQUE SPECIFICATIONS table at end of article.

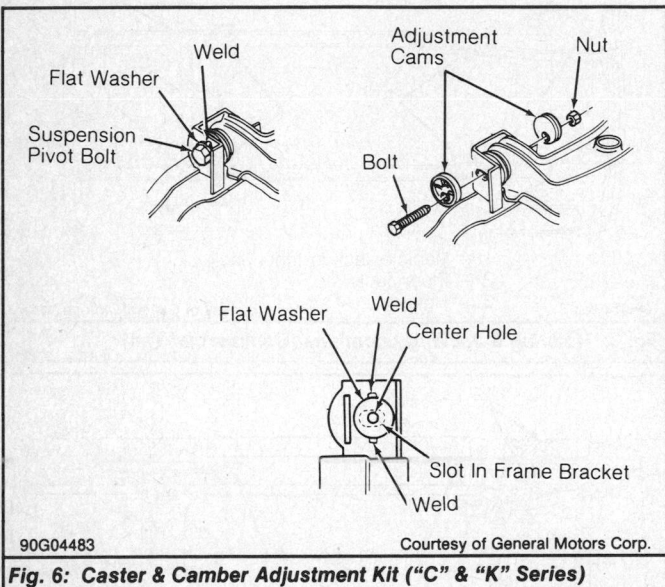

90G04483　　　　　　　　Courtesy of General Motors Corp.

Fig. 6: Caster & Camber Adjustment Kit ("C" & "K" Series)

Astro, Commercial Van, Safari, Van & "S" Series – Camber and caster angle may be adjusted using shims. *See Fig. 7.* Loosen upper control arm shaft-to-frame nuts. Remove original shims from bolts and add or remove shims to meet specification. See WHEEL ALIGNMENT SPECIFICATIONS table at end of article. Tighten nuts to specification when servicing is complete. See TORQUE SPECIFICATIONS table at end of article.

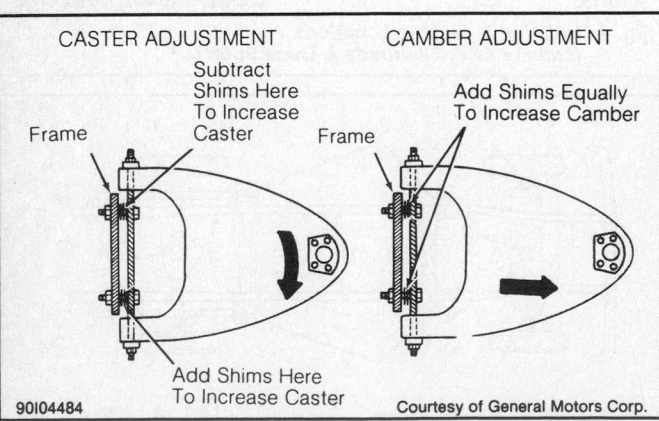

90I04484　　　　　　　　Courtesy of General Motors Corp.

Fig. 7: Adjusting Caster & Camber (Astro, Commercial Van, Safari, Van & "S" Series)

Lumina APV, Silhouette & Trans Sport – 1) Caster is not adjustable. Measure caster to check for bent or damaged parts. See WHEEL ALIGNMENT SPECIFICATIONS table at end of article. Replace damaged components if necessary.

2) For camber adjustment, loosen both strut-to-knuckle bolts enough to allow movement. *See Fig. 8.* Adjust camber to specification by moving top of wheel in or out. See WHEEL ALIGNMENT SPECIFICATIONS table at end of article. Tighten strut-to-knuckle bolts to specification. See TORQUE SPECIFICATIONS table at end of article.

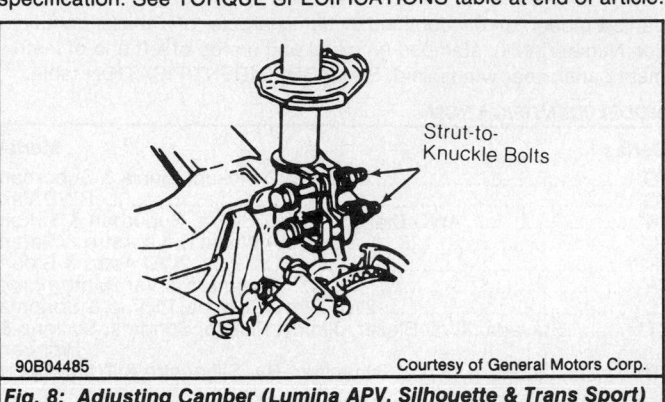

90B04485　　　　　　　　Courtesy of General Motors Corp.

Fig. 8: Adjusting Camber (Lumina APV, Silhouette & Trans Sport)

"T" Series – Caster and camber adjustments are made by means of cams on upper control arm frame attaching bolts. *See Fig. 9.* Loosen upper control arm-to-frame attaching nuts. Rotate cam by rotating bolt head. Adjust caster and camber to specification. See WHEEL ALIGNMENT SPECIFICATIONS table at end of article. Tighten nuts to specification. See TORQUE SPECIFICATIONS table at end of article.

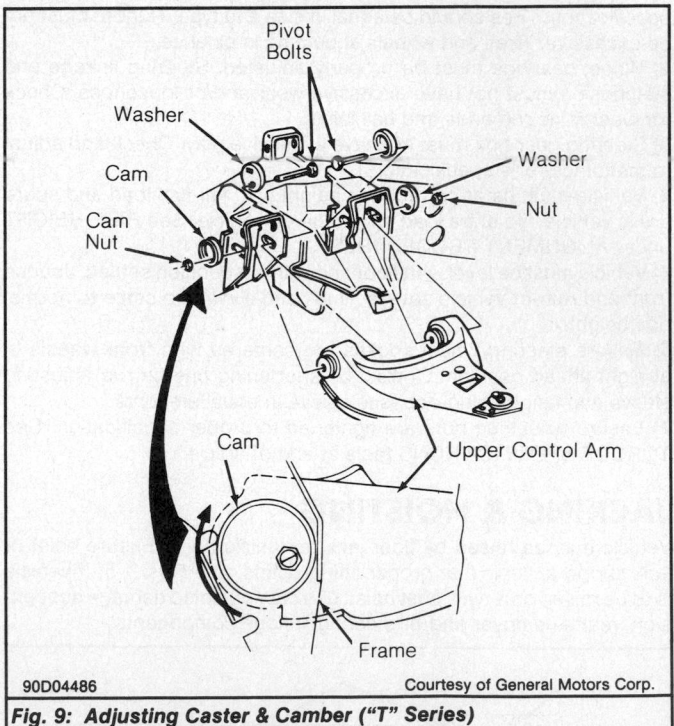

90D04486　　　　　　　　Courtesy of General Motors Corp.

Fig. 9: Adjusting Caster & Camber ("T" Series)

TOE-IN ADJUSTMENT

NOTE: Tie rod adjuster parts often become rusted in service. If torque required to remove nut from bolt after break-away exceeds 84 INCH lbs. (9 N.m), discard nuts and bolts and replace with correct numbered parts.

1) Center steering wheel and hold with steering wheel clamp. Loosen tie rod lock nuts or adjustment sleeve clamp bolts. Rotate inner tie rods or adjustment sleeves to align toe to specification. See WHEEL ALIGNMENT SPECIFICATIONS table at end of article.

2) Ensure number of threads showing on each tie rod or inside each adjustment sleeve is nearly equal. Ensure tie rod ends are square before tightening lock nuts. Tighten tie rod lock nuts or adjustment sleeve clamp bolts to specification. See TORQUE SPECIFICATIONS table at end of article.

RIDE HEIGHT

1) Proper ride height is necessary for correct wheel alignment. Ensure tires are correctly inflated, cargo compartment is empty and fuel tank is full. Bounce vehicle several times to normalize ride height.

2) Most vehicles provide front wheel alignment specifications which allow camber and caster adjustment for a large range of ride heights. See RIDE HEIGHT SPECIFICATIONS table. Ride height measurement points are shown in illustrations. *See Figs. 10-15.*

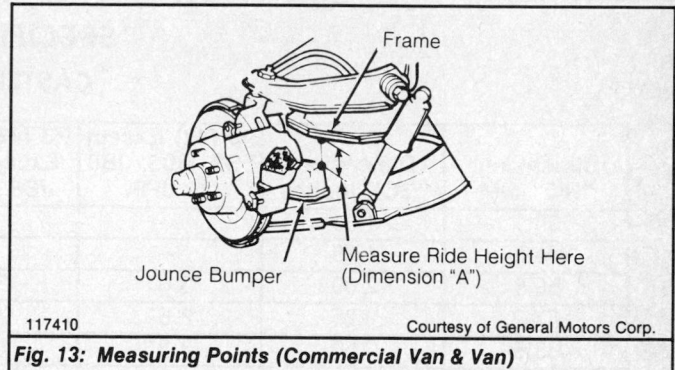

Fig. 13: *Measuring Points (Commercial Van & Van)*

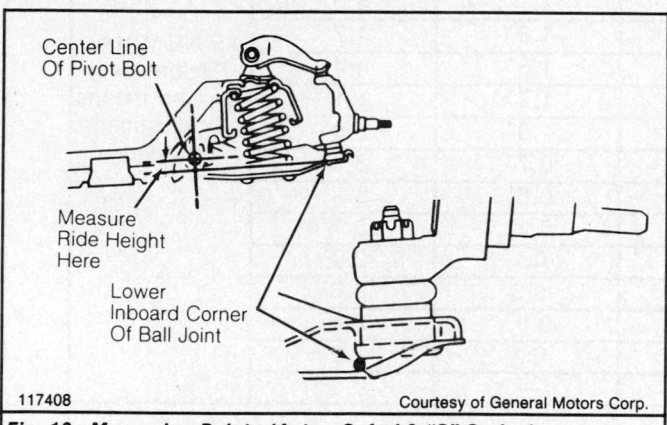

Fig. 10: *Measuring Points (Astro, Safari & "S" Series)*

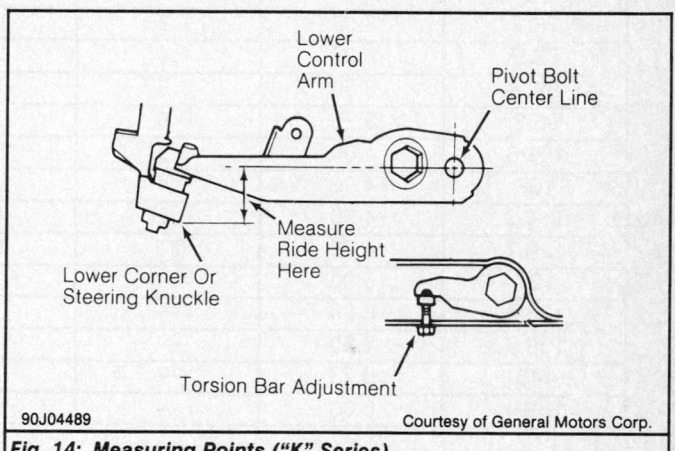

Fig. 14: *Measuring Points ("K" Series)*

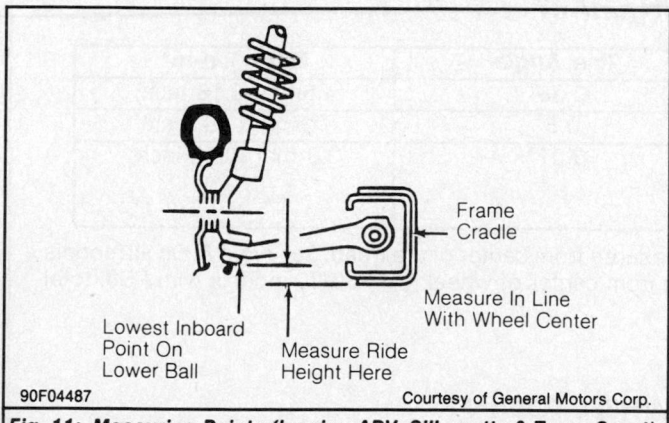

Fig. 11: *Measuring Points (Lumina APV, Silhouette & Trans Sport)*

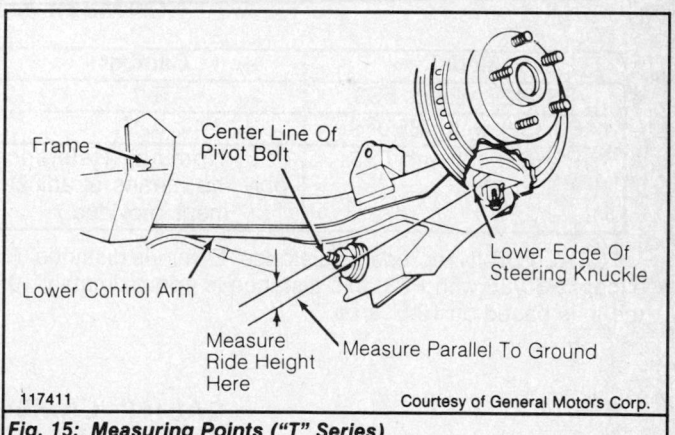

Fig. 15: *Measuring Points ("T" Series)*

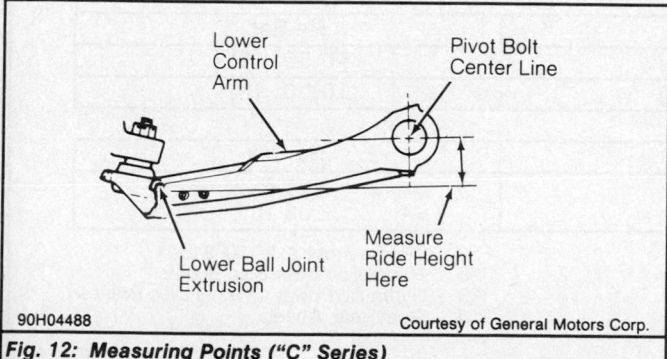

Fig. 12: *Measuring Points ("C" Series)*

RIDE HEIGHT SPECIFICATIONS

Application	Ride Height Dimension INCH (mm)
Astro & Safari	
2WD	3.1 ± 0.2 (80 ± 6.0)
4WD	5.4 ± 0.2 (136 ± 6.0)
"C" & "K" Series	
C15/35	3.7 ± 0.2 (95 ± 6.0)
K15/25	6.2 ± 0.2 (157 ± 6.0)
K35	5.7 ± 0.2 (145 ± 6.0)
Commercial Van & Van	[1]
Lumina APV, Silhouette & Trans Sport	0 ± .4 (0 ± 10)
"S" Series	2.8 ± 0.2 (73 ± 6.0)
"T" Series	4.8 ± 0.2 (122 ± 6.0)

[1] – Ride height is not adjustable.

1992 WHEEL ALIGNMENT
Specifications & Procedures (Cont.)

SPECIFICATIONS
CASTER CHART

Dimension "BC" MM	Dimension "BC" Inches	P3 (42) Except FS3, R05, JB8 or JF9	P3 (42) w/R05 Except FS3, JB8 or JF9	P3 (42) W/JB8 or JF9 Except FS3	P3 (32) w/JB8 or JF9 Except FS3	P3 (32, 42) w/FS3
38.1	1.50	—	—	—	—	
44.5	1.75	—	—	—	—	
50.8	2.00	3.0°	2.5°	3.2°	—	
57.2	2.25	2.6°	2.2°	2.9°	—	
63.5	2.50	2.3°	1.9°	2.6°	5.5°	
70	2.75	2.0°	1.6°	2.4°	5.3°	
76.2	3.00	1.7°	1.3°	2.1°	5.0°	+5 NOMINAL (References only, no means of adjustment provided.)
82.5	3.25	1.4°	1.1°	1.8°	4.7°	
88.9	3.50	1.2°	0.8°	1.5°	4.4°	
95.3	3.75	0.9°	0.5°	1.2°	4.1°	
101.6	4.00	0.6°	0.3°	1.0°	3.8°	
108	4.25	0.4°	0.0°	0.7°	3.6°	
114.3	4.50	0.2°	-0.2°	0.5°	3.3°	
120.7	4.75	-0.1°	-0.4°	0.2°	3.1°	
127	5.00	—	—	-0.1°	2.9°	
133.4	5.25	—	—	-0.3°	2.6°	
139.7	5.50	—	—	0.5°	2.4°	
146	5.75	—	—	-0.7°	2.2°	
152.4	6.00	—	—	—	2.0°	

CAMBER & TOE-IN CHART

Model	Camber	Toie Angle	Total Toe-In*
P3 (42) without FS3	0.1°	0.36°	4.5mm (0.18 inch)
P3 (32) with JB8/JF9	0.1°	0.5°	1.5mm (.06 inch)
P3 (32, 42) with FS3	+1.5° Nominal (Reference only, no means of adjustment provided.)	0.07°	3.0 mm (0.12 inch)

* TOTAL TOE-IN represents distance "E" minus distance "F" as measured from center of tire tread. *See Fig. 17.* On all models except P30/35 with FS3, this distance is approximately 10 inches from center of wheel. On P30/35 models with FS3, total toe-in is based on 19.5" tires.

CASTER, CAMBER & WHEEL TOE-IN
ALIGNMENT SETTING TOLERANCES

	Check	Re-Set
Caster	±1.00° (1)	±0.50° (2)
Camber	±0.75° (1)	±0.50° (2)

Total Toe-In	Check	Re-Set
P all	±.23° ±.12 in.	±.12° ±.06 in.

(1) Left and right to be equal within 1° 0'.
(2) Left and right to be equal within 0° 30'.

FS3 – I-Beam Front Axle (5000 lbs.)
JB8 – Hydraulic Power Disc Brakes
JF9 – Hydraulic Power 4-Wheel Disc Brakes
R05 – Dual Rear Wheels

92B21916 92C21917 92D21918

Courtesy of General Motors Corp.

Fig. 16: *Caster Specifications (Commercial Van)*

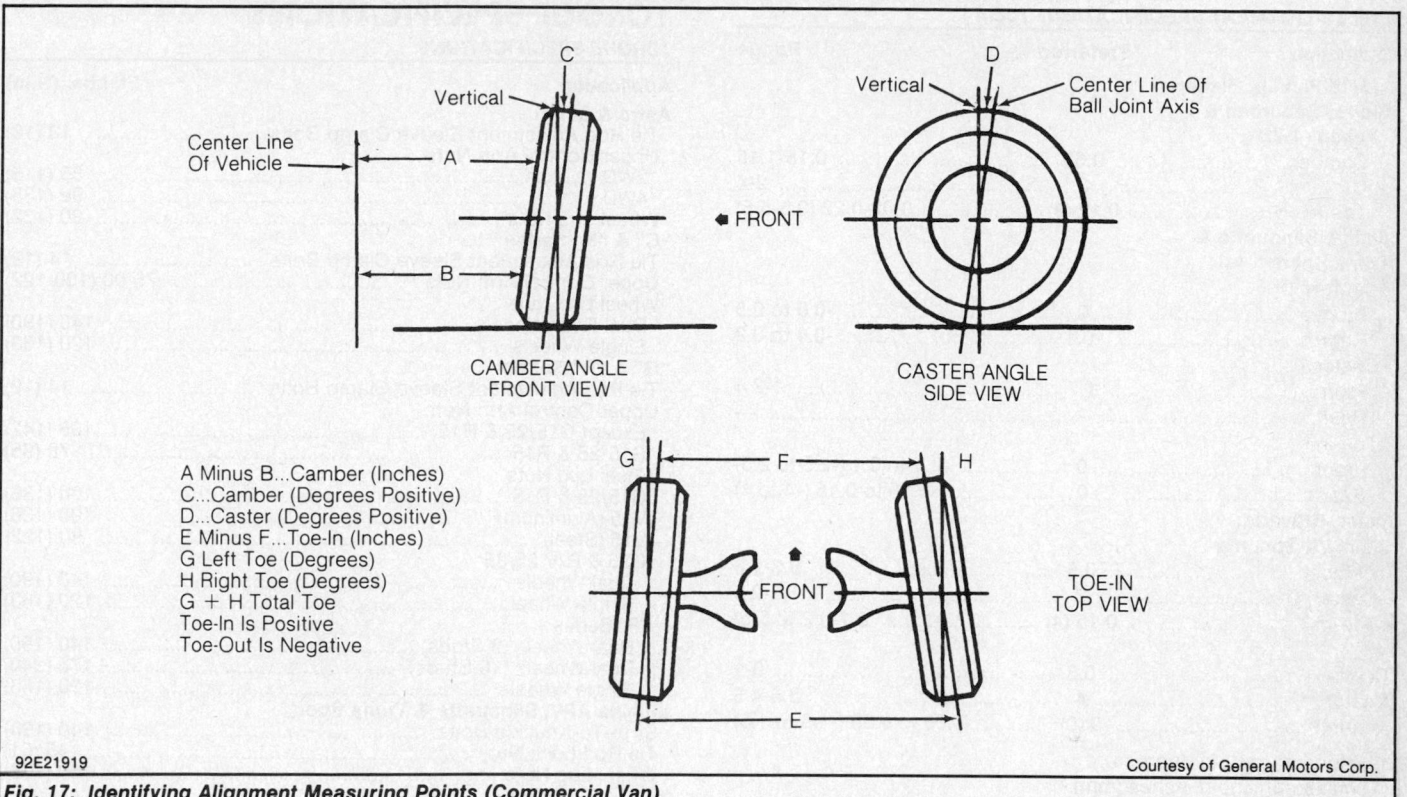

A Minus B...Camber (Inches)
C...Camber (Degrees Positive)
D...Caster (Degrees Positive)
E Minus F...Toe-In (Inches)
G Left Toe (Degrees)
H Right Toe (Degrees)
G + H Total Toe
Toe-In Is Positive
Toe-Out Is Negative

92E21919

Courtesy of General Motors Corp.

Fig. 17: Identifying Alignment Measuring Points (Commercial Van)

Caster varies with ride height. Measure distance between frame crossmember and lower control arm jounce bracket (Dimension "A"). See Fig. 13.

Dimension "A"		
Inches	**(MM)**	**CASTER**
1.50	**(38.1)**	**3.4°**
1.75	**(44.5)**	**3.2°**
2.00	**(50.8)**	**3.0°**
2.25	**(57.2)**	**2.0°**
2.50	**(63.5)**	**2.7°**
2.75	**(70.0)**	**2.5°**
3.00	**(76.2)**	**2.3°**
3.25	**(82.5)**	**2.2°**
3.50	**(88.9)**	**2.0°**
3.75	**(95.3)**	**1.8°**
4.00	**(101.6)**	**1.7°**
4.25	**(108.0)**	**1.5°**
4.50	**(114.3)**	**1.4°**
4.75	**(120.7)**	**1.3°**
5.00	**(127.0)**	**1.2°**
5.25	**(133.4)**	**1.1°**
5.50	**(139.7)**	**1.0°**
5.75	**(146.0)**	**0.9°**
6.00	**(152.4)**	**0.08°**

92H21920

Courtesy of General Motors Corp.

Fig. 18: Caster Specifications (Van)

WHEEL ALIGNMENT SPECIFICATIONS

NOTE: Wheel alignment specification for Syclone and Typhoon is not available from manufacturer.

WHEEL ALIGNMENT SPECIFICATIONS

Application	Preferred	Range
Astro/Safari		
Camber [1] [3]		
2WD	0.8	0.3-1.5
4WD	0.89	0.49-1.29
Caster [1] [3]		
2WD	2.7	2.2-3.2
4WD	2.0	1.5-2.5
Toe-In [2]		
2WD	.1 (2.5)	0.05-0.15 (1.5-4)
4WD	-0.05 (-1.5)	-0.1-0 (-2.5-0)
C 15/25 Pickup, Sierra &		
Suburban (2WD)		
Camber [1] [3]	0.5	0-1
Caster [1] [3]	3.75	2.75-4.75
Toe-In [2]	0.12 (3)	0.02-0.22 (0.5-5.5)
Commercial Van [3] [4] [5]		

[1] – Measurement in degrees.

[2] – Measurement in inches (mm).

[3] – Left and right adjustments must be within 0.5 degree of each other.

[4] – See Fig. 16 for explanation of Regular Production Option (RPO) codes.

[5] – See Figs. 16 and 17 for caster specifications.

1992 WHEEL ALIGNMENT
Specifications & Procedures (Cont.)

WHEEL ALIGNMENT SPECIFICATIONS (Cont.)

Application	Preferred	Range
K 15/25 Pickup, Blazer, Sierra, Suburban & Yukon (4WD)		
Camber [1][3]	0.65	0.15-1.15
Caster [1][3]	3	2-4
Toe-In [2][4]	0.12 (3)	0.02-0.22 (0.5-5.5)
Lumina, Silhouette & Trans Sport		
Camber [1][5]		
Front	0	-0.5 to 0.5
Rear	-0.1	-0.4 to 0.2
Caster [1]		
Front	1.7	1-2.4
Rear	---	---
Toe-In [2]		
Front	0	-0.1 to 0.1 (-2.5 to 2.5)
Rear	0	-0.15 to 0.15 (-4 to 4)
Blazer, Bravada, Jimmy & Sonoma		
Camber [1][3]	0.8	0.3-1.3
Caster [1][3]	2	1.5-2.5
Toe-In [2]	0.15 (4)	0.1-0.2 (2.5-5)
Van		
Camber [1]	0.5	0-1
Caster [1][6]	4	3.5-4.5
Toe-In [2]	0 (0)	-0.05 to 0.05 (-1.5 to 1.5)

[1] – Measurement in degrees.

[2] – Measurement in inches (mm).

[3] – Left and right adjustments must be within 0.5 degree of each other.

[4] – Toe-in on left and right side must be set equally per wheel. Steering wheel must be held in straight-ahead position within plus or minus 5.0 degrees.

[5] – Left and right adjustments must be within .07 degree of each other.

[6] – See Fig. 18 for caster specifications.

TORQUE SPECIFICATIONS

TORQUE SPECIFICATIONS

Application	Ft. Lbs. (N.m)
Astro & Safari	
Tie Rod Adjustment Sleeve Clamp Bolts	13 (18)
Upper Control Arm Nuts	
2WD	85 (115)
4WD	99 (135)
Wheel Lug Nuts	90 (122)
"C" & "K" Series	
Tie Rod Adjustment Sleeve Clamp Bolts	14 (19)
Upper Control Arm Nuts [1]	75-90 (100-122)
Wheel Lug Nuts	
Dual Rear Wheels	140 (190)
Single Wheels	120 (163)
"G" & "P" Series	
Tie Rod Adjustment Sleeve Clamp Bolts	14 (19)
Upper Control Arm Nuts	
Except G15/25 & R15	105 (142)
G15/25 & R15	70 (95)
Wheel Lug Nuts	
G15/25 & R15	100 (136)
V15 (Aluminum)	100 (136)
V15 (Steel)	90 (122)
G35 & R/V 25/35	
Dual Wheels	140 (190)
Single Wheels	120 (163)
"P" Series	
Dual Wheels (8 Studs)	140 (190)
Dual Wheels (10 Studs)	[2] 175 (240)
Single Wheels	120 (163)
Lumina APV, Silhouette & Trans Sport	
Strut-To-Knuckle Bolts	140 (190)
Tie Rod Lock Nut	45 (61)
Wheel Lug Nuts	100 (136)
"S" & "T" Series	
Tie Rod Adjustment Sleeve Clamp Bolts	14 (19)
Upper Control Arm Nuts	
"S" Series	65 (88)
"T" Series	70 (95)
Wheel Lug Nuts	
Aluminum	90 (122)
Steel	73 (99)

[1] – Adjustment Kit (G.M. 15538596) must be used on "C" and "K" Series vehicles.

[2] – Tighten in 2 steps. Initially tighten all studs to 140 ft. lbs. (190 N.m), and then tighten all studs to 175 ft. lbs. (240 N.m).

Lumina APV, Silhouette, Trans Sport

DESCRIPTION

Front suspension is a combination strut and spring design. The control arms pivot from the frame. *See Fig. 1.* The frame has isolation mounts to the body and conventional rubber bushing for control arm pivots. The upper end of the strut is isolated by a rubber mount and contains a bearing to allow for wheel turning.

The lower end of the steering knuckle pivots on a ball joint riveted to the control arm. The ball joint is fastened to the steering knuckle with a pinch bolt.

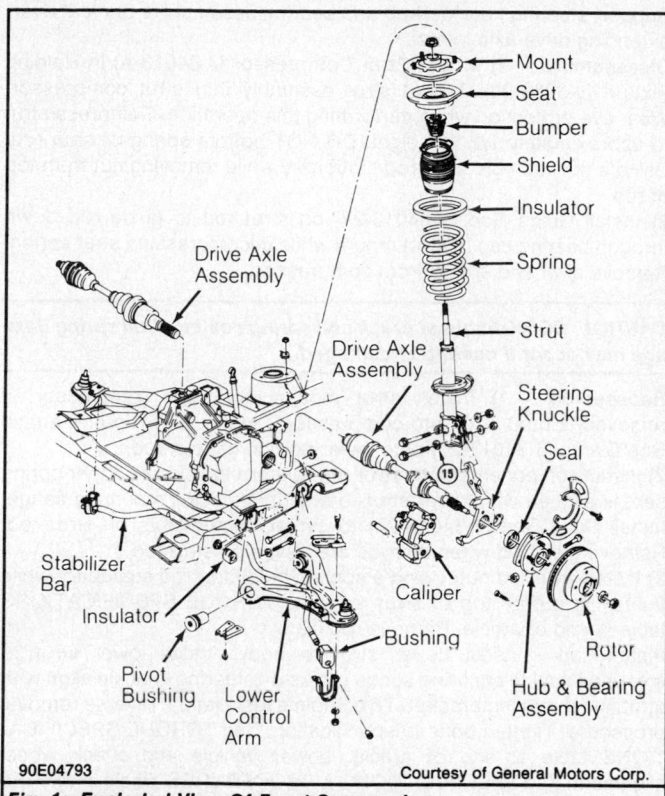

90E04793   Courtesy of General Motors Corp.

Fig. 1: Exploded View Of Front Suspension

Labels (top to bottom): Mount, Seat, Bumper, Shield, Insulator, Spring, Strut, Steering Knuckle, Seal

Drive Axle Assembly, Drive Axle Assembly, Stabilizer Bar, Insulator, Pivot Bushing, Lower Control Arm, Bushing, Caliper, Rotor, Hub & Bearing Assembly

ADJUSTMENTS & INSPECTION

WHEEL ALIGNMENT
SPECIFICATIONS & PROCEDURES

NOTE: See SPECIFICATIONS & PROCEDURES article in WHEEL ALIGNMENT.

FRONT WHEEL BEARINGS

Front bearings are pre-adjusted and lubricated, requiring no routine maintenance or adjustment. Front wheel bearings are serviceable only by complete replacement of hub and bearing assembly.

RIDING HEIGHT

NOTE: See SPECIFICATIONS & PROCEDURES article in WHEEL ALIGNMENT.

BALL JOINT CHECKING

Raise and support vehicle. Allow suspension to hang freely. Inspect ball joint seals for cracks or tears. Replace ball joint if seal is damaged. Grasp tire at top and bottom. Move top of tire using an in-and-out motion. Note horizontal movement of the knuckle relative to the con-

trol arm. Replace ball joint if any looseness exists. Ball stud tightness in steering knuckle boss should be checked by shaking wheel and looking for looseness at stud end. Repair or replace as necessary.

REMOVAL & INSTALLATION

CAUTION: When servicing suspension, use Inner Drive Joint Seal Protector (J-34754). Modify protector by removing 3 tabs on inside surface. DO NOT overextend drive axle joints, or internal parts may separate.

BALL JOINT

Removal – 1) Raise and support vehicle. Place jack stands under frame. Lower vehicle slightly so that weight of vehicle rests on jack stands and not on control arms. Remove front wheel assemblies. Install Inner Drive Joint Seal Protector (J-34754 – modified) on drive axle joints.
2) Remove pinch bolt securing ball joint to steering knuckle. Separate ball joint from steering knuckle. Tap ball joint with mallet to loosen (if necessary).
3) Drill out ball joint retaining rivets. DO NOT damage drive axle seals when removing rivets. Loosen stabilizer bar bushing assembly nut. Remove ball joint from control arm.
Installation – 1) Install ball joint in control arm. Install and tighten retaining bolts as shown in instructions included with ball joint kit. Position steering knuckle over ball joint. Use NEW pinch bolt and nut whenever ball joint is separated from steering knuckle.
2) Align notch in ball joint with steering knuckle bolt hole, and install NEW pinch bolt. Install NEW pinch bolt nut. To complete installation, reverse removal procedure. Tighten bolts to specification. See TORQUE SPECIFICATIONS table at end of article. Lower vehicle and check wheel alignment. See SPECIFICATIONS & PROCEDURES article in WHEEL ALIGNMENT.

STEERING KNUCKLE

Removal – 1) Raise and support vehicle. Place jack stands under frame. Lower vehicle slightly so that weight of vehicle rests on jack stands and not on control arms. Remove front wheel assemblies. Install Inner Drive Joint Seal Protector (J-34754 – modified) on drive axle joints.
2) Disconnect stabilizer bar from control arm. See STABILIZER BAR & BUSHING ASSEMBLY under REMOVAL & INSTALLATION. Remove hub and bearing assembly. See WHEEL HUB/ROTOR & BEARINGS under REMOVAL & INSTALLATION. *See Fig. 1.* Remove pinch bolt and separate ball joint from steering knuckle. See BALL JOINT under REMOVAL & INSTALLATION.

CAUTION: DO NOT overextend drive axle joints, or internal parts may separate.

3) With a sharp tool, scribe reference marks on steering knuckle along lower outboard strut radius. *See Fig. 2* (VIEW A). Also, scribe reference marks on inboard side of strut mounting bracket along curve of steering knuckle (VIEW B), and across strut mounting bracket and steering knuckle interface (VIEW C).
4) Remove strut-to-steering knuckle retaining bolts. Remove steering knuckle.
Installation – 1) Install NEW bearing seal (if removed). Install steering knuckle to strut ensuring scribe marks on steering knuckle align with strut and mounting bracket. Position steering knuckle over ball joint. Use NEW pinch bolt and nut whenever ball joint is separated from steering knuckle. Align notch in ball joint with steering knuckle bolt hole, and install NEW pinch bolt. Install NEW pinch bolt nut.
2) To complete installation, reverse removal procedure. Tighten bolts and nuts to specification. See TORQUE SPECIFICATIONS table at end of article. Lower vehicle and check wheel alignment. See SPECIFICATIONS & PROCEDURES article in WHEEL ALIGNMENT.

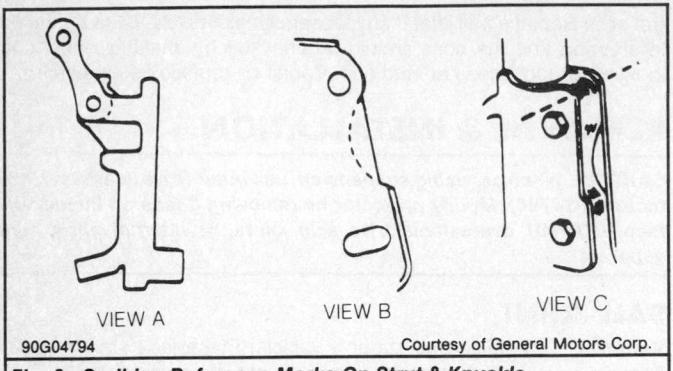

VIEW A   VIEW B   VIEW C

90G04794   Courtesy of General Motors Corp.

Fig. 2: Scribing Reference Marks On Strut & Knuckle

WHEEL HUB/ROTOR & BEARINGS

Removal – 1) Raise and support vehicle. Place jack stands under frame. Lower vehicle slightly so that weight of vehicle rests on jack stands and not on control arms. Remove front wheel assemblies. Install Inner Drive Joint Seal Protector (J-34754 – modified) on drive axle joints.

2) Remove hub-to-drive axle nut and washer. *See Fig. 3.* Remove brake caliper. DO NOT disconnect brake line. Support caliper to prevent brake hose damage.

3) Remove rotor. Using Front Hub Spindle Remover (J-28733-A), separate hub from drive axle shaft. Remove hub and bearing retaining bolts. Remove splash shield, hub and bearing assembly and "O" ring.

4) Using punch, tap seal toward engine. Using side cutters, cut seal off of drive axle after seal has been removed from steering knuckle.

Installation – 1) Using Inner Hub Seal Installer (J-28671) or Inner Hub Seal Installer w/JA Power Heavy Duty Brakes (J-34657-A), install NEW seal into steering knuckle from wheel side of steering knuckle. Lubricate seal with grease.

2) Install "O" ring on hub and bearing assembly. *See Fig. 3.* Hub and bearing are replaced as an assembly. DO NOT damage seal during hub and bearing assembly installation.

3) Install hub and bearing assembly into steering knuckle. Install rotor. Install brake caliper. Install hub-to-drive axle nut and washer. To complete installation, reverse removal procedure. Tighten bolts and nuts to specification. See TORQUE SPECIFICATIONS table at end of article. Lower vehicle and check wheel alignment. See SPECIFICATIONS & PROCEDURES article in WHEEL ALIGNMENT.

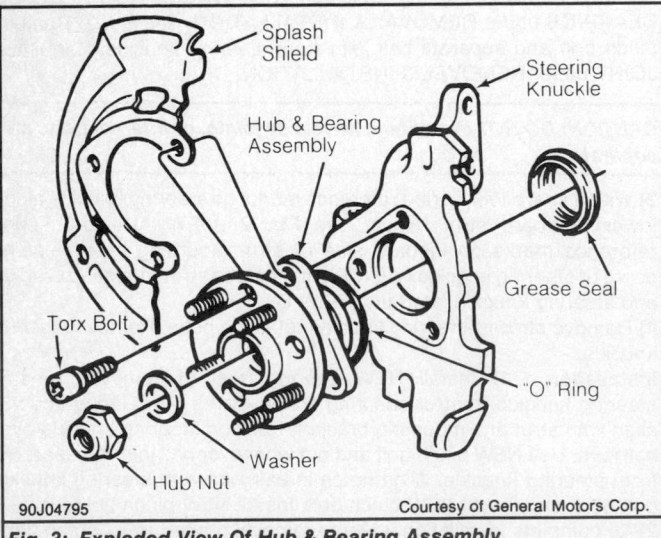

Splash Shield

Steering Knuckle

Hub & Bearing Assembly

Grease Seal

Torx Bolt

"O" Ring

Washer

Hub Nut

90J04795   Courtesy of General Motors Corp.

Fig. 3: Exploded View Of Hub & Bearing Assembly

STRUT ASSEMBLY

Removal – 1) Remove upper strut-to-body mount nuts. Raise and support vehicle. Place jack stands under frame. Lower vehicle slightly

so that weight of vehicle rests on jack stands and not on control arms. Remove front wheel assemblies. Install Inner Drive Joint Seal Protector (J-34754 – modified) on drive axle joints.

CAUTION: Support steering knuckle/hub and bearing assembly during strut removal to prevent tension from being applied to brake hose. DO NOT overextend drive axle joints.

2) Remove brake line bracket from strut. Scribe strut-to-mounting bracket outline on steering knuckle for reassembly reference. *See Fig. 2.* Remove lower strut-to-steering knuckle bolts and remove strut assembly from vehicle. DO NOT chip or scratch coil spring coating. Support steering knuckle/hub and bearing assembly to prevent over-extending drive axle joints.

Disassembly – 1) Mount Strut Compressor (J-34013-A) in Holding Fixture (J-3289-20). Mount strut assembly into strut compressor. Wear eye protection while performing this operation. Compress strut to approximately 1/2 its height. DO NOT bottom spring or strut rod. Using a socket, hold strut rod stationary while removing nut from top of rod.

2) Install Guide Rod (J-34013-27) on strut rod to guide rod down through bearing cap of strut mount while decompressing strut spring. Remove strut and spring from compressor.

CAUTION: DO NOT chip or crack coil spring coating. Coil spring damage may occur if coating is damaged.

Reassembly – 1) Install strut mount into strut compressor, if removed. Mount strut into compressor. Extend strut rod and attach Rod Clamp (J-34013-20) onto lower portion of strut rod.

2) Install components onto strut rod. Ensure flat side of upper spring seat is aligned with lower strut-to-steering knuckle mounting flange. Install Guild Rod (J-34013-27) to center components on strut rod. Remove guild rod when threads are visible on strut rod.

3) Install strut rod nut. Using a socket, hold strut rod stationary while tightening nut on top of strut rod. See TORQUE SPECIFICATIONS table at end of article. Remove rod clamp.

Installation – Install upper strut to body. Install lower strut to steering knuckle ensuring scribe marks on steering knuckle align with strut and mounting bracket. To complete installation, reverse removal procedure. Tighten bolts to specification. See TORQUE SPECIFICATIONS table at end of article. Lower vehicle and check wheel alignment. See SPECIFICATIONS & PROCEDURES article in WHEEL ALIGNMENT.

CONTROL ARM

Removal – 1) Raise and support vehicle. Place jack stands under frame. Lower vehicle slightly so that weight of vehicle rests on jack stands and not on control arms. Remove front wheel assemblies. Install Inner Drive Joint Seal Protector (J-34754 – modified) on drive axle joints.

2) Remove stabilizer bar from control arm. See STABILIZER BAR & BUSHING ASSEMBLY under REMOVAL & INSTALLATION. Remove pinch bolt and separate ball joint from steering knuckle. See BALL JOINT under REMOVAL & INSTALLATION. Remove control arm mounting bolts and remove control arm.

Installation – To install, reverse removal procedure. Install NEW ball joint pinch bolt and nut. Tighten control arm bolts with vehicle weight on control arms. Tighten bolts to specification. See TORQUE SPECIFICATIONS table at end of article. Lower vehicle and check wheel alignment. See SPECIFICATIONS & PROCEDURES article in WHEEL ALIGNMENT.

NOTE: Control arm bolts must be tightened to specification with vehicle weight on control arms.

CONTROL ARM BUSHINGS

Removal & Installation – Remove control arm. See CONTROL ARM under REMOVAL & INSTALLATION. Use control arm bushing service tools to change bushings in control arm. *See Fig. 4.*

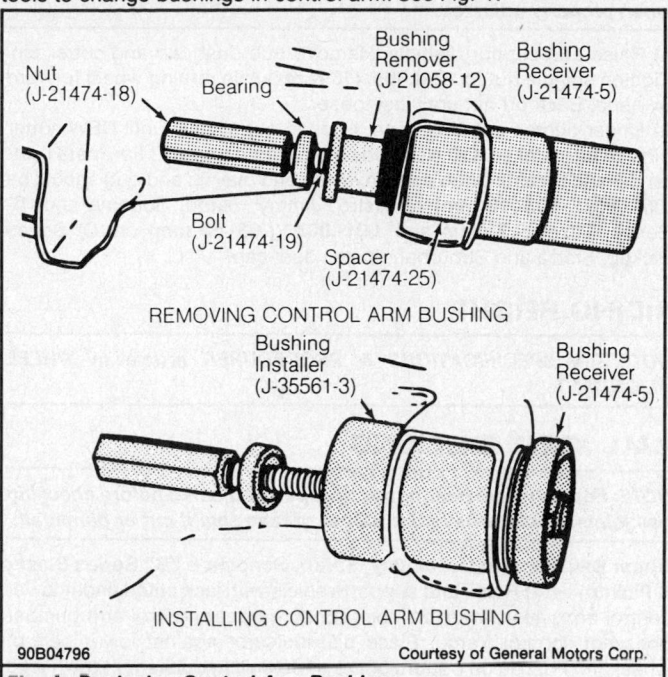

REMOVING CONTROL ARM BUSHING

INSTALLING CONTROL ARM BUSHING

90B04796   Courtesy of General Motors Corp.

Fig. 4: Replacing Control Arm Bushings

STABILIZER BAR & BUSHING ASSEMBLY

Removal – Raise and support vehicle. Allow suspension to hang freely. Remove stabilizer bar bushing clamps and bushing from control arms. Remove stabilizer bar reinforcement plates from frame. Remove stabilizer bar and bushings from vehicle. Inspect and replace all rubber bushings showing signs of wear, damage or deterioration.
Installation – To install, reverse removal procedure. Install bushings with slit facing towards front of vehicle. During installation, loosely assemble all fasteners and ensure stabilizer bar is centered from side to side. Tighten bolts and nuts to specification. See TORQUE SPECIFICATIONS table at end of article.

TORQUE SPECIFICATIONS

TORQUE SPECIFICATIONS

Application	Ft. Lbs. (N.m)
Ball Joint-To-Steering Knuckle Pinch Bolt Nut	33 (45)
Brake Caliper Bolts	38 (51)
Brake Line Bracket Bolt	13 (17)
Control Arm-To-Crossmember Pivot Bolt Nuts	61 (83)
Hub & Bearing Retaining Bolts	70 (95)
Hub-To-Drive Axle Nut	185 (260)
Stabilizer Bar	
Bushing Clamp-To-Control Arm Nuts	33 (45)
Reinforcement Plate-To-Frame Bolts	40 (55)
Strut Assembly	
Rod Nut	65 (85)
Strut-To-Steering Knuckle Bolts	140 (190)
Strut-To-Upper Body Mount Nuts	18 (25)
Wheel Lug Nuts	100 (140)

1992 SUSPENSION
Front – 2WD Coil Spring – Except Van

**Astro, Jimmy, Safari, Sierra,
Sonoma, Suburban, "C" Series Pickup,
"S" Series Blazer & Pickup**

DESCRIPTION

Independent front suspension consists of upper and lower control arms with steering knuckle mounted between ball joints. *See Fig. 1.* On Astro, Jimmy, Safari, Sonoma and "S" Series Blazer & Pickup, upper control arm is mounted on pivot shaft. On "C" Series Pickup, Sierra and Suburban, upper control arm is mounted directly to frame with pivot bolts. On all models, lower control arm is mounted directly to frame with pivot bolts.

Coil springs are mounted between lower control arm and a formed seat in suspension crossmember. Shock absorbers fit between lower control arm and frame. A stabilizer bar is mounted to frame side rails and connected to lower control arms.

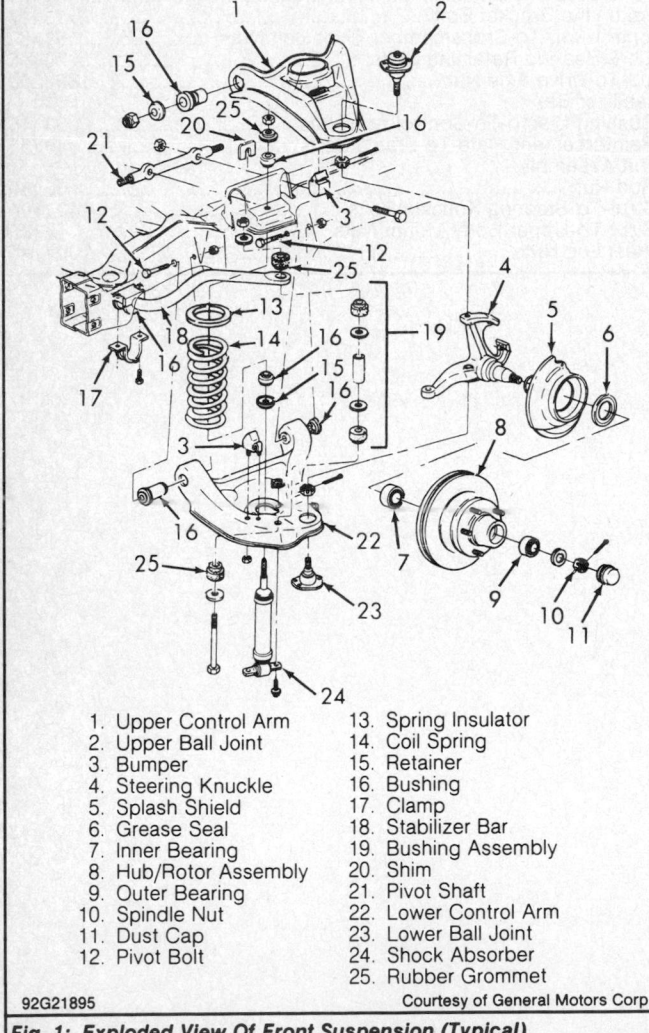

1. Upper Control Arm	13. Spring Insulator
2. Upper Ball Joint	14. Coil Spring
3. Bumper	15. Retainer
4. Steering Knuckle	16. Bushing
5. Splash Shield	17. Clamp
6. Grease Seal	18. Stabilizer Bar
7. Inner Bearing	19. Bushing Assembly
8. Hub/Rotor Assembly	20. Shim
9. Outer Bearing	21. Pivot Shaft
10. Spindle Nut	22. Lower Control Arm
11. Dust Cap	23. Lower Ball Joint
12. Pivot Bolt	24. Shock Absorber
	25. Rubber Grommet

92G21895   Courtesy of General Motors Corp.

Fig. 1: Exploded View Of Front Suspension (Typical)

ADJUSTMENTS & INSPECTION

WHEEL ALIGNMENT
SPECIFICATIONS & PROCEDURES

NOTE: See SPECIFICATIONS & PROCEDURES article in WHEEL ALIGNMENT.

FRONT WHEEL BEARINGS

CAUTION: Never preload tapered roller bearings, or damage to bearings will result. Bearings are designed to have a slightly loose feel when properly adjusted.

1) Raise and support vehicle. Remove hub dust cap and cotter pin. Tighten spindle nut to **12 ft. lbs. (16 N.m)** while turning wheel forward by hand. Back off nut until just loose.

2) Finger tighten nut until snug. Loosen nut slightly until NEW cotter pin can be installed. DO NOT loosen nut more than 1/2 flat. Install cotter pin and measure hub end play. Hub end play (in and out) should be **.001-.005" (.03-.13 mm)** on Astro, Jimmy, Safari, Sonoma and "S" Series Blazer & Pickup and **.001-.008" (.03-.20 mm)** on "C" Series Pickup, Sierra and Suburban. Install dust cap.

RIDING HEIGHT

NOTE: See SPECIFICATIONS & PROCEDURES article in WHEEL ALIGNMENT.

BALL JOINT CHECKING

NOTE: Ensure wheel bearings are properly adjusted before checking ball joints. Replace ball joint rubber grease seal if cut or damaged.

Upper Ball Joint (Astro, Jimmy, Safari, Sonoma & "S" Series Blazer & Pickup) – 1) Raise and support vehicle with jack stand under lower control arm, near lower ball joint. Ensure upper control arm bumper does not contact frame. Place dial indicator against lower part of wheel rim. Push in on bottom of tire while pulling outward at top. Read dial indicator, then reverse push/pull procedure.

2) Lateral (horizontal) deflection should not exceed **.125" (3.18 mm)**. If deflection is excessive, replace ball joint.

3) With ball joint disconnected from steering knuckle, check to see if ball joint can be rotated by finger pressure. Replace if ball joint can be twisted.

Lower Ball Joint (Astro, Jimmy, Safari, Sonoma & "S" Series Blazer & Pickup) – 1) Wear indicator is built into ball joint. Wear is indicated by position of the 1/2" diameter round boss that grease fitting is threaded into. A NEW ball joint has a boss projection of **.050" (1.27 mm)** beyond cover surface.

2) With vehicle weight on wheels, ensure wear indicator protrudes beyond surface of ball joint cover. Replace ball joint if wear indicator is recessed or even with housing.

Upper & Lower Ball Joints ("C" Series Pickup, Sierra & Suburban) –
1) Raise and support vehicle with jack stand under lower control arm, near lower ball joint. Place a dial indicator on spindle hub.

2) Pry tire and wheel assembly between lower control arm and outer race to measure vertical movement. Note dial indicator reading. If reading exceeds **.08" (2.0 mm)**, replace loose ball joint.

REMOVAL & INSTALLATION

WHEEL HUB/ROTOR & BEARINGS

Removal – 1) Raise and support vehicle. Remove wheel and tire assembly. Remove brake caliper and wire aside. DO NOT allow brake caliper to hang by brake line. Remove dust cap, cotter pin, spindle nut and washer. Carefully remove hub/rotor assembly to avoid damage to spindle threads.

2) Remove outer bearing, inner grease seal and inner bearing. Clean bearings and inspect bearings and races for damage. If races required removal from hub, drive old races from hub using hammer and Wheel Bearing Race Remover (J-29117).

Installation – 1) To install, reverse removal procedure. Pack bearings with high-temperature bearing grease. Install NEW grease seal until seal is even with hub surface. Lubricate seal lip and hub cavity with wheel bearing grease.

2) Tighten bolts and nuts to specification. See TORQUE SPECIFICATIONS table at end of article. Adjust wheel bearings. See FRONT WHEEL BEARINGS under ADJUSTMENTS & INSPECTION. Lower vehicle and check wheel alignment. See SPECIFICATIONS & PROCEDURES article in WHEEL ALIGNMENT.

SHOCK ABSORBERS

Removal – Raise and support vehicle. Remove wheel and tire assembly. Hold upper stem from turning while removing upper stem retaining nut, retainer and rubber grommet at top of shock absorber. Remove shock absorber-to-lower control arm bolts and nuts. Lower shock absorber from vehicle.

NOTE: Purging air from non-spiral groove shock is not required as reservoir has gas-charged cell. Spiral groove shock has air-charged cell and air must be purged.

Inspection – **1)** On spiral groove shock, purge air from pressure chamber by mounting shock in vise (top end up) and fully extending unit. Reverse position (top end down) and fully collapse unit. Repeat procedure several times.

2) Bench check shock unit by mounting in vise with top end up (top end down on gas-charged shocks). DO NOT clamp vise on reservoir tube or mounting threads. Check rubber grommets for deterioration and replace as necessary.

3) Operate shock by hand at various rates of speed and note resistance. Rebound force is normally stronger than compression force. If resistance is not smooth and constant, replace shock.

Installation – To install, reverse removal procedure. Tighten bolts and nuts to specification. See TORQUE SPECIFICATIONS table at end of article.

STABILIZER BAR

Removal – Raise and support vehicle. Remove wheel and tire assembly. Remove stabilizer bar-to-frame retaining bolts and clamps. See Fig. 1. Disconnect stabilizer bar from frame. Remove stabilizer bar-to-lower control arm retaining bolt, nut and washers. Disconnect stabilizer bar from lower control arm and remove rubber grommets and bushing assembly. Remove stabilizer bar and bushings from vehicle. Check all rubber bushings for excessive wear, deterioration or damage. Replace as necessary.

Installation – To install, reverse removal procedure. Bushings should be installed with slit area toward front of vehicle. Apply rubber lubricant to bushings to aid in installation. Tighten bolts and nuts to specification. See TORQUE SPECIFICATIONS table at end of article.

COIL SPRINGS

Removal – **1)** Raise and support vehicle with jack stand under frame, with control arms hanging free. Remove wheel and tire assembly. Remove shock absorber. See SHOCK ABSORBERS under REMOVAL & INSTALLATION.

2) Install Spring Remover (J-23028-01) on floor jack. Position assembly under lower control arm so bushings seat in grooves of spring remover.

WARNING: Securely bolt Spring Remover (J-23028-01) to floor jack, and install safety chain through lower control arm and coil spring to prevent personal injury.

3) Remove stabilizer bar-to-lower control arm retaining bolt, nut and washers. Disconnect stabilizer bar from lower control arm and remove rubber grommets and bushing assembly. Raise floor jack to release spring tension on lower control arm pivot bolts. Install safety chain around coil spring and through lower control arm.

4) Remove lower control arm pivot bolts and nuts (rear bolt and nut first). Carefully lower floor jack until all tension is released from coil spring. Remove safety chain and coil spring from vehicle.

NOTE: DO NOT apply force on lower control arm and ball joint to remove coil spring. Coil spring can easily be removed by maneuvering spring.

Installation – **1)** Position coil spring onto lower control arm. Ensure spring insulator is in place. Raise control arm with spring remover and floor jack. Ensure coil spring is properly positioned, with end of lower spring coil covering one drain hole in lower control arm, and clear of or partially covering other drain hole.

NOTE: Coil spring must be positioned with tape at lowest position. Bottom of spring is coiled helical, and top is coiled flat with a gripper notch near end of spring coil.

2) Install lower control arm pivot bolts and nuts (front bolt and nut first). Pivot bolts must be installed with nuts toward rear of vehicle. To complete installation, reverse removal procedure. Tighten bolts and nuts to specification. See TORQUE SPECIFICATIONS table at end of article. Lower vehicle and check wheel alignment. See SPECIFICATIONS & PROCEDURES article in WHEEL ALIGNMENT.

STEERING KNUCKLE

Removal – **1)** Raise and support vehicle with jack stand under frame, with control arms hanging free.

NOTE: DO NOT place jack stand under lower control arm. Spring tension is needed to break loose ball joint stud.

2) Remove wheel and tire assembly. Remove brake caliper and wire aside. DO NOT allow brake caliper to hang by brake line. Remove hub/rotor assembly. Remove splash shield. Remove cotter pin and nut from tie rod end. Use Tie Rod Remover (J-6627-A) to separate tie rod end from steering knuckle.

3) If replacing steering knuckle, carefully remove steering knuckle grease seal. Position floor jack under lower control arm between ball joint and spring seat. Raise floor jack until lower control arm is just supported.

CAUTION: Support lower control arm with floor jack during removal and installation of steering knuckle.

4) Remove cotter pins and nuts from upper and lower ball joints. Using Ball Joint Separator (J-23742), separate ball joint studs from steering knuckle. See Fig. 2. Raise upper control arm to disengage ball joint stud from steering knuckle. Remove steering knuckle.

Inspection – Inspect tapered holes in steering knuckle for out-of-round, deformation or damage. Inspect spindle for worn or damaged threads. Replace steering knuckle as necessary.

CAUTION: When installing upper and lower ball joint stud nuts, DO NOT loosen nut to install cotter pin. Stud nuts may be tightened up to 40 ft. lbs. (54 N.m) in excess of torque specification.

Installation – **1)** To install, reverse removal procedure. Install NEW grease seal on steering knuckle (if removed). Tighten ball joint stud nuts to align cotter pin holes as necessary. Install tie rod end stud into steering knuckle.

2) Install Steering Linkage Installer (J-29193) or (J-29194). Tighten steering linkage installer to 40 ft. lbs. (54 N.m) to seat tie rod taper. Remove steering linkage installer and install tie rod end stud nut.

3) To complete installation, reverse removal procedure. Adjust wheel bearings. See FRONT WHEEL BEARINGS under ADJUSTMENTS & INSPECTION. Tighten bolts and nuts to specification. See TORQUE SPECIFICATIONS table at end of article. Lower vehicle and check wheel alignment. See SPECIFICATIONS & PROCEDURES article in WHEEL ALIGNMENT.

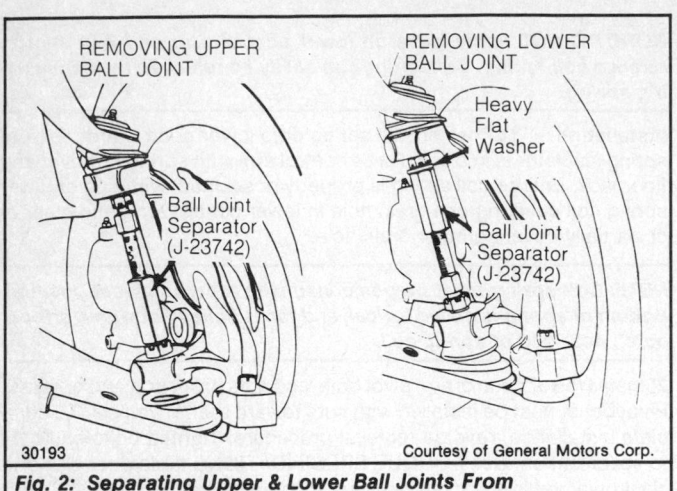

REMOVING UPPER BALL JOINT

REMOVING LOWER BALL JOINT

Heavy Flat Washer

Ball Joint Separator (J-23742)

Ball Joint Separator (J-23742)

30193 Courtesy of General Motors Corp.

Fig. 2: Separating Upper & Lower Ball Joints From Steering Knuckle

UPPER BALL JOINT

Removal – **1)** Raise and support vehicle with jack stand under lower control arm, between ball joint and spring seat. Jack stand must remain under lower control arm during upper ball joint servicing to maintain lower control arm and coil spring positioning.

2) Remove wheel and tire assembly. Remove brake caliper and wire aside. DO NOT allow brake caliper to hang by brake line. Remove grease fitting and cotter pin from upper ball joint stud. Remove upper ball joint stud nut.

3) Install Ball Joint Separator (J-23742) between upper and lower ball studs. See Fig. 2. Extend bolt on ball joint separator to loosen ball joint stud from steering knuckle. Remove ball joint separator. Separate ball joint from steering knuckle.

4) Using drill and 1/8" (3.18 mm) drill bit, drill 1/4" (6.35 mm) deep hole in ball joint retaining rivets. Using 1/2" (12.7 mm) drill bit, drill out rivet heads. Using a hammer and small punch, drive out rivets and remove upper ball joint from upper control arm.

CAUTION: When installing upper and lower ball joint stud nuts, DO NOT loosen nut to install cotter pin. Stud nuts may be tightened up to 40 ft. lbs. (54 N.m) in excess of torque specification.

Installation – To install, reverse removal procedure. Use NEW nuts and bolts to install ball joint into upper control arm. Install grease fitting and lubricate NEW ball joint. Tighten bolts and nuts to specification. See TORQUE SPECIFICATIONS table at end of article. Lower vehicle and check wheel alignment. See SPECIFICATIONS & PROCEDURES article in WHEEL ALIGNMENT.

LOWER BALL JOINT

Removal – **1)** Raise and support vehicle with jack stand under lower control arm between ball joint and spring seat. Jack stand must remain under lower control arm during lower ball joint servicing to maintain lower control arm and coil spring positioning.

2) Remove wheel and tire assembly. Remove brake caliper and wire aside. DO NOT allow brake caliper to hang by brake line. Remove grease fitting, rubber grease seal and cotter pin from lower ball joint stud. Remove lower ball joint stud nut.

3) Install Ball Joint Separator (J-23742) between upper and lower ball studs. See Fig. 2. Extend bolt on ball joint separator to loosen ball joint stud from steering knuckle. Remove ball joint separator. Separate ball joint from steering knuckle.

4) Place a wooden block between upper control arm and frame to keep steering knuckle assembly out of the way. Assemble on lower control arm, "C" Clamp (J-9519-00) and Removers (J-9519-7 and J-9519-28) from Ball Joint Remover/Installer Set (J-9519-D). See Fig. 3. Remove ball joint from lower control arm.

CAUTION: When installing upper and lower ball joint stud nuts, DO NOT loosen nut to install cotter pin. Stud nuts may be tightened up to 40 ft. lbs. (54 N.m) in excess of torque specification.

Installation – **1)** Assemble on lower control arm, "C" Clamp (J-9519-30) and Installer (J-9519-16) from ball joint remover/installer set. See Fig. 3. Reverse removal procedure to install ball joint into lower control arm. Ensure bleed vent in rubber grease seal is facing forward. Install grease fitting and lubricate NEW ball joint.

2) To complete installation, reverse removal procedure. Tighten bolts and nuts to specification. See TORQUE SPECIFICATIONS table at end of article. Lower vehicle and check wheel alignment. See SPECIFICATIONS & PROCEDURES article in WHEEL ALIGNMENT.

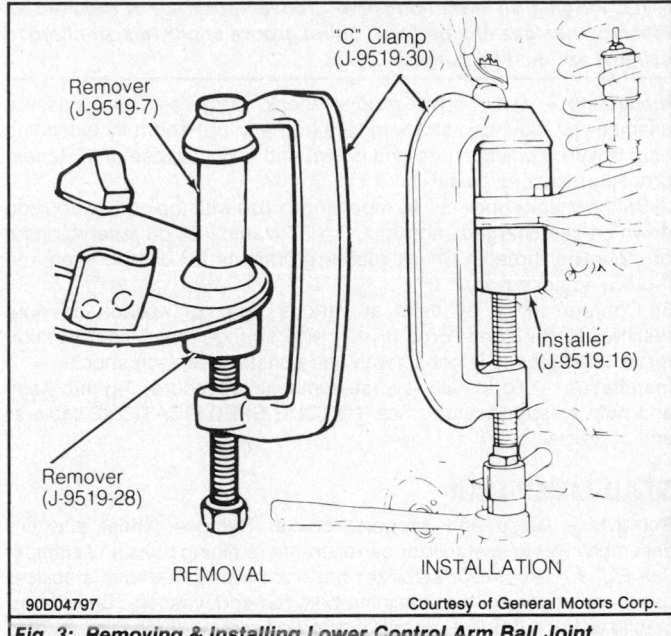

"C" Clamp (J-9519-30)

Remover (J-9519-7)

Installer (J-9519-16)

Remover (J-9519-28)

REMOVAL INSTALLATION

90D04797 Courtesy of General Motors Corp.

Fig. 3: Removing & Installing Lower Control Arm Ball Joint

UPPER CONTROL ARM

Removal (Astro, Jimmy, Safari, Sonoma & "S" Series Blazer & Pickup – 1) Note location of alignment shims for reassembly. Remove upper control arm pivot shaft-to-frame nut and shim. See Fig. 1. Raise and support vehicle with jack stand under lower control arm, between ball joint and spring seat. Ensure jack stand remains under lower control arm during upper control arm servicing to maintain lower control arm and coil spring positioning.

2) Remove wheel and tire assembly. Remove grease fitting and cotter pin from upper ball joint stud. Remove upper ball joint stud nut. Install Ball Joint Separator (J-23742) between upper and lower ball studs. See Fig. 2. Extend bolt on ball joint separator to loosen ball joint stud from steering knuckle. Remove ball joint separator. Separate ball joint from steering knuckle.

3) Lift upper control arm, and remove upper control arm pivot shaft-to-frame bolts. Remove upper control arm.

Removal ("C" Series Pickup, Sierra & Suburban) – 1) Raise and support vehicle with jack stand under lower control arm, between ball joint and spring seat. Ensure jack stand remains under lower control arm during upper control arm servicing to maintain lower control arm and coil spring positioning.

2) Remove wheel and tire assembly. Remove air cleaner extension (if necessary). Remove brake line bracket from upper control arm. Remove grease fitting and cotter pin from upper ball joint stud. Remove upper ball joint stud nut. Install Ball Joint Separator (J-23742) between upper and lower ball studs. See Fig. 2. Extend bolt on ball joint separator to loosen ball joint stud from steering knuckle. Remove ball joint separator. Separate ball joint from steering knuckle.

3) Remove upper control arm-to-frame pivot bolts and nuts. Remove upper control arm.

Installation – 1) To Install, reverse removal procedure. On "C" Series Pickup, Sierra and Suburban without pivot shaft, ensure upper control arm pivot bolt heads face each other, and are tightened to specification with vehicle at riding height.

2) On Astro, Jimmy, Safari, Sonoma and "S" Series Blazer & Pickup, ensure holes in upper control arm shaft align with holes in frame. Ensure alignment shims are installed in original position.

3) On all models, tighten bolts and nuts to specification. See TORQUE SPECIFICATIONS table at end of article. Lower vehicle and check wheel alignment. See SPECIFICATIONS & PROCEDURES article in WHEEL ALIGNMENT.

UPPER CONTROL ARM BUSHINGS

NOTE: Upper control arm bushings are not replaceable on "C" Series Pickup, Sierra and Suburban. Upper control arm and bushings are serviced as an assembly.

Pivot Shaft Bushing Replacement (Astro, Jimmy, Safari, Sonoma & "S" Series Blazer & Pickup) – 1) Remove upper control arm from vehicle. See UPPER CONTROL ARM under REMOVAL & INSTALLATION. Place upper control arm in soft-jawed vise. Remove nuts and retainers from ends of pivot shaft.

2) Using Bushing Remover (J-22269-1), a slotted washer and a short piece of pipe (slightly larger than bushing), press bushing and pivot shaft from upper control arm. Repeat procedure for opposite bushing.

3) To install, place pivot shaft in upper control arm. Using Bushing Installer (J-22269-1) and small piece of pipe with the same outer diameter as bushing, press NEW bushing into upper control arm and onto pivot shaft.

4) Ensure each bushing is positioned .48-.52" (12.8-13.8 mm) from face of control arm to bushing outer sleeve. Repeat procedure for bushing on opposite end. Install nuts and retainers onto upper control arm pivot shaft ends.

LOWER CONTROL ARM

Removal – 1) Raise and support vehicle with jack stand under frame, with control arms hanging free. Remove wheel and tire assembly. Remove coil spring. See COIL SPRINGS under REMOVAL & INSTALLATION. Separate lower ball joint from steering knuckle. See LOWER BALL JOINT under REMOVAL & INSTALLATION.

2) Separate lower control arm from steering knuckle and carefully maneuver out of opening in splash shield. Remove lower control arm-to-frame pivot bolts and nuts (rear bolt and nut first). Remove lower control from vehicle.

Installation – 1) To install, reverse removal procedure. Use NEW nuts on lower control arm pivot bolts. Install lower control arm pivot bolts and nuts (front bolt and nut first). Ensure lower control arm pivot bolts are installed with bolt heads facing toward front of vehicle, and are tightened to specification with vehicle at riding height.

2) Tighten bolts and nuts to specification. See TORQUE SPECIFICATIONS table at end of article. Lower vehicle and check wheel alignment. See SPECIFICATIONS & PROCEDURES article in WHEEL ALIGNMENT.

LOWER CONTROL ARM BUSHINGS

NOTE: Bushing replacement procedure for "C" Series Pickup is not available from manufacturer.

Front Bushing Replacement (Astro, Jimmy, Safari, Sonoma & "S" Series Blazer & Pickup) – 1) Remove lower control arm from vehicle. See LOWER CONTROL ARM under REMOVAL & INSTALLATION. Place lower control arm in soft-jawed vise. Using a blunt chisel, drive front bushing flare down even with rubber of bushing.

2) Install lower control arm bushing service set. On Astro and Safari, service set includes Receiver (J-21474-5), Nut (J-21474-18), Bolt (J-21474-19), Remover (J-21474-23) and Spacer (J-23737). See Fig. 4.

3) On Jimmy, Sonoma and "S" Series Blazer & Pickup, service set includes Receiver (J-21474-5), Nut (J-21474-18), Bolt (J-21474-19),

Remover (J-21474-23) and Spacer (J-22222-5). See Fig. 4. On all models, tighten nut until front bushing is removed from lower control arm.

4) To install front bushing, assemble control arm bushing service set. On Astro and Safari, use Installer (J-21474-20) and Spacer (J-21474-12) with other removal tools of service set. See Fig. 5.

5) On Jimmy, Sonoma and "S" Series Blazer & Pickup, use Remover/Installer (J-21474-8) with other removal tools of service set to install NEW bushing. See Fig. 4. Position NEW front bushing into lower control arm with lip side of bushing on outside of lower control arm. Tighten nut until bushing is fully seated into lower control arm.

6) Flare front bushings after installation. On Astro and Safari, install Flaring Die (J-21474-2), Installer (J-21474-13), Nut (J-21474-18), Bolt (J-21474-19) and Spacer (J-23737). See Fig. 6.

7) On Jimmy, Sonoma and "S" Series Blazer & Pickup, install Flaring Die (J-21474-2), Spacer (J-21474-12), Installer (J-21474-13) and Nut (J-21474-18). See Fig. 6. On all models, turn nut on flaring die until bushing is flared approximately 45 degrees. Remove bushing flaring die and service tools.

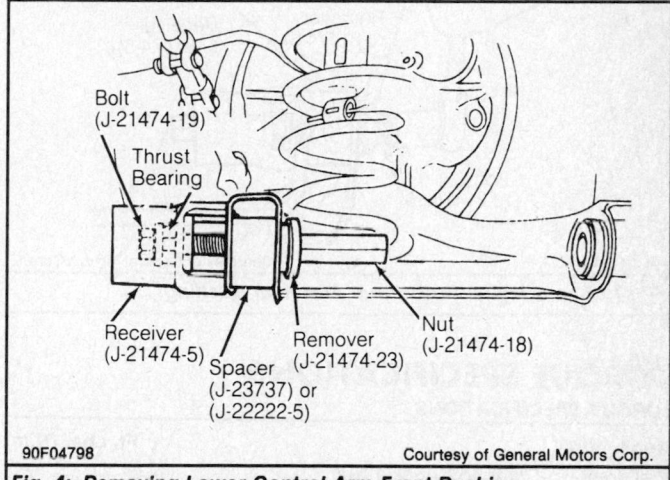

90F04798   Courtesy of General Motors Corp.

Fig. 4: Removing Lower Control Arm Front Bushing

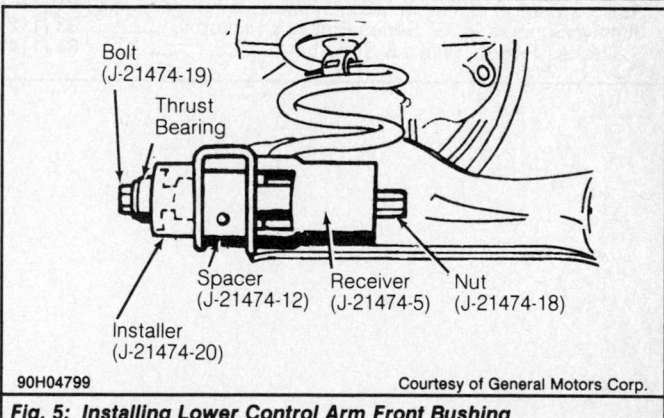

90H04799   Courtesy of General Motors Corp.

Fig. 5: Installing Lower Control Arm Front Bushing (Astro & Safari)

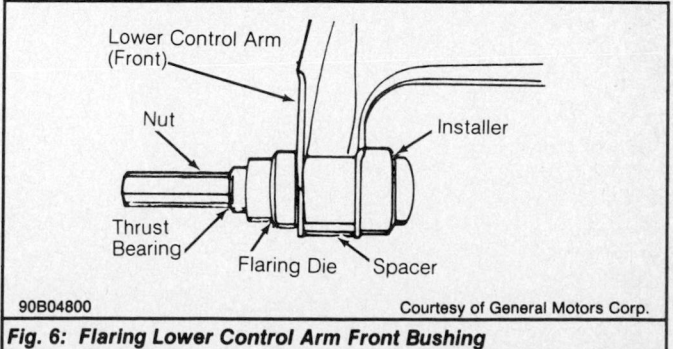

90B04800   Courtesy of General Motors Corp.

Fig. 6: Flaring Lower Control Arm Front Bushing

Rear Bushing Replacement (Astro, Jimmy, Safari, Sonoma & "S" Series Blazer & Pickup) – **1)** Remove lower control arm from vehicle. See LOWER CONTROL ARM under REMOVAL & INSTALLATION. Place lower control arm in soft-jawed vise.

2) Install Receiver (J-21474-5), Remover (J-21474-8), Spacer (J-21474-12), Nut (J-21474-18), Bolt (J-21474-19). See Fig. 7. Tighten nut until rear bushing is removed from lower control arm.

3) Assemble control arm bushing service set. Install Nut (J-21474-18), Bolt (J-21474-19), Spacer (J-21474-12) and Receiver (J-21474-5). On Astro and Safari, also use Installer (J-21474-20). Position NEW rear bushing into lower control arm with lip side of bushing on outside of lower control arm. Tighten nut until bushing is fully seated into lower control arm.

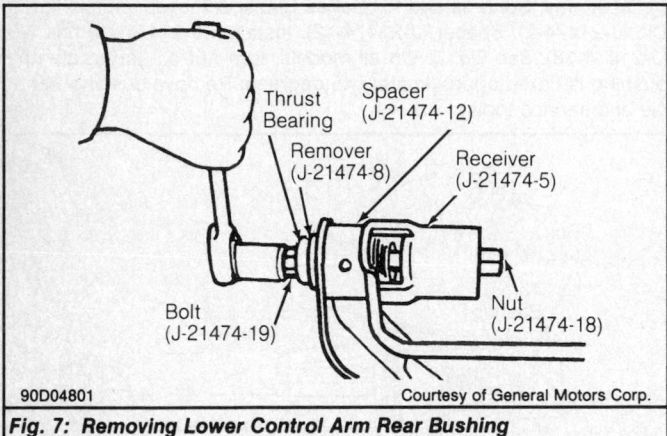

90D04801   Courtesy of General Motors Corp.

Fig. 7: Removing Lower Control Arm Rear Bushing

TORQUE SPECIFICATIONS

TORQUE SPECIFICATIONS

Application	Ft. Lbs. (N.m)
Ball Joint-To-Steering Knuckle Nut	
Lower	
Astro & Safari	81 (110)
Jimmy, Sonoma, & "S" Series Blazer & Pickup	83 (112)
"C" Series Pickup, Sierra & Suburban	84 (114)

TORQUE SPECIFICATIONS (Cont.)

Application	Ft. Lbs. (N.m)
Upper	
Astro & Safari	65 (88)
Jimmy, Sonoma, & "S" Series Blazer & Pickup	61 (83)
"C" Series Pickup, Sierra & Suburban	84 (114)
Lower Control Arm-To-Frame Pivot Bolt Nuts	
Astro & Safari	[1] 96 (130)
Jimmy, Sonoma, & "S" Series Blazer & Pickup	
Front Bolt	[1] 94 (127)
Rear Bolt	[1] 66 (89)
"C" Series Pickup, Sierra & Suburban	[1] 121 (164)
Shock Absorber-To-Frame Nut	
Astro & Safari	11 (15)
"C" Series Pickup, Jimmy, Sierra, Sonoma, Suburban & "S" Series Blazer & Pickup	10 (14)
Shock Absorber-To-Lower Control Arm Bolts	
Astro & Safari	18 (24)
"C" Series Pickup, Jimmy, Sierra, Sonoma, Suburban & "S" Series Blazer & Pickup	20 (27)
Splash Shield Bolts	
Astro, Jimmy, Safari, Sonoma & "S" Series Blazer & Pickup	10 (14)
"C" Series Pickup, Sierra & Suburban	19 (26)
Stabilizer Bar	
To-Frame Bolts	
Astro & Safari	13 (18)
"C" Series Pickup, Jimmy, Sierra, Sonoma, Suburban & "S" Series Blazer & Pickup	24 (33)
To-Lower Control Arm Nut	
Astro & Safari	[2] 27 (37)
"C" Series Pickup, Jimmy, Sierra, Sonoma, Suburban & "S" Series Blazer & Pickup	[2] 13 (18)
Tie Rod End-To-Steering Knuckle Nut	
Astro, Jimmy, Safari, Sonoma & "S" Series Blazer & Pickup	35 (47)
"C" Series Pickup, Sierra & Suburban	40 (54)
Upper Ball Joint-To-Control Arm Nuts	
Astro & Safari	22 (30)
Jimmy, Sonoma, & "S" Series Blazer & Pickup	17 (23)
"C" Series Pickup, Sierra & Suburban	18 (24)
Upper Control Arm Pivot Shaft Nuts	85 (115)
Upper Control Arm Pivot Shaft-To-Frame Nuts	65 (88)

[1] – Tighten to specifications with weight of vehicle on its wheels.
[2] – Obtain torque by running nut to unthreaded portion of bolt.

Commercial Van, Van

MODEL IDENTIFICATION

Vehicle model can be identified by fifth character of Vehicle Identification Number (VIN), stamped on metal pad on top of left end of instrument panel, near windshield. See MODEL IDENTIFICATION table.

MODEL IDENTIFICATION

Series [1]	Model
"G"	RWD Van
"P"	Commercial Van/Motorhome

[1] – Vehicle series is fifth character of VIN.

DESCRIPTION

Independent front suspension consists of upper and lower control arms with steering knuckle mounted between ball joints. *See Fig. 1.* Control arms are mounted on pivot shafts. Coil springs are mounted between lower control arm and a formed seat in suspension crossmember. Some models have urethane air cylinders inside the coil springs. Shock absorbers fit between lower control arm and frame. A stabilizer bar is mounted to frame side rails and connected to lower control arms.

ADJUSTMENTS & INSPECTION

WHEEL ALIGNMENT
SPECIFICATIONS & PROCEDURES

NOTE: See SPECIFICATIONS & PROCEDURES article in WHEEL ALIGNMENT.

FRONT WHEEL BEARINGS

CAUTION: Never preload tapered roller bearings, or damage to bearings will result. Bearings are designed to have a slightly loose feel when properly adjusted.

1) Raise and support vehicle. Remove hub dust cap and cotter pin. Tighten spindle nut to **12 ft. lbs. (16 N.m)** while turning wheel forward by hand. Back off nut until just loose.
2) Finger tighten nut until snug. Loosen nut slightly (no more than 1/2 flat) until NEW cotter pin can be installed. Install NEW cotter pin and measure hub end play. Hub end play (in and out) should be **.001-.005"** **(.03-.13 mm)** when properly adjusted. Install dust cap.

RIDING HEIGHT

NOTE: See SPECIFICATIONS & PROCEDURES article in WHEEL ALIGNMENT.

BALL JOINT CHECKING

Upper Ball Joint – 1) Upper ball joint is spring-loaded in socket to minimize looseness and compensate for normal wear. Raise and support vehicle with jack stand under lower control arm. Remove wheel and tire assembly.
2) Inspect ball joint for lateral shake by gripping hub/rotor assembly at top and bottom, and moving spindle inward and outward. Replace ball joint if any lateral movement exists.
3) Check ball joint, only with ball joint disconnected from steering knuckle, to see if ball joint can be rotated by finger pressure. Replace if ball joint can be twisted. Inspect upper ball joint rubber grease seal for cracks, cuts or tears. Replace as necessary.
Lower Ball Joint – 1) Lower ball joint wear may be checked without disassembling ball joint stud. Raise and support vehicle at wheel and hub with jack stand.
2) Measure distance between top of ball joint stud and tip of lower grease fitting. *See Fig. 2.* Move support to lower control arm and allow wheel and hub to hang free.
3) Measure distance again. If difference between measurements exceeds **.094" (2.38 mm)**, replace ball joint. Inspect lower ball joint rubber grease seal for cracks, cuts or tears. Replace as necessary.

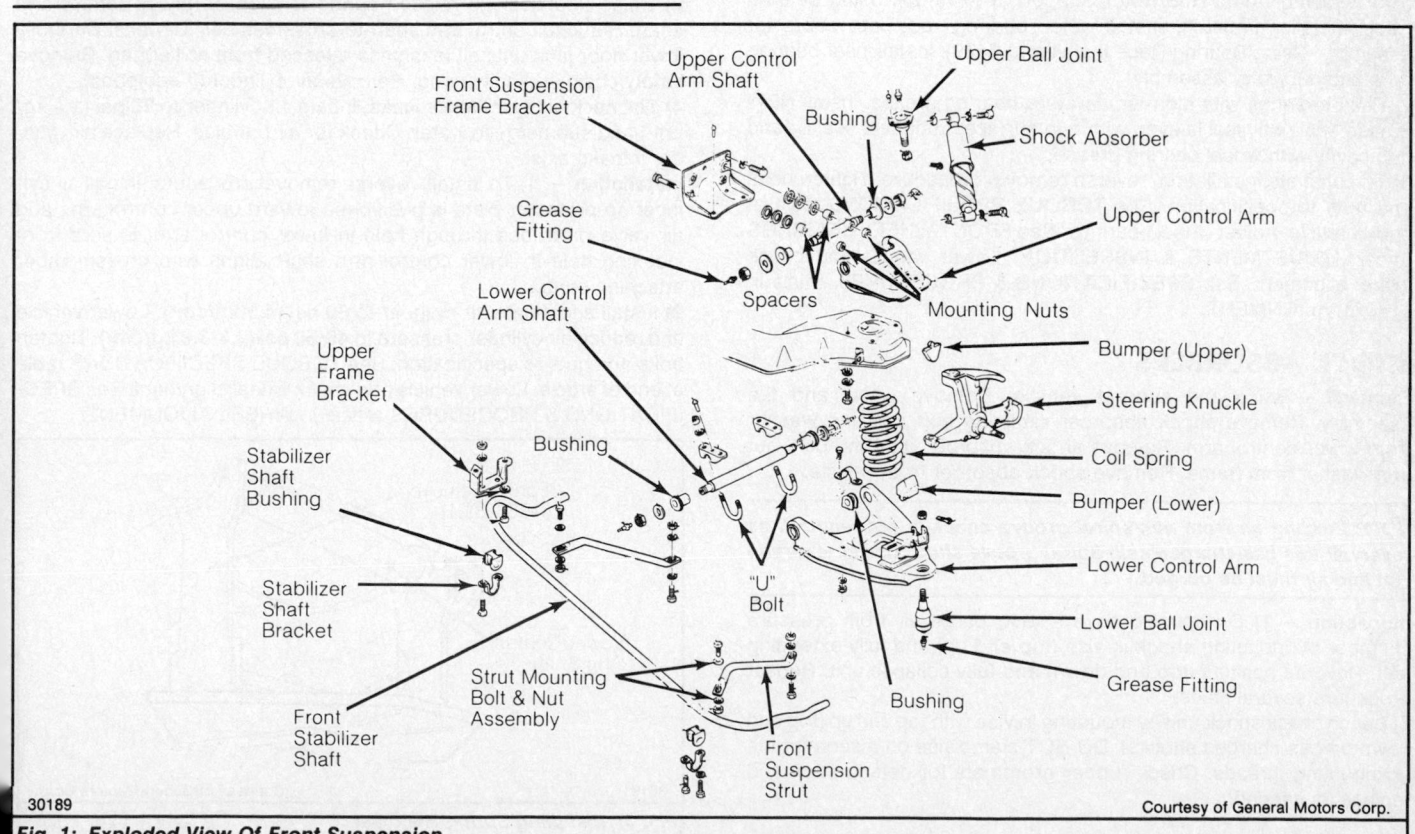

30189

Courtesy of General Motors Corp.

Fig. 1: Exploded View Of Front Suspension

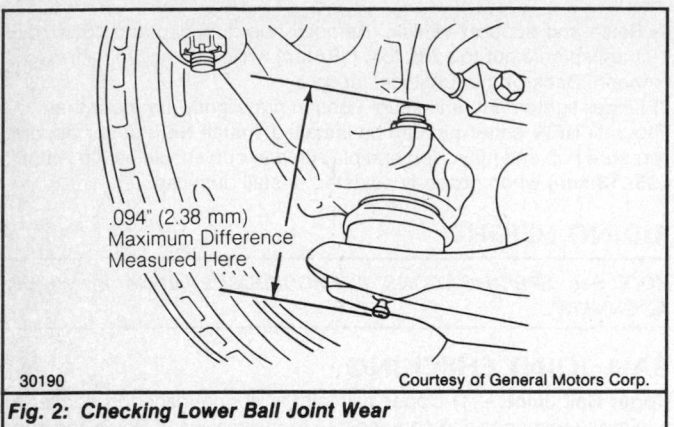

.094" (2.38 mm)
Maximum Difference
Measured Here

30190   Courtesy of General Motors Corp.

Fig. 2: Checking Lower Ball Joint Wear

REMOVAL & INSTALLATION

WARNING: When battery is disconnected, vehicle computer and memory systems may lose memory data. Driveability problems may exist until computer systems have completed a relearn cycle. See COMPUTER RELEARN PROCEDURES article in GENERAL INFORMATION before disconnecting battery.

WHEEL HUB/ROTOR & BEARINGS

Removal – 1) Raise and support vehicle. Remove wheel and tire assembly. Remove brake caliper and hang aside with wire. DO NOT allow brake caliper to hang by brake line.
2) Remove dust cap, cotter pin, spindle nut and washer. Carefully remove hub/rotor assembly to avoid damage to spindle threads. Remove outer bearing, inner grease seal and inner bearing.
3) Clean bearings and inspect bearings and races for damage. If races require removal from hub, drive old races from hub using a hammer and a brass drift inserted through notches of hub.
Installation – 1) To install, reverse removal procedure. Place hub/rotor assembly onto Hub/Rotor Support (J-9746-02). Using Bearing Race Installer (J-8457), install outer bearing race into hub/rotor assembly. Using Bearing Race Installer (J-8449), install inner bearing race into hub/rotor assembly.
2) Pack bearings with high-temperature bearing grease. Install NEW grease seal until seal is even with hub surface. Lubricate seal lip and hub cavity with wheel bearing grease.
3) To complete installation, reverse removal procedure. Tighten bolts and nuts to specification. See TORQUE SPECIFICATIONS table at end of article. Adjust wheel bearings. See FRONT WHEEL BEARINGS under ADJUSTMENTS & INSPECTION. Lower vehicle and check wheel alignment. See SPECIFICATIONS & PROCEDURES article in WHEEL ALIGNMENT.

SHOCK ABSORBERS

Removal – Raise and support vehicle. Remove wheel and tire assembly. Remove shock absorber retaining bolt, nut and washer from lower control arm. Remove shock absorber retaining bolt, nut and washer from frame. Remove shock absorber from vehicle.

NOTE: Purging air from non-spiral groove shock is not required as reservoir has gas-charged cell. Spiral groove shock has air-charged cell and air must be purged.

Inspection – 1) On spiral groove shock, purge air from pressure chamber by mounting shock in vise (top end up) and fully extending unit. Reverse position (top end down) and fully collapse unit. Repeat procedure several times.
2) Bench check shock unit by mounting in vise with top end up (top end down on gas-charged shocks). DO NOT clamp vise on reservoir tube or mounting threads. Check rubber grommets for deterioration and replace as needed.

3) Operate shock by hand at various rates of speed and note resistance. Rebound force is normally stronger than compression force. If resistance is not smooth and constant, replace shock.
Installation – To install, reverse removal procedure. Tighten bolts and nuts to specification. See TORQUE SPECIFICATIONS table at end of article.

STABILIZER BAR

Removal – Raise and support vehicle. Remove wheel and tire assembly. Remove stabilizer bar-to-frame retaining bolts, washers and clamps. Disconnect stabilizer bar from frame. Remove stabilizer bar-to-lower control arm retaining bolts, nuts, washers and clamps. Disconnect stabilizer bar from lower control arms. Remove stabilizer bar and bushings from vehicle. Check all rubber bushings for excessive wear, deterioration or damage. Replace as necessary.
Installation – To install, reverse removal procedure. Bushings should be installed with slit area toward front of vehicle. Apply rubber lubricant to bushings to aid in installation. Tighten bolts and nuts to specification. See TORQUE SPECIFICATIONS table at end of article.

COIL SPRINGS

Removal – 1) Raise and support vehicle with jack stand under frame, with control arms hanging free. Remove wheel and tire assembly. Disconnect shock absorber and stabilizer bar at lower control arm. Install Spring Remover (J-23028-01) on floor jack. *See Fig. 3.* Position assembly under lower control arm so shaft seats in grooves of spring remover.

WARNING: Securely bolt Spring Remover (J-23028-01) to floor jack, and install safety chain through lower control arm and coil spring to prevent personal injury.

2) If air cylinders are installed in coil springs, remove valve cap and valve core. Pry on air cylinder to release air pressure. Reinstall valve core and valve cap to retain vacuum condition. Push air cylinder upward toward top of spring as far as possible. Install safety chain around coil spring and through lower control arm.
3) Raise floor jack to release spring tension on lower control arm shaft. Remove control arm shaft-to-crossmember "U" bolts. Carefully lower floor jack until all tension is released from coil spring. Remove safety chain and coil spring. Remove air cylinder (if equipped).
4) To check air cylinder for leaks, inflate air cylinder to **20 psi (1.4 kg/cm²)** and submerge in water. Check for air bubbles. Replace air cylinder if leaks exist.
Installation – 1) To install, reverse removal procedure. Install air cylinder so protector plate is positioned toward upper control arm, and air valve protrudes through hole in lower control arm. Ensure front indexing hole in lower control arm shaft aligns with crossmember attaching studs.
2) Install and inflate air cylinder to **60 psi (4.3 kg/cm²)**. Lower vehicle and reduce air cylinder pressure to **40-50 psi (2.8-3.6 kg/cm²)**. Tighten bolts and nuts to specification. See TORQUE SPECIFICATIONS table at end of article. Lower vehicle and check wheel alignment. See SPECIFICATIONS & PROCEDURES article in WHEEL ALIGNMENT.

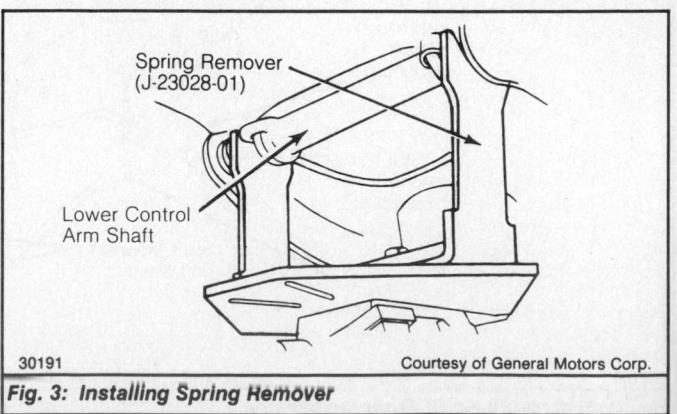

Spring Remover
(J-23028-01)

Lower Control
Arm Shaft

30191   Courtesy of General Motors Corp.

Fig. 3: Installing Spring Remover

STEERING KNUCKLE

Removal – **1)** Raise and support vehicle with jack stand under frame, with control arms hanging free.

NOTE: DO NOT place jack stands under lower control arm. Spring tension is needed to break loose ball joint stud.

2) Remove wheel and tire assembly. Remove brake caliper and hang aside with wire. DO NOT allow brake caliper to hang by brake line. Remove hub/rotor assembly. Remove splash shield. Remove cotter pin and nut from tie rod end. Use Tie Rod Remover (J-6627-A) to separate tie rod end from steering knuckle.

3) If replacing steering knuckle, carefully remove steering knuckle grease seal. Position floor jack under lower control arm between ball joint and spring seat. Raise floor jack until lower control arm is just supported.

CAUTION: Lower control arm must be supported with floor jack during removal and installation of steering knuckle.

4) Remove cotter pins and nuts from upper and lower ball joints. Using Ball Joint Separator (J-23742), separate ball joint studs from steering knuckle. *See Fig. 4.* Raise upper control arm to disengage ball joint stud from steering knuckle. Remove steering knuckle.

Inspection – Inspect tapered holes in steering knuckle for out-of-round, deformation or damage. Inspect spindle for worn or damaged threads. Replace steering knuckle as necessary.

CAUTION: When installing upper and lower ball joint stud nuts, NEVER loosen nut to install cotter pin. Stud nuts may be tightened up to 40 ft. lbs. (54 N.m) in excess of specified torque specification.

Installation – **1)** To install, reverse removal procedure. Install NEW grease seal on steering knuckle (if removed). Tighten ball joint stud nuts to align cotter pin holes as necessary. Install tie rod end stud into steering knuckle.

2) Install Steering Linkage Installer (J-29193) or (J-29194). Tighten steering linkage installer to **40 ft. lbs. (54 N.m)** to seat tie rod taper. Remove steering linkage installer and install tie rod end stud nut.

3) To complete installation, reverse removal procedure. Adjust wheel bearings. See FRONT WHEEL BEARINGS under ADJUSTMENTS & INSPECTION. Tighten bolts and nuts to specification. See TORQUE SPECIFICATIONS table at end of article. Lower vehicle and check wheel alignment. See SPECIFICATIONS & PROCEDURES article in WHEEL ALIGNMENT.

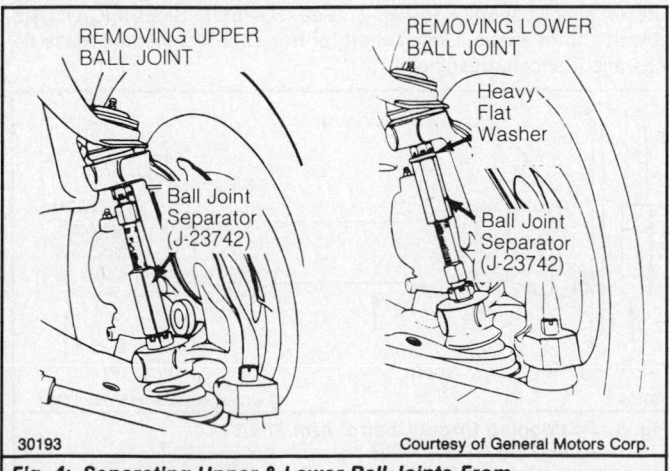

30193   Courtesy of General Motors Corp.

Fig. 4: Separating Upper & Lower Ball Joints From Steering Knuckle

UPPER BALL JOINT

Removal – **1)** Raise and support vehicle with jack stand under lower control arm between ball joint and spring seat. Jack stand must remain under lower control arm during upper ball joint servicing to maintain lower control arm and coil spring positioning.

2) Remove wheel and tire assembly. Remove brake caliper and hang aside with wire. DO NOT allow brake caliper to hang by brake line. Remove grease fitting and cotter pin from upper ball joint stud. Loosen ball joint stud nut 2 turns. DO NOT remove nut at this time.

3) Install Ball Joint Separator (J-23742) between upper and lower ball joint studs. *See Fig. 4.* Extend bolt on ball joint separator to loosen ball joint stud from steering knuckle. Remove ball joint separator and ball joint stud nut. Separate ball joint from steering knuckle.

4) Using drill and 1/8" (3.18 mm) drill bit, drill 1/4" (6.35 mm) deep hole in ball joint retaining rivets. Using 1/2" (12.7 mm) drill bit, drill out rivet heads. Using a hammer and small punch, drive out rivets and remove upper ball joint from upper control arm.

CAUTION: When installing upper and lower ball joint stud nuts, NEVER loosen nut to install cotter pin. Stud nuts may be tightened up to 40 ft. lbs. (54 N.m) in excess of specified torque specification.

Installation – To install, reverse removal procedure. Use NEW nuts and bolts to install ball joint into upper control arm. Install grease fitting and lubricate NEW ball joint. Tighten bolts and nuts to specification. See TORQUE SPECIFICATIONS table at end of article. Lower vehicle and check wheel alignment. See SPECIFICATIONS & PROCEDURES article in WHEEL ALIGNMENT.

LOWER BALL JOINT

Removal – **1)** Raise and support vehicle with jack stand under lower control arm between ball joint and spring seat. Jack stand must remain under lower control arm during lower ball joint servicing to maintain lower control arm and coil spring positioning.

2) Remove wheel and tire assembly. Remove brake caliper and hang aside with wire. DO NOT allow brake caliper to hang by brake line. Remove grease fitting, rubber grease seal and cotter pin from lower ball joint stud. Loosen ball joint stud nut 2 turns. DO NOT remove nut at this time.

3) Install Ball Joint Separator (J-23742) between upper and lower ball studs. *See Fig. 4.* Extend bolt on ball joint separator to loosen ball joint stud from steering knuckle. Remove ball joint separator. Separate ball joint from steering knuckle.

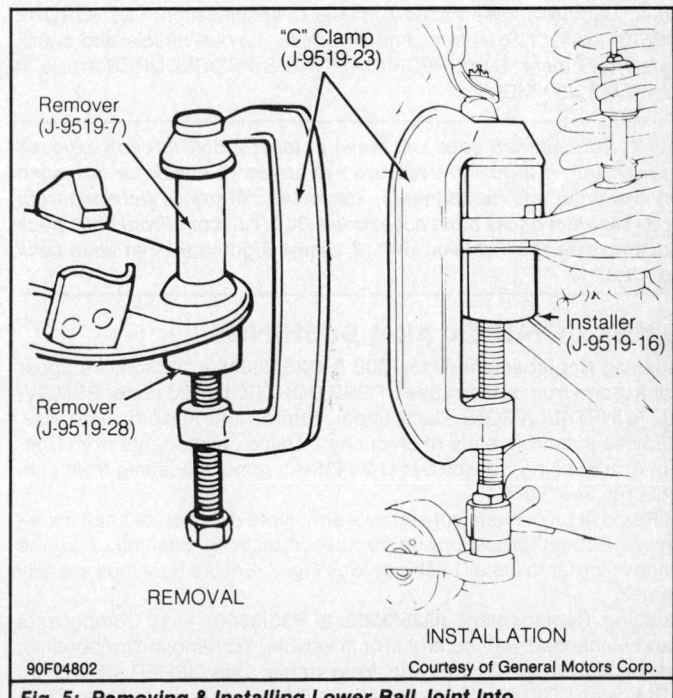

90F04802   Courtesy of General Motors Corp.

Fig. 5: Removing & Installing Lower Ball Joint Into Lower Control Arm

4) Place a wooden block between upper control arm and frame to keep steering knuckle assembly out of the way. Assemble on control arm, "C" Clamp (J-9519-23) and Removers (J-9519-7 and J-9519-28) from Ball Joint Remover/Installer Set (J-9519-D). *See Fig. 5.* Remove ball joint from lower control arm.

CAUTION: When installing upper and lower ball joint stud nuts, NEVER loosen nut to install cotter pin. Stud nuts may be tightened up to 40 ft. lbs. (54 N.m) in excess of specified torque specification.

Installation – **1)** Assemble on control arm, "C" Clamp (J-9519-23) and Installer (J-9519-16) from ball joint remover/installer set. *See Fig. 5.* Reverse removal procedure to install ball joint into lower control arm. Ensure bleed vent in rubber grease seal is facing forward. Install grease fitting and lubricate NEW ball joint.

2) To complete installation, reverse removal procedure. Tighten bolts and nuts to specification. See TORQUE SPECIFICATIONS table at end of article. Lower vehicle and check wheel alignment. See SPECIFICATIONS & PROCEDURES article in WHEEL ALIGNMENT.

UPPER CONTROL ARM

Removal – **1)** Raise and support vehicle with jack stand under lower control arm between ball joint and spring seat. Jack stand must remain under lower control arm during upper control arm servicing to maintain lower control arm and coil spring positioning.

2) Remove wheel and tire assembly. Remove brake line bracket from upper control arm. Remove grease fitting and cotter pin from upper ball joint stud. Loosen ball joint stud nut. Using Ball Joint Separator (J-23742), position large cupped end of separator over upper ball stud nut, and position pilot-threaded end of tool onto lower ball stud. *See Fig. 4.*

3) Extend bolt on ball joint separator to loosen ball joint stud from steering knuckle. Remove ball joint separator and stud nut. Separate upper ball joint from steering knuckle.

4) Remove upper control arm pivot shaft-to-frame nuts. Remove upper control arm alignment shims and spacers. Tape alignment shims together and tag location for reassembly. Remove frame bracket bolts and washers. Remove upper control arm from frame bracket.

Installation – To install, reverse removal procedure. Ensure alignment shims are installed in original position, with concave and convex sides together. Tighten bolts and nuts to specification. See TORQUE SPECIFICATIONS table at end of article. Lower vehicle and check wheel alignment. See SPECIFICATIONS & PROCEDURES article in WHEEL ALIGNMENT.

NOTE: Normal shim pack will leave at least 2 bolt threads exposed beyond nut. If 2 bolt threads are not exposed, check for damaged control arms and components. Thickness difference between front and rear shim packs must not exceed .30" (7.6 mm). Front shim pack thickness must be at least .24" (6.1 mm). Tighten thinner shim pack nut first.

UPPER CONTROL ARM BUSHINGS

Bushing Replacement (G15/1500 & G25/2500) – **1)** Remove upper control arm from vehicle. See UPPER CONTROL ARM under REMOVAL & INSTALLATION. Place upper control arm in soft-jawed vise. Remove nuts from ends of pivot shaft. Using components from Control Arm Bushing Service Set (J-24435-A), remove bushing from control arm. *See Fig. 6.*

2) Remove pivot shaft from control arm. Note direction of shaft installation. Repeat procedure to remove remaining bushing. Reverse removal order to install bushings. *See Fig. 7.* Ensure bushings are fully seated.

Bushing Replacement (G35/3500 & P35/3500) – **1)** Components can be changed with control arm in vehicle. To remove components, disconnect upper control arm from frame. See UPPER CONTROL ARM under REMOVAL & INSTALLATION. Unscrew bushings and slide pivot shaft out of upper control arm. Remove grease fitting. Remove inner seals from between bushings and pivot shaft.

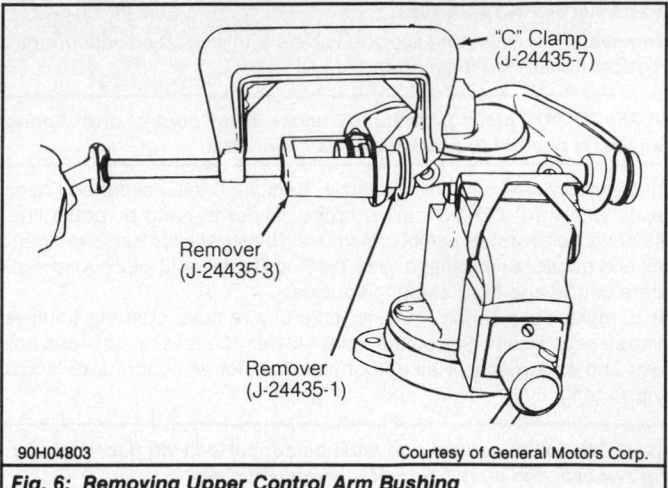

90H04803 Courtesy of General Motors Corp.

Fig. 6: Removing Upper Control Arm Bushing (G15/1500 & G25/2500)

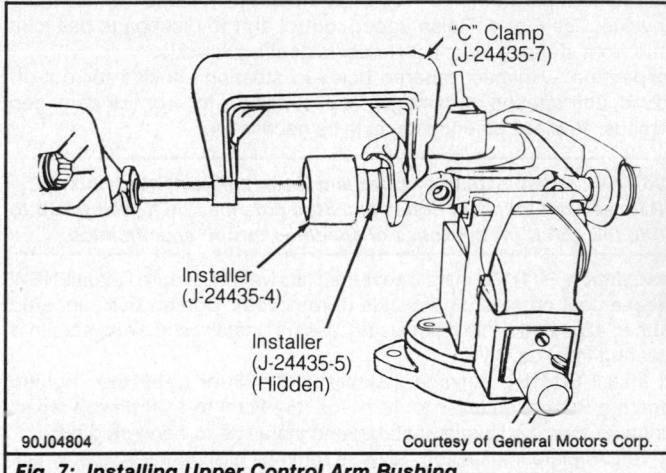

90J04804 Courtesy of General Motors Corp.

Fig. 7: Installing Upper Control Arm Bushing (G15/1500 & G25/2500)

2) To install, slide NEW seal onto each end of upper control arm pivot shaft. Install pivot shaft into upper control arm. Install NEW bushings. Adjust pivot shaft until centered in control arm, then tighten bushing nuts to specification. *See Fig. 8.* See TORQUE SPECIFICATIONS table at end of article. Check shaft for free rotation. Install grease fittings and lubricate bushings.

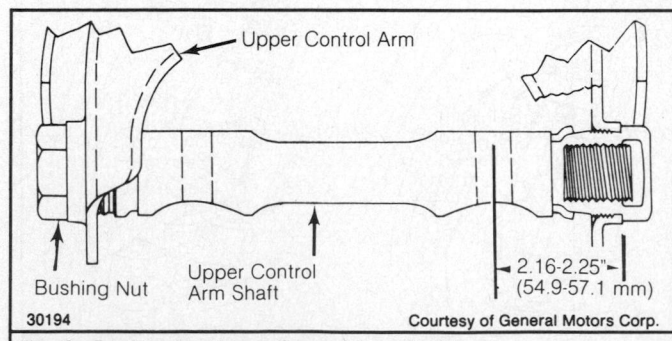

30194 Courtesy of General Motors Corp.

Fig. 8: Positioning Upper Control Arm Shaft (G35/3500 & P35/3500)

LOWER CONTROL ARM

WARNING: Securely bolt Spring Remover (J-23028-01) to floor jack, and install safety chain through lower control arm and coil spring to prevent personal injury.

Removal – 1) Raise and support vehicle with jack stand under lower control arm between ball joint and spring seat. Jack stand must remain under lower control arm during upper control arm servicing to maintain lower control arm and coil spring positioning.

2) Remove wheel and tire assembly. Remove brake caliper. Remove coil spring. See COIL SPRINGS under REMOVAL & INSTALLATION. Support inboard end of control arm. Remove cotter pin from lower ball joint stud. Loosen ball joint stud nut one turn.

3) Using Ball Joint Separator (J-23742), position large cupped end of separator over upper ball stud nut, and position pilot-threaded end of tool onto lower ball stud. See Fig. 4.

4) Extend bolt of ball joint separator to separate ball stud from steering knuckle. Remove ball joint separator and stud nut. Separate lower ball joint from steering knuckle. Remove lower control arm.

Installation – To install, reverse removal procedure. Ensure front indexing hole in lower control arm shaft aligns with crossmember attaching studs. Tighten bolts and nuts to specification. See TORQUE SPECIFICATIONS table at end of article. Lower vehicle and check wheel alignment. See SPECIFICATIONS & PROCEDURES article in WHEEL ALIGNMENT.

LOWER CONTROL ARM BUSHINGS

Bushing Replacement (G15/1500 & G25/2500) – 1) Remove lower control arm. See LOWER CONTROL ARM under REMOVAL & INSTALLATION. Remove nuts and washers from control arm shaft.

2) Install control arm in press for rear bushing removal. Press on front of lower control arm shaft and remove rear bushing. Remove lower control arm shaft.

3) Using Bushing Remover (J-24435-3), Spacer (J-24435-2 and J-24435-6) and "C" Clamp (J-24435-7), remove front bushing.

4) Use Installer (J-24435-4), Spacer (J-24435-6) and "C" Clamp (J-24435-7) to install NEW front bushing. See Fig. 9. Stake front bushing in at least 2 areas.

5) Align outer tube hole so it faces front or toward staked bushing. Install lower control arm shaft and repeat procedure to install remaining bushing. Install washers and nuts on lower control arm shaft. Install lower control arm.

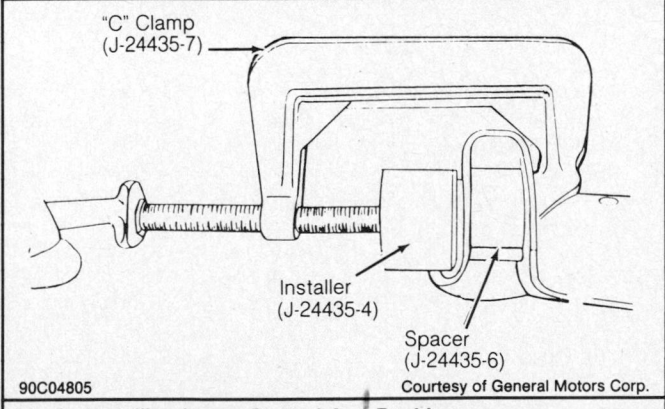

Fig. 9: Installing Lower Control Arm Bushing
(G15/1500 & G25/2500)

Bushing Replacement (G35/3500 & P35/3500) – 1) Raise and support vehicle under frame, with control arms hanging free. Remove wheel and tire assembly. Disconnect shock absorber and stabilizer bar at lower control arm.

2) Place jack under lower control arm. Jack must be positioned inward of coil spring and in depression areas of control arm. Install safety chain over upper control arm on inside of stabilizer bar and outside of shock absorber.

3) Remove lower control arm "U" bolt nuts and washers. Slowly lower the control arm from frame releasing coil spring tension. Remove grease fittings. Remove bushing nuts and remove lower control arm shaft from control arm. Remove seals located between bushing and lower control arm shaft.

4) To install, slide NEW seals onto lower control arm shaft. Install shaft into lower control arm. Adjust shaft until centered in control arm, then tighten bushing nuts to specification. See Fig. 10. See TORQUE SPECIFICATIONS table at end of article. Check shaft for free rotation. Install grease fittings and lubricate bushings.

5) Install lower control arm. Ensure front indexing hole in lower control arm shaft aligns with crossmember attaching stud. To complete installation, reverse removal procedure. Tighten bolts and nuts to specification. See TORQUE SPECIFICATIONS table at end of article. Lower vehicle and check wheel alignment. See SPECIFICATIONS & PROCEDURES article in WHEEL ALIGNMENT.

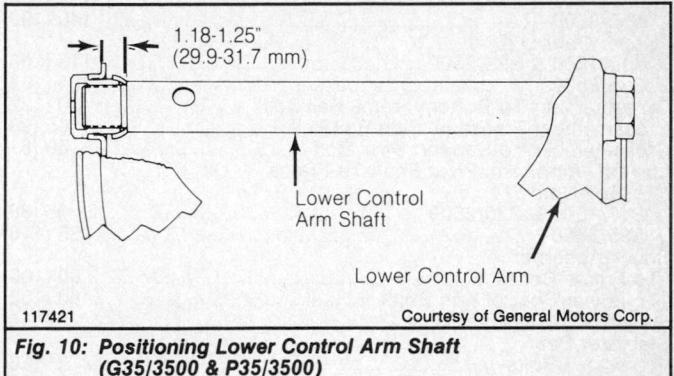

Fig. 10: Positioning Lower Control Arm Shaft
(G35/3500 & P35/3500)

CROSSMEMBER & SUSPENSION UNIT

NOTE: Front suspension components may be serviced separately as previously outlined or, if extensive repairs are necessary, crossmember and suspension unit can be removed as an assembly.

Removal – 1) Disconnect battery negative cable. Raise and support vehicle. Remove wheel and tire assembly. Remove brake line bracket from upper control arm.

2) Support vehicle with jack stands at frame side rails, and lower hoist. Clean area around brake line fitting. Remove brake line from brake caliper and plug openings.

3) Disconnect tie rod end from steering knuckle. Remove stabilizer bar and shock absorber from lower control arm. Remove brake line bracket bolt from front suspension crossmember.

CAUTION: Brake line clips must be disconnected from front suspension unit, or severe damage to brake line will result when unit is lowered from vehicle.

4) Remove engine mount support bracket-to-front suspension crossmember bolts. Remove crossmember-to-lower frame rail bolts. Raise hoist and support suspension crossmember. Support engine.

NOTE: Support engine BEFORE lowering front suspension unit.

5) Remove upper control arm bracket-to-frame side rail bolts. Suspension unit is now disconnected. Lower hoist and remove front suspension unit from vehicle.

Installation – To install, reverse removal procedure. Lubricate suspension components. Bleed brake system. Tighten bolts and nuts to specification. See TORQUE SPECIFICATIONS table at end of article. Lower vehicle and check wheel alignment. See SPECIFICATIONS & PROCEDURES article in WHEEL ALIGNMENT.

TORQUE SPECIFICATION

TORQUE SPECIFICATIONS

Application	Ft. Lbs. (N.m)
Van	
Ball Joint-To-Steering Knuckle Nut	
Lower	90 (122)
Upper	
G15/1500 & G25/2500	50 (68)
G35/3500	90 (122)
Control Arm Pivot Shaft Nuts	
Lower Control Arm	
G15/1500 & G25/2500	115 (156)
G35/3500	1 140 (190)
Upper Control Arm	
G15/1500 & G25/2500	115 (156)
G35/3500	1 125 (169)
Crossmember-To-Bottom Frame Rail Bolt	90 (122)
Crossmember-To-Frame Side Rail Bolt	65 (88)
Crossmember-To-Support Strut Bolt	60 (81)
Lower Control Arm Pivot Shaft-To-Frame	
"U" Bolt Nuts	
G15/1500 & G25/2500	65 (88)
G35/3500	85 (115)
Shock Absorber	
To-Frame Bolts	80 (108)
To-Lower Control Arm Bolts	80 (108)
Splash Shield Bolts	10 (14)
Stabilizer Bar	
To-Frame Bolts	21 (28)
To-Lower Control Arm Nuts	24 (33)
Suspension Bumper	15 (20)
Tie Rod End-To-Steering Knuckle Nut	46 (62)
Upper Ball Joint-To-Control Arm Nuts	18 (24)
Upper Control Arm Pivot Shaft-To-Frame Nuts	
G15/1500 & G25/2500	70 (95)
G35/3500	105 (142)

TORQUE SPECIFICATIONS (Cont.)

Application	Ft. Lbs. (N.m)
Commercial Van	
Ball Joint-To-Steering Knuckle Nut	
Lower	90 (122)
Upper	90 (122)
Control Arm Pivot Shaft Nuts	
Lower Control Arm	1 280 (380)
Upper Control Arm	1 190 (257)
Crossmember-To-Bottom Frame Rail Bolt	
Motorhome	215 (291)
"P" Series With Disc Brakes	130 (176)
All Others	90 (122)
Crossmember-To-Frame Side Rail Bolt	
"P" Series With Disc Brakes & Motorhome	100 (136)
All Others	65 (88)
Crossmember-To-Support Strut Bolt	60 (81)
Lower Control Arm Pivot Shaft-To-Frame	
"U" Bolt Nuts	85 (115)
Shock Absorber	
To-Frame Bolts	140 (190)
To-Lower Control Arm Bolts	59 (80)
Splash Shield Bolts	10 (14)
Stabilizer Bar	
To-Frame Bolts	24 (33)
To-Lower Control Arm Nuts	24 (33)
Suspension Bumper	19 (26)
Tie Rod End-To-Steering Knuckle Nut	46 (62)
Upper Ball Joint-To-Control Arm Nuts	18 (24)
Upper Control Arm Pivot Shaft-To-Frame Nuts	105 (142)

1 – This is control arm pivot shaft bushing nut.

**Astro, Bravada, Jimmy, Safari,
Sierra, Sonoma, Suburban,
Syclone, Typhoon, Yukon,
"K" Series Blazer & Pickup,
"T" Series Blazer & Pickup**

DESCRIPTION

Independent front suspension consists of upper and lower control arms with steering knuckle mounted between ball joints. *See Fig. 1.* Shock absorbers fit between lower control arm and frame. A stabilizer bar is mounted to frame side rails and connected to lower control arms.

Torsion bars are used in place of coil springs. Front of torsion bar attaches to lower control arm. Rear of torsion bar attaches to adjustable arm at torsion bar support crossmember. Adjustments to trim height are made here.

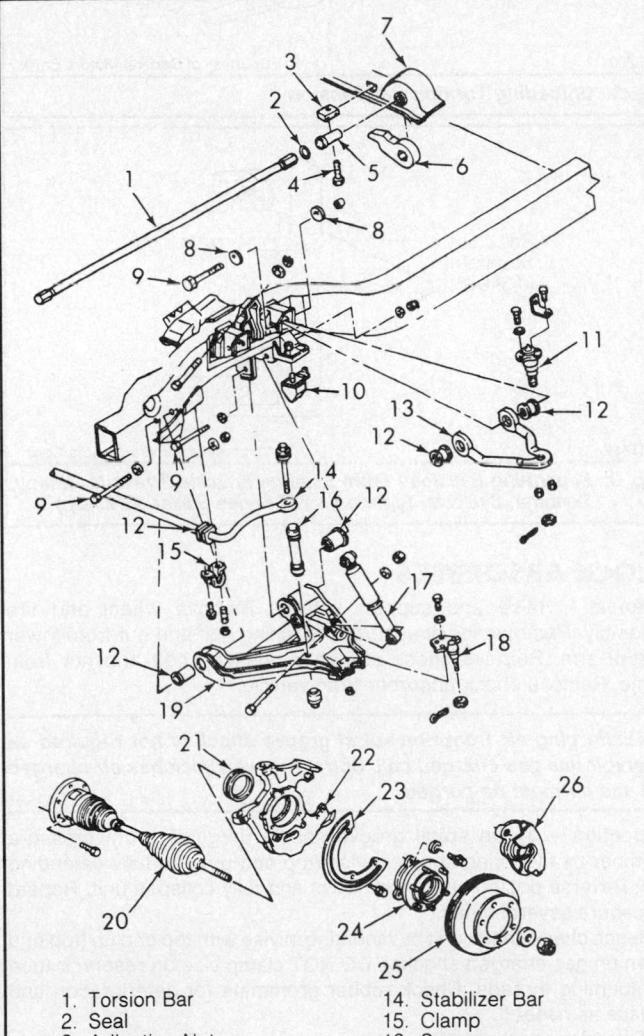

1. Torsion Bar	14. Stabilizer Bar
2. Seal	15. Clamp
3. Adjusting Nut	16. Spacer
4. Adjusting Bolt	17. Shock Absorber
5. Anchor Adapter	18. Lower Ball Joint
6. Adjusting Arm	19. Lower Control Arm
7. Support	20. Drive Axle
8. Alignment Adjustment Cam	21. Grease Seal
9. Pivot Bolt	22. Steering Knuckle
10. Bumper	23. Splash Shield
11. Upper Ball Joint	24. Hub & Bearing Assembly
12. Bushing	25. Rotor
13. Upper Control Arm	26. Brake Caliper

92H21896   Courtesy of General Motors Corp.

*Fig. 1: Exploded View Of Front Suspension
(Astro & Safari – Other Models Similar)*

ADJUSTMENTS & INSPECTION

WHEEL ALIGNMENT SPECIFICATIONS & PROCEDURES

NOTE: See SPECIFICATIONS & PROCEDURES article in WHEEL ALIGNMENT.

FRONT WHEEL BEARINGS

Front wheel bearings are sealed, pre-adjusted and require no maintenance unless wheel hub and bearing assembly is removed. See WHEEL HUB & BEARINGS under REMOVAL & INSTALLATION.

RIDING HEIGHT

NOTE: See SPECIFICATIONS & PROCEDURES article in WHEEL ALIGNMENT.

BALL JOINT CHECKING

NOTE: Replace ball joint rubber grease seal if cut or damaged.

Upper Ball Joint (Astro, Bravada, Jimmy, Safari, Sonoma, Syclone, Typhoon & "T" Series Blazer & Pickup) – 1) Raise and support vehicle with jack stand under lower control arm, near lower ball joint. Ensure upper control arm bumper does not contact frame. Place dial indicator against lower part of wheel rim. Push in on bottom of tire while pulling outward at top. Read dial indicator, then reverse push/pull procedure.

2) Lateral (horizontal) deflection should not exceed .125" (3.18 mm). If deflection is excessive, replace ball joint.

3) Check ball joint, only with ball joint disconnected from steering knuckle, to see if ball joint can be rotated by finger pressure. Replace if ball joint can be twisted.

Lower Ball Joint (Astro, Bravada, & Safari) – 1) Wear indicator is built into ball joint. Wear is indicated by position of the 1/2" diameter round boss that grease fitting is threaded into. A NEW ball joint has a boss projection of .050" (1.27 mm) beyond cover surface.

2) With vehicle weight on wheels, ensure wear indicator protrudes beyond surface of ball joint cover. Replace ball joint if wear indicator is recessed or even with housing.

Lower Ball Joint (Jimmy, Sonoma, Syclone, Typhoon & "T" Series Blazer & Pickup) – 1) Raise and support vehicle with jack stand under lower control arm, near lower ball joint. Place a dial indicator on spindle hub.

2) Pry tire and wheel assembly between lower control arm and outer race to measure vertical movement. Note dial indicator reading. If reading exceeds .125" (3.18 mm), replace loose ball joint.

Upper & Lower Ball Joints ("K" Series Blazer & Pickup, Sierra, Suburban & Yukon) – 1) Raise and support vehicle with jack stand under lower control arm, near lower ball joint. Place a dial indicator on spindle hub.

2) Pry tire and wheel assembly between lower control arm and outer race to measure vertical movement. Note dial indicator reading. If reading exceeds .08" (2.0 mm), replace loose ball joint.

REMOVAL & INSTALLATION

WARNING: When battery is disconnected, vehicle computer and memory systems may lose memory data. Driveability problems may exist until computer systems have completed a relearn cycle. See COMPUTER RELEARN PROCEDURES article in GENERAL INFORMATION before disconnecting battery.

WHEEL HUB & BEARINGS

NOTE: Darkened areas on bearing assembly are caused by heat treatment process and do not indicate a need for replacement.

Removal – 1) Raise and support vehicle. Remove wheel and tire assembly. Install Axle Shaft Boot Seal Protector (J-28712) to drive axle shaft boot to protect drive axle during repair. Depress brake caliper piston, detach brake caliper and wire aside. Remove brake rotor. *See Fig. 1.* Remove drive axle shaft nut cotter pin, retainer, drive axle shaft nut and washer. Slide hub and bearing assembly off drive axle shaft.

2) Inspect steering knuckle grease seal for cuts, distortion and wear. Inspect steering knuckle, hub and bearing for damage. Replace as necessary. If wheel hub stud must be replaced, use Wheel Stud Remover (J-6627-A).

Installation – 1) To install NEW wheel hub stud, lubricate hub bore and install stud. Place 4 washers on stud and install stud nut with flat side to washers. Tighten stud nut to draw stud into hub bore. Remove nut and washers. Install hub and bearing assembly onto drive axle shaft.

2) To complete installation, reverse removal procedure. Tighten bolts and nuts to specification. Depress brake pedal several times to extend caliper piston after installation.

STEERING KNUCKLE

Removal – 1) Raise and support vehicle. Unload torsion bar tension. *See Fig. 2.* Count exact number of tool turns for reassembly reference. Slide, but DO NOT remove, torsion bar forward.

2) Remove wheel and tire assembly. Install Axle Shaft Boot Seal Protector (J-28712) to drive axle shaft boot to protect drive axle during repair. Depress brake caliper piston, detach brake caliper and wire aside. Remove brake rotor.

3) Remove drive axle shaft nut cotter pin, retainer, drive axle shaft nut and washer. Slide hub and bearing assembly off drive axle shaft. Remove splash shield. Remove cotter pin and tie rod end stud nut. Using Universal Steering Linkage Puller (J-24319-01), separate tie rod end from steering knuckle.

4) On Astro, "K" Series Blazer & Pickup, Safari, Sierra, Suburban and Yukon, remove bolts connecting drive axle shaft to differential drive flange. Press drive axle shaft splines out of hub. Remove drive axle from vehicle. Remove upper and lower ball joint stud cotter pins. Separate upper and lower ball joint studs from steering knuckle using Ball Joint Separator (J-36607).

5) On Bravada, Jimmy, Sonoma, Syclone, Typhoon and "T" Series Blazer & Pickup, remove upper and lower ball joint stud cotter pins. Place Ball Joint Separator (J-34026) over upper ball joint stud. Loosen ball joint stud nut. *See Fig. 3.* Back off nut until nut contacts tool. Continue backing off nut until nut forces ball stud out of steering knuckle. Remove spacer. Repeat procedure to separate lower ball joint from steering knuckle.

6) On all models, remove steering knuckle from vehicle. Inspect steering knuckle grease seal for cuts, distortion and wear. Inspect steering knuckle, hub and bearing for damage. Replace as necessary.

Installation – 1) Using hammer and Steering Knuckle Seal Installer (J-28574), install NEW steering knuckle grease seal into steering knuckle. Install spacer (if equipped). Install steering knuckle onto upper and lower ball joint studs.

CAUTION: When installing upper and lower ball joint stud nuts, tighten nut to align cotter pin hole. DO NOT tighten ball joint stud nuts more than an additional 1/6 turn to align cotter pin hole. Complete tightening of ball joint stud nuts with vehicle at proper riding height specification.

---

2) Install ball joint stud nuts and cotter pins. Install drive axle (if removed). Install tie rod end onto steering knuckle. Install tie rod end stud nut and cotter pin. Install splash shield. Install hub and bearing assembly onto drive axle shaft and into steering knuckle.

3) To complete installation, reverse removal procedure. Tighten bolts and nuts to specification. See TORQUE SPECIFICATIONS table at end of article. Lower vehicle. Check wheel alignment and adjust ride height. See SPECIFICATIONS & PROCEDURES article in WHEEL ALIGNMENT.

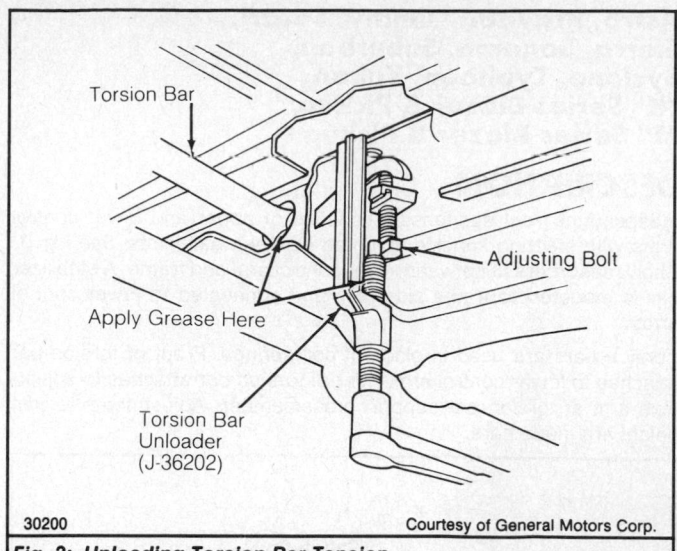

30200   Courtesy of General Motors Corp.

Fig. 2: Unloading Torsion Bar Tension

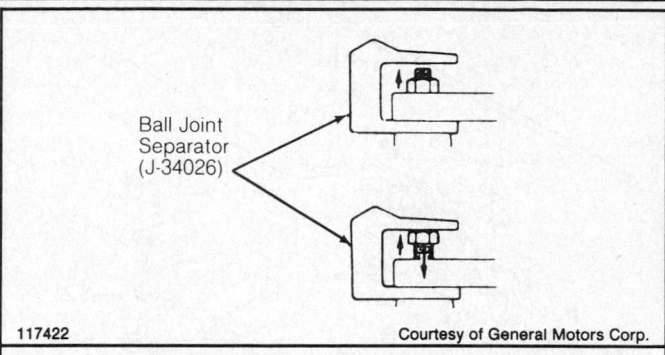

117422   Courtesy of General Motors Corp.

Fig. 3: Separating Ball Joint From Steering Knuckle (Bravada, Jimmy, Sonoma, Syclone, Typhoon & "T" Series Blazer & Pickup)

SHOCK ABSORBERS

Removal – Raise and support vehicle. Remove wheel and tire assembly. Remove shock absorber retaining bolt and nut from lower control arm. Remove shock absorber retaining bolt and nut from frame. Remove shock absorber from vehicle.

NOTE: Purging air from non-spiral groove shock is not required as reservoir has gas-charged cell. Spiral groove shock has air-charged cell and air must be purged.

Inspection – 1) On spiral groove shock, purge air from pressure chamber by mounting shock in vise (top end up) and fully extending unit. Reverse position (top end down) and fully collapse unit. Repeat procedure several times.

2) Bench check shock unit by mounting in vise with top end up (top end down on gas-charged shocks). DO NOT clamp vise on reservoir tube or mounting threads. Check rubber grommets for deterioration and replace as needed.

3) Operate shock by hand at various rates of speed and note resistance. Rebound force is normally stronger than compression force. If resistance is not smooth and constant, replace shock.

Installation – To install, reverse removal procedure. Tighten bolts and nuts to specification. See TORQUE SPECIFICATIONS table at end of article.

STABILIZER BAR

NOTE: Keep right and left side stabilizer bar components separate for installation in original locations.

Removal – 1) Raise and support vehicle. Remove wheel and tire assembly. Remove stabilizer bar-to-frame bolts, nuts and clamps. On Bravada, Jimmy, Sonoma, Syclone, Typhoon and "T" Series Blazer & Pickup, remove stabilizer bar-to-lower control arm bolts, nuts and clamps.

2) On Astro, "K" Series Blazer & Pickup, Safari, Sierra, Suburban and Yukon, remove stabilizer bar-to-lower control arm bolt, nut and spacer. Remove stabilizer bar from vehicle. Remove stabilizer bar bushings.

3) Inspect bushings for deformation and deterioration. Check stabilizer bar and clamps for excessive wear and damage. Replace as necessary.

Installation – 1) Unload torsion bar tension. *See Fig. 2.* Count exact number of tool turns for reassembly reference. Slide, but DO NOT remove, torsion bar forward.

2) To install, reverse removal procedure. Install NEW bushings on stabilizer bar. Ensure split in bushing faces toward front of vehicle. Tighten bolts and nuts to specification. See TORQUE SPECIFICATIONS table at end of article. Lower vehicle. Check wheel alignment and adjust ride height. See SPECIFICATIONS & PROCEDURES article in WHEEL ALIGNMENT.

UPPER BALL JOINT

Removal – 1) Raise and support vehicle under lower control arms. Remove wheel and tire assembly. Remove steering knuckle. See STEERING KNUCKLE under REMOVAL & INSTALLATION. Remove brake line and brackets from upper control arm (if equipped).

2) To remove upper ball joint from upper control arm, using drill and 1/8" (3.18 mm) drill bit, drill 1/4" (6.35 mm) deep hole in ball joint retaining rivets. Using 1/2" (12.7 mm) drill bit, drill out rivet heads. Using a hammer and small punch, drive out rivets and remove ball joint from upper control arm.

CAUTION: When installing upper ball joint stud nut, tighten nut to align cotter pin hole. DO NOT tighten ball joint stud nut more than an additional 1/6 turn to align cotter pin hole. Complete tightening of upper ball joint stud nut with vehicle at proper riding height specification.

Installation – To install, reverse removal procedure. Use NEW nuts and bolts to install ball joint to upper control arm. Lubricate NEW ball joint. Tighten bolts and nuts to specification. See TORQUE SPECIFICATIONS table at end of article. Lower vehicle. Check wheel alignment and adjust ride height. See SPECIFICATIONS & PROCEDURES article in WHEEL ALIGNMENT.

LOWER BALL JOINT

Removal – 1) Raise and support vehicle under lower control arms. Remove wheel and tire assembly. Remove steering knuckle. See STEERING KNUCKLE under REMOVAL & INSTALLATION. Remove brake line and brackets from lower control arm (if equipped).

2) On Bravada, Jimmy, Sonoma, Syclone, Typhoon and "T" Series Blazer & Pickup, to remove lower ball joint from lower control arm, using drill and 1/8" (3.18 mm) drill bit, drill 1/4" (6.35 mm) deep hole in ball joint retaining rivets. Using 1/2" (12.7 mm) drill bit, drill out rivet heads. Using a hammer and small punch, drive out rivets and remove ball joint from lower control arm.

3) On Astro, "K" Series Blazer & Pickup, Safari, Sierra, Suburban, and Yukon, to remove lower ball joint from lower control arm, using drill and 1/8" (3.18 mm) drill bit, drill 1/4" (6.35 mm) deep hole in ball joint retaining rivets. Using 1/2" (12.7 mm) drill bit, drill out rivet heads. Using 5/16" (8 mm) drill bit, drill hole 2/3 the length of rivet shank. Using 5/16" (8 mm) punch, drive out rivets and remove ball joint from lower control arm.

CAUTION: When installing lower ball joint stud nut, tighten nut to align cotter pin hole. DO NOT tighten ball joint stud nut more than an additional 1/6 turn to align cotter pin hole. Complete tightening of lower ball joint stud nut with vehicle at proper riding height specification.

Installation – To install, reverse removal procedure. Use NEW nuts and bolts to install ball joints to lower control arm. Lubricate NEW ball joint. Tighten bolts and nuts to specification. See TORQUE SPECIFICATIONS table at end of article. Lower vehicle. Check wheel alignment and adjust ride height. See SPECIFICATIONS & PROCEDURES article in WHEEL ALIGNMENT.

UPPER CONTROL ARM

Removal – 1) Raise and support vehicle under lower control arms. Remove wheel and tire assembly. On Astro, "K" Series Blazer & Pickup, Safari, Sierra, Suburban and Yukon, disconnect battery negative cable. Remove air cleaner extension (if necessary). Remove brake line and brackets from upper control arm.

2) On all models, remove upper ball joint stud cotter pin. On Bravada, Jimmy, Sonoma, Syclone, Typhoon and "T" Series Blazer & Pickup, place Ball Joint Separator (J-34026) over upper ball joint stud. Loosen ball joint stud nut. *See Fig. 3.* Back off nut until nut contacts tool. Continue backing off nut until nut forces ball stud out of steering knuckle. Remove spacer.

3) On Astro, "K" Series Blazer & Pickup, Safari, Sierra, Suburban and Yukon, remove upper ball joint stud nut and separate upper ball joint stud from steering knuckle using Ball Joint Separator (J-36607).

4) On all models, mark alignment adjustment cams for reassembly reference. Remove upper control arm pivot bolts, cams/washers and nuts. Remove upper control arm from vehicle. *See Figs. 4 and 5.* Replace bushings and/or bumper as necessary.

Installation – 1) If upper control arm bumper is deteriorated or damaged, install NEW bumper. Mount upper control arm on vehicle. On Bravada, Jimmy, Sonoma, Syclone, Typhoon and "T" Series Blazer & Pickup, install pivot bolts, alignment adjustment cams and NEW pivot bolt nuts. On Astro, "K" Series Blazer & Pickup, Safari, Sierra, Suburban and Yukon, install pivot bolts, washers and NEW pivot bolt nuts.

CAUTION: When installing upper ball joint stud nut, tighten nut to align cotter pin hole. DO NOT tighten ball joint stud nut more than an additional 1/6 turn to align cotter pin hole. Complete tightening of upper ball joint stud nut with vehicle at proper riding height specification.

---

2) On all models, ensure pivot bolts heads are facing inward. Connect steering knuckle to upper ball joint studs. To complete installation, reverse removal procedure. Tighten bolts and nuts to specification. See TORQUE SPECIFICATIONS table at end of article. Lower vehicle. Check wheel alignment and adjust ride height. See SPECIFICATIONS & PROCEDURES article in WHEEL ALIGNMENT. Complete tightening of upper control arm pivot bolts and nuts with vehicle at proper riding height specification.

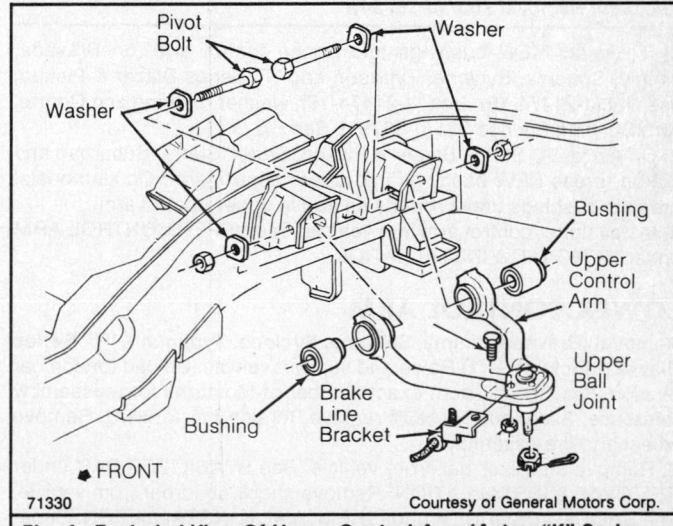

71330　　　　　　Courtesy of General Motors Corp.

Fig. 4: Exploded View Of Upper Control Arm (Astro, "K" Series Blazer & Pickup, Safari, Sierra, Suburban & Yukon)

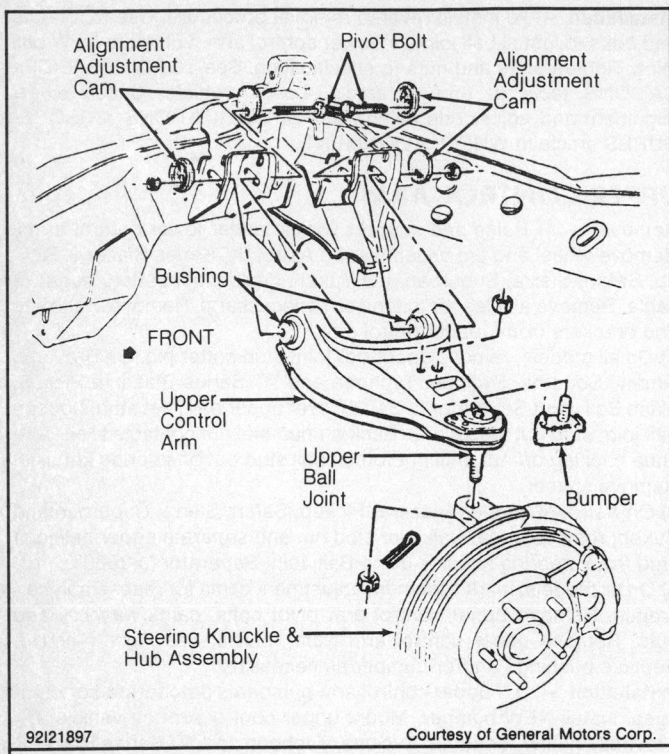

92I21897   Courtesy of General Motors Corp.

Fig. 5: Exploded View Of Upper Control Arm (Bravada, Jimmy, Sonoma, Syclone, Typhoon & "T" Series Blazer & Pickup)

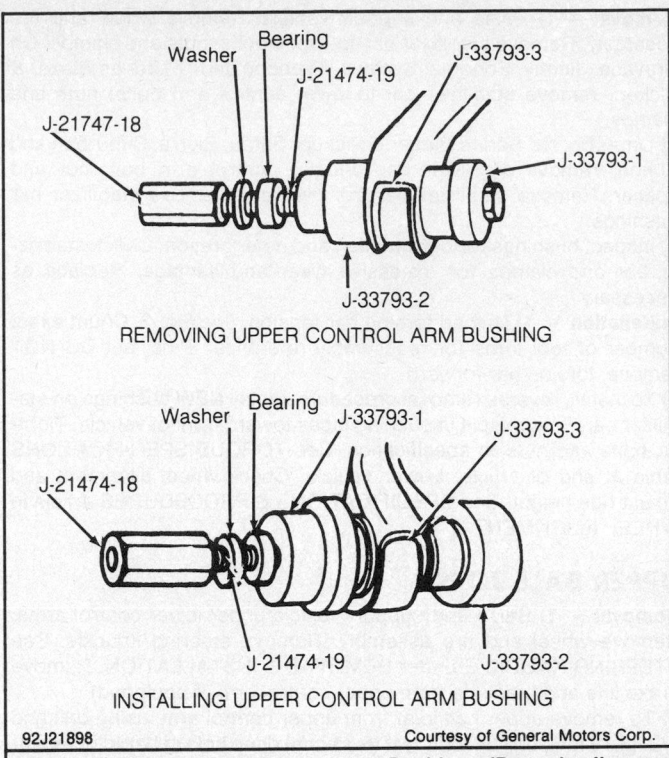

92J21898   Courtesy of General Motors Corp.

Fig. 6: Replacing Upper Control Arm Bushings (Bravada, Jimmy, Sonoma, Syclone, Typhoon & "T" Series Blazer & Pickup)

UPPER CONTROL ARM BUSHINGS

Bushing Replacement – 1) Remove upper control arm from vehicle. See UPPER CONTROL ARM under REMOVAL & INSTALLATION. Place upper control arm in soft-jawed vise.

2) On Astro, "K" Series Blazer & Pickup, Safari, Sierra, Suburban and Yukon, press bushings out of upper control arm. On Bravada, Jimmy, Sonoma, Syclone, Typhoon and "T" Series Blazer & Pickup, press bushings out of upper control arm using Nut (J-21474-18), Bolt (J-21474-19), washer, bearing and Control Arm Bushing Service Set (J-33793). See Fig. 6.

NOTE: On Astro, "K" Series Blazer & Pickup, Safari, Sierra, Suburban and Yukon, alignment angles are preset at factory. Knockouts MUST be removed before installation of alignment adjustment cams using Knockout Removal Tool (J-38794).

3) To install NEW bushings into upper control arm, on Bravada, Jimmy, Sonoma, Syclone, Typhoon and "T" Series Blazer & Pickup, use Nut (J-21474-18), Bolt (J-21474-19), washer, bearing and Control Arm Bushing Service Set (J-33793). See Fig. 6.
4) On Astro, "K" Series Blazer & Pickup, Safari, Sierra, Suburban and Yukon, press NEW bushings into upper control arm. On all models, press in bushings until properly seated in upper control arm.
5) Install upper control arm into vehicle. See UPPER CONTROL ARM under REMOVAL & INSTALLATION.

LOWER CONTROL ARM

Removal (Bravada, Jimmy, Sonoma, Syclone, Typhoon & "T" Series Blazer & Pickup) – 1) Raise and support vehicle. Unload torsion bar tension. See Fig. 2. Count exact number of tool turns for reassembly reference. Slide, but DO NOT remove, torsion bar forward. Remove wheel and tire assembly.
2) Remove stabilizer bar from vehicle. See STABILIZER BAR under REMOVAL & INSTALLATION. Remove shock absorber from vehicle. See SHOCK ABSORBER under REMOVAL & INSTALLATION. Separate lower ball joint from steering knuckle. See LOWER BALL JOINT under REMOVAL & INSTALLATION.

3) Remove lower control arm pivot bolts, nuts and washers. Remove lower control arm from vehicle. See Fig. 1. Replace bushings and/or bumper as necessary.
Removal (Astro & Safari) – 1) Raise and support vehicle. Unload torsion bar tension. See Fig. 2. Count exact number of tool turns for reassembly reference. Slide, but DO NOT remove, torsion bar forward. Remove adjusting arm.
2) Remove wheel and tire assembly. Remove front splash shield bolts enabling splash shield to be rotated for access to tie rod end and stabilizer bar. Remove stabilizer bar from vehicle. See STABILIZER BAR under REMOVAL & INSTALLATION. Remove shock absorber from vehicle. See SHOCK ABSORBER under REMOVAL & INSTALLATION.
3) Using Universal Steering Linkage Puller (J-24319-01), separate inner tie rod end from relay rod. Remove drive axle shaft nut cotter pin, retainer, drive axle shaft nut and washer. Remove bolts connecting drive axle shaft to differential drive flange. Press drive axle shaft splines out of hub. Remove drive axle from vehicle.
4) Remove cotter pin and lower ball joint stud nut. Separate lower ball joint stud from steering knuckle using Ball Joint Separator (J-36607). Remove lower control arm pivot bolts, nuts and washers. Remove lower control arm and torsion bar from vehicle as an assembly. See Fig. 1. Remove torsion bar from lower control arm. Replace bushings and/or bumper as necessary.
Removal ("K" Series Blazer & Pickup, Sierra, Suburban & Yukon) – 1) Raise and support vehicle. Unload torsion bar tension. See Fig. 2. Count exact number of tool turns for reassembly reference. Slide, but DO NOT remove, torsion bar forward. Remove adjusting arm.
2) Remove wheel and tire assembly. Install Axle Shaft Boot Seal Protector (J-28712) to drive axle shaft boot to protect drive axle during repair. Depress brake caliper piston, detach brake caliper and wire aside. Remove brake rotor.
3) Remove drive axle shaft nut cotter pin, retainer, drive axle shaft nut and washer. Remove shock absorber-to-lower control arm bolt, nut and washers. Compress shock absorber. Using Universal Steering Linkage Puller (J-24319-01), separate inner tie rod end from relay rod. Remove stabilizer bar from vehicle. See STABILIZER BAR under REMOVAL & INSTALLATION.

4) Remove bolts connecting drive axle shaft to differential drive flange. Press drive axle shaft splines out of hub. Remove drive axle from vehicle. Remove cotter pin and upper ball joint stud nut. Separate upper ball joint stud from steering knuckle using Ball Joint Separator (J-36607).

5) Remove lower control arm pivot bolts, nuts and washers. Remove lower control arm and steering knuckle from vehicle as an assembly. *See Fig. 1.* Replace bushings and/or bumper as necessary.

Installation – 1) To install, reverse removal procedure. Install front leg of lower control arm onto vehicle, then rear leg. Install lower control arm pivot bolts, washers and NEW nuts, with bolts heads facing forward on Astro, "K" Series Blazer & Pickup, Safari, Sierra, Suburban and Yukon. Pivot bolt heads should be installed facing rear on Bravada, Jimmy, Sonoma, Syclone, Typhoon and "T" Series Blazer & Pickup.

CAUTION: When installing upper ball joint stud nut, tighten nut to align cotter pin hole. DO NOT tighten ball joint stud nut more than an additional 1/6 turn to align cotter pin hole. Complete tightening of upper ball joint stud nut with vehicle at proper riding height specification.

---

2) Tighten bolts and nuts to specification. See TORQUE SPECIFICATIONS table at end of article. Lower vehicle. Check wheel alignment and adjust ride height. See SPECIFICATIONS & PROCEDURES article in WHEEL ALIGNMENT. Complete tightening of lower control arm pivot bolts and nuts with vehicle at proper riding height specification.

LOWER CONTROL ARM BUSHINGS

Bushing Replacement – 1) Remove lower control arm from vehicle. See LOWER CONTROL ARM under REMOVAL & INSTALLATION. Place lower control arm in soft-jawed vise.

NOTE: On "K" Series Blazer, K15 and K25 Pickup and Sierra, Suburban and Yukon, lower control arm bushings are NOT replaceable. Complete replacement of lower control arm and bushings as an assembly is required.

---

2) On Astro, K35 Series Pickup, Safari and Sierra K3500, using a punch, unbend crimps on front bushing. Press front and rear bushings out of lower control arm using Ball Joint "C" Clamp (J-9519-23) and Control Arm Bushing Service Set (J-36618).

3) On Bravada, Jimmy, Sonoma, Syclone, Typhoon and "T" Series Blazer & Pickup, press front and rear bushings out of lower control arm using a washer, bearing and Control Arm Bushing Service Set (J-21474). *See Fig. 7.*

4) To install, reverse removal procedure. *See Fig. 7.* On Astro, K35 Series Pickup, Safari and Sierra K3500, crimp front bushing after installation. On all models, press in bushings until properly seated in lower control arm.

5) Install lower control arm into vehicle. See LOWER CONTROL ARM under REMOVAL & INSTALLATION.

TORSION BARS & SUPPORT

Removal – 1) Raise and support vehicle. Remove wheel and tire assembly. Unload torsion bar tension. *See Fig. 2.* Mark adjusting bolt setting. Using Torsion Bar Unloading Tool (J-36202), increase tension on adjusting arm. Remove torsion bar adjusting bolt, counting number of turns for reassembly reference. Remove torsion bar adjusting nut. Slowly relieve torsion bar tension.

2) Remove unloading tool. Slide torsion bar forward. Remove torsion bar adjusting arm. Remove support mounting bolts, nuts and washers. Remove support retainer, spacer and rubber insulator. *See Fig. 8.*

3) On Astro, "K" Series Blazer & Pickup, Safari, Sierra, Suburban and Yukon, slide torsion bar support rearward. Slide torsion bar rearward and pull down to remove from lower control arm. Mark right and left torsion bars for reassembly reference. Torsion bars must be reinstalled in same location and direction as removed.

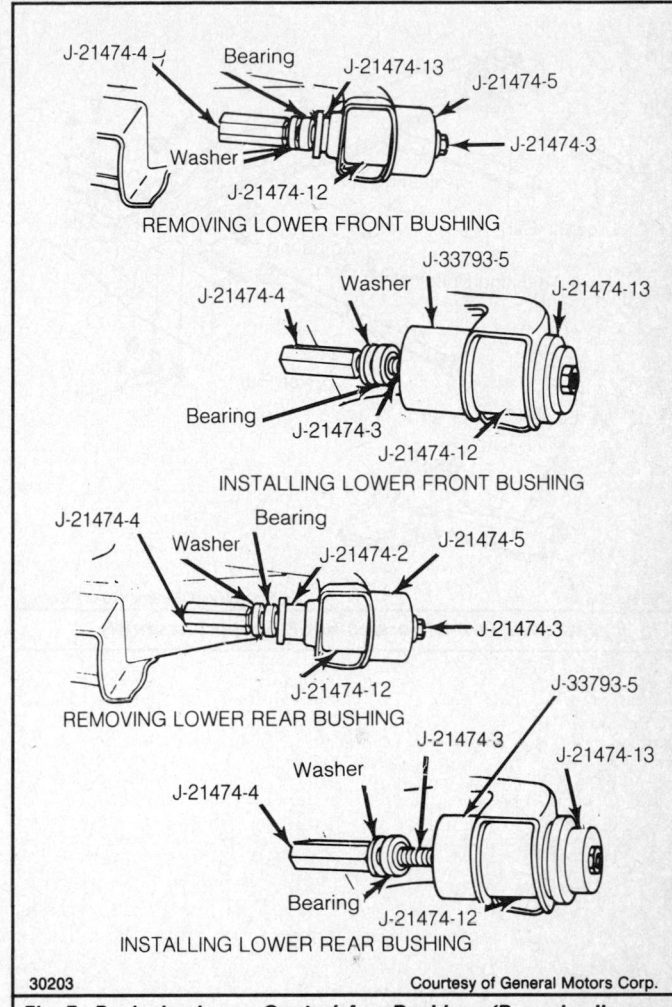

REMOVING LOWER FRONT BUSHING

INSTALLING LOWER FRONT BUSHING

REMOVING LOWER REAR BUSHING

INSTALLING LOWER REAR BUSHING

30203   Courtesy of General Motors Corp.

Fig. 7: Replacing Lower Control Arm Bushings (Bravada, Jimmy, Sonoma, Syclone, Typhoon & "T" Series Blazer & Pickup)

4) On Bravada, Jimmy, Sonoma, Syclone, Typhoon and "T" Series Blazer & Pickup, disconnect muffler flange from catalytic converter. Loosen rear exhaust hanger and lower rear exhaust. Remove torsion bar support. Slide torsion bar rearward and remove from lower control arm.

5) On all models, inspect torsion bars, adjusting arms, retainers, rubber insulators and support for bend, cracks, deterioration or damage. Check adjusting bolt and nut for damage or stripped threads. Replace as necessary.

Installation – 1) Install torsion bar rubber insulators, spacer and support retainer onto support. Install support assembly onto frame, slightly behind mounting holes.

2) On Bravada, Jimmy, Sonoma, Syclone, Typhoon and "T" Series Blazer & Pickup, install rear exhaust and rear exhaust hanger. Connect muffler flange to catalytic converter.

3) On all models, install adjusting arm and seal onto torsion bar. Slide torsion bar into lower control arm in original position. Slide torsion bar support forward, engaging rear of torsion bar in support. Install support mounting bolts, nuts and washers. Tighten bolts and nuts to specification. See TORQUE SPECIFICATIONS table at end of article.

4) Install adjusting bolt and nut on each torsion bar. Add tension to torsion bar with Torsion Bar Unloading Tool (J-36202). Ensure adjusting bolt is positioned to setting marked before removal. Release tension on unloading tool until tension is taken up by adjusting bolt. Remove unloading tool.

5) Lower vehicle. Check wheel alignment and adjust ride height. See SPECIFICATIONS & PROCEDURES article in WHEEL ALIGNMENT.

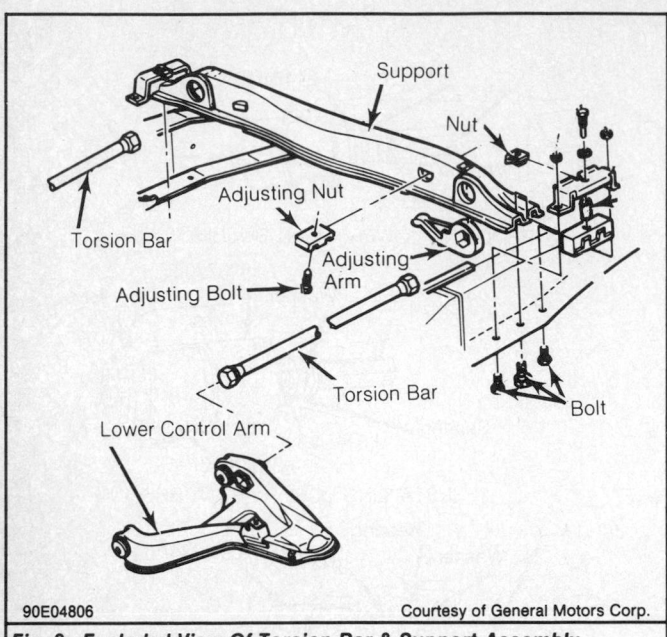

90E04806   Courtesy of General Motors Corp.

Fig. 8: Exploded View Of Torsion Bar & Support Assembly

TORQUE SPECIFICATIONS
TORQUE SPECIFICATIONS

Application	Ft. Lbs. (N.m)
Astro & Safari	
Ball Joint-To-Control Arm Nuts [5]	22 (30)
Ball Joint-To-Steering Knuckle Nut [1][5]	
Lower	92 (125)
Upper	94 (128)
Drive Axle Shaft Nut	173 (234)
Drive Axle Shaft-To-Differential Drive Flange Bolts	60 (80)
Hub & Bearing-To-Steering Knuckle Bolts	66 (90)
Lower Control Arm-To-Frame Pivot Bolt Nuts [2][3][5]	135 (185)
Shock Absorber Nuts [4]	66 (89)
Splash Shield Bolts	12 (16)
Stabilizer Bar Clamp-To-Frame Bolts	12 (16)
Stabilizer Bar Spacer Bolt	22 (33)
Tie Rod End-To-Steering Knuckle Nut	35 (47)
Torsion Bar Retainer-To-Support Nuts	
Center Nut	18 (24)
Edge Nuts	46 (62)
Upper Control Arm-To-Frame Pivot Bolt Nuts [2][5]	88 (120)
"K" Series Blazer & Pickup, Sierra, Suburban & Yukon	
Ball Joint-To-Control Arm Nuts [5]	
Lower	45 (60)
Upper	
K15 & K25 Series Pickup and Sierra, Suburban & Yukon	17 (23)
K35 Series Pickup & Sierra K35	52 (70)
Ball Joint-To-Steering Knuckle Nut [1][5]	
Lower	94 (128)
Upper	84 (115)
Drive Axle Shaft Nut	173 (234)
Drive Axle Shaft-To-Differential Drive Flange Bolts	60 (80)
Hub & Bearing-To-Steering Knuckle Bolts	133 (180)
Lower Control Arm-To-Frame Pivot Bolt Nuts [2][3][5]	135 (185)
Shock Absorber Nuts [4]	66 (89)
Splash Shield Bolts	19 (26)
Stabilizer Bar Clamp-To-Frame Bolts	13 (18)
Stabilizer Bar Spacer Nut	12 (16)
Tie Rod End-To-Steering Knuckle Nut	35 (47)
Torsion Bar Retainer-To-Support Nuts	
Center Nut	18 (24)
Edge Nuts	46 (62)
Upper Control Arm-To-Frame Pivot Bolt Nuts [2][5]	139 (188)
Bravada, Jimmy, Sonoma, Syclone, Typhoon & "T" Series Blazer & Pickup	
Ball Joint-To-Control Arm Nuts [5]	17 (23)
Ball Joint-To-Steering Knuckle Nut [1][5]	
Lower	83 (112)
Upper	61 (83)
Drive Axle Shaft Nut	181 (245)
Hub & Bearing/Shield-To-Steering Knuckle Bolts	86 (117)
Lower Control Arm-To-Frame Pivot Bolts [4][5]	148 (201)
Lower Control Arm-To-Frame Pivot Bolt Nuts [2][4][5]	92 (125)
Shock Absorber Nuts [3]	54 (73)
Stabilizer Bar Clamp-To-Frame Bolts	35 (47)
Stabilizer Bar-To-Lower Control Arm Bolts	24 (33)
Tie Rod End-To-Steering Knuckle Nut	35 (47)
Torsion Bar Retainer-To-Support Bolts	26 (35)
Torsion Bar Retainer-To-Support Nut	25 (34)
Upper Control Arm-To-Frame Pivot Bolt Nuts [5]	70 (95)

[1] – Tighten nut to align cotter pin hole. DO NOT tighten nut more than an additional 1/6 turn to align cotter pin hole.
[2] – Use NEW nuts during reassembly.
[3] – Install both bolts with nuts facing rear of vehicle.
[4] – Install upper/rear bolt with nut facing rear of vehicle. Install lower/front bolt with nut facing front of vehicle.
[5] – Complete tightening of bolts and/or nuts with vehicle at proper riding height specification.

Commercial Van, C35 Pickup

DESCRIPTION

Leaf spring assembly attaches to front axle with "U" bolts. A kingpin is used to attach the steering knuckle to the front axle. The kingpin is part of bearing cap and rides in a tapered roller bearing. *See Fig. 1.*

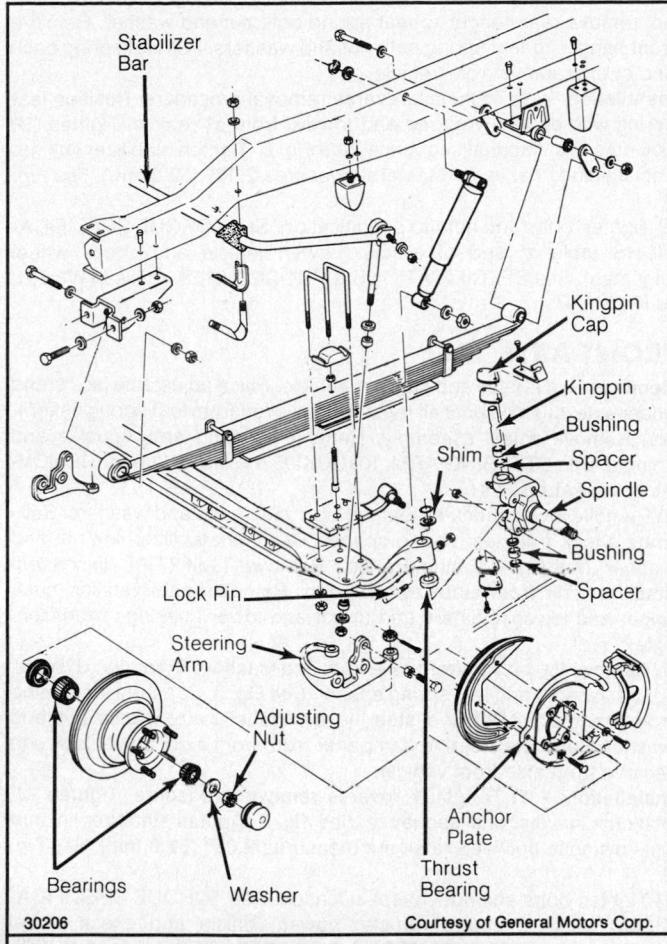

Fig. 1: Exploded View Of Front Suspension (Commercial Van – C35 Pickup Similar)

30206   Courtesy of General Motors Corp.

ADJUSTMENTS & INSPECTION

WHEEL ALIGNMENT
SPECIFICATIONS & PROCEDURES

On Commercial Van, caster and camber are designed into front axle assembly and are nonadjustable. Toe-in can be adjusted. See SPEC-IFICATIONS & PROCEDURES article in WHEEL ALIGNMENT.

FRONT WHEEL BEARINGS

Raise and support vehicle. Remove bearing cap and cotter pin. To seat bearing, tighten adjusting nut to **12 ft. lbs. (16 N.m)** while rotating wheel. Back off adjusting nut approximately one flat. Check rotor and hub end play. End play should be **.0005-.0080" (.013-.203 mm)**. Install cotter pin and bearing cap. If hole in spindle and slot in adjusting nut do not line up, back off adjusting nut one additional flat.

REMOVAL & INSTALLATION

WHEEL HUB/ROTOR & BEARINGS

Removal – Raise and support vehicle. Remove wheel assembly. Remove brake caliper and support aside. DO NOT allow caliper to hang by brake line. Remove bearing cap and cotter pin. *See Fig. 1.*

Remove adjusting nut, washer, outer bearing and wheel hub/rotor assembly. Remove grease seal and inner bearing (if necessary). Using a brass drift, remove bearing races (if necessary).

Inspection – Wash all bearings in solvent and check for cracked bearing cages and worn, chipped or pitted rollers. Wash hub I.D. and inspect bearing races for cracks, scoring or looseness in hub. Replace components as needed.

NOTE: Always replace bearings and races as matched sets. Install NEW grease seal whenever wheel hub is disassembled. Before assembly, ensure all parts are thoroughly lubricated.

Installation – Install outer bearing race using Bearing Installer (J-29040). Install inner bearing race, using 3" (76.2 mm) diameter rod. DO NOT use a bar larger than specified as it may damage bearing seal seat. Pack wheel bearings with wheel bearing grease. To complete installation, reverse removal procedure. Adjust wheel bearings. See FRONT WHEEL BEARINGS under ADJUSTMENTS.

SPINDLE

NOTE: For spindle removal, see STEERING ARM, KNUCKLE & KINGPIN under REMOVAL & INSTALLATION.

STEERING ARM, KNUCKLE & KINGPIN

Removal – **1)** Raise and support vehicle. Remove wheel assembly. Remove brake caliper and support aside. DO NOT allow caliper to hang by brake line. Remove wheel hub/rotor assembly. See WHEEL HUB/ROTOR & BEARINGS under REMOVAL & INSTALLATION.

2) Remove mounting bolts, nuts and washers. Remove anchor plate, splash shield and steering arm. *See Fig. 1.* Steering arm can hang by tie rod end. Remove upper and lower kingpin cap bolts, washers, brake line bracket, kingpin caps and gaskets from steering knuckle.

3) Remove lock pin nut and washer. Tap out lock pin. Using a drift, remove kingpin, spacers and bushings. Remove steering knuckle and spindle assembly. Remove dust seal, shim and thrust bearing. *See Fig. 1.*

Installation – **1)** Install NEW kingpin bushings. Ream bushings to **1.1804-1.1820" (29.982-30.023 mm)**. Lubricate thrust bearing. Install steering knuckle, thrust bearing, shim and dust seal. Lubricate kingpin.

2) Install kingpin and spacers. Install lock pin, washer and nut. Install gaskets, kingpin caps, brake line bracket, washers and bolts into steering knuckle. To complete installation, reverse removal procedure.

3) Tighten bolts and nuts to specification. See TORQUE SPECIFICA-TIONS table at end of article. Lower vehicle and check wheel alignment. See SPECIFICATIONS & PROCEDURES article in WHEEL ALIGNMENT.

SHOCK ABSORBER

Removal & Installation – Raise and support vehicle. Remove wheel assembly. Remove upper shock-to-frame rail nuts and washers. *See Fig. 1.* Remove lower shock-to-leaf spring spacer nuts and washers. Separate shock from frame rail and leaf spring spacer and remove from vehicle. To install, reverse removal procedure. Tighten nuts to specifications. See TORQUE SPECIFICATIONS table at end of article.

STABILIZER BAR & LINK

Removal – **1)** Raise and support vehicle. Remove wheel assembly. Remove stabilizer link nuts and washers. Using Tie Rod Remover (J-6627-A), disconnect stabilizer links from stabilizer bar end. Remove nuts, washers and bracket bolts attaching stabilizer brackets and bushings to frame rail. *See Fig. 2.*

2) Remove stabilizer bar from vehicle. Remove bushings from stabilizer bar. Remove stabilizer link nuts, upper and lower retainers and upper and lower bushings from front axle. Inspect rubber bushings for excessive wear or deterioration. Check bar and links for damage. Replace as necessary.

Installation – 1) Install upper retainer and bushing onto stabilizer link. Install stabilizer link into front axle. Install lower bushing, retainer and link nut. Tighten link nut until distance between retainers measures **2.08" (52.8 mm)**. See Fig. 2.

2) Place stabilizer bar and bushings in position on frame and install brackets over bushings. Ensure brackets are positioned properly over bushings. Install bracket bolts, washers and nuts. Connect stabilizer bar to stabilizer link. Install washers and nuts.

3) To complete installation, reverse removal procedure. Tighten all bolts and nuts to specification. See TORQUE SPECIFICATIONS at end of article.

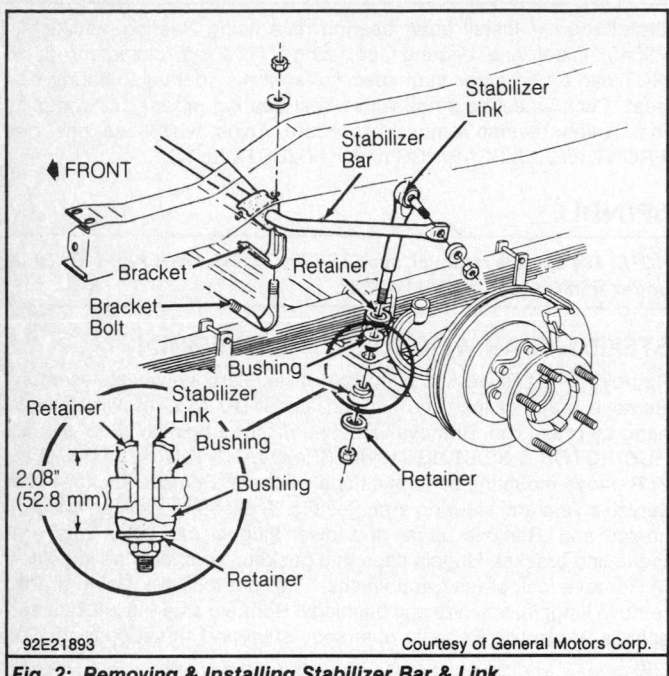

92E21893   Courtesy of General Motors Corp.

Fig. 2: Removing & Installing Stabilizer Bar & Link

LEAF SPRING & BUSHINGS

Removal – 1) Raise and support vehicle. Place adjustable jack stand under axle. Lift axle until all tension is relieved from leaf spring assembly. Remove wheel assembly. Remove shock absorber. See SHOCK ABSORBER under REMOVAL & INSTALLATION.

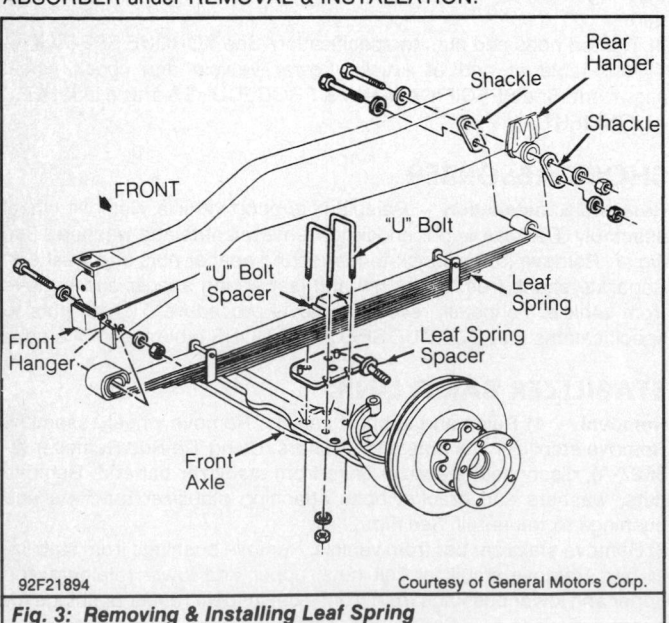

92F21894   Courtesy of General Motors Corp.

Fig. 3: Removing & Installing Leaf Spring (Commercial Van – C35 Pickup Similar)

2) Remove stabilizer link nut and washer. See Fig. 2. Using Tie Rod Remover (J-6627-A), disconnect stabilizer link from stabilizer bar end. Remove stabilizer link nuts, upper and lower retainers and upper and lower bushings from front axle. Remove "U" bolt-to-front axle nuts and washers. Remove "U" bolts, "U" bolt spacer and leaf spring spacer.

3) Separate leaf spring from front axle. On Commercial Van, remove shackle-to-leaf spring bolt, nut and washers. See Fig. 3. On C35 Pickup, remove rear hanger-to-leaf spring bolt, nut and washer. Remove front hanger-to-leaf spring bolt, nut and washers. Pull leaf spring back and out to remove from vehicle.

Installation – 1) To install, reverse removal procedure. Position leaf spring with double wrapped end toward front of vehicle. Tighten "U" bolt nuts in a diagonal sequence. See Fig. 3. Tighten stabilizer link nut until distance between retainers measures **2.08" (52.8 mm)**. See Fig. 2.

2) Tighten bolts and nuts to specification. See TORQUE SPECIFICATIONS table at end of article. Lower vehicle and check wheel alignment. See SPECIFICATIONS & PROCEDURES article in WHEEL ALIGNMENT.

FRONT AXLE

Removal – 1) Raise and support vehicle. Place adjustable jack stand under axle. Lift axle until all tension is relieved from leaf spring assembly. Remove wheel assembly. Remove steering arm, knuckle and spindle. See STEERING ARM, KNUCKLE & KINGPIN under REMOVAL & INSTALLATION.

2) Remove lower shock-to-leaf spring spacer nuts and washers. Separate shock from leaf spring spacer. Remove stabilizer link nut and washer. See Fig. 2. Using Tie Rod Remover (J-6627-A), disconnect stabilizer link from stabilizer bar end. Remove stabilizer link nuts, upper and lower retainers and upper and lower bushings from front axle.

3) Remove "U" bolt-to-front axle nuts and washers. Remove "U" bolts, "U" bolt spacer and leaf spring spacer. See Fig. 3. Separate leaf spring from front axle. Remove steering dampener-to-front axle nut and washer. Separate steering dampener from front axle. Lower jack and remove front axle from vehicle.

Installation – 1) To install, reverse removal procedure. Tighten "U" bolt nuts in a diagonal sequence. See Fig. 3. Tighten stabilizer link nut until distance between retainers measures **2.08" (52.8 mm)**. See Fig. 2.

2) Tighten bolts and nuts to specification. See TORQUE SPECIFICATIONS table at end of article. Lower vehicle and check wheel alignment. See SPECIFICATIONS & PROCEDURES article in WHEEL ALIGNMENT.

TORQUE SPECIFICATIONS
TORQUE SPECIFICATIONS

Application	Ft. Lbs. (N.m)
Anchor Plate & Steering Arm-To-Steering Knuckle Nut	230 (312)
Kingpin Lock Pin Nut	29 (39)
Leaf Spring-To-Front Hanger Nut	92 (125)
Leaf Spring-To-Rear Hanger Nut	92 (125)
Leaf Spring-To-Shackle Nut	92 (125)
Leaf Spring "U" Bolt Nuts	80 (108)
Shock Absorber-To-Frame Rail Nut	136 (184)
Shock Absorber-To-Leaf Spring Spacer Nut	37 (50)
Splash Shield-To-Anchor Plate Bolt	12 (16)
Stabilizer Bar-To-Frame Bolt	21 (28)
Stabilizer Bar-To-Link Nut	50 (68)
Steering Dampener-To-Front Axle Nut	
Commercial Van	35 (47)
C35 Pickup	33 (45)
Tie Rod End Stud Nut	
Commercial Van	162 (220)
C35 Pickup	66 (90)
	INCH Lbs. (N.m)
Kingpin Cap Bolts	62 (7)

**Lumina APV, Silhouette,
Trans Sport, Typhoon**

DESCRIPTION

Rear level control automatically adjusts rear height of vehicle regardless of load. System is activated when ignition is on and weight is added or removed from vehicle.

Electronic Level Control (ELC) consists of a compressor, air drier, exhaust solenoid, compressor relay, height sensor, air adjustable shock absorbers and connecting air lines. Air drier contains a moisture absorbing chemical and pressure maintaining valves. Valves maintain minimum system pressure of approximately 7-14 psi (.5-.9 kg/cm²).

On Lumina APV, Silhouette and Trans Sport, a provision is made so ELC compressor can be used for other purposes, such as inflating tires, etc. The inflation equipment consists of inflator switch, inflator solenoid valve assembly and inflation timer relay.

OPERATION

RAISING VEHICLE

When weight is added to vehicle, height sensor arm rotates upward, grounding compressor relay circuit. After a time delay of approximately 8-15 seconds, compressor relay turns air compressor on, causing vehicle to rise.

As vehicle rises, height sensor rotates downward to curb height position. When vehicle is within 1" (25.4 mm) of curb height, height sensor opens ground circuit to compressor relay, turning compressor off.

LOWERING VEHICLE

When weight is removed from vehicle, height sensor arm rotates downward. After a time delay of approximately 8-15 seconds, downward rotation of the arm grounds exhaust solenoid valve circuit. Energizing exhaust solenoid valve causes air to vent through air drier and out of exhaust solenoid valve.

As vehicle lowers, height sensor arm rotates upward to curb height position. When vehicle is within 1" (25.4 mm) of curb height, height sensor opens exhaust solenoid valve circuit, causing exhaust solenoid valve to close.

AIR REPLENISHMENT

In order to ensure the system is operating with at least minimum air pressure, the height sensor commands an air replenishment cycle each time the ignition is cycled on. An internal timer circuit is activated when ignition is turned on. After a delay of approximately 35-45 seconds, compressor turns on for 3-5 seconds to ensure residual system pressure.

If weight is added or removed from vehicle during 35-45 second delay, air replenishment cycle will be overridden and vehicle will rise or lower after normal time delay.

INFLATOR

On Lumina APV, Silhouette and Trans Sport, when inflator switch is turned on, it grounds the inflation timer relay. This operates the inflator solenoid valve assembly, turning on the compressor through the ELC relay. The inflator solenoid valve assembly redirects compressed air from the suspension to the inflator hose.

The inflation timer relay limits inflation operation to 10 minutes each time the inflator switch is operated.

ADJUSTMENTS

HEIGHT SENSOR

1) Place vehicle on level surface, with gas tank full and NO load in vehicle. Turn ignition switch to ON position. Bounce vehicle 3 times to normalize suspension. To increase vehicle riding height, loosen lock bolt on sensor arm. Move plastic arm upward, and tighten lock nut.

2) To lower riding height, loosen lock nut, move plastic arm down and tighten lock nut. There is a total of 5 degrees adjustment on sensor. One degree adjustment provides 1/4" change in height at bumper. If adjustment cannot be made, problem is with rear springs or suspension. See Fig. 1.

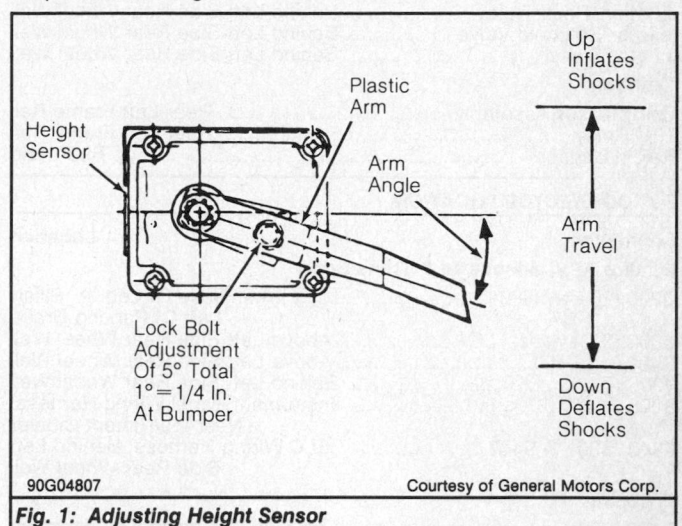

90G04807   Courtesy of General Motors Corp.

Fig. 1: Adjusting Height Sensor

RIDING HEIGHT

NOTE: See RIDE HEIGHT in SPECIFICATIONS & PROCEDURES article in WHEEL ALIGNMENT.

TROUBLE SHOOTING

Perform SYSTEM OPERATIONAL TEST and SYSTEM LEAK TEST under TESTING to determine if electrical fault exists. Refer to WIRING DIAGRAMS and ELC COMPONENT LOCATION, ELC CONNECTOR LOCATION and ELC CIRCUIT IDENTIFICATION tables to locate and identify circuits, components, etc.

VEHICLE LOADED, WILL NOT RISE

Leaks in air lines, fittings or shock absorbers. Pinched lines between compressor and shock absorbers. Defective height sensor. Compressor inoperative. Loose or damaged electrical connections to sensor or compressor.

VEHICLE LOADED, RISES, THEN LEAKS DOWN

Severe leak in lines, fittings or shock absorbers. Internal leak in motor.

VEHICLE LOADED, RISES PARTIALLY

Height sensor out of adjustment. Compressor or wiring defective.

VEHICLE RISES WHEN LOADED, LEAKS DOWN WHEN DRIVING

Defective drier or compressor. Pinched air lines or leaks in fittings or air lines.

VEHICLE RIDES HIGH

Height sensor out of adjustment. Drier plugged or air lines pinched. Poor electrical connections.

ELC COMPONENT LOCATION

Component	Location
Lumina APV, Silhouette & Trans Sport	
Compressor Assembly	Behind Left Side Rear Wheel
ELC Relay	Behind Left Side Rear Wheel Well
Fuse Block	Behind Instrument Panel Compartment Door
Height Sensor	Mounted To Center Of Rear Crossmember
Inflation Timer Relay	Behind Left Side Rear Wheel Well
Inflator Solenoid Valve	Behind Left Side Rear Wheel Well
Inflator Switch	Behind Left Side Rear Wheel Well
Typhoon	
Compressor Assembly	Rear Left Frame Rail
ELC Relay	Rear Left Frame Rail
Height Sensor	Rear Axle

ELC CONNECTOR LOCATION

Connector	Location
Lumina APV, Silhouette & Trans Sport	
C200 (26 Cavities)	Near Base Of Left "A" Pillar, Left Of Parking Brake
C302 (2 Cavities)	Above Left Side Rear Wheel Well
G401	Above Left Side Rear Wheel Well
P300	Behind Left Side Rear Wheel Well
S208	Instrument Panel Wiring Harness, Near Instrument Cluster
S300, S303 & S407	ELC Wiring Harness, Behind Left Side Rear Wheel Well
Typhoon	
C112	Left Side Of Engine Compartment
C465	Compressor Assembly
C466	Height Sensor

ELC CIRCUIT IDENTIFICATION

Circuit Number	Wire Color	Location
Lumina APV, Silhouette & Trans Sport		
39	Pink/Black	Fuse Block To Height Sensor
150	Black	Compressor Assembly To Ground
		Inflator Solenoid Valve To Ground
		Inflator Switch To Ground
		Inflation Timer Relay To Ground
		Height Sensor To Ground
320	White	Compressor Assembly To Height Sensor
321	Yellow	ELC Relay To Height Sensor To Inflation Timer Relay
322	Dark Green	ELC Relay To Compressor Assembly
340	Orange	Fuse Block To ELC Relay
		Fuse Block To Compressor Assembly
		Fuse Block To Inflation Timer Relay
1248	Light Blue	Inflation Timer Relay To Height Sensor
1249	Dark Blue	Inflation Timer Relay To Inflator Solenoid Valve
1250	White	Inflation Timer Relay To Inflator Switch
1267	Purple	Inflation Timer Relay To Inflator Switch
Typhoon		
39	Pink	C112 To Height Sensor
87	Dark Green	ELC Relay To Compressor Assembly
150	Black	C112 To Compressor Assembly
		C112 To Height Sensor
320	White	Compressor Assembly To Height Sensor
321	Yellow	ELC Relay To Height Sensor
340	Orange	C112 To ELC Relay
		C112 To Compressor Assembly
		C112 To Height Sensor

TESTING

SYSTEM OPERATIONAL TEST

1) Unload vehicle. With ignition off, check riding height. Turn ignition on. Add 300 lbs. (136 kg) load to rear passenger compartment. Compressor should start operating after a time delay of approximately 8-15 seconds. Vehicle should rise to within 1" (25.4 mm) of curb height.
2) Remove load from passenger compartment. Exhaust should start within 8-15 seconds. Within 3 1/2 minutes, exhaust should stop and vehicle should be within 1" (25.4 mm) of curb height.

SYSTEM LEAK TEST

1) Install Pressure Gauge (J-22124-A) in line between air drier assembly and existing line to shocks. *See Fig. 2.* Install gauge so shut-off valve is on compressor side of gauge. With shut-off valve open, apply shop air pressure through the fill valve until gauge reaches 100 psi (7.03 kg/cm²).
2) If a leak is indicated, close shut-off valve and continue to watch for a pressure drop. If pressure continues to drop, leak is external from the compressor. Leak test all connections. If pressure stops decreasing after shut-off valve is closed, leak is in the compressor assembly.
3) Check compressor for leaks. If pressure builds up rapidly but vehicle does not rise, check for pinched air line, and stuck air binding shocks.

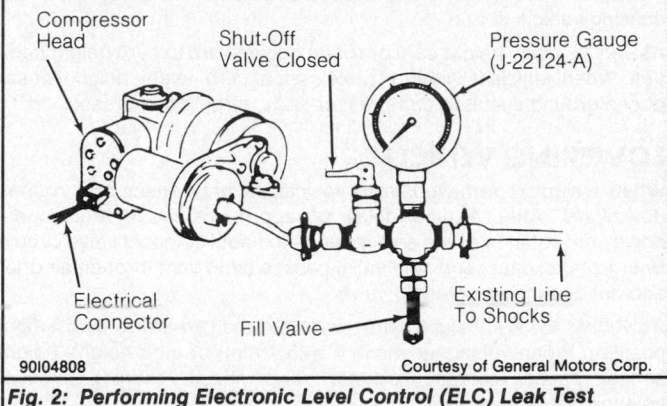

90I04808   Courtesy of General Motors Corp.

Fig. 2: Performing Electronic Level Control (ELC) Leak Test

COMPRESSOR PERFORMANCE TEST

1) Disconnect pressure line from air drier and attach Pressure Gauge (J-22124-A) to air drier fitting. Disconnect electrical connector from compressor motor and exhaust solenoid terminals. *See Fig. 2.*
2) Connect 12-volt power supply to compressor through ammeter. Current draw must not exceed 14 amps. Replace compressor if current draw is greater than 14 amps. Allow pressure to reach 100 psi (7.03 kg/cm²) minimum, and shut off compressor. Allow pressure to stabilize.
3) If pressure leaks down below 90 psi (6.33 kg/cm²) before holding steady but does not reach zero psi, replace head assembly. If pressure leaks down to zero psi, perform compressor/drier leak test. Repair as necessary.
4) If compressor output is less than 110 psi (7.73 kg/cm²), perform compressor/drier leak test. If no leak is found, replace compressor. See COMPRESSOR/DRIER LEAK TEST under TESTING.
5) If compressor does not operate, replace compressor. If compressor operates correctly, reconnect wiring and air lines.

NOTE: If compressor is allowed to run to maximum output pressure of 180 psi (12.7 kg/cm²), solenoid exhaust valve will act as a relief valve. This gives a false indication of system leakage.

COMPRESSOR/DRIER LEAK TEST

1) Attach Pressure Gauge (J-22124-A) to drier fitting. Allow pressure to reach 100 psi (7.03 kg/cm²) minimum and shut off compressor.

2) Using soap and water solution. Check for pressure leaks at locations shown. *See Fig. 3.* Torque compressor head bolts if necessary. See TORQUE SPECIFICATIONS table at end of article.

HEIGHT SENSOR OPERATION TEST

1) To reset height sensor timer circuits, cycle ignition off, then on. Raise vehicle on hoist. Ensure rear axle housing is supported as close to ride height specification as possible. Check all wiring for good connections. Disconnect link from height sensor arm.

2) Move sensor arm upward. *See Fig. 1.* After an 8-15 second delay, the compressor should run and shock absorbers should start to inflate. As soon as shock absorber air boots fill, stop compressor by moving sensor actuator arm down.

3) Move sensor arm below position where compressor stopped running. There should be an 8-15 second delay before shock absorbers start to deflate, and lower vehicle. Replace height sensor if it does not function properly.

SENSOR ACTUATOR ARM TEST

Raise vehicle. Ensure link is attached to actuator arm correctly, and actuator arm is properly aligned. *See Fig. 1.*

INFLATOR SWITCH DOES NOT ACTIVATE COMPRESSOR MOTOR

Lumina APV, Silhouette & Trans Sport – 1) Using digital volt/ohm meter (DVOM), measure voltage between inflation timer relay terminal "E" (Yellow wire) and ground. If voltage is not present, go to next step. If voltage measures battery voltage, go to step **6)**.

2) Measure voltage between ELC relay terminal No. 2 (Yellow wire) and ground. If voltage is not present, go to next step. If voltage measures battery voltage, repair open in circuit No. 321 (Yellow wire) between ELC relay and inflation timer relay.

3) Using test light, backprobe between ELC relay terminals No. 1 & 5 (Orange wires) and ground. If test light lights, go to next step. If test light does not light, repair open in circuit No. 340 (Orange wires) between ELC relay and fuse block.

4) Connect a fused jumper between ELC relay terminal No. 1 (Orange wire) and terminal No. 4 (Dark Green wire). If compressor motor starts, check for poor connections at ELC relay terminals No. 1 and No. 4. If connections are okay, replace ELC relay. If compressor motor does

not start, with jumper still connected, disconnect compressor. Using test light, backprobe between body harness side of compressor terminal "B" (Dark Green wire) and ground. If test light lights, go to next step. If test light does not light, repair open in circuit No. 322 (Dark Green wire) between compressor and ELC relay.

5) With fused jumper connected as in step **4)**, connect test light to body harness side of compressor between terminal "B" (Dark Green wire) and terminal "D" (Black wire). If test light does not light, repair open in circuit No. 150 (Black wire) between compressor and ground. If test light lights, check for poor connections at compressor terminals "B" and "D". If connections are okay, replace compressor motor.

6) Using DVOM, measure voltage between inflation timer relay terminal "D" (Orange wire) and ground. If voltage measures battery voltage, go to next step. If voltage is not present, check for poor connection at inflation timer relay terminal "D", or for open in circuit No. 340 (Orange wire) between inflation timer relay and fuse.

7) Using DVOM, measure voltage between inflation timer relay terminal "D" (Orange wire) and terminal "H" (Black wire). If voltage is present, go to next step. If voltage is not present, repair open in circuit No. 150 (Black wire) between inflation timer relay and ground.

8) Disconnect inflator switch. Connect a fused jumper between inflator switch terminal "A" (White wire) and terminal "B" (Black wire). If compressor does not start, go to next step. If compressor motor starts, check for poor connections at inflator switch terminal "A" and "B". If connections are okay, replace inflator switch.

9) With fused jumper connected as in step **7)**, using DVOM, measure voltage between inflation timer relay terminal "F" (White wire) and ground. If voltage is not present, check for poor connections at inflation timer relay terminals "E" (Yellow wire), "F" (White wire) and "H" (Black wire). If connections are okay, replace inflation timer relay. If voltage measures battery voltage, check for open in circuit No. 1250 (White wire) or circuit No. 150 (Black wire) between inflation timer relay, inflator switch and ground.

INFLATOR SWITCH ACTIVATES COMPRESSOR MOTOR, BUT HIGH PRESSURE AIR IS NOT AVAILABLE AT AIR HOSE

Lumina APV, Silhouette & Trans Sport – 1) Turn inflator switch to ON position. Using test light, backprobe between inflation timer relay terminal "C" (Dark Blue wire) and ground. If test light lights, go to next

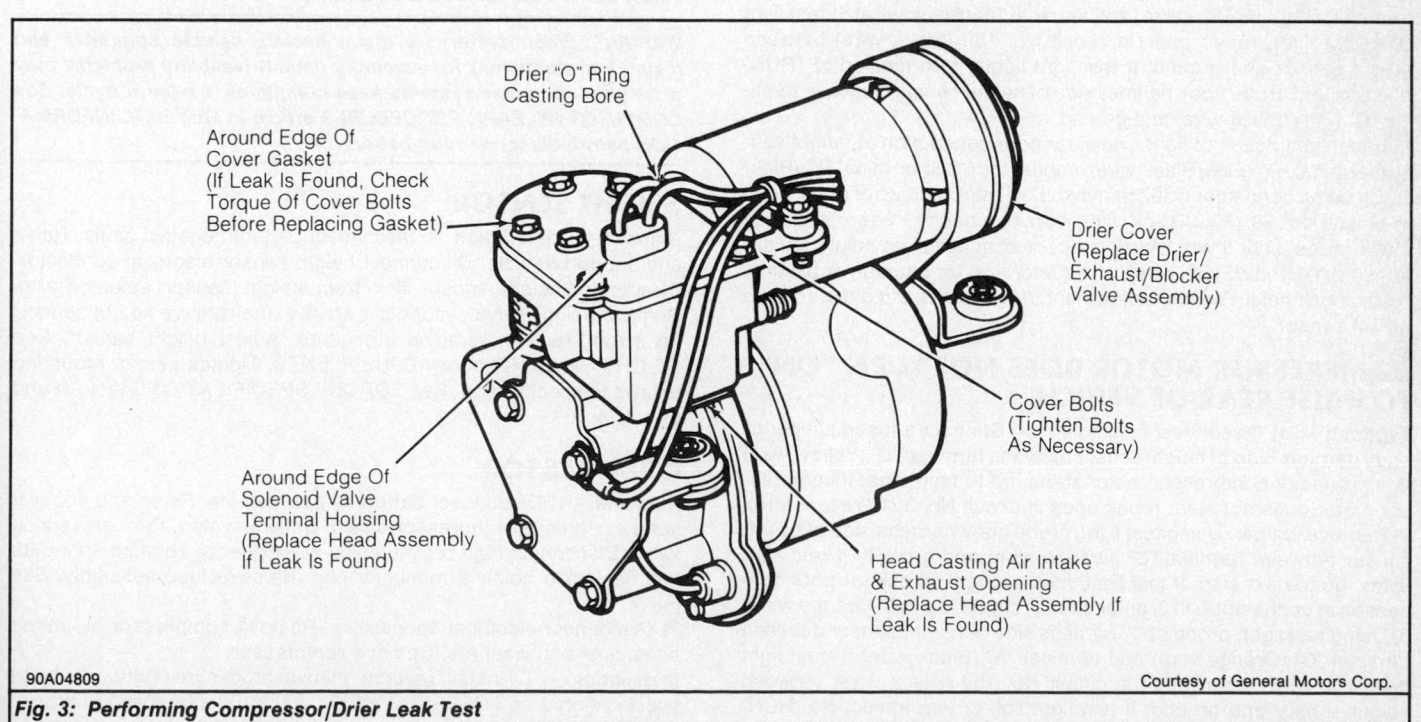

90A04809

Courtesy of General Motors Corp.

Fig. 3: Performing Compressor/Drier Leak Test

step. If test light does not light, check for poor connection at inflation timer relay terminal "C", or for open in circuit No. 340 (Orange wire). If connection and wire are okay, replace inflation timer relay.

2) Connect test light between inflator solenoid valve assembly terminal "A" (Dark Blue wire) and terminal "B" (Black wire). If test light does not light, check for open in circuit No. 1249 (Dark Blue wire) or circuit No. 150 (Black wire) between inflation timer relay, inflator solenoid valve assembly and ground. If test light lights, check for poor connections at inflator solenoid valve assembly terminals "A" and "B". If connections are okay, replace inflator solenoid valve assembly.

INFLATOR SWITCH ACTIVATES COMPRESSOR MOTOR, BUT WILL NOT TURN COMPRESSOR MOTOR "OFF"

Lumina APV, Silhouette & Trans Sport – 1) Disconnect inflation timer relay. Connect test light between inflation timer relay terminal "D" (Orange wire) and terminal "A" (Purple wire). Press and hold inflator switch to OFF position.

2) If test light does not light, check for poor connection at inflator switch terminal "C" (purple wire), or for open in circuit No. 1267 (Purple wire). If connection and wire are okay, replace inflator switch.

3) If test light lights, check for poor connection at inflation timer relay terminal "A" (Purple wire). If connection is okay, replace inflation timer relay.

COMPRESSOR MOTOR DOES NOT TURN "ON" TO RAISE REAR OF VEHICLE, BUT INFLATOR SWITCH OPERATES NORMALLY

Lumina APV, Silhouette & Trans Sport – 1) Disconnect height sensor. Connect a fused jumper to body harness side of height sensor between terminal "B" (Yellow wire) and ground. If compressor motor starts, go to next step. If compressor motor does not start, repair open in circuit No. 321 (Yellow wire).

2) Remove jumper. Using test light, probe body harness side of height sensor between terminal "C" (Light Blue wire) and ground. If test light lights, go to next step. If test light does not light, check for poor connection at inflation timer relay terminal "B" (Light Blue wire), or for open in circuit No. 1248 (Light Blue wire). If connection and wire are okay, replace inflation timer relay.

3) Using test light, probe body harness side of height sensor between terminal "C" (Light Blue wire) and terminal "A" (Black wire). If test light does not light, repair open in circuit No. 150 (Black wire) between height sensor and ground. If test light lights, turn ignition to "RUN" position and probe body harness side of height sensor between terminal "D" (Pink/Black wire) and ground.

4) If test light does not light, check for poor connection at height sensor terminal "D" (Pink/Black wire), connector C200 terminal D1 (Pink/Black wire), connector C302 terminal "D" (Pink/Black wire) or for open in circuit No. 39 (Pink/Black wire) between height sensor and fuse block. If test light lights, check for poor connection at height sensor terminal "D" (Pink/Black wire), or actuator arm for damage or binding. Also, check height sensor adjustment. If all checks are okay, replace height sensor.

COMPRESSOR MOTOR DOES NOT TURN "ON" TO RAISE REAR OF VEHICLE

Typhoon – 1) Disconnect height sensor. Connect a fused jumper to body harness side of height sensor between terminal "B" (Yellow wire) and ground. If compressor motor starts, go to next step. If compressor motor does not start, repair open in circuit No. 321 (Yellow wire).

2) Remove jumper. Using test light, probe body harness side of height sensor between terminal "C" (Orange wire) and ground. If test light lights, go to next step. If test light does not light, check for poor connection at connector C112, or for open in circuit No. 340 (Orange wire).

3) Using test light, probe body harness side of height sensor between terminal "C" (Orange wire) and terminal "A" (Black wire). If test light does not light, repair open in circuit No. 150 (Black wire) between height sensor and ground. If test light lights, turn ignition to "RUN" position and probe body harness side of height sensor between terminal "D" (Pink wire) and ground.

4) If test light does not light, check for open in circuit No. 39 (Pink wire) between height sensor and connector C112. If test light lights, check for poor connection at height sensor terminal "D" (Pink wire), or actuator arm for damage or binding. Also, check height sensor adjustment. If all checks are okay, replace height sensor.

ELECTRONIC LEVEL CONTROL SYSTEM DOES NOT VENT TO LOWER REAR OF VEHICLE

1) Disconnect height sensor. Connect a fused jumper to body harness side of height sensor between terminal "E" (White wire) and ground. Vent solenoid should click and vent air. If vent solenoid does not operate, go to next step. If vent solenoid operates, check for poor connection at height sensor terminal "E", or actuator arm for damage or binding. Also, check height sensor adjustment. If all checks are okay, replace height sensor.

2) Does fuse in fused jumper blow? If fuse blows, repair short to voltage on circuit No. 320 (White wire). If fuse does not blow, with jumper still connected, disconnect compressor assembly. Connect test light to body harness side of compressor assembly between terminal "C" (Orange wire) and terminal "A" (White wire).

3) If test light lights, check for poor connections at compressor assembly terminals "A" and "C". If connections are okay, replace vent solenoid. If test light does not light, check for open in circuit No. 340 (Orange wire) or No. 320 (White wire).

COMPRESSOR MOTOR RUNS CONTINUOUSLY OR FOR MAXIMUM RUN TIME, THEN STOPS

1) Turn ignition switch to OFF position. Disconnect compressor assembly and height sensor. Connect test light to body harness side of height sensor between terminal "E" (White wire) and battery voltage. If test light does not light, go to next step. If test light lights, repair short to ground in circuit No. 320 (White wire).

2) Reconnect height sensor. Connect test light to body harness side of compressor assembly between terminal "A" (White wire) and battery voltage. If test light lights, replace height sensor. If test light does not light, check electronic level control system for air leaks. Also, check height sensor adjustment. If all checks are okay, replace vent solenoid.

REMOVAL & INSTALLATION

WARNING: When battery is disconnected, vehicle computer and memory systems may lose memory data. Driveability problems may exist until computer systems have completed a relearn cycle. See COMPUTER RELEARN PROCEDURES article in GENERAL INFORMATION before disconnecting battery.

HEIGHT SENSOR

Removal & Installation – Disconnect battery negative cable. Raise and support vehicle. Disconnect height sensor electrical connector. Disconnect height sensor link from height sensor actuator arm. Remove height sensor mounting screws and remove height sensor. To install, reverse removal procedure. Adjust height sensor. See HEIGHT SENSOR under ADJUSTMENTS. Tighten sensor mounting screws to specification. See TORQUE SPECIFICATIONS table at end of article.

COMPRESSOR

Removal – 1) Disconnect battery negative cable. Raise and support vehicle. Remove compressor shield. Deflate system through service valve. Disconnect high pressure line at air drier by rotating spring 90 degrees while holding connector end. Remove tube assembly. *See Fig. 4.*

2) Disconnect electrical connectors. Remove compressor mounting bolts, nuts and washers. Remove compressor.

Installation – To install, reverse removal procedure. Tighten bolts to specification. See TORQUE SPECIFICATIONS table at end of article. Turn ignition on and allow system to cycle. Check for leaks using soap and water solution.

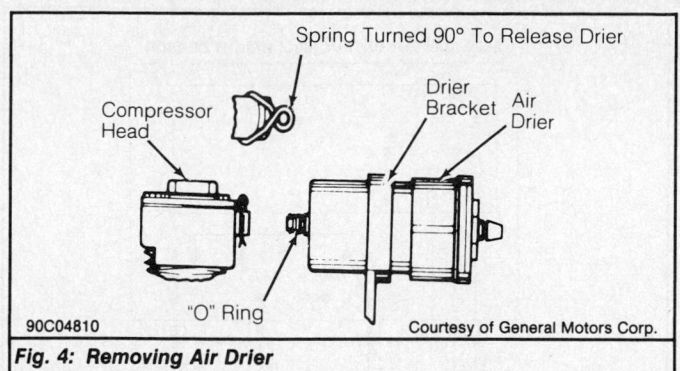

Fig. 4: Removing Air Drier

AIR DRIER

Removal – Disconnect battery negative cable. Raise and support vehicle. Remove bolts retaining air drier and bracket to compressor. Disconnect air drier from compressor by rotating spring 90 degrees. Remove air drier.

Installation – Lubricate "O" ring and install in port of compressor head. Return spring to its original position. Install air drier on compressor head assembly. If difficulty arises when installing air drier in compressor head assembly, rotate slightly while apply pressure. Check system for leaks.

AIR LINE REPAIR

If a leak is found in air line, it is not necessary to replace entire line. Air line can be repaired by splicing in a service coupling at leak area. Inflate system to 100 psi (7.03 kg/cm²). Use a soap and water solution to locate leak. Deflate system through service valve and cut out leaking area. Install service coupling and tighten tube nuts to **72 INCH lbs. (8 N.m)**. *See Fig. 5.* Inflate system and check for leaks using a soap and water solution.

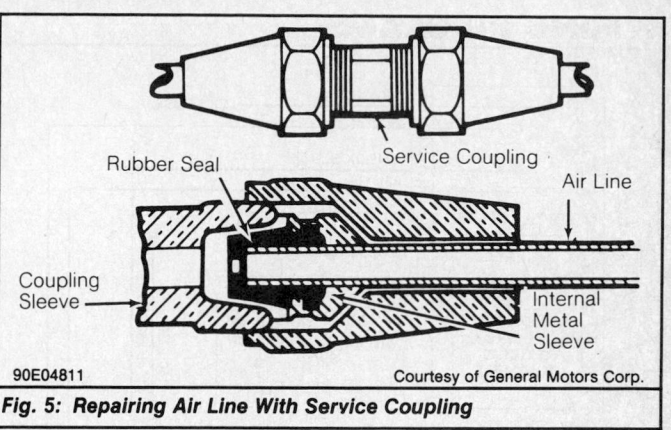

Fig. 5: Repairing Air Line With Service Coupling

TORQUE SPECIFICATIONS
TORQUE SPECIFICATIONS

Application	Ft. Lbs. (N.m)
Typhoon	
Compressor Mounting Bolts	18 (24)
Compressor Mounting Nuts	70 (95)

	INCH Lbs. (N.m)
Lumina APV, Silhouette & Trans Sport	
Compressor Bracket Mounting Screws	35 (4)
Compressor Head Bolts	35 (4)
Compressor Mounting Screws	35 (4)
Compressor Relay Mounting Screws	27 (3)
Height Sensor Link Nuts	53 (6)
Height Sensor Mounting Screws	35 (4)
Typhoon	
Compressor Bracket Mounting Screws	44 (5)
Compressor Head Bolts	35 (4)
Height Sensor Mounting Screws	31 (3.5)

WIRING DIAGRAMS

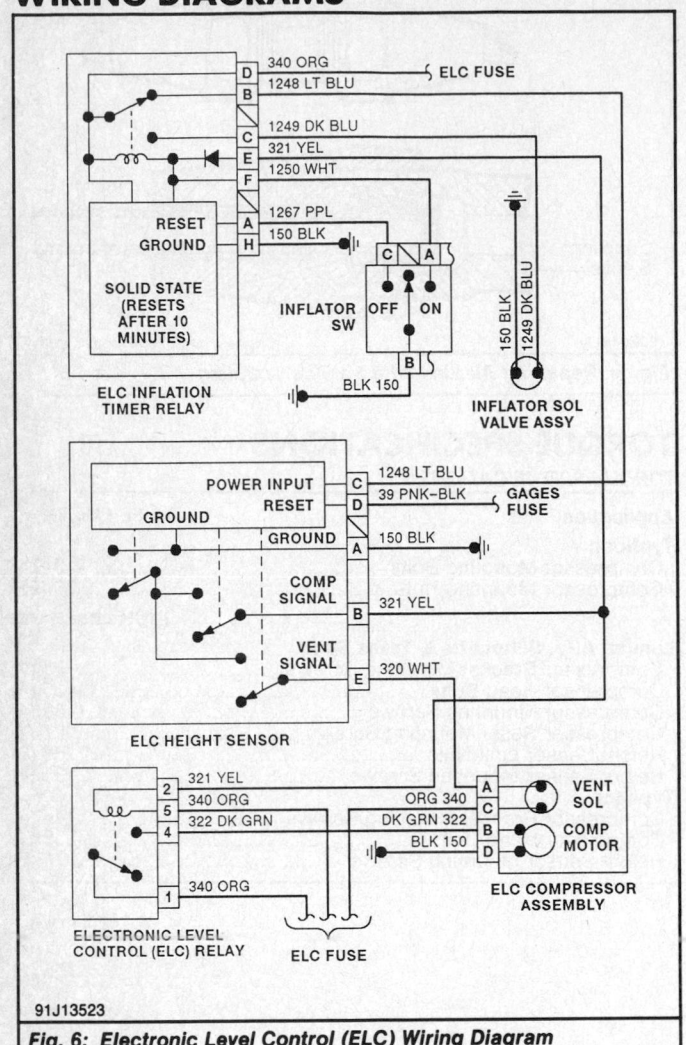

Fig. 6: Electronic Level Control (ELC) Wiring Diagram (Lumina APV, Silhouette & Trans Sport)

91J13523

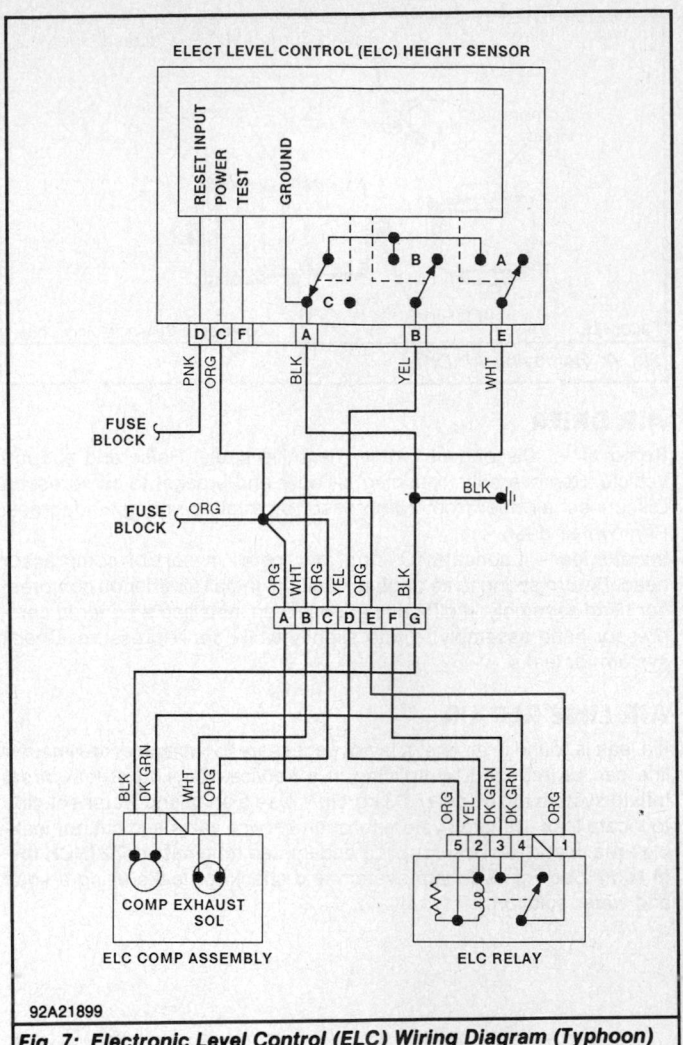

Fig. 7: Electronic Level Control (ELC) Wiring Diagram (Typhoon)

92A21899

Astro, Bravada, Commercial Van, Jimmy, Lumina APV, Safari, Sierra, Silhouette, Sonoma, Suburban, Syclone, Trans Sport, Typhoon, Van, Yukon, "C" & "K" Series Blazer & Pickup, "S" & "T" Series Blazer & Pickup

DESCRIPTION

All models use collapsible steering columns. All columns have integral ignition switch and locking device. Optional tilt wheel is available with both automatic and manual transmissions.

REMOVAL & INSTALLATION

WARNING: When battery is disconnected, vehicle computer and memory systems may lose memory data. Driveability problems may exist until computer systems have completed a relearn cycle. See COMPUTER RELEARN PROCEDURES article in GENERAL INFORMATION before disconnecting battery.

NOTE: Use only specified screws. Using screws that are too long may prevent column from compressing under impact.

STEERING WHEEL & HORN PAD

Removal – Disconnect negative battery cable. Remove horn pad. Remove snap ring and steering wheel retaining nut. Disconnect horn lead assembly (if equipped). Mark steering wheel and shaft for reassembly reference. Using Steering Wheel Puller (J-1859-03), remove steering wheel.

NOTE: To prevent damage to canceling cam and switch assembly, turn signal switch must be in neutral position before steering wheel is installed.

Installation – Before installing steering wheel, ensure turn signal switch is in neutral position. Install steering wheel onto steering shaft aligning marks made during removal. DO NOT misalign steering wheel more than .79" (20 mm) from horizontal centerline. Connect horn lead assembly (if equipped). Install and tighten steering wheel retaining nut to **30 ft. lbs. (41 N.m).** Install snap ring and horn pad. Connect negative battery cable.

STEERING COLUMN

NOTE: Some procedures do not apply to all models.

Removal – **1)** Disconnect negative battery cable. Disconnect transmission shift linkage from column shift tube levers. Mark position of pot joint to steering shaft. Remove upper intermediate shaft bolt and nut from steering shaft.

2) Remove steering column support bracket bolts and nuts. Remove support bracket. Remove steering column seal bolts and seal. Remove steering wheel. See STEERING WHEEL & HORN PAD. Disconnect electrical connectors at column harness.

3) Disconnect start/neutral switch and back-up light switch electrical connectors (if equipped). Disconnect transmission indicator cable (if equipped). On column shift models, rotate column so shift lever can clear dash opening. On all models, remove steering column assembly.

Installation – To install, reverse removal procedure. Tighten bolts and screws to specifications. See TORQUE SPECIFICATIONS table at end of article.

INTERMEDIATE SHAFT

Removal – Set front wheels in straight-ahead position. Mark pot joint to steering shaft position. Mark rag joint to steering gear worm shaft position. Remove intermediate shaft shield screw (if equipped) and remove shield (if equipped). Remove upper and lower intermediate shaft bolts and nut. Remove intermediate shaft. On Astro and Safari, remove steering gear for removal access of intermediate shaft.

Installation – To install, reverse removal procedure. Tighten bolts, nut and screw to specification. See TORQUE SPECIFICATIONS table at end of article.

SWITCHES & LOCK CYLINDER

NOTE: Removal and installation procedures for steering column switches and lock cylinder are contained within appropriate steering column overhaul procedure. See STANDARD COLUMN or TILT COLUMN under OVERHAUL.

OVERHAUL

WARNING: When battery is disconnected, vehicle computer and memory systems may lose memory data. Driveability problems may exist until computer systems have completed a relearn cycle. See COMPUTER RELEARN PROCEDURES article in GENERAL INFORMATION before disconnecting battery.

NOTE: Use only specified screws. Using screws that are too long may prevent column from compressing under impact.

NOTE: Although columns are similar, some procedures do not apply to all steering column.

STANDARD COLUMN

Disassembly (Column Shift) – **1)** Disconnect battery negative cable. Remove steering column from vehicle. See STEERING COLUMN under REMOVAL & INSTALLATION. Remove steering wheel. See STEERING WHEEL & HORN PAD under REMOVAL & INSTALLATION. Remove shaft lock cover. *See Fig. 1.* Using Lock Plate Compressor (J-23653-C), compress lock plate and pry retaining ring from groove in steering shaft. *See Fig. 2.* Discard retaining ring. Remove lock plate. Remove turn signal cancelling cam.

2) Remove upper bearing spring. Remove thrust washer. Place turn signal in up (right turn) position. Remove turn signal/combination switch lever and hazard switch lever. Remove switch actuator arm screw and switch actuator arm. Remove 3 turn signal switch retaining screws. Remove steering column support bracket bolts and support bracket.

3) Disconnect turn signal switch electrical connector. Remove 2 wiring protectors and carefully pull wiring through steering column. Remove turn signal switch and allow to hang free.

4) Remove buzzer switch. Place key in lock cylinder and turn to LOCK position. Remove lock retaining screw, being careful not to drop screw down column. *See Fig. 3.* Pull lock cylinder from housing.

5) Remove second retaining ring from steering shaft. Remove steering shaft. Disconnect dimmer switch electrical connector. Remove dimmer switch retaining screws and remove dimmer switch. Remove dimmer switch actuator rod. Remove ignition switch retaining screw and remove ignition switch.

6) Remove 4 steering column housing-to-steering column retaining screws. Remove column housing from column. Remove upper bearing retainer. Remove shift lever gate screws and remove shift lever gate. Remove ignition switch actuator rack and spring and bolt assembly from steering column housing. Remove spring and bolt assembly from ignition switch actuator rack. Remove switch actuator rod from actuator rack. Remove spring thrust washer from spring and bolt assembly.

7) Remove switch actuator sector. Remove rack preload spring. Remove housing cover end cap screw and housing cover end cap. Remove washer/wiper switch actuator pivot pin. Remove wiper/washer switch actuator retaining bushing from housing. Remove horn circuit contact from bearing retaining bushing. Remove bearing assembly.

8) Remove lower bearing adapter clip from bottom of steering column. Remove lower bearing adapter retainer. Remove adapter and bearing assembly. Remove shift tube return spring. Remove spring thrust washer.

9) Remove gearshift lever bowl and bowl shroud assembly from upper steering column. Separate gearshift lever bowl from bowl shroud. Remove shift lever spring from gearshift lever bowl. Remove shift tube assembly from bottom of steering column. Remove bowl lower bearing from upper shift tube assembly.

Reassembly – 1) To reassemble, reverse disassembly procedure. Lubricate adapter and bearing assembly with lithium grease before installation. Ensure first tooth of ignition actuator rack is positioned between first and second tooth of actuator sector. *See Fig. 4.* With actuator rack fully inserted, block tooth of actuator sector will be positioned within block tooth of actuator rack. *See Fig. 4.*

2) Install second retaining ring onto steering shaft. Lubricate steering shaft with lithium grease, and install shaft into steering column. Install turn signal switch electrical connector through housing. Install upper bearing retainer. Install steering column housing to steering column and tighten screws in clockwise sequence.

3) Install 2 wiring protectors. Install steering column support bracket and support bracket bolts. Move ignition switch slider to far left position and then back 1 detent to right. *See Fig. 5.* Ignition switch should now be in OFF/LOCK position.

NOTE: *Install ignition switch with switch in OFF/LOCK position. New ignition switch will be pinned in OFF/LOCK position; plastic pin must be removed after installation of ignition switch to steering column.*

4) Install ignition switch onto steering column. Install dimmer switch actuator rod. Connect dimmer switch to actuator rod. Place a 3/32" drill bit into hole on dimmer switch. Position dimmer switch onto steering column and push against actuator rod to remove lash. Remove drill bit and tighten dimmer switch retaining screws. Connect ignition switch and dimmer switch electrical connectors.

5) To complete installation, reverse remaining disassembly procedure. Lubricate turn signal cancelling cam with synthetic grease before installation. Using Lock Plate Compressor (J-23653-C), install NEW shaft lock retaining ring. *See Fig. 2.* Ensure retaining ring is fully seated in groove on steering shaft.

6) Carefully pull down on turn signal electrical wiring to remove any possible kinks within steering column. Tighten bolts and screws to specification. See TORQUE SPECIFICATIONS table at end of article.

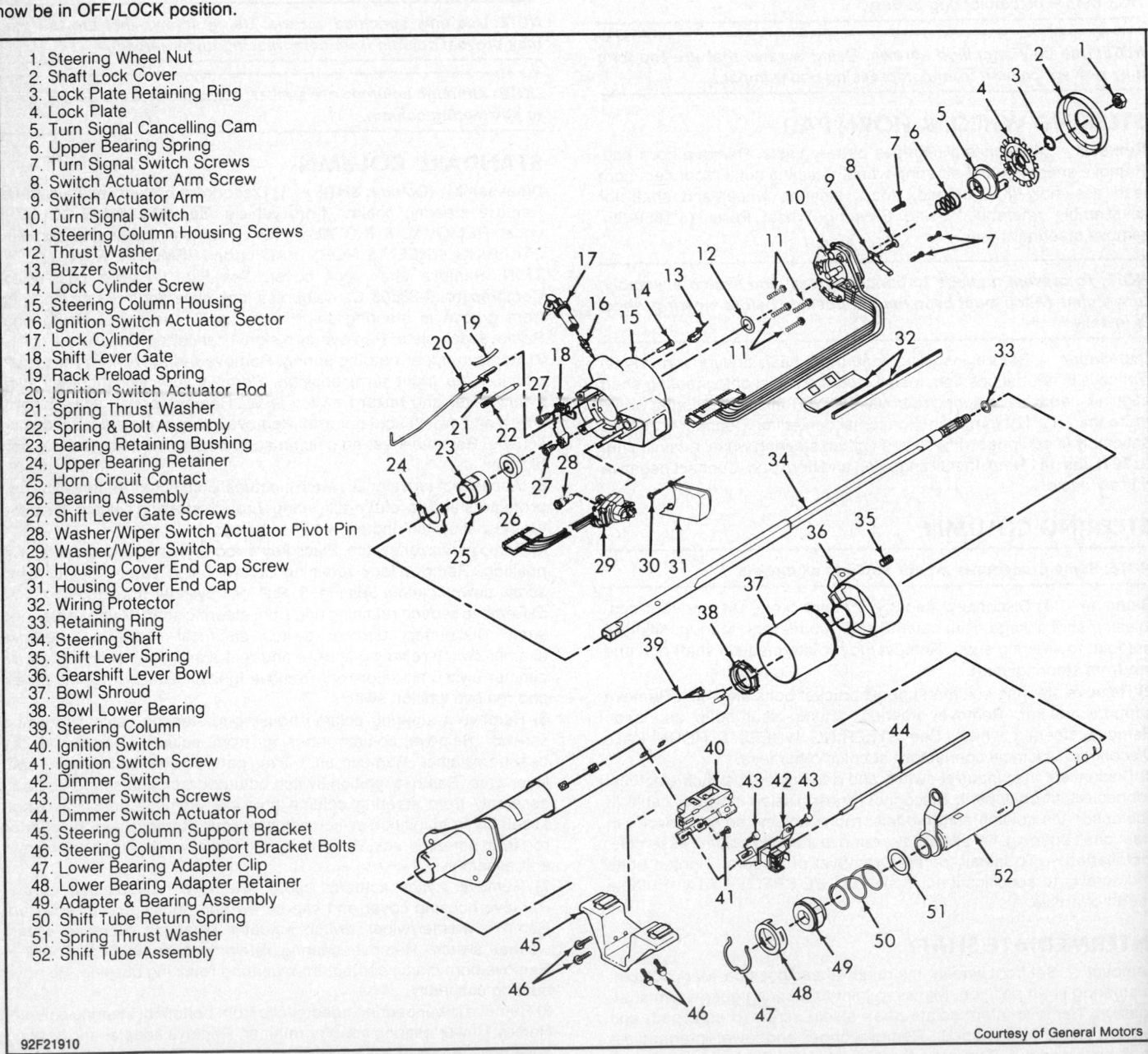

1. Steering Wheel Nut
2. Shaft Lock Cover
3. Lock Plate Retaining Ring
4. Lock Plate
5. Turn Signal Cancelling Cam
6. Upper Bearing Spring
7. Turn Signal Switch Screws
8. Switch Actuator Arm Screw
9. Switch Actuator Arm
10. Turn Signal Switch
11. Steering Column Housing Screws
12. Thrust Washer
13. Buzzer Switch
14. Lock Cylinder Screw
15. Steering Column Housing
16. Ignition Switch Actuator Sector
17. Lock Cylinder
18. Shift Lever Gate
19. Rack Preload Spring
20. Ignition Switch Actuator Rod
21. Spring Thrust Washer
22. Spring & Bolt Assembly
23. Bearing Retaining Bushing
24. Upper Bearing Retainer
25. Horn Circuit Contact
26. Bearing Assembly
27. Shift Lever Gate Screws
28. Washer/Wiper Switch Actuator Pivot Pin
29. Washer/Wiper Switch
30. Housing Cover End Cap Screw
31. Housing Cover End Cap
32. Wiring Protector
33. Retaining Ring
34. Steering Shaft
35. Shift Lever Spring
36. Gearshift Lever Bowl
37. Bowl Shroud
38. Bowl Lower Bearing
39. Steering Column
40. Ignition Switch
41. Ignition Switch Screw
42. Dimmer Switch
43. Dimmer Switch Screws
44. Dimmer Switch Actuator Rod
45. Steering Column Support Bracket
46. Steering Column Support Bracket Bolts
47. Lower Bearing Adapter Clip
48. Lower Bearing Adapter Retainer
49. Adapter & Bearing Assembly
50. Shift Tube Return Spring
51. Spring Thrust Washer
52. Shift Tube Assembly

92F21910

Courtesy of General Motors

Fig. 1: Exploded View Of Standard (Column Shift) Steering Column

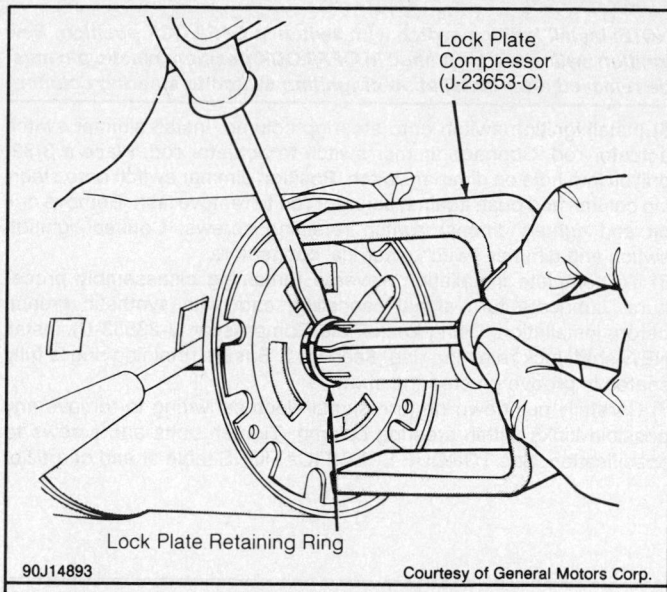

90J14893   Courtesy of General Motors Corp.

Fig. 2: Removing Shaft Lock Plate & Retaining Ring

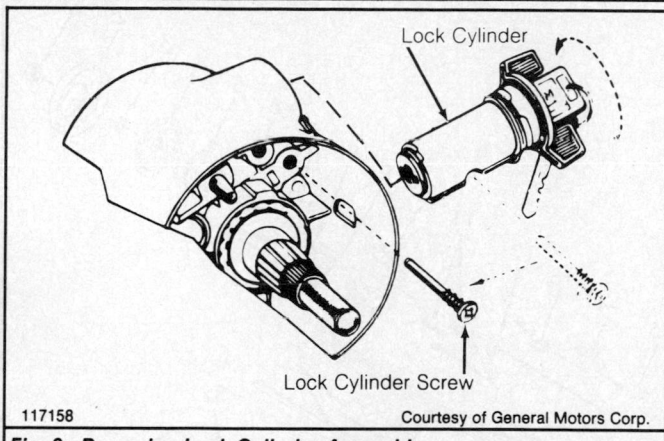

117158   Courtesy of General Motors Corp.

Fig. 3: Removing Lock Cylinder Assembly

Disassembly (Floor Shift) – **1)** Disconnect battery negative cable. Remove steering column from vehicle. See STEERING COLUMN under REMOVAL & INSTALLATION. Remove steering wheel. See STEERING WHEEL & HORN PAD under REMOVAL & INSTALLATION. Remove shaft lock cover. *See Fig. 6.* Using Lock Plate Compressor (J-23653-C), compress lock plate and pry retaining ring from groove in steering shaft. *See Fig. 2.* Discard retaining ring. Remove lock plate. Remove turn signal cancelling cam.

2) Remove upper bearing spring. Remove thrust washer. Place turn signal in up (right turn) position. Remove turn signal/combination switch lever and hazard switch lever. Remove switch actuator arm screw and switch actuator arm. Remove 3 turn signal switch retaining screws. Remove steering column support bracket bolts and support bracket.

3) Disconnect turn signal switch electrical connector. Remove 2 wiring protectors and carefully pull wiring through steering column. Remove turn signal switch and allow to hang free.

4) Remove buzzer switch. Place key in lock cylinder and turn to LOCK position. Remove lock retaining screw, being careful not to drop screw down column. *See Fig. 3.* Pull lock cylinder from housing.

5) Remove second retaining ring from steering shaft. Remove steering shaft. Disconnect dimmer switch electrical connector. Remove dimmer switch retaining screws and remove dimmer switch. Remove dimmer switch actuator rod. Remove ignition switch retaining screw and remove ignition switch.

6) Remove 4 steering column housing-to-steering column retaining screws. Remove column housing, gearshift lever bowl and bowl

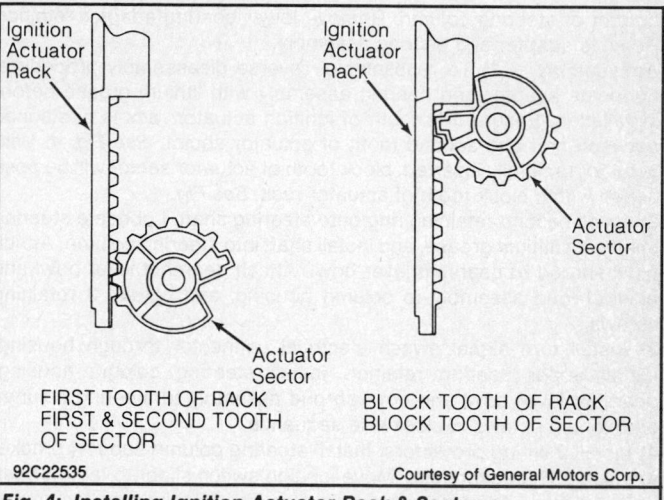

92C22535   Courtesy of General Motors Corp.

Fig. 4: Installing Ignition Actuator Rack & Sector

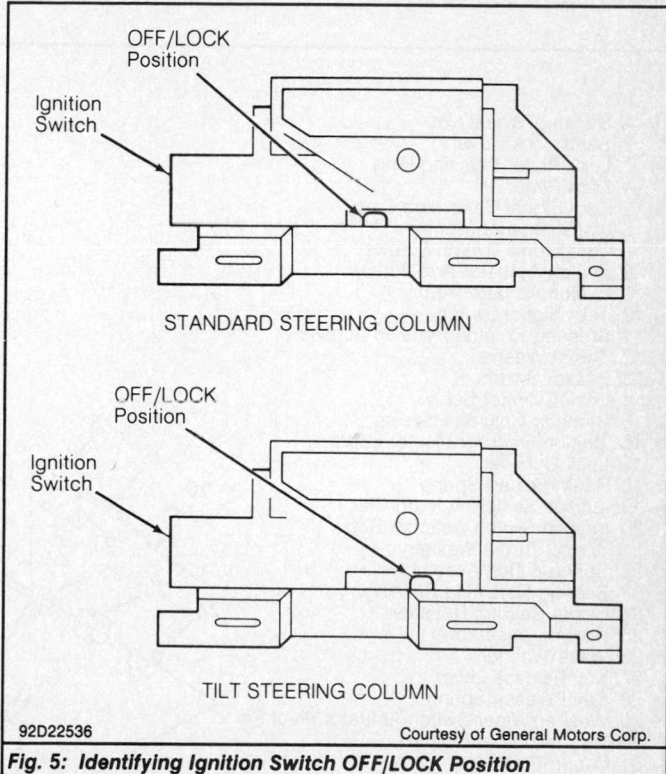

92D22536   Courtesy of General Motors Corp.

Fig. 5: Identifying Ignition Switch OFF/LOCK Position

shroud assembly from column. Remove upper bearing retainer. Remove 3 gearshift lever bowl-to-column housing retaining screws. Separate gearshift lever bowl from column housing and bowl shroud from gearshift lever bowl.

NOTE: *Key release lever is under spring tension. Use care during removal so as not to lose wave washer and key release lever spring.*

---

7) Carefully remove wave washer, key release lever and key release spring. Remove ignition switch actuator rack and spring and bolt assembly from steering column housing. Remove spring and bolt assembly from ignition switch actuator rack. Remove switch actuator rod from actuator rack. Remove spring thrust washer from spring and bolt assembly.

8) Remove switch actuator sector. Remove rack preload spring. Remove washer/wiper switch actuator pivot pin. Remove wiper/washer switch. Remove bearing retaining bushing from housing. Remove bearing assembly. Remove lower bearing adapter clip from bottom of steering column. Remove lower bearing adapter retainer. Remove adapter and bearing assembly.

Reassembly – 1) To reassemble, reverse disassembly procedure. Lubricate adapter and bearing assembly with lithium grease before installation. Ensure first tooth of ignition actuator rack is positioned between first and second tooth of actuator sector. *See Fig. 4.* With actuator rack fully inserted, block tooth of actuator sector will be positioned within block tooth of actuator rack. *See Fig. 4.*

2) Install second retaining ring onto steering shaft. Lubricate steering shaft with lithium grease, and install shaft into steering column. Attach bowl shroud to gearshift lever bowl. Attach gearshift lever bowl and bowl shroud assembly to column housing, and tighten 3 retaining screws.

3) Install turn signal switch electrical connector through housing. Install upper bearing retainer. Install steering column housing, gearshift lever bowl and bowl shroud assembly to steering column, and tighten screws in clockwise sequence.

4) Install 2 wiring protectors. Install steering column support bracket and support bracket bolts. Move ignition switch slider to far left position and then back 1 detent to right. *See Fig. 5.* Ignition switch should now be in OFF/LOCK position.

NOTE: Install ignition switch with switch in OFF/LOCK position. New ignition switch will be pinned in OFF/LOCK position; plastic pin must be removed after installation of ignition switch to steering column.

5) Install ignition switch onto steering column. Install dimmer switch actuator rod. Connect dimmer switch to actuator rod. Place a 3/32" drill bit into hole on dimmer switch. Position dimmer switch onto steering column and push against actuator rod to remove lash. Remove drill bit and tighten dimmer switch retaining screws. Connect ignition switch and dimmer switch electrical connectors.

6) To complete installation, reverse remaining disassembly procedure. Lubricate turn signal cancelling cam with synthetic grease before installation. Using Lock Plate Compressor (J-23653-C), install NEW shaft lock retaining ring. *See Fig. 2.* Ensure retaining ring is fully seated in groove on steering shaft.

7) Carefully pull down on turn signal electrical wiring to remove any possible kinks within steering column. Tighten bolts and screws to specification. See TORQUE SPECIFICATIONS table at end of article.

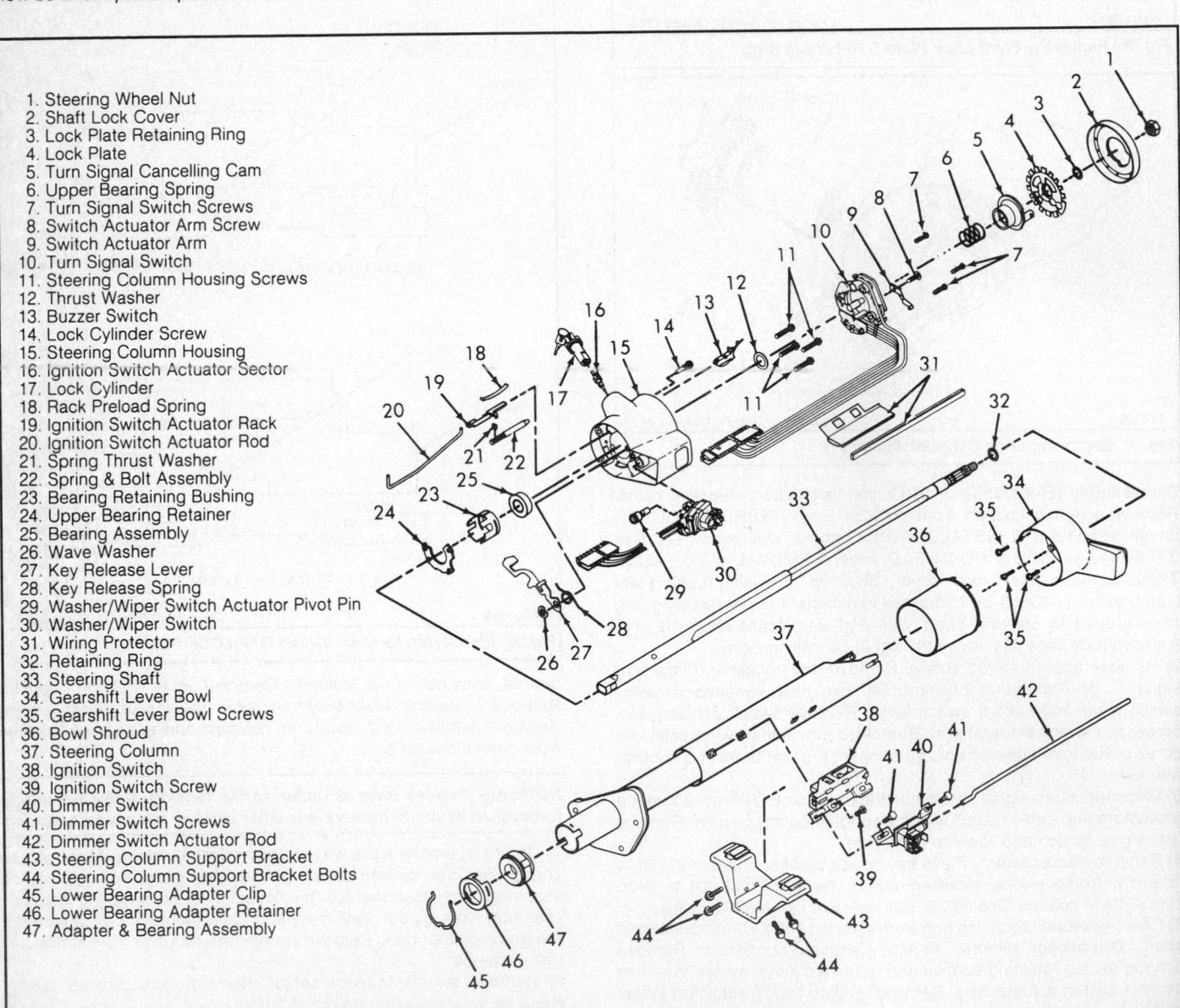

1. Steering Wheel Nut
2. Shaft Lock Cover
3. Lock Plate Retaining Ring
4. Lock Plate
5. Turn Signal Cancelling Cam
6. Upper Bearing Spring
7. Turn Signal Switch Screws
8. Switch Actuator Arm Screw
9. Switch Actuator Arm
10. Turn Signal Switch
11. Steering Column Housing Screws
12. Thrust Washer
13. Buzzer Switch
14. Lock Cylinder Screw
15. Steering Column Housing
16. Ignition Switch Actuator Sector
17. Lock Cylinder
18. Rack Preload Spring
19. Ignition Switch Actuator Rack
20. Ignition Switch Actuator Rod
21. Spring Thrust Washer
22. Spring & Bolt Assembly
23. Bearing Retaining Bushing
24. Upper Bearing Retainer
25. Bearing Assembly
26. Wave Washer
27. Key Release Lever
28. Key Release Spring
29. Washer/Wiper Switch Actuator Pivot Pin
30. Washer/Wiper Switch
31. Wiring Protector
32. Retaining Ring
33. Steering Shaft
34. Gearshift Lever Bowl
35. Gearshift Lever Bowl Screws
36. Bowl Shroud
37. Steering Column
38. Ignition Switch
39. Ignition Switch Screw
40. Dimmer Switch
41. Dimmer Switch Screws
42. Dimmer Switch Actuator Rod
43. Steering Column Support Bracket
44. Steering Column Support Bracket Bolts
45. Lower Bearing Adapter Clip
46. Lower Bearing Adapter Retainer
47. Adapter & Bearing Assembly

Courtesy of General Motors

92E22537

Fig. 6: Exploded View Of Standard (Floor Shift) Steering Column

TILT COLUMN

Disassembly (Column Shift) – **1)** Disconnect negative battery cable. Remove steering column from vehicle. See STEERING COLUMN under REMOVAL & INSTALLATION. Remove steering wheel. See STEERING WHEEL & HORN PAD under REMOVAL & INSTALLATION. Remove shaft lock cover. See Fig. 7. Using Lock Plate Compressor (J-23653-C), compress lock plate and pry retaining ring from groove in steering shaft. See Fig. 2. Discard retaining ring. Remove lock plate. Remove turn signal cancelling cam.
2) Remove upper bearing spring. Remove upper bearing race seat and inner race. Place turn signal in up (right turn) position. Remove turn signal/combination switch lever and hazard switch lever. Remove switch actuator arm screw and switch actuator arm. Remove 3 turn signal switch retaining screws. Remove steering column support bracket bolts and support bracket.
3) Disconnect turn signal switch electrical connector. Remove 2 wiring protectors and carefully pull wiring through steering column. Remove turn signal switch and allow to hang free.
4) Remove buzzer switch. Place key in lock cylinder and turn to LOCK position. Remove lock retaining screw, being careful not to drop screw down column. See Fig. 3. Pull lock cylinder from housing.
5) Remove 3 column housing cover screws. Remove tilt lever. Remove column housing cover. Remove column housing cover end cap and dimmer switch rod actuator assembly. Separate dimmer switch rod actuator from end cap. Remove washer/wiper switch actuator pivot pin. Remove washer/wiper switch.
6) Using screwdriver, push down and turn counterclockwise to release and remove tilt spring retainer. Remove tilt spring and spring guide. Using Pivot Pin Remover (J-21854-01), remove tilt pivot pins from steering column. Reinstall tilt lever. Pull back on tilt lever and pull column housing down and away separating housing from column.
7) Remove bearing assembly. Remove shaft lock bolt spring screw, lock bolt spring and shaft lock bolt. Remove ignition switch actuator rack and rack preload spring. Remove drive shaft. Remove switch actuator sector. Using Lock Shoe/Release Lever Pin Remover/Installer (J-22635), remove release lever pin. Remove shoe release lever and release lever spring.
8) Lock Shoe/Release Lever Pin Remover/Installer (J-22635), remove lock shoe dowel pin. Remove lock shoes and lock shoe springs from column housing. Mark upper steering shaft to lower steering shaft for reassembly reference. Tilt lower steering shaft up to 90-degree angle and separate from upper steering shaft. Rotate upper steering shaft centering sphere 90 degrees and slip out of upper shaft. Remove joint preload spring from centering sphere.
9) Remove 4 steering column housing support screws. Remove steering column housing support and dimmer switch actuator rod assembly. Remove dimmer switch actuator rod from column housing support. Remove shift lever gate retaining screws, and remove shift lever gate from column housing support.
10) Disconnect dimmer switch electrical connector. Remove dimmer switch retaining screws and dimmer switch. Remove ignition switch retaining screw and ignition switch. Remove ignition switch actuator rod. Remove shift tube retaining ring and thrust washer.
11) Remove lower bearing adapter clip from bottom of steering column. Remove lower bearing adapter retainer. Remove adapter and bearing assembly. Using Shift Tube Remover (J-23072), remove shift tube assembly from bottom of steering column.
12) Remove gearshift lever bowl lock plate and wave washer. Remove gearshift lever bowl and bowl shroud assembly from upper steering column. Separate gearshift lever bowl from bowl shroud. Remove shift lever spring from gearshift lever bowl.
Reassembly – **1)** To reassemble, reverse disassembly procedure. Using Shift Tube Installer (J-23073), install shift tube assembly into bottom of steering column. Lubricate adapter and bearing assembly with lithium grease before installation. Lubricate gearshift lever bowl wave washer with lithium grease before installation.
2) Install joint preload spring onto centering sphere. Lubricate upper steering shaft centering sphere with lithium grease. Insert centering sphere into upper steering shaft and rotate 90 degrees. Tilt lower steering shaft up to 90-degree angle and attach to upper steering shaft aligning marks made during disassembly procedure.

NOTE: Ensure upper and lower steering shafts are properly assembled with marks made during disassembly properly aligned. Failure to properly assemble steering shafts will cause steering wheel to be incorrectly positioned by 180 degrees.

3) Lubricate steering shaft with lithium grease and install shaft into steering column. Move ignition switch slider to far right position and then back one detent to left. See Fig. 5. Ignition switch should now be in OFF/LOCK position.

NOTE: Install ignition switch with switch in OFF/LOCK position. New ignition switch will be pinned in OFF/LOCK position; plastic pin must be removed after installation of ignition switch to steering column.

4) Install ignition switch onto steering column. Install dimmer switch actuator rod. Connect dimmer switch to actuator rod. Place a 3/32" drill bit into hole on dimmer switch. Position dimmer switch onto steering column and push against actuator rod to remove lash. Remove drill bit and tighten dimmer switch retaining screws. Connect ignition switch and dimmer switch electrical connectors.
5) Using Lock Shoe/Release Lever Pin Remover/Installer (J-22635), install lock shoe dowel pin and release lever pin. Lubricate bearing assembly with lithium grease, and install assembly into column housing using Steering Column Hanging Bearing Installer (J-38630) and Driver (J-8092).
6) Install tilt lever. Position column housing onto column housing support engaging ignition switch actuator rack in housing with pin on end of ignition switch actuator rod in housing support. Pull back on tilt lever and push column housing onto column housing support. Release tilt lever engaging lock shoes onto lock shoe dowel pin. Remove tilt lever.
7) Lubricate tilt pivot pins with lithium grease and firmly press pins into column housing until seated. Lubricate tilt spring guide and tilt spring with lithium grease and install into housing. Using screwdriver, push down and turn clockwise to install and lock tilt spring retainer into column housing.
8) Install washer/wiper switch. Install washer/wiper switch actuator pivot pin. Lubricate dimmer switch actuator rod with lithium grease and install onto end cap. Install housing cover end cap into column housing cover. Install column housing cover onto steering column housing and tighten screws in counterclockwise sequence beginning with screw in 12 o'clock position. Install tilt lever.
9) To complete installation, reverse remaining disassembly procedure. Lubricate turn signal cancelling cam with synthetic grease before installation. Using Lock Plate Compressor (J-23653-C), install NEW shaft lock retaining ring. See Fig. 2. Ensure retaining ring is fully seated in groove on steering shaft.
10) Carefully pull down on turn signal electrical wiring to remove any possible kinks within steering column. Tighten bolts and screws to specification. See TORQUE SPECIFICATIONS table at end of article.
Disassembly (Floor Shift) – **1)** Disconnect negative battery cable. Remove steering column from vehicle. See STEERING COLUMN under REMOVAL & INSTALLATION. Remove steering wheel. See STEERING WHEEL & HORN PAD under REMOVAL & INSTALLATION. Remove shaft lock cover. See Fig. 8. Using Lock Plate Compressor (J-23653-C), compress lock plate and pry retaining ring from groove in steering shaft. See Fig. 2. Discard retaining ring. Remove lock plate. Remove turn signal cancelling cam.
2) Remove upper bearing spring. Remove upper bearing race seat and inner race. Place turn signal in up (right turn) position. Remove turn signal/combination switch lever and hazard switch lever. Remove switch actuator arm screw and remove switch actuator arm. Remove 3 turn signal switch retaining screws. Remove steering column support bracket bolts and support bracket.
3) Disconnect turn signal switch electrical connector. Remove 2 wiring protectors and carefully pull wiring through steering column. Remove turn signal switch and allow to hang free.
4) Remove buzzer switch. Place key in lock cylinder and turn to LOCK position. Remove lock retaining screw, being careful not to drop screw down column. See Fig. 3. Pull lock cylinder from housing.

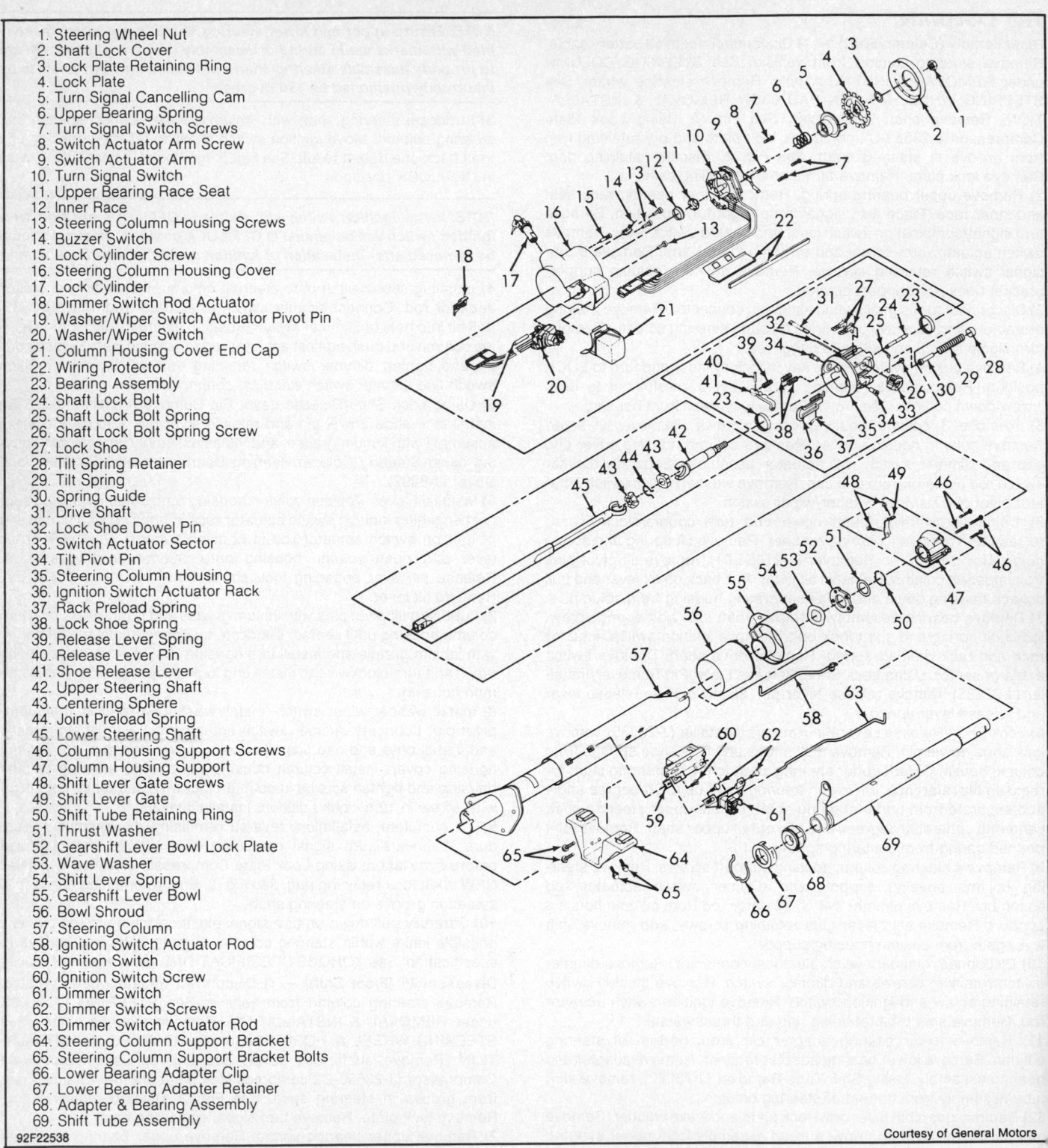

1. Steering Wheel Nut
2. Shaft Lock Cover
3. Lock Plate Retaining Ring
4. Lock Plate
5. Turn Signal Cancelling Cam
6. Upper Bearing Spring
7. Turn Signal Switch Screws
8. Switch Actuator Arm Screw
9. Switch Actuator Arm
10. Turn Signal Switch
11. Upper Bearing Race Seat
12. Inner Race
13. Steering Column Housing Screws
14. Buzzer Switch
15. Lock Cylinder Screw
16. Steering Column Housing Cover
17. Lock Cylinder
18. Dimmer Switch Rod Actuator
19. Washer/Wiper Switch Actuator Pivot Pin
20. Washer/Wiper Switch
21. Column Housing Cover End Cap
22. Wiring Protector
23. Bearing Assembly
24. Shaft Lock Bolt
25. Shaft Lock Bolt Spring
26. Shaft Lock Bolt Spring Screw
27. Lock Shoe
28. Tilt Spring Retainer
29. Tilt Spring
30. Spring Guide
31. Drive Shaft
32. Lock Shoe Dowel Pin
33. Switch Actuator Sector
34. Tilt Pivot Pin
35. Steering Column Housing
36. Ignition Switch Actuator Rack
37. Rack Preload Spring
38. Lock Shoe Spring
39. Release Lever Spring
40. Release Lever Pin
41. Shoe Release Lever
42. Upper Steering Shaft
43. Centering Sphere
44. Joint Preload Spring
45. Lower Steering Shaft
46. Column Housing Support Screws
47. Column Housing Support
48. Shift Lever Gate Screws
49. Shift Lever Gate
50. Shift Tube Retaining Ring
51. Thrust Washer
52. Gearshift Lever Bowl Lock Plate
53. Wave Washer
54. Shift Lever Spring
55. Gearshift Lever Bowl
56. Bowl Shroud
57. Steering Column
58. Ignition Switch Actuator Rod
59. Ignition Switch
60. Ignition Switch Screw
61. Dimmer Switch
62. Dimmer Switch Screws
63. Dimmer Switch Actuator Rod
64. Steering Column Support Bracket
65. Steering Column Support Bracket Bolts
66. Lower Bearing Adapter Clip
67. Lower Bearing Adapter Retainer
68. Adapter & Bearing Assembly
69. Shift Tube Assembly

92F22538

Courtesy of General Motors

Fig. 7: Exploded View Of Tilt (Column Shift) Steering Column

---

5) Remove 3 column housing cover screws. Remove tilt lever. Remove column housing cover. Remove column housing cover end cap and dimmer switch rod actuator assembly. Separate dimmer switch rod actuator from end cap. Remove washer/wiper switch actuator pivot pin. Remove washer/wiper switch.

6) Using screwdriver, push down and turn counterclockwise to release and remove tilt spring retainer. Remove tilt spring and spring guide. Using Pivot Pin Remover (J-21854-01), remove tilt pivot pins from steering column. Reinstall tilt lever. Pull back on tilt lever and pull column housing down and away, separating housing from column.

7) Remove bearing assembly. Remove shaft lock bolt spring screw, lock bolt spring and shaft lock bolt. Remove ignition switch actuator rack and rack preload spring. Remove drive shaft. Remove switch actuator sector. Using Lock Shoe/Release Lever Pin Remover/Installer (J-22635), remove release lever pin. Remove shoe release lever and release lever spring.

8) Using Lock Shoe/Release Lever Pin Remover/Installer (J-22635), remove lock shoe dowel pin. Remove lock shoes and lock shoe springs from column housing. Mark upper steering shaft to lower steering shaft for reassembly reference. Tilt lower steering shaft up

90-degree angle and separate from upper steering shaft. Rotate upper steering shaft centering sphere 90 degrees and slip out of upper shaft. Remove joint preload spring from centering sphere.

9) Remove 4 steering column housing support screws. Remove steering column housing support and dimmer switch actuator rod assembly. Remove dimmer switch actuator rod from column housing support. Remove shift lever gate retaining screws and remove shift lever gate from column housing support.

10) Disconnect dimmer switch electrical connector. Remove dimmer switch retaining screws and remove dimmer switch. Remove ignition switch retaining screw and remove ignition switch and actuator rod. Separate ignition switch actuator rod from switch. Remove lock plate from steering column support. Remove key release lever and key release spring from gearshift bowl shroud. Separate key release spring and release lever finger pad from key release lever.

11) Remove gearshift bowl shroud from steering column. Remove lower bearing adapter clip from bottom of steering column. Remove lower bearing adapter retainer, adapter and bearing assembly.

Reassembly – 1) To reassemble, reverse disassembly procedure. Lubricate adapter and bearing assembly with lithium grease before installation. Install joint preload spring onto centering sphere. Lubricate upper steering shaft centering sphere with lithium grease. Insert centering sphere into upper steering shaft and rotate 90 degrees. Tilt lower steering shaft up to 90-degree angle and attach to upper steering shaft aligning marks made during disassembly procedure.

NOTE: Ensure upper and lower steering shafts are properly assembled with marks made during disassembly properly aligned. Failure to properly assemble steering shafts will cause steering wheel to be incorrectly positioned by 180 degrees.

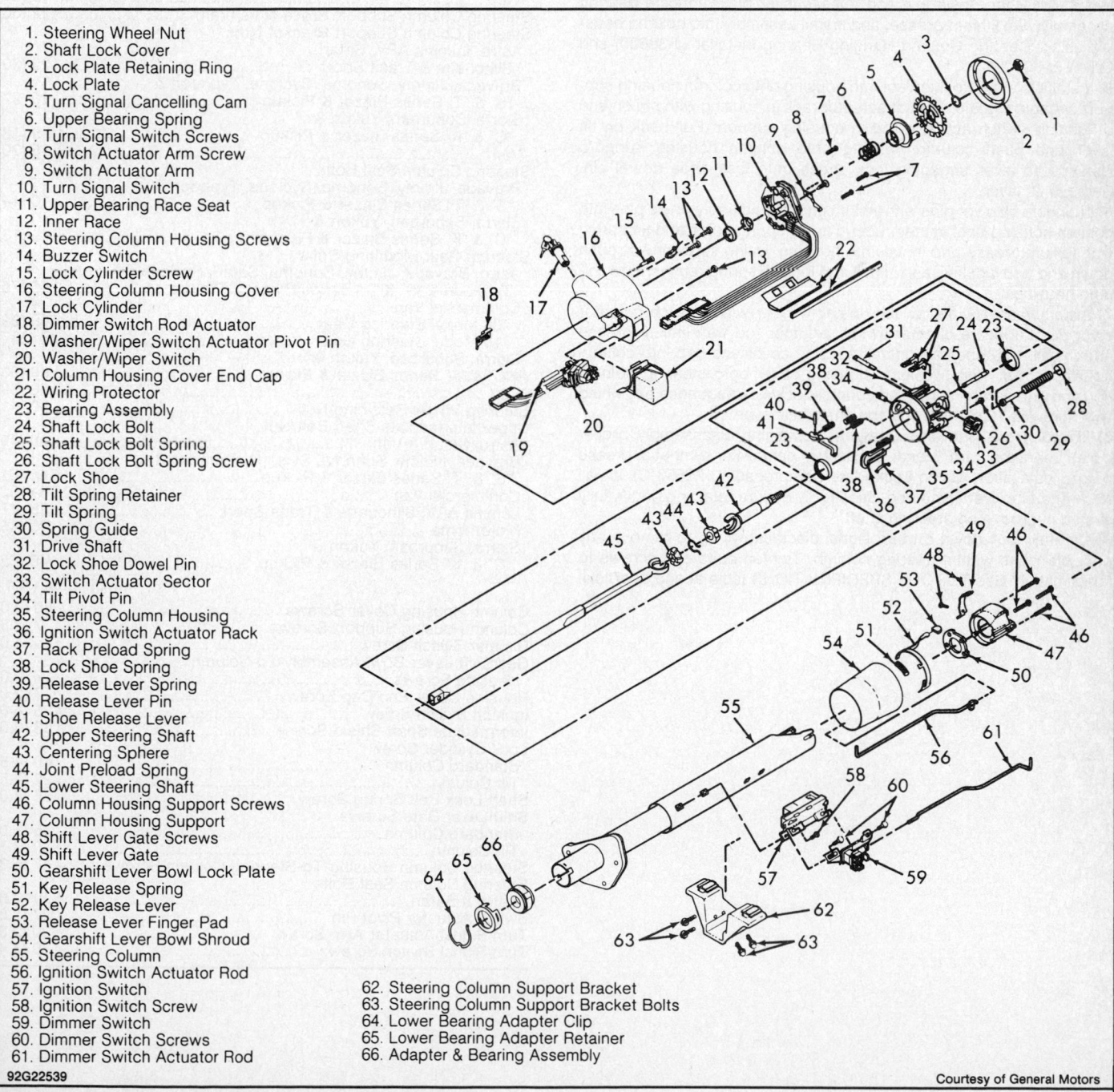

1. Steering Wheel Nut
2. Shaft Lock Cover
3. Lock Plate Retaining Ring
4. Lock Plate
5. Turn Signal Cancelling Cam
6. Upper Bearing Spring
7. Turn Signal Switch Screws
8. Switch Actuator Arm Screw
9. Switch Actuator Arm
10. Turn Signal Switch
11. Upper Bearing Race Seat
12. Inner Race
13. Steering Column Housing Screws
14. Buzzer Switch
15. Lock Cylinder Screw
16. Steering Column Housing Cover
17. Lock Cylinder
18. Dimmer Switch Rod Actuator
19. Washer/Wiper Switch Actuator Pivot Pin
20. Washer/Wiper Switch
21. Column Housing Cover End Cap
22. Wiring Protector
23. Bearing Assembly
24. Shaft Lock Bolt
25. Shaft Lock Bolt Spring
26. Shaft Lock Bolt Spring Screw
27. Lock Shoe
28. Tilt Spring Retainer
29. Tilt Spring
30. Spring Guide
31. Drive Shaft
32. Lock Shoe Dowel Pin
33. Switch Actuator Sector
34. Tilt Pivot Pin
35. Steering Column Housing
36. Ignition Switch Actuator Rack
37. Rack Preload Spring
38. Lock Shoe Spring
39. Release Lever Spring
40. Release Lever Pin
41. Shoe Release Lever
42. Upper Steering Shaft
43. Centering Sphere
44. Joint Preload Spring
45. Lower Steering Shaft
46. Column Housing Support Screws
47. Column Housing Support
48. Shift Lever Gate Screws
49. Shift Lever Gate
50. Gearshift Lever Bowl Lock Plate
51. Key Release Spring
52. Key Release Lever
53. Release Lever Finger Pad
54. Gearshift Lever Bowl Shroud
55. Steering Column
56. Ignition Switch Actuator Rod
57. Ignition Switch
58. Ignition Switch Screw
59. Dimmer Switch
60. Dimmer Switch Screws
61. Dimmer Switch Actuator Rod
62. Steering Column Support Bracket
63. Steering Column Support Bracket Bolts
64. Lower Bearing Adapter Clip
65. Lower Bearing Adapter Retainer
66. Adapter & Bearing Assembly

92G22539

Courtesy of General Motors

Fig. 8: Exploded View Of Tilt (Floor Shift) Steering Column

2) Lubricate steering shaft with lithium grease and install shaft into steering column. Move ignition switch slider to far right position and then back one detent to left. *See Fig. 5.* Ignition switch should now be in OFF/LOCK position.

NOTE: Install ignition switch with switch in OFF/LOCK position. New ignition switch will be pinned in OFF/LOCK position; plastic pin must be removed after installation of ignition switch to steering column.

3) Install ignition switch onto steering column. Install dimmer switch actuator rod. Connect dimmer switch to actuator rod. Place a 3/32" drill bit into hole on dimmer switch. Position dimmer switch onto steering column and push against actuator rod to remove lash. Remove drill bit and tighten dimmer switch retaining screws. Connect ignition switch and dimmer switch electrical connectors.

4) Using Lock Shoe/Release Lever Pin Remover/Installer (J-22635), install lock shoe dowel pin and release lever pin. Lubricate bearing assembly with lithium grease, and install assembly into column housing using Steering Column Hanging Bearing Installer (J-38630) and Driver (J-8092).

5) Install tilt lever. Position column housing onto column housing support engaging ignition switch actuator rack in housing with pin on end of ignition switch actuator rod in housing support. Pull back on tilt lever and push column housing onto column housing support. Release tilt lever engaging lock shoes onto lock shoe dowel pin. Remove tilt lever.

6) Lubricate tilt pivot pins with lithium grease and firmly press pins into column housing until seated. Lubricate tilt spring guide and tilt spring with lithium grease and install into housing. Using screwdriver, push down and turn clockwise to install and lock tilt spring retainer into column housing.

7) Install washer/wiper switch. Install washer/wiper switch actuator pivot pin. Lubricate dimmer switch actuator rod with lithium grease and install onto end cap. Install housing cover end cap into column housing cover. Install column housing cover onto steering column housing and tighten screws in counterclockwise sequence beginning with screw in 12 o'clock position. Install tilt lever.

8) To complete installation, reverse remaining disassembly procedure. Lubricate turn signal cancelling cam with synthetic grease before installation. Using Lock Plate Compressor (J-23653-C), install NEW shaft lock retaining ring. *See Fig. 2.* Ensure retaining ring is fully seated in groove on steering shaft.

9) Carefully pull down on turn signal electrical wiring to remove any possible kinks within steering column. Tighten bolts and screws to specification. See TORQUE SPECIFICATIONS table at end of article.

TORQUE SPECIFICATIONS

TORQUE SPECIFICATIONS

Application	Ft. Lbs. (N.m)
Lower Intermediate Shaft Bolt	
Astro, Safari & Van	30 (41)
Bravada, Jimmy, Sonoma, Syclone, Typhoon & "S" & "T" Series Blazer & Pickup	26 (35)
Commercial Van	75 (102)
Lumina APV, Silhouette & Trans Sport	35 (47)
Motorhome	33 (45)
Sierra, Suburban, Yukon & "C" & "K" Series Blazer & Pickup	22 (30)
Steering Column Support Bracket Bolts	
Bravada, Jimmy, Sonoma, Syclone, Typhoon & "S" & "T" Series Blazer & Pickup	22 (30)
Commercial Van	18 (25)
Lumina APV, Silhouette & Trans Sport	21 (29)
Van	15 (20)
Steering Column Support Brace Nuts (Van)	22 (30)
Steering Column Support Bracket Nuts	
Astro, Lumina APV, Safari, Silhouette & Trans Sport	22 (30)
Bravada, Jimmy, Sonoma, Syclone, Typhoon & "S" & "T" Series Blazer & Pickup	20 (27)
Sierra, Suburban, Yukon & "C" & "K" Series Blazer & Pickup	9 (13)
Van	15 (20)
Steering Column Seal Bolts	
Bravada, Jimmy, Sonoma, Syclone, Typhoon & "S" & "T" Series Blazer & Pickup	10 (14)
Sierra, Suburban, Yukon & "C" & "K" Series Blazer & Pickup	9 (13)
Steering Gear Mounting Bolts	
Astro, Bravada, Jimmy, Sonoma, Safari, Syclone, Typhoon & "S" & "T" Series Blazer & Pickup	55 (75)
Commercial Van	
708 Model Steering Gear	66 (89)
710 Model Steering Gear	175 (237)
Sierra, Suburban, Yukon & "C" & "K" Series Blazer & Pickup	69 (93)
Van	66 (89)
Steering Wheel Retaining Nut	30 (41)
Upper Intermediate Shaft Bolt/Nut	
Astro, Safari & Van	30 (41)
Bravada, Jimmy, Sonoma, Syclone, Typhoon & "S" & "T" Series Blazer & Pickup	45 (61)
Commercial Van	75 (102)
Lumina APV, Silhouette & Trans Sport	35 (47)
Motorhome	33 (45)
Sierra, Suburban, Yukon & "C" & "K" Series Blazer & Pickup	46 (62)

	INCH Lbs. (N.m)
Column Housing Cover Screws	80 (9.0)
Column Housing Support Screws	77 (8.8)
Dimmer Switch Screw	35 (4.0)
Gearshift Lever Bowl Assembly-To-Column	
Housing Screws	17 (2.0)
Housing Cover End Cap Screw	17 (2.0)
Ignition Switch Screw	35 (4.0)
Intermediate Shaft Shield Screw	53 (6.0)
Lock Cylinder Screw	
Standard Column	40 (4.5)
Tilt Column	22 (2.5)
Shaft Lock Bolt Spring Screw	35 (4.0)
Shift Lever Gate Screws	
Standard Column	45 (5.0)
Tilt Column	33 (3.7)
Steering Column Housing-To-Steering Column Screws	47 (5.3)
Steering Column Seal Bolts	
Astro & Safari	89 (10.0)
Switch Actuator Pivot Pin	27 (3.0)
Turn Signal Actuator Arm Screw	20 (2.3)
Turn Signal Switch Screws	30 (3.4)

Jimmy, Sonoma, "S" & "T" Series Blazer & Pickup

DESCRIPTION & OPERATION

Steering gear is a recirculating ball-type consisting of a ball nut connected to steering worm and in-mesh with sector gear. Proper engagement between sector and ball nut is obtained by adjusting screw. Worm bearing adjuster can be turned to provide proper preloading of upper and lower bearings. See Fig. 1.

Steering linkage connects steering gear to front wheels through pitman arm. Steering linkage consists of pitman arm, idler arm, relay rod and tie rods. See Figs. 2 and 3. Tie rod ends connect to relay rod by ball studs. Adjuster tubes between inner and outer tie rod ends are used to adjust toe. 4WD models have a shock absorber attached to relay rod.

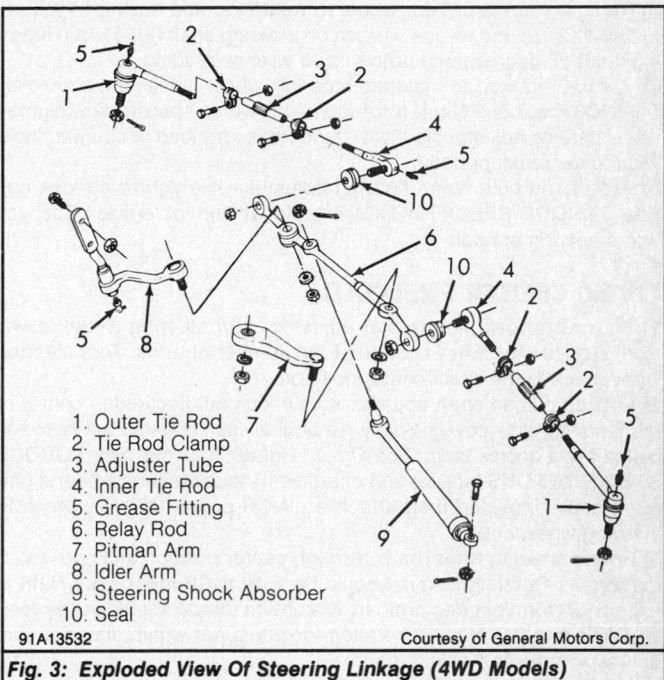

1. Outer Tie Rod
2. Tie Rod Clamp
3. Adjuster Tube
4. Inner Tie Rod
5. Grease Fitting
6. Relay Rod
7. Pitman Arm
8. Idler Arm
9. Steering Shock Absorber
10. Seal

91A13532   Courtesy of General Motors Corp.

Fig. 3: Exploded View Of Steering Linkage (4WD Models)

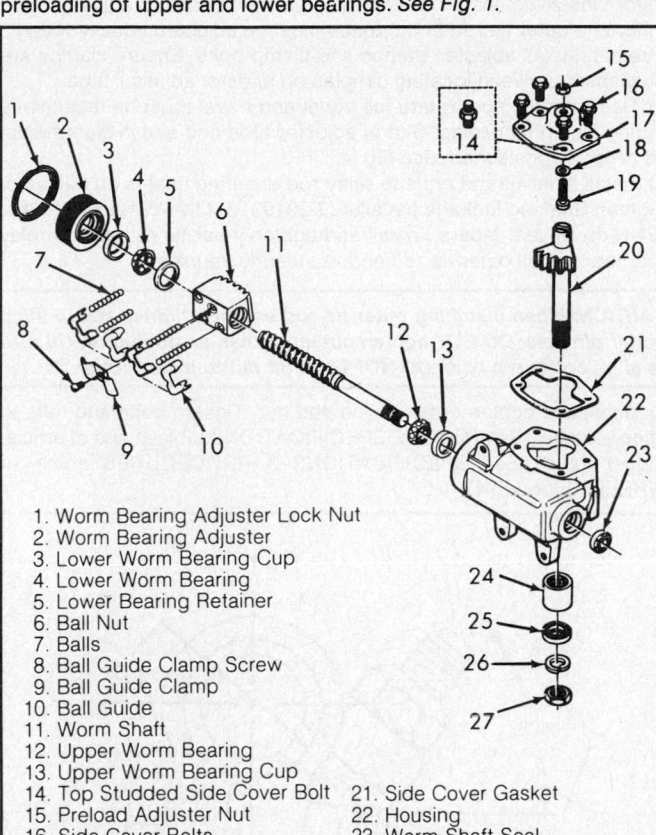

1. Worm Bearing Adjuster Lock Nut
2. Worm Bearing Adjuster
3. Lower Worm Bearing Cup
4. Lower Worm Bearing
5. Lower Bearing Retainer
6. Ball Nut
7. Balls
8. Ball Guide Clamp Screw
9. Ball Guide Clamp
10. Ball Guide
11. Worm Shaft
12. Upper Worm Bearing
13. Upper Worm Bearing Cup
14. Top Studded Side Cover Bolt
15. Preload Adjuster Nut
16. Side Cover Bolts
17. Side Cover
18. Preload Adjuster Shim
19. Preload Adjuster
20. Pitman Shaft
21. Side Cover Gasket
22. Housing
23. Worm Shaft Seal
24. Pitman Shaft Needle Bearing
25. Pitman Shaft Seal
26. Spring Washer
27. Pitman Arm Nut

91F13529   Courtesy of General Motors Corp.

Fig. 1: Exploded View Of Steering Gear

LUBRICATION

FLUID TYPE

Manufacturers recommend General Motors Steering Lubricant (1051052). DO NOT use EP chassis lube.

FLUID LEVEL CHECK

Steering gear is filled at factory with steering gear lubricant. Lubricant should NOT be changed and steering gear housing should NOT be drained. Additional lubricant should NOT be added to housing.

Steering gear should be inspected for seal leakage of solid grease during service intervals. Housing should be filled with specified lubricant only if a seal is replaced or steering gear is overhauled. DO NOT overfill system.

ADJUSTMENTS

WARNING: When battery is disconnected, vehicle computer and memory systems may lose memory data. Driveability problems may exist until computer systems have completed a relearn cycle. See COMPUTER RELEARN PROCEDURES article in GENERAL INFORMATION before disconnecting battery.

NOTE: Adjust worm bearing preload before performing over-center preload adjustment.

WORM BEARING PRELOAD

1) Inspect shock absorbers, wheel alignment, wheel balance and tire pressure for damage or steering problems before adjusting steering gear. Disconnect battery negative cable. Raise and support vehicle. On 4WD models, remove flexible coupling-to-intermediate shaft retaining screw and remove flexible coupling.
2) On all models, mark relationship of pitman arm-to-pitman shaft. Remove pitman arm nut and spring washer. Remove pitman arm

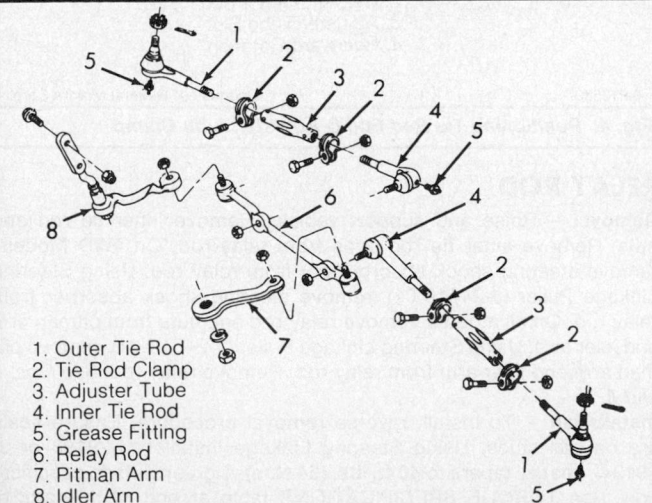

1. Outer Tie Rod
2. Tie Rod Clamp
3. Adjuster Tube
4. Inner Tie Rod
5. Grease Fitting
6. Relay Rod
7. Pitman Arm
8. Idler Arm

91J13531   Courtesy of General Motors Corp.

Fig. 2: Exploded View Of Steering Linkage (2WD Models)

using Puller (J-6632-01) or Remover (J-29107). Loosen worm bearing adjuster lock nut. Back off worm bearing adjuster 1/4 turn. *See Fig. 1.*

CAUTION: DO NOT turn steering wheel hard against stop with steering linkage disconnected or steering gear may be damaged.

3) Remove horn cap. Turn wheel to right stop and back off 1/2 turn. Install INCH-pound torque wrench on steering shaft nut. Rotate steering shaft 90 degrees and note torque wrench reading.

4) Torque required to maintain steering wheel movement should be **5-8 INCH lbs. (.6-.9 N.m).** If torque is not within specification, tighten worm bearing adjuster clockwise to increase preload or counterclockwise to decrease preload.

5) Adjust and hold worm bearing adjuster while tightening lock nut. See TORQUE SPECIFICATIONS table at end of article. Recheck worm bearing preload.

OVER-CENTER PRELOAD

1) With worm bearing preload adjusted, turn steering wheel slowly from stop-to-stop while counting total number of turns. Turn steering wheel back to the exact center position.

2) Loosen pitman shaft adjuster screw lock nut (located in center of pitman shaft side cover) clockwise until all lash is taken out between ball nut and sector teeth. *See Fig. 1.* Tighten lock nut. See TORQUE SPECIFICATIONS table at end of article. Rotate steering wheel slightly off center position then attach an INCH-pound torque wrench to steering wheel nut.

3) Rotate steering wheel back through center position and note rotating torque. Rotating torque should be **4-10 INCH lbs. (.5-1.1 N.m)** in excess of worm bearing preload. Maximum torque should not exceed **16 INCH lbs. (1.8 N.m).** If rotating torque is not within specification, adjust pitman shaft adjuster screw.

CAUTION: If maximum torque is exceeded, rotate pitman shaft adjuster screw counterclockwise and adjust by rotating lock nut clockwise.

4) After all adjustments are completed, install pitman arm onto pitman shaft. Ensure pitman arm-to-pitman shaft reference marks are aligned. Install pitman arm spring washer and nut. On 4WD models, install flexible coupling and flexible coupling-to-intermediate shaft retaining screw. Tighten bolts and nuts to specifications. See TORQUE SPECIFICATIONS table at end of article.

REMOVAL & INSTALLATION

WARNING: When battery is disconnected, vehicle computer and memory systems may lose memory data. Driveability problems may exist until computer systems have completed a relearn cycle. See COMPUTER RELEARN PROCEDURES article in GENERAL INFORMATION before disconnecting battery.

STEERING GEAR

Removal – 1) Position front wheels in straight-ahead position and note position of steering wheel. Disconnect battery negative cable. On 4WD models, remove flexible coupling-to-intermediate shaft retaining screw and remove flexible coupling. On 2WD models, remove shield from intermediate shaft. On all models, remove lower clamp bolt and lower clamp from worm shaft.

2) Mark relationship of pitman arm-to-pitman shaft. Remove pitman arm nut and spring washer. Remove pitman arm using Puller (J-6632-01) or Remover (J-29107). Remove steering gear mounting bolts and washers. Remove steering gear.

Installation – To install, reverse removal procedure. Check position of steering wheel. Ensure lower clamp bolt hole is aligned with groove in worm shaft. Ensure pitman arm-to-pitman shaft reference marks are aligned. Tighten bolts and nuts to specification. See TORQUE SPECIFICATIONS table at end of article.

INNER & OUTER TIE ROD ENDS

Removal – Raise and support vehicle. Remove cotter pins and outer tie rod end nuts. Remove inner tie rod end nuts. Using Wheel Stud and Tie Rod Remover (J-6627-A), remove outer tie rod ball studs from steering knuckle and inner tie rod ball studs from relay rod. Loosen adjuster tube clamp bolts and clamps. Unscrew and remove tie rod ends from adjuster tube.

Installation – 1) Lubricate tie rod end threads with chassis lubricant before installing. Install inner and outer tie rod ends to adjuster tube. Inner and outer tie rod end threads must be adjusted equally within 3 threads. Install adjuster clamps and clamp bolts. Ensure clamps are positioned between locating dimples on ends of adjuster tube.

2) Tie rod ends must rotate full travel and travel must be maintained during clamp tightening. Slot in adjuster tube and slot in clamp must be properly positioned. *See Fig. 4.*

3) Install inner tie rod ends to relay rod ensuring seal is on ball stud. Tighten Steering Linkage Installer (J-29193) or (J-29194) to **40 ft. lbs. (54 N.m)** to seat tapers. Install and tighten inner tie rod end-to-relay rod nuts. Install outer tie rod end to steering knuckle.

CAUTION: When installing outer tie rod end nut, tighten nut to align cotter pin hole. DO NOT tighten nut more than an additional 1/6 turn to align cotter pin hole. DO NOT back off nut to insert cotter pin.

4) Install and tighten outer tie rod end nut. Tighten bolts and nuts to specifications. See TORQUE SPECIFICATIONS table at end of article. Adjust toe-in. See SPECIFICATIONS & PROCEDURES article in WHEEL ALIGNMENT.

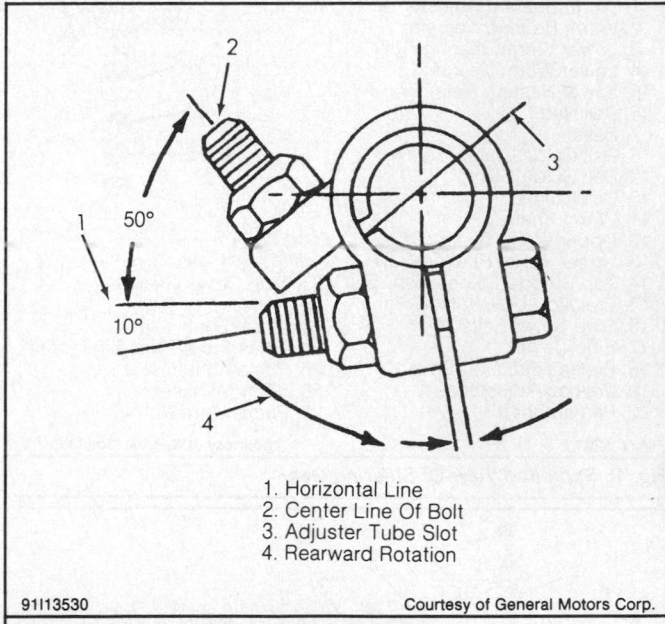

1. Horizontal Line
2. Center Line Of Bolt
3. Adjuster Tube Slot
4. Rearward Rotation

91I13530   Courtesy of General Motors Corp.

Fig. 4: Positioning Tie Rod End & Adjuster Tube Clamp

RELAY ROD

Removal – Raise and support vehicle. Remove inner tie rod end nuts. Remove inner tie rod ends from relay rod. On 4WD Models, remove steering shock absorber nut from relay rod. Using Steering Linkage Puller (J-24319-01), remove steering shock absorber from relay rod. On all models, remove relay rod end nuts from pitman arm and idler arm. Using Steering Linkage Puller (J-24319-01), remove pitman arm and idler arm from relay rod. Remove relay rod. *See Figs. 2 and 3.*

Installation – To install, reverse removal procedure. Ensure seals are on ball studs. Using Steering Linkage Installer (J-29193 or J-29194), seat all tapers to **40 ft. lbs. (54 N.m).** Tighten nuts to specification. See TORQUE SPECIFICATIONS table at end of this article. Adjust toe-in. See SPECIFICATIONS & PROCEDURES article in WHEEL ALIGNMENT.

IDLER ARM

NOTE: Replace idler arm assembly if an up and down force of 25 ft. lbs. (110 N.m), applied at relay rod end of idler arm, produces a lash of more than 1/8" (3 mm) for a total of 1/4" (6 mm) in straight-ahead position. See Fig. 5.

Removal – Raise and support vehicle. Remove idler arm-to-frame nut and bolt. Remove idler arm nut and spring washer from relay rod. Using Steering Linkage Puller (J-24319-01), remove idler arm from relay rod. Remove idler arm. *See Figs. 2 and 3.*

Installation – To install, reverse removal procedure. Ensure seal is on ball stud. Using Steering Linkage Installer (J-29193 or J-29194), seat tapers to **40 ft. lbs. (54 N.m).** Tighten nuts to specification. See TORQUE SPECIFICATIONS table at end of article. Adjust toe-in. See SPECIFICATIONS & PROCEDURES article in WHEEL ALIGNMENT.

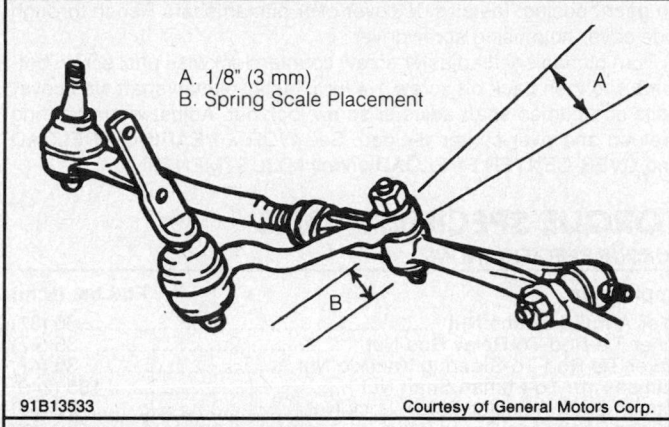

A. 1/8" (3 mm)
B. Spring Scale Placement

91B13533   Courtesy of General Motors Corp.

Fig. 5: Checking Idler Arm Play

PITMAN ARM

Removal – **1)** Raise and support vehicle. Disconnect air induction assembly. Slide up intermediate shaft cover. Mark intermediate shaft for reassembly. Remove intermediate shaft. Disconnect oil filter lines at crossmember bracket. Remove splash shield.
2) Remove pitman arm nut and spring washer from relay rod. Using Steering Linkage Puller (J-24319-01), remove pitman arm from relay rod.
3) Remove lower steering gear bolts. LOOSEN upper steering gear bolt. Rotate steering gear for pitman arm clearance at crossmember and support with block of wood.
4) Mark relationship of pitman arm-to-pitman shaft position. Remove pitman arm nut and spring washer from pitman shaft. Using Remover (J-6632-01) or Puller (J-29107), remove pitman arm from pitman shaft. *See Figs. 2 and 3.*

Installation – To install, reverse removal procedure. Ensure pitman arm-to-pitman shaft reference marks are aligned. Ensure seal is on ball stud. Using Steering Linkage Installer (J-29193 or J-29194), seat tapers to **40 ft. lbs. (54 N.m).** Tighten nuts to specification. See TORQUE SPECIFICATIONS table at end of article.

PITMAN SHAFT SEAL

NOTE: Pitman shaft seal may be replaced without removing steering gear from vehicle.

Removal – **1)** Position front wheels in straight-ahead position and note position of steering wheel. Disconnect battery negative cable. Mark relationship of pitman arm-to-pitman shaft. Remove pitman arm nut and spring washer. Remove pitman arm using Puller (J-6632-01) or Remover (J-29107).
2) Remove pitman shaft side cover bolts. Remove pitman shaft and side cover assembly from housing. Pry pitman shaft seal from housing using a screwdriver. DO NOT damage housing bore. Remove pitman shaft adjuster screw lock nut. Remove pitman shaft side cover from sector assembly by turning adjuster screw clockwise.

3) Inspect gear lubricant for contamination. If lubricant is contaminated in any way, gear must be removed and overhauled.
Installation – **1)** Lubricate NEW pitman shaft seal with steering gear lubricant. Position seal in pitman shaft bore and tap it into place using a 1" (25 mm) pipe or socket.
2) Install pitman shaft into steering gear ensuring center tooth of sector enters center tooth space of ball nut. Fill gear housing with lubricant, and install NEW side cover gasket on gear housing. Install side cover over pitman shaft. Reach through side cover hole using screwdriver.
3) Turn pitman shaft adjuster screw counterclockwise until screw bottoms and then back off screw 1/4 turn. Install pitman shaft side cover bolts and pitman shaft adjuster screw lock nut. Adjust worm bearing preload and over-center preload. See WORM BEARING PRELOAD and OVER-CENTER PRELOAD under ADJUSTMENTS.
4) Install pitman arm on pitman shaft. Ensure pitman arm-to-pitman shaft reference marks are aligned. Tighten bolts and nuts to specification. See TORQUE SPECIFICATIONS table at end of article.

STEERING SHOCK ABSORBER

Removal (4WD) – Remove steering shock absorber nut from relay rod. Using Steering Linkage Puller (J-24319-01), remove steering shock absorber from relay rod. Remove steering shock absorber-to-frame cotter pin, nut and bolt. Remove steering shock absorber. *See Fig. 3.*
Installation – To install, reverse removal procedure. Ensure seal is on ball stud. Using Steering Linkage Installer (J-29193 or J-29194), seat tapers to **40 ft. lbs. (54 N.m).** Tighten nuts to specification. See TORQUE SPECIFICATIONS table at end of article.

OVERHAUL

DISASSEMBLY

1) Place steering gear in vise, clamping onto one mounting tab. Worm shaft should be in a horizontal position. Rotate worm shaft from stop to stop while counting total number of turns. Turn worm shaft back to exact center position.
2) Loosen pitman shaft adjuster screw lock nut. Remove pitman shaft side cover bolts. Remove pitman shaft and side cover assembly from housing.
3) Loosen worm bearing adjuster lock nut. Remove worm bearing adjuster with lower bearing cup, bearing and bearing retainer. *See Fig. 1.* Remove ball nut and worm shaft assembly.

CAUTION: DO NOT allow ball nut to rotate down to either end of worm shaft, as ball guide ends may be damaged.

4) Remove remaining upper bearing and bearing cup from housing. Using screwdriver, pry lower bearing retainer from worm bearing adjuster assembly and remove lower bearing. Remove pitman shaft adjuster screw lock nut.
5) Hold pitman shaft side cover from sector assembly by turning adjuster screw clockwise. Remove pitman shaft adjuster screw and shim from pitman shaft. Pry out and discard both pitman shaft and worm shaft seals. Remove pitman shaft needle bearing and worm shaft upper bearing only if replacement is necessary.

CLEANING & INSPECTION

Clean components with solvent and dry with compressed air. Inspect bearings and cups for signs of wear. Inspect pitman shaft fit at side cover. Check ball nut and worm shaft assembly for wear and straightness. Inspect housing for burrs.

COMPONENT SERVICE

Pitman Shaft Bearing Replacement – Support steering gear in an arbor press. Using Bearing Remover (J-6278), drive pitman shaft needle bearing from housing. Install NEW needle bearing into housing using Bearing Installer (J-35469 and J-8092).

Worm Shaft Lower Bearing Replacement (In Worm Bearing Adjuster) – Using slide hammer and Puller (J-29369-1), remove lower bearing retainer, bearing and bearing cup from worm bearing adjuster. Using Bearing Installer (J-35365), install bearing cup, lower bearing and bearing retainer in worm bearing adjuster.

Worm Shaft Upper Bearing Replacement (In Housing) – Using a hammer and punch, remove upper bearing and bearing cup from housing. Using Bearing Installer (J-35365), install NEW upper bearing and bearing cup in housing.

Ball Nut & Worm Shaft Assembly – Ball nut disassembly is only necessary if binding or tightness exists while rotating worm shaft. If disassembly is required, proceed to step **1**).

CAUTION: Note number of balls located in each circuit of ball nut. Correct amount must be installed in each circuit. Note direction of ball nut installation on worm shaft.

---

1) Remove ball guides retaining clamp. Pull guides from ball nut while catching balls in clean pan. DO NOT lose balls. Turn nut over and rotate worm shaft until all balls have been removed.

2) Remove worm shaft from ball nut. Wash parts, and inspect worm, nut grooves and ball bearings for indentations. Check ball guides for damage at ends where they deflect or pick up balls from helical path on worm shaft.

3) Measure distance between ball grooves of worm gear. Distance between grooves determines amount of balls to be installed in each circuit. See BALL USAGE table.

BALL USAGE

Groove Distance In. (mm)	Balls Per Circuit
.04 (1.0)	25
.10 (2.5)	27
.20 (5.0)	27

4) To reassemble ball nut and worm shaft, install ball nut with narrow end of ball nut teeth upward on right side (looking from steering wheel end of worm shaft). Install worm shaft. Ensure worm shaft is aligned with grooves in ball nut.

5) Install guides in ball nut. Install proper amount of balls in one guide hole while rotating worm shaft. Repeat procedure for remaining guide. Install guide clamps and bolts.

REASSEMBLY

1) Place steering gear housing in a vise with worm shaft bore horizontal and side cover opening facing upward. All seals, bushings and worm shaft bearing cups should be installed.

2) Place upper ball bearing over worm shaft. Install worm shaft and ball nut assembly into housing and up through the upper bearing cup and seal. Install lower bearing, bearing cup and bearing retainer in worm bearing adjuster.

3) Install worm shaft and worm bearing adjuster in housing. Tighten worm bearing adjuster until a slight amount of worm shaft end play exists. Install pitman shaft adjuster screw and shim in slotted end of pitman shaft.

4) Using feeler gauge, check clearance between adjuster screw and pitman shaft when holding adjuster screw upward. Clearance should not exceed .002" (.05 mm). If clearance exceeds specification, a different thickness shim should be installed.

5) Rotate worm shaft until ball nut is at center of its travel. Install pitman shaft into steering gear ensuring center tooth of sector enters center tooth of ball nut.

6) Fill gear housing with lubricant, and install NEW side cover gasket on gear housing. Install side cover over pitman shaft. Reach through side cover hole using screwdriver.

7) Turn pitman shaft adjuster screw counterclockwise until screw bottoms and then back off screw 1/4 turn. Install pitman shaft side bolts and pitman shaft adjuster screw lock nut. Adjust worm bearing preload and over-center preload. See WORM BEARING PRELOAD and OVER-CENTER PRELOAD under ADJUSTMENTS.

TORQUE SPECIFICATIONS
TORQUE SPECIFICATIONS

Application	Ft. Lbs. (N.m)
Idler Arm-To-Frame Nut	60 (81)
Inner Tie Rod-To-Relay Rod Nut	35 (47)
Outer Tie Rod-To-Steering Knuckle Nut	35 (47)
Pitman Arm-To-Pitman Shaft Nut	185 (249)
Pitman Shaft Adjuster Screw Lock Nut	22 (30)
Pitman Shaft Side Cover Bolts	32 (43)
Relay Rod-To-Idler Arm Nut	
2WD	35 (47)
4WD	60 (81)
Relay Rod-To-Pitman Arm Nut	
2WD	35 (47)
4WD	60 (81)
Steering Gear Lower Clamp Bolt	30 (41)
Steering Gear Mounting Bolts	55 (75)
Steering Shock Absorber	
To-Frame Nut	26 (35)
To-Relay Rod Nut	45 (61)
Tie Rod Adjuster Tube Clamp Bolt	14 (19)
Worm Bearing Adjuster Lock Nut	85 (115)

	INCH Lbs. (N.m)
Flexible Coupling Retaining Screw	50 (5.6)

Astro, Bravada, Commercial Van, Jimmy, Safari, Sierra, Sonoma, Suburban, Syclone, Typhoon, Van, Yukon, "C" & "K" Series Blazer & Pickup, "S" & "T" Series Blazer & Pickup

DESCRIPTION & OPERATION

Steering gear is a variable ratio, recirculating ball-type which acts as a rolling thread between worm shaft and rack piston. The worm shaft is supported at the lower end by a thrust bearing with 2 races. It is supported at the upper end by a bearing assembly in the adjuster plug. Control valves, located inside steering gear housing, direct power steering fluid to either side of rack piston. See Fig. 1.

Steering linkage connects steering gear to front wheels through pitman arm. Steering linkage consists of pitman arm, idler arm, relay rod and tie rods. See Figs. 2-12. Tie rod ends connect to relay rod by ball studs. Adjuster tubes between inner and outer tie rod ends are used to adjust toe. Some models have a shock absorber attached to relay rod.

Two different types of vane-type power steering pumps are used. The Model P pump is mounted inside the reservoir. See Fig. 20. The Model TC pump is mounted below the reservoir. See Fig. 21. On both models, the vanes are driven by a rotor and move fluid from the intake to the pressure cavities of pump ring.

LUBRICATION

FLUID TYPE

Manufacturer recommends General Motors Power Steering Fluid (1050017) or an equivalent meeting G.M. Specification No. 9985010. Failure to use proper fluid will cause hose and seal damage, resulting in fluid leaks.

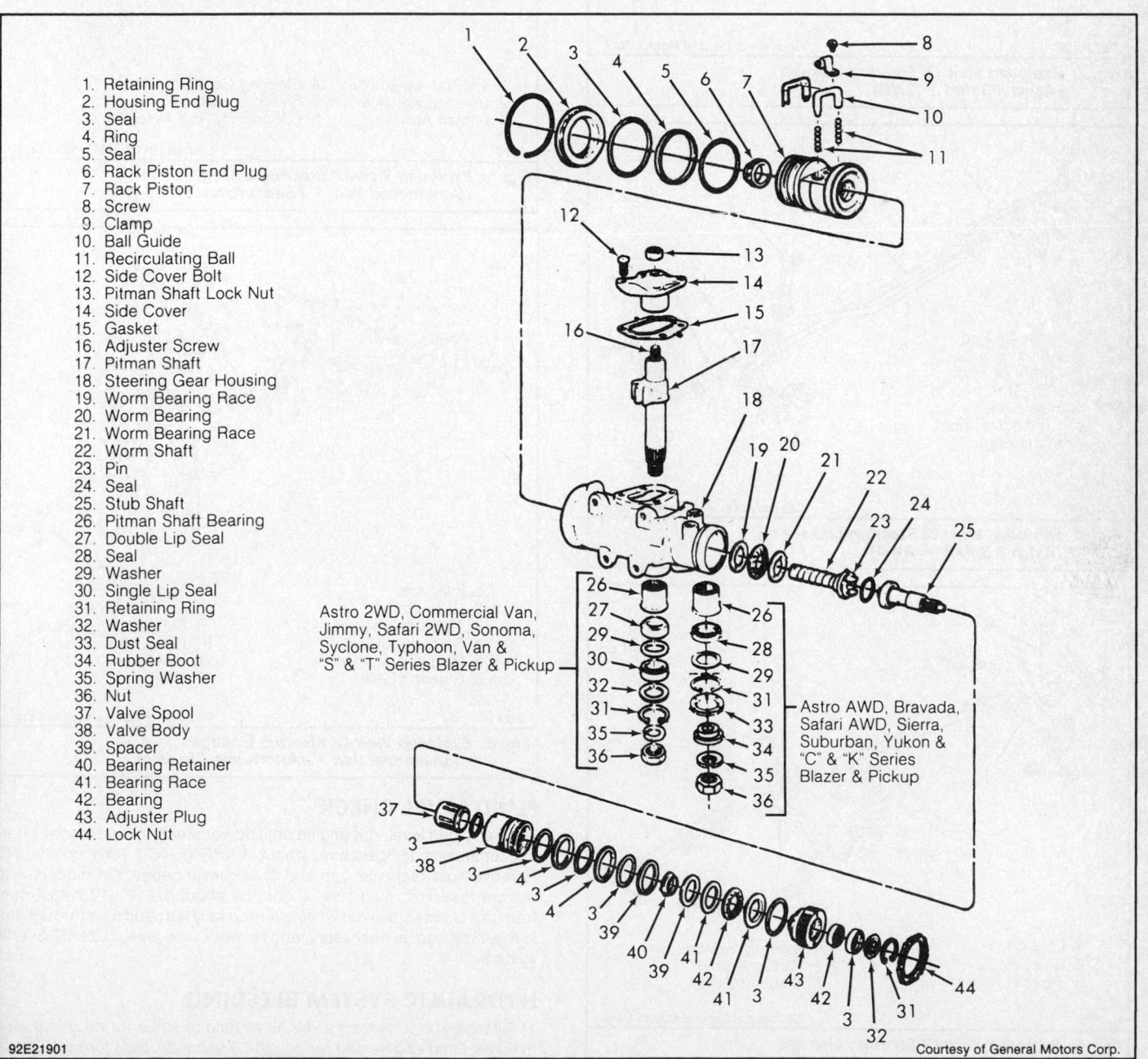

1. Retaining Ring
2. Housing End Plug
3. Seal
4. Ring
5. Seal
6. Rack Piston End Plug
7. Rack Piston
8. Screw
9. Clamp
10. Ball Guide
11. Recirculating Ball
12. Side Cover Bolt
13. Pitman Shaft Lock Nut
14. Side Cover
15. Gasket
16. Adjuster Screw
17. Pitman Shaft
18. Steering Gear Housing
19. Worm Bearing Race
20. Worm Bearing
21. Worm Bearing Race
22. Worm Shaft
23. Pin
24. Seal
25. Stub Shaft
26. Pitman Shaft Bearing
27. Double Lip Seal
28. Seal
29. Washer
30. Single Lip Seal
31. Retaining Ring
32. Washer
33. Dust Seal
34. Rubber Boot
35. Spring Washer
36. Nut
37. Valve Spool
38. Valve Body
39. Spacer
40. Bearing Retainer
41. Bearing Race
42. Bearing
43. Adjuster Plug
44. Lock Nut

Astro 2WD, Commercial Van, Jimmy, Safari 2WD, Sonoma, Syclone, Typhoon, Van & "S" & "T" Series Blazer & Pickup

Astro AWD, Bravada, Safari AWD, Sierra, Suburban, Yukon & "C" & "K" Series Blazer & Pickup

92E21901

Courtesy of General Motors Corp.

Fig. 1: Exploded View Of Power Steering Gear

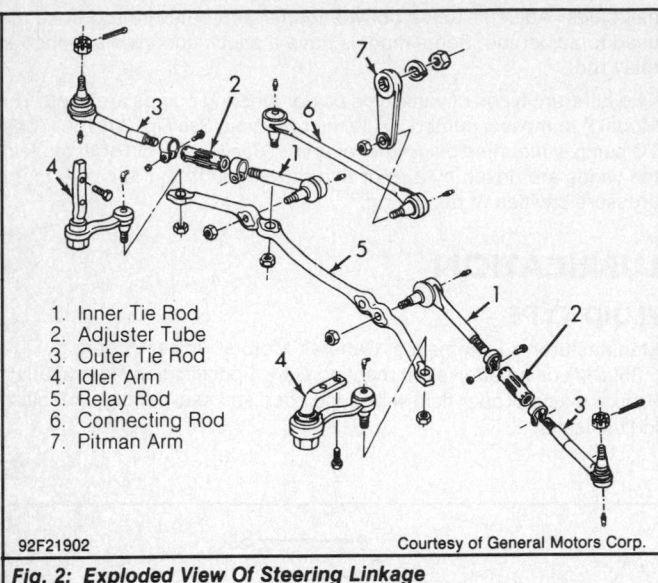

1. Inner Tie Rod
2. Adjuster Tube
3. Outer Tie Rod
4. Idler Arm
5. Relay Rod
6. Connecting Rod
7. Pitman Arm

92F21902   Courtesy of General Motors Corp.

Fig. 2: Exploded View Of Steering Linkage (Astro & Safari – 2WD)

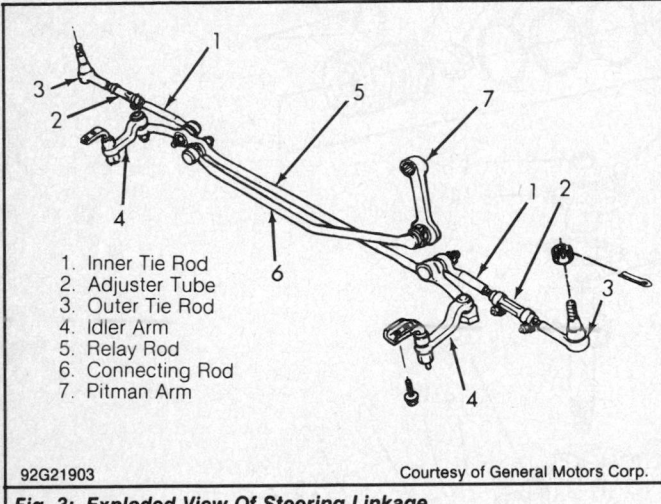

1. Inner Tie Rod
2. Adjuster Tube
3. Outer Tie Rod
4. Idler Arm
5. Relay Rod
6. Connecting Rod
7. Pitman Arm

92G21903   Courtesy of General Motors Corp.

Fig. 3: Exploded View Of Steering Linkage (Astro & Safari – AWD)

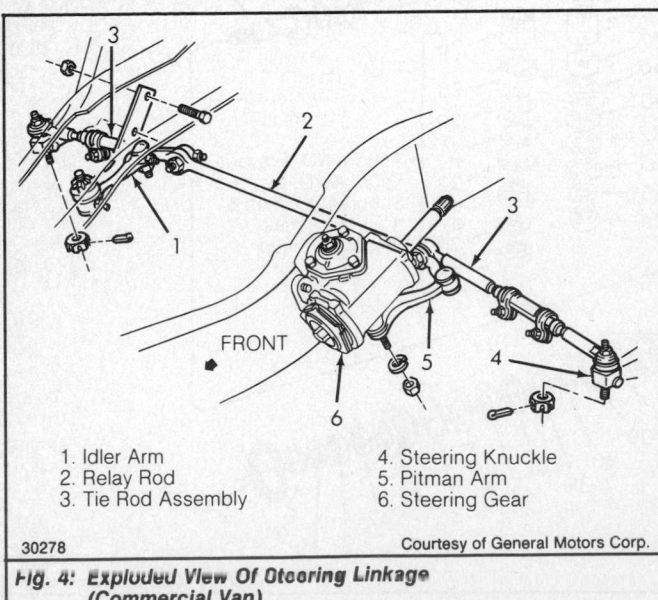

1. Idler Arm   4. Steering Knuckle
2. Relay Rod   5. Pitman Arm
3. Tie Rod Assembly   6. Steering Gear

30278   Courtesy of General Motors Corp.

Fig. 4: Exploded View Of Steering Linkage (Commercial Van)

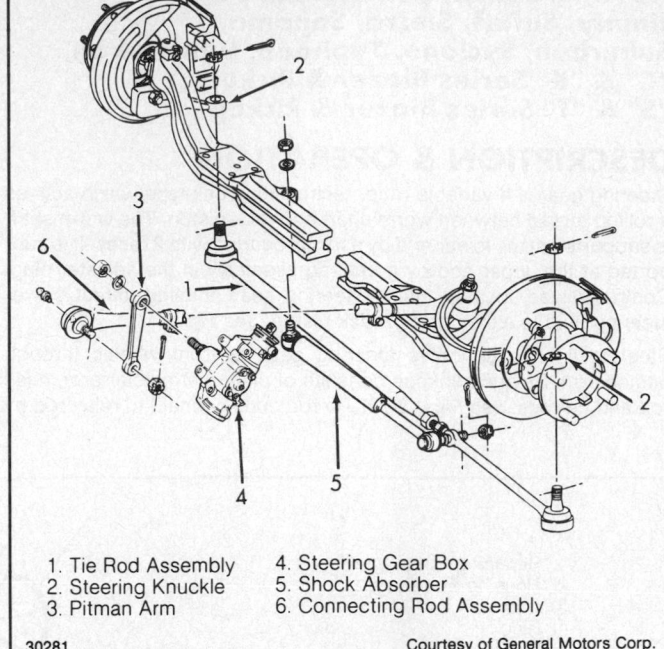

1. Tie Rod Assembly   4. Steering Gear Box
2. Steering Knuckle   5. Shock Absorber
3. Pitman Arm   6. Connecting Rod Assembly

30281   Courtesy of General Motors Corp.

Fig. 5: Exploded View Of Steering Linkage (Commercial Van – I-Beam Axle)

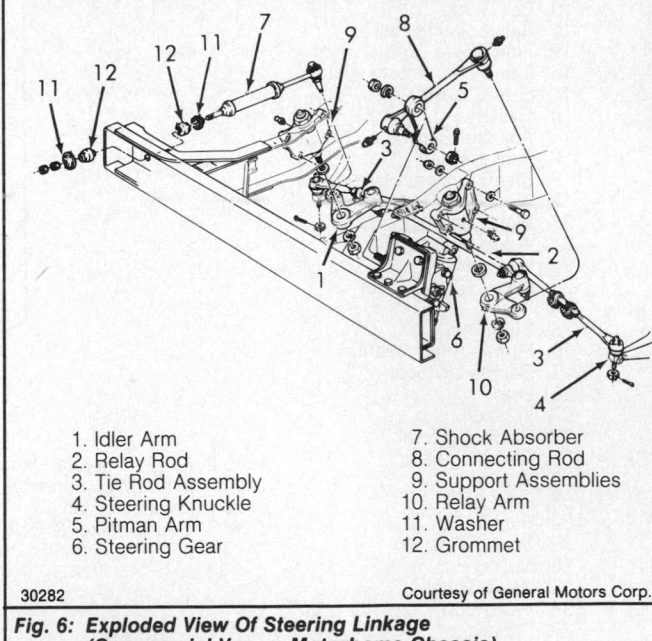

1. Idler Arm   7. Shock Absorber
2. Relay Rod   8. Connecting Rod
3. Tie Rod Assembly   9. Support Assemblies
4. Steering Knuckle   10. Relay Arm
5. Pitman Arm   11. Washer
6. Steering Gear   12. Grommet

30282   Courtesy of General Motors Corp.

Fig. 6: Exploded View Of Steering Linkage (Commercial Van – Motorhome Chassis)

FLUID LEVEL CHECK

To check fluid level, run engine until power steering fluid reaches normal operating temperature, about 170°F (77°C). Turn engine off. Remove fluid reservoir cap and check level gauge. On models with remote reservoir, fluid level should be about 1/2"-1" (12.7-25.4 mm) from top of reservoir with wheels turned fully left. Add fluid through fluid reservoir cap as necessary, and recheck fluid level. DO NOT overfill system.

HYDRAULIC SYSTEM BLEEDING

1) Fill reservoir to correct level. Allow fluid to settle for no less than 2 minutes. Start engine and run for 30-60 seconds, then turn off. Check fluid level and add fluid (as necessary). Repeat procedure until fluid level in reservoir remains constant.

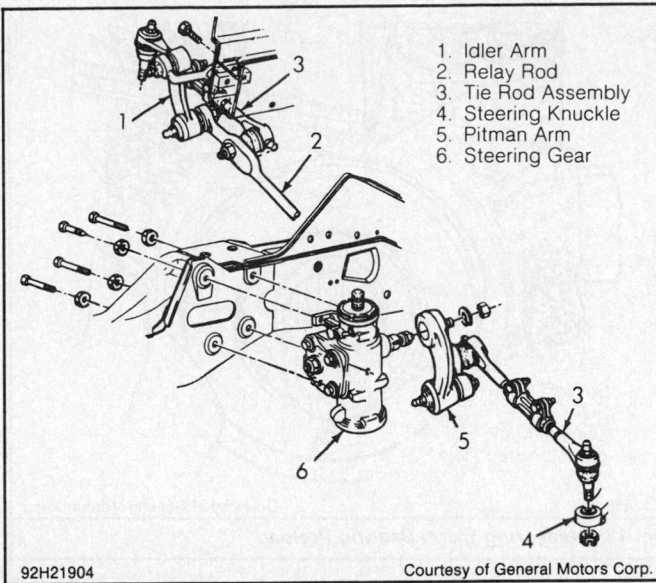

1. Idler Arm
2. Relay Rod
3. Tie Rod Assembly
4. Steering Knuckle
5. Pitman Arm
6. Steering Gear

92H21904   Courtesy of General Motors Corp.

Fig. 7: Exploded View Of Steering Linkage (Van)

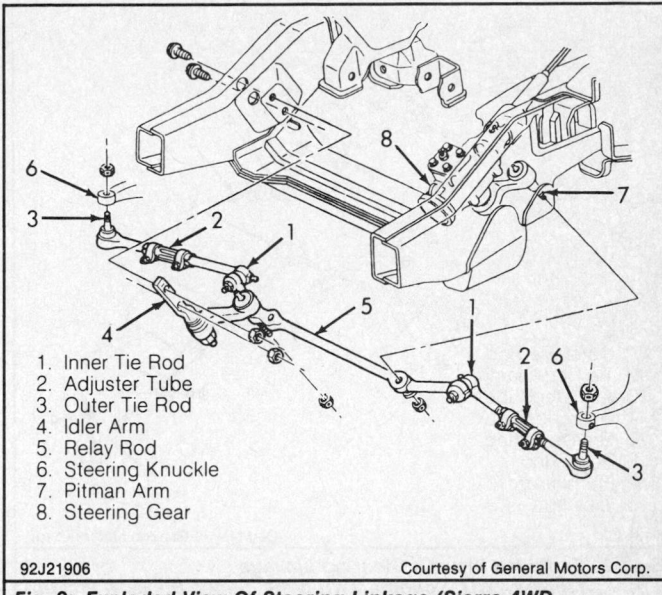

1. Inner Tie Rod
2. Adjuster Tube
3. Outer Tie Rod
4. Idler Arm
5. Relay Rod
6. Steering Knuckle
7. Pitman Arm
8. Steering Gear

92J21906   Courtesy of General Motors Corp.

Fig. 9: Exploded View Of Steering Linkage (Sierra 4WD, Suburban 4WD, Yukon & "K" Series Blazer & Pickup)

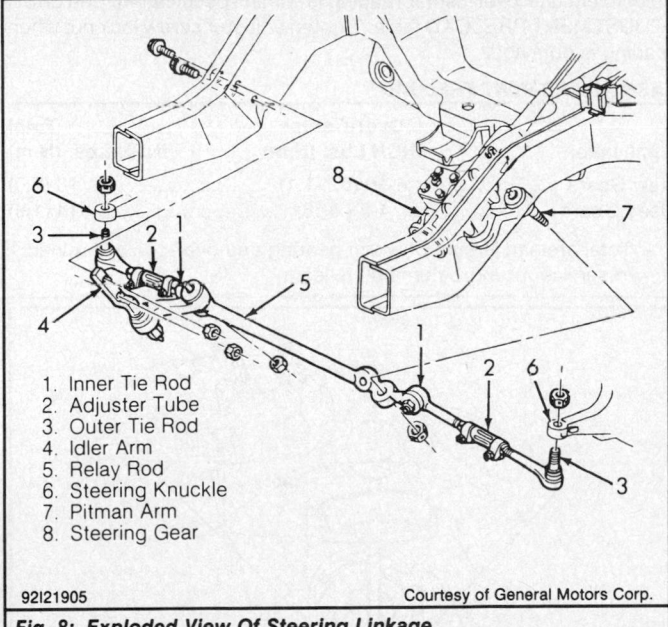

1. Inner Tie Rod
2. Adjuster Tube
3. Outer Tie Rod
4. Idler Arm
5. Relay Rod
6. Steering Knuckle
7. Pitman Arm
8. Steering Gear

92I21905   Courtesy of General Motors Corp.

Fig. 8: Exploded View Of Steering Linkage (Sierra 2WD, Suburban 2WD & "C" Series Blazer & Pickup)

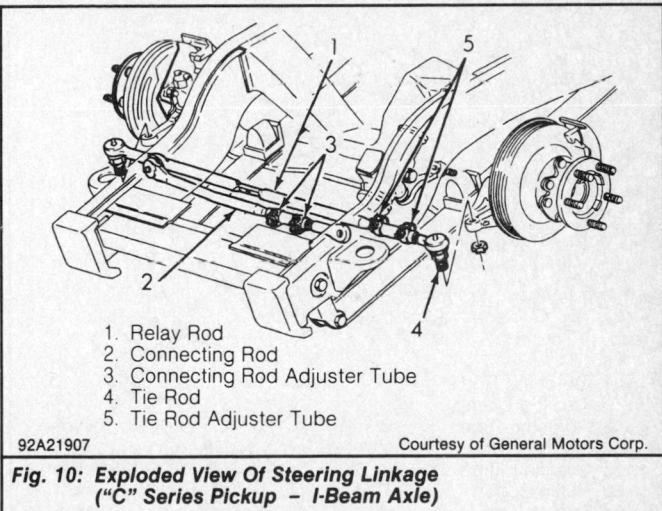

1. Relay Rod
2. Connecting Rod
3. Connecting Rod Adjuster Tube
4. Tie Rod
5. Tie Rod Adjuster Tube

92A21907   Courtesy of General Motors Corp.

Fig. 10: Exploded View Of Steering Linkage ("C" Series Pickup – I-Beam Axle)

2) Raise and support vehicle with both front wheels off the ground. Start engine. Turn wheels right and left, lightly contacting stops. Check fluid level and add fluid (as necessary).

3) Lower vehicle. Turn wheels right and left, slowly from lock to lock. Turn off engine. Check fluid level and add fluid (as necessary). If fluid is foamy, allow vehicle sit for a few minutes, repeat bleeding procedure.

ADJUSTMENTS

NOTE: Adjust worm bearing preload before performing over-center preload adjustment.

POWER STEERING PUMP BELT

BELT TENSION (Tension in Lbs. Using V-Belt Tension Gauge)

Application	New Belt	Used Belt
Serpentine Belt	[1]	[1]
"V" Belt	146	67

[1] – Serpentine belts are equipped with self-tensioner; adjustment is not required.

WORM BEARING PRELOAD

1) Remove steering gear from vehicle before performing preload adjustments and mount in vise. See STEERING GEAR under REMOVAL & INSTALLATION. Remove worm bearing adjuster lock nut. *See Fig. 1.* Using spanner wrench, turn adjuster plug clockwise until plug is seated in housing. Torque should be about **20 ft. lbs. (27 N.m).**

2) Index mark housing even with one hole in adjuster plug. *See Fig. 13.* Measure back 1/2" counterclockwise from first index mark. Mark housing with second index mark. Rotate adjuster plug back counterclockwise until hole in adjuster plug aligns with second index mark on housing. Install and tighten adjuster plug lock nut. Ensure adjuster plug remains in position.

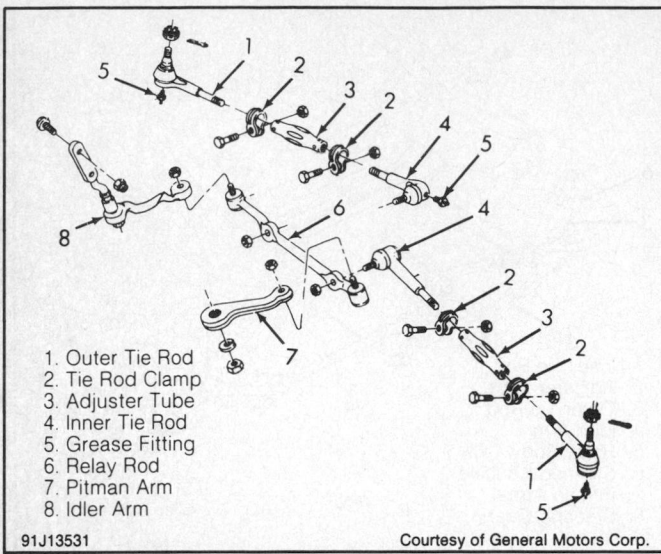

1. Outer Tie Rod
2. Tie Rod Clamp
3. Adjuster Tube
4. Inner Tie Rod
5. Grease Fitting
6. Relay Rod
7. Pitman Arm
8. Idler Arm

91J13531   Courtesy of General Motors Corp.

Fig. 11: Exploded View Of Steering Linkage (Jimmy 2WD, Sonoma 2WD & "S" Series Blazer & Pickup)

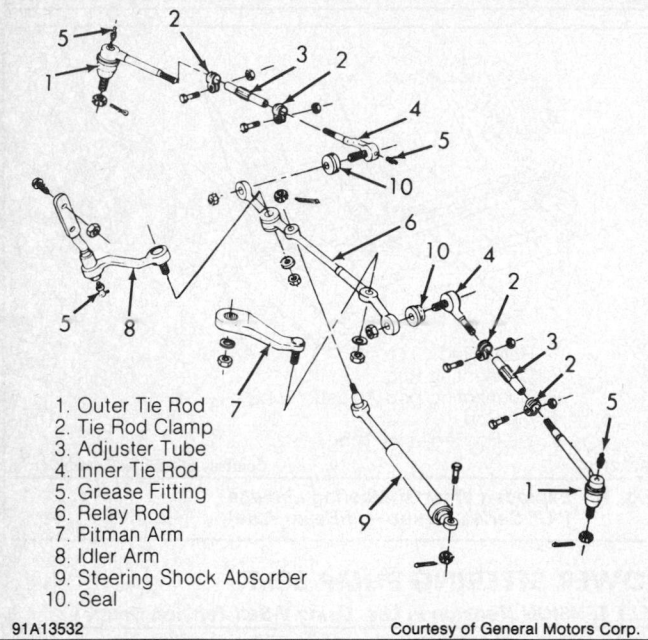

1. Outer Tie Rod
2. Tie Rod Clamp
3. Adjuster Tube
4. Inner Tie Rod
5. Grease Fitting
6. Relay Rod
7. Pitman Arm
8. Idler Arm
9. Steering Shock Absorber
10. Seal

91A13532   Courtesy of General Motors Corp.

Fig. 12: Exploded View Of Steering Linkage (Bravada, Jimmy 4WD, Sonoma 4WD, Syclone, Typhoon & "T" Series Blazer & Pickup)

OVER-CENTER PRELOAD

1) With worm bearing preload adjusted, rotate stub shaft slowly from stop to stop while counting total number of turns. With stub shaft positioned at either stop, rotate stub shaft back 2/3 total number of turns counted. Stub shaft should be back to the exact center position. Flat on stub shaft should be facing upward and parallel to side cover and master spline on pitman shaft should be aligned with adjuster screw.

2) Turn pitman shaft adjuster screw counterclockwise until extended, then back off one full turn. Place INCH-pound torque wrench in vertical position on end of stub shaft. Measure gear over-center torque by rotating torque wrench attached to stub shaft in a 90 degree arc, 45 degrees on each side of center. See Fig. 14. Record highest degree of arc on each side of center. Record highest reading.

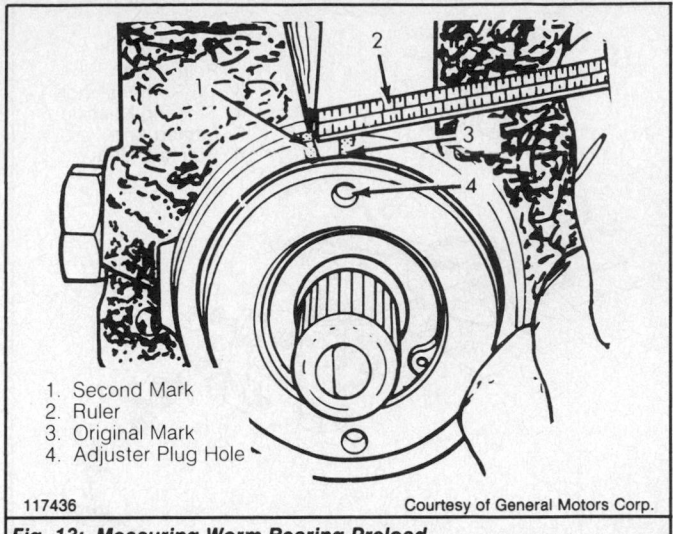

1. Second Mark
2. Ruler
3. Original Mark
4. Adjuster Plug Hole

117436   Courtesy of General Motors Corp.

Fig. 13: Measuring Worm Bearing Preload

3) Turn adjuster screw in until torque required to rotate stub shaft is 6-10 INCH lbs. (.6-1.1 N.m) greater than reading in step **2)**. Continue adjustment until over-center reading is within specification. See LASH ADJUSTMENT PRELOAD table. Tighten adjuster screw lock nut when reading is obtained.

LASH ADJUSTMENT PRELOAD

Application	Over-Center INCH Lbs. (N.m)	[1] Total INCH Lbs. (N.m)
New Gears	6-10 (0.7-1.1)	18 (2.0)
Used Gears [2]	4-5 (.5-.6)	14 (1.6)

[1] – Total preload is sum of worm bearing and over-center preload.
[2] – In service for more than 400 miles.

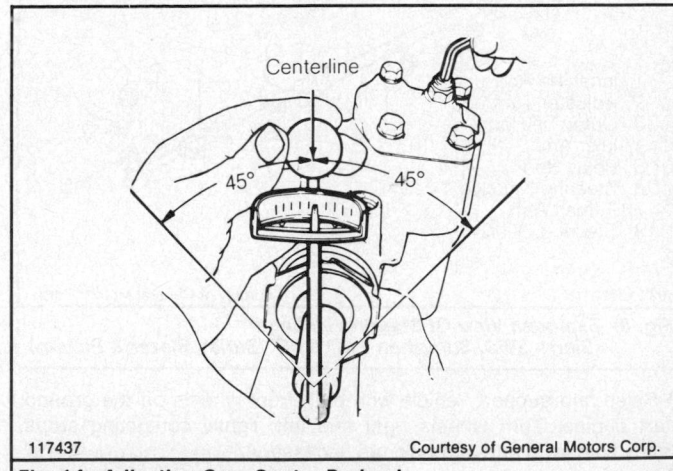

117437   Courtesy of General Motors Corp.

Fig. 14: Adjusting Over-Center Preload

TROUBLE SHOOTING

NOTE: See TROUBLE SHOOTING article in GENERAL INFORMATION.

TESTING

HYDRAULIC SYSTEM PRESSURE TEST

1) Ensure belt tension is correct. Disconnect high pressure line from power steering pump. Connect Power Steering Pressure Gauge (J-5176-D) hose to power steering pump fitting. Connect other hose from valve side of tester to steering gear inlet.

PUMP SPECIFICATIONS

Note: Idle pressure is 80-125 psi (6-9 kg/cm²).

Vehicle	Part Number	Model	Minimum Output [1]		Maximum Output [2]		Relief Valve Settings			
							Minimum		Maximum	
			GPM [3]	L/Min. [4]	GPM [3]	L/Min. [4]	PSI	kPa	PSI	kPa
Van	7841731	132-P-222	1.32	5.00	3.1-3.5	11.7-13.2	1350	9308	1450	9998
	26001536	132-P-267	1.32	5.00	3.1-3.5	11.7-13.2	1200	8274	1300	8964
Commercial Van	7839808	132-P-154	1.32	5.00	2.4-2.8	9.1-10.6	1200	8274	1300	8964
	7839809	132-P-155	1.32	5.00	2.4-2.8	9.1-10.6	1200	8274	1300	8964
	7839812	132-P-158	1.32	5.00	2.4-2.8	9.1-10.6	1350	9308	1450	9998
	7842032	132-P-226	1.32	5.00	3.1-3.5	11.7-13.2	1200	8274	1300	8964
	7842033	132-P-227	1.32	5.00	3.1-3.5	11.7-13.2	1200	8274	1300	8964
	7842490	132-P-231	1.32	5.00	2.4-2.8	9.1-10.6	1350	9308	1450	9998
	7842491	132-P-232	1.32	5.00	3.1-3.5	11.7-13.2	1200	8274	1300	8964

[1] – Output of Power Steering Fluid at 32°C (90°F) temperature when operating pump at 465 rpm against 4585-5068 kPa (665-735 psi) pressure.
[2] – Output of Power Steering Fluid at 32°C (90°F) temperature when operating pump at 1500 rpm against 345 kPa (50 psi) pressure.
[3] – Gallons Per Minutes
[4] – Liters Per Minute

92B21908

Courtesy of General Motors Corp.

Fig. 15: Pump Pressure Specifications (Commercial Van & Van)

2) Open valve on pressure gauge. Check fluid level, and add fluid (as necessary). Check for possible leaks at pressure gauge connections. Bleed air from system. See HYDRAULIC SYSTEM BLEEDING under LUBRICATION. Run engine until fluid reaches normal operating temperature of 150-170°F (66-77°C). Check fluid level, and add fluid (as necessary).
3) Note pressure reading with valve open and engine idling. Pressure should be **80-125 psi (6-9 kg/cm²)**. If pressure exceeds 200 psi (14 kg/cm²), check hoses for restrictions and poppet valve for proper assembly.

___

CAUTION: To prevent pump damage, DO NOT hold gauge valve closed for more than 5 seconds.

___

4) Completely close and open valve 3 times. Record highest reading each time. Readings should be within specifications. On Commercial Van and Van, see *Fig. 15*; on all other models, see PRESSURE TEST SPECIFICATIONS table.
5) If pressure readings are within specifications and within 50 psi (4 kg/cm²) of each other, pump is operating properly. On Commercial Van and Van, see *Fig. 15*; on all other models, see PRESSURE TEST SPECIFICATIONS table.
6) If readings are within specifications but not within 50 psi (4 kg/cm²) of each other, flow control valve in pump is sticking. Remove valve, but DO NOT disassemble it. Clean valve using crocus cloth or fine hone. Flush system if it is dirty. If it is exceptionally dirty, disassemble and clean pump and steering gear.
7) If pressure is constant but more than 100 psi (7 kg/cm²) below specifications, clean or replace flow control valve in pump. If readings are still low, replace pump.
8) If pressure readings are as specified, turn steering wheel from stop to stop with valve open. Record highest pressure with wheels at both stops. If highest pressure is not equal to highest pressure recorded in step **2)**, steering gear is leaking internally. Repair or replace assembly.
9) Turn engine off. Remove tester. Reconnect pressure hose. Check fluid level. Bleed hydraulic system. See HYDRAULIC SYSTEM BLEEDING under LUBRICATION.

PRESSURE TEST SPECIFICATIONS

Application	Idle Pressure psi (kg/cm²)	Relief Pressure psi (kg/cm²)
Astro & Safari	80-125 (6-9)	1250-1350 (87-95)
C15/25 & "K" Series	80-125 (6-9)	1200-1300 (84-91)
C35	80-125 (6-9)	1465-1515 (103-106)
C35 (With Hydro-Boost)	80-125 (6-9)	1350-1450 (95-102)
Bravada, "S" & "T" Series	80-125 (6-9)	1100-1200 (77-84)

REMOVAL & INSTALLATION

STEERING GEAR

Removal (Astro & Safari) – **1)** Remove hood latch and upper radiator fan shroud. Remove power steering pump belt. Remove fan assembly from water pump. Remove lower radiator fan shroud. Center steering gear. Raise and support vehicle.
2) Place drain pan under steering gear assembly. Disconnect return and feed lines from steering gear. Cap ends of lines and steering gear fittings. Remove intermediate shaft-to-steering shaft bolt and separate intermediate shaft from steering shaft.
3) Mark relationship of pitman arm-to-pitman shaft. Remove pitman arm nut and spring washer. Remove pitman arm using Puller (J-24319-01) or Remover (J-29107). Remove steering gear mounting bolts and washers. Remove steering gear.
Removal (Syclone & Typhoon) – **1)** Center steering gear. Raise and support vehicle. Place drain pan under steering gear assembly, and charge air cooler radiator. Disconnect return and feed lines from steering gear. Cap ends of lines and steering gear fittings. Remove shield from intermediate shaft. Mark alignment of lower clamp to intermediate shaft. Remove lower clamp bolt, and separate intermediate shaft from steering gear. Remove intermediate shaft-to-steering shaft bolt, and separate intermediate shaft from steering shaft.
2) Raise and support vehicle. Remove charge air cooler radiator. Mark relationship of pitman arm-to-pitman shaft. Remove pitman arm nut and spring washer. Remove pitman arm using Puller (J-24319-01) or Remover (J-29107). Remove steering gear mounting bolts and washers. Remove steering gear.

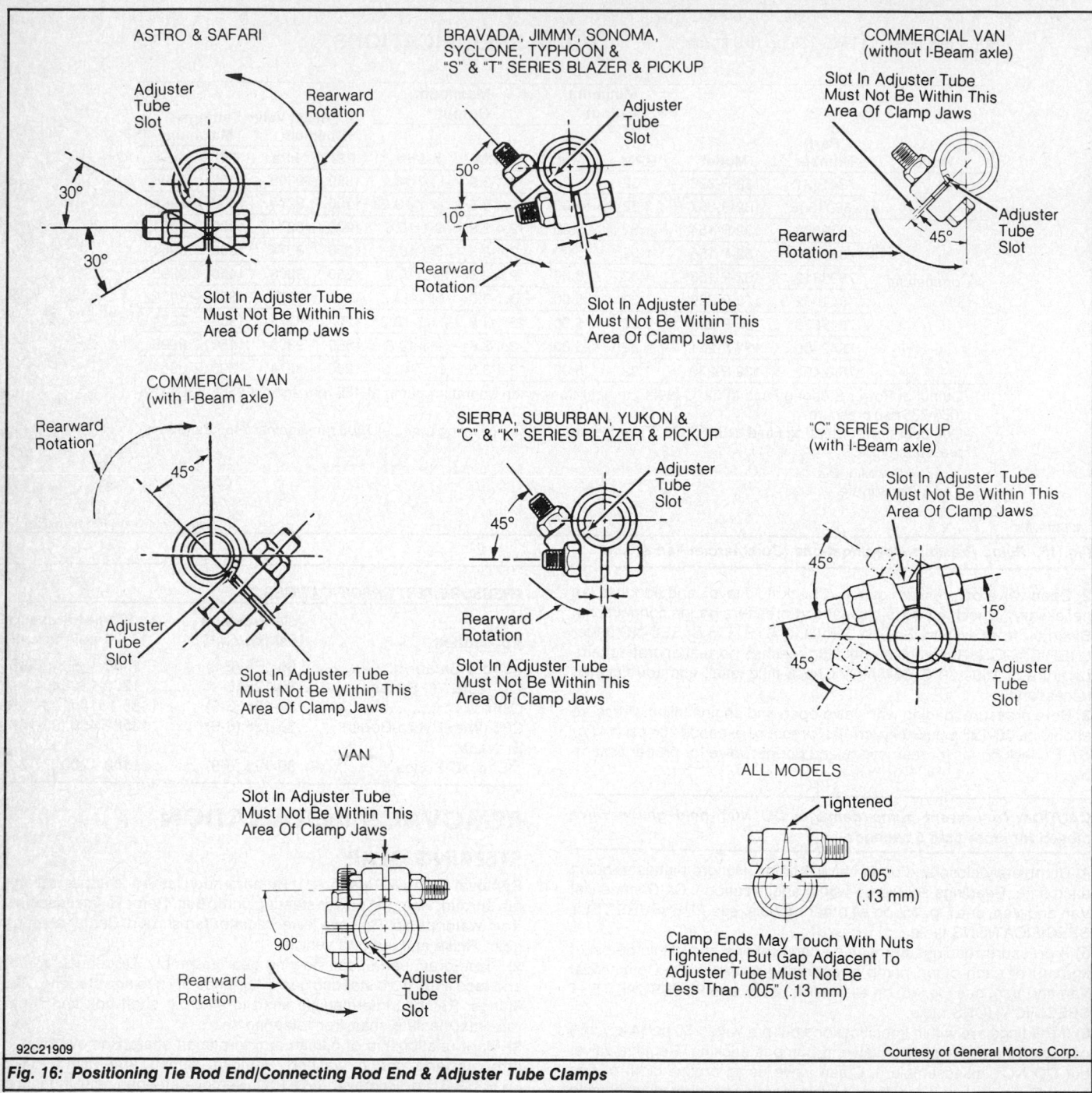

Fig. 16: Positioning Tie Rod End/Connecting Rod End & Adjuster Tube Clamps

Removal (Except Astro, Safari, Syclone & Typhoon) – 1) Center steering gear. Raise and support vehicle. Place drain pan under steering gear assembly. Disconnect return and feed lines from steering gear. Cap ends of lines and steering gear fittings. Remove flexible coupling-to-intermediate shaft retaining screw and remove flexible coupling (if equipped) or remove shield from intermediate shaft (if equipped).

2) Mark alignment of lower clamp to steering shaft. Remove lower clamp bolt from steering shaft. Mark relationship of pitman arm-to-pitman shaft. Remove pitman arm nut and spring washer. Remove pitman arm using Puller (J-6632-01) or Remover (J-29107). Remove steering gear mounting bolts and washers. Remove steering gear.

Installation (All Models) – To install, reverse removal procedure. Ensure lower clamp bolt hole is aligned with groove in worm shaft (if equipped). Ensure pitman arm-to-pitman shaft reference marks are aligned. Tighten bolts and nuts to specifications. See TORQUE SPEC-IFICATIONS table at end of article. Fill reservoir (if necessary). Bleed air from system. See HYDRAULIC SYSTEM BLEEDING under LUBRICATION.

POWER STEERING PUMP

Removal (Astro & Safari) – 1) Unload power steering pump belt tensioner. Remove power steering pump belt. Remove hood latch and upper radiator fan shroud. Using Pulley Remover (J-29785-A), remove pulley from pump shaft.

NOTE: DO NOT discharge A/C system.

2) On A/C equipped models, remove A/C compressor and secure aside. Place drain pan under steering pump assembly. Disconnect return and feed lines from steering pump. Cap ends of lines and steering pump fittings. Remove pump mounting bolts and remove pump.

Removal (Syclone & Typhoon) – 1) Remove air cleaner and duct. Remove upper radiator fan shroud. Unload power steering pump belt tensioner. Remove power steering pump belt. Remove radiator fan and water pump pulley. Using Pulley Remover (J-25034-B), remove pulley from pump shaft.

2) Raise and support vehicle. Remove left wheel and tire assembly. Remove left wheelwell panel. Place drain pan under steering pump assembly. Remove hose bracket bolt. Disconnect return and feed lines from steering pump. Cap ends of lines and steering pump fittings.

3) Remove pump-to-front bracket bolts. Remove pump rear bracket-to-alternator bolts. Remove pump and rear bracket assembly. Remove rear bracket-to-pump nuts and separate bracket from pump.

Removal (Except Astro, Safari, Syclone & Typhoon) – 1) Place drain pan under steering pump assembly. Disconnect return and feed lines from steering pump. Cap ends of lines and steering pump fittings.

2) Unload power steering pump belt tensioner (if equipped). Remove power steering pump belt. Remove bracket mounting nuts and remove bracket (if equipped). Using Pulley Remover (J-25034-B), remove pulley from pump shaft. Remove pump mounting bolts and remove pump.

Installation (All Models) – 1) To install, reverse removal procedure. Use Pulley Installer (J-25033-B) to install pulley. Install pulley flush with end of pump shaft plus or minus .010" (.25 mm). Tighten bolts and nuts to specifications. See TORQUE SPECIFICATIONS table at end of article. Fill reservoir (if necessary). Bleed air from system. See HYDRAULIC SYSTEM BLEEDING under LUBRICATION.

INNER & OUTER TIE ROD ENDS

Removal – Raise and support vehicle. Remove cotter pins and outer tie rod end nuts. Remove inner tie rod end nuts. Using Wheel Stud and Tie Rod Remover (J-6627-A), remove outer tie rod ball studs from steering knuckle and inner tie rod ball studs from relay rod. On Commercial Van with I-Beam Axle, remove shock absorber from tie rod. On all models, loosen adjuster tube clamp bolts and clamps. Unscrew and remove tie rod ends from adjuster tube.

Installation – 1) Lubricate tie rod end threads with chassis lubricant before installing. Install inner and outer tie rod ends to adjuster tube. Inner and outer tie rod end threads must be adjusted equally within 3 threads. Install adjuster clamps and clamp bolts. Ensure clamps are positioned between locating dimples on ends of adjuster tube.

2) Tie rod ends must rotate full travel and travel must be maintained during clamp tightening. See Fig. 16. Slot in adjuster tube and slot in clamp must be positioned as shown in Fig. 16.

3) Install inner tie rod ends to relay rod ensuring seal is on ball stud. Tighten Steering Linkage Installer (J-29193 or J-29194) to **40 ft. lbs. (54 N.m)** to seat tapers. Install and tighten inner tie rod end-to-relay rod nuts. Install outer tie rod end to steering knuckle.

CAUTION: When installing outer tie rod end nut, tighten nut to align cotter pin hole. DO NOT tighten nut more than an additional 1/6 turn to align cotter pin hole. DO NOT back off nut to insert cotter pin.

---

4) Install and tighten outer tie rod end nut. Tighten bolts and nuts to specifications. See TORQUE SPECIFICATIONS table at end of article. Adjust toe-in. See SPECIFICATIONS & PROCEDURES article in WHEEL ALIGNMENT.

RELAY ROD

Removal – 1) Raise and support vehicle. Remove inner tie rod end nuts. Remove inner tie rod ends from relay rod (if equipped). On models without inner tie rods, remove tie rod end-to-steering knuckle nuts. Separate tie rod ends from steering knuckle.

2) On all models, remove steering shock absorber nut from relay rod (if equipped). Using Steering Linkage Puller (J-24319-01), remove steering shock absorber from relay rod (if equipped). Remove connecting rod nut and remove connecting rod from relay rod (if equipped).

3) Remove relay rod end nuts from pitman arm and idler arm. Using Steering Linkage Puller (J-24319-01), remove pitman arm and idler arm from relay rod. Remove relay rod. See Figs. 2-12.

Installation – Reverse removal procedure. Ensure seals are on ball studs. Using Steering Linkage Installer (J-29193 or J-29194), seat all tapers to **40 ft. lbs. (54 N.m)**. Tighten nuts to specification. See TORQUE SPECIFICATIONS table at end of article. Adjust toe-in. See SPECIFICATIONS & PROCEDURES article in WHEEL ALIGNMENT.

IDLER ARM

NOTE: Replace idler arm assembly if an up and down force of 25 ft. lbs. (110 N.m), applied at relay rod end of idler arm, produces a lash of more than 1/8" (3 mm) for a total of 1/4" (6 mm) in straight-ahead position. See Fig. 17.

Removal – Raise and support vehicle. Remove idler arm-to-frame nut and bolt. Remove idler arm nut and spring washer from relay rod. Using Steering Linkage Puller (J-24319-01), remove idler arm from relay rod. Remove idler arm. See Figs. 2-12.

Installation – To install, reverse removal procedure. Ensure seal is on ball stud. Using Steering Linkage Installer (J-29193 or J-29194), seat tapers to **40 ft. lbs. (54 N.m)**. Tighten nuts to specification. See TORQUE SPECIFICATIONS table at end of article. Adjust toe-in. See SPECIFICATIONS & PROCEDURES article in WHEEL ALIGNMENT.

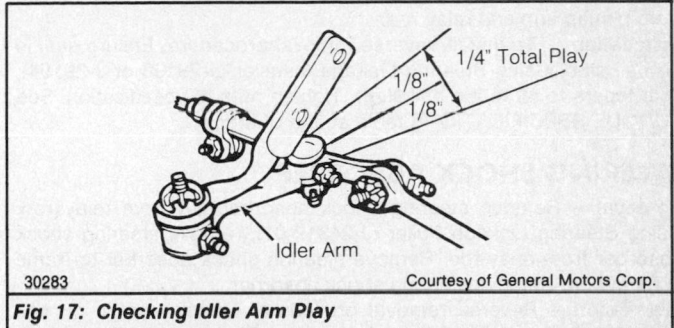

1/4" Total Play
1/8"
1/8"
Idler Arm
30283
Courtesy of General Motors Corp.

Fig. 17: Checking Idler Arm Play

PITMAN ARM

Removal (Bravada, Jimmy, Sonoma, Syclone, Typhoon & "S" & "T" Series Blazer & Pickup) – 1) Raise and support vehicle. Disconnect air induction assembly. Slide up intermediate shaft cover. Mark intermediate shaft for reassembly. Remove intermediate shaft. Disconnect oil filter lines at crossmember bracket. Remove splash shield.

2) Remove pitman arm nut and spring washer from relay rod. Using Steering Linkage Puller (J-24319-01), remove pitman arm from relay rod.

3) Remove lower steering gear bolts. LOOSEN upper steering gear bolt. Rotate steering gear for pitman arm clearance at crossmember, and support gear using block of wood.

4) Mark relationship of pitman arm-to-pitman shaft position. Remove pitman arm nut and spring washer from pitman shaft. Using Remover (J-6632-01) or Puller (J-29107), remove pitman arm from pitman shaft. See Figs. 11 and 12.

Removal (All Other Models) – 1) Raise and support vehicle. Remove pitman arm nut from relay rod (if equipped). Using Steering Linkage Puller (J-24319-01), remove pitman arm from relay rod (if equipped). Remove pitman arm nut from connecting rod (if equipped). Using Steering Linkage Puller (J-24319-01), remove pitman arm from connecting rod (if equipped).

2) Mark relationship of pitman arm-to-pitman shaft position. Remove pitman arm nut and spring washer from pitman shaft. Using Remover (J-6632-01) or Puller (J-29107), remove pitman arm from pitman shaft. See Figs. 2-10.

Installation (All Models) – To install, reverse removal procedure. Ensure pitman arm-to-pitman shaft reference marks are aligned. Ensure seal is on ball stud. Using Steering Linkage Installer (J-29193 or J-29194), seat tapers to **40 ft. lbs. (54 N.m)**. Tighten nuts to specification. See TORQUE SPECIFICATIONS table at end of article.

CONNECTING ROD

Removal (Models With I-Beam Axle) – Raise and support vehicle. Remove connecting rod nuts from pitman arm and steering arm. Using Steering Linkage Puller (J-24319-01), remove connecting rod from pitman arm and steering arm. Mark position of adjuster tube and direction of bolt installation. Loosen adjuster tube clamp bolts and clamps. Unscrew and remove connecting rod ends from adjuster tube.

Installation – 1) Lubricate connecting rod end threads with chassis lubricant before installing. Install connecting rod ends to adjuster tube. Connecting rod end threads must be adjusted equally within 3 threads. Install adjuster clamps and clamp bolts. Slot in adjuster tube and slot in clamp must be properly positioned. *See Fig. 16.*

2) Connecting rod ends must rotate full travel and travel must be maintained during clamp tightening. *See Fig. 16.* Install connecting rod end to pitman arm ensuring seal is on ball stud. Tighten Steering Linkage Installer (J-29193 or J-29194) to **40 ft. lbs. (54 N.m)** to seat tapers. Install and tighten connecting rod-to-pitman arm nut.

3) Install connecting rod end to steering arm. Install and tighten connecting rod-to-steering arm nut. Tighten bolts and nuts to specification. See TORQUE SPECIFICATIONS table at end of article. Adjust toe-in. See SPECIFICATIONS & PROCEDURES article in WHEEL ALIGNMENT.

Removal (Except Models With I-Beam Axle) – Raise and support vehicle. Remove connecting rod nuts from pitman arm and relay rod. Using Steering Linkage Puller (J-24319-01), remove connecting rod from pitman arm and relay rod.

Installation – To install, reverse removal procedure. Ensure seal is on ball stud. Using Steering Linkage Installer (J-29193 or J-29194), seat tapers to **40 ft. lbs. (54 N.m)**. Tighten nuts to specification. See TORQUE SPECIFICATIONS table at end of article.

STEERING SHOCK ABSORBER

Removal – Remove steering shock absorber nut from relay rod. Using Steering Linkage Puller (J-24319-01), remove steering shock absorber from relay rod. Remove steering shock absorber-to-frame nut and bolt. Remove steering shock absorber.

Installation – Reverse removal procedure. Ensure seal is on ball stud. Using Steering Linkage Installer (J-29193 or J-29194), seat tapers to **40 ft. lbs. (54 N.m)**. Tighten nuts to specification. See TORQUE SPECIFICATIONS table at end of article.

OVERHAUL

STEERING GEAR

Disassembly – 1) Mount steering gear in vise, clamping onto one mounting tab. Pitman shaft should be in a vertical position. Insert punch through housing access hole to unseat retaining ring. Using screwdriver, pry retaining ring out of groove in housing.

2) Rotate stub shaft counterclockwise to force housing end plug from housing. Remove seals and ring. Using Rack Piston Arbor (J-21552) and socket, remove rack piston end plug from rack piston.

3) Remove side cover bolts. Remove pitman shaft nut and spring washer from lower end of shaft retaining pitman arm. Remove pitman shaft and side cover assembly. Remove pitman shaft adjuster screw lock nut. Remove pitman shaft cover. Remove gasket from side cover.

4) Remove pitman shaft lower dust seal and rubber boot (if equipped). Using snap ring pliers, remove pitman shaft lower retaining ring. Remove pitman shaft lower seals and washer. Using Pitman Shaft Bearing Puller (J-6278), remove pitman shaft bearing from housing.

5) Insert Rack Piston Arbor (J-21552) into end of rack piston assembly until arbor seats into end of worm shaft. Threaded arbor will keep recirculating balls from falling out of rack piston. Rotate stub shaft counterclockwise, forcing rack piston onto arbor. Remove rack piston and arbor assembly. Ensure arbor is fully inserted so recirculating balls will not fall out.

6) Remove adjuster plug lock nut. Using spanner wrench, remove adjuster plug. Remove valve body, stub shaft, worm shaft, seal, bearing races and worm bearing assembly from housing. If further disassembly is required, see appropriate component under OVERHAUL.

Inspection – Clean components using solvent, and blow dry. Avoid wiping valve components using cloth. Lint may cause binding of mechanism. DO NOT steam clean hydraulic parts.

Reassembly – 1) Lubricate components with power steering fluid before reassembly. Install valve body, stub shaft and worm shaft assembly into housing.

2) Place seal protector over stub shaft. Install adjuster plug until it seats against valve body. Remove seal protector from housing. Loosely install adjuster plug lock nut. Insert rack piston (with arbor to retain recirculating balls) into housing. Align worm shaft and rack piston. Turn stub shaft clockwise to engage worm. Maintain pressure on arbor until worm is fully engaged. Remove arbor.

3) Install NEW pitman shaft side cover gasket. Thread pitman shaft side cover onto adjuster screw until it bottoms. Back off 1/2 turn. Install pitman shaft so that center sector gear tooth meshes with center groove in rack piston. Install side cover bolts.

4) Install adjuster screw lock nut halfway onto pitman shaft. Install rack piston end plug in rack piston. Install housing end plug seals, ring, end plug and retainer ring. Adjust worm shaft bearing preload and over-center preload. See WORM BEARING PRELOAD and OVER-CENTER PRELOAD under ADJUSTMENTS.

ADJUSTER PLUG

Disassembly – Using snap ring pliers, remove adjuster plug retaining ring. Remove adjuster plug washer and seal. Using screwdriver, pry up bearing retainer at raised area. Using Bearing Remover (J-8524-1) and Driver (J-7079-2), remove bearing from adjuster plug.

Inspection – Inspect bearings and races for scoring, pitting and wear. Inspect adjuster plug threads for damage.

Reassembly – Using Bearing Remover (J-8524-1) and Driver (J-7079-2), install bearing into adjuster plug. Install bearing retainer. Lubricate seal with power steering fluid. Install adjuster plug seal, washer and retaining ring.

NOTE: Retainer projections must not extend beyond washer when retaining ring is seated. Adjuster plug washer must be free to rotate.

WORM SHAFT, STUB SHAFT & VALVE BODY

Disassembly – 1) Mark position of worm bearing races and bearing to worm shaft. Mark position of worm shaft notches to valve body. Remove worm shaft from valve body and stub shaft assembly. Remove stub shaft seal. Remove worm bearing races and bearing from worm shaft.

2) Lightly tap end of stub shaft against wood block until shaft cap is free of valve body. Pull stub shaft outward until drive pin hole is visible. *See Fig. 18.*

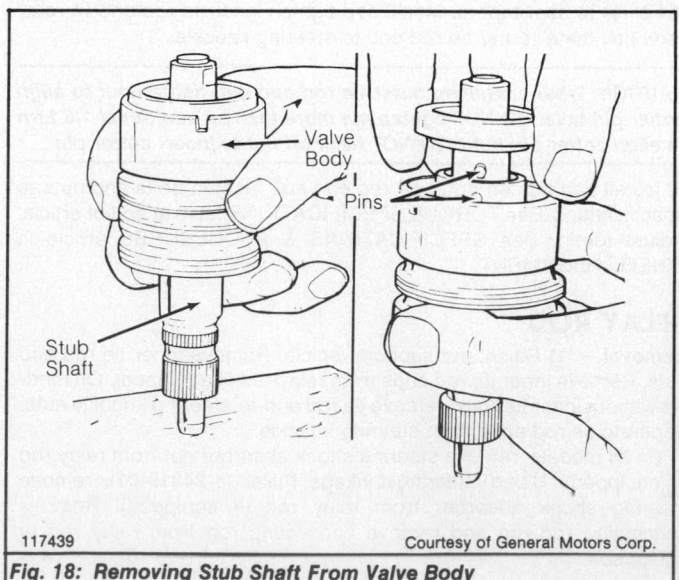

117439   Courtesy of General Motors Corp.

Fig. 18: Removing Stub Shaft From Valve Body

CAUTION: DO NOT pull shaft more than 1/4" (6 mm) or spool valve may become cocked in valve body.

3) Disengage drive pin. Remove stub shaft from valve body. Rotate and remove valve spool from valve body. If binding occurs, realign valves.

CAUTION: DO NOT force stub shaft or valve spool out of valve body.

4) Remove spool valve seal. Remove valve body rings and seals.

Inspection – 1) Clean components using solvent, and blow dry. Inspect stub shaft for nicks and burrs. Remove nicks and burrs using crocus cloth if possible. Inspect shaft pin for wear and cracks.

2) Check valve spool fit in valve body. Remove nicks and burrs using crocus cloth if possible. Lubricate valve spool with power steering fluid. Rotate valve spool in valve body. If valve spool does not rotate freely, replace complete valve and stub shaft assembly.

3) Valve assembly is balanced during assembly. If replacing any components other than rings or seals, replace complete valve and stub shaft assembly.

Reassembly – 1) Lubricate valve body components with power steering fluid. Install NEW rings and seals. Lubricate spool valve seals with power steering fluid and install on valve spool. Carefully insert valve spool into valve body.

2) Push valve spool through valve body until locating pin hole is visible at opposite end of valve body, and valve spool is flush with notched end of valve body. Install stub shaft into valve spool and valve body.

3) Align stub shaft locating pin with valve spool locating hole. Align notch in stub shaft cap with pin in valve body. Install stub shaft seal into valve body.

CAUTION: Before installing assembled valve body into gear housing, ensure valve body stub shaft locating pin is fully engaged in stub shaft cap notch. DO NOT allow stub shaft to disengage from valve body pin.

4) Install bearing and races on worm shaft aligning marks made during disassembly. *See Fig. 1.* Install worm shaft onto valve body and stub shaft assembly aligning notches made during disassembly.

RACK PISTON BALLS

Disassembly – Remove ball guide clamp screws and clamps. Remove ball guides. Remove all recirculating balls from rack piston. *See Fig. 1.*

Inspection – Clean components using solvent, and blow dry. Inspect rack piston grooves for scoring. Inspect ball bearings for damage. If any ball bearings are damaged, replace entire set. Check ball guides for cracks or dented ends. Inspect rack piston teeth for chips, cracks, dents and scoring. If rack piston is damaged, replace rack piston and worm shaft as an assembly.

Reassembly – 1) Lubricate seals and ring with power steering fluid and carefully install onto rack piston. Install worm shaft into rack piston until worm shaft touches piston shoulder. While turning worm shaft counterclockwise, insert ball bearings into rack piston.

NOTE: Ensure light and dark colored balls are installed alternately; Black balls are .0005" (.013 mm) smaller than Silver balls.

2) Install 6 balls in ball guide, alternating ball colors. Bearings in guide must be in sequence with bearings in rack piston. Hold balls in place with chassis lubricant. Install return ball guide assembly into position.

3) Install clamp. Tighten clamp screws. *See Fig. 19.* Insert Rack Piston Arbor (J-21552) into rack piston until it contacts worm shaft. Maintain pressure on arbor, and back worm shaft out of rack piston. DO NOT allow ball bearings to drop out.

POWER STEERING PUMP

Disassembly (Model P) – 1) Using Puller (J-29785-A), remove pulley from shaft if not previously removed. Remove union fitting and "O" ring. Remove reservoir retaining bolts. Remove reservoir and "O" rings from housing.

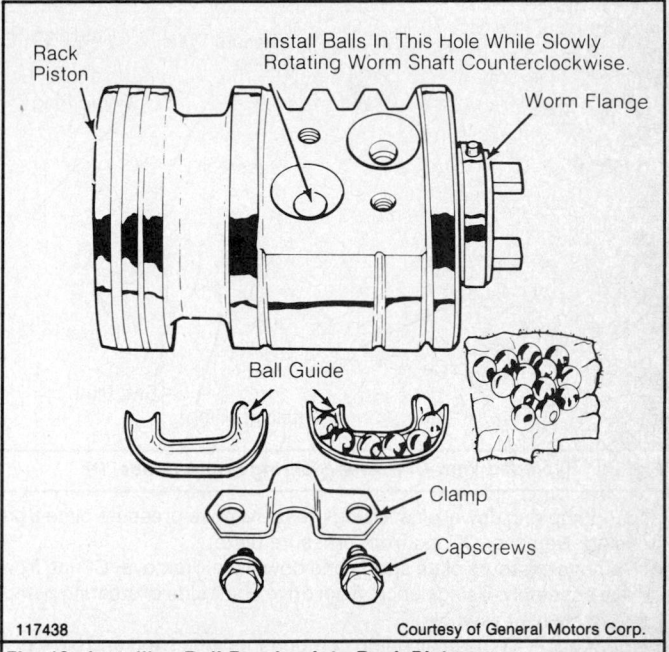

Fig. 19: *Installing Ball Bearing Into Rack Piston*

2) Using punch and screwdriver, remove end plate retaining ring. Remove end plate and pressure plate spring. *See Fig. 20.* Remove "O" ring, flow control valve, and spring. Using soft-faced hammer, tap end of drive shaft to loosen pressure plate.

3) Remove pressure plate, pump ring, vanes, retaining ring, rotor, and thrust plate assembly from housing. Remove drive shaft. Using a screwdriver, pry drive shaft seal from housing. Remove dowel pins and seals.

Inspection – 1) Clean all pump components with solvent and blow dry. Inspect flow control valve assembly for wear, scoring, burrs and other damage. Inspect seal bore for burrs, nicks and score marks.

2) Inspect machined surfaces of body for scratches or burrs. Check "O" ring mating surfaces. Inspect drive shaft for excessive wear.

3) Inspect pump ring for roughness. Check thrust plate and pressure plate for scoring and wear. Ensure vanes slide freely but fit snugly into slots. If vanes are loose in slots, replace rotor and/or vanes.

Reassembly – 1) Lubricate all "O" rings, seals, pump ring, rotor and vanes with power steering fluid. Using socket, press NEW drive shaft seal into housing.

2) Install dowel pins and all "O" rings. Install drive shaft and thrust plate. Install pump rotor into housing with counterbore facing drive shaft side of steering pump.

3) Install NEW drive shaft retaining ring, ensuring ring is seated in groove. Install vanes with rounded edges toward pump ring. Install pump ring and pressure plate. Install "O" ring, flow control valve, and spring.

4) Install pressure plate spring, end plate, and retaining ring. Install seals and reservoir. Install union fitting, "O" ring, and reservoir retaining bolts.

Disassembly (Model TC) – 1) Clamp front hub in soft-jawed vise. Pry tab outward and remove reservoir clips (if equipped). *See Fig. 21.* Remove reservoir or return tube and "O" ring. Using Pulley Remover (J-25034-B), remove pulley from shaft if not previously removed.

2) Remove union fitting, "O" ring, flow control valve and spring. Note location of large lug side of retaining ring before removal. Remove retaining ring. Remove drive shaft and bearing assembly. Measure and note clearance between drive shaft and bearing collar. Press bearing from drive shaft. Using screwdriver, remove drive shaft seal from housing.

3) Remove thrust plate retaining ring by inserting punch into access hole and disengaging retaining ring. Using a 5/8" bar stock or brass drift, press pressure plate and remove thrust plate from drive shaft side of steering pump. Remove "O" ring, pump ring, pump rotor, vanes

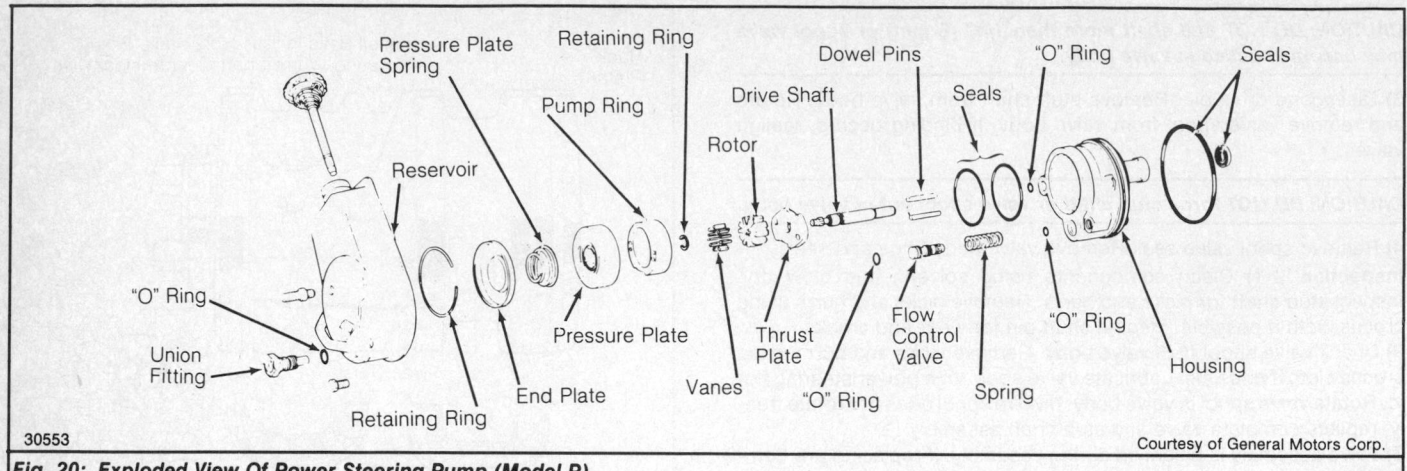

Fig. 20: Exploded View Of Power Steering Pump (Model P)

Courtesy of General Motors Corp.

30553

and 2 pump ring dowel pins. Using press, remove pressure plate from housing. Remove "O" ring from pressure plate.

4) Remove pressure plate spring and dowel pin. Remove "O" ring from sleeve assembly. Using punch, from drive shaft side of steering pump, remove sleeve assembly.

Inspection – 1) Clean all pump components in solvent and blow dry. Inspect flow control valve assembly for wear, scoring, burrs or other damage. Inspect seal bore for burrs, nicks or score marks.

2) Inspect machined surfaces of body for scratches or burrs. Check "O" ring mating surfaces. Inspect drive shaft for wear.

3) Inspect pump ring for roughness. Check thrust plate and pressure plate for scoring and wear. Ensure vanes slide freely but fit snugly into slots. If vanes are loose in slots, replace rotor and/or vanes.

Reassembly – 1) Lubricate all "O" rings, seals, pump ring, rotor and vanes with power steering fluid. Install NEW sleeve assembly. Using press, seat sleeve assembly into pump housing from pressure plate side of steering pump. See Fig. 21. Lubricate NEW "O" ring with power steering fluid and install into groove of sleeve assembly.

2) Install dowel pin and pressure plate spring into housing. Lubricate NEW "O" ring with power steering fluid and install into groove of pressure plate. Reference mark top of pressure plate directly over dowel pin hole located on under side of pressure plate. Align mark on pressure plate to dowel pin previously installed into steering pump housing. Install pressure plate into housing engaging, dowel pin into pressure plate dowel pin hole.

3) Install 2 pump ring dowel pins. Install pump rotor into housing with counterbore facing drive shaft side of steering pump. Install vanes into slots of pump rotor. Install pump ring on 2 pump ring dowel pins. Lubricate NEW "O" ring with power steering fluid and install into groove of steering pump housing.

4) Lubricate outer edge of thrust plate. Install thrust plate into housing aligning dimples in thrust plate to steering pump bolt holes. Ensure thrust plate engages 2 pump ring dowel pins. Press thrust plate on far enough to install thrust plate retaining ring. Install thrust plate retaining ring into groove in housing with ring opening centered with bolt hole in steering pump nearest to access hole.

5) Lubricate NEW drive shaft seal with power steering fluid, and install seal into pump housing using socket. Install bearing onto drive shaft, pressing bearing to shoulder of drive shaft or to within clearance measurement made between drive shaft shoulder and inner bearing race during disassembly.

6) Install drive shaft and ball bearing assembly into steering pump. Rotate drive shaft engaging shaft serration with steering pump rotor. Install retaining ring onto housing.

7) Install flow control spring and control valve assembly into housing. Install NEW "O" ring onto union fitting. Install union fitting into steering pump and tighten to specification. See TORQUE SPECIFICATIONS table. Install return tube or reservoir using NEW "O" ring.

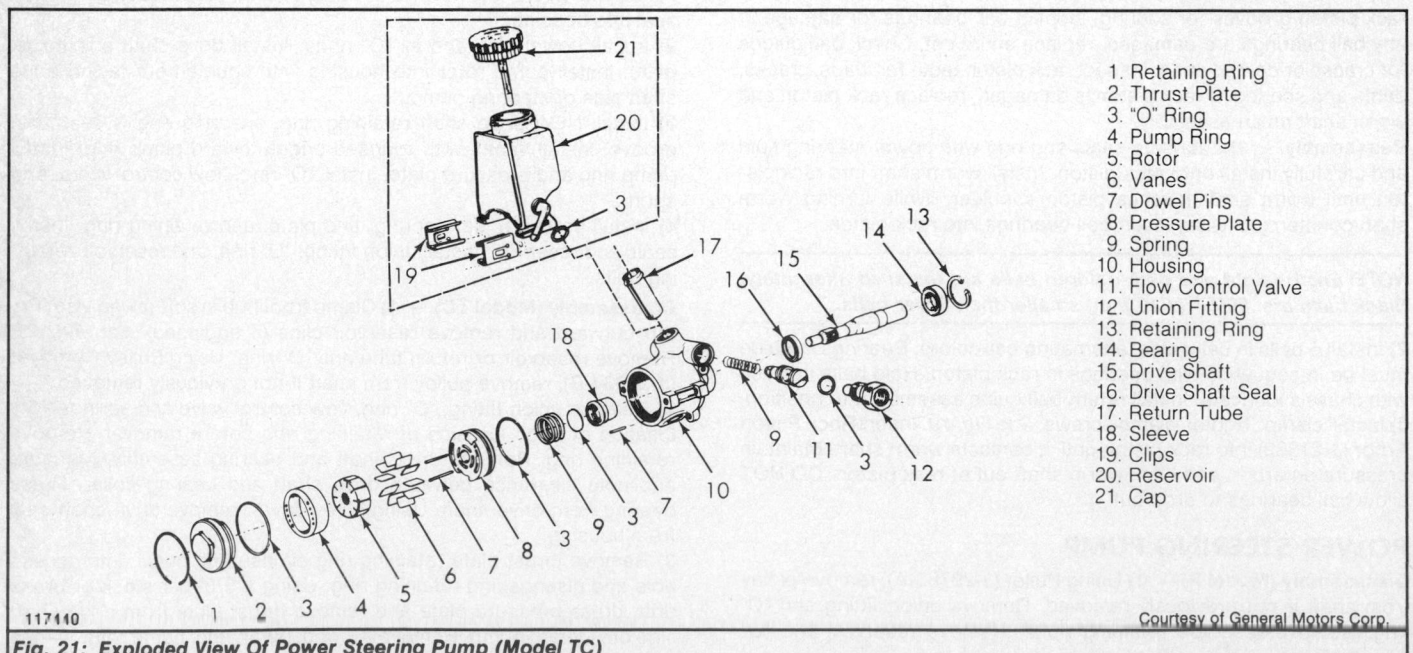

1. Retaining Ring
2. Thrust Plate
3. "O" Ring
4. Pump Ring
5. Rotor
6. Vanes
7. Dowel Pins
8. Pressure Plate
9. Spring
10. Housing
11. Flow Control Valve
12. Union Fitting
13. Retaining Ring
14. Bearing
15. Drive Shaft
16. Drive Shaft Seal
17. Return Tube
18. Sleeve
19. Clips
20. Reservoir
21. Cap

Fig. 21: Exploded View Of Power Steering Pump (Model TC)

Courtesy of General Motors Corp.

117110

TORQUE SPECIFICATIONS

TORQUE SPECIFICATIONS

Application	Ft. Lbs. (N.m)
Adjuster Plug Lock Nut	78-81 (106-110)
Connecting Rod Adjuster Clamp Nut	
Models With I-Beam Axle	50 (68)
Connecting Rod-To-Pitman Arm Nut	
Astro & Safari	35 (47)
Commercial Van With I-Beam Axle & Motorhome	70 (95)
"C" Series Pickup With I-Beam Axle	36 (49)
Connecting Rod-To-Relay Rod Nut	
Astro & Safari	35 (47)
Motorhome	70 (95)
Connecting Rod-To-Tie Rod Nut	
"C" Series Pickup With I-Beam Axle	77 (104)
Idler Arm Mounting Bolts	
Astro & Safari	
AWD	102 (138)
2WD	78 (106)
Bravada, Jimmy, Sonoma, Syclone, Typhoon &	
"S" & "T" Series Blazer & Pickup	60 (81)
Commercial Van	30 (41)
Van	35 (47)
Sierra, Suburban, Yukon &	
"C" & "K" Series Blazer & Pickup	78 (106)
Idler Arm-To-Relay Rod Nut	
Astro & Safari	35 (47)
Bravada, Syclone & Typhoon	60 (81)
Commercial Van, Motorhome & Van	66 (89)
Jimmy, Sonoma & "S" & "T" Series Blazer & Pickup	
2WD	35 (47)
4WD	60 (81)
Sierra, Suburban, Yukon &	
"C" & "K" Series Blazer & Pickup	40 (54)
Intermediate Shaft-To-Stub Shaft Bolt	
Astro & Safari	29 (39)
Bravada, Jimmy, Sonoma, Syclone, Typhoon &	
"S" & "T" Series Blazer & Pickup	26 (35)
Commercial Van	
With I-Beam Axle	80 (108)
Without I-Beam Axle	75 (102)
Sierra, Suburban, Yukon &	
"C" & "K" Series Blazer & Pickup	30 (41)
Syclone & Typhoon	27 (37)
Van	46 (62)
Pitman Arm-To-Relay Rod Nut	
Bravada, Jimmy, Sonoma, Syclone, Typhoon &	
"S" & "T" Series Blazer & Pickup	60 (81)
Commercial Van & Van	66 (89)
Sierra, Suburban, Yukon &	
"C" & "K" Series Blazer & Pickup	40 (54)
Pitman Arm-To-Steering Gear Nut	
Commercial Van With I-Beam Axle & Motorhome	125 (169)
All Other Models	184 (249)
Pitman Shaft Adjuster Screw Lock Nut	
Bravada	20 (27)
Commercial Van & Van	35 (47)
All Other Models	32 (43)
Rack Piston End Plug	110 (149)
Relay Arm-To-Relay Rod Nut	
Motorhome	66 (89)
Shock Absorber-To-Frame Bolt	
Bravada, Jimmy, Sonoma, Syclone, Typhoon &	
"T" Series Blazer & Pickup	26 (35)
Commercial Van With I-Beam Axle	35 (47)
Motorhome	8 (11)
Sierra, Suburban, Yukon &	
"C" & "K" Series Blazer & Pickup	30 (41)
"C" Series Pickup With I-Beam Axle	33 (45)

TORQUE SPECIFICATIONS (Cont.)

Application	Ft. Lbs. (N.m)
Shock Absorber-To-Idler Arm Nut	
Motorhome	46 (62)
Shock Absorber-To-Relay Rod Nut	45-46 (61-62)
Shock Absorber-To-Tie Rod Nut	
Models With I-Beam Axle	46 (62)
Side Cover Bolts	
Bravada	40 (54)
Commercial Van & Van	45 (61)
All Other Models	48 (65)
Steering Gear Mounting Bolts	
Astro, Bravada, Jimmy, Sonoma, Safari, Syclone,	
Typhoon & "S" & "T" Series Blazer & Pickup	55 (75)
Commercial Van	
708 Model Steering Gear	66 (89)
710 Model Steering Gear	175 (237)
Sierra, Suburban, Yukon &	
"C" & "K" Series Blazer & Pickup	69 (93)
Van	66 (89)
Steering Pump Mounting Bolts	
Astro, Bravada, Safari, Sierra, Suburban,	
Syclone, Typhoon, Yukon &	
"C" & "K" Series Blazer & Pickup	36 (49)
Commercial Van	
4.3L & 5.7L	25 (34)
6.2L Diesel	32 (43)
7.4L	36 (49)
Jimmy, Sonoma & "S" & "T" Series Blazer & Pickup	
2.5L	20 (27)
2.8L & 4.3L	36 (49)
Van	
4.3L, 5.0L, 5.7L & 7.4L Engine	36 (49)
6.2L Diesel	32 (43)
Tie Rod Adjuster Clamp Nut	
"C" Series Pickup With I-Beam Axle	50 (68)
All Other Models	14 (19)
Tie Rod Jam Nut	
Commercial Van With I-Beam Axle	277 (375)
Tie Rod-To-Relay Rod Nut	
Astro, Bravada, Jimmy, Safari, Sonoma, Syclone,	
Typhoon & "S" & "T" Series Blazer & Pickup	35 (47)
Commercial Van, Motorhome & Van	66 (89)
Sierra, Suburban, Yukon &	
"C" & "K" Series Blazer & Pickup	40 (54)
Tie Rod-To-Steering Arm Nut	
Sierra, Suburban, Yukon &	
"C" & "K" Series Blazer & Pickup	40 (54)
"C" Series Pickup With I-Beam Axle	66 (89)
Tie Rod-To-Steering Knuckle Nut	
Astro & Safari	
AWD	37 (50)
2WD	35 (47)
Bravada, Jimmy, Sonoma, Syclone, Typhoon &	
"S" & "T" Series Blazer & Pickup	35 (47)
Commercial Van, Motorhome & Van	46 (62)
Commercial Van With I-Beam Axle	162 (220)
Union Fitting	55 (75)

Lumina APV, Silhouette, Trans Sport

DESCRIPTION & OPERATION

Power rack and pinion steering system uses a rotary control valve to direct hydraulic fluid to either side of rack piston. Rack piston is integral with rack gear and converts hydraulic pressure to linear force. This force assists rack gear to move either left or right. Power rack and pinion steering gear consists of an input pinion gear, steering rack gear, tube housing and a rotary valve assembly.

Power steering system uses a belt-driven, vane type pump with an integral reservoir. A pressure relief valve inside the flow control valve limits pump pressure. TC series pump uses a ball bearing assembly on the drive shaft.

LUBRICATION

CAPACITY

Fluid capacity is about 1.5 pts. (.7L).

FLUID TYPE

Manufacturer recommends General Motors Power Steering Fluid (1050017) or an equivalent meeting G.M. Specification No. 9985010. Failure to use proper fluid will cause hose and seal damage, resulting in fluid leaks.

FLUID LEVEL CHECK

To check fluid level, remove fluid reservoir cap and check level gauge or check level indicator on transparent reservoir. Fluid level should be at FULL HOT mark when fluid temperature is 170°F (77°C) or hot to touch and FULL COLD mark when fluid temperature is 70°F (21°C). Add fluid through fluid reservoir cap as necessary, and recheck fluid level. DO NOT overfill system.

HYDRAULIC SYSTEM BLEEDING

NOTE: If air was introduced into hydraulic system during servicing, system must be bled. Aerated fluid, which appears Light Tan in color, results in poor steering performance and may cause pump damage.

1) Raise and support vehicle with engine off. Turn front wheels to full left position. Fill reservoir to FULL COLD mark. Turn front wheels from side to side several times without hitting stops. Maintain fluid level at FULL COLD mark. When fluid is clear and free of bubbles, start engine and recheck fluid level. Add fluid as necessary.
2) Return front wheels to center position and lower vehicle. Allow vehicle to idle for 2-3 minutes. Road test vehicle to ensure power steering is functioning properly. After road test, check that fluid level is at FULL HOT mark. Check system for leaks.

ADJUSTMENTS

POWER STEERING PUMP BELT

Serpentine belt is self-adjusting within tensioner operating limits.

RACK BEARING PRELOAD

1) With steering gear installed, raise and support vehicle. Position wheels in straight-ahead position. Loosen adjuster plug lock nut. *See Fig. 1.* Rotate adjuster plug clockwise until it bottoms in housing.
2) Back off adjuster plug 50-70 degrees (approximately one flat). Tighten adjuster plug lock nut to specification. See TORQUE SPECIFICATIONS table at end of article. DO NOT allow adjusting plug to rotate while tightening lock nut.

NOTE: Ensure steering wheel returns to center position after adjusting rack bearing preload.

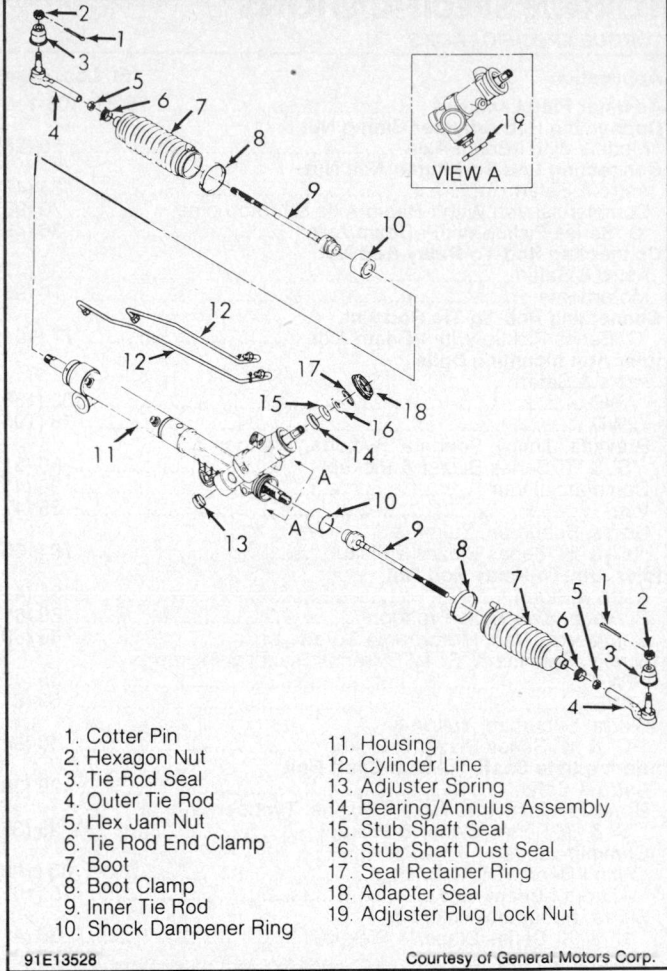

1. Cotter Pin	11. Housing
2. Hexagon Nut	12. Cylinder Line
3. Tie Rod Seal	13. Adjuster Spring
4. Outer Tie Rod	14. Bearing/Annulus Assembly
5. Hex Jam Nut	15. Stub Shaft Seal
6. Tie Rod End Clamp	16. Stub Shaft Dust Seal
7. Boot	17. Seal Retainer Ring
8. Boot Clamp	18. Adapter Seal
9. Inner Tie Rod	19. Adjuster Plug Lock Nut
10. Shock Dampener Ring	

91E13528   Courtesy of General Motors Corp.

Fig. 1: Exploded View Of Rack & Pinion Steering Gear

TROUBLE SHOOTING

NOTE: See TROUBLE SHOOTING article in GENERAL INFORMATION.

TESTING

NOTE: Incorrect fluid level and idle speed and damaged pump pulley can affect test results. If any of these conditions exists, correct them before testing power steering system.

HYDRAULIC SYSTEM PRESSURE TEST

1) Disconnect high pressure line from power steering pump. Attach a spare pressure hose to power steering pump fitting. Connect Power Steering Pressure Gauge (J-5176-D) to spare hose. On 3.8L, Adapter (J-38049-38) must also be attached to hose. On all models, connect other hose from valve side of tester to steering gear inlet. Open valve on pressure gauge.
2) Check fluid level, and add fluid (as necessary). Check for possible leaks at pressure gauge connections. Bleed air from system. See HYDRAULIC SYSTEM BLEEDING under LUBRICATION. Run engine until fluid reaches operating temperature. Check fluid level, and add fluid (as necessary). Note pressure reading with valve open and engine idling. Pressure should be **80-125 psi (5.6-8.8 kg/cm²)**. If pressure exceeds 200 psi (14 kg/cm²), check hoses for restrictions and poppet valve for proper assembly.

CAUTION: To prevent pump damage, DO NOT hold gauge valve closed for more than 5 seconds.

3) Completely close and open valve 3 times. Record reading each time. Readings should be within 50 psi (3.5 kg/cm²) of each other. If pressure readings are as specified and within 50 psi (3.5 kg/cm²) of each other, pump is operating properly.

4) If pressure readings are as specified but not within 50 psi (3.5 kg/cm²) of each other, flow control valve in pump is sticking. Remove valve, but DO NOT disassemble it. Clean valve using crocus cloth or fine hone. Flush system if it is dirty. If it is exceptionally dirty, disassemble and clean pump and steering gear.

5) If pressure readings are as specified, with valve open, turn steering wheel from stop to stop. Record highest pressure with wheels at both stops. If highest pressure is not equal to highest pressure recorded in step 3), rack and pinion assembly is leaking internally. Repair or replace assembly.

6) Turn engine off. Remove tester and spare hose. Reconnect pressure hose. Check fluid level. Bleed hydraulic system. See HYDRAULIC SYSTEM BLEEDING under LUBRICATION.

REMOVAL & INSTALLATION

OUTER TIE ROD END

Removal – Remove cotter pin and nut from outer tie rod end at steering knuckle. Using Steering Linkage Remover (J-24319-01), separate tie rod end from steering knuckle. Loosen lock nut on inner tie rod. Unscrew outer tie rod from inner tie rod. Note number of turns required for removal.

CAUTION: When installing tie rod end nut, tighten nut to align cotter pin hole. DO NOT tighten nut more than an additional 1/6 turn or 52 ft. lbs. (71 N.m) to align cotter pin hole. DO NOT back off nut to insert cotter pin.

Installation – To install, reverse removal procedure. Install tie rod to same number of turns required during removal. Adjust toe-in. See SPECIFICATIONS & PROCEDURES article in WHEEL ALIGNMENT. Ensure boot is not twisted or puckered. Tighten tie rod lock nut and tie rod-to-steering knuckle nut to specifications. See TORQUE SPECIFICATIONS table at end of article.

INNER TIE ROD END

Removal – 1) Remove steering gear. See STEERING GEAR. Remove boot and breather tube. See BOOT & BREATHER TUBE. Remove shock damper ring from inner tie rod, and slide back on rack. See Fig. 2.

CAUTION: Hold rack during inner tie rod removal to prevent damage to internal gears of rack.

2) Place wrenches on flats of rack and inner tie rod housing. See Fig. 2. Rotate inner tie rod housing counterclockwise until tie rod separates from rack.

Installation – 1) To install, ensure all surfaces are clean. Install shock dampener ring onto rack. Place wrenches on flats of rack and inner tie rod housing. See Fig. 2. Install inner tie rod onto rack. Ensure tie rod rocks freely in housing before staking inner tie rod assembly to rack. Support rack and inner tie rod housing.

2) Stake both sides of inner tie rod housing to flats on rack. Insert .01" (.25 mm) feeler gauge between rack and tie rod housing stake. Feeler gauge must not pass between rack and housing stake.

3) Slide and engage shock damper ring over inner tie rod housing. Lubricate boot contact areas on inner tie rod end and housing with grease before installing boot. Install boot and breather tube, aligning reference mark with mark on housing. Install NEW boot seal clamps. Using Clamp Pliers (J-22610), tighten boot clamps. Ensure boot is not twisted or puckered.

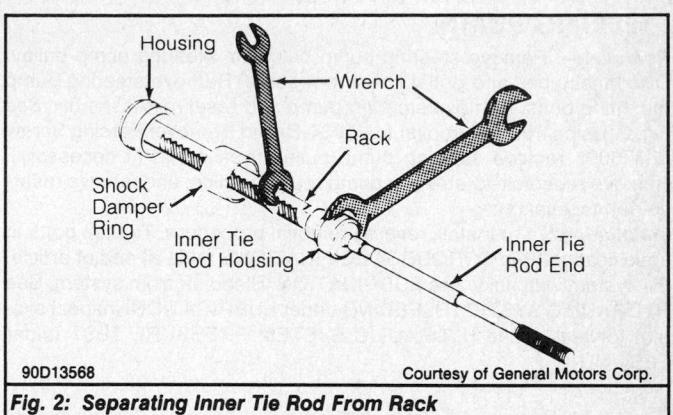

Fig. 2: Separating Inner Tie Rod From Rack

4) To complete installation, reverse removal procedure. Tighten bolts and nuts to specifications. See TORQUE SPECIFICATIONS table at end of article.

BOOT & BREATHER TUBE

Removal – Remove outer tie rod end. See OUTER TIE ROD END. Remove outer tie rod lock nut from inner tie rod. See Fig. 1. Remove tie rod end clamp. Using side cutters, remove boot clamps. Mark location of breather tube on steering gear housing for reassembly reference. Remove boot and breather tube.

Installation – 1) To install, ensure all surfaces are clean. Lubricate boot contact areas on inner tie rod end and housing with grease before installing boot. Install boot and breather tube, aligning reference mark with mark on housing.

2) Install NEW boot seal clamps. Using Clamp Pliers (J-22610), tighten boot clamps. Ensure boot is not twisted or puckered. To complete installation, reverse removal procedure.

STEERING GEAR

CAUTION: Disconnect steering column intermediate shaft before removing steering gear to prevent damage to steering gear and intermediate shaft.

Removal – 1) Remove air cleaner. Remove dust boot from steering gear. Remove intermediate shaft-to-steering gear pinion shaft pinch bolt. Separate intermediate shaft from steering gear pinion shaft.

NOTE: If necessary, remove intermediate shaft-to-steering column shaft pinch bolt. Separate intermediate shaft from steering column shaft before disconnecting intermediate shaft from steering gear pinion shaft.

2) Disconnect pressure and return hydraulic line assemblies at steering gear. Raise and support vehicle. Remove wheel and tire assembly. Remove cotter pin and nut from outer tie rod end at steering knuckle. Using Steering Linkage Remover (J-24319-01), separate tie rod end from steering knuckle.

3) Remove remaining brackets and clips on crossmember. Support body using jackstands to allow for lowering of frame about 5" (127 mm) for steering gear removal. Support frame using jack. Remove rear frame-to-body bolts.

4) Disconnect stabilizer bar from lower control arm before rear of frame can be lowered (if necessary). Lower rear of frame about 5" (127 mm). DO NOT lower rear of frame too far or engine components will be damaged by contacting the cowl.

5) Remove steering gear mounting bolts and nuts. Remove steering gear through left wheel opening.

Installation – Reverse removal procedure. Install NEW frame-to-body bolts. Tighten bolts and nuts to specification. See TORQUE SPECIFICATIONS table at end of article. Fill system with fluid. See LUBRICATION. Bleed air from system. See HYDRAULIC SYSTEM BLEEDING under LUBRICATION. Inspect system for leaks. See HYDRAULIC SYSTEM PRESSURE TEST under TESTING.

STEERING PUMP

Removal – Remove steering pump belt from steering pump pulley. Disconnect inlet and outlet lines from pump. Remove steering pump mounting bolts. Remove steering pump and reservoir assembly. *See Fig. 3.* Using Pulley Remover (J-25034-B) and Remover Forcing Screw (J-37609), remove steering pump pulley from pump (if necessary). Remove reservoir-to-steering pump retaining clips, and remove reservoir (if necessary).

Installation – To install, reverse removal procedure. Tighten bolts to specification. See TORQUE SPECIFICATIONS table at end of article. Fill system with fluid. See LUBRICATION. Bleed air from system. See HYDRAULIC SYSTEM BLEEDING under LUBRICATION. Inspect system for leaks. See HYDRAULIC SYSTEM PRESSURE TEST under TESTING.

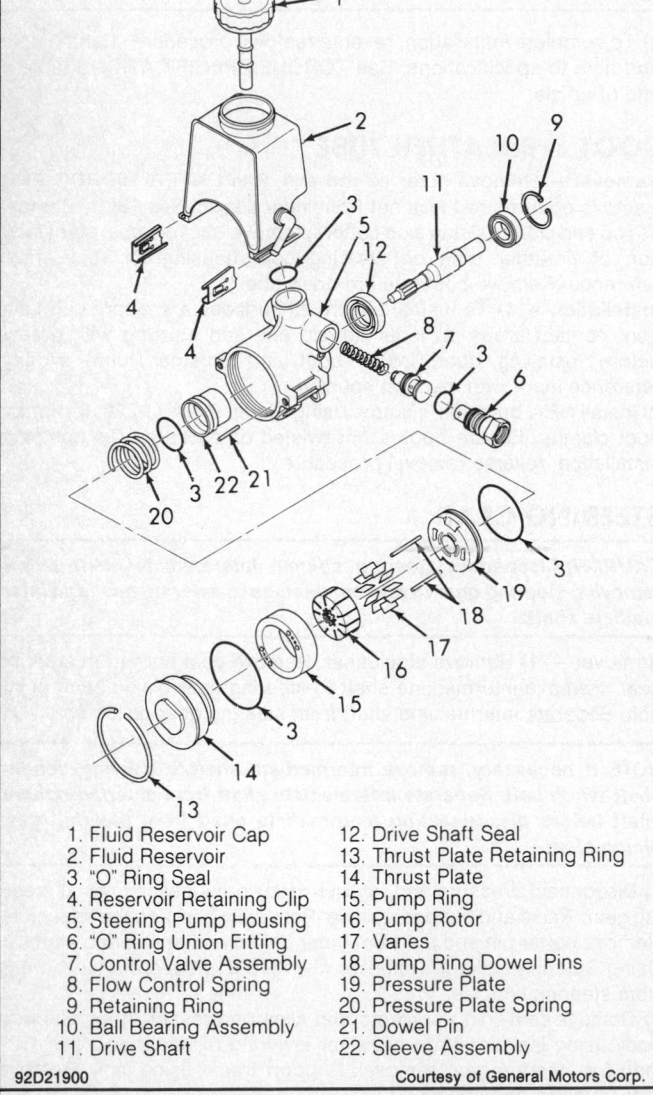

1. Fluid Reservoir Cap
2. Fluid Reservoir
3. "O" Ring Seal
4. Reservoir Retaining Clip
5. Steering Pump Housing
6. "O" Ring Union Fitting
7. Control Valve Assembly
8. Flow Control Spring
9. Retaining Ring
10. Ball Bearing Assembly
11. Drive Shaft
12. Drive Shaft Seal
13. Thrust Plate Retaining Ring
14. Thrust Plate
15. Pump Ring
16. Pump Rotor
17. Vanes
18. Pump Ring Dowel Pins
19. Pressure Plate
20. Pressure Plate Spring
21. Dowel Pin
22. Sleeve Assembly

92D21900 Courtesy of General Motors Corp.

Fig. 3: Exploded View Of TC Series Power Steering Pump

OVERHAUL

PINION SEAL, DUST SEAL & BEARING/ANNULUS ASSEMBLY

Disassembly – **1)** Remove steering gear. See STEERING GEAR under REMOVAL & INSTALLATION. Remove adjuster plug lock nut, adjuster plug, spring and rack bearing. *See Fig. 1.*

2) Remove seal retainer ring from top of steering gear. Remove dust cover from bottom of steering gear. Hold pinion shaft, and remove pinion shaft lock nut from bottom of pinion shaft.

NOTE: DO NOT remove pinion from housing. Press pinion assembly far enough to only allow seals and bearing/annulus assembly removal. Removal of pinion assembly is not required.

3) Arbor press must be used to remove seals and bearing/annulus assembly. DO NOT hammer on pinion shaft, as drive pin in pinion shaft will be damaged. Using arbor press, press on threaded end of pinion. Press dust seal, shaft seal and bearing/annulus assembly from steering gear. *See Fig. 1.*

Reassembly – **1)** Install pinion shaft lock nut on bottom of pinion shaft. While holding pinion shaft, tighten lock nut to specification. See TORQUE SPECIFICATIONS table at end of article. Install dust cover.

2) Install bearing/annulus assembly on pinion shaft. Install Seal Protector (J-29810) on pinion shaft. Apply small amount of grease between stub shaft seal and dust seal. Install stub shaft seal and dust seal over seal protector and slide into steering gear. Install seal retainer ring into groove on steering gear.

3) Lubricate seal area with grease. Coat rack bearing, spring and adjuster plug with lithium grease. Install rack bearing, spring and adjuster plug in steering gear.

4) Position rack in center of steering gear. Rotate adjuster plug clockwise until it bottoms in steering gear. Back off adjuster plug 50-70 degrees (approximately one flat). *See Fig. 1.*

5) Using INCH-pound torque wrench, check torque required to rotate pinion. Maximum torque should be **16 INCH lbs. (1.8 N.m)**. Tighten adjuster plug lock nut to specification. See TORQUE SPECIFICATIONS table at end of article. DO NOT allow adjusting plug to rotate while tightening lock nut. Install steering gear. See STEERING GEAR under REMOVAL & INSTALLATION.

STEERING PUMP

Disassembly – **1)** Remove steering pump. See STEERING PUMP under REMOVAL & INSTALLATION. Remove "O" ring union fitting from steering pump. *See Fig. 3.* Remove "O" ring seal from "O" ring union fitting. Remove control valve assembly and flow control spring from steering pump housing.

2) Remove retaining ring from pump housing. Remove drive shaft and ball bearing assembly from steering pump housing. Measure clearance between drive shaft shoulder and inner bearing race. Remove bearing from drive shaft. Remove drive shaft seal from pump housing.

3) Remove thrust plate retaining ring from housing. Using a 5/8" bar stock or brass drift, from drive shaft side of steering pump, press pressure plate and remove thrust plate. Remove "O" ring seal, pump ring, pump rotor, vanes and 2 pump ring dowel pins. Using press, remove pressure plate from housing. Remove "O" ring seal from pressure plate.

4) Remove pressure plate spring and dowel pin. Remove "O" ring seal from sleeve assembly. Using punch, remove sleeve assembly from drive shaft side of steering pump.

Reassembly – **1)** Clean steering pump components in power steering fluid. Inspect components for scoring and pitting. Install NEW sleeve assembly. Using press, seat sleeve assembly into pump housing from pressure plate side of steering pump. *See Fig. 3.* Lubricate NEW "O" ring seal with power steering fluid and install into groove of sleeve assembly.

2) Install dowel pin and pressure plate spring into housing. Lubricate NEW "O" ring seal with power steering fluid and install into groove of pressure plate. Reference mark top of pressure plate directly over dowel pin hole located on under side of pressure plate. Align mark on pressure plate to dowel pin previously installed into steering pump housing. Install pressure plate into housing engaging dowel pin into pressure plate dowel pin hole.

3) Install 2 pump ring dowel pins. Install pump rotor into housing with counterbore facing drive shaft side of steering pump. Install vanes into slots of pump rotor. Install pump ring on 2 pump ring dowel pins. Lubricate NEW "O" ring seal with power steering fluid, and install it into groove of steering pump housing.

4) Lubricate outer edge of thrust plate. Install thrust plate into housing, aligning dimples in thrust plate to steering pump bolt holes. Ensure thrust plate engages 2 pump ring dowel pins. Press thrust plate on far enough to install thrust plate retaining ring. Install thrust plate retaining ring into groove in housing with ring opening centered with bolt hole in steering pump nearest to access hole.

5) Lubricate NEW drive shaft seal with power steering fluid, and install into pump housing using socket. Install bearing onto drive shaft, pressing bearing to shoulder of drive shaft or to within clearance measurement made between drive shaft shoulder and inner bearing race during disassembly.

6) Install drive shaft and ball bearing assembly into steering pump. Rotate drive shaft engaging shaft serration with steering pump rotor. Install retaining ring onto housing.

7) Install flow control spring and control valve assembly into housing. Install NEW "O" ring seal onto "O" ring union fitting. Install "O" ring union fitting into steering pump; tighten to specification. See TORQUE SPECIFICATIONS table. Install steering pump. See STEERING PUMP under REMOVAL & INSTALLATION.

TORQUE SPECIFICATIONS
TORQUE SPECIFICATIONS

Application	Ft. Lbs. (N.m)
Adjuster Plug Lock Nut	50 (68)
Frame-To-Body Bolts	[1] 103 (140)
Inner Tie Rod	74 (100)
Intermediate Shaft Pinch Bolts	35 (47)
Lines-To-Steering Gear	18 (24)
"O" Ring Union Fitting	55 (75)
Pinion Shaft Lock Nut	22 (30)
Steering Gear Mounting Bolts	70 (95)
Steering Pump Mounting Bolts	
3.1L	18 (25)
3.8L	20 (27)
Tie Rod End Lock Nut	50 (68)
Tie Rod-To-Steering Knuckle Nut	[2] 30 (41)

[1] – Use NEW bolt. DO NOT reuse bolts.
[2] – Maximum torque to align cotter key hole is 52 ft. lbs. (71 N.m).

Astro, Bravada, Commercial Van, Jimmy, Lumina APV, Safari, Sierra, Silhouette, Sonoma, Suburban, Syclone, Trans Sport, Typhoon, Van, Yukon, "C" & "K" Series Blazer & Pickup, "S" & "T" Series Blazer & Pickup

IDENTIFICATION

AUTOMATIC TRANSMISSION APPLICATIONS

Model	Transmission
Astro & Safari	Hydra-Matic 4L60
Bravada, Jimmy, Sonoma, Syclone, Typhoon & "S" & "T" Series Blazer & Pickup	Hydra-Matic 4L60
Commercial Van	Hydra-Matic 4L80-E
Lumina APV, Silhouette & Trans Sport	Hydra-Matic 3T40 & 4T60-E
Sierra, Suburban, Van, Yukon & "C" & "K" Series Blazer & Pickup	Hydra-Matic 4L60 & 4L80-E

LUBRICATION

SERVICE INTERVALS

Bravada, Lumina APV, Silhouette & Trans Sport – Check transmission fluid level at each engine oil change. Under normal driving conditions, change transmission fluid and filter every 100,000 miles. Under severe driving conditions, change fluid and filter every 15,000 miles.

Except Bravada, Lumina APV, Silhouette & Trans Sport – Check transmission fluid level at each engine oil change. Under normal griving conditions, on vehicles under 8600 Gross Vehicle Weight Rating (GVWR), change transmission fluid and filter at 30,000 mile intervals. On vehicles over 8600 GVWR, change transmission fluid and filter at 24,000 miles.

If vehicle is used in severe service conditions (commercial use, trailer pulling, constant stop-and-go driving), change fluid and filter every 15,000 miles on vehicles under 8600 GVWR and at 12,000 miles on vehicles over 8600 GVWR.

Transfer Case – Check transfer case fluid every oil change or every 12 months. Check more frequently under severe conditions.

CHECKING FLUID LEVEL

NOTE: Vehicle must be at normal operating temperature (180-200 degrees) when checking fluid level. One pint of fluid raises level from ADD to FULL mark on dipstick in a hot transmission. DO NOT overfill.

Transmission – With vehicle parked on a level surface and engine at idle, move selector lever through all positions, ending in Park. Let vehicle idle for 3 minutes with accessories off. Remove dipstick, wipe clean and check fluid level. Fluid level should be between ADD and FULL marks on dipstick.

If vehicle has been operated for an extended time at high speed, in city traffic, or pulling a trailer, an accurate fluid level cannot be immediately determined. Transmission must cool for about 30 minutes after vehicle is parked before fluid level can be accurately checked.

Transfer Case – Remove fill plug. Check fluid level. If level is not up to fill plug opening, add fluid until fluid reaches bottom of plug opening.

RECOMMENDED FLUID

Transmissions and transfer cases use Dexron-IIE ATF. Although Dexron-IIE is recommended, Dexron-II may still be used. Dexron-II will eventually be replaced with Dexron-IIE.

FLUID CAPACITY

Transfer Case & Transmission – The transmission refill capacities are approximate. See TRANSMISSION REFILL CAPACITIES and TRANSFER CASE REFILL CAPACITIES tables. Determine correct fluid level by marks on dipstick. DO NOT overfill.

TRANSMISSION REFILL CAPACITIES

Application	Refill Qts. (L)	Dry Fill Qts. (L)
Hydra-Matic 3T40	4.0 (3.8)	7 (6.6)
Hydra-Matic 4L60	5.0 (4.8)	11.2 (10.6)
Hydra-Matic 4T60-E	6.0 (5.7)	7.1 (6.7)
Hydra-Matic 4L80-E	5.0 (4.7)	11.5 (10.9)

TRANSFER CASE REFILL CAPACITIES

Application	Capacity
New Process Model 231 & 233	2.2 Pts. (1.1L)
New Process Model 241	4.6 Pts. (2.2L)
Borg-Warner Model 4401, 4470 & 4472	2.9 Pts. (1.4L)

DRAINING & REFILLING

Transmission – 1) Raise and support vehicle. Loosen transmission oil pan bolts. Slowly pry pan loose with a large screwdriver and allow fluid to drain. Remove oil pan and gasket. Remove filter or filter screen. Replace paper element filter (if used) and seal.

2) Clean filter screen (if equipped) and pan with solvent. Blow dry with compressed air. Install oil pan with new gasket. Tighten bolts to specification. See TORQUE SPECIFICATIONS at end of article.

3) Add 3 quarts of Dexron-IIE. Start engine and recheck level. Add fluid until level is between FULL and ADD marks on dipstick. Test drive vehicle and recheck fluid level.

Transfer Case – Remove drain plug from transfer case. Remove fill plug for easier draining. With fluid fully drained, reinstall drain plug. Fill transfer case to fill plug opening with Dexron-IIE.

ADJUSTMENTS

THROTTLE VALVE (T.V.) CABLE

Hydra-Matic 3T40, 4L60 & 4T60-E – Depress readjust tab on cable adjuster and hold. *See Fig. 1.* Move slider back through fitting away from throttle body lever until slider stops at fitting. Release readjust tab and open throttle body lever to full throttle stop. This automatically adjusts slider to correct setting.

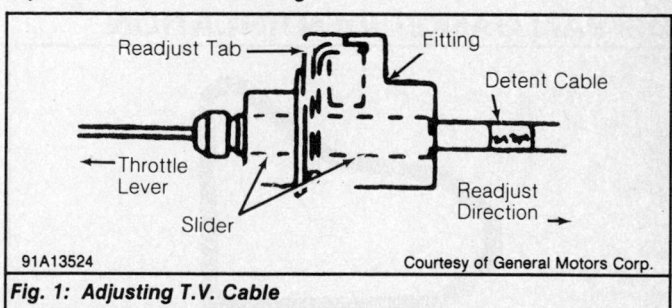

91A13524   Courtesy of General Motors Corp.

Fig. 1: Adjusting T.V. Cable

SHIFT LINKAGE

Commercial Van – 1) Remove clevis pin retaining clip and clevis pin. *See Fig. 2.* Move shift lever arm at transmission fully forward and then pull back 2 detents to Neutral position.

2) Loosen jam nut and adjust cable end to align with shift lever arm at transmission. Reinstall clevis pin and clip. Check adjustment, engine should start in Park and Neutral only.

Lumina APV, Silhouette & Trans Sport – 1) To adjust shift cable, place shift lever in Neutral. Turn transaxle lever clockwise from Park through Reverse to Neutral.

2) Place shift control assembly in Neutral position. Push tab on cable adjuster to adjust cable in cable mounting bracket.

Except Commercial Van, Lumina APV, Silhouette & Trans Sport – 1) Ensure shift tube and lever are free in steering column. To adjust linkage, remove screw and spring washer from swivel. Turn transmission lever clockwise to stop, then counterclockwise 2 detents. This is Neutral position.

2) Place selector lever in Neutral. Locate proper position using mechanical stops, NOT shift indicator pointer. Hold swivel against shift lever. Install spring washer and screw. Tighten finger tight. Avoid applying force in either direction (along shift rod or lever) while tightening screw to specification. See TORQUE SPECIFICATIONS at end of article.

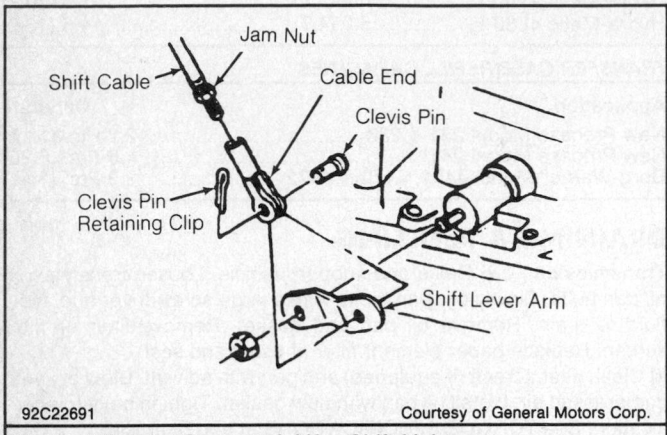

92C22691   Courtesy of General Motors Corp.

Fig. 2: Adjusting Commercial Van Shift Linkage

NEUTRAL SAFETY SWITCH

Trans. Mounted Switch (Lumina APV, Silhouette & Trans Sport) –
1) Raise and support vehicle and loosen switch mounting bolts. Align hole in switch lever with hole in switch assembly. Insert a 3/32" gauge pin through switch holes to hold switch in Neutral position.
2) With selector lever on transmission in Neutral detent position, tighten switch mounting bolts and remove gauge pin. Lower vehicle and check operation of switch.

___

NOTE: Neutral safety switch adjustment information for all models except Lumina APV, Silhouette and Trans Sport is not available from manufacturer.

OIL PAN GASKET IDENTIFICATION

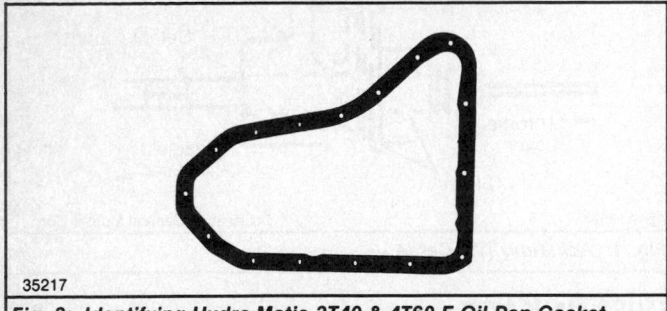

35217

Fig. 3: Identifying Hydra-Matic 3T40 & 4T60-E Oil Pan Gasket

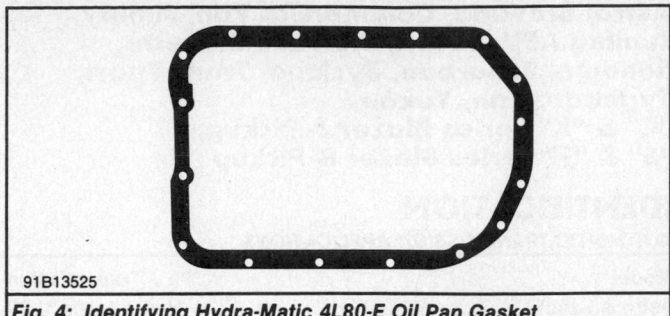

91B13525

Fig. 4: Identifying Hydra-Matic 4L80-E Oil Pan Gasket

121173

Fig. 5: Identifying Hydra-Matic 4L60 Oil Pan Gasket

TORQUE SPECIFICATIONS
TORQUE SPECIFICATIONS

Application	Ft. Lbs. (N.m)
Oil Pan Bolts	
4L60 & 4L80-E	15 (20)
4T60-E	13 (18)
Neutral Safety Switch	
Lumina APV, Silhouette & Trans Sport	
3T40	22 (30)
4T60-E	15 (20)
Shift Linkage Spring Washer Screw	
Astro, Safari & Van	26 (35)
Bravada, Jimmy, Sonoma, Syclone, Typhoon &	
"S" & "T" Series Blazer & Pickup	18 (24)
Sierra, Suburban, Yukon &	
"C" & "K" Series Blazer & Pickup	18 (24)
	INCH Lbs. (N.m)
Oil Pan Bolts 3T40	96 (11)

Commercial Van, Jimmy, Sierra, Sonoma, Suburban, Yukon, "C" & "K" Series Blazer & Pickup, "S" & "T" Series Blazer & Pickup

IDENTIFICATION

MANUAL TRANSMISSION APPLICATION

Vehicle Model	Transmission Model (RPO)
Commercial Van	NVG 4500 109 MM 5-Speed O/D (MT8)
Jimmy, Sonoma & "S" & "T" Series Blazer & Pickup	Borg-Warner T5 77 MM 5-Speed (MW1) NVG 5LM60 85 MM 5-Speed O/D (MY2)
Sierra, Suburban, Yukon & "C" & "K" Series Blazer & Pickup	NVG 5LM60 85 MM 5-Speed O/D (MG5) NVG 4500 109 MM 5-Speed O/D (MT8)

LUBRICATION

SERVICE INTERVALS

NOTE: There are 2 light duty truck emission control classifications: Light Duty (up to 8600 lbs. Gross Vehicle Weight) and Heavy Duty (vehicles more than 8600 lbs. GVW).

Transmission – On all light duty vehicles, check transmission fluid level every 12 months or 7500 miles. On heavy duty vehicles, check fluid level every 12 months or 6000 miles. Periodic draining and refilling is not required.

Transfer Case – Check transfer case fluid at every oil change or every 12 months. Under severe conditions, check more frequently.

CHECKING FLUID LEVEL

Transmission & Transfer Case – Remove filler plug. Fluid should be level with bottom of filler plug hole. Add as necessary.

RECOMMENDED FLUID

RECOMMENDED FLUID

Application	Fluid Type
Borg-Warner T5 77 MM 5-Speed	[1] Dexron-IIE ATF
NVG 5LM60 85 MM 5-Speed O/D	API GL5 (SAE 80W-90)
NVG 4500 109 MM 5-Speed O/D	GM Man. Trans. Syn. Fluid (12345871)
Transfer Cases	[1] Dexron-IIE ATF

[1] – Although Dexron-IIE is recommended, Dexron-II may still be used. Dexron-II will eventually be replaced with Dexron-IIE.

FLUID CAPACITY

NOTE: Capacities listed in the following chart are approximations only. Correct fluid level should be determined by level at filler plug hole rather than by amount added.

TRANSMISSION REFILL CAPACITIES

Application	Pts. (L)
Borg-Warner (T5) 5-Speed	4.2 (2.0)
NVG 5LM60 5-Speed O/D	4.2 (2.0)
NVG 4500 5-Speed O/D	8.4 (4.0)

TRANSFER CASE REFILL CAPACITIES

Application	Pts. (L)
New Process Model 231 & 233	2.5 (1.2)
New Process Model 241	4.6 (2.2)
Borg-Warner Model 4401	2.9 (1.4)
Borg-Warner Model 4470	6.6 (3.1)

ADJUSTMENTS

NOTE: Manual transmissions have no shift rods. The shift lever mounts directly to top of transmission and is not adjustable.

Astro, Bravada, Commercial Van, Jimmy, Lumina APV, Safari, Sierra, Silhouette, Sonoma, Suburban, Syclone, Trans Sport, Typhoon, Van, Yukon, "C" & "K" Series Blazer & Pickup, "S" & "T" Series Blazer & Pickup

IDENTIFICATION

AUTOMATIC TRANSMISSION APPLICATIONS

Model	Transmission
Astro & Safari	Hydra-Matic 4L60
Bravada, Jimmy, Sonoma, Syclone, Typhoon & "S" & "T" Series Blazer & Pickup	Hydra-Matic 4L60
Commercial Van	Hydra-Matic 4L80-E
Lumina APV, Silhouette & Trans Sport	Hydra-Matic 3T40 & 4T60-E
Sierra, Suburban, Van, Yukon & "C" & "K" Series Blazer & Pickup	Hydra-Matic 4L60 & 4L80-E

MANUAL TRANSMISSION APPLICATION

Vehicle Model	Transmission Model (RPO)
Commercial Van	NVG 4500 109 MM 5-Speed O/D (MT8)
Jimmy, Sonoma & "S" & "T" Series Blazer & Pickup	Borg-Warner T5 77 MM 5-Speed (MW1) NVG 5LM60 85 MM 5-Speed O/D (MY2)
Sierra, Suburban, Yukon & "C" & "K" Series Blazer & Pickup	NVG 5LM60 85 MM 5-Speed O/D (MG5) NVG 4500 109 MM 5-Speed O/D (MT8)

TRANSFER CASE APPLICATIONS

Model	Transfer Case
Astro, Bravada, Safari Syclone, & Typhoon	BW-4472
Jimmy, Sonoma, "T" Series Blazer & Pickup	NP-231 & NP-233
Sierra, Suburban, Yukon & "K" Series Blazer & Pickup	NP-241
K30 & Sierra 3500 (Some)	BW-4401 & BW-4470

MANUAL TRANSMISSION

NOTE: For manual transmission replacement procedures, see CLUTCH article.

TRANSFER CASE (A/T)

WARNING: When battery is disconnected, vehicle computer and memory systems may lose memory data. Driveability problems may exist until computer systems have completed a relearn cycle. See COMPUTER RELEARN PROCEDURES article in GENERAL INFORMATION before disconnecting battery.

BW-4401 & BW-4470

Removal) – 1) Disconnect negative battery cable. Place transfer case in 4H position. Raise vehicle. Remove skid plate. Drain fluid from transfer case. Mark front drive shaft and flange for reassembly reference. Remove front drive shaft.

2) Remove left strut rod. Mark rear drive shaft and flange for reassembly reference. Remove rear drive shaft. Disconnect electrical connectors from transfer case. Disconnect shift linkage at transfer case.

3) Support transfer case and remove transfer case-to-transmission adapter bolts. Remove transfer case by moving transfer case rearward until it is free of transmission output shaft. Remove old gasket material.

Installation – To install, reverse removal procedure. Install a NEW gasket and fill transfer case with Dexron-IIE.

BW-4472

Removal – 1) Disconnect negative battery cable. Raise and support vehicle on hoist. Drain transfer case. Mark rear drive shaft components for reassembly reference. Disconnect rear drive shaft from differential and remove from vehicle.

2) Mark front drive shaft components for reassembly reference. Disconnect front drive shaft from transfer case and differential. Remove front drive shaft from vehicle. Disconnect breather hose and electrical connectors from transfer case.

3) Support transfer case and remove transfer case mount and support bracket. Remove transfer case-to-transmission adapter bolts. Move transfer case to rear and lower assembly from vehicle.

Installation – Position NEW gasket on transfer case adapter with gasket sealer. To complete installation, reverse removal procedure and fill transfer case with Dexron-IIE.

NP-241

Removal – 1) Disconnect negative battery cable. Raise and support vehicle on hoist. Remove skid plate. Drain transfer case. Mark rear drive shaft components for reassembly reference. Disconnect and remove rear drive shaft from vehicle.

2) Mark front drive shaft components for reassembly reference. Disconnect and remove front drive shaft from vehicle. Disconnect vent hose and electrical connectors from transfer case. Disconnect speedometer cable and shift linkage at transfer case. Remove transfer case strut rod (if equipped).

3) Support transfer case and remove bolts attaching transfer case to transmission adapter. Move transfer case to rear until input shaft clears adapter. Lower transfer case assembly from vehicle.

Installation – To install, reverse removal procedure. Install a NEW gasket and fill transfer case with Dexron-IIE.

NP-231 & NP-233

Removal – 1) Disconnect negative battery cable. Move transfer case shift lever to 4H position. Raise vehicle and remove skid plate. Drain transfer case. Mark front and rear output shaft yokes and drive shafts for reassembly reference and remove shafts.

2) Disconnect speedometer cable and vacuum harness from transfer case. Disconnect shift linkage from case. Remove catalytic converter hanger bolts at converter and loosen front catalytic converter clamp.

3) Raise transmission and transfer case assembly with jack and remove transmission mount bolts. Remove catalytic converter front bracket. Lower transmission and transfer case. Support transfer case alone and remove transmission-to-transfer case bolts.

4) Remove shift lever bracket from transfer case adapter in order to reach upper left attaching bolt. Separate transfer case from transmission adapter and remove from vehicle.

Installation – To install, reverse removal procedure. Always use a NEW gasket between transfer case and adapter and fill transfer case with Dexron-IIE.

AUTOMATIC TRANSMISSION

WARNING: When battery is disconnected, vehicle computer and memory systems may lose memory data. Driveability problems may exist until computer systems have completed a relearn cycle. See COMPUTER RELEARN PROCEDURES article in GENERAL INFORMATION before disconnecting battery.

4L60 & 4L80-E

Removal – 1) Disconnect negative battery cable and remove air cleaner. Disconnect Throttle Valve (T.V.) cable from throttle linkage. Raise and support vehicle. Drain transmission fluid. Disconnect shift linkage at transmission.

WARNING: ALWAYS relieve fuel pressure before disconnecting any fuel injection related component. DO NOT allow fuel to contact electrical components.

2) Mark rear drive shaft for installation reference and remove from vehicle. Mark front drive shaft and remove from transfer case, if equipped. Hold rag over disconnect area and relieve fuel line pressure. Remove fuel lines.

3) Remove transmission support bracket attaching bolts at converter. Position transmission jack under transmission and raise slightly. Remove transmission crossmember-to-mount bolts, crossmember-to-frame bolts and vibration damper (if equipped). Slide crossmember rearward and remove from vehicle.

CAUTION: When lowering transmission to gain clearance for additional component removal, use care not to stretch or damage transmission lines, cables or wires.

4) Remove dipstick tube and seal. Disconnect speedometer cable at transmission. Disconnect vacuum modulator line (if equipped). Lower transmission enough to gain access and disconnect all electrical leads at transmission and electrical harness clips on transmission. Disconnect oil cooler lines and cap openings.

5) Disconnect transfer case shifter and move aside. Note location of transmission support brackets before removal for reassembly reference. Remove transmission support brackets. Remove torque converter cover and mark flywheel and torque converter to maintain original balance. Remove torque converter-to-flywheel bolts.

6) Support engine and remove transmission-to-engine bolts. Disconnect transmission assembly, being careful not to damage any cables, lines or linkage. Install Torque Converter Holding Strap (J-21366) and remove transmission from vehicle.

Installation – To install, reverse removal procedure. Mount vibration damper (if equipped) at a 90 degree angle to centerline of transmission.

3T40 & 4T60-E

Removal – **1)** Disconnect negative battery cable and remove. Remove air intake duct. Remove cruise control cable, vacuum hoses and servo assembly. Remove shift control linkage and manual lever at transaxle.

2) Remove all wiring connectors at transaxle. Remove fuel line retainers. Remove vacuum modulator hose at transaxle.

WARNING: ALWAYS relieve fuel pressure before disconnecting any fuel injection related component. DO NOT allow fuel to contact electrical components.

3) Cover surrounding areas with a shop rag while relieving fuel pressure. Remove fuel lines. Drain coolant and remove radiator and fan assembly. Remove throttle cables from throttle body.

4) Remove torque strut and bracket from engine. Disconnect wiring harness at ECM and pull through firewall. Separate engine wiring harness from body connectors and lay harness on engine.

5) Remove A/C compressor from bracket and tie off to lower tie bar. Remove vapor hoses from canister. Remove starter assembly. Remove power steering lines from frame rail and disconnect as required for removal.

6) Raise and support vehicle. Remove front wheels and stabilizer shaft. Disconnect tie rod ends at steering knuckle. Remove lower control arm ball joints from steering knuckles.

7) Remove drive axles from transaxle and support them to body. See FWD AXLE SHAFTS article in DRIVE AXLES. Remove intermediate steering shaft pinch bolt. Remove torque converter cover and remove converter-to-flexplate bolts.

8) Separate exhaust pipe at rear manifold. Support engine/frame/transaxle assembly (with hydraulic table). Remove frame bolts.

NOTE: When lowering engine/frame/transaxle assembly, ensure ALL lines, wiring and attaching components are free and unobstructed.

9) Lower engine/frame/transaxle assembly. Remove transaxle mounts and exhaust crossover pipe. Remove transaxle-to-engine bolts, ensuring bolt from engine side is also removed.

Installation – To install, reverse removal procedure. Tighten all nuts and bolts to specification. See appropriate TORQUE SPECIFICATIONS table. Refill coolant and adjust transaxle fluid level with Dexron-IIE. Adjust cables as necessary and check for fluid leaks.

TORQUE SPECIFICATIONS

TORQUE SPECIFICATIONS (3T40)

Application	Ft. Lbs. (N.m)
Cooler Lines-To-Radiator	20 (27)
Cooler Lines-To-Transaxle	16 (22)
Crossmember-To-Frame Bolts	56 (76)
Dipstick Tube-To-Engine	14 (19)
Flexplate-To-Torque Converter Bolts	35 (47)
Transaxle Mounts Bolts	22 (30)
Transaxle Mount-To-Bracket Nut	35 (47)
Transaxle-To-Engine Bolts	55 (75)

	INCH Lbs. (N.m)
Converter Cover Housing	48 (5)
T.V. Cable	80 (9)

TORQUE SPECIFICATIONS (4T60-E)

Application	Ft. Lbs. (N.m)
Cooler Lines-To-Radiator	20 (27)
Cooler Pipe & Tube Nut	30 (41)
Crossmember-To-Frame Bolts	56 (76)
Flexplate-To-Torque Converter Bolts	46 (62)
Transaxle Mounts Bolts	52 (71)
Transaxle Mount-To-Bracket Nut	30 (41)
Transaxle-To-Engine Bolts	55 (75)

	INCH Lbs. (N.m)
Converter Cover Housing	62 (7)
T.V. Cable	80 (9)

TORQUE SPECIFICATIONS (4L60)

Application	Ft. Lbs. (N.m)
Cooler Lines-To-Transmission	18 (24)
Crossmember-To-Frame Bolts	56 (76)
Dipstick Tube-To-Engine	23 (31)
Flexplate-To-Torque Converter Bolts	46 (62)
Transmission-To-Engine Bolts	23 (31)

	INCH Lbs. (N.m)
T.V. Cable	80 (9)
Converter Housing Cover	88 (10)

TORQUE SPECIFICATIONS (4L80-E)

Application	Ft. Lbs. (N.m)
Cooler Lines-To-Transmission	28 (38)
Crossmember-To-Frame Bolts	56 (76)
Dipstick Tube-To-Engine	33 (45)
Flexplate-To-Torque Converter Bolts	33 (45)
Transmission-To-Engine Bolts	33 (45)

	INCH Lbs. (N.m)
Converter Housing Cover	62 (7)
Speed Sensor-To-Case	96 (11)

TORQUE SPECIFICATIONS (TRANSFER CASES)

Application	Ft. Lbs. (N.m)
Transfer Case-To-Adapter Bolts	
BW-4472	38 (52)
All Others	24 (33)
Transmission-To-Adapter Bolts	
BW-4472	38 (52)
All Others	24 (33)

JEEP

1992 JEEP CONTENTS

NOTE: Includes 1991-92 Cruise Control Systems and 1993 Grand Cherokee.

GENERAL INFORMATION [1]

ENGINE PERFORMANCE

ENGINE PERFORMANCE (Cont.)

1992 ENGINE PERFORMANCE
Jeep Introduction

1992 MODEL COVERAGE

MODEL	BODY CODE	ENGINE [1]	ENGINE ID	FUEL SYSTEM	IGNITION SYSTEM
Cherokee	XJ	2.5L (HX)	P	PFI [2]	Magnetic
		4.0L (MX)	S	PFI [2]	Magnetic
Comanche	MJ	2.5L (HX)	P	PFI [2]	Magnetic
		4.0L (MX)	S	PFI [2]	Magnetic
Grand Cherokee [3]	ZJ	4.0L (MX)	S	PFI [2]	Magnetic
Wrangler	YJ	2.5L (HX)	P	PFI [2]	Magnetic
		4.0L (MX)	S	PFI [2]	Magnetic

[1] – Fourth and fifth characters of engine code (on block) identify engine. See ENGINE CODE LOCATION.
[2] – Sequential Multi-Point Fuel Injection.
[3] – 1993

VIN DEFINITION

1J4FJ35S9NL000001

① ② ③ ④ ⑤ ⑥ ⑦ ⑧ ⑨ ⑩ ⑪ ⑫ ⑬ ⑭ ⑮ ⑯ ⑰

① Indicates Nation of Origin.
② Indicates Manufacturer.
③ Indicates Vehicle Type.
④ Indicates GVWR.
⑤ Indicates Vehicle Line.
⑥ Indicates Vehicle Series.
⑦ Indicates Body Type.
⑧ **Indicates Engine Code.**
⑨ Indicates Check Digit.
⑩ **Indicates Model Year.**
⑪ Indicates Assembly Plant.
⑫ ⑬ ⑭ ⑮ ⑯ ⑰ Indicates Plant Sequential Number.

ENGINE CODE LOCATION

2.5L (HX) – On machined surface, on right side of cylinder block, between cylinders No. 3 and No. 4.
4.0L (MX) – On machined surface, on right side of cylinder block, between cylinders No. 2 and No. 3.

MODEL YEAR VIN CODE APPLICATION

VIN Code	Model Year
N	1992
P	1993

1992 ENGINE PERFORMANCE
Emission Applications

1992 JEEP EMISSION SYSTEMS

Engine & Fuel System	Emission Control Systems & Devices
Cherokee, Comanche, Grand Cherokee [1], Wrangler 2.5L (PFI) & 4.0L (PFI)	[2] **CCV, EVAP, TWC, FR, SPK, O_2, CEC, EMR, CE** EVAP-CPCV, EVAP-PRRV, EVAP-VC, SPK-CC, SPK-TCS,

[1] – 1993 models.
[2] – No PCV valve is used.

NOTE: Major emission control systems are listed above in bold type; components are listed in light type.

CCV – Crankcase Ventilation
CE – Check Engine Light
CEC – Computerized Engine Control
EMR – Emission Maintenance Reminder Light
EVAP – Evaporative Emission Control

EVAP-CPCV – Canister Purge Control Valve
EVAP-PRRV – Pressure Relief/Rollover Valve
EVAP-VC – EVAP System Vapor Canister
FR – Fill Pipe Restrictor
O_2 – Oxygen Sensor

PFI – Multi-Port Fuel Injection
SPK – Spark Controls
SPK-CC – SPK Computer Controlled
SPK-TCS – SPK Transmission Controlled
TWC – Three-Way Catalyst

**Cherokee, Comanche,
Grand Cherokee (1993), Wrangler**

INTRODUCTION

Use this article to quickly find specifications related to servicing and on-vehicle adjustments. This is a quick-reference article for when you are familiar with an adjustment procedure and only need a specification.

CAPACITIES

BATTERY SPECIFICATIONS

Application & Group [1]	Cold Crank Amps @ 0°F (-18°C)
Standard Duty	390
Heavy Duty	475

[1] – All models use group 58 battery.

FLUID CAPACITIES

Application	[1] Quantity
Crankcase [2]	
2.5L	5.0 qts. (4.7L)
4.0L	6.0 qts. (5.7L)
Cooling System (Includes Heater)	
2.5L	
Cherokee & Comanche	10.0 Qts. (9.5L)
Wrangler	9.0 Qts. (8.5L)
4.0L	
Cherokee & Comanche	12.0 Qts. (11.4L)
Grand Cherokee	
Heavy Duty Cooling System	10.5 Qts. (9.9L)
Standard Duty Cooling System	9.0 Qts. (8.5L)
Wrangler	10.5 Qts. (9.9L)
Automatic Transmission (Mercon Or Dexron-II) [3]	
AW-4	8.5 Qts. (8.0L)
32RH	8 Qts. (7.6L)
Manual Transmission (API GL-5 75W-90)	
AX-4 (4-Speed)	7.8 Pts. (3.7L)
AX-5 (2WD 5-Speed)	7.4 Pts. (3.5L)
AX-5 (4WD 5-Speed)	7.0 Pts. (3.3L)
AX-15 (5-Speed)	6.7 Pts. (3.2L)
Front/Rear Axles (API GL-5 75W-90)	
Cherokee [4]	2.5 Pts. (1.2L)
Comanche & Wrangler [5][6]	2.5 Pts. (1.2L)
Comanche & Wrangler (H/D Axle) [5][6]	3.0 Pts. (1.4L)
Grand Cherokee [5][6]	3.0 Pts. (1.4L)
Transfer Case (Mercon or Dexron-II)	
Command-Trac 231	
Except Wrangler	2.2 Pts. (1.0L)
Wrangler	3.3 Pts. (1.5L)
Model 249	3.0 Pts. (1.4L)
Selec-Trac 242	3.0 Pts. (1.4L)

[1] – Fluid capacities listed are approximate. Always fill to FULL mark.
[2] – Includes oil filter.
[3] – Drain and refill capacity only. Does not include torque converter.
[4] – With trailer towing package (5000 lbs.), use 75W-140 synthetic gear oil.
[5] – With trailer towing package use API GL-5 80W-140.
[6] – With limited slip differential, add 2 ounces of friction modifier.

QUICK-SERVICE

SERVICE INTERVALS & SPECIFICATIONS

REPLACEMENT INTERVALS

Component	Miles
Oil & Filter	7500
Air Filter	30,000
Coolant	52,500
Fuel Filter	30,000
Oxygen Sensor	75,000
Spark Plugs	30,000

BELT ADJUSTMENT
(Tension In Lbs. (kg) Using Belt Tension Gauge)

Application	Tension
Serpentine Belt	
New Belts	180-200 (81.72-90.8)
Used Belts	140-160 (63.56-72.64)
V-Belt	
New Belts	120-160 (54.48-72.64)
Used Belts	90-115 (40.86-52.21)

MECHANICAL CHECKS

ENGINE COMPRESSION

Check engine compression with engine at normal operating temperature at specified cranking speed, all spark plugs removed (on dual plugs, remove exhaust side only) and throttle wide open.

NOTE: Compression pressure and cylinder pressure variation for 2.5L and 4.0L engines are not available from manufacturer.

COMPRESSION RATIO

Application	Specification
2.5L	
Cherokee & Comanche	9.2:1
Wrangler	9.1:1
4.0L	8.8:1

VALVE CLEARANCE

NOTE: All models are equipped with hydraulic lifters. No adjustments are required.

IGNITION SYSTEM

IGNITION COIL
IGNITION COIL RESISTANCE – Ohms @ 68°F (20°C)

Application	Primary Ohms	Secondary Ohms
Diamond Coil	.95-1.20	11,300-15,300
Toyodenso Coil	.95-1.20	11,300-13,300

HIGH TENSION WIRE RESISTANCE
HIGH TENSION WIRE RESISTANCE

Application	Ohms
All Wires	250-1000 per inch

SPARK PLUGS
SPARK PLUG TYPE

Application	Specification
2.5L & 4.0L	Champion RC-12 LYC

SPARK PLUG SPECIFICATIONS

Application	Gap In. (mm)	Torque Ft. Lbs. (N.m)
2.5L & 4.0L	.035 (.89)	27 (36.6)

FIRING ORDER & TIMING MARKS

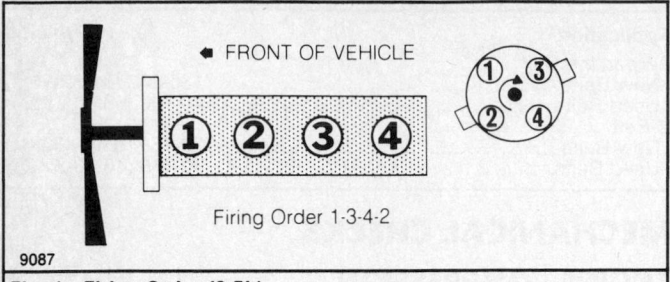

Firing Order 1-3-4-2

9087

Fig. 1: Firing Order (2.5L)

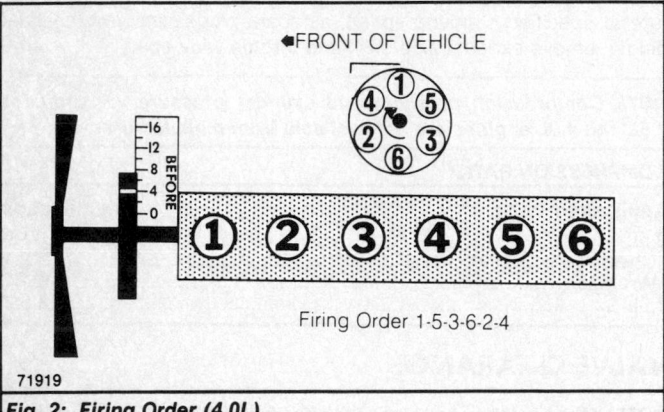

Firing Order 1-5-3-6-2-4

71919

Fig. 2: Firing Order (4.0L)

IGNITION TIMING

All models are equipped with Single Board Engine Controller II computerized ignition. SBEC-II controls ignition timing. No adjustment is possible.

DISTRIBUTOR SPECIFICATIONS

All models are equipped with Single Board Engine Controller II computerized ignition. Distributor's only function is to distribute high voltage to appropriate spark plug. No adjustments are required.

FUEL SYSTEM

FUEL PUMP

NOTE: Fuel pump performance refers to fuel pressure and volume availability, not regulated fuel pressure.

FUEL PUMP PERFORMANCE

Application	Pressure psi (kg/cm²)	Min. Vol. In 30 Sec.
2.5L & 4.0L	39 (2.70)	1 pt. (.47L)

REGULATED FUEL PRESSURE

Application	psi (kg/cm²)
2.5L & 4.0L (At Idle)	
With Vacuum	31 (2.18)
Without Vacuum	39 (2.70)

INJECTOR RESISTANCE

INJECTOR RESISTANCE – Ohms @ 68°F (20°C)

Application	Specification
2.5L & 4.0L	12.8-15.2

IDLE SPEED & MIXTURE

NOTE: Idle mixture is controlled by the Single Board Engine Controller II (SBEC-II). Adjustment is not required or possible.

THROTTLE POSITION SENSOR (TPS)

2.5L & 4.0L – Output voltage (center terminal of TPS) should be .20-1.2 volts with closed throttle. TPS is not adjustable.

**Cherokee, Comanche,
Grand Cherokee (1993), Wrangler**

ENGINE MECHANICAL

Before performing any on-vehicle adjustments to fuel or ignition systems, ensure engine mechanical condition is okay.

VALVE CLEARANCE

All models are equipped with hydraulic valve lifters. No adjustments are required.

IGNITION TIMING

All Jeep vehicles are equipped with Single Board Engine Controller-II computerized ignition system. SBEC-II controls ignition timing. Adjustment is not required or possible.

IDLE SPEED & MIXTURE

All Jeep vehicles are equipped with Single Board Engine Controller-II computerized ignition system. SBEC-II controls idle speed and air/fuel mixture. Adjustments are not required or possible.

THROTTLE POSITION SENSOR (TPS)

1) Turn ignition on. Check TPS output voltage at sensor wiring harness center terminal. At idle, output voltage should be greater than 200 millivolts.
2) Gradually open throttle plate. Output voltage should gradually increase as throttle plate is opened. At wide open throttle, output voltage must be less than 4.8 volts.
3) If voltages are not as specified, make sure 5-volt input and ground circuits between TPS and engine controller are okay. Repair circuits, if necessary. If TPS output voltages are still not as specified, replace TPS. Adjustment is not required or possible.

NOTE: Also see appropriate throttle position sensor tests in SELF-DIAGNOSTICS article.

1992 ENGINE PERFORMANCE
Theory & Operation

**Cherokee, Comanche,
Grand Cherokee (1993), Wrangler**

INTRODUCTION

This article covers basic description and operation of engine performance-related systems and components. Read this article before diagnosing vehicles or systems with which you are not completely familiar.

COMPUTERIZED ENGINE CONTROLS

SINGLE BOARD ENGINE CONTROLLER-II

The Single Board Engine Controller-II (SBEC-II) is a dual microprocessor that receives various signals from engine sensors and provides the necessary signals to control engine sub-systems. The SBEC-II has a voltage converter that converts battery voltage to regulated 5-volt or 8-volt outputs. The regulated 5-volt output is used to power Manifold Absolute Pressure (MAP) sensor, Throttle Position Sensor (TPS) and logic circuits. The regulated 8-volt output is used to power crankshaft position sensor and synchronization signal generator in distributor.

The ignition and fuel injection systems are controlled by the SBEC-II. Based on present engine operating conditions, the engine controller is programmed to provide a precise amount of fuel and the correct ignition timing to meet existing engine speed and load requirements.

The engine controller adjusts ignition timing based on inputs it receives from synchronization sensor generator, MAP sensor, coolant temperature sensor, throttle position sensor, vehicle speed sensor, transmission gear selection (automatic transmissions only), and brake switch.

The engine controller adjusts idle speed based on inputs it receives from throttle position sensor, vehicle speed sensor, transmission gear selection (automatic transmissions only), A/C clutch switch, and brake switch.

The engine controller also controls the speed (cruise) control system and alternator charge rate by controlling the alternator field.

NOTE: Components are grouped into 2 categories. The first category covers INPUT DEVICES, which control or produce voltage signals that are monitored by the SBEC-II. The second category covers OUTPUT SIGNALS, which are components controlled by the SBEC-II.

INPUT DEVICES

Vehicles are equipped with different combinations of input devices. Not all devices are used on all models. To determine the input device usage on a specific model, see appropriate wiring diagram in WIRING DIAGRAMS article. The available input signals include the following:

A/C Pressure Switch & Evaporator Switch – When A/C switch is in ON position and A/C low pressure switch and evaporator switch are closed, an A/C select signal is sent to engine controller. If A/C low pressure switch or evaporator switch opens, the engine controller will not receive an A/C select signal.

When A/C function is selected (A/C switch on), the A/C request signal provides information to the engine controller from the A/C temperature control thermostat (evaporator switch). This signal indicates evaporator temperature is in the proper range for A/C operation.

The A/C request signal is used by engine controller to determine required Automatic Idle Speed (AIS) motor position and to activate or deactivate A/C compressor clutch. When engine controller receives an A/C request signal, it repositions the AIS motor to increase idle speed. The increased idle speed compensates for additional engine load caused by engagement of A/C compressor.

On 4.0L engine, whenever A/C compressor clutch is energized, engine controller also energizes the radiator (cooling) fan relay. This occurs regardless on engine coolant temperature.

Alternator Output – The engine controller keeps charging system voltage at 13.4-15.0 volts. Charging system voltage will be adjusted by engine controller based on battery temperature sensor, located within engine controller housing. The voltage determined by engine controller as final goal for charging system is called "control" voltage. The control voltage will be used to determine alternator field control and to detect if charging system is operating properly.

If sensed voltage is lower than "control" voltage, engine controller will alter duty cycle and ground alternator (rotor) field for a longer period of time and create a higher alternator output which should raise sensed voltage level. If sensed voltage is higher than "control" voltage, engine controller will alter duty cycle and lower alternator output which should lower sensed voltage level.

Battery Voltage Signal – The engine controller uses a battery voltage signal to determine vehicle's battery voltage level. The engine controller uses this information to determine injector pulse width and alternator field control.

The engine controller uses battery voltage level to regulate alternator field (rotor) duty cycle and alter fuel injector pulse width according to available voltage. If battery voltage drops, engine controller will increase injector on time to compensate for the reduced fuel flow of injector caused by the lower voltage. This will permit injector to deliver proper amount of fuel to the engine.

Brake Switch – The brake switch is mounted on steering column support bracket, under instrument panel. The engine controller uses the brake switch to determine when brakes are being applied or not. When brakes are applied (brake switch on) and if engine controller sees a TPS opening and a lower speed sensor rate, it recognizes a deceleration condition and opens up the Automatic Idle Speed (AIS) motor. The brake switch signal will also disengage speed (cruise) control operation, if it was engaged.

Coolant Temperature Sensor – The coolant temperature sensor is mounted on top of engine, next to thermostat housing. It provides an analog signal to the engine controller that is used to calculate injector pulse width and ignition timing when engine is cold. Input from the coolant temperature sensor will also affect Automatic Idle Speed (AIS) motor position and spark advance operation.

Crankshaft Position Sensor – The Hall Effect type crankshaft position sensor is mounted on transaxle bellhousing. The sensor reads slots (4 per cylinder) on flywheel/flex plate. The signal generated provides engine speed and crankshaft position information to engine controller. The engine controller uses this information to determine proper fuel injection and ignition timing.

When a flywheel/flex plate slot passes the crankshaft position sensor magnet, output voltage of the Hall Effect sensor goes high (5 volts). When the metal between the slots is aligned with sensor, output voltage goes low (.3 volts).

This high/low voltage signal is generated and sent to engine controller each time one of the slots passes the crankshaft position sensor. The engine controller uses this information to determine when to energize the injectors for fuel delivery to the proper cylinders.

Ignition Circuit – When ignition key is turned to the ON position, the engine controller receives a signal that the ignition circuit has been activated. The engine controller will start looking at the input signals.

Manifold Absolute Pressure (MAP) Sensor – The MAP sensor is mounted on engine compartment firewall. The MAP sensor is used by engine controller to calibrate amount of air/fuel mixture supplied to the engine. This sensor measures manifold absolute pressure and ambient barometric pressure when ignition switch is first turned on, during engine cranking, and at wide open throttle.

The MAP sensor transmits a low voltage signal (1.5-2.1 volts) at idle when manifold vacuum is high, and a higher voltage signal (3.9-4.8 volts) during open throttle when manifold vacuum is low.

Input voltage (from the engine controller) to MAP sensor ranges from 4.8-5.1 volts. Adjustments made as a result of this input will usually affect injector pulse width, ignition timing, idle speed and upshift indicator light.

Manifold Air Temperature (MAT) Sensor – The MAP sensor is located on intake manifold, with sensor element extending into the air stream. The sensor measures the temperature of air entering the intake manifold. This sensor provides an analog voltage signal to engine controller. This signal is used to compensate for changes in air density due to temperature.

The MAT sensor is a Negative Temperature Coefficient (NTC) thermistor-type sensor. Its internal resistance varies opposite with temperature. At cold temperatures, the resistance is high. As temperature increases, its resistance decreases.

Oxygen (O_2) Sensor – The heated oxygen sensor detects amount of oxygen content of the exhaust gases and produces a voltage signal. Engine controller uses this signal to monitor system output signals which control air/fuel mixture.

Variations in voltage signal from O_2 sensor serve as air/fuel ratio indicators. Changes occur because oxygen sensor voltage input to engine controller varies. When oxygen content is low (rich mixture), voltage signal will be approximately one volt. When oxygen content is high (lean mixture), voltage signal will be approximately 0.1 volt.

The O_2 sensor contains a ceramic heater in the sensor housing. The heater operates on 12 volts. The heater is used in cold starts to help O_2 sensor heat up quicker and to maintain the O_2 sensor's Zirconia semiconductor at its operational temperature of 932-1112°F (500-600°C).

In "closed loop" operation, engine controller monitors O_2 sensor input (along with other sensors) and adjusts the injector pulse width accordingly. During "open loop" operation, engine controller ignores O_2 sensor input and adjust injector pulse width to a pre-programmed value based on the other sensor inputs.

Park/Neutral Switch – On vehicles equipped with automatic transmission, a gear position indicator signal is sent to engine controller when gear selector lever has been moved to the Drive range. This signal comes from the Park/Neutral switch (Neutral safety switch on AW-4) and allows engine controller to adjust idle speed, fuel injector pulse width, and ignition timing advance.

Power Steering Switch – On 2.5L vehicles with power steering, a power steering switch is used. The switch is located on pressure line, next to power steering pump.

The power steering switch sends a signal to engine controller when pressures in system rise above 250-300 psi (17.6-21.1 kg/cm²) and engine RPM is low. The engine controller, through AIS motor, will raise the idle speed to prevent engine from stalling.

Serial Communications Interface Receive – The Serial Communications Interface (SCI) receive circuit is the serial data circuit that is used when diagnosing vehicle with Chrysler's Diagnostic Readout Box-II (DRB-II). The engine controller receives data from the DRB-II through this SCI receive circuit.

Speed (Cruise) Control Switches – The speed (cruise) control switches provide 3 separate inputs to the engine controller. The ON/OFF switch informs engine controller that speed control system has been activated. The SET switch informs engine controller that a set vehicle speed has been selected. The RESUME switch informs engine controller that the previously selected set speed has been selected.

Start (Cranking) Signal – The start (cranking) signal from starter relay signals engine controller when starter is engaged. When engine controller determines that starter is engaged, it starts looking at inputs from crankshaft position sensor and synchronization signal generator.

The engine controller then uses these signals to determine spark timing and whether the first fuel injection should occur at cylinder No. 4 or 1 (4-cylinder) or cylinder No. 3 or 4 (6-cylinder). Once synchronization has been established, the engine controller energizes the proper injector and provides the ignition output needed to start the engine.

Synchronization Signal Generator – The synchronization signal generator is located in distributor. This Hall Effect type sensor works in conjunction with engine speed signal of crankshaft position sensor providing engine controller with inputs necessary to establish and maintain proper fuel injector firing order.

When leading of pulse ring enters the sync signal generator, change in the magnetic field causes a 5-volt reference signal to be induced. On 4-cylinder engines, this indicates to the engine controller that piston No. 4 will be the next piston at Top Dead Center (TDC). On 6-cylinder engine, it indicates that piston No. 3 will be at TDC.

When trailing edge of pulse ring leaves the sync signal generator, the collapse of the magnetic field causes reference signal to drop to zero volts. On 4-cylinder engines, this indicates that piston No. 1 will be the next piston at TDC. On 6-cylinder engine, it indicates that piston No. 4 will be at TDC.

Throttle Position Sensor (TPS) – The TPS is mounted on throttle body and monitors opening angle of throttle valve. It contains a potentiometer operated by the opening and closing of throttle plate. Engine controller uses TPS input signal to determine throttle position under all operating conditions and adjust fuel injector pulse width and ignition timing accordingly.

The engine controller supplies a 5-volt reference signal to TPS. The TPS output voltage (input signal to engine controller) represents throttle blade position. The TPS output voltage varies from one volt at minimum throttle opening (idle) to 4 volts at wide open throttle.

Vehicle Speed Sensor – The vehicle speed sensor is located on transaxle extension housing (2WD models) or on transfer case extension housing (4WD models). The engine controller uses vehicle speed (distance) sensor to detect if vehicle is moving and at what speed it is moving.

The sensor is an 8-pole switch which provides a pulse or switching rate, proportional to vehicle speed, to the engine controller. By comparing the number of pulses to time elapsed, the controller determines vehicle speed and distance traveled.

The vehicle speed sensor generates 8 pulses per sensor revolution. This signal, along with a closed throttle signal from the TPS sensor, indicates a closed throttle deceleration to the engine controller.

Under deceleration conditions, engine controller adjusts the Automatic Idle Speed (AIS) motor to maintain desired MAP value. During idle (vehicle stopped), the engine controller adjusts the AIS motor to maintain a desired engine speed.

The vehicle speed (distance) sensor input is also used to maintain speed (cruise) control operation and as a reference for Emission Maintenance Reminder (EMR) light.

Vehicle Theft Alarm – Cherokee is equipped with vehicle theft alarm. The theft alarm module will provide a signal to engine controller to enable it to start the engine. With theft alarm module activated, no signal though the communication bus will be sensed by the engine controller and the engine will not start. The engine controller controls ignition and fuel delivery to the engine.

OUTPUT SIGNALS

NOTE: Vehicles are equipped with different combinations of computer-controlled components. Not all components listed below are used on every vehicle. For theory and operation on each output component, refer to the system indicated after component.

A/C Compressor Clutch Relay – See MISCELLANEOUS CONTROLS.
Alternator Light – See MISCELLANEOUS CONTROLS.
Automatic Shutdown Relay – See FUEL DELIVERY.
Automatic Idle Speed (AIS) Motor – See IDLE SPEED.
Ballast Resistor – See FUEL DELIVERY.
Ballast Resistor By-Pass Relay – See FUEL DELIVERY.
CHECK ENGINE Light – See SELF-DIAGNOSTIC SYSTEM.
Emission Maintenance Reminder (EMR) Light – See EMISSION SYSTEMS.
Fuel Injectors – See FUEL DELIVERY.
Fuel Pump Relay – See FUEL DELIVERY.
Ignition Coil – See IGNITION SYSTEM.
Injection Timing – See FUEL DELIVERY.
Radiator (Cooling) Fan Relay – See MISCELLANEOUS CONTROLS.

Serial Communication Interface Transmit – See MISCELLANEOUS CONTROLS.

Speed (Cruise) Control Solenoids – See MISCELLANEOUS CONTROLS.

Tachometer – See MISCELLANEOUS CONTROLS.

Upshift Light – See MISCELLANEOUS CONTROLS.

FUEL SYSTEM

FUEL DELIVERY

Automatic Shutdown Relay – The Automatic Shutdown (ASD) relay is located in power distribution center near the battery or next to radiator coolant recovery bottle.

The ASD relay is used by the engine controller to supply voltage to fuel pump, fuel injectors and ignition coil. The relay contacts are normally open.

Power is supplied to relay coil when the ignition switch is turned on. The engine controller controls the ground circuit, which energizes the coil and closes the relay contacts.

The engine controller will only ground the relay when ignition switch is in the RUN or START positions and some activity is sensed through the crankshaft position sensor and the synchronization signal in the distributor. If the engine controller senses the RPM signal has stopped, it will remove the ground from relay coil, which will cause the contacts to open and remove power from the circuit.

Ballast Resistor – Cherokee and Comanche models have a ballast resistor located between fuel pump relay and the fuel pump. Its purpose is to reduce voltage to the fuel pump. This reduces fuel pump noise during operation. Ballast resistor is mounted on fender panel, next to washer fluid reservoir.

When fuel pump relay is energized, voltage is supplied to fuel pump through the ballast resistor. During start and wide open throttle conditions, ballast resistor is by-passed and fuel pump receives its voltage from ballast resistor by-pass relay.

NOTE: Wrangler models DO NOT use a ballast resistor or ballast resistor by-pass relay in the fuel pump circuit. The engine controller operates fuel pump through the fuel pump relay during all operating conditions.

Ballast Resistor By-Pass Relay – Cherokee and Comanche models have a ballast resistor by-pass relay located on a bracket next to power distribution center (next to coolant recovery bottle). By switching the ground circuit on or off, the engine controller can control fuel pump (power) feed. The ballast resistor by-pass relay receives its voltage from fuel pump relay.

Normally, voltage is supplied to fuel pump through a ballast resistor. At wide open throttle, fuel pump receives voltage through the ballast resistor by-pass relay, which speeds up fuel pump to compensate for higher fuel demand.

Fuel Pump (Electric) – All models are equipped with a gear/rotor type electric pump. Pump is driven by a permanent magnet, 12-volt electric motor that is immersed in fuel tank. The pump is an integral part of the fuel gauge sending unit.

Fuel system pressure is maintained at about 31 psi (2.2 kg/cm²) when pump is operating and vacuum applied to fuel pressure regulator. With no vacuum applied to fuel pressure regulator, fuel pressure should be 39-41 psi (2.7-2.9 kg/cm²) or higher. When fuel pump is not operating, fuel pressure is maintained at 19-39 psi (1.3-2.7 kg/cm²) by fuel pump outlet check valve and the fuel pressure regulator.

Fuel Pump Relay – Cherokee, Comanche and Grand Cherokee models have a fuel pump relay located in the power distribution center, next to coolant recovery bottle. On Wrangler, the fuel pump relay is located in power distribution center next to battery.

The feed side of the relay coil is powered by the ignition switch. The relay is energized by the engine controller by grounding the other side of the relay coil. The relay contacts are normally open and will close when the engine controller provides a ground path for the relay coil.

The fuel pump circuit is completed during cranking and whenever the engine is running. If the ignition key is turned to the RUN position, the fuel pump will operate for 1-3 seconds and then shut off. If the engine controller DOES NOT receive a crank or run signal, it deactivates the fuel pump by opening the relay coil ground circuit. The 1-3 second time limit is used to prevent unnecessary operation of the fuel pump once the system is pressurized. If the engine were running, the engine controller would maintain the fuel pump relay coil ground allowing continuous operation of the fuel pump.

FUEL CONTROL

Fuel Injectors – The fuel injectors are controlled electronically by the engine controller. Because each injector is connected to 12 volts, the injector is energized when connected to ground through the engine controller. The engine controller also controls the amount of time the injector is energized (pulse width). Pulse width is based on various inputs and is calculated by the engine controller. The fuel injectors are sequentially energized, by firing order, by the engine controller.

With injector connected to a pressurized fuel supply, a fine mist will spray from the injector nozzle into the intake manifold. The injector uses an electromagnet and spring pressure to open or close the fuel metering plunger. When connected to battery voltage, the coil of wire in the injector becomes an electromagnet. The magnetic field generated will overcome spring pressure and raise the plunger off its seat. When the injector circuit is opened by the engine controller, the magnetic field collapses and spring pressure forces the plunger against its seat.

Whenever an injector is opened, it will always spray a consistent amount of fuel for a given amount of pressure. Because pressure drop across the injector is fixed and the fuel flow rate constant, the only control variable is the amount of time injector is open. By controlling the time the injector is open (pulse width), the engine controller can decrease pulse width for engine idle or it can increase pulse width at wide open throttle.

Injection Timing – All engines use a sequential port fuel injection system. This means that the injectors have a specific firing order and fuel injection is timed to piston movement. The spark plugs and injectors are fired in the same order: 1-3-4-2 on 2.5L and 1-5-3-6-2-4 on 4.0L.

In order for the engine controller to fire the injectors in a specific order timed to crankshaft and piston movement, it has to establish a reference point. Establishing the reference point requires engine controller inputs from the crankshaft position sensor and synchronization signal generator.

The crankshaft position sensor is located on transmission bellhousing and provides the engine controller with crankshaft angle and speed. The engine controller converts crankshaft speed into engine RPM and crankshaft angle into piston position.

On 2.5L engine, the slotted flywheel/drive plate, rotating past the sensor, contains 2 groups of 4 slots located 180 degrees apart. Each group of slots represents the position of two of the pistons. Pistons No. 1 and 4 approach TDC at the same time and use the same flywheel slot, while piston No. 3 is matched with piston No. 2.

On 4.0L engine, the slotted flywheel/drive plate, rotating past the sensor, contains 3 groups of 4 slots located 120 degrees apart. Each group of slots represents the position of two of the pistons. Pistons No. 1 and 6 approach TDC at the same time and use the same flywheel slot. Pistons No. 2 and 5 are matched, while piston No. 3 is matched with piston No. 4.

The engine controller, through the crankshaft position sensor, knows that two pistons are approaching TDC and uses the sync signal generator to determine which injector/spark plug to fire. *See Fig. 1.*

IDLE SPEED

Automatic Idle Speed (AIS) Motor – The AIS motor is mounted on throttle body and is used by the engine controller to adjust engine idle speed. The throttle plate regulates off idle engine speed by controlling the amount of air allowed to enter the intake manifold and is mechanically operated by the accelerator cable.

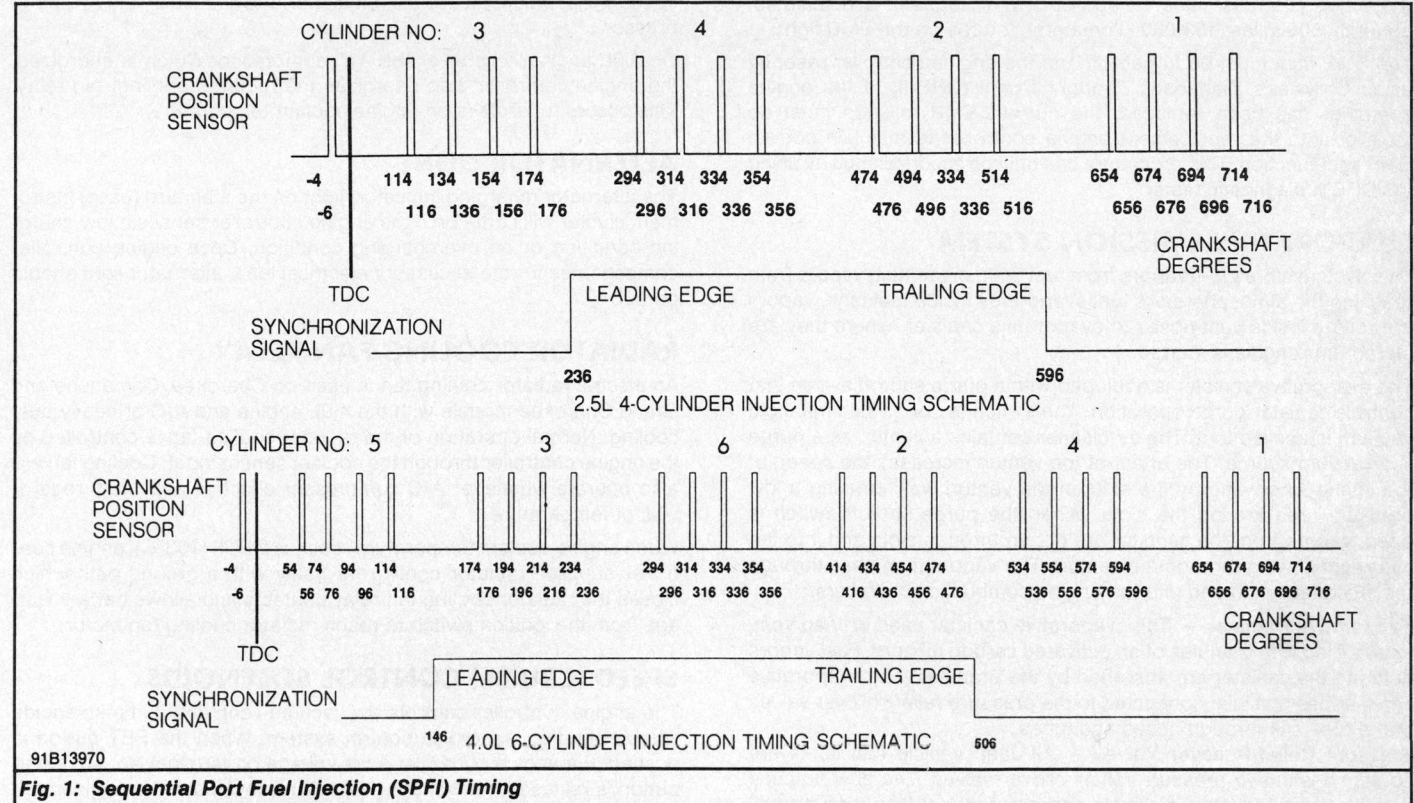

Fig. 1: Sequential Port Fuel Injection (SPFI) Timing

The engine controller and idle stepper motor adjust engine idle by regulating the size of an air by-pass passage that routes air past the closed throttle plate. The amount of air flowing through the by-pass circuit depends on engine operating conditions at idle.

When the engine is cold, the engine controller increases engine speed by retracting the stepper motor pintle, thus allowing more air to enter the intake manifold. To maintain the proper air/fuel mixture, more fuel is also injected into the intake manifold. The increased air/fuel mixture, in turn, raises the engine idle speed. As the engine warms up, the engine controller will extend the stepper motor pintle into the air passage to reduce the amount of air by-passing the throttle plate.

IGNITION SYSTEM

SBEC-II CONTROLLED IGNITION SYSTEM

All engines use a Single Board Engine Controller-II (SBEC-II) based ignition system. Base ignition timing is NOT adjustable with this system. The SBEC-II controlled ignition system consists of coolant temperature sensor, crankshaft position sensor, distributor (includes rotor and synchronization sensor), ignition coil, manifold absolute pressure sensor, Single Board Engine Controller-II, and throttle position sensor.

Coolant Temperature Sensor – See INPUT DEVICES.
Crankshaft Position Sensor – See INPUT DEVICES.
Distributor – Distributor consists of cap, rotor, and synchronization signal generator. The distributor does not have built-in centrifugal or vacuum advance mechanisms to advance ignition timing. Ignition timing advance is electronically controlled by the engine controller. See SYNCHRONIZATION SIGNAL GENERATOR under INPUT DEVICES.
Ignition Coil – The ignition coil is constructed of epoxy-embedded windings and is not oil filled. Battery voltage is supplied to the ignition coil positive terminal. The engine controller receives inputs from the appropriate sensors. Based on these inputs, it then determines the proper ignition timing and interrupts the ignition coil ground signal to trigger secondary voltage of the ignition coil.

Manifold Absolute Pressure Sensor – See INPUT DEVICES.
Manifold Air Temperature Sensor – See INPUT DEVICES.
Single Board Engine Controller-II – The engine controller opens and closes the ignition coil ground circuit to adjust ignition timing according to engine operating conditions. The amount of electronic spark advance provided by the engine controller is determined by coolant temperature sensor, crankshaft position sensor (engine RPM), manifold absolute pressure sensor and throttle position sensor inputs. See COMPUTERIZED ENGINE CONTROLS for additional information.
Throttle Position Sensor – See INPUT DEVICES.

EMISSION SYSTEMS

CRANKCASE VENTILATION (CCV) SYSTEM

Engines on all models use a crankcase ventilation system. The CCV system performs the same function as a conventional PCV system, but does not use a vacuum controlled valve. On 2.5L engine, a fitting on the driver's side of the cylinder head cover contains a metered orifice that is connected to manifold vacuum. On 4.0L engine, a molded vacuum tube connects manifold vacuum to the top of the cylinder head cover. The molded vacuum tube contains a fixed, calibrated orifice that meters the amount of crankcase vapors drawn out of the engine.

On both engines, a fresh air supply hose from the air cleaner is connected to the cylinder head cover. When the engine is operating, fresh air enters the engine and mixes with crankcase vapors. Manifold vacuum then draws the crankcase vapors/air mixture through the fixed orifice and into the engine by intake manifold vacuum.

EMISSION MAINTENANCE REMINDER LIGHT

The Emission Maintenance Reminder (EMR) light on instrument cluster indicates to vehicle owner components of the vehicle's emission system are scheduled for service or replacement.

The emission maintenance reminder function is built into the engine controller. The engine controller reads vehicle speed (distance) sensor and stores mileage information in a resettable memory. When the engine controller sees the appropriate mileage has accumulated, about 82,500 miles (133,000 kilometers), it turns on the EMR light.

The EMR light must be turned off and the engine controller reset by using Chrysler's Diagnostic Readout Box-II (DRB-II). If the engine controller has been replaced, the current EMR mileage must be installed into the replacement engine controller to maintain correct EMR light function. This procedure can only be accomplished by using the DRB-II diagnostic tester.

EVAPORATIVE EMISSION SYSTEM

This system stores fuel vapors from fuel tank, preventing vapors from reaching the atmosphere. As fuel evaporates inside fuel tank, vapors are routed inside vent hoses to evaporative canister, where they are stored until engine is started.

The evaporative canister is equipped with a purge shutoff switch that controls canister purge operation. The switch is open when manifold vacuum is applied to it. The air cleaner contains a venturi as a purge line vacuum source. The effect of the venturi increases the speed of the intake air flowing by the slots in the venturi wall, creating a low pressure area around the slots. When the purge shutoff switch is open, vapors from the canister are drawn through slots and into the airstream flowing through the venturi. The vapors then pass through the intake manifold and into the engine combustion chambers.

Evaporative Canister – The evaporative canister used in Jeep vehicles is filled with granules of an activated carbon mixture. Fuel vapors entering the canister are absorbed by the granules. The evaporative canister has one inlet connected to the pressure relief/rollover valves of the fuel tank through hoses and tubes.

Pressure Relief/Rollover Valves – All Jeep vehicle fuel tanks are equipped with two pressure relief/rollover valves. The dual function valves relieve fuel tank pressure and prevent fuel flow through fuel tank vent hoses in the event of a vehicle rollover. The valve consists of a plunger, spring, orifice and guide plate. The valve is normally open, allowing fuel vapors to vent to the canister where they are stored.

If bottom of plunger is contacted by sloshing fuel in fuel tank, the plunger seats in the guide plate, preventing liquid fuel from reaching the evaporative canister. In a vehicle rollover, the valve is inverted. This forces the plunger against the guide plate and fuel is prevented from flowing through the valve orifice and into fuel tank vent tube.

SELF-DIAGNOSTIC SYSTEM

CHECK ENGINE LIGHT

The CHECK ENGINE light lets the driver know if the engine controller has recorded a system or sensor malfunctions. CHECK ENGINE light will come on if vehicle goes into a "limp-in" mode. The CHECK ENGINE can also be used to display fault codes. By cycling the ignition on, off, on, off and on within 5 seconds, the engine controller will display the fault codes in a series of flashes representing numbers. For additional information, see SELF-DIAGNOSTICS article.

MISCELLANEOUS CONTROLS

NOTE: Although not considered true engine performance-related systems, some controlled devices may affect driveability if they malfunction.

A/C COMPRESSOR CLUTCH RELAY

The engine controller controls the A/C compressor clutch through a relay. This allows the engine controller to receive an A/C select signal when driver moves mode lever into A/C position. The engine controller also receives a request signal from the A/C temperature control thermostat (evaporator switch).

The engine controller then adjusts idle speed using the AIS motor. Only then can the engine controller activate the A/C compressor clutch through the A/C compressor clutch relay. The increased idle

speed will compensate for the additional load caused by the A/C compressor.

On 4.0L engine, whenever the A/C compressor clutch is energized, the engine controller also energizes the radiator (cooling) fan relay. This occurs regardless on engine coolant temperature.

ALTERNATOR LIGHT

The alternator (charging indicator) light on the standard (base) instrument cluster will come on if the engine controller senses a low charging condition or an overcharging condition. Once engine controller compensates for the accessory electrical load, alternator light should go out.

RADIATOR COOLING FAN RELAY

An electric radiator cooling fan is used on Cherokee, Comanche and Grand Cherokee models with the 4.0L engine and A/C or heavy duty cooling. Normal operation of the radiator cooling fan is controlled by the engine controller through the coolant sensor input. Cooling fan will also operate whenever A/C compressor clutch is activated, regardless of temperature.

When engine coolant temperature reaches 217°F (103°C), engine controller supplies radiator cooling fan relay with a ground path which closes the radiator cooling fan relay contacts and allows battery voltage from the ignition switch to reach radiator cooling fan motor.

SPEED (CRUISE) CONTROL SOLENOIDS

The engine controller controls the vacuum vent, and dump solenoids when operating the cruise control system. When the SET button is pushed, the engine controller sees voltage on terminal No. 48. When button is released, the voltage signal is removed and the engine controller locks in a set speed for the system. The set speed becomes the target for the cruise control system to maintain. The cruise control system will not permit speeds higher than 85 MPH to be set.

The engine controller energizes the vacuum solenoids located in the cruise control servo assembly to open the throttle to maintain the set speed. To increase set speed, the engine controller grounds the vacuum solenoid through terminal No. 33 of the engine controller. The solenoid receives battery voltage with ignition on and as long as the brakes are off. The vacuum solenoid is spring loaded to block vacuum from getting into the servo diaphragm. When energized, vacuum solenoid is pulled open, allowing vacuum to enter servo diaphragm and open throttle.

At the same time vacuum solenoid is being commanded to open the throttle, the engine controller must supply a ground to the vent solenoid. The vent solenoid is spring loaded so that when it is not energized, it bleeds vacuum from the servo chamber. The vent solenoid receives battery voltage with ignition switch on and as long as the brakes are off. When the engine controller supplies the vent solenoid with a ground, the solenoid blocks the leakage of vacuum from the servo chamber. To increase throttle opening, the engine controller grounds the vacuum solenoid. To reduce throttle opening, the engine controller grounds the vent solenoid.

Anytime the brakes are applied, the brake switch will interrupt power supply to the dump solenoid which causes it to vent vacuum as the vent and vacuum solenoids return to their relaxed (non-energized) positions by opening their ground circuits. The dump solenoid is reset when the brakes are released but the engine controller will only reactivate the vacuum and vent solenoids when the RESUME switch is pushed.

UPSHIFT INDICATOR LIGHT

Vehicles equipped with a manual transmission have an upshift light located in the instrument cluster. The upshift light is controlled by the engine controller and will illuminate the light to inform the driver when to shift to the next higher gear for best fuel economy. The engine controller determines which gear should be used by observing and remembering RPM and manifold absolute pressure values. A high gear switch is NOT used in the transmission.

Cherokee, Comanche, Grand Cherokee (1993), Wrangler

INTRODUCTION

The following diagnostic steps will help prevent overlooking a simple problem. This is also where to begin diagnosis for a no-start condition.

The first step in diagnosing any driveability problem is verifying the customer's complaint with a test drive under the conditions the problem reportedly occurred.

Before entering self-diagnostics, perform a careful and complete visual inspection. Most engine control problems result from mechanical breakdowns, poor electrical connections or damaged/misrouted vacuum hoses. Before condemning the computerized system, perform each test listed in this article.

NOTE: *Perform all voltage tests with a Digital Volt-Ohmmeter (DVOM) with a minimum 10-megohm input impedance, unless stated otherwise in test procedure.*

PRELIMINARY INSPECTION & ADJUSTMENTS

VISUAL INSPECTION

Visually inspect all electrical wiring, looking for chafed, stretched, cut or pinched wiring. Ensure electrical connectors fit tightly and are not corroded. Ensure vacuum hoses are properly routed and are not pinched or cut. See VACUUM DIAGRAMS article to verify routing and connections. Inspect air induction system for possible vacuum leaks.

MECHANICAL INSPECTION

Compression – Check engine mechanical condition with a compression gauge, vacuum gauge or engine analyzer. See engine analyzer manual for specific instructions.

WARNING: *DO NOT use ignition switch during compression tests on fuel injected vehicles. Crank engine with a remote starter. Fuel injectors on many models are triggered by ignition switch during cranking mode, which can create a fire hazard or contaminate the engine's oiling system.*

COMPRESSION RATIO

Application	Specification
2.5L	
Cherokee & Comanche	9.2:1
Wrangler	9.1:1
4.0L	8.8:1

NOTE: *Compression pressure and cylinder pressure variation are not available from manufacturer.*

Exhaust System Backpressure – The exhaust system can be checked with a vacuum or pressure gauge. Remove O_2 sensor. Connect a 0-5 psi pressure gauge and run engine at 2500 RPM. If exhaust system backpressure is greater than 1 3/4 - 2 psi, exhaust system or catalytic converter is plugged.

If a vacuum gauge is used, connect vacuum gauge hose to intake manifold vacuum port and start engine. Observe vacuum gauge. Open throttle part way and hold steady. If vacuum gauge reading slowly drops after stabilizing, check exhaust system for restriction.

FUEL SYSTEM

WARNING: *When battery is disconnected, vehicle computer and memory systems may lose memory data. Driveability problems may exist until computer systems have completed a relearn cycle. See COMPUTER RELEARN PROCEDURES article in GENERAL INFORMATION before disconnecting battery.*

FUEL PRESSURE

Basic diagnosis of fuel system should begin with determining fuel system pressure.

WARNING: *ALWAYS relieve fuel pressure before disconnecting any fuel injection-related component. DO NOT allow fuel to contact engine or electrical components.*

Fuel Pressure Release – Disconnect negative battery cable. Remove fuel filler cap. Remove cap from pressure test port on fuel rail. Position shop towels to soak up any spilled fuel. Using a small screwdriver or pin punch, push test port valve in to relieve fuel pressure. *See Fig. 1.* Install cap over test port. Reconnect negative battery cable.

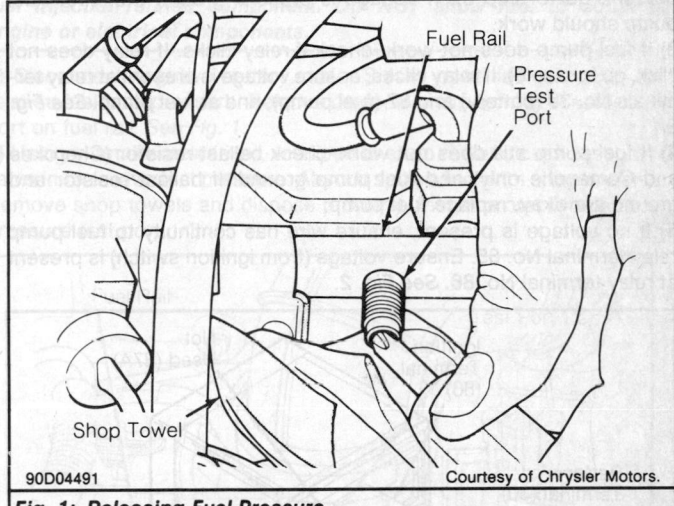

90D04491   Courtesy of Chrysler Motors.

Fig. 1: Releasing Fuel Pressure

Deadhead Pressure – 1) Relieve fuel pressure. See FUEL PRESSURE RELEASE. Connect a 0-60 psi (0-4.2 kg/cm²) fuel pressure gauge to the pressure test port fitting on fuel rail.
2) Remove fuel pump relay (located in power distribution center). Using a jumper wire, connect terminals No. 30 and 87. *See Fig. 2.* Note fuel pressure gauge, and momentarily pinch fuel return line.
3) Fuel pressure should be at least 53 psi (3.7 kg/cm²). DO NOT allow pressure to exceed 60 psi (4.2 kg/cm²). Release fuel return line.
Fuel System Pressure Test – 1) Relieve fuel pressure. See FUEL PRESSURE RELEASE. Connect a 0-60 psi (0-4.2 kg/cm²) fuel pressure gauge to the pressure test port fitting on fuel rail.
2) Remove vacuum line from fuel pressure regulator. Start vehicle and note gauge reading. Reconnect vacuum line and note gauge reading. See FUEL SYSTEM PRESSURE SPECIFICATIONS table. Ensure pressure readings are as specified. If fuel pressure is not higher with vacuum line disconnected, inspect pressure regulator vacuum line for cause of no vacuum.
3) If fuel pressure is too high, inspect fuel return line for kinks and blockage. If fuel pressure is low, momentarily pinch fuel return line. If pressure remains low, inspect fuel supply line, fuel filter and fuel rail inlet for blockage. If fuel pressure rises, replace fuel pressure regulator.

FUEL SYSTEM PRESSURE SPECIFICATIONS

Application	psi (kg/cm²)
Vacuum Line Disconnected	39 (2.7)
Vacuum Line Connected	31 (2.2)

Fuel System Rest Pressure – 1) Relieve fuel pressure. See FUEL PRESSURE RELEASE. Connect a 0-60 psi (0-4.2 kg/cm²) fuel pressure gauge to the pressure test port fitting on fuel rail. Start engine and note reading on pressure gauge. Shut engine off.
2) Wait 30 minutes and check fuel pressure. Fuel pressure should be within 20 psi (1.4 kg/cm²) of first reading. If pressure is not as indicated, check fuel system for leaks at fuel pressure regulator, fuel pump check valve or fuel injectors.

Most tests available in this mode provide an audible or visual indication of device operation (click of relay contacts, spray fuel, etc.). With the exception of an intermittent condition, if a device functions properly during its test, it can be assumed that device, wiring and its driver circuit are functioning properly.

ADJUSTMENTS Mode – This function allows user to erase fault codes. Function also allows user to perform Emission Maintenance Reminder (EMR) memory test and reset EMR light and mileage.

DRB-II Volt/Ohmmeter Mode – 1) To access volt/ohmmeter mode of DRB-II, connect Red volt/ohmmeter test lead to Red port, located on top right side of DRB-II.

NOTE: Because DRB-II is grounded through engine diagnostic connector, only one volt/ohmmeter test lead is required when using volt/ohmmeter option. The DRB-II volt/ohmmeter mode should only be used when diagnostic tests require the use of this option.

2) To access voltmeter, press VOLT/OHM key once. DRB-II is now in voltmeter mode. Touch test probe to connector or wire to be measured. Read voltage on DRB-II display. When voltage testing is completed, press VOLT/OHM key 3 times to exit voltmeter mode.

3) To access ohmmeter, press VOLT/OHM key twice. DRB-II is now in ohmmeter mode. Touch test probe to connector or wire to be measured. Read resistance to circuit ground on DRB-II display. When resistance testing is complete, press VOLT/OHM key twice to exit ohmmeter mode.

DRB-II Continuity Meter Mode – To access continuity meter, press VOLT/OHM key 3 times. Display will read NO CONTINUITY. Touch test probe to connector or wire to be measured. Read continuity on DRB-II display. When continuity testing is complete, press VOLT/OHM key once to exit continuity meter mode.

VEHICLES TESTED Mode – 1) Vehicles tested mode is used to show what vehicles are covered by DRB-II cartridge. To access vehicles tested mode, ensure ignition is off.

2) Connect DRB-II to engine diagnostic connector. Connector is located on left side (right side on Grand Cherokee) of engine compartment, near engine controller. *See Figs. 2 and 3.* Turn ignition switch to RUN position.

3) Copyright information and diagnostic program version will appear on screen for a few seconds. After a few seconds DRB-II menu will appear. At DRB-II menu, press "1" (VEHICLES TESTED) key. Press ENTER key. DRB-II will display vehicles covered by cartridge. Screen will display for 5 seconds and return to DRB-II menu.

HOW TO USE Mode – 1) To access HOW TO USE mode, ensure ignition is off. Attach DRB-II to engine diagnostic connector. Connector is located on left side (right side on Grand Cherokee) of engine compartment, near engine controller. *See Figs. 2 and 3.* Turn ignition switch to RUN position.

2) Copyright information and diagnostic program version will appear on screen for a few seconds. After a few seconds DRB-II menu will appear. At DRB-II menu, press "2" (HOW TO USE) key. Press ENTER key. A series of screens will be displayed explaining use of DRB-II keys used to move through engine diagnostic program.

CONFIGURE Mode – 1) Configure option allows user to VIEW or CHANGE DRB-II display to US/METRIC, KEY CLICK, KEY REPEAT, or REMOTE DISPLAY. All selections made under CONFIGURE option remain active until user changes selection.

2) To access CONFIGURE mode, ensure ignition is off. Attach DRB-II to engine diagnostic connector. Connector is located on left side (right side on Grand Cherokee) of engine compartment, near engine controller. *See Figs. 2 and 3.* Turn ignition switch to RUN position.

3) Copyright information and diagnostic program version will appear on screen for a few seconds. After a few seconds DRB-II menu will appear. At DRB-II menu, press "3" (CONFIGURE) key. Press ENTER key. DRB-II will display CONFIGURE menu.

4) Selecting VIEW from CONFIGURE menu allows user to view setting of CONFIGURE functions. Selecting CHANGE from CONFIGURE menu allows user to change setting of CONFIGURE functions.

5) Selecting US/METRIC function allows user to have sensor, input/output values displayed in either US/METRIC units. Selecting KEY CLICK allows user to have a Green light come on or have a beeper sound whenever a DRB-II key is pressed.

6) If REPEAT KEY function is on, the down/up arrow key will scroll the DRB-II display repeatedly. If REPEAT KEY function is off, the down/up arrow will scroll the DRB-II display only one item at a time. Selecting REMOTE DISPLAY function allows user to have DRB-II screen displayed on another screen.

DRB-II PROBLEMS & ERROR MESSAGES

Blank DRB-II Message Screen – 1) Connect DRB-II to a different vehicle. If message screen is still blank, DRB-II or cable adapter are faulty. Substitute to find faulty component.

2) If message screen is not blank, DRB-II and cable adapter are functioning properly. Inspect diagnostic connector for proper wire placement, damaged terminals or pushed out pins. Repair as necessary.

3) If diagnostic connector is okay, use a DVOM to check resistance between ground and Black wire (Black/Tan wire on Grand Cherokee; Black/Yellow wire on Wrangler) at engine diagnostic connector. If resistance is 10 ohms or more, repair open in Black wire (Black/Tan wire on Grand Cherokee; Black/Yellow wire on Wrangler).

NO RESPONSE Message – 1) Ensure ignition is OFF and disconnect DRB-II. Using a DVOM, check resistance of Pink wire (Black wire on Grand Cherokee; Black/Red wire on Wrangler) between engine controller terminal No. 25 and engine diagnostic connector. *See Fig. 4.*

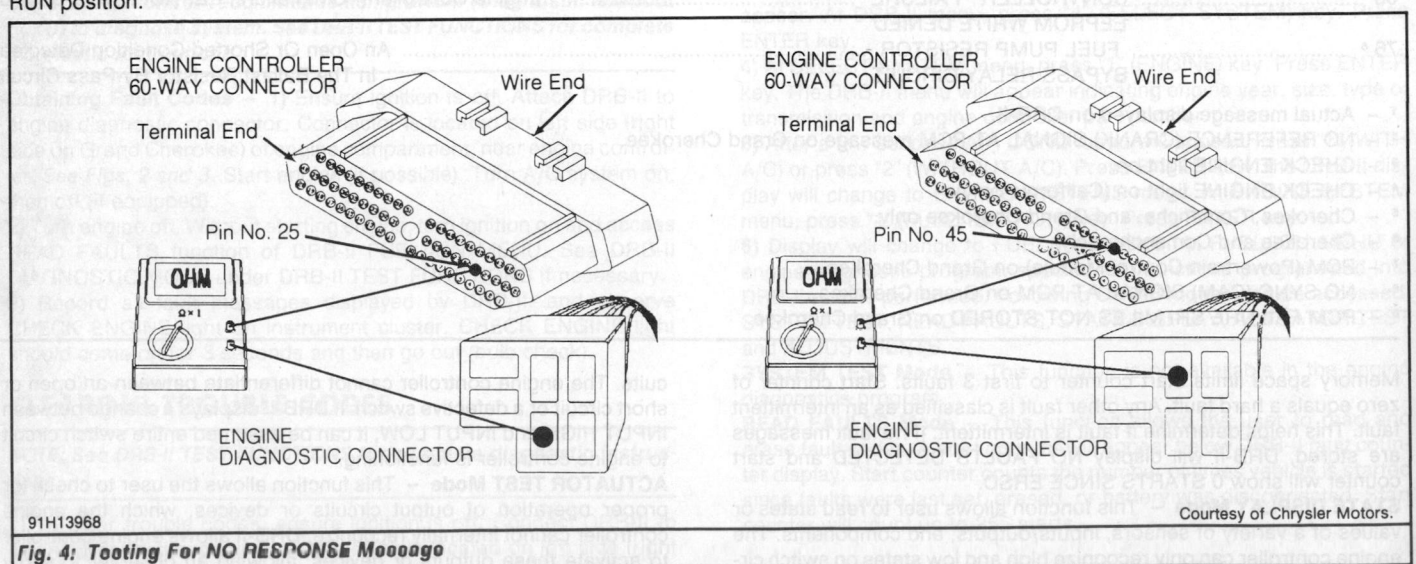

ENGINE CONTROLLER
60-WAY CONNECTOR
Wire End
Terminal End
Pin No. 25
OHM
Ω×1
ENGINE DIAGNOSTIC CONNECTOR

ENGINE CONTROLLER
60-WAY CONNECTOR
Wire End
Terminal End
Pin No. 45
OHM
Ω×1
ENGINE DIAGNOSTIC CONNECTOR

91H13968

Fig. 4: Testing For NO RESPONSE Message

If resistance is 10 ohms or more, repair open Pink wire (Black wire on Grand Cherokee; Black/Red wire on Wrangler).

2) If resistance is less than 10 ohms, check resistance of Light Green wire (Black/Yellow wire on Grand Cherokee; Black/Pink wire on Wrangler) between engine controller terminal No. 45 and engine diagnostic connector. If resistance is 10 ohms or more, repair open Light Green wire (Black/Yellow wire on Grand Cherokee; Black/Pink wire on Wrangler).

3) If resistance is less than 10 ohms, turn ignition off and disconnect DRB-II, DRB-II cartridge, and adapter cable. Find a second vehicle identical in equipment to vehicle being tested.

4) Connect DRB-II to substitute (second) vehicle and use DRB-II as you did on original vehicle. If message screen is still blank, adapter cable or DRB-II (including cartridge) is faulty. Substitute adapter cable with a known good cable to find faulty component.

5) If it is determined that adapter cable, DRB-II and cartridge are okay, replace engine controller. Reset EMR mileage and, on vehicles equipped with factory theft alarm, start vehicle at least 20 times to enable theft alarm system.

Other Error Messages – If BAD FRAMING, CARTRIDGE ERROR, LOW BATTERY, BAD OP CODE, HIGH BATTERY, RAM TEST FAILURE, COMMAND REJECTED or KEYPAD TEST FAILURE message is displayed, there is a DRB-II to vehicle communications system breakdown.

EMISSION MAINTENANCE REMINDER (EMR) MEMORY TEST

NOTE: Perform EMR memory test only if referred here by diagnostic tests.

1) To perform EMR memory check, ensure ignition is off. Attach DRB-II to engine diagnostic connector. Connector is located on left side (right side on Grand Cherokee) of engine compartment, near engine controller. *See Figs. 2 and 3.* Turn ignition switch to RUN position.

2) Copyright information and diagnostic program version will appear on screen for a few seconds. After a few seconds DRB-II menu will appear. At FUEL/IGN MENU, press "5" (ADJUSTMENTS) key. Press ENTER key. At ADJUSTMENTS menu, press "4" (EMR MEMORY CHK) key. Press ENTER key. The DRB-II display will read EMR MEMORY CHECK ARE YOU SURE? (ENTER TO CONTINUE).

3) Press ENTER key. The DRB-II will display EMR MEMORY TEST WRITE TEST [-------] and after a few seconds IS INSTRUMENT PANEL MILEAGE BETWEEN XXXXX AND XXXXX? (PRESS YES OR NO). If vehicle mileage is within specification, EMR memory check is complete. Press YES key. If vehicle mileage is not within specification, go to next step.

4) Press NO key. DRB-II will display ENTER MILEAGE SHOWN ON INSTRUMENT PANEL (USE ENTER TO END) XXXXXXX. Enter vehicle mileage. DO NOT enter tenths. When correct vehicle mileage is entered, press ENTER key.

5) DRB-II will ask for verification of mileage entry. If mileage entry was accurate, press ENTER key. DRB-II will display EMR MEMORY CHECK COMPLETE. Vehicle must travel at least 8 miles for reset to occur.

EMISSION MAINTENANCE REMINDER (EMR) LIGHT RESET PROCEDURE

Emission Maintenance Reminder (EMR) light is designed to be a reminder to service vehicle emissions control system. It is not an emissions warning system, only a reminder to perform necessary emissions servicing.

Components to be serviced include PCV valve, oxygen sensor and some vacuum-operated components. EMR light will illuminate after a predetermined mileage.

1) To reset EMR light, ensure ignition is off. Connect DRB-II to engine diagnostic connector. Connector is located on left side (right side on Grand Cherokee) of engine compartment, near engine controller. *See Figs. 2 and 3.* Turn ignition switch to RUN position.

2) Copyright information and diagnostic program version will appear on screen for a few seconds. After a few seconds DRB-II menu will appear. At FUEL/IGN MENU, press "5" (ADJUSTMENTS) key. Press ENTER key.

3) At ADJUSTMENTS menu, press "3" (RESET EMR LIGHT) key. Press ENTER key. Display will read RESET EMR LIGHT ARE YOUR SURE? (ENTER TO RESET). Press ENTER key.

EMISSION MAINTENANCE REMINDER (EMR) MILEAGE TRANSFER

NOTE: Perform mileage transfer procedure only if engine controller is being replaced.

1) When engine controller is replaced, vehicle mileage must be copied from odometer to replacement engine controller memory. Transfer of vehicle mileage will enable new engine controller to operate EMR light properly.

2) To transfer mileage to new engine controller, ensure ignition is off. Connect DRB-II to engine diagnostic connector. Connector is located on left side (right side on Grand Cherokee) of engine compartment, near engine controller. *See Figs. 2 and 3.* Turn ignition switch to RUN position.

3) Copyright information and diagnostic program version will appear on screen for a few seconds. After a few seconds DRB-II menu will appear. At FUEL/IGN MENU, press "5" (ADJUSTMENTS) key. Press ENTER key. At ADJUSTMENTS menu, press "4" (EMR MEMORY CHK) key. Press ENTER key. The DRB-II display will read EMR MEMORY CHECK ARE YOU SURE? (ENTER TO CONTINUE).

4) Press ENTER key. The DRB-II will display EMR MEMORY TEST WRITE TEST [-------] and after a few seconds IS INSTRUMENT PANEL MILEAGE BETWEEN XXXXX AND XXXXX? (PRESS YES OR NO). If vehicle mileage is within specification, EMR memory check is complete. Press YES key. If vehicle mileage is not within specification, go to next step.

5) Press NO key. DRB-II will display ENTER MILEAGE SHOWN ON INSTRUMENT PANEL (USE ENTER TO END) XXXXXXX. Enter vehicle mileage. DO NOT enter tenths. When correct vehicle mileage is entered, press ENTER key.

6) DRB-II will ask for verification of mileage entry. If mileage entry was accurate, press ENTER key. DRB-II will display EMR MEMORY CHECK COMPLETE. Vehicle must travel at least 8 miles for reset to occur.

THEFT ALARM SYSTEM

NOTE: If SECURITY light comes and remains on with ignition on, Chrysler Collision Detection (CCD) bus communication with engine controller has been lost. After servicing vehicle, ensure system operates properly. A malfunctioning theft alarm system may keep engine from starting.

SELF-DIAGNOSTIC TEST

Cherokee & Grand Cherokee – Turn ignition switch to ACCY position 3 times and leave in ACCY position to enter self-diagnostic mode. To stop self-diagnostic mode, return ignition switch to OFF position.

After entering self-diagnostic mode, the headlights, parking lights, and taillights will flash to verify theft alarm system operation. The horn should also sound twice.

While in self-diagnostic mode, it is recommended that illuminated entry module be removed. Otherwise its necessary to wait 30 seconds after opening or closing each door. Begin theft alarm system self-diagnosis as follows:

1) Close ALL doors. Enter self-diagnostic mode and remove illuminated entry module. Module is located on a bracket behind instrument panel. Open and close each door and hood. The horn should sound when door jamb (hood) switch closes and again when switch opens. Wait one second before closing and opening doors (hood).

2) Actuate power door locks and remote keyless entry (if equipped) in both the lock and unlock position. The horn should sound after each actuation. Rotate key in each door lock to the unlock position. The horn should sound when door jamb switch closes and again when switch opens. Wait one second before closing and opening doors.

3) Place ignition switch in RUN position. Horn should sound to indicate proper operation of ignition input and exit theft alarm system self-diagnostic mode.

4) If horn does not sound, it indicates a switch failure, an open/shorted circuit (lack of switch input), or a security alarm module failure. Check switch and wiring harness continuity. Service theft alarm system based on following self-diagnostics test results:

NOTE: A functional engine controller that has been used in a vehicle equipped with theft alarm system CANNOT be used in another vehicle that is NOT equipped with theft alarm system. If engine controller has been replaced, start vehicle at least 20 times to enable theft alarm system.

PARKING LIGHTS & TAILLIGHTS DO NOT FLASH

Cherokee – 1) Turn ignition switch to RUN position and then OFF. Check for battery voltage at Pink/Light Green wire at terminal No. 21 of security alarm module. Security alarm module is located on driver's side of A/C-heater housing.

2) If battery voltage is present, replace security alarm module and retest system. If battery voltage is NOT present, repair wiring harness and retest system.

Grand Cherokee – 1) Check for battery voltage at Red/Black wire at terminal No. 6 of lamp outage module. Lamp outage module is located behind instrument panel.

2) If battery voltage is present, repair open wiring harness to taillights. If battery voltage is NOT present, check for battery voltage at Tan/Pink wire at terminal No. 14 of security alarm module. Security alarm module is located behind instrument panel.

3) If battery voltage is present, repair wiring harness between module and taillights. After repairs, retest system. If battery voltage is NOT present, replace security alarm module and retest system.

ALL EXTERIOR LIGHTS DO NOT FLASH, BUT WORK NORMALLY

Cherokee & Grand Cherokee – 1) Turn ignition switch to RUN position and then OFF. Check if flash to pass switch operates properly (lightly pull and release turn signal lever). If flash to pass feature works properly (headlights come on and remain on until lever is release), go to next step. If flash to pass feature does not work properly, check for blown fuse. Replace fuse and retest system.

2) Check for battery voltage at Pink/Light Green wire (Light Green/Black wire on Grand Cherokee) at terminal No. 21 of security alarm module. Security alarm module is located on driver's side of A/C-heater housing (behind instrument panel on Grand Cherokee). If battery voltage is present, replace security alarm module and retest system. If battery voltage is NOT present, repair wiring harness and retest system.

HEADLIGHTS DO NOT FLASH, BUT WORK NORMALLY

Cherokee – 1) Check (backprobe) for battery voltage at terminal No. 7 of security alarm module (Tan/Pink wire). Security alarm module is located on driver's side of A/C-heater housing. If battery voltage is present, go to next step. If battery voltage is NOT present, turn ignition switch to RUN position and then OFF. Replace security alarm module and retest system.

2) Turn ignition switch to RUN position and then OFF. Disconnect security alarm module relay. Relay is taped to wiring harness, near driver's side kick panel. Check relay continuity between Black and

Tan/Pink wire terminals. If continuity exists, go to next step. If no continuity exists, replace relay and retest system.

3) Check continuity between relay connector and ground (Black wire). If no continuity exists, repair open Black (ground) wire and retest system. If continuity exists, check continuity of Tan/Pink wire between relay connector and terminal No. 7 of security alarm module. If no continuity exists, repair open Tan/Pink wire.

Grand Cherokee – 1) Check for battery voltage at terminal No. 1 of security alarm module relay (Light Green/Black wire). If battery voltage is present, go to next step. If battery voltage is NOT present, go to step **6)**.

2) Check for battery voltage at terminal No. 3 of security alarm module relay (Black wire). If battery voltage is NOT present, go to next step. If battery voltage is present, go to step **5)**.

3) Turn ignition switch to RUN position and then OFF. Check continuity between terminals No. 3 (Black wire) and 5 (Tan/Pink wire) of security alarm module relay. If no continuity exists, replace relay and retest system.

4) Check continuity between terminal No. 14 (Tan/Pink wire) of security alarm module and terminal No. 5 of security alarm module relay. If no continuity exists, repair open Tan/Pink wire and retest system. If continuity exists, replace security alarm module and retest system.

5) Turn ignition switch to RUN position and then OFF. Check continuity between ground and terminal No. 3 (Black wire) of security alarm module relay. If no continuity exists, repair open Black (ground) wire and retest system. If continuity exists, replace relay, retest system, and go to step **7)**.

6) If battery voltage was NOT present in step **1)**, repair open Light Green/Black wire between fuse No. 7 and security alarm module relay. After repairs, retest system.

7) If system now operates properly, test is complete. If system still does NOT operate properly, check continuity between relay connector terminal No. 2 (Red/Orange wire) and headlights. if continuity exists, replace relay and retest system. If no continuity exists, repair open Red/Orange wire and retest system.

HORN DOES NOT SOUND TWICE

Cherokee & Grand Cherokee – Turn ignition switch to RUN position and then OFF. Check if horn operates normally. If horn does not operate, repair horn circuit. If horn operates normally, check continuity of Black/Red wire (Gray/Orange wire on Grand Cherokee) between horn and terminal No. 12 (terminal No. 6 on Grand Cherokee) of security alarm module. Security alarm module is located on driver's side of A/C-heater housing (behind instrument panel on Grand Cherokee). If continuity exists, replace security alarm module. If no continuity exists, repair open Black/Red (Gray/Orange) wire and retest system.

HORN SOUNDS TWICE AND HEADLIGHTS, PARKING LIGHTS & TAIL LIGHTS FLASH

Cherokee & Grand Cherokee – 1) Ensure that doors, liftgate, and hood are closed. Verify SECURITY light is flashing. If SECURITY light is not flashing, check bulb and wiring harness. Repair or replace as necessary. If bulb and wiring are okay, replace security alarm module and retest system.

2) If SECURITY light is flashing, turn ignition switch to OFF position. Remove illuminated entry module from vehicle. Module is located on a bracket behind instrument panel.

3) Check theft alarm switches by opening and closing doors and liftgate. Horn should sound one time, at each switch, to ensure proper operation. Replace switch(es) or repair wiring harness as necessary. If switches are okay, check hood switch by opening and closing hood.

4) Replace hood switch or repair wiring harness as necessary. If hood switch is okay, unlock (with key) each front door and liftgate one at a time to test disarm switches. Replace switch(es) or repair wiring harness as necessary and retest system.

5) If disarm switches are okay, cycle power door locks to lock and then unlock position. Replace door lock switch(es), lock/unlock relay(s), or repair wiring harness as necessary and retest system.

6) If power door locks operate properly, lock and unlock vehicle with keyless entry transmitter. Replace keyless entry transmitter, receiver, or repair wiring harness as necessary and retest system.

7) If keyless entry system operates properly, turn ignition switch to ON position and wait 30 seconds. If SECURITY light comes on and stays on, repair or replace CCD bus and wiring as necessary and retest system. If SECURITY light remains off, theft alarm system is operating properly. Reconnect illuminated entry module

SUMMARY

If no hard fault codes or only pass codes are present, driveability symptoms exist or intermittent codes exist, proceed to TROUBLE SHOOTING – NO CODES article for diagnosis by symptom (i.e. ROUGH IDLE, NO START, etc.) or intermittent diagnostic procedures.

CONNECTOR IDENTIFICATION

CONNECTOR IDENTIFICATION DIRECTORY

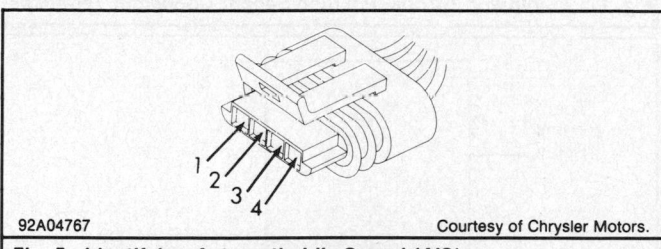

92A04767   Courtesy of Chrysler Motors.

Fig. 5: *Identifying Automatic Idle Speed (AIS) Motor Connector Terminals*

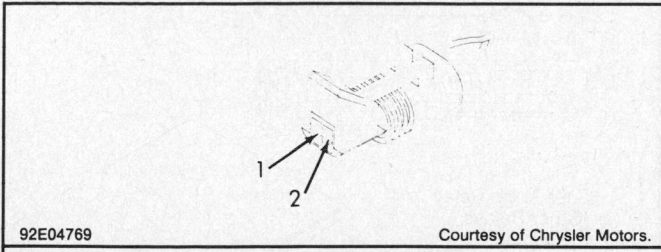

92E04769   Courtesy of Chrysler Motors.

Fig. 6: *Identifying Charge Temperature Sensor & Coolant Temperature Sensor Connector Terminals*

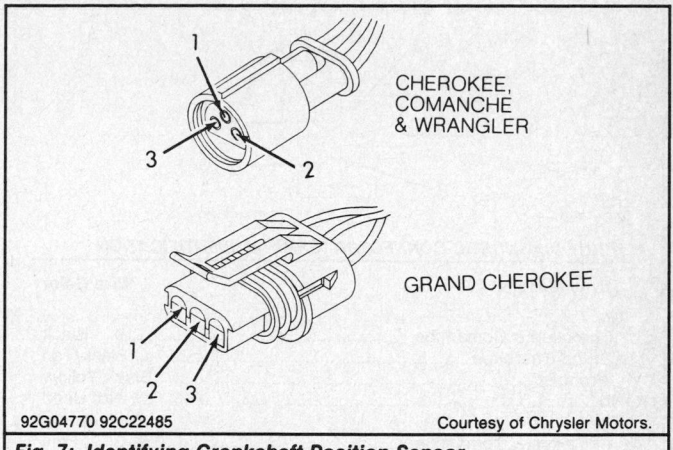

CHEROKEE, COMANCHE & WRANGLER

GRAND CHEROKEE

92G04770 92C22485   Courtesy of Chrysler Motors.

Fig. 7: *Identifying Crankshaft Position Sensor Connector Terminals*

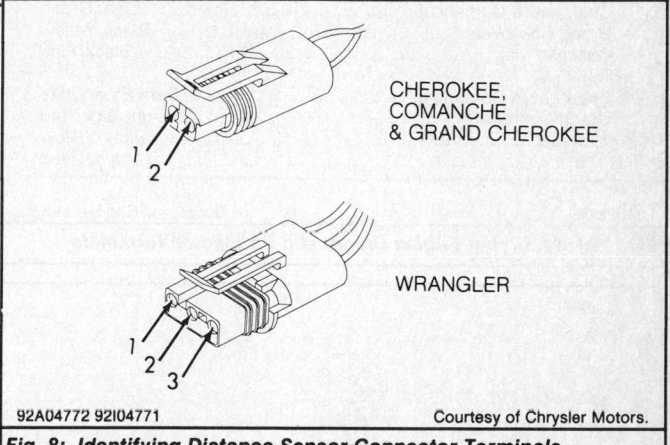

CHEROKEE, COMANCHE & GRAND CHEROKEE

WRANGLER

92A04772 92I04771   Courtesy of Chrysler Motors.

Fig. 8: *Identifying Distance Sensor Connector Terminals*

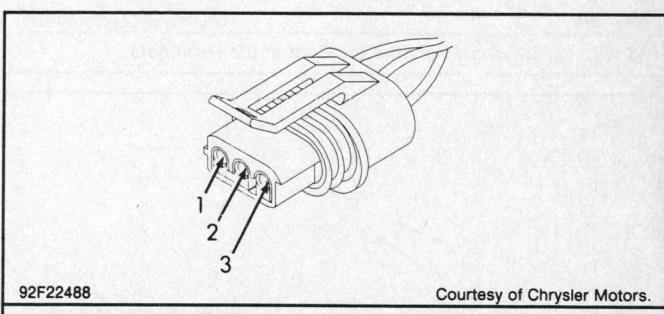

92F22488   Courtesy of Chrysler Motors.

Fig. 9: *Identifying Distributor Sync Pick-Up Connector Terminals*

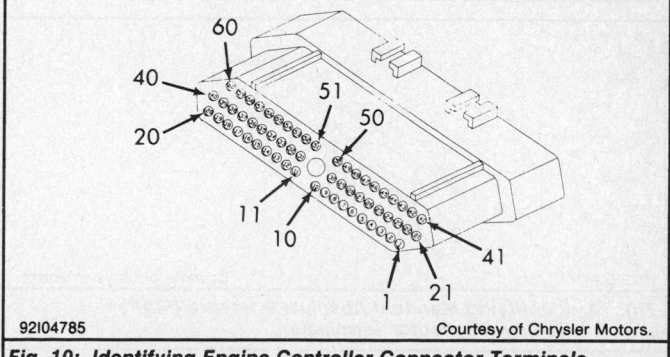

92I04785   Courtesy of Chrysler Motors.

Fig. 10: *Identifying Engine Controller Connector Terminals*

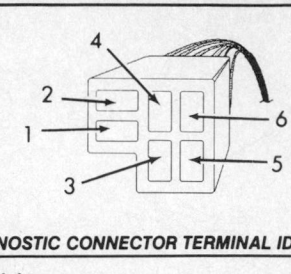

ENGINE DIAGNOSTIC CONNECTOR TERMINAL IDENTIFICATION

Cavity & Model	Wire Color
No. 1	
Cherokee & Comanche	Black
Grand Cherokee	Black/Tan
Wrangler	Black/Yellow
No. 2	Not Used
No. 3	
Cherokee & Comanche	Pink
Grand Cherokee	Black
Wrangler	Black/Red
No. 4	
Cherokee & Comanche	Light Green
Grand Cherokee	Black/Yellow
Wrangler	Black/Pink
No. 5	
Cherokee & Comanche	Dark Blue/White
Grand Cherokee	Light Blue/Red
Wrangler	white/Yellow
No. 6	Not Used

92D22486   Courtesy of Chrysler Motors.

Fig. 11: Identifying Engine Diagnostic Connector Terminals

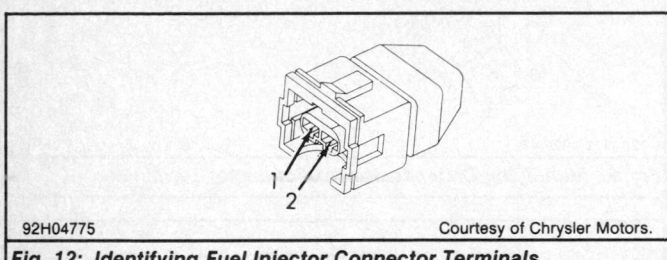

92H04775   Courtesy of Chrysler Motors.

Fig. 12: Identifying Fuel Injector Connector Terminals

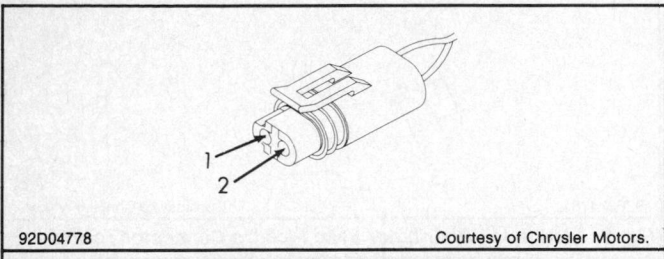

92D04778   Courtesy of Chrysler Motors.

Fig. 13: Identifying Ignition Coil Connector Terminals

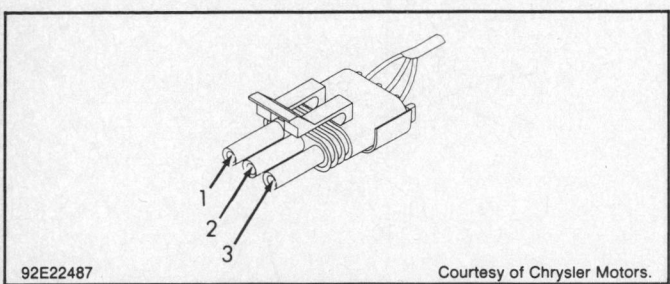

92E22487   Courtesy of Chrysler Motors.

Fig. 14: Identifying Manifold Absolute Pressure (MAP) Sensor Connector Terminals

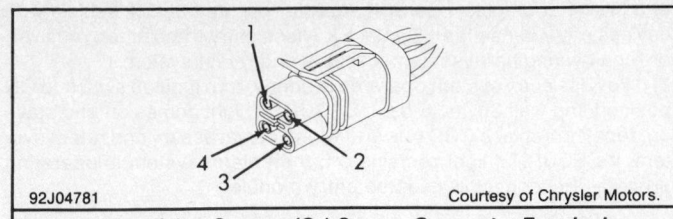

92J04781   Courtesy of Chrysler Motors.

Fig. 15: Identifying Oxygen (O₂) Sensor Connector Terminals

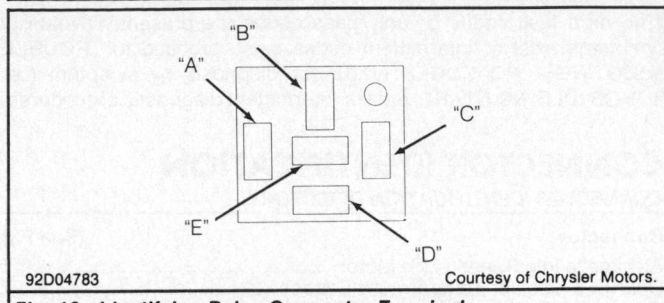

92D04783   Courtesy of Chrysler Motors.

Fig. 16: Identifying Relay Connector Terminals

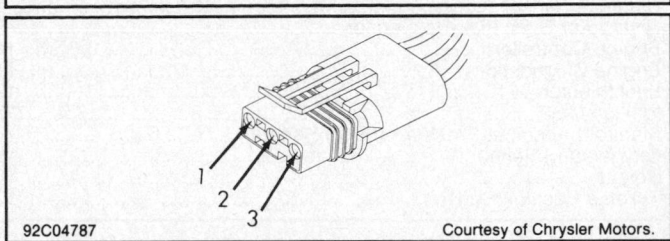

92C04787   Courtesy of Chrysler Motors.

Fig. 17: Identifying Throttle Position Sensor Connector Terminals

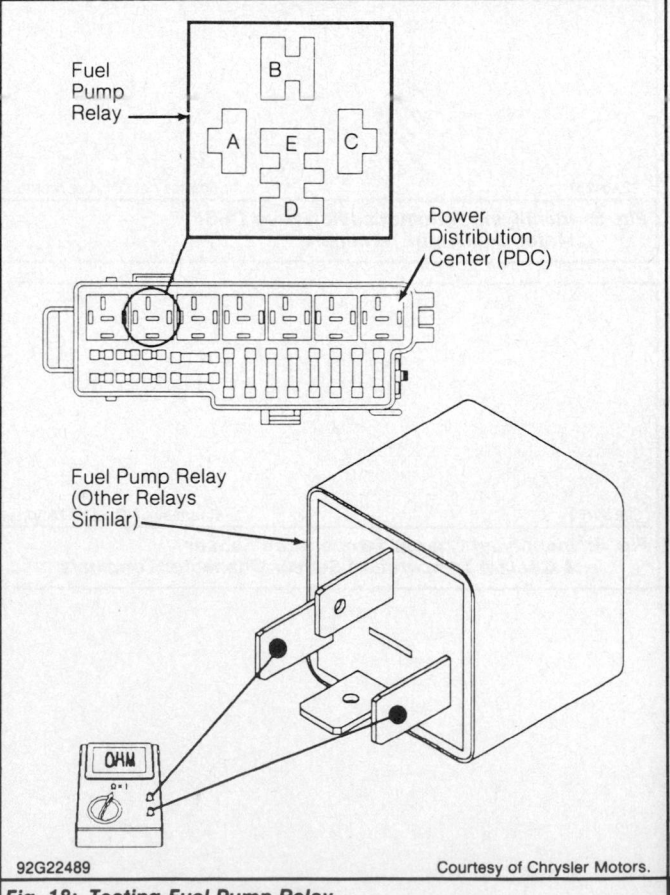

92G22489   Courtesy of Chrysler Motors.

Fig. 18: Testing Fuel Pump Relay

SELF-DIAGNOSTIC TESTS

WARNING: *When battery is disconnected, vehicle computer and energy systems may lose memory data. Driveability problems may exist until computer systems have completed a relearn cycle. See* COMPUTER RELEARN PROCEDURES *article in* GENERAL INFORMATION *before disconnecting battery.*

TEST NS-1A

QUALIFYING NO START CONDITION

NOTE: For connector terminal identification, see CONNECTOR IDENTIFICATION at beginning of article. For appropriate wiring diagram, see WIRING DIAGRAMS article in ENGINE PERFORMANCE.

1) Perform visual inspection of vehicle. See VISUAL INSPECTION under SELF-DIAGNOSTIC SYSTEM. Ensure battery is fully charged. Using DRB-II, erase faults and reset adaptive memory. Try to start engine by cranking for at least 10 seconds. Ensure key is turned off before each attempt to start engine. Turn ignition on. Using DRB-II, read faults.

2) If DRB-II displays a fault message, perform appropriate test. See DRB-II FAULT MESSAGES table. If DRB-II does not display any fault message, go to step 3).

DRB-II FAULT MESSAGES

DRB-II Message	Test No.
AUTOMATIC IDLE SPEED MOTOR CIRCUITS	NS-6A
AUTO SHUTDOWN RELAY CONTROL CIRCUIT	NS-10A
COOLANT VOLTAGE & TPS VOLTAGE HIGH	[1]
INJECTOR CONTROL CIRCUIT FAULT	NS-5A
INTERNAL CONTROLLER FAILURE or	
CONTROLLER FAILURE SPI COMMUNICATIONS	[2]
NO ASD RELAY VOLTAGE SENSE	
AT CONTROLLER	NS-11A
NO REFERENCE SIGNAL DURING CRANKING	NS-9A
NO RESPONSE	NS-8A
NO SYNC PICK-UP SIGNAL	NS-9B

[1] – Repair open Black/Light Blue wire (Brown/Red wire on Wrangler) to engine controller terminal No. 4.
[2] – Replace engine controller. Perform VERIFICATION TEST VER-1.

3) Try to start engine by cranking for at least 10 seconds. Ensure key is turned off before each attempt to start engine. If engine starts and stalls, perform TEST NS-2A. If engine does not start and stall, turn ignition off. Disconnect any spark plug wire from spark plug.

4) Insert an insulated screwdriver in cable terminal. Hold screwdriver a maximum of 1/4" away from a good ground. Watch for spark while cranking engine for 10 seconds. Consider 1-2 sparks as a no-spark condition. If a good spark occurs, perform TEST NS-2A.

5) If a good spark does not occur, turn ignition off. Disconnect coil secondary wire from distributor. Hold coil wire a maximum of 1/4" away from a good ground. Watch for spark while cranking engine for 10 seconds. If there is good spark, repair secondary ignition system (distributor cap, rotor or spark plug wires). Perform VERIFICATION TEST VER-1.

6) If a good spark does not occur, turn ignition off. Remove coil secondary wire. Using a DVOM, measure coil secondary wire resistance. If resistance is greater than 15,000 ohms, replace coil secondary wire. Perform VERIFICATION TEST VER-1. If resistance is 15,000 ohms or less, remove distributor cap. Watch for rotor to turn while cranking engine. If rotor does not turn, repair distributor drive system. Perform VERIFICATION TEST VER-1.

7) If rotor turned, reinstall distributor cap. Disconnect ignition coil connector. Using DRB-II, actuate fuel system. With fuel system actuating, place DRB-II in voltmeter mode. Probe Dark Green/Orange wire (Dark Green/Black wire on Wrangler) in ignition coil harness connector. If voltage is not greater than 10 volts, repair Dark Green/Orange (Dark Green/Black) wire between coil and ASD relay splice. Perform VERIFICATION TEST VER-1.

8) If voltage is 10 volts or more, probe Gray wire (Gray/White wire on Grand Cherokee; Yellow/Black wire on Wrangler) in ignition coil harness connector. If voltage is greater than 10 volts, go to step 11). If voltage is 10 volts or less, turn ignition off. Disconnect engine controller connector. Place DRB-II in ohmmeter mode. Probe Gray wire (Gray/White wire on Grand Cherokee; Yellow/Black wire on Wrangler) in engine controller connector terminal No. 19.

TEST NS-1A (Cont.)

9) If resistance is less than 10 ohms, repair Gray wire (Gray/White wire on Grand Cherokee; Yellow/Black wire on Wrangler) for a short to ground. Perform VERIFICATION TEST VER-1. If resistance is 10 ohms or more, check resistance of Gray wire (Gray/White wire on Grand Cherokee; Yellow/Black wire on Wrangler) between coil harness connector and engine controller connector terminal No. 19.

10) If resistance is greater than 10 ohms, repair open Gray wire (Gray/White wire on Grand Cherokee; Yellow/Black wire on Wrangler). Perform VERIFICATION TEST VER-1. If resistance is 10 ohms or less, replace engine controller. Perform VERIFICATION TEST VER-1.

11) Turn ignition off. Using a DVOM, check ignition coil primary circuit resistance. If resistance is not .8-1.3 ohms at 75°F (24°C), replace ignition coil. Perform VERIFICATION TEST VER-1.

12) If resistance is .8-1.3 ohms at 75°F (24°C), check ignition coil secondary circuit resistance (coil – terminal and coil tower). If resistance is not 10,000-16,000 ohms, replace ignition coil. Perform VERIFICATION TEST VER-1. If resistance is 10,000-16,000 ohms, reconnect ignition coil connector. Perform TEST NS-9A.

TEST NS-2A

INSPECTING FUEL SYSTEM

NOTE: For connector terminal identification, see CONNECTOR IDENTIFICATION at beginning of article. For appropriate wiring diagram, see WIRING DIAGRAMS article in ENGINE PERFORMANCE. If vehicle is equipped with factory theft alarm, use DRB-II to read theft alarm status. If DRB-II displays FUEL ON, go to step 1). If not, check theft alarm system. See THEFT ALARM SYSTEM at beginning of this article.

1) Ensure throttle is at idle position. Using DRB-II, read TPS sensor voltage. If voltage is more than 1.5 volts, replace throttle position sensor. Perform VERIFICATION TEST VER-1. If voltage is 1.5 volts or less, disconnect fuel injector No. 1 connector.

2) Place DRB-II in voltmeter mode and actuate ASD fuel system. Probe Dark Green/Orange wire (Dark Green/Black wire on Grand Cherokee and Wrangler). If voltage is 10 volts or less on both wires, repair Dark Green/Orange (Dark Green/Black wire on Grand Cherokee) between injector connector and harness splice. Perform VERIFICATION TEST VER-1. If voltage is more than 10 volts on both wires, turn ignition off.

WARNING: **Fuel system must be opened and may be under high pressure.**

3) Install fuel pressure gauge in fuel supply line, on fuel rail near fuel pressure regulator. Ensure fuel tank is at least 1/4 full. Reconnect injector connector. Turn ignition on. Using DRB-II, actuate ASD fuel system. Listen for fuel pump operation at fuel tank. If fuel pump operation cannot be heard, go to TEST NS-7A.

4) If fuel pump operation can be heard, read fuel pressure gauge. If fuel pressure is more than 43 psi, perform TEST NS-4B. If fuel pressure is less than 35 psi, perform TEST NS-4A. If fuel pressure is not less than 35 or more than 43 and vehicle starts/stalls repeatedly, perform TEST NS-12A. If vehicle does not start and stall repeatedly, perform TEST NS-3A.

TEST NS-3A

INSPECTING MECHANICAL SYSTEM

NOTE: For connector terminal identification, see CONNECTOR IDENTIFICATION at beginning of article. For appropriate wiring diagram, see WIRING DIAGRAMS article in ENGINE PERFORMANCE.

1) Turn ignition off. Check spark plug wires for proper firing order. If firing order is not correct, reconnect wires in correct firing order. Perform VERIFICATION TEST VER-1. If firing order is correct, remove all spark plugs and inspect tips for fuel (flooding). Clean spark plugs as necessary. Reinstall spark plugs. Connect timing light to engine.

2) Check ignition timing while cranking engine. If ignition timing is 0-25 degrees BTDC, go to step 3). If timing is not 0-25 degrees BTDC, replace engine controller. Perform VERIFICATION TEST VER-1.

TEST NS-3A (Cont.)

3) Locate cylinder No. 1 on distributor cap and mark housing for reference. Position piston in cylinder No. 1 to Top Dead Center (TDC) of compression stroke. Remove distributor cap and check if rotor is pointing to mark on distributor housing. Reposition distributor housing into correct alignment, if necessary, and go to next step.

4) Turn ignition off. Disconnect engine controller connector and MAP sensor connector. Using a DVOM, check resistance of Violet/White wire (Brown/Yellow wire on Wrangler) between MAP sensor and engine controller connectors.

5) If resistance is 10 ohms or more, repair open Violet/White wire (Brown/Yellow wire on Wrangler). Perform VERIFICATION TEST VER-1. If resistance is less than 10 ohms, check valve timing and engine compression. If valve timing and engine compression are okay, replace MAP sensor. Perform VERIFICATION TEST VER-1. If valve timing and engine compression are not okay, repair engine as necessary. Perform VERIFICATION TEST VER-1.

TEST NS-4A

CORRECTING FUEL DELIVERY

WARNING: Fuel system must be opened and may be under high pressure.

1) Measure and record fuel pressure gauge reading at fuel rail. Turn ignition off. Remove fuel pressure gauge and reconnect fuel line. Install fuel pressure gauge in fuel line between fuel tank and fuel filter. Turn ignition on. Using DRB-II, actuate ASD fuel system. Record fuel pressure gauge reading.

2) Compare fuel pressure gauge readings. If fuel pressure is not at least 10 psi more, go to step 3). If fuel pressure is at least 10 psi more, go to step 4).

CAUTION: DO NOT allow fuel pressure to exceed 70 psi.

3) Watch fuel pressure gauge while gently squeezing fuel return hose. If fuel pressure is greater than 35 psi, replace fuel pressure regulator. Perform VERIFICATION TEST VER-1. If fuel pressure is 35 psi or less, replace fuel pump and filter sock assembly. Perform VERIFICATION TEST VER-1.

4) Inspect fuel lines between fuel filter and fuel rail for restriction. If fuel lines are restricted, repair lines as necessary. Perform VERIFICATION TEST VER-1. If lines are not restricted, replace fuel filter. Perform VERIFICATION TEST VER-1.

TEST NS-4B

CORRECTING FUEL DELIVERY

WARNING: Fuel system must be opened and may be under high pressure.

1) Ensure fuel tank is at least 1/4 full. Relieve fuel system pressure. Remove fuel return hose from fuel rail. Connect a 6 foot long piece of fuel hose to fuel rail return fitting. Place other end of hose into an approved gasoline container (minimum 2 gallon capacity). Turn ignition on. Using DRB-II, actuate ASD fuel system.

2) Read fuel pressure gauge. If fuel pressure is 43 psi or more, replace fuel pressure regulator. Perform VERIFICATION TEST VER-1. If fuel pressure is less than 43 psi, turn ignition off. Reconnect fuel return hose. Disconnect fuel return hose from fuel tank. Connect 6 foot long piece of fuel hose to disconnected fuel return hose. Place other end of fuel hose into an approved gasoline container (minimum 2 gallon capacity).

3) Turn ignition on. Using DRB-II, actuate ASD fuel system. Read fuel pressure gauge. If fuel pressure is less than 43 psi, replace fuel return assembly in fuel tank. Perform VERIFICATION TEST VER-1. If fuel pressure is 43 psi or more, repair restricted fuel return line between fuel rail and fuel tank. Perform VERIFICATION TEST VER-1.

TEST NS-5A

REPAIRING FAULT
"FUEL INJECTOR CONTROL CIRCUIT"

NOTE: For connector terminal identification, see CONNECTOR IDENTIFICATION at beginning of article. For appropriate wiring diagram, see WIRING DIAGRAMS article in ENGINE PERFORMANCE.

1) Turn ignition off. Disconnect fuel injector No. 1 connector. Turn ignition on. Using DRB-II, actuate ASD fuel system. Place DRB-II in voltmeter mode. Probe Dark Green/Orange wire (Dark Green/Black on Grand Cherokee and Wrangler) in injector harness connector.

2) If voltage is less than 10 volts, repair open Dark Green/Orange wire (Dark Green/Black wire on Grand Cherokee and Wrangler). Perform VERIFICATION TEST VER-1. If voltage is 10 volts or more, replace engine controller. Perform VERIFICATION TEST VER-1.

TEST NS-6A

REPAIRING FAULT
"AUTOMATIC IDLE SPEED MOTOR CIRCUIT"

NOTE: For connector terminal identification, see CONNECTOR IDENTIFICATION at beginning of article. For appropriate wiring diagram, see WIRING DIAGRAMS article in ENGINE PERFORMANCE.

1) Disconnect Automatic Idle Speed (AIS) motor connector. Turn ignition on. Using DRB-II, actuate AIS motor. Place DRB-II in voltmeter mode. Probe Gray/Red wire (Yellow/Black wire on Grand Cherokee; Dark Green/Black wire on Wrangler) in AIS motor harness connector. When normal, voltage will switch from less than one volt to more than 10 volts.

2) If voltage stayed less than one volt, repair Gray/Red wire (Yellow/Black wire on Grand Cherokee; Dark Green/Black wire on Wrangler) for a short to ground. Perform VERIFICATION TEST VER-1. If voltage stayed more than 10 volts, repair Gray/Red wire (Yellow/Black wire on Grand Cherokee; Dark Green/Black wire on Wrangler) for a short to voltage. Perform VERIFICATION TEST VER-1.

3) If voltage did NOT stay less than one volt or more than 10 volts, probe Yellow/Black wire (Violet/Black wire on Grand Cherokee; Pink/Black wire on Wrangler) in AIS motor harness connector.

4) If voltage stayed less than one volt, repair Yellow/Black wire (Violet/Black wire on Grand Cherokee; Pink/Black wire on Wrangler) for a short to ground. Perform VERIFICATION TEST VER-1. If voltage stayed more than 10 volts, repair Yellow/Black wire (Violet/Black wire on Grand Cherokee; Pink/Black wire on Wrangler) for a short to voltage. Perform VERIFICATION TEST VER-1.

5) If voltage did NOT stay less than one volt or more than 10 volts, probe Brown/White wire (Red/Yellow wire on Wrangler) in AIS motor harness connector. If voltage stayed less than one volt, repair Brown/White wire (Red/Yellow wire on Wrangler) for a short to ground. Perform VERIFICATION TEST VER-1. If voltage stayed more than 10 volts, repair Brown/White wire (Red/Yellow wire on Wrangler) for a short to voltage. Perform VERIFICATION TEST VER-1.

6) If voltage did NOT stay less than one volt or more than 10 volts, probe Violet/Black wire (Gray/Red wire on Grand Cherokee; Dark Blue/Yellow wire on Wrangler) in AIS motor harness connector. If voltage stayed less than one volt, repair Violet/Black wire (Gray/Red wire on Grand Cherokee; Dark Blue/Yellow wire on Wrangler) for a short to ground. Perform VERIFICATION TEST VER-1.

7) If voltage stayed more than 10 volts, repair Violet/Black wire (Gray/Red wire on Grand Cherokee; Dark Blue/Yellow wire on Wrangler) for a short to voltage. Perform VERIFICATION TEST VER-1. If voltage did NOT stay less than one volt or more than 10 volts, turn ignition off. Reconnect AIS motor. Disconnect engine controller 60-pin connector.

8) Using a DVOM, measure resistance between engine controller connector terminals No. 39 and 59. If resistance is less than 35 ohms, replace AIS motor. Perform VERIFICATION TEST VER-1. If resistance is 35 ohms or more, go to next step.

9) Using a DVOM, measure resistance between engine controller connector terminals No. 40 and 60. If resistance is less than 35 ohms, replace AIS motor. Perform VERIFICATION TEST VER-1. If resistance is 35 ohms or more, go to next step.

10) Using a DVOM, measure resistance between engine controller connector terminals No. 39 and 60. If resistance is less than 10 ohms, repair

TEST NS-6A (Cont.)

wires (terminals No. 1 and 2 of AIS harness connector) for a short to each other. *See Fig. 5.* Perform VERIFICATION TEST VER-1.

11) If resistance in step **10)** was 10 ohms or more, check if resistance is less than 75 ohms (between terminals No. 39 and 60). If resistance is less than 75 ohms, go next step. If resistance is 75 ohms or more, go to step **13)**.

12) Using a DVOM, measure resistance between engine controller connector terminals No. 59 and 60. If resistance is less than 10 ohms, repair wires (terminals No. 2 and 4 of AIS harness connector) for a short to each other. Perform VERIFICATION TEST VER-1. If resistance is 10 ohms or more, repair wires (terminals No. 1 and 3 of AIS harness connector) for a short to each other. Perform VERIFICATION TEST VER-1.

13) If resistance in step **11)** was 75 ohms or more, check if resistance is less than 120 ohms (between terminals No. 39 and 60). If resistance is less than 120 ohms, repair wires (terminals No. 3 and 4 of AIS harness connector) for a short to each other. Perform VERIFICATION TEST VER-1. If resistance is 120 ohms or more, replace engine controller. Perform VERIFICATION TEST VER-1.

TEST NS-7A

INSPECTING FUEL PUMP

NOTE: For connector terminal identification, see CONNECTOR IDENTIFICATION at beginning of article. For appropriate wiring diagram, see WIRING DIAGRAMS article in ENGINE PERFORMANCE.

1) Using DRB-II, stop actuation test. Using DRB II, actuate ASD relay. Touch fuel pump relay to check for operation. If fuel pump relay does not pulsate, perform TEST NS-7B. If fuel pump relay pulsates, stop actuation test. Disconnect fuel pump relay. Turn ignition on. Place DRB-II in voltmeter mode. Probe Red wire (Pink/Yellow wire on Wrangler) in fuel pump relay connector.

2) If voltage is 10 volts or less, repair Red wire (Pink/Yellow wire on Wrangler) for an open circuit to splice. Perform VERIFICATION TEST VER-1. If voltage is greater than 10 volts, disconnect fuel pump harness connector. Reconnect fuel pump relay. Using DRB-II, actuate fuel system. Place DRB-II in voltmeter mode. Probe Dark Green/Red wire (Orange/Black wire on Grand Cherokee and Wrangler) in fuel pump connector. If voltage is more than 10 volts, go to step **6)**.

3) If voltage is 10 volts or less, turn ignition off. Disconnect fuel pump relay. Using a DVOM, check resistance between fuel pump relay connector Dark Green/Black wire (Orange/Dark Blue on Grand Cherokee; Orange/Black on Wrangler) and fuel pump connector Dark Green/Red wire (Orange/Black on Grand Cherokee and Wrangler).

4) If resistance is less than 10 ohms, replace fuel pump relay. Perform VERIFICATION TEST VER-1. If resistance is 10 ohms or more (Cherokee or Comanche), go to next step. If resistance is 10 ohms or more, repair open between fuel pump relay connector Orange/Dark Blue wire (Orange/Black on Wrangler) and fuel pump connector Orange/Black wire. Perform VERIFICATION TEST VER-1.

5) Disconnect ballast resistor. Ballast resistor is located next to windshield washer fluid reservoir. Using a DVOM, measure resistance across ballast resistor. If resistance is 10 ohms or more, replace ballast resistor. Perform VERIFICATION TEST VER-1. If resistance is less than 10 ohms, repair Dark Green/Black wire between fuel pump relay and fuel pump. Perform VERIFICATION TEST VER-1.

6) Using DRB-II, stop actuation test. Place DRB-II in ohmmeter mode. Probe Black wire (Tan/Black wire on Wrangler) in fuel pump connector. If resistance is less than 5 ohms, replace fuel pump. Perform VERIFICATION TEST VER-1. If resistance is 5 ohms or more, repair Black wire (Tan/Black wire on Wrangler) wire for an open circuit to ground. Perform VERIFICATION TEST VER-1.

TEST NS-7B

INSPECTING FUEL PUMP

NOTE: For connector terminal identification, see CONNECTOR IDENTIFICATION at beginning of article. For appropriate wiring diagram, see WIRING DIAGRAMS article in ENGINE PERFORMANCE.

1) Turn ignition off. Disconnect fuel pump relay. Turn ignition on. Probe Dark Blue wire (Light Blue/Red wire on Grand Cherokee; White/Yellow wire on Wrangler) in fuel pump relay connector. If voltage is 10 volts or less, repair Dark Blue wire (Light Blue/Red wire on Grand Cherokee; White/Yellow wire on Wrangler) for an open circuit to splice. Perform VERIFICATION TEST VER-1.

2) If voltage is more than 10 volts, measure resistance across fuel pump relay terminals "A" and "C". *See Fig. 18.* If resistance is 100 ohms or more, replace fuel pump relay. Perform VERIFICATION TEST VER-1. If resistance is less than 100 ohms, repair open Dark Blue wire (Pink wire on Grand Cherokee; Orange/Dark Green wire on Wrangler) between fuel pump relay connector and splice. Perform VERIFICATION TEST VER-1.

TEST NS-8A

REPAIRING "NO RESPONSE" CONDITION

NOTE: For connector terminal identification, see CONNECTOR IDENTIFICATION at beginning of article. For appropriate wiring diagram, see WIRING DIAGRAMS article in ENGINE PERFORMANCE.

1) Turn ignition off. Disconnect Throttle Position Sensor (TPS). Turn ignition on. Place DRB-II in voltmeter mode. Probe Violet/White wire (Brown/Yellow wire on Wrangler) at TPS harness connector. If voltage is more than 6 volts, repair open at engine controller connector terminals No. 5, 11 and 12. Perform VERIFICATION TEST VER-1.

2) If voltage is 6 volts or less, check if voltage is less than 4.4 volts. If voltage is 4.4 volts or less, go to next step. If voltage is more than 4.4 volts, reconnect TPS connector. Disconnect MAP sensor connector. Probe Violet/White wire (Brown/Yellow wire on Wrangler) at MAP sensor connector. If voltage is more than 4.4 volts, see NO RESPONSE MESSAGE under DRB-II PROBLEMS & ERROR MESSAGES in under SELF-DIAGNOSTIC SYSTEM. If voltage is 4.4 volts or less, replace TPS. Perform VERIFICATION TEST VER-1.

3) Disconnect MAP sensor connector. Probe Violet/White wire (Brown/Yellow wire on Wrangler) at TPS connector. If voltage is more than 4.4 volts, replace MAP sensor. Perform VERIFICATION TEST VER-1. If voltage is 4.4 volts or less, turn ignition off. Disconnect and inspect engine controller connector. Repair connector as necessary and go to next step.

4) Place DRB-II in ohmmeter mode. Probe engine controller connector terminal No. 6 Violet/White wire (Brown/Yellow wire on Wrangler). If resistance is less than 10 ohms, repair short to ground in Violet/White (Brown/Yellow) wire. Perform VERIFICATION TEST VER-1.

5) If resistance is 10 ohms or more, turn ignition on. Place DRB-II in voltmeter mode. Probe engine controller connector terminal No. 9 Dark Blue wire (Light Blue/Red wire on Grand Cherokee; White/Yellow wire on Wrangler). If voltage is 10 volts or less, repair open Dark Blue (Light Blue/Red; White/Yellow) wire between engine controller connector terminal No. 9 and ignition switch. Perform VERIFICATION TEST VER-1.

6) If voltage is more than 10 volts, probe engine controller connector terminal No. 3 Red wire (Pink/Yellow wire on Wrangler). If voltage is more than 10 volts, replace engine controller. Perform VERIFICATION TEST VER-1. If voltage is 10 volts or less, go to next step.

7) Turn ignition off. Place DRB-II in ohmmeter mode. Probe engine controller connector terminal No. 3 Red wire (Pink/Yellow wire on Wrangler). If resistance is less than 10 ohms, repair Red (Pink/Yellow) wire for a short to ground between battery and engine controller connector terminal No. 3.

8) If resistance is 10 ohms or more, inspect fuse and fused circuit between battery and engine controller connector terminal No. 3. If fuse is okay, repair open repair Red wire (Pink/Yellow wire on Wrangler) between battery and engine controller connector terminal No. 3. If fuse is NOT okay, go to next step.

9) Disconnect Auto Shutdown (ASD) relay. Place DRB-II in ohmmeter mode. Probe Dark Green/Orange wire (Dark Green/Black wire on Grand

TEST NS-8A (Cont.)

Cherokee and Wrangler) in ASD relay connector. If resistance is 10 ohms or less, go to step **12**).

10) If resistance is more than 10 ohms, reconnect ASD relay. Disconnect fuel pump relay, fuel pump connector, and oxygen sensor connector. Probe Dark Green/Black wire (Orange/Dark Blue wire on Grand Cherokee; Orange/Black wire on Wrangler) in fuel pump relay connector. If resistance is less than 10 ohms, repair short to ground in Dark Green/Black wire (Orange/Blue wire on Grand Cherokee; Orange/Black wire on Wrangler).

11) If resistance is 10 ohms or more, probe both White wires at oxygen sensor connector. If resistance for either wire is 10 ohms or more, replace fuel pump relay connector. Perform VERIFICATION TEST VER-1. If resistance for either wire is less than 10 ohms, replace oxygen sensor. Perform VERIFICATION TEST VER-1.

12) Disconnect ignition coil connector. If resistance is more than 10 ohms, replace ignition coil. Perform VERIFICATION TEST VER-1. If resistance is 10 ohms or less, go to next step.

13) Disconnect fuel injector No. 1 connector. If resistance is more than 10 ohms, replace fuel injector No. 1. Perform VERIFICATION TEST VER-1. If resistance is 10 ohms or less, go to next step.

14) Disconnect fuel injector No. 2 connector. If resistance is more than 10 ohms, replace fuel injector No. 2. Perform VERIFICATION TEST VER-1. If resistance is 10 ohms or less, go to next step.

15) Disconnect fuel injector No. 3 connector. If resistance is more than 10 ohms, replace fuel injector No. 3. Perform VERIFICATION TEST VER-1. If resistance is 10 ohms or less, go to next step.

16) Disconnect fuel injector No. 4 connector. If resistance is more than 10 ohms, replace fuel injector No. 4. Perform VERIFICATION TEST VER-1. If resistance is 10 ohms or less (4-cylinder engine), go step **19**). If resistance is 10 ohms or less (6-cylinder engine), go to next step.

17) Disconnect fuel injector No. 5 connector. If resistance is more than 10 ohms, replace fuel injector No. 5. Perform VERIFICATION TEST VER-1. If resistance is 10 ohms or less, go to next step.

18) Disconnect fuel injector No. 6 connector. If resistance is more than 10 ohms, replace fuel injector No. 6. Perform VERIFICATION TEST VER-1. If resistance is 10 ohms or less, go to next step.

19) Disconnect alternator. Probe Dark Green/Orange wire (Dark Green/Black wire on Grand Cherokee and Wrangler) in ASD relay connector. If resistance is more than 10 ohms, replace alternator. Perform VERIFICATION TEST VER-1. If resistance is 10 ohms or less, repair Dark Green/Orange wire (Dark Green/Black wire on Grand Cherokee and Wrangler) for a short to ground. Perform VERIFICATION TEST VER-1.

TEST NS-9A

REPAIRING FAULT
"NO REFERENCE SIGNAL DURING CRANKING"

NOTE: For connector terminal identification, see CONNECTOR IDENTIFICATION at beginning of article. For appropriate wiring diagram, see WIRING DIAGRAMS article in ENGINE PERFORMANCE.

1) Disconnect crank position sensor. Turn ignition on. Place DRB-II in voltmeter mode. Probe Gray/Black wire (Red/Light Green wire on Grand Cherokee; Red/Dark Green wire on Wrangler) in crank position sensor connector. If voltage is greater than 4.5 volts, go to step **4**). If voltage is 4.5 volts or less, turn ignition off. Disconnect engine controller 60-pin connector.

2) Place DRB-II in ohmmeter mode. Probe Gray/Black wire (Red/Light Green on Grand Cherokee; Red/Dark Green wire on Wrangler) in crank position sensor connector. If resistance is less than 10 ohms, repair Gray/Black wire (Red/Light Green wire on Grand Cherokee; Red/Dark Green wire on Wrangler) for a short to ground. Perform VERIFICATION TEST VER-1. If resistance is 10 ohms or more, go to next step.

3) Using a DVOM, check continuity of Gray/Black wire (Red/Light Green on Grand Cherokee; Red/Dark Green wire on Wrangler) between engine controller connector terminal No. 24 and crank position sensor connector. If resistance is less than 10 ohms, replace engine controller. Perform VERIFICATION TEST VER-1. If resistance is 10 ohms or more, repair open Gray/Black wire (Red/Light Green wire on Grand Cherokee; Red/Dark Green wire on Wrangler). Perform VERIFICATION TEST VER-1.

4) Probe Orange wire (White/Black wire on Grand Cherokee and Wrangler) in crank position sensor connector. If voltage is 7.5 volts or less

TEST NS-9A (Cont.)

(except Wrangler), go to step **6**). If voltage is 7.5 volts or less (Wrangler), go to step **8**). If voltage is greater than 7.5 volts (all models), go to next step.

5) Turn ignition off. Probe Black/Light Blue wire (Brown/Red wire on Wrangler) in crank position sensor connector. If resistance is less than 10 ohms, replace crank position sensor. Perform VERIFICATION TEST VER-1. If resistance is 10 ohms or more, repair open Black/Light Blue wire (Brown/Red wire on Wrangler) between engine controller connector terminal No. 4 and crank position sensor connector. Perform VERIFICATION TEST VER-1.

6) Turn ignition off. Disconnect engine controller 60-pin connector. Place DRB-II in ohmmeter mode. Probe engine controller connector terminal No. 7 (Black/White wire on Grand Cherokee; Orange wire on all other models). If resistance is less than 10 ohms, repair Orange wire (Black/White wire on Grand Cherokee) for a short to ground. Disconnect battery quick disconnect. Reconnect battery quick disconnect. Perform VERIFICATION TEST VER-1.

7) If resistance is 10 ohms or more, check Orange wire (White/Black wire on Grand Cherokee) for continuity between engine controller connector terminal No. 7 and crank position sensor connector using a DVOM. If resistance is less than 10 ohms, replace engine controller. Perform VERIFICATION TEST VER-1. If resistance is 10 ohms or more, repair Orange wire (White/Black wire on Grand Cherokee) between engine controller connector terminal No. 7 and crank position sensor connector. Perform VERIFICATION TEST VER-1.

8) Disconnect distance (speed) sensor. Place DRB-II in voltmeter mode. Probe White/Black wire in crank position sensor connector. If voltage is greater than 7.5 volts, replace distance (speed) sensor. Perform VERIFICATION TEST VER-1. If voltage is 7.5 volts or less, go to next step.

9) Turn ignition off. Disconnect engine controller 60-pin connector. Place DRB-II in ohmmeter mode. Probe engine controller connector terminal No. 7 (White/Black wire). If resistance is less than 10 ohms, repair White/Black wire for a short to ground. Disconnect battery quick disconnect. Reconnect battery quick disconnect. Perform VERIFICATION TEST VER-1.

10) If resistance is 10 ohms or more, check White/Black wire for continuity between engine controller connector terminal No. 7 and distributor sync pick-up sensor connector using a DVOM. If resistance is less than 10 ohms, replace engine controller. Perform VERIFICATION TEST VER-1. If resistance is 10 ohms or more, repair White/Black wire between engine controller connector terminal No. 7 and sync sensor connector. Perform VERIFICATION TEST VER-1.

TEST NS-9B

REPAIRING FAULT "NO SYNC PICK-UP SIGNAL"

NOTE: For connector terminal identification, see CONNECTOR IDENTIFICATION at beginning of article. For appropriate wiring diagram, see WIRING DIAGRAMS article in ENGINE PERFORMANCE.

1) Ensure distributor shaft turns when engine is cranked. If shaft does not turn, repair as necessary. Perform VERIFICATION TEST VER-1. If shaft turns, disconnect distributor sync pick-up sensor. Turn ignition on. Place DRB-II in voltmeter mode. Probe Tan/Yellow wire (Gray/Black wire on Grand Cherokee and Wrangler) in distributor sync pick-up connector. If voltage is more than 4.5 volts, go to step **4**).

2) If voltage is 4.5 volts or less, turn ignition off. Disconnect engine controller 60-pin connector. Place DRB-II in ohmmeter mode. Probe Tan/Yellow wire (Gray/Black wire on Grand Cherokee and Wrangler) in distributor sync pick-up connector. If resistance is less than 10 ohms, repair Tan/Yellow wire (Gray/Black wire on Grand Cherokee and Wrangler) for a short to ground. Perform VERIFICATION TEST VER-1.

3) If resistance is 10 ohms or more, check Tan/Yellow wire (Gray/Black wire on Grand Cherokee and Wrangler) for continuity between engine controller connector terminal No. 44 and distributor sync pick-up sensor connector using a DVOM. If resistance is less than 10 ohms, replace engine controller. Perform VERIFICATION TEST VER-1. If resistance is 10 ohms or more, repair open Tan/Yellow wire (Gray/Black wire on Grand Cherokee and Wrangler). Perform VERIFICATION TEST VER-1.

4) Probe Orange wire (White/Black wire on Grand Cherokee and Wrangler) in distributor sync pick-up connector. If voltage is 7.5 volts or less (except Wrangler), go to step **6**). If voltage is 7.5 volts or less (Wrangler), go to step **8**). If voltage is greater than 7.5 volts (all models), go to next step.

TEST NS-9B (Cont.)

5) Turn ignition off. Place DRB-II in ohmmeter mode. Probe Black/Light Blue wire (Brown/Red wire on Wrangler) in distributor sync pick-up connector. If resistance is less than 10 ohms, replace distributor sync pick-up. Perform VERIFICATION TEST VER-1. If resistance is 10 ohms or more, repair open Black/Light Blue wire (Brown/Red on Wrangler) between sensor connector and splice. Perform VERIFICATION TEST VER-1.

6) Turn ignition off. Disconnect engine controller 60-pin connector. Place DRB-II in ohmmeter mode. Probe engine controller connector terminal No. 7 Orange wire (Black/White wire on Grand Cherokee). If resistance is less than 10 ohms, repair Orange wire (Black/White wire on Grand Cherokee) for a short to ground. Disconnect battery quick disconnect. Reconnect battery quick disconnect. Perform VERIFICATION TEST VER-1.

7) If resistance is 10 ohms or more, check Orange wire (White/Black wire on Grand Cherokee) for continuity between engine controller connector terminal No. 7 and distributor sync pick-up sensor connector using a DVOM. If resistance is less than 10 ohms, replace engine controller. Perform VERIFICATION TEST VER-1. If resistance is 10 ohms or more, repair Orange wire (White/Black on Grand Cherokee) between engine controller connector terminal No. 7 and distributor sync pick-up sensor connector. Perform VERIFICATION TEST VER-1.

8) Disconnect distance (speed) sensor. Place DRB-II in voltmeter mode. Probe Orange wire (White/Black wire on Grand Cherokee) in distributor sync pick-up sensor connector. If voltage is greater than 7.5 volts, replace distance (speed) sensor. Perform VERIFICATION TEST VER-1. If voltage is 7.5 volts or less, go to next step.

9) Turn ignition off. Disconnect engine controller 60-pin connector. Check Orange wire (White/Black wire on Grand Cherokee) for continuity between engine controller connector terminal No. 7 and distributor sync pick-up sensor connector using a DVOM. If resistance is less than 10 ohms, replace engine controller. Perform VERIFICATION TEST VER-1. If resistance is 10 ohms or more, repair Orange wire (White/Black wire on Grand Cherokee) between engine controller connector terminal No. 7 and distributor sync pick-up sensor connector. Perform VERIFICATION TEST VER-1.

TEST NS-10A

REPAIRING FAULT "AUTO SHUTDOWN RELAY CONTROL CIRCUIT"

NOTE: For connector terminal identification, see CONNECTOR IDENTIFICATION at beginning of article. For appropriate wiring diagram, see WIRING DIAGRAMS article in ENGINE PERFORMANCE.

1) Turn ignition on. Disconnect Auto Shutdown (ASD) relay. Place DRB-II in voltmeter mode. Probe Dark Blue wire (Light Blue/Red wire on Grand Cherokee; White/Yellow wire on Wrangler) in ASD relay connector. If voltage is more than 10 volts, go to next step. If voltage is 10 volts or less, repair open Dark Blue wire (Light Blue/Red wire on Grand Cherokee; White/Yellow wire on Wrangler) wire from ignition switch. Perform VERIFICATION TEST VER-1.

2) Using a DVOM, check resistance between Dark Blue wire (Light Blue/Red wire on Grand Cherokee; White/Yellow on Wrangler) at ASD relay. If resistance is 100 ohms or more, replace ASD relay. Perform VERIFICATION TEST VER-1. If resistance is less than 100 ohms, go to next step.

3) Turn ignition off. Disconnect engine controller 60-pin connector. Using a DVOM, check resistance of Dark Blue/Yellow wire (Pink wire on Grand Cherokee; Orange/Dark Green on Wrangler) between engine controller connector terminal No. 51 and ASD relay connector.

4) If resistance is less than 10 ohms, replace engine controller. Perform VERIFICATION TEST VER-1. If resistance is 10 ohms or more, repair open Dark Blue/Yellow wire (Pink wire on Grand Cherokee; Orange/Dark Green wire on Wrangler). Perform VERIFICATION TEST VER-1.

TEST NS-11A

REPAIRING FAULT "NO ASD RELAY VOLTAGE SENSE AT CONTROLLER"

NOTE: For connector terminal identification, see CONNECTOR IDENTIFICATION at beginning of article. For appropriate wiring diagram, see WIRING DIAGRAMS article in ENGINE PERFORMANCE.

1) Disconnect ASD relay. Turn ignition on. Place DRB-II in voltmeter mode. Probe Red wire (Pink/Yellow wire on Wrangler) in ASD relay connector. If voltage is 10 volts or less, repair open Red wire (Pink/Yellow wire on Wrangler) to splice. Perform VERIFICATION TEST VER-1. If voltage is more than 10 volts, probe Dark Blue wire (Light Blue/Red wire on Grand Cherokee; White/Yellow wire on Wrangler) in ASD relay connector. If voltage is 10 volts or less, repair open Dark Blue wire (Light Blue/Red on Grand Cherokee; White/Yellow on Wrangler) between ASD relay connector and ignition switch. Perform VERIFICATION TEST VER-1.

2) If voltage is more than 10 volts, turn ignition off. Disconnect engine controller 60-pin connector. Using a DVOM, check resistance of Dark Green/Orange wire (Dark Green/Black wire on Grand Cherokee and Wrangler) between engine controller connector terminal No. 57 and ASD relay connector. If resistance is 10 ohms or more, repair open Dark Green/Orange wire (Dark Green/Black wire on Grand Cherokee and Wrangler) between ASD relay and engine controller. Perform VERIFICATION TEST VER-1.

3) If resistance is less than 10 ohms, check resistance of Dark Blue/Yellow wire (Pink wire on Grand Cherokee; Orange/Dark Green wire on Wrangler) between engine controller connector terminal No. 51 and ASD relay connector. If resistance is 10 ohms or more, repair open Dark Blue/Yellow wire (Pink wire on Grand Cherokee; Orange/Dark Green on Wrangler) between ASD relay and engine controller. Perform VERIFICATION TEST VER-1.

4) If resistance is less than 10 ohms, reconnect engine controller 60-pin connector. Substitute a known good relay for ASD relay. DO NOT use fuel pump relay. Try to start engine. If engine starts, repair is complete. Perform VERIFICATION TEST VER-1. If engine did not start, replace engine controller. Perform VERIFICATION TEST VER-1.

TEST NS-12A

INSPECTING AIS MOTOR OPERATION

NOTE: For connector terminal identification, see CONNECTOR IDENTIFICATION at beginning of article. For appropriate wiring diagram, see WIRING DIAGRAMS article in ENGINE PERFORMANCE.

1) Turn ignition on. Using DRB-II, actuate AIS motor. Disconnect AIS motor. Place DRB-II in voltmeter mode. Probe AIS motor connector Gray/Red wire (Yellow/Black wire on Grand Cherokee; Dark Green/Black wire on Wrangler). If voltage stays less than one volt, perform TEST NS-12B.

2) If voltage does not stay less one volt, probe Brown/White wire (Red/Yellow wire on Wrangler) at AIS motor connector. If voltage stays less than one volt, perform TEST NS-12C. If voltage does not stay less than one volt, probe Violet/Black wire (Gray/Red wire on Grand Cherokee; Dark Blue/Yellow wire on Wrangler) at AIS motor connector. If voltage stays less than one volt, perform TEST NS-12D.

3) If voltage does not stay less than one volt, probe Yellow/Black wire (Violet/Black wire on Grand Cherokee; Pink/Black wire on Wrangler) at AIS motor connector. If voltage stays less than one volt, perform TEST NS-12E. If voltage did not stay less than one volt, stop AIS motor test. Turn ignition off.

4) Remove AIS motor from throttle body. Reconnect AIS motor connector. Turn ignition on. Using DRB-II, actuate AIS motor. If AIS motor tip moves in and out, perform TEST NS-13A. If AIS motor tip does not move in and out, replace AIS motor. Perform VERIFICATION TEST VER-1.

TEST NS-12B

INSPECTING AIS MOTOR OPERATION

NOTE: For connector terminal identification, see CONNECTOR IDENTIFICATION at beginning of article. For appropriate wiring diagram, see WIRING DIAGRAMS article in ENGINE PERFORMANCE.

Turn ignition off. Disconnect and inspect engine controller 60-pin connector. Repair connector as necessary. Perform VERIFICATION TEST VER-1. If connector is okay, check resistance of Gray/Red wire (Yellow/Black wire on Grand Cherokee; Dark Green/Black wire on Wrangler) between AIS motor connector and engine controller connector terminal No. 39 using a DVOM. If resistance is less than 10 ohms, replace engine controller. Perform VERIFICATION TEST VER-1. If resistance is 10 ohms or more, repair open Gray/Red wire (Yellow/Black wire on Grand Cherokee; Dark Green/Black wire on Wrangler) wire. Perform VERIFICATION TEST VER-1.

TEST NS-12C

INSPECTING AIS MOTOR OPERATION

NOTE: For connector terminal identification, see CONNECTOR IDENTIFICATION at beginning of article. For appropriate wiring diagram, see WIRING DIAGRAMS article in ENGINE PERFORMANCE.

Turn ignition off. Disconnect and inspect engine controller 60-pin connector. Repair connector as necessary. Perform VERIFICATION TEST VER-1. If connector is okay, check resistance of Brown/White wire (Red/Yellow wire on Wrangler) between AIS motor connector and engine controller connector terminal No. 40 using a DVOM. If resistance is less than 10 ohms, replace engine controller. Perform VERIFICATION TEST VER-1. If resistance is 10 ohms or more, repair open Brown/White wire (Red/Yellow wire on Wrangler). Perform VERIFICATION TEST VER-1.

TEST NS-12D

INSPECTING AIS MOTOR OPERATION

NOTE: For connector terminal identification, see CONNECTOR IDENTIFICATION at beginning of article. For appropriate wiring diagram, see WIRING DIAGRAMS article in ENGINE PERFORMANCE.

Turn ignition off. Disconnect and inspect engine controller 60-pin connector. Repair connector as necessary. Perform VERIFICATION TEST VER-1. If connector is okay, check resistance of Violet/Black wire (Gray/Red wire on Grand Cherokee; Dark Blue/Yellow wire on Wrangler) between AIS motor connector and engine controller connector terminal No. 59 using a DVOM. If resistance is less than 10 ohms, replace engine controller. Perform VERIFICATION TEST VER-1. If resistance is 10 ohms or more, repair open Violet/Black wire (Gray/Red wire Grand Cherokee; Dark Blue/Yellow on Wrangler). Perform VERIFICATION TEST VER-1.

TEST NS-12E

INSPECTING AIS MOTOR OPERATION

NOTE: For connector terminal identification, see CONNECTOR IDENTIFICATION at beginning of article. For appropriate wiring diagram, see WIRING DIAGRAMS article in ENGINE PERFORMANCE.

Turn ignition off. Disconnect and inspect engine controller 60-pin connector. Repair connector as necessary. Perform VERIFICATION TEST VER-1. If connector is okay, check resistance of Yellow/Black wire (Violet/Black wire on Grand Cherokee; Pink/Black wire on Wrangler) between AIS motor connector and engine controller connector terminal No. 60 using a DVOM. If resistance is less than 10 ohms, replace engine controller. Perform VERIFICATION TEST VER-1. If resistance is 10 ohms or more, repair open Yellow/Black wire (Violet/Black on Grand Cherokee; Pink/Black on Wrangler). Perform VERIFICATION TEST VER-1.

TEST NS-13A

CORRECTING START & STALL CONDITION

At this point in diagnostic procedure, all engine control systems have been determined to be operating as designed and are not the cause of the no-start or start-and-stall problem. Following additional items should be checked as possible causes:
- Check if any MITCHELL® TECHNICAL SERVICE BULLETINS (TSBs) apply to vehicle.
- Check engine valve timing.
- Check engine compression.
- Check for exhaust system restriction.
- Ensure PCV system is functioning properly.
- Check camshaft and crankshaft sprockets.
- Check torque converter stall speed.
- Check for fuel contamination.
- Check secondary ignition circuit for abnormal scope pattern.

TEST DR-1A

CHECKING SYSTEM FOR FAULTS

NOTE: For connector terminal identification, see CONNECTOR IDENTIFICATION at beginning of article. For appropriate wiring diagram, see WIRING DIAGRAMS article in ENGINE PERFORMANCE. Battery must be fully charged and at rated capacity before performing any driveability test procedure. If vehicle starts and stalls repeatedly, perform TEST NS-2A. If vehicle stalls when A/C is turned on, perform TEST NF-9A.

1) Turn ignition on. Connect DRB-II to engine diagnostic connector. Read fault messages. If DRB-II displays fault messages, go to step 4). If DRB-II does not display fault messages, start engine. Allow engine to reach normal operating temperature. Set engine speed manually to 2000 RPM for at least 10 seconds, and return engine to idle.

2) On A/T models, apply brakes. Shift gear selector through all gears and return to PARK position. Using DRB-II, read fault messages. If no fault messages are displayed, go to next step. If fault messages are displayed, go to step 4).

3) On all models, check MITCHELL® TECHNICAL SERVICE BULLETINS (TSBs) for any pertinent information if DRB-II still displays NO FAULTS. If a TSB exists, perform corrective action. If driveability problem continues after performing TSB procedure or if no TSB information was found, perform TEST NF-1A.

NOTE: ENGINE COLD TOO LONG fault message may set erroneously if ambient temperature is extremely cold.

4) If fault message is INTERNAL CONTROLLER FAILURE or CONTROLLER FAILURE, replace Single Board Engine Controller (SBEC). Perform VERIFICATION TEST VER-2. If fault message is ENGINE COLD TOO LONG, check engine cooling system. Repair cooling system as necessary. Perform VERIFICATION TEST VER-3.

5) If either of these fault messages are NOT displayed, see DRB-II FAULT MESSAGES table. Select fault message and corresponding test. Correct all hard fault messages before proceeding to intermittent fault message.

NOTE: A false fault code may set if vehicle being tested is not equipped with these options.

DRB-II FAULT MESSAGES

DRB-II Message	[1] Hard Fault	[2] Intermittent Fault
A/C CLUTCH RELAY CIRCUIT	DR-22A	DR-33A
AUTOMATIC IDLE SPEED (AIS) MOTOR CIRCUIT	DR-15A	DR-31A
CHARGE TEMPERATURE VOLTAGE HIGH	DR-26A	DR-30A
CHARGE TEMPERATURE VOLTAGE LOW	DR-27A	DR-30A
CONTROLLER FAILURE EEPROM WRITE DENIED	DR-28A	DR-28A

[1] – Key counter is "0".
[2] – Key counter is more than "0"

TEST DR-1A (Cont.)

DRB-II FAULT MESSAGES (Cont.)

DRB-II Message	[1] Hard Fault	[2] Intermittent Fault
CONTROLLER FAILURE EMR MILES NOT STORED	DR-28A	DR-28A
COOLANT SENSOR VOLTAGE TOO HIGH	DR-11A	DR-30A
COOLANT SENSOR VOLTAGE TOO LOW	DR-12A	DR-30A
FUEL PUMP RESISTOR BY-PASS RELAY CIRCUIT	DR-24A	DR-33A
INJECTOR NO. 1 CONTROL CIRCUIT	DR-16A	DR-32A
INJECTOR NO. 2 CONTROL CIRCUIT	DR-17A	DR-32A
INJECTOR NO. 3 CONTROL CIRCUIT	DR-18A	DR-32A
INJECTOR NO. 4 CONTROL CIRCUIT	DR-19A	DR-32A
INJECTOR NO. 5 CONTROL CIRCUIT	DR-20A	DR-32A
INJECTOR NO. 6 CONTROL CIRCUIT	DR-21A	DR-32A
MAP SENSOR VOLTAGE TOO HIGH	DR-5A	DR-30A
MAP SENSOR VOLTAGE TOO LOW	DR-4A	DR-30A
NO ASD RELAY VOLTAGE SENSE AT CONTROLLER	DR-25A	DR-34A
NO CHANGE IN MAP FROM START TO RUN	DR-3A	DR-30A
NO VEHICLE SPEED SIGNAL	DR-6A	DR-6A
O_2 SENSOR SHORTED TO VOLTAGE	DR-8A	DR-30A
O_2 SENSOR SIGNAL STAYS ABOVE CENTER (RICH)	DR-9A	DR-30A
O_2 SENSOR SIGNAL STAYS AT CENTER	DR-7A	DR-30A
O_2 SENSOR SIGNAL STAYS BELOW CENTER (LEAN)	DR-10A	DR-30A
RADIATOR FAN RELAY CIRCUIT	DR-23A	DR-33A
SLOW CHANGE IN IDLE MAP SIGNAL	DR-2A	DR-30A
THROTTLE POSITION SENSOR VOLTAGE HIGH	DR-13A	DR-30A
THROTTLE POSITION SENSOR VOLTAGE LOW	DR-14A	DR-30A

[1] – Key counter is "0".
[2] – Key counter is more than "0".

TEST DR-2A

CODE 13, REPAIRING FAULT "SLOW OR NO CHANGE IN IDLE MAP SIGNAL"

NOTE: For connector terminal identification, see CONNECTOR IDENTIFICATION at beginning of article. For appropriate wiring diagram, see WIRING DIAGRAMS article in ENGINE PERFORMANCE.

1) Turn ignition on. Tee a vacuum gauge into MAP sensor vacuum hose. Start engine. Observe vacuum gauge reading. If vacuum reading is zero in. Hg at idle, repair plugged or restricted hose to MAP sensor. Perform VERIFICATION TEST VER-2. If vacuum reading is not zero in. Hg at idle, snap throttle open and closed while observing vacuum gauge.

2) If vacuum gauge does not instantly drop to zero and return, repair restricted vacuum hose to MAP sensor. Perform VERIFICATION TEST VER-2. If vacuum reading instantly drops to zero and returns, turn ignition off. Disconnect and inspect MAP sensor connector. Repair connector if damaged. Perform VERIFICATION TEST VER-2.

3) If MAP sensor connector is okay, turn ignition on. Place DRB-II in voltmeter mode. Probe Violet/White wire (Brown/Yellow wire on Wrangler) at MAP sensor connector. If voltage is less than one volt, repair open Violet/White wire (Brown/Yellow wire on Wrangler). Perform VERIFICATION TEST VER-2. If voltage is one volt or more, replace MAP sensor. Perform VERIFICATION TEST VER-2.

TEST DR-3A

CODE 13, REPAIRING FAULT "SLOW OR NO CHANGE IN MAP FROM START TO RUN"

Turn ignition on. Tee a vacuum gauge into MAP sensor vacuum hose. Start engine. While at idle, read vacuum gauge. If reading is zero in. Hg at idle, repair leak in vacuum hose to MAP sensor. Perform VERIFICATION TEST VER-2. If reading is not zero in. Hg at idle, repair restriction in vacuum hose to MAP sensor. Perform VERIFICATION TEST VER-2.

TEST DR-4A

CODE 14, REPAIRING FAULT "MAP VOLTAGE TOO LOW"

NOTE: For connector terminal identification, see CONNECTOR IDENTIFICATION at beginning of article. For appropriate wiring diagram, see WIRING DIAGRAMS article in ENGINE PERFORMANCE.

1) Turn ignition off. Disconnect MAP sensor connector. Turn ignition on. Using DRB-II, read MAP sensor voltage. If MAP sensor voltage is more than 4.5 volts, replace MAP sensor. Perform VERIFICATION TEST VER-2.

2) If MAP sensor voltage is 4.5 volts or less, turn ignition off. Disconnect engine controller 60-pin connector. Place DRB-II in ohmmeter mode. Probe Dark Green/Red wire (Red/White wire on Grand Cherokee and Wrangler) at MAP sensor connector.

3) If resistance is less than 10 ohms, repair short to ground in Dark Green/Red wire (Red/White wire on Grand Cherokee and Wrangler). Perform VERIFICATION TEST VER-2. If resistance 10 ohms or more, replace engine controller. Perform VERIFICATION TEST VER-2.

TEST DR-5A

CODE 14, REPAIRING FAULT "MAP VOLTAGE TOO HIGH"

NOTE: For connector terminal identification, see CONNECTOR IDENTIFICATION at beginning of article. For appropriate wiring diagram, see WIRING DIAGRAMS article in ENGINE PERFORMANCE.

1) Turn ignition off. Disconnect and inspect MAP sensor connector. Repair connector if damaged. Perform VERIFICATION TEST VER-2. If MAP sensor connector is okay, go to next step.

2) Connect a jumper wire between Black/Light Blue wire (Brown/Red wire on Wrangler) and Dark Green/Red wire (Red/White wire on Grand Cherokee and Wrangler) at MAP sensor connector. Turn ignition on. Read MAP sensor voltage. If voltage is less than one volt, replace MAP sensor. Perform VERIFICATION TEST VER-2.

3) If MAP sensor voltage is one volt or more, remove jumper wire. Connect jumper wire between Dark Green/Red wire (Red/White wire on Grand Cherokee and Wrangler) at MAP sensor connector and ground. If voltage is less than one volt, repair open Black/Light Blue wire (Brown/Red wire on Wrangler). Perform VERIFICATION TEST VER-2.

4) If voltage is one volt or more, disconnect and inspect engine controller 60-pin connector. Repair connector if damaged. Perform VERIFICATION TEST VER-2. If engine controller connector is okay, go to next step.

5) Using a DVOM, check resistance of Dark Green/Red wire (Red/White wire on Grand Cherokee and Wrangler) between MAP sensor connector and engine controller connector terminal No. 1. If resistance is 10 ohms or more, repair open Dark Green/Red wire (Red/White on Grand Cherokee and Wrangler). Perform VERIFICATION TEST VER-2. If resistance is less than 10 ohms, replace engine controller. Perform VERIFICATION TEST VER-2.

TEST DR-6A

CODE 15, REPAIRING FAULT
"NO VEHICLE SPEED SIGNAL"

NOTE: For connector terminal identification, see CONNECTOR IDENTIFICATION at beginning of article. For appropriate wiring diagram, see WIRING DIAGRAMS article in ENGINE PERFORMANCE. On Wrangler, DO NOT perform TEST DR-6A, go directly to TEST DR-6B.

1) Turn ignition off. Disconnect and inspect distance (speed) sensor connector. Repair connector if damaged. Perform VERIFICATION TEST VER-2. If connector is okay, go to next step.

2) Turn ignition on. Connect a jumper wire to one terminal of distance (speed) sensor connector. Monitor vehicle speed on DRB-II while tapping open end of jumper wire to other distance sensor harness connector terminal.

3) If DRB-II shows vehicle speed to be more than zero MPH, replace distance sensor. Perform VERIFICATION TEST VER-2. If vehicle speed is zero MPH, place DRB-II in ohmmeter mode. Probe Black/Light Blue wire at distance sensor connector.

4) If resistance is 10 ohms or more, repair open Black/Light Blue wire. Perform VERIFICATION TEST VER-2. If resistance is less than 10 ohms, turn ignition off. Disconnect and inspect engine controller connector terminal No. 47. Repair connector if damaged. Perform VERIFICATION TEST VER-2. If connector is okay, go to next step.

5) Turn ignition on. Place DRB-II in voltmeter mode. Probe White/Orange wire at engine controller connector terminal No. 47. If voltage is more than 4 volts, go to step **7)**. If voltage is 4 volts or less, check if speedometer works. If speedometer works, repair open White/Orange wire between distance sensor and engine controller connector. Perform VERIFICATION TEST VER-2.

6) If speedometer does not work, turn ignition off. Place DRB-II in ohmmeter mode. Probe White/Orange wire at engine controller connector terminal No. 47. If resistance is less than 5 ohms, repair short to ground in White/Orange wire. Perform VERIFICATION TEST VER-2. If resistance is 5 ohms or more, repair open White/Orange wire between sensor and splice. Perform VERIFICATION TEST VER-2.

7) Probe White/Orange wire at distance sensor connector. If voltage is more than 4 volts, replace engine controller. Perform VERIFICATION TEST VER-2. If voltage is 4 volts or less, repair open White/Orange wire between distance sensor and engine controller connector. Perform VERIFICATION TEST VER-2.

TEST DR-6B

CODE 15, REPAIRING FAULT
"NO VEHICLE SPEED SIGNAL"

NOTE: For connector terminal identification, see CONNECTOR IDENTIFICATION at beginning of article. For appropriate wiring diagram, see WIRING DIAGRAMS article in ENGINE PERFORMANCE.

1) Turn ignition off. Disconnect and inspect distance (speed) sensor connector. Repair connector if damaged. Perform VERIFICATION TEST VER-2. If connector is okay, go to next step.

2) Turn ignition on. Place DRB-II in voltmeter mode. Probe White/Black wire at distance sensor connector. If voltage is more than 7 volts, go to next step. If voltage is 7 volts or less, repair open White/Black wire between sensor and splice. Perform VERIFICATION TEST VER-2.

3) Connect a jumper wire to Dark Blue wire terminal of distance (speed) sensor connector. Monitor vehicle speed on DRB-II while tapping open end of jumper wire to Brown/Red wire terminal at distance sensor harness connector.

4) If DRB-II shows vehicle speed to be more than zero MPH, replace distance (speed) sensor. Perform VERIFICATION TEST VER-2. If vehicle speed is zero MPH, place DRB-II in ohmmeter mode. Probe Brown/Red wire at distance sensor connector.

5) If resistance is 10 ohms or more, repair open Brown/Red wire. Perform VERIFICATION TEST VER-2. If resistance is less than 10 ohms, turn ignition off. Disconnect and inspect engine controller connector terminal No. 47. Repair connector if damaged. Perform VERIFICATION TEST VER-2. If connector is okay, go to next step.

6) Turn ignition on. Place DRB-II in voltmeter mode. Probe Dark Blue wire at engine controller connector terminal No. 47. If voltage is more

TEST DR-6B (Cont.)

than 4 volts, go to step **8)**. If voltage is 4 volts or less, check if speedometer works. If speedometer works, repair open Dark Blue wire between distance sensor and engine controller connector. Perform VERIFICATION TEST VER-2.

7) If speedometer does not work, turn ignition off. Place DRB-II in ohmmeter mode. Probe Dark Blue wire at engine controller connector terminal No. 47. If resistance is less than 5 ohms, repair short to ground in Dark Blue wire. Perform VERIFICATION TEST VER-2. If resistance is 5 ohms or more, repair open Dark Blue wire between sensor and splice. Perform VERIFICATION TEST VER-2.

8) Probe Dark Blue wire at distance sensor connector. If voltage is more than 4 volts, replace engine controller. Perform VERIFICATION TEST VER-2. If voltage is 4 volts or less, repair open Dark Blue wire between distance sensor and engine controller connector. Perform VERIFICATION TEST VER-2.

TEST DR-7A

CODE 21, REPAIRING FAULT
"OXYGEN (O₂) SENSOR SIGNAL STAYS AT CENTER"

NOTE: For connector terminal identification, see CONNECTOR IDENTIFICATION at beginning of article. For appropriate wiring diagram, see WIRING DIAGRAMS article in ENGINE PERFORMANCE.

1) Turn ignition off. Disconnect and inspect oxygen sensor connector. Repair connector if damaged. Perform VERIFICATION TEST VER-2. If connector is okay, turn ignition on. Connect a jumper wire to Black/Dark Green wire (Black/Orange wire on Grand Cherokee; Gray wire on Wrangler) at sensor connector.

2) Connect other end of jumper wire to positive battery terminal. Read oxygen sensor voltage. If voltage is less than one volt, go to step **4)**. If voltage is one volt or more, go to next step.

3) Disconnect jumper wire. Turn ignition off. Place DRB-II in ohmmeter mode. Probe Black/Light Blue wire (Brown/Red wire on Wrangler) at sensor connector. If resistance is 10 ohms or more, repair open Black/Light Blue wire (Brown/Red on Wrangler). Perform VERIFICATION TEST VER-2. If resistance is less than 10 ohms, replace oxygen sensor. Perform VERIFICATION TEST VER-2.

4) Disconnect jumper wire. Turn ignition off. Disconnect and inspect engine controller connector. Repair connector if damaged. Perform VERIFICATION TEST VER-2. If engine controller connector is okay, go to next step.

5) Using a DVOM, check resistance of Black/Dark Green wire (Black/Orange wire on Grand Cherokee; Gray wire on Wrangler) between sensor connector and engine controller connector terminal No. 41. If resistance is less than 10 ohms, replace engine controller. Perform VERIFICATION TEST VER-2. If resistance is 10 ohms or more, repair open Black/Dark Green wire (Black/Orange wire on Grand Cherokee; Gray wire on Wrangler). Perform VERIFICATION TEST VER-2.

TEST DR-8A

CODE 21, REPAIRING FAULT
"OXYGEN (O₂) SIGNAL SHORTED TO VOLTAGE"

NOTE: For connector terminal identification, see CONNECTOR IDENTIFICATION at beginning of article. For appropriate wiring diagram, see WIRING DIAGRAMS article in ENGINE PERFORMANCE.

1) Start engine, and let it idle for 2 minutes. Using DRB-II, read oxygen sensor voltage. If voltage is more than 1.3 volts, go to step **3)**. If voltage is 1.3 volts or less, read sensor voltage while wiggling sensor wiring harness.

2) If voltage is more than 1.3 volts while wiggling sensor wiring harness, repair short to voltage in Black/Dark Green wire (Black/Orange wire on Grand Cherokee; Gray wire on Wrangler). Perform VERIFICATION TEST VER-2. If voltage stays less than 1.3 volts while wiggling sensor wiring harness, replace engine controller. Perform VERIFICATION TEST VER-2.

TEST DR-8A (Cont.)

3) Disconnect oxygen sensor connector. If voltage is less than one volt with sensor disconnected, replace oxygen sensor. Perform VERIFICATION TEST VER-2. If voltage is more than one volt with sensor disconnected, repair Black/Dark Green wire (Black/Orange wire on Grand Cherokee; Gray wire on Wrangler) for a short to Dark Green/Black wire (Orange/Dark Blue wire on Grand Cherokee).

4) After repairing short between wires, reconnect oxygen sensor connector. Using DRB-II, reset adaptive fuel value. Start engine, and let it idle for 2 minutes. Using DRB-II, read oxygen sensor value. If oxygen sensor switches from rich to lean, test is complete. Perform VERIFICATION TEST VER-2. If oxygen sensor does not switch from rich to lean, replace oxygen sensor. Perform VERIFICATION TEST VER-2.

TEST DR-9A

CODE 52, REPAIRING FAULT
"OXYGEN (O₂) SIGNAL STAYS ABOVE CENTER (RICH)"

1) Start engine. Allow engine to reach normal operating temperature. Turn engine off. Allow engine to "hot soak" for 5 minutes. Remove spark plugs, keeping them in order according to cylinder. Inspect spark plugs for wet tips or fuel fouling.

2) If any spark plug is wet or fuel fouled, replace leaking injector(s) at corresponding cylinder(s). Perform VERIFICATION TEST VER-2. If spark plug(s) are wet or fuel fouled, inspect air cleaner filter and inlet ducts for restrictions. Clean or repair as necessary. Perform VERIFICATION TEST VER-2. If no restrictions exist, perform TEST NF-11A.

TEST DR-10A

CODE 51, REPAIRING FAULT
"OXYGEN (O₂) SIGNAL STAYS BELOW CENTER (LEAN)"

Code 51 may set for several reasons not related to oxygen sensor or oxygen sensor circuits. If Code 51 sets, perform TEST NF-1A.

TEST DR-11A

CODE 22, REPAIRING FAULT
"COOLANT SENSOR VOLTAGE TOO HIGH"

NOTE: For connector terminal identification, see CONNECTOR IDENTIFICATION at beginning of article. For appropriate wiring diagram, see WIRING DIAGRAMS article in ENGINE PERFORMANCE.

1) Turn ignition off. Disconnect and inspect coolant temperature sensor connector. Repair connector if damaged. Perform VERIFICATION TEST VER-2. If coolant temperature sensor connector is okay, go to next step.

2) Connect a jumper wire between wires at coolant temperature sensor connector. Turn ignition on. Using DRB-II, read coolant temperature sensor voltage. If voltage is less than one volt, replace coolant temperature sensor. Perform VERIFICATION TEST VER-2.

3) If voltage is one volt or more, remove jumper wire. Connect a jumper wire between ground and Tan/Black wire (Tan wire on Wrangler) at coolant temperature sensor connector. Read coolant temperature sensor voltage. If voltage is less than one volt, repair open Black/Light Blue wire (Brown/Red wire on Wrangler). Perform VERIFICATION TEST VER-2.

4) If voltage is one volt or more, disconnect and inspect engine controller 60-pin connector. Repair connector if damaged. Perform VERIFICATION TEST VER-2. If connector is okay, go to next step.

5) Using a DVOM, check resistance of Tan/Black wire (Tan wire on Wrangler) between coolant temperature sensor connector and engine controller connector terminal No. 2. If resistance is less than 10 ohms, replace engine controller. Perform VERIFICATION TEST VER-2. If resistance is 10 ohms or more, repair open Tan/Black wire (Tan wire on Wrangler). Perform VERIFICATION TEST VER-2.

TEST DR-12A

CODE 22, REPAIRING FAULT
"COOLANT SENSOR VOLTAGE TOO LOW"

NOTE: For connector terminal identification, see CONNECTOR IDENTIFICATION at beginning of article. For appropriate wiring diagram, see WIRING DIAGRAMS article in ENGINE PERFORMANCE.

1) Turn ignition on. Using DRB-II, read coolant temperature sensor voltage. Disconnect coolant temperature sensor. If voltage changed to more than 4 volts with sensor disconnected, replace coolant temperature sensor. Perform VERIFICATION TEST VER-2. If voltage did not change to more than 4 volts with sensor disconnected, go to next step.

2) Turn ignition off. Disconnect engine controller 60-pin connector. Place DRB-II in ohmmeter mode. Probe Tan/Black wire (Tan wire on Wrangler) at engine controller connector terminal No. 2. If resistance is less than 10 ohms, repair Tan/Black wire (Tan wire on Wrangler) for short to Black/Light Blue wire (Brown/Red wire on Wrangler) or ground. Perform VERIFICATION TEST VER-2. If resistance is 10 ohms or more, replace engine controller. Perform VERIFICATION TEST VER-2.

TEST DR-13A

CODE 24, REPAIRING FAULT
"THROTTLE POSITION SENSOR (TPS) VOLTAGE HIGH"

NOTE: For connector terminal identification, see CONNECTOR IDENTIFICATION at beginning of article. For appropriate wiring diagram, see WIRING DIAGRAMS article in ENGINE PERFORMANCE.

1) Turn ignition off. Disconnect and inspect TPS connector. Repair TPS connector if damaged. Perform VERIFICATION TEST VER-2. If TPS connector is okay, go to next step.

2) Turn ignition on. Connect a jumper wire between Orange/Dark Blue wire (Yellow/Dark Green wire on Wrangler) and Black/Light Blue wire (Brown/Red wire on Wrangler) at TPS connector. Using DRB-II, read TPS voltage. If voltage is less than one volt, replace TPS. Perform VERIFICATION TEST VER-2.

3) If voltage is one volt or more, remove jumper wire. Connect jumper wire between ground and Orange/Dark Blue wire (Yellow/Dark Green wire on Wrangler) at TPS connector. Using DRB-II, read TPS voltage. If voltage is less than one volt, repair open Black/Light Blue wire (Brown/Red wire on Wrangler). Perform VERIFICATION TEST VER-2.

4) If voltage is one volt or more, turn ignition off. Disconnect and inspect engine controller 60-pin connector. Repair connector if damaged. Perform VERIFICATION TEST VER-2. If connector is okay, go to next step.

5) Using a DVOM, check resistance of Orange/Dark Blue wire (Yellow/Dark Green wire on Wrangler) between TPS connector and engine controller connector terminal No. 22. If resistance is less than 10 ohms, replace engine controller. Perform VERIFICATION TEST VER-2. If resistance is 10 ohms or more, repair open Orange/Dark Blue wire (Yellow/Dark Green wire on Wrangler) wire. Perform VERIFICATION TEST VER-2.

TEST DR-14A

CODE 24, REPAIRING FAULT
"THROTTLE POSITION SENSOR (TPS) VOLTAGE LOW"

NOTE: For connector terminal identification, see CONNECTOR IDENTIFICATION at beginning of article. For appropriate wiring diagram, see WIRING DIAGRAMS article in ENGINE PERFORMANCE.

1) Turn ignition off. Disconnect TPS connector. Turn ignition on. Place DRB-II in voltmeter mode. Probe Violet/White wire (Brown/Yellow wire on Wrangler) at TPS connector. If voltage is less than one volt, repair open Violet/White wire (Brown/Yellow wire on Wrangler). Perform VERIFICATION TEST VER-2.

2) If voltage is one volt or more, probe Orange/Dark Blue wire (Yellow/Dark Green wire on Wrangler) at TPS connector. If voltage is one volt or more, replace TPS. Perform VERIFICATION TEST VER-2. If voltage is less than one volt, go to next step.

TEST DR-14A (Cont.)

3) Turn ignition off. Disconnect engine controller 60-pin connector. Place DRB-II in ohmmeter mode. Probe Orange/Dark Blue (Yellow/Dark Green) wire at engine controller connector terminal No. 22. If resistance is less than 10 ohms, repair short to ground in Orange/Dark Blue (Yellow/Dark Green) wire. Perform VERIFICATION TEST VER-2. If resistance is 10 ohms or more, replace engine controller. Perform VERIFICATION TEST VER-2.

TEST DR-15A

CODE 25, REPAIRING FAULT
"AUTOMATIC IDLE SPEED MOTOR CIRCUITS"

NOTE: For connector terminal identification, see CONNECTOR IDENTIFICATION at beginning of article. For appropriate wiring diagram, see WIRING DIAGRAMS article in ENGINE PERFORMANCE.

1) Disconnect Automatic Idle Speed (AIS) motor connector. Turn ignition on. Using DRB-II, actuate AIS motor. Place DRB-II in voltmeter mode. Probe AIS motor connector Gray/Red wire (Yellow/Black wire on Grand Cherokee; Dark Green/Black on Wrangler).

2) Under normal conditions, voltage will switch from less than one volt to more than 10 volts. If voltage stays less than one volt, repair short to ground in Gray/Red wire (Yellow/Black wire Grand Cherokee; Dark Green/Black on Wrangler). Perform VERIFICATION TEST VER-2.

3) If voltage stays more than 10 volts, repair short to voltage in Gray/Red wire (Yellow/Black wire on Grand Cherokee; Dark Green/Black on wire Wrangler). Perform VERIFICATION TEST VER-2. If voltage does not stay less than one volt or more than 10 volts, probe Yellow/Black wire (Violet/Black wire on Grand Cherokee; Pink/Black wire on Wrangler) at AIS motor connector.

4) If voltage stays less than one volt, repair short to ground in Yellow/Black wire (Violet/Black wire on Grand Cherokee; Pink/Black wire on Wrangler). Perform VERIFICATION TEST VER-2. If voltage stays more than 10 volts, repair short to voltage in Yellow/Black wire (Violet/Black wire on Grand Cherokee; Pink/Black wire on Wrangler). Perform VERIFICATION TEST VER-2. If voltage does not stay less than one volt or more than 10 volts, probe Brown/White wire (Red/Yellow wire on Wrangler) at AIS connector.

5) If voltage stays less than one volt, repair short to ground in Brown/White wire (Red/Yellow wire on Wrangler). Perform VERIFICATION TEST VER-2. If voltage stays more than 10 volts, repair short to voltage in Brown/White wire (Red/Yellow wire on Wrangler). Perform VERIFICATION TEST VER-2. If voltage does not stay less than one volt or more than 10 volts, probe Violet/Black wire (Gray/Red wire on Grand Cherokee; Dark Blue/Yellow wire on Wrangler) at AIS connector terminal.

6) If voltage stays less than one volt, repair short to ground in Violet/Black wire (Gray/Red wire Grand Cherokee; Dark Blue/Yellow wire Wrangler). Perform VERIFICATION TEST VER-2. If voltage stays more than 10 volts, repair short to voltage in Violet/Black wire (Gray/Red wire on Grand Cherokee; Dark Blue/Yellow wire Wrangler). VERIFICATION TEST VER-2. If voltage does not stay less than one volt or more than 10 volts, go to next step.

7) Turn ignition off. Reconnect AIS motor connector. Disconnect engine controller 60-pin connector. Using a DVOM, check resistance between terminals No. 39 and 59 of engine controller connector. If resistance is less than 35 ohms, replace AIS motor. Perform VERIFICATION TEST VER-2.

8) If resistance is 35 ohms or more, check resistance between terminals No. 40 and 60 of engine controller connector. If resistance is less than 35 ohms, replace AIS motor. Perform VERIFICATION TEST VER-2.

9) If resistance is 35 ohms or more, check resistance between engine controller terminals No. 39 and 60. If resistance is less than 10 ohms, repair Gray/Red wire (Yellow/Black wire on Grand Cherokee; Dark Green/Black on Wrangler) for a short to Yellow/Black wire (Violet/Black wire on Grand Cherokee; Pink/Black wire on Wrangler). Perform VERIFICATION TEST VER-2.

10) If resistance in step 9) was more than 75 ohms but less than 120 ohms, repair Brown/White wire (Red/Yellow wire on Wrangler) for a short to Violet/Black wire (Gray/Red on Grand Cherokee; Dark Blue/Yellow wire on Wrangler). Perform VERIFICATION TEST VER-2. If resistance is more than 120 ohms, replace engine controller. Perform VERIFICATION TEST VER-2.

TEST DR-15A (Cont.)

11) If resistance in step 9) was more than 10 ohms but less than 75 ohms, check resistance between engine controller connector terminals No. 59 and 60. If resistance is less than 10 ohms, repair Violet/Black wire (Gray/Red wire on Grand Cherokee; Dark Blue/Yellow wire on Wrangler) for a short to Yellow/Black (Violet/Black; Pink/Black) wire. Perform VERIFICATION TEST VER-2. If resistance is 10 ohms or more, repair Gray/Red wire (Yellow/Black wire on Grand Cherokee; Dark Green/Black wire on Wrangler) for a short to Brown/White wire (Red/Yellow wire on Wrangler). Perform VERIFICATION TEST VER-2.

TEST DR-16A

CODE 27, REPAIRING FAULT
"INJECTOR NO. 1 CONTROL CIRCUIT"

NOTE: For connector terminal identification, see CONNECTOR IDENTIFICATION at beginning of article. For appropriate wiring diagram, see WIRING DIAGRAMS article in ENGINE PERFORMANCE.

1) Turn ignition off. Disconnect and inspect fuel injector No. 1 connector. Repair connector if damaged. Perform VERIFICATION TEST VER-2. If connector is okay, measure fuel injector resistance using a DVOM. If resistance is not 13-16 ohms, replace injector. Perform VERIFICATION TEST VER-2. If resistance is 13-16 ohms (except Wrangler), go to next step. If resistance is 13-16 ohms (Wrangler), perform TEST DR-16B.

2) Turn ignition on. With DRB-II, actuate fuel system. Place DRB-II in voltmeter mode. Probe Dark Green/Orange wire (Dark Green/Black wire on Grand Cherokee) at injector No. 1 connector. If voltage is 10 volts or less, repair open Dark Green/Orange wire (Dark Green/Black wire on Grand Cherokee) between injector connector and harness splice. Perform VERIFICATION TEST VER-2. If voltage is more than 10 volts, go to next step.

3) Turn ignition off. Disconnect and inspect engine controller 60-pin connector. Repair connector if damaged. Perform VERIFICATION TEST VER-2. If connector is okay, place DRB-II in ohmmeter mode. Check resistance of White/Dark Blue wire at engine controller connector terminal No. 16. If resistance is less than 10 ohms, repair White/Dark Blue wire for a short to ground. Perform VERIFICATION TEST VER-2.

4) If resistance is 10 ohms or more, check resistance of White/Dark Blue wire between fuel injector No. 1 connector and engine controller connector terminal No. 16 using a DVOM. If resistance is 10 ohms or more, repair open White/Dark Blue wire. Perform VERIFICATION TEST VER-2. If resistance is less than 10 ohms, replace engine controller. Perform VERIFICATION TEST VER-2.

TEST DR-16B

CODE 27, REPAIRING FAULT
"INJECTOR NO. 1 CONTROL CIRCUIT"

NOTE: For connector terminal identification, see CONNECTOR IDENTIFICATION at beginning of article. For appropriate wiring diagram, see WIRING DIAGRAMS article in ENGINE PERFORMANCE.

1) Turn ignition on. Using DRB-II, actuate fuel system. Place DRB-II in voltmeter mode. Probe Dark Green/Black wire at injector No. 1 connector. If voltage is 10 volts or less, repair open Dark Green/Black wire between injector connector and harness splice. Perform VERIFICATION TEST VER-2. If voltage is more than 10 volts, go to next step.

2) Turn ignition off. Disconnect and inspect engine controller 60-pin connector. Repair connector if damaged. Perform VERIFICATION TEST VER-2. If connector is okay, place DRB-II in ohmmeter mode. Check resistance of Light Blue wire at engine controller connector terminal No. 16. If resistance is less than 10 ohms, repair Light Blue wire for a short to ground. Perform VERIFICATION TEST VER-2.

3) If resistance is 10 ohms or more, check resistance of Light Blue wire between fuel injector No. 1 connector and engine controller connector terminal No. 16 using a DVOM. If resistance is 10 ohms or more, repair open Light Blue wire. Perform VERIFICATION TEST VER-2. If resistance is less than 10 ohms, replace engine controller. Perform VERIFICATION TEST VER-2.

TEST DR-17A

CODE 27, REPAIRING FAULT
"INJECTOR NO. 2 CONTROL CIRCUIT"

NOTE: For connector terminal identification, see CONNECTOR IDENTIFICATION at beginning of article. For appropriate wiring diagram, see WIRING DIAGRAMS article in ENGINE PERFORMANCE.

1) Turn ignition off. Disconnect and inspect fuel injector No. 2 connector. Repair connector if damaged. Perform VERIFICATION TEST VER-2. If connector is okay, measure fuel injector resistance using a DVOM. If resistance is not 13-16 ohms, replace injector. Perform VERIFICATION TEST VER-2. If resistance is 13-16 ohms (except Wrangler), go to next step. If resistance is 13-16 ohms (Wrangler), perform TEST DR-17B.

2) Turn ignition on. With DRB-II, actuate fuel system. Place DRB-II in voltmeter mode. Probe Dark Green/Orange wire at injector No. 2 connector. If voltage is 10 volts or less, repair open Dark Green/Orange wire between injector connector and harness splice. Perform VERIFICATION TEST VER-2. If voltage is more than 10 volts, go to next step.

3) Turn ignition off. Disconnect and inspect engine controller 60-pin connector. Repair connector if damaged. Perform VERIFICATION TEST VER-2. If connector is okay, place DRB-II in ohmmeter mode. Check resistance of Tan wire at engine controller connector terminal No. 15. If resistance is less than 10 ohms, repair Tan wire for a short to ground. Perform VERIFICATION TEST VER-2.

4) If resistance is 10 ohms or more, check resistance of Tan wire between fuel injector No. 2 connector and engine controller connector terminal No. 15 using a DVOM. If resistance is 10 ohms or more, repair open Tan wire. Perform VERIFICATION TEST VER-2. If resistance is less than 10 ohms, replace engine controller. Perform VERIFICATION TEST VER-2.

TEST DR-17B

CODE 27, REPAIRING FAULT
"INJECTOR NO. 2 CONTROL CIRCUIT"

NOTE: For connector terminal identification, see CONNECTOR IDENTIFICATION at beginning of article. For appropriate wiring diagram, see WIRING DIAGRAMS article in ENGINE PERFORMANCE.

1) Turn ignition on. Using DRB-II, actuate fuel system. Place DRB-II in voltmeter mode. Probe Dark Green/Black wire at injector No. 2 connector. If voltage is 10 volts or less, repair open Dark Green/Black wire between injector connector and harness splice. Perform VERIFICATION TEST VER-2. If voltage is more than 10 volts, go to next step.

2) Turn ignition off. Disconnect and inspect engine controller 60-pin connector. Repair connector if damaged. Perform VERIFICATION TEST VER-2. If connector is okay, place DRB-II in ohmmeter mode. Check resistance of Light Green wire at engine controller connector terminal No. 15. If resistance is less than 10 ohms, repair Light Green wire for a short to ground. Perform VERIFICATION TEST VER-2.

3) If resistance is 10 ohms or more, check resistance of Light Green wire between fuel injector No. 2 connector and engine controller connector terminal No. 15 using a DVOM. If resistance is 10 ohms or more, repair open Light Green wire. Perform VERIFICATION TEST VER-2. If resistance is less than 10 ohms, replace engine controller. Perform VERIFICATION TEST VER-2.

TEST DR-18A

CODE 27, REPAIRING FAULT
"INJECTOR NO. 3 CONTROL CIRCUIT"

NOTE: For connector terminal identification, see CONNECTOR IDENTIFICATION at beginning of article. For appropriate wiring diagram, see WIRING DIAGRAMS article in ENGINE PERFORMANCE.

1) Turn ignition off. Disconnect and inspect fuel injector No. 3 connector. Repair connector if damaged. Perform VERIFICATION TEST VER-2. If connector is okay, measure fuel injector resistance using a DVOM. If resistance is not 13-16 ohms, replace injector. Perform VERIFICATION TEST VER-2. If resistance is 13-16 ohms (except Wrangler), go to next step. If resistance is 13-16 ohms (Wrangler), perform TEST DR-18B.

TEST DR-18A (Cont.)

2) Turn ignition on. Using DRB-II, actuate fuel system. Place DRB-II in voltmeter mode. Probe Dark Green/Orange wire (Dark Green/Black wire on Grand Cherokee) at injector No. 3 connector. If voltage is 10 volts or less, repair open Dark Green/Orange wire (Dark Green/Black wire on Grand Cherokee) between injector connector and harness splice. Perform VERIFICATION TEST VER-2. If voltage is more than 10 volts, go to next step.

3) Turn ignition off. Disconnect and inspect engine controller 60-pin connector. Repair connector if damaged. Perform VERIFICATION TEST VER-2. If connector is okay, place DRB-II in ohmmeter mode. Check resistance of Yellow/White wire at engine controller connector terminal No. 14. If resistance is less than 10 ohms, repair Yellow/White wire for a short to ground. Perform VERIFICATION TEST VER-2.

4) If resistance is 10 ohms or more, check resistance of Yellow/White wire between fuel injector No. 3 connector and engine controller connector terminal No. 14 using a DVOM. If resistance is 10 ohms or more, repair open Yellow/White wire. Perform VERIFICATION TEST VER-2. If resistance is less than 10 ohms, replace engine controller. Perform VERIFICATION TEST VER-2.

TEST DR-18B

CODE 27, REPAIRING FAULT
"INJECTOR NO. 3 CONTROL CIRCUIT"

NOTE: For connector terminal identification, see CONNECTOR IDENTIFICATION at beginning of article. For appropriate wiring diagram, see WIRING DIAGRAMS article in ENGINE PERFORMANCE.

1) Turn ignition on. Using DRB-II, actuate fuel system. Place DRB-II in voltmeter mode. Probe Dark Green/Black wire at injector No. 3 connector. If voltage is 10 volts or less, repair open Dark Green/Black wire between injector connector and harness splice. Perform VERIFICATION TEST VER-2. If voltage is more than 10 volts, go to next step.

2) Turn ignition off. Disconnect and inspect engine controller 60-pin connector. Repair connector if damaged. Perform VERIFICATION TEST VER-2. If connector is okay, place DRB-II in ohmmeter mode. Check resistance of Tan/Yellow wire at engine controller connector terminal No. 14. If resistance is less than 10 ohms, repair Tan/Yellow wire for a short to ground. Perform VERIFICATION TEST VER-2.

3) If resistance is 10 ohms or more, check resistance of Tan/Yellow wire between fuel injector No. 3 connector and engine controller connector terminal No. 14 using a DVOM. If resistance is 10 ohms or more, repair open Tan/Yellow wire. Perform VERIFICATION TEST VER-2. If resistance is less than 10 ohms, replace engine controller. Perform VERIFICATION TEST VER-2.

TEST DR-19A

CODE 27, REPAIRING FAULT
"INJECTOR NO. 4 CONTROL CIRCUIT"

NOTE: For connector terminal identification, see CONNECTOR IDENTIFICATION at beginning of article. For appropriate wiring diagram, see WIRING DIAGRAMS article in ENGINE PERFORMANCE.

1) Turn ignition off. Disconnect and inspect fuel injector No. 4 connector. Repair connector if damaged. Perform VERIFICATION TEST VER-2. If connector is okay, measure fuel injector resistance using a DVOM. If resistance is not 13-16 ohms, replace injector. Perform VERIFICATION TEST VER-2. If resistance is 13-16 ohms (except Wrangler), go to next step. If resistance is 13-16 ohms (Wrangler), perform TEST DR-19B.

2) Turn ignition on. Using DRB-II, actuate fuel system. Place DRB-II in voltmeter mode. Probe Dark Green/Orange wire at injector No. 4 connector. If voltage is 10 volts or less, repair open Dark Green/Orange wire between injector connector and harness splice. Perform VERIFICATION TEST VER-2.

3) If voltage is more than 10 volts, turn ignition off. Disconnect and inspect engine controller 60-pin connector. Repair connector if damaged. Perform VERIFICATION TEST VER-2. If connector is okay, place DRB-II in ohmmeter mode. Check resistance of Light Blue/Brown wire at engine controller connector terminal No. 13. If resistance is less than 10 ohms, repair Light Blue/Brown wire for a short to ground. Perform VERIFICATION TEST VER-2.

TEST DR-19A (Cont.)

4) If resistance is 10 ohms or more, check resistance of Light Blue/Brown wire between fuel injector No. 4 connector and engine controller connector terminal No. 13 using a DVOM. If resistance is 10 ohms or more, repair open Light Blue/Brown wire. Perform VERIFICATION TEST VER-2. If resistance is less than 10 ohms, replace engine controller. Perform VERIFICATION TEST VER-2.

TEST DR-19B

CODE 27, REPAIRING FAULT
"INJECTOR NO. 4 CONTROL CIRCUIT"

NOTE: For connector terminal identification, see CONNECTOR IDENTIFICATION at beginning of article. For appropriate wiring diagram, see WIRING DIAGRAMS article in ENGINE PERFORMANCE.

1) Turn ignition on. Using DRB-II, actuate fuel system. Place DRB-II in voltmeter mode. Probe Dark Green/Black wire at injector No. 4 connector. If voltage is 10 volts or less, repair open Dark Green/Black wire between injector connector and harness splice. Perform VERIFICATION TEST VER-2. If voltage is more than 10 volts, go to next step.

2) Turn ignition off. Disconnect and inspect engine controller 60-pin connector. Repair connector if damaged. Perform VERIFICATION TEST VER-2. If connector is okay, place DRB-II in ohmmeter mode. Check resistance of Yellow wire at engine controller connector terminal No. 13. If resistance is less than 10 ohms, repair Yellow wire for a short to ground. Perform VERIFICATION TEST VER-2.

3) If resistance is 10 ohms or more, check resistance of Yellow wire between fuel injector No. 4 connector and engine controller connector terminal No. 13 using a DVOM. If resistance is 10 ohms or more, repair open Yellow wire. Perform VERIFICATION TEST VER-2. If resistance is less than 10 ohms, replace engine controller. Perform VERIFICATION TEST VER-2.

TEST DR-20A

CODE 27, REPAIRING FAULT
"INJECTOR NO. 5 CONTROL CIRCUIT"

NOTE: For connector terminal identification, see CONNECTOR IDENTIFICATION at beginning of article. For appropriate wiring diagram, see WIRING DIAGRAMS article in ENGINE PERFORMANCE.

1) Turn ignition off. Disconnect and inspect fuel injector No. 5 connector. Repair connector if damaged. Perform VERIFICATION TEST VER-2. If connector is okay, measure fuel injector resistance using a DVOM. If resistance is not 13-16 ohms, replace injector. Perform VERIFICATION TEST VER-2. If resistance is 13-16 ohms (except Wrangler), go to next step. If resistance is 13-16 ohms (Wrangler), perform TEST DR-20B.

2) Turn ignition on. Using DRB-II, actuate fuel system. Place DRB-II in voltmeter mode. Probe Dark Green/Orange wire (Dark Green/Black wire on Grand Cherokee) at injector No. 5 connector. If voltage is 10 volts or less, repair open Dark Green/Orange wire (Dark Green/Black wire on Grand Cherokee) between injector connector and harness splice. Perform VERIFICATION TEST VER-2.

3) If voltage is more than 10 volts, turn ignition off. Disconnect and inspect engine controller 60-pin connector. Repair connector if damaged. Perform VERIFICATION TEST VER-2. If connector is okay, place DRB-II in ohmmeter mode. Check resistance of Pink/Black wire (Gray wire on Grand Cherokee) at engine controller connector terminal No. 38. If resistance is less than 10 ohms, repair Pink/Black wire (Gray wire on Grand Cherokee) for a short to ground. Perform VERIFICATION TEST VER-2.

4) If resistance is 10 ohms or more, check resistance of Pink/Black wire (Gray wire on Grand Cherokee) between fuel injector No. 5 connector and engine controller connector terminal No. 38 using a DVOM. If resistance is 10 ohms or more, repair open Pink/Black wire (Gray wire on Grand Cherokee). Perform VERIFICATION TEST VER-2. If resistance is less than 10 ohms, replace engine controller. Perform VERIFICATION TEST VER-2.

TEST DR-20B

CODE 27, REPAIRING FAULT
"INJECTOR NO. 5 CONTROL CIRCUIT"

NOTE: For connector terminal identification, see CONNECTOR IDENTIFICATION at beginning of article. For appropriate wiring diagram, see WIRING DIAGRAMS article in ENGINE PERFORMANCE.

1) Turn ignition on. Using DRB-II, actuate fuel system. Place DRB-II in voltmeter mode. Probe Dark Green/Black wire at injector No. 5 connector. If voltage is 10 volts or less, repair open Dark Green/Black wire between injector connector and harness splice. Perform VERIFICATION TEST VER-2. If voltage is more than 10 volts, go to next step.

2) Turn ignition off. Disconnect and inspect engine controller 60-pin connector. Repair connector if damaged. Perform VERIFICATION TEST VER-2. If connector is okay, place DRB-II in ohmmeter mode. Check resistance of White wire at engine controller connector terminal No. 38. If resistance is less than 10 ohms, repair White wire for a short to ground. Perform VERIFICATION TEST VER-2.

3) If resistance is 10 ohms or more, check resistance of White wire between fuel injector No. 5 connector and engine controller connector terminal No. 38 using a DVOM. If resistance is 10 ohms or more, repair open White wire. Perform VERIFICATION TEST VER-2. If resistance is less than 10 ohms, replace engine controller. Perform VERIFICATION TEST VER-2.

TEST DR-21A

CODE 27, REPAIRING FAULT
"INJECTOR NO. 6 CONTROL CIRCUIT"

NOTE: For connector terminal identification, see CONNECTOR IDENTIFICATION at beginning of article. For appropriate wiring diagram, see WIRING DIAGRAMS article in ENGINE PERFORMANCE.

1) Turn ignition off. Disconnect and inspect fuel injector No. 6 connector. Repair connector if damaged. Perform VERIFICATION TEST VER-2. If connector is okay, measure fuel injector resistance using a DVOM. If resistance is not 13-16 ohms, replace injector. Perform VERIFICATION TEST VER-2. If resistance is 13-16 ohms (except Wrangler), go to next step. If resistance is 13-16 ohms (Wrangler), perform TEST DR-21B.

2) Turn ignition on. Using DRB-II, actuate fuel system. Place DRB-II in voltmeter mode. Probe Dark Green/Orange wire (Dark Green/Black wire on Grand Cherokee) at injector No. 6 connector. If voltage is 10 volts or less, repair open Dark Green/Orange wire (Dark Green/Black wire on Grand Cherokee) between injector connector and harness splice. Perform VERIFICATION TEST VER-2.

3) If voltage is more than 10 volts, turn ignition off. Disconnect and inspect engine controller 60-pin connector. Repair connector if damaged. Perform VERIFICATION TEST VER-2. If connector is okay, place DRB-II in ohmmeter mode. Check resistance of Light Green/Black wire (Brown/Yellow wire on Grand Cherokee) at engine controller connector terminal No. 58. If resistance is less than 10 ohms, repair Light Green/Black (Brown/Yellow) wire for a short to ground. Perform VERIFICATION TEST VER-2.

4) If resistance is 10 ohms or more, check resistance of Light Green/Black wire (Brown/Yellow wire on Grand Cherokee) between fuel injector No. 6 connector and engine controller connector terminal No. 58 using a DVOM. If resistance is 10 ohms or more, repair open Light Green/Black wire (Brown/Yellow wire on Grand Cherokee) wire. Perform VERIFICATION TEST VER-2. If resistance is less than 10 ohms, replace engine controller. Perform VERIFICATION TEST VER-2.

TEST DR-21B

CODE 27, REPAIRING FAULT
"INJECTOR NO. 6 CONTROL CIRCUIT"

NOTE: For connector terminal identification, see CONNECTOR IDENTIFICATION at beginning of article. For appropriate wiring diagram, see WIRING DIAGRAMS article in ENGINE PERFORMANCE.

1) Turn ignition on. Using DRB-II, actuate fuel system. Place DRB-II in voltmeter mode. Probe Dark Green/Black wire at injector No. 6 connector. If voltage is 10 volts or less, repair open Dark Green/Black wire between injector connector and harness splice. Perform VERIFICATION TEST VER-2. If voltage is more than 10 volts, go to next step.

TEST DR-21B (Cont.)

2) Turn ignition off. Disconnect and inspect engine controller 60-pin connector. Repair connector if damaged. Perform VERIFICATION TEST VER-2. If connector is okay, place DRB-II in ohmmeter mode. Check resistance of Brown/Dark Green wire at engine controller connector terminal No. 58. If resistance is less than 10 ohms, repair Brown/Dark Green wire for a short to ground. Perform VERIFICATION TEST VER-2.

3) If resistance is 10 ohms or more, check resistance of Brown/Dark Green wire between fuel injector No. 6 connector and engine controller connector terminal No. 58 using a DVOM. If resistance is 10 ohms or more, repair Brown/Dark Green wire. Perform VERIFICATION TEST VER-2. If resistance is less than 10 ohms, replace engine controller. Perform VERIFICATION TEST VER-2.

TEST DR-22A

CODE 33, REPAIRING FAULT
"A/C CLUTCH RELAY CIRCUIT"

NOTE: For connector terminal identification, see CONNECTOR IDENTIFICATION at beginning of article. For appropriate wiring diagram, see WIRING DIAGRAMS article in ENGINE PERFORMANCE.

1) Turn ignition on. Using DRB-II, actuate A/C clutch relay. If relay is clicking, perform TEST DR-33A. If relay is not clicking, remove the A/C clutch relay and inspect connector. Repair connector if damaged. Perform VERIFICATION TEST VER-2. If connector is okay, substitute A/C relay with a known good relay. DO NOT use a relay from power distribution center.

2) Using DRB-II, actuate A/C relay. If relay is clicking, repair is complete. Perform VERIFICATION TEST VER-2. If relay is not clicking (except Grand Cherokee), remove substitute relay and go to next step. If relay is not clicking (Grand Cherokee), remove substitute relay and perform TEST DR-22B.

3) Place DRB-II in voltmeter mode. Probe Dark Blue/White wire (White/Black wire on Wrangler) at A/C relay connector terminal. If voltage is 10 volts or less, repair open Dark Blue/White wire (White/Black wire on Wrangler). Perform VERIFICATION TEST VER-2. If voltage is more than 10 volts, go to next step.

4) Turn ignition off. Disconnect and inspect engine controller connector. Repair connector if damaged. Perform VERIFICATION TEST VER-2. If connector is okay, place DRB-II in ohmmeter mode. Probe Dark Blue/Orange wire (Dark Blue/White wire on Wrangler) at engine controller connector terminal No. 34. If resistance is less than 10 ohms, repair short to ground in Dark Blue/Orange wire (Dark Blue/White wire on Wrangler). Perform VERIFICATION TEST VER-2. If resistance is 10 ohms or more, go to next step.

5) Using a DVOM, check resistance of Dark Blue/Orange wire (Dark Blue/White wire on Wrangler) between the engine controller connector terminal No. 34 and A/C relay connector terminal. If resistance is 10 ohms or more, repair open Dark Blue/Orange wire (Dark Blue/White wire on Wrangler). Perform VERIFICATION TEST VER-2. If resistance is less than 10 ohms, go to next step.

6) Reconnect A/C clutch relay. Turn ignition on. Place DRB-II in voltmeter mode. Probe Dark Blue/Orange wire (Dark Blue/White wire on Wrangler) at engine controller connector terminal No. 34. If voltage is more than 10 volts, replace engine controller. Perform VERIFICATION TEST VER-2. If voltage is 10 volts or less, replace A/C clutch relay. Perform VERIFICATION TEST VER-2.

TEST DR-22B

CODE 33, REPAIRING FAULT
"A/C CLUTCH RELAY CIRCUIT"

NOTE: For connector terminal identification, see CONNECTOR IDENTIFICATION at beginning of article. For appropriate wiring diagram, see WIRING DIAGRAMS article in ENGINE PERFORMANCE.

1) Using DRB-II, actuate ASD fuel system test. Place DRB-II in voltmeter mode. Probe Orange/Dark Blue wire at A/C relay connector terminal. If voltage is 10 volts or less, repair open Orange/Dark Blue wire. Perform VERIFICATION TEST VER-2. If voltage is more than 10 volts, go to next step.

TEST DR-22B (Cont.)

2) Turn ignition off. Disconnect and inspect engine controller connector. Repair connector if damaged. Perform VERIFICATION TEST VER-2. If connector is okay, place DRB-II in ohmmeter mode. Probe Dark Blue/Red wire at engine controller connector terminal No. 34. If resistance is less than 10 ohms, repair short to ground in Dark Blue/Red wire. Perform VERIFICATION TEST VER-2. If resistance is 10 ohms or more, go to next step.

3) Using a DVOM, check resistance of Dark Blue/Red wire between engine controller connector terminal No. 34 and A/C relay connector terminal. If resistance is 10 ohms or more, repair open Dark Blue/Red wire. Perform VERIFICATION TEST VER-2. If resistance is less than 10 ohms, go to next step.

4) Reconnect A/C clutch relay. Turn ignition on. Connect a jumper wire between ground and Pink wire at engine controller connector terminal No. 51. Place DRB-II in voltmeter mode. Probe Dark Blue/Red wire at engine controller connector terminal No. 34. If voltage is more than 10 volts, replace engine controller. Perform VERIFICATION TEST VER-2. If voltage is 10 volts or less, replace A/C clutch relay. Perform VERIFICATION TEST VER-2.

TEST DR-23A

CODE 35, REPAIRING FAULT
"RADIATOR FAN RELAY CIRCUIT"

NOTE: For connector terminal identification, see CONNECTOR IDENTIFICATION at beginning of article. For appropriate wiring diagram, see WIRING DIAGRAMS article in ENGINE PERFORMANCE.

1) Turn ignition on. Using DRB-II, actuate radiator fan relay. If relay is clicking, perform TEST DR-33A. If relay is not clicking, remove radiator fan relay and inspect connector. Repair connector as necessary. Perform VERIFICATION TEST VER-2. If connector is okay, go to next step.

2) Substitute radiator fan relay with a known good relay. DO NOT use a relay from power distribution center. Using DRB-II, actuate radiator fan relay. If relay is clicking, repair is complete. Perform VERIFICATION TEST VER-2. If relay is not clicking, go to next step.

3) Remove substitute relay. Place DRB-II in voltmeter mode. Probe Dark Blue/White wire at relay connector terminal. If voltage is 10 volts or less, repair open Dark Blue/White wire. Perform VERIFICATION TEST VER-2. If voltage is more than 10 volts, go to next step.

4) Turn ignition off. Disconnect and inspect engine controller connector. Repair connector as necessary. Perform VERIFICATION TEST VER-2. If connector is okay, place DRB-II in ohmmeter mode. Probe Dark Blue/Pink wire at engine controller connector terminal No. 31. If resistance is less than 10 ohms, repair short to ground in Dark Blue/Pink wire. Perform VERIFICATION TEST VER-2. If resistance is 10 ohms or more, go to next step.

5) Using a DVOM, check resistance of Dark Blue/Pink wire between engine controller connector terminal No. 31 and relay connector terminal. If resistance is 10 ohms or more, repair open Dark Blue/Pink wire. Perform VERIFICATION TEST VER-2. If resistance is less than 10 ohms, go to next step.

6) Reconnect radiator fan relay. Turn ignition on. Place DRB-II in voltmeter mode. Probe Dark Blue/Pink wire at engine controller connector terminal No. 31. If voltage is more than 10 volts, replace engine controller. Perform VERIFICATION TEST VER-2. If voltage is 10 volts or less, replace radiator fan relay. Perform VERIFICATION TEST VER-2.

TEST DR-24A

CODE 76, REPAIRING FAULT
"FUEL PUMP RESISTOR BY-PASS
RELAY CIRCUIT"

NOTE: For connector terminal identification, see CONNECTOR IDENTIFICATION at beginning of article. For appropriate wiring diagram, see WIRING DIAGRAMS article in ENGINE PERFORMANCE.

1) Turn ignition on. Using DRB-II, actuate ballast resistor by-pass relay. If relay is clicking, perform TEST DR-33A. If relay is not clicking, remove by-pass relay and inspect connector. Repair connector as necessary. Perform VERIFICATION TEST VER-2. If connector is okay, go to next step.

TEST DR-24A (Cont.)

2) Substitute by-pass relay with a known good relay. DO NOT use a relay from power distribution center. Using DRB-II, actuate by-pass relay. If relay is clicking, repair is complete. Perform VERIFICATION TEST VER-2. If relay is not clicking, go to next step.

3) Remove substitute relay. Place DRB-II in voltmeter mode. Probe Dark Blue/White wire at relay connector terminal. If voltage is 10 volts or less, repair open Dark Blue/White wire. Perform VERIFICATION TEST VER-2. If voltage is more than 10 volts, go to next step.

4) Turn ignition off. Disconnect and inspect engine controller connector. Repair connector as necessary. Perform VERIFICATION TEST VER-2. If connector is okay, place DRB-II in ohmmeter mode. Probe Red/Dark Blue wire at engine controller connector terminal No. 37. If resistance is less than 10 ohms, repair short to ground in Red/Dark Blue wire. Perform VERIFICATION TEST VER-2. If resistance is 10 ohms or more, go to next step.

5) Using a DVOM, check resistance of Red/Dark Blue wire between engine controller connector terminal No. 37 and relay connector terminal. If resistance is 10 ohms or more, repair open Red/Dark Blue wire. Perform VERIFICATION TEST VER-2. If resistance is less than 10 ohms, go to next step.

6) Reconnect ballast resistor by-pass relay. Turn ignition on. Place DRB-II in voltmeter mode. Probe Red/Dark Blue wire at engine controller connector terminal No. 37. If voltage is more than 10 volts, replace engine controller. Perform VERIFICATION TEST VER-2. If voltage is 10 volts or less, replace by-pass relay. Perform VERIFICATION TEST VER-2.

TEST DR-25A

CODE 42, REPAIRING FAULT
"NO ASD VOLTAGE SENSE AT CONTROLLER"

NOTE: For connector terminal identification, see CONNECTOR IDENTIFICATION at beginning of article. For appropriate wiring diagram, see WIRING DIAGRAMS article in ENGINE PERFORMANCE.

1) Turn ignition off. Disconnect Auto Shutdown (ASD) relay. Disconnect and inspect engine controller 60-pin connector. Repair connector as necessary. Perform VERIFICATION TEST VER-2. If connector is okay, go to next step.

2) Using a DVOM, check resistance of Dark Green/Orange wire (Dark Green/Black wire on Grand Cherokee and Wrangler) between engine controller connector terminal No. 57 and ASD relay terminal.

3) If resistance is less than 10 ohms, replace engine controller. Perform VERIFICATION TEST VER-2. If resistance is 10 ohms or more, repair open Dark Green/Orange wire (Dark Green/Black wire on Grand Cherokee and Wrangler). Perform VERIFICATION TEST VER-2.

TEST DR-26A

CODE 46, REPAIRING FAULT
"CHARGE TEMP VOLTAGE HIGH"

NOTE: For connector terminal identification, see CONNECTOR IDENTIFICATION at beginning of article. For appropriate wiring diagram, see WIRING DIAGRAMS article in ENGINE PERFORMANCE.

1) Turn ignition on. Using DRB-II, select charge temperature sensor voltage. Disconnect charge temperature sensor. Connect a jumper wire across sensor harness connector terminals. Read sensor voltage. If voltage is less than one volt, replace charge temperature sensor. Perform VERIFICATION TEST VER-2.

2) If voltage is one volt or more, remove jumper wire. Connect jumper wire between ground and Black/Red wire (Tan/Dark Blue wire on Wrangler) at charge temperature sensor harness connector. Read sensor voltage. If voltage is less than one volt, repair open Black/Light Blue wire (Brown/Red wire on Wrangler). Perform VERIFICATION TEST VER-2.

3) If voltage is one volt or more, turn ignition off. Disconnect and inspect engine controller connector. Repair connector as necessary. Perform VERIFICATION TEST VER-2. If connector is okay, check resistance of Black/Red wire (Tan/Dark Blue wire on Wrangler) between engine controller connector terminal No. 21 and charge temperature sensor connector using a DVOM.

TEST DR-26A (Cont.)

4) If resistance is less than 10 ohms, replace engine controller. Perform VERIFICATION TEST VER-2. If resistance is 10 ohms or more, repair open Black/Red wire (Tan/Dark Blue wire on Wrangler). Perform VERIFICATION TEST VER-2.

TEST DR-27A

CODE 47, REPAIRING FAULT
"CHARGE TEMP VOLTAGE LOW"

NOTE: For connector terminal identification, see CONNECTOR IDENTIFICATION at beginning of article. For appropriate wiring diagram, see WIRING DIAGRAMS article in ENGINE PERFORMANCE.

1) Turn ignition on. Using DRB-II, select charge temperature sensor voltage. Disconnect charge temperature sensor. Read sensor voltage. If voltage is more than 4 volts, replace charge temperature sensor. Perform VERIFICATION TEST VER-2. If voltage is 4 volts or less, turn ignition off. Disconnect and inspect engine controller connector. Repair connector as necessary. Perform VERIFICATION TEST VER-2.

2) If connector is okay, place DRB-II in ohmmeter mode. Probe Black/Red wire (Tan/Dark Blue wire on Wrangler) at engine controller connector terminal No. 21. If resistance is 10 ohms or more, replace engine controller. Perform VERIFICATION TEST VER-2. If resistance is less than 10 ohms, repair short to ground in Black/Red wire (Tan/Dark Blue wire on Wrangler). Perform VERIFICATION TEST VER-2.

TEST DR-28A

REPAIRING FAULT
CODE 62, "CONTROLLER FAILURE EMR MILES NOT STORED" OR
CODE 63, "CONTROLLER FAILURE EEPROM WRITE DENIED"

1) Turn ignition on. Using DRB-II, perform EMR memory test. If DRB-II displays WRITE FAILURE, replace engine controller. Perform VERIFICATION TEST VER-2. If DRB-II displays WRITE REFUSED, go to step 3). If DRB-II displays EMR MILEAGE INVALID, update mileage and retest EMR mileage. Perform VERIFICATION TEST VER-2.

2) If DRB-II does not display WRITE FAILURE, WRITE REFUSED or EMR MILEAGE INVALID, compare EMR mileage stored with instrument panel odometer. If mileage is the same, retest EMR memory. Perform VERIFICATION TEST VER-2. If mileage is not the same, update mileage and retest EMR memory. Perform VERIFICATION TEST VER-2.

3) Engine controller was busy. Using DRB-II, perform EMR memory test again. Retest EMR memory 2 or more times if necessary. If WRITE REFUSED is displayed, replace engine controller. Perform VERIFICATION TEST VER-2. If WRITE REFUSED is no longer displayed, test is complete. Perform VERIFICATION TEST VER-2.

TEST DR-30A

INTERMITTENT TEST FOR SENSOR VOLTAGE

NOTE: For connector terminal identification, see CONNECTOR IDENTIFICATION at beginning of article. For appropriate wiring diagram, see WIRING DIAGRAMS article in ENGINE PERFORMANCE.

1) If intermittent fault is SLOW CHANGE OR NO CHANGE IN MAP, perform TEST DR-30B. Otherwise, start engine. Using DRB-II, monitor suspect sensor circuit voltage while wiggling sensor connector and wiring. If engine stalls or voltage becomes erratic, repair sensor wiring or connector. Perform VERIFICATION TEST VER-2.

2) If engine does not stall or voltage does not become erratic, wiggle sections of wiring harness between suspect sensor and engine controller. Wait 5 seconds before moving to next section of harness. If engine stalls or sensor voltage becomes erratic, repair harness where wiggling caused erratic reading. Perform VERIFICATION TEST VER-2. If engine does not stall or voltage is not erratic, test is complete. Perform VERIFICATION TEST VER-2.

TEST DR-30B

INTERMITTENT MAP SENSOR SIGNAL CHANGE

NOTE: For connector terminal identification, see CONNECTOR IDENTIFICATION at beginning of article. For appropriate wiring diagram, see WIRING DIAGRAMS article in ENGINE PERFORMANCE.

1) Start engine. Using DRB-II, set engine speed to 1400 RPM and read MAP sensor voltage. Wiggle MAP sensor wiring harness while monitoring voltage. If engine stalls or voltage becomes erratic, repair MAP sensor wiring or connector. Perform VERIFICATION TEST VER-2.

2) If engine does not stall or voltage is not erratic, turn ignition off. Install a vacuum "T" into MAP sensor vacuum hose. Connect a vacuum gauge to "T". Start engine. Snap throttle open and closed while observing vacuum gauge.

3) If vacuum drops rapidly to zero in. Hg, test is complete. Perform VERIFICATION TEST VER-2. If vacuum does not drop rapidly to zero in. Hg, repair MAP sensor vacuum hose restrictions as necessary. Perform VERIFICATION TEST VER-2.

TEST DR-31A

INTERMITTENT AIS MOTOR CIRCUIT FAULT

1) Turn ignition on. Using DRB-II, erase faults and actuate AIS motor. Read secondary indicators while actuating AIS motor. Wiggle AIS motor connector. If fault indicator returns, repair AIS motor wiring or connector. Perform VERIFICATION TEST VER-2.

2) If fault indicator does not return, wiggle sections of wiring harness between AIS motor and engine controller. Wait 5 seconds before moving to next section of wiring harness.

3) If fault indicator returns, repair wiring harness where wiggling caused fault indicator to return. Perform VERIFICATION TEST VER-2. If fault indicator does not return, test is complete. Perform VERIFICATION TEST VER-2.

TEST DR-32A

INTERMITTENT INJECTOR CONTROL CIRCUIT FAULT

NOTE: For connector terminal identification, see CONNECTOR IDENTIFICATION at beginning of article. For appropriate wiring diagram, see WIRING DIAGRAMS article in ENGINE PERFORMANCE.

1) Using DRB-II, erase fault codes. Start engine. Using DRB-II, select SECONDARY INDICATORS. Wiggle wiring harness from suspect fuel injector to engine controller. If fault indicator returns, repair harness where wiggling caused indicator to return. Perform VERIFICATION TEST VER-2.

2) If fault indicator does not return, visually inspect related harness connectors. Look for broken, bent, pushed-out, or corroded terminals. Visually inspect related harnesses. Look for chafed, pierced, or partially broken wires. Repair wiring and/or connectors as necessary. Test is complete. Perform VERIFICATION TEST VER-2.

TEST DR-33A

INTERMITTENT RELAY OR SOLENOID FAULT

1) Turn ignition on. Using DRB-II, erase faults and actuate suspect relay (solenoid). Read secondary indicators while actuating relay (solenoid). Wiggle connector at intermittent relay (solenoid).

2) If fault indicator returns, repair relay (solenoid) wiring or connector. Perform VERIFICATION TEST VER-2. If fault indicator does not return, wiggle sections of wiring harness between relay (solenoid) and engine controller. Wait 5 seconds before moving to next section of wiring harness.

3) If fault indicator returns, repair wiring harness where wiggling caused fault indicator to return. Perform VERIFICATION TEST VER-2. If fault indicator does not return, test is complete. Perform VERIFICATION TEST VER-2.

TEST DR-34A

INTERMITTENT ASD SENSE CIRCUIT FAULT

1) Turn ignition on. Using DRB-II, erase fault codes and select ACTUATE ASD RELAY. Using DRB-II, select SECONDARY INDICATORS. Observe secondary indicators while wiggling wires and connectors of ASD relay circuit. If ASD fault returns, repair harness or connector where wiggling caused fault indicator to return. Perform VERIFICATION TEST VER-2.

2) If ASD fault does not return, visually inspect related harness connectors. Look for broken, bent, pushed-out, or corroded terminals. Visually inspect related harnesses. Look for chafed, pierced, or partially broken wires. Repair wiring and/or connectors as necessary. Test is complete. Perform VERIFICATION TEST VER-2.

TEST NF-1A

NO FAULT TEST CODE MENU

Check MITCHELL® TECHNICAL SERVICE BULLETINS (TSBs) for any pertinent information. If a TSB exists, perform corrective action. If TSB does not exist or if driveability problem still exists after performing TSB, check suspect system and perform indicated test. See NO FAULT CODE TEST MENU table. If system causing driveability problem is not known, perform TEST NF-2A through TEST NF-13A in sequence until problem is found.

NO FAULT CODE TEST MENU

Application	Test
Checking Coolant & TPS Calibrations	NF-4A
Checking Engine Controller Grounds	NF-9A
Checking Engine Mechanical Condition	NF-11A
Checking Engine Vacuum	NF-10A
Checking Fuel Pressure	NF-3A
Checking Idle Speed Motor Operation	NF-7A
Checking MAP Sensor Calibration	NF-5A
Checking Oxygen (O_2) Sensor Switching	NF-6A
Checking Park/Neutral Switch (A/T Only)	NF-8A
Checking Secondary Ignition & Timing	NF-2A

TEST NF-2A

CHECKING SECONDARY IGNITION & TIMING

1) Turn engine off. Connect engine analyzer to engine. Start engine and let it idle. Set scope to read display or parade pattern. Follow equipment manufacturer's procedure for pattern analysis.

2) If secondary ignition pattern is not okay, repair indicated component in secondary ignition system. Perform VERIFICATION TEST VER-2. If secondary ignition pattern is okay, disconnect any spark plug wire. Observe secondary kilovolt (kv) line.

3) If open circuit secondary voltage is less than 25 kilovolts, replace ignition coil. Perform VERIFICATION TEST VER-2. If open circuit secondary voltage is at least 25 kilovolts, reinstall spark plug wire. Ensure engine temperature is more than 180°F (82°C) before proceeding to next step.

4) Using DRB-II, read total spark advance. Increase engine speed to 2000 RPM. If spark advance does not change with increase in RPM, replace engine controller. Perform VERIFICATION TEST VER-2. If spark advance changes with increase in RPM, test is complete.

TEST NF-3A

CHECKING FUEL PRESSURE

WARNING: High fuel pressure may be present in fuel lines. Open fuel system with caution. See FUEL PRESSURE RELEASE procedure in SELF-DIAGNOSTICS article.

1) Relieve fuel pressure. Connect fuel pressure gauge to fuel rail. Turn ignition on. Using DRB-II, actuate ASD fuel system test. If fuel pressure is 35-45 psi, test is complete. If fuel pressure is not 35-45 psi, record fuel pressure reading. If pressure is more than 45 psi, perform TEST NF-3B.

2) If fuel pressure is less than 45 psi, stop ASD fuel system actuation test. Turn ignition off. Inspect fuel lines for kinks or restrictions. Repair fuel lines as necessary. Perform VERIFICATION TEST VER-2. If lines are not kinked or restricted, release fuel pressure. Remove fuel pressure gauge.

TEST NF-3A (Cont.)

3) Install fuel pressure gauge between fuel tank and fuel filter. Turn ignition on. Using DRB-II, actuate ASD fuel system test. If fuel pressure is at least 5 psi more than recorded fuel pressure, in step 1), replace fuel filter. Perform VERIFICATION TEST VER-2.

CAUTION: DO NOT allow fuel pressure to exceed 50 psi in step 4).

4) If fuel pressure is not at least 5 psi more than recorded fuel pressure, gently squeeze fuel return hose while observing fuel pressure gauge. If fuel pressure increases, replace fuel pressure regulator. Perform VERIFICATION TEST VER-2. If fuel pressure does not increase, replace fuel pump and sock assembly. Perform VERIFICATION TEST VER-2.

TEST NF-3B

CHECKING FUEL SYSTEM

WARNING: High fuel pressure may be present in fuel lines. Open fuel system with caution. See FUEL PRESSURE RELEASE procedure in SELF-DIAGNOSTICS article.

1) Using DRB-II, stop fuel system actuation test. Relieve fuel pressure. Ensure fuel tank is at least 1/4 full before proceeding. Remove fuel return line from fuel pump at fuel tank. Connect Fuel Pressure Test Adapter (6541) to fuel return line. Place other end of adapter hose into an approved 2-gallon gasoline can.

2) Turn ignition on. Using DRB-II, actuate ASD fuel system test. Observe fuel pressure gauge. If fuel pressure is 35-45 psi, repair fuel return line for a restriction at fuel tank. Perform VERIFICATION TEST VER-2. If fuel pressure is not 35-45 psi, stop ASD fuel system actuation test. Relieve fuel pressure.

3) Reconnect fuel return line to fuel tank. Disconnect fuel return line from fuel rail. Attach fuel pressure test adapter to fuel return line fitting. Place other end of adapter hose into an approved 2-gallon gasoline can. Turn ignition on. Using DRB-II, actuate ASD fuel system test. Observe fuel pressure gauge.

4) If fuel pressure is 35-45 psi, repair restricted fuel return line to fuel tank. Perform VERIFICATION TEST VER-2. If fuel pressure is not 35-45 psi, check fuel damper line for restrictions. Replace fuel pressure damper line if necessary. Perform VERIFICATION TEST VER-2. If damper line is free of restrictions, replace fuel pressure regulator. Perform VERIFICATION TEST VER-2.

TEST NF-4A

CHECKING COOLANT SENSOR & TPS CALIBRATIONS

1) Start engine. Allow engine to reach normal operating temperature. Using DRB-II, read coolant temperature sensor value. If temperature is 180-220°F (82-104°C), turn engine off and go to next step. If temperature is not as specified, replace coolant temperature sensor. Perform VERIFICATION TEST VER-2.

2) Turn ignition on. Using DRB-II, read TPS voltage with throttle fully closed and against throttle stop. If reading is more than 1.5 volts with throttle closed, replace TPS. Perform VERIFICATION TEST VER-2. If reading is 1.5 volts or less with throttle closed, monitor TPS voltage while slowly opening throttle to wide open position.

3) If voltage change is not a smooth transition, replace TPS. Perform VERIFICATION TEST VER-2. If voltage change is a smooth transition, check if maximum voltage is at least 3.4 volts with throttle wide open. If maximum voltage is not at least 3.4 volts, replace TPS. Perform VERIFICATION TEST VER-2.

4) If maximum voltage is at least 3.4 volts, start engine and let it idle. Using DRB-II, read minimum throttle voltage. If reading is not 0-1.5 volts, replace TPS. Perform VERIFICATION TEST VER-2. If reading is 0-1.5 volts, test is complete.

TEST NF-5A

CHECKING MAP SENSOR CALIBRATION

1) Turn engine off. Install vacuum "T" in MAP sensor vacuum hose. Connect vacuum gauge to "T". Start engine and let it idle. Using DRB-II, read MAP (vacuum) gauge. If DRB-II vacuum reading is within one in. Hg of teed-in vacuum gauge reading, test is complete.

2) If DRB-II vacuum reading is not as specified, turn engine off. Disconnect vacuum gauge from MAP sensor. Connect a hand-held vacuum pump to MAP sensor. Apply 5 in. Hg of vacuum to MAP sensor. Using DRB-II, read and record MAP sensor voltage.

3) Increase vacuum to MAP sensor to 20 in. Hg. Using DRB-II, read and record MAP sensor voltage. Subtract voltage recorded at 20 in. Hg from voltage recorded at 5 in. Hg.

4) If difference is between 2.3 and 2.9 volts, repair restriction in vacuum hose to MAP sensor. Perform VERIFICATION TEST VER-2. If voltage difference is not between 2.3 and 2.9 volts, replace MAP sensor. Perform VERIFICATION TEST VER-2.

TEST NF-6A

CHECKING OXYGEN (O_2) SENSOR SWITCHING

1) Allow engine to reach normal operating temperature. Using DRB-II, read O_2 sensor state for one minute (at idle). If O_2 sensor state is switching (rich to lean), system is functioning properly. Test is complete. If O_2 sensor state is not switching, check if O_2 sensor is locked on lean. If O_2 sensor is locked on lean, perform TEST NF-6B. If O_2 sensor is not locked on lean, go to next step.

2) Turn engine off. Allow engine to "hot soak" for 5 minutes. Remove spark plugs, keeping them in order according to cylinder. Inspect spark plugs for wet tips or fuel fouling.

3) If ANY spark plug is wet or fuel fouled, replace leaking injector(s) at corresponding cylinder(s). Perform VERIFICATION TEST VER-3. If NO spark plug is wet or fuel fouled, inspect air cleaner filter and inlet ducts for restrictions. Clean or repair as necessary. Perform VERIFICATION TEST VER-3. If no restrictions exist, perform TEST NF-11A.

TEST NF-6B

CHECKING OXYGEN (LOCKED LEAN)

NOTE: For connector terminal identification, see CONNECTOR IDENTIFICATION at beginning of article. For appropriate wiring diagram, see WIRING DIAGRAMS article in ENGINE PERFORMANCE.

1) Allow engine to idle. Inspect engine for vacuum leaks. Repair vacuum leaks as necessary. Perform VERIFICATION TEST VER-3. If no vacuum leaks exist, read O_2 sensor signal voltage.

2) If voltage is more than .10 volt, go to step 4). If voltage is less than .10 volt, turn ignition off. Disconnect O_2 sensor connector and engine controller connector. Place DRB-II in ohmmeter mode. Probe Black/Dark Green wire (Black/Orange wire on Grand Cherokee; Gray wire on Wrangler) at engine controller connector terminal No. 41.

3) If resistance is less than 10 ohms, repair short to ground in Black/Dark Green wire (Black/Orange wire on Grand Cherokee; Gray wire on Wrangler). Perform VERIFICATION TEST VER-3. If resistance is 10 ohms or more, replace O_2 sensor. Perform VERIFICATION TEST VER-3.

4) Turn engine off and replace O_2 sensor. Turn ignition on. Using DRB-II, reset adaptive fuel value. Start engine and allow it to reach normal operating temperature.

5) Read O_2 sensor state. If O_2 sensor state is switching (rich to lean), repair is complete. Perform VERIFICATION TEST VER-3. If O_2 sensor state is not switching, perform TEST NF-10A.

TEST NF-7A

CHECKING IDLE SPEED MOTOR OPERATION

NOTE: For connector terminal identification, see CONNECTOR IDENTIFICATION at beginning of article. For appropriate wiring diagram, see WIRING DIAGRAMS article in ENGINE PERFORMANCE.

1) Using DRB-II, set engine speed to 1100 RPM. If engine speed can be set to 1050-1150 RPM, test is complete. If engine speed cannot be set to 1050-1150 RPM, return engine to normal idle speed. Disconnect and inspect idle speed motor connector. Repair connector if damaged. Perform VERIFICATION TEST VER-2.

2) If connector is okay, place DRB-II in voltmeter mode. Open and close throttle while probing Gray/Red wire (Yellow/Black wire on Grand Cherokee; Dark Green/Black wire on Wrangler) at idle speed motor connector. If voltage is less than one volt, perform TEST NF-7B. If voltage is more than one volt, go to next step.

3) Open and close throttle while probing Yellow/Black wire (Violet/Black wire on Grand Cherokee; Pink/Black wire on Wrangler) at idle speed motor connector. If voltage is less than one volt, perform TEST NF-7B. If voltage is more than one volt, go to next step.

4) Open and close throttle while probing Brown/White wire (Red/Yellow wire on Wrangler) at idle speed motor connector. If voltage is less than one volt, perform TEST NF-7B. If voltage is more than one volt, go to next step.

5) Open and close throttle while probing Violet/Black wire (Gray/Red wire on Grand Cherokee; Dark Blue/Yellow wire on Wrangler) at idle speed motor connector. If voltage is less than one volt, perform TEST NF-7B. If voltage is more than one volt, inspect engine for vacuum leaks. Repair vacuum leaks as necessary. Perform VERIFICATION TEST VER-2. If no vacuum leaks exist, replace idle speed motor. Perform VERIFICATION TEST VER-2.

TEST NF-7B

CHECKING IDLE SPEED MOTOR OPERATION

NOTE: For connector terminal identification, see CONNECTOR IDENTIFICATION at beginning of article. For appropriate wiring diagram, see WIRING DIAGRAMS article in ENGINE PERFORMANCE.

1) Turn engine off. Disconnect and inspect engine controller connector. Repair connector as necessary. Perform VERIFICATION TEST VER-2. If connector is okay, go to next step.

2) Using a DVOM, check continuity between idle speed motor connector terminal No. 1 and engine controller connector terminal No. 39, and motor connector terminal No. 2 and controller connector terminal No. 60.

3) Also check continuity between idle speed motor connector terminal No. 3 and controller connector terminal No. 40, and motor connector terminal No. 4 and controller connector terminal No. 59.

4) If resistance is less than 10 ohms for each circuit, replace engine controller. Perform VERIFICATION TEST VER-2. If resistance is 10 ohms or more for any circuit, repair open wire in that circuit. Perform VERIFICATION TEST VER-2.

TEST NF-8A

CHECKING PARK/NEUTRAL SWITCH INPUT (A/T ONLY)

NOTE: For connector terminal identification, see CONNECTOR IDENTIFICATION at beginning of article. For appropriate wiring diagram, see WIRING DIAGRAMS article in ENGINE PERFORMANCE.

1) Using DRB-II, read park/neutral switch input state. While observing DRB-II display, move gear selector in and out of Park and Reverse positions. If display shows P/N and D/R, system is functioning properly. If display does not show P/N and D/R (Grand Cherokee and Wrangler with AW-4 auto. trans.), service or replace park/neutral switch. If display does not show P/N and D/R (all other applications), go to next step.

TEST NF-8A (Cont.)

2) Turn ignition off. Place gear selector in Park position. Disconnect engine controller connector. Disconnect battery quick disconnect cable (at battery). Place DRB-II in ohmmeter mode. Probe Black/Tan wire (Black/White wire on Grand Cherokee and Wrangler) at engine controller connector terminal No. 30. While observing DRB-II display, move gear selector in and out of Park and Reverse positions.

3) If display switches from less than 5 ohms to more than 5 ohms, replace engine controller. Perform VERIFICATION TEST VER-2. If display always stays less than 5 ohms, repair short to ground in Black/Tan wire (Black/White wire on Grand Cherokee and Wrangler). Perform VERIFICATION TEST VER-2. If display does not always stay less than 5 ohms, go to next step.

4) Disconnect park/neutral switch connector. Using a DVOM, check resistance of Black/Tan wire (Black/White wire on Grand Cherokee and Wrangler) between park/neutral switch connector and engine controller connector terminal No. 30. If resistance is less than 10 ohms, replace park/neutral switch. Perform VERIFICATION TEST VER-2. If resistance is 10 ohms or more, repair open Black/Tan wire (Black/White wire on Grand Cherokee and Wrangler). Perform VERIFICATION TEST VER-2.

TEST NF-9A

CHECKING ENGINE CONTROLLER GROUNDS

NOTE: For connector terminal identification, see CONNECTOR IDENTIFICATION at beginning of article. For appropriate wiring diagram, see WIRING DIAGRAMS article in ENGINE PERFORMANCE.

1) Turn ignition off. Disconnect and inspect engine controller connector. Repair connector as necessary. Perform VERIFICATION TEST VER-2. If connector is okay, go to next step.

2) Place DRB-II in ohmmeter mode. Probe Black wire (Black/Tan wire on Grand Cherokee; Black/Yellow wire on Wrangler) at engine controller connector terminal No. 5. If resistance is less than one ohm, go to next step. If resistance is one ohm or more, repair open Black wire (Black/Tan wire on Grand Cherokee; Black/Yellow wire on Wrangler). Perform VERIFICATION TEST VER-2.

3) Probe Black/Tan wire (Black wire on Wrangler) at engine controller connector terminal No. 11. If resistance is less than one ohm, go to next step. If resistance is one ohm or more, repair open Black/Tan wire (Black wire on Wrangler). Perform VERIFICATION TEST VER-2.

4) Probe Black/Tan wire (Black wire on Wrangler) at engine controller connector terminal No. 12. If resistance is less than one ohm, reconnect engine controller connector. Test is complete. If resistance is one ohm or more, repair open Black/Tan wire (Black wire on Wrangler). Perform VERIFICATION TEST VER-2.

TEST NF-10A

CHECKING ENGINE VACUUM

Connect a vacuum gauge to engine. Start engine and let it idle. Normal vacuum reading will vary depending on altitude. Observe vacuum gauge reading at idle. If vacuum gauge reading is not a steady 13-22 in. Hg of vacuum, perform TEST NF-11A. If vacuum gauge reading is a steady 13-22 in. Hg of vacuum, test is complete.

TEST NF-11A

PERFORMING NO FAULT MECHANICAL TEST

At this point in diagnostic test procedure, all engine control systems have been determined to be operating as designed and not causing a driveability problem. Following additional items should be checked as possible causes:

NOTE: If coming to this test from O₂ sensor test and rich or lean condition is not corrected after checking the following items, replace engine controller. Perform VERIFICATION TEST VER-3.

- Check if any MITCHELL® TECHNICAL SERVICE BULLETINS (TSBs) apply to vehicle.
- Check engine vacuum. It must be at least 13 in. Hg in Neutral.
- Check valve timing.
- Check engine compression.
- Check for exhaust system restriction.
- Ensure PCV system is functioning properly.
- Check camshaft and crankshaft sprockets.
- Check torque converter stall speed.
- Check power brake booster for internal vacuum leak.
- Check for fuel contamination.
- Ensure injector control wire is connected to correct fuel injector and injector is not plugged or restricted.

VERIFICATION TEST VER-1

1) Inspect vehicle to ensure all engine components are connected. Reassemble and reconnect components as necessary. Attempt to start engine. If engine does not start, return to TEST NS-1A.

2) If engine starts and engine controller was changed, write vehicle's EMR mileage into replacement engine controller. This will enable new engine controller to operate Emission Maintenance Reminder (EMR) light properly. No-start condition is corrected and repair is now complete.

3) If engine starts and engine controller has not been changed, connect DRB-II to engine diagnostic connector, and erase faults. If no-start condition has been corrected and fault messages have been erased. Repair is now complete.

4) If repaired fault resets, repair is NOT complete. Check all pertinent MITCHELL® TECHNICAL SERVICE BULLETINS (TSBs), and return to TEST DR-1A if necessary. If another fault exists, return to TEST DR-1A and follow path specified by other fault. If no other faults exist, repair is now complete.

VERIFICATION TEST VER-2

If VERIFICATION TEST VER-3 was performed previously, perform VERIFICATION TEST VER-3 again. Inspect vehicle to ensure all engine components are connected. Reassemble and reconnect components as necessary. If another fault was read previously and not corrected, return to TEST DR-1A and follow path specified by other fault. If engine controller was replaced, perform the following steps:

1) Start vehicle at least 20 times to enable factory theft alarm system (if equipped). Write vehicle's EMR mileage into replacement engine controller. This will enable new engine controller to operate Emission Maintenance Reminder (EMR) light properly. Connect DRB-II to engine diagnostic connector and erase faults.

2) Start engine and allow it to reach normal operating temperature. Raise engine speed to 2000 RPM for at least 10 seconds. Allow engine to idle. On A/T equipped models, apply brake and cycle transmission through all gear ranges. Place gear selector in Park position. On A/C equipped models, turn on A/C system. Set blower to low speed.

3) On all models, turn engine off. Start engine and allow it to idle for at least 2 minutes. Turn engine off. Using DRB-II, read fault messages. If repaired fault resets, repair is NOT complete. Check all pertinent MITCHELL® TECHNICAL SERVICE BULLETINS (TSBs), and return to TEST DR-1A if necessary. If another fault exists, return to TEST DR-1A and follow path specified by other fault. If no other faults exist, repair is now complete.

VERIFICATION TEST VER-3

Inspect vehicle to ensure all engine components are connected. Reassemble and reconnect components as necessary. If another fault was read previously and not corrected, return to TEST DR-1A and follow path specified by other fault. If engine controller was replaced, perform the following steps:

1) Start vehicle at least 20 times to activate factory theft alarm (if equipped). Write vehicle's EMR mileage into replacement engine controller. This will enable new engine controller to operate Emission Maintenance Reminder (EMR) light properly. Connect DRB-II to engine diagnostic connector and erase faults.

2) On A/C equipped models, turn on A/C system. Set blower to low speed. Drive vehicle for at least 5 minutes and attain a speed of at least 40 MPH. Ensure transmission shifts through all gears. Upon completion of road test, turn engine off. Restart engine and let it idle for at least 2 minutes.

3) Turn engine off. Connect DRB-II to engine diagnostic connector and read fault messages. If repaired fault has reset, repair is NOT complete. Check all pertinent MITCHELL® TECHNICAL SERVICE BULLETINS (TSBs), and return to TEST DR-1A if necessary. If another fault exists, return to TEST DR-1A and follow path specified by other fault. If no other faults exist, repair is now complete.

Cherokee, Grand Cherokee (1993)

DESCRIPTION

CCD BUS

The CCD bus is a twisted pair of wires traveling from module to module receiving and delivering coded information. The code identifies the message and its importance. When multiple messages attempt to access CCD bus at once, code assigns priority ranking.

The 2 twisted wires used by the CCD bus system are called Bus "+" and Bus "–". Both wires carry approximately 2.5 volts.

SELF-DIAGNOSTIC SYSTEM

PRETEST INSPECTION

Before proceeding with diagnosis, the following precautions must be followed:

- Vehicle must have a fully charged battery and functional charging system.
- Only perform test steps indicated. It is NOT necessary to perform all steps in a test.
- VEHICLE COMMUNICATIONS tests should only be used when instructed to do so by another test. Always start at TEST 1A: BLANK DRB-II MESSAGE SCREEN.
- Always perform VERIFICATION TEST after repairs are made.
- At the end of each test step, reconnect all wires and install any components removed for testing.
- Use extreme care when connecting or disconnecting wiring during testing to prevent accidental grounding or shorting.
- DO NOT use a test light in place of a voltmeter.
- Always disconnect DRB-II after use.
- Always disconnect DRB-II before charging battery.

DIAGNOSTIC PROCEDURE

DRB-II PROBLEMS & ERROR MESSAGES

If a problem exists with the operation of DRB-II, DRB-II displays a blank screen, CCD bus failure message or NO RESPONSE, RAM TEST FAILURE, CARTRIDGE ERROR, KEYPAD TEST FAILURE, HIGH BATTERY or LOW BATTERY error message appears, refer to SELF-DIAGNOSTIC TESTS. Always start at TEST 1A: BLANK DRB-II MESSAGE SCREEN.

BODY CONTROL SYSTEM CONNECTORS

NOTE: For terminal identification of body control system connectors, see Figs. 1-6.

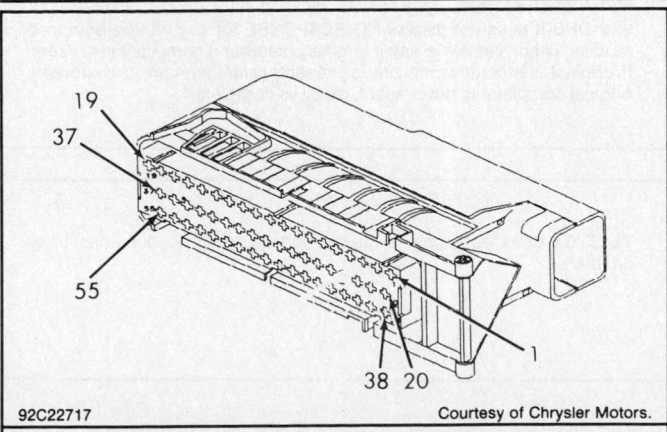

Fig. 1: Identifying Anti-Lock Brake System (ABS) Controller Connector Terminals

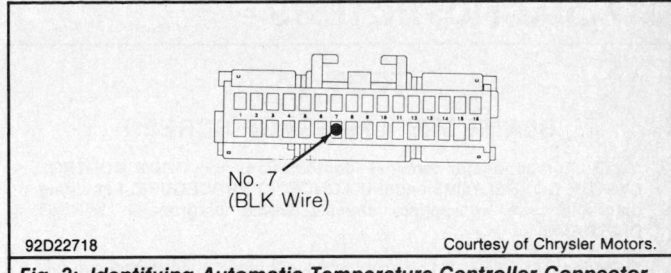

Fig. 2: Identifying Automatic Temperature Controller Connector Terminals

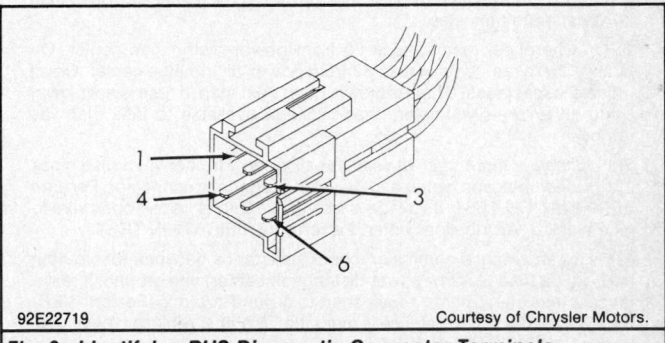

Fig. 3: Identifying BUS Diagnostic Connector Terminals

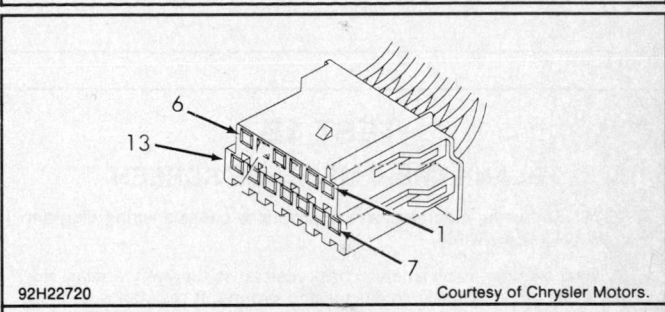

Fig. 4: Identifying Compass/Mini-Trip Connector Terminals

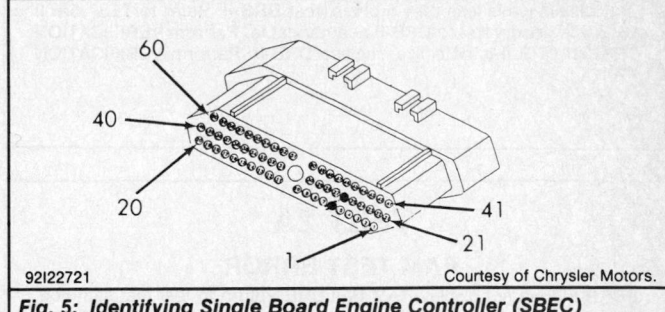

Fig. 5: Identifying Single Board Engine Controller (SBEC) Connector Terminals

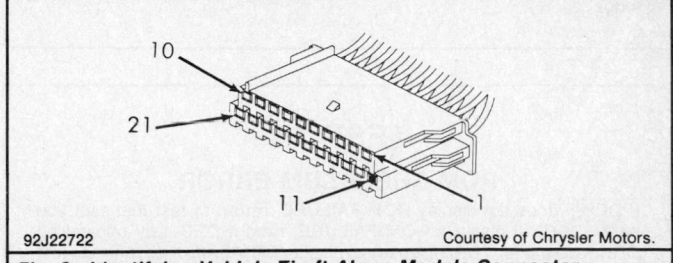

Fig. 6: Identifying Vehicle Theft Alarm Module Connector Terminals

SELF-DIAGNOSTIC TESTS

TEST 1A

BLANK DRB-II MESSAGE SCREEN

NOTE: For connector terminal identification, see BODY CONTROL SYSTEM CONNECTORS under DIAGNOSTIC PROCEDURE. For wiring diagrams, see appropriate chassis wiring diagram in WIRING DIAGRAMS.

1) Disconnect DRB-II. Using an external voltmeter, check voltage at terminal No. 5 at Chrysler Collision Detection (CCD) bus diagnostic connector. Connector is located underneath dash at left side of steering column. If voltage is more than 10 volts, Perform TEST 1B. If voltage is less than 10 volts, go to next step.

2) On Cherokee, remove fuse F5 from power distribution center. On Grand Cherokee, remove fuse F2 from power distribution center. On all models inspect fuse. If fuse is blown, go to next step. If fuse is not blown, using an external voltmeter, check voltage available to fuse that was removed.

3) If voltage is more than 10 volts, repair open wire between fuse block or power distribution center and CCD bus diagnostic connector. Perform VERIFICATION TEST. If voltage is less than 10 volts, repair open wire to fuse block or distribution center. Perform VERIFICATION TEST.

4) Using an external ohmmeter, check resistance between fuse output terminal (at fuse block or power distribution center) and ground. If resistance is less than 5 ohms, repair short to ground in wiring. Perform VERIFICATION TEST. If resistance is more than 5 ohms, replace blown fuse. Perform VERIFICATION TEST.

TEST 1B

BLANK DRB-II MESSAGE SCREEN

NOTE: For wiring diagrams, see appropriate chassis wiring diagram in WIRING DIAGRAMS.

1) Using an external ohmmeter, check resistance between terminal No. 3 at CCD bus diagnostic connector and ground. If resistance is more than 5 ohms, repair open in wiring to terminal No. 3. Perform VERIFICATION TEST.

2) If resistance is less than 5 ohms, test DRB-II. Refer to TEST 5A. If DRB-II is good, replace DRB-II adapter cable. Perform VERIFICATION TEST. If DRB-II is defective, replace DRB-II. Perform VERIFICATION TEST.

TEST 2A

RAM TEST ERROR

If DRB-II does not display RAM FAILURE, return to test that sent you here. If DRB-II displays RAM FAILURE, reboot DRB-II by reinstalling DRB-II cartridge. If DRB-II does not display RAM FAILURE, return to test that sent you here. If DRB-II displays RAM FAILURE, replace DRB-II cartridge.

TEST 3A

ROM CHECKSUM ERROR

If DRB-II does not display ROM FAILURE, return to test that sent you here. If DRB-II displays ROM FAILURE, reboot DRB-II by reinstalling DRB-II cartridge. If DRB-II does not display ROM FAILURE, return to test that sent you here. If DRB-II displays ROM FAILURE, replace DRB-II.

TEST 4A

KEYPAD TEST FAILURE MESSAGE

NOTE: DO NOT touch DRB-II keypad during following test.

If DRB-II does not display KEYPAD TEST FAILURE, return to test that sent you here. If DRB-II displays KEYPAD TEST FAILURE, reboot DRB-II by reinstalling DRB-II cartridge. If DRB-II does not display KEYPAD TEST FAILURE, return to test that sent you here. If DRB-II displays KEYPAD TEST FAILURE, replace DRB-II.

TEST 5A

TESTING DRB-II

Although the manufacturer is the only one equipped to physically test the DRB-II for proper operation, you should be able to determine the state of your DRB-II by using the following substitution techniques and the process of elimination.

1) Turn ignition switch to OFF position. Disconnect DRB-II adapter cable and DRB-II cartridge. Locate a second vehicle with identical equipment to original vehicle. Connect DRB-II assembly to second vehicle and turn ignition switch to ON position. Use DRB-II as it was used on first vehicle. If DRB-II results are not the same as before, problem is not with the DRB-II. Return to test that sent you here.

2) If same problem still exists as before substituting vehicles, DRB-II has a defective adapter cable or DRB-II cartridge. If a second DRB-II cartridge for the same vehicle is available, try substituting DRB-II cartridge. If DRB-II now functions correctly, original DRB-II cartridge is defective. Use the good DRB-II cartridge and return to test that sent you here.

3) If DRB-II still does not function correctly, substitute a second DRB-II adapter cable. If a second DRB-II adapter cable of same type is not available, use a SCI or CCD adapter cable. If DRB-II now functions correctly, DRB-II has a defective adapter cable. Use the good adapter cable and return to test that sent you here.

4) If DRB-II still does not work, substitute a second DRB-II. If a second DRB-II is not available, send DRB-II in for repair. If DRB-II now functions correctly, original DRB-II is defective. Use the good DRB-II and return to test that sent you here.

VERIFICATION TEST

1) Reconnect all components and connectors that have been disconnected. Connect DRB-II, if not already connected. Turn ignition switch to ON position with engine off. If DRB-II display is blank, perform TEST 1A.

2) If DRB-II displays a bus failure message on DRB-II, perform bus failure message test displayed. See TEST 7A. If DRB-II displays NO RESPONSE for any vehicle equipped module, perform NO RESPONSE test. See TEST 20A.

3) If DRB-II does not display NO RESPONSE for any vehicle equipped module, check vehicle to see if original customer's complaint is present. If original customer complaint is present, retest system. If customers original complaint is not present, repair is complete.

TEST 6A does not apply to these models. No procedure has been omitted.

TEST 7A
BUS FAILURE MESSAGES

Select error message and corresponding test from BUS FAILURE MESSAGES table. Proceed to self-diagnostic test indicated. Each specific error message is diagnosed by following a specific testing sequence. It is not necessary to perform all tests to diagnose an individual error message.

BUS FAILURE MESSAGES

Message	Test No.
BUS BIAS LEVEL TOO HIGH	14A
BUS BIAS LEVEL TOO LOW	13A
BUS (+) OPEN	16A
BUS (-) OPEN	17A
BUS (+) & (-) OPEN	18A
BUS (+) & BUS (-) SHORTED TOGETHER	11A
SHORT TO BATTERY	8A
SHORT TO GROUND	10A
SHORT TO 5 VOLTS	9A
NO BUS BIAS	15A
NOT RECEIVING BUS MESSAGES CORRECTLY	19A
NO TERMINATION	12A

TEST 8A
SHORT TO BATTERY ON BUS

NOTE: For connector terminal identification, see BODY CONTROL SYSTEM CONNECTORS under DIAGNOSTIC PROCEDURE. For wiring diagrams, see appropriate chassis wiring diagram in WIRING DIAGRAMS.

CAUTION: Always turn ignition switch to OFF position prior to disconnecting or connecting any module connector.

1) Using DRB-II, answer the question whether a module is present or not. Disconnect Anti-Lock Brake System (ABS) controller connector (if equipped). On Cherokee, controller is located to right of steering column. On Grand Cherokee, controller is located in left front of engine compartment. On all models, check connector condition and clean or repair connector as necessary. If DRB-II does not display SHORT TO BATTERY, replace ABS controller. Perform VERIFICATION TEST.

2) If DRB-II displays SHORT TO BATTERY, disconnect Single Board Engine Controller (SBEC) connector. On Cherokee, SBEC is located at left front of engine compartment. On Grand Cherokee, SBEC is located at right rear of engine compartment. On all models, check connector condition and clean or repair connector as necessary.

3) If DRB-II does not display SHORT TO BATTERY, replace SBEC. Perform VERIFICATION TEST. If DRB-II displays SHORT TO BATTERY, disconnect compass/mini-trip module connector (if equipped). Connector is located in overhead console. Check connector condition and clean or repair connector as necessary. If DRB-II does not display SHORT TO BATTERY, perform TEST 8B.

4) If DRB-II displays SHORT TO BATTERY, disconnect vehicle theft module (if equipped). On Cherokee, module is located to right of steering column. On Grand Cherokee, module is located behind glove box. On all models, check connector condition and clean or repair connector as necessary. If DRB-II does not display SHORT TO BATTERY, perform TEST 8C.

5) If DRB-II displays SHORT TO BATTERY, disconnect automatic temperature controller (if equipped). Check connector condition and clean or repair connector as necessary. If DRB-II does not display SHORT TO BATTERY, perform TEST 8D. If DRB-II displays SHORT TO BATTERY, using an external voltmeter, measure voltage between terminal No. 1 (Violet/Brown wire) of CCD bus diagnostic connector and ground.

6) If voltage is more then 10 volts, repair short to battery in Violet/Brown wire. Perform VERIFICATION TEST. If voltage is less than 10 volts, repair short to battery in White/Black wire or White/Gray wire. Perform VERIFICATION TEST.

TEST 8B
SHORT TO BATTERY ON BUS

NOTE: For connector terminal identification, see BODY CONTROL SYSTEM CONNECTORS under DIAGNOSTIC PROCEDURE. For wiring diagrams, see appropriate chassis wiring diagram in WIRING DIAGRAMS.

Ensure all doors, trunk and hood are closed. Put DRB-II in ohmmeter mode. Probe terminal No. 5 (Black/Orange wire) of compass/mini-trip module connector. If resistance is less than 5 ohms, replace compass/mini-trip module. Perform VERIFICATION TEST. If resistance is more than 5 ohms, repair open Black/Orange wire. Perform VERIFICATION TEST.

TEST 8C
SHORT TO BATTERY ON BUS

NOTE: For connector terminal identification, see BODY CONTROL SYSTEM CONNECTORS under DIAGNOSTIC PROCEDURE. For wiring diagrams, see appropriate chassis wiring diagram in WIRING DIAGRAMS.

Turn ignition switch to OFF position. Put DRB-II in ohmmeter mode. Probe terminal No. 11 (Black wire) of vehicle theft alarm module connector. If resistance is less than 5 ohms, replace vehicle theft alarm module. Perform VERIFICATION TEST. If resistance is more than 5 ohms, repair open Black wire. Perform VERIFICATION TEST.

TEST 8D
SHORT TO BATTERY ON BUS

NOTE: For connector terminal identification, see BODY CONTROL SYSTEM CONNECTORS under DIAGNOSTIC PROCEDURE. For wiring diagrams, see appropriate chassis wiring diagram in WIRING DIAGRAMS.

Turn ignition switch to OFF position. Put DRB-II in ohmmeter mode. Probe terminal No. 7 (Black wire) of automatic temperature controller connector. If resistance is less than 5 ohms, replace automatic temperature controller module. Perform VERIFICATION TEST. If resistance is more than 5 ohms, repair open Black wire. Perform VERIFICATION TEST.

TEST 9A
SHORT TO 5 VOLTS ON BUS

NOTE: For connector terminal identification, see BODY CONTROL SYSTEM CONNECTORS under DIAGNOSTIC PROCEDURE. For wiring diagrams, see appropriate chassis wiring diagram in WIRING DIAGRAMS.

CAUTION: Always turn ignition switch to OFF position prior to disconnecting or connecting any module connector.

1) Using DRB-II, answer the question whether a module is present or not. Disconnect compass/mini-trip module connector (if equipped). Connector is located in overhead console. Check connector condition and clean or repair connector as necessary. If DRB-II does not display SHORT TO 5 VOLTS, replace compass/mini-trip module. Perform VERIFICATION TEST.

2) If DRB-II displays SHORT TO 5 VOLTS, disconnect Anti-Lock Brake System (ABS) controller connector (if equipped). On Cherokee, controller is located to right of steering column. On Grand Cherokee, controller is located in left front of engine compartment. On all models, check connector condition and clean or repair connector as necessary. If DRB-II does not display SHORT TO 5 VOLTS, replace ABS controller. Perform VERIFICATION TEST.

TEST 9A (Cont.)

3) If DRB-II displays SHORT TO 5 VOLTS, disconnect automatic temperature controller (if equipped). Check connector condition and clean or repair connector as necessary. If DRB-II does not display SHORT TO 5 VOLTS, replace automatic temperature controller. Perform VERIFICATION TEST. If DRB-II displays SHORT TO 5 VOLTS, disconnect Single Board Engine Controller (SBEC) connector.

4) Check connector condition and clean or repair connector as necessary. Using an external ohmmeter, check resistance between terminals No. 6 (Violet/White wire) and No. 26 (Violet/Brown wire) at SBEC connector. If resistance is less than 1000 ohms, repair short in Violet/Brown and Violet/White wires. Perform VERIFICATION TEST.

5) If resistance is more than 1000 ohms, check resistance between terminals No. 46 (White/Black wire on Cherokee or White/Gray on Grand Cherokee) and No. 6 (Violet/White wire) of SBEC connector. If resistance is less than 1000 ohms, repair short in White/Black or White/Gray wire and Violet/Black wire. Perform VERIFICATION TEST.

6) If resistance is more than 1000 ohms, turn ignition switch to ON position. If DRB-II does not display SHORT TO 5 VOLTS, replace SBEC. Perform VERIFICATION TEST. If DRB-II displays SHORT TO 5 VOLTS, replace vehicle theft alarm module. Perform VERIFICATION TEST. If DRB-II displays SHORT TO 5 VOLTS, replace instrument cluster. On Cherokee, module is located to right of steering column. On Grand Cherokee, module is located behind glove box. Perform VERIFICATION TEST.

TEST 10A

SHORT TO GROUND ON BUS

NOTE: For connector terminal identification, see BODY CONTROL SYSTEM CONNECTORS under DIAGNOSTIC PROCEDURE. For wiring diagrams, see appropriate chassis wiring diagram in WIRING DIAGRAMS.

CAUTION: Always turn ignition switch to OFF position prior to disconnecting or connecting any module connector.

1) Using DRB-II, answer the question whether a module is present or not. Disconnect Anti-Lock Brake System (ABS) controller connector (if equipped). On Cherokee, controller is located to right of steering column. On Grand Cherokee, controller is located in left front of engine compartment. Check connector condition and clean or repair connector as necessary.

2) If DRB-II does not display SHORT TO GROUND, replace ABS controller. Perform VERIFICATION TEST. If DRB-II displays SHORT TO GROUND, disconnect Single Board Engine Controller (SBEC) connector. Check connector condition and clean or repair connector as necessary.

3) If DRB-II does not display SHORT TO GROUND, replace SBEC. Perform VERIFICATION TEST. If DRB-II displays SHORT TO GROUND, disconnect compass/mini-trip module connector (if equipped). Connector is located in overhead console. Check connector condition and clean or repair connector as necessary. If DRB-II does not display SHORT TO GROUND, replace compass/mini-trip module. Perform VERIFICATION TEST.

4) If DRB-II displays SHORT TO GROUND, disconnect vehicle theft alarm module (if equipped). On Cherokee, module is located to right of steering column. On Grand Cherokee, module is located behind glove box. On all models, check connector condition and clean or repair connector as necessary. If DRB-II does not display SHORT TO GROUND, replace vehicle theft alarm module. Perform VERIFICATION TEST.

5) If DRB-II displays SHORT TO GROUND, disconnect automatic temperature controller (if equipped). On Cherokee, module is located to right of steering column. On Grand Cherokee, module is located behind glove box. Check connector condition and clean or repair connector as necessary. If DRB-II does not display SHORT TO GROUND, replace automatic temperature controller. Perform VERIFICATION TEST.

6) If DRB-II displays SHORT TO GROUND, disconnect DRB-II. Using an external ohmmeter, check resistance between terminal No. 1 (Violet/Brown wire) of CCD bus diagnostic connector and ground. If resistance is less than 5 ohms, repair short to ground in Violet/Brown wire. Perform VERIFICATION TEST. If resistance is more than 5 ohms, repair short to ground in White/Black or White/Gray wire. Perform VERIFICATION TEST.

TEST 11A

BUS (+) & (-) SHORTED TOGETHER ON BUS

NOTE: For connector terminal identification, see BODY CONTROL SYSTEM CONNECTORS under DIAGNOSTIC PROCEDURE. For wiring diagrams, see appropriate chassis wiring diagram in WIRING DIAGRAMS.

CAUTION: Always turn ignition switch to OFF position prior to disconnecting or connecting any module connector.

NOTE: A common cause of this message is a low battery condition

1) Using DRB-II, answer whether a module is present or not. Disconnect Anti-Lock Brake System (ABS) controller connector (if equipped). On Cherokee, controller is located to right of steering column. On Grand Cherokee, controller is located in left front of engine compartment.

2) Check connector condition, and clean or repair connector as necessary. If DRB-II does not display BUS (+) and BUS (-) SHORTED TOGETHER, replace ABS controller. Perform VERIFICATION TEST. If DRB-II displays BUS (+) and BUS (-) SHORTED TOGETHER, disconnect Single Board Engine Controller (SBEC) connector.

3) If DRB-II does not display BUS (+) and BUS (-) SHORTED TOGETHER, replace SBEC. Perform VERIFICATION TEST. If DRB-II displays BUS (+) and BUS (-) SHORTED TOGETHER, disconnect compass/mini-trip module connector (if equipped). Connector is located in overhead console. If DRB-II does not display BUS (+) and BUS (-) SHORTED TOGETHER, replace compass/mini-trip module. Perform VERIFICATION TEST.

4) If DRB-II displays BUS (+) and BUS (-) SHORTED TOGETHER, disconnect vehicle theft alarm module (if equipped). On Cherokee, module is located to right of steering column. On Grand Cherokee, module is located behind glove box. Check connector condition and clean or repair connector as necessary. If DRB-II does not display BUS (+) and BUS (-) SHORTED TOGETHER, replace vehicle theft alarm module. Perform VERIFICATION TEST.

5) If DRB-II displays BUS (+) and BUS (-) SHORTED TOGETHER, disconnect automatic temperature controller connector (if equipped). If DRB-II does not display BUS (+) and BUS (-) SHORTED TOGETHER, replace automatic temperature controller. Perform VERIFICATION TEST.

6) If DRB-II displays BUS (+) and BUS (-) SHORTED TOGETHER, disconnect DRB-II. Using an external ohmmeter, check resistance between terminals No. 1 (Violet/Brown wire) and No. 6 (White/Black wire on Cherokee or White/Gray wire on Grand Cherokee) of CCD bus diagnostic connector.

7) If resistance is less than 20 ohms, repair short between White/Black or White/Gray wire and Violet/Black wire. Perform VERIFICATION TEST. If resistance is more than 20 ohms, test DRB-II. Refer to TEST 5A.

TEST 12A

NO TERMINATION ON BUS

NOTE: For connector terminal identification, see BODY CONTROL SYSTEM CONNECTORS under DIAGNOSTIC PROCEDURE. For wiring diagrams, see appropriate chassis wiring diagram in WIRING DIAGRAMS.

1) Turn ignition switch to OFF position. Disconnect Anti-Lock Brake System (ABS) controller connector (if equipped). On Cherokee, controller is located to right of steering column. On Grand Cherokee, controller is located in left front of engine compartment. Check connector condition and clean or repair connector as necessary.

2) Using an external ohmmeter, check resistance between terminals No. 23 and 42 of ABS controller. If resistance is not 100-140 ohms, replace ABS controller and go to next step. If resistance is 100-140 ohms, go to next step.

3) Check resistance at Violet/Brown wire between terminals No. 23 of ABS controller connector and No. 1 at CCD bus diagnostic connector. If resistance is more than 5 ohms, repair open Violet/Brown wire and go to next step. If resistance is less than 5 ohms, go to next step.

TEST 12A (Cont.)

4) Check resistance of White/Black wire on Cherokee or White/Gray wire on Grand Cherokee between terminals No. 42 of ABS controller connector and No. 6 at CCD bus diagnostic connector. If resistance is more than 5 ohms, repair open in White/Black or White/Gray wire to Violet/Brown wire and go to next step. If resistance is less than 5 ohms, go to next step.

5) Disconnect Single Board Engine Controller (SBEC) connector. Check connector condition and clean or repair connector as necessary. Using an external ohmmeter, check resistance between terminals No. 26 and 46 at SBEC. If resistance is not 100-140 ohms, replace SBEC and go to next step. If resistance is 100-140 ohms, go to next step.

6) Check resistance at Violet/Brown wire between terminals No. 1 at CCD bus diagnostic connector and No. 26 at SBEC connector. If resistance is more than 5 ohms, repair open Violet/Brown wire and go to next step. If resistance is less than 5 ohms, go to next step.

7) Check resistance at White/Black wire on Cherokee or White/Gray wire on Grand Cherokee between terminals No. 6 at CCD bus diagnostic connector and No. 46 at SBEC connector. If resistance is more than 5 ohms, repair open in White/Black or White/Gray wire and go to next step. If resistance is less than 5 ohms, go to next step.

8) Disconnect vehicle theft module (if equipped). On Cherokee, module is located to right of steering column. On Grand Cherokee, module is located behind glove box. On all models, check connector condition and clean or repair connector as necessary.

9) Using an external ohmmeter, check resistance between terminals No. 1 and 2 of vehicle theft alarm module. If resistance is not 100-140 ohms, replace vehicle theft alarm module and go to next step. If resistance is 100-140 ohms, go to next step.

10) Check resistance at Violet/Brown wire between terminals No. 1 at CCD bus diagnostic connector and No. 2 at vehicle theft alarm module connector. If resistance is more than 5 ohms, repair open Violet/Brown wire and go to next step. If resistance is less than 5 ohms, go to next step.

11) Check resistance at White/Black wire on Cherokee or White/Gray wire on Grand Cherokee between terminals No. 6 at CCD bus diagnostic connector and No. 1 at vehicle theft alarm module connector. If resistance is more than 5 ohms, repair open in White/Black or White/Gray wire. Perform VERIFICATION TEST.

12) If resistance is less than 5 ohms, test DRB-II. Refer to TEST 5A. Replace DRB-II and/or adapter cable as necessary. Perform VERIFICATION TEST. If DRB-II is good, perform TEST 20A.

TEST 13A

BUS BIAS LEVEL TOO LOW ON BUS

NOTE: For connector terminal identification, see BODY CONTROL SYSTEM CONNECTORS under DIAGNOSTIC PROCEDURE. For wiring diagrams, see appropriate chassis wiring diagram in WIRING DIAGRAMS.

NOTE: A common cause of this failure is ignition switch is in OFF position.

1) If ignition switch was in the OFF position when performing TEST 7A, turn ignition switch to ON position with engine off. Perform VERIFICATION TEST. If ignition switch was not in the OFF position when performing TEST 7A, check if battery is fully charged. If battery is not fully charged, charge battery. Perform VERIFICATION TEST.

2) If battery is fully charged, disconnect DRB-II. Using an external voltmeter, check voltage at terminal No. 1 (Violet/Brown wire) at CCD bus diagnostic connector. If voltage is not 2.1-2.7 volts, go to step **4)**.

3) If voltage is 2.1-2.7 volts, check voltage at terminal No. 6 (White/Black wire on Cherokee or White/Gray wire on Grand Cherokee) at CCD bus diagnostic connector. If voltage is not 2.1-2.7 volts, perform TEST 13B. If voltage is 2.1-2.7 volts, test DRB-II. Refer to TEST 5A. Perform VERIFICATION TEST.

4) If voltage at Violet/Brown wire is not 2.1-2.7 volts in step **2)**, turn ignition switch to OFF position. Disconnect Anti-Lock Brake System (ABS) controller connector (if equipped). On Cherokee, controller is located to right of steering column. On Grand Cherokee, controller is located in left front of engine compartment. Check connector condition and clean or repair connector as necessary.

TEST 13A (Cont.)

5) Using an external ohmmeter, check resistance between terminals No. 23 and 42 of ABS controller. If resistance is not 100-140 ohms, replace ABS controller. Perform VERIFICATION TEST. If resistance is 100-140 ohms, check resistance at Violet/Brown wire between terminals No. 1 at CCD bus diagnostic connector and No. 23 of ABS controller connector. If resistance is more than 5 ohms, repair open Violet/Brown. Perform VERIFICATION TEST.

6) If resistance is less that 5 ohms, disconnect Single Board Engine Controller (SBEC) connector. Check connector condition and clean or repair connector as necessary. Check resistance between terminals No. 26 and 46 at SBEC. If resistance is not 100-140 ohms, replace SBEC. Perform VERIFICATION TEST.

7) If resistance is 100-140 ohms, check resistance at Violet/Brown wire between terminals No. 1 at CCD bus diagnostic connector and No. 26 at SBEC connector. If resistance is more than 5 ohms, repair open Violet/Brown wire. Perform VERIFICATION TEST. If resistance is less than 5 ohms, go to next step

8) Disconnect vehicle theft module (if equipped). On Cherokee, module is located to right of steering column. On Grand Cherokee, module is located behind glove box. On all models, check connector condition and clean or repair connector as necessary. Check resistance between terminals No. 1 and 2 of vehicle theft alarm module.

9) If resistance is not 100-140 ohms, replace vehicle theft alarm module. Perform VERIFICATION TEST. If resistance is 100-140 ohms, check resistance at Violet/Brown wire between terminals No. 1 at CCD bus diagnostic connector and No. 2 of vehicle theft alarm module connector. If resistance is more than 5 ohms, repair open Violet/Brown wire. Perform VERIFICATION TEST. If resistance is less than 5 ohms, perform TEST 20A.

TEST 13B

BUS BIAS LEVEL TOO LOW ON BUS

NOTE: For connector terminal identification, see BODY CONTROL SYSTEM CONNECTORS under DIAGNOSTIC PROCEDURE. For wiring diagrams, see appropriate chassis wiring diagram in WIRING DIAGRAMS.

1) Turn ignition switch to OFF position. Disconnect Anti-Lock Brake System (ABS) controller connector (if equipped). On Cherokee, controller is located to right of steering column. On Grand Cherokee, controller is located in left front of engine compartment.

2) Check connector condition and clean or repair connector as necessary. Using an external ohmmeter, check resistance between terminals No. 23 and 42 of ABS controller. If resistance is not 100-140 ohms, replace ABS controller. Perform VERIFICATION TEST.

3) If resistance is 100-140 ohms, check resistance at White/Black wire on Cherokee or White/Gray wire on Grand Cherokee between terminals No. 6 at CCD bus diagnostic connector and No. 42 at ABS controller connector. If resistance is more than 5 ohms, repair open White/Black or White/Gray wire. Perform VERIFICATION TEST.

4) If resistance is less than 5 ohms, disconnect Single Board Engine Controller (SBEC) connector. Check connector and clean or repair connector as necessary. Using an external ohmmeter, check resistance between terminals No. 26 and 46 at SBEC. If resistance is not 100-140 ohms, replace SBEC. Perform VERIFICATION TEST.

5) If resistance is 100-140 ohms, check resistance at White/Black wire on Cherokee or White/Gray wire on Grand Cherokee between terminals No. 6 at CCD bus diagnostic connector and No. 46 at SBEC connector. If resistance is more than 5 ohms, repair open White/Black or White/Gray wire. Perform VERIFICATION TEST.

6) If resistance is less than 5 ohms, disconnect vehicle theft module (if equipped). On Cherokee, module is located to right of steering column. On Grand Cherokee, module is located behind glove box. On all models, check connector condition and clean or repair connector as necessary. Check resistance between terminals No. 1 and 2 of vehicle theft alarm module.

7) If resistance is not 100-140 ohms, replace vehicle theft alarm module. Perform VERIFICATION TEST. If resistance is 100-140 ohms, check resistance at White/Black wire on Cherokee or White/Gray wire on Grand Cherokee between terminals No. 6 at CCD bus diagnostic connector and No. 1 of vehicle theft alarm module connector.

8) If resistance is more than 5 ohms, repair open White/Black or White/Gray wire. Perform VERIFICATION TEST. If resistance is less than 5 ohms, perform TEST 20A.

TEST 14A

BUS BIAS LEVEL TOO HIGH ON BUS

NOTE: For connector terminal identification, see BODY CONTROL SYSTEM CONNECTORS under DIAGNOSTIC PROCEDURE. For wiring diagrams, see appropriate chassis wiring diagram in WIRING DIAGRAMS.

1) Turn ignition switch to ON position. Disconnect DRB-II. Using an external voltmeter, check voltage at terminal No. 1 (Violet/Brown wire) at CCD bus diagnostic connector. If voltage is not 2.1-2.7 volts, proceed to step 3).

2) If voltage is 2.1-2.7 volts, check voltage at terminal No. 6 (White/Black wire on Cherokee or White/Gray wire on Grand Cherokee) at CCD bus diagnostic connector. If voltage is not 2.1-2.7 volts, perform TEST 14B. If voltage is 2.1-2.7 volts, test DRB-II. Refer to TEST 5A. Perform VERIFICATION TEST.

3) If voltage at Violet/Brown wire is not 2.1-2.7 volts in step 1), turn ignition switch to OFF position. Disconnect Anti-Lock Brake System (ABS) controller connector (if equipped). On Cherokee, controller is located to right of steering column. On Grand Cherokee, controller is located in left front of engine compartment.

4) On all models, check connector condition and clean or repair connector as necessary. Using an external ohmmeter, check resistance between terminals No. 23 and 42 at ABS controller. If resistance is not 100-140 ohms, replace ABS controller. Perform VERIFICATION TEST. If resistance is 100-140 ohms, go to next step.

5) Check resistance at Violet/Brown wire between terminals No. 1 at CCD bus diagnostic connector and No. 23 at ABS controller connector. If resistance is more than 5 ohms, repair open Violet/Brown wire. Perform VERIFICATION TEST. If resistance is less than 5 ohms, go to next step.

6) Disconnect Single Board Engine Controller (SBEC) connector. Check connector condition and clean or repair connector as necessary. Check resistance between terminals No. 26 and 46 at SBEC. If resistance is not 100-140 ohms, replace SBEC. Perform VERIFICATION TEST.

7) If resistance is 100-140 ohms, check resistance at Violet/Brown wire between terminals No. 1 at CCD bus diagnostic connector and No. 26 at SBEC connector. If resistance is more than 5 ohms, repair open Violet/Brown wire. Perform VERIFICATION TEST. If resistance is less than 5 ohms, disconnect vehicle theft module (if equipped).

8) On Cherokee, module is located to right of steering column. On Grand Cherokee, module is located behind glove box. On all models, check connector condition and clean or repair connector as necessary. Check resistance between terminals No. 1 and 2 of vehicle theft alarm module.

9) If resistance is not 100-140 ohms, replace vehicle theft alarm module. Perform VERIFICATION TEST. If resistance is 100-140 ohms, check resistance at Violet/Brown wire between terminals No. 1 at CCD bus diagnostic connector and No. 2 of vehicle theft alarm module connector.

10) If resistance is more than 5 ohms, repair open Violet/Brown wire. Perform VERIFICATION TEST. If resistance is less than 5 ohms, perform TEST 20A.

TEST 14B

BUS BIAS LEVEL TOO HIGH ON BUS

NOTE: For connector terminal identification, see BODY CONTROL SYSTEM CONNECTORS under DIAGNOSTIC PROCEDURE. For wiring diagrams, see appropriate chassis wiring diagram in WIRING DIAGRAMS.

1) Turn ignition switch to OFF position. Disconnect Anti-Lock Brake System (ABS) controller connector (if equipped). On Cherokee, controller is located to right of steering column. On Grand Cherokee, controller is located in left front of engine compartment.

2) On all models, check connector condition and clean or repair connector as necessary. Using an external ohmmeter, check resistance between terminals No. 23 and 42 at ABS controller. If resistance is not 100-140 ohms, replace ABS controller. Perform VERIFICATION TEST.

3) If resistance is 100-140 ohms, check resistance at White/Black wire on Cherokee or White/Gray wire on Grand Cherokee between terminals No. 6 at CCD bus diagnostic connector and No. 42 of ABS controller connector. If resistance is more than 5 ohms, repair open White/Black or White/Gray wire. Perform VERIFICATION TEST. If resistance is less than 5 ohms, go to next step.

TEST 14B (Cont.)

4) Disconnect Single Board Engine Controller (SBEC) connector. Check connector condition and clean or repair connector as necessary. Using an external ohmmeter, check resistance between terminals No. 26 and No. 46 at SBEC. If resistance is not 100-140 ohms, replace SBEC. Perform VERIFICATION TEST.

5) If resistance is 100-140 ohms, check resistance at White/Black wire on Cherokee or White/Gray wire on Grand Cherokee between terminals No. 6 at CCD bus diagnostic connector and No. 46 at SBEC connector. If resistance is more than 5 ohms, repair open White/Black or White/Gray wire. Perform VERIFICATION TEST. If resistance is less than 5 ohms, go to next step.

6) Disconnect vehicle theft module (if equipped). On Cherokee, module is located to right of steering column. On Grand Cherokee, module is located behind glove box. On all models, check connector condition and clean or repair connector as necessary. Check resistance between terminals No. 1 and 2 of vehicle theft alarm module.

7) If resistance is not 100-140 ohms, replace vehicle theft alarm module. Perform VERIFICATION TEST. If resistance is 100-140 ohms, check resistance at White/Black wire on Cherokee or White/Gray wire on Grand Cherokee between terminals No. 6 at CCD bus diagnostic connector and No. 1 of vehicle theft alarm module connector.

8) If resistance is more than 5 ohms, repair open White/Black or White/Gray wire. Perform VERIFICATION TEST. If resistance is less than 5 ohms, perform TEST 20A.

TEST 15A

NO BUS BIAS ON BUS

NOTE: For connector terminal identification, see BODY CONTROL SYSTEM CONNECTORS under DIAGNOSTIC PROCEDURE. For wiring diagrams, see appropriate chassis wiring diagram in WIRING DIAGRAMS.

1) If DRB-II is not connected to correct diagnostic connector, connect DRB-II to CCD bus diagnostic connector. Perform VERIFICATION TEST. If DRB-II is connected to CCD bus diagnostic connector, turn ignition switch to OFF position. Disconnect Anti-Lock Brake System (ABS) controller connector (if equipped). On Cherokee, controller is located to right of steering column. On Grand Cherokee, controller is located in left front of engine compartment.

2) On all models check connector condition and clean or repair connector as necessary. Using an external ohmmeter, check resistance between terminals No. 23 and 42 of ABS controller. If resistance is not 100-140 ohms, replace ABS controller. Perform VERIFICATION TEST. If resistance is 100-140 ohms, go to next step.

3) Check resistance at Violet/Brown wire between terminals No. 1 at CCD bus diagnostic connector and No. 23 of ABS controller connector. If resistance is more than 5 ohms, repair open Violet/Brown wire and go to next step. If resistance is less than 5 ohms, go to next step.

4) Check resistance of White/Black wire on Cherokee or White/Gray wire on Grand Cherokee between terminals No. 6 at CCD bus diagnostic connector and No. 42 of ABS controller connector. If resistance is more than 5 ohms, repair open White/Black or White/Gray wire. Perform VERIFICATION TEST. If resistance is less than 5 ohms, go to next step.

5) Disconnect Single Board Engine Controller (SBEC) connector. Check connector condition and repair or replace connector as necessary. Using an external ohmmeter, check resistance between terminals No. 26 and No. 46 at SBEC.

6) If resistance is not 100-140 ohms, replace SBEC. Perform VERIFICATION TEST. If resistance is 100-140 ohms, check resistance at Violet/Brown wire between terminals No. 1 at CCD bus diagnostic connector and No. 26 at SBEC connector. If resistance is more than 5 ohms, repair open Violet/Brown wire and go to next step. If resistance is less than 5 ohms, go to next step.

7) Check resistance at White/Black wire on Cherokee or White/Gray wire on Grand Cherokee between terminals No. 6 at CCD bus diagnostic connector and No. 46 at SBEC connector. If resistance is more than 5 ohms, repair open White/Black or White/Gray wire. Perform VERIFICATION TEST. If resistance is less than 5 ohms, go to next step.

8) Disconnect vehicle theft module (if equipped). On Cherokee, module is located to right of steering column. On Grand Cherokee, module is located behind glove box. On all models, check connector condition and clean or repair connector as necessary. Check resistance between terminals No. 1 and 2 of vehicle theft alarm module.

TEST 15A (Cont.)

9) If resistance is not 100-140 ohms, replace vehicle theft alarm module. Perform VERIFICATION TEST. If resistance is 100-140 ohms, check resistance at Violet/Brown wire between terminals No. 1 at CCD bus diagnostic connector and No. 2 of vehicle theft alarm module connector. If resistance is more than 5 ohms, repair open Violet/Brown wire and go to next step. If resistance is less than 5 ohms, go to next step.

10) Check resistance at White/Black wire on Cherokee or White/Gray wire on Grand Cherokee between terminals No. 6 at CCD bus diagnostic connector and No. 1 of vehicle theft alarm module connector. If resistance is more than 5 ohms, repair open White/Black or White/Gray wire. Perform VERIFICATION TEST.

11) If resistance is less than 5 ohms, test DRB-II. Refer to TEST 5A. Replace DRB-II and/or adapter cable as necessary. Perform VERIFICATION TEST. If DRB-II and adapter cable are good, perform TEST 20A.

TEST 16A

BUS (+) OPEN ON BUS

NOTE: For connector terminal identification, see BODY CONTROL SYSTEM CONNECTORS under DIAGNOSTIC PROCEDURE. For wiring diagrams, see appropriate chassis wiring diagram in WIRING DIAGRAMS.

1) If DRB-II is not connected to correct diagnostic connector, connect DRB-II to CCD bus diagnostic connector. Perform VERIFICATION TEST. If DRB-II is connected to CCD bus diagnostic connector, turn ignition switch to OFF position. Disconnect Anti-Lock Brake System (ABS) controller connector (if equipped). On Cherokee, controller is located to right of steering column. On Grand Cherokee, controller is located in left front of engine compartment.

2) On all models, check connector condition and clean or repair connector as necessary. Using an external ohmmeter, check resistance between terminals No. 23 and 42 of ABS controller. If resistance is not 100-140 ohms, replace ABS controller. Perform VERIFICATION TEST.

3) If resistance is 100-140 ohms, check resistance at Violet/Brown wire between terminals No. 1 at CCD bus diagnostic connector and No. 23 of ABS controller connector. If resistance is more than 5 ohms, repair open Violet/Brown wire and go to next step. If resistance is less than 5 ohms, go to next step.

4) Using an external ohmmeter, check resistance of White/Black wire on Cherokee or White/Gray wire on Grand Cherokee between terminals No. 42 of ABS controller connector and No. 6 of CCD bus diagnostic connector. If resistance is more than 5 ohms, repair open White/Black or White/Gray wire. Perform VERIFICATION TEST.

5) If resistance is less than 5 ohms, disconnect Single Board Engine Controller (SBEC) connector. Check connector condition and clean or repair connector as necessary. Using an external ohmmeter, check resistance between terminals No. 26 and No. 46 at SBEC.

6) If resistance is not 100-140 ohms, replace SBEC. Perform VERIFICATION TEST. If resistance is 100-140 ohms, check resistance at Violet/Brown wire between terminals No. 1 at CCD bus diagnostic connector and No. 26 at SBEC connector. If resistance is more than 5 ohms, repair open Violet/Brown wire and go to next step. If resistance is less than 5 ohms, go to next step.

7) Check resistance at White/Black wire on Cherokee or White/Gray wire on Grand Cherokee between terminals No. 6 at CCD bus diagnostic connector and No. 46 at SBEC connector. If resistance is more than 5 ohms, repair open White/Black or White/Gray wire. Perform VERIFICATION TEST.

8) If resistance is less than 5 ohms, disconnect vehicle theft module (if equipped). On Cherokee, module is located to right of steering column. On Grand Cherokee, module is located behind glove box. On all models, check connector condition and clean or repair connector as necessary. Check resistance between terminals No. 1 and 2 of vehicle theft module.

9) If resistance is not 100-140 ohms, replace vehicle theft alarm module. Perform VERIFICATION TEST. If resistance is 100-140 ohms, check resistance at Violet/Brown wire between terminals No. 1 at CCD bus diagnostic connector and No. 2 of vehicle theft alarm module connector. If resistance is more than 5 ohms, repair open Violet/Brown wire and go to next step. If resistance is less than 5 ohms, go to next step.

TEST 16A (Cont.)

10) Check resistance at White/Black wire on Cherokee or White/Gray wire on Grand Cherokee between terminals No. 6 at CCD bus diagnostic connector and No. 1 of vehicle theft alarm module connector. If resistance is more than 5 ohms, repair open White/Black or White/Gray wire. Perform VERIFICATION TEST.

11) If resistance is less than 5 ohms, test DRB-II. Refer to TEST 5A. Replace DRB-II and/or adapter cable as necessary. Perform VERIFICATION TEST. If DRB-II and adapter cable are good, perform TEST 20A.

TEST 17A

BUS (-) OPEN ON BUS

NOTE: For connector terminal identification, see BODY CONTROL SYSTEM CONNECTORS under DIAGNOSTIC PROCEDURE. For wiring diagrams, see appropriate chassis wiring diagram in WIRING DIAGRAMS.

1) If DRB-II is not connected to correct diagnostic connector, connect DRB-II to CCD bus diagnostic connector. Perform VERIFICATION TEST. If DRB-II is connected to CCD bus diagnostic connector, turn ignition switch to OFF position. Disconnect Anti-Lock Brake System (ABS) controller connector (if equipped). On Cherokee, controller is located to right of steering column. On Grand Cherokee, controller is located in left front of engine compartment.

2) On all models check connector condition and clean or repair connector as necessary. Using an external ohmmeter, check resistance between terminals No. 23 and 42 of ABS controller. If resistance is not 100-140 ohms, replace ABS controller. Perform VERIFICATION TEST.

3) If resistance is 100-140 ohms, check resistance at Violet/Brown wire between terminals No. 1 at CCD bus diagnostic connector and No. 23 of ABS controller connector. If resistance is more than 5 ohms, repair open Violet/Brown wire and go to next step. If resistance is less than 5 ohms, go to next step.

4) Check resistance of White/Black wire on Cherokee or White/Gray wire on Grand Cherokee between terminals No. 6 at CCD bus diagnostic connector and No. 42 of ABS controller connector. If resistance is more than 5 ohms, repair open White/Black or White/Gray wire. Perform VERIFICATION TEST.

5) If resistance is less than 5 ohms, disconnect Single Board Engine Controller (SBEC) connector. Check connector condition and clean or repair connector as necessary. Using an external ohmmeter, check resistance between terminals No. 26 and No. 46 at SBEC. If resistance is not 100-140 ohms, replace SBEC. Perform VERIFICATION TEST. If resistance is 100-140 ohms, go to next step.

6) Check resistance at Violet/Brown wire between terminals No. 1 at CCD bus diagnostic connector and No. 26 at SBEC connector. If resistance is more than 5 ohms, repair open Violet/Brown wire and go to next step. If resistance is less than 5 ohms, go to next step.

7) Check resistance at White/Black wire on Cherokee or White/Gray wire on Grand Cherokee between terminals No. 6 at CCD bus diagnostic connector and No. 46 at SBEC connector. If resistance is more than 5 ohms, repair open White/Black or White/Gray wire. Perform VERIFICATION TEST.

8) If resistance is less than 5 ohms, disconnect vehicle theft module (if equipped). On Cherokee, module is located to right of steering column. On Grand Cherokee, module is located behind glove box. On all models, check connector condition and clean or repair connector as necessary. Check resistance between terminals No. 1 and 2 of vehicle theft alarm module.

9) If resistance is not 100-140 ohms, replace vehicle theft alarm module. Perform VERIFICATION TEST. If resistance is 100-140 ohms, check resistance at Violet/Brown wire between terminals No. 1 at CCD bus diagnostic connector and No. 2 of vehicle theft alarm module connector. If resistance is more than 5 ohms, repair open Violet/Brown wire and go to next step. If resistance is less than 5 ohms, go to next step.

10) Check resistance at White/Black wire on Cherokee or White/Gray wire on Grand Cherokee between terminals No. 6 at CCD bus diagnostic connector and No. 1 of vehicle theft alarm module connector. If resistance is more than 5 ohms, repair open White/Black or White/Gray wire. Perform VERIFICATION TEST.

11) If resistance is less than 5 ohms, test DRB-II. Refer to TEST 5A. Replace DRB-II and/or adapter cable as necessary. Perform VERIFICATION TEST. If DRB-II and adapter cable are good, perform TEST 20A.

TEST 18A

BUS (+) & BUS (-) OPEN ON BUS

NOTE: For connector terminal identification, see BODY CONTROL SYSTEM CONNECTORS under DIAGNOSTIC PROCEDURE. For wiring diagrams, see appropriate chassis wiring diagram in WIRING DIAGRAMS.

1) If DRB-II is not connected to correct diagnostic connector, connect DRB-II to CCD bus diagnostic connector. Perform VERIFICATION TEST. If DRB-II is connected to CCD bus diagnostic connector, turn ignition switch to OFF position. Disconnect Anti-Lock Brake System (ABS) controller connector (if equipped). On Cherokee, controller is located to right of steering column. On Grand Cherokee, controller is located in left front of engine compartment.

2) On all models, check connector condition and clean or repair connector as necessary. Using an external ohmmeter, check resistance between terminals No. 23 and 42 of ABS controller. If resistance is not 100-140 ohms, replace ABS controller. Perform VERIFICATION TEST.

3) If resistance is 100-140 ohms, check resistance at Violet/Brown wire between terminals No. 1 at CCD bus diagnostic connector and No. 23 of ABS controller connector. If resistance is more than 5 ohms, repair open Violet/Brown wire and go to next step. If resistance is less than 5 ohms, go to next step.

4) Check resistance of White/Black wire on Cherokee or White/Gray wire on Grand Cherokee between terminals No. 6 at CCD bus diagnostic connector and No. 42 of ABS controller connector. If resistance is more than 5 ohms, repair open White/Black or White/Gray wire. Perform VERIFICATION TEST. If resistance is less than 5 ohms, go to next step.

5) Disconnect Single Board Engine Controller (SBEC) connector. Check connector condition and clean or repair connector as necessary. Using an external ohmmeter, check resistance between terminals No. 26 and 46 at SBEC. If resistance is not 100-140 ohms, replace SBEC. Perform VERIFICATION TEST. If resistance is 100-140 ohms, go to next step.

6) Check resistance at Violet/Brown wire between terminals No. 1 at CCD bus diagnostic connector and No. 26 at SBEC connector. If resistance is more than 5 ohms, repair open Violet/Brown wire and go to next step. If resistance is less than 5 ohms, go to next step.

7) Check resistance at White/Black wire on Cherokee or White/Gray wire on Grand Cherokee between terminals No. 6 at CCD bus diagnostic connector and No. 46 at SBEC connector. If resistance is more than 5 ohms, repair open White/Black or White/Gray wire. Perform VERIFICATION TEST.

8) If resistance is less than 5 ohms, disconnect vehicle theft module (if equipped). On Cherokee, module is located to right of steering column. On Grand Cherokee, module is located behind glove box. On all models, check connector condition and clean or repair connector as necessary. Check resistance between terminals No. 1 and 2 of vehicle theft alarm module.

9) If resistance is not 100-140 ohms, replace vehicle theft alarm module. Perform VERIFICATION TEST. If resistance is 100-140 ohms, check resistance at Violet/Brown wire between terminals No. 1 at CCD bus diagnostic connector and No. 2 of vehicle theft alarm module connector. If resistance is more than 5 ohms, repair open Violet/Brown wire and go to next step. If resistance is less than 5 ohms, go to next step.

10) Check resistance at White/Black wire on Cherokee or White/Gray wire on Grand Cherokee between terminals No. 6 at CCD bus diagnostic connector and No. 1 of vehicle theft alarm module connector. If resistance is more than 5 ohms, repair open White/Black or White/Gray wire. Perform VERIFICATION TEST.

11) If resistance is less than 5 ohms, test DRB-II. Refer to TEST 5A. Replace DRB-II and/or adapter cable as necessary. Perform VERIFICATION TEST. If DRB-II and adapter cable are good, perform TEST 20A.

TEST 19A

NOT RECEIVING BUS MESSAGES CORRECTLY ON BUS

NOTE: For connector terminal identification, see BODY CONTROL SYSTEM CONNECTORS under DIAGNOSTIC PROCEDURE. For wiring diagrams, see appropriate chassis wiring diagram in WIRING DIAGRAMS.

1) If DRB-II is not connected to correct diagnostic connector, connect DRB-II to CCD bus diagnostic connector. Perform VERIFICATION TEST. If DRB-II is connected to CCD bus diagnostic connector, turn ignition switch to OFF position. Disconnect Anti-Lock Brake System (ABS) controller connector (if equipped). On Cherokee, controller is located to right of steering column. On Grand Cherokee, controller is located in left front of engine compartment.

2) On all models, check connector condition and clean or repair connector as necessary. Using an external ohmmeter, check resistance between terminals No. 23 and 42 of ABS controller. If resistance is not 100-140 ohms, replace ABS controller. Perform VERIFICATION TEST.

3) If resistance is 100-140 ohms, check resistance at Violet/Brown wire between terminals No. 1 at CCD bus diagnostic connector and No. 23 of ABS controller connector. If resistance is more than 5 ohms, repair open Violet/Brown wire and go to next step. If resistance is less than 5 ohms, go to next step.

4) Check resistance of White/Black wire on Cherokee or White/Gray wire on Grand Cherokee between terminals No. 6 at CCD bus diagnostic connector and No. 42 of ABS controller connector. If resistance is more than 5 ohms, repair open White/Black or White/Gray wire. Perform VERIFICATION TEST. If resistance is less than 5 ohms, go to next step.

5) Disconnect Single Board Engine Controller (SBEC) connector. Check connector condition and clean or repair connector as necessary. Using an external ohmmeter, check resistance between terminals No. 26 and 46 at SBEC. If resistance is not 100-140 ohms, replace SBEC. Perform VERIFICATION TEST. If resistance is 100-140 ohms, go to next step.

6) Check resistance at Violet/Brown wire between terminals No. 1 at CCD bus diagnostic connector and No. 26 at SBEC connector. If resistance is more than 5 ohms, repair open Violet/Brown wire and go to next step. If resistance is less than 5 ohms, go to next step.

7) Check resistance at White/Black wire on Cherokee or White/Gray wire on Grand Cherokee between terminals No. 6 at CCD bus diagnostic connector and No. 46 at SBEC connector. If resistance is more than 5 ohms, repair open White/Black or White/Gray wire. Perform VERIFICATION TEST.

8) If resistance is less than 5 ohms, disconnect vehicle theft module (if equipped). On Cherokee, module is located to right of steering column. On Grand Cherokee, module is located behind glove box. On all models, check connector condition and clean or repair connector as necessary. Check resistance between terminals No. 1 and 2 of vehicle theft alarm module.

9) If resistance is not 100-140 ohms, replace vehicle theft alarm module. Perform VERIFICATION TEST. If resistance is 100-140 ohms, check resistance at Violet/Brown wire between terminals No. 1 at CCD bus diagnostic connector and No. 2 of vehicle theft alarm module connector. If resistance is more than 5 ohms, repair open Violet/Brown wire and go to next step. If resistance is less than 5 ohms, go to next step.

10) Check resistance at White/Black wire on Cherokee or White/Gray wire on Grand Cherokee between terminals No. 6 at CCD bus diagnostic connector and No. 1 of vehicle theft alarm module connector. If resistance is more than 5 ohms, repair open White/Black or White/Gray wire. Perform VERIFICATION TEST.

11) If resistance is less than 5 ohms, test DRB-II. Refer to TEST 5A. Replace DRB-II and/or adapter cable as necessary. Perform VERIFICATION TEST. If DRB-II and adapter cable are good, perform TEST 20A.

TEST 20A

NO RESPONSE MESSAGES

NOTE: For connector terminal identification, see BODY CONTROL SYSTEM CONNECTORS under DIAGNOSTIC PROCEDURE. For wiring diagrams, see appropriate chassis wiring diagram in WIRING DIAGRAMS.

There are 3 ways to get to this test:

1) The DRB-II is currently connected to the CCD bus diagnostic connector and you have selected ENGINE from the main menu. Perform VERIFICATION TEST.

2) A self-diagnostic test brought you here.

3) The DRB-II displayed NO RESPONSE message when an attempt was made to read information from a module. Perform VERIFICATION TEST.

NOTE: It is possible to monitor the SBEC for an ACTIVE ON BUS message only at the CCD bus diagnostics connector. Monitor the SBEC for a NO RESPONSE message by selecting SYSTEM TEST under any of the module test selection menus.

If step 1) is the reason you came to this test, you must either select an appropriate selection from the DRB-II menu (BODY, ABS, OR TRANSMISSION) or, if you want to perform engine tests, connect DRB-II to the engine diagnostic connector located in the engine compartment.

If step 2) is the reason you came to this test, you must verify that you can access all the modules that are on the vehicle. Perform tests as necessary. See NO RESPONSE MESSAGE table.

NO RESPONSE MESSAGE

Module	Test No.
Compass/Mini-Trip Module	21A
Single Board Engine Controller	22A

If step 3) is the reason you came to this test, perform test as necessary in the order than they appear. See NO RESPONSE MESSAGE table. The DRB-II will also show a NO RESPONSE message when you are trying to access a module that is not on the vehicle.

TEST 21A

TESTING COMPASS/MINI-TRIP MODULE FOR NO RESPONSE

NOTE: For connector terminal identification, see BODY CONTROL SYSTEM CONNECTORS under DIAGNOSTIC PROCEDURE. For wiring diagrams, see appropriate chassis wiring diagram in WIRING DIAGRAMS.

1) Turn ignition switch to OFF position. Disconnect compass/mini-trip module connector. Connector is located in overhead console. Check connector condition and clean or repair connector as necessary. Turn ignition switch to ON position. Put DRB-II in voltmeter mode. Measure voltage at terminal No. 7 (Yellow/Dark Green wire) of compass/mini-trip module connector.

2) If voltage is more than 10 volts, replace compass/mini-trip module. Perform VERIFICATION TEST. If voltage is less than 10 volts, remove and inspect fuse No. 19 from fuse block. If fuse is blown, go to step 4). If fuse is okay, probe input terminal (in fuse block) to fuse No. 19.

3) If voltage is more than 10 volts, repair open in Yellow/Dark/Green wire between fuse block and compass/mini-trip connector. Perform VERIFICATION TEST. If voltage is less than 10 volts, repair open Orange/Black wire between ignition switch and fuse block. Perform VERIFICATION TEST.

4) Put DRB-II in ohmmeter mode. Probe output terminal (in fuse block) from fuse No. 19. If resistance is less than 5 ohms, repair short to ground in Yellow/Dark Green wire and replace fuse No. 19. Perform VERIFICATION TEST. If resistance is more than 5 ohms, replace fuse No. 19. Reconnect compass/mini-trip module connector.

5) Turn ignition switch to On position. Remove and recheck fuse No. 19. If fuse is blown, replace compass/mini-trip module. Perform VERIFICATION TEST. If fuse is okay, repair is complete. Perform VERIFICATION TEST.

TEST 21B

TESTING COMPASS/MINI-TRIP MODULE FOR NO RESPONSE

NOTE: For connector terminal identification, see BODY CONTROL SYSTEM CONNECTORS under DIAGNOSTIC PROCEDURE. For wiring diagrams, see appropriate chassis wiring diagram in WIRING DIAGRAMS.

1) Turn ignition switch to OFF position. Put DRB-II in ohmmeter mode. Probe terminal No. 5 (Black/Orange wire) of compass/mini-trip module connector. If resistance is more than 5 ohms, repair open Black/Orange wire. Perform VERIFICATION TEST. If resistance is less than 5 ohms, disconnect DRB-II.

2) Using an external ohmmeter, check resistance at Violet/Brown wire between terminals No. 1 of CCD bus diagnostic connector and No. 12 of compass/mini-trip module connector. If resistance is more than 5 ohms, repair open in Violet/Brown wire. Perform VERIFICATION TEST.

3) If resistance is less than 5 ohms, check resistance between terminals No. 6 (White/Black wire on Cherokee or White/Gray wire on Grand Cherokee) of CCD bus diagnostic connector and No. 11 (White/Black wire) of compass/mini-trip module connector. If resistance is more than 5 ohms, repair open in White/Black or White/Gray wire. Perform VERIFICATION TEST. If resistance is less than 5 ohms, replace compass/mini-trip module. Perform VERIFICATION TEST.

TEST 22A

TESTING BODY CONTROLLER FOR NO RESPONSE

NOTE: For connector terminal identification, see BODY CONTROL SYSTEM CONNECTORS under DIAGNOSTIC PROCEDURE. For wiring diagrams, see appropriate chassis wiring diagram in WIRING DIAGRAMS.

1) Turn ignition switch to OFF position. Disconnect Single Board Engine Controller (SBEC) connector. Check connector condition and clean or repair connector as necessary. Using an external ohmmeter, check resistance between terminals No. 26 and 46 at SBEC. If resistance is not 100-140 ohms, replace SBEC. Perform VERIFICATION TEST.

2) If resistance is 100-140 ohms, check resistance at Violet/Brown wire between terminals No. 1 at CCD bus diagnostic connector and No. 26 at SBEC connector. If resistance is more than 5 ohms, repair open Violet/Brown wire. Perform VERIFICATION TEST. If resistance is less than 5 ohms, go to next step.

3) Check resistance at White/Black wire on Cherokee or White/Gray wire on Grand Cherokee between terminals No. 6 at CCD bus diagnostic connector and No. 46 at SBEC connector. If resistance is more than 5 ohms, repair open White/Black or White/Gray wire. Perform VERIFICATION TEST. If resistance is less than 5 ohms, replace SBEC. Perform VERIFICATION TEST.

1992 ENGINE PERFORMANCE
Trouble Shooting – No Codes

Cherokee, Comanche, Grand Cherokee (1993), Wrangler

INTRODUCTION

Before diagnosing symptoms or intermittent faults, perform steps in BASIC DIAGNOSTIC PROCEDURES and SELF-DIAGNOSTICS articles. Use this article to diagnose driveability problems existing when a hard fault code is not present or vehicle is not equipped with a self-diagnostic system.

NOTE: *Some manufacturer driveability problems may have been corrected by manufacturer with a revised computer calibration chip or computer control unit. Check with manufacturer for latest chip or computer application.*

Symptom checks can direct the technician to malfunctioning component(s) for further diagnosis. A symptom should lead to a specific component, system test or an adjustment.

Use intermittent test procedures to locate driveability problems that do not occur when the vehicle is being tested. These test procedures should also be used if a soft (intermittent) trouble code was present, but no problem was found during self-diagnostic testing.

NOTE: *For specific testing procedures, see SYSTEM & COMPONENT TESTING - FUEL INJECTED article. For specifications, see ON-VEHICLE ADJUSTMENTS or SERVICE & ADJUSTMENT SPECIFICATIONS article.*

SYMPTOMS

SYMPTOM DIAGNOSIS

Symptom checks cannot be used properly unless problem occurs while vehicle is being tested. To reduce diagnostic time, ensure steps in BASIC DIAGNOSTIC PROCEDURES and SELF-DIAGNOSTICS articles were performed before diagnosing a symptom. Following are some symptoms available for diagnosis.

- Engine Does Not Operate Smoothly Or Misfires At High Speed
- Engine Fails To Start, No Spark At Plugs
- Engine Backfires, Fails To Start
- Engine Continues To Run With Key Off
- Engine Runs Only With Key In Start Position
- Excessive Fuel Consumption
- Intermittent Spark

ENGINE DOES NOT OPERATE SMOOTHLY OR MISFIRES AT HIGH SPEED

- Ensure distributor cap is dry inside.
- Ensure distributor cap is not cracked or carbon tracked.
- Check spark plugs.
- Check ignition system wires and connections.
- See BASIC DIAGNOSTIC PROCEDURES article.

ENGINE FAILS TO START, NO SPARK AT PLUGS

- Ensure distributor cap is not cracked or carbon tracked.
- Check for defective rotor.
- Check for corroded wires and connections.
- See BASIC DIAGNOSTIC PROCEDURES article.

ENGINE BACKFIRES, FAILS TO START

- Ensure distributor cap is not cracked or carbon tracked.
- Ensure ignition wires are connected in proper firing order.
- Check for moisture in distributor cap.
- See BASIC DIAGNOSTIC PROCEDURES article.

ENGINE CONTINUES TO RUN WITH KEY OFF

- Check for defective starter motor solenoid.
- Check for shorted diode in alternator warning light circuit.
- See SYSTEM & COMPONENT TESTING article.

ENGINE RUNS ONLY WITH KEY IN START POSITION

- See SYSTEM & COMPONENT TESTING article.

EXCESSIVE FUEL CONSUMPTION

- Check for vacuum leaks.
- Check air filter.
- See BASIC DIAGNOSTIC PROCEDURES article.
- See SYSTEM & COMPONENT TESTING article.

INTERMITTENT SPARK

- Check for loose or corroded distributor and coil terminals.
- See BASIC DIAGNOSTIC PROCEDURES article.

INTERMITTENTS

INTERMITTENT PROBLEM DIAGNOSIS

Intermittent fault testing requires duplicating circuit or component failure to identify the problem. These procedures may lead to the computer setting a fault code (on some systems) which may help in diagnosis.

If problem vehicle does not produce fault codes, monitor voltage or resistance values using a DVOM, while attempting to reproduce conditions causing intermittent fault. A change in status on DVOM will indicate a fault has been located.

Use a DVOM to pinpoint faults. When monitoring voltage, ensure ignition switch is in ON position or engine is running. Ensure ignition switch is in OFF position or negative battery cable is disconnected when monitoring circuit resistance. Status changes on DVOM during test procedures will indicate area of fault.

TEST PROCEDURES

Intermittent Simulation – To reproduce conditions creating an intermittent fault, use following methods:
- Lightly vibrate component.
- Heat component.
- Wiggle or bend wiring harness.
- Spray component with water.
- Remove/apply vacuum source.

Monitor circuit/component voltage or resistance while simulating intermittent. If engine is running, monitor for self-diagnostic codes. Use test results to identify a faulty component or circuit.

Cherokee, Comanche, Grand Cherokee (1993), Wrangler

INTRODUCTION

Before testing separate components or systems, perform procedures in BASIC DIAGNOSTIC PROCEDURES article. Since many computer-controlled and monitored components set a trouble code if they malfunction, also perform procedures in SELF-DIAGNOSTICS article.

NOTE: Testing individual components does not isolate possible short or open circuits. Perform all voltage tests with a Digital Volt-Ohmmeter (DVOM) with a minimum 10-megohm input impedance, unless stated otherwise in test procedure. Use ohmmeter to isolate wiring harness short or open circuits.

COMPUTERIZED ENGINE CONTROLS

SINGLE BOARD ENGINE CONTROLLER

Power & Ground Circuits – Check power and ground circuits using a DVOM and appropriate wiring diagram in WIRING DIAGRAMS article.

ENGINE SENSORS & SWITCHES

Camshaft Position Sensor (Synchronization Signal Generator) – **1)** Use an analog voltmeter. DO NOT remove distributor connector from distributor. Insert voltmeter leads into backside of distributor wiring harness connector to make contact with terminals. Ensure that connector is not damaged when inserting test probes.
2) Insert positive voltmeter lead into synchronization signal output Tan/Yellow wire on Cherokee and Comanche (Gray/Black wire on Grand Cherokee and Wrangler) at distributor wiring harness connector.
3) Insert negative voltmeter lead into ground Black/Blue wire (Brown/Red wire on Wrangler) at distributor wiring harness connector. Set voltmeter to 15-volt DC scale.
4) With distributor cap removed, manually rotate engine until pulse ring enters sync signal generator. Turn ignition switch to ON position. With pulse positioned in the sync generator, reading should be about 5 volts.
5) If no voltage is indicated, check voltmeter leads for good connections If connections are okay and there is still no voltage, check for voltage at Orange supply wire on Cherokee and Comanche (White/Black wire on Grand Cherokee and Wrangler).
6) If no voltage is indicated at supply wire, remove engine controller and check voltage at pin No. 7. Engine controller is located on left side of engine compartment. If there is no voltage at engine controller, see appropriate synchronization sensor/circuit tests in SELF-DIAGNOSTICS article.
7) If voltage is indicated at engine controller pin No. 7, but not at supply wire, check continuity of supply wire between the distributor connector and the engine controller. If no continuity exists, repair wiring harness as necessary.
8) If supply wire is okay, check continuity between sync signal output wire at the distributor connector and pin No. 44 at engine controller. If no continuity exists, repair wiring harness as necessary.
9) If sync signal output wire is okay, check continuity between ground circuit wire at the distributor connector and ground. If no continuity exists, repair wiring harness as necessary. If ground wire is okay, go to next step.
10) While observing voltmeter, crank engine. Voltmeter needle should fluctuate from 0-5 volts while the engine is cranking. This verifies that stator in distributor is operating properly and that a sync (pulse) signal is being generated. If voltmeter does not fluctuate, replace synch sensor stator.

Charge Air Temperature Sensor (Grand Cherokee) – See MANIFOLD AIR TEMPERATURE (MAT) SENSOR.

Coolant Temperature Sensor – **1)** Disconnect coolant temperature sensor. Using DVOM, check sensor resistance. Resistance should be as specified in COOLANT TEMPERATURE SENSOR & MANIFOLD AIR TEMPERATURE SENSOR RESISTANCE table. Replace sensor if necessary.
2) Check continuity between engine controller wiring harness terminal No. 2 and sensor connector terminal. Also check continuity between engine controller wiring harness terminal No. 4 and sensor connector terminal. Repair wiring if an open circuit is indicated.

NOTE: Also see appropriate coolant temperature sensor tests in SELF-DIAGNOSTICS article.

COOLANT TEMPERATURE SENSOR & MANIFOLD AIR TEMPERATURE SENSOR RESISTANCE

Temperature °F (°C)	Minimum Ohms	Maximum Ohms
-40 (-40)	291,490	381,710
-4 (-20)	85,850	108,390
14 (-10)	49,250	61,430
32 (0)	29,330	35,990
50 (10)	17,990	21,810
68 (20)	11,370	13,610
77 (25)	9120	10,880
86 (30)	7370	8750
104 (40)	4900	5750
122 (50)	3330	3880
140 (60)	2310	2670
158 (70)	1630	1870
176 (80)	1170	1340
194 (90)	860	970
212 (100)	640	720
230 (110)	480	540
248 (120)	370	410

Crankshaft Position Sensor (Except Grand Cherokee) – **1)** Disconnect crankshaft position sensor. On Cherokee and Comanche, connect ohmmeter across sensor terminal "A" (Orange/Dark Blue wire) and terminal "B" (Black/Light Blue wire). On Wrangler, connect ohmmeter across sensor terminal "A" (Brown/Red wire) and terminal "B" (Red/Green wire).
2) Ohmmeter should read 125-275 ohms with engine hot. Replace sensor if reading is not as specified. Also see appropriate crankshaft position sensor tests in SELF-DIAGNOSTICS article.

Crankshaft Position Sensor (Grand Cherokee) – **1)** Disconnect crankshaft position sensor. Connect ohmmeter across sensor terminal "2" (Black/Light Blue wire) and terminal "3" (Red/Light Green wire).
2) Ohmmeter should indicate an open circuit. Replace sensor if reading is not as specified. Also see appropriate crankshaft position sensor tests in SELF-DIAGNOSTICS article.

Manifold Absolute Pressure (MAP) Sensor – **1)** Inspect MAP sensor vacuum hose connections at throttle body and sensor. Replace or repair vacuum hose if necessary.
2) Turn ignition on, engine off. Using DVOM, check MAP sensor output voltage. On Cherokee and Comanche, connect DVOM to MAP sensor terminal "B" (Dark Green/Red wire). On Grand Cherokee, connect DVOM to MAP sensor terminal "2" (Red/White wire). On Wrangler, connect DVOM to MAP sensor terminal "B" (Red/White wire).
3) Output voltage should be 4-5 volts. Voltage should drop to 1.5-2.1 volts with a hot engine operating in Neutral and at idle speed. Also check for output voltage at engine controller wiring harness terminal No. 1. If voltage is not as specified in step 2), repair wiring harness if necessary.
4) With ignition on, check MAP sensor supply voltage at sensor connector terminal "C" (Violet wire on Cherokee and Comanche or Brown/Yellow wire on Wrangler). On Grand Cherokee, check MAP sensor supply voltage at sensor connector "3" (Violet/White wire). Supply voltage should be 4.5-5.5 volts. Also check for supply voltage

at engine controller wiring harness terminal No. 6. If supply voltage is not as specified, repair wiring harness if necessary.

5) Check continuity of MAP sensor ground circuit at sensor connector terminal "A" (Black/Light Blue wire on Cherokee and Comanche or Brown/Red wire on Wrangler) and engine controller wiring harness terminal No. 4. On Grand Cherokee, check continuity of MAP sensor ground circuit at sensor connector terminal "1" (Black/Light Blue wire) and engine controller wiring harness terminal No. 4. Repair wiring harness if necessary.

6) Check continuity of MAP sensor ground circuit at engine controller wiring harness terminal No. 4 and engine controller wiring harness terminal No. 11. If ohmmeter indicates an open circuit, go to next step. If ground connection is okay, replace the engine controller.

NOTE: If terminal No. 4 has a short circuit to 12 volts, correct this condition before replacing engine controller. If necessary, perform appropriate MAP sensor tests in SELF-DIAGNOSTICS article.

7) Check for defective sensor ground connection. Connection is located on right side of engine block, at oil dipstick tube mounting block. Repair connection as necessary.

Manifold Air Temperature (MAT) Sensor – 1) Disconnect coolant temperature sensor. Using DVOM, check sensor resistance. Resistance should be as specified in COOLANT TEMPERATURE SENSOR & MANIFOLD AIR TEMPERATURE SENSOR RESISTANCE table. If resistance is not as specified, replace sensor.

2) Check resistance between engine controller wiring harness terminal No. 21 and sensor connector terminal. Also check resistance between engine controller wiring harness terminal No. 4 and sensor connector terminal. Repair wiring if resistance is greater than 1 ohm.

Oxygen (O₂) Sensor (Heating Element) – 1) Disconnect oxygen sensor connector. Using an ohmmeter, check sensor heating element resistance.

2) On Comanche and Cherokee, connect ohmmeter to Black/Tan and Dark Green/Black sensor wires. On Wrangler, connect ohmmeter to Black and Dark Green/Black sensor wires.

3) Heating element resistance should be 5-7 ohms. Replace oxygen sensor if ohmmeter reads infinity.

Park/Neutral Switch (AW-4 Auto. Trans.) – 1) Disconnect park/neutral switch. Ensure continuity exists between terminals "B" and "C" with transmission in Park or Neutral. *See Fig. 1.*

2) Ensure continuity exists between terminals "A" and "E" with transmission in Reverse. *See Fig. 1.* Ensure continuity exists between terminals "A" and "G" with transmission in 3rd gear.

3) Ensure continuity exists between terminals "A" and "H" with transmission in 1st or 2nd gear. *See Fig. 1.* If switch fails continuity tests, replace park/neutral switch.

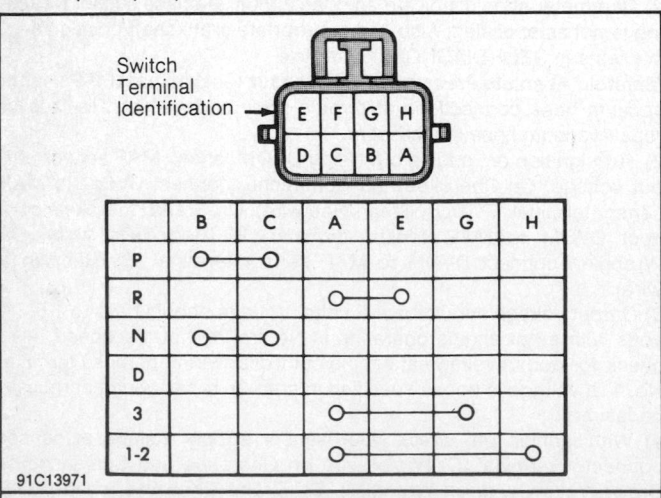

Fig. 1: Testing Park/Neutral Switch Continuity (AW-4 Auto. Trans.)

NOTE: Also see appropriate park/neutral switch input test procedures in SELF-DIAGNOSTICS article.

Park/Neutral Switch (32RH Auto. Trans.) – 1) Disconnect park/neutral switch. Check continuity between switch center terminal and transmission case. Continuity should exist only when transmission is in Park or Neutral.

2) Shift transmission into Reverse. Check continuity between the 2 outside terminals on switch. Continuity should exist only when transmission is in Reverse. Check continuity between each outer terminal and transmission case.

3) Continuity should not exist between either terminal and case while in Reverse. If switch continuity tests are okay, check gearshift adjustment or back-up light circuit. If switch fails continuity tests, replace park/neutral switch.

Throttle Position Sensor (TPS) – 1) Turn ignition on. Check TPS output voltage at sensor wiring harness center terminal. At idle, output voltage should be greater than 200 millivolts.

2) Gradually open throttle plate. Output voltage should gradually increase as throttle plate is opened. At wide open throttle, output voltage must be less than 4.8 volts.

NOTE: Also see appropriate throttle position sensor tests in SELF-DIAGNOSTICS article.

Vehicle Speed Sensor – See appropriate vehicle speed sensor tests in SELF-DIAGNOSTICS article.

MODULES, MOTORS & RELAYS
MODULES

Theft Alarm Module (Cherokee & Grand Cherokee) – 1) Turn ignition key to ACCY position 3 times and leave in ACCY position to activate Security Alarm Module (SAM) self-diagnostics. If parking lights and tail lights do not flash, go to step **2)**. If headlights do not flash, go to step **6)**. If horn does not sound twice, go to step **7)**. If horn sounds and headlights, parking lights and tail lights flash, go to step **8)**.

NOTE: For identifying circuits referred to in testing, see appropriate wiring diagram in WIRING DIAGRAMS article.

2) Check accessory and parking light fuses. Replace fuses, if necessary. If fuses are okay, disconnect SAM connector. Security alarm module is located on driver's side of A/C-heater housing.

NOTE: If SECURITY light comes and remains on with ignition on, the Chrysler Collision Detection (CCD) bus communication with the engine controller has been lost. After servicing vehicle ensure that system operates properly. A malfunctioning anti-theft system may keep engine from starting.

3) Check wiring side of SAM connector for battery voltage at battery, accessory, and headlight feed wires. Also check ground circuits for both ground wires.

4) If battery voltages and ground circuits are NOT okay, repair wiring harness and retest system. If battery voltages and ground circuits are okay, check for battery voltage at ignition feed wire of SAM connector.

5) If battery voltage is present, replace security alarm module and retest system. If battery voltage is not present, repair wiring harness and retest system.

6) Check headlight wiring harness and headlight relay. If wiring harness and relay are okay, replace security alarm module. If wiring harness and relay are NOT okay, repair wiring harness or replace relay and retest system.

7) Check horn, horn fuse and wiring harness. If horn, horn fuse and wiring harness are okay, replace security alarm module and retest system. If horn, horn fuse and wiring harness are not okay, repair wiring harness or replace fuse or horn and retest system.

8) Verify that SECURITY light is flashing. If SECURITY light is not flashing, check bulb and wiring harness. Repair or replace as necessary. If bulb and wiring are okay, replace security alarm module and retest system.

9) If SECURITY light is flashing, turn ignition key to OFF position. Remove illuminated entry relay from vehicle. Relay is located on a bracket behind instrument panel.

10) Check theft alarm switches by opening and closing doors and liftgate. Replace switch(es) or repair wiring harness as necessary. If switches are okay, check hood switch by opening and closing hood.

11) Replace hood switch or repair wiring harness as necessary. If hood switch is okay, unlock (with key) each front door and liftgate one at a time to test disarm switches. Replace switch(es) or repair wiring harness as necessary and retest system.

12) If disarm switches are okay, cycle power door locks to lock position and then unlock. Replace door lock switch(es), lock/unlock relay(s) or repair wiring harness as necessary and retest system.

13) If power door locks operate properly, lock and unlock vehicle with keyless entry transmitter. If power door locks do not operate properly, replace keyless entry transmitter, receiver or repair wiring harness as necessary and retest system.

14) If keyless entry system operates properly, turn ignition key to ON position and wait 30 seconds. If SECURITY light comes on and stays on, repair or replace CCD bus and wiring as necessary and retest system. If SECURITY light remains off, theft alarm system is operating properly.

NOTE: A functional SBEC-II that has been used in a vehicle equipped with theft alarm system CANNOT be used in another vehicle that is NOT equipped with theft alarm system.

MOTORS

Automatic Idle Speed (AIS) Motor – See IDLE CONTROL SYSTEM.

RELAYS

A/C Compressor Clutch Relay – See A/C COMPRESSOR CLUTCH under MISCELLANEOUS CONTROLS.

Automatic Shutdown (ASD) Relay – See appropriate ASD relay tests in SELF-DIAGNOSTICS article.

Fuel Pump Relay – See FUEL PUMP RELAY under FUEL DELIVERY.

Radiator (Cooling) Fan Relay – See RADIATOR (COOLING) FAN under MISCELLANEOUS CONTROLS.

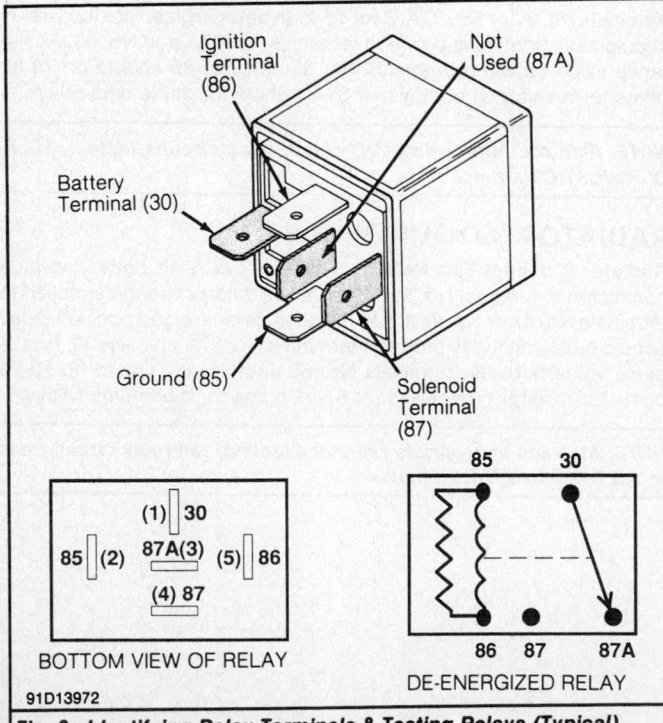

Fig. 2: Identifying Relay Terminals & Testing Relays (Typical)

Starter Motor Relay – Some relays have battery voltage supplied to terminal No. 30. Others have battery voltage supplied to terminals No. 87 or 87A. See Fig. 2. In de-energized position, relay should have continuity between terminals No. 87A and No. 30. Resistance value between terminals No. 85 and No. 86 should be 70-80 ohms for resistor type relays or 81-91 ohms for diode type relays.

FUEL SYSTEM

FUEL DELIVERY

NOTE: Also see appropriate fuel delivery system or fuel injector control circuit tests in SELF-DIAGNOSTICS article.

Fuel System Pressure Test – **1)** Remove cap from pressure test port in fuel rail. See Fig. 3. Using a shop towel to absorb any spilled fuel, connect a 0-60 psi (0-4.22 kg/cm²) fuel pressure gauge to pressure fitting on fuel rail. Dispose of shop towel properly. Disconnect vacuum hose from fuel pressure regulator. Start engine.

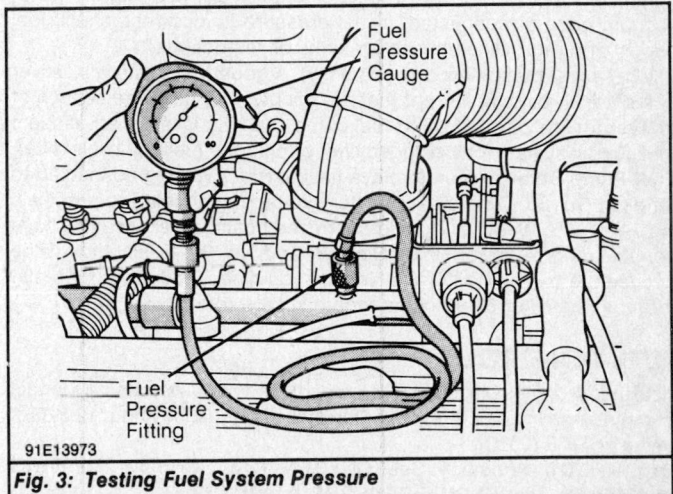

Fig. 3: Testing Fuel System Pressure

2) Pressure should be approximately 39 psi (2.74 kg/cm²) with vacuum hose disconnected and 31 psi (2.18 kg/cm²) with vacuum hose connected to fuel pressure regulator.

3) If fuel pressure is not 8-10 psi (.56-.70 kg/cm²) higher with vacuum hose disconnected from fuel pressure regulator, inspect vacuum hose for blockage, leaks, kinks or other damage.

CAUTION: Fuel pressure will rise as high as 95 psi (6.7 kg/cm²) when fuel return line is pinched shut. Turn engine off IMMEDIATELY after pinching off fuel return line.

4) If fuel pressure is low, restart vehicle and let engine idle. Momentarily pinch hose section of fuel return line and IMMEDIATELY turn engine off. Note pressure reading on gauge.

5) If fuel pressure rises, replace fuel pressure regulator. If fuel pressure remains low, inspect fuel supply line, fuel filter, and fuel rail inlet for blockage. If fuel pressure rises above specifications, check fuel return line for kinks or blockage.

Fuel Pressure Leak Down Test – **1)** Remove cap from pressure test port in fuel rail. See Fig. 3. Connect a 0-60 psi (0-4.22 kg/cm²) fuel pressure gauge to pressure fitting on fuel rail. Start and run engine at idle.

2) Turn engine off and note fuel pressure reading on gauge. Leave fuel pressure gauge connected. Allow 30 minutes to elapse and then compare fuel pressure reading to reading taken when engine was off.

3) A pressure drop up to 20 psi (1.4 kg/cm²) to a range of 19-39 psi (1.3-2.7 kg/cm²) is within specification. If pressure drop is correct, the fuel pump outlet check valve and fuel pressure regulator are operating correctly.

CAUTION: Fuel pressure will rise as high as 95 psi (6.7 kg/cm²) when fuel return line is pinched shut. Turn engine off IMMEDIATELY after pinching off fuel return line.

4) If pressure drop is greater than 20 psi (1.4 kg/cm²), restart vehicle and let engine idle. Momentarily pinch shut hose section of fuel return line and IMMEDIATELY turn engine off. Note pressure reading on gauge. Allow 30 minutes to elapse and then compare fuel pressure reading to reading taken when engine was turned off.

5) If fuel pressure drops to about 20 psi (1.4 kg/cm²), replace fuel pressure regulator. If fuel pressure drops more than 20 psi (1.4 kg/cm²), fuel pressure is bleeding off past outlet check valve in fuel pump. Fuel pump must be replaced.

Fuel Pump Capacity Test – 1) Remove cap from pressure test port in fuel rail. *See Fig. 3.* Connect a 0-60 psi (0-4.22 kg/cm²) fuel pressure gauge to pressure fitting on fuel rail. Start and run engine at idle. Note fuel pressure.

2) Pressure should be roughly 31 psi (2.18 kg/cm²) with vacuum hose connected to fuel pressure regulator and 39 psi (2.74 kg/cm²) with vacuum hose disconnected. If fuel pressure is incorrect, check fuel supply and return lines/hoses for kinks or restrictions.

3) Check fuel pump flow rate (capacity). A good fuel pump will deliver at least 2.11 pints (1 liter) of fuel per minute with the hose section of fuel return line pinched off. If fuel pump capacity is incorrect, inspect fuel supply system for a plugged filter or plugged fuel pump inlet filter.

Fuel Pump Relay – Some relays have battery voltage connected to terminal No. 30. Others have battery voltage connected to terminals No. 87 or 87A. *See Fig. 2.* In de-energized position, relay should have continuity between terminals No. 87A and No. 30. Resistance value between terminals No. 85 and No. 86 should be 70-80 ohms for resistor type relays, or 81-91 ohms for diode type relays.

FUEL CONTROL

Fuel Injectors – Disconnect injector from wiring harness. Connect ohmmeter on injector terminals. Resistance should be about 12.8-15.2 ohms at 68°F (20°C).

Oxygen (O₂) Sensor – See OXYGEN (O₂) SENSOR (HEATING ELEMENT) under ENGINE SENSORS & SWITCHES.

IDLE CONTROL SYSTEM

Automatic Idle Speed (AIS) Motor – 1) Set parking brake and block drive wheels. Route all Exerciser Tester (7558) cables away from cooling fans, drive belt, pulleys, and exhaust components. Adjust engine idle speed to normal before disconnecting exerciser.

2) With ignition off, disconnect AIS motor connector at throttle body. Plug in exerciser tester harness connector into AIS motor. Connect Red clip of exerciser to battery positive terminal.

3) Connect Black clip to battery negative terminal. Red light on exerciser will flash if exerciser is properly connected. Start engine. Move exerciser switch to HIGH position. Engine speed should increase. Move switch to LOW position. Engine speed should decrease.

4) If engine idle speed changes while using exerciser, AIS motor is working properly. Return engine speed to normal idle and disconnect exerciser from idle speed stepper motor.

5) If engine idle did not change, turn ignition off. DO NOT disconnect exerciser from stepper motor. Remove AIS motor from throttle body. With ignition off, cycle the exerciser switch between HIGH and LOW positions. Pintle should move in and out of motor.

CAUTION: When checking AIS motor operation with motor removed from throttle body, DO NOT extend pintle more than 1/4" (6.35 mm), as pintle may separate from motor. The AIS motor must be replaced if pintle separates from motor.

6) If pintle still does not move, replace AIS motor. Start engine and test replacement motor. If pintle now operates properly, check AIS motor bore in throttle body and clean if necessary. Reinstall AIS motor and retest.

7) If throttle body is clear of obstructions, use Chrysler's Diagnostic Readout Box II (DRB-II) tester and appropriate AIS (idle speed stepper) motor tests in SELF-DIAGNOSTICS article.

IGNITION SYSTEM

TIMING CONTROL SYSTEMS

Ignition timing is electronically controlled by Single Board Engine Controller-II (SBEC-II). Base ignition timing is NOT adjustable with this system. SBEC-II controlled ignition system consists of coolant temperature sensor, crankshaft position sensor, distributor (includes rotor and synchronization sensor), ignition coil, manifold absolute pressure sensor and throttle position sensor. See ENGINE SENSORS & SWITCHES for component testing.

EMISSION SYSTEMS & SUB-SYSTEMS

CRANKCASE VENTILATION SYSTEM

System and component testing information is not available from manufacturer.

FUEL EVAPORATION

System and component testing information is not available from manufacturer.

MISCELLANEOUS CONTROLS

A/C COMPRESSOR CLUTCH

A/C Compressor Clutch Relay – Some relays have battery voltage supplied to terminal No. 30. Other haves battery voltage supplied to terminals No. 87 or No. 87A. *See Fig. 2.* In de-energized position, relay should have continuity between terminals No. 87A and No. 30. Resistance value between terminals No. 85 and No. 86 should be 70-80 ohms for resistor type relays, or 81-91 ohms for diode type relays.

NOTE: Also see appropriate A/C clutch relay circuits tests in SELF-DIAGNOSTICS article.

RADIATOR (COOLING) FAN

Radiator (Cooling) Fan Relay – Some relays have battery voltage connected to terminal No. 30. Other haves battery voltage supplied to terminals No. 87 or No. 87A. *See Fig. 2.* In de-energized position, relay should have continuity between terminals No. 87A and No. 30. Resistance value between terminals No. 85 and No. 86 should be 70-80 ohms for resistor type relays, or 81-91 ohms for diode type relays.

NOTE: Also see appropriate radiator (cooling) fan relay circuit tests in SELF-DIAGNOSTICS article.

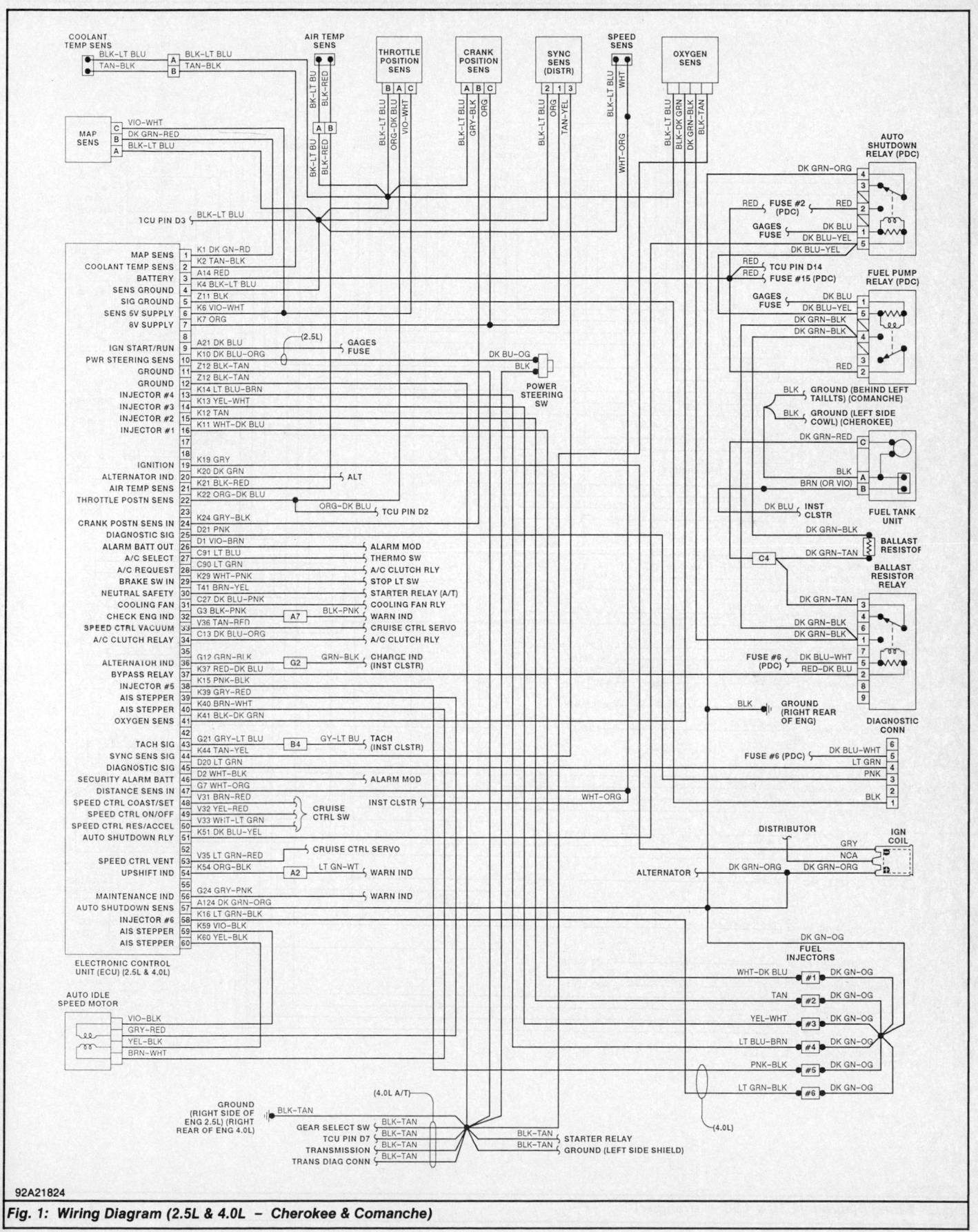

Fig. 1: Wiring Diagram (2.5L & 4.0L — Cherokee & Comanche)

92A21824

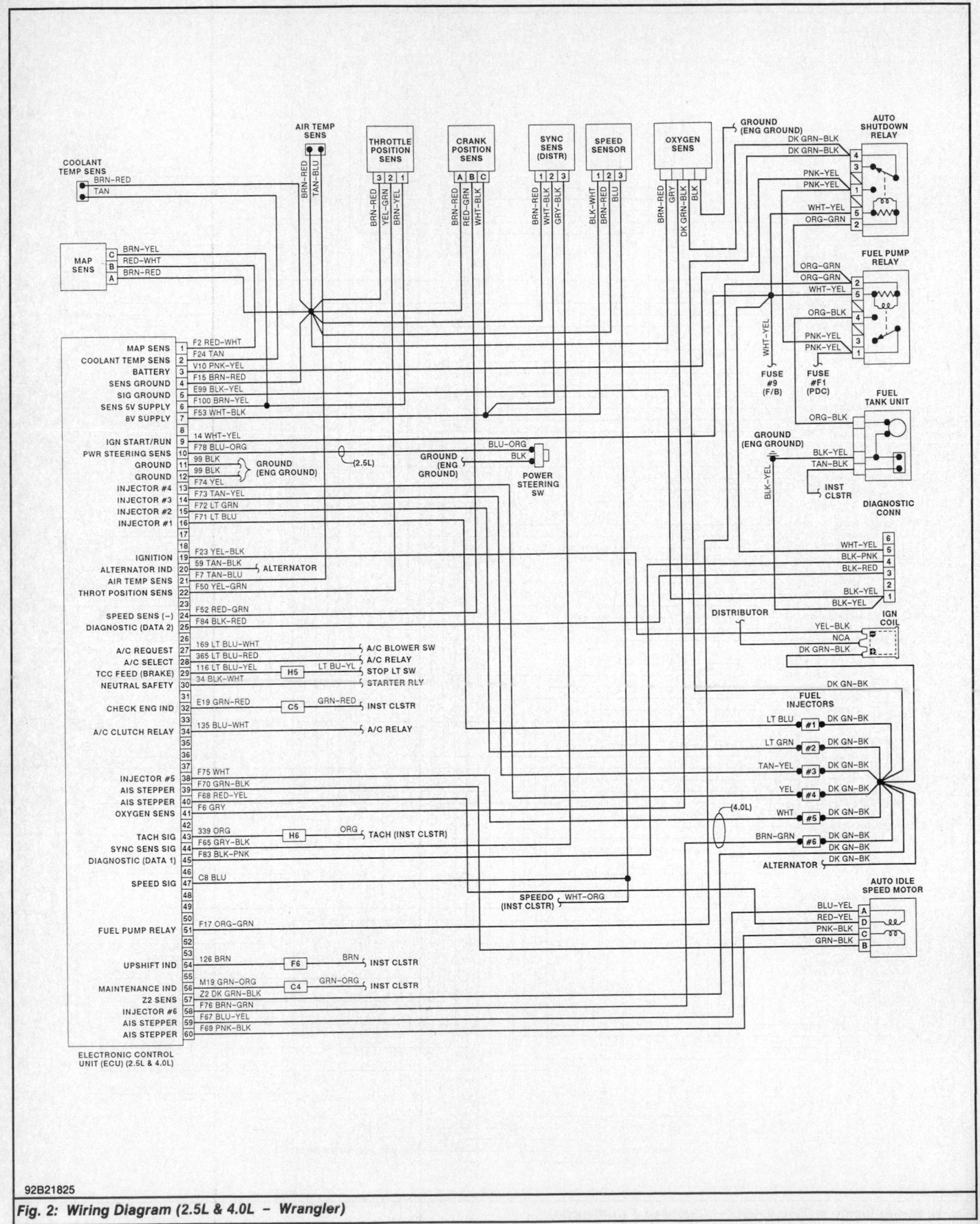

Fig. 2: Wiring Diagram (2.5L & 4.0L - Wrangler)

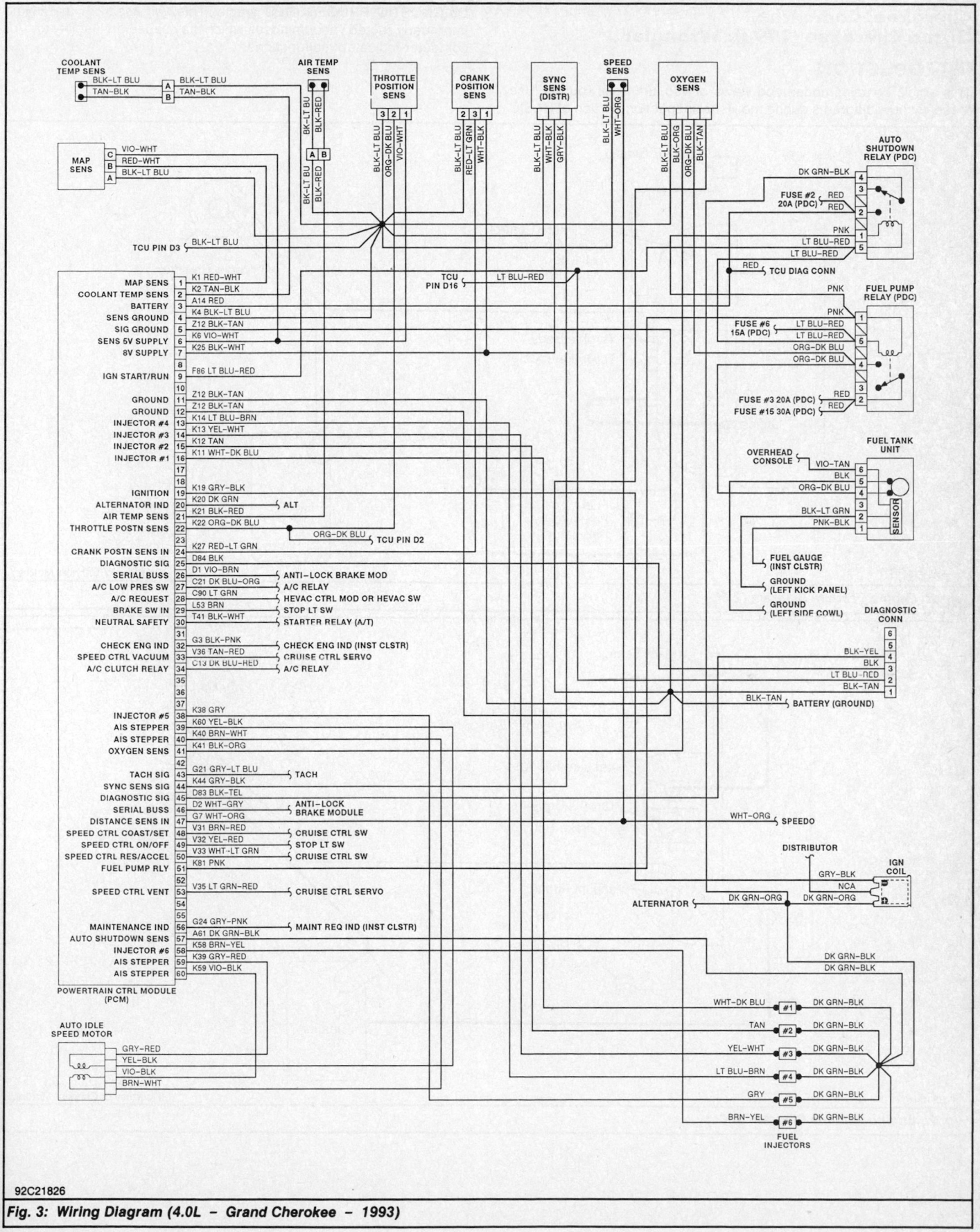

Fig. 3: Wiring Diagram (4.0L – Grand Cherokee – 1993)

1992 ENGINE PERFORMANCE
Vacuum Diagrams

**Cherokee, Comanche,
Grand Cherokee (1993), Wrangler**

INTRODUCTION

This article contains underhood views of vacuum hose routing. Use these vacuum diagrams during the visual inspection portion of BASIC

DIAGNOSTIC PROCEDURES article. This will assist in identifying improperly routed vacuum hoses which may cause driveability and/or computer-indicated malfunctions.

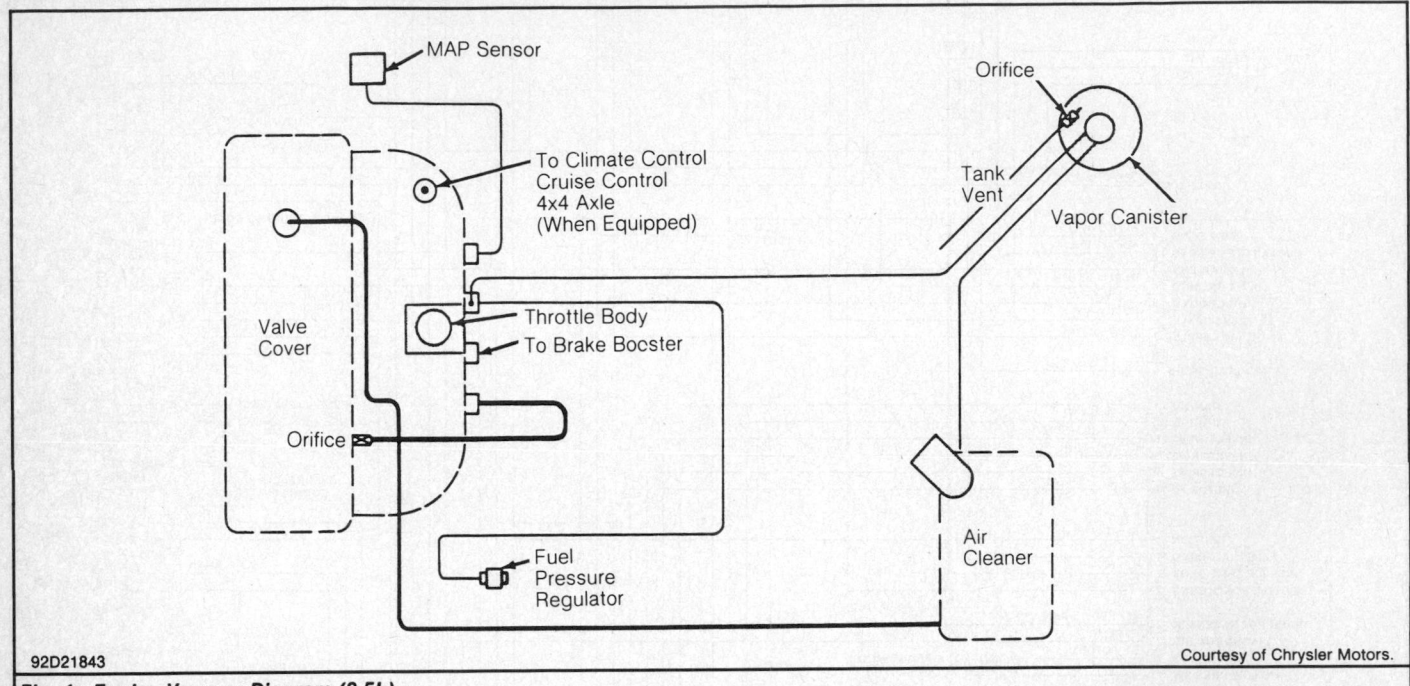

92D21843

Courtesy of Chrysler Motors.

Fig. 1: Engine Vacuum Diagram (2.5L)

92E21844

Courtesy of Chrysler Motors.

Fig. 2: Engine Vacuum Diagram (4.0L)

**Cherokee, Comanche,
Grand Cherokee (1993), Wrangler**

WARNING: When battery is disconnected, vehicle computer and memory systems may lose memory data. Driveability problems may exist until computer systems have completed a relearn cycle. See COMPUTER RELEARN PROCEDURES article in GENERAL INFORMATION before disconnecting battery.

INTRODUCTION

Removal, overhaul and installation procedures are covered in this article. If component removal and installation is primarily an unbolt and bolt-on procedure, only a torque specification may be furnished.

IGNITION SYSTEM

SYNCHRONIZATION SIGNAL GENERATOR

Removal & Installation – 1) Remove distributor cap, rotor, and distributor. Remove pulse ring mounting screws and remove pulse ring. Using pin punch and hammer, remove distributor gear roll pin.
2) Using a rubber mallet, tap distributor shaft out until distributor gear and shim are removed. Slide shaft out of distributor housing. Remove sync (synchronization) signal generator stator mounting screws and positioning arm.
3) Slide wiring harness grommet out of distributor housing. Remove synch signal generator. To install, reverse removal procedure.

FUEL SYSTEM

FUEL SYSTEM PRESSURE RELEASE

WARNING: ALWAYS relieve fuel pressure before disconnecting any fuel injection-related component. DO NOT allow fuel to contact engine or electrical components.

1) Disconnect negative battery cable. Remove fuel filler cap. Remove cap from pressure test port on fuel rail. *See Fig. 1.* Place shop towels around pressure test port to absorb spilled fuel.
2) Press the test port valve with a small screwdriver or punch wrapped in shop towels. Remove shop towels and dispose of properly. Install pressure test port cap.

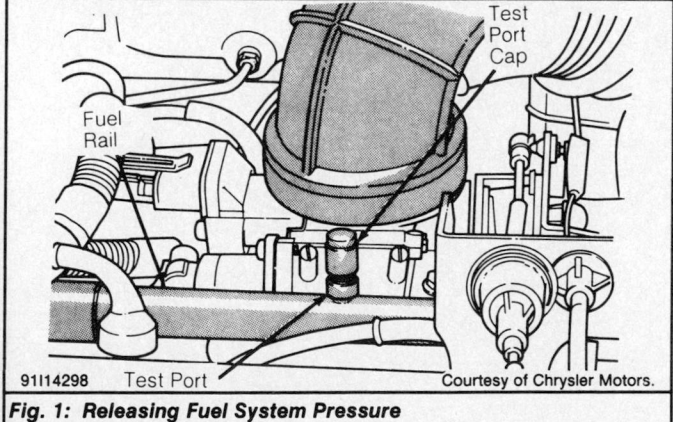
91I14298   Test Port   Courtesy of Chrysler Motors.
Fig. 1: Releasing Fuel System Pressure

FUEL HOSES & CLAMPS

Removal – 1) Quick-connect fittings are used on inlet and outlet ports of fuel rail. Fitting consists of 2 "O" rings, spacer, and "O" ring retainer.
2) To disconnect quick-connect fitting, squeeze tabs against tube and pull fitting of hose/fitting assembly. Retainer should stay on fuel tube when tube is disconnected. The "O" rings and spacer should remain in connector.
Servicing Quick-Connect Fitting – A repair kit with replacement "O" ring, spacer, and retainer is available. *See Fig. 2.* To service quick-con-

nect fitting, push disposable plug/kit assembly into quick-connect fitting until a "click" is heard. Grasp end of disposable plug and pull outward to remove it from fitting.
Installation – When installing and connecting fitting, push fuel tube into quick-connect fitting until a "click" is heard. Ensure connection is secure by firmly pulling on fuel tube. Tube should be locked in place.

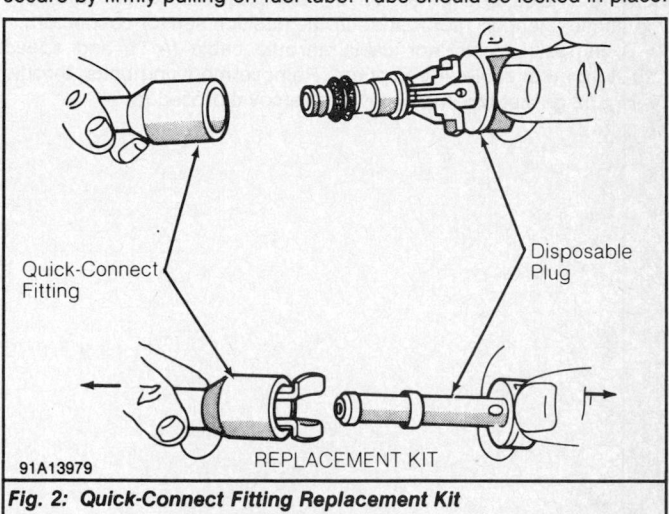
91A13979
Fig. 2: Quick-Connect Fitting Replacement Kit

FUEL RAILS & INJECTORS

Removal & Installation – 1) Relieve fuel system pressure. See FUEL SYSTEM PRESSURE RELEASE under FUEL SYSTEM. Remove and tag injector wiring harness connectors from each injector. Disconnect vacuum hose from fuel pressure regulator.
2) Disconnect fuel supply and fuel return lines. Remove fuel rail mounting bolts. On automatic transmission vehicles, it may be necessary to remove throttle line pressure cable and bracket.
3) Gently rock fuel rail until all injector are clear from intake manifold. Remove injector retaining clips and remove injectors. To install, reverse removal procedure. Ensure fuel injectors are properly seated in intake manifold.

FUEL FILTER

Removal & Installation – Relieve fuel pressure. See FUEL SYSTEM PRESSURE RELEASE under FUEL SYSTEM. Raise and support vehicle. Locate filter along driver-side frame rail. On Wrangler, remove fuel filter protection shield. Remove hose and clamps from both sides of filter. Remove retaining strap and remove filter. To install, reverse removal procedure.

FUEL PUMP

Removal & Installation (Cherokee & Comanche) – 1) Relieve fuel system pressure. See FUEL SYSTEM PRESSURE RELEASE under FUEL SYSTEM. Remove fuel tank filler cap, and siphon fuel out of fuel tank. Raise and support vehicle. Disconnect fuel gauge sending unit connector.
2) Disconnect fuel tank vent hose and return hoses from fuel pump/fuel gauge sending unit. Using drift punch and hammer, carefully remove fuel pump lock ring counterclockwise. Remove fuel pump/fuel gauge sending unit and "O" ring. To install, reverse removal procedure.
Removal & Installation (Wrangler) – 1) Relieve fuel system pressure. See FUEL SYSTEM PRESSURE RELEASE under FUEL SYSTEM. Remove fuel tank filler cap, and siphon fuel out of fuel tank. Raise and support vehicle. Disconnect filler vent hose and fuel filler hose from tank.
2) Disconnect fuel gauge sending unit connector. Remove tie straps securing connector harness to fuel supply and return tubes. Disconnect fuel tank vent hose from vent tube.
3) Remove fuel tank shield or skid plate (if equipped). Support fuel tank with floor jack, and remove support strap nuts. Lower fuel tank.

Remove mounting bolts, gasket, and fuel pump/fuel gauge sending unit. To install, reverse removal procedure.

THROTTLE BODY

Removal & Installation – 1) Disconnect negative battery cable. Remove air cleaner snorkel from throttle body. Disconnect automatic idle speed (stepper) motor and throttle position sensor connectors. **2)** Disconnect accelerator cable, throttle cable (A/T), and speed (cruise) control cable (if equipped). Remove mounting bolts, throttle body, and gasket. To install, reverse removal procedure.

TORQUE SPECIFICATIONS
TORQUE SPECIFICATIONS

Application	Ft. Lbs. (N.m)
Automatic Idle Speed Motor	[1]
Coolant Temperature Sensor	21 (28)
Crankshaft Position Sensor	[1]
Fuel Rail Bolts	20 (27)
Ignition Coil	[1]
Manifold Absolute Pressure Sensor	[1]
Manifold Air Temperature Sensor	20 (27)
Oxygen (O_2) Sensor	23 (31)
Power Steering Pressure Switch	[1]
Throttle Position Sensor	[1]
Vehicle Speed Sensor	[1]

	INCH Lbs. (N.m)
Fuel Filter Strap Bolt	108 (12)
Single-Board Engine Controller-II	[2] 9 (1)
Throttle Body Bolts	108 (12)

[1] – Torque specification is not available from manufacturer.
[2] – Tighten 60-pin connector screws to 35 INCH Lbs. (4 N.m).

1992 ELECTRICAL
Alternators – Nippondenso

**Cherokee, Comanche,
Grand Cherokee (1993), Wrangler**

DESCRIPTION

Charging system consists of a Single Board Engine Controller-II (SBEC-II), alternator, CHECK ENGINE light and battery. Voltage regulation is controlled within the SBEC-II and cannot be serviced.

The SBEC-II monitors charging system input and output to ensure correct operation. The SBEC-II stores any charging system failures in memory and outputs fault code(s) when on-board diagnostics are entered.

The SBEC-II monitors several different engine control system circuits. If a problem is detected within a monitored circuit, a fault code is stored in the SBEC-II memory. The CHECK ENGINE light will illuminate and system may enter limp-in mode. In limp-in mode, engine controller compensates for component or circuit failure by using information from other sources until repairs are made.

NOTE: Fault codes remain in memory for 50 engine starts. Fault is erased from memory if failure does not reoccur.

ADJUSTMENTS

BELT TENSION

*BELT ADJUSTMENT
(Tension In Lbs. (kg) Using Belt Tension Gauge)*

Application	Lbs. (kg)
Serpentine Belt	
New Belts	180-200 (81.72-90.8)
Used Belts	140-160 (63.56-72.64)
"V" Belt	
New Belt	120-160 (54-73)
Used Belt	90-115 (41-52)

TROUBLE SHOOTING

PRELIMINARY CHECKS

Visually inspect wiring and drive belts. If charging system is not working, check the following areas: Ensure drive belts are properly tightened. Ensure 12 volts exist at alternator field terminal with ignition on. Ensure battery cables, alternator ground cables and alternator and terminal block connections are clean and tight. Ensure alternator field circuit is not grounded (overcharging).

UNSTEADY OR LOW CHARGING

Check for loose alternator belt, defective alternator, loose alternator ground wire or corroded battery terminals.

OVERCHARGING

Check for grounded alternator field wiring or faulty alternator.

ON-VEHICLE TESTING

ALTERNATOR OUTPUT

Output Wire Resistance (Voltage Drop) Test – 1) Ensure battery is charged. Turn ignition off. Disconnect negative battery cable. Connect a 0-150 DC ammeter and a voltmeter (0-18 volts) to vehicle's charging system. *See Fig. 1.*
2) Connect a carbon pile rheostat between battery terminals. Ensure carbon pile is in OFF position before connecting leads.
3) Connect one end of jumper wire to ground and other end to alternator field terminal Dark Green wire (Tan/Black wire on Wrangler) on rear side of alternator. *See Fig. 2.* Connect negative battery cable.

CAUTION: Alternator has 2 field terminals. DO NOT connect jumper wire to alternator field terminal Dark Green/Red wire (Dark Green/Black wire on Wrangler).

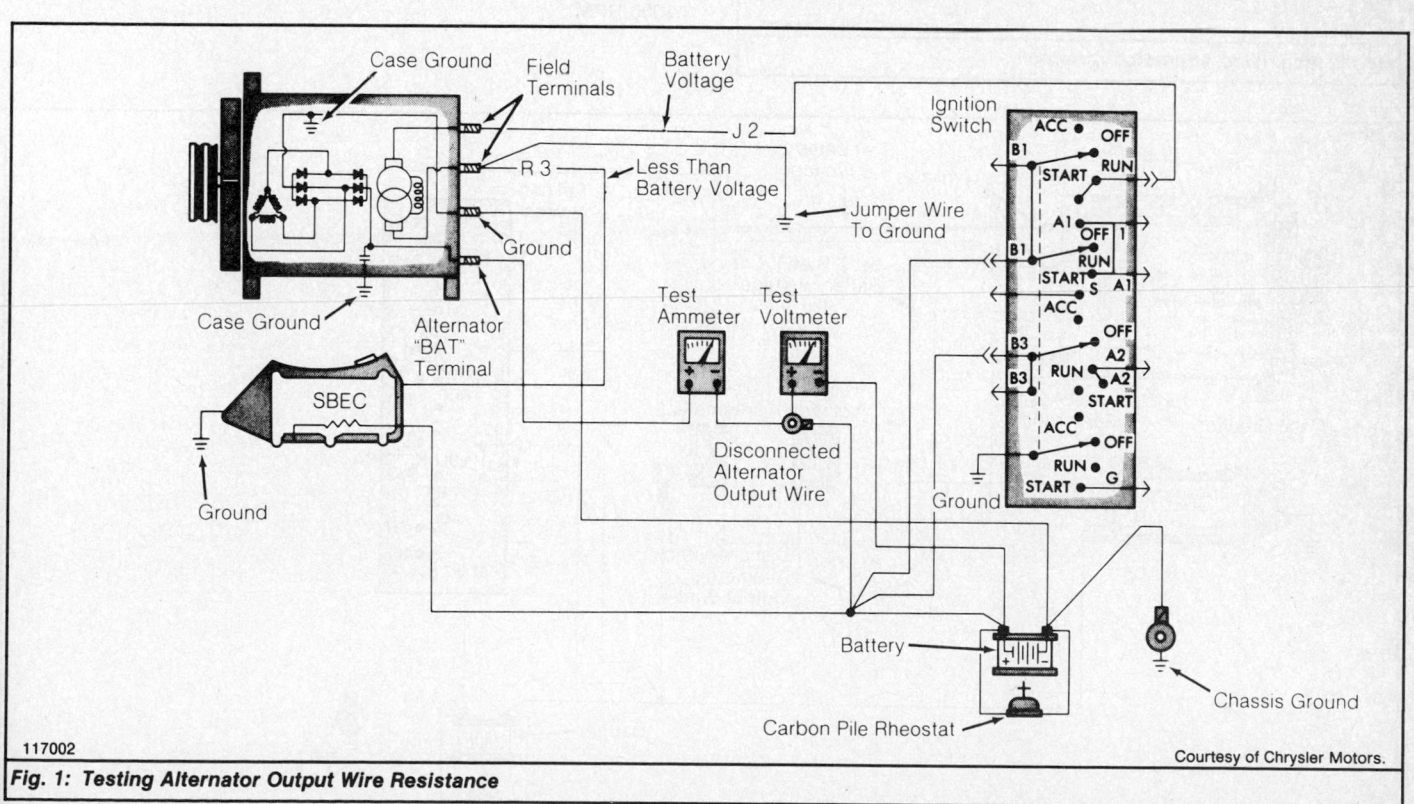

117002   Courtesy of Chrysler Motors.

Fig. 1: Testing Alternator Output Wire Resistance

4) Start engine. Reduce engine speed to idle. Adjust engine speed and carbon pile to maintain 20 amps current flow. Observe voltmeter reading. Voltage drop should be .5 volt or less.

5) If voltage drop is more than .5 volt, inspect, clean and tighten all connections between alternator BAT (B+) terminal and positive battery post. If wire resistance (voltage drop) is okay, test is complete. Remove all test equipment.

Current Output Test – **1)** Ensure battery is charged. Turn ignition off. Disconnect negative battery cable. Connect a 0-150 DC ammeter and a voltmeter (0-18 volts) to vehicle's charging system. *See Fig. 3.*

2) Connect a carbon pile rheostat between battery terminals. Ensure carbon pile is in OFF position before connecting leads.

3) Connect one end of jumper wire to ground and other end to alternator field terminal Dark Green wire (Tan/Black wire on Wrangler) on rear side of alternator. *See Fig. 2.* Connect negative battery cable.

CAUTION: Alternator has 2 field terminals. DO NOT connect jumper wire to alternator field terminal Dark Green/Red wire (Dark Green/Black wire on Wrangler).

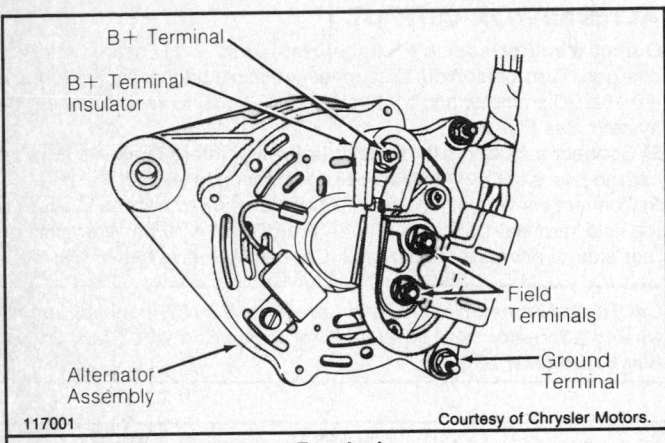

B+ Terminal

B+ Terminal Insulator

Field Terminals

Alternator Assembly

Ground Terminal

117001

Courtesy of Chrysler Motors.

Fig. 2: Identifying Alternator Terminals

4) Start engine and reduce engine speed to idle. Adjust carbon pile and engine speed until engine speed is 1250 RPM and voltmeter reads 15 volts. DO NOT allow voltage to read more than 16 volts.

5) Ammeter should read within 10 amps of rating listed on back of the alternator. If reading is not as specified, replace alternator. Remove all test equipment.

ENTERING ON-BOARD DIAGNOSTICS

CAUTION: Before entering on-board diagnostics, check charging system for other problems. See PRELIMINARY CHECKS under TROUBLE SHOOTING. DO NOT connect DRB-II to vehicle with battery charger connected, as damage to DRB-II may result.

Reading Trouble Codes – Trouble codes may be read by using the CHECK ENGINE light on the instrument panel or using the DRB-II. See CHECK ENGINE LIGHT DIAGNOSTIC MODE and DIAGNOSIS USING DRB-II. A more complete diagnosis is possible using the DRB-II.

NOTE: The SBEC-II CANNOT diagnose every charging system problem. If a fault still exists after performing self-diagnostic procedures, go to ON-VEHICLE TESTING.

Trouble Code Explanation – **1)** See CHARGING SYSTEM FAULT CODES table for charging-related faults.

2) Code 41 will set if the alternator field control fails to switch properly. SBEC-II monitors this circuit whenever ignition is on.

3) If battery temperature sense voltage goes out of range, Code 44 will set in memory. SBEC-II monitors this circuit any time ignition is on.

4) If battery voltage is more than one volt above desired control voltage for more than 20 seconds, a Code 46 will be set in memory. SBEC-II monitors this signal whenever the engine is running.

5) If battery is more than one volt below desired control voltage for more than 20 seconds, Code 47 will be set. Code 47 will also set if no significant change in voltage is detected during alternator test. The SBEC-II monitors this signal whenever engine speed is more than 1500 RPM.

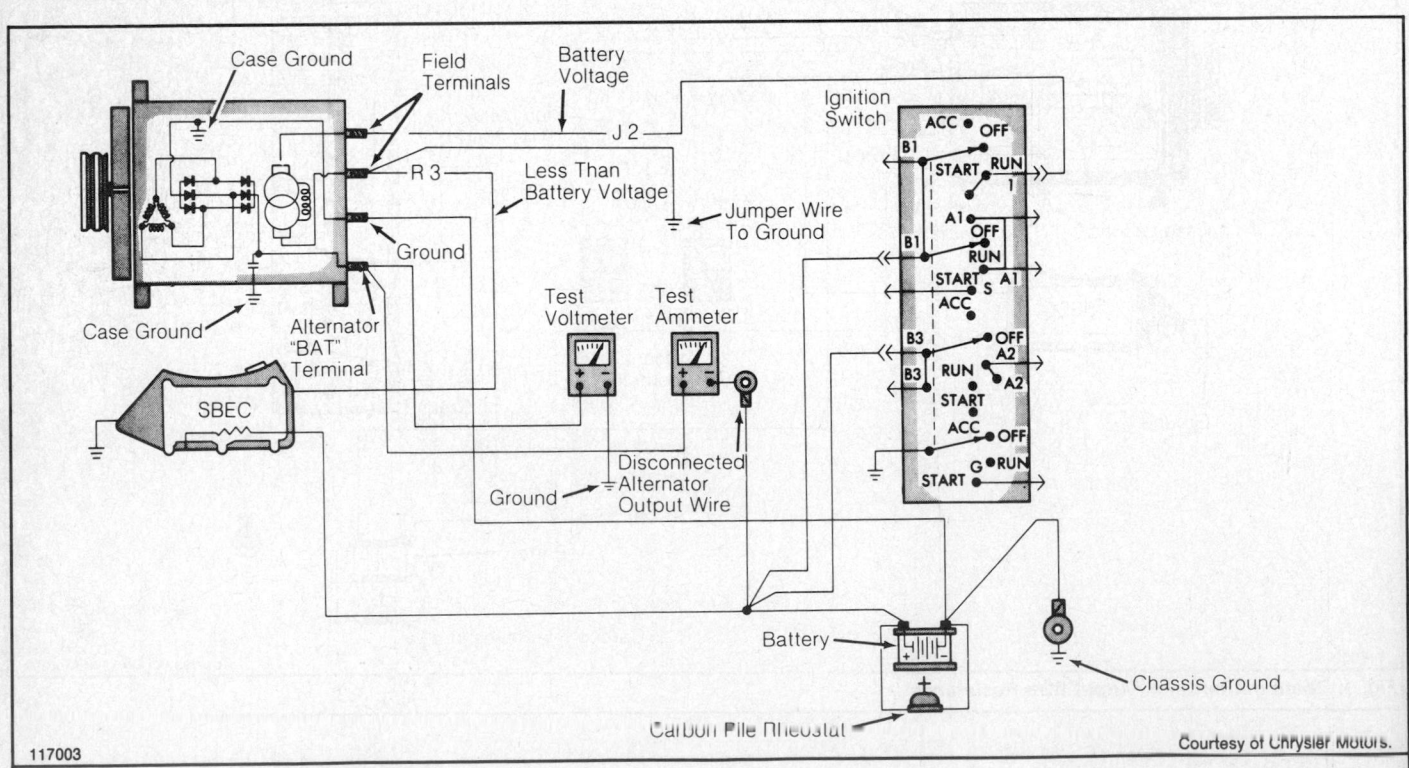

117003

Courtesy of Chrysler Motors.

Fig. 3: Testing Alternator Current Output

CHARGING SYSTEM FAULT CODES

Code	Circuit	CHECK ENGINE Light Status
41 [1]	Alternator Field Control	On
44 [1]	[2] Battery Temp. Sensor	On
46 [1]	High Battery Voltage	On
47 [1]	Low Battery Voltage	Off
55	End of Diagnostic Mode	Off

[1] – This code will cause limp-in mode.
[2] – Sensor inside SBEC-II. If failed, replace SBEC-II.

NOTE: Only charging system-related codes are listed here. For engine-related codes, see appropriate SELF-DIAGNOSTICS article in ENGINE PERFORMANCE.

CHECK ENGINE Light Diagnostic Mode – 1) Start engine (if possible). On models equipped with automatic transmission, place foot on brake and cycle transmission shift lever through all positions, ending in Park. On all models, turn A/C switch on and then off (if equipped).

2) Turn engine off. Without starting engine, turn ignition on, off, on, off and on. CHECK ENGINE light will come on for 2 seconds as a bulb check, followed by fault codes. Record 2-digit fault codes as displayed by flashing CHECK ENGINE light.

3) Once CHECK ENGINE light begins to flash fault codes, it cannot be stopped. Repeat step **1)** to enter diagnostic mode. Code 55 indicates end of fault code display. For more information on vehicle self-diagnostics, see appropriate SELF-DIAGNOSTICS article in ENGINE PERFORMANCE.

4) Refer to CHARGING SYSTEM FAULT CODES table to relate trouble code number to a system fault description (DRB-II display). Once trouble area is known, go to appropriate charging system test.

NOTE: CHECK ENGINE light CANNOT be used to perform actuation test mode, sensor test modes or engine running test. Fault codes can only be erased using DRB-II. Fault codes will be erased from SBEC-II memory after 50 key starts if fault does not reoccur.

Diagnosis Using DRB-II – The DRB-II is used as part of a charging system diagnostic procedure. Perform BATTERY TEST and CHARGING VERIFICATION (CH-VER) test.

Erasing Fault Codes – 1) To erase faults, press ATM key. At DRB-II display, press "2" (ERASE) key. DRB-II will display ERASE FAULTS ARE YOU SURE? (ENTER TO ERASE). Press ENTER key.

2) When DRB-II is finished erasing fault codes, it will display FAULTS ERASED. This display will remain until ATM key is pressed. After ATM key is pressed, display will return to CHARGING MENU screen.

DRB-II TEST FUNCTIONS

NOTE: DO NOT touch DRB-II keypad during DRB-II power-up sequence, or an error message will result.

1) To diagnose system with DRB-II, DRB-II must be in CHARGING MENU. At CHARGING MENU, fault codes and DRB-II test functions can be used.

2) To get to CHARGING MENU, turn ignition off. Attach DRB-II to engine diagnostic connector. Connector is located in engine compartment, near SBEC-II. Turn ignition switch to RUN position.

3) All DRB-II character positions will illuminate and copyright information will appear on screen for several seconds.

4) After several seconds DRB-II menu will appear. At DRB-II menu, press "4" (SELECT SYSTEM) key. Press ENTER key. At SELECT SYSTEM menu, press "1" (ENGINE) key. Press ENTER key. DRB-II menu will appear, indicating engine year and size, type of transmission and SBEC-II part number.

5) After several seconds AIR COND menu will appear. Press "1" (WITH A/C) or press "2" (WITHOUT A/C). DRB-II display will change to ENGINE SYSTEMS menu. At ENGINE SYSTEMS menu, press "2" (CHARGING) key. Press ENTER key.

6) Display will change to CHARGING MENU. At CHARGING menu of engine diagnostic program, specific test functions programmed into DRB-II can be performed. Following DRB-II modes can be accessed: SYSTEM TEST, READ FAULTS, STATE DISPLAYS, ACTUATOR TEST and ADJUSTMENTS.

READ FAULTS Mode – This allows technician to read and erase fault codes. Fault counter will appear along with fault displayed on DRB-II. For example, DRB-II will display 1 OF 2 FAULTS. SBEC-II will store up to 8 fault messages.

Faults are numbered in reverse order of setting. Most recent fault to occur will be number one. Vehicles without A/C will always have A/C CLUTCH RELAY CKT (circuit) stored in memory. This fault will always be number one if vehicle is not equipped with A/C. If no fault messages are stored, DRB-II will display NO FAULTS DETECTED and start counter will show 0 STARTS SINCE ERS.

A start counter will appear below DRB-II fault counter display. Start counter counts the number of times vehicle is started since faults were last set, erased or battery was disconnected. This helps determine if fault is intermittent.

Memory space limits start counter to first 3 faults. Start counter of zero equals a hard fault. Start counter of more than zero indicates an intermittent fault. Start counter will count up to 255 starts. If no fault messages are stored, DRB-II will display NO FAULTS DETECTED and start counter will show 0 STARTS SINCE ERS.

STATE DISPLAYS Mode – This allows technician to read status or values of sensors, inputs/outputs and components. SBEC-II can only recognize high and low status on switch circuits. SBEC-II cannot detect the difference between an open or short circuit or a defective switch. If DRB-II displays a change between INPUT HIGH and INPUT LOW, it can be assumed that the entire switch circuit to SBEC-II is working.

ACTUATOR TEST Mode – This function allows the technician to check operation of output circuits or devices, which SBEC-II cannot detect. DRB-II allows SBEC-II to activate these outputs or devices, so technician can check for proper operation.

Most of the tests available in this mode provide an audible or visual indication of device operation (click of relay contacts, spray fuel, etc.). With the exception of an intermittent condition, if a device functions properly during its test, it can be assumed that the device, its wiring and driver circuit are working properly.

ADJUSTMENTS Mode – This function allows the user to erase fault codes. Function also allows user to reset Emission Maintenance Reminder (EMR) light and mileage.

DRB-II Volt/Ohmmeter Mode – To access volt/ohmmeter mode of DRB-II, connect Red volt/ohmmeter test lead to Red port, located on right-top side of DRB-II.

NOTE: Because DRB-II is grounded through engine diagnostic connector, only one volt/ohmmeter test lead is required when using volt/ohmmeter option.

To access voltmeter, press VOLT/OHM key once. DRB-II is now in voltmeter mode. Touch test probe to connector or wire to be measured. Read voltage on DRB-II display. When voltage testing is complete, press VOLT/OHM key 3 times to exit voltmeter mode.

To access ohmmeter, press VOLT/OHM key twice. DRB-II is now in ohmmeter mode. Touch test probe to connector or wire to be measured. Read resistance to circuit ground on DRB-II display. When resistance testing is complete, press VOLT/OHM key twice to exit ohmmeter mode.

DRB-II Continuity Meter Mode – Press VOLT/OHM key 3 times. Display will read NO CONTINUITY. Touch test probe to connector or wire to be measured. Read continuity on DRB-II display. When continuity testing is complete, press VOLT/OHM key once to exit continuity meter mode.

VEHICLES TESTED Mode – Mode is used to show what vehicles are covered by DRB-II cartridge. To access VEHICLES TESTED mode, turn ignition off. Attach DRB-II to engine diagnostic connector. Connector is located in engine compartment, near SBEC-II.

Turn ignition switch to RUN position. All DRB-II character positions will illuminate and copyright information will appear on screen for several seconds. After several seconds DRB-II menu will appear.

At DRB-II menu, press "1" (VEHICLES TESTED) key. Press ENTER key. DRB-II will display vehicles covered by cartridge. Screen will display for 5 seconds and return to DRB-II menu.

HOW TO USE Mode – Enter DRB-II menu display. Refer to VEHICLES TESTED MODE. At DRB-II menu, press "2" (HOW TO USE) key. Press ENTER key. A series of screens will be displayed explaining the use of DRB-II keys used to move through engine diagnostic program.

BATTERY TEST

NOTE: Perform PRELIMINARY CHECKS under TROUBLE SHOOTING before proceeding. If battery shows signs of freezing or leakage, battery posts are loose or battery has low electrolyte level, DO NOT test.

1) If battery has a built-in hydrometer, go to step **2)**. Turn ignition and all accessories off. Ensure battery voltage is 12.3 volts or more. If voltage is less than 12.3 volts, charge battery and go to step **3)**.

2) If battery hydrometer is Green, go to step **3)**. If battery hydrometer is Yellow or a bright color, replace battery and perform CHARGING VERIFICATION (CH-VER) test. If battery hydrometer is dark in color, charge battery and go to next step.

3) Ensure battery cables, terminals and posts are clean and tight. Perform a battery load test by applying a 300-amp load for 15 seconds. Wait 15 seconds to allow battery to stabilize. Apply a load equal to 50 percent of battery cold cranking rating for 15 seconds and record minimum voltage reading.

4) See MINIMUM BATTERY VOLTAGE table. If battery is below voltage, replace battery and perform CHARGING VERIFICATION (CH-VER) test. If voltage reading is okay, go to next step.

MINIMUM BATTERY VOLTAGE

Battery Temperature	Minimum Volts
70°F (21°C) Or More	9.6
60°F (16°C)	9.5
50°F (10°C)	9.4
40°F (4°C)	9.3
30°F (-1°C)	9.1
20°F (-7°C)	8.9
10°F (-12°C)	8.7
0°F (-18°C)	8.5

5) Reconnect battery cables. Inspect alternator belt tension and condition. Replace belt as necessary. Start engine. Set engine speed to 2000 RPM for 30 seconds. Turn ignition off. Connect DRB-II. Turn ignition on with engine off. Read faults.

6) If DRB-II displays BATTERY TEMP SENSOR OUT OF LIMIT, replace SBEC-II and perform CHARGING VERIFICATION (CH-VER) test. If DRB-II displays other messages, go to appropriate test. If DRB-II does not display any faults, there are either no fault messages or faults are intermittent. Go to TEST CH-5, CHECKING FOR INTERMITTENT PROBLEMS.

TEST CH-2, ALTERNATOR FIELD NOT SWITCHING PROPERLY (CODE 41)

NOTE: Perform BATTERY TEST before proceeding.

1) Put DRB-II in voltmeter mode and probe Dark Green/Red wire (Dark Green/Black wire on Wrangler) at back of alternator. If voltage is less than 10 volts, repair open circuit from ignition switch. If voltage is 10 volts or more, probe Dark Green wire (Tan/Black wire on Wrangler) at back of alternator. If voltage is less than 10 volts, go to next step. If voltage is 10 volts or more, go to step **4)**.

2) Turn ignition off. Disconnect and inspect SBEC-II connector. If connector is damaged, repair as necessary. If connector is okay, turn ignition on and probe Dark Green wire (Tan/Black wire on Wrangler) at back of alternator. If voltage is 10 volts or more, replace SBEC-II. Perform CHARGING VERIFICATION (CH-VER) test.

3) If voltage is less than 10 volts, turn ignition off and put DRB-II in ohmmeter mode. Probe Dark Green wire (Tan/Black wire on Wrangler) in alternator harness. If resistance less than 10 ohms, repair Dark Green wire (Tan/Black wire on Wrangler) for short to ground. If resistance is 10 ohms or more, replace alternator. Perform CHARGING VERIFICATION (CH-VER) test.

4) Turn ignition off. Disconnect and inspect SBEC-II connector. If connector is damaged, repair as necessary. If connector is okay, turn ignition on and put DRB-II in voltmeter mode. Probe cavity No. 20. *See Fig. 4.* If voltage is 10 volts or more, replace SBEC-II. Perform CHARGING VERIFICATION (CH-VER) test. If voltage is less than 10 volts, repair open circuit in Dark Green wire (Tan/Black wire on Wrangler). Perform CHARGING VERIFICATION (CH-VER) test.

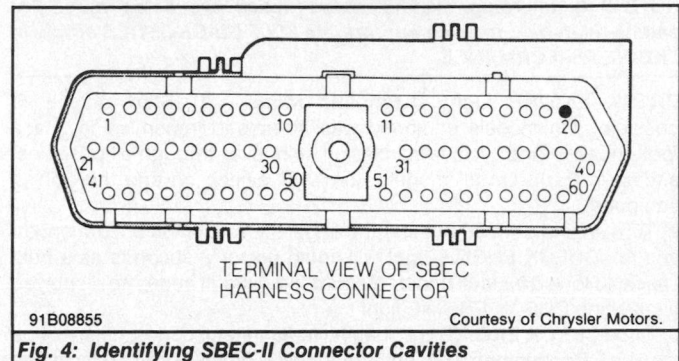

TERMINAL VIEW OF SBEC
HARNESS CONNECTOR

91B08855   Courtesy of Chrysler Motors.

Fig. 4: Identifying SBEC-II Connector Cavities

TEST CH-3, CHARGING SYSTEM VOLTAGE LOW (CODE 47)

NOTE: Perform BATTERY TEST before proceeding.

1) If alternator voltage is 15.1 volts or more, replace SBEC-II. If less than 15.1 volts, ensure no resistance is present between alternator BAT (B+) and battery positive terminal.

CAUTION: Ensure all wires are clear of moving parts.

2) Check alternator case for good connection to ground and to negative battery cable. If the ground is good, manually set engine speed to 1600 RPM. Compare voltage on DRB-II and voltage on an external meter. If difference is 1.0 volt or more, replace alternator. If difference is less than 1.0 volt, go to TEST CH-5, CHECKING FOR INTERMITTENT PROBLEMS.

TEST CH-4, CHARGING SYSTEM VOLTAGE HIGH (CODE 46)

NOTE: Perform BATTERY TEST before proceeding.

1) Turn ignition on. Put DRB-II in voltmeter mode. Probe Dark Green wire (Tan/Black wire on Wrangler) at back of alternator. If voltage is 10.0 volts or more, go to step **4)**. If voltage is less than 10.0 volts, turn ignition off. Disconnect SBEC-II connector, inspect and repair if necessary.

2) If connector is okay, turn ignition on. Probe Dark Green wire (Tan/Black wire on Wrangler) at back of alternator. If voltage is 10.0 volts or more, replace SBEC-II. Perform CHARGING VERIFICATION (CH-VER) test. If voltage is less than 10.0 volts, go to next step.

3) Turn ignition off. Disconnect alternator harness from alternator. Put DRB-II in ohmmeter mode. Probe Dark Green wire (Tan/Black wire on Wrangler) in alternator harness. If resistance is less than 10.0 ohms, repair Dark Green wire (Tan/Black wire on Wrangler) for short to ground. If resistance is 10.0 ohms or more, replace alternator. Perform CHARGING VERIFICATION (CH-VER) test.

4) With ignition on and engine off, read voltage. If voltage is less than 13.0 volts, replace SBEC-II. Perform CHARGING VERIFICATION (CH-VER) test. If voltage is 13.0 volts or more, start engine and read voltage. Compare voltage readings before and after engine is running. Watch for up to 5 minutes, for a 1.0-volt difference.

5) If voltage difference is 1.0 volt or more, replace SBEC-II. Perform CHARGING VERIFICATION (CH-VER) test. If voltage difference is less than 1.0 volt, go to TEST CH-5, CHECKING FOR INTERMITTENT PROBLEMS.

TEST CH-5, CHECKING FOR INTERMITTENT PROBLEMS

NOTE: *Perform TEST CH-4, CHARGING SYSTEM VOLTAGE HIGH (CODE 46) before proceeding.*

1) Actuate the alternator field. Put DRB-II in voltmeter mode. Probe the Dark Green wire (Tan/Black wire on Wrangler) at back of alternator. Voltage should cycle from zero to battery voltage every 1.4 seconds.
2) While watching the DRB-II, wiggle wires between alternator and SBEC-II. If there is any interruption in the voltage cycle, repair wire at point at which cycle was interrupted. If there is no interruption of voltage cycle, test is complete. Perform CHARGING VERIFICATION (CH-VER) test.

CHARGING VERIFICATION (CH-VER)

1) Ensure all engine components are connected. If SBEC-II has been changed and if vehicle is equipped with a factory theft alarm system, start vehicle at least 20 times so alarm will activate when desired.

2) Write Emission Maintenance Reminder (EMR) mileage into new SBEC-II. Connect DRB-II to engine diagnostic connector, and erase faults. Recheck system for fault codes.
3) If fault codes reset, charging system still needs repair. Check all pertinent MITCHELL® TECH SERVICE BULLETINS, and return to BATTERY TEST.

BENCH TESTING

NOTE: *Alternators are not repairable; replace if necessary.*

TORQUE SPECIFICATIONS
TORQUE SPECIFICATIONS

Application	Ft. Lbs. (N.m)
Alternator Mounting Bolts	28 (38)
Idler Pulley (Power Steering)	20 (27)

1992 ELECTRICAL
Starters – Bosch & Mitsubishi

Cherokee, Comanche, Grand Cherokee (1993), Wrangler

DESCRIPTION

Both Bosch and Mitsubishi starters are permanent-magnet type. A planetary gear train transmits power between starter motor and pinion shaft. Both starters are 12-volt units with solenoid mounted on starter housing.

TROUBLE SHOOTING

STARTER MOTOR NOISE

NOTE: To diagnose starter motor noise, see Fig. 1.

ON-VEHICLE TESTING

COLD CRANKING TEST

NOTE: Ensure battery is fully charged and engine is at operating temperature. A cold engine increases starter draw amperage.

1) Connect battery load/charging system tester to battery, and connect remote starter switch to starter relay. Set voltmeter selector to 18-volt position. Adjust ammeter reading to zero.
2) Disconnect coil wire from distributor cap. Attach coil wire to ground to prevent engine from starting. Crank engine, and note cranking voltage and amperage. Replace or repair starter if it is not to specifications. See appropriate STARTER SPECIFICATIONS table at end of article.

STARTER RELAY TEST

1) Place transmission selector in Park or Neutral (automatic only). Ensure Black/Tan wire (Black/White wire on Wrangler) has continuity to ground. Turn ignition switch to start position. Starter solenoid should work.
2) If starter solenoid does not work, check if relay clicks. If starter relay does not click, go to step 4). If relay clicks, ensure voltage is present at relay terminals No. 30 (battery) and 87 (starter solenoid). Also ensure voltage is present at starter solenoid.
3) If starter solenoid still does not work, check starter solenoid ground. If ground is okay, replace starter solenoid.

4) Ensure neutral safety switch wire has continuity to starter relay terminal No. 85. Ensure voltage from ignition switch is present at relay terminal No. 86.
5) If starter relay still does not work, check resistance between relay terminals No. 86 and 85. If resistance is not 70-80 ohms, replace starter relay.

SOLENOID TEST

Continuity Test – 1) Disconnect wire from solenoid field coil terminal (large terminal connected to starter body). Using an ohmmeter, test for continuity between field terminal and solenoid terminal (small terminal).
2) If continuity exists, solenoid is okay. If continuity does not exist, solenoid has open circuit. Replace solenoid.
Functional Test – 1) With a fully charged battery, connect a heavy gauge jumper wire between battery terminal and solenoid terminal wire connector at starter relay. If engine cranks, solenoid is okay.
2) If engine does not crank, check battery cable for voltage to starter solenoid BAT terminal. Jump starter relay terminals as in step 1), checking for voltage at solenoid terminal No. 50. Repair as necessary. If engine still does not crank, repair or replace starter.

BENCH TESTING

ARMATURE TEST

Short Circuit – Place armature in a growler. While rotating armature slowly, hold growler's blade parallel to and touching armature core. Blade vibrates if armature is shorted. Replace shorted armature.

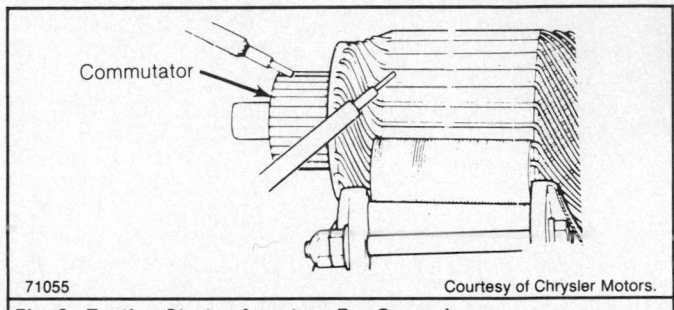

71055   Courtesy of Chrysler Motors.

Fig. 2: Testing Starter Armature For Ground

CONDITION	POSSIBLE CAUSE	CORRECTION
1. VERY HIGH FREQUENCY WHINE BEFORE ENGINE STARTS; ENGINE STARTS OK.	1. Excessive distance between pinion gear and flywheel/drive plate gear.	1. Shim starter motor toward flywheel/drive plate.
2. VERY HIGH FREQUENCY WHINE AFTER ENGINE STARTS WITH IGNITION KEY RELEASED. ENGINE STARTS OK.	2. Insufficient distance between starter motor pinion gear and flywheel/drive plate runout can cause noise to be intermittent.	2. Shim starter motor away from flywheel/drive plate. Inspect flywheel/drive plate for damage; bent, unusual wear, and excessive runout. Replace flywheel/drive plate as necessary.
3. A LOUD "WHOOP" AFTER ENGINE STARTS WHILE STARTER MOTOR IS ENGAGED.	3. Most probably cause is defective overrunning clutch. Clutch replacement normally corrects this condition	3. Replace overrunning clutch or drive assembly.
4. A "RUMBLE," "GROWL," OR "KNOCK" AS STARTER MOTOR COASTS TO STOP AFTER ENGINE STARTS.	4. Most probable cause is bent or unbalanced starter motor armature. Armature replacement normally corrects this condition.	4. Replace starter motor armature.

Courtesy of Chrysler Motors.

Fig. 1: Diagnosing Starter Motor Noise

Ground – Using growler or a self-powered test light, touch one lead to armature shaft and other lead to each commutator bar. *See Fig. 2.* If light glows at any point during procedure, armature is grounded. Replace grounded armature.

DRIVE CLUTCH CHECK

While holding drive clutch housing, rotate pinion. Drive pinion should rotate smoothly in only one direction (pinion should engage and lock in opposite direction). If drive unit does not operate properly or if pinion is worn or burred, replace drive clutch.

REMOVAL & INSTALLATION

STARTER

Removal & Installation (2.5L) – **1)** Disconnect negative battery cable. Remove exhaust pipe clamp from bracket. *See Fig. 3.* On Che-

rokee and Comanche models with automatic transmission, remove nut and bolt from forward end of brace rod. Remove brace rod and bracket.

2) On vehicles with manual transmission, remove nut, bolt and bracket from bellhousing. On all models, disconnect battery cable and solenoid wire from starter solenoid. To install, reverse removal procedure.

Removal & Installation (4.0L) – Disconnect negative battery cable. Raise and support vehicle. Disconnect starter battery cable and solenoid feed wire. Remove starter from flywheel housing. To install, reverse removal procedure.

OVERHAUL

NOTE: For exploded views of starters, see Figs. 4 and 5.

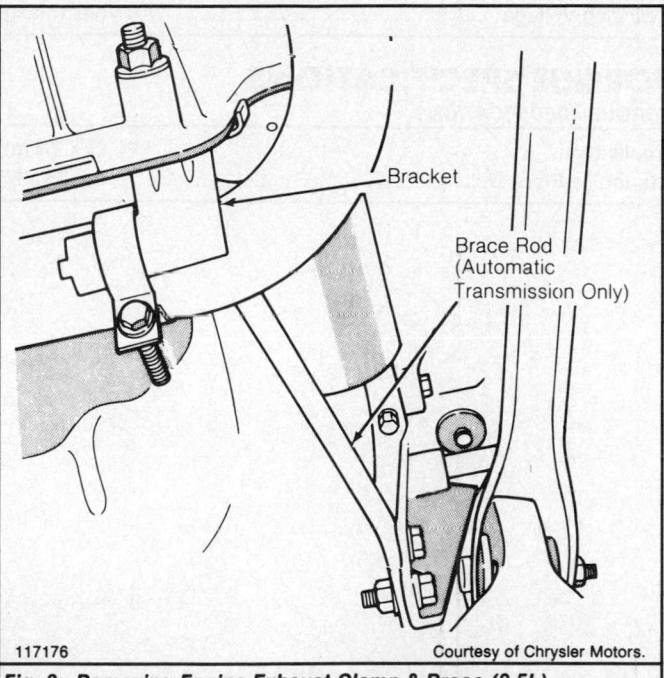

117176   Courtesy of Chrysler Motors.

Fig. 3: Removing Engine Exhaust Clamp & Brace (2.5L)

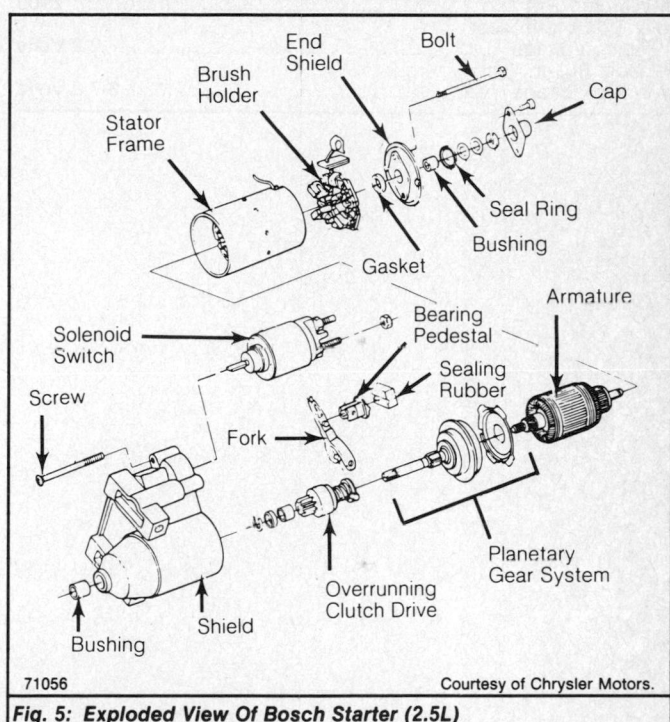

71056   Courtesy of Chrysler Motors.

Fig. 5: Exploded View Of Bosch Starter (2.5L)

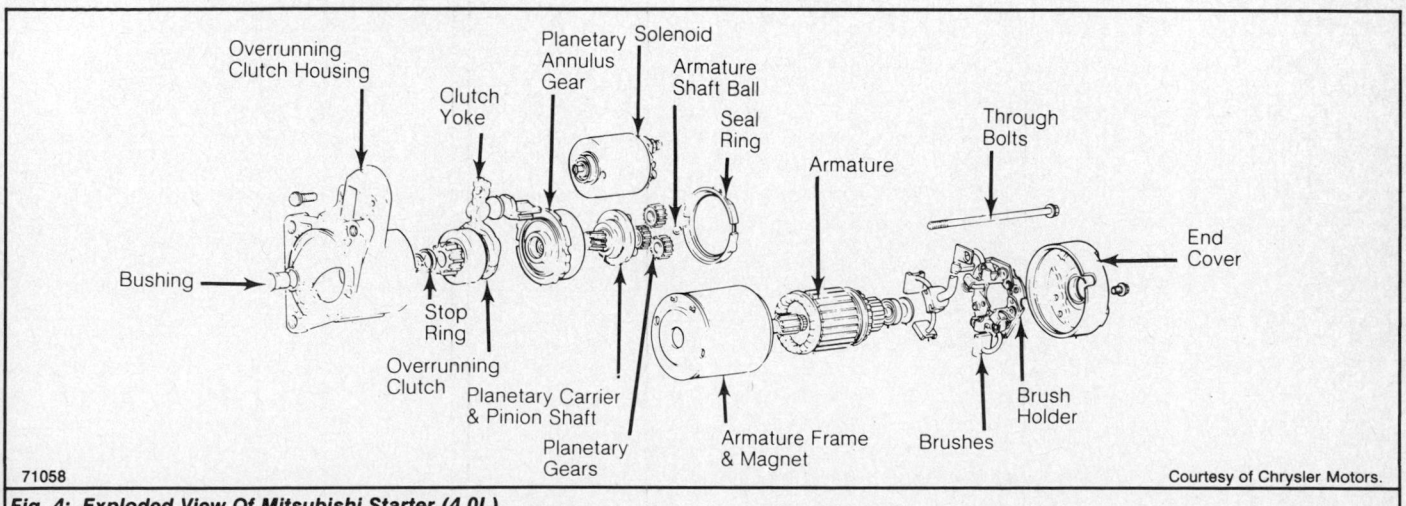

71058   Courtesy of Chrysler Motors.

Fig. 4: Exploded View Of Mitsubishi Starter (4.0L)

STARTER SPECIFICATIONS
BOSCH STARTER SPECIFICATIONS

Application	Specification
Carbon Brush	
Minimum Length	.314" (8.0 mm)
Commutator	
Diameter	1.23-1.27" (31.2-32.3 mm)
Runout	.0004" (.01 mm)
Armature	
Core Runout	.002" (.05 mm)
End Play	.002" (.05 mm)
Cranking Test	
Test Voltage	12.5
Minimum Voltage	9.6
Amps	160
No-Load Test @ 11.5 Volts	
Maximum Amps	75
Minimum RPM	2900
Solenoid Hold-In Test	
Winding Voltage	.2-2 Volts
Solenoid Pull-In Test	
Winding Voltage	6-7.3 Volts

MITSUBISHI STARTER SPECIFICATIONS

Application	Specification
Carbon Brush	
Minimum Length	.354" (9 mm)
Commutator	
Diameter	1.118-1.161" (28.4-29.5 mm)
Runout	.001" (.03 mm)
Armature	
Core Runout	.003" (.08 mm)
End Play	.023" (.58 mm)
Cranking Test	
Test Voltage	12.5
Minimum Voltage	9.6
Amps	130
No-Load Test @ 11.5 Volts	
Maximum Amps	80
Minimum RPM	2500
Solenoid Hold-In Test	
Winding Voltage	3.5 Volts (Min.)
Solenoid Pull-In Test	
Winding Voltage	7.8 Volts (Max.)

TORQUE SPECIFICATIONS
TORQUE SPECIFICATIONS

Application	Ft. Lbs. (N.m)
Starter-To-Block Bolts	33 (45)

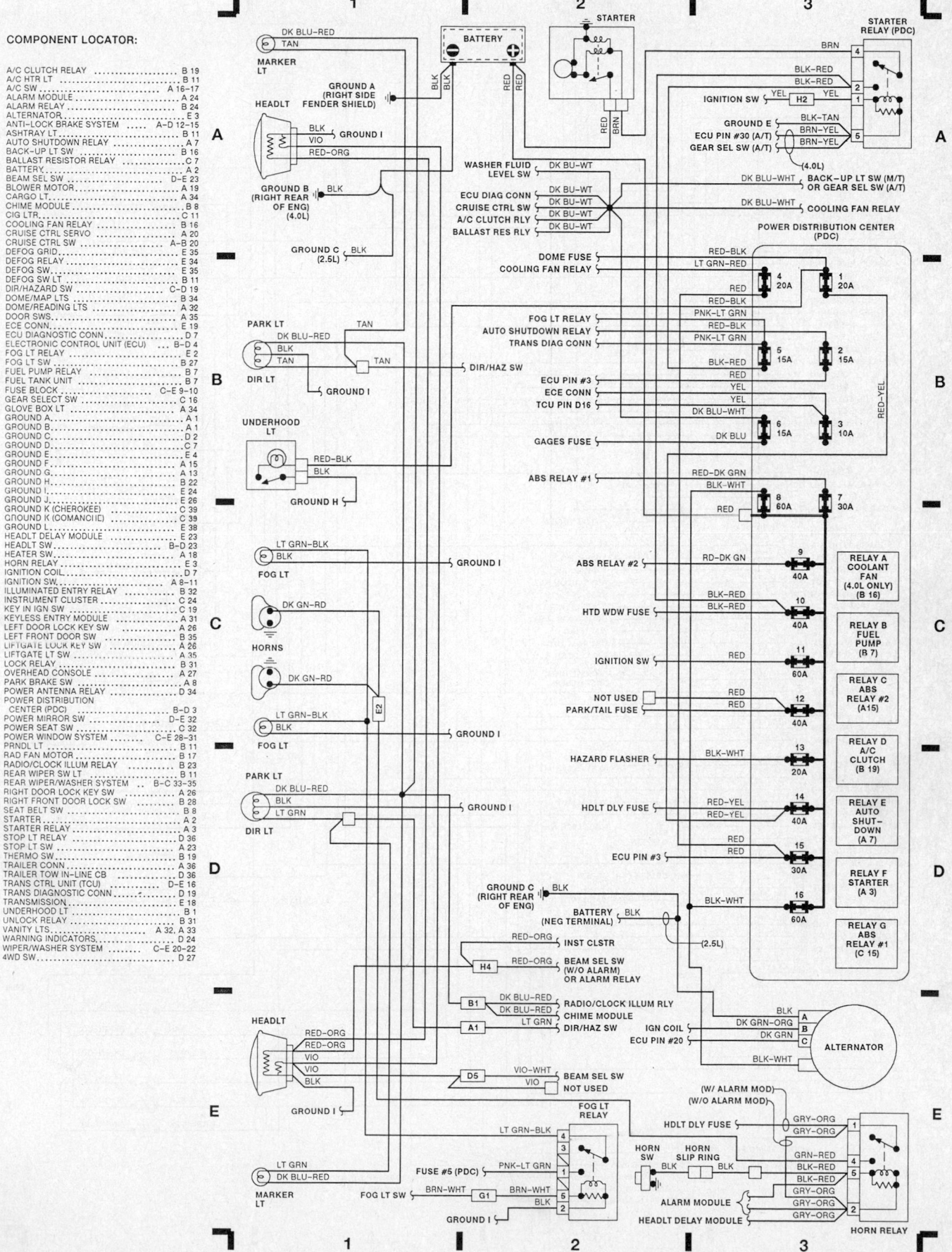

COMPONENT LOCATOR:

A/C CLUTCH RELAY .... B 19
A/C HTR LT .... B 11
A/C SW .... A 16-17
ALARM MODULE .... A 24
ALARM RELAY .... B 24
ALTERNATOR .... E 3
ANTI-LOCK BRAKE SYSTEM ..... A-D 12-15
ASHTRAY LT .... B 11
AUTO SHUTDOWN RELAY .... A 7
BACK-UP LT SW .... B 16
BALLAST RESISTOR RELAY .... C 7
BATTERY .... A 2
BEAM SEL SW .... D-E 23
BLOWER MOTOR .... A 19
CARGO LT .... A 34
CHIME MODULE .... B 8
CIG LTR .... C 11
COOLING FAN RELAY .... B 16
CRUISE CTRL SERVO .... A 20
CRUISE CTRL SW .... A-B 20
DEFOG GRID .... E 35
DEFOG RELAY .... E 34
DEFOG SW .... E 35
DEFOG SW LT .... B 11
DIR/HAZARD SW .... C-D 19
DOME/MAP LTS .... B 34
DOME/READING LTS .... A 32
DOOR SWS. .... A 35
ECE CONN. .... E 19
ECU DIAGNOSTIC CONN. .... D 7
ELECTRONIC CONTROL UNIT (ECU) . B-D 4
FOG LT RELAY .... E 2
FOG LT SW .... B 27
FUEL PUMP RELAY .... B 7
FUEL TANK UNIT .... B 7
FUSE BLOCK .... C-E 9-10
GEAR SELECT SW .... C 16
GLOVE BOX LT .... A 34
GROUND A. .... A 1
GROUND B. .... A 1
GROUND C. .... D 2
GROUND D. .... C 7
GROUND E. .... E 4
GROUND F. .... A 15
GROUND G. .... A 13
GROUND H. .... B 22
GROUND I. .... E 24
GROUND J. .... E 26
GROUND K (CHEROKEE) .... C 39
GROUND K (COMANCHE) .... C 39
GROUND L. .... E 38
HEADLT DELAY MODULE .... E 23
HEADLT SW .... B-D 23
HEATER SW .... A 18
HORN RELAY .... E 3
IGNITION COIL .... D 7
IGNITION SW. .... A 8-11
ILLUMINATED ENTRY RELAY .... B 32
INSTRUMENT CLUSTER .... C 24
KEY IN IGN SW .... C 19
KEYLESS ENTRY MODULE .... A 31
LEFT DOOR LOCK KEY SW .... A 26
LEFT FRONT DOOR SW .... B 35
LIFTGATE LOCK KEY SW .... A 26
LIFTGATE LT SW .... A 35
LOCK RELAY .... B 31
OVERHEAD CONSOLE .... A 27
PARK BRAKE SW .... A 8
POWER ANTENNA RELAY .... D 34
POWER DISTRIBUTION
   CENTER (PDC) .... B-D 3
POWER MIRROR SW .... D-E 32
POWER SEAT SW .... C 32
POWER WINDOW SYSTEM .... C-E 28-31
PRNDL LT .... B 11
RAD FAN MOTOR .... B 17
RADIO/CLOCK ILLUM RELAY .... B 23
REAR WIPER SW LT .... B 11
REAR WIPER/WASHER SYSTEM .. B-C 33-35
RIGHT DOOR LOCK KEY SW .... A 26
RIGHT FRONT DOOR LOCK SW ...... A 28
SEAT BELT SW .... B 8
STARTER .... A 2
STARTER RELAY .... A 3
STOP LT RELAY .... D 36
STOP LT SW .... A 23
THERMO SW .... B 19
TRAILER CONN .... A 36
TRAILER TOW IN-LINE CB .... D 36
TRANS CTRL UNIT (TCU) .... D-E 16
TRANS DIAGNOSTIC CONN. .... D 19
TRANSMISSION .... E 18
UNDERHOOD LT .... B 1
UNLOCK RELAY .... B 31
VANITY LTS. .... A 32, A 33
WARNING INDICATORS .... D 24
WIPER/WASHER SYSTEM .... C-E 20-22
4WD SW .... D 27

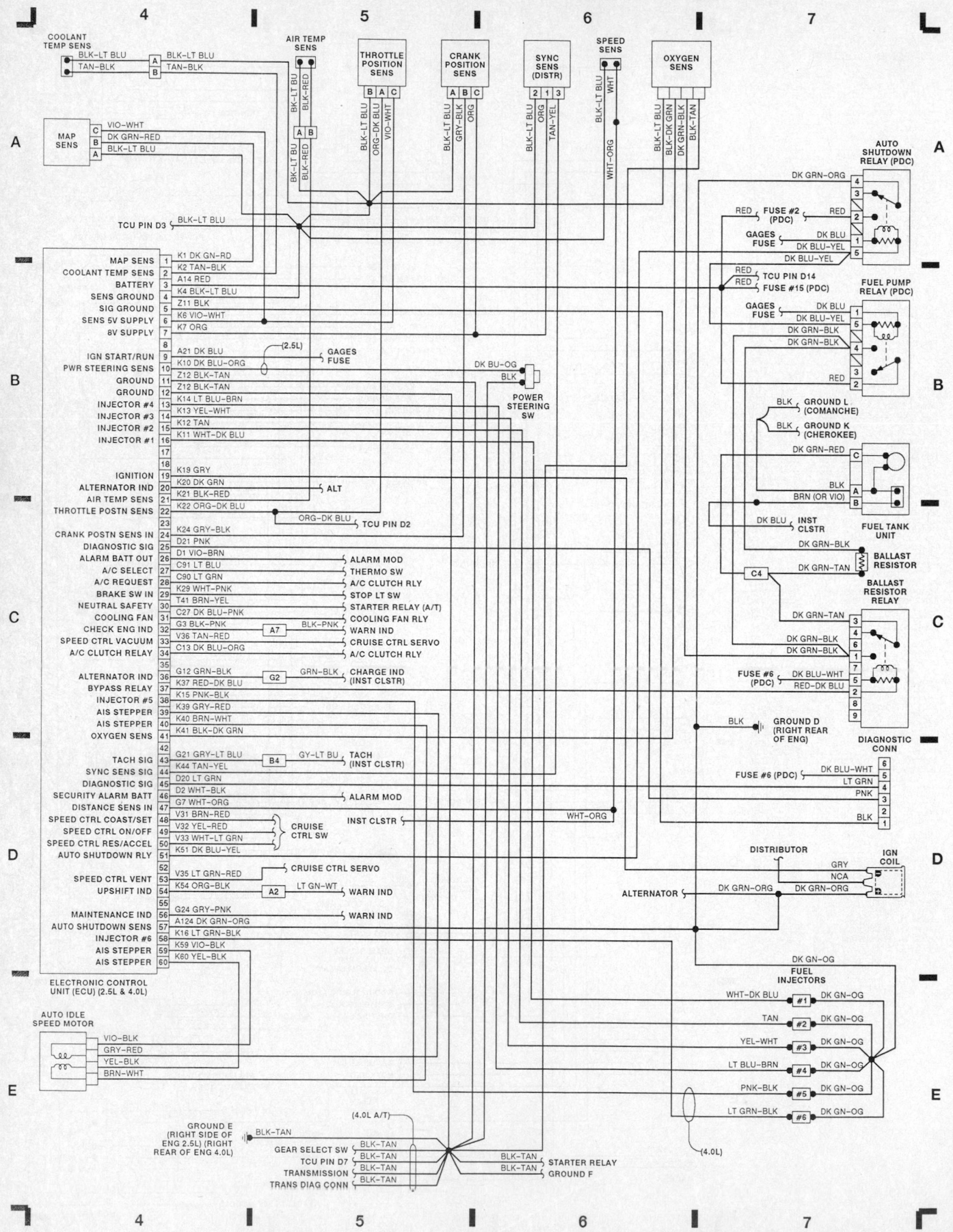

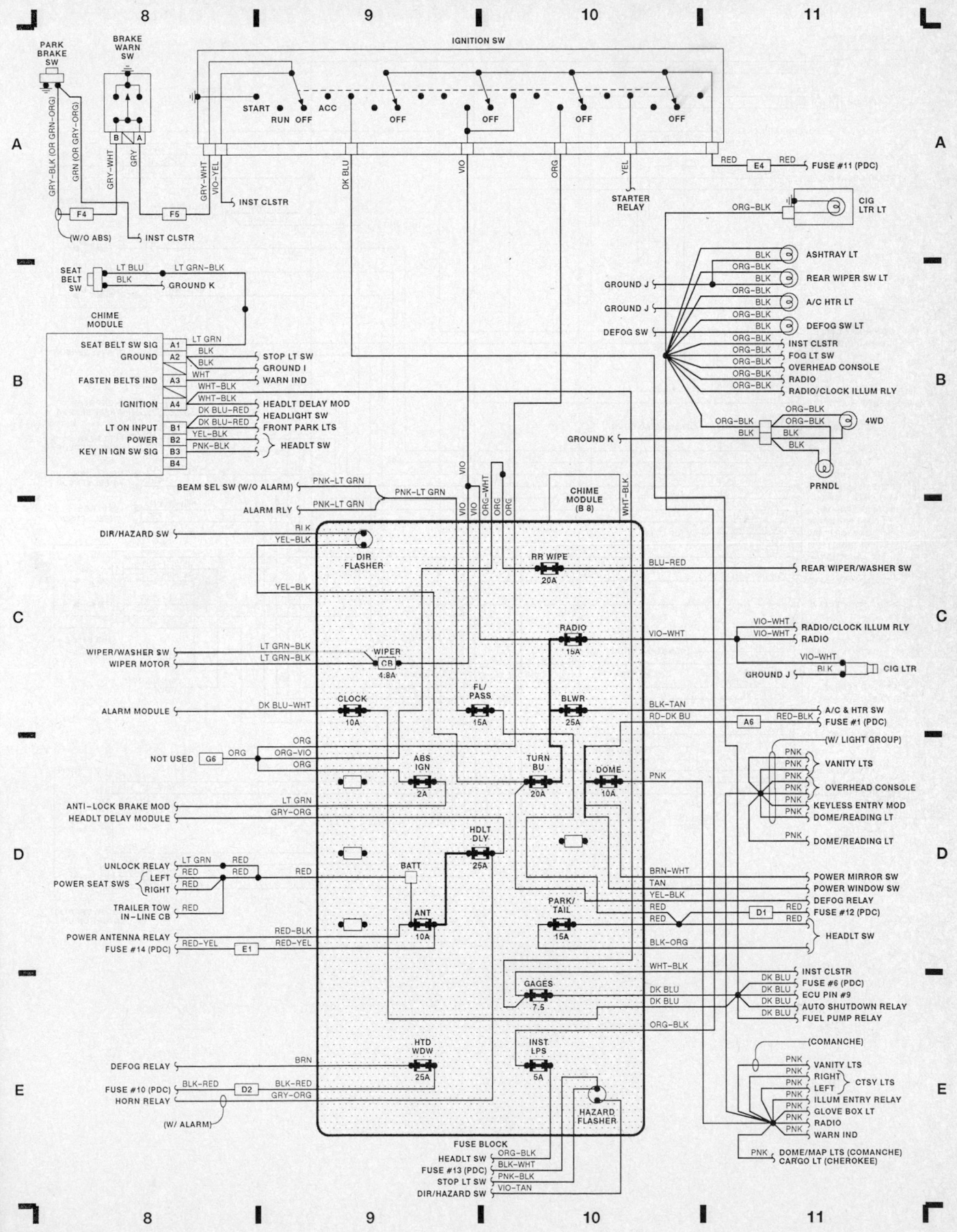

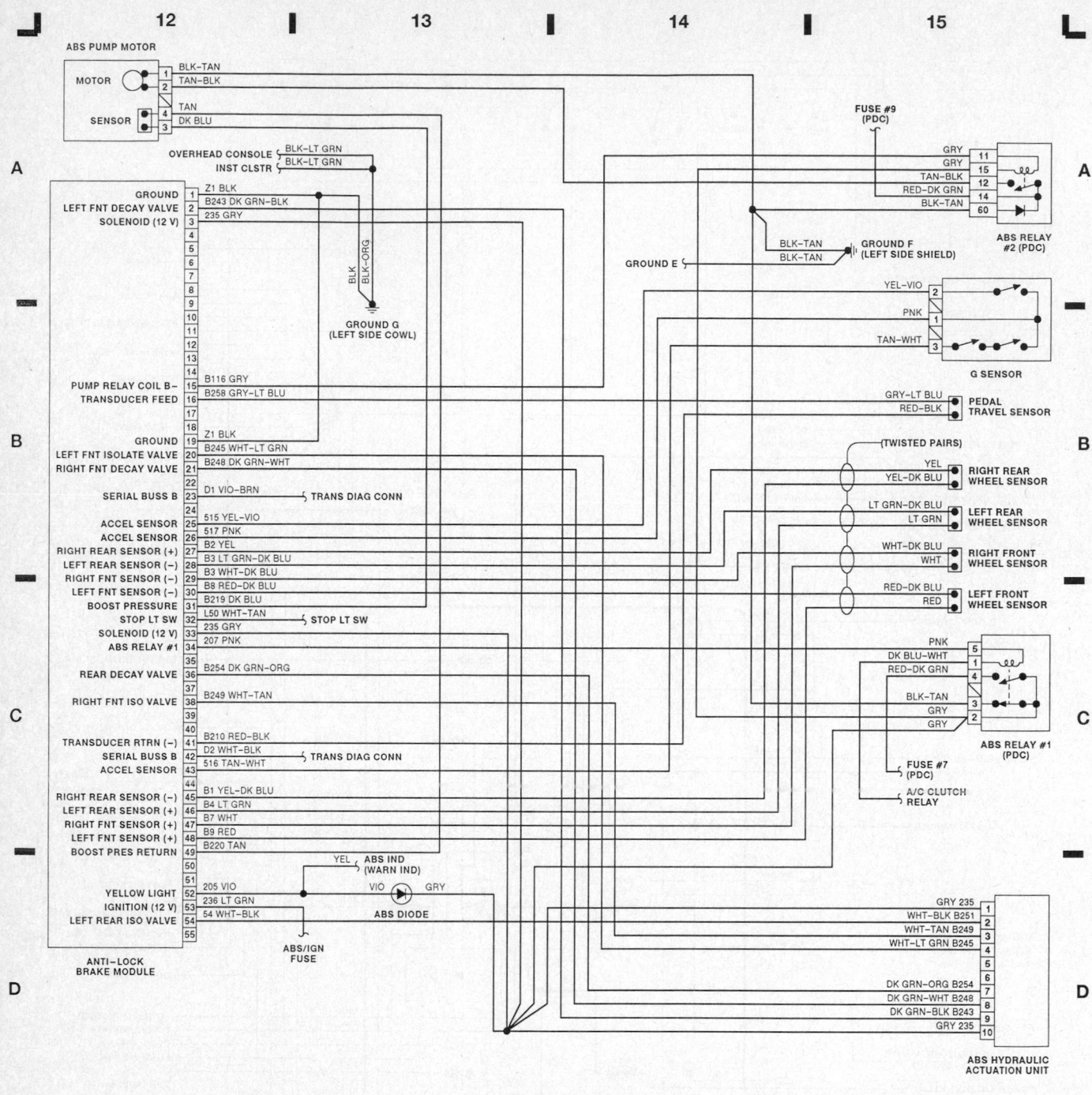

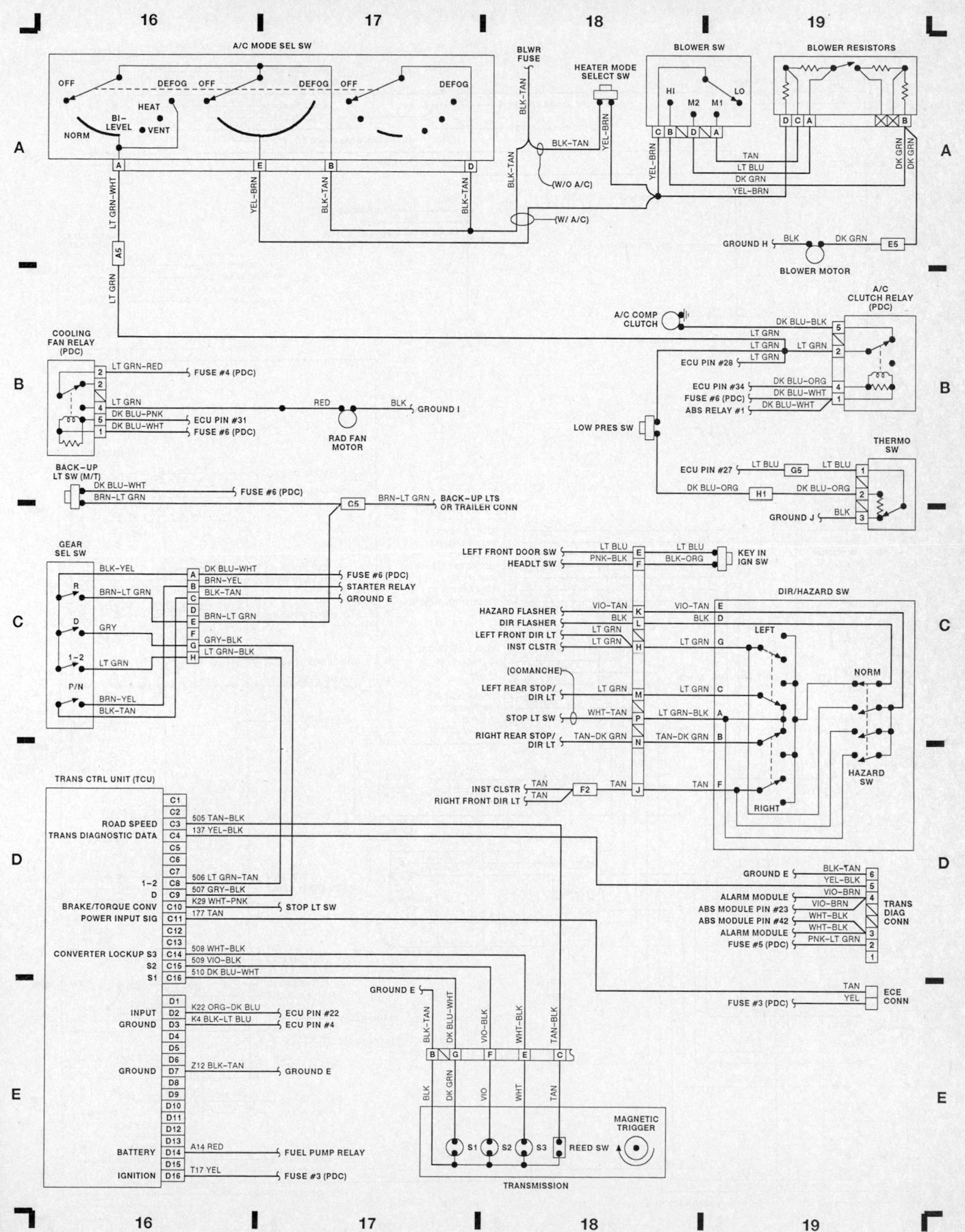

1992 WIRING DIAGRAMS
Cherokee & Comanche (Cont.)

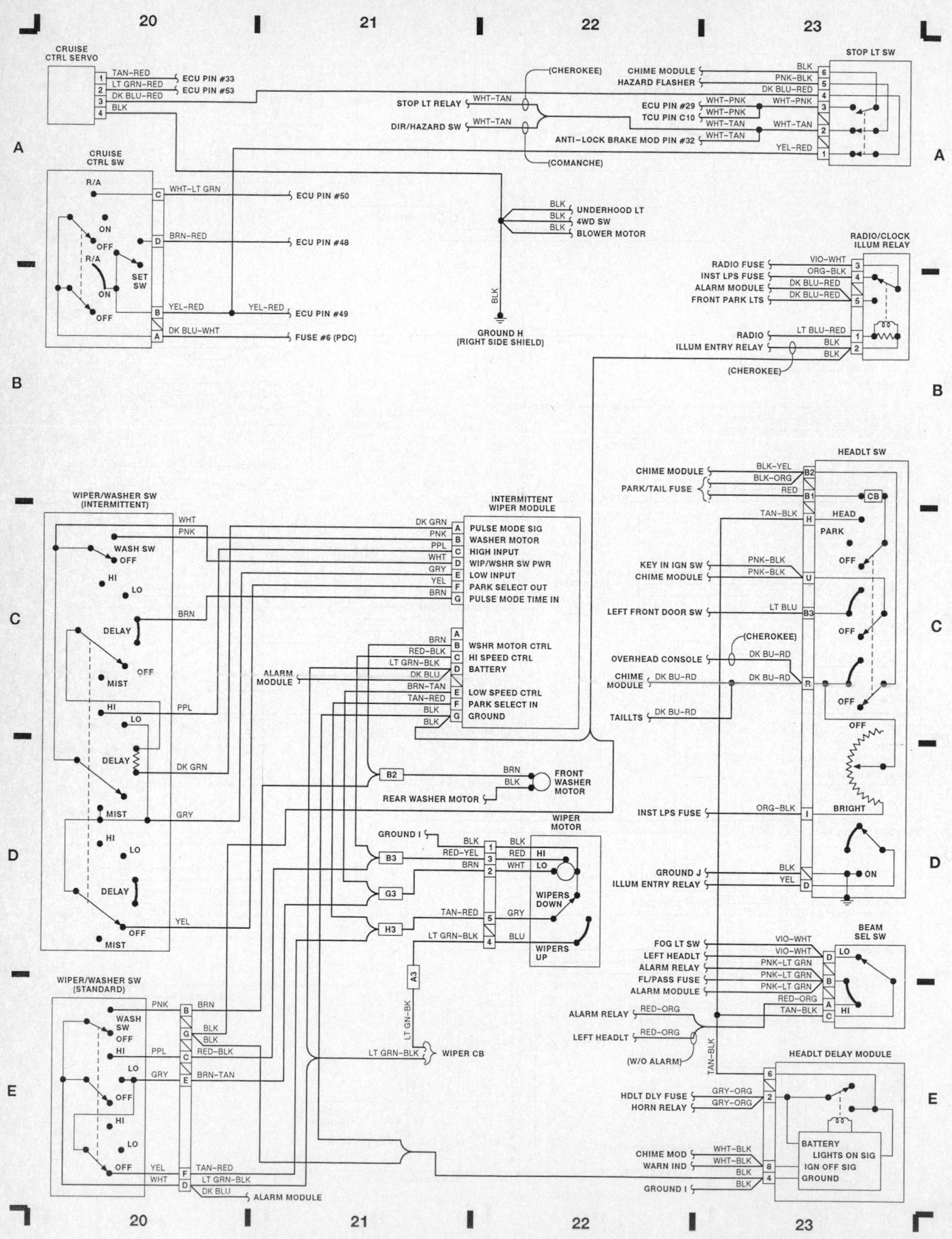

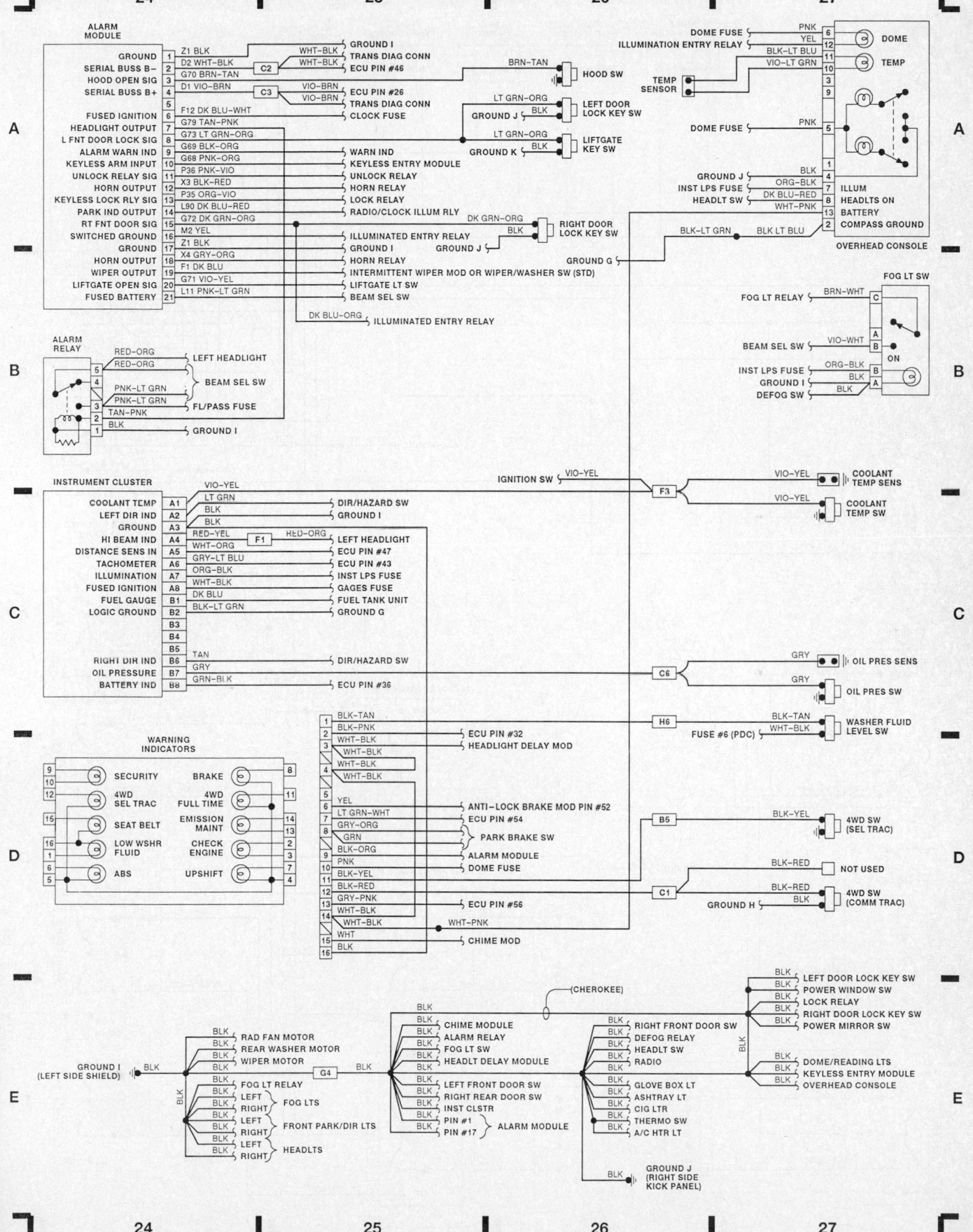

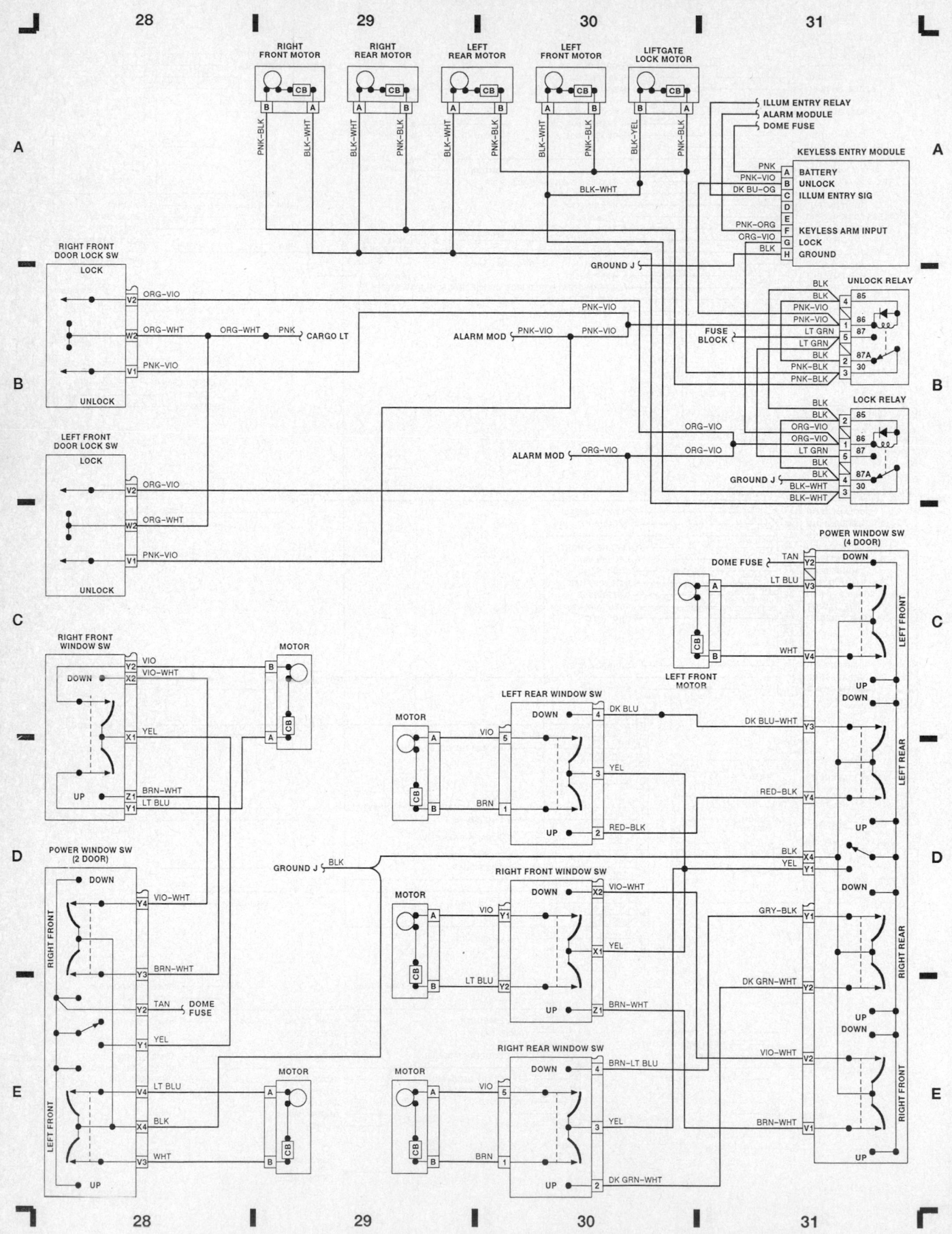

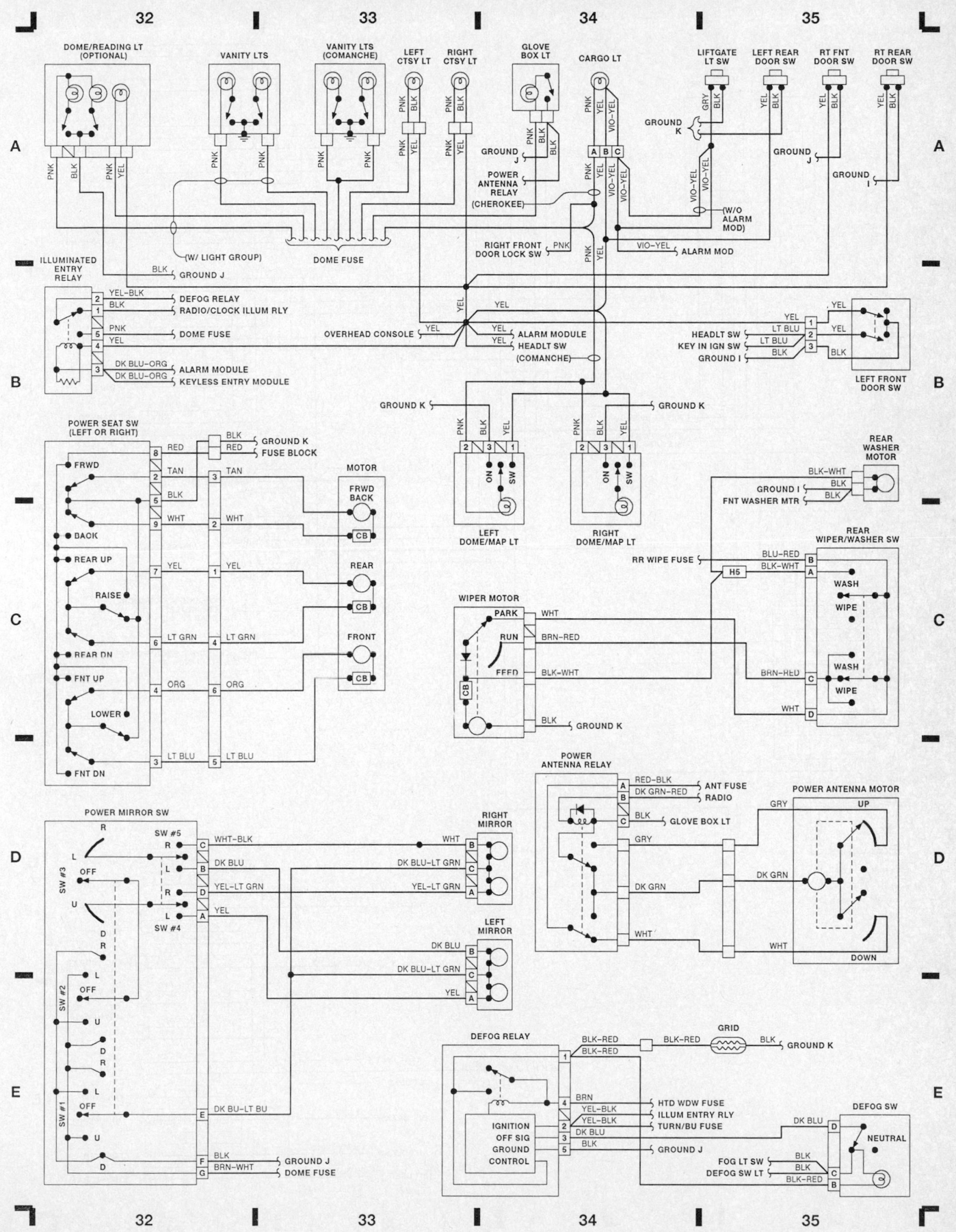

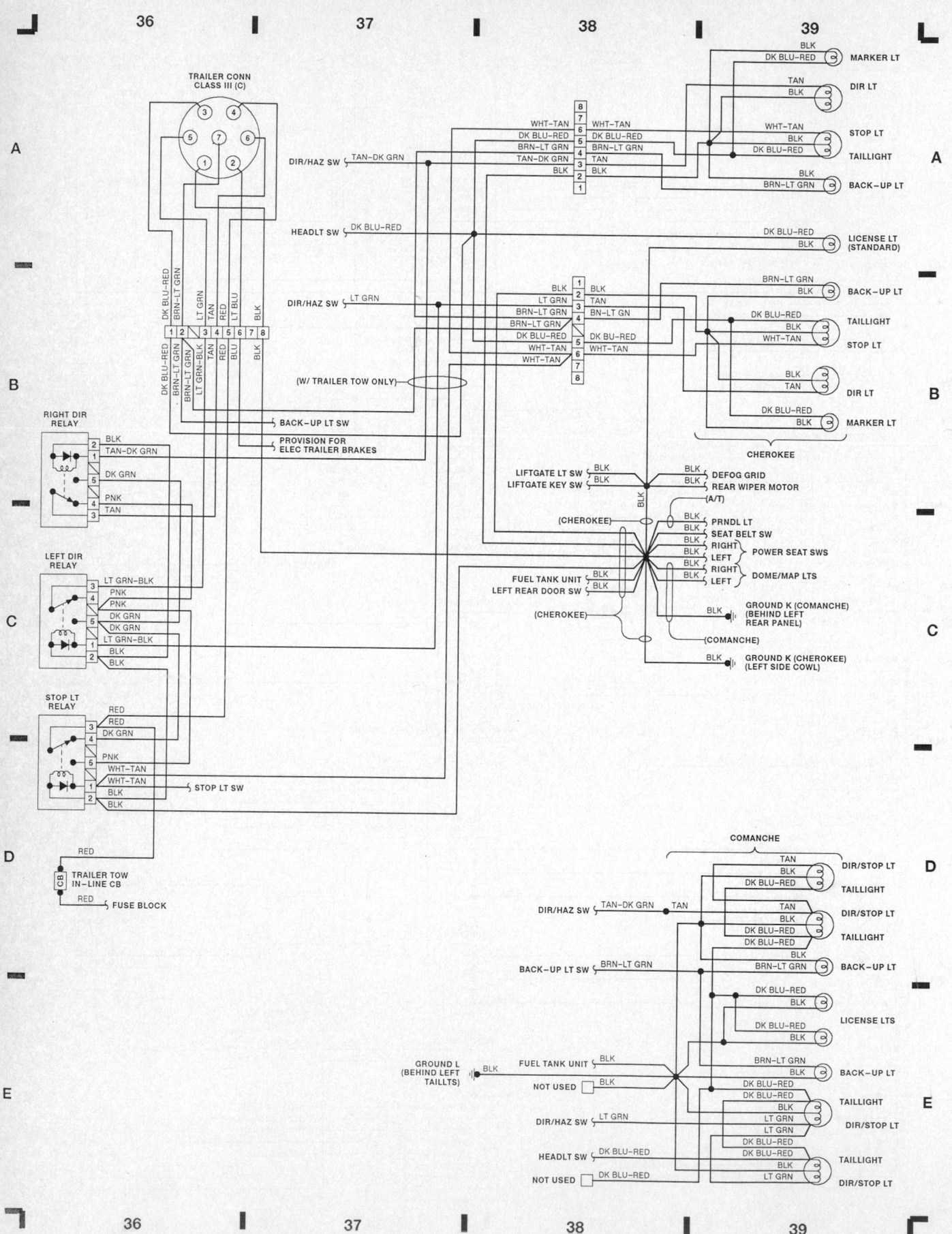

1993 WIRING DIAGRAMS
Grand Cherokee

COMPONENT LOCATOR:

A/C-HEATER SYSTEMS .... A-E 16-19
AIRBAG MODULE .... D-E 12
ALARM MODULE .... A 28
ALARM RELAY .... B 28
ALTERNATOR .... E 3
ANTI-LOCK BRAKE SYSTEM ..... A-D 12-15
AUTO SHUTDOWN RELAY .... A 7
BATTERY .... A 1-2
BRAKE WARN SW .... A 8
CONVENIENCE CENTER CHIME .... E 28
CRUISE CTRL SYSTEM .... A 24-27
DEFOG GRID .... B 38-39
DEFOG RELAY .... B-C 37-38
DEFOG/OVERDRIVE SW .... B-C 39
DIMMER SW .... E 23
DIR FLASHER .... E 21
DIR/HAZ SW .... E 20
DOOR SWS .... B-E 31
DOOR SWS .... A-B 38-39
ENG/MET SW .... B 31
ENGINE COOLANT LEVEL SENS .... E 31
FOG LT RELAY .... E 2
FUEL PUMP RELAY .... B 7
FUEL TANK UNIT .... B 7
FUSE BLOCK .... C-D 8-11
GLOVE BOX LT/SW .... B 8
GROUND A .... A 1
GROUND B .... A 1
GROUND C .... E 1
GROUND D .... E 11
GROUND E .... D 8
GROUND F .... E 15
GROUND G .... B 13
GROUND H .... A-B 23
GROUND I .... A 41
HAZ FLASHER .... D-E 21
HEADLIGHT SW .... B-D 23
HOOD SW .... A 29-30
HORN RELAY/SW .... E 3
I/P DIMMING MOD .... E 23
I/P ILLUMINATION LTS .... C 20-21
IGN COIL .... D 7
IGN SW/LT .... E 30
IGNITION SW .... A 9-10
ILLUM ENTRY RELAY .... B 36
INSTRUMENT CLUSTER .... B-D 28-30
INTERIOR LTS .... A-B 36-39
INTERIOR MIRROR .... B-C 11
KEYLESS ENTRY MODULE .... A 35
LEFT FRONT DOOR KEY SW .... A 29
LIFTGATE AJAR SW .... E 31
LIFTGATE KEY CYLINDER SW .... A 30
LT OUTAGE MODULE .... B-C 42-43
OVERHEAD CONSOLE .... A 31
PCM DIAG CONN .... C 7
POWER ANTENNA SYSTEM .... D 38-39
POWER DISTRIBUTION
CENTER (PDC) .... A-D 3
POWER DOOR LOCK SYSTEM ... A-B 32-35
POWER MIRROR SYSTEM .... D-E 36-38
POWER SEAT SYSTEM .... B-C 39-37
POWER WINDOW SYSTEM .... C-E 32-35
POWERTRAIN CTRL MODULE (PCM) .. A-D 4
RELAY CENTER .... F 9-10
RIGHT FRONT DOOR KEY SW ..... A-B 29-30
STARTER RELAY .... A 3
STOP/DIR LT RELAYS .... B-D 40
TRAILER TOW CB .... C 41
TRANSMISSION/TRANSFER
CASE SYSTEMS .... A-B 20-23
ULTRALIGHT SENTINEL .... C-D 20
UNDERHOOD LT .... A 1-2
VEHICLE INFORMATION CENTER .... C-D 31
WASHER FLUID LEVEL SENS .... E 31
WIPER/WASHER SYSTEMS .... C-E 24-27

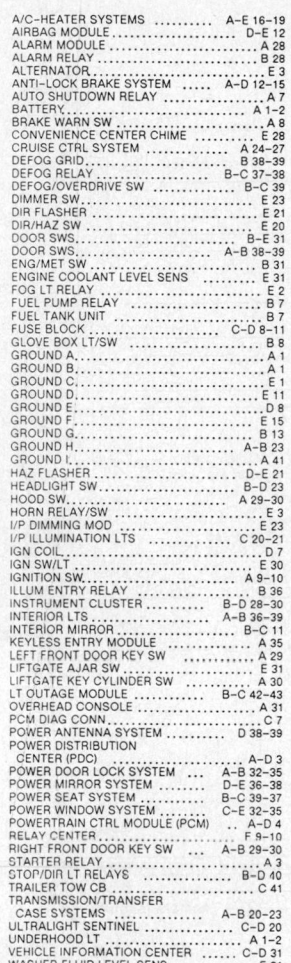

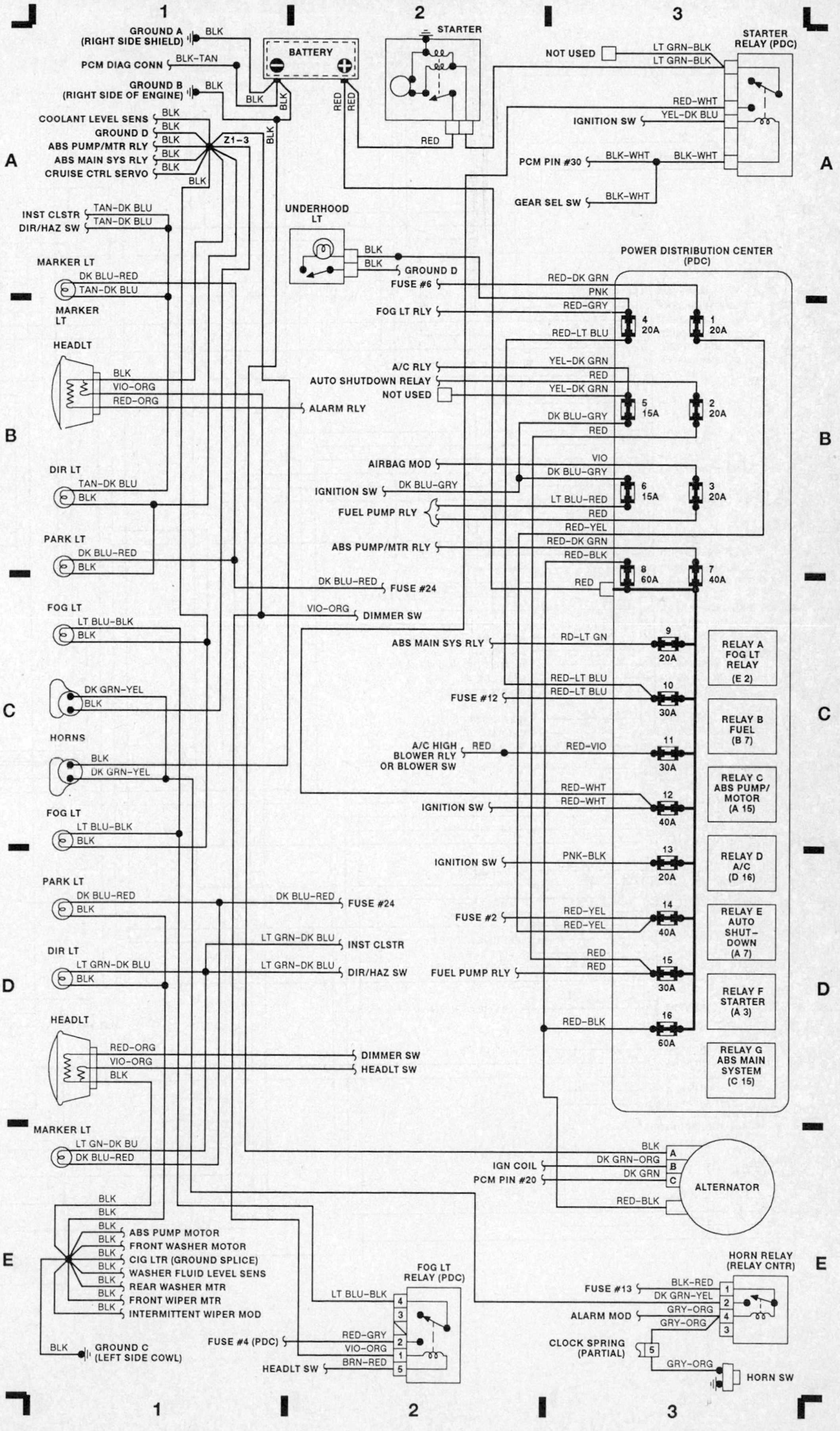

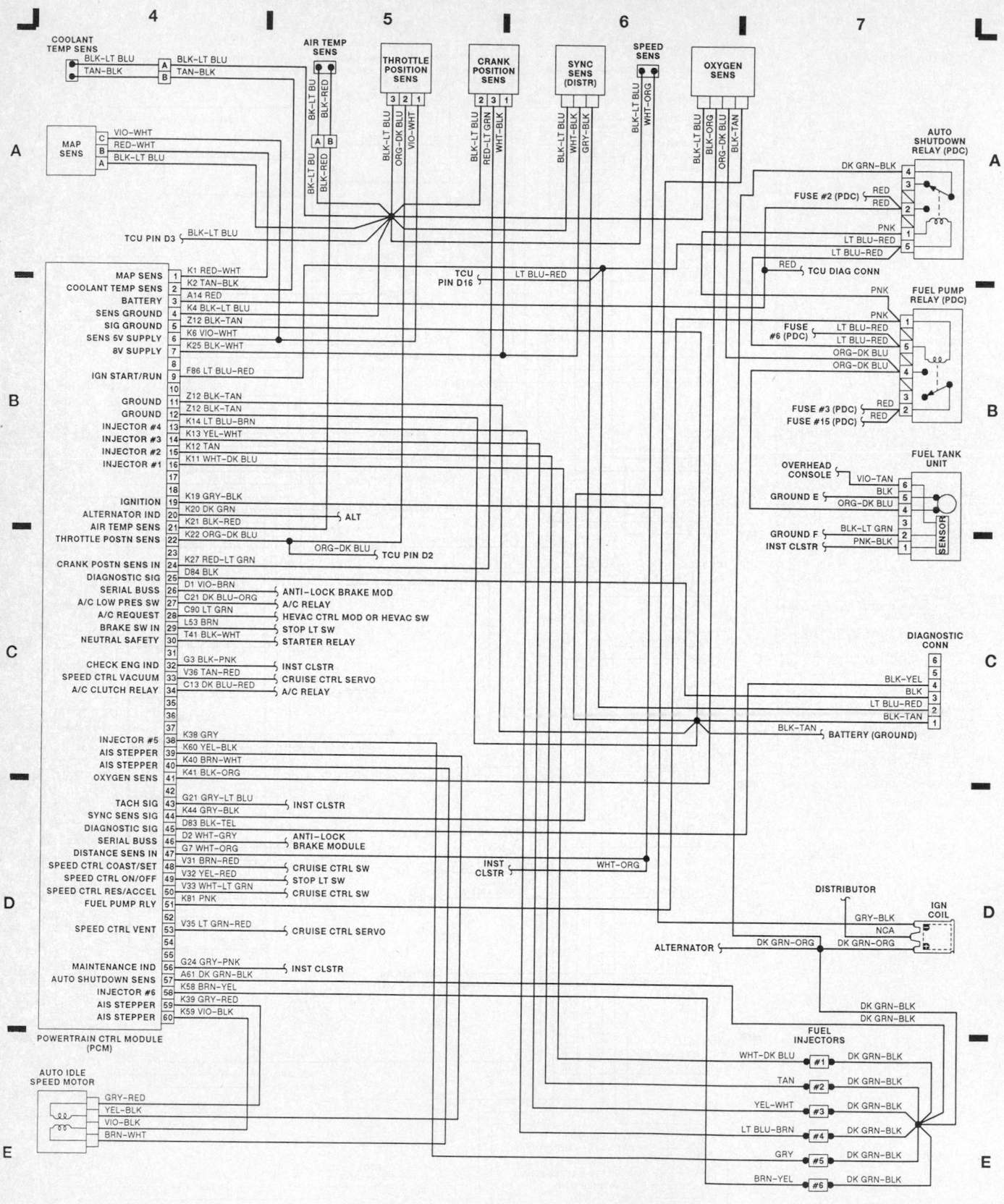

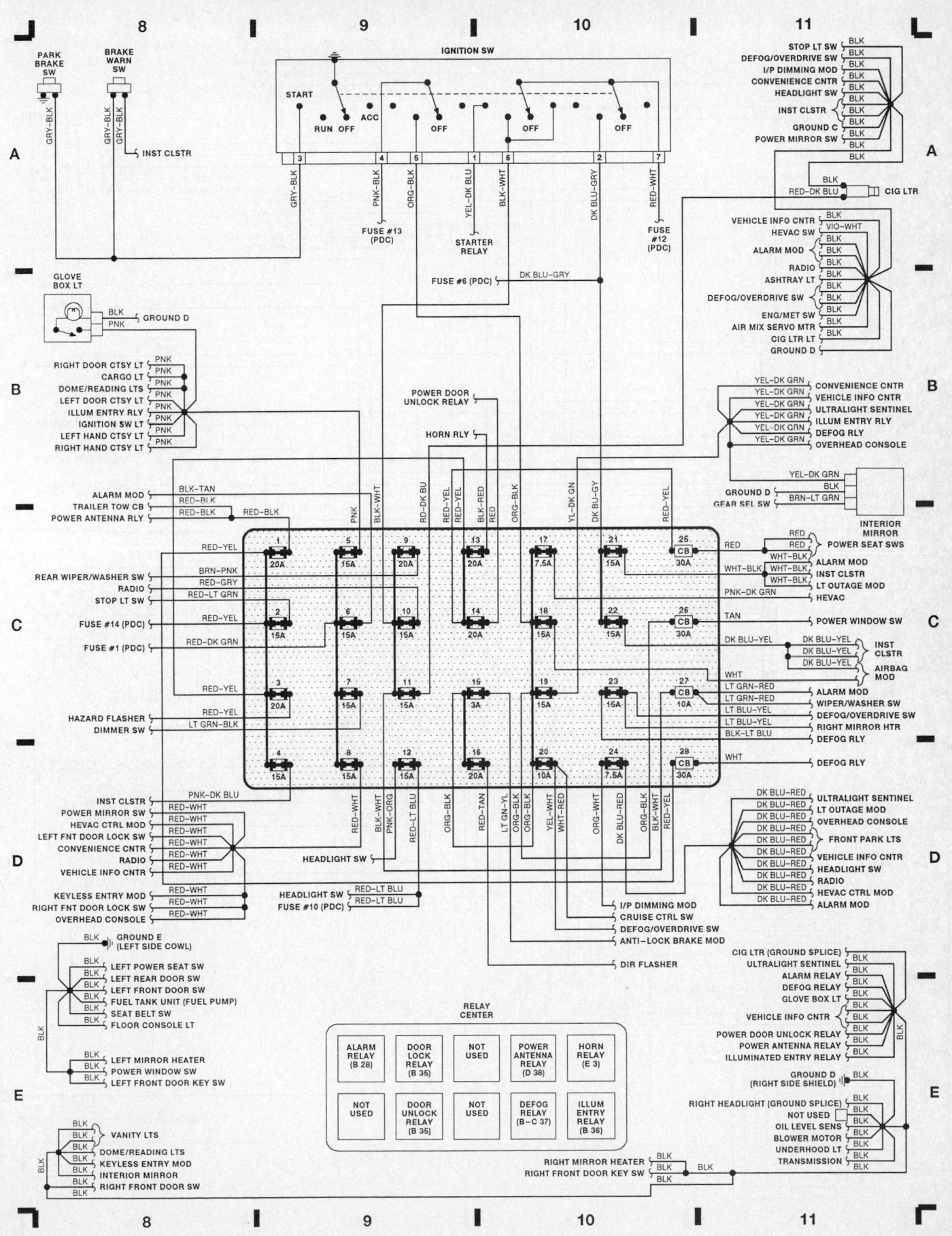

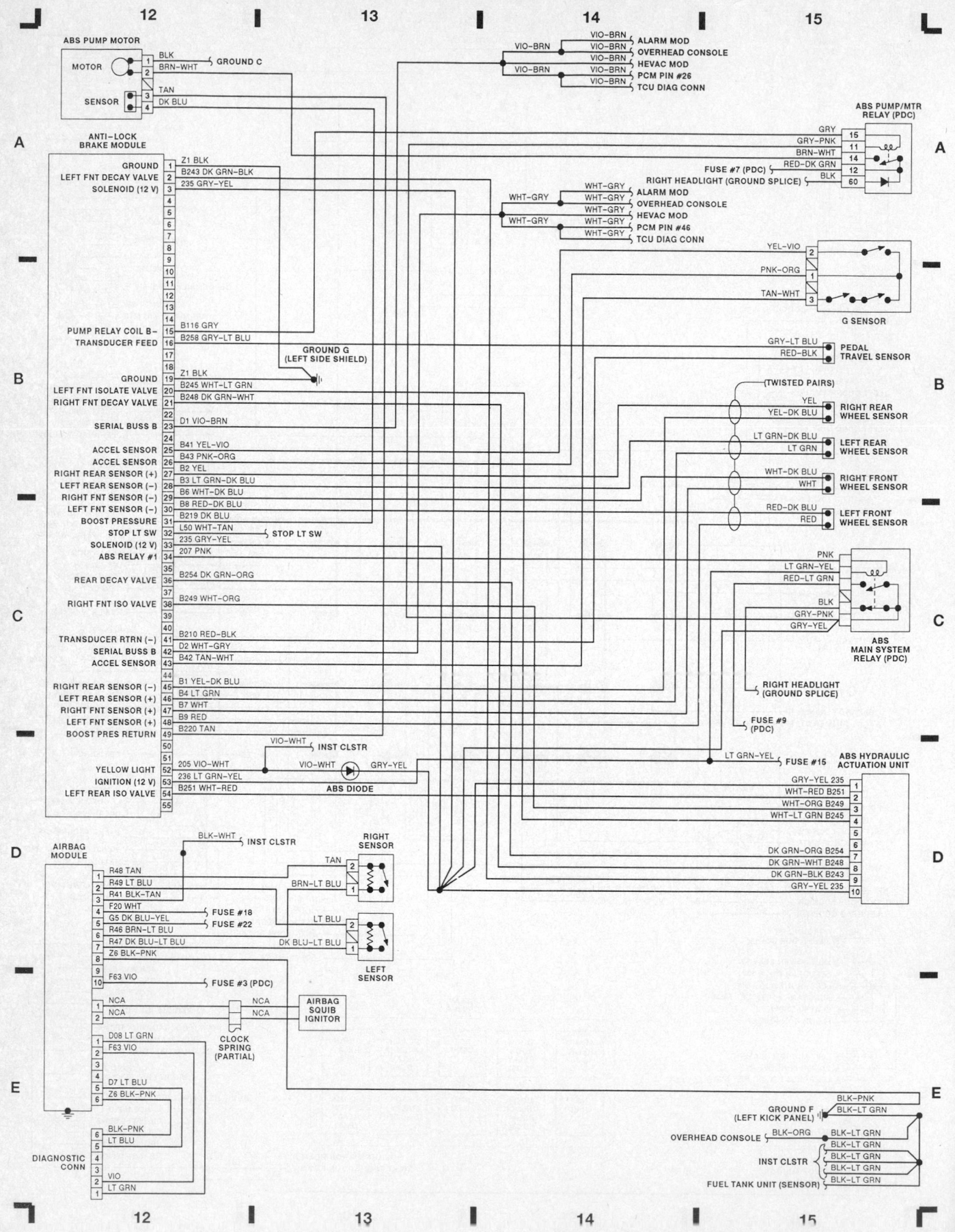

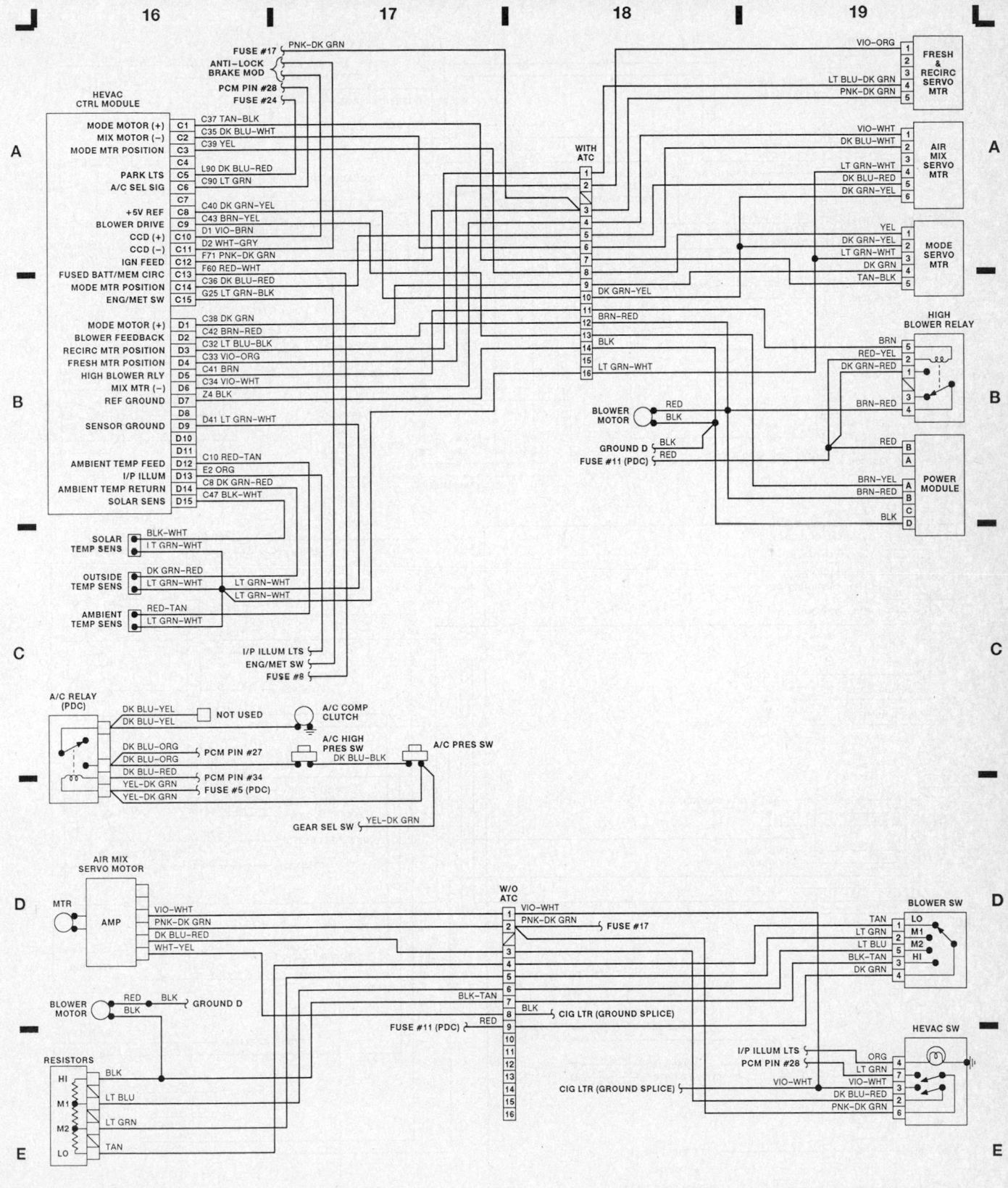

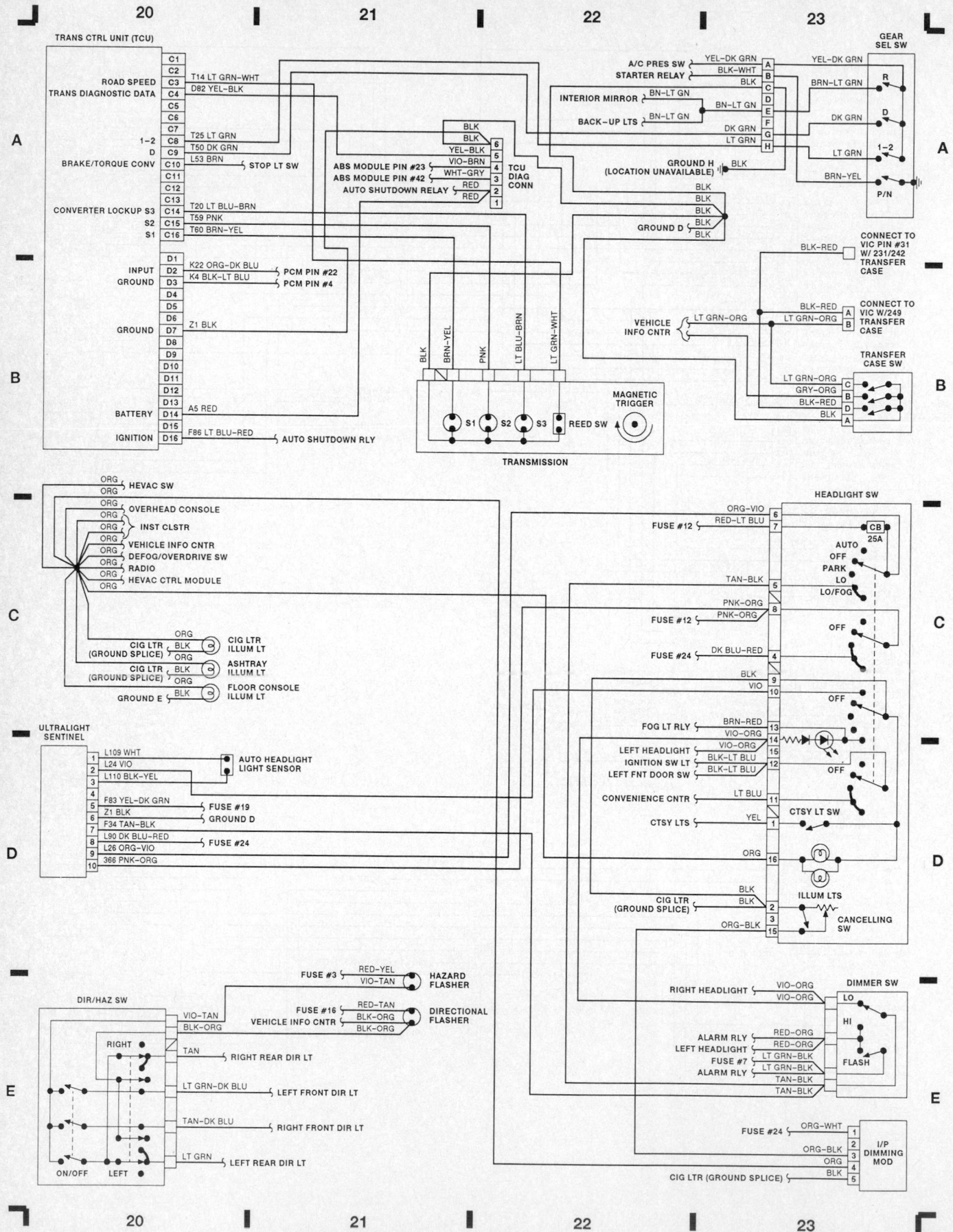

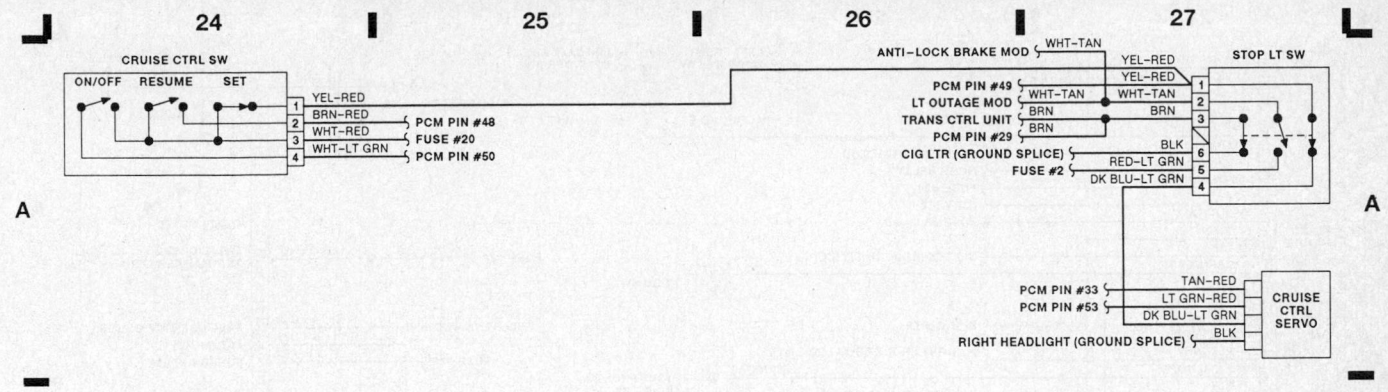

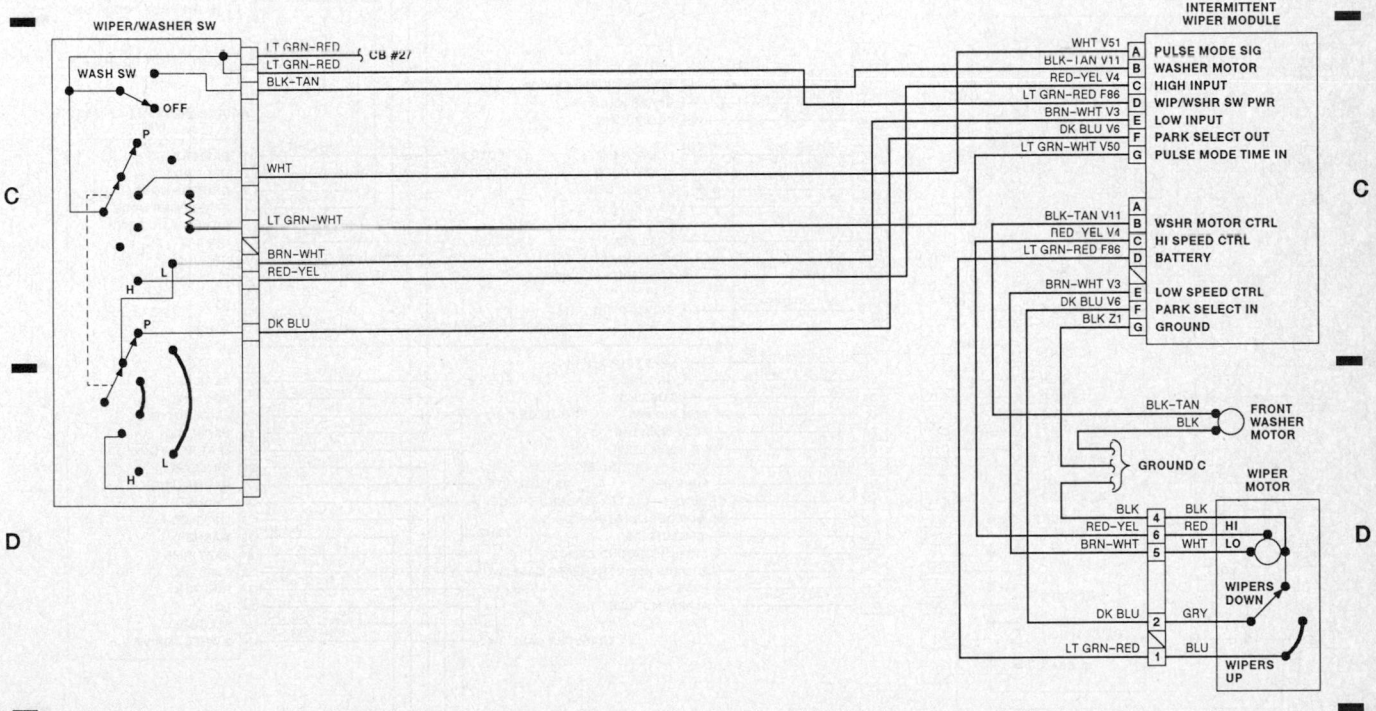

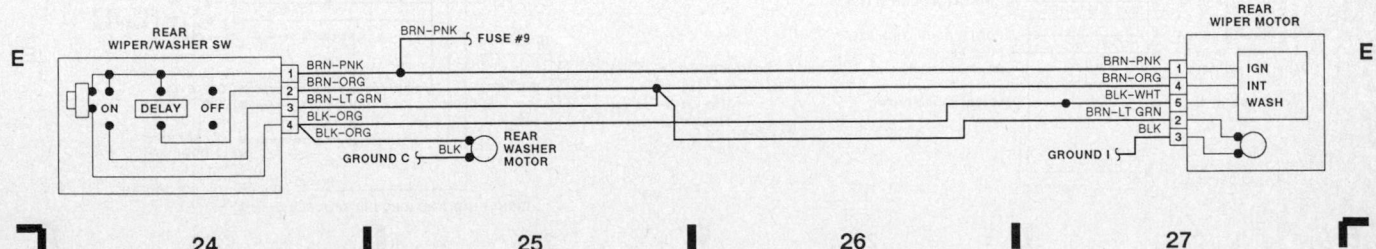

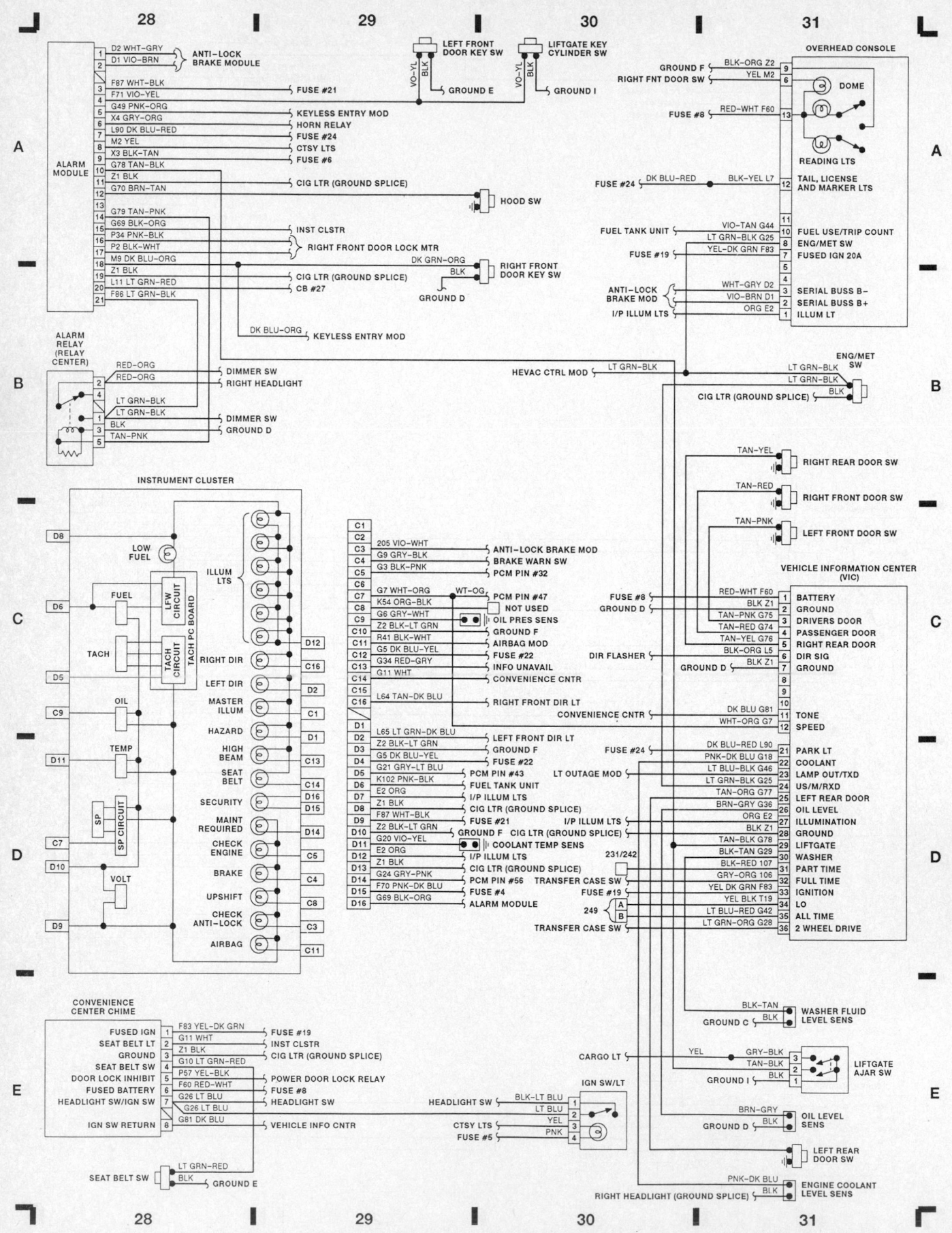

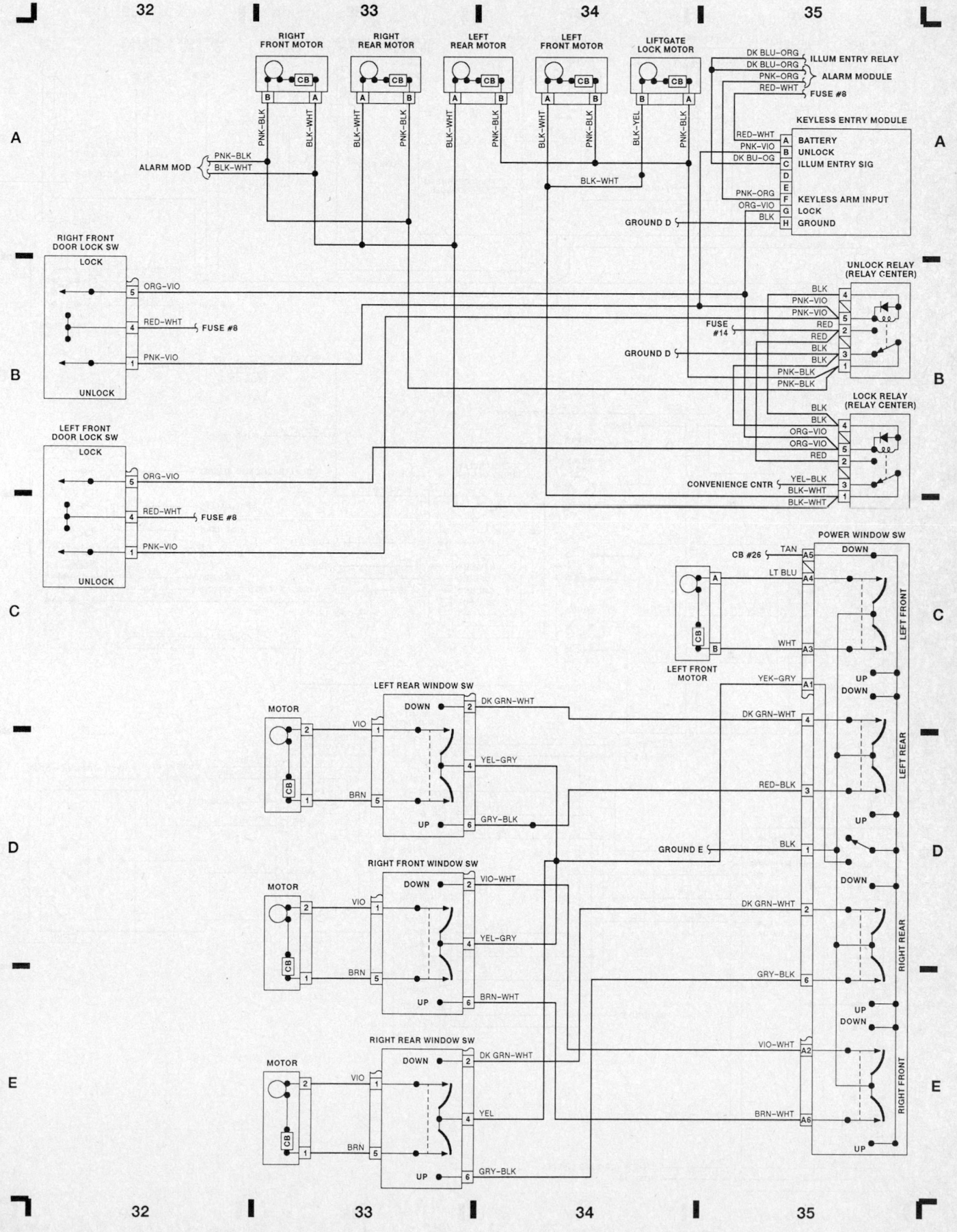

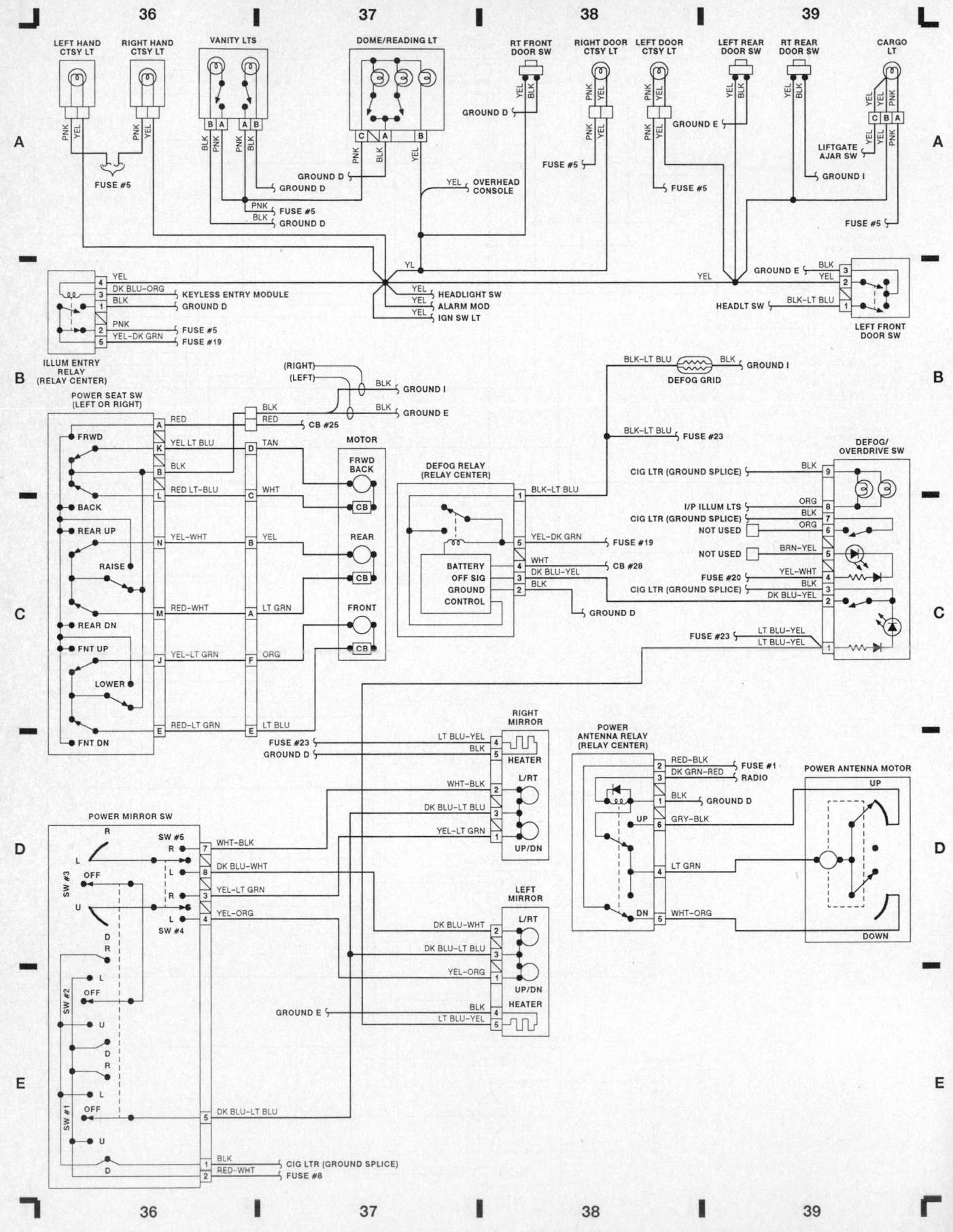

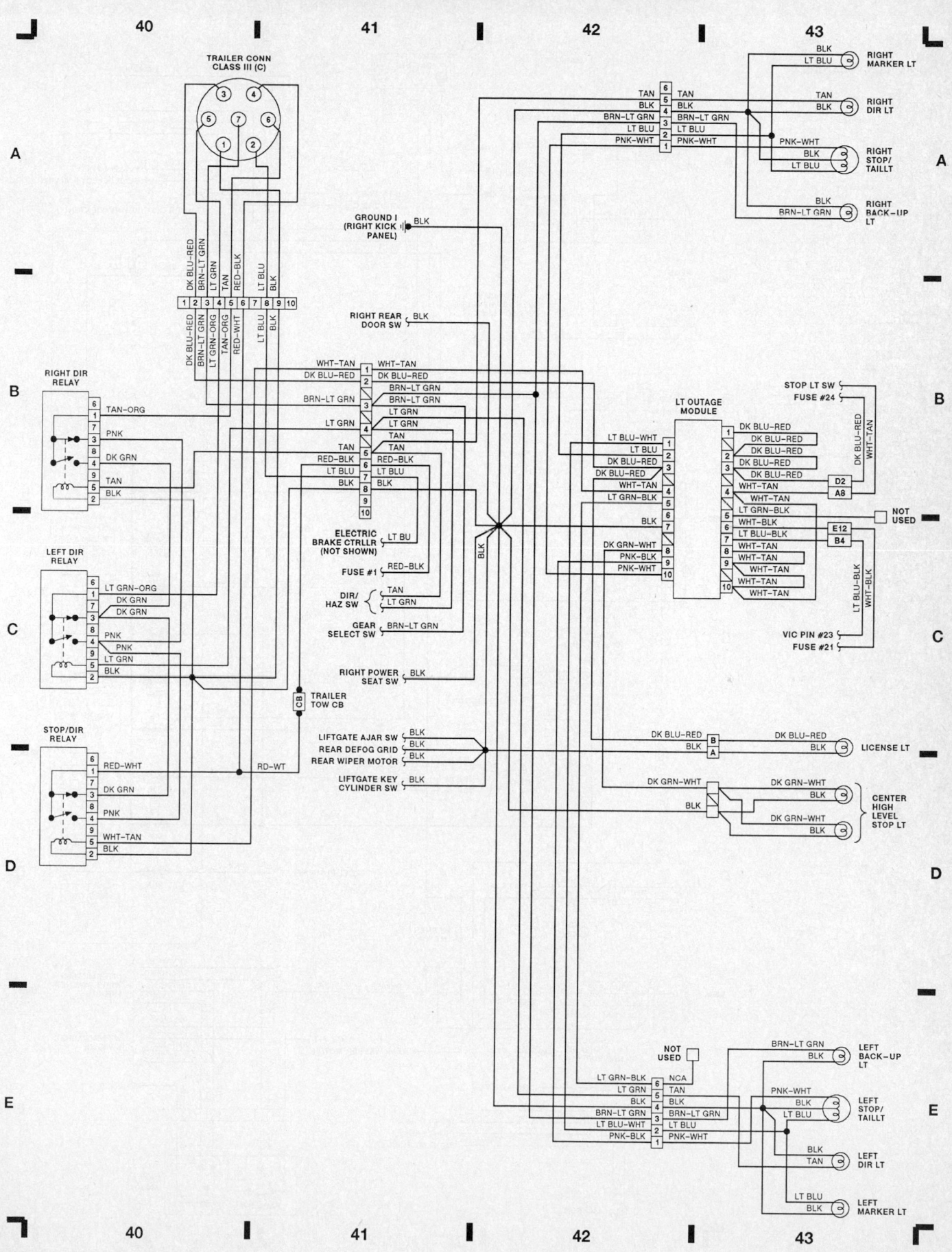

1992 WIRING DIAGRAMS
Wrangler

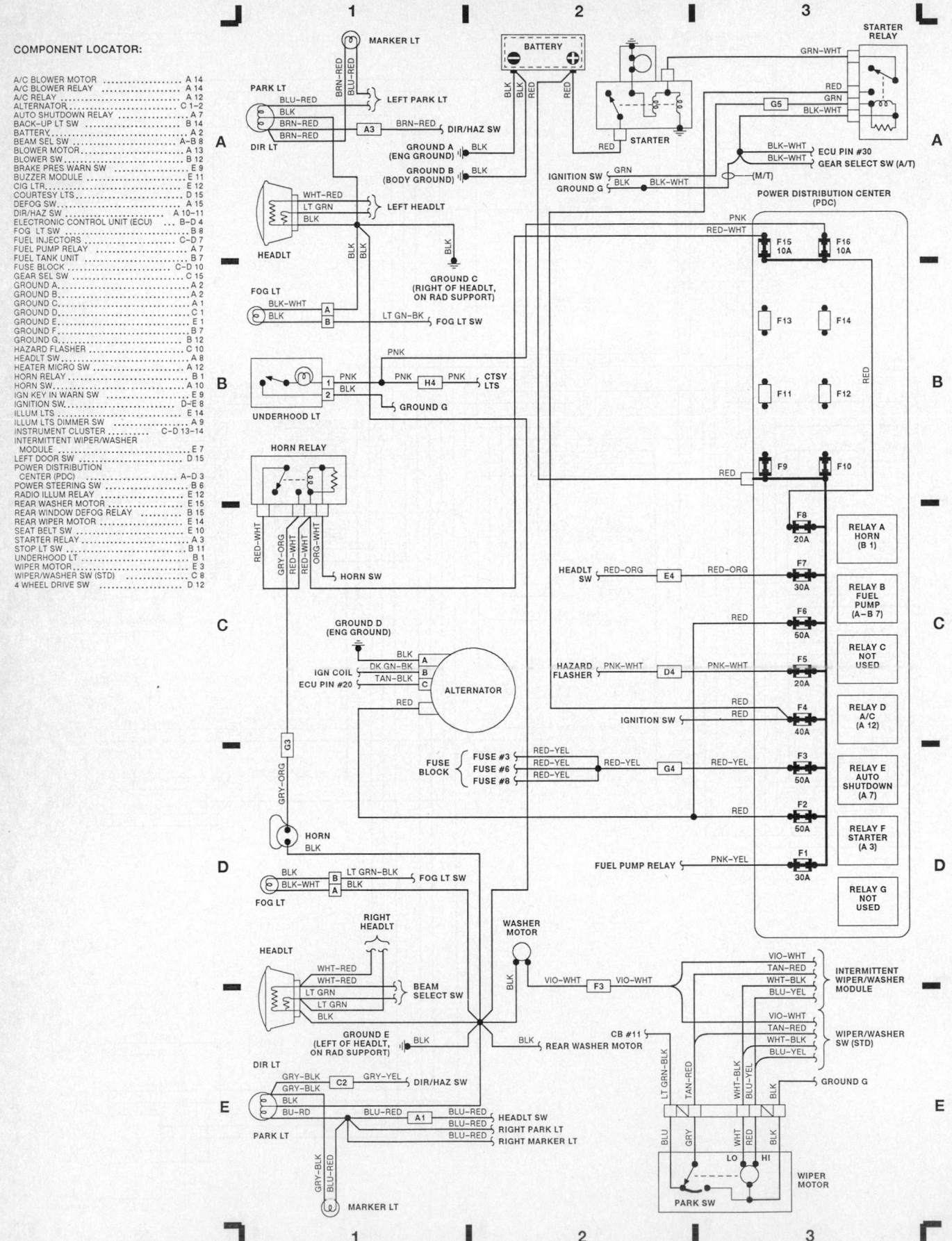

COMPONENT LOCATOR:

A/C BLOWER MOTOR .... A 14
A/C BLOWER RELAY .... A 14
A/C RELAY .... A 12
ALTERNATOR .... C 1–2
AUTO SHUTDOWN RELAY .... A 7
BACK-UP LT SW .... B 14
BATTERY .... A 2
BEAM SEL SW .... A–B 8
BLOWER MOTOR .... A–B 13
BLOWER SW .... B 12
BRAKE PRES WARN SW .... E 9
BUZZER MODULE .... E 11
CIG LTR .... E 12
COURTESY LTS .... D 15
DEFOG SW .... A 15
DIR/HAZ SW .... A 10–11
ELECTRONIC CONTROL UNIT (ECU) ... B–D 4
FOG LT SW .... B 8
FUEL INJECTORS .... C–D 7
FUEL PUMP RELAY .... A 7
FUEL TANK UNIT .... B 7
FUSE BLOCK .... C–D 10
GEAR SEL SW .... C 15
GROUND A .... A 2
GROUND B .... A 2
GROUND C .... A 1
GROUND D .... C 1
GROUND E .... E 1
GROUND F .... B 7
GROUND G .... B 12
HAZARD FLASHER .... C 10
HEADLT SW .... A 8
HEATER MICRO SW .... A 12
HORN RELAY .... B 1
HORN SW .... A 10
IGN KEY IN WARN SW .... E 9
IGNITION SW .... D–E 8
ILLUM LTS .... E 14
ILLUM LTS DIMMER SW .... A 9
INSTRUMENT CLUSTER .... C–D 13–14
INTERMITTENT WIPER/WASHER
    MODULE .... E 7
LEFT DOOR SW .... D 15
POWER DISTRIBUTION
    CENTER (PDC) .... A–D 3
POWER STEERING SW .... B 6
RADIO ILLUM RELAY .... E 12
REAR WASHER MOTOR .... E 15
REAR WINDOW DEFOG RELAY ... B 15
REAR WIPER MOTOR .... E 14
SEAT BELT SW .... E 10
STARTER RELAY .... A 3
STOP LT SW .... B 11
UNDERHOOD LT .... B 1
WIPER MOTOR .... E 3
WIPER/WASHER SW (STD) .... C 8
4 WHEEL DRIVE SW .... D 12

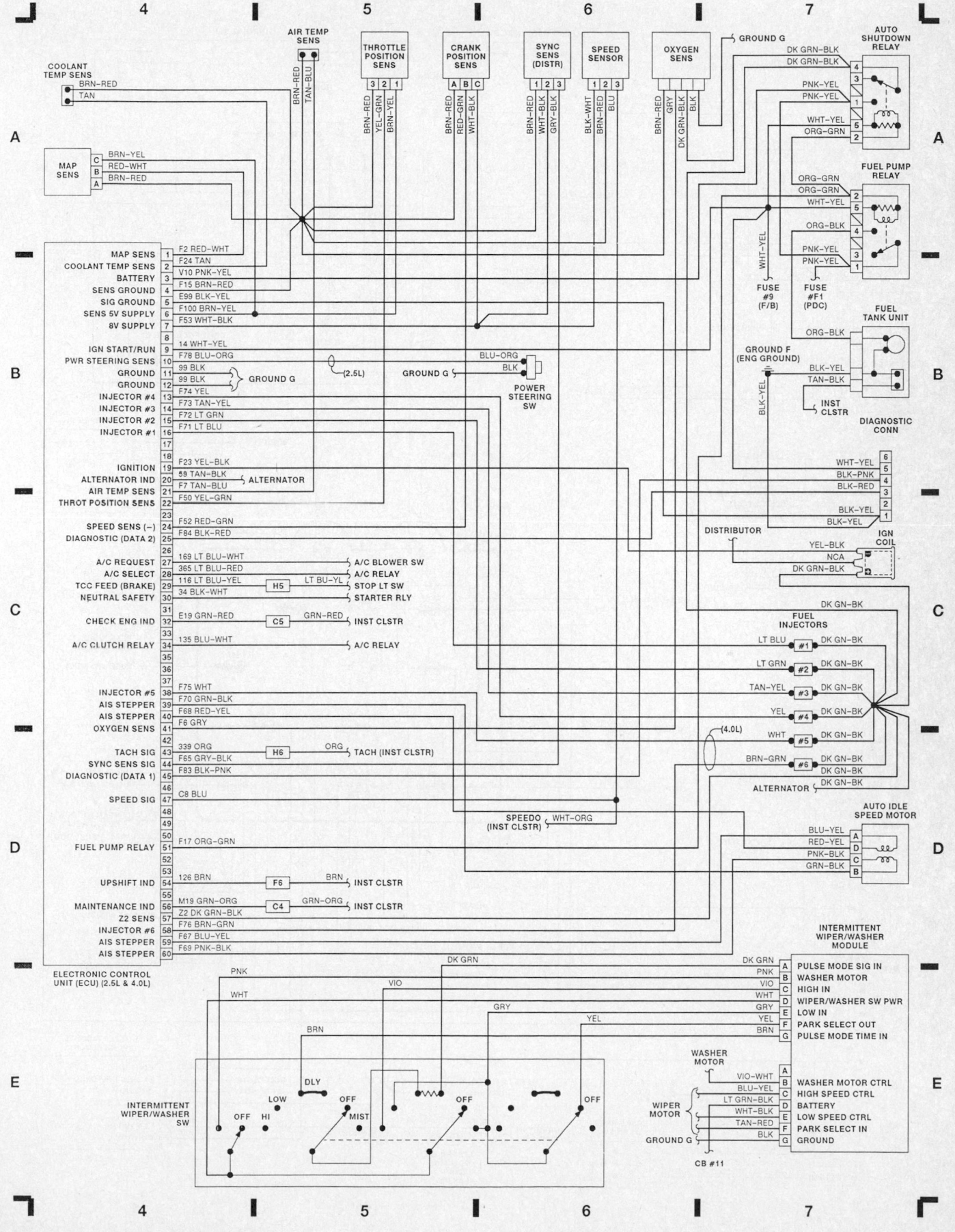

1992 WIRING DIAGRAMS
Wrangler (Cont.)

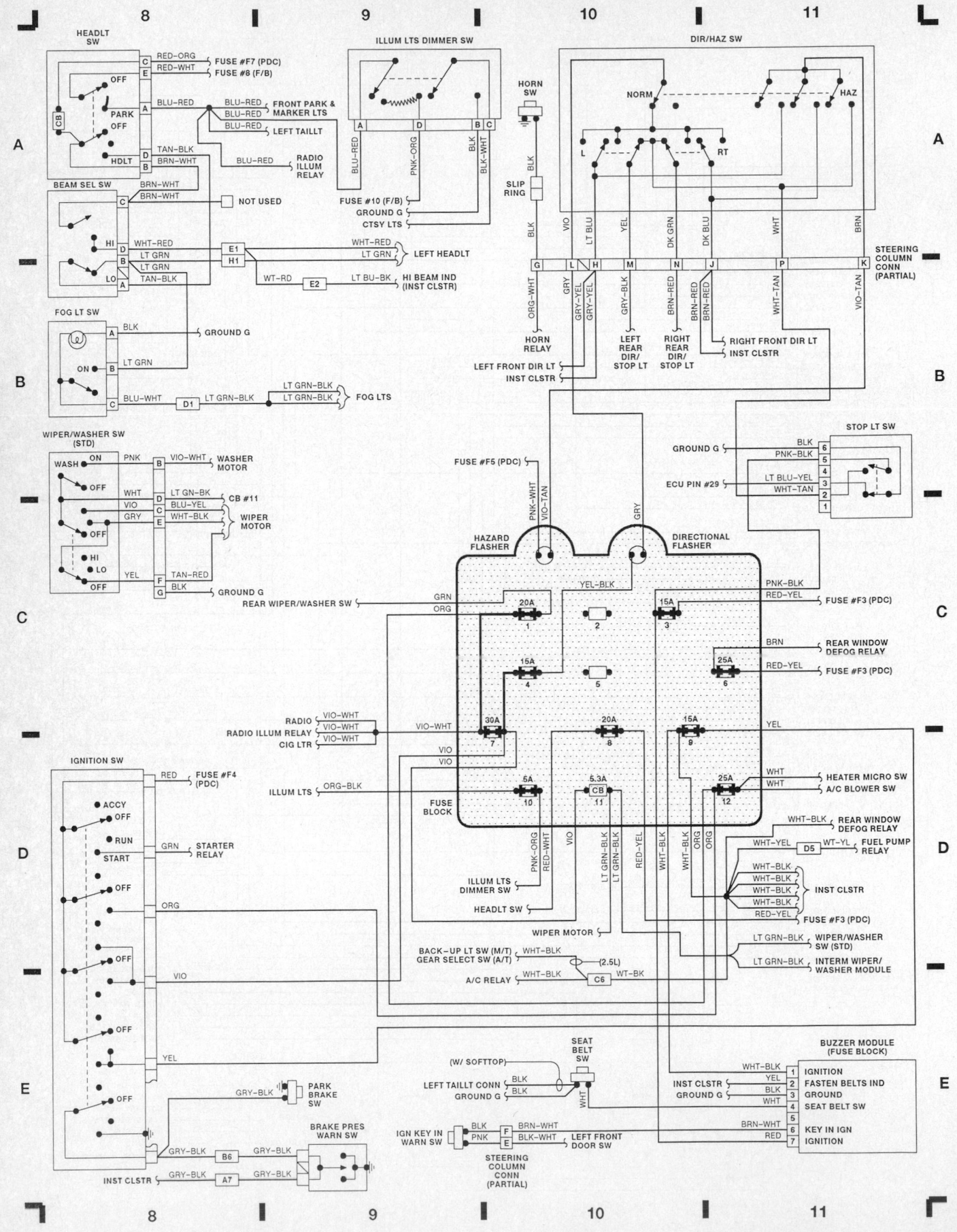

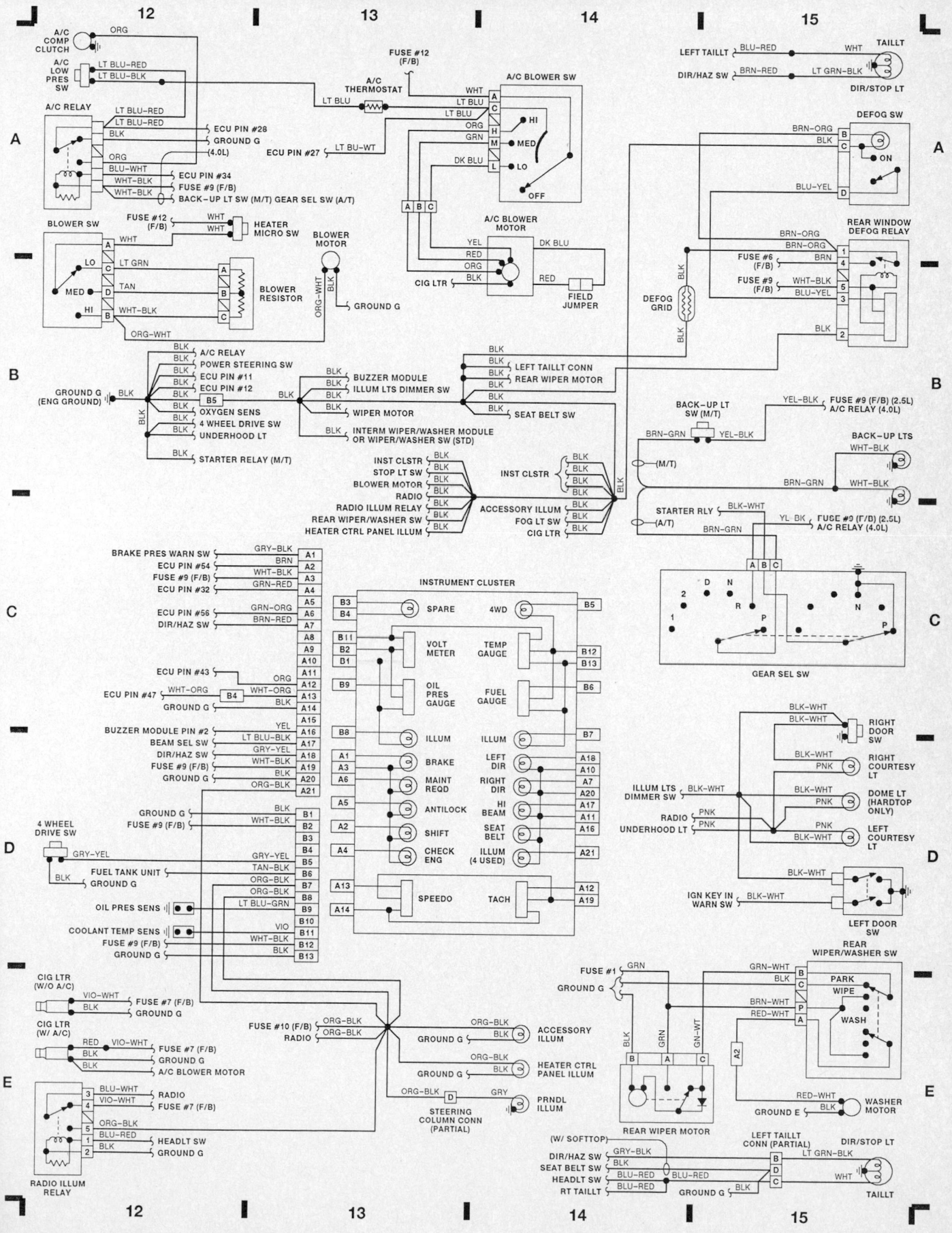

Cherokee, Comanche

DESCRIPTION

The cruise control system is electronically controlled and vacuum operated. The electronic control is integrated into the Single Board Engine Controller (SBEC). System consists of SBEC, servo, cruise control switch panel, vacuum reservoir, distance (speed) sensor, brakelight switch and park/neutral switch (automatic transmission). System controls are located on the steering wheel and consist of ON/OFF, RESUME/ACCEL, and SET/DECEL or SET/COAST buttons.

OPERATION

SYSTEM CONTROLS

To Set Speed Control – Press ON/OFF button to turn cruise control system on. Accelerate to desired speed (minimum of 35 MPH) and depress SET/DECEL or SET/COAST button. Vehicle speed will be maintained.

To Disengage Speed Control – Depress brake pedal or clutch pedal. The ON/OFF button may also be used, but set speed will be erased from memory. If clutch pedal is used to disengage cruise control, engine speed will increase before cruise control cuts out.

To Resume Previous Speed – If set speed has not been erased from memory and vehicle speed is more than 30 MPH, press RESUME/ACCEL button.

To Increase Speed – With cruise control system on, increase set speed by pressing and releasing RESUME/ACCEL button within one second. Each press and release of button will cause an increase of 2 MPH. For example, 3 presses would result in a speed increase of 6 MPH. To increase speed gradually, press RESUME/ACCEL button until desired speed is reached. When button is released, new set speed will be maintained.

To Decrease Speed – With cruise control system on, decrease set speed by pressing SET/DECEL or SET/COAST button. Vehicle speed will gradually decrease. Releasing button will set a new set speed as long as vehicle speed is still more than 35 MPH.

NOTE: Speed control system will automatically disengage when vehicle speed drops to less than 35 MPH or rises to more than 85 MPH.

SELF-DIAGNOSTIC SYSTEM

SYSTEM DIAGNOSTICS

The self-diagnostic capabilities of this system, if properly utilized, can simplify testing. The cruise control system is monitored by Single Board Engine Controller (SBEC).

If a problem is sensed with a monitored circuit, a fault code is stored in the SBEC. Once codes are known, refer to FAULT CODES to determine the questionable circuit. Test circuits and repair or replace components as required. If problem is repaired or ceases to exist, the SBEC cancels that fault code after 50 ignition on/off cycles. To clear codes, refer to CLEARING FAULT CODES.

A specific fault code results from a particular system failure. It is NOT necessarily the reason for that failure. The fault code does not condemn a specific component. The fault code calls out a probable malfunction area.

SERVICE PRECAUTIONS

Before proceeding with diagnosis, the following precautions must be followed:

* Vehicle must have a fully charged battery and functional charging system.
* Probe SBEC 60-pin connector from pin side. DO NOT backprobe SBEC connector.
* DO NOT cause short circuits when performing electrical tests. This will set additional fault codes, making diagnosis of original problem more difficult.

* Always repair lowest fault code number (CHECK ENGINE light) or first fault displayed (DRB-II) first.
* Always perform VERIFICATION TEST SP-VER after repairs are made.

VISUAL INSPECTION

Always perform a visual inspection before attempting to diagnose cruise control system problems. A visual inspection may quickly identify cause of a malfunction and eliminate the need for diagnostic testing. A thorough visual inspection includes checking for disconnected or faulty wiring harness connectors, leaking or misrouted vacuum hoses, corroded battery terminals or bare wires.

DIAGNOSTIC PROCEDURE

NOTE: When using self-diagnostic tests for diagnosis, DO NOT skip any steps or incorrect diagnosis may result. Always start with TEST SP-1A.

Always perform a visual inspection before attempting to diagnose engine control system problems. See VISUAL INSPECTION. Enter on-board diagnostics and retrieve fault codes. See ENTERING ON-BOARD DIAGNOSTICS. If fault codes are NOT present and/or DRB-II (Diagnostic Readout Box II) is used, proceed to TEST SP-1A.

ENTERING ON-BOARD DIAGNOSTICS

NOTE: Although other scan testers are available, manufacturer recommends using DRB-II (Diagnostic Readout Box II) to diagnose the system. CHECK ENGINE light function can be used, but has limited diagnostic usage.

CHECK ENGINE Light Diagnostic Mode – **1)** With key inserted in ignition switch, cycle ignition switch to ON position 3 times. On third cycle, leave ignition switch in ON position. Record 2-digit fault codes as displayed by flashing CHECK ENGINE light.

2) For example, Code 34 is displayed as a series of 3 flashes in rapid succession, a 4-second pause, then 4 flashes in rapid succession. After a slightly longer pause, other codes stored are displayed in numerical order.

3) When CHECK ENGINE light begins to flash fault codes, it cannot be stopped. If you lose count, it will be necessary to start over. Code 55 indicates end of fault code display.

4) Refer to FAULT CODES table to translate trouble code number to a system fault description (DRB-II display). Once trouble area is identified, refer to TEST SP-1A to diagnose problem.

NOTE: If fault code exists that is not related to cruise control system, see appropriate SELF-DIAGNOSTICS article in ENGINE PERFORMANCE.

DRB-II Diagnostic Mode – **1)** Connect DRB-II to engine diagnostic connector. Connector is located in engine compartment, near SBEC. Start engine. Turn ignition switch to ON position. Enter SPEED CONTROL MENU. See SPEED CONTROL MENU under DRB-II TEST FUNCTIONS.

2) At SPEED CONTROL MENU, press "2" (READ FAULTS) key. Press ENTER key. After fault codes are accessed, refer to TEST SP-1A to diagnose problem. If no fault codes are present, see TROUBLE SHOOTING.

3) To erase fault codes while in this mode, press ATM key. At DRB-II display, press "2" (ERASE) key. DRB-II will display ERASE FAULTS ARE YOU SURE? (ENTER TO ERASE). Press ENTER key.

4) When DRB-II is finished erasing fault codes, it will display FAULTS ERASED. This display will remain until ATM key is pressed. After ATM key is pressed, display will return to SPEED CONTROL MENU screen.

CLEARING FAULT CODES

NOTE: Fault codes can also be cleared in READ FAULTS option of DRB-II. To ensure that all faults are read, it is advisable to use READ FAULTS option to erase fault codes. See DRB-II DIAGNOSTIC MODE under ENTERING ON-BOARD DIAGNOSTICS.

1) If DRB-II is not available, go to step 3). If DRB-II is available, enter SPEED CONTROL MENU. See DRB-II TEST FUNCTIONS. At SPEED CONTROL menu, press "5" (ADJUSTMENTS) key. Press ENTER key. At ADJUSTMENTS menu, press "1" (ERASE FAULTS) key. Press ENTER key.
2) DRB-II will display ERASE FAULTS ARE YOU SURE? (ENTER TO ERASE). Press ENTER key. When DRB-II is finished erasing fault codes, screen will display FAULTS ERASED.
3) If DRB-II is not available, fault codes may be cleared by disconnecting negative battery cable for at least 15 seconds, allowing SBEC to clear fault codes.

WARNING: When battery is disconnected, vehicle computer and energy systems may lose memory data. Driveability problems may exist until computer systems have completed a relearn cycle. See COMPUTER RELEARN PROCEDURES article in GENERAL INFORMATION before disconnecting battery.

DRB-II TEST FUNCTIONS

SPEED CONTROL MENU

1) In order to perform cruise control system tests using DRB-II, the DRB-II must be in the SPEED CONTROL MENU. At SPEED CONTROL MENU, fault codes and DRB-II test functions can be accessed.
2) To reach SPEED CONTROL MENU, turn ignition off. Connect DRB-II to engine diagnostic connector. Connector is located in engine compartment, near SBEC. Turn ignition switch to RUN position.

NOTE: DO NOT touch DRB-II keypad during DRB-II power-up sequence or an error message will result.

3) All DRB-II character positions will illuminate and copyright information will appear on screen for a few seconds. If DRB-II screen is blank or any error messages appear, refer to DRB-II PROBLEMS & ERROR MESSAGES under DRB-II TEST FUNCTIONS in appropriate SELF-DIAGNOSTICS article in ENGINE PERFORMANCE.
4) After a few seconds DRB-II menu will appear. At DRB-II menu, press "4" (SELECT SYSTEM) key. Press ENTER key. At SELECT SYSTEM menu, press "1" (ENGINE) key. Press ENTER key. DRB-II menu will appear indicating engine year, size, type of transmission and SBEC part number.
5) After a few seconds AIR COND menu will appear. Press "1" (WITH A/C) or press "2" (WITHOUT A/C). DRB-II display will change to ENGINE SYSTEMS menu. At ENGINE SYSTEMS menu, press "3" (SPEED CONTROL) key. Press ENTER key.
6) Display will change to SPEED CONTROL menu. At SPEED CONTROL MENU, specific test functions programmed into DRB-II can be performed. The following DRB-II modes can be accessed: SYSTEM TEST, READ FAULTS, STATE DISPLAYS, ACTUATOR TEST and ADJUSTMENTS.

NOTE: For more information on DRB-II test functions, see appropriate SELF-DIAGNOSTICS article in ENGINE PERFORMANCE.

TROUBLE SHOOTING

NO CRUISE CONTROL WHEN SET BUTTON IS PRESSED & RELEASED

Fuse blown. No vacuum at servo. Speed control cable is disconnected. Brakelight switch out of adjustment. Faulty electrical circuit. Faulty neutral safety switch input to SBEC. Defective servo. Faulty SBEC.

CRUISE CONTROL ENGAGES WITHOUT ACTUATING CRUISE SET BUTTON

Faulty electrical circuit or control switch. Defective servo.

CRUISE CONTROL ENGAGES WHEN ENGINE IS STARTED

Faulty electrical circuit. Defective servo.

ERRATIC SPEED OR ENGINE SHUTS OFF

Poor engine performance (surge). Defective distance (speed) sensor. Vacuum leak. Faulty servo. Faulty SBEC.

CRUISE CONTROL DISENGAGES ON ROUGH ROAD

Brakelight switch out of adjustment. Faulty electrical circuit.

ENGINE DOES NOT RETURN TO NORMAL IDLE

Kinked or damaged cruise control cable. Faulty throttle linkage.

NO RESUME WHEN RESUME BUTTON IS PRESSED

Defective switch. Faulty electrical circuit.

CRUISE CONTROL DOES NOT DISENGAGE WITH BRAKE PEDAL DEPRESSED

Defective or improperly adjusted brakelight switch. Speed control cable is kinked or damaged. Faulty electrical circuit.

TESTING

BRAKELIGHT SWITCH

Disconnect brakelight switch 6-pin connector. Using an ohmmeter, check for continuity at switch side of connector terminals. See TESTING BRAKELIGHT SWITCH table. If continuity is not as specified, check brakelight switch adjustment. If switch adjustment is okay, replace defective brakelight switch.

FAULT CODES
FAULT CODES

Code	Display On DRB-II	Fault Condition
15	NO VEHICLE SPEED SIGNAL	No Vehicle Distance (Speed) Sensor Signal Detected During Road Load Conditions
34	SPEED CONTROL SOLENOID CIRCUITS	An Open Or Shorted Condition Detected In Cruise Control Vacuum Or Vent Solenoid Circuits
77	SPEED CONTROL POWER RELAY CIRCUIT	An Open Or Shorted Condition Detected In Cruise Control Power Relay Circuit

TESTING BRAKELIGHT SWITCH

Brake Pedal Position	Check Between Terminals No.	Continuity
Released	1 & 4	Yes
	3 & 6	Yes
	2 & 5	No
Depressed	1 & 4	No
	3 & 6	No
	2 & 5	Yes

CRUISE CONTROL CIRCUIT

1) Disconnect Single Board Engine Controller (SBEC) 60-pin connector. Connect negative lead of voltmeter to a good chassis ground near SBEC. Turn ignition switch to ON position. Depress and hold cruise control switch in OFF position.

2) Touch positive lead of voltmeter to terminal No. 53 (Light Green/Red wire) at SBEC connector. Voltage should be zero volts with cruise control switch off and battery voltage with cruise control switch on. If voltage is not as specified, repair Light Green/Red wire as necessary. If voltage is as specified, go to next step.

3) Measure voltage at terminal No. 33 (Tan/Red wire) at SBEC connector. Voltage should be zero volts with cruise control switch off and battery voltage with cruise control switch on. If voltage is not as specified, repair Tan/Red wire as necessary. If voltage is as specified, go to next step.

4) Measure voltage at terminal No. 48 (Brown/Red wire) at SBEC connector with switch in specified position. Voltage reading should be as follows:

- Zero volts with cruise control switch off.
- Battery voltage with cruise control switch on.
- Pressing cruise control SET button should cause voltage to change from battery voltage to zero volts.

If voltage is as specified, go to next step. If voltage is not as specified, check cruise control switch. See CRUISE CONTROL SWITCH. If cruise control switch is defective, replace switch. If cruise control switch is okay, repair Brown/Red wire as necessary.

5) Measure voltage at terminal No. 50 (White/Light Green wire) at SBEC connector. Voltage should be zero volts with cruise control switch in OFF or ON positions. With cruise control switch on, depress RESUME button.

6) Voltage at terminal No. 50 should indicate battery voltage. If voltage is as specified, go to next step. If voltage is not as specified, check cruise control switch. See CRUISE CONTROL SWITCH. Replace cruise control switch, if defective. If cruise control switch is okay, repair White/Light Green wire as necessary.

7) Measure voltage at terminal No. 49 (Yellow/Red wire) at SBEC connector. Voltage should be zero volts with cruise control switch off and battery voltage with cruise control switch on. If voltage is as specified, go to next step. If voltage is not as specified, repair Yellow/Red wire as necessary.

CRUISE CONTROL SERVO

1) Turn ignition switch to ON position. Position cruise control switch to ON position. Disconnect servo 4-pin connector. Using a voltmeter, measure voltage at terminal No. 2 (Blue/Red wire) at servo connector. If battery voltage is not present, check for loose connections, brakelight switch adjustment, or repair main harness as necessary.

2) Connect a jumper wire between male and female terminals of Blue/Red wire. Other three male terminals from servo should indicate battery voltage. If not, replace servo.

3) Using an ohmmeter, connect one lead to ground and other lead to Black wire terminal in 4-pin main harness connector. Ohmmeter should indicate continuity. If not, repair ground circuit as necessary.

CRUISE CONTROL SWITCH

Remove cruise control switch. Using an ohmmeter, check cruise control switch. If cruise control switch does not test as specified, replace switch. See TESTING CRUISE CONTROL SWITCH table.

TESTING CRUISE CONTROL SWITCH

Switch Position	Check Between Terminals No.	Ohms
OFF	3 & 4	5890-6510
OFF	1 & 3	[1]
ON	1 & 4	5890-6510
ON	1 & 3	[2]
ON/SET	3 & 4	1020-1130
ON/RESUME	3 & 4	2040-2260

[1] – No continuity should exist.
[2] – Continuity should exist.

SERVO VACUUM TEST

1) Remove cruise control cable from throttle body. Disconnect cruise control servo 4-pin connector. Disconnect vacuum hose at servo. Apply battery voltage to terminal No. 2 (Dark Blue/Red wire) at servo connector. Using jumper wire, ground remaining 3 terminals at servo connector.

2) Connect hand-held vacuum pump to servo vacuum nipple. Apply 10-15 in. Hg of vacuum. Cruise control cable should pull in and hold as long as vacuum is applied. If servo does not test as specified, replace servo.

VACUUM SUPPLY

1) Disconnect vacuum hose at cruise control servo. Install vacuum gauge to disconnected vacuum hose. Start engine and observe gauge. Vacuum reading should be a minimum of 10 in. Hg. Turn engine off. Vacuum should continue to hold at a minimum of 10 in. Hg.

2) If vacuum is not as specified, check for kinked or leaking vacuum lines, defective check valve, defective vacuum reservoir and/or poor engine performance. If no problems are found, check servo. See CRUISE CONTROL SERVO.

REMOVAL & INSTALLATION

CRUISE CONTROL SERVO

Removal – Remove cruise control cable mounting bracket from servo. Remove servo mounting bracket from battery tray. Disconnect wiring harness connector and vacuum hose from servo. Pull cable away from servo to expose retaining clip. Remove retaining clip and cable. Remove servo.

Installation – With throttle in full open position, align hole in cruise control cable sleeve with hole in servo pin. Install retaining clip. To complete installation, reverse removal procedure.

CRUISE CONTROL SWITCH

Removal & Installation – Turn ignition switch to OFF position. Remove 2 screws from back of steering wheel. Rock switch back and forth and remove switch from steering wheel. Disconnect cruise control switch connector. To install switch, reverse removal procedure.

CONNECTOR IDENTIFICATION

CONNECTOR IDENTIFICATION DIRECTORY

Connector	See Fig.
Brakelight Switch	1
Cruise Control Relay	2
Cruise Control Servo	3
Cruise Control Switch	4
Distance Sensor	5
Single Board Engine Controller (SBEC)	6

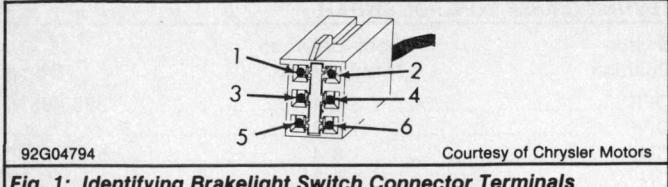

92G04794   Courtesy of Chrysler Motors

Fig. 1: Identifying Brakelight Switch Connector Terminals

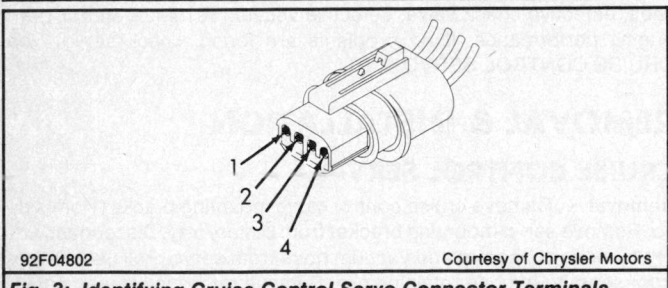

Relay Center

Cruise Control Relay Connector

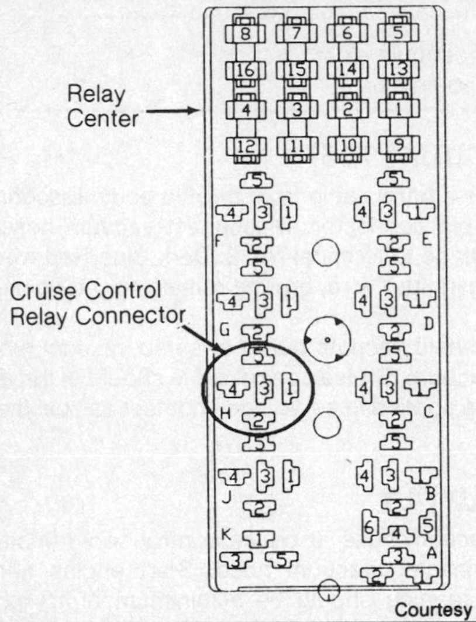

92D04801   Courtesy of Chrysler Motors

Fig. 2: Identifying Cruise Control Relay Connector Terminals

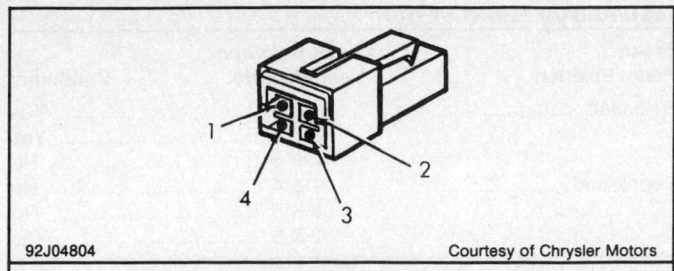

92J04804   Courtesy of Chrysler Motors

Fig. 4: Identifying Cruise Control Switch Connector Terminals

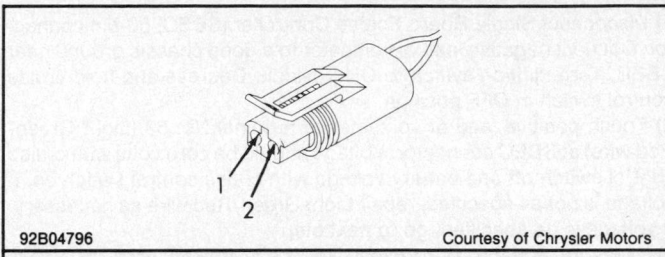

92B04796   Courtesy of Chrysler Motors

Fig. 5: Identifying Distance Sensor Connector Terminals

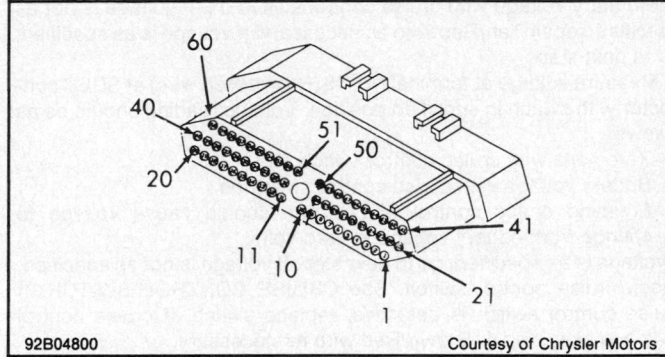

92B04800   Courtesy of Chrysler Motors

Fig. 6: Identifying Single Board Engine Controller (SBEC) Connector Terminals

92F04802   Courtesy of Chrysler Motors

Fig. 3: Identifying Cruise Control Servo Connector Terminals

SELF-DIAGNOSTIC TESTS

TEST SP-1A

READING FAULT CODES

1) Ensure battery is fully charged. Start engine. Allow engine to idle. Using DRB-II, read engine RPM.

2) If DRB-II reading does not correspond with engine speed, go to DRB-II PROBLEMS & ERROR MESSAGES under DRB-II TEST FUNCTIONS in appropriate SELF-DIAGNOSTICS article in ENGINE PERFORMANCE. If DRB-II reading corresponds with engine speed, turn engine off. Put ignition switch in ON position.

3) Read faults with DRB-II. If DRB-II display shows SPEED CONTROL SOLENOID CIRCUIT, perform TEST SP-2A. If DRB-II display shows NO VEHICLE SPEED SIGNAL, perform TEST SP-3A. If DRB-II display does not show a fault, perform TEST SP-4A.

TEST SP-2A

REPAIRING POWER & GROUND SUPPLY FOR OPEN TO SERVO SOLENOIDS

1) While listening to cruise control servo, cycle cruise control ON/OFF switch. If cruise control servo clicks when cycling ON/OFF switch, perform TEST SP-2B. If cruise control servo does not click when cycling ON/OFF switch, disconnect cruise control servo 4-pin connector.

2) Inspect connector. If connector is not okay, repair connector as necessary. Perform VERIFICATION TEST SP-VER. If connector is okay, put cruise control ON/OFF switch in ON position. Place DRB-II in voltmeter mode.

3) Ensure brake pedal is not depressed during following step. Probe Dark Blue/Red wire at cruise control servo connector. If voltage is less than 10 volts, go to step 5). If voltage is 10 volts or more, go to next step.

4) Place DRB-II in ohmmeter mode. Probe terminal No. 1 (Black wire) at cruise control servo connector. If resistance is 10 ohms or more, replace cruise control servo. If resistance is less than 10 ohms, repair short to ground in Black wire. Perform VERIFICATION TEST SP-VER.

5) If voltage is less than 10 volts at Dark Blue/Red wire in step 3), ensure brake pedal is not depressed. Backprobe Dark Blue/Red wire at brake-light switch connector. If voltage is 10 volts or more, repair open in Dark Blue/Red wire. Perform VERIFICATION TEST SP-VER. If voltage is less than 10 volts, go to next step.

6) Backprobe Yellow/Red wire at brakelight switch connector. If voltage is 10 volts or more, adjust or replace brakelight switch as necessary. Perform VERIFICATION TEST SP-VER. If voltage is less than 10 volts, repair open in Yellow/Red wire. Perform VERIFICATION TEST SP-VER.

TEST SP-2B

CODE 34, CRUISE CONTROL VACUUM SOLENOID CONTROL CIRCUIT

1) Turn ignition switch to OFF position. Disconnect and inspect Single Board Engine Controller (SBEC) connector. If connector is not okay, repair connector as necessary. Perform VERIFICATION TEST SP-VER. If connector is okay, turn ignition switch to ON position.

2) Put cruise control ON/OFF switch in ON position. Place DRB-II in voltmeter mode. Probe terminal No. 33 (Tan/Red wire) at SBEC connector. If voltage is 10 volts or more, perform TEST SP-2C. If voltage is less than 10 volts, disconnect cruise control servo connector. Inspect connector.

3) If connector is not okay, repair connector as necessary. Perform VERIFICATION TEST SP-VER. If connector is okay, place DRB-II in ohmmeter mode. Probe Tan/Red wire in servo connector. If resistance is less than 10 ohms, repair short to ground in Tan/Red wire. Perform VERIFICATION TEST SP-VER. If resistance is 10 ohms or more, go to next step.

4) Using an external ohmmeter, check resistance at Tan/Red wire between terminal No. 33 at SBEC connector and terminal No. 4 at cruise control servo connector. If resistance is less than 10 ohms, replace cruise control servo. Perform VERIFICATION TEST SP-VER. If resistance is 10 ohms or more, repair open Tan/Red wire. Perform VERIFICATION TEST SP-VER.

TEST SP-2C

CODE 34, CRUISE CONTROL SOLENOID CIRCUIT

1) Probe terminal No. 53 (Light Green/Red wire) at Single Board Engine Controller (SBEC) connector. If voltage is 10 volts or more, replace SBEC. Perform VERIFICATION TEST SP-VER. If voltage is less than 10 volts, disconnect cruise control 4-pin servo connector. Inspect connector.

2) If connector is not okay, repair connector as necessary. Perform VERIFICATION TEST SP-VER. If connector is okay, put DRB-II in ohmmeter mode. Probe terminal No. 3 (Light Green/Red wire) at servo connector. If resistance is less than 10 ohms, repair short to ground in Light Green/Red wire. Perform VERIFICATION TEST SP-VER. If resistance is 10 ohms or more, go to next step.

3) Using an external ohmmeter, check resistance at Light Green/Red wire between terminal No. 53 at SBEC connector and terminal No. 3 at cruise control servo connector. If resistance is less than 10 ohms, replace cruise control servo. Perform VERIFICATION TEST SP-VER. If resistance is 10 ohms or more, repair open Light Green/Red wire. Perform VERIFICATION TEST SP-VER.

TEST SP-3A

CODE 15, NO VEHICLE SPEED SIGNAL

1) Turn ignition switch to OFF position. Disconnect vehicle distance sensor connector. Inspect connector. If connector is not okay, repair connector as necessary. Perform VERIFICATION TEST SP-VER.

2) If connector is okay, turn ignition switch to ON position. Connect a jumper wire to one terminal of distance sensor connector. Using DRB-II, monitor car speed while tapping open end of jumper wire to the other distance sensor connector terminal.

3) If DRB-II display shows car speed to be more than zero, replace distance sensor. Perform VERIFICATION TEST SP-VER. If car speed is zero, put DRB-II in voltmeter mode. Probe terminal No. 1 (White/Orange wire) at distance sensor connector.

4) If voltage is less than 4 volts, go to next step. If voltage is 4 volts or more, turn ignition switch to OFF position. Put DRB-II in ohmmeter mode. Probe terminal No. 2 (Black/Light Blue wire) at distance sensor. If resistance is less than 10 ohms, replace SBEC. If resistance is 10 ohms or more, repair open Black/Light Blue wire.

5) Turn ignition switch to OFF position. Place DRB-II in ohmmeter mode. Probe terminal No. 1 (White/Orange wire) at distance sensor connector. If resistance is 10 ohms or more, perform TEST SP-3B. If resistance is less than 10 ohms, disconnect instrument panel 50-pin connector at firewall. Probe terminal No. 1 (White/Orange wire) at distance sensor connector.

6) If resistance is less than 10 ohms, repair White/Orange wire for a short to ground in engine wiring harness. Perform VERIFICATION TEST SP-VER. If resistance is 10 ohms or more, repair open White/Orange wire. Perform VERIFICATION TEST SP-VER.

TEST SP-3B

CODE 15, NO VEHICLE SPEED SIGNAL

1) Disconnect Single Board Engine Controller (SBEC) connector. Inspect connector. If connector is not okay, repair connector as necessary. Perform VERIFICATION TEST SP-VER. If connector is okay, go to next step.

2) Using an external ohmmeter, check resistance at White/Orange wire between terminal No. 47 at SBEC connector and terminal No. 1 at distance sensor connector. If resistance is less than 10 ohms, replace SBEC. Perform VERIFICATION TEST SP-VER. If resistance is 10 ohms or more, repair open White/Orange wire. Perform VERIFICATION TEST SP-VER.

TEST SP-4A

TESTING CRUISE CONTROL SWITCHES

1) Using DRB-II, read inputs monitor. While watching ON/OFF input, cycle ON/OFF switch several times. If DRB-II display does not correspond with switch position, perform TEST SP-6A.

2) If DRB-II display does correspond with switch position, place cruise control ON/OFF switch in ON position. While watching RESUME input, cycle RESUME switch several times. If DRB-II display does not correspond with switch position, perform TEST SP-8A. If DRB-II display does correspond with switch position, go to next step.

3) While watching SET input on DRB-II display, cycle SET switch several times. If DRB-II display does not correspond with switch position, perform TEST SP-10A. If DRB-II display does correspond with switch position, cycle brake pedal several times, while watching BRAKE input display.

4) If DRB-II display does not correspond with brake pedal position, perform TEST SP-11A. If DRB-II display does correspond with brake pedal position, check if vehicle is equipped with a manual transmission. If vehicle is equipped with manual transmission, perform TEST SP-13A. If vehicle is not equipped with manual transmission, go to next step.

5) With ignition switch in ON position and engine not running, cycle gear lever several times between "P", "R", "N" and "D", while watching PARK/NEUTRAL input. If DRB-II display does not correspond with selector position, perform TEST SP-12A. If DRB-II display does correspond with selector position, perform TEST SP-13A.

TEST SP-5A

NOTE: Test SP-5A applies to passenger cars only. No test procedures are missing.

TEST SP-6A

TESTING CRUISE CONTROL ON/OFF SWITCH

1) Turn ignition switch to ON position. Put DRB-II in voltmeter mode. Probe both ends of cruise control fuse. If voltage at both ends of fuse is 10 volts or more, perform TEST SP-6B. If voltage is 10 volts or more at input side of fuse only, go to next step. If voltage is less than 10 volts at input side of fuse, repair open in Dark Blue wire between ignition switch and speed control fuse. Perform VERIFICATION TEST SP-VER.

2) Put cruise control ON/OFF switch in OFF position. Replace cruise control fuse. Probe end of fuse (White/Red wire) that had less than 10 volts. If voltage is less than 10 volts, repair short to ground in White/Red wire. Perform VERIFICATION TEST SP-VER. If voltage is 10 volts or more, go to next step.

3) Put cruise control ON/OFF switch in ON position. Probe end of fuse (White/Red wire at output side) that previously had less than 10 volts. If voltage is 10 volts or more, test is complete. Perform VERIFICATION TEST SP-VER. If voltage is less than 10 volts, put cruise control ON/OFF switch in OFF position. Turn ignition switch to OFF position.

4) Disconnect Single Board Engine Controller (SBEC) connector. Inspect connector. If connector is not okay, repair connector as necessary. Perform VERIFICATION TEST SP-VER. If connector is okay, place DRB-II in ohmmeter mode. Probe terminal No. 48 (Brown/Red wire) at SBEC connector. Record resistance reading. Probe terminal No. 50 (White/Light Green wire) at SBEC connector.

5) If resistance is 10 ohms or more at both terminals No. 48 and 50, repair short to ground in Yellow/Red wire between SBEC connector and cruise control ON/OFF switch. Perform VERIFICATION TEST SP-VER. If resistance is less than 10 ohms at both terminals No. 48 and 50, go to next step.

6) Disconnect cruise control ON/OFF switch connector. Probe terminal No. 48 (Brown/Red wire) at SBEC connector. If resistance is less than 10 ohms, repair short to ground in Brown/Red wire. Perform VERIFICATION TEST SP-VER. If resistance is 10 ohms or more, probe terminal No. 50 (White/Light Green wire) at SBEC connector.

7) If resistance is less than 10 ohms, repair short to ground in White/Red wire. Perform VERIFICATION TEST SP-VER. If resistance is 10 ohms or more, replace cruise control switch. Perform VERIFICATION TEST SP-VER.

TEST SP-6B

TESTING CRUISE CONTROL ON/OFF SWITCH

1) Place DRB-II in voltmeter mode. With cruise control switch connector connected, probe terminal No. 1 (Dark Blue wire) at cruise control switch connector. See Fig. SP-6B. If voltage is less than 10 volts, repair open in White/Red wire between cruise control fuse and cruise control switch. Perform VERIFICATION TEST SP-VER.

2) If voltage is 10 volts or more, put cruise control ON/OFF switch in ON position. Probe terminal No. 2 (Yellow/Red wire) at cruise control connector. If voltage is less than 10 volts, replace cruise control switch. Perform VERIFICATION TEST SP-VER. If voltage is 10 volts or more, turn ignition switch to OFF position.

3) Disconnect Single Board Engine Controller (SBEC) connector. Inspect connector. If connector is not okay, repair connector as necessary. Perform VERIFICATION TEST SP-VER. If connector is okay, turn ignition switch to ON position.

4) Probe terminal No. 49 (Yellow/Red wire) at SBEC connector. If voltage is 10 volts or more, replace SBEC. Perform VERIFICATION TEST SP-VER. If voltage is less than 10 volts, repair open Yellow/Red wire. Perform VERIFICATION TEST SP-VER.

92A04809

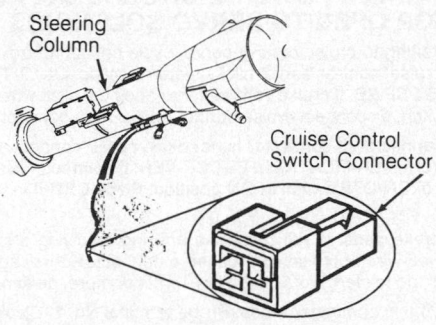

Steering Column

Cruise Control Switch Connector

Fig. SP-6B: Locating Cruise Control Switch Connector

TEST SP-7A

NOTE: Test SP-7A applies to passenger cars only. No test procedures are missing.

TEST SP-8A

TESTING CRUISE CONTROL RESUME SWITCH

1) Put cruise control ON/OFF switch in the ON position. Place DRB-II in voltmeter mode. Hold down RESUME button and probe terminal No. 3 (White/Light Green wire) at cruise control switch connector. See Fig. SP-6B. If voltage is less than 10 volts, replace cruise control switch. Perform VERIFICATION TEST SP-VER.

2) If voltage is 10 volts or more, turn ignition switch to OFF position. Disconnect Single Board Engine Controller (SBEC) connector. Inspect connector. If connector is not okay, repair connector as necessary. Perform VERIFICATION TEST SP-VER. If connector is okay, go to next step.

3) Turn ignition switch to ON position. Hold down RESUME button and probe terminal No. 50 (White/Light Green wire) at SBEC connector. If voltage is 10 volts or more, replace SBEC. Perform VERIFICATION TEST SP-VER. If voltage is less than 10 volts, repair open White/Light Green wire. Perform VERIFICATION TEST SP-VER.

TEST SP-9A

NOTE: Test SP-9A applies to passenger cars only. No test procedures are missing.

TEST SP-10A

TESTING CRUISE CONTROL SET SWITCH

1) Put cruise control ON/OFF switch in the ON position. Place DRB-II in voltmeter mode. Probe Brown/Red wire at cruise control switch connector (with connector connected). If voltage is less than 10 volts, replace cruise control switch. Perform VERIFICATION TEST SP-VER.

2) If voltage is 10 volts or more, hold down cruise control SET button and probe Brown/Red wire at cruise control switch connector. If voltage is 10 volts or more, replace cruise control switch. Perform VERIFICATION TEST SP-VER. If voltage is less than 10 volts, go to next step.

3) Turn ignition switch to OFF position. Disconnect Single Board Engine Controller (SBEC). Inspect connector. If connector is not okay, repair connector as necessary. Perform VERIFICATION TEST SP-VER. If connector is okay, turn ignition switch to ON position.

4) Probe terminal No. 48 (Brown/Red wire) at SBEC connector. If voltage is 10 volts or more, replace SBEC. If voltage is less than 10 volts, replace SBEC. Perform VERIFICATION TEST SP-VER. If voltage is 10 volts or more, replace cruise control switch. Perform VERIFICATION TEST SP-VER.

TEST SP-11A

CHECKING BRAKELIGHT SWITCH CIRCUITS FOR OPENS

1) If DRB-II display shows RE at all times, perform TEST SP-11B. If DRB-II does not show RE at all times, disconnect brakelight switch connector. Inspect connector. If connector is not okay, repair connector as necessary. Perform VERIFICATION TEST SP-VER.

2) If connector is okay, connect a jumper wire between terminals No. 1 (White/Pink wire) and No. 2 (Black wire) at brakelight switch connector. Using DRB-II, read inputs monitor. if DRB-II display does not show RE, go to step 4).

3) If DRB-II display shows RE, check brakelight switch adjustment. If brakelight switch is adjusted correctly, replace brakelight switch. Perform VERIFICATION TEST SP-VER. If brakelight switch is not adjusted correctly, adjust brakelight switch. Perform VERIFICATION TEST SP-VER.

4) If DRB-II display does not show RE in step 2), connect jumper wire between terminal No. 1 (White/Pink wire) and ground. Using DRB-II, read inputs monitor. If DRB-II display shows RE, repair open in Black wire.

5) If DRB-II does not show RE, turn ignition switch to OFF position. Remove jumper wire. Disconnect Single Board Engine Controller (SBEC) connector. Inspect connector. If connector is not okay, repair connector as necessary. Perform VERIFICATION TEST SP-VER.

6) If connector is okay, using an external ohmmeter, check resistance at White/Pink wire between terminal No. 29 at SBEC connector and terminal No. 1 at brakelight switch connector. If resistance is 10 ohms or more, repair open White/Pink wire. Perform VERIFICATION TEST SP-VER. If resistance is less than 10 ohms, replace SBEC. Perform VERIFICATION TEST SP-VER.

TEST SP-11B

CHECKING BRAKELIGHT SWITCH CIRCUITS FOR SHORTS

1) Disconnect brakelight switch connector. Using DRB-II, read inputs monitor. If DRB-II display shows PR, go to step 3). If DRB-II display does not show PR, turn ignition switch to OFF position. Disconnect Single Board Engine Controller (SBEC) connector. Place DRB-II in ohmmeter mode. Probe terminal No. 29 (White/Pink wire) at SBEC connector.

2) If resistance is less than 10 ohms, repair short to ground in White/Pink wire. Perform VERIFICATION TEST SP-VER. If resistance is 10 ohms or more, replace SBEC. Perform VERIFICATION TEST SP-VER.

3) If DRB-II display shows PR in step 1), check brakelight switch adjustment. If brakelight switch is adjusted correctly, replace brakelight switch. Perform VERIFICATION TEST SP-VER. If brakelight switch is not adjusted correctly, adjust brakelight switch. Perform VERIFICATION TEST SP-VER.

TEST SP-12A

CHECKING PARK/NEUTRAL SAFETY SWITCH

1) Disconnect park/neutral safety switch connector at transmission. Inspect connector. If connector is not okay, repair connector as necessary. Perform VERIFICATION TEST SP-VER. If connector is okay, using DRB-II read inputs monitor.

2) If DRB-II display shows D/R, replace park/neutral safety switch. Perform VERIFICATION TEST SP-VER. If DRB-II display does not show D/R, turn ignition switch to OFF position. Disconnect and inspect Single Board Engine Controller (SBEC) connector. If connector is not okay, repair connector as necessary. Perform VERIFICATION TEST SP-VER.

3) If connector is okay, place DRB-II in ohmmeter mode. Probe terminal No. 30 (Brown/Yellow wire) at SBEC connector. If resistance is less than 10 ohms, repair short to ground in Brown/Yellow wire. Perform VERIFICATION TEST SP-VER. If resistance is 10 ohms or more, replace SBEC. Perform VERIFICATION TEST SP-VER.

TEST SP-13A

CHECKING CRUISE CONTROL SERVO OPERATION

1) Disconnect and inspect 4-pin cruise control servo connector. If connector is not okay, repair connector as necessary. Perform VERIFICATION TEST SP-VER. If connector is okay, place DRB-II in ohmmeter mode. Probe terminal No. 1 (Black wire) at cruise control servo connector.

2) If resistance is 10 ohms or more, repair open Black wire. Perform VERIFICATION TEST SP-VER. If resistance is less than 10 ohms, reconnect cruise control servo connector. Check if vehicle is equipped with a vacuum reservoir. If vehicle is equipped with vacuum reservoir, perform TEST SP-13B.

3) If vehicle is not equipped with a vacuum reservoir, disconnect cruise control servo vacuum hose. Using an alternative source of constant vacuum supply, connect a vacuum supply hose to servo. Using DRB-II, actuate servo solenoids. If throttle fully opens and closes, perform TEST SP-14A.

4) If throttle does not fully open and close, using DRB-II, stop actuation test. Inspect cruise control servo cable condition. If cruise control servo cable condition okay, replace cruise control servo. Perform VERIFICATION TEST SP-VER. If cruise control servo cable condition is not okay, repair cable as necessary. Perform VERIFICATION TEST SP-VER.

TEST SP-13B

CHECKING CRUISE CONTROL SERVO OPERATION

1) Start engine. Turn engine off. Turn ignition switch to ON position. Using DRB-II, actuate servo solenoids. If throttle fully opens and closes, perform TEST SP-14A. If throttle does not fully open and close, using DRB-II, stop actuation test.

2) Disconnect vacuum hose at cruise control servo. Using an alternative source of constant vacuum supply, connect a vacuum supply hose to servo. Using DRB-II, actuate servo solenoids. If throttle fully opens and closes, repair vacuum leak or restriction between servo and vacuum source. Perform VERIFICATION TEST SP-VER.

3) If throttle does not fully open and close, using DRB-II, stop actuation test. Inspect cruise control servo cable condition. If cruise control servo cable condition is okay, replace cruise control servo. Perform VERIFICATION TEST SP-VER. If cruise control servo cable condition is not okay, repair cable as necessary. Perform VERIFICATION TEST SP-VER.

TEST SP-14A
CHECKING FOR INTERMITTENT FAULTS

1) Reconnect and reassemble all previously tested components. Connect DRB-II to engine diagnostic connector so DRB-II display can be seen from driver's seat. Road test vehicle. Using DRB-II, read cutout monitor on DRB-II display. If DRB-II display shows erratic vehicle speed, replace distance sensor. Perform VERIFICATION TEST SP-VER.

2) If DRB-II display does not show erratic vehicle speed, put cruise control ON/OFF switch in ON position. With vehicle at a minimum of 35 MPH, depress and release cruise control SET switch. If DRB-II display shows S/C DENIED, see appropriate DENIED MESSAGE in DRB-II INTERMITTENT FAULT MESSAGES table and correct problem as necessary.

DRB-II INTERMITTENT FAULT MESSAGES

Denied Message	Problem To Correct
BRAKE	Open Circuit At Terminal No. 29 At SBEC
CLUTCH	RPM/Vehicle Speed Ratio Is Not Constant
ON/OFF	Lack Of Voltage At Terminal No. 49 At SBEC
P/N	Ground Exists At Terminal No. 30 At SBEC
RPM/SPD	RPM/Speed Ratio Is Not Constant
SPEED	Vehicle Speed As Read By Distance Sensor Is Less Than 35 MPH
RPM	Engine RPM Is Excessively High
SOL/FLT	Fault In Servo Vent Or Vacuum Solenoid Circuit That Is Either Maturing Or Set

3) If DRB-II display shows S/C ALLOWED and cruise control is operative, perform the following:

- Check for cruise control disengagement without driver command by driving vehicle under various road conditions.
- If cruise control disengages without driver command, read cutout monitor S/C DENIED message on DRB-II display. See appropriate DENIED MESSAGE in DRB-II INTERMITTENT FAULT MESSAGES table and repair as necessary.
- If cruise control does not disengage without driver command, read DRB-II cutout monitor display. Compare GOAL value with SPEED value. If the 2 values are not within 2 MPH of each other, replace SBEC.

VERIFICATION TEST SP-VER
CRUISE CONTROL VERIFICATION

Reconnect and reassemble all previously tested components. If Single Board Engine Controller has been changed, perform the following:

- If vehicle is equipped with factory theft alarm, start vehicle at least 20 times so alarm system may be activated when desired.
- Write vehicle's odometer mileage to memory location within replacement SBEC. This will enable new SBEC to operate Emission Maintenance Reminder (EMR) light properly. See MILEAGE TRANSFER under DRB-II TEST FUNCTIONS in appropriate SELF-DIAGNOSTICS article in ENGINE PERFORMANCE.
- Connect DRB-II to engine diagnostic connector and erase faults.

To ensure no other faults remain, perform the following:

1) Road test vehicle at a speed of above 35 MPH. Put cruise control ON/OFF switch in ON position. Depress and release SET switch. If cruise control did not engage, repair is not complete. Check all pertinent MITCHELL® TECHNICAL SERVICE BULLETINS (TSBs) and return to TEST SP-1A, if necessary.

2) Depress and release SET switch. If vehicle speed did not increase by 2 MPH, repair is not complete. Check all pertinent MITCHELL® TECHNICAL SERVICE BULLETINS (TSBs) and return to TEST SP-1A, if necessary.

3) Depress and release brake pedal. If cruise control did not disengage, repair is not complete. Check all pertinent MITCHELL® TECHNICAL SERVICE BULLETINS (TSBs) and return to TEST SP-1A, if necessary.

4) Bring vehicle speed back up to 35 MPH. Depress RESUME/ACCEL switch. If cruise control did not resume the previously set speed, repair is not complete. Check all pertinent MITCHELL® TECHNICAL SERVICE BULLETINS (TSBs) and return to TEST SP-1A, if necessary.

5) Hold down SET switch. If vehicle did not decelerate, repair is not complete. Check all pertinent MITCHELL® TECHNICAL SERVICE BULLETINS (TSBs) and return to TEST SP-1A, if necessary.

6) Ensure vehicle speed is greater than 35 MPH and release SET switch. If vehicle did not adjust and set to new vehicle speed, repair is not complete. Check all pertinent MITCHELL® TECHNICAL SERVICE BULLETINS (TSBs) and return to TEST SP-1A, if necessary.

7) Turn ON/OFF switch to OFF position. If cruise control did not disengage, repair is not complete. Check all pertinent MITCHELL® TECHNICAL SERVICE BULLETINS (TSBs) and return to TEST SP-1A, if necessary.

8) If vehicle successfully passed all previous tests, cruise control system is now functioning correctly. Repair is complete.

WIRING DIAGRAM

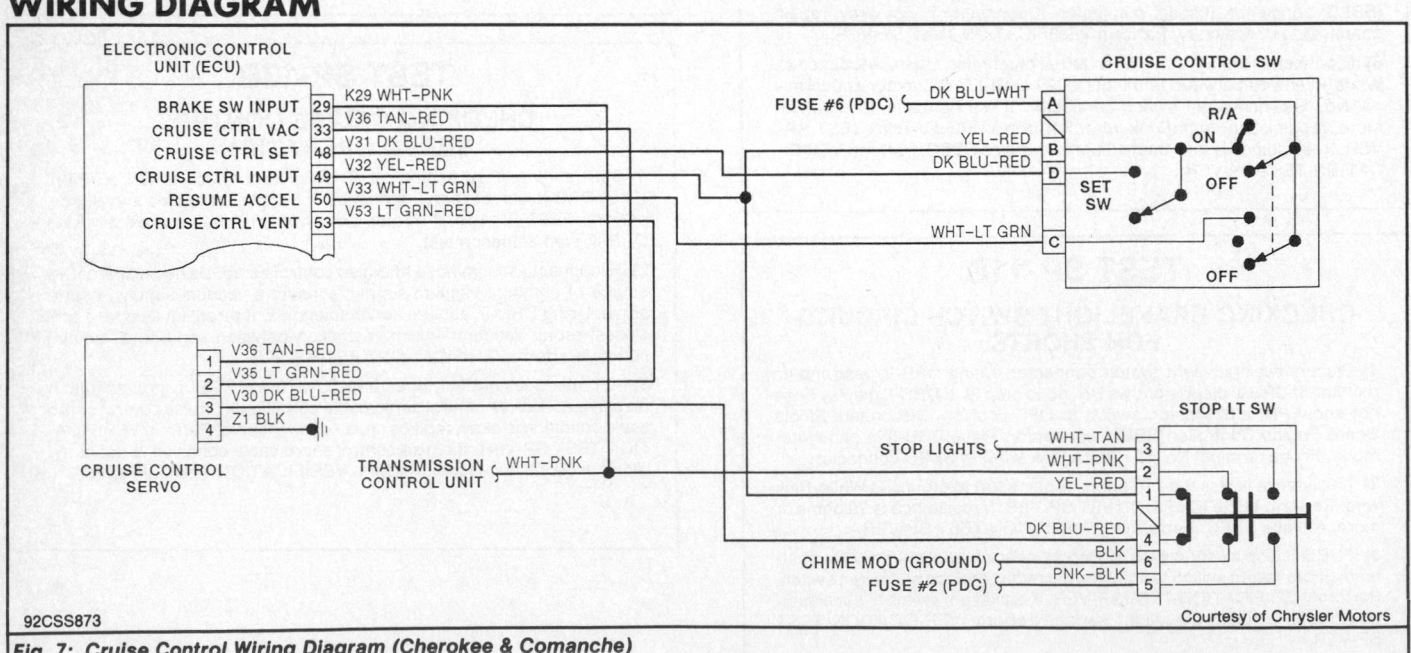

92CSS873

Courtesy of Chrysler Motors

Fig. 7: Cruise Control Wiring Diagram (Cherokee & Comanche)

Cherokee, Comanche

DESCRIPTION

The cruise control system is electronically controlled and vacuum operated. The electronic control is integrated into the Single Board Engine Controller (SBEC). System consists of SBEC, servo, cruise control switch panel, vacuum reservoir, distance sensor, brakelight switch and Park/Neutral switch (automatic transmission). System controls are located on the steering wheel and consist of ON/OFF, RESUME/ACCEL, and SET/DECEL or SET/COAST buttons.

OPERATION

SYSTEM CONTROLS

To Set Cruise Control – Press ON/OFF button to turn cruise control system on. Accelerate to desired speed (minimum of 35 MPH) and press SET/DECEL or SET/COAST button. Vehicle speed will be maintained.

To Disengage Cruise Control – Press brake pedal or clutch pedal. The ON/OFF button may also be used, but set speed will be erased from memory. If clutch pedal is used to disengage cruise control, engine speed will increase before cruise control cuts out.

To Resume Previous Speed – If set speed has not been erased from memory and vehicle speed is more than 30 MPH, press RESUME/ACCEL button.

To Increase Speed – With cruise control system on, increase set speed by rapidly pressing and releasing RESUME/ACCEL button. Each pressing of button will cause a speed increase of 2 MPH. For example, 3 presses would result in an increased speed of 6 MPH. To increase speed gradually, press RESUME/ACCEL button until desired speed is reached. When button is released, new set speed will be maintained.

To Decrease Speed – With cruise control system on, decrease set speed by pressing SET/DECEL or SET/COAST button. Vehicle speed will gradually decrease. Releasing button will set a new speed as long as vehicle speed is still more than 35 MPH.

NOTE: Cruise control system will automatically disengage when vehicle speed drops to less than 35 MPH or rises to more than 85 MPH.

SELF-DIAGNOSTIC SYSTEM

SYSTEM DIAGNOSTICS

The self-diagnostic capabilities of this system, if properly utilized, can simplify testing. Cruise control system is monitored by Single Board Engine Controller (SBEC).

If a problem is sensed with a monitored circuit, a fault code is stored in SBEC. Once codes are known, refer to FAULT CODES table to determine questionable circuit. Test circuits and repair or replace components as required. If problem is repaired or ceases to exist, SBEC cancels that fault code after 50 ignition on/off cycles. To clear codes, refer to CLEARING FAULT CODES.

A specific fault code results from a particular system failure. It is NOT necessarily the reason for that failure. Fault code does not condemn a specific component. Fault code calls out a probable malfunction area.

SERVICE PRECAUTIONS

Before proceeding with diagnosis, the following precautions must be observed:

- Vehicle must have a fully charged battery and functional charging system.
- Probe SBEC 60-pin connector from pin side. DO NOT backprobe SBEC connector.
- DO NOT cause short circuits when performing electrical tests. This will set additional fault codes, making diagnosis of original problem more difficult.

- Always repair lowest fault code number (CHECK ENGINE light) or first fault displayed (DRB-II) before repairing others.
- Always perform appropriate VERIFICATION TEST SP-VER after repairs are made.

VISUAL INSPECTION

Perform a visual inspection before attempting to diagnose cruise control system problems. A visual inspection may quickly identify cause of a malfunction and eliminate need for diagnostic testing. A thorough visual inspection includes checking for disconnected or faulty wiring harness connectors, leaking or misrouted vacuum hoses, corroded battery terminals or bare wires.

DIAGNOSTIC PROCEDURE

NOTE: When using self-diagnostic tests for diagnosis, DO NOT skip any steps or incorrect diagnosis may result. Always start with TEST SP-1A.

Perform a visual inspection before attempting to diagnose engine control system problems. See VISUAL INSPECTION. Enter on-board diagnostics and retrieve fault codes. See ENTERING ON-BOARD DIAGNOSTICS. If fault codes are NOT present and/or DRB-II (Diagnostic Readout Box II) is used, proceed to TEST SP-1A.

ENTERING ON-BOARD DIAGNOSTICS

NOTE: Although other scan testers are available, manufacturer recommends using DRB-II (Diagnostic Readout Box II) to diagnose system. CHECK ENGINE light function can be used, but has limited diagnostic abilities.

CHECK ENGINE Light Diagnostic Mode – 1) With key inserted in ignition switch, cycle ignition switch to ON position 3 times. On third cycle, leave ignition switch in ON position. Record 2-digit fault codes as displayed by flashing CHECK ENGINE light.

2) For example, Code 34 is displayed as a series of 3 flashes in rapid succession, followed by a 4-second pause, then 4 flashes in rapid succession. After a slightly longer pause, other stored codes are displayed in numerical order.

3) When CHECK ENGINE light begins to flash fault codes, it cannot be stopped. If you lose count, it will be necessary to start over. Code 55 indicates end of fault code display.

4) Refer to FAULT CODES table to translate trouble code number to a system fault description (DRB-II display). Once trouble area is identified, refer to TEST SP-1A to diagnose problem.

NOTE: If fault code exists that is not related to cruise control system, see appropriate SELF-DIAGNOSTICS article in ENGINE PERFORMANCE.

DRB-II Diagnostic Mode – 1) Connect DRB-II to engine diagnostic connector. Connector is located in engine compartment, near SBEC. Start engine. Turn ignition switch to ON position. Enter SPEED CONTROL MENU. See SPEED CONTROL MENU under DRB-II TEST FUNCTIONS.

2) At SPEED CONTROL MENU, press "2" (READ FAULTS) key. Press ENTER key. After fault codes are accessed, refer to TEST SP-1A to diagnose problem. If no fault codes are present, see TROUBLE SHOOTING.

3) To erase fault codes while in this mode, press ATM key. At DRB-II display, press "2" (ERASE) key. DRB-II will display ERASE FAULTS ARE YOU SURE? (ENTER TO ERASE). Press ENTER key.

4) When DRB-II is finished erasing fault codes, it will display FAULTS ERASED. This display will remain until ATM key is pressed. After ATM key is pressed, display will return to SPEED CONTROL MENU screen.

1992 SAFETY EQUIPMENT
Cruise Control Systems (Cont.)

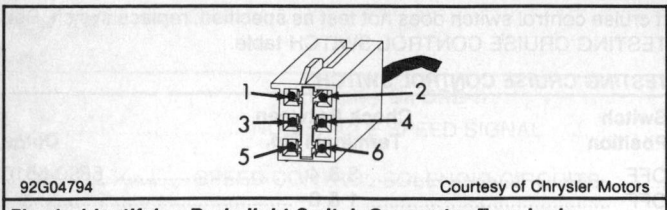

Fig. 1: Identifying Brakelight Switch Connector Terminals

92G04794   Courtesy of Chrysler Motors

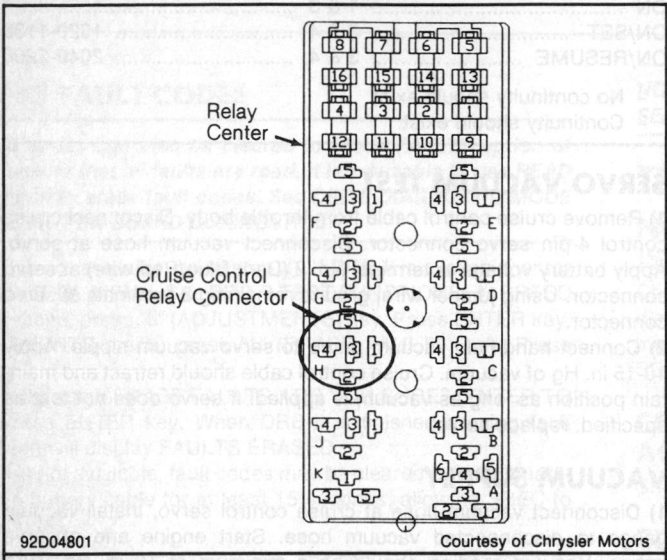

Fig. 2: Identifying Cruise Control Relay Connector Terminals

92D04801   Courtesy of Chrysler Motors

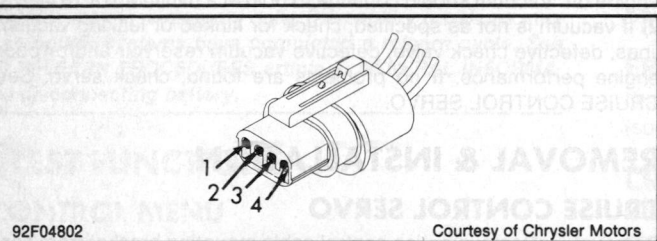

Fig. 3: Identifying Cruise Control Servo Connector Terminals

92F04802   Courtesy of Chrysler Motors

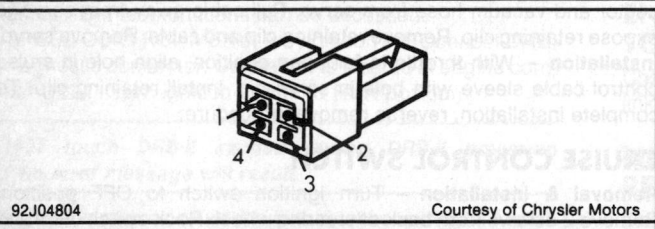

Fig. 4: Identifying Cruise Control Switch Connector Terminals

92J04804   Courtesy of Chrysler Motors

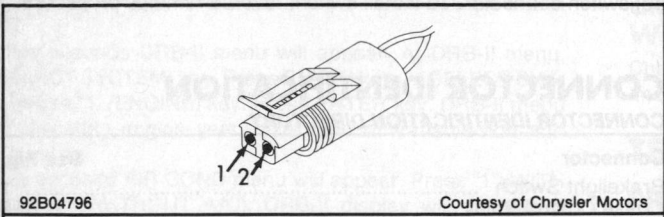

Fig. 5: Identifying Distance Sensor Connector Terminals

92B04796   Courtesy of Chrysler Motors

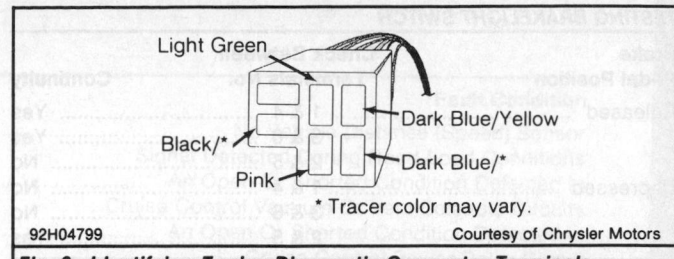

Fig. 6: Identifying Engine Diagnostic Connector Terminals

92H04799   Courtesy of Chrysler Motors

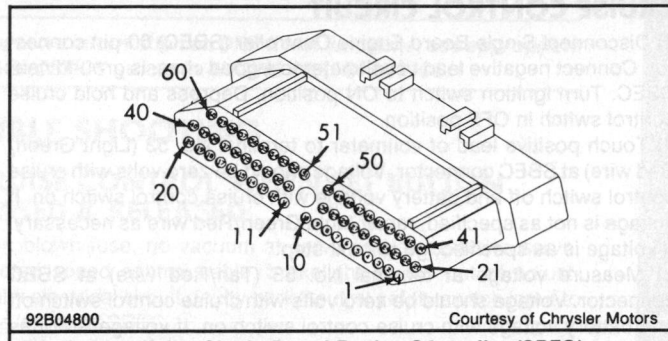

Fig. 7: Identifying Single Board Engine Controller (SBEC) Connector Terminals

92B04800   Courtesy of Chrysler Motors

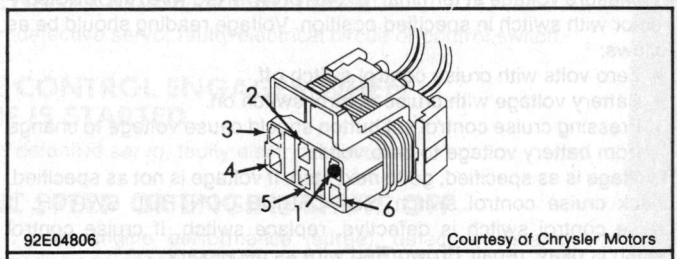

Fig. 8: Identifying Park/Neutral Safety Switch Connector Terminals

92E04806   Courtesy of Chrysler Motors

WIRING DIAGRAMS

For wiring diagrams, see appropriate chassis wiring diagram in WIRING DIAGRAMS.

SELF-DIAGNOSTIC TESTS

NOTE: In the following self-diagnostic tests, illustrations are courtesy of Chrysler Motors. For connector terminal identification, see CONNECTOR IDENTIFICATION table.

TEST SP-1A
READING FAULT CODES

1) Ensure battery is fully charged. Start engine. Allow engine to idle. Using DRB-II, read engine RPM.

2) If DRB-II reading does not correspond with engine speed, go to DRB-II PROBLEMS & ERROR MESSAGES under DRB-II TEST FUNCTIONS in appropriate SELF-DIAGNOSTICS article in ENGINE PERFORMANCE. If DRB-II reading corresponds with engine speed, turn engine off. Turn ignition switch to ON position.

3) Read fault codes with DRB-II. If DRB-II display shows SPEED CONTROL SOLENOID CIRCUIT, perform TEST SP-2A. If DRB-II display shows NO VEHICLE SPEED SIGNAL, perform TEST SP-3A. If DRB-II display does not show a fault codes, perform TEST SP-4A.

TEST SP-2A

REPAIRING POWER & GROUND SUPPLY FOR OPEN TO SERVO SOLENOIDS

1) While listening to cruise control servo, cycle cruise control ON/OFF switch. If cruise control servo clicks when cycling ON/OFF switch, perform TEST SP-2B. If cruise control servo does not click when cycling ON/OFF switch, disconnect cruise control servo 4-pin connector.

2) Inspect connector. If connector is not okay, repair connector as necessary. Perform VERIFICATION TEST SP-VER. If connector is okay, put cruise control ON/OFF switch in ON position. Place DRB-II in voltmeter mode.

3) Ensure brake pedal is not pressed during following step. Probe Dark Blue/tracer wire at cruise control servo connector. Color of tracer may vary. If voltage is less than 10 volts, go to step 5). If voltage is more than 10 volts, go to next step.

4) Place DRB-II in ohmmeter mode. Probe Black wire at cruise control servo connector. If resistance is more than 10 ohms, replace cruise control servo. If resistance is less than 10 ohms, repair short to ground in Black wire. Perform VERIFICATION TEST SP-VER.

5) If voltage is less than 10 volts at Dark Blue/tracer wire in step 3), ensure brake pedal is not pressed. Backprobe Dark Blue/tracer wire at brakelight switch connector. If voltage is more than 10 volts, repair open in Dark Blue/tracer wire between cruise control switch and brakelight switch. Perform VERIFICATION TEST SP-VER.

6) If voltage is less than 10 volts, backprobe Yellow/Red wire at brakelight switch connector. If voltage is more than 10 volts, adjust or replace brakelight switch as necessary. Perform VERIFICATION TEST SP-VER. If voltage is less than 10 volts, repair open in Yellow/Red wire to brakelight switch connector. Perform VERIFICATION TEST SP-VER.

TEST SP-2B

CODE 34, CRUISE CONTROL VACUUM SOLENOID CONTROL CIRCUIT

1) Turn ignition switch to OFF position. Disconnect and inspect Single Board Engine Controller (SBEC) connector. If connector is not okay, repair connector as necessary. Perform VERIFICATION TEST SP-VER. If connector is okay, turn ignition switch to ON position.

2) Turn cruise control ON/OFF switch to ON position. Place DRB-II in voltmeter mode. Probe terminal No. 33 (Tan/Red wire) at SBEC connector. If voltage is more than 10 volts, perform TEST SP-2C. If voltage is less than 10 volts, disconnect cruise control servo connector. Inspect connector.

3) If connector is not okay, repair connector as necessary. Perform VERIFICATION TEST SP-VER. If connector is okay, place DRB-II in ohmmeter mode. Probe Tan/Red wire in servo connector. If resistance is less than 10 ohms, repair short to ground in Tan/Red wire. Perform VERIFICATION TEST SP-VER. If resistance is more than 10 ohms, go to next step.

4) Using an external ohmmeter, check resistance at Tan/Red wire between terminal No. 33 at SBEC connector and terminal No. 4 at cruise control servo connector. If resistance is less than 10 ohms, replace cruise control servo. Perform VERIFICATION TEST SP-VER. If resistance is more than 10 ohms, repair open in Tan/Red wire. Perform VERIFICATION TEST SP-VER.

TEST SP-2C

CODE 34, CRUISE CONTROL VENT SOLENOID CONTROL CIRCUIT

1) Probe terminal No. 53 (Light Green/Red wire) at Single Board Engine Controller (SBEC) connector. If voltage is more than 10 volts, replace SBEC. Perform VERIFICATION TEST SP-VER. If voltage is less than 10 volts, disconnect and inspect cruise control 4-pin servo connector.

2) If connector is not okay, repair connector as necessary. Perform VERIFICATION TEST SP-VER. If connector is okay, put DRB-II in ohmmeter mode. Probe terminal No. 3 (Light Green/Red wire) at servo connector. If resistance is less than 10 ohms, repair short to ground in Light Green/Red wire. Perform VERIFICATION TEST SP-VER. If resistance is more than 10 ohms, go to next step.

TEST SP-2C (Cont.)

3) Using an external ohmmeter, check resistance at Light Green/Red wire between terminal No. 53 at SBEC connector and terminal No. 3 at cruise control servo connector. If resistance is less than 10 ohms, replace cruise control servo. Perform VERIFICATION TEST SP-VER. If resistance is more than 10 ohms, repair open in Light Green/Red wire. Perform VERIFICATION TEST SP-VER.

TEST SP-3A

CODE 15, NO VEHICLE SPEED SIGNAL

1) Turn ignition switch to OFF position. Disconnect vehicle distance sensor connector. Inspect connector. If connector is not okay, repair connector as necessary. Perform VERIFICATION TEST SP-VER.

2) If connector is okay, turn ignition switch to ON position. Connect a jumper wire to one terminal of distance sensor connector. Using DRB-II, monitor car speed while tapping open end of jumper wire to other distance sensor connector terminal.

3) If DRB-II display shows car speed to be more than zero, replace distance sensor. Perform VERIFICATION TEST SP-VER. If car speed is zero, turn ignition switch to OFF position. Place DRB-II in ohmmeter mode. Probe Black/Light Blue wire at distance sensor connector.

4) If resistance is more than 10 ohms, repair open in Black/Light Blue wire. Perform VERIFICATION TEST SP-VER. If resistance is less than 10 ohms, disconnect Single Board Engine Controller (SBEC) connector. Inspect connector. If connector is not okay, repair connector as necessary. Perform VERIFICATION TEST SP-VER.

5) If connector is okay, turn ignition switch to ON position. Put DRB-II in voltmeter mode. Probe terminal No. 47 (White/Orange wire) at SBEC connector.

6) If voltage is more than 4 volts, go to step 8). If voltage is less than 4 volts, check if speedometer works. If speedometer works, repair open in White wire between distance sensor connector and SBEC connector. Perform VERIFICATION TEST SP-VER.

7) If speedometer does not work, turn ignition switch to OFF position. Place DRB-II in ohmmeter mode. Probe terminal No. 47 (White/Orange wire) at SBEC connector. If resistance is less than 10 ohms, repair short to ground in White/Orange wire. Perform VERIFICATION TEST SP-VER. If resistance is more than 10 ohms, repair open in White/Orange wire. Perform VERIFICATION TEST SP-VER.

8) If voltage at White/Orange wire is more than 4 volts in step 6), probe White wire at distance sensor connector. If voltage is more than 4 volts, replace SBEC. Perform VERIFICATION TEST SP-VER.

9) If voltage is less than 4 volts, repair open in White or White/Orange wire between distance sensor and SBEC connector. Perform VERIFICATION TEST SP-VER.

TEST SP-4A

CHECKING CRUISE CONTROL SWITCHES

1) Using DRB-II, read inputs monitor. While watching ON/OFF input, cycle ON/OFF switch several times. If DRB-II display does not correspond with switch position, perform TEST SP-6A.

2) If DRB-II display does correspond with switch position, place cruise control ON/OFF switch in ON position. While watching RESUME input, cycle resume switch several times. If DRB-II display does not correspond with switch position, perform TEST SP-6A. If DRB-II display does correspond with switch position, go to next step.

3) While watching SET input, cycle set switch several times. If DRB-II display does not correspond with switch position, perform TEST SP-8A. If DRB-II display does correspond with switch position, cycle brake pedal several times, while watching BRAKE input.

4) If DRB-II display does not correspond with brake pedal position, perform TEST SP-11A. If DRB-II display does correspond with brake pedal position, check if vehicle is equipped with a manual transmission. If vehicle is equipped with manual transmission, perform TEST SP-12A. If vehicle is not equipped with manual transmission, go to next step.

5) With ignition switch in ON position and engine not running, cycle gear lever several times between "P", "R", "N" and "D", while watching PARK/NEUTRAL input. If DRB-II display does not correspond with selector position, perform TEST SP-13A. If DRB-II display does correspond with selector position, perform TEST SP-12A.

TEST SP-5A

NOTE: Test SP-5A applies to passenger cars only. No test procedures are missing.

TEST SP-6A

CHECKING CRUISE CONTROL RESUME SWITCH CIRCUIT

1) Turn ignition switch to OFF position. Disconnect Single Board Engine Controller (SBEC) connector. Inspect connector. If connector is not okay, repair connector as necessary. Perform VERIFICATION TEST SP-VER.

2) If connector is okay, turn ignition switch to ON position. Place DRB-II in voltmeter mode. Probe terminal No. 50 (White/Light Green wire) at SBEC connector. If voltage is more than 10 volts, replace cruise control switch. Perform VERIFICATION TEST SP-VER. If voltage is less than 10 volts, go to next step.

3) Access cruise control switch connector. See Fig. SP-6A. While holding RESUME switch down, backprobe White/Light Green wire at cruise control switch connector. If voltage is less than 10 volts, replace cruise control switch. If voltage is more than 10 volts, go to next step.

4) Continue to hold RESUME switch down and probe terminal No. 50 (White/Light Green wire) at SBEC connector. If voltage is less than 10 volts, repair open in White/Light Green wire. Perform VERIFICATION TEST SP-VER. If voltage is more than 10 volts, replace SBEC. Perform VERIFICATION TEST SP-VER.

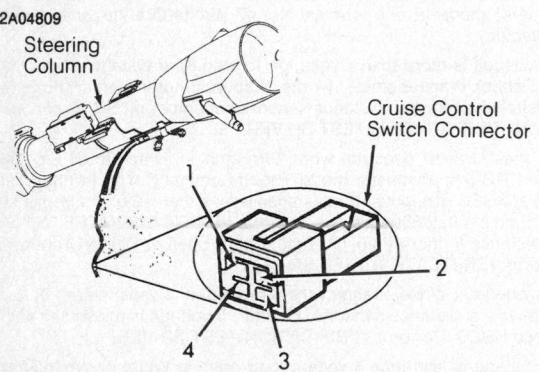

92A04809

Steering Column

Cruise Control Switch Connector

Fig. SP-6A: Locating Cruise Control Switch Connector

TEST SP-7A

NOTE: Test SP-7A applies to passenger cars only. No test procedures are missing.

TEST SP-8A

CHECKING CRUISE CONTROL SET SWITCH CIRCUIT

1) Turn ignition switch to OFF position. Disconnect Single Board Engine Controller (SBEC). Inspect connector. If connector is not okay, repair connector as necessary. Perform VERIFICATION TEST SP-VER. If connector is okay, turn ignition switch to ON position. Place DRB-II in voltmeter mode.

2) Probe terminal No. 48 (Brown/Red wire) at SBEC connector. If voltage is more than 10 volts, replace cruise control switch. Perform VERIFICATION TEST SP-VER. If voltage is less than 10 volts, access cruise control switch connector. See Fig. SP-6A. While holding SET switch down, backprobe terminal No. 3 (Brown/Red wire) at cruise control switch connector.

TEST SP-8A (Cont.)

3) If voltage is less than 10 volts, replace cruise control switch. Perform VERIFICATION TEST SP-VER. If voltage is more than 10 volts, continue to hold SET switch down and probe terminal No. 48 (Brown/Red wire) at SBEC connector.

4) If voltage is less than 10 volts, repair open in Brown/Red wire. Perform VERIFICATION TEST SP-VER. If voltage is more than 10 volts, replace SBEC. Perform VERIFICATION TEST SP-VER.

TESTS SP-9A & SP-10A

NOTE: Tests SP-9A and SP-10A apply to passenger cars only. No test procedures are missing.

TEST SP-11A

CHECKING BRAKELIGHT SWITCH CIRCUITS FOR OPEN

1) If DRB-II display shows RELEASED at all times, perform TEST SP-11B. If DRB-II does not show RELEASED at all times, disconnect brakelight switch connector. Inspect connector. If connector is not okay, repair connector as necessary. Perform VERIFICATION TEST SP-VER.

2) If connector is okay, connect a jumper wire between terminal No. 1 (White/Pink wire) and terminal No. 2 (Black wire) at brakelight switch connector. Using DRB-II, read inputs monitor. if DRB-II display does not show RELEASED, go to step 4).

3) If DRB-II display shows RELEASED, check brakelight switch adjustment. If brakelight switch is adjusted correctly, replace brakelight switch. Perform VERIFICATION TEST SP-VER. If brakelight switch is not adjusted correctly, adjust brakelight switch. Perform VERIFICATION TEST SP-VER.

4) If DRB-II display does not show RELEASED in step 2), connect jumper wire between terminal No. 1 (White/Pink wire) at brakelight switch connector and ground. Using DRB-II, read inputs monitor.

5) If DRB-II display shows RELEASED, repair open in Black wire. If DRB-II does not show RELEASED, turn ignition switch to OFF position. Remove jumper wire. Disconnect Single Board Engine Controller (SBEC) connector. Inspect connector. If connector is not okay, repair connector as necessary. Perform VERIFICATION TEST SP-VER.

6) If connector is okay, using an external ohmmeter, check resistance between terminal No. 1 (White/Pink wire) at brakelight switch connector and terminal No. 29 (White/Pink wire) at SBEC connector. If resistance is more than 10 ohms, repair open in White/Pink wire. Perform VERIFICATION TEST SP-VER. If resistance is less than 10 ohms, replace SBEC. Perform VERIFICATION TEST SP-VER.

TEST SP-11B

CHECKING BRAKELIGHT SWITCH CIRCUITS FOR SHORTS

1) Disconnect brakelight switch connector. Using DRB-II, read inputs monitor. If DRB-II display shows PRESSED, go to step 3). If DRB-II display does not show PRESSED, turn ignition switch to OFF position. Disconnect Single Board Engine Controller (SBEC) connector. Place DRB-II in ohmmeter mode. Probe terminal No. 29 (White/Pink wire) at SBEC connector.

2) If resistance is less than 10 ohms, repair short to ground in White/Pink wire. Perform VERIFICATION TEST SP-VER. If resistance is more than 10 ohms, replace SBEC. Perform VERIFICATION TEST SP-VER.

3) If DRB-II display shows PRESSED in step 1), check brakelight switch adjustment. If brakelight switch is adjusted correctly, replace brakelight switch. Perform VERIFICATION TEST SP-VER. If brakelight switch is not adjusted correctly, adjust brakelight switch. Perform VERIFICATION TEST SP-VER.

TEST SP-12A

CHECKING CRUISE CONTROL SERVO OPERATION

1) Disconnect and inspect 4-pin cruise control servo connector. If connector is not okay, repair connector as necessary. Perform VERIFICATION TEST SP-VER. If connector is okay, place DRB-II in ohmmeter mode. Probe terminal No. 1 (Black wire) at cruise control servo connector.

2) If resistance is more than 10 ohms, repair open Black wire. Perform VERIFICATION TEST SP-VER. If resistance is less than 10 ohms, reconnect cruise control servo connector. Check if vehicle is equipped with a vacuum reservoir. If vehicle is equipped with vacuum reservoir, perform TEST SP-12B.

3) If vehicle is not equipped with a vacuum reservoir, disconnect cruise control servo vacuum hose. Connect vacuum gauge to disconnected servo vacuum hose. Start engine. If gauge does not show a minimum of 10 in. Hg of vacuum, repair vacuum leak or restriction between servo and vacuum source. Perform VERIFICATION TEST SP-VER.

4) If gauge does show a minimum of 10 in. Hg of vacuum, turn engine off. Turn ignition switch to ON position. Using an alternative source of constant vacuum supply, connect a vacuum supply hose to servo. Using DRB-II, actuate servo solenoids. If throttle fully opens and closes, perform TEST SP-14A.

5) If throttle does not fully open and close, using DRB-II, stop actuation test. Inspect cruise control servo cable condition. If cruise control servo cable condition is okay, replace cruise control servo. Perform VERIFICATION TEST SP-VER. If cruise control servo cable condition is not okay, repair cable as necessary. Perform VERIFICATION TEST SP-VER.

TEST SP-12B

CHECKING VACUUM TO CRUISE CONTROL SERVO

1) Start engine. Turn engine off. Turn ignition switch to ON position. Using DRB-II, actuate servo solenoids. If throttle fully opens and closes, perform TEST SP-14A. If throttle does not fully open and close, use DRB-II and stop actuation test.

2) Disconnect vacuum hose at cruise control servo. Using an alternative source of constant vacuum supply, connect a vacuum supply hose to servo. Using DRB-II, actuate servo solenoids. If throttle fully opens and closes, repair vacuum leak or restriction between servo and vacuum source. Perform VERIFICATION TEST SP-VER.

3) If throttle does not fully open and close, using DRB-II, stop actuation test. Inspect cruise control servo cable condition. If cruise control servo cable condition is okay, replace cruise control servo. Perform VERIFICATION TEST SP-VER. If cruise control servo cable condition is not okay, repair cable as necessary. Perform VERIFICATION TEST SP-VER.

TEST SP-13A

CHECKING PARK/NEUTRAL SAFETY SWITCH

1) Disconnect Park/Neutral safety switch connector at transmission. Inspect connector. If connector is not okay, repair connector as necessary. Perform VERIFICATION TEST SP-VER. If connector is okay, use DRB-II and read inputs monitor.

2) If DRB-II display shows D/R, replace Park/Neutral safety switch. Perform VERIFICATION TEST SP-VER. If DRB-II display does not show D/R, turn ignition switch to OFF position. Disconnect and inspect Single Board Engine Controller (SBEC) connector. If connector is not okay, repair connector as necessary. Perform VERIFICATION TEST SP-VER.

3) If connector is okay, place DRB-II in ohmmeter mode. Probe terminal No. 30 (Black/Tan or Brown/Yellow wire) at SBEC. If resistance is less than 10 ohms, repair short to ground in Black/Tan or Brown/Yellow wire. Perform VERIFICATION TEST SP-VER. If resistance is more than 10 ohms, replace SBEC. Perform VERIFICATION TEST SP-VER.

TEST SP-14A

CHECKING FOR INTERMITTENT FAULTS

1) Reconnect and reassemble all previously tested components. Connect DRB-II to engine diagnostic connector so DRB-II display can be seen from driver's seat. Road test vehicle. Using DRB-II, read cutout monitor on DRB-II display. If DRB-II display shows erratic vehicle speed, replace distance sensor. Perform VERIFICATION TEST SP-VER.

2) If DRB-II display does not show erratic vehicle speed, put cruise control ON/OFF switch in ON position. With vehicle speed at a minimum of 35 MPH, press and release cruise control set switch. If DRB-II display shows S/C DENIED, see appropriate DENIED MESSAGE in DRB-II INTERMITTENT FAULT MESSAGES table and correct problem as necessary.

DRB-II INTERMITTENT FAULT MESSAGES

Denied Message	Problem To Correct
BRAKE	Open Circuit At Terminal No. 29 At SBEC
CLUTCH	RPM/Vehicle Speed Ratio Is Not Constant
ON/OFF	Lack Of Voltage At Terminal No. 23 Or No. 49 At SBEC
P/N	Ground Exists At Terminal No. 30 At SBEC
RPM/SPD	RPM/Speed Ratio Is Not Constant
SPEED	Vehicle Speed As Read By Distance Sensor Is Less Than 35 MPH
RPM	Engine RPM Is Excessively High
SOL/FLT	Fault In Servo Vent Or Vacuum Solenoid Circuit That Is Either Maturing Or Set

3) If DRB-II display shows S/C ALLOWED and cruise control is operative, perform the following:

- Check for cruise control disengagement without driver command by driving vehicle under various road conditions.
- If cruise control disengages without driver command, read cutout monitor S/C DENIED message on DRB-II display. See appropriate DENIED MESSAGE in DRB-II INTERMITTENT FAULT MESSAGES table and repair as necessary.
- If cruise control does not disengage without driver command, read cutout monitor on DRB-II display. Compare GOAL value with SPEED value. If values are not within 2 MPH of each other, replace SBEC.

VERIFICATION TEST SP-VER

CRUISE CONTROL VERIFICATION

Reconnect and reassemble all previously tested components. If Single Board Engine Controller (SBEC) has been changed, perform the following:

- If vehicle is equipped with factory theft alarm, start vehicle at least 20 times so alarm system may be activated when desired.
- Write vehicle's odometer mileage to memory location within replacement SBEC. This will enable new SBEC to operate Emission Maintenance Reminder (EMR) light properly. See MAINTENANCE REMINDER (EMR) MILEAGE TRANSFER under SELF-DIAGNOSTIC SYSTEM in appropriate SELF-DIAGNOSTICS article in ENGINE PERFORMANCE.
- On all models, connect DRB-II to engine diagnostic connector and erase faults.

To ensure no other fault remains, perform the following:

1) Road test vehicle at a speed above 35 MPH. Put cruise control ON/OFF switch in ON position. Press and release SET switch. If cruise control did not engage, repair is not complete. Check all pertinent MITCHELL® TECHNICAL SERVICE BULLETINS (TSBs) and return to TEST SP-1A, if necessary.

2) Press and release SET switch. If vehicle speed did not increase by 2 MPH, repair is not complete. Check all pertinent MITCHELL® TECHNICAL SERVICE BULLETINS (TSBs) and return to TEST SP-1A, if necessary.

3) Press and release brake pedal. If cruise control did not disengage, repair is not complete. Check all pertinent MITCHELL® TECHNICAL SERVICE BULLETINS (TSBs) and return to TEST SP-1A, if necessary.

VERIFICATION TEST SP-VER (Cont.)

4) Bring vehicle speed back up to 35 MPH. Press RESUME/ACCEL switch. If cruise control did not resume previously set speed, repair is not complete. Check all pertinent MITCHELL® TECHNICAL SERVICE BULLETINS (TSBs) and return to TEST SP-1A, if necessary.

5) Hold down SET switch. If vehicle did not decelerate, repair is not complete. Check all pertinent MITCHELL® TECHNICAL SERVICE BULLETINS (TSBs) and return to TEST SP-1A, if necessary.

6) Ensure vehicle speed is greater than 35 MPH and release SET switch. If vehicle did not adjust to new vehicle speed, repair is not complete. Check all pertinent MITCHELL® TECHNICAL SERVICE BULLETINS (TSBs) and return to TEST SP-1A, if necessary.

7) Turn ON/OFF switch to OFF position. If cruise control did not disengage, repair is not complete. Check all pertinent MITCHELL® TECHNICAL SERVICE BULLETINS (TSBs) and return to TEST SP-1A, if necessary.

8) If vehicle successfully passed all previous tests, cruise control system is now functioning correctly. Repair is complete.

Cherokee, Grand Cherokee (1993), Wrangler

DESCRIPTION & OPERATION

System consists of 2 vertical bus bars and horizontal rows of heating elements fused to inside of rear glass. On Cherokee, power circuit to grid is protected by fuse No. 18 (25 amp) located in fuse box. Power for relay is protected by fuse No. 8 (20 amp) located in fuse box.

On Grand Cherokee, power circuit to grid is protected by circuit breaker No. 28 (30 amp) located in fuse box. Power for relay is protected by fuse No. 19 (15 amp) located in fuse box. Fuse No. 23, located in fuse box, controls power to switch light and side mirrors.

On Wrangler, power circuit to grid is protected by fuse No. 6 (25 amp) located in fuse box. Power for relay is protected by fuse No. 9 (15 amp) located in fuse box.

TESTING

NOTE: For terminal identification, see appropriate chassis wiring in WIRING DIAGRAMS.

SYSTEM TESTING

1) On Wrangler, check fuses No. 6 and 9. On Cherokee, check HTD/WDW and TURN fuses. On Grand Cherokee, check fuses No. 19 and 23 and circuit breaker No. 28. Replace as necessary.
2) If fuses are okay, check voltage at fuse No. 6 (Wrangler), HTD/WDW fuse (Cherokee) or fuse No. 28 (Grand Cherokee). If voltage is not present, replace fuse.
3) Check ignition side of fuse No. 9 (Wrangler), TURN fuse (Cherokee) or fuse No. 19 (Grand Cherokee) for voltage. If battery voltage is not present, check for an open circuit from ignition switch.

DEFOGGER SWITCH TEST

Cherokee & Wrangler – 1) Disconnect defogger switch connector. Turn ignition switch to RUN position. Measure voltage at defogger switch connector terminal "D". About 5 volts should be present. If about 5 volts are not present, repair open circuit from relay.
2) Measure resistance across switch terminals "B" and "D". *See Figs. 1 and 2.* With switch button depressed, almost zero ohms should be present. Measure resistance across switch terminals "D" and "C". With switch button depressed, zero ohms should be present. Measure resistance across switch terminals "B" and "C". Almost zero ohms should be present.
Grand Cherokee – 1) Disconnect defogger switch connector. Using a jumper wire, apply 12 volts to switch terminal No. 1. Using another jumper wire, connect terminal No. 3 of switch to ground. If switch indicator lights, go to next step. If indicator does not light, replace switch.
2) Remove jumper wires. Connect an ohmmeter between switch terminals No. 2 and 3. Depress switch. Ohmmeter should indicate 10 ohms. If ohmmeter does not indicate 10 ohms, replace switch. If ohm-

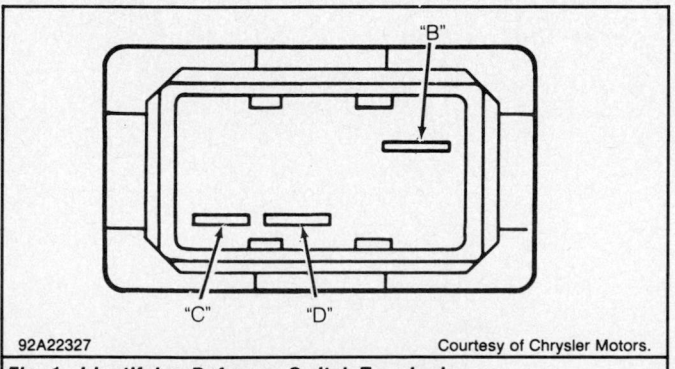

92A22327   Courtesy of Chrysler Motors.
Fig. 1: Identifying Defogger Switch Terminals

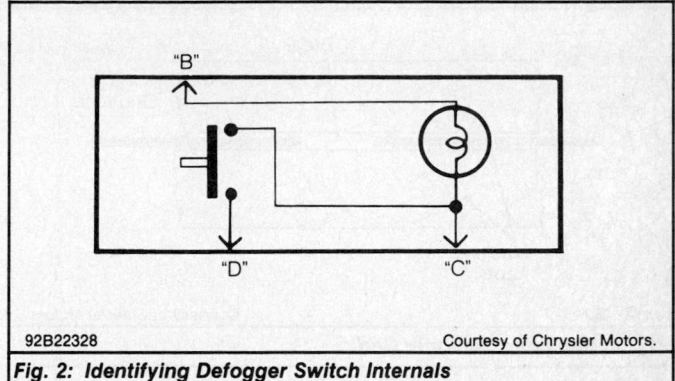

92B22328   Courtesy of Chrysler Motors.
Fig. 2: Identifying Defogger Switch Internals

meter indicates 10 ohms, check for an open circuit between terminal No. 1 and fuse No. 23, between terminal No. 3 and ground and between relay terminals No. 2 and 3.

DEFOGGER RELAY TEST

1) Disconnect defogger relay connector. Turn ignition switch to RUN position. Measure voltage at relay connector terminal No. 4 (Cherokee and Wrangler) or No. 5 (Grand Cherokee). Battery voltage should be present. If battery voltage is not present, repair open circuit to fuse No. 9 (Grand Cherokee and Wrangler) or HTD/WDW fuse (Cherokee).
2) Measure voltage at relay connector terminal No. 4. Battery voltage should be present. If battery voltage is not present, repair open circuit from fuse No. 6 (Wrangler), TURN fuse (Cherokee) or circuit breaker No. 28 (Grand Cherokee).
3) Turn ignition switch to OFF position. Check resistance between relay connector terminal No. 1 and left (driver side) of defogger grid. Zero ohms should be present. If zero ohms are not present, repair open circuit between relay connector and left side of defogger grid.
4) Measure resistance between relay connector terminal No. 5 (Cherokee and Wrangler) or No. 2 (Grand Cherokee) and ground. Zero ohms should be present. If zero ohms are not present, repair open circuit between relay connector and ground.
5) Reconnect relay connector. Turn ignition switch to RUN position. Measure voltage at terminal No. 3. About 5 volts should be present. If about 5 volts are not present, replace defogger relay.

GRID FILAMENT TEST

1) Turn defogger on. Turn ignition switch to RUN position. Measure voltage at left (driver side) of defogger grid. Battery voltage should be present. If battery voltage is not present, repair open circuit from defogger relay.
2) Turn ignition switch to OFF position. Measure resistance from right side of defogger grid to ground. Zero ohms should be present. If zero ohms are not present, repair open circuit between right side of defogger grid and ground.

ON-VEHICLE SERVICE

GRID FILAMENT REPAIR

1) Mark location of broken or open grid on exterior surface of glass using a marking pen. Using fine steel wool, lightly rub area to be repaired inside rear window. Clean area using alcohol.
2) Place 2 strips of masking tape to inside surface of rear window, above and below break in grid. *See Fig. 3.* Thoroughly mix conductive epoxy. Apply epoxy on grid break, overlapping both ends of break.
3) Carefully remove masking tape from grid line. Allow epoxy to cure 24 hours at room temperature or use a heat gun for 15 minutes. Hold gun about 10" from damaged area.

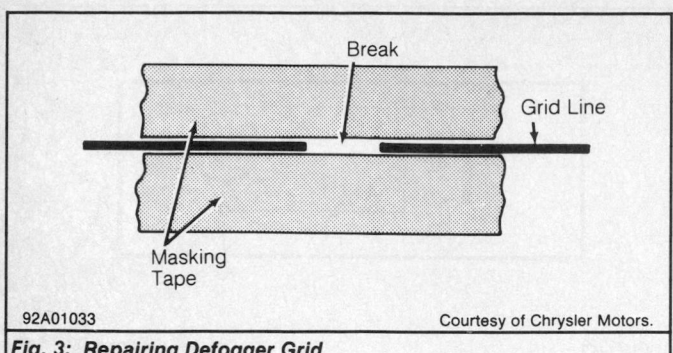

Fig. 3: Repairing Defogger Grid

92A01033   Courtesy of Chrysler Motors.

REMOVAL & INSTALLATION

DEFOGGER SWITCH

Removal & Installation (Cherokee) – Disconnect negative battery cable. Remove instrument panel bezel. Remove switch housing panel. Disconnect switch connector. Depress switch mounting tabs, and remove switch. To install, reverse removal procedure.

Removal & Installation (Grand Cherokee) – **1)** Disconnect negative battery cable. Remove ash tray. Remove 6 screws retaining center cluster bezel. Remove center bezel. Remove 2 screws holding dash pad located behind top of center bezel.

2) Pry defroster grille out of dash pad. Unplug sensors and set defroster grille aside. Remove 4 screws in defroster duct opening holding dash pad. Remove 3 screws above instrument panel cluster holding dash pad.

3) Open glove box, and remove 2 screws holding dash pad. Remove dash pad by pulling upward and unsnapping end clips. With driver's door open, remove one screw from side of lower trim panel. Remove one screw from bottom of lower trim panel and pull panel off. Ensure clip is disengaged holding panel to instrument panel.

4) Remove 4 screws holding steering column cover. Remove 3 screws holding bottom of bezels. Remove 2 screws holding top of end and switch pod bezels. Remove end bezel. Remove 2 screws holding left side of switch pod bezel. Remove 3 screws holding right side of switch pod bezel.

5) Pull switch pod bezel out far enough to remove switch connectors. Disconnect connectors from each switch pod and remove bezel. Remove switch attaching screws and switch. To install, reverse removal procedure.

Removal & Installation (Wrangler) – Disconnect negative battery cable. Remove 6 instrument panel shroud screws. Slide shroud toward steering wheel. Remove 3 defogger switch bezel screws. Disconnect defogger switch connector. Squeeze ends of switch to release plastic retaining fingers. To install, reverse removal procedure.

DEFOGGER RELAY

Removal & Installation (Cherokee) – Rear defogger relay is Red and located behind instrument panel, to right of steering column. Remove lower instrument panel trim panel. Remove relay from connector.

Removal & Installation (Grand Cherokee) – Rear defogger relay is Red and located in relay center, in glove box. Remove relay from connector.

Removal & Installation (Wrangler) – Rear defogger relay is Red and located behind driver-side kick panel. Remove relay from connector.

WIRING DIAGRAMS

See appropriate chassis wiring diagram in WIRING DIAGRAMS.

Cherokee, Comanche, Wrangler

DESCRIPTION

Instrument panel is supplied voltage through gauges fuse. A printed circuit on rear of instrument cluster distributes voltage to gauges and indicators.

Emission Maintenance Timer – Emission Maintenance Timer and Indicator Light activate when mileage reaches scheduled maintenance interval of 82,500 miles. Timer can be reset using DRB-II.

TESTING

GAUGE TESTING

Compare resistance values of malfunctioning gauge to specifications. See OIL PRESSURE GAUGE RESISTANCES, FUEL GAUGE RESISTANCES and TEMPERATURE GAUGE RESISTANCES tables.

OIL PRESSURE GAUGE RESISTANCES

Oil pressure (psi)	Ohms
Cherokee & Comanche	
0	1
40	46
80	87
Wrangler	
0	1
40	46
80	90

FUEL GAUGE RESISTANCES

Application	Ohms
Cherokee & Comanche	
Empty	105
1/2 Full	33
Full	5
Wrangler	
Empty	0
1/2 Full	44
Full	89

TEMPERATURE GAUGE RESISTANCES

Application & Test Temperature	Ohms
Cherokee & Comanche	
100°F (38°C)	1365.0
220°F (104°C)	93.5
260°F (127°C)	55.1
Wrangler	
100°F (82°)	1365.0
210°F (99°C)	115.0
240°F (116°C)	55.1

CHEROKEE & COMANCHE

NOTE: To locate instrument cluster connectors and terminals, see Figs. 1 and 2.

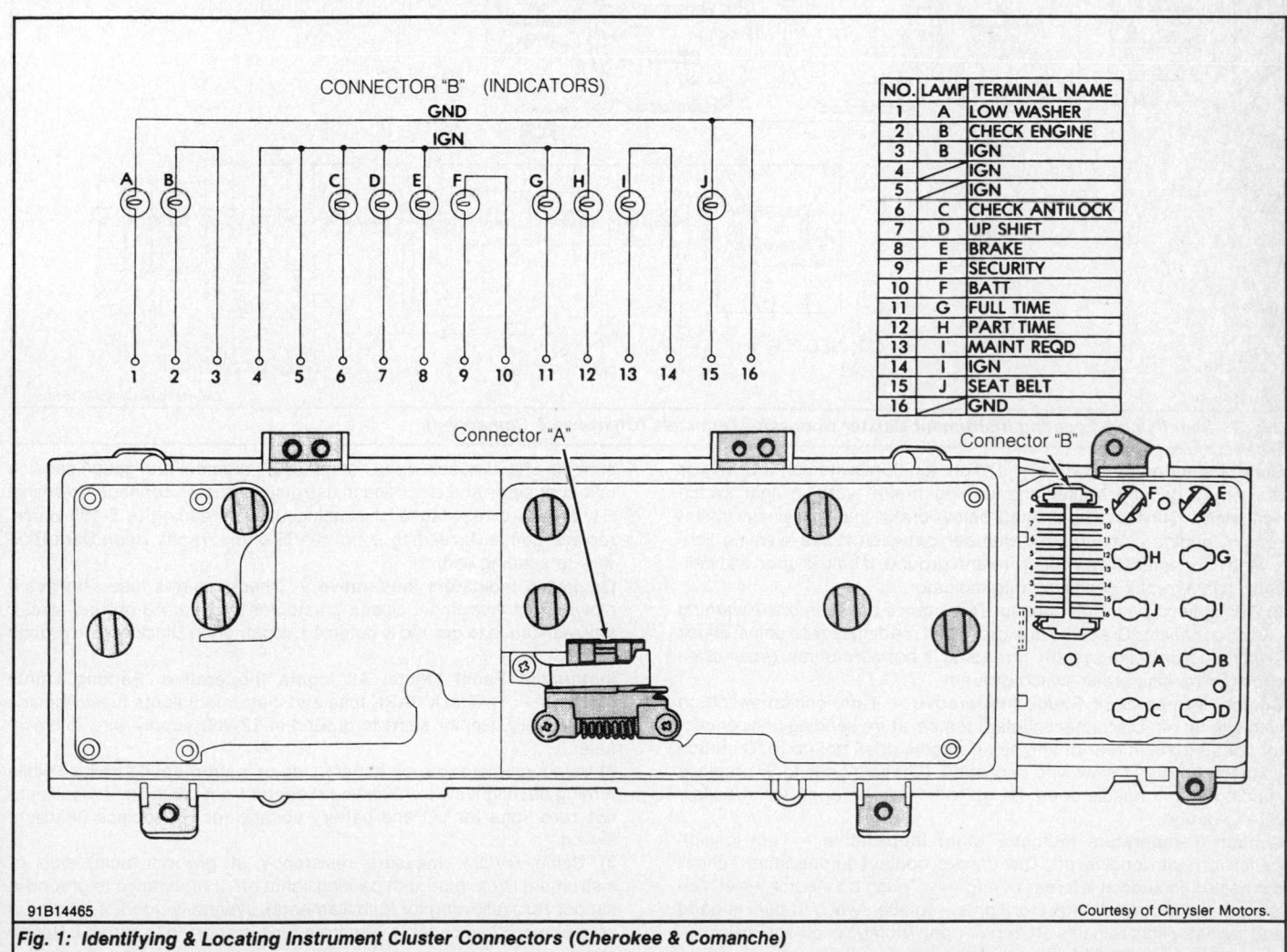

NO.	LAMP	TERMINAL NAME
1	A	LOW WASHER
2	B	CHECK ENGINE
3	B	IGN
4		IGN
5		IGN
6	C	CHECK ANTILOCK
7	D	UP SHIFT
8	E	BRAKE
9	F	SECURITY
10	F	BATT
11	G	FULL TIME
12	H	PART TIME
13	I	MAINT REQD
14	I	IGN
15	J	SEAT BELT
16		GND

91B14465

Courtesy of Chrysler Motors.

Fig. 1: Identifying & Locating Instrument Cluster Connectors (Cherokee & Comanche)

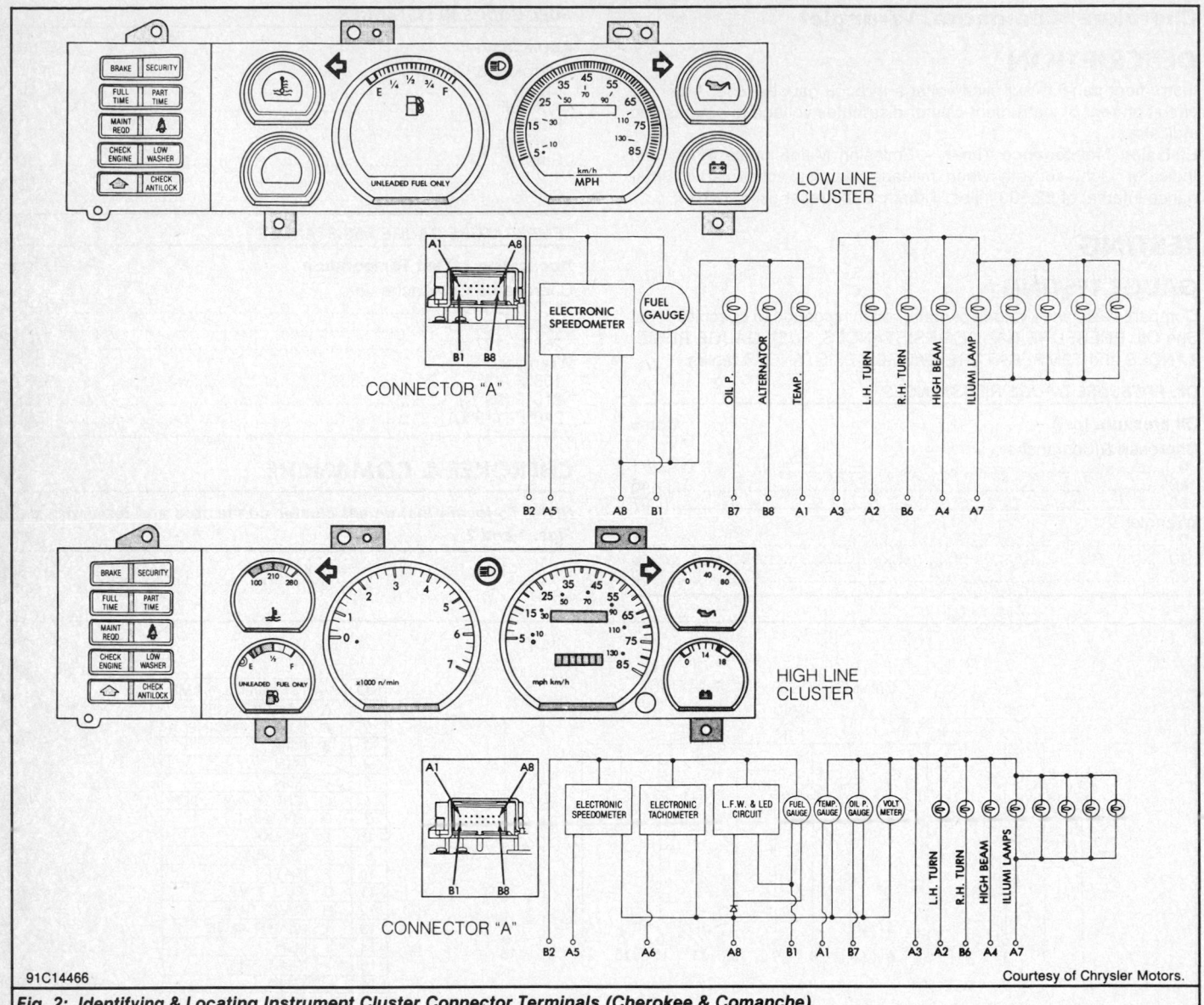

91C14466   Courtesy of Chrysler Motors.

Fig. 2: Identifying & Locating Instrument Cluster Connector Terminals (Cherokee & Comanche)

Brake Indicator Inoperative – 1) Turn ignition switch on with engine off. Apply parking brake, and unplug brake warning light switch connector. Connector is located below brake master cylinder at left rear of engine compartment. Jumper between brake warning light switch connector Gray/White wire and ground. If bulb is good and indicator lights, repair open circuit to indicator.

2) With ignition switch off, measure resistance between brake warning switch connector Gray wire and ground. If reading is zero ohms, check switch and/or brake system. If reading is not zero ohms, repair open circuit to parking brake switch ground.

Coolant Temperature Gauge Inoperative – Turn ignition switch on with engine off. Disconnect coolant temperature sending unit connector (located at left rear of engine). If needle does not go to "C", touch connector Violet/Yellow wire to ground. If needle goes to "H", replace sending unit. If needle does not go to "H", repair open Violet/Yellow wire to gauge.

Coolant Temperature Indicator Light Inoperative – Turn ignition switch on with engine off. Disconnect coolant temperature sender connector (located at left rear of engine). Touch connector Violet/Yellow wire to ground. If indicator lights, replace switch. If bulb is good and indicator light remains off, repair open Violet/Yellow wire to instrument cluster terminal A1.

Fuel Gauge Inoperative – With ignition on and engine off, disconnect fuel gauge sending unit connector. If needle goes to "E", replace sending unit. If needle does not go to "E", connect fuel gauge sending unit connector and disconnect instrument cluster connector terminal B1. Measure resistance of sending unit. If reading is 5-105 ohms, replace gauge. If reading is not 5-105 ohms, repair open Dark Blue wire to sending unit.

Gauges & Indicators Inoperative – Check gauges fuse. Replace if blown. Test instrument cluster connector terminal A3 ground wire. If any resistance to ground is detected, repair open Black wire in ground circuit.

Instrument Panel Lights: All Lights Inoperative, Parking Lights Working – 1) Check PARK fuse and instrument lights fuse. Replace if necessary. Repair short to ground in 12-volt supply wire to blown fuse.

2) Using voltmeter, probe battery side of instrument lights fuse while turning headlight switch dimming rheostat from LO to HI. If results are not zero volts for LO and battery voltage for HI, replace headlight switch.

3) Using DVOM, measure resistance at ground (bulb) side of instrument lights fuse with parking lights off. If resistance to ground is almost zero (allowing for bulb filaments), system is good. If reading is zero ohms, 12 volt supply wire from fuse is shorted to ground. Repair short.

Low Fuel Warning Light Inoperative – Turn ignition on with engine off. Disconnect wire to terminal B1 of instrument cluster connector.

Wait 10 seconds. If indicator light glows, system is good. Replace sending unit. If indicator light does not glow, replace low fuel warning module (on back of instrument cluster).

Oil Pressure Gauge Inoperative – **1)** Turn ignition on with engine off. Disconnect oil pressure sender connector, located on right side of engine, next to distributor. If needle goes to "H", system is good.

2) If needle does not go to "H", touch oil pressure sending unit connector Gray wire to ground. If needle goes to "L", replace sending unit. If needle does not go to "L", repair open in Gray wire circuit to gauge (instrument cluster terminal B7).

Oil Pressure Indicator Inoperative – Turn ignition on with engine off. Touch oil pressure switch connector Gray wire to ground. If light glows, replace switch. If light does not glow and bulb is good, repair open in Gray wire to instrument cluster connector terminal B7.

Part Time Or 4WD Indicator Inoperative – **1)** Apply parking brake. Start engine. Place 4WD selector lever in 4WD LOCK or 4WD position. Unplug 4WD switch, and touch harness connector Black/Yellow wire to ground. If indicator light glows, wiring system is good. Check 4WD switch operation, and replace switch if defective.

2) If indicator light does not glow and bulb is good, repair open in Black/Yellow wire circuit to indicator light.

Tachometer Inoperative – Tachometer input is from engine ECU pin No. 43. Check Gray/Light Blue wire for short or open circuits. If wire is okay, see appropriate SELF-DIAGNOSTICS article.

Voltmeter (Gauge) Inoperative – Turn ignition on with engine off. If voltmeter does not indicate battery voltage, measure voltage at instrument cluster connector terminal No. A8. If battery voltage is present at terminal No. A8, replace voltmeter. If battery voltage is not present at terminal No. A8, repair open White/Black wire circuit to gauges fuse.

WRANGLER

NOTE: To locate instrument cluster connectors and terminals, see Figs. 3 and 4.

All Gauges Inoperative – **1)** Check power supply to gauges with ignition on and engine off. If power is not present, check fuse No. 9 and replace as necessary. Turn ignition switch to RUN position, and measure voltage at battery side of fuse No. 9. Battery voltage should be present. If battery voltage is not present, repair open from ignition switch.

2) Disconnect gauge package connector. Turn ignition switch to OFF position, and measure resistance from instrument cluster connector terminals No. 1 and 13 to ground. Ohmmeter should indicate zero ohms. If resistance is not zero ohms, repair open to ground.

3) Turn ignition switch to RUN position, and measure voltage at instrument cluster connector terminals No. 2 and 12. Voltmeter should indicate battery voltage. If battery voltage is not present, repair open circuit from fuse panel.

Coolant Temperature Sending Unit – Turn ignition switch to RUN position. Disconnect coolant temperature sending unit connector from coolant temperature sending unit. Touch connector to engine block. Gauge should indicate at high end of scale. When connector is not touching ground, gauge should read at low end of scale. If gauge is okay, replace sending unit. If gauge is not okay, check circuit between sending unit and gauge for an open circuit. If wiring is okay, replace gauge.

Fuel Gauge Sending Unit – **1)** Turn ignition switch to RUN position. Disconnect fuel gauge sending unit connector from fuel gauge sending unit near tank. Ground center wire of body harness side of

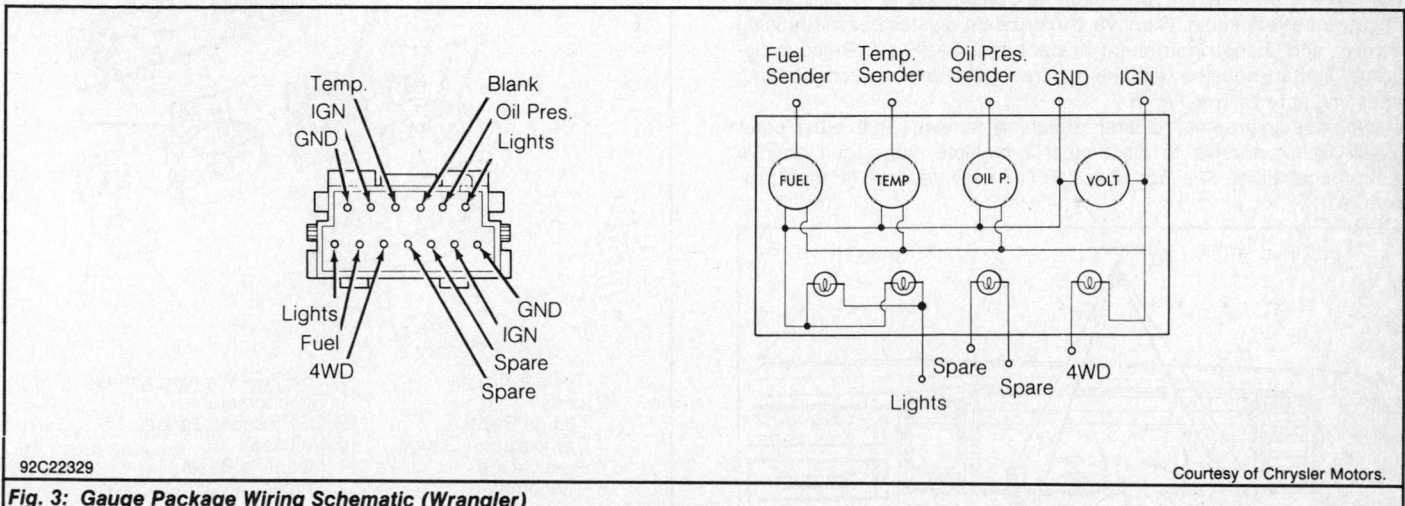

92C22329

Courtesy of Chrysler Motors.

Fig. 3: Gauge Package Wiring Schematic (Wrangler)

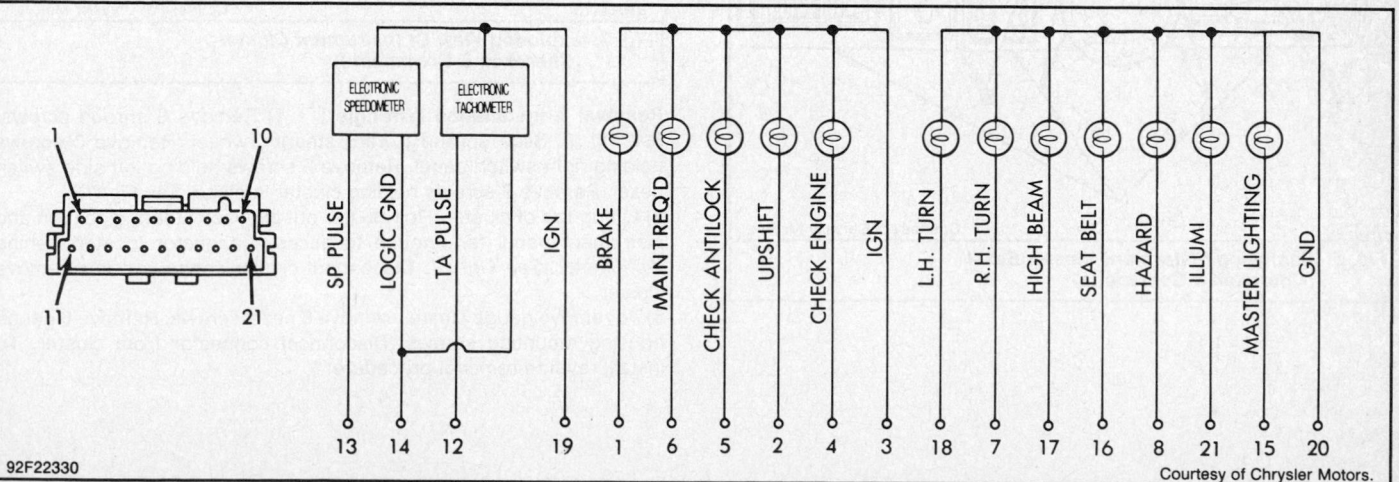

92F22330

Courtesy of Chrysler Motors.

Fig. 4: Indicator Light Wiring Schematic (Wrangler)

connector (Tan/Black wire). If gauge reads at low end of scale, go to next step. If gauge does not read at low end of scale, check circuit between connector and gauge. If circuit is okay, replace gauge.

2) Turn ignition switch to OFF position. Measure resistance from fuel gauge sending unit connector center terminal to ground. See FUEL GAUGE RESISTANCES table. If resistances are not to specification, replace sending unit. If sending unit is okay, repair open circuit from fuel gauge sending unit connector to ground.

Oil Pressure Sending Unit – 1) Turn ignition switch to RUN position. Disconnect oil pressure sending unit connector from oil pressure sending unit. Touch connector to ground. Gauge should read at low end of scale. When connector is not touching ground, gauge should read at high end of scale. If gauge is okay, replace sending unit.

2) If gauge is not okay, check circuit between sending unit and gauge for an open circuit. If wiring is okay, replace gauge.

Printed Circuit Check – 1) Turn ignition switch to RUN position. Disconnect gauge package connector. Measure resistance from gauge package terminal No. 12 (fuel and coolant temperature gauge) or from terminal No. 2 (voltmeter and oil pressure gauge) to gauge battery terminal. Ohmmeter should read zero ohms. If resistance is not zero ohms, replace printed circuit.

2) Measure resistance from gauge package terminal No. 13 (fuel and coolant temperature gauge) or from terminal No. 1 (voltmeter and oil pressure gauge) to gauge ground terminal. Ohmmeter should read zero ohms. If resistance is not zero ohms, replace printed circuit.

REMOVAL & INSTALLATION

INSTRUMENT CLUSTER

Removal & Installation (Cherokee & Comanche) – 1) Disconnect negative battery cable. Remove 4 instrument cluster bezel attaching screws, and unsnap instrument cluster bezel. See Fig. 5. Remove cigarette lighter housing attaching screw. Remove switch housing attaching screws. See Fig. 6.

2) Remove instrument cluster attaching screws. Pull out cluster assembly far enough to disconnect 2 multiple plugs, and remove instrument cluster. See Figs. 7 and 8. To install, reverse removal procedure.

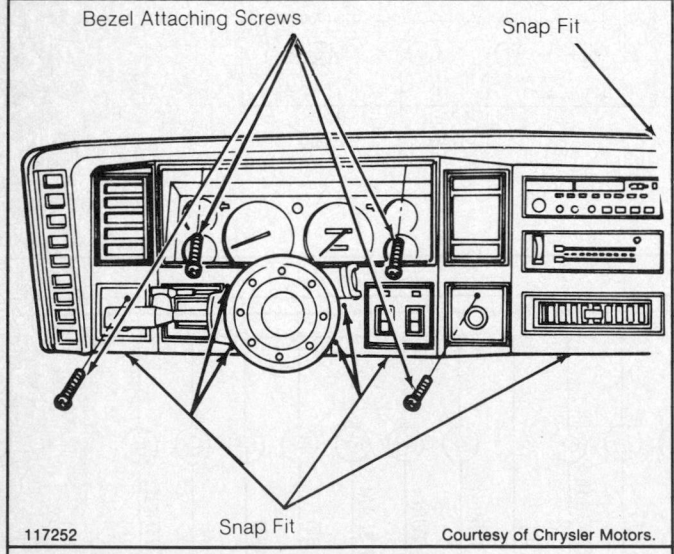

Fig. 5: Removing Instrument Cluster Bezel (Cherokee & Comanche)

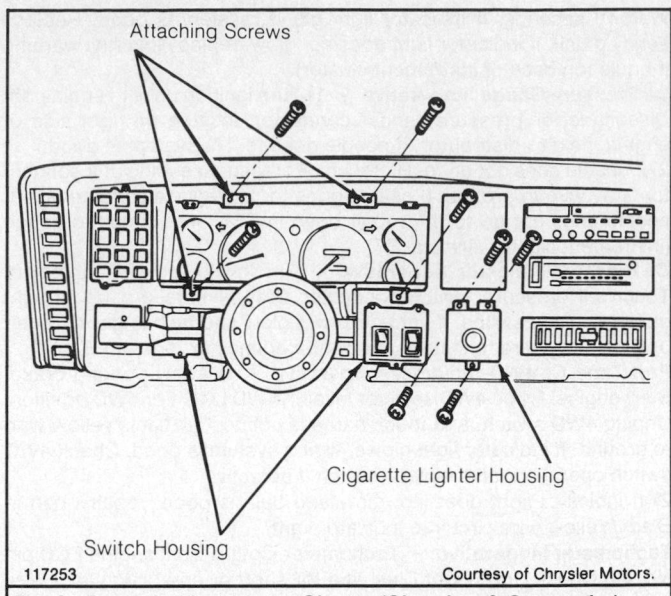

Courtesy of Chrysler Motors.

Fig. 6: Removing Instrument Cluster (Cherokee & Comanche)

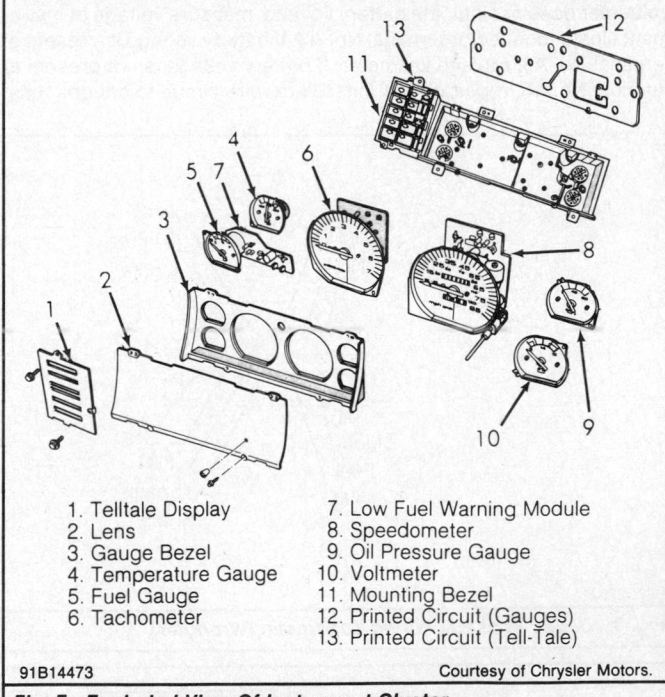

1. Telltale Display
2. Lens
3. Gauge Bezel
4. Temperature Gauge
5. Fuel Gauge
6. Tachometer
7. Low Fuel Warning Module
8. Speedometer
9. Oil Pressure Gauge
10. Voltmeter
11. Mounting Bezel
12. Printed Circuit (Gauges)
13. Printed Circuit (Tell-Tale)

91B14473 Courtesy of Chrysler Motors.

Fig. 7: Exploded View Of Instrument Cluster (Cherokee & Comanche)

Removal & Installation (Wrangler) – 1) Remove 6 shroud screws. See Fig. 9. Slide shroud toward steering wheel. Remove 3 screws holding right switch panel. Remove 3 screws holding left side switch bezel. Remove 2 screws holding cluster in place. See Fig. 10.

2) Lift up top of cluster. Roll cluster out between steering column and instrument panel far enough to access connector located behind tachometer. See Fig. 11. Disconnect cluster connector, and remove cluster.

3) To remove gauge cluster, remove 6 bezel screws. Remove 6 gauge housing mounting screws. Disconnect connector from cluster. To install, reverse removal procedure.

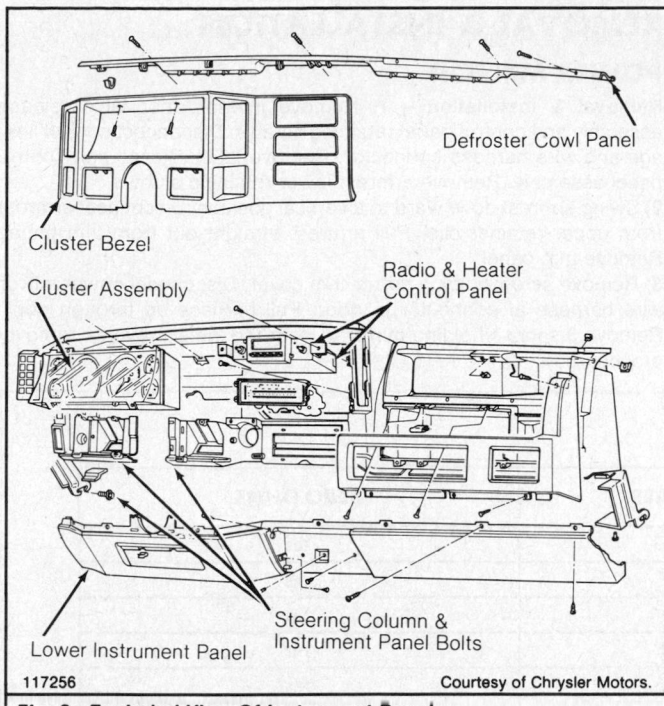

Fig. 8: Exploded View Of Instrument Panel (Cherokee & Comanche)

117256   Courtesy of Chrysler Motors.

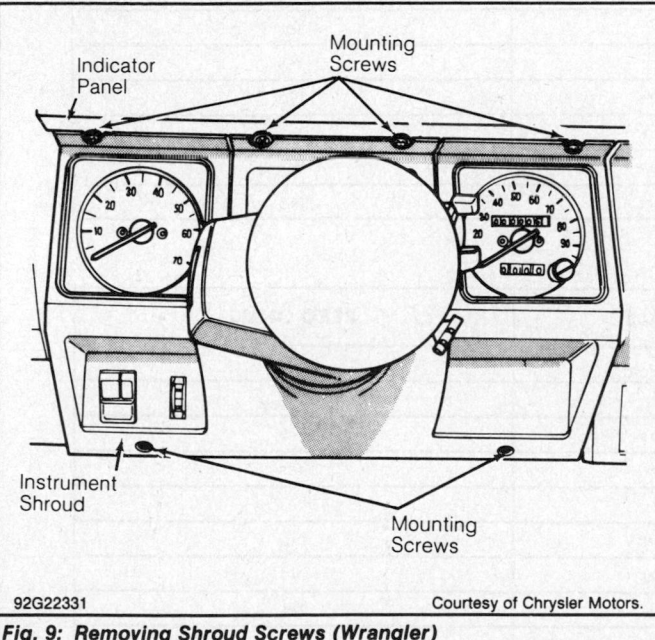

92G22331   Courtesy of Chrysler Motors.

Fig. 9: Removing Shroud Screws (Wrangler)

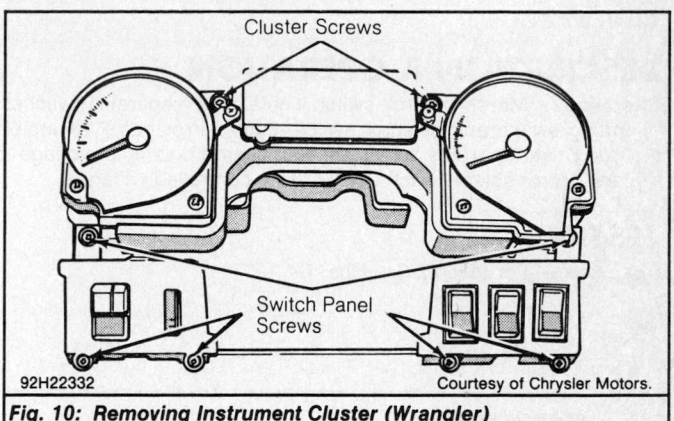

92H22332   Courtesy of Chrysler Motors.

Fig. 10: Removing Instrument Cluster (Wrangler)

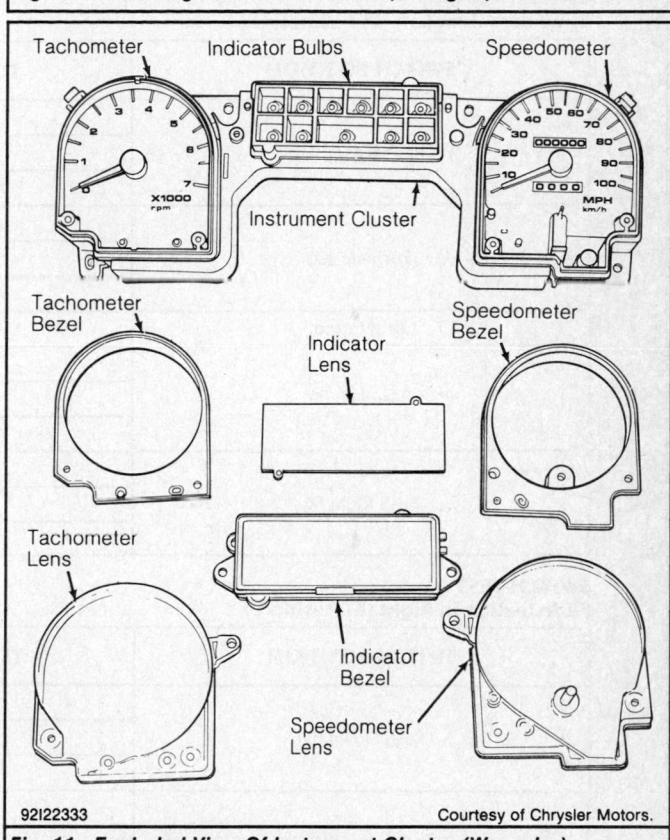

92I22333   Courtesy of Chrysler Motors.

Fig. 11: Exploded View Of Instrument Cluster (Wrangler)

WIRING DIAGRAMS

See appropriate chassis wiring diagram in WIRING DIAGRAMS.

1992 SAFETY EQUIPMENT
Power Mirrors

Cherokee

DESCRIPTION & OPERATION

Cherokee – Mirror control switch contains 2 separate switches: operating switch and selector switch. Each mirror has 2 reversible motors. Driver operates 3 switches that control polarity of voltage to motors. Mirror select switch directs these controlled voltages.

TESTING

Cherokee – For testing, *See Figs. 1-4.*

REMOVAL & INSTALLATION

POWER MIRROR

Removal & Installation – 1) Remove interior door latch release assembly and control panel retaining screws. Disconnect control linkage and wire harness connector. Remove latch release and control panel assembly. Remove armrest lower retaining screws.
2) Swing armrest downward to a vertical position. Disconnect armrest from upper retainer clip. Pull armrest straight out from trim panel. Remove trim panel.
3) Remove screw holding mirror trim cover. Disconnect power mirror wire harness at connector in door. Pull harness up through door. Remove 3 screws holding mirror to door. To install, reverse removal procedure.

SWITCH TEST
Slide Switch in Left (L) Position

SWITCH POSITION	TERMINALS	ZERO OHMS
Push Down (D)	A and G	Yes
	E and F	Yes
	All Others	No
Push Up (U)	A and F	Yes
	E and G	Yes
	All Others	No
Off (Normal)	All Others	No
Push Left (L)	B and G	Yes
	E and F	Yes
	All Others	No
Push Right (R)	B and F	Yes
	E and G	Yes
	All Others	No

SWITCH TEST
Slide Switch in Right (R) Position

SWITCH POSITION	TERMINALS	ZERO OHMS
Push Down (D)	D and G	Yes
	E and F	Yes
	All Others	No
Push Up (U)	D and F	Yes
	E and G	Yes
	All Others	No
Off (Normal)	All Others	No
Push Left (L)	C and G	Yes
	E and F	Yes
	All Others	No
Push Right (R)	C and F	Yes
	E and G	Yes
	All Others	No

Courtesy of Chrysler Motors

Fig. 1: Testing Power Mirror Switch

1. POWER INPUT—Fuse

TEST	OK	NOT OK
Open Door	Dome Lamps light	Check Dome fuse

2. POWER MIRROR SWITCH ASSEMBLY—Remove switch, unplug switch connector

TEST	OK	NOT OK
Mirror switch connector terminal F	Zero ohms	Repair open to Splice G
Mirror switch connector terminal G	Battery voltage	Repair open to Dome fuse
Jumper test leads terminal E to terminal F	—	Next step
Jumper test leads terminal G to: terminal A terminal B terminal C terminal D	Mirror moves. If OK, replace switch	Repair open to test motor and/or replace motor

Courtesy of Chrysler Motors

Fig. 2: Trouble Shooting Power Mirror

WIRING DIAGRAMS

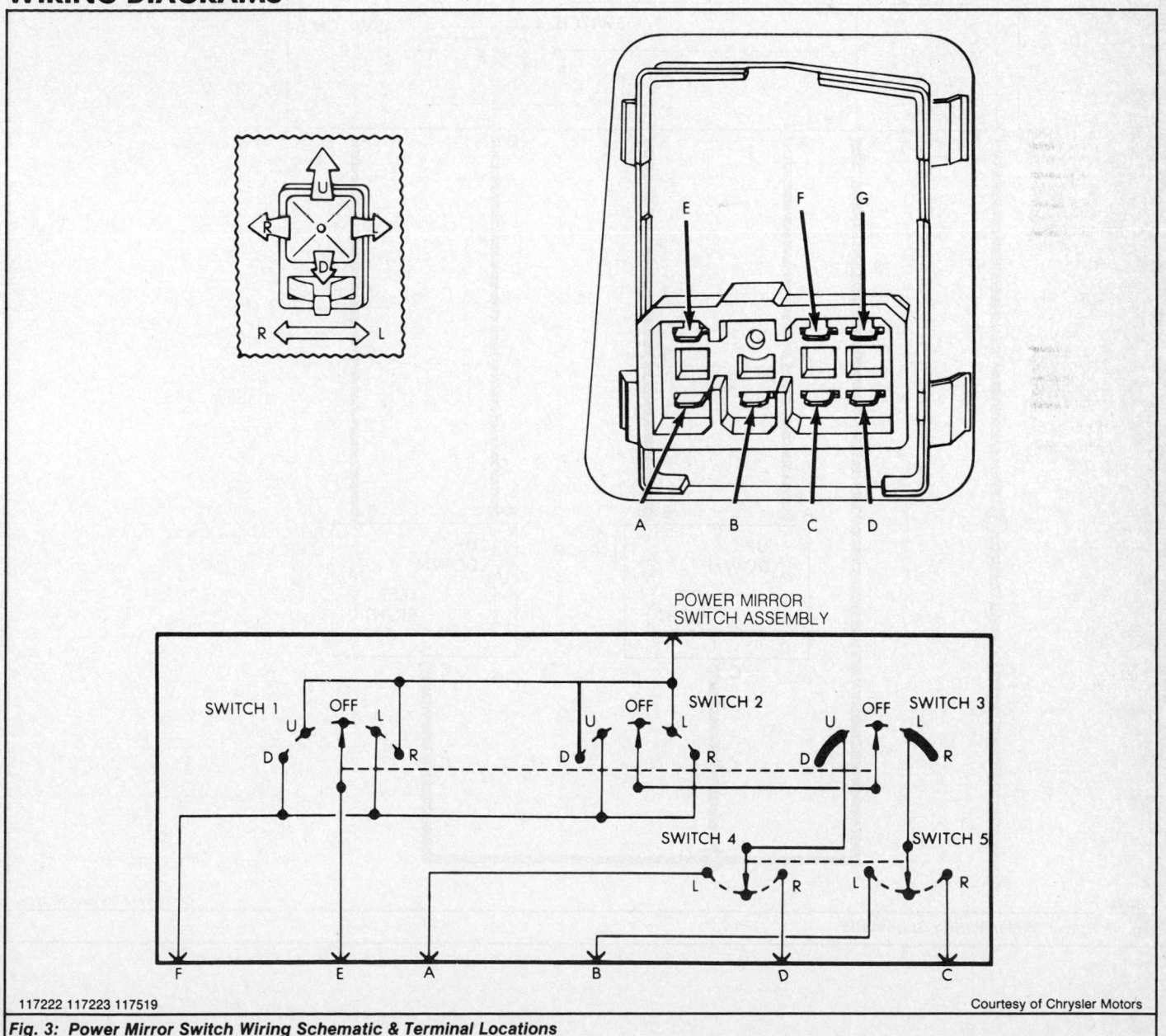

Fig. 3: Power Mirror Switch Wiring Schematic & Terminal Locations

117222 117223 117519

Courtesy of Chrysler Motors

1992 SAFETY EQUIPMENT
Power Mirrors (Cont.)

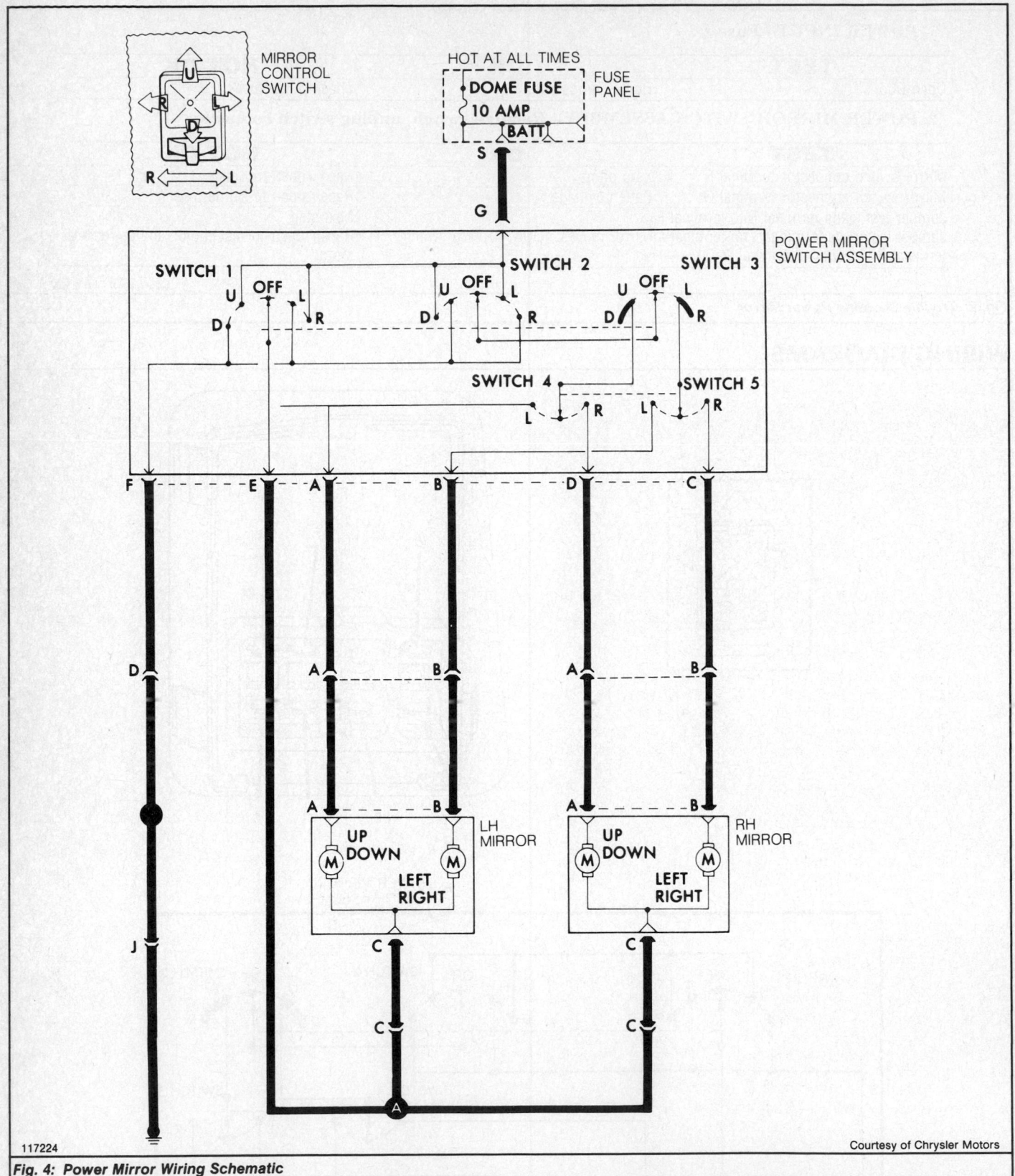

Fig. 4: Power Mirror Wiring Schematic

117224

Courtesy of Chrysler Motors

Cherokee, Comanche, Wrangler

TESTING

HEADLIGHT DIMMER SWITCH

1) Position headlight switch in ON position. Position dimmer switch in HIGH or LOW beam position.

2) Measure voltage between dimmer switch connector voltage supply terminal and vehicle body ground. Voltmeter should indicate battery voltage. If not, repair open circuit in wire harness between headlight switch and dimmer switch.

3) Position dimmer switch in LOW beam position. Measure voltage between dimmer switch connector low beam voltage out terminal and vehicle body ground. Voltmeter should indicate battery voltage. If not, replace dimmer switch.

4) Position dimmer switch in HIGH beam position. Measure voltage between dimmer switch connector high beam voltage out terminal and vehicle body ground. Voltmeter should indicate battery voltage. If not, replace dimmer switch.

HAZARD SWITCH

Cherokee & Comanche – 1) Ensure fuse for hazard flasher is good. Measure voltage at fuse side of flasher (side terminal). If battery voltage is present, go to next step. If battery voltage is not present, repair open circuit between fuse and hazard flasher.

2) Replace hazard flasher. Lights should flash. If lights do not flash, measure voltage at turn signal switch connector between Violet/Tan wire and ground. If battery voltage is present, replace hazard/turn signal combination switch. If battery voltage is not present, repair open in Violet/Tan wire.

Wrangler – Ensure fuse for hazard flasher is good. Measure voltage at battery side of hazard fuse flasher terminal "A". If battery voltage is not present, repair open circuit from fuse No. 5.

HEADLIGHT SWITCH

1) Place headlight switch in ON position. Measure voltage between headlight switch connector voltage supply terminal and ground. Voltmeter should indicate battery voltage. If not, repair open circuit in wire harness between fuse and switch connector terminal.

2) Measure voltage between headlight switch connector voltage supply terminal and ground. Battery voltage should be present. If not, repair open circuit in wire harness between fuse and switch connector terminal.

3) Measure voltage between headlight switch connector battery voltage out terminal and ground. Voltmeter should indicate battery voltage. If not, replace headlight switch.

HORN

Cherokee & Comanche – 1) Inspect headlight delay fuse, and replace if necessary. Relay contacts should click when horn switch is depressed. If relay clicks, go to step 4). If relay does not click, remove relay located on bracket (3 relays) behind instrument panel. Measure voltage at relay connector between Gray/Orange wire and ground. If battery voltage is present, go to next step. If battery voltage is not present, repair open in Gray/Orange wire.

2) Depress horn switch. Measure resistance at relay connector between Black/Red wire and ground. If reading is zero ohms, go to next step. If reading is not zero ohms, repair horn switch ground.

3) Measure resistance at relay connector between Green/Red wire and ground. Reading should be almost zero ohms (horn resistance). If resistance is okay, replace relay. If resistance is not okay, repair open in circuit between relay and horns (Green/Red wire).

4) Disconnect horn connector. Depress horn switch. Measure voltage at horn connector between Green/Red wire and ground. If battery voltage is not present, go to next step. If battery voltage is present, replace horns.

5) Measure resistance between horn bracket and chassis ground. Resistance should be zero ohms. If resistance is not zero ohms,

check mounting screw for corrosion and repair or replace as necessary.

Wrangler – 1) Check 10-amp fuse (fuse No. F15) located in fuse block below flashers. Replace fuse as necessary. Relay contacts should click when horn switch is depressed. If relay does not click, go to next step. If relay clicks, go to step 5).

2) Remove relay. Relay is taped in wiring harness above fuse panel. Measure voltage at relay connector between Red/White wire and ground. If battery voltage is present, go to next step. If battery voltage is not present, repair open in Red/White wire.

3) Depress horn switch. Measure resistance at relay connector between Orange/White wire and ground. If reading is almost zero ohms, go to next step. If reading is not almost zero ohms, repair horn switch ground.

4) Measure resistance at relay connector between Gray/Orange wire and ground. Reading should be almost zero ohms (horn resistance). If resistance is okay, replace relay. If resistance is not okay, repair open in Gray/Orange wire between relay and horns.

5) Disconnect horn connector. Depress horn switch. Measure voltage at horn connector between Gray/Orange wire and ground. If battery voltage is not present, go to next step. If battery voltage is present, replace horns.

6) Measure resistance at horn connector between Black wire and chassis ground. Reading should be zero ohms. If reading is not zero ohms, repair open in Black wire to ground.

ILLUMINATED VANITY MIRROR

Cherokee – 1) Remove and inspect dome light fuse and replace as necessary. If dome light does not operate, repair open circuit in wiring harness from splice.

2) If dome light operates, measure voltage between Pink wire on switch connector and vehicle body ground. Voltmeter should indicate battery voltage. If battery voltage is not present, repair open circuit in wiring harness from splice.

3) Connect a jumper wire from ground side of switch to a good ground. Measure resistance to ground. Ohmmeter should indicate about zero ohms. If resistance is not about zero ohms, repair open circuit in wiring harness to ground.

IGNITION SWITCH

1) Remove ignition switch. See IGNITION SWITCH under REMOVAL & INSTALLATION. Using an ohmmeter or self-powered test light, check ignition positions for continuity between terminals. See IGNITION SWITCH TERMINAL CONNECTIONS table. See Fig. 1.

2) Identify ignition switch slide bar positions by locating alignment hole in flat portion of switch, adjacent to terminals. Starting from alignment hole end of switch, positions are ACC, OFF-LOCK, OFF, ON and START. Each position has a detent stop except START position, which is spring loaded. There should be no resistance between any 2 connected terminals. If switch does not function as specified, replace switch.

IGNITION SWITCH TERMINAL CONNECTIONS

Switch Position	Continuity Between	Circuit Result
ACC	A & B 2	Connected
OFF–LOCK		Open
OFF		Open
ON	I 1 & B 1 [1]	Connected
	A & B 2 [1]	Connected
	I 3 & B 3 [1]	Connected
START	I 1, B 1 & S	Connected
	G 1 & G 2	Grounded

[1] – Terminals B 1, B 2 and B 3 are all connected to battery circuit.

117284

Fig. 3: Ren

1. Steer
2. Wash
3. Lock
4. Snap
5. Lock
6. Horn
7. Cance

71355

Fig. 4: Expl

1992 SAFETY EQUIPMENT
Wiper/Washer Systems

**Cherokee, Comanche,
Grand Cherokee (1993), Wrangler**

DESCRIPTION & OPERATION

All models use a standard wiper system with a 2-speed motor and electric washers. An optional system provides an intermittent cycle. Optional rear wiper/washer system is available on Cherokee, Grand Cherokee and Wrangler.

ADJUSTMENTS

WIPER ARM ADJUSTMENT

Except Wrangler – Ensure wiper shafts are in park position. Install driver side wiper arm onto pivot shafts so that end of wiper arm is .9-2" (23-52 mm) above lower windshield reveal molding. Install passenger side wiper arm so that its end is 1.3-2.4" (33-62 mm) above reveal molding. Blades should be parallel to lower reveal molding after installation. Install rear wiper arm (if equipped) so that midpoint of blade is .6-1.4" (15-35 mm) above lower window seal.

Wrangler – Ensure wiper shafts are in park position. Install both wiper arms onto pivot shafts so that end of wiper arms are 4 1/4-5 1/8" (108-130 mm) above lower windshield reveal molding. Blades should be parallel to each other after installation.

TESTING

FRONT WIPER MOTOR TEST

Cherokee, Comanche & Grand Cherokee – 1) Unplug wiper motor connector. Check for continuity between harness connector terminal No. 1 (Black wire) and ground. If no continuity exists, repair open circuit in Black wire to ground. Reconnect wiring to motor.

2) Turn ignition switch to accessory position. With wiper switch in any position, check for battery voltage at harness connector terminal No. 4 (Light Green/Black wire). If battery voltage is not present, repair open circuit in Light Green/Black wire from fuse panel.

3) Set wiper switch to LO. Check for battery voltage at harness connector terminal No. 2 (Brown wire). If battery voltage is present, replace wiper motor. If battery voltage is not present, repair open circuit in Brown wire to wiper switch.

4) Set wiper switch to HI. Check for battery voltage at harness connector terminal No. 3 (Red/Yellow wire). If battery voltage is present, replace wiper motor. If battery voltage is not present, repair open circuit in Red/Yellow wire to wiper switch.

5) Check for battery voltage at harness connector terminal No. 5 (Tan/Red wire). Set wiper switch to OFF. Battery voltage should be present until wipers park, then drop to zero volts. If voltage is as specified, replace motor. If voltage is not as specified, repair open circuit in Tan/Red wire to wiper switch.

Wrangler – 1) Unplug wiper motor connector. Check for continuity between harness connector terminal "E" (Black wire) and ground. If no continuity exists, repair open circuit in Black wire to ground. Reconnect wiring to motor.

2) Turn ignition switch to accessory position. With wiper switch in any position, check for battery voltage at harness connector terminal "B" (Light Green/Black wire). If battery voltage is not present, repair open circuit in Light Green/Black wire from circuit breaker.

3) Set wiper switch to LO. Check for battery voltage at harness connector terminal "A" (White/Black wire). If battery voltage is present, replace wiper motor. If battery voltage is not present, repair open circuit in White/Black wire to wiper switch.

4) Set wiper switch to HI. Check for battery voltage at harness connector terminal "H" (Blue/Yellow wire). If battery voltage is present, replace wiper motor. If battery voltage is not present, repair open circuit in Blue/Yellow wire to wiper switch.

5) Check for battery voltage at harness connector terminal "D" (Tan/Red wire). Set wiper switch to OFF. Battery voltage should be present until wipers park, then drop to zero volts. If voltage is as specified, replace motor. If voltage is not as specified, repair open circuit in Tan/Red wire to wiper switch.

FRONT WIPER SWITCH TEST

NOTE: All terminals specified in this test are on wiper switch connector for vehicles with standard wipers. For vehicles with intermittent wipers, specified terminals are on switch side connector of intermittent module. Module is on lower instrument panel cover, near steering column.

1) Turn ignition on. Check for battery voltage on terminal "D" White wire). If no voltage exists, repair open circuit in White wire from circuit breaker.

2) Set wiper switch to LO. Measure voltage at terminal "E" (Gray wire). If meter does not indicate battery voltage, replace switch.

3) Set wiper switch to HI. Measure voltage at terminal "C" (Purple wire). If meter does not indicate battery voltage, replace switch.

4) Measure voltage at terminal "F" (Yellow wire). Meter should indicate battery voltage. Set wiper switch to OFF. Meter should indicate battery voltage until wipers park, then drop to zero volts. If voltage is not as specified, replace switch.

5) For models with intermittent wipers, disconnect switch side connector from module. With an ohmmeter, measure resistance between terminals "A" (Dark Green wire) and "D" (White wire) while rotating switch from minimum to maximum delay. If resistance does not vary smoothly between 0-500,000 ohms, replace switch.

6) For models with intermittent wipers, disconnect switch side connector from module. With an ohmmeter, measure resistance between terminals "A" (Dark Green wire) and "G" (Brown wire) while rotating switch from minimum to maximum delay. If resistance does not vary smoothly between 0-500,000 ohms, replace switch.

FRONT WASHER MOTOR TEST

1) Unplug washer pump connector, under washer reservoir in engine compartment. Check for continuity between harness connector terminal "A" and ground. *See Fig. 1.* If no continuity exists, repair open circuit in Black wire to ground.

2) Connect a jumper wire between terminal "A" on washer pump and a known good ground. Supply battery voltage to washer pump terminal "B", using a jumper wire with a 15-amp in-line fuse. Replace pump if it does not operate.

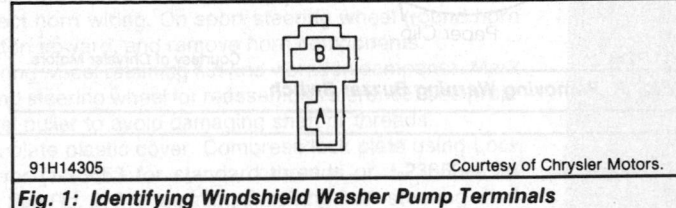

91H14305   Courtesy of Chrysler Motors.

Fig. 1: Identifying Windshield Washer Pump Terminals

REAR WIPER MOTOR TEST

Cherokee & Grand Cherokee – 1) Unplug harness connector at rear wiper motor. Check for continuity between Black wire on harness connector and ground. If there is no continuity, repair open circuit in Black wire to ground. Reconnect wiring to motor.

2) Turn ignition on. With rear wiper switch in any position, check for battery voltage at White wire at harness connector. If battery voltage is not present, repair open circuit in White wire from rear wiper switch.

3) Set rear wiper switch to WIPE. Check for battery voltage at Brown/Red wire at harness connector. If battery voltage is present, replace wiper motor. If battery voltage is not present, repair open circuit in Brown/Red wire to rear wiper switch.

Wrangler – 1) Unplug harness connector at rear wiper motor. Check for continuity between terminal "B" (Black wire) at harness connector and ground. If there is no continuity, repair open circuit in Black wire to ground. Reconnect wiring to motor.

2) Turn ignition on. With rear wiper switch in any position, check for battery voltage at terminal "A" (Green wire) at harness connector. If battery voltage is not present, repair open circuit in Green wire from rear wiper switch.

3) Set rear wiper switch to WIPER. Check for battery voltage at terminal "C" (Green/White wire) at harness connector. If battery voltage is present, replace wiper motor. If battery voltage is not present, repair open circuit in Green/White wire to rear wiper switch.

REAR WIPER SWITCH TEST

NOTE: Testing information for Grand Cherokee was not available from manufacturer at time of publication.

Cherokee – 1) Turn ignition on. Check for battery voltage at terminal "B" (Light Blue/Red wire) at rear wiper switch harness connector. If no voltage exists, repair open circuit in Light Blue/Red wire to fuse panel.
2) With rear wiper switch in any position, check for battery voltage at terminal "D" (White wire). If no voltage is indicated at terminal "D" (White wire), replace switch.
3) With switch in WASH position, check for battery voltage at terminal "C" (Brown/Red wire). Repeat test with switch in WIPE position. If no voltage is indicated in each position, replace switch.
4) With switch in WASH position, check for battery voltage at terminal "A" (Black/White wire). If no voltage is indicated, replace switch.
Wrangler – 1) Unplug harness connector at rear wiper switch. Check for continuity between Black wire at harness connector and ground. If no continuity exists, repair open circuit in Black wire to ground.
2) Turn wiper switch off. Check for continuity between Green/White and Black wires at switch connector. If no continuity exists, replace switch. Reconnect wiring to switch.
3) Turn ignition on. Check for battery voltage at Brown/White wire at harness connector. If no voltage exists, replace fuse or repair open circuit in Brown/White wire to fuse panel.
4) With switch in WASH position, check for battery voltage at Green/White wire at harness connector. Repeat test with switch in WIPER position. If no voltage exists, replace switch.
5) With switch in WASH position, check for battery voltage at Red/White wire at harness connector. If no voltage exists, replace switch.

REAR WASHER MOTOR TEST

1) Unplug washer pump connector, under washer reservoir in engine compartment. Check for continuity between harness connector terminal "A" (Black wire) and ground. If no continuity exists, repair open circuit in Black wire to ground.
2) Connect a jumper wire between terminal "A" on washer pump and a good ground. Supply battery voltage to washer pump terminal "B", using a jumper wire with a 15-amp in-line fuse. See Fig. 1. Pump should operate. If pump is inoperative, replace pump.

REMOVAL & INSTALLATION

FRONT WIPER MOTOR

Removal & Installation (Except Wrangler) – Remove wiper arms. Remove cowl trim. Disconnect washer hose. Remove cowl mounting bracket nuts and pivot pin screws. Disconnect wiring. Remove wiper motor. To install, reverse removal procedure. Adjust wiper blades. See WIPER ARM ADJUSTMENT under ADJUSTMENTS.
Removal & Installation (Wrangler) – 1) Remove top, if installed. Remove windshield hold-down bolts from lower corners of instrument panel. Remove wiper motor mounting screws. Disconnect wiper linkage drive arm. Remove wiper motor wire harness retaining clip. Pull motor and drive arm out through access hole.
2) Pry drive arm from motor pivot. DO NOT remove pivot attaching nut. Remove intermittent module bracket screws. Reach behind instrument panel to disconnect wiper motor harness. Remove wiper motor. To install, reverse removal procedure. Adjust wiper blades. See WIPER ARM ADJUSTMENT under ADJUSTMENTS.

FRONT WIPER SWITCH

Removal (Except Grand Cherokee) – 1) Disconnect negative battery cable. For vehicles with optional steering wheel, push and turn horn button to remove it. Remove retaining screws, bushing, receiver, flexplate and insulator. On all models, remove 3 retaining screws and steering wheel cover.

2) Disconnect horn wiring. Remove grounding pin by pulling it out gently. Remove steering wheel retaining nut and vibration damper. Mark steering shaft and steering wheel for reassembly reference. Using steering wheel puller, remove steering wheel.

CAUTION: Lock plate is retained by a high pressure spring. DO NOT remove snap ring without using a compressor tool.

3) Remove lock plate cover. Compress lock plate with Lock Plate Compressor (C4156). Remove lock plate retaining ring, lock plate, canceling cam and spring. On vehicles with optional steering wheel, remove horn button components from cancelling cam. Discard lock plate retaining ring.
4) Remove hazard warning switch knob, dimmer switch actuating arm screw and turn signal switch attaching screws. On Cherokee and Comanche, remove lower instrument panel trim panel. On Wrangler, remove steering column shroud screws. Slide shroud toward steering wheel. On all models, apply pressure upward to shroud and downward to instrument panel to free holding tabs.
5) Remove cover under steering column. Remove PRNDL clip (if equipped). Remove 2 nuts and 4 bolts from steering column bracket. Loosen steering column brace nut at kick panel. Ease steering column downward.
6) Unplug wiper switch connector. Tape wires to wiper connector to ease harness removal. Remove wiring harness cover from column. Pull turn signal switch out from column far enough for access to retaining screws.
7) Turn ignition switch on. Insert paper clip below key warning buzzer retainer to flatten retainer. Remove key warning buzzer and retaining clip as an assembly. DO NOT try to remove warning buzzer and retaining clip separately; clip could fall into column jacket.
8) Remove ignition lock cylinder retaining screw and lock cylinder. Remove attaching screws, housing and shroud. Ensure dimmer switch rod, lock pin and lock rack do not fall out. Remove turn signal/wiper switch lever from housing. Remove wiper switch cover from rear of housing. Remove pivot screw and wiper switch.
Installation – 1) Install new switch. Push dimmer switch rod to ensure it is connected. Position housing to column. Ensure nylon spring retainer is forward of lock rack retaining slot. Position first tooth of gear so that it engages with first tooth of lock rack.
2) Install housing attaching screws and key lock cylinder. Carefully tighten screws while mating housing to column. Turn key to ensure lock pin extends fully when ignition switch is locked.
3) To complete installation, reverse removal procedure. Install NEW lock plate retaining ring. Ensure wires are flat against inside column. Ensure PRNDL cable clip is installed so that pointer aligns properly. Reinstall steering wheel and tighten nut to **25 ft. lbs. (34 N.m)**.
Removal & Installation (Grand Cherokee) – 1) Disconnect negative battery cable. Remove tilt lever (if equipped). Remove upper and lower steering column trim covers. Remover knee blocker. Remove steering column mounting nuts.
2) Lower steering column to gain access to rear of multifunction switch. Using Remover (TTXR20B2), remove tamper-proof mounting screws. Gently pull multifunction switch away from steering column. Loosen connector screw sufficiently to remove connector. Screw will remain in connector. Remove connector. To install, reverse removal procedure. Install NEW tamper-proof switch mounting screws. Tighten multifunction switch mounting screws to **17 INCH lbs. (2 N.m)**.

FRONT WASHER MOTOR

Removal & Installation – Remove reservoir mounting screws and reservoir. Disconnect hose from pump. Drain reservoir. Remove filter nuts from inside reservoir. Remove washer pump motor. To install, reverse removal procedure.

REAR WIPER MOTOR

Removal & Installation (Cherokee & Grand Cherokee) – Remove wiper arm. Slide clip along hose to remove it from hose mounting. Disconnect hose. Remove pivot pin retaining nut. Remove liftgate trim panel. Disconnect wiring harness. Remove hinge nut securing motor to top. Remove wiper motor. To install, reverse removal procedure.

Removal & Installation (Wrangler) – Remove wiper arm. Remove pivot shaft retaining nut and trim cover. Unplug electrical connector. Remove mounting screws and wiper motor. To install, reverse removal procedure.

REAR WIPER SWITCH

Removal & Installation (Cherokee) – Disconnect negative battery cable. Remove 4 instrument bezel retaining screws. Pull bezel away from snap attachments. Remove switch housing panel. Unplug switch connector. Press mounting tabs and remove switch. To install, reverse removal procedure.

Removal & Installation (Grand Cherokee) – **1)** Disconnect negative battery cable. Remove ash tray. Remove screws securing center cluster bezel. Remove cluster center bezel. Remove dash pad retaining screws behind top of center bezel. Gently pry defroster grille out of dash pad. Unplug sensors from grille (if equipped). Set defroster grille aside.

2) Remove screws holding defroster duct, instrument cluster and glove box to dash pad. Pulling up and out to unsnap end clips, remove dash pad. With driver's door open, remove left side trim cover, steering column cover and knee bolster. Remove steering column retaining nuts.

3) Remove screws securing bottom of end bezel and switch pod bezel. Remove screws retaining top of end bezel and switch pod bezel. Remove end bezel. Starting on the left side, remove remaining switch pod bezel retaining screws. Pull switch pod bezel out sufficiently to disconnect switch connectors.

4) Disconnect switch connectors. Remove switch pod bezel. Remove switch retaining screws. Remove switch. To install, reverse removal procedure.

Removal & Installation (Wrangler) – Disconnect negative battery cable. Remove 6 instrument panel shroud screws. Slide shroud toward steering wheel. Pull bulb socket from bulb retainer. Press shroud upward and indicator panel downward to release holding tabs. Place shroud under steering column. Remove switch housing panel. Press switch mounting tabs and remove switch. To install, reverse removal procedure.

REAR WASHER MOTOR

Removal & Installation (Cherokee & Wrangler) – Remove reservoir mounting screws and reservoir. Disconnect hose from pump. Drain reservoir. Remove filter nuts from inside reservoir. Remove washer pump motor. To install, reverse removal procedure.

Removal & Installation (Grand Cherokee) – Rear washer pump is located next to front washer pump. See FRONT WASHER MOTOR.

WIRING DIAGRAMS

See appropriate chassis wiring diagram in WIRING DIAGRAMS.

Cherokee, Comanche, Wrangler

NOTE: For repair procedures not covered in this article, see ENGINE OVERHAUL PROCEDURES article in GENERAL INFORMATION.

ENGINE IDENTIFICATION

Engine can be identified by eighth character of Vehicle Identification Number (VIN). The VIN is stamped on a plate attached to top left corner of instrument panel.

Engine code is on a machined surface on right side of cylinder block between cylinders No. 3 and 4. This code may be required when ordering replacement parts.

ENGINE IDENTIFICATION CODE

Engine	Code
2.5L PFI	P

Some engines are manufactured with oversize or undersize components. These engines are identified by a letter code stamped on oil filter boss near distributor. Letters are decoded as follows:

- "B" indicates all cylinder bores .010" (.25 mm) oversize.
- "C" indicates all camshaft bearing bores .010" (.25 mm) oversize.
- "M" indicates all main bearing journals .010" (.25 mm) undersize.
- "P" indicates one or more connecting rod journals .010" (.25 mm) undersize.
- "PM" indicates all crankshaft main bearing journals and one or more connecting rod journals .010" (.25 mm) undersize.

ADJUSTMENTS

VALVE CLEARANCE ADJUSTMENT

Engine is equipped with hydraulic valve lifters. No valve adjustment is required.

REMOVAL & INSTALLATION

NOTE: For reassembly reference, label all electrical connectors, vacuum hoses and fuel lines before removal. Also place mating marks on engine hood and other major assemblies before removal.

WARNING: When battery is disconnected, vehicle computer and memory systems may lose memory data. Driveability problems may exist until computer systems have completed a relearn cycle. See COMPUTER RELEARN PROCEDURES article in GENERAL INFORMATION before disconnecting battery.

FUEL PRESSURE RELEASE

CAUTION: Fuel system is under constant pressure. This pressure must be released before disconnecting or servicing any fuel supply or return system component. Wear proper eye protection when releasing fuel system pressure.

Disconnect negative battery cable. Remove fuel filler cap. Remove cap from pressure test port on fuel rail. *See Fig. 1.* Place shop towels around pressure test port to absorb spilled fuel. Press test port valve with a small screwdriver or punch wrapped in shop towels. Remove shop towels and dispose of properly. Install pressure test port cap.

CAUTION: Always replace "O" rings, spacers and retainers whenever fuel system quick-connect fittings are disconnected. Ensure fuel connections are secure by verifying that only retainer tabs protrude from connectors, and by pulling on tubes to verify that they are secure.

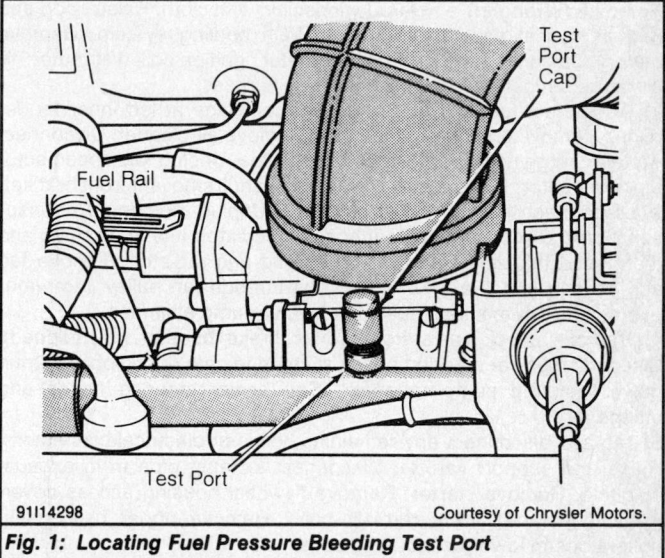

91I14298   Courtesy of Chrysler Motors.

Fig. 1: Locating Fuel Pressure Bleeding Test Port

COOLING SYSTEM BLEEDING

CAUTION: Engine coolant may be hot. Avoid scalding by using care. Carefully release system pressure before removing radiator cap or drain cock.

Refill cooling system. Remove coolant temperature sensor to bleed air from system while filling.

ENGINE

Removal (Cherokee & Comanche) – 1) Remove battery and air cleaner. Remove hood. Drain cooling system. Remove radiator hoses, coolant recovery hose and fan shroud. Disconnect transmission fluid cooler lines (if equipped).

2) Discharge A/C system (if equipped). Discharge A/C system using approved refrigerant recovery/recycling equipment. Remove A/C condenser (if equipped) and radiator. Remove fan. To maintain pulley and water pump alignment, install a 5/16" x 1/2" bolt through fan pulley into water pump flange.

3) Disconnect heater hoses, throttle linkage, cruise control cable (if equipped) and throttle valve rod. Disconnect wires from starter solenoid and all fuel injection harness connections.

4) Release fuel pressure. See FUEL PRESSURE RELEASE. Disconnect fuel supply and return lines at throttle body. Disconnect TDC sensor wire connector. Remove A/C service valves and cap compressor ports (if equipped).

5) Remove vacuum check valve from power brake booster (if equipped). Disconnect power steering hoses at steering gear (if equipped). Drain power steering pump reservoir. Cap power steering hoses and fittings.

6) Tag and disconnect any remaining hoses or electrical connectors. Raise and support vehicle. Disconnect exhaust pipe from exhaust manifold. Remove starter and flywheel cover.

7) On automatic transmission equipped models, mark converter and flexplate for installation reference. Remove converter-to-flexplate bolts. On all models, remove upper bellhousing bolts and loosen bottom bolts. Remove engine mount bolts.

8) Remove engine shock damper bracket. Lower vehicle. Attach lifting device to engine. Raise engine from front supports. Place support under bellhousing. Remove remaining bellhousing bolts. Remove engine.

Removal (Wrangler) – **1)** Pad windshield with cloth. Raise hood and rest it against windshield frame. Drain cooling system. Remove battery. Disconnect wiring from alternator, ignition coil, distributor, oil pressure sender and fuel injection wire harness.

2) Disconnect fuel line quick-connect couplings at left inner fender panel. Remove engine ground strap. Remove air cleaner. Disconnect vacuum purge hose from vapor canister tee. Unplug idle speed actuator connector. Disconnect throttle cable and remove it from bracket.

3) Disconnect throttle rod at bellcrank. Unplug oxygen (O₂) sensor connector. Disconnect coolant hoses at radiator, intake manifold and thermostat housing. Remove fan shroud and radiator. Remove fan and spacer. Install a 5/16" x 1/2" bolt through fan pulley into water pump flange to maintain pulley and water pump alignment.

4) Remove check valve from power brake booster (if equipped). Disconnect power steering hoses at steering gear (if equipped). Drain power steering pump reservoir. Cap power steering hoses and fittings.

5) Tag and disconnect any remaining hoses or electrical connectors. Raise and support vehicle. Disconnect exhaust pipe from exhaust manifold. Remove starter. Remove flywheel housing access cover. Remove engine mount through-bolts. Remove upper bellhousing bolts. Loosen lower bellhousing bolts.

6) Lower vehicle. Attach lifting device to engine. Raise engine from front supports. Place support under bellhousing. Remove remaining bellhousing bolts. Lift engine from engine compartment.

Installation (All Models) – Remove engine mount cushions from brackets to aid alignment of engine and transmission. To complete installation, reverse removal procedure. Adjust throttle and cruise control linkage (if equipped). Tighten bolts to specification. See TORQUE SPECIFICATIONS table at end of article. Refill and check fluid levels.

INTAKE MANIFOLD

Removal – **1)** Disconnect negative battery cable. Remove air inlet hose at throttle body and air cleaner. Remove power steering pump with hoses attached and wire it aside.

2) Release fuel pressure. See FUEL PRESSURE RELEASE. Remove power steering pump brackets at water pump and intake manifold. Disconnect fuel supply and return lines at fuel rail.

3) Disconnect accelerator cable. Unplug cruise control connector at throttle body, using finger pressure only. Remove crankcase ventilation and manifold pressure sensor hoses. Tag and disconnect all wiring and hoses.

4) Remove bolts No. 2 through 5 securing intake manifold to cylinder head. *See Fig. 2.* Slightly loosen bolt No. 1 and nuts No. 6 and 7. Remove intake manifold. Drain coolant from manifold.

Installation – Ensure all gasket surfaces are clean. Install intake manifold. Finger tighten all bolts. Tighten intake manifold bolts to specification in correct sequence. *See Fig. 2.* Also see TORQUE SPECIFICATIONS table at end of article. To complete installation, reverse removal procedure. Fill and bleed cooling system.

EXHAUST MANIFOLD

Removal – Disconnect negative battery cable. Remove intake manifold. See INTAKE MANIFOLD. Raise and support vehicle. Disconnect exhaust pipe from exhaust manifold. Lower vehicle. Remove retaining nuts and bolts. Remove exhaust manifold.

Installation – **1)** Clean all gasket surfaces. Install intake and exhaust manifolds together, using NEW gasket. Ensure exhaust manifold is centrally located over end studs and spacer. Tighten bolt No. 1 to specification. See TORQUE SPECIFICATIONS table at end of article. Tighten bolts No. 2 through 5 to specification in sequence. *See Fig. 2.*

2) Install new spacers over cylinder head studs. Tighten nuts No. 6 and 7 to specification. To complete installation, reverse removal procedure. Start engine and check for leaks.

CYLINDER HEAD

Removal – **1)** Disconnect negative battery cable. Drain cooling system. Remove accessory drive belt. Remove A/C compressor (if equipped) and wire it aside. DO NOT discharge A/C system. Remove air cleaner.

2) Remove A/C compressor mounting bracket-to-cylinder head bolts. Loosen A/C compressor mounting bracket-to-cylinder block bolts. Disconnect upper radiator hose and heater hoses. Remove valve cover.

3) Remove rocker arms, bridges, pivots and push rods. Tag all parts for installation reference. See ROCKER ARMS. Remove manifolds. See INTAKE MANIFOLD and EXHAUST MANIFOLD.

4) Tag and disconnect spark plug wires. Remove spark plugs. Remove cylinder head bolts. Remove cylinder head. Stuff clean lint-free shop towels into cylinder bores.

Inspection – **1)** Inspect cylinder head for cracks or damage. Using straightedge, check cylinder head for warpage across bolt holes and diagonals. Resurface or replace cylinder head if warpage exceeds specification or damage exists. See CYLINDER HEAD table under ENGINE SPECIFICATIONS at end of article.

2) Cylinder head bolts may be REUSED ONLY ONCE. If this is the first time cylinder head has been removed, put a dab of paint on the head of each bolt. If the bolts already have paint on them, or if it is unknown whether they have been used before, DISCARD THEM and replace with NEW bolts.

Installation – **1)** Clean carbon from combustion chambers and tops of pistons. Ensure all gasket surfaces, head bolts and head bolt holes are clean. Install NEW cylinder head gasket with numbers or word TOP upward. DO NOT apply sealant to cylinder head gasket. Ensure all holes align properly.

2) Install cylinder head. Apply sealing compound to threads of cylinder head bolt No. 7 before installation. Install cylinder head bolts. Tighten all bolts in 3 stages and in sequence to specification. *See Fig. 3.* See TORQUE SPECIFICATIONS table at end of article.

NOTE: During the final tightening sequence, bolt No. 7 will be tightened to a lower torque than the others.

---

3) To complete installation, reverse removal procedure. Install all valve train components into their original locations. Refill cooling system. Remove coolant temperature sensor to bleed air from system while filling.

FRONT COVER OIL SEAL

Removal & Installation – **1)** Remove drive belt. Remove vibration damper. Remove radiator shroud. Remove seal from front cover. Apply sealant to outer diameter of new seal. Coat crankshaft lightly with oil.

2) Drive seal into front cover, using Front Cover Aligner/Seal Installer (6139). Lightly coat seal contact area of vibration damper with oil. Lubricate vibration damper bolt with oil before installation. Reverse removal procedure to complete installation. See TORQUE SPECIFICATIONS table at end of article.

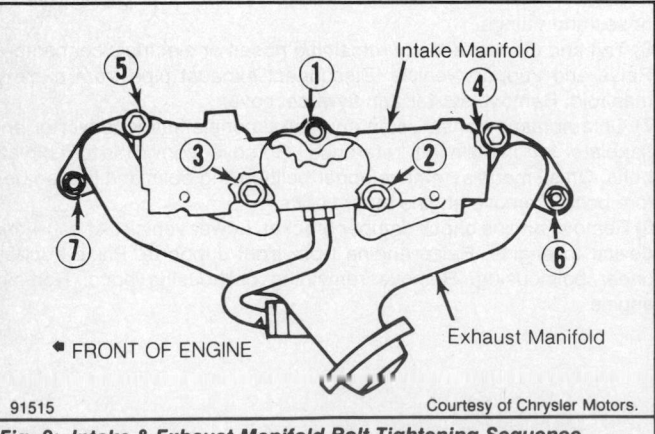

FRONT OF ENGINE

Intake Manifold

Exhaust Manifold

91515   Courtesy of Chrysler Motors.

Fig. 2: Intake & Exhaust Manifold Bolt Tightening Sequence

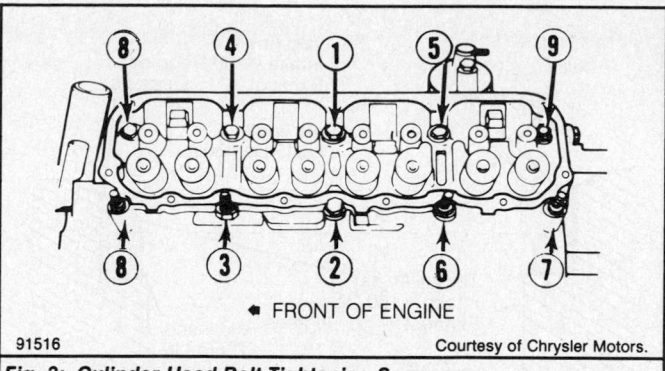

Fig. 3: Cylinder Head Bolt Tightening Sequence

◀ FRONT OF ENGINE

91516

Courtesy of Chrysler Motors.

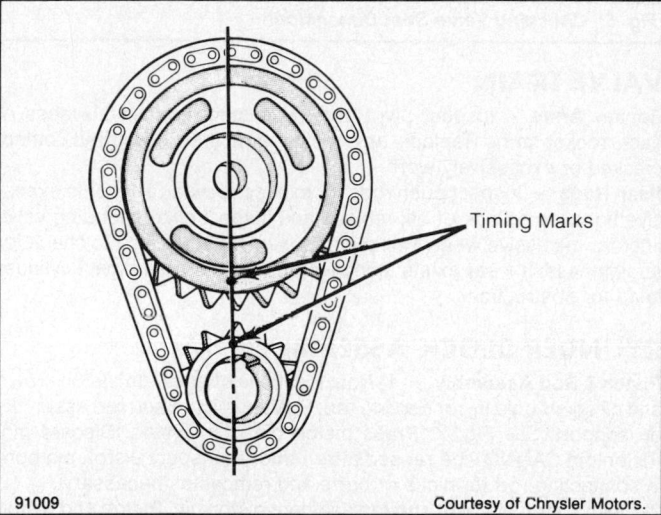

Timing Marks

91009

Courtesy of Chrysler Motors.

Fig. 4: Aligning Sprocket Timing Marks

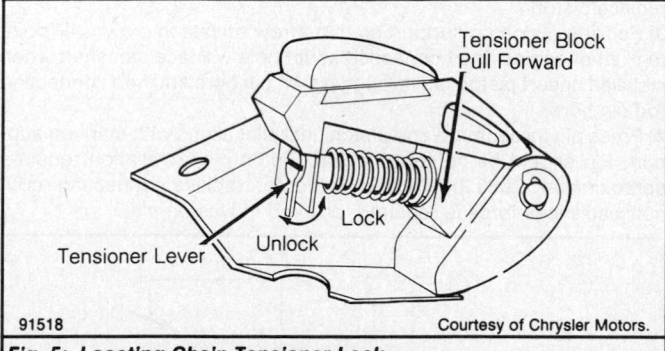

Tensioner Block
Pull Forward

Lock

Tensioner Lever

Unlock

91518

Courtesy of Chrysler Motors.

Fig. 5: Locating Chain Tensioner Lock

TIMING CHAIN & SPROCKETS

Removal – 1) Disconnect negative battery cable. Remove drive belt, fan and hub assembly. Remove fan shroud. Remove accessory drive brackets attached to timing case cover. Remove A/C compressor (if equipped) with hoses attached and wire it aside. DO NOT discharge A/C system. Remove alternator bracket assembly from cylinder head.
2) Remove vibration damper retaining bolt and washer. Remove vibration damper and key. Remove front cover retaining bolts and front cover. Cut oil pan gasket flush with face of cylinder block. Remove cut-off pieces.
3) Rotate crankshaft until timing marks on crankshaft and camshaft sprockets align. See Fig. 4. Remove oil slinger and camshaft sprocket retaining bolt. Remove sprockets and chain as an assembly. Remove front cover oil seal.

Installation – 1) Turn tensioner lever down to unlock position. Pull tensioner block toward lever to compress spring. Turn lever up to lock position. See Fig. 5. Install timing chain and sprockets as an assembly. Ensure timing marks align. Install camshaft sprocket retaining bolt and washer. Tighten to specification. See TORQUE SPECIFICATIONS table at end of article.

NOTE: Ensure chain tensioner is in unlock (down) position before installing front cover.

2) Verify proper installation by rotating crankshaft until timing mark on camshaft is at approximately one o'clock position. Timing sprockets are installed correctly if there are 20 timing chain pins between timing marks on both sprockets.
3) Clean all gasket surfaces. Install oil slinger. Apply sealing compound to both sides of front cover gasket. Install gasket onto cylinder block. Replace front section of oil pan seal with similar piece cut from new seal.
4) Coat new seal with RTV sealant and place into position. Apply sealant where oil pan and cylinder block meet. Place front cover onto cylinder block. Place Front Cover Aligner/Seal Installer (6139) in front engine cover seal area.
5) Install cover retaining bolts, and tighten to specification. To complete installation, reverse removal procedure. Lubricate vibration damper retaining bolt before installation, and tighten to specification. See TORQUE SPECIFICATIONS table at end of article.

ROCKER ARMS

Removal – Remove valve cover. See CYLINDER HEAD under REMOVAL & INSTALLATION. Alternately loosen cap screws one turn at a time to prevent damaging bridges. Remove bridges, pivots, rocker arms and push rods. Tag all parts for reassembly reference.
Installation – 1) Lubricate push rod ends with MOPAR Engine Oil Supplement (4318002). Install push rods into their original locations. Ensure bottom end of each push rod is centered in valve lifter.
2) Lubricate pivot contact area of each rocker arm with engine oil supplement. Install rocker arms, pivots and bridges into their original locations. Loosely install cap screws, then tighten alternately one turn at a time to specification. Reverse removal procedure to complete installation.
3) Pour remaining engine oil supplement over entire valve train. Supplement must remain in engine oil for at least 1000 miles (1600 km), but need not be drained until next scheduled oil change.

CAMSHAFT

Removal – 1) Disconnect negative battery cable. Drain cooling system. Discharge A/C system (if equipped). Remove A/C condenser (if equipped) and radiator. Mark distributor and engine block for installation reference. Remove distributor and ignition wiring. Remove rocker arms, bridges, pivots and push rods. See ROCKER ARMS.
2) Remove valve lifters using Hydraulic Valve Lifter Remover/Installer (C-4129-A). Tag each valve lifter for installation reference. Remove timing chain and sprockets. See TIMING CHAIN & SPROCKETS. Remove camshaft.
Inspection – Inspect lobes, journals, bearings and distributor drive gear for wear. If camshaft sprocket or chain rubs against engine front cover, examine oil pressure relief holes in rear camshaft journal and ensure they are free of debris.
Installation – 1) Lubricate camshaft and dip valve lifters into MOPAR Engine Oil Supplement (4318002). Install camshaft. Reverse removal procedure to complete installation.
2) Pour remaining oil supplement over entire valve train. Supplement must remain in engine oil for at least 1000 miles (1600 km), but need not be drained until next scheduled oil change. Refill cooling system. Adjust ignition timing. Check for leaks.

REAR CRANKSHAFT OIL SEAL

Removal – Remove transmission, clutch housing and flywheel or flexplate. Pry oil seal from housing. Avoid damage to surrounding area.

Installation – Coat outer lip of replacement seal with engine oil. Using Seal Installer (6271), install seal flush with cylinder block. Use only new bolts when installing flywheel or flexplate. Ensure felt lip is inside flywheel mounting surface to avoid tearing seal. To complete installation, reverse removal procedure. Tighten flywheel or flexplate bolts to specification, then an additional 60 degrees. See TORQUE SPECIFICATIONS table at end of article.

WATER PUMP

Removal – Disconnect negative battery cable. Drain cooling system. Remove fan shroud and drive belts. Remove fan assembly. Disconnect heater hoses and lower radiator hose at water pump. Remove water pump retaining bolts. Remove water pump.

Installation – Install water pump. Tighten bolts to specification. See TORQUE SPECIFICATIONS table at end of article. Ensure pump turns freely. Ensure belt is installed correctly to prevent engine overheating because water pump rotates in wrong direction. To complete installation, reverse removal procedure. Fill and purge air from cooling system. Remove coolant temperature sensor to bleed air from system while filling.

OIL PAN

Removal – 1) Disconnect negative battery cable. Raise and support vehicle. Drain engine oil. Disconnect exhaust pipe at exhaust manifold. Disconnect exhaust pipe hanger at catalytic converter and lower exhaust pipe. Remove starter. Remove flywheel access cover.

2) Position jackstand directly under vibration damper. Place wooden block between damper and jackstand. Remove through bolts from engine mounts. Raise engine enough to remove oil pan. Remove oil pan retaining bolts. Remove oil pan.

Installation – Install new seals and gaskets. To complete installation, reverse removal procedure. Tighten oil pan bolts to specification. See TORQUE SPECIFICATIONS table at end of article. Fill crankcase. Start engine and check for leaks.

OVERHAUL

CYLINDER HEAD

Inspection – Inspect for cracks in combustion chambers, coolant passages, ports and exhaust valve seats. Using straightedge, check cylinder head for warpage in several areas. Repair or replace cylinder head if warpage exceeds specification or damage exists. See CYLINDER HEAD table under ENGINE SPECIFICATIONS at end of article.

Valve Springs – Use Valve Spring Tester (J-22738-02) to test each valve spring. Measure free length of each valve spring. Replace valve springs that do not meet specifications. See VALVES & VALVE SPRINGS table under ENGINE SPECIFICATIONS at end of article.

Valve Stem Oil Seals – Replace valve stem oil seals if they have deteriorated or whenever valves are serviced. Oil seals are marked INT and EXH for intake and exhaust valves, respectively. Oversize oil seals must be used with valves having .015" (.38 mm) oversize stems.

Valve Guides – Measure diameter of valve guide approximately 3/8" (10 mm) from valve spring side of head, both parallel and at right angle to long axis of head. If difference between measurements exceeds .0025" (.063 mm), or if diameter exceeds specification by .003" (.08 mm), ream valve guide for oversize valve stem. See CYLINDER HEAD table under ENGINE SPECIFICATIONS at end of article. Reface valve seats after reaming valve guides.

Valve Seats – Reface valve seats to specification. Remove only enough metal to provide smooth finish. Use tapered stones to obtain specified seat width. *See Fig. 6.* Seat width runout should not exceed .0025" (.063 mm) after refacing. See CYLINDER HEAD table under ENGINE SPECIFICATIONS at end of article.

Valves – Reface valves to specification. At least 1/32" (.79 mm) margin must remain after refacing valve. Valve stem tip can be resurfaced and chamfered when worn. DO NOT remove more than .01" (.25 mm). See VALVES & VALVE SPRINGS table under ENGINE SPECIFICATIONS at end of article.

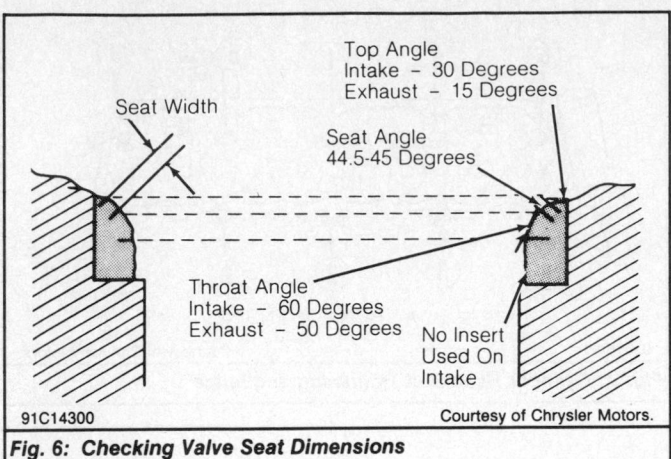

Fig. 6: **Checking Valve Seat Dimensions**

VALVE TRAIN

Rocker Arms – Inspect pivot and valve stem contact surfaces of each rocker arm. Replace any rocker arm that is scuffed, pitted, cracked or excessively worn.

Push Rods – Inspect push rods for excessive wear. If wear is excessive because of lack of oil, replace and inspect corresponding valve lifter for excessive wear. Roll push rods on a flat surface to check for straightness. If wear exists along length of push rod, inspect cylinder head for obstruction.

CYLINDER BLOCK ASSEMBLY

Piston & Rod Assembly – 1) Note locations of arrow on piston crown and oil squirt hole in connecting rod. Position piston and rod assembly on support. *See Fig. 7.* Press piston pin from piston. Discard pin. Piston pin CANNOT be reused after removal. Inspect piston pin bore in connecting rod for nicks or burrs and remove as necessary.

2) Clean piston pin bore and replacement piston pin. Piston and piston pin must be at room temperature when measuring fit. Piston pin should fall through piston at room temperature. If pin jams in pin bore, replace piston.

3) Position piston on support so that arrow on piston crown will point to front of engine and connecting squirt hole will face camshaft when installed. Insert piston pin through piston pin bore and into connecting rod pin bore.

4) Press pin through rod and piston until pilot aligns with mark on support. Pin should be centered in rod. Piston pin installation requires approximately 2000 lbs. (900 kg) of force. Replace connecting rod if noticeably less force is required or if rod moves on pin.

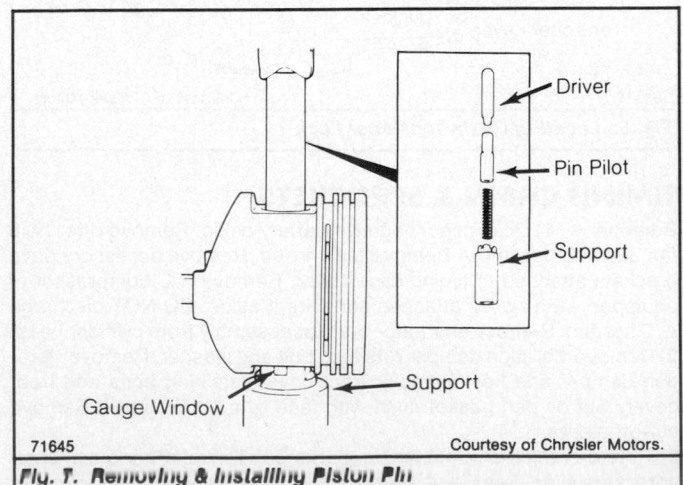

Fig. 7: **Removing & Installing Piston Pin**

Fitting Pistons – Measure cylinder bore 2 5/16" (59 mm) below top of bore. Measure piston diameter at right angle to piston pin at center line of pin. Piston clearance is difference between measurements. Pistons up to .004" (.10 mm) undersize may be enlarged by knurling or shot peening. Replace pistons if clearance is greater than .004" (.10 mm) or more.

Piston Rings – Install piston rings. DO NOT interchange piston rings. Top ring has a Gray scraping surface; second ring is Black. Ensure ring end gap and side clearance are within specifications. Position ring end gaps in specified area. Ring gaps may vary 20 degrees from locations illustrated. *See Fig. 8.* Also see PISTONS, PINS & RINGS table under ENGINE SPECIFICATIONS at end of article.

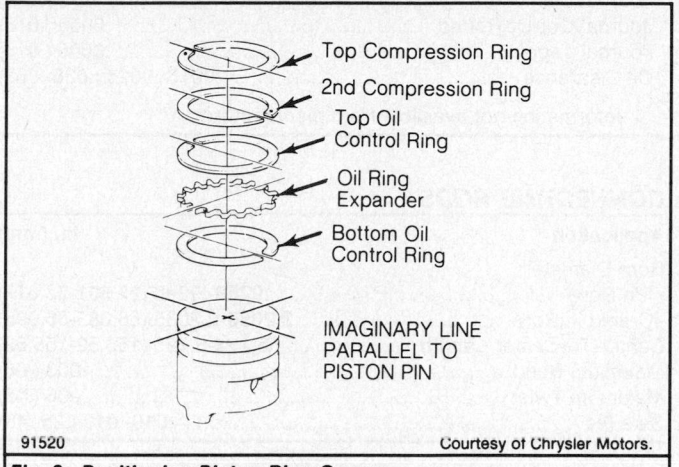

Top Compression Ring
2nd Compression Ring
Top Oil Control Ring
Oil Ring Expander
Bottom Oil Control Ring

IMAGINARY LINE PARALLEL TO PISTON PIN

91520   Courtesy of Chrysler Motors.

Fig. 8: Positioning Piston Ring Gaps

Rod Bearings – **1)** Inspect bearings for wear or damage. Replace as necessary. Using Plastigage, check bearing clearance. See CRANKSHAFT, MAIN & CONNECTING ROD BEARINGS table under ENGINE SPECIFICATIONS at end of article. Bearings are available for standard and undersize applications.
2) If necessary, different size upper and lower bearings may be combined to obtain correct oil clearance. Tighten bolts to specification. Check rod side play. Rotate crankshaft to ensure freedom of movement. See TORQUE SPECIFICATIONS table at end of article. See CRANKSHAFT, MAIN & CONNECTING ROD BEARINGS table.

NOTE: Never combine bearing inserts that differ by more than .001" (.03 mm) in size. Odd size inserts must be on bottom (rod cap) side.

Crankshaft & Main Bearings – **1)** Inspect bearings for damage or wear. Replace as necessary. Using Plastigage, measure bearing clearance. See CRANKSHAFT, MAIN & CONNECTING ROD BEARINGS table under ENGINE SPECIFICATIONS at end of article. Bearings are available in standard and undersize. If necessary, different size upper and lower bearings may be installed to obtain correct oil clearance. Lubricate bearings before installation.

NOTE: If different size bearings are installed, the odd size bearings must all be uniform in location (upper or lower). Never combine bearing inserts that differ by more than .001" (.03 mm).

2) Install upper bearing inserts. Install bearing caps and lower inserts. Tighten bearing caps No. 1, 3, 4 and 5 in 3 stages to specification. Pry crankshaft to front or rear and tighten bolts for cap No. 2 to specification in 3 stages. Rotate crankshaft to ensure freedom of movement after tightening each cap. See TORQUE SPECIFICATIONS table at end of article. See CRANKSHAFT, MAIN & CONNECTING ROD BEARINGS table.

Thrust Bearing – Check crankshaft end play. If end play is not within specification, replace bearing No. 2. If end play is still not within specification, replace crankshaft. See CRANKSHAFT, MAIN & CONNECTING ROD BEARINGS table under ENGINE SPECIFICATIONS at end of article.

Cylinder Block – **1)** Measure cylinder bore diameter crosswise to cylinder block near top of bore. Repeat measurement at bottom of bore. Subtract smaller diameter from larger diameter to determine taper. Repeat measurements for each cylinder.
2) Repeat measurements with measuring device rotated 120 degrees. Repeat this step for a total of 3 measurements. Cylinder out-of-round is the difference between measurements. Repeat for each cylinder.
3) Bore and hone cylinders for oversize pistons if taper or out-of-round exceeds specification. Move hone up and down to provide a 60-degree crosshatch pattern. DO NOT use a rigid hone or exceed 10 strokes per cylinder. See CYLINDER BLOCK table under ENGINE SPECIFICATIONS at end of article.

ENGINE OILING

ENGINE LUBRICATION SYSTEM

A distributor-driven pump supplies oil through a full-flow oil filter to an oil gallery on right side of block and intersecting lifter bores. Oil then flows to camshaft and crankshaft bearings. The rocker arms receive oil through the push rods and lifters.

Crankcase Capacity – Crankcase capacity is **4 qts. (3.8L)** with oil filter change.

Oil Pressure – Normal oil pressure should be **25-35 psi (1.8-2.5 kg/cm²)** at 800 RPM or **37-75 psi (2.6-5.3 kg/cm²)** at 1600 RPM. Oil pressure relief occurs at 75 psi (5.3 kg/cm²).

OIL PUMP

Removal & Disassembly – Remove oil pump retaining bolts. DO NOT move oil pick-up pipe in pump body. If oil pick-up pipe is moved, pick-up pipe must be replaced to ensure an airtight seal. Remove pump cover. Disassemble pump.

Inspection – **1)** Inspect for wear and damage. Place Plastigage across full width of each gear. Temporarily install cover, and tighten bolts to **70 INCH lbs. (8 N.m)**. Remove cover. Examine Plastigage to determine end clearance.
2) Rotate gears, and measure clearance between each tooth and oil pump body, directly opposite point of mesh. Replace oil pump if not within specification. See OIL PUMP SPECIFICATIONS table.

OIL PUMP SPECIFICATIONS

Application	In. (mm)
Gear End Clearance	.002-.006 (.05-.15)
Gear-to-Body Clearance	.002-.004 (.05-.10)

Reassembly & Installation – **1)** Apply sealant to pick-up pipe and pump cover area prior to installation. To install pick-up tube, use Pipe Installer (7624). Ensure pick-up pipe support bracket is aligned with pump cover bolt. If relief valve is replaced, ensure replacement valve is same diameter as that removed.
2) Fill pump cavity with petroleum jelly. Install cover. Tighten cover bolts to specification. Check pump gears for freedom of rotation. Install new gasket and oil pump. Tighten retaining bolts to specification. See TORQUE SPECIFICATIONS table.

TORQUE SPECIFICATIONS

TORQUE SPECIFICATIONS

Application	Ft. Lbs. (N.m)
Camshaft Sprocket Bolt	80 (108)
Connecting Rod Cap Nuts	33 (45)
Cylinder Head Bolts [1]	
Stage 1	22 (30)
Stage 2	45 (61)
Stage 3	[2] 110 (149)
Drive Plate-To-Converter Bolts	50 (68)
Exhaust Manifold Bolts [3]	
Bolt No. 1	30 (41)
Bolt No. 2-5	23 (31)
Nut No. 6 & 7	30 (41)
Fan Bolts	18 (24)
Flexplate-To-Crankshaft Bolts	[4] 50 (68)
Flywheel-To-Crankshaft Bolts	[4] 50 (68)
Intake Manifold Bolts [3]	
Bolt No. 1	30 (41)
Bolt No. 2-5	23 (31)
Nut No. 6 & 7	30 (41)
Main Bearing Cap Bolts	
Stage 1	40 (54)
Stage 2	70 (95)
Stage 3	80 (108)
Oil Pump Retaining Bolts	
Long	17 (23)
Short	10 (14)
Oxygen (O_2) Sensor	35 (48)
Pulley-To-Vibration Damper Bolts	20 (27)
Rocker Arm Bolts	21 (28)
Throttle Body-To-Intake Bolts	16 (22)
Vibration Damper Bolt	[5] 80 (108)
Water Pump Bolts	22 (30)

Application	INCH Lbs. (N.m)
Front Cover-To-Block Bolts	62 (7)
Oil Pan Bolts	
1/4" X 20	114 (13)
5/16" X 18	156 (18)
Oil Pump Cover Bolts	70 (8)
Valve Cover Bolts	85 (10)

[1] – Tighten in sequence. *See Fig. 3.*
[2] – All except bolt No. 7. Tighten bolt No. 7 to 100 ft. lbs (136 N.m).
[3] – Tighten bolts in sequence. *See Fig. 2.*
[4] – Tighten to specification and an additional 60 degrees.
[5] – With bolt cleaned and threads lubricated with oil.

ENGINE SPECIFICATIONS

GENERAL SPECIFICATIONS

Application	Specification
Displacement	150 Cu. In. (2.5L)
Bore	3.88" (98.6 mm)
Stroke	3.19" (81.0 mm)
Compression Ratio	
Cherokee & Comanche	9.2:1
Wrangler	9.1:1
Fuel System	PFI
Horsepower @ RPM	
Cherokee & Comanche	130 @ 5250
Wrangler	123 @ 5250
Torque Ft. Lbs. @ RPM	
Cherokee & Comanche	149 @ 3000
Wrangler	139 @ 3250

CRANKSHAFT, MAIN & CONNECTING ROD BEARINGS

Application	In. (mm)
Crankshaft	
End Play	.0015-.0065 (.038-.165)
Runout	[1]
Main Bearings	
Journal Diameter	2.4996-2.5001 (63.490-63.503)
Journal Out-Of-Round	.0005 (.013)
Journal Taper	.0005 (.013)
Oil Clearance	.0010-.0025 (.025-.063)
Connecting Rod Bearings	
Journal Diameter	2.0934-2.0955 (53.172-53.226)
Journal Out-Of-Round	.0005 (.013)
Journal Taper	.0005 (.013)
Oil Clearance	.0015-.0025 (.038-.063)

[1] – Information not available from manufacturer.

CONNECTING RODS

Application	In. (mm)
Bore Diameter	
Pin Bore	.9288-.9298 (23.591-23.617)
Crankpin Bore	2.2080-2.2085 (56.083-56.096)
Center-To-Center Length	6.123-6.127 (155.52-155.62)
Maximum Bend	.003 (.08)
Maximum Twist	.006 (.15)
Side Play	.010-.019 (.25-.48)

PISTONS, PINS & RINGS

Application	In. (mm)
Piston	
Clearance	.0013-.0021 (.033-.053)
Diameter	[1]
Pins	
Diameter	.9304-.9309 (23.63-23.64)
Piston Fit	.0004-.0006 (.010-.015)
Rod Fit	Press Fit
Rings	
No. 1 & 2	
End Gap	.010-.020 (.25-.51)
Side Clearance	.001-.003 (.03-.08)
No. 3 (Oil)	
End Gap	.015-.055 (.38-1.40)
Side Clearance	.001-.010 (.03-.24)

[1] – Information not available from manufacturer. Replace pistons if piston clearance exceeds .004" (.10 mm).

CYLINDER BLOCK

Application	In. (mm)
Cylinder Bore	
Standard Diameter	3.875-3.877 (98.42-98.48)
Maximum Taper	.001 (.03)
Maximum Out-Of-Round	.001 (.03)
Minimum Deck Height	9.320 (236.73)
Maximum Deck Warpage	.008 (.20)

VALVES & VALVE SPRINGS

Application	Specification
Intake Valves	
Face Angle	45°
Head Diameter	1.90" (48.3 mm)
Minimum Margin	.031" (.79 mm)
Minimum Refinish Length	4.889" (124.18 mm)
Stem Diameter	.311-.312" (7.89-7.92 mm)
Valve Tip Maximum Refinish	.010" (.25 mm)
Exhaust Valves	
Face Angle	45°
Head Diameter	1.50" (38.1 mm)
Minimum Margin	.031" (.79 mm)
Minimum Refinish Length	4.927" (125.15 mm)
Stem Diameter	.311-.312" (7.90-7.92 mm)
Valve Tip Maximum Refinish	.010" (.25 mm)
Valve Springs	
Free Length	2.0" (51 mm)
Installed Height	[1]
Out-Of-Square	[1]
	Lbs. @ In. (kg @ mm)
Pressure	
Valve Closed	80-90 @ 1.64 (36.3-40.8 @ 40.8)
Valve Open	200 @ 1.216 (90.7 @ 30.9)

[1] – Information not available from manufacturer.

CYLINDER HEAD

Application	Specification
Cylinder Head Height	[1]
Maximum Warpage	.008" (.20 mm)
Valve Seats	
Intake Valve	
Seat Angle	44.5 45°
Seat Width	.040-.060" (1.02-1.52 mm)
Maximum Seat Runout	.0025" (.063 mm)
Exhaust Valve	
Seat Angle	44.5-45°
Seat Width	.040-.060" (1.02-1.52 mm)
Maximum Seat Runout	.0025" (.063 mm)
Seat Bore Diameter	[1]
Valve Guides	
Intake Valve	
Valve Guide I.D.	.313-.314" (7.95-7.98 mm)
Valve Stem-To-Guide Oil Clearance	.001-.003" (.03-.08 mm)
Exhaust Valve	
Valve Guide I.D.	.313-.314" (7.95-7.98 mm)
Valve Stem-To-Guide Oil Clearance	.001-.003" (.03-.08 mm)

[1] – Information not available from manufacturer.

CAMSHAFT

Application	In. (mm)
Bore Diameter	[1]
End Play	[2] 0 (0)
Journal Diameter	
No. 1.	2.029-2.030 (51.54-51.56)
No. 2.	2.019-2.020 (51.28-51.31)
No. 3.	2.009-2.010 (51.03-51.05)
No. 4.	1.999-2.000 (50.78-50.80)
Journal Runout	[3]
Lobe Height	[1]
Lobe Lift	.265 (6.73)
Oil Clearance	.001-.003 (.03-.08)

[1] – Information not available from manufacturer.
[2] – Engine running.
[3] – Information not available from manufacturer. Manufacturer specifies .001" (.03 mm) maximum base circle runout.

VALVE LIFTERS

Application	In. (mm)
Bore Diameter	.9055-.9065 (22.987-23.025)
Lifter Diameter	.9040-.9045 (22.962-22.974)
Oil Clearance	.001-.002 (.03-.05)

Cherokee, Comanche, Grand Cherokee (1993), Wrangler

NOTE: For repair procedures not covered in this article, see ENGINE OVERHAUL PROCEDURES article in GENERAL INFORMATION.

ENGINE IDENTIFICATION

The Vehicle Identification Number (VIN) is located on the upper left side of the dash and is visible through the windshield. The eighth character identifies engine size.

ENGINE IDENTIFICATION CODE

Engine	Code
4.0L PFI	S

Some engines are manufactured with oversize or undersize components. These engines are identified by a letter code stamped on a boss between ignition coil and distributor. Letters are decoded as follows:

- "B" indicates all cylinder bores are .010" (.25 mm) oversize.
- "C" indicates all camshaft bearing bores are .010" (.25 mm) oversize.
- "M" indicates all main bearing journals are .010" (.25 mm) undersize.
- "P" indicates one or more connecting rod journals are .010" (.25 mm) undersize.
- "PM" indicates all main journals and one or more rod journal are .010" (.25 mm) undersize.

ADJUSTMENTS

VALVE CLEARANCE ADJUSTMENT

Engine is equipped with hydraulic valve lifters. No valve adjustment is required.

REMOVAL & INSTALLATION

NOTE: For reassembly reference, label all electrical connectors, vacuum hoses and fuel lines before removal. Also place mating marks on engine hood and other major assemblies before removal.

FUEL PRESSURE RELEASE

CAUTION: Fuel system is under constant pressure. This pressure must be released before disconnecting or servicing any fuel supply or return system component. Wear proper eye protection when releasing fuel system pressure.

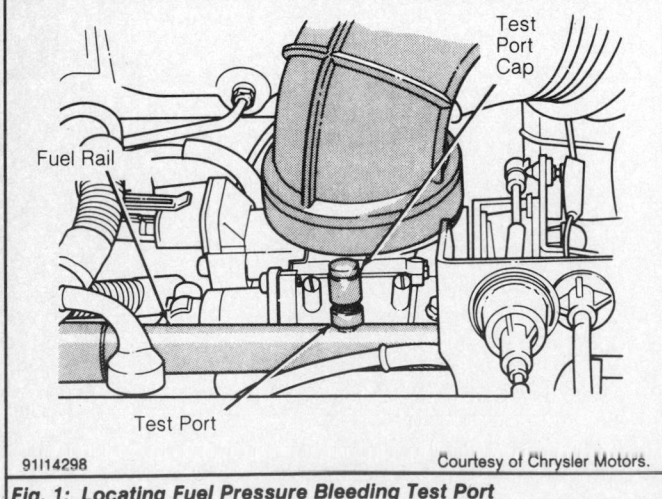

91114298   Courtesy of Chrysler Motors.

Fig. 1: Locating Fuel Pressure Bleeding Test Port

Disconnect negative battery cable. Remove fuel filler cap. Remove cap from pressure test port on fuel rail. *See Fig. 1.* Place shop towels around pressure test port to absorb spilled fuel. Press test port valve with a small screwdriver or punch wrapped in shop towels. Remove shop towels and dispose of properly. Install pressure test port cap.

CAUTION: Always replace "O" rings, spacers and retainers whenever fuel system quick-connect fittings are disconnected. Ensure fuel connections are secure by verifying that only retaining tabs protrude from connectors, and by pulling on tubes to verify that they are locked into place.

COOLING SYSTEM BLEEDING

CAUTION: Engine coolant may be hot. Avoid scalding by using care. Carefully release system pressure before removing radiator cap or drain cock.

ENGINE

Removal (Cherokee, Comanche & Grand Cherokee) – 1) Remove hood. Disconnect battery cables. Remove battery. Remove air cleaner. Unplug quick-connect vacuum hose fittings at intake manifold. Drain cooling system. Remove radiator hoses and radiator support. Disconnect harness from electric fan motor (if equipped). Remove fan shroud and fan. Disconnect transmission cooler lines (if equipped). Remove radiator.

2) Discharge A/C system (if equipped). Discharge A/C system using approved refrigerant recovery/recycling equipment. Remove A/C service valves. Cap compressor ports. Remove A/C condenser. Disconnect heater hoses at water pump and thermostat housing. Disconnect cruise control (if equipped) and throttle linkage. Disconnect distributor wiring, oil pressure sender wire and fuel injection wire harness at each injector. Tag connectors for installation reference.

3) Disconnect line pressure cable to A/T (if equipped). Release fuel pressure. See FUEL PRESSURE RELEASE. Disconnect fuel supply quick-connect fittings at fuel rail. Remove fuel line bracket from intake manifold. Remove check valve from power brake booster (if equipped). Disconnect power steering hoses at steering gear (if equipped). Drain power steering pump reservoir. Cap power steering hoses and fittings.

4) Tag and disconnect any remaining vacuum hoses and electrical connectors as required. Raise and support vehicle. Disconnect exhaust pipe from exhaust manifold. Remove starter and flywheel cover. Disconnect oxygen (O_2) sensor. Disconnect engine speed sensor.

5) On A/T models, mark converter and flexplate for installation reference. Remove converter-to-flexplate bolts. Remove upper and loosen lower bellhousing bolts. Remove engine mount bracket bolts. Lower vehicle.

6) Attach lifting device to engine. Lift engine from front supports. Place support under bellhousing. Remove remaining bellhousing bolts. Remove engine.

Removal (Wrangler) – 1) Pad windshield with cloth. Raise hood and rest it against windshield frame. Drain cooling system. Disconnect battery cables. Remove battery. Disconnect wiring from alternator, ignition coil, distributor, oil pressure sender and fuel injection wire harness. Disconnect wires at starter solenoid and injector harness connector.

2) Disconnect fuel line quick-connect couplings at fuel rail. Remove fuel line bracket from intake manifold. Remove engine ground strap. Remove air cleaner. Disconnect vacuum purge hose from vapor canister tee. Unplug idle speed actuator connector. Disconnect throttle cable and remove it from bracket.

3) Disconnect throttle rod at bellcrank. Disconnect cruise control cable (if equipped). Unplug oxygen (O_2) sensor connector. Disconnect coolant hoses at radiator, intake manifold and thermostat housing. Remove fan shroud and radiator. Remove fan and spacer. Install a 5/16" x 1/2" bolt through fan pulley into water pump flange to maintain pulley and water pump alignment.

4) Remove check valve from power brake booster (if equipped). Disconnect power steering hoses at steering gear (if equipped). Drain power steering pump reservoir. Cap power steering hoses and fittings.

5) Tag and disconnect any remaining hoses or electrical connectors. Raise and support vehicle. Disconnect exhaust pipe from exhaust manifold. Remove starter. Remove flywheel housing access cover. Remove engine mount through-bolts. Remove upper bellhousing bolts. Loosen lower bellhousing bolts.

6) Lower vehicle. Attach lifting device to engine. Raise engine from front supports. Place support under bellhousing. Remove remaining bellhousing bolts. Lift engine from engine compartment.

Installation (All Models) – 1) Remove engine mount cushions from brackets to aid alignment of engine and transmission. Replace fuel line quick-connect "O" rings, spacers and retainers.

2) Be careful not to damage trigger wheel on flywheel when installing engine into vehicle with automatic transmission. To complete installation, reverse removal procedure. Adjust throttle and cruise control linkage (if equipped). Tighten bolts to specification. See TORQUE SPECIFICATIONS table at end of article. Check and refill fluid levels.

INTAKE MANIFOLD

Removal – 1) Disconnect negative battery cable. Remove air inlet from throttle plate assembly. Remove air cleaner. Disconnect throttle and cruise control (if equipped) cables. Disconnect line pressure cable to A/T (if equipped).

2) Unplug all electrical connectors from intake manifold. Release fuel system pressure. See FUEL PRESSURE RELEASE. Disconnect fuel line quick-connect fittings at fuel rail. Loosen accessory drive belt and tensioner.

3) Remove power steering pump and bracket. Wire pump aside. Remove fuel rail retaining bolts. Remove fuel rail and injector assembly. Raise and support vehicle. Disconnect exhaust pipe from exhaust manifold. Lower vehicle. Remove retaining bolts. Remove intake and exhaust manifolds as an assembly.

Installation – 1) Ensure all gasket surfaces are clean. Install NEW gasket. Install exhaust manifold and tighten bolt No. 3 finger tight. Install intake manifold and remaining bolts loosely. Replace fuel line quick-connect "O" rings, spacers and retainers.

2) Tighten bolts to specification and in proper sequence. See Fig. 2. Reverse removal procedure to complete installation. See TORQUE SPECIFICATIONS table at end of article.

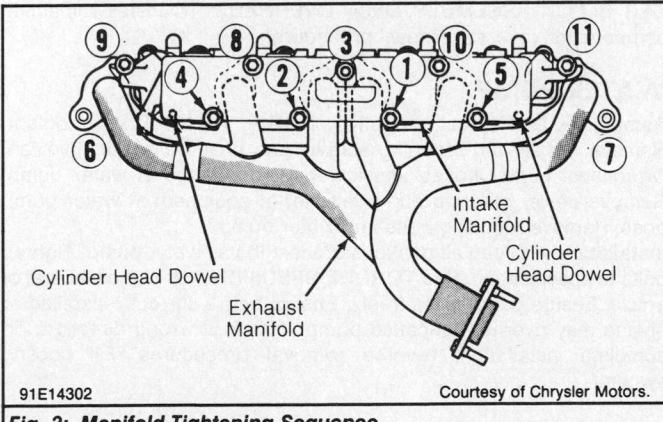

91E14302   Courtesy of Chrysler Motors.

Fig. 2: Manifold Tightening Sequence

EXHAUST MANIFOLD

Removal & Installation – Remove exhaust manifold with intake manifold. See INTAKE MANIFOLD.

CYLINDER HEAD

Removal – 1) Disconnect negative battery cable. Drain cooling system. Remove air cleaner and fuel pipe. Remove molded hoses from cylinder head cover. Remove cylinder head cover.

2) Remove rocker arms, bridges, pivots and push rods. See ROCKER ARMS. Tag all parts for reassembly reference. Loosen serpentine drive belt at power steering pump (if equipped) or at idler pulley. Remove alternator bracket-to-cylinder head bolt. Disconnect power steering pump bracket. DO NOT disconnect hoses. Wire power steering pump aside.

3) Remove manifolds. See INTAKE MANIFOLD and EXHAUST MANIFOLD. Remove A/C compressor bracket bolts from cylinder head (if equipped). Loosen through bolt at bottom of A/C compressor bracket. Remove A/C compressor, and wire it aside.

4) Tag and disconnect spark plug wires. Remove spark plugs. Disconnect temperature sending unit. Remove ignition coil and bracket assembly.

5) Remove cylinder head bolts. Pull bolt No. 14 out as far as possible and hold in position using tape. Bolt No. 14 cannot be removed until head is moved forward. Remove cylinder head. Stuff clean lint-free shop towels into cylinder bores.

Inspection – 1) Inspect cylinder head for cracks and damage. Using straightedge, check cylinder head for warpage across bolt holes and diagonals. Repair or replace cylinder head if warpage exceeds specification or damage exists. See CYLINDER HEAD table under ENGINE SPECIFICATIONS at end of article.

2) Cylinder head bolts may only be reused once. If this is first time cylinder head has been removed, put a dab of paint on head of each bolt. If bolts already have paint on them or if it is unknown whether bolts have been used before, discard bolts and replace them with new head bolts.

Installation – 1) Clean carbon from combustion chambers and tops of pistons. Ensure all gasket surfaces, head bolts and head bolt holes are clean. Install new cylinder head gasket with numbers or word "TOP" upward. DO NOT apply gasket sealant to cylinder head gasket. Ensure all holes are aligned. Install cylinder head bolt No. 14, and hold in raised position using tape. Cylinder head bolt No. 14 cannot be installed after head is in position on block. Install cylinder head.

2) Apply sealant to threads of cylinder head bolt No. 11 before installation. Install cylinder head bolts. Tighten all bolts to specification in 3 stages and in sequence. During final tightening stage, bolt No. 11 will be tightened to a lower torque than others. See Fig. 3. See TORQUE SPECIFICATIONS table at end of article.

3) To install remaining components, reverse removal procedure. Install all valve train components into original locations. Adjust A/T linkage. Refill cooling system. Start engine, and check for leaks.

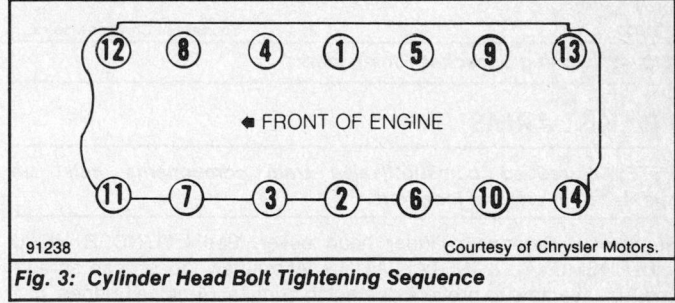

91238   Courtesy of Chrysler Motors.

Fig. 3: Cylinder Head Bolt Tightening Sequence

FRONT COVER OIL SEAL

Removal – 1) Disconnect negative battery cable. Remove drive belts, fan shroud, fan and hub assembly. Remove accessory drive pulley. Remove vibration damper retaining bolt and washer.

2) Using Puller (8068), remove vibration damper and key. Using appropriate seal remover, remove front cover oil seal.

Installation – 1) Position seal on Seal Installer (6139), with seal open end facing toward cover. Apply thin coat of RTV sealant on outside diameter of seal. Lightly coat crankshaft with engine oil.

2) Position installer over end of crankshaft. Insert draw screw into end of crankshaft. Tighten draw screw nut until seal is fully seated in front cover. Remove installer. Check seal for proper installation. To complete installation, reverse removal procedure.

TIMING CHAIN & SPROCKETS

Removal – 1) Disconnect negative battery cable. Remove drive belts, fan shroud, fan and hub assembly. Remove accessory drive pulley. Remove vibration damper retaining bolt and washer.

2) Using Puller (8068), remove vibration damper and key. Remove alternator bracket assembly and A/C compressor bracket (if equipped). Remove oil pan-to-front cover bolts. Remove cover-to-block retaining bolts. Remove front cover. Take care that tension spring and thrust pin do not fall out of camshaft preload bolt into oil pan. Remove tension spring and thrust pin from preload bolt. Rotate crankshaft until timing marks on sprockets are aligned. *See Fig. 4.* Remove preload bolt. Remove timing chain and sprockets as an assembly.

Installation – 1) Install timing chain and sprockets as an assembly. Ensure timing marks align. Lubricate tension spring, thrust pin and thrust pin bore with MOPAR Engine Oil Supplement (4318002) before installation. Install preload bolt and washer. Tighten to specification.

2) Verify proper installation by rotating crankshaft until timing mark on camshaft is at approximately one o'clock position. Timing sprockets are installed correctly if 15 timing chain pins are between timing marks on both sprockets.

3) Install NEW front cover oil seal. Cut oil pan gasket tabs even with face of cylinder block. Remove tabs. Remove gasket from oil pan. Remove crankshaft oil seal from front cover. Clean front cover, oil pan and cylinder block gasket surfaces. Install front cover. To install remaining components, reverse removal procedure. See TORQUE SPECIFICATIONS table at end of article.

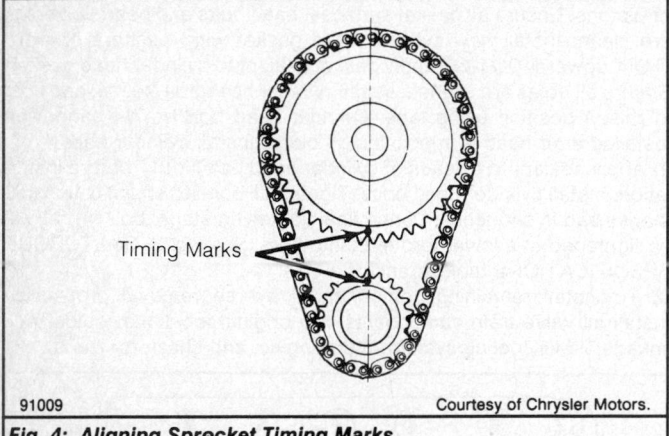

91009   Courtesy of Chrysler Motors.

Fig. 4: Aligning Sprocket Timing Marks

ROCKER ARMS

NOTE: All reused camshaft/valve train components must be reinstalled in original locations.

Removal – Remove cylinder head cover. See CYLINDER HEAD under REMOVAL & INSTALLATION. Alternately loosen cap screws one turn at a time to prevent damaging bridges. Remove bridges, pivots, rocker arms and push rods. Tag all parts for installation reference.

Installation – 1) Install all reused components into original locations. Ensure bottom ends of push rods are centered in valve lifters. Lubricate pivot contact area of rocker arms with MOPAR Engine Oil Supplement (4318002). Install cap screws loosely, and then tighten alternately one turn at a time to specification. See TORQUE SPECIFICATIONS table at end of article.

2) Reverse removal procedure to complete installation. Pour remaining engine oil supplement over entire valve train. Supplement must remain in engine oil for at least 1000 miles (1600 km). Refill cooling system. Adjust ignition timing. Check for leaks.

CAMSHAFT

Removal – 1) Disconnect negative battery cable. Drain cooling system. Remove radiator and A/C condenser (if equipped), but DO NOT discharge system. Mark distributor and engine block for installation reference. Remove distributor and ignition wiring. Remove cylinder head. See CYLINDER HEAD under REMOVAL & INSTALLATION.

2) Remove valve lifters using Hydraulic Valve Lifter Remover/Installer (C-4129-A). Tag each valve lifter for installation reference. Remove timing chain and sprockets. See TIMING CHAIN & SPROCKETS. Remove front bumper and/or grille as required. Remove camshaft.

Inspection – Inspect lobes, journals, bearings and distributor drive gear for wear. Inspect valve lifters for abnormal wear. If camshaft sprocket or chain rubs against engine front cover, examine oil pressure relief holes in rear camshaft journal and ensure they are free of debris. Replace components as necessary. If camshaft requires replacement, valve lifters MUST also be replaced.

Installation – 1) Lubricate camshaft and dip valve lifters into MOPAR Engine Oil Supplement (4318002). Install camshaft. Reverse removal procedure to complete installation.

2) Pour remaining engine oil supplement over entire valve train. Supplement must remain in engine oil for at least 1000 miles (1600 km). Refill cooling system. Adjust ignition timing. Check for leaks.

REAR CRANKSHAFT OIL SEAL

Removal – 1) Remove transmission, clutch housing and flywheel or flexplate. Remove oil pan. See OIL PAN.

2) Remove rear main bearing cap and push upper seal from groove. Ensure crankshaft is not damaged. Remove lower half of seal from bearing cap.

Installation – 1) Clean surface of crankshaft. Apply thin coat of oil to crankshaft and seal lip. Position upper seal into groove in cylinder block so lip of seal faces front of engine. Place lower half into bearing cap.

2) Coat both ends of lower seal end tabs with sealant. DO NOT apply sealant to lip of seal. Coat outer curved surface of lower seal with soap and lip of seal with engine oil. Position lower seal into bearing cap recess and seat firmly. Coat both chamfered edges of rear main bearing cap with sealant. DO NOT apply sealant to mating surfaces of bearing cap or cylinder block.

3) Install rear main cap in original position. Tighten bolts in 3 stages to specification. See CRANKSHAFT & MAIN BEARINGS under CYLINDER BLOCK ASSEMBLY under OVERHAUL. To install remaining components, reverse removal procedure.

WATER PUMP

Removal – Disconnect negative battery cable. Drain coolant. Remove fan shroud retaining screws and drive belts. Remove fan. Disconnect heater hoses and lower radiator hose at water pump. Remove power steering pump bracket (if equipped) at water pump boss. Remove retaining bolts and water pump.

Installation – Clean all gasket surfaces. Install water pump. Tighten bolts to specification. See TORQUE SPECIFICATIONS table at end of article. Ensure pump turns freely. Ensure belt is correctly installed or engine may overheat because pump rotates in wrong direction. To complete installation, reverse removal procedures. Fill cooling system.

OIL PAN

Removal – 1) Disconnect negative battery cable. Raise and support vehicle at side sills. Drain engine oil. Disconnect exhaust pipe at exhaust manifold. Disconnect exhaust hanger at catalytic converter. Lower exhaust pipe. Remove starter. Remove flywheel access cover.

2) Position jackstand directly under vibration damper. Place wooden block between vibration damper and jackstand. Remove through bolts from engine mounts. Raise engine enough to remove oil pan. Remove oil pan retaining bolts. Remove oil pan by sliding it to rear.

Installation – Ensure all gasket surfaces are clean. Install NEW front and rear seals and side rail gaskets. Coat inside surface of rear seal with soap. To complete installation, reverse removal procedure. Tighten oil pan bolts to specification. See TORQUE SPECIFICATIONS table at end of article. Fill crankcase. Start engine. Check for leaks.

OVERHAUL

CYLINDER HEAD

Cylinder Head Service – Inspect for cracks in combustion chambers, coolant passages, ports and exhaust valve seats. Using straightedge, check cylinder head for warpage across bolt holes and diagonals. Resurface or replace cylinder head if warpage exceeds specification or damage exists. See CYLINDER HEAD table under ENGINE SPECIFICATIONS at end of article.

Valve Springs - Use Valve Spring Tester C-647 (J-22738-02) to test each valve spring. Measure free length of each valve spring. Replace valve springs that do not meet specifications. See VALVES & VALVE SPRINGS table under ENGINE SPECIFICATIONS at end of article.

Valve Stem Oil Seals - Replace valve stem oil seals if they have deteriorated or whenever valves are serviced. Oil seals are marked "INT" and "EXH" for intake and exhaust valves, respectively.

Valve Guides – Measure diameter of valve guide approximately 3/8" (10 mm) from valve spring side of head, both parallel and at right angles to long axis of head. If difference between measurements exceeds .0025" (.063 mm), or if diameter exceeds specification by .003" (.08 mm), ream valve guide for oversize valve stem. Valve seats MUST be refaced after reaming valve guides. See CYLINDER HEAD table under ENGINE SPECIFICATIONS at end of article.

Valve Seats – Reface valve seats to specification. Remove only enough metal to provide smooth finish. Use tapered stones to obtain specified seat width. See Fig. 5. Seat width runout should not exceed .0025" (.063 mm) after refacing. See CYLINDER HEAD table under ENGINE SPECIFICATIONS at end of article.

Valves – Reface valves to specification. At least .031" (.79 mm) margin must remain after refacing valve. Valve stem tip can be resurfaced and chamfered when worn. DO NOT remove more than .01" (.25 mm). See VALVES & VALVE SPRINGS table under ENGINE SPECIFICATIONS at end of article.

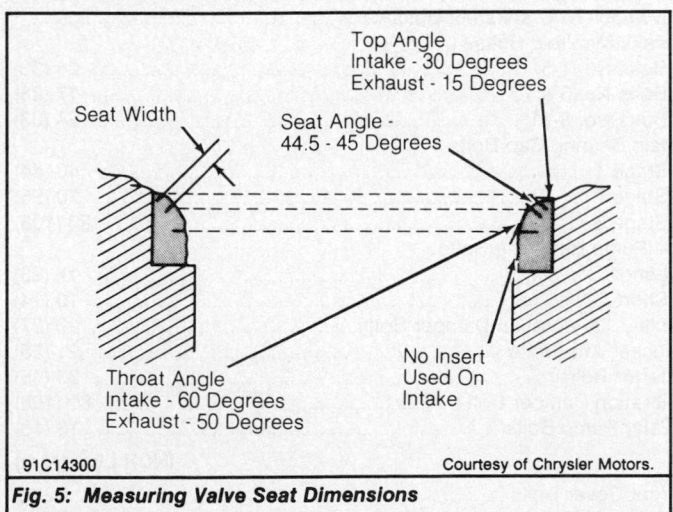

Fig. 5: Measuring Valve Seat Dimensions

VALVE TRAIN

Rocker Arms – Inspect pivot and valve stem contact surfaces of each rocker arm. Replace any rocker arm that is scuffed, pitted, cracked or excessively worn.

Push Rods – Inspect push rods for excessive wear. If wear is excessive due to lack of lack of oil, replace and inspect corresponding valve lifters for excessive wear. Roll push rods on a flat surface to check for straightness. If wear exists along length of push rod, inspect cylinder head for obstruction.

CYLINDER BLOCK ASSEMBLY

Piston & Rod Assembly – **1)** Position piston on support. See Fig. 6. Press piston pin from piston. Discard pin. Piston pin CANNOT be reused after removal. Inspect piston pin bore in connecting rod for nicks and burrs and remove as necessary. Clean and dry piston pin bore and new piston pin.

2) Clean piston pin bore and replacement piston pin. Piston and piston pin must be at room temperature when measuring fit. Piston pin should fall through piston at room temperature. If pin jams in pin bore, replace piston.

3) Ensure arrow on piston crown is pointing up. Insert piston pin through piston pin bore and into connecting rod pin bore. Assemble connecting rod and piston so oil squirt hole faces camshaft and arrow on piston points to front of engine when installed.

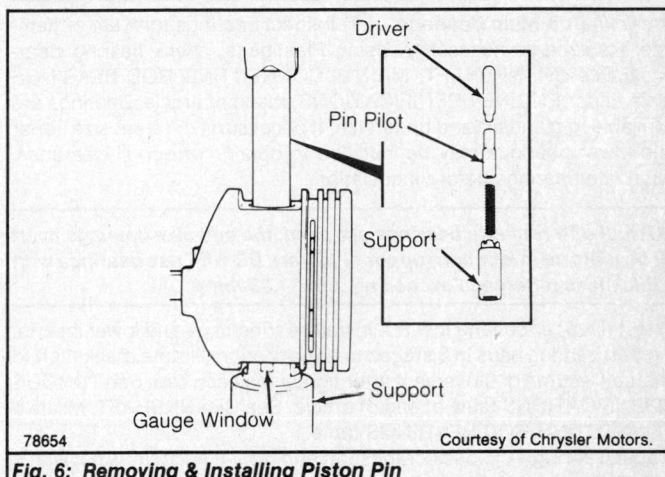

Fig. 6: Removing & Installing Piston Pin

4) Press pin through rod and piston until pilot indexes with mark on support. Pin should be centered in rod. Piston pin installation requires approximately 2000 lbs. (900 kg) of force. Replace connecting rod if noticeably less force is required, or if rod moves on pin.

Fitting Pistons – Measure cylinder bore 2 5/16" (59 mm) below top of bore. Measure piston diameter at right angle to piston pin at center line of pin. Piston clearance is difference between measurements. Pistons up to .004" (.10 mm) undersize may be enlarged by knurling or shot peening. Replace pistons if they are .004" (.10 mm) or more undersize.

Piston Rings – Install piston rings. Ensure ring end gap and side clearance are within specifications. Position ring end gaps in specified area. DO NOT interchange compression rings. Top ring has Gray scraping surface; second ring has Black scraping surface. Ring gaps may vary 20 degrees from positions illustrated. See Fig. 7. See PISTONS, PINS & RINGS table under ENGINE SPECIFICATIONS at end of article.

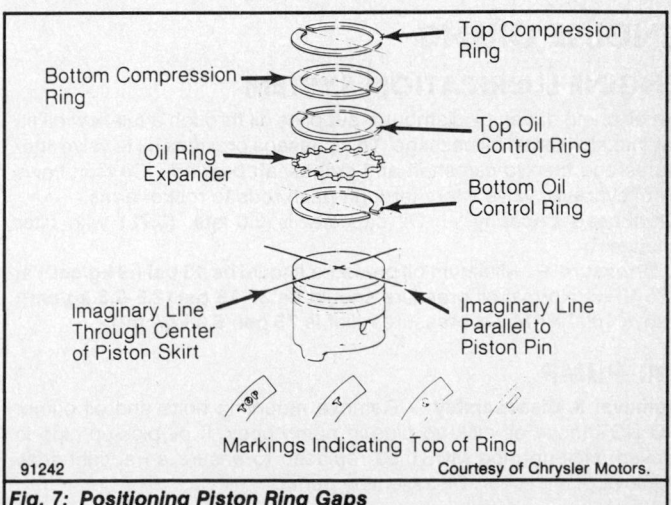

Fig. 7: Positioning Piston Ring Gaps

Rod Bearings – **1)** Inspect bearings for wear or damage. Replace as necessary. Using Plastigage, check bearing clearance. See CRANKSHAFT, MAIN & CONNECTING ROD BEARINGS table under ENGINE SPECIFICATIONS at end of article. Bearings are available for standard and undersize applications.

2) If necessary, different size upper and lower bearings may be combined to obtain correct oil clearance. Lubricate bearing surfaces with oil before installation. Tighten bolts to specification. Check rod side play. Rotate crankshaft to ensure freedom of movement. See TORQUE SPECIFICATIONS table at end of article. See CRANKSHAFT, MAIN & CONNECTING ROD BEARINGS table.

NOTE: Avoid combining bearing inserts in excess of .001" (.03 mm) difference in size. Odd size inserts must be on bottom (rod cap) side.

Crankshaft & Main Bearings – **1)** Inspect bearings for wear or damage. Replace as necessary. Using Plastigage, check bearing clearance. See CRANKSHAFT, MAIN & CONNECTING ROD BEARINGS table under ENGINE SPECIFICATIONS at end of article. Bearings are available in standard and undersize. If necessary, different size upper and lower bearings may be installed to obtain correct oil clearance. Lubricate bearings before installation.

NOTE: If different size bearings are used, the odd size bearings must all be uniform in location (upper or lower). DO NOT use bearings with a thickness difference exceeding .001" (.03 mm).

2) Install upper bearing inserts. Install bearing caps and lower inserts. Tighten bearing caps in 3 stages to specification. Rotate crankshaft to ensure freedom of movement after tightening each cap. See TORQUE SPECIFICATIONS table at end of article. See CRANKSHAFT, MAIN & CONNECTING ROD BEARINGS table.

Thrust Bearing – Check crankshaft end play. If end play is not within specification, replace thrust bearing. If end play is still not within specification, replace crankshaft.

Cylinder Block – **1)** Thoroughly clean all gasket surfaces. Using a tap, clean head bolt holes. Clean oil gallery by blowing compressed air into oil filter adapter, filter by-pass, oil gallery and crankshaft oil feed holes.

2) Measure cylinder bore diameter crosswise to cylinder block about 1/2" below top of bore. Repeat measurement at bottom of bore. Subtract smaller diameter from larger diameter to determine taper. Repeat measurements for each cylinder.

3) Repeat measurements with measuring device rotated 120 degrees. Repeat this step for a total of 3 measurements. Cylinder out-of-round is difference between measurements. Repeat for each cylinder.

4) Bore and hone cylinders for oversize pistons if taper or out-of-round exceeds specification. Move hone up and down to provide a 60-degree crosshatch pattern. DO NOT use a rigid hone or exceed 10 strokes per cylinder. See CYLINDER BLOCK table under ENGINE SPECIFICATIONS at end of article.

ENGINE OILING

ENGINE LUBRICATION SYSTEM

An oil pump driven by distributor supplies oil through a full-flow oil filter into an internal oil passage. This passage provides oil to valve lifter bores and then to camshaft and crankshaft bearings. Oil then flows from hydraulic valve lifters through push rods to rocker arms.

Crankcase Capacity – Oil capacity is **6.0 qts. (5.7L)** with filter change.

Oil Pressure – Minimum oil pressure should be **13 psi (.9 kg/cm²)** at 600 RPM. Normal oil pressure should be **37-75 psi (2.6-5.3 kg/cm²)** above 1600 RPM. Oil pressure relief is **75 psi (5.3 kg/cm²)**.

OIL PUMP

Removal & Disassembly – Remove mounting bolts and oil pump. DO NOT move oil pick-up pipe in pump body. If oil pick-up pipe is moved, pick-up pipe MUST be replaced to ensure an airtight seal. Remove pump cover. Disassemble pump.

Inspection – Inspect for wear or damage. Place Plastigage across full width of each gear. Install cover temporarily and tighten bolts to **70 INCH lbs. (8 N.m)**. Remove cover. Examine Plastigage to determine end clearance. Measure clearance between each tooth and oil pump body directly opposite point of mesh. Replace oil pump if not within specifications. See OIL PUMP SPECIFICATIONS table.

OIL PUMP SPECIFICATIONS

Application	In. (mm)
Gear End Clearance	.002-.006 (.05-.15)
Gear-to-Body Clearance	.002-.004 (.05-.10)

Reassembly & Installation – **1)** Apply sealant to pick-up pipe and pump cover area prior to installation. To install pick-up pipe use Pipe Installer (7624). Ensure pick-up pipe support bracket aligns with pump cover bolt. If relief valve is replaced, ensure replacement valve is the same diameter as that removed.

2) Fill pump cavity with petroleum jelly. Install cover. Tighten cover bolts to specification. Check pump gears for freedom of rotation. Install new gasket and oil pump. Tighten retaining bolts to specification. See TORQUE SPECIFICATIONS table.

TORQUE SPECIFICATIONS

TORQUE SPECIFICATIONS

Application	Ft. Lbs. (N.m)
Camshaft Sprocket Preload Bolt	80 (108)
Connecting Rod Cap Nut	33 (45)
Converter-To-Flexplate Bolts	[3]
Cylinder Head Bolts [1]	
Stage 1	22 (30)
Stage 2	45 (61)
Stage 3	[2] 110 (149)
Exhaust Manifold Bolts [2]	
Bolts No. 1-5	24 (33)
Bolts No. 6 & 7	17 (23)
Bolts No. 8-11	24 (33)
Fan Bolt	18 (24)
Flexplate-To-Crankshaft Bolts	55 (75)
Flywheel-To-Crankshaft Bolts	[3]
Intake Manifold Bolts [2]	
Bolts No. 1-5	24 (33)
Bolts No. 6 & 7	17 (23)
Bolts No. 8-11	24 (33)
Main Bearing Cap Bolts	
Stage 1	40 (54)
Stage 2	70 (95)
Stage 3	80 (108)
Oil Pump Retaining Bolts	
Long	17 (23)
Short	10 (14)
Pulley-To-Vibration Damper Bolts	20 (27)
Rocker Arm Bolts	21 (28)
Starter Bolts	33 (45)
Vibration Damper Bolt [4]	80 (108)
Water Pump Bolts	13 (18)
	INCH Lbs. (N.m)
Front Cover Bolts	62 (7)
Oil Pan Bolts	
1/4" X 20	114 (13)
5/16" X 18	156 (18)
Oil Pump Cover Bolts	70 (8)
Valve Cover Bolts	80 (10)

[1] – All bolts except No. 11. Tighten bolt No. 11 to 100 ft. lbs (136 N.m) *See Fig. 3.*

[2] – Tighten in sequence. *See Fig. 2.*

[3] – Information not available from manufacturer.

[4] – With bolt cleaned and threads lubricated with oil.

ENGINE SPECIFICATIONS

GENERAL SPECIFICATIONS

Application	Specification
Displacement	242 Cu. In. (4.0L)
Bore	3.88" (98.5 mm)
Stroke	3.41" (86.6 mm)
Compression Ratio	8.8:1
Fuel System	PFI
Horsepower @ RPM	
Cherokee, Comanche & Grand Cherokee	190 @ 4750
Wrangler	180 @ 4750
Torque Ft. Lbs. @ RPM	
Cherokee, Comanche & Grand Cherokee	225 @ 4000
Wrangler	220 @ 4000

CRANKSHAFT, MAIN & CONNECTING ROD BEARINGS

Application	In. (mm)
Crankshaft	
End Play	.0015-.0065 (.038-.165)
Runout	[1]
Main Bearings	
Journal Diameter	2.4996-2.5001 (63.489-63.502)
Journal Out-Of-Round	.0005 (.013)
Journal Taper	.0005 (.013)
Oil Clearance	.0010-.0025 (.025-.064)
Connecting Rod Bearings	
Journal Diameter	2.0934-2.0955 (53.170-53.230)
Journal Out-Of-Round	.0005 (.013)
Journal Taper	.0005 (.013)
Oil Clearance	.0015-.0025 (.038-.064)

[1] – Information not available from manufacturer.

CONNECTING RODS

Application	In. (mm)
Bore Diameter	
Pin Bore	.9288-.9298 (23.591-23.617)
Crankpin Bore	2.2080-2.2085 (56.083-56.096)
Center-To-Center Length	6.123-6.127 (155.52-155.62)
Maximum Bend	.003 (.08)
Maximum Twist	.006 (.15)
Side Play	.010-.019 (.25-.48)

PISTONS, PINS & RINGS

Application	In. (mm)
Pistons	
Clearance	.0013-.0021 (.033-.053)
Diameter	[1]
Pins	
Diameter	.9306-.9307 (23.637-23.640)
Piston Fit	.0004-.0006 (.010-.015)
Rod Fit	Press Fit
Rings	
No. 1	
End Gap	.010-.020 (.25-.51)
Side Clearance	.0010-.0032 (.025-.081)
No. 2	
End Gap	.010-.020 (.25-.51)
Side Clearance	.0017-.0032 (.043-.081)
No. 3 (Oil)	
End Gap	.010-.025 (.25-.64)
Side Clearance	.001-.009 (.03-.23)

[1] – Information not available from manufacturer. Replace pistons if piston clearance exceeds .004" (.10 mm).

CYLINDER BLOCK

Application	In. (mm)
Cylinder Bore	
Standard Diameter	3.8751-3.8775 (98.42-98.48)
Maximum Taper	.001 (.03)
Maximum Out-Of-Round	.001 (.03)
Minimum Deck Height	9.429-9.435 (239.49-239.64)
Maximum Warpage	.008 (.20)

VALVES & VALVE SPRINGS

Application	Specification
Intake Valves	
Face Angle	45°
Head Diameter	1.91" (48.5 mm)
Minimum Margin	.031" (.79 mm)
Minimum Refinish Length	4.822" (122.47 mm)
Stem Diameter	.312" (7.93 mm)
Valve Tip Maximum Refinish	.010" (.25 mm)
Exhaust Valves	
Face Angle	45°
Head Diameter	1.5" (38 mm)
Minimum Margin	.031" (.79 mm)
Minimum Refinish Length	4.837" (122.86 mm)
Stem Diameter	.312" (7.93 mm)
Valve Tip Maximum Refinish	.010" (.25 mm)
Valve Springs	
Free Length	1.82" (46.2 mm)
Installed Height	[1]
Out-Of-Square	[1]

	Lbs. @ In. (kg @ mm)
Pressure	
Valve Closed	66-74 @ 1.625 (29.96-33.59 @ 41.2)
Valve Open	205-220 @ 1.2 (93.07-99.88 @ 30.48)

[1] – Information not available from manufacturer.

CYLINDER HEAD

Application	Specification
Cylinder Head Height	[1]
Maximum Warpage	.008" (.20 mm)
Valve Seats	
Intake Valve	
Seat Angle	44.5°
Seat Width	.040-.060" (1.02-1.52 mm)
Maximum Seat Runout	.0025" (.064 mm)
Seat Bore Diameter	[1]
Exhaust Valve	
Seat Angle	44.5°
Seat Width	.040-.060" (1.02-1.52 mm)
Maximum Seat Runout	.0025" (.064 mm)
Seat Bore Diameter	[1]
Valve Guides	
Intake Valve	
Valve Guide Cylinder Head Bore I.D.	[1]
Valve Guide I.D.	.312" (7.9 mm)
Valve Guide Installed Height	[1]
Valve Stem-To-Guide Oil Clearance	.001-.003" (.03-.08 mm)
Exhaust Valve	
Valve Guide Cylinder Head Bore I.D.	[1]
Valve Guide I.D.	.312" (7.9 mm)
Valve Guide Installed Height	[1]
Valve Stem-To-Guide Oil Clearance	.001-.003" (.03-.08 mm)

[1] – Information not available from manufacturer.

CAMSHAFT

Application	In. (mm)
Bore Diameter	[1]
End Play [2]	0 (0)
Journal Diameter	
No. 1.	2.029-2.030 (51.54-51.56)
No. 2.	2.019-2.020 (51.28-51.31)
No. 3.	2.009-2.010 (51.03-51.05)
No. 4.	1.999-2.000 (50.78-50.80)
Journal Runout	[3]
Lobe Height	[1]
Lobe Lift	.253 (6.43)
Oil Clearance	.001-.003 (.03-.08)

[1] – Information not available from manufacturer.
[2] – Engine running.
[3] – Information not available from manufacturer. Manufacturer specifies .001" (.03 mm) maximum base circle runout.

VALVE LIFTERS

Application	In. (mm)
Bore Diameter	.9050-.9065 (22.987-23.025)
Lifter Diameter	.9040-.9045 (22.962-22.974)
Oil Clearance	.001-.0025 (.025-.063)

Cherokee, Comanche, Grand Cherokee (1993), Wrangler

SPECIFICATIONS

BELT ADJUSTMENT

Loosen rear mounting bolts of idler pulley or power steering pump (if equipped). Loosen power steering pivot bolt and lock nut (if equipped). Turn adjusting bolt to tighten belt to specification. See BELT TENSION table under BELT TENSION. Tighten bolts and lock nut to **20 ft. lbs. (27 N.m)**. For serpentine belt routing, *see Fig. 1.*

BELT TENSION

BELT TENSION
Tension in Lbs. (kg) Using Strand Tension Gauge

Application	New Belt	Used Belt
Serpentine Belt	180-200 (82-91)	140-160 (64-73)
"V" Belt	120-160 (54-73)	90-115 (41-52)

COOLING SYSTEM SPECIFICATIONS

COOLING SYSTEM SPECIFICATIONS

Application	Specification
Coolant Replacement Interval	[1] 24 months
Coolant Capacity	
Cherokee & Comanche	
2.5L	10.0 qts. (9.5L)
4.0L	12.0 qts. (11.4L)
Grand Cherokee	
Standard Cooling System	9.0 qts. (8.5L)
Heavy Duty Cooling System	10.5 qts. (9.9L)
Wrangler	
2.5L	9.0 qts. (8.5L)
4.0L	10.5 qts. (9.9L)
Pressure Cap	12-16 psi
Thermostat Opens	
Starts	195°F (90°C)
Fully Open	218°F (103°C)

[1] – Manufacturer recommends replacing original coolant at 36 months or 52,500 miles, whichever occurs first.

ELECTRIC COOLING FAN

On Cherokee and Comanche 4.0L engine and heavy-duty cooling and/or air conditioning, an auxiliary electric fan operates whenever engine temperature exceeds 190°F (88°C), or whenever air conditioner is on. If Single Board Engine Controller II (SBEC-II) detects a fan control circuitry problem, a fault code will set.

NOTE: For more information on vehicle self-diagnostics, see appropriate SELF-DIAGNOSTICS article in ENGINE PERFORMANCE.

TROUBLE SHOOTING & TESTING

Electric Cooling Fan Circuit – **1)** Ensure fuses No. 4 and 6 on Power Distribution Center (PDC), near battery, are good. Ensure fan operates. See MOTOR under COMPONENT TESTING. Remove cooling fan relay from PDC. Start engine. Using a test light, check for power at terminal No. 2 (Light Green/Red wire) of PDC. If test light does not illuminate, repair open circuit in Light Green/Red wire between terminal No. 2 and fuse No. 4.

2) Connect a jumper wire between terminal No. 2 (Light Green/Red wire) and terminal No. 4 (Light Green wire) on PDC. If fan does not operate, leave jumper wire connected. Unplug fan connector on left side of fan shroud.

3) Using a test light, check for power at Light Green wire on fan harness connector. If no power exists, repair Light Green wire between fan harness connector and terminal No. 4 on PDC. If power exists at Light Green wire, repair open circuit in Black wire on fan harness connector and ground.

4) Turn ignition off. Reconnect fan motor connector. Remove jumper wires. Reinstall relay. Connect Diagnostic Readout Box II (DRB-II) to

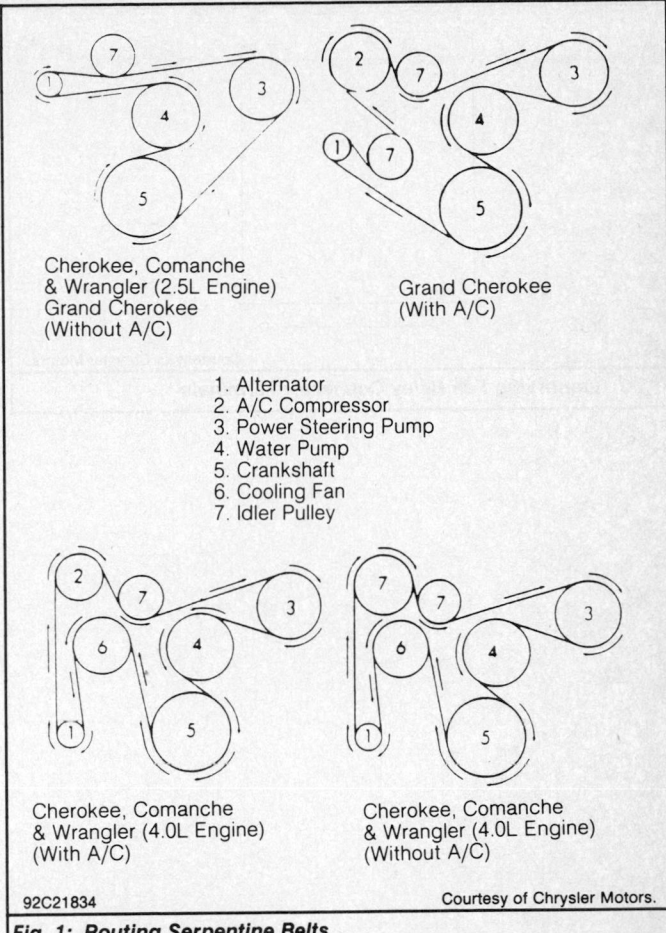

1. Alternator
2. A/C Compressor
3. Power Steering Pump
4. Water Pump
5. Crankshaft
6. Cooling Fan
7. Idler Pulley

Cherokee, Comanche & Wrangler (2.5L Engine) Grand Cherokee (Without A/C)

Grand Cherokee (With A/C)

Cherokee, Comanche & Wrangler (4.0L Engine) (With A/C)

Cherokee, Comanche & Wrangler (4.0L Engine) (Without A/C)

92C21834   Courtesy of Chrysler Motors.

Fig. 1: Routing Serpentine Belts

engine diagnostic connector. Connector is located in engine compartment, next to SBEC-II.

5) Start engine. Energize fan relay circuit by warming engine until coolant temperature is higher than **190°F (88°C)**, or by turning air conditioning on (if equipped). If relay clicks but fan does not operate, check for poor relay connections at socket. If connections are okay, test relay. See RELAY under COMPONENT TESTING.

6) If relay does not click, put DRB-II into voltmeter mode. Measure voltage at cavity A1 (Dark Blue/White wire) in relay connector. If voltage is less than 10 volts, repair open circuit in Dark Blue/White wire between cavity A1 and fuse No. 6. If voltage is 10 volts or more, turn ignition off and reconnect relay.

7) Unplug connector from SBEC-II. Examine connector. If connector is okay, turn ignition on. With DRB-II in voltmeter mode, measure voltage at terminal No. 31 on SBEC-II harness connector. If voltage is 10 volts or more, replace SBEC-II. If voltage is less than 10 volts, repair open circuit in Dark Blue/Pink wire between SBEC-II terminal No. 31 and PDC terminal No. 5.

COMPONENT TESTING

Motor – Unplug fan motor connector at left side of fan shroud. Connect a jumper wire from terminal "B" (Black wire) of fan motor connector to a known good engine ground. Using another jumper with a 25-amp in-line fuse, supply battery power to terminal "A" (Red wire) of fan motor connector. Service fan motor if it does not run.

Relay – **1)** Remove relay from Power Distribution Center (PDC). Connect a self-powered test light between terminals No. 2 and 4 on relay. *See Fig. 2.* Test light should indicate no continuity. Leave test light connected.

2) Using a jumper wire, connect relay terminal No. 5 to a good ground. Using another jumper with a 15-amp in-line fuse, supply battery power to terminal No. 1 of relay. If test light does not indicate continuity, replace relay.

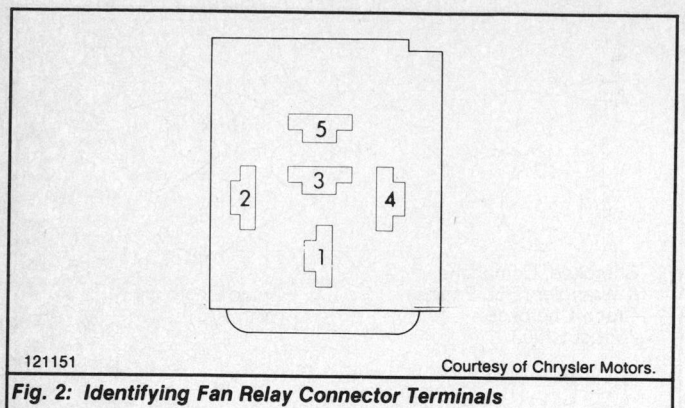

121151

Courtesy of Chrysler Motors.

Fig. 2: Identifying Fan Relay Connector Terminals

WIRING DIAGRAM

Also see appropriate chassis wiring diagram in WIRING DIAGRAMS.

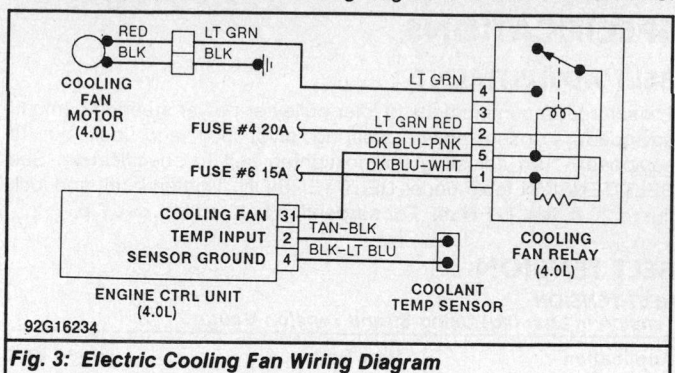

92G16234

Fig. 3: Electric Cooling Fan Wiring Diagram

Cherokee, Comanche, Grand Cherokee (1993), Wrangler

DESCRIPTION

The clutch assembly consists of a single dry-disc driven plate and a one-piece diaphragm spring-type clutch cover. The clutch is actuated through a hydraulic master cylinder and a slave cylinder.

On Cherokee, Comanche and Wrangler models, slave cylinder and clutch release bearing are combined in an assembly. Slave cylinder and clutch release bearing must be replaced as a complete unit. On Grand Cherokee models, slave cylinder and clutch release bearing are of conventional design and may be serviced separately.

ADJUSTMENTS

HYDRAULIC SYSTEM BLEEDING

Cherokee, Comanche & Wrangler – 1) Fill master cylinder reservoir with DOT 3 brake fluid. Raise and support vehicle. Attach bleeder hose to bleeder screw on bleed line of slave cylinder. *See Fig. 1.* Place other end of hose in glass container 1/2 full of brake fluid. Loosen bleeder screw while holding bleeder screw fitting.

CAUTION: DO NOT allow bleed line to bend or flex when loosening bleeder screw.

---

2) Have an assistant depress clutch pedal to the floor. Tighten bleeder screw and release clutch pedal. Repeat bleeding procedure until fluid entering container is free of bubbles. DO NOT allow reservoir to run out of fluid during bleeding. Refill clutch master cylinder reservoir.
Grand Cherokee – Bleeding procedure not available from manufacturer.

NOTE: No other adjustments are necessary or possible.

TROUBLE SHOOTING

NOTE: See TROUBLE SHOOTING article in GENERAL INFORMATION.

REMOVAL & INSTALLATION

TRANSMISSION

Removal (Cherokee, Comanche & Wrangler) – 1) Place transmission in 1st or 3rd gear. Raise and support vehicle. Drain fluid from transfer case. Support the engine with adjustable jack stand. Remove rear crossmember.
2) Disconnect transmission shift linkage, speedometer cable, transfer case vacuum lines, electrical wiring and clutch hydraulic lines. Plug hydraulic lines to prevent fluid loss and contamination. Place reference mark on drive shaft yokes and transfer case yokes for reassembly reference. Disconnect drive shafts.
3) Support transfer case with jack and lower (NOT MORE than 3 inches). Reaching up and around transmission case, move boot upward to access shift lever retainer.

NOTE: DO NOT remove shift lever from floor pan boot.

---

4) Disengage shift lever from transmission by pressing down and turning retainer counterclockwise to release it. Lift retainer out of transmission shift tower. Remove clutch housing to engine bolts. Remove transmission and transfer case.
Installation – To install, reverse removal procedure. Fill transmission with proper lubricant. Fill and bleed hydraulic clutch system. See HYDRAULIC SYSTEM BLEEDING under ADJUSTMENTS.
Removal (Grand Cherokee) – 1) Shift transmission into neutral. Raise and support vehicle. Remove skid plate. Mark drive shafts for installation reference. Remove drive shafts. Disconnect transfer case shaft linkage. Disconnect wire harness and vent hoses from transmission and transfer case. Drain fluid from transfer case.

2) Support the engine with adjustable jack stand. Support transmission on jack. Secure transmission on jack with safety chains. Remove rear crossmember. Support transfer case. Remove transfer case mounting bolts. Remove transfer case.
3) Disconnect speedometer cable, vacuum lines, and engine timing sensor. Remove clutch slave cylinder from clutch housing. Hang slave cylinder aside with wire. Lower transmission slightly (NOT MORE than 3 inches). Reaching up and around transmission case, move boot upward to access shift lever retainer.

NOTE: DO NOT remove shift lever from floor pan boot.

---

4) Disengage shift lever from transmission by pressing down and turning retainer counterclockwise to release it. Lift retainer out of transmission shift tower. Remove clutch housing-to-engine bolts. Remove transmission.
Installation – To install, reverse removal procedure. Tighten bolts to specification. See TORQUE SPECIFICATIONS table at end of article. Fill transmission with proper lubricant.

CLUTCH ASSEMBLY

Removal – Remove transmission. See TRANSMISSION. Mark clutch cover and flywheel for reassembly reference. Evenly loosen clutch cover bolts until clutch cover spring tension is released. Remove cover bolts, clutch cover and clutch disc.
Installation – Replace all worn or damaged parts. Align clutch cover with reference marks on flywheel. Using clutch alignment shaft, align clutch disc. Tighten each cover bolt a few turns at a time to specification. See TORQUE SPECIFICATIONS table at end of article.

NOTE: Flywheel cannot be resurfaced. If service is required, replace flywheel.

CLUTCH MASTER CYLINDER

Removal – Disconnect hydraulic line at master cylinder. On Grand Cherokee, disconnect hydraulic line from remote reservoir to master cylinder. Plug all hydraulic lines and openings. On all models, remove cotter pin or spring clip holding push rod on clutch pedal. Slide push rod off pedal pivot. Remove master cylinder retaining nuts. Remove master cylinder.
Installation – To install, reverse removal procedure. Bleed hydraulic system. See HYDRAULIC SYSTEM BLEEDING under ADJUSTMENTS.

CLUTCH SLAVE CYLINDER

Removal (Cherokee, Comanche & Wrangler) – 1) Drain clutch master cylinder. Disconnect line at clutch master cylinder and clutch slave cylinder lines. Remove transmission and transfer case. Remove insulator bolts and slide insulator and bracket off lines. *See Fig. 1.*

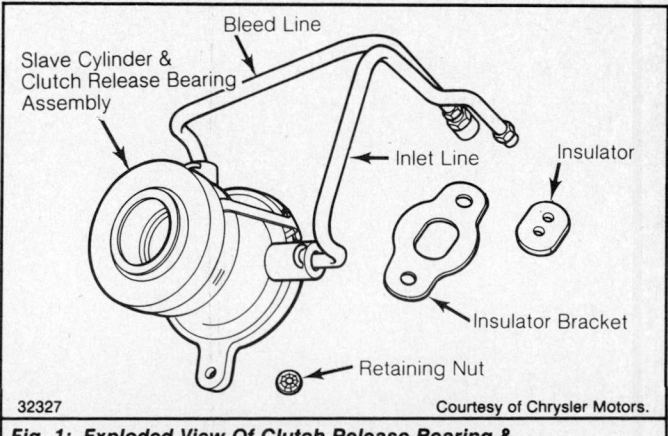

32327

Courtesy of Chrysler Motors.

Fig. 1: Exploded View Of Clutch Release Bearing & Slave Cylinder (Cherokee, Comanche & Wrangler)

2) Remove retaining nut. Pry nut upward and off mounting pin on transmission front case. Remove assembly.

Installation – To install, reverse removal procedure. Bleed hydraulic system. See HYDRAULIC SYSTEM BLEEDING under ADJUSTMENTS.

Removal & Installation (Grand Cherokee) – Disconnect hydraulic line at slave cylinder. Plug line to prevent fluid loss and contamination. Remove slave cylinder mounting bolts. Remove slave cylinder. To install, reverse removal procedure.

PILOT BEARING

Removal & Installation – Remove clutch assembly. Using slide hammer and internal puller, remove pilot bearing. To install, lubricate pilot bearing with wheel bearing grease. Using clutch alignment shaft, install pilot bearing. Reverse removal procedure to install remaining components.

OVERHAUL

CLUTCH MASTER & SLAVE CYLINDERS

NOTE: No overhaul procedures are available. Replace defective or leaking units with new parts.

TORQUE SPECIFICATIONS

TORQUE SPECIFICATIONS

Application	Ft. Lbs. (N.m)
Clutch Cover Bolt	
4-Cylinder	23 (31)
6-Cylinder	40 (54)
Clutch Housing-To-Engine Bolt	
Except Grand Cherokee	28 (38)
Grand Cherokee	45 (61)
Clutch Housing-To-Transmission Bolts	27 (37)
Crossmember-To-Frame Bolt	30 (41)
Master Cylinder Mounting Nut	19 (26)
Rear Support-To-Crossmember Bolt	33 (45)

1992 DRIVE AXLES
Axle Ratio Identification

Cherokee, Comanche, Grand Cherokee (1993), Wrangler

The axle build date and manufacturer's number are stamped on the passenger side axle tube, near housing cover. The axle assembly part number, gear ratio and identification tag are attached to the left side of the housing cover.

AXLE RATIO & IDENTIFICATION

Axle Ratio	Pinion/Ring Gear Tooth Combinations	Ring Gear Diameter
Front Axle [1]		
3.07:1	14/43	7 1/8 In. (181 mm)
3.55:1	11/39	7 1/8 In. (181 mm)
4.10:1	9/37	7 1/8 In. (181 mm)
Rear Axle		
2.72:1 [2]	18/49	8 1/2 In. (216 mm)
3.07:1 [3]	14/43	7 9/16 In. (192 mm)
3.07:1 [2]	14/43	8 1/2 In. (216 mm)
3.31:1 [2]	13/43	8 1/2 In. (216 mm)
3.54:1 [2]	13/46	8 1/2 In. (216 mm)
3.55:1 [3]	11/39	7 9/16 In. (192 mm)
3.55:1 [4]	11/39	8 1/4 In. (209 mm)
4.09:1 [2]	11/45	8 1/2 In. (216 mm)
4.10:1 [3]	9/37	7 9/16 In. (192 mm)

[1] – Model 30 axle used on all models.
[2] – Model 44 axle used on Comanche optional Metric Ton Package.
[3] – Model 35 axle used on all models.
[4] – Optional rear axle for Cherokee models only.

1992 DRIVE AXLES
Front Axles

Cherokee, Comanche, Grand Cherokee (1993), Wrangler

DESCRIPTION

Model 30 axle is used on all 4WD applications. Cherokee and Comanche utilize either Command-Trac or Selec-Trac 4WD system. Wrangler uses only Command-Trac 4WD system. Grand Cherokee uses a full time 4WD system.

Command-Trac is a part time system designed for off-road use. Command-Trac uses a vacuum operated axle disconnect mechanism to control 4WD operation.

Selec-Trac is a combination part time/full time system designed for both highway and off-road use. Transfer case shifter is used to control 4WD operation.

REMOVAL & INSTALLATION

NOTE: This article covers removal and installation, and overhaul of front axle components. For information on the differential, see the 7 1/8", 7 9/16", 8 1/4" & 8 1/2" RING GEAR article in DRIVE AXLES.

AXLE ASSEMBLY

Removal (Cherokee, Comanche & Grand Cherokee) – **1)** Raise and support vehicle under frame. Remove wheels. Remove disc brake calipers. Hang calipers aside with wire. Remove rotors and brake shields.
2) Disconnect breather tube at axle. On models with Command-Trac, remove vacuum harness from shift motor. Remove vent hose from differential housing. Remove stabilizer bar link, tie rod and drag link.
3) Remove front drive shaft. Disconnect shock absorbers and steering damper. If equipped with Anti-Lock Brake System (ABS), disconnect brake sensor.
4) Disconnect track bar. Position jack under axle. Disconnect upper and lower control arms at axle. Lower and remove axle slowly to release coil spring pressure.
Installation – Raise axle into position while guiding coil springs into position. Connect upper and lower control arms to axle. To complete installation, reverse removal procedure.
Removal (Wrangler) – **1)** Raise vehicle. Position supports under frame rails at rear of front springs. Remove wheels. Remove brake calipers and hang aside with wire. Remove brake rotors. Disconnect Command-Trac vacuum harness.
2) Mark front drive shaft and axle yoke for reassembly. Disconnect front drive shaft at axle yoke. Secure shaft to frame with wire. Disconnect tie rods at steering knuckles. Remove shock absorbers. Remove retaining nuts and bolts from track bars at axle shaft tube brackets. Disconnect breather tube at axle. Disconnect stabilizer bar link bolts at spring brackets.
3) Support axle and raise jack slightly to relieve spring tension. Remove spring "U" bolts and brackets. Loosen nuts attaching spring rear shackles to springs. Remove bolts attaching spring front shackles. Lower springs to floor. Remove axle assembly.
Installation – To install, reverse removal procedure.

AXLE SHAFT

Removal – **1)** Raise and support vehicle. Remove wheels, caliper and rotor. Remove cotter pin, lock nut and axle hub nut.
2) Remove hub-to-steering knuckle bolts. Remove hub and rotor shield from steering knuckle. Remove left axle shaft from axle tube. On models with Command-Trac, disconnect vacuum harness. Remove vacuum motor housing. *See Fig. 1.*
3) Remove right axle shaft from axle tube. Ensure shift collar remains on intermediate shaft.

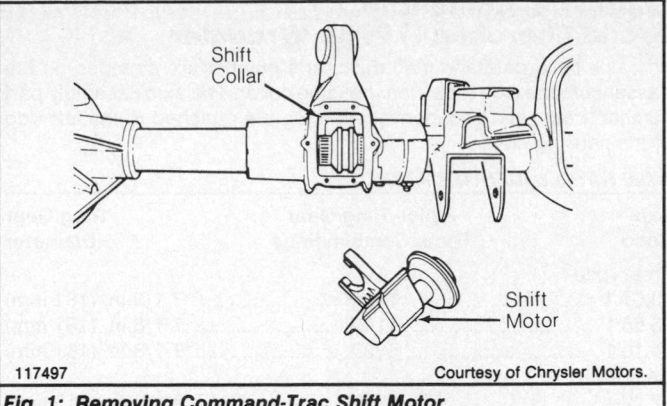

Fig. 1: *Removing Command-Trac Shift Motor*

Installation – **1)** Install right and left axle shafts in axle tubes. On models with Command-Trac, ensure shift collar is correctly positioned on intermediate axle shaft.
2) Ensure outer axle shaft is completely engaged with shift collar and joined with intermediate axle shaft. *See Fig. 1.* Install shift motor. Ensure fork engages with shaft collar.
3) On all models, lubricate hub bore in steering knuckle with wheel bearing grease. Install rotor shield. Install hub on axle. Slide hub into steering knuckle hub bore. Tighten hub bolts. Install washer and hub nut. Tighten hub nut to specification. See TORQUE SPECIFICATIONS table at end of article. Install retainer and cotter pin. Install rotor, caliper and wheel. Lower vehicle.

INTERMEDIATE AXLE SHAFT

Removal & Installation (Cherokee, Comanche & Wrangler) – Remove outer axle. Remove differential cover and drain fluid. Remove intermediate shaft retaining clip. *See Fig. 2.* Remove intermediate shaft. To install, reverse removal procedure. Fill differential housing with 2.5 pts. (1.2L) of SAE 75W-90 gear oil.

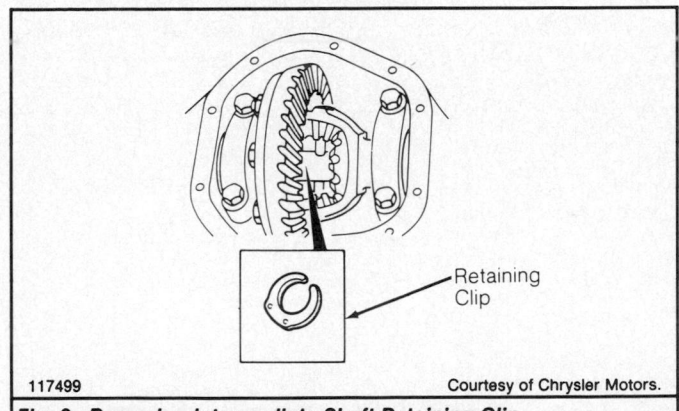

Fig. 2: *Removing Intermediate Shaft Retaining Clip*

HUB & BEARING

Removal – Raise and support vehicle. Remove wheel, caliper and rotor. Remove cotter pin, nut retainer, hub nut and washer. Remove hub-to-knuckle bolts. Remove hub from steering knuckle. *See Fig. 3.*
Installation – Apply wheel bearing grease to hub bore in steering knuckle and install hub and bearings. To complete installation, reverse removal procedure.

NOTE: Hub bearings CANNOT be serviced. If defective, the complete hub assembly must be replaced.

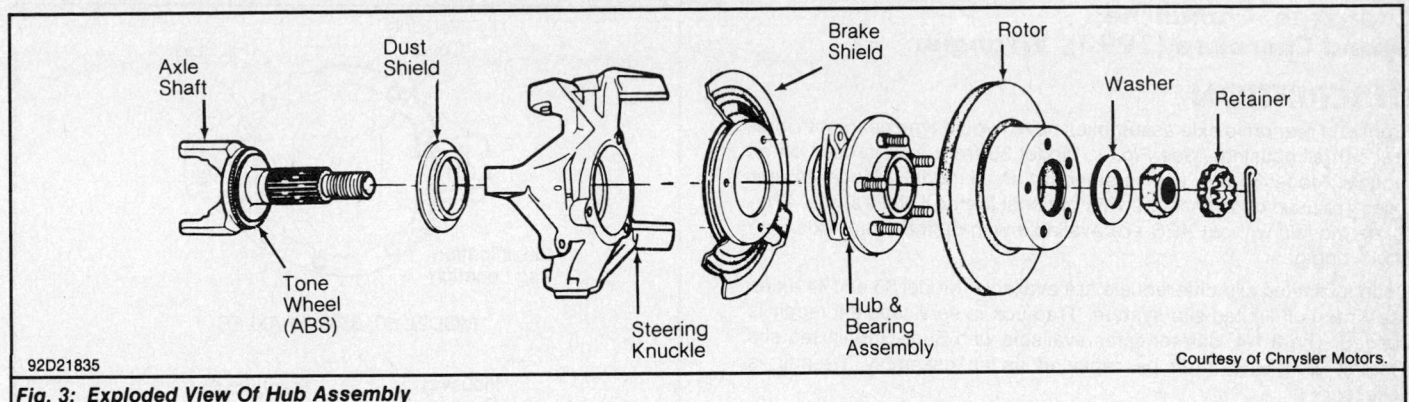

Fig. 3: Exploded View Of Hub Assembly

Courtesy of Chrysler Motors.

OVERHAUL

AXLE SHAFT OUTER "U" JOINT

Remove axle shaft. Remove bearing cap and snap rings. Press out bearings caps from yoke. To install, reverse removal procedure. Pack replacement bearing caps 1/3 full of bearing grease.

TORQUE SPECIFICATIONS

TORQUE SPECIFICATIONS

Applications	Ft. Lbs. (N.m)
Cherokee & Comanche	
Axle Yoke Nut	210 (285)
Hub Bolt	75 (102)
Hub Nut	175 (237)
Lower Control Arm Bolt	133 (180)
Track Bar Axle Bracket Nut	63 (85)
Track Bar Frame Nut	55 (75)
"U" Joint Strap Bolt	14 (19)
Upper Control Arm Bolt	55 (75)
Grand Cherokee	
Hub Bolt	75 (102)
Hub Nut	175 (237)
Spring Pivot Bolt	100 (136)
Track Bar Axle Bracket Nut	74 (100)
Track Bar Ball Stud Nut	60 (81)
Upper Control Arm Bolt	55 (75)
Wrangler	
Axle Yoke Nut	210 (285)
Frame Bracket	105 (142)
Hub Bolt	75 (102)
Hub Nut	175 (237)
Shackle Bolt	95 (129)
Track Bar Axle Nut	74 (100)
Track Bar Frame Nut/Bolt	125 (169)
"U" Bolt At Axle Tube Retaining Nut	90 (122)
"U" Joint Strap Bolt	14 (19)
	INCH Lbs. (N.m)
Vacuum Shift Motor Bolt	98 (11)

1992 DRIVE AXLES
7 1/8", 7 9/16", 8 1/4" & 8 1/2" Ring Gears

**Cherokee, Comanche,
Grand Cherokee (1993), Wrangler**

DESCRIPTION

Front and rear drive axle assemblies have hypoid type gears with integral carrier housings. *See Fig. 1.* Model 30 front axle is used on all models. Model 35 rear axle is standard on all models. Model 44 rear axles are used on Comanche with optional Metric Ton Package. Cherokee models without ABS are available with optional rear axle with 8 1/4" ring gear.

Optional limited slip differentials are available. Model 35 and 44 axles use Trac-Lok limited slip system. Trac-Lok is serviceable if repair is needed. The 8 1/4" differential is available with Sure-Grip limited slip system. Sure-Grip must be replaced as an assembly if repair is necessary.

AXLE RATIO & IDENTIFICATION

Axle build date and manufacturer number are stamped on passenger-side axle tube near housing cover. Axle assembly part number, gear ratio and identification tag is attached to housing cover bolts. See AXLE RATIO & IDENTIFICATION table. *See Fig. 2.*

AXLE RATIO & IDENTIFICATION

Axle Ratio	Pinion/Ring Gear Tooth Combinations	Ring Gear Diameter
Front Axle [1]		
3.07:1	14/43	7 1/8 In. (181 mm)
3.55:1	11/39	7 1/8 In. (181 mm)
4.10:1	9/37	7 1/8 In. (181 mm)
Rear Axle		
2.72:1 [2]	18/49	8 1/2 In. (216 mm)
3.07:1 [3]	14/43	7 9/16 In. (192 mm)
3.07:1 [2]	14/43	8 1/2 In. (216 mm)
3.31:1 [2]	13/43	8 1/2 In. (216 mm)
3.54:1 [2]	13/46	8 1/2 In. (216 mm)
3.55:1 [3]	11/39	7 9/16 In. (192 mm)
3.55:1 [4]	11/39	8 1/4 In. (209 mm)
4.09:1 [2]	11/45	8 1/2 In. (216 mm)
4.10:1 [3]	9/37	7 9/16 In. (192 mm)

[1] – Model 30 axle used on all models.
[2] – Model 44 axle used on Comanche optional Metric Ton Package.
[3] – Model 35 axle used on all models.
[4] – Optional rear axle for Cherokee models only.

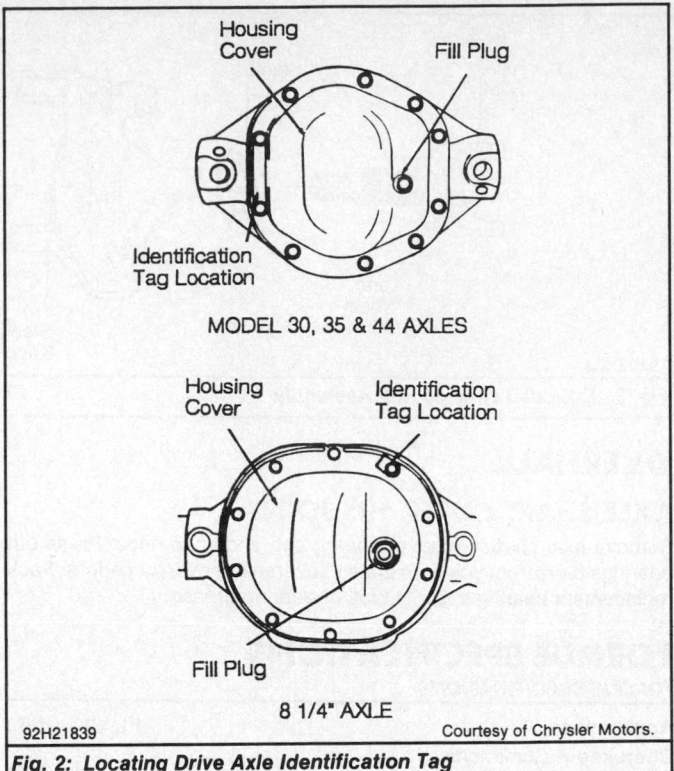

MODEL 30, 35 & 44 AXLES

8 1/4" AXLE

92H21839   Courtesy of Chrysler Motors.

Fig. 2: Locating Drive Axle Identification Tag

REMOVAL & INSTALLATION

REAR AXLE SHAFT, BEARING, SEALS & RETAINER

NOTE: To service front axle shaft, bearings, seals and retainer, see FRONT AXLES article.

Removal – 1) Raise and support vehicle. Remove rear wheel(s). Remove brake drum. Clean axle housing cover. Loosen cover bolts and drain oil. Remove cover.

2) Remove differential pinion-shaft lock screw or spring clips. Remove pinion shaft from differential. Push axle in. Remove "C" clip from axle

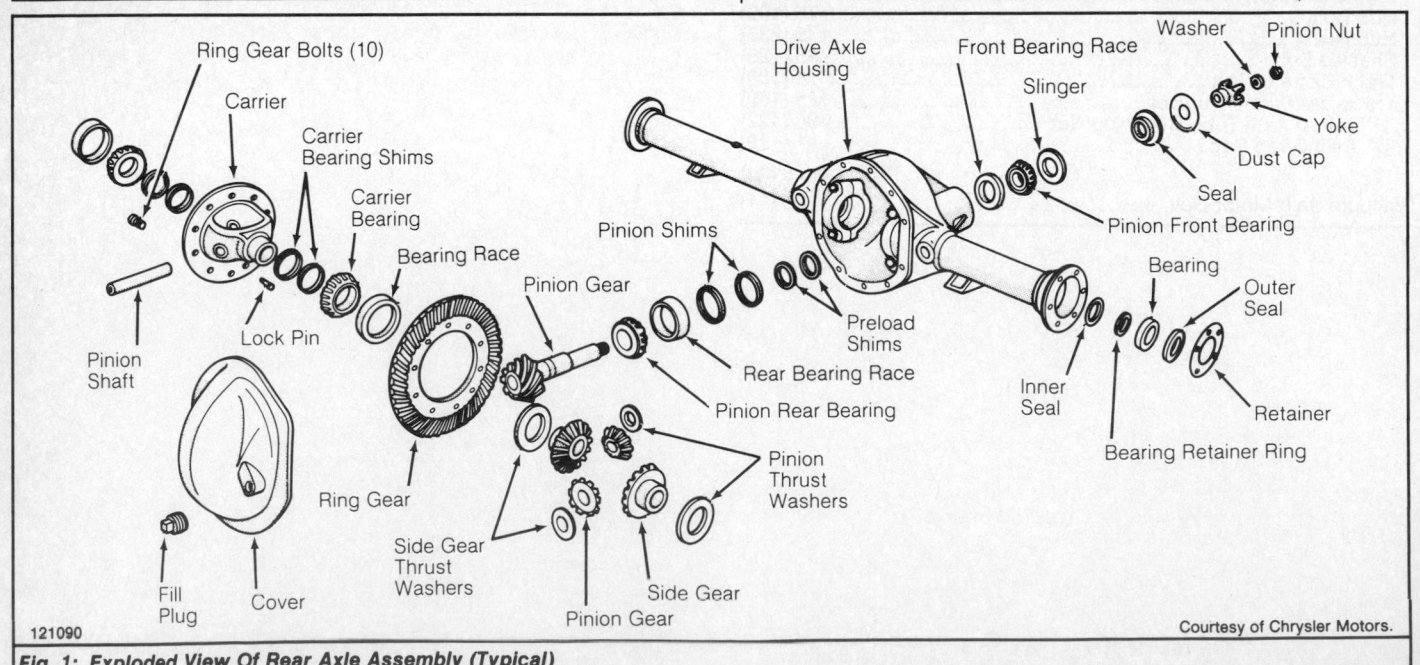

121090

Fig. 1: Exploded View Of Rear Axle Assembly (Typical)

Courtesy of Chrysler Motors.

1992 DRIVE AXLES
7 1/8", 7 9/16", 8 1/4" & 8 1/2" Ring Gears (Cont.)

JEEP
7-5

at pinion gear. Remove axle from tube. Remove axle shaft seal and bearing from axle tube.

Installation – **1)** Grease bearing and install in axle tube. Apply wheel bearing grease to axle shaft seal. Install seal in axle tube. Install axle shaft.

2) Install axle "C" clip. Pull axle out to seat "C" clip. Install pinion shaft. Install lock screw and tighten to specification. Install pinion shaft spring clips (if equipped). Apply RTV to axle housing cover. Tighten cover bolts to specification. See TORQUE SPECIFICATIONS table at end of article. Fill with gear oil.

NOTE: On vehicles with Trac-Lok (limited slip) differentials, slowly drive vehicle in 10-12 "figure 8" patterns to distribute lubricant to clutch and bearing assembly.

PINION SEAL & YOKE

Removal – **1)** Raise and support vehicle. Remove wheels and brake rotor/drums. Stamp or paint a reference mark at rear propeller shaft to axle yoke. Disconnect and remove propeller shaft. Rotate yoke three or four times.

2) Measure amount of torque needed (in INCH lbs.) to rotate pinion gear. Record torque reading for installation procedure. Remove pinion nut and discard. DO NOT reuse nut.

3) Index mark yoke-to-pinion position for installation. Remove pinion yoke. Using Universal Gear Puller (J-22888), remove yoke. Remove pinion seal, and wipe surface of seal bore clean.

Installation – **1)** Coat pinion seal with axle oil and install. Align and install yoke on pinion shaft. On Cherokee, Comanche and Wrangler axles, install NEW pinion nut and tighten only enough to remove end play. DO NOT tighten pinion nut further yet.

CAUTION: DO NOT overtighten or loosen and retighten pinion nut. If required preload torque is exceeded, the collapsible pinion spacer will have to replaced and pinion preload reset.

2) Place an INCH-pound torque wrench on pinion nut. Rotate pinion and note rotating torque. Hold yoke with Yoke Support Wrench (J-8614-1). Tighten pinion nut until preload torque is same as amount recorded during removal, plus 5 INCH lbs. (.56 N.m). Pinion nut torque should equal or exceed torque specification. See TORQUE SPECIFICATIONS table at end of article.

3) Align and install propeller shaft. Tighten "U" joint clamp bolts. Install brake drum/rotors and wheels. Tighten lug nuts to specification. See TORQUE SPECIFICATIONS table. Check oil level.

DRIVE AXLE HOUSING

Removal – **1)** Raise and support vehicle on frame rails. Remove wheels. Index mark propeller shaft and axle yoke for installation reference. Remove propeller shaft.

2) Disconnect rear track bar (if equipped) at axle bracket. Remove axle vent tube at axle. Disconnect parking brake cables at equalizer (rear axle). Remove shock absorbers. Disconnect brake hose(s).

3) On Cherokee, Comanche and Grand Cherokee, support axle housing. Disconnect upper and lower control arms at axle. Lower and remove assembly to release coil spring pressure. Remove coil springs. Lower and remove axle housing assembly from vehicle.

4) On Wrangler, loosen, but DO NOT remove, bolts attaching spring eyes to frame brackets and shackles. Support axle housing. Remove spring "U" bolts and tie plates. Raise axle housing just enough to relieve weight from springs.

5) Remove bolts attaching springs to frame bracket and shackles. Lower springs to the floor. Lower jack slowly, and remove axle housing assembly from vehicle.

Installation – Align spring mounting points, and place axle in position. To install, reverse removal procedure.

DIFFERENTIAL CARRIER & PINION

Removal (Except Cherokee 8 1/4" Ring Gear) – **1)** Raise and support vehicle. Remove axle housing cover and drain oil. Index mark

drive axle and propeller shaft yokes for installation. Remove propeller shaft.

2) Remove wheels, brake rotor/drums and axle shafts. Mount Housing Spreader (J-24385-01) on axle housing. Mount Dial Indicator (J-8001). Spread housing enough to remove differential carrier. *See Fig. 3.*

CAUTION: DO NOT spread housing more than .02" (.5 mm) or damage to housing may result.

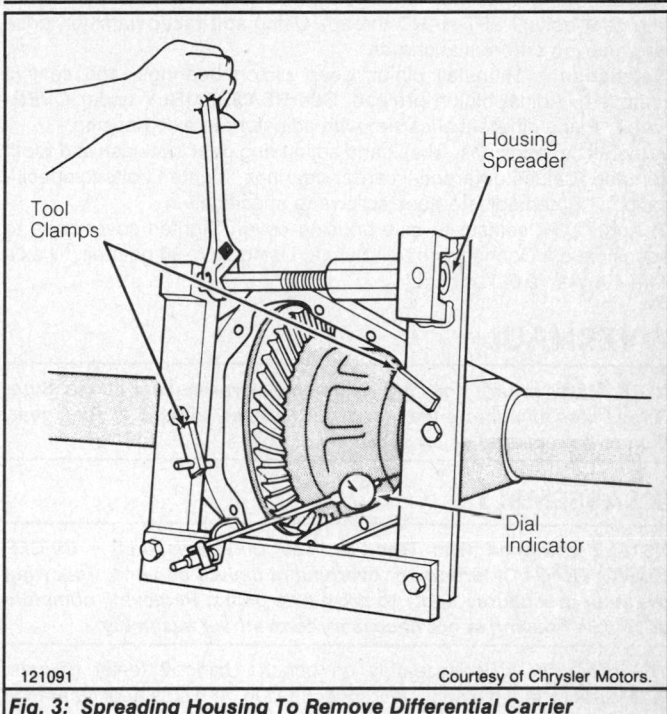

121091   Courtesy of Chrysler Motors.

Fig. 3: Spreading Housing To Remove Differential Carrier

3) Index mark bearing caps for installation reference. Loosen bearing caps until almost out. Pry differential carrier loose. Remove bearing caps. Remove differential carrier. Remove housing spreader. Check pinion preload and remove pinion gear assembly. See PINION SEAL & YOKE.

Installation – **1)** Install pinion gear, pinion bearings and seal (if removed), and adjust pinion preload. See REASSEMBLY under OVERHAUL. Spread housing as during removal.

2) Place differential carrier with bearing races and shims in axle housing. Using a mallet, tap outer edges of drive axle bearing races to seat differential carrier. Remove housing spreader.

3) Install bearing caps. Tighten bolts to specification. See TORQUE SPECIFICATIONS table at end of article. Check and adjust ring gear backlash and tooth contact. If pinion gear, bearings or seal was serviced, adjust pinion preload.

4) Apply RTV sealant to axle housing cover. Tighten cover bolts. Connect propeller shaft. Fill axle with 2.5 pts. (1.2L) 75W-90 gear oil.

NOTE: For differentials with Trac-Lok or Sure-Grip, add friction modifier (limited slip additive).

Removal (Cherokee 8 1/4" Ring Gear) – **1)** Raise and support vehicle. Remove wheels and brake drums. Mark propeller shaft for reassembly. Remove propeller shaft. Drain oil and remove housing cover. Remove pinion shaft lock screw. Remove pinion shaft.

2) Push axle shafts in and remove "C" clips. Remove axles. Measure and record differential side play, ring gear runout and pinion gear preload.

3) Mark differential gear and carrier at point of maximum runout. Side play should not exist. If ring gear runout exceeds .005" (.13 mm), replace differential carrier.

4) Remove pinion yoke and seal. Mark side bearing caps and axle housing for reassembly. Remove adjuster locks. Loosen but do not remove bearing caps. Insert Hex Adjuster (C-4164) through axle tube and loosen hex adjuster on each side.

5) Remove bearing caps, adjusters and differential carrier. Keep all bearing races, bearings and adjusters together. Using brass drift, hammer pinion shaft out of housing.

6) Drive pinion bearing races out of housing. Remove shim(s) from behind rear races, and record thickness. Remove bearing from pinion shaft using Bearing Puller (C-293-PA) and Bearing Remover Adapter (C-293-42).

7) Mount differential carrier in soft-jawed vise. Remove and discard ring gear bolts (LEFT-HAND thread). Using soft-faced hammer, drive ring gear off differential carrier.

Installation – 1) Install pinion gear, pinion bearings, and seal (if removed). Adjust pinion preload. See REASSEMBLY under OVER-HAUL. Place differential carrier with adjusters in axle housing.

2) Install bearing caps. Check and adjust ring gear backlash and tooth contact. Preload differential carrier bearings. Tighten bolts to specification. Tighten adjuster lock screws to specification.

3) Apply RTV sealant to axle housing cover. Tighten cover bolts to specification. Connect propeller shaft. Using 75W-90 gear oil, fill axle with 4.4 pts. (2.0L) of fluid.

OVERHAUL

NOTE: Manufacturer does not recommend overhaul of optional Sure-Grip limited slip differential used on Cherokee with 8 1/4" Ring gear. It must be replaced as an assembly.

DISASSEMBLY

NOTE: If equipped with Trac-Lok, see DIFFERENTIALS – SPICER (DANA) TRAC-LOK article for overhaul of limited slip unit. Following overhaul procedures apply to drive axle gears. Removing complete drive axle housing is not necessary to overhaul assembly.

1) Place drive axle assembly on bench. Using 2 feeler gauges, measure carrier side gear clearance. *See Fig. 4.* If side gear clearance exceeds specification, replace both side gear thrust washers. See SIDE GEAR CLEARANCE SPECIFICATIONS table.

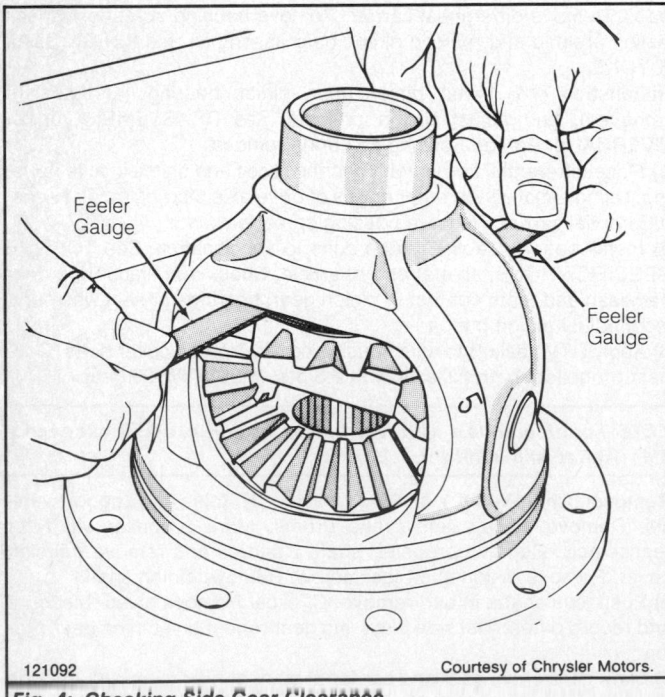

121092   Courtesy of Chrysler Motors.

Fig. 4: Checking Side Gear Clearance

SIDE GEAR CLEARANCE SPECIFICATIONS

Application	Maximum Clearance In. (mm)
Models 30 & 44	.006 (.15)
Model 35	.007 (.18)
8 1/4" Ring Gear	[1]

[1] - Specification is not available from manufacturer.

2) Remove and discard ring gear bolts (LEFT-HAND thread on Cherokee 8 1/4" rear axle). Remove ring gear. Remove pinion gears and thrust washers. Remove side gears and thrust washers.

3) On all axles, remove yoke nut, washer and pinion yoke. Keep pinion nut for pinion depth adjustment slinger during reassembly. Remove pinion gear, pinion bearings and preload shims. Discard collapsible spacer.

4) On all axles, remove pinion seal and rear pinion bearing race. Remove and retain pinion depth shim located under rear bearing race. Remove pinion front bearing race. Press off pinion gear rear bearing from pinion gear using Bearing Press Plate (J-22912-01) and hydraulic press. *See Fig. 5.* On front axles, remove inner axle housing seals.

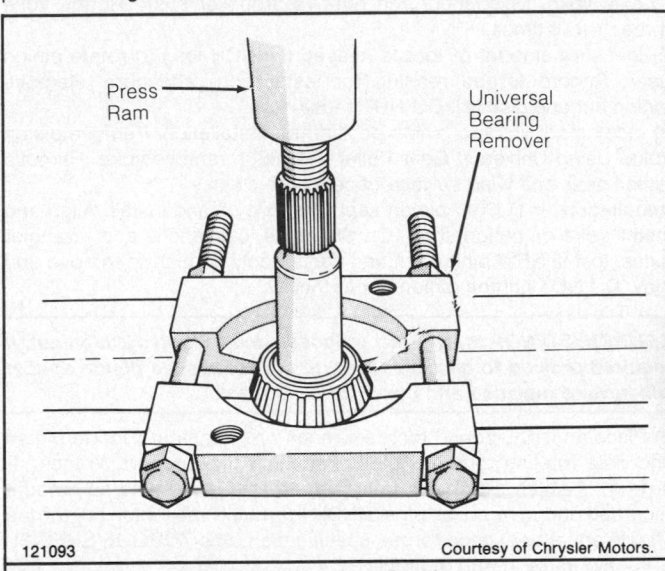

Press → Ram

Universal Bearing Remover

121093   Courtesy of Chrysler Motors.

Fig. 5: Pressing Off Pinion Gear Rear Bearing

CLEANING & INSPECTION

Clean and inspect all parts. Replace any worn, cracked, chipped or broken parts. Replace ring and pinion gears as a complete set if either gear is worn or damaged. If necessary, axle and differential pinion gears must be replaced as a complete set. Inspect carrier case for wear and cracks, and replace it if necessary.

REASSEMBLY

NOTE: Ensure correct shims are chosen to obtain proper ring gear backlash and bearing preload before reassembly. See ADJUST-MENTS.

Pinion Gear – 1) Install oil slinger (front axle). Press rear bearing on pinion gear shaft. Place original shim (or see ADJUSTMENTS) in rear bearing bore, and install rear bearing race.

NOTE: Chamfered side of shim must be installed toward bottom of rear bearing bore.

2) On all axles, install front bearing race into housing. Install pinion gear. Install front bearing over pinion gear. Apply oil to seal. Install seal, yoke, washer and original pinion nut. Tighten nut to remove bearing end play only.

3) Remove original pinion nut, washer, yoke and front bearing. Install NEW collapsible spacer on pinion. Reinstall components and front oil slinger (if equipped) in order using NEW pinion nut.

1992 DRIVE AXLES
7 1/8", 7 9/16", 8 1/4" & 8 1/2" Ring Gears (Cont.)

JEEP
7-7

4) Preload pinion bearing. See PINION SEAL & YOKE under REMOVAL & INSTALLATION. Using an INCH-pound torque wrench, check pinion bearing preload by measuring torque needed to rotate pinion gear. Ensure pinion bearing preload is **15-35 INCH lbs. (1.3-4.0 N.m)**. If preload is not within specification, see PINION BEARING PRELOAD under ADJUSTMENTS.

Differential Carrier – 1) Assemble side gears with thrust washers and install into carrier. Replace side gear thrust washers if one or both side clearance checked during disassembly was greater than specification. See SIDE GEAR CLEARANCE SPECIFICATIONS table under DISASSEMBLY.

2) Install carrier pinion gears and thrust washers into carrier. Using Bearing Puller (J-22888) and Thrust Pad (J-22888-9), remove carrier bearings. *See Fig. 6.* Note if shims are used between carrier bearing and carrier.

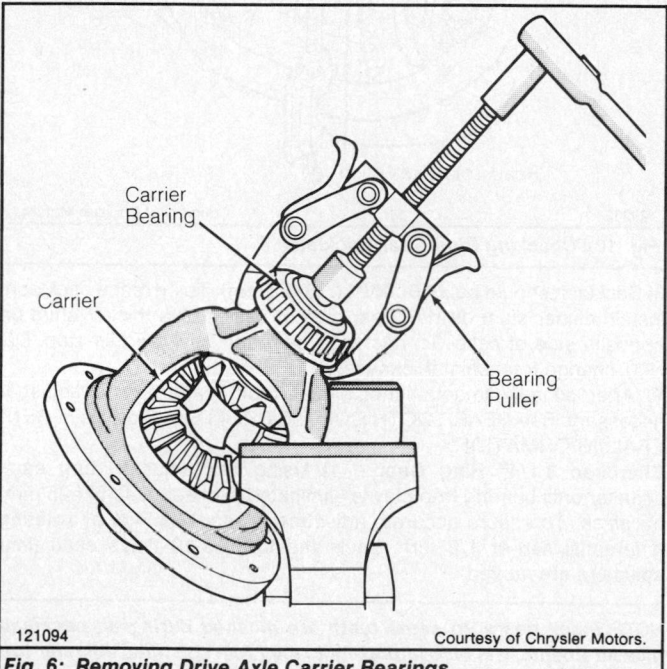

121094   Courtesy of Chrysler Motors.
Fig. 6: Removing Drive Axle Carrier Bearings

3) Install shims (if equipped), and press carrier bearings onto carrier. Using heat lamp, heat ring gear to 250°F (121°C). Install ring gear on carrier. Install NEW ring gear bolts (LEFT-HAND thread on Cherokee with 8 1/4" rear axle).

4) Tighten ring gear bolts to specification. To complete reassembly, see DIFFERENTIAL CARRIER & PINION under REMOVAL & INSTALLATION. Check ring gear backlash. See RING GEAR BACKLASH under ADJUSTMENTS.

ADJUSTMENTS

NOTE: Ring and pinion gears are serviced as matched set only. They are identified by numbers etched on gear and pinion. See Fig. 7. First 2 numbers identify matched set. Second number on pinion gear is pinion depth variance. This number indicates amount (in thousandths of an inch) gear set varied from standard setting. See PINION GEAR STANDARD DEPTH SPECIFICATIONS table.

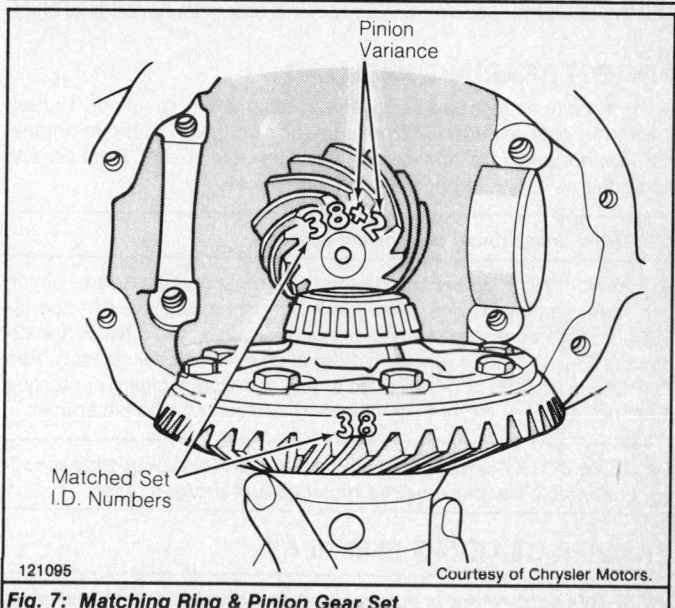

121095   Courtesy of Chrysler Motors.
Fig. 7: Matching Ring & Pinion Gear Set

PINION GEAR STANDARD DEPTH SPECIFICATIONS

Application	Standard Depth In. (mm)
Front Axle (Models 30)	2.250 (57.15)
Rear Axle	
Model 35	2.095 (53.29)
Model 44	2.625 (66.67)
8 1/4" Ring Gear	1

¹ – Specification is not available from manufacturer.

OLD PINION MARKING	NEW PINION MARKING								
	−4	−3	−2	−1	+0	+1	+2	+3	+4
+4	+0.008	+0.007	+0.006	+0.005	+0.004	+0.003	+0.002	+0.001	0
+3	+0.007	+0.006	+0.005	+0.004	+0.003	+0.002	+0.001	0	−0.001
+2	+0.006	+0.005	+0.004	+0.003	+0.002	+0.001	0	−0.001	−0.002
+1	+0.005	+0.004	+0.003	+0.002	+0.001	0	−0.001	−0.002	−0.003
0	+0.004	+0.003	+0.002	+0.001	0	−0.001	−0.002	−0.003	−0.004
−1	+0.003	+0.002	+0.001	0	−0.001	−0.002	−0.003	−0.004	−0.005
−2	+0.002	+0.001	0	−0.001	−0.002	−0.003	−0.004	−0.005	−0.006
−3	+0.001	0	−0.001	−0.002	−0.003	−0.004	−0.005	−0.006	−0.007
−4	0	−0.001	−0.002	−0.003	−0.004	−0.005	−0.006	−0.007	−0.008

Courtesy of Chrysler Motors.
Fig. 8: Selecting Correct Pinion Starting Shim From Pinion Variance Chart

JEEP
7-8

1992 DRIVE AXLES
7 1/8", 7 9/16", 8 1/4" & 8 1/2" Ring Gears (Cont.)

DETERMINING CORRECT PINION STARTING SHIM

1) If original ring and pinion is being installed, use original shim. If new parts (gear set) is being installed, use following steps to determine best starting shim thickness.

2) Check numbers etched on drive pinion and ring gear. Measure thickness of original pinion shim. Note variance number on pinion gear. *See Fig. 7.* Note where old and new pinion marking columns intersect on chart. *See Fig. 8.*

3) Intersecting figure represents amount needed to add or subtract from original shim. For example, if old pinion is +1 and new pinion is -3, intersecting figure is +.004" (+.10 mm). Add this amount to original shim. If old pinion is -3 and new pinion is -2, intersecting figure is -.001" (-.025 mm). *See Fig. 8.* Subtract this amount from original shim.

PINION BEARING PRELOAD

1) Apply oil to seal. Install seal, yoke, washer and original nut. Tighten pinion nut only enough to remove bearing end play. Remove original nut, washer and yoke and install new collapsible spacer. Reassemble components, including oil slinger (if equipped).

CAUTION: Never reuse collapsible spacer.

---

2) Place an INCH-pound torque wrench on pinion nut. Rotate pinion and note rotating torque. Hold yoke with Yoke Support Wrench (J-8614-1). Tighten pinion nut until preload torque is 15-25 INCH lbs. (2-3 N.m). Pinion nut torque should equal or exceed specification. See TORQUE SPECIFICATIONS table at end of article. If pinion nut torque does not equal or exceed specification, replace collapsible spacer.

CAUTION: DO NOT overtighten pinion nut. If preload torque is exceeded, collapsible spacer must be replaced and preload reset.

CARRIER BEARING END PLAY

NOTE: This adjustment is not required on Cherokee 8 1/4" rear axle.

---

1) Place bearing race over each carrier bearing. Install carrier assembly (without ring gear) into axle housing. Install a .142" (3.60 mm) shim on outer side of each carrier bearing race.

2) Install bearing caps and tighten bolts finger tight. Mount dial indicator to housing. *See Fig. 9.* Using a pry bar between shims and housing, move assembly to one side. Zero dial indicator. Pry assembly to opposite side. Record indicator reading. DO NOT zero or read indicator while prying.

3) Indicator reading (when divided by 2; one for each side) is thickness of shims required. Shims are available in .002" (.050 mm) increments.

4) When all side play is eliminated, check drive gear face of carrier for runout by rotating carrier and reading dial indicator. Runout should not exceed .002" (.050 mm). Remove carrier from housing, and retain shims. *See Fig. 9.*

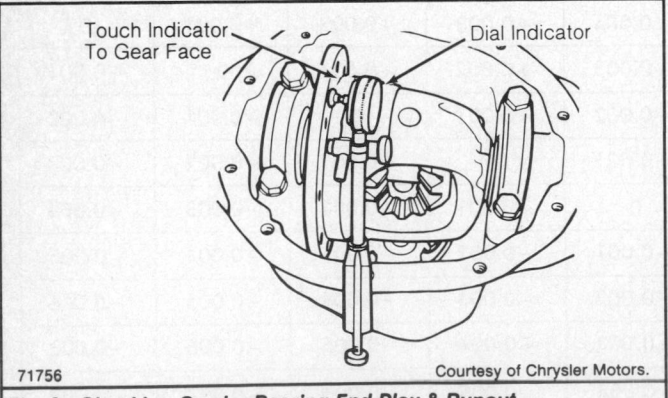

71756   Courtesy of Chrysler Motors.

Fig. 9: Checking Carrier Bearing End Play & Runout

RING GEAR BACKLASH

All Except Cherokee 8 1/4" Ring Gear – 1) Install carrier assembly into housing using shims selected to remove end play. Tighten bearing cap bolts evenly to specification.

2) Attach a dial indicator to housing so button of indicator contacts drive side of ring gear tooth. Rock ring gear, and note backlash. *See Fig. 10.*

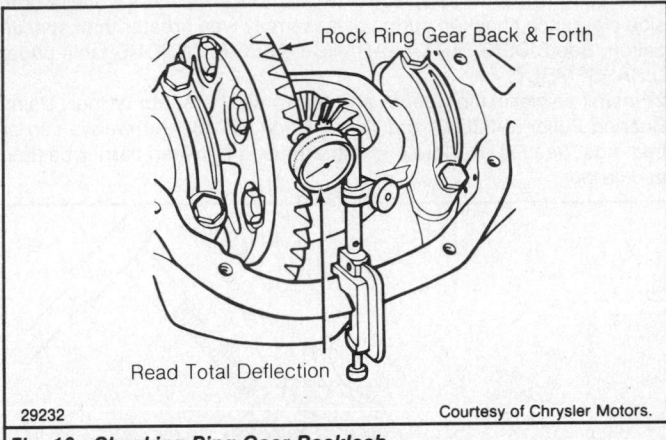

Rock Ring Gear Back & Forth

Read Total Deflection

29232   Courtesy of Chrysler Motors.

Fig. 10: Checking Ring Gear Backlash

3) Backlash should be .005-.009" (.13-.23 mm). To increase backlash, install thinner shim on ring gear side of case and a thicker shim on opposite side of case. To decrease backlash, reverse this step. DO NOT change total shim thickness.

4) After all adjustments, check gear tooth pattern, and adjust if necessary. See GEAR TOOTH CONTACT PATTERNS article in GENERAL INFORMATION.

Cherokee 8 1/4" Ring Gear – 1) Using hex adjuster, turn each adjuster until bearing free play is eliminated with about .010" (.25 mm) backlash. To ensure accurate adjustment, seat bearings by rotating differential carrier 1/2 turn, back and forth, 5-10 times each time adjusters are moved.

NOTE: Index gears so same teeth are meshed during all backlash measurements. It is also important to maintain specified adjuster torque to obtain accurate differential bearing preload.

---

2) Mount dial indicator on flange. Position indicator stem against drive side of ring gear. Check backlash every 90 degrees to find point of minimum backlash. Mark each position so backlash readings will be taken with same teeth meshed. Rotate ring gear to point of minimum backlash.

3) Tighten each adjuster to 10 ft. lbs. (14 N.m). Seat bearings as in step 1. Measure backlash. If necessary, back out right or left adjuster and turn in right or left adjuster until backlash is .003-.004" (.08-.10 mm). Tighten and seat carrier bearings each time adjusters are moved.

4) Tighten bearing cap bolts to 100 ft. lbs. (136 N.m). Using hex adjuster, tighten right adjuster to 70 ft. lbs. (95 N.m). Seat bearings, and continue to tighten adjuster until torque remains constant at 70 ft. lbs. (95 N.m).

5) Check backlash again with indicator. If backlash is not between .005-.008" (.13-.20 mm), increase torque on right adjuster and seat bearings. Continue until backlash is .005-.008" (.13-.20 mm). Tighten left adjuster to 70 ft. lbs. (95 N.m), and seat bearings. With adjustments completed, install adjuster locks. Make sure lock teeth are engaged in adjuster threads. Tighten lock bolts to specification.

6) After all adjustments, check gear tooth pattern and adjust if necessary. See GEAR TOOTH CONTACT PATTERNS article in GENERAL INFORMATION.

1992 DRIVE AXLES
7 1/8", 7 9/16", 8 1/4" & 8 1/2" Ring Gears (Cont.)

JEEP
7-9

CARRIER BEARING PRELOAD

NOTE: Pre-loading carrier bearings may change backlash setting. Recheck backlash and adjust as necessary.

1) Preload carrier bearings by adding **.004" (.10 mm)** to each existing shim. Mount Housing Spreader (J-24385-01) on axle housing. Mount Dial Indicator (J-8001). Spread housing enough to remove differential. *See Fig. 3.*

CAUTION: DO NOT spread housing more than .02" (.5 mm), or damage to housing may result.

2) Position carrier assembly into axle housing bearing bores. Tap bearing races until fully seated in housing. Remove housing spreader. Install bearing caps, aligning marks made at disassembly. Install and tighten bolts. Recheck ring gear backlash.
Cherokee 8 1/4" Ring Gear – Carrier bearings are preloaded during backlash adjustment. See RING GEAR BACKLASH.

TORQUE SPECIFICATIONS

TORQUE SPECIFICATIONS

Application	Ft. Lbs. (N.m)
Axle Housing Cover	20 (27)
Differential Carrier Bearing Caps	
7 1/8" & 7 9/16" Ring Gear	57 (77)
8 1/4" Ring Gear	100 (136)
8 1/2" Ring Gear	80 (108)
Leaf Spring Front Eye Bolts	105 (142)
Leaf Spring Shackle Bolts	95 (129)
Leaf Spring "U" Bolt Nuts	90 (122)
Pinion Yoke Nut	
Except 8 1/4" Ring Gear	200 (271)
8 1/4" Ring Gear	210 (285)
Propeller Shaft "U" Joint Clamp Bolts	14 (19)
Ring Gear Bolts	
Except 8 1/4" Ring Gear	80 (108)
8 1/4" Ring Gear	70 (95)
Wheel Lug Nuts	75 (102)

	INCH Lbs. (N.m)
Adjuster Lock Screws	
Cherokee (8 1/4" Ring Gear)	90 (10)
Pinion Shaft Lock Bolt	102 (11)

1992 DRIVE AXLES
Differentials – Spicer (Dana) Trac-Lok

Cherokee, Comanche, Grand Cherokee (1993), Wrangler

DESCRIPTION

The Trac-Lok positive traction differential is a 2-pinion, single-case type. Under normal conditions, torque to each rear wheel is divided evenly. When vehicle is driven on snow, ice or mud, torque will transfer to the wheel with the greatest traction.

LUBRICATION

NOTE: Use 75W-90 GL-5 plus Trac-Lok additive (friction modifier).

DIAGNOSIS & TESTING

Most common Trac-Lok condition is chatter when turning corners. Incorrect or contaminated oil is usual cause.

Changing axle oil (with Trac-Lok additive) should correct the condition. After changing Trac-Lok differential oil, make 10 or 12 slow figure 8 turns. If chatter persists, the clutch packs must be inspected for damage.

REMOVAL & INSTALLATION

NOTE: This article covers overhaul of Trac-Lok (positive traction) unit. For all other information, see 7 1/8", 7 9/16", 8 1/4" & 8 1/2" RING GEAR article in DRIVE AXLES.

OVERHAUL

Disassembly – 1) Using 2 screwdrivers, remove pinion snap rings. Using a brass drift and a hammer, remove pinion shaft from case. *See Fig. 1.* Install Step Plate (C-4487-1) in side gear. Grease centering hole of step plate. Position Gear Rotator (C-4487-4) in pinion shaft hole. Coat threads of Forcing Screw (C-4487-2) with oil.

2) Insert Threaded Adapter (C-4487-3) into side gear opposite step plate. Insert Forcing Screw (C-4487-2) through threaded adapter.

Thread screw through adapter until it contacts centering hole in step plate. Tighten forcing screw sufficiently to relieve clutch pack tension. Remove pinion thrust washers.

3) Loosen forcing screw until all clutch pack tension is relieved. Using gear rotator, engage side gear teeth and rotate side gears until pinions can be removed.

4) Remove step plate, threaded adapter, gear rotator, forcing screw, side gears and clutch packs. Remove clutch pack retainer clips. Mark clutch packs for reassembly reference.

Reassembly – 1) Lightly oil clutch discs. Assemble clutch pack discs. *See Fig. 2.* Assemble clutch packs on side gears.

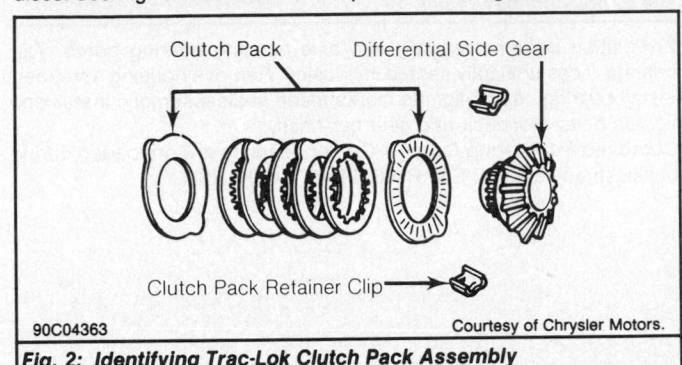

Clutch Pack   Differential Side Gear

Clutch Pack Retainer Clip

90C04363   Courtesy of Chrysler Motors.

Fig. 2: Identifying Trac-Lok Clutch Pack Assembly

2) Install clutch pack and side gear in side of case. Ensure retaining clips remain seated in case pockets. Install step plate in clutch pack just installed.

3) Install remaining side gear and clutch pack in case. Hold assembly in position. Install rotating tool and forcing screw.

4) Tighten forcing screw and compress clutch packs. Install pinions. Rotate side gear with tool pawl until each pinion is aligned with pinion shaft bore.

5) Install pinion thrust washers. Remove tools. Install pinion shaft. Install snap rings on pinion shaft. Position ring gear on differential case. Install NEW ring gear bolts and tighten to **52 ft. lbs. (70 N.m)**.

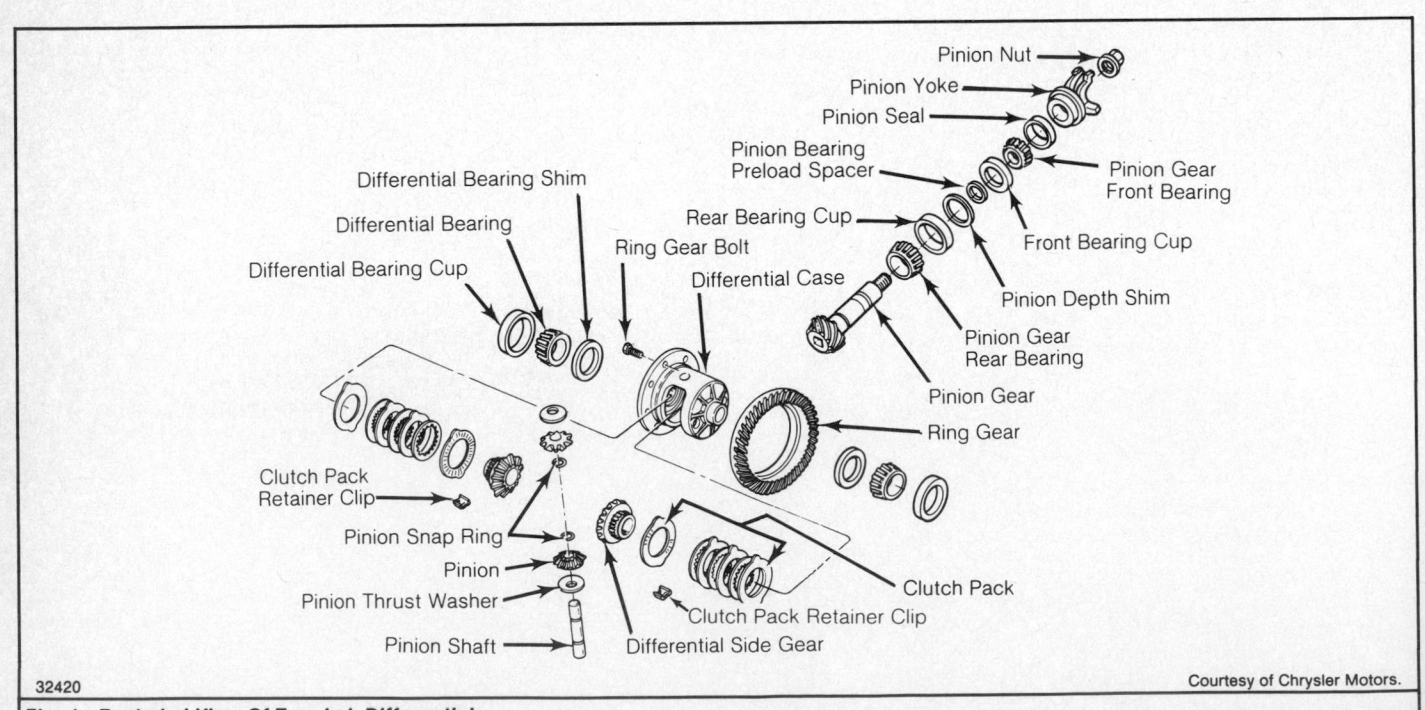

32420

Courtesy of Chrysler Motors.

Fig. 1: Exploded View Of Trac-Lok Differential

Cherokee, Comanche, Grand Cherokee (1993), Wrangler

DESCRIPTION

The Command-Trac locking hub is used (when equipped) on all 4WD models except Grand Cherokee. This system can be shifted between 2WD and 4WD high range, from inside the vehicle, while vehicle is moving. Command-Trac utilizes a vacuum operated shift motor to engage or disengage front drive axle shaft. The vehicle speed must be reduced to 2-3 MPH, to shift into or out of 4WD low range. See Fig. 1.

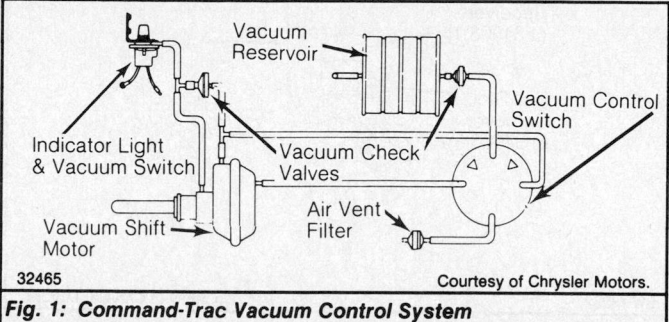

Fig. 1: Command-Trac Vacuum Control System

Selec-Trac locking hub is used on some 4WD Cherokee and Comanche models. Selec-Trac utilize a non-disconnect front axle. Engagement of 2WD or 4WD is accomplished at transfer case by means of mechanical shift linkage. System allows full or part time 4WD. Selec-Trac can be shifted into 2WD or 4WD modes from inside the vehicle at any speed.

NOTE: *Grand Cherokee DOES NOT use Command-Trac or Selec-Trac 4WD system.*

TROUBLE SHOOTING

2WD TO 4WD

Place mode select switch in 4WD position while driving vehicle 2-3 MPH (Command-Trac). Axle shift should be accompanied by a ratcheting sound followed by an audible mechanical engagement. Transfer case should shift after axle shifts, accompanied by hissing sound from mode selector switch.

4WD TO 2WD

1) Place mode select switch in 2WD position. Transfer case should shift to 2WD and not allow shifting into 4WD or LO range. Axle should shift after transfer case shifts.
2) To determine if front axle has completed a shift out of 4WD into 2WD, position mode select switch back to 4WD position while operating vehicle at slow speed. If vehicle shifts into 2WD, axle will ratchet. If shift is not completed, transfer case will shift into 4WD and hissing sound will come from mode select switch.

ON-VEHICLE TESTING

FRONT AXLE SHIFT MOTOR

1) Raise and support vehicle. Remove vacuum harness from front axle shift motor. Apply **15 in. Hg** to front port of shift motor. See Fig. 2. Rotate right front wheel to disengage axle (2WD operation).

2) Replace shift motor if it does not hold vacuum for at least 30 seconds. If shift motor holds vacuum, remove vacuum pump. Connect vacuum pump to shift motor rear port and cap indicator light switch port. See Fig. 2. Apply 15 in. Hg to shift motor.
3) Replace shift motor if it does not hold vacuum for at least 30 seconds. If shift motor holds vacuum, remove cap from indicator light switch port.
4) If vacuum is present, shift motor is okay. If no vacuum is present, cap indicator light switch port and reapply **15 in. Hg** to shift motor rear port. Rotate right front wheel to make sure axle shafts are engaged (4WD operation).
5) Axles must be completely engaged to open indicator light switch port. If vacuum is now present at indicator light switch port, shift motor is okay. If not, replace shift motor or repair shifter mechanism.

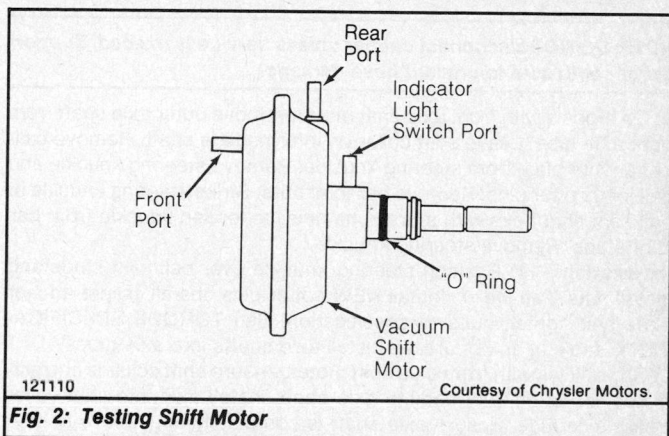

Fig. 2: Testing Shift Motor

REMOVAL & INSTALLATION

AXLE SHIFT MOTOR & HOUSING

Removal – 1) Raise and support vehicle. Place a drain pan under shift housing. Disconnect vacuum harness. Remove housing bolts. Remove motor and housing. See Fig. 3.
2) Mark shift fork and housing for reassembly. Remove shift fork and motor snap rings. Remove shift motor from housing. See Fig. 2.

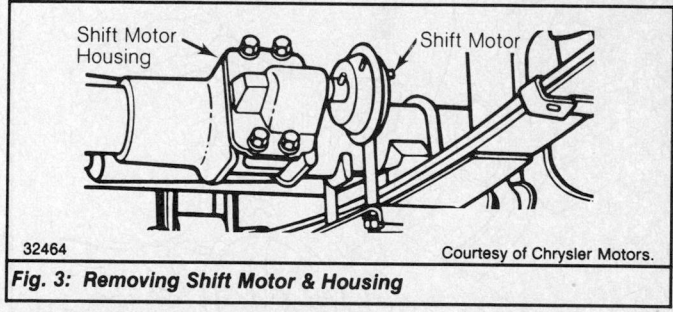

Fig. 3: Removing Shift Motor & Housing

Installation – Install NEW "O" ring on motor shaft. Assemble shift motor shift fork onto shaft. Position motor and housing on axle. Add axle oil to shift motor housing. Install shift fork in shift collar and install housing bolts. Connect vacuum harnesses.

1992 DRIVE AXLES
4WD Steering Knuckles

**Cherokee, Comanche,
Grand Cherokee (1993), Wrangler**

DESCRIPTION

Open-end steering knuckles pivot on ball joints and allow wheels to turn.

REMOVAL & INSTALLATION

Removal – 1) Raise and support vehicle. Remove wheel, disc brake caliper, rotor, cotter pin, nut retainer, and axle hub nut. Remove hub-to-steering knuckle attaching bolts. Remove hub and rotor shield from steering knuckle. Remove axle shaft from axle tube. See FRONT AXLES article.

NOTE: DO NOT disconnect caliper unless service is needed. Support caliper with wire to prevent hose damage.

---

2) On models with front axle shift motor, remove outer axle shaft from right axle tube. Leave shift collar on intermediate shaft. Remove caliper anchor plate from steering knuckle. Remove steering knuckle and ball joint cotter pins. Remove ball joint nuts. Strike steering knuckle at ball joint stud boss with a brass hammer to loosen knuckle from ball joint studs. Remove steering knuckle.

Installation – 1) Position steering knuckle over ball joint studs and install nuts. *See Fig. 1.* Install NEW cotter pins. Install caliper anchor plate and tighten bolts to specification. See TORQUE SPECIFICATIONS table at end of article. Install axle shafts into axle tubes.

2) On vehicles with front axle shift motor, ensure shift collar is correctly positioned on intermediate axle shaft, install axle into shift collar inside axle tube. Ensure axle shaft is completely engaged with shift collar.

3) On all models, apply bearing grease to spindle hub bore in steering knuckle and install rotor shield and hub. Tighten spindle hub bolts. Install hub washer and nut. Tighten hub nut to specification. Install hub nut retainer and install NEW cotter pin. Install rotor, caliper and wheel. Lower vehicle.

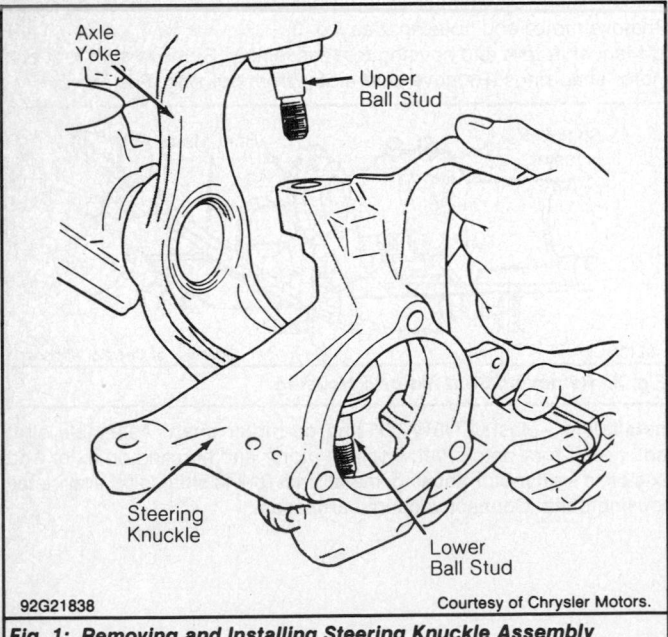

92G21838   Courtesy of Chrysler Motors.

Fig. 1: Removing and Installing Steering Knuckle Assembly

OVERHAUL

Removal (Upper Ball Joint) – Place steering knuckle in soft jawed vise, place Receiver (J-34503-1) on top of upper ball joint. Place Ball Stud Remover (J-34503-3) in "C" clamp. Place "C" clamp and remover under upper ball joint and tighten "C" clamp screw to remove ball joint. *See Fig. 2.*

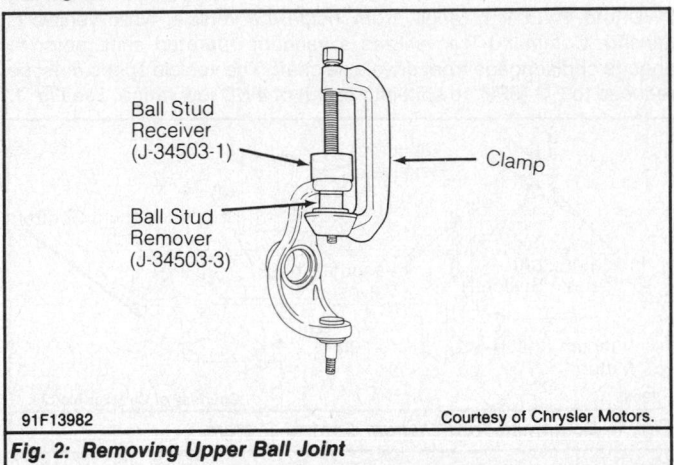

91F13982   Courtesy of Chrysler Motors.

Fig. 2: Removing Upper Ball Joint

Installation – Place Ball Stud Installer (J-34503-5) on top of upper ball joint. Place Ball Stud Support (J-34503-12) between "C" clamp and yoke. Tighten "C" clamp screw and seat ball joint. *See Fig. 3.*

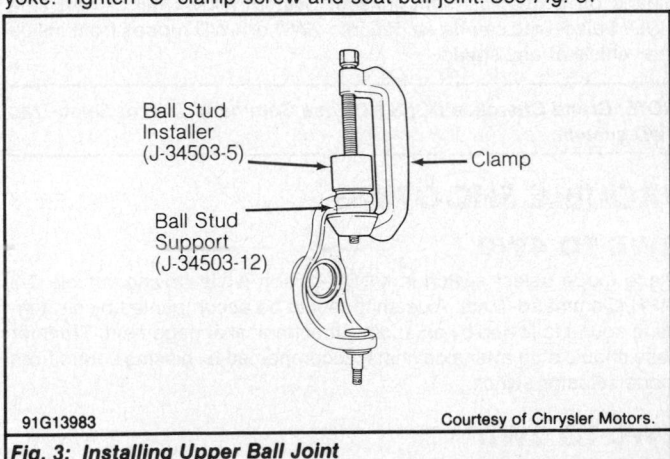

91G13983   Courtesy of Chrysler Motors.

Fig. 3: Installing Upper Ball Joint

Removal (Lower Ball Joint) – Place Ball Stud Receiver (J-34503-1) on "C" clamp screw and Ball Stud Remover (J-34503-3) between top of yoke and "C" clamp. Press lower ball joint into receiver.

Installation – Place Installation Cup (J-34503-4) on "C" clamp screw and Ball Stud Support (J-34503-12) between top of yoke and "C" clamp. Tighten "C" clamp screw until lower ball joint is seated in yoke.

TORQUE SPECIFICATIONS

TORQUE SPECIFICATIONS

Application	Ft. Lbs. (N.m)
Ball Joint Nuts	75 (102)
Caliper Anchor Plate	77 (104)
Spindle Hub Bolts	75 (102)
Axle Hub-To-Shaft nut	175 (237)
Wheel Lug Nuts	
Except Grand Cherokee	75 (102)
Grand Cherokee	88 (120)

Cherokee, Comanche,
Grand Cherokee (1993), Wrangler

DESCRIPTION

Propeller shafts are balanced, one-piece, tubular steel shafts with universal joints at each end. Single Cardan universal joints contain a spider, 4 bearing caps with needle bearings, seals and clips. Double Cardan universal joints contains 2 spiders joined together, 8 bearing caps with needle bearings, seals and clips. *See Fig. 1.*

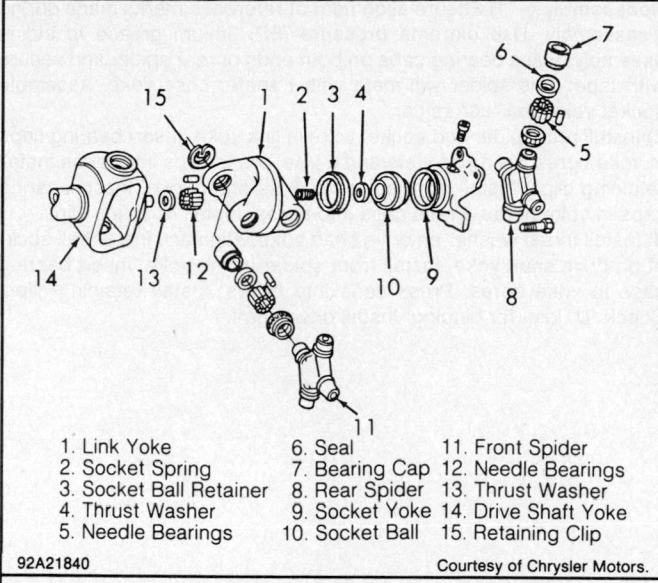

1. Link Yoke
2. Socket Spring
3. Socket Ball Retainer
4. Thrust Washer
5. Needle Bearings
6. Seal
7. Bearing Cap
8. Rear Spider
9. Socket Yoke
10. Socket Ball
11. Front Spider
12. Needle Bearings
13. Thrust Washer
14. Drive Shaft Yoke
15. Retaining Clip

92A21840   Courtesy of Chrysler Motors.

Fig. 1: Exploded View Of Double Cardan Universal Joint

INSPECTION

VIBRATION

Tires & Wheels – Check tire inflation and wheel balance. Check for foreign objects in tread, damaged tread, mismatched treads or tire sizes. Check for tires that are out of round. Replace or repair as necessary.
Engine & Transmission Mounts – Tighten mounting bolts. Replace mounts if soft or separated.
Drive Shaft – Check shaft for damage or dents. Check for undercoating on shaft. If present, clean shaft.
Universal Joints – Check for defective or damaged "U" joints. Check for loose bolts and worn bearings.

DRIVE SHAFT RUNOUT

Remove any dirt from area around shaft where dial indicator is placed. Measure shaft runout about 3" from weld-seam on each end of shaft. With dial indicator mounted perpendicular to drive shaft, rotate shaft several times. Record runout measurement. Repeat procedure at opposite end and center of drive shaft. See DRIVE SHAFT RUNOUT table. If runout is not equal to or less than specification, replace drive shaft.

DRIVE SHAFT RUNOUT

Application	In. (mm)
Front & Rear of Shaft	.010 (.25)
Center of Shaft	.015 (.38)

DRIVE SHAFT ANGLE

NOTE: *If drive shaft angle is excessive, vibration may result.*

1) Check condition of springs, engine and transmission mounts. Ensure all mounting fasteners are tight. To ensure proper riding

height, fuel tank should be full and vehicle should be empty of cargo. Raise and support vehicle so suspension bears weight of vehicle and wheels can rotate freely.
2) Remove clips from "U" joint cap bore. Ensure bearing caps are clean. Joint bearing cap to be measured must be straight down. Place Inclinometer (J-23498-A) on bearing cap. Center bubble in sight glass. Record measurement. Rotate drive shaft 90 degrees. Repeat procedure. Subtract smaller figure from larger figure to obtain "U" joint angle.
3) Repeat procedure outlined in step 2) at opposite end of drive shaft. Compare "U" joint angle measurements. Difference of "U" joint angles MUST be within specification. See UNIVERSAL JOINT ANGLE table. If not with specification, adjust "U" joint angle. See SHAFT ANGLE under ADJUSTMENTS.

UNIVERSAL JOINT ANGLE

Application	Degrees
Double Cardan Universal Joint	
2.5L Engine	0-2.5
4.0L Engine	0-1.5
Single Cardan "U" Joint	0-1.5

ADJUSTMENTS

SHAFT ANGLE

Cherokee, Comanche & Grand Cherokee (Front) – 1) Adjust drive pinion gear shaft angle "A" at the lower suspension arms with shims. Adding shims will decrease pinion gear shaft angle "A" but will increase caster angle. *See Fig. 2.*
2) Adjustment of angle "A" is more important than caster angle. When angle "A", angle "B" and vehicle height are correct, angle "C" will also be correct.

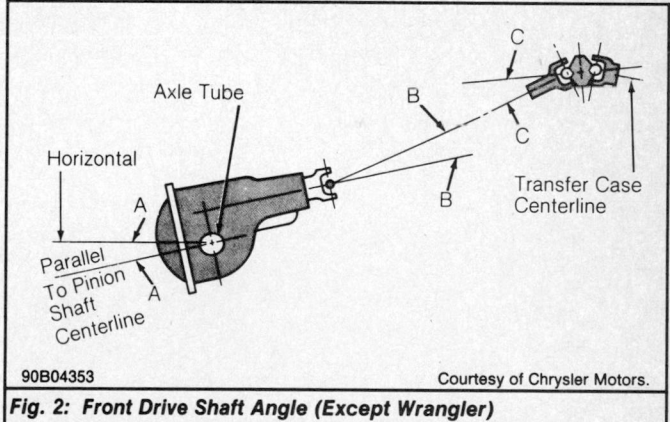

90B04353   Courtesy of Chrysler Motors.

Fig. 2: Front Drive Shaft Angle (Except Wrangler)

Wrangler (Front) – 1) Raise vehicle and place jack stands under frame. Place a hydraulic jack under differential housing. Raise jack to support weight of axle.
2) Loosen spring "U" bolt nuts, and install tapered shims between springs and axle spring bracket to correct angle. Torque spring "U" bolt nuts to **52 ft. lbs. (70 N.m)** for Cherokee and Comanche or **100 ft. lbs. (136 N.m)** for all others.

NOTE: *Adjustment procedure for rear shaft angle not available from manufacturer.*

OVERHAUL

NOTE: *If joints are rusted or corroded, apply penetrating oil before disassembly.*

SINGLE CARDAN UNIVERSAL JOINT

Disassembly – Scribe or paint marks on yokes and drive shaft for reassembly reference. Remove bearing cap retainer clips. Using sockets and vise as a press, remove bearing caps retaining spider to drive shaft and yoke. Remove spider. Inspect caps for cracks or defective needle bearings. Check spider for scores or excessive wear. If defective, replace complete unit.

CAUTION: DO NOT place shaft or slip yoke tube in vise. Clamp only the forged portions in vise.

Reassembly – 1) Clean universal joint bores and yoke. Apply grease to yoke bores, bearing caps, bearings and spider contact surfaces.
2) Place spider into yoke and tap bearing cap, seal and bearings into yoke far enough to hold spider. Place a socket (smaller than cap) on side cap and place in vise.
3) Tighten vise until caps are seated in yoke. Rotate spider to make sure no binding occurs. Install cap clips and repeat procedure on remaining caps.

DOUBLE CARDAN UNIVERSAL JOINT

NOTE: Double cardan universal joints are not serviceable. If defective, they must be replaced as an assembly.

Disassembly – 1) Scribe or paint marks on yokes and drive shaft for reassembly reference. Remove bearing cap retainer clips. Using sockets and vise as a press, remove bearing caps retaining front spider to link yoke. Remove drive shaft yoke from link yoke. *See Fig. 1.*
2) Remove bearing caps retaining rear spider in link yoke. Remove rear spider and socket yoke from link yoke. Remove bearing caps retaining front spider in drive shaft yoke. Remove front spider from drive shaft yoke.

Inspection – Check all component for cracks, scores and excessive looseness. If any defect is found replace complete "U" joint assembly.

Reassembly – 1) Ensure alignment of reference marks made during disassembly. Use extreme pressure (EP) lithium grease to aid in assembly. Place bearing caps on both ends of rear spider and secure with tape. This spider will mate with transfer case yoke. Assemble socket yoke and rear spider.
2) Install rear spider and socket yoke in link yoke. Insert bearing caps in yoke bores. Using sockets and a vise, press caps into bores Install retaining clips. Install front spider in drive shaft yoke. Insert bearing caps in yoke bores. Press caps into bores. Install retaining clips.
3) Install thrust washer on drive shaft yoke. Align and install ball socket on drive shaft yoke. Install front spider in link yoke. Insert bearing caps in yoke bores. Press caps into bores. Install retaining clips. Check "U" joint for binding. Install drive shaft.

Cherokee, Grand Cherokee (1993)

DESCRIPTION

The Teves Anti-Lock Brake System (ABS) consists of acceleration switch, Controller Anti-Lock Brake (CAB), CHECK ANTI-LOCK warning light, Hydraulic Control Unit (HCU), main relay, master cylinder, pedal travel sensor, pump motor relay, pump motor sensor, vacuum booster, 4 wheel speed sensors and axle shaft tone (pulse) rings.

During ABS operation, front wheels are controlled individually and rear wheels are controlled together. ABS modulates brake fluid pressure during high pedal pressure and high vehicle deceleration to prevent wheel lock-up.

NOTE: For more information on brake system, see DISC & DRUM article in BRAKES.

OPERATION

The Teves Anti-Lock Brake System (ABS) is activated during hard braking to prevent wheel lock-up. Wheel lock-up does not mean wheel has stopped, but wheel is turning slower than vehicle speed. When ignition is on, before vehicle is moved, Controller Anti-Lock Brake (CAB) performs a static system initialization. When vehicle speed reaches approximately 6 MPH, CAB briefly cycles pump to verify operation. Hydraulic Control Unit (HCU) solenoids are checked continuously.

When ABS is activated, vibrations and pulsations may be felt in brake pedal and solenoid valves clicking and pump motor running may be heard. Some wheel slip is required for best braking performance. This wheel slip may be heard as tire chirping. Do not confuse tire chirping with tire skidding. When vehicle is braked heavily, wheels will lock-up below 3 MPH. When braking on rough road surfaces, ABS may activate detecting wheel lock-up tendencies from wheel hop.

CAUTION: See ANTI-LOCK BRAKE SAFETY PRECAUTIONS article in GENERAL INFORMATION.

BLEEDING BRAKE SYSTEM

NOTE: Use only DOT 3 brake fluid from a sealed container. DO NOT use DOT 5 silicone brake fluid.

1) Ensure ignition is off. Clean master cylinder reservoir cover and surrounding area. Ensure reservoir is full. Bleeding sequence is master cylinder, Hydraulic Control Unit (HCU) valve body (at fluid lines), right rear wheel, left rear wheel, right front wheel and left front wheel.
2) After bleeding master cylinder, position shop towel below 4 hydraulic control unit brake pipes. Using flare wrench, slightly open hydraulic control unit brake pipe fittings individually.
3) DO NOT allow brake fluid to contact paint or electrical connectors. Slowly depress brake pedal. Close hydraulic control unit brake pipe fitting and release brake pedal. Repeat process until no air escapes from brake pipe fitting. Repeat procedure for remaining 3 brake lines.
4) Ensure master cylinder reservoir is full. Raise and support vehicle. Bleed all 4 wheel calipers. Attach a clear hose to right rear caliper bleeder valve and submerge other end of hose in container of brake fluid.

NOTE: DO NOT pump brake pedal while bleeding brakes. Pumping brake pedal compresses air into tiny bubbles throughout system making bleeding more difficult.

5) Open bleeder valve. Slowly depress brake pedal. Close bleeder valve and release brake pedal. Wait 5 seconds. Repeat process until no air bubbles are seen from hose. Tap lightly on cylinder/caliper housing to free trapped air. Close bleeder valve. Repeat process until no air bubbles are seen from hose. Repeat procedure on left rear, right front and left front bleeder valves. Ensure reservoir is full.

6) Using DRB-II, follow prompts and perform BLEED BRAKES procedure. After performing BLEED BRAKES procedure using DRB-II, repeat steps 1)-5). Ensure master cylinder reservoir is full.

ADJUSTMENTS

REAR WHEEL SPEED SENSOR

See REAR WHEEL SPEED SENSOR under REMOVAL & INSTALLATION.

REMOVAL & INSTALLATION

ABS MAIN SYSTEM RELAY

Removal & Installation – ABS main system relay is located on right side of engine compartment in Power Distribution Center (PDC). Turn ignition off. Remove cover from PDC. Locate and remove ABS main system relay from PDC. *See Fig. 1.* To install, reverse removal procedure.

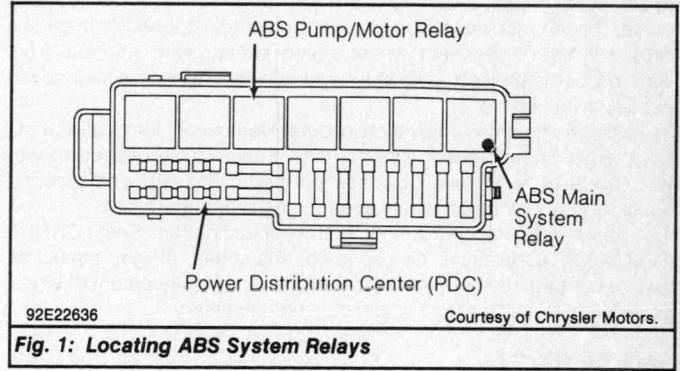

ABS Pump/Motor Relay

ABS Main System Relay

Power Distribution Center (PDC)

92E22636
Courtesy of Chrysler Motors.

Fig. 1: Locating ABS System Relays

ABS PUMP/MOTOR RELAY

Removal & Installation – ABS pump/motor relay is located on right side of engine compartment in Power Distribution Center (PDC). Turn ignition off. Remove cover from PDC. Locate and remove ABS pump/motor relay from PDC. *See Fig. 1.* To install, reverse removal procedure.

CONTROLLER ANTI-LOCK BRAKE (CAB)

Removal & Installation (Cherokee) – Turn ignition off. CAB is located under instrument panel to right of steering column. Remove screws attaching CAB mounting bracket to vehicle. Disconnect CAB electrical connector. Disconnect security alarm module electrical connector. Security alarm module is mounted on opposite side of mounting bracket. Remove CAB and mounting bracket. *See Fig. 2.* To install, reverse removal procedure. If a new CAB is being installed, transfer mounting bracket to new CAB.

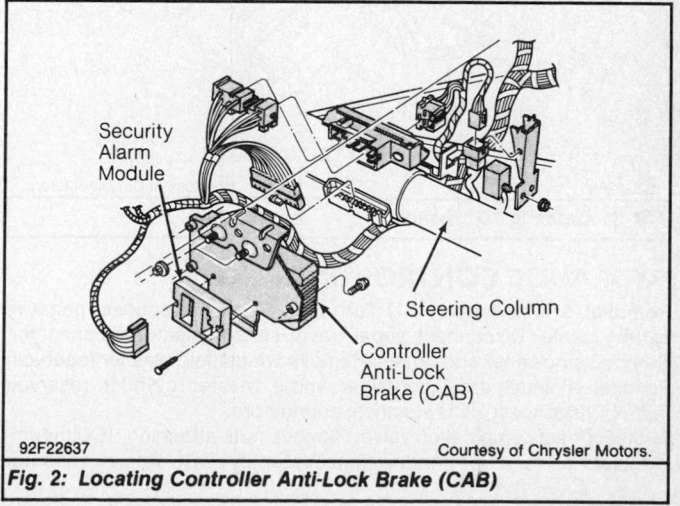

Security Alarm Module

Steering Column

Controller Anti-Lock Brake (CAB)

92F22637
Courtesy of Chrysler Motors.

Fig. 2: Locating Controller Anti-Lock Brake (CAB)

CAUTION: DO NOT force CAB electrical connector onto CAB. CAB pins are easily damaged.

Removal & Installation (Grand Cherokee) – Turn ignition off. Disconnect negative battery cable. CAB is located on driver side inner fender panel. Remove screws attaching CAB to fender panel bracket. Remove CAB from bracket for access to CAB electrical connector. Release strap securing harness connector to CAB. Tilt CAB electrical connector upward to disengage. Slide CAB electrical connector from retaining tangs. Remove CAB from vehicle. To install, reverse removal procedure.

FRONT WHEEL SPEED SENSOR

Removal & Installation – **1)** Turn ignition off. Raise and support vehicle. Remove wheel and tire assembly. Clean area surrounding wheel speed sensor prior to removal. Remove bolt attaching wheel speed sensor to steering knuckle.

2) Unseat grommet retaining wheel speed sensor wire in wheel well panel. Disconnect wheel speed sensor electrical connector in engine compartment. Disconnect wheel speed sensor wire harness from clips on body, chassis, and steering knuckle. Remove wheel speed sensor from vehicle.

3) To install, reverse removal procedure. Remove all kinks and twists from wheel speed sensor wire harness. Ensure wheel speed sensor wire harness is installed in clips on body, chassis and steering knuckle. Use Loctite on wheel speed sensor mounting bolt.

4) Tighten wheel speed sensor bolt to specification. See TORQUE SPECIFICATIONS table. Air gap is not adjustable. Air gap should be **.040" (1.3 mm)**. If air gap is not to specification, replacement of wheel speed sensor and/or tone wheel may be necessary.

"G" SWITCH

Removal & Installation – Turn ignition off. Disconnect negative battery cable. Tilt rear seat assembly forward to access "G" switch. Disconnect "G" switch electrical connector. Remove "G" switch mounting bolts. Remove "G" switch. See Fig. 3. To install, reverse removal procedure. Ensure arrow on top of "G" switch is facing toward front of vehicle.

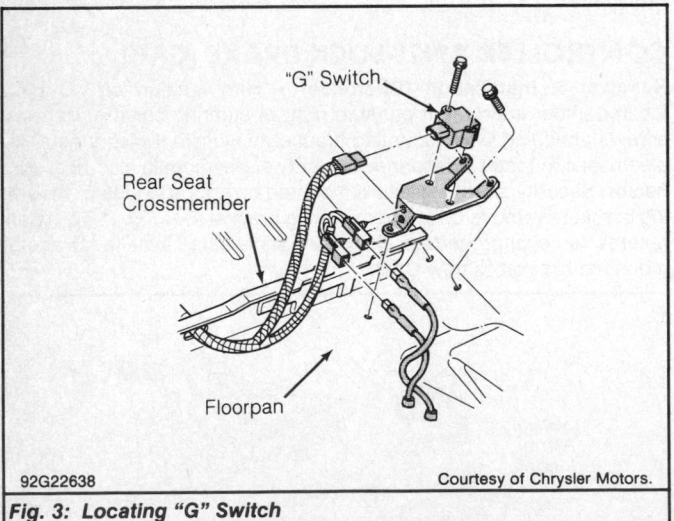

92G22638   Courtesy of Chrysler Motors.

Fig. 3: Locating "G" Switch

HYDRAULIC CONTROL UNIT (HCU)

Removal & Installation – **1)** Turn ignition off. Disconnect negative battery cable. Disconnect pedal travel sensor electrical connector. Remove air cleaner and hoses. Remove windshield washer reservoir. Position a small drain container under master cylinder reservoir hoses. Disconnect HCU electrical connectors.

2) Disconnect combination valve. Remove nuts attaching HCU mounting bracket to inner fender panel. Identify HCU brake lines for

reassembly reference. Disconnect brake lines from HCU. Remove HCU from vehicle. See Fig. 4. To install, reverse removal procedure. Bleed brake system. See BLEEDING BRAKE SYSTEM.

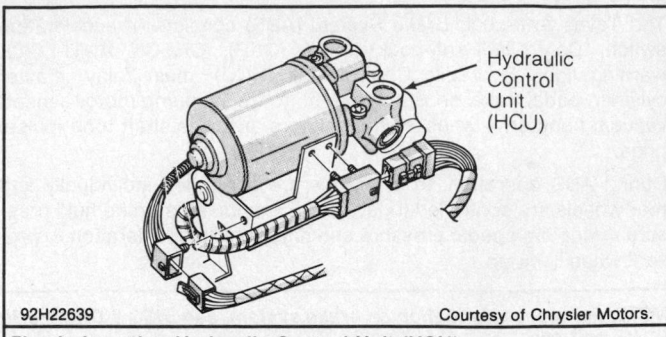

92H22639   Courtesy of Chrysler Motors.

Fig. 4: Locating Hydraulic Control Unit (HCU)

PEDAL TRAVEL SENSOR

Removal & Installation – Turn ignition off. Disconnect pedal travel sensor electrical connector. Pump brake pedal to exhaust all vacuum from vacuum booster. Unseat pedal travel sensor retaining ring. Remove pedal travel sensor from vacuum booster. See Fig. 5. To install, reverse removal procedure. Ensure color dot on face of vacuum booster matches color of plunger tip. If colors are different, replace plunger tip to match color dot on vacuum booster.

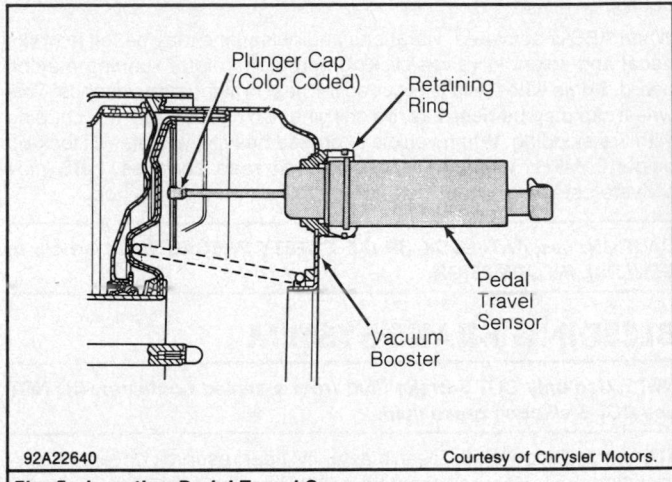

92A22640   Courtesy of Chrysler Motors.

Fig. 5: Locating Pedal Travel Sensor

REAR WHEEL SPEED SENSOR

Removal – **1)** Turn ignition off. Raise and fold rear seat to access rear wheel speed sensor connectors. Disconnect rear wheel speed sensor electrical connector. Push rear wheel speed sensor grommet and wire harness through floorpan on vehicle.

2) Raise and support vehicle. Remove wheel and brake drum. Remove clips attaching rear wheel speed sensor wire harness to brake lines. Unseat rear wheel speed sensor grommet from brake backing plate. Remove rear wheel speed sensor mounting bolt. Push rear wheel speed sensor through grommet opening in backing plate. Remove rear wheel speed sensor from vehicle.

Installation – **1)** If original wheel speed sensor is being installed, go to step **3)**. If a NEW wheel speed sensor is being installed, position wheel speed sensor until cardboard spacer contacts tone wheel.

2) Use Loctite on wheel speed sensor mounting bolt. Tighten wheel speed sensor mounting bolt to specification. See TORQUE SPECIFICATIONS table. Spin rear axle by hand until cardboard spacer is peeled from sensor face. Air gap adjustment should be correct. Using a brass feeler gauge, check air gap adjustment. Air gap should be **.043" (1.1 mm)**. If air gap is not correct, adjust as necessary. Go to step **4)**.

3) Remove any remaining pieces of cardboard from sensor face. Install wheel speed sensor. Using a brass feeler gauge, adjust air gap. Air gap should be .043" (1.1 mm). Use Loctite on wheel speed sensor mounting bolt. Tighten wheel speed sensor mounting bolt to specification. See TORQUE SPECIFICATIONS table.

4) Remove all kinks and twists from wheel speed sensor wire harness. Ensure wheel speed sensor wire harness is installed in clips on brake lines. To complete installation, reverse removal procedure.

TORQUE SPECIFICATIONS

TORQUE SPECIFICATIONS

Application	Ft. Lbs. (N.m)
Combination Valve Brake Line Fittings	13-18 (18-24)
Front Speed Sensor Bolt	11 (15)
HCU Brake Line Fittings	10-12 (14-16)
Master Cylinder Brake Line Fittings	11-13 (15-18)
Rear Speed Sensor Bolt	11 (15)
Wheel Lug Nuts	88 (119)
	INCH Lbs. (N.m)
CAB Mounting Bolts	75-115 (9-13)
"G" Switch Bolt	17-32 (2-4)
HCU Bracket Mounting Bolts	92-112 (10-13)

DIAGNOSIS & TESTING

NOTE: DRB-II and appropriate cartridge is necessary for diagnosing ABS system.

WARNING LIGHTS

Amber ABS Warning Light – After engine start-up, ABS warning light glows as part of a self-check feature. ABS warning light normally will light for 2-3 seconds and then go out. If ABS warning light remains illuminated after engine start-up, diagnosis will be necessary to determine which component or circuit is malfunctioning.

Red BRAKE Warning Light – With ignition on, Red BRAKE warning light will glow when low brake fluid level is detected or parking brake switch is closed. BRAKE warning light normally indicates a hydraulic or mechanical failure is present.

PRE-DIAGNOSTIC INSPECTION

1) Check master cylinder reservoir for correct fluid level. Inspect Hydraulic Control Unit (HCU) for leakage and wiring damage. Check caliper piston for activation and release. Check all brakes to verify no drag exists.

2) Check speed sensors for correct mounting and alignment. Inspect wire harness for correct routing. Ensure connectors are not damaged and have good contact.

3) Verify all wheel bearings are not worn or causing wheel wobble. Ensure all tires are in good condition and properly inflated. After performing pre-diagnostic inspection, perform TEST-1A under SELF-DIAGNOSTIC TESTS using DRB-II. *See Figs. 6 and 7.*

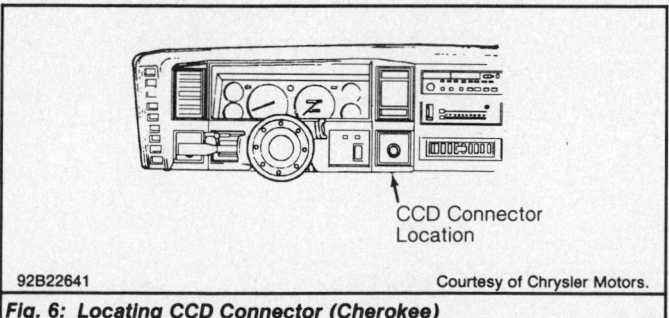

92B22641   Courtesy of Chrysler Motors.

Fig. 6: Locating CCD Connector (Cherokee)

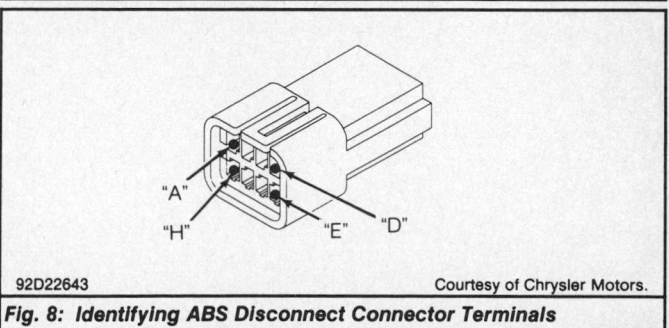

92C22642   Courtesy of Chrysler Motors.

Fig. 7: Locating CCD Connector (Grand Cherokee)

INTERMITTENTS

Most intermittent problems are caused by faulty electrical connections or wiring; however, a sticking relay or solenoid can cause a failure.

When intermittent failure is encountered, check for fault messages stored in CAB. If fault messages are found, inspect related components and circuitry for poor connections. If no trouble codes are found, inspect suspect circuits as follows:

* Check for poor mating of connector halves, or terminals not fully seated in connector body (backed-out).
* Check for improperly formed or damaged terminals. Carefully reform all connector terminals of problem circuit to increase contact tension.
* Check for poor terminal-to-wire connection.
* Check for hydraulic system leaks.

CLEARING FAULT MESSAGES

DRB-II – Using DRB-II, select ADJUSTMENTS. Press "1" (ERASE FAULTS key). Press ENTER key. DRB-II will display ERASE FAULTS ARE YOU SURE? (ENTER TO ERASE). Press ENTER key. DRB-II will display ERASE FAULTS TURN KEY OFF. Turn ignition off. Turn ignition on. DRB-II will display ERASE FAULTS FAULTS ERASED. Faults are now erased.

Ignition Cycle Default – If no fault codes occur for 50 driving cycles, any existing fault messages will be cleared from CAB memory. A drive cycle occurs when ignition is turned on and vehicle is driven faster than 10 MPH.

CONNECTOR IDENTIFICATION

CONNECTOR IDENTIFICATION DIRECTORY

Connector	Figure
ABS Disconnect Connector	8
ABS Main System Relay Socket Connector	9
ABS Pump/Motor Relay Socket Connector	10
Controller Anti-Lock Brake (CAB) Connector	11
"G" Switch Connector	12
Hydraulic Control Unit (HCU) Connector	13
Pump/Motor Connector	14

92D22643   Courtesy of Chrysler Motors.

Fig. 8: Identifying ABS Disconnect Connector Terminals

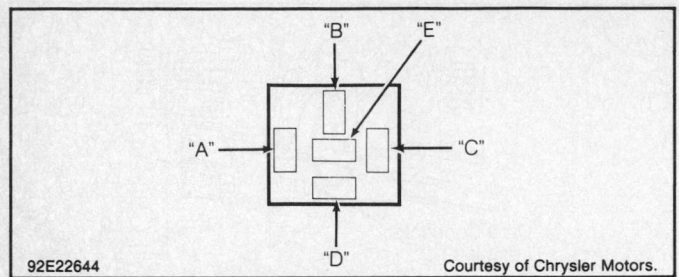

Fig. 9: Identifying ABS Main System Relay Connector Terminals

Courtesy of Chrysler Motors.

92E22644

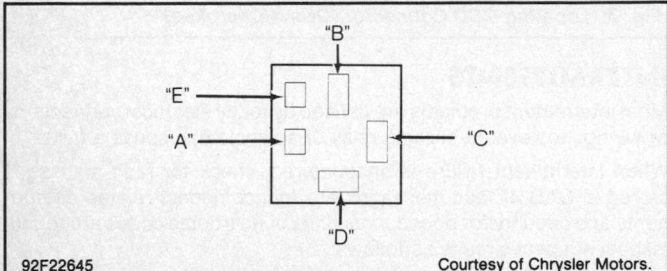

Fig. 10: Identifying ABS Pump/Motor Relay Connector Terminals

Courtesy of Chrysler Motors.

92F22645

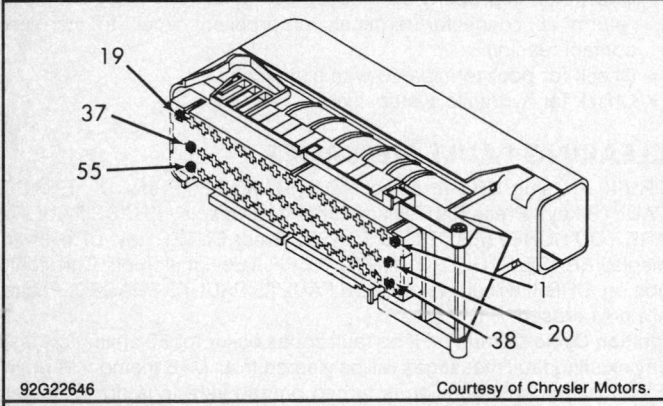

Fig. 11: Identifying Controller Anti-Lock Brake (CAB) Connector Terminals

Courtesy of Chrysler Motors.

92G22646

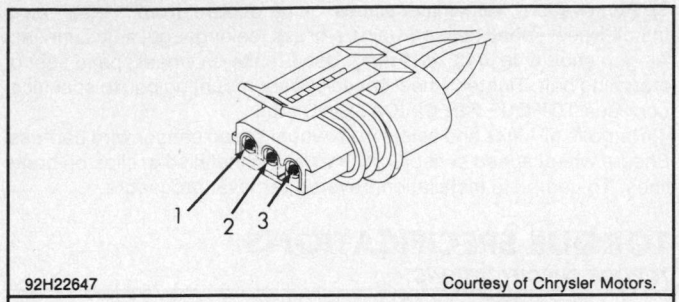

Fig. 12: Identifying "G" Switch Connector Terminals

Courtesy of Chrysler Motors.

92H22647

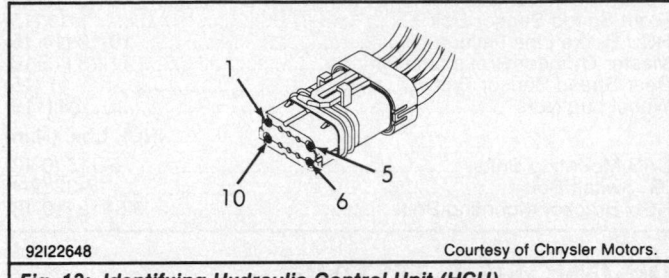

Fig. 13: Identifying Hydraulic Control Unit (HCU) Connector Terminals

Courtesy of Chrysler Motors.

92I22648

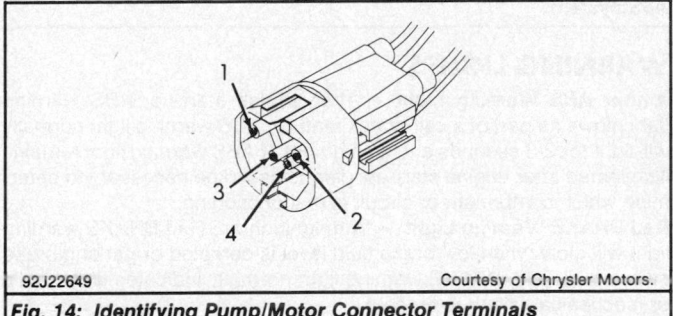

Fig. 14: Identifying Pump/Motor Connector Terminals

Courtesy of Chrysler Motors.

92J22649

WIRING DIAGRAMS

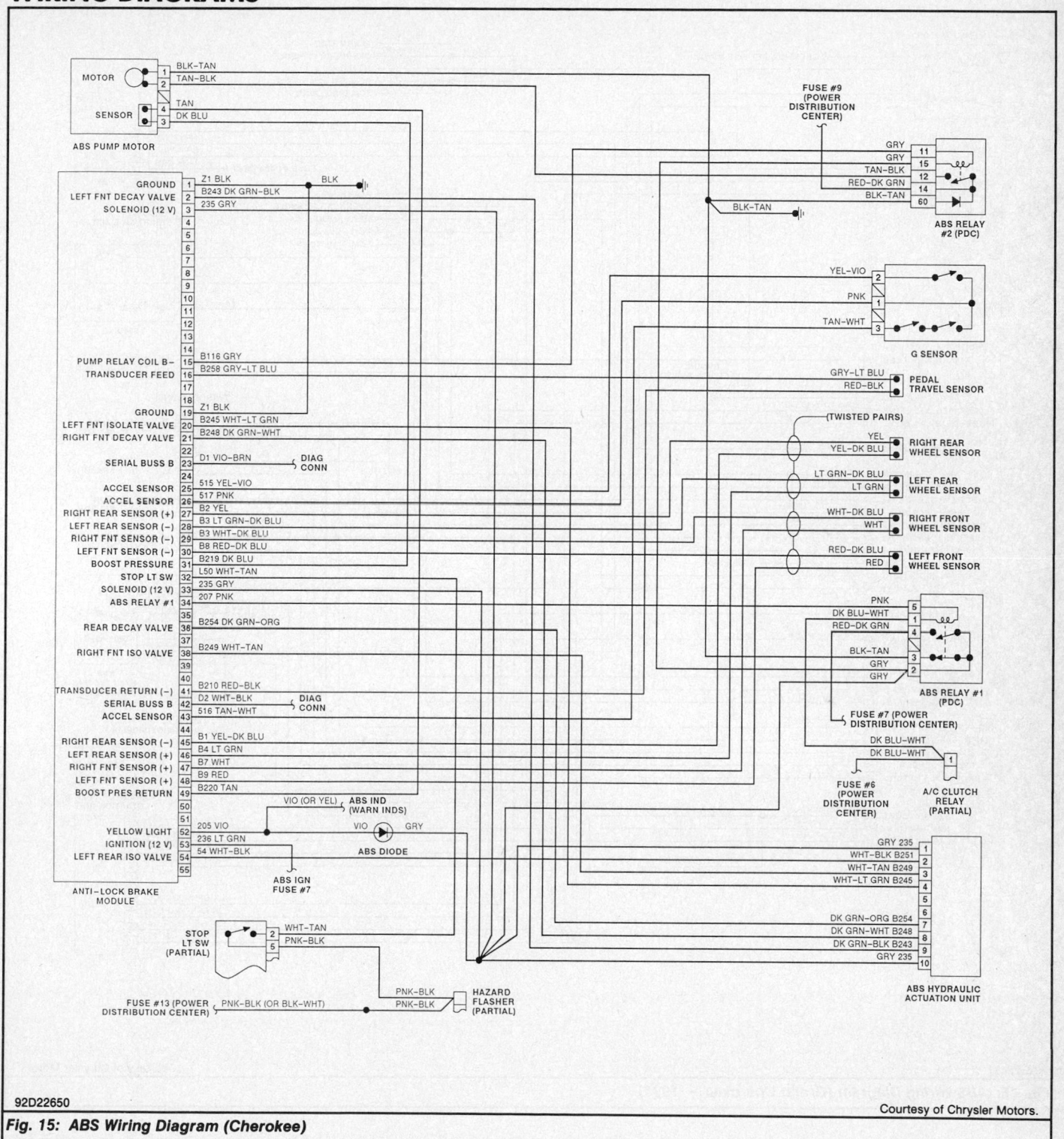

92D22650

Courtesy of Chrysler Motors.

Fig. 15: ABS Wiring Diagram (Cherokee)

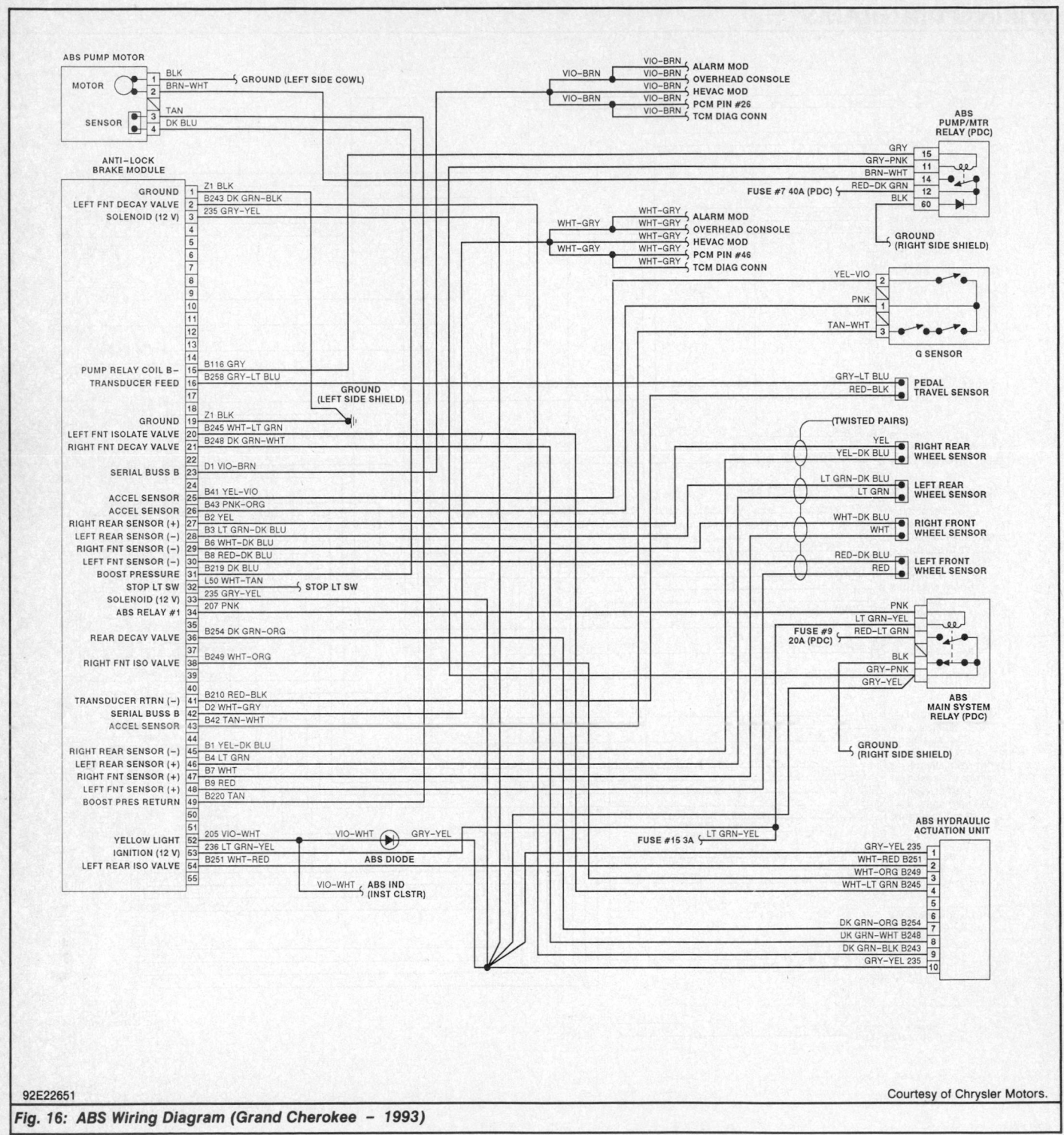

92E22651

Courtesy of Chrysler Motors.

Fig. 16: ABS Wiring Diagram (Grand Cherokee – 1993)

SELF-DIAGNOSTIC TESTS

NOTE: Connector and terminal identification illustrations in following tests are provided courtesy of Chrysler Motors.

NOTE: For connector terminal identification in following tests, see CONNECTOR IDENTIFICATION under DIAGNOSIS & TESTING. For wire color and terminal identification, see WIRING DIAGRAMS.

TEST 1A
READING FAULT MESSAGES

Using DRB-II, read fault messages and perform appropriate test listed in FAULT MESSAGES table. If DRB-II displays NO RESPONSE message, perform TEST 23A. If other DRB-II related communication problems exist, see VEHICLE COMMUNICATIONS article in ENGINE PERFORMANCE. If multiple fault messages are present, fault repairs must be performed in order in which they are displayed. If no fault messages are present, perform VERIFICATION TEST VER-1A.

FAULT MESSAGES

Fault Message	Perform Test
CONTROLLER FAILURE	2A
"G" SWITCH NOT PROCESSABLE	3A
HYDRAULIC FAILURE	4A
LEFT FRONT INLET VALVE	5A
LEFT FRONT OUTLET VALVE	6A
LEFT FRONT SENSOR CIRCUIT FAILURE	7A
LEFT FRONT SENSOR CONTINUITY>25 MPH	7A
LEFT FRONT SENSOR CONTINUITY<25 MPH	7A
LEFT FRONT SENSOR SIGNAL MISSING	7A
LEFT FRONT WHEEL SPEED COMPARISON	7A
REAR INLET VALVE	9A
REAR OUTLET VALVE	10A
LEFT REAR SENSOR CIRCUIT FAILURE	11A
LEFT REAR SENSOR CONTINUITY>25 MPH	11A
LEFT REAR SENSOR CONTINUITY<25 MPH	11A
LEFT REAR SENSOR SIGNAL MISSING	11A
LEFT REAR WHEEL SPEED COMPARISON	11A
MAIN RELAY/POWER CIRCUIT FAILURE	13A
PEDAL TRAVEL SENSOR CIRCUIT	14A
PUMP MOTOR CIRCUIT NOT WORKING PROPERLY	15A
RIGHT FRONT INLET VALVE	16A
RIGHT FRONT OUTLET VALVE	17A
RIGHT FRONT CIRCUIT FAILURE	18A
RIGHT FRONT SENSOR CONTINUITY>25 MPH	18A
RIGHT FRONT SENSOR CONTINUITY<25 MPH	18A
RIGHT FRONT REAR SENSOR SIGNAL MISSING	18A
RIGHT FRONT WHEEL SPEED COMPARISON	18A
RIGHT REAR SENSOR CIRCUIT FAILURE	20A
RIGHT REAR SENSOR CONTINUITY>25 MPH	20A
RIGHT REAR SENSOR CONTINUITY<25 MPH	20A
RIGHT REAR SENSOR SIGNAL MISSING	20A
RIGHT REAR WHEEL SPEED COMPARISON	20A
ABS WARNING LAMP ILLUMINATION PROBLEM	22A
NO RESPONSE	23A

TEST 2A
CONTROLLER FAILURE

If DRB-II displays CONTROLLER FAILURE, replace Controller Anti-Lock Brake (CAB). Perform VERIFICATION TEST VER-1A.

TEST 3A
"G" SWITCH NOT PROCESSABLE

1) Ensure "G" switch sensor assembly is properly installed. If not properly installed, repair as necessary and perform VERIFICATION TEST VER-1A. If "G" switch is properly installed, turn ignition off. Disconnect and inspect CAB 55-pin connector and "G" switch sensor 3-pin connector. Repair connectors as necessary.

2) Turn ignition on. With DRB-II in voltmeter mode, probe "G" switch connector terminals individually. If voltage is present, repair short to voltage in that "G" switch circuit. Perform VERIFICATION TEST VER-1A. If voltage is not present at any terminals, go to next step.

3) With DRB-II in ohmmeter mode, probe "G" switch connector terminals individually with remaining lead connected to chassis ground. If resistance at any terminal is less than 5 ohms, repair short to ground in that circuit. Perform VERIFICATION TEST VER-1A.

4) If resistance at each terminal is more than 5 ohms, connect jumper wire between ground and "G" switch terminals No. 1-3. Check for continuity to ground on CAB terminals No. 25, 26 and 43. If continuity to ground does not exist, repair open in that circuit. Perform VERIFICATION TEST VER-1A. If continuity to ground exists, replace CAB. Perform VERIFICATION TEST VER-1A.

TEST 4A
HYDRAULIC FAILURE

1) Inspect brake system for hydraulic leaks, and repair as necessary. If brake system is okay, using DRB-II, read fault messages. If DRB-II displays PUMP/MOTOR NOT WORKING PROPERLY, perform TEST 15A. If DRB-II does not display PUMP/MOTOR NOT WORKING PROPERLY, using DRB-II, erase fault messages.

2) Using DRB-II, monitor read faults display for 4 minutes. If any fault messages are displayed, perform TEST 1A. If no fault messages are displayed, depress brake pedal. Using DRB-II, actuate any of the outlet valves and actuate pump motor.

3) If brake pedal came back up, perform TEST 14A. If brake pedal did not come back up, check if pump/motor turned on when actuated by DRB-II. If pump/motor is on, replace pump/motor assembly. If pump/motor is off, perform TEST 15A.

TEST 5A
LEFT FRONT INLET VALVE

1) Disconnect and inspect hydraulic unit 10-pin connector. Repair connector as necessary. Turn ignition on. With DRB-II in voltmeter mode, probe terminal No. 4 (White/Light Green wire) of hydraulic unit connector. If voltage is present, repair short to voltage in White/Light Green wire. Perform VERIFICATION TEST VER-1A.

2) If voltage is not present, turn ignition off. Disconnect and inspect CAB 55-pin connector. Repair connector as necessary. With DRB-II in ohmmeter mode, probe terminal No. 4 (White/Light Green wire) of hydraulic unit connector. If resistance is less than 5 ohms, repair short to ground in White/Light Green wire.

3) If resistance is more than 5 ohms, check resistance of White/Light Green wire between terminals No. 20 of CAB connector and No. 4 of hydraulic unit connector using an external ohmmeter. If resistance is less than 5 ohms, repair short to ground in White/Light Green wire. Perform VERIFICATION TEST VER-1A. If resistance is more than 5 ohms, replace CAB, Perform VERIFICATION TEST VER-1A.

TEST 6A
LEFT FRONT OUTLET VALVE

1) Disconnect and inspect hydraulic unit 10-pin connector. Repair connector as necessary. Turn ignition on. With DRB-II in voltmeter mode, probe terminal No. 9 (Dark Green/Black wire) of hydraulic unit connector. If voltage is present, repair short to voltage in Dark Green/Black wire. Perform VERIFICATION TEST VER-1A.

2) If voltage is not present, turn ignition off. Disconnect and inspect CAB 55-pin connector. Repair connector as necessary. With DRB-II in ohmmeter mode, probe terminal No. 9 (Dark Green/Black wire) of hydraulic unit connector. If resistance is less than 5 ohms, repair short to ground in Dark Green/Black wire.

3) If resistance is more than 5 ohms, check resistance of Dark Green/Black wire between terminals No. 2 of CAB connector and No. 9 of hydraulic unit connector using an external ohmmeter. If resistance is less than 5 ohms, repair short to ground in Dark Green/Black wire. Perform VERIFICATION TEST VER-1A. If resistance is more than 5 ohms, replace CAB. Perform VERIFICATION TEST VER-1A.

TEST 7A
LEFT FRONT SENSOR CIRCUIT FAILURE

1) Using DRB-II, read and record all speed sensor fault messages. If DRB-II does not display LEFT FRONT SENSOR CIRCUIT FAILURE, perform TEST 8A. If DRB-II displays LEFT FRONT SENSOR CIRCUIT FAILURE, inspect left front wheel speed sensor for damage. If sensor is damaged, repair or replace sensor as necessary. If sensor is okay, turn ignition off.

2) Disconnect and inspect CAB 55-pin connector. Repair connector as necessary. Turn ignition on. With DRB-II in voltmeter mode, probe terminal No. 48 (Red wire) of CAB connector. If voltage is present, repair short to battery in Red wire. Perform VERIFICATION TEST VER-1A.

3) If voltage is not present, put DRB-II in ohmmeter mode. Probe terminal No. 48 (Red wire) of CAB connector. If resistance is less than 5 ohms, repair short to ground in Red wire. Perform VERIFICATION TEST VER-1A. If resistance is more than 5 ohms, go to next step.

4) Using an external ohmmeter, check resistance between terminals No. 48 (Red wire) and 30 (Red/Dark Blue wire) of CAB connector. If resistance is 900-1300 ohms, replace CAB. Perform VERIFICATION TEST VER-1A. If resistance is not 900-1300 ohms, disconnect and inspect left front wheel speed sensor connector.

5) Using an external ohmmeter, check resistance between left wheel speed sensor connector terminals. If resistance is not 900-1300 ohms, replace wheel speed sensor. If resistance is 900-1300 ohms, check resistance of Red wire between terminals No. 48 of CAB connector and No. 1 of left front wheel speed sensor connector using an external ohmmeter.

6) If resistance is more than 5 ohms, repair open Red wire. Perform VERIFICATION TEST VER-1A. If resistance is less than 5 ohms, repair open Red/Dark Blue wire. Perform VERIFICATION TEST VER-1A.

TEST 8A
LEFT FRONT SENSOR

1) Inspect left front wheel speed sensor for damage. Repair or replace sensor as necessary. If sensor is okay, check left front sensor tone (pulse) ring for damage. Repair or replace tone ring as necessary. If tone ring is okay, inspect left front wheel speed sensor wiring harness for damage.

2) Repair or replace wiring as necessary. If wiring harness is okay, disconnect and inspect left front wheel speed sensor connector. Repair connector as necessary. Using an external ohmmeter, check resistance between left front wheel speed sensor connector terminals.

3) If resistance is not 900-1300 ohms, replace wheel speed sensor. Perform VERIFICATION TEST VER-1A. If resistance is 900-1300 ohms, replace CAB. Perform VERIFICATION TEST VER-1A.

TEST 9A
REAR INLET VALVE

1) Disconnect and inspect hydraulic unit 10-pin connector. Repair connector as necessary. Turn ignition on. With DRB-II in voltmeter mode, probe No. 2 (White/Black wire on Cherokee or White/Red wire on Grand Cherokee) of hydraulic unit connector. If voltage is present, repair short to voltage in White/Black or White/Red wire. Perform VERIFICATION TEST VER-1A.

2) If voltage is not present, turn ignition off. Disconnect and inspect CAB 55-pin connector. Repair connector as necessary. With DRB-II in ohmmeter mode, probe terminal No. 2 of hydraulic unit connector. If resistance is less than 5 ohms, repair short to ground in White/Black or White/Red wire.

3) If resistance is more than 5 ohms, check resistance of between terminals No. 54 of CAB connector and No. 4 of hydraulic unit connector using an external ohmmeter. If resistance is less than 5 ohms, repair short to ground in White/Black or White/Red wire. Perform VERIFICATION TEST VER-1A. If resistance is more than 5 ohms, replace CAB. Perform VERIFICATION TEST VER-1A.

TEST 10A
REAR OUTLET VALVE

1) Disconnect and inspect hydraulic unit 10-pin connector. Repair connector as necessary. Turn ignition on. With DRB-II in voltmeter mode, probe terminal No. 7 (Dark Green/Orange wire) of hydraulic unit connector. If voltage is present, repair short to voltage in Dark Green/Orange wire. Perform VERIFICATION TEST VER-1A.

2) If voltage is not present, turn ignition off. Disconnect and inspect CAB 55-pin connector. Repair connector as necessary. With DRB-II in ohmmeter mode, probe terminal No. 7 (Dark Green/Orange wire) of hydraulic unit connector. If resistance is less than 5 ohms, repair short to ground in Dark Green/Orange wire.

3) If resistance is more than 5 ohms, check resistance of Dark Green/Orange wire between terminals No. 36 of CAB connector and No. 7 of hydraulic unit connector using an external ohmmeter. If resistance is less more than 5 ohms, repair open Dark Green/Orange wire. Perform VERIFICATION TEST VER-1A. If resistance is less than 5 ohms, go to next step.

4) Using an external ohmmeter, check resistance between terminals No. 7 and 10 of hydraulic control unit connector. If resistance is not 3-5 ohms, replace hydraulic control unit. Perform VERIFICATION TEST VER-1A. If resistance is 3-5 ohms, replace CAB. Perform VERIFICATION TEST VER-1A.

TEST 11A
LEFT REAR SENSOR CIRCUIT FAILURE

1) Using DRB-II, read and record all speed sensor fault messages. If DRB-II does not display LEFT REAR SENSOR CIRCUIT FAILURE, perform TEST 12A. If DRB-II displays LEFT REAR SENSOR CIRCUIT FAILURE, inspect left rear wheel speed sensor for damage. If sensor is damaged, repair or replace sensor as necessary. If sensor is okay, turn ignition off.

2) Disconnect and inspect CAB 55-pin connector. Repair connector as necessary. Turn ignition on. With DRB-II in voltmeter mode, probe terminal No. 46 (Light Green wire) of CAB connector. If voltage is present, perform TEST 11B.

3) If voltage is not present, put DRB-II in ohmmeter mode. Probe terminal No. 46 (Light Green wire) of CAB connector. If resistance is less than 5 ohms, perform TEST 11C. If resistance is more than 5 ohms, using an external ohmmeter, check resistance between terminals No. 46 (Light Green wire) and No. 28 (Light Green/Dark Blue wire) of CAB connector.

4) If resistance is 900-1300 ohms, replace CAB. Perform VERIFICATION TEST VER-1A. If resistance is not 900-1300 ohms, disconnect and inspect left rear wheel speed sensor connector. Using an external ohmmeter, check resistance between left rear wheel speed sensor connector terminals. If resistance is not 900-1300 ohms, replace wheel speed sensor.

5) If resistance is 900-1300 ohms, connect a jumper wire between terminal No. 46 (Light Green wire) of CAB connector and ground. With DRB-II in ohmmeter mode, probe Light Green wire of left rear wheel speed sensor connector. If resistance is more than 5 ohms, perform TEST 11D. If resistance is less than 5 ohms, perform TEST 11E.

TEST 11B

LEFT REAR SENSOR CIRCUIT FAILURE

1) On Cherokee, repair short to battery in Light Green wire. Perform VERIFICATION TEST VER-1A. On Grand Cherokee, disconnect and inspect ABS 8-pin disconnect connector. Connector is located behind left side kick panel. Repair connector as necessary. With DRB-II in voltmeter mode, probe Light Green wire of ABS disconnect connector.

2) If voltage is not present, repair short to battery in Light Green wire between wheel speed sensor and CAB disconnect connector. Perform VERIFICATION TEST VER-1A. If voltage is present, repair short to battery in Light Green wire between ABS disconnect connector and CAB 55-pin connector. Perform VERIFICATION TEST VER-1A.

TEST 11C

LEFT REAR SENSOR CIRCUIT FAILURE

1) On Cherokee, repair short to ground in Light Green wire. Perform VERIFICATION TEST VER-1A. On Grand Cherokee, disconnect and inspect CAB 8-pin disconnect connector. Connector is located behind left side kick panel. Repair connector as necessary. With DRB-II in ohmmeter mode, probe Light Green wire of ABS disconnect connector.

2) If resistance is more than 5 ohms, repair short to ground in Light Green wire between wheel speed sensor and ABS disconnect connector. Perform VERIFICATION TEST VER-1A. If resistance is less than 5 ohms, repair short to ground in Light Green wire between ABS disconnect connector and CAB 55-pin connector. Perform VERIFICATION TEST VER-1A.

TEST 11D

LEFT REAR SENSOR CIRCUIT FAILURE

1) On Cherokee, repair open in Light Green wire. Perform VERIFICATION TEST VER-1A. On Grand Cherokee, disconnect and inspect CAB 8-pin disconnect connector. Connector is located behind left side kick panel. Repair connector as necessary. With DRB-II in ohmmeter mode, probe Light Green wire of ABS disconnect connector.

2) If resistance is less than 5 ohms, repair open in Light Green wire between wheel speed sensor and ABS disconnect connector. Perform VERIFICATION TEST VER-1A. If resistance is more than 5 ohms, repair open in Light Green wire between ABS disconnect connector and CAB 55-pin connector. Perform VERIFICATION TEST VER-1A.

TEST 11E

LEFT REAR SENSOR CIRCUIT FAILURE

1) On Cherokee, repair open in Light Green/Dark Blue wire. Perform VERIFICATION TEST VER-1A. On Grand Cherokee, disconnect and inspect ABS 8-pin disconnect connector. Connector is located behind left side kick panel. Repair connector as necessary. Connect a jumper wire between terminal No. 28 (Light Green/Dark Blue wire) of ABS disconnect connector and ground. With DRB-II in ohmmeter mode, probe Light Green/Dark Blue wire of ABS disconnect connector.

2) If resistance is less than 5 ohms, repair open in Light Green/Dark Blue wire between wheel speed sensor and ABS disconnect connector. Perform VERIFICATION TEST VER-1A. If resistance is more than 5 ohms, repair open in Light Green/Dark Blue wire between ABS disconnect connector and CAB 55-pin connector. Perform VERIFICATION TEST VER-1A.

TEST 12A

LEFT REAR SENSOR

1) Inspect left rear wheel speed sensor. If speed sensor is damaged, contaminated or loose, repair or replace speed sensor as necessary. If speed sensor is okay, inspect left rear tone (pulse) ring for damaged teeth or excessive runout. Runout should not exceed .003" (.08 mm). Repair or replace tone ring as necessary.

TEST 12A (Cont.)

2) If tone ring is okay, using a feeler gauge, check left rear wheel sensor-to-tone ring clearance. If clearance is not .036-.050" (.91-1.27 mm), repair as necessary. If clearance is .036-.050" (.91-1.27 mm), inspect left rear wheel speed sensor inspect left front wheel speed sensor wiring harness for damage.

3) Repair or replace wiring as necessary. If wiring harness is okay, disconnect and inspect left rear wheel speed sensor connector. Repair connector as necessary. Using an external ohmmeter, check resistance between left rear wheel speed sensor connector terminals.

4) If resistance is not 900-1300 ohms, replace wheel speed sensor. Perform VERIFICATION TEST VER-1A. If resistance is 900-1300 ohms, replace CAB. Perform VERIFICATION TEST VER-1A.

TEST 13A

MAIN RELAY/POWER CIRCUIT FAILURE

1) Check ABS system fuse in Power Distribution Center (PDC). If fuse is not okay, perform TEST 13B. If fuse is okay, go to next step.

2) Check if charging system is overcharging. If charging system is operating properly, go to next step. If charging system is not operating properly, repair as necessary. Perform VERIFICATION TEST VER-1A.

3) Temporarily replace ABS main relay with another 5-terminal relay from PDC. Using DRB-II, erase ABS fault messages. Cycle ignition off and on. Using DRB-II, read ABS fault messages. If MAIN RELAY POWER CIRCUIT FAILURE message is displayed, go to next step. If fault is not displayed, replace ABS main relay. Perform VERIFICATION TEST VER-1A.

4) Install replacement 5-terminal relay back into PDC, leaving ABS main relay disconnected (removed). With DRB-II in voltmeter mode, probe fused battery feed Red/Dark Green wire (Red/Light Green wire on Grand Cherokee) at ABS main relay socket. If voltage is more than 9 volts, go to next step. If voltage is less than 9 volts, repair open Red/Dark Green wire (Red/Light Green on Grand Cherokee) wire to ABS fuse in PDC. Perform VERIFICATION TEST VER-1A.

5) Turn ignition off. Disconnect and inspect CAB 55-pin connector. Repair connector as necessary. Ensure ABS main relay is still disconnected. Using an external ohmmeter, check continuity of Pink wire between CAB connector terminal No. 34 and ABS main relay socket. If resistance is less than 5 ohms, go to next step. If resistance is more than 5 ohms, repair open Pink wire to ABS main relay. Perform VERIFICATION TEST VER-1A.

6) Check continuity of Gray wire (Gray/Yellow wire on Grand Cherokee) between CAB connector terminal No. 3 and ABS main relay socket. If resistance is less than 5 ohms, go to next step. If resistance is more than 5 ohms, repair open Gray wire (Gray/Yellow wire on Grand Cherokee) wire to ABS main relay. Perform VERIFICATION TEST VER-1A.

7) Check continuity of Gray wire (Gray/Yellow wire on Grand Cherokee) between CAB connector terminal No. 33 and ABS main relay socket. If resistance is less than 5 ohms, replace CAB. Perform VERIFICATION TEST VER-1A. If resistance is more than 5 ohms, repair open Gray wire (Gray/Yellow wire on Grand Cherokee) wire to ABS main relay. Perform VERIFICATION TEST VER-1A.

TEST 13B

MAIN RELAY/POWER CIRCUIT FAILURE

1) Remove ABS system fuse from Power Distribution Center (PDC). Remove ABS main relay from PDC, and inspect connector. Repair connector as necessary. With DRB-II in ohmmeter mode, probe fused battery feed Red/Dark Green wire (Red/Light Green wire on Grand Cherokee) at ABS main relay socket. If resistance is less than 5 ohms, repair Red/Dark Green wire (Red/Light Green wire on Grand Cherokee) wire for a short to ground. Perform VERIFICATION TEST VER-1A. If resistance is more than 5 ohms, go to next step.

2) Remove ABS pump/motor relay from PDC, and inspect connector. Repair connector as necessary. Using an external ohmmeter, measure resistance of ABS pump/motor relay coil. See Fig. 13B. If resistance is 35-65 ohms, go to next step. If resistance is not 35-65 ohms, replace ABS pump/motor relay. Perform VERIFICATION TEST VER-1A.

TEST 13B (Cont.)

3) Disconnect HCU 10-pin connector. With DRB-II in ohmmeter mode, probe Red/Dark Green wire (Red/Light Green on Grand Cherokee) at ABS main relay socket. If resistance is less than 5 ohms, repair Red/Dark Green wire (Red/Light Green on Grand Cherokee) wire for a short to ground. Perform VERIFICATION TEST VER-1A. If resistance is more than 5 ohms, go to next step.

4) Reconnect all disconnected components. Install a new ABS fuse in PDC and cycle ignition off and on. Inspect ABS fuse in PDC. If fuse is okay (does not blow), perform TEST 13C. If fuse is not okay (blows), replace hydraulic control unit. Perform VERIFICATION TEST VER-1A.

92J22490

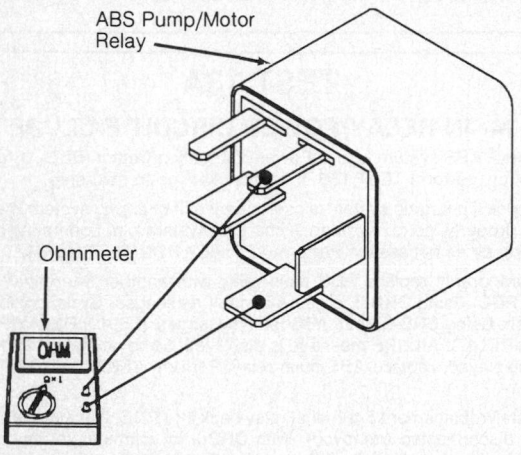

ABS Pump/Motor Relay

Ohmmeter

Fig. 13B: Measuring ABS Pump/Motor Relay Resistance

TEST 13C

MAIN RELAY/POWER CIRCUIT FAILURE

1) Ensure DRB-II is NOT in TEVES ABS DIAGNOSTIC MODE. Road test vehicle, making several ABS stops. Inspect ABS fuse in PDC. If fuse is okay (does not blow), ABS system is operating properly at this time. Perform VERIFICATION TEST VER-1A.

2) If fuse is not okay (blows), inspect ABS wiring harness for damage. If wiring harness is okay, replace hydraulic control unit. Perform VERIFICATION TEST VER-1A. If wiring harness is damaged, repair wiring harness as necessary. Perform VERIFICATION TEST VER-1A.

TEST 14A

PEDAL TRAVEL SENSOR CIRCUIT

1) Inspect pedal travel sensor connector. Sensor is located on right side of brake booster. If connector is disconnected and/or damaged, repair connector as necessary and perform VERIFICATION TEST VER-1A. If connector is properly connected and NOT damaged, go to next step.

2) Turn ignition off. Disconnect and inspect CAB 55-pin connector. Repair connector as necessary. Turn ignition on. Disconnect and inspect pedal travel sensor connector. Repair connector as necessary. With DRB-II in voltmeter mode, probe Gray/Light Blue wire at sensor connector. If no voltage is present, go to next step. If any voltage is present, repair Gray/Light Blue wire for a short to battery voltage. Perform VERIFICATION TEST VER-1A.

3) With DRB-II in ohmmeter mode, probe Gray/Light Blue wire at pedal travel sensor connector. If resistance is less than 5 ohms, repair Gray/Light Blue wire for a short to ground. Perform VERIFICATION TEST VER-1A. If resistance is more than 5 ohms, go to next step.

4) Using an external ohmmeter, measure resistance between CAB connector terminal No. 16 and pedal travel sensor connector Gray/Light Blue wire. If resistance is less than 5 ohms, go to next step. If resistance is more than 5 ohms, repair open Gray/Light Blue wire to pedal travel sensor. Perform VERIFICATION TEST VER-1A.

TEST 14A (Cont.)

5) Using an external ohmmeter, measure resistance between CAB connector terminal No. 41 and pedal travel sensor connector Red/Black wire. If resistance is less than 5 ohms, go to next step. If resistance is more than 5 ohms, repair open Red/Black wire to pedal travel sensor. Perform VERIFICATION TEST VER-1A.

6) Remove pedal travel sensor from brake booster. Check if sensor plunger cap color matches dot color on booster (near sensor). If colors match, go to next step. If colors do not match, replace pedal travel sensor. Perform VERIFICATION TEST VER-1A.

7) Using an external ohmmeter, measure resistance of pedal travel sensor while slowly depressing sensor plunger. If sensor resistance is as specified, replace CAB. See PEDAL TRAVEL SENSOR RESISTANCE table. Perform VERIFICATION TEST VER-1A. If sensor resistance is not as specified, replace pedal travel sensor. Perform VERIFICATION TEST VER-1A.

PEDAL TRAVEL SENSOR RESISTANCE

Plunger Position	Ohms
Step 1 (Rest)	236-262
Step 2	414-458
Step 3	534-592
Step 4	655-725
Step 5	776-858
Step 6	980-1084
Step 7	Infinity

TEST 15A

PUMP MOTOR CIRCUIT NOT WORKING PROPERLY

1) Inspect ABS pump/motor fuse from Power Distribution Center (PDC). If fuse is okay, go to next step. If fuse is not okay (blown), perform TEST 15B.

2) Remove ABS pump/motor relay from PDC, and inspect connector. Repair connector as necessary. With DRB-II in voltmeter mode, probe Red/Dark Green wire at ABS pump/motor relay socket. If voltage is more than 9 volts, go to next step. If voltage is less than 9 volts, repair open Red/Dark Green wire to ABS pump/motor relay.

3) Connect a jumper wire between Red/Dark Green wire and Tan/Black wire (Brown/White wire on Grand Cherokee) at ABS pump/motor relay socket. Inspect ABS pump/motor fuse. If fuse is okay (does not blow), go to next step. If fuse is not okay (blows), perform TEST 15B.

4) Listen for ABS pump/motor operation. If ABS pump/motor is running, go to next step. If ABS pump/motor is not running, perform TEST 15C.

5) Turn ignition off. Remove jumper wire used in step 3), and ensure ABS main relay is installed in PDC. With DRB-II in ohmmeter mode, probe Gray wire (Gray/Pink wire on Grand Cherokee) at ABS pump/motor relay socket. If resistance is less than 5 ohms, go to next step. If resistance is more than 5 ohms, repair open Gray wire (Gray/Pink wire on Grand Cherokee) wire between ABS pump/motor relay socket and ABS main relay. Perform VERIFICATION TEST VER-1A.

6) Using an external ohmmeter, measure resistance of ABS pump/motor relay coil. *See Fig. 13B.* If resistance is 35-65 ohms, go to next step. If resistance is not 35-65 ohms, replace ABS pump/motor relay. Perform VERIFICATION TEST VER-1A.

7) Disconnect and inspect CAB 55-pin connector. Repair connector as necessary. Turn ignition on. With DRB-II in voltmeter mode, probe Gray wire (Gray/Pink wire on Grand Cherokee) at ABS pump/motor relay socket. If no voltage is present, go to next step. If any voltage is present, repair Gray wire (Gray/Pink wire on Grand Cherokee) for a short to battery voltage. Perform VERIFICATION TEST VER-1A.

8) With DRB-II in ohmmeter mode, probe Gray wire at ABS pump/motor relay socket. If resistance is less than 5 ohms, repair Gray wire for a short to ground. Perform VERIFICATION TEST VER-1A. If resistance is more than 5 ohms, go to next step.

9) Using an external ohmmeter, measure resistance between CAB connector terminal No. 15 and ABS pump/motor relay socket Gray wire (Gray/Pink wire on Grand Cherokee). If resistance is less than 5 ohms, go to next step. If resistance is more than 5 ohms, repair open Gray wire (Gray/Pink wire on Grand Cherokee) to relay socket. Perform VERIFICATION TEST VER-1A.

TEST 15A (Cont.)

10) Turn ignition off. Reinstall ABS pump/motor relay in PDC. Apply battery voltage to CAB connector terminal No. 15, and go to next step.

11) Ensure ignition is off. With DRB-II in voltmeter mode, probe Tan/Black wire (Brown/White wire on Grand Cherokee) at ABS pump/motor 4-pin harness connector. If voltage is more than 9 volts, perform TEST 15D. If voltage is less than 9 volts, replace ABS pump/motor relay. Perform VERIFICATION TEST VER-1A.

TEST 15B

PUMP MOTOR CIRCUIT NOT WORKING PROPERLY

1) Remove ABS pump/motor relay, if installed, from Power Distribution Center (PDC). Remove jumper wire from ABS pump/motor relay socket (if installed). Turn ignition off, and go to next step.

2) With DRB-II in ohmmeter mode, probe Tan/Black wire (Brown/White wire on Grand Cherokee) at ABS pump/motor relay socket. If resistance is less than 5 ohms, repair Tan/Black wire (Brown/White wire on Grand Cherokee) for a short to ground. If resistance is more than 5 ohms, go to next step.

3) Using an external ohmmeter, check ABS pump/motor relay diode. Attach ohmmeter positive and negative leads as shown. See Fig. 15B. If continuity exists, replace ABS pump/motor relay. Perform VERIFICATION TEST VER-1A. If no continuity exists, replace ABS pump/motor assembly. Perform VERIFICATION TEST VER-1A.

92A22491

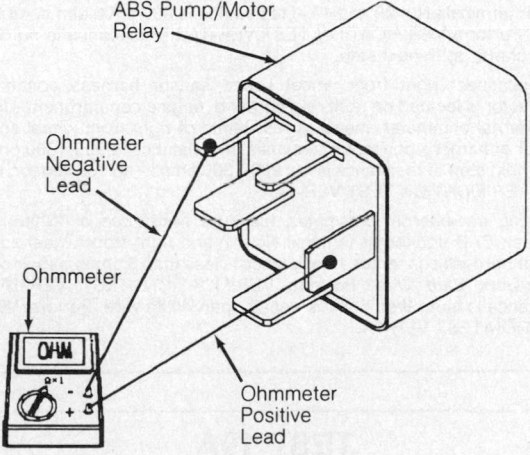

ABS Pump/Motor Relay

Ohmmeter Negative Lead

Ohmmeter

Ohmmeter Positive Lead

Fig. 15B: Checking ABS Pump/Motor Relay Diode

TEST 15C

PUMP MOTOR CIRCUIT NOT WORKING PROPERLY

1) Disconnect ABS pump/motor 4-pin connector at hydraulic control unit. Ensure jumper wire is still connected between Red/Dark Green wire and Tan/Black wire (Brown/White wire on Grand Cherokee) at ABS pump/motor relay socket.

2) With DRB-II in voltmeter mode, probe Tan/Black wire (Brown/White wire on Grand Cherokee) at ABS pump/motor 4-pin harness connector. If voltage is more than 9 volts, go to next step. If voltage is less than 9 volts, repair open Tan/Black wire (Brown/White wire on Grand Cherokee) to 4-pin harness connector. Perform VERIFICATION TEST VER-1A.

3) With DRB-II in ohmmeter mode, probe Black/Tan ground wire (Black ground wire on Grand Cherokee) at ABS pump/motor 4-pin harness connector. If resistance is less than 5 ohms, replace ABS pump/motor assembly. Perform VERIFICATION TEST VER-1A. If resistance is more than 5 ohms, repair Black/Tan ground wire (Black ground wire on Grand Cherokee). Perform VERIFICATION TEST VER-1A.

TEST 15D

PUMP MOTOR CIRCUIT NOT WORKING PROPERLY

1) Using an external ohmmeter, measure resistance of ABS pump/motor speed sensor. If sensor resistance is 10-35 ohms, go to next step. If resistance is not 10-35 ohms, replace ABS pump/motor assembly. Perform VERIFICATION TEST VER-1A.

2) Turn ignition on. With DRB-II in voltmeter mode, probe Tan wire at ABS pump/motor 4-pin harness connector. If any voltage is present, repair ABS pump/motor speed sensor Tan wire for a short to battery voltage. Perform VERIFICATION TEST VER-1A. If no voltage is present, go to next step.

3) With DRB-II in voltmeter mode, probe Dark Blue wire at ABS pump/motor 4-pin harness connector. If any voltage is present, repair ABS pump/motor speed sensor Dark Blue wire for a short to battery voltage. Perform VERIFICATION TEST VER-1A. If no voltage is present, go to next step.

4) With DRB-II in ohmmeter mode, probe Tan wire at ABS pump/motor 4-pin harness connector. See Fig. 15D. If resistance is less than 5 ohms, repair ABS pump/motor speed sensor Tan wire for a short to ground. Perform VERIFICATION TEST VER-1A. If resistance is more than 5 ohms, go to next step.

5) With DRB-II in ohmmeter mode, probe Dark Blue wire at ABS pump/motor 4-pin harness connector. If resistance is less than 5 ohms, repair ABS pump/motor speed sensor Dark Blue wire for a short to ground. Perform VERIFICATION TEST VER-1A. If resistance is more than 5 ohms, go to next step.

6) Using an external ohmmeter, measure resistance of Tan wire between CAB connector terminal No. 49 and ABS pump/motor 4-pin harness connector. If resistance is less than 5 ohms, go to next step. If resistance is more than 5 ohms, repair open ABS pump/motor speed sensor Tan wire. Perform VERIFICATION TEST VER-1A.

7) Using an external ohmmeter, measure resistance of Dark Blue wire between CAB connector terminal No. 31 and ABS pump/motor 4-pin harness connector. If resistance is less than 5 ohms, replace CAB. Perform VERIFICATION TEST VER-1A. If resistance is more than 5 ohms, repair open ABS pump/motor speed sensor Dark Blue wire. Perform VERIFICATION TEST VER-1A.

92B22492

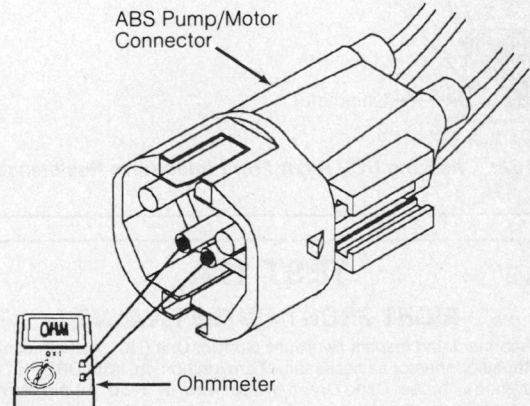

ABS Pump/Motor Connector

Ohmmeter

Fig. 15D: Checking ABS Pump/Motor Sensor Resistance

TEST 16A

RIGHT FRONT INLET VALVE

1) Disconnect and inspect Hydraulic Control Unit (HCU) 10-pin connector. Repair connector as necessary. Turn ignition on. With DRB-II in voltmeter mode, probe White/Tan wire (White/Orange wire on Grand Cherokee) at HCU 10-pin harness connector. If no voltage is present, go to next step. If any voltage is present, repair White/Tan wire (White/Orange wire on Grand Cherokee) for a short to battery power. Perform VERIFICATION TEST VER-1A.

2) Turn ignition off. Disconnect and inspect CAB 55-pin connector. Repair connector as necessary. With DRB-II in ohmmeter mode, probe White/Tan wire (White/Orange wire on Grand Cherokee) at HCU 10-pin harness connector. If resistance is more than 5 ohms, go to next step. If resistance is less than 5 ohms, repair White/Tan wire (White/Orange wire on Grand Cherokee) for a short to ground. Perform VERIFICATION TEST VER-1A.

3) Using an external ohmmeter, measure resistance of White/Tan wire (White/Orange wire on Grand Cherokee) between CAB connector terminal No. 38 and HCU 10-pin harness connector. If resistance is less than 5 ohms, go to next step. If resistance is more than 5 ohms, repair open White/Tan wire (White/Orange wire on Grand Cherokee). Perform VERIFICATION TEST VER-1A.

4) Using an external ohmmeter, measure resistance of right front inlet valve between terminals No. 3 and 5 at HCU connector. *See Fig. 16A.* If resistance is 5-8 ohms, replace CAB. Perform VERIFICATION TEST VER-1A. If resistance is not 5-8 ohms, replace hydraulic control unit. Perform VERIFICATION TEST VER-1A.

92C22493

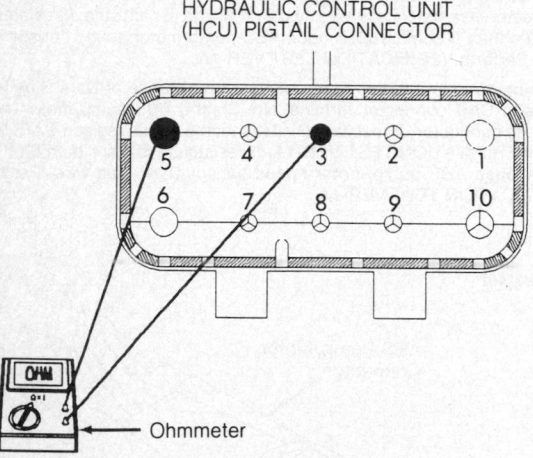

HYDRAULIC CONTROL UNIT
(HCU) PIGTAIL CONNECTOR

Ohmmeter

Fig. 16A: Checking HCU Right Front Inlet Valve Resistance

TEST 17A

RIGHT FRONT OUTLET VALVE

1) Disconnect and inspect Hydraulic Control Unit (HCU) 10-pin connector. Repair connector as necessary. Turn ignition on. With DRB-II in voltmeter mode, probe Dark Green/White wire at HCU 10-pin harness connector. If no voltage is present, go to next step. If any voltage is present, repair Dark Green/White wire for a short to battery power. Perform VERIFICATION TEST VER-1A.

2) Turn ignition off. Disconnect and inspect CAB 55-pin connector. Repair connector as necessary. With DRB-II in ohmmeter mode, probe Dark Green/White wire at HCU 10-pin harness connector. If resistance is more than 5 ohms, go to next step. If resistance is less than 5 ohms, repair Dark Green/White wire for a short to ground. Perform VERIFICATION TEST VER-1A.

3) Using an external ohmmeter, measure resistance of Dark Green/White wire between CAB connector terminal No. 21 and HCU 10-pin harness connector. If resistance is less than 5 ohms, go to next step. If resistance is more than 5 ohms, repair open Dark Green/White wire. Perform VERIFICATION TEST VER-1A.

TEST 17A (Cont.)

4) Using an external ohmmeter, measure resistance of right front outlet valve between terminals No. 8 and 10 at HCU connector. *See Fig. 16A.* If resistance is 3-5 ohms, replace CAB. Perform VERIFICATION TEST VER-1A. If resistance is not 3-5 ohms, replace hydraulic control unit. Perform VERIFICATION TEST VER-1A.

TEST 18A

RIGHT FRONT SENSOR CIRCUIT FAILURE

1) Using DRB-II, read and record all wheel speed sensor faults. If RIGHT FRONT SENSOR CIRCUIT FAILURE message is displayed, go to next step. If message is not displayed, perform TEST 19A.

2) Inspect right front wheel speed sensor for damage. If sensor is okay, go to next step. If sensor is damaged, repair or replace as necessary. Perform VERIFICATION TEST VER-1A.

3) Turn ignition off. Disconnect and inspect CAB 55-pin connector. Repair connector as necessary. Turn ignition on. with DRB-II in voltmeter mode, probe White wire at CAB connector terminal No. 47. If no voltage is present, go to next step. If any voltage is present, repair White wire for a short to battery power. Perform VERIFICATION TEST VER-1A.

4) With DRB-II in ohmmeter mode, probe White wire at CAB connector terminal No. 47. If resistance is more than 5 ohms, go to next step. If resistance is less than 5 ohms, repair White wire for a short to ground. Perform VERIFICATION TEST VER-1A.

5) Using an external ohmmeter, measure resistance of right front wheel speed sensor between White/Dark Blue wire and White wire at CAB connector terminals No. 29 and 47. If resistance is 900-1300 ohms, replace CAB. Perform VERIFICATION TEST VER-1A. If resistance is not 900-1300 ohms, go to next step.

6) Disconnect right front wheel speed sensor harness connector. Connector is located on right rear corner of engine compartment. Using an external ohmmeter, measure resistance of right front wheel speed sensor at harness connector terminals. If resistance is 900-1300 ohms, go to next step. If resistance is not 900-1300 ohms, replace sensor. Perform VERIFICATION TEST VER-1A.

7) Using an external ohmmeter, measure resistance of White wire between CAB connector terminal No. 47 and right front wheel speed sensor harness connector. If resistance is less than 5 ohms, repair open White/Dark Blue wire. Perform VERIFICATION TEST VER-1A. If resistance is more than 5 ohms, repair open White wire. Perform VERIFICATION TEST VER-1A.

TEST 19A

RIGHT FRONT SENSOR

1) Inspect right front wheel speed sensor for damage. If sensor is okay, go to next step. If sensor is damaged, repair or replace as necessary. Perform VERIFICATION TEST VER-1A.

2) Inspect right front wheel speed sensor tone (pulse) ring for damaged teeth or excessive runout. Runout should not exceed .003" (.08 mm). Repair or replace tone ring as necessary. Perform VERIFICATION TEST VER-1A. If tone ring is okay, go to next step.

3) Using a feeler gauge, check right front wheel sensor-to-tone ring clearance. If clearance is .036-.050" (.91-1.27 mm), go to next step. If clearance is not .036-.050" (.91-1.27 mm), repair as necessary. Perform VERIFICATION TEST VER-1A.

4) Inspect right front wheel speed sensor wiring harness for damage. If wiring harness is okay, go to next step. If wiring harness is damaged, repair wiring harness as necessary. Perform VERIFICATION TEST VER-1A.

5) Disconnect right front wheel speed sensor harness connector. Connector is located on right rear corner of engine compartment. Using an external ohmmeter, measure resistance of right front wheel speed sensor at harness connector terminals. If resistance is 900-1300 ohms, replace CAB. Perform VERIFICATION TEST VER-1A. If resistance is not 900-1300 ohms, replace sensor. Perform VERIFICATION TEST VER-1A.

TEST 20A

RIGHT REAR SENSOR CIRCUIT FAILURE

1) Using DRB-II, read and record all wheel speed sensor faults. If RIGHT REAR SENSOR CIRCUIT FAILURE message is displayed, go to next step. If message is not displayed, perform TEST 21A.

2) Inspect right rear wheel speed sensor for damage. If sensor is okay, go to next step. If sensor is damaged, repair or replace as necessary. Perform VERIFICATION TEST VER-1A.

3) Turn ignition off. Disconnect and inspect CAB 55-pin connector. Repair connector as necessary. Turn ignition on. Using DRB-II in voltmeter mode, probe Yellow wire at CAB connector terminal No. 27. If no voltage is present, go to next step. If any voltage is present, perform TEST 20B.

4) Using DRB-II in ohmmeter mode, probe Yellow wire at CAB connector terminal No. 27. If resistance is more than 5 ohms, go to next step. If resistance is less than 5 ohms, perform TEST 20C.

5) Using an external ohmmeter, measure resistance of right rear wheel speed sensor between Yellow wire and Yellow/Dark Blue wire at CAB connector terminals No. 27 and 45. If resistance is 900-1300 ohms, replace CAB. Perform VERIFICATION TEST VER-1A. If resistance is not 900-1300 ohms, go to next step.

6) Disconnect right rear wheel speed sensor. Using an external ohmmeter, measure resistance of right rear wheel speed sensor. If resistance is 900-1300 ohms, go to next step. If resistance is not 900-1300 ohms, replace sensor. Perform VERIFICATION TEST VER-1A.

7) Connect a jumper wire between ground and Yellow/Dark Blue wire at CAB connector terminal No. 45. Using an external ohmmeter, measure resistance of Yellow wire at right rear wheel speed sensor harness connector. If resistance is less than 5 ohms, perform TEST 20E. If resistance is more than 5 ohms, perform TEST 20D.

TEST 20B

RIGHT REAR SENSOR CIRCUIT FAILURE

1) On Cherokee, repair Yellow wire for a short to battery power. Perform VERIFICATION TEST VER-1A. On Grand Cherokee, disconnect and inspect ABS 8-pin disconnect connector. Connector is located behind left kick panel. Repair connector as necessary. With DRB-II in voltmeter mode, probe Yellow wire of ABS disconnect connector.

2) If no voltage is present, repair Yellow wire for a short to battery power between right rear wheel speed sensor and ABS disconnect connector. Perform VERIFICATION TEST VER-1A. If any voltage is present, repair Yellow wire for a short to battery power between ABS disconnect connector and CAB 55-pin connector. Perform VERIFICATION TEST VER-1A.

TEST 20C

RIGHT REAR SENSOR CIRCUIT FAILURE

1) On Cherokee, repair Yellow wire for a short to ground. Perform VERIFICATION TEST VER-1A. On Grand Cherokee, disconnect and inspect ABS 8-pin disconnect connector. Connector is located behind left side kick panel. Repair connector as necessary. With DRB-II in ohmmeter mode, probe Yellow wire of ABS disconnect connector.

2) If resistance is less than 5 ohms, repair Yellow wire for a short to ground between right rear wheel speed sensor and ABS disconnect connector. Perform VERIFICATION TEST VER-1A. If resistance is more than 5 ohms, repair Yellow wire for a short to ground between ABS disconnect connector and CAB 55-pin connector. Perform VERIFICATION TEST VER-1A.

TEST 20D

RIGHT REAR SENSOR CIRCUIT FAILURE

1) On Cherokee, repair open Yellow wire to right rear wheel speed sensor. Perform VERIFICATION TEST VER-1A. On Grand Cherokee, disconnect and inspect ABS 8-pin disconnect connector. Connector is located behind left kick panel. Repair connector as necessary. With DRB-II in ohmmeter mode, probe Yellow wire of ABS disconnect connector.

2) If resistance is less than 5 ohms, repair open Yellow wire between right rear wheel speed sensor and ABS disconnect connector. Perform VERIFICATION TEST VER-1A. If resistance is more than 5 ohms, repair open Yellow wire between ABS disconnect connector and CAB 55-pin connector. Perform VERIFICATION TEST VER-1A.

TEST 20E

RIGHT REAR SENSOR CIRCUIT FAILURE

1) On Cherokee, repair open Yellow/Dark Blue wire to right rear wheel speed sensor. Perform VERIFICATION TEST VER-1A. On Grand Cherokee, disconnect and inspect ABS 8-pin disconnect connector. Connector is located behind left side kick panel. Repair connector as necessary. Connect a jumper wire between ground and Yellow wire at CAB connector terminal No. 27. With DRB-II in ohmmeter mode, probe Yellow/Dark Blue wire of ABS disconnect connector.

2) If resistance is less than 5 ohms, repair open Yellow/Dark Blue wire between right rear wheel speed sensor and ABS disconnect connector. Perform VERIFICATION TEST VER-1A. If resistance is more than 5 ohms, repair open Yellow/Dark Blue wire between ABS disconnect connector and CAB 55-pin connector. Perform VERIFICATION TEST VER-1A.

TEST 21A

RIGHT REAR SENSOR

1) Inspect right rear wheel speed sensor for damage. If sensor is okay, go to next step. If sensor is damaged, repair or replace as necessary. Perform VERIFICATION TEST VER-1A.

2) Inspect right rear wheel speed sensor tone (pulse) ring for damaged teeth and excessive runout. Runout should not exceed .003" (.08 mm). Repair or replace tone ring as necessary. Perform VERIFICATION TEST VER-1A. If tone ring is okay, go to next step.

3) Using a feeler gauge, check right rear wheel sensor-to-tone ring clearance. If clearance is .036-.050" (.91-1.27 mm), go to next step. If clearance is not .036-.050" (.91-1.27 mm), repair as necessary. Perform VERIFICATION TEST VER-1A.

4) Inspect right rear wheel speed sensor wiring harness for damage. If wiring harness is okay, go to next step. If wiring harness is damaged, repair wiring harness as necessary. Perform VERIFICATION TEST VER-1A.

5) Disconnect right rear wheel speed sensor. Using an external ohmmeter, measure resistance of right rear wheel speed sensor. If resistance is 900-1300 ohms, replace CAB. Perform VERIFICATION TEST VER-1A. If resistance is not 900-1300 ohms, replace sensor. Perform VERIFICATION TEST VER-1A.

TEST 22A

ABS WARNING LIGHT ILLUMINATION PROBLEM

1) Using DRB-II, read ABS fault codes. If any fault codes are present, perform TEST 1A. Turn ignition off. Remove ABS main relay from PDC, and inspect connector. Repair connector as necessary. Turn ignition on. If ABS warning light comes on, go to next step. If warning light does not come on, perform VERIFICATION TEST VER-1C.

NOTE: A main relay/power circuit failure fault will set with ABS main relay removed.

TEST 22A (Cont.)

2) Using DRB-II in ohmmeter mode, probe Black/Tan ground wire (Black ground wire on Grand Cherokee) at ABS main relay socket. If resistance is less than 5 ohms, go to next step. If resistance is more than 5 ohms, repair open Black/Tan ground wire (Black ground wire on Grand Cherokee). Perform VERIFICATION TEST VER-1A.

3) Turn ignition off. Disconnect and inspect CAB 55-pin connector. Repair connector as necessary. Using DRB-II in voltmeter mode, probe Gray wire (Gray/Yellow wire on Grand Cherokee) at ABS main relay socket. If no voltage is present, go to next step. If any voltage is present, replace ABS main relay. Perform VERIFICATION TEST VER-1A.

4) Remove ABS diode. Diode is taped to wiring harness, near CAB (near ABS 8-pin disconnect connector on Grand Cherokee). Connect a jumper wire between Gray wire (Gray/Pink wire on Grand Cherokee) and Black/Tan wire (Black/Tan wire on Grand Cherokee) at ABS main relay socket.

5) Using DRB-II in ohmmeter mode, probe Gray wire (Gray/Pink wire on Grand Cherokee) at ABS diode connector. If resistance is less than 5 ohms, go to next step. If resistance is more than 5 ohms, repair open Gray wire (Gray/Pink Wire on Grand Cherokee) between relay splice and diode. Perform VERIFICATION TEST VER-1A.

6) Remove jumper wire used in step 4). Turn ignition on. If ABS warning light does not come on, go to next step. If ABS warning light comes on, repair Violet wire (Violet/White wire on Grand Cherokee) for a short circuit to ground between CAB connector terminal No. 52 and ABS diode.

7) Connect a jumper wire between ground and Violet wire (Violet/White wire on Grand Cherokee) at CAB connector terminal No. 52. Using DRB-II in ohmmeter mode, probe Violet wire (Violet/White wire on Grand Cherokee) at ABS diode connector. If resistance is less than 5 ohms, replace ABS diode. Perform VERIFICATION TEST VER-1A. If resistance is more than 5 ohms, repair open Violet wire (Violet/White wire on Grand Cherokee) between ABS warning light and diode. Perform VERIFICATION TEST VER-1A.

TEST 23A
NO RESPONSE MESSAGE

1) On Cherokee, remove and inspect fuse No. 7. If fuse is blown, check for possible short to ground in Light Green wire between ignition switch and terminal No. 53 of CAB connector. If fuse is okay, go to next step. On Grand Cherokee, remove and inspect fuse No. 15. If fuse is blown, check for possible short to ground in Light Green/Yellow wire between ignition switch and terminal No. 53 of CAB connector. If fuse is okay, go to next step.

2) On all models, turn ignition off. Disconnect and inspect CAB 55-pin connector. Repair connector as necessary. Turn ignition on. With DRB-II in voltmeter mode, probe terminal No. 53 (Light Green wire on Cherokee or Light Green/Yellow wire on Grand Cherokee) of CAB connector.

3) If voltage is less than 9 volts, repair open in Light Green wire (Cherokee) or Light Green/Yellow wire (Grand Cherokee). Perform VERIFICATION TEST VER-1A. If voltage is more than 9 volts, put DRB-II in ohmmeter mode. Probe terminal No. 1 (Black wire) of CAB connector. If resistance is more than 5 ohms, repair open Black wire. Perform VERIFICATION TEST VER-1A.

4) If resistance is less than 5 ohms, probe terminal No. 19 (Black wire) of CAB connector. If resistance is more than 5 ohms, repair open Black wire. Perform VERIFICATION TEST VER-1A. If resistance is less than 5 ohms, check resistance of Violet/Brown wire between terminals No. 4 of CCD bus diagnostic connector and No. 23 of CAB connector using an external ohmmeter.

5) If resistance is more than 5 ohms, repair open in Violet/Brown wire. Perform VERIFICATION TEST VER-1A. If resistance is less than 5 ohms, using an external ohmmeter, check resistance of White/Black wire on Cherokee or White/Gray wire on Grand Cherokee between terminals No. 3 of CCD bus diagnostic connector and No. 42 of CAB connector.

6) If resistance is more than 54 ohms, repair open in White/Black wire (Cherokee) or White/Gray wire (Grand Cherokee). Perform VERIFICATION TEST VER-1A. If resistance is less than 5 ohms, reconnect CAB 55-pin connector. Using DRB-II, try to access ABS TEVES diagnostics. If DRB-II does not display NO RESPONSE, system is functioning properly. If DRB-II displays NO RESPONSE, replace CAB. Perform VERIFICATION TEST VER-1A.

VERIFICATION TEST VER-1A
SYSTEM VERIFICATION TEST

1) Disconnect all previously connected jumper wires. Reconnect all previously disconnected connectors. Reinstall all previously removed relays. Replace any blown fuses. Using DRB-II, erase fault messages. Cycle ignition off and then on. Using DRB-II, monitor read faults display for 3 minutes. If DRB-II displays any faults, perform TEST 1A.

2) If DRB-II does not display any faults, using DRB-II, read brakelight switch input. Depress brake pedal. If DRB-II does not display PRESSED, perform VERIFICATION TEST VER-1B. If DRB-II displays PRESSED, using DRB-II, read "G" SWITCH input. If DRB-II does not display "G" SWITCH #1 CLOSED, "G" SWITCH #2 CLOSED, perform TEST 3A.

3) If DRB-II displays No. 1 and 2 "G" switch CLOSED, with DRB-II in ABS TEVES diagnostic mode, check ANTI-LOCK warning light. If warning light is off, perform, VERIFICATION TEST VER-1C. If warning light is flashing, depress brake pedal. Using DRB-II, actuate left front outlet valve.

4) If brake pedal "drop" was not felt when valve was actuated, replace hydraulic control unit. Perform VERIFICATION TEST VER-1A. If brake pedal "drop" was felt when valve was actuated, release brake pedal. Depress brake pedal. Using DRB-II, actuate right front outlet valve.

5) If brake pedal "drop" was not felt when valve was actuated, replace hydraulic control unit. Perform VERIFICATION TEST VER-1A. If brake pedal "drop" was felt when valve was actuated, release brake pedal. Depress brake pedal. Using DRB-II, actuate rear outlet valve.

6) If brake pedal "drop" was not felt when valve was actuated, replace hydraulic control unit. Perform VERIFICATION TEST VER-1A. If brake pedal "drop" was felt when valve was actuated, road test vehicle for a minimum of 5 minutes and perform several anti-lock braking stops.

7) Using DRB-II, read fault messages. If DRB-II displays any faults, perform TEST 1A. If DRB-II displays no faults, system is operating properly.

VERIFICATION TEST VER-1B
BRAKELIGHT SWITCH SENSOR CIRCUIT

1) Check brakelight operation. If brakelights are not operating properly, repair as necessary. Perform VERIFICATION TEST VER-1A. If brakelights are operating properly, turn ignition off. Disconnect and inspect CAB 55-pin connector. Repair connector as necessary.

2) Depress brake pedal. With DRB-II in voltmeter mode, probe terminal No. 32 (White/Tan wire) of CAB connector. If voltage is less than 9 volts, repair open White/Tan wire. Perform VERIFICATION TEST VER-1A. If voltage is more than 9 volts, replace CAB. Perform VERIFICATION TEST VER-1A.

VERIFICATION TEST VER-1C
ANTI-LOCK WARNING LIGHT CIRCUIT

1) Set parking brake. If Red BRAKE warning light is off, repair fused ignition feed circuit to warning lights. Perform VERIFICATION TEST VER-1A. If Red BRAKE warning light is on, turn ignition off. Disconnect and inspect CAB 55-pin connector. Repair connector as necessary.

2) Turn ignition on. Connect a jumper wire between terminal No. 52 (Violet wire on Cherokee or Violet/White wire on Grand Cherokee) and ground. Check ANTI-LOCK warning light. If ANTI-LOCK warning light is on, replace CAB. Perform VERIFICATION TEST VER-1A.

3) If ANTI-LOCK warning light is off, inspect ANTI-LOCK warning light bulb. Replace bulb as necessary. Perform VERIFICATION TEST VER-1A. If bulb is okay, repair open Violet wire (Cherokee) or Violet/White wire (Grand Cherokee). Perform VERIFICATION TEST VER-1A.

Cherokee, Comanche, Grand Cherokee (1993), Wrangler

DESCRIPTION

Floating caliper disc brake assembly uses a single piston caliper which floats on 2 bolts. As brake pedal is depressed, hydraulic pressure passes through a proportioning valve to brake caliper piston.

This force is transmitted to inboard brake pad, forcing it against braking surface of rotor. Pressure then moves outer caliper housing and pad inward on caliper mounting bolts, forcing outer pad against outer braking surface of rotor.

A combination proportioning valve/pressure differential switch is used on all models. Proportioning valve is not serviceable. Valve must be replaced if it malfunctions. Comanche models also use a height sensing proportioning valve. When vehicle is loaded, height sensing valve adjusts front and rear brake proportioning to maintain brake balance. As vehicle load increases (resulting in decreased vehicle height), higher brake line pressure to rear brakes is provided. Height sensing proportioning valve is not serviceable and must be replaced if it malfunctions.

WARNING: Use of aftermarket load leveling kits, air shocks or modifications changing axle-to-frame distance will provide a false reading to height sensing proportioning valve. These modifications can result in unsatisfactory brake performance, which can result in an accident.

A pressure differential brake warning light switch is used to warn vehicle operator that one side of the hydraulic system has failed. When hydraulic pressure is equal in both front and rear systems, switch piston remains centered and does not contact terminal in switch. If one side of brake system fails, hydraulic pressure moves piston toward failed side. Shoulder of piston contacts switch terminal, grounding brake warning light.

Proportioning valve operates by restricting hydraulic pressure to rear brakes at a given ratio when system hydraulic pressure reaches a certain point. This improves front-to-rear brake balance during high speed braking, when a percentage of rear weight is transferred to front wheels. Valve reduces rear brake pressure and delays rear wheel skid. On light brake application, valve allows full hydraulic pressure to rear brakes.

BLEEDING BRAKE SYSTEM

NOTE: Brake bleeding procedures for models with anti-lock brakes are not covered in this article. See ANTI-LOCK article for proper procedure.

BLEEDING SEQUENCE

Before bleeding system, exhaust all vacuum from power unit by depressing brake pedal several times. When bleeding disc brakes, air may tend to cling to caliper walls. Lightly tap caliper, while bleeding, to aid in removal of air.

Fill master cylinder with clean brake fluid. Fluid should meet DOT 3 specifications. Bleed master cylinder with bleeder valves (if equipped). Bleed wheel cylinders and calipers in sequence. See BRAKE LINE BLEEDING SEQUENCE table.

BRAKE LINE BLEEDING SEQUENCE

Application	Sequence
All Models	RR, LR, RF, LF

MASTER CYLINDER BLEEDING

Bench Bleeding – **1)** Master cylinder must be bled before installation to prevent excessive amounts of air from entering hydraulic system, creating poor brake operation.

2) Place master cylinder in soft-jawed vise. DO NOT tighten vise enough to damage master cylinder. Install bleed tubes in both outlets of master cylinder. *See Fig. 1.*
3) Fill master cylinder with clean brake fluid. Fluid should meet DOT 3 specifications. Ensure end of bleed tubes are submerged in brake fluid.
4) Using proper size rod, apply and release master cylinder until no air bubbles exist in brake fluid flow. When all air bubbles are gone from master cylinder, cap outlet ports. Install reservoir cover and seal. Install master cylinder and bleed on vehicle.

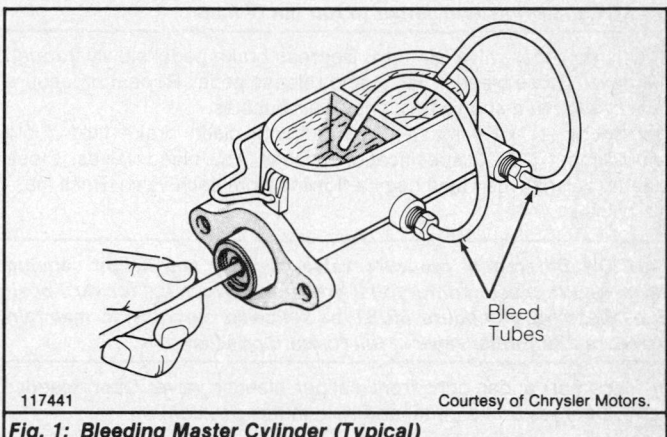

Bleed Tubes

117441   Courtesy of Chrysler Motors.

Fig. 1: Bleeding Master Cylinder (Typical)

On-Vehicle Bleeding – **1)** Install master cylinder on vehicle after bench bleeding. Remove bleeder lines and install brake lines. DO NOT tighten brake lines yet.
2) Slowly force brake pedal to floor and hold in this position. Tighten brake lines, and release brake pedal. Repeat procedure until no air bubbles exist at brake lines. Tighten brake lines. Check for leaks.

PRESSURE BLEEDING

CAUTION: Front brake metering valve is located in front end of combination valve. Valve stem MUST be pressed inward or held outward slightly to bleed front brakes.

NOTE: Comanche brake system MUST be bled manually.

1) Clean master cylinder cap and surrounding area. Remove cap. With pressure tank at least 1/2 full, connect to master cylinder with adapters. Attach bleed hose to first bleeder valve to be serviced. See BRAKE LINE BLEEDING SEQUENCE table under BLEEDING SEQUENCE.
2) Place other end of hose in clean glass jar partially filled with clean brake fluid so end of hose is submerged in fluid.
3) Open release valve on pressure bleeder. Follow equipment manufacturer's pressure instructions or see PRESSURE BLEEDER SETTINGS table. Open bleeder valve 3/4 turn, and note fluid flow.
4) Close bleeder screw when fluid is free of bubbles. Repeat procedure on remaining wheels in proper sequence. Check brake pedal operation after bleeding has been completed.
5) Remove pressure bleeding equipment and valve retainer from hold-off valve. Ensure master cylinder is full of fluid. Check for leaks.

PRESSURE BLEEDER SETTINGS

Application	psi (kg/cm²)
All Models	15-20 (1.1-1.4)

MANUAL BLEEDING

NOTE: Grand Cherokee is equipped with anti-lock brake system. See ANTI-LOCK – TEVES article for bleeding procedure.

Cherokee & Wrangler – 1) Fill master cylinder with clean brake fluid. Fluid should meet DOT 3 specifications. Open ALL bleed valves. Close bleeder valves when fluid begins flowing from each valve. Refill master cylinder.

2) Install bleed hose to first bleeder valve to be serviced. See BRAKE LINE BLEEDING SEQUENCE table under BLEEDING SEQUENCE. Submerge other end of hose in clean glass jar partially filled with clean brake fluid. *See Fig. 2.*

NOTE: Ensure bleeder valve is closed when brake pedal is released. DO NOT allow master cylinder to run out of fluid.

3) Open bleeder valve 3/4 turn. Depress brake pedal slowly through full travel. Close bleeder valve, and release pedal. Repeat procedure until flow of fluid shows no signs of air bubbles.

Comanche – 1) Fill master cylinder with clean brake fluid. Fluid should meet DOT 3 specifications. Open ALL bleed valves. Close bleeder valves when fluid begins flowing from each valve. Refill master cylinder.

CAUTION: Differential pressure valve circuitry and height sensing valve require placing differential pressure valve in full forward position. Bleeding procedure MUST be followed carefully to maintain pressure differential valve in full forward position.

2) Place pan under right front caliper bleeder valve. Open bleeder valve. Depress brake pedal and hold in this position.

NOTE: Right front bleeder valve MUST remain open throughout rear brake bleeding procedure.

3) Start engine. Brake warning light should illuminate, indicating differential pressure valve is in forward position. Turn engine off. Release brake pedal. Install bleed hose to left rear bleeder valve. Submerge other end of hose in clean glass jar partially filled with clean brake fluid. *See Fig. 2.*

4) Open bleeder valve 3/4 turn. Depress brake pedal slowly through full travel. Close bleeder valve, and release pedal. Repeat procedure until flow of fluid shows no signs of air bubbles. Refill master cylinder. Repeat procedure at right rear wheel. Close bleeder valve at right front caliper.

5) Bleed right front bleeder valve. Bleed left front bleeder valve. Refill master cylinder. Check brake operation before moving vehicle. Pedal should be at normal height and exhibit NO sponginess.

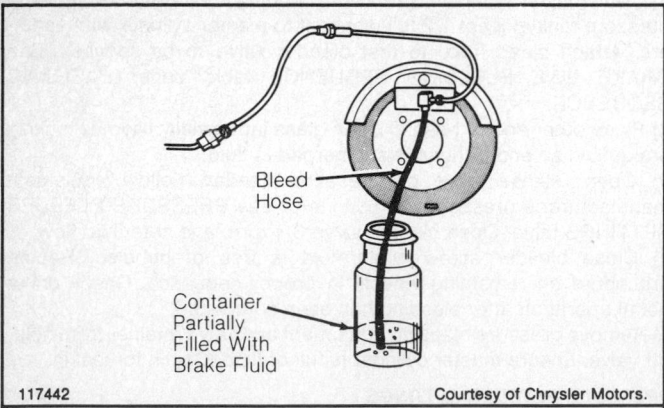

117442   Courtesy of Chrysler Motors.

Fig. 2: Bleeding Brakes (Manual Procedure)

ADJUSTMENTS

BRAKE PEDAL

Brake pedal push rod length is preset by manufacturer. No adjustment is possible.

HEIGHT SENSING PROPORTIONING VALVE

WARNING: Vehicle must be unloaded and on level surface for accurate valve adjustment. Proportioning valve bushing must also be replaced during adjustment. Failure to observe these precautions can result in unsatisfactory brake performance, which can result in an accident.

1) Unload vehicle. Position vehicle on level surface. Raise and support vehicle. Do not allow wheels to hang free. Remove nut attaching lever to valve shaft. *See Fig. 3.*

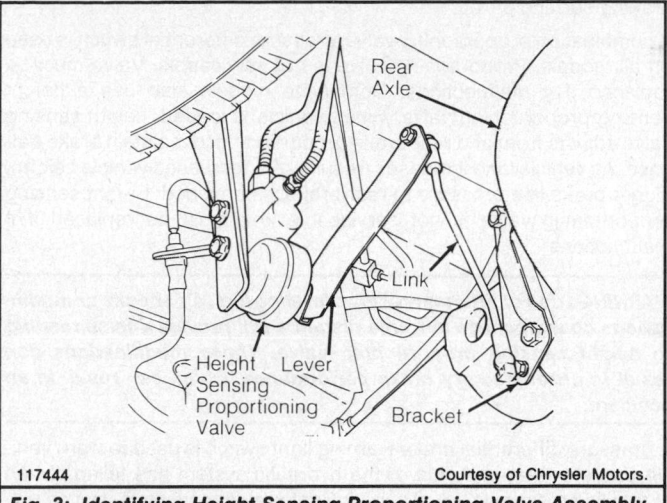

117444   Courtesy of Chrysler Motors.

Fig. 3: Identifying Height Sensing Proportioning Valve Assembly (Comanche)

2) Pull lever and retainer off valve shaft, and remove old bushing. Discard bushing. Clean threads and splines on valve shaft. If valve link was disconnected from axle bracket or lever, reconnect link.

NOTE: Do not attempt adjustment with link disconnected. Link must be connected to avoid false reading to valve after installation.

3) Loosen valve mounting bolts 2 turns. Turn valve shaft until shaft flat is approximately at 5:50 o'clock position. *See Fig. 4.* Install Valve Adjusting Gauge (6439). Position gauge on mounting bolt and shaft. *See Fig. 5.*

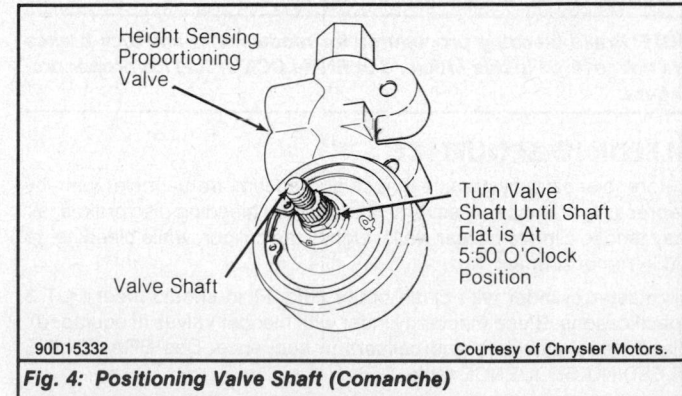

90D15332   Courtesy of Chrysler Motors.

Fig. 4: Positioning Valve Shaft (Comanche)

4) No clearance between gauge, shaft and bolts should exist. Gauge must be seated on shaft flat. Install retainer (if removed) in lever. Install NEW bushing in retainer and lever. Start bushing and lever on valve shaft.

5) Press bushing and lever onto shaft with Bushing Installer (6229) or "C" clamp and a socket. *See Fig. 6.* Remove adjustment gauge and bushing installer. Tighten valve mounting bolts to **118 INCH lbs. (13 N.m).** Install and tighten lever attaching nut to **100 INCH lbs. (11 N.m).**

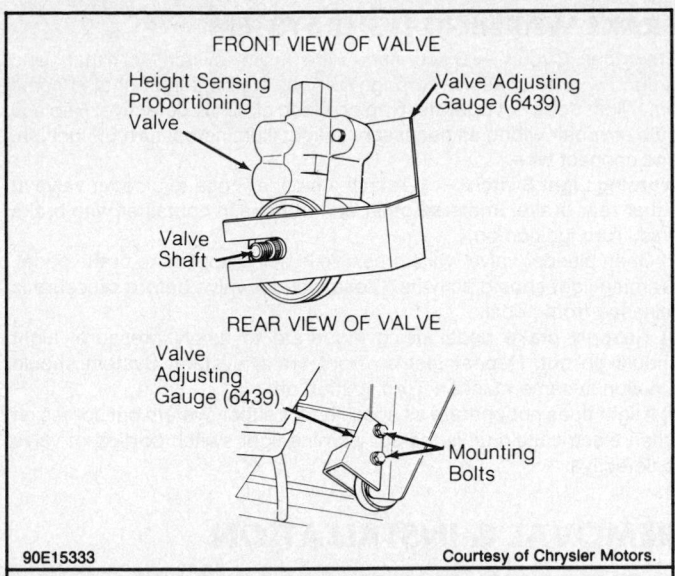

Height Sensing Proportioning Valve

Valve Adjusting Gauge (6439)

FRONT VIEW OF VALVE

Valve Shaft

REAR VIEW OF VALVE

Valve Adjusting Gauge (6439)

Mounting Bolts

90E15333   Courtesy of Chrysler Motors.

Fig. 5: Installing Valve Adjusting Gauge (Comanche)

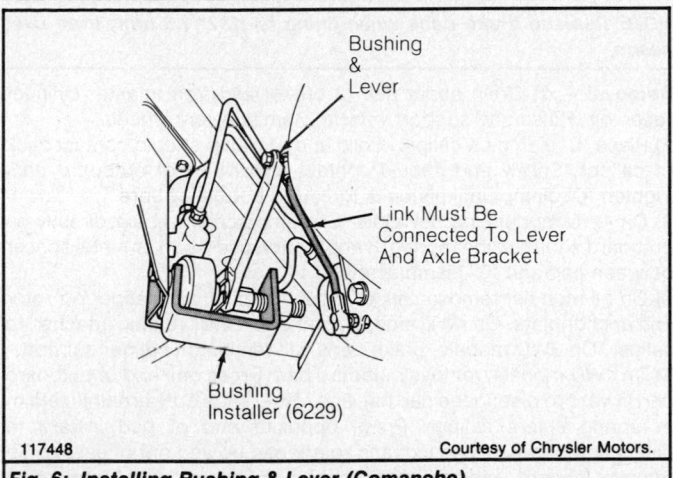

Bushing & Lever

Link Must Be Connected To Lever And Axle Bracket

Bushing Installer (6229)

117448   Courtesy of Chrysler Motors.

Fig. 6: Installing Bushing & Lever (Comanche)

PARKING/EMERGENCY BRAKE

Cherokee, Comanche & Wrangler – 1) Adjust rear brakes. See REAR BRAKE SHOES under ADJUSTMENTS. Check cable for binding, kinking or fraying. Replace cable as required. Apply and release parking brake 5 times.

2) Place parking brake lever in fifth notch. Raise and support vehicle. Position Adjustment Gauge (J-34651) on one of rear parking brake cables. See Fig. 7. Apply and hold a torque of **50 INCH lbs. (6 N.m)** on adjustment gauge, and note position of gauge pointer.

3) If adjustment gauge pointer is not within okay band, turn parking brake cable equalizer adjustment nut in or out until pointer is within okay band. Remove tools, and lower vehicle. Ensure proper parking brake operation.

Grand Cherokee – 1) Adjust rear brakes. See REAR BRAKE SHOES under ADJUSTMENTS. Check cable for binding, kinking or fraying. Replace cable as required.

2) Fully apply parking brake. Raise and support vehicle. Mark position of adjusting nut on threaded end of cable tensioner. Tighten adjusting nut about **1/2" (13 mm)**. Replace tensioner if there are not enough threads for proper adjustment.

3) Lower vehicle until wheels are about 6 in. off floor. Release parking brake. Verify that rear wheels rotate freely and no drag is felt. Lower vehicle, and ensure parking brake operates properly.

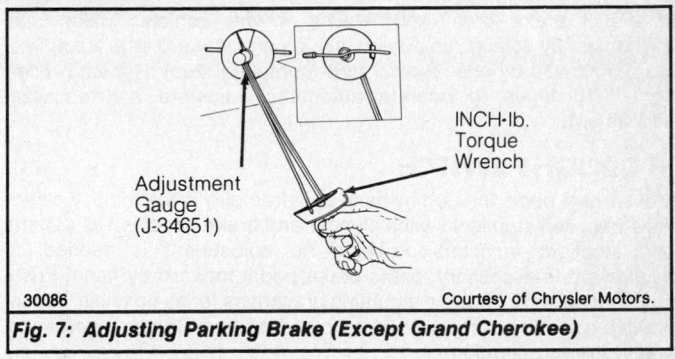

INCH·lb. Torque Wrench

Adjustment Gauge (J-34651)

30086   Courtesy of Chrysler Motors.

Fig. 7: Adjusting Parking Brake (Except Grand Cherokee)

REAR BRAKE SHOES

NOTE: Brakes are self-adjusting. Under normal circumstances, manual adjustment is only required if shoes are removed. Replace brake shoes when lining is 1/16" on bonded linings and 1/32" from rivet on riveted linings.

1) Raise and support vehicle. Remove wheels and brake drums. Ensure right and left automatic adjuster lever and cable are properly connected.

2) Insert Brake Shoe Adjustment Gauge (J-21177-01) in drum. See Fig. 8. Expand gauge until inner legs contact drum braking surface. Lock gauge in position.

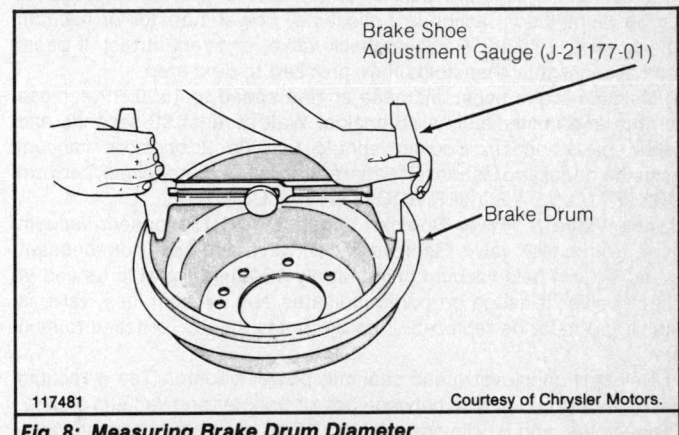

Brake Shoe Adjustment Gauge (J-21177-01)

Brake Drum

117481   Courtesy of Chrysler Motors.

Fig. 8: Measuring Brake Drum Diameter

3) Reverse brake shoe adjustment gauge, and install it on brake shoes. See Fig. 9. Position gauge legs at shoe centers. If gauge does not fit (too loose or too tight), adjust brake shoes accordingly.

4) Turn star adjuster wheel (by hand) to expand or retract brake shoes. Continue adjustment until gauge outside legs have a slight drag on shoes. Repeat procedure on opposite brake shoe assembly.

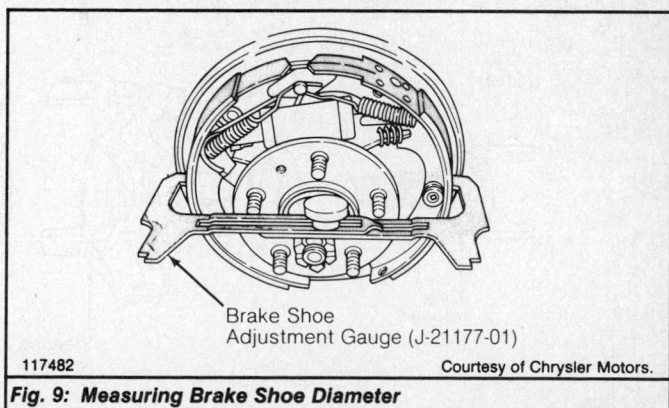

Brake Shoe Adjustment Gauge (J-21177-01)

117482   Courtesy of Chrysler Motors.

Fig. 9: Measuring Brake Shoe Diameter

5) Install brake drum and wheels. Lower vehicle. Make final adjustment by driving vehicle and making one forward stop (complete stop), followed by one reverse stop (complete stop). Repeat procedure 8-10 times to operate automatic adjusters and equalize adjustment.

STOPLIGHT SWITCH

Move brake pedal forward by hand until free play is taken up. If clearance between stoplight switch plunger and brake pedal is 1/8" (3 mm) and stoplight functions properly, no adjustment is needed. If adjustment is necessary, press brake pedal forward by hand. Push stoplight switch forward in mounting bracket as far as possible. Grasp brake pedal and pull rearward to stop and release. Recheck clearance and stoplight operation.

TESTING

POWER BOOSTER

Master Cylinder/Power Booster – 1) Start engine, and check power booster vacuum hose for leaks. Repair as required. Stop engine, and place gear selector in Neutral. Pump brake pedal until all vacuum reserve is depleted.

2) Press and hold brake pedal under light foot pressure. If pedal does not hold firm and falls away, master cylinder is leaking internally. Repair or replace as required. If brake pedal holds firm, proceed to next step.

3) While holding light pressure on pedal, start engine, and note pedal action. If no pedal action is noticeable, power booster or vacuum check valve is faulty. Replace check valve, and repeat test. If pedal falls away slightly then holds firm, proceed to next step.

4) Release brake pedal. Increase engine speed to 1500 RPM, close throttle and immediately stop engine. Wait at least 90 seconds and retest pedal action. Booster should provide 2 or more vacuum assisted pedal applications. If pedal action is not as specified, perform CHECK VALVE & POWER BOOSTER VACUUM test.

Check Valve & Power Booster Vacuum – 1) Disconnect vacuum hose from check valve. Remove check valve and seal from booster. Using a hand-held vacuum pump, apply 15-20 in. Hg at large end of check valve. If gauge on pump indicates any vacuum loss, valve is faulty and must be replaced. If gauge holds steady, proceed to next step.

2) Reinstall check valve and seal into power booster. Tee a vacuum gauge into vacuum hose between power booster and vacuum source. Start engine, and let idle one minute. Clamp hose shut between vacuum source and power booster.

3) Stop engine, and observe vacuum gauge. If vacuum drops more than 1 in. Hg within 15 seconds, booster diaphragm or check valve is faulty. Replace as required.

BRAKE WARNING LIGHT SYSTEM

Electrical Circuit – Disconnect wire from switch terminal, and ground wire to chassis. Turn ignition on. Warning light should come on. If light does not operate, bulb or wiring circuit is defective. Replace bulb or repair wiring as necessary. If light illuminates, turn off ignition, and connect wire.

Warning Light Switch – 1) Attach a bleeder hose to bleeder valve at either rear brake. Immerse other end of hose in container with brake fluid. Turn ignition on.

2) Open bleeder valve while pressure is being applied to brake pedal. Warning light should activate. Close bleeder valve before pressure is released from pedal.

3) Reapply brake pedal using moderate to heavy pressure. Light should go out. Repeat test on front brake system. System should function in same manner. Turn ignition off.

4) If light does not operate as specified for either system but comes on when electrical circuit is tested, warning light switch portion of valve is defective.

REMOVAL & INSTALLATION

FRONT BRAKE CALIPER & BRAKE PADS

NOTE: Replace brake pads when lining is 1/32" (.8 mm) from rivet heads.

Removal – 1) Drain about half of brake fluid from master cylinder reservoir. Raise and support vehicle. Remove front wheels.

2) Place "C" clamp on caliper. Solid end of clamp should contact back of caliper. Screw end should contact metal part of outboard pad. Tighten "C" clamp until piston is forced to bottom of bore.

3) On 4WD models, do not allow "C" clamp screw to bear directly on outboard shoe retainer spring. If necessary, use wood or metal spacer between pad and "C" clamp screw.

4) On all models, remove caliper mounting pins. Lift caliper off rotor and anchor plate. On 4WD models, brake pads will remain attached to caliper. On 2WD models, brake pads will remain on caliper support.

5) On 4WD models, remove outboard pad. Press one end of outboard pad inward to disengage pad lug, and rotate shoe outward until retainer spring clears caliper. Press opposite end of pad inward to disengage opposite pad lug, and rotate pad up and out of caliper. To remove inboard pad, grasp ends of pad, and tilt pad outward to release springs from caliper piston. Remove pad from piston.

6) On 2WD models, hold lower anti-rattle clip against support bracket and remove outboard brake pad from caliper support. Remove inboard brake pad and both anti-rattle clips from caliper support.

7) On all models, disconnect brake line at caliper, and cap hole to prevent contamination while removing caliper from vehicle.

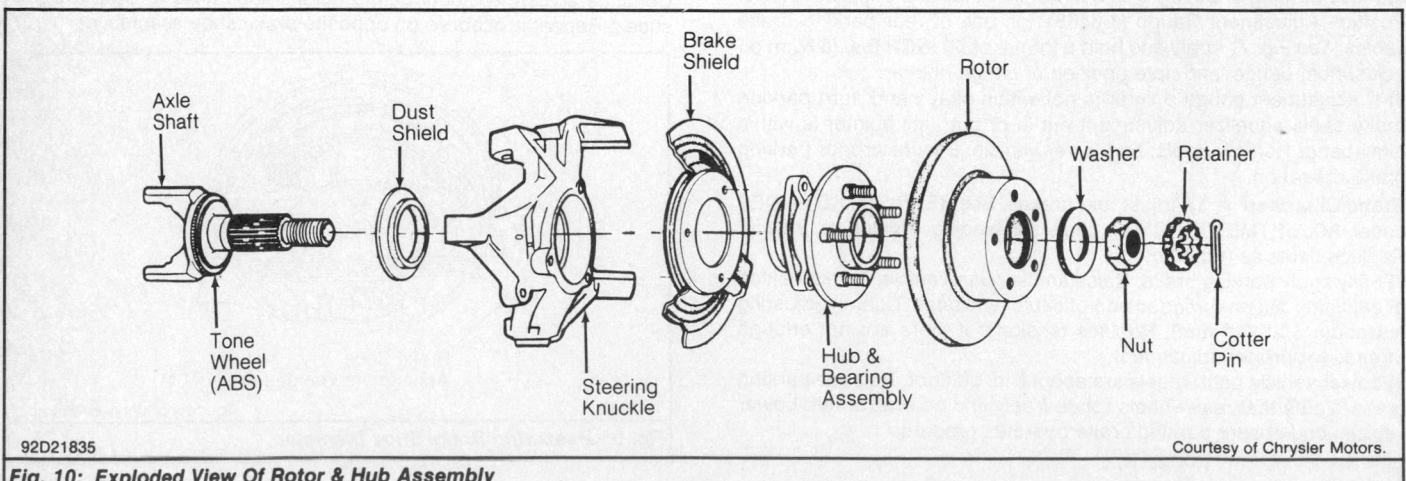

92D21835   Courtesy of Chrysler Motors.

Fig. 10: Exploded View Of Rotor & Hub Assembly

Installation – 1) To install, reverse removal procedure. Apply a light coat of multipurpose grease to caliper sliding surfaces. Lubricate caliper mounting pins and bushings with silicone.

2) Torque caliper mounting pins to specification. See TORQUE SPECIFICATIONS table at end of article. Add brake fluid to reservoir. Apply brakes until brake pedal is firm. Check brake fluid level.

ROTOR

NOTE: DO NOT disconnect brake hose from caliper unless caliper is to be disassembled.

Removal (2WD) – 1) Raise and support vehicle. Remove front wheels. Remove caliper. See FRONT BRAKE CALIPER & BRAKE PADS under REMOVAL & INSTALLATION. Suspend caliper from frame or suspension with wire.

2) Remove cap, cotter pin, nut retainer, adjusting nut and front bearing from spindle. Remove rotor from spindle. Remove grease seal and rear bearing from hub.

Installation – 1) Clean, inspect and repack wheel bearings. Replace grease seal. Coat spindle, bearing races and rotor hub cavity with grease. Clean rotor surface as required.

2) To install, reverse removal procedure. Tighten spindle nut to specification while rotating rotor to seat bearings. See TORQUE SPECIFICATIONS table at end of article. Apply brakes until brake pedal is firm. Check brake fluid level.

Removal & Installation (4WD) – Raise and support vehicle. Remove front wheels. Remove caliper. See FRONT BRAKE CALIPER & BRAKE PADS under REMOVAL & INSTALLATION. Suspend caliper from frame or suspension. Remove retainers securing rotor to hub. Remove rotor from hub. To install, reverse removal procedure. *See Fig. 10.*

REAR BRAKE SHOES

Removal (Cherokee, Comanche, Grand Cherokee & Wrangler) – 1) Raise and support vehicle. Remove wheels and brake drum. Remove "U" clip and washer from parking brake lever pivot pin. Place Wheel Cylinder Clamp (J-8002) over wheel cylinder.

2) Remove primary and secondary shoe return springs, hold-down spring and retainers and pins. *See Fig. 11 or 12.* Remove self-adjuster lever, adjuster and adjuster spring from brake shoes.

3) Remove brake shoes. Disconnect parking brake cable from parking brake lever, and remove lever.

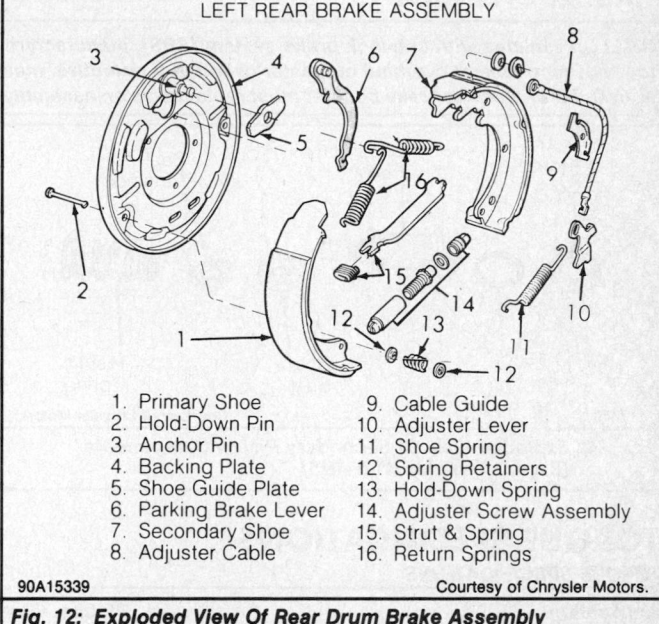

1. Primary Shoe
2. Hold-Down Pin
3. Anchor Pin
4. Backing Plate
5. Shoe Guide Plate
6. Parking Brake Lever
7. Secondary Shoe
8. Adjuster Cable
9. Cable Guide
10. Adjuster Lever
11. Shoe Spring
12. Spring Retainers
13. Hold-Down Spring
14. Adjuster Screw Assembly
15. Strut & Spring
16. Return Springs

90A15339   Courtesy of Chrysler Motors.

Fig. 12: Exploded View Of Rear Drum Brake Assembly (Comanche W/Heavy-Duty Suspension & Grand Cherokee)

Installation – 1) Lubricate backing plate ledges, anchor pin, cable guide, self-adjuster screw assembly, parking brake lever and lever pivot pin with white lithium grease. *See Fig. 11 or 12.*

2) Connect parking brake lever to secondary brake shoe with washer and "U" clip. Crimp ends of clip to secure clip on pivot. Remove wheel cylinder clamp. Position brake shoes on brake support plate, and install hold-down springs.

3) Install parking brake lever strut and spring. Install cable guide plate and adjuster cable on anchor pin. Install primary return spring. Install guide to secondary brake shoe. Install secondary return spring.

4) Install adjuster screw, spring and lever. Connect lever to cable. Using Brake Shoe Adjustment Gauge (J-21177-01), preset brake shoe adjustment. See REAR BRAKE SHOES under ADJUSTMENTS. Install brake drums. Install wheels, and lower vehicle. Check brake fluid. Road test vehicle.

OVERHAUL

CALIPER

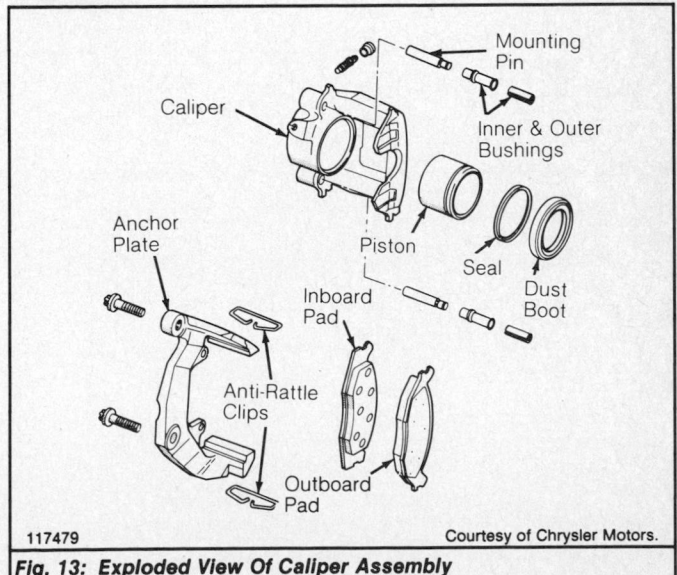

Mounting Pin
Caliper
Inner & Outer Bushings
Anchor Plate
Piston
Seal
Dust Boot
Inboard Pad
Anti-Rattle Clips
Outboard Pad

117479   Courtesy of Chrysler Motors.

Fig. 13: Exploded View Of Caliper Assembly

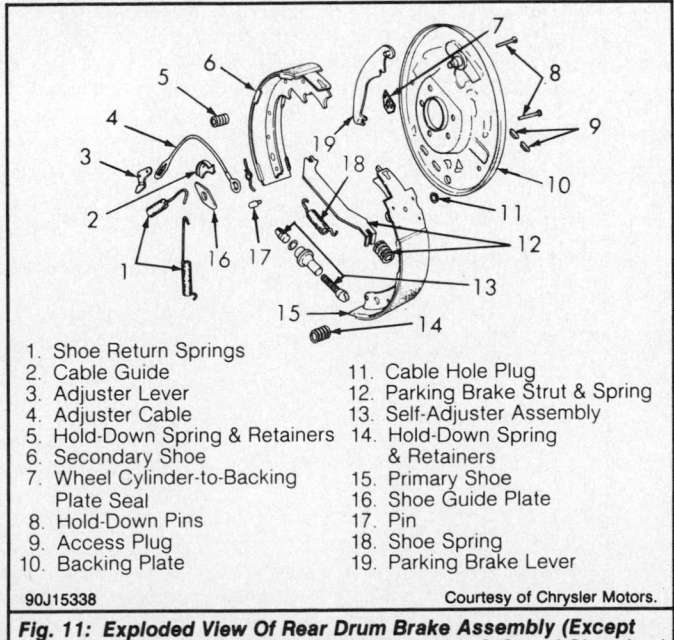

1. Shoe Return Springs
2. Cable Guide
3. Adjuster Lever
4. Adjuster Cable
5. Hold-Down Spring & Retainers
6. Secondary Shoe
7. Wheel Cylinder-to-Backing Plate Seal
8. Hold-Down Pins
9. Access Plug
10. Backing Plate
11. Cable Hole Plug
12. Parking Brake Strut & Spring
13. Self-Adjuster Assembly
14. Hold-Down Spring & Retainers
15. Primary Shoe
16. Shoe Guide Plate
17. Pin
18. Shoe Spring
19. Parking Brake Lever

90J15338   Courtesy of Chrysler Motors.

Fig. 11: Exploded View Of Rear Drum Brake Assembly (Except Comanche W/Heavy-Duty Suspension & Grand Cherokee)

MASTER CYLINDER

NOTE: On vehicles with anti-lock brake system (ABS), manufacturer does not recommend overhaul of master cylinder. If defective, master cylinder and power brake booster must replaced as an assembly.

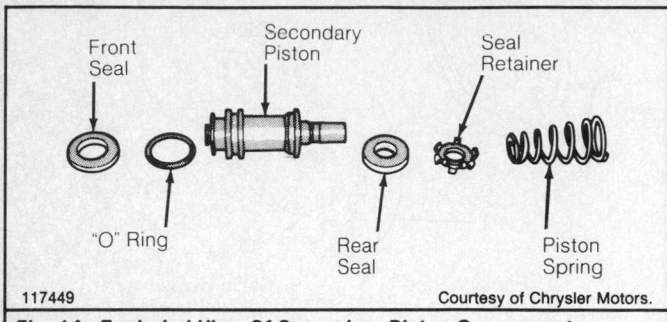

117449   Courtesy of Chrysler Motors.

Fig. 14: Exploded View Of Secondary Piston Components (Except Vehicles With ABS)

TORQUE SPECIFICATIONS

TORQUE SPECIFICATIONS

Application	Ft. Lbs. (N.m)
Backing Plate Bolt	32 (43)
Brake Hose-To-Caliper	23 (31)
Brake Line-To-Master Cylinder	15 (21)
Brake Line-To-Wheel Cylinder	13 (18)
Caliper Mounting Pins	
2WD	25-35 (34-47)
4WD	7-15 (10-20)
Master Cylinder-To-Power Booster Nuts	15 (21)
Wheel Bearing	[1] 17-25 (23-34)
Wheel Lug Nuts	
Except Grand Cherokee	75 (102)
Grand Cherokee	88 (120)

	INCH Lbs. (N.m)
Wheel Cylinder Bolts	
Except Comanche (Model 44 Rear Axle)	72-156 (8-18)
Comanche (Model 44 Rear Axle)	130-230 (15-24)

[1] – Tighten bearing nut while rotating wheel. Loosen nut 1/2 turn, and retighten to 19 INCH lbs. (2 N.m).

DISC BRAKE SPECIFICATIONS

DISC BRAKE ROTOR SPECIFICATIONS

Application	In. (mm)
Disc Diameter	11.02 (279.9)
Lateral Runout	
Except Grand Cherokee	.003 (.08)
Grand Cherokee	.005 (.13)
Parallelism	.0005 (.013)
Original Thickness	[1]
Minimum Refinish Thickness	
Cherokee & Comanche	
2WD	.86 (22)
4WD	.89 (23)
Grand Cherokee & Wrangler	.89 (23)

[1] – Information not available from manufacturer.

DRUM BRAKE SPECIFICATIONS

DRUM BRAKE SPECIFICATIONS

Application	In. (mm)
Drum Diameter	
Cherokee & Wrangler	9.00 (228.6)
Comanche	
Heavy Duty Suspension	10.00 (254.0)
Standard Suspension	9.00 (228.6)
Grand Cherokee	[1]
Drum Width	[1]
Maximum Drum Refinish Diameter	
Cherokee & Wrangler	9.050 (230.00)
Comanche	
Heavy Duty Suspension	10.06 (255.5)
Standard Suspension	9.050 (230.00)
Grand Cherokee	[1]
Wheel Cylinder Diameter	[1]
Master Cylinder Diameter	[1]

[1] – Information is not available from manufacturer.

**Cherokee, Comanche,
Grand Cherokee (1993), Wrangler**

RIDING HEIGHT ADJUSTMENT

Before adjusting alignment, check riding height. Riding height must be checked with vehicle on level floor and tires properly inflated. Bounce vehicle several times and allow suspension to settle. Visually inspect vehicle for signs of abnormal height from front to rear or side to side. Check passenger and luggage compartments for extra heavy items and remove if present. If riding height difference from side to side is more than 1" (25.4 mm), check all suspension components and repair or replace as necessary.

JACKING & HOISTING

FLOOR JACK

Vehicle may be raised by positioning jack under front or rear frame rails. *See Fig. 1.*

NOTE: Use sub-frame rail lift points to hoist vehicle. Never raise vehicle with jack under axle tubes, body side sills, steering linkage components, propeller shafts, engine/transmission oil pans, fuel tank or front suspension arms.

EMERGENCY JACKING

Except Wrangler – Park vehicle on a firm, level surface. Block tire diagonally opposite tire being changed. Place automatic transmission in Park, manual transmission in Reverse. Set parking brake. Position emergency jack under front or rear axle housing. Raise vehicle.
Wrangler – Park vehicle on a firm, level surface. Block tire diagonally opposite tire being changed. Place automatic transmission in Park, manual transmission in Reverse. Set parking brake. Position emergency jack under front or rear axle housing "U" bolts. Raise vehicle.

HOIST

Vehicle may be raised on single or twin-post swiveling arm, or ramp-type drive hoists. If using swiveling arm hoist, ensure lifting pads are positioned evenly at sub-frame lift points. *See Fig. 1.* All hoists should be equipped with proper adapters to support vehicle at frame rails only.

WHEEL ALIGNMENT PROCEDURES

CAMBER MEASUREMENT

Check camber to determine if any components are bent or damaged. Camber angle is NOT adjustable. If angle not to specification, components causing the problem must be replaced. See ALIGNMENT SPECIFICATIONS at end of article. Camber is NOT adjustable.

CASTER ADJUSTMENT

Check caster angle. See ALIGNMENT SPECIFICATIONS at end of article. If caster is not to specifications, adjust by adding or removing

shims at rear of lower control arms on Cherokee, Comanche and Grand Cherokee, or between front axle pads and spring brackets on Wrangler. *See Fig. 2 or 3.*

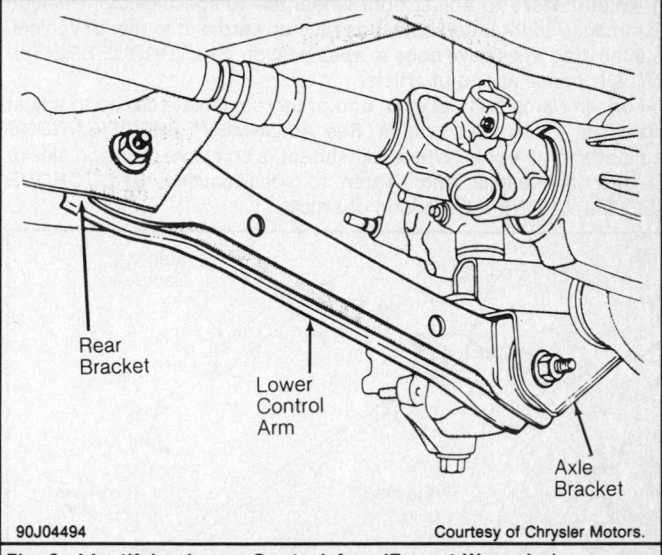

Fig. 2: Identifying Lower Control Arm (Except Wrangler)

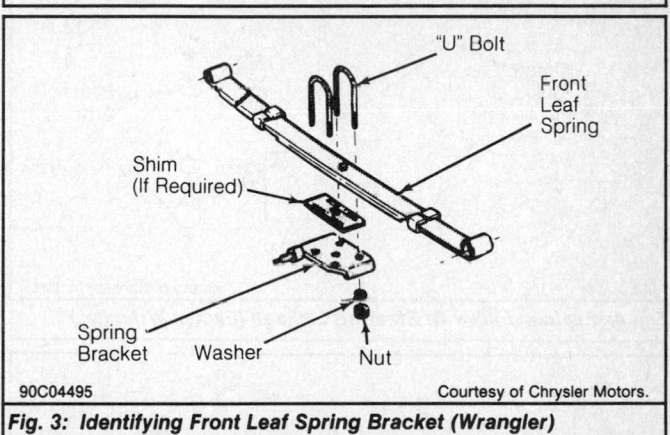

Fig. 3: Identifying Front Leaf Spring Bracket (Wrangler)

NOTE: On 4WD vehicles, shim adjustment will change caster angle and front drive shaft angle. If both angles cannot be adjusted to specifications, drive shaft angle has priority and should be adjusted for its specified angle. See appropriate article in DRIVE AXLES.

TOE-IN ADJUSTMENT

Except Wrangler – 1) Center front wheels straight ahead. Measure toe and compare to specifications. See ALIGNMENT SPECIFICATIONS at end of article.

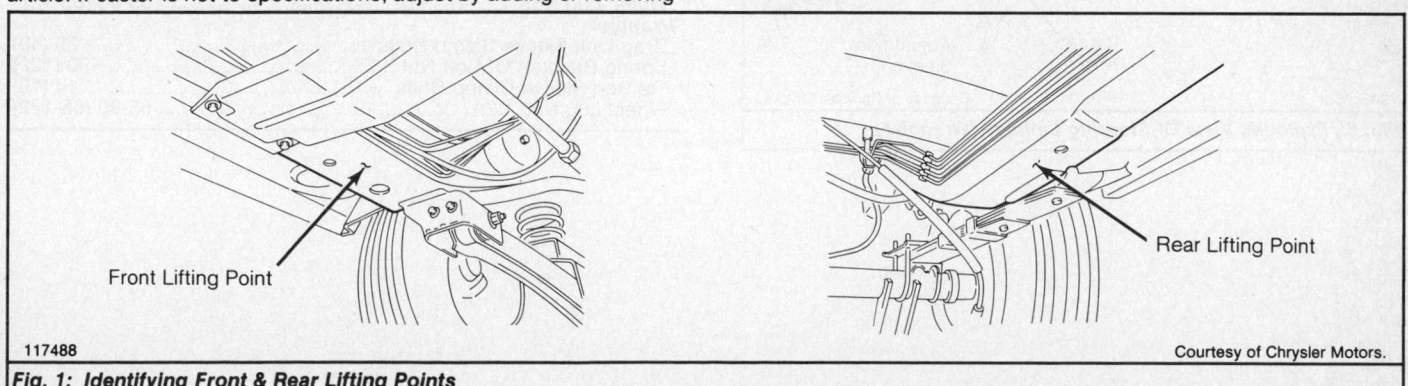

Fig. 1: Identifying Front & Rear Lifting Points

2) Center steering wheel by counting the turns required to hit left and right steering stops. Center steering wheel mid-way between stops. Loosen drag link adjustment sleeve clamp bolts. *See Fig. 4.*

3) Rotate sleeve to adjust right wheel toe to specification. Position clamp bolts so threaded bolt ends face upward and to rear of vehicle. Tighten drag link sleeve bolts to specification. See TORQUE SPECIFICATIONS table at end of article.

4) Loosen clamp bolts at each end of tie rod. Rotate tie rod to adjust left wheel to toe specification. See ALIGNMENT SPECIFICATIONS table at end of article. When adjustment is complete, position sleeve as described earlier and tighten to specifications. See TORQUE SPECIFICATIONS table at end of article.

Wrangler – 1) Center front wheels straight ahead and lock steering wheel in centered position. Measure toe and compare to specifications. See ALIGNMENT SPECIFICATIONS table at end of article.

2) Loosen tie rod adjustment sleeve clamp bolts. *See Fig. 5.* Rotate sleeve to adjust toe to specification. See ALIGNMENT SPECIFICATIONS table at end of article. After adjustment, position clamp bolts so threaded ends face rearward and are angled upward. Tighten sleeve clamp to specification. See TORQUE SPECIFICATIONS table at end of article.

3) If necessary, steering wheel can be centered by adjusting the drag link adjustment sleeve. When adjustment is complete, position sleeve as described earlier and tighten to specifications. See TORQUE SPECIFICATIONS table at end of article.

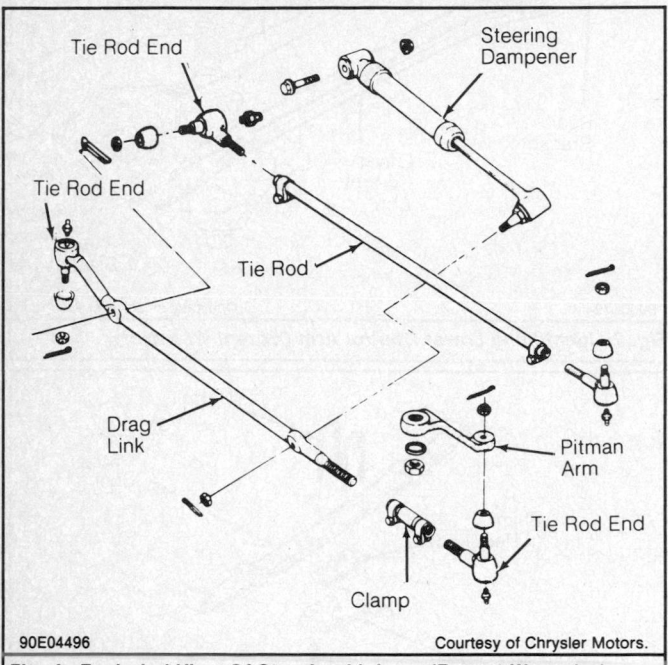

90E04496   Courtesy of Chrysler Motors.

Fig. 4: Exploded View Of Steering Linkage (Except Wrangler)

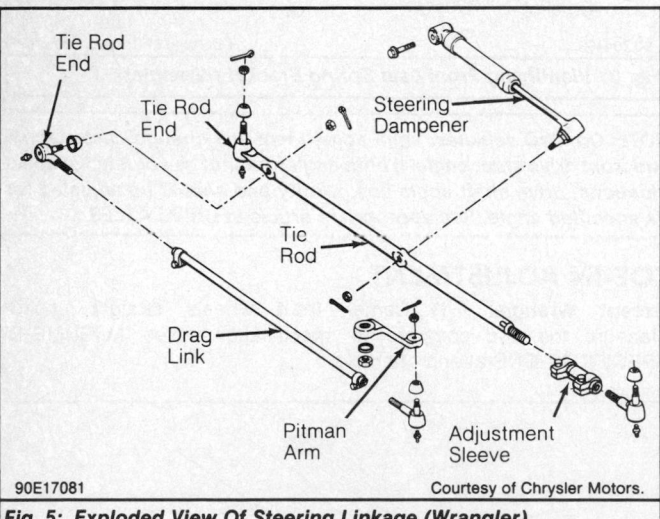

90E17081   Courtesy of Chrysler Motors.

Fig. 5: Exploded View Of Steering Linkage (Wrangler)

ALIGNMENT SPECIFICATIONS
WHEEL ALIGNMENT SPECIFICATIONS

Application	Preferred	Range
Cherokee & Comanche		
Camber [1]	0	−0.75 To 0.5
Caster [1]	6	5 To 9
Toe-In [1]	0	−0.1 To 0.1
Toe-In [2]	0	−0.05 To 0.05
Toe-Out On Turns [1]	33	33
Grand Cherokee		
Camber [1]	−0.5	0 To −1
Caster [1]	7	6.5 To 7.5
Toe-In [1]	0.5	0.1 To 0.9
Toe-In [2]	[3]	[3]
Toe-Out On Turns [1]	33	33
Wrangler		
Camber [1]	0	−0.5 To 0.5
Caster [1]		
Manual Transmission	8	6.5 To 9
Automatic Transmission	6.5	5.25 To 7.25
Toe-In [1]	0	−0.24 To 0.24
Toe-In [2]	0	−0.12 To 0.12
Toe-Out On Turns [1]	33	33

[1] – Measurement in degrees.
[2] – Measurement in inches (mm).
[3] – Specification not available from manufacturer.

TORQUE SPECIFICATIONS
TORQUE SPECIFICATIONS

Application	Ft. Lbs. (N.m)
Cherokee & Comanche	
Drag Link Sleeve Clamp Bolts	14 (19)
Lower Control Arm Nuts	133 (180)
Tie Rod Sleeve Clamp Bolts	36 (49)
Wheel Lug Nut	65-90 (88-122)
Grand Cherokee	
Drag Link Sleeve Clamp Bolts	36 (49)
Lower Control Arm Nuts	130 (176)
Tie Rod Sleeve Clamp Bolts	25 (34)
Wheel Lug Nut	65-90 (88-122)
Wrangler	
Drag Link Sleeve Clamp Bolts	36 (49)
Spring Bracket "U" Bolt Nut	90 (122)
Tie Rod Sleeve Clamp Bolts	14 (19)
Wheel Lug Nut	65-90 (88-122)

Cherokee, Comanche, Grand Cherokee (1993), Wrangler

DESCRIPTION

Cherokee, Comanche and Grand Cherokee front suspensions consist of axle, 2 coil springs, track bar, stabilizer bar and upper and lower control arms. Track bar is used to minimize front axle side-to-side movement. Stabilizer bar and shock absorbers control suspension spring movement.

Wrangler models use leaf spring front suspension with shock absorbers, stabilizer bar and a track bar.

ADJUSTMENTS & INSPECTION

WHEEL ALIGNMENT SPECIFICATIONS & PROCEDURES

NOTE: See SPECIFICATIONS & PROCEDURES article in WHEEL ALIGNMENT.

WHEEL BEARING

NOTE: Wheel bearings on all 4WD models are nonadjustable. If wheel bearings require service, see WHEEL BEARINGS under REMOVAL & INSTALLATION.

2WD Models (Cherokee & Comanche) – **1)** Raise and support vehicle. Turn wheel by hand while placing fingers of free hand on rotor shield. If any roughness is detected proceed to WHEEL BEARINGS under REMOVAL & INSTALLATION. Remove wheel and tire assembly. See Fig. 1.
2) Remove hub dust cap, cotter pin and nut retainer. Ensure bearings are thoroughly packed with lithium grease. Rotate hub and rotor assembly by hand, tighten retainer nut to **21 ft. lbs. (29 N.m)** to seat bearings.
3) Loosen retainer nut 1/2 turn while rotating hub. Then retighten nut to **19 INCH lbs. (2 N.m)**. Install nut retainer and new cotter pin. Clean hub dust cap and coat inside with clean grease. Reverse removal procedure for remaining components.

REMOVAL & INSTALLATION

WHEEL BEARINGS

Removal (2WD Models) – **1)** Raise and support vehicle. Remove wheel assembly. Remove brake caliper and suspend caliper with wire. DO NOT allow caliper to hang on brake hose.
2) Remove hub dust cap, cotter pin, nut retainer, nut, washer and outer wheel bearing. Remove rotor and hub assembly. Pry grease seal from hub. Remove inner wheel bearing.
Inspection – Clean bearings and hub in solvent and dry with compressed air. Inspect bearings and races for damage or excessive wear.
Installation – To install, reverse removal procedure. Pack bearings with wheel bearing grease. Adjust wheel bearings. See WHEEL BEARING under ADJUSTMENT.

NOTE: On 4WD models, front wheel bearings cannot be serviced separately. If defective, hub and bearing must be replaced as an assembly. See HUB & BEARING under REMOVAL & INSTALLATION in FRONT AXLES article.

SHOCK ABSORBER

Removal & Installation – With vehicle at normal ride height, remove nut, washer and rubber grommet from top of shock absorber. Raise and support vehicle. Remove lower shock mounting bolts from axle housing bracket. Remove shock absorber. Inspect units for damage or leakage. To install, reverse removal procedure.

STEERING KNUCKLE

Removal – **1)** Raise and support vehicle. Remove wheel, disc brake caliper, rotor, cotter pin, nut retainer, and axle hub nut. Remove hub-to-steering knuckle attaching bolts. Remove hub and rotor shield from steering knuckle. Remove axle shaft from axle tube. See FRONT AXLES article.

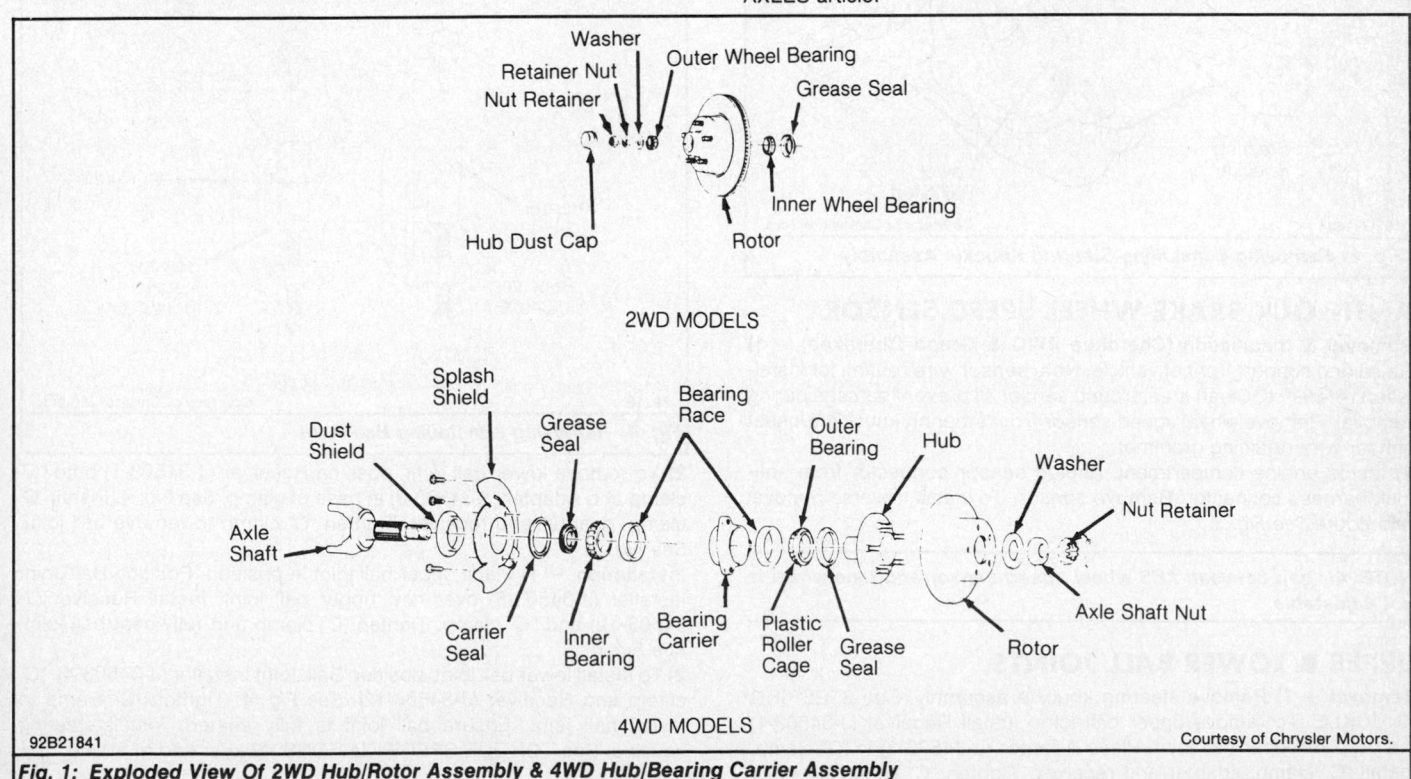

92B21841

Courtesy of Chrysler Motors.

Fig. 1: Exploded View Of 2WD Hub/Rotor Assembly & 4WD Hub/Bearing Carrier Assembly

NOTE: DO NOT disconnect caliper unless service is needed. Support caliper with wire to prevent hose damage.

2) On models with front axle shift motor, remove outer axle shaft from right axle tube. Leave shift collar on intermediate shaft. Remove caliper anchor plate from steering knuckle. Remove steering knuckle and ball joint cotter pins. Remove ball joint nuts. Strike steering knuckle at ball joint stud boss with a brass hammer to loosen knuckle from ball joint studs. Remove steering knuckle. See Fig. 2.

Installation – 1) Position steering knuckle over ball joint studs and install nuts. Tighten to specification. Install NEW cotter pins. Install caliper anchor plate and tighten bolts to specification. See TORQUE SPECIFICATIONS table at end of article. Install axle shafts into axle tubes.

2) On vehicles with front axle shift motor, ensure shift collar is correctly positioned on intermediate axle shaft, install axle into shift collar inside axle tube. Ensure axle shaft is completely engaged with shift collar.

3) On all models, apply bearing grease to spindle hub bore in steering knuckle and install rotor shield and hub. Tighten spindle hub bolts. Install hub washer and nut. Tighten hub nut to specification. Install hub nut retainer and install NEW cotter pin. Install rotor, caliper and wheel. Lower vehicle.

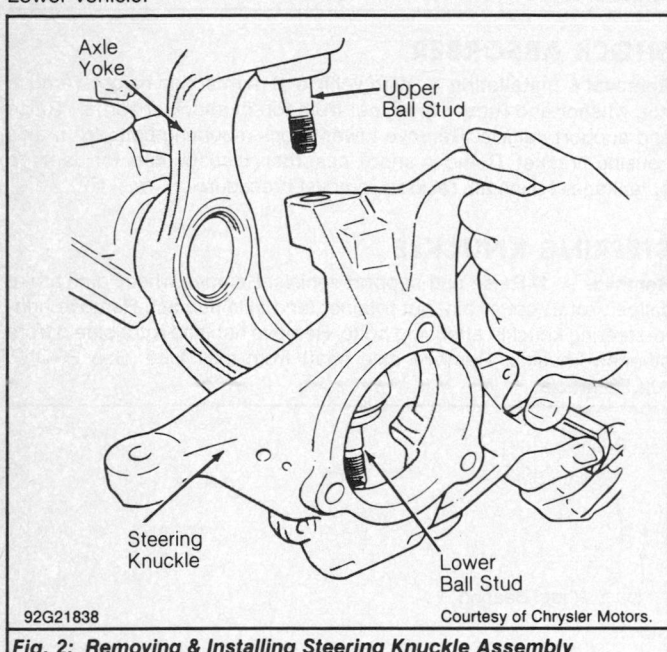

Fig. 2: Removing & Installing Steering Knuckle Assembly

ANTI-LOCK BRAKE WHEEL SPEED SENSOR

Removal & Installation (Cherokee 4WD & Grand Cherokee) – 1) Raise and support front of vehicle. Note sensor wire routing for installation reference. Clean area around sensor to prevent damage during removal. Remove wheel speed sensor from steering knuckle. Unseat sensor wire retaining grommet.

2) Inside engine compartment, unplug sensor connector from anti-lock harness connector. Remove sensor. To install, reverse removal procedure. See Fig. 3.

NOTE: Air gap between ABS wheel speed sensor and tone wheel is not adjustable.

UPPER & LOWER BALL JOINTS

Removal – 1) Remove steering knuckle assembly. See STEERING KNUCKLE. To remove upper ball joint, install Receiver (J-34503-1) over top of upper ball joint. Place Adapter (J-34503-3) in "C" clamp. Install "C" clamp, adapter and receiver. Tighten "C" clamp screw to remove ball joint. See Fig. 4.

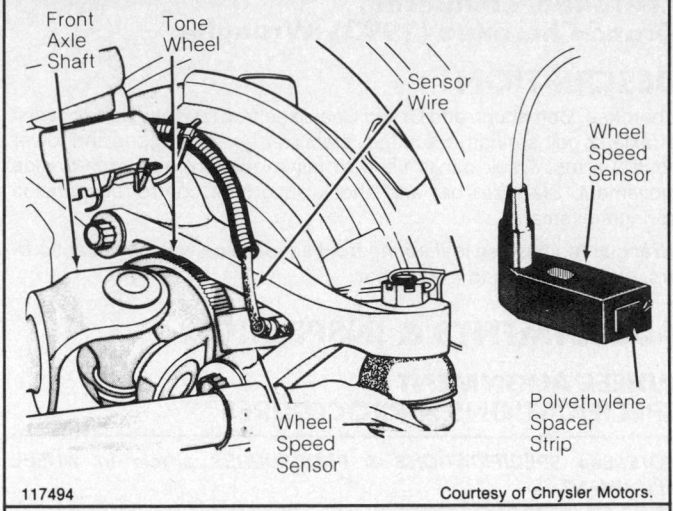

Fig. 3: Locating Anti-Lock Brake Wheel Speed Sensor

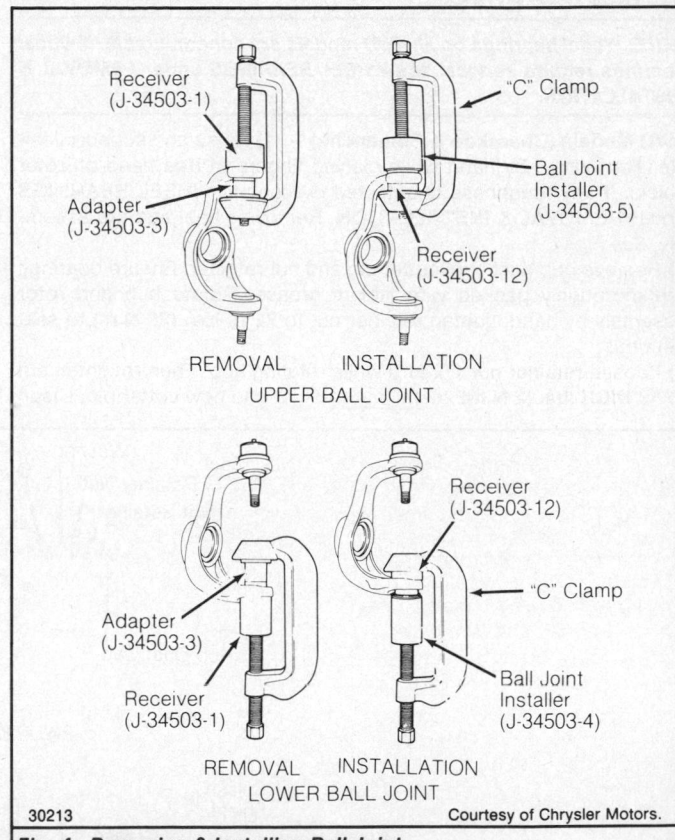

Fig. 4: Removing & Installing Ball Joint

2) To remove lower ball joint, position Receiver (J-34503-1) onto "C" clamp and Adapter (J-34503-3) at base of clamp. See Fig. 4. Install "C" clamp, adapter and receiver. Tighten "C" clamp to remove ball joint. See Fig. 4.

Installation – 1) Place upper ball joint in position. Position Ball Joint Installer (J-34503-5) over new upper ball joint. Install Receiver (J-34503-12) and "C" clamp. Tighten "C" clamp and fully seat ball joint. See Fig. 4.

2) To install lower ball joint, position Ball Joint Installer (J-34503-4), "C" clamp and Receiver (J-34503-12). See Fig. 4. Tighten "C" clamp to install ball joint. Ensure ball joint is fully seated. Install steering knuckle. See TORQUE SPECIFICATIONS table at end of article.

COIL SPRING

Removal & Installation – **1)** Raise and support vehicle on frame rails. Remove wheel assembly. On 4WD models, Place reference mark on drive shaft and front axle flanges. Disconnect drive shaft at front axle. **2)** Place jack stand under axle housing. Disconnect lower control arms at axle housing. Disconnect stabilizer bar links and lower shock absorber mounting bolts at axle housing. Disconnect track bar at frame rail bracket. Disconnect tie rod from pitman arm. **3)** Lower axle housing to relieve spring pressure. Remove spring retainer mounting bolt. Remove spring retainer and coil spring. Note component location for reassembly reference. To install, reverse removal procedure.

LEAF SPRING

Removal & Installation – **1)** Raise and support vehicle. Raise axle assembly with jack to relieve spring tension. On Wrangler, remove wheels and loosen stabilizer bar link nut. On all other models, remove stabilizer bar link from spring bracket. **2)** On all models, remove spring "U" bolts and plate. Remove spring-to-front shackle bolt and spring-to-rear frame hanger bolt. Remove spring. To install, reverse removal procedure. Ensure spring center bolt is seated in axle housing. Tighten spring-to-front shackle bolt and spring-to-rear frame hanger bolt with vehicle at normal operating height. See TORQUE SPECIFICATIONS table at end of article.

UPPER CONTROL ARM & AXLE HOUSING PIVOT BUSHING

Removal & Installation – **1)** Raise vehicle and remove upper control arm mounting bolt from axle housing. Disconnect control arm mounting bolt at frame rail. Remove upper control arm. Repeat procedure for opposite control arm. **2)** Inspect control arm for damage or distortion and replace as needed. Check pivot bushings for excessive distortion, deterioration or wear. **3)** If pivot bushing requires replacement, on 2WD models, install Spacer (J-33581-3) between ears of control arm bracket on axle housing. See Fig. 5.

NOTE: Spacer (J-33581-3) is not used on 4WD models as solid control arm brackets are used. DO NOT attempt to remove upper control arm pivot bushing on 2WD models without spacer. Axle bracket will be distorted if spacer is not used.

---

4) Install Bushing Remover/Installer Set (J-35581, which includes Spacer J-35581-3, Remover/Installer J-35581-2, Receiver J-35581-1, Bolt J-21474-19 and Nut J-21474-18) onto pivot bushing. See Fig. 5. **5)** Rotate nut to press bushing from axle housing and into receiver. See Fig. 5. Once bushing is removed, remove bushing remover/installer components.

CAUTION: On 2WD models, spacer must remain installed for bushing installation.

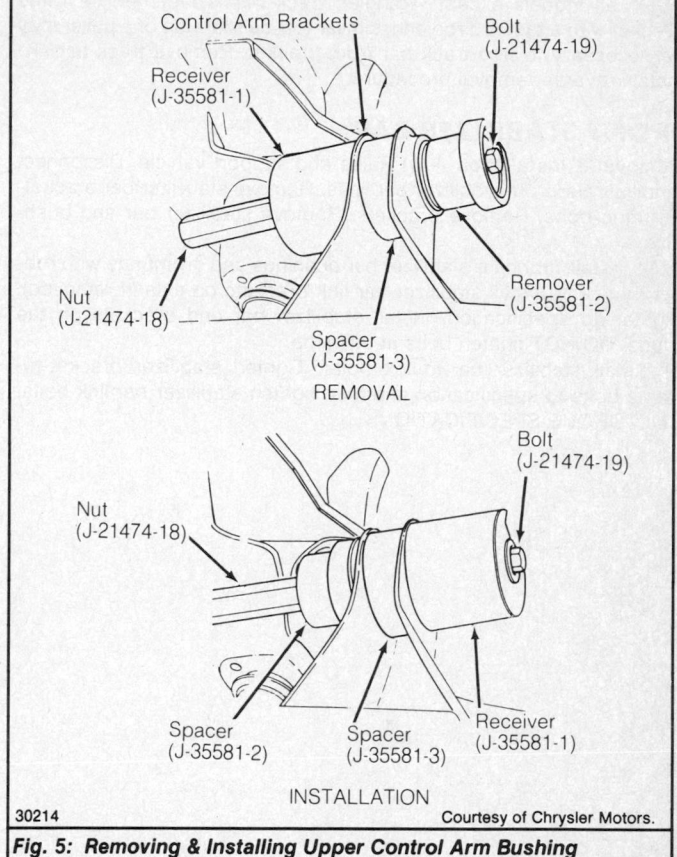

Fig. 5: Removing & Installing Upper Control Arm Bushing

6) Position bushing on Remover/Installer (J-35581-2) and Nut (J-21474-18). Position bushing and installer components in control arm bracket. Assemble remaining installer components. See Fig. 5. **7)** Rotate nut to press bushing into housing until fully seated in bore. See Fig. 5. Remove bushing installer components. To install upper control arm, reverse removal procedure.

LOWER CONTROL ARM

Removal & Installation – Raise and support vehicle. Disconnect lower control arm mounting bolts at axle housing and frame brackets. Remove lower control arm. To install, reverse removal procedure.

TRACK BAR

Removal & Installation – **1)** Raise and support vehicle. Remove cotter pin (if used) and nut at frame rail bracket. Remove track bar-to-axle housing bracket.

2) On all models except Wrangler, track bar is fastened to frame bracket with a tapered rod end, similar to a tie rod. Use of a puller may be necessary to free track bar from bracket. Remove track bar. To install, reverse removal procedure.

FRONT STABILIZER BAR

Removal & Installation – 1) Raise and support vehicle. Disconnect stabilizer bar from stabilizer bar links. Remove stabilizer bar bracket-to-frame bolts. Remove brackets. Remove stabilizer bar and bushings.

2) To install, lubricate stabilizer bar bushings and grommets with rubber lubricant. Install stabilizer bar link brackets on axle (if removed). Tighten to specification. Install stabilizer bar and brackets on the frame. DO NOT tighten bolts at this time.

3) Install stabilizer bar-to-link bolts. Tighten stabilizer bracket-to-frame bolts to specification and then tighten stabilizer bar link bolts. See TORQUE SPECIFICATIONS.

TORQUE SPECIFICATIONS
TORQUE SPECIFICATIONS

Application	Ft. Lbs. (N.m)
Cherokee, Comanche & Grand Cherokee	
Axle Shaft Nut	175 (237)
Axle Shift Motor Bolt	[1]
Ball Joint Nut	75 (102)
Bearing Assembly-To-Steering Knuckle Bolt	75 (102)
Brake Caliper	
Mounting Bolt	77 (104)
Mounting Pin	30 (41)
Control Arm Bolt	
Upper	
At Axle	55 (75)
At Frame	66 (90)
Lower	133 (180)
Shock Absorber Nut (Lower)	14 (19)
Stabilizer Bar	
Frame Bolt	55 (75)
Link Bolt	27 (37)
Stabilizer Bar Link-To-Bracket Bolt	70 (95)
Tie Rod-To-Steering Knuckle Nut	35 (47)
Track Bar	
Frame Rail Bracket Nut	63 (85)
Axle Mount Bolt	74 (100)
Wheel Bearing Outer Lock Nut	50 (68)
Wheel Lug Nut	75 (102)
Wheel Speed Sensor Bolt	11 (15)
Wrangler	
Axle Shaft Nut	175 (237)
Ball Joint Nut	75 (102)
Bearing Assembly-To-Steering Knuckle Bolt	75 (102)
Brake Caliper	
Mounting Bolt	77 (104)
Mounting Pin	30 (41)
Shock Absorber	
Lower Bolt	45 (61)
Upper Stud Nut	10 (14)
Spring-To-Frame Bracket Bolt	105 (142)
Spring-To-Front Shackle Bolt	95 (129)
Spring "U" Bolt Nut	90 (122)
Stabilizer Bar	
Link Bolt	45 (61)
Mounting Bracket Bolt	55 (75)
Stabilizer Bar Link-To-Spring Bracket Nut	45 (61)
Tie Rod-To-Steering Knuckle Nut	35 (47)
Track Bar Bolt	74 (100)
Wheel Bearing Outer Lock Nut	50 (68)
Wheel Lug Nut	75 (102)
	INCH Lbs. (N.m)
Axle Shift Motor Bolt	101 (11)
Shock Absorber Nut (Upper)	96 (10)

Cherokee, Comanche, Grand Cherokee (1993), Wrangler

DESCRIPTION & OPERATION

All models use collapsible steering columns. All columns have integral ignition switch and locking device. Optional tilt wheel is available with both A/T and M/T models. Transmission shift linkage is integral on all models except those with floor shift. *See Figs. 1 and 2.*

Grand Cherokee models are equipped with driver-side air bag. Steering column on Grand Cherokee models is serviced only as an assembly, except for steering wheel, switches and wiring.

WARNING: On models with Supplemental Restraint System (SRS), air bag system MUST be disabled before servicing ANY steering column component. Disabling system will prevent accidental air bag deployment, resulting in possible serious injury or property damage.

AIR BAG DISABLING

BEFORE servicing ANY steering column or air bag component, disconnect and shield negative (ground) battery cable. Wait 2 MINUTES to allow air bag system capacitor to deplete its residual charge. Proceed with steering column service.

REMOVAL & INSTALLATION
HORN PAD & STEERING WHEEL

Removal & Installation (Except Grand Cherokee) – 1) Disconnect negative battery cable. Place wheels in straight-ahead position. On models with standard steering wheel, remove horn button retaining screws from rear of steering wheel. Disconnect wiring from horn button and remove.

2) On models with sport steering wheel (round horn button), remove horn button by pulling button upward. If necessary, remove horn internal components. Place components in order of removal.

3) Remove steering wheel retaining nut. Reference mark steering wheel and steering shaft. Using puller, remove steering wheel. To install, reverse removal procedure. Align marks made during removal. Tighten steering wheel retaining nut to specification. See TORQUE SPECIFICATIONS table at end of article.

Removal & Installation (Grand Cherokee) – 1) Disable air bag system. See AIR BAG DISABLING. Ensure steering wheel is in straight-ahead position. Remove nuts mounting air bag module to steering wheel. Remove screws securing cruise control switch to steering wheel. Disconnect wiring connectors. Remove air bag module and cruise control switch assembly.

2) Pry trim covers from back of steering wheel and remove horn switch mounting screws. Disconnect horn wires. Remove horn switch.

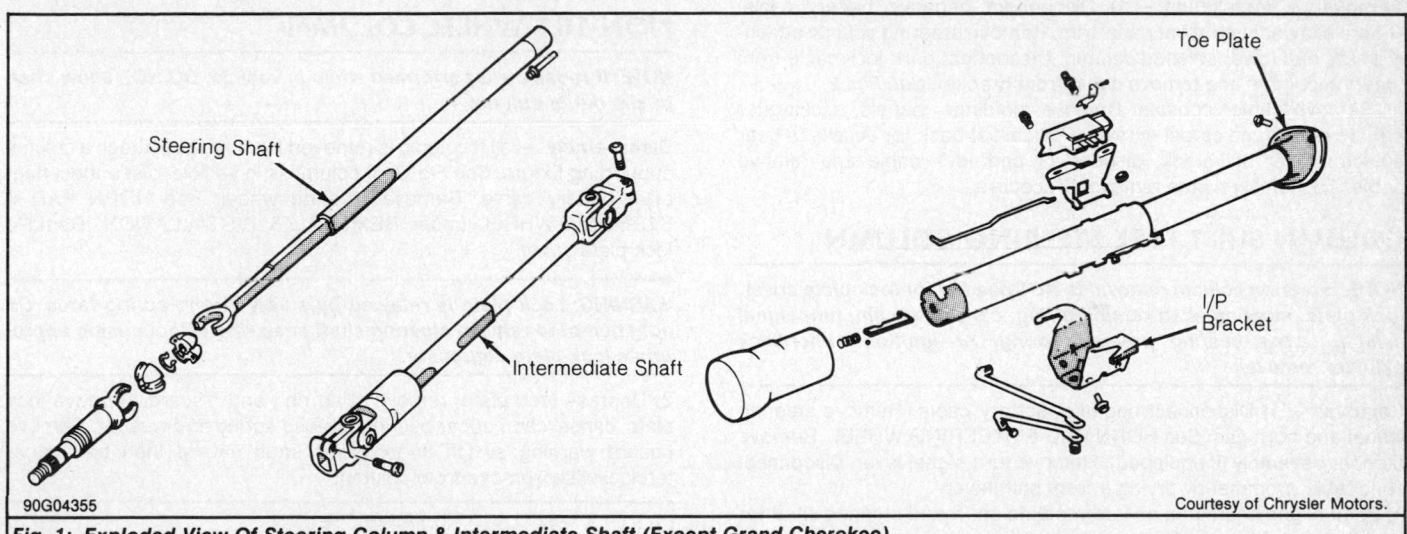

Fig. 1: Exploded View Of Steering Column & Intermediate Shaft (Except Grand Cherokee)

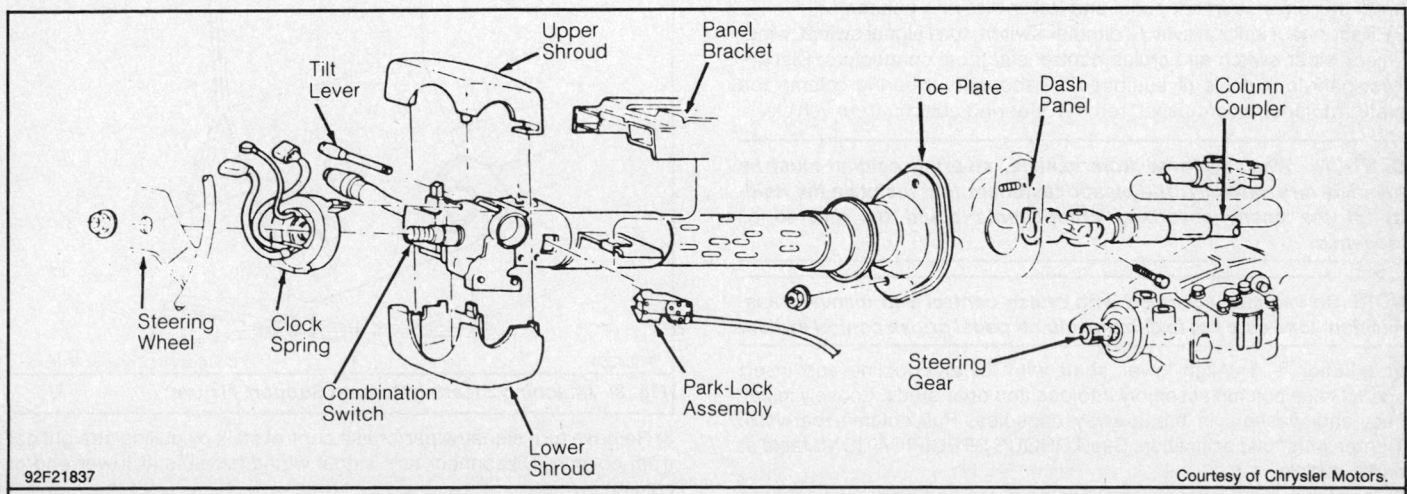

Fig. 2: Exploded View Of Steering Column (Grand Cherokee)

3) Remove steering wheel retaining nut. Reference mark steering wheel and steering shaft. Using puller, remove steering wheel. To install, reverse removal procedure. Align marks made during removal. Tighten steering wheel retaining nut to specification.

COMBINATION SWITCH

Installation & Removal (Grand Cherokee) – 1) Disable air bag system. See AIR BAG DISABLING. Remove tilt lever (if equipped). Remove upper and lower steering column covers. Remove steering panel trim panel and knee bolster. Remove steering column-to-mounting bracket retaining nuts. Lower steering column. See Fig. 2.

2) Using Tamper Proof Torx Bit (TTXR20B2), remove combination switch retaining screws. Gently roll combination switch away from column. Unscrew connector retaining screw from combination switch. Screw will remain in connector. Disconnect connector. Remove switch. To install, reverse removal procedure.

PARK-LOCK CABLE

NOTE: Park-Lock (Shifter/Ignition Interlock on Grand Cherokee) cable mechanism is used on all models equipped with floor shift and AW4 transmission (except Wrangler). Park-Lock system locks shifter in PARK position when key switch is in LOCK or ACCESSORY position.

Removal & Installation – 1) Disconnect negative battery cable. Remove lower instrument panel trim. Remove steering column attaching nuts and lower steering column. Disconnect park-lock cable from steering column and remove cable from bracket. See Fig. 2.

2) Remove center console. Remove moldings, panels, accelerator pedal bracket and carpet screws. Pull carpet back for access to gear selector lever bell-crank, disconnect park-lock cable and remove cable. To install, reverse removal procedure.

COLUMN SHIFT TYPE STEERING COLUMN

NOTE: Steering column removal is NOT needed for lock plate cover, lock plate, steering shaft retaining ring, canceling cam, turn signal switch, upper bearing preload spring, or ignition switch/lock cylinder removal.

Removal – 1) Disconnect negative battery cable. Remove steering wheel and horn pad. See HORN PAD & STEERING WHEEL. Remove damper assembly (if equipped). Remove turn signal lever. Disconnect shift cable grommet by prying it from shift lever.

2) Paint alignment marks on intermediate shaft and steering shaft for installation reference. Disconnect steering shaft from intermediate shaft. If necessary, remove lower part of instrument panel, disconnect bracket from instrument panel and lower steering column.

3) Disconnect ignition switch, dimmer switch, turn signal switch, windshield wiper switch and cruise control electrical connectors. Disconnect park-lock cable (if equipped). Disconnect steering column toe plate from instrument panel, remove steering column from vehicle.

CAUTION: When removed from vehicle, steering column must be handled very carefully. The plastic fasteners that maintain the rigidity of the energy-absorbing components could be sheared or loosened.

NOTE: On vehicles equipped with cruise control and manual transmission, take care not to damage clutch pedal cruise control switch.

Installation – 1) Align lower shaft with lower coupling and insert shaft. Raise column assembly into position onto studs. Loosely install nuts and washers in break-away capsules. Pull column rearward. Tighten nuts to specification. See TORQUE SPECIFICATIONS table at end of article.

2) Install new shift lever grommet using pliers and back-up washer to snap grommet into place. Use a multipurpose grease to aid installation. Connect gearshift cable rod to shift lever by snapping rod into grommet with pliers.

3) Adjust linkage. Place steering wheel on shaft with master splines aligned. Place damper assembly inside steering wheel (if equipped). Install steering wheel retaining nut. Tighten to specification.

4) Install horn pad assembly. Connect electrical connectors at steering column jacket. Connect negative battery cable. Test operation of lights and horn.

5) On models with automatic transmission, install gearshift indicator pointer. Slowly move gearshift lever from Low to Park position, pausing briefly at each position. Readjust pointer as required. Install instrument panel steering column cover.

FLOOR SHIFT TYPE STEERING COLUMN

Removal & Installation – Removal procedure is same as for column shift with following exceptions: In place of rotating shift bowl, a plastic shroud is fixed to lock housing. Shroud covers jacket and lock inhibitor assembly with a tab holding it in place. Replace shroud by removing key/lock housing from jacket.

OVERHAUL

NOTE: Manufacturer does not recommend overhaul of steering column on Grand Cherokee; if service is required, replace steering column as an assembly. Steering wheel, switches and wiring can be serviced separately.

NON-TILT WHEEL COLUMN

NOTE: If repairs are performed while in vehicle, DO NOT allow shaft to slip out of column.

Disassembly – 1) If column is removed from vehicle, attach a column supporting fixture. See Fig. 3 . If column is in vehicle, disconnect negative battery cable. Remove steering wheel. See HORN PAD & STEERING WHEEL under REMOVAL & INSTALLATION. Remove lock plate cover.

WARNING: Lock plate is retained by a very strong spring force. Do not attempt to remove steering shaft snap ring without using appropriate lock plate depressor.

2) Depress lock plate, remove snap ring and discard. Remove lock plate, cancel cam, upper bearing preload spring and washer. Remove hazard warning switch knob, press knob inward then turn counterclockwise, remove from column.

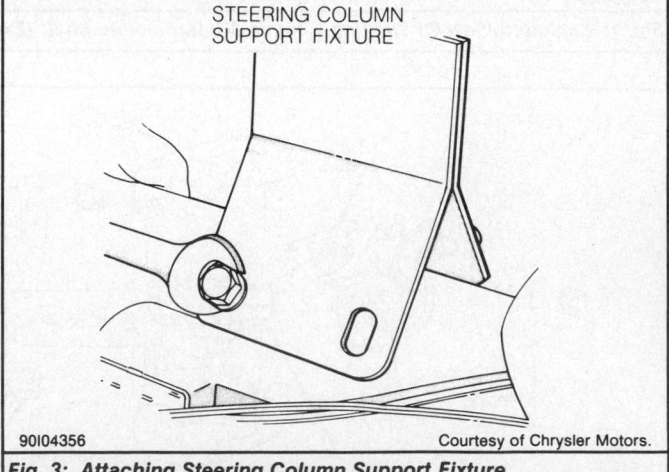

STEERING COLUMN
SUPPORT FIXTURE

90I04356   Courtesy of Chrysler Motors.

Fig. 3: Attaching Steering Column Support Fixture

3) Remove turn signal/wiper/cruise control stalk by pulling straight out from column. Disconnect turn signal wiring harness at lower end of column.

4) Remove turn signal/dimmer retaining screws and remove switch. Guide harness and switch up and out of column. Remove all other wire harnesses in steering column.

NOTE: Wrap tape around turn signal wire harness to prevent entanglement during removal.

5) Turn ignition to ON position. Remove key warning buzzer and contacts as a unit with needle nose pliers. Insert a small screwdriver into right hand slot adjacent to switch attaching screw boss. Depress spring latch located at bottom of slot and pull cylinder out of column.
6) On models equipped with floor shift, proceed to step **10**. On column shift models, remove gear selector lever upper pivot pin, selector lever and upper bearing thrust washer. Remove four screws attaching key/lock cylinder housing to steering column, remove key/lock cylinder housing.
7) Remove thrust cap and ignition switch actuating rod and rack. Remove rack preload spring, shaft lock bolt and spring from housing. Remove shift lever detent plate from housing. *See Fig. 4.*

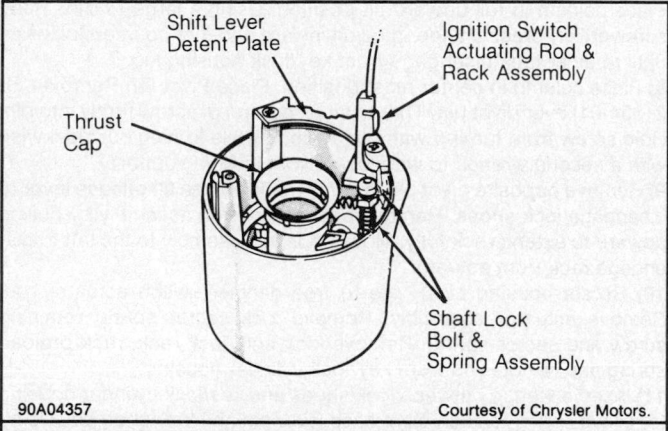

90A04357   Courtesy of Chrysler Motors.
Fig. 4: Identifying Key/Lock Cylinder Housing

8) Use punch to exert force on block tooth to disengage and remove lock sector. Remove gear selector lever housing and shroud from steering shaft. Remove gear selector lever spring from housing.

NOTE: Steering column must be removed from vehicle for further disassembly.

9) Remove steering shaft, if not removed earlier. Remove spring clip from lower bearing retainer, remove retainer, lower bearing, and adapter. Slide out shift tube.
10) On models equipped with floor shift, remove screws attaching key/lock cylinder and shroud to column jacket. Remove dimmer switch arm, disengage remote rod from lock rack. Remove key/lock cylinder housing to shroud screws and separate.

11) Remove and separate wave washer from key release lever pivot. Remove lock rack, lock bolt and preload spring. Use punch to exert force on block tooth to disengage and remove lock sector. Remove gear selector lever housing and shroud from steering shaft.
12) Remove steering shaft, if not removed earlier. Remove spring clip from lower bearing retainer, remove retainer, lower bearing and adapter. Slide out shift tube.
Reassembly – 1) Coat all friction surfaces with grease. Insert key sector through key/lock cylinder hole. Install lock sector shaft. Ensure sector turns freely. Install lock rack preload spring. Assemble lock bolt and rod and install assembly in housing. Mate assembly with lock sector gear teeth. Install shift lever detent plate on housing. *See Fig. 5.*
2) Install thrust cap and ignition switch actuating rod on housing. Insert gear selector lever housing lower bearing and align indentations in shell with projections on housing. Install gear selector spring in housing.
3) Install gear selector lever housing and shroud on column. Rotate housing to ensure that bearing is seated. With gear selector housing in Park position and lock rack pulled downward, position and seat key/lock cylinder housing on column. Tighten 4 screws to **40 INCH lbs. (4.5 N.m)**.
4) Insert shift tube in lower end of column and rotate until shift tube upper key slides into gear selector housing keyway. On models equipped with floor shift, proceed to step **10**). On column shift models, proceed to next step.
5) Install key/lock cylinder housing and shroud on steering column, place key in ignition cylinder and rotate until key is aligned with keyway in housing. Insert cylinder into housing far enough to contact switch actuator. Press inward and rotate cylinder. When aligned, cylinder will move inward and spring-loaded retainer will snap into place. Cylinder is now locked in column.
6) Turn key/lock cylinder to ON position and install key/lock buzzer switch. Move ignition switch to ACC position then back 2 clicks to OFF position. The remote rod hole in ignition switch should be centered. Insert remote rod in ignition switch slider hole. Tighten ignition switch mounting screws to **35 INCH lbs. (4 N.m)**.
7) Install lower bearing, adapter, retainer and spring clip at lower end of column. Install steering shaft into lower end of column and route through into upper bearing. Position turn signal switch and wire harness in key/lock housing. Fold wires against connector and feed down through column. Install wiper wiring harness and route through column. Align and secure turn signal switch. Tighten screws to **35 INCH lbs. (4 N.m)**.
8) Install dimmer switch actuator arm and tighten screw to **35 INCH lbs. (4 N.m)**. Route cruise control wiring harness in column (if equipped). Install turn signal/wiper/dimmer/cruise control switch stalk on column by pressing straight in. Position thrust washer, upper bearing preload spring and cancel cam on steering column.

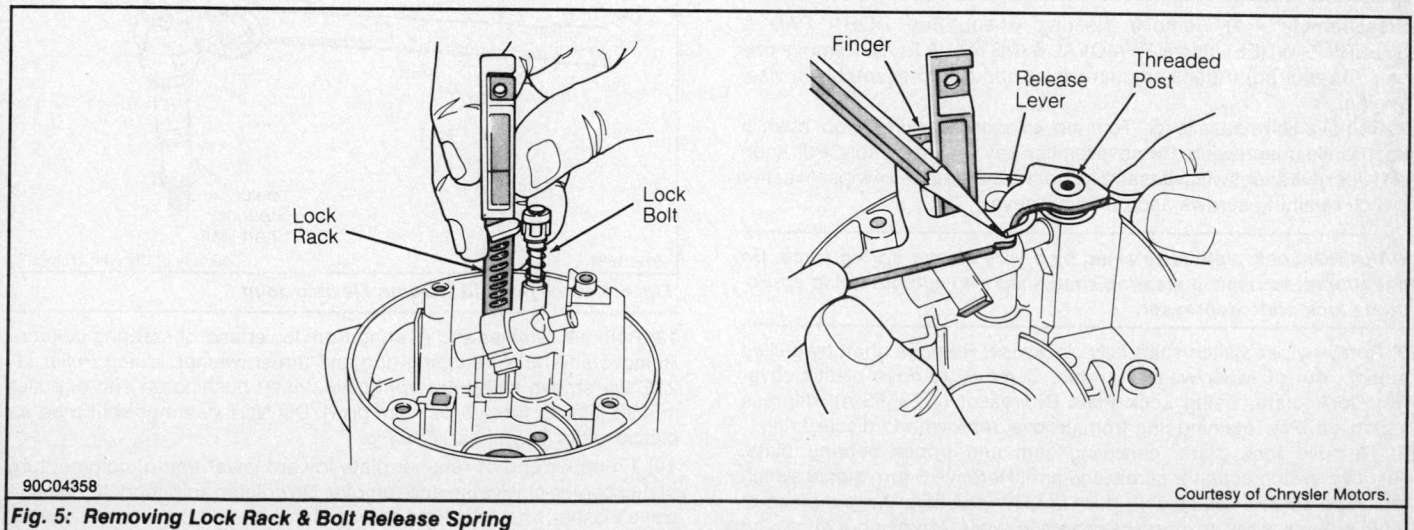

90C04358   Courtesy of Chrysler Motors.
Fig. 5: Removing Lock Rack & Bolt Release Spring

9) Install hazard warning switch knob. Place lock plate on shaft, depress lock plate with depressor and install new snap ring. Install steering wheel. See HORN PAD & STEERING WHEEL under REMOVAL & INSTALLATION. Tighten steering wheel nut to specification. See TORQUE SPECIFICATIONS table at end of article.

10) On models equipped with floor shift, install key release lever return spring over threaded pivot post on housing. Insert key release finger in lock rack slot and position hole in lever over threaded pivot post. *See Fig. 5.* Ensure inner end of spring contacts release lever.

11) Raise key release lever slightly. Install lever spring between lever and boss on housing. Lubricate and place wave washer on threaded pivot post. Position shroud on key/lock housing. Tighten screws to **18 INCH lbs. (2 N.m).**

12) Insert short, hooked end of remote rod in lock rack. Install assembled key/lock housing on steering column and tighten screws to **60 INCH lbs. (7 N.m).** Install key/lock cylinder housing and shroud on steering column, place key in ignition cylinder and rotate until key is aligned with keyway in housing.

13) Insert cylinder into housing far enough to contact switch actuator. Press inward and rotate cylinder. When parts align, cylinder will move inward and spring-loaded retainer will snap into place. Cylinder is now locked in column.

14) Turn key/lock cylinder to ON position and install key/lock buzzer switch. Move ignition switch slider to ACC position, then back 2 clicks to OFF position. The remote rod hole in ignition switch should be centered. Insert remote rod in ignition switch slider hole and tighten ignition switch to column screws to **35 INCH lbs. (4 N.m).**

15) Install lower bearing, adapter, retainer and spring clip at lower end of column. Install steering shaft into lower end of column and insert into upper bearing. Position turn signal switch and wire harness in key/lock housing. Fold wires against connector and feed down through column jacket. Install wiper wiring harness and route through column. Align and secure turn signal switch. Tighten screws to **35 INCH lbs. (4 N.m).**

16) Install dimmer switch actuator arm and tighten screw to **35 INCH lbs. (4 N.m).** Route cruise control wiring harness in column (if equipped). Install turn signal/wiper/dimmer/cruise control switch stalk on column by pressing straight in. Position thrust washer, upper bearing preload spring and canceling cam on steering column.

17) Install hazard warning switch knob. Place lock plate on shaft, compress plate and install new snap ring. Ensure that new snap ring is completely seated in groove before removing depressor. Install steering wheel. Tighten steering wheel nut to specification.

TILT WHEEL COLUMN

NOTE: Tilt steering can be disassembled in vehicle down to the column jacket. If further repairs are needed, column must be removed from vehicle.

Disassembly – 1) Remove steering wheel. See HORN PAD & STEERING WHEEL under REMOVAL & INSTALLATION. Remove column (if required). Attach column fixture and clamp assembly in vise. *See Fig. 3.*

2) Remove tilt release lever. To remove hazard warning knob, push in knob while unscrewing. Remove ignition key light assembly. Pull knob off wiper/washer switch assembly. Remove 2 sleeve-to-wiper/washer switch retaining screws and remove sleeve.

WARNING: Lock plate is retained by a very strong spring force. Do not attempt to remove steering shaft snap ring without using appropriate lock plate depressor.

3) Rotate wiper switch shaft fully clockwise. Remove shaft by pulling straight out of wiper/washer switch. Carefully remove plastic cover from lock plate. Using Lock Plate Depressor (J-23653-A), depress lock plate. Pry retaining ring from groove, remove and discard ring.

4) Remove lock plate, canceling cam and upper bearing plate. Remove switch actuator screw and arm. Remove 3 turn signal switch attaching screws. Place shift bowl in LOW position. Wrap a piece of tape around wires to prevent snagging while removing switch and remove switch.

5) Turn key/lock cylinder to ON position. Using needle nose pliers, remove key warning buzzer switch and contacts as one unit. Remove spring and switch. DO NOT allow spring to fall into steering column. Insert a small screwdriver into the right-hand slot adjacent to switch attaching screw boss. Depress spring latch located at bottom of slot and remove key/lock cylinder.

6) Remove 3 key/lock cylinder housing cover screws and remove housing cover. Remove wiper/washer switch. Tilt lever opening shield and dimmer switch actuator rod may be removed from cap (if necessary). Remove dimmer switch mounting screws and remove switch. With ignition switch in ACC position, remove ignition switch mounting screws and remove switch.

WARNING: Tilt spring guide retainer has strong spring force.

7) Remove upper bearing race and bearing seat from steering shaft. Place column in full upward tilt position. Using a large Phillips head screwdriver, press tilt spring guide inward and turn counterclockwise until retainer tabs disengage from key/lock housing lug.

8) Place column in center most position. Place Pivot Pin Remover (J-21854-01) over pivot pin. Thread small portion of screw firmly into pin. Hold screw from turning with one wrench while turning nut clockwise with a second wrench to withdraw pivot pin from support.

9) Remove opposite pivot pin in same manner. Use tilt release lever to disengage lock shoes. Remove bearing housing assembly by pulling upward to extend rack fully. Move housing assembly to the left to disengage rack from actuator.

10) Rotate housing clockwise to free dimmer switch actuator rod. Remove actuator assembly. Remove lock sector spring retaining screw and sector spring. Remove lock bolt, lock rack, rack preload spring and remote rod from key/lock cylinder housing.

11) Insert a wedge between lock shoes and key/lock cylinder housing to relieve spring tension tilt release lever pin and lock shoe pin. Using a punch, remove tilt release lever pin and lock shoe pin. Remove lock shoes, spring and wedge. Remove upper and lower bearings and races from key/lock cylinder housing if required.

NOTE: Bearings and races only require removal if damaged. Remove races with hammer and punch and discard. DO NOT reuse components.

12) Remove steering shaft from upper end of steering column. Separate upper and lower steering shaft by folding shaft 90 degrees at flex joint and detaching shaft sections. *See Fig. 6.* Remove steering column support from column. Remove shift gate from steering support (if required).

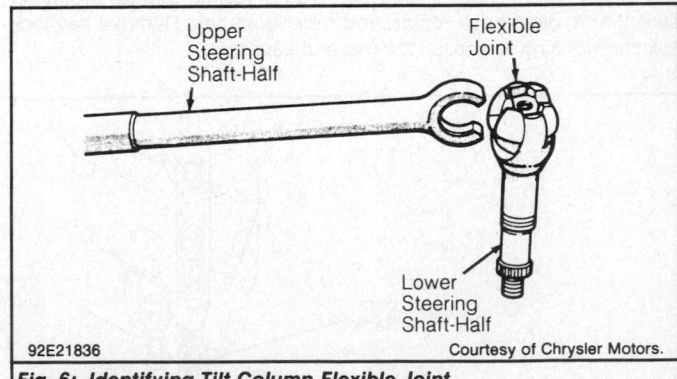

Upper Steering Shaft-Half

Flexible Joint

Lower Steering Shaft-Half

92E21836   Courtesy of Chrysler Motors.

Fig. 6: Identifying Tilt Column Flexible Joint

13) Remove retainer and bearing from lower end of steering column. Remove shift tube retaining ring and thrust washer. Using Puller (J-23072), remove shift tube from bowl. Insert bushing on end of puller in shift tube to force tube from bowl. DO NOT hammer shift tube as plastic joints may shear. *See Fig. 7.*

14) Tilt upper end of retainer plate toward lower end of column, turn plate counter-clockwise and remove. On column shift models, remove wave washer and shift tube spring. Remove shift bowl from steering column jacket. On floor shift models, remove column shroud from col-

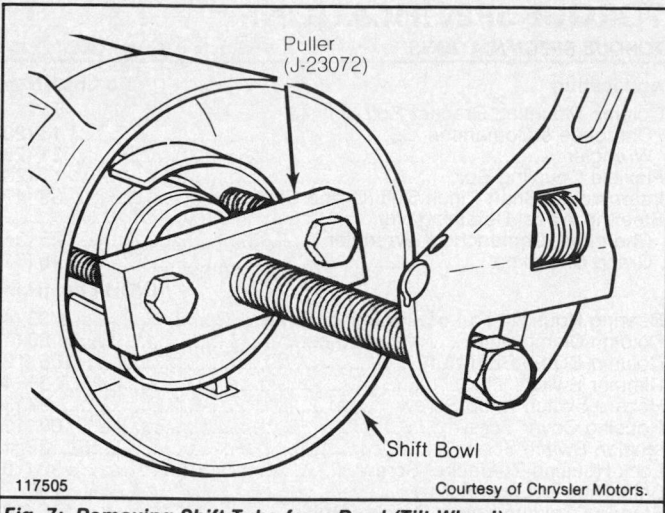

Courtesy of Chrysler Motors.

Fig. 7: Removing Shift Tube from Bowl (Tilt Wheel)

umn jacket. Remove key release lever and spring from column shroud.

WARNING: *Use only original or exact replacement screws, bolts and nuts to assemble steering column. Use of incorrect hardware could keep column from compressing in a collision. Column-to-instrument panel attaching nuts MUST be tightened to correct torque so that column will break away on impact.*

Reassembly – **1)** During reassembly, coat all friction surfaces with multipurpose grease. If reassembling a floor shift type column, proceed to step **3)**. To reassemble column shift type column, install shift bowl on steering column jacket. Install shift tube spring, wave washer and retainer plate in shift bowl. Insert shift tube through lower end of column jacket and align tube key spline with shift bowl keyway.
2) Install Installer (J-23073-01) and pull shift tube into bowl. *See Fig. 8.* Install shift tube thrust washer and retainer plate snap ring. Install column lower bearing. Attach shift gate to steering column support. Install steering column support assembly into column and tighten retaining screws alternately and evenly to **60 INCH lbs. (7 N.m).**

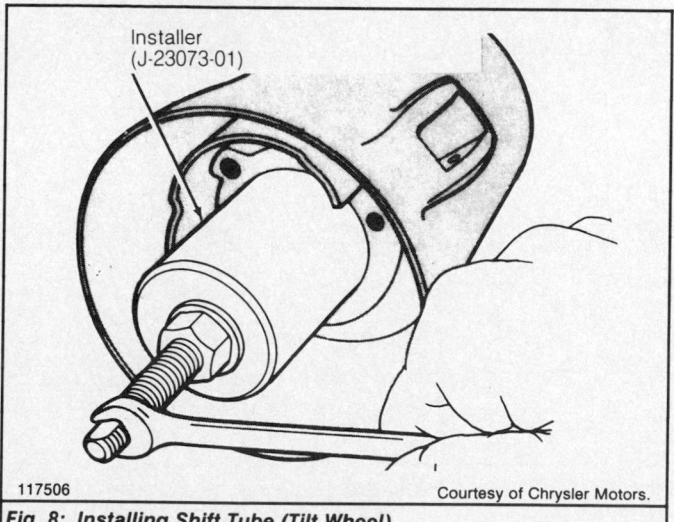

Courtesy of Chrysler Motors.

Fig. 8: Installing Shift Tube (Tilt Wheel)

3) To reassemble floor shift type column, position key release lever spring onto lever and install assembly into column shroud. Install shroud onto steering column jacket. Install retainer plate into column jacket notches.

4) Install column support into column jacket by aligning "V" on support with "V" notch in column jacket. To completely seat support, press key release lever downward while pressing support into place. Install steering column support retaining screws and tighten alternately and evenly to **60 INCH lbs. (7 N.m).**

NOTE: Remaining steps apply to either column shift type or floor shift type columns.

5) Install remote rod in column support rod slot. Install dimmer and ignition switches. Install new races and bearings in key/lock cylinder housing if old components were removed. Using a .18" (4.5 mm) diameter rod to aid in alignment, install lock shoes, lock shoe springs and lock shoe pin.
6) Install tilt release lever, lever spring and lever pin in key/lock cylinder housing. Insert wedge between housing and lever to relieve spring tension and ease pin installation.
7) Install lock bolt in key/lock cylinder housing and engage it in lock sector cam surface. Install lock rack, rack preload spring and replacement shim in key/lock cylinder housing. Mate square block tooth on lock rack to like tooth on lock sector. Tighten screws to **35 INCH lbs. (4 N.m).**
8) Retain lock shoes in disengaged position and install key/lock housing on column support. Align pivot pin holes in key/lock cylinder housing with those in column support and install pivot pins. Seat pins fully using a hammer and punch.

CAUTION: Press housing down firmly while installing pivot pins to avoid damage to holes in column support.

9) Place key/lock cylinder housing in full upward tilt position. Lubricate tilt spring guide and spring with chassis lube. Insert tilt spring guide and spring into key/lock cylinder housing. Using a large Phillips head screwdriver, install spring retainer into key/lock cylinder housing lugs.
10) Install key/lock cylinder housing cover and tighten screws to **60 INCH lbs. (7 N.m).** Install gear selector indicator light assembly (if equipped). Route dimmer switch harness down through column.
11) Insert key/lock cylinder into housing far enough to contact switch actuator. Press inward and rotate cylinder. When aligned, cylinder will move inward and spring-loaded retainer will snap into place. Cylinder is now locked in column. Turn key/lock cylinder to ON position. Install key/lock buzzer switch.
12) Install turn signal switch, but DO NOT install switch retaining screws at this time. Install windshield wiper harness and switch and route harness down through column jacket. Route cruise control harness (if equipped), down through column jacket.
13) Install turn signal switch stalk by pushing straight into column. Install hazard warning knob on hazard warning switch. Install turn signal retaining screws and tighten to **35 INCH lbs. (4 N.m).** Install upper bearing race in key/lock cylinder housing.
14) Install cruise control harness (if equipped). Install upper bearing preload spring, canceling cam and lock plate. Depress lock plate with depressor and install new snap ring. *See Fig. 9.* Install lock plate cover. Install gear selector lever and retaining pin (if equipped).
15) Install steering wheel. See HORN PAD & STEERING WHEEL under REMOVAL & INSTALLATION. Turn key/lock cylinder to OFF position, move ignition switch downward to eliminate lash, and install switch retaining screws. Tighten screws to **35 INCH lbs. (4 N.m).**
16) Depress dimmer switch slightly and insert 3/32" drill bit into adjustment hole. Loosen retaining screws, move switch upward to remove lash, and retighten screws to **35 INCH lbs. (4 N.m).** Remove drill bit and test dimmer switch operation in all column tilt positions.
17) Install steering column. See appropriate type column under REMOVAL & INSTALLATION. Reconnect negative battery cable. Test ignition switch in all tilt positions. Ensure vehicle starts only in Park and Neutral.

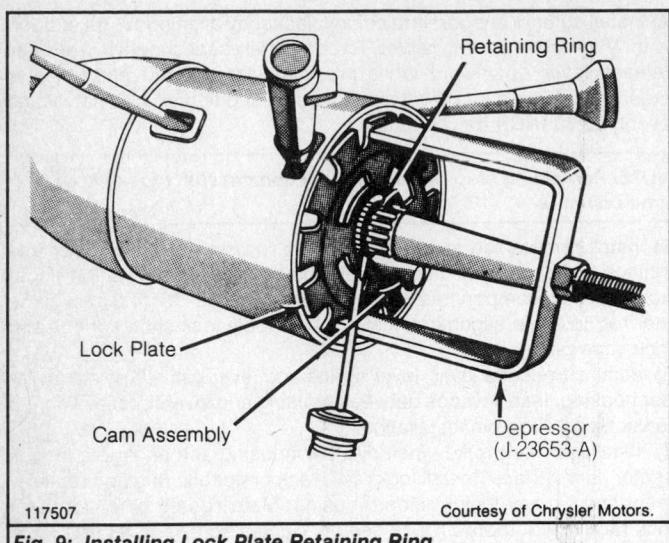

Fig. 9: Installing Lock Plate Retaining Ring

117507   Courtesy of Chrysler Motors.

TORQUE SPECIFICATIONS
TORQUE SPECIFICATIONS

Application	Ft. Lbs. (N.m)
Column Mounting Bracket Bolt	
Cherokee & Comanche	15 (20)
Wrangler	21 (28)
Flexible Coupling Bolt	17 (23)
Intermediate Shaft Pinch Bolt (Grand Cherokee)	35 (47)
Steering Wheel Retaining Nut	
Cherokee, Comanche & Wrangler	25 (34)
Grand Cherokee	45 (61)
	INCH Lbs. (N.m)
Bearing Housing-To-Lock Housing Screw	35 (4)
Column Clamp Stud	20 (2)
Column Clamp Stud Nut	106 (12)
Dimmer Switch	35 (4)
Hazard Switch Knob Screw	27 (3)
Housing Cover Screw	100 (11)
Ignition Switch Screw	35 (4)
Lock Housing-To-Jacket Screw	90 (10)
Shift Tube Support Screw	60 (7)
Steering Column Lower Bracket Bolt	106 (12)
Toe Plate	
Cherokee & Comanche	66 (7)
Grand Cherokee	105 (12)
Wrangler	192 (22)
Tilt Release Spring Retaining Screw	35 (4)
Turn Signal Retaining Plate Screw	33 (4)
Upper Bracket Nut	106 (12)

Comanche, Wrangler

DESCRIPTION & OPERATION

Steering gear is a recirculating ball-type consisting of a ball nut connected to steering worm and in mesh with sector gear. Proper engagement of sector gear and ball nut is obtained by adjusting screw. Worm bearing adjuster can be turned to provide proper preloading of upper and lower bearings.

LUBRICATION

Use multipurpose chassis lubricant.

ADJUSTMENTS

NOTE: Adjust worm bearing preload prior to performing over-center preload adjustment. If steering gear is removed, install INCH-pound. torque wrench on worm shaft to check preload adjustments.

WORM BEARING PRELOAD

1) Raise and support vehicle. Place reference mark on pitman arm and sector shaft. Remove pitman arm retaining nut. Using Puller (7998), remove pitman arm from sector shaft. Loosen sector shaft adjuster screw lock nut and back out adjuster screw 2-3 turns. *See Fig. 1.*

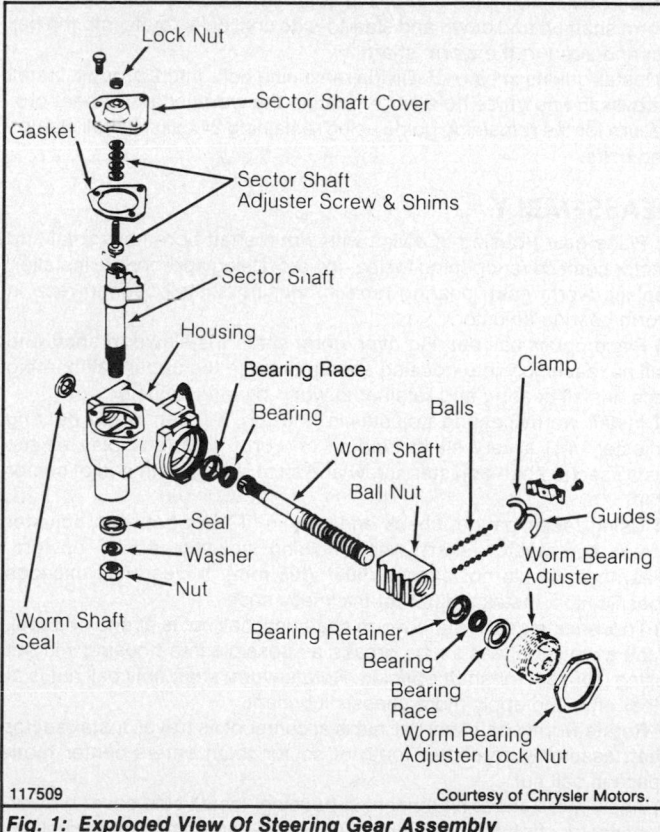

Lock Nut
Sector Shaft Cover
Gasket
Sector Shaft Adjuster Screw & Shims
Sector Shaft
Housing
Bearing Race
Clamp
Bearing
Balls
Worm Shaft
Ball Nut
Guides
Seal
Worm Bearing Adjuster
Washer
Nut
Worm Shaft Seal
Bearing Retainer
Bearing
Bearing Race
Worm Bearing Adjuster Lock Nut

117509
Courtesy of Chrysler Motors.

Fig. 1: Exploded View Of Steering Gear Assembly

2) Remove horn button. Turn wheel to the right stop, turn wheel back 1/2 turn. Using an INCH-pound torque wrench on steering shaft nut, rotate steering shaft from right stop through a 90-degree arc and note torque wrench reading. Torque required to maintain wheel movement should be **5-8 INCH lbs. (.6-1 N.m)**.

NOTE: If rotating torque is exceptionally high, check steering column/shaft alignment. If alignment is okay, disassemble steering gear and repair as required.

3) If torque reading is not as specified, loosen worm bearing adjuster lock nut. *See Fig. 1.* Rotate worm bearing adjuster clockwise to increase preload or counterclockwise to decrease preload.
4) Hold worm bearing adjuster while tightening lock nut to **50 ft. lbs. (68 N.m)**. Recheck worm bearing preload. Adjust over-center preload.

OVER-CENTER PRELOAD

1) With worm bearing preload adjusted, turn worm shaft slowly from stop-to-stop while counting total number of turns. Turn shaft back to the exact center position.
2) Loosen lock nut and turn sector shaft adjuster screw in until all lash is taken out of sector shaft. Tighten lock nut. Rotate worm shaft slightly off center (1/2 turn). Attach an INCH-pound torque wrench to worm shaft or steering wheel nut.
3) Rotate worm shaft back through center position and note rotating torque. Rotating torque should be **4-10 INCH lbs. (.4-1.1 N.m)** in excess of worm bearing preload. Maximum torque should not exceed **18 INCH lbs. (2 N.m)**. If rotating torque is not within specification, adjust sector shaft adjuster screw.

REMOVAL & INSTALLATION

STEERING GEAR

Removal & Installation – 1) Remove body trim panel sand skid plate to access steering gear (if necessary). Disconnect intermediate shaft from steering gear. Raise and support vehicle. Disconnect drag link from pitman arm. Stabilizer bar may require removal for access to drag link.
2) Mark pitman arm and sector shaft for installation reference. Remove pitman arm retaining nut. Using Puller (7998), remove pitman arm. Remove steering gear mounting bolts and remove gear assembly. On Comanche, adapter plate is removed with steering gear assembly. On Wrangler, adapter plate remains in vehicle.
3) To install, reverse removal procedure. Ensure all reference marks are aligned. Stake pitman arm nut against the shaft in several areas to provide safe retention.

TIE ROD END

Removal & Installation – 1) Remove cotter pins and retaining nuts at both ends of tie rod and remaining steering components. *See Figs. 2 and 3.* Disconnect steering damper from tie rod. Using puller, separate tie rod ends from steering knuckles and steering linkage.

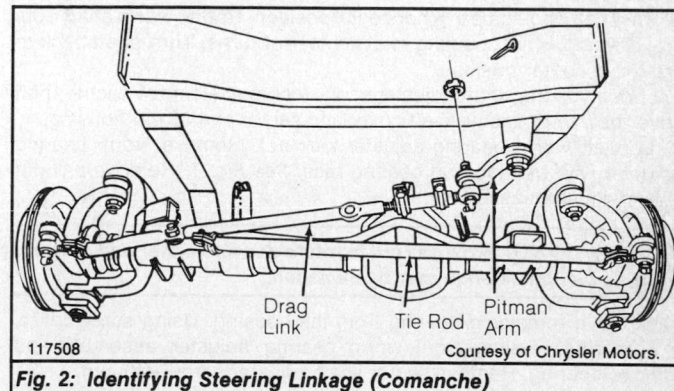

Drag Link
Tie Rod
Pitman Arm

117508
Courtesy of Chrysler Motors.

Fig. 2: Identifying Steering Linkage (Comanche)

2) Loosen clamp bolts at adjusting sleeve. Remove tie rod ends from adjusting sleeve. Note number of turns required to remove tie rod, for assembly reference.
3) To install, reverse removal procedure. Adjusting sleeve clamp bolts should be installed with threaded end of bolt toward rear of vehicle and angled slightly upward. Check and adjust toe-in. See SPECIFICATIONS & PROCEDURES article in WHEEL ALIGNMENT.

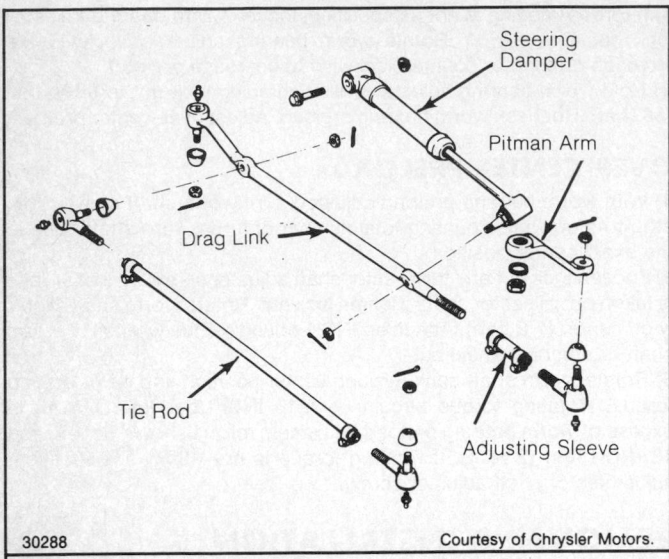

30288   Courtesy of Chrysler Motors.

Fig. 3: Exploded View Of Steering Linkage (Wrangler)

STEERING DAMPER

Removal & Installation – Place front wheels in straight-ahead position. Remove cotter pins and retaining nuts and bolts at both ends of steering damper and steering linkage. *See Fig. 3.* Remove steering damper assembly and rubber bushings. To install, reverse removal procedure.

DRAG LINK

Removal & Installation – Separate steering damper from drag link. Remove cotter pins and nuts from both ends of drag link. Using a puller, separate drag link from pitman arm and tie rod. To install, reverse removal procedure. Ensure wheels are in straight-ahead position and pitman arm is centered prior to installation.

OVERHAUL

DISASSEMBLY

1) Place steering gear in a vise, clamping onto one mounting tab. Worm shaft should be in a horizontal position. Rotate worm shaft from stop-to-stop while counting total number of turns. Turn shaft back to the exact center position.
2) Loosen sector shaft adjuster screw lock nut. Remove sector shaft cover bolts. Lift sector shaft cover and sector shaft from housing.
3) Loosen worm bearing adjuster lock nut. Remove worm bearing adjuster with bearing and bearing race. *See Fig. 1.* Remove ball nut and worm shaft assembly.

CAUTION: DO NOT allow ball nut to rotate down to either end of worm shaft as ball guide ends may be damaged.

4) Remove remaining bearing from the housing. Using screwdriver, pry bearing retainer from worm bearing adjuster assembly and remove bearing. Remove sector shaft adjuster screw lock nut.
5) Hold sector shaft cover and turn sector shaft adjuster screw clockwise to remove sector shaft cover. Remove sector shaft adjuster screw and shim from sector shaft. Pry out and discard both sector shaft and worm shaft seals.

CLEANING & INSPECTION

Clean components with solvent and dry with compressed air. Inspect bearings and races for signs of wear. Check ball nut and worm shaft assembly for wear and straightness.

COMPONENT SERVICE

Worm Shaft Bearing Race (In Worm Bearing Adjuster) – Using slide hammer and puller, remove bearing race from worm bearing adjuster. Using proper installer, install bearing race in worm bearing adjuster.
Worm Shaft Bearing Race (In Housing) – Using a hammer and punch, remove bearing race from the housing. Using proper diameter installer, install new bearing race in the housing.
Ball Nut & Worm Shaft Assembly – Ball nut disassembly is necessary only if binding or tightness exists while rotating worm shaft. If disassembly is required, proceed as follows:
1) Remove ball guide retaning clamp. Position clean pan under ball nut. Pull guides from ball nut letting balls fall in pan. Turn ball nut over and rotate worm shaft until all balls (50) are removed.
2) Remove worm shaft from the ball nut. Wash parts and inspect worm, nut grooves, and ball bearings for indentations. Check ball guides for damage at ends where they deflect or pick up balls from helical path on worm shaft.
3) To reassemble ball nut and worm shaft, hold the ball nut with helical grooved bore in a horizontal position with ball guide holes facing upward.
4) Position ball nut so that wider/deeper side of the teeth is closer to the sector shaft cover opening after installation. Install worm shaft. Ensure worm shaft is aligned with grooves in the ball nut.
5) Rotate worm shaft until same number of shaft threads exist on both ends of ball nut. Install one ball in each guide hole on ball nut. Move worm shaft up and down and side-to-side until balls rotate into the ball nut and support the worm shaft.
6) Install guides in ball nut. Divide remaining balls into 2 groups. Install 24 balls in one guide hole while rotating the worm shaft. Repeat procedure for the remaining guide using remaining 24 balls. Install clamps and bolts.

REASSEMBLY

1) Place gear housing in a vise with worm shaft bore horizontal and sector shaft cover opening facing upward. Using appropriate installer, replace worm shaft bearing race in housing. Install bearing race in worm bearing adjuster.
2) Place upper ball bearing over worm shaft. Install worm shaft and ball nut assembly into housing and up through the upper ball bearing race. Install bearing and retainer in worm bearing adjuster.
3) Install worm bearing adjuster in housing. Tighten worm bearing adjuster until a very slight amount of worm shaft end play exists. Install sector shaft adjuster screw and shim in "T" slot in end of sector shaft.
4) Using feeler gauge, check end play in "T" slot between adjuster screw and sector shaft when holding adjuster screw upward. Clearance should not exceed .002" (.05 mm). If clearance exceeds specification, install a different thickness shim.
5) To lubricate gear, rotate worm shaft until ball nut is at end of travel. Pack as much chassis lube grease as possible into housing without losing it out sector shaft opening. Rotate worm shaft until ball nut is at other end, and apply more chassis lubricant.
6) Rotate worm shaft until ball nut is at center of its travel. Install sector shaft assembly so center tooth of sector teeth enters center tooth space in ball nut.
7) Apply more chassis lubricant in housing. Install side cover gasket. Coat sector shaft adjuster screw with a non-hardening thread sealant. Install side cover over sector shaft by reaching through cover with a screwdriver.
8) Turn adjuster screw until sector shaft cover almost contacts the gasket. Install cover retaining bolts finger tight only. Turn sector shaft adjuster screw until sector shaft cover is tight against gasket and then loosen 1/2 turn. Loosely install a NEW lock nut on adjuster screw.
9) Lightly lubricate all seals with grease. Wrap sector shaft treads with single layer of tape. Install sector shaft seal in the housing. Remove tape. Install worm shaft seal. Ensure seals are fully seated.
10) Tighten sector shaft cover bolts to specification. Adjust worm bearing preload and over-center preload. See WORM BEARING PRELOAD and OVER-CENTER PRELOAD under ADJUSTMENTS.

TORQUE SPECIFICATIONS

TORQUE SPECIFICATIONS

Application	Ft. Lbs. (N.m)
Drag Link Clamp Bolt	
Comanche	36 (49)
Wrangler	34 (46)
Drag Link-To-Pitman Arm Nut	60 (81)
Drag Link-To-Steering Knuckle Nut (Comanche)	35 (47)
Drag Link-To-Tie Rod Nut (Wrangler)	35 (47)
Pitman Arm-To-Sector Shaft Nut	185 (251)
Sector Shaft Adjuster Screw Lock Nut	25 (34)
Sector Shaft Cover Bolt	45 (61)
Steering Damper-To-Axle Bracket Bolt	55 (75)
Steering Damper-To-Drag Link Nut(Comanche)	55 (75)
Steering Damper-To-Tie Rod Nut (Wrangler)	53 (72)
Steering Gear-To-Frame Bolt	
Comanche	70 (95)
Wrangler	75 (102)
Tie Rod Clamp Bolt	
Comanche	22 (30)
Wrangler	25 (34)
Tie Rod End Stud Nut	35 (47)
Worm Bearing Adjuster Lock Nut	50 (68)

Cherokee, Comanche, Grand Cherokee (1993), Wrangler

DESCRIPTION & OPERATION

Steering gear is a variable ratio, recirculating ball type. Power assist is provided by a belt driven hydraulic pump. Control valves are located inside steering gear housing.

Two types of Saginaw vane-type power steering pumps are used to provide hydraulic pressure for a recirculating ball type steering gear. Some applications utilize a pump submerged in reservoir housing. Other applications are equipped with a remote reservoir mounted on left fender apron. See POWER STEERING APPLICATIONS table. Manufacturer does not recommend overhaul of power steering pump. If service is required, pump should be replaced as an assembly.

Pump vanes are driven by a rotor and move fluid from the intake to the pressure cavities of pump ring. Centrifugal force moves vanes against inside surface of pump ring to pick up residual oil. As more oil is picked up, it is forced into cavities of thrust plate, into 2 crossover holes in pump ring and pressure plate, and into a high pressure area between pressure plate and housing end plate.

Filling the high pressure area causes oil to flow under the vanes in slots of the rotor. This forces vanes to follow inside oval surface of pump ring. As vanes rotate to small area of pump ring, oil is forced out from between vanes.

POWER STEERING APPLICATIONS

Application	Type
Cherokee, Comanche & Grand Cherokee	
2.5L	Non-Submerged
4.0L	Submerged
Wrangler	Non-Submerged

LUBRICATION

CAPACITY

Information is not available from manufacturer.

FLUID TYPE
RECOMMENDED FLUID

Application	Type
All Models	Mopar Power Steering Fluid

FLUID LEVEL CHECK

Power steering fluid level is checked using dipstick attached to reservoir cap. Check fluid with engine stopped and fluid hot or cold. Depending on fluid temperature, level must be at HOT or COLD mark on dipstick. Use ONLY Mopar power steering fluid.

HYDRAULIC SYSTEM BLEEDING

1) Fill reservoir. Operate engine until fluid reaches operating temperature of 170°F (77°C). Turn wheels to full left position. Check fluid, and add if necessary.
2) Start and operate engine at fast idle. Recheck reservoir level. Add fluid if necessary. Turn wheels from side to side without contacting stops. Maintain fluid level just above pump body.
3) After air is removed, return wheels to straight-ahead position. Run engine 2-3 minutes. Road test vehicle. Recheck fluid level.

ADJUSTMENTS

POWER STEERING PUMP BELT

Using belt tension gauge, check power steering belt tension. See BELT TENSION SPECIFICATIONS table. If adjustment is required, loosen power steering pump rear mounting bolts. Loosen pivot bolt. Tighten adjuster bolt to increase belt tension. Loosen adjuster bolt to decrease belt tension. Tighten mounting and pivot bolts. Recheck belt tension.

BELT TENSION SPECIFICATIONS [1]

Application	New Belt	Used Belt
Serpentine Belt	180-200	140-160
V-Belt	120-160	90-115

[1] – Tension specifications in Lbs. using Burroughs tension gauge.

WORM SHAFT THRUST BEARING PRELOAD

CAUTION: Always adjust worm shaft bearing preload before adjusting sector shaft over-center preload torque.

1) Remove steering gear from vehicle. See STEERING GEAR under REMOVAL & INSTALLATION. Rotate gear lock-to-lock several times to drain fluid. Loosen adjuster plug lock nut. See Fig. 1. Using spanner wrench, turn adjuster plug clockwise until plug is seated in housing. Torque will be about 20 ft. lbs. (27 N.m)

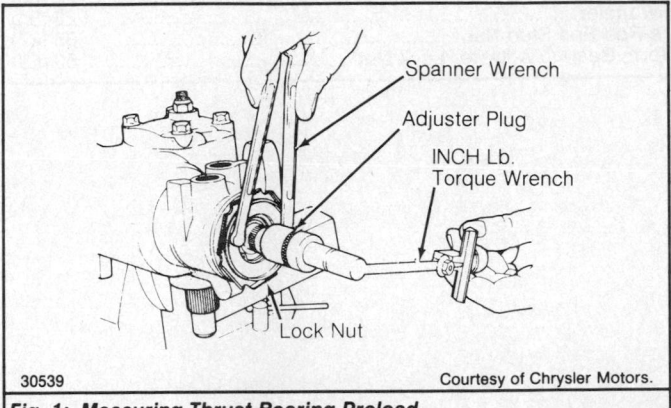

30539   Courtesy of Chrysler Motors.

Fig. 1: Measuring Thrust Bearing Preload

2) Index mark housing opposite one hole in adjuster plug. On Cherokee, Comanche and Comanche models, measure about 1/4" (6 mm) counterclockwise from mark. On Grand Cherokee models, measure about 1/2" (13 mm) counterclockwise from mark. Mark housing. Rotate plug counterclockwise until hole in adjuster aligns with second mark.
3) Tighten lock nut to 80 ft. lbs. (108 N.m). Ensure adjuster plug remains in position. Attach INCH Lb. torque wrench to end of stub shaft. Turn stub shaft to right stop, and then back 1/4 turn.
4) Using torque wrench, measure rotational torque required to turn shaft. Take reading with handle of torque wrench nearly vertical while turning it counterclockwise at an even rate. On Cherokee, Comanche and Wrangler models, reading should be 4-10 INCH lbs. (.5-1.1 N.m). On Grand Cherokee models, readings should be 6-10 INCH lbs. (.6-1.1 N.m),
5) If torque wrench reading is not within specifications, adjustment cap may not be correctly adjusted, steering gear may be assembled incorrectly or thrust bearings and races may be defective.

SECTOR SHAFT OVER-CENTER PRELOAD

CAUTION: Always adjust worm shaft bearing preload before adjusting sector shaft over-center preload torque.

1) Rotate stub shaft from stop-to-stop and count turns. To center steering gear, rotate shaft in reverse direction 1/2 number turned during stop-to-stop. Attach an INCH lb. torque wrench to stub shaft. Measure sector shaft over-center preload torque by turning torque wrench in a 45-degree arc on each side of vertical center. Record highest over-center rotational torque reading.
2) Rotational torque required to turn stub shaft should be 6-10 INCH lbs. (.6-1.2 N.m) greater than rotational torque specified for worm shaft. See WORM SHAFT THRUST BEARING PRELOAD.

3) If adjustment necessary, loosen adjustment on sector shaft adjuster screw until shaft has no preload. *See Fig. 2.* Tighten adjuster screw until required preload is obtained. Ensure adjustment screw does not move and tighten adjuster screw lock nut to **36 ft. lbs. (49 N.m)**. Recheck preload.

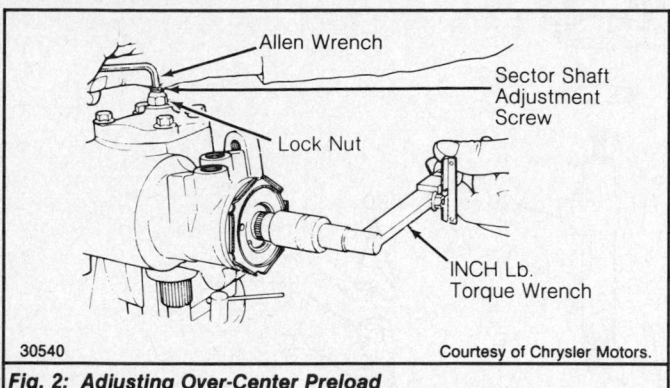

Fig. 2: Adjusting Over-Center Preload

TESTING

HYDRAULIC SYSTEM PRESSURE TEST

1) With belt tension correct, disconnect power steering pump pressure hose. Keep hose end raised to prevent fluid loss. Install Pressure Tester (7617) between power steering pump and steering gear.

2) Open valve. Run engine until fluid reaches normal operating temperature of **170°F (77°C)**. Check fluid level. Add fluid if necessary.

3) Note pressure reading with valve open and engine idling. Pressure should be less than **125 psi (9 kg/cm²)**. If pressure exceeds **125 psi (9 kg/cm²)**, check hoses for restrictions and poppet valve for proper assembly.

4) Close and reopen gate valve completely 3 times. Record highest reading each time. DO NOT close valve longer than 5 seconds. Note if pressure is within specifications. See PRESSURE TEST SPECIFICATIONS table.

5) If all readings are within specifications and 50 psi (3.5 kg/cm²) of each other, pump operation is normal.

6) If readings exceed specifications or are not within 50 psi (3.5 kg/cm²) of each other, flow control valve in pump is sticking. Remove flow control valve. Clean or replace valve as necessary.

7) If readings are below specifications, clean or replace flow control valve. If pressures are still low, replace pump.

8) If readings are all within specifications, open valve, and turn steering wheel from right stop to left stop. Record pressure. DO NOT hold wheel against stops longer than 5 seconds.

9) Compare both readings to pump output pressure reading obtained. Readings should be same as pump output pressure. If readings are low, steering gear is leaking internally. Repair or replace as required.

PRESSURE TEST SPECIFICATIONS

Application	Idle Pressure psi (kg/cm²)	Relief Pressure psi (kg/cm²)
Wrangler	Less Than 125 (9)	1050-1150 (74-81)
All Others	Less Than 125 (9)	1350-1450 (95-102)

REMOVAL & INSTALLATION

POWER STEERING PUMP

Removal & Installation – 1) Loosen and remove pump drive belt. Place pan under power steering pump. Disconnect pressure and return hoses from pump. Cap ends to prevent excessive fluid loss or contamination.

2) Remove bracket-to-engine bolts. Remove pivot bolt. Remove pump and mounting bracket as an assembly. To install, reverse removal procedure. Fill and bleed system. See HYDRAULIC SYSTEM BLEEDING under LUBRICATION.

STEERING GEAR

Removal – 1) Center steering gear. Disconnect intermediate shaft. Raise and support vehicle. Place drain pan under steering gear assembly. Disconnect hydraulic hoses from gear. Cap ends to prevent excessive fluid loss or contamination. Disconnect steering linkage from pitman arm.

2) Remove pitman arm from gear. Remove flexible coupling clamp bolt. Remove steering gear-to-frame bolts. Remove gear from flexible coupling and frame.

Installation – To install, reverse removal procedure. Fill pump reservoir. Bleed air from system. See HYDRAULIC SYSTEM BLEEDING under LUBRICATION.

TIE ROD END

Removal & Installation – 1) Remove cotter pins and retaining nuts at tie rod end. *See Figs. 3 and 4.* If necessary, disconnect steering damper from tie rod. Using puller, separate tie rod end from steering knuckle or steering linkage.

2) Loosen clamp bolts at adjusting sleeve. Remove tie rod end from adjusting sleeve. Note number of turns required to remove tie rod end for installation reference.

3) To install, reverse removal procedure. Adjusting sleeve clamp bolts should be installed with threaded end of bolt toward rear of vehicle and angled slightly upward. Check and adjust toe-in. See SPECIFICATIONS & PROCEDURES article in WHEEL ALIGNMENT.

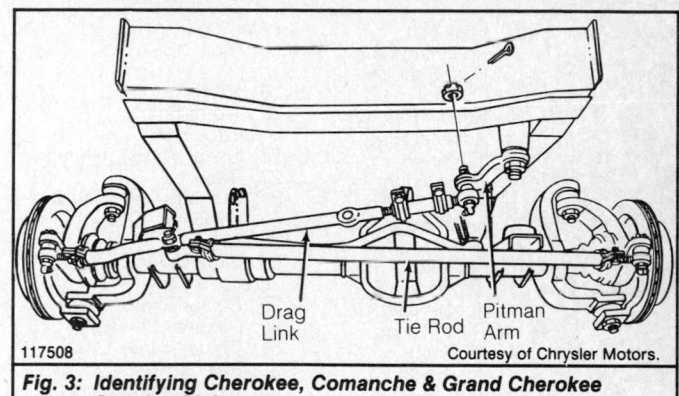

Fig. 3: Identifying Cherokee, Comanche & Grand Cherokee Steering Linkage

Fig. 4: Exploded View Of Steering Linkage (Wrangler)

STEERING DAMPER

Removal & Installation – Place front wheels in straight-ahead position. Remove cotter pins and retaining nuts and bolts at ends of damper and steering linkage. *See Figs. 3 and 4.* Remove damper assembly and rubber bushings. To install, reverse removal procedure.

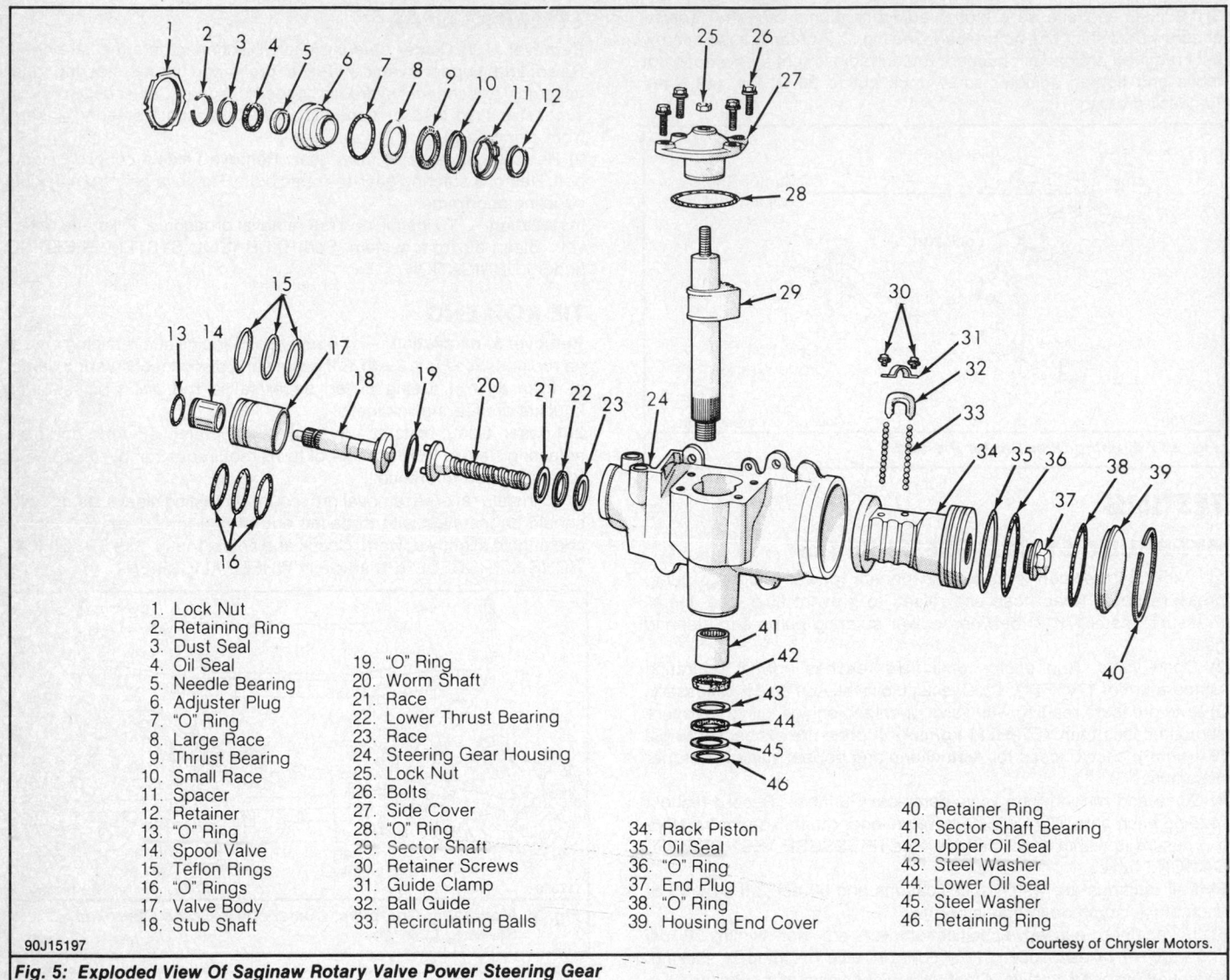

1. Lock Nut
2. Retaining Ring
3. Dust Seal
4. Oil Seal
5. Needle Bearing
6. Adjuster Plug
7. "O" Ring
8. Large Race
9. Thrust Bearing
10. Small Race
11. Spacer
12. Retainer
13. "O" Ring
14. Spool Valve
15. Teflon Rings
16. "O" Rings
17. Valve Body
18. Stub Shaft

19. "O" Ring
20. Worm Shaft
21. Race
22. Lower Thrust Bearing
23. Race
24. Steering Gear Housing
25. Lock Nut
26. Bolts
27. Side Cover
28. "O" Ring
29. Sector Shaft
30. Retainer Screws
31. Guide Clamp
32. Ball Guide
33. Recirculating Balls

34. Rack Piston
35. Oil Seal
36. "O" Ring
37. End Plug
38. "O" Ring
39. Housing End Cover

40. Retainer Ring
41. Sector Shaft Bearing
42. Upper Oil Seal
43. Steel Washer
44. Lower Oil Seal
45. Steel Washer
46. Retaining Ring

Courtesy of Chrysler Motors.

90J15197

Fig. 5: Exploded View Of Saginaw Rotary Valve Power Steering Gear

DRAG LINK

Removal & Installation – Raise and support vehicle. Separate steering damper from drag link. *See Figs. 3 and 4.* Remove cotter pins and nuts from both ends of drag link. Using a puller, separate drag link from steering linkage. To install, reverse removal procedure. Before installation, ensure wheels are in straight ahead position and pitman arm is centered.

OVERHAUL

STEERING GEAR

Disassembly – 1) Cap all openings in gear. Clean gear exterior completely. Mount gear in vise so sector shaft points downward. *See Fig. 5.* Rotate housing end plug retainer ring until one end of plug is over hole in housing.

2) Force end of ring from groove in housing. Remove ring. Rotate stub shaft counterclockwise to force housing end cover from housing. Rotate stub shaft clockwise 1/2 turn to draw rack piston inward.

CAUTION: DO NOT rotate stub shaft more than necessary to remove plug as ball bearings will fall out of worm and rack piston assembly.

3) Remove end plug. Remove lock nut from sector shaft adjuster. Remove side cover. Remove and discard "O" ring or gasket from cover. Turn stub shaft until sector shaft teeth are centered in housing.

4) Using a soft-faced hammer, tap end of sector shaft to free shaft from housing. Remove sector shaft. Remove adjuster plug lock nut. Using a spanner wrench, remove adjuster plug.

5) Insert Rack Piston Arbor (C-4175) into end of rack piston assembly until arbor contacts worm shaft. Threaded arbor keeps recirculating balls from falling out of rack piston. Turn stub shaft counterclockwise to force rack piston onto arbor. Remove rack piston and arbor as an assembly.

6) Take care to keep arbor fully inserted so recirculating balls do not fall out. Remove stub shaft and valve body from housing. Remove worm shaft, worm shaft lower thrust bearing and washers from housing.

Inspection – 1) Clean all internal parts in solvent, and dry with compressed air. DO NOT steam clean hydraulic parts. Avoid wiping valve parts with cloth. Lint may cause binding of mechanism.

2) If further disassembly is required, see ADJUSTER PLUG, RACK PISTON & WORM SHAFT ASSEMBLY, VALVE BODY ASSEMBLY or HOUSING ASSEMBLY under OVERHAUL.

Reassembly – 1) Lubricate all parts with power steering fluid before reassembly. Install lower thrust bearing and washers on worm shaft. *See Fig. 6.*

NOTE: *If conical thrust washers are used, ensure tapered surfaces are parallel to each other and cupped sides face toward stub shaft.*

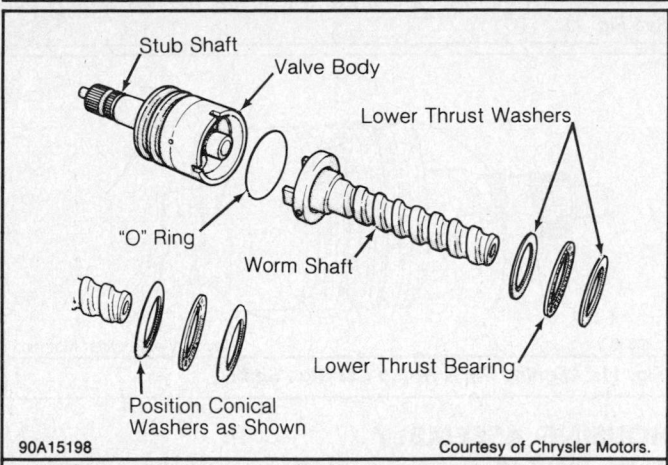

Fig. 6: **Exploded View Of Valve Body & Worm Shaft Assembly**

2) Place worm shaft in valve body. Install NEW "O" ring in valve body. Align notch in valve body with pin in worm shaft. Install valve body and worm assembly into housing. Installation is correct when fluid return port in housing is fully visible.

3) Place seal protector over stub shaft. Using NEW "O" ring, install adjuster plug until it seats against valve body. Remove seal protector from housing.

4) Loosely install adjuster plug lock nut. Insert rack piston (with arbor to retain recirculating balls) into housing. Align worm and rack piston. Turn stub shaft clockwise to engage worm. Maintain pressure on arbor until worm is fully engaged.

5) Rotate stub shaft clockwise to align middle rack groove in rack piston with center of sector shaft roller bearing. Remove arbor. Install a NEW side cover seal.

6) Thread side cover onto adjuster screw until bottomed. Back off 1/2 turn. Install sector shaft so center gear tooth meshes with center groove in rack piston. Install cover attaching bolts.

7) Install adjuster lock nut halfway onto sector shaft. Install piston and plug in rack piston. Install housing end cover "O" ring, end plug and retainer ring. Adjust worm shaft thrust bearing preload and sector shaft over-center preload. See WORM SHAFT THRUST BEARING PRELOAD and SECTOR SHAFT OVER-CENTER PRELOAD under ADJUSTMENTS.

ADJUSTER PLUG

Disassembly – 1) Using a screwdriver, carefully remove and discard thrust bearing retainer. Remove spacer, thrust bearing and bearing races. *See Fig. 7.* Remove and discard adjuster plug "O" ring.

2) Remove retaining ring. Remove and discard dust seal. Pry oil seal from adjuster plug, and discard seal. Inspect needle bearing. If necessary, press bearing from spacer end of adjuster plug.

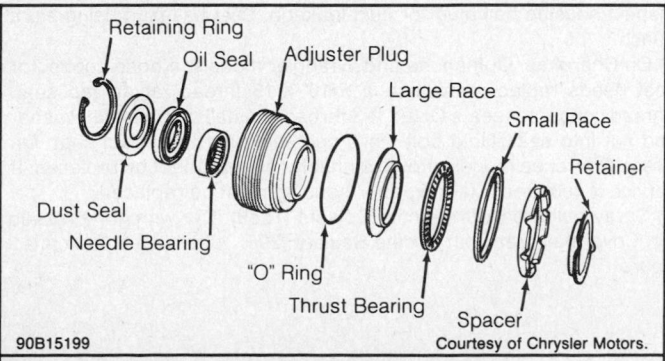

Fig. 7: **Exploded View Of Adjuster Plug Assembly**

Inspection – Inspect thrust bearing for cracks. Check rollers for pitting, scoring and cracking. Check thrust races and spacer for damage. Replace parts as necessary.

Reassembly – 1) Press needle bearing into adjuster plug (identification end facing arbor) until bearing bottoms in bore. Install oil seal with spring in seal facing adjuster plug. Install dust seal into adjuster plug.

2) Rubber face of dust seal must face away from plug. Install retaining ring and NEW adjuster plug "O" ring. Assemble thrust bearing, thrust bearing race and spacer on adjuster plug. Flanges of both thrust bearing races face away from plug. Install spacer. Using a punch, tap NEW retainer into position.

RACK PISTON & WORM SHAFT ASSEMBLY

Disassembly – Remove guide clamp, place complete unit on clean surface and remove ball guide. Remove arbor from rack piston. Remove and retain 24 recirculating balls. Remove Teflon piston rings and "O" ring seal.

Inspection – 1) Clean and dry all parts. Inspect worm shaft and rack piston grooves for scoring. Inspect recirculating balls for damage. If any ball bearings are damaged, replace entire set. Check ball guides for pinched ends.

2) Inspect lower thrust bearing races for cracking, scoring and pitting. If either race is damaged, replace worm shaft and rack piston as an assembly. Inspect rack piston teeth for chips, cracks, dents and scoring.

Reassembly – 1) Lubricate NEW Teflon seal and "O" ring with power steering fluid, and carefully install onto rack piston. Install worm shaft into rack piston until worm shaft touches piston shoulder.

2) Turning worm shaft counterclockwise, insert recirculating balls into rack piston hole nearest piston ring. *See Fig. 8.* Install 18 recirculating balls in ball guide, beginning with a Black ball, and then alternating between Silver and Black. After installing each ball, press it down to provide space for next ball. Worm shaft will spiral outward as each ball is inserted.

3) Split ball guide halves, and fill one half with petroleum jelly. Install 6 remaining recirculating balls in ball guide half maintaining alternating pattern. Reassemble guide, and install in rack piston. Ensure end balls in guide are alternate of end balls in rack piston.

4) Install clamp, and tighten attaching bolts to **10 ft. lbs. (14 N.m).** Insert Rack Piston Arbor (C-4175) into rack piston until it contacts worm shaft. Maintaining pressure on arbor, back worm shaft completely out of rack piston. DO NOT allow recirculating balls to drop out.

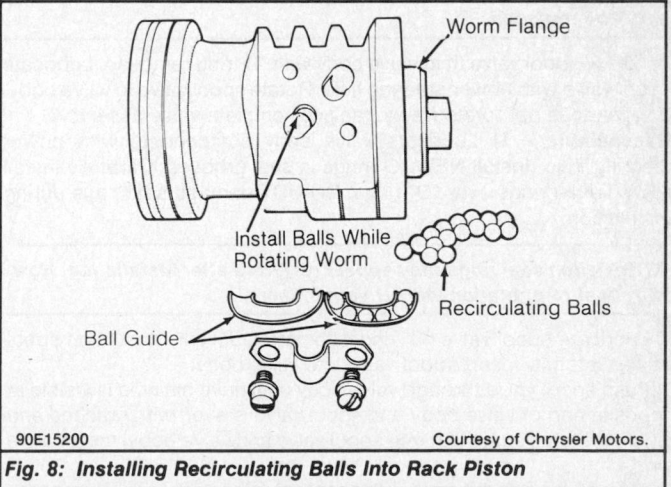

Fig. 8: **Installing Recirculating Balls Into Rack Piston**

VALVE BODY ASSEMBLY

Disassembly – 1) Remove and discard stub shaft cap "O" ring. Lightly tap end of stub shaft against wood block until shaft cap is free of valve body. Pull stub shaft outward until drive pin hole is visible. *See Fig. 9.*

CAUTION: DO NOT pull shaft more than 1/4" (6 mm) or spool valve may cock in valve body.

2) Disengage drive pin. Remove stub shaft from valve body and spool valve assembly with a twisting motion. *See Fig. 10.* If binding occurs, realign valve.

CAUTION: DO NOT force stub shaft or spool valve from valve body.

3) Remove spool valve from valve body with twisting motion. Remove and discard all "O" and Teflon rings.

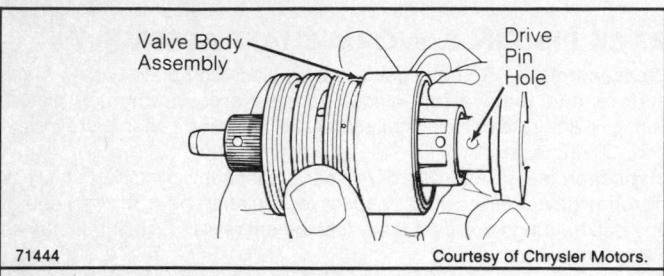

Fig. 9: **Pulling Shaft From Valve Body**

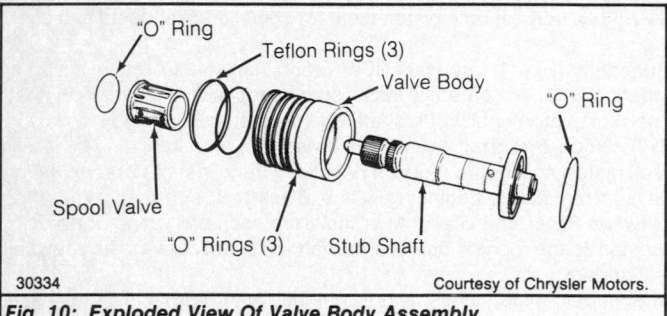

Fig. 10: **Exploded View Of Valve Body Assembly**

Inspection – 1) Wash all parts in solvent, and blow dry. Check for evidence of leaks between stub shaft and torsion bar. Check for nicks and scores on stub shaft. If possible, smooth stub shaft using crocus cloth. Check notch in valve body skirt for wear.

NOTE: Valve body is precision built unit with selectively fitted and balanced components. If any component is faulty, entire assembly MUST be replaced.

2) Check spool valve fit in valve body with "O" ring removed. Lubricate spool valve with power steering fluid. Rotate spool valve in valve body. If valve does not rotate freely, replace complete valve assembly.

Reassembly – 1) Lubricate valve body components with power steering fluid. Install NEW "O" rings in seal grooves. Carefully install NEW Teflon rings over "O" rings. DO NOT damage seal rings during installation.

NOTE: Teflon seal rings may appear distorted after installation. However, heat of operation will straighten them.

2) Lubricate spool valve "O" ring with petroleum jelly. Install on spool valve. Carefully insert spool valve into valve body.

3) Push spool valve through valve body until drive pin hole is visible at opposite end of valve body and spool valve is even with notched end of valve. Install stub shaft into spool valve and valve body. Install drive pin.

4) Align stub shaft drive pin with spool valve locating hole. Align notch in stub shaft cap with pin in valve body. Press stub shaft and spool valve into valve body. Install stub shaft cap "O" ring into valve body. *See Fig. 6.*

CAUTION: Before installing valve body into gear housing, ensure valve body stub shaft locating pin is fully engaged in stub shaft cap notch. DO NOT allow stub shaft to disengage from valve body pin. See Fig. 11.

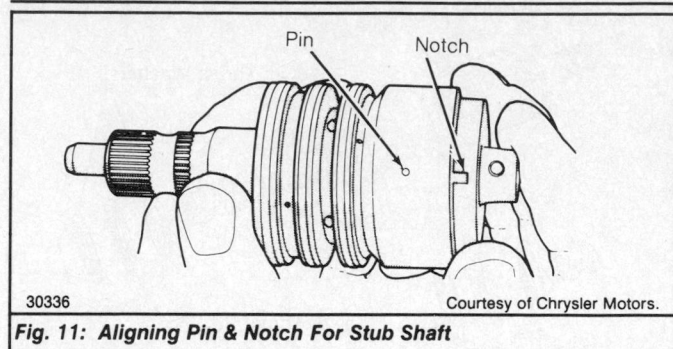

Fig. 11: **Aligning Pin & Notch For Stub Shaft**

HOUSING ASSEMBLY

Disassembly – Remove sector shaft seal retaining ring. Remove steel washer. Remove lower oil seal, steel washer and upper oil seal from housing. *See Fig. 12.* Press sector shaft bearing out of housing from lower end.

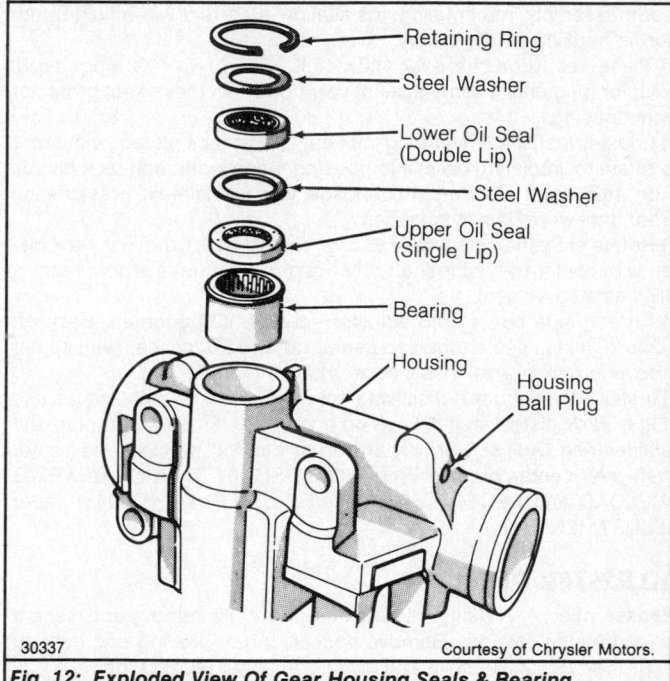

Fig. 12: **Exploded View Of Gear Housing Seals & Bearing**

Inspection – 1) If housing bore is severely worn, scored or pitted, replace housing. Minor scratches may be removed using crocus cloth. Inspect housing ball plug for fluid leakage. Seat ball plug using blunt punch.

2) On Cherokee, Comanche and Wrangler models, if hose connector seat needs replacement, use a 5/16" X 18 thread tap to tap seat. Thread connector seats ONLY 2-3 threads. Install bolt with flat washer and nut into seat. Hold bolt while tightening nut to extract seat. On Grand Cherokee models, hose connector seats cannot be replaced. If service is required, steering gear housing must be replaced.

3) Spray ball area with Loctite Solvent (7559). Dry with compressed air. Cover ball area with Loctite Sealant (290). Allow sealant to cure 2 hours.

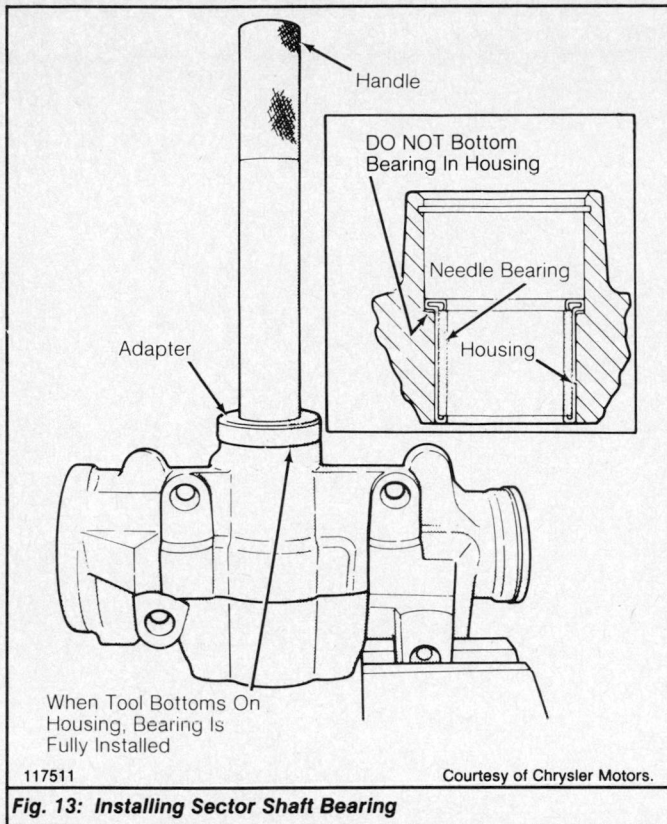

Fig. 13: **Installing Sector Shaft Bearing**

117511 Courtesy of Chrysler Motors.

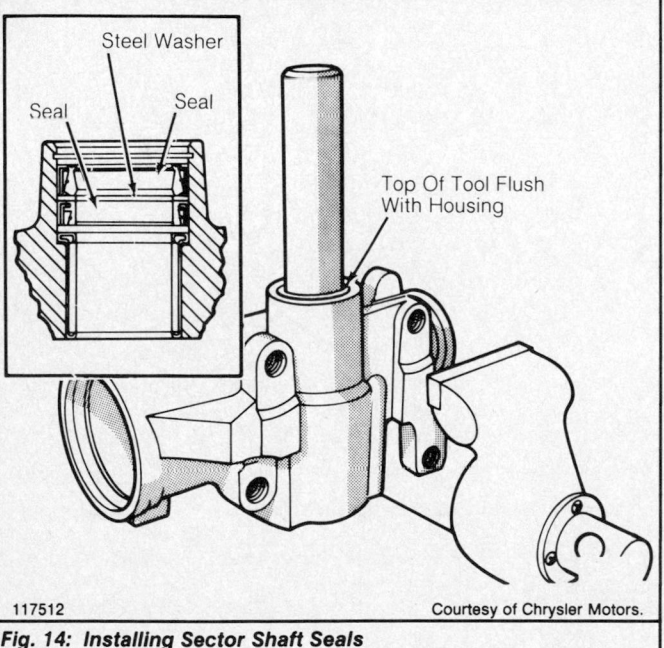

Fig. 14: **Installing Sector Shaft Seals**

117512 Courtesy of Chrysler Motors.

4) Inspect all retaining ring, bearing and seal surfaces in housing. If any surface is worn or damaged, replace housing.

Reassembly – 1) Install sector shaft bearing in steering housing using Handle (8015) and Adapter (7614). *See Fig. 13.* Position bearing so identification marks face away from adapter. Press in bearing until adapter bottoms against housing. DO NOT bottom bearing in housing.

2) Install lower oil seal, steel washer and upper oil seal on handle and adapter used to install bearing. *See Fig. 14.* Lips of both seals should face toward housing bore.

3) Install steel washer and retaining ring in housing. Using handle and adapter, drive in seals until retaining ring seats in groove. Ensure hose connector seat bores are clean. Press NEW hose connector seats in bores (if removed).

TORQUE SPECIFICATIONS
TORQUE SPECIFICATIONS

Application	Ft. Lbs. (N.m)
Adjuster Plug Lock Nut	80 (108)
Drag Link Clamp Bolt	
Cherokee & Comanche	14 (19)
Grand Cherokee	30 (41)
Wrangler	36 (49)
Drag Link-To-Pitman Arm Nut	60 (81)
Drag Link-To-Steering Knuckle Nut	
Cherokee & Comanche	35 (47)
Drag Link-To-Tie Rod Nut (Wrangler)	35 (47)
Pitman Arm Attaching Nut	185 (251)
Pressure & Return Hose Fitting	21 (28)
Pump Bracket-To-Engine Bolt	
Cherokee, Comanche & Wrangler	33 (45)
Grand Cherokee	30 (41)
Pump Pivot Bolt	20 (27)
Pump-To-Bracket Bolt	20 (27)
Rack Piston End Plug	
Cherokee, Comanche & Wrangler	50 (68)
Grand Cherokee	75 (102)
Sector Shaft Adjuster Lock Nut	36 (49)
Side Cover Bolt	45 (61)
Steering Damper-To-Axle Bracket Bolt	55 (75)
Steering Damper-To-Drag Link Nut	35 (47)
Steering Damper-To-Tie Rod Nut (Wrangler)	53 (72)
Steering Gear-To-Frame Bolt	
Cherokee & Comanche	70 (95)
Grand Cherokee	100 (136)
Wrangler	75 (102)
Tie Rod Clamp Bolt	
Cherokee, Comanche & Grand Cherokee	22 (30)
Wrangler	25 (34)
Tie Rod End Stud Nut	35 (47)

Cherokee, Comanche, Grand Cherokee (1993), Wrangler

IDENTIFICATION

JEEP AUTOMATIC TRANSMISSION APPLICATIONS

Model	Transmission
Cherokee, Comanche & Grand Cherokee	Aisin Warner AW-4
Wrangler	Chrysler 32RH (Formerly 999)

121175

Fig. 1: AW-4 Oil Pan Gasket Identification

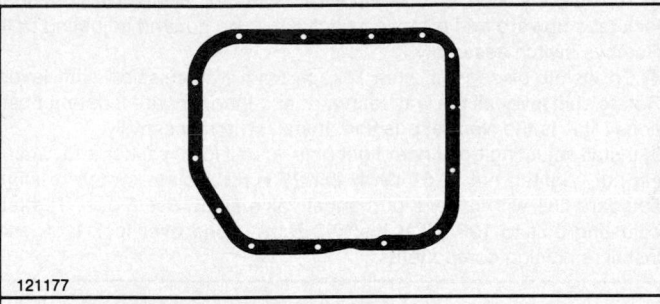

121177

Fig. 2: 32RH Oil Pan Gasket Identification

LUBRICATION

SERVICE INTERVALS

Transmission – Check fluid level and condition of fluid at 7500 mile intervals. Change fluid, replace filter and adjust bands at 30,000 miles or 30 month intervals.
Transfer Case – Check transfer case fluid every 7500 miles and replace fluid every 30,000 miles or 30 month intervals.

CHECKING FLUID LEVEL

Transmission – Park vehicle on a level surface and apply parking brake. With engine idling at normal operating temperature, move transmission selector lever through all gears, ending in Neutral (Park for AW-4 transmission). Check fluid level. Fluid level should be between FULL and ADD mark on dipstick. Add fluid as needed. DO NOT overfill.
Transfer Case – Remove fill plug. Check oil level. If level is not up to bottom of fill plug opening, add lubricant.

RECOMMENDED FLUID

Transmission – Aisin Warner AW-4 transmissions and transfer cases use Mercon type ATF. Chrysler 32RH transmissions use Dexron-II type ATF.
Transfer Case – Transfer cases use same fluid as attached transmission.

FLUID CAPACITY

NOTE: Transmission and converter capacities are approximate. Fluid level should always be determined by reading on dipstick, rather than amount of fluid added.

TRANSMISSION REFILL CAPACITIES

Application	Qts. (L)
All Models	8.5. (8.0)

TRANSFER CASE REFILL CAPACITIES

Application	Pts. (L)
Model 231	
Wrangler	3.3 (1.5)
All Others	2.2 (1.0)
Model 242	3.0 (1.4)
Model 249	3.0 (1.4)

DRAINING & REFILLING

Transmission – 1) Position large drain pan under transmission. Loosen oil pan bolts, tap pan to break it loose and allow fluid to drain. Remove pan and oil filter. Install NEW filter on bottom of valve body and tighten retaining screws to **35 INCH lbs. (4 N.m).** Clean oil pan and install with NEW gasket. Tighten bolts to **150 INCH lbs. (17 N.m).**
2) Refill transmission with approximately 5 qts. (4.7L) of ATF. Start engine and allow to run at curb idle. With vehicle on level surface, engine idling and parking brake applied, move shift selector lever through all gear ranges, ending in Neutral (Park for AW-4 transmission).
3) Recheck fluid level when transmission reaches normal operating temperature. Add fluid to FULL mark on dipstick.
Transfer Case – Remove drain plug from transfer case. Remove fill plug for easier draining. With fluid fully drained, reinstall drain plug. Fill transfer case and install fill plug. Tighten drain plug and fill plug to **20 ft. lbs. (27 N.m).**

ADJUSTMENTS

NOTE: Bands on the AW-4 transmission are not adjustable. If slippage occurs, bands must be replaced.

KICKDOWN (FRONT) BAND

32RH – 1) Locate kickdown band adjusting screw on left side of case (near throttle lever shaft). *See Fig. 3.* Loosen adjusting screw lock nut and back off 4-5 turns. Ensure adjusting screw turns freely in case.
2) Tighten adjusting screw to **72 INCH lbs. (8 N.m).** If Adapter Extension (J-24063) is used, tighten adjusting screw to **50 INCH lbs. (5 N.m).** Back off adjusting screw 2 1/2 turns. Hold adjusting screw and tighten lock nut to **30 ft. lbs. (41 N.m).**

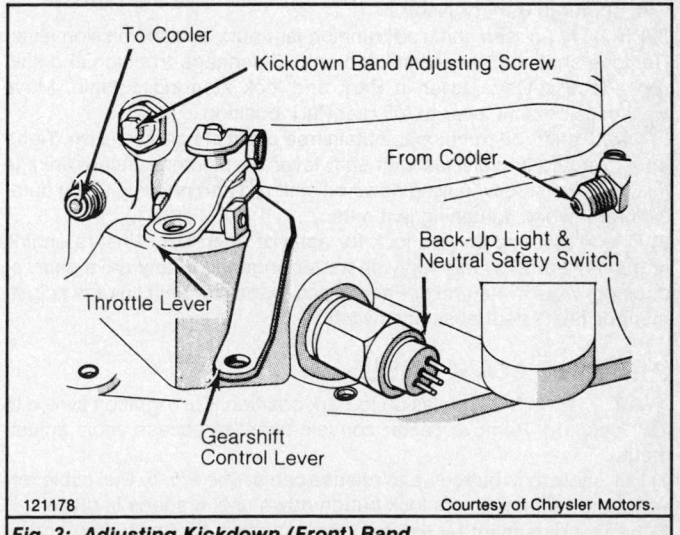

121178   Courtesy of Chrysler Motors.

Fig. 3: Adjusting Kickdown (Front) Band

LOW-REVERSE (REAR) BAND (TYPICAL)

32RH – 1) Raise and support vehicle. Drain transmission fluid and remove oil pan. Locate low-reverse band adjusting screw on rear servo lever. *See Fig. 4.* Loosen adjusting screw lock nut. Back off lock nut 5-6 turns.

2) Tighten adjusting screw to **72 INCH lbs. (8 N.m)**. Back off adjusting screw 4 turns. Hold adjusting screw and tighten lock nut to **25 ft. lbs. (34 N.m)**. Install oil pan and fill transmission with fluid.

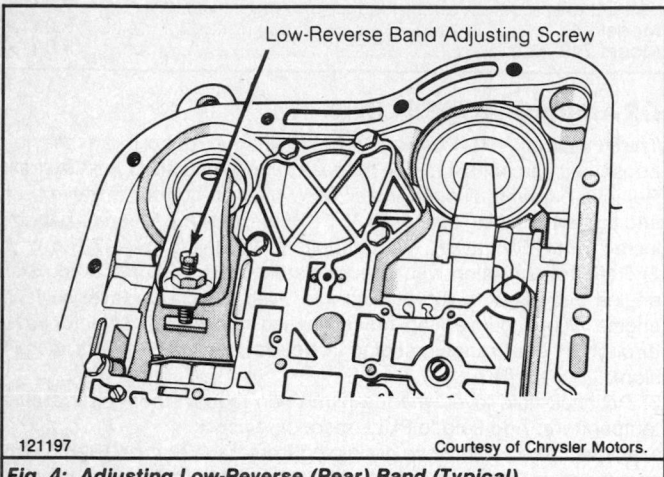

Low-Reverse Band Adjusting Screw

121197   Courtesy of Chrysler Motors.

Fig. 4: Adjusting Low-Reverse (Rear) Band (Typical)

THROTTLE CABLE

1) With ignition off, fully retract cable plunger. Press cable button down and push cable plunger inward.

2) Rotate throttle lever to wide open throttle position. Cable will ratchet to correct position. Release throttle lever. Cable is now adjusted.

SHIFT LINKAGE

AW-4 – 1) Place gearshift lever in Park and raise vehicle. Using a small screwdriver, unlock shift control cable by releasing "U" shaped cable adjuster clamp. Remove cable from mounting bracket.

2) Move transmission shift lever rearward until fully seated into Park detent. Ensure that drive shaft cannot be rotated. Snap control cable into cable mounting bracket and replace "U" shaped cable adjuster clamp.

3) Lower vehicle and verify engine starting. Engine should start only with shifter in Park or Neutral.

32RH – 1) Loosen shift rod trunnion jam nuts at transmission lever. Remove shift rod-to-bellcrank lock pin. Disengage trunnion and shift rod. Place selector lever in Park and lock steering column. Move transmission shift lever to full rear Park position.

2) Adjust shift rod trunnion to obtain free pin fit in bellcrank arm. Tighten jam nuts. On vehicles with shift lever on column, ensure linkage lash is eliminated by pulling down on shift rod and pushing up on outer bellcrank when tightening jam nuts.

3) Check steering column lock for ease of operation. Ensure engine starts in Neutral or Park only. If starter engages in any drive gear, or does not work in Neutral or Park, check for proper shift linkage adjustment or faulty neutral safety switch.

PARKING LOCK CABLE

AW-4 – 1) Shift transmission to Park position. Turn ignition switch to lock position. Remove center console bezel to access cable adjustment.

2) Pull cable lock button up to release cable. *See Fig. 5.* Pull cable forward and release. Press lock button down until it snaps in place.

3) Verify adjustment by trying to move shifter. Shifter button and/or shifter should not move.

4) Turn ignition on. Move shifter to Neutral. If ignition switch cannot be turned to Lock position, cable is adjusted. Repeat this step with shifter in Drive.

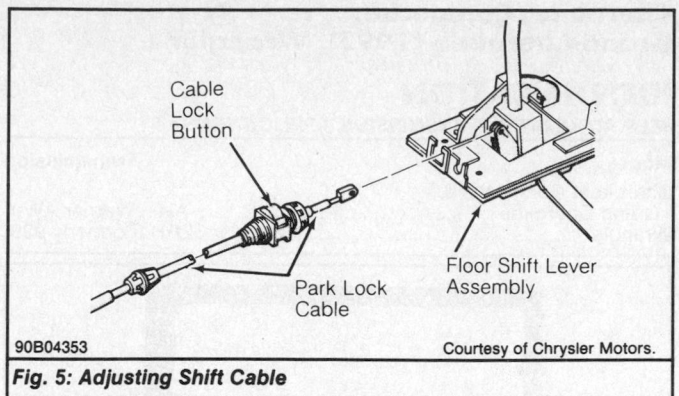

Cable Lock Button

Park Lock Cable

Floor Shift Lever Assembly

90B04353   Courtesy of Chrysler Motors.

Fig. 5: Adjusting Shift Cable

NEUTRAL SAFETY SWITCH

AW-4 – 1) With transmission linkage properly adjusted, switch allows starter operation in Park or Neutral only.

2) To test switch, remove wire connector. Using ohmmeter, check that continuity exists between proper terminals with transmission at specified gear range. *See Fig. 6.* Replace switch if faulty.

3) To replace switch, disconnect wire connector. Bend switch washer lock tabs upward and remove switch retaining nut and adjusting bolt. Remove switch assembly.

4) To install, disconnect shift linkage from transmission shift lever. Rotate shift lever all the way rearward and then forward 2 detent positions. This is the Neutral position. Install switch assembly.

5) Install adjusting bolt finger tight only. Install lock washer and retaining nut. Tighten nut to **61 INCH lbs. (7 N.m)**. Rotate switch to align standard line with groove of manual valve shaft. *See Fig. 6.* Tighten adjusting bolt to **108 INCH lbs. (13 N.m)**. Bend over lock tabs and install remaining components.

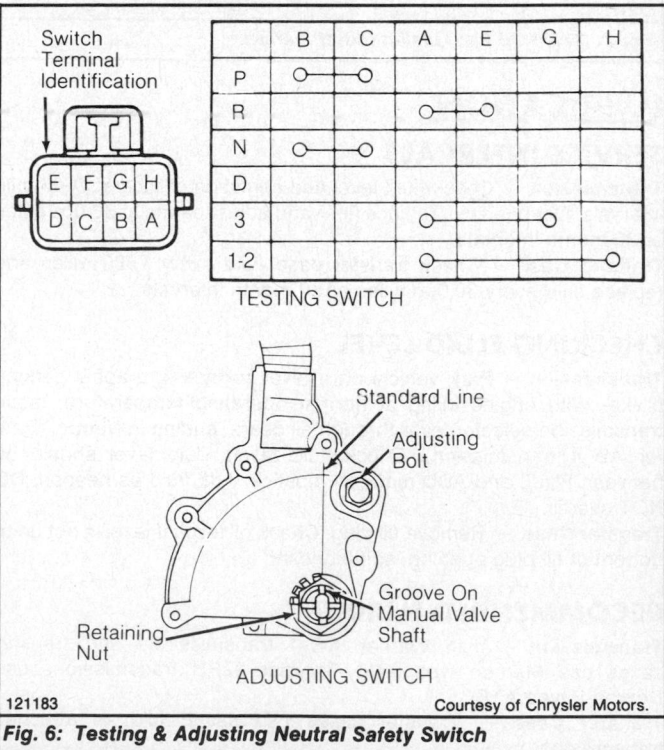

Switch Terminal Identification

	B	C	A	E	G	H
P	○—	—○				
R			○—	—○		
N	○—	—○				
D						
3			○—	—○		
1-2			○—			—○

E F G H
D C B A

TESTING SWITCH

Standard Line

Adjusting Bolt

Groove On Manual Valve Shaft

Retaining Nut

ADJUSTING SWITCH

121183   Courtesy of Chrysler Motors.

Fig. 6: Testing & Adjusting Neutral Safety Switch

32RH – 1) With transmission linkage properly adjusted, switch should allow starter operation in Park or Neutral only.

2) To test switch, remove wire harness and test for continuity between center pin of switch and transmission case. Continuity should only exist when transmission is in Park or Neutral.

3) Shift transmission into Reverse. Check for continuity between 2 outer switch terminals. Continuity should exist with transmission in Reverse only. With transmission in Reverse, check continuity between each outer switch terminal and transmission case. No continuity should exist between terminals and transmission case.

4) To replace switch, disconnect wire connector and unscrew switch from case. Move selector lever to Park and Neutral positions and check that switch operating fingers are centered in switch opening.

5) Install switch and new seal in case. Tighten switch to **24 ft. lbs. (33 N.m)**. Check fluid level and add as needed.

TORQUE SPECIFICATIONS

TORQUE SPECIFICATIONS

Application	Ft. Lbs. (N.m)
Kickdown (Front) Band Lock Nut	30 (41)
Low-Reverse (Rear) Band Lock Nut	25 (34)
Neutral Safety Switch (32RH)	24 (33)
Oil Pan Bolts	13 (18)
Transfer Case Fill Plug	20 (27)

	INCH Lbs. (N.m)
Filter	
AW-4	84 (10)
32RH	35 (4)
Kickdown (Front) Band	[1] 72 (8)
Low-Reverse (Rear) Band	72 (8)
Neutral Safety Switch (AW-4)	
Retaining Nut	61 (7)
Adjusting Bolt	108 (13)

[1] – If adapter extension is used, tighten to 50 INCH Lbs. (5 N.m). See text for complete adjusting procedure.

Cherokee, Comanche, Grand Cherokee (1993), Wrangler

IDENTIFICATION
MANUAL TRANSMISSION APPLICATIONS

Model	Transmission
4-Cylinder	Aisin AX4 4-Speed
	Aisin AX5 5-Speed Overdrive
6-Cylinder	Aisin AX15 5-Speed Overdrive

LUBRICATION

SERVICE INTERVALS

Transmission – Check fluid level at 7500 mile intervals. Change fluid at 30,000 miles or 30 month intervals.
Transfer Case – Check transfer case fluid every 7500 miles and replace fluid every 30,000 miles or 30 month intervals.

CHECKING FLUID LEVEL

Transmission – Remove fill plug. Check oil level. If level is not up to bottom of fill plug opening, add lubricant.
Transfer Case – Remove fill plug. Check oil level. If level is not up to bottom of fill plug opening, add lubricant.

RECOMMENDED FLUID

Use Mercon type ATF in transfer cases. Use SAE 75W-90 gear lube with API rating of GL-5 in transmissions.

FLUID CAPACITIES
TRANSMISSION REFILL CAPACITIES

Application	Pts. (L)
AX-4 (4-Speed)	7.8 (3.7)
AX-5 (2WD 5-Speed)	7.4 (3.5)
AX-5 (4WD 5-Speed)	7.0 (3.3)
AX-15 (5-Speed)	6.7 (3.2)

TRANSFER CASE REFILL CAPACITIES

Application	Pts. (L)
Model 231	
Cherokee & Comanche	2.2 (1.0)
Wrangler	3.3 (1.5)
Model 242	3.0 (1.4)
Model 249	3.0 (1.4)

DRAINING & REFILLING

Transmission – Position drain pan under transmission. Remove drain plug from transmission. Remove fill plug for easier draining. With fluid fully drained, reinstall drain plug. Fill transmission and install fill plug.
Transfer Case – Position drain pan under transfer case. Remove drain plug from transfer case. Remove fill plug for easier draining. With fluid fully drained, reinstall drain plug. Fill transfer case and install fill plug. Tighten drain plug and fill plugs to **20 ft. lbs. (27 N.m)**.

ADJUSTMENTS
SHIFT LINKAGE

NOTE: Transmissions require no external shift linkage adjustments.

TORQUE SPECIFICATIONS
TORQUE SPECIFICATIONS

Application	Ft. Lbs. (N.m)
Drain Plug	20 (27)
Fill Plug	20 (27)

Cherokee, Comanche, Grand Cherokee (1993), Wrangler

MANUAL TRANSMISSION

NOTE: For manual transmission replacement procedures, see appropriate CLUTCHES article.

AUTOMATIC TRANSMISSION

Removal (Cherokee, Comanche & Grand Cherokee) – 1) Raise vehicle. Drain fluid and remove upper half of transmission fill tube.

2) Disconnect cooler lines at transmission. Press fitting release tabs and pull cooler line and fitting out of case. Plug all openings to prevent fluid loss and contamination. Support engine with safety stand.

3) Support transmission/transfer case assembly with jack. Disconnect or remove following: transmission and transfer case shift linkage; necessary exhaust components; speedometer cable; front and rear propeller shaft; transmission wire harnesses; transfer case vacuum and wire harnesses.

4) Remove rear crossmember. Disconnect necessary vacuum and fluid hoses and transmission throttle cable at engine. On 1992 models, remove crankshaft position sensor.

5) On all models, remove starter. Remove converter-to-drive plate and converter housing-to-engine bolts.

6) Secure transmission (and transfer case assembly on 4WD models) to transmission jack with safety chains. Remove transmission/transfer case assembly.

NOTE: Remove transfer case from transmission if transmission is to be overhauled.

Installation – 1) To install, reverse removal procedures. On 4WD models, connect transfer case shift linkage and vacuum hoses. Install NEW "O" ring seal on upper half of transmission fill tube. Connect upper and lower tube halves.

2) Tighten all bolts to specification and fill transmission with MOPAR Mercon Type ATF fluid. See TORQUE SPECIFICATIONS table at end of article.

Removal (Wrangler) – 1) Disconnect fan shroud and transmission fill tube upper bracket. Raise vehicle. Remove converter inspection cover and fill tube. Plug fill tube hole to prevent fluid loss and contamination. Remove starter.

2) Mark drive shafts for reassembly. Disconnect shafts at transfer case and wire to frame rails. DO NOT allow shafts to hang free as damage to universal joints may result. Disconnect exhaust pipes from exhaust manifolds, if necessary. Drain transfer case lubricant. Disconnect speedometer cable from transmission.

3) Disconnect all shift and throttle linkages and wiring from transmission and transfer case. Mark converter drive plate and converter for reassembly. Remove torque converter-to-drive plate bolts. Rotate crankshaft to gain access to bolts.

4) Support transmission/transfer case assembly with jack and secure with chain. Remove bolts and rear transmission crossmember. Lower transmission enough to disconnect cooler lines at transmission. Remove transmission-to-engine retaining bolts and slowly slide transmission assembly away from engine.

5) Hold converter in position while lowering transmission assembly from vehicle. Separate transmission from transfer case.

Installation – To install, reverse removal procedures. DO NOT tighten exhaust pipe attaching bolts until crossmember has been installed and transmission jack has been removed. Ensure all index marks made at removal are aligned. Tighten all bolts to specification and fill transmission and transfer case with fluid.

TORQUE SPECIFICATIONS

Application	Ft. Lbs. (N.m)
Cherokee, Comanche & Grand Cherokee	
Converter Housing Bolts	
10 mm	25 (34)
12 mm	42 (57)
Dust Cover Bolts	13-17 (18-23)
Filler Tube Bracket Bolt	37-47 (50-64)
Torque Converter-To-Drive Plate Bolts	22 (30)
Transfer Case-To-Transmission Bolts	22-30 (30-41)
Transmission-To-Engine Bolts	37-47 (50-64)
Transmission-To-Rear Mount Bolts	44-66 (60-81)
Wrangler	
Cooler Line Nut	13 (18)
Drive Plate-To-Converter Bolts	22 (30)
Drive Plate-To-Crankshaft Bolts	55 (75)
Filler Tube Bracket Bolt	24 (33)
Transfer Case-To-Transmission Bolts	22-30 (30-41)
Transmission-To-Engine Bolts	30 (41)

1992 LATEST CHANGES & CORRECTIONS CONTENTS

LATEST CHANGES & CORRECTIONS
For 1992 & Earlier Models

NOTE: Latest Changes and Corrections represents a collection of last-minute information and relevant technical service bulletins. Read this section and make notations in appropriate manuals for easy reference later.

CHRYSLER MOTORS

ENGINE PERFORMANCE

⟨1⟩ *1990 3.9L, 5.2L & 5.9L ENGINES: IGNITION TIMING* – Please note that ignition timing specifications have been revised as follows:

IGNITION TIMING (Degrees BTDC @ RPM)

Application	Man. Trans.	Auto. Trans.
3.9L, 5.2 & 5.9L	8-12 [1]	8-12 [1]

[1] – With engine at idle RPM.

This revision applies to the following publications:
ENGINE PERFORMANCE SERVICE & REPAIR supplement and DOMESTIC LIGHT TRUCKS & VANS REPAIR manual.
- 1990 – Page CHRY 1-3

SAFETY EQUIPMENT

⟨2⟩ *ALL 1991 MODELS: REVISED ILLUSTRATION* – Please note that *Fig. 1*, illustrating rear widow defogger control switch/timer relay terminals, has been revised. For revised illustration, see the 1992 publication.
This revision applies to the following publications:
ELECTRICAL SERVICE & REPAIR supplement and DOMESTIC LIGHT TRUCKS & VANS SERVICE & REPAIR manual.
- 1991 – Page CHRY 4-11

ENGINES

⟨3⟩ *1990-91 3.9L & 5.9L ENGINES: CRANKSHAFT SPECIFICATION* – Please note that the following main bearing journal diameter specification has been revised:

CRANKSHAFT, MAIN & CONNECTING ROD BEARINGS

Application	In. (mm)
Main Bearing	
Journal Diameter	
3.9L & 5.2L	2.4995-2.5005 (63.487-63.513)

This revision applies to the following publications:
ENGINE, CLUTCH & DRIVE AXLE SERVICE & REPAIR supplement and DOMESTIC LIGHT TRUCKS & VANS SERVICE & REPAIR manual.
- 1990 – Page CHRY 5-33
- 1991 – Page CHRY 5-37

BRAKES

⟨4⟩ *1991 DAKOTA, PICKUP, RAMCHARGER & RWD VAN: ABS TESTING* – Please note that step **6)** of TEST 5 – DIAGNOSTIC CONNECTOR CHECK, has been revised. For revised procedure, see the 1992 publication.
This revision applies to the following publications:
CHASSIS SERVICE & REPAIR supplement and DOMESTIC LIGHT TRUCKS & VANS SERVICE & REPAIR manual.
- 1991 – Page CHRY 8-66

⟨5⟩ *1991 DAKOTA, PICKUP, RAMCHARGER & RWD VAN: ABS SELF-DIAGNOSTICS* – Please note that CODE 9 and CODE 10 test procedures have been revised. For revised procedure, see the 1992 publication.
This revision applies to the following publications:
CHASSIS SERVICE & REPAIR supplement and DOMESTIC LIGHT TRUCKS & VANS SERVICE & REPAIR manual.
- 1991 – Page CHRY 8-68

FORD MOTOR CO.

ENGINE PERFORMANCE

⟨6⟩ *1992 BRONCO, F150 & F250: CONTINUOUS MEMORY CODE 173 (HEGO RICH)* – If pass code is received during KOEO and KOER but Code 173 is present in continuous memory, ECA is performing HEGO test during open loop operation. No driveabliity symptoms will be present; however, CHECK ENGINE light will come on and HEGO switching will not occur until HEGO test is complete.
If Code 173 is present, perform appropriate CIRCUIT TEST. See SELF-DIAGNOSTICS – EEC-IV article. If Code 173 is still present, replace ECA. Gap spark plugs to .052-.056" (1.3-1.4 mm). Obtain and complete an AUTHORIZED MODIFICATION DECAL. Place decal near Vehicle Emission Control Information (VECI) decal in engine compartment.

⟨7⟩ *ALL 1991 MODELS: SELF-DIAGNOSTICS* – Please note that CIRCUIT TEST TC has been revised. For revised procedure, refer to the 1992 publication.
This revision applies to the following publications:
ENGINE PERFORMANCE SERVICE & REPAIR supplement and DOMESTIC LIGHT TRUCKS & VANS SERVICE & REPAIR manual.
- 1991 – Page FORD 1-88 through FORD 1-92

ELECTRICAL

⟨8⟩ *1991 AEROSTAR, EXPLORER, RANGER (EXCEPT 2.9L): STARTER SOLENOID* – Starter solenoid test procedures have been discontinued. Please disregard references to this procedure.
This revision applies to the following publications:
ELECTRICAL SERVICE & REPAIR supplement and DOMESTIC LIGHT TRUCKS & VANS SERVICE & REPAIR manual.
- 1991 – Page FORD 2-21

SAFETY EQUIPMENT

⟨9⟩ *1991 EXPLORER & RANGER: WIPER/WASHER SYSTEMS* – Please note that WIPER SWITCH CONTINUITY TEST, previously not included, is now available. Refer to the 1992 publication for testing procedure. This addition applies to the following publications:
ELECTRICAL SERVICE & REPAIR supplement and· DOMESTIC LIGHT TRUCKS & VANS SERVICE & REPAIR manual.
- 1991 – Page FORD 4-35

ENGINES

⟨10⟩ *1991 EXPLORER & RANGER 4.0L: CRANKSHAFT SPECIFICATIONS* – Please note that crankshaft end play specifications have been revised as follows:

CRANKSHAFT, MAIN & CONNECTING ROD BEARINGS

Application	In. (mm)
Crankshaft	
End Play	
Standard	.012-.016 (.30-.40)
Service Limit	.012 (.30)

This revision applies to the following publications:
ENGINE, CLUTCH & DRIVE AXLE SERVICE & REPAIR supplement and DOMESTIC LIGHT TRUCKS & VANS SERVICE & REPAIR manual.
- 1991 – Page FORD 5-31

DRIVE AXLES

⟨11⟩ *1990-91 MODELS WITH 7 1/2" RING GEAR DIFFERENTIAL: REVISED DISASSEMBLY PROCEDURE* – Please note that steps **2)** through **5)** of DIFFERENTIAL ASSEMBLY – DISASSEMBLY have been revised as follows:

2) Place reference mark on drive shaft flanges for reassembly reference. Remove drive shaft. Install plug in transmission extension housing to prevent oil leakage.

3) Check and record ring gear runout. See RING GEAR RUNOUT under RING GEAR & DIFFERENTIAL CASE RUNOUT CHECKING PROCEDURE. Place reference mark on bearing cap and differential housing assembly for reassembly reference.

CAUTION: Ensure bearing cap location is marked for reassembly reference. Bearing caps must be installed in original location. Arrow or triangle area between bolt holes on bearing cap must point away from ring gear (toward axle shaft end of housing).

4) Loosen bearing cap retaining bolts. Pry differential case, bearing races and preload shims until loose in bearing caps. Remove retaining bolts, bearing caps and differential case.

CAUTION: Mark bearing races and preload shim location for reassembly reference if components are to be reused. Components must be installed in original location. Use care not to damage rear anti-lock brake sensor when removing differential case.

This revision applies to the following publications:
ENGINE, CLUTCH & DRIVE AXLE SERVICE & REPAIR supplement and DOMESTIC LIGHT TRUCKS & VANS SERVICE & REPAIR manual.
- 1990 – Page FORD 7-3
- 1991 – Page FORD 7-3

12▷ *1989-91 MODELS WITH 8 3/4" & 10 1/4" RING GEAR DIFFERENTIAL: REVISED PINION DEPTH ADJUSTMENT PROCEDURE* – Please note that step **3)** and **4)** of pinion depth adjustment has been revised as follows:

3) Ensure pinion depth measuring tools are properly installed and tightened. Apply a light film of oil to pinion bearings. Rotate gauge block several times to seat bearings.

4) Tighten tool handle to **20 ft. lbs. (27 N.m)**. Final position of gauge block should be 45 degrees above axle shaft centerline. Clean differential bearing bores thoroughly and install gauge tube.
This revision applies to the following publications:
ENGINE, CLUTCH & DRIVE AXLE SERVICE & REPAIR supplement and DOMESTIC LIGHT TRUCKS & VANS SERVICE & REPAIR manual.
- 1989 – Page FORD 9-3
- 1990 – Page FORD 7-8
- 1991 – Page FORD 7-9

13▷ *1991 AEROSTAR: REVISED ILLUSTRATION* – Please note that *Fig. 1*, illustrating differential and drive axle shaft, has been revised. For revised illustration, see the 1992 publication.
This revision applies to the following publications:
CHASSIS SERVICE & REPAIR supplement and DOMESTIC TRUCKS & VANS SERVICE & REPAIR manual.
- 1991 – Page FORD 7-44

GENERAL MOTORS

ENGINE PERFORMANCE

14▷ *1985 DELCO-REMY HIGH ENERGY IGNITION (HEI): REVISED ELECTRONIC SPARK CONTROL (ESC) TEST PROCEDURE* – Please note that step **2)** under DETONATION PROBLEMS has been revised as follows:

2) If no retard occurs, backprobe 10-pin connector at ESC controller located in passenger compartment. Connect voltmeter leads between pins "B" and "K" of connector. With engine operating at 2000 RPM, voltage should read 80 millivolts (.08 volts). If voltage is correct, go to step **5)**.
This revision applies to the following publications:
ENGINE PERFORMANCE SERVICE & REPAIR supplement and DOMESTIC TRUCKS & VANS SERVICE & REPAIR manual.
- 1985 – Page GM 4-26

15▷ *1989-91 6.2L DIESEL: NO START – COLD TEST PROCEDURES* – Please note that test procedures have been revised. For revised procedure, see SYSTEM & COMPONENT TESTING article in the 1992 publication.
This revision applies to the following publications:
ENGINE PERFORMANCE SERVICE & REPAIR supplement and DOMESTIC TRUCKS & VANS SERVICE & REPAIR manual.
- 1989 – Page GM 2-21
- 1990 – Page GM 1-65
- 1991 – Page GM 1-97

16▷ *1989-91 6.2L DIESEL: DIESEL COLD ADVANCE SYSTEM CHECK TEST PROCEDURES* – Please note that test procedures have been revised and new information has been added. For revision and additional information, see SYSTEM & COMPONENT TESTING article in the 1992 publication.
This revision applies to the following publications:
ENGINE PERFORMANCE SERVICE & REPAIR supplement and DOMESTIC TRUCKS & VANS SERVICE & REPAIR manual.
- 1989 – Page GM 1A-79
- 1990 – Page GM 1-65
- 1991 – Page GM 1-97

17▷ *1992 LUMINA 3.8L, SILHOUETTE 3.8L & TRANSPORT 3.8L: INTERMITTENT DRIVEABILITY, CRUISE CONTROL OR INSTRUMENT PANEL PROBLEMS* – The ground strap, located under the DIS coil pack, can come loose causing intermittent problems. If intermittent problems are present, clean and tighten ground strap nut to **12 ft. lbs. (17 N.m)**. *See Fig. 1*.

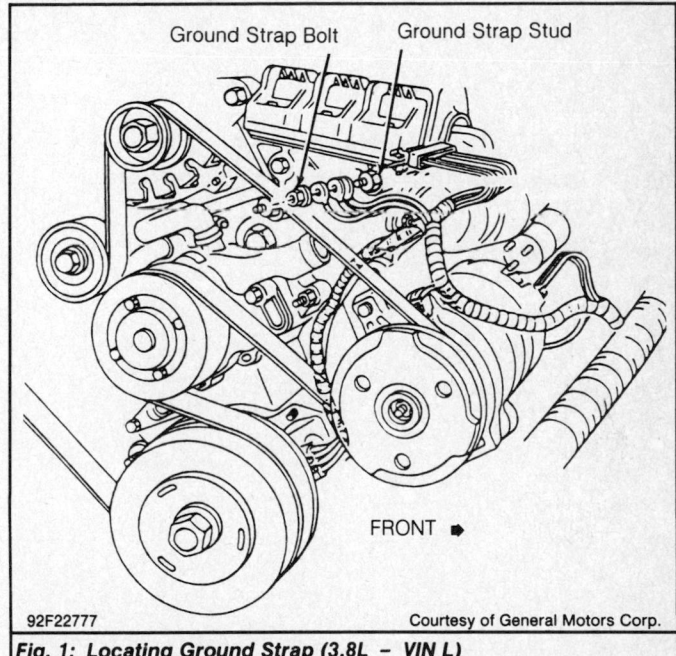

92F22777   Courtesy of General Motors Corp.
Fig. 1: Locating Ground Strap (3.8L – VIN L)

SAFETY EQUIPMENT

18▷ *1991 LUMINA APV: INSTRUMENT PANEL TESTING* – Please note that step **2)** of ALL GAUGES INOPERATIVE testing procedure under INSTRUMENT CLUSTER, has been revised as follows:

2) Connect test light between instrument cluster connector terminal "K" and ground. If light does not come on, repair open in Pink/Black wire. If test light comes on, connect test light between connector terminals "K" and "M". If test light does not comes on, repair open in Black/White wire. If test light comes on, go to next step.
This revision applies to the following publications:
ELECTRICAL SERVICE & REPAIR supplement and DOMESTIC TRUCKS & VANS SERVICE & REPAIR manual.
- 1991 – Page GM 4-9

LATEST CHANGES & CORRECTIONS
For 1992 & Earlier Models (Cont.)

STEERING

19▷ *1991 C35: POWER STEERING* – Please note that system power steering pressure specifications have been revised. For revised specifications, see PRESSURE TEST SPECIFICATIONS table.

PRESSURE TEST SPECIFICATIONS

Application	Idle Pressure psi (kg/cm²)	Relief Pressure psi (kg/cm²)
C35	80-125 (6-9)	1465-1515 (103-106)
C35 (with Hydro-Boost)	80-125 (6-9)	1350-1450 (95-102)

This revision applies to the following publications:
CHASSIS SERVICE & REPAIR supplement and DOMESTIC TRUCKS & VANS SERVICE & REPAIR manual.
- 1991 – Page GM 11-10

JEEP

ENGINE PERFORMANCE

20▷ *1991 2.5L & 4.0L ENGINES: EMISSION SYSTEM APPLICATION* – Please disregard references to Thermostatic Air Cleaner (TAC) and Exhaust Gas Recirculation (EGR).

This revision applies to the following publications:
ENGINE PERFORMANCE SERVICE & REPAIR supplement and DOMESTIC LIGHT TRUCKS & VANS SERVICE & REPAIR manual.
- 1991 – Page JEEP 1-1

TRANSMISSION SERVICING

21▷ *ALL 1990-91 MODELS: AUTOMATIC TRANSMISSION* – Please note that low-reverse (rear) band adjustment procedure has been revised as follows:

Loadflite 727 & 999 – 1) Raise vehicle, drain transmission fluid and remove oil pan. Locate adjusting screw on rear servo lever. Loosen adjusting screw lock nut and back off about 5-6 turns.
2) Tighten adjusting screw to **72 INCH lbs. (8 N.m)** then back off adjusting screw 4 turns on 999 and 2 turns on 727. Hold adjusting screw in place and tighten lock nut to **25 ft. lbs. (34 N.m)**. Install oil pan and fill transmission with fluid.

This revision applies to the following publications:
ENGINE, CLUTCH DRIVE AXLE SERVICE & REPAIR supplement and DOMESTIC TRUCKS & VANS SERVICE & REPAIR manual.
- 1990 – Page JEEP 12-2
- 1991 – Page JEEP 12-2

NOTES

NOTES

NOTES

NOTES

NOTES

NOTES

NOTES

NOTES

NOTES

NOTES

NOTES

NOTES

NOTES

NOTES

NOTES

NOTES

NOTES

NOTES

COMMENTS AND SUGGESTIONS

Please let us know if you have any comments or recommended changes to this book. Mail this postage-paid card today. We'd like to hear from you!

☐ Domestic Cars ☐ Imported Cars & Trucks ☐ Domestic Light Trucks ☐ Medium & Heavy Duty Trucks
☐ Engine Performance ☐ Electrical ☐ Engine ☐ Chassis ☐ Transmission
☐ Air Conditioning ☐ Electrical Component Locators ☐ Other _____

Section No. _____ Page No. _____ Vehicle Model & Year _____

Comments: _____
_____
_____

Name _____ Company _____

Address _____ City _____ State _____ Zip _____

Phone (___) _____ Date _____ THANK YOU

ADT92

COMMENTS AND SUGGESTIONS

Please let us know if you have any comments or recommended changes to this book. Mail this postage-paid card today. We'd like to hear from you!

☐ Domestic Cars ☐ Imported Cars & Trucks ☐ Domestic Light Trucks ☐ Medium & Heavy Duty Trucks
☐ Engine Performance ☐ Electrical ☐ Engine ☐ Chassis ☐ Transmission
☐ Air Conditioning ☐ Electrical Component Locators ☐ Other _____

Section No. _____ Page No. _____ Vehicle Model & Year _____

Comments: _____
_____
_____

Name _____ Company _____

Address _____ City _____ State _____ Zip _____

Phone (___) _____ Date _____ THANK YOU

ADT92

Be sure to fill out this form completely.

COMMENTS AND SUGGESTIONS

Please let us know if you have any comments or recommended changes to this book. Mail this postage-paid card today. We'd like to hear from you!

☐ Domestic Cars ☐ Imported Cars & Trucks ☐ Domestic Light Trucks ☐ Medium & Heavy Duty Trucks
☐ Engine Performance ☐ Electrical ☐ Engine ☐ Chassis ☐ Transmission
☐ Air Conditioning ☐ Electrical Component Locators ☐ Other _____

Section No. _____ Page No. _____ Vehicle Model & Year _____

Comments: _____
_____
_____

Name _____ Company _____

Address _____ City _____ State _____ Zip _____

Phone (___) _____ Date _____ THANK YOU

ADT92

Be sure to fill out this form completely.

BUSINESS REPLY MAIL

FIRST CLASS   PERMIT NO. 3701   SAN DIEGO, CA

POSTAGE WILL BE PAID BY ADDRESSEE

MITCHELL INTERNATIONAL
P.O. Box 26260
San Diego, California 92196-9984

NO POSTAGE
NECESSARY
IF MAILED
IN THE
UNITED STATES

BUSINESS REPLY MAIL

FIRST CLASS   PERMIT NO. 3701   SAN DIEGO, CA

POSTAGE WILL BE PAID BY ADDRESSEE

MITCHELL INTERNATIONAL
P.O. Box 26260
San Diego, California 92196-9984

NO POSTAGE
NECESSARY
IF MAILED
IN THE
UNITED STATES

BUSINESS REPLY MAIL

FIRST CLASS   PERMIT NO. 3701   SAN DIEGO, CA

POSTAGE WILL BE PAID BY ADDRESSEE

MITCHELL INTERNATIONAL
P.O. Box 26260
San Diego, California 92196-9984

TO PASS THE ASE TESTS, TAKE THE INSIDE TRACK.

In the race for ASE certification, it pays to take the <u>smartest</u> route to the finish line. Mitchell leads the way with eight easy-to-understand, easy-to-afford ASE Certification Test preparation books designed to help you pass with flying colors.

ASE certification is important to your career. It can mean more money. More prestige. More employment opportunities. When you pass your ASE tests, you join the elite of your profession.

Because of the importance – and cost – of your ASE test, you want to do your very best on test day. The key to passing is focused preparation. You need to concentrate on the information that will matter most. You need to know what to expect when you enter the room where the test will be given. And you need to have a clear plan, or strategy, for success.

That's where Mitchell can help.

One Book For Each Test

There are eight Mitchell ASE Test Preparation Guides in all – one for each ASE test area: Engine Repair, Automatic Transmission/Transaxle, Manual Drive Train and Axles, Suspension and Steering, Brakes, Electrical Systems, Heating and Air Conditioning, Engine Performance.

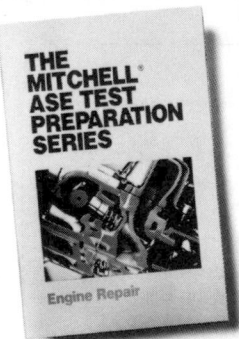

Each book is packed with fact, theory, sample tests, and plenty of illustrations. It offers real-world examples of repair problems and solutions from Mitchell's exclusive quick fix database.

It also includes helpful tips on "How to Study," "The Night Before the Test," "Test Day," and even "Guessing." You learn all about the ASE test itself. When it's given. How it's written. The confidentiality of your results. How to certify. And how to recertify.

Not Just Answers, But Reasons

The sample tests in the Mitchell ASE Test Preparation Guides are multiple choice, just like the ASE exams. The sample tests contain the same number of questions – in the same proportions – as the ASE tests. So you can practice under simulated exam conditions.

All the answers are provided, of course. But that's just the beginning. Your Mitchell Guide explains *why* each answer is right...and the other choices are wrong. The result: A deeper understanding of the sometimes subtle differences that separate correct answers from incorrect ones.

A Winning Strategy

Often, a test is passed the same way a race is won – with a clear strategy. Mitchell experts have analyzed the various ASE tests and mapped out test-taking strategies to help you earn your highest possible score.

To order, call: 1-800-648-8010 (In the 619 area, call 578-6550.)

WE SUPPORT
VOLUNTARY TECHNICIAN
CERTIFICATION THROUGH

National Institute for
**AUTOMOTIVE
SERVICE
EXCELLENCE**

The Leader in Professional Estimating and Repair Information.

ADT92

MITCHELL'S TECHNICAL SEMINAR PROGRAMS

Mitchell's Technical Seminars teach technicians how to quickly diagnose and repair new import and domestic vehicles with their many computer-controlled operations. These advanced technical updates for automotive professionals will increase your knowledge, sharpen your skills, and teach you new techniques that can help you repair computerized vehicles quickly and correctly.

All Mitchell Technical Seminars are highly concentrated sessions that tackle real-world diagnostic situations. Classes include:

- Electronic Ignition Systems: Conventional and Distributorless
- Feedback Carburetors
- Electronic Fuel Injection Systems
- On-Board Computer Diagnosis
- Using the DVOM and Scan Tool For Diagnostics

Seven separate Mitchell Technical Seminars are offered:

Asian I EFI Driveability Diagnosis Seminar

Shows how to diagnose driveability problems related to Nissan, Toyota, and Mitsubishi ignition and fuel injection systems, plus how to enter and use computer diagnostics.

Asian II EFI Driveability Diagnosis Seminar

Shows how to diagnose driveability problems related to Acura, Honda, and Mazda ignition and fuel injection systems, plus how to enter and use computer diagnostics.

INTRODUCING MITCHELL'S *NEW* ELECTRICAL TROUBLESHOOTING SEMINAR...

When you want to repair vehicles right the first time, the most valuable tools you have are your Digital Volt Ohmmeter, Lab scope, up-to-date technical data, and training. This new seminar provides the practical, hands-on training you need to solve circuit problems in ignition systems, mass airflow, and speed density systems.

Chrysler FBC/EFI Seminar

Answers your questions on computer-controlled fuel injected or carbureted engines. Includes information on how to diagnose the Chrysler SMEC system.

Ford MCU/EEC Seminar

Learn to diagnose and repair both feedback carbureted and fuel injected engines, including vehicles equipped with distributorless ignition systems.

GM CCC/TBI Seminar

Gain the knowledge and confidence needed to work on computer-controlled carburetor or throttle body injected engines. An excellent program for technicians who are beginning to learn how to diagnose GM computer systems.

GM DIS/PFI Seminar

Provides answers to your toughest GM problems related to distributorless ignition systems or port fuel injected engines.

SIGN UP FOR YOUR SEMINAR TODAY

Ask your Mitchell sales representative for details, or call for more information.

1-800-854-7030 *or*
619-578-6550
extension 8570.

The Leader in Professional Estimating and Repair Information.

ADT92